Webster's Third New International Dictionary

OF THE ENGLISH LANGUAGE
UNABRIDGED

A Merriam-Webster

REG. U.S. PAT. OFF.

VOLUME III

S to Z

and Britannica World Language Dictionary

17·68

ENCYCLOPÆDIA BRITANNICA, INC.

Chicago, London, Toronto, Geneva, Sydney, Tokyo, Manila

This volume contains the final portion
of *Webster's Third New International Dictionary of the English Language,* letters S through Z,
followed by the *Britannica World Language Dictionary.*

Part I of the *Britannica World Language Dictionary,* beginning at page 2679,
comprises a list of about 6,000 most commonly used words in English with their closest equivalents
in six other important languages.

In Part II the same list of words is repeated in each of
the other six languages, with the English equivalents.
There are also grammar sections for the other languages.

1s \'es\ *n, pl* **s's** *or* **ss** \'es∂z\ *often cap, often attrib* **1 a :** the 19th letter of the English alphabet **b :** an instance of this letter printed, written, or otherwise represented — see LONG S **c :** a speech counterpart of orthographic *s* (as *s* in *sister, basin,* or French *sang*) **2 :** a printer's type, a stamp, or some other instrument for reproducing the letter *s* **3 :** someone or something distinctively or conveniently designated *s* esp. as the 18th or when *j* is used for the 10th the 19th in order or class **4 a** [*satisfactory*] **:** a grade assigned by a teacher or examiner rating a student's work as satisfactory **b :** one graded or rated with an *s* **5 :** something having the shape of the letter S (an *S* curve in the road)

2s *abbr, often cap* **1** sabbath **2** sacral **3** sacred **4** saeculum **5** saint **6** sand **7** satang **8** scalar **9** schilling **10** school **11** science **12** scribe **13** seaman **14** search **15** seat **16** second; secondary **17** secretary **18** section **19** see **20** semi **21** senate **22** September **23** [L *sepultus*] buried **24** series **25** set **26** sharp **27** shilling **28** ship **29** side **30** sign; signed **31** [L *signa*] write **32** signature **33** signor **34** silicate **35** silver **36** silversmith **37** simplex **38** [L *sine*] without **39** sine **40** single **41** singular **42** [L *sinister*] left **43** sink **44** sire **45** slip **46** slow **47** small **48** smooth **49** snow **50** socialist **51** society **52** [L *socius* or *sodalis*] fellow **53** soft **54** sol **55** solid **56** solidus **57** solo **58** solubility **59** son **60** soprano **61** sou **62** south; southerly; southern **63** special **64** species **65** speed **66** sphere; spherical **67** staff **68** standard **69** station **70** statute **71** steamer **72** steel **73** stem **74** stere **75** stock **76** straight **77** subito **78** subject **79** submarine **80** substantive **81** succeeded **82** sucre **83** sun **84** superb **85** superior **86** surfaced **87** surplus **88** survey **89** switch **90** symmetrical

3s *symbol, cap* **1** sulfur **2** entropy **3** the subject of a proposition in logic

1s- — see SYM-

2s- \'sekən,derē, 'es\ *abbr, usu ital* secondary — esp. in names of organic radicals ⟨*s*-butyl⟩

1-s \s *after a voiceless consonant sound, z after a voiced consonant sound or a vowel sound*\ *n pl suffix* [ME *-es, -s,* fr. OE *-as,* nom. & acc. pl. ending of some masc. nouns; akin to OS *-os,* nom. & acc. pl. ending of some masc. nouns, and prob. to Skt (Vedic) *-āsas,* nom. pl. ending of some masc. nouns] **1 a** — used to form the plural of most nouns that do not end in *s, z, sh, ch,* or postconsonantal *y* ⟨*heads*⟩ ⟨*books*⟩ ⟨*boys*⟩ ⟨*beliefs*⟩ ⟨*parades*⟩ ⟨*states*⟩ — compare 1-ES 1 **b** — used to form the plural of proper nouns that end in postconsonantal *y* ⟨*Italys*⟩ ⟨*Marys*⟩ **c** — used to form the plural of abbreviations, numbers, letters, and symbols used as nouns ⟨MCs⟩ ⟨4s⟩ ⟨#s⟩ and often preceded by an apostrophe ⟨B's⟩ ⟨&'s⟩ **2** [ME *-es, -s,* gen. sing. ending of nouns] — used to form the possessive of singular nouns (boy's) of plural nouns not ending in *s* ⟨children's⟩, of some pronouns ⟨anyone's⟩, and of word groups functioning as nouns ⟨the man in the corner's hat⟩ or pronouns ⟨someone else's⟩

2-s *n suffix* — used to form nicknames expressing affection or familiarity ⟨Moms⟩ ⟨Dads⟩ or designating a characteristic feature or activity of the person named ⟨Fats⟩ ⟨Freckles⟩ ⟨Cuddles⟩ ⟨Smiles⟩ or an object characteristically associated with the person named ⟨Boots⟩ ⟨Sparks⟩

3-s \s\ *vb suffix* [ME (Northern & North Midland dial.) *-es,* fr. OE (Northumbrian dial.) *-es, -as,* 2d pers. sing. pres. indic. ending — more at -EST] — used to form the third person singular present of most verbs that do not end in *s, z, sh, ch,* or postconsonantal *y* ⟨falls⟩ ⟨takes⟩ ⟨plays⟩ — compare 2-ES 1 **2** *substand* — used to form the historical present first person singular ⟨then I says to him⟩ — compare 2-ES 2

-'s \s *after voiceless consonant sounds other than* s, sh, ch; *z after vowel sounds or voiced consonant sounds other than* z, zh, j; *əz after* s, sh, ch, z, zh, j\ *n suffix or pron suffix* [ME *-s, -es,* gen. sing. ending of nouns, fr. OE *-es,* gen. sing. ending of some masc. & neut. nouns; akin to OHG *-es,* gen. sing. ending of some masc. & neut. nouns, ON *-s,* Goth *-is,* Gk *-ou,* Gk (Homeric) *-oo, -oio,* Skt *-asya*] — used to form the possessive of singular nouns ⟨boy's⟩, of plural nouns not ending in *s* ⟨children's⟩, of some pronouns ⟨anyone's⟩, and of word groups functioning as nouns ⟨the man in the corner's hat⟩ or pronouns ⟨someone else's⟩

-s' \like 1-s\ *n pl suffix* [ME *-s,* alter. of *-es* — more at -ES'] — used to form the plural possessive of most nouns that do not end in *s, z, sh, ch,* or postconsonantal *y* ⟨girls'⟩ ⟨workers'⟩ ⟨voters'⟩

1's \like -'s\ *vb* [contr. of *is, has, does*] **1 :** 1IS ⟨she's here⟩ **2 :** HAS ⟨he's seen them⟩ **3 :** DOES ⟨what's he want?⟩ ⟨what's it mean?⟩

2's \s\ *pron* [by contr.] **:** US — used with *let* ⟨let's⟩

3's \like -'s\ *adj* [by contr.] *archaic* **:** HIS ⟨I cut off's head —Shak.⟩

4's \before a vowel sound: z; before a consonant sound that can follow word-initial s in English: s; before a voiced consonant that does not follow word-initial s: z or (with alteration of the voiced to the corresponding voiceless consonant) s\ *n* [contr. of *God's,* gen. of *God*] **:** God's — often used in mild oaths ⟨'sblood⟩ ⟨'sdeath⟩

5's \z\ *conj* [by contr.] *dial* **:** AS ⟨so's you can come⟩

6's *or* **'se** *also* **s'** \s\ *vb* [contr. of *so*] *dial Brit* **:** SHALL ⟨I'se repeat each poor man's prayer —Robert Burns⟩

sa \'sä, ˌsä\ *dial var of* SO

SA *abbr* **1** salt added **2** seaman apprentice **3** *often not cap* [L *secundum artem*] according to art **4** semiannual **5** semiautomatic **6** sex appeal **7** *often not cap* [L *sine anno*] without year **8** small arms **9** [F] société anonyme **10** *often not cap* [L *sub anno*] under the year **11** subject to approval

SAA *abbr* small arms ammunition

saa·di·an \'sädēən\ *n -s usu cap* [*Saadi,* 16th and 17th cent. dynasty of sherifs in Morocco + E *-an*] **:** a member of a dynasty of sherifs of Arab descent ruling Morocco between 1550 and 1688 and noted for their splendid tombs in Marrakech

1saa·nen \'sänən, 'zä-\ *n* [fr. *Saanen,* locality in southwest Switzerland] **1** *usu cap* **:** a Swiss breed of white or light-colored usu. hornless short-haired dairy goats **2** *often cap* **:** an animal of the Saanen breed

2saanen \"\ *also* **saanen cheese** *n -s often cap* **:** a cheese similar to Emmental cheese that is cooked longer, keeps without year **:** small arms **9** [F] société anonyme **10** to three years to cure, and keeps longer

saar·land·er \'särˌlandər, 'zˌl\ *n -s often cap* [G *saarländer,* fr. *Saarland,* coal-producing and industrial region in southwest Germany + G *-er*] **:** a native or inhabitant of Saarland

sab *abbr, often cap* sabbath

SAB *abbr* **1** science advisory board **2** soprano, alto, baritone

sa·ba \'säbä\ *n -s* [Tag *saba*] **1** [Tag *saba*] **:** a common cooking banana (*Musa sapientum* var. *compressa*) in the Philippines **2 :** fine textile from the fiber of the saba plant

sab·a·dil·la \ˌsabə'dilə, -ˌdē(y)ə\ *also* **ceb·a·dil·la** \ˌseb-\ *n -s* [Sp *cebadilla,* dim. of *cebada* barley, fr. *cebo* feed, fr. L *cibus* food — more at CIBARIAL] **1 :** a Mexican plant (*Schoenocaulon officinale*) of the family Liliaceae — called also *cevadilla* **2 :** the seeds of the sabadilla plant used as a source of veratrine and in the preparation of an insecticide used esp. for stock and for garden crops

sab·a·dine \'sabəˌdēn, -ˌdən\ *n -s* [ISV *sabad-* (fr. NL *Sabadilla*) — syn. of *Schoenocaulon,* fr. E *sabadilla*) + *-ine*] **:** a crystalline alkaloid $C_{29}H_{51}NO_8$ that is found in sabadilla seeds

sab·a·dine \'sabəˌdēn\ *n -s* [ISV *sabadine* + *-ine*] **:** CEVINE

1sa·bae·an \sə'bēən\ *adj, usu cap* [L *sabaeus,* fr. Gk *sabaios,* fr. *Saba* Sheba, ancient kingdom in southwestern Arabia, fr. Ar *Saba'*) + E *-an*] **1 :** of or relating to the ancient people and kingdom of Saba flourishing in southwestern Arabia from about 950 to 115 B.C., attaining their prime about the middle of the first millennium B.C., and

anciently renowned for wealth and trade (as in spices) — compare HIMYARITE, MINAEAN **2 :** of or relating to the language and alphabet of the Sabaeans

2sabaean *or* **sabean** \"\ *n -s* **1** *cap* **a :** a native or inhabitant of Saba in southern Arabia **b :** the Semitic language of the Sabaean people that is a form of South Arabic **2** *usu cap* **:** MANDAEAN

sa·bai grass \sə'bī-\ *n* [Hindi *sabai*] **:** BHABAR 1

sabakha *var of* SEBKHA

sa·bal \'sabəl, -bl\ *n* [NL] **1** *cap* **:** a small genus of American dwarf fan palms having creeping horizontal or subterranean stems and long petioled leaves with obscure or rudimentary midribs — see CABBAGE PALMETTO **2 -s :** the partly dried ripe fruit of the saw palmetto used as a diuretic

sa·ba·lo \'sabəˌlō\ *n -s* [AmerSp *sábalo,* fr. Sp, shad, perh. of Celt origin; akin to OIr *sam* summer — more at SUMMER] **1 :** TARPON **2** *also* **sa·ba·lo·te** \ˌsabō'lōdˌē\ [*sabalo* fr. AmerSp *sábalo,* fr. Sp, shad; dialect alter. fr. AmerSp, fr. *sábalo*] **:** MILKFISH 1

sabal palmetto *n* **:** CABBAGE PALMETTO

sa·ba·na \sä'bänə, -'v‖, ‖a-\ *n -s* [Sp — more at SAVANNA] **:** SAVANNA 2

sa·ba·thé's cycle \ˌsabəˈtäz-\ *n, usu cap S* [prob. fr. the name *Sabathé*] **:** a cycle of operations in internal-combustion engines in which the combustion takes place partly explosively and partly at constant pressure and which resembles partly the Otto cycle and partly the Diesel cycle

sabaton *var of* SABBATON

sa·ba·yon \ˌsäbäˈyōⁿ\ *n, pl* **sabayons** \"\ [F, modif. of It *zabaione* zabaglione, perh. of Illyrian origin; akin to the source of LL *sabaia,* an Illyrian drink made from grain; akin to OE *sæp* sap — more at SAP] **:** ZABAGLIONE

sab·bat \'sabət\ *n -s often cap* [F, lit., sabbath, fr. L *sabbatum* — more at SABBATH] **:** a midnight assembly of witches and sorcerers held in medieval and Renaissance times at intervals (as on Walpurgis Night, Halloween) to renew allegiance to the devil sometimes present in a form like a goat and to celebrate rites (as the Black Mass) and orgies — called also *sabbath, witches' sabbath*

1sab·ba·tar·i·an \ˌsabə'terēən, -ta(r)-,-tär-\ *n -s often cap* [L *sabbatarius,* n., sabbatarian (fr. *sabbatum* sabbath + *-arius* -ary) + E *-an,* n. suffix] **1 :** one who regards and keeps the seventh day of the week as holy in conformity with the letter of the decalogue ⟨were strict Sabbatarians, would not even read Sunday papers —*Time*⟩ **2 :** one who favors strict observance of the sabbath **3 :** a member of a non-Jewish religious sect originating in Russia distinguished by observance of Jewish rites and festivals including Saturday as the day of rest

2sabbatarian \"\ *adj, often cap* [LL *sabbatarius,* adj., sabbatarian (fr. L *sabbatum* sabbath + *-arius* -ary) + E *-an,* adj. suffix] **1 :** of or relating to the sabbath or to sabbatarians ⟨~ regulations⟩ **2 :** rigidly strict in the manner advocated by sabbatarians ⟨a soberer crowd . . . almost ~ in its decorousness —Robert Lynd⟩

sab·ba·tar·i·an·ism \ˌ‖,‖,ˌnizəm\ *n -s often cap* **:** the principles and practices of sabbatarians; *esp* **:** the puritanical suppression on Sunday of all avoidable work and enjoyment as an enforcement of pious devotion and sobriety

sab·bath \'sabəth\ *n -s often attrib* [ME *sabath, sabat,* fr. OF *sabat, sabbat* & OE *sabat,* fr. L *sabbatum,* fr. Gk *sabbaton,* fr. Heb *shabbāth,* fr. *shābath* to rest] **1** *often cap* **a** (1) *also* **sabbath day** [ME *sabat day,* fr. *sabat* sabbath + *day*] **:** the day of rest and solemn assembly observed as sacred to God by Jews and some Christian churches on the seventh day of the week from sunset Friday until sunset Saturday ⟨six days thou shalt labor and do all thy work: but the seventh day is the ~ of the Lord thy God; in it thou shalt not do any work —Deut 5:13–14 (AV)⟩ (2) **:** some other Scriptural period (as the sabbatical year) of solemn rest or cessation from usual activity ⟨the tenth day of this seventh month is the day of atonement; it shall be for you . . . a ~ of solemn rest —Lev 23:27–32 (RSV)⟩ ⟨six years shall you sow in your field . . . but in the seventh year there shall be a ~ of solemn rest for the land —Lev 25:3–4 (RSV)⟩ **b** *also* **sabbath day :** the day of rest and public worship observed on Sunday by most Christian churches in commemoration of the resurrection of Christ on the first day of the week; *specif* **:** the Lord's Day observed strictly as a day of solemn rest and devotion continuing the Old Testament Sabbath **c :** the day of the week regularly set aside by some other religion for public observances ⟨although it was Friday, the Moslem *Sabbath,* people were at work —Francis Ofner⟩ **2** *often cap* **:** a time of rest or repose **:** a cessation of effort, pain, or care **3** *sometimes cap* **:** SABBAT

sab·bath·ar·i·an \ˌsabə'therēən\ *n -s often cap* [by alter. (influence of SABBATH)] **:** SABBATARIAN

sabbath–day house *n, often cap S* **:** a house formerly built (as in colonial Connecticut) near a church and heated on winter Sundays as a place for worshipers living at a distance to warm themselves and eat between morning and afternoon services in an unheated church

sabbath–day's journey *n, often cap S* **:** a distance of 2000 cubits that under rabbinic law a Jew might travel on the sabbath from the walled limits of a town or city

sab·bath·less \'sabəthləs\ *adj, often cap* **:** having no sabbath ⟨Sabbathless Satan —Charles Lamb⟩

1sab·bath·ly \-thlē\ *adv, often cap* [*sabbath* + *-ly,* adv. suffix] **:** every sabbath

2sabbathly \"\ *adj, often cap* [*sabbath* + *-ly,* adj. suffix] **:** occurring every sabbath

sabbath school *n, often cap 1st S* **:** a school held on the sabbath for purposes of religious education; *also* **:** the pupils or teachers and pupils of such a school

sab·ba·tia \sə'bāsh(ē)ə, -shə\ *n -s* [NL, fr. Liberatus *Sabbati,* 18th cent. Ital. botanist + NL *-ia*] **1** *cap* **:** a genus of smooth slender No. American herbs (family Gentianaceae) with opposite leaves and showy white or rose-pink cymose flowers — see MARSH PINK **2 -s :** any plant of the genus Sabbatia — see AMERICAN CENTAURY

1sab·ba·tian \sə'bāshən\ *n -s usu cap* [*Sabbatius,* 4th cent. A.D. Novatian presbyter + E *-an*] **:** one of the followers of the Novatian presbyter Sabbatius who held that Easter and the feast of the Passover should be kept at the same time by Christians and Jews

2sab·ba·ti·an \ˌsabəˈtīən\ *or* **shab·ba·thai·an** *or* **shab·be·thai·an** \ˌshabəˈtīən\ *n -s usu cap* [Sabbatian (latinized form of the name of Sabbatai Zebi †1676 Hebrew mystic) + E *-an; shabbathaian, shabbethaian* fr. *Shabbethai* (Sabbatai Zebi) + E *-an*] **:** a follower of the cabalist Sabbatai Zebi who proclaimed himself the Messiah and was accepted as such by many Jews — compare DÖNMEH

1sab·bat·i·cal \sə'bad-ə‖kəl, -ˌdˌ‖, -ˌĭk-‖, -ĭk\ *adj* [*sabbatical,* fr. LL *sabbaticus* sabbatical (fr. Gk *sabbatikos,* fr. *sabbaton* sabbath + *-ikos* -ic) + E *-al; sabbatic* fr. LL *sabbaticus*] **1** *sometimes cap* **:** of, relating to, or suited to the sabbath ⟨~ laws⟩ ⟨~ peace⟩ **2 :** having the character of a recurring period of rest or renewal

2sabbatical \"\ *n -s* **:** SABBATICAL YEAR 2 **:** LEAVE (studied in Europe on his ~)

sabbatical year *n* **1** *often cap S* **:** a year of rest for the land observed every seventh year in ancient Judea by allowing the fields and vineyards to lie without tilling, sowing, pruning, or reaping from autumn to autumn in accordance with a Levitical commandment — compare JUBILEE **2** *or* **sabbatical leave :** a leave with full or half pay granted (as every seventh year) to one holding an administrative or professional position (as college professor) for rest, travel, or research

sab·ba·tine \'sabəˌtīn, -ˌtēn\ *adj, usu cap* [ML *sabbatinus* of the sabbath, fr. L *sabbatum* sabbath + *-inus* -ine] **:** of, relating to, or constituting an indulgence granted the Carmelite order and its confraternities based orig. on a spurious bull of 1322 promising liberation from Purgatory the Saturday after death, ratified in modified form by later popes, and promising the intercession of the Virgin Mary to those observing given conditions ⟨the Sabbatine privilege⟩

sab·ba·tism \ˌ-ˌtizəm\ *n -s* [LL *sabbatismus* celebration of the sabbath, fr. Gk *sabbatismos,* fr. *sabbatizein* to keep the sabbath] **:** the strict observance of the sabbath

sab·ba·ti·za·tion \ˌsabəd-əˈzāshən, -bə,tīˈz-\ *n -s often cap*

[ML *sabbatization-, sabbatizatio,* fr. LL *sabbatizatus* (past part. of *sabbatizare*) + -ion] **:** the act or process of sabbatizing

sab·ba·tize \'sabəˌtīz\ *vb* -ED/-ING/-S *sometimes cap* [ME *sabbatisen,* fr. LL *sabbatizare,* fr. Gk *sabbatizein,* fr. *sabbaton* sabbath + *-izein* -ize — more at SABBATH] *vi* **:** to keep the sabbath ~ *vt* **:** to keep as the sabbath

sab·ba·ton *or* **sab·a·ton** \'sabəˌtän\ *n -s* [ME *sabaton, sabatoun,* fr. OProv *sabato, sabaton,* fr. *sabata* shoe — more at SABOT] **:** a piece of armor covering the foot; *specif* **:** a solleret broad and blunted at the toes

sabbats *pl of* SABBAT

sab·be·ka \'sabəkə\ *n -s* [Aram *šabbĕkhā*] **:** TRIGON

sab–cat \'sab,-\ [*sabotage* + *cat*] **:** SABOTEUR

1sa·be \'savē, -vi\ *vb* sabed; sabed; sabeing; sabes [Sp, 2nd pers. (formal) & 3d pers. sing. pres. indic. of *saber* to know — more at SAVVY] **:** SAVVY

2sabe \"\ *n -s* **:** SAVVY

sabean *usu cap, var of* SABEAN

sa·bel·la \sə'belə\ *n* [NL, fr. L *sabulum* sand + NL *-ella* — more at SAND] **1** *cap* **:** a genus (the type of the family Sabellidae) of tube-dwelling marine polychaete worms with the prostomial palps modified into semicircular plumose gills **2 -s :** any worm of the genus *Sabella* — **sa·bel·li·form** \-lə,form\ *adj* — **sabel·loid** \sə'be,loid, 'sabə,l-\ *adj or n*

sab·el·lar·ia \ˌsabə'la(r)ēə\ *n, cap* [NL, prob. fr. *Sabella* + *-aria*] **:** a genus (the type of the family Sabellariidae) of tube-dwelling marine polychaete worms with greatly developed peristome and the posterior end of the body tapering like a tail

1sab·el·lar·i·id \ˌ-ˌ‖ˌ‖rēəd\ *adj* [NL *Sabellariidae*] **:** of or relating to the Sabellariidae

2sabellariid \"\ *n -s* [NL *Sabellariidae*] **:** a worm of the family Sabellariidae

sab·el·la·ri·idae \ˌsabələ'rīəˌdē, sə,bel-\ *n pl, cap* [NL, fr. *Sabellaria,* type genus + *-idae*] **:** a family of typically colonial and sometimes reef-building polychaete worms — see SABELLARIA

1sa·bel·li·an \sə'belēən\ *n -s usu cap* [ME, fr. LL *sabellianus,* fr. *Sabellius,* 3d cent. A.D. Roman Christian prelate and theologian + L *-anus* -an] **:** a follower of Sabellius, a leader of the Modalistic Monarchians in the 3d century who held in general that there is one divine essence and that the Father, the Logos, and the Holy Spirit are three different manifestations of the one God; *also* **:** a Modalistic Monarchian

2sabellian \"\ *adj, usu cap* **1 :** of or relating to the Sabellians **2 :** of or adhering to Modalistic Monarchianism

3sa·bel·li·an \"\ *n -s cap* [*Sabellus,* n., Sabine + E *-an,* n. suffix] **1 :** a member of one of a group of early Italian peoples comprising Sabines, Samnites, and others **2 :** one or all of a number of poorly known languages or dialects of ancient central Italy that are presumably closely related to Oscan and Umbrian

4sabellian \"\ *adj, usu cap* [L *Sabellus,* n., Sabine + E *-an,* adj. suffix] **:** of, relating to, or forming the Sabellians or their languages or dialects

sa·bel·li·an·ism \sə'belēə,nizəm\ *n -s usu cap* **:** the theological doctrines of the Sabellians **:** MODALISTIC MONARCHIANISM — compare PATRIPASSIANISM

sa·bel·lic \sə'belik\ *adj, usu cap* [L *sabellicus* of the Sabines, fr. *Sabellus,* n., Sabine + *-icus* -ic] **:** 3SABELLIAN

1sa·bel·lid \sə'beləd\ *adj* [NL *Sabellidae,* family of worms, fr. *Sabella,* type genus + *-idae*] **:** of or relating to the genus *Sabella* or the family Sabellidae

2sabellid \"\ *n -s* [NL *Sabellidae*] **:** a worm of the family *Sabella* or the family Sabellidae

1sa·ber *or* **sa·bre** \'sābə(r)\ *n -s* [F *sabre,* modif. of G dial.

saber 1

sabel, fr. MHG *sabel, sebel,* of Slav origin; akin to Russ *sablya* saber, Pol *szabla*] **1 :** a heavy military sword with a usu. curved blade having a cutting edge, a thick back, and a guard for the hand and used esp. by cavalry men **2 a :** a light fencing or dueling sword with an arc-shaped guard and tapering flexible blade of fluted H section that is not more than 41⅜ inches long and has one full cutting edge and an 8-inch cutting edge on the back at the tip — compare ÉPÉE, FOIL **b :** the art or practice of fencing with the saber that limits the target to the trunk and counts hits by cut as well as thrust

2saber *or* **sabre** \"\ *vt* sabered *or* sabred; sabered *or* sabred; sabering *or* sabring \-b(ə)riŋ\ sabers *or* sabres **:** to strike, cut, or kill with a saber

saberbill \'‖,‖,‖\ *n* **1 :** CURLEW **2 :** So. American dendrocolaptine bird of the genus *Campylorhamphus* having a long decurved bill

saber fish *n* **:** CUTLASS FISH

saber leg *n* **:** an incurved chair leg square in cross section — see LEG illustration

saber-legged \'‖,‖·(‖)‖\ *adj* **:** being sickle-hocked

saber rattling *n* **:** an ostentatious, offensive, or threatening display of military power or prowess

saber saw *n* **:** a portable electric jigsaw

saber shin *n* **:** a tibia with a pronounced anterior convexity that occurs in congenital syphilis

sabertooth \'‖,‖·‖\ *n* **:** SABER-TOOTHED TIGER

saber-toothed \'‖,‖·‖\ *adj* **:** having long trenchant canine teeth **:** MACHAIRODONT

saber-toothed tiger *n* **1 :** any of numerous extinct cats widely distributed in the Oligocene through the Pleistocene of both the Old and New World, differing from the typical cats chiefly in the extreme development of the upper canines into curved swordlike piercing or slashing weapons and in enlargement of the gape with corresponding muscular and skeletal changes, and constituting a distinct felid subfamily that reaches its climax in the New World Pleistocene genus *Smilodon* **2 :** any of various chiefly No. American and Miocene or Pliocene cats of *Nimravus* and related genera that resemble but are less specialized than the typical saber-toothed tigers — called also *false saber-toothed tiger*

saberwing \'‖,‖·‖\ *n* **:** any of various So. American hummingbirds of the genera *Campylopterus* and *Eupetomena* in which the outer primaries are strongly falcate

sabes *pres 3d sing of* SABE, *pl of* SABE

sa·bha \'sə'bä\ *n -s* [Hindi *sabhā,* fr. Skt — more at SIB] **1 :** a public meeting in India **:** ASSEMBLY **2 :** an organized group in India **:** SOCIETY, COUNCIL

1sa·bia \'säbēə\ *n, cap* [NL, prob. fr. native name in India] **:** a genus (the type of the family Sabiaceae) of tropical Asiatic erect or climbing shrubs having alternate petioled leaves and small axillary regular flowers and having the stamens, petals, and sepals opposite throughout

2sa·bia \sə'byä\ *n -s* [Pg *sabiá,* fr. Tupi] **:** any of several thrushes of the genus *Mimus* popular as songbirds in Brazil

sa·bi·a·ce·ae \ˌsäbē'āsē,ē\ *n pl, cap* [NL, fr. *Sabia,* type genus + *-aceae*] **:** a family of tropical shrubs and trees (order Sapindales) having small paniculate flowers with a compressed or lobed ovary of two or three cells and fruit consisting of one-seeded nutlets — **sa·bi·a·ceous** \ˌ‖ˌ‖āshəs\ *adj*

1sa·bi·an \'sābēən, 'säb-\ *n -s usu cap* [Ar *Ṣābi'* Sabian + E *-an*] **1 :** one of a group mentioned in the Koran as entitled to Muslim religious toleration along with Jews and Christians and usu. identified with the Mandaeans or the Elkesaites **2 :** a Syrian pagan of a Hauranitic group orig. of star worshipers claiming toleration from the Muslim conquerors under the pretense of belonging to the Sabian group tolerated by the Koran and including scholars and astronomers noted under the caliphate

2sabian \"\ *adj, usu cap* **:** of or relating to the Sabians

sa·bi·an·ism \ˌ-ˌnizəm\ *n -s usu cap* **:** the religion of the Sabians

sab·i·cu *or* **sabicu wood** \'sabəˌkü, ˌsabə'kü\ [AmerSp *sabicú*] **1 :** the hard dark brown wood of a West Indian tree (*Lysiloma sabicu*) resembling mahogany in texture and valued for furniture making **2 :** the tree that yields sabicu wood

sabin \'säbən, 'sab-\ *n -s* [after Wallace C. W. *Sabine* †1919 Am. physicist] **:** a unit of acoustic absorption equivalent to

the absorption by one square foot of a perfect absorber (as an open window)

sa·bi·na \sə'bīnə, -bēnə\ *or* **sab·ine** \'sabən\ *n* -s [L *sabina*] : SAVIN 1

sab·i·nane \'sabə,nān\ *n* -s [ISV *sabin-* (fr. NL *sabina* — specific epithet of the savin *Juniperus sabina* — fr. L *sabina* savin) + *-ane*] : THUJANE

¹sabine \'sā,bīn, 'sa,b-\ *n* -s *usu cap* [ME *Sabyn*, fr. L *Sabinus*, n. & adj.] **1** : a member of an ancient people inhabiting chiefly the Apennines northeast of Latium and conquered and incorporated by Rome in 290 B.C. — compare SAMNITE **2** : the Italic language of the Sabine people

²sabine \"\ *adj, usu cap* [L *Sabinus*] : of or relating to the Sabines

sab·i·nene \'sabə,nēn\ *n* -s [ISV *sabin-* (fr. NL *sabina*) + *-ene*] : a liquid bicyclic unsaturated terpene hydrocarbon $C_{10}H_{16}$ found esp. in savin oil that is the isomer of thujene containing a double bond outside of the rings; 4(10)-thujene

sabine pine \'sā|bən-, 'sa|, |,bīn-\ *n* [after Joseph *Sabine* †1837 Brit. horticulturist] *n, usu cap S* **1** : DIGGER PINE **2** : TORREY PINE

sabine's gull \-nz-\ *n, usu cap S* [after Sir Edward *Sabine* †1883 Brit. physicist and explorer] : a small gull (*Xema sabini*) breeding in arctic regions that has a dark gray head, black collar, white wing tips, and a slightly forked tail

sa·bi·no \sə'bē(,)nō\ *n* -s [AmerSp *sabino, sabina*, fr. Sp *sabina* savin, fr. L] **1 a** (1) : a bald cypress (*Taxodium distichum*) (2) : AHUEHUETE **b** : ROCK CEDAR **2** : a Puerto Rican forest tree (*Magnolia splendens*) with hard heavy durable wood that is used for furniture and general construction

sa·bir \sə'bi(ə)r\ *n* -s [F, fr. the word for "know" in a concocted lingua franca used by Molière †1673 Fr. playwright in his comedy *Le Bourgeois Gentilhomme* (1670) as the vehicle of a song (of which the first two lines are *Se ti sabir, Ti respondir* meaning "if you know, answer"), prob. fr. Sp *saber* to know — more at SAVVY] : a French-based pidgin language of No. Africa

sabkha *var of* SEBKHA

¹sa·ble \'sābəl\ *n* -s *see sense 2a* [ME, sable (heraldic color, color, animal, and fur), fr. MF, fr. OF (animal and fur), fr. MLG *sabel*, fr. MHG *zabel, zobel*, fr. OHG *zobel*, of Slav origin; akin to Russ *sobol'* sable (animal and fur), Pol *sobol*; perh. akin to Skt *śabara, śabala* spotted — more at CERBERUS] **1 a** : the heraldic color black **b** : the color black **c** : black clothing worn as a sign of mourning — usu. used in pl. **2 a** *or pl* **sable** (1) : a carnivorous mammal (*Martes zibellina*) of northern Europe and parts of northern Asia that attains a length of about 18 inches exclusive of the tail, varies from yellowish to dark brown above with grayish markings on the face and tawny on the throat and underparts, and is one of the most valued of fur-bearing animals esp. for its very dark skin (2) : any of various related animals; *esp* : PINE MARTEN **b** (1) : the fur or pelt of a sable (2) : a trimming or article of this fur ⟨she wore her ~s with a tailored suit⟩ — usu. used in pl. **3** *or* **sable's hair pencil** : an artist's brush of sable hair **4** : SABLE ANTELOPE **5 a** : the color of the fur of the sable **b** : WOODBARK

²sable \"\ *adj* [ME, fr. *sable*, n.] **1 a** : of the heraldic color black — abbr. *sa* **b** : black in color : dressed in black : darkened as by night ⟨down the ~ flood we glided —Charlotte Brontë⟩ **c** *of a dog* : having a black-shaded outer coat over an undercoat of lighter color **2 a** : SAD, GLOOMY, DISMAL **b** : darkly mysterious or threatening **3** : SATANIC ⟨his ~ majesty⟩

sable antelope *n* : a large handsome nearly extinct antelope (*Hippotragus niger*) of eastern and southern Africa that has large curved annulated horns, a tufted tail, and a slight mane and is glossy black in the male except for the white underparts and facial markings — called also *black buck, sable*

sablefish \'==,=\ *n* : a large elongated slaty gray to nearly black scorpaenid food fish (*Anoplopoma fimbria*) of the Pacific coast from Alaska to southern California that is a leading market fish usu. sold fresh but sometimes smoked or salted and has a liver rich in vitamins — called also *black cod, blue cod, candlefish*

sa·ble·ness *n* -ES : the quality or state of being sable : BLACKNESS, GLOOMINESS

sa·bly \'sāb(ə)lē\ *adv* [²*sable* + *-ly*] : in a sable manner : BLACKLY, DARKLY

sa·bo·ra \sä'bó(,)rä\ *n, pl* **sabora·im** \,säbó'rä,im\ *often cap* [Aram *sābhōrā*, lit., thinker, fr. *sēbhār* to think, intend] : one of the Jewish rabbis active in the Babylonian academies during the 6th century who completed the revision of the Babylonian Talmud — compare AMORA, TANNA

sa·bo·ra·ic \,säbə'rāik\ *adj, often cap* : of or relating to the saboraim

sabot \(')sa¦bō, sə'bō, *in sense 1b often* 'sabət\ *n* -s [F, fr. MF, alter. (influenced by *bot, bote* boot) of *savate* old shoe; akin to It *ciabatta* old shoe, Sp *zapato* shoe, OProv *sabata*] **1 a** : a wooden work shoe worn in various European countries (as Germany, France, Belgium, Holland) — compare CLOG **b** (1) *or* **sabot strap** : a strap or wide band of leather or other material fitting across the instep in a shoe esp. of the sandal type (2) : a shoe having a sabot strap **2 a** : a thick circular disk of wood for holding the cartridge bag and projectile of fixed ammunition for smoothbore cannon **b** : a piece of soft metal formerly attached to a projectile for a muzzle-loading rifle to take the grooves of the rifling **c** : a thrust-transmitting light-weight carrier that positions a missile or subcaliber projectile in a tube and is normally discarded when free of the tube

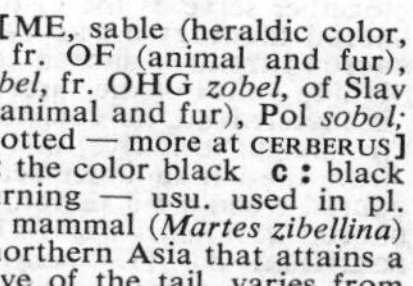

sabot 1 b (2)

¹sab·o·tage \'sabə,täzh, -täj *sometimes* |j *or* ,==='=\ *n* -s [F, fr. *saboter* to botch, do in a clumsy or slipshod way, sabotage (fr. *sabot*) + *-age*] **1** : malicious destruction of or damage to property with the intention of injuring a business or impairing the economic system or weakening a government or nation in time of war or national emergency ⟨a synthetic resin to be used for the ~ of their gasoline supplies in the event the Germans were able to invade Britain —*Current Biog.*⟩: as **a** : destruction of property (as tools of production or materials) or deliberate slowing down of work or interference with production in any way during a labor dispute **b** : the crime in time of war or declared national emergency of willfully injuring or destroying the U.S. or any nation associated with it in preparing for or carrying on war or national defense **2** : willful effort by indirect means to hinder, prevent, undo, or discredit (as a plan or activity) : deliberate subversion ⟨~ of the project by disgruntled officials⟩; *broadly* : any act or process tending to hamper or hurt ⟨if a racing man can cruise in his boat, if the cruising bug is given a chance to bite him, his racing career is in serious danger of ~ —Peter Heaton⟩

²sabotage \"\ *vt* -ED/-ING/-S : to practice sabotage on : WRECK, DESTROY, DAMAGE ⟨in a war between rival cab companies . . . cabs are *sabotaged* and riders kidnapped —*TV Guide*⟩ ⟨had sought to ~ the meeting by sending misleading telegrams to members —*Call*⟩

sab·o·teur \R ¦sabə¦tər (+ *vowel* -¦tər-), -¦tú(ə)r; -R -¦tə, -¦tuə, + *vowel in a word following without pause* -¦tər-, -¦tə, -¦tú(ə)r, + *vowel* -¦tú *also* -¦tər\ *n* -s [F, fr. *saboter* + *-eur* -or] : one that engages in sabotage ⟨~s . . . plant bombs resembling lumps of coal in our locomotive tenders —*Combat Forces Jour.*⟩ ⟨rain, wind, and sun are not the only ~s . . . which imperil the winning of blue ribbons —D.S.Boyer⟩

sa·bo·tier \,sabə¦tyā\ *n, pl* **sabotiers** \-ā(z)\ [F, fr. MF, fr. *sabot* + *-ier* -eer] : one that makes sabots

sa·bra \'säbrə, -(,)brä\ *n* -s [NHeb *ṣābrāh*] **1** : the reddish prickly edible fruit of various cacti (genus *Opuntia*) growing on the coastal plains of Palestine; *broadly* : INDIAN FIG, PRICKLY PEAR **2** : a native-born Israeli

sabre *var of* SABER

sa·bre·tache \'sabə(r),tash, 'sab-, -taash,-taish\ *n* -s [F, fr. G *säbeltasche*, fr. *säbel* saber (fr. MHG *sabel, sebel*) + *tasche* pocket, fr. OHG *tasca* purse, fr. (assumed) VL *tasca* task, remuneration — more at SABER, TASK] : a flat leather case formerly worn suspended on the left from the saber belt by men of some cavalry units

sa·breur \sə'brər(·), sa'b-\ *n* -s [F, fr. *sabrer* to strike with a saber (fr. *sabre* saber) + *-eur* -or] **1** : one that carries a saber : CAVALRYMAN **2** : one that fences with a saber

sab·u·lous \'sabyələs\ *also* **sab·u·lose** \-,lōs\ *also* **sab·u·line** \-,līn, -lən\ *adj* [*sabulous, sabulose* fr. L *sabulosus*, fr. *sabulum* sand + *-osus* -ose; *sabuline* fr. L *sabulum* + E *-ine* — more at SAND] : SANDY, GRITTY, ARENACEOUS

sa·bur·ra \sə'bərə\ *n* -s [NL, fr. L, sand, ballast; akin to L *sabulum* sand] **1** : SORDES **2** : SAND COLIC — **sa·bur·ral** \-rəl\ *adj*

sa·bu·tan \¦säbə¦tän\ *n* -s [Tag *sabután*] : a coarse fiber or straw from a species of *Pandanus* used in making hats and mats in the Philippines

sab·zi \(,)səb'zē\ *n* -s [Hindi *sabzī*, lit., greenness, fr. Per] **1** *India* : a green vegetable **2** *India* : the larger leaves and the seed capsules of Indian hemp used for making bhang

¹sac \'sak\ *n* -s [F, lit., bag, fr. L *saccus* — more at SACK] **1** : a pouch within an animal or plant; *specif* : a soft-walled cavity usu. having a narrow opening or none at all and containing in many cases a special fluid ⟨a synovial ~⟩ ⟨a lachrymal ~⟩ **2** : SACK 5

²sac *usu cap, var of* SAUK

SAC *abbr* Strategic Air Command

sa·cae \'sā,sē, 'sä,kī\ *n pl, usu cap* [L, fr. Gk *Sakai*] : an ancient people settled in the eastern part of Iran

sa·ca·huis·te \,sakə'wistē, ,säk-\ *also* **sa·ca·huis·ta** \-stə\ *or* **sa·ca·guis·ta** \-kə'wistə\ *n* -s [AmerSp *zacahuiscle*, of AmerInd origin; akin to Nahuatl *zacatl* coarse grass] : a bear grass (*Nolina texana*) having a thick caudex and long linear leaves and used in some areas for forage though reputed to have buds and blossoms that are poisonous to livestock

sac-a-lait \'sakə,lā, ,==''=\ *n* -s [LaF *sac-à-lait*, by folk etymology (influence of F *sac* bag, F *à* to, for, and F *lait* milk) fr. Choctaw *sakli* trout] **1** : WHITE CRAPPIE **2** : WARMOUTH **3** : KILLIFISH

sac·a·line *also* **sach·a·line** \'sakələn, -,lēn\ *n* -s [irreg. fr. *Sakhalin*, island in the Sea of Okhotsk, eastern U.S.S.R.] : a coarse herb (*Polygonum sachalinense*) of Sakhalin and cultivated in the U.S. as forage and for lawn decoration

¹sa·ca·ton \'sakə,tōn\ *n* -s [AmerSp *zacatón*, fr. *zacate* coarse grass, fr. Nahuatl *zacatl*] : a coarse perennial grass (*Sporobolus wrightii*) of the southwestern U.S. useful for hay in alkaline regions

²sacaton \"\ *adj, usu cap* [*Sacaton*, town in southern Arizona] : of or belonging to a Hohokam culture in southern Arizona A.D. 900–1150 characterized by rectangular excavated floors with rounded corners, and red-on-buff pottery with intricate fabric design decoration

sacbrood \'=,=\ *n* [¹*sac* + *brood*] : a virus disease of the honeybee affecting the larvae and causing them to shrivel and become scalelike

sacc- *or* **sacci-** *or* **sacco-** *comb form* [NL, fr. L *sacc-, sacci-* bag, fr. *saccus*] : sac ⟨saccate⟩ ⟨sacciform⟩ ⟨Saccomys⟩

sac·cade \sa'käd, sə'k-\ *n* -s [F, fr. MF, fr. *saquer, sachier* to pull, draw + *-ade*] : a quick violent check of a horse by a single pull or twitch of the reins

sac·cad·ic \-dik\ *adj* [*saccade* + *-ic*] : of or relating to a sudden movement : JERKY

saccadic movement *n* : the quick movement of the eyes by which the gaze is transferred from one fixation point to another

sac·cam·mi·na \sə'kamənə, sa'k-\ *n, cap* [NL] : a genus of foraminiferans having a thick arenaceous test often in the shape of a pear, spindle, or sphere, having survived from the Ordovician to the present time, and making up with their remains various Carboniferous strata

sac·cate \'sa,kāt\ *adj* [NL *saccatus*, fr. *sacc-* + L *-atus* -ate] **1** : having the form of a sac or pouch **2** : ENCYSTED

sac·cat·ed \-ād·əd\ *adj* [*saccate* + *-ed*] : SACCATE

acchar- *or* **sacchari-** *or* **saccharo-** *comb form* [L *saccharum*, fr. Gk *sakcharon*, fr. Pali *sakkharā*, fr. Skt *śarkarā* gravel, grit, sugar — more at SUGAR] **1** : sugar ⟨saccharic⟩ ⟨sacchariferous⟩ ⟨saccharometer⟩ **2** : saccharine and ⟨saccharomucilaginous⟩

sac·cha·rase \'sakə,rās, -āz\ *n* -s [ISV *sacchar-* + *-ase*] : INVERTASE

sac·cha·rate \-,rāt, -rət\ *n* -s [*saccharic* (in *saccharic acid*) + *-ate*] **1** : a salt or ester of saccharic acid **2** : a metallic derivative of a sugar usu. with a bivalent metal (as calcium, strontium, or barium); *esp* : SUCRATE — not used systematically

sac·cha·rat·ed \-,rād·əd\ *adj* [*sacchar-* + *-ate*, v. suffix + *-ed*] : mixed or combined with sucrose

sac·char·ic \sə'karik, (')sa¦k-\ *adj* [*sacchar-* + *-ic*] : of, relating to, or obtained from saccharine substances

saccharic acid *n* **1** : a deliquescent solid dicarboxylic acid $HOOC(CHOH)_4COOH$ that is obtained by oxidation of glucose or its derivatives (as sucrose) by nitric acid and that readily undergoes inner esterification to a lactone — called also *glucaric acid* **2** : either of two dicarboxylic acids from the other hexoses having the pair of central hydroxyl groups on opposite sides of the molecule similarly to glucose ⟨manno-saccharic acid⟩ ⟨ido-saccharic acid⟩ — compare MUCIC ACID

sac·cha·ride \'sakə,rīd, -rəd\ *n* -s [ISV *sacchar-* + *-ide*] : a simple sugar, combination of sugars, or polymerized sugar : CARBOHYDRATE — see DISACCHARIDE, MONOSACCHARIDE, OLIGOSACCHARIDE, POLYSACCHARIDE, TRISACCHARIDE

sac·cha·rif·er·ous \¦sakə¦rif(ə)rəs\ *adj* [*sacchar-* + *-ferous*] : producing or containing sugar

sac·chari·fi·ca·tion \sə,karəfə'kāshən, sa,kar-, ,sakər-\ *n* -s [ISV *sacchar-* + *-fication*] : the process of saccharifying

sac·chari·fy \sə'karə,fī, sa'kar-, 'sakər-\ *vt* -ED/-ING/-ES [ISV *sacchar-* + *-fy*] : to hydrolyze (a sugar derivative or complex carbohydrate) into a simple soluble fermentable sugar (as glucose or maltose) — compare DEXTRINIZE

saccharifying enzyme *n* : AMYLASE 2 b

sac·cha·rim·e·ter \,sakə'rimad·ə(r)\ *n* [ISV *sacchar-* + *-meter*] : a device for measuring the amount of sugar in a solution; *esp* : a polarimeter particularly adapted for distinguishing different kinds of sugar in solution — compare SACCHAROMETER — **sac·chari·met·ric** \¦sakərə¦me·trik, sə¦kar-, sa¦kar-\ *or* **sac·chari·met·ri·cal** \-trəkəl\ *adj* — **sac·cha·rim·e·try** \,sakə'rimə·trē\ *n* -ES

sac·cha·rin \'sak(ə)rən\ *n* -s [ISV *sacchar-* + *-in*] : a crystalline cyclic imide $C_6H_4(CO)(SO_2)NH$ that is remarkable for its sweetness varying from 200 to 700 times that of sucrose in solutions of varying concentration, that is made usu. from the amide of *ortho*-toluenesulfonic acid, and that is used often in the form of its soluble sodium derivative as a sweetening agent (as in cases of diabetes and obesity) but that has no food value — called also *benzosulfimide, gluside*

sac·cha·rin·at·ed \-rə,nād·əd\ *adj* [*saccharine* + *-ate*, v. suffix + *-ed*] : mixed with or containing saccharine matter : SACCHARATED

sac·cha·rine \'sak(ə)rən, -kə,rēn, -kə,rīn\ *adj* [L *saccharum* sugar + E *-ine* — more at SACCHAR-] **1 a** : of, relating to, or of the nature of sugar ⟨~ taste⟩ ⟨~ fermentation⟩ **b** : yielding or containing sugar ⟨~ vegetables⟩ **2** : overly or unpleasantly sweet ⟨~ flavor⟩ **3** : unpleasantly or ingratiatingly pleasant, agreeable, gentle, or friendly ⟨a ~ smile⟩ ⟨~ poetry⟩

sac·cha·rin·ic acid \,sakə¦rinik-\ *n* [*saccharinic* ISV *saccharin* + *-ic*] : any of several polyhydroxy acids formed from sugars by alkaline treatment as though by internal oxidation and reduction so that one carbon no longer holds an oxygen and in many instances with branching of the carbon skeleton

sac·cha·rin·i·ty \,sakə'rinəd·ē\ *n* -ES : the quality or state of being saccharine : SWEETNESS

sac·cha·ro·genesis \,sakərō+\ *n* [*sacchar-* + *genesis*] : the formation of sugar esp. by saccharification

sac·cha·ro·gen·ic \,sakərō¦jenik\ *adj* [*sacchar-* + *-genic*] : producing sugar — compare DEXTRINOGENIC

¹sac·cha·roid \'sakə,rȯid\ *also* **sac·cha·roi·dal** \¦==¦rȯid°l\ *adj* [*saccharoid* ISV *sacchar-* + *-oid*; *saccharoidal* fr. *saccharoid* + *-al*] : CRYSTALLINE, GRANULAR ⟨~ stone⟩

²saccharoid \"\ *n* -s : a saccharoid substance

sac·cha·ro·lyt·ic \¦sakərō¦lid·ik\ *adj* [*sacchar-* + *-lytic*] *of a microorganism* : breaking down sugars as a source of energy in metabolism

sac·cha·rom·e·ter \,sakə'rämad·ə(r)\ *n* [*sacchar-* + *-meter*] : a device for measuring the amount of sugar in a solution: as **a** : a hydrometer with a special scale (as a Brix scale or Baumé scale) for use where the presence of other dissolved solids does not interfere **b** : a tube arranged for the collection and measurement of the gas evolved in the fermentation of sugars (as in urine) — compare SACCHARIMETER — **sac·cha·ro·met·ric** \¦sakərə¦me·trik, sə¦kar-, sa¦kar-\ *adj* — **sac·cha·rom·e·try** \,sakə'rämə·trē\ *n* -ES

sac·cha·ro·my·ces \,sakərō'mī(,)sēz\ *n, cap* [NL *Saccharomycet-, Saccharomyces*, fr. *sacchar-* + *-mycet-, -myces*] : a genus of usu. unicellular yeasts (family Saccharomycetaceae) distinguished by their sparse or absent mycelium and their facility in reproducing asexually by budding — see BREWERS' YEAST, WINE YEAST

sac·cha·ro·my·ce·ta·ce·ae \¦sakərō,mīsə'tāsē,ē\ *n pl, cap* [NL, fr. *Saccharomycet-, Saccharomyces*, type genus + *-aceae*] : a family of ascomycetous fungi (order Endomycetales) comprising the typical yeasts that form asci or reproduce by budding and that typically produce alcoholic fermentation in carbohydrate substrates — **sac·cha·ro·my·ce·ta·ceous** \¦=====¦tāshəs\ *adj*

sac·cha·ro·my·ce·ta·les \,====¦tā(,)lēz\ *n pl, cap* [NL, fr. *Saccharomycet-, Saccharomyces* + *-ales*] *in some classifications* : an order of Fungi comprising the yeasts and various chiefly parasitic molds that are now usu. included in the order Moniliales

sac·cha·ro·my·cete \¦sakərō¦mī,sēt, -,mī¦sēt\ *n* -s [ISV *saccharomycete*] : a yeast fungus — **sac·cha·ro·my·ce·tic** \-ēd·ik\ *adj*

sac·cha·rose \'sakə,rōs *also* -ōz\ *n* -s [ISV *sacchar-* + *-ose*] **1** : SUCROSE — compare SUGAR 1 **2** : any of the compound sugars including the disaccharides and trisaccharides; *esp* : DISACCHARIDE

sac·cha·rum \'sakərəm\ *n* [NL, fr. L, sugar — more at SACCHAR-] **1** *cap* : a genus of large grasses of the Old World tropics resembling reeds and having expanded panicles with very small paired spikelets intermixed with numerous silky hairs — see SUGARCANE **2** -s [L] : SUGAR: as **a** : SUCROSE **b** : INVERT SUGAR

sacci- — see SACC-

sac·ci·form \'sak(s)ə,fȯrm\ *adj* [ISV *sacc-* + *-form*] : resembling a pouch

sacco- — see SACC-

sac·co·branchiata \¦sa(,)kō+\ [NL, fr. *sacc-* + *Branchiata*] *syn of* ASCIDIACEA

sac·co·derm \'sakō,dərm\ *adj* [*sacc-* + Gk *derma* skin — more at DERM-] : having a cell wall consisting of a single piece and lacking vertical pores in the wall — used of desmids of the family Mesotaeniaceae; distinguished from *placoderm*

sac·co·la·bi·um \,sakō'lābēəm\ *n* [NL, fr. *sacc-* + *labium*] **1** *cap* : a genus of epiphytic orchids of the East Indies and the Malay archipelago having racemose flowers with a flat spreading perianth and a lip with a saccate base **2** *pl* **saccolabia** \-ēə\ *or* **saccolabiums** : any plant or flower of the genus *Saccolabium*

sac·co·my·idae \,sakō'mīə,dē\ [NL, fr. *Saccomys* + *-idae*] *syn of* HETEROMYIDAE

sac·co·my·ina \,sakō,mī'īnə, -,mē'īnə, -,mē'ēnə\ [NL, fr. *Saccomys* + *-ina*] *syn of* GEOMYOIDEA

sac·co·my·oid \¦sakō¦mī,ȯid\ *or* **sac·co·my·oi·de·an** \-ī-¦ȯidēən\ *adj* [*saccomyoid* fr. NL *Saccomyoidea*; *saccomyoidean* fr. NL *Saccomyoidea* + E *-an*] : GEOMYOID

sac·co·my·oi·dea \¦=====¦ȯidēə\ [NL, fr. *Saccomys* + *-oidea*] *syn of* GEOMYOIDEA

sac·co·mys \'sakō,mis\ [NL, fr. *sacc-* + *-mys*] *syn of* HETEROMYS

sac·co·rhi·za \,sakə'rīzə\ *n* [NL, fr. *sacc-* + *-rhiza*] **1** *cap* : a small genus of marine brown algae (family Laminariaceae) having above the holdfast a swelling that resembles a bulb and is formed by whorls of tentacular outgrowths **2** -s : SEA FURBELOW

saccos *var of* SAKKOS

sac·cu·lar \'sakyələ(r)\ *adj* [ISV *saccul-* (fr. NL *sacculus*) + *-ar*] : being like a sac

sac·cu·late \-lət, -,lāt\ *adj* [NL *sacculus* + E *-ate*] : SACCULATED

sac·cu·lat·ed \-,lād·əd\ *adj* [NL *sacculus* + E *-ate* + *-ed*] : furnished with or formed of a sac : having a series of saclike expansions

sac·cu·la·tion \,sakyə'lāshən\ *n* -s [NL *sacculus* + E *-ation*] **1** : the quality or state of being sacculated **2** : the process of developing or segmenting into sacculate structures **3** : a sac or sacculate structure; *esp* : one of a linear series of such structures ⟨intestinal ~s⟩

sac·cule \'sa(,)kyül\ *n* -s [NL *sacculus*, fr. L, small bag, fr. *saccus* bag + *-ulus* — more at SACK] : a little sac; *specif* : the smaller chamber of the membranous labyrinth of the ear — compare UTRICLE

sac·cu·li·na \,sakyə'līnə, -lēnə\ *n* [NL, fr. *sacculus* + *-ina*] **1** *cap* : a genus of parasitic barnacles (order Rhizocephala) **2** -s : any parasite of the genus *Sacculina*

sac·cu·lo·utricular \¦sakyə(,)lō+\ *adj* [*sacculo-* (fr. NL *sacculus*) + *utricular*] : UTRICULOSACCULAR

sac·cu·lus \'sakyələs\ *n, pl* **saccu·li** \-,lī, -,lē\ [NL] : SACCULE

sac·cus \'sakəs\ *n, pl* **sac·ci** \-a,kī, -a(,)kē, -ak,sī\ [NL, fr. L, bag — more at SACK] : SAC

sa·cel·lum \sə'keləm, sə'se-\ *n, pl* **sacel·la** \-lə\ [L, pagan Roman sacellum, dim. of *sacrum* sanctuary, sacred object, fr. neut. of *sacer* sacred] **1** : a small monumental chapel in a church **2** : an unroofed space in an ancient Roman building consecrated to a divinity

sac·er·do·cy \'sasə(r),dōsē, 'sakə-\ *n* -ES [L *sacerdotium*, fr. *sacerdot-, sacerdos* priest] **1** : PRIESTHOOD **2** : priestly office, character, or order

sac·er·do·tal \¦sasə(r)¦dōd·°l, ¦sakə-, -ōt°l\ *adj* [ME, fr. MF, fr. L *sacerdotalis*, fr. *sacerdot-, sacerdos* priest (fr. *sacer* sacred + *-dot-, -dos* — akin to L *facere* to make, do) + *-alis* -al — more at SACRED, DO] **1 a** : of or relating to priests or a priesthood : PRIESTLY ⟨~ literature⟩ ⟨~ vestments⟩ **b** : belonging to a priesthood ⟨a ~ teacher⟩ **2** : of, relating to, or suggesting sacerdotalism ⟨a ~ emphasis in tribal religions⟩ — **sac·er·do·tal·ly** \-ōd·°lē, -ōt°lē, -°li\ *adv*

sac·er·do·tal·ism \,===¦==,izəm\ *n* -s [ISV *sacerdotal* + *-ism*] **1** : a belief that assumes a necessity for an authorized priesthood as a mediator between men and their divine needs or aspirations or the doctrine based on such an assumption **2** : undue emphasis on the need for or the authority of a priesthood or of priests

¹sac·er·do·tal·ist \-əst\ *n* -s [*sacerdotal* + *-ist*] : one who upholds sacerdotalism

²sacerdotalist \¦==¦===\ *adj* : of or relating to sacerdotalism

sac·er·do·tal·ize \,===¦==,īz\ *vt* -ED/-ING/-S **1** : to make sacerdotal **2** : to subject to sacerdotalism

sac·er·dot·i·cal \¦==¦dōd·əkəl, -¦däd-\ *adj* [L *sacerdot-, sacerdos* priest + E *-ical*] : SACERDOTAL

sac fry *n* : YOLK FRY

sac fungus *n* [so called fr. the fact that the spores are formed in a sac] : a fungus of the class Ascomycetes : ASCOMYCETE

sachaline *var of* SACALINE

sa·chem \'sāchəm\ *n* -s [Narraganset & Pequot *sachima, sachimau*] **1** : a No. American Indian chief; *specif* : the supreme chief of a confederation among the Algonquian tribes of the north Atlantic coast **2** : the leader of a political party; *specif* : one of the 12 governors of the Tammany Society — **sa·chem·ic** \(')sā¦chemik, 'sāchəm-\ *adj*

sa·chem·ship \'sāchəm,ship\ *n* : the office or authority of a sachem

sa·cher torte \'s|äkə(r)-, 'z|\ *n, usu cap S* [G *sachertorte*, fr. *Sacher* (name of a family of 19th and 20th cent. Austrian hotel and restaurant proprietors) + G *torte*] : a torte made of butter, eggs, confectioner's sugar, toasted bread crumbs, chocolate, and spices, baked in layers, put together with apricot jam, and frosted with chocolate — compare LINZER TORTE

sa·chet \(')sa¦shā\ *n* -s [F, fr. OF, dim. of *sac* bag — more at SAC] **1** : a small bag or packet; *esp* : a small bag containing a perfumed powder that is used to scent clothes (as in drawers, closets, trunks) **2** *or* **sachet powder** : a perfumed powder that is often used in small bags

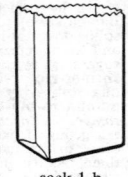

sack 1 b

¹sack \'sak\ n -s [ME sak sack, bag, sackcloth, fr. OE sacc, sæcc; akin to MD & OHG sac sack, bag, ON sekkr sack, bag, Goth sakkus sackcloth; all fr. a prehistoric Gmc word borrowed fr. L saccus sack, bag & LL saccus sackcloth; L saccus & LL saccus both fr. Gk sakkos sack, bag, sackcloth, of Sem origin; akin to Heb śaq sack, bag, sackcloth] **1 a** : a large usu. rectangular bag of coarse strong material (as canvas or burlap) used to store and ship goods (as grain, fruit, coal) **b** : a small container made of paper, plastic, or other similar material used to contain various kinds of merchandise (as foodstuffs); specif : a paper bag **c** : a canvas bag for holding mail (as parcel post or second or third class mail) — called also mail sack **2** archaic : SACKCLOTH, SACKING **3 a** : a sack with its contents **b** : the amount contained in a sack; esp : such an amount as fixed for a certain commodity (as flour, wool) and sometimes used as a unit of measure **4** : the punishment (as in ancient Rome) whereby an offender is sewn in a sack and drowned — used with the **5 a** : a woman's loose-fitting dress; specif : a gown or overdress of the late 17th and early 18th centuries often made with a Watteau back **b** : a short coat or jacket usu. loose-fitting and made in outdoor and indoor styles for women and children — see DRESSING SACK **c** : SACQUE 2 **d** : SACK COAT **6 a** : DISMISSAL — usu. used with get or give (an employee who gets the ~) **b** : REJECTION — usu. used with get or give (she gave the ~ to successive suitors) **7 a** : HAMMOCK, BUNK **b** : BED **8** : a base in the game of baseball **9** : SAC 1

²sack \"\ vt -ED/-ING/-s [ME sakken, fr. sak, n.] **1** : to put or place in a sack (as for storage or shipment) (~ potatoes in the field) (~ corn) **2** archaic : to kill (as a condemned person) by drowning within a sewn-up sack **3** : to carry off : GAIN : to make an enormous profit) — sometimes used with up **4** : to dismiss (as from employment) esp. summarily (~ a dilatory worker) syn see DISMISS — **sack the rear** : to follow a drive in logging and roll in logs that have lodged or grounded — **sack the slide** : to return to a slide logs that have jumped out

³sack \"\ n -s [modif. of MF sec dry (in vin sec dry wine), fr. L siccus; akin to OE sion, seon to strain, filter, OHG sīhan, ON sia to strain, filter, Gk hikmas moisture, Skt secate he pours] : a usu. dry white wine imported to England from the south of Europe (as from Jerez, Spain, and the Canary islands) during the 16th and 17th centuries

⁴sack \"\ n -s [MF sac, fr. OIt sacco, lit., bag, fr. L saccus — more at ¹SACK] **1** : the plundering or looting of a captured town by its conquerors (a city put to the ~) (the ~ of Rome) **2** : PLUNDER, LOOT

⁵sack \"\ vt -ED/-ING/-s **1** : to plunder (as a town) after capture **2** : to strip (as an overpowered person or unprotected building) of valuables : LOOT syn see RAVAGE

sack·age \'sakij\ n -s : the action of sacking or pillaging

sack-bearer \'₌,₌⁼\ n : any of various caterpillars that are larvae of moths of the family Mimallonidae

sack borer n : a device used in mining for sinking shafts in soft ground by boring to the full size with a very large tool resembling an auger behind the cutters of which large sacks are attached to catch material as it is removed

sack·but \'sak(,)bət\ n -s [MF saquebute, saqueboute, sackbut, hooked lance, fr. OF, hooked lance, fr. saquer, sachier to pull + bouter to push, thrust, butt — more at BUTT] **1 a** : the medieval trombone **b** : a player on such a trombone **2** [influenced in meaning by Aram śabbĕkhā trigon (in Dan 3:5)] : TRIGON

sackcloth \'₌,₌⁼\ n [ME sakcloth, fr. sak sack, bag, sackcloth + cloth] **1** : a coarse cloth made of goat hair or camel hair or of flax, hemp, or cotton and used for sacks or garments **2** : a garment of sackcloth; esp : one worn as a sign of mourning, distress, penitence, or protest — **in sackcloth and ashes** : in a spirit of sorrow, repentance, or humility (this, then, is an essay about education by a layman . . . and it is not written in sackcloth and ashes —M.B.Smith)

sack cloud n : a well-developed mammatocumulus

sack coat n : a man's single-breasted or double-breasted jacket with a straight unfitted back

¹sack·er \'sakə(r)\ n -s [¹sack + -er] : one that sacks : PILLAGER, LOOTER

²sacker \"\ n -s [²sack + -er] : one that sacks : as **a** : a device for sacking **b** : BAGGER

³sacker \"\ n -s [¹sack + -er] : a baseball player whose position in the field is one of the three bases : BASEMAN — usu. used with first, second, or third (a hard-hitting first ~)

sack·et \'sakət\ n -s [ME sakett, fr. MF saquet, sachet small bag — more at SACHET] **1** Scot : a small sack or wallet **2** Scot : a small person esp. of a rascally or stupid nature

sack·ful \'sak,fu̇l\ n, pl **sackfuls** also **sacks·ful** \-k,fu̇lz, -ks,fu̇l\ : the quantity that fills or would fill a sack

sack in vi, slang : to go to bed

¹sack·ing \'sakiŋ, -kēŋ\ n -s [fr. gerund of ⁵sack] : an act or action of plundering or vanquishing; also : decisive victory

²sacking \"\ n -s [¹sack + -ing] : material for sacks : a coarse fabric (as burlap or gunny)

sack·less \'sakləs\ adj [ME sakles, fr. OE sacleas, fr. sacu fault, conflict, action at law + -leas -less — more at SAKE] **1** obs : free from accusation : UNMOLESTED **2** archaic : INNOCENT **3** chiefly Scot **a** : WEAK, DISPIRITED **b** : HARMLESS

sack moth n : the adult of a sack-bearer

sack out vi, slang : to go to sleep

sack race n : a race run by persons each with his legs in a sack

sacks pl of SACK, pres 3d sing of SACK

sack suit n : a man's suit having a sack coat

sack-winged \'₌,wiŋd\ adj : having wings resembling or furnished with formations resembling sacks — used esp. of tropical American bats (family Emballonuridae) with a glandular pouch near the front edge of the wing

sac·like \'₌,₌⁼\ adj : having the form of or suggesting a sac

saco·glos·sa \,sakə'gläsə, ,säk-, -lòsə\ n pl, cap [NL, fr. saco- (fr. Gk sakos shield) + -glossa; akin to Skt tvak skin, hide] in some classifications : a division of Opisthobranchia including sea slugs (family Elysiidae) that are usu. placed in the suborder Nudibranchia

sacque \'sak\ n [alter. of ¹sack] **1** : SACK 5a, 5b **2** : a jacket for a small baby

sacque 2

¹sacr- or **sacro-** comb form [ME sacr-, fr. MF & L; MF, fr. L, fr. sacr-, sacer — more at SACRED] **1** : sacred : something sacred (sacral) **2** : sacred and (sacropictorial)

²sacr- or **sacro-** comb form [NL, fr. sacrum] **1** : sacrum (sacral) **2** : sacrum and (sacrococcyx) : sacral and (sacrotuberous)

sacra pl of SACRUM

sacrad \'sā,krad, 'sakrəd, 'sā,krad\ adv [²sacr- + -ad] : toward the sacrum

¹sacral \'sakrəl, 'sā-\ adj [NL sacralis, fr. ²sacr- + L -alis -al] : of, relating to, or lying near the sacrum

²sacral \"\ n : a sacral vertebra or sacral nerve

³sacral \"\ adj [ISV ¹sacr- + -al] : HOLY, SACRED (~ and secular authorities) (~ laws)

sacral canal : the part of the spinal canal lying in the sacrum

sacral index n : the ratio of the breadth of the sacrum to its length multiplied by 100

sacral·iza·tion \,sakrəli'zāshən, ,sāk-, -,lī'z-\ n -s [ISV ¹sacral + -ization] : incorporation (as of the last lumbar vertebra or any of its parts) into the sacrum; specif : a congenital anomaly in which the fifth lumbar vertebra is fused to the sacrum in varying degrees

sacral·ize \'sakrə,līz\ vt -ED/-ING/-s [³sacral + -ize] : to sanctify or make holy by means of a religious sanction (~ a crisis of life)

sacral nerve n : any of the spinal nerves of the sacral region having anterior and posterior branches that pass out through foramina in the sacrum

sacral plexus n : a nerve plexus supplying the posterior limb and pelvic region and in man being formed by the lumbosacral trunk and the first, second, and third sacral nerves

---

sacral promontory n : the inwardly projecting anterior part of the body of the first sacral vertebra

sac·ra·ment \'sakrəmənt\ n -s [ME sacrement, sacrament, fr. OF & LL; OF sacrement, sacrament, fr. LL sacramentum, fr. L, oath of allegiance, solemn obligation, sacramentum, fr. sacrare to consecrate + -mentum -ment — more at SACRED] **1** : a religious act, ceremony, or practice that is considered especially sacred as a sign or a symbol of a deeper reality; esp : one of various Christian acts, ceremonies, or practices distinguished from other Christian rites as having been instituted, observed, or recognized by Jesus Christ **2** usu cap : the Christian Eucharist, Holy Communion, or Lord's Supper; specif : the consecrated Host in Roman Catholicism **3 a** : something sacred in character or significance : a spiritual sign, seal, or bond (as a covenant held to exist between God and man) **b** : something that has the significance of a deeply religious act or observance

²sacrament \-,ment, -₌mənt — see ¹SACRAMENT\ vt -ED/-ING/-s : to make holy or sacred (~ed covenant)

¹sac·ra·men·tal \,sakrə'mentᵊl\ adj [ME, fr. LL sacramentalis, fr. sacramentum + L -alis -al] **1** : of or relating to sacred rites; specif : of or relating to the Christian sacraments or one of them (as the Eucharist) **2** : of the nature of a sacrament : characterized by or connected with belief in the sacraments (~ bread) (~ marriage) (~ doctrine) **3** : solemnly binding, bound, or motivated by or as if by a covenant (a ~ obligation) **4** : possessed of the dignity or aura of a religious rite : SACRED (an almost ~ atmosphere) **5** : of or relating to a sacramentum — **sac·ra·men·tal·ly** \-ᵊlē,-ᵊli\ adv

²sacramental \"\ n : a ceremony, action, or sacred object (as in the Roman Catholic Church) resembling or related to a sacrament (as liturgical prayers and holy water) but held to have originated in ecclesiastical custom rather than to have been instituted by Christ

sac·ra·men·ta·lia \,₌₌₌₌'men'tālyə, -₌mən-, -lēə\ n pl [LL, neut. pl. of sacramentalis] : sacramental things

sac·ra·men·tal·ism \-'mentᵊl,izəm\ n -s **1** : the doctrine and use of the sacraments; esp : the attaching of great importance to the sacraments **2** : the doctrine that sacraments are inherently efficacious and indispensable to salvation and capable of conferring grace on a recipient's soul **3** : the view that all nature and all life are full of spiritual meaning and symbolic of the unseen and eternal

sac·ra·men·tal·ist \-ᵊst\ n -s **1** : one who holds that the sacraments are inherently efficacious and capable of conferring grace on the recipient's soul **2** : one versed in or placing great emphasis upon religious ritual and the role and function of sacraments

sac·ra·men·tal·i·ty \,₌₌₌(,)men'taləd·ē, -,mən-\ n -ES : sacramental nature or quality

sacramental wine n : wine conforming to prescribed standards of the Christian church and used in its Holy Sacrament

sac·ra·men·tan \,sakrə'mentⁿ\ n -s cap [Sacramento, California + E -an] : a native or resident of Sacramento, California

¹sac·ra·men·tar·i·an \,₌₌(,)men-'terēən, -₌mən-, -ta(ə)r-\ n -s [¹sacrament + -arian] usu cap [trans. of G sakramentierer, sakramentierer] **1** : one who interprets sacraments as visible symbols that are not inherently efficacious and not supernaturally potent but of great symbolic significance **2** : SACRAMENTALIST

²sacramentarian \,₌₌(,)₌₌₌\ adj, usu cap **1** : of or relating to the Sacramentarians **2** : of or relating to the sacraments or to sacramentalism

sac·ra·men·tar·i·an·ism \-ēə,nizəm\ n -s : SACRAMENTALISM 2

¹sac·ra·men·ta·ry \,₌₌'mentərē\ n -ES usu cap [¹sacrament + -ary; trans. of G sakramenter, sakramentierer] : SACRAMENTARIAN 1

²sacramentary \,₌₌'₌₌₌\ adj [LL sacramentarius, fr. sacramentum sacrament + L -arius -ary] **1** : of or relating to a sacrament : SACRAMENTAL **2** [¹sacramentary] : SACRAMENTARIAN

³sacramentary \,₌₌'₌₌₌\ n -ES [LL sacramentarium, fr. neut. of sacramentarius, adj.] : an early service book of the Western church known in many specific forms and containing typically the celebrant's part of the mass together with prayers for baptisms, ordinations, blessings, and consecrations

sacrament chapel n : a chapel in which the Eucharistic Host is preserved

sac·ra·men·ter \,₌₌'mentə(r)\ n -s usu cap [G sakramenter, fr. sakrament sacrament (fr. MHG sacrament, fr. LL sacramentum) + -er] : SACRAMENTARIAN

sacrament house n : an ambry or tabernacle for holding the reserved Eucharist — compare PYX

sac·ra·men·tism \,₌₌'men₌izəm, -n₌tīzəm\ n -s : SACRAMENTARIANISM

sac·ra·men·tize \,₌₌'men,tīz, -n,tīz\ vt -ED/-ING/-s : to administer the sacraments

sac·ra·men·to \,sakrə'men(,)tō, -n(,)tō̇\ adj, usu cap [Sacramento, California] : of or from Sacramento, the capital of California (Sacramento schools) : of the kind or style prevalent in Sacramento

sacramento cat n, usu cap S [Sacramento river, northwest California] : HORNED POUT

sacramento perch n, usu cap S : a primitive centrarchid sunfish of the Sacramento and San Joaquin river basins that resembles a perch and is the only freshwater percoid fish native to the Pacific coast region of America

sacramento pike n, usu cap S : SQUAWFISH

sacramento salmon n, usu cap 1st S : KING SALMON

sacramento sturgeon n, usu cap 1st S : WHITE STURGEON

sacramento sucker n, usu cap 1st S : a sucker (Catostomus occidentalis) of the streams of California that reaches a length of one foot

sacraments pl of SACRAMENT, pres 3d sing of SACRAMENT

sacrament sunday n, usu cap both Ss : a Sunday of the year on which the Lord's Supper is celebrated

sac·ra·men·tum \,sakrə'mentəm\ n, pl **sacramen·ta** \-tə\ [L — more at SACRAMENT] : a deposit of money by way of pledge made by each party to a civil action and forfeited to the state by the loser

¹sa·crar·i·um \sə'kra(a)rēəm\ n, pl **sacrar·ia** \-ēə\ [ML, fr. L, pagan Roman sacrarium, fr. sacr-, sacer sacred + -arium] **1 a** : SANCTUARY 1a(2) **b** : SACRISTY **c** : PISCINA 2 **2** [L] **a** : an ancient Roman shrine or sanctuary in a temple or private house holding sacred objects : ORATORY, CHAPEL **b** : an ancient Roman building erected for the performance of religious rites by a sacred person

²sacrarium \"\ n, pl **sacraria** [NL, fr. ²sacr- + -arium] : SYNSACRUM

sacrary n -ES [ME sacrarie, fr. MF & ML & L; MF sacraire Christian sanctuary, fr. ML sacrarium, fr. L, pagan Roman sacrarium, holy place or temple in general] obs : SACRARIUM

sacrate vt -ED/-ING/-s [L sacratus, past part. of sacrare] obs : CONSECRATE — **sacration** n -s

¹sa·cred \'sākrəd\ adj [ME, fr. past part. of sacren to consecrate, fr. OF sacre, fr. L sacrare, fr. sacr-, sacer sacred, holy, cursed; akin to L sancire to make sacred, Hitt saklais rite, custom] **1** : CONSECRATED (the ~ elements of the Eucharist) **2 a** : dedicated or set apart (as to the honor or veneration of a deity, group, or person) — usu. used with to (a tree ~ to Jupiter) **b** : devoted exclusively to the service or use (as of a particular person, purpose, or group) — usu. used with to (a fund ~ to charity) (a study ~ to the chairman) **3 a** : holy or hallowed esp. by association with the divine or consecrated : worthy of religious veneration (the ~ name of Jesus) (Jerusalem's ~ soil) (a ~ memory) **b** : entitled to reverence and respect : VENERABLE (~ old age) **4** : religious in nature, association, or use : not secular or profane (~ vestments) (~ history) **5** obs : ACCURSED, CONSUMING **6** : organized around ceremonial and traditionalistic values and patterns to the exclusion of new ones (a ~ society of medieval times) — contrasted with secular

²sacred n -s obs : a sacred rite or oblation

sacred ape n : SACRED MONKEY

sacred baboon n : a baboon (Papio hamadryas) venerated by the ancient Egyptians

---

sacred bamboo n : NANDINA 2

sacred bark n **1** : CASCARA SAGRADA **2** : CASCARA BUCKTHORN

sacred bean n **1** : seed of the Indian lotus **2** : INDIAN LOTUS

sacred beetle n : the scarabaeus which was held sacred by the Egyptians

sacred book n : any book (as the Bible) regarded by a religious body as an authoritative source or divinely inspired statement of its faith, history, and practices

sacred bo tree n : PIPAL

sacred cow n [so called fr. the veneration of cows in India] : a person or thing so well established in and venerated by a society that it seems unreasonably immune from ordinary criticism even of the honest or justified kind

sacred ear or **sacred earflower** n : the fragrant spicy flower of a Mexican and Central American shrub or small tree (Cymbopetalum penduliflorum) having the shape of an ear and prized by the Aztecs for flavoring chocolate and for its supposed tonic properties

sacred fig n : PIPAL

sacred fish n : any of several fishes of the genus Mormyrus (as M. oxyrhynchus) that inhabit the river Nile and that were held in veneration by the ancient Egyptians because they were thought to have devoured a part of the body of the god Osiris

sacred girdle n : the kusti of the Parsis

sacred ibis n : an ibis (Threskiornis aethiopica) common in the Nile basin about two feet long and chiefly white and black with naked head and neck that was venerated by the ancient Egyptians

sacred lotus n : INDIAN LOTUS

sa·cred·ly adv : in a sacred manner

sacred monkey n : any of several monkeys held sacred by natives of the regions they inhabit (as the hanuman, the rhesus monkey, or the sacred baboon)

sacred mushroom n : MESCAL BUTTON

sa·cred·ness n -ES : the quality or state of being sacred

sacred order n : MAJOR ORDER — usu. used in pl.

sacred shirt n : the shirt worn by Parsis with the kusti which together serve as the distinguishing marks of a Parsi

sacred theology n : REVEALED THEOLOGY

sacred thread or **sacred cord** n : a cotton thread with which a Hindu youth of the three twice-born castes and some Sudras is invested at the ceremony of initiation (as at the age of from eight to twelve) and which is worn constantly thereafter from the left shoulder across the body to the right

sacred weed n : a vervain (Verbena officinalis)

sacred writ n, usu cap S&W : SCRIPTURE

sacrifical adj [L sacrificalis, fr. sacrificus sacrificial (fr. sacri- — fr. sacr-, sacer sacred — + -ficus -fic) + -alis -al] obs : SACRIFICIAL

sac·ri·fi·ca·tion \,sakrəfə'kāshən\ n -s [L sacrification-, sacrificatio, fr. sacrificatus (past part. of sacrificare to sacrifice) + -ion-, -io -ion] : a making of a sacrifice

sac·ri·fi·ca·tor \'₌₌₌,kād·ə(r)\ n -s [MF sacrificateur, fr. LL sacrificator, fr. L sacrificatus (past part. of sacrificare to sacrifice) + -or] : SACRIFICER; esp : PRIEST

sac·ri·fi·ca·to·ry \,sə'krifəkə,tōrē, sa'k-; 'sakrəfək-; chiefly Brit 'sakrifə,kātəri, -ā'trī\ adj [L sacrificatus (past part. of sacrificare to sacrifice, fr. sacr-, sacer sacred — + -ificare -fy) + E -ory] : of or relating to sacrifice esp. of the mass

¹sac·ri·fice \'sakrə,fīs also -fəs or -,fīz sometimes esp before pl ending -,fīs\ n -s [ME sacrifise, sacrifice, fr. OF, fr. L sacrificium, fr. sacri- (fr. sacr-, sacer sacred) + -ficium (akin to L -ficare -fy) — more at SACRED] **1** : an act or action of making an offering of animal or vegetable life, of food, drink, or incense, or of some precious object to a deity or spiritual being **b** : something consecrated and offered to God or to a divinity or an immolated victim or an offering of any kind laid on an altar or otherwise presented in the way of religious thanksgiving, atonement, or conciliation **2 a** : the crucifixion of Christ; specif : the voluntary offering by Christ of himself to reconcile God and man ★ often cap : the sacramental repetition of Jesus Christ's death on the cross held by some Christians to be Christ's repeatable offering of himself to God on behalf of men (Eastern Orthodoxy's Bloodless Sacrifice) **3 a** : destruction or surrender of something for the sake of something else : giving up of some desirable thing in behalf of a higher object **b** : something given up or lost (the ~s made by parents) **4 a** : LOSS, DEPRIVATION (the ~ of a whole regiment) (flood victims who suffered the ~ of their homes) **b** : financial loss (as incurred from selling goods marked down for immediate sale) **5** : SACRIFICE HIT

²sac·ri·fice \-,fīs also -,fīz sometimes -fəs or esp before əz & iŋ endings -,fīs\ vb -ED/-ING/-s [ME sacrifisen, sacrificen, fr. sacrifise, sacrifice, n.] vt **1** : to offer (as a sacrificial victim) as a sacrifice : make a sacrifice or religious oblation : IMMOLATE (Abraham about to ~ Isaac) **2** : to suffer loss of, give up, renounce, injure, or destroy often for an ideal or belief or for an advantageous or beneficial end (~ lives for the sake of freedom) **3** : to sell at a loss (the owner ~d his house) ~ vi **1** : to offer up or perform rites of a sacrifice **2** : to make a sacrifice hit in baseball syn see FORGO

sacrifice bunt n : SACRIFICE HIT

sacrifice fly n : a fly in baseball that enables a base runner to score after the catch and that gives the batter credit for a run batted in but is not recorded as an official time at bat

sacrifice hit n : a bunt in baseball laid down with less than two out that enables a base runner to advance a base while the batter is put out at first base and that is not recorded as an official time at bat — abbr. SH

sac·ri·fic·er \-ə(r)\ n -s : one that sacrifices; specif : a sacrificing priest

sac·ri·fi·cial \,sakrə'fishəl\ adj [L sacrificium sacrifice + E -al] **1** : of, relating to, or of the nature of, or involving sacrifice **2** : of or relating to the anodes that are consumed in preventing electrolytic corrosion of the metal protected

sac·ri·fi·cial·ly \-shəlē, -li\ adv : in a sacrificial manner

sacrificial theory n : a modern theory of the atonement derived from the New Testament epistle to the Hebrews and holding that Christ as both son of God and sinless representative of man has offered on the cross a life of perfect obedience which becomes the expiation cleansing all sin-stained souls — compare SATISFACTION THEORY

sacrificing adj : SACRIFICIAL

sac·ri·lege \'sakrəlij\ n -s [ME, fr. OF, fr. L sacrilegium, fr. sacrilegus one that steals that which is sacred, fr. sacri- (fr. sacr-, sacer sacred) + -legus (fr. legere to gather, steal) — more at SACRED, LEGEND] **1** : the crime of stealing, misusing, violating, or desecrating that which is sacred, holy, or dedicated to sacred uses **2** : the unworthy or irreverent use of sacred persons, places, or things : the profanation of that which is dedicated to God or to sacred purposes syn see PROFANATION

sac·ri·le·gious \÷'sakrə'lijəs, -lēj-\ adj [sacrilege + -ious] : committing sacrilege : characterized by or involving sacrilege : polluted with sacrilege (~ robbers) (~ acts) syn see IMPIOUS

sac·ri·le·gious·ly adv : in a sacrilegious manner

sa·cring \'sākriŋ\ n [ME sacringe, fr. gerund of sacren to consecrate — more at SACRED] : the act or action of consecrating: **a** archaic : the consecration of the eucharistic elements in the service of the mass **b** archaic : the consecration of a king or bishop) to office or orders

sacring bell n [ME sacringe bell, fr. sacringe sacring + belle bell] **1** : a small hand bell made sometimes of silver and rung at the elevation in mass **2** : the tolling of the church bell announcing the elevation

sacrist \'sakrəst, 'sā-\ n -s [ML sacrista] : SACRISTAN

sac·ris·tan \'sakrəstən\ n -s [ME, fr. ML sacristanus, fr. sacrista (fr. L sacr-, sacer sacred + -ista -ist) + L -anus -an — more at SACRED] : an officer of a church in charge of the sacristy, of the utensils or movables, and sometimes of the parish in general; also : SEXTON

sac·ris·ty \'sakrəstē, -ti\ n -ES [ML sacristia, fr. sacrista + L -ia -y] : a room in or attached to a church where the sacred utensils and vestments are kept : VESTRY

sacro- — see SACR-

sacro·coc·cyg·e·us \,sa(,)krō also 'sä(-÷\ n [NL, fr. ²sacr- + coccygeus] : either the anterior muscle or the posterior muscle extending between the sacrum and coccyx

sacro·coccyx \"+\ n [NL, fr. ²sacr- + coccyx] : the fused sacrum and coccyx

[1]sacro·iliac \ˌsakrōˈileˌak *also* ˈsāk-\ *adj* [ISV [2]*sacr-* + *iliac*] **:** of, relating to, or affecting the sacroiliac ⟨~ distress⟩

[2]sacroiliac \"\ *n* -s **:** the region of juncture of the sacrum and ilium; *also* **:** the firm fibrocartilage joint between these bones

sacro·lum·balis \ˌ==ˌləmˈbaləs, -bäl-,-bäl-\ *n* -ES [NL, fr. [2]*sacr-* + *lumbalis*, adj., lumbar, fr. *lumb-* + *L -alis* -al] **:** ILIOCOSTALIS

sac·ro·sanct \ˈsakrō saŋ(k)t, -rə,s-, -ˌsaiŋ-\ *adj* [L *sacrosanctus*, prob. fr. *sacro* by a sacred rite (abl. of *sacrum* sacred thing, sacred rite, fr. neut. of *sacer* sacred) + *sanctus* (past part. of *sancire* to make sacred) — more at SACRED] **:** most holy or sacred **:** INVIOLABLE; *also* **:** overly or unpleasantly holy or sacred

sac·ro·sanc·ti·ty \ˌ==ˈsaŋ(k)təd·ē, -ˈsaiŋ-, -tətē, -i\ *n* -ES **:** the quality or state of being sacrosanct

sacro·sciatic foramen \ˌsa|(ˌ)krō *also* ˌsā|+...-\ *n* [*sacrosciatic* prob. fr. (assumed) NL *sacrosciaticus*, fr. NL [2]*sacr-* + LL *sciaticus* sciatic] **:** SCIATIC FORAMEN

sacrosciatic notch *n* **:** SCIATIC NOTCH

sacro·spinalis \ˌsa(ˌ)krō *also* ˌsā(-+\ *n* [NL, fr. [2]*sacr-* + LL *spinalis*, adj., spinal] **:** a muscle extending the length of the back and neck consisting of many distinct parts attached to the crest of the ilium, the vertebrae, and the ribs

sacro·spinous \"+\ *adj* [[2]*sacr-* + *spinous*] **:** of or relating to a ligament on each side passing from the back of the sacrum to the spine of the ischium and converting the greater sciatic notch of the innominate bone into the greater sciatic foramen

sacro·tuberous \"+\ *adj* [[2]*sacr-* + *tuberous*] **:** of or relating to a ligament on each side passing from the back of the sacrum to the tuberosity of the ischium and converting the lesser sciatic notch of the innominate bone into the lesser sciatic foramen

sacrum \ˈsakrəm, ˈsāk-\ *n, pl* **sacra** \-rə\ [NL, fr. LL (in *os sacrum* last bone of the spine, trans. of Gk *hieron osteon*), fr. L, neut. of *sacer* sacred] **:** the part of the vertebral column that is directly connected with or forms a part of the pelvis by articulation with the ilia, that consists of a single vertebra or of several more or less consolidated, that has in the transverse processes expanded ends fused into a solid bony mass on each side, and that in man forms the dorsal wall of the pelvis and consists of five united vertebrae diminishing in size to the apex which bears the coccyx — compare SYNSACRUM

sacs *pl of* SAC

[1]sad \ˈsad, ˈsaa(ə)d\ *adj* **sadder**; **saddest** [ME, fr. OE *sæd;* akin to OHG *sat* sated, ON *sathr, saddr*, Goth *sads*, L *satur* sated, *satis* enough, Gk *haden* to satiety, enough, Skt *asinva* insatiable] **1 a** *obs* **:** SATED, SATISFIED, SURFEITED **b** *obs* (1) **:** firmly established in status or determination **:** SETTLED, FIXED ⟨settled in his face I see ~ resolution —John Milton⟩ (2) **:** capable of steadfast resistance **:** STOUT, VALIANT **c** *archaic* **:** maturely steady **:** GRAVE, SERIOUS ⟨a *sadder* and a wiser man he rose the morrow morn —S.T.Coleridge⟩ **2 a** *obs* **:** SOLID, COMPACTED **b** *dial Brit, of soil* **:** not friable **c** *chiefly Midland, of food* **:** HEAVY, SOGGY — used esp. of baked goods that do not rise **3 a :** affected with or expressive of grief or unhappiness **:** DOWNCAST, GLOOMY, MOURNFUL ⟨feeling ~ because his pet had died⟩ ⟨a ~ song about his disappointed love⟩ **b** (1) **:** causing or associated with grief or unhappiness **:** DEPRESSING ⟨heard the ~ news of their army's defeat⟩ ⟨gay clothes in ~ weather was sound sense —Audrey Barker⟩ ⟨the long ~ notes of taps —J.M.Virden⟩ (2) **:** giving occasion for regret or dismay **:** DEPLORABLE ⟨those war years were leading to a ~ relaxation of morals —C.W.Cunnington⟩ ⟨~ to say, the funds were exhausted⟩ **c :** of little worth **:** contemptibly bad **:** SORRY, POOR, INFERIOR ⟨some of these stories are good, but many are ~ drivel —Norman Douglas⟩ **4 a** *archaic* **:** DEEP, DARK ⟨a dark greenish color, growing *sadder* . . . as the plant decays, till it approaches a black —Robert Plot⟩ **b :** of a dull somber color or shade **:** DRAB ⟨~ browns and blacks⟩

[2]sad \"\ *adv, archaic* **:** SADLY ⟨so ~ forlorn —John Keats⟩

sa·dang *or* **sa'·dang** \ˈsäˌdaŋ\ *n* -s *usu cap* **1 :** an Indonesian people inhabiting the mountainous northern part of So. Celebes and sometimes considered a subdivision of the Toradja people **2 :** a member of the Sadang people

sad·den \ˈsadᵊn, ˈsaad-\ *vb* **saddened**; **saddened**; **saddening** \-d(ᵊ)niŋ\ **saddens** *vt* **:** to make sad **:** *a dial chiefly Eng* **:** to make firm, solid, or thick **b :** to make gloomy in spirits or appearance **:** DEPRESS ⟨his old age was ~*ed* by the dissoluteness of his eldest son —M.L.Bonham⟩ **c :** to make dark or dull ⟨~ cloth in dyeing⟩ ~ *vi* **1 :** to become or grow sad (as in spirits) **2 :** to make a person or thing sad

sad·den·ing·ly *adv* **:** in a saddening manner

saddhu *var of* SADHU

sad·dish \ˈsa(a)dish\ *adj* **:** somewhat sad

[1]sad·dle \ˈsadᵊl\ *n* -s [ME *sadel*, fr. OE *sadol, sadul;* akin to OHG *satul* saddle, ON *söthull;* all fr. a prehistoric Gmc word perh. borrowed fr. an eastern IE word represented by OSlav *sedlo* saddle; akin to L *sedēre* to sit — more at SIT] **1 a** (1) **:** a seat shaped to fit the inside contours of the buttocks of a rider on horseback and made of a leather-covered wooden frame that is padded to comfortably span a horse's back, raised in front and rear, provided with stirrups, and secured by a girth passing under the belly of the horse ⟨a journey of 63 miles in the ~ —*Sacramento (Calif.) Bee*⟩ ⟨few horses are worked under ~ . . . for fear they will break down —A.J.Liebling⟩ — see ENGLISH SADDLE, MCCLELLAN SADDLE, STOCK SADDLE (2) **:** a padded part of a harness centered on a horse's back, fastened with a girth, and used to keep the breeching in place and to carry guides for the reins (3) **:** an adaptation of a riding saddle — see PACKSADDLE **b :** a seat similarly designed to be straddled on a bicycle, tricycle, motorcycle, or similar vehicle — see BICYCLE illustration **c :** the part of a gymnastics side horse between the pommels **2 :** a device mounted as a support and often shaped to fit the object held: as **a :** a hollowed block of wood attached to a spar on a ship as a crutch for another spar **b :** a block over which the cables of a suspension bridge pass or to which they are anchored **c :** the part of a gun carriage that supports the trunnions **d** (1) **:** a sliding carriage for a tool or work-holding table on a machine tool (as a lathe or a milling machine) (2) **:** the part of a binder's sewing machine on which the sections of a book are spread and placed for sewing **e :** CHAIR 5a **f :** a seating for a cylindrical steam boiler **g :** the part of a partial denture that carries an artificial tooth and has connectors for adjacent teeth attached to its ends **h :** a fitting mounted on a pipe (as a gas or sewer main) for attaching a new connection (as a service line) where no branch has been provided and the main is not thick enough for direct connection **i :** a transverse log with a depression cut in it to guide logs along a skid road **j :** a fired clay support for ceramic ware during a glazing fire **3 a** (1) **:** a ridge connecting two higher elevations **:** a low point in the crest line of a ridge (2) **:** COL 2 **b :** SADDLE REEF **c :** a minor upfold along the axis of a syncline **d :** a minor downfold along the axis of an anticline **4 :** a part or marking of an animal suggesting the saddle of a horse in form or position: **a** (1) **:** HINDSADDLE ⟨a ~ of mutton⟩ (2) **:** both sides of the unsplit back of a carcass including both loins **:** the undivided loins prepared for roasting (3) **:** the lower part of the back with the hind legs of a frog **b** (1) **:** a colored marking on the back of an animal (2) **:** a portion of a suture in a cephalopod shell that forms an angle or curve whose convexity is directed toward the orifice of the shell — opposed to *lobe* (3) **:** the rear part of a male fowl's back extending to the tail and covered by long narrow feathers resembling the true hackle — see COCK illustration (4) **:** the clitellum of an earthworm (5) **:** EPHIPPIUM 2 **5 a :** CRICKET 5 **b :** the metal covering of a roll on a metal-covered roof **c** *or* **saddleback** \ˈ==ˌ=\ **:** a ridge that divides a coaling hatch of a ship so that the coal is diverted into the bunkers at each side **6 :** a two-number combination selected to appear among the numbers that will win in a lottery **7 :** a strip of thin board or metal covering the floor joint on the threshold of a door **:** SILL **8 :** a bridging piece between a pair of cylinders in a locomotive **9 :** the central part of the backbone of the binding of a book **10 a :** an ornamental piece or pair of pieces of leather extending across the instep of a shoe and often contrasting in color or design **b :** SADDLE SHOE **11 :** a canvas jacket used on turkey hens to prevent injury during treading **12 :** a folded paper attached over a bag closure to label or strengthen (as for hanging on display) — called also *header* — **in the saddle** *adv (or adj)* **1 :** in a position to dictate **:** in control ⟨back *in the saddle* as chairman of the board —Bennett Cerf⟩ **2 :** on top in the act of coitus

[2]saddle \"\ *vb* **saddled**; **saddled**; **saddling** \-d(ᵊ)liŋ\ **saddles** [ME *sadelen, sadlen*, fr. OE *sadelian;* akin to OHG *gisatilen* to saddle, ON *söthla;* denominative fr. the root of OE *sadol* saddle] *vt* **1 :** to put a saddle upon ⟨*saddled* their horses and mounted and rode up to the door —Irving Bacheller⟩ — often used with *up* **2 a :** to place under a burden or encumbrance **:** weigh down with an onerous responsibility or restriction — usu. used with *with* ⟨finds himself *saddled* with a woman he does not want —Vernon Jarratt⟩ ⟨the taxpayers of the nation would be *saddled* with the tremendous burden of the additional costs —*U. S. Code*⟩ ⟨*saddling* the nation with restrictive laws —*New Republic*⟩ **b :** to place (an onerous responsibility, restriction, or reputation) on a person or group — usu. used with *on* ⟨the military attempt to ~ on labor the responsibility for shortages —*Atlantic*⟩ ⟨~ tighter government and military control on the nation —Lindesay Parrott⟩ **3 :** to put in place, support, join, or shape by or as if by means of a saddle **4 :** to put on like a saddle **:** to cause to straddle ⟨barn swallows which . . . *saddled* their nest in the loop of a rope —John Burroughs⟩ ⟨~ the stag's carcass on a pony⟩ **5 :** to send (a horse that one has trained) into a race ⟨the trainer who has *saddled* the greatest number of winners —Harry Disston⟩ ~ *vi* **1 :** to mount a saddled horse **2 :** to put a saddle on an animal ⟨had to ~ for him the first few times⟩ — often used with *up* **syn** see BURDEN

[3]saddle \"\ *adj* [[1]*saddle*] **1 a :** of or attached to a saddle ⟨a ~ holster⟩ **b :** designed for use while riding horseback ⟨a ~ coat⟩ ⟨a ~ rifle⟩ **2 :** ridden with or suitable for riding with a saddle ⟨a ~ pony⟩ ⟨bareback bronc riding and ~ bronc riding⟩ **3 :** caused by riding or by being under a saddle ⟨~ soreness⟩ ⟨a ~ irritation⟩ **4 :** resembling a saddle in shape or position ⟨~ fuel tanks⟩ **5 a :** riding horseback **:** MOUNTED ⟨a ~ preacher⟩ **b :** of or relating to horsemanship with a saddle horse ⟨won the five-gaited ~ championship⟩

[1]saddleback \ˈ==ˌ=\ *n* [[1]*saddle* + *back*] **1 :** something saddle-backed in outline: as **a** (1) **:** SADDLE ROOF (2) **:** a coping with a slope on the two sides **b :** a hill or ridge having a concave outline at the top **c :** SADDLE OYSTER **d :** two supporting members (as of timber) placed in the form of an inverted V **2 :** an animal having a marking on the back suggesting a saddle: as **a :** the male harp seal **b :** BLACK-BACKED GULL **c :** HOODED CROW **d :** a passerine bird (*Philesturnus carunculatus*) native to New Zealand that is related to the huia and when mature has black plumage with a chestnut-colored band on the back and wings **e** *usu cap* **:** an animal of either of two British breeds (Essex Saddleback and Wessex Saddleback) of medium-sized black swine distinguished by a white band crossing the back at the shoulder and descending on to each forefoot **3** *Brit* **:** a size of wrapping paper measuring 45 by 36 inches

[2]saddleback \"\ *adj* **:** SADDLE-BACKED

saddleback caterpillar *n* **:** a caterpillar that is the larva of a cup moth (*Sibine stimulea*), has urticating hairs and usu. a green and brown saddle-shaped mark on the back, and feeds on cherry and oak in the southeastern U.S.

saddle–backed \ˈ==ˌ=\ *adj* **1 :** having the outline of the upper part concave **b :** having an upper outline in the form of an arch or an inverted V **2** *of a horse* **:** having a depression behind the withers **3 :** having a marking that suggests a saddle

saddle–backed jackal *n* **:** BLACK-BACKED JACKAL

saddleback roof *n* **:** SADDLE ROOF

saddleback stitch *n* **:** SADDLE STITCH

[1]saddlebag \ˈ==ˌ=\ *n* [[1]*saddle* + *bag*] **1 a :** a large bag or pouch of leather or a textile fabric carried hanging from one side of a saddle and commonly one of a pair united by a band or strap and so hung that the weight is evenly distributed **b :** one of a pair of similar pouches carried one on each side of the rear wheel of a bicycle or motorcycle **2 :** an upholstering cloth imitating the hand-knotted texture of oriental saddlebags and popular in the late Victorian period **3** *or* **saddlebag house :** a double cabin with two units separated by several feet but covered by one roof

[2]saddlebag \"\ *vi* **:** to catch on an obstruction and swing around it ⟨a barge that *saddlebagged* on a bridge pier⟩

saddle bar *n* **1 :** one of the slender horizontal iron bars to which the lead panels of a glazed window are secured **2 :** a side bar of the tree of a saddle connecting the pommel and cantle on each side

saddle–bill \ˈ==ˌ=\ *or* **saddle–billed stork** \ˈ==ˌ=-\ *n* **:** a large black-and-white West African stork (*Ephippiorhynchus senegalensis*) having the bill red with a black median band — called also *jabiru*

saddle blanket *n* **:** a blanket folded beneath a saddle to prevent galling the horse

saddle block anesthesia *or* **saddle block** *n* **:** spinal anesthesia confined to the perineal area

saddle board *n* **:** a strip of wood or metal covering the ridge of a roof

saddle boiler *n* **:** a boiler with an arched base serving as a flue

saddlebow \ˈ==ˌ=\ *n* [ME *sadelbowe*, fr. OE *sadulboga*, fr. *sadol, sadul* saddle + *boga* bow] **:** the arch in the front or the pieces forming the front of a saddle

saddle brown *n* **:** SADDLE TAN

saddle–check chair *n* **:** an English wing chair of the 18th century

saddlecloth \ˈ==ˌ=\ *n* [ME *sadylclow*, fr. *sadyl, sadel* saddle + *clow, cloth* cloth] **1 :** a cloth formerly placed under a saddle and extending out behind; *also* **:** HOUSING **2 :** a cloth bearing a racehorse's number and placed over the saddle

saddled *past of* SADDLE

saddle embolus *n* **:** an embolus that straddles the branching of an artery blocking both branches — called also *rider embolus*

saddle flange *n* **:** a pipe flange curved to fit snugly against a cylindrical pipe or tank and used esp. to repair a leak

saddle fungus *n* **:** a fungus of the genus *Helvella* having a saddle-shaped fruiting body

saddle graft *n* **:** a plant graft made by fitting a deep cleft in the end of the scion over a wedge in the end of a stock of similar diameter so that the two cambiums are in contact — see GRAFT illustration

saddle gun *n* **:** a light hand-operated dusting machine designed to be carried on the back of a mule or horse

saddle head *n* **:** a head with a depressed or sunken crown caused by premature closure of the sphenoparietal suture

saddle horn *n* **:** the hornlike prolongation of the pommel of a stock saddle which is usu. made of leather-covered metal and to which the rope or lasso of a cowhand is commonly made fast

saddle horse *n* **1 :** a horse suited for or trained for riding typically with a strong back, well-rounded body with long sloping pasterns and shoulders, a stylish carriage, and several gaits (as the walk, trot, and canter); *specif* **:** AMERICAN SADDLE HORSE — compare HARNESS HORSE, HUNTER, JUMPER **2** *dial* **:** LEAD HORSE

saddle iron *n* **:** a strip of iron used to brace the open bottom of a stage flat (as for a door, arch, or fireplace)

saddle joint *n* **1 :** a joint formed in sheet-metal roofing by bending up the edge of a sheet and folding it downward over the turned-up edge of the next sheet **2 :** a joint in a weathered course of masonry (as a coping or sill) between adjoining stones whose ends are cut higher than the surface of the weathering between **3 :** a joint (as the carpometacarpal of the thumb) with saddle-shaped articular surfaces that are convex in one direction and concave in another and that permit movements in all directions except axial rotation

saddle key *n* **:** a key for securing a member to a machine shaft that fits into a keyway in the secured member and is concave to grip the shaft by friction — compare FLAT KEY, SUNK KEY

saddleleaf \ˈ==ˌ=\ *n* **:** TULIP TREE 1

saddle leather *n* **1 :** vegetable tanned cattlehide usu. tan in color for saddlery **2 :** cattlehide leather for handbags and fancy leather goods colored and finished to resemble saddle leather

sad·dle·less \ˈsadᵊl(l)ᵊs\ *adj* [ME *sadulles*, fr. *sadul, sadel* saddle + *-les* -less] **:** having no saddle

saddlelike \ˈ==ˌ=\ *adj* **:** resembling or suggesting a saddle (as in shape)

saddlemaker \ˈ==ˌ==\ *n* [ME *sadlemaker*, fr. *sadle, sadel* saddle + *maker*] **:** SADDLER 1

saddlenose \ˈ==ˌ=\ *n* **:** a nose marked by depression of the bridge resulting from injury or disease

saddle–notched joint \ˈ==ˌ=-\ *n* **:** a joint made for the overlapping of round logs in log construction by scooped depressions in the members

saddle oyster *n* **1 :** a windowpane oyster (*Placuna sella*) of the Indian and Pacific oceans having a broad arch like a saddle **2 :** a mollusk of *Anomia* or a related genus

saddle pile *n* **:** a sheet pile driven into the ground and made concave on the top edge to support a sewer pipe or the like in soft ground

saddle point *n* **1 :** a point on a curved surface at which the curvatures in two mutually perpendicular planes are of opposite signs — compare ANTICLASTIC **2 :** a value of a function of two variables which is a maximum with respect to one and a minimum with respect to the other

saddle quern *n* **:** METATE

sad·dler \ˈsadlə(r)\ *n* -s [ME *sadelere*, fr. *sadel* saddle + *-ere* -er] **1 :** one that makes, repairs, or sells saddles and other furnishings for saddle horses **2 :** SADDLE HORSE 1 **3 :** the male harp seal **4** [[2]*saddle* + *-er*] **:** one that saddles

saddle reef *n* **:** one of a nearly vertical succession of saddle-shaped ore deposits straddling anticlinal or synclinal folds

saddle rock \ˈ==ˌ=\ *n* [perh. fr. *Saddle Rock*, rock in Little Neck Bay, Long Island, N.Y.] *Northeast* **:** a large prime oyster

saddle roof *n* **:** a roof (as of a tower) having two gables and one ridge — called also *saddleback, saddleback roof*

sad·dlery \ˈsadlərē, -dᵊlrē, -ri\ *n* -ES **1 :** the skill or employment of a saddler **2 :** saddles and other furnishings for saddle horses **:** TACK **3 :** a place where saddlery is sold or stored

saddles *pl of* SADDLE, *pres 3d sing of* SADDLE

saddle seam *n* **:** a seam used esp. in shoes that is made by sewing together the edges of two pieces of leather placed with their inner sides facing and then opening them out so that the cut edges and stitching show

saddle seat *n* **:** a slightly concave chair seat (as of a Windsor chair) with sometimes a thickened ridge at the center front

saddle–sew \ˈ==ˌ=\ *vt* **:** to fasten together the leaves of (as a book) by a method resembling saddle stitching but using thread instead of wire

saddle–shaped \ˈ==ˌ=\ *adj* **1 :** bent down at the sides so as to give the upper part a rounded form **2 :** having the form of an anticlinal fold

saddle shell *n* **:** JINGLE SHELL

saddle shoe *or* **saddle oxford** *n* **:** an oxford-style shoe having a saddle of a color or leather contrasting with that of the rest of the shoe

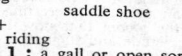

saddle shoe

saddle skirt *n* **:** the part of a saddle extending down on the flank of a horse — usu. used in pl.

saddle soap *n* **:** a mild soap made with some added unsaponified oil and used in the form of an aqueous paste or bar for cleansing and conditioning leather

saddlesore \ˈ==ˌ=\ *adj* [[1]*saddle* + *sore*, adj.] **:** sore and stiffened from riding

saddle sore *n* [[1]*saddle* + *sore*, n.] **1 :** a gall or open sore developing on the back of a horse at points of pressure from an ill-fitting or improperly adjusted saddle **2 :** an irritation or sore on parts of the rider chafed by the saddle

[1]saddle stitch *n* **1 :** a stitch made by placing the center of the fold (as of a magazine or pamphlet) across the saddle of the stitcher and driving wire staples through and clinching them on the inside — called also *saddleback stitch, saddle-wire stitch* **2 :** an even or uneven running stitch usu. set in from an edge that is used as a decorative trimming on clothing and leather articles

[2]saddle stitch *vt* **:** to secure (as a magazine or pamphlet) with a saddle stitch

saddle stone *n* **:** APEX STONE

saddle tan *n* **:** a moderate brown that is redder, lighter, and stronger than coffee, lighter, stronger, and slightly yellower than chestnut brown, and yellower, lighter, and stronger than auburn

saddle tank *n* **:** a water tank straddling the boiler of a locomotive (as a small switch engine) and designed to increase the weight on the drivers

sad·dle·tree \ˈsadᵊl·(ˌ)trē, -ˌtri\ *n* [ME *sadeltre*, fr. *sadel* saddle + *tre, tree* tree] **1 :** the frame of a saddle **2** [[1]*saddle* + *tree;* fr. the shape of the leaves] **:** TULIP TREE 1

saddle–wire \ˈ==ˌ=\ *vt* **:** to secure (as a magazine or pamphlet) with a saddle stitch

saddle–wire stitch *n* **:** SADDLE STITCH 1

saddling *pres part of* SADDLE

sad·du·ca·ic \ˌsajəˈkāik, ˌsadyə-, -əˈsā-\ *adj, usu cap* [*sadducee* + *-aic* (as in *pharisaic*)] **:** SADDUCEAN

sad·du·ce·an *or* **sad·du·cae·an** \ˌ==ˈsēən\ *adj, usu cap* [LL *sadducaeus* Sadducee + E *-an*] **:** of, relating to, or characteristic of the Sadducees ⟨the *Sadducean* party⟩ ⟨*Sadducean* materialism⟩

sad·du·cee \ˈ==ˌsē\ *n* -s [ME *saducee*, fr. OE *sadduce*, fr. LL *sadducaeus*, fr. Gk *saddoukaios*, fr. LHeb *ṣāddūqī*, prob. fr. *Ṣadoq* Zadok, high priest of Israel during the reign of King David and supposed founder of the sect] **1** *usu cap* **:** a member of a party or sect among the Jews from the 2d century B.C. to the latter part of the 1st century A.D. consisting largely of the priestly aristocracy, opposing politically and doctrinally the Pharisees, interpreting the law more literally and less strictly than the Pharisees, rejecting the authority of the other parts of Scripture and the rabbinic tradition, and denying the resurrection, personal immortality, retribution in a future life, and the existence of angels, spirits, and demons **2** *often cap* **:** one who denies immortality and tends to materialism or religious indifferentism

sad·du·cee·ism \-ēˌizəm\ *n* -s *usu cap* **:** the tenets, disposition, or point of view of the Sadducees

sade \ˈsād\ *vb* -ED/-ING/-S [ME *saden, sadden* to weary, become weary or satiated, fr. OE *sadian* to satiate, become weary or satiated; akin to OHG *satōn* to become satiated; denominative fr. the root of E [1]*sad*] *dial Eng* **:** WEARY

sa·dha·na \ˈsädənə\ *n* -s [Skt *sādhana;* akin to Skt *sādhu* going straight to a goal] **1 :** Hindu religious training or discipline through which an individual attains samadhi **2 :** Hindu or Buddhist spiritual training through which an individual worships a formed image as a mediate step to the worship of a formless deity or principle **3 :** the tantric evocation of a deity by means of spells and ritual for the purpose of getting control of the deity

sa·dhe *also* **sa·de** \ˈsä(ˌ)de, -)dē\ *n* -s [Heb *ṣādhē*] **1 :** the eighteenth letter of the Hebrew alphabet — symbol צ or ץ; see ALPHABET table **2 :** the letter of the Phoenician or of any of various other Semitic alphabets corresponding to Hebrew sadhe

sa·dhu *or* **sad·dhu** \ˈsä(ˌ)dü\ *n* -s [Skt *sādhu*, fr. *sādhu*, adj., straight, going straight to a goal, good; akin to Gk *ithys* straight, direct — more at ATHROGENIC] **:** a Hindu mendicant ascetic claiming great mystic powers, wearing a saffron robe or abjuring all clothing, and often practicing extreme mortification (as burying oneself alive) **:** holy man

sadic \ˈsādik, ˈsad-, -dēk *sometimes* ˈsäd- *or* ˈsȧd-\ *adj* [F *sadique*, fr. Comte de *Sade* + F *-ique* -ic] **:** SADISTIC

sad·iron \ˈsaˌdī(ə)rn, -īən\ *n* [[1]*sad* + *iron;* fr. its heaviness and solidity in contrast with a box iron] **:** a flatiron pointed at both ends and having a removable handle

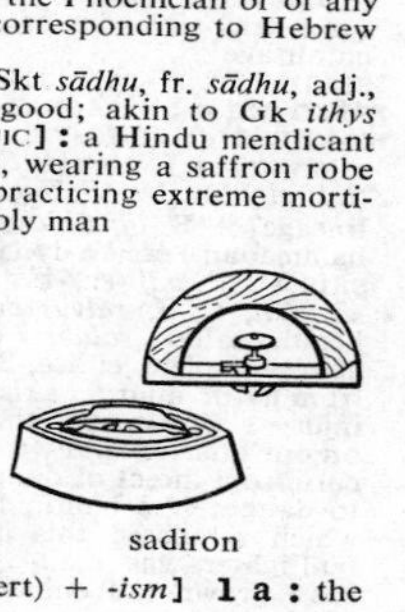
sadiron

sadism \ˈsāˌdizəm, ˈsaˌd- *sometimes* ˈsäˌd- *or* ˈsȧˌd-\ *n* -s [ISV *sad-* (fr. Comte Donatien Alphonse François de *Sade* †1814 Fr. soldier and pervert) + *-ism*] **1 a :** the

infliction of pain upon a love object as a means of obtaining sexual release — compare MASOCHISM **b :** the satisfaction of outwardly directed destructive impulses as a source of libidinal gratification **2 a :** delight in physical or mental cruelty **b :** excessive cruelty

sadist \ˈ-dəst\ *n* -S [ISV *sad-* (fr. Comte de *Sade*) + *-ist*] **:** one who makes a practice of sadism **:** a sadistic person

sa·dis·tic \səˈdistik, -tēk *also* säˈd- *or* saˈd- *sometimes* säˈd- *or* sāˈd-\ *adj* **:** of or characterized by sadism ⟨homosexual practices accompanied by strong ~ and masochistic fantasies —Charles Anderson⟩ ⟨a leg . . . sawed off in sections by a ~ surgeon —*New Yorker*⟩ — **sa·dis·ti·cal·ly** \-tək(ə)lē, -tēk-, -li\ *adv*

¹sad·ly \ˈsadlē, ˈsaad-, -li\ *adv* [ME, fr. ¹*sad* + *-ly*] **:** in a sad manner or way: **a** *obs* **:** in earnest **:** SERIOUSLY, GRAVELY, SOBERLY **b :** with sorrow or so as to cause sorrow **:** SORROWFULLY ⟨stood ~ beside the grave⟩ **c :** BADLY, DEPLORABLY ⟨a sedan . . . one of whose fenders is ~ banged up —*New Yorker*⟩

²sadly \"\ *adj, dial Eng* **:** suffering from poor health **:** POORLY ⟨the master's well . . . but the missus is very ~ —Samuel Butler †1902⟩

sad·ness *n* -ES [ME *sadnesse* seriousness, firmness, fr. ¹*sad* + *-nesse* -ness] **1 :** the quality or state of being sad **:** SORROWFULNESS, UNHAPPINESS, GLOOMINESS **2 :** an instance (as a mood or an appearance) of being sad **:** something sorrowful, gloomy, or depressing ⟨she talked about death as she spoke . . . of any of the ~*es* of nature —Willa Cather⟩

syn DEPRESSION, MELANCHOLY, MELANCHOLIA, DEJECTION, GLOOM, BLUES, DUMPS: SADNESS is a general term usu. without implications about cause or intensity of unhappy feeling ⟨conscious of a profound *sadness* which was not grief —Arnold Bennett⟩ ⟨a certain sense of desolation and *sadness* —A.C.Benson⟩ DEPRESSION may indicate a brooding, listless, sullen, or despondent condition in which one usu. feels let down, disheartened, enervated, or inadequate ⟨never before, in any mood of *depression*, had she given evidence of suicidal thoughts —Havelock Ellis⟩ ⟨many youngsters are conscious of a vast *depression* when entering the portals of a university; they feel themselves inadequate to cope with the wisdom of the ages garnered in the solid walls —G.D.Brown⟩ MELANCHOLY now is likely to indicate a mood or mental condition marked by sad and serious pensiveness ⟨the wit, the gaiety of spirit tinged with a tender *melancholy* —W.H.Hudson †1922⟩ MELANCHOLIA may indicate a settled deep depression verging on insanity ⟨the excited phase is called mania and its counterpart is known as *melancholia*. In the former there is a slaphappy hilarity and a disregard of the conventional restraints, while the latter phase is marked by mournful and self-accusatory ideas and a countenance disfigured by despair —R.S.Ellery⟩ DEJECTION is close to DEPRESSION but may apply to a more temporary mood and suggest a natural cause or logical reason ⟨it was the last of the regiment's stay in Meryton, and all the young ladies in the neighborhood were drooping apace. The *dejection* was almost universal —Jane Austen⟩ ⟨these notable victories of the mind, from which so much was hoped, have had for result not so much increased happiness as disquiet, have made for *dejection* rather than rejoicing —W.M.Dixon⟩ GLOOM may suggest the dark and dispiriting overall atmosphere or effect of depression or dejection ⟨the leaden *gloom* of one who has lost all that can make life interesting, or even tolerable —Thomas Hardy⟩ ⟨the *gloom* that now lay over it in a dead and menacing quietude and stagnation —Walter de la Mare⟩ BLUES simply indicates low spirits ⟨suffering from a sharp attack of the *blues*. A feeling of depression and foreboding had taken possession of him. The present seemed empty and futile, the future dark with intangible calamity —F.W.Crofts⟩ DUMPS, now usu. used only in the phrase *in the dumps*, may indicate a deeper, more sullen and cheerless state than that indicated by BLUES ⟨in the *dumps* about his stock market losses⟩

sa·do \ˈsäˌdō, ˈsä(ˌ)dō\ *n* -S [Malay, modif. of F *dos-à-dos*] **:** a Javanese carriage like the dos-à-dos

sado·masochism \ˌsā(ˌ)dō, ˌsa(-, ˌsä(-, ˌsā(-+\ *n* [ISV *sadism* + *-o-* + *masochism*] **:** the derivation of pleasure from the infliction of physical or mental pain either on others or on oneself **:** sadism and masochism conceived as two aspects of an underlying destructive tendency

sado·masochist \"+\ *n* **:** one that is given to sadomasochism — **sado·masochistic** \"+\ *adj*

sad sack *n* **1 :** a meek inept unmilitary serviceman who blunders his way resignedly finding the odds always against him in military life **2 :** a hopelessly inept person **:** a ludicrous misfit

sadware \ˈ=,=\ *n* [¹*sad* + *ware;* fr. its heaviness and solidity] **1 :** flat and usu. cold-pressed or hammered pieces (as plates) of fine pewter as distinguished from vessels (as mugs or measures) **2 :** LEY PEWTER

sae \(ˈ)sā\ *chiefly Scot var of* SO

SAE *abbr* **1** *often not cap* self-addressed envelope **2** standard average European

sae·beins \(ˈ)sāˌbēnz, -binz\ *conj* [by alter.] *Scot* **:** so being

saecular *var of* SECULAR

saec·u·lum \ˈsekyələm\ *n, pl* **saecu·la** \-lə\ [L, breed, generation, age — more at SECULAR] **:** a period of long duration **:** AGE

saeng·er·bund *or* **säng·er·bund** \ˈzeŋə(r),bu̇nt, ˈse-\ *n* [G *sängerbund*, fr. *sänger* singer (fr. MHG *senger*) + *bund* association, club — more at MINNESINGER, BUND] **:** a German choral society; *specif* **:** a choral society having as members chiefly persons of German descent

saeng·er·fest *or* **säng·er·fest** \-ˌfest\ *n* -S [G *sängerfest*, fr. *sänger* singer + *fest* festival — more at -FEST] **:** a singing festival of a saengerbund

saennegrass *var of* SENNEGRASS

sae number \ˌe,sā'ē-\ *n, usu cap S&A&E* [Society of *A*utomotive *E*ngineers] **:** a number in a standard series from 10 to 70 for grading lubricating oil as to viscosity ⟨the higher the *SAE number* the greater the viscosity⟩

sa·eta \säˈäd·ə\ *n* -S [Sp, lit., arrow, fr. L *sagitta*] **:** an unaccompanied partly improvised piercing Andalusian song of lamentation or penitence sung during the religious procession on Good Friday

sae·ter *also* **se·ter** \ˈsed·ə(r), ˈsād-\ *n* -S [Norw *seter, sæter*, fr. ON *setr, sætr;* akin to ON *sitja* to sit — more at SIT] **1 :** a pasture high in the mountains of Norway or northern Sweden where herds are kept in summer and butter and cheese are made **2 :** a hut built on a saeter as a shelter for the dairymaids and equipment

saf *abbr* safety

SAF *abbr* strategic air force

sa·far \səˈfär\ *n* -S *usu cap* [Ar *ṣafar*] **:** the second month of the Muhammadan year — see MONTH table

¹sa·fa·ri \səˈfärē, -ˈfār-, -ri *also* -ˈfar-\ *n* -S [Swahili, trip, journey, fr. Ar *safarīya*] **1 :** the caravan of a hunting or other expedition esp. in East Africa with men, vehicles, animals, and equipment **2 a :** a hunting or other expedition in East Africa esp. on foot **b :** an adventurous expedition elsewhere in the world ⟨arctic ~⟩ **c :** a long carefully planned trip (as a campaign tour or a legislative junket) usu. with a large entourage

²safari \"\ *vi* -ED/-ING/-S **:** to journey in a safari

safari ant *n* **:** FORAGING ANT

sa·fa·wid *or* **sa·fa·vid** \səˈfäˌwēd\ *also* **sa·fa·vi** \-ä(ˌ)wē\ *n* -S *usu cap* [*Safawid*, fr. Ar *ṣafawīy* descended from *Ṣafī-al-Dīn* (fr. *Ṣafī-al-Dīn* †1334 Persian saint of Arab lineage) + E *-id; Safavi* fr. Ar *ṣafawīy*] **:** a member of a Muhammadan Persian dynasty founded in 1502 by Shah Ismail

¹safe \ˈsāf\ *adj* -ER/-EST [ME *sauf, saf, save*, fr. OF *sauf, saf, sal*, fr. L *salvus* safe, whole, healthy; akin to L *salus* health, safety, *salubris* healthful, salutary, *solidus* solid, Gk *holos* complete, entire, Skt *sarva* unharmed, entire] **1 :** freed from harm, injury, or risk **:** no longer threatened by danger or injury **:** UNHARMED, UNHURT ⟨the rocks were to windward on our quarter, and we were ~ —Frederick Marryat⟩ **2 :** secure from threat of danger, harm, or loss: as **a :** not exposed to danger ⟨the bullfighters had been developing a technique which simulated this appearance of danger . . . while the bullfighter was really ~ —Ernest Hemingway⟩ ⟨the trees have grown tall enough to be ~ from trampling —*Amer. Guide Series: La.*⟩ **b (1) :** successful in reaching base ⟨the batter was ~ at first on a close play⟩ **(2) :** enabling a batter in baseball to reach base ⟨a ~ hit to deep short⟩ **c :** secure from loss to the opposition in an election ⟨if a poll shows that a state or district is ~, there may be no reason for spending money . . . for . . . party propaganda —D.D.McKean⟩ **d :** not liable to decipherment ⟨a ~ code⟩ **3 :** affording protection from danger **:** securing from harm ⟨a ~ margin of national revenue must be kept for possible defense needs —*Current Biog.*⟩ ⟨a ~ haven⟩ **4** *obs, of mental or moral faculties* **:** HEALTHY, SOUND ⟨are his wits ~ —Shak.⟩ **5 a (1) :** not threatening danger **:** HARMLESS ⟨other animals . . . instinctively realize when a party of lions may be regarded as ~ —James Stevenson-Hamilton⟩ **(2)** *archaic* **:** made incapable of doing harm (as by being placed in confinement or under custody) **b :** unlikely to produce controversy or contradiction ⟨the ~, sane, and sanitary cliché —S.H.Adams⟩ ⟨it is *safer* to generalize about institutions than individuals —Harry Levin⟩ **c :** free from contaminating qualities **:** not liable to corrupt or injure ⟨a ~ vaccine⟩ ⟨a ~ book for young people⟩ **d** *of a part of a file* **:** left without teeth so that only one surface of an object is cut when filing near a corner or in a narrow slot **6 a :** not liable to take risks **:** CAUTIOUS ⟨the ~ man usually has been preferred to the audacious —C.E.Silcox⟩ **b :** of known and reliable opinions and actions ⟨a ~ man, unlikely to give trouble —Osbert Sitwell⟩

syn SECURE: SAFE can imply that one has run a risk without incurring harm or damage ⟨to arrive home *safe* after a rough trip⟩ ⟨to see the children *safe* in bed⟩ or can apply to persons or possessions whose situation or position involves no risk ⟨a *safe* place to live⟩ ⟨remain *safe* in an air raid shelter all night⟩, or to such things as bridges, vehicles, or policies so designed or constructed that they expose one to no risk ⟨a bridge not *safe* for heavy trucks⟩ ⟨a *safe* political position⟩ SECURE, sometimes interchangeable with SAFE, usu. implies freedom from anxiety or apprehension of danger and often freedom from all hazards, or it can apply to something conducive to such a frame of mind or such freedom ⟨feel *secure* only among close friends⟩ ⟨a *secure* harbor⟩ ⟨a good bank account often can help make one *secure*⟩ ⟨make your investments *secure*⟩ ⟨a *secure* place for himself in the academic world⟩

²safe \"\ *n* -S [ME *saue*, fr. *sauf, saf*, adj.] **1 :** a place or receptacle to keep articles safe: as **a :** a ventilated or refrigerated chest or closet for securing provisions from pests and the effects of weather **b :** a metal box or chest sometimes built into a wall or vault to protect money or other valuables against fire or burglary **2 :** a tray under a fixture (as a bath or roof tank) to catch drippings or overflow **3 :** CONDOM

safe 1 b

³safe \"\ *adv* -ER/-EST [¹*safe*] **:** SAFELY, SECURELY ⟨play ~⟩ ⟨hit ~⟩ ⟨land me ~ on Canaan's side —William Williams †1791⟩ — often used in combination ⟨*safe*-hidden⟩ ⟨*safe*-moored⟩

⁴safe *vt* -ED/-ING/-S [¹*safe*] *obs* **:** to make safe

safe \ˈsāf\ *Scot var of* SAVE

safe–conduct \ˈ=ˈ=(ˌ)=\ *n* [ME *sauf conduit, saf conduit*, fr. OF *sauf conduit*, fr. *sauf* safe + *conduit* conduct — more at SAFE, CONDUCT] **1 :** a privilege granted by a military or other authority to an enemy, neutral, or other person not otherwise protected to move within or through or perform specified activities within a designated area **2 :** a document similar to a passport authorizing safe-conduct

safecracker \ˈ=,==\ *n* **:** one that breaks open safes to steal

safecracking \ˈ=,==\ *n* **:** the act or process of breaking into a safe esp. by explosives to burglarize it

safe–deposit \ˈ==ˌ==\ *adj* **:** of, providing, or constituting a box or vault for the storage of valuables in safety

safe edge *n* **:** a smooth uncut edge on a file or rasp

safe–edge file *n* **:** a file that is left uncut on at least one edge and used for filing near a corner so as not to cut the surface at right angles

¹safeguard \ˈ=,=\ *n* [ME *saufgarde*, fr. MF *salvegarde, saufegarde*, fr. OF, fr. *salve, sauve* (fem. of *salf, sauf* safe) + *garde* guard — more at SAFE, GUARD] **1 a** *obs* **:** SAFE-CONDUCT **1 b :** SAFE-CONDUCT 2 **2 a :** a written order issued by a military commander or other authority guaranteeing the safety of specified persons or property **b :** a guard furnished by a military commander or other authority to protect persons or property **3** *archaic* **:** PROTECTION, DEFENSE ⟨if you do fight in ~ of your wives —Shak.⟩ **4 :** a means of protection against something undesirable ⟨necessary ~*s* against the conviction of innocent persons —F.A.Ogg & P.O.Ray⟩ ⟨this diversification is considered a ~ against crises —G.G.Weigend⟩ **5** *archaic* **:** a protective petticoat worn outside a riding habit

²safeguard \"\ *vt* **:** to provide a safeguard for **:** PROTECT ⟨a clause ~*ing* the right of habeas corpus —Irving Brant⟩ ⟨~ the layman against being victimized by quacks —H.G. Rickover⟩ **syn** see DEFEND

safehold \ˈ=,=\ *n* **:** a refuge esp. from attack

safekeeping \ˈ=ˈ==\ *n* [ME *safe kepyng*] **1 :** the act or process of preserving in safety from injury, loss, or escape ⟨systematic provision is made for the ~ of work slips —*Nat'l Miller*⟩ **2 :** the state of being preserved in safety from injury, loss, or escape ⟨had his various business papers and his will in ~ —Glenway Wescott⟩

safelight \ˈ=,=\ *n* **1 :** a color filter under which a sensitive paper, plate, or film may be manipulated and developed without danger of fogging and which usu. consists of colored gelatin protected by glass plates or laminated in plastic **2 :** a darkroom lamp with its filter

safe·ly *adv* [ME *savely, saufly, safly*, fr. *sauf, saf, save* safe + *-ly* — more at SAFE] **:** in a safe manner **:** with safety

saf·en \ˈsāfən\ *vt* -ED/-ING/-S [¹*safe* + *-en*] **:** to make safe; *specif* **:** to reduce the phytotoxic effect of by adding a safener ⟨the use of lime to ~ arsenical sprays⟩

saf·en·er \-f(ə)nə(r)\ *n* -S **:** a chemical used in an insecticidal or fungicidal spray to prevent damage to trees and foliage by the other ingredients in the spray

safe·ness *n* -ES [ME *savenes, safnes*, fr. *sauf, save, saf* safe + *-nes* -ness] **:** the quality or state of being safe

safe period *n* **:** a portion of the human female sexual cycle during which conception is least likely to occur and which usu. includes several days immediately before and after the menstrual period and the period itself — compare RHYTHM METHOD

safe–pledge *n, obs* **:** a surety for the appearance of a person at a given time

safer *comparative of* SAFE

safes *pl of* SAFE, *pres 3d sing of* SAFE

safest *superlative of* SAFE

¹safe·ty \ˈsāftē, -ti *sometimes* ÷-fəd- *or* ÷-fət-\ *n* -ES *often attrib* [ME *sauvete, saufte, safte*, fr. MF *sauveté, sauvete*, fr. OF, fr. *salve, sauve* (fem. of *salf, sauf* safe) + *-té* -ty — more at SAFE] **1 :** the condition of being safe **:** freedom from exposure to danger **:** exemption from hurt, injury, or loss ⟨the only ~ against being deceived lies in . . . refusal to bear arms —W.R.Inge⟩ ⟨ferried in ~ across the river⟩ **2** *obs* **:** CUSTODY ⟨hold him in ~ till the prince come hither —Shak.⟩ **3 a** *archaic* **:** a means of protection **:** SAFEGUARD **b (1) :** a locking or interrupting device on a military apparatus (as a mine, missile, weapon) that prevents it from being fired accidentally **(2) :** the condition of a firearm when the safety is in action ⟨to carry a piece at ~⟩ **c :** a device (as an elevator cable break or a drop hammer trip) applied to equipment to reduce hazard from component failure or personal contact **d :** CONDOM **4 a :** the quality or state of not presenting risks **:** SAFENESS ⟨people have a tendency to choose the ~ of the middle-ground reply —S.L.Payne⟩ ⟨the captain of an airplane was held responsible for the . . . ~ of his ship —E.K.Gann⟩ **b :** the quality or state of being financially secure ⟨~ of principal⟩ **5 :** knowledge of or skill in methods of avoiding accident or disease ⟨an expert in traffic ~⟩ **6 :** any of several plays in various sports: **a :** a billiard shot made with no attempt to score and intended to leave the balls in an unfavorable position for the opponent **b (1) :** a football play in which the ball is downed by the offensive team behind its own goal line **(2) :** a score made by a safety that counts two points for the opposing team — compare TOUCHBACK **c :** BASE HIT **d :** the act of hitting the ball across the back line and not between the goal posts by one of the defending side in a polo match **7 :** a member of a defensive backfield in football who occupies the deepest position in order to receive a kick or defend against a pass made by the opposing team or to stop a ballcarrier who has broken away

²safety \"\ *vt* -ED/-ING/-ES **:** to protect against failure, breakage, or other accident: as **a :** to secure (a nut on an airplane) against loosening by vibration **b :** to engage the safety of (a weapon)

safety arch *n* **:** an undecorated arch used for purely constructional reasons

safety belt *n* **:** a belt for fastening a person to some object: as **a :** one used to prevent a person from falling while working at a height **b :** one used in an airplane or vehicle to prevent injury in a crash

safety bicycle *n* **:** a bicycle made with equal or nearly equal wheels usu. 28 inches in diameter and driven by pedals connected to the rear wheel by a multiplying gear

safety bolt *n* **:** a bolt to fasten a door or gate; *esp* **:** a bolt that cannot be moved from the other side of the door or gate

safety button *n* **:** a medallion worn by nuclear energy workers to warn of excess exposure to radiation

safety cage *n* **:** a cage for an elevator or mine lift that has appliances to check the fall if the rope breaks

safety catch *n* **:** a device in an elevator or hoisting appliance to ensure safety from falling in case the mechanism fails to operate properly

safety chain *n* **1 a :** a normally slack chain for preventing excessive movement between a railroad car truck and a car body in sluing **b :** a heavy chain by which railroad cars may be connected to protect against accidental uncoupling **2 :** a small chain used as a secondary safeguard on a piece of jewelry (as a watch or bracelet) **3 :** a chain formed of sheet metal links with an elongated hole through each broad end and constructed by a repeated series of doubling a link upon itself, slipping the next link through the two now superimposed holes of the first, and doubling it

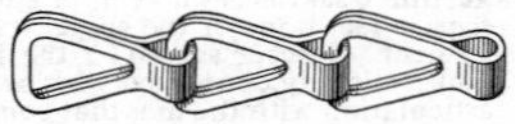
safety chain 3

safety curtain *n* **:** an asbestos or metal theater curtain to be lowered in case of fire

safety–deposit *adj* **:** SAFE-DEPOSIT

safety disk *n* **:** a thin copper disk over the steam boiler end of an escape pipe designed to break and permit escape of steam under excessive pressure

safety dog *n* **:** a dog in a lathe equipped with safety setscrews

safety edge *n* **:** SAFE EDGE

safety explosive *n* **:** a permissible explosive

safety factor *n* **:** FACTOR OF SAFETY

safety film *n* **:** photographic film having a support of cellulose acetate or other somewhat noninflammable material

safety–fund system *n* **:** a system under which banks are required by law to have or provide a fund (as a common fund provided for by a small tax) as a pledge for the redemption of their circulation

safety fuse *n* **1 :** a fuse that burns slowly for communicating fire to a detonator or blasting cap and that consists usu. of a train of fine black powder surrounded by a tight wrapping **2 :** CARTRIDGE FUSE

safety glass *n* **1 :** LAMINATED GLASS **2 :** glass that is strengthened by tempering and that when struck breaks into relatively harmless granules rather than large jagged pieces **3 :** WIRE GLASS

safety hanger *n* **:** a strap or loop under a piece of railroad rolling stock to stop broken rods and other matter from falling on the track

safety hasp *n* **:** a hasp that is used with a padlock and has a slotted plate fitting over the staple to prevent its removal when locked

safety hat *n* **:** a shallow domed hat of steel or a similar material worn (as by miners and sandhogs) to protect the top of the head

safety hoist *or* **safety lift** *n* **1 a :** a hoisting gear that does not overhaul when the tension is released on the fall **2 :** a hoisting gear that is provided with a special attachment to prevent overhauling

safety ink *n* **:** indelible ink

safety island *also* **safety isle** *n* **:** an area within a roadway from which vehicular traffic is excluded (as by pavement markings or curbing) in order to provide an area of safety for pedestrians or to channel traffic flow

safety lamp *n* **:** a miner's lamp constructed to avoid explosion in an atmosphere containing inflammable gas usu. by enclosing the flame in fine wire gauze that by its cooling effect prevents the flame from passing

safety link *n* **1 :** a device used for the same purpose as a safety chain **2 :** a link in a chain designed to fail at rated stress and protect the rest of the links against overstress

safety lock *n* **:** a lock specially devised to prevent picking

safe·ty·man \-ˌman, -ˌmaa(ə)n\ *n* **:** SAFETY 7

safety match *n* **:** a match capable of being struck and ignited only on a specially prepared friction surface

safety nut *n* **:** LOCKNUT

safety paper *n* **:** a paper (as the silk-fibered paper of the U. S. currency or the watermarked paper of Bank of England notes) difficult to duplicate or so made that erasures or changes in matter written or printed on it are readily detectable

safety pin *n* **:** a pin used esp. for fastening clothes and made in the form of a clasp with a guard covering the point so that it will not prick the wearer

safety pinion *n* **:** a center pinion gear of a watch that unscrews when the mainspring breaks and relieves the pressure on the delicate train wheel teeth and arbor pivots

safety plug *n* **:** a fusible metal plug set in a boiler shell to release steam when the plug reaches a predetermined temperature due to excessive pressure in the boiler

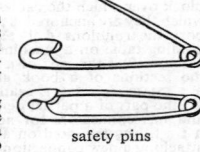

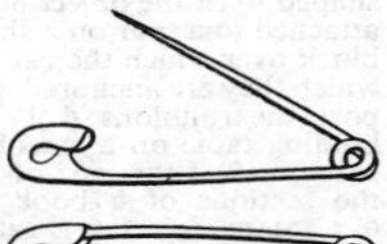
safety pins

safety rail *n* **:** GUARDRAIL

safety razor *n* **:** a razor provided with a guard for the blade to prevent deep cuts in the skin — see RAZOR illustration

safety shoe *n* **1 :** a shoe with a reinforced toe cap to minimize foot injuries caused by dropped articles **2 :** a shoe with a sole of material incapable of sparking for work near combustibles or explosives

safety stop *n* **:** any of various devices to stop an undesirable motion or action: as **a :** an attachment for an elevator to prevent accidental falling **b :** a device that closes a supply valve and stops an engine in case of accident to the governor belt **c :** a contrivance to prevent a pulley tackle from overhauling **d :** a device in a lathe to prevent a carriage from colliding with the headstock **e :** a system for stopping trains automatically if they try to pass a stop signal **f :** a stop motion for textile machinery

safety straps *n pl* **:** a harness affixed to the seat of a vehicle and passed over the shoulders or legs; *esp* **:** one used in an airplane in addition to a safety belt to provide more widely distributed restraint of the body in moments of rapid acceleration or deceleration

safety switch *n* **:** an electric switch completely enclosed in a metal box with an external control handle and so designed that the box cannot be opened while the switch is closed and the switch cannot be closed while the box is open

safety switchboard *n* **:** a dead-front switchboard with an enclosure on the back and sides to prevent access to the live parts

safety tread *n* **:** a surface on a floor or deck (as at the top and bottom of a ladder) designed to prevent slipping

safety tube *n* **:** a tube to prevent explosion or to control delivery of gases by an automatic valvular connection with the outer air; *esp* **:** a safety funnel tube — compare FUNNEL TUBE

safety valve *n* **1 a :** an automatic escape or relief valve (as for a steam boiler or hydraulic system) held shut by an arrangement exerting a definite usu. adjustable pressure so that the valve lift and the steam, water, or other contents escape when the pressure exceeds a predetermined amount **b :** a similar valve opening inward to admit air to a vessel in which the pressure is less than that of the atmosphere and prevent collapse **2 :** something that serves as an outlet for an excess or pressure ⟨wit is the best *safety valve* modern man has evolved —A.A.Brill⟩ ⟨emigration can serve as a *safety valve* for transitory problems of critical population pressure —*President's Commission on Immigration & Naturalization*⟩

safety zone *n* **:** a safety island for pedestrians or for street car or bus passengers

saffi *var of* SAPHIE

saf·fi·an \ˈsafēən\ *n* -s [Russ *saf'yan*, fr. Turk *sahtiyan*, fr. Per *sakhtiyān* goatskin, fr. *sakht* hard, strong] **:** a leather made of goatskins or sheepskins tanned with sumac and dyed with bright colors

saf·flor \ˈsa,flȯ(ə)r, ═ˈ═\ *n* -s [fr. *safflor* (safflower)] **:** CARTHAMUS RED

saf·flor·ite \ˈsaflə,rīt\ *n* -s [G *saflorit*, fr. *saflor* zaffer (modif. — influenced by *saflor* safflower — of It *zaffera*) + G *-it* -ite — more at ZAFFER] **:** a mineral $CoAs_2$ that consists of a cobalt arsenide, is isomorphous with loellingite and dimorphous with smaltite, and occurs in tin-white masses

saf·flow·er \ˈsa,flau̇(ə)r, -au̇ə\ *also* **saf·flor** \-lō(ə)r, -ō(ə)\ *n* -s [MF *saffleur, safleur*, fr. OIt *saffiore, zaffrole*, fr. Ar *aṣfar* yellow, a yellow plant] **1 :** an Old World herb (*Carthamus tinctorius*) that resembles a thistle, is widely grown for its oil, and has large vivid red or orange flower heads **2 :** a dye prepared from the flower heads of the safflower and now used chiefly in the Orient for dyeing silk and cotton light red — see CARTHAMIN **3 :** a drug consisting of the dried florets of the safflower and used in medicine in place of saffron

safflower carmine *n* **:** a commercial preparation of carthamin

safflower oil *n* **:** an edible drying oil obtained from the seeds of the safflower

safflower red *n* **:** CARTHAMUS RED

¹saf·fron \ˈsafrən *sometimes* -f(ə)rn\ *n* -s [ME *saffran, saffroun, saffron*, fr. OF *safran*, fr. ML *safranum*, fr. Ar *za'farān*] **1** *or* **saffron crocus :** a crocus (*Crocus sativus*) with purple flowers widely cultivated throughout southern Europe for the drug and dyestuff that it yields **2 :** a deep orange-colored substance consisting of the aromatic pungent dried stigmas of saffron and used to color and flavor foods and formerly as a dyestuff and as a stimulant antispasmodic emmenagogue in medicine **3** *or* **saffron yellow :** a moderate orange to orange yellow — called also *croceus* **4 :** any of several saffron-colored substances used in alchemy ⟨CROCUS 2a ⟨antimony ~⟩ **5 :** SAFFLOWER 1, 3 **6** *also* **saffron tree :** SATINLEAF

²saffron \"\ *vt* -ED/-ING/-S **:** to color or flavor with or as if with saffron

saffron plum *n* **:** a buckthorn (*Bumelia angustifolia*) of southern Florida and the West Indies that is a small often shrubby tree with heavy hard close-grained wood and a sweet edible fruit resembling a small plum

saffron thistle *n* **:** SAFFLOWER; *also* **:** a related European herb (*Carthamus lanatus*) with yellow flower heads that is naturalized and a troublesome weed in Australia

saffronwood \ˈ══,═\ *n* **1 :** the yellowish wood of a southern African timber tree (*Elaeodendron croceum*) **2 :** the tree that yields saffronwood

saf·frony \-nē\ *adj* **:** YELLOWISH

safing *pres part of* SAFE

saf·ra·nine *also* **saf·ra·nin** *or* **saf·fra·nine** \ˈsafrə,nēn, -,nən\ *n* -s *sometimes cap* [ISV *safran-* (fr. F or G *safran* saffron) + *-ine*] **:** any of a class of red to blue azine dyes that for the most part are diamino derivatives of *N*-phenylphenazine: as **a :** PHENOSAFRANINE **b** *or* **safranine O** *or* **safranine T :** a basic dye made by oxidation of a mixture of *ortho*-toluidine, *para*-tolylenediamine, and aniline and used chiefly in dyeing paper, as a desensitizer in photography, and as a biological stain — see DYE table I (under *Basic Red 2*)

saf·ra·no·phile \ˈsafrənō,fīl\ *or* **saf·ra·no·phil** \-,fil\ *adj* [*safranine* + *-o-* + *-phile, -phil*] *of cells* **:** staining readily with safranine

saf·ra·no pink \ˈsafrə,nō-\ *n* [fr. *Safrano*, a variety of rose, fr. F *safran* saffron] **:** a moderate yellowish pink that is yellower and paler than coral pink and redder and duller than peach pink

saf·role \ˈsa,frōl\ *also* **saf·rol** \-rōl, -rȯl\ *n* -s [ISV *safr-* (fr. F or G *safran* saffron) + *-ole, -ol*] **:** a poisonous oily cyclic ether $C_{10}H_{10}O_2$ that is the principal component of sassafras oil and occurs also in other essential oils (as camphor oil) and that is used chiefly for perfuming and flavoring; 4-allyl-1,2-methylenedioxy-benzene — compare ISOSAFROLE

saft \ˈsäft, ˈsȧft, ˈsaft\ *chiefly Scot var of* SOFT

¹sag \ˈsag, ˈsaa(ə)g, ˈsaig\ *vb* **sagged; sagged; sagging; sags** [ME *saggen*, prob. of Scand origin; akin to Sw *sacka* to sag, settle down, Norw dial. *sakka* to sink, prob. derivatives fr. the stem of ON *sökkva* to sink — more at SINK] *vi* **1 a :** to sink or settle gradually from an established or normal position ⟨frame store buildings . . . left to ~ and gather cobwebs since lumbering operations stopped —*Amer. Guide Series: Calif.*⟩ **b :** to decline in intensity or vigor ⟨spirits had *sagged* almost to the breaking point —W.H.Waggoner⟩ **c :** to decline from a thriving position ⟨oil shares *sagged* owing to lack of fresh support —*Financial Times (London)*⟩ ⟨cloth output and prices ~ despite the . . . comeback in apparel —*Wall Street Jour.*⟩ **2 a :** to hang loosely **:** lose tautness (as from age or fatigue) ⟨when his face *sagged* like this, worriment claimed it —O.B. Chidsey⟩ **b :** to lie or hang unevenly **:** droop to one side ⟨the chair . . . *sagged* on one rocker —Ellen Glasgow⟩ **c :** to bend downward in the middle under its own or applied pressure ⟨a black reticule that *sagged* under the weight of shapeless objects —Allen Tate⟩ ⟨the clothesline *sagged* between its poles⟩ **d :** to fall from the lack or removal of muscular control ⟨he *sagged* flabbily to his knees —George Orwell⟩ **e :** to flow after application to a vertical or sloping surface and produce irregular films — used of a paint or varnish **3 :** to move ahead at a feeble plodding pace ⟨the depression *sagged* along —Don Baines⟩ **4 :** DRIFT — used chiefly in the phrase *sag to leeward* **5 :** to fail to stimulate or retain interest ⟨his latest picture had *sagged* at the box office —E.L.Acken⟩ ⟨though it ~s in the middle, the novel is readable throughout —Walter Havighurst⟩ ~ *vt* **:** to cause to sag: as **a :** to cause (as a ship or timber) to curve downward in the middle usu. as a result of improper loading or supporting **b :** to leave slack in (an electrical transmission line) to compensate for changes in temperature **syn** see DROOP

²sag \"\ *n* -s **1 :** a tendency to drift (as of a ship to leeward) **:** DRIFT **2 :** a drop or depression below the surrounding area: **:** as **a :** a pass or gap in a ridge or mountain range **:** SADDLE **b :** a depression in an otherwise flat or gently sloping land surface **c :** a minor downwarped structure often with faults on one or more sides **d :** a sunken area in a roadbed or pipeline **3 a :** a distortion of an airship in which the center bends down and both ends rise **b :** a bending of an object (as a chain) under its own weight or applied pressure **c :** a curve in the line of chained logs in a log boom caused by wind or current **4 :** a temporary economic decline (as in the price of a particular commodity)

³sag \ˈsag\ *dial Brit var of* SEDGE

⁴sag \"\ *chiefly dial var of* SAW

¹saga *pl of* SAGUM

²sa·ga \ˈsägə, ˈsȧgə *sometimes* ˈsagə\ *n* -s [ON, story, legend, history, saga — more at SAW] **1 a :** a prose narrative sometimes of legendary content but typically dealing with prominent figures and events of the heroic age in Norway and Iceland esp. as recorded in Icelandic manuscripts of the late 12th and 13th centuries **b :** the saga as a literary genre **2 :** any of various historical or fictional narratives: as **a :** a modern retelling usu. in verse or highly stylized prose of the events of the Icelandic sagas or of similar subjects ⟨I have called it a novel but in fact it is a prose ~ of the wanderings of the Vikings —M.R.Ridley⟩ **b :** an episodic story centering about a usu. heroic figure of earlier ages with factual or fictional details drawn from various sources ⟨one of the old knightly ~s⟩ **c :** a series of legends that embodies in detail the esp. oral history of a people ⟨the great ~ of the patriarchs —A.P. Davies⟩ **d :** a long detailed narrative usu. without psychological or historical depth (as of a particular occupation, area, historical event, period, or person) ⟨a ~ of the Indian Territory at the turn of the nineteenth century —*Current Biog.*⟩ ⟨that ~ of the farm which has occupied so many American novelists —*Times Lit. Supp.*⟩ ⟨the great ~ of the winning of the West⟩ ⟨the ~ of the colonel who piloted the plane that dropped the atomic bomb —John McCarten⟩ **e** *also* **saga novel :** ROMAN-FLEUVE **3 :** an occupation, life, series of events, or location suitable as a subject for a saga ⟨~ of the cattle industry —*Amer. Guide Series: Texas*⟩ **syn** see MYTH

sa·ga·ci·ate \səˈgashē,āt, -gāsh-, -gashə,wāt\ *vi* -ED/-ING/-S [prob. fr. *sagacity* + *-ate*] *chiefly South* **:** to get along **:** THRIVE

sa·ga·cious \səˈgāshəs\ *adj* [L *sagac-, sagax* sagacious + E *-ious*; akin to L *sagire* to perceive quickly or keenly — more at SEEK] **1** *obs* **:** quick or keen in sense perceptions ⟨a dog ~ in scent⟩ ⟨~ of his quarry —John Milton⟩ **2 a :** possessing quick intellectual perceptions **:** of keen penetration and judgment **:** discerning and farsighted in judging men and means ⟨a natively ~, intuitively understanding humanitarian —H.F. Wilkins⟩ **b :** caused by keen intellectual perception or penetration **:** indicating acute discernment ⟨a ~ marketing of his product —Lucius Garvin⟩ **syn** see SHREWD

sa·ga·cious·ly *adv* **:** in a sagacious manner

sa·ga·cious·ness *n* -ES **:** SAGACITY

sa·gac·i·ty \səˈgasəd·ē, -ˈgaas-, -ətē, -i\ *n* -ES [MF or L; MF *sagacité*, fr. L *sagacitat-, sagacitas*, fr. *sagac-, sagax* + *-itat-, -itas* -ity] **1 a :** the quality of being sagacious **:** quickness or acuteness of sense perceptions **:** keenness of discernment or penetration with soundness of judgment **:** ability to see what is relevant and significant ⟨a man of exceptional intelligence and unusual political ~ —Brian Crozier⟩ **b :** a sagacious remark or judgment **2** *archaic* **:** acuteness of smell

sa·gai \səˈgī\ *or* **sagai tatar** *n, pl* **sagai** *or* **sagai tatars** *usu cap S&T* **1 :** a group composed of the Beltir, the Koibal, and other peoples on the Abakan river that speak a Turkic dialect **2 :** a member of the Sagai people

sa·gaie \səˈgī\ *n* -s [F *sagaie, zagaie* assegai, sagaie, fr. MF *azagaie* assegai — more at ASSEGAI] **:** a Paleolithic bone javelin point

sa·ga·man \ˈsägə,man, -,mən\ *n, pl* **sagamen** [trans. of ON *sǫgumathr*] **:** a narrator of a saga

sa·ga·mi·té \səˌgamə'tā\ *n* -s [CanF, of Algonquian origin; akin to Cree *kisāgamitew* the liquid is hot, Nipissing *kijagamite*] **1 :** HULLED CORN **2 :** a thin porridge of hulled corn

sag·a·more \ˈsagə,mō(ə)r, -mȯ(ə)r, -mōə, -mȯ(ə)\ *n* -s [Abnaki *sāgimau*, lit., he prevails over] **1 :** a subordinate or war chief of the Algonquian Indians of the north Atlantic coast **2 :** SACHEM 1

sag and swell *n* **:** an undulating topography (as of a moraine)

sagapen *n* -s [L *sagapenum*] *obs* **:** SAGAPENUM

sag·a·pe·num \,sagəˈpēnəm\ *n* -s [L, fr. Gk *sagapēnon*, a plant (*Ferula persica*), sagapenum] **:** a bitter yellowish or brownish oleo-gum-resin of strong odor derived from plants of the genus *Ferula* in Arabia and Persia and formerly used similarly to asafetida and galbanum

sag·a·thy \ˈsagəthē\ *n* -ES [origin unknown] **:** a fine twilled worsted fabric similar to serge used esp. formerly for clothing and curtains

¹sage \ˈsāj\ *adj* -ER/-EST [ME, fr. OF, fr. (assumed) VL *sapius*, fr. L *sapere* to taste, have good taste, have sense, be wise; akin to OE *sefa* mind, OS *sebo* mind, *afsebbian* to perceive, OHG *antseffen, intseffen* to notice, Oscan *sipus* knowing, Arm *ham* juice, taste; basic meaning: to taste] **1 a :** eminent in wisdom **:** wise through reflection and experience **:** prudent and philosophic in judgment and views ⟨the wise reasoning of a certain ~ magistrate —George Berkeley⟩ **b** *archaic* **:** GRAVE, SOLEMN ⟨among the ~ and somber figures that would put his unsophisticated cheerfulness to shame —Nathaniel Hawthorne⟩ **2 :** proceeding from or characterized by wisdom, prudence, and good judgment ⟨providing ~ guidance to nonponderous writing —*Saturday Rev.*⟩ **syn** see WISE

²sage \"\ *n* -s [ME, fr. MF, fr. *sage*, adj.] **1 :** one (as a profound philosopher or eminently wise counselor) distinguished for wisdom ⟨this excellent book considers six ~s . . . whose vision springs from a vivid conception of the principles governing the workings of the world —*Times Lit. Supp.*⟩ **2 :** a mature or venerable man rich in experience and sound in judgment ⟨one of the ancient ~s of our law —B.N.Cardozo⟩ **3** *often cap, Confucianism* **:** a truly natural man who is virtuous and wise and has attained the highest perfection of man

³sage \"\ *n* -s *often attrib* [ME *sauge, sage*, fr. MF *saulge, sauge*, fr. L *salvia*, fr. *salvus* safe, whole, healthy; fr. its use as a medicinal herb — more at SAFE] **1 a :** a half shrubby mint (*Salvia officinalis*) with grayish green pungent and aromatic leaves that are much used in flavoring foods and as a mild tonic and astringent; *broadly* **:** a plant of the genus *Salvia* — compare BLUE SAGE, CLARY, SCARLET SAGE **b (1) :** SAGEBRUSH (2) **:** the sagebrush regions of the western U.S. ⟨~ dog⟩ ⟨~ riders⟩ **c :** any of several plants felt to resemble the true sage — usu. used in combination; see BETHLEHEM SAGE, JERUSALEM SAGE **2 :** SAGE GREEN

SAGE \ˈsāj\ *abbr or n* -s [*s*emi*a*utomatic *g*round *e*nvironment] **:** a ground air defense system in which reporting devices feed into an electronic computer that digests, memorizes, and displays the air situation shown by the reports and then when decision for action is fed into it translates the decision into orders to the various air defense combat units

sage·brush \ˈsāj,brəsh\ *n* [³*sage* + *brush*] **:** any of several No. American hoary undershrubs of the genus *Artemisia*; *esp* **:** a common plant (*A. tridentata*) having a bitter juice and an odor resembling sage and often covering vast tracts of alkaline plains in the western U.S. — called also *big sagebrush, blue sage*

sage·brush·er \-shə(r)\ *n* -s [*sagebrush* + *-er*] **:** an inhabitant of or a camper in a sagebrush region of the western U.S.

sagebrush green *n* **:** a dark greenish gray that is yellower and darker than Muscovite and yellower and deeper than castor gray

sagebrush lizard *n* **:** a small variable lizard (*Sceloporus graciosus*) of dry uplands of western No. America

sagebrush rabbit *n* **:** a rather small grayish cottontail (*Sylvilagus nuttallii*) of western No. America

sage cheese *n* **:** a mottled green cheese similar to cheddar flavored with chopped sage leaves or sage extract

sage chippy *or* **sagebrush chippy** *n* **:** BREWER SPARROW

sage cock *n* **:** SAGE GROUSE; *specif* **:** a male sage grouse

sage grass *n* **:** a grass of the genus *Andropogon*

sage gray *n* **1 :** a grayish green **2 :** a light olive gray to light grayish olive that is very slightly greener and deeper than beach

sage green *n* **:** a variable color averaging a grayish yellow green that is greener and deeper than mermaid, stronger and very slightly yellower and lighter than palmetto, and deeper and slightly greener than celadon

sage grouse *n* **:** a very large grouse (*Centrocercus urophasianus*) native to the dry sagebrush plains of western No. America having mottled gray, black, and buff plumage and flesh often poor and bitter from feeding on the buds of the sagebrush

sage hen *n* **1 :** SAGE GROUSE; *specif* **:** the female sage grouse **2** *usu cap S&H* **:** NEVADAN — used as a nickname

sage-king \ˈ═ˈ═\ *n, often cap S&K, Confucianism* **1 :** an ideal ruler of antiquity who by combining the virtue and wisdom of a sage with the power of a king exemplified perfection in government **2 :** an exemplary mythological ruler of prehistoric China

sage·ly *adv* [ME, fr. *sage* + *-ly*] **:** in a sage manner

sage mullein \ˈ═-\ *also* **sageleaf mullein** \ˈ═,═-\ *n* **:** JERUSALEM SAGE

sa·gene \ˈsä,zhen\ *n* -s [Russ *sazhen'*; akin to Russ *syagat'* to reach for, grasp, OSlav *sęgnǫti* to grasp, Latvian *segt* to cover — more at SAGUM] **:** a Russian unit of length equal to 7 feet

sage·ness *n* -ES [¹*sage* + *-ness*] **:** the quality or state of being sage

sag·e·nite \ˈsajə,nīt\ *n* -s [F *sagénite*, fr. L *sagena* large fishing net + F *-ite* — more at SEINE] **:** a mineral consisting of an acicular rutile that occurs in reticulated forms and is often embedded in quartz or other minerals

sag·e·nit·ic \══ˈnid·ik\ *adj* **:** containing sagenite or similar acicular crystals ⟨~ tourmaline⟩ — used esp. of quartz

sage of bethlehem *usu cap B* [fr. *Bethlehem*, Palestine] **1 :** SPEARMINT **2 :** LUNGWORT 2a

sage oil *n* **:** either of two essential oils from sage: **a :** the yellowish or greenish yellow oil with a penetrating odor of sage obtained from the leaves of the common sage (*Salvia officinalis*) and used chiefly in flavoring **b :** the pale yellow oil with an odor like that of ambergris obtained from the flowers of clary (*Salvia sclarea*) and used chiefly in perfumery — called also *clary sage oil*

sager *comparative of* SAGE

sage rabbit *or* **sage hare** *n* **:** SAGEBRUSH RABBIT

sag·e·re·tia \,sajəˈrēsh(ē)ə, -ēd·ēə\ *n, cap* [NL, fr. Augustin *Sageret* †1852 French agronomist + NL *-ia*] **:** a genus of American and Asiatic shrubs (family Rhamnaceae) having opposite branches, sometimes edible fruit, and opposite leaves that in a Chinese member (*S. theezans*) are used locally as a substitute for tea

sages *pl of* SAGE

sagest *superlative of* SAGE

sage sparrow *n* **:** a sparrow (*Amphispiza belli*) that inhabits esp. sagebrush regions in western No. America

sage tea *n* **:** a beverage prepared by infusion of sage leaves

sage thrasher *n* **:** a thrasher (*Oreoscoptes montanus*) that inhabits sagebrush in western No. America and is pale grayish brown above and white spotted with brownish below

sage willow *n* **:** a willow shrub (*Salix tristis*) of the eastern U.S. growing in dry ground and having linear-oblong leaves that are white-tomentose beneath — called also *dwarf gray willow*

sagey *var of* SAGY

sagged *past of* SAG

¹sag·ger *or* **sag·gar** \ˈsagə(r)\ *n* -s [prob. alter. of *safeguard*] **1 a :** a box made of fire clay in which delicate ceramic pieces are placed while being fired either for biscuit or for glaze **b :** the clay of which saggers are made **2 :** a box in which cast-iron articles are packed in contact with hematite ore or mill scale to be converted to malleable cast iron in an annealing furnace

²sagger \"\ *vt* -ED/-ING/-S **:** to treat (as stoneware) in a sagger

sag·ger·man \ˈ══mən\ *n, pl* **saggermen :** one who forms saggers on a potter's wheel or loads them with pottery to be fired

sagging *n* -s [ME, fr. gerund of *saggen* to sag — more at SAG] **1 :** an arching downward in the middle (as of a ship after being strained) — compare HOGGED **2 :** a defect in the enamel of a piece of ceramics caused by flow down a vertical surface

¹sag·gy \ˈsagē\ *adj* [¹*sag* + *-y*] *chiefly dial* **:** SEDGY

²saggy \"\ *adj* -ER/-EST [¹*sag* + *-y*] **:** characterized or caused by sagging

sagier *comparative of* SAGY

sagiest *superlative of* SAGY

sa·gi·na \səˈjīnə\ *n, cap* [NL, fr. L *sagina* action of stuffing or fattening food, fatness, nourishment; fr. the supposed nutritive value of plants of this genus] **:** a genus of small herbs (family Caryophyllaceae) native to temperate and cool regions that have subulate leaves and small whitish sometimes apetalous flowers with the styles equal in number to the four or five sepals and alternating with them

sag·i·nate \ˈsajə,nāt\ *vt* -ED/-ING/-S [L *saginatus*, past part of *saginare* to fatten, fr. *sagina*] *archaic* **:** FATTEN — **sag·i·na·tion** \══ˈnāshən\ *n* -s

sa·ging \ˈsä,gēŋ\ *n* -s [Tag] *Philippines* **:** BANANA

sa·git·ta \səˈjid·ə\ *n* [NL, fr. L, arrow, prob. of non-IE origin] **1** -s **:** the distance from the midpoint of an arc to the midpoint of its chord **2** -s **:** the larger of the two large otoliths found in the ear of most fishes **3 a** *cap* **:** the chief genus of Chaetognatha including the largest and several common arrowworms **b** *pl* **sagittas** \-d·əz\ *or* **sagit·tae** \-d·,ē\ **:** any arrowworm of the genus *Sagitta*

sag·it·tal \ˈsajəd·ᵊl, -ətᵊl\ *adj* [L *sagitta* + E *-al*] **1 a :** of or relating to the suture between the parietal bones of the skull **b :** of, relating to, or situated in the median plane of the body or any plane parallel thereto **2 :** of, relating to, or shaped like an arrow or arrowhead — **sag·it·tal·ly** \-ᵊlē\ *adv*

sagittal arc *n* **:** the arc from the nasion to the opisthion along the sagittal line of the skull

sagittal crest *n* **:** an elevated bony ridge that develops along the sagittal suture of many mammals esp. in old age

sagittal diameter *n* **1 :** the distance between the glabella and the opisthocranion **2 :** the distance between the midpoint of the sacral promontory and the midpoint of the posterior ridge of the pubic symphysis

sagittal fontanelle *n* **:** an unossified space in the region of the parietal foramina usu. closed at birth

sagittal sinus *n* **:** either of two venous sinuses of the dura mater: **a :** one passing backward in the convex attached margin of the falx cerebri and ending at the internal occipital protuberance by fusion with the transverse sinus — called also *superior sagittal sinus* **b :** one lying in the posterior two thirds of the concave free margin of the falx cerebri and ending posteriorly by joining the great cerebral vein to form the straight sinus — called also *inferior sagittal sinus*

sagittal suture *n* **:** the deeply serrated articulation between the two parietal bones in the median plane of the top of the head

sag·it·tar·ia \,sajəˈta(a)rēə\ *n, cap* [NL, fr. L *sagitta* + NL *-aria*] **:** a genus of aquatic herbs (family Alismataceae) of temperate and tropical regions having basal often sagittate or hastate leaves and scapose flowers with 3 sepals and 3 deciduous white petals — see ARROWHEAD, WAPATOO

sag·it·tar·i·us \,sajəˈta(a)rēəs, -ter-, -tär-\ *n, pl* **sagittar·ii** \-ē,ī\ [ME, fr. ML, fr. L, a constellation, fr. *sagittarius* archer, fr. *sagitta* arrow + *-arius* -ary] **1** *usu cap* **:** the ninth sign of the zodiac — see SIGN table, ZODIAC illustration **2** [L] **:** ARCHER

sag·it·tary \ˈsajə,terē\ *n* -ES [ME *sagitary*, fr. ML *sagittarius*] **1** *obs* **:** SAGITTARIUS **2 :** CENTAUR

sag·it·tate \ˈsajə,tāt\ *adj* [L *sagitta* arrow + E *-ate*] **1 :** shaped like an arrowhead **2** *of a leaf* **:** elongated, triangular, and having the two basal lobes prolonged downward — see LEAF illustration

sa·git·to·cyst \səˈjid·ə,sist, ˈsajəd·ō,-\ *n* [NL *sagitta* + E *-o-* + *cyst*] **:** a capsule having a spindle-shaped needle produced by epidermal cells of certain turbellarians

sag·it·toid \ˈsajə,tȯid\ *adj* [NL *Sagitta* + E *-oid*] **:** of, relating to, or resembling an arrowworm

sag·less \ˈsagləs\ *adj* [²*sag* + *-less*] **:** having no sag

sa·go \ˈsā(,)gō\ *n* -s [Malay *sagu*] **1 :** SAGO PALM **2 :** a dry granulated or powdered starch prepared from the pithy trunks of several tropical palms (as the sago) and used as a thickening agent in foods (as a pudding) and as textile stiffening

sago fern *n* **:** SILVER TREE FERN

sa·goin \səˈgȯin\ *n* -s [F *sagoin*, fr. Pg *sagüi, sagüi, sagüim*, fr. Tupi *saguí, sauin, saguim*] **:** MARMOSET; *esp* **:** one of the genus *Callithrix*

sago palm *n* **1 :** a plant that yields sago: as **a :** any of various lofty pinnate-leaved Indian and Malaysian palms of the genus *Metroxylon* (as *M. laeve* or *M. rumphii*) **b :** a Malaccan palm (*Phoenix farinifera*) **c :** GEBANG PALM **d :** any of several Indian palms: (1) **:** GOMUTI (2) **:** JAGGERY PALM (3) **:** PALMYRA **e :** CABBAGE PALM 1b **2 a :** a cycad (*Cycas revoluta*) with recurved leaves that have revolute edges **b :** COONTIE

sago pondweed *n* **:** a No. American pondweed (*Potamogeton pectinatus*) having sharply acute leaves and seeds that provide feed for wild fowl

sag·o·weer \ˈsagə,wi(ə)r\ *n* -s [D *sagoweer, saguweer*, fr. Pg *sagüeiro*, fr. *sagu, sagú* sago (fr. Malay *sagu*) + *-eiro* -ary (fr. L *-arius*)] **:** GOMUTI

sa·gra \ˈsāgrə, ˈsag-\ *n, cap* [NL] **:** a genus of chrysomelid beetles comprising the kangaroo beetles

sags *pres 3d sing of* SAG, *pl of* SAG

sa·gua·ro *also* **sa·hua·ro** *or* **su·war·ro** \səˈ(g)wä(,)rō, -ˈgw-, -ˈ(h)wä-\ *n* -s [MexSp *saguaro, sahuaro*, prob. fr. Opata *sahuaro*] **:** an arborescent cactus (*Carnegiea gigantea*) occurring in desert regions of the southwestern U.S. and Mexico, having a tall columnar simple or sparsely branched trunk, attaining a height of 60 feet or more, and bearing white flowers and edible fruit

sa·gum \ˈsāgəm\ *n, pl* **sa·ga** \-gə\ [L, fr. Gaulish; akin to MIr *sēn* snare, W *hoenyn* snare, Latvian *segt* to cover, Skt

sajati he fastens, sticks; basic meaning: to touch, stick] : a square or rectangular cloak made of coarse wool, fastened usu. on the right shoulder, and worn esp. by Gauls, early Germans, and soldiers of ancient Rome

sa·gu·ran \sə'gü,rän\ *n, pl* **sa·gu·ra·nes** \,sägü'rä,näs\ [native name in the Philippines] *Philippines* : a textile made from the fiber of leaves of the talipot palm and used esp. for packing

sagy *also* **sagey** \'sājē\ *adj* **sagier; sagiest** [³*sage* + -*y*] : perfumed or seasoned with sage

sa·haj·da·ri \sə,häj'därē\ *n* -s *usu cap* [native name in India] : one of a sect of Sikhs observing many Hindu customs but emphasizing a special regard for Guru Nanak and his teachings

sa·hap·ti·an \sə'haptēən\ *or* **sa·hap·tin** \-tən\ *usu cap, var of* SHAHAPTIAN

¹**sa·ha·ra** \sə'ha(a)rə, -'herə, -'hārə, -'hārə\ *adj, usu cap* [fr. the *Sahara* desert, vast region of wasteland and oases in northern Africa] : of or relating to the Sahara desert ⟨a *Sahara* oasis⟩

²**sahara** \"\ *n* -s [fr. the *Sahara* desert] **1** *usu cap* : something regarded as arid, barren, or deserted ⟨the *Sahara* of the early morning streets⟩ ⟨turned bookman and for twenty-one years wandered . . . in the *Sahara* of medieval scholarship —V.L. Parrington⟩ **2** *often cap* : SIENNA BROWN

sa·ha·ran \-rən\ *also* **sa·ha·ri·an** \-rēən\ *adj, usu cap* [*Sahara* desert + E -*an*, -*ian*] : of, relating to, characteristic of, or likened to the Sahara desert ⟨a day of *Saharan* temperature⟩ ⟨a *Saharan* landscape of blighted fields⟩

sa·ha·ran·pur \sə'härən,pů(ə)r\ *adj, usu cap* [fr. *Saharanpur*, India] : of or from the city of Saharanpur, India : of the kind or style prevalent in Saharanpur

sa·heh·wa·mish \sə'hāwə,mish\ *n, pl* **sahehwamish** *or* **sahehwamishes** *usu cap* **1 a** : a Salishan people about the inlets at the southern end of Puget Sound, Washington **b** : a member of such people **2** : a dialect related to Skagit

sa·hib \'sä,(h)ib, 'sȧ,-, -(h)ēb\ *also* **sa·heb** \-,(h)eb\ *n* -s [Hindi *ṣāhib*, lit., master, lord, fr. Ar] **1** : SIR, MASTER — used as a term of respect esp. among Hindus and Muslims in colonial India when addressing or speaking of a European of some social status and as a general title affixed to the name or official title of a European ⟨colonel-*sahib*⟩ or affixed to the title of a man of rank ⟨raja ~⟩ **2** : EUROPEAN; *typically* : a European official or settler in a largely non-European population ⟨the prewar white ~ sat under a punkah pulled by tireless little Asians —Peggy Durdin⟩

sa·hi·bah *or* **sa·hi·ba** \'säēbə\ *n* -s [Hindi *ṣāhiba*, fr. Per, fem. of *ṣāhib* master, lord, fr. Ar] : LADY, MISTRESS

sa·hid·ic \sə'hidik\ *n, usu cap* [Ar *ṣa'īdīy* of Upper Egypt, fr. *aṣ-ṣa'īd* Upper Egypt] : a Coptic dialect of southern Egypt

sa·hi·wal \'sä(h)ə,väl\ *n* [fr. *Sahiwal*, town in western Pakistan] **1** *usu cap* : an Indian breed of humped short-horned solid-colored dairy cattle **2** -s *often cap* : any animal of the Sahiwal breed

sah·lin·ite \'sälə,nīt\ *n* -s [prob. fr. Sw *sahlinit*, fr. Carl *Sahlin*, 20th cent. Swed. scientist + Sw -*it* -ite] : a mineral $Pb_{14}(AsO_4)_2O_9Cl_4$ composed of an arsenate, oxide, and chloride of lead

sa·ho \'sä(,)hō\ *n, pl* **saho** *or* **sahos** *usu cap* **1 a** : a Hamitic people of northeastern Ethiopia **b** : a member of such people **2** : the Cushitic language of the Saho people

saib·ling \'zīplin, 'sībl-\ *n* -s [G, fr. G dial. (Bavaria), alter. of *sälmling*, fr. *salm* salmon (fr. OHG *salmo*, fr. L) + -*ling*] **1** : a char (*Salvelinus alpinus*) of mountain streams of Europe **2** : SUNAPEE TROUT

sa·ic \sä'ēk, 'sāik\ *n* -s [F *saïque*, fr. Turk *şayka*] : a ketch common in the Levant

saice \'sīs\ *var of* SYCE

said \'sed\ *adj* [fr. *said*, past part. of *say*] : AFOREMENTIONED

saidest *or* **saidst** *archaic past of* SAY

sa·if *var of* SEIF

¹**sai·ga** \'sīgə\ *n* -s [ML] : a small silver coin issued under the Merovingians and current in France before the introduction of the denier

²**saiga** \"\ *n* -s [Russ *saĭga*, fr. Fagatai *saigak*] : a sheeplike antelope (*Saiga tartarica*) of Siberia and eastern Russia having the nasal region inflated and the nostrils widely separated and in the male having lyrate annulated horns and tufts of long hair beneath the eyes and ears

sai·gon \(')sī'gän\ *adj, usu cap* [fr. *Saigon*, So. Vietnam] : of or from Saigon, the capital of So. Vietnam : of the kind or style prevalent in Saigon

saigon cinnamon *n, usu cap S* : the bark of an Indo-Chinese tree (*Cinnamomum loureirii*)

¹**sail** \'sāl, *esp before pause or consonant* -āəl\ *n* -s *see sense 1b* [ME *seil, sail*, fr. OE *segl*; akin to OFris *seil* sail, OS *segel*, OHG *segal*, ON *segl* sail, *sægr* piece torn off of something, strip, *sǫg* saw — more at SAW] **1 a** : an extent of canvas or other fabric by means of which the wind is used to propel ships through the water; *collectively* : the sails of a ship ⟨boats large enough to carry ~ —Thor Heyerdahl⟩ **b** *pl usu* **sail** : SAILING SHIP ⟨saw one ~, a brig —Arnold Bennett⟩ ⟨its mackerel fleet comprised seventy ~ —Elizabeth Coatsworth⟩ ⟨a good many ~s in the bay —G.W.Brace⟩ **2** : an extent of fabric used in propelling a wind-driven vehicle (as an iceboat) **3** : something that resembles a sail: as **a** : the extended surface of the arm of a windmill **b** : a wing of a bird (as a hawk) **c** : FIN **d** : TENTACLE **e** : a streamlined conning tower on a submarine **4** *Africa* : BUCK SAIL **5** [²*sail*] **a** (1) *obs* : sailing ability ⟨finding his ship but ill of ~ —William Monson⟩ (2) : the handling and navigation of ships under sail as distinct from under steam **b** (1) : a passage by a sailing ship : CRUISE ⟨a ~ upon the bay⟩ ⟨a ~ around the world⟩ (2) : the distance coverable in a specified period of sailing ⟨two days' ~ from port⟩ **c** *obs* : a group sailing together ⟨a large ~ of ducks passed here —Jonathan Swift⟩ — **under sail 1** : in motion with sails set **2** : propelled by sails

²**sail** \"\ *vb* -ED/-ING/-S [ME *seilen, sailen*, fr. OE *seglian, seglan*; akin to MLG *segelen* to sail, MHG *segelen, sigelen*, ON *sigla*; denominative fr. the stem of E ¹*sail*] *vi* **1 a** (1) : to travel on water in a ship propelled by the wind (2) : to travel in a ship propelled by steam or other means ⟨~ down the river by steamer⟩ **b** : to take trips in or manage a sailboat for pleasure : YACHT **2 a** : to move forward (as of a ship on water) by the action of wind upon sails **b** : to move forward on water by the action of steam or other motive power **c** : to move without visible effort through or on the water ⟨the swan ~*ing* on the lake⟩ **3** : to begin a water voyage ⟨~ with the tide⟩ **4** : to glide through the air without apparent exertion ⟨the white clouds ~*ed* across the sky —William Black⟩ **5** : to travel or go in any of various manners: as **a** : to stride in a stately, pompous, or proud manner ⟨~*ed* gracefully into the room —L.C.Douglas⟩ **b** : to move without effort ⟨held the door for us and we ~*ed* through —P.E.Deutschman⟩ **c** : to move or arrive so as to attract attention or create a disturbance ⟨~ up in their big new car⟩ **6 a** : to begin vigorously to do something : attack with gusto — used with *in* or *into* ⟨coffee and sandwiches, which I ~*ed* into with . . . gratitude —H.A. Chippendale⟩ **b** : to attack a person with words or blows — used with *in* or *into* ⟨with questions and complaints, one after another ~*ed* into him —A.R.Williams⟩ ~ *vt* **1 a** : to move or travel upon (water) by means of sail, steam, or other motive power ⟨trawlers ~*ing* the fishing grounds⟩ ⟨the first man to ~ these waters⟩ **b** : to fly through : glide or move smoothly through ⟨gray hawks . . . ~*ing* the sky —J.M.Synge⟩ **2** : to direct or manage the motion of (a ship or glider) ⟨tugboats and the men who ~ them —*advt*⟩ **3** : to cause to move smoothly through the air ⟨~ a discus⟩

sail·age \-lij\ *n* -s [¹*sail* + -*age*] : the sails of a ship

sail arm *n* : WHIP 5

sailboat \'ₛ,ₛ\ *n* : a boat usu. propelled by sail

sail burton *n* : a top burton with a tail block seized to the lower hook and the hauling part rove through this tail block and thence through a snatch block on deck so that the lead of the hauling part serves to guy a sail clear and keep it from twisting when bending sails

sailcloth \'ₛ,ₛ\ *n* [ME *seilcloth, sailcloth*, fr. *seil, sail* + *cloth*] **1 a** : a strong heavy canvas for sails, tents, or upholstery **b** : a lightweight canvas for clothing or curtains **2** : a piece of sailcloth

sail·er \-lə(r)\ *n* -s [ME, fr. *seilen, sailen* to sail + -*er* — more at SAIL] : a sailing or other ship or a sailboat esp. having specified sailing qualities ⟨failed sadly . . . as a ~ and was shorn of her topmasts —R.B.O'Brien⟩ ⟨a smart ~⟩

sailfin \'ₛ,ₛ\ *or* **sailfin mollie** *n* : a topminnow (*Mollienisia latipinna*) of the southern U.S. and Mexico that is predominantly olive green with black markings and fins of lavender, orange, and blue and that has the dorsal fin greatly enlarged in the male

sailfish \'ₛ,ₛ\ *n* **1** : any of several large pelagic fishes constituting a genus (*Istiophorus*) related to the swordfish but having teeth, scales, pelvic fins of a few rays, and a very large dorsal fin highest at or behind its middle — see ATLANTIC SAILFISH, PACIFIC SAILFISH **2** : BASKING SHARK

sailflying \'ₛ,ₛₛ\ *n* : the action of flying in a sailplane

sail hook *n* : a small hook used to hold cloth while a sail is being made

sailing *n* -s [ME *seiling, sailing*, fr. gerund of *seilen, sailen* to sail — more at SAIL] **1 a** : the technical skill of managing a ship; *esp* : the skill of directing a ship to a given place according to the rules of navigation : NAVIGATION **b** : the method of determining the course to be followed, the direction and distance to be sailed to reach a given point, and the position of a ship from dead reckoning **2 a** (1) : the sport or pastime of navigating or riding in a sailboat (2) : the conditions under which one may sail ⟨the ~ was excellent last month⟩ **b** : a trip or voyage in a ship ⟨make a fast ~⟩ **c** : a departure from a port; *esp* : a scheduled departure of a liner

sailing boat *n* : SAILBOAT

sailing day *n* **1** : the day of departure of a passenger ship **2** : the day that cargo will no longer be received on a cargo ship

sailing master *n* **1** : a ship's officer in charge of navigation **2** : a warrant officer (as formerly in the U.S. Navy) in charge of navigating a ship and of stowage

sailing ship *n* : a ship propelled by sail

sail·less \'sā(ə)lləs\ *adj* : having no sail

sail lizard *n* : any of several large agamid lizards of the genus *Hydrosaurus* of the Moluccas and the Philippines that have a crested tail

sail loft *n* : a loft or room where sails are cut out and made

sailmaker \'ₛ,ₛₛ\ *n* : one who cuts, assembles, and sews sails and canvas parts for ships; *specif* : a warrant officer (as formerly in the U.S. Navy) in charge of all sails and articles of canvas

sailmaker's mate *n* : a petty officer (as formerly in the U.S. Navy) assisting or acting as a sailmaker and in charge of all canvas (as bags, hammocks, or awnings)

sailmaker's splice *n* : a tapered splice joining two ropes of different sizes

sail needle *n* : a large needle triangular in section for sewing sailcloth

sail·or \'sālə(r)\ *n* -s [alter. (influenced by -*or*) of *sailer*] **1 a** : one that sails; *esp* : one that takes part in or understands the practical operation of a ship : MARINER **b** : a member of a ship's crew other than an officer **2** *archaic* : SAILER **3** : a traveler by water ⟨so bad a ~ that he nearly died of seasickness —Robert Graves⟩ **4** *or* **sailor hat** : a man's hat of stiff straw with a low flat crown and a straight circular brim; *also* : a woman's hat usu. of straw of somewhat similar shape

sailor 4

sailor blue *n* : a moderate purplish blue that is lighter and stronger than marine blue and bluer and duller than average cornflower or gentian blue

sailor collar *n* : a broad collar having a square flap across the back and tapering to a V in front

sail·or·ing \-ləriŋ\ *n* -s [*sailor* + -*ing*] : the life, occupation, or duties of a sailor : SAILORIZING

sail·or·iz·ing \-lə,rīziŋ\ *n* -s [*sailor* + -*ize* + -*ing*] : the practice or art of sailing esp. as a seaman : the work of a sailor

sail·or·less \-lə(r)ləs\ *adj* : having no sailor

sail·or·ly *adj* : having the characteristics of a sailor

sail·or·man \-(r)mən, -(r),man\ *n, pl* **sailormen** : SAILOR, SEAMAN

sailor's-choice \'ₛₛₛ'ₛ\ *n, pl* **sailor's-choice** : any of several small grunts of the western Atlantic: as **a** : PINFISH a,b **b** : a pigfish (*Orthopristis chrysopterus*) **c** (1) : a ronco (*Haemulon parra*) (2) : MARGATE a

sailor's-knot \'ₛₛₛ,ₛ\ *n, pl* **sailor's-knots** : a wild geranium (*Geranium maculatum*)

sailor's skin *n* : skin of exposed portions of the body marked by warty thickening, pigmentation, and presenile keratosis and often considered to be precancerous and to lead to formation of epitheliomas

sailor's-tobacco \'ₛₛₛₛ'ₛ(,)ₛ\ *n, pl* **sailor's-tobaccos** : a mugwort (*Artemisia vulgaris*)

sailor suit *n* : a boy's outfit of middy blouse and bell-bottom trousers copied from a sailor's uniform

sailor tie *n* : a 2-eyelet low shoe with a ribbon tie

sailor suit

sail-over \'ₛ,ₛₛ\ *n* -s : OVERHANG b

¹**sailplane** \'ₛ,ₛ\ *n* [²*sail* + *plane*] : a glider with a wing load small enough to enable it to rise in an upward air current : a soaring glider

²**sailplane** \"\ *vi* : to fly in a sailplane

sails *pl of* SAIL; *pres 3d sing of* SAIL

sailship \'ₛ,ₛ\ *n* : SAILING SHIP

sail track *n* : a track on the afterside of a mast to which the edge of the sail is attached that takes the place of mast hoops

sail yard *n* : a yard or spar on which a sail is spread

saim \'sām\ *n* -s [ME *seim, saim*, fr. (assumed) VL *sagimen*, alter. of L *sagina* action of stuffing or fattening, food, fatness] *dial chiefly Brit* : animal fat; *specif* : LARD

sai·mi·ri \sī'mirē\ *n* [Pg, fr. Guarani *çai miri*, lit., little monkey] **1** -s : SQUIRREL MONKEY **2** *cap* [NL, fr. Pg] : a genus of small arboreal gregarious So. American monkeys comprising the squirrel monkeys

sain \'sān\ *vt* -ED/-ING/-S [ME *seynen, sainen, sanen*, fr. OE *segnian*, fr. LL *signare* — more at SIGN] **1** *dial Brit* **a** : to cross (oneself) esp. as a blessing against evil influence **b** : BLESS **2** *chiefly dial* : to save from evil by invocation or blessing

sa·i·ne·te \,sīē'nā(,)tā\ *n* -s [Sp, small piece of fat, tidbit, relish, entremés, dim. of *sain* fat, grease, fr. (assumed) VL *saginum*, alter. of L *sagina* action of stuffing or fattening, food, fatness] : ENTREMÉS 2

sain·foin \'sān,fōin\ *or* **san·foin** \'san-\ *n* -s [F *sainfoin*, fr. MF, fr. *sain* healthy (fr. L *sanus* healthy, sane) + *foin* hay, fr. L *fenum, faenum*; fr. its use as a medicinal herb — more at SANE, FENNEL] **1** : a Eurasian perennial herb (*Onobrychis viciaefolia*) having pinnate leaves and spicate pink flowers **2** : an American tick trefoil (*Desmodium canadense*) **3** : a perennial herb (*Psoralea onobrychis*) of the central U. S.

¹**saint** \'sānt, *when a name follows* (,)sānt *or* sənt, *when a name follows that begins with a consonant chiefly Brit* sən\ *n* -s [ME, fr. MF, fr. LL *sanctus*, fr. L, sacred, pure, holy, fr. past part. of *sancire* to make sacred, ordain, establish — more at SACRED] **1 a** : one officially recognized or acknowledged as preeminent for consecration, holiness, and piety esp. through canonization by one of the branches of the Christian church ⟨*Saint* Matthew⟩ **b** : an image of a saint ⟨the ~ was cast . . . eighty-two years ago —Norman Douglas⟩ **2 a** : one of the spirits of the departed in heaven **b** : ANGEL ⟨*Saint* Michael the archangel⟩ **3 a** : one of God's chosen people (1) : ISRAELITE, JEW; *esp* : one who strictly practices his religion ⟨Israel's ~s did not defer the day —O.J.Baab⟩ (2) : one belonging to the entire company of baptized Christians ⟨with all the ~s —2 Cor 1:1 (RSV)⟩ **b** *usu cap* : a member of any of various religious bodies ⟨on either side of the preacher several female *Saints* —E.T.Clark⟩: as (1) : PURITAN ⟨any news of the *Saints* in Amsterdam —Ben Jonson⟩ (2) : LATTER-DAY SAINT **4 a** : a person consecrated or single-heartedly dedicated to holiness, religion, or a religious task : a holy or godly person ⟨a great ~ who has given up his life for the sanctification of the Name —Maurice Samuel⟩ ⟨some local ~, a creature who made an annual pilgrimage to some shrine —G.A.Wagner⟩ **b** : one eminent for piety, virtue, or purity of conscience ⟨the calm, serene face of an elderly ~ at a funeral service —A.N. Meckel⟩ **c** : one spiritually reborn and sanctified or undergoing spiritual rebirth ⟨a cry of victory broke through the moaning as a ~ was born —J.C.Brauer⟩ **d** : one slightly or considerably more charitable, patient, self-denying, or virtuous than the average ⟨a reign of the ~s which ordinary mortals could not live up to —A.L.Rowse⟩ ⟨the patience of a ~⟩ **5** : a person honored after death for virtue, piety, or martyrdom ⟨the Muslim ~s⟩ **6** : a member of a 19th century English party zealously advocating emancipation of slaves **7** : a founder, illustrious example, or benefactor of an art, movement, school, or way of life ⟨became the first precursors of symbolism and were afterwards placed among its ~s —Edmund Wilson⟩

²**saint** \'sānt\ *vt* -ED/-ING/-S [ME *sainten*, fr. *saint*, n.] **1** *archaic* : to make blessed in or as if in heaven : BEATIFY **2** : to recognize or designate as a saint; *specif* : to enroll among the saints by an official act : CANONIZE **3** : to make (as a person) an object of veneration or reverence : ENSHRINE

saint an·drew \-'an(,)drü\ *n, usu cap S&A* [after *St. Andrew* †60 A.D., one of the twelve apostles, patron saint of Scotland] : a Scottish gold coin first issued by Robert III (1390–1406) having a representation of St. Andrew on the reverse and a lion rampant over the shield of Scotland on the obverse — called also *lion*

saint andrew's cross *n, usu cap S&A* [so called fr. the tradition that St. Andrew was crucified on a cross of this type] **1 a** : a figure of a cross having the form of two intersecting oblique bars : SALTIRE 2 **b** : such a figure extending to and cut off by the boundaries of the area on which it is depicted — used esp. in describing flags; compare SALTIRE 1 **2** : CRUX DECUSSATA 1

Saint Andrew's cross

saint-andrew's-cross \(')ₛ'ₛ(,)ₛ'ₛ\ *n, usu cap S&A* [*St. Andrew's cross*] : a No. American and West Indian woody plant (*Ascyrum hypericoides*) with petals arranged as a St. Andrew's cross

saint andrew's day *n, usu cap S&A&D* : November 30 observed in New Zealand as a statutory bank holiday

saint-ann's-bark \-'anz,-\ *n, usu cap S&A* [after *St. Ann* (Anne), mother of the Virgin Mary] : RED BARK

saint an·tho·ny's cross \-'an(t)thənēz-\ *n, usu cap S&A* [after *St. Anthony* †*ab*A.D.350 Egyptian abbot regarded as the founder of Christian monasticism who traditionally wore a tau cross on his cloak] **1** : a T-shaped cross : TAU CROSS 1 **2** : CRUX COMMISSA 1

saint anthony's fire *n, usu cap S&A* [so called fr. the belief that such diseases could be cured through the intercession of St. Anthony] : any of several inflammations or gangrenous conditions (as erysipelas or ergotism) of the skin

saint au·gus·tine grass \-'ògə,stēn-\ *n, usu cap S&A* [after *St. Augustine* — more at AUGUSTINIAN] **1** : a perennial much-branched creeping grass (*Stenotaphrum secundatum*) of the southern U.S. valuable as a sand binder and sod grass — called also *buffalo grass* **2** : a grass (*Manisuris rugosa*) similar to St. Augustine grass

saint aus·tin's summer \-'òstənz-\ *or* **saint au·gus·tine's summer** \-ò'gəstənz-\ *n, usu cap S&A* [after *St. Austin* (*Augustine*); prob. fr. the proximity of his feast day (Aug. 28)] *Brit* : Indian summer when occurring in September

saint bar·na·bas' day \-'bärnəbəs(əz)-\ *n, usu cap S&B* [after *St. Barnabas* — more at BARNABY BRIGHT] : BARNABY BRIGHT

saint-bar·na·by's-thistle \-,bärnəbēz,-\ *n, usu cap S&B* [after *St. Barnabas* — more at BARNABY'S THISTLE] : BARNABY'S THISTLE

saint be·noit \-ben'wä\ *n, often cap S&B* [prob. fr. F *St. Benoît*, after *St. Benoît* (Benedict) the Black †1589 Sicilian monk] : NEGRO 2

saint ber·nard \-bər'närd, -bə'nȧd\ *n, usu cap S&B* [fr. the hospice of Grand *St. Bernard*, alpine pass between Switzerland and Italy where such dogs were first bred] **1** : a Swiss alpine breed of powerful tall imposing dogs used esp. formerly in aiding lost travelers and having a massive head, deep stop, short muzzle, large button ears, short and strong neck, sloping shoulders, broad back that slopes gently from the haunches to the rump, well-developed hindquarters, and a long blunt-ended tail **2** *pl* **saint bernards** : any dog of the St. Bernard breed

saint-ber·nard's-lily \-,bərnərdz,-\ *n, usu cap S&B* [prob. after *St. Bernard* of Clairvaux †1153 Fr. ecclesiastic] : an Old World herb (*Anthericum liliago*) with long recurved linear leaves commonly cultivated for its racemose greenish white flowers

saint-bru·no's-lily \-,brü(,)nōz,-\ *n, usu cap S&B* [prob. after *St. Bruno* of Querfurt †1009 Ger. archbishop & missionary] : a European alpine plant (*Paradisea liliastrum*) of the family Liliaceae resembling the asphodel with fascicled fleshy roots, radical leaves, and funnel-shaped white flowers

saint-cath·er·ine's flower \-'kath(ə)rənz-\ *n, usu cap S&C* [after *St. Catherine* of Alexandria †*ab*307 Christian martyr who was tortured on a spiked wheel] **1** [so called fr. the fancied resemblance of the styles to the spikes on Catherine's wheel] : LOVE-IN-A-MIST 1 **2** : POINSETTIA

saint cuth·bert's beads \-'kəthbə(r)ts-\ *n pl, usu cap S&C* [after *St. Cuthbert* †687 English monk] : joints of fossil crinoid stems

saint cuthbert's duck *n, usu cap S&C* : EIDER DUCK

saint-dab·e·oc's-heath \-'dabē,äks,-\ *n, usu cap S&D* [after *St. Dabeoc* (Beoc), 5th or 6th cent. Brit. monk who founded a monastery in Ireland] : IRISH HEATH

saint·dom \'sāntdəm\ *n* -s : the quality or state of being a saint

sainted *adj* **1** : of, relating to, befitting, or resembling a saint ⟨the enthron'd gods on ~ seats —John Milton⟩ **2** : SAINTLY, VIRTUOUS, PIOUS ⟨spiritual and moral stature of their ~ predecessors —K.S.Latourette⟩ **3** : entered into heaven : DEAD ⟨one of our long departed, ~ ministers —Sara King⟩

saint ed·ward's crown \-'edwə(r)dz-\ *n, usu cap S&E* [after *St. Edward* (Edward the Confessor) †1066 king of England] : IMPERIAL CROWN 1a

saint elmo's fire *or* **saint elmo's light** \-'el(,)mōz-\ *or* **saint ulmo's fire** *or* **saint ulmo's light** \-'əl(,)mōz-\ *n, usu cap S&E&U* [after *St. Elmo* or *Ulmo* (*Erasmus*) †303 Ital. bishop and martyr, patron saint of sailors] : a flaming phenomenon sometimes seen in stormy weather at prominent points on an airplane (as at the wing tips) or ship (as at the masthead or yardarms) and on land (as at the tops of trees or steeples) that is of the nature of a brush discharge of electricity which is reddish when positive and bluish when negative — called also *corposant*

saint-errant \'ₛ'ₛₛ\ *n, pl* **saints-errant** *or* **saint-errants** [¹*saint* + *errant* (as in *knight-errant*)] : a wandering saint : a missionary saint

saint-étienne *or* **saint-etienne** \saⁿtātyen\ *adj, usu cap S&E* [fr. *St.-Étienne*, France] : of or from the city of St.-Étienne, France : of the kind or style prevalent in St.-Étienne

saint·foin \'sānt,fōin\ *n* -s [F, alter. of *sainfoin* — more at SAINFOIN] : SAINFOIN

saint george's day \-'jȯrjəz-\ *n, usu cap S&G&D* [after *St. George* †*ab*303 Cappadocian Christian martyr, patron saint of England] : April 23 observed as a bank holiday in New Zealand

saint george's duck *n, usu cap S&G, Brit* : a European sheldrake (*Tadorna tadorna*)

saint george's mushroom *n, usu cap S&G* : HORSE MUSHROOM; *also* : a related mushroom (*Agaricus gambosus*)

saint george's round *n, usu cap S&G* : an archery round of 36 arrows fired at 100 yards, 80 yards, and 60 yards respectively

saint he·le·na tea \(,)sānt°l'ēnə, -thə'lēnə\ *n, usu cap S&H* [fr. *St. Helena*, island in the south Atlantic ocean] : a shrub (*Frankenia portulacifolia*) of St. Helena whose leaves are used as a substitute for tea

saint hel·ens \-'helənz\ *adj, usu cap S&H* [fr. *St. Helens*, England] : of or from the county borough of St. Helens,

sails: fore-and-aft and square

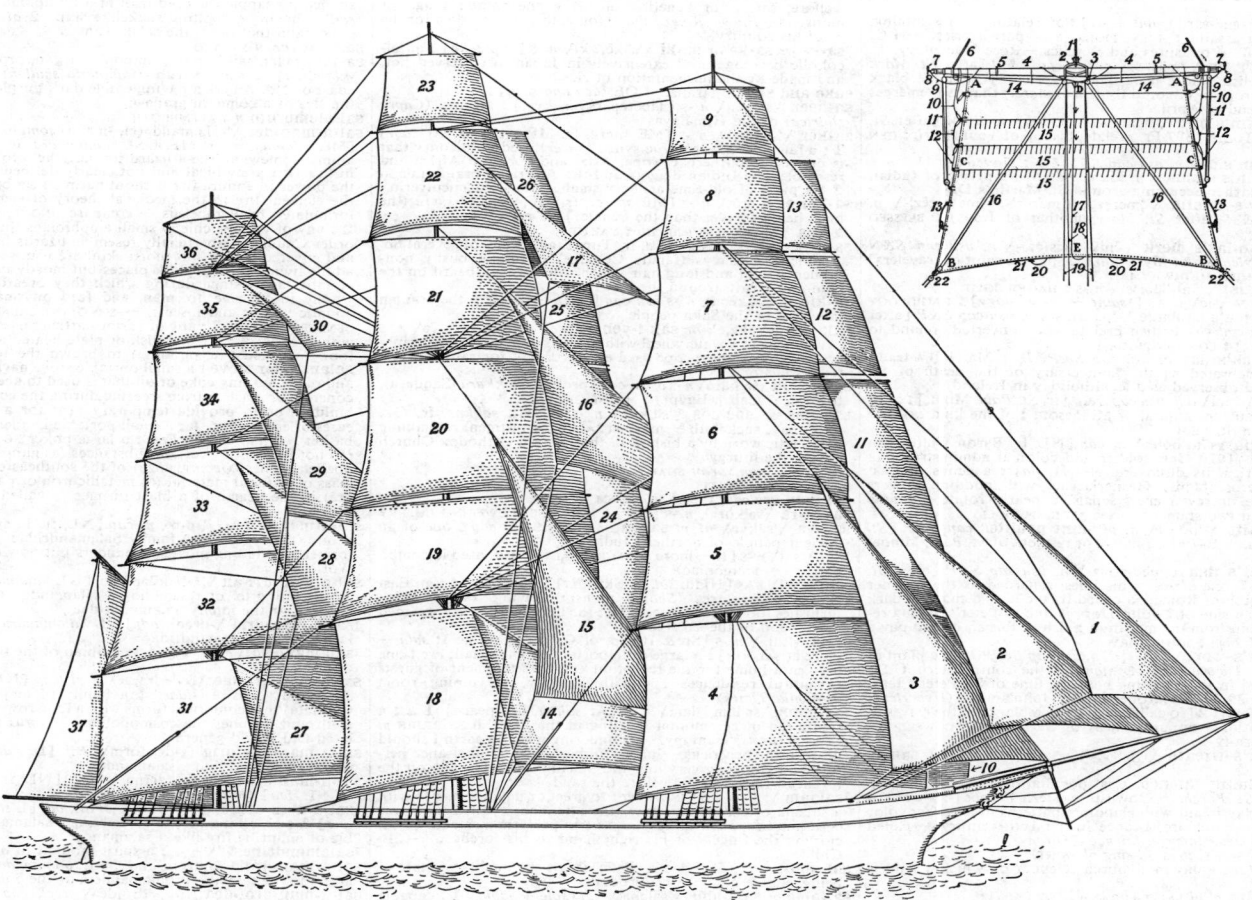

SCHOONER'S SAILS
(an inner and an outer jib are sometimes fitted instead of one jib)
1 flying jib, *2* jib, *3* forestaysail, *4* foresail, *5* fore gaff-topsail, *6* main-topmast staysail, *7* mainsail, *8* main gaff-topsail

FULL-RIGGED SHIP under ALL PLAIN SAIL to skysails, with all staysails and all port studding sails
(sometimes an inner jib and outer jib are fitted instead of one jib, and also an upper and lower main-topmast staysail instead of one staysail, the upper stay leading just below the foretop; double topgallant sails are sometimes fitted)
1 flying jib, *2* jib, *3* fore-topmast staysail, *4* foresail, *5* lower fore-topsail, *6* upper fore-topsail, *7* fore-topgallant sail, *8* fore-royal, *9* fore-skysail, *10* lower studding sail (never on the main), *11* fore-topmast studding sail, *12* fore-topgallant studding sail, *13* fore-royal studding sail, *14* main staysail, *15* main-topmast staysail, *16* main-topgallant staysail, *17* main-royal staysail, *18* mainsail, *19* lower main topsail, *20* upper main topsail, *21* main-topgallant sail, *22* main royal, *23* main skysail, *24* main-topmast studding sail, *25* main-topgallant studding sail, *26* main-royal studding sail, *27* mizzen staysail, *28* mizzen-topmast staysail, *29* mizzen-topgallant staysail, *30* mizzen-royal staysail, *31* mizzen sail (crossjack), *32* lower mizzen topsail, *33* upper mizzen topsail, *34* mizzen-topgallant sail, *35* mizzen royal, *36* mizzen skysail, *37* spanker
SMALL DIAGRAM: parts of a square sail (topsail) *1* tye, *2* yoke, *3* quarter block, *4* stirrup for footrope, *5* burton bolt, *6* lift, *7* boom ring, *8* pacific iron, *9* Flemish horse, *10* bull earing, *11* reef tackle, *12* reef earing, *13* bowline bridle, *14* footrope, *15* reef point, *16* clew line, *17* bunt whip, *18* topgallant sheet, *19* reef tackle, *20* buntline, *21* buntline toggle, *22* sheet, *A* head-earing cringle, *B* clew, *C* leech, *D* head, *E* foot

Lancashire, England : of the kind or style prevalent in St. Helens

saint·hood \'sānt,hu̇d\ *n* [¹*saint* + *-hood*] **1** : the quality or state of being a saint **2** : saints as a group

saint-ig·na·tius's-bean \-ig¦nāsh(ē)əs(əz)¦-\ *n, usu cap S&I* [after *St. Ignatius* of Loyola (Íñigo de Oñez y Loyola) †1556 Span. soldier and ecclesiastic, founder of the Jesuits] : the greenish straw-colored seed of a Philippine woody vine (*Strychnos ignatii*) like nux vomica in its action and uses — see STRYCHNINE

sainting *pres part of* SAINT

saint·ish \'sāntish\ *adj* [¹*saint* + *-ish*] : somewhat saintly

saint-ja·cob's-dipper \-¦jākəbz¦-\ *n, usu cap S&J* [prob. after the Hebrew patriarch *Jacob* who first met his future wife Rachel by a well (Gen 29:9 ff.)] : PITCHER PLANT a

saint-james's-lily \-¦jāmz(əz)¦-\ *n, usu cap S&J* [prob. after *St. James* the Greater, one of Jesus's twelve apostles] : JACOBEAN LILY

saint john's \-'jänz\ *adj, usu cap S&J* [fr. *St. John's*, Newfoundland] : of or from St. John's, the capital of Newfoundland : of the kind or style prevalent in St. John's

saint-john's-bread \(¦)=¦=¦=\ *n, usu cap S&J* [after *St. John* the Baptist, known as the precursor of Christ; prob. in allusion to John's preaching in the wilderness of Judea and subsisting on honey and locusts (Mt 3:4 & Mk 1:6), the carob being also called *locust bean*, and *locust* (tree) being confused with *locust* (grasshopper)] : CAROB 1b

saint john's eve *n, usu cap S&J & sometimes cap E* **1** : the evening before St. John the Baptist's Day **2** : MIDSUMMER EVE

saint john's fire *n, usu cap S&J* : a fire lighted on the night of St. John the Baptist's Day to ward off sickness and ill luck — compare NEEDFIRE

saint-john's-wort \(¦)=¦=¦=\ *n, usu cap S&J* [after *St. John* the Baptist; fr. its being gathered on St. John's eve to be used to ward off evil spirits and as a medicinal herb] : a plant of the genus *Hypericum* — see HYPERICISM, KLAMATH WEED

saint-john's-wort family *n, usu cap S&J* : GUTTIFERAE

saint john the baptist's day *usu cap S&J&B&D* : June 24

saint-jo·seph's-lily \-¦jōzəfs¦-\ *n, usu cap S&J* [after *St. Joseph*, husband of Mary, mother of Jesus, often depicted with a lily in his hand] : MADONNA LILY

saint law·rence skiff \-'lȯrən(t)s-, -'lärən(t)s-\ *n, usu cap 1st S&L* : SKIFF 3

saint·less \'sāntləs\ *adj* : having no patron saint

saint·li·ly \'sāntlәlē\ *adv* : in a saintly manner

saint·li·ness \-tlēnəs, -lin-\ *n* -ES : the quality or state of being saintly : SANCTITY

saint·ling \-tliŋ\ *n* -S [¹*saint* + *-ling*] : an unimportant or young saint

saint lou·is \-'lüəs *sometimes* -'lüē *or* -'lüi\ *adj, usu cap S&L* [fr. *St. Louis*, Mo.] : of or from the city of St. Louis, Mo. : of the kind or style prevalent in St. Louis

saint lou·i·san \-üəsən\ *n, pl* **saint louisans** *cap S&L* [*St. Louis* + E *-an*] : a native or resident of St. Louis, Mo.

saint louis encephalitis *n, usu cap S&L* [so called fr. its having first occurred in epidemic form in St. Louis in 1933] : a No. American viral encephalitis

saint lu·cie cherry \-lü'sē-, -'==-\ *n, usu cap S&L* [prob. fr. *St. Lucie* (St. Lucia), largest of the Windward islands in the eastern West Indies] : MAHALEB

saint lucie grass *n, usu cap S&L* [fr. *St. Lucie* island] : a Bermuda grass that proliferates from aboveground runners

saint lu·cy's day \-'lüsēz-\ *n, usu cap S&L* [after *St. Lucy* †303 Sicilian Christian martyr] : LUCY LIGHT

saint luke's summer \-'lüks-\ *n, usu cap 1st S&L* [after *St. Luke* the Evangelist †*ab*74, whose feast day is Oct. 18] : a period of Indian summer weather occurring around St. Luke's Day

saint·ly *adj* -ER/-EST [¹*saint* + *-ly*] : of, relating to, resembling, or befitting a saint : HOLY, PIOUS ⟨a ~ parish priest —H.O. Taylor⟩ ⟨full of treasures and ~ relics —Rose Macaulay⟩

saint mark's fly \-'märks-\ *n, usu cap S&M* [after *St. Mark* the Evangelist, whose feast day is April 25] : a large black angular European bibionid fly (*Bibio marci*) that usu. emerges about the end of April

saint mar·tin's bird \-'märt°nz-\ *n, usu cap S&M* [after *St. Martin* of Tours †397 Fr. prelate, bishop of Tours] *Brit* : HEN HARRIER

saint martin's day *n, usu cap S&M&D* : November 11

saint martin's summer *n, usu cap S&M* : a period of Indian summer weather occurring around St. Martin's Day

saint-mary's-thistle \-¦merēz¦-, -¦mārēz¦-, -¦ma(a)rēz¦-\ *n, usu cap S&M* [after *St. Mary*, mother of Jesus] : BLESSED THISTLE

saint nich·o·las's clerk \-'nik(ə)ləs(əz)-\ *n, usu cap S&N* [after *St. Nicholas* of Myra †*ab*352, patron saint of travelers] *archaic* : THIEF, HIGHWAYMAN

saint·ol·o·gist \sānt·'äləjəst\ *n* -S : HAGIOLOGIST

saint·ol·o·gy \-jē\ *n* -ES [¹*saint* + *-o-* + *-logy*] : HAGIOLOGY

saint-pat·rick's cabbage \-'pa·triks-\ *n, usu cap S&P* [after *St. Patrick* †*ab*461 British prelate who converted Ireland to Christianity] : LONDON PRIDE 1

saint patrick's day *n, usu cap S&P&D* : March 17 traditionally celebrated as the anniversary of the death of St. Patrick and observed as a legal holiday in Ireland

saint paul \-'pȯl\ *adj, usu cap S&P* [fr. *St. Paul*, Minn.] : of or from St. Paul, the capital of Minnesota : of the kind or style prevalent in St. Paul

saint·pau·lia \sānt'pȯlēə\ *n, cap* [NL, fr. Baron Walter von *Saint Paul* †1910 Ger. soldier and colonial administrator in eastern Africa, its discoverer + NL *-ia*] : a genus of East African herbs (family Gesneriaceae) with nodding flowers having five or seven erect sepals, a nearly rotate bilabiate corolla, and two stamens — see AFRICAN VIOLET

saint paul·ite \-'pȯ,līt\ *n, pl* **saint paulites** *cap S&P* [*St. Paul*, Minn. + E *-ite*] : a native or resident of St. Paul, Minnesota

saint pe·ter's fish \-'pēd·ə(r)z-\ *n, usu cap S&P* [after *St. Peter* †*ab*67, one of Jesus' disciples, regarded as the founder of the Church of Rome; so called fr. the legend that the dark spot on each side of a John Dory is due to Peter's having removed a coin from the mouth of a fish of this species to pay a tax (Mt 17:27)] : JOHN DORY

saint-peter's-wort \(¦)=¦=¦=\ *n, usu cap S&P* **1 a** : a plant of the genus *Ascyrum* (as *A. stans* of the southeastern U.S.) **b** [so called fr. its blooming near the time of St. Peter's feast day (June 29)] : a European Saint-John's-wort (*Hypericum quadrangulum*) **2** [so called fr. the resemblance of the leaves to keys, traditional appurtenances of St. Peter] : COWSLIP 1a **3** : SNOWBERRY 1

saint-peter's-wreath \(¦)=¦=¦=\ *n, usu cap S&P* : BRIDAL WREATH 1

saint-porchaire faïence \¦saⁿ,pȯr¦sha(a)(ə)r-\ *n, usu cap S&P* [fr. *St.-Porchaire*, town in western France] : a ware of pale buff clay inlaid with elaborate patterns in a darker color made at St.-Porchaire, France in the 16th century — called also *Henri Deux faïence*, *faïence d'Oiron*

saints *pl of* SAINT, *pres 3d sing of* SAINT

saint's day *n* : a day in a church calendar on which a saint is commemorated

saints-errant *pl of* SAINT-ERRANT

saint·ship \'sānt,ship\ *n* [¹*saint* + *-ship*] : the quality or state of being a saint or saintly; *specif* : the quality or state of being canonized

¹saint-si·mo·ni·an \¦sānt,sī¦mōnēən\ *adj, usu cap both Ss* [Count de *St.-Simon* (Claude Henri de Rouvroy) †1825 Fr. philosopher and social scientist + E *-ian*] : of or relating to St.-Simon or Saint-Simonianism

²saint-simonian \"\ *n* -S *usu cap both Ss* : a follower of St.-Simon or an adherent of Saint-Simonianism

saint-si·mo·ni·an·ism \-ē·ə,nizəm\ *n* -S *usu cap both Ss* : a socialistic system in which the state owns all property and the laborer is entitled to share according to the quality and amount of his work

saint-si·mon·ism \(¦)sānt'sīmə,nizəm\ *n* -S *usu cap both Ss* [Count *St.-Simon* + E *-ism*] : SAINT-SIMONIANISM

saint thom·as tree \-'täməs-\ *n, usu cap S & 1st T* [after *St. Thomas*, one of Jesus' disciples; fr. the tradition that the red spots on the flowers were caused by drops of Thomas' blood falling on such a shrub when he was martyred in India] : a tropical Asiatic and African shrub (*Bauhinia tomentosa*) with tomentose to glabrate branchlets, lower leaf surfaces, and pods and yellow flowers with a red or brownish blotch that is grown as an ornamental and found as an escape in the West Indies

saint ulmo's fire *or* **saint ulmo's light** *usu cap S&U, var of* SAINT ELMO'S FIRE

saint val·en·tine's day \-'valən·,tīnz-\ *n, usu cap S&V&D* [after *St. Valentine* †*ab*270 Ital. priest] : Feb. 14 observed as a festival in honor of St. Valentine and as a day for sending love tokens or valentines

saint vi·tus's dance \-'vīd·əs(əz)-, -'vītəs(əz)-\ *n, usu cap S&V* [after *St. Vitus*, 3d cent. Christian child martyr who was invoked by sufferers from chorea] : CHOREA

¹sair \'sā(ə)r\ *Scot var of* SORE

²sair \"\ *Scot var of* SERVE

sair·ly \-rlī\ *Scot var of* SORELY

sairve \'särv\ *Scot var of* SERVE

sairy \'sārī\ *chiefly Scot var of* SORRY

sais \'sīs\ *var of* SYCE

¹sa·ite \'sā,īt\ *n* -S *cap* [L *Saites*, fr. Gk *Saītēs*, fr. *Saïs*, city in ancient Egypt + Gk *-itēs* -ite] : a native or inhabitant of Saïs

²saite \"\ *or* **sa·it·ic** \sā'id·ik\ *adj, usu cap* [*Saite* fr. ¹*Saite*; *Saitic* fr. L *Saiticus*, fr. Gk *Saitikos*, fr. *Saitēs* + *-ikos* -ic] **1** : of or relating to Saïs or its inhabitants **2** : of or relating to the XXVIth Dynasty of ancient Egypt

saith \(')seth, 'sāəth\ *archaic pres 3d sing of* SAY

saithe \'sāth\ *n, pl* **saithe** [of Scand origin; akin to ON *seithr* coalfish; perh. akin to ON *sītha* side — more at SIDE] : POLLACK

sai·va \'sīvə\ *or* **shai·va** \'shīvə\ *n* -S *usu cap* [Skt *Śaiva*, fr. *Śiva* (Siva), one of the principal deities of Hinduism] : a worshiper of Siva

sai·vism *or* **shai·vism** \-ī,vizəm\ *or* **shi·va·ism** \'shēvə,izəm\ *n* -S *usu cap* [*Saiva* or *Shaiva* + *-ism*] : SIVAISM

sai·vite *or* **shai·vite** \'shī,vīt\ *or* **shi·vite** \'shē,v-\ *n* -S *usu cap* [*Saiva* + *-ite*] : SAIVA

sa·jou \sə'jü\ *n* -S [F, fr. Tupi *sai-guaçú*, lit., big monkey] **1** : CAPUCHIN 3b **2** : SPIDER MONKEY

sa·ka \'säkə\ *n, pl* **saka** *usu cap* : any of various nomadic peoples formerly inhabiting the steppelands north of the Iranian plateau

¹sa·kai \'sä,kī\ *n, pl* **sakai** *usu cap* **1 a** : a forest people of Malaya comprising a number of small tribes **b** : a member of such people **2** : the Mon-Khmer language of the Sakai people

²sakai \"\ *adj, usu cap* [fr. *Sakai*, Japan] : of or from the city of Sakai, Japan : of the kind or style prevalent in Sakai

sa·ka·ki \sə'käkē\ *n* -S [Jap] : a small Japanese and Indian evergreen shrub (*Cleyera japonica*) of the family Theaceae having alternate leaves, bisexual white fragrant flowers, and globose red berries that is used as an ornamental

sa·ka·la·va \,säkə'lävə\ *n, pl* **sakalava** *or* **sakalavas** *usu cap* : a people in western Madagascar — compare MALAGASY

¹sake \'sāk\ *n* -S [ME, dispute, accusation, fault, guilt (the phrase *for someones sake* meaning orig. "because of someone's guilt"), fr. OE *sacu* fault, guilt, conflict, action at law; akin to OHG *sahha* action at law, cause, reason, ON *sök* action at law, guilt, crime, cause, sake, Goth *sakjo* quarrel, *sakan* to quarrel — more at SEEK] **1** : END, PURPOSE ⟨suppose, for the ~ of argument⟩ ⟨no desire to strike . . . for the ~ of striking —*Wall Street Jour.*⟩ **2 a** : the good, advantage, or enhancement of an object, ideal, emotion, or other entity ⟨toil for the ~ of money⟩ ⟨keeps . . . its ornate old bar, mostly for sentiment's ~ —Green Peyton⟩ ⟨the highest ends — those to be pursued for their own ~s —Harry Bear⟩ **b** : the good, advantage, or well-being of a person or group : personal or social welfare, safety, or benefit ⟨for her ~ he contends against monsters —*Encyc. Americana*⟩ ⟨for both our ~s⟩ ⟨died for the ~ of his country⟩

²sa·ke *or* **sa·ké** *or* **sa·ki** \'säkē, -ki\ *n* -S [Jap *sake*] : an alcoholic beverage used extensively in Japan, usu. served hot, and made by the fermentation of rice

sake and soke *n* [trans. of OE *sacu ond sōcn*] : SOKE

sa·keen \sə'kēn\ *n* -S [Tibetan *skyin, kyin*] : an ibex (*Capra sibirica*) of the Himalayas

sa·ker \'sākə(r)\ *n* -S [ME *sagre*, fr. MF *sacre*, fr. Ar *ṣaqr*] **1** : a falcon (*Falco cherrug* syn. *F. sacer*) used in falconry that is native to southern Europe, Asia, and northern Africa and resembles the Indian luggars and the American prairie falcon **2** : a piece of old-time artillery smaller than a demiculverin

sa·ker·et \-ərət\ *n* -S [ME *sacret*, fr. MF, dim. of *sacre* (the male being smaller than the female)] : a male saker

sa·kha \'säkə\ *n* -S *usu cap* : YAKUT

sa·ki \'sakē, 'säkē\ *n* -S [F, fr. Tupi *sagui*] : any of several So. American monkeys (family Cebidae) having a bushy nonprehensile tail and long hair which usu. forms a beard on the chin and a ruff around the face

sa·ki·an \'säkēən\ *n* -S *usu cap* [*Saka* + *-ian*] : the Iranian language of the Saka people

sa·ki·eh \'sakē,e\ *or* **sak·i·yeh** \-ē,ye\ *or* **sak·ia** \-ēə\ *n* -S [Ar *sāqiyah*] : a waterwheel with buckets attached to its periphery or to an endless rope used esp. in Egypt for raising water from wells or pits

sak·ka·ra \sə'kärə\ *n* -S *often cap* [prob. fr. *Sakkara* (Saqqara), town near Cairo, Egypt] : MOUSE GRAY

sak·kos *or* **soc·cos** \'sä,kȯs\ *n* -ES [NGk *sakkos*, fr. Gk, sack, bag, sackcloth — more at SACK] : a vestment resembling a dalmatic worn by a bishop in the Eastern Orthodox Church during the liturgy

sakta *usu cap, var of* SHAKTA

sakti *var of* SHAKTI

saktism *usu cap, var of* SHAKTISM

sa·ku·ra \sə'ku̇rə\ *n* -S [Jap] : JAPANESE FLOWERING CHERRY

sak·ya \'säkyə\ *n, pl* **sakya** *or* **sakyas** *usu cap* : one of an ancient people of northern India

¹sal \'sal\ *n* -S [L — more at SALT] : SALT — usu. used in combination ⟨~ ammoniac⟩

²sal \'säl\ *n* -S [Hindi *sāl*, fr. Skt *śāla*] **1** *or* **sal tree** : an East Indian timber tree (*Shorea robusta*) having foliage which furnishes food for lac insects **2** : the light brown close-grained hard wood of the sal tree

sa·la \'sälə\ *n* -S [Sp & It; Sp, of Gmc origin like It *sala* — more at SALOON] : a large or important room or hall; *esp* : one used in a home for the reception and entertainment of guests ⟨beautiful residences . . . with balcony, ~, dining room —*Manila Times*⟩

¹sa·laam \sə'läm, -lam\ *n* -S [Ar *salām*, lit., peace] **1 a** : a salutation or ceremonial greeting in the East **b salaams** *pl* : COMPLIMENTS ⟨sent my ~s, wondering what on earth I should do with the peacocks —Janet Dunbar⟩ **2** : an obeisance performed by bowing very low and placing the right palm on the forehead ⟨made his ~ before the rajah⟩

²salaam \"\ *vb* -ED/-ING/-S *vt* : to greet or pay homage to with a salaam or ceremonial bow ⟨the attendant opened the door, ~*ed* him in —J.A.Phillips⟩ ~ *vi* : to perform a salaam ⟨~*ed*, curving the fingers of his right hand to his forehead —C.B. Child⟩

sal·abil·i·ty \,sālə'biləd·ē, -ilətē, -i\ *n* : the quality or state of being salable ⟨the ~ of a product⟩

sal·able *or* **sale·able** \'sāləbəl\ *adj* [*sale* + *-able*] **1** : capable of being sold : fit to be sold : MARKETABLE, VENDIBLE ⟨write a ~ story⟩ ⟨little boys . . . find ~ bottles —W.A.White⟩ ⟨develop ~ skills —M.B.Smith⟩ **2** *archaic* : susceptible to bribery : VENAL — **sal·able·ness** *n* -ES

sa·la·cious \sə'lāshəs\ *adj* [L *salac-*, *salax* fond of leaping, lustful (fr. *salire* to leap) + E *-ious* — more at SALLY] **1 a** *archaic, of a food* : tending to arouse sexual appetite : APHRODISIAC **b** : inciting to sexual desire or imagination : LASCIVIOUS, OBSCENE ⟨a collection of ~ poems —Malcolm Cowley⟩ **2** : marked by lecherousness or lewdness : LUSTFUL ⟨the ~ rooster⟩ ⟨their erotic skill is emphasized with ~ eagerness —Jack Morpurgo⟩ — **sa·la·cious·ly** *adv* — **sa·la·cious·ness** *n* -ES

sa·lac·i·ty \sə'lasəd·ē, -asətē, -aas-, -i\ *n* -ES [MF or L; MF *salacité*, fr. L *salacitat-*, *salacitas*, fr. *salac-*, *salax* + *-itat-*, *-itas* -ity] : the quality or state of being salacious : SALACIOUSNESS ⟨handled sex in his novels with a mere suggestion of ~⟩

sal·a·cot *or* **sal·a·kot** \'salə,kät\ *n* -S [Sp & Tag; Sp *salacot*, fr. Tag *salakót*] : a broad-brimmed Philippine hat woven from strips of cane or from palm leaves

sal·ad \'saləd\ *n* -S *often attrib* [ME *selad*, *salade*, fr. MF *salade*, fr. OProv *salada*, fr. fem. of *salat*, past part. of *salar* to salt, fr. *sal* salt, fr. L — more at SALT] **1 a** : a cooked or uncooked food prepared with a savory or piquant dressing and usu. served cold: as (1) : green usu. raw vegetables or herbs (as lettuce, endive, romaine) to which tomato, cucumber, or radish is often added and which are served with dressing (2) : meat, fish, shellfish, eggs, fruits or vegetables singly or in combination that are sliced, cut in pieces, shredded, or minced, are often set in a mold with gelatin, and are served cold with a dressing **b** *South & Midland* : cooked greens (as poke or turnip tops) seasoned during or after cooking **2** : a green vegetable or herb grown for salad; *esp* : LETTUCE **3** : an incongruous mixture : HODGEPODGE ⟨its incredible ~ of verbless sentences, historic presents, twisted quotations —Kingsley Amis⟩

sa·lada \sə'lädə, -ladə\ *n* -S [MexSp, fr. Sp, fem. of *salado*, past part. of *salar* to salt, fr. *sal* salt, fr. L] : a salt-covered plain in the Southwest where a lake has evaporated

saladang *var of* SELADANG

salad burnet *n* : a European common garden burnet (*Sanguisorba minor*) sometimes eaten as a salad — called also *burnet bloodwort*

salad days *n pl* : days of youthful inexperience or indiscretion ⟨my *salad days* when I was green in judgment, cold in blood —Shak.⟩ ⟨has long since lived down his *salad days* —John Gunther⟩

salad dressing *n* : a savory liquid or semisolid cooked or uncooked food used as a dressing for salads: as **a** : FRENCH DRESSING **b** : MAYONNAISE 1a **c** : a semisolid dressing made of eggs, a fat (as vegetable oil), vinegar or lemon juice, and seasonings cooked with a starch (as wheat, rye, or tapioca flour)

salade *var of* SALLET

sal·a·de·ro hide \¦salə¦de(,)rō-\ *n* [*saladero* fr. Sp, salting plant, fr. *salado* + *-ero* (fr. L *-arius* -ary)] : a cattlehide from Argentina corresponding to a U.S. small packer hide — compare FRIGORIFICO 2

salad fork *n* : a short broad four-tined fork used in eating salad or pastry

salad fork

sal·ad·ing \'saladiŋ\ *n* -S *chiefly Brit* : vegetables or herbs for salad

sa·la·do \sə'lä(,)dō\ *also* **sa·la·do·an** \-ädəwən\ *adj, usu cap* [*salado* fr. *Salado*, an ancient Indian people of Arizona, fr. Sp, fr. *Río Salado* (Salt river), Arizona; *saladoan* fr. *Salado* Indians + E *-an*] : of or relating to a culture in central Arizona about A.D. 1100 to 1450 giving evidence of a merging of Mogollon and Anasazi traits

salad oil *n* **1** : an oil for salad dressing **2** : an edible vegetable oil (as corn or sesame oil) other than olive oil

salad plate *n* **1** : a plate about seven inches in diameter chiefly for individual servings of salad **2** : a salad mixture on a bed of lettuce served as a main dish esp. in restaurants

salad tree *n* : REDBUD

salaeratus *var of* SALERATUS

sa·la·gra·ma \,shälə'grämə\ *or* **sa·li·gram** \'shälə,gräm\ *or* **sa·li·gra·ma** \,shälə'grämə\ *n* -S [Skt *Śālagrāma*, a village in ancient India] : a fossil ammonite held by Hindus to be a representative of Vishnu

salah *var of* SALAT

sa·lai \sə'lī, 'sa,lī\ *also* **salai tree** *n* -S [Hindi *śallak*, *sallak*, fr. Skt *śallakī*] : an East Indian tree (*Boswellia serrata*) yielding resin that is used as an incense and as a medicine

sa·lak \sə'lak\ *n* -S [native name in Malaya] **1** : the pear-shaped pineapple-flavored fruit of a Philippine palm (*Zalacca edulis*) having a twisting snakelike skin **2** *also* **salak palm** : the palm that bears the salak fruit

salakot *var of* SALACOT

sa·lal \sə'lal, sa'l-\ *n* -S [Chinook Jargon, prob. fr. Chinook *-klkwšala*] : a small shrub (*Gaultheria shallon*) of the Pacific coast of No. America having edible dark purple berries about the size of a common grape

sal alembroth *n* : ALEMBROTH

sal·a·man·der \'salə,mandə(r), -maan- *sometimes* ,==¦==\ *n* -S [ME *salamandre*, fr. MF, fr. L *salamandra*, fr. Gk] **1 a** : an animal somewhat like a lizard formerly held to be able to live in fire **b** : a mythical and not clearly defined animal having the power to endure fire without harm **c** : a being inhabiting the element fire in the medieval theory of elementals esp. as formulated by Paracelsus — compare GNOME, SYLPH, UNDINE **2** : any of various chiefly small amphibians that comprise the order Caudata, superficially resemble lizards but are scaleless and covered with a soft moist skin, are usu. semiterrestrial as adults living in moist dark places but mostly pass through an aquatic larval stage during which they breathe by gills, are wholly inoffensive to man, and feed on small animals (as aquatic worms and insects) — see GIANT SALAMANDER, HELLBENDER 1, NEWT **3** : any of various articles used in connection with fire: as **a** : a metal disk or plate heated and held over a food (as pastry or pudding) to brown the top of it **b** *or* **salamander stove** : a small portable stove having no chimney and often burning coke or oil that is used to keep materials (as concrete or plaster) from freezing during the construction of a building or to provide temporary heat for a greenhouse in cases of emergency **c** : a small portable incinerator (as a wire basket) **d** *dial chiefly Eng* : a large poker **e** : an iron used red hot for igniting certain substances (as gunpowder) **4** : the pocket gopher (*Geomys tuza*) of the southeastern U.S. **5** : a mass of unfused material (as metallic iron or partially reduced ore) in the hearth of a blast furnace — called also *shadrach*, *sow*

sal·a·man·dra \,==¦=drə\ *n, cap* [NL, fr. L, salamander] : a genus (the type of the family Salamandridae) of amphibians formerly including most salamanders but now only a few Old World species

sal·a·man·dri·an \¦==¦=drēən\ *adj* [NL *Salamandra* + E *-ian*] : of, relating to, or resembling a salamander, the genus *Salamandra*, or the family Salamandridae

¹sal·a·man·drid \-drəd\ *adj* [NL *Salamandridae*] : of or relating to the Salamandridae

²salamandrid \"\ *n* -S : an amphibian of the family Salamandridae

sal·a·man·dri·dae \,==¦=drə,dē\ *n pl, cap* [NL, fr. *Salamandra*, type genus + *-idae*] : a family of amphibians (order Caudata) that comprises forms with a long row of prevomerine teeth and includes the cosmopolitan *Triturus* and several related Old World genera

sal·a·man·dri·form \-drə,fȯrm\ *adj* [L *salamandra* + E *-iform*] : shaped like a salamander

sal·a·man·dri·na \,==,=¦drīnə, -rēnə\ *n* [NL, fr. L *salamandra* + NL *-ina*] *syn of* MUTABILIA

¹sal·a·man·drine \¦==¦=drən, -,drīn\ *adj* [L *salamandra* + E *-ine*] **1** : of, relating to, or resembling a salamander **2** : capable of enduring fire like a salamander

²salamandrine \"\ *n* -S : a spirit thought to live in fire

sal·a·man·droid \-,drȯid\ *adj* [NL *Salamandroidea*] : of, relating to, or resembling salamanders or the Salamandroidea

sal·a·man·droi·dea \,==,=¦drȯidēə\ *n pl, cap* [NL, fr. L *salamandra* + *-oidea*] : a suborder of Caudata comprising salamanders of numerous and varied form (as the aquatic newts and the lungless terrestrial plethodonts) that have in common teeth on the roof of the mouth behind the internal openings of the nostrils — compare PLETHODON

sal·am·bao \¦saləm¦bau̇\ *n* -S [PhilSp, fr. Tag *salambáw*] : a large Philippine fishing net supported by a long bamboo cross-piece mounted on a raft

sa·la·mi \sə'lämē, -lám-, -mi\ *n* -S [It, pl. of *salame* salami, fr. *salare* to salt, fr. *sale* salt, fr. L *sal* — more at SALT] : highly seasoned sausage made of pork and beef in various proportions either air-dried, hard, and of good keeping qualities or fresh, soft, and requiring refrigeration until consumed

¹sal·a·min·i·an \¦salə¦minēən\ *adj, usu cap* [L *Salaminius* Salaminian (fr. Gk *Salaminios*, fr. *Salamin-*, *Salamis*, city in ancient Cyprus) + E *-an*] : of or relating to Salamis, Cyprus

²salaminian \"\ *n* -S *cap* : a native or inhabitant of ancient Salamis, Cyprus

sal ammoniac *n* [ME *sal armoniak*, fr. L *sal ammoniacus*, fr. *sal* salt + *ammoniacus* of Ammon — more at SALT, AMMONIA] **1 :** ammonium chloride esp. when purified by sublimation **2 :** a mineral NH_4Cl consisting of native ammonium chloride

sal·am·pore *also* **sal·em·pore** \'salәm,pō(ә)r\ *n* -s [origin unknown] **:** a colored cotton cloth with woven stripe and check designs made in India and England usu. for export to Africa and So. America

sal·an·gane \'salәn,gan, -gān\ *n* -s [F, fr. Tag & Bisayan *salangan*] **:** any of several swifts producing edible nests — compare EDIBLE BIRD'S NEST

sa·lan·gid \sә'lanjәd\ *n* -s [NL *Salangidae*] **:** a fish of the family Salangidae

sa·lan·gi·dae \-jә,dē\ *n pl, cap* [NL, fr. *Salang-, Salanx*, type genus (fr. Gk, a kind of fish) + *-idae*] **:** a family of small slender translucent salmonoid fishes of China and Japan — see ICEFISH

[1]**sa·lar** \sә'lär\ *n, pl* **salar** *or* **salars** *usu cap* **1 :** a Moslem people of Chinese Turkestan speaking a Turkic dialect **2 :** a member of the Salar people

[2]**salar** \"\ *adj, usu cap* **:** of, relating to, or characteristic of the Salar

[3]**salar** \"\ *n* -s [AmerSp, fr. Sp, to salt — more at SALADA] **:** a salt-encrusted depression (as in the nitrate fields of Chile) that may or may not be the basin of an evaporated lake — compare SALADA, SALINA

sa·lar·i·at \sә'la(a)rēәt, -ē,at\ *n* -s [F, blend of *salaire* salary (fr. L *salarium*) and *prolétariat* — more at SALARY, PROLETARIAT] **:** the class or body of salaried persons usu. as distinguished from wage earners — compare PROLETARIAT ⟨the wage-labor force and ~ —J.S.Coleman⟩

sal·a·ried \'sal(ә)rēd, -rid\ *adj* **1 :** receiving a salary ⟨the ~ staff⟩ ⟨to point out that the ~ manager of a public or private monopoly is quite unlikely to behave like a Victorian entrepreneur —Peter Wiles⟩ — contrasted with *hourly-rated* **2 :** calling for the payment of a salary ⟨a ~ position⟩

[1]**sal·a·ry** \'sal(ә)rē, -ri\ *n* -ES *often attrib* [ME *salarie*, fr. L *salarium* money given to soldiers for salt, pension, stipend, salary, fr. neut. of *salarius* of salt, fr. *sal* salt + *-arius* -ary — more at SALT] **1 :** fixed compensation paid regularly (as by the year, quarter, month, or week) for services **:** STIPEND; *esp* **:** such compensation paid to holders of official, executive, or clerical positions — often distinguished from *wage* **2** *obs* **a :** remuneration for services given **:** FEE, HONORARIUM ⟨why, this is hire and ~, not revenge —Shak.⟩ **b :** REWARD, RECOMPENSE **syn** see WAGE

[2]**salary** \"\ *vt* -ED/-ING/-S **1 :** to pay (as a person) for something done **:** RECOMPENSE, REWARD ⟨would string wretched rhymes even when not *salaried* for them —Isaac D'Israeli⟩ **2 a :** to pay a salary to (a person) ⟨the academicians were *salaried* by the Crown —S.F.Mason⟩ **b :** to attach a salary to (a position)

[3]**salary** \"\ *dial var of* CELERY

salary savings insurance *or* **salary allotment insurance** *also* **salary deduction insurance** *n* **:** an individual life insurance policy for which the premium is deducted from an employee's pay and remitted by his employer directly to the company

salas *pl of* SALA

[1]**sal·at** \'salәt\ *archaic & dial var of* SALAD

[2]**sa·lat** \sә'lät\ *also* **sa·lah** \-lä\ *n* -s [Ar *ṣalāt*] **:** a ritual prayer of Muslims made five times daily in a standing position alternating with inclinations and prostrations as the worshiper faces toward Mecca

sal·band \'sal,band; 'säl,bänt, 'zäl-\ *n* -s [G, lit., selvage, fr. MHG *selbende, selpende*, fr. *selp* self (fr. OHG *selb*) + *ende* end, fr. OHG *enti* — more at SELF, END] **:** the border of an igneous mass (as a dike) usu. characterized by a finer grain or even glassy texture produced by the chilling of the molten rock by the cold country rock

sal·chow \'sal,kōv\ *n* -s *usu cap* [after Ulrich *Salchow*, 20th cent. Swed. skating champion] **:** a figure-skating jump with a takeoff from the back inside edge of one skate followed by a full turn in the air and a landing on the back outside edge of the opposite skate

sal·cio·nal \'salshәnᵊl\ *n* -s [by alter.] **:** SALICIONAL

[1]**sal·did** \'saldәd\ *adj* [NL *Saldidae*] **:** of or relating to the Saldidae

[2]**saldid** \"\ *n* -s **:** a bug of the family Saldidae

sal·di·dae \-ldә,dē\ *n pl, cap* [NL, fr. *Salda*, type genus + *-idae*] **:** a widely distributed family of predacious aquatic bugs

[1]**sale** \'sāl, *esp before pause or consonant* -āәl\ *n* -s [ME, fr. OE *sala*, fr. ON — more at SELL] **1 :** the act of selling **:** a contract transferring the absolute or general ownership of property from one person or corporate body to another for a price (as a sum of money or any other consideration); *specif* **:** a present transfer of such ownership of and title to all of or a part interest in personal property (as existing identifiable movable and tangible or fungible goods) under a contract by the seller to the buyer for a price paid or payable in money or other personal property — distinguished from *gift* ⟨arranged the ~ of a large estate to a syndicate of home builders⟩ **2 :** exhibition for selling **:** the status of being purchasable — usu. used in the phrases *for sale* and *on sale* ⟨put a house up for ~⟩ ⟨on ~ at most stationery stores⟩ **3 a :** opportunity of selling or being sold **:** DEMAND, MARKET ⟨counting on a large ~ for their latest publication⟩ **b :** distribution (as of goods or services) by selling ⟨the average total ~ for books in this category —*Saturday Rev.*⟩ **4 :** public disposal to the highest bidder **:** AUCTION ⟨art dealers flocking to the ~ of a famous collection of early Renaissance masters⟩ **5 a :** a selling off of goods (as surplus or shopworn stock) at bargain prices ⟨a clearance ~⟩ ⟨rummage ~⟩ **b :** an advertised disposal of marked-down goods ⟨a dress bought at a department-store ~⟩ **6 sales** *pl* **a :** operations and activities involved in promoting and selling goods or services ⟨a ~s department⟩ ⟨vice-president in charge of ~s⟩ **b :** gross receipts ⟨~s were over five million dollars⟩ — **on sale or return :** on approval

[2]**sale** \"\ *adj* [ME, fr. *sale*, n.] **1 :** made for selling rather than home use **:** PURCHASABLE ⟨~ bread⟩ ⟨~ milk⟩ ⟨~ ware⟩ **2 :** produced in large quantities for the trade **:** READY-MADE ⟨~ doors⟩ ⟨~ tools⟩ **3 :** SELLING ⟨special ~ price⟩

saleable *var of* SALABLE

sale-and-leaseback \,=='=,=\ *n* **:** LEASEBACK

sa·lée·ite \sә'lā,īt\ *n* -s [F, fr. A. *Salée*, 20th cent. Frenchman + F *-ite*] **:** a mineral $Mg(UO_2)_2(PO_4)_2.10H_2O$ that is a hydrous phosphate of magnesium and uranium and is isomorphous with autunite and torbernite

sa·le·le \sә'lālē\ *n* -s [Samoan] **:** a small dusky silver or silvery bronze percoid fish (*Dules rupestris*) widely distributed chiefly in fresh or brackish water in the tropical Indo-Pacific area from eastern Africa to Hawaii

[1]**sa·lem** \'sālәm\ *adj, usu cap* [fr. *Salem*, Ore.] **:** of or from Salem, the capital of Oregon ⟨a *Salem* lawyer⟩ **:** of the kind or style prevalent in Salem

[2]**salem** \"\ *adj, usu cap* [fr. *Salem*, India] **:** of or from the city of Salem, India **:** of the kind or style prevalent in Salem

salem grass \"-\ *n, usu cap S* [prob. fr. *Salem*, Mass.] **:** VELVET GRASS

salempore *var of* SALAMPORE

salem rocker *n, usu cap S* [fr. *Salem*, Mass.] **:** an early 19th century rocking chair with heavy scrolled seat and arms and a back of slender curved spindles and scrolled and often painted and stenciled top rail

sale note *n* **:** a memorandum given by a broker to a buyer or seller of goods stating that the specified goods have been sold by him for the account of a named seller to a named buyer

salep \'salәp, sә'lep\ *also* **saleb** \'salәb, sә'leb\ *n* -s [F or Sp *salep*, fr. Ar *sahlab*, alter. of *khusy ath-tha'lab*, lit., the fox's testicles] **:** the dried tubers of various European orchids (genus *Orchis*) or East Indian orchids (genus *Eulophia*) containing gum and starch and being used for food (as tapioca) and as a demulcent

sal·e·ra·tus *also* **sal·ae·ra·tus** \,salә'rādәs\ *n* -ES [NL *sal aeratus*, fr. L *sal* salt + *aeratus* aerated, fr. L *aer-* + *-atus* -ate, fr. the carbon dioxide that is evolved upon treatment with acids] **:** either of two salts used as leavening agents: **a :** POTASSIUM BICARBONATE **b :** SODIUM BICARBONATE

sales \'sā(ә)lz\ *adj* [fr. pl. of [1]*sale*] **:** of, relating to, or used in selling ⟨~ quota⟩ ⟨~ manager⟩

sales agency *n* **1 :** the commission or authorization of a sales agent **2 :** the place of business of a sales agent

sales agent *n* **:** one who is authorized or appointed by a manufacturer to sell or distribute his products within a given territory but who is in business for himself, takes title to the goods, and does not act as agent for a principal

sales check *n* **:** a strip or piece of paper used by retail stores as a memorandum, record, or receipt of a purchase or sale

salesclerk \'=,=\ *n* **:** a salesman or saleswoman employed in a store

sales engineer *n* **1 :** an engineer who sells equipment and manufactured products by estimating from plans and computing cost of installation and often establishes liaison between designers and contractors for the manufacture of machines and equipment suited to each situation and for efficient operation when installed **2 :** an engineer attached to a sales department to assist salesmen with technical information and advice

salesgirl \'=,=\ *n* **:** SALESWOMAN

[1]**sa·le·sian** \sә'lēzhәn, -ēsh-\ *adj, usu cap* [St. Francis de *Sales* †1622 Savoyard ecclesiastic + E *-ian*] **1 :** of or relating to St. Francis de Sales **2 :** of or relating to the Salesians

[2]**salesian** \"\ *n* -s *cap* **:** a member of the Society of St. Francis de Sales founded as a Roman Catholic religious congregation in the 19th century by St. John Bosco in Turin and devoted chiefly to education

sales·ite \'sāl,zīt\ *n* -s [Reno *Sales* *b*1876 Am. geologist + E *-ite*] **:** a mineral $Cu(IO_3)(OH)$ consisting of a basic copper iodate found at Chuquicamata, Chile

saleslady \'=,==\ *n* **:** SALESWOMAN ⟨*salesladies* will tell you that husbands don't know their wives' fundamental measurements —S.L.Payne⟩

sales·man \'sā(ә)lzmәn\ *n, pl* **salesmen :** one that sells: **a :** one employed to sell goods or services either within a given territory or in a store — see SALESCLERK, TRAVELING SALESMAN; compare DETAIL MAN **b :** one who seeks to persuade others to accept or approve an idea, system of thought, or course of action ⟨the new *salesmen* of popular religion —M.W.Straight⟩ ⟨ambassadors in overalls can be the best *salesmen* of democracy —A.E.Stevenson †1965⟩

sales·man·ship \-,ship\ *n* **1 :** the skill or art of selling ⟨a course in ~⟩ **2 :** the act or process of selling ⟨large sums spent in ~⟩ **3 :** ability or effectiveness in selling (as goods) or in presenting persuasively (as ideas) ⟨saw . . . that his tales were not all ~ —Wendell Willkie⟩ ⟨stated that bad ~ . . . was mainly responsible for the party's defeat —Cecil Harden⟩

salespeople \'=,==\ *n pl* **:** persons employed to sell goods or services; *esp* **:** the corps of salesmen and saleswomen of a particular business concern

salesperson \'=,==\ *n* **:** a person employed to sell merchandise to customers in a store; *specif* **:** SALESCLERK

sales promotion *n* **:** activities and devices designed to create goodwill and sell a product; *esp* **:** selling activities (as use of displays, sampling, demonstrations, fashion shows, contests, coupons, premiums, and special sales) that supplement advertising and personal selling, coordinate them, and make them effective

sales register *n* **:** CASH REGISTER

sales representative *n* **:** REPRESENTATIVE 3e

sales resistance *n* **1 :** the power, capacity, or disposition to resist buying goods or services offered for sale ⟨surveys . . . to determine the presumptive *sales resistance* of potential purchasers —Charles Merz⟩ **2 :** disinclination to accept or approve (as new ideas or proposals) ⟨millions were spent . . . to hammer away at the *sales resistance* of voters —*Nation*⟩ ⟨*sales resistance* to the author's ideas is likely to be still more gratuitously stimulated by elementary infelicities of idiom —Randolph Quirk⟩

salesroom *also* **saleroom** \'=,=\ *n* **:** a place where goods are displayed for sale **:** SHOWROOM; *esp* **:** an auction room

sales slip *n* **:** SALES CHECK

sales talk *n* **:** argument often accompanied by demonstration used to persuade others to buy a product or service or to accept an idea or proposal ⟨memorized the *sales talk* he hoped would bring in large orders⟩ ⟨a glib *sales talk* that produced unanimous agreement⟩

sales tax *n* **:** a tax on the privilege or freedom of making sales of tangible personal property that is usu. measured by a percentage (as 3%) of the purchase price, is collected for the government imposing the tax by the seller, and is distinguished from a tax imposed on the property itself

saleswoman \'=,==\ *n, pl* **saleswomen :** a woman employed to sell merchandise esp. in a store

salet *var of* SALLET

saleyard \'=,=\ *n* **:** a yard in which livestock is sold

sal·fern \'salfә(r)n\ *or* **salfern stoneseed** *n* [origin unknown] **:** CORN GROMWELL

sal·ford \'sȯlfә(r)d\ *adj, usu cap* [fr. *Salford*, Lancashire, England] **:** of or from the county borough of Salford, Lancashire **:** of the kind or style prevalent in Salford

sali- *comb form* [L, fr. *sal* — more at SALT] **:** salt ⟨*sali*ferous⟩ ⟨*sali*meter⟩

[1]**sa·lian** \'sālēәn, -lyәn\ *adj, usu cap* [LL *Salii*, a division of the Franks (fr. the *Sala* — Ijssel — river) + E *-an*] **:** of or relating to a Frankish people dwelling early in the 4th century A.D. on the Ijssel river — see SALIC LAW

[2]**salian** \"\ *adj, usu cap* [L *Salii*, priests of Mars in ancient Rome (fr. *salire* to leap) + E *-an* — more at SALLY] **:** of or relating to the Salii of ancient Rome ⟨*Salian* hymns⟩

saliant *var of* SALIENT

salic \'sā|lik, 'sal, |lēk\ *also* **sa·lique** \", sә'lēk, sa|\ *adj, usu cap* [MF or ML; MF *salique*, fr. ML *Salicus*, fr. LL *Salii* Salian Franks + L *-icus* -ic] **:** SALIAN

sal·i·ca·ce·ae \,salә'kāsē,ē\ *n pl, cap* [NL, fr. *Salic-, Salix*, type genus + *-aceae*] **:** a family of dioecious trees or shrubs (order Salicales) having small apetalous flowers in catkins — see SALIX

sal·i·ca·les \-ā(,)lēz\ *n pl, cap* [NL, fr. *Salic-, Salix* + *-ales*] **:** an order of dicotyledonous plants coextensive with the family Salicaceae

salices *pl of* SALIX

sal·i·cet \'salә'set\ *n* -s [G, fr. L *salic-, salix* willow + F *-et*, dim. suffix — more at SALLOW] **:** a soft-toned labial pipe-organ stop similar to the salicional but of 4-foot or 2-foot pitch

sal·i·ce·tum \,salә'sēdәm\ *n, pl* **salicetums** \-d·әmz\ *or* **salice·ta** \-d·ә\ [L *salictum, salicetum*, fr. *salic-, salix* willow] **:** a collection or plantation of living willows

sal·i·cin \'salәsәn\ *n* -s [F *salicine*, fr. L *salic-, salix* willow + F *-ine* — more at SALLOW] **:** a bitter white crystalline beta-glucoside $C_{13}H_{18}O_7$ esp. in the bark and leaves of several willows and poplars yielding saligenin and glucose on hydrolysis and formerly used in medicine as an antipyretic, antirheumatic, and tonic — compare POPULIN

sa·li·cio·nal \sә'lishәnᵊl\ *n* -s [G, fr. L *salic-, salix* willow + *-ion* + *-al*] **:** a soft-toned labial pipe-organ stop usu. of 8-foot pitch

salic law *or* **salique law** *n, usu cap S* **:** a law or rule held to derive orig. from the legal code of the Salian Franks excluding females from the line of succession to a throne ⟨they would hold up this *Salique* law to bar your Highness claiming from the female —Shak.⟩

sal·i·cor·nia \,salә'kȯ(r)nēә\ *n* [NL, fr. F *salicorne* glasswort (fr. Catal *salicorn*, fr. *sali-* — fr. L — + *corn* horn, fr. L *cornu*) + NL *-ia* — more at HORN] **1** *cap* **:** a genus of fleshy maritime herbs (family Chenopodiaceae) having thick jointed leafless stems bearing minute flowers in the form of a spike that are succeeded by utricles containing a single seed — see GLASSWORT **2** -s **:** any plant of the genus *Salicornia*

salicyl- *or* **salicylo-** *comb form* [ISV, fr. *salicyl* salicyloyl] **:** related to salicylic acid ⟨*salicyl*amide⟩ ⟨*salicylo*yl⟩

sal·i·cyl alcohol \'salәsәl-\ *n* [*salicyl* salicyloyl, fr. F *salicyle*, fr. *salicine* + *-yle* -yl] **:** SALIGENIN

sal·i·cyl·aldehyde \'===+\ *n* [ISV *salicyl-* + *aldehyde*] **:** an oily liquid phenolic aldehyde HOC_6H_4CHO that has a bitter almond odor, that is found esp. in oils from spirea plants but that is usu. made by reaction of phenol, sodium hydroxide, and chloroform, and that is used chiefly in perfumery and in making coumarin; *ortho*-hydroxy-benzaldehyde

sal·i·cyl·amide \,salә'silә,mīd, -mәd\ *n* [ISV *salicyl-* + *amide*] **:** the crystalline amide $HOC_6H_4CONH_2$ of salicylic acid made usu. by reaction of methyl salicylate with ammonia and used chiefly as an analgesic, antipyretic, and antirheumatic

sal·i·cyl·anilide \'salәsәl+\ *n* [ISV *salicyl-* + *anilide*] **:** a crystalline compound $HOC_6H_4CONHC_6H_5$ made usu. by reaction of salicylic acid or methyl salicylate with aniline and used as a fungicidal agent esp. in the external treatment of ringworm of the scalp and in the prevention of mildew in cotton fabrics and cordage

sa·lic·y·late \sә'lisә,lāt, -is(ә)lәt, -i,slāt\ *n* -s [ISV *salicyl-* + *-ate*] **:** a salt or ester of salicylic acid; *also* **:** SALICYLIC ACID

sa·lic·y·lat·ed \-ād·әd\ *adj* **:** treated with salicylic acid

sal·i·cyl·ic acid \,salә¦silik-\ *n* [*salicylic* ISV *salicyl* salicyloyl + *-ic*] **:** a crystalline phenolic acid HOC_6H_4COOH of sweetish acrid taste found in many plants and in most fruits often in the form of its methyl ester but usu. made by reaction of phenol, sodium hydroxide, and carbon dioxide and used chiefly in making pharmaceuticals and dyes, as an antiseptic and disinfectant esp. in treating skin diseases, and in the form of salts and other derivatives as an analgesic and antipyretic and in the treatment of rheumatism; *ortho*-hydroxybenzoic acid — compare ASPIRIN

salicylic aldehyde *n* **:** SALICYLALDEHYDE

sa·lic·y·lide \sә'lisә,līd, -lәd\ *n* -s [ISV *salicyl-* + *-ide*] **:** any of several anhydrides of salicylic acid; *esp* **:** a crystalline compound $(OC_6H_4CO)_4$ formed by condensation of four molecules of salicylic acid

sal·i·cyl·ism \'salәsә,lizәm, sә'lisә,l-\ *n* -s [ISV *salicyl-* + *-ism*] **:** a toxic condition produced by the excessive intake of salicylic acid or salicylates and marked by ringing in the ears, nausea, and vomiting

sal·i·cyl·iza·tion \,salәsәlә'zāshәn, -lәsә,lī'z-, -lә,silә'z-; sә,lisәlә'z-, -isә,lī'z-\ *n* -s **1 :** the act or process of administering salicylates until a patient is salicylized **2 :** the condition of being salicylized

sal·i·cyl·ize \'salәsә,līz, sә'lisә,l-\ *vt* -ED/-ING/-S [*salicyl-* + *-ize*] **:** to treat (a patient) with salicylic acid or its compounds until physiological effects are produced

sal·i·cyl·o·yl \,salә'silә,wil\ *or* **sa·lic·y·lyl** \sә'lisә,lil\ *n* -s [*salicyl-* + *-yl*] **:** the radical $HOC_6H_4CO—$ of salicylic acid

sal·i·cyl·uric acid \,salәsәl¦yu̇|rik-, -ә¦lu̇|\ *n* [ISV *salicyl-* + *-uric*] **:** a crystalline acid $C_9H_9NO_4$ found in the urine after the administration of salicylic acid or one of its derivatives; *ortho*-hydroxy-hippuric acid

sa·lience \'sālyәn(t)s, -lēәn- *sometimes* 'sal-\ *or* **sa·lien·cy** \-nsē,-nsi\ *n, pl* **saliences** *also* **saliencies 1 :** the quality or state of being salient: as **a :** physical prominence **:** PROJECTION, PROTRUSION ⟨the ~ of a buttress⟩ **b :** STRIKINGNESS, EMPHASIS ⟨elements of *saliency* and color —Carl Van Doren⟩ ⟨wherever she turned her eyes detail took on an uncanny ~ —Elizabeth Bowen⟩ **2 :** a striking point or feature **:** HIGHLIGHT ⟨seize a ~ of characteristic and . . . present it picturesquely —*Nineteenth Century & After*⟩

[1]**sa·lient** \-nt\ *adj* [L *salient-, saliens*, pres. part. of *salire* to leap, spring — more at SALLY] **1** *or* **saliant** *heraldry, of a beast* **a :** rampant but leaning forward as if leaping **b :** being in a leaping position with both hind feet on the ground **2 :** moving by leaps or springs **:** JUMPING ⟨a ~ animal⟩ ⟨a ~ fish⟩; *specif* **:** of or relating to the Salientia ⟨a ~ amphibian⟩ **3 :** spouting forth **:** jetting upward ⟨a ~ spring⟩ ⟨a ~ fountain⟩ **4 a :** projecting above or beyond a general line, surface, or level **:** jutting upward or outward **:** PROTUBERANT ⟨his nose was ~ and pointed —Elinor Wylie⟩ ⟨not on the level ground but on a ~ corner . . . of earth —Thomas Hardy⟩ **b :** standing out conspicuously **:** PROMINENT, STRIKING ⟨~ features⟩ ⟨~ traits⟩ ⟨will suffice to give its ~ points only —*Rev. of Religion*⟩ ⟨pick the ~ details out of dull verbiage —J.P.Marquand⟩ **syn** see NOTICEABLE

[2]**salient** \"\ *n* -s **1 :** SALIENT ANGLE; *specif* **:** an offensive bulge into enemy-held territory ⟨~s . . . so arranged that any one bastion could come to the aid of another by means of cross fire —Lewis Mumford⟩ ⟨a front line . . . has ~s and reentrants all along its length, depending on the progress of the fighting at different points —*Infantry Jour.*⟩ **2 :** something (as a promontory or cape along a shoreline or an abrupt change in the profile of a stream course) that projects outward or upward from its surroundings

salient angle *n* **:** an angle pointing outward; *specif* **:** an angle in a fortification (as a bastion) or in a battle line with its apex toward the enemy — opposed to *reentering angle*; see BASTION illustration

sa·li·en·tia \,sālē'ench(ē)ә, ,sal-, -ntēә\ *n pl, cap* [NL, fr. L, neut. pl. of *salient-, saliens*] **:** an order of Amphibia comprising the frogs, toads, and tree toads all of which are distinguished by complete absence of a tail in the adult stage and by possession of long strong hind limbs well suited to leaping and swimming

[1]**sa·li·en·tian** \¦==¦ench(ē)әn, -¦entēәn\ *adj* [NL *Salientia* + E *-an*] **:** of or relating to the Salientia

[2]**salientian** \"\ *n* -s **:** an amphibian of the order Salientia

sa·lient·ly *adv* **:** in a salient manner **:** OUTSTANDINGLY, CONSPICUOUSLY ⟨~ characteristic⟩ ⟨~ lacking⟩

salient point *n* **1** *archaic* **:** starting point **:** SOURCE **2 :** a prominent feature or detail

salient pole *n* **:** a magnet pole that projects toward the armature of an electric machine — compare CONSEQUENT POLE

sa·lif·er·ous \sә'lif(ә)rәs, (')sa¦l-\ *adj* [*sali-* + *-ferous*] **:** producing, impregnated with, or containing salt ⟨~ formations⟩

sal·i·fi·able \'salә,fīәbәl, ,==¦===\ *adj* **:** capable of being salified

sal·i·fi·ca·tion \,salәfә'kāshәn\ *n* -s [prob. fr. F, fr. *sali-* + *-fication*] **1 :** the act, process, or result of salifying **2 :** the state of being salified

sal·i·fy \'salә,fī\ *vt* -ED/-ING/-ES [F *salifier*, fr. *sali-* + *-fier* -fy] **1 :** to combine or impregnate with a salt **:** SALINIZE **2 :** to form a salt with **:** convert into a salt ⟨~ a base by treatment with an acid or an acid by treatment with a base⟩

sal·i·gen·in \,salә'jenәn, sә'lijәnәn\ *n* -s [ISV *salicin* + *-genin*] **:** a crystalline phenolic alcohol $HOC_6H_4CH_2OH$ that is obtained usu. by hydrolysis of salicin or by reduction of salicylamide or salicylaldehyde and that acts as a local anesthetic; *ortho*-hydroxy-benzyl alcohol — called also *salicyl alcohol*

saligram *or* **saligrama** *var of* SALAGRAMA

sa·lim·e·ter \sә'limәd·ә(r)\ *n* [*sali-* + *-meter*] **:** a hydrometer specially graduated so as to indicate directly the percentage of a salt (as common salt) in a brine or other salt solution

salin- *or* **salini-** *or* **salino-** *comb form* [[1]*saline*] **1 :** salt **:** saline ⟨*salini*ze⟩ ⟨*salini*form⟩ ⟨*salino*meter⟩ **2 :** saline and ⟨*salino*sulfureous⟩

sa·li·na \sә'līnә, -lēnә\ *n* -s [Sp, fr. L *salinae*, pl., saltworks, salt pits, fr. fem. pl. of *salinus* of salt — more at SALINE] **1 :** a salt-encrusted playa or flat **:** SALADA **2 :** a salt marsh, pond, or lake

sa·li·nan \sә'lēnәn\ *n, pl* **salinan** *or* **salinans** *usu cap* [*Salinas* river, western Calif. + E *-an*] **1 a :** an Indian people of southwestern California **b :** a member of such people **2 :** a language of the Salinan people **3 :** a language family of the Hokan stock comprising only the Salinan language

sal·i·nar \'salә¦när\ *adj, usu cap* [fr. *Salinar*, locality in northern Peru, its type site] **:** of or relating to a culture in northwestern Peru about the 6th century A.D. characterized by irrigated agriculture, use of the llama, weaving and metallurgy, adobe houses, reed-bundle boats, and distinctive pottery

sa·li·na·tion \,salә'nāshәn, sә,lī-\ *n* -s [*salin-* + *-ation*] **:** treatment with salt or salt solution

[1]**sa·line** \'sā,lēn, -līn\ *adj* [ME *salyne*, fr. L *salinus*, fr. *sal* salt + *-inus* -ine — more at SALT] **1 :** consisting of or containing salt **:** SALIFEROUS ⟨~ deposits⟩ ⟨a ~ solution⟩ **2 :** of, relating to, or resembling salt **:** SALTY ⟨a ~ taste⟩ ⟨~ compounds⟩ ⟨the ~ properties of the water —Alice Duncan-Kemp⟩ **3 :** consisting of or relating to the salts of the alkali metals or of magnesium ⟨a ~ cathartic⟩

[2]**sa·line** \'sā,lēn, -,līn, *in sense 1 often* sә'lēn\ *n* -s [partly fr. ME *salyne*, fr. L *salinae*, pl., saltworks; partly fr. [1]*saline* — more at SALINA] **1 a :** a spring of salt water **b :** a natural deposit of common salt or of any other soluble salt (as left by the evaporation of a lake) **c :** SALINA 2 **2 a** (1) **:** a metallic salt; *esp* **:** a salt of potassium, sodium, or magnesium with a cathartic action (2) **:** an aqueous solution of one or more such salts **b** *also* **sa·lin** \'salәn\ **:** a crude potash obtained from beet residues and similar sources **3 salines** *pl* **:** the naturally oc-

curring soluble salts (as common salt, sodium carbonate, sodium nitrate, potassium salts, borax) **4 :** a saline solution used in physiology; *esp* **:** physiological salt solution for mammals

saline dome *n* **:** SALT DOME

sal·i·nel·la \ˌsalə'nelə\ *n, cap* [NL, fr. L *salinus* + NL *-ella;* fr. the fact that it is found in salines and raised in saline aquariums] **:** a genus of minute animals of doubtful relationship having the body composed of a single layer of cells surrounding a central digestive cavity — compare MESOZOA

sal·i·nelle \ˌsalə'nel\ *n* -s [F, dim. of *saline* saltworks, fr. L *salinae*, pl. — more at SALINA] **:** a mud volcano that erupts saline mud

sa·line·ness \'sāˌlēnnəs, -līnn-\ *n* -ES **:** SALINITY

saline soil *n* **:** soil containing enough soluble salts (as 0.2 percent) to interfere with crop growth

saline water *n* **:** water containing salt; *esp* **:** mineral water containing sodium chloride, sodium sulfate, and magnesium sulfate

sa·lin·i·fi·ca·tion \səˌlinəfə'kāshən\ *n* -s [*salin-* + *-fication*] **:** the act or process of becoming or causing to become saline ⟨the . . . ~ of many agricultural soils —*Science*⟩

sa·lin·i·form \sə'linəˌfȯrm\ *adj* [*salin-* + *-form*] **:** having the form or qualities of a salt

sal·i·nim·e·ter \ˌsalə'nimədə(r)\ *n* [*salin-* + *-meter*] **:** SALINOMETER

sa·lin·i·ty \sā'linəd·ē, sə'l-, -nətē, -i\ *n* -ES [¹*saline* + *-ity*] **1 :** the quality or state of being saline **:** SALTINESS **2 a :** concentration (as in a solution) of salt ⟨marine animals . . . adjust themselves to changing *salinities* —R.E.Coker⟩

salinity current *n* **:** an oceanic current the flow of which is caused or controlled by its relatively greater density due to excessive salinity

sa·lin·iza·tion \ˌsāˌlēnə'zāshən, -līn-\ *n* -s **:** the process by which salts accumulate in soil

sa·lin·ize \'=ˌlēˌnīz, -ˌlī-\ *vt* -ED/-ING/-s [*salin-* + *-ize*] **:** to impregnate or treat (as a soil) with salt

sa·lin·o·gen·ic \ˌsāˌlēnə'jenik, -ˌlīn-; səˌlēn-, -ˌlīn-\ *adj* [*salin-* + *-genic*] **:** capable of forming salts ⟨~ dyes⟩

sal·i·nom·e·ter \ˌsalə'nämǝd·ə(r)\ *n* [ISV *salin-* + *-meter*] **:** an instrument for measuring the amount of salt in a solution; *esp* **:** SALIMETER

salique *usu cap, var of* SALIC

salis·bury steak \'sȯlzˌberē-, -ˌb(ə)rē, -ri-\ *n, usu cap 1st S* [after J. H. *Salisbury*, 19th cent. Eng. physician who advocated dietary reform] **:** ground beef mixed with egg, milk, bread crumbs and seasonings, formed into patties, and broiled, fried, or braised

sa·lish \'sālish\ *n* -ES *usu cap* **1 :** a language stock of the Mosan phylum — compare SKAGIT **2 :** the peoples speaking Salish dialects — **salish·an** \-shən, 'sal-\ *adj, usu cap*

salite \'saˌlīt, 'sä,-\ *n* -s [G *salit*, fr. *Sala*, Västmanland, Sweden + G *-it* -ite] **:** a mineral $(Mg,Fe)_2Si_2O_6$ consisting of a diopside with more magnesium than iron

¹**sa·li·va** \sə'līvə\ *n* -s [L — more at SALLOW] **:** a viscous colorless somewhat opalescent secretion that is usu. slightly alkaline in reaction, contains water, mucin, protein, salts, and often a starch-splitting enzyme, is secreted into the mouth by salivary glands, and serves to lubricate ingested food and often to begin the breakdown of starches — see PTYALIN

²**sá·li·va** \'säləvə\ *n, pl* **sáliva** *or* **sálivas** *usu cap* [Sp, of AmerInd origin] **1 :** a people of the Orinoco valley, Venezuela **2 :** a member of the Sáliva people

sal·i·val \sə'līvəl\ *adj* [ML *salivalis*, fr. L *saliva* + *-alis* -al] **:** SALIVARY

¹**sal·i·vant** \'saləvənt\ *adj* [L *salivant-, salivans*, pres. part. of *salivare* to spit out, salivate, fr. *saliva*] **:** causing or increasing the flow of saliva **:** MOUTH-WATERING

²**salivant** \"\ *n* -s **:** a salivant drug or agent **:** SIALAGOGUE

sal·i·var·i·um \ˌsalə'va(a)rēəm\ *n, pl* **salivar·ia** \-ēə\ *or* **salivariums** [NL, fr. L *saliva* + *-arium*] **:** a small pocket within the oral cavity of an insect containing the opening of the salivary duct

sal·i·vary \'saləˌverē, -ri\ *adj* [L *salivarius* slimy, fr. *saliva* + *-arius* -ary] **:** of or relating to saliva or the glands that secrete it **:** producing or carrying saliva

salivary chromosome *n* **:** one of the very large polytene chromosomal strands made up of many chromatids that are typical of the salivary gland cells of various insects

salivary corpuscles *n pl* **:** degenerating lymphocytes originating in the tonsils and passing into the saliva in the mouth

salivary gland *n* **:** any of various glands discharging a fluid secretion into the mouth cavity that in man comprise the large compound racemose parotid, sublingual, and submaxillary glands and in snakes include the venom glands; *specif* **:** a gland that secretes saliva

sal·i·vate \'saləˌvāt, *usu* -ād·+V\ *vb* -ED/-ING/-s [L *salivatus*, past part. of *salivare* to spit out, salivate, fr. *saliva*] *vt* **:** to produce an abnormal flow of saliva in **:** produce ptyalism in (as by the use of mercury) ~ *vi* **:** to secrete or have a flow of saliva esp. in excess **:** DRIVEL, DROOL, SLAVER

saliva test *n* **:** a test of a sample of saliva taken from a race horse at the end of a race to determine whether or not the horse is doped

sal·i·va·tion \ˌsalə'vāshən\ *n* -s [MF or LL; MF *salivation*, fr. LL *salivation-, salivatio*, fr. L *salivatus* + *-ion-, -io* -ion] **:** the act or process of salivating; *esp* **:** excessive secretion of saliva often accompanied with soreness of the mouth and gums

sa·li·vous \sə'līvəs\ *adj* [L *salivosus*, fr. *saliva* + *-osus* -ous] **:** relating to saliva **:** being or made up of saliva ⟨~ discharge⟩

salix \'sāliks, 'sal-\ *n* [NL, fr. L, willow — more at SALLOW] **1** *cap* **:** a genus (the type of the family Salicaceae) of shrubs and trees that have the bracts of the ament entire and only 2 to 10 stamens and that are widely distributed in temperate and cold regions — compare OSIER 1, POPULUS, SALLOW, WILLOW **2** *pl* **sal·i·ces** \'saləˌsēz, 'sāl-\ **:** any plant of the genus *Salix*

salk vaccine \'sȯ(l)k-\ *n, usu cap S* [after Jonas *Salk* b1914 Amer. physician and bacteriologist] **:** a vaccine consisting of three strains of poliomyelitis virus grown on embryonated eggs and treated with formaldehyde for inactivation

sall \səl, (ˌ)sal\ *chiefly dial var of* SHALL

salle \'sal\ *n* -s [F, hall, of Gmc origin; akin to OHG *sal* house, hall — more at SALOON] *Brit* **:** a sorting room in a paper mill

sal·lee *or* **sal·ly** \'salē\ *n, pl* **sallees** *or* **sallies** [native name in Australia] **1** *Austral* **:** any of several wattles **2** *Austral* **:** BLACK SALLY

sal·lee·man \'salēmən\ *also* **sallee-rover** \-lēˌrōvə(r)\ *n, pl* **salleemen** *also* **sallee-rovers** [*Sallee* (Salé), seaport in Morocco + E *man* or *rover*] **1 :** a Moorish pirate ship **2** *also* **sallyman :** VELELLA

sal·len·ders \'saləndə(r)z\ *n pl but usu sing in constr* [origin unknown] **:** an eczematous eruption occurring on the hind leg of a horse in front of the hock — compare MALANDERS

¹**sal·let** *or* **sal·et** \'salət\ *or* **sa·lade** \sə'läd, -lad\ *n* -s [ME *sallet, salet*, fr. MF *sallade*, prob. fr. OIt *celata*, fr. fem. of *celato* (past part. of *celare* to hide), fr. L *celatus*, past part. of *celare* to conceal, hide — more at HELL] **:** a light helmet common during the 15th century of simple form with or without a visor and with a projection over the neck

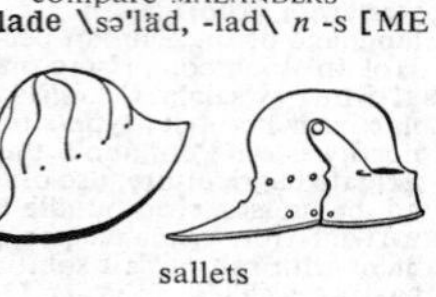
sallets

²**sallet** \"\ *chiefly dial var of* SALAD

sal·ley \'salē\ *chiefly dial var of* ¹SALLOW

¹**sal·low** \'sa(ˌ)lō, -lə; -ləw, -lō+V\ *n* -s [ME *salwe, sallow*, fr. OE *seal-, sealh;* akin to OHG *salha, salaha* sallow, MLG *salwīde*, ON *selja* sallow, L *salix* willow, MIr *sail* willow, and perh. to OE *salu* dusky, dark — more at ²SALLOW] **1 :** any of various Old World and chiefly Eurasiatic willows having broad leaves and including both shrubs and trees some of which are important sources of charcoal, tanbark, and wood for small implements; *esp* **:** a small northern or alpine Old World shrubby or arborescent much-branched willow (*Salix caprea*) with strongly fissured bark **2 :** a willow twig or shoot

²**sallow** \"\ *adj* -ER/-EST [ME *salowe*, fr. OE *salu, salo* dusky, dark, sallow; akin to OE *sōl* dark, dirty, OHG *salo* murky, dirty gray, ON *sölr* dirty, OIr *sal, saile* dirt, L *saliva* spittle, Skt *sāra, sāla* gray; basic meaning: dirty gray] **1 :** having any of several colors averaging a grayish greenish yellow that is paler than the color hay **2 :** of a grayish greenish yellow color suggesting sickliness — usu. used of the skin or complexion

³**sallow** \"\ *vt* -ED/-ING/-s **:** to make (as the complexion) sallow ⟨malarial poison had . . . ~*ed* his skin —Irving Bacheller⟩

sal·low·ish \-ləwish, -lōish\ *adj* **:** somewhat sallow ⟨a ~ complexion⟩

sal·low·ness *n* -ES **:** the quality or state of being sallow

sallow thorn *n* [¹*sallow*] **:** SEA BUCKTHORN

sal·lowy \-ləwē, -lōē\ *adj* [¹*sallow* + *-y*] **:** full of sallows

¹**sal·ly** \'salē, -li\ *n* -ES [MF *saillie*, fr. OF, fr. fem. of *sailli*, past part. of *saillir* to jump, rush forward, fr. L *salire* to jump, leap; akin to MIr *saltraid* he tramples, Gk *hallesthai* to leap, Lith *salti* to flow, and perh. to Skt *ucchalati* he jumps up; basic meaning: to jump] **1 a :** an action of rushing or bursting forth; *specif* **:** a sortie of troops from a defensive position to attack the enemy ⟨making a ~ against the besieging force⟩ ⟨sudden *sallies* of solo voices —Irving Kolodin⟩ **b** *dial chiefly Eng* **:** an action of leaping forth **:** BOUND, SPRING ⟨every ~ of the boat —Richard Steele⟩ **2 a :** a brief outbreak into activity or expression (as of affection or temper) **:** OUTBURST ⟨fretted with *sallies* of his mother's kisses —William Wordsworth⟩ ⟨those *sallies* of passion so common in princes —W.H.Prescott⟩ **b :** a boldly witty or imaginative saying (as in conversation or in a written passage) **:** flight of fancy **:** QUIP ⟨the cheap roar which would follow such a . . . ~ —Arnold Bennett⟩ ⟨a volume full of bright and sometimes brilliant *sallies* —*Saturday Rev.*⟩ **3 a :** a venture or excursion usu. off the beaten track **:** JAUNT, TRIP ⟨a ~ into the country⟩ ⟨the first spectacular *sallies* into unknown space —*Swiss Industry & Trade*⟩ **b** *archaic* **:** a bold violation of custom or propriety **:** ESCAPADE ⟨a ~ of youth⟩ **4 :** a projection esp. of a rafter notched to fit over a plate or horizontal beam so as to jut beyond it **5 a :** HANDSTROKE 2 **b :** ²GRIP 6b

²**sally** \"\ *vb* -ED/-ING/-s *vi* **1 a :** to leap or rush out **:** burst forth **:** issue suddenly (as troops from a fortified place to attack besiegers) ⟨would ~ out in their canoes and capture passing vessels —*Amer. Guide Series: Mich.*⟩ **b** *archaic* **:** ISSUE, SPURT, JET, SPRING ⟨his warm blood *sallied* from the wound —William Cowper⟩ **2 :** to set out (as from one's home or station) — usu. used with *forth* ⟨tightening the belt of his overcoat, he *sallied* forth —John Galsworthy⟩ ~ *vt* **:** to cause (a ship) to roll by having the crew run or move weights from side to side ⟨bluejackets raced from the port side to the starboard side and back, ~*ing* ship . . . to free her ample bottom from the sucking mud —*Time*⟩

³**sally** \"\ *chiefly dial var of* ¹SALLOW

⁴**sally** \"\ *n* -ES [prob. fr. the name *Sally*] **1** *Irish* **:** the European house wren **2** *Brit* **:** STONE FLY

⁵**sally** \"\ *var of* SALLEE

sally-bloom \'==ˌ=\ *n* [³*sally* + *bloom*] **:** FIREWEED b

sally gate *n* [¹*sally*] **:** a minor gate or passage (as in the wall of a fort) used to avoid opening major gates

sal·ly light·foot \ˌsalē'līt,fu̇t\ *n, pl* **sally lightfoots** *usu cap S&L* [*sally* fr. the name *Sally*] **:** a common active crab (*Grapsus grapsus*) living among rocks near or below the tide line in the West Indies and adjacent mainland

sally lunn \-'lən\ *n, pl* **sally lunns** *usu cap S&L* [after *Sally Lunn*, 18th cent. English baker] **:** a slightly sweetened bread raised with yeast or baking powder, baked as a thin loaf or as muffins, and eaten hot with butter

sally picker \'==,==\ *n* [³*sally*] **1 :** CHIFFCHAFF **2 :** WILLOW WREN **3** *Irish* **:** SEDGE WARBLER

sally port *n* [¹*sally*] **1 a :** a large gate or passage in a fortified place suitable for the use of troops making a sortie **b :** a similar passage esp. through the lower story of buildings (as barracks) forming a quadrangle **2** *usu* **sally-port** \'==,=\ **a :** a large port on each quarter of a fire ship for escape of the men after the firing of the train **b :** a large port in a three-decker warship

sally saw *n, usu cap 1st S* [prob. fr. ³*sally*] **:** a portable circular saw that consists of a regularly perforated toothed disk power-driven through a gear which engages the perforations

sallywood \'==,=\ *n* [³*sally* + *wood*] **1 :** WILLOW WOOD **2 :** MOUNTAIN HOLLY 1

sal·ma·gun·di *also* **sal·ma·gun·dy** \ˌsalmə'gəndē, -di\ *n* -ES [F *salmigondis*] **1 :** a salad plate consisting of chopped or sliced meats, anchovies, hard-cooked eggs, pickled vegetables, olives, radishes, endive, and watercress that are arranged in rows for color and flavor contrast and dressed with a salad dressing **2 :** a heterogeneous mixture **:** MEDLEY, POTPOURRI ⟨no ~ made of things, amusements, lust for power, can assuage our gnawing hunger to create —B.I.Bell⟩

sal·ma·naz·ar \ˌsalmə'nazə(r)\ *n* -s *usu cap* [after *Salmanasar* IV (Shalmaneser), 8th cent. B.C. king of Assyria mentioned in the Bible (2 Kings 17:3)] **:** an oversize wine bottle holding about 12 quarts ⟨a ~ of champagne⟩

sal·mi *also* **sal·mis** \'sal(ˌ)mē\ *n, pl* **salmis** \-ēz\ [F *salmis*, short for *salmigondis*] **1 :** a ragout of half roasted game stewed in a rich sauce **2 :** leftover game or domestic duck or goose reheated in a rich brown sauce

sal·mi·ac \'salmēˌak\ *n* -s [G *salmiak*, modif. of L *sal ammoniacus* — more at AMMONIA] **:** SAL AMMONIAC

sal·mine \'salˌmēn\ *n* -s [ISV *salm-* (fr. NL *Salmo*) + *-ine*] **:** a protamine obtained from the sperm of fishes of the genus *Salmo* and used chiefly in the form of its sulfate to reverse the anticoagulant effect of heparin or as the protamine component of protamine zinc insulin

sal·mo \'sal(ˌ)mō\ *n, cap* [NL, fr. L, salmon] **:** a genus of fishes (family Salmonidae) comprising the Atlantic salmon (*S. salar*) and various trouts of Europe and western No. America and formerly the Pacific salmons (genus *Oncorhynchus*) and the European and American chars (genus *Salvelinus*)

salm·on \'samən *sometimes* 'säm- *or* 'sȧm-\ *n, pl* **salmon** *also* **salmons** *often attrib* [ME *salmoun, samoun*, fr. MF *saumon, samon*, fr. L *salmon-, salmo*] **1 a :** a large isospondylous anadromous game fish (*Salmo salar*) that frequents coastal waters of the northern Atlantic and ascends adjacent streams of Europe and No. America to spawn, is extremely variable in appearance esp. at different ages and under different conditions of life, commonly attains a weight of 15 pounds, and is noted for its gaminess as a sport fish and the quality of its flesh as a table fish — see GRILSE, PARR, SMOLT; LANDLOCKED SALMON, OUANANICHE **b :** any of various other anadromous fishes of the family Salmonidae; *esp* **:** a fish of the genus *Oncorhynchus* that lives in and breeds in rivers tributary to the northern Pacific — often used with a qualifying term; see DOG SALMON, KING SALMON, HUMPBACK SALMON, SILVER SALMON, SOCKEYE **2 :** any of various fishes of families other than Salmonidae having some point of resemblance (as pink flesh) to a true salmon: as **a :** AUSTRALIAN SALMON **b :** BARRAMUNDA a **c :** any of several sciaenid fishes; *esp* **:** GEELBEC 2 **d :** WALLEYED PIKE **3 :** the flesh of a salmon used as food either fresh or cured and smoked **4 :** the variable color of salmon's flesh averaging a strong yellowish pink that is darker and slightly yellower than salmon pink, yellower and deeper than melon, and yellower than peach red

salmonbass \'==,=\ *n* **:** KABELJOU

salmonberry \'==—*see* -BERRY\ *n* **1 a :** a large red-flowered raspberry (*Rubus spectabilis*) native to the northern Pacific coast **b :** the salmon-colored edible berry of this plant **2 a :** a white-flowered raspberry (*R. parviflorus*) of western No. America that is closely related to the purple-flowering raspberry **b :** the fruit of this plant **3 :** CLOUDBERRY

salmon boat *n* **:** a carvel-built open double-ended cat-rigged sailboat used for fishing on the Columbia river and along the Pacific coast to Alaska

salmon brick *n* **:** an underburned brick

salmon cloud *n* **:** NOAH'S ARK 2

salmon disease *n* **:** a disease of salmon and related fishes and their eggs caused by a water mold of the genus *Saprolegnia*

sal·mo·nel·la \ˌsalmə'nelə\ *n* [NL, fr. Daniel E. *Salmon* †1914 American veterinarian + NL *-ella*] **1** *cap* **:** a genus of aerobic gram-negative rod-shaped nonspore-forming usu. motile bacteria (family Enterobacteriaceae) that grow well on artificial media and form acid and gas on many carbohydrates but not on lactose, sucrose, or salicin, that are all pathogenic for man and other warm-blooded animals, and that are chiefly associated with various types of food poisoning, with acute gastrointestinal inflammation, or with diseases of the genital tract — see FOWL TYPHOID, PULLORUM DISEASE, TYPHOID **2** *pl* **salmonellas** \-ləz\ *or* **salmonella** \-lə\ *also* **salmonellae** \-(ˌ)lē\ *sometimes cap* **:** any bacterium of the genus *Salmonella*

sal·mo·nel·lal \ˌ==ˌneləl\ *adj* [NL *Salmonella* + E *-al*] **:** of, relating to, or caused by salmonellas

sal·mo·nel·lo·sis \ˌsalməˌnel'ōsəs\ *n, pl* **salmonello·ses** \-ōˌsēz\ [NL, fr. *Salmonella* + *-osis*] **:** infection with or disease caused by bacteria of the genus *Salmonella* typically marked by gastroenteritis but often complicated by septicemia, meningitis, endocarditis, and various focal lesions (as in the kidneys) — compare FOOD POISONING, FOWL TYPHOID, ⁵KEEL, NECROTIC ENTERITIS, PARATYPHOID, PULLORUM DISEASE, TYPHOID

salmonfly \'==,=\ *n* **:** any of several stone flies (esp. *Pteronarcys californica*)

salmon grouper *n* **:** any of various reddish rockfishes (as the bocaccio) of the genus *Sebastodes* of the Pacific coast of No. America

salmon gum *n* **1 :** an Australian tree (*Eucalyptus salmonophloia*) with dense hard fine-grained salmon-colored wood **2 :** the wood of the salmon gum tree

salmon herring *n, Austral* **:** MILKFISH 1

¹**salmo·nid** \'sa(l)mənəd, -ˌnid *also* 'säm- *or* 'sȧm-\ *adj* [NL *Salmonidae*] **:** of or relating to the Salmonidae

²**salmonid** \"\ *n* -s **:** a fish of the family Salmonidae

sal·mon·i·dae \sal'mänəˌdē\ *n pl, cap* [NL, fr. *Salmon-*, *Salmo*, type genus + *-idae*] **:** a family of soft-finned fishes (suborder Salmonoidea) including as generally understood the salmons, trouts, chars, and whitefishes all of which are elongate and shapely and have the last vertebrae upturned

sal·mon·i·form \-nəˌfȯrm\ *adj* [*salmon* + *-iform*] **:** resembling a salmon

salmon ladder *or* **salmon leap** *or* **salmon stair :** FISH LADDER

¹**salmo·noid** \'sa(l)məˌnȯid *also* 'säm- *or* 'sȧm-\ *adj* [NL *Salmonoidea*] **1 :** like or related to the Salmonidae **2 :** of or relating to Salmonoidea

²**salmonoid** \"\ *n* -s **:** a salmonoid fish

sal·mo·noi·dea \ˌsalmə'nȯidēə\ *n pl* [NL, fr. *Salmon-, Salmo* + *-oidea* or *-oidei*] **:** a suborder of soft-finned fishes (order Isospondyli) that includes the salmons and trouts and numerous other forms (as the graylings, smelts, and capelins) having an adipose fin

salmon oil *n* **:** a fatty oil obtained usu. from the waste from the canning of salmon and used chiefly in dressing leather and in soap

salmon peal *or* **salmon peel** *n* **:** GRILSE

salmon pink *n* **:** a strong yellowish pink that is yellower and stronger than melon, yellower and lighter than peach red, lighter and much yellower than madder scarlet, and lighter and slightly redder than average salmon

salmon poisoning *also* **salmon disease** *n* **:** a highly fatal febrile disease of dogs and various other fish-eating mammals that resembles canine distemper and is thought due to a rickettsia transmitted by encysted larvae of a fluke (*Troglotrema salmincola*) ingested with the flesh of infested salmon or trout — compare BLACKHEAD 3

salmon shark *n* **:** PORBEAGLE

salm·ons·ite \'sa(l)mənˌzīt\ *n* -s [Frank A. *Salmons*, 20th cent. Am. mineralogist + E *-ite*] **:** a mineral $Mn_9Fe_2(PO_4)_8 \cdot 14H_2O$(?) consisting of a hydrous manganese iron phosphate occurring in buff-colored cleavable masses (sp. gr. 2.9)

salmon trout *n* **1 a :** a European sea trout (*Salmo trutta*) **b :** LAKE TROUT **b c :** any of numerous large trout of western No. America: as (1) **:** CUTTHROAT TROUT (2) **:** STEELHEAD TROUT **2 :** a half-grown Australian salmon of the size preferred for food

salmon wheel *n* **:** a device for catching salmon in large quantities consisting of a large revolving wheel suspended in the water and turned by the current to which are attached scoop nets that catch the fish passing beneath

sal·mo·per·cae \ˌsalmō'pərˌsē, -rˌkē, -rˌkī\ *n pl, cap* [NL, fr. L *salmo* salmon + *percae*, pl. of *perca* perch — more at PERCH] **:** a small order that comprises No. American freshwater fishes in some respects intermediate between the Ostariophysi and the Percomorphi and includes the pirate perch and the trout-perches

salm·wood \'säm,=\ *n* [*salm* (origin unknown) + *wood*] **:** PRINCEWOOD 1

salmatron \'==\ *n* [*sal* + *natron*] **:** crude sodium carbonate

sal·oid \'saˌlȯid\ *n* -s [*sal* + *-oid*] **:** an insoluble salt of an acidoid in soil

sal·ol \'saˌlȯl, -lōl\ *n* -s [fr. *Salol*, a trademark] **:** PHENYL SALICYLATE

sa·lom·e·ter \sə'lämǝd·ə(r)\ *n* [L *sal* salt + *-o-* + *-meter* — more at SALT] **:** SALIMETER

sa·lo·mó·ni·ca \ˌsalə'mänəkə\ *n* -s [Sp, fr. fem. of *salomónico* of Solomon (in the Bible), fr. *Salomón* Solomon + *-ico* -ic; fr. the belief that a similar column in St. Peter's Cathedral in Rome came fr. Solomon's temple — more at SOLOMON] **:** a twisted architectural column

sa·lon \(')sa'lōⁿ, sə'län, (')sa'län *also* sə'lōn *or* (')sa'lōn *or* (')sa'lōⁿ *sometimes* (')sa'läⁿ *or* sə'lōⁿ\ *n, pl* **salons** \-ōⁿ(z), -änz, -ōnz, -äⁿ(z)\ *often attrib* [F — more at SALOON] **1 a :** a usu. spacious and elegant apartment or living room (as in a fashionable French home) **2 :** a fashionable assemblage that is held by custom at the home of a usu. socially prominent person and takes its character from the kind of notables (as literary figures, artists, or statesmen) who frequent it ⟨literary ~*s* . . . have flourished in Paris since the days of Louis XIV —Malcolm Cowley⟩ ⟨witty favorite of Society . . . and mistress of a brilliant ~ —*advt*⟩ **3 a :** an apartment or hall for the exhibition of works of art (as paintings and sculptures) **b** *usu cap* (1) **:** an annual exhibition of such works; *esp* **:** one held by a national society of artists (2) **:** an annual exhibition usu. international in scope of outstanding photographs, color slides, and transparencies **4 :** a business establishment or shop having stylishness ⟨a shoe ~⟩ ⟨a beauty ~⟩ ⟨a reducing ~⟩

sa·lon·i·ca *or* **sa·lon·i·ka** \sə'länəkə *also* ˌsalə'nēkə\ *adj, usu cap* [fr. *Salonica*, Greece] **:** of or from the city of Salonica, Greece ⟨*Salonica* businessmen⟩ **:** of the kind or style prevalent in Salonica

salon music *n* **:** instrumental music of a light, pleasing, and often sentimental character suitable for the drawing room rather than the concert hall

sa·loon \sə'lün\ *n* -s [F *salon*, fr. It *salone*, aug. of *sala* hall, room, of Gmc origin; akin to OE *sele* hall, house, OS *seli*, MD *sale*, OHG *sal*, ON *salr* hall, house, Goth *saljan* to stay at an inn, *salithwos* inn; akin to OSlav *selitva* dwelling, Lith *sala* village] **1 :** a spacious, lofty, and elegant apartment (as in a palace or manor house) for the reception and entertainment of guests **:** a large and elaborate drawing room **:** SALON 1 ⟨the gilden ~*s* in which the first magnates of the realm . . . gave banquets and balls —T.B.Macaulay⟩ **2 :** SALON 2 **3 a :** a usu. elaborately decorated apartment or hall (as a ballroom, gaming room, exhibition room, or a ship's dining hall) **b :** a large cabin for the social use of passengers (as on shipboard) **c :** a business establishment characterized by fanciness (as a shop or an amusement hall) **:** SALON 4 ⟨a shaving ~⟩ ⟨hair-dressing ~⟩ ⟨a billiard ~⟩ ⟨a dancing ~⟩ ⟨went out . . . to play at some ice-cream ~ —Betty Smith⟩ **d :** a room or public establishment in which alcoholic beverages are sold and consumed **:** BARROOM, TAPROOM **4** *Brit* **a :** a railroad car approximating the American parlor car in arrangement and function **b :** SEDAN 2a

sa·loon·atic \sə'lünəˌtik\ *n* -s [blend of *saloon* and *lunatic*] **:** an enthusiastic advocate of saloons and drinking ⟨people who . . . are neither bonehead drys nor ~*s* —*N.Y.Evening Jour.*⟩

saloon deck *n* **:** a deck on which a ship's saloon is located

sa·loon·ist \sə'lünəst\ *n* -s **:** SALOONKEEPER

saloonkeeper \=='==\ *n* **:** a person who owns or manages a saloon

saloon pistol *or* **saloon rifle** *n, Brit* : a small light pistol or rifle used chiefly in a shooting gallery

sa·loop \sə'lüp\ *also* **salop** \'saləp, sə'läp\ *n* -s [modif. of F or Sp *salep* — more at SALEP] **1** : SALEP **2** : a common sassafras (*Sassafras albidum molle*) **3** : a hot drink made from an infusion of powdered salep or sassafras with milk and sugar

sal·op \'saləp\ *adj, usu cap* [fr. county of *Salop*, England] : SHROPSHIRE

¹sa·lo·pi·an \sə'lōpēən\ *adj, usu cap* [county of *Salop* + E *-ian*] : of or relating to Salop or Shropshire in England

²salopian \"\ *n* -s *cap* : a native or inhabitant of Shropshire

salopian ware *n, usu cap S* **1** : Roman pottery found in Shropshire that is usu. made of red or white clay **2** : a modern somewhat coarse and opaque porcelaneous Shropshire ware first made toward the end of the 18th century

salp \'salp\ *n* -s [NL *Salpa*] : SALPA 2

sal·pa \'salpə\ *n* [NL, fr. L *salpa*, a kind of stockfish, fr. Gk *salpē*] **1** *cap* : a genus (the type of the family Salpidae) of transparent barrel-shaped or fusiform free-swimming oceanic tunicates that are abundant in warm seas and that exist in two forms one of which lives solitary and reproduces by budding from an internal organ a series of hermaphroditic individuals of the other kind that are united side by side in a chain or cluster and usu. carry each only a single egg destined to develop into an individual of the solitary kind **2** *pl* **sal·pae** \-(,)pē, -,pī\ *or* **salpas** : any tunicate of the genus *Salpa* or family Salpidae

¹sal·pid \'salpəd\ *or* **sal·pid·i·an** \(')sal¦pidēən\ *adj* [*salpid* fr. NL *Salpidae*; *salpidian* fr. NL *Salpidae* + E *-ian*] : of or relating to the Salpidae

²salpid \"\ *or* **salpidian** \"\ *n* -s : a tunicate of the family Salpidae

sal·pi·dae \'salpə,dē\ *n pl, cap* [NL, fr. *Salpa*, type genus + *-idae*] : a small family of tunicates (order Thaliacea) of which *Salpa* is the chief and in some classifications the sole genus

sal·pi·form \'salpə,fȯrm\ *adj* [NL *Salpa* + E *-iform*] : resembling a salpa

sal·pi·glos·sis \,salpə'gläsəs, -glȯs-\ *n* [NL, irreg. fr. Gk *salpinx* trumpet + *glōssa* tongue — more at GLOSS (explanation)] **1** *cap* : a small genus of Chilean herbs (family Solanaceae) having large funnel-shaped variously colored and often showily marked flowers with a tubular 5-cleft calyx **2** -ES : any plant of the genus *Salpiglossis*

salping- *or* **salpingo-** *comb form* [NL, fr. *salping-*, *salpinx*] **1** : salpinx ‹*salping*ectomy› ‹*salping*emphraxis› ‹*salping*itis› **2** : fallopian tube ‹*salpingo*tomy› ‹*salpingo*rrhaphy› **3 a** : fallopian tube and ‹*salpingo*-oophorectomy› ‹*salpingo*-uterostomy› **b** : eustachian and ‹*salpingo*nasal› ‹*salpingo*palatine› ‹*salpingo*pharyngeal›

sal·pin·gec·to·my \,salpən'jektəmē\ *n* -ES [ISV *salping-* + *-ectomy*] : the excision of a salpinx (as a fallopian or eustachian tube)

salpinges *pl of* SALPINX

sal·pin·gi·an \(')sal¦pinjēən\ *adj* [*salping-* + *-ian*] : of or relating to a salpinx

sal·pin·gi·on \sal'pinjē,än\ *n* -s [NL, fr. Gk, tube, dim. of *salping-*, *salpinx* trumpet — more at SALPINX] : the apex of the petrous portion of the temporal bone

sal·pin·gi·tis \,salpən'jīdəs\ *n* -ES [NL, fr. *salping-* + *-itis*] : inflammation of a salpinx (as a fallopian or a eustachian tube)

sal·pin·gog·ra·phy \-n'gägrəfē\ *n* -ES [ISV *salping-* + *-graphy*] : visualization of a fallopian tube by roentgenography following injection of an opaque medium

salpingo-oophorectomy \sal¦piŋ(,)gō+\ *n* [ISV *salping-* + *oophorectomy*] : excision of a fallopian tube and an ovary

sal·pin·go·palatine \"+\ *adj* [*salping-* + *palatine*] : of or relating to the eustachian tubes and the palate

sal·pin·go·pharyngeal \"+\ *adj* [*salping-* + *pharyngeal*] : of or relating to the eustachian tubes and pharynx

sal·pinx \'sal(,)piŋ(k)s\ *n, pl* **sal·pin·ges** \sal'pin(,)jēz\ [NL, fr. Gk, trumpet] **1** : EUSTACHIAN TUBE **2** : FALLOPIAN TUBE

sal·poid \'sal,pȯid\ *adj* [NL *Salpa* + E *-oid*] : of, relating to, or resembling salpae

sal prunella *n* [¹*sal* + *prunella* (angina)] : potassium nitrate fused and cast in balls, cakes, or sticks

salps *pl of* SALP

sals *pl of* SAL

salse \'sal(t)s\ *n* -s [F, fr. It *salsa*, lit., sauce, fr. ML *salsa* salty condiment, salt — more at SAUCE] : MUD VOLCANO

sal·si·fy \'salsəfē, -,fī\ *n* -ES [F *salsifis*, fr. It *salsefica*, *salsefrica*, alter. of *sassefica*, *sassefrica*, fr. LL *saxifrica*, any of various herbs, fr. L *saxum* rock + *-i-* + *-frica* (fr. *fricare* to rub) — more at SAX, FRICTION] : a European biennial herb (*Tragopogon porrifolius*) with long-peduncled heads of purple ray flowers and a long fusiform edible root — called also *oyster plant*, *vegetable oyster*

sal·sil·la \sal'silə\ *n* -s [NL *salsilla* (specific epithet of *Bomarea salsilla*), fr. fem. of *salsillus* salty, fr. L *salsus* salted, fr. past part. of *sallere* to salt] : a tropical American plant of the genus *Bomarea*; *esp* : one (as *B. salsilla* or *B. edulis*) with edible roots that are sometimes boiled and used as a substitute for potatoes

sal soda *n* [¹*sal*] : SODIUM CARBONATE a(3)

sal·so·la \sal'sōlə\ *n, cap* [NL, fr. It, a plant of the genus *Salsola*, fr. *salso* salty, fr. L *salsus* — more at SAUCE] : a large genus of mostly Old World herbs or shrubs of the family Chenopodiaceae with variously shaped often prickly leaves and small greenish flowers whose 4- to 5-parted perianth remains investing the utricle — see BARILLA, RUSSIAN THISTLE, SALTWORT

sal·so·la·ceous \¦salsə¦lāshəs\ *adj* [NL *Salsola* + E *-aceous*] : of, relating to, or resembling the genus *Salsola*

sal·su·gi·nous \(')sal¦süjənəs\ *adj* [L *salsugin-*, *salsugo* saltiness (fr. *salsus* salty) + E *-ous* — more at SAUCE] : HALOPHYTIC

¹salt \'sȯlt, *chiefly Brit* 'säl-\ *n* -s [ME, fr. OE *sealt*; akin to OFris, OS, ON, & Goth *salt*, OHG *salz*, L *sal* salt, Gk *hals* salt, sea, Arm *al* salt, Skt *salila* sea] **1 a** : a colorless or white crystalline compound NaCl consisting of sodium chloride that occurs abundantly in nature both solid in minerals (as halite) and in solution, that has various uses (as for seasoning food, preserving meat, manufacturing sodium, chlorine, and their compounds, making glass and soap, and refrigerating), that constitutes about 2.6 percent of seawater, is found in small quantities in fresh water, and is present in all animal fluids and esp. in urine, that is obtained commercially from deposits in the earth or by evaporation of natural brines (as seawater), and that in the commercial form usu. contains small quantities of the deliquescent salts magnesium chloride and calcium chloride that cause it to attract moisture — called also *common salt* **b** : any of numerous substances (as sal ammoniac, sal prunella, sal soda) resembling common salt (as in appearance, incombustibility, or taste) **c salts** *pl* (1) : a mineral or saline mixture (as Epsom salts, Rochelle salt, or Glauber's salt) used as an aperient or cathartic (2) : SMELLING SALTS **d** : one of the three primary elements of matter in alchemy representing in contrast to mercury and sulfur the principle of fixity and solidity **e** : any of a class of compounds typified by common salt that are derived from acids by replacement of part or all of the acid hydrogen by a metal or radical acting like a metal, that may be formed by the reaction of acids with bases either with or without elimination of water, with metallic oxides, or with metals and also in other ways (as by direct union of their elements), that for the most part are dominantly ionic in character and have high melting points, and that in solution or in the fused state conduct an electric current and thereby undergo decomposition ‹sodium bisulfate and sodium sulfate are sodium ~s of sulfuric acid› — compare ¹ACID 2a(2), ¹BASIC 3c, DOUBLE SALT, ¹NORMAL 10c; -ATE, -IDE, -ITE **2** : a container for salt at table : SALTCELLAR, SALTSHAKER ‹the roly-poly ~s and peppers that bob right up again if you tip them over —*House Beautiful*› — often used in the phrases *above the salt* and *below the salt* alluding to the former custom of seating persons of higher rank above and those of lower rank below a large saltcellar placed near the middle of a long table **3** : sustenance or support provided (as by a host or employer) : FOOD, HOSPITALITY, KEEP — used often in the phrase *to be worth one's salt* **4 a** : an ingredient or element that gives savor, piquancy, or zest : FLAVOR ‹a people . . . full of life, vigor, and the ~ of personality —Clifton Fadiman› **b** : sharpness of wit : PUNGENCY ‹a wit which has kept something of its ~ —A.T.Quiller-Couch› **c** : COMMON SENSE, EARTHINESS ‹the speech with the most ~ and the least jargon —Colin Simpson› **d** : corrective allowance : RESERVE, SKEPTICISM ‹take all the political and economic references with a healthy amount of ~ —*New Republic*› — often used in the phrase *take with a grain of salt* **e** : the sprinkling of people thought to set a model of excellence for or to give tone to the rest — usu. used in the phrase *the salt of the earth* ‹we no longer accept these country gentlemen . . . as the ~ of the earth —W.S.Maugham› **5 a** : SALT MARSH **b salts** *pl, chiefly dial* : marshes flooded by the tide **6** : SAILOR; *esp* : an experienced seaman — often used with *old* ‹a tale worthy of an old ~›

²salt \"\ *vt* -ED/-ING/-S [ME *salten*, fr. OE *sealtan*; akin to OHG *salzan* to salt, ON *salta*, Goth *saltan*; all fr. a prehistoric Gmc v. fr. the n. represented by E ¹*salt*] **1 a** : to add salt to : sprinkle, rub, impregnate, or season with salt ‹~ the food› ‹~ the icy sidewalk› ‹the spray ~*ing* our faces —Franc Shor› **b** : to preserve (as fish or meat) with salt or in brine ‹~ mackerel› ‹~ beef› **2 a** : to give flavor or piquancy to ‹employs an irreverent humor to ~ her shrewd observations —James Kelly› ‹~*ed* the work with highly readable case histories —*Saturday Rev.*› **b** : to make bitter ‹their lives had been ~*ed* by the taste of death —J.P.Bishop› **3 a** : to enrich (as a mine) artificially usu. with fraudulent intent by secretly placing valuable mineral in some of the working places : PLANT 4b **b** : to enrich or impoverish either intentionally or accidentally ‹samples taken from a mine or claim for test purposes› ‹~*ing* a barren claim . . . thereby setting off a rush that drew 5000 miners into the area on a fruitless search —Oscar Lewis› **c** : to give to (something for sale or upon which a sale is based) an appearance of value, profitableness, or genuineness by fraudulent means ‹~*ing* the books of a business› **4** : to supply (as an animal) with salt : feed salt to ‹the field where cattle are ~*ed*› **5 a** : to sprinkle as if with salt ‹~*ing* clouds with silver iodide crystals› **b** : to intersperse with : scatter among ‹party organizations . . . are heavily ~*ed*, almost inevitably, with men of affairs —W.S.White› **c** : GRAY ‹experience has . . . ~*ed* his hair —Truman Capote›

³salt \"\ *adj* -ER/-EST [ME, fr. OE *sealt* (akin to ON *saltr* salt), fr. *sealt*, n.] **1 a** : full of, impregnated with, or containing salt : SALINE, SALTY ‹~ tears› ‹~ butter› ‹a ~ solution› **b** : smelling or tasting of salt ‹tasted the water, and it was ~*er* than the waters of the sea —Elinor Wylie› ‹with the sea all around her, and the ~, cold air —William Black› **c** : being or inducing one of the four basic taste sensations — compare BITTER, SOUR, SWEET **2** : cured or seasoned with salt : SALTED ‹~ beef› **3 a** : overflowed with or impregnated by salt water **b** : growing in or native to a salt marsh **c** *of soil or rock* : mixed with salt : BARREN **4 a** : SHARP, PUNGENT ‹a ~ wit —John Buchan› **b** : BITTER ‹a great and ~ reproach —Stephen Crane›

⁴salt \"\ *adj* [by shortening & alter. fr. *assaut*, fr. ME *a sawt*, fr. MF *a saut*, lit., on the jump, fr. *a* at, on + *saut* jump, fr. L *saltus*, fr. *saltus*, past part. of *salire* to jump, leap — more at SALLY] **1** *obs, of a female animal* : being in heat **2** *obs, of a person* : LUSTFUL, LASCIVIOUS ‹his ~ and most hidden loose affection —Shak.›

sal·ta \'saltə, 'sȯl-\ *n* -s [G, fr. L, jump!, imper. of *saltare* to jump, dance] : a game for two played on a board of 100 squares in which the object is to move one's men into the positions orig. occupied by the opponent's men

saltando *adv (or adj)* [It, jumping, fr. L *saltandum*, gerund of *saltare* to jump, dance] : ARCO SALTANDO

salt-and-pepper \¦=¦=¦==\ *adj* : PEPPER-AND-SALT

¹sal·tant \'saltᵊnt, 'sȯl-, -ltənt\ *adj* [L *saltant-*, *saltans*, pres. part. of *saltare* to jump, leap, dance, fr. *saltus*, past part. of *salire* to jump, leap — more at SALLY] : DANCING, LEAPING

²saltant \"\ *n* -s : a mutant individual or strain; *esp* : one produced in a fungal or bacterial culture

sal·ta·rel·lo \,saltə're(,)lō, ,sȯl-\ *also* **sal·ta·rel·la** \-elə\ *n* -s [It *saltarello*, fr. *saltare* to jump, fr. L] **1** : an Italian dance characterized by a lively hop step at the beginning of each measure **2** : music for this dance or having its rhythm in quick triple or sextuple time and being characterized typically by skips and dotted triple rhythm **3** : a jack of a harpsichord

sal·tate \'sal,tāt, 'sȯl-\ *vi* -ED/-ING/-S [L *saltatus*, past part. of *saltare* to jump, leap, dance] **1** : to move by jumps or leaps **2** : to undergo or exhibit evolutionary saltation **syn** see JUMP

sal·ta·tion \-'tāshən\ *n* -s [L *saltation-*, *saltatio*, fr. *saltatus* + *-ion-*, *-io* -ion] **1 a** : the action of leaping or jumping ‹ordained for ~, their hinder legs do far exceed the other —Sir Thomas Browne› **b** : DANCING ‹continued his ~ without . . . intermission —Sir Walter Scott› **2** *obs* : a flow in spurts — used of arterial blood **3 a** : an advance by leaps rather than by continuous gradations : a sudden or abrupt change; *specif* : the reputed direct transformation of one form into another in the course of evolution : DISCONTINUOUS VARIATION, MACROEVOLUTION **b** : the production of saltants **c** : SALTANT **4** : the transportation of particles by currents of water or air in such a manner that they move along in a series of short intermittent leaps — compare TRACTION TRANSPORT **syn** see JUMP

sal·ta·to \säl'täd·(,)ō\ *adv (or adj)* [It (past part. of *saltare* to jump, leap), fr. L *saltatus*, past part. of *saltare* to jump, leap, dance — more at SALTANT] : ARCO SALTANDO

sal·ta·tor \sal'tād·ə(r), sȯl-, '=,==\ *n* [NL, fr. L *saltator* dancer, fr. *saltatus* + *-or*] **1** *cap* : a large genus of Neotropical birds of relatively large size and plain coloration that are classified with either the finches or the tanagers **2** -s : any bird of the genus *Saltator*

sal·ta·to·ria \,saltə'tōrēə, ,sȯl-\ *n pl, cap* [NL, fr. L, neut. pl. of *saltatorius*] : a suborder of Orthoptera that is often considered a separate order, comprises insects with the hind legs usu. adapted for leaping, and includes the grasshoppers, crickets, and related forms — compare CURSORIA

sal·ta·to·ri·al \¦==¦==al\ *adj* [L *saltatorius* + E *-al*] **1** : of, relating to, or marked by leaping or dancing : SALTATORY ‹~ exercises› ‹the bow's ~ elasticity —Paul Hindemith› **2** : capable of or adapted for leaping ‹~ legs›

sal·ta·to·ri·an \-ən\ *adj* [L *saltatorius* + E *-an*] : SALTATORY 1

sal·ta·to·ry \'==,tōrē\ *adj* [L *saltatorius*, fr. *saltatus* + *-orius* -ory] **1** : of or relating to dancing ‹the ~ art› **2** : characterized by movement in leaps and bounds ‹~ thinking› ‹~ insects› **3** : proceeding by leaps rather than by gradual transitions : DISCONTINUOUS ‹a ~ advance› ‹~ relations between terms› — compare DISCONTINUOUS VARIATION

saltatory evolution *n* : evolution by sudden variation or by periods of active variation with intervening inactive periods : MACROEVOLUTION — compare SALTATION 3a

salt away *or* **salt down** *vt* **1** : to prepare (as meat or eggs) with or pack in salt for preserving **2** : to lay away (as money) : invest safely : SAVE ‹*salt away* part of their . . . income each year for retirement —*Wall Street Jour.*› ‹making quite a little . . . *salting down* my commissions —Elisabeth Thomas›

saltbox *or* **saltbox house** *n* : a type of frame dwelling much used in colonial New England having two stories in front and one behind and having the roof double-sloping with the longer and lower slope to the rear

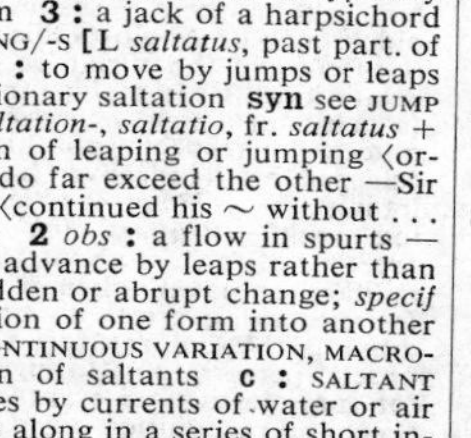

saltbox

saltbush \'=,=\ *n* : any of various shrubby plants of the family Chenopodiaceae that thrive in dry alkaline soil; *esp* : any of numerous oraches that are important browse plants in dry parts of the western U.S., Australia, and southern Africa and are sometimes cultivated for forage and for soil stabilization

salt cake *n* **1** : anhydrous sodium sulfate Na_2SO_4; *esp* : a crude form obtained usu. by reaction in a furnace of sulfuric acid on common salt in the manufacture of hydrochloric acid and used chiefly in the sulfate process for wood pulp and in making glass and chemicals **2** : a substance made by reaction of soda ash and sulfur and used in the sulfate pulp process

saltcat \'=,kat\ *n* [ME, prob. fr. *salt* + *cat*] : a lump of salt; *specif* : a mixture chiefly of salt, meal, and lime that is attractive to pigeons

salt cedar *n, Southwest* : TAMARIX 2

saltcellar \'=,==\ *n* : a vessel usu. of glass or silver used on the table for holding salt

salt-desert cavy *n* : a mara (*Dolichotis salinicola*) of the Argentine salt marshes

salt dome *n* : a domical anticline in sedimentary rocks having a mass of rock salt as its core and being forced up in plastic form by earth stresses from an underlying bed of salt

sal·teaux \'sal,tō, 'sȯl-\ *n pl but sing or pl in constr, usu cap* [F, irreg. fr. *Sault* Ste. Marie, Ontario] **1 a** : an Algonquian people of the vicinity of Sault Ste. Marie, Ontario **b** : a member of such people **2** : a dialect of Ojibwa

salted *adj* [fr. past part. of ²*salt*] *of an animal* : immune against a contagious disease because of prior infection and recovery from it : PREMUNE

salt eel *n* **1** *obs* : the end of a rope used as a whip **2** *obs* : a flogging with a rope's end

¹salt·er \'sȯltə(r), *chiefly Brit* 'säl-\ *n* -s [ME, fr. OE *sealtere*, fr. *sealt* salt + *-ere* -er — more at SALT] **1 a** : one that manufactures or deals in salt **b** *Brit* : DRYSALTER **2** [²*salt* + *-er*] : one that salts something (as meat, fish, cheese, hides) to season or preserve it **3** : a vessel or trough in which meat is salted **4** : a brook trout (*Salvelinus fontinalis*) that has become catadromous

²salter *comparative of* SALT

sal·tern \'sȯltə(r)n\ *n* -s [OE *sealtern*, fr. *sealt* salt + *ern*, *ærn*, *ren* house — more at SALT, REST] : a building or place where salt is made by boiling or evaporation : SALTWORKS

salt·ery \'sȯltərē\ *n* -ES [¹*salt* + *-ery*] **1** : SALTWORKS **2** : an establishment in which fish are salted for market

saltest *superlative of* SALT

salt·fat \'=,fat\ *also* **salt·foot** \-,fu̇t\ *n* [*saltfat* fr. ME, fr. OE *sealtfæt*, fr. *sealt* salt + *fæt* vat, vessel, jar; *saltfoot* alter. of *saltfat* — more at SALT, VAT] *archaic Scot* : SALTCELLAR

salt flat *n* : the salt-encrusted bottom of an evaporated lake or pond

salt glaze *n* : a stoneware glaze produced by vaporizing common salt in the fire of the kiln at the height of the firing so that the sodium of the salt reacts with silicates of the ware to form a coating of glassy acid-resistant mixed silicate of sodium and aluminum — **salt-glazed** *adj*

salt grass *n* : any of various grasses native to salt meadows or other markedly alkaline habitats: as **a** : a rigid erect No. American dioecious perennial grass (*Distichlis spicata*); *broadly* : any grass of the genus *Distichlis* **b** : any of several spartinas; *esp* : a perennial rhizomatous grass (*Spartina patens*) of wet brackish areas of eastern No. America **c** : FEATHER GRASS 2

salt hay *n* : hay made from salt grass or grass growing on tidal marshes; *specif* : BLACK GRASS 1

salt horse *n* : salted meat (as beef or pork)

¹sal·ti·cid \'saltəsəd, 'sȯl-, -tə,sid\ *adj* [NL *Salticidae*] : of or relating to the Salticidae

²salticid \"\ *n* -s : a spider of the family Salticidae

sal·tic·i·dae \sal'tisə,dē, sȯl-\ *n pl, cap* [NL, fr. *Salticus*, type genus (fr. LL *salticus* dancing, fr. L *saltare* to jump, leap, dance + *-icus* -ic) + *-idae* — more at SALTANT] : a family of small spiders that stalk and leap upon their prey — see JUMPING SPIDER

¹sal·tier \'sal,ti(ə)r, 'sȯl-, -tī(ə)r\ *archaic var of* SALTIRE

²saltier *comparative of* SALTY

sal·ti·er·ra \,saltē'erə, ,sȯl-\ *n* -s [Sp, fr. *sal* salt (fr. L) + *tierra* earth, fr. L *terra* — more at SALT, TERRACE] : salt left by evaporation of some shallow inland lakes

saltiest *superlative of* SALTY

¹sal·ti·grade \'saltə,grād, 'sȯl-\ *adj* [L *saltus* leap + E *-i-* + *-grade* — more at SALT (in heat)] : having the feet or legs adapted to leaping — usu. used of spiders (as members of the family Salticidae)

²saltigrade \"\ *n* -s : a saltigrade spider

salt·i·ly \'sȯltəlē, -li, *chiefly Brit* 'säl-\ *adv* : in a salty manner

sal·tim·ban·co \,saltəm'baŋ(,)kō, ,sȯl-\ *or* **sal·tim·ban·que** *also* **sal·tim·bank** \'==,baŋk\ *n* -s [F & It; F *saltimbanque*, fr. It *saltimbanco*, lit., one that jumps upon a bench, fr. *saltare* to jump (fr. L) + *in* (fr. L) + *banco* bench, of Gmc origin; akin to OHG *bank* bench — more at SALTANT, IN, BENCH] : MOUNTEBANK

sal·tine \(')sȯl¦tēn\ *n* -s [¹*salt* + *-ine*] : a thin crisp cracker sprinkled with salt

salt·i·ness \'sȯltēnəs, -tin-, *chiefly Brit* 'säl-\ *n* -ES : the quality or state of being salty ‹the ~ of the sea air› ‹humor . . . usually flavored late in life with a sardonic ~ —J.C.Fitzpatrick›

salt·ing \-tiŋ\ *n* -s [fr. gerund of ²*salt*] *chiefly Brit* : land flooded regularly by tides — often distinguished from *salt marsh*; usu. used in pl.

¹sal·tire \'sal,tī(ə)r, 'sȯl-\ *n* -s [ME *sawturoure*, *sawtire*, fr. MF *saultoir*, *sautoir* X-shaped animal barricade that can be jumped over by people, saltire, fr. *saulter*, *sauter* to jump, fr. L *saltare* — more at SALTANT] **1** *heraldry* : an ordinary consisting of a cross formed by a bend dexter and a bend sinister crossing in the center of the field **2** : an X-shaped cross; *esp* : SAINT ANDREW'S CROSS 1 — **in saltire** : in position so as to suggest the form of a saltire: **a** *of a pair of heraldic bearings* : one bendwise and the other bendwise sinister so as to cross each other ‹two crosiers *in saltire*› **b** *of four heraldic bearings* : in diagonal position so as to converge toward or meet at a common center ‹four hands conjoined *in saltire*› **c** *of five or more heraldic bearings* : arranged as if along the arms of a saltire ‹five dice *in saltire* argent› — **per saltire** : divided into four parts by two diagonal lines crossing each other

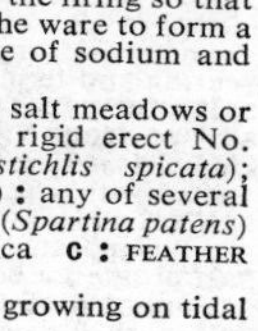

saltire 1

²saltire \"\ *adj* : shaped like an X ‹a ~ stretcher›

saltire cross *n* : SALTIRE

sal·tire·wise \-,wīz\ *also* **sal·tire·ways** \-,wāz\ *adv* **1** : in saltire **2** : per saltire **3** : with the arms extending diagonally

salt·ish \'sȯltish, -tēsh, *chiefly Brit* 'säl-\ *adj* [ME, fr. *salt* + *-ish*] **1** : of, relating to, or impregnated with salt **2** : somewhat salty — **salt·ish·ly** *adv* — **salt·ish·ness** *n* -ES

salt junk *n* : dried salted beef

salt lake *n* : an inland body of saline water having no outlet to the sea

salt lake city \¦=¦==¦==\ *or* **salt lake** \'=,=\ *adj, usu cap S&L&C* [fr. *Salt Lake City*, Utah] : of or from Salt Lake City, the capital of Utah ‹a *Salt Lake City* smelter› : of the kind or style prevalent in Salt Lake City

salt lak·er \'=,lākə(r)\ *n, cap S&L* [*Salt Lake (City)* + E *-er*] : a native or resident of Salt Lake City, Utah

salt·less \'=ləs\ *adj* **1** : having no salt **2** : lacking liveliness or flavor : INSIPID ‹a dull, ~ life›

salt·less·ness *n* -ES : the quality or state of being saltless

salt lick *n* : LICK 3

saltlike \'=,=\ *adj* : resembling a salt esp. in ionic character ‹~ carbides, hydrides, and nitrides›

salt·ly *adv* [³*salt* + *-ly*] : in a salty manner ‹~ bitter›

salt·man \'=mən\ *n, pl* **saltmen** : BRINEMAN 2

salt marsh *n* [ME *saltmersh*, fr. *salt* + *mersh* marsh — more at MARSH] : flat land that is subject to intermittent or occasional overflow by salt water, contains water that is brackish to strongly saline, and supports a vegetation of halophytic plants usu. consisting chiefly of grasses

salt-marsh caterpillar *n* : a hairy caterpillar that is the larva of an American moth (*Estigmene acrea*) of the family Arctiidae and that is destructive to various crop plants

salt-marsh fleabane *n* : any of various herbs (genus *Pluchea*) growing chiefly in salt marshes

salt-marsh gerardia *n* : SEASIDE GERARDIA

salt-marsh grass *n* : SALT GRASS

salt-marsh hen *n* : CLAPPER RAIL

salt-marsh mosquito *n* : any of various mosquitoes that breed in the brackish water of salt marshes but include some forms (as *Aedes sollicitans*) which migrate inland for miles

salt-marsh moth *n* : the moth of the salt-marsh caterpillar

salt-marsh terrapin *n* : DIAMONDBACK TERRAPIN

salt meadow *n* : a meadow subject to flooding by salt water

salt-meadow grass *n* : SALT GRASS

saltmouth \'=,=\ *n* : a widemouthed bottle with glass stopper for holding chemicals (as crystallized salts)

salt·ness *n* -ES [ME *saltnesse*, fr. OE *sealtnes*, fr. *sealt* salt + *-nes* -ness — more at SALT] **:** the quality or state of being salt or salty: as **a :** SALINITY ⟨the ~ of the sea water⟩ **b :** PUNGENCY ⟨the ~ of a speech⟩
salt of amber : SUCCINIC ACID
salt of hartshorn 1 : AMMONIUM CHLORIDE **2 :** AMMONIUM CARBONATE C
salt of lemon *or* **salts of lemon :** either of two salts: **a :** POTASSIUM OXALATE b **b :** POTASSIUM TETROXALATE
salt of phosphorus : MICROCOSMIC SALT
salt of saturn *usu cap 2d S* **:** LEAD ACETATE a
salt of soda : SODIUM CARBONATE
salt of sorrel *or* **salts of sorrel :** either of two salts: **a :** POTASSIUM OXALATE b **b :** POTASSIUM TETROXALATE
salt of tartar : POTASSIUM CARBONATE; *esp* **:** a pure form made orig. by heating cream of tartar
salt of vitriol : ZINC SULFATE
salt of wisdom : ALEMBROTH
salt of wormwood : POTASSIUM CARBONATE; *esp* **:** an impure form obtained orig. from the ashes of wormwood (*Artemisia absinthium*)
salt out *vt* **:** to precipitate, coagulate, or separate as a liquid layer or gas (a dissolved substance or lyophilic sol as a soap or protein) from a solution by the addition of salt, esp. common salt; *broadly* **:** to produce similar effects on by the addition usu. of an electrolyte other than a salt ~ *vi* **1** *of a saline solution* **:** to deposit salt **2 :** to become deposited by or separated from a solution ⟨albumin and gelatin both *salt out* reversibly in the presence of high concentrations of the salts —J.W.McBain⟩
salt pan *n* [ME *salt panne*] **1 :** an undrained natural depression in which water gathers and leaves a deposit of salt on evaporation **2 :** a large pan for making salt by evaporation
salt·pe·tre *also* **salt·pe·ter** \sȯlt¦pēd·ə(r), -ētə-, *in rapid speech* -l'p-; '⸗,⸗⸗\ *n* [alter. (influenced by ¹*salt*) of earlier *salpeter*, fr. ME *salpetre, salpeter*, fr. MF *salpetre*, fr. ML *sal petrae*, fr. L *sal* salt + *petrae*, gen. of *petra* rock, fr. Gk] **1 :** POTASSIUM NITRATE **2 :** CHILE SALTPETER **3 :** an efflorescence of salts sometimes formed on the surface of tobacco leaves during curing and fermentation
saltpeter paper *n* **:** TOUCH PAPER
salt·pe·trous \(')sȯl(t)¦pē·trəs\ *adj* [modif. of F *salpêtreux*, fr. MF *salpetreux*, fr. *salpetre* + *-eux* -ous] **:** relating to, impregnated with, or resembling saltpeter
salt pit *n* [ME *salte pitte*] **:** a pit in which seawater is received and evaporated
salt plug *n* **:** a body of rock salt; *specif* **:** the core of a salt dome
salt–poor diet *n* **:** LOW-SODIUM DIET
salt pork *n* **:** pork cured in salt or brine; *specif* **:** cured pork from the belly, back, or side consisting largely of fat — compare BACON 3, FATBACK, SIDE MEAT, SOWBELLY, WHITE MEAT
salt tree *n* [²*sal*] **:** ²SAL 1
salt reed grass *n* **:** a tall reedlike grass (*Spartina cynosuroides*) common in salt meadows
salt rheum *n* **:** ECZEMA
salt–rheum weed *n* **:** a turtlehead (*Chelone glabra*)
salt–rising bread \'⸗,⸗⸗-\ *n* **:** bread raised by a portion of the sponge of sourdough held over from a previous baking
salt river \'⸗¦⸗⸗\ *n, usu cap S&R* [fr. *Salt river*, Ky., that in the early 19th cent. flowed through a region notorious for its backward backwoods quality] **:** a river symbolizing the route to oblivion for defeated political candidates or parties — usu. used in the phrase *row up Salt River*
salts *pl of* SALT, *pres 3d sing of* SALT
saltshaker \'⸗,⸗⸗\ *n* **1 :** a container with a perforated top for sprinkling salt on food **2 :** a pressure-operated microphone that can receive sounds equally well from all directions
salt–sick \'⸗,⸗\ *also* **salt sickness** *n, South* **:** cobalt deficiency disease of cattle **:** PINE
salt spoon *n* **:** a miniature spoon used with an open saltcellar for individual service
salt stain *n* **:** a mark on leather caused by bacterial action during the process of salting
salt tree *n* **1 :** a small tree (*Halimodendron argenteum*) of the family Leguminosae growing in the Caspian salt plains and Siberia **2 :** an East Indian tamarisk (*Tamarix orientalis*) with frequently salt-encrusted twigs
sal·tus \'saltəs, 'sȯl-\ *n* -ES [NL, fr. L, leap, jump — more at SALT (in heat)] **:** a break of continuity; *specif* **:** an omission of a necessary step of a proof in logic
salt water *n* [ME] **1 a :** water impregnated with salt; *esp* **:** the water of the ocean and of certain seas and lakes **b :** SEA **2 :** fused sodium sulfate that appears as a layer on top of the melt in glassmaking
saltwater \'⸗¦⸗\ *adj* [*salt water*] **1 :** of or belonging to salt water **:** living in or taken from salt water ⟨~ fish⟩ ⟨~ terrapin⟩ **2 :** consisting of salt as opposed to fresh water ⟨a ~ lake⟩ **3 :** taking place in or on salt water ⟨~ plunge⟩ **4 :** accustomed to navigating in salt waters ⟨~ sailor⟩ **5 :** of or relating to the sea ⟨~ songs⟩
saltwater crocodile *n* **:** a large man-eating crocodile (*Crocodylus porosus*) of East Asia and Indonesia that reputedly attains a length of 30 feet and that is a saltwater or brackish water species common about the outlets of rivers but also encountered far from land — called also *estuarine crocodile*
saltwater muskellunge *or* **saltwater pike** *n* **:** GREAT BARRACUDA
saltwater sheldrake *n* **:** RED-BREASTED MERGANSER
saltwater taffy *n* **:** a pulled candy made from white sugar and variously flavored and colored
saltwater trout *n* **:** either of two weakfishes: **a :** GRAY TROUT 1 **b :** SPOTTED WEAKFISH
saltweed \'⸗,⸗\ *n* **1 :** TOAD RUSH **2 :** SAMPHIRE 4 **3 :** an annual silvery weed (*Atriplex argentea*) found in various alkaline and dry regions of No. America
salt well *n* **:** a bored or driven well from which brine is obtained
saltworks \'⸗,⸗\ *n pl but sing or pl in constr* **:** a plant where salt is made on a commercial scale (as by extraction from seawater or the brine of salt springs)
saltwort \'⸗,⸗\ *n* **1 :** a plant of the genus *Salsola* (as *S. kali, S. soda*) used in the manufacture of soda ash — see BARILLA **2 :** GLASSWORT 1 **3 :** a low-growing strong-smelling coastal shrub (*Batis maritima*) of warm parts of the New World
saltwort family *n* **:** BATIDACEAE
salty \'sȯltē, -ti, *chiefly Brit* 'säl-\ *adj* -ER/-EST [ME, fr. *salt* + *-y*] **1 :** of, seasoned with, or containing salt **:** SALINE ⟨~ tears⟩ ⟨~ butter⟩ ⟨small, ~ bays —*Amer. Guide Series: Md.*⟩ **2 :** smacking of the sea or nautical life ⟨a ~ flavor lent by salvaged anchors . . . and other old marine gear —*Amer. Guide Series: Del.*⟩ **3 a :** engagingly provocative **:** PIQUANT ⟨the *saltiest* . . . autobiography of our time —E.A.Weeks⟩ **b :** EARTHY, RACY ⟨~ . . . talk among men in a livery stable —H.S.Canby⟩ **c :** CAUSTIC ⟨penetrating and ~ in his criticism —August Heckscher⟩ **d :** EXPERIENCED, SOPHISTICATED ⟨trying out his . . . lingo to show us how ~ he was —L.M.Uris⟩ **4** *of a horse* **:** hard to manage **:** INTRACTABLE ⟨able to keep a hot seat on a ~ bronc —F.B.Gipson⟩
sa·lu·bri·ous \sə'lübrēəs\ *adj* [L *salubris* salubrious + E *-ous* — more at SAFE] **1 :** favorable to or promoting health or well-being **:** INVIGORATING ⟨~ food⟩ ⟨a ~ climate⟩ ⟨the ~ mountain air and water —C.B.Davis⟩ **2 a :** spiritually wholesome **:** SALUTARY ⟨brought a ~ excitement . . . to American literary life —Charles Angoff⟩ **b :** conducive to good results **:** BENEFICIAL ⟨has received much publicity as a more ~ environment for the operation of textiles —*Textile Industries*⟩ **syn** see HEALTHFUL
sa·lu·bri·ous·ly *adv* **:** in a salubrious manner **:** with salubrious effects
sa·lu·bri·ous·ness *n* -ES **:** the quality or condition of being salubrious
sa·lu·bri·ty \-brəd·ē\ *n* -ES [ME *salubrite*, fr. L *salubritas*, fr. *salubris* + *-itas* -ity] **:** the quality or state of being salubrious **:** HEALTHFULNESS, WHOLESOMENESS ⟨expatiating on the ~ of the cold bath —Robert Lynd⟩ ⟨the ~ of their walk is sadly tinctured by carbon monoxide —Lewis Mumford⟩
salue *vt* -ED/-ING/-S *obs* [ME *saluen*, fr. OF *saluer*, fr. L *salutare* — more at SALUTE] **:** GREET, SALUTE
sa·lu·ki \sə'lükē\ *n* [Ar *salūqīy* of Saluq, ancient city in southern Arabia, fr. *Salūq* Saluq] **1** *usu cap* **:** an old No. African and Asiatic breed of tall slender swift-footed keen-eyed hunting dogs having long narrow skulls, long silky ears, straight forelegs, strong widely set hind legs, a long well-feathered tail, and a smooth silky coat ranging from white or cream to black and tan **2** *or* **sloughi** *or* **slughi** \'slügē\ -S *often cap* **:** a dog of the Saluki breed
sa·lung \sə'ləŋ\ *n, pl* **salung** *or* **salungs** [Siamese *saliṅ*] **1 :** an old Siamese silver coin equal to ¼ tical **2 :** the unit of value represented by a silver salung
sal·u·tar·i·ly \¦salyə¦terəlē, -li\ *adv* **:** in a salutary manner
sal·u·tar·i·ness \'⸗⸗,terēnəs, -rin-, ,⸗⸗'⸗⸗\ *n* -ES **:** the quality or state of being salutary
sal·u·tary \'salyə,terē, -ri\ *adj* [modif. (influenced by E *-ary*) of MF *salutaire*, fr. L *salutaris*, fr. *salut-, salus* health, safety + *-aris* -ar] **1 :** promoting health **:** CURATIVE, RESTORATIVE ⟨~ exercise⟩ ⟨~ medicine⟩ ⟨the ~ mineral or herb —Walter Pater⟩ **2 :** producing a wholesome, corrective, or ultimately beneficial effect **:** REMEDIAL ⟨~ influence⟩ ⟨a ~ rebuke⟩ ⟨~ suffering⟩ ⟨the ~ discovery that even encyclopedias may disagree —Frances Eldredge⟩ ⟨~ shock to middle-class complacency —Roy Lewis & Angus Maude⟩ **syn** see HEALTHFUL
sal·u·ta·tion \,salyə'tāshən\ *n* -S [ME *salutacioun*, fr. L *salutation-, salutatio*, fr. *salutatus* (past part. of *salutare* to salute) + *-ion-, -io* -ion — more at SALUTE] **1 a :** an act or action of saluting (as by expressing goodwill or courtesy) ⟨the polite ~*s* of the lounging natives —Mary Austin⟩ **b :** a gesture or ceremony (as a bow, kiss, or handshake) of greeting ⟨all classes . . . observe the old forms of ~: men embrace —*Amer. Guide Series: Texas*⟩ **c :** a speech of honor or praise **:** TRIBUTE ⟨the speaker's ~ to the modern dance⟩ **d :** SALUTE 4 ⟨~ to the flag⟩ **e :** the word or phrase (as *Dear Sir* or *Mr. Chairman, Ladies and Gentlemen*) that conventionally comes immediately before the body of a letter or at the opening of a speech and that expresses the writer's or speaker's greeting to the person addressed **2** *archaic* **:** a naval salute (as by the firing of guns or lowering of flags) — **sal·u·ta·tion·al** \¦⸗⸗¦tāshən³l, -shnəl\ *adj*
sa·lu·ta·to·ri·an \sə,lüd·ə'tōrēən, -üta-, -'tȯr-\ *n* -S [²*salutatory* + *-an*] **:** the graduating student who is usu. second highest in rank and who in some institutions pronounces the salutatory oration — compare VALEDICTORIAN
sa·lu·ta·to·ri·ly \⸗¦⸗⸗¦rəlē, -li\ *adv* **:** in a salutatory manner
¹**sa·lu·ta·to·ry** \⸗¦⸗⸗,rē, -ri\ *adj* [ML *salutatorius*, fr. L *salutatus* (past part. of *salutare* to salute) + *-orius* -ory] **:** containing or expressing salutations **:** speaking a welcome — used esp. of the oration that often introduces commencement exercises
²**salutatory** \"\ *n* -ES **:** a salutatory oration delivered at the commencement exercises of an educational institution
¹**sa·lute** \sə'lüt, *usu* -üd.+V\ *vb* -ED/-ING/-S [ME *saluten*, fr. L *salutare*, fr. L *salut-, salus* health, safety, greeting — more at SAFE] *vt* **1 a :** to address with expressions of kind wishes, courtesy, or honor ⟨*saluted* him cheerfully by his name —Charles Dickens⟩ **b** *archaic* **:** to hail with the title or epithet of ⟨*saluted* the fathers of their country —John Milton⟩ **c :** to appear, come forth, or burst into song as if to welcome ⟨the lark ~*s* the dawn⟩ ⟨the peeping crocus ~*s* the spring⟩ **d :** to become apparent to (one of the senses) **:** impress itself upon ⟨a moist pungent odor of perfumes *saluted* his nose —James Joyce⟩ **2 a :** to give a sign of respect, courtesy, or goodwill to ⟨*saluted* the old man in the doorway —Kay Boyle⟩ **b :** to compliment by a customary or conventional act of ceremony ⟨*saluted* her in the style of the French dancing master —Meridel Le Sueur⟩ **c :** to make the sign of formal greeting to (an opponent) in fencing **d :** to bow to (one's partner) in square dancing **:** HONOR 4, ADDRESS 10c **3 a :** to honor (as a person, nation, or event) by a conventional military or naval act or ceremony **b :** to show respect and recognition to (a military superior) by assuming a position prescribed by drill regulations **c :** to express high approval or commendation of **:** PRAISE ⟨~ a tradition of leadership —A.E.Stevenson b.1900⟩ ~ *vi* **:** to make a salute
²**salute** \"\ *n* -S [ME *salut*, fr. MF, fr. L *salut-, salus* health, safety, greeting] **1 :** a speech or gesture expressing welcome, recognition, or courtesy **:** GREETING, SALUTATION ⟨did not return my ~ —L.C.Douglas⟩ ⟨his morning ~ for the tenement mothers —Seamus Brady⟩ **2 :** an old French or Anglo-Gallic gold coin bearing the figure of the Virgin receiving the angel's salutation **3 a :** a sign, token, or ceremony (as a kiss or a bow) expressing goodwill, compliment, or respect ⟨took his ~ on the cheek⟩ ⟨clasped his hands over his head in a prize-fighter's ~ —*Time*⟩ ⟨participate in ~ to selling week —*Printers' Ink*⟩ **b :** the formal greeting of fencers about to engage **4 a :** a military or naval token of respect or honor (as presenting arms, discharging cannon, or dipping the colors) for a distinguished or official person, for a foreign vessel or flag, or for some festival or event **b :** a mark of respect and recognition given (as with the hand, rifle, or sword) by military personnel in a manner prescribed by regulations and varying according to circumstances **c :** the position (as of the hand, rifle, or sword) or the entire attitude of a person saluting a superior ⟨stand at ~⟩ **5 :** FIRECRACKER 1 ⟨a string of one-inch ~*s* —*Time*⟩

salute 4c

salute state *n* **:** a state whose ruler is entitled by treaty with a dominant foreign power to a salute of a specified number of guns
salute to the union : a salute of one gun for each state in the U.S. fired only on Independence Day at noon
sal·u·tif·er·ous \¦salyə¦tif(ə)rəs\ *adj* [L *salutifer* salutary (fr. *salut-, salus* + *-ifer* -iferous) + E *-ous*] **:** SALUTARY ⟨fell into a ~ sleep —Hugh McCrae⟩
salv *abbr* **1** salvage **2** *often cap* [LL *salvator*] savior
sal·va·ble \'salvəbəl\ *adj* [LL *salvare* to save + E *-able* — more at SAVE] **1 :** capable of being saved **:** admissible to salvation **2 :** SALVAGEABLE
¹**sal·va·dor** \'salvə,dȯ(ə)r, ,⸗⸗'⸗\ *adj, usu cap* [fr. El *Salvador*, republic in Central America] **:** EL SALVADOR
²**salvador** \"\ *adj, usu cap* [fr. *Salvador*, Brazil] **:** of or from the city of Salvador, Brazil **:** of the kind or style prevalent in Salvador
sal·va·do·ra \,salvə'dōrə, -dȯrə\ *n, cap* [NL, after Juan *Salvador* †1681 Span. botanist] **:** a genus (the type of the family Salvadoraceae) of trees and shrubs of Africa and southern Asia having opposite leaves and small panicled flowers with a bell-shaped corolla — see TOOTHBRUSH TREE
sal·va·do·ra·ce·ae \,salvə,də'rāsē,ē\ *n pl, cap* [NL, fr. *Salvadora*, type genus + *-aceae*] **:** a family (order Primulales) of shrubs and trees related to the Oleaceae but having four stamens and four petals
sal·va·do·ra·ceous \¦⸗⸗⸗¦rāshəs\ *adj* [NL *Salvadoraceae* + E *-ous*] **:** of, relating to, or resembling the Salvadoraceae
¹**sal·va·do·ran** \,salvə'dōrən, -dȯr-\ *also* **sal·va·dor·ian** \-rēən\ *adj, usu cap* [El *Salvador*, Central America + E *-an* or *-ian*] **1 :** of, relating to, or characteristic of the Central American republic of El Salvador **2 :** of, relating to, or characteristic of Salvadorans
²**salvadoran** \"\ *also* **salvadorian** \"\ *n* -S *cap* **:** a native or inhabitant of El Salvador
¹**sal·vage** \'salvij, -vēj\ *archaic var of* SAVAGE
²**salvage** \"\ *n* -S *often attrib* [F, fr. MF, fr. *salver, sauver* to save + *-age* — more at SAVE] **1 a :** the compensation paid for saving a ship or its cargo from the perils of the sea or for the lives and property rescued in a wreck; *specif* **:** the compensation allowed to those who under no duty voluntarily save a ship or lives of those belonging to it from peril ⟨awarded the shipping company a large ~ payment⟩ **b :** the act of saving or rescuing a ship or its cargo; *specif* **:** the act of one or more persons who under no duty voluntarily save a ship or its cargo or wreck or in some cases the lives of persons belonging to it from a marine peril or retake and restore it or its cargo when captured in war — compare MILITARY SALVAGE **c :** the act of saving or rescuing property in danger (as from fire) ⟨had little time for the ~ of his effects⟩ **2 a :** property saved from destruction in a wreck; *specif* **:** the part of the property that survives a marine peril and is saved ⟨~ from the stricken vessel lay on the dock⟩ **b :** something extracted (as from wreckage, ruins, or rubbish) as valuable or having further usefulness ⟨the sale of ~ to the poor⟩; *specif* **:** warehouse grain damaged by fire, smoke, or water **c** (1) **:** insured goods rescued from destruction or loss (2) **:** the value of such goods (3) **:** the proceeds from the sale of such goods **3 :** something (as an organ, tissue, or patient) saved by preventive or therapeutic measures in medicine ⟨fetal ~⟩ ⟨lung ~⟩ ⟨the ~ rate in tuberculosis⟩
³**salvage** \"\, *esp in pres part* -vəj\ *vt* -ED/-ING/-S **1 :** to rescue or save esp. from wreckage or ruin ⟨*salvaged* torpedoed vessels —Rachel L. Carson⟩ ⟨materials *salvaged* from crashed airplanes —*Amer. Fabrics*⟩ ⟨expect this teacher . . . to ~ the present or potential hoodlums —A.H.Grommon⟩ ⟨*salvaging* a marriage threatened chiefly by alcohol —J.J.Espey⟩ **2 :** to save (an organ, tissue, or patient) by preventive or therapeutic measures ⟨a *salvaging* operation⟩ ⟨a *salvaged* cancer patient⟩
sal·vage·abil·i·ty \,⸗⸗ə'biləd·ē\ *n* **:** the quality or state of being salvageable
sal·vage·able \'⸗⸗əbəl\ *adj* **:** capable of being salvaged ⟨~ cargo⟩ ⟨a ~ criminal⟩
salvage boat *n* **:** a boat engaged in salvage activities
salvage corps *n* **:** a body of men maintained by fire-insurance companies to protect goods, merchandise, and effects from destruction by fire or from water or chemicals used in fighting fire — called also *fire patrol*
salvage cover *n* **:** a waterproof sheet for protecting goods from damage by water, smoke, or weather during or after a fire
salvage cutting *n* **:** a cutting made to remove injured or killed trees for the primary purpose of recovering usable material before it becomes worthless — compare SANITATION CUTTING
salvage loss *n* **:** the difference between the amount of the proceeds of what is saved after salvage charges have been deducted and the total value of the property loss
salvage man *n* [¹*salvage*] *archaic* **:** one clad in foliage to represent a savage (as in medieval and Renaissance pageantry and mumming)
sal·vag·er \-vijə(r), -vēj-\ *n* -S **:** one that salvages **:** SALVOR
salvage value *n* **:** an amount estimated as expected to be realized or actually realized on sale of a fixed asset at the end of its useful life — used in calculating depreciation
Sal·var·san \'salvə(r),san, -,saa(ə)n\ *trademark* — used for arsphenamine
sal·va·tel·la \,salvə'telə\ *n, pl* **salvatel·lae** \-e(,)lē, -e,lī\ [ME, fr. ML, fr. LL *salvatus* (past part. of *salvare* to save) + L *-ella*, dim. suffix] *archaic* **:** a vein on the back of the little finger and hand formerly considered esp. effective for bloodletting
sal·va·tion \sal'vāshən\ *n* -S [ME *salvacioun, sauvacioun*, fr. OF *salvation, sauvation*, fr. LL *salvation-, salvatio*, fr. *salvatus* (past part. of *salvare* to save) + L *-ion-, -io* -ion — more at SAVE] **1 :** the saving of man from the power and effects of sin: as **a :** his deliverance from the condition of spiritual isolation and estrangement to a reconciled relationship of community with God and fellowmen **:** redemption from spiritual lostness to religious fulfillment and restoration to the fullness of God's favor **b :** redemption from ultimate damnation through divine agency **c :** the deliverance of the soul from sin or the spiritual consequences of sin **:** the saving of a person's soul from eternal punishment and its admission into heavenly beatitude **2 :** liberation from ignorance or illusion **:** deliverance from clinging to the phenomenal world of appearance and final union with ultimate reality ⟨~ in Hinduism implies deliverance from samsara⟩ **3** *Christian Science* **:** the realization of the supremacy of infinite Mind over all bringing with it the destruction of the illusion of sin, sickness, and death **4 :** preservation esp. from destruction, disintegration, or failure **:** final deliverance esp. from dangers, difficulties, or deficiencies ⟨~ from alcoholism —H.C.Webster⟩ ⟨pursuit of individual ~ through hard work —W.H.Whyte⟩ ⟨seeks in religion ~ from the evils and dangers of the times —H.J.Morgenthau⟩ **5 :** the agent, the means, or the course of spiritual experiences determining the soul's redemption ⟨Christ is our ~⟩ ⟨preach ~⟩ **6 :** something that saves or delivers from danger or difficulty **:** the source, cause, or means of preservation ⟨tourism is their only economic ~ —T.H.Fielding⟩ ⟨arboreal habitat was the evolutionary ~ of the primates —Weston La Barre⟩
sal·va·tion·al \-shən³l, -shnəl\ *adj* **:** of, relating to, or conducive to salvation ⟨a ~ religion⟩ ⟨the individual psyche in different stages of its ~ career —Joseph Katz⟩ ⟨elect him back to the ~ office he had resigned —Janet Flanner⟩
sal·va·tion·ism \-shə,nizəm\ *n* -S **1 :** religious teaching in which the saving of the soul is particularly emphasized **2 :** the doctrine of the salvation of the soul esp. as taught by those stressing the need of open conversion **3 a** *usu cap* **:** the doctrine and practices of the Salvation Army organized in the 19th century on military lines as an international evangelistic and philanthropic movement **b :** the zeal of a Salvationist
sal·va·tion·ist \-sh(ə)nəst\ *n* -S *often attrib* **1** *usu cap* **:** a soldier or officer of the Salvation Army ⟨national commander of the *Salvationists*⟩ ⟨posted to *Salvationist* stations⟩ **2 :** an advocate of salvationism ⟨a militant ~⟩ **3 :** EVANGELIST ⟨street-corner ~*s*⟩
¹**salvatory** *n* -ES [ML *salvatorium*, any receptacle for keeping property safe, fr. LL *salvare* to save, keep safe + L *-orium* -ory — more at SAVE] *obs* **:** a box or receptacle for ointment
²**sal·va·to·ry** \'salvə,tōrē\ *adj* [*salvation* + *-ory*] **:** conducive to salvation, saving, or safety ⟨the book . . . was vastly less significant or ~ than the sanctified wafer —H.B.Alexander⟩
sal·va ver·i·ta·te \'säl,wä,werə'täd·ē\ *adv* [L, the truth being safe] **:** in accordance with a principle attributed to Leibniz by which two expressions are said to be synonymous if the substitution of one for the other does not change the truth value or meaning of any context in which either expression appears
¹**salve** \'sav, 'saa(ə)v, 'säv, 'sȧv, *Brit sometimes* 'salv\ *n* -S [ME *salf, salve*, fr. OE *sealf*; akin to OS *salba* salve, MLG & MD *salve*, OHG *salba* salve, Gk *elpos* oil, fat, *elphos* butter, *olpē* oil flask, Skt *sarpis* melted butter, ghee, Alb *gjalpë* butter] **1 :** an unctuous adhesive composition or substance to be applied to wounds or sores **:** a healing ointment **2 :** something likened to a salve: as **a :** something (as an influence, agency, or statement) remedial, comforting, or soothing ⟨a ~ for sin⟩ ⟨a ~ to wounded feelings⟩ **b :** something (as praise or flattery) applied or laid on like a salve **3 :** any ointment or cerate prepared with a base (as of a fat, oil, wool fat, petrolatum, wax, or resin) ⟨a blistering or antiseptic ~⟩
²**salve** \"\ *vt* -ED/-ING/-S [ME *salven*, fr. OE *sealfian*; akin to OS *salbon* to salve, anoint, MLG & MD *salven*, OHG *salbōn*, Goth *salbōn*; denominative fr. the root of E ¹*salve*] **1** *archaic* **:** to apply salve to (as a wound) **:** ANOINT **2 :** to heal, cure, or soothe (as a disease, sin, grief) with or as if with a salve **:** to provide a remedy or consolation for ⟨the character of the work did not ~ the Prologue's sting —H.O.Taylor⟩ **3** *obs* **:** to cover up (as something festering, ugly, or disgraceful) **:** gloss over **4 :** QUIET, ALLAY, ASSUAGE ⟨did not exacerbate her emotional unfulfillment . . . but *salved* it by writing historical novels —*Times Lit. Supp.*⟩ ⟨give him a raise in salary to ~ his feelings —Upton Sinclair⟩
³**salve** \'sa(l)v, -aa(ə)-,-ai-,-ȧ-\ *vt* -ED/-ING/-S [ML *salvare*, fr. LL, to save — more at SAVE] **1** *obs* **:** to provide a hypothesis or offer a solution or explanation of **:** SOLVE, RESOLVE ⟨what may we do then to ~ this seeming inconsistence —John Milton⟩ **2** *obs* **:** to make (as a doctrine) capable of a rational or reasonable explanation **:** justify with arguments **:** SUPPORT ⟨lest my liking might too sudden seem, I would have *salved* it with a longer treatise —Shak.⟩ **3** *obs* **:** to save or maintain intact (as one's honor or an oath) **:** preserve the credit or integrity of **:** SAFEGUARD ⟨to ~ his credit . . . still will be tempting him who foils him still —John Milton⟩
⁴**salve** *n* -S [F — more at SALVO] *obs* **:** SALVO
⁵**salve** \'salv\ *vt* -ED/-ING/-S [back-formation fr. ²*salvage*] **:** to save (as a ship or its cargo) from destruction or loss **:** SALVAGE ⟨a lifeboat was sent to the wreck . . . and it spent the morning *salving* bedding, crockery, and a small amount of clothing —J.H.Marsh⟩ ⟨the campaign for *salving* and processing kitchen scraps —V.C.Fishwick⟩
salve bug \salve *like* ¹SALVE\ *n* [¹*salve*, so called fr. its traditional use by fishermen in preparing a salve] **:** a large stout isopod crustacean (*Aega psora*) parasitic on the halibut and codfish
sal·ve·line \'salvə,līn, -lēn\ *adj* [NL *Salvelinus*] **:** of or relating to the genus *Salvelinus*
sal·ve·li·nus \,salvə'līnəs, -lēn-\ *n, cap* [NL, fr. G dial. *sälbling*, a char (*Salvelinus alpinus*), alter. of *sälmling* — more at SAIBLING] **:** a genus of fishes (family Salmonidae) distinguished

chiefly by their small scales and boat-shaped vomer with teeth only at the end and including a common European fish (*S. alpinus*) and the American brook trout and Dolly Varden

salve mull *n* **:** ²MULL 2

sal·ver \'salvə(r)\ *n* -s [modif. (influenced by *-er*) of F *salve*, fr. Sp *salva* sampling of food to detect poison, small tray, fr. *salvar* to save, sample food to detect poison, fr. LL *salvare* to save — more at SAVE] **:** a tray of any of a wide range of sizes for a variety of purposes but used esp. for serving food or beverages **:** SERVER, WAITER ⟨pad over the turf to them with a ~ of iced tea —G.A.Wagner⟩ ⟨brought the second post on a silver ~ —Virginia Woolf⟩ ⟨milk and dates were served . . . in great brass ~*s* with decorated conical covers —*N.Y.Times*⟩

sal·ver·form \'salvə(r),fȯrm\ *or* **salver–shaped** \'==,=\ *adj* **:** tubular with a spreading limb — used of a gamopetalous corolla

sal·via \'salvēə\ *n* [NL, fr. L, sage — more at SAGE] **1** *cap* **:** a large and widely distributed genus (family Labiatae) of herbs or shrubs varying greatly in habit and in the size and color of the flowers but having a 2-lipped open calyx and two anthers of which one is erect and perfect and the other spreading and sterile — see ²CLARY, SAGE 1a **2** -s **:** any plant of the genus *Salvia*

salvia blue *n* **:** a strong blue that is redder and less strong than Sèvres and redder and paler than cerulean blue

sal·via·nin \-vēənən, -,nin\ *n* -s [NL *Salvia* + anthocyanin] **:** an anthocyanin extracted from salvia and Oswego tea in the form of its chloride $C_{36}H_{38}ClO_{17}$ that yields pelargonidin chloride as one product of hydrolysis

sal·vif·ic \(')sal'vifik\ *or* **sal·vif·i·cal** \-fəkəl\ *adj, sometimes cap* [*salvific* fr. LL *salvificus*, fr. *salvus* saved (fr. L healthy, safe) + L *-ificus* -ific; *salvifical* fr. LL *salvificus* + E *-al*] **:** having the intent to save or admit to salvation ⟨trusted in the *Salvific* Will —W.H.Gardner⟩ ⟨the ~ life and death of Christ —E.A.Walsh⟩ — **sal·vif·i·cal·ly** \-fək(ə)lē\ *adv*

sal·vin·ia \sal'vinēə\ *n, cap* [NL, fr. Antonio M. *Salvini* †1729 Ital. linguist + NL *-ia*] **:** a small genus (the type of the family Salviniaceae) of widely distributed water ferns having distichous leaves borne mostly on simple stems — see FLOATING MOSS

sal·vin·i·a·ce·ae \(,)sal,vinē'āsē,ē\ *n pl, cap* [NL, fr. *Salvinia*, type genus + *-aceae*] **:** a small family that comprises water ferns with branching stems bearing small leaves and one-celled sporocarps containing either megasporangia or microsporangia and that in some classifications constitutes with the Marsileaceae a distinct order but is usu. included in Filicales

¹**sal·vo** \'sal(,)vō\ *n, pl* **salvos** *or* **salvoes** [modif. of It *salva*, fr. F *salve*, fr. MF, fr. L, imper. (used as a greeting) of *salvēre* to be in good health, fr. *salvus* healthy, safe — more at SAFE] **1 :** a simultaneous discharge of fire weapons: as **a :** a firing of several pieces of artillery all together either in action for increased effect or with blank charges as a salute **b** (1) **:** a simultaneous discharge of two or more guns of the same naval battery at one target (2) **:** a series of shots by an artillery battery with each gun firing one round in turn after a prescribed interval (3) **:** the projectiles so discharged in their flight **c** (1) **:** the release all at one time of a rack of bombs or rockets (as from an airplane) (2) **:** the bombs or rockets so released (3) **:** several bombs or rockets released simultaneously from each of several airplanes — compare STICK 17a, VOLLEY 1a **2 :** SALUTE, TRIBUTE ⟨received ~*s* of praise from three of the four leading . . . critics —Janet Flanner⟩ **3 :** a sudden eruption or explosion (as of laughter, cheers, or handclaps) **:** BURST 2b ⟨laughed heartily, in great ~*s* —S.E.White⟩ ⟨a stirring ~ of applause —*Time*⟩ **4 :** a game for two players in which each has a cross-ruled diagram on which he blacks in groups of squares to represent ships with the object of trying to locate and hit an enemy fleet by calling out numbered squares at random — called also *battleships*

²**salvo** \"\ *vb* -ED/-ING/-S *vt* **:** to release a salvo of ⟨electronic gear . . . automatically ~*s* rockets —*advt*⟩ ~ *vi* **:** to fire a salvo ⟨the rest of the fleet ~*ed* steadily into the jungle —*Sat. Eve. Post*⟩

³**salvo** \"\ *n* -s [L, abl. of *salvus* healthy, safe, intact (as in *salvo jure* with the right intact, saving the right) — more at SAFE] **1 :** a mental reservation **:** PROVISO ⟨a ~ for the rights of their order —David Hume †1776⟩ **2** *archaic* **:** a way out of a difficulty **:** EXPLANATION ⟨we have a ~ for that —Samuel Foote⟩ **3 :** a means of safeguarding (as one's name or honor) or of quieting or allaying (as the conscience) **:** SALVE 2

sal vo·la·ti·le \,salvə'ladᵊl,(,)ē\ *n* [NL, lit., volatile salt] **1 :** AMMONIUM CARBONATE c **2 :** an aromatic solution of ammonium carbonate in alcohol or ammonia water or both — compare AROMATIC SPIRIT OF AMMONIA, SMELLING SALTS

sal·vor \'salvər, -,vȯ(ə)r\ *n* -s [*salvage* + *-or*] **:** one that engages in salvage **:** SALVAGER ⟨the ~ in offshore work has no time for hesitation . . . as to the salvage method necessary —*Marine Engineering & Shipping Rev.*⟩

salvy *pronunc at* ¹SALVE + ē *or* i\ *adj* -ER/-EST [¹*salve* + *-y*] **:** resembling salve in texture or oiliness ⟨~ butter⟩

Sal·yr·gan \'salə(r),gan\ *trademark* — used for mersalyl

salz·burg \'sȯl\|z,bərg, 'säl\|, 'sal\|, 'säl\|, \|ts,b-, -bürg, -bōg, -bəig,-büəg, *G* 'zälts,bürk *or* -rk\ *adj, usu cap* [fr. *Salzburg*, Austria] **:** of or from the city of Salzburg, Austria **:** of the kind or style prevalent in Salzburg

salz·git·ter \'zälts,gid·ə(r)\ *adj, usu cap* [fr. *Salzgitter*, Germany] **:** of or from the city of Salzgitter, Germany **:** of the kind or style prevalent in Salzgitter

¹**sam** \'sam\ *dial Brit var of* SAME

²**sam** \"\ *n* -s *usu cap* [fr. *Uncle Sam*, imaginary character supposed to represent the U.S. government] **:** KNOW-NOTHING 2

³**sam** \"\ *or* **samm** *vb* **sammed; sammed; samming; sams** *or* **samms** [perh. fr. E dial. *sam* half-cooked, moist, short for *sam-sodden*] **:** SAMMY

⁴**sam** \"\ *n* -s *often cap* [prob. by shortening and alter. fr. earlier *salmon*, fr. the name *Salomon, Solomon* used in oaths] *slang Brit* **:** OATH ⟨swop my solemn ~ —John Masefield⟩

sam- \(')sam\ *prefix* [ME, fr. OE; akin to OHG *sāmi-* half — more at SEMI-] *dial Eng* **:** half ⟨*sam*-ripe⟩ ⟨*sam*-sodden⟩

sa·ma \'sämə\ *n* -s [AmerSp] **:** MUTTONFISH 1

sa·mad·era \sə'madərə; ,samə'dirə, -'derə\ *n, cap* [NL, fr. Sinhalese *samadarā*, a tree of Ceylon] **:** a genus of East Indian and African trees (family Simaroubaceae) having flowers with a 3- to 5-parted perianth and 6 to 10 included stamens and a fruit that is a dry drupe — see NIEPA

sa·madh \sə'mäd\ *n* -s [Hindi *samādh*, lit., contemplation, self-immolation, fr. Skt *samādhi* — more at SAMADHI] **:** a tomb built in India over the grave of a holy mendicant

sa·ma·dhi \sə'mädē\ *n* -s [Skt *samādhi*, lit., application, contemplation, fr. *sam* together + *ā* to, towards + *-dhi* (akin to *dadhāti* he puts, places) — more at SAME, ACHARYA, DO] **1** *Hinduism* **a :** a state of deep concentration resulting in union with or absorption into ultimate reality — compare RAJA-YOGA **b :** a religious trance **2** *Buddhism* **:** the meditative concentration that is the final step of the Eightfold Path **3** *Jainism* **:** spiritual self-fulfillment **:** ENLIGHTENMENT

sa·maj \sə'mäj\ *n* -ES *usu cap* [Hindi *samāj* meeting, assembly, fr. Skt *samāja*, fr. *sam* together + *ajati* he drives — more at SAME, AGENT] **:** a Hindu religious association **:** SOCIETY

sa·mal \sə'mäl\ *n, pl* **samal** *or* **samals** *usu cap* [Bisayan] **1 a :** a Moro people inhabiting southwestern Mindanao and the Sulu archipelago **b :** a member of such people **2 :** the Austronesian language of the Samal people

sa·man \sə'män\ *n* -s [Sp *samán*, fr. Carib *zamang*] **:** RAIN TREE

sa·man·du·ra \sə'mandərə, ,samən'dùrə\ [NL, fr. Sinhalese *samadarā, samandarā*, a plant of Ceylon] *syn of* SAMADERA

sa·man·go monkey \sə'maŋ(,)gō-\ *n* [of Bantu origin] **:** a dark-colored forest-dwelling monkey (*Cercopithecus labiatus*) common in parts of southern Africa that resembles but is larger than the vervet

sa·ma·nid \sə'mänəd, 'samən-\ *n, pl* **samanids** \-dz\ *or* **sama·ni** \-nē\ *usu cap* [*Saman*, eponymous ancestor of the first ruler of the dynasty + E *-id*] **:** a member of a 9th and 10th century Persian dynasty ruling from Bokhara and encouraging literature and art

sa·mar \sə'mär, 'sä,mär\ *n, pl* **samar** [Bengali *chumar, chamar*] **:** a caste of tanners among the Hindus of Bengal

sam·a·ra \'samərə, sə'ma(a)rə\ *n* -s [NL, fr. L *samara, samera* seed of the elm] **:** a dry indehiscent usu. one-seeded winged fruit (as of an ash or elm tree) — called also *key, key fruit*; see FRUIT illustration

samarang *usu cap, var of* SEMARANG

sam·a·ri·form \'samərə,fȯrm, sə'ma(a)r-\ *adj* [NL *samara* + E *-iform*] **:** having the form of a samara

¹**sa·mar·i·tan** \sə'marətᵊn, -mer-, -rətən,-rəd·ən\ *n* -s [ME, fr. LL *samaritanus*, fr. *samaritanus* of the inhabitants of Samaria, fr. Gk *samaritēs* inhabitant of Samaria (fr. *Samaria*, district of ancient Palestine + Gk *-itēs* -ite) + L *-anus* -an] **1** *cap* **a :** a native or inhabitant of Samaria in ancient Palestine — compare ISRAELITE 1a **b :** the dialect of Hebrew used by the Samaritans **2** *usu cap* **:** a member of a dwindling sect in Nablus similar in doctrine to the Jews except for their centralization of worship at Mount Gerizim and the limitation of their Scriptures to the Pentateuch **3** *often cap* [so called fr. the parable of the good Samaritan, Lk 10: 30–37] **:** a compassionate person **:** one who is ready to help the distressed

²**samaritan** \"\ *adj* [LL *samaritanus* of the inhabitants of Samaria] **1** *usu cap* **:** of or relating to Samaria or the Samaritans **2 :** COMPASSIONATE

sa·mar·i·tan·ism \-ᵊn,izəm, -ə,ni-\ *n* -s [¹*samaritan* + *-ism*] **1** *usu cap* **a :** the religious doctrine of the Samaritans **b :** an expression characteristic of the Samaritan dialect **2** *often cap* **:** a compassionate character or deed

sa·mar·i·um \sə'ma(a)rēəm\ *n* -s [NL, fr. F *samarskite* + NL *-ium* — more at SAMARSKITE] **:** a pale gray lustrous metallic element of the rare-earth group that occurs associated esp. with cerium, yttrium, and neodymium in rare-earth minerals and that is bivalent and trivalent in red-brown and pale yellow compounds respectively — symbol *Sm*; see ELEMENT table

¹**samar·kand** \'samər,kand *also* 'sämər,känd *or* 'sä,mär,känd *sometimes* =(,)=¦=\ *n* -s *usu cap* [fr. *Samarkand*, city or region of Uzbek S.S.R.] **:** a medium-sized oriental rug from Chinese Turkestan usu. tied in Sehna knots and made with a field typically blue, red, or golden brown, often with a fretwork effect and five medallions in the corners and the center, and with Chinese motifs (as dragons or stiff floral forms)

²**samarkand** \"\ *adj, usu cap* [fr. *Samarkand*, city of central Uzbek S.S.R.] **:** of or from the city of Samarkand, U.S.S.R. **:** of the kind or style prevalent in Samarkand

samar–leyte \,sä,mär'lād·ē\ *n, pl* **samar–leyte** *or* **samar–leytes** *usu cap S&L* [fr. *Samar*, island of the Visaya group, central Philippines + *Leyte*, island of the Visaya group] **1 a :** a Bisayan people inhabiting Samar and eastern Leyte, Philippines **b :** a member of such people **2 :** an Austronesian language of the Samar-Leyte people that is often considered a dialect of Bisayan

sa·ma·rra \sə'märə, -marə\ *n* -s [ML, garment worn by those condemned by the Inquisition, fr. OSp *zamarra* sheepskin coat worn by shepherds, prob. of Iberian origin; akin to Basque *zamar* sheepskin] **:** SANBENITO 2

sa·mar·ran \-rən\ *adj, usu cap* [*Samarra*, town of north central Iraq + E *-an*] **:** of or belonging to an aeneolithic culture of Mesopotamia following the Hassunan and characterized by black-on-buff pottery

samar·skite \sə'mär,skīt, 'samər-\ *n* -s [F, fr. Col. von *Samarski* 19th cent. Russ. mine official + F *-ite*] **:** a velvet-black commonly metamict orthorhombic mineral with splendent vitreous or resinous luster consisting of an oxide of rare earths, uranium, iron, lead, thorium, columbium, tantalum, titanium, and tin — compare HJELMITE

samas *pl of* SAMA

¹**sam·ba** \'sambə, 'säm-,'saam-,'säm-\ *n* -s [Pg, of African origin] **1 a :** a Brazilian dance of African origin characterized by a sprightly step pattern in duple time and by a bouncy dip and spring upward of the torso with a bending of the knee at each beat of the music **b :** music in ²⁄₄ time for dancing the samba **2 a :** a variation of canasta using three decks and six jokers and including in the possible melds a seven-card natural sequence worth 1500 points, game being 10,000 points **b :** a seven-card natural sequence meld in samba **3** [native name in Nigeria] **:** OBECHE

²**samba** \"\ *vi* -ED/-ING/-S **:** to dance the samba ⟨trying to conga, rumba, and ~ —*Time*⟩

¹**sam·bal** \(')säm¦bäl\ *n* -s [Malay] **:** a condiment made typically of peppers, pickles, grated coconut, salt fish, or fish roe and eaten esp. with curry and rice in and around Indonesia and Malaya

²**sam·bal** \"\ *also* **sam·ba·li** \säm'bälē\ *or* **zam·bal** \(')säm-¦bäl\ *n, pl* **sambal** *or* **sambals** *also* **sambali** *or* **sambalis** *or* **zambal** *or* **zambals** *usu cap* [Tag *Sambál, Sambali*] **1 a :** a people of Zambales province, western Luzon, Philippines **b :** a member of such people **2 :** the Austronesian language of the Sambal people

sam·ba·qui \,sambə'kē\ *n* -s [Pg, fr. Tupi & Guarani *sambaqui, tambaqui*, fr. *tamba* shell + *qui* hill] **:** one of the prehistoric kitchen middens found on the coast of Brazil

sam·bar *or* **sam·bur** *also* **sam·bhar** *or* **sam·bhur** \'sämbə(r), 'sam-\ *n* -s [Hindi *sābar*, fr. Skt *śambara*] **:** a large Asiatic deer (*Cervus unicolor* or *Rusa unicolor*) having long coarse hair on the throat and the antlers strong and three-pointed; *esp* **:** a dark brown Indian deer (*C. u. unicolor*) — called also *elk*

sam·bho·ga·ka·ya \səm,bōgə'käyə\ *n* -s [Skt *sambhogakāya*, fr. *sambhoga* delight in sexual union (fr. *sam* together + *bhoga* enjoyment, fr. *bhuṅkte, bhuñjati* he enjoys) + *kāya* body; akin to Skt *cinoti* he gathers, heaps up, piles in order — more at SAME, FUNCTION, POET] **:** the body of bliss worshiped as deity in the Buddhist doctrine of trikaya

sam·bo \'sam(,)bō, 'saam-\ *n* -s [AmerSp *zambo* Negro, mulatto, perh. fr. Kongo *nzambu* monkey] **1 :** ZAMBO **2** *often cap* **:** NEGRO — usu. used disparagingly

sam browne belt *or* **sam browne** \,sa\|m,braùn-, ,saa\|\ *n, usu cap S&1stB* [after Sir Samuel James *Browne* †1901 Brit. army officer] **:** a leather belt for a dress uniform supported by a light strap passing over the right shoulder ⟨a Mountie's *Sam Browne* —Andrew Bishop⟩

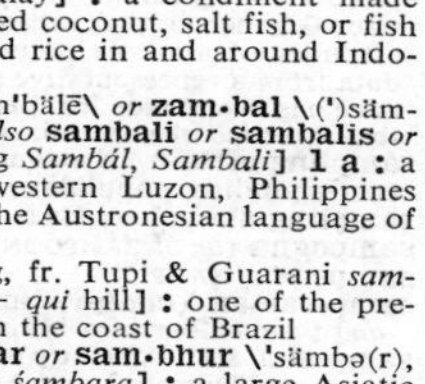

Sam Browne belt

sam·bu·ca \sam'b(y)ükə\ *n* -s [L, fr. Gk *sambykē*, of Sem origin; akin to Aram *śabbĕkhā* trigon] **:** TRIGON

sam·bu·cus \-kəs\ *n, cap* [NL, fr. L, elder tree] **:** a genus of shrubs, trees, or rarely herbs (family Caprifoliaceae) that are native to temperate regions and have pinnate leaves with serrate or incised leaflets, white or pink flowers in thyrsoid cymes with the corolla regular, rotate, and 3- to 5-lobed and with five stamens, and a black or red berrylike fruit

sam·buk *also* **sam·bouk** *or* **sam·buq** \(')sam¦bük\ *n* -s [Ar *sanbūq*] **:** a small Arab dhow

sam·bul *var of* SUMBUL

sam·bu·nigrin \,samb(y)ə'nīgrən, -nig-\ *n* -s [NL *Sambucus nigra*, species of elder (fr. *Sambucus* + L *nigra*, fem. of *niger* black) + ISV *-in* — more at NEGRO] **:** a crystalline glucoside $C_6H_5CH(CN)OC_6H_{11}O_5$ that occurs esp. in the berries of the common elder, that on complete hydrolysis yields benzaldehyde, hydrocyanic acid, and glucose, and that racemizes in alkaline solution to prulaurasin — compare AMYGDALIN, PRUNASIN

¹**same** \'sām\ *adj* [ME, fr. ON *samr, sami*; akin to OE (*swā*) *same* likewise, OHG & Goth *sama* same, L *similis* like, *semone*, *simul* together, at the same time, Gk *homos* same, *heis*, *hen* one, *hama* together, Skt *sama* level, equal, same, *sam* together] **1 a :** resembling in every way **:** not different in relevant essentials at one time ⟨we must not expect to be all happy in the ~ degree —James Boswell⟩ **b :** conforming in every respect — used with *as* ⟨eat the ~ rations as the captain —H.A.Chippendale⟩ ⟨gave him the ~ answer as before⟩ **2 a :** being one without addition, change, or discontinuance **:** having one nature or individuality **:** of like nature or identity **:** IDENTICAL, SELFSAME ⟨you can't do the ~ thing all the time —Jimmy Cannon⟩ ⟨speakers and hearers, who may be one and the ~ persons —Gilbert Ryle⟩ **b :** being the one under discussion or already referred to ⟨the committee backing the fare increase is the ~ committee that recently issued an urgent plea to curb inflation⟩ — often used as an intensive ⟨used six quotations from this ~ book⟩ **3 :** corresponding so closely as to be indistinguishable **:** closely similar **:** COMPARABLE ⟨mother and son have the ~ black eyes⟩ ⟨the way two different drivers treat . . . the ~ sets of tires —R.L.Rosekrans⟩ ⟨the form is diverse; the essence is the ~ —Havelock Ellis⟩

syn SAME, SELFSAME, VERY, IDENTICAL, IDENTIC, EQUIVALENT, EQUAL, and TANTAMOUNT can apply to one thing not different from another or things not differing from each other. SAME may imply, and SELFSAME always implies, that the things under consideration are only one thing ⟨the systems of all three countries conform to the *same* standards of . . . justice and fair play —John Moylan⟩ ⟨in efficiency, one method may be the *same* as another⟩ ⟨each question was directed to the *selfsame* urgent end —E.M.Lustgarten⟩ ⟨voted out of power . . . by the *selfsame* people who had put them into office in the first place —B.F. Fairless⟩ VERY can often be no different from SELFSAME ⟨what others have thought about the *very* problems that face us now —C.F.Strubbe⟩ ⟨here in this *very* town there was once a cafe —Carson McCullers⟩ ⟨the *very* man I was looking for⟩ IDENTICAL implies selfsameness or absolute agreement in all details ⟨consists of several hundred *identical* shacks arranged in rows —*Amer. Guide Series: Pa.*⟩ ⟨we are not *identical* with our former self —Alexis Carrel⟩ IDENTIC is the same as IDENTICAL but has a chiefly diplomatic or governmental provenience ⟨collective or *identic* notes utilized by the powers in making joint representation to a government —G.H.Stuart⟩ ⟨the resolution is *identic* with a resolution enacted last year —*U.S. Code*⟩ ⟨the president in *identic* letters addressed to the attorney general, the secretary of war and the secretary of the navy, notified them of his approval —F.A.Howard⟩ EQUIVALENT applies to things estimated against each other and implies amounting to the same thing ⟨instead of matching it with an *equivalent* folly, we wish to offer an alternative —Herbert Agar⟩ ⟨the voters, who for practical purposes are *equivalent* to the people —W.J.Shepard⟩ ⟨the accumulation of property is therefore *equivalent* to a concentration of power or sovereignty over the lives of those who need the goods owned by others —M.R.Cohen⟩ EQUAL signifies identical in some specific way, as in height, amount, or effectiveness ⟨in many counties cattle and sheep are of almost *equal* importance —*Amer. Guide Series: Nev.*⟩ ⟨when our men have *equal* weapons in their hands —Sir Winston Churchill⟩ ⟨the picture cannot be painted if the significant and the insignificant are given *equal* prominence —B.N.Cardozo⟩ ⟨two boys *equal* in size and age⟩ TANTAMOUNT is the same as EQUIVALENT but applies only to one of two equivalent things, usu. nonmaterial ⟨an article of faith, the denial of which is *tantamount* to treason —Archibald MacLeish⟩ ⟨failure to publish is *tantamount* to suppression —R.H. Rovere⟩ ⟨production of coal is *tantamount* to the destruction of stored energy —W.P.Webb⟩

²**same** \"\ *pron* [ME, fr. ¹*same*] **1 a :** something identical with or similar to another ⟨an actual apple or a picture of the ~ —Einar Haugen⟩ ⟨the rules . . . are the ~ which govern professional big-league play —C.L.Biemiller⟩ ⟨when by sheer luck you strike a wedding . . . and when by more of the ~ you reach Vienna on a feast day —Claudia Cassidy⟩ **b** *obs* **:** something that is a counterpart — used with *that* ⟨such was thy zeal to Israel then, the ~ that now to me —John Milton⟩ **2 :** something that has previously been defined or described ⟨ran up big bills . . . but was not very strong on paying ~ —Bennett Cerf⟩ ⟨each house shall keep a journal of its proceedings, and from time to time publish the ~ —*U.S.Constitution*⟩ ⟨have in his possession gold certificates after ~ had been registered at Washington —F.A.Limpert⟩ — **the same** *adv* **:** in the same manner ⟨*to* and *two* are spelled differently but pronounced *the same*⟩ ⟨a woman's shoulder muscles are not attached *the same* as a man's —Deems Taylor⟩

³**same** \"\ *adv* [¹*same*] **:** in the same manner **:** the same ⟨may be applied with . . . connector strips, ~ as any other wallboard —*Stonewall Board*⟩

same here *adv* **:** similarly with me ⟨said she wanted a soda and I said *same here*⟩

sa·mekh *or* **sa·mech** *also* **sa·mek** \'sä(,)mek, -ek\ *n* -s [Heb *sāmekh*, lit., a support] **1 :** the 15th letter of the Hebrew alphabet — symbol ס; see ALPHABET table **2 :** a letter of the Phoenician or of any of various other Semitic alphabets corresponding to the Hebrew samekh

sam·el *also* **sam·mel** \'saməl\ *adj* [prob. akin to OE *sam-*half and to OE *ǣlan* to burn — more at SAM-, ANNEAL] **:** soft and crumbling — used of bricks that lie outermost in the kiln and are in consequence not thoroughly burned; compare PLACE BRICK

same·ly \'sāmlē\ *adj* [¹*same* + *-ly*] **:** MONOTONOUS, UNVARIED

sam·en \'sāmən\ *adj* [by alter.] *Scot* **:** SAME

same·ness \'sāmnəs\ *n* -ES **1 :** the quality or state of being the same **:** IDENTITY, SIMILARITY ⟨the ~*es*, the traits of mankind which are general —H.W.Taylor⟩ **2 :** unvarying homogeneity **:** MONOTONY, UNIFORMITY ⟨~ of food — oats and hay continuously —Robert Chawner⟩ ⟨the sun-browned ~ of outlying rangelands —*Amer. Guide Series: Texas*⟩

samgha *var of* SANGHA

sa·mhain eve \'saùən-, 'säwən-\ *n, usu cap S&E* [IrGael *samhain* feast of All Saints + E *eve*] **:** HALLOWEEN

sam hill \'sam¦hil\ *n, often cap S&H* [prob. euphemism for *hell*] **:** DEVIL, DEUCE ⟨just what in the *Sam Hill* was he going to do —Norman Mailer⟩

sam·hi·ta \'səmhi¦tä\ *n* -s *usu cap* [Skt *saṁhitā*, lit., combination, fr. *sam* together + *hita*, past part. of *dadhāti* he puts, places — more at SAME, DO] **:** any of the four basic canonical books of Hindu scriptures comprising hymns, prayers, and liturgical formulas and including the Rig-Veda, the Yajur-Veda, the Sama-Veda, and the Atharva-Veda

sa·mia \'sāmēə\ *n, cap* [NL, fr. L, the Samian goddess (epithet of Juno or Saturnia), fr. fem. of *samius* Samian] **:** a genus of large saturniid moths — see CYNTHIA MOTH

¹**sa·mi·an** \'sāmēən\ *adj, usu cap* [L *samius* Samian (fr. Gk *samios*, fr. *Samos*) + E *-an*] **:** of or relating to the island of Samos in the Aegean sea ⟨fill high the bowl with *Samian* wine —Lord Byron⟩

²**samian** \"\ *n* -s *cap* **:** a native or inhabitant of Samos

samian ware *n, usu cap S* **:** ARRETINE WARE

sam·iel \səm'yel\ *n* -s [Turk *samyeli*, fr. *sam* poisonous + *yel* wind] **:** SIMOOM

sam·i·res·ite \,samə're,sīt, sə'mirə,s-\ *n* -s [F *samirésite*, fr. *Samirésy*, hill near Antsirabe, Madagascar + F *-ite*] **:** BETAFITE

sam·i·sen \'samə,sen\ *also* **sam·si·en** \-msē,en\ *or* **sham·i·sen** \'shamə-,sen\ *n, pl* **samisen** *or* **samisens** [Jap *samisen*, fr. Chin (Pek) *san*¹ *hsien*², fr. *san*¹ three + *hsien*² string] **:** a 3-stringed Japanese musical instrument resembling a banjo

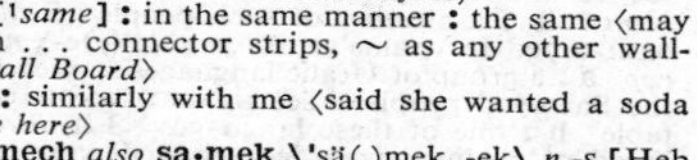

samisen

samite \'sa,mīt, 'sā,-\ *n* -s [ME *samit*, fr. MF, fr. ML *examitum, samitum*, fr. (assumed) MGk *hexamiton* (whence OSlav *oksamitŭ* velvet), fr. Gk, neut. of *hexamitos* of six threads, fr. *hexa-* + *mitos* thread of the warp — more at DIMITY] **:** a rich medieval fabric of silk interwoven sometimes with gold or silver threads and used or worn only by ecclesiastics and nobles ⟨an arm rose up from out the bosom of the lake clothed in white ~, mystic, wonderful —Alfred Tennyson⟩

samkhya *usu cap, var of* SANKHYA

sam·let \'samlət\ *n* -s [irreg. fr. *salmon* + *-let*] **:** a fingerling salmon **:** PARR

samm *var of* SAM

sam·ma \'samə\ *n* -s *usu cap* **:** one of a number of Rajput peoples in the lower Sind in early Indian history

sammarinese *usu cap, var of* SAN MARINESE

sammed *past of* SAM

sammel *var of* SAMEL

sam·mer \'samə(r)\ *n* -s [³*sam* + *-er*] **:** one that sams leather — called also *sammier, sammy man*

sam·mi·er \'samēə(r)\ *n* -s [²*sammy* + *-er*] **:** SAMMER

samming *pres part of* SAM

¹**sam·my** \'samē\ *adj* [perh. alter. of E dial. *sam* half-cooked, moist — more at SAM] **1** *dial* **:** CLAMMY, SODDEN **2** *dial* **:** WATERY

²sammy \"\ *or* **sam·mie** \"\ *vb* **sammied; sammied; sammying** *or* **sammieing; sammies** [alter. of ³*sam*] *vt* : to moisten (leather) before staking : SAM ~ *vi* : to make rough-tanned leather evenly moist throughout

³sammy \"\ *n* -ES [fr. *Sammy*, nickname for *Samuel*] *dial Eng* : SIMPLETON

sammy man *n* [²*sammy*] : SAMMER

sam·na·ni \səm'nänē\ *n, pl* **samnani** *or* **samnanis** *usu cap* **1 a** : a people of Samnan in north central Iran **b** : a member of such people **2** : the Iranian language of the Samnani people

sam·nite \'sam,nīt\ *n* -S *cap* [L *Samnites* (pl.) Samnites, fr. *Samnium*, country in ancient central Italy] **1** : a people of ancient Samnium in ancient central Italy speaking the Oscan language **2** : a gladiator of ancient Rome bearing the arms and oblong shield of the Samnites

¹sa·mo·an \sə'mōən\ *adj, usu cap* [*Samoa*, group of islands in southwest central Pacific ocean + E *-an*] : of or relating to Samoa or the Samoans

²samoan \"\ *n* -S *cap* **1** : a native or inhabitant of Samoa **2** : the Polynesian language of the Samoan people

sam·o·gi·tian \,samə'gishən, -mə'ji-\ *n* -S *cap* **1** : a Lithuanian of the lowlands in the western part of the Kaunas district **2** : the language of the Samogitian people constituting one of the two linguistic divisions of Lithuanian

sa·mo·gon \¦sämə¦gȯn\ *also* **sa·mo·gon·ka** \-ȯŋkə\ *n* -S [Russ, prob. fr. *samo-* self (akin to OE *same*) + *peregon*, *peregonka* distillation] : illicitly distilled Russian vodka : HOME BREW

sa·mo·hu \sə'mō(,)hü\ *n* -S [native name in So. America] **1** : FLOSS-SILK TREE **2** : the ashy gray light soft lumber of the floss-silk tree

sam·o·lus \'saməl əs\ *n, cap* [NL, fr. L, a plant growing in wet places, of Gaulish origin] : a small genus of mainly tropical herbs (family Primulaceae) having small white flowers with a perigynous corolla including five stamens and five staminodia — see BROOKWEED

sa·mos·a·te·nian \sə,mäsə'tēnēən\ *n* -S *usu cap* [LL Paulus *Samosatenus* Paul of Samosata (fr. Gk *samosatēnos* of Samosata, fr. *Samosata*, city of ancient Syria) + E *-ian*] : PAULIANIST

sam·o·there \'samə,thi(ə)r\ *n* -S [NL *Samotherium*] : an ungulate or fossil of the genus *Samotherium*

sam·o·the·ri·um \,samə'thirēəm\ *n, cap* [NL, fr. *Samos*, island in the Aegean sea + *-therium*] : a genus of extinct ungulates of the Miocene of Greece related to the giraffe but having a shorter neck and no median frontal knob

¹sam·o·thra·cian \,samə'thrāshən\ *n* -S *cap* [L *samothracius* of Samothrace (fr. Gk *samothrakios*, fr. *Samothrakē* Samothrace, island in the Aegean sea) + E *-an*] : a native or inhabitant of the Greek island of Samothrace in the Aegean sea

²samothracian \¦==¦==\ *adj, usu cap* [L *samothracius*] : of, relating to, or constituting the religious cult centering around the Cabiri of ancient Greece

sam·o·var \'samə,vär, -,vå(r *sometimes* ,==ˈ=\ *n* -S [Russ, fr. *samo-* self (akin to OE *same*) + *varit'* to boil, cook] **1** : a usu. copper urn with a spigot at its base and a central tube for live charcoal used esp. in Russia to boil water for tea **2** : a similar urn of metal or china with an alcohol lamp or other device for heating the contents

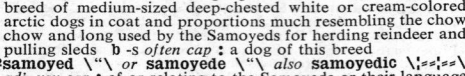

samovar 1

¹sam·o·yed *also* **sam·o·yede** \'samə,yed, 'sa,mȯi(y)ed, sə'mȯi(y)əd\ *n* [Russ *samoed*] **1** *pl* **samoyed** *or* **samoyeds** *cap* **a** : a Finno-Asian people of the Nenets district of the Arkhangelsk region of the U.S.S.R. scattered along the coasts and islands from the White sea to the Taimyr peninsula — called also *Nentsi* **b** : a member of such people **2** *also* **sam·o·yed·ic** \,samə'yedik, ,sa,mȯi'(y)e-\ *n* -S *cap* **a** : a group of Uralic languages spoken by the Samoyed people — see URALIC LANGUAGES table **b** : one of these languages **3 a** *usu cap* : a Siberian breed of medium-sized deep-chested white or cream-colored arctic dogs in coat and proportions much resembling the chow chow and long used by the Samoyeds for herding reindeer and pulling sleds **b** -S *often cap* : a dog of this breed

²samoyed \"\ *or* **samoyede** \"\ *also* **samoyedic** \¦==¦==\ *adj, usu cap* : of or relating to the Samoyeds or their language

samp \'samp\ *n* -S [Narraganset *nasaump* corn mush, soup] : coarse hominy or a boiled cereal made from it

sam·pa·gui·ta \,sampə'gēd·ə\ *n* -S [PhilSp, fr. Tag *sampaga* Arabian jasmine + Sp *-ita* dim. suffix] *Philippines* : ARABIAN JASMINE

sam·pa·loc \'sampə,läk\ *n* -S [Tag *sampalok*] *Philippines* : TAMARIND

sam·pan *also* **san·pan** \'sam,pan, 'saam,paa(ə)n\ *n* -S [Chin (Pek) *san¹ pan³*, fr. *san¹* three + *pan³* board, plank] **1 a** : a flat-bottomed wedge-shaped Chinese skiff with low transom bow and rising transom stern with a pronounced rake, usu. having a mat roofing over the cabin, sometimes equipped with a sail but usu. propelled by two short oars in oarlocks consisting of twisted rattan, and used principally for river and harbor traffic **b** : a small open Chinese boat **2** : a Japanese boat with a broad flat keel, a long raking sharp bow and vertical square stern propelled by a single scull or a group of sculls, by square sails on one to three masts, or by an engine **3** *Hawaii* : a boat built on oriental lines, propelled by a diesel motor, and widely used in Hawaiian fishery

sam·phire \'sam,fī(ə)r\ *n* -S [alter. (perh. influenced by *camphire*) of earlier *sampere*, *sampiere*, fr. MF (*herbe de*) *Saint Pierre*, lit., St. Peter's herb] **1** : a fleshy European seacoast plant (*Crithmum maritimum*) of the family Umbelliferae that is sometimes pickled **2** : a common glasswort (*Salicornia europaea*) that is sometimes pickled **3** : SEA OXEYE **4** : a tropical American fleshy herb (*Philoxerus vermicularis*) of the family Amaranthaceae with dense heads of white flowers that is common along beaches

¹sam·ple \'sampəl, 'saam-,'saim-, 'sâm-\ *n* -S [ME, fr. MF *essample* — more at EXAMPLE] **1** *obs* : one that is worthy of imitation : EXAMPLE ⟨liv'd in court . . . most prais'd, most lov'd, a ~ to the youngest —Shak.⟩ **2 a** : a representative portion of a whole : a small segment or quantity taken as evidence of the quality or character of the entire group or lot ⟨the ~ of the . . . Nordic race with which he identifies himself —Ruth Benedict⟩ ⟨knowledge of the deep ocean floor comes from . . . bottom ~*s* —F.P.Shepard⟩ **b** : one displaying characteristics typical of its kind : SPECIMEN ⟨the collection of ~*s* for museum displays —R.W.Murray⟩ ⟨molded caps over the windows and the original broad porch make it an excellent ~ of its period —*Amer. Guide Series: Conn.*⟩ **c** (1) : a trial package of a product distributed without cost to potential consumers (2) : a unit of merchandise used for demonstration or display ⟨floor ~⟩ **3** : one that serves to illustrate the full range or scope : INDICATION, INSTANCE ⟨offering listeners ~*s* from the whole tradition of world drama —Leslie Rees⟩ ⟨contrasting ~*s* of church-state policy —Paul Blanshard⟩ **4 a** : a part (as of a population) used for purposes of investigating and comparing properties ⟨poll a national ~ as a means of predicting elections⟩ **b** : SAMPLING ⟨results of the ~ . . . must be translated and interpreted —W.E.Deming⟩ **syn** see INSTANCE

²sample \"\ *vt* **sampled; sampled; sampling** \-p(ə)liŋ\ **samples 1** *obs* **a** : to make comparable to : find a counterpart for : MATCH ⟨she seemed to be *sampled* for him —Henry Lord⟩ ⟨this notion . . . nowhere else *sampled* in any Greek author —Joseph Mede⟩ **b** : SYMBOLIZE ⟨some way ~ that, which no way we can express —Henry Montagu⟩ **c** : COPY ⟨a model . . . must be *sampled* in Jerusalem —Joseph Hall⟩ **2 a** : to take a sample of : assess by examining a small portion : TEST ⟨inspectors . . . ~ a year's output of fifty million parts —Bryan Morgan⟩ ⟨achievement tests . . . each *sampling* a different area —*Univ. of State of N. Y. Bull.*⟩ **b** : to yield in sample ⟨good ore, two feet of which ~*s* more than . . . 30 ounces of silver —*N.Y.Sun*⟩ **c** : to become acquainted with through personal experiment : try out : EXPERIENCE ⟨rail fans will . . . adjust their itineraries this summer to ~ the shiny new equipment —P.J.C.Friedlander⟩ ⟨~ the pleasures of the simple life —Thomas Cadett⟩ **d** : to dip into : glance through : SKIM ⟨~ the literature of social science⟩ ⟨surrounds himself with books . . . and ~*s* them as a dowager might a box of chocolates —*Time*⟩ **3** : to give an impression or show an example of : EXEMPLIFY, REPRESENT ⟨manuscripts are so extensive . . . that it would be a heavy task to undertake even to ~ them adequately —*Times Lit. Supp.*⟩ ⟨denims are *sampled* in red —*Women's Wear Daily*⟩ **4** : to take samples from (a given population) and from them make statistical estimates of the trait or attitude measured ⟨polling organizations *sampled* the electorate at intervals —*Americana Annual*⟩

³sample \"\ *adj* **1** : serving as an illustration or example ⟨~ question⟩ ⟨designed a ~ three-bedroom house —*N.Y.Times*⟩ **2 a** : exemplifying a whole body or lot ⟨~ ore⟩ ⟨~ copy⟩ **b** : making, examining, showing, or distributing samples ⟨~ cutter⟩ ⟨~ tester⟩ ⟨~ card⟩ ⟨~ passer⟩ **3** : of an exploratory nature : EXPERIMENTAL ⟨~ tunnels have already indicated the proximity of fossils —R.W.Murray⟩ **4** : of or relating to a statistical sample ⟨was courteous enough to check his attendances for us during a random ~ week —Ernest & Pearl Beaglehole⟩

sam·ple·ite \-pə,līt\ *n* -S [Mat *Sample* 20th cent. Am. mine superintendent in Chile + *-ite*] : a mineral $NaCaCu_5(PO_4)_4Cl.5H_2O$ consisting of hydrous phosphate and chloride of sodium, calcium, and copper

sam·ple·man \'=pəlmən, -,man\ *n, pl* **samplemen** [¹*sample* + *man*] : a maker, distributor, or tester of samples : SAMPLER

sample post *n* [¹*sample*] : a postal service for international mail provided by Universal Postal Union regulations and allowing special rates on trade samples

¹sam·pler \-plə(r)\ *n* -S [ME, fr. OF *essamplaire*, fr. LL *exemplarium* — more at EXEMPLAR] **1** *obs* : an original model or characteristic sample : ARCHETYPE, EXAMPLE ⟨Christ's baptism was the perfect ~ and pattern of ours —Daniel Featley⟩ **2 a** : a practical example of needlework patterns; *esp* : a piece of cloth with rows of different embroidery stitches worked across it **b** : a decorative square or rectangular piece of needlework typically having the alphabet, numbers, family names and dates, and a motto embroidered on it in various stitches as an example of skill

²sam·pler \-p(ə)lə(r)\ *n* -S [²*sample* + *-er*] **1** : one that collects or examines samples: as **a** (1) : one that determines the quality of a product by testing samples taken from it ⟨cotton ~⟩ ⟨grain ~⟩ (2) : one that prepares samples ⟨the ~ extracts olives from the barrels for the inspector⟩ **b** : a customs inspector who compares samples of merchandise with discharge permits and endorses the permits if there are no discrepancies **c** : a mechanical device for obtaining a small quantity of something for testing or analysis ⟨grab ~*s* . . . are designed to take a surface sample of the bottom —J.D. Isaacs⟩ **2 a** : one that contains representative specimens or selections ⟨a fiction ~ from the work of a notable . . . writer —Harvey Breit⟩ ⟨cities became . . . ~*s* of the past styles of every country but our own —*Amer. Guide Series: Va.*⟩ **b** : a trial package or assortment intended to introduce a product to potential customers ⟨a connoisseur's ~ containing small packets of six choice teas⟩ ⟨each preparation has its . . . niche in the ~ —*Phoenix Flame*⟩ **3** : one engaged in statistical sampling ⟨a ~ of public opinion⟩

sample room *n* [¹*sample*] : a room in which samples are displayed; *esp* : a hotel room in which salesmen display merchandise for the inspection of buyers for retail stores

sampling *n* -S *often attrib* [fr. gerund of ²*sample*] **1 a** : an act or instance of obtaining a sample ⟨improved technic . . . for blood ~ —*advt*⟩ ⟨the purpose of ~ is to determine the average mineral values in the deposit —J.D.Forrester⟩ **b** : assessment of the quality or character of a whole by examination of a sample : TESTING ⟨periodic ~ of the stored grain is necessary to be sure it is not molding⟩ **c** : personal investigation : TRIAL ⟨experimental ~, as with edibles, . . . played a part in the transformation of our material environment —Lewis Mumford⟩ **2** : SAMPLE ⟨those who would like to find out what the French do in commerce and industry can get complete ~*s* at the . . . fair —*N.Y.Times*⟩ ⟨this inventory is far from complete, but it is an adequate ~ —Abram Kardiner⟩ ⟨ask a ~ of people why they didn't buy one client's product —Vance Packard⟩ **3** : the introduction of a product or promotion of its sale by distributing at no cost or at a reduced price a trial package in regular or specially designed smaller size **4** : the act, process, or technique of determining traits or attitudes of a whole population by collecting and analyzing data from a representative segment of it : SURVEY ⟨after allowance has been made for the quantitative and qualitative bias of the ~, series of generalizations are drawn —Sidney Hook⟩

sampling error *n* : the chance difference of a statistic from the corresponding population constant of which it is an estimate

sampling shovel *n* : SPLIT SHOVEL

sampogna *var of* ZAMPOGNA

samps *pl of* SAMP

samp·sae·an \sam(p)'sēən\ *n* -S *usu cap* [LGk *sampsaios* + E *-an*] : a member of a branch of the Elkesaites

samp·son fish \'sa|m(p)sən-, 'saa|, 'sai|\ *n, usu cap S* [fr. the name *Sampson*] : an Australian fish (*Seriola hippos*) of the family Carangidae

sampson fox *or* **samson fox** \"-\ *n, usu cap S* [prob. after *Samson*, judge of Israel; fr. his tying torches to the tails of foxes to set fire to the grain of the Philistines, Judg 15:4–5] : a red fox having a coat in which the guard hairs are lacking and the under fur is woolly and scorched looking due to genetic variation

sampson snakeroot *or* **sampson's snakeroot** *also* **samson snakeroot** *n, usu cap 1st S* [fr. the name *Sampson* or *Samson*] **1** : an aromatic herb (*Psoralea psoralioides*) of the southeastern U.S. with a root having tonic properties — called also *babroot, Congo root* **2** : any of several American gentians of the genus *Dasystephana*

sams *pl of* SAM, *pres 3d sing of* SAM

sam·sa·ra \sən'sārə\ *also* **sansara** \sən'-\ *n* -S [Skt *saṁsāra*, lit., passing through, fr. *sam* together, completely + *sarati* it runs, flows — more at SAME, SERUM] **1** *Hinduism & Buddhism* : the indefinitely repeated cycles of birth, misery, and death caused by karma : TRANSMIGRATION **2** *Hinduism & Buddhism* : ever-changing finite temporal existence : life in society — contrasted with *Nirvana*

sam scratch \'samz'krach, -m'sk-\ *n, usu cap both Ss* : OLD NICK

sam·shu \'sam¦shü, -¦syü\ *n* -S [perh. fr. Chin (Pek) *shao¹ chiu³* spirits that will burn, samshu, fr. *shao¹* to burn + *chiu³* wine, spirits] : an alcoholic liquor distilled in China usu. from rice or large millet

samsien *var of* SAMISEN

sam·ska·ra \səmz'kärə, -m'sk-\ *n* -S [Skt *saṁskāra*, lit., putting together, making perfect, purifying, fr. *sam* together + *karoti* he makes, does — more at SAME, KARMA] **1** : a purificatory Hindu ceremony **2** *Hinduism & Buddhism* : a mental conformation or latent karmic tendency shaping one's present life

sam·skrit *or* **sam·skrt** \'samz,krit, -m,sk-\ *n* -S *cap* [Skt *saṁskṛta* — more at SANSKRIT] : SANSKRIT

sam–sodden \'sam,säd³n\ *adj* [fr. (assumed) ME *sam-soden*, fr. OE, fr. *sam-* + *soden*, past part. of *sēothan* to boil — more at SEETHE] *dial Eng* : half cooked

sam·son \'sam(p)sən, 'saam-,'saim-\ *n* -S [after *Samson*, judge of Israel famed for his strength, Judg 13:24–16:31] **1** *usu cap* : a mighty man ⟨we proclaimed him a *Samson* who might pull down the pillars of our temple —R.H.Jackson⟩ **2** : SAMSON POST

sam·so·ni·an \(')=¦sōnēən\ *also* **sam·son·ic** \(')=¦sänik\ *adj, usu cap* [*Samson*, judge of Israel + E *-ian*, *-ic*] : of heroic strength or proportions : MIGHTY ⟨a *Samsonian* attempt to demolish the gigantic structure —Douglas Watt⟩

sam·son·ite \'= sə,nīt\ *n* -S [G *samsonit*, fr. the *Samson* mine, Sankt Andreasberg, Harz Mts., Germany + G *-it* -ite] : a mineral $Ag_4MnSb_2S_6$ consisting of a silver manganese antimony sulfide and occurring in steel-black monoclinic prismatic crystals

samson post *n, often cap S* [after *Samson*, judge of Israel; prob. fr. his pulling down the pillars of the palace of the Philistines, Judg 16:25–30] **1 a** : a post resting on the keelson and supporting a deck beam of a ship **b** : a post for use in securing a cable (as the anchor cable) **c** : KING POST 2 **2** : an upright post that supports the walking beam in an oil derrick **3** : a heavy timber with a chain and hook used for moving logs

samum *var of* SIMOOM

sa·mu·rai \'sam(y)ə,rī, 'sämə-, ,==ˈ=\ *n, pl* **samurai** *or* **samurais** [Jap] **1 a** : a military retainer of a Japanese daimyo practicing the chivalric code of Bushido, privileged to wear two swords, and having the power of life and death over commoners **b** : the warrior aristocracy of Japan — see SHIZOKU **2** : a professional soldier ⟨used by the militarists to spread the idea of Japan as a nation of ~ —D.C.Buchanan⟩

sam·vat \'səm(,)vət\ *n* -S *usu cap* [Skt *saṁvat* year, short for *saṁvatsara*, fr. *sam* together + *vatsara* year — more at SAME, WETHER] : an era of Hindu chronology used in northern India

¹san \'san\ *n* -S [Gk (Doric), of Sem origin; akin to Heb *sīn* sin] : a sibilant letter of the original Greek alphabet used in numerical notation to represent the numeral 900

²san \'sän\ *n pl, usu cap* [Hottentot (Nama dial.)] : BUSHMEN

³san \'san\ *n* -S [by shortening] : SANATORIUM

san *abbr* sanitary; sanitation

sa·n'a \(')sä¦nä\ *adj, usu cap* [fr. *San'a*, city in central Yemen] : of or from San'a, the capital of Yemen : of the kind or style prevalent in San'a

sanable *adj* [L *sanabilis*, fr. *sanare* to cure + *-abilis* -able] *obs* : capable of being healed or cured : susceptible of remedy

san·ad *also* **sun·nud** \'sə,nəd\ *n* -S [Ar *sanad* support] **1** : an Indian government charter, warrant, diploma, patent or deed **2** : a letter having the force of an edict or ordinance in India

san an·to·ni·an \,sanən·'tōnēən, -nan-, -naan-\ *n* -S *cap S&A* [*San Antonio*, Texas + E *-an*] : a native or resident of San Antonio, Texas

san an·to·nio \¦==¦tōnē,ō *sometimes* -¦tōn\ *adj, usu cap S&A* [fr. *San Antonio*, city in So. central Texas] : of or from the city of San Antonio, Texas : of the kind or style prevalent in San Antonio ⟨the *San Antonio* climate⟩

san·a·tar·i·um \,sanə'ta(a)rēəm, -'ter-, -'tār-\ *n, pl* **sanatariums** \-mz\ *or* **sanatar·ia** \-ēə\ [NL, alter. (influenced by *sanitarium*) of *sanatorium*] : SANATORIUM

sanation *n* -S [ME *sanacioun*, fr. L *sanation-*, *sanatio*, fr. *sanatus* (past part. of *sanare* to cure) + *-ion-*, *-io* -ion] *obs* : the act or process of healing

san·a·tive \'sanəd·iv\ *adj* [ME *sanatif*, fr. MF, fr. LL *sanativus*, fr. L *sanatus* (past part. of *sanare* to cure) + *-ivus* -ive] : having the power to cure or heal : BENEFICIAL, RESTORATIVE ⟨flooded with the bright ~ light of day —C.I.Glicksberg⟩ ⟨a little of the ~ calmness of conservatism —Raymond English⟩

san·a·to·ri·um \,sanə'tōrēəm, -'tȯr-\ *n, pl* **sanatoriums** \-mz\ *or* **sanato·ria** \-ēə\ [NL, fr. LL, neut. of *sanatorius* sanatory] **1** : an establishment that provides therapy by physical agents (as hydrotherapy, light therapy) combined with diet, exercise, and other measures for treatment or rehabilitation **2 a** : an institution for rest and recuperation esp. for invalids and convalescents **b** : an establishment for the treatment of the sick esp. if suffering from chronic disease (as alcoholism, tuberculosis, nervous or mental disease) requiring protracted care

san·a·to·ry \'sanə,tōrē\ *adj* [LL *sanatorius*, fr. L *sanatus* (past part. of *sanare* to cure, fr. *sanus* healthy) + *-orius* -ory] : conducive to health : tending to cure : CURATIVE ⟨~ mineral baths at a spa⟩

san·be·ni·to \,sanbə'nēd·(,)ō\ *n* -S [Sp *sambenito*, fr. *San Benito* St. Benedict †*ab*543 founder of monasticism in western Europe; fr. its resemblance to the scapular believed to have been introduced by St. Benedict] **1** : a sackcloth coat worn by penitents on being reconciled to the church **2** : a Spanish Inquisition garment resembling a scapular and either of yellow with red crosses for the penitent or of black with painted devils and flames for the impenitent condemned to an auto-da-fé

san blas \san'bläs\ *n, pl* **san blas** *usu cap S&B* [fr. *San Blas* islands, archipelago off the north coast of Panama] **1 a** : a Cunan people of the islands off the north coast of Panama **b** : a member of such people **2** : a Chibchan language of the San Blas people

san·born·ite \'sanbə(r),nīt\ *n* -S [Frank *Sanborn* †1945 Am. mineralogist + E *-ite*] : a mineral $BaSi_2O_5$ consisting of a rare triclinic barium silicate

san car·los \san'kär,lōs\ *n, pl* **san carlos** *usu cap S&C* [fr. *San Carlos* Reservation, eastern Arizona] **1 a** (1) : a subdivision of the Apache including the Cibecue, the Tonto, and the White Mountain Apaches (2) : a group of Apache bands including the Pinal **b** : a member of such subdivision or group **2** : the language of the San Carlos people

¹san·cho \'saŋ(,)kō\ *n* -S [of African origin; akin to Ewe *saŋku³* stringed instrument, guitar, Twi *ō¹sā¹ŋkū³* guitar] : a primitive guitar with fiber strings played by both West African and American negroes

²san·cho \'san(,)chō\ *n* -S [Sp *Sancho*, proper name] : the nine of trumps in sancho pedro

san·cho pan·za \¦san(,)chō'panzə, 'sän . . . 'pänzə\ *n, usu cap S&P* [fr. *Sancho Panza*, commonsensical peasant squire of Don Quixote in the satiric novel *Don Quixote de la Mancha* (1605, 1615) by Miguel de Cervantes Saavedra †1616 Span. novelist] : one that occupies a position analogous to the squire of Don Quixote ⟨his realistic colleagues, the *Sancho Panzas* of jurisprudence —M.R.Cohen⟩

sancho pedro *n* : pedro in which the 9 and 5 of trumps are counted at face value and the 10 of trumps counts game — called also *pedro sancho*

san·cord \'san,kȯrd\ *n* -S [Afrik] : a small reddish deep-sea scorpaenid fish (*Helicolenus maculatus*) of southern Africa

sancta *pl of* SANCTUM

sanc·ti·fi·ca·tion \,saŋ(k)təfə'kāshən, ,saiŋ-\ *n* -S [LL *sanctification-*, *sanctificatio*, fr. *sanctificatus* (past part. of *sanctificare* to make holy) + *-ion-*, *-io* -ion] **1 a** : an act of sanctifying or of being sanctified; *specif* : an act or process of growth in God's grace by which men are set free from the bondage of sin and exalted to a supreme love of God and service to his Kingdom under the inspiration of the Holy Spirit **b** : the state of thus being purified : HOLINESS **2** : development of or increasing adherence to a body of normative rules and standards — contrasted with *secularization*

sanc·ti·fied \'saŋ(k)tə,fīd, 'saiŋ-\ *adj* [ME, fr. past part. of *sanctifien* to sanctify] **1 a** : made holy : made free of sin or free from the bondage of sin **b** : set apart to sacred duty or use **2** : made to have the air of sanctity : SANCTIMONIOUS

sanc·ti·fi·er \-ī(ə)r, -īə\ *n* -S [*sanctify* + *-er*] **1** : one that sanctifies **2** : HOLY SPIRIT

sanc·ti·fy \-,fī\ *vt* -ED/-ING/-ES [ME *sanctifien*, *seintifien*, fr. MF *sanctifier*, *saintifier*, fr. LL *sanctificare*, fr. L *sanctus* holy + *-ficare* -fy — more at SAINT] **1** : to make sacred or holy : set apart to a sacred purpose or to religious use : CONSECRATE, HALLOW ⟨God blessed the seventh day and *sanctified* it —Gen 2:3 (AV)⟩ **2** : to make free from sin : cleanse from moral corruption and pollution : PURIFY **3** : to impart or impute sacredness, inviolability, title to reverence, venerability, or respect to : give sanction to ⟨what mankind has *sanctified* with usage —R.M.Weaver⟩ **4** : to make efficient as the means of holiness : make productive of holiness or piety ⟨observe the day of the sabbath, to ~ it —Deut 5:12 (DV)⟩

sanc·ti·mo·ni·al \,saŋ(k)tə'mōnēəl\ *n* -S [LL *sanctimonialis*, fr. *sanctimonialis* holy, pious, fr. L *sanctimonia* sanctimony + *-alis* -al] : NUN

sanc·ti·mo·ni·ous \¦saŋ(k)tə¦mōnēəs, ¦saiŋ-, -nyəs\ *adj* [L *sanctimonia* sanctimony + E *-ous*] **1** : affecting piousness : hypocritically devout : displaying high-mindedness with intent to impress ⟨easy to be ~ about loyalty —C.P.Curtis⟩ ⟨a woman who was religious without being ~ —G.S.Stokes⟩ **2** *archaic* : possessing sanctity : HOLY, SACRED **syn** see DEVOUT

sanc·ti·mo·ni·ous·ly *adv* : in a sanctimonious manner ⟨~ criticizing the situation —Chester Bowles⟩

sanc·ti·mo·ni·ous·ness *n* -ES : the quality or state of being sanctimonious ⟨almost reek of ~ —Kenneth Roberts⟩

sanc·ti·mo·ny \'saŋ(k)tə,mōnē, 'saiŋ-, -ni\ *n* -ES [MF *sanctimonie*, fr. L *sanctimonia*, fr. *sanctus* holy] **1** *obs* : devoutness of intent : HOLINESS **2** *obs* : SACREDNESS **3** : outward or artificial saintliness : assumed or pretended holiness : hypocritical devoutness ⟨its religiousness is . . . free of pomp and ~ —*Time*⟩

¹sanc·tion \'saŋ(k)shən, 'saiŋ-\ *n* -S [MF or L; MF *sanction*, fr. L *sanction-*, *sanctio*, fr. *sanctus* (past part. of *sancire* to decree, make sacred) + *-ion-*, *-io* -ion — more at SACRED] **1 : a**

formal decree; *esp* **:** an ecclesiastical decree **2 a** *obs* **:** a solemn agreement **:** OATH **b :** something that makes an oath binding ⟨the solemnity of the administration of the oath with its august ~s —L.P.Stryker⟩ **3 :** the detriment, loss of reward, or other coercive intervention that is annexed to a violation of a law as a means of enforcing the law and may consist in the direct infliction of injury or inconvenience (as in the punishments of crime) or in mere coercion, restitution, or undoing of what was wrongly accomplished (as in the judgments of civil actions) or may take the form of a reward which is withheld for failure to comply with the law **4 :** solemn or ceremonious ratification or acceptance ⟨must be divine ~ for all human laws —V.L.Parrington⟩ **5 :** a consideration, principle, or influence (as the findings of conscience or the principle of the golden rule or the goal of perfection) that impels to moral action or determines the moral judgment as valid ⟨the ~ that a religion can add to social ethics —Alfred Cobban⟩ ⟨poetry is one of the ~s of life —S.F.Morse⟩ **6 a :** explicit permission or recognition by one in authority that gives validity to the act of another person or body ⟨functioning under the ~ of the state —W.A.Robinson⟩ ⟨so firmly established as not to need the ~ of formal statute —F.B.Simkins⟩ ⟨received his father's ~ and authority —George Meredith⟩ **b :** encouragement or approbation given usu. by an authoritative person, by custom, or by tradition ⟨not as yet received the ~ of tradition —J.L.Lowes⟩ ⟨allows them to become accessories to any crime that has social ~ —Anthony West⟩ **7 :** something that authorizes, confirms, or countenances ⟨their chief ~ was his personal prestige —John Buchan⟩ **8 :** a coercive measure adopted usu. by several nations in concert for forcing a nation violating international law to desist or yield to adjudication esp. by withholding loans or limiting trade relations or by military force or blockade **9 :** a mechanism of social control that punishes deviancy from or rewards conformance to the normative standards of behavior existing in a society ⟨in some societies shame and ridicule may operate as the principal ~⟩ ⟨lives in a world . . . with inescapable pressures in the form of ~s —T.D.McCown⟩ **10 :** a restrictive measure used to punish a specific action or to prevent some future activity ⟨establishing ~s against the violators of labor legislation —*Current Biog.*⟩

[2]**sanction** \"\ *vb* **sanctioned; sanctioned; sanctioning** \-sh(ə)niŋ\ **sanctions** *vt* **1 :** to make valid or binding **:** ratify, confirm, or put into effect typically by decree, fiat, or other formal procedure ⟨the fact . . . would not justify this court in ~*ing* an error —R.B.Taney⟩ ⟨the vicar became reasonable and ~*ed* the marriages —*Amer. Guide Series: Ariz.*⟩ **2 :** to establish, maintain, encourage, or permit usu. by some authoritative approval or consent ⟨~*ed* by his job to drive . . . constantly in an automobile —Bernard De Voto⟩ ⟨use words ~*ed* by long tradition —John Dewey⟩ **3 :** to annex a sanction or penalty to the violation of (as a right, obligation, or command) **4 :** to define as original and fundamental law antecedent to any possible violation, penalty, or sanction — used chiefly in the phrase *sanctioned rights* ~ *vi* **:** to arise as a preventive of violation of a sanctioned right or obligation — used chiefly in the phrase *sanctioning rights* **syn** see APPROVE

sanc·tion·ative \-shə,nād·iv, -,nəd-\ *adj* [[1]*sanction* + *-ative*] **:** involving or implying sanction **:** serving or tending to sanction ⟨the functions of the guardian were either administrative or ~ —Edward Poste⟩

sanc·tion·er \-sh(ə)nə(r)\ *n* -s **:** one that sanctions

sanc·ti·tude \'saŋ(k)tə,tüd\ *n* -s [ME *sanctitud*, fr. L *sanctitudo*, fr. *sanctus* holy + *-i-* + *-tudo* -tude] **:** pure and saintly character **:** HOLINESS, SACREDNESS

sanc·ti·ty \'saŋ(k)təd-ē, 'saiŋ-, -tətē, -i\ *n* -ES [ME *saunctite*, *sauntite*, fr. MF *saincteté*, *sainctité*, fr. L *sanctitat-*, *sanctitas*, fr. *sanctus* holy + *-itat-*, *-itas* -ity — more at SAINT] **1 a :** holiness of life and character **:** SAINTLINESS, GODLINESS **b sanctities** *pl* **:** sacred excellences or principles ⟨no pretense of *sanctities*⟩ ⟨with no regard for rules or *sanctities* —*Christian Century*⟩ **2 a :** the quality or state of being holy or sacred **:** a religious binding force **:** INVIOLABILITY, SACREDNESS ⟨things whose ~ it would be insane even to question —T.O.Heggen⟩ ⟨the problem of ~ of boundaries —P.C.Nash⟩ **b sanctities** *pl* **:** sacred objects, obligations, or rights

sanc·to·ral \'saŋ(k)tərəl\ *adj* [ML *sanctorale*] **:** of or relating to the sanctorale

sanc·to·ra·le \,saŋ(k)tə'rālē\ *n* -s [ML, fr. neut. of ML *sanctoralis* of saints, fr. *sanctor-* (fr. LL *sanctus* saint, fr. L, holy) + L *-alis* -al] **:** the part of the breviary and missal that contains the offices proper to the saints' days — compare *temporale*

sanc·to·ri·um \,saŋ(k)'tōrēəm\ *n* -s [NL, fr. LL *sanctus* saint + L *-orium* -ory] **:** SHRINE

sanc·tu·ar·ied \'saŋ(k)chə,werēd\ *adj* **:** having or furnishing a sanctuary

sanc·tu·a·rize \'saŋ(k)chəwə,rīz\ *vt* -ED/-ING/-S [[1]*sanctuary* + *-ize*] **:** to shelter by a sanctuary or sacred privileges ⟨no place indeed should murther ~; revenge should have no bounds —Shak.⟩

[1]**sanc·tu·ary** \'saŋ(k)chə,werē, 'saiŋ-, -ri\ *n* -ES [ME *sanctuarie*, *seintuarie*, fr. MF *saintuarie*, *saintuarie*, fr. LL *sanctuarium*, fr. L *sanctus* holy + *-arium* -ary] **1 a :** a consecrated place **:** one devoted to the keeping of sacred things: as (1) **:** the temple at Jerusalem or the most retired part of it, in which was kept the ark of the covenant and into which no person was permitted to enter except the high priest and he only once a year to intercede for the people; *also* **:** the most sacred part of the tabernacle — compare HOLY OF HOLIES (2) **:** the most sacred part of any religious building **:** the part of a Christian church in which the altar is placed or the room in which general worship services are held (3) **:** a house consecrated to the worship of God **:** a church, temple, or other building for worship (4) **:** a place consecrated to some god esp. by the ancient Greeks and Romans that might be open (as in a grove) or enclosed and often built around an enclosure containing a temple, shrines, and a theater **b** *obs* **:** HEAVEN **c :** something resembling a sanctuary **:** a place held to be sacrosanct ⟨I hold a ~ in their hearts — Charles Dickens⟩ ⟨this ~ where scrap gold and silver are melted —*Amer. Guide Series: N. Y. City*⟩ **2 a :** a sacred and inviolable asylum; a place of refuge and protection **b :** immunity from law by entering such a place **c :** the right or privilege of conferring such immunity ⟨the ancient privilege of ~ was transferred to the Christian temples —Edward Gibbon⟩ **3 :** a place of resort for those who seek relief **:** a refuge from turmoil and strife **:** HAVEN ⟨her bedroom, that ~ whither she could take refuge in tears —J.C. Snaith⟩ ⟨his quest is the . . . ~ from the modern world —F.R. Leavis⟩ **4 :** a place of refuge for birds or for game or other animals where predatory animals may be controlled and hunting is not allowed — compare PRESERVE 3

[2]**sanctuary** \"\ *vt* -ED/-ING/-ES **:** SANCTUARIZE

sanctuary ring *or* **sanctuary knocker** *n* **:** a ring on a church door, ensuring sanctuary to any laying hold of it

sanc·tum \'saŋ(k)təm, 'saiŋ-\ *n*, *pl* **sanctums** \-mz\ *also* **sanc·ta** \-tə\ [L, neut. of *sanctus* holy] **1 a :** a sacred place **b :** an object of religious regard **:** something hallowed — often used in pl. **2 :** a study, office, or place of retreat where one is free from intrusion ⟨an editor's ~⟩

sanctum sanc·to·rum \-saŋ(k)'tōrəm, -saiŋ-, -'tȯr-\ *n* [LL, trans. of Gk *to hagion tōn hagiōn*, trans. of Heb *qōdhesh haqqōdhāshīm*] **1 :** the most holy place **:** HOLY OF HOLIES **2 :** SANCTUM 2

sanc·tus \'saŋ(k)təs, 'saiŋ-, 'säŋ-\ *n* -ES *often cap* [ME, fr. ML, first word of the conclusion of the eucharistic preface, fr. LL *Sanctus, sanctus, sanctus* Holy, holy, holy, opening of a hymn sung by the angels in Isa 6:3, trans. of Gk *hagios, hagios, hagios*, trans. of Heb *qādhōsh, qādhōsh, qādhōsh*] **:** the last part of the preface of most Christian liturgies commencing with the words *Sanctus, Sanctus, Sanctus* or *Holy, Holy, Holy* — called also *tersanctus*

sanctus bell *n*, *usu cap S* [ME] **:** a bell rung at the Sanctus in a highly liturgical church service

[1]**sand** \'sand, 'saa(ə)nd\ *n* -s [ME *sond*, *sand*, fr. OE; akin to OHG *sant* sand, ON *sandr*, L *sabulum*, Gk *psammos* sand, *psēphos* pebble, *psēn* to rub, Skt *babhasti* he chews] **1 a** (1) **:** a loose material consisting of small but easily distinguishable grains usu. less than two millimeters in diameter, most commonly of quartz resulting from the disintegration of rocks, and commonly used for making mortar and glass, as an abrasive, or for molds in founding (2) **:** a mass of this material esp. on a beach or a desert **b :** a most unstable material or medium that will make futile all effort or endeavor ⟨be like a foolish man who built his house upon the ~ —Mt 7:26 (RSV)⟩ **2 a :** a tract, region, or deposit of sand **:** BEACH, SHORE — often used in pl. ⟨we shall fight them on the ~s —Sir Winston Churchill⟩ **b :** a sand bank or sand bar — often used in pl. **c :** a grain of sand — often used in pl. **d :** sandy soil — often used in pl. **3 a :** the sand in an hourglass; *also* **:** a grain of it **b** (1) **:** a moment or interval of time (2) **:** the moments of an existence or a life — usu. used in pl. ⟨the ~s of this government run out very rapidly —H.J.Laski⟩ **4 :** a sandstone or unconsolidated sand formation containing oil **:** an oil-producing formation ⟨can produce oil from one ~ and gas from another in the same well —W.F.Cloud⟩ **5 :** firm resolution **:** COURAGE, STAMINA ⟨hasn't got ~ enough to talk back to her⟩ **6 :** a variable color averaging a yellowish gray that is darker and slightly greener and stronger than average natural and redder and deeper than ivory tint **7 :** gritty particles in various body tissues or fluids — compare BRAIN SAND **8 :** tailings esp. from a cyanide mill or stamp mill **9 :** a circular footscraping used as a jazz dance step ⟨doing a slow ~ on the uncarpeted section of the floor —Eugene Brown⟩ **syn** see FORTITUDE

[2]**sand** \"\ *vt* -ED/-ING/-S [ME *sanden*, fr. *sand*, n.] **1 :** to sprinkle or powder with or as if with sand ⟨~*ed* the ink to dry it and sealed the letter⟩ ⟨100 miles of public road will remain to be plowed and ~*ed* —David Anderson⟩ ⟨a clear night ~*ed* with stars —R.H.Newman⟩ **2 :** to cover with sand: as **a :** to fill (as harbors) with sand esp. by the action of currents **b :** to treat (as clay soil) with an overspread layer of sand **3 :** to adulterate with sand for purposes of fraud **4 :** to smooth by grinding or rubbing with an abrasive; *specif* **:** to rub or polish with sandpaper ⟨the stain . . . will have to be ~*ed* out —Erle Stanley Gardner⟩

[1]**san·dal** \'sand°l, 'saan-\ *n* -s [ME *sandalie*, fr. L *sandalium* (pl. *sandalia*), fr. Gk *sandalion* little sandal, dim. of *sandalon* sandal] **1 :** a shoe consisting essentially of a sole fastened to the foot by means of straps or thongs passing over the instep and around the ankle **2 :** a low-cut shoe that is usu. fastened to the foot by means of an ankle strap and has openwork in the upper **3 :** a strap or latchet to hold on a slipper or low shoe by passing across the foot or around the ankle **4 :** a rubber overshoe cut very low either with an entire sole and a strip across the instep or with a sole for the fore part of the foot and a strip back of the heel — compare TOE RUBBER

[2]**sandal** \"\ *vt* **sandaled** *or* **sandalled; sandaled** *or* **sandalled; sandaling** \-d(°)liŋ\ **sandals 1 :** to provide with sandals **:** put sandals on **2 :** to fasten with a sandal

[3]**sandal** \"\ *n* -s [ME, fr. MF, fr. ML *sandalum*, *santalum*, fr. LGk *santalon*, *sandanon*, fr. or akin to Skt *candana* sandalwood, of Dravidian origin; akin to Tamil *cāntu* sandal tree] **:** SANDALWOOD 1a

[4]**sandal** \"\ *n* -s [Ar *ṣandal*, fr. Per *sandal* skiff] **:** a narrow two-masted boat used on the Barbary coast and on the Nile

sandal brick *n* **:** PLACE BRICK

sandaled *or* **sandalled** *adj* **:** wearing sandals ⟨the measured footfalls of his ~ feet —H.W.Longfellow⟩ ⟨went ~ or even barefoot —David Garnett⟩

sandaling *n* -s [fr. gerund of [2]*sandal*] **:** material woven in elastic strips for sandals

sandal tree *also* **sandal** *n* -s [[3]*sandal*] **1 :** SANTOL **2 :** SANDALWOOD 1a

sandalwood \'==,=\ *n* [[3]*sandal* + *wood*] **1 a** (1) **:** a compact close-grained fragrant yellowish wood that is the heartwood of an Indo-Malayan parasitic tree, has insect repelling properties, and is much used for ornamental carving and cabinetwork and esp. for chests and other containers (2) **:** the tree (*Santalum album*) that produces sandalwood **b** (1) **:** any of several other trees of the genus *Santalum* or family Santalaceae (as the Polynesian *S. freycetiarum*, the Hawaiian *S. pyrularium*, or the Australian *Eucarya spicata* and *Exocarpus latifolia*) that have wood similar to or similarly used to the true sandalwood — usu. used with a qualifying term; see SCRUB SANDALWOOD (2) **:** the wood of a tree resembling true sandalwood **2 a :** any of various trees of families other than Santalaceae with usu. fragrant wood that is felt to resemble the true sandalwood: as (1) **:** FALSE SANDALWOOD 1 (2) **:** BASTARD SANDALWOOD 2a(1) (3) **:** PINK MAHOGANY (4) **:** MAIRE a (5) **:** a Russian buckthorn (*Rhamnus dahuriea*) whose wood yields a dye for leather (6) **:** SCENTWOOD **b :** the wood of such a tree; *also* **:** RED SANDALWOOD 1 **3 :** a moderate brown that is lighter and slightly stronger than chestnut brown, yellower, lighter, and less strong than bay, yellower and lighter than auburn, and yellower, less strong, and slightly lighter than toast brown

sandalwood english *n*, *usu cap S&E* **:** an English-based pidgin language used in the Pacific islands

sandalwood family *n* **:** SANTALACEAE

sandalwood oil *n* **1 :** an essential oil obtained from sandalwood: as **a :** a pale yellow somewhat viscous aromatic liquid obtained from the sandalwood (*Santalum album*) usu. from Mysore, India, and used chiefly in perfumes and soaps and esp. formerly in medicine — called also *East Indian sandalwood oil, santal oil* **b :** a similar oil obtained from a sandalwood (*Eucarya spicata*) in Western Australia — called also *Australian sandalwood oil* **2 :** AMYRIS OIL

san·dan \'sandən\ *n* -s [Nepali *sādan*] **:** an East Indian timber tree (*Ougeinia dalbergioides*) of the family Leguminosae, having hard wood, yielding a valuable red gum, and having bark that is used in various native remedies

san·da·rac *also* **san·da·rach** \'sandə,rak\ *n* -s [L *sandaraca*, *sandaracha* red coloring matter, beebread, fr. Gk *sandarakē*, *sandarachē* realgar, red pigment derived from realgar, beebread; prob. akin to Skt *candana* sandalwood — more at SANDAL] **1 :** REALGAR **2 :** SANDARAC TREE 1 **3 a :** a brittle faintly aromatic translucent resin obtained esp. from the African sandarac tree usu. in the form of small pale yellow dusty tears and used chiefly in making varnish and as incense — compare [6]POUNCE 1 **b :** a similar resin from Australian cypress pines

sandarac tree *n* **1 :** a large cypress pine (*Callitris articulata*) of northern Africa that yields a hard durable fragrant wood much used in building (as in the roof of Cordova Cathedral) — see SANDARAC 3, THYINE WOOD **2 :** an Australian cypress pine that yields sandarac

san·da·we \sän'dä(,)we\ *n*, *pl* **sandawe** *or* **sandawes** *usu cap* **1 a :** a Negro African people of Tanganyika **b :** a member of such people **2 :** the language of the Sandawe people related to Khoisan

sand badger *n* **1** *or* **sand bear :** HOG-NOSED BADGER **2 :** a Japanese badger (*Meles anakuma*)

[1]**sandbag** \'=,=\ *n* [[1]*sand* + *bag*] **:** a bag filled with sand: as **a :** one used in a pile to form a wall, a revetment, a field fortification, or as a protection for buildings **b :** one used as a weapon swinging at the end of a staff or beam of a quintain or only partially filled for use as a club **c :** one used as ballast in boats and aircraft **d :** one used as a cover for a crevice to exclude drafts **e :** one used to prop a patient in position (as in bed or on an operating table)

[2]**sandbag** \"\ *vt* **1 :** to bank, stop up, or weight with sandbags ⟨workers were hurriedly building and *sandbagging* new bomb shelters —*N.Y. Times*⟩ **2 a :** to hit or stun with a sandbag **b :** to coerce by crude means ⟨was really too young to come out but . . . had *sandbagged* her family into it —Al Hine⟩ **3 :** to trap (another poker player) by checking a strong hand and then raising if he bets ~ *vi* **:** to check with a strong hand in a game of poker with intent to raise the ante if another player bets

sand·bag·ger \"+ə(r)\ *n* [[2]*sandbag* + *-er*] **1 a :** one who uses a sandbag; *esp* **:** a robber who stuns his victim with a sandbag **b :** one who uses tactics resembling those of a sandbagger ⟨been one of the best . . . ~s, persuading employers to come through with jobs —C.H.Upton⟩ **2 :** a light-draft sailboat with sandbags for ballast **3 :** one that sandbags in poker

sandbank \'=,=\ *n* [[1]*sand* + *bank*] **:** a large deposit of sand in a mound, hillside, bar, or shoal

sandbar \'=,=\ *n* [[1]*sand* + *bar*] **:** a bar or ridge of sand built up to or near to the surface by currents in a river or in coastal waters

sandbar willow *n* **:** any of various willows that flourish along streams or on alluvial land: as **a :** a much-branched chiefly eastern No. American shrubby willow (*Salix interior*) with lanceolate leaves that are silky when young **b :** a shrubby chiefly western No. American willow (*Salix exigua*) having leaves permanently silky but otherwise resembling the eastern sandbar willow

sand bass *n* **1 a :** a California sea bass (*Paralabrax nebulifer*) that is greenish above and silvery below **b :** KELP BASS **2 a :** GREEN SUNFISH **b :** WHITE BASS 1

sand bath *n* [[1]*sand* + *bath*] **1 :** a bath of sand in which laboratory vessels to be heated are partly immersed **2 :** a shallow or deep pan usu. of iron for holding the sand

sandbeach grape \'=,=-\ *n* [*sandbeach* fr. [1]*sand* + *beach*] **:** SAND GRAPE

sand bellows *n pl but sing in constr* **:** a blower for sanding surfaces

sand belt *n* **:** a belt surfaced with an abrasive usu. for grinding or polishing

sand-belt machine *n* **:** BELT SANDER

sand·berg bluegrass \'san(d),bərg-\ *n*, *usu cap S* [after J. H. *Sandberg*, 19th cent. Am. botanist] **:** a densely tufted bluegrass (*Poa secunda*) of No. America esp. of the Northwestern U. S. having slender culms, usu. folded leaf blades, and somewhat appressed branches

sand binder *n* **:** a grass or other plant that grows in sand which it holds in place by its rootstocks and roots

sand bird *n* **:** a shore bird

sand blackberry *n* **:** a stiff thorny blackberry (*Rubus cuneifolius*) of the eastern U. S. having leaves white-tomentose beneath and sweet fruit

[1]**sandblast** \'=,=\ *n* [[1]*sand* + *blast*] **1 a :** a stream of sand forcibly projected by air or steam usu. for engraving, cutting, or cleaning glass, stone, or other hard materials, for cleaning and sharpening files, or for removing scale from metals **b :** the apparatus used to apply it **2 :** a gust of wind carrying sand **3 :** an irresistible destructive action suggestive of a blast of sand ⟨against ~ of time and spoliation of man —Robert Bridges †1930⟩

[2]**sandblast** \"\ *vt* **:** to engrave, cut, or clean with a high-velocity stream of sand

sand·blast·er \"+ə(r)\ *n* [[1]*sandblast* + *-er*] **:** one that sandblasts: as **a :** one that cleans objects of metal or similar material with an abrasive blast **b :** one that cleans stone, brick, or metal structures with a spray of sand **c :** one that guided by a stencil cuts lettering and designs on stone monuments or buildings with a blast of sand or shot — called also *blastman* **d :** one that frosts panes of glass by sandblasting one side **e :** one that sandblasts designs onto glass articles (as vases)

sand-blight *n*, *Austral* **:** BLIGHT 5

sand-blind \'=,=\ *adj* [ME, prob. by folk etymology fr. (assumed) *samblind*, fr. OE *sam-* half + *blind* — more at SAM-, BLIND] **:** having poor eyesight **:** PURBLIND ⟨are they lazy or *sand-blind* from their own investigations —*Saturday Rev.*⟩ — compare GRAVEL-BLIND

sand block *n* **:** a block to which sandpaper is attached

sandblow \'=,=\ *n* [[1]*sand* + *blow*] **:** an area of coarse sandy soil denuded of vegetation by wind action

sand blower *n* **:** SAND BELLOWS

sand bluestem *n* **:** a tall American grass (*Andropogon hallii*) used for forage and in soil conservation having creeping rhizomes and racemes of flowers that are conspicuously villous with grayish to pale golden hairs

sand boa *n* **:** any of various small burrowing boas (genera *Eryx* or *Gongylophis*) of the sandy regions of Africa and Asia having rough keeled scales and a very blunt tail

sandboard \'=,=\ *n* [[1]*sand* + *board*] **:** the board that runs over and parallel with the axle of a wagon with the ends resting upon the hounds

sand bobber *n* **:** one who smooths and polishes silverware or jewelry by means of pumice and oil and a leather buffing wheel

sand boil *n* **:** a bubbling spring sometimes several feet in diameter that bursts through the ground at the back of a river levee and is caused by the water in the river at flood stages being forced under the levee through a pervious stratum of sand or silt

sand borer *n* **1 :** a common small Australian anomuran crustacean (*Upogebia simsoni*) that burrows in sandy beaches **2 :** any of several whitings (genus *Sillago*) of the western Pacific ocean

sandbox \'=,=\ *n* [[1]*sand* + *box*] **1 :** a box or other receptacle containing loose sand: as **a :** a shaker for sprinkling sand upon wet ink **b :** SAND DOME **c :** a box that is large enough to sit in and contains sand for children to play in **2 :** SAND MOLD **3 a :** SANDBOX TREE **b :** its explosive pod often filled with shot and used as a paperweight

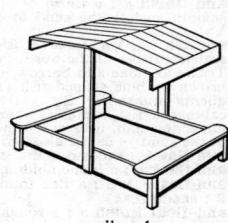

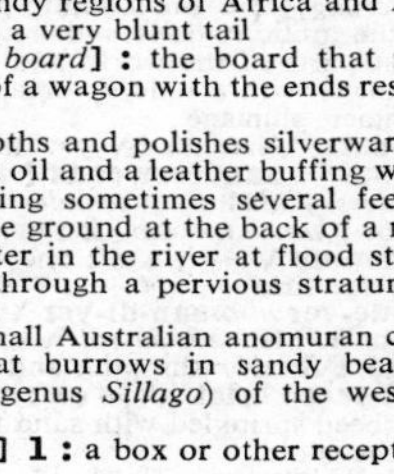
sandbox 1c

sandbox tree *n* **:** a tropical American tree (*Hura crepitans*) having a depressed many-celled woody capsule which when completely dry bursts with a loud report and scatters the seeds — compare YELLOW SANDBOX

sandboy \'=,=\ *n* [[1]*sand* + *boy*] **1 :** a peddler of sand at a seashore resort — used chiefly in the phrase *happy as a sandboy* **2 :** any of various hopping insects (as a sand flea) found on sandy beaches **3 a :** one who sprinkles sand on bricks to prevent their sticking together in the kiln **b :** an operator of a machine for separating floor tiles from the sand that held them in the saggers

sand brier *n* **:** HORSE NETTLE

sand bug *n* **:** a common bait bug (*Emerita talpoida*)

sandbur *also* **sandburr** \'=,=\ *n* [[1]*sand* + *bur*, *burr*] **:** any of several weeds growing in waste places and having burry fruit: as **a :** BUFFALO BUR **b :** an annual bristly herb (*Franseria acanthicarpa*) of western No. America related to the cocklebur **c** *also* **sandbur grass :** BUR GRASS

sand-burned \'=,=\ *adj* **:** having a hard skin due to the silica of sand combining with the surface of metal when metal is poured into a mold at too high a temperature — used of a casting

S and C *abbr* **1** shipper and carrier **2** sized and calendered

sand-calcite \'=,=\ *n* **:** a calcite crystal containing a large proportion of sand grains as inclusions

[1]**sand-cast** \'=,=\ *adj* **:** cast in a mold made of sand

[2]**sand-cast** \"\ *vt* **:** to make (a casting) by pouring metal in a sand mold (as in ordinary founding)

sand casting *n* **:** a casting made in a mold of sand

sand cat *n* **:** a desert-dwelling wildcat

sand cay *n* **:** a small sandy island that is not elongate and is parallel with the shore

sand cherry *n* **:** any of several usu. small straggling No. American cherries that grow esp. on dry sandy land: as **a :** a low-growing cherry (*Prunus pumila*) of the northern U. S. and Canada with minute scarcely edible shiny purplish black fruit **b :** a small strongly rooted shrub (*P. cuneata* or *P. susquehanae*) of eastern No. America **c :** WESTERN SAND CHERRY

sand clam *n* **:** SOFT-SHELL CLAM

sand clock *n* **:** SANDGLASS

sand cock *n*, *Brit* **:** REDSHANK

sand colic *also* **sand disease** *n* **:** distention with resulting catarrh of the stomach and small intestines in horses and cattle caused by the ingestion of sand with feed and water

sand collar *n* **:** the mass of eggs embedded in sand and jellylike matter that is produced by a moon shell and is shaped like a thin collar or bottomless saucer open at one side

sand column *n* **:** DUST DEVIL

sand cone *n* **1 :** a low pinnacle of ice on a glacier protected from melting by a veneer of sand **2 :** a cone-shaped mass of sandy debris deposited esp. in an alluvial cone

sand crab *n* **1 a** (1) : LADY CRAB 1 (2) : an Australian swimming crab (*Ovalipes bipustulatus*) **b** : a crab of *Ocypode* or a related genus **2** : BAIT BUG
sand crack *n* : a fissure or lesion in the hoof wall of a horse often causing lameness — see QUARTER CRACK, TOE CRACK
sand crater *n* : an opening in the earth from which sand and water are erupted during an earthquake
sand cricket *n* : any of several large clumsy terrestrial grasshoppers of the genus *Stenopelmatus* (family Stenopelmatidae) that resemble crickets and are found in sandy plains of the western U. S.
sand crystal *n* : a large calcite crystal found in sandstone and loaded with inclusions of detrital sand
sandculture \ˈ=,==\ *n* [¹*sand* + *culture*] : hydroponics in which the roots of plants are established in sand
sand cusk *n* : CUSK EEL
sand dab *n* : any of several flatfishes: as **a** : RUSTY DAB **b** : a fish of the genus *Citharichthys* (family Bothidae) of the Pacific coast of No. America including several small but excellent food fishes
sand darter *n* : DARTER; *esp* : a small translucent fish (*Ammocrypta beanii*) of the Gulf states
sand dollar *n* **1** : any of numerous flat circular sea urchins of the order Exocycloida which live on sandy bottoms (as *Echinarachnius parma* of the American coast) **2** : STAR CACTUS
sand dome *n* : the sandbox of a locomotive whose contents are used for sanding the rails to give added friction to the wheels
sand drift *n* : an accumulation of sand that drifts down wind in the lee of some obstruction and is usu. smaller than a dune
sand dropseed *n* : an erect smooth grass (*Sporobolus cryptandrus*) found in sandy places in eastern No. America
sand drown *n* [so called fr. its occurrence on sandy soils subject to leaching in heavy rainfall areas] : a magnesium deficiency disease of tobacco characterized by chlorosis
sand dune *n* **1** : DUNE 1 **2** : DRAB 2a
san·de \ˈsän(,)dā\ *n* -s *usu cap* [Mende *sāneˈ*] : a Liberia and Sierra Leone secret custom by which young girls are secluded in a separate camp for a variable period of months and trained in the duties and responsibilities of adult society
sanded *adj* [fr. past part. of ²*sand*] **1** *obs* : having a sand color **2 a** : formed or composed of sand : SANDY ⟨the ~ plains —George Farwell⟩ **b** : sprinkled with sand **3** : rolled in granulated sugar ⟨~ gumdrops⟩
sanded plaster *n* : plaster to which properly graded sand is added at the mill
sand eel *n* **1** : SAND LAUNCE **2** : a slender soft-finned fish (*Gonorhynchus gonorhynchus* or *G. grayi*) of the Indo-Pacific having small spiny scales, a single barbel in the produced snout, and the eyes beneath the skin
san·dek \ˈsän,dek\ *or* **san·dik** \-dēk\ *n* -s [Yiddish *sandik*, fr. LHeb *sandiqōs*, *sindiqās*, prob. modif. of LGk *synteknos* godfather, fr. Gk, foster brother, fr. *synteknoun* to breed, bring up children together, fr. *syn-* + *teknon* child — more at THANE] : a person who holds the Jewish infant on his knees during the circumcision ceremony
san·de·ma·ni·an \,sandəˈmānēən\ *n* -s *usu cap* [Robert *Sandeman* †1771 Scot. religious leader + E *-an*] : GLASSITE
sand·er \ˈsandə(r), ˈsaan-\ *n* -s [²*sand* + *-er*] : one that sands: as **a** : a device on a locomotive or electric car operated by a steam or air blast for sanding the rails to give added friction to the driving wheels **b** : SAND BELLOWS **c** : a sand spreader for asphalted or icy roads **d** : SANDING MACHINE **e** : one that by hand or by machine sands surfaces (as of wood, metal, plastic) to smooth, clean, or roughen them in preparation for finishing
sand·er·ling \ˈsandə(r)liŋ\ *n* -s [¹*sand* + *-erling* (as in *underling*)] : a small sandpiper (*Crocethia alba*) that breeds in the arctic regions and migrates south along the coasts of most parts of the world and that has largely gray and white plumage with a reddish breast as a distinction of the adult's summer plumage
san·ders \ˈsandə(r)z\ *or* **sanderswood** \ˈ==,=\ *n*, *pl* **sanderses** *or* **sanderswoods** [*sanders* alter. of earlier *saunders*; *sanderswood* alter. of *saunderswood* — more at SAUNDERSWOOD] **1** *obs* : SANDALWOOD **2** : RED SANDALWOOD 1a
sander-up \ˈ==ˈ=\ *n* -s : one who beds greenware in sand and clay for firing
san·de·ver *also* **san·di·ver** \ˈsandəvə(r)\ *n* -s [ME *saundiver*, prob. fr. MF *sain de voirre* grease of glass] : GLASS GALL
S and FA *abbr* shipping and forwarding agent
sand-faced brick \ˈ=,=-\ *n* : a face brick shaped in a mold that has been sprinkled with sand to prevent the clay from sticking to the mold
sand finish *n* : a finish of plastering made by rubbing to a smooth surface the sand or mortar coat — **sand-finished** \ˈ=ˈ==\ *adj*
sandfish \ˈ=,=\ *n* [¹*sand* + *fish*] **1** : either of two small silvery scaleless fishes of the north Pacific that constitute the family Trichodontidae and burrow in the sand **2** : a small grayish brown or blue striped fish (*Diplectrum formosum*) that frequents sand shores **3** : SAND EEL 2 **4** : an elongated cylindrical marine fish (genus *Gonorhynchus*) that has a short barbel under the chin, lives over sandy bottoms, and burrows freely in the sand — called also *beaked salmon*
sand flag *n* : sandstone that splits up into flagstones
sand flask *n* : a frame holding a sand mold
sand flea *n* **1 a** : a flea found in sandy places **b** : CHIGOE **2** : BEACH FLEA
sand-float finish *n* : a rough sand finish made in plastering with a wooden float
sand flotation *n* : CHANCE PROCESS
sand flounder *n* : any of various flounders frequenting sandy bottom : SAND FLUKE; *esp* : WINDOWPANE
sand fluke *n* : a flounder frequenting a sandy bottom: as **a** : SMEAR DAB **b** : a small flounder (*Hippoglossoides platessoides*) common on both coasts of the north Atlantic
sand fly *n* : any of various small biting two-winged flies of the families Psychodidae, Simuliidae, and Ceratopogonidae; *esp* : a fly of the genus *Phlebotomus*
sand-fly bush *n* : an Australian tree (*Zieria smithii*) of the family Rutaceae that has aromatic foliage and small white flowers in loose cymes and bark which is used for tanning and dyeing
sand-fly fever *n* : PHLEBOTOMUS FEVER
sand food *n* : a low root-parasitic brownish leguminous herb (*Ammobroma sonorae*) of the Colorado desert having flowers in a saucer-shaped head, all parts but the flower head buried in the sand, and edible stems and tubers resembling sweet potatoes
sand fox *n* : any of several small African foxes; *esp* : a tawny desert-dwelling No. African fox (*Vulpes rüppelli* syn. *V. pallida*)
sand gall *n* : SAND PIPE
sandglass \ˈ=,=\ *n* [¹*sand* + *glass*] : an instrument for measuring time by the running of sand that is similar to an hourglass ⟨three-minute ~*es* . . . to help time our breakfast eggs —A.L. Kroeber⟩
sandgoby \ˈ=,=\ *n* [¹*sand* + *goby*] : any of various sand-dwelling gobies; *esp* : a common European fish (*Gobius minutus*) with variable coloration that makes it almost invisible in the sandy tide pools which it frequents
sand grape *n* : a shrubby wild grape (*Vitis rupestris*) of the southeastern U. S. having sweet black fruit with or without bloom
sand grass *n* : a grass growing in sand: as **a** : a tufted grass (*Triplasis purpurea*) with stiff awl-shaped leaves on the Atlantic coast of the U. S. **b** : a perennial grass (*Calamovilfa longifolia*) **c** : a salt grass (*Distichlis spicata*)
sandgrouse \ˈ=,=\ *n* [¹*sand* + *grouse*] : any of numerous birds constituting the family Pteroclididae, inhabiting arid parts of southern Europe, Asia, and Africa, resembling the related pigeons in structure but having precocial young that are downy and ready to run when hatched, and being strong fliers with long pointed wings and tail — see PAINTED SANDGROUSE, PALLAS'S SANDGROUSE, PIN-TAILED SANDGROUSE
S and H *abbr* Sundays and holidays
san·dhi \ˈsandē, ˈsaan-, ˈsän-, -di *sometimes* ˈsən-\ *n* -s [Skt *saṁdhi*, lit., placing together, fr. *sam* together + *dadhāti* he places — more at SANSKRIT, DO] : modification of the sound of a morpheme (as a word or affix) conditioned by the context in which it is uttered ⟨pronunciation of *the* as \thə\ in *the cow* and as \thē\ in *the old cow*, pronunciation of *-ed* as \d\ in *glazed* and as \t\ in *paced*, occurrence of *a* in *a cow* and of *an* in *an old cow*, and occurrence of *'ll* in *he'll go* and of *will* in *he will if he can* are examples of ~⟩ — used orig. of Sanskrit but now of any language
sand hill *n* [ME *sond hylle*, fr. OE *sondhyll*, fr. *sond* sand + *hyll* hill — more at SAND, HILL] **1** : a natural elevation or ridge of sand : DUNE **2 sandhills** *pl* : a region of sand hills
sandhill \ˈ=,=\ *adj* [*sand hill*] : of or relating to a region of sand hills ⟨certain types of pines will thrive even in the ~ areas —*Amer. Guide Series: Nebr.*⟩
sandhill crane *n* **1** : a rare crane (*Grus canadensis*) of eastern and central No. America that is chiefly bluish gray overcast with ocherous **2** : LITTLE BROWN CRANE
sand·hill·er \"+ə(r)\ *n* -s : one that lives in a sandhill region
sandhill rosemary *n* : a small aromatic heathlike evergreen shrub (*Ceratiola ericoides*) of the family Empetraceae with reddish whorled axillary flowers
sandhog \ˈ=,=\ *n* [¹*sand* + *hog*] : a laborer who works under compressed air esp. in the driving of tunnels by the pneumatic caisson method
sand hole *n* **1** : a small hole in a casting **2** : a water hole in sand
sand hopper *n* : BEACH FLEA
¹**san·dia** \sänˈdēə\ *n* -s [Sp *sandía*, fr. Ar (*baṭṭīha*) *sindīya* melon of Sind, fr. *baṭṭīha* melon + *sindīya* of Sind, fr. *Sind*, region in the northwestern part of the Indian subcontinent, fr. Hindi; akin to Skt *sindhu* river — more at INDIA] : WATERMELON
²**san·dia** \sanˈdēə, sän-\ *or* **san·di·as** \-əz\ *n*, *pl* **sandia** or **sandias** *usu cap* [fr. *Sandia*, pueblo in central New Mexico] **1** : a Tanoan people occupying a pueblo in New Mexico **2** : a member of the Sandia people
³**sandia** \"\ *adj*, *usu cap* [fr. *Sandia* mountains, east of the Rio Grande, New Mexico, where remains of this culture were found] : of or belonging to a pre-Folsom hunting culture in New Mexico characterized by leaf-shaped spear points longer, thicker, and heavier than Folsom points and having a side shoulder at the base as an aid in hafting
sandia man *n*, *usu cap S* : one of a western No. American prehistoric people known only from hearths, flint projectile points, and scrapers and thought to be antecedent to Folsom man
san di·e·gan \,sandēˈāgən\ *n* -s *cap S&D* [*San Diego*, Calif. + E *-an*] : a native or resident of San Diego, California
san di·e·go \ˈ==ˈā(,)gō\ *adj*, *usu cap S&D* [fr. *San Diego*, city in southwestern California] : of or from the city of San Diego, Calif. ⟨the *San Diego* fishing fleet⟩ : of the kind or style prevalent in San Diego
sandier *comparative of* SANDY
sandies *pl of* SANDY
sandiest *superlative of* SANDY
sandik *var of* SANDEK
sand-in \ˈ=ˈ=\ *vt* [²*sand*] : to use (abrasive paper) to curve the contact face of a dynamo brush to conform to the curvature of the commutator
sand·i·ness \ˈsandēnəs, ˈsaand-, -din-\ *n* -ES [¹*sandy* + *-ness*] : the quality or state of being sandy
sanding *n* -s [fr. gerund of ²*sand*] **1** : a sprinkling, covering, or mixing with sand **2** : a smoothing or polishing esp. with sandpaper **3** : a fraudulent practice of feeding poultry with a paste of coarse sand to increase the apparent live weight
sanding disk *or* **sanding drum** *n* : a disk or drum with an attached abrasive for power tool application in sanding
sanding machine *n* : a machine provided with a moving surface coated with abrasive material
sandiver *var of* SANDEVER
san·dix *also* **san·dyx** \ˈsandiks\ *n* -ES [L *sandix*, *sandyx* vermilion, fr. Gk *sandyx*; akin to Skt *sindūra* vermilion] : any of various red pigments; *esp* : ORANGE MINERAL
¹**sand jack** *n* : a device consisting essentially of a sandbox and a series of plungers for gradually lowering into position a heavy weight (as a bridge section) supported by the plungers by running out the sand below
²**sand jack** *n* : BLUEJACK
sand jet *n* : SANDBLAST 1a
sandkey \ˈ=,=\ *n* [¹*sand* + *key*] : SAND CAY
sand·krui·per \ˈsan(d),krōipə(r)\ *n* -s [part trans. of Afrik *zand kruiper*, lit., sand creeper, fr. *zand* sand + *kruiper* creeper, fr. D, fr. *kruipen* to creep, fr. MD *crupen*; akin to ON *krjūpa* to creep — more at CREEP] : any of several small So. African viviparous rays (genus *Rhinobatus*) of sandy shallow seas that are considered excellent food fishes
sandlapper \ˈ=,==\ *n* [¹*sand* + *lapper*] : one living in a lowland area esp. in the southeastern U.S.
sand lark *n* **1** : any of numerous Asiatic larks (genus *Alaudula*) having short toes **2** *Brit* : a small sandpiper or plover (as a ring plover, the sanderling, and the common European sandpiper) **3** : an Australian plover (*Charadrius ruficapillus*)
sand launce *or* **sand lance** *n* : any of several small elongate marine teleost fishes of the genus *Ammodytes* (family Ammodytidae) that do not exceed six or eight inches in length, associate in large schools, and remain buried in sandy beaches at ebb tide
sand leaf *n* : a small leaf near the base of the tobacco stalk often bearing grains of sand
sand leek *n* : ROCAMBOLE
sand lily *n* : a spring herb (*Leucocrinum montanum*) native to western No. America and used as an ornamental with narrow linear leaves and fragrant salver-shaped flowers
sand-lime \ˈ=ˈ=\ *adj* : made from mixed sand and lime
sand-lime brick *n* : brick made of sand and lime that is pressed into molds and steamed
sand line *n* : the rope attached to the bailer in well drilling
sand·ling \ˈsan(d)liŋ\ *n* -s [¹*sand* + *-ling*] : a small flounder : DAB
sand lizard *n* **1** : a common and widely distributed European lizard (*Lacerta agilis*) **2** : RACE RUNNER **3** : any of several iguanid lizards (as of the genera *Callisaurus*, *Holbrookia*, or *Uta*) that are common in arid sandy regions
sand lob *n* : LUGWORM
¹**sandlot** \ˈ=,=\ *adj* [¹*sand* + *lot*] **1** : of or relating to a lot or piece of sandy ground esp. as the scene of unorganized sports for boys from city streets **2** [so called fr. a sandlot laid out for building on the west side of San Francisco where adherents of the movement held meetings] : of, relating to, or characteristic of a 19th century workingmen's movement in California opposed esp. to Chinese immigration ⟨people of the ~ type of orators . . . favor the treatment of the Chinese proposed by the legislation —T.J.Geary⟩
²**sandlot** \"\ *n* : a vacant lot or piece of ground esp. when used as the scene of unorganized sports for boys from city streets
sand·lot·ter \"+ə(r)\ *n* : one who plays on a sandlot : one whose training began in the sandlots or something resembling the sandlots
sand lovegrass *n* : a fine-stemmed bunch grass (*Eragrostis trichodes*) found native on sandy soils chiefly in the southern Great Plains area of No. America and used as a forage grass
sandman \ˈ=,=\ *n*, *pl* **sandmen 1** : the genie of folklore who makes children sleepy supposedly by sprinkling sand in their eyes **2** : a worker who screens, mixes, or loads sand : one who sands surfaces with an abrasive
sand martin *n*, *Brit* : BANK SWALLOW
sand mason *n* : a terebellid worm (*Lanice conchilega*) that builds a dwelling tube of grains of sand
sand mat *n* : any of several flat spreading plants of the genus *Euphorbia* that grow in desert areas of the U.S.
sand·mey·er reaction \ˈsan(d),mī(ə)r-\ *n*, *usu cap S* [after Traugott *Sandmeyer* †1922 Swiss chemist] : a reaction for preparing aromatic halides or cyanides from a salt with a cuprous halide or cyanide as catalyst ⟨*ortho*-bromo-toluene can be made from *ortho*-toluene-diazonium bromide by the *Sandmeyer reaction*⟩
sandmite \ˈ=,=\ *n* [¹*sand* + *mite*] : a mite of the genus *Halotydeus*; *esp* : a mite (*H. destructor*) that is a serious pest of vegetable crops in Australia and southern Africa
sand mold *n* : a mold made of sand and used in sand-casting
sand-molding \ˈ=,==\ *n* : the molding of brick in molds that have been sanded on the inside to prevent sticking in soft-mud process brickmaking — compare SLOP-MOLDING
sand mole *n* : MOLE RAT c
sand monitor *n* : a large Egyptian lizard (*Varanus griseus*) that inhabits dry localities
sand mullet *n*, *Austral* : either of two mullets: **a** : a sea mullet (*Mugil dobula*) **b** : a small brownish green pink flushed mullet (*Myxus elongatus*) common in warm shallow waters
sand myrtle *n* : a highly variable low-branching evergreen shrub (*Leiophyllum buxifolium*) of the family Ericaceae that has coriaceous leaves and small pink or white flowers in terminal clusters and occurs in upland regions of the southeastern U.S.
sand·nat·ter \ˈsan(d),nad·ə(r)\ *n* -s [G, fr. *sand* (fr. OHG *sant* sand) + *natter* adder, fr. OHG *nātara* — more at SAND, ADDER] **1** : SAND BOA **2** : SAND VIPER c
sand oat *n* : WILD OAT 1a
sand painting *n* : a Navaho and Pueblo Indian ceremonial design made of various colored sands, powdered minerals, and vegetable materials upon a flat surface of sand or buckskin and frequently used in healing rites and religious ceremonies — called also *dry painting*
¹**sand·pa·per** \ˈsan(d),pāpə(r), ˈsaan-\ *n* [¹*sand* + *paper*] : paper covered on one side with sand or other abrasive material glued fast and used for smoothing and polishing — compare GARNET PAPER
²**sandpaper** \"\ *vt* **sandpapered; sandpapered; sandpapering** \-āp(ə)riŋ\ **sandpapers** : to rub with or as if with sandpaper ⟨boards are planed and ~*ed* until perfectly smooth —Madge Reese⟩ ⟨the sharp edges of his temper had been ~*ed* down by success —Malcolm Cowley⟩
sand·pa·per·er \-āp(ə)rə(r)\ *n* : one that sandpapers
sandpaper fig *n* : any of several Australian figs with harsh rough leaves; *esp* : PURPLE FIG
sandpaper tree *n* : any of several trees having very rough leaves: as **a** : CHAPARRO 3 **b** : a tree (*Dillenia scabrella*) of Asia
sand·pa·pery \-rē\ *adj* [¹*sandpaper* + *-y*] : resembling the sound of sandpaper on wood : GRATING, HARSH ⟨~ sound of the maracas —Ludwig Bemelmans⟩ ⟨tried to make his ~ voice sound nonchalant —H.N.Hempel⟩
sand partridge *n* : any of several small partridges of the genus *Ammoperdix* related to the red-legged partridge, inhabiting southern Asia and northeastern Africa, and frequenting sandy wastes with which its colors harmonize
sand pea *n* : BEACH PEA
sand pear *n* **1** : SNOW PEAR **2 a** : a Chinese pear (*Pyrus pyrifolia*) with large white flowers and in some strains edible fruit that is cultivated as an ornamental, is sometimes used as a stock for grafting horticultural pears, and has been hybridized with the common pear esp. to impart disease resistance **b** : any of various cultivated pears that contain numerous stone cells in the fruit and are usu. hybrids between the common horticultural pears and the Chinese sand pear
sandpeep \ˈ=,=\ *n* [¹*sand* + *peep* (sandpiper)] : a very small sandpiper
sand pig *n* : HOG-NOSED BADGER
sand pigeon *n* : SANDGROUSE
sand pike *n* : SAUGER
sand pile *n* : a filling of sand that is rammed hard in a deep round hole, is made by driving and withdrawing a wooden pile, and is sometimes used as a means of preparing foundations in soft soil
sandpile \ˈ=,=\ *n* [¹*sand* + *pile*] : a pile of sand; *esp* : sand for children to play in ⟨~ and building blocks —*New Republic*⟩
sand pillar *n* : DUST DEVIL
sand pine *n* **1** : a pine (*Pinus clausa*) common along the coast of Florida and Alabama with smooth bark, leaves in pairs, and spiny-tipped cones **2** : LODGEPOLE PINE a
sand pink *n* : a caespitose herb (*Dianthus armerius*) native to Europe and Asia, having bluish green leaves in spreading mats and flowers with deeply fringed corolla lobes, and widely cultivated as an ornamental
sand pipe *n* **1** : a pipe containing sand or serving as a channel for sand (as on a locomotive) **2** : a tubular cavity from a few inches to many feet in depth formed by solution esp. in calcareous rocks and often filled with gravel and sand
sandpiper \ˈ=,==\ *n* [¹*sand* + *piper*] **1** : any of numerous small limicoline birds (as the common European sandpiper *Actitis hypoleucos* and the spotted sandpiper of America) that are distinguished from the related plovers chiefly by the bill which is moderately long and often soft and sensitive at the tip but not of the extreme length characteristic of the typical snipe, that have moderately long legs and necks and plumage usu. streaked with brown, gray, or blackish above but more or less extensively white below, and that frequent sandy and muddy shores breeding mostly in the arctic regions but migrating extensively into temperate latitudes — see BAIRD'S SANDPIPER, LEAST SANDPIPER, SEMIPALMATED SANDPIPER, WHITE-RUMPED SANDPIPER **2** : SAND PRIDE
sandpit \ˈ=,=\ *n* [ME *sond pitt*, fr. *sond* sand + *pitt* pit — more at SAND, PIT] : a pit dug in sandy soil esp. as a place for procuring sand
sand plain *n* : an outwash plain usu. of rather small extent composed chiefly of sand deposited by meltwater from a glacier
sand plover *n* : RING PLOVER
sand plum *n* : a western American variety (*Prunus angustifolia watsonii*) of the Chickasaw plum with thick-skinned fruit
sand pocket mouse *n* : a common light-colored pocket mouse (*Perognathus penicillatus pricei*) of the Arizona desert
sand prey *n* : SAND PRIDE
sand pride *n* : a small European freshwater lamprey (*Petromyzon planeri*)
sand pump *n* : a pump for removing wet sand, mud, or silt: as **a** : a centrifugal pump used on a floating dredging machine **b** : a simple plunger pump with a nonreturn valve at the bottom usu. used for cleaning out a borehole
san·dra \ˈsandrə\ *n* -s [NL (specific epithet of the pike perch *Lucioperca sandra*), fr. G *zander*] : ZANDER
sandragon *var of* SANGDRAGON
sand rat *n* : any of various rodents native to sandy or desert areas: as **a** : POCKET GOPHER **b** : either of two small nearly naked African mole rats (genus *Heterocephalus*) **c** : any of several African cricetid rodents (genus *Psammomys*) **d** : a southern European rodent (*Meriones longifrons*) related to the typical gerbils
sand reed *n* **1** : BEACH GRASS **2** : SAND SEDGE
sand reef *n* : a low ridge of sand that borders the shore, is built up by waves and currents, and in many places encloses a lagoon
sand reel *n* : a windlass to lower and raise the bailer in a well-boring rig
sandrock \ˈ=,=\ *n* [¹*sand* + *rock*] : SANDSTONE 1
sand rocket *n* : a European yellow flowered annual weed (*Diplotaxis muralis*) adventive in No. America
sand roll *n* **1** : a roll cast in a sand mold **2** : a take-up roll that guides newly-woven cloth
sand roller *n* : TROUT-PERCH
sand runner *n* **1** : a small plover : SANDPIPER **2** : any of certain freshwater mussels that dig trails at the surface of the sand; *esp* : YELLOWBACK
sands *pl of* SAND, *pres 3d sing of* SAND
sand sage *n* : a sage (*Artemisia filifolia*) occurring as a troublesome weed on the rangelands of the U.S. and having the leaves 3-parted into filiform segments
sandsailer \ˈ=,==\ *n* [¹*sand* + *sailer*] : a 3-wheeled wind-driven craft that carries two persons, is equipped with a single sail, steered with a tiller over the rear wheel, and is used esp. on firmly packed beach sand — **sandsailing** \ˈ=,==\ *n*
sand saucer *n* : SAND COLLAR
S and SC *abbr* sized and supercalendered
sand screw *n* : an amphipod crustacean (*Lepidactylis arenarius*) which burrows in the sandy seabeaches of Europe and America
sand sedge *n* : a European maritime sedge (*Carex arenaria*) that is naturalized along the Atlantic coast of the U.S. and has a rootstock with the properties of sarsaparilla
sand shadow *n* : SAND DRIFT
sand shark *n* : any of numerous elasmobranch fishes native to sandy bottoms and usu. to shallow seas: as **a** : a shark

of the genus *Carcharias* — see NURSE SHARK 3 **b :** a fish of the family Rhinobatidae; *esp* **:** GUITARFISH
sand shell *n* **:** SAND RUNNER 2
sand shilling *n, Austral* **:** SAND DOLLAR
sandshoe \ˈ=,=\ *n* [¹*sand* + *shoe*] **1 :** a shoe designed for wear in sandy ground **2** *Brit* **:** CANVAS SHOE
sand skink *n* **:** any of several Old World lizards of the family Scincidae
sand skipper *n* **:** BEACH FLEA
sand smelt *n* **:** SILVERSIDES 1
sand snake *n* **1 :** SAND BOA **2 :** any snake of an Old World boigid genus (*Psammophis*) with large eyes and variable color pattern common in sandy areas of northern Africa and Asia **3 :** any of a genus (*Chilomeniscus*) of small No. American colubrid burrowing snakes
sand snipe *n* **:** SANDPIPER
sandsoap \ˈ=,=\ *n* [¹*sand* + *soap*] **:** a gritty soap for all-purpose cleaning
sand sole *n* **:** a common brownish speckled flatfish (*Psettichthys melanostichus*) of the Pacific coast of No. America
sandspit \ˈ=,=\ *n* [¹*sand* + *spit*] **:** ¹SPIT 2
sand spout *n* **:** DUST DEVIL
sandspur \ˈ=,=\ *n* [¹*sand* + *spur*] **:** BUR GRASS
sand spurry *or* **sand spurrey** *n* **:** any weed of the genus *Spergularia; esp* **:** a Eurasian prostrate herb (*S. rubra*) with tiny pink flowers that is commonly naturalized in eastern No. America
sand squeteague *n* **:** a weakfish (*Cynoscion arenarius*) of the Gulf of Mexico
sand star *n* **:** BRITTLE STAR
sandstay \ˈ=,=\ *n* [¹*sand* + *stay*] **:** SAND BINDER; *specif* **:** an Australian shrub or small tree (*Leptospermum laevigatum*) that is very effective as a sand binder
sandstone \ˈ=,=\ *n* [¹*sand* + *stone*] **1 :** a sedimentary rock made up of sand that usu. consists of quartz more or less firmly united by some cement (as silica, iron oxide, or calcium carbonate) and that varies in color being commonly red, yellow, brown, gray, or white — see GRIT 2, OLD RED SANDSTONE **2 :** a light grayish brown to reddish brown that is lighter and slightly stronger than wood rose and stronger and slightly darker than misty morn — called also *cream beige, tawny birch*
sandstorm \ˈ=,=\ *n* [¹*sand* + *storm*] **:** a storm of wind that drives clouds of sand along a desert
sand-struck brick \ˈ=,=-\ *n* **:** brick made by the sand-molding method of the soft-mud process — compare WATER-STRUCK BRICK
sand sturgeon *n* **:** SHOVELNOSE STURGEON
sand sucker *n* **1 :** CORBINA 1 **2 :** SAND PUMP a
sand swallow *n* **:** BANK SWALLOW
S and T *abbr* supply and transport
sand table *n* **1 a :** a usu. reinforced table with raised edges holding sand for children to mold **b :** a table bearing a relief model of a section of terrain built to scale of hardened sand that usu. reproduces the contours, streams, trees, and buildings for the study of military tactics **2 :** an inclined table used for concentrating ores that typically has the separating surface in motion and a continuous feed and discharge and that uses the motion to separate the ores into layers with the heavy material being shifted for further treatment
sand trap *n* **1 :** a device for separating sand from water **2 :** an artificial hazard on a golf course often near a green consisting of a depression containing sand — see BUNKER
sand trout *n* **:** the sand squeteague or a related weakfish (*Cynoscion nothus*)
sand tube *n* **:** a tube made of sand; *specif* **:** a tubular fulgurite formed in sand
san·dun·ga \sänˈdüŋgə\ *n* -s [MexSp] **:** a Mexican couple dance in which the woman waltzes holding her skirt spread while the man shuffles around her
sand up *vb* [²*sand*] *vt* **:** to choke with sand (as in a well producing sand mixed with oil or gas) ~ *vi* **:** to become choked with sand ⟨the well . . . had *sanded up* —Edwin Corle⟩
san·dust \ˈsan,dəst\ *n* [prob. blend of *sand* and *dust*] **:** a moderate yellowish pink that is much yellower, less strong, and slightly lighter than coral pink, yellower and duller than peach pink, and yellower, less strong, and slightly darker than average peach
sand verbena *n* **:** a western American herb of the genus *Abronia* having flowers resembling the verbena (esp. *A. latifolia* and *A. umbellata* of the Pacific coast)
sand vine *n* **:** a scrambling vine (*Ampelanus albidus*) of the southeastern U.S. related to the milkweeds and having a milky juice, opposite leaves deeply cordate at the base, and small whitish flowers in axillary cymes succeeded by large follicles
sand violet *n* **:** any of several violets found commonly in sandy soil: as **a :** either of two violets (*Viola arenaria* and *V. hirta*) **b :** BIRD'S-FOOT VIOLET
sand viper *n* **:** any of various snakes that burrow into the sand: as **a :** HOGNOSE SNAKE **b :** HORNED VIPER **c :** a common viper (*Vipera ammodytes*) of southeastern Europe
sand wasp *n* **:** any of various wasps that dig burrows in sand; *esp* **:** a wasp of the genus *Bembix*
sand wedge *n* **:** a golfing iron with considerable loft and a wide flange for use in blasting from a sand trap
sandweed \ˈ=,=\ *n* [¹*sand* + *weed*] **1 :** SANDWORT **2 :** SPURRY 1
sandweld \ˈ=,=\ *vt* [¹*sand* + *weld*] **:** to weld with a flux of fused sand which is hammered or squeezed out
sand whiting *n* **:** any of several marine fishes: as **a :** KING WHITING **b :** SAND BORER **2 c :** an Australian whiting (*Sillago ciliata*)
¹**sand·wich** \ˈsan,(d)wich, ˈsaan- *sometimes esp before a syllable-increasing suffix* -ij\ *n* -ES [after John Montagu, 4th Earl of *Sandwich* †1792 Eng. diplomat] **1 a :** two slices of bread usu. buttered with a thin layer (as of meat, cheese, or savory mixture) spread between them **b :** food consisting of a filling placed upon one slice or between two or more slices of a variety of bread or something that takes the place of bread (as a cracker, cookie, or cake) **2 :** something resembling a sandwich: two similar objects enclosing a different one **3 :** composite structural material most commonly consisting of thin high-strength facings bonded to a thicker light low-strength central core
²**sandwich** \"\ *vt* -ED/-ING/-ES **1 :** to put together like a sandwich ⟨heavy metals (such as lead) and light metals (such as beryllium) are ~*ed* to stop more radiation with less overall weight —*Newsweek*⟩ **2 a :** to insert or place between two or more things ⟨~ the film of metal between two layers of glass —Peter Latham⟩ ⟨song and skit specialties ~*ed* between the longer numbers —*Amer. Guide Series: La.*⟩ **b :** to make a place for **:** CROWD ⟨leisure . . . ~*ed* into the wee hours after an exhausting day —Graenum Berger⟩ ⟨~*es* her writing in with home chores —*Current Biog.*⟩ **3 :** to enclose in the manner of a sandwich ⟨safety spectacles . . . with double lenses ~*ing* a thin layer of the plastic —Harland Manchester⟩
sandwich beam *also* **sandwich girder** *n* **:** FLITCH BEAM
sandwich board *n* **:** two usu. hinged boards designed for hanging from the shoulders with one board before and one behind and used esp. for advertising

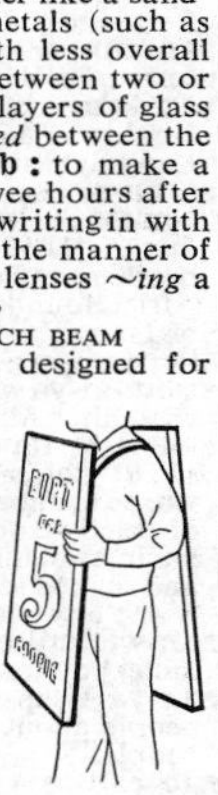

sandwich board

sandwich glass *n, usu cap S* [fr. *Sandwich*, Mass.] **:** blown, molded, or pressed glass made by the Boston and Sandwich Glass Company between 1825 and 1886 and now widely collected esp. in some of its lacy pressed forms
sandwich man *n* **:** one who advertises or pickets a place of business by wearing a sandwich board
sandwich panel *n* **:** structural panel material fabricated by bonding several laminations
sandwich tern *n* [*Sandwich*, Kent, England] **:** a rather large tern (*Thalasseus sandvicensis*) that occurs in its typical form in Europe and is represented in No. and Central America by a variety (*T. s. acuflavidus*)
sand widgeon *n, Brit* **:** GADWALL
sand wireworm *n* **:** the larva of an elaterid beetle (*Horistonotus uhlerii*) destructive to corn and cotton in the southern U.S.
sandworm \ˈ=,=\ *n* [¹*sand* + *worm*] **1 :** any of various sand-dwelling polychaete worms: as **a :** CLAM WORM **b :** LUGWORM **c :** a worm (genus *Sabellaria*) that constructs a tube similar to that of the sand mason **2 :** CHIGOE
sandwort \ˈ=,=\ *n* [¹*sand* + *wort*] **1 :** a plant of the genus *Arenaria* growing usu. in dry sandy soil **2 :** a plant of the genus *Moehringia* (esp. *M. lateriflora*)
¹**sandy** \ˈsandē, ˈsaan-, -di\ *adj, usu* -ER/-EST [ME, fr. OE *sandig*, fr. *sand* + *-ig* -y — more at SAND] **1 :** consisting of, abounding in, or containing sand **:** full of sand **:** covered or sprinkled with sand ⟨confined to the rocky region and ~ pools —W.H.Dowdeswell⟩ **2 :** of the color sand ⟨~ hair⟩ **3 :** resembling sand: as **a :** lacking stability **:** being without firmness **:** UNSOUND ⟨the foundation on which to base a friendship was too ~⟩ **b :** lacking interest **:** DRY, STALE ⟨a criticism . . . that it contained long ~ stretches —A.W.Long⟩ **c :** full of pluck **:** possessing grit ⟨the . . . cool and ~ regular army man —A.J.Mekeel⟩ **4** *archaic* **:** of or relating to the time measured by the sand in a sandglass ⟨ere the glass . . . finish the process of his ~ hour —Shak.⟩ **5 a :** that grains like sand — used of varnish, paint, chemicals **b :** containing lactose crystals — used of ice cream
²**sandy** \"\ *n* -ES [¹*sand* + *-y* (n. suffix)] **1** *Brit* **:** RING PLOVER **2 :** SAND CRAB 1a(2)
³**sandy** \"\ *n, pl* **sandys** *or* **sandies** *usu cap* [fr. *Sandy*, nickname for *Alexander*, a common Scottish Christian name] **:** SCOTCHMAN
sandy beige *n* **:** SLATE GRAY
sandy blight *n, Austral* **:** BLIGHT 5
sandy·ish \-dēish\ *adj* [¹*sandy* + *-ish*] **:** somewhat sandy
sandy laverock *n* **1** *Scot* **:** RING PLOVER **2 :** the common European sandpiper
sandy loam *n* **:** a loam consisting of less than 7 percent clay, less than 50 percent silt, and between 43 and 50 percent sand
sandy mockingbird *n* **:** BROWN THRASHER
sandyx *var of* SANDIX
¹**sane** \ˈsān\ *adj, usu* -ER/-EST [L *sanus* healthy, sane] **1 :** free from hurt or disease **:** HEALTHY **2 :** mentally sound **:** possessing a rational mind **:** having the mental faculties in such condition as to be able to anticipate and judge of the effect of one's actions **3 :** proceeding from a sound mind **:** being without delusions or prejudice **:** free of ignorance **:** LOGICAL, RATIONAL, SENSIBLE ⟨his . . . school reports were models of ~ educational thinking —Caroline Ticknor⟩ ⟨a more ~ collection of people I have never worked with —Denis Johnston⟩ **syn** see WISE
²**sane** \"\ *dial var of* SAIN
sane·ly *adv* **:** in a sane manner ⟨speak more ~ about . . . affairs —*Time*⟩
san fe·lipe \,sanfəˈlēpē\ *n, pl* **san felipe** *or* **san felipes** *usu cap S&F* [fr. *San Felipe*, pueblo in north central New Mexico] **1 :** a Keres people occupying a pueblo in New Mexico **2 :** a member of the San Felipe people
sanfoin *var of* SAINFOIN
san·ford's brown \ˈsanfə(r)dz-\ *n, often cap S* [fr. the name *Sanford*] **:** a brownish orange that is stronger than spice or gold pheasant
san fran·cis·can \,sanfrənˈsiskən, ,saan-, -ran-, -raan- *sometimes* -fərn-\ *n* -s *cap S&F* [*San Francisco*, Calif. + E *-an*] **:** a native or resident of San Francisco, Calif.
san fran·cis·co \;==ˈsi(,)skō\ *adj, usu cap S&F* [fr. *San Francisco*, city in western California] **:** of or from the city of San Francisco, Calif. ⟨the *San Francisco* hills⟩ **:** of the kind or style prevalent in San Francisco
¹**sang** [ME, fr. OE] *past of* SING
²**sang** \ˈsaŋ\ *Scot var of* SONG
³**sang** \"\ *n* -s [F, fr. MF, fr. L *sanguen*, var. of *sanguin-, sanguis* blood] *chiefly Scot* **:** BLOOD — usu. used as a mild oath
⁴**sang** \"\ *n* -s [by shortening & alter. fr. *ginseng*] *chiefly Midland* **:** a ginseng (*Panax quinquefolium*)
⁵**sang** \ˈsəŋ\ *n* -s [Chin (Pek) *sheng*¹] **1 :** SHENG **2** [Per, prob. fr. Chin *sheng*¹] **:** a Persian harp of the middle ages
san·ga *also* **san·gu** \ˈsaŋgə\ *n* -s [Amharic *sangā*] **:** any of various African cattle: as **a :** an eastern and southern African breed of long-horned small-humped cattle **b :** a western African crossbreed of zebu and native cattle
san·ga·mon \ˈsaŋgəmən\ *also* **san·ga·mo·ni·an** \,saŋgəˈmōnēən\ *adj, usu cap* [*sangamon* fr. *Sangamon* river & *Sangamon* County, central Illinois; *sangamonian* fr. *Sangamon*, river & county + E *-an*] **:** belonging to the third interglacial interval during the glacial epoch in No. America
san·gar *or* **sun·gar** \ˈsaŋgə(r), ˈsəŋ-\ *n* -s [Hindi *saṅgar*] **1** *also* **san·ger** \"\ **:** a small breastwork or rifle pit to hold a few men often constructed of boulders around a natural hollow **2 :** a primitive wooden bridge with stone piers
san·ga·ree \,saŋgəˈrē\ *n* -s [Sp *sangría*, lit., action or effect of bleeding, fr. *sangre* blood, modif. of L *sanguin-, sanguis* blood] **:** a tall drink usu. of wine but sometimes of ale, beer, or strong alcoholic liquor that is sweetened, poured into a tumbler of cracked ice, and garnished with nutmeg
san·ga–san·ga \ˈsaŋgəˈsaŋgə\ *n* -s [native name in the Belgian Congo] **:** a tropical African tree (*Ricinodendron africanum*) of the family Euphorbiaceae that has small greenish flowers in dense cymes and nuts that yield an oil
sang de boeuf \sänˈdəbə̄f\ *n* [F, oxblood] **1 :** an opaque claret red to brownish red reduced copper glaze developed in China during the K'ang Hsi period and used chiefly on porcelain wares **2 :** OXBLOOD
sang·drag·on \ˈsaŋ,dragən\ *also* **san·drag·on** \ˈsan,-\ *n* [obs. E, dragon's blood, fr. ME *sandragoun*, modif. of MF *sang-dragon*, contr. of *sang-de-dragon*, lit., blood of dragon, fr. *sang* blood + *de* of (fr. L, from, away) + *dragon*, fr. OF — more at DE-, DRAGON] **:** AMBOYNA
sängerbund *var of* SAENGERBUND
sängerfest *var of* SAENGERFEST
sang·froid \(ˈ)saŋˈfrwä, (ˈ)säŋ-, (ˈ)sänⁿ-, -wäd\ *n* -s [F *sang-froid*, lit., cold blood, fr. MF, fr. *sang* blood + *froid* cold, fr. L *frigidus* — more at SANG, FRIGID] **:** extraordinary often cold-blooded self-possession or imperturbability esp. under strain ⟨with gigantic ~ I performed one of her own dances for her —Agnes de Mille⟩ **syn** see EQUANIMITY
sang·gil *also* **san·gil** \säŋˈgēl\ *n* -s *usu cap* **:** SANGIR
sangh \ˈsaŋ, ˈsəŋ\ *n* -s [Hindi *sāg*, lit., association, fr. Skt *saṅga*, fr. *sajati* he adheres to, sticks — more at SAGUM] **:** an association or society having as its object the unification of the different groups in Hinduism and the prevention of the conversion of Hindus to Christianity or Islam
san·gha *also* **sam·gha** \ˈsəŋgə\ *n* -s [Skt *saṅgha*] **1 :** a Buddhist religious community or monastic order **2 :** a Jain monastic community
sang·ir \ˈsäŋ,i(ə)r\ *also* **sang·i·rese** \,säŋəˈrēz, -ēs\ *n, pl* **sangir** *or* **sangirs** *also* **sangirese** *usu cap* **1 a :** a predominantly Muslim people inhabiting the Sangir islands, Indonesia, and the southern coastal regions of Mindanao — called also *Sanggil* **b :** a member of such people **2 :** an Austronesian language of the Sangir people
san·gley \säŋˈglā\ *n* -s [Chin (Pek) *shang*¹*lü*³ merchant guest] **:** a Chinese trader in the Philippines
sang·li·er \ˈsaŋlēə(r)\ *n* -s [ME *senglere*, fr. MF *sengler*, *sanglier*, fr. ML *singularis*, fr. L, single, solitary — more at SINGULAR] **:** a wild boar
san·go \ˈsäŋ(,)gō\ *n* -s *usu cap* **:** a trade language widely used in French Equatorial Africa belonging to the Adamawa-Eastern branch of the Niger-Congo family
san·go·an \ˈsäŋgəwən\ *adj, usu cap* [*Sango* Bay, Uganda, where remains of the culture were found + E *-an*] **:** of or belonging to a modified Acheulean culture of central Africa characterized by a hand-ax altered so that it might be used as a pick
san·gra·do \sänˈgrä(,)dō\ *n* -ES [after Doctor *Sangrado*, physician (whose panacea was copious bloodletting and drinking of hot water) in the picaresque novel *Gil Blas* (*L'Histoire de Gil Blas de Santillane*, 1715–35) by Alain René Lesage †1747 Fr. novelist and playwright] *archaic* **:** one who pretends to a knowledge of medicine **:** QUACK
san·gree·root \ˈsaŋgrē,-\ *n* [*sangree* (alter. of *snagrel*) + *root*] **:** VIRGINIA SNAKEROOT
sangs *pl of* SANG
sang·sue \ˈsaŋ,sü\ *n* -s [F, fr. L *sanguisuga* bloodsucker, leech, fr. *sanguis* blood + *-suga* (fr. *sugere* to suck) — more at SUCK] **:** ¹LEECH 2 a
sangu *var of* SANGA
sangui- *comb form* [MF, fr. L, fr. *sanguis*] **:** blood ⟨*sanguimotor*⟩
san·guic·o·lous \saŋˈgwikələs\ *adj* [*sangui-* + *-colous*] **:** HEMATOBIC
san·gui·fi·ca·tion \,saŋgwəfəˈkāshən\ *n* -s [MF, fr. L *sangui-* (fr. *sanguis* blood) + MF *-fication*] **:** conversion (as of food) into blood **:** HEMATOPOIESIS
sanguify *vb* -ED/-ING/-ES [*sangui-* + *-fy*] *vi, obs* **:** to produce blood ~ *vt, obs* **:** to change into blood
san·gui·motor \ˈsaŋgwə+\ *adj* [*sangui-* + *motor*] **:** of or relating to the circulation of blood
san·gui·nar·ia \,saŋgwəˈna(a)rēə\ *n* [NL, fr. L, an herb that stanches blood, fr. fem. of *sanguinarius* sanguinary] **1** *cap* **:** a genus of scapose perennial herbs (family Papaveraceae) having reddish juice and capsules that are dehiscent to their base — see BLOODROOT **2** -s **:** the dried rhizome and roots of a plant of the genus *Sanguinaria* used as an expectorant and emetic
san·gui·nar·i·ly \ˈ;saŋgwə;nerəlē\ *adv* **:** in a sanguinary manner
san·guin·a·rine \saŋˈgwinə,rēn, -,rən\ *n* -s [ISV *sanguinar-* (fr. NL *Sanguinaria*, genus name of the bloodroot *Sanguinaria canadensis*) + *-ine*] **:** a poisonous bitter crystalline alkaloid $C_{20}H_{15}NO_5$ obtained esp. from bloodroot
san·gui·nary \ˈsaŋgwə,nerē, -ri\ *adj* [L *sanguinarius*, fr. *sanguin-, sanguis* blood + *-arius* -ary] **1 :** willing or even anxious to shed blood **:** BLOODTHIRSTY, MURDEROUS ⟨went after the collaborators with a ~ fury that drenched the land with blood —G.W.Johnson⟩ **2 :** attended by, prompting, or concerning much bloodshed **:** BLOODY ⟨this bitter and ~ war waged under conditions of incredible hardship —T.H.D. Mahoney⟩ **3 :** consisting of blood ⟨a ~ stream⟩
sanguinary ant *n* **:** a slave-making ant (*Formica sanguinea*) widely distributed over the northern hemisphere
¹**san·guine** \ˈsaŋgwən\ *adj* [ME *sanguin*, fr. MF, fr. L *sanguineus* of blood, bloody, bloodred, fr. *sanguin-, sanguis* blood + *-eus* -eous] **1 a :** red like blood **:** of the color blood red ⟨cedar logs whose ~ color made . . . a fantastic wreath of flames —Elinor Wylie⟩ **b :** of the heraldic color murrey **2 a :** consisting of or relating to blood **b :** SANGUINARY 1 **c** *of the complexion* **:** RUDDY ⟨his complexion was fresh and ~ —Elinor Wylie⟩ **3 a :** having blood as the predominating bodily humor **b :** having the bodily conformation and temperament thought to be characteristic of such predominance and marked by sturdiness, high color, and an appearance of cheerful spiritedness **4 :** anticipating the best **:** marked by eager hopefulness **:** ardently or confidently optimistic ⟨his ~ temper and fearlessness of mind —Jane Austen⟩ ⟨too ~ about success —Ernest Beaglehole⟩ ⟨a ~ happy-go-lucky habit of thought —J.G.Cozzens⟩ **syn** see CONFIDENT
²**sanguine** \"\ *n* -s **1 a :** BLOOD RED **b :** the heraldic color murrey **2 :** a sanguine humor or temperament ⟨the ~ and melancholic are temperaments of feeling —A.L.Kroeber⟩ **3 a :** a type of red crayon usu. of red hematite **b :** a drawing in red crayon, red chalk, or similar medium
³**sanguine** *vt* -ED/-ING/-S *obs* **:** ENSANGUINE
san·guine·ly *adv* **:** in a sanguine manner
san·guine·ness *n* -ES **:** SANGUINITY
san·guin·e·ous \saŋˈgwinēəs, sanˈ-\ *adj* [L *sanguineus*] **1 :** BLOODRED **2 :** of, relating to, or involving bloodshed **:** BLOODTHIRSTY ⟨~ histories of queens —W.M.Thackeray⟩ **3 a :** of or relating to blood **:** constituting or containing blood **b** *obs, of an animal* **:** having blood or a circulatory system **4 a** *archaic* **:** characterized by a plethora of blood ⟨~ fever⟩ **b :** FULL-BLOODED, SANGUINE 3b ⟨a ~ temperament⟩
sanguini- *comb form* [fr. ¹*sanguine*] **:** SANGUINO- ⟨*sanguinicolous*⟩
sanguinian *n* -s [ME *sanguinien*, fr. MF, fr. *sanguin* sanguine + *-ien* -ian] *obs* **:** one that has a sanguine temperament
sanguinicolous \;saŋgwə;nikələs\ *adj* [*sanguini-* + *-colous*] **:** SANGUICOLOUS
san·guin·i·ty \saŋˈgwinəd·ē, sanˈ-, -ətē, -i\ *n* -ES [¹*sanguine* + *-ity*] **:** the quality or state of being sanguine ⟨~ about the financial interests . . . of government officials —*New Republic*⟩
san·gui·niv·o·rous \,saŋgwəˈniv(ə)rəs\ *adj* [*sanguini-* + *-vorous*] **:** HEMATOPHAGOUS
sanguino- *comb form* [F, fr. *sanguin* sanguine, fr. MF] **:** blood ⟨*sanguinopurulent*⟩
san·guin·o·lent \saŋˈgwinᵊlənt\ *adj* [L *sanguinolentus* bloody, bloodred, fr. *sanguin-, sanguis* blood] **:** of, containing, or tinged with blood ⟨~ sputum⟩
san·gui·no·purulent \,saŋgwənō+\ *adj* [*sanguino-* + *purulent*] **:** containing blood and pus ⟨~ discharge⟩
san·gui·nous \ˈsaŋgwənəs\ *adj* [L *sanguin-, sanguis* blood + E *-ous*] **:** SANGUINEOUS
san·gui·sor·ba \,saŋgwəˈsȯrbə\ *n, cap* [NL, fr. *sangui-* + *-sorba* (fr. L *sorbēre* to absorb); fr. its styptic quality — more at ABSORB] **:** a small genus of herbs (family Rosaceae) native to temperate regions with odd-pinnate stipulate leaves and small apetalous flowers in dense terminal spikes or clusters — see BURNET 2
san·guiv·o·rous \saŋˈgwiv(ə)rəs\ *adj* [*sangui-* + *-vorous*] **:** feeding on blood
san·he·drin \(ˈ)sanˈhēdrən, sänˈ-, -ˈhed-; ˈsan(h)ē,drin, -nə,-, -,drən\ *or* **san·he·drim** \-rəm, -rim\ *n* -s *usu cap* [Mishnaic Heb *sanhedhrīn* (*gĕdhōlāh*) (great) Sanhedrin, fr. Gk *synedrion*, lit., council, council chamber, fr. *synedros* sitting in council, fr. *syn-* + *hedra* seat — more at SIT] **1 :** the supreme council and tribunal of the ancient Jewish nation consisting of 70–72 members and having jurisdiction over religious matters and important civil and criminal cases **2 :** one of the provincial councils of the ancient Jews consisting of 23 members and having jurisdiction over minor civil and criminal cases
san hemp \ˈsan-, ˈsən-\ *n* [*san* fr. Hindi, sunn — more at SUNN] **:** SUNN
san·i·cle \ˈsanəkəl\ *n* -s [ME, fr. MF, fr. ML *sanicula*] **:** any of several plants reputed to have healing powers: as **a :** a plant of the genus *Sanicula* having a root that is used esp. in folk medicine as an anodyne or astringent — called also *black snakeroot* **b :** AMERICAN SANICLE **c :** YORKSHIRE SANICLE
sa·nic·u·la \səˈnikyələ\ *n, cap* [NL, fr. ML, sanicle, prob. dim. of L *sanus* healthy] **:** a genus of chiefly American herbs (family Umbelliferae) having palmately compound leaves, unisexual flowers in panicled umbels, and fruit covered with hooked bristles
san·i·dine \ˈsanə,dēn, -,dən\ *n* -s [G *sanidin*, fr. Gk *sanid-, sanis* board + G *-in* -ine; fr. its tabular crystals] **:** a variety of orthoclase in often transparent crystals in eruptive rock (as trachyte) that is thought to form at higher temperatures than adularia — called also GLASSY FELDSPAR — **san·i·din·ic** \;==ˈdinik\ *adj*
sa·ni·es \ˈsānē,ēz\ *n, pl* **sanies** [L] **1 :** a thin blood-tinged seropurulent discharge from ulcers or infected wounds — compare ICHOR **2** *archaic* **:** a watery vital bodily fluid; *esp* **:** one comparable to blood
san·i·fi·ca·tion \,sanəfəˈkāshən\ *n* -s [L *sanus* healthy + E *-i-* + *-fication*] **:** the act or process of making sanitary
san·i·fy \ˈsanə,fī\ *vt* -ED/-ING/-ES [L *sanus* healthy + E *-ify*] **:** to make healthful **:** provide with sanitary conditions and equipment
san il·de·fon·so \sa,nildəˈfän(t)(,)sō\ *n, pl* **san ildefonso** *or* **san ildefonsos** *usu cap S&I* [fr. *San Ildefonso*, pueblo in central New Mexico] **1 :** a Tanoan people occupying a pueblo in New Mexico **2 :** a member of the San Ildefonso people
sa·nio's beam \ˈsänē,ōz-\ *n, usu cap S* [prob. after Karl Gustav *Sanio*, 19th cent. Ger. botanist] **:** CRASSULA
sa·ni·ous \ˈsānēəs\ *adj* [L *saniosus*, fr. *sanies* + *-osus* -ose] **:** thin and seropurulent with a slightly bloody tinge ⟨the ~ discharge from an ulcer⟩
¹**san·i·tar·i·an** \,sanəˈta(a)rēən, -ter-, -tär-\ *n* -s [¹*sanitary* + E *-an* (n. suffix)] **:** one skilled in matters of sanitary science and public health ⟨milk ~⟩
²**sanitarian** \;==;===\ *adj* [¹*sanitary* + E *-an* (adj. suffix)] **:** of or relating to sanitary science or public health
san·i·tar·i·ly \,sanəˈterəlē, -li\ *adv* **:** in a sanitary manner **:** with regard to sanitation ⟨the peculiar, ~ dubious, but often delicious foods —Joseph Alsop⟩
san·i·tar·ium \,sanəˈta(a)rēəm, -ter-, -tär-\ *n, pl* **sanitariums** \-mz\ *also* **sanitar·ia** \-ēə\ [NL, fr. L *sanitat-, sanitas* health + *-arium* -ary] **:** SANATORIUM

[1]san·i·tary \'sanə,terē, -ri\ *adj* [F *sanitaire*, fr. L *sanitas* health + F *-aire* -ary] **:** of or relating to health **:** for or relating to the preservation or restoration of health **:** occupied with measures or equipment for improving conditions that influence health **:** free from or effective in preventing or checking an agent (as filth or infection) injurious to health **:** HYGIENIC **syn** see HEALTHFUL

[2]sanitary \"\ *n* -ES **:** a water closet, urinal, or similar equipment fitted with sanitary plumbing

sanitary can *n* **:** PACKER'S CAN

sanitary cordon *n* [trans. of *cordon sanitaire*] **:** CORDON SANITAIRE

sanitary engineer *n* **:** an engineer whose training or occupation is in sanitary engineering

sanitary engineering *n* **:** a branch of civil engineering concerned primarily with the maintenance of environmental conditions (as pure water supply, waste disposal, insect control, nuisance abatement) conducive to public health

sanitary fill *n* **:** the disposition of garbage by spreading in layers and covering with ashes or dirt to a depth sufficient to control rats, flies, and odors

sanitary napkin *n* **:** a disposable absorbent pad of cellulose or similar filler in a gauze covering used to absorb the flow from uterus or vagina during menstruation or postpartum

sanitary sewer *n* **:** a sewer to dispose of sewage but not water from ground, surface, or storm

sanitary ware *n* **:** plumbing articles (as sinks, baths, lavatories, showers, toilet bowls)

san·i·tate \'sanə,tāt\ *vt* -ED/-ING/-S [back-formation fr. *sanitation*] **:** to make sanitary **:** provide with sanitary appliances

san·i·ta·tion \,sanə'tāshən\ *n* -S [[1]*sanitary* + *-ation*] **1 :** the act or process of making sanitary **2 :** the application of measures to make environmental conditions favorable to health **3 :** the maintenance of a healthy population of a wild species by the selective action of predators in removing weak or unfit individuals

sanitation cutting *n* **:** a cutting made to remove trees that have been injured or killed (as by fire or wind) primarily to prevent spread of disease or insects — compare SALVAGE CUTTING

san·i·ta·tion·ist \-sh(ə)nəst\ *n* -S **:** SANITARIAN

san·i·ti·za·tion \,sanədə'zāshən\ *n* -S **:** the act or process of sanitizing

san·i·tize \'sanə,tīz\ *vt* -ED/-ING/-S [L *sanitat-*, *sanitas* health + E *-ize*] **:** to make sanitary (as by cleaning or sterilizing)

san·i·tiz·er \-zə(r)\ *n* -S **:** a sanitizing agent esp. for use in connection with food

san·i·to·ri·um \,sanə'tōrēəm, -tȯr-\ *n, pl* **sanitoriums** \-mz\ *also* **sanito·ria** \-ēə\ [NL, alter. (influenced by *sanitarium*) of *sanatorium*] **:** SANATORIUM

san·i·ty \'sanəd·|ē, -ət|, |i\ *n* -ES [ME *sanite*, fr. L *sanitat-* *sanitas* health, sanity, fr. *sanus* healthy, sane + *-itat-*, *-itas* -ity] **:** the quality or state of being sane: as **a :** a healthy state of body **b :** soundness or health of mind

san ja·cin·to day \¦sanjə¦sin(,)tō-\ *n, usu cap S&J&D* [fr. the battle of *San Jacinto*, fr. *San Jacinto*, river in southeastern Texas near the mouth of which Americans under Gen. Sam Houston decisively defeated Mexicans under Santa Anna] **:** April 21 observed as a legal holiday by the state of Texas in commemoration of the battle of San Jacinto in 1836

san·jak \san'jak, '≠,≠\ *n* -S [earlier *sangiac*, fr. Turk *sancàk*, lit., flag, standard] **:** a district or subdivision of a vilayet — compare MUTESSARIF

san joa·quin fever \¦sanwȯ¦kēn-, -wä¦-\ *also* **san joaquin valley fever** *n, usu cap S&J&V* [after *San Joaquin* Valley, central California, where it was endemic] **:** COCCIDIOIDOMYCOSIS

san jo·sé *or* **san jo·se** \¦san(h)ō¦zā, -nə¦-\ *adj, usu cap S&J* [fr. *San José*, Costa Rica] **:** of or from San José, the capital of Costa Rica **:** of the kind or style prevalent in San José

san jose scale *n, usu cap 1st S&J* [after *San Jose*, California, where it first appeared in the U.S.] **:** a scale insect (*Aspidiotus perniciosus*) that is prob. native to eastern Asia but widely distributed in warm and temperate areas, has become one of the most damaging plant pests in the U.S., and is esp. destructive to apple, pear, and other fruit trees

[1]san juan \(')san¦(h)wän\ *adj, usu cap S&J* [fr. *San Juan*, Puerto Rico] **:** of or from San Juan, the capital of Puerto Rico **:** of the kind or style prevalent in San Juan

[2]san juan \"\ *n, pl* **san juan** *or* **san juans** *usu cap S&J* [fr. *San Juan*, pueblo in northern New Mexico] **1 :** a Tanoan people occupying a pueblo in New Mexico **2 :** a member of the San Juan people

san jua·ne·ro \,san(h)wə'ne(,)rō\ *n* -S *cap S&J* [AmerSp, fr. *San Juan* + Sp *-ero* (fr. L *-arius* -ary)] **:** a native or resident of San Juan, esp. San Juan, Puerto Rico

san·jua·ni·to \,san(h)wə'nēd·(,)ō\ *n* -S [AmerSp, fr. dim. of *San Juan* St. John] **:** an Ecuadorian couple dance resembling but more melancholy than the marinera of Peru

[1]sank [ME, fr. OE *sanc*] *past of* SINK

[2]sank \'saŋk\ *n* -S [Skt *śaṅkha* — more at CONCH] **:** CHANK

san·khya *also* **sam·khya** \'säŋkyə\ *n* -S *usu cap* [Skt *sāṁkhya*, lit., based on calculation, philosophical method, fr. *saṁkhyā* calculation, number, fr. *saṁkhyāti* he counts up] **:** one of the earliest of the major orthodox systems of Hindu philosophy resting on a metaphysical dualism that exists between the ultimates of prakriti and purusha whose contact produces the phenomenal world and whose disentangling represents the process of individual salvation

san luis po·to·sí *or* **san luis potosi** \sän'lwē,spōd·ə'sē\ *adj, usu cap S&L&P* [fr. *San Luis Potosí*, city in central Mexico] **:** of or from the city of San Luis Potosí, Mexico **:** of the kind or style prevalent in San Luis Potosí

[1]san mar·i·nese \(,)san¦marə¦nēz, -ēs\ *or* **sam·mar·i·nese** \(,)sa(m)¦ma-\ *n, pl* **san marinese** \"\ *or* **san marine·si** \,≠,≠≠'nāzē\ *or* **sammarinese** *or* **sammarinesi** *usu cap S&M* [*San Marino*, republic on the Italian peninsula + E *-ese* (n. suffix)] **:** a native or inhabitant of the Republic of San Marino

[2]san marinese \"\ *or* **sammarinese** \"\ *adj, usu cap S&M* [*San Marino* + E *-ese* (adj. suffix)] **:** of or relating to San Marino or the San Marinese

san ma·ri·no \¦sanmə¦rē(,)nō\ *adj, usu cap S&M* [fr. *San Marino*, republic on the Italian peninsula in southern Europe] **:** of or from the Republic of San Marino, in Italy **:** of the kind or style prevalent in San Marino

san·mar·tin·ite \san'märtᵊn,īt\ *n* -S [Sp *sanmartinita*, fr. *San Martín*, town in Argentina + Sp *-ita* -ite] **:** a tungstate of zinc, iron, and calcium closely related to wolframite

sann \'san, 'sən\ *n* -S [Hindi *san* — more at SUNN] **:** SUNN

san·na \'sanə\ [by contr. & alter.] *Scot* **:** shall not

sannhemp \'≠,≠\ *n* [*sann* + *hemp*] **:** SUNN

san·nup \'sa,nəp\ *n* -S [Abnaki *senanbe*] **:** a married male American Indian — compare SQUAW

sann·ya·si \,sən'yäsē\ *or* **sann·ya·sin** \-sᵊn\ *n* -S [Hindi *sannyāsī*, fr. Skt *saṁnyāsin* abandoning, fr. *sam* together + *ni* down + *asyati* he throws — more at SANSKRIT, NETHER] **:** a wandering mendicant Hindu ascetic **:** HOLY MAN, MONK; *specif* **:** one belonging to a Brahman or Jain order comprising men in the fourth ashrama

sanpan *var of* SAMPAN

san pe·dro fish \san'pē(,)drō-, -'pā(,)drō-\ *n, usu cap S&P* [after Point *San Pedro*, Calif.] **:** OPAH

san·poil \'san,pȯil\ *n, pl* **sanpoil** *or* **sanpoils** *usu cap* **1 a :** a Salishan people of northeastern Washington **b :** a member of such people **2 :** a dialect of Okanagon

SANR *abbr, often not cap* subject to approval no risk

san·ron \'sän,rōn\ *n* -S *usu cap* [Jap] **:** a Japanese Buddhist school founded in A.D. 625 and based on Madhyamika principles

[1]sans \'sanz, 'saa(ə)nz, 'sänz\ *prep* [ME *saun*, *saunz*, *sans*, fr. MF *san*, *sanz*, *sans*, fr. OF *sen*, *senz*, *sens*, partly fr. L *sine* without, and partly modif. (influenced by L *sine*) of L *absentia* in the absence of, abl. of *absentia* absence — more at SUNDER, ABSENCE] **:** deprived or destitute of **:** WITHOUT ⟨her face seen in repose . . . ~ the liveliness of her eyes revealed her age —Eugene Walter⟩

[2]sans *pl of* SAN

[3]sans \'sanz\ *n* -ES [by shortening] **:** SANS SERIF

sansa *var of* ZANZA

san sal·va·dor \san'salvə,dȯ(ə)r\ *adj, usu cap both Ss* [fr. *San Salvador*, El Salvador] **:** of or from San Salvador, the capital of El Salvador **:** of the kind or style prevalent in San Salvador

san·sar \'san(t)sə(r)\ *n* -S [modif. of Ar *ṣarṣar*] **:** SARSAR

sansara *var of* SAMSARA

sans·cu·lotte \,sanzk(y)ə'lät, -nsk-\ *n* -S [F *sans-culotte*, lit., without breeches; prob. fr. the fact that members of the republican party had rejected short breeches as being peculiar to the upper classes and had adopted instead other articles of dress, esp. pantaloons] **1 :** one belonging to the extreme republican party in France at the time of the Revolution **2 :** a political extremist or radical; *esp* **:** one who believes in violence to attain an end

sans·cu·lotte·rie \-ä·trē\ *n* -S [F *sans-culotterie*, fr. *sans-culotte* + *-erie* -ery] **:** SANSCULOTTISM

sans·cu·lot·tic \¦≠≠¦läd·ik\ *adj* [*sansculotte* + *-ic*] **:** relating to or involving sansculottism **:** RADICAL, REVOLUTIONARY

sans·cu·lot·tish \-ish\ *adj* [*sansculotte* + *-ish*] **:** SANSCULOTTIC

sans·cu·lot·tism \,≠≠'läd·,izəm\ *n* -S [F *sans-culottisme*, fr. *sans-culotte* + *-isme* -ism] **:** extreme republican principles **:** the principles or practice of the sansculottes

sans·cu·lot·tize \-,īz\ *vb* [*sansculotte* + *-ize*] *vt* **:** to make sansculottic ~ *vi* **:** to uphold radical principles

san se·bas·tián *or* **san se·bas·tian** \¦sansə¦bas(h)chən\ *adj, usu cap both Ss* [fr. *San Sebastián*, city in northern Spain] **:** of or from the city of San Sebastián, Spain **:** of the kind or style prevalent in San Sebastián

sans égal \säⁿzāgäl\ *n* [F, lit., without equal] **:** bagatelle in which each player uses four balls and another ball is spotted

san·sei \(')sän¦sā\ *n, pl* **sansei** *also* **sanseis** *often cap* [Jap *san* third + *sei* generation] **:** a son or daughter of nisei or kibei parents who is born and educated in America and esp. in the U.S.

san·se·vie·ria \,san(t)sə'virēə\ *n* [NL, fr. Raimondo di Sangro †1774 Ital. scholar and prince of *San Severo* + NL *-ia*] **1** *cap* **:** a genus of tropical chiefly Asiatic and African herbs (family Liliaceae) having sword-shaped leaves which are mottled or striped with various shades of green or yellow, white or yellowish flowers on jointed pedicels, a 3-celled ovary, and a 1- to 3-seeded berry — see BOWSTRING HEMP **2** *or* **san·se·vie·ra** \-rə\ -S **:** any plant of the genus *Sansevieria*

[1]san·skrit \'sanz,krit, 'saan-, -n,sk-, *usu* -id·+V\ *n* -S *cap* [Skt *saṁskṛta*, lit., prepared, cultivated, refined, fr. *sam* together (akin to *sama* same) + *karoti* he makes, does — more at SAME, KARMA] **1 :** an ancient Indic language that is the classical language of India and of Hinduism as described by the Indian grammarians (as Panini) — called also *classical Sanskrit* **2 :** classical Sanskrit together with the older Vedic and various later modifications of classical Sanskrit

[2]sanskrit \"\ *adj, usu cap* **1 :** of, relating to, or written in Sanskrit **2 :** derived from or relating to classical Indian culture

san·skrit·ic \(')sanz¦krid·|ik, (')saan-, -n¦sk-, -it|, |ēk\ *n* -S *usu cap* [*sanskrit* + *-ic*] **1 :** INDIC **2 :** a group of Indic languages developed directly from Sanskrit — see INDO-EUROPEAN LANGUAGES table

san·skrit·ist \'sanz,krid·əst, 'saan-, -n,sk-, -itə-\ *n* -S *usu cap* [ISV *sanskrit* + *-ist*] **:** a specialist in Sanskrit

san·skrit·iza·tion \,sanz,krid·ə'zāshən\ *n* -S *usu cap* [*sanskritize* + *-ation*] **1 :** the assimilation of a language to Sanskrit in vocabulary, syntax, or style **2 :** the assimilation of a culture to that of Brahminical Hinduism

san·skrit·ize \'sanzkrə,tīz\ *vt* -ED/-ING/-S *often cap* [*sanskrit* + *-ize*] **:** to modify (a word, phrase, or language) to conform to characteristics distinctive of Sanskrit ⟨the interpreters' grasp of Hindi is said to be sound but their vocabulary is highly *Sanskritized* —Christopher Rand⟩

sans ser·if \sanz'serəf\ *or* **san·ser·if** \san'-\ *n* [prob. fr. [1]*sans* + modif. of D *schreef* stroke, line — more at SERIF] **:** a letter or typeface with no serifs — called also *doric*, *gothic*, *grotesque*

[1]sant \'sant\ *n* -S [perh. modif. of MF *cent* hundred — more at CENT] **:** a card game similar to piquet and popular in the 15th and 16th centuries **:** CENT

[2]sant \"\ *vi* [origin unknown] *chiefly Scot* **:** VANISH

[3]sant *var of* SUNT

san·ta \'santə, 'saan-\ *n* -S *usu cap* [by shortening] **:** SANTA CLAUS

[1]san·ta ana \¦santə¦anə\ *n, pl* **santa ana** *or* **santa anas** *usu cap S&A* [fr. *Santa Ana*, pueblo in north central New Mexico] **1 a :** a Keres people occupying a pueblo in New Mexico **b :** a member of such people **2 :** the language of the Santa Ana people

[2]santa ana \"\ *n, usu cap S&A* [fr. *Santa Ana* mountains, range in southwestern California where the wind is channeled through the Santa Ana canyon whence it spreads over the coastal plain] **:** a strong hot dry foehn wind from the north, northeast, or east in southern California

san·ta cla·ra \¦santə¦kla(a)rə\ *n, pl* **santa clara** *or* **santa claras** *usu cap S&C* [fr. *Santa Clara*, pueblo in northern New Mexico] **1 :** a Tanoan people occupying a pueblo in New Mexico **2 :** a member of the Santa Clara people

san·ta claus \'santə,klȯz, 'saan-, -tē,-\ *n, usu cap S&C* [fr. *Santa Claus*, legendary Christmas figure, modif. of D *Sinterklaas*, alter. of *Sint Nikolaas* St. Nicholas *fl* 4th cent. A.D. bishop of Myra, in Lycia, Asia Minor who is considered as patron saint of children and who is fabled as having provided three maidens with dowry by throwing in at their window purses of gold] **:** the religious and holiday spirit of Christmas personified

san·ta cruz \¦santə¦krüz\ *adj, usu cap S&C* [fr. *Santa Cruz* de Tenerife, Spain] **:** of or from the city of Santa Cruz de Tenerife, in the Canary islands, Spain **:** of the kind or style prevalent in Santa Cruz de Tenerife

san·ta fe \¦santə¦fā, *in sense 2* ¦sän-\ *adj, usu cap S&F* **1** [fr. *Santa Fe*, city in north central New Mexico] **:** of or from Santa Fe, the capital of New Mexico ⟨*Santa Fe* stores⟩ **:** of the kind or style prevalent in Santa Fe **2** [fr. *Santa Fe*, city in east central Argentina] **:** of or from the city of Santa Fe, Argentina **:** of the kind or style prevalent in Santa Fe

san·ta fe·an \-āən\ *n* -S *cap S&F* [*Santa Fe*, New Mexico + E *-an*] **:** a native or resident of Santa Fe, New Mexico

san·ta ger·tru·dis \,santə,gər·'trüdəs\ *n, usu cap S&G* [after *Santa Gertrudis*, section of the King Ranch, Kingsville, Texas] **1 :** a breed of cherry-red beef cattle developed from a Brahman-Shorthorn cross and valuable because of their hardiness in hot climes and their thrifty growth on grass feeding **2 :** an animal of the Santa Gertrudis breed

[1]san·tal \'santᵊl\ *n* -S [F, red sandalwood, fr. MF, fr. ML *sandalum*, *santalum* sandalwood — more at SANDAL] **:** a crystalline compound $C_{16}H_{12}O_6$ derived from flavone and obtained from red sandalwood and camwood

[2]san·tal \,sən·'täl\ *n, pl* **santal** *or* **santals** *usu cap* **:** a member of a Kolarian people in southeastern Bihar and adjacent Bengal

san·ta·la·ce·ae \,santə'lāsē,ē\ *n pl, cap* [NL, fr. *Santalum*, type genus + *-aceae*] **:** a family of mostly tropical herbs, shrubs, or rarely trees (order Santalales) that have clustered apetalous monoecious or dioecious flowers, the ovary partly inferior and the fruit a nut or drupe and that include some members which are stem or root parasites — **san·ta·la·ceous** \¦≠≠¦lāshəs\ *adj*

san·ta·la·les \,≠≠'lā(,)lēz\ *n pl, cap* [NL, fr. *Santalum* + *-ales*] **:** an order of dicotyledonous plants which are distinguished by having a one-celled inferior ovary and many of which are parasitic or partly parasitic

san·ta·lene \'santə,lēn\ *n* -S [ISV *santal-* (fr. NL *Santalum*) + *-ene*] **:** either of two liquid unsaturated hydrocarbons $C_{15}H_{24}$ occurring in East Indian sandalwood oil: **a :** a tricyclic sesquiterpene — called also *alpha-santalene* **b :** a bicyclic sesquiterpene — called also *beta-santalene*

san·ta·li \,sən·'tälē\ *n* -S *usu cap* **:** the Munda language of the Santal people

san·ta·lin \'santᵊlən\ *n* -S [ISV *santal-* (fr. NL *Santalum*) + *-in*] **:** a red crystalline compound constituting the chief coloring matter in red sandalwood and camwood

santal oil *n* **:** SANDALWOOD OIL 1a

san·ta·lol \'santə,lȯl, -,lōl\ *n* -S [ISV *santal-* (fr. NL *Santalum*) + *-ol*] **:** a mixture of two liquid isomeric sesquiterpene alcohols $C_{15}H_{23}OH$ derived from the santalenes and constituting the chief constituent of sandalwood oil; *also* **:** either of these alcohols distinguished as alpha and beta

san·ta lu·cia fir \¦santəlü¦sēə-\ *n, usu cap S&L* [after *Santa Lucia* range, southwestern California] **:** a pyramidal California evergreen tree (*Abies venusta*) with spiny pointed leaves and cones that have long spines protruding from the scale bracts — called also *bristlecone fir*

san·ta·lum \'santᵊləm\ *n, cap* [NL, fr. ML *sandalum*, *santalum* sandalwood] **:** a small genus (the type of the family Santalaceae) of Indo-Malayan parasitic trees having coriaceous leaves and small perfect flowers in terminal panicles — see SANDALWOOD

santalwood \'≠≠,≠\ *n* [alter. (influenced by [1]*santal*) of *sandalwood*] **:** SANDALWOOD

san·ta ma·ria tree \¦santəmə¦rēə-\ *n, usu cap S&M* [*santa maria* fr. Sp, fr. *Santa Maria* St. Mary] **:** an evergreen tropical American tree (*Calophyllum calaba*) that yields a durable straight close-grained timber and a fluid balsam like copaiba — called also *Calaba*

san·tana \san·'tanə\ *n* -S *usu cap* [by contr.] **:** SANTA ANA

san·tan·der \¦san·,tän¦der\ *adj, usu cap* [fr. *Santander*, city in northern Spain] **:** of or from the city of Santander, Spain **:** of the kind or style prevalent in Santander

san·ta·ya·ni·an \¦säntə¦yänēən\ *adj, usu cap* [George *Santayana* †1952 Am. poet and philosopher + E *-an*] **:** of or relating to the philosopher and aesthetician George Santayana or his theories and esp. his realism and separation of essence from existence

san·tee \san·'tē\ *n, pl* **santee** *or* **santees** *usu cap* **:** either of two Siouan peoples: **a :** a large number of small groups located in the Carolinas **b** (1) **:** a division of the Dakota people (2) **:** a dialect of Dakota

san·tene \'san·,tēn\ *n* -S [ISV *sant-* (fr. NL *Santalum*) + *-ene*] **:** a liquid unsaturated terpene C_9H_{14} derived from norbornane and found esp. in East Indian sandalwood oil and various pine-needle oils

san·te·none \'santə,nōn\ *n* -S [ISV *santene* + *-one*] **:** a crystalline bicyclic ketone $C_9H_{14}O$ that is the lower homolog of camphor and occurs in East Indian sandalwood oil

san·thali \,sən·'tälē\ *n, pl* **santhali** *or* **santhalis :** SANTALI

san·ti·a·go \¦santē¦ä(,)gō\ *adj, usu cap* [fr. *Santiago*, city in central Chile] **1 :** of or from Santiago, the capital of Chile **:** of the kind or style prevalent in Santiago **2** [fr. *Santiago* de Cuba, city on south coast of Cuba] **:** of or from the city of Santiago de Cuba, Cuba **:** of the kind or style prevalent in Santiago de Cuba

san·tims \'säntəmz\ *n, pl* **san·ti·mi** \-təmē\ [Latvian, fr. F *centime* — more at CENTIME] **1 :** a unit of value of Latvia equivalent to 1/100 lat between 1922 and 1940 **2 :** a coin representing one santims

san·tir \san·'ti(ə)r\ *also* **san·tour** \-tu̇(ə)r\ *n* -S [Ar *sinṭīr*, *sanṭīr*, *sanṭūr*, fr. Gk *psaltērion* psaltery, harp — more at PSALTER] **:** a Persian dulcimer that is played with two curved sticks

santo \'sän·(,)tō\ *n* -S [Sp, fr. LL *sanctus* — more at SAINT] **1 :** SAINT **2 :** a saint's image; *esp* **:** a painted or carved wooden image usu. found in New Mexico ⟨had carved crude ~*s* of the Virgin and St. Joseph and the Child —Ann Ehidester⟩

[1]san·to do·min·gan \¦santōdə¦miŋgən\ *adj, usu cap S&D* [*Santo Domingo* (former name of the Dominican Republic) + E *-an*] **:** of or relating to Santo Domingo or the Dominican Republic

[2]santo domingan \"\ *n, cap S&D* **:** a native or inhabitant of Santo Domingo

san·to do·min·go \-ŋ(,)gō\ *n, pl* **santo domingo** *or* **santo domingos** *usu cap S&D* [fr. *Santo Domingo*, pueblo in central New Mexico] **1 a :** a Keres people occupying a pueblo in New Mexico **b :** a member of such people **2 :** the language of the Santo Domingo people

san·tol \sän·'tōl\ *n* -S [Tag *santól*] **:** an Indo-Malayan tree (*Sandoricum indicum* or *S. koetjape*) of the family Meliaceae that yields a reddish wood and that is sometimes cultivated for its red acid fruits which are used esp. in preserves and pickles

san·to·li·na \,santə'līnə\ *n* [NL, alter. of L *santonica*] **1** *cap* **:** a genus of Mediterranean undershrubs (family Compositae) having dissected leaves resembling those of the yarrow and clustered flower heads that lack ray flowers — see LAVENDER COTTON **2** -S **:** any plant of the genus *Santolina*

[1]san·ton \'santᵊn, -tən\ *n* -S [F, fr. Sp *santón*, aug. of *santo* saint] **1 :** a saint in Muslim countries **:** a dervish regarded by the people as a saint **2 :** HERMIT

[2]san·ton \säⁿtōⁿ\ *n* -S [F, fr. Prov *santoun*, lit., little saint, fr. *sant* saint, fr. LL *sanctus* saint, fr. L, holy — more at SAINT] *in southern France* **:** a small clay image usu. of a saint

san·ton·i·ca \san·'tänəkə\ *n* -S [NL, fr. L (*herba*) *santonica*, an herb, prob. wormwood, fem. of *santonicus* of or belonging to the Santoni, fr. *Santoni* a people of Aquitania + L *-icus* -ic] **1 :** a European wormwood (*Artemisia pauciflora*) **2 :** an anthelmintic drug consisting of the unexpanded dried flower heads of the santonica or a closely related plant (as Levant wormseed)

san·to·nin \'santᵊnən, -tən-\ *n* -S [ISV *santon-* (fr. NL *santonica*) + *-in*] **:** a poisonous slightly bitter crystalline compound $C_{15}H_{18}O_3$ that is a bicyclic sesquiterpenoid ketonic lactone occurring in santonica and in other plants of the genus *Artemisia* and used esp. formerly as an anthelmintic

san·to ni·ño \'säntō'nēn(,)yō\ *n* [Sp, lit., holy child] **:** an image of the Christ child

san·to·rin earth \¦santə¦rēn-\ *or* **santorin** *n, usu cap S* [fr. *Santorin*, Greek island in the Aegean] **:** a volcanic tuff from the island of Santorin consisting principally of a fine light gray siliceous material used for making cement

san·to·ri·ni's cartilage \¦santə¦rēnēz-, ¦sän-\ *n, usu cap S* [after Giovanni D. *Santorini* †1737? Ital. anatomist] **:** CORNICULATE CARTILAGE

santorini's duct *n, usu cap S* [after Giovanni D. *Santorini* †1737? Ital. anatomist] **:** DUCT OF SANTORINI

[1]san·tos \'santəs\ *adj, usu cap* [fr. *Santos*, city in southeastern Brazil] **:** of or from the city of Santos, Brazil **:** of the kind or style prevalent in Santos

[2]santos \"\ *n* -ES [after *Santos*, Brazil, principal shipping port for coffee in Brazil] **1** *or* **santos coffee** *usu cap S* **:** Brazilian coffee that is produced chiefly in São Paulo and is characterized by moderate body and somewhat acid flavor — see BOURBON 5 **2** *often cap* **:** DARK BEAVER

santour *var of* SANTIR

sants *pl of* SANT, *pres 3d sing of* SANT

san ts'ai \'sän'tsī\ *n* [Chin(Pek) *san*[1] *ts'ai*[3] three-color] **:** a 3-color enamel-glazed ceramic ware produced during the Ming dynasty and later

sa·nu·si *also* **se·nus·si** \sə'nüsē\ *n, pl* **sanusi** *or* **sanusis** *also* **senussi** *or* **senussis** *usu cap* [after Muhammad ibn Ali as-*Sanūsī* †1859 Algerian religious leader, founder of the Sanusi brotherhood] **:** a member of a Muslim brotherhood of No. Africa founded in 1837 who observes a strict and ascetic type of Islamic orthodoxy combined with a militant aggressiveness in pursuance of political goals

sa·nu·si·ya *or* **sa·nu·si·yah** \-ē(y)ə\ *n pl, usu cap* [Ar *Sanūsīya*, after Muhammad as-*Sanūsī* †1859] **:** SANUSIS

san·vi·ta·lia \,sanvə'tālēə\ *n* [NL, prob. fr. F. *Sanvitali* †1761 Ital. mathematician (or fr. the *Sanvitali* family, many of whose members were famous) + NL *-ia*] **1** *cap* **:** a small genus of chiefly tropical American annual herbs (family Compositae) having small heads with yellow or white rays, a flat receptacle, and naked or awn-tipped achenes — see CREEPING ZINNIA **2** -S **:** any plant of the genus *Sanvitalia*

san·wa millet \'säŋwə-\ *n* [Hindi *sāwā*, fr. Skt *śyāmāka* millet] **:** JAPANESE MILLET

san·ya \'sänyə\ *n, pl* **sanya** *or* **sanyas** *usu cap* **1 :** a Tlingit people about Cape Fox, Alaska **2 :** a member of the Sanya people

são pau·lo \(')sau̇ⁿ(m)¦pau̇(,)lü\ *adj, usu cap S&P* [fr. *São Paulo*, Brazil] **:** of or from the city of São Paulo, Brazil **:** of the kind or style prevalent in São Paulo

saora *usu cap, var of* SAURA

sao·shyant \'sau̇shyənt\ *n* -S *usu cap* [Av, savior] **:** one of three deliverers of later Zoroastrian eschatology appearing at thousand year intervals and each inaugurating a new order of things and a special period of human progress

¹sap \'sap\ *n* -s [ME, fr. OE *sæp;* akin to OHG *saf* sap, MD *sap*] **1 a :** the fluid part of a plant; *specif* **:** a watery solution of gases (as carbon dioxide), salts and other materials from the soil, and organic products of metabolism that circulates through the vascular system, carries raw materials to the peripheral chlorophyll-bearing cells, translocates the products of metabolism to other parts of the plant for use or storage, and is a major commercial source of sugar in sugarcane, various palms, and the sugar maple **b (1) :** a body fluid (as blood, lymph, saliva, or semen) essential to life or health or characteristic of a healthy, fresh, or vigorous condition **(2) :** bodily health and vigor **:** VITALITY ⟨the ~ of youth, the sapience of age⟩ **c** *chiefly Scot* **:** a beverage taken with solid food **d :** moisture in stone **2 a :** SAPWOOD **b saps** *pl* **:** lumber containing much sapwood and inferior in quality to firsts and seconds **3 a** *Brit* **:** GRIND 3 **b :** a person unusually liable to be taken in (as by his own sentimentality or gullibility or by a deliberate trick) **:** SIMPLETON, FOOL ⟨fleecing one ~ at a time —Alva Johnston⟩ **4 :** outside stone (as in a quarry) softened by weathering **5 :** a blackjack, policeman's club, or other object used as a bludgeon ⟨his ~ made of rocks in a sock —Frank McIntyre⟩

²sap \"\ *n* -s [MF & OIt; MF *sape, sappe* spade, hoe, fr. OIt *zappa,* perh. fr. OIt dial. *zappo* goat] **1 a** *obs* **:** the act or process of undermining an enemy fortification **b :** the act or process of digging a trench from within **c :** the act or process of weakening or destroying by stealth or devious methods ⟨an endeavor by slow ~ to weaken the authority of some of the writers —C.J.Ellicott⟩ **2 a :** a trench prolonged in the desired direction by digging away the earth at its head from within the trench itself and usu. throwing the earth up as a parapet on the exposed flank and on the end as additional protection to the working party — compare FLYING SAP **b :** a trench or gallery dug from an attacker's lines to a point beneath an enemy's fortifications to gain entrance or to destroy them with explosives

³sap \"\ *vb* **sapped; sapped; sapping; saps** [MF *saper, sapper,* prob. fr. OIt *zappare,* fr. *zappa* spade, hoe] *vi* **:** to proceed by or execute a sap ~ *vt* **1 :** to subvert by digging or eroding the substratum or foundation **:** UNDERMINE ⟨the village . . . may be slowly *sapped* away by ants moving blindly over the earth —David Garnett⟩ **2 a :** to diminish gradually the supply or intensity of ⟨his driving ambition . . . was slowly *sapping* away his fundamental decency and idealism —F.G.Slaughter⟩ ⟨old organisms do produce some substance which ~*s* their vigor —Waldemar Kaempffert⟩ **b :** to exhaust the energy or vitality of ⟨it isn't merely danger which ~*s* these young men —Frederic Morton⟩ **3 :** to operate against or pierce by a sap **syn** see WEAKEN

⁴sap \"\ *vb* **sapped; sapped; sapping; saps** [¹*sap*] *vt* **1 a :** to drain or deprive of its sap **b :** to draw off (sap) **2 :** to heat flue-cured tobacco to a high temperature for a short interval after its being hung in a barn to drive off moisture and start the curing **3 :** to knock out with a sap ⟨whether a guy fell or whether he was *sapped* —*Police Gazette*⟩ ~ *vi, Brit* **:** to act the sap **:** GRIND

sap *abbr* sapwood

SAP *abbr* **1** semi-armor-piercing **2** soon as possible

sa·pa \'sāpə\ *n* -s [L; akin to L *sapere* to taste, have good taste — more at SAGE] **:** grape juice evaporated to a syrupy consistency or to the consistency of honey and used esp. in the 16th century as a cough cure **:** MUST

sap·a·jou \'sapə,jü, ,sapə'zhü\ *n* -s [F, fr. Tupi] **1 :** CAPUCHIN 3b **2 :** SPIDER MONKEY

sa·pan \sə'pan, 'sa,pan\ *n* -s [Malay *sapang*] **:** the heartwood of sappanwood formerly used as an astringent

sapanwood *var of* SAPPANWOOD

sap cavity *n* [¹*sap*] **:** VACUOLE

sap chafer *n* **:** any of various sap-feeding flower beetles esp. of the family Cetoniidae

sap-drawer \'=,=(=)\ *n* **:** one of the small lower branches left on a topworked or frameworked tree to nourish the roots until new growth is well established

sa·pe·le mahogany *or* **sapele** *also* **sa·pe·li** \sə'pēlē\ *n* -s [*sapele, sapeli* fr. native name in West Africa] **1 :** MAHOGANY 1b(2) **2 :** a tree (esp. *Entandrophragma cylindricum*) that produces sapele mahogany

sa·peque *also* **sa·pek** \sə'pek\ *n* -s [F *sapèque,* fr. Malay *sa pek, sa pe,* fr. *sa* one + *pek, pe* pie (currency)] **:** ²CASH; *esp* **:** a cash formerly issued by France for use in Indochina

sa·per·da \sə'pərdə\ *n* [NL, prob. fr. Gk *saperdēs,* a fish, prob. perch] **1** *cap* **:** a genus of long-horned beetles containing several whose larvae are destructive borers — see APPLE TREE BORER, LINDEN BORER **2** -s **:** any beetle of the genus *Saperda*

sap flow *n* **:** TRANSPIRATION STREAM

sap·ful \'sapfəl\ *adj* [¹*sap* + *-ful*] **:** SAPPY 1a

sap green *n* **1 :** a dull green lake prepared from buckthorn berries — compare LOKAO **2 a :** a strong yellow green **b :** a light olive color that is greener and less strong than citrine and darker than grape green — called also *bladder green, verd vessie*

sap gum *n* **1 :** sapwood from the sweet gum or lumber sawed from it **2 :** SWEET GUM **3 :** lumber sawed from a tree of the genus *Nyssa*

¹saphead \'=,=\ *n* [¹*sap* + *head*] **:** a weak-minded stupid person **:** SAP 3b

²saphead \"\ *n* [²*sap* + *head*] **:** the end of a sap at which digging is in progress

sa·phe·na \sə'fēnə\ *n* -s *often attrib* [ME, fr. ML, fr. Ar *ṣāfin*] **:** SAPHENOUS VEIN

sa·phe·nous \-nəs\ *adj* [*saphena* + *-ous*] **:** of, relating to, associated with, situated near, or being the two chief superficial veins of the leg ⟨the ~ opening gives passage to the long saphenous vein through the fascia lata⟩

saphenous vein *n* **:** either of two chief superficial veins of the leg: as **a :** one originating in the foot and passing up the medial side of the leg and through the saphenous opening to join the femoral vein — called also *internal saphenous vein, long saphenous vein* **b :** one originating similarly and passing up the back of the leg to join the popliteal at the knee — called also *external saphenous vein, short saphenous vein*

saph·ie *also* **saf·fi** \'safē\ *n* -s [Mandingo *safaye*] **:** a West African talisman, amulet, or charm

sa·phir d'eau \sa'fi(ə)r'dō\ *n, pl* **saphirs d'eau** \-i(ə)r(z)'-\ [F] **:** WATER SAPPHIRE

sa·pi·ao \,säpē'aù\ *or* **sapiao net** *n* -s [native name in the Philippines] **:** a round haul net of the Philippines made of cotton twine and used for catching small pelagic fishes

sap·id \'sapəd\ *adj* [L *sapidus* tasty, savory, fr. *sapere* to taste, have good taste — more at SAGE] **1 a :** affecting the organs of taste **:** possessing flavor **b :** having a strong esp. agreeable flavor **:** SAVORY **2 :** agreeable to the mind **syn** see PALATABLE

sa·pid·i·ty \sə'pidəd.ē, -dətē, -i\ *n* -ES **:** the quality or state of being sapid **:** SAVOR, SAVORINESS **syn** see TASTE

sa·pi·ence \'sāpēən(t)s, 'sap-\ *n* -s [ME, fr. MF, fr. L *sapientia,* fr. *sapient-, sapiens* (pres. part.) + *-ia* -y] **1 a :** the quality of being sapient **:** profound knowledge **:** WISDOM, SAGENESS ⟨the perspective of four or five decades informing his judgment with a clarity and authority which are what we mean by ~ — E.A.Weeks⟩ **b** *obs* **:** wisdom regarding ultimate principles in speculative or theoretical rather than practical knowledge ⟨wisdom . . . may denote either ~, a habit of knowing what is true; or prudence, a disposition of choosing what is good — Isaac Barrow⟩ **2 :** exactness and discrimination in expression

sapi·ens \'sapēənz, 'sāp- *also* -ē,enz *or* -ē,en(t)s\ *adj* [NL (specific epithet of *Homo sapiens*), fr. L, knowing] **:** of, relating to, resembling, or being recent man (*Homo sapiens*) as distinguished from various fossil men

¹sapi·ent \'sāpēənt, 'sap-\ *adj* [ME, fr. MF, fr. L *sapient-, sapiens,* pres. part. of *sapere* to have sense, be wise — more at SAGE] **:** possessing or expressing great sagacity and discernment **:** SAGE ⟨valuable insights and ~ advice to educators — H.A.Larrabee⟩ ⟨eyes that were ~ and almost ironical — T.W.Duncan⟩ ⟨a ~ author⟩ **syn** see WISE

²sapient \"\ *n, archaic* **:** a sapient person

sapi·en·tial \,=='enchəl\ *adj* [ME *sapiencial,* fr. LL *sapientialis,* fr. L *sapientia* wisdom + *-alis* -al] **:** characterized by or peculiar to wisdom ⟨the ~ attitude . . . replaced the imprecatory attitude —Joseph Frank⟩ ⟨attributing a ~ function to prudence —V.J.Bourke⟩

sapiential books *n* **:** the biblical books of Proverbs, Ecclesiastes, Canticle of Canticles, Wisdom, and Ecclesiasticus

sapi·ent·ly *adv* **:** in a sapient manner

sa·pin \sa'paⁿ\ *n* -s [ME, fr. MF, fr. L *sapinus, sappinus,* of Gaulish origin; akin to W *syb-wydd* fir, Corn *sib-nit* silver fir; akin to OSlav *sokŭ* sap] **:** FIR 1

sa·pin·da \sə'pində\ *n* -s [Skt *sapiṇḍa,* lit., having the same lump, fr. *sa-* one and the same (akin to *sama* same) + *piṇḍa* lump of rice offered to deceased ancestors; fr. the fact that the lump is offered to the three nearest ancestors and the crumbs to the next three — more at SAME] **:** a person considered in his relation to any of his three or sometimes six nearest lineal male ancestors or descendants

sap·in·da·ce·ae \,sapən'dāsē,ē\ *n pl, cap* [NL, fr. *Sapindus,* type genus + *-aceae*] **:** a large family of chiefly tropical and predominantly Old World woody plants (order Sapindales) with alternate and usu. pinnate or trifoliolate leaves that lack stipules, small flowers commonly in axillary or terminal panicles, and a fruit that may be capsular, drupaceous, or made up of samaras — **sap·in·da·ceous** \;==;dāshəs\ *adj*

sap·in·da·les \,=='dā(,)lēz\ *n pl, cap* [NL, prob. fr. *Sapindus* + *-ales*] **:** an order of dicotyledonous plants having the stamens inserted on a disk and the ovary with one or two ovules in each cell

sa·pin·dus \sə'pindəs\ *n, cap* [NL, prob. fr. L *sapo* soap + *Indus* of India, India, fr. Gk *Indos* — more at SAPONACEOUS, INDIA] **:** a genus of tropical and subtropical trees (family Hippocastanaceae) having simply pinnate leaves, flowers nearly regular, and fruit a globose or 2- to 3-lobed berry — see SOAPBERRY; compare SAPINDACEAE

sa·pit \sä'pēt\ *n* -s [Moro, prob. modif. of E *sailboat*] **:** a decorated sailboat of Sulu Archipelago

sa·pi·um \'sāpēəm\ *n, cap* [NL, prob. fr. L *sapinus* fir] **:** a genus of tropical trees and shrubs (family Euphorbiaceae) having poisonous milky juice, alternate entire leaves and apetalous flowers in spikes — see CHINESE TALLOW TREE

sa·pi·u·tan \;säpē'üt'n\ *n* -s [Malay *sapi hutan* wild cattle, fr. *sapi* cow + *hutan* forest, wild] **:** ANOA

sa·ple \'sāpəl\ *n* -s [by alter.] **:** SABLE

sap·less \'sapləs\ *adj* [¹*sap* + *-less*] **1 a :** destitute of sap or other vital juices **:** DRY ⟨the wood dry and splintered and dead, the rats and roaches scurrying along the ~ planks —Norman Mailer⟩ **b :** barren and unproductive from lack of moisture ⟨a rock, barren, and herbless, and ~ —E.G.Bulwer-Lytton⟩ **2 :** lacking vitality **:** LIFELESS, FEEBLE ⟨my mother's hair at this time was full of gray and her body looked ~ —Nadine Gordimer⟩ **3 :** being without substantial value **:** INSIPID ⟨a somewhat ~ tale of a poor little rich girl and a rich little poor boy —Florence Bullock⟩ — **sap·less·ness** *n* -ES

sap·ling \'saplin, -lēn\ *n* -s [ME, fr. ¹*sap* + *-ling*] **1 :** a young tree; *specif* **:** a young forest tree not over four inches in diameter at breast height **2 :** YOUTH ⟨a young foolish ~ —Shak.⟩ **3 :** a greyhound whelped prior to a running season but in the same calendar year

sap·ling·hood \-,hùd\ *n* **:** the state of being a sapling

¹sa·po \'sä,pō\ *n* -s [AmerSp, fr. Sp, toad] **:** TOADFISH

²sa·po \'sā,pō\ *n* -s [L] **:** ¹SOAP 1; *esp* **:** a sodium soap — compare CASTILE

sap·o·dil·la \,sapə'dilə, -dē(y)ə\ *also* **sap·o·til·la** \-'tilə, -tē(y)ə\ *or* **sap·o·ti·lha** \-'tilyə\ *n* -s [*sapodilla, sapotilla* fr. Sp *zapotillo,* dim. of *zapote* sapodilla plum; *sapotilha* fr. Pg, prob. fr. Sp *zapotillo* — more at SAPOTA] **1 :** a large tree (*Achras zapota*) found throughout tropical No. America but naturalized throughout the tropical world with hard reddish durable wood and handsome evergreen foliage and latex that yields chicle **2** *or* **sapodilla plum :** the fruit of the sapodilla with a rough brownish skin and very sweet brownish pulp — called also *chico, chicozapote, nispero*

sapodilla family *n* **:** SAPOTACEAE

sap·o·gen·in \,sapə'jenən; sə'päjənən, -,nēn\ *n* -s [ISV *saponin* + *-genin*] **:** the nonsugar portion of a saponin obtained by hydrolysis or in a few cases found free in plants and characterized by either a triterpenoid usu. pentacyclic structure (as in quillaic acid) or by a steroid structure usu. having a spiro acetal side chain (as in diosgenin) ⟨interest in the steroidal ~*s* has been increasing in recent years because of their usefulness as starting materials in the synthesis of steroidal hormones —Stephen Kaufmann⟩

sap·o·na·ceous \,sapə'nāshəs\ *adj* [NL *saponaceus,* fr. L *sapon-, sapo* soap (of Gmc origin) + *-aceus* -aceous; akin to OE *sāpe* soap — more at SOAP] **1 :** resembling soap **:** having the qualities of soap **:** SOAPY **2 :** liable to slip away **:** ingratiating but evasive **:** ELUSIVE — **sap·o·na·ceous·ness** *n* -ES

sa·po·nar·ia \,==na(ə)rēə\ *n, cap* [NL, fr. ML, fem. of *saponarius* of soap, fr. L *sapon-, sapo* soap + *-arius* -ary] **:** a genus of Old World herbs (family Caryophyllaceae) having large flowers with a tubular or gibbous calyx, five clawed petals, and a 4-valved capsular fruit — see SOAPWORT

sap·o·nary \'==,nerē\ *n* -ES [NL *Saponaria*] **:** SOAPWORT 1

sa·po·nat·ed \'==;nād·əd\ *adj* [L *sapon-, sapo* soap + E *-ate* + *-ed*] **:** treated or combined with a soap ⟨~ cresol solution⟩

sa·po·ni \sə'pōnē\ *n, pl* **saponi** *or* **saponis** *usu cap* **1 :** an extinct Siouan people of central Virginia **2 :** a member of the Saponi people

sa·pon·i·fi·able \sə'pänə,fīəbəl, ,==='===\ *adj* **:** capable of being saponified

sa·pon·i·fi·ca·tion \=,===fə'kāshən\ *n* -s [F, fr. *saponifier* to saponify, after such pairs as F *identifier* to identify: *identification*] **1 a :** the act, process, or result of soapmaking **:** conversion into soap **:** the hydrolysis of a fat by alkali with the formation of salts of the fatty acids together with glycerol **b :** the hydrolysis of a fat or wax **2 a :** the hydrolysis esp. by alkali of an ester into the corresponding alcohol and acid or salt of the acid **b :** the hydrolysis of an organic compound esp. by alkali

saponification value *or* **saponification number** *n* **:** a measure of the total free and combined acids esp. in a fat, wax, or resin expressed as the number of milligrams of potassium hydroxide required for the complete saponification of one gram of substance

sa·pon·i·fi·er \sə'pänə,fī(ə)r, -fīə\ *n* -s **:** one that saponifies: as **a :** a reagent used to cause saponification **b :** an apparatus for saponifying fats

sa·pon·i·fy \-,fī\ *vb* -ED/-ING/-ES [F *saponifier,* fr. L *sapon-, sapo* soap + *-ifier* -ify] *vt* **:** to convert (as a fat or fatty acid) into soap **:** subject to saponification ~ *vi* **:** to undergo saponification

sap·o·nin \'sapənən\ *n* -s [F *saponine,* fr. L *sapon-, sapo* soap + *-ine* -in] **1 :** any of numerous glycosides that occur in many plants (as soapbark, soapwort, or sarsaparilla), that are characterized by their properties of foaming in water solution and producing hemolysis when solutions are injected into the bloodstream, and that on hydrolysis yield a triterpenoid or steroid sapogenin and one or more sugars (as glucose, galactose, or xylose) **2 :** a yellowish to white acrid hygroscopic amorphous substance that in powder form causes sneezing, that is extracted esp. from soapbark or soapwort, that contains a triterpenoid saponin as the active ingredient, and that is used chiefly as a foaming and emulsifying agent and detergent

sap·o·nite \-,nīt\ *n* -s [Sw *saponit,* fr. L *sapon-, sapo* soap + Sw *-it* -ite — more at SAPONACEOUS] **:** a mineral consisting of a hydrous magnesium aluminosilicate occurring in soft soapy masses and filling veins and cavities in serpentine, diabase, and other rocks (sp. gr. 2.24–2.30)

sa·por \'sāpə(r)\ *n* -s [ME, fr. L — more at SAVOR] **:** a property (as bitterness) affecting the sense of taste **:** SAVOR, FLAVOR

sap·o·rif·ic \;sapə;rifik\ *adj* [NL *saporificus,* fr. L *sapor* savor + *-i-* + *-ficus* -fic] **:** having the power to produce the sensation of taste

sap·o·rous \'sapərəs\ *adj* [LL *saporosus,* fr. L *sapor* savor + *-osus* -ose] **:** of, relating to, or capable of exciting the sensation of taste **:** having flavor; *esp* **:** agreeable in taste **syn** see PALATABLE

sapos *pl of* SAPO

¹sa·po·ta \sə'pōd·ə\ [NL, fr. Sp *zapote*] *syn of* ACHRAS

²sapota \"\ *n* -s [earlier *sapote,* fr. Sp *zapote,* fr. Nahuatl *tzapotl*] **:** SAPODILLA

sap·o·ta·ce·ae \,sapə'tāsē,ē\ *n pl, cap* [NL, fr. *Sapota* (syn. of *Achras*) + *-aceae*] **:** a family of trees or shrubs (order Ebenales) that are widely distributed in tropical regions and have milky juice, coriaceous leaves, and axillary flowers with stamens in two or three whorls borne on the corolla and often in alternation with staminodia and a superior 2-celled to many-celled ovary followed by often edible fleshy fruits — **sap·o·ta·ceous** \;==;tāshəs\ *adj*

sapota gum *n* **:** chicle obtained from the sapodilla

sa·po·te \sə'pōd·ē\ *or* **za·po·te** \zə-,sə-\ *n* -s [Sp *zapote*] **1 a :** MARMALADE TREE; *also* **:** its fruit **b :** SAPODILLA **2** *Philippines* **:** a date plum (*Diospyros ebenaster*)

sapotilla *or* **sapotilha** *var of* SAPODILLA

sap·o·toxin \,sapə+\ *n* [*saponin* + *toxin*] **:** any of various highly poisonous saponins

sap·pan·wood *or* **sa·pan·wood** \sə'pan,=, 'sa,pan,=\ *also* **sap·pan** *n* -s [*sappanwood, sapanwood* fr. Malay *sapang* + E *wood; sappan* fr. Malay *sapang*] **1 :** a red soluble brazilwood obtained from an East Indian tree (*Caesalpinia sappan*) **2 :** a tree that yields sappanwood

sap·pare \'sa,pa(a)(ə)r, -pe(ə)r\ *n* -s [F, perh. modif. of E *sapphire*] **:** CYANITE

sapped *past of* SAP

¹sap·per \'sapə(r)\ *n* -s [³*sap* + *-er*] **:** one that saps: as **a :** a member of a military engineer unit organized, trained, and equipped primarily to execute sapping and other field fortification work **b :** an engineer that lays, detects, and disarms mines

²sapper \"\ *n* -s [⁴*sap* + *-er*] **:** a sucking insect that punctures plants to feed on the sap (as various bugs or plant lice)

¹sap·phic \'safik, -fēk\ *adj* [L *sapphicus,* fr. Gk *sapphikos,* fr. *Sapphō* Sappho *fl ab* 600 B.C. Greek lyric poetess of Lesbos + *-ikos* -ic] **1** *usu cap* **:** of or relating to the Greek lyric poetess Sappho **2** *sometimes cap* [so called fr. the reputed lesbian group associated with Sappho] **:** of or relating to erotic indulgence **3** *sometimes cap* [so called fr. being the verse forms used by Sappho] **:** of, relating to, or consisting of a four line strophe of three primarily trochaic lines made up of five equal beats of which the middle is a dactyl and the others are of two syllables and followed by an adonic

²sapphic \"\ *n* -s *sometimes cap* **1 :** a sapphic strophe **2 :** a line of verse having the metrical pattern of one of the first three lines of a sapphic strophe **3 :** a verse composed of sapphic strophes

¹sap·phire \'sa,fī(ə)r, -fīə\ *n* -s [ME *saphir, safir,* fr. OF *safir,* fr. L *sapphirus,* fr. Gk *sappheiros,* fr. Heb *sappīr,* fr. Skt *śanipriya,* lit., dear to the planet Saturn, fr. *Śani* (the planet) Saturn + *priya* dear — more at FREE] **1 a :** a precious stone of transparent rich blue corundum of great value **b (1) :** a pure variety of corundum in transparent or translucent crystals used as gems **(2) :** a gem from a corundum crystal **2 a :** a variable color averaging a deep purplish blue that is bluer and deeper than hyacinth blue or Mazarine blue and stronger than cyanine blue (sense 1b) **b :** a dark blue that is greener than Peking blue, greener, lighter, and stronger than Japan blue, and greener and stronger than Flemish blue **3 :** a hummingbird of the genus *Hylocharis* native to So. America and having a bright blue throat and breast

²sapphire \"\ *adj* [ME *saphir,* fr. *saphir,* n., sapphire] **1 :** of or resembling sapphire **2 :** of the color sapphire blue **:** SAPPHIRINE

sapphireberry \'=,=- — *see* BERRY\ *n* **:** ASIATIC SWEETLEAF

sapphire gurnard *n* **:** SAPPHIRINE GURNARD

sapphire quartz *n* **:** a rare blue variety of quartz

sapphirewing \'=,=,=\ *n* **:** a So. American hummingbird (*Pterophanes cyanopterus*) with blue wings

sap·phir·ic \sə'firik\ *adj* **:** having the nature of or resembling a sapphire

¹sap·phir·ine \'safərən, -,rīn, -,rēn\ *adj* [ME *saphirin,* fr. L *sapphirinus,* fr. Gk *sappheirinos,* fr. *sappheiros* sapphire + *-inos* -ine] **1 :** made of sapphire **2 :** resembling sapphire esp. in color

²sapphirine \"\ *n* -s [G *saphirin,* fr. *saphir* sapphire (fr. MHG *saphīr,* fr. OIt *saffiro,* fr. L *sapphirus*) + *-in* -ine] **:** a mineral $(MgFe)_{15}(Al,Fe)_{34}Si_7O_{80}$ consisting of a green or pale blue magnesium aluminum iron silicate and oxide and occurring usu. in granular form (hardness 7.5, sp. gr. 3.42–3.48)

sapphirine gurnard *n* **:** a European gurnard (*Trigla hirundo*) having the pectoral fins much blotched with a rich blue

sap·phism \'sa,fizəm\ *n* -s *sometimes cap* [*Sappho fl ab* 600 B.C. Greek poetess of Lesbos + E *-ism;* fr. the belief that Sappho was homosexual] **:** sensual desire of a woman for other women **:** LESBIANISM

sap·phist \-,fəst\ *n* -s *sometimes cap* [*Sappho fl ab* 600 B.C. + E *-ist*] **:** LESBIAN 2

sap·pho \'sa,fō\ *n* [NL, after *Sappho fl ab* 600 B.C. Greek lyric poetess, fr. L, fr. Gk *Sapphō*] **1** *cap* **:** a genus of hummingbirds comprising a single So. American showy bird (*S. sparganura*) with a forked tail **2** *also* **sappho comet** -s *usu cap S* **:** any hummingbird of the genus *Sappho*

sap pine *n* **1 :** a pitch pine (*Pinus rigida*) **2 :** LOBLOLLY

sap·pi·ness \'sapēnəs, -pin-\ *n* -ES [*sappy* + *-ness*] **1 :** the state of being full of or smelling of sap **2 :** the quality or state of being sappy **:** FOOLISHNESS

sapping *pres part of* SAP

sap·ples \'sapəlz\ *n pl* [prob. dim. (pl.) of E dial. (Sc) *saip* soap, fr. OE *sāpe* — more at SOAP] *Scot* **:** SUDS

sap·po·ro \sə'pōr(,)ō, -pó(,)rō\ *adj, usu cap* [fr. *Sapporo,* Japan] **:** of or from the city of Sapporo, Japan **:** of the kind or style prevalent in Sapporo

sap·py \'sapē, -pi\ *adj* -ER/-EST [ME *sapy,* fr. OE *sæpig,* fr. *sæp* sap + *-ig* -y — more at SAP] **1 a :** abounding with sap **b** *dial* **:** SUCCULENT, JUICY **c** *dial* **:** becoming putrid **:** TAINTED **d** *dial* **:** extremely damp **:** SODDEN **e** *of wool* **:** having a superabundance of yolk **f** *of a feather* **:** immature and with blood in the quill **2 a :** resembling sapwood **b :** consisting largely of sapwood **3 a :** foolishly or immaturely sentimental **:** MAWKISH **b :** lacking in good sense **:** FOOLISH, SILLY **c :** somewhat effeminate **:** FOPPISH **4** *chiefly Scot* **a :** fond of drinking **b :** cheerful as the result of drinking

sappy spot *n* **:** a portion of wood or lumber showing the effects of decay

sapr- *or* **sapro-** *comb form* [Gk, fr. *sapros;* perh. akin to Lith *šupti* to rot] **1 :** rotten **:** putrid ⟨*sapr*emia⟩ ⟨*sapro*stomous⟩ **2 :** dead or decaying organic matter ⟨*sapr*odontia⟩ ⟨*sapro*phyte⟩ **3 :** saprophytic ⟨*Sapro*legnia⟩ **4 :** sapropel ⟨*sapro*coll⟩ ⟨*sapro*dil⟩

sa·pre·mia \sə'prēmēə\ *n* -s [NL, fr. *sapr-* + *-emia*] **:** a toxic state resulting from the presence in the blood of toxic products of putrefactive bacteria and often accompanying gangrene of a part of the body — **sa·pre·mic** \-mik\ *adj*

sap·robe \'sa,prōb\ *or* **sap·ro·bi·ont** \,sa,prō'bī,änt, sə'prōbē,ä-\ *n* -s [*saprobe* ISV *sapr-* + *-be* (fr. Gk *bios* life); *saprobiont* ISV *sapr-* + *-biont* — more at QUICK] **:** a saprobic organism

sa·pro·bic \sə'prōbik, -präb-\ *adj* [ISV *saprobe* + *-ic*] **:** SAPROPHYTIC; *esp* **:** living in or being an environment rich in organic matter and relatively free from oxygen ⟨~ organisms living in sewage⟩ — compare KATHAROBIC — **sa·probi·cal·ly** \-bək(ə)lē\ *adv*

sap·ro·coll \'saprə,käl\ *n* -s [ISV *sapr-* + *-coll*] **:** gelatinous sapropel

sap·ro·dil \-,dil\ *n* -s [prob. fr. *sapr-* + *-dil* (fr. *dilute*)] **:** a sapropel found in the Tertiary

sap·ro·gen \'saprəjən, -,jen\ *n* -s [ISV *sapr-* + *-gen*] **:** an organism (as a fungus) living upon nonliving organic matter and capable of producing its decay; *also* **:** PERTHOPHYTE

sap·ro·gen·e·sis \;saprə+\ *n* [NL, fr. *sapr-* + *genesis*] **:** a part of the life cycle during which a pathogenic organism is living saprophytically or in a dormant state (as the ascospore stage of the apple scab fungus)

sap·ro·gen·ic \;==;jenik\ *adj* [*sapr-* + *-genic*] **1 :** capable of producing decay or putrefaction (as any of various saprophytic bacteria) — compare SAPROPHILOUS **2 a :** of or relating to the production of putrefaction **b :** occurring or produced in or upon putrefying matter

sap·ro·ge·nic·i·ty \,==jə'nisəd·ē\ *n* -ES **:** the capacity for becoming saprogenic

sa·prog·e·nous \sə'präjənəs\ *adj* [*sapr-* + *-genous*] **:** SAPROGENIC

sap·ro·leg·nia \ˌsaprəˈlegnēə\ *n* [NL, fr. *sapr-* + Gk *legnon* border + NL *-ia*] **1** *cap* **:** a genus (the type of the family Saprolegniaceae of the order Saprolegniales) of fungi having a stout tubular multinucleate much-branched thallus without constrictions, producing dimorphic zoospores, growing in water chiefly on plant debris and animal remains, and including one form (*S. ferax*) that attacks living fish, tadpoles, and spawn and causes the white fungus disease **2** -s **:** any fungus of the genus *Saprolegnia*

sap·ro·leg·ni·a·les \ˌ==ˌlegnēˈā(ˌ)lēz\ *n pl, cap* [NL, fr. *Saprolegnia* + *-ales*] **:** an order of chiefly aquatic fungi (class Phycomycetes) having a well-developed mycelium, both sexual and asexual reproduction, biflagellate zoospores, and no periplasm in the oogonia and comprising the water molds — see DIPLANETIC — **sap·ro·leg·ni·ous** \ˌ==¦legnēəs\ *adj*

sap·ro·lite \ˈsaprəˌlīt\ *n* -s [*sapr-* + *-lite*] **:** disintegrated somewhat decomposed rock that lies in its original place — compare GEEST, MANTLEROCK — **sap·ro·lit·ic** \ˌ==¦lid·ik\ *adj*

sap·ront \ˈsaˌpränt\ *n* -s [contr. of *saprobiont*] **:** SAPROBE

sap·ro·pel \ˈsaprəˌpel\ *n* -s [ISV *sapr-* + *-pel* (fr. Gk *pēlos* clay, mud) — more at PEL-] **1 :** a slimy sediment of marine, estuarine, or lacustrine deposition consisting largely of organic debris derived from aquatic plants and animals **2 :** KEROGEN

sap·ro·pel·ic \ˌ==¦pelik\ *adj* [ISV *sapropel* + *-ic*] **1 :** living in mud or ooze composed chiefly of decaying organic matter (as various freshwater protozoa) **2 :** of, relating to, or derived from sapropel ⟨the organic carbon may be humic (coaly) or ∼ (bituminous) —F.J.Pettijohn⟩

sap·ro·pel·ite \ˈ==ˌpeˌlīt, ˌ==ˈ=ˌ=\ *n* -s [*sapropel* + *-ite*] **:** a coal or oil shale formed from sapropel

¹**sa·proph·a·gan** \səˈpräfəgən\ *n* -s [(assumed) NL *saprophaga* + E *-an*] **:** a saprophagous individual

²**saprophagan** \"\ *adj* **:** SAPROPHAGOUS

sa·proph·a·gous \-gəs\ *adj* [prob. fr. (assumed) NL *saprophagus*, fr. *sapr-* + *-phagus* -phagous] **:** feeding on decaying matter

sa·proph·i·lous \səˈpräfələs\ *also* **sap·ro·phile** \ˈsaprəˌfīl\ *adj* [ISV *sapr-* + *-philous* or *-phile*] **:** SAPROPHYTIC; *specif* **:** thriving in decaying matter ⟨∼ bacteria⟩

sap·ro·phyte *also* **sap·ro·phite** \ˈsaprəˌfīt\ *n* -s [ISV *sapr-* + *-phyte*, *-phite* (alter. of *-phyte*)] **1 :** a plant living on dead or decaying organic matter — compare AUTOPHYTE, PERTHOPHYTE **2 :** an organism engaging in saprophytic nutrition — compare PARASITE

¹**sap·ro·phyt·ic** \ˌ==¦fid·ik\ *adj* [*saprophyte* + *-ic*] **:** obtaining food by absorbing dissolved organic material **:** obtaining nourishment osmotically from the products of organic breakdown and decay ⟨∼ plants and animals⟩ — compare AUTOTROPHIC, HOLOPHYTIC, HOLOZOIC; see SAPROZOIC — **sap·ro·phyt·i·cal·ly** \-ək(ə)lē\ *adv*

²**saprophytic** \"\ *n* -s **:** a saprophytic organism

sap·ro·phyt·ism \ˈ==ˌfīdˌizəm, -ˌfīˌtiz-\ *n* -s [*saprophyte* + *-ism*] **:** the condition of feeding saprophytically

sap·ro·spi·ra \ˌsaprəˈspīrə\ *n, cap* [NL, fr. *sapr-* + L *spira* coil — more at SPIRE] **:** a genus of large free-living or commensal aquatic spirochetes (family Spirochaetaceae) having neither crista nor flagella

sap rot *n* **:** a disintegration (as caused by wood-destroying fungi) of sapwood

sap·ro·zo·ic \ˌsaprəˈzōik\ *adj* [*sapr-* + *-zoic*] **:** SAPROPHYTIC — used of animals (as protozoans) — **sap·ro·zo·on** \ˌ==ˈzōˌän\ *n, pl* **sapro·zoa** \-zōə\

saps *pl of* SAP, *pres 3d sing of* SAP

sap·sa·go \sapˈsāˌgō, ˈsapsəˌgō\ *n* -s [modif. of G *schabziger*, fr. *schaben* to scrape (fr. OHG *skaban*) + G dial. *ziger, zieger* whey, whey cheese, fr. MHG *ziger*, prob. fr. a Celt compound whose 1st constituent is akin to OW *dou* two, and whose 2d constituent is akin to MIr *guirim* I warm up; fr. the milk's being heated twice in the cheese-making process; akin to L *duo* two, and to OE *wearm* warm — more at SHAVE, TWO, WARM] **:** a hard green cheese that is made from skim-milk curd, partly ripened, and then mixed with dried powdered leaves of blue melilot for color and flavor

sap·sap \ˈsäpˌsäp\ *n, pl* **sapsap** [native name in the Philippines] **:** any of several small slimy-bodied percoid fishes (genus *Leiognathus*) *esp* **:** a common market fish (*L. equulus*) of the Philippines

sap shield *n* **:** a steel plate used as a shield by a sapper or other advanced worker in places where earth thrown up is inadequate for his defense

sap stain *n* **1 :** a discoloration in sapwood caused by any of various fungi **2 :** a discoloration in newly sawn sapwood due to oxidizing enzymes — compare BLUE STAIN

sapstreak \ˈ=ˌ=\ *n* [¹*sap* + *streak*] **:** a fungous disease of sugar maple caused by a fungus (*Endoconidiophora virescens*) and characterized by death of the crown from the top down and radial water-soaked reddish or gray streaks across the sapwood

sap stream *n* **:** TRANSPIRATION STREAM

sapsucker \ˈ=ˌ==\ *n* [¹*sap* + *sucker*] **1 :** any of several small American woodpeckers of the genus *Sphyrapicus*; *specif* **:** YELLOW-BELLIED SAPSUCKER — see RED-BREASTED SAPSUCKER **2 :** any of various small woodpeckers of genera other than *Sphyrapicus*

sap tie *n* **:** a railroad crosstie having sapwood wider than one-fourth the width of the tie on the top at a point between 20 and 40 inches from the middle of the tie

sap·u·caia *or* **sap·u·ca·ja** *also* **sap·u·ca·ya** \ˌsapəˈkīə\ *n* -s [Pg *sapucaia*, fr. Tupi *zabucáya, sapucáya*] **1 :** a tree of the genus *Lecythis* — see SAPUCAIA NUT **2 :** the hard heavy durable timber of various sapucaias that is used for ties, in heavy construction, and to a limited extent in cabinetmaking

sapucaia nut *n* **:** the oily edible seed of various sapucaias esp. of Brazil and British Guiana that resemble but are often considered superior to Brazil nuts and yield a high percentage of oil — compare MONKEY POT

sapucaia–nut family *n* **:** LECYTHIDACEAE

sap·u·cai·nha \-ˈkīnyə\ *n* -s [Pg, dim. of *sapucaia*] **:** a tall central and southern Brazilian tree (*Carpotroche brasiliensis*) of the family Flacourtiaceae with a nut that yields an oil used in the treatment of leprosy

sapwood \ˈ=ˌ=\ *n* [¹*sap* + *wood*] **:** the younger softer living or physiologically active outer portion of wood that lies between the cambium and the heartwood and is more permeable, less durable, and usu. lighter in color than the heartwood to which it is ultimately converted — called also *alburnum*

sapwood rot *n* **:** SAP ROT

sa·pyg·i·dae \səˈpijəˌdē\ *n pl, cap* [NL, fr. *Sapyga*, type genus (fr. Gk *saos* whole + *pygē* rump) + *-idae* — more at PYG-] **:** a family of parasitic wasps

SAR *abbr* **1** search and rescue **2** semiautomatic rifle

¹**sa·ra** \ˈsärə\ *n, pl* **sara** *or* **saras** *usu cap* **1 :** a people on the Shari river in central Africa **2 :** a member of the Sara people

²**sa·ra** \səˈrō\ *n, pl* **sara** [earlier *Saraw* Cheraw — more at CHERAW] **:** CHERAW

sa·rab·a·ite \səˈrabəˌīt\ *n* -s *usu cap* [ME *Serabite*, fr. LL *Sarabaïta*] **:** one of various vagrant and independent eastern monks in the early church

¹**sar·a·band** *or* **sar·a·bande** \ˈsarəˌband, -baa(ə)nd *also* ˈser-\ *n* -s [F *sarabande*, fr. Sp *zarabanda*] **1 :** a stately court dance of the 17th and 18th centuries resembling the minuet and evolved from a slow Spanish dance of oriental origin **2 :** the music for the saraband in slow triple time characterized usu. by an accent on the second beat; *specif* **:** a movement of the classical suite (as of Handel or Bach)

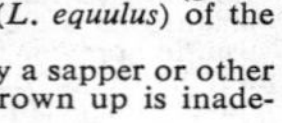

rhythms for saraband

²**saraband** \"\ *or* **ser·e·bend** \ˈserəˌbend\ *n* -s *usu cap* [fr. *Saravan*, district in Iran] **:** a Persian rug of fairly fine weave and short pile usu. having rows of small cashmere palmettes in delicate hues set in a drop repeat on a mellow red ground

sar·a·cen \ˈsarəsən *also* ˈser-\ *n* -s *usu cap* [ME *Saracen*, fr. LL *Saracenus*, fr. LGk *Sarakēnos*] **1 :** a nomadic people of the deserts between Syria and Arabia — usu. used in pl. ⟨crusaders fighting the *Saracens*⟩ **2 :** a member of the Saracen people; *specif* **:** ARAB

sar·a·cen·ic \ˌ==¦senik, -nēk\ *or* **sar·a·cen** \ˈ==sən\ *adj, usu cap* [*saracenic* fr. ML *saracenicus*, fr. LL *Saracenus* Saracen + L *-icus* -ic] **:** of, relating to, or having the characteristics of the Saracens

saracenic architecture *n, usu cap S* **:** the architecture of the Muhammadans consisting chiefly of mosques and tombs and characterized by decorated surfaces, bulbous domes, and horseshoe, pointed, and multifoil arches — compare MOORISH ARCHITECTURE

saracen's comfrey *or* **saracen's consound** *n, usu cap S* **:** a ragwort (*Senecio saracenicus*) believed to have been used by the Saracens to heal wounds

saracen's head *n, usu cap S* **:** MOOR'S HEAD 1b

saracen stone *or* **saracen's stone** *n, usu cap 1st S* **:** SARSEN

sa·ra·da \ˈshärəˌdä, -ˌdə\ *n* -s *usu cap* [after *Sāradā* Nandan, said to have first reduced Kashmiri to writing] **:** an older alphabet of Kashmir that is akin to the Devanagari

sar·a·gos·sa \ˌsarəˈgäsə *also* ¦ser- *or* -gȯsə\ *adj, usu cap* [fr. *Saragossa*, city in northeastern Spain] **:** of or from the city of Saragossa, Spain **:** of the kind or style prevalent in Saragossa

sar·ah *also* **sara** \ˈserə, ˈsa(a)rə, ˈsärə\ *n* -s *usu cap* [prob. fr. the feminine name *Sarah*] **:** PAINTED TRILLIUM

sa·ra·je·vo *or* **se·ra·je·vo** \ˈsärəyeˌvō, -yə,-, -vō; ¦särə¦yā(ˌ)vō, ¦sar-, ¦ser-, -ye(-\ *adj, usu cap* [fr. *Sarajevo*, city in central Yugoslavia] **:** of or from the city of Sarajevo, Yugoslavia **:** of the kind or style prevalent in Sarajevo

sar·a·kolle \ˌsarəˈkäl\ *also* **sar·a·kole** \-kōl\ *n, pl* **sarakolle** *or* **sarakolles** *also* **sarakole** *or* **sarakoles** *usu cap* **1 :** a people of the French Sudan claiming descent from light-skinned ancestors of the Ghana empire and speaking a Mandingo dialect **2 :** a member of the Sarakolle people

sar·a·mac·ca \ˌsarəˈmakə\ *n* -s *usu cap* [fr. *Saramacca*, river and district in central Surinam] **:** an English based Creole language of Surinam

sar·a·mac·can·er \-nə(r)\ *n* -s *usu cap* [D, fr. *Saramacca*, river and district in central Surinam] **:** a member of a Negro people living in Surinam

sa·ran \səˈran, -raa(ə)n\ *n* -s [fr. *Saran*, a trademark] **:** a tough flexible thermoplastic made by polymerizing or usu. copolymerizing vinylidene chloride that can be formed into waterproof and chemically resistant filaments, staple fibers, fabrics, pipe, film, molded parts, and protective coatings

sa·rang·ean \səˈraŋēən\ *n, pl* **sarangean** *or* **sarangeans** *usu cap* [*Sarang* native name in Seistan + E *-an*] **1 :** an early people inhabiting a region adjacent to the lower Gilmend river in southwestern Afghanistan **2 :** a member of the Sarangean people

sar·an·gous·ty \ˌsaranˈgüstē\ *n* -ES [Per *sar-angushti* thin paste for painting the tips of fingers, fr. *sari angusht* fingertip, fr. *sar* head + *angusht* finger, toe] **:** stucco made waterproof for protection against dampness

sa·ra·pe *or* **se·ra·pe** \səˈräpē\ *n* -s [MexSp *sarape*] **:** a woolen blanket often of bright geometric patterns worn by Spanish-American men as a cloak or poncho

saras *pl of* SARA

sar·a·to·ga \ˌsarəˈtōgə *also* ˌser-; *attrib* ¦==¦==\ *n* -s *usu cap* [fr. *Saratoga* Springs, N.Y.] **1 :** a variation of Michigan in which the same number of chips is placed on each boodle card by each player **2 :** SARATOGA TRUNK **3 :** a box or container used in the transfer or temporary storage of tobacco

saratoga chip *or* **saratoga potato** *n, usu cap S* [after *Saratoga* Springs, N.Y.] **:** POTATO CHIP

saratoga chop *n, usu cap S* **:** a boneless shoulder chop of lamb rolled and skewered with the cut surfaces left exposed — see LAMB illustration

saratoga cocktail *n, usu cap S* **:** a cocktail consisting of brandy, sweet vermouth, bitters, and sometimes a fruit juice (as of lemon or pineapple)

saratoga spittlebug *n, usu cap 1st S* **:** a cercopid bug (*Aphrophora saratogensis*) that feeds on pines in northern U.S.

saratoga trunk *n, usu cap S* **:** a large traveling trunk usu. with a rounded top

sar·a·to·gi·an \ˌ==ˈtōgēən\ *n* -s *cap* [*Saratoga* Springs, N.Y. + E *-an*] **:** a native or resident of Saratoga Springs, New York

sa·ra·tov \səˈrädˌəf, -dˌəv\ *adj, usu cap* [fr. *Saratov*, U.S.S.R.] **:** of or from the city of Saratov, U.S.S.R. **:** of the kind or style prevalent in Saratov

sara·wak bean \səˈräwə(k)-, -äˌwak-, ÷ˈsarəˌvak-\ *n, usu cap S* [after *Sarawak*, northwestern Borneo] **:** a plant (*Dolichos hosei*) introduced into Australia for forage and hay

sar·ba·cane \ˈsärbəˌkān, -bəkən\ *also* **sar·bi·can** \ˈsärbəkən\ *n* -s [F *sarbacane*, fr. MF, alter. (influenced by *cane* reed, cane) of *sarbatenne*, fr. OSp *cerbatana*, fr. Ar *zarbaṭāna*, *zabaṭāna* — more at CANE] **:** BLOWGUN 1

sarc- *or* **sarco-** *comb form* [Gk *sark-*, *sarko-*, fr. *sark-*, *sarx*] **:** flesh ⟨*sarcic*⟩ ⟨*sarcidium*⟩ ⟨*sarcoblast*⟩ ⟨*sarcosepsis*⟩

-sarc \ˌsärk, ˌsȧk\ *n comb form* -s [Gk *sark-*, *sarx* flesh] **:** flesh **:** fleshy material ⟨*ectosarc*⟩ ⟨*perisarc*⟩

sar·casm \ˈsärˌkazəm, ˈsȧˌk-\ *n* -s [F *sarcasme*, fr. LL *sarcasmos*, fr. Gk *sarkasmos*, fr. *sarkazein* to tear flesh like dogs, bite the lips in rage, speak bitterly, sneer, fr. *sark-*, *sarx* flesh; akin to Av *thwarǝs-* to cut] **1 :** a keen or bitter taunt **:** a cutting gibe or rebuke often delivered in a tone of contempt or disgust ⟨speech full of reproachful ∼*s*⟩ **2 :** the use of caustic or stinging remarks or language often with inverted or ironical statement on occasion of an offense or shortcoming with intent to wound the feelings **syn** see WIT

sar·cast \-kast\ *n* -s [prob. back-formation fr. *sarcastical*] **:** an adept in sarcasm

sar·cas·tic \(ˈ)¦==¦kastik, -¦kaas-, -tēk\ *also* **sar·cas·ti·cal** \-təkəl, -tēk-\ *adj* [fr. *sarcasm*, after such pairs as E *enthusiasm: enthusiastic, enthusiastical*] **1 :** expressive of or characterized by sarcasm **:** marked by contempt or disgust ⟨made a profound and ∼ bow, turned on his heel and left the room —W.H.Hudson †1922⟩ ⟨making the ∼ comment that his popularity with his fellow workers depends on his not producing more than they⟩ **2 :** given to the use of sarcasm **:** CAUSTIC ⟨was as a stump speaker ∼ . . . as often as he was argumentative —Carl Sandburg⟩

syn SATIRIC, IRONIC *or* IRONICAL, SARDONIC: SARCASTIC may describe whatever is bitter, cutting, and marked by intent to wound by taunting, mocking, deriding, or making ridiculous ⟨laughed in her face, with a horrid *sarcastic* demoniacal laughter, that almost sent the schoolmistress into fits —W.M.Thackeray⟩ SATIRIC applies to attempts to censure, castigate, or expose to open ridicule weaknesses, faults, or excesses ⟨a *satiric* picture, too, an intermittent glimpse into the smallness of human nature —John Erskine †1951⟩ ⟨the *satiric* theme of the rustic staring wildly about him in the town —G.G.Coulton⟩ IRONIC or IRONICAL applies to amusing, piquant, startling, or surprising difference between what is said and what is intended or between what is given out and accepted and what is really true ⟨it is an *ironic* likelihood that had he written less he would be held in higher esteem —Dorothy S. Davis⟩ ⟨a man so excessively ugly that he went by the *ironical* appellation of "beauty" —Herman Melville⟩ SARDONIC may apply to what manifests scorn, mockery, or derision and arises from disbelief in or doubt about values or motives ⟨continued to grin with a *sardonic* humor, with a cynical mockery and defiance —Jack London⟩ ⟨came to the funeral, full of calm, *sardonic* glee, and without being asked —Arnold Bennett⟩

sar·cas·ti·cal·ly \-tək(ə)lē, -tēk-, -li\ *adv* **:** in a sarcastic manner ⟨skilled ability to catalog ∼ the interiors of middle-class American homes and offices —*Time*⟩ ⟨you weren't very particular about the roomers you took, we said, ∼ —Helen S. Rush & Mary Sherkanowski⟩

sar·cas·tic·ness *or* **sar·cas·ti·cal·ness** *n* -ES [*sarcasticness* fr. *sarcastic* + *-ness*; *sarcasticalness* fr. *sarcastical* + *-ness*] **:** the quality or state of being sarcastic

sar·cee *also* **sar·see** *or* **sar·ci** *or* **sarsi** \ˈsärsē\ *n, pl* **sarcee** *or* **sarcees** *usu cap* [prob. fr. Blackfoot (Siksika) *sa arsi* not good] **1 a :** an Athapaskan people of the upper Saskatchewan and Athabaska river valleys in Alberta, Canada **b :** a member of such people **2 :** the language of the Sarcee people

sar·cel \ˈsärsəl\ *n* -s [ME *sercell*, fr. MF *cercel*, fr. L *circellus* small ring, dim. of *circus* ring — more at CIRCLE] **:** a pinion feather of a hawk's wing

sar·celle \(ˈ)sär¦sel\ *n* -s [ME *sarcell*, *cercelle*, fr. MF *cercelle*, fr. (assumed) VL *cercedula*, fr. L *querquedula*, a duck, prob. teal, prob. modif. of Gk *kerkithalis* heron; akin to Skt *kṛkara* partridge, Gk *korak-*, *korax* raven — more at RAVEN] **:** TEAL

sar·cel·ly \(ˈ)sär¦selē\ *also* **cer·ce·lée** \", ¦sərsə¦lā\ *adj* [*sarcelly* modif. of MF *cercelee*, fr. OF, fem. of *cercelé*, past part. of *cerceler* to curl, fr. *cercle* curl, circle — more at CIRCLE] **:** RECERCELÉE

¹**sarce·net** *or* **sarse·net** *also* **sars·net** \ˈsärsnət\ *n* -s [ME *sarcenet*, fr. AF *sarzinett*, fr. *Sarzin* Saracen (fr. LL *Saracenus*) + *-ett* (fr. OF *-et*) — more at SARACEN] **:** a soft thin silk of oriental origin made in plain or twill weaves used since the medieval period for dresses, veilings, or trimmings

²**sarcenet** *or* **sarsenet** \"\ *adj* **:** like sarcenet in softness **:** TEMPERED ⟨*darn(ed)* and *hail Columbia* and *goodness gracious*, and suchlike ∼ surety for one's oaths, have largely given way to their undisguised originals —J.W.Clark b. 1907⟩

sar·ci·na \ˈsärsənə, -rkənə\ *n* [NL, fr. L, bundle; akin to L *sarcire* to patch, mend — more at EXORCISE] **1** *cap* **:** a genus of bacteria (family Micrococcaceae) that are mostly harmless saprophytes but include a few serious brewery pests and that have cells which under favorable conditions divide in three directions into cubical masses **2** *pl* **sarcinas** *or* **sarci·nae** \-səˌnē, -kəˌnī\ **:** any bacterium of the genus *Sarcina*

¹**sar·cle** \ˈsärkəl\ *vt* [MF *sarcler*, fr. LL *sarculare*, fr. L *sarculum* hoe; akin to L *sarire* to hoe, weed — more at ASSART] *obs* **:** to weed or cultivate (crops) with a sarcle

²**sarcle** \"\ *n* -s [L *sarculum*] **:** an ancient hoe

sar·cob·a·tus \särˈkäbəd·əs\ *n, cap* [NL, fr. *sarc-* + Gk *batos* prickly bush] **:** a small genus of branching spiny shrubs (family Chenopodiaceae) that are found on alkali plains and deserts of the western U.S. and have monoecious flowers of which the staminate are borne in aments while the pistillate are solitary and winged fruits containing a single seed — see GREASEWOOD 1

sar·co·carp \ˈsärkəˌkärp\ *n* -s [F *sarcocarpe*, fr. *sarc-* + *-carpe* -carp] **1 :** MESOCARP; *esp* **:** one that is thickened and fleshy (as in the peach) **2 :** a fleshy fruit

sar·co·cele \ˈsärkəˌsēl\ *n* -s [NL, fr. Gk *sarkokēlē*, fr. *sark-* sarc- + *kēlē* tumor — more at -CELE] **:** a fleshy swelling of the testicle resembling a tumor

sar·co·ceph·a·lus \ˌsärkəˈsefələs\ *n, cap* [NL, fr. *sarc-* + *-cephalus*] **:** a genus of tropical trees and shrubs (family Rubiaceae) — see NEGRO PEACH, OPEPE

sar·co·coc·ca \ˌsärkəˈkäkə\ *n, cap* [NL, fr. *sarc-* + *-cocca* (fr. Gk *kokkos* grain, seed)] **:** a small genus of evergreen Asiatic shrubs (family Buxaceae) that are cultivated for their foliage and their black or red showy fruit and have alternate entire leaves and inconspicuous whitish flowers in heads or racemes

sar·co·col \ˈsärkəˌkäl\ *n* -s [ME, fr. L *sarcocolla*] **:** SARCOCOLLA 2

sar·co·col·la \ˌsärkəˈkälə\ *n* [NL, fr. L, gum of the milk vetch (*Astragalus fasiculifolius*), fr. Gk *sarkokolla*, fr. *sark-* sarc- + *kolla* gum — more at PROTOCOL] **1** *cap* **:** a small genus of shrubs (family Penaeaceae) native to southern Africa and having axillary or spicate red flowers with a long perianth tube and four reflexed lobes **2** -s **:** a gummy exudate believed to be obtained from either of two shrubs of the genus *Penaea* (*P. mucronata* and *P. sarcocolla*) but also held to be obtained from either of two milk vetches (*Astragalus fasiculifolius* and *A. sarcocolla*) and occurring in small yellowish or brownish red grains with a bittersweet and acrid taste

sar·co·cyst \ˈsärkəˌsist\ *n* [NL *sarcocystis*] **:** SARCOCYSTIS 2; *specif* **:** the large intramuscular cyst of a sarcocystis

sar·co·cys·tid·e·an *or* **sar·co·cys·tid·i·an** \¦särkōsə¦stidēən\ *adj or n* [NL *Sarcocystid-*, *Sarcocystis* + E *-an*] **:** SARCOSPORIDIAN

sar·co·cys·tis \ˌsärkəˈsistəs\ *n* [NL, fr. *sarc-* + *-cystis*] **1** *cap* **:** the chief and characteristic genus of the order Sarcosporidia **2** *pl* **sarcocystis** *or* **sarcocystises :** any organism of the genus *Sarcocystis; broadly* **:** SARCOSPORIDIAN

¹**sar·co·cys·toid** \¦särkə¦siˌstȯid\ *adj* [NL *Sarcocystis* + E *-oid*] **:** resembling or related to the genus *Sarcocystis*

²**sarcocystoid** \"\ *n* -s **:** a sarcocystoid organism

sar·co·cyte \ˈsärkəˌsīt\ *n* -s [*sarc-* + *-cyte*] **:** the outer clear layer of ectoplasm lying between the myocyte and epicyte or cuticle in gregarines

sar·code \ˈsärˌkōd\ *n* -s [F, fr. Gk *sarkōdes* fleshlike substance, fr. neut. of *sarkōdēs* fleshy] **:** PROTOPLASM

sar·cod·ic \(ˈ)sär¦kädik\ *or* **sar·co·dous** \-kōdəs\ *adj* [*sarcodic* ISV *sarcode* + *-ic*; *sarcodous* fr. *sarcode* + *-ous*] **:** relating to or resembling protoplasm

sar·co·dic·ty·um \ˌsärkōˈdiktēəm, -ikshēəm\ *n* -s [NL, fr. *sarc-* + Gk *diktyon* net — more at DICTY-] **:** a network of protoplasm on the surface of the calymma of a radiolarian

sar·co·di·na \ˌsärkəˈdīnə, -dēnə\ *n pl, cap* [NL, fr. Gk *sarkōdēs* fleshy part, fleshlike substance + NL *-ina*] **:** a class of Protozoa commonly including the subclasses Rhizopoda and Actinopoda and comprising forms whose chief character in common is the formation of pseudopodia that ordinarily serve as the organs for locomotion and for taking food — **sar·co·din·i·an** \¦==¦dinēən\ *adj*

sar·coglia \(ˈ)sär¦käglēə, ¦särkə¦glīə\ *n* -s [NL, fr. *sarc-* + *-glia*] **:** the granular protoplasmic substance marking the junction of a motor nerve and a muscle cell

¹**sar·coid** \ˈsärˌkȯid\ *adj* [Gk *sarkoeidēs*, fr. *sark-* sarc- + *-oeidēs* -oid] **:** of or resembling flesh

²**sarcoid** \"\ *n* -s [ISV *sarc-* + *-oid*] **1 :** a disease of horses and mules characterized by the formation of nodules in the skin **2 :** a nodule characteristic of sarcoid or of sarcoidosis

sar·coid·osis \ˌsärˌkȯiˈdōsəs\ *n, pl* **sarcoido·ses** \-ōˌsēz\ [NL, fr. ISV *sarcoid* + NL *-osis*] **:** a chronic disease of unknown cause characterized by the formation of nodules resembling true tubercles in the lymph nodes, lungs, bones, skin and other organs

sar·co·lactic acid \¦särkə+ . . . -\ *n* [*sarcolactic* fr. *sarc-* + *lactic*] **:** the dextrorotatory L-form of lactic acid occurring in muscle

sar·co·lem·ma \ˌsärkəˈlemə\ *n* [NL, fr. *sarc-* + Gk *lemma* rind, husk — more at LEMMA] **:** the thin transparent homogeneous sheath enclosing a striated muscular fiber — **sar·co·lem·mal** \¦==¦leməl\ *adj*

sar·col·o·gy \särˈkäləjē\ *n* -ES [Gk *sarko-* (fr. *sark-*, *sarx* flesh) + E *-logy*] **1** *archaic* **:** the anatomy of the soft parts — distinguished from *osteology* **2 :** a theory that a part of the animal body taken into the human system nourishes or affects a corresponding part — compare DOCTRINE OF SIGNATURES, ORGANOTHERAPY

sar·col·y·sis \särˈkäləsəs\ *n* [NL, fr. *sarc-* + *-lysis*] **:** the lysis of muscular tissue

sar·co·ma \särˈkōmə, sȧˈk-\ *n, pl* **sarcomas** \-məz\ *or* **sarcoma·ta** \-məd·ə\ [NL, fr. Gk *sarkōmat-*, *sarkōma* fleshy growth, fr. *sarkoun* to grow flesh, become fleshy, fr. *sark-*, *sarx* flesh — more at SARCASM] **:** a malignant neoplasm arising in connective tissue and esp. in bone, cartilage, or striated muscle that spreads by extension into neighboring tissue or by way of the bloodstream — compare CARCINOMA, TUMOR

sar·co·ma·gen·ic \==¦==¦jenik\ *adj* [NL *sarcoma* + E *-genic*] **:** producing sarcoma

sar·co·ma·toid \ˈ=ˈ==ˌtȯid\ *adj* [NL *sarcomat-*, *sarcoma* + E *-oid*] **:** resembling a sarcoma

sar·co·ma·to·sis \(ˌ)=ˌ==ˈtōsəs\ *n, pl* **sarcomato·ses** \-ōˌsēz\ [NL, fr. *sarcomat-*, *sarcoma* + *-osis*] **:** a disease characterized by the presence and spread of sarcomas

sar·coma·tous \(ˈ)sär¦käməd·əs, (ˈ)sȧ¦k-, -kōm-, -mətəs\ *adj* [NL *sarcomat-*, *sarcoma* + E *-ous*] **:** of, relating to, or resembling sarcoma

sar·co·mere \ˈsärkəˌmi(ə)r\ *n* -s [*sarc-* + *-mere*] **:** a transverse segment of a striated muscle fibril held in some theories to be the fundamental contractile unit

¹**sar·coph·a·ga** \särˈkäfəgə\ *n pl, cap* [NL, fr. *sarc-* + *-phaga*] *in former classifications* **:** an artificial division of marsupials comprising the Didelphidae and Dasyuridae

²**sarcophaga** \"\ *n, cap* [NL, fr. fem. of L *sarcophagus* flesh-eating, fr. Gk *sarkophagos*] **:** the type genus of Sarcophagidae comprising typical flesh flies

¹**sar·coph·a·gid** \-fəgəd, -fəjəd\ *adj* [NL *Sarcophagidae*] **:** of or relating to the Sarcophagidae

²**sarcophagid** \"\ *n* -s **:** a two-winged fly of the family Sarcophagidae

sar·co·phag·i·dae \ˌsärkəˈfajəˌdē\ *n pl, cap* [NL, fr. *Sarcophaga*, type genus + *-idae*] **:** a family of two-winged flies (superfamily Muscoidea) that includes flesh flies, some that

cause myiases, and others that develop in organic materials (as manure)

sar·coph·a·gine \sär'käfə,gīn, -,jīn\ *adj* [NL *Sarcophagidae* + E *-ine*] : of, like, or relating to the family Sarcophagidae

sar·coph·a·gous \(')sär¦käfəgəs\ *or* **sar·co·phag·ic** \¦särkə¦fajik\ *adj* [*sarcophagous* fr. L *sarcophagus* flesh-eating, fr. Gk *sarkophagos; sarcophagic* fr. L *sarcophagus* + E *-ic*] : CARNIVOROUS

sar·coph·a·gus \sär'käfəgəs, sȧ'k-\ *n, pl* **sarcopha·gi** \-fə,gī, -fə,jī, -fə,gē\ *also* **sarcophaguses** \-fəgəsəz\ [L *sarcophagus (lapis)* limestone used for coffins, fr. Gk (*lithos*) *sarkophagos*, lit., flesh-eating stone, fr. *sark-* sarc- + *-phagos* (fr. *phagein* to eat) — more at BAKSHEESH] **1** *obs* : a limestone used among the Greeks for the construction of coffins and held to disintegrate the flesh of bodies deposited in it **2** [L, fr. Gk *sarkophagos*, fr. *sarkophagos (lithos)* limestone used for coffins] : a coffin made of stone, often ornamented with sculpture, and usu. placed in a church, tomb, or vault **3** : a kind of wine cooler forming part of or standing near a sideboard and used chiefly in the 18th century

sar·coph·a·gy \sär'käfəjē\ *n* -ES [Gk *sarkophagia*, fr. *sarkophagos* flesh-eating + *-ia* -y] : the practice of eating flesh

sar·co·phile \'särkə,fīl\ *n* -S [*sarc-* + *-phile*] : a carnivorous animal; *esp* : TASMANIAN DEVIL

sar·coph·i·lous \(')sär¦käfələs\ *adj* [*sarc-* + *-philous*] : fond of flesh

sar·coph·i·lus \=ˈ==ləs\ *n, cap* [NL, fr. *sarc-* + *-philus*] : a genus of marsupial mammals consisting of the Tasmanian devil

sar·co·plasm \'särkə,plazəm\ *n* [NL *sarcoplasma*] : the hyaline semifluid substance between the fibrils of striated muscular fibers — **sar·co·plas·mic** \¦==¦plazmik\ *adj*

sar·co·plas·ma \,==ˈplazmə\ *n, pl* **sarcoplasma·ta** \-mədə\ [NL, fr. *sarc-* + *plasma*] : SARCOPLASM

sar·cop·side \sär'käpsəd\ *n* -S [G *sarkopsid*, fr. *sark-* sarc- + Gk *ōps* face, eye + G *-id* -ide; fr. the fleshlike color it exhibits — more at EYE] : a mineral $(Fe,Mn,Ca)_7(PO_4)_4F_2$(?) consisting of a fluoride and phosphate of calcium, manganese, and iron

sar·copsyl·la \,sär,käp'silə, -rkō's-\ [NL, fr. *sarc-* + Gk *psylla* flea — more at PSYLLA] *syn of* TUNGA

sar·cop·tes \sär'käp(,)tēz\ *n, cap* [NL, fr. *sarc-* + Gk *koptein* to cut off — more at CAPON] : a genus of itch mites that is the type of the family Sarcoptidae

sar·cop·tic \(')sär¦käptik\ *adj* [NL *Sarcoptes* + E *-ic*] : of, relating to, or caused by itch mites of the family Sarcoptidae ⟨~ infection⟩

sar·cop·ti·cide \sär'käptə,sīd\ *n* -S [*sarcoptic* + *-cide*] : an agent used for killing itch mites

sarcoptic mange *n* : a mange caused by mites (genus *Sarcoptes*) burrowing in the skin esp. of the head and face — called also *barn itch*; compare CHORIOPTIC MANGE

¹sar·cop·tid \(')sär¦käptəd\ *adj* [NL *Sarcoptidae*] : of or relating to the Sarcoptidae : SARCOPTIC

²sarcoptid \"\ *n* -S : a mite of the family Sarcoptidae

sar·cop·ti·dae \sär'käptə,dē\ *n pl, cap* [NL, fr. *Sarcoptes*, type genus + *-idae*] : a family of small whitish itch mites that attack the skin of man and other mammals

sar·cop·toid \sär'käp,tȯid\ *adj* [NL *Sarcoptoidea*] : of, relating to, or having the characteristics of the Sarcoptoidea : resembling or related to the Sarcoptidae

sar·cop·toi·dea \,sär,käp'tȯidēə\ *n pl, cap* [NL, fr. *Sarcoptes* + *-oidea*] *in some classifications* : a superfamily of mites containing Sarcoptidae and related families

sar·co·ram·phus \,särkə'ram(p)fəs\ *n, cap* [NL, fr. *sarc-* + Gk *rhamphos* beak — more at RHAMPH-] : a genus of vultures usu. including only the king vulture

sar·co·sine \'särkə,sēn, -kəsən\ *n* -S [ISV *sarcos-* (irreg. fr. Gk *sark-, sarx* flesh) + *-ine*; orig. formed as G *sarkosin* — more at SARCASM] : a sweetish crystalline amino acid CH_3NHCH_2COOH formed by the decomposition of creatine or made synthetically from methylamine (as by reaction with chloroacetic acid) and used in making an antienzyme agent for toothpaste formulations; *N*-methyl-glycine

sar·co·so·ma \,särkə'sōmə\ *or* **sar·co·some** \'särkə,sōm\ *n* -S [NL *sarcosoma*, fr. *sarc-* + *-soma*] **1** : the fleshy portion of an anthozoan as distinguished from the skeleton **2** *usu sarcosome* : one of the granular interfibrillar bodies of a striated muscle fiber that are sometimes considered to have a nutritive function

sar·co·so·mal \¦särkə¦sōməl\ *adj* [NL *sarcosoma* + E *-al*] : of or relating to sarcosomas

sar·co·spor·i·da \,särkə'spȯrədə\ [NL, fr. *sarc-* + *-spora* + *-ida*] *syn of* SARCOSPORIDIA

sar·co·spo·rid·ia \,sär(,)kōspə'ridēə\ *n pl, cap* [NL, fr. *sarc-* + *-sporidia*] : an order of Acnidosporidia comprising imperfectly known parasites of the muscles of vertebrates — see SARCOCYSTIS

¹sar·co·spo·rid·i·an \¦=(,)==¦==ēən\ *adj* [NL *Sarcosporidia* + E *-an*] : of or relating to the Sarcosporidia

²sarcosporidian \"\ *n* -S : a parasite of the order Sarcosporidia : SARCOCYSTIS

sar·co·spo·rid·i·o·sis \=(,)==,=dē'ōsəs\ *n, pl* **sarcosporidio·ses** \-ō,sēz\ [NL, fr. *Sarcosporidia* + *-osis*] : infestation with or disease caused by protozoans of the order Sarcosporidia

sar·co·style \'särkə,stīl\ *n* [*sarc-* + *-style*] **1** : a muscle fibril **2** : the dactylozooid of a calyptoblastic hydroid

sar·co·testa \¦särkə+\ *n* [NL, fr. *sarc-* + *testa*] : the outer and usu. soft fleshy part of the testa in various seeds (as of a cycad)

sar·co·theca \"+\ *n* [NL, fr. *sarc-* + *theca*] : the theca of a sarcostyle of a hydrozoan

sar·cous \'särkəs\ *adj* [*sarc-* + *-ous*] : of, relating to, or consisting of muscle tissue : FLESHY

sar·cu·ra \sär'kyu̇rə\ *n pl, cap* [NL, fr. *sarc-* + *-ura*] *in some classifications* : a suborder or other division of rays that have a thick tail, two dorsal fins, and a caudal fin and include the guitarfishes and often the electric rays — compare MASTICURA

¹sard \'särd\ *n* -S [F *sarde*, fr. L *sarda*, prob. modif. of Gk *sardion*, perh. fr. *Sardeis* Sardis, capital of the ancient kingdom of Lydia] : a deep orange-red variety of chalcedony similar to but darker than carnelian and classed by some as a variety of carnelian — called also *sardine, sardius*

²sard \"\ *n* -S *cap* [It *Sardo*, fr. L *Sardus* of Sardinia, Sardinian, fr. Gk *Sardō* Sardinia] : SARDINIAN

sar·da \'särdə\ *n, cap* [NL, fr. L, a fish, perh. sardine] : a genus of marine fishes (family Scombridae) comprising the common bonitos

sar·da·na \sär'dänə\ *n* -S *sometimes cap* [Sp, fr. Catal] **1** : a Catalan dance in which participants form a ring and move alternately to the left and right with long and short steps **2** : the music for the sardana usu. arranged in quick 6/8 time and played on the fife and tabor

sar·da·na·pa·lian \¦särdᵊnə¦pālyən, -pāl-, -lēən\ *adj, usu cap* [*Sardanapalus* legendary last king of the Assyrian empire (fr. L, fr. Gk *Sardanapalos*) + E *-an*] : of, relating to, or characterized by the luxuriously sensual nature or way of life attributed to the Assyrian king Sardanapalus

sardar *var of* SIRDAR

sar·delle \sär'delə, (')sär¦del\ *or* **sar·del** \(')sär¦del\ *n, pl* **sar·del·len** \=ˈdelən\ *or* **sar·delles** \(')=¦delz\ *or* **sardels** \(')=¦delz\ [G *sardelle* & Yiddish *sardel*, fr. It *sardella*, dim. of *sarda* sardine, fr. L] : SARDINE : a fish related to the sardine — compare ANCHOVY

¹sar·di·an \'särdēən\ *adj, usu cap* [L *sardianus*, fr. Gk *sardianos*, fr. *Sardeis* Sardis, capital of the ancient kingdom of Lydia in Asia Minor] **1** : of, relating to, or characteristic of the ancient city of Sardis in Asia Minor **2** : of, relating to, or characteristic of Sardians

²sardian \"\ *n* -S *cap* : a native or resident of ancient Sardis

sardian nut *n, usu cap S* : CHESTNUT 1b

¹sar·dine \'sär,dīn, -dᵊn\ *n* -S [ME, fr. LL (*lapis*) *sardinus* Sardian (stone), fr. Gk *sardinos* (*lithos*), perh. fr. *Sardeis* Sardis, capital of Lydia] : SARD

²sar·dine \(')sär¦dēn, (')sȧd-\ *n, pl* **sardines** *also* **sardine** [ME *sardeine*, fr. MF *sardine*, fr. L *sardina*, prob. fr. Gk *sardinos*] **1 a** : any of several small or immature clupeid fishes: (1) : the young of the European pilchard (*Sardinia pilchardus*) when of a size suitable for preserving for food (2) : any of various similar young of closely related fishes (as *Sardinops caerulea* of the Pacific coast of No. America, *Sardinella anchovia* of the tropical Atlantic and Caribbean area, or *Sardinia neopilchardus* of Australia and New Zealand) (3) : any of various small or immature herrings that resemble or are used similarly to the true sardines — compare BRISLING, SILD **b** : a similar but more distantly related fish (as an anchovy) — not used technically and in some jurisdictions not legally acceptable without a qualifying term **2** *sardines pl but sing in constr* : a game in which one person hides from others who try to find him and the first to do so hides with him, the second hides with the first two, and so on until all are crowded into the hiding spot

sardine oil *n* : a yellow drying oil obtained from sardines and used chiefly as a lubricant, in fat-liquoring leather, and in soap — compare PILCHARD OIL

¹sar·din·i·an \sär'dinēən, sȧ'd-, -inyən\ *n* -S *cap* [*Sardinia*, island in the Mediterranean west of the Italian peninsula + E *-an*] **1** : a native or inhabitant of Sardinia **2** : the Romance language of central and southern Sardinia

²sardinian \(')=¦=(=)=\ *adj, usu cap* [in sense 1, alter. (influenced by L *sardinianus* of Sardinia) of *sardonian;* in other senses, fr. L *sardinianus*, fr. *Sardinia* + *-anus* -an] **1** *obs* : SARDONIC ⟨*Sardinian* laughter⟩ **2 a** : of, relating to, or characteristic of the island of Sardinia in the Mediterranean sea **b** : of, relating to, or characteristic of Sardinians **3** : of, relating to, or characteristic of the Sardinian language

sar·di·nier \,sär,dēn¦yā\ *n, pl* **sardiniers** \-ā(z)\ [F, fr. *sardine* (fr. MF) + *-ier* -er] : a boat built for sardine fishing

sar·di·us \'särdēəs\ *n* -ES [LL, fr. (*lapis*) *sardius* Sardian (stone), fr. Gk *sardios* (*lithos*), perh. fr. *Sardeis* Sardis, capital of Lydia] : SARD

sar·do·ni·an \(')sär¦dōnēən\ *adj* [MF *sardonien*, fr. Gk *sardonios* sardonic + MF *-ien* -ian] *archaic* : SARDONIC

¹sar·don·ic \(')sär¦dänik, (')sȧ¦d-, -nēk\ *also* **sar·don·i·cal** \-nəkəl, -nēk-\ *adj* [*sardonic* fr. F *sardonique*, fr. MF, fr. Gk *sardonios, sardanios* derisive, sardonic + MF *-ique* -ic; *sardonical* fr. F *sardonique* + E *-al;* perh. akin to MBret *huersin* & W *chwarddu* to laugh] : expressive of or characterized by derision or scorn : disdainfully or skeptically humorous : CYNICAL ⟨got a ~ twist to his mouth, the way of a man who feels that the breaks are against him —Mary Austin⟩ ⟨his rebellion is the bitter, ~ laughter of all great satirists —Franz Schoenberner⟩ ⟨with a ~ smile —W.S.Maugham⟩ ⟨predominant mood was reflected in the bright and bitter humor, the ~ portrayal of human futility —D.S.Savage⟩ ⟨the enemy seemed to take a ~ delight in picking Sunday for his most savage forays —Irwin Shaw⟩ ⟨the rather ~ aphorism that there's nothing like a pension to induce longevity —*St. Louis Post-Dispatch*⟩ **syn** see SARCASTIC

²sardonic \"\ *n* -S : a sardonic expression or remark — often used in pl. ⟨light ~s about a reprobate —*Time*⟩ ⟨the advertisement — whose impish ~s may be placed in early evidence —K.N.Cameron⟩

sar·don·i·cal·ly \-nək(ə)lē, -nēk-, -li\ *adv* : in a sardonic manner : with a sardonic attitude ⟨some say ~ that combat pay is good and that one can do quite well out of this war —Thomas Griffith⟩ ⟨was heard to say ~ that . . . they preached a good many things they themselves did not believe —A.W.Long⟩

sardonic grin *or* **sardonic laugh** *n* [trans. of NL *risus sardonicus*] : RISUS SARDONICUS

sar·don·i·cism \=ˈ=nə,sizəm\ *n* -S : sardonic quality or humor ⟨speaks her lines with impeccable artifice and gets all the withering ~ out of them —Brooks Atkinson⟩

sar·don·yx \(')sär¦däniks, (')sȧ¦d-, -nēks *sometimes* 'särdᵊniks *or* 'sȧd-\ *n* -ES [ME *sardonix*, fr. L *sardonyx*, fr. Gk, prob. fr. *sardion* sard + *onyx* onyx, nail — more at SARD, NAIL] : an onyx marked by parallel layers of sard and of mineral of another color

sar·doo·dle·dom \sär'düdᵊldəm\ *n* -S *usu cap* [*sardoodle-* (blend of Victorien *Sardou* †1908 Fr. playwright criticized by G. B. Shaw †1950 Eng. playwright for the supposed staginess of his plays and E ¹*doodle*) + *-dom*] : mechanically contrived plot structure and stereotyped or unrealistic characterization in drama : STAGINESS, MELODRAMA ⟨the authors of the world's great plays are not mere tricksters in *Sardoodledom* —John Mason Brown⟩

sards *pl of* SARD

sare \'sār\ *chiefly Scot var of* SORE

sa·rep·ta mustard \sə'reptə-\ *n* [after *Sarepta* (former name of Krasnoarmeisk), oblast near Stalingrad, U.S.S.R.] : a Russian mustard (*Brassica besseriana*) grown commercially in No. America as the source of a brownish black mustard

sar·gas·so \sär'ga(,)sō, sȧ'g-, -gaa(-\ *n* -S [Pg *sargaço*, prob. fr. *sargaço, sargaça* rockrose, perh. fr. L *salicastrum*, a wild vine found in willow-thickets, fr. *salic-, salix* willow — more at SALLOW] **1** *also* **sargasso weed** : a seaweed of the genus *Sargassum* : GULFWEED **2** : a mass of floating vegetation consisting chiefly of sargasso

sargasso weed fish *n, usu cap S* : SARGASSUM FISH

sar·gas·sum \-səm\ *n* [NL, fr. ISV *sargasso*] **1** *cap* : a genus of brown algae that have branching thalli with lateral outgrowths differentiated as leafy segments, air bladders, or spore-bearing structures, that develop initially along tropical shores from which they break away to drift in the open ocean (as the Sargasso sea) and reproduce vegetatively for indefinite periods, and that are usu. placed in the family Fucaceae but are sometimes isolated in a separate family — see GULFWEED **2** -S : any plant of the genus *Sargassum*

sargassum crab *or* **sargasso crab** *n, usu cap S* : GULF-WEED CRAB

sargassum fish *n* : any of several small fantastically formed and colored fishes of genus *Histrio* (family Antennariidae) that float about in the open ocean with the masses of sargassum

sargassum pipefish *n* : a large pipefish (*Syngnathus pelagicus*) that lives among gulfweed

sarge \'särj, 'sȧj\ *n* -S [by shortening] : SERGEANT

sar·gent cypress \-jənt-\ *also* **sargent's cypress** *n, usu cap S* [prob. after Charles Sprague *Sargent* †1927 Am. dendrologist] : a shrub or bushy tree (*Cupressus sargentii*) of western No. America having dark green acute glandular pitted leaves

sargent juniper *also* **sargent's juniper** *n, usu cap S* [prob. after Charles Sprague *Sargent* †1927] : a low spreading Chinese juniper (*Juniperus chinensis sargentii*) that has needle-pointed leaves on many conspicuous twigs and is used as an ornamental

sar·go \'sär(,)gō\ *n* -S [Sp, fr. L *sargus*, a sea fish, fr. Gk *sargos*] **1** : any of several sparid fishes of *Diplodus* and related genera; *esp* : either of two pinfishes (*D. argenteus* and *Lagodon rhomboides*) **2** : a small silvery grunt (*Anisotremus davidsonii*) of the coast of southern California and adjacent Mexico

sa·ri *or* **sa·ree** \'särē, 'sär-, -rī, -rē\ *n* -S [Hindi *sārī*, fr. Skt *śāṭī*] : a garment worn chiefly by Hindu women that consists of a lightweight cloth of 5 to 7 yards in length draped gracefully and loosely so that one end forms a skirt and the other a head or shoulder covering

sa·rin \zä'rēn\ *n* -S [G] : a corrosive volatile organic phosphorus ester $CH_3PFO(OC_3H_7)$ that acts as a nerve gas

sa·rin·da \sə'rində\ *n* -S [Hindi *sārindā*] : a bowed stringed musical instrument of India

sark \'särk\ *n* -S [ME (Sc) *serk*, fr. OE *serc, serce;* akin to ON *serkr* shirt and perh. to OHG *saruh* bathtub, cupboard, chest] *dial chiefly Brit* : a body garment for either sex : SHIRT

sark·ful \-,fu̇l\ *n* -S [*sark* + *-ful*] *Scot* : a quantity filling or sufficient to fill a shirt

sark·ing \'särkən, -kiŋ\ *n* -S [ME (Sc), fr. gerund of *serken* to clothe in a shirt, sheathe, fr. *serk* shirt] **1** *chiefly Scot* : thin boards for sheathing (as under shingles or slates) **2** *Scot* : linen shirting

sar·ki·nite \'särkə,nīt\ *n* -S [Sw *sarkinit*, fr. *sarkin-* (fr. Gk *sarkinos* fleshlike, fr. *sark-, sarx* flesh) + *-it* -ite — more at SARCASM] : a mineral $Mn_2(AsO_4)(OH)$ consisting of a hydrous manganese arsenate occurring in flesh red greasy monoclinic crystals (hardness 4-5, sp. gr. 4.2)

sark·it \'särkət\ *adj* [fr. past part. of obs. E (Sc) *sark*, v., to clothe in a shirt, fr. ME (Sc) *serken*] *Scot* : provided with a shirt

sar·lak *or* **sar·lyk** \'särlək\ *n* -S [Russ *sarlyk, sarluk*, fr. Mongolian *sarlug*] : YAK

¹sar·ma·tian \(')sär¦māshən\ *adj, usu cap* [*Sarmatia*, anciently a region north of the Black sea + E *-an*] **1 a** : of, relating to, or characteristic of ancient Sarmatia **b** : of, relating to, or characteristic of the Sarmatians **2** : of, relating to, or characteristic of the Sarmatian language

²sarmatian \"\ *n* -S *cap* [*Sarmatia* + E *-an*, n. suffix] **1** : a native or inhabitant of ancient Sarmatia **2** : the language of the Sarmatians that is now presumed to be Iranian

sar·ma·tier \¦zärmə¦ti(ə)r, ¦sär-\ *n* -S [G, prob. fr. *Sarmatien* Sarmatia + *tier* animal, beast, fr. OHG *tior* wild animal — more at DEER] : PERWITSKY

sar·ment \'särmənt\ *n* -S [ME, fr. L *sarmentum* twig; akin to L *sarpere* to prune — more at ASSART] **1** : CUTTING, SCION **2** : a slender prostrate running stem : RUNNER

sar·men·ta·ceous \¦särmən¦tāshəs\ *adj* [*sarment* + *-aceous*] : SARMENTOSE

sar·men·tif·er·ous \-tif(ə)rəs\ *adj* [*sarment* + *-iferous*] : SARMENTOSE

sar·men·to·cymarin \sär¦mentō+\ *n* [*sarmento-* (fr. NL *sarmentosus* — specific epithet of *Strophanthus sarmentosus* —, fr. L, sarmentose) + *cymarin*] : a crystalline steroid cardiac glycoside $C_{30}H_{46}O_8$ found in the seeds of several plants of the genus *Strophanthus* (as *S. sarmentosus*)

sar·men·to·gen·in \sär,mentō'jenən, ,särmən·'täjənən\ *n* -S [*sarmento-* (in *sarmentocymarin*) + *-genin*] : a crystalline steroid lactone $C_{23}H_{34}O_5$ closely related to digitoxigenin, found in several plants of the genus *Strophanthus*, obtained esp. by hydrolysis of sarmentocymarin, and used in a synthesis of cortisone

¹sar·men·tose \sär'ment·,ōs, -n·,tōs, 'särmən·,tōs\ *adj* [L *sarmentosus*, fr. *sarmentum* twig + *-osus* -ose] **1** : producing slender prostrate branches or runners **2** : of the nature of or resembling a sarment

²sarmentose \" *also* -ōz\ *n* -S [*sarment-* (in *sarmentocymarin*) + *-ose*] : a sugar $C_7H_{14}O_4$ that is obtained from sarmentocymarin by hydrolysis and that is stereoisomeric with cymarose and closely related to digitalose

sar·men·tous \(')sär¦mentəs\ *adj* [L *sarmentosus*] : SARMENTOSE

sar·men·tum \sär'mentəm\ *n, pl* **sarmen·ta** \-tə\ [L, twig] : SARMENT 2

sar·mi·en·tite \,särmē'ent·,īt, -n·,tīt\ *n* -S [Sp *sarmientita*, fr. *Sarmiento*, town in Argentina + Sp *-ita* -ite] : a mineral $Fe_2(AsO_4)(SO_4)(OH).5H_2O$ consisting of a hydrous basic arsenate and sulfate of iron

sa·rod *also* **sa·rode** \sə'rōd\ *n* -S [Hindi *sarod*, fr. Per] : a stringed instrument of India resembling a waisted lute

sa·ron \'sä,rän, sə'rän\ *n* -S [Jav] : a metallophone of seven bronze plates used in the Javanese gamelan

sa·rong \sə'rȯŋ, -räŋ\ *n* -S [Malay (*kain*) *sarong*, fr. *kain* cloth + *sarong* sheath, covering] **1 a** : a loose skirt that is made of a long strip of cloth wrapped around the body and held in place by tucking or rolling at the waist and is worn chiefly by men and women of the Malay archipelago and the Pacific islands **b** : cloth for such garments; *esp* : printed cotton **2** : a close-fitting outer garment or dress copied from the sarong that is worn by western women and usu. draped in the front

sar·os \'sa(a),räs\ *n* -ES [Gk, fr. Assyr-Bab *shāru*] : a Babylonian lunar cycle of 6585.32 days at the end of which the centers of sun and moon return so nearly to their relative positions at the beginning that all the eclipses of the period recur approximately as before though in longitudes about 120 degrees west of the regions where they were visible in the saros immediately preceding

saros series *n* : a series of eclipses occurring at intervals of a saros that consists of about 50 lunar eclipses in a period of about 870 years or about 70 solar eclipses in a period of about 1200 years — called also *eclipse series*

sar·o·tham·nus \,sarə'thamnəs\ [NL, fr. Gk *saron* brush, broom (fr. *sairein* to sweep) + *thamnos* bush, shrub] *syn of* CYTISUS

sa·roth·rum \sə'räthrəm\ *n* -S [NL, fr. Gk *sarōtron* broom, fr. *saroun* to sweep clean, fr. *saron* broom] : the pollen brush of a bee

sa·rouk *or* **sa·ruk** \sə'rük\ *n* -S *usu cap* [fr. *Saruk, Sarouk*, village near Hamadan, western Iran] : a Persian carpet of fine compact weave, mellow colors, and fluid often medallion designs — compare KASHAN

sar·pler \'särplər\ *or* **sar·pli·er** \-lēər\ *n* -S [ME *sarpler*, fr. MF *sarpilliere*] **1** *obs* : a weight for a bale of wool usu. estimated as 80 tods or 2240 lbs. **2** : a covering or wrapper of coarse cloth (as sackcloth)

sar·ra·ce·nia \,sarə'sēnēə\ *n* [NL, fr. Michel *Sarrazin*, †1734 Fr.-Canadian physician and naturalist + NL *-ia*] **1** *cap* : a genus (the type of the family Sarraceniaceae) of American bog herbs having tubular leaves with an arched or hooded flap at the apex and solitary flowers with a style shaped like an umbrella — see PITCHER PLANT **2** -S : any plant of the genus *Sarracenia*

sar·ra·ce·ni·a·ce·ae \-,sēnē'āsē,ē\ *n pl, cap* [NL, fr. *Sarracenia*, type genus + *-aceae*] : a family of insectivorous plants (order Sarraceniales) having basal tubular leaves with a thin lamina like a wing at the inner margin and a hood or other appendage at the apex and large conspicuous pentamerous flowers — **sar·ra·ce·ni·a·ceous** \¦==¦==¦āshəs\ *adj*

sar·ra·ce·ni·al \¦==¦sēnēəl\ *adj* [NL *Sarraceniales*] : of, relating to, or having the characteristics of the order Sarraceniales

sar·ra·ce·ni·a·les \,==,==ˈā(,)lēz\ *n pl, cap* [NL, fr. *Sarracenia* + *-ales*] : an order of dicotyledonous plants constituting the families Sarraceniaceae, Nepenthaceae, and Droseraceae and having scapose flowers and leaves that secrete a viscous fluid and are variously modified to serve as insect traps

sar·ra·zin \'sarəzən\ *n* -S [F *sarrasin*, fr. (*blé*) *sarrasin* Saracen (wheat), fr. MF, fr. *Sarrasin, Sarrazin* Saracen, fr. LL *Saracenus* — more at SARACEN] : BUCKWHEAT

¹sar·row \'sarə, -a(,)rō\ *also* **sar·ra** \-arə\ *dial Eng var of* SORROW

²sarrow \"\ *or* **sarra** \"\ *vb* [by alter.] *dial Eng* : SERVE

sar·ruso·phone \sə'rüzə,fōn, -'rəsə-\ *n* [*Sarrus*, 19th cent. Fr. bandmaster + *-o-* + *-phone*] : a metal wind instrument with a double reed and a tube of wide conical bore played like the bassoon and sometimes used in place of it or a contrabassoon — **sar·ruso·phon·ist** \-nəst\ *n* -S

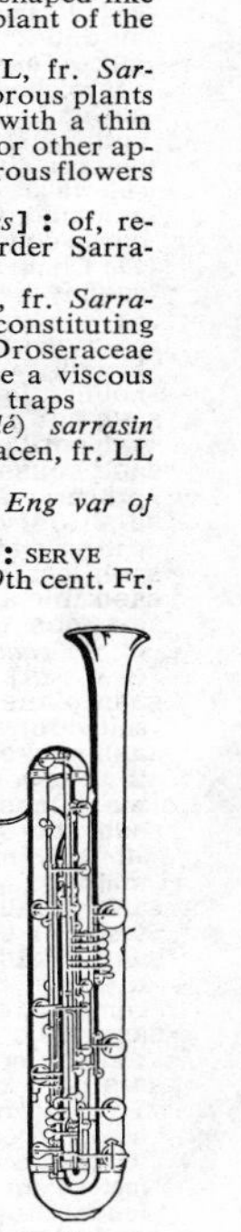

sarrusophone

sar·sa·pa·ril·la \,sas(ə)pə'rilə, ,saa|, *also* ,sär| *or* ,sȧ| *or* =ˈsprilə *or* -relə, *dial with f instead of p*\ *n* -S [Sp *zarzaparrilla*, fr. *zarza* bush + *parrilla*, dim. of *parra* vine] **1 a** : any of various Mexican, Central American, or So. American plants of the genus *Smilax* (as *S. officinalis, S. papyracea*, and *S. aristolochiaefolia*) **b** : the dried roots of a sarsaparilla plant used as a flavoring or olfactory agent in the form of an infusion, extract, or syrup **2** : any of various plants resembling or used as a substitute for sarsaparilla — see INDIAN SARSAPARILLA, WILD SARSAPARILLA **3** : a sweetened carbonated beverage similar to root beer with the predominant flavor from birch oil and sassafras

sar·sar \'särsər\ *n* -S *usu cap* [Ar *ṣarṣar*] : a whistling violently cold wind

sar·sa·sap·o·gen·in \,sasə,sapə'jenən, ,särs-, ,==sə'päjənən\ *n* -S [*sarsasaponin* + *-genin*] : a crystalline steroid sapogenin $C_{27}H_{44}O_3$ obtained esp. by hydrolysis of sarsasaponin

sar·sa·sap·o·nin \¦==+\ *also* **sar·saponin** \(')sär, (')sa+\ *n* [*sarsasaponin* fr. *sarsa* (short for *sarsaparilla*) + *saponin; sarsaponin* blend of *sarsa* and *saponin*] : a saponin $C_{45}H_{74}O_{17}$ obtained from Mexican sarsaparilla root

sarsee *or* **sarsi** *usu cap, var of* SARCEE

sar·sen \'särsᵊn\ *n* -S [short for *sarsen stone*, alter. of *Saracen stone*, i.e., a pagan stone or monument] : a large loose residual mass of stone left after the erosion of a once continuous bed or layer; *specif* : one of the large sandstone blocks scattered over the English chalk downs — called also *druid stone*

sarsenet *also* **sarsnet** *var of* SARCENET

sar·sia \'särsēə, -rshə\ *n, cap* [NL] : a widely distributed genus of small hydrozoan medusae with four tentacles

sar·son \'särs°n\ *n* -s [Hindi *sarsõ*, fr. Skt *sarṣapa*] : an Indian colza (*Brassica campestris sarson*)

¹sart \'särt\ *adj* [by alter.] *dial Eng* : SOFT

²sart \"\, *n, pl* **sart** *or* **sarts** *usu cap* [Kirghiz] **1** : a trading and town-dwelling people constituting the Iranian populations of central and southwestern Asia **2** : a member of the Sart people

sar·tain \'särt°n, 'sät-\ *dial var of* CERTAIN

sar·to·ri·al \(')sär|'tōrēəl, (')sä|t-, -tȯr-\ *adj* [L *sartor* patcher, tailor + E -*ial*] **1** : of, relating to, or characteristic of a tailor ⟨sitting ~ in fashion⟩ **2** : of or relating to dress or to tailored clothes ⟨native sandals, a sport shirt which was whole once upon a time, and an outrageously battered final straw sombrero . . . completed a strange ~ picture —Lawrence Dame⟩ ⟨his well-known ~ fancies —Gladwin Hill⟩ ⟨acquired more of the statesman's ~ appearance —*Current Biog.*⟩ ⟨~ elegance⟩ —

sar·to·ri·al·ly \-ōlē,-əli\ *adv*

sar·to·rite \'särtə̇ˌrīt\ *n* -s [Wolfgang *Sartorius* von Waltershausen †1876 Ger. geologist + E -*ite*] : a mineral PbAs₂S₄ consisting of a dark gray crystalline compound of lead, arsenic, and sulfur

sar·to·ri·us \sär|'tōrēəs\ *n, pl* **sarto·rii** \-ē,ī\ [NL, fr. L *sartor* tailor, fr. *sartus* (past part. of *sarcire* to mend) + -*or*— more at EXORCISE] : a muscle that arises from the anterior end of the iliac crest, crosses the front of the thigh obliquely to insert on the upper part of the inner surface of the tibia, assists in rotating the leg to the position assumed in sitting like a tailor, and is the longest muscle in man

sar·tri·an \'sär-trēən\ *adj, usu cap* [Jean Paul *Sartre* b1905 + E -*an*] : of, relating to, or characteristic of the French philosopher, novelist, and dramatist Jean Paul Sartre or his existentialist theories

saruk *usu cap, var of* SAROUK

sar·um \'sa(a)rəm\ *adj, usu cap* [fr. *Sarum* (now *Old Sarum*), extinct borough and city near Salisbury in the county of Wiltshire, England] : of or relating to Sarum, diocese of Salisbury, England, in the late medieval period ⟨*Sarum* missal⟩ ⟨*Sarum* office⟩ ⟨*Sarum* rubric⟩ ⟨*Sarum* Use⟩

sa·rus \'säros\ *or* **sarus crane** *n, pl* **saruses** *or* **sarus cranes** [Hindi *sāras*, fr. Skt *sārasa*, lit., of a lake, fr. *saras* lake, fr. *sarati* it runs, flows — more at SERUM] : a crane (*Grus antigone or Antigone antigone*) of the Indian and Malay region

sar·vas·ti·va·din \sə(r)ˌvästə̇'väd°n\ *n* -s *usu cap* [Hindi *sarvāstivādin* adherent of a school of Buddhism that flourished in northern India in the 5th cent. B.C., fr. *sarvāstivāda* doctrine that everything exists, fr. *sarva* entire + *asti* is + *vāda* doctrine — more at SAFE, IS] : a member of an early realist school of Buddhism that affirms the existence of all material, mental, or other elements of experience

sar·wan \'sär,wän\ *n* -s [Per *sārwān*, fr. *sār* camel + -*wān* keeping, guarding] : a camel driver

SAS *abbr* sodium aluminum sulfate in the anhydrous form

sa·sak *or* **sas·sak** \'sä,säk, sȯ'säk\ *n, pl* **sasak** *or* **sasaks** *or* **sassak** *or* **sassaks** *usu cap* [Malay *sasak*] **1 a** : an Indonesian people inhabiting Lombok Island, Indonesia **b** : a member of the Sasak people **2** : the Austronesian language of the Sasak people

sasanian *usu cap, var of* SASSANIAN

sa·san·qua \sə'saŋkwə\ *n* -s [Jap *sasankwa*] : a shrub (*Camellia sasanqua*) of China and Japan often cultivated for its fragrant evergreen leaves and white or red flowers and for seeds that yield tea-seed oil

sa·se·bo \'säsȯˌbō, sä'(ˌ)bō\ *adj, usu cap* [fr. *Sasebo*, Japan] : of or from the city of Sasebo, Japan : of the kind or style prevalent in Sasebo

¹sash \'sash, -aa(ə)-,-ai-\ *n* -ES [Ar *shāsh* muslin] **1** *obs* : an oriental turban **2** : any of various bands worn about the waist or over one shoulder, fastened with a loop, knot, or bow, and used as an accessory of dress, a symbol of an honorary or military order, or other distinctive badge — see CUMMERBUND

²sash \"\, *n, pl* **sash** *also* **sashes** *often attrib* [prob. modif. of F *châssis* frame, chassis (taken as a pl.) — more at CHASSIS] **1** : the framework in which panes of glass or other usu. transparent or translucent material are set for installation in a window or door or for covering a hotbed, cold frame, greenhouse, or other glazed enclosure — see CASEMENT 2a; *also* : a movable part of a window ⟨raise the ~ for ventilation⟩ **2** : the frame in which a sash saw or gang saw is stretched or mounted — called also *gate*

³sash \"\ *vt* -ED/-ING/-ES : to furnish (as a door or window) with a sash ⟨a door half ~ed with glass —Sir Walter Scott⟩

⁴sash \"\ *vt* -ED/-ING/-ES [¹*sash*] : to fasten, trim, or adorn with a sash ⟨~ed in at the waist —Oliver La Farge⟩

¹sa·shay \sa'shā *also* (')sī,-\ *vi* -ED/-ING/-S [alter. of ²*chassé*] **1** : CHASSÉ **2 a** : WALK, GLIDE, GO ⟨after the work was through and we all ~ed to the chuck wagon —Will James⟩ ⟨~ down to your ship or station library —*All Hands*⟩ ⟨~s down the center aisle to the stage —John Kobler⟩ ⟨~ed complacently through his duties without any qualms about serious opposition for his job —*Time*⟩ **b** : to strut or move about in an ostentatious or conspicuous manner ⟨putting on a dress that reveals the hidden glories of her shape, and ~ing around like a . . . model —Wolcott Gibbs⟩ **c** : to proceed or move in a diagonal or sideways manner ⟨having to ~ from oasis to oasis along the littered sidewalks —*New Yorker*⟩ ⟨the drive ~s from one side of a mountain to the other —V.H.Lawn⟩ ⟨~s to the right and come down on him from that angle —R.G.Hubler & J.A. De Chant⟩

²sashay \"\ *n* -s [¹*sashay* + ³CHASSÉ 2] : TRIP, EXCURSION, VENTURE ⟨a ~ I took with friends —A.B.Guthrie⟩ ⟨scrubbing his own cartridge belt after every ~ in the field —James Jones⟩ ⟨permits himself cautious ~s into such subjects as history, education, politics, love —*New Yorker*⟩

sash bar *n* : BAR 1d⟨3⟩

sash cord *n* : the cord used to attach a weight to a window sash

sash house *n* : a simple greenhouse made of sash and designed primarily for starting young plants

sa·shi·mi \'säshōmē\ *n* -s [Jap] : raw fish served as an appetizer and usu. accompanied by a condiment

sash·less \'sashlə̇s\ *adj* [²*sash* + -*less*] : lacking a sash

sash line *n* : a rope used in erecting telegraph poles

sa·shoon \(')sȯ'shün\ *n* -s [prob. modif. of obs. F *chausson*, fr. F *chausse* tight-fitting breeches, chausses — more at CHAUSSES] : a pad worn on the leg under the boot

sash plane *n* : a carpenter's plane with a notched cutter esp. suited for trimming the inside of door and sash frames

sash pocket *n* **1** : the hollow in a pulley stile for a sash weight **2** : a removable section of a pulley stile giving access to a sash weight and sash cord

sash saw *n* : a strip of steel that is toothed on one edge, stretched in a frame, and used for sawing in small water-power mills

sash weight *n* : an iron bar or cylinder attached to a window sash as a counterweight

sash window *n* : a window consisting of sash usu. double-hung to slide vertically in a window frame — compare CASEMENT WINDOW

sasin \'säsᵊn, 'sasᵊn\ *n* -s [origin unknown] : BLACK BUCK 1

sa·sine \'sāsᵊn\ *n* -s [alter. of *seisin*] **1** *Scots law* : the seisin or possession of feudal property; *also* : the formality by which it is acquired by the tenant **2** : the instrument or deed by which the transfer of feudal property is proved

[diagram: window/sash, caption:] **sash windows**

sas·katch·e·wan \sȯ'skachȯwȯn *also* sa'sk- *or* -,wän\ *adj, usu cap* [fr. *Saskatchewan*, province in western Canada] : of or from the province of Saskatchewan : of the kind or style prevalent in Saskatchewan

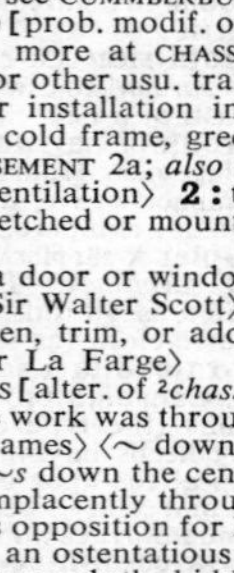

sas·ka·toon \ˌsaskȯ'tün\ *n* -s [fr. *Saskatoon*, city in central Saskatchewan, Canada] : JUNEBERRY; *esp* : a widely distributed shrubby Juneberry (*Amelanchier alnifolia*) of the northern and western U.S. and adjacent Canada that has leaves like those of an alder and sweet usu. purple fruit

¹sass \'sas, -aa(ə)-,-ai-,-ȧ-\ *n* [alter. of ¹*sauce*] *chiefly Midland* : fresh garden vegetables — called also *garden sass*

²sass \"\ *n* [by alter.] *chiefly Midland* : ¹SAUCE 5

³sass \"\ *n* -ES [back-formation fr. ¹*sassy*] : BACK TALK ⟨takes

---

no ~ from her pupils⟩ ⟨a past master of ~ —*TV Guide*⟩

⁴sass \"\ *vt* -ED/-ING/-ES : to talk impudently or disrespectfully to (an elder or superior) ⟨did not yell or ~ their mothers —Sally Carrighar⟩ ⟨call her a bum and she ~es them back —Polly Adler⟩

sas·sa·by \'sasəbē *or* **tses·se·be** *or* **tses·se·by** \'(t)sesəbē\ *n, pl* **sassabies** *or* **tsessebes** *or* **tsessebies** [Tswana *tshêsêbê*] : a large So. African antelope (*Damaliscus lunatus*) similar to the hartebeest that is dark purplish red with the back and face nearly black and has regularly curved horns

sas·sa·fac \'sasə,fak\ *also* **sas·sa·frack** \-frak\ *chiefly Midland var of* SASSAFRAS

sas·sa·fras \'sas(ə)ˌfras, 'saas(ə)ˌfraa(ə)s, 'sais(ə)ˌfrais\ *n* [NL, fr. Sp *sasafrás*] **1 a** *cap* : a small genus of aromatic No. American and Asiatic trees (family Lauraceae) with soft yellow wood, ovate entire or 1- to 3-lobed leaves, dioecious yellow flowers in umbellate racemes, a 6-lobed perianth, and nine stamens in three rows **b** -ES : a tall widely distributed tree (*S. albidum*) of eastern No. America with mucilaginous twigs and leaves — see TREE illustration **2** -ES : the dried bark of the root of the American sassafras used as a diaphoretic, a flavoring agent, an aromatic stimulant, or as a source of an aromatic volatile oil used in perfumes **3** -ES **a** : any of several Australian trees of the family Monimiaceae with aromatic bark used esp. for flavoring: as (1) : a medium-sized tree (*Atherosperma moschatum*) with soft grayish to nearly black wood used esp. in cabinetry and for carving or turning (2) : a tree (*Daphnandra micrantha*) with pale yellowish easily worked wood and a bark rich in physiologically active alkaloids (3) : an often large tree (*Doryphora sassafras*) with starry white flowers and bright glossy foliage that yields a yellowish wood suitable for flooring **b** : the bark of any of these trees

sassafras laurel *n* : CALIFORNIA LAUREL

sassafras oil *n* : a yellow or reddish yellow aromatic essential oil obtained from the roots and stumps of American sassafras and used chiefly in flavoring and perfuming and as a disinfectant — compare OCOTEA CYMBARUM OIL

sassafras pith *or* **sassafras medulla** *n* : the dried pith of the American sassafras formerly used in making a mucilage added to eye lotions for its emollient properties

sassafras tea *n* : a tea made from the dried bark of roots of the American sassafras

sassak *usu cap, var of* SASAK

¹sas·sa·nian *or* **sa·sa·nian** \sə'sānēən, sa's-, -ānyən\ *adj, usu cap* [*Sassan*, grandfather of Ardashir I *fl ab* A.D. 226 who founded the Sassanid dynasty + E -*an*] : of, relating to, or having the characteristics of the Sassanid dynasty of ancient Persia and esp. the art forms or architecture developed during the period of the dynasty

²sassanian \"\ *also* **sassanide** \"\ *adj, usu cap* : SASSANIAN

¹sas·sa·nid *also* **sas·sa·nide** \sȯ'sänə̇d, -'san-\ *n, pl* **sassanids** \-dz\ *or* **sas·san·i·dae** \sȯ'sanəˌdē\ *also* **sassanides** \-'sänə̇dz, -'san-\ *usu cap* [NL *Sassanidae*, pl., Sassanids, fr. *Sassan*, grandfather of Ardashir I + -*idae*] : a member of a dynasty of Persian kings succeeding the Arsacids and commencing with Ardashir I in A.D. 226 and ending with Yazdegerd III in the middle of the 7th century

²sassanid \"\ *also* **sassanide** \"\ *adj, usu cap* : SASSANIAN

sasse \'sas\ *n* -s [D *sas*] *archaic* : SLUICE, LOCK

sas·se·nach \'sasᵊn,ȧk, -,nᵊȯl, -,nȧᵊ\ *n* -s *often cap* [Ir *Sasanach*, of Gmc origin; akin to OE *Seaxan* Saxons] : a typical Englishman or something considered typical of England — often used disparagingly by Scots and Irish ⟨a dreadful *Sassenach* concoction —I.A.Bremner⟩

sas·sin·ger \'sasə̇njə(r)\ *n* -s [by alter.] *dial* : SAUSAGE

sas·so·lite \'sasə,līt\ *also* **sas·so·lin** \-,lən\ *n* -s [*sassolite* fr. *Sasso*, Tuscany, Italy + E -*lite*; *sassolin* fr. G, fr. *Sasso*, Italy + connective -*l-* + G -*in* -ine] : a mineral B(OH)₃ consisting of native boric acid and usu. occurring in small pearly scales as an incrustation

sass·wood \'sa,swu̇d\ *or* **sas·sy·wood** \'sasē,wu̇d\ *n* [*sass-wood* alter. of *sassywood; sassywood* fr. *sassy* (prob. of African origin) + *wood*] : a western African tree (*Erythrophleum guineense*) of the family Leguminosae having a poisonous bark and yielding a hard strong insect-resistant wood

sas·sy \'saˌsē, 'saaȯ, 'saiᵊ, 'sȧᵊ\ *adj* -ER/-EST [alter. of *saucy*] **1 a** : given to back talk : FRESH, IMPERTINENT ⟨were polite and . . . not the ~ type —*Boston Herald*⟩ ⟨~ kids —Barbara B. Jamison⟩ **b** : physically vigorous : SPIRITED, JAUNTY ⟨the timber mechanic, that fat and ~ plutocrat of the modern logging camps —J.F.Stevens⟩ ⟨feel like I can jump over a six-foot fence and getting very ~ —*Time*⟩ **2** : distinctively smart or stylish ⟨a ~ black-and-white bow tie —Jean Stafford⟩ ⟨woven into his own nostalgic or ~ musical style —E.T.Canby⟩ ⟨rocketed from a pulp-type blood-and-thunder book to a ~ slick with top-name contributors —*Newsweek*⟩

sassy bark \"+\ [*sassy* prob. of African origin; akin to Twi *ɛsɛ³sɛ³* plane tree, Ewe *se³se³wu³* African oak] : the bark of the sasswood that is used locally as an ordeal poison

¹sas·te·an \'sastēən\ *n* -s *usu cap* [alter. of *shastan*] : a subdivision of the Shastan language family comprising the Shasta language

²sastean \"\ *adj, usu cap* [alter. of *shastan*] : SHASTAN

sastra \'sastrə\ *var of* SHASTRA

sas·tru·ga *or* **zas·tru·ga** \'sastrəgə, 'z|, -äs-, -ˌgä; zᵊ'strügə\ *n, pl* **sastru·gi** *or* **zastru·gi** \-(ˌ)gē\ [Russ *zastruga* groove] : a wavelike ridge of hard snow usu. formed on a level surface by the wind parallel to its direction and occurring in great numbers in the snowfields of the arctic and antarctic regions — usu. used in pl. ⟨the crisscrossing and fan-tailed form of the *sastrugi* —R.E.Byrd⟩

¹sat [ME, alter. of OE *sæt*] *past of* SIT

²sat \'sȧt\ *Scot var of* SALT

³sat \'sȯt\ *n* -s [Skt, fr. *sat* being — more at SOOTH] *Hinduism* : eternal and immutable existence : the pure essence of being

sat *abbr* saturate; saturated; saturation

sa·tan \'sāt°n *also* -ˌtȧn\ *n* -s *usu cap* [ME *Satan, Sathan*, fr. OE *Satan, Satanas*, fr. LL, fr. Gk, fr. Heb *śāṭān* devil, adversary] **1** *also* **sata·nas** \'sad·ᵊnᵊs, 'sᵊtᵊn-\ : DEVIL 1 **2 a** *obs* : a minion of the archfiend ⟨the very places from which the *Satans* by transgression fell —John Bunyan⟩ **b** : a wicked person : FIEND ⟨that villainous abominable misleader of youth . . . that old white-bearded *Satan* —Shak.⟩

sa·tang \sȯ'täŋ\ *n, pl* **satang** *or* **satangs** \-ŋz\ [Thai *satāň*] **1** : a monetary unit of Thailand equal to ¹⁄₁₀₀ baht — see MONEY table **2** : a coin representing one satang

sa·tan·ic \sȯ'tanik, (')sᵊt-, -nēk\ *adj* [LGk *satanikos*, fr. Gk *Satan, Satanas* Satan + -*ikos* -ic] **1 a** : of, relating to, or characteristic of Satan or his minions ⟨in secular history ~ interference is more conspicuous than divine guidance —E.E.Aubrey⟩ ⟨~ pride in the powerful negation of God —E.J.Simmons⟩ **b** : resembling Satan in appearance : MEPHISTOPHELIAN, SATURNINE ⟨a pointed ~ face⟩ ⟨herds of ~ black goats —Mollie Panter-Downes⟩ **c** : DERISIVE ⟨the sound of faint ~ mirth —Gordden Link⟩ **2 a** : characterized by extreme cruelty or viciousness : DIABOLICAL, FIENDISH ⟨not only the ape and the tiger, but what is far worse — perverted and ~ man —Walter Moberly⟩ **b** : of a hideous or forbidding aspect : GHOULISH, INFERNAL ⟨the black ~ landscapes of the Midlands —H.C.Darby⟩ ⟨mills which are dark and ~ with the glare and smoke of the furnaces —Sam Pollock⟩ **c** : of an excruciating nature : HELLISH ⟨battle against . . . ~ conditions of climate —J.S.Bradford⟩ **3** : of a repellent or demented nature : AWFUL, DEMONIAC ⟨hoped that his other hat . . . would be smaller and paler than the ~ thing he had always worn pulled down over his eyes —Elinor Wylie⟩ ⟨irreverent, slightly ~, and resolutely bawdy —C.J.Rolo⟩ **4** : of, relating to, or constituting a group of 19th century writers castigated as immoral by their more pious contemporaries ⟨a ~ spirit of pride and audacious impiety —Robert Southey⟩

sa·tan·i·cal \-nᵊkəl, -nēk-\ *adj* [*satan* + -*ical*] *archaic* : SATANIC

sa·tan·i·cal·ly \-k(ȯ)lē, -li\ *adv* : in a satanic manner : to a satanic degree ⟨~ handsome⟩ ⟨~ arrogant⟩

sa·tan·ism \'sāt°n,izəm *also* -ᵊtᵊn,i-\ *n* -s *often cap* [*satan* + -*ism*] **1** : innate wickedness : DIABOLISM ⟨the ~ of Hitlers and Mussolinis —Walter Moberly⟩ **2** : obsession with or affinity for evil ⟨both in her verse and her one solitary stupendous novel we find . . . this *Satanism* embodied and expressed —J.A. Bramley⟩; *specif* : the worship of Satan reputedly practiced by

---

various writers in Paris in the 1890s marked by the travesty of Christian rites ⟨interpretation of *Satanism* as an offshoot of the belief in two coequal and coeternal principles of good and evil . . . deriving ultimately from Zoroastrianism —*Times Lit. Supp.*⟩

sa·tan·ist \-t°nᵊst, -tᵊn-\ *n* -s *usu cap* [ML *satanista*, fr. LL *Satan, Satanas* + L -*ista* -ist] **1 a** *archaic* : one that is regarded as inherently evil ⟨atheistical Satanists, or evil-seekers —*Fraser's Mag.*⟩ **b** : EUCHITE **2** : an adherent of Satan or Satanism : DIABOLIST ⟨a *Satanist* . . . contemplating anatomical experiments out of his unique sadism —A.J.Guérard⟩

sa·tan·i·ty \sᵊ'tanəd·ē\ *n* -ES [*satan* + -*ity*] : SATANISM

sa·tan·ize \'sāt°n,īz, -tᵊnᵊz\ *vt* -ED/-ING/-S [*satan* + -*ize*] : to make satanic ⟨a thirst for blood is the characteristic of . . . *satanized* man —*Dublin Rev.*⟩

satan monkey *n* : a small black bearded So. American monkey (*Pithecia satanas*)

sa·tan·o·pho·bia \ˌsāt°nȯ'fōbēȯ, -tᵊn-; sȯ,tan-, sā,tan-\ *n* [*satan* + -*o-* + *phobia*] : abnormal fear of Satan

satan's mushroom *n, usu cap S* : a large usu. brownish yellow pore fungus (*Boletus satanus*) that occurs esp. in open woodland and is reputedly somewhat poisonous

SATB *abbr* soprano, alto, tenor, bass

satch·el \'sachəl\ *n* -s [ME *sachel*, fr. MF, fr. L *sacellus*, dim. of *saccus* bag — more at SACK] **1** : a small bag usu. of leather or canvas with a flat bottom and often having a shoulder strap ⟨the whining schoolboy, with his ~ and shining morning face —Shak.⟩ ⟨people think that the stork brings babies, that the doctor brings the children in his ~ —Morris Fishbein⟩ ⟨picking up . . . the little canvas furlough ~ —James Jones⟩ **2** : something that resembles a satchel ⟨from above two heavy ~s of flesh peered a pair of pale blue, bloodshot eyes —Eric Ambler⟩ ⟨candy ~s —*advt*⟩

satchel charge *n* : several blocks of explosive usu. taped to a board fitted with a rope or wire loop for use as a handle

sat-chromosome \'sat-; ,e,sā|tē-\ *n, usu cap S & A & T* [SAT abbr. of NL *Sine Acido Thymonucleico* without thymonucleic acid] **1** : a chromosome including the nucleolus organizer **2** : a chromosome with one or more satellites

satd *abbr* saturated

¹sate [ME, alter. of ¹*sat*] *archaic past of* SIT

²sate \'sāt, *usu* -ȧd-+V\ *vt* -ED/-ING/-S [prob. short for ²*satiate*] **1 a** : to cloy with overabundance : GLUT, SURFEIT ⟨lust, though to a radiant angel link'd, will ~ itself in a celestial bed —Shak.⟩ ⟨engulfed in enough celluloid adventure to ~ any escapist for a decade —John McCarten⟩ **b** : to appease (as a thirst or violent emotion) by indulging to the full ⟨the sort of rage that only the obliteration of a world could ~ —Clellon Holmes⟩ **2** : SATIATE 1a ⟨~ people's desire to understand the past —J.D.Hart⟩ **3** *obs* : SATURATE **syn** see SATIATE

sated *adj* [fr. past part. of ²*sate*] : SATIATED

sa·teen \sa'tēn, (')sa|tēn, sᵊ|t-\ *n* -s [alter. (influenced by -*een* & ²-*ine*) of ¹*satin*] : a smooth durable lustrous fabric usu. made of cotton in satin weave and in various weights for fine and work clothing, curtains, and linings

sateen weave *n* : satin weave used on cotton fabrics

sateenwood \ˈsᵊ,ᵊ,ᵊ\ *n* [*sateen* + *wood*] : a yellow satiny wood derived from an Amazonian tree (*Euxylophora paraensis*) of the family Rutaceae and widely used in Brazil in combination with acapu for parquetry

sate·less \'sātlᵊs\ *adj* [²*sate* + -*less*] *archaic* : INSATIATE

¹sat·el·lite \'sad·ᵊl,līt, -atᵊl- *sometimes* 'sat,līt\ *n, usu -ᵊd-+V\ *n* [MF, fr. L *satellit-, satelles* attendant, bodyguard, prob. of Etruscan origin; akin to the source of L *Satellius*, a Roman name] **1** : a hired agent or obsequious follower : MINION, SYCOPHANT ⟨armed ~s of great men, were forced to seek an independent source of livelihood —G.E.Fussell⟩ ⟨no ~ on whom he could bestow recognition with a maestro bow —Marjorie Brace⟩ **2 a** : a celestial body orbiting another of larger size : secondary planet : MOON ⟨Jupiter has twelve ~s, and Saturn probably has millions of them in its rings —*Time*⟩ **b** : a man-made object or vehicle intended to orbit the earth, the moon, or another celestial body and usu. instrumented for the transmission of space data ⟨such far-soaring objects as missiles, ~s, and lunar probes —*Newsweek*⟩ ⟨talks of a manned ~ to be used for meteorological observation —J.K. Hutchens⟩ **3 a** : one that resembles a celestial satellite ⟨the central sun he became for a host of surrounding ~s —Irving Kolodin⟩ ⟨in both the film and radio firmaments Ireland tends to be a ~ of Great Britain —Paul Blanshard⟩ **b** : one that is subject to external influence: as (1) : a political entity within the sphere of influence of a stronger power ⟨when demoralized, disorganized, ideologically confused groups collaborate with a powerful, tightly organized world conspiracy . . . they do not become allies but only ~s or puppets —Edmond Taylor⟩ ⟨~s have sovereignty, although they lack supremacy —H.D. Lasswell & Abraham Kaplan⟩ ⟨conversion of local regions into ~s poses a threat deadly to our liberties —D.D.Eisenhower⟩ (2) : a subordinate area or suburban community dependent upon a metropolis for economic support ⟨economic activities of the ~s are closely geared to those of the central city —C.D.Harris & E.L.Ullman⟩ ⟨an associated or subsidiary enterprise ⟨the hotel moved two blocks away . . . and immediately attracted new shops as ~s —Hal Burton⟩ ⟨a main base in the Little America area from which two ~s . . . will be supplied —Glen Jacobsen⟩ **4** : one that is secondary or adjacent: as **a** (1) : a short segment separated from the main body of a chromosome by a constriction — called also *trabant* (2) : the secondary or later member of a chain of gregarines in syzygy (3) : a bodily structure lying near or associated with another (as a vein accompanying an artery) **b** : a smaller lesion accompanying a main one and situated nearby **c** : a spectral line of low intensity having a frequency close to that of another stronger line to which it is closely related (as by having a common energy level) **d** : an auxiliary airfield of limited facilities serving as a dispersal point for a main air base and as a base of operations if the main field is put out of action **5** : one that accompanies : COMPLEMENT ⟨maize and its ~s — squashes and beans —A.L.Kroeber⟩

²satellite \"\ *also* **sat·el·lit·ic** \ˌsad·ᵊl'id·ik, 'satᵊl-, -ˌlit\ *adj* **1** : of, relating to, or being a satellite ⟨globular star clusters are ~ systems —G.W.Gray b.1898⟩ ⟨the earth ~ vehicle program —*New Republic*⟩ ⟨the Kremlin could launch four ~ armies against them and still disclaim responsibility —H.F.Armstrong⟩ ⟨T chromosomes are characterized by having a ~ end —Leona Schnell⟩ **2** : dominated by or dependent upon an external power : SUBORDINATE, RELATED ⟨did not take as much as four days . . . to obtain from its vassal ~ regimes acceptance of new measures —W.H.Chamberlin⟩ ⟨a survey of the governmental relationships between that city and its ~ communities —Robert Shaplen⟩ ⟨~ industries which can supply them with parts and components —Darrell Berrigan⟩ **3 a** : being in close proximity or association : ADJACENT, ANCILLARY ⟨guarded by a formidable barrier of ~ peaks —*Times Lit. Supp.*⟩ ⟨a large, angry boil ~ surrounded by a crop of what the doctors call ~ boils —S.M.Spencer⟩ ⟨a central library and ~ departmental libraries —*Library Science Abstracts*⟩ **b** : of a correlative nature : CONCOMITANT ⟨characters . . . correlated with growth —J.W.MacArthur⟩

sat·el·lit·ed \'sad·ᵊl,īd·ᵊd *sometimes* 'sat,lēn-, -ᵊl- -ed⟩ : having a satellite ⟨a ~ chromosome⟩

satellite sphinx *n* : a large handsomely colored sphinx (*Pholus pandorus*) whose larva feeds on the grapevine

sat·el·lit·ism \'sad·ᵊl,īd·ˌizᵊm *sometimes* 'satᵊl-\ *n* -s [¹*satellite* + -*ism*] **1** : the practice of or belief in acquiring political satellites **2** : the growth of bacteria of one sort in culture about colonies of another sort that supply needed micronutrients or growth factors

sat·el·lit·osis \ˌsad·ᵊl,īd·'ōsᵊs, ,satᵊlī-\ *n, pl* **satellit·oses** \-ō,sēz\ [NL, fr. ISV *satellite* + NL -*osis*] : a condition accompanying degenerative or inflammatory diseases of the central nervous system and characterized by a grouping of satellite cells around gangliocytes in the brain

sa·tem \'säˌtem, -ᵊtᵊm\ *adj* [Av *satəm* hundred; fr. the fact that the initial sound of Av *satəm* (pronounced approximately \'säˌtem\) represents an IE palatal stop; akin to Skt *śatam* hundred — more at HUNDRED] : belonging to or constituting a part of the Indo-European language family in which the palatal stops became palatal or alveolar fricatives — opposed to *centum*

sates *pres 3d sing of* SATE

satg *abbr* saturating

sathan *obs var of* SATAN

sati *var of* SUTTEE

sa·tia·ble \ˈsāshəbəl *sometimes* -shēəb-\ *adj* [LL satiabilis satisfying, fr. L satiare to satisfy, satiate + -abilis -able] : capable of being appeased or satisfied

¹sa·ti·ate \ˈsāsh(ē)ət\ *adj* [ME saciat, fr. L satiatus, past part. of satiare to satiate] : SATIATED ⟨that ... moment after dinner —D.L.Morgan⟩

²sa·ti·ate \ˈsāshēˌāt, *usu* -ˌad-+V\ *vt* -ED/-ING/-S [L satiatus, past part. of satiare to satiate, fr. satis enough — more at SAD] **1 a** : to satisfy (as an appetite or desire) fully ⟨in reviewing a novel, you should try to ... titillate rather than ~ the reader's interest —Raymond Walters b.1912⟩ **b** : SATE **1 2** *obs* : SATURATE

syn SATE, SURFEIT, CLOY, PALL, GLUT, GORGE: SATIATE is the most general term, referring chiefly to the fact of repletion, without specifying manner or consequence. Both SATIATE and SATE were formerly used in the sense of merely to satisfy completely; both terms, but esp. SATE, now usu. imply overindulgence to the point where there is no longer any pleasure in what once seemed desirable ⟨a vast sameness of sweetness, satiating but never satisfying —Winifred Bambrick⟩ ⟨our generation is so overwhelmed by information ... that curiosity becomes sated, discrimination dulled —W.R.Parker⟩ SURFEIT implies feeding, supplying, or indulging to excess, with consequent revulsion or disgust ⟨other poems have other crimes, and long before the reader has finished with them he is surfeited —J.G.Southworth⟩ CLOY stresses the aversion resulting from an excess of normally gratifying experience ⟨all breathing human passion far above, that leaves a heart highsorrowful and cloy'd —John Keats⟩ PALL emphasizes loss of power to attract and a consequent waning of interest ⟨the vision palled, and Wells, the lifelong Utopian, despaired of man —Karl Meyer⟩ GLUT suggests a full supply or sometimes oversupply not necessarily resulting in extinction of desire; often (except in the economic sense of a glutted market) it suggests a constantly renewed greed, limited only by physical necessity ⟨glutted, but not sated with blood —Jane Porter⟩ GORGE suggests a greed, whether for material or spiritual goods, that is intensified by gratification and is only abated though not necessarily satisfied when the bursting point is reached ⟨the more she heard, the more she wanted to know; there was no gorging her to satiety —Samuel Butler †1902⟩ where food is the object, GORGE may suggest prolonged and unrestrained stuffing ⟨fell upon eggs and bacon and gorged till he could gorge no more —Rudyard Kipling⟩

satiated *adj* [fr. past part. of ²satiate] : filled to satiety : surfeited ⟨to the point of indifference or aversion : BORED, GLUTTED ⟨went and went again, never ~ with the theme —R.M.Lovett⟩ ⟨preaching continues until about 9 o'clock at night, when the people, ... and satiated, begin to leave —Amer. Guide Series: Tenn.⟩

sa·ti·a·tion \ˌsāsh(ē)ˈāshən\ *n* -s [L satiatus (past part. of satiare to satiate) + E -ion] **1** : the quality or state of being satiated ⟨the fundamental precept of the fight for longevity is avoidance of ~ —A.A.Bogomolets⟩ **2** : the act or process of achieving gratification ⟨~ of wants⟩

sa·ti·e·ty \səˈtīəd-ē, -ḍē, |tˌ, |ē *also* ˈsāsh(ē)ə\ *n* -ES [MF satiete, fr. L satietat-, satietas, fr. satis enough] **1** : the quality or state of being fed to or beyond capacity : FULLNESS, SURFEIT ⟨gorged to ~ after a big Thanksgiving dinner⟩ **2 a** *obs* : full measure ⟨a ~ of joy, and an uninterrupted happiness —Joseph Addison⟩ **b** *archaic* : a completely adequate or more than adequate amount or extent ⟨had miracles even to ~ —J.H.Newman⟩ **3 a** : excessive gratification of a desire ⟨gave one of the soldiers leave to be drunk six weeks, in hopes of curing him by ~ —William Cowper⟩ **b** : the quality or state of being cloyed by overindulgence ⟨when natural pleasures had been indulged in to ~, pleasures ... were imported from the East to stimulate the exhausted appetite —J.A.Froude⟩

¹sat·in \ˈsatⁿn\ *n* -s [ME, fr. MF satin, satanin, zatanin, zatany, prob. fr. Ar zaytūnī, fr. Zaytūn, a seaport in China during the Middle Ages, prob. Zayton, Zaitun, described by Marco Polo as one of the great ports of the East in the 13th cent. and isu. identified with Tsinkiang (formerly Chuanchow), seaport city in Fukien Province, southeastern China] **1 a** : a smooth sleek fabric in satin weave with a very lustrous face and a dull back woven of silk and other fibers (as rayon, nylon, cotton) and used in various weights esp. for lingerie, dresses, and upholstery **2** : something that resembles satin in texture or appearance ⟨parts finished in metallic ~ —Sweet's Catalog Service⟩

²satin \"\ *adj* **1** : made of or covered with satin ⟨~ shoes⟩ ⟨carried the crown on a ~ cushion⟩ **2** : resembling satin in lustrous finish, smooth appearance, or soft slippery feel ⟨roses break their ~ flake upon my garden floor —Emily Dickinson⟩ ⟨the master bedroom is finished in ~ plywood —Amer. Builder⟩

³satin \"\ *vt* -ED/-ING/-S : SATINIZE

sat·i·nay \ˈsatⁿnˌā\ *n* -s [F satiné satiny] : the wood of an Australian tree (Syncarpia hillii) of the family Myrtaceae resembling satiné in color and grain and being used for veneer and fine furniture

satin-back *or* **satin-backed** \ˌ≠≠,≠\ *adj* : having a satin weave surface on the back and any of various weaves on the front — used of reversible fabrics

satin bowerbird *or* **satin bird** *n* : a bowerbird (Ptilonorhynchus violaceus) of southeast Australia having feathered nostrils and being in the fully adult male a glossy violet blue and in the female a light gray green

¹sat·i·né \ˌsatⁿ'ā\ *n* -s [F, satiny, fr. past part. of satiner to satinize, fr. satin, n., fr. MF] **1** : a timber tree (Brosimum paraense) of Brazil and the Guianas **2** : the heavy hard lustrous red wood of satiné used for cabinetwork, veneers and furniture because of its golden sheen

²satine *var of* SATEEN

sat·in·et *also* **sat·in·ette** \ˌsatⁿˈet\ *n* -s [F satinet, fr. satin, n. + -et] **1** : a thin silk satin or an imitation satin usu. of silk and cotton or wool and cotton used chiefly for clothing **2 a** : a variation of satin weave used in making satinet

satinfin \ˈ≠≠,≠\ *or* **satinfin shiner** *n* [²satin + fin] : a common minnow (Notropis analostanus) of the northeastern U.S. or a related fish (N. spilopterus) of the eastern and central U.S., both having the lower fins largely white

satinflower \ˈ≠≠,≠\ *n* [²satin + flower] **1** : HONESTY 3 **2** : BLUE-EYED GRASS **3** : COMMON CHICKWEED **4** : FLANNELFLOWER 1 : a plant or flower of the genus Godetia

satin flycatcher *also* **satin sparrow** *n* : a flycatcher (Myiagra cyanoleuca) of Tasmania and Australia that in the male is iridescent greenish black above and white below with greenish black throat — called also shining flycatcher

sating *pres part of* SATE

satin glass *n* : usu. colored or opaque and often cased ornamental glassware given a satinized finish by treatment with hydrofluoric acid vapor

satin grass *n* : any of several American grasses of the genus Muhlenbergia (as M. mexicana and M. racemosa)

sat·in·ize \ˈsatⁿnˌīz\ *vt* -ED/-ING/-S [¹satin + -ize] : to give a satiny finish to ⟨glass ... satinized by plunging in a bath of hydrofluoric acid vapor —C.W.Drepperd⟩

satinleaf \ˈ≠≠,≠\ *n* [²satin + leaf] : CAIMITILLO

satin moth *n* : a tussock moth (Stilpnotia salicis) that is native to Europe but has become established in several parts of the U.S. and Canada whose adults have white satiny wings and whose blackish white-marked larvae feed on the foliage of the poplar and willow

satinpod \ˈ≠≠,≠\ *n* [²satin + pod] : HONESTY 3, LUNARIA

satin spar *or* **satin stone** *n* : a fine fibrous calcite or gypsum with a satiny luster

satin stitch *n* : a padded or unpadded embroidery stitch that is nearly alike on both sides and worked in various lengths and parallel lines so closely and evenly as to resemble satin fabric

satin walnut *n* : SWEET GUM 1

satin weave *n* : a weave in which the warp yarns are floated over the weft yarns or the weft over the warp and are interlaced at widely spread regular or irregular intervals thereby forming a smooth compact unbroken surface

satin white *n* : a white pigment made usu. by precipitating an aluminum sulfate with calcium hydroxide, consisting essentially of calcium sulfate and aluminum hydroxide and used chiefly in coating paper and as a base for organic pigments

satinwood \ˈ≠≠,≠\ *n* [²satin + wood] **1 a** : an East Indian tree (Chloroxylon swietenia) of the family Meliaceae **b** : the very hard yellowish brown wood of this tree which has a satiny luster and is used esp. for fine cabinetwork and farming tools **2 a** : any of several trees with wood felt to resemble the East Indian satinwood: as (1) : a rather small yellowwood (Zanthoxylum coriaceum) of southern Florida and the West Indies with very heavy pale orange wood used locally for furniture and implements; also : a similar Australian tree (Z. brachyacanthum) with deep yellow wood (2) : ORANGE JESSAMINE (3) Austral : SASSAFRAS 3a(2) **b** : the wood of such

sat·iny \ˈsat(ⁿ)nē, -ni\ *adj* [¹satin + -y] **1** : having the soft texture or lustrous smoothness of satin ⟨the acorns ... were green and ~ —Josephine Johnson⟩ ⟨waters of the harbor were a ~ light blue —Kenneth Roberts⟩ **2** : richly sensuous ⟨the ~ sandalwood scent that came from the splendid coffin —Thomas Wolfe⟩

sat·ire \ˈsaˌtī(ə)r, -īə\ *n* -s [MF, fr. L satira, satura satirical poetry, poetic medley, fr. (lanx) satura full plate, plate filled with various fruits, mixture, medley, fr. lanx plate + satura, fem. of satur full of food, sated — more at BALANCE, SAD] **1 a** : an ancient Roman commentary in verse on some prevailing vice or folly **b** : a usu. topical literary composition holding up human or individual vices, folly, abuses, or shortcomings to censure by means of ridicule, derision, burlesque, irony, or other method sometimes with an intent to bring about improvement ⟨a farcical ~ about ... adultery and lateachieved maturity —Orville Prescott⟩ **c** : LAMPOON ⟨diabolically good ~s of single authors —Anthony Boucher⟩ **d** : an expression of satire in another form ⟨dance ~⟩ ⟨visual ~ ... abetted by hilarious sound effects —M.S.Dworkin⟩ ⟨an ungainly person, whose clothes were a continual ~ on his professional skill —Bayard Taylor⟩ **2 a** : a branch of literature ridiculing vice or folly ⟨~ ... flourishes in a stable society and presupposes homogeneous moral standards —Evelyn Waugh⟩ ⟨the constructive purpose to which the humor and underlying hopefulness of good ~ give nourishment —J.R.Newman⟩ **b** *obs* : SATIRIST **3** : railery used to convey rebuke or criticism : caustic comment ⟨essay into these paragraphs he packed his dry wit and his easy, good-natured ~ on the follies of the day —Eleanor Sickels⟩ ⟨a brilliant writer with a rare talent for corrosive ~ —C.J.Rolo⟩ *syn* see WIT

sa·tir·ic \səˈtirik, -rēk\ *or* **sa·tir·i·cal** \-rəkəl, -rēk-\ *adj* [satiric fr. MF satirique, fr. LL satiricus, fr. L satira satire + -icus -ic; satirical fr. MF satirique + E -al] **1** : of, relating to, characterized by, or based on satire ⟨a ~ poet⟩ ⟨~ awareness of the ... contradictory behavior of the whites —C.I.Glicksberg⟩ ⟨a ~ portrait of a ... soldier who makes life simple by limiting his horizon —Henry Hewes⟩ ⟨noted for her ~ oils and drawings —Amer. Guide Series: La.⟩ **2** : fond of satire ⟨skilled at ironic comment ⟨witty, eloquent, and satirical in his sermons —G.H.Genzmer⟩ ⟨a flair for drawing and a nice satirical sense —Merle Miller⟩ **3 a** : bearing a device satirizing a political or social issue ⟨satirical coin⟩ **b** : circulated for propaganda purposes ⟨satirical token⟩ ⟨satirical medal⟩ *syn* see SARCASTIC

sa·tir·i·cal·ly \-rək(ə)lē, -rēk-, -li\ *adv* : in a satirical manner

sa·tir·i·cal·ness *n* -ES *archaic* : the quality or state of being satirical

satirism *n* -s [satire + -ism] *obs* : expression of satire

sat·i·rist \ˈsad-ərəst, -atə-\ *n* -s [satire + -ist] : one that satirizes; *esp* : a satirical writer

sat·i·rize \-ˌrīz\ *vb* -ED/-ING/-S *see -ize in Explan Notes* [F satiriser, fr. MF, fr. satire + -iser -ize] *vi* : to utter or write satires : comment satirically esp. in literary form ⟨it is as bad a fault in history to panegyrize, as to ~ without reason —Roger North⟩ *vt* : to censure or ridicule by means of satire ⟨makes use of allegory and fantasy to ~ the society of his time —Amer. Guide Series: N.Y.City⟩

sat·i·riz·er \-zə(r)\ *n* -s [satirize + -er] : one that satirizes

sat·is·da·tion \ˌsad-əsˈdāshən\ *n* -s [L satisdation-, satisdatio, fr. satisdatus, past part. of satisdare to give security, give enough, fr. satis enough + dare to give — more at SAD, DATE] *Roman & civil law* : the giving of security esp. by a guarantor on behalf of a debtor sometimes in form of a cautio

sat·is·fac·tion \ˌsad-əsˈfakshən, ˌsatə-\ *n* -s [ME satisfaccion, fr. MF satisfaction, fr. LL satisfaction-, satisfactio penitence, penance, fr. L satisfaction-, fr. satisfactus (past part. of satisfacere to satisfy) + -ion-, -io ion — more at SATISFY] **1 a** : reparation for sin made by performing the penance imposed by a confessor ⟨the good works required of penitent sinners in ~ for their offenses —K.S.Latourette⟩ **b** : fulfillment of the demands of divine justice on behalf of mankind ⟨the voluntary death of Christ ... accomplished this ~ —Encyc. Americana⟩ — compare ATONEMENT 2 **2 a** : complete fulfillment of a need or want : attainment of a desired end ⟨if for this night he entreat you to his bed, give him promise of ~ —Shak.⟩ ⟨primitive art quickly flowers into full ~ of some aesthetic craving —A.N.Whitehead⟩ ⟨when the cause of the arthritis can be definitely determined ... the condition can be treated with much more ~ —Morris Fishbein⟩ **b** : the quality or state of being satisfied : CONTENTMENT, PLEASURE ⟨~ in able work accomplished and recognized —Johnson O'Connor⟩ ⟨derive a melancholy ~ from the conviction that they are on the losing side —Elmer Davis⟩ ⟨the ~ derived from a sense of sharing in creative activities —John Dewey⟩ **c** : a cause or means of enjoyment : GRATIFICATION ⟨children ... found it a novelty and a ~ to work on the soil —Martha Sharp⟩ ⟨journeyed to Kentucky ... to pay off his debts, an action that gave him one of the greatest ~s of his life —W.J.Ghent⟩ **3 a** (1) : compensation for a loss or injury : ATONEMENT, RESTITUTION ⟨promised to have the fellows punished, and ~ to be made —Daniel Defoe⟩ (2) *obs* : payment for service given ⟨operation of writing, for which it directed the scribe to receive a ~ —William Blackstone⟩ (3) : opportunity to vindicate one's honor ⟨ready for his fighting a duel⟩ ⟨if ... you will give me your card, I will see that you shall shortly have the ~ you require —Thomas Medwin⟩ **b** (1) : the discharge of a legal obligation or settlement of a claim : execution of an accord ⟨~ of a mortgage⟩ (2) : a legal document showing that such an obligation has been met **c** : fulfillment of an essential condition ⟨~ of the foreign language distribution requirement —College of William & Mary Cat.⟩ **4 a** : dissipation of doubt or ignorance : CONVICTION, ENLIGHTENMENT ⟨the charge must be proved to the ~ of the court⟩ ⟨for your private ~ ... I will let you know —Shak.⟩ ⟨his investigation was a legitimate ~ of congressional curiosity —Brian Gilbert⟩ **b** : satisfactory proof ⟨I doubt not but to give you ~ that I am not worthy of this wrong —Itinerary⟩

satisfaction piece *n* : a formal written acknowledgment by the holder of a mortgage or judgment of its satisfaction with an authorization for its discharge of record

satisfaction theory *n* : a theory of the atonement in scholastic theology: according to the requirements of divine justice God and man could not be reconciled until human guilt was punished or acceptable satisfaction was made and Christ made such satisfaction by freely and vicariously suffering and dying — see PENAL THEORY; compare GOVERNMENTAL ATONEMENT, MORAL THEORY, RANSOM THEORY, SACRIFICIAL THEORY

sat·is·fac·to·ri·ly \ˌsad-əsˈfakt(ə)rəlē, -rəli, -li\ *adv* : in a satisfactory manner

sat·is·fac·to·ri·ness \-rēnəs, -rin-\ *n* -ES : the quality or state of being satisfactory

sat·is·fac·to·ry \ˌ≠≠ˈfakt(ə)rē, -ri\ *adj* [LL satisfactorius, fr. satisfactus (past part. of satisfacere to satisfy) + -orius -ory] **1** *archaic* : fulfilling the requirements of divine justice ⟨the ~ ... and propitiatory sacrifice of Christ Jesus —William Gouge⟩ **2** : sufficient to meet a condition or obligation ⟨~ scores on the medical college admission test —Bull. of Meharry

Med. Coll.⟩ 3 : giving satisfaction: as **a** : capable of dispelling doubt or ignorance : CONVINCING, INFORMATIVE ⟨very ~ evidence that around the tenth century A.D. the stories ... were almost identical —E.R.Leach⟩ ⟨the most ~ and trustworthy ... book on the subject —Zechariah Chafee⟩ **b** : adequate to meet a need or want ⟨breast milk is the best food for an infant ... provided the supply is ~ —Morris Fishbein⟩ **2** : producing pleasure or contentment : ENJOYABLE, GRATIFYING ⟨a ~ pet is an animal ... that is not an annoyance to owner or guests —Doris Bryant⟩ ⟨found that ... the sphere and the cone were ~ objects in themselves —Herbert Read⟩ ⟨particularly are the declines in infantile mortality ~ —R.C.Geary⟩ **d** : having all the necessary qualities for effective use ⟨a number of fountain pens had been patented previously, but to his mind none of them was ~ —C.W.Mitman⟩

sat·is·fi·able \ˈ≠≠,sfīəbəl, ≠≠ˈ≠≠≠\ *adj* [satisfy + -able] : capable of being satisfied

satisfied *adj* [fr. past part. of satisfy] **1** : full of contentment : PLEASED, GRATIFIED ⟨a ~ customer⟩ **2** : paid in full : DISCHARGED ⟨a ~ mortgage⟩ **3** : persuaded by argument or evidence : CONVINCED ⟨there is great force in this argument, and the court is not ~ —John Marshall⟩

sat·is·fi·er \ˈ≠≠,sfī(ə)r, -īə\ *n* -s [satisfy + -er] : one that satisfies

sat·is·fy \ˈsad-ə,sfī, -atə-\ *vb* -ED/-ING/-ES [ME satisfien, fr. MF satisfier, modif. (influenced by MF -fier-fy) of L satisfacere, fr. satis enough + facere to do, make — more at SAD, DO] *vt* **1 a** : to carry out the terms of (as a contract) : DISCHARGE ⟨the property would be insufficient to ~ ... the lien —G.A.Parks⟩ ⟨helpless to ... defend a suit because he has no money to ~ court fees —J.M.Maguire⟩ **b** : to meet a financial obligation to (a creditor) ⟨had to sell land ... to ~ his creditors —T.J.Wertenbaker⟩ **c** *obs* : to recompense for services : REMUNERATE ⟨not a compositor's duty; especially where he has no expectation of being satisfied for it —Philip Luckombe⟩ **2 a** *obs* : to serve as compensation for (a loss or injury) : AVENGE, REQUITE **b** (1) : to do penance for (a sin) (2) : to make atonement or reparation to (an injured party) : INDEMNIFY ⟨conclude a treaty to ~ Indians deprived of their hereditary lands⟩ **3 a** : to make happy : PLEASE ⟨in the position of having to ~ teachers and critics —R.M.Weaver⟩ ⟨farmers ... were satisfied with the administration's flexible farm support program —Wall Street Jour.⟩ ⟨a picture, in whatever degree it be realistic or nonrealistic, should ... ~ the eye —C.W.H.Johnson⟩ **b** : to gratify to the full : APPEASE, SATIATE ⟨satisfied his omnivorous appetite for reading in the village library —A.C.Cole⟩ ⟨the men in the capital ... do their utmost to gauge and to ~ the desires of the nation —Lester Markel⟩ **4 a** : to persuade by argument or evidence : CONVINCE ⟨took me a long time to ~ them ... that my engagements prevented me from presiding —O.S.J.Gogarty⟩ ⟨not satisfied that I have penetrated this allegory —Paul Pickrel⟩ **b** : to put an end to (doubt or uncertainty) : DISPEL ⟨many a world-renowned lecturer came up the Mississippi ... to ~ his curiosity —Amer. Guide Series: Minn.⟩ **c** : to answer or express fully (a question or two in the unquiet heads which do not ~ the romantic illusion he has created —I.L.Salomon⟩ ⟨cloying repetitions that do not ~ —W.L.Sullivan⟩ **5 a** : to conform to (accepted criteria or requirements) : FULFILL, MEET ⟨if a consignment does not ~ all the conditions ... it is graded down —Farmer's Weekly (So. Africa)⟩ ⟨able ... to ~ the demands of a moral, Victorian society —Ruth R. Chapman⟩ ⟨an explanation which might ~ these statements and be true to the evidence —H.Lovegrove⟩ **b** : to comply with (an academic requirement) ⟨courses ... taken to ~ the distribution requirements —Official Register of Harvard Univ.⟩ **c** : to provide a solution for; *specif* : to substitute an expression for an unknown quantity in (an equation) so that the resulting equation is true **d** : to serve as an embodiment of : give concrete expression to : EXEMPLIFY ⟨the first American foundation which satisfies the definition —F.E.Andrews⟩ ⟨a social regime can come into enduring existence only as it satisfies some elements of human nature not previously afforded expression —John Dewey⟩ **6** : to respond to by chemical union ⟨to ~ valences⟩ ~ *vi* **1** *archaic* : to do penance : ATONE; *specif* : to fulfill the requirements of divine justice **2** : to be a source of pleasure or gratification : PLEASE, SUFFICE ⟨where the play seems not to ~ is in the full release of emotions —Leslie Rees⟩

syn CONTENT: SATISFY usu. implies full appeasement of a desire, longing, need, or requirement ⟨satisfy curiosity⟩ ⟨satisfy an appetite⟩ ⟨satisfy the desire for power —W.G.Walter⟩ ⟨the needs which such an effort purports to satisfy —Abram Kardiner⟩ CONTENT usu. implies gratification of a desire or longing to the point where one is not disquieted or disturbed even though every wish is not fully realized ⟨must content myself with adducing some fresh evidence on the subject —J.G.Frazer⟩ ⟨contented with the same food, clothing and lodging which satisfied them in former times —Adam Smith⟩

syn SATISFY, FULFILL, MEET, ANSWER all imply the ability to measure up to a set of criteria or requirements. SATISFY often implies adequacy to a practical extent or for a stated purpose ⟨went a long way toward satisfying the long-standing claims of his critics —Time⟩ ⟨a culture which will satisfy our needs —J.B.Conant⟩ ⟨finding the way to satisfy her demands —A.S.Iglehart⟩ FULFILL, when it is not interchangeable with SATISFY, may connote more abundance or richness of qualification ⟨fulfill the requirement for graduation⟩ ⟨fulfill his greatest need⟩ ⟨fulfill all conditions imposed upon a candidate for office⟩ MEET implies an exactness of agreement between a requirement and what is submitted to fill it ⟨the instruments met all the criteria with above-average ratings —Helen Vodicka⟩ ⟨the student has not met all financial obligations to the University —Loyola Univ. Bull.⟩ ⟨the provisions were sufficiently flexible to meet the needs of men with very large families —R.A.Billington⟩ ANSWER usu. though not necessarily implies the simple satisfaction of a demand, need, or purpose often in a temporary or expedient manner and may imply some falling short in completeness or fullness of qualification ⟨answer a need⟩ ⟨though a sharp knife should be used, a dull one will answer the purpose⟩ ⟨answer in some way the demands of a growing child for good counseling⟩ *syn* see in addition PAY

satisfying *adj* : SATISFACTORY 3 — **sat·is·fy·ing·ly** *adv*

sat·is·fy·ing·ness *n* -ES : SATISFACTION

sat·is·pas·sion \ˌsad-əˈspashən\ *n* [L satis enough + E passion (sense 1); influenced by ML satis pati to suffer enough] : penitential suffering

sative *adj* [L sativus, fr. satus (past part. of serere to sow) + -ivus -ive — more at SOW] *obs* : SOWN, CULTIVATED

satn *abbr* saturation

sa·to·ri \səˈtōrē\ *n* -s [Jap] : sudden enlightenment and a state of consciousness attained by intuitive illumination representing the spiritual goal of Zen Buddhism

sa·trae \ˈsātrē\ *n pl, usu cap* [NL, fr. Gk Satrai] : an ancient people of Thrace living on Mount Pangaeus without ever being subjugated by a conqueror

satrap \ˈsāˌtrap *also* ˈsaˌtrap, *chiefly Brit* ˈsaˈtrəp\ *n* -s [ME, fr. L satrapes, fr. Gk satrapēs, fr. OPer xshathrapāvan, lit., protector of the dominion, a compound whose first constituent is akin to Skt kṣatra might, power, kṣayati he rules, and whose second constituent is akin to Skt pāti he protects — more at CHECK, FUR] **1 a** : the governor of a province in ancient Persia **b** : the viceroy of a sovereign power ⟨~s who represented the king in Ireland —O.S.J.Gogarty⟩ ⟨Soviet leaders and their East German ~s —Newsweek⟩ **2 a** : one having authority ⟨the ~s of Yale University saw nothing wrong in allowing one of its lecture halls to be used —Amer. Mercury⟩ **b** : a subordinate often subservient official or supporter : HENCHMAN ⟨political ~s who battled for senators in the legislature —W.A.White⟩

sat·ra·py \ˈsāˌtrapē, ˈsaˌtrap-, ˈsaˈtrəp-, ˈsaˌtrap-, -pi\ *n* -ES [F satrapie, fr. L satrapia, satrapea, fr. Gk satrapeia, fr. satrapēs satrap + -ia -y] **1 a** : a territory governed by a satrap ⟨the Greek city was no mere ~ of a faraway king —C.H.McIlwain⟩ **b** : the sphere of influence of a powerful individual ⟨views ... unions outside his ~ with the loathing of a highcaste Hindu for an untouchable —Joe Miller⟩ **2 a** : a hierarchy of satraps ⟨the most unappetizing man in the Hitler ~ —New Yorker⟩

sats *pl of* SAT

satin stitch

sat·sop \'sat,säp\ *n, pl* **satsop** *or* **satsops** *usu cap* **1 :** a Salishan people of the Satsop river valley in southwestern Washington **2 :** a member of the Satsop people

sat·su·ma \sat'sümə, 'satsəmə\ *n* -s [fr. *Satsuma*, former province in southern Kyushu, Japan] **1** *or* **satsuma ware** *usu cap S* **:** a hard fine-grained buff Japanese pottery first produced about the end of the 16th century, orig. decorated with monochrome glazes, and from the late 18th century finished with increasingly ornate overglaze enamels and gilding **2** *or* **satsuma orange :** any of several cultivated mandarin trees having medium-sized largely seedless fruits with thin smooth skin

sat·ta·gyd·i·an \,sad·ə'jidēən, -'gi-\ *n, pl* **sattagydian** *or* **sattagydians** *usu cap* **1 :** an ancient people of the Punjab **2 :** a member of the Sattagydian people

sat·tle \'satᵊl\ *dial Brit var of* SETTLE

satt·va \'sətvə\ *n* -s [Skt, lit., existence, fr. *sat, sant* existing, true, good — more at SOOTH] **:** the purity and wisdom constituting one of the three gunas of Sankhya philosophy and leading to true enlightenment — compare RAJAS, TAMAS

sa·tu·ra \'säd·ərə\ *n, pl* **satu·rae** \-,rī\ [L — more at SATIRE] **:** a rudimentary type of stage show with musical accompaniment performed in ancient Rome prior to the introduction of formal Latin comedy

sat·u·ra·ble \'sach(ə)rəbəl\ *adj* [LL *saturabilis*, fr. L *saturare* to saturate + *-abilis* -able] **:** capable of being saturated

saturable reactor *also* **saturable core reactor** *n* **:** an AC reactor coil of variable but limited impedance because of magnetic core saturation by means of an auxiliary DC excitation coil — abbr. *SR*

¹sat·u·rant \'sachərənt\ *adj* [L *saturant-, saturans*, pres. part. of *saturare* to saturate] **:** impregnating to the full **:** SATURATING

²saturant \"\ *n* -s **:** a substance used to saturate another

¹sat·u·rate \'sachə,rāt, *usu* -ād·+V\ *vt* -ED/-ING/-S [L *saturatus*, past part. of *saturare* to fill, saturate, fr. *satur* full of food, satiated — more at SAD] **1 :** to cloy with overabundance **:** SATE, SURFEIT ⟨a surfeit of war and massive injustice have *saturated* our capacity for moral indignation —John Barkham⟩ **2 :** to satisfy the affinity of (a substance) **:** cause to combine till there is no further tendency to combine **:** NEUTRALIZE ⟨~ an acid with an alkali⟩ **3 a :** to infuse thoroughly or cause to be pervaded **:** SOAK, STEEP ⟨~ a sponge with water⟩ ⟨the whole house was *saturated* with the aroma —Ellen Glasgow⟩ ⟨moonglow . . . ~s an empty sky —Henry Miller⟩ **b :** to fill completely **:** IMBUE ⟨the novel . . . is *saturated* with individualism and liberal culture —V.S.Pritchett⟩ ⟨this little town with its giant elms is *saturated* with . . . traditions —E.A.Weeks⟩ ⟨literary men ~ themselves in attitudes that have become irrelevant —H.J.Muller⟩ **c :** to load to capacity **:** CROWD, DELUGE ⟨jet operations already ~ all air space between 20,000 ft. and 40,000 ft. —*Time*⟩ ⟨the two-million-dollar . . . campaign, which *saturated* radio and television for two weeks before election day —Robert Bendiner⟩; *specif* **:** to furnish to an amount which meets present and prospective demands at current prices ⟨believed that 8000 machines . . . would about ~ the market —Bryan Morgan⟩ **d** (1) **:** to overwhelm (an air defense system) by sending in so many airplanes in a unit of time that detecting and tracking equipment becomes erratic (2) **:** to blanket (a target area) with bombs or projectiles to the point of utter destruction **4 a :** to impregnate with a vapor to the maximum degree possible at the existing temperature and pressure ⟨~ air with water vapor⟩ **b :** to dissolve in (a solvent) as much of a solute as can be held in solution at the existing temperature and pressure **c :** to magnetize (a substance) until further increase of magnetizing force produces no increase in magnetization **d :** to increase the voltage on (a vacuum tube or other device) until further voltage increase produces no change in current **syn** see PERMEATE

²sat·u·rate \'sach(ə)rət, *usu* -əd·+V\ *adj* [L *saturatus*, past part. of *saturare* to saturate] **:** SATURATED ⟨seaweed can loll in the water, buoyed by it and even ~ with it —D.C.Peattie⟩ ⟨words . . . have become enriched by many associations, ~ with many colors —Havelock Ellis⟩ ⟨a ~ solution of silver⟩

³saturate *n* -s **:** a saturated chemical compound

saturated *adj* [fr. past part. of ¹*saturate*] **1 :** brought to a state of full contentment or development **:** SATISFIED, PERFECTED ⟨as well-*saturated* guests, we should . . . willingly recede from the table —Henry More⟩ ⟨exaggerate the differences between . . . ~ and emergent cultures —Edward Sapir⟩ **2 a :** steeped in moisture **:** SOAKED, SOGGY ⟨the top of the ~ zone is called the groundwater table —V.C.Finch & G.T.Trewartha⟩ **b :** completely penetrated **:** ABSORBED, PERVADED ⟨listened to jazz in a smoke-*saturated* room —Molly L. Bar-David⟩ ⟨a ~ knowledge which . . . has entered the very bloodstream of his thought —H.M.Wriston⟩ **3 a** *of a solution* **:** having the greatest concentration that can remain under given conditions (as of temperature and pressure) in the presence of the dissolved substance **b** *of a chemical compound* **:** not tending to form addition products — used esp. of organic compounds containing only single bonds between carbon atoms ⟨paraffin hydrocarbons are ~ compounds⟩ ⟨~ fatty acids⟩ **4 a :** impregnated to the maximum degree ⟨water . . . permanently ~ with oxygen —W.H.Dowdeswell⟩ ⟨a magnetically ~ steel bar⟩ **b :** having high saturation **:** PURE, VIVID — used of a color **c :** containing the greatest possible amount of combined silica — used of a mineral or rock **5 :** filled to capacity **:** fully supplied ⟨500 millions of . . . folk live in a continent which is now essentially ~ —Griffith Taylor⟩ ⟨possible results of such an operation . . . would have but little effect on an already ~ market —*Amer. Guide Series: Wash.*⟩

saturated steam *n* **1 :** water vapor in equilibrium with liquid water at or above the normal boiling point **2 :** WET STEAM

saturated vapor *n* **:** vapor at the temperature of the boiling point corresponding to its pressure and so incapable of being compressed or cooled without condensing — compare EQUILIBRIUM 1c

saturating felt *n* **:** a felt paper for impregnation with asphalt or other waterproofing compound

sat·u·ra·tion \,sachə'rāshən\ *n* -s *often attrib* [LL *saturation-, saturatio*, fr. L *saturatus* (past part. of *saturare* to saturate) + *-ion-, -io* -ion] **1 :** complete satiety or glut **:** CONTENTMENT, SURFEIT ⟨moving from stable ~ to . . . restlessness, and instability —A.L.Kroeber⟩ ⟨become familiar, to the point of ~ . . . with the subject matter —John Dewey⟩ **2 :** conversion of an unsaturated chemical compound to a saturated one — compare HYDROGENATION **3 a :** the quality or state of being soaked or steeped **:** PERMEATION ⟨water . . . fills all pores and openings within the zone of ~ —A.M.Bateman⟩ ⟨that ~ with the years that for Europe is synonymous with cultural meaning —Harold Rosenberg⟩ **b :** impregnation to the maximum extent: as (1) **:** the presence in air of as much water vapor per unit volume as possible at a given temperature (2) **:** magnetization to the point beyond which a further increase in the intensity of the magnetizing force will produce no further magnetization and only an equal increase in the magnetic flux density in the body (3) **:** the condition in which all the electrons in an electron tube flow to the plate as fast as they are emitted by the filament, an increase of plate or grid voltage producing no increase of current **c :** the quality or state of being filled to capacity ⟨without drastic regulation of traffic, our streets . . . will reach a point of ~ —Hal Burton⟩ **4 a :** chromatic purity **:** freedom from dilution with white **:** INTENSITY, VIVIDNESS ⟨a dull red lacking in ~⟩ **b** (1) **:** degree of difference from the gray having the same lightness — used of an object color (2) **:** degree of difference from the achromatic light-source color of the same brightness — used of a light-source color **5 a :** the supplying of a market with goods sufficient to meet all present and prospective demands at current prices ⟨falling off of refrigerator sales due to market ~⟩ **b :** widespread coverage of an area (as by personnel or promotional material) ⟨spot announcements used in metropolitan areas in varying degrees of ~⟩ ⟨~ of a tough neighborhood with police patrols⟩ **c :** the ratio of public acceptance ⟨electric cooking . . . has been developed to a ~ of 23 percent —*Electric World*⟩ **d :** the limit of consumer capacity ⟨television set ownership . . . is now less than forty percent short of ~ —Philip Minoff⟩ **6 :** a concentration of military forces or firepower sufficient to overwhelm or completely wipe out enemy defenses ⟨a logical target for quick ~ by parachute troops —George Weller⟩ **7 :** the supposed increased resemblance to the sire of successive offspring of the same parents — compare TELEGONY

saturation bombing *n* **:** AREA BOMBING

saturation current *n* **:** the limiting current through an ionized gas or an electron tube such that further increase of voltage produces no further increase in current

saturation curve *n* **:** a magnetization curve for a process carried to saturation

saturation factor *n* **:** a measure of the saturation of a magnetizable body that is the ratio of a small percentage increase in excitation to the percentage increase in magnetic flux produced thereby and that is usu. applied to the magnetic excitation of dynamoelectric machines at rated speed and voltage

saturation point *n* **:** the point at which saturation is reached: as **a** (1) **:** the limit of response to desire or stimulus ⟨killing . . . reaches a *saturation point* when the hunter ceases to want to hunt —*Nature Mag.*⟩ ⟨the boy has reached the *saturation point* and does not respond to the training school program any longer —Erwin Schepses⟩ (2) **:** the maximum level of provocation or of injurious effect ⟨the mother . . . reached a *saturation point* with the screaming child —Jessie Chamberlin⟩ ⟨a person has . . . reached the *saturation point* of aging between 70 and 80 and, from there on, he will age only very slowly —Martin Gumpert⟩ **b :** a limit of acceptance ⟨immigration . . . has not reached a *saturation point* —D.D.McKean⟩; *specif* **:** the point in a flow of goods or money at which the market will take no more except at a decrease in price ⟨houses will be built until the *saturation point* is reached —Brendon Shea⟩ **c :** the maximum degree of impregnation; *specif* **:** DEW POINT **d :** the maximum number of a kind of organism that can be carried on a particular range under optimum conditions — compare CARRYING CAPACITY

saturation pressure *n* **:** the pressure of a vapor which is in equilibrium with its liquid (as steam with water); *specif* **:** the maximum pressure possible by water vapor at a given temperature

sat·u·ra·tor \'sachə,rād·ə(r), -ātə-\ *n* -s [¹*saturate* + *-or*] **:** one that saturates: as **a :** a tank containing sulfuric acid through which vapors are passed in the carbonization of coal to remove ammonia with the formation of ammonium sulfate **b :** HUMIDIFIER 1 **c :** a device for injecting water spray into heated compressed air to cool the air **d :** an operator of a machine for saturating roofing felt with hot asphalt

sat·ur·day \'sad·ə(r)dē, -atə-, -(r)(,)dā, *in rapid speech* 'saddē *or* 'sardē *or* 'satdē *or* -di\ *n* -s *usu cap* [ME *saterday*, fr. OE *sæterdæg, sæterndæg*; akin to OFris *sāterdei* Saturday, MD *saterdach*, MLG *sāterdach*; all fr. a prehistoric WGmc compound whose first constituent was borrowed fr. L *Saturnus* Saturn and whose second constituent is represented by OE *dæg* day; trans. of L *Saturni dies* — more at DAY] **:** the seventh day of the week **:** the day following Friday

sat·ur·days \-z\ *adv, usu cap* **:** on Saturday repeatedly **:** on any Saturday

sat·u·re·ia \,sachə'rē(y)ə, ,sad·ə'-\ *n, cap* [NL, fr. L, savory (mint)] **:** a genus of aromatic herbs or shrubs (family Labiatae) that are nearly all native to southern Europe and that have small entire leaves, bracted purple flowers in axillary or terminal clusters, and oblong or oval nutlets — see SAVORY, WILD BASIL, YERBA BUENA

sat·u·re·ja \-ē(y)ə, -ējə\ [NL] *syn of* SATUREIA

sat·urn \'sad·ə(r)n, -atə-\ *n* -s *usu cap* [ME *saturne*, fr. ML *saturnus*, fr. L *Saturnus* Saturn (the planet), fr. *Saturnus* Saturn (the god); prob. fr. the sluggishness associated with the planet Saturn by astrologists] *archaic* **:** ⁴LEAD 1a

sat·ur·na·lia \,sad·ə(r)'nālyə, ,satə-, -lēə\ *n pl but sing or pl in constr* [L, fr. neut. pl. of *saturnalis* of or relating to Saturn, fr. *Saturnus* Saturn + *-alis* -al] **1** *usu cap* **:** the festival of Saturn in ancient Rome beginning on Dec. 17 and celebrated with feasting, exchange of gifts, and tumultuous revelry and presided over by a king chosen by lot ⟨a survival of the ancient *Saturnalia* or of some other pagan rite of orgiastic nature —C.B. Kelland⟩ **2** *sing, pl* **saturnalias** *also* **saturnalia** *sometimes cap* **a :** an unrestrained often licentious celebration or spectacle **:** ORGY ⟨the ~ of an American Legion convention turning Cleveland into Paris for a week —D.W.Brogan⟩ ⟨a ~ of blood and crime in which . . . the guilty are not punished for the most flagrant violation —Sheldon Glueck⟩ ⟨pilferings of . . . rum from her barroom for his noisy ~s —Wilmon Menard⟩ **b :** an excess of emotion or immorality ⟨rushed in a ~ of faith to spell out its . . . consequences for the solitary soul —S.E. Whicher⟩ ⟨sacrifice of the state, in a veritable ~ of corruption —C.G.Bowers⟩

sat·ur·na·lian \¦==¦nālyən, -lēən\ *adj* **1** *usu cap* **:** of or relating to the ancient Roman Saturnalia **2** *often cap* **:** characterized by unrestrained emotion or licentious indulgence **:** ORGIASTIC ⟨feast days with their . . . games and merrymakings and their generally *Saturnalian* aspect —Hutton Webster⟩

sat·ur·nals \sə'tərnᵊlz, 'sad·ər-\ *n pl, usu cap* [L *Saturnalia* + E *-s* (pl. suffix)] *archaic* **:** SATURNALIA

sa·tur·nia \sə'tərnēə\ *n, cap* [NL, fr. L, daughter of the Roman god Saturn (epithet of the goddess Juno), fr. fem. of *saturnius* of Saturn, fr. *Saturnus* Saturn] **:** a genus of wild silk moths that is the type of the family Saturniidae

¹sa·tur·ni·an \sə'tərnēən\ *adj, usu cap* [L *Saturnius* Saturnian (fr. *Saturnus* sixth major planet from the sun and the most remote planet known to the ancients, fr. *Saturnus* Roman god connected with the sowing of seed) + E *-an*] **1 :** of, relating to, resembling, or influenced by the planet Saturn **2** *archaic* **:** of or relating to the god Saturn or his flourishing era conceived of as a golden age ⟨a new social order . . . to bring back the ~ era to the world —Thomas Carlyle⟩

²saturnian \"\ *n* -s *usu cap* **1 :** a hypothetical inhabitant of the planet Saturn **2 :** one that has a well-developed Mount of Saturn and a long and large finger of Saturn and that is usu. held by palmists to be characterized by prudence, sobriety, cynicism, and often gloom ⟨the *Saturnian* is predisposed to suicide as an end to his woes —W.G.Benham⟩ **3 :** SATURNIAN VERSE

saturnian verse *n, usu cap S* **:** the ancient Latin verse used before the adoption of Greek verse forms

¹sa·tur·ni·id \sə'tərnēəd\ *adj* [NL *Saturniidae*] **:** of or relating to the Saturniidae

²saturniid \"\ *n* -s **:** a moth of the family Saturniidae

sat·ur·ni·idae \,sad·ər'nīə,dē\ *n pl, cap* [NL, fr. *Saturnia*, type genus + *-idae*] **:** an important and widely distributed family of moths including some of the largest insects known, having a stout hairy body, strong wide wings, and antennae which are bipectinate to the tip, having larvae which spin silken cocoons, and comprising among others the io, polyphemus, luna, and cecropia moths, the pernyi and tussah silkworms, and the Atlas moth

sat·ur·nine \'sad·ə(r),nīn, -atə-\ *adj* [ME, prob. fr. (assumed) ML *saturninus*, fr. L *Saturnus* Saturn + *-inus* -ine; perh. fr. the planet's remoteness from the sun] **1 a** *archaic* **:** born under or influenced astrologically by the planet Saturn **:** SLOW, SLUGGISH ⟨~ heavy-headed blunderers —Thomas Nash⟩ **b :** of a moody or surly character **:** MOROSE, SULLEN ⟨a ~, almost misanthropic young genius —Bruce Bliven b. 1889⟩ ⟨driven to ~ and scornful silence by . . . godless conversation —Elinor Wylie⟩ **c :** having a sardonic aspect **:** DEVILISH, WRY ⟨the face was ~ and swarthy, and the sensual lips . . . twisted with disdain —Oscar Wilde⟩ ⟨~ philosophical laughter —E.K.Brown⟩ **2 a** *archaic* **:** of or relating to lead ⟨acetate of lead and other ~ preparations —A.B.Garrod & E.B.Baxter⟩ **b :** of, relating to, or produced by lead poisoning ⟨victims of ~ poisoning —Thomas Stevenson⟩ **syn** see SULLEN

sat·ur·nin·i·ty \¦==¦ninəd·ē, -ətē, -i\ *n* -ES **:** the quality or state of being saturnine

sat·urn·ism \'==,nizəm\ *n* -s [*saturn* + *-ism*] **:** LEAD POISONING

saturn line *n, usu cap S* **:** LINE OF FATE

saturn red *or* **saturnine red** *n* **:** RED LEAD

saturns *pl of* SATURN

sat·ya·gra·ha \(,)sə'tyägrəhə, (,)sət'y-; 'sə·tyə,grəhə, 'sət·y-\ *n* -s *often cap* [Skt *satyāgraha*, lit., insistence on truth, fr. *satya* reality, truth (fr. *sat, sant* existing, true) + *āgraha* clinging to, obstinate inclination for (fr. *ā* to + *grbhnāti* he seizes) — more at SOOTH, ACHARYA, GRAB] **:** reliance on truth **:** the Gandhian method of achieving social and political reform by means of tolerance and active goodwill coupled with a firmness in one's cause expressed through nonviolent passive resistance and noncooperation

sat·ya·gra·hi \-(,)hē\ *n* -s *often cap* [Skt *satyāgrahin*, fr. *satyāgraha*] **:** one that practices satyagraha

satyr \'sād·ə(r), |tə- *also* 'sa|\ *n* -s [ME, fr. L *satyrus*, fr. Gk *satyros*] **1 a** *often cap* **:** an ancient Greek sylvan deity often represented as having certain attributes of a horse or goat and having a fondness for Dionysian revelry **b :** ORANGUTAN **c :** a hairy demon of the desert ⟨wild beasts shall meet with hyenas, the ~ shall cry to his fellow —Isa 34:14 (RSV)⟩ **2 :** a lecherous man **:** one having satyriasis ⟨he is neither a eunuch nor a ~ —Raymond Chandler⟩ **3 :** any of numerous butterflies (family Satyridae) that are commonly brown and gray often with ocelli on the wings and have the veins of the fore wings usu. much swollen at the base

saty·ri·a·sis \,sā|d·ə'rīəsəs, ,sa|, |tə-\ *n, pl* **satyria·ses** \-ə,sēz\ [LL, fr. Gk, fr. *satyros* satyr + *-iasis*] **:** excessive or abnormal sexual craving in the male — compare NYMPHOMANIA

sa·tyr·ic \(')sā¦tirik, sə't-\ *adj* [F *satyrique*, fr. Gk *satyrikos*, fr. *satyros* satyr + *-ikos* -ic] **:** of, relating to, or having the characteristics of a satyr ⟨the ~ old goat who pursues young girls —*Sat. Eve. Post*⟩

sa·tyr·i·cal \-rəkəl\ *adj* [L *satyrus* satyr + E *-ical*] *archaic* **:** SATYRIC

¹satyr·id \'sād·ərəd, 'satə-\ *adj* [NL *Satyridae*] **:** of or relating to the Satyridae

²satyrid \"\ *n* -s **:** a butterfly of the family Satyridae

sa·tyr·i·dae \sə'tirə,dē\ *n pl, cap* [NL, fr. *Satyrus*, type genus (fr. L, satyr) + *-idae*] **:** a widely distributed family of butterflies common near the edges of woods

satyr·ine \'sād·ə,rīn, 'sad-·\ *adj* [*satyr* + *-ine*] **:** of or relating to the genus *Satyrus*

satyr·ism \-,rizəm\ *n* -s [*satyr* + *-ism*] **:** SATYRIASIS

satyr orchid *n* [so called fr. the ancient Greek and Roman belief that certain kinds of orchids were aphrodisiac] **:** a terrestrial orchid (*Coeloglossum bracteatum*) of the cooler parts of No. America and Europe having broad usu. ovate leaves and long-bracted green very irregular flowers

satyr play *n* **:** an ancient Greek drama usu. composed and performed in conjunction with a trilogy of tragedies but having a less elevated subject and diction and having a chorus representing a ribald band of satyrs

sat-zone \'sat,-; ,e,sā'tē,-\ *n* -s *usu cap S&A&T* [*sat* abbr. of NL *Sine Acido Thymonucleico* without thymonucleic acid] **:** NUCLEOLUS ORGANIZER

sa·u·ba ant \sə'übə-\ *n* [*sauba* fr. Pg *saúba, saúva*, fr. Tupi *saúba, isaúba*] **:** any of several tropical leaf-cutting ants esp. of the genus *Atta* that live in immense subterranean colonies and cultivate a fungus upon leaves and other vegetable material collected by the workers

¹sauce \'sȯs; *usu in senses 4&7, dial in other senses* 'sas *or* 'saa(ə)s *or* 'sais; *dial* 'särs *or* 'sás\ *n* -s [ME, fr. MF *sauce, sausse*, fr. L *salsa*, fem. of *salsus* salted, fr. past part. of *sallere* to salt, fr. *sal* salt — more at SALT] **1 :** a condiment or composition of condiments and appetizing ingredients eaten with food as a relish ⟨barbecue ~⟩ **2 :** a fluid, semifluid, or sometimes semisolid accompaniment of solid food: **a :** meat or fish stock or milk or cream thickened with flour or other starch, usu. flavored with a concentrate (as from roast meat), seasoned with a variety of condiments or spices, and used for fish, meat, eggs, or vegetables — see ³ALLEMANDE, BÉCHAMEL, BROWN SAUCE, VELOUTÉ **b :** a variously flavored sweetened mixture served as a topping with a dessert: as (1) **:** one composed of water, milk, cream, or fruit juice with sugar and other ingredients added and thickened with flour or other starch or with eggs ⟨butterscotch ~⟩ ⟨lemon ~⟩ ⟨custard ~⟩ (2) **:** one composed of eggs and butter without other liquid **3 :** something that adds zest or piquancy ⟨fame is only one of the ~s of life —A.C.Benson⟩ **4 :** vegetables eaten with meat or as a relish **5 :** stewed or canned fruit eaten as an accompaniment with other food or as a dessert ⟨blueberry ~⟩ ⟨cranberry ~⟩ **6 :** a solution used in some manufacturing processes (as moistening layers of tobacco) **:** PICKLE **7 :** pert or insolent language or actions **:** SAUCINESS ⟨it never pays to stand any ~ —Arnold Bennett⟩ **8** *slang* **:** intoxicating drinks **:** LIQUOR ⟨been off the ~ for fourteen months —John O'Hara⟩

²sauce \'sȯs; *usu in sense 4b, dial in other senses* 'sas *or* 'saa(ə)s *or* 'sais; *dial* 'särs *or* 'sás\ *vt* -ED/-ING/-S [ME *saucen*, fr. *sauce*, n.] **1 :** to dress (food) with something intended to give a higher relish **:** SEASON, FLAVOR **2 a** *archaic* **:** to modify the harsh or unpleasant characteristics of **:** TEMPER ⟨a slice of the densest cloud within his reach, ~*d* with moonshine —Nathaniel Hawthorne⟩ **b :** to add interesting qualities to **:** give zest to **:** make piquant or attractive ⟨technicalities *sauced* and seasoned by songs, recitations, and tales of adventure —Llewellyn Howland⟩ **3** *obs* **:** FLOG **4 a** *dial chiefly Eng* **:** REBUKE **b :** to address in bitter, pert, or tart language **:** be impudent or saucy to

sauce–alone \'=;=,=\ *n* -s **:** GARLIC MUSTARD

sauceboat \'=,=\ *n* **:** GRAVY BOAT

saucebox \'=,=\ *n* **:** a saucy impudent person

saucedish \'=,=\ *n* **:** a small round shallow dish for serving stewed fruit or other food

sauce·less \'=·ləs\ *adj* **:** having no sauce

sauce·pan \'=,= *also chiefly Brit* -pən\ *n* [¹*sauce* + *pan*] **:** a deep cooking utensil with a long handle used for stewing or boiling — compare SAUCEPOT

sauce pi·quante \,sȯspē'känt, ,sōs-, -äⁿt\ *n, pl* **sauces piquantes** \"\ [F] **1 :** PIQUANT SAUCE **2 :** something that stimulates interest or curiosity or intensifies appreciation

saucepot \'=,=\ *n* [¹*sauce* + *pot*] **:** a deep cooking utensil with two hand grips opposite each other used for stewing or boiling — compare SAUCEPAN

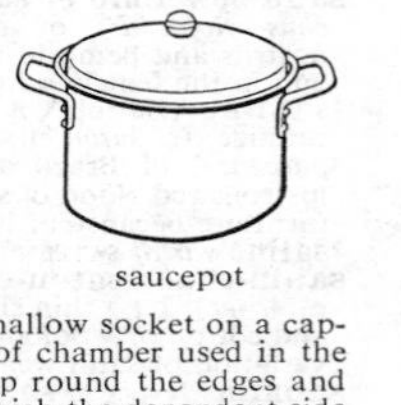

saucepot

¹sau·cer \'sȯsə(r), *dial* 'sas- *or* 'saas- *or* 'sais- *or* 'särs- *or* 'sás-\ *n* -s [ME, fr. MF *saussier*, fr. *sausse* sauce + *-ier* -er] **1** *obs* **:** a dish or plate to contain sauces at table **2 a :** a small shallow dish usu. with a slightly depressed center for holding a cup at table **b :** SAUCEDISH **3 :** something likened to a saucer in shape: as **a :** a saucer-shaped part of a plant **b :** a shallow socket on a capstan **c :** the base of the usual form of chamber used in the manufacture of sulfuric acid turned up round the edges and partly filled with chamber acid into which the dependent side dips to form a seal **d :** a shallow depression in a landscape ⟨a town . . . set in a ~ formed by a range of hills —Hamilton Basso⟩ **e :** FLYING SAUCER

²saucer \"\ *vt* -ED/-ING/-S *dial* **:** to pour into a saucer ⟨~*ed* her coffee and blew on it —H.E.Giles⟩

saucer dome *n* **:** a dome that is less than a hemisphere in form or that shows less than a hemisphere on the exterior

saucer eye *n* **:** a large round staring eye — **saucer–eyed** \'=;=¦=\ *adj*

saucer–eye porgy \'=;=¦=-\ *n* **:** a porgy (*Calamus calamus*) of the West Indies and southern Florida that is silvery and blue with longitudinal golden-yellow stripes and reaches a length of one foot

saucer·ful \'==,fu̇l\ *n, pl* **saucerfuls** \-(r),fu̇lz\ *also* **saucers·ful** \-(r)z,fu̇l\ **:** the content of a saucer

sau·cer·iza·tion \,==rə'zāshən, -,rī'z-\ *n* -s **:** the operation of saucerizing

sau·cer·ize \'==,rīz\ *vt* -ED/-ING/-S [¹*saucer* + *-ize*] **:** to form a shallow depression by excavation of tissue to promote granulation and healing of (a wound)

sau·cer·less \'==,ləs\ *adj* **:** lacking a saucer

saucer magnolia *n* **:** a large shrub or small tree (*Magnolia soulangeana*) native to Asia and Europe and widely used esp. in eastern No. America as a spring-blooming ornamental that bears large open flowers which are purplish or rose-colored on the outside and white within

sauces *pl of* SAUCE, *pres 3d sing of* SAUCE

sau·cier \(')sōs¦yā, (')sōs-\ *n* -s [F, fr. *sauce* (fr. MF) + *-ier* -er — more at SAUCE] **:** an assistant chef who specializes in preparing sauces and soups

sau·ci·ly \-səlē, -li — *see* SAUCY\ *adv* **:** in a saucy manner

sau·ci·ness \-sēnəs, -sin-\ *n* -ES **:** the quality or state of being saucy

saucing *pres part of* SAUCE

sau·cis·son \¦sōsē¦sōⁿ\ *also* **sau·cisse** \sō'sēs\ *n, pl* **saucissons** \-ōⁿ(z)\ *also* **sau·cisses** \-ēs(əz)\ [*saucisson* fr. F, fr. It *salsiccione*, aug. of *salsiccia* large sausage, powder bag

shaped like a sausage, fr. LL *salsicia* sausage; *saucisse* fr. F, fr. LL *salsicia* — more at SAUSAGE] **1 :** a tube of paper or canvas filled with powder and used as a fuse **2 :** a large fascine

sau·con·ite \ˈsȯkə,nīt\ *n* -s [Upper *Saucon*, Lehigh County, Penn., its locality + E *-ite*] **:** a montmorillonitic mineral $Zn_3Si_4O_{10}(OH)_2.nH_2O$ consisting of a basic hydrous zinc aluminum silicate isomorphous with saponite

saucy \ˈsasē, ˈsaa|, ˈsai| (*usu. in sense 1b*), ˈsȯ|, -si, *dial* ˈsär| *or* ˈsȧ|\ *adj* -ER/-EST [¹*sauce* + *-y*] **1 a** *archaic* **:** grossly disrespectful ⟨speak to him like a ∼ lackey —Shak.⟩ **b :** expressive of or marked by impertinent boldness or forwardness **:** IMPUDENT ⟨sometimes ∼, he was by no means an agreeable fellow traveler —S.C.Brownstein & Mitchel Weiner⟩ **c :** amusingly or unobjectionably forward or impertinent **2** *dial chiefly Eng* **:** overly fastidious esp. with regard to food **3** *Scot* **:** DISDAINFUL, SCORNFUL **4 :** SMART, TRIM ⟨a ∼ ship⟩ ⟨a ∼ automobile⟩

¹**sau·di** \ˈsau̇dē, säˈüdē\ *adj, usu cap* [fr. *Saudi* Arabia, kingdom in southwestern Asia, after Abdul-Aziz Ibn-*Saud* †1953 king of Saudi Arabia who founded the Saudi dynasty] **1 :** SAUDI ARABIAN **2 :** of, relating to, or characteristic of the Saudi dynasty or its supporters

²**saudi** \"\ *n* -s *usu cap* **1 :** SAUDI ARABIAN **2 :** a member or supporter of an Arabian dynasty

saudi ara·bia \-əˈrābēə *also* -byə\ *adj, usu cap S&A* [fr. *Saudi Arabia*, southwestern Asia] **:** of or from the kingdom of Saudi Arabia **:** of the kind or style prevalent in Saudi Arabia **:** SAUDI ARABIAN

¹**saudi arabian** *adj, usu cap S&A* [*Saudi Arabia* + E *-an*] **1 :** of, relating to, or characteristic of Saudi Arabia **2 :** of, relating to, or characteristic of the people of Saudi Arabia

²**saudi arabian** *n, cap S&A* **:** a native or inhabitant of Saudi Arabia

sau·er·bra·ten \ˈsau̇(ə)r,brätᵊn, ˈzau̇-\ *n* -s [G, fr. *sauer* sour (fr. OHG *sūr*) + *braten* roast meat, alter. (influenced by *braten* to roast, fr. OHG *brātan*) of MHG *brāte* meat without waste, soft edible meat, fr. OHG *brāto*; akin to OHG *brādam* breath, heat — more at SOUR, BREATH, BRAWN] **:** oven-roasted or pot-roasted beef marinated in a vinegar solution with peppercorns, garlic, onions, and bay leaves before cooking

sauer·kraut *also* **sour·crout** *or* **sour·krout** \ˈsau̇(ə)r,krau̇t, -au̇ə,k-, *usu* -əd·+V\ *n* -s [G *sauerkraut*, fr. *sauer* sour (fr. OHG *sūr*) + *kraut* cabbage, fr. OHG *krūt* herb, cabbage; akin to OS *krūd* cabbage, MD *cruut* cabbage, herb, and perh. to Goth *qairu* thorn, L *veru* spit, Gk *bryein* to swell, Av *gravastick* — more at SOUR] **:** cabbage cut fine and allowed to ferment in a brine made of its own juice with salt

sau·ger \ˈsȯgə(r)\ *n* -s [origin unknown] **1 :** a small pike perch (*Stizostedion canadense*) similar to the walleye but without a black blotch on the dorsal fin that is an important food fish in parts of Canada and is distributed from the Hudson Bay drainage east to New Brunswick, west to Montana, and south through much of the Mississippi drainage **2 :** WALLEYE

saugh *or* **sauch** \ˈsau̇k, ˈsȯk, ˈsäk\ *n* -s [ME (Sc) *sauch*, fr. OE *salh*, var. of *sealh* sallow — more at SALLOW] *chiefly Scot* **:** SALLOW

saught \ˈsau̇kt\ *n* -s [ME *saght, saht*, fr. OE *seht, seaht*, fr. or akin to ON *sātt, sætt* agreement, covenant, peace; akin to ON *sækja* to seek — more at SEEK] *archaic* **:** PEACE, QUIET, EASE

sauk \ˈsȯk\ *or* **sac** \", ˈsak\ *n, pl* **sauk** *or* **sauks** *or* **sac** *or* **sacs** *usu cap* [Fox (Sauk dial.) *Osākiwūg*, lit., people of the outlet] **1 a :** an Indian people of the Fox river valley and shores of Green Bay, Wisconsin **b :** a member of such people **2 :** a dialect of Fox

saul \ˈsȯl\ *chiefly dial var of* SOUL

sauld \ˈsȯld\ *Scot past of* SELL

saul·ie \ˈsȯli\ *n* -s [origin unknown] *Scot* **:** a hired mourner

sault *n* -s [ME *saut*, fr. OF, fr. L *saltus*, fr. *saltus*, past part. of *salire* to leap — more at SALLY] **1** *obs* **:** LEAP, JUMP; *specif* **:** a leap in the manege **2** \ˈsü\ **:** a fall or rapid in a river

saul·teur \süˈtər(·)\ *n* -s *usu cap* [F, fr. *Sault* Ste. Marie, city in Ontario, Canada, near which the Salteaux lived in the 17th cent. + F *-eur* -or] **:** a member of the Salteaux people

sau·mont \ˈsȯmənt\ *Scot var of* SALMON

sau·na \ˈsau̇nə\ *n* -s [Finn] **1 :** a Finnish bath in steam from water thrown on heated stones **2 :** a bathhouse designed for a sauna

saun·ders·wood \ˈsȯndə(r)z,=, ˈsän-\ *n* [obs. E *saunders* sandalwood (fr. MF *sandre*, alter. of *sandal*) + *wood* — more at SANDAL] **:** SANDALWOOD

¹**saun·ter** \ˈsȯntə(r), ˈsän-, ˈsän-\ *vi* **sauntered**; **sauntered**; **sauntering** \-ntəriŋ, -n·triŋ\ **saunters** [prob. fr. ME *santren* to muse, brood] **1 :** to walk about idly and in a leisurely manner ⟨I ∼*ed* along the docks . . . not knowing what to do or where to go —H.A.Chippendale⟩ **2** *obs* **:** to travel around aimlessly from place to place **3** *archaic* **:** DAWDLE, IDLE

²**saunter** \"\ *n* -s **1 :** a leisurely strolling gait **2 :** an idle aimless walk **:** STROLL

saun·ter·er \-ntərə(r), -n·trə(r)\ *n* -s **:** one that saunters

saun·ter·ing·ly *adv* **:** in a sauntering manner

saur- *or* **sauro-** *comb form* [NL, fr. Gk, fr. *sauros*] **:** lizard

sau·ra *also* **sao·ra** \ˈsau̇rə\ *n, pl* **saura** *also* **saora** *usu cap* **1 :** a forest people of the mountains of the Eastern Ghats, India **2 :** a member of the Saura people

-sau·ra \ˈsȯrə\ *n comb form* [NL, fr. Gk *saura, sauros*] **:** lizard — in generic names ⟨*Chamaesaura*⟩

sau·ra·se·ni \,sau̇rəˈsānē\ *n* -s *cap* [Skt *Śaurasenī*] **:** the central Prakrit language of northern India

sau·rau·ia \sȯˈrȯyə\ *n, cap* [NL, fr. Count F. J. von *Saurau* †1832 Austrian statesman + NL *-ia*] **:** a genus of trees and shrubs (family Dilleniaceae) with toothed parallel-veined leaves and paniculate pentamerous flowers followed by a baccate fruit that is edible in some Mexican species

sau·rel \ˈsȯrəl\ *n* -s [F, fr. LL *saurus* horse mackerel, fr. Gk *sauros*] **:** any of several elongated compressed fishes (genus *Trachurus*) with a series of bony plates extending the full length of the lateral line: as **a :** a horse mackerel (*Trachurus trachurus*) **b :** JACK MACKEREL a

sau·ria \ˈsȯrēə\ *n pl, cap* [NL, fr. *saurus* lizard (fr. Gk *saura, sauros* horse mackerel, lizard) + *-ia*; akin to Gk *saulos* straddling, waddling, *saukros* delicate, graceful, *psaukros* nimble, *psauein* to touch, graze, and prob. to Gk *psēn* to rub — more at SAND] **1** *in former classifications* **:** a division of Reptilia comprising the lizards, crocodilians, and various extinct elongated limbed reptiles that superficially resemble lizards **2** *in some classifications* **:** a suborder of Squamata coextensive with Lacertilia

-sau·ria \ˈsȯrēə\ *n pl comb form* [NL, fr. *-saurus* + *-ia*] **:** lizards **:** animals resembling lizards — in names of higher taxa ⟨*Pterosauria*⟩ ⟨*Ankylosauria*⟩

¹**sau·ri·an** \ˈsȯrēən\ *adj* [NL *Sauria* + E *-an*] **1 :** of or relating to the Sauria **2 :** resembling a lizard

²**saurian** \"\ *n* -s **1 :** a reptile of the group Sauria **2 :** a reptile that resembles a lizard

sauries *pl of* SAURY

sau·rii \ˈsȯrē,ī\ [NL, fr. Gk *saura, sauros* lizard] *syn of* SAURIA

saur·is·chia \sȯˈriskēə\ *n pl, cap* [NL, fr. *saur-* + L *ischium* hip joint + NL *-ia* — more at ISCHIUM] **:** an order of Reptilia including those dinosaurs in which the pelvis is triradiate and the pubes meet in a ventral symphysis — see SAUROPODA, THEROPODA — **saur·is·chi·an** \sȯˈriskēən\ *adj or n*

¹**sau·ro·dont** \ˈsȯrə,dänt\ *adj* [NL *Saurodontidae*] **:** of or relating to the Saurodontidae

²**saurodont** \"\ *n* -s **:** a fish of the family Saurodontidae

sau·ro·don·ti·dae \,=ˈdäntə,dē\ *n pl, cap* [NL, fr. *Saurodont-, Saurodon*, type genus (fr. *saur-* + *-odon*) + *-idae*] **:** a family of extinct Cretaceous clupeoid fishes with powerful jaws and a single row of compressed knifelike teeth

sau·rog·na·thism \sȯˈrägnə,thizəm\ *n* [*saurognathous* + *-ism*] **:** the quality or state of being saurognathous

sau·rog·na·thous \(ˈ)=ˈ==thəs\ *adj* [*saur-* + *-gnathous*] **1 :** of, relating to, or being an arrangement of the bones of the palate (as in certain woodpeckers) in which the maxillopalatals are short and the vomer is divided longitudinally and represented by a pair of slender rods **2 :** having a saurognathous palate

¹**sau·roid** \ˈsȯ,rȯid\ *adj* [NL *Sauroidei*] **:** of or relating to the Sauroidei

²**sauroid** \"\ *n* -s **:** a fish of the group Sauroidei

sau·roi·dei \sȯˈrȯidē,ī\ *n pl, cap* [NL, fr. Gk *sauroeidēs* like a lizard, fr. *saur-* + *-oeidēs* -oid] *in former classifications* **:** a group of ganoid fishes having flat rhomboidal scales, reptile-like teeth, and a bony skeleton

sau·roph·a·gous \(ˈ)sȯˈräfəgəs\ *adj* [*saur-* + *-phagous*] **:** feeding on lizards

¹**sau·ro·pod** \ˈsȯrə,päd\ *adj* [NL *Sauropoda*] **:** of or relating to the Sauropoda

²**sauropod** \"\ *n* -s **:** a dinosaur of the suborder Sauropoda

sau·rop·o·da \sȯˈräpədə\ *n pl, cap* [NL, fr. *saur-* + *-poda*] **:** a suborder of Saurischia consisting of herbivorous dinosaurs with a long neck and tail, small head, and more or less plantigrade 5-toed limbs all used in walking, including the most gigantic of land animals of any period, and known from the Middle Jurassic into the Cretaceous — **sau·rop·o·dous** \(ˈ)=ˈ===dəs\ *adj*

sau·rop·sid \sȯˈräpsəd\ *n* -s [NL *Sauropsida*] **:** a vertebrate of the group Sauropsida

sau·rop·si·da \-psədə\ *n pl, cap* [NL, fr. *saur-* + Gk *opsis* appearance + NL *-ida* — more at OPTIC] *in some esp former classifications* **:** a group of vertebrates comprising the reptiles and birds — compare ICHTHYOPSIDA, MAMMALIA — **sau·rop·si·dan** \(ˈ)=ˈ=sədən\ *adj or n* — **sau·rop·sid·i·an** \,=,=ˈsidēən\ *adj*

sau·rop·te·ryg·ia \sȯ,räptəˈrijēə\ *n pl, cap* [NL, fr. *saur-* + *pteryg-* + *-ia*] **:** an order of Reptilia comprising forms more or less completely adapted to a marine environment and usu. including the suborders Nothosauria and Plesiosauria — **sau·rop·te·ryg·i·an** \=,=ˈ=rijēən\ *adj or n*

sau·ror·ni·thes \sȯ,rȯ(r)ˈnī(,)thēz\ [NL, fr. *saur-* + *-ornithes*] *syn of* ARCHAEORNITHES

sau·ru·ra·ce·ae \,sȯrəˈrāsē,ē\ *n pl, cap* [NL, fr. *Saururus*, type genus + *-aceae*] **:** a family of perennial herbs (order Piperales) having small flowers destitute of perianth in terminal spikes and with an ovary of several separate carpels — **sau·ru·ra·ceous** \,=;=ˈrāshəs\ *adj*

sau·ru·rae \sȯˈru̇,rē\ [NL, fr. *saur-* + *-urae*, fem. pl. of *-urus*] *syn of* ARCHAEORNITHES

sau·ru·rus \-,rəs\ *n, cap* [NL, fr. *saur-* + *-urus*] **:** a genus (the type of the family Saururaceae) of herbs having alternate cordate leaves and racemes of white flowers with four to eight stamens and an ovary of four carpels coalescent into a capsule in fruit — see LIZARD'S-TAIL

-sau·rus \ˈsȯrəs\ *n comb form* [NL, fr. Gk *saura, sauros* — more at SAURIA] **:** lizard — in generic names in zoology ⟨*Brontosaurus*⟩ ⟨*Icthyosaurus*⟩

sau·ry \ˈsȯrē, -ri\ *n* -ES [NL *saurus* lizard + E *-y* — more at SAURIA] **1 :** a slender long-beaked fish (*Scombresox saurus*) that is related to the needlefishes, is found in the temperate parts of the Atlantic north to Cape Cod and the French coast, about southern Africa, and possibly off the southern coasts of Australia and New Zealand, reaches a length of 18 inches, swims in large schools, and often leaps from the water when pursued by larger fishes **2 :** a fish (*Cololabis saira*) that is similar to but smaller than the closely related saury and is widely distributed in the Pacific

sau·sage \ˈsȯ|sij, |sēj, *chiefly Brit* ˈsä|, *dial* ˈsa| *or* ˈsä|\ *n* -s [ME *sausige*, fr. ONF *saussiche*, fr. LL *salsicia*, fr. L *salsus* salted — more at SAUCE] **1 a :** highly seasoned finely divided meat that is usu. a mixture (as of beef or pork), is often extended (as with cereal or milk solids), is stuffed in casings of prepared animal intestine or synthetic material which are tied shut at both ends to form a single cylindrical unit or at intervals to form links, and is used either fresh or cured; *also* **:** a single unit of sausage **b :** SAUSAGE MEAT **2 :** SAUCISSON **3** *or* **sausage balloon :** a captive observation or barrage balloon **4 :** GERMAN — usu. used disparagingly **5 :** material (as crude rubber or alumina catalyst) formed in the shape of a sausage

sausage bassoon *n* **:** RACKETT

sausage bull *n* **:** a mature male bovine suitable for producing meat for sausage, bologna, or similar manufactured products

sausage curl *n* **:** a curl shaped like a sausage

sausage meat *n* **:** pork sausage in bulk

sausage tree *n* **:** a tropical African tree (*Kigelia africana*) of the family Bignoniaceae often cultivated in tropical countries for its brownish red bell-shaped flowers and long sausage-shaped fruits

sausage turning *n* **:** a continuous turning used esp. in 19th century American furniture

sausage turning

sau·sin·ger \|sənjə(r)\ *n* [by alter.] *dial* **:** SAUSAGE

saus·su·rea \sȯˈsu̇rēə\ *n, cap* [NL, after H. Bénédict de *Saussure* †1799 and his son N. Théodore de *Saussure* †1845 Swiss naturalists] **:** a genus of herbs (family Compositae) found mostly in temperate and cool regions of Eurasia with heads of blue or purple flowers that resemble thistles — see COSTUSROOT

saus·su·rite \ˈsȯsə,rīt\ *n* -s [F, fr. H. Bénédict de *Saussure* †1799 + F *-ite*] **:** a mineral consisting of a tough compact substance that is white, greenish, or grayish, is produced in part at least by alteration of feldspar, and consists chiefly of zoisite or epidote — **saus·su·rit·ic** \,=;=ˈrid·ik\ *adj*

saus·su·ri·tiza·tion \sȯ,su̇rəd·əˈzāshən, -d·,īˈz-\ *n* -s [ISV *saussurite* + *-ization*] **:** the process of converting feldspar into saussurite

saus·su·ri·tize \=ˈ=rə,tīz\ *vt* -ED/-ING/-S [back-formation fr. *saussuritization*] **:** to convert (feldspar) into saussurite

saut \ˈsät, ˈsȯt\ *chiefly Scot var of* SALT

saut de basque \,sōdə-\ *n, pl* **sauts de basque** \"\ [F, lit., Basque leap] **:** a jump in ballet in which the dancer turns in the air with the foot of one leg drawn up to the knee of the other

¹**sau·té** \(ˈ)sō|tā, (ˈ)sȯ-\ *n* -s [F, past part. of *sauter* to jump, fr. MF, fr. L *saltare* to dance, freq. of *salire* to leap — more at SALLY] **:** a sautéed dish

²**sauté** *also* **sau·te** \"\ *vt* **sautéed** *or* **sautéd**; **sautéed** *or* **sautéd**; **sautéing**; **sautés :** to fry in very little fat — distinguished from *deep fry*

³**sauté** \(ˈ)=ˈ=\ *adj* **:** fried in very little fat **:** SAUTÉED

⁴**sauté** \"\ *adj* [F, fr. past part. of *sauter* to jump] *of a ballet step* **:** executed with a jump

sau·te·relle \,sōd·əˈrel, sōˈtrel\ *n* -s [F, lit., little jumper, dim. of *sauteur* jumper] **:** an instrument used (as by masons) to trace and form angles

sau·terne \sōˈtərn, sȯˈ-, -te(ə)rn\ *n* -s *often cap* [F *sauternes*, fr. *Sauternes*, commune in southwestern France, where it is made] **1 a** *also* **sauternes**, *pl* **sauternes :** a usu. semisweet golden-colored table wine produced from grapes that are allowed to become overripe and modified by a mold (*Botrytis cinerea*) before fermentation **b :** a similar California or New York wine **2 :** a light brown that is redder, stronger, and slightly darker than cork, yellower and deeper than French nude, and yellower and stronger than French beige — called also *Tuscan tan*

sau·teur \(ˈ)sō|tər\ *n* -s [F, jumper, fr. *sauter* to jump + *-eur* -or] **:** a leatherjacket (*Oligoplites saurus*)

sau·til·lé \sōtēyā\ *adv (or adj)* [F, past part. of *sautiller* to hop, skip, fr. *sauter* to jump] **:** ARCO SALTANDO

sau·toir \sōˈtwär, -wȧ(r, ˈ== *also* -wō(ə)r *or* -wȯ(ə)\ *n* -s [F, fr. MF *sautoir, saultoir* saltire — more at SALTIRE] **1 :** a chain, ribbon, or scarf worn about the neck with the ends forming a St. Andrew's cross in front **2 :** a long gold chain often set with precious stones usu. with a pendant hanging from it

sa·u·va ant \səˈüvə-\ *n* [sauva fr. Pg *saúba, saúva*, fr. Tupi *saúba, isaúba*] **:** SAUBA ANT

sau·va·ge·sia \,sōvəˈjēzēə, -ēzhə\ *n, cap* [NL, fr. Pierre A. Boissier de la Croix de *Sauvages* †1795 Fr. botanist + NL *-ia*] **:** a genus of chiefly tropical American herbs or undershrubs (family Ochnaceae) having alternate leaves, fringed stipules, and small pentamerous flowers with an outer row of staminodia which is filiform and an inner row of staminodia which is petaloid

sauve \ˈsȯv\ *dial Eng var of* SALVE

sauve·garde \ˈsōv,gärd\ *n* -s [F, lit., safeguard, fr. MF *saufegarde, salvegarde* — more at SAFEGUARD] **:** MONITOR 3

sauve qui peut \,sōv,kēˈpə, -ˈpər(·), -ˈpə̄\ *n* [F, save himself who can] **:** a complete rout

sav *abbr* savings

sav·able *or* **save·able** \ˈsāvəbəl\ *adj* [ME *sauvable*, fr. MF, fr. OF *sauver* to save + *-able* — more at SAVE] **:** capable of being saved

¹**sav·age** \ˈsavij, -vēj\ *adj, usu* -ER/-EST [ME *sauvage, savage*, fr. MF *sauvage, salvage*, fr. ML *salvaticus*, alter. of L *silvaticus* of the woods, wild, fr. *silva* wood, grove] **1 a :** not domesticated or under human control **:** UNTAMED ⟨the dog that is kept in a good home is usually watched carefully, kept from contact with ∼ dogs —Morris Fishbein⟩ ⟨in time the ∼ bull doth bear the yoke —Shak.⟩ **b :** marked by cruelty **:** FEROCIOUS, FIERCE ⟨the victim of a ∼ attack that left him crippled⟩ ⟨his tone containing the ∼ satisfaction of a cat purring over a freshly caught mouse —Erle Stanley Gardner⟩ **c :** enraged with anger or pain **:** FURIOUS ⟨when I was left at home I was ∼ at not being let go —G.B.Shaw⟩ ⟨the mother bird flew about over me, squealing in a very angry, ∼ manner —John Burroughs⟩ **d :** violent and extreme in action, manner, or effect **:** DEVASTATING, RELENTLESS ⟨lashed out with all the oratorical fury and ∼ invective at his command —Sidney Warren⟩ ⟨what must happen in the *savagest* fury of a hurricane is left to the imagination —T.M.Longstreth⟩ ⟨a ∼ flu epidemic —Mollie Panter-Downes⟩ **2 a :** of, relating to, or characteristic of an unsettled and uncultivated place or region **:** RUGGED, WILD ⟨there was something sylvan and ∼ in the mountains on the farther side —George Borrow⟩ ⟨seldom have I seen such ∼ scenery associated with such placid beauty —Douglas Carruthers⟩ **b** *archaic* **:** growing wild **:** not cultivated ⟨∼ berries of the wood —John Dryden⟩ **3 :** BOORISH, RUDE ⟨the ∼ bad manners of most motorists —M.P.O'Connor⟩ **4 a :** UNCIVILIZED ⟨think that we have gained much over ∼ people in our notion of murder —W.G.Sumner⟩ ⟨civilized countries are more accessible than ∼ ones —Elinor Wylie⟩ **b :** of, belonging to, or produced by a primitive or a primitive people ⟨his ∼ bones were small and delicate —David Garnett⟩ ⟨in delineation of animal life they are thus superior to modern ∼ fine art —*Encyc. Americana*⟩ **syn** see BARBARIAN, FIERCE

²**savage** \"\ *n* -s **1 :** SALVAGE MAN **2 a :** a person living in a primitive state or belonging to a primitive society **:** PRIMITIVE ⟨almost universally the children of ∼*s* are contented and well behaved —W.D.Wallis⟩ **b :** one who acts with cruelty or ferocity **:** a brutal or inhumane person ⟨a ∼ who murdered in cold blood⟩ **c :** a completely undisciplined or unmannerly person ⟨the disagreeable person, however cultured, is a ∼ —F.A.Swinnerton⟩ **3 :** a wild or ferocious animal; *esp* **:** a vicious horse

³**savage** \"\ *vt* -ED/-ING/-S **1 :** to make savage ⟨a solvent to the bitterness that had *savaged* him —Angus Mowat⟩ **2 :** to attack or treat violently or brutally ⟨a plump young man whose bare toes in their sandals must have been cruelly *savaged* in the crowd —Alan Moorehead⟩ ⟨the ugly habit of *savaging* mercilessly those who have somehow raised his dander —*Times Lit. Supp.*⟩ **3** *of an animal* **:** to bite or trample furiously ⟨his horse must have gone crazy, thrown him and *savaged* him on the ground —Robert Graves⟩ ⟨set up an irritation which started the dog *savaging* itself —*Veterinary Record*⟩

sav·age·dom \-dəm\ *n* -s [¹*savage* + *-dom*] **:** SAVAGERY

sav·age·ly *adv* [ME *savagelich*, fr. ¹*savage* + *-lich* -ly] **:** in a savage manner ⟨struck her ∼⟩ ⟨a ∼ funny book⟩

sav·age·ness *n* -ES [ME *savagenes*, fr. ¹*savage* + *-nes* -ness] **:** the quality or state of being savage

sav·age·rous \ˈsavij(ə)rəs, -vēj-\ *adj* [*savagery* + *-ous*] *slang* **:** barbarously savage

sav·age·ry \-j(ə)rē, -ri\ *n* -ES [¹*savage* + *-ry*] **1 a :** the quality of being savage **:** savage disposition or action ⟨this outburst of ∼ that was to prove his undoing —Harold Helfer⟩ ⟨the ∼ of her methods of warfare —*Times Lit. Supp.*⟩ **b :** an act of cruelty or violence ⟨during the *savageries* of the blitz —Christopher Morley⟩ **2 :** the state or condition of being uncivilized ⟨it is only somewhere between ∼ and civilization that love is born —J.W.Krutch⟩ **3 :** WILDNESS ⟨the splendor of the seascape, the ∼ of the mountains —Claudia Cassidy⟩

sav·ag·ism \ˈsavi,jizəm, -vē,-, -və,-\ *n* -s [¹*savage* + *-ism*] **:** SAVAGERY

sa·van \(ˈ)saˈväⁿ, (ˈ)sȧ|v-, səˈv-, (ˈ)sȧ|v-\ *n* -s [modif. of obs. F *savans*, pl. of F *savant* — more at SAVANT] **:** SAVANT

sav·a·nil·la \,savəˈnilə, -nē(y)ə\ *n* -s [prob. fr. *Savanilla*, former seaport, Colombia] **:** TARPON

savanilla rhatany *n* [after *Savanilla*, former seaport, Colombia] **:** the root of a shrub (*Krameria ixina*) as distinguished from rhatany obtained from other plants of the genus *Krameria*

sa·van·na *or* **sa·van·nah** \səˈvanə\ *n* -s [earlier *zavana*, fr. Sp, fr. Taino *zabana*] **1 :** a treeless plain **:** an open, level region — used esp. of land in the southeastern U.S. **2 :** a tropical or subtropical grassland usu. containing scattered trees or shrubs that develops in areas in which heavy rainfall is interrupted by a distinct dry season, that is often maintained by human action (as of periodic burning or heavy grazing), and that tends to pass on the one hand into steppes and on the other into savanna woodland

savanna blackbird *n* **:** ANI

savanna flower *n* **:** a West Indian plant of the genus *Echites*

sa·van·nah \səˈvanə\ *adj, usu cap* [fr. *Savannah*, Ga.] **:** of or from the city of Savannah, Ga. ⟨the *Savannah* cotton market⟩ **:** of the kind or style prevalent in Savannah

savannah grass *n* **:** a stoloniferous tropical American grass (*Axonopus compressus*) related to carpet grass but with broader leaves and pointed sterile lemmos and sometimes cultivated for pasture

sa·van·nah·ian \-nəyən\ *n* -s *cap* [*Savannah*, Ga. + E *-an*] **:** a native or resident of Savannah, Ga.

savannah sparrow *n, cap 1st S* [after *Savannah*, Ga., where it was discovered] **:** a small streaked brown-and-white No. American sparrow (*Passerculus sandwichensis*) inhabiting fields and meadows

savanna woodland *n* **:** a usu. tropical open woodland in which the undergrowth is of the xerophilous type

sa·vant \(ˈ)sa|vänt, (ˈ)sȧ|v-, səˈv-, (ˈ)sä|v-, -ˈväⁿ; səˈvant, -ˈvaa(ə)nt; ˈsavənt\ *n* -s [F, fr. pres. part. of *savoir* to know, fr. L *sapere* to have sense, be wise — more at SAGE] **:** a man of learning; *esp* **:** a person with detailed knowledge in some specialized field (as of science or literature) **:** SCHOLAR

sav·a·ra \ˈsavərə, ˈsəv-\ *n, pl* **savara** *or* **savaras** *usu cap* **1 a :** a people of northeastern Madras **b :** a member of such people **2 :** the Munda language of the Savara people

sav·a·rin \ˈsavərən\ *n* -s [F, after Anthelme Brillat-*Savarin* †1826 Fr. politician, writer, and gourmet] **:** a brioche baked in a ring mold and covered with nuts and fruit (as almonds and citron)

sa·vate \səˈvat\ *n* -s [F, lit., old shoe, fr. MF — more at SABOT] **:** a form of boxing in which blows are delivered with either the feet or the hands

sav·a·tion \sāˈvāshən\ *n* -s [¹*save* + *-ation*] *dial Eng* **:** an act of saving

¹**save** \ˈsāv\ *vb* -ED/-ING/-S [ME *saven*, fr. OF *sauver, salver*, fr. LL *salvare*, fr. L *salvus* safe — more at SAFE] *vt* **1 a :** to deliver from sin **:** rescue from condemnation and spiritual death and bring into spiritual life ⟨Christ Jesus came into the world to ∼ sinners —1 Tim 1:15 (RSV)⟩ **b** (1) **:** to rescue or deliver from danger or harm **:** make safe ⟨any human life is to be *saved* if it can be *saved* —Harvey Flack⟩ ⟨risked his life to ∼ his friend from drowning⟩ ⟨the retailers who were *saved* by wholesalers during the depression —J.I.Grant⟩ ⟨God ∼ the king⟩ — used formerly in phrases of greeting ⟨God ∼ you⟩ ⟨∼ you⟩ (2) *obs* **:** to spare instead of slaying **:** permit to live **c** (1) **:** to maintain intact **:** PRESERVE, SAFEGUARD ⟨∼ his honor⟩ ⟨∼ her reputation⟩ ⟨∼ his credit⟩ ⟨∼ appearances⟩ ⟨∼ face⟩ (2) **:** to preserve in a specified state or condition — used esp. in the phrase *save harmless* ⟨agreed to indemnify and ∼ harmless the contractor from any and all loss —*Federal Supplement*⟩ **d :** to deliver from an anticipated or likely danger, difficulty, or annoyance ⟨vaccinate children to ∼ them from smallpox⟩ ⟨grasped him by the arm to ∼ him from falling⟩ **e :** to rescue or deliver from destruction ⟨*saved* the Union⟩ ⟨put out the fire and *saved* the house⟩ **f :** to preserve or guard from injury, destruction, or loss ⟨∼ the paint from cracking⟩ ⟨∼ the coat from damage by moths⟩ **2 a :** to put by as a store or reserve **:** ACCUMULATE, HOARD ⟨∼*s* part of his salary each week⟩ **b** (1) **:** to put aside for a particular purpose or occasion ⟨∼*s* his best suit for special dates⟩ ⟨∼*s* her best dishes for company⟩ (2) **:** to keep for the

use of another ⟨his outgrown clothing was *saved* for his younger brother⟩ ⟨*saved* a seat for his wife⟩ (3) : to keep in reserve : hold in abeyance ⟨*saving* him for another spot in this story —Green Peyton⟩ **c** (1) : to keep from being spent, wasted, or lost ⟨walks to work to ~ carfare⟩ ⟨~s several dollars a week by careful shopping⟩ ~s *time* by taking a short cut⟩ (2) : to preserve in serviceable condition by careful or sparing use ⟨his youthful hose well *saved* —Shak.⟩ (3) : to use or manage with discretion : CONSERVE, HUSBAND ⟨cut down on his reading in order to ~ his eyes⟩ ⟨his doctor warned him to ~ his strength⟩ ⟨*saving* himself to become a great pitcher —John Lardner⟩ **3 a** : to make unnecessary : enable one to avoid : AVOID ⟨it ~s a 50-mile detour —*Ford Times*⟩ ⟨*saved* them the trouble of looking for a parking place⟩ **b** (1) : to keep from being lost to an opponent ⟨a fine relief pitcher who has *saved* many games⟩ (2) : to prevent an opponent from scoring or winning (as a goal, wager, trick, or card) **c** *chiefly Brit* : to avoid missing : be in time for : CATCH ⟨~ the train⟩ ⟨~ the mail⟩ **4** *archaic* : to account for : EX-PLAIN — used with *appearances* or *phenomena* ⟨these were the phenomena which they had to ~ —Benjamin Farrington⟩ ~ *vi* **1** : to rescue or deliver someone ⟨bow hither out of heaven and see and ~ —A.E.Housman⟩ **2 a** : to accumulate savings : put by money ⟨would rather ~ than spend⟩ — often used with *up* ⟨started to ~ up for a trip abroad⟩ **b** : to avoid unnecessary waste or expense : ECONOMIZE ⟨~s on food by using leftovers⟩ **c** : to last in good condition : KEEP ⟨doesn't buy as much bread as she used to, because it doesn't ~ —F.C. Othman⟩ **3** : to make a save ⟨the visiting goalie went to the ice to ~ —*N. Y. Times*⟩ **syn** see RESCUE — **save ground** *of a racehorse* : to run along the inside rail — **save one's bacon** : to preserve or rescue something of vital importance ⟨as one's life, livelihood, or reputation⟩ from loss or harm ⟨the pilots of my section *saved my bacon* many times when I have been attacked from behind —Keith Ayling⟩, is forced to compromise these beliefs in order to *save his economic bacon* —Louis Bromfield⟩

²save \"\ *n* -s : the act or an instance of saving ⟨the goalie went down on all fours and smothered the shot to make a honey of a ~ —Cortland Fitzsimmons⟩ ⟨the audience is teased with the hope of a sentimental ~ —*Time*⟩

³save \"\ *prep* [ME *save, sauf, saf,* fr. OF *sauf, saf, salf,* fr. *sauf, saf, salf,* adj., safe — more at SAFE] **1** : with the exception of : BARRING ⟨the two poems have nothing in common — the title —T.O.Mabbott⟩ ⟨has a boomtown psychology in every respect — zoning —Hal Burton⟩ **2** : other than : BUT, EX-CEPT ⟨no question ~ in the minds of prejudiced people⟩ ⟨without duties ~ to eat and sleep⟩ ⟨dark ~ for one light⟩

⁴save \"\ *conj* [ME *save, sauf, saf, sauf, saf, salf,* adj., safe] **1** : were it not : ONLY — used with *that* ⟨a similar system is followed in the cheese factories, ~ that the farmers usually bring in their own milk —*McGill News*⟩ **2** : BUT, EXCEPT — used before a word often taken to be the subject of a clause ⟨no one knows about it ~ she⟩ ⟨all the conspirators ~ only he —Shak.⟩ **3** : UNLESS ⟨~ they could be plucked asunder, all my quest were but in vain —Alfred Tennyson⟩

saveable *var of* SAVABLE

¹save-all \"₌₌\ *n* -s **1** : something that prevents waste, loss, or damage: as **a** : a device to hold a candle end in a candlestick and permit it to burn to the very end **b** (1) : a small sail sometimes set under the foot of another sail or between two sails (2) : a net hung between ship and pier for safety purposes (2) : a receptacle for catching waste products for further utilization: as (1) : a small sluice used in gold dredging to catch the drippings from the buckets as they go into the well after discharging (2) : a device in papermaking that operates on the principle of sedimentation, flotation, or filtration to recover most of the fiber and filler from white water **d** *dial* : OVERALLS, PINAFORE **2** *chiefly dial* : MISER **3** *chiefly dial* : a contribution box or child's bank

²save-all \(')₌₌\ *adj* : MISERLY

saved \"\ *adj* [ME, fr. past part. of *saven* to save — more at SAVE] **1** : rescued from eternal punishment ⟨a ~ soul⟩ **2** : kept unused or unspent : HOARDED ⟨~ money⟩ — often used with *up* ⟨*saved*-up scraps of food⟩

sa·ve·lha \sə'velyə\ *n* -s [Pg, dim. of *savel* shad, prob. of Celt origin; akin to OIr *sam, samrad* summer — more at SUMMER] **1** : MENHADEN **2** : a fish (*Brevoortia pectinata*) of the south Atlantic closely related to the menhaden

sav·e·loy \'savə̇,lȯi, ₌₌'₌\ *n* -s [modif. of F *cervelas,* fr. obs. F *cervelat,* fr. MF, fr. OIt *cervellata* Milanese sausage, pig's brains, fr. *cervello* brain, fr. L *cerebellum,* dim. of *cerebrum* brain — more at CEREBRAL] *Brit* : a cooked dry sausage

sa·vels·berg process \'sāvȯlz,bərg-\ *n, usu cap S* [prob. fr. the name *Savelsberg*] : BLAST ROASTING

sav·er \'sāvə(r)\ *n* -s [ME, fr. *saven* to save + *-er*] : one that saves: as **a** : SAVIOR **b** : one who economizes or hoards : one who withholds part of his income from consumption for investment or deposit in a bank **c** : something that prevents loss or waste — often used in combination ⟨labor-*saver*⟩ ⟨money-*saver*⟩ ⟨time-*saver*⟩ **d** *slang* : a hedging bet on a horse race **e** : a marginally applied patch to correct an erroneously cut slot in a hand-sorted punched card

saves *pres 3d sing of* SAVE, *pl of* SAVE

sav·in *or* **sav·ine** \'savə̇n\ *n* -s [ME, fr. OE *safine, savine &* OF *savine,* fr. L *sabina*] **1** : a mostly prostrate Eurasian evergreen juniper (*Juniperus sabina*) with dark foliage and small berries having a glaucous bloom and with bitter acrid tops that are sometimes used in folk medicine (as for amenorrhea or as an abortifacient) — called also *cover-shame, red-shame;* see SAVIN OIL **2 a** : CREEPING JUNIPER 2 **b** : RED CEDAR 1a **3** : any of several trees, shrubs, or shrubby herbs somewhat resembling plants of the genus *Juniperus*

¹sav·ing \'sāviṅ, -vēṅ\ *n* -s [ME, fr. gerund of *saven* to save — more at SAVE] **1** : preservation from danger or destruction : DELIVERANCE ⟨work's the ~ of mankind —Eden Phillpotts⟩ **2** : the act or an instance of economizing : reduction in cost ⟨a ~ on fuel⟩ ⟨a ~ of ten percent in maintenance costs⟩ **3 a** *savings pl* : money put by ⟨keeps her ~s under the mattress⟩ ⟨has her ~s invested in stocks⟩ **b** : the excess of income over consumption expenditures — often used in pl.

²saving \"\ *prep* [ME, fr. pres. part. of *saven* to save] **1** : EX-CEPT, SAVE ⟨without disrespect to ⟨there are men in these modern times, ~ your presence, that can't visit a privy without searching out for a meaning behind it —Mary Deasy⟩ ⟨who, ~ your reverence, is the devil himself —Shak.⟩

³saving \"\ *conj* : EXCEPT, SAVE

⁴saving \"\ *adj* [fr. pres. part. of ¹*save*] **1 a** : serving to rescue, preserve, or protect; *specif* : leading to salvation ⟨a ~ faith⟩ **b** : serving to keep from or compensate for error or weakness : REDEEMING ⟨a scholar of vision and insight with a fund of ~ common sense —Geoffrey Bruun⟩ ⟨a ~ sense of humor⟩ **2** : characterized by thriftiness : ECONOMICAL ⟨wealthy by inheritance but ~ by constitution —Ellen Glasgow⟩ **3** *archaic* : bringing neither profit nor loss **4** : embodying or expressing an exception or reservation

saving arch *n* : SAFETY ARCH

saving clause *n* : a clause in an instrument or law exempting something from its operation or providing that the rest of it will stand if part is held invalid **2** : a statement making a reservation or expressing a condition

saving grace *n* : a redeeming quality or factor ⟨shrank at the thought of leaving even a place so austere as this parish house, whose *saving grace* was that he kept busy here —Marcia Davenport⟩

sav·ing·ly \"\ *adv* **1** : in a saving manner : FRUGALLY ⟨has few wants and lives ~⟩ **2** : in a manner that brings salvation : so as to redeem

sav·ing·ness *n* -ES : the quality or state of being saving : FRUGALITY

savings account *n* : an account in a bank or savings and loan association on which interest or interest dividends are usu. paid and from which withdrawals can be made usu. only by presentation of a passbook or by written authorization on prescribed forms — distinguished from *checking account*

savings and loan association *n* : a cooperative association formed under federal and state law in the U. S. that solicits savings in the form of share capital, invests its funds in mort-

gages, and permits deposits in and withdrawals from share accounts similar to those allowed for savings accounts in banks — called also *cooperative bank, mutual loan association*

savings bank *n* : a banking institution organized to receive savings accounts only on which accrued interest is periodically paid to depositors

savings bank life insurance *n* : life insurance sold over the counter by mutual savings banks as authorized by law in some states

savings bond *n* : a nontransferable registered U. S. bond issued in denominations of $25 to $1,000

savings deposit *n* : a bank deposit usu. of an individual or a nonprofit organization drawing regular interest and payable on 30 days notice

savings stamp *n* : a stamp of a small denomination issued by a savings bank or a government to be purchased and accumulated with others (as on a card) for deposit in a bank or exchange for an interest-bearing obligation when a specified amount has been reached

savin oil *n* : a pungent essential oil from the tops of a savin (*Juniperus Sabina*) that causes inflammation of the skin and mucous membrane

sav·ior *or* **sav·iour** \'sāvyə(r) *also* -,yȯ(ə)r *or* -ȯ(ə)\ *n* -s [ME *saviour, saveour,* fr. MF *sauveour, saveour,* fr. LL *salvator,* fr. *salvatus* (past part. of *salvare* to save) + L *-or* — more at SAVE] **1** : one that preserves or delivers from danger or destruction ⟨this modest leader and ~ died, almost forgotten by the people he had served and saved —Harrison Smith⟩ ⟨atomic energy as a possible ~ of our culture —Waldemar Kaempffert⟩ **2** *usu cap* : one who brings salvation ⟨for I am the Lord your God, the Holy One of Israel, your *Savior* —Isa 43:3 (RSV)⟩ ⟨our Lord and *Savior* Jesus Christ⟩

sav·ior·ess \-yərə̇s\ *n* -ES [*savior* + *-ess*] : a female savior

sav·ior·hood \'sāvyə(r),hu̇d\ *n* [*savior* + *-hood*] : the quality or state of being a savior

sav·ior·ship \-,ship\ *n* [*savior* + *-ship*] : SAVIORHOOD

sa·voir faire \,sav,wär'fa(a)l(ə)r, -fe[, -wȧ]l'f ... ,)ə\ *n* [F *savoir-faire,* lit., knowing how to do] : a seemingly instinctive ability to act appropriately in a particular situation; *esp* : adroitness in social relationships ⟨manifested a deplorable lack of *savoir faire,* and shattered harmony on an occasion on which harmony was above all things to be desired —*Spectator*⟩ **syn** see TACT

savoir vivre \-'vēvr(ᵊ), -v(rə)\ *n* [F *savoir-vivre,* lit., knowing how to live] : ability to live elegantly : observance of the usages of fashionable society

savona·ro·la chair \,savə̇|nə'rōlə-, so,vä|\ *n, usu cap S* [after Girolamo *Savonarola* †1498 Ital. religious reformer] : a folding X-shaped chair of Italian Renaissance style that has interlaced curved slats pivoted at their intersections — called also *scissors chair*

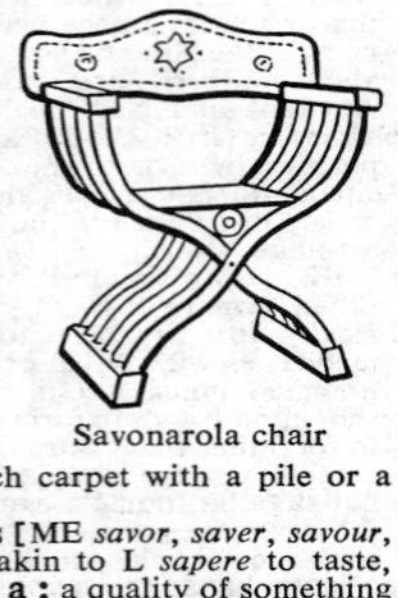

sa·vonne·rie \,savon'rē, ₌₌₌'₌\ *adj, usu cap* [F (*La*) *Savonnerie,* carpet factory manufacturing savonnerie carpets established in 1628 on the site of a former soap factory at Chaillot, near the Seine, in Paris, fr. *savonnerie* soap factory, fr. L *sapon-, sapo* — + *-ier -er*) + *-ie -y* — more at SAPONACEOUS] : of, relating to, or being a handmade one-piece French carpet with a pile or a woven tapestry

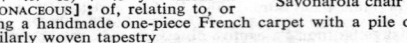
Savonarola chair

¹sa·vor *also* **sa·vour** \'sāvə(r)\ *n* -s [ME *savor, saver, savour,* fr. OF *savor, savour,* fr. L *sapor;* akin to L *sapere* to taste, have good taste — more at SAGE] **1 a** : a quality of something that affects the sense of taste or smell ⟨if the salt have lost his ~, wherewith shall it be salted —Mt 5:13 (AV)⟩ ⟨rosemary and rue; these keep seeming and ~ all the winter long —Shak.⟩ **b** : a particular flavor or smell ⟨described the ~ of the durian as a rich butterlike custard, highly flavored with almonds —V. G. Heiser⟩ ⟨a kettle from which issued the ~ of cooking mutton fat —Willa Cather⟩ **2** : a distinctive quality ⟨an odd blend of bitter naturalism and quiet humor that gives it a ~ quite its own —Anthony Boucher⟩ ⟨contributed their share to the ~ of local life —*Amer. Guide Series: Del.*⟩ **d** : a qualifying flavor : SMACK, TINGE ⟨refreshing our minds with a ~ of the antique, primeval world —Laurence Binyon⟩ **2** : a taste for something : RELISH ⟨lost his ~ for food —Rex Ingamells⟩ **3 a** : power to affect the sense of taste or smell ⟨in his illness, food and drink lost their ~ for him⟩ **b** : power to arouse interest or zest ⟨times change, and the sprightliest wit may lose its ~ —V.L.Parrington⟩ **4** *archaic* : REPUTATION, REPUTE **5** *obs* : CHARACTER, SORT ⟨this admiration . . . is much o' the ~ of other your new pranks —Shak.⟩ **syn** see TASTE

²savor *also* **savour** \"\ *vb* **savored** *also* **savoured; savoring** *also* **savouring** \-v(ə)riṅ\ **savors** *also* **savours** [ME *savowren,* fr. OF *savourer, savorer,* fr. LL *saporare,* fr. L *sapor* savor] *vi* **1** *archaic* : to be agreeable ⟨what is loathsome to the young ~s well to thee and me —Alfred Tennyson⟩ **2** : to have a specified smell or to smell of a specified substance ⟨the very doors and windows ~ vilely —Shak.⟩ ⟨the solemn vestments, ~ing of naphthalene —Norman Douglas⟩ **3** : to partake of a quality or state : indicate a presence or influence : SMACK — used with *of* ⟨the argument ~s of cynicism —V.L.Parrington⟩ ⟨an intense dislike of anything ~ing of regimentation —Chilton Williamson⟩ ~ *vt* **1 a** : to give a salt taste to ⟨the salt that ~s the sea —F.K.Lane⟩ **b** : to give flavor to : SEASON ⟨the salt of danger ~ing nights and days —*Atlantic*⟩ **2 a** : to have experience of : TASTE ⟨once before, he had ~ed politics —Ellery Sedgwick⟩ **b** *archaic* : to be conscious of the odor of : SMELL ⟨wisdom and goodness to the vile seem vile, filths ~ but themselves —Shak.⟩ **c** : to taste or smell with pleasure : RELISH ⟨~ing the succulent watermelon —Jane Nickerson⟩ ⟨walk around . . . ~ing the wild roses —Ann Panners⟩ **d** : to take conscious pleasure in : appreciate or enjoy with deliberate awareness ⟨this is a book to ~ on leisurely summer days —Pamela Taylor⟩ ⟨he decided to hold it back and thus ~ a little longer the pleasure of the surprise —T.B.Costain⟩ **3** *archaic* : to care for : LIKE ⟨thou ~est not the things that be of God, but those that be of men —Mt 16:23 (AV)⟩

savored *adj* [fr. past part. of ²*savor*] : having or indicating a particular savor — usu. used in combination ⟨surrounded by his evil-*savored* companions —Agnes M. Lawson⟩

sa·vor·er \'sāv(ə)rə(r)\ *n* -s : one that savors ⟨a ~, content to taste and retaste what was best or most flavorsome in the volumes he cherished —John Mason Brown⟩

sa·vor·i·ly \-v(ə)rəlē, -rē|ē\ *adv* [ME, fr. ¹*savory* + *-ly*] **1** : in a relishing manner : with appetite ⟨would eat our plain food ~ —Charles Lamb⟩ **2** : in a savory manner : APPETIZINGLY ⟨how ~ he described the strawberry —R.L.Cook⟩

sa·vor·i·ness \-v(ə)rēnə̇s, -rin-\ *n* -ES [ME *saverinesse,* fr. *savery* savory + *-nesse -ness*] : the quality or state of being savory

sa·vor·ing·ly \"\ *adv* : in a relishing manner ⟨get slowly ~ mellow drunk —James Jones⟩

sa·vor·less \'sāvə(r)ləs\ *adj* [ME *savourless,* fr. *savour* savor + *-less* — more at SAVOR] : lacking savor — **sa·vor·less·ness** *n* -ES

savorly *adv* [ME *saverly,* fr. *saver* savor + *-ly*] *obs* : with keen relish, feeling, or understanding

sa·vor·ous \'sāvə(r)əs\ *adj* [ME, fr. MF *savoureus, saverous,* fr. LL *saporosus,* fr. L *sapor* savor + *-osus -ose*] : having savor : FLAVORFUL ⟨written in rich, lusty, ~ English prose —Frances Winwar⟩ — **sa·vor·ous·ly** *adv*

sa·vor·some \-və(r)səm\ *adj* : FLAVORSOME

¹sa·vory \'sāv(ə)rē, -ri\ *adj* [ME *savory, savery, savure,* fr. OF *savouré,* past part. of *savourer* to savor — more at SAVOR] **1 a** : AGREEABLE, PLEASANT ⟨an exceedingly varied and ~ travel book —*Newsweek*⟩ **b** : morally attractive : EDIFYING, WHOLESOME ⟨his fallen partner has proved to be none too ~ a character —John Paterson⟩ ⟨scandals don't make very ~ reading —Green Peyton⟩ **2 a** : agreeable to the taste : APPETIZING ⟨fruit more ~ than berries —John Burroughs⟩ **b** : pleasing in smell : FRAGRANT ⟨a wooden tray... smelling of rich cedarwood and varnish —Elizabeth M. Roberts⟩

c : having a stimulating taste ⟨a ~ dish⟩ ⟨~ jelly⟩ **syn** see PALATABLE

²savory \"\ *n* -ES *Brit* : a cooked or uncooked dish of stimulating flavor served usu. at the end of dinner but sometimes as an appetizer before the meal

³savory \"\ *n* -ES [ME *saverey,* prob. alter. (influenced by *savery,* adj., savory) of OE *sætherie,* fr. L *satureia*] : any of several aromatic mints of the genus *Satureia* — see SUMMER SAVORY, WINTER SAVORY

savour *var of* SAVOR

sa·voy \sə'vȯi *also esp attrib* 'sa,vȯi\ *n* -s [F (*chou de*) *Savoie* cabbage of Savoy] **1** *also* **savoy cabbage** : a cabbage having a compact head with wrinkled and curled leaves **2** : a spinach having wrinkled leaves

¹sa·voy·ard \sə'vȯiə̇rd, sə'vȯi,(y)ärd, ,sa,vȯi'(y)ärd, F sȧvȯyȧȧr *or* sȧvwȧyȧȧr\ *n* -s *cap* [F, fr. *Savoie* Savoy, region in southeastern France + F *-ard*] : a native or inhabitant of Savoy

²savoyard \"\ *adj, usu cap* **1** : of, relating to, or characteristic of Savoy, France **2** : of, relating to, or characteristic of the people of Savoy

³savoyard \"; *often pronounced in French fashion like the preceding although not from French*\ *n* -s *usu cap* [*Savoy,* theater in London specially built in 1881 by Richard D'Oyly Carte †1901 Eng. operatic impresario for the presentation of the operas of W.S.Gilbert †1911 Eng. playwright and A.S. Sullivan †1900 Eng. composer + E *-ard*] : a devotee, performer, or producer of the comic operas of W.S.Gilbert and A.S.Sullivan

savoy cake *n, usu cap S* [fr. *Savoy,* region in France] **1** *or* **savoy finger** *or* **savoy biscuit** : LADYFINGER 2 **2** : a large spongecake often baked or cut in fancy shape

savoy disease *n, usu cap S* [so called fr. the resemblance of the leaves to those of savoy cabbage] : a virus disease of plants transmitted by a lace bug (*Piesma cinerea*) and marked by wrinkling of leaves

sa·voyed \sə'vȯid *also* ,sa'vȯid\ *adj* [*savoy* + *-ed*] : curled and wrinkled; *specif* : abnormally wrinkled as a result of disease (as a virus infection) — used of leaves or plants

sa·voy·ing \sə'vȯiiṅ, ,sa,vȯi-\ *n* -s [*savoy* + *-ing*] : a savoyed quality or state

savs *abbr* savings

sav·vi·ness \'savēnəs, -vin-\ *n* -ES : the quality or state of being savvy

¹sav·vy \'savē, -vi\ *vb* -ED/-ING/-ES [modif. of Sp *sabe,* 2d pers. (formal) & 3d pers. sing. pres. indic. of *saber* to know, fr. L *sapere* to have sense, be wise — more at SAGE] *vt, slang* : COMPREHEND, UNDERSTAND ⟨he *savvied* them, they fitted into his language —Will James⟩ ~ *vi, slang* : to understand the meaning or implication of something heard : get the point ⟨I take care of myself — ~? —S.V.Benét⟩

²savvy \"\ *n* -ES *slang* : expertness in a particular field based on experience and native ability : practical grasp : KNOW-HOW, SHREWDNESS ⟨political ~⟩ ⟨business ~⟩ ⟨baseball ~⟩

³savvy \"\ *adj* [²*savvy*] *slang* : characterized by shrewdness and practical grasp ⟨most of them are pretty ~ fellows: they know the answers —J.S.Childers⟩

¹saw [ME *saugh* (past sing.), *sawen* (past pl.), fr. OE *seah* (past sing.), *sāwon* (past pl.)] *past* or *substand past part of* SEE

²saw \'sȯ\ *n* -s [ME *sawe,* fr. OE *sagu, sage;* akin to OHG *sega, saga* saw, ON *sög* saw, L *secare* to cut, *securis* ax, *secula* sickle, OSlav *sěšti* to cut, *sekyra* ax, Alb *shatë* mattock; basic meaning: to cut] **1a** (1) : a manually operated or power-driven tool used to cut hard material (as wood, metal, or bone) and usu. consisting of a thin flat blade or plate of tempered steel with a continuous series of teeth on the edge and mounted in a handle or frame (2) : a saw blade **b** : any of various tools or devices without teeth that cut by wearing out a kerf: as (1) : HELICOIDAL SAW (2) : a soft steel disk revolved at high speed to cut metal (as armor plate) **c** : a tool or machine having a saw for cutting **2a** : the ovipositor of a sawfly **b** : the snout of a sawfish

³saw \"\ *vb* **sawed; sawed** *also* **sawn; sawing; saws** [ME *sawen,* fr. *sawe* saw] *vt* **1 a** : to cut with a saw ⟨~ timber⟩ ⟨~ marble⟩ ⟨~ the log in two⟩ **b** : to cut into pieces as if with a saw ⟨about 20 carbines and tommy guns practically ~ed him in half —Bill Alcine⟩ **c** : to cut kerfs across ⟨the back of an unbound hand-sewn book⟩ to receive the cords that secure the covers in order to prevent the cords from raising ridges on the covered backbone — usu. used with *in* **2** : to produce or form by cutting with or as if with a saw ⟨solid wheels ~ed from the trunks of cottonwood trees —*Amer. Guide Series: Texas*⟩ **3 a** : to cut through as though using a saw ⟨a fir tree ~ed the air with its creaking branches —Elizabeth Taylor⟩ ⟨do not ~ the air too much with your hand —Shak.⟩ **b** : to give the motion of a saw to ⟨~ing the towel across his back —A.P.Gaskell⟩ ~ *vi* **1 a** : to use a saw ⟨he ~s well⟩ **b** : to cut with or as if with a saw ⟨a machine that can ~ in many patterns⟩ ⟨the river that ~ed through the rising mountain barrier —*Amer. Guide Series: Wash.*⟩ **2** : to admit of being cut with a saw ⟨the timber ~s smoothly⟩ **3 a** : to make motions as though using a saw ⟨~ed at the reins⟩ **b** : to play on a stringed instrument with a bow ⟨the cellist ~ed away⟩ — **saw alive** *or* **saw through and through** : to make all cuts on a log parallel — **saw gourds** *South & Midland* : SNORE — **saw wood 1** *slang* : to attend to one's affairs : mind one's business ⟨said nothing and *sawed wood* and drank his coffee —Helen Reilly⟩ **2** *slang* : SNORE

⁴saw \"\ *n* -s [ME *sawe,* fr. OE *sagu* speech, talk, discourse; akin to OHG & ON *saga* tale, saga, account, OE *secgan* to say — more at SAY] : a traditional saying : MAXIM, PROVERB ⟨the old ~ that ignorance is bliss —M.W.Childs⟩

sa·wah \'sä,wȯ\ *n* -s [Malay] : a wet or irrigated rice field in Indonesia

sa·wa·li \sə'wälē\ *n* -s [Tag *sawali*] : a coarse twilled matting of flattened bamboo strips used in the Philippines for partitions, walling, and baskets

sa·wan \'säwȯn\ *n* -s *usu cap* [Hindi *sāwan,* fr. Skt *śrāvaṇa*] : a month of the Hindu year — see MONTH table

sa·wa·ra cypress \'säwərə-\ *n* [Jap *sawara*] : a Japanese evergreen tree (*Chamaecyparis pisifera*) used for timber and as the source of many horticultural forms of retinispora

saw arbor *n* : MANDREL 4

saw·back \'₌,₌\ *n* [²*saw* + *back*] : something that has a serrate dorsal outline; *specif* : a mountain range or crest that has sharp peaks of about equal height

saw·bel·ly \'₌,₌₌\ *n* [²*saw* + *belly*] **1** : ALEWIFE 1a **2** : GIZZARD SHAD

saw·bill \'₌,₌\ *n* [²*saw* + *bill*] : a bird with a serrate beak; *esp* : MERGANSER

saw bill *n* : a list given to a sawyer of sizes to be sawed from logs

saw·billed \'₌,₌\ *adj* : having a serrated bill

saw·bones \'₌,₌₌\ *n, pl* **sawbones** *or* **sawboneses** [³*saw* + *bones*] *slang* : a physician or surgeon ⟨the usual anecdotal memoir churned out by the ~ who takes pen instead of tongue depressor in hand —*Saturday Rev.*⟩

saw brier *n* : any of several prickly plants of the genus *Smilax:* as **a** : BULLBRIER **b** : a Bahamian brier (*S. havanensis*) **c** : CATBRIER

saw·buck \'₌,₌\ *n* [²*saw* + *buck;* trans. of D *zaagbok*] **1** : SAWHORSE **2** [prob. so called fr. the Roman numeral X that suggests the crossed ends of a sawhorse] *slang* : a 10-dollar bill

sawbuck table *n* : a table with X-shaped supports

saw·bwa \'sȯbwä\ *n* -s [Burmese *cdbwä*] : the hereditary ruler of a Shan state of Burma

saw cabbage palm *n* : SAW PALMETTO b

saw·der \'sȯdə(r)\ *vt* -ED/-ING/-s [origin unknown] : FLATTER

¹saw·dust \'₌,₌\ *n* [²*saw* + *dust*] **1 a** : dust or small fragments (as of wood or stone) made by a saw in cutting ⟨the floor was covered with ~⟩ **b** : flimsy stuffing ⟨a man made of ~⟩ **2** *or* **sawdust liver** : a cattle abnormality of undetermined cause characterized by the presence of small granular light-colored areas scattered through the liver

sawbuck table

²sawdust \"\ *vt* **:** to strew or carpet with sawdust
³sawdust \"\ *adj* **1 :** covered or stuffed with sawdust ⟨the ~ ring⟩ ⟨a ~ doll⟩ **2 :** of, relating to, or connected with an enterprise (as a circus or revival meeting) conducted under a tent ⟨a ~ performer⟩ ⟨a ~ preacher⟩ **3 :** having no real substance : not solid ⟨she asks vital questions, but she gives ~ answers —*Saturday Rev.*⟩ ⟨a ~ Caesar⟩
sawdust trail *n* [so called fr. the practice of going down a sawdust-covered aisle to the altar in a revival tent meeting as a sign of repentance or conversion] **1 :** the path of conversion to a gospel or belief ⟨when a notorious grizzled old sinner hits the *sawdust trail*, the hallelujahs shake the tabernacle —Beverly Smith⟩ ⟨drew the students back down the *sawdust trail* to the old-time Congregationalism —*Amer. Guide Series: Conn.*⟩ **2 :** the circuit of revival meetings ⟨five of the biggest attractions on the *sawdust trail* —Furman Bisher⟩
saw·dusty \'sȯ(,)dəstē, -ti\ *adj* [¹*sawdust* + *-y*] **1 :** filled with, resembling, or smelling of sawdust ⟨the ~, soapy-smelling dark of the shop —Angus Wilson⟩ **2 :** lacking inherent interest or appeal : WEARISOME ⟨the old formal, dogmatic, ~ conning of the grammar book —Eric Partridge⟩
sawed *adj* [fr. past part. of ³*saw*] **1 :** cut with a saw ⟨~ boards⟩ ⟨~ bone⟩ **2 :** SERRATE ⟨~ edges⟩
saw-edged \'=¦=\ *adj* **:** having a toothed or badly nicked edge
sawed-off \'=¦=\ *adj* **1 :** having an end sawed off ⟨a *sawed-off* shotgun⟩ ⟨a *sawed-off* baseball bat which in peaceful times served as a rolling pin —Rose Feld⟩ **2 :** of less than average height : PINT-SIZE ⟨a little *sawed-off* mountaineer lugging a rifle longer than he was —F.B.Gipson⟩
saw·er \'sȯ(ə)r, -ȯə\ *n* -s [ME, fr. *sawen* to saw + *-er* — more at SAW] **:** one that saws : SAWYER
saw fern *n* **:** a widely distributed fern (*Blechnum serrulatum*) with erect stiff fronds that often grows in dense colonies in tropical marshes and is esp. common in Florida and the West Indies
saw file *n* **:** a usu. triangular file for sharpening saw teeth
sawfish \'=,=\ *n* **:** any of several large elongate viviparous fishes constituting the family Pristidae, having a flattened and much elongated snout with a row of stout toothlike structures inserted along each edge, and living in warm shallow seas and about river mouths principally in tropical America and Africa — see PRISTIDAE
sawfly \'=,=\ *n* **1 :** any of numerous hymenopterous insects constituting a superfamily Tenthredinoidea, having the female usu. with a pair of serrated blades in her ovipositor that are used to make the incisions in leaves and stems of plants in which the eggs are laid, developing from larvae that resemble lepidopterous caterpillars but usu. have more numerous prolegs, and including many destructive pests of plants that feed on foliage or mine in leaves and stems **2 :** any of various other hymenopterous insects of similar habits and form
saw gate *or* **saw frame** *n* **:** a stretching frame for a saw or gang of saws
saw gin *n* **:** a cotton gin in which the lint is drawn by the teeth of revolving circular saws through a grating of vertical ribs too closely spaced for the seeds to pass with the lint being removed from the saw teeth by rotating brushes or a blast or air
saw grass *n* **:** any of various sedges having the edges of the leaves set with minute sharp teeth: as **a :** a European sedge (*Cladium mariscus*) **b :** a sedge (*C. jamaicensis*) of southern U.S. and the West Indies — compare RAZOR GRASS
sawhorse \'=,=\ *n* [²*saw* + *horse*] **1 :** a rack shaped like a double St. Andrew's cross that is used to support wood while it is being sawed — called also *buck*, *sawbuck* **2 :** a flat-topped trestle usu. used in pairs to support something (as wood that is being sawed)

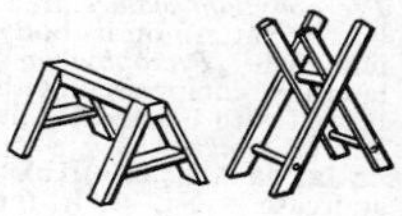
sawhorses

sawing *adj* [fr. pres. part. of ³*saw*] **:** having a rasping quality ⟨a ~ sound⟩ ⟨a ~ voice⟩
sawl \'sȯl\ *dial chiefly Brit var of* SOUL
sawlike \'=,=\ *adj* **:** resembling a saw or the teeth of a saw ⟨a ~ snout⟩ ⟨~ teeth⟩
sawlog \'=,=\ *n* **:** a log of suitable size for sawing into lumber
saw·man \'=,mən\ *n, pl* **sawmen :** one who saws or who repairs saws
sawmill \'=,=\ *n* [²*saw* + *mill*] **1 :** a plant having power-driven machinery for sawing logs **2 :** a machine used for sawing logs
sawmiller \'=,==\ *n* **:** one who operates a sawmill
sawmilling \'=,==\ *n* **:** the process of operating a sawmill
sawn *past part of* SAW
¹**saw·ney** \'sȯnē, -ni\ *n* -s [prob. alter. of *zany*] *chiefly Brit* **:** FOOL, SIMPLETON
²**sawney** \"\ *n* -s *usu cap* [alter. of ³*sandy*] **:** SCOTCHMAN — usu. used disparagingly
³**sawney** *also* **saw·ny** \"\ *adj* [¹*sawney*] *chiefly Brit* **:** naïvely or sentimentally foolish : SILLY
saw palmetto *n* **:** any of several palms with spiny-toothed leafstalks: as **a :** a common stemless palm (*Serenoa repens*) of the southern U.S. **b :** a palm (*Paurotis wrightii*) of the West Indies and southern Florida
sawpit \'=,=\ *n* [ME *sawe pitt*, fr. *sawe* saw + *pitt* pit — more at SAW, PIT] **:** a pit over which timber is laid to be sawed with a long two-handled saw operated by two men of whom one stands above the timber and the other below it
saws *pl of* SAW, *pres 3d sing of* SAW
saw-scaled viper \'=¦=-\ *n* **:** a small but fierce and aggressive desert-dwelling viper (*Echis carinatus*) found from No. Africa to India, having roughly keeled lateral scales, and being exceedingly venomous and responsible for many deaths esp. in India — called also *kupper*
saw set *n* **:** an instrument used to give set to sawteeth
sawsetter \'=,==\ *n* [²*saw* + *setter*] **:** one that sets the teeth of saws
saw shark *n* **:** any of several small sharks (family Pristiophoridae) found along the shores of southern Africa, eastern Asia, and Australia and having a snout like that of a sawfish but smaller teeth not embedded in sockets and lateral rather than ventral gill openings
saw sharpener *also* **sawsharper** \'=,==\ *n* [so called fr. the grating noise made by the male] **:** GREAT TIT
sawt \'sät, 'sȯt\ *chiefly Scot var of* SALT
saw table *n* **:** an iron or wooden table having a slot in which a circular saw operates : a saw bench
sawtimber \'=,==\ *n* **:** timber suitable for sawing into lumber
¹**sawtooth** \'=,=\ *n* [²*saw* + *tooth*] **:** a tooth of a saw or one of the teeth of an animal or machine shaped or arranged like the teeth of a saw
²**sawtooth** \"\ *adj* **1 :** SAW-TOOTHED **2 :** having a wave form resembling the teeth of a saw and of a quantity that varies periodically either gradually or gradually and abruptly between two peak values — used esp. of voltages and currents
sawtooth building *n* **:** a building having a sawtooth roof
saw-toothed \'=¦=\ *adj* **1 :** having teeth like those of a saw **:** having pointed teeth ⟨a *saw-toothed* shark⟩ **2 :** having serrations : SERRATE ⟨*saw-toothed* mountains pierced by valleys —*Lamp*⟩
saw-toothed grain beetle *n* **:** a minute widely distributed cucujid beetle (*Oryzaephilus surinamensis*) that feeds esp. on stored cereal products
sawtooth roof *also* **sawtooth** *n* **:** a roof composed of two or more parallel simple roofs resembling in section the teeth of a saw and ordinarily having one slope of each member steeper than the other to receive glazing
sawtooth roulette *n* **:** a zigzag stamp roulette that produces a sawtooth pattern on the edge of a detached stamp

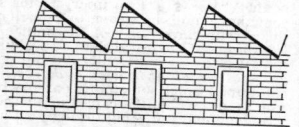

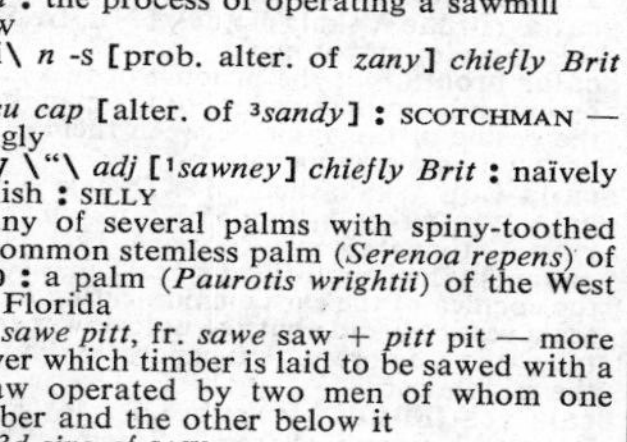
sawtooth roof

saw tree *n* **:** a tree suitable for sawing
sawway \'=,=\ *n* [²*saw* + *way*] **:** the path of a saw in cutting
saw-whet owl \'=,=-\ *also* **saw-whet** *n* **:** a very small No. American owl (*Cryptoglaux acadica*) that is largely dark brown above and white beneath with vertical brown stripes on the breast, has a rasping metallic call suggesting the filing of a saw, and feeds chiefly on small rodents
sawwort \'=,=\ *n* [²*saw* + *wort*] **1 :** any of various plants constituting a genus (*Serratula*) of the family Compositae; *esp* **:** a plant (*S. tinctoria*) the serrate leaves of which yield a yellow dye **2 :** a plant of the genus *Saussurea* **3 :** a button snakeroot (*Liatris spicata*)
saw·yer \'sȯyə(r), 'sȯiə-\ *n* -s [ME *sawier, sawyer*, fr. *sawen* to saw + *-ier* *-er* — more at SAW] **1 a :** one that saws logs or timber (as in lumbering or in a sawmill) **b :** either of the two men who work together at sawing timber over a sawpit — see BOTTOM SAWYER, TOP SAWYER **c :** one that saws a particular material (as wood, ivory, or metal) esp. for use in manufacturing **2** *or* **sawyer beetle :** any of several large longicorn beetles whose larvae bore large holes in timber or dead wood esp. of various conifers — see PINE SAWYER **3 :** a tree fast in the bed of a stream with its branches projecting to the surface and bobbing up and down with the current — distinguished from *planter*
¹**sax** \'saks\ *or* **seax** \'saəks\ *n* -ES [ME *sexe* knife, short sword, fr. OE *seax, sæx;* akin to OHG *sahs* knife, ON *sax* knife, sword, L *saxum* rock, OE *sagu* saw — more at SAW] **:** a knifelike chopping tool used for trimming the edges of roof slates and having a pointed pick at the back for making nail holes
²**sax** \'saks\ *dial Brit var of* SIX
³**sax** \"\ *n* -ES [by shortening] **:** SAXOPHONE
sax·a·tile \'saksə,tīl\ *adj* [L *saxatilis*, fr. *saxum* rock] **:** SAXICOLOUS
sax·aul \'sak,sȯl\ *n* -s [prob. native name in Turkistan] **:** a leafless xerophytic shrub or tree (*Haloxylon ammondendron*) of the family Chenopodiaceae of Asia that has green or greenish branches and is used for stabilization of desert soils
saxboard \'=,=\ *n* [¹*sax* + *board*] **:** the uppermost strake of an open boat
saxe blue \'saks-\ *also* **saxe** *n* -s *often cap S* [F *Saxe* Saxony] **:** a grayish blue that is redder and paler than electric, greener and slightly lighter than copenhagen, redder, lighter, and stronger than Gobelin, and greener, lighter, and stronger than old china
sax·horn \'saks+,-\ *n* [Antoine Joseph (known as Adolphe) *Sax* †1894 Belgian maker of musical instruments, its inventor + E *horn*] **:** one of a complete family of conical-bore brass-wind musical instruments with valves that are characterized by fullness and evenness of tone and large compass and are made in sizes grading from soprano to bass

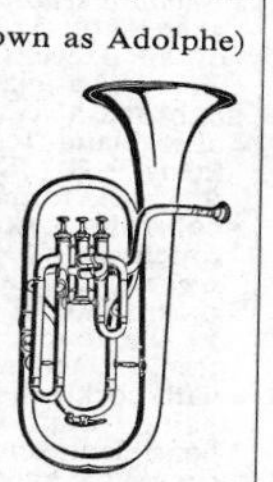
saxhorn

saxi- *comb form* [L, fr. *saxum;* akin to L *secare* to cut — more at SAW] **:** rock ⟨*saxicolous*⟩
sax·i·ca·vous \¦saksē¦kāvəs\ *adj* [NL *saxicavus*, fr. *saxi-* + *-cavus* (fr. L *cavare* to make hollow) — more at EXCAVATE] **:** boring in rock — used esp. of a mollusk; compare LITHOPHAGOUS
¹**sax·ic·o·la** \sak'sikələ\ *n, cap* [NL, fr. *saxi-* + *-cola*] **:** a genus of Old World passerine birds including the whinchat, stonechat, and related birds
²**saxicola** \"\ [NL] *syn of* ²OENANTHE
sax·ic·o·line \(')sak¦sikə,līn, -lən\ *adj* [NL *Saxicola* + E *-ine*] **:** of or relating to the genus *Saxicola*
sax·ic·o·lous \(')sak¦sikələs\ *also* **sax·ic·o·line** \-,līn, -lən\ *or* **sax·i·cole** \'saksə,kōl\ *adj* [*saxi-* + *-colous* or *-coline* or *-cole*] **:** inhabiting or growing among rocks
sax·if·ra·ga \sak'sifrəgə\ *n, cap* [NL, fr. LL, saxifrage] **:** a genus (the type of the family Saxifragaceae) of usu. perennial herbs of diverse habit of arctic and temperate regions having pentamerous often showy flowers with a 2-celled ovary followed by a 2-beaked follicle and often having basal tufted leaves — see LONDON PRIDE
sax·i·fra·ga·ce·ae \,saksəfrə'gāsē,ē\ *n pl, cap* [NL, fr. *Saxifraga*, type genus + *-aceae*] **:** a widely distributed family of herbs (order Rosales) of variable habit usu. distinguished by the free ovary with two carpels, by having as many or twice as many stamens as petals, and by the absence of staminodia — **sax·i·fra·ga·ceous** \¦==¦==¦gāshəs\ *adj*
sax·i·frage \'saksəfrij, -rēj\ *n* -s [ME, fr. MF, fr. LL *saxifraga*, fr. L *saxifraga (herba)*, lit., rock-breaking herb, fr. *saxifraga* (fem. of *saxifragus* rock-breaking, fr. *saxi-* + *-fragus*, fr. *frangere* to break) + *herba* herb; fr. its growing in crevices of rocks — more at BREAK] **1 :** a plant of the genus *Saxifraga*— called also *breakstone* **2 :** any of various plants felt to resemble a saxifrage — usu. used with a qualifying term; see BURNET SAXIFRAGE, GOLDEN SAXIFRAGE
saxifrage family *n* **:** SAXIFRAGACEAE
saxifrage pink *n* **:** a tufted European perennial herb (*Tunica saxifraga*) of the family Caryophyllaceae that has clustered subulate leaves and is adventive in No. America
sax·if·ra·gous \(')sak¦sifrəgəs\ *adj* [L *saxifragus* rock-breaking] *of a plant* **:** growing in crevices of and promoting splitting of rock
sax·i·frax \'saksə,fraks\ *n* -ES [modif. (influenced by LL *saxifraga* saxifrage) of Sp *sasafrás* sassafras — more at SAXIFRAGE] **:** SASSAFRAS
sax·ig·e·nous \(')sak¦sijənəs\ *adj* [LL *saxigenus*, fr. *saxi-* + *-genus* (fr. *gignere* to beget) — more at KIN] **:** SAXICOLOUS
¹**sax·on** \'saksən\ *n* -s [ME, fr. LL *Saxones* Saxons (sing. *Saxo*), of Gmc origin; akin to OE *Seaxe, Seaxan*, pl., Saxons] **1** *cap* **a** (1) **:** a member of a Germanic people entering and conquering England with the Angles and Jutes in the 5th century A.D. and merging with them to form the Anglo-Saxon people (2) **:** an Englishman or Lowlander as distinguished from a Welshman, Irishman, or Highlander — compare SASSENACH **b :** a native or inhabitant of Saxony, Germany **2** *cap* **a :** the Germanic language or dialect of any of the Saxon peoples **b :** the Germanic element in the English language esp. as distinguished from the French and Latin **3** *usu cap* [prob. so called fr. its originating in Saxony] **:** a firework having a brilliant turning fire that produces the appearance of a revolving sun
²**saxon** \"\ *adj, usu cap* **1 a :** of, relating to, or characteristic of the Anglo-Saxons **:** belonging to the period of English history between the Anglo-Saxon invasions and the Norman Conquest in 1066 **b :** of Anglo-Saxon origin ⟨the *Saxon* words have a simple vigor which no other vocabulary at our disposal could secure —Barrett Wendell⟩ **2 a :** of, relating to, or characteristic of Saxony **b :** of, relating to, or characteristic of the people of Saxony
³**saxon** \"\ *dial var of* SEXTON
saxon blue *n, usu cap S* **1 :** a dye made by dissolving indigo in sulfuric acid **2** *or* **saxony blue :** SMALT 1
sax·o·nian \(')sak¦sōnēən, -nyən\ *adj, usu cap* [ML *Saxonia* Saxony (fr. LL *Saxon-, Saxo* Saxon + L *-ia* -y) + E *-an*] **:** SAXON 2 a
sax·on·ic \(')sak¦sänik\ *adj, usu cap* [¹*saxon* + *-ic*] **:** of or relating to the Anglo-Saxons
sax·on·ism \'saksə,nizəm\ *n* -s *usu cap* [¹*saxon* + *-ism*] **:** ANGLO-SAXONISM
sax·on·ist \-,nəst\ *n* -s *usu cap* [¹*saxon* + *-ist*] **:** a specialist in Old English or in Saxon history or culture
sax·on·ize \-,nīz\ *vt* -ED/-ING/-S *sometimes cap* [ML *saxonizare*, fr. LL *Saxon-, Saxo* Saxon + *-izare* -ize] **:** ANGLO-SAXONIZE
sax·on·ly *adv, usu cap* **:** in a Saxon manner
saxon wheel *or* **saxony wheel** *n, usu cap S* [so called fr. its being the invention of a 16th cent. German wood-carver] **:** a flax-spinning treadle machine in which the bobbin lags behind the fly with the spindle giving the twist to the yarn and the difference of speeds of the spindle and bobbin causing the bobbin to be wound
sax·o·ny \'saksənē, -ni\ *n* -ES *often cap* [fr. *Saxony*, former German state in central Germany] **1 a :** any of various fine soft woolen fabrics orig. made in Saxony of merino wool and usu. having a firm texture and small clear patterns **b :** a fine knitting yarn of closely-twisted three-ply wool **2 :** a Wilton jacquard carpet woven with moderately tight twisted pile yarns
saxony green *n, often cap S* **:** COBALT GREEN 2
sax·o·phone \'saksə,fōn\ *n* [F, fr. Antoine J. (known as Adolphe) *Sax* †1894 Belgian maker of musical instruments, its inventor + F *-phone*] **1 :** a wind instrument that combines the reed mouthpiece of a clarinet with a usu. curved conical metal tube made in various sizes, that is equipped with finger keys, and that is used esp. in military bands and dance orchestras **2 :** a flue or reed pipe-organ stop so constructed as to imitate the saxophone — **sax·o·phon·ic** \¦==¦fänik\ *adj*

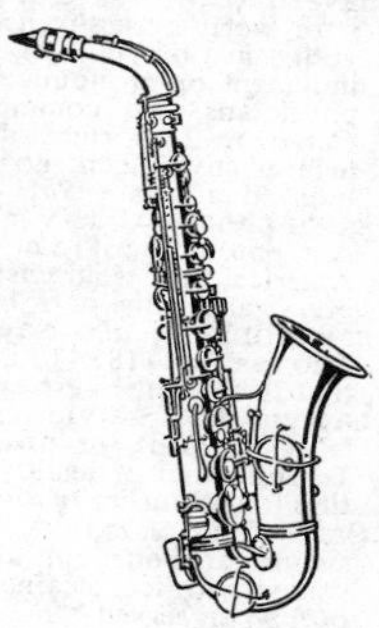
saxophone

sax·o·phon·ist \-,fōnəst *chiefly Brit* sak'säfənəst\ *n* -s **:** a player on the saxophone
sax·tuba \'saks+,-\ *n* [Antoine J. *Sax* †1894 + E *tuba*] **:** a bass saxhorn
¹**say** \(')sā, *South also* (¦)se\ *vb, past* **said** \(')sed, səd\ *or archaic* **said·est** \'sedəst\ *or* **saidst** \'sedzt, -edst, -etst\ *past part* **said**; *pres part* **saying** \'sāiŋ\ *pres 1st sing* **say** *or chiefly dial* **says** \(')sez, səz\ *2d sing* **say**; *3d sing* **says** \(')sez, səz\ *or archaic* **saith** \(')seth, 'sā(ə)th\ *pl* **say** [ME *sayen, seyen, seggen*, fr. OE *secgan;* akin to OHG *sagēn* to say, ON *segja* to say, OIr *insce* speech, OL *insece* tell, relate, 2d pers. sing. pres. imper., Gk *enepein, ennepein* to tell, speak, Lith *sakyti* to say] *vt* **1 a :** to express in words **:** DECLARE, STATE ⟨~ what you mean in clear, simple language⟩ ⟨he ~*s* that it's raining outside⟩ ⟨the book ~*s* nothing about the background of these events⟩ ⟨it ~*s* drive carefully⟩ **b :** to state as a common opinion or belief **:** ALLEGE ⟨the school is *said* to be the country's largest endowed trade school —*Amer. Guide Series: Minn.*⟩ ⟨wages are *said* to be as high in the other colonies as in New York —Adam Smith⟩ **c :** to announce as a decision or opinion : state positively : ASSERT ⟨nobody can ~ at this point what the results of the test will be⟩ ⟨he's a good ball-player if he ~*s* it himself⟩ **d :** to state as something to be accomplished : ORDER ⟨if the human beings under his direction don't do what he ~*s*, then he is a failure as a manager —J.I. Miller⟩ ⟨no sooner *said* than done⟩ **e** *slang* **:** to state effectively or forcefully ⟨you *said* \'sed\ it⟩ **2 a :** UTTER, PRONOUNCE ⟨a meek little person who couldn't ~ boo⟩ ⟨can't ~ two words without stopping to think⟩ ⟨make one copy of the list, ~*ing* each outline to yourself as you write —C.I.Blanchard & C.E.Zoubek⟩ — often used to introduce a direct quotation **b :** RECITE, REPEAT ⟨I stood up to ~ my repetition —Rex Ingamells⟩ ⟨*said* his prayers⟩ **3 a :** INDICATE, SHOW ⟨the clock ~*s* five minutes after twelve⟩ ⟨the smug look on his face *said* that he was confident of success⟩ **b :** to give expression to : COMMUNICATE ⟨wanted to produce sculpture which really *said* something —Agnes Allen⟩ ⟨the artist with something new to ~ —Selden Rodman⟩ **4** *dial Eng* **:** to answer esp. with advice or admonition **5 :** ASSUME, SUPPOSE ⟨let us ~ that such an offer is made. Would you accept it⟩ ~ *vi* **1 :** to express oneself : SPEAK, DECLARE ⟨did he really ~ so⟩ ⟨a man, they ~, of great ability⟩ **2** *archaic* **:** to finish speaking ⟨when I have *said*, make answer to us both —Shak.⟩ **3** *archaic* **:** to make a recital — **not to say :** to use a milder expression than ⟨his manner was discourteous, *not to say* offensive⟩ — **say for oneself :** to offer as an excuse or justification ⟨what have you got to *say for yourself*⟩ — **say nothing of :** to leave out of consideration (an important or essential factor) ⟨the expedition will be expensive, to *say nothing of* the danger⟩ — **say uncle :** to admit defeat : give up ⟨forced his opponent to *say uncle*⟩ — **that is to say :** in other words : in effect
²**say** \'sā, *South also* 'se\ *n, pl* **says** \'sāz, *South also* 'sez\ **1** *archaic* **:** something that is said : SAYING, STATEMENT ⟨ere the fatal hour I said the ~ that placed me in thy power —W.S.Gilbert⟩ **2 a :** a full expression of opinion : all that one wants to say ⟨that gentleman had said his ~ and now chose to be silent —Max Peacock⟩ **b :** an opportunity to express one's views or intentions ⟨feel that if such a person is dissatisfied with the conduct of affairs he should resign before having his ~ —Zechariah Chafee⟩ **3 a :** a right or power to influence action or decision : VOICE ⟨had no ~ in the upbringing of his son —W.C.DeVane⟩ ⟨bound-up babies voice complaints but have no ~ about their clothing —*Better Homes & Gardens*⟩ **b :** a right or power of final decision : supreme authority — used with *the* ⟨they will have the ~ shortly about what shall be done —E.S.Martin⟩ ⟨he had the ~ over more than $50 billion —*Newsweek*⟩ **4** *chiefly dial* **:** CONVERSATION, TALK
³**say** \"\ *adv* [fr. imper. of ¹*say*] **1 :** ABOUT, APPROXIMATELY ⟨the property is worth, ~, four million dollars⟩ ⟨the car was going, ~, sixty miles an hour⟩ **2 :** for instance : by way of example : AS ⟨if we compress any gas, ~ oxygen⟩
⁴**say** \'sā\ *n, pl* **says** \'sāz\ [ME *say, saie*, fr. OF *saie*, a cloth, fr. (assumed) VL *sagia*, fr. L *sagum* — more at SAGUM] **1 :** a fine woolen cloth resembling serge formerly worn esp. by Quakers and members of religious orders **2** *obs* **:** SILK
⁵**say** \"\ *vb* [ME *sayen*, short for *assayen* to assay — more at ASSAY] *chiefly dial* **:** ASSAY
⁶**say** \"\ *n* [ME (Sc dial.), of Scand origin; akin to ON *sār* large vessel, Dan *saa* tub, Sw *så* bucket; akin to OE *sā* tub, bucket] *chiefly Scot* **:** BUCKET
sa·ya \'säyə\ *n* -s [Sp, fr. *saya* man's cloak, sagum, fr. (assumed) VL *sagia*, fr. L *sagum* cloak, sagum] **:** an ankle-length outer skirt tied at the waist that is worn by women in the Philippines and Spanish America
say·able \'sāəbəl\ *adj* [¹*say* + *-able*] **1 :** capable of being said ⟨what he felt was not easily ~⟩ **2 :** capable of being spoken effectively or easily ⟨the piece is ~ like a speech in a great play —J.M.Barzun⟩
sa·yal brown \sä'yäl-\ *n* [Sp *sayal* sackcloth, fr. *saya* man's cloak, sagum] **:** a light brown that is yellower and deeper than blush and deeper than cork
sa·yan samoyedic \'säyən-\ *n, usu cap both Ss* [fr. *Sayan* mountains, range between the Tuva and Irkutsk regions in Siberia] **:** KAMASIN 2
say blister beetle \'sā-\ *n, usu cap S* [after Thomas *Say* †1834 Am. entomologist] **:** a blister beetle (*Pomphopoea sayi*) that is often destructive to apple and other fruit blossoms in parts of northern No. America
say·bolt viscosity \'sā,bōlt-\ *n, usu cap S* [after George M. *Saybolt* †1924 Am. chemist] **:** viscosity as determined by the number of seconds required for an oil heated to 130° F for lighter oils and 210° F for heavier oils to flow through a standard orifice and fill a 60 milliliter flask
say·ee \(')sā¦ē\ *n* -s [¹*say* + *-ee*] **:** one to whom something is said ⟨the disaccords between sayer and ~ as to just how much has been said —I.A.Richards⟩
say·er \'sāə(r), 'seə-\ *n* -s [ME, fr. *sayen* to say + *-er* — more at SAY] **1 :** one that says ⟨he is a ~ rather than a doer⟩ **2** *archaic* **:** POET ⟨find some sense which no pen yet from singer, ~, ever has extracted —Robert Browning⟩
say·ing \'sāiŋ, -ēēŋ\ *n* -s [ME, fr. gerund of *sayen* to say] **1 :** the act of speaking or asserting ⟨he is better at ~ than at doing⟩ **2 :** something that is said: as **a :** a wise or witty statement attributed to a specific usu. well-known person ⟨a collection of the ~*s* of great statesmen⟩ ⟨often quotes the ~*s* of his father⟩ **b :** a commonly repeated statement : ADAGE, PROVERB ⟨no ~ was ever more true than the old adage that without his tools the workman is helpless —T.F.McNally⟩
say·nète \(')sā¦net\ *n* -s [F, fr. Sp *sainete*, lit., tidbit, delicacy, relish, spice, fr. *sain* grease, fat, fr. (assumed) VL *saginum*, fr. L *sagina* stuffing, food, fatness, fodder] **:** ENTREMES 2
sa·yo·na·ra \,säyə'närə, ,sīə'-, -näd·ə\ *n* -s [Jap] **:** GOOD-BYE
say over *vt* **:** to repeat from memory ⟨practiced *saying* his speech over until he was letter-perfect⟩
says *pres 3d sing or chiefly dial pres 1st sing of* SAY, *pl of* SAY

say's law \'sāz-\ *n, usu cap S & often cap L* [after Jean Baptiste *Say* †1832 Fr. economist] **:** a statement in economics: production creates not only the supply of goods but also the demand for them

say-so \'ₛ,ₛ\ *n* -s **1 a :** one's unsupported assertion **:** one's bare word or assurance ⟨you think the jury will find him guilty, just on your *say-so* —H.L.Davis⟩ **b :** an authoritative judgment or pronouncement **:** DICTUM ⟨on the *say-so* of the physicians, the commission granted the extension —Saul Carson⟩ **2 :** a right of final decision **:** AUTHORITY, SAY ⟨the federal government no longer has any *say-so* in the island's internal affairs —*Sat. Eve. Post*⟩

say's phoebe \'sāz-\ *n, usu cap S* [after Thomas *Say* †1834 Am. entomologist] **:** a phoebe (*Sayornis saya*) of western No. America that is grayish brown above with cinnamon buff breast and belly, dark brown head, and black tail

say stinkbug *also* **say's stinkbug** *n, usu cap 1st S* [after Thomas *Say* †1834] **:** a common stinkbug (*Chlorochroa sayi*) that is a serious pest esp. on grains in parts of western U. S.

say·yid *also* **sa·yid** *or* **sey·yid** *or* **se·yid** \'sī(y)əd, 'sīd, 'sä(y)əd, 'säd\ *or* **si·di** \'sēdē\ *n* -s [Ar *sayyid*] **1 :** an Islamic chief or leader **2 :** LORD, SIR — used as a courtesy title for a Muslim of outstanding achievement or noble lineage

Saz·e·rac \'sazə,rak\ *trademark* — used for a cocktail consisting of bourbon, absinthe flavoring, bitters, and sugar stirred with ice, strained, and flavored with a twist of lemon peel when served

sb *abbr* **1** stilb **2** substantive

SB *abbr or n* -s [NL *scientiae baccalaureus*] Bachelor of Science

SB *abbr* **1** sales book **2** savings bank **3** separately binned **4** shipping board **5** short bill **6** signal boatswain **7** simultaneous broadcast **8** small bonds **9** southbound **10** splash block **11** standard bead **12** statement of billing **13** steamboat **14** stolen base **15** stretcher bearer **16** stuffing box **17** switchboard

Sb *symbol* [L *stibium*] antimony

SBA *abbr* standard beam approach

sbj *abbr* subjunctive

s brake *n, cap S* **:** a brake for two consecutive wheels having a brake block at each end of an S-shaped lever

sbrinz \'sprints, 'zbr-\ *n, usu cap* [It *sbrinze, sbrinzo,* fr. *Sbrinze Sbrinzo* Brienz, commune of Bern canton, Switzerland] **:** a hard cheese suitable for grating

sc *abbr* **1** scale **2** scene **3** science **4** scilicet **5** screen **6** screw **7** scruple **8** [L *sculpsit*] he or she carved or engraved it

SC *abbr* **1** salvage charges **2** sanitary corps **3** school certificate **4** security council **5** see copy **6** self-closing **7** self-contained **8** [L *Senatus consulto*] by the decree of the Senate **9** service ceiling **10** sharp cash **11** ship's cook **12** signal corps **13** single case **14** single column **15** single comb **16** *often not cap* single crochet **17** *often not cap* small capital; small capitals **18** special circular **19** special constable **20** spreading coefficient **21** staff college **22** staff corps **23** statement of charges **24** steel casting **25** submarine chaser **26** sugar coated **27** summary court **28** super-calendered **29** superimposed current **30** supply corps **31** supreme court **32** swimming club

Sc *symbol* scandium

¹scab \'skab, 'skaa(ə)b\ *n* -s [ME *scab, scabbe,* of Scand origin; akin to OSw *skabbr* scab; akin to OE *sceabb* scab, L *scabies* mange, *scabere* to scratch — more at SHAVE] **1** *archaic* **:** a disease of the skin forming pustules or scales **2 :** scabies of domestic animals; *esp* **:** PSOROPTIC MANGE **3 :** CRUST 3e(1) **4 a :** a mean contemptible person **:** SCOUNDREL **b** (1) **:** one who refuses to join a union (2) **:** a member of a union who refuses to strike or returns to work before a strike has ended (3) **:** a worker who accepts employment or replaces a union worker during a strike (4) **:** one who works for lower wages than or under conditions contrary to those prescribed by a union — compare BLACKLEG, STRIKEBREAKER **c :** RAT 2b(1) **5 a :** any of various bacterial or fungous diseases of plants characterized by crustlike spots — see APPLE SCAB, POTATO SCAB, WHEAT SCAB **b :** one of the crusty spots in any of these diseases **6 :** a short piece of timber nailed or bolted to two abutting timbers to splice them together **7 a :** a slight irregular protuberance on a casting caused by a break in the mold **b :** a part of a surface of a wire or strip damaged by an adhesion of scale or other matter **8 :** a defect in enamel resembling a scab on skin **9 :** a piece of a target broken off from the rear opposite the place struck

²scab \"\ *vb* **scabbed; scabbed; scabbing; scabs** *vi* **1 :** to become covered with a scab **:** form a scab ⟨the wound *scabbed* over⟩ **2 :** to act as a scab ⟨trying to ~ against their own fellow musicians —*Internat'l Musician*⟩ **3 :** to throw off a piece from the rear opposite the place struck ⟨data bearing on the *scabbing* of metals under explosive attack —*Bull. of Amer. Physical Society*⟩ ~ *vt* **1 :** to label or treat (someone) as a scab **:** label (a job or a shop) as such that anyone working will be treated as a scab **2 :** to break off (a piece) from the rear of a target opposite the place struck ⟨bombs *scabbed* the concrete⟩

¹scab·bard \'skabə(r)d\ *n* -s [ME *scauberc, scaubert* fr. AF *escaubers, escauberz* (pl.), of Gmc origin, fr. a compound whose first element is akin to OHG *skār* blade and whose second element is akin to OHG *bergan* to shelter, hide — more at SHEAR, BURY] **1 a :** a usu. leather or metal sheath in which the blade of a sword, dagger, bayonet, or other cutting weapon is enclosed when not in use **b :** a sheath for carrying a hand weapon (as a carbine) or a tool (as a saw) for ready use ⟨methods of buckling a ~ to a saddle —William Curtis⟩ ⟨angler's pliers in leather ~ —*advt*⟩ — compare HOLSTER **2** [prob. fr. MLG *schalbort* thin board, fr. *schale* shell + *bort* board; akin to E ¹*scale* and to E *board*] **:** SCALEBOARD

²scabbard \"\ *vt* -ED/-ING/-S **1 :** to put in a scabbard **2** *archaic* **:** to beat with a scabbard as punishment

scabbard fish *n* **:** a cutlass fish esp. of the genus *Lepidopus; usu* **:** an elongated silvery food fish (*L. caudatus*) that is esp. abundant in southern seas

scab·bard·less \-dləs\ *adj* **:** lacking a scabbard

scabbed \'skabəd, -bd\ *adj* [ME, fr. ¹*scab* + *-ed*] **1 :** affected with scab ⟨~ potatoes⟩ **2 :** MEAN, PALTRY — **scabbed·ness** *n* -ES

scab·bi·ly \-bəlē\ *adv* **:** in a scabby manner

scab·bi·ness \-bēnəs\ *n* -ES **:** the condition of being scabby

scab·ble \'skabəl\ *or* **scap·ple** \-apəl\ *vt* -ED/-ING/-S [ME *scaplen,* fr. MF *escapler* to dress timber] **1 :** to work or shape roughly (as stone before leaving the quarry) **2 :** to dress (as stone) in any way short of fine tooling or rubbing

scabbled rubble *n* [fr. past part. of *scabble*] **:** undressed stone masonry from which only the roughest irregularities have been removed before laying in a wall

scab·bler \-b(ə)lə(r)\ *or* **scap·pler** \-p(ə)lə(r)\ *n* -s [*scabble* or *scapple* + *-er*] **1 :** a quarryman who scabbles stone slabs to make blocks of uniform size and to reduce shipping weight **2 :** a stonecutter who points blocks to approximate dimensions for finishing

scab·bling \-b(ə)liŋ\ *n* -s [fr. gerund of *scabble*] **:** a fragment or chip of stone

scab·by \'skabē, 'skaab-, -bi\ *adj* -ER/-EST [¹*scab* + *-y*] **1 a :** covered with scabs **:** full of scabs **:** consisting of scabs ⟨~ skin⟩ **b :** affected with scab ⟨a ~ animal⟩ ⟨~ potatoes⟩ **2 :** MEAN, SCURRILOUS, CONTEMPTIBLE ⟨a ~ trick⟩ **3 :** marred with scabs **:** SCALY ⟨temple of brick and rubble and ~ plaster —Aldous Huxley⟩ ⟨wrought-iron gates ~ with rust —Gerald Durrell⟩ ⟨a ~ casting⟩ **4 :** marked by a blotched appearance suggestive of scab ⟨landscape ~ with old mine workings —Sylvia T. Warner⟩ **5 :** like a scab in form or appearance ⟨dark land finally began to wear thin . . . leach white . . . and leave wide ~ places —*Survey Graphic*⟩

scabby mouth *n, Austral & NewZeal* **:** SORE MOUTH

sca·ber·u·lous \skə'berələs\ *adj* [L *scaber* scabrous + E *-ulous* dim. suffix — more at SCABROUS] **:** minutely scabrous

sca·bia \'skābēə\ *n* -s [prob. back-formation fr. ¹*scabious* (taken as a pl.)] *dial Eng* **:** SCABIOUS

scab·i·ci·dal \¦skabə¦sīdᵊl\ *adj* [*scabies* + *-cidal*] **1 :** destroying the itch mite causing scabies **2 :** of or relating to a scabicide

scab·i·cide \'skabə,sīd\ *or* **sca·bi·et·i·cide** \,skābē'ed·ə,sīd\ *n* -s [*scabicide* fr. *scabies* + *-cide; scabieticide* fr. *scabietic* + *-cide*] **:** a drug that destroys the itch mite causing scabies

sca·bies \'skābēz\ *n, pl* **scabies** [L, roughness, scurf, mange, itch; akin to L *scabere* to scratch, scrape — more at SHAVE] **:** itch or mange caused by mites esp. when marked by the formation of exudative crusts

sca·bi·et·ic \¦skābē¦ed·ik\ *also* **sca·bet·ic** \skə'bed·ik\ *adj* [*scabies* + *-etic*] **:** of, relating to, or infected with scabies **:** MANGY

sca·bi·o·sa \,skābē'ōsə, ,skab-\ *n* [NL, fr. ML, scabious] **1** *cap* **:** a large genus of Old World herbs (family Dipsacaceae) having terminal heads of flowers subtended by a leafy involucre and flowers with a 5-cleft often bilabiate corolla and four stamens **2** -s **:** any plant of the genus *Scabiosa*

¹sca·bi·ous \'skābēəs\ *n* -ES [ME *scabiose,* fr. ML *scabiosa* (*herba*), fr. L, fem. of *scabiosus* scabious, mangy; fr. its supposed efficacy in the treatment of scabies] **1 :** a plant of the genus *Scabiosa:* as **a :** SWEET SCABIOUS **b :** FIELD SCABIOUS **2 :** any of several fleabanes (genus *Erigeron*): as **a :** HORSE-WEED 1 **b :** DAISY FLEABANE **3 :** BLUE SCABIOUS

²scabious \"\ *adj* [L *scabiosus* scurfy, scabby, mangy, fr. *scabies* + *-osus* -ous] **1 :** consisting of scabs **:** SCABBY **2 :** of, relating to, or like scabies ⟨~ eruptions⟩

scab·ish \'skabish\ *n* -ES [alter. of ¹*scabious*] **1 :** FIELD SCABIOUS **2 a :** an evening primrose (*Oenothera biennis*) **b :** either of two sundrops (*O. fruticosa* and *O. glauca*)

scabland \'ₛ,ₛ\ *n* [¹*scab* + *land*] **1 :** an elevated tract of bare or shallow-soiled rocky land (as the top of a butte or mesa) in the Northwest caused esp. (as on the Columbia lava plateau) by denudation of the soil mantle or prevention of its formation ⟨gray ~ lifting against the sky —H.L.Davis⟩ — see SCABROCK **2 :** a region characterized by scablands traversed or isolated by postglacial dry stream channels ⟨area of approximately 1,500,000 acres of sage and ~ —*Amer. Guide Series: Wash.*⟩ — often used in pl. ⟨the channeled ~*s* of eastern Washington⟩

scab mite *n* **:** any of several small mites that cause scab; *esp* **:** one of the genus *Psoroptes*

sca·bres·cent \skə'bresᵊnt\ *adj* [*scabrous* + *-escent*] **:** becoming minutely scabrous

scab·rid \'skabrəd\ *adj* [LL *scabridus,* fr. L *scabrēre* to be rough, be scurfy, fr. *scabr-, scaber* rough, scurfy — more at SCABROUS] **:** somewhat rough in texture — **sca·brid·i·ty** \skə'bridəd·ē\ *n* -ES

scab·rin \'skabrən\ *n* -s [NL *scabra* (specific epithet of *Heliopsis scabra*) (fr. L, fem. of *scaber* rough) + E *-in* — more at SCABROUS] **:** an insecticidal material obtained from the roots of an oxeye (*Heliopsis scabra*) that contains an isobutylamide of a mixture of unsaturated fatty acids

scabrock \'ₛ,ₛ\ *n* [¹*scab* + *rock*] **1 :** an area or outcropping of scabland ⟨following the tongues of ~ between the cultivated fields —H.L.Davis⟩ ⟨two-acre patch of ~ —W.M.Mason⟩ **2 :** rock forming or scattered over the surface of scabland

scab·rous \'skabrəs *sometimes* 'skāb-\ *adj* [L *scabr-, scaber* rough, scurfy + E *-ous;* akin to L *scabies* roughness, mange, *scabere* to scratch, scrape — more at SHAVE] **1** *obs* **:** HARSH, UNMUSICAL **2 :** DIFFICULT, KNOTTY ⟨a ~ problem⟩ **3 :** rough to the touch **:** having small raised dots, scales, or points **:** SCALY, PRICKLY, SCURFY, SCABBY ⟨a ~ leaf⟩ ⟨cold sand ~ with cockles —J.M.Brinnin⟩ ⟨patches of darker plaster, of ~ paint —Edith C. Rivett⟩ **4 :** unpleasant, repulsive, or reprehensible in some way: as **a :** dealing with or characterized by suggestive, indecent, or scandalous themes **:** RISQUÉ, SALACIOUS ⟨scandal sheets did their best to improve on a sufficiently ~ text —Simeon Strunsky⟩ ⟨burly, arrogant, swashbuckling toper and ~ gossip —Douglas Bush⟩ ⟨belongs to a ~ genre of writing —Georges Duthuit⟩ ⟨witty, malicious, often ~ character studies —Peter Forster⟩ **b :** inclined to or indicative of licentious or corrupt habits **:** of depraved manners ⟨a ~ resort crowd⟩ ⟨soberest note in this ~, boomtown atmosphere —Davenport Steward⟩ **c :** encrusted or blotched with dirt or other foreign matter **:** FROWZY, GRIMY, SQUALID ⟨shell of the house is ~ with lichen and mildew —James Reynolds⟩ **syn** see ROUGH

scab·rous·ly *adv* **:** in a scabrous manner

scab·rous·ness *n* -ES **:** the quality or state of being scabrous

scabs *pl of* SCAB, *pres 3d sing of* SCAB

scabwort \'ₛ,ₛ\ *n* [ME, fr. ¹*scab* + *wort*] **:** ELECAMPANE

scac·chite \'ska,kīt\ *n* -s [It *scacchite,* fr. Arcangelo *Scacchi* †1894 Ital. mineralogist + It *-ite*] **:** a mineral $MnCl_2$ consisting of native manganese chloride found in volcanic regions

¹scad \'skad, 'skaa(ə)d\ *n, pl* **scad** *also* **scads** [origin unknown] **1 :** any of several carangid fishes: as **a :** BIG-EYED SCAD **b :** MACKEREL SCAD **c :** ROUND SCAD **2 :** CATALUFA

²scad \"\ *n* [origin unknown] *Scot* **:** a faint gleam of color or light

³scad \'skȧd\ *chiefly Scot var of* SCALD

⁴scad *also* **skad** \'skad\ *n* -s [prob. alter. of E dial. *scald,* fr. ²*scald*] **1 a :** a large number or quantity ⟨hooked a ~ of little fish —*Field & Stream*⟩ ⟨costs a ~ of money —Theodore Morrison⟩ **b scads** *pl* **:** a great abundance ⟨~*s* of money⟩ ⟨~*s* of guests⟩ ⟨~*s* of time⟩ ⟨~*s* of opportunities⟩ **2** *archaic* **:** DOLLAR, COIN — usu. used in pl. ⟨staggerin' along, jinglin' the ~*s* they had won —Bret Harte⟩

scad·dle *also* **skad·dle** \'skadᵊl\ *adj* [alter. of earlier *scathel* harmful, dangerous, of Scand origin; akin to OHG *skadal, skatal* harmful, Goth *skathuls,* OE *sceathian* to injure — more at SCATHE] **1** *dial Eng* **:** FIERCE, WILD **2** *dial Eng, of an animal* **:** badly behaved **:** SKITTISH

scae·na \'sēnə\ *n, pl* **scae·nae** \-ē,nē\ [L — more at SCENE] **:** the stage of a Roman theater — compare CAVEA

scae·vo·la \'sēvələ\ *n* [NL, after C. Mucius *Scaevola* 6th cent. B.C. Roman hero] **1** *cap* **:** a genus of shrubs (family Goodeniaceae) having flowers with the corolla tube split, anthers free, and an indehiscent succulent drupaceous fruit **2** -s **:** any plant of the genus *Scaevola*

scaf·fie \'skafi\ *n* -s [prob. by alter.] *Scot* **:** SCAVENGER

¹scaf·fold \'skafəld *also* -a,fōld\ *n* -s [ME, fr. ONF *escafaut,* modif. (perh. influenced by assumed ONF *escache* stilt) of (assumed) VL *catafalicum* — more at SKATE, CATAFALQUE] **1 a** (1) **:** a usu. temporary or movable platform (as a plank) supported by a wood or metal framework, jacks, poles, or brackets or suspended (as by ropes and tackle) and used by workmen (as bricklayers, painters, or miners) to stand or sit on and to support tools and material when working at considerable heights above floor or ground (2) **:** such a platform together with the structure that supports it — compare TRESTLE **b** (1) **:** a platform on which a criminal stands for execution esp. by hanging or beheading (2) **:** the penalty of death by execution esp. by hanging or beheading; *broadly* **:** CAPITAL PUNISHMENT — used with *the* ⟨condemned to the ~⟩ **c** *archaic* **:** a usu. temporary stand on which a public spectacle (as a dramatic performance) is staged **d** *obs* **:** a stand for spectators at a public spectacle (as a tournament or dramatic performance) **e** *chiefly New Eng* **:** a barn loft for storing hay or grain **:** HAYLOFT **f :** any platform at a considerable height above ground or floor level ⟨~*s* were used by some American Indians to dispose of the dead⟩ ⟨on the ~ the fishermen kept dip nets for the smaller trout —Julian Dana⟩ **g :** a supporting framework ⟨~ of a ski slide⟩ ⟨plantation bell hanging in a ~ separate and apart from the church —*Amer. Guide Series: La.*⟩ **2 :** an accumulation of adherent partly fused material forming an obstruction above the tuyeres in a blast furnace **3 :** FRAMEWORK 4; *also* **:** SCAFFOLD BRANCH

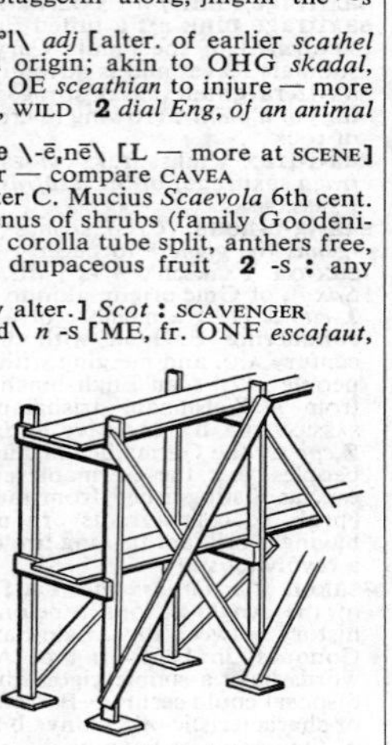

scaffold 1a(2)

²scaffold \"\ *vb* -ED/-ING/-S *vt* **1 a :** to place on or support by means of a scaffold **b :** to suspend (fresh-cut tobacco plants) upon a portable rack to wilt before hanging in the curing barn **2 a :** to furnish with a scaffold or scaffolding **:** erect scaffolding in front of or against ⟨the opera's ~*ed* shell —Leigh White⟩ **b :** to support (as an argument) by scaffolding ⟨book could well be ~*ed* more strongly with explanation and comment —Roland Mathias⟩ ~ *vi* **:** to form a scaffold esp. in smelting

scaf·fold·age \-dij\ *n* -s [¹*scaffold* + *-age*] **:** SCAFFOLD, SCAFFOLDING

scaffold branch *or* **scaffold limb** *n* [¹*scaffold*] **:** one of the main branches forming the framework of a tree or shrub

scaf·fold·er \-də(r)\ *n* -s [²*scaffold* + *-er*] **:** one who erects scaffolding

scaf·fold·ing \-diŋ, -dēŋ\ *n* -s [ME, fr. ¹*scaffold* + *-ing*] **1 a :** a system of scaffolds ⟨go up ladders and walk about ~*s* —J.D.Beresford⟩ ⟨erected the steel ~ to support the roof forms —*Civil Engineering*⟩ **b :** materials for scaffolds **2** [fr. gerund of ²*scaffold*] **a :** the construction of scaffolds **b** (1) **:** the formation of a scaffold in the smelting of ores (2) **:** SCAFFOLD 2 **3 a :** a framework serving as a supporting structure, base, or outline for something (as a literary work or a part of an organism) ⟨use of the epic as a ~ for his stories —Robert Halsband⟩ ⟨comprehending the naked ~ of an idea rather than its architectural fulfillment —H.V.Gregory⟩ ⟨cartilaginous skeleton serves as a temporary ~ for a skeleton of much harder material —Norbert Wiener⟩ **b :** evidence or explanatory matter tending to confirm, validate, or bolster something (as an argument) ⟨book . . . a little overequipped with the ~ of research —H.J.Laski⟩

scagl·io·la \skal'yōlə\ *n* -s [It, lit., little chip, dim. of *scaglia* scale, chip, of Gmc origin; akin to Goth *skalja* tile — more at SHELL] **:** an imitation of ornamental marble consisting of a base of finely ground gypsum mixed with glue, variegated on its surface while soft (as with marble, spar, or granite dust) and subsequently polished, and used for floors, columns, and other ornamental interior work

scaith \'skāth\ *dial Brit var of* SCATHE

¹sca·la \'skālə\ *n, pl* **sca·lae** \-ā,lē\ [NL, fr. LL, ladder, staircase — more at SCALE] **:** any of the three spiral canals of the cochlea

²scala \"\ [NL, fr. LL, ladder, staircase; fr. the resemblance of the shell to a spiral staircase] *syn of* EPITONIUM

³scala \"\ *n* -s [*Scala*] **:** a mollusk of the genus *Epitonium* **:** WENTLETRAP

scal·able \'skāləbəl\ *adj* [⁷*scale* + *-able*] **:** capable of being scaled — **scal·able·ness** *n* -ES — **scal·ably** \-blē\ *adv*

sca·lade \skə'läd\ *or* **sca·la·do** \-ä(,)dō\ *n* -s [obs. It *scalada,* fr. *scalare* to scale (fr. *scala* ladder, staircase, fr. LL) + *-ada* -ade — more at SCALE] *archaic* **:** ESCALADE

scal·age \'skālij, -lēj\ *n* -s [⁷*scale* + *-age*] **1 :** an allowance or percentage by which something (as listed weights, bulks, or prices of goods) is scaled down to compensate for loss (as by shrinkage or abrasion) **2 :** the act of scaling in weight, quantity, or dimensions **3 :** the amount that logs or timber scale

scala me·dia \-'mēdēə\ *n, pl* **scalae medi·ae** \-dē,ē\ [NL, lit., middle scala] **:** the membranous spiral canal containing the essential organ of hearing — compare COCHLEA

¹sca·lar \'skālə(r)\ *adj* [L *scalaris* of a ladder or staircase, fr. *scalae* stairs, ladder — more at SCALE] **1 :** arranged like a ladder **:** having an uninterrupted series of steps **:** GRADUATED, SCALARIFORM ⟨~ chain of authority in business organization⟩ ⟨~ cells⟩ **2** [prob. fr. ⁶*scale* + *-ar*] **:** describable by a number that can be represented by a point on a scale ⟨a ~ quantity⟩

²scalar \"\ *n* -s **1 a :** an undirected quantity in vector analysis and quaternions **:** a quantity fully described by a number — distinguished from *vector* **b :** a scalar number **2 :** a quantity (as mass or time) that has magnitude but does not involve any concept of direction — compare VECTOR 1b

sca·la·re \skə'la(a)rē, -lärə\ *n* -s [NL, specific epithet of *Pterophyllum scalare,* fr. L, neut. of *scalaris* of a ladder; fr. the barred pattern on its body] **:** a popular cichlid tropical aquarium fish (*Pterophyllum scalare*) of So. American origin laterally compressed with large pointed fins and strikingly barred with black and silver; *also* **:** a very similar but smaller fish (*P. eimekei*)

sca·lar·ia \skə'la(a)rēə\ [NL, fr. L *scalaris* of a ladder or staircase + NL *-ia;* fr. the resemblance of the shell to a spiral staircase] *syn of* EPITONIUM

sca·lar·i·an \-ēən\ *adj* [NL *Scalaria* + E *-an*] **:** SCALARIFORM 2

sca·lar·i·form \skə'la(a)rə,fȯrm\ *adj* [NL *scalariformis,* fr. L *scalaris* of a ladder + *-formis* -form] **1 :** resembling a ladder **:** having transverse bars or markings like the rounds of a ladder ⟨~ cells in plants⟩ **2 :** of or relating to the genus *Epitonium* or related forms — **sca·lar·i·form·ly** \ₛ¦ₛₛₛ¦lē\ *adv*

scalariform conjugation *n* **:** sexual union between cells in adjacent filaments of an alga — compare LATERAL CONJUGATION

scalariform-pitted tracheid \ₛ'ₛₛ,ₛ,ₛₛ-\ *n* **:** a tracheid having a ladderlike arrangement of pits

scal·a·ri·idae \,skalə'rīə,dē\ [NL, fr. *Scalaria,* type genus + *-idae*] *syn of* EPITONIIDAE

scalar product *n* **:** the product of two vectors that is obtained by multiplying the product of the magnitudes of the vectors by the cosine of the angle between them — called also *inner product;* compare DOT PRODUCT

sca·la·tion \skā'lāshən\ *n* -s [⁵*scale* + *-ation*] **:** LEPIDOSIS 2

scala tym·pa·ni \-'timpə,nī, -,nē\ *n, pl* **scalae tym·pa·no·rum** \-,timpə'nōrəm, -'nȯrəm\ [NL, lit., scala of the tympanum] **:** the lymph-filled spiral canal below the scala media in the cochlea of the ear communicating at its upper end with the scala vestibuli and abutting at its lower end upon the secondary tympanic membrane that separates the fenestra cochleae from the middle ear

scala ves·tib·u·li \-ve'stibyə,lī, -,lē\ *n, pl* **scalae ves·tib·u·lo·rum** \-ve,stibyə'lōrəm, -'lȯrəm\ [NL, lit., scala of the vestibule] **:** the lymph-filled spiral canal above the scala media in the cochlea of the ear connecting with the fenestra vestibuli and receiving vibrations from the stapes

scal·a·wag *or* **scal·ly·wag** *also* **scal·la·wag** *or* **skal·a·wag** \'skalə,wag, -lē,w-, -waa(ə)g, -waig\ *n* -s [origin unknown] **1 :** RASCAL, SCAMP, REPROBATE ⟨hand a quarter to a bewhiskered old ~ —James Thurber⟩ ⟨something good to say about the worst *scallywag* —John Buchan⟩ **2 :** an animal of little value esp. because of poor feeding, smallness, or age **3 :** a white Southerner acting as a Republican in the time of reconstruction after the Civil War

scal·a·wag·gery \-garē\ *n* -ES [*scalawag* + *-ery*] **:** the conduct or doings of a scalawag

¹scald \'skȯld\ *vb* -ED/-ING/-S [ME *scalden* to burn with hot liquid, fr. ONF *escalder,* fr. LL *excaldare* to wash in warm water, fr. L *ex-* + *calida, calda* warm water, fr. fem. of *calidus, caldus* warm — more at CAULDRON] *vt* **1 :** to burn with hot liquid or steam **:** pain or injure by contact with any hot fluid or irritating chemicals **2 a :** to subject to the action of boiling water or steam (as for loosening hair or feathers on a slaughtered animal, for loosening skin of fruits or vegetables, or for stopping enzyme action or bacterial growth) ⟨~ a tomato before peeling it⟩ ⟨~ dishes⟩ — compare BLANCH, PARBOIL **b :** to immerse in a boiling liquid or chemical **c :** to bring (a liquid) to a temperature just below the boiling point ⟨~ milk⟩ **d :** to cook (a slurry of grain meal and water) as the first step in the mashing process by pouring boiling water over the meal or by using live steam to heat the mixture usu. in a pressure cooker **3 :** to affect as painfully as by the application of boiling water ⟨tears that ~ the cheek⟩ **4 :** SCORCH ⟨sun-*scalded* ground —Myrtle R. White⟩ **5** *chiefly Irish* **:** WORRY, TORMENT ⟨it ~*s* my heart⟩ ~ *vi* **1 :** to produce the effects of boiling water or scorching heat **:** inflict agonizing pain ⟨a desert of dry ~*ing* sand —Daniel Defoe⟩ **2 a :** to suffer the effects of boiling water or scorching heat **b :** to be affected by scald ⟨the apples ~*ed* severely in storage⟩

²scald \"\ *n* -s **1 :** an injury to the skin or flesh caused by some hot liquid, by steam, or by irritating chemicals ⟨dressed the ~ with carron oil —A.J.Cronin⟩ **2 a :** a process of subjection (as of food or dishes) to scalding **b :** the act of scalding ⟨shorter ~*s* apparently did not completely inactivate the enzymes —*Biol. Abstracts*⟩ **3** *dial chiefly Eng* **:** the hot bath or solution in which something is or may be scalded **4** *dial chiefly Eng* **:** a piece of land (as part of a larger field) that is prone to scorching and too rapid drying **5 :** any of several plant diseases marked esp. by discoloration suggesting injury by heat: as **a :** CRANBERRY SCALD **b :** a burning and browning of plant tissues resulting from high temperatures or from the combined actions of high temperature and intense light **c :** a browning of bean plants caused by excess of manganese

uptake **d :** a storage discoloration of apples or pears due to the volatile products given off by the ripening tissues that is now almost wholly controlled by the use of oiled wrappings which absorb these substances **6 :** a nonspecific inflammation of the feet of sheep often the forerunner of foot rot — **get a good scald on** *dial* **:** to have good success with

³scald \"\ *adj* [*scall* + *-ed*] **1** *archaic* **:** SCABBY, SCURFY ⟨powder or meal was first used . . . to conceal their ~ heads —Tobias Smollett⟩ **2** *archaic* **:** SCURVY, SHABBY, CONTEMPTIBLE ⟨~ rogues⟩

⁴scald *n* -s [alter. (influenced by ³*scald*) of *scall*] **:** scurf on the head **:** a scabby spot or condition caused by disease

⁵scald \'skäd\ *chiefly Scot var of* SCOLD

⁶scald *var of* SKALD

⁷scald \'skōld\ *adj* [by shortening] **:** SCALDED ⟨like coffee covered with ~ cream —Charles Kingsley⟩

scald crow *n* [prob. fr. ³*scald*] *Irish* **:** HOODED CROW

¹scalded *adj* [fr. past part. of ¹*scald*] **1 a :** cooked, burned, or treated with boiling liquid ⟨~ meal⟩ **b :** heated to just below the boiling point ⟨~ milk⟩ **2** *chiefly Austral* **:** composed of hard bare or eroded ground ⟨~ plains⟩

²scalded *adj* [⁴*scald* + *-ed*] **:** affected with scald ⟨~ fruit⟩ ⟨a sheep's ~ foot⟩

¹scald·er \'skȯldə(r)\ *n* -s [¹*scald* + *-er*] **:** one that scalds: as **a :** a cannery worker who sterilizes raw fruit by scalding it with lye and water **b :** a machine used for scalding

²scald·er \'skädə(r)\ *vt* -ED/-ING/-S [prob. freq. of ¹*scald*] *dial Eng* **:** SCALD

³scald·er \'skȯldə(r)\ *n* -s [NL, fr. ON *skāld* skald] *archaic* **:** SKALD

scaldfish \'=,=\ *n* [prob. fr. ³*scald*] **:** ²MEGRIM a

scald head *n* [³*scald*] *archaic* **:** any of several diseases of the scalp characterized by falling out of the hair and by pustules the discharge of which forms scales

scaldic *var of* SKALDIC

¹scald·ing \'skȯldiŋ, -dēŋ\ *n* -s [ME, fr. gerund of *scalden* to scald] **1 :** the act or process of burning or treating with steam or hot liquid (as for cooking, cleansing, bathing, or rinsing) **2 scaldings** *pl, archaic* **:** boiling-hot liquid **3 :** ²SCALD 5 **4 :** a dark discoloration of tobacco leaves resulting from a too rapid increase in temperature during the early stages of curing

²scalding \"\ *adj* [fr. pres. part. of ¹*scald*] **1 :** causing the sensation of scalding or burning ⟨coffee felt ~ all the way down —Wirt Williams⟩ ⟨the ~ pie in my mouth —J.W.Ellison b.1929⟩ **2 :** BOILING ⟨sprayed with ~ water to extract the tanning properties —*Amer. Guide Series: Pa.*⟩ **3 :** SCORCHING, ARDENT ⟨succumb to a dusky oasis from the ~ sun —Claudia Cassidy⟩ **4 :** BITING, STINGING, SCATHING ⟨series of ~ articles —Christopher Isherwood⟩ ⟨a very ~ letter —Virginia D. Dawson & Betty D. Wilson⟩ ⟨a ~ comment on human avarice —*Time*⟩

scalds *pres 3d sing of* SCALD, *pl of* SCALD

¹scale \'skāl, *esp before pause or consonant* -āəl\ *n* -s [ME *scale, scole*, fr. ON *skāl* bowl, scale of a balance; akin to OHG *scāla* cup, bowl, *scala* husk, shell — more at SHELL] **1** *dial* **:** a drinking vessel **:** CUP, BOWL ⟨offered him a ~ of beer —Peter Abrahams⟩ **2 a :** either pan or tray of a balance **b :** BALANCE 1a(1)— usu. used in pl. sometimes with *pair* ⟨weighed on the only pair of ~*s* in the hamlet —Flora Thompson⟩ and sometimes sing. in constr. ⟨weighing something on a big brass ~*s* —Helen Eustis⟩ **c :** an instrument or machine for weighing ⟨bathroom ~⟩ ⟨counter ~⟩ ⟨livestock ~⟩ — often used in pl. but sometimes sing. in constr.; see COMPUTING SCALE, CYLINDER SCALE, PLATFORM SCALE, SPRING SCALE **3 a :** the position where a grave decision (as for life or death) is called for or a turning point is imminent **:** BALANCE — often used in pl. ⟨you never forget that your life, as well as his, is in the ~*s* —E.L.Beach⟩ **b :** the process or situation in which something (as a force or set of values) is opposed to or contrasted with other like things or an established or assumed standard for such things ⟨weight of his authority was thrown into the ~ against the teachings —Harvey Graham⟩ — usu. used in pl. ⟨weighed his own life and the life of his neighbors in the ~*s* —V.L.Parrington⟩ ⟨rig the ~*s* heavily in favor of the values you see the need of preserving —G.O.Williams⟩ **4 :** WEIGHT, SIZE — used esp. of livestock ⟨new breed is cherry red, possesses lots of ~ —L.M.Winters⟩

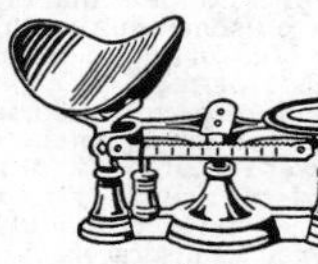

counter scale

²scale \"\ *vb* -ED/-ING/-S *vt* **1 a :** to weigh in scales **b** *obs* **:** MEASURE, COMPARE ⟨*scaling* his present bearing with his past —Shak.⟩ **2 :** to make or to lay out so as to be of exact weight, quantity, or dimensions; *specif* **:** to divide into exact parts by weight ⟨~ dough into loaves⟩ **~** *vi* **:** to have a specified weight on scales ⟨at 19 he *scaled* 12 stone —G.E.Odd⟩ ⟨a dog *scaling* 50 pounds⟩ — often used with *in* ⟨man *scaling* in at over 200 pounds⟩

³scale \"\ *n* -s [ME, fr. ON *skāli*; akin to ON *sky* cloud — more at SKY] *dial chiefly Eng* **:** HUT

⁴scale \"\ *vb* -ED/-ING/-S [ME *skailen, scalen*, prob. of Scand origin; akin to ON *skilja* to separate, divide — more at SKILL] *vt* **1** *chiefly Scot* **:** DISPERSE, SCATTER ⟨~ a crowd⟩ **2** *chiefly Scot* **:** to spread esp. wastefully **3** *chiefly Scot* **:** SPILL ⟨~ her tea⟩ **~** *vi, chiefly Scot* **:** DISPERSE, SCATTER

⁵scale \"\ *n* -s [ME *scale, skale*, fr. MF *escale*, of Gmc origin; akin to OE *scealu* husk, shell, scale of a balance — more at SHELL] **1 a :** a small, more or less flattened, rigid, and definitely circumscribed plate forming part of the external body covering of an animal, in fishes consisting of dermal bony tissue, in recent forms being commonly in imbricated rows with their posterior edges partly overlapping, and in reptiles and on the legs of birds being horny, circumscribed, and slightly differentiated areas of the epidermis — see FISH illustration **b :** any of various usu. flattened and more or less chitinized outgrowths of the body wall of an insect (as those clothing the wings of most moths and butterflies) **c :** the scaly covering of a scaled animal **:** a coating of scales **d :** a plate of similar structure making up wool fiber and distinguishing it from hair **2 scales** *pl* **:** impediments to seeing rightly ⟨I hope in time the ~*s* will be taken off the eyes of the landlord —William Ellis⟩ **3 :** a small thin dry lamina shed (as in many skin diseases) from the skin **4 :** a thin outer lamina or layer removable as a peel or in flakes or chips: as **a** (1) **:** a black scaly coating of oxide (as magnetic oxide) forming on the surface of iron when heated for processing (as by hammering or rolling) — called also *iron scale, mill scale;* see HAMMER SCALE (2) **:** a similar coating forming on other metals **b :** a film of tartar encrusting the teeth **c :** a hard incrustation that is deposited esp. on the inside of a vessel (as a boiler) in which water is heated, that in the case of hard water commonly contains calcium sulfate as the principal component, and that is objectionable because it is a nonconductor of heat **5 a :** one of the modified leaves serving in most seed plants to protect a bud before expansion — see BUD SCALE **b :** a thin, membranous, chaffy, or woody bract ⟨the ~ of an alder catkin⟩ ⟨the cone ~ of a pine⟩ **c :** RAMENTUM 2a **d :** the small appendage at the base of the petal in some plants of the family Caryophyllaceae **e :** one of the disklike trichomes making up the characteristic silvery or scurfy pubescence of the foliage in some plants (as Russian olive) **6 a :** one of the small overlapping usu. metal pieces forming the outer surface of scale armor ⟨representations of Byzantine warriors nearly always show corselets of ~*s* —J.G.Mann⟩ **b :** SCALE ARMOR **7 :** either of the pieces fastened one on each side of the tang of a cutting instrument (as a knife) to form the outside of the handle **8 a** *or* **scale insect** *also* **scale louse** *or* **scale bug :** any of numerous small very prolific insects constituting Coccidae and related families of the suborder Homoptera, having young that suck the juices of plants, adult males that lack mouthparts and do not feed and have a single pair of wings, and adult females that are usu. permanently attached to the host plant, structurally degenerate with most of the external differentiation lost, similar to a scale on the surface of the host, and often obscured by a waxy or powdery secretion that protects the female and her eggs, and including many extremely destructive pests of economic plants as well as a few that yield valuable products — compare COCHINEAL, LAC **b :** infestation with or disease caused by scale insects ⟨our roses are full of ~ this year⟩ ⟨a promising citrus plantation had been destroyed by ~⟩ **9 :** SCALE WAX

⁶scale \"\ *vb* -ED/-ING/-S [ME *scalen*, fr. ⁵*scale*] *vt* **1 a :** to remove the scales from (as by scraping) ⟨~ a fish⟩ **b :** to remove scale from ⟨~ a boiler⟩ **c :** to take off the surface of **:** PEEL, HUSK ⟨~ chestnuts⟩ **d :** to loosen and remove fragments from (as a rock surface) ⟨~ a rock wall after blasting⟩ **2 :** to take off in thin layers or scales **:** remove as if consisting of a scale **:** peel off esp. in pieces ⟨~ tartar from the teeth⟩ — often used with *off* ⟨~ off the bark of a tree⟩ ⟨flames that *scaled* off the soft stone carvings of the interior —F.L.Paxson⟩ **3** *obs* **:** to clean (as the inside of a cannon) by the explosion of a small quantity of powder **4 :** to form scale on **:** cover with scale ⟨water ~*s* a boiler⟩ **5 :** to throw (as a thin flat stone) so that the edge cuts the air or so that it skips (as on a water surface) **:** SKIM, SAIL ⟨took off his hat, *scaled* it across the room —Burt Arthur⟩ ⟨*scaled* the letter . . . across the broad-topped walnut desk —Don Tracy⟩ ⟨*scaled* the discus 194 feet 6 inches —*N.Y.Times*⟩ **~** *vi* **1 :** to separate and come off in thin layers or laminae **:** FLAKE ⟨some sandstone ~*s* by exposure⟩ — often used with *off* ⟨bark that ~*s* off readily⟩ **2 :** to shed scales or fragmentary surface matter **:** EXFOLIATE, SPALL ⟨*scaling* skin⟩ ⟨a *scaling* wall of rock⟩ **3 :** to become encrusted with a hard deposit — used esp. of vessels or pipes containing water or chemical solutions

⁷scale \"\ *n* -s [ME, ladder, staircase, line marked by graduations, fr. LL *scala* ladder, staircase, fr. L *scalae* (pl.) stairs, rungs of a ladder, ladder; akin to L *scandere* to climb — more at SCAN] **1 a** (1) **:** an indication of the relationship between the distances on a map, chart, or plan and the corresponding actual distances usu. in the form of a direct statement (as 1 inch to 1 mile), a representative fraction (as 1/250,000 or 1:250,000), a graphic measure (as a bar or line), or a line subdivided at selected intervals (2) **:** a series of spaces marked off by lines or dots and used for measuring distances, amounts, or quantities **b :** a mathematical instrument consisting of a strip (as of wood, plastic, or metal) with one or more sets of spaces graduated and numbered on its surface and used esp. for measuring or laying off distances and dimensions (as in drawing or plotting) — see ARCHITECTS' SCALE, ENGINEER'S SCALE; compare RULE **c :** a basis for a numeral system ⟨the decimal ~⟩ ⟨the binary ~⟩ **d :** one of the measures on a typewriter by which paper is aligned and centered, margin and tabulator stops set, or characters centered **2 a** *obs* **:** LADDER **b** *obs* **:** a flight of stairs **:** STAIRCASE **c** *archaic* **:** a means of ascending or descending ⟨in th' ascending ~ of heav'n the stars that usher evening rose —John Milton⟩ **3 a :** a graduated series of musical tones ascending or descending in order of pitch according to a specified scheme of their intervals and varying in pitch arrangement and size of intervals according to the number of tones to the octave ⟨descending ~⟩ ⟨minor ~⟩ ⟨major ~⟩ **b :** a scale on a given keynote ⟨the ~ of G⟩ ⟨played the ~ of D minor⟩ **c :** the compass of a voice or instrument **d :** the width of an organ pipe in proportion to its length that may be increased to give full and sonorous tones and decreased to give thin edgy tones **4 :** a graduated or ordered series of degrees, stages, or classes **:** a scheme of comparative rank or order (as of forms of life) ⟨the ~ of being⟩ ⟨a ~ of taxation⟩ ⟨color ~⟩**: a :** a set of graduated wage rates or a wage consistent with such rates ⟨workmen were paid the union ~⟩ **b :** the full range of tones of a photographic material expressed in terms of the brightnesses recorded, the exposure given, or the resultant range of densities **c :** a table for calculating cost based on size ⟨engravers' ~⟩ ⟨electrotypers' ~⟩ **5 a :** relative dimensions without difference in proportion of parts **:** size or degree of the parts or components in any complex thing compared with other like things; *esp* **:** the relative proportion of the linear dimensions of parts (as of a drawing or model) to the dimensions of the corresponding parts of the object that is represented ⟨a map on a ~ of an inch to a mile⟩ **b :** a distinctive relative size, extent, or degree ⟨despite high-*scale* national employment —*Current History*⟩ — often used with *on* ⟨much of the artist's sculpture is on a large ~ —*Current Biog.*⟩ ⟨printing color reproductions on a commercial ~ —*Encyc. Americana*⟩ ⟨gambling on a grand ~⟩ **6 :** a standard for reference in estimating or judging ⟨a ~ to measure degrees of crime⟩ **7 a :** relative size of esp. architectural parts as compared with the whole or with the human figure ⟨importance of ~ and detailing to the layout as a whole —*Architectural Rev.*⟩ ⟨~ is produced by introducing into the design some unit which acts as a visual measuring rod —T.F.Hamlin⟩ ⟨harmony of ~ . . . in a room —Mildred J. O'Brien⟩ **b :** proper or intended size, proportion, and relationship with reference to other elements and to the whole or to the setting ⟨the one essential to remember in carrying out the necessary periodic replanting in the park is ~ —S.Lang⟩ ⟨in our time, ~ has survived splendor —Alfred Frankfurter⟩ **8 :** a series of tests graded from easy to difficult or of performances graded from bad to good to be used in rating individual intellectual or emotional behavior or attitudes ⟨rating ~⟩ ⟨intelligence ~⟩ ⟨achievement ~⟩ — **in scale :** in conformity to its due proportion in a fixed scale ⟨a building that is *in scale* with its surroundings⟩ — **out of scale :** not in conformity to its due proportion in a fixed scale — **to scale** *adv* **:** according to the proportions of an established scale of measurement ⟨floor plans drawn *to scale*⟩

⁸scale \"\ *vb* -ED/-ING/-S [ME *scalen*, fr. *scale*, n., ladder] *vt* **1 a :** to attack with or take by means of scaling ladders ⟨~ a castle wall⟩ ⟨~ a walled town⟩ **b :** to climb up or reach by means of a ladder ⟨*scaling* the girl's bedchamber —E.A.Poe⟩ ⟨firemen *scaled* the building⟩ **c :** to ascend or go over by climbing or as if by climbing **:** clamber up ⟨*scaling* the mighty barrier of the Alps —G.F.Maclear⟩ ⟨climbers *scaled* the mountain face⟩ ⟨wildcats might ~ the fence —Zane Grey⟩ **d :** to press one's way up into or over typically with or as if with strong flight ⟨falcon *scaling* the sky⟩ **e :** to reach the highest point of or surmount typically with strong effort ⟨~ the moral and esthetic heights in the novel —Lionel Trilling⟩ **2 :** to treat according to a scale with gradation or in proportion: **a :** to arrange in a graduated series ⟨~ a test⟩ **b :** to measure by or as if by a scale: as (1) **:** to measure (logs) to ascertain the number of board feet (2) **:** to estimate the yield of (standing timber) in board feet **c :** to pattern, make, regulate, set, or estimate according to some proportion, rate, standard, or control **:** increase or reduce according to a fixed ratio ⟨a production schedule *scaled* to actual need⟩ ⟨~ the prices of tickets for a theatrical performance⟩ — often used with *down* or *up* ⟨~ up imports⟩ ⟨~ down the output of a mine⟩ **d :** to crop, reduce, or enlarge (as a pictorial illustration) to fit a given space or layout; *also* **:** to determine the dimensions of (as an illustration) that will result from such scaling **~** *vi* **1 :** to climb by or as if by a ladder ⟨firemen given the command to ~⟩ **2 :** to rise in a graduated series ⟨windows *scaling* beside a stairway⟩ **3 a :** MEASURE ⟨this tree . . . probably ~*s* no more than about 50 feet —Alexander Tewnion⟩ **b** *of a log, tree, or stand of timber* **:** to yield an estimated number of board feet ⟨growth ~*s* from forty to sixty thousand board feet an acre —*Nature Mag.*⟩ **4 :** to sing or play a musical scale **:** rise high in pitch ⟨high with the last line *scaled* her voice —Alfred Tennyson⟩ **syn** see ASCEND

⁹scale \"\ *n* -s [⁸*scale*] **1** *obs* **:** ESCALADE **2 :** an estimate of the amount of sound lumber in logs or standing timber

¹⁰scale \"\ *adj* [⁷*scale*] **:** drawn or constructed to scale ⟨~ map⟩ ⟨~ drawing⟩ ⟨~ model of an automobile⟩

¹¹scale *n* -s [F or It; F *escale*, fr. It *scala*, ladder, landing place, fr. LL, ladder, staircase — more at ⁷SCALE] *obs* **:** a landing place **:** PORT

scale armor *n* [⁵*scale*] **:** armor made of small metallic scales overlapping and fastened upon leather or cloth

scaleback \'=,=\ *n* [⁵*scale* + *back*] **:** SCALE WORM

scale bark *n* **1 :** SHAGBARK HICKORY **2 :** RHYTIDOME

scaleboard \'=,=\ *n* [⁵*scale* + *board*] **1** *archaic* **:** thin strips of sheet iron used by printers as leads; *also* **:** thin strips of material (as wood or paperboard) placed in an imposed form before locking up **2 a :** thin wooden boards once used for book covers **b :** a thin leaf of wood used for veneering

scale bug *n* [⁵*scale*] **:** ⁵SCALE 8a

scale carp *n* **:** a normally scaled variety of the common carp — compare LEATHER CARP, MIRROR CARP

scale caterpillar *n* **:** a lepidopterous larva that feeds on scale insects; *esp* **:** the larva of a small moth (*Laetilia coccidivora*) of the family Pyralididae

Sca·le·cide \'skālə,sīd\ *trademark* — used for an agent that destroys scale insects

¹scaled \'skāld, *esp before pause or consonant* -āəld\ *adj* [ME, fr. ⁵*scale* + *-ed*] **1 a :** covered with scales or a scalelike structure ⟨~ fish⟩ ⟨~ reptile⟩ ⟨~ moth⟩ or with scalelike parts that overlap in the manner of roof tiles ⟨the ~ bud of a beech tree⟩ **b :** covered with tiles overlapping like scales **c :** having a surface pattern or texture resembling scales ⟨~ jewelry⟩ **2 :** having feathers that in appearance or arrangement somewhat resemble scales — see SCALED DOVE, SCALED QUAIL

²scaled \"\ *adj* [fr. past part. of ⁶*scale*] **:** lacking scales **:** having had the scales removed ⟨~ herring⟩

³scaled \"\ *adj* [⁷*scale* + *-ed*] **:** furnished with or adjusted to a scale ⟨traveled . . . over ~ highways —*From Australia*⟩ ⟨chose delicately ~ antiques —*This Week Mag.*⟩

scaled dove *or* **scale dove** *n* [¹*scaled*] **:** any of several doves (genus *Scardafella*) of tropical America that are pale gray below and usu. light grayish brown above with dark-margined feathers — compare INCA DOVE

¹scale–down \'=,=\ *n* -s [⁶*scale* + *down*] **:** a reduction according to a fixed ratio ⟨a *scale-down* of debts⟩

²scale–down \"\ *adj* **:** characterized by a reduction according to a fixed ratio ⟨*scale-down* investment buying⟩

scaled quail *or* **scaled partridge** *n* [¹*scaled*] **:** a crested partridge (*Callipepla squamata*) of the southwestern U.S. and northern Mexico that is largely grayish brown above with pale bluish gray black-tipped breast feathers — called also *blue quail*

scale duck *n* [⁵*scale*] **1** *dial Brit* **:** SHELDRAKE **2** *dial Brit* **:** MERGANSER

scale effect *n* [⁷*scale*] **:** the correction necessary to apply to measurements made on a model in a wind tunnel in order to deduce corresponding values for the full-sized object

scale fern *n* [⁵*scale*] **:** a small European fern (*Ceterach officinarum*) with chaffy coriaceous fronds

scale fly *n* **:** the winged male of a scale

scale hopper *n* [¹*scale*] **:** a bin mounted on a scale so that its contents can be weighed

scale house *n* **:** a shelter for the beam of an outdoor scale

scale insect *or* **scale louse** *n* [⁵*scale*] **:** ⁵SCALE 8a

scale leaf *n* **:** a scalelike structure that is morphologically a leaf often reduced in size (as a bud scale, various bracts, or the leaves of various conifers)

scale·less \'skā(ə)lləs\ *adj* [partly fr. ⁷*scale* + *-less;* partly fr. ⁵*scale* + *-less*] **:** lacking a scale **:** destitute of scales

scalelike \'=,=\ *adj* [⁵*scale* + *like*] **:** resembling a scale ⟨~ design⟩; *specif* **:** reduced to a minute appressed element resembling a scale ⟨~ leaves⟩

scale·man \'=mən\ *n, pl* **scalemen** [¹*scale* + *man*] **1 :** one who repairs scales **2 :** one whose work is weighing goods or ingredients sometimes with automatic scales **3** [⁶*scale* + *man*] **:** a worker who removes scale from newly-processed iron and steel equipment

scale moss *n* **:** LEAFY LIVERWORT

sca·lene \(')skā¦lēn\ *adj* [LL *scalenus*, fr. Gk *skalēnos* uneven, unequal, scalene; akin to Gk *skolios* crooked — more at CYLINDER] **1** *of a triangle* **:** having the sides unequal — see TRIANGLE illustration **2** [NL *scalenus*] **:** of, relating to, or being a scalenus muscle

sca·le·no·he·dral \skā¦lēnə¦hēdrəl\ *adj* [NL *scalenohedron* + E *-al*] **:** of, relating to, or having the form of a scalenohedron ⟨~ crystal⟩ ⟨~ calcite⟩

sca·le·no·he·dron \=,==ˈhēdrən\ *n, pl* **scalenohedrons** \-nz\ *or* **scalenohe·dra** \-rə\ [NL, fr. Gk *skalēnos* scalene + NL *-hedron*] **:** a hemihedral form bounded ideally by scalene triangles: **a** *in the hexagonal system* **:** one of 12 faces resembling a double 6-sided pyramid **b** *in the tetragonal system* **:** one of 8 faces somewhat resembling the disphenoid

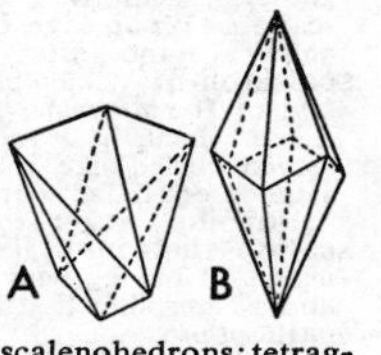

scalenohedrons: tetragonal, *A;* ditrigonal or hexagonal, *B*

sca·le·nous \skā'lēnəs\ *adj* [LL *scalēnus*] **:** SCALENE

sca·le·nus \skā'lēnəs\ *n, pl* **scale·ni** \-ē,nī, -ē,nē\ [NL, fr. LL or Gk; LL *scalenus* scalene, fr. Gk *skalēnos* uneven, scalene] **:** any of usu. three deeply situated muscles on each side of the neck each extending from the transverse processes of two or more cervical vertebrae to the first or second rib

scalepan \'=,=\ *n* [¹*scale* + *pan*] **:** a pan of a scale for weighing

¹scal·er \'skālə(r)\ *n* -s [⁸*scale* + *-er*] **1 :** one that climbs (as a wall or mountain) or attacks or captures (as a castle) by climbing **2 :** one that measures by means of a scale: as **a :** one that scales logs or standing timber **b :** an electronic device that operates a recorder (as of nuclear disintegrations or cosmic rays) after a specified number of impulses appearing too rapidly for individual recording

²scaler \"\ *n* -s [⁶*scale* + *-er*] **1 :** one that removes scale (as from metal) **2 :** one that removes scales (as from fish)

³scaler \"\ *n* -s [²*scale* + *-er*] **:** one that weighs goods with scales

scale rule *n* [⁷*scale*] **:** a graduated stick having the number of board feet in logs of given diameters and lengths marked upon it and used in scaling logs or timber — compare LOG RULE, LOG SCALE

scales *pl of* SCALE, *pres 3d sing of* SCALE

scales·man \'skā(ə)lzmən\ *n, pl* **scalesmen** [¹*scale*] **:** SCALEMAN 2

scaletail \'=,=\ *also* **scale–tailed squirrel** \'=,=-\ *n* [⁵*scale*] **:** a rodent of the genus *Anomalurus* having horny scales under the base of the tail

scale tank *n* [¹*scale*] **:** a tank for spirit mounted on a scale so that the contents can be weighed

¹scale–up \'=,=\ *n* -s [⁶*scale* + *up*] **:** an increase according to a fixed ratio ⟨a *scale-up* of wages⟩

²scale–up \'=,=\ *adj* **:** characterized by an increase according to a fixed ratio ⟨*scale-up* buying in cotton futures⟩

scale wax *n* [⁵*scale*] **:** partly refined paraffin wax obtained by sweating slack wax so that only a small percentage of oil remains — called also *paraffin scale*

scalewing \'=,=\ *n* [⁵*scale* + *wing*] **:** MOTH, BUTTERFLY

scalewise \'=,=\ *adv* (*or adj*) [⁷*scale* + *-wise*] **:** in the manner of a scale ⟨diatonic tones are used ~ —*Down Beat*⟩ ⟨in some of the organ works, he was hypnotized by ~ movement —W.H.Mellers⟩

scale worm *n* [⁵*scale*] **:** any of numerous chaetopod worms of *Polynoe* and related genera that have two rows of large elytra along the back — called also *scaleback*

scaley *var of* SCALY

scalier *comparative of* SCALY

scaliest *superlative of* SCALY

scal·i·ness \'skālēnəs, -lin-\ *n* -ES **:** the quality or state of being scaly

¹scaling *n* -s [fr. *gerund of* ⁸*scale*] **1 :** an attack, conquest, or ascent by or as if by means of ladders **2 :** a measurement, arrangement, or adjustment according to a scale **3 :** a system of trading by buying or selling at specified price intervals on a rise or fall in the market in order to average one's costs or profits

²scaling *n* -s [fr. gerund of ⁶*scale*] **1 a :** the act or process of removing scales (as from fish) **b :** the act or process of removing scale (as from the teeth or from metal) **2 a :** deposition of scale (as in steam condensers) **b :** falling scale or fragments of it **3 :** scaly structure, markings, or arrangement **:** LEPIDOSIS

scaling circuit *n* [*scaling* (fr. pres. part. of ⁸*scale*) + *circuit*] **:** ¹SCALER 2b

scall \'skȯl\ *n* -s [ME, fr. ON *skalli* bald head; perh. akin to ON *skāl* bowl — more at SCALE] **:** a scurf or scabby disease esp. of the scalp

scallawag *var of* SCALAWAG

scalled \'skȯld\ *or* **scall** \'skȯl\ *archaic var of* ³SCALD

¹scal·lion \'skalyən\ *or* **scul·lion** \'skəl-\ *n* -s [ME *scalone, scaloun*, fr. AF *scalun*, fr. (assumed) VL *escalonia*, fr. L *ascalonia* (*caepa*) Ascalonian onion, fr. fem. of *ascalonius* of Ascalon, fr. *Ascalon-, Ascalo* Ascalon, seaport in southern

Palestine] **1 :** SHALLOT **2 :** LEEK **3 :** an onion forming a thick basal portion without a normal bulb as a result of disease, attacks of insects, or unfavorable environmental conditions **4 :** GREEN ONION

[2]scallion \"\ *vi* -ED/-ING/-S *of an onion* **:** to form a scallion

[1]scal·lom \ˈskaləm\ *n* -S [origin unknown] **:** a straight rod like a stake but usu. thinner with the ends secured by being twisted round another rod used in basketry esp. to serve as a foundation (as for fitching or randing)

[2]scallom \"\ *vt* -ED/-ING/-S **:** to join (as the end of a scallom) to a rod by twisting **:** PLAIT

[1]scal·lop \ˈskäləp, ˈskal-\ *also* **scol·lop** \ˈskäləp\ *n* -S [ME *scalop*, fr. MF *escalope* shell, of Gmc origin; akin to MD *schelpe* shell — more at SCALP] **1 a :** any of many marine bivalve mollusks of the family Pectinidae that have the shell characteristically radially ribbed and the edge undulated, the mantle edges bearing well-developed ocelli, a single large adductor muscle which is esteemed a great delicacy and is the only part commonly used as food and that usu. do not attach themselves but are able to swim by opening and closing the valves — see BAY SCALLOP, GIANT SCALLOP **b :** the adductor muscle of scallop (as the bay scallop and giant scallop) cooked and served as food — usu. used in pl. **2** *or* **scallop shell a :** one of the valves of the shell of a scallop **b :** a dish (as a baking dish) shaped like one of these valves **3 a** (1) **:** one of a usu. continuous series of curves forming an edge or design (as on cloth, leather, or metal) ⟨pillowcases with small ∼*s*⟩ ⟨gables trimmed with ∼*s*⟩ (2) **:** a small sharply defined curve esp. in a series ⟨sunken road winding in ∼*s* —Ellen Glasgow⟩ ⟨cigarettes traced little ∼*s* in the darkness —Howard Hunt⟩ ⟨rising and falling ∼*s* of the waves —J.E.Macdonnell⟩ **b :** a row or design of scallops **:** SCALLOPING ⟨an edging consisting of small ∼*s*⟩ **c :** a decorative motif in the form of a scallop shell **:** ESCALLOP **4** *or* **scallop squash :** CYMLING **5** [F *escalope* — more at SCALLOPINI] **:** a thin slice of boneless meat

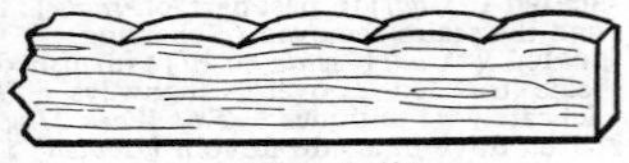

scallops 3a(1)

[2]scallop \"\ *also* **scollop** \"\ *vb* -ED/-ING/-S *vt* **1** *or* **escallop** [*escallop* fr. earlier *escallop* scallop shell, alter. (influenced by MF *escalope* shell) of [1]*scallop*] **:** to bake in a sauce usu. covered with seasoned bread or cracker crumbs ⟨∼ the potatoes⟩ ⟨oysters ∼*ed*⟩ ⟨∼*ed* peaches⟩ **2 a :** to shape, cut, or finish an edge or border in scallops **b :** to form scallops in ⟨concentrated settlement ∼*s* the eastern border of the country —P.E.James⟩ ∼ *vi* **1 :** to cook by scalloping ⟨veal . . . tucked into the oven to ∼ —T.H.Fielding⟩ **2 :** to gather or dredge scallops

scallop budding *n* **:** a mode of budding by paring off a strip of bark from the stock and applying the bud with its wood directly to the surface thus formed

scal·loped \-pt\ *adj* [[1]*scallop* + *-ed*] **:** having or forming a wavy edge, border, or design ⟨∼ neckline⟩ ⟨battlement-*scalloped* walls and turrets —Jerome Ellison⟩ ⟨lofty sierra arising from all around the ∼ shore —S.E.Morison⟩ — compare INVECTED

scal·lop·er \-pə(r)\ *n* -S [[2]*scallop* + *-er*] **1 a :** one that dredges for or gathers scallops **b** *or* **scallop dragger :** a boat equipped and used to dredge for scallops **2 :** one that finishes cloth (as for awnings, clothing, or embroidery) with scallops or scalloped designs

scalloping *n* -S [fr. gerund of [2]*scallop*] **1 :** the act or work of gathering scallops **2 a :** the act or work of making ornamental scallops **b :** an edge, border, or design of scallops ⟨between an empty sea and a firm ∼ of sand —P.H.Newby⟩

scal·lo·pi·ni \ˌskäləˈpēnē\ *n* -S [modif. (influenced by [1]*scallop*) of It *scaloppine*, pl. of *scaloppina*, dim. of *scaloppa* thin slice of meat, fr. F *escalope*, perh. fr. E [1]*scallop*; fr. its being served curled like a shell] **:** thin slices of meat (as veal) sautéed or coated with flour and fried

scallop shell *n* **1 :** SCALLOP 2 **2 :** PILGRIM SCALLOP

scallop-shell moth *n* **:** a yellow-and-brown moth (*Calocalpe undulata*) having wing markings like those on a scallop shell and a caterpillar that feeds esp. on cherry leaves

scalls *pl of* SCALL

scallywag *var of* SCALAWAG

scal·ma \ˈskalmə\ *n* -S [NL, fr. OHG *scalmo* pestilence] **:** a mild virus disease of the horse marked by inflammation of the pharynx, larynx, and bronchi and by a severe cough

sca·lo·gram \ˈskāləˌgram\ *n* [[6]*scale* + *-o-* + *-gram*] **:** an arrangement of items (as of a psychological or sociological test) in ascending order of difficulty ⟨analysis by ∼⟩

sca·lops \ˈskāˌläps\ [NL, fr. Gk *skalops*, mole] *syn of* SCALOPUS

scal·o·pus \ˈskaləpəs\ *n, cap* [NL, fr. Gk *skalops* mole, lit., digger — more at SHELF] **:** a genus of insectivores including the common mole of the eastern U.S.

[1]scalp \ˈskalp, ˈskau̇p\ *n* -S [ME, of Scand origin; akin to ON *skālpr* sheath, MD *schelpe* shell, and prob. to OHG *skala* husk, shell — more at SCALE] **1** *chiefly Scot* **:** SKULL, HEAD **2 :** the part of the integument of the human head usu. covered with hair; *broadly* **:** this part including the skin, the dense subcutaneous tissue, the occipitofrontalis muscle with the galea aponeurotica, the loose subaponeurotic tissue, and the cranial periosteum **3 a :** a part of the human scalp with attached hair cut or torn from an enemy as a token of victory by Indian warriors of No. America or their white adversaries **b** (1) **:** an act of capitulation (as a resignation) demanded or obtained (as in retaliation for some act or line of action) ⟨senators clamored for the secretary's ∼⟩ ⟨civic airport boosters were calling for ∼*s* —Joseph Wechsberg⟩ (2) **:** one whose compliance or defeat is sought or obtained as a means of advancing one's cause or enhancing one's status ⟨a society leader adding ∼*s*⟩ (3) **:** something symbolizing the result of punitive action and becoming a tally in a series ⟨boxer who has added four more ∼*s* to his belt⟩ **4** *chiefly Scot* **a :** a projecting mass of bare ground or rock ⟨grassy ∼ of the hill . . . that stood clear of the . . . pine forest —G.K.Chesterton⟩ **b :** a bank (as a bed of oysters) uncovered by the sea at low tide **5 a :** the part of an animal (as a wolf or a fox) corresponding to the human scalp; *also* **:** the part of a hide (as an ear or tail) surrendered when collecting a bounty whether restricted to this area or not ⟨some country shires pay bonuses on wombat ∼*s* —Bill Beatty⟩ **b :** the skin of the head and part of the neck of an animal preserved so as to be suitable for mounting either over the natural skull or an artificial model — compare DOLLYHEAD **c :** the whole upper part of the head of a whale **6 :** a small profit taken by a speculator in a quick transaction **7** [[2]*scalp*] **a :** a sieve or other device for scalping a material (as wheat) **b :** the coarse portion of a material (as wheat) that is removed by scalping

[2]scalp \"\ *vb* -ED/-ING/-S *vt* **1 a :** to deprive of the scalp **:** cut or tear the scalp from the head of **b** (1) **:** to remove a top layer or growth from ⟨seed spots one foot square were ∼*ed* free of sod and litter —*Amer. Midland Naturalist*⟩ ⟨most of the land had been ∼*ed* for pine lumber —Lenard Kaufman⟩ (2) **:** to cause (as a top layer) to be removed ⟨if sod is heavy, it should be ∼*ed* off before planting the shrubs —R.E.Trippensee⟩ ⟨∼ weeds⟩ **c :** ROSS ⟨splitting out clapboards and laying them on the ∼*ed* joists —Conrad Richter⟩ **d :** to remove a desired constituent from (a material) with the residue left as waste ⟨wasteful refiners ∼ petroleum —Lalia P. Boone⟩ **2 :** to screen or sift (as grain, meal, or ore) in order to remove foreign materials or to separate out coarser grades **3 a :** to buy and sell so as to make small quick profits ⟨∼ stocks⟩ ⟨∼ grain⟩ **b :** to obtain and resell (as theater tickets) at prices usu. greatly above the stated rates without official sanction as a speculation ⟨speculators were ∼*ing* tickets at double the going price —Dean Jennings⟩ ⟨possible . . . to ∼ tickets even for a free-admission television show —Arthur Godfrey⟩ ⟨newsboys bought copies by the armload, ∼*ed* them for as much as $1 each —*Time*⟩ **4 a :** to deprive (as a politician or officeholder) of position or influence **b :** to triumph over esp. in a spectacular fashion ⟨∼ a tennis opponent⟩ **c :** to hold up to ridicule **:** polish off **:** HUMILIATE **5 :** to machine the surface from (semifinished metal products) before further fabrication ⟨∼ billets⟩ ∼ *vi* **1 :** to remove or obtain scalps esp. as tokens of victory **2 a :** to make a small usu. quick profit by slight fluctuations of the market **b :** to scalp tickets

[3]scalp \"\ *vi* -ED/-ING/-S [L *scalpere* to dig, scratch, carve, cut — more at SHELF] *of a horse* **:** to cut the coronary cushion or quarters esp. when traveling at high speed

scalp dance *n* [[1]*scalp*] **:** an American Indian victory dance often by women around a pole with enemy scalps or with scalp-surmounted sticks in hand

[1]scal·pel \ˈskalpəl, -ˌkau̇p-, (ˈ)skalˈpel\ *n* -S [L *scalpellum*,

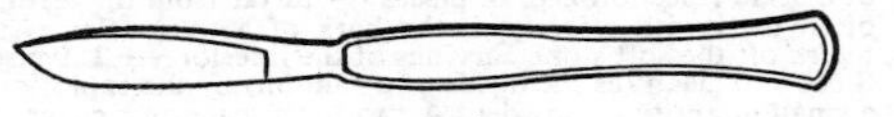

scalpel

scalpellus, dim. of *scalprum*, *scalper* chisel, knife, fr. *scalpere* to carve, cut — more at SHELF] **:** a small straight knife with a thin keen blade used esp. for dissecting; *also* **:** a detachable blade of such a knife

[2]scalpel \"\ *vt* **scalpeled** *also* **scalpelled; scalpeled** *also* **scalpelled; scalpeling** *also* **scalpelling; scalpels :** to cut with a scalpel **:** DISSECT

scal·pel·lar \skalˈpelə(r)\ *adj* [NL *scalpellum* + E *-ar*] **:** of, relating to, or being a scalpellum

scal·pel·lum \-ləm\ *n, pl* **scalpel·la** \-lə\ [NL, fr. L, scalpel] **:** any of four slender piercing organs in the proboscis of true bugs or bloodsucking two-winged flies corresponding to the mandibles and the first pair of maxillae

[1]scalp·er \ˈskalpə(r), -kau̇p-\ *n* -S [[1]*scalp* + *-er*] **:** one that scalps: as **a :** a slaughterhouse worker who skins animals' heads **b :** any of various machines or devices used in scalping grain **c** (1) **:** a speculator who seeks to make small profits on quick transactions (2) **:** a speculator who obtains and resells something (as theater tickets) at prices usu. greatly above the stated rates **d :** ROSSER

[2]scalper \"\ *n* -S [L, chisel, knife — more at SCALPEL] **:** SCORPER

[3]scalper \"\ *also* **scalping boot** *n* -S [*scalper* fr. [3]*scalp* + *-er; scalping* fr. gerund of [3]*scalp*] **:** a light leather or rubber toe boot worn by a horse on the hind foot to prevent scalping

scalp halloo *or* **scalp yell** *n* **:** the shout of an American Indian before, while, or after scalping an enemy

scalping *n* -S [fr. gerund of [2]*scalp*] **1 a :** an act of scalping **b :** the process of scalping **2 scalpings** *pl* **:** foreign matter removed by scalping ⟨oat ∼*s* from wheat⟩

scalp·less \-pləs\ *adj* **:** deprived of the scalp

scalp lock *n* **:** a long tuft of hair on the crown of the otherwise shaved head of a warrior of some tribes of American Indians

scal·pri·form \ˈskalprəˌfȯrm\ *adj* [L *scalprum* chisel, knife + E *-iform* — more at SCALPEL] **:** shaped like a chisel ⟨∼ incisor⟩

scal·prum \ˈskalprəm\ *n, pl* **scal·pra** \-rə\ [NL, fr. L, chisel, knife — more at SCALPEL] **:** the front or cutting edge of an incisor tooth

scalps *pl of* SCALP, *pres 3d sing of* SCALP

scaly *also* **scaley** \ˈskālē, -li\ *adj* **scalier; scaliest** [[4]*scale* + *-y*] **1 a :** covered or abounding with scales ⟨∼ fish⟩ ⟨∼ trunks of trees⟩ **b :** covered with scale ⟨a ∼ boiler⟩ **c :** composed of scales ⟨∼ armor⟩; *specif* **:** composed of imbricated scales ⟨a ∼ bud⟩ **d :** composed of or forming scale ⟨a ∼ encrustation⟩ **e :** cleaving off in flakes at the surface ⟨∼ stone⟩ **2 :** consisting of scaly animals **:** being a scaly animal **3 a :** MEAN, DESPICABLE, STINGY ⟨a ∼ fellow⟩ **b :** POOR, INFERIOR ⟨a ∼ piece of road —Hamlin Garland⟩ **4 :** infested with scale insects ⟨∼ fruit⟩

scaly anteater *n* **:** PANGOLIN; *esp* **:** a southern African pangolin (as the Cape armadillo)

scaly bark *n* **: 1 a** *or* **scaly-bark hickory :** SHAGBARK HICKORY **b :** any of several rough-barked Australian eucalypts; *esp* **:** a rather small tree (*Eucalyptus squamiata*) with dark scaly bark, lanceolate leaves, and coarse reddish wood used chiefly for fuel **2 :** either of two abnormal conditions characterized by roughened scaly bark: **a :** LEPROSIS **b :** PSOROSIS

scaly blazing star *n* **:** a button snakeroot (*Liatris squarrosa*) having purple heads with scaly involucrate bracts

scaly fern *n* **:** SCALE FERN

scaly-finned \ˌ==ˈ=\ *adj* **:** having scales on the fins — compare SPINY-FINNED

scaly leg *n* **:** a disease of poultry caused by the scaly-leg mite producing an abnormal rough hard scaliness on the featherless parts of the legs — sometimes used in pl. but sing. or pl. in constr.

scaly-leg mite *n* **:** a minute round flattened whitish mite (*Knemidocoptes mutans*) of the family Sarcoptidae that burrows beneath the leg scales of poultry and various other birds

scaly mistletoe *n* **:** a plant of the genus *Arceuthobium*

scaly spleenwort *n* **:** SCALE FERN

scalytail \ˈ==ˌ=\ *n* [*scaly* + *tail*] **:** SCALETAIL

[1]scam·ble \ˈskambəl\ *vb* **scambled; scambled; scambling** \-b(ə)liŋ\ **scambles** [origin unknown] *vi* **1** *obs* **:** to struggle with others for largess thrown to a crowd; *broadly* **:** to struggle greedily and indecorously for something **2** *chiefly dial* **:** to get on somehow **:** stumble along **3** *dial Eng* **:** to loll around **:** SPRAWL, SHAMBLE ∼ *vt* **1** *dial* **:** to scrape together **:** COLLECT **2** *dial Eng* **:** to trample down

[2]scam·ble \ˈskam(b)əl\ *n* -S *dial Eng* **:** BOTCH, MESS

[3]scamble \"\ *dial Brit var of* SHAMBLE

scam·bler \ˈskamblər\ *n* -S [origin unknown] *Scot* **:** a meal-time visitor **:** SPONGER

[1]scambling *n* [origin unknown] *dial* **:** a picked up meal

[2]scambling *adj* [fr. pres. part. of [1]*scamble*] **1** *obs* **:** BRAWLING, QUARRELSOME **2 :** carelessly done **:** MAKESHIFT, SHODDY **3 :** irregularly spread out **:** SCATTERED, RAMBLING ⟨a town ∼ in all directions⟩ **4 :** awkwardly formed or executed **:** SHAMBLING ⟨little clean punching and a lot of holding in a ∼ bout —*Sunday Independent* (*Dublin*)⟩

sca·mil·lus \skəˈmiləs\ *n* -ES [L, lit., little bench, dim. of *scamnum* bench, stool] **:** a second plinth below the base of an Ionic or Corinthian column usu. without moldings and of smaller size horizontally than the pedestal

scam·mo·ni·ate \skəˈmōnēət, -ēˌāt\ *adj* [NL *scammoniatus*, fr. L *scammonia* + *-atus* -ate] **:** made with scammony

scam·mo·ny \ˈskamənē\ *n* -ES [ME *scamonie*, fr. L *scammonia*, fr. Gk *skammōnia*] **1 a :** a twining plant (*Convolvulus scammonia*) native to Asia Minor and having a thick root two or three feet long, sagittate leaves, and white flowers **b :** a tropical American morning glory (*Ipomoea orizabensis*) **2 a :** the dried root of scammony **b :** the resin obtained as an exudation from the living root of scammony or prepared by extracting the dried root with alcohol and precipitating with water and used as a drastic cathartic **c :** IPOMOEA 3

scammonyroot \ˈ===ˌ=\ *n* [*scammony* + *root*] **:** MAN-OF-THE-EARTH 1

sca·moz·zi \skəˈmȯtsē\ *n* -S *usu cap* [after Vincenzo *Scamozzi* †1616 Ital. architect] **:** a variation of the Ionic order with the volutes of the capital radiating at 45 degrees used esp. in colonial buildings

[1]scamp \ˈskamp, -aa(ə)mp, -aimp\ *n* -S [obs. *scamp* to roam about idly, perh. short for *scamper*] **1** *archaic* **:** HIGHWAYMAN **2 a :** a scheming person **:** RASCAL, ROGUE ⟨an insincere but ambitious ∼ —Lucien Warner⟩ **b :** a usu. young person given to impish playful tricks ⟨a shocking young ∼ of a rover —W.S.Gilbert⟩ **3** [so called fr. its ability to steal bait without being caught] **:** a West Indian grouper (*Mycteroperca falcata*)
syn see VILLAIN

[2]scamp \"\ *vt* -ED/-ING/-S [perh. of Scand origin; akin to ON *skammr* short — more at SCANT] **:** to perform in a hasty, neglectful, or imperfect manner **:** do or make superficially **:** SKIMP, SCANT ⟨the book is brief, but never hurried or ∼*ed* —Crane Brinton⟩

[1]scam·per \ˈskampə(r), -aam-, -aim-\ *vi* -ED/-ING/-S [prob. fr. obs. D *schampen* to flee, fr. MF *escamper*, fr. It *scampare*, fr. (assumed) VL *excampare* to decamp, fr. L *ex-* + *campus* field — more at CAMP] **1 :** to run away **:** FLEE **2 :** to run nimbly and usu. playfully about ⟨a gray squirrel is ∼*ing* from limb to limb —D.J.Malcolm⟩

[2]scamper \"\ *n* -S **:** a playful scurrying run

scam·per·er \-p(ə)rə(r)\ *n* -S **:** one that scampers

scamping *n* -S [fr. gerund of [2]*scamp*] **1 :** the intentional failure of an employee to perform his task properly **2 :** the act or practice of an employee in exceeding his usual rate of output for the purpose of gaining a personal advantage over his fellows or contrary to their mutual understanding of a proper rate of production **3 :** the act or practice of an employer in attracting labor from competitors underhandedly

scamp·ish \ˈskampish\ *adj* [[1]*scamp* + *-ish*] **:** of or like a scamp **:** ROGUISH ⟨∼ conduct⟩ — **scamp·ish·ness** *n* -ES

[1]scan \ˈskan, -aa(ə)n\ *vb* **scanned; scanned; scanning; scans** [ME *scannen*, fr. LL *scandere* to climb, scan verses, fr. L, to climb; akin to Gk *skandalon* trap, stumbling block, offense, Skt *skandati* he leaps, MIr *scendim* I leap] *vt* **1 a :** to analyze (verse) so as to exhibit rhythmic and esp. metrical structure **b :** to indicate rhythmic or metrical structure of (verse) **2** *archaic* **:** to test the correctness, importance, or value of **:** judge critically ⟨know then thyself, presume not God to ∼ —Alexander Pope⟩ **3 a** (1) **:** to make an intensive examination of (a small area) ⟨*scanning* each vein of rock for the telltale glint of yellow metal —R.A.Billington⟩ ⟨*scanned* their faces as they passed —Joseph Conrad⟩ ⟨*scanned* closely the claims of individuals as against the state —B.R.Trimble⟩ (2) **:** to check (as a magnetic wire or tape or a punched card) for recorded data esp. by means of an electronic device **b :** to make a thorough search of (a wide area) usu. by eye (as by moving one's eyes in repeated sweeping motions from side to side) ⟨*scanning* the forest with binoculars, on the lookout for fire —Isaac Rosenfeld⟩ ⟨∼ the field of medicine —Sara Jordan⟩ **c :** to look through or over hastily ⟨read several and ∼ the rest —Kermit Ely⟩ ⟨*scanned* the film advertisements —D.M.Davin⟩ **4** *archaic* **:** DISCERN ⟨not wise enough to ∼ his best concerns aright —William Cowper⟩ **5** *obs* **:** to explain the meaning of **:** INTERPRET **6 a :** to subject (as an image or picture) to scanning **b :** to cause a narrow beam of light to shine through (a sound track) or to traverse (an object) in order to translate light modulations into a corresponding electrical current **c :** to direct a succession of radar beams so that they traverse (a prescribed area) in searching for a target ∼ *vi* **1 :** to scan verse **2 :** to admit of being scanned **:** conform to or reveal a definite metrical pattern **syn** see SCRUTINIZE

[2]scan \"\ *n* -S **1 :** the act or process of scanning **:** a close searching look ⟨the captain spins the periscope, making a quick ∼ of the situation —E.L.Beach⟩ **2 :** range of vision **:** APPREHENSION ⟨the authors' ∼ was limited —*Current Biog.*⟩ **3 :** a radar display

scandahoovian *cap, var of* SCANDIHOOVIAN

[1]scan·dal \ˈskandᵊl, -aan-\ *n* -S [LL *scandalum* stumbling block, offense, fr. Gk *skandalon* — more at SCAN] **1 a** (1) **:** discredit brought upon religion by unseemly conduct in a religious person (2) **:** offense, doubt, or bewilderment occasioned to a person's religious feelings by another's lapse in ethics or religion ⟨abstained from decorating their private chapels . . . lest ∼ should be given to weaker brethren —T.B.Macaulay⟩ (3) **:** conduct that causes or encourages a lapse of faith or of religious obedience in another ⟨his bad example is a constant ∼ to all who knew him in the days of his fidelity —D.J.Corrigan⟩ **b :** something that prevents the reception of religious or other faith or serves as justification for a lapse from faith or morals **:** OFFENSE ⟨one ∼ of Christendom, the great schism, had indeed been overcome —S.E.Morison & H.S.Commager⟩ ⟨the ∼ of the apparent contradiction of reason with itself —Edward Caird⟩ **2 a :** loss of or damage to reputation caused by actual or apparent violation of morality or propriety ⟨a soldier should not bring ∼ upon the uniform⟩ **b** *archaic* **:** a disgraceful usu. baseless accusation or imputation ⟨an improbable ∼ flung upon the nation by a few bigoted . . . scribblers —Jonathan Swift⟩ **3 a :** a circumstance or action that offends propriety or established moral conceptions or disgraces those associated with or involved in it ⟨the man's life is an open ∼ —Willa Cather⟩ ⟨an early history of ∼ and mismanagement —*Amer. Guide Series: N.Y. City*⟩ **b :** a person whose conduct offends propriety or morality ⟨under no temptation to nominate men who will be either drones or ∼*s* —*Spectator*⟩ **4 :** gossip or utterance of gossip that emphasizes true or false details damaging to another's reputation ⟨the political harridans . . . would attack every possible leader with ∼ and abuse and falsehood —H.G.Wells⟩ **5 :** anger, indignation, chagrin, bewilderment, or incredulity brought about by a flagrant violation of morality, propriety, or religious opinion ⟨to the ∼ and grief of her sisters, made up her mind not to go to church any more —Margaret Deland⟩ ⟨his marriage would give the gravest ∼ to millions —*Manchester Guardian Weekly*⟩ **6 :** something alleged in an equity pleading that is impertinent and is reproachful to a person or derogates from the dignity of the court or is contrary to good manners **:** an immaterial allegation that is slanderous **syn** see DETRACTION

[2]scandal \"\ *vt* -ED/-ING/-S **1** *obs* **:** to bring reproach or scandal upon **:** DISGRACE **2** *chiefly dial* **:** to spread scandal concerning **:** DEFAME, SLANDER

scan·dal·iza·tion \ˌskandᵊləˈzāshən\ *n* -S **:** the act of scandalizing or the condition of being scandalized

[1]scan·dal·ize \ˈskandᵊlˌīz, -aan-\ *vt* -ED/-ING/-S [partly fr. MF *scandaliser* to cause to stumble, shock, fr. LL *scandalizare* to cause to stumble, fr. Gk *skandalizein*, fr. *skandalon* stumbling block, offense; partly fr. [1]*scandal* + *-ize*] **1 :** to speak falsely or maliciously of **:** DEFAME, MALIGN **2** *archaic* **:** to bring into reproach **:** DISHONOR, DISGRACE **3 :** to offend the feelings, conscience, or propriety of by an action considered immoral, criminal, or unseemly ⟨*scandalized* his brethren by espousing euthanasia, sterilization, easy divorce —*Time*⟩

[2]scandalize \"\ *vt* [alter. of earlier *scantelize* to shorten, curtail, fr. [2]*scantle* + *-ize*] **1 :** to lower the peak and haul up the tack or clew of (a fore-and-aft sail) in order to reduce the size or to spill the sail **2 :** to reduce sail on (a mizzenmast) when before the wind so that the sails on the mainmast may have the full force of the wind

scan·dal·iz·er \-zə(r)\ *n* -S [[1]*scandalize* + *-er*] **:** one that utters scandal

scandalmonger \ˈ==ˌ==\ *n* [[1]*scandal* + *monger*] **:** a person who circulates scandal

scan·dal·ous \ˈskandᵊləs, -aan-\ *adj* [MF *scandaleux*, fr. ML *scandalosus*, fr. LL *scandalum* stumbling block + L *-osus* -ous] **1 a** *obs* **:** constituting a spiritual or moral lapse endangering by example faith or morals **b** *obs, of a clergyman* **:** endangering faith or morals through conduct or views **2 :** containing shocking or defamatory information **:** LIBELOUS ⟨only read it for the ∼ passages —Arnold Bennett⟩ **3 :** offensive to public or individual sense of propriety or morality **:** exciting reprobation ⟨considered the publisher a ∼ person, and had refused to meet him —W.B.Yeats⟩ ⟨rumors about the ∼ treatment of the native population —H.O.Mackey⟩ — **scan·dal·ous·ly** *adv* — **scan·dal·ous·ness** *n* -ES

scandals *pl of* SCANDAL, *pres 3d sing of* SCANDAL

scandal sheet *n* **:** a newspaper or periodical dealing to a large extent in scandal and gossip

scan·da·lum mag·na·tum \ˈskandᵊləm,magˈnādəm\ *n, pl* **scanda·la magnatum** \-ᵊlə,-\ [ML, lit., slander of magnates] **:** a defamatory speech or writing published to the injury of a peer, judge, or other great officer of England

scan·da·roon \ˌskandəˈrün\ *n* -S [fr. *Scandaroon*, now *İskenderon*, seaport of southern Turkey] **:** a long-bodied long-legged domestic pigeon of the carrier type with a curved bill and solid-colored or varied plumage

scan·dent \ˈskandənt\ *adj* [L *scandent-*, *scandens*, pres. part. of *scandere* to climb — more at SCAN] **:** CLIMBING ⟨plant of a creeping or ∼ nature —*Farmer's Weekly* (*So. Africa*)⟩

[1]scan·di·an \ˈskandēən\ *adj, usu cap* [L *Scandia*, ancient name of the southern Scandinavian peninsula, + E *-an*] **1 a :** of or relating to Scandia **b :** SCANDINAVIAN **2 :** of or relating to the languages of Scandinavia

[2]scandian \"\ *n* -S *cap* **:** SCANDINAVIAN

scan·di·hoo·vi·an *or* **scan·da·hoo·vi·an** \ˌskandəˈhüvēən\ *n* -S *cap* [alter. of *Scandinavian*] **1 :** a Scandinavian individual esp. living in the U. S. — usu. used disparagingly **2 :** a Scandinavian language as spoken in the U. S. esp. by rural people

[1]scan·di·na·vi·an \ˌskandəˈnāvēən, -aand-, -vyən\ *adj, usu cap* [*Scandinavia*, ancient name of the country of the Norsemen + E *-an*] **:** of or relating to Scandinavia, its peoples, or languages

[2]scandinavian \"\ *n* -S *cap* **1 a :** a native or inhabitant of

Scandinavia; *esp* **:** a member of the tall blond dolichocephalic dominant race **b :** one that is of Scandinavian descent **2 :** the No. Germanic languages

scan·di·um \'skandēəm\ *n* -s [NL, fr. L *Scandia*, ancient name of southern Scandinavian peninsula + NL *-ium*] **:** a white trivalent metallic element sparsely but widely distributed in combined form in association with the rare-earth metals with which it is sometimes included and found esp. in various Scandinavian minerals (as thortveitite) — symbol *Sc;* see ELEMENT table

scan·dix \'skandiks\ *n, cap* [NL, fr. L, chervil, fr. Gk *skandix*] **:** a small genus of Eurasian herbs (family Umbelliferae) with finely dissected leaves, white flowers, and wingless long-beaked fruit and with obscure oil tubes — see LADY'S COMB

SC and S *abbr* strapped, corded, and sealed

scan·mag \'skan,mag\ *n* -s [*scan*dalum *mag*natum] **:** SCANDAL

scan·na·ble \'skanəbəl\ *adj* [¹*scan* + *-able*] **:** capable of being scanned

scanned *past of* SCAN

scan·ner \'skanə(r), -aan-\ *n* -s **:** one that scans: as **a :** one that scans verse **b :** a device used for scanning (as in television, facsimile, or radar) **c :** a device that automatically checks a process or condition and may initiate a desired corrective action ⟨electronic ~ that can monitor up to 25 different production points, checking such variables as temperature, pressure, liquid level, and rate of flow —*Dun's Rev.*⟩ **d :** a device for sensing recorded data; *esp* **:** such a device that is operated photoelectrically ⟨a punched-card ~⟩

¹**scanning** *n* -s [ME, fr. gerund of *scannen* to scan] **1 :** SCANSION **2 :** minute, thorough, critical, or judicial examination **3 :** the process of analyzing by means of an electron beam that moves usu. in successive lines the light and dark values that constitute a picture or image and of translating these values into corresponding electrical values for transmission by facsimile or television; *also* **:** the reverse process by means of which a receiver synthesizes the picture or image

²**scanning** *adj* [fr. pres. part. of ¹*scan*] **:** minutely scrutinizing

scanning disk *n* [²*scanning*] **:** a rotating disk with a number of spirally arranged holes near its edge which permit a light beam to sweep over successive portions of a picture or object

scanning speech *n* **:** speech characterized by regularly recurring pauses between words or syllables

scans *pres 3d sing of* SCAN, *pl of* SCAN

scan·sion \'skanchən, -aan-\ *n* -s [LL *scansion-, scansio*, fr. L, act of climbing, fr. (assumed) L *scansus* (past part. of L *scandere* to climb) + L *-ion-, -io* -ion — more at SCAN] **1 a :** the analysis of a rhythmic structure (as a verse) so as to show the elements or units of which its rhythm is composed and esp. to identify some unifying recurrent element or unit **b :** the division of a rhythmic series into such units; *esp* **:** the division of a metrical series into its component feet **2 :** the product or result of scansion **:** a particular description or representation of a given rhythmic or esp. metrical structure ⟨two possible ~s of this verse are printed⟩

scan·sion·ist \-chənəst\ *n* -s [*scansion* + *-ist*] **:** one who practices or is skilled in the art of scansion

scan·so·res \skan'sō,rēz\ *n pl, cap* [NL, lit., climbers, pl. of *scansor*, fr. (assumed) L *scansus* (past. part. of L *scandere* to climb) + L *-or* — more at SCAN] *in former classifications* **:** an order of birds having the toes two before and two behind and including the parrots, woodpeckers, cuckoos, trogons, and toucans

scan·so·ri·al \skan'sōrēəl, -'sȯr-\ *adj* [L *scansorius* (fr. — assumed — L *scansus* + L *-orius* -ory) + E *-al*] **1 :** relating to, capable of, or adapted for climbing **2 :** of or relating to the Scansores

scansorial barbet *n* **:** a barbet of the family Capitonidae

¹**scant** \'skant, -aa(ə)nt, -aint\ *n* -s [ME, fr. ON *skamt*, fr. neut. of *skammr* short] *chiefly dial* **:** scanty supply **:** SCARCITY

²**scant** \"\ *adj* -ER/-EST [ME, fr. ON *skamt*, neut. of *skammr* short; akin to OHG *scam* short, L *capon-, capo* capon — more at CAPON] **1 a** *dial* **:** excessively frugal **:** PARSIMONIOUS **b** *dial* **:** wisely sparing **:** not prodigal **:** CHARY ⟨from this time be something ~*er* of your maiden presence —Shak.⟩ **2 a :** barely or scarcely sufficient ⟨likely to pay ~ attention to proportion or design —Ben Riker⟩ ⟨desiccated stalks offer ~ browsing to cattle —*N.Y. Times Mag.*⟩; *specif* **:** lacking a trifle of or not quite coming up to a stated measure ⟨had seen him, three ~ months ago —Donn Byrne⟩ ⟨a ~ chance of one man in ten surviving the torpedoing —*English Digest*⟩ ⟨many insulating boards are cut ~ in width and length —P.D.Close⟩ **b :** lacking in amplitude or quantity **:** MEAGER, SCANTY ⟨amaryllis is tall-stemmed, and has ~ foliage —G.M.Fosler⟩ ⟨a truly ~ black lace underskirt —Lois Long⟩ **3 a :** having a small or insufficient supply ⟨he's fat, and ~ of breath —Shak.⟩ **b :** somewhat wanting or weak in a particular area ⟨this small book . . . is a good bit too ~ in documentation —*New Yorker*⟩ **4** *of a wind* **:** having such a direction or force that a sailing ship can barely hold its course even close-hauled

syn see MEAGER

³**scant** \"\ *adv* [ME, fr. ²*scant*] *dial* **:** SCARCELY, HARDLY

⁴**scant** \"\ *vt* -ED/-ING/-S [²*scant*] **1 :** to provide with a meager or inadequate portion, supply, or allowance ⟨shall not allow myself to be circumscribed and ~*ed* of elbowroom —J.R.Lowell⟩ ⟨~*ed* in my allowance —Clara Reeve⟩ **2 :** to make small, narrow, thin, or meager **:** reduce the size or quantity of ⟨has not hesitated to expand rather than ~ the meaning of the original —*Saturday Rev. (London)*⟩ **3 :** to provide an incomplete supply of **:** fail to give in full **:** WITHHOLD ⟨to ~ one's service was the cardinal sin —V.L.Parrington⟩ **4 :** to give scant attention to **:** SLIGHT ⟨vitally interdependent aims, and neither can be ~*ed* without the other suffering —Fredson Bowers⟩ ⟨a subject ~*ed* in too many grammars —A.F.Hubbell⟩

scant·ies \-tēz\ *n pl* [blend of ²*scant* and *panties*] **:** abbreviated panties for women

scant·i·ly \-tᵊlē, -tᵊli, -təl-\ *adv* [*scanty* + *-ly*] **:** in a scanty manner

scant·i·ness \-tēnəs, -tin-\ *n* -ES **:** the quality or state of being scanty

¹**scantle** *vt* -ED/-ING/-S [freq. of ⁴*scant*] **1** *obs* **:** to cut down the supply of **2** [prob. back-formation fr. ¹*scantling*] *obs* **:** to adjust to a standard of measure

²**scan·tle** \'skantᵊl\ *n* -s [prob. fr. ¹*scantle*] **1** *obs* **:** a small portion **:** SCANTLING **2 :** a gage for measuring slates

¹**scant·ling** \'skantliŋ, -aan-, -ain-, -lēŋ\ *n* -s [alter. (influenced by *-ling*) of earlier *scantillon* mason's or carpenter's gage, dimension, fr. ME *scantilon*, fr. ONF *escantillon*] **1 a** *obs* **:** the measure or dimension of something (as the caliber of a bullet or shot) **b :** the breadth and thickness of timber and stone used in building **c :** the dimensions of a frame, strake, or other structural part used in shipbuilding **d** *obs* **:** the quantity, amount, or degree of a quality, capacity, or ability **e** *obs* **:** a measure that confines to a comparatively small size or quantity **:** LIMIT, SCOPE ⟨this . . . is to measure truth by a wrong standard, and to circumscribe her by too narrow a ~ —T.P. Blomt⟩ **2 a** *archaic* **:** SPECIMEN, SAMPLE **b** *obs* **:** a rough draft **:** a rude sketch or outline **3 :** something that has a measure or is measured out: as **a :** an allotted portion **b :** a small quantity, amount, or proportion **:** MODICUM ⟨able to devote but a ~ of his philosophical labor to the problem —John Baillie⟩ **c :** a small piece of lumber (as an upright piece in house framing) **d :** a piece of yard lumber that is under 8 inches wide and from 2 inches to 6 inches thick **e :** yellow pine lumber that varies in size from 2 in. x 2 in. to 5 in. x 8 in.

²**scantling** \"\ *adj* [fr. pres. part. of ¹*scantle*] *archaic* **:** SCANTY

scantling number *or* **scantling numeral** *n* [¹*scantling*] **:** a number variously computed from a ship's dimensions and used in reference to a tabulated scheme specifying the size of structural material required to entitle a ship according to its type to a classification or grading with respect to seaworthiness

scant·ly *adv* [ME, fr. ²*scant* + *-ly*] **1 :** BARELY, SCARCELY **2 :** in small or inadequate measure **:** SCANTILY

scant·ness *n* -ES [ME *scantnesse*, fr. ²*scant* + *-nesse* -ness] **:** the quality or state of being scant **:** INSUFFICIENCY

scant-o-grace \'skantə,grās\ *n* [²*scant* + *o'* + *grace*] *Scot* **:** ROGUE

scanty \'skantē, -aan-, -ain-, -ti\ *adj* -ER/-EST [¹*scant* + *-y*] **1 a :** meager or barely sufficient **:** lacking in amplitude, abundance, or extension ⟨the peasant whose nervous system is best adapted to thrive on ~ nutriment —Brooks Adams⟩ ⟨used to acquire much of his ~ wardrobe by barter —Dwight Macdonald⟩ **b :** somewhat less than is needed **:** INSUFFICIENT, SCANT ⟨his own ~ cavalry . . . would . . . be unequal to the weight which would be thrown on them —J.A.Froude⟩ ⟨issuing bills of credit to supplement the ~ currency —V.L. Parrington⟩ **c :** thinly spread in time or space **:** SPARSE ⟨a desert range with ~ vegetation —G.R.Stewart⟩ ⟨the grass does not renew itself after the rains become ~ —Samuel Van Valkenburg & Ellsworth Huntington⟩ **2 :** giving small portions **:** PARSIMONIOUS **syn** see MEAGER

scap·a·no·rhyn·chus \,skapənō'riŋkəs\ *n, cap* [NL, fr. Gk *skapanē* spade + NL *-o-* + *-rhynchus;* akin to Gk *skaptein* to dig — more at CAPON] **:** a genus of galeoid sharks comprising the goblin sharks and related extinct forms and known from the Lower Cretaceous onward

scap·a·nus \'skapənəs\ *n, cap* [NL, fr. Gk *skapaneus* digger; akin to Gk *skaptein* to dig] **:** a genus of insectivores (family Talpidae) comprising the common mole of the western U. S.

¹**scape** \'skāp\ *vb* -ED/-ING/-S [ME *scapen*, short for *escapen* — more at ESCAPE] **:** ESCAPE

²**scape** \"\ *n* -s [ME, fr. *scapen* to scape] **1** *dial* **a :** ESCAPE **b :** a means of escape **2 a** *obs* **:** a breach of morals **:** TRANSGRESSION **b** *obs* **:** an inadvertent error **:** SLIP **3 :** ESCAPEMENT

³**scape** \"\ *n* -s [L *scapus* shaft of a column, stalk — more at SHAFT] **1 :** a peduncle arising at or beneath the surface of the ground in an acaulescent plant (as the bloodroot, tulip, or primrose); *broadly* **:** a flower stalk **2 a :** the shaft of a column **b :** APOPHYGE **3 :** STEM, SHAFT: as **a :** the basal joint of an insect antenna esp. when longer than the other joints **b :** the shaft of a feather **c :** the peduncle of the balancer of a dipterous insect

⁴**scape** \"\ *n* -s [back-formation fr. *landscape*] **:** a scenic view (as of sea, land, or sky)

⁵**scape** \"\ *n* -s [imit.] **1 :** the cry or note of a flushed snipe **2 :** SNIPE

-scape \,skāp\ *n comb form* -s [*landscape*] **:** view **:** pictorial representation of a (specified) type of view ⟨city*scape*⟩ ⟨water*scape*⟩

scapegallows \'≈,≈(,)≈\ *n* [¹*scape* + *gallows*] **:** one who has narrowly escaped the gallows for his crimes

¹**scapegoat** \'≈,≈\ *n* [¹*scape* + *goat;* intended as trans. of Heb *'azāzēl* (prob. name of a demon), as if *'ēz 'ōzēl* goat that departs, Lev 16:8 (AV)] **1 :** a goat upon whose head are symbolically placed the sins of the people after which he is suffered to escape into the wilderness as part of the ceremony prescribed by Biblical law for Yom Kippur **2 :** an animal or person to whom sins, ill luck, or other evils are ceremonially attached and who symbolically bears them away by being sacrificed or exiled **3 a :** a person or thing bearing the blame for others ⟨made a ~ and relieved for a failure not his own —H.W.Baldwin⟩ **b :** a person, group, race, or institution against whom is directed the irrational hostility and unrelieved aggression of others ⟨the wholesale hunting for ~*s* at whom all can throw invectives —Walter Coutu⟩

²**scapegoat** \"\ *vt* -ED/-ING/-S **:** to displace aggression or project guilt upon ⟨the minority groups in the country conveniently ~*ed* —H.H.Long⟩

scape·goat·er \"+ə(r)\ *n* -s [²*scapegoat* + *-er*] **:** one that makes a scapegoat of something or somebody

scape·goat·ism \"+,izəm\ *n* -s [¹*scapegoat* + *-ism*] **:** the casting of blame upon others **:** the attribution of failure to the malign activities of an individual or group

scapegrace \'≈,≈\ *n* [¹*scape* + *grace*] **:** a reckless unprincipled person **:** REPROBATE

scap·el \'skapəl\ *n* -s [NL *scapellus*, dim. of L *scapus* stalk — more at SHAFT] **:** CAULICLE

scape·less \'skāpləs\ *adj* [³*scape* + *-less*] **:** lacking a scape

scape·ment \'skāpmənt\ *n* -s [¹*scape* + *-ment*] **:** ESCAPEMENT

scape wheel *n* [²*scape*] **:** ESCAPE WHEEL

scaph- *or* **scapho-** *comb form* [scaphoid] **1 :** scaphoid ⟨*scapho*cephaly⟩ **2 :** scaphoid and ⟨*scapho*lunar⟩

sca·pha \'skafə\ *n* -s [NL, fr. L, light boat, skiff, fr. Gk *skaphē* trough, bowl, skiff — more at SCAPHOID] **:** an elongated depression of the ear that separates the helix and antihelix

sca·phan·der \skə'fandə(r)\ *n, cap* [NL *Scaphandr-, Scaphander*, fr. *scaph-* + *-ander*] **:** a genus (the type of the family Scaphandridae) of gastropods having an external ovoid shell with a concealed spire

sca·phan·dri·dae \-drə,dē\ *n pl, cap* [NL *Scaphandr-, Scaphander*, type genus + *-idae*] **:** a family of gastropods (suborder Tectibranchia) comprising the canoe shells

sca·phi·o·pod·i·dae \,skāfēō'pädə,dē\ *n pl, cap* [NL, fr. *Scaphiopod-, Scaphiopus*, type genus, + *-idae*] *in some classifications* **:** a family of toads that comprises the American spadefoot toads and is now usu. included in the cosmopolitan family Pelobatidae

sca·phi·o·pus \skə'fīəpəs\ *n, cap* [NL *Scaphiopod-, Scaphiopus*, fr. Gk *skapheion* spade + NL *-pus;* akin to Gk *skaptein* to dig — more at CAPON] **:** a genus of toads comprising the American spadefoot toads and being placed in the family Pelobatidae or sometimes made the type of Scaphiopodidae

scaph·ite \'ska,fīt\ *n* -s [NL *Scaphites*] **:** a fossil cephalopod of *Scaphites* or a related genus

sca·phi·tes \skə'fīd·(,)ēz\ *n, cap* [NL, fr. *scaph* + *-ites*] **:** a genus (the type of the family Scaphitidae) comprising Cretaceous ammonoid cephalopods that have all the whorls coiled in an involute spiral except the last which is straight for a distance and then bent back toward the coiled part — **scaph·i·toid** \'skafə,tȯid\ *adj*

scaph·o·ce·phal·ic \,skafōsə'falik\ *or* **scaph·o·ceph·a·lous** \,skafə'sefələs\ *adj* [ISV *scaph-* + *-cephalic* or *-cephalous*] **:** of, relating to, or exhibiting scaphocephaly

scaph·o·ceph·a·lism \,skafə'sefə,lizəm\ *n* -s [ISV *scaph-* + *-cephalism*] **:** SCAPHOCEPHALY

scaph·o·ceph·a·ly \-fəlē\ *n* -ES [ISV *scaph-* + *-cephaly*] **:** a congenital deformity of the skull in which the vault is narrow, elongated, and boat-shaped because of premature ossification of the sagittal suture

scaph·o·ce·rite \,skafə'si,rīt\ *n* -s [*scaph-* + Gk *keras* horn + E *-ite* — more at HORN] **:** a flattened plate on the second joint of the antennae of many crustaceans — **scaph·o·ce·rit·ic** \,skafəsə'rid·ik\ *adj*

sca·phog·na·thite \skə'fägnə,thīt\ *n* [*scaph-* + *gnathite*] **:** a thin leaflike appendage of the second maxilla of decapod crustaceans — **sca·phog·na·thit·ic** \,≈;≈≈'thid·ik\ *adj*

¹**scaph·oid** \'ska,fȯid\ *adj* [NL *scaphoides*, fr. Gk *skaphoeidēs*, fr. *skaphē* trough, bowl, light boat, skiff + *-oeidēs* -oid; prob. akin to Gk *skaptein* to dig — more at CAPON] **1 :** shaped like a boat **:** NAVICULAR **2 :** characterized by concavity ⟨the ~ abdomen in some serious diseases⟩

²**scaphoid** \"\ *n* -s [NL *scaphoides*, fr. *scaphoides* boat-shaped] **:** the navicular of the carpus or tarsus

sca·phoi·de·us \skə'fȯidēəs\ *n, cap* [NL, fr. *scaphoides* scaphoid] **:** a genus of leafhoppers including one (*S. luteolus*) that feeds on and transmits phloem necrosis to elm trees

¹**scapho-lunar** \¦skafō+\ *adj* [*scaph-* + *lunar*] **:** relating to or composed of the navicular and lunar bones of the carpus

²**scapholunar** \"\ *n* **:** a bone in the carpus of many carnivorous mammals that is made up of the fused navicular and lunar

¹**scaph·o·pod** \'skafə,päd\ *adj* [NL *Scaphopoda*] **:** of or relating to the Scaphopoda

²**scaphopod** \"\ *n* -s **:** a mollusk of the class Scaphopoda

sca·phop·o·da \skə'fäpədə\ *n pl, cap* [NL, fr. *scaph-* + *-poda*] **:** a small class of Mollusca comprising bilaterally symmetrical marine forms that have a tapering tubular shell open at both ends, a pointed or spade-shaped foot for burrowing, many long slender prehensile oral tentacles about a mouth containing a radula, a rudimentary heart, no gills, and separate sexes whose reproductive products escape through the right kidney — see TOOTH SHELL; compare GASTROPODA — **sca·phop·o·dous** \-dəs\ *adj*

scapi *pl of* SCAPUS

scapi- *comb form* [L *scapus* shaft of a column, stalk — more at SHAFT] **:** scape **:** stem **:** shaft ⟨*scapi*form⟩ ⟨*scapi*gerous⟩

sca·pi·form \'skāpə,fȯrm, 'skap-\ *adj* [*scapi-* + *-form*] **:** resembling a scape esp. in being a stem without leaves

scap net \'skap-\ *n* [prob. alter. of *scoop net*] **:** a scoop net for catching bait (as fish or shrimp)

sca·poid \'skā,pȯid\ *adj* [L *scap*us shaft, stalk + E *-oid* — more at SHAFT] **:** SCAPIFORM

sca·po·lite \'skāpə,līt\ *n* -s [F, fr. L *scapus* shaft + F *-o-* + *-lite;* fr. the prismatic shape of its crystals] **1 :** a mineral of the scapolite group that is intermediate in composition between meionite and marialite, contains 46 to 54 percent of silica, and resembles feldspar when massive but has a fibrous appearance and higher specific gravity (sp. gr. 2.66–2.73) — called also *wernerite* **2 :** a member of the scapolite group

scapolite group *n* **:** a group of minerals crystallizing in the dipyramidal class of the tetragonal system, being white or grayish white in color when pure, and consisting essentially of silicates of aluminum, calcium, and sodium (hardness 5–6.5, sp. gr. 2.5–2.8)

scap·o·li·tiza·tion \,skapə,lid·ə'zāshən\ *n* -s [*scapolite* + *-ization*] **:** the process or state of alteration by which a mineral (as feldspar) is converted into scapolite

sca·pose \'skā,pōs\ *adj* [NL *scapus* + E *-ose*] **:** bearing, resembling, or consisting of a scape

scapple *var of* SCABBLE

scappler *var of* SCABBLER

scapul- *or* **scapulo-** *comb form* [L *scapula*] **1 :** scapula ⟨*scapul*ectomy⟩ ⟨*scapulo*pexy⟩ **2 :** scapular and ⟨*scapulo*-axillary⟩

scap·u·la \'skapyələ\ *n, pl* **scapu·lae** \-yə,lē\ *or* **scapulas** [NL, fr. L, shoulder blade, shoulder; prob. akin to Gk *skaptein* to dig — more at CAPON] **1 a :** either of a pair of large essentially flat and triangular bones lying one in each dorsal lateral part of the thorax, forming the principal bone of the corresponding half of the shoulder girdle, divided into unequal parts by an obliquely transverse ridge that terminates in the acromion, providing articulation for the humerus, and articulating with the corresponding clavicle or coracoid — called also *shoulder blade, shoulder bone;* see CORACOID PROCESS, GLENOID CAVITY; BAT illustration **b** (1) **:** HYPERCORACOID (2) **:** SUPRACLAVICLE **2 a :** TEGULA 1a **b :** a pleuron of the mesothorax of an insect **c :** the trochanter of either of the anterior pair of legs of an insect **d :** PATAGIUM 2a

¹**scap·u·lar** \-lə(r)\ *n* -s [ME *scapulare*, fr. LL, fr. L *scapula* shoulder] **1 a :** a sleeveless outer garment of a monk's habit that falls over the shoulders and down the front and back usu. almost to the feet and may include the cowl **b :** a badge of membership in an order usu. worn over the shoulders **2 a :** SCAPULA **b :** a scapular feather — see BIRD illustration

²**scapular** \"\ *adj* [NL *scapularis*, fr. *scapula* + L *-aris* -ar] **1 :** of or relating to the shoulder or the scapula **2 :** of, relating to, or constituting the short feathers overlying the base of the wing of a bird

scapular arch *n* **:** PECTORAL GIRDLE

scap·u·la·re \,skapyə'la(a)rē\ *n* -s [NL, fr. neut of *scapularis* scapular] **1 :** the scapular region of a bird **2 :** POSTTEMPORAL

scapular index *n* **:** the ratio of the length of the scapula to its breadth multiplied by 100

scap·u·lary \'skapyə,lerē\ *n* -ES [ME *scapelarie*, fr. ML *scapularium*, fr. L *scapula* shoulder + *-arium* -ary] **:** SCAPULAR 1

scap·u·late \'skapyələt, -,lāt\ *adj* [*scapul*et + *-ate*] **:** having scapulets

scap·u·lat·ed \-,lād·əd\ *adj* [NL *scapulat*us scapulated (fr. *scapula* + L *-atus* -ate) + E *-ed*] **:** having conspicuous and usu. distinctively colored scapular feathers

scap·u·let *or* **scap·u·lette** \'skapyə,let\ *n* -s [G *scapulette*, fr. NL *scapula* + G *-ette*] **:** a fold at the bases of the lobes of the manubrium of many rhizostomous medusae

scap·u·li·man·cy *also* **scap·u·lo·mancy** \'skapyələ,man(t)sē\ *n* -ES [*scapul-* + *-i-* + *-mancy*] **:** divination by observation of a shoulder blade usu. as blotched or cracked from a fire

sca·pus \'skāpəs\ *n, pl* **sca·pi** \-ā,pī\ [NL, fr. L, shaft of a column, stalk — more at SHAFT] **:** STEM, SHAFT, COLUMN: as **a :** SCAPE 3b **b :** the basal part of a polyp **c :** the main stem of a sea pen

¹**scar** \'skär, 'skȧ(r\ *n* -s [ME *skerre, skar*, fr. ON *sker* skerry; akin to ON *skera* to cut — more at SHEAR] **1 a :** an isolated or protruding rock **b :** a steep rocky eminence **:** a bare place on the side of a mountain or steep bank of earth **2 :** a hard cinder **:** furnace slag **:** CLINKER

²**scar** \"\ *n* -s [ME *scar, escare*, fr. MF *escare* scab, fr. LL *eschara*, fr. Gk, hearth, fireplace, scab] **1 :** a mark left in the skin or an internal organ by new connective tissue that replaces tissue injured (as by a burn, ulcer, incision) — compare CICATRIX **2 a** (1) **:** a mark left on a stem or branch by a fallen leaf or harvested fruit or on a seed by separation of the funicle (2) **:** CATFACE **b :** CICATRIX 2 **3 :** a mark or indentation resulting from damage or wear ⟨the ~*s* of bullets on the . . . church door —Kay Boyle⟩ **4 :** a lasting effect of a disturbing experience (as of dishonor, lapse of integrity, or a wound to the feelings by affliction, loss, or disappointment) **:** a remaining painful memory or maladjustment following an emotional or social trauma ⟨one of his men had been killed . . . in a manner that left a ~ upon his mind —H.G.Wells⟩

³**scar** \"\ *vb* **scarred; scarred; scarring; scars** *vt* **1 :** to mark with a scar **:** MAR, DISFIGURE **2 :** to leave a lasting ill effect on ⟨two events that *scarred* the man — the inquiry into his conduct as governor . . . and the death of his wife —G.W. Johnson⟩ ⟨the weariness, the disdain and passion that *scarred* his mind —Anne D. Sedgwick⟩ ~ *vi* **1 :** to form a scar **2 :** to become scarred

⁴**scar** \'skär\ *adj* [ON *skjarr*] *chiefly Scot* **:** SCARED, SHY

⁵**scar** \"\ *dial var of* SCARE

scar·ab \'skarəb *also* -ker-\ *n* -s [MF *scarabée*, fr. L *scarabaeus;* prob. akin to Gk *karabos* horned beetle — more at CARAVEL] **1** *or* **scarab beetle :** any of various usu. rather large beetles that have the clypeus expanded to cover the mouthparts, are typically dung beetles, and constitute the family Scarabaeidae; *esp* **:** SCARABAEUS 1a **2 :** a conventionalized representation of a scarabaeus commonly in stone or faience usu. having an inscription on the flat underside symbolizing the sun-god Khepera and widely used in ancient Egypt as a talisman, an ornament, and a symbol (as on a mummy) of resurrection — called also *scarabaeus*

scar·a·bae·id \,skarə'bēəd\ *adj* [NL *Scarabaeidae*] **:** of or relating to the Scarabaeidae; *broadly* **:** SCARABAEOID

scar·a·bae·i·dae \-ēə,dē\ *n pl, cap* [NL, fr. *Scarabaeus*, type genus + *-idae*] **:** a family of stout-bodied lamellicorn beetles now usu. restricted to beetles (as the tumblebugs or scarabaeus) of subsocial habits that feed on dung but sometimes esp. formerly extended to include the plant-feeding rhinoceros beetles, flower beetles, leaf chafers and others that are usu. placed in separate families — compare CETONIIDAE, DUNG BEETLE, MELOLONTHIDAE, RUTELINIDAE

scar·a·bae·i·doid \¦≈≈'bēə,dȯid\ *adj* [NL *Scarabaeidae* + E *-oid*] **:** SCARABAEOID

scar·a·bae·i·form \-,fȯrm\ *adj* [*scarabae*us + E *-iform*] **:** resembling a scarabaeid beetle or its larva

¹**scar·a·bae·oid** \,≈≈'bē,ȯid\ *n* -s [*scarabae*us + E *-oid*] **1 :** a beetle of Scarabaeidae or a closely related family **:** SCARABAEUS **2 :** SCARABOID

²**scarabaeoid** \¦≈≈¦≈\ *adj* [*scarabaeus* + E *-oid*] **1 :** of, relating to, or constituting the third instar in the development of a blister beetle in which it resembles the larva of a scarabaeid beetle **2 :** of or relating to the Scarabaeoidea

scar·a·bae·oi·dea \,skarəbē'ȯidēə\ *n pl, cap* [NL, fr. *Scarabaeus* + *-oidea*] *in many classifications* **:** a superfamily of Polyphaga that is equivalent to the most inclusive concept of Scarabaeidae or to the superfamily Lamellicornia

scar·a·bae·us \,skarə'bēəs\ *n* [L — more at SCARAB] **1 a** *pl* **scarabaeuses** \-ēəsəz\ *or* **scara·baei** \-ē,ī\ **:** a large black or nearly black dung beetle (*Scarabaeus sacer*) of the countries bordering on the Mediterranean that with perhaps also one or more related beetles was regarded by the ancient Egyptians as symbolic of resurrection and immortality **b** *cap* [NL, fr. L, scarab] **:** a genus containing the scarabaeus and related beetles and being the type of the family Scarabaeidae **2** -ES **:** SCARAB 2

scar·a·bee \'skarə,bē\ *n* -s [MF *scarabée* — more at SCARAB] **:** SCARAB 1

scar·a·be·idae \,skarə'bēə,dē\ [NL, fr. *Scarabaeus* + *-idae*] *syn of* SCARABAEIDAE

scarab green *n* : a brilliant green that is bluer and stronger than emerald (sense 2a)

¹scar·a·boid \'skarə,bȯid\ *n* -s [*scarab* + *-oid*] : a gem engraved only on the flat oval base and somewhat rounded on the back but with no imitation of the beetle ⟨a Greek ~ of the late 6th and 5th centuries B.C.⟩

²scaraboid \"\ *adj* [*scarab* + *-oid*] **1** : SCARABAEOID **2** : of or resembling a scarab; *esp* : of or forming a scaraboid

scar·a·mouch *or* **scar·a·mouche** \'skarə,müsh *also* -ker- *or* -müch-\ *n* -s [F *Scaramouche*, fr. It *Scaramuccia*, fr. *scaramuccia* skirmish — more at SKIRMISH] **1** *usu cap* : a stock character in the Italian commedia dell' arte characterized orig. in burlesque of a Spanish don by boastfulness and poltroonery **2** *a* : a cowardly buffoon : NE'ER-DO-WELL **b** : RASCAL, SCAMP

scar·bo·rough lily \'skär(ə)rə-\ *n, usu cap S* [fr. *Scarborough*, municipal borough of Yorkshire, England] : a plant (*Vallota speciosa*) of southern Africa resembling the amaryllis and having bright red flowers

scarborough warning *n, usu cap S* [fr. *Scarborough*, Yorkshire, England] *Brit* : a very short notice or warning or none at all

scarb-tree \'skärb,trē\ *n* [prob. alter. of obs. *scrab-tree*, fr. *scrab* crab apple (prob. alter. of Scand origin) + *tree*] : WILDING 1a

¹scarce \'ske(ə)rs, 'ska(ə)|, |əs, *dial* 'skij *or* 'skərs *or* 'skȯs *or* 'skäs\ *adj* -ER/-EST [ME *scars*, fr. ONF *escars*, *scars*, fr. (assumed) VL *excarpsus*, lit., plucked out, alter. of L *excerptus*, past part. of *excerpere* to pluck out, excerpt — more at EXCERPT] **1 a** : deficient in quantity or number compared with the demand : not plentiful or abundant ⟨butter is cheap when it is plentiful, and dear when it is ~ —G.B.Shaw⟩ ⟨snappy looking gals are ~ as hen's teeth out here —*Star Detective*⟩ : RARE ⟨collects ~ Japanese prints⟩ **b** : not provided in sufficient abundance to be free **2** *obs* : PARSIMONIOUS, STINGY, FRUGAL

²scarce \"\ *adv* [ME *scars*, fr. *scars*, adj.] : SCARCELY, BARELY, HARDLY ⟨would have ~ arrived before she would find some excuse to leave —W.B.Yeats⟩ ⟨cities of the period were ~ more than towns —J.T.Adams⟩

scarce·ly *adv* [ME *scarsly*, fr. *scars* scarce + *-ly*] **1** *obs* : in a sparing manner : STINGILY **2** : by a narrow margin (as of quantity, time, or space) : only just : BARELY ⟨had ~ rung the bell when the door flew open —Agnes S. Turnbull⟩; *also* : only just if at all or as much or as many ⟨seemed ~ to notice what passed ... as if he were in some partial coma —Elizabeth M. Roberts⟩ ⟨~ more than a stone's throw from the square are the great flour mills —*Amer. Guide Series: Minn.*⟩ : almost not ⟨~ ever wore this mantle —Arnold Bennett⟩ ⟨~ anything left to sell⟩ ⟨it seemed to the child that it was after midnight ... but it was ~ eleven o'clock —Margaret Deland⟩ ⟨a guide who knew ~ a word of English⟩ — sometimes used in nonstandard construction with a superfluous negative ⟨wasn't ~ eleven o'clock yet⟩ ⟨ain't ~ 15 years old⟩ **3** *archaic* : with difficulty ⟨if the righteous ~ be saved, where shall the ... sinner appear —1 Pet 4:18 (AV)⟩ **4 a** : certainly not ⟨could ~ interfere between another man and his own beast —Owen Wister⟩ **b** : probably not — used to mitigate the force of the speaker's certainty ⟨there could ~ have been found a leader better equipped for the work —V.L. Parrington⟩

scarce·ment \'skersmənt, -kə(ə)r-\ *n* -s [obs. *scarce* to diminish (fr. ME *scarsen*, fr. *scars* scarce) + *-ment*] : an offset or retreat in the thickness of a wall or bank of earth

scarce·ness *n* -ES [ME *scarsnes*, fr. *scars* scarce + *-nes* -ness] : the quality or state of being scarce : SCARCITY

scar·ci·ty \'ske(ə)rsəd·ē, 'ska(ə)|, |əs, -ət͡ɛ, -i\ *n* -ES [ME *scarsetee*, fr. ONF *escarseté*, fr. *escars* scarce + *-eté* -ity — more at SCARCE] : the quality or condition of being scarce: **a** *obs* : SPARINGNESS, NIGGARDLINESS, PARSIMONY **b** : smallness of quantity or number in proportion to the wants or demands ⟨a ~ of grain⟩ ⟨the ~ of teachers⟩ : very limited supply ⟨the ~ of radium⟩ **c** : lack of provisions for the support of life : a period of such want ⟨a drought-struck area suffers ~⟩ **d** *obs* : the condition of lacking an adequate supply (as of the necessities of life) : PENURY, POVERTY **e** *obs* : a state of imperfection : INADEQUACY **f** : RARENESS, UNCOMMONNESS ⟨praise ... owes its value to its ~ —Samuel Johnson⟩

scarcity economics *n pl but usu sing in constr* : an economic theory that allegedly justifies limitations of output so as to assure profits

¹scare \'ske(ə)r, 'ska(ə)|, |ə, *dial* 'skij\ *vb* **scared** \|(ə)rd, |əd\ *or dial* **scart** \|(ə)rt, |ət\ **scared** *or dial* **scart; scaring; scares** [ME *skerren*, *skeren*, fr. ON *skirra*, fr. *skjarr* shy, timid] *vt* **1** : to strike with sudden fear : FRIGHTEN, ALARM, PANIC **2 a** : to drive or impel or evoke by fright ⟨rattlesnakes used to ~ me to death —Ben Hogan⟩ ⟨a scream that *scared* away the burglar⟩ ⟨an aloofness that ~s off suitors⟩ ⟨~ a confession out of the suspect by threats⟩ ⟨a pet mouse that *scared* the wits out of his mother⟩ : cause to become by fright ⟨a wild midnight ride that *scared* him stiff⟩ **b** : to cause (as bird pests) to go away in fright : frighten off ⟨from *scaring* birds, to ... child graduated through the many tasks of mixed farming —*Times Lit. Supp.*⟩ **c** : to frighten (game) from cover — used with *out* or *up* ⟨sent a beater ahead to ~ out the partridge⟩ ~ *vi* **1** : to become scared : take alarm ⟨a woman who ~s easily at the sight of a mouse⟩ **2** : to produce fright *syn* see FRIGHTEN

²scare \"\ *n* -s [ME *skere*, fr. *skeren* to scare] **1** : a sensation or state of sudden fear (fired over their heads to throw a ~ into them) : an instance of being scared: as **a** : a sudden fright produced by a trifling cause or originating in a mistake ⟨given quite a ~ by hearing the news of a boy's drowning before they set out returned⟩ **b** : a widespread state of exaggerated or mistaken alarm : PANIC ⟨the frontier situation and British arbitrary naval seizures produced a war ~ in the spring of 1794 —S.F.Bemis⟩ **2** : something that causes fright ⟨~s were made of poles wrapped with reeds hung with potsherds —C.D.Forde⟩

³scare \"\ *adj* **1** : tending to cause fright or widespread alarm ⟨~ stories that tuna caught in the Pacific are dangerously radioactive —*U.S. News & World Report*⟩ **2** : affected by or due to fright or panic ⟨a refuge for ~ money from unsettled parts of the world —*Christian Science Monitor*⟩

scarebabe \'ˌ₌ˌ\ *n* [¹*scare* + *babe*] : a thing to scare a baby : BOGEY

scarebug *n* [²*scare* + *bug*] *obs* : BUGBEAR

scare buying *n* : buying in advance of need in anticipation of possible shortages ⟨as just after the outbreak of a war⟩

scarecrow \'ˌ₌ˌ\ *n* [¹*scare* + *crow*] **1 a** : an object typically suggesting a human figure set up to frighten crows or other birds away from crops **b** : something that frightens without harming **2** : a person whose appearance suggests that of a scarecrow ⟨in a state of fear, fright, or panic ⟨~ that he will fall into the hands of the wrong kind of girl⟩ : FRIGHTENED ⟨~ to death of mature responsibilities —*Time*⟩ *syn* see AFRAID

scared *adj* -ER/-EST [fr. past part. of ¹*scare*] : thrown into or living in a state of fear, fright, or panic

scared·ness *n* -ES : the quality or state of being scared

scaredy-cat \'skerdē,kat, -di,-\ *n* [*scared* + *-y* + *cat*] : an unduly fearful person

scare·ful \'ˌ₌fəl\ *or* **scare·some** \'ˌ₌səm\ *adj* [²*scare* + *-ful* or *-some*] *dial* : DREADFUL, ALARMING

¹scarehead \'ˌ₌ˌ\ *n* [²*scare* + *head*] : an extraordinarily large or sensational newspaper headline; *esp* : one designed to arouse anxiety

²scarehead \"\ *vt* : to provide (a news story) with a scarehead

scare headline *n* [³*scare*] : SCAREHEAD

scaremonger \'ˌ₌ˌ₌\ *n* [²*scare* + *monger*] : a person who circulates frightening reports of impending disaster : ALARMIST — **scaremongering** \'ˌ₌ˌ₌ˌ\ *n* -s

scar end *n* [²*scar*] : the unfinished end of a breakwater or similar structure under construction

scar·er \'skerə(r, 'ska(ə)rə\ *n* -s : one that scares ⟨rooks ... haunted the newly sown fields, and rose in clouds at the ~'s shout —Adrian Bell⟩

scares present 3d sing of SCARE, pl of SCARE

scare up *vt* : to find by persistent effort : bring to light or get together with labor : scrape up ⟨managed to *scare up* enough food to fill a freight car —Rice⟩ ⟨*scare up* a light supper for unexpected guests⟩

scarey *var of* SCARY

¹scarf \'skärf, 'skȧf\ *n, pl* **scarves** \ˌvz, ˌvz\ *or* **scarfs** [ONF *escarpe* sash, sling, prob. alter. of OF *escrepe* wallet suspended from the shoulder, fr. ML *scrippum* pilgrim's scrip — more at SCRIP] **1 a** : a piece of cloth made in varying widths and lengths and worn for decoration or warmth across the shoulders, around the neck, over the head, or about the waist ⟨a narrow knitted ~ for sports wear and a long lace one for evening wear⟩ **b** : a square or triangle of cloth for similar uses **c** : a fur or set of furs for women's wear **2 a** : a military or official sash usu. indicative of rank or office : TIPPET **3 c** : a band of crape worn over the shoulder by mourners at a funeral **3** : a usu. oblong decorative cloth covering for the top of a table, sideboard, or bureau

²scarf \"\ *vt* -ED/-ING/-S **1** : to wrap, cover, or adorn with or as if with a scarf **2** : to wrap or throw on (a scarf or mantle) loosely

³scarf *also* **scarph** \'skärf, 'skȧf\ *n* -s [ME *skarf*, prob. of Scand origin; akin to Sw *skarv* seam, scarf, ON *skarfr* scarf — more at SCORPION] **1** : either of the chamfered or cutaway ends that fit together to form a scarf joint **2** : SCARF JOINT **3** : a groove cut along a whale's body preliminary to cutting away the blubber **4** : the beveled face of a stump or log produced by the undercut in tree felling **5** : a crease made in a piece of veneer wood or heavy paper to facilitate folding or bending in the making of a plant band

⁴scarf *or* **scarph** \"\ *vb* -ED/-ING/-S *vt* **1** : to unite (as pieces of timber) by a scarf joint **2** : to form a scarf on esp. for a joint **3** : FLENSE **4** : to put a taper in (a leaf spring) ~ *vi* **1** : to become united by a scarf joint **2** : to unite members with a scarf joint

⁵scarf *or* **scarfe** \'skärf\ *n* -s [of Scand origin; akin to ON *skarfr* cormorant] *Scot* : CORMORANT

⁶scarf \"\ *vb* -ED/-ING/-S [perh. alter. of ²*scarp*] *vi* : to remove defects (as seams, scab, scale) from the surface of unfinished steel (as a bar, ingot, billet, bloom) with oxyacetylene flame or abrasive powder ~ *vt* : to smooth by scarfing

scarf cloud *n* [¹*scarf*] : a wispy cloud forming above and later mantling the sides of a rising cumulus

scarfed \'skärft\ *or* **scarved** \-rvd\ *adj* [¹*scarf* + *-ed*] : having or wearing a scarf

scarf·er *or* **scarph·er** \'skärfə(r)\ *n* -s [⁴*scarf* + *-er*] : one that scarfs: as **a** : one that scarfs parts (as of shoes or metal pieces) so that smooth joints may be formed **b** : an operator of a machine for beveling the edges of skelp

scarf joint *n* [³*scarf*] : a joint made by chamfering, halving, notching, or otherwise cutting away two pieces to correspond to each other and securing them together after overlapping (as by gluing, bolting, riveting, welding, brazing)

scarfpin \'ˌ₌ˌ\ *n* [¹*scarf* + *pin*] : TIEPIN

scarfskin \'ˌ₌ˌ\ *n* [¹*scarf* + *skin*] : EPIDERMIS; *esp* : that forming the cuticle of a nail

scarfweld *n* [³*scarf* + *weld*] : a welded scarf joint in metal

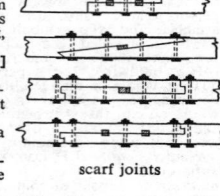

scarf joints

¹scar·id \-rəd\ *adj* [NL *Scaridae*] : of or relating to the Scaridae

²scarid \"\ *n* -s : a fish of the family Scaridae

scar·i·dae \'skarə,dē\ *n pl, cap* [NL fr. *Scarus*, type genus + *-idae*] : a family of marine percoid fishes closely resembling the Labridae but having the teeth of the jaws more or less coalescent and comprising the true parrot fishes

scarier *comparative of* SCARY

scariest *superlative of* SCARY

scar·i·fi·ca·tion \ˌskar(ə)rəfəˈkāshən, ˌsker-\ *n* -s [ME, fr. LL *scarification-, scarificatio*, fr. *scarificatus* (past part. of *scarificare* to scarify) + L *-ion-, -io* -ion] **1** : the act or process of scarifying **2** : a mark or group of marks made by scarifying

scar·i·fi·ca·tor \'ˌ₌₌₌ˌkād·ə(r\ *n* -s [NL, fr. LL *scarificatus* + L *-or*] : an instrument for making superficial cuts in the skin; *esp* : one containing several lancets moved by a spring

scar·i·fi·er \'ska(ə)rəˌf(ə)r, 'sker-, -ˌī-\ *n* -s : one that scarifies: as **a** : SCARIFICATOR : a machine that tears up and partially pulverizes surface soil **c** : an implement or machine that tears up the surface of a road prior to resurfacing

¹scar·i·fy \-ˌfī\ *vb* -ED/-ING/-ES [MF *scarifier*, fr. LL *scarificare*, alter. (influenced by L *-ficare* -fy) of L *scarifare*, fr. Gk *skariphasthai* to scratch an outline, sketch — more at SCRIBE, -FY] *vt* **1** : to make a number of cuts, scratches, or scars on: as **a** : to make a number of small incisions in (the superficial skin or mucous membrane) with a lancet or scarificator (as for drawing blood or inoculating) **b** : to mark with scars : CICATRIZE **2** : to lacerate the feelings of : censure mercilessly : FLAY ⟨in a brilliant tirade ... he denounces, *scarifies*, slaps the pedantic schoolmasters —Gilbert Highet⟩ **3** : to break up and loosen the surface of (as a field or road) **4** : to treat (hard-coated seed) by mechanical abrasion or with acid to facilitate water absorption and hasten germination ~ *vi* **1** : to make cuts, scratches, or scars on skin or mucous membrane **2** : to subject a person to cutting criticism or some other painful experience **3** : to break up and loosen a hard surface ⟨if the road has become deeply rutted or pitted it is necessary to ~ at least to the depth of the deepest holes —L.I.Hewes & C.H.Oglesby⟩

²scarify \"\ *vt* -ED/-ING/-ES [¹*scare* + *-ify*] *dial* : SCARE, FRIGHTEN

scar·i·ly \'skerəlē, 'ska(ə)r-, -li\ *adv* : in a scary manner : in a frightened or frightening way

scar·i·ness \-rēn-\ *n* -ES : the quality or state of being scary

scaring *pres part of* SCARE

scar·i·ous \'ska(ə)rēəs\ *also* **scar·i·ose** \-ē,ōs\ *adj* [NL *scariosus*] : thin and membranous in texture ⟨a bract⟩

scar·la·ti·na \ˌskärlə'tēnə, -kȧl-\ *n* -s [NL, fr. ML *scarlata*, *scarlatum* piece of cloth, scarlet] : SCARLET FEVER — **scar·la·ti·nal** \-'tēn³l\ *adj*

scar·la·ti·ni·form \ˌ₌₌'tēnə,fȯrm, -tin-\ *adj* [NL *scarlatina* + E *-iform*] : resembling the rash of scarlet fever

scar·la·ti·no·gen·ic \-,jenik\ *adj* [NL *scarlatina* + *-o-* + E *-genic*] : causing scarlet fever ⟨a ~ streptococcus⟩

scar·la·ti·noid \-'tē,nȯid, skär'lat³n,ȯid\ *adj* [NL *scarlatina* + E *-oid*] : SCARLATINIFORM

scar·less \'skärləs\ *adj* [*scar* + *-less*] : having or leaving no scar

¹scar·let \'skärlət, 'skȧl-, *usu* -ləd-+V\ *n* -s [ME *scarlet, scarlat*, fr. OF or ML; OF *escarlate*, fr. ML *scarlata, scarlatum, scarleta, scarletum*, fr. Per *saqalāt* kind of rich cloth] **1 a** *obs* (1) : a rich cloth of bright color (2) *or* **scarlet in grain** [*scarlet in grain*, ME, fr. *scarlet* + *in grain* — more at GRAIN] : a cloth of a fast-dyed red **b** : cloth or clothes of a scarlet color ⟨arrayed in ~⟩; *specif* : a costume of scarlet color signifying official or professional rank or worn as a uniform **c** : persons wearing scarlet (as at a fox hunt) **2 a** : any of various bright reds ⟨summer flowers had given place to the ~s and mauves of autumn —Frances Towers⟩ **b** *or* **scarlet red** : a vivid red that is yellower and slightly paler than apple red, yellower and lighter than carmine, yellower and duller than Castilian red, yellower and paler than madder crimson, and bluer, less strong, and slightly darker than pimento — called also *French scarlet*, *Venetian scarlet*

²scarlet \"\ *adj* [ME, fr. ¹*scarlet*] **1 a** : of the color scarlet **b** : clad in scarlet **c** : having the face reddened by emotion (as embarrassment, anger) : RED-FACED ⟨turned ~ with rage⟩ **2** [so called fr. its use in Isa 1:18 and Rev 17:1–6] **a** : glaringly offensive : FLAGRANT, HEINOUS ⟨bent upon sinning in flagrant and ~ fashion —G.W.Johnson⟩ **b** : of, characterized by, or associated with sexual immorality; *specif* : of or practicing prostitution ⟨in the mining camps ... the inevitable influx of ~ women who became the hostesses of the gambling dens and night clubs —Mabel Elliott⟩

scarlet admiral *n* : RED ADMIRAL

scarlet-berried elder \'ˌ₌₌₌ — ₌-\ *n* : RED-BERRIED ELDER

scarletberry \'ˌ₌₌ — *see* BERRY\ *n* **1** : BITTERSWEET 2a **2** : the fruit of the scarletberry

scarlet bugler *n* **1** : a pentstemon (*Pentstemon centranthifolius*) native to southwestern No. America, used as an ornamental, and having thick leaves and long tubular scarlet

flowers **2** : a cactus of the genus *Cleistocactus* having long tubular bright-red flowers

scarlet bush *n* : SCARLET HAMELIA

scarlet clematis *n* : a showy woody vine (*Clematis texensis*) of Texas with solitary nodding scarlet flowers

scarlet cup *n* : any of various red fungi of the genus *Peziza*

scarlet-day *n* : a ceremonial occasion at a British university marked by the wearing of official robes of scarlet

scarlet eggplant *n* : TOMATO EGGPLANT

scarlet elder *n* : RED-BERRIED ELDER

scarlet fever *n* : an acute contagious febrile disease caused by a hemolytic streptococcus and characterized by inflammation of the nose, throat, and mouth sometimes with strawberry tongue and a generalized toxemia accompanied by a rash marked by flushing of the skin with red spots and followed in a week or two by desquamation of the skin

scarlet fritillary *n* : a bulbous herb (*Fritillaria recurva*) with scarlet-and-yellow flowers

scarlet gaura *n* : an erect perennial herb (*Gaura coccinea*) of central No. America with alternate lanceolate leaves and rather sparse terminal leafy spikes of bright red flowers

scarlet hamelia *n* : a tropical American shrub (*Hamelia erecta*) having edible fruit and often cultivated for its showy scarlet or crimson flowers

scarlet haw *n* : any of several hawthorns; *esp* : a common American tree or shrub (*Crataegus biltmoriana*) with showy white flowers in corymbs and bright-red fruit

scarlet ibis *n* : an ibis (*Eudocimus ruber*) of South and Central America that is an intense scarlet with black-tipped wings

scarlet lake *n* : BLOOD RED

scarlet larkspur *n* : a perennial herb (*Delphinium cardinale*) of southern California with bright-scarlet flowers

scarlet letter *n* [fr. the novel *The Scarlet Letter* (1850) by Nathaniel Hawthorne †1864 Am. novelist] : a scarlet A worn as a punitive mark of adultery

scarlet lightning *n* [by folk etymology fr. *scarlet lychnis*] : MALTESE CROSS 2

scarlet lobelia *n* : CARDINAL FLOWER

scar·let·ly *adv* : in a scarlet manner : FLAGRANTLY

scarlet lychnis *n* : MALTESE CROSS 2

scarlet macaw *n* : a macaw (*Ara macao*) that is the largest and showiest of Mexican parrots and has predominantly scarlet or vermilion plumage with bright yellow wing coverts, deep purplish remiges, and azure blue lower back, rump, and tail coverts

scarlet madder *n* : MADDER SCARLET

scarlet maple *n* : RED MAPLE

scarlet mite *n* : any of numerous bright red carnivorous mites found among grass and weeds including some with young that are parasitic on spiders and insects — compare CHIGGER 2

scarlet monkey flower *n* : a perennial herb (*Mimulus cardinalis*) of the western U. S. with showy scarlet 2-lipped flowers

scarlet oak *n* : an oak (*Quercus coccinea*) having close-grained wood, deeply 7-lobed leaves that turn scarlet in autumn, and an acorn with a deep cup

scarlet ocher *n* : INDIAN RED 2b

¹scarlet pimpernel *n* : a common pimpernel (*Anagallis arvensis*) having scarlet, white, or purplish flowers that close at the approach of rainy or cloudy weather — called also *poor man's weatherglass*, *red pimpernel*

²scarlet pimpernel *n* [fr. *The Scarlet Pimpernel*, assumed name of hero of *The Scarlet Pimpernel* (1905), romance by Baroness Emmuska Orczy †1947 Eng. novelist and playwright] : a person who rescues others from mortal danger by smuggling them across a border

scarlet plume *n* : a Mexican shrub (*Euphorbia fulgens*) often cultivated for its scarlet-bracted flowers

scarlet red *n* **1** : SCARLET 2b **2** *also* **scarlet red medicinal** : SUDAN IV

scarlet runner *also* **scarlet runner bean** *n* : a tropical American high-climbing bean (*Phaseolus coccineus*) with large bright red flowers and red-and-black seeds that is grown widely as an ornamental and is a preferred food bean in Great Britain

scarlets *pl of* SCARLET

scarlet sage *n* : any of several red-flowered salvias; *esp* : a well-known garden bedding plant (*Salvia splendens*) of Brazil with long racemes of intense scarlet flowers — compare SAGE 1a

scarlet snake *n* **1** : a small slender colubrid snake (*Cemophora coccinea*) of the southern U. S. having the back transversely striped with black, red, and yellow **2** *also* **scarlet king snake** : a king snake (*Lampropeltis elapsoides*) having marks like those of the scarlet snake

scarlet strawberry *n* : VIRGINIA STRAWBERRY

scarlet sumac *n* : SMOOTH SUMAC 1

scarlet tanager *n* : a common American tanager (*Piranga olivacea*) of which the adult male is scarlet with black wings and tail and the female and young are chiefly olive — called also *redbird*, *red robin*

scarlet trumpet *n* : STANDING CYPRESS

scarlet vermilion *n* : a strong reddish orange that is yellower and paler than paprika or poppy, redder and darker than fire red, and less strong and slightly lighter than average coral red

¹scarn \'skärn\ *archaic var of* SCORN

²scarn \"\ *n* -s [of Scand origin; akin to ON *skarn* dung — more at SCAT-] *dial Eng* : DUNG

¹scar·oid \'ska(ə),rȯid\ *adj* [NL *Scarus* + E *-oid*] : resembling or related to the Scaridae

²scaroid \"\ *n* -s : a scaroid fish

sca·ro·la \skə'rōlə\ *or* **sca·role** \-ˈōl\ *n* -s [It *scariola, scarola*, fr. OIt *scariola* — more at ESCAROLE] : ESCAROLE

¹scarp *or* **scarpe** \'skärp\ *n* -s [ONF *escarpe* sash, sling — more at SCARF] *heraldry* : a diminutive of the bend sinister half its width

²scarp \'skärp, 'skȧp\ *n* -s [It *scarpa*, prob. of Gmc origin; akin to OE *scearp* sharp — more at SHARP] **1** : a nearly vertical sometimes walled side of a ditch below the parapet of a fortification — called also *escarp*; compare COUNTERSCARP **2 a** : a line of cliffs produced by faulting or erosion — see FAULT-LINE SCARP, FAULT SCARP **b** : a low steep slope along a beach caused by wave erosion

³scarp \"\ *vt* -ED/-ING/-S **1** : to cut so as to form a scarp ⟨cut down vertically or to a steep slope ⟨~ the face of a ditch⟩ ⟨~ a coast into rugged cliffs⟩

scar·pa's fascia \'skärpəz-\ *n, usu cap S* [after Antonio *Scarpa* †1832, Ital. anatomist & surgeon] : the superficial fascia of the groin

scarpa's foramen *n, usu cap S* [after Antonio *Scarpa*] : either of two canals opening into the incisive foramen in the median plane and transmitting the nasopalatine nerves

scarpa's triangle *also* **scarpa's trigone** *n, usu cap S* [after Antonio *Scarpa*] : an area in the upper anterior part of the thigh bounded by Poupart's ligament, the sartorius, and the adductor longus

scarp·er \'skȧpə(r\ *vi* -ED/-ING/-S [perh. fr. It *scappare* to flee, escape, fr. (assumed) VL *excappare* — more at ESCAPE] *Brit* : to run away : make off

scarph *var of* SCARF

scarpher *var of* SCARFER

scarp·let \'skärplət\ *n* -s [²*scarp* + *-let*] : a fault scarp only a few inches or at most a few feet high : earthquake rent

scarpside \'ˌ₌ˌ\ *n* : the side of a scarp

scarred *past of* SCAR

scar·rer \'skärə(r\ *n* -s [²*scar* + *-er*] : one that shaves blemishes from leather

scarring *n* [fr. gerund of ²*scar*] : a marking resulting from being scarred

scar·row \'ska(ə)‚rō\ *n* -s [of Scand origin; akin to ON *skæra* twilight, Gk *skia* shadow — more at SCENE] *Scot* : a shadowy or faint light

¹scar·ry \'skärē\ *adj* [¹*scar* + *-y*] : characterized by bare and rugged projections of rock ⟨the ~ flank of the mountain⟩

²scarry \"\ *adj* -ER/-EST [²*scar* + *-y*] : bearing marks of wounds : SCARRED

scars *pl of* SCAR, *pres 3d sing of* SCAR

¹scart \'skärt\ *vb* -ED/-ING/-ES [ME *skarten*, alter. of *scratten* to scratch] *chiefly Scot* : SCRATCH, SCRAPE

²scart \"\ *n* -s *chiefly Scot* : SCRATCH, MARK; *esp* : one made in writing

3scart \"\ or **scarth** \-rth\ *n* -s [ME *scarth*, of Scand origin; akin to ON *skarfr* cormorant] *chiefly Scot* : CORMORANT

4scart *dial past of* SCARE

scarth \'skärth\ *n* -s [of Scand origin; akin to ON *skarth* notch, mountain pass — more at SHARD] *dial Eng* : a bare rough rock

scar tissue *n* : the connective tissue forming a scar and composed chiefly of fibroblasts in recent scars and largely of dense collagenous fibers in old scars

scar·us \'ska(a)rəs\ *n* [L, fr. Gk *skaros*; prob. akin to Gk *skairein* to skip, leap] **1** -ES : a parrot fish (*Sparisoma cretense*) of the Mediterranean of excellent table quality and highly esteemed by the ancient Romans **2** *cap* [NL, fr. L, parrot fish] : the type genus of Scaridae comprising fishes with the teeth completely consolidated so that the jaws have the appearance of a bird's beak — compare PARROT FISH

scarved *var of* SCARFED

scarves *pl of* SCARF

scary *also* **scarey** \'skerē, 'ska(a)r-, -ri, *dial* 'skir-\ *adj* **scarier**; **scariest** [2*scare* + *-y*] **1** : causing fright : ALARMING ⟨this . . . ~ picture story of a jungle tiger who waits to pounce on an unsuspecting camel —Katharine T. Kinkead⟩ **2** : easily scared : TIMID ⟨a sudden movement or sharp noise could cause a stampede in the ~ half-wild cattle⟩ **3** : SCARED, ALARMED, FRIGHTENED ⟨while I'm waiting, I get a little ~ and think I ought to call the cops —Bant Singer⟩

1scat \'skat\ *n* -s [ON *skattr* tribute — more at SCEAT] : a crown tax in the Shetland and Orkney islands for the use (as for pasturage) of commons

2scat \"\ *n* -s [prob. imit.] **1** *dial Eng* : a sudden shower of rain **2** [perh. fr. 3*scat*] *dial* : SMASH, BANG, SMACK

3scat \"\ *vt* **scat**; **scat**; **scatting**; **scats** [perh. short for 1*scatter*] **1** *chiefly dial* : SCATTER ⟨~ his bones abroad, so as not one hangs to another —Eden Phillpotts⟩ **2** *chiefly dial* : SMASH, BEAT ⟨~ me across the face with a tar brush —*Manchester Guardian Weekly*⟩

4scat \", *usu* -ad·+V\ *vi* **scatted**; **scatted**; **scatting**; **scats** **1** : to go away quickly : leave hurriedly ⟨you just ~ off to bed, young lady —Oakley Hall⟩ — often used interjectionally to drive away an animal (as a cat) **2** : to move with more than ordinary speed ⟨only advertised 125 hp, but the car would ~ in any man's language —*Motor Life*⟩

5scat *var of* SKAT

6scat *also* **skat** \'skat, *usu* -ad·+V\ *n* -s [Gk *skat-*, *skōr* excrement — more at SCAT-] : an animal fecal dropping

7scat \"\ *n* -s [by shortening fr. NL *Scatophagus*, former generic name, fr. Gk *skatophagos* scatophagous] : ARGUSFISH

8scat \"\ *n* -s [perh. imit.] : singing with meaningless syllables instead of words used esp. in jazz for an instrumental effect — compare BOP, RIFF

9scat \"\ *vi* **scatted**; **scatted**; **scatting**; **scats** : to improvise or repeat meaningless syllables to a melody : sing scat

scat- *or* **scato-** *comb form* [Gk *skato-*, fr. *skat-*, *skōr* excrement; akin to OE *scearn* dung, ON *skarn* dung, L mu*scerda* mouse dropping, and prob. to Russ *sor* filth] : ordure ⟨*scato*logy⟩

scatback \'=,=\ *n* [5*scat* + *back*] : a backfield player in football who is an esp. fast and elusive runner

1scathe \'skāth\ *also* **scath** \'skath\ *n*, *pl* **scathes** [ME *scath*, *skathe*, fr. ON *skathi*; akin to OE *sceatha* malefactor, injury, OHG *scado* damage, injury, harm, Goth *skathis*, Gk *askēthēs* unharmed] **1** : HARM, INJURY, DAMAGE ⟨all the British bombers were able to return safely to their base . . . without ~ —*Manchester Guardian Weekly*⟩ **2** *chiefly dial* : a source of regret : PITY, MISFORTUNE

2scathe \"\ *also* **scath** \"\ *vt* **scathed**; **scathed**; **scathing**; **scathes** *also* **scaths** [ME *scathen*, *skathen*, fr. ON *skatha*; akin to OE *sceathian* to injure, OHG *scadōn*; denominative fr. the root of OE *sceatha* injury] **1** : to do harm to : INJURE, DAMAGE; *specif* : to injure by scorching or withering with fire or lightning ⟨a giant oak which heaven's fierce flame had *scathed* —P.B.Shelley⟩ **2** : to assail with withering denunciation ⟨bombarding her with rhetoric and . . . *scathing* her with sarcasm —Jean Stafford⟩

scathe·ful \'skāthfəl\ *adj* [1*scathe* + *-ful*] : HARMFUL, PERNICIOUS

scathe·less \-thləs\ *adj* [ME *scathles*, fr. *scath* scathe + *-les* -less] : being without scathe, injury, or damage : UNHARMED ⟨too excited to stop and shoot, and so they got away ~ —T.E. Lawrence⟩ — **scathe·less·ly** *adv*

scathing *adj* [fr. pres. part. of 2*scathe*] : bitterly severe ⟨silenced him with a ~ look⟩ ⟨braved his ~ scorn⟩ ⟨looked as though he had been through some ~ ordeal —Agnes M. Cleaveland⟩ — **scath·ing·ly** *adv*

scatole *var of* SKATOLE

scat·o·log·i·cal \¦skad·ᵊl¦äjəkəl, -atᵊl-, -jēk-\ *also* **scat·o·log·ic** \-jik, -jēk\ *adj* [*scatology* + *-ical*, *-ic*] **1** : of or relating to the study of excrement ⟨~ data⟩ **2** : marked by an interest in excrement or obscenity ⟨of the obscene rhymes contributed by the younger children, the ~ rather than the sexual element prevailed —Brian Sutton-Smith⟩ **3** : of or relating to excrement or excremental functions ⟨~ terms⟩

sca·tol·o·gy *also* **ska·tol·o·gy** \skə'täləjē, ska'- -ji\ *n* -ES [*scatology* fr. *scat-* + *-logy*; *skatology*, alter. (influenced by Gk *skato-* scat-) of *scatology*] **1** : the study of excrement; *specif* : analysis of animal diet by examination of fecal droppings **2** : obscene literature **3** : interest in things filthy or obscene (as in literature)

scat·o·phag·i·dae \,skad·ə'fajə,dē\ *n*, *cap* [NL, fr. *Scatophaga*, type genus, (fr. Gk *skatophagos* scatophagous) + *-idae*] : a family of round-headed pollinose muscoid flies that comprise the typical dung flies

sca·toph·a·gous \skə'täfəgəs\ *adj* [Gk *skatophagos*, fr. *skat-*, *skōr* excrement + *phagein* to eat — more at SCAT-, BAKSHEESH] : habitually feeding on dung : COPROPHAGOUS ⟨a ~ beetle⟩

sca·toph·a·gy \-fəjē\ *n* -ES [*scat-* + *-phagy*] : the practice of eating excrement or other filth as a religious ceremonial rite or as a pathological obsession

scats *pl of* SCAT, *pres 3d sing of* SCAT

scatt \'skat\ *n* -s [of Scand origin; akin to ON *skattr* tribute — more at SCEAT] *archaic* : TAX, TRIBUTE ⟨laying waste the kingdom, seizing ~ and treasure —H.W.Longfellow⟩

scatted *past of* SCAT

1scat·ter \'skad·ə(r), -atə-\ *vb* -ED/-ING/-S [ME *scateren*] *vt* **1** *archaic* : to fling away heedlessly : SQUANDER **2 a** : to cause (a group or collection) to separate into various widely removed parts ⟨approaching cars that ~*ed* the players to both sides of the street⟩ ⟨a gust that ~*ed* the pile of leaves in all directions⟩ ⟨heirs who ~*ed* his library of Colonial history by selling the books when they needed money⟩ **b** : to cause (as a mist) to vanish as if by scattering ⟨combating prejudice and ~*ing* the clouds of ignorance —Julius May⟩ **3** : to place (as buildings) here and there : distribute at irregular and widely separate intervals ⟨~ defense factories instead of concentrating them in a single area easily obliterated by one bombing⟩ ⟨a child who ~*s* his toys all over the house⟩ **4 a** : to spread widely and at random by or as if by throwing: SOW, BROADCAST ⟨plant the seed in rows or ~ it over the plot⟩ : DISSEMINATE ⟨~ tracts from train windows —Roger Pippett⟩ ⟨the editors fled . . . ~*ing* flames of discontent along the way —R.A.Billington⟩ : DIFFUSE ⟨the writers have ~*ed* sentiment and glamor over the story with a lavish hand —*Irish Digest*⟩ **b** (1) : to overspread haphazardly with something : SPRINKLE ⟨a battle that ~*ed* the field with dead and wounded⟩ ⟨~*ed* the pages of her book with famous names⟩ (2) : to spread at random over : BESTREW ⟨small floating shapes of paper . . . ~*ing* the water like a countless flock of inch-long ducks —William Sansom⟩ **5 a** : to reflect irregularly and diffusely (as from a piece of ground glass) **b** : to diffuse or disperse (a beam of radiation) in a random manner as a result of collision of the particles, photons, or waves with particles of the medium traversed **6** : to divide into ineffectually small portions : make ineffectual by excessive division ⟨was cautious about ~*ing* his strength and frequently had to curb the ambitions of his sons to go into other lines of business —Frank Kent⟩ ~ *vi* **1 a** : to separate and go in various directions ⟨a flock of pigeons feeding that ~*ed* when a dog approached⟩ **b** : to vanish as if by scattering ⟨clouds ~ after a storm⟩ **2** : to occur or fall at irregular widely separated intervals : spread at random over a surface or through a space or substance ⟨that fine chain of lakes which ~ up and down the center of Florida, like bright beads —Marjory S. Douglas⟩ **3** : to cause something to scatter; *esp* : to cause the shot of a shotgun to spread widely when fired

syn SCATTER, DISPERSE, DISSIPATE, and DISPEL can mean in common to cause a group or mass to separate or break up. SCATTER may imply a force which drives, usu. rapidly, in different directions or may imply only throwing so that the units spread out and fall at random ⟨*scatter* a mob with tear gas bombs⟩ ⟨*scatter* seed over a lawn⟩ ⟨the brief yarns *scattered* so profusely through his first novel —Dayton Kohler⟩ ⟨the serious composer must, through necessity, *scatter* his energy and diffuse his efforts by spending innumerable hours in teaching —David Ewen⟩ ⟨a shower of dried mud was *scattered* over her clothes —Ellen Glasgow⟩ DISPERSE usu. implies a wider separation and a complete breaking up of a mass or group ⟨the clouds *dispersed*, driven into fragments by the wind⟩ ⟨the bureau was dismembered, its staff *dispersed* —V.G.Heiser⟩ ⟨when this simple meal was finished, the Webster family *dispersed* to entertain itself —Robertson Davies⟩ ⟨the nature of their employment and adjustment tended to *disperse* the refugees through the whole nation —Oscar Handlin⟩ DISSIPATE stresses the idea of complete disintegration or dissolution, as by evaporation or squandering, and a consequent vanishing ⟨from the far-off wooded hills the haze . . . had not yet *dissipated* —D.H.Lawrence⟩ ⟨this hysteria can be *dissipated* —Kenneth Leslie⟩ ⟨other freedoms will be *dissipated* along with that of the press —Hal O'Flaherty⟩ DISPEL stresses the driving away by or as if by scattering, stressing very little the idea of separation of parts ⟨*dispel* all remnants of your influenza —G.B.Shaw⟩ ⟨*dispel* the notion that social life is a peculiarity of the higher organisms —A.N.Whitehead⟩ ⟨truth and frankness *dispel* difficulties —Bertrand Russell⟩ ⟨had not *dispelled* her apprehension and her distrust —Jean Stafford⟩ **syn** see in addition STREW

2scatter \"\ *n* -s **1** : the act or process of scattering **2** : a small supply or number scattered, irregularly distributed, or carelessly strewn about ⟨there was a ~ of rain on the windows —Dorothy Whipple⟩ ⟨a ~ of applause⟩ **3** : the state or extent of being scattered; *specif* : the dispersion of observations in a frequency distribution measured by the coefficient of variation **4** : SCATTERING 2b

3scatter \"\ *adj* [1*scatter* & 2*scatter*] **1** : of, characterized by, or effecting scatter ⟨~ analysis⟩ ⟨~ dose⟩ ⟨~ arm⟩ **2** : adapted to being placed here and there

4scatter \"\ *n* -s [origin unknown] **1** *slang* : SALOON **2** *slang* : HANGOUT, JOINT

scat·ter·able \-ərəbəl\ *adj* : that can be scattered

scat·ter·ation \,skad·ə'rāshən\ *n* -s [1*scatter* + *-ation*] **1** : the act or process of scattering ⟨while there are many reasons for the centrifugal whirl of people and business from the older cities, the automobile has been the greatest factor in the ~ —*N.Y.Times*⟩ **2** : the state of being scattered **3** : something scattered ⟨a tract of land, edged on its two coasts with a ~ of islands —Colin Simpson⟩

scatter bomb *n* [3*scatter*] : an incendiary bomb containing a bursting charge that scatters the burning incendiary agent over a considerable area

scatter-bomb \'==,=\ *vb* [*scatter bomb*] *vt* : to bomb with scatter bombs ~ *vi* : to bomb a target so that the bombs land in a loose or random pattern

scatterbrain \,==,=\ *n* [1*scatter* + *brain*] : a flighty thoughtless person : a person who is incapable of concentration or attention

scatterbrained \'==,=\ *adj* : having the characteristics of a scatterbrain

scatter diagram *n* [3*scatter*] : a two-dimensional graph in rectangular coordinates consisting of points whose coordinates represent corresponding values of two variables whose relationship is being studied — called also *scattergram*, *scattergraph*, *scatterplot*

scattered *adj* [fr. past part. of 1*scatter*] **1 a** : marked by disorganized dispersion : DISUNITED ⟨the growth of modern science from an activity of ~ individuals —John Pfeiffer⟩ **b** : marked by distraction : RAMBLING ⟨~ thoughts⟩ **2 a** : separated by or occurring at wide irregular intervals ⟨only ~ remarks on the subject are to be found in the literature —David Abercrombie⟩ ⟨~ showers⟩ : widely separated ⟨four ~ states — Utah, Texas, Michigan, and New Jersey —Arthur Geddes⟩ **b** : irregular in position : having no fixed or definite arrangement — used of leaves or branches **3** *obs* : negligently tossed aside or dropped ⟨loose now and then a ~ smile —Shak.⟩ **4** : having the parts disorganized or widely separated ⟨a ~ story⟩ : spread over a wide area ⟨a ~ village⟩ ⟨serves the ~ population in this mountain region —*Amer. Guide Series: Tenn.*⟩

scattered clouds *n pl* : clouds covering one tenth to one half of the sky

scat·tered·ly *adv* : in a scattered manner

scat·tered·ness *n* -ES : the quality or state of being scattered

scat·ter·er \'skad·ərə(r), -atər-\ *n* -s : one that scatters

scattergood \'==,=\ *n* [1*scatter* + *good*] : a wasteful person : SPENDTHRIFT

scat·ter·gram \'skad·ə(r),gram\ *n* [2*scatter* + *-gram*] : SCATTER DIAGRAM

scat·ter·graph \-raf, -råf\ *n* [2*scatter* + *-graph*] : SCATTER DIAGRAM

scatter-gun \'==,=\ *n* [1*scatter* + *gun*] : SHOTGUN

1scattering *n* -s [ME *scatering*, fr. *scateren* to scatter + *-ing*] **1** : an act or process in which something scatters or is scattered **2** : something scattered: as **a** : a small number or quantity interspersed here and there ⟨a ~ of visitors⟩ **b** : the random change in direction of a beam or ray due to collision of the particles, photons, or waves constituting the radiation with the particles of the medium traversed

2scattering *adj* [fr. pres. part. of 1*scatter*] **1** : going in various directions **2** : found or placed far apart and in no order : occurring at irregular intervals ⟨~ shots⟩ **3** : divided among many or several ⟨~ votes⟩ — **scat·ter·ing·ly** *adv*

scattering coefficient *n* : the fractional rate in the transmission of radiation through a scattering medium (as of light through fog) at which the flux density of radiation decreases by scattering in respect to the thickness of the medium traversed

scat·ter·ling \'skad·ə(r)liŋ\ *n* -s [1*scatter* + *-ling*] *archaic* : VAGRANT

scatter pin *n* [1*scatter*] : a small pin used as jewelry and worn usu. in groups of two or more on a woman's dress

scatterplot \'==,=\ *n* [3*scatter* + *plot*] : SCATTER DIAGRAM

scatter rug *n* [1*scatter*] : a rug of such a size that several can be used (as to fill vacant places) in a room

scatters *pres 3d sing of* SCATTER, *pl of* SCATTER

scatter shot *n* : shot loaded for firing in a weapon built to fire a solid projectile through its rifled bore — compare SHOTGUN

scattershot \'==,=\ *adj* [*scatter shot*] : extending over a wide undiscriminating range : broadly haphazard : randomly inclusive : SHOTGUN ⟨~ approaches . . . provide services for groups or masses of individuals —R.P.Capes⟩ ⟨disgusted by his ~ accusations⟩

scat·tery \'skad·ərē\ *adj* [1*scatter* + *-y*] : marked by scattering : SCATTERED

scatting *pres part of* SCAT

scat·ty \'skati\ *adj* -ER/-EST [prob. fr. *scatt*erbrain + *-y*] *Brit* : CRAZY

scat·u·la \'skachələ\ *n*, *pl* **scatu·lae** \-chə,lē\ [ML] : a flat rectangular box used in dispensing powders and pills

sca·tu·ri·ent \skə'tu̇rēənt\ *adj* [L *scaturient-*, *scaturiens*, fr. pres. part. of *scaturire* to gush out, fr. *scatere* to bubble, gush, be abundant — more at SHAD] : gushing forth : OVERFLOWING, EFFUSIVE

scaud \'skåd, 'sko̊d\ *chiefly Scot var of* SCALD

scauld \'skåd\ *Scot var of* SCOLD

scaum \'skåm, 'sko̊m\ *vt* -ED/-ING/-S [origin unknown] *chiefly Scot* : BURN, SCORCH

scaup \'skåp, 'sko̊p\ *dial var of* SCALP

scaup duck \'sko̊p-\ *or* **scaup** *n*, *pl* **scaup** *or* **scaups** [*scaup*, perh. alter. of 1*scalp*; fr. its fondness for shellfish] : any of several ducks of the genus *Aythya*: as **a** : GREATER SCAUP **b** : LESSER SCAUP

scauper *var of* SCORPER

1scaur \'skär\ *chiefly Scot var of* 4SCAR

2scaur \"\ *chiefly Scot var of* 1SCAR

scav·age \'skavij\ *n* -s [ME *skawage*, fr. ONF *escauwage* inspection, fr. *escauwer* to inspect (of Gmc origin) + *-age*; akin to OE *scēawian* to look at, see, inspect — more at SHOW] : a duty exacted in 14th, 15th, and 16th century England of nonresident merchants by mayors, sheriffs, or corporations on goods shown for sale

scavager *n* -s [ME *skawager*, fr. *skawage* scavage + *-er*; fr. the fact that the official charged with collecting the toll was later made responsible for keeping the streets clean] *obs* : SCAVENGER

scav·enge \'skavənj\ *vb* -ED/-ING/-S [back-formation fr. *scavenger*] *vt* **1 a** (1) : to dislodge or gather and remove (dirt, waste, or impurities) from cast-off matter ⟨sea gulls . . . ~ the remains of the daily fish market —Arnold Bennett⟩ (2) : to remove (burned gases) from the cylinder of an internal combustion engine by special means (as a long exhaust pipe or piston-controlled ports in the cylinder wall) **b** (1) : to remove dirt, waste, or impurities from (as a street or chemical solution) (2) : to clean and purify (molten metal) by taking up foreign elements (as oxygen) in chemical union **2 a** : to extract or collect (something for use) from discarded material ⟨with no food, money, or work permits, . . . his friends headed south, eating anything they could ~ —*Time*⟩ **b** : to extract or collect usable material from ⟨lighted false beacons for mariners and *scavenged* the wreckage down to the boots of the drowned sailors —Robert Hatch⟩ **3** : to hunt in for wanted or usable material obtainable at no cost ⟨he gathered material for . . . settings by *scavenging* museums, textile and rubber factories —Stephen Winship⟩ ~ *vi* **1** : to remove dirt, waste, or impurities from a space or substance **2** : to remove the burned gases from the cylinder of an internal-combustion engine after a working stroke **3** : to extract or collect something for use from material regarded as useless ⟨another way of gathering parts is by *scavenging* off wrecked vehicles —*Infantry Jour.*⟩ : appropriate for use what otherwise would go to waste : exploit leavings **4** : to search about for wanted or usable material usu. obtainable at no cost : HUNT — usu. used with *for* ⟨women who ~ for scrap brass on the artillery range⟩

scavenge pipe *n* : a return pipe for oil from an internal-combustion engine to a tank

1scav·eng·er \-jə(r)\ *n* -s [alter. of *scavager*] **1** : a former English official charged orig. with the collection of scavage and later with various other duties including that of keeping the streets clean **2** *chiefly Brit* : a person employed to remove dirt and refuse from the streets of a municipality : STREET CLEANER **3** : one that scavenges: as **a** : a garbage collector **b** : JUNKMAN **c** : one that collects the refuse about a logging camp **d** : a chemically active substance either present in or added to a mixture to make innocuous or to remove an undesirable substance ⟨calcium . . . is already being used as a ~ in melting steel, copper, nickel, lead —A.M.Bateman⟩ ⟨the tin compound acts also as a ~ for hydrogen chloride —A.S. Kenyon⟩ — compare GETTER **4 a** : an organism that devours refuse, carrion, or matter injurious to the general health **b** : SCAVENGER BEETLE **c** : a small mottled green marine percoid food fish (*Lethrinus nebulosus*) of warm shallow waters of the Indo-Pacific area

2scavenger \"\ *vi* -ED/-ING/-S : to clean up filth (as street refuse)

scavenger beetle *n* [1*scavenger*] : a beetle (as of the family Hydrophilidae) that feeds on decaying substances

scavenger hunt *n* : a party contest in which couples are sent out with a time limit to acquire without buying one or several articles that are somewhat difficult to obtain

scavenger pump *n* : a pump to return used oil to a tank for cooling, purification, or storage

scavenger roll *n* : a roller in a textile machine for collecting loose fibers or fluff

scav·en·ger's daughter \'skavənjə(r)z-\ *n* [*scavenger's* gen. of 1*scavenger*, by wordplay fr. Leonard *Skevington* or *Skeffington*, 16th cent. lieutenant of the Tower of London, inventor of the instrument] : an instrument of torture that so compressed the body as to force blood to flow from the nostrils and ears and sometimes from the hands and feet

scav·en·gery \'skavənjərē\ *n* -ES [*scavenger* + *-y*] : the removal of dirt, garbage, and other refuse from streets of a municipality

scavenging *also* **scavenge** *adj* [*scavenging* fr. *scavenging* act of cleaning (fr. gerund of *scavenge* to clean; *scavenge* fr. *scavenge* to clean] : of or relating to the process of removing used oil and waste gases from an engine cylinder ⟨a ~ pump⟩ ⟨the ~ stroke⟩

scaw \'sko̊\ *n* -s [of Scand origin; akin to ON *skagi* headland] *archaic* : HEADLAND, PROMONTORY

scawt·ite \'sko̊,tīt\ *n* -s [*Scawt* Hill, Antrim, Northern Ireland + E *-ite*] : a mineral $Ca_6Si_4O_{11}(CO_3)_3$ consisting of a silicate and carbonate of calcium

sca·zon \'skāzᵊn\ *n* -s [L *scazont-*, *scazon*, fr. Gk *skazont-*, *skazōn*, lit., one that limps, fr. pres. part. of *skazein* to limp — more at SHANK] : a classical verse with a limping or halting movement: **a** : CHOLIAMB **b** : a trochaic tetrameter with protraction in the seventh foot : HIPPONACTEAN

sca·zon·tic \skā'zäntik\ *adj* [L *scazont-*, *scazon* + E *-ic*] : composed in scazons

ScB *abbr or n* -s [NL *scientiae baccalaureus*] Bachelor of Science

scd *abbr* **1** schedule **2** screwed

ScD *abbr or n* -s [NL *scientiae doctor*] : a doctor of science

SCE *abbr* standard calomel electrode

sceat \'sha(ə)t\ *or* **sceat·ta** \-ad·ə\ *or* **skeat** \-a(ə)t\ *n*, *pl* **sceats** *or* **sceattas** [OE *sceat*, *sceatt* sceat, property, money; akin to OHG *scaz* property, money, ON *skattr* tribute, Goth *skatts* coin] : a small thick Anglo-Saxon coin of silver or rarely of gold or of copper — see STYCA

scel- *or* **scelo-** *comb form* [NL, fr. Gk *skelos* — more at CYLINDER] : leg ⟨*scel*algia⟩ ⟨*Scelo*porus⟩

scel·er·at \'selə,rat\ *n* -s [F *scélérat*, fr. L *sceleratus*, fr. *sceleratus*, past part. of *scelerare* to pollute, defile, fr. *sceler-*, *scelus* crime — more at CYLINDER] *archaic* : VILLAIN, ROGUE, CRIMINAL

scelerate *adj* [L *sceleratus*, past part. of *scelerare*] *obs* : notably wicked

sceleton *obs var of* SKELETON

scel·i·do·saur \'selədō,so̊(ə)r\ *n* -s [NL *Scelidosaurus*] : a dinosaur of the genus *Scelidosaurus*

1scel·i·do·sau·roid \¦===¦so̊,ro̊id\ *adj* [NL *Scelidosaurus* + E *-oid*] : like or related to the scelidosaurs

2scelidosauroid \"\ *n* -s : a scelidosauroid dinosaur

scel·i·do·sau·rus \,==='so̊rəs\ *n*, *cap* [NL, fr. *scelid-* (fr. Gk *-skelid-*, *-skelis* leg — as in *periskelid-*, *periskelis* band worn on the leg, anklet — fr. *skelos* leg) + *-o-* + *-saurus* — more at CYLINDER] : a genus of European Lower Jurassic dinosaurs (suborder Stegosauria) having a dermal armor of longitudinal series of small tubercles and scutes on the back and tail

scel·i·do·the·ri·um \,==='thirēəm\ *n*, *cap* [NL, fr. *scelid-* (fr. Gk *-skelid-*, *-skelis* leg) + *-o-* + *-therium*] : a genus of extinct Pleistocene four-toed So. American edentates smaller than and intermediate in characters between those of the genera *Megatherium* and *Mylodon*

scel·i·on·i·dae \,selē'änə,dē\ *n pl*, *cap* [NL, fr. *Scelion-*, *Scelio*, type genus (prob. fr. L *scelion-*, *scelio* scoundrel, fr. *scelus* crime) + *-idae*] : a cosmopolitan family of serphoid wasps that are mostly very small, dark, and shining, have elbowed usu. 11-segmented or 12-segmented antennae, and include many economically important parasites of pest insects

scel·i·phron \'selə,frän, sə'lifrən\ *n*, *cap* [NL, fr. Gk *skeliphron*, neut. of *skeliphros* dry, parched; akin to Gk *skellein* to dry up — more at SKELETON] : a genus of wasps (family Sphecidae) comprising many common mud daubers and having the first segment of the abdomen narrowed into a long smooth round petiole

sce·lop·o·rus \sə'läpərəs\ *n* [NL, fr. *scel-* (fr. Gk *skelos* leg) + *-porous* (fr. Gk *poros* passage, pore); fr. the large femoral pores — more at FARE] **1** *cap* : a large genus of small iguanid lizards of No. and Central America including the pine and sagebrush lizards **2** -ES : any lizard of the genus *Sceloporus*

1sce·na \'shānə, -(,)nä\ *n* -s [It, fr. L *scaena*, *scena* stage] **1** : a scene in an opera **2** : an accompanied dramatic recitative usu. followed by one or more sections resembling an aria that

forms a part of an opera or sometimes an independent musical composition

²sce·na \'sēnə, 'skānə\ *n, pl* **sce·nae** \-ē(,)nē, -ā,nī\ [L *scaena, scena*] : ²SKENE

sce·nar·io \sə'na(a)rē,ō, -ner-, -när-, -nar-, -nər- *sometimes* shə-\ *n* -s [It, fr. L *scaenarium*, fr. *scaena* stage + *-arium*] **1** *pl also* **sce·nari** \-rē, -ri\ **a** : an outline or synopsis of a play; *esp* : a plot outline used by actors of the commedia dell'arte **b** : the book of an opera **2 a** : SCREENPLAY **b** : SHOOTING SCRIPT

sce·nar·io·ist \-rē,ōəst\ *n* -s : SCENARIST

sce·nar·ist \-rəst\ *n* -s [ISV *scenario* + *-ist*] : a writer of scenarios

sce·nar·ize \-,rīz\ *vt* -ED/-ING/-S [*scenario* + *-ize*] : to make a scenario of (as a story, book)

sce·na·ry \'sēn(ə)rē, -ri\ *n* -ES [It *scenario* scenery, scenario] **1** *obs* : the disposition of the scenes in which the action (as of a play or poem) is laid **2** *archaic* : SCENERY 1, 2

¹scend \'send\ *vi* -ED/-ING/-S [alter. (influenced by *ascend*) of *send*] : to rise or heave upward under the influence of a natural force (as waves in a seaway) — used esp. of a ship; compare PITCH

²scend \"\ *n* -s **1** : an upward movement or displacement (as of a ship in a seaway) **2** : the lift of a wave : SEND

¹scene \'sēn\ *n* -s [MF, stage, fr. L *scaena, scena*, fr. Gk *skēnē* booth, tent, skene, stage; akin to Gk *skia* shadow, Skt *chāyā* color, shadow — more at SHINE] **1** : one of the subdivisions or units of a dramatic presentation: as **a** : a division of an act during which there is no change of place or lapse of continuity of time; *esp* : a division in a classical Roman or French drama in which there is no change of persons and which ends with the entrance or exit of one or more characters **b** : a part of a drama or narrative featuring a single item (as a situation or dialogue) ⟨a famous mad ~⟩ **c** : ¹SCENA 2 **d** (1) : an episode in a motion picture consisting of a shot or a succession of related shots in which a single continuous action is represented (2) : a single sequence of continuous action in a television presentation consisting of one or more shots **2 a** : the material objects (as hangings, sets, furnishings) that impart an air of reality to the background of a dramatic representation : stage scenery : STAGE SET ⟨a ~ shifter⟩ — often used in pl. ⟨went back of the ~s⟩ **b** : a real or imaginary prospect likened to that presented by stage scenery : VIEW, SIGHT, VISTA ⟨a sylvan ~⟩ ⟨the current ~⟩ **3 a** : the place in which represented action (as in a play or story) is laid : surroundings amid which anything is set before the imagination **b** : the place of occurrence or action : LOCALE ⟨the ~ of a historic event⟩ ⟨the ~ of this disaster⟩ **4** : the stage on which a play is presented esp. in an ancient Greek or Roman theater **5 a scenes** *pl, obs* : a theatrical presentation : a drama or other play **b** *archaic* : the drama as an art or profession **6 a** : one of a sequence of actions and events esp. as represented in literature or art ⟨~s of revelry and despair⟩ ⟨each ~ more stirring than the last⟩ **b** : an episode viewed in real or imagined action ⟨their parting was a sad ~⟩ **7 a** : an exhibition of passionate or explosive and usu. irate emotion (as between individuals) ⟨a tempestuous ~ of tears and remorse⟩ **b** : an affected display of passion or temper ⟨made a ~ to get her own way⟩ — **behind the scenes** *adv* **1** : in a position to see without being seen : out of public view : in secret ⟨a decision reached *behind the scenes*⟩ **2** : in a position to see the hidden agencies or workings ⟨made cynical by what went on *behind the scenes*⟩

²scene \"\ *vt* -ED/-ING/-S : to provide with scenes or scenery

scene cloth *n* : a painted hanging (as a backdrop or drop curtain) for a theatrical stage

scenecraft \'=,=\ *n* : the art of furnishing fitting scenes or stage settings for plays

scene·des·mus \,sēnə'dezməs, ,sen-\ *n, cap* [NL, fr. Gk *skēnē* tent + *desmos* bond, fetter, fr. *dein* to bind — more at SCENE, DIADEM] : a genus (the type of the family Scenedesmaceae of the order Chlorococcales) of colonial green algae having groups of four or eight or rarely sixteen ellipsoid, fusiform, or oblong cells arranged side by side and frequently with more or less conspicuous appendages esp. on the two end cells

scene dock *n* : a space near the stage in a theater where scenery is stored

sceneman *n, pl* **scenemen** *obs* : SCENESHIFTER

scene painter *n* : one that paints scenery: as **a** : a painter of theatrical scenery **b** : an artist specializing in scenic subjects

scene plot *n* : a list and description of the scenes of a play

sce·nery \'sēn(ə)rē, -ri\ *n* -ES [alter. (influenced by *-ery*) of *scenary*] **1** : the representation of the place of an action or occurrence; *specif* : the representation of the scene of action on a stage consisting usu. of painted scenes or hangings with their accessories **2** : a view of picturesque spots and expanses esp. in open country : the general aspect of a landscape : the array of impressive natural prospects and imposing features of a particular place ⟨preferred ~ to historical landmarks⟩ ⟨mountain ~⟩ **3 a** : a picturesque view or landscape **b** : a picture representing such a view

sce·nery·less \-ləs\ *adj* : lacking scenery ⟨a ~ stage⟩ : presented without the use of scenery ⟨a ~ production of a play⟩

sceneshifter \'=,==\ *n* : a worker who moves the scenes in a theater — called also *grip*

scene-stealer \'=,==\ *n* : an actor who skillfully or ostentatiously diverts attention to himself when he is not intended to be the center of attention

scenewright \'=,=\ *n* [¹*scene* + *wright*] : a designer and maker of theatrical scenery

¹sce·nic \'sēnik, -nēk *sometimes* 'sen-\ *adj* [L *scaenicus, scenicus*, fr. Gk *skēnikos*, fr. *skēnē* stage + *-ikos* -ic — more at SCENE] **1 a** : of or relating to the stage, a stage setting, or stage representation : of, resembling, or suited to stage representation : DRAMATIC ⟨~ writers⟩ ⟨~ effects⟩ **b** : of, relating to, or concerned with stage scenery ⟨a ~ triumph⟩ ⟨~ carpenters⟩ **2 a** : of or relating to natural scenery ⟨~ beauties⟩ **b** : affording or abounding in attractive scenery ⟨a ~ route⟩ **3** : representing graphically an action, event, or episode ⟨a ~ bas-relief⟩ ⟨~ wallpapers⟩ — often opposed to *decorative*

²scenic \"\ *n* -s : something stressing the beauties of nature or naturalistic ornamentation: as **a** : a scenic wallpaper usu. depicting a single continuous scene without repetition **b** : a motion picture the chief interest of which is in the natural scenery depicted **c** : a photograph featuring scenery rather than figures

sce·ni·cal \-nəkəl, -nēk-\ *adj* [ME, fr. L *scaenicus, scenicus* scenic + E *-al*] **1** : SCENIC 1; *esp* : characteristic of or resembling a stage performance ⟨a ~ situation⟩ **2** *obs* : having the illusory quality of a stage scene : IMAGINARY, UNREAL

sce·ni·cal·ly \-k(ə)lē, -li\ *adv* **1** : in a theatrical manner **2** : in regard to scenery

scenic artist *n* : SCENE PAINTER

scenic railway *n* : a miniature railway (as in an amusement park) with artificial scenery along the way

sce·nite \'sē,nīt\ *adj or n* [L *scenites*, n., fr. Gk *skēnitēs*, fr. *skēnē* tent + *-itēs* -ite — more at SCENE] *archaic* : NOMAD

sce·no·graph \'sēnə,graf, -rāf\ *n* [back-formation fr. *scenographer, scenographic, scenography*] : a perspective representation

sce·nog·ra·pher \sē'nägrəfə(r)\ *n* -s [LGk *skēnographos* scene painter (fr. Gk *skēno-* — fr. *skēnē* stage — + *-graphos* -grapher) + E *-er*] : a practicer of scenography

sce·no·graph·ic \,sēnə¦grafik\ *also* **sce·no·graph·i·cal** \-fəkəl\ *adj* [*scenographic* fr. Gk *skēnographikos*, fr. *skēnographia* + *-ikos* -ic; *scenographical* fr. *scenographic* + *-al*] : of, relating to, or conforming to scenography — **sce·no·graph·i·cal·ly** \-fək(ə)lē\ *adv*

sce·nog·ra·phy \sē'nägrəfē\ *n* -ES [Gk *skēnographia* scene painting, fr. *skēno-* (fr. *skēnē* stage) + *-graphia* -graphy] **1** : the art or act of representing a body on a perspective plane : representation of an object from a point of view not on a principal axis — compare ORTHOGRAPHIC PROJECTION **2** : the art of perspective representation applied to the painting of stage scenery (as by the Greeks)

sce·no·pin·i·dae \,sēnə'pinə,dē\ *n pl, cap* [NL, fr. *Scenopinus*, type genus (perh. modif. of Gk *skēnopoios* one that makes tents, fr. *skēno-* — fr. *skēnē* tent — + *poiein* to make) + *-idae* — more at SCENE, POET] : a family of small elongated two-winged flies that sometimes congregate about windows — see WINDOW FLY

¹scent \'sent\ *vb* -ED/-ING/-S [ME *senten*, fr. MF *sentir* to feel, have the odor of, fr. L *sentire* to feel, perceive — more at SENSE] *vt* **1 a** : to perceive by the olfactory organs : SMELL ⟨a hound ~*ing* game⟩ **b** : to get or have an inkling of : detect the existence of ⟨~ a plot⟩ ⟨~ the morning air — Shak.⟩ **2** : to imbue or fill with odor agreeable or disagreeable ⟨the air ~*ed* with wild thyme⟩ **3** : to perceive through touch or by the mind ~ *vi* **1** : to yield an odor of some specified kind ⟨this ~*s* of sulfur⟩; *also* : to bear indication or suggestions — used with *of* ⟨the very air ~*s* of treachery⟩ **2** : to use the olfactory organ in seeking or tracking prey ⟨dogs ~ after rabbits⟩

²scent \"\ *n* -s [ME *sent*, fr. *senten*, v.] **1** : emanations or effluvia from a substance that affect the sense of smell pleasantly or unpleasantly: as **a** : an odor left by an animal on a surface passed over ⟨dogs follow the ~⟩; *also* : a course of pursuit : track of discovery ⟨throw one off the ~⟩ **b** : a characteristic or particular odor; *esp* : one that is agreeable ⟨the ~ of flowers⟩ **2 a** *obs* : perception through touch or by the mind **b** : power of smelling : sense of smell ⟨a keen ~⟩ — used chiefly of a lower animal **c** : power of detection ⟨a ~ for heresy⟩ : NOSE **3** : a premonitory indication : INKLING, INTIMATION ⟨a ~ of trouble⟩ **4** *chiefly Brit* : PERFUME 2 **5** : bits of paper dropped by the hares in the game of hare and hounds to mark their course **6** : a mixture prepared for use as a lure on and around a trap (as for an animal) or in water (as for fish) **syn** see FRAGRANCE, SMELL

scent bag *n* **1** : a small scented pad or bag; *esp* : SACHET **2** : a scent gland when pouched in form; *also* : a sac receiving the secretion of a scent gland

scent·ed \'sentəd\ *adj* [partly fr. ²*scent* + *-ed*, partly fr. past part. of ¹*scent*] : having scent: as **a** : having the sense of smell ⟨a keen-*scented* hound⟩ **b** : PERFUMED ⟨over-*scented* girls⟩ **c** : having or exhaling an odor ⟨a ~ flower⟩ ⟨clean-*scented* laundry⟩

scented fern *n* **1** : HAY-SCENTED FERN **2** : a tansy (*Tanacetum vulgare*)

scented satinwood *n* : COACHWOOD 2

scented tea *n* : tea that is fragrant usu. through being packed with or fired with flowers; *esp* : JASMINE TEA

scent·er \-tə(r)\ *n* -s : one that scents

scent gland *n* : a gland (as in the beaver or the civet cat) secreting an odoriferous substance — compare MUSK BAG

scent·less \'sentləs\ *adj* **1** : lacking the sense of smell **2** : emitting no odor ⟨~ wisps of straw⟩ **3 a** : holding no scent ⟨a ~ stretch of rocky ground⟩ **b** : yielding no scent ⟨a ~ day⟩ — **scent·less·ness** *n* -ES

scentless camomile *or* **scentless mayweed** *n* : CORN MAYWEED 2

scent scale *n* : ANDROCONIUM

scentwood \'=,=\ *n* : a fragrant Australian and Tasmanian shrub or small tree (*Alyxia buxifolia*) of the family Apocynaceae

scepsis *var of* SKEPSIS

¹scep·ter \'septə(r)\ *n* -s *see -er in Explan Notes* [ME *ceptre, septre, sceptre*, fr. OF *ceptre*, fr. L *sceptrum*, fr. Gk *skēptron* staff, scepter — more at SHAFT] **1 a** : a staff or baton borne by a sovereign as a ceremonial emblem of authority : a royal mace **b** : a representation (as in heraldry) of a scepter **2** : royal or imperial authority : SOVEREIGNTY

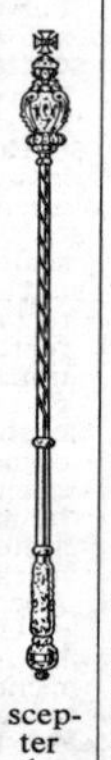

scepter 1a

²scepter \"\ *vt* -ED/-ING/-S **1** : to endow with the scepter : invest with royal authority **2** : to ratify by touching with the scepter

scep·tered \-tə(r)d\ *adj* **1** : invested with a scepter or sovereign authority **2** : belonging or relating to a sovereign or to royalty : ROYAL, REGAL

scep·ter·less \-tə(r)ləs\ *adj* **1** : having no scepter **2** : subject to no royal sovereignty

sceptic *var of* SKEPTIC

scep·tral \'sept(ə)rəl\ *adj* : resembling or relating to a scepter or to royal authority

scerne *vt* [by shortening & alter.] *obs* : DISCERN

sceu·o·pho·rion \,skevə'fōr,yōn\ *n, pl* **sceuopho·ria** \-yə\ [MGk *skeuophorion*, fr. Gk, yoke placed over the shoulders for carrying pails, fr. *skeuos* vessel, utensil + *-phorion* (fr. *pherein* to carry) — more at SKEUOMORPH, BEAR] : a receptacle used in the Eastern Orthodox Church and corresponding to the pyx

sceu·o·phy·la·cium \,skyüōfə'lāsh(ē)əm\ *n* -s [MGk *skeuophylakion*, fr. Gk, storehouse, fr. *skeuos* vessel, utensil + *phylakion, phylakeion* fort, fr. *phylak-, phylax* guard] : a sacristy in the early church and in the Eastern Orthodox Church

sceu·o·phy·lax \skyü'äfə,laks, ,skevō'fē,läks\ *n* -ES [LGk *skeuophylak-, skeuophylax*, fr. Gk, keeper of a storehouse, fr. *skeuos* vessel, utensil + *phylak-, phylax* guard] : a sacristan in the early church and in the Eastern Orthodox Church

sch *abbr* **1** schedule **2** schilling **3** scholar **4** scholium **5** school **6** schoolhouse **7** schooner

schaap·ste·ker *or* **skaap·ste·ker** \'skäp,stikə(r), -tēk-\ *n* -s [Afrik *skaapsteker*, fr. *skaap* sheep (fr. D *schaap*, fr. MD *schaep*) + *steker* one that stings or pricks, fr. D, fr. *steken* to sting, prick + *-er*; akin to OHG *stehhan* to sting, prick — more at SHEEP, STICK] : any of several inoffensive and generally harmless African back-fanged snakes: as **a** : a snake (*Trimerorhinus rhombeatus*) irregularly marked in shades of brown — called also *spotted schaapsteker* **b** : a related snake (*T. tritaeniatus*) having two or three dark longitudinal bands on the grayish brown back — called also *striped schaapsteker* **c** : a sand snake of the genus *Psammophis*

schab·zie·ger *also* **schab·zi·ger** \'shäp(t),sēgə(r)\ *n* -s *usu cap* [G *schabziger* — more at SAPSAGO] : SAPSAGO

schacht·ism \'shäk,tizəm, -äk,t-\ *also* **schact·ian·ism** \-tēə,niz-\ *n* -s *usu cap* [*schachtism* fr. Hjalmar *Schacht* b1877 Ger. financier + E *-ism*; *schachtianism* fr. Hjalmar *Schacht* + E *-an* + *-ism*; fr. Schacht's use of such policies as acting minister of national economy in Germany 1934–37] : trade and finance policies including exchange controls, bilateral trade agreements, multiple exchange rates, and other practices designed to benefit one nation at the expense of others

scha·den·freu·de \'shäd°n,frȯidə\ *n* -s [G, fr. *schaden* damage, injury, harm (fr. OHG *scado*) + *freude* joy, fr. OHG *frewida*, fr. *frō* happy — more at SCATHE, FROLIC] : enjoyment obtained from the mishaps of others

schaef·fe·ria \shā'firēə\ *n* [NL, fr. Jacob Christian *Schäffer* †1790 Ger. naturalist + NL *-ia*] **1** *cap* : a small genus of chiefly tropical American shrubs or occasionally small trees (family Celastraceae) having dioecious tetramerous flowers, coriaceous leaves, dry drupaceous fruits containing two seeds without an aril, and hard fine-grained yellow wood that has been used as a substitute for boxwood **2** -s : any plant of the genus *Schaefferia*

schaef·fer's acid *or* **schäf·fer's acid** \'shāfə(r)z-\ *n, usu cap S* [after L. *Schaeffer*, 19th cent. Ger. chemist] : a crystalline naphtholsulfonic acid $HOC_{10}H_6SO_3H$ used as a dye intermediate; 2-naphthol-6 sulfonic acid

schaeffer's salt *or* **schäffer's salt** *n, usu cap 1st S* : the sodium salt $HOC_{10}H_6SO_3Na$ of Schaeffer's acid

schaer·beek \'skär,bāk\ *adj, usu cap* [fr. *Schaerbeek*, Belgium] : of or from the city of Schaerbeek, Belgium : of the kind or style prevalent in Schaerbeek

scha·far·zik·ite \'shäfə(r),zi,kīt\ *n* -s [G *schafarzikit*, fr. Ferenc *Schafarzik* †1927 Hung. mineralogist + G *-it* -ite] : a mineral $Fe_5Sb_4O_{11}$ consisting of an oxide of iron and antimony and occurring in red to brown prismatic acicular crystals

scha·fer method *or* **schae·fer method** \'shāfə(r)-\ *n, usu cap S* [after Sir Edward A. Sharpey-*Schafer* †1935 Eng. physiologist] : PRONE PRESSURE METHOD

schafs·kopf \'shaf,skȯpf\ *also* **schaf·kopf** \-f,k-\ *n* -s [G, schafskopf, blockhead, sheep's head, fr. *schaf* sheep (fr. OHG *scāf*) + *kopf* head, fr. OHG, drinking vessel — more at SHEEP, CUP] : SHEEPSHEAD 3

schai·rer·ite \'shīrə,rīt\ *n* -s [John F. *Schairer* b1904 Am. physical chemist + E *-ite*] : a mineral $Na_3(SO_4)(F,Cl)$ consisting of a rare sodium sulphate with fluorine and chlorine and occurring in colorless rhombohedral crystals

schal·ler·ite \'shalə,rīt\ *n* -s [Waldemar T. *Schaller* b1882 Am. mineralogist + E *-ite*] : a mineral $Mn_8Si_6O_{18}(AsO_3)$-$(OH).3½H_2O$(?) consisting of a hydrous basic silicate and arsenite of manganese

schal·mei *or* **schal·mey** \(')shäl¦mī\ *n* -s [G *schalmei*, fr. MHG *schalmīe*, fr. OF *chalemie* — more at SHAWM] **1** : SHAWM **2** : CHALUMEAU 4

schal·stein \'shäl,s(h)tīn\ *n* -s [G, fr. *schale* husk, shell (fr. OHG *scala*) + *stein* stone, fr. OHG — more at SCALE, STONE] : a slaty rock formed by the compression and metamorphism of basaltic or andesitic tuff or lava : slaty greenstone

schap·bach·ite \'shäp,bä,kīt\ *n* -s [G *schapbachit*, fr. *Schapbach*, Baden, Germany + G *-it* -ite] : MATILDITE; *also* : a high-temperature polymorph of matildite

schap·pe \'shäpə\ *or* **chappe** \'shap\ *n* -s [G dial. (Swiss) *schappe* raw silk waste] : a yarn or fabric of spun silk; *also* : an imitation of it (as in rayon or nylon)

schap·ping \-piŋ\ *n* -s : a European method for fermenting and removing the gum from silk wastes

schap·ska \'shäpskə\ *n* -s [F, modif. of Pol *czapka* cap] : a flat-topped cavalry helmet

schar·ding·er dextrin \'shärdiŋə(r)-\ *n, usu cap S* [after Franz *Schardinger*, 20th cent. Austrian chemist] : any of several nonreducing water soluble low-molecular-weight polysaccharides formed by cultivation of a bacillus (*Bacillus macerans*) upon starch solutions

schardinger enzyme *n, usu cap S* : XANTHINE OXIDASE

scharf \'shärf\ *n* -s [G, fr. *scharf*, adj., sharp, fr. OHG *scarf* — more at SHARP] : a mixture stop in a pipe organ with a bright and penetrating tone

schatchen *var of* SHADCHAN

schechina *usu cap, var of* SHEKINAH

sched *abbr* schedule

sched·i·asm \'skedē,azəm, 'sked-\ *n* -s [Gk *schediasma* caprice, fr. *schediazein* to do offhand, fr. *schedios* temporary, extemporaneous, impromptu; akin to Gk *echein* to have — more at SCHEME] *archaic* : an extemporaneous action (as in writing) : something done offhand

sched·i·us \-dēəs\ *n, cap* [NL, perh. fr. Gk *schedios* temporary, extemporaneous, impromptu] : a genus of minute chalcid flies including egg parasites of economic pests (as the gypsy moth)

sched·u·lar \'skejələ(r), -(,)jül-\ *adj* : of or relating to a schedule

¹sched·ule \'ske(,)jül, -jəl *sometimes* -(,)jül *or* -,jüəl, *Canadian* " *or* 'she(,)j|, *Brit* 'she(,)dy| *or* 'she(,)j|\ *n* -s [alter. (influenced by LL *schedula*) of earlier *cedule, sedule*, fr. ME, fr. MF, note, slip of paper, fr. LL *schedula* slip of paper, fr. L *scheda, scida* leaf of paper or papyrus (fr. assumed Gk *schidē* split piece of wood, fr. Gk *schizein* to split) + *-ula* — more at SHED] **1 a** *obs* : a piece of written matter : DOCUMENT; *esp* : a supplementary slip appended to a document **b** : an appended statement of supplementary details usu. accompanying a legal or legislative document and often taking the form of a detailed list of relevant matters **2** : a written or printed formal list (as a catalog or inventory or calendar of events) ⟨a ~ of freight rates⟩ ⟨a ~ of social events⟩: as **a** : a detailed list of a bankrupt's creditors, liabilities, and assets ⟨filed a ~ with his bankruptcy petition⟩ **b** : a transportation timetable **c** : an executive's record of matters (as assignments of subordinate personnel) handled or to be handled **d** : a student's program of studies **e** : a list of questions designed to elicit objective data for a statistical study **3** : a usu. written plan or proposal for future procedure typically indicating the objective proposed, the time and sequence of each operation, and the materials required ⟨planned a new ~ of operations for the factory⟩ ⟨their ~ allowed for only 50 percent of last year's production⟩ ⟨laid out a ~ for building the new school⟩ **4** : a body of items requiring to be dealt with usu. at a particular time or within an indicated period ⟨a lecturer with a very heavy ~⟩ ⟨my ~ for tomorrow⟩ — **on schedule** : at the time indicated in a schedule : at the due or proper time ⟨winter arrived *on schedule*⟩ ⟨an *on schedule* presentation⟩

²schedule \"\ *vt* -ED/-ING/-S **1 a** : to place in a schedule ⟨~ a new train⟩ **b** : to make a schedule of ⟨*scheduled* his income and debts⟩ **2** : to add in or as a schedule or appendix **3** : to appoint, assign, or designate to do or receive something at a fixed time in the future ⟨*scheduled* a meeting for the next week⟩

schedule bond *n* : a fidelity bond that covers as principals only those employees specifically designated by name or by position

scheduled caste *or* **scheduled class** *n* : UNTOUCHABLES

scheduled disease *n, Brit* : a notifiable disease

sched·ul·er \-lə(r)\ *n* -s : a preparer of a schedule

schedule rate *n* : an insurance merit rating derived from an analysis of the physical characteristics of a risk according to a schedule of charges and credits

schee·le's green \'shāləz-, -lēz-\ *n* [after Karl W. *Scheele* †1786 Swed. chemist] **1** *usu cap S* : a poisonous yellowish green pigment consisting essentially of a copper arsenite and used esp. formerly in paints **2** *often cap S* : a strong yellow green to yellowish green — called also *English green, Swedish green*

schee·lite \'shā,līt\ *n* -s [G *scheelit*, fr. Karl W. *Scheele* + G *-it* -ite] : a native calcium tungstate $CaWO_4$ that is isomorphous with powellite, occurs as a white or yellow to brownish when impure tetragonal mineral in tabular and massive forms, and is a commercial source of tungsten and tungsten compounds

schef·fer·ite \'shefə,rīt\ *n* -s [Sw *schefferit*, fr. H. T. *Scheffer* †1759 Swed. chemist + Sw *-it* -ite] : a mineral $(Ca,Mn)(Mg,Fe,Mn)Si_2O_6$ that is a brown to black variety of pyroxene containing manganese and frequently much iron

schef·flera \'sheflərə\ *n* -s [NL *Schefflera*, genus of plants, fr. J. C. *Scheffler*, 18th cent. Ger. botanist] : any of several shrubby tropical plants of the family Araliaceae that are cultivated for their showy digitately compound foliage

sche·her·a·za·di·an \shə¦herə¦zädēən, she¦h- *sometimes* -zäd-\ *adj* [*Scheherazade*, fictitious queen represented as narrator of the stories in the *Arabian Nights' Entertainments* + E *-an*] : suited to a tale of the fabled queen Scheherazade : strangely fabulous

scheib·ler's reagent \'shīb|lə(r)z-, -īp|\ *n, usu cap S* [after Karl *Scheibler* †1899 Ger. chemist] : a solution of phosphotungstic acid or its sodium salt used as a precipitant for alkaloids

schei·ner speed \'shīnə(r)-\ *n, usu cap 1st S* [after Julius *Scheiner* †1913 Ger. astrophysicist] : the speed of photographic material based on the exposure required to obtain a just-detectable density and indicated by a system of numbers

schel·ling \'skeliŋ\ *n* -s [D, fr. MD *schellinc*; akin to OE *scilling* shilling — more at SHILLING] : an old silver or sometimes billon coin of the Low Countries usu. current at six stivers but varying from five to eight

schel·ling·ian \(')she,liŋēən, shə'l-, -linj(ē)ən\ *adj, usu cap* [Friedrich Wilhelm Joseph von *Schelling* †1854 Ger. philosopher + E *-an*] : of or relating to Schelling or his system of idealism that makes the ego and the world two poles of the Absolute

schel·ly \'sheli\ *n* -s [origin unknown] *dial Eng* : GWYNIAD

schelm \'skelm\ *n* -s [Afrik *skelm*, fr. D *schelm* — more at SKELLUM] *Africa* : ROGUE, RASCAL

schel·orib·a·tes \,skelə'ribə,tēz\ *n, cap* [NL, fr. *schel-* (prob. fr. Gk *schelides* ribs of beef) + *Oribates* (syn. of *Oribata*, type genus of the mite family Oribatidae); akin to Gk *skelos* leg — more at CYLINDER, ORIBATOIDEA] : a genus of oribatid mites containing some that are intermediate hosts of several tapeworms of ruminants

schel·to·pu·sik *or* **shel·to·pu·sic** *or* **shel·to·pu·sick** \,sheltō¦p(y)üzik\ *n* -s [Russ *zheltopuzik*, fr. *zhelto* yellow (akin to OE *geolu* yellow) + *-puzik* fr. *puzo* belly) — more at YELLOW] : an anguid lizard (*Ophisaurus apus* or *Pseudopus apus*) chiefly of southeastern Europe and Asia Minor that resembles the glass snake of America

sche·ma \'skēmə\ *n, pl* **schema·ta** \-mədə, -mətə\ [G, fr. Gk *schēmat-, schēma* shape, figure, manner — more at SCHEME] **1** : a general representation produced according to Kantianism by the imagination working with the pure form of time by which the understanding is able to apply a category to particular representations of sense ⟨the universal following in time of something, A, by something else, B, is the ~ of cause and effect⟩ **2 a** : a diagrammatic depiction of a typical or average situation ⟨a ~ of the reflex arc⟩; *broadly* : an abridged

or generalized presentation : a framework of reference : OUT-LINE, PLAN **b** : a syllogistic figure in logic **3 a** : a nonconscious adjustment of the brain to the afferent impulses indicative of bodily posture that is a prerequisite of appropriate bodily movement and of spatial perception **b** : the organization of experience in the mind or brain

¹sche·mat·ic \(')ske̅'mad̶.ik, ski̅'m-, -at̶, |ek̶\ *adj* [NL *schematicus,* fr. L *schemat-, schema* shape, figure, manner (fr. Gk *schēmat-, schēma*) + *-icus -ic*] : of, relating to, or constituting a scheme or schema: as **a** : corresponding to an established or formalized conception ⟨a ∼ arrangement⟩ ⟨∼ drawing⟩ **b** : showing part for part in a model or diagram ⟨a ∼ eye⟩ **c** : employing or constituting a scheme of conventional symbols ⟨a ∼ wiring diagram⟩ ⟨using ∼ symbols⟩

²schematic \"\ *n* -s : a schematic drawing or diagram

sche·mat·i·cal·ly \|ək(ə)le̅, |ek̶-, -li\ *adv* : in a schematic manner

sche·ma·tism \'ske̅mə,tizəm\ *n* -s [NL *schematismus,* fr. Gk *schēmatismos* configuration, assumption of a manner, fr. *schēmatizein* to assume a certain form, put into a systematic arrangement] **1 a** : the disposition of constituents in a pattern or according to a scheme; *also* : a particular systematic disposition of parts **b** : the inclination to arrange or present schematically **2** [G *schematismus,* fr. NL] : the process by which the imagination according to Kantianism mediates between a category or abstract concept of the understanding and a particular content of sense experience by providing a general plan for the application of the concept to the content of sense — compare SCHEMA 1

sche·ma·tist \-mət̶əst, -məd̶·ə̇-\ *n* -s [fr. *schematism,* after such pairs as E *deism: deist*] **1** : one that makes modifications to suit an established or preconceived system **2** *obs* : one given to forming schemes : PROJECTOR, SCHEMER

sche·ma·ti·za·tion \,ske̅mə̇t̶ə̇'zā̇shən, -məd̶-ə̇'z-, -mə,tī̇'z-\ *n* -s : an act or instance or the product of schematizing

sche·ma·tize \'ske̅mə,tīz\ *vt* -ED/-ING/-S [Gk *schēmatizein* to assume a certain form, put into a systematic arrangement, fr. *schēmat-, schēma* shape, figure, manner + *-ize* -ize] **1** : to form or to form into a scheme or schemes : make or put into a systematic arrangement **2** : to express or depict schematically; *usu* : to convert (an art subject) into nonnaturalistic symbols or decorative motifs : STYLIZE, CONVENTIONALIZE

sche·ma·tiz·er \-zə(r)\ *n* -s : one that schematizes

sche·ma·to·gram \'ske̅'mad̶ə,gram, 'ske̅mə̇tə-\ *n* [Gk *schēmat-, schēma* shape, figure, manner + E -o- + *-gram*] : a tracing made with a schematograph

sche·ma·to·graph \-raf, -räf\ *n* [Gk *schēmat-, schēma* shape, figure, manner + E -o- + *-graph*] : an apparatus for tracing in reduced form the outline of a person in recording posture

¹scheme \'ske̅m\ *n* -s [L *schema, schemat-, schema* shape, figure, manner, figure of speech, fr. Gk *schēmat-, schēma;* akin to OE *sige* victory, OHG *sigu, ON sigr,* Goth *sigis* victory, Gk *echein, schein* to have, hold, Skt *sahas* strength, victory] **1** *obs* **a** : FIGURE OF SPEECH **b** : FORM, SEMBLANCE **c** : POMP, SHOW **2 a** *archaic* : a mathematical or astronomical diagram; *sometimes* : a representation of the astrological aspects of the planets at a particular time **b** : a graphic sketch, design, or outline : a delineated plan ⟨sketched a small ∼ of the watershed⟩ **c** : a diagram or table showing metrical structure or rhyme arrangement (as of a stanza) **3 a** : a concise statement in an outline, table, or list : EPITOME (2) : a preparatory outline or draft **b** : a plan reduced to a precise and definite often tabulated form; *also* : a tabulation of a plan or set of directions **4** : a plan or program of something to be done : a planned undertaking ⟨a business ∼⟩ ⟨a new ∼ for rural electrification⟩: as **a** : a crafty or unethical project ⟨a ∼ to get control of the government⟩ ⟨∼s to evade taxes⟩ **b** : a visionary project ⟨a head full of ∼s and wild ideas⟩ **c** : a combination of elements (as thoughts, theories, considerations) that are connected, adjusted, and integrated by design : a systematic plan : SYSTEM ⟨worked out a new ∼ of philosophical interpretations⟩ ⟨wholly changed his ∼ of life⟩ **d** : a planned and often mildly mischievous diversion : LARK, ESCAPADE **e** *chiefly Brit* : a governmental or official plan or project ⟨a contributory pension ∼⟩; *also* : the product of such a scheme ⟨obtained their irrigation water from the new ∼⟩ **5** : a complexity (as in nature or social institutions) that suggests or reveals systematic design ⟨attain their rightful place in the ∼ of things —S.L.A.Marshall⟩ *syn* see PLAN, SYSTEM

²scheme \"\ *vb* -ED/-ING/-S *vt* **1** : to devise or contrive a scheme for : accomplish by clever contriving : DESIGN, PROJECT, PLOT ⟨*scheming* an escape⟩ — often used with *out* ⟨*schemed* out a plot against the king⟩ **2** : to confine within the arbitrary bounds of a system or formula; *also* : to employ in or under a scheme ∼ *vi* : to form plans or designs : devise intrigue *syn* see ¹PLAN

scheme arch \'ske̅m-\ *also* skeen arch *or* skene arch \'ske̅n-\ *n* [*scheme, skeen, skene* of unknown origin] : DIMINISHED ARCH

scheme·less \'ske̅mləs\ *adj* : lacking a plan or plot ⟨∼ tales⟩

schem·er \-mə(r)\ *n* -s : one that forms schemes (as a plotter or intriguer) : PROJECTOR

sche·mery \'ske̅mərē\ *n* -ES : deceptive contriving : MACHINATION

scheming *adj* : given to forming schemes ⟨a busy ∼ brain⟩ : tending to artful contriving : shrewdly devising and intriguing ⟨a ∼ wife⟩ — compare DESIGNING — **schem·ing·ly** *adv*

sche·mist \'ske̅məst\ *n* -s : SCHEMER; *also* : an advocate of a particular scheme

sche·moz·zle \shə'mäzəl\ *n* -s [modif. of Yiddish *shlimazel* bad luck, difficulty, misfortune, fr. *shlim* bad, ill (fr. MHG *slimp* awry, not right) + *mazel* luck, fate, fr. LHeb *mazzāl* luck, fate, star — more at SLIM] **1** *slang* : a confused situation or affair : MESS, MUDDLE **2** *slang* : QUARREL, ROW

schemy \'ske̅mē\ *adj* : SCHEMING, ARTFUL

sche·nec·ta·dy putter \skə'nektəd̶·, -di\ *n, usu cap S* [*Schenectady,* city in eastern New York] : a golf putter in which the shaft is fastened near the center of the head

schenk beer \'shenk-\ *n* [part trans. of G *schenkbier,* fr. *schenken* to pour out (fr. OHG *skenken*) + *bier* beer; fr. the fact that it is put on draft soon after it is made — more at NUNCHEON] : a beer brewed in the winter by the bottom-fermentation process for immediate consumption and not stored like lager

sche·pel \'skāpəl\ *n* -s [D, fr. MD; akin to OHG *sceffil* bushel, *skepfen* to shape, form, create — more at SHAPE] **1** *also* skip·ple \'skipəl\ : an old Dutch unit of dry measure equal to ¼ muid or about ¾ bushel **2** : a modern Dutch unit of capacity equal to one decaliter

sche·pen \'skāpə(n)\ *n* -s [D, fr. MD, fr. MD *schepene;* akin to OHG *sceffino* magistrate, *skepfen* to shape, form, create] : a municipal officer in Holland and in Dutch settlements analogous to an English alderman

sche·ring bridge \'sheriŋ, -'shā\ *n, usu cap S* [after H. *Schering,* 20th cent. Ger. engineer, the inventor] : an alternating-current bridge used to measure the energy loss in dielectrics and to determine the capacitance of condensers — compare WHEATSTONE BRIDGE

scherm \'ske(ə)rm, 'skərm\ *n* -s [Afrik *skerm,* fr. D *scherm* screen, curtain, fr. MD, screen, fence, protection; akin to OHG *skerm, skirm* shield, L *corium* skin, hide — more at CUIRASS] *Africa* : SCREEN, FENCE ⟨a brushwood ∼⟩; *also* : a plot enclosed by a scherm

¹scher·zan·do \skert'sän(.)dō̇, skeət-, -'san-, -'sän-, -'saan-\ *adj* [It, verbal of *scherzare* to joke, of Gmc origin; akin to MHG *scherzen* to joke, have a good time, leap for joy — more at CARDINAL] : PLAYFUL, JESTING — used as a direction in music indicating style and tempo ⟨allegretto ∼⟩

²scherzando \"\ *n* -s : a passage or movement in scherzando style

scher·zo \'skert(,)sō̇, -eət-\ *n, pl* scherzos \-ōz\ *also* scherzi \-(,)sē̇\ [It, lit., joke, fr. *scherzare* to joke — more at SCHERZANDO] : a sprightly humorous instrumental musical composition or movement that is commonly in quick triple time and usu. in ternary form — compare MINUET

scher·zo·so \(,)sō̇(.)sō̇\ *adj* [It, fr. *scherzo* + *-oso* -ose (fr. L *-osus*)] : SCHERZANDO

sche·sis \'ske̅səs, -ke̅\ *n, pl* scheses \|,se̅z\ [Gk, condition, quality, relation; akin to Gk *echein, schein* to have, hold — more at SCHEME] *obs* : general state or disposition of the body

or mind or of one thing with regard to other things : HABITUDE, RELATION

sche·tel·i·gite \shə'telə,gīt\ *n* -s [Norw *scheteligit,* fr. Jacob *Schetelig* †1935 Norw. mineralogist + Norw *-it* -ite] : a mineral (Ca,Y,Sb,Mn)₂(Ti,Ta,Cb)₂O₆(O,OH) that is an oxide of calcium, rare earth metals, antimony, manganese, titanium, columbium, and tantalum

scheuch·ze·ria \shȯikt'sirē̇ə\ *n, cap* [NL, fr. Johann Jakob *Scheuchzer* †1733 and his brother Johann *Scheuchzer* †1738 Swiss botanists + NL *-ia*] : a monotypic genus (the type of the family Scheuchzeriaceae) of bog herbs that are found throughout the north temperate zone and that have leafy stems with white or greenish racemose flowers, several carpels, and fruits resembling follicles

scheuch·ze·ri·a·ce·ae \(,)shȯikt,sirē̇'āse̅,ē̇\ *n pl, cap* [NL *Scheuchzeria,* type genus + *-aceae*] : a family of monocotyledonous plants (order Naiadales) coextensive with the genus *Scheuchzeria*

schia·vo·ne \skya'vōnē̇\ *n* -s [It, lit., Slavonian; fr. its use by the Slavonian guards of the doge of Venice] : a two-edged basket-hilted sword

schick test \'shik-\ *n, usu cap S* [after Béla *Schick* †1967 Am. pediatrician] : a test for susceptibility to diphtheria performed by injecting a suitable amount of diphtheria toxin into the skin upon which susceptible persons develop an area of redness and slight infiltration followed by some desquamation while immune persons show no reaction

schie·dam \'ske̅,dam, -däm, ⸴-'\ *n* -s *sometimes cap* [*Schiedam,* city in southwestern Netherlands, fr. its locality] : a strongly flavored gin

schie·le's pivot \'she̅lē̇z-\ *n, usu cap S* [after Christian *Schiele,* 19th cent. Eng. engineer] : a pivot having a curved surface which is generated by the revolution of a tractrix about its axis, wearing uniformly, but wasting 50 percent more energy than a flat pivot

schiff base \'shif-\ *n, usu cap S* [after Hugo *Schiff* †1915 Ger. chemist] : any of a class of bases of the general formula RR′C=NR″ that are obtained typically by condensation of an aldehyde or ketone with a primary amine (as aniline) with elimination of water, that usu. polymerize readily if made from aliphatic aldehydes, and that are used chiefly as intermediates in organic synthesis and in some cases as accelerators of vulcanization and as dyes : AZOMETHINE; *esp* : ANIL — compare ALDIMINE, KETIMINE

schiff·li \'shiflē̇\ *n* -s [G dial. (Swiss), lit., small ship, dim. of G *schiff* ship, fr. OHG *skif;* prob. fr. the shape of its shuttles — more at SHIP] : a complex power machine for working embroidery designs and lace patterns on textiles ⟨∼ embroidery⟩

schiff reaction *n, usu cap S* : a reaction that is used as a test for aldehydes and consists in the formation by them of a reddish violet color with a solution of fuchsine decolorized with sulfurous acid

schiff reagent *n, usu cap S* : a solution of fuchsine decolorized by treatment with sulfur dioxide that gives a useful test for aldehydes because they restore the reddish violet color of the dye — compare FEULGEN REACTION

schih \'she̅\ *n* -s [native name in northern Africa] : dry grasslands of northern Africa

schill *chiefly Scot var of* SHILL

schil·ler \'shilə(r)\ *n* -s [G, play of colors, iridescence, fr. MHG *schiler* iridescent taffeta, fr. *schilhen* to squint, twinkle (fr. OHG *scilihen* to squint) + *-er;* akin to OE *bescȳlan* to look sidelong, MLG *schelen* to peer out; causative-denominatives fr. the root of OE *sceol* wry, squinting — more at CYLINDER] **1** : the bronzy iridescent luster of a mineral (as hypersthene or schiller spar) due to minute inclusions or cavities in parallel position and sometimes resulting from alteration **2** : lustrously or resplendently iridescent coloration (as of a beetle)

schil·ler·iza·tion \,shilərə'zāshən, -,rī'z-\ *n* -s : the alteration of orthorhombic pyroxene and sometimes diallage in such a way that minute inclusions of secondary minerals are developed that reflect light simultaneously

schil·ler·ize \'shilə,rīz\ *vt* -ED/-ING/-S : to impart a schiller to (a mineral) by the development (as by solution and infiltration) of inclusions or cavities

schiller spar *n* [part trans. of G *schillerspat,* fr. *schiller* play of colors, iridescence + *spat* spar] : an altered enstatite characterized by a schiller on its chief cleavage face, occurring as green or brown foliated masses in igneous rocks, and having a composition approximately that of serpentine

schil·ling \'shiliŋ, -lēŋ\ *n* -s [G, fr. OHG *skilling,* a gold coin — more at SHILLING] **1 a** : a subsidiary unit of value formerly used in some of the northern states of Germany **b** : a corresponding coin **2 a** : the basic monetary unit of Austria since 1925 — see MONEY table **b** : a coin representing one schilling

schil·ling index \"-\ *n, usu cap S* [after Victor Theodor Adolf Georg *Schilling* b1883 Ger. physician] : an age classification of blood neutrophils into myelocytes, metamyelocytes, stab cells, and mature neutrophils on the basis of increasing irregularity or lobulation of the nucleus — compare ARNETH INDEX

schi·ma \'ski̅mə\ *n, cap* [NL, prob. modif. of Gk *skiasma* shadow, fr. *skiazein* to overshadow, fr. *skia* shadow — more at SHINE] : a small genus of East Indian and eastern Asian evergreen trees and shrubs (family Theaceae) that are sometimes cultivated in warm regions for their showy often fragrant white flowers

schim·mel \'skiməl\ *n* -s [Afrik *skimmel* gray horse, mildew, fr. D *schimmel;* akin to OHG *scimbalōn* to become moldy, MLG *schimmel* gray horse, mildew, OE *scīnan* to shine — more at SHINE] *chiefly dial* : a gray or grayish horse

schin·dy·le·sis \,skində'lēsəs\ *n, pl* schindyle·ses \-ē̇,sēz\ [NL, fr. Gk *schindylēsis* act or process of splitting into fragments; akin to Gk *schizein* to split — more at SHED] : an articulation in which one bone is received into a groove or slit in another

schin·dy·let·ic \,skində'led̶·ik\ *adj* [fr. *schindylesis,* after such pairs as E *narcosis: narcotic*] : exhibiting or joined in schindylesis

schi·nop·sis \ski̅'näpsəs\ *n, cap* [NL, fr. *Schinus* + *-opsis*] : a genus of So. American deciduous to half-evergreen trees (family Anacardiaceae) with extremely hard heavy durable reddish to reddish brown heartwood that is an important source of tannins — see QUEBRACHO 1b

schi·nus \'ski̅nəs\ *n, cap* [NL, fr. Gk *schinos* mastic tree] : a genus of tropical American trees (family Anacardiaceae) with odd-pinnate leaves and small dioecious white flowers in panicles — see PEPPER TREE

schip·per·ke \'skipə(r)kē̇, -kə\ *n* [Flem, dim. of *schipper* boatman, skipper, fr. MD; fr. the use of such dogs as watch-dogs on boats — more at SKIPPER] **1** *usu cap* : a Belgian breed of small stocky black dogs with foxy head and erect triangular ears developed originally chiefly for use as a watchdog on canalboats **2** : a dog of the Schipperke breed

schir·mer·ite \'shərmə,rīt\ *n* -s [J. H. L. *Schirmer,* 19th cent. Am. mint superintendent + E *-ite*] : a mineral PbAg₄Bi₄S₉ consisting of a sulfide of bismuth, silver, and lead

schirrhus *var of* SCIRRHUS

schi·san·dra \skə'zandrə, -'sa-\ *n, cap* [NL, irreg. fr. *schiz- + -andra*] : a genus of aromatic woody vines or shrubs (family Magnoliaceae) including one in No. America and others in eastern Asia and having the leaves often evergreen, unisexual flowers in axillary clusters with the petals and sepals undifferentiated, and a fruit that is an elongated spike crowded with berries

-schi·sis \\ *n comb form, pl* -schi·ses \-ə,sēz\ *also* -schi·sis·es \NL, fr. Gk *schisis* cleavage, fr. *schizein* to split] : breaking up of attachments or adhesions : fissure ⟨gastro-*schisis*⟩

schism \'sizəm, ÷'ski-\ *n* -s *among clergymen usu* 'si-\ *n* -s [alter. (influenced by LL *schisma*) of earlier *scisme,* fr. ME, fr. MF & LL; MF *cisme,* fr. LL *schismat-, schisma,* fr. Gk, cleft, division, fr. *schizein* to split — more at SHED] **1** : DIVISION, SEPARATION; *specif* : DISCORD, DISHARMONY ⟨there should be no ∼ in the body —1 Cor 12:25 (AV)⟩ **2 a** : formal division or separation in the Christian church or from a church or religious body : breach of unity among people of the same religious faith **b** : the offense of seeking to produce division

in a church **c** : a schismatic body or sect **d** *obs* : a schismatic opinion **3 a** *obs* : a condition of disagreement in opinion : mutual hostility **b** : a division of a group into two discordant groups ⟨a ∼ in a political party⟩; *also* : a condition of opposition or divergence (as between abstract principles) ⟨the widening ∼ between pure and applied science⟩ **4** *archaic* : a tear in fabric (as clothing) **5** *archaic* : FACTION, CLIQUE *syn* see BREACH

schis·ma \'skizmə\ *n, pl* schisma·ta \-məd̶·ə\ [LL *schismat-, schisma* minute interval in music, schism] : the interval between an acoustical pure and an equally tempered fifth — see DIASCHISMA

¹schis·mat·ic \siz'mad̶·ik, ÷ski-, -at̶, |ek̶\ *n* -s [alter. (influenced by LL *schismaticus*) of earlier *scismatyke,* fr. ME *scismatike,* fr. MF *scismatique,* fr. LL *schismaticus,* fr. *schismat-, schisma* schism + L *-icus -ic*] : one who creates or takes part in schism : one who separates from a church or religious communion on account of a difference of opinion — compare HERETIC

²schismatic \(')ᵔᵔ|ᵔᵔ\ *adj* [alter. (influenced by LL *schismaticus*) of earlier *scismatyke,* fr. ME *scismatike,* fr. LL *schismaticus,* fr. *schismat-, schisma* schism + L *-ic -ic*] : of, relating to, or characteristic of schism : implying schism : having the nature of or tending to schism : separated from some body by schism : guilty of schism ⟨∼ opinions⟩ ⟨∼ sects⟩

schis·mat·i·cal \|əkəl, |ek̶-\ *adj* [alter. (influenced by LL *schismaticus*) of earlier *scismatical,* fr. obs. E *scismatyke,* adj. + E *-al*] : SCHISMATIC — **schis·mat·i·cal·ness** *n* -ES

schis·mat·i·cal·ly \-k(ə)lē̇, -li\ *adv* [alter. (influenced by LL *schismaticus*) of earlier *scismatically,* fr. obs. E *scismatical* + E *-ly*] : in a schismatic manner : so as to schismatize

schis·ma·tist \'ᵔ,mət̶əst, -məd̶·ə̇-\ *n* -s [prob. fr. *schismatize,* after such pairs as E *colonize: colonist*] : SCHISMATIC

schis·ma·tize \-mə,tīz\ *vb* -ED/-ING/-S [prob. fr. ²*schismatic,* after such pairs as E *harmonic: harmonize*] *vi* : to take part in schism; *esp* : to make a breach of union (as in the church) ∼ *vt* : to induce into schism

schismless *adj, obs* : free from schismatic disorder

schist *also* shist \'shist\ *n* -s [F *schiste,* fr. L *schistos,* adj., that splits easily, fr. Gk, divided, divisible, fr. *schizein* to split — more at SHED] : a metamorphic crystalline rock having a closely foliated structure, admitting of division along approximately parallel planes, and differing from gneisses in containing no essential feldspar and usu. in having finer laminations

schis·tic \-tik\ *adj* : SCHISTOSE

schis·to- *comb form* [NL, fr. Gk *schistos* divided, divisible] : cleft : divided ⟨*Schisto*cephalus⟩

schis·to·ceph·a·lus \,shistə'sefələs\ *n, cap* [NL, fr. *schisto- + -cephalus*] : a genus of tapeworms closely related to and resembling those of the genus *Ligula* in appearance and behavior

schis·to·cer·ca \,shistə'sərkə\ *n, cap* [NL, fr. *schisto- + -cerca* (fr. Gk *kerkos* tail)] : a genus of large migratory locusts

schis·to·cyte \'ᵔᵔᵔᵔ,sīt\ *n* -s [ISV *schisto- + -cyte*] **1** : a very small red blood cell **2** : a fragmenting red blood cell

schis·toid \'shi,stȯid\ *adj* [ISV *schist + -oid*] : resembling schist

schist oil *n* : oil distilled from bituminous schists

schis·tor·rha·chis \shi̅'stȯrəkəs *sometimes* ski-\ *n* -ES [NL, fr. *schisto- + -rrhachis*] : SPINA BIFIDA

schis·tose *also* shist·ose \'shi,stōs *also* -ōz\ *or* schist·ous \-,stəs\ *adj* [*schistose, schist + -ose; schistous* fr. F *schisteux,* fr. *schiste* schist + *-eux -ous*] : of or relating to schist : having the character or structure of a schist

schis·tos·i·ty \shi̅'stäsəd̶·ē\ *n* -ES : the quality or state of being a schist

schis·to·so·ma \,shistə'sōmə *sometimes* ,ski-\ *n* [NL *Schistosomat-, Schistosoma,* fr. *schisto- + -somat-, -soma -soma*] **1** *cap* : the type genus of the family Schistosomatidae comprising digenetic trematodes parasitic in the visceral veins of man and other mammals — see SCHISTOSOMIASIS **2** -s : any worm of the genus *Schistosoma* : SCHISTOSOME

schis·to·so·mat·i·dae \,shistə,sō'mad̶·ə,dē\ *n pl, cap* [NL, fr. *Schistosomat-, Schistosoma,* type genus + *-idae*] : a family of slender elongated digenetic trematodes (superfamily Schistosomatoidea) in which the sexes are separate and marked sexual dimorphism is usu. present — see SCHISTOSOMA

schis·to·so·ma·toi·dea \,shistə,sō(,)mad̶·ə'tȯidē̇ə\ *n pl, cap* [NL, fr. *Schistosomat-, Schistosoma* + *-oidea*] : a superfamily of digenetic trematodes that lack a metacercaria and have instead a furcocercous cercaria that actively penetrates the skin of a definitive host — compare SCHISTOSOME DERMATITIS

¹schis·to·some \'ᵔᵔᵔ,sōm\ *adj* [NL *Schistosoma*] : of or relating to the genus *Schistosoma* ⟨∼ morphology⟩ : caused by schistosomes

²schistosome \"\ *n* -s [NL *Schistosoma*] : a trematode of the genus *Schistosoma* or broadly of the family Schistosomatidae — called also *blood fluke*

schistosome dermatitis *n* : an itching inflammation caused by invasion of the skin by furcocercous cercariae of various schistosomes that are not normally parasites of man — called also *swimmer's itch;* see STAGNICOLA

schis·to·so·mi·a·sis \,shistə,sō'mīəsəs *sometimes* ,ski-\ *n, pl* schistosomi·a·ses \-,ī,sēz\ [NL, fr. *Schistosoma* + *-iasis*] : infestation with or disease caused by schistosomes; *specif* : a severe endemic disease of man in much of Asia, Africa, and So. America that is caused by any of three schistosomes (*Schistosoma haematobium, S. mansoni,* and *S. japonicum*) which multiply in snail intermediate hosts and are disseminated into fresh waters as furcocercous cercariae that bore into the body when in contact with infested water, migrate through the tissues to the visceral venous plexuses (as of the bladder or intestine) where they attain maturity, and cause much of their injury through hemorrhage and damage to tissues resulting from the passage of the usu. spined eggs to the intestine and bladder whence they pass out to start a new cycle of infection in snail hosts — compare SCHISTOSOME DERMATITIS

schistosomiasis hae·ma·to·bi·um \-,hēmə'tōbē̇əm\ *n* [schistosomiasis + NL *haematobium* (specific epithet of *Schistosoma haematobium,* fr. L *haemat-* hemat- + NL *-bium,* neut. of *-bius* having a (specified) mode of life — more at -BIUS] : schistosomiasis caused by the worm (*Schistosoma haematobium*) occurring over most of Africa and in Asia Minor and predominantly involving infestation of the veins of the urinary bladder

schistosomiasis ja·pon·i·ca \-jə'pänəkə\ *n* [NL, *schistosomiasis + japonica,* fem. of *japonicus* Japanese (of which the neut. *japonicum* is the specific epithet of *Schistosoma japonicum*), fr. *Japonia* Japan, country off the eastern coast of Asia + L *-icus -ic*] : schistosomiasis caused by the worm (*Schistosoma japonicum*) occurring chiefly in eastern Asia and the Pacific islands and predominantly involving infestation of the portal and mesenteric veins

schistosomiasis man·so·ni \-'man(t)sə,nī\ *n* [schistosomiasis + NL *mansoni* (specific epithet of *Schistosoma mansoni*), gen. of *Mansoni,* latinization of the name of Sir Patrick *Manson* †1922 Brit. physician and parasitologist] : schistosomiasis caused by the worm (*Schistosoma mansoni*) occurring chiefly in central Africa and eastern So. America and predominantly involving infestation of the mesenteric and portal veins

schis·to·so·moph·o·ra \,shistəsō'mäfərə *sometimes* ,ski-\ *n, cap* [NL, fr. *Schistosoma* + *-phora*] : a genus of Oriental freshwater snails (family Bulimidae) including important intermediate hosts of the schistosome (*Schistosoma japonicum*) esp. in the Philippines — compare ONCOMELANIA

schis·to·som·u·lum \,shistə'sämyələm\ *n, pl* schistosomu·la \-lə\ [NL, fr. *Schistosoma* + *-ulum*] : an immature schistosome in the body of the definitive host

schists *pl of* SCHIST

schiz- *or* schizo- *comb form* [NL, fr. Gk *schizo-,* fr. *schizein* to split — more at SHED] **1** : split : cleft : divided ⟨*schiz*axon⟩ **2** : characterized by or involving cleavage ⟨*schizo*genesis⟩ : produced by cleavage ⟨*schizo*coel⟩ ⟨*schizo*phrenia⟩

schi·zaea \skə'zē̇ə\ *n, cap* [NL, irreg. fr. Gk *schizein* to split] : a genus (the type of the family Schizaeaceae) of small leptosporangiate ferns with filiform or linear fronds and the sporangia in close distichous spikes — see CURLY GRASS

schiz·ae·a·ce·ae \ˌskizēˈāsēˌē\ *n pl, cap* [NL, fr. *Schizaea*, type genus + *-aceae*] **:** a small family of mainly tropical ferns of various habit with simple or pinnate fronds and ovoid sessile sporangia in spikes or panicles — **schiz·ae·a·ceous** \ˌskizēˈāshəs\ *adj*

schiz·af·fin \ˈskitsəˌfēn\ *adj* [ISV *schiz-* + *-affin* (fr. *affinity*)] **:** ASTHENIC 2

schi·zan·dra \skəˈzandrə\ *syn of* SCHISANDRA

schi·zan·thus \-ˈzan(t)thəs\ *n* [NL, fr. *schiz-* + *-anthus*] **1** *cap* **:** a genus of Chilean herbs (family Solanaceae) having finely divided leaves and showy variegated flowers with an irregular laciniate corolla and two exserted stamens — see BUTTERFLY FLOWER **2** -ES **:** any plant of the genus *Schizanthus*

schiz·axon \(ˈ)skiz, skəz+\ *n* [NL, fr. *schiz-* + *axon*] **:** an axon that splits into nearly equal branches; *esp* **:** an axon of a sensory neuron entering the spinal cord and being so split

schizo \ˈskit(ˌ)sō *sometimes* -i(d)(ˌ)zō\ *n* -s [short for *schizophrenic*] **:** a schizophrenic individual

schizo-affective \ˌ≈(ˌ)≈+\ *adj* [*schiz-* + *affective*] **:** exhibiting symptoms of both schizophrenia and manic-depressive psychosis

schizo·carp \ˈskizōˌkärp\ *n* -s [ISV *schiz-* + *-carp*] **:** a dry compound fruit that splits at maturity into several indehiscent one-seeded carpels — see MERICARP; FRUIT illustration — **schizo·car·pic** \ˌ≈≈ˈkärpik\ *adj* — **schizo·car·pous** \-pəs\ *adj*

schizo·coel *also* **schizo·coele** \ˈ≈≈ˌsēl\ *n* -s [*schiz-* + *-coele*] **:** a perivisceral cavity that arises by the splitting of the mesoblast of the embryo — compare ENTEROCOELE — **schizo·coe·lic** \ˌ≈≈ˈsēlik\ *adj* — **schizo·coe·lous** \-ləs\ *adj*

schizo·din·ic \ˌ≈≈ˈdinik\ *adj* [*schiz-* + Gk *ōdinein* to be in labor + E *-ic*; akin to Gk *odynē* pain — more at ANODYNE] **:** discharging genital products by rupture

schi·zog·a·my \skəˈzägəmē\ *n* -ES [ISV *schiz-* + *-gamy*] **:** reproduction involving division of the body into a sexual and an asexual individual (as in some chaetopod worms)

schizo·genesis \ˌskizō+\ *n* [NL, fr. *schiz-* + L *genesis*] **:** reproduction by fission

schizo·ge·net·ic \ˌ≈≈jəˈned·ik\ *or* **schizo·gen·ic** \-ˈjenik\ *adj* [*schiz-* + *-genetic* or *-genic*] **:** SCHIZOGENOUS — **schizo·ge·net·i·cal·ly** \-d·ək(ə)lē\ *adv*

schi·zog·e·nous \skəˈzäjənəs\ *adj* [*schiz-* + *-genous*] **:** of, relating to, or formed by fission: as **a :** SCHIZOGONOUS **b :** formed by splitting, delamination, or separation of adjacent cell walls ⟨~ intercellular spaces in plants⟩ — compare LYSIGENOUS — **schi·zog·e·nous·ly** *adv*

schi·zog·na·thae \skəˈzägnəˌthē\ *n pl, cap* [NL, fr. *schiz-* + *-gnathae*] *in former classification* **:** a suborder of carinate birds consisting of those (as the pigeons, gallinaceous birds, penguins, gulls, cranes, shorebirds) with a schizognathous palate

schi·zog·na·thism \-ˌthizəm\ *n* -s [*schizognathous* + *-ism*] **:** the condition of being schizognathous

schi·zog·na·thous \-thəs\ *adj* [*schiz-* + *-gnathous*] **:** constituting or having an arrangement of the bones of the palate in which the vomer is narrow and pointed in front and separated by a space on each side from the usu. long narrow maxillopalatals which do not unite with each other or with the vomer — used of birds

schizo·go·ni·a·les \ˌskizəˌgōnēˈā(ˌ)lēz\ *n pl, cap* [NL, fr. *schiz-* + *goni-* + *-ales*] **:** a monotypic order of green algae (class Chlorophyceae) having a filamentous, flat and expanded, or solid cylindrical body made of uninucleate cells with single stellate chloroplasts

schi·zog·o·nous \skəˈzägənəs\ *also* **schizo·gon·ic** \ˌskizəˈgänik\ *adj* [*schizogonous* fr. *schizogony* + *-ous; schizogonic* ISV *schizogon-* (fr. NL *schizogonia*) + *-ic*] **:** of, relating to, or reproducing by schizogony ⟨~ protozoans⟩

schi·zog·o·ny \skəˈzägənē\ *n* -ES [NL *schizogonia*, fr. *schiz-* + L *-gonia* -gony] **:** asexual reproduction by multiple segmentation of an enlarged trophozoite that is characteristic of many sporozoans (as the malaria parasite) — compare SPOROGONY

schizo·gregarinae \ˌski(ˌ)zō+\ *n* [NL, fr. *schiz-* + *Gregarinae*] *syn of* SCHIZOGREGARINARIA

schizo·gregarinaria \"+\ *n pl, cap* [NL, fr. *schiz-* + *Gregarinaria*] **:** a suborder of Gregarinida comprising sporozoans that possess both sexual reproduction and asexual schizogony — compare EUGREGARININA

schizo·gregarine \"+\ *n* -s [NL *Schizogregarinae*] **:** a sporozoan of the suborder Schizogregarinaria

schizo·gregarinida \"+\ [NL, fr. *schiz-* + *Gregarinida*] *syn of* SCHIZOGREGARINARIA

¹**schiz·oid** \ˈskitˌsȯid *sometimes* -i(d)ˌzȯid\ *adj* [ISV *schiz-* + *-oid*] **1 :** characterized by, resulting from, or possessed of a split personality **2 :** disintegrating into mutually contradictory or antagonistic parts ⟨conflicting values make ours a ~ culture⟩ ⟨a ~ foreign policy⟩

²**schizoid** \"\ *n* -s **:** a schizoid individual ⟨extreme devotion to religious pursuits . . . is common among ~*s* —R.S.Banay⟩

schiz·oid·ism \-ˌdizəm\ *n* -s **:** the state of being split off (as in schizoid personality and schizophrenia) from one's social and vital environment

schizoidmanic \ˌ≈≈ˈ≈≈\ *also* **schizo·manic** \ˌskitsō *sometimes* -i(d)zō-\ *adj* [*schizoidmanic* fr. ¹*schizoid* + *manic; schizomanic* fr. *schiz-* + *manic*] **:** schizo-affective and usu. with predominantly manic features

schizoid personality *n* **:** a personality disorder characterized by shyness, withdrawal, inhibition of emotional expression, and apparent diminution of affect, displaying an active fantasy life often evidenced by eccentric behavior or by artistic creativeness and sometimes by nomadism or by religiosity but not necessarily going on to intellectual or emotional deterioration or regression, and generally being in actual or potential contact with reality

schiz·o·lite \ˈskizəˌlīt\ *n* -s [Dan *schizolit*, fr. *schiz-* + *-lit* -lite] **:** a manganese-containing variety of pectolite

schizo·lysigenous \ˌski(ˌ)zō+\ *adj* [blend of *schizogenous* and *lysigenous*] **:** formed both schizogenously and lysigenously — **schizo·ly·sig·e·nous·ly** *adv*

schiz·o·me·ria \ˌskizəˈmirēə\ *n, cap* [NL, fr. *schiz-* + Gk *meros* part + NL *-ia* — more at MERIT] **:** a small genus of trees (family Cunoniaceae) of Australia and New Guinea with strong hard wood — see ASH

schizo·my·cete \ˌskizəˈmīˌsēt, -ˌmīˈsēt\ *n* -s [NL *Schizomycetes*] **:** an organism of the class Schizomycetes **:** BACTERIUM

schizo·my·ce·tes \-ˌmīˈsēd·ēz\ *n pl, cap* [NL, fr. *schiz-* + *-mycetes*] **:** a class of unicellular or noncellular organisms lacking true chlorophyll, comprising the bacteria, being classed among the fungi, kept separate, or grouped with the blue-green algae in a distinct division — see PROTOPHYTA, SCHIZOPHYTA; compare BACTERIOCHLOROPHYLL — **schizo·my·cet·ic** \ˌ≈≈ˌmīˈsed·ik\ *adj* — **schizo·my·ce·tous** \-sēd·əs\ *adj*

schizo·my·coph·y·ta \ˌ≈≈ˌmīˈkäfəd·ə\ [NL, fr. *schiz-* + *myc-* + *-phyta*] *syn of* SCHIZOPHYTA

schizo·nemertea \ˌski(ˌ)zō+\ *n pl, cap* [NL, fr. *schiz-* + *Nemertea*] *in some classifications* **:** a group of nemerteans comprising those having a deep slit along each side of the head and a proboscis devoid of stylets — **schizo·nemertean** \"+\ *or* **schizo·nemertine** \"+\ *adj or n*

schizont \ˈskīˌzänt, -ki,z-\ *n* -s [ISV *schiz-* + *-ont*] **:** a multinucleate cell in some sporozoans that is formed by the growth of a trophozoite in a cell of the host and that segments directly into merozoites — compare SCHIZOGONY, SPORONT

schi·zon·ti·ci·dal \skəˈzäntəˈsīdᵊl\ *adj* **:** of or relating to a schizonticide

schi·zon·ti·cide \≈ˈ≈≈ˌsīd\ *n* -s [*schizont* + *-i-* + *-cide*] **:** an agent selectively destructive of the schizont of a sporozoan parasite (as of malaria)

schiz·o·pel·mous \ˌskizōˈpelməs\ *adj* [*schiz-* + *-pelmous*] **:** having the two flexor tendons of the toes separate and the flexor of the hallux going to the first toe only

schizo·pet·a·lon \ˌ≈≈ˈped·əlˌän\ *n, cap* [NL, fr. *schiz-* + Gk *petalon* leaf — more at PETAL] **:** a genus of So. American annual herbs (family Cruciferae) having lobed or sometimes pinnatifid leaves, racemose flowers with unequally cut long-clawed petals, and narrow pods

schizo·pha·sia \ˌskitsōˈfāzh(ē)ə *sometimes* -i(d)zō-\ *n* -s [NL, fr. *schiz-* + *-phasia*] **:** the disorganized speech characteristic of schizophrenia

schi·zoph·o·ra \skəˈzäfərə\ *n pl, cap* [NL, fr. *schiz-* + *-phora*] **:** a suborder or other division of Diptera consisting mainly of the Acalyptratae and Calyptratae

schiz·o·phrene \ˈskitsəˌfrēn *sometimes* -i(d)zə-\ *n* -s [ISV, prob. back-formation fr. NL *schizophrenia*] **:** SCHIZOPHRENIC

schiz·o·phre·nia \ˌskitsəˈfrēnēə *sometimes* -i(d)zəˈf- *or* -fren-\ *n* -s [NL, fr. *schiz-* + *-phrenia*] **1 :** a psychotic disorder of unknown complex etiology that occurs as simple, paranoid, catatonic, or hebephrenic, is characterized by disturbance in thinking involving a distortion of the usual logical relations between ideas, a separation between the intellect and the emotions so that the patient's feelings or their manifestations seem inappropriate to his life situation, and a reduced tolerance for the stress of interpersonal relations so that the patient retreats from social intercourse into his own fantasy life and commonly into delusions and hallucinations, and may when untreated or unsuccessfully treated go on to marked deterioration or regression in the patient's behavior though often unaccompanied by further intellectual loss **2 :** SPLIT PERSONALITY — **schiz·o·phre·ni·ac** \-nēˌak\ *n* -s — **schiz·o·phrenic** \ˌ≈≈ˈfrenik *also* -rēn- *sometimes* -rin-\ *adj or n*

schizophrenic reaction *n* **:** SCHIZOPHRENIA 1

schiz·o·phren·i·form \ˌ≈≈ˈfrenəˌfȯrm\ *adj* [*schizophreni-* (fr. *schizophrenia*) + *-form*] **:** similar to schizophrenia in appearance or manifestations

schiz·o·phreno·gen·ic \ˌ≈≈ˌfrēnəˈjenik, -ren-\ *adj* [*schizophrenia* + *-o-* + *-genic*] **:** causative of or tending to produce schizophrenia

schiz·o·phy·ce·ae \ˌskizəˈfīsēˌē\ [NL, fr. *schiz-* + *-phyceae*] *syn of* MYXOPHYCEAE

schi·zoph·y·ta \skəˈzäfəd·ə\ *n pl, cap* [NL, fr. *schiz-* + *-phyta*] *in some classifications* **:** a division comprising the blue-green algae and bacteria (classes Myxophyceae and Schizomycetes) and characterized by unicellular or loosely colonial and often filamentous organization, by lack of a readily identifiable condensed nucleus, and by reproduction chiefly or wholly by fission — **schizo·phyt·ic** \ˌskizəˈfid·ik\ *adj*

schizo·phyte \ˈskizəˌfīt\ *n* -s [NL *Schizophyta*] **:** one of the Schizophyta

schizo·pod \ˈskizəˌpäd\ *n* -s [NL *Schizopoda*] **:** a crustacean of the order Euphausiacea or Mysidacea

schi·zop·o·da \skəˈzäpədə\ *n pl, cap* [NL, fr. *schiz-* + *-poda*] *in former classifications* **:** an order or other division of Malacostraca that is now divided between the orders Euphausiacea and Mysidacea — **schi·zop·o·dous** \-dəs\ *adj*

schi·zop·o·dal \-dᵊl\ *adj* [NL *Schizopoda* + E *-al*] **:** having biramous thoracic appendages

schizo·rhinal \ˌskizəˈrīnᵊl\ *adj* [*schiz-* + *rhin-* + *-al*] **:** having each of the bones forming the posterior contour of the osseous external nares deeply cleft instead of rounded ⟨pigeons, most shore birds, and various other birds are ~⟩ — opposed to *holorhinal*

schizos *pl of* SCHIZO

schizo·saccharomyces \ˌski(ˌ)zō+\ *n, cap* [NL, fr. *schiz-* + *Saccharomyces*] **:** a genus (coextensive with the family Schizosaccharomycetaceae of the order Endomycetales) of fungi comprising the fission yeasts and characterized by division of each cell into two daughter cells of similar size — compare BUDDING YEAST

schizo·the·cal \ˌskizəˈthēkəl\ *adj* [*schiz-* + *thec-* + *-al*] **:** having the horny envelope of the tarsus divided into plates that resemble large firm scales ⟨most birds are ~⟩

schizo·thoracic \ˌski(ˌ)zō+\ *adj* [*schiz-* + *thorac-* + *-ic*] **:** having the prothorax large and loosely articulated to the remainder of the thorax ⟨~ insects⟩

schiz·o·thyme \ˈskitsəˌthīm *sometimes* -i(d)zə-\ *n* -s [ISV, prob. back-formation fr. NL *schizothymia*] **:** an individual exhibiting or characterized by schizothymia

schiz·o·thy·mia \ˌ≈≈ˈthīmēə\ *n* -s [NL, fr. *schiz-* + *-thymia*] **:** an introvert tendency or temperament that while remaining within the bounds of normality somewhat resembles schizophrenia (as in a tendency to autistic thinking) — opposed to *cyclothymia* — **schiz·o·thy·mic** \ˌ≈≈ˈthīmik\ *also* **schiz·o·thy·mous** \-məs\ *adj*

schiz·o·tryp·a·num \ˌskizōˈtripənəm\ *n, cap* [NL, fr. *schiz-* + Gk *trypanon* auger — more at TRYPAN-] *in some classifications* **:** a genus of flagellates comprising the trypanosome of Chagas' disease — used when the organism is viewed as generically distinct from *Trypanosoma*

schizo·zo·ite \ˌskizəˈzōˌīt\ *n* -s [*schiz-* + Gk *zōion* animal + E *-ite* — more at ZO-] **:** MEROZOITE

schl *abbr* school

schlä·ger \ˈshlāgə(r)\ *n, pl* **schläger** [G, lit., one that strikes or beats, fr. *schlagen* to strike, beat (fr. OHG *slahan*) + *-er* — more at SLAY] **:** a long straight basket-hilted blunt-ended sword that is sharpened only near the end and is used in duels by German university students

schle·miel *or* **schle·mihl** *or* **shle·miel** \shləˈmē(ə)l\ *n* -s [Yiddish *shlumiel*, prob. fr. the name Heb *Shĕlūmīel* Shelumiel (Num 1:6)] *slang* **:** an unlucky bungling person **:** a foolish gullible person **:** NE'ER-DO-WELL

schlemm's canal \ˈshlemz-\ *n, usu cap S* [after Friedrich S. *Schlemm* †1858 Ger. anatomist] **:** a circular canal lying in the substance of the sclerocorneal junction of the eye and draining the aqueous humor from the anterior chamber into the anterior ciliary veins

schlen·ter \ˈs(h)lentə(r)\ *n* -s [modif. of Afrik *slenter*, fr. D, trick] *Africa* **:** IMITATION, FAKE — used esp. of a diamond

schlepp \ˈshlep\ *vb* -ED/-ING/-S [Yiddish *shlepen* to drag, fr. MHG *sleppen, slēpen*, fr. MLG *slēpen*; akin to MD *slepen* to drag, OHG *sleifen*; causative fr. the root of MD *slīpen* to whet, polish, MLG *slīpen* to whet, polish, OHG *slīfan* to slide, whet; akin to OE *slipor* slippery — more at SLIPPERY] *slang* **:** DRAG, HAUL; *also* **:** STEAL

schlich \ˈshlik, -iḵ\ *n* -s [G, slime, mud, fr. MHG *slich* — more at SLICK] **:** SLIME 2d

schlie·ren \ˈshlirən\ *n pl* [G, fr. G dial. *schlieren*, pl. of *schlier*, lit., ulcer, fr. MHG *slier, sliere*; prob. akin to MHG *slier* mud — more at SLUR] **1 :** small masses or streaks that differ in mineral composition from the main body of an igneous rock but graduate insensibly into it **2 :** regions or streaks in a transparent medium (as a fluid) that have a density and hence a refractive index differing from that of the bulk of the medium and often resulting from pressure or temperature differences and that are detected esp. by photographing the passage of a beam of light (as in the shock waves of a projectile) — **schlie·ric** \-rik\ *adj*

schli·ma·zel *or* **schli·mazl** *or* **shli·ma·zel** *or* **shli·mazl** \shləˈmäzəl\ *n* -s [Yiddish *shlimazel* consistently unlucky person, bad luck, misfortune — more at SCHEMOZZLE] *slang* **:** a consistently unlucky person

schlip·pe's salt \ˈshlipəz-\ *n, usu cap 1st S* [after Karl Friedrich von *Schlippe* †1867 Ger. chemist] **:** a crystalline salt $Na_3SbS_4.9H_2O$ used as an intensifier in photography; sodium thioantimonate

schloop \ˈshlüp\ *n* -s [imit.] **:** a swishing sound ending in a plop

schloss \ˈshlȯs\ *n* -ES [G, castle, lock, fr. MHG *sloz*, fr. OHG, lock, bolt — more at SLOT] **:** a German castle or manor house

schmaltz *or* **schmalz** \ˈshmȯlts, -mäl-, *in sense 2* -ä-\ *n* -ES [Yiddish *shmalts*, lit., rendered fat, fr. MHG *smalz*, fr. OHG; akin to OHG *smelzan* to melt — more at SMELT] **1 a :** extremely sentimental music **b :** sentimentalism in artistic expression **c :** something notably florid or showy of its kind **2** *slang* **:** the rendered fat of poultry

schmaltzy *or* **schmalzy** \-tsē\ *adj, sometimes* -ER/-EST **:** marked by schmaltz **:** excessively sentimental

schmeiss \ˈshmīs\ *n* -ES [G *schmeissen* to fling, throw away, fr. MHG *smīzen* to stroke, smear, strike, fr. OHG *-smīzan* (in *bismīzan* to defile, stain) — more at SMITE] **:** a bid in klaberjass that requires the opponent to accept the bidder's trump suit or abandon the hand

schmelz *or* **schmelze** \ˈshmelts\ *n, pl* **schmelz·es** \-tsəz\ [G *schmelz* enamel, fr. OHG *smelzi*; akin to OHG *smelzan* to melt] **:** any of various decorative glasses; *esp* **:** a glass colored red with metallic salts and used to flash white glass

schmidt camera \ˈshmit\ *n, usu cap S* [after B. *Schmidt* †1935 Ger. optician] **:** a camera embodying a Schmidt system and a film or plate holder and used extensively in astronomy and in photofluorography

schmidt system *n, usu cap S* **:** an optical system that utilizes an objective composed of a concave spherical mirror having in front of it a transparent correction plate carefully figured to offset the spherical aberration of the mirror

schmidt telescope *n, usu cap S* **:** a photographic astronomical reflecting telescope embodying a Schmidt system so that the curved focal surface is free of significant spherical aberration and coma over a wide angular field

schmier·ka·se \ˈshmi(ə)rˌkäzə\ *n* -s [G *schmierkäse* — more at SMEARCASE] **:** COTTAGE CHEESE

schmitt box \ˈshmit-\ *n, sometimes cap S* [after P. Jerome *Schmitt* †1904 Am. priest who designed it] **:** a wooden pest-proof box for storing pinned insects

schmo *or* **schmoe** \ˈshmō\ *n, pl* **schmoes** [prob. modif. of Yiddish *shmok* fool, fr. Slovenian *šmok*] *slang* **:** JERK 5

¹**schmooze** *also* **schmoose** \ˈshmüz\ *vi* -ED/-ING/-S [Yiddish *shmuesn* to talk, chat, fr. *shmues* talk, chat, fr. Heb *shĕmūʽōth* news, rumors, report, pl. of *shĕmūʽāh* rumor, report, fr. *shāmōʽa* to hear, listen] *slang* **:** to chatter esp. in jargon or cant

²**schmooze** \"\ *n* -s [Yiddish *shmues* talk, chat] *slang* **:** JARGON

schnap·per \ˈshnapə(r)\ *n* -s [alter. (influenced by G *schnapper* snapper, fr. MHG *snapper* gossipy or quarrelsome person, fr. *snappen* to snap + *-er*) of *snapper*] **:** SNAPPER 3c

schnapps *also* **schnaps** \ˈshnaps\ *n, pl* **schnapps** [G *schnaps*, lit., dram of liquor, fr. LG *snaps* dram, mouthful, fr. *snappen* to snap, fr. MLG — more at SNAP] **:** any of various distilled liquors; *esp* **:** strong Holland gin

schnau·zer \ˈshnaůzə(r), -aůtsə-\ *n* [G, fr. *schnauze* snout, muzzle + *-er*; fr. the mustache and beard — more at SNOUT] **1** *usu cap* **:** an old German breed of terriers occurring in three varieties differing only in size that have a long head with small ears and heavy eyebrows, mustache, and beard and a wiry coat of pepper-and-salt, black, or black and tan **2** -s **:** a dog of this breed

schnec·ke \ˈshnekə\ *n, pl* **schnec·ken** \-kən\ [G, lit., snail, fr. OHG *snecko* — more at SNAIL] **:** a cinnamon bun made of rich yeast-leavened dough that is rolled up like a jelly roll, cut into crosswise slices, and baked cut side down — usu. used in pl.

¹**schnei·der** \ˈshnīdə(r)\ *n* -s [G, lit., tailor, fr. MHG *snīdære*, fr. *snīden* to cut (fr. OHG *snīdan*) + *-ære* -er (fr. OHG *-āri*); akin to OE *snīthan* to cut, ON *snītha* to cut, Goth *sneithan* to reap, Czech *snět* bough] **1 a :** the taking of 91 or more points by the bidder in skat or schafskopf or of 90 or more by the opponents **b :** failure of the loser of a game of gin rummy to score any point **c :** the winning of a game of sixty-six by a player before his opponent has scored 33 points **2 :** the scoring effect of a schneider (as the doubling of the winner's score)

²**schneider** \"\ *vt* -ED/-ING/-S **:** to cause (an opponent) to lose by a schneider

schnei·de·ri·an membrane \(ˈ)shnīˈdirēən-\ *n, usu cap S* [*schneiderian* fr. Conrad Victor *Schneider* †1680 Ger. anatomist + E *-an*] **:** modified mucous membrane forming the epithelial part of the olfactory organ

schnei·der index \ˈshnīdə(r)-\ *n, usu cap S* [after Edward Christian *Schneider* †1954 Am. biologist] **:** a measure of comparative circulatory efficiency based on determination of pulse rates under several test conditions (as reclining, standing, or after exercise), time required for rate to alter with change of state, and accompanying variations in systolic pressure

schnell \ˈshnel\ *adv (or adj)* [G, fr. OHG *snel*, adj., strong, bold, agile — more at SNELL] **:** in a rapid manner **:** QUICKLY — used as a direction in music

schnitz *or* **snits** *also* **snitz** \ˈshnits\ *n, pl* **schnitz** *or* **snits** *also* **snitz** [PaG, *schnitz*, pl. of *schnutz* section of dried fruit, alter. of G *schnitz* slice, cut, fr. MHG *sniz*; akin to OHG *snīdan* to cut] **:** sliced dried fruit; *esp* **:** sliced dried apples

schnitz and knepp \ˌ≈ənkəˈnep, -ənˈknep\ *n* [PaG *gnepp*, pl. of *gnopp* button, lump, fr. MHG dial. *knopp*; akin to OHG *knopf* knot, lump — more at KNOP] **:** a dish consisting of dried apples and dumplings boiled with or without smoked ham

schnit·zel \ˈshnitsəl\ *n* -s [G, cutlet, shaving, chip, fr. MHG *snitzel* small slice, dim. of *sniz* slice, cut] **:** a veal cutlet variously seasoned and garnished

schnitz un knepp \ˌshnitsən-\ *n* [PaG *schnitz un gnepp*] **:** SCHNITZ AND KNEPP

schnook \ˈshnůk\ *n* -s [origin unknown] *slang* **:** a stupid or suggestible person **:** a person of no importance **:** DOLT

schnorkel *also* **schnorchel** *var of* SNORKEL

schnor·rer \ˈshnōrər, -nȯr-\ *n* -s [Yiddish *shnorer*, fr. *shnoren* to beg (fr. MHG *snurren* to hum, whir, of imit. origin) + *-er* (fr. MHG *-ære*, fr. OHG *-āri*); fr. the sound of the musical instrument used by strolling beggars] *slang* **:** BEGGAR

schnoz·zle \ˈshnäzəl\ *n* -s [prob. modif. of Yiddish *shnoitsl*, dim. of *shnoits* snout, fr. G *schnauze* snout, muzzle — more at SNOUT] *slang* **:** NOSE

schnur·ke·ra·mik \ˈshnů(ə)rkəˌrämik\ *n* -s [G, fr. *schnur* string, cord (fr. OHG *snuor*) + *keramik* ceramics, fr. F *céramique* — more at NARROW, CERAMIC] **:** a Neolithic pottery decorated by imprints of string or cord

schochet *var of* SHOHET

schoen·feld's purple \ˈshō[n,feld(z)-, ˈshə(r)|, -lts-\ *n, often cap S* [prob. fr. the name *Schoenfeld*] **:** a dark purplish red that is bluer and paler than pansy purple and bluer, lighter, and stronger than raisin, Bokhara, or dahlia purple (sense 1)

schoe·no·cau·lon \ˌskēnəˈkōˌlän\ *n, cap* [NL, fr. *schoeno-* (fr. Gk *schoinos* rush, reed) + *-caulon* (fr. Gk *kaulos* stem) — more at HOLE] **:** a genus of bulbous American herbs (family Liliaceae) having linear basal leaves and white flowers with exserted stamens — see SABADILLA

schoe·nus \ˈskēnəs\ *n, cap* [NL, fr. Gk *schoinos* rush, reed] **:** a genus of stout sedges (family Cyperaceae) chiefly Australasian but including a few from Europe and the warm or tropical parts of No. America and having few-flowered spikelets in a spike or head, flowers without a perianth of bristles, and nutlets lacking a beak

schoep·ite \ˈskeˌpīt, ˈskə(r)ˌp-\ *n* -s [Alfred *Schoep*, 20th cent. Belg. mineralogist + E *-ite*] **:** a mineral prob. $4UO_3.9H_2O$ that is a hydrous uranium oxide and is found esp. in the Belgian Congo

schoi·nob·a·tes \skȯiˈnäbəˌtēz\ *n, cap* [NL, fr. Gk *schoinobatēs* ropedancer, fr. *schoinos* rush, reed, rope + *-batēs* one that goes (fr. *bainein* to go, walk) — more at COME] **:** a genus of marsupials comprising the large flying phalangers of Australia

schok·ker \ˈskäkə(r)\ *n* -s [D] **:** a large Dutch cutter, yawl, or ketch-rigged pleasure boat

scho·la \ˈskōlə\ *n, pl* **scho·lae** \-ˌlē, -ˌlī\ *also* **scholas** [L] **1 a :** an ancient Roman school **b :** a private room in an ancient Roman residence **c :** a lecture hall or meeting room (as of a guild or corporation) **2** [LL, fr. L] **:** an ancient Roman association of persons (as military men) sharing a common interest or profession

schola can·to·rum \ˌ≈≈ˌkanˈtōrəm\ *n, pl* **scholae cantorum** [ML, school of singers] **1 :** a singing school; *specif* **:** the choir or choir school of a monastery or of a cathedral **2 :** the part of an ecclesiastical edifice reserved to the choir

schol·ar \ˈskälə(r)\ *n* -s [ME *scoler*, fr. OE *scolere* & OF *escoler*, fr. ML *scholaris*, fr. LL, adj., of a school, fr. L *schola* school + *-aris* -ar — more at SCHOOL] **1 a :** one who attends a school or studies under a teacher **:** PUPIL, STUDENT — used esp. in combination ⟨Sunday school ~⟩ **b :** one under the training of a particular master ⟨a ~ of the learned doctor⟩ **2 a :** one who by long systematic study (as in a university) has gained a high degree of mastery in one or more of the academic disciplines; *esp* **:** one who has engaged in advanced study and acquired the minutiae of knowledge in some special field along with accuracy and skill in investigation and powers of critical analysis in interpretation of such knowledge ⟨a noted Shakespeare ~⟩ ⟨was a ~. He knew the right books, knew them to the core and how to use them —H.S.Canby⟩ **b :** a learned person; *esp* **:** one who has the attitudes (as curiosity, perseverance, initiative, originality, integrity) considered essential for learning ⟨using the word ~ . . . to include

all those . . . endeavoring to be original thinkers in any field of learning —J.B.Conant⟩ ⟨the self-dedication of ~s to concerns unrelated to individual profit —Lynn White⟩ **c** *dial* **:** a person knowing how to read and write **3 :** a holder of a scholarship

schol·arch \'skä,lärk\ *n* -s [LGk *scholarchēs*, fr. Gk *scholē* school + *-archēs* -arch — more at SCHOOL] **1 :** the head of a school; *esp* **:** the leader of an Athenian school of philosophy **2** [F *scolarque* & G *scholarch*, fr. LGk *scholarchēs*] *archaic* **:** a school inspector in France or Germany

schol·ar·dom \'skälə(r)dəm\ *n* -s **:** the realm of scholarship **:** the whole body of scholars

scho·lar·i·an \skä'lerēən\ *n* -s [LL *scholarius* scholarian (fr. *schola* ancient Roman association of persons sharing a common interest or profession + L *-arius* -ary) + E *-an*] **:** a member of the Roman imperial guard

schol·ar·ism \'skälə,rizəm\ *n* -s **:** scholastic often pedantic learning

scho·lar·i·ty \skä'larəd·ē\ *n* -ES [ML *scholaritat-*, *scholaritas*, fr. *scholaris* scholar + L *-tat-*, *-tas* -ty] *archaic* **:** status as scholar

schol·ar·less \'skälə(r)ləs\ *adj* **:** lacking students ⟨a ~ tutor⟩

scholarlike \'=,=\ *adj* **:** SCHOLARLY

schol·ar·li·ly \'skälə(r)lәlē, -əli\ *adv* **:** in a scholarly manner **:** so as to be scholarly

schol·ar·li·ness \-)lēnəs, -)lin-\ *n* -ES **:** the quality or state of being scholarly

¹schol·ar·ly \'skälə(r)lē, -)li\ *adj, sometimes* -ER/-EST [*scholar* + *-ly*, adj. suffix] **:** like, characteristic of, or suitable to a scholar: as **a :** concerned with academic study and esp. with research ⟨contact between the craft and ~ elements of the profession —S.F.Mason⟩ ⟨the author of ~ and reference works —Charlton Laird⟩ **b :** exhibiting the methods and attitudes of a scholar ⟨his method was laborious and ~; it was not exceptional for him to spend three years in research, travel, and sketching, to produce a single canvas —*Amer. Guide Series: Calif.*⟩ **c :** having the manner and appearance of a scholar ⟨never academic — still less pedantic — but always ~; with the effect of profound learning ever so lightly worn —Ronald Storrs⟩

²scholarly \"\ *adv* [*scholar* + *-ly*, adv. suffix] **:** in the manner or character of or as befits a scholar

schol·ar·ship \'skälə(r),ship\ *n* **1 :** a sum of money or its equivalent offered (as by an educational institution, a public agency, or a private organization or foundation) to enable a student to pursue his studies at a school, college, or university — compare FELLOWSHIP **2 :** the character, qualities, or attainments of a scholar: as **a :** scholastic achievement **:** LEARNING ⟨Dante, whose ~ was . . . considerable, appears to have known no more than a word or two of Greek —Gilbert Highet⟩ ⟨devices employed by schools . . . for their supposed influence on ~ are . . . marks on report cards —H.R.Douglass⟩ **b :** methods, attitudes, and traditions characterizing a scholar ⟨if by ~ we mean all of the activities and attitudes encompassed in the sincere search for truth —Hugh & Mabel Smythe⟩ **3 :** the body of learning and esp. of research available in a particular field ⟨acquaint themselves with the actual nature of religious ~ —George Hedley⟩ **syn** see KNOWLEDGE

scho·lasm \'skō,lazəm\ *n* -s [fr. ¹*scholastic*, after such pairs as E *enthusiastic*: *enthusiasm*] **:** a pedantic or academic expression

¹scho·las·tic \skə'lastik -laas-, -tēk *also* skō'l- *or* skä'l-\ *adj* [in sense 1, fr. ML *scholasticus*, fr. L, of a school, fr. Gk *scholastikos* enjoying leisure, devoting one's leisure to learning, academic, fr. (assumed) Gk *scholastos* (verbal of Gk *scholazein* to have leisure, give lectures, keep a school, fr. *scholē* leisure, lecture, school) + Gk *-ikos* -ic; in other senses, fr. L *scholasticus* — more at SCHOOL] **1 a** *often cap* **:** of or relating to the Schoolmen of the medieval period ⟨~ theology⟩ ⟨~ philosophy⟩ **b** (1) **:** characterized by or suggestive of the logic or methods of the medieval Schoolmen (2) **:** characterized by excessive subtlety **:** PEDANTIC, FORMAL **2** *obs* **:** academically trained **:** BOOK-LEARNED **3 a :** of, relating to, or associated with a school ⟨~ standards⟩ ⟨during the ~ holidays⟩ ⟨a sense that ~ teaching is not divorced from the practical world —Bertrand Russell⟩ **b :** having the characteristics of, belonging to, or befitting a scholar **:** SCHOLARLY ⟨a thorough and ~ piece of work⟩ **c :** designed for scholars ⟨an honorary ~ fraternity⟩

²scholastic \"\ *n* -s [ML *scholasticus*, fr. *scholasticus*, adj.] **1 a** *usu cap* **:** a Christian philosopher of the medieval period **:** SCHOOLMAN **b** (1) **:** one who deals with philosophical or theological problems in the spirit of Scholasticism (2) **:** PEDANT, FORMALIST **2** [¹*scholastic*] *obs* **:** SCHOLAR, STUDENT **3** [NL *scholasticus*, fr. L *scholasticus*, adj.] **:** a student in a scholasticate **4** [¹*scholastic*] **:** one who advocates or practices scholastic or traditional methods in art **5 scholastics** *pl* **:** scholastic practices or methods **:** scholastic philosophy or theology; *broadly* **:** PEDANTRY ⟨dry and lifeless ~s —P.A. Sorokin⟩

scho·las·ti·cal \-təkəl, -tēk-\ *adj or n* [ML & L *scholasticus* scholastic + E *-al*] *archaic* **:** SCHOLASTIC

scho·las·ti·cal·ly \-k(ə)lē, -li\ *adv* **:** in a scholastic manner **:** in respect to school or scholarship

scho·las·ti·cate \-tə,kāt, -təkət\ *n* -s [NL *scholasticatus*, fr. *scholasticus*, n., scholastic + L *-atus* -ate] **:** a school of general study for those preparing for membership in a Roman Catholic religious order

scho·las·ti·cism \-tə,sizəm\ *n* -s **1** *usu cap* **:** a philosophical movement dominant in western Christian civilization from the Carolingian period in the 9th century until the rise of Cartesianism in the 17th century; *specif* **:** the philosophical systems and speculative tendencies of various medieval Christian thinkers who working on a background of fixed religious dogma sought to solve anew general philosophical problems (as of faith and reason, will and intellect, realism and nominalism, and the provability of the existence of God) initially under the influence of the mystical and intuitional tradition of patristic philosophy and esp. Augustinianism and later under that of Aristotle — compare OCKHAMISM, SCOTISM, THOMISM; see NEO-SCHOLASTICISM **2 :** close adherence to traditional teachings or methods prescribed by schools or sects; *specif* **:** a viewpoint dominated by scholastic modes of thought

scho·las·ti·cize \-tə,sīz\ *vi* -ED/-ING/-S **:** to favor or employ scholastic principles or arguments **:** become influenced by scholasticism

scho·li·ast \'skōlē,ast\ *n* -s [MGk *scholiastēs*, fr. *scholiazein* to write scholia on, fr. Gk *scholion*] **:** a maker of scholia **:** COMMENTATOR, ANNOTATOR — **scho·li·as·tic** \¦==¦astik\ *adj*

scho·li·on \'skōlē,än, -ēən\ *n, pl* **scho·lia** \-ēə\ *also* **scholions** [Gk] **:** SCHOLIUM

scho·li·um \-ēəm\ *n, pl* **scho·lia** \-ēə\ *also* **scholiums** [NL *scholium*, fr. Gk *scholion*, dim. of *scholē* lecture — more at SCHOOL] **1 :** a marginal annotation **:** an explanatory remark or comment (as on the text of a classic by an early grammarian) **2 :** a remark or observation subjoined but not essential to a demonstration or a train of reasoning ⟨explanatory *scholia* inserted by the editors of Euclid's *Elements*⟩

schom·burgk·ia \(')shäm¦bərkēə, -bůr-\ *n, cap* [NL, fr. Robert H. *Schomburgk* †1865 Brit. traveler and explorer + NL *-ia*] **:** a genus of So. American epiphytic orchids having showy racemose flowers borne either on a scape from pseudobulbs or on a long fleshy stem

schön·fels·ite \'shōn,fel,zīt, 'shə(r)n-\ *n* -s [G *schönfelsit*, fr. *Altschönfels*, Saxony, Germany + G *-it* -ite] **:** a perknite with phenocrysts of olivine and augite in a dense groundmass of titanomagnetite, orthorhombic pyroxene, apatite, interstitial brown glass, and traces of basic plagioclase

¹school \'skül\ *n* -s [ME *scole*, fr. OE *scōl*, fr. L *schola* leisure devoted to learning, lecture, school, fr. Gk *scholē* leisure, learned discussion, lecture, school; akin to Gk *echein*, *schein* to have, hold — more at SCHEME] **1 a** (1) **:** an organized body of scholars and teachers associated for the pursuit and dissemination of knowledge (as in a particular advanced field) and constituting a college esp. of a medieval university (2) **schools** *pl* **:** the academic or learned world **:** UNIVERSITIES — usu. used with the definite article ⟨the view accepted by the ~s⟩ (3) *usu cap, obs* **:** SCHOOLMEN — usu. used in pl. **b** (1) **:** the body of pupils or students attending a school ⟨the new teacher is liked by the whole ~⟩ (2) **:** the members of a school including both faculty and students ⟨the ~ had a holiday⟩ ⟨the ~ participated in a fire drill⟩ **c** (1) **:** the disciples or followers of a teacher (2) **:** persons who hold a common doctrine or accept the same teachings or follow the same intellectual methods **:** a sect or denomination (as in philosophy, theology, medicine, or politics) ⟨belonged to the radical ~ of economists⟩ (3) **:** people forming a distinguishable group or class and sharing common principles, canons, precepts, or a common body of opinion or practice ⟨a gentleman of the old ~⟩ ⟨other ~s of opinion⟩ (4) **:** a group (as of painters, sculptors, or musicians) under a common local or personal influence producing a general similarity in their work ⟨the Wagnerian ~⟩; *also* **:** the artists or art of a country or region ⟨paintings of the Flemish ~⟩ **d** *Brit* **:** a body of gamblers or thieves **:** GANG **2 a :** an organized source of education or training: as (1) **:** an institution for the teaching of children **:** an elementary or secondary school (2) **:** an institution for specialized higher education usu. within a university ⟨the ~ of medicine at the state university⟩ (3) **:** COLLEGE, UNIVERSITY ⟨the excellent east coast ~s⟩ (4) **:** an establishment for teaching a particular skill or group of skills ⟨a ~ of design⟩ ⟨a fencing ~⟩ ⟨a beauticians' ~⟩ **b :** a place where instruction is given: (1) **:** a place where lectures are held; *esp* **:** a place for lectures in logic, metaphysics, and theology in the medieval period (2) **:** a building or hall where examinations for degrees and honors are held at an English university (3) **:** a building or group of buildings in which a school is conducted ⟨the new ~ is very elaborate⟩ ⟨the most beautiful ~ in the area⟩ (4) **:** an area (as an enclosure or covered ring) where horses are schooled **:** a riding school **c :** something that is a source of instruction ⟨the ~ of experience⟩ **3 a :** the process of being instructed or educated in institutions for teaching the young ⟨found ~ very difficult⟩ **b :** attendance at a school ⟨he quit ~⟩ ⟨during her last year of ~⟩ **4 :** a session of a school ⟨there will be no ~ on Friday⟩ ⟨late for ~⟩ ⟨kept in after ~⟩ **5 :** an administrative unit in a private school comprising several consecutive grades or forms ⟨a lower ~⟩ ⟨boys in the upper ~⟩ **6 a :** a final examination for the bachelor of arts degree (as at Oxford University) **b :** an honors course (as at Oxford University) **7 a :** a book of instruction (as in a particular system of execution in music) **b :** a system of instruction or execution **8 :** the regulations governing military drill of individuals or of a unit of a given size or kind; *also* **:** the exercises carried out in accordance with such regulations ⟨the ~ of the soldier⟩

²school \"\ *vb* -ED/-ING/-S *vt* **1 :** to educate or provide with education in an institution of learning **:** send to school ⟨the boy was ~*ed* at great cost to his family⟩ **2 :** to give teaching or training to: **a :** to teach or drill in a specific knowledge, attitude, or skill ⟨well ~*ed* in languages⟩ ⟨our parents have ~*ed* us in the principle of the rights of the individual⟩ **b :** to instruct, stabilize, or inure by practice, long or repeated experience, or subjection to systematic discipline — usu. used with *in* ⟨~ oneself in patience⟩ ⟨~*ing* a horse in the five gaits⟩ ⟨~ an athlete in timing⟩ **c :** to make tractable (as by teaching, admonition, or chastisement) **d :** to educate, cultivate, or advance mentally or culturally by formal instruction in or as if in a school ⟨~*ed* his mind with travel and study⟩ **e** (1) *archaic* **:** to reprove for error or fault **:** set right **:** CHIDE, ADMONISH; *also* **:** to dictate to (2) *obs* **:** to punish by way of giving a lesson ~ *vi* **1 :** to go to school **2 :** to ride or course cross-country ⟨~*ing* over meadows and hills⟩ **syn** see TEACH

³school \"\ *adj* **1 :** of or relating to a school ⟨~ traditions⟩ **:** connected with or employed in connection with a school ⟨a ~ library⟩ ⟨the ~ superintendent⟩ **2 a :** of the kind taught in school ⟨~ studies⟩; *sometimes* **:** superficially and incompletely mastered ⟨amateurish ~ French⟩ **b :** of the kind taught or practiced in a school of horsemanship **:** trained in a school of horsemanship **:** SCHOOLED ⟨a ~ gait⟩ **3 a :** of or relating to the Schoolmen ⟨~ theology⟩ **:** of the kind employed by the Schoolmen ⟨~ arguments⟩ **b :** being or involving mere abstractions or quibbling **:** having no practical application or value ⟨~ language⟩ ⟨a ~ name⟩

⁴school \"\ *n* -s [ME *scole*, fr. MD *schole* group esp. of fish or animals of one kind, multitude; akin to OE *scolu* multitude, troop, *sciell* shell — more at SHELL] **1 :** a large number of one kind of fish or other aquatic animals swimming or feeding together ⟨a ~ of dolphins⟩ **2 :** a large group or flock (as of birds or people) ⟨too busy receiving the congratulations of a ~ of admirals for us to buttonhole her —*New Yorker*⟩

⁵school \"\ *vi, of fishes* **:** to swim and feed together in large numbers ⟨bluefish are ~*ing*⟩

school·able \'skülәbәl\ *adj* **:** suitable for school or schooling: **a :** sufficiently tractable or intelligent to warrant training ⟨a quiet ~ beast⟩ **b :** of an age to attend school ⟨~ children⟩

school age *n* **:** the period of life during which a child is considered mentally and physically fit to attend school and is commonly required to do so by law — **school-ager** \'skü,lājə(r)\ *n*

schoolbag \'=,=\ *n* **:** a bag usu. of cloth in which a pupil may carry school books, school supplies, and miscellaneous objects needed at school or for homework

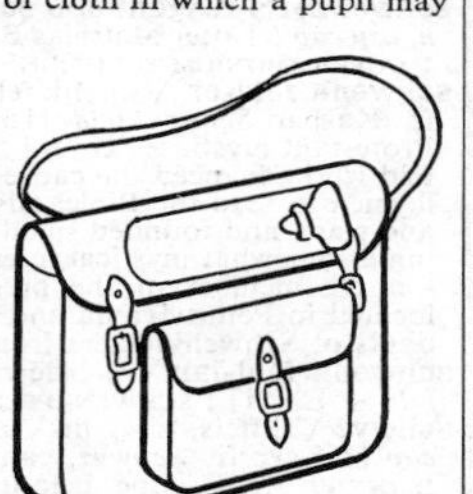

schoolbag

school bass \'=¦bas\ *n* **:** a small or immature channel bass

school board *n* **:** a local board of education

schoolboy \'=,=\ *n* **:** a boy attending school

school·boy·ish \'=,=ish, -ēsh\ *adj* **:** suited to or resembling that of a young boy ⟨an immature ~ laugh⟩

school·boy·ish·ness *n* **:** behavior suited to a young boy **:** immature or childish conduct

school bus *n* **:** a vehicle that is either publicly owned or privately owned and operated for compensation, that is usu. conspicuously marked with the words *school bus*, and that is used for transporting children to or from school or on activities connected with school

school canter *n* **:** a precisely balanced and strongly collected slow canter performed with long clean reaching strides

school certificate *or* **school leaving certificate** *n* **:** a certificate awarded in the British Commonwealth to students 16 years or older who have completed the secondary school course and passed a special examination — called also GENERAL CERTIFICATE OF EDUCATION

schoolchild \'=,=\ *n, pl* **schoolchildren :** a child who attends school

school committee *n* **:** SCHOOL BOARD

schoolcraft \'=,=\ *n, archaic* **:** knowledge purveyed by school

schooldame \'=,=\ *n* **:** the keeper of a dame school **:** SCHOOLMISTRESS

school district *n* **:** an area within a state sometimes coinciding with a township but having its own board and power of taxation and serving as the smallest unit for administration of a public-school system

school divine *n* **:** SCHOOLMAN 1b

school doctor *n* **1** *obs* **:** SCHOOLMAN 1b **2 :** a physician employed to make periodic examinations of the children of a school or of the schools of a community

school·dom \'sküldәm\ *n* -s **:** school affairs; *also* **:** those concerned with their administration

schooled *past of* SCHOOL

school edition *n* **:** an edition of a book issued esp. for use in schools and usu. differing from the ordinary edition in having a simplified, condensed, or otherwise emended text and glossarial or explanatory matter

school·er \'skülə(r)\ *n* -s **:** a pupil in school — usu. used in combination

school·ery \'skül(ə)rē\ *n* -ES *archaic* **:** matters taught in or as if in a school **:** SCHOOLING

schoolfellow \'=,(,)=\ *n* [ME *scollfelau*, fr. *scoll*, *scole* school + *felau*, *felawe* fellow] **:** SCHOOLMATE

school figure *n* **:** one of a progressive series of fundamental figure skating movements that are executed in a prescribed pattern in the form of a 2-lobed or 3-lobed figure eight and constitute 60 percent of championship competition

schoolgirl \'=,=\ *n* **:** a girl attending school

school·girl·ish \'=,=ish, -ēsh\ *adj* **:** suited to or resembling that of a young girl ⟨a dress too ~ for office wear⟩ ⟨~ chatter⟩

schoolhouse \'=,=\ *n* [ME *scolehous*, fr. *scole* school + *hous* house] **1 :** a building used as a school and esp. as an elementary school ⟨little red ~⟩ **2 a :** the headmaster's residence at some British schools **b :** the group of boys boarding in the headmaster's household

schooling *n* -s [ME *scoling*, fr. *scole* school + *-ing*] **1 a :** instruction in or attendance at school ⟨had to interrupt his ~ to go to work⟩ **:** education in an institution of learning ⟨the state now takes responsibility for ~⟩ **b :** training, guidance, or discipline derived from experience or contact with experts ⟨a long and arduous ~ as a performer in several of the best bands —Irving Kolodin⟩ **2** *archaic* **:** chastisement for correction **:** REPROOF, REPRIMAND **3 :** tuition or tuition and maintenance in a school **:** the cost of instruction and maintenance ⟨pay a boy's ~⟩ **4 :** the training of a horse for service ⟨~ a horse to lead⟩ ⟨gave the filly thorough ~ in the gaits⟩: as **a :** the teaching and exercising of horse and rider in the formal techniques of equitation and coordination therein (as in a riding school) **b :** the teaching and exercising of a horse in jumping techniques **c :** the training of a race horse to break from a starting gate

school·ing·ly *adv* [*schooling* (pres. part. of ²*school*) + *-ly*] **:** in a manner intended to teach or admonish

school·ish \-lish,-lēsh\ *adj* **:** characteristic of schools: as **a :** remote from life **:** PEDANTIC **b :** following scholastic traditions **:** ACADEMIC

schoolkeeper \'=,=\ *n* **:** one that keeps a school: **a :** the proprietor of a private school **b :** a teacher in a school and usu. in a small or elementary school **c** *chiefly Brit* **:** the janitor of a school

school land *n* **:** government lands set aside for the support of public schools — usu. used in pl. ⟨bought up *school lands* in the newly opened area⟩

school leaver *n, chiefly Brit* **:** a pupil who has recently left school usu. without completing his course — compare GRADUATE

school·less \'sküllәs\ *adj* **:** lacking a school or schooling ⟨~ children⟩

school·man \'skülmәn, -,man, -,maa(ә)n\ *n, pl* **schoolmen 1 a :** one skilled in the niceties of academic disputation **b** *usu cap* **:** a philosopher or divine of the schools of the medieval period **:** SCHOLASTIC **2 :** one professionally engaged in education through the schools **:** a teacher or administrative officer of an educational institution **3 a :** an orthodox follower of a school (as of philosophy or politics) **b :** an adherent of neo-scholasticism

school·marm *or* **school·ma'am** *R* '=,mä(r)m, *-R* -,mȧm, *R & -R* -,mam, -,maa(ә)m\ *n* -s **1 :** a woman schoolteacher esp. in an old-type rural or small-town school ⟨the New England ~ of 50 years ago⟩ **2 :** a person either male or female who exhibits characteristics (as pedantry and priggishness) popularly attributed to schoolteachers ⟨the Puritan ~s who once kept the tang of the city streets out of our . . . language —Edgar Kemler⟩ **3 a :** a forked tree **b :** a log cut from the fork of such a tree

school·marm·ish \-ish, -ēsh\ *adj* **:** resembling or typical of a schoolmarm

¹schoolmaster \'=,==\ *n* [ME *scolemaister*, fr. *scole* school + *maister* master] **1 :** a male schoolteacher: as **a :** the teacher of an old-type rural or small-town school ⟨in colonial New England, the ~ was boarded around⟩ **b :** the headmaster of a school **c :** a master or preceptor in a school **d** *obs* **:** a private tutor **2 :** one acting as a teacher or resembling a teacher in effect or behavior: as **a :** one having a guiding or inspiring influence ⟨the ~ of medieval Europe⟩ **b :** one exhibiting the pedantry and despotism popularly attributed to old-time schoolteachers **3 :** a reddish brown edible snapper (*Lutjanus apodus*) of the tropical Atlantic and the Gulf of Mexico with large scales, vertical greenish bars on the sides, and greenish orange fins — called also *black snapper*

²schoolmaster \"\ *vt* **:** to train or instruct in the manner of a schoolmaster; *esp* **:** to force into conformity by constant supervision or faultfinding ⟨the children, obviously much ~*ed*, had lost their natural initiative⟩ ⟨purists who would ~ the language⟩ ~ *vi* **:** to be or act as a schoolmaster **:** teach as a means of livelihood ⟨returned to ~*ing*⟩

³schoolmaster \"\ *n* [⁴*school* + *master*] **:** a member of a school of fishes or whales that appears to be the leader

school·mas·ter·hood \'=,==,hůd\ *n* **:** the position or state of a schoolmaster

school·mas·ter·ish \-ish\ *adj* **:** suggestive of a schoolmaster esp. in pedantry — **school·mas·ter·ish·ly** *adv* — **school·mas·ter·ish·ness** *n* -ES

school·mas·ter·ly \-lē,-li\ *adj* **:** resembling or characteristic of a schoolmaster

school·mas·ter·ship \-,ship\ *n* **:** the status or position of a schoolmaster

school·mas·tery \-ē,-i\ *n* **:** the work or practice of a schoolmaster; *specif* **:** insistence upon obedience to authority even in petty details

schoolmate \'=,=\ *n* **:** an associate or companion at school

schoolmistress \'=,=\ *n* [ME *scolemaystress*, fr. *scole* school + *maystress*, *maistresse* mistress] **:** a female schoolteacher

school·mis·tressy \-ē,-i\ *adj* **:** resembling or characteristic of a schoolmistress

school of thought : a group sharing a common point of view in respect to some matter ⟨belongs to the liberal *school of thought*⟩; *also* **:** a point of view recognized as held but not necessarily accepted ⟨there are two *schools of thought* about this question⟩

schoolroom \'=,=\ *n* **:** a room in which pupils are instructed ⟨the sewing room became a ~ when we were kept home by minor ailments⟩ ⟨the new elementary school has 12 ~s together with offices, service rooms, and an auditorium⟩

schools *pl of* SCHOOL, *pres 3d sing of* SCHOOL

school section *n* **:** a section of public land set apart in a surveyed township by the U. S. government for the maintenance of public schools

school shark *n, Austral* **:** SOUPFIN SHARK, TOPE

school ship *n* **:** a ship used as a nautical training school for apprentices being educated at public expense

school sister of no·tre dame \-,nōd·ə(r)'dām, -ō·trə'd- *also* -dȧm *or* -dām *sometimes* -dam *or* -daa(ə)m\ *n, usu cap both Ss&N&D* [F *Notre Dame* Our Lady (the Virgin Mary)] **:** a member of a Roman Catholic religious congregation founded in France by St. Peter Fourier in 1597 and devoted chiefly to education

school system *n* **:** the aggregate of the public schools of an area under the administration of an executive officer who represents and is responsible to the board of education for that area

schoolteacher \'=,==\ *n* **:** a person who teaches in a school

school·teach·er·ish \'=,==ish\ *adj* **:** resembling a schoolteacher or what a schoolteacher is felt to be; *often* **:** PRISSY, PEDANTIC, FINICKY

school·teach·er·ly \-lē\ *adj* **:** SCHOOLTEACHERY

school·teach·ery \-ē\ *adj* **:** resembling or characteristic of a schoolteacher **:** prim and formal in manner and esp. in speech

schoolteaching *n* **:** the occupation or profession of teaching school

school tie *n* **:** OLD SCHOOL TIE

schooltime \'=,=\ *n* **1 :** the time for beginning a session of school **:** the time during which school is held **2 :** the period of life spent in school or in study — usu. used in pl. ⟨~s are looked back on as the best part of a life⟩ **3 :** a period of training ⟨this life is our ~⟩ ⟨put in a year's ~ to qualify for his license⟩

¹school·ward \'skülwə(r)d\ *also* **school·wards** \-dz\ *adv* **:** toward school ⟨moving ~ at a snail's pace⟩

²schoolward \"\ *adj* **:** directed or extending toward school ⟨took his ~ way⟩

schoolwork \'=,=\ *n* **:** matter studied in school or assigned in school to be studied either in or out of school ⟨found her ~ increasingly difficult⟩ — compare HOMEWORK 2a

school year *n* **:** ACADEMIC YEAR

schoo·ner \'skünə(r) *sometimes* -kůn-\ *n* -s [origin unknown] **1 :** a fore-and-aft rigged boat having two masts with a smaller sail on the foremast and with the mainmast stepped nearly amidships, sometimes carrying square topsails on one or both

masts or even a forecourse, and adapted to sailing close to the wind; *broadly* : any of various larger fore-and-aft rigged ships with three to seven masts — see SAIL illustration **2 a** : a large tall drinking glass (as for beer or ale) **b** : a British measure used esp. for beer or ale **3** : PRAIRIE SCHOONER

schooner rig *n* : FORE-AND-AFT RIG — **schooner-rigged** \'==,=\ *adj*

schoop process \'shōp-\ *n, usu cap S* [after Max Ulrich *Schoop* †1956 Swiss engineer] : a process in which objects or surfaces are coated with zinc or other metal by spraying them with the molten metal shot from a nozzle by compressed air

scho·pen·hauerean·ism \,shōpən¦hau̇rēə,nizəm, ,==,hau̇-'irēə,n-, ,==,hau̇'rēə,n-\ *n* -s *usu cap* : SCHOPENHAUERISM

scho·pen·hauerian \,shōpən¦hau̇rēən, ¦==,hau̇¦irēən\ *also* **scho·pen·hauerean** \", ¦==,hau̇ə¦rēən\ *adj, usu cap* [Arthur *Schopenhauer* †1860 Ger. philosopher + E *-an*] : of or relating to Schopenhauer or his doctrines

scho·pen·hauer·ism \'==,hau̇(ə),rizəm\ *n* -s *usu cap* [Arthur *Schopenhauer* + E *-ism*] : the philosophy of Arthur Schopenhauer who taught that the essential or absolute reality is a blind and restless will manifesting itself as a will to live and that life is an evil to be cured only by overcoming the will to live — compare VOLUNTARISM

schorl *also* **shorl** \'shȯr(ə)l\ *or* **schorl·ite** \-r,līt\ *n* -s [*schorl, shorl* fr. G *schörl; schorlite* fr. G *schorlit*, irreg. fr. *schörl* + *-it* -ite] **1** : TOURMALINE; *esp* : tourmaline of a common black iron-rich variety **2** *archaic* : any of several dark-colored minerals other than tourmaline

schor·la·ceous \(')shȯr¦lāshəs\ *adj* : being, containing, or resembling schorl

schor·lo·mite \'shȯrlə,mīt\ *n* -s [*schorl* + Gk *homos* same + E *-ite* — more at SAME] : a mineral $Ca_3(Fe,Ti)_2[(Si,Ti)O_4]_3$ consisting of an iron calcium titanate and silicate related to garnet and occurring usu. in black masses with vitreous luster (hardness 7–7.5, sp. gr. 3.81–3.88)

schorly \'shorlē\ *adj* : containing or mingled with schorl ⟨~ granite⟩

schotten–baumann reaction \,shät³n¦bau̇mən-, -,män-\ *n, usu cap S&B* [after Carl *Schotten* †1910 Ger. chemist and *Baumann*, 19th cent. Ger. chemist] : acylation (as conversion of an alcohol to an ester, of an amine to an amide, or of hydroxylamine to a hydroxamic acid) by an acid chloride in the presence of alkali

[1]**schot·tische** \'shäd-¦ish, -ät¦, ¦esh, *chiefly Brit* shä'tesh\ *n* -s [G, fr. *schottische*, weak nom. sing. masc. of *schottisch* Scottish, fr. MHG *schottesch*, fr. *Schotte* Scotchman + *-esch* -ish (fr. OHG *-isc*); akin to OE *Scottas* (pl.) Scotchmen — more at SCOT] **1** : a round dance in duple measure characterized by gliding and hopping steps and similar to but slower than the polka **2** : music for the schottische

[2]**schottische** \"\ *vi* -ED/-ING/-S : to dance a schottische

schott·ky defect \'shätkē-\ *n, usu cap S* [after Walter *Schottky* b1886 Ger. physicist] : a defect in a crystal lattice created by removing an ion from its normal site and placing it on the crystal surface

schottky effect *n, usu cap S* : the increase of the thermionic current in a vacuum tube with the increase of the applied potential between the cathode and anode due to a lowering of the energy required to remove electrons from the cathode

schout \'skau̇t\ *n* -s [D, fr. MD *schoutete* count's or bishop's agent with judicial powers in civil cases; akin to OE *sculthēta* bailiff, OHG *sculdheizo* magistrate; all fr. a prehistoric WGmc compound noun whose first constituent is represented by OE *scyld* debt, obligation and whose second constituent is akin to OE *hātan* to command — more at SHALL, HIGHT] **1** : a Dutch bailiff or sheriff **2** : a person vested in the former Dutch colonies of America with local judicial functions

schouw \'skau̇, 'skōu̇\ *n* -s [D, schouw, scow — more at SCOW] : a light-draft open pleasure boat of the Netherlands

schr *abbr* schooner

schra·dan \'shrā,dan\ *n* -s [Gerhard *Schrader* b1903 Ger. chemist + E *-an*] : an almost odorless viscous liquid $\{[(CH_3)_2N]_2PO\}_2O$ made from phosphorus oxychloride, dimethylamine, and sodium ethoxide and used chiefly in emulsions as a systemic insecticide — called also *octamethylpyrophosphoramide, OMPA*

schra·der's bromegrass \'shrādə(r)z-\ *n, usu cap S* [prob. fr. the name *Schrader*] : RESCUE GRASS

schre·bera \shrēbərə, shrə'birə\ [NL, fr. J. C. D. von *Schreber* †1810 Ger. botanist] *syn of* HARTOGIA

schrei·ber·site \'shrībə(r),zīt\ *n* -s [G *schreibersit*, irreg. fr. Karl F. A. von *Schreiber* †1852 Austrian museum director + G *-it* -ite] : a mineral $(Fe,Ni)_3P$ consisting of a phosphide of iron and nickel and occurring in meteorites

schrei·ner finish \,shrīnə(r)-\ *n, often cap S* [prob. fr. the name *Schreiner*] : a finish imparted to cotton fabrics by schreinerizing

schrei·ner·ize \'shrīnə,rīz\ *or* **schrei·ner** \-nə(r)\ *vt* -ED/-ING/-S [*schreinerize* prob. fr. the name *Schreiner* + E *-ize*; *schreiner* prob. fr. the name *Schreiner*] : to calender (cotton fabric) with rollers engraved all over with very fine lines in order to produce a lustrous surface

schrik \'skrik\ *n* -s [Afrik *skrik*, fr. D *schrik*, fr. *schrikken* to be frightened, fr. MD *schricken* to be frightened, stride; akin to OHG *scricken* to jump, MHG *scherzen* to leap for joy — more at CARDINAL] *southern Africa* : a sudden fright : PANIC

schrö·ding·er atom \'shrā¦diŋər-\ *n, usu cap S* [after Erwin *Schrödinger* b1887 Ger. physicist] : a conception of atomic structure in which a nucleus of positive electricity is embedded in and surrounded by concentric spherical shells of diffuse negative electricity

schrödinger equation *also* **schrödinger wave equation** *n, usu cap S* : an equation that describes the wave nature of elementary particles and is fundamental to the description of the properties of all matter; *specif* : a common formulation of this equation

$$\frac{\delta^2\psi}{\delta x^2}+\frac{\delta^2\psi}{\delta y^2}+\frac{\delta^2\psi}{\delta z^2}+\frac{8\pi^2 m}{h^2}[W-V]\psi=0$$

where ψ $(x\ y\ z)$ is the wave function, m is the mass of the elementary particle, h is the Planck constant, W is the total energy, and V is the potential energy

schroec·king·er·ite \'shrekiŋə,rīt, 'shrə(r)k-\ *n* -s [G *schröckingerit*, fr. J. von *Schröckinger*, 19th cent. Austrian mineralogist + G *-it* -ite] : a mineral $NaCa_3(UO_2)(CO_3)_3(SO_4)F.10H_2O$ that is a hydrous carbonate, sulfate, and fluoride of calcium, sodium, and uranyl

schro·ther \'shrōd-ə(r), -räthə(r)\ *n* -s [perh. modif. of G *schröter* one that cuts or chops or crushes, fr. MHG *schrōtære* tailor, mintmaster, fr. *schrōten* to cut, hew, chop (fr. OHG *scrōtan* to cut) + *-ære* -er (fr. OHG *-āri*) — more at SHRED] : SHREDDER c

schrund *n* -s [G, crack — more at BERGSCHRUND] : BERGSCHRUND

schuet·zen·fest \'shütsən,fest, 'shitsən-, 'shætsən-\ *n* -s [G *schützenfest*, fr. *schütz, schütze* marksman, archer (fr. OHG *scutzo* archer) + *fest* festival; akin to OE *scytta* archer, ON *skyti* archer, OE *scēotan* to shoot — more at SHOOT, -FEST] : a shooting match : an entertainment or a picnic where marksmanship is practiced

schuet·zen rifle \-tsən-\ *n, usu cap S* [G *schützen*, pl. of *schütz, schütze* marksman] : an extremely accurate single-shot rifle having a heavy barrel, a stock with elaborate butt plate and grip, precision sights, and a palm rest

schuff·ner's dots \'shu̇¦fnə(r)z-, 'shü¦, 'shæ¦\ *n pl, usu cap S* [prob. after Wilhelm August Paul *Schüffner* †1949 Du. physician] : punctate granulations present in red blood cells invaded by the tertian malaria parasite

schuh·platt·ler \'shü,plätlə(r)\ *n* -s *often cap* [G, fr. G dial. *schuochplattlar*, fr. *schuochplattln* to slap the soles of one's shoes (fr. *schuoch* shoe — fr. OHG *scuoh* — + *plattln* to strike two flat objects together, fr. G *platte* slab, fr. OHG *platta* stone slab, fr. ML, flat object, fr. assumed VL, fem. of *plattus* flat) + *-ar* -er (fr. OHG *-āri*) — more at SHOE, PLATE] : a Bavarian courtship dance in which before the couple dances together the woman calmly does steps resembling those of a waltz while the man dances vigorously about her swinging his arms and slapping his thighs and the soles of his feet

schul *var of* SHUL

schüller–christian disease *n, usu cap S&C* : HAND-SCHÜLLER-CHRISTIAN DISEASE

schul·ten·ite \'shu̇lt³n,īt\ *n* -s [Baron August B. de *Schulten* †1912 Ger. scientist + E *-ite*] : a mineral $PbHAsO_4$ consisting of a lead hydrogen arsenate and occurring in colorless tabular orthorhombic crystals

schultz–dale reaction \'shu̇¦lts'dā(ə)l-, 'shü¦\ *n, usu cap S&D* [after Werner *Schultz* b1878 Ger. physician and Sir Henry Hallett *Dale* b1875 Eng. physiologist] : a reaction of anaphylaxis carried out in vitro with isolated tissues (as a guinea pig uterus)

schult·ze powder \'shu̇¦ltsə-, 'shü¦\ *n, usu cap S* [after Edward *Schultze*, 19th cent. Ger. chemist who invented it] : a propellant of the smokeless powder type consisting essentially of nitrated pellets of wood impregnated with barium nitrate and potassium nitrate

schu·mann region \'shümən-, -,män-\ *n, usu cap S* [after Viktor *Schumann* †1913 Ger. physicist] : the portion of the ultraviolet spectrum lying approximately between 1850 and 1200 angstroms

schun·gite \'shu̇ŋ,gīt\ *n* -s [G *schungit*, fr. *Schunga, Shunga*, northwest U.S.S.R. + G *-it* -ite] : an amorphous carbon that occurs in schists

[1]**schuss** \'shu̇s, 'shüs\ *n* -ES [G, lit., shot, fr. OHG *scuz* — more at SHOT] **1** : a straight high-speed run on skis **2** : a straightaway skiing course : an area in a fall line on which a straight downhill run may be made

[2]**schuss** \"\ *vb* -ED/-ING/-ES *vt* : to make a schuss over ⟨~ a slope⟩ ~ *vi* : to ski directly down a slope

schuyt \'skīt, 'skȯit, 'skät, *D* 'skœit\ *n* -s [D *schuit*, fr. MD *schute* — more at SCOUT] : a bluff-bowed Dutch boat fitted with leeboards, used chiefly on canals and for coasting, and sometimes square-rigged but usu. sloop-rigged

schwa *also* **shwa** \'shw¦ä, ¦a *also* 'shf¦ *or* 'shv¦ *or* shə'w¦ *or* shə'v¦ *or* 'sw¦ *or* 'sv¦ *or* 'sf¦\ *n* -s [G, fr. Heb *shĕwā'*] **1** : a faint indistinct vowel sound like that of *e* in English *quiet* that is indicated in Hebrew by two perpendicular dots (as :) and in transliteration by *ĕ* or by a superior dot or small superior *e* **2 a** : an unstressed mid-central vowel that is the usual sound of the first and last vowels of the English word *America* **b** : the symbol ə commonly used for this vowel and sometimes also for a similarly articulated stressed vowel (as in American English *cut*)

schwann·ian \'shwänēən, 'shfä-,'shvä-\ *adj* [Theodor *Schwann* †1882 Ger. naturalist + E *-an*] : of, relating to, or made up of Schwann's cells; *also* : NEURILEMMAL

schwan·no·ma \-'nōmə\ *n, pl* **schwannomas** \-məz\ *or* **schwannoma·ta** \-məd-ə\ [NL, fr. Theodor *Schwann* + NL *-oma*] : NEURILEMMOMA

schwann's cell \'shw¦änz-, 'shf¦, 'shv¦\ *n, usu cap S* : a cell of the neurilemma

schwann's sheath *or* **schwann tube** *n, usu cap S* : NEURILEMMA 1

schwar·me·rei \,shfermə¦rī, ¦shve-\ *n* -s [G *schwärmerei*, fr. *schwärmen* to be enthusiastic, be fanatical or heretical, swarm (said of bees), fr. MHG *swermen, swarmen* to swarm, fr. *swarm* swarm (of bees), fr. OHG *swaram* — more at SWARM] : excessive unbridled enthusiasm or attachment

schwartz·brot *or* **schwarz·brot** \'shfärts,brōt, 'shvä-\ *n* -s [G *schwarzbrot*, fr. *schwarz* black (fr. OHG *swarz*) + *brot* bread, fr. OHG *brōt* — more at SWART, BREAD] : BLACK BREAD

schwart·zem·berg·ite \'shwȯrtsəm,bər,gīt\ *n* -s [*Schwartzemberg*, 19th cent. Chilean mineral assayer + E *-ite*] : a mineral $Pb_5(IO_3)Cl_3O_3$ that is an iodate, chloride, and oxide of lead

schwarz \'shwȯrts, 'shfärts, 'shvä-\ *n* -ES [G, fr. *schwarz*, adj., black] : the winning of all the tricks in skat or schafskopf; *also* : the scoring effect of this which adds two multipliers in skat and triples the score in schafskopf

schwed·ler's maple \'shwedlə(r)z-\ *n, usu cap S* [prob. fr. the name *Schwedler*] : a commonly cultivated maple that is a variety (*Acer platanoides schwedleri*) of the Norway maple with the foliage bronzy red in early spring and later becoming green

schwe·gel \'shfāgel, 'shvā-\ *n* -s [G, fr. OHG *swegala*; akin to OE *swegl*horn, a wind instrument, Goth *swiglon* to play the flute] **1** : WIND INSTRUMENT; *specif* : PIPE **2** : a flue organ pipe

schwein·furt green *or* **schwein·furth green** \'shf¦īn,fu̇rt-, 'shv¦\ *n, usu cap S* [*Schweinfurt*, Bavaria, Germany] : PARIS GREEN 1

schwei·zer·deutsch \'shfītsə(r),dȯich, 'shvī-\ *n* -ES *usu cap* [G, fr. *schweizer* of or belonging to Switzerland (fr. *Schweiz* Switzerland, country in central Europe) + *deutsch* German, fr. OHG *thiutisc, diutisc*, fr. *thiutisc, diutisc*, adj., German — more at DUTCH] : SCHWYZERTÜTSCH

schwei·zer's reagent *also* **schweit·zer's reagent** \-tsə(r)z-\ *n, usu cap S* [after Matthias E. *Schweizer* †1860 Ger. chemist] : CUPRAMMONIUM SOLUTION

schwenk·feld·er \'shfeŋk,feldə(r), 'shve-\ *n* -s *usu cap* [G, fr. Kaspar *Schwenkfeld* †1561 Ger. Silesian nobleman and Protestant mystic + G *-er*] : a follower of Kaspar Schwenkfeld who advanced the cause of the Reformation, encouraged laymen to read the Bible, advocated the separation of church and state, and founded small spiritual communities emphasizing a somewhat mystical interpretation of the Christian faith; *esp* : a member of the present-day Schwenkfelder Church located in Pennsylvania and composed principally of descendants of Schwenkfelders from Europe

schwenk·feld·ian \(')=¦=dēən\ *n* -s *usu cap* [Kaspar *Schwenkfeld* + E *-an*] : SCHWENKFELDER

schwyz \'shf¦ēts, 'shv¦, ¦its\ *also* **schwyz·er** \-tsə(r)\ *n pl, usu cap* [*schwyz* fr. *Schwyz*, canton in east central Switzerland; *schwyzer* fr. G, one belonging to the canton Schwyz, fr. *Schwyz* + G *-er*] : BROWN SWISS

schwyz·er dutsch \'shfētsə,tüech, 'shvē-\ *n, usu cap S&D* [modif. of G dial. (Swiss) *schwyzertütsch*] : SCHWYZERTÜTSCH

schwyz·er·tütsch \-,tüech\ *n* -ES *usu cap* [G dial. (Swiss), fr. *schwyzer* of or belonging to Switzerland (fr. *Schwyz* Switzerland, country in central Europe) + *tütsch* German, fr. OHG *thiutisc, diutisc*] : a dialect of German spoken in Switzerland

sci- *or* **scio-** *also* **scia-** *or* **skia-** *comb form* [NL, fr. Gk *ski-, skio-*, fr. *skia* — more at SCENE] : shadow ⟨*scio*gram⟩ ⟨*scio*ptic⟩ ⟨*scia*lytic⟩ ⟨*skia*scope⟩

sci *abbr* science; scientific

sci·ae·na \sī'ēnə\ *n, cap* [NL, fr. L, a fish, fr. Gk *skiaina*, a fish, prob. the maigre] : the type genus of Sciaenidae comprising somewhat elongated marine fishes with a conical head, terminal or subterminal mouth, and no barbels and including numerous croakers some of which are favored as food or sport fishes — see BLACK CROAKER, MAIGRE, MULLOWAY

[1]**sci·ae·nid** \-nəd\ *adj* [NL *Sciaenidae*] : of or relating to the Sciaenidae

[2]**sciaenid** \"\ *n* -s : a fish of the family Sciaenidae

sci·ae·ni·dae \-nə,dē\ *n pl, cap* [NL, fr. *Sciaena*, type genus + *-idae*] : a large, economically important, and widely distributed family of carnivorous percoid fishes comprising the croakers, being nearly all marine along the sandy shores of warm temperate seas, usu. having the air bladder large and complicated and used to produce a sound, and including various large fishes valued as food — see SCIAENA

[1]**sci·ae·noid** \-,nȯid\ *n* -s [NL *Sciaena* + E *-oid*] : a sciaenoid fish

[2]**sciaenoid** \"\ *adj* : resembling or related to the Sciaenidae

scia·lyt·ic \¦sīə¦lid-ik\ *adj* [*sci-* + *-lytic*] : dispersing or dispelling shadows ⟨a ~ lamp⟩

sci·am·a·chy \sī'aməkē\ *n* -ES [Gk *skiamachia*, fr. *skia* shadow + *-machia* -machy] : a fighting with a shadow : a mock or futile combat (as with an imaginary foe)

sci·an \'shēən\ *adj, usu cap* [It *Scio* Chios, island in the Aegean sea + E *-an*] : CHIAN

sciaphilous *var of* SCIOPHILOUS

scia·pod \'sīə,päd\ *also* **skia·pod** \'skī-\ *n* -s [L *Sciapodes* Sciapods, fr. Gk *Skiapodes*, fr. *skia* shadow + *pod-, pous* foot — more at SCENE, FOOT] : one of a mythological people having feet big enough for use as sunshades and living according to classic Greek mythology in Libya or according to medieval legend in which they were one-footed sometimes in India

sci·ap·o·dous \(')sī¦apədəs\ *adj* [L *Sciapodes* + E *-ous*] : having very large feet

sci·a·ra \'sīərə\ *n* [NL, fr. Gk *skiaros* shady, dark-colored, fr. *skia* shadow] **1** *cap* : a genus (the type of the family Sciaridae) of minute and usu. blackish fungus gnats typically with highly gregarious larvae that are often destructive to mushrooms and seedlings — see ARMYWORM **2** -s : any insect of the genus *Sciara*

[1]**sci·a·rid** \-rəd\ *adj* [NL *Sciaridae*] : of or relating to the Sciaridae

[2]**sciarid** \"\ *n* -s : a fly of the family Sciaridae : FUNGUS GNAT

sci·ar·i·dae \sī'arə,dē\ *n pl, cap* [NL, fr. *Sciara*, type genus + *-idae*] : a family of minute usu. dark or blackish two-winged flies some of which are destructive to mushrooms and to seedlings of higher plants — see FUNGUS GNAT, SCIARA; compare MYCETOPHILIDAE

[1]**sci·at·ic** \(')sī¦ad-¦ik, -at¦, ¦ēk\ *adj* [MF *sciatique*, fr. LL *sciaticus*, alter. of L *ischiadicus* of pain in the hip — more at ISCHIADIC] **1** : of or relating to the hip : situated in the region of or affecting the hip : ISCHIAL **2** : of, relating to, or caused by sciatica : afflicted with sciatica ⟨~ pains⟩ ⟨a ~ patient⟩

[2]**sciatic** \"\ *n* -s : a sciatic part (as a nerve or artery)

sci·at·i·ca \sī'ad-¦əkə, -at¦, ¦ēkə\ *n* -s [ME, fr. ML, fr. fem. of LL *sciaticus* sciatic] : pain along the course of a sciatic nerve or its branches and esp. in the leg caused by compression, inflammation, or reflex mechanisms; *broadly* : pain in the lower back, buttocks, hips, or adjacent parts — not used technically

sci·at·i·cal \(')=¦==kəl\ *adj* [*sciatica* + *-al*] : caused by or affected with sciatica ⟨becoming increasingly ~⟩

sciatic artery *n* : the gluteal artery that arises in the ischial region of each side of the body

sciatic foramen *n* : either of two foramina on each side leading from the pelvis to the gluteal and peroneal regions and transmitting respectively (1) the sciatic nerve, superior and inferior gluteal, pudendal, and other nerves, associated vessels, and the piriformis muscle and (2) the tendon of the internal obturator muscle and the pudendal vessels and nerve — called also (1) *greater sciatic foramen* (2) *lesser sciatic foramen*

sci·at·icky \sī'ad-əkē\ *adj* [*sciatica* + *-y*] *dial* : affected with sciatica

sciatic nerve *n* : the largest nerve in the body arising from the sacral plexus on each side and passing out of the pelvis through the greater sciatic foramen and thence down the back of the thigh to its lower third where it divides into the tibial and peroneal nerves

sciatic notch *n* : any of four notches on the dorsal border of the innominate bone comprising a greater above and a lesser below the spine of the ischium on each side of the body

sciatic vein *n* : any of the veins accompanying the sciatic arteries : a gluteal vein

sci·ence \'sīən(t)s, *in rapid speech often* -īn-\ *n* -s [ME, fr. MF, fr. L *scientia* knowledge, science, fr. *scient-, sciens* (pres. part. of *scire* to know) + *-ia* -y; akin to L *scindere* to cut, split — more at SHED] **1 a** : possession of knowledge as distinguished from ignorance or misunderstanding : knowledge as a personal attribute ⟨I speak from ~ and the voice is fate —Alexander Pope⟩ **b** : knowledge possessed or attained through study or practice ⟨~ crown my age —Thomas Gray⟩ **2 a** : a branch or department of systematized knowledge that is or can be made a specific object of study ⟨the basic tool ~*s* of reading, writing, and ciphering⟩ ⟨learned in the ~ of theology⟩ **b** : something (as a sport or technique) that may be studied or learned like systematized knowledge ⟨skilled in the ~ of evading work⟩ ⟨little interested in cards and such like ~⟩: as (1) *obs* : a trained skill (as in an occupation) (2) : FENCING (3) : BOXING **c** : studies mainly in the works of ancient and modern philosophers formerly taught as a group or field of specialization (as at Oxford University) **d** : any of the individual subjects taught at an educational institution in one of the departments of natural science ⟨required to take two ~*s* to complete a minor⟩ ⟨students majoring in a ~⟩ — compare HUMANITY 3c **3 a** : accumulated and accepted knowledge that has been systematized and formulated with reference to the discovery of general truths or the operation of general laws : knowledge classified and made available in work, life, or the search for truth : comprehensive, profound, or philosophical knowledge; *esp* : knowledge obtained and tested through use of the scientific method **b** : such knowledge concerned with the physical world and its phenomena : NATURAL SCIENCE **4** : a branch of study that is concerned with observation and classification of facts and esp. with the establishment or strictly with the quantitative formulation of verifiable general laws chiefly by induction and hypotheses ⟨mathematical ~⟩ **5** : a system based or purporting to be based upon scientific principles : a method (as of arrangement, functioning) reconciling practical or utilitarian ends with scientific laws ⟨husbandry is a ~⟩ ⟨a student of culinary ~⟩ **6** *usu cap* : CHRISTIAN SCIENCE **syn** see KNOWLEDGE

sci·enced \-n(t)st\ *adj, archaic* : skilled in science : LEARNED

science fiction *n* : fiction dealing principally with the impact of actual or imagined science upon society or individuals; *broadly* : literary fantasy including a scientific factor as an essential orienting component

science of language : LINGUISTICS

science of religion : the descriptive study of religion that examines all religions phenomenologically, historically, psychologically, and sociologically : HISTORY OF RELIGIONS, COMPARATIVE RELIGION

sci·ent \'sīənt\ *adj* [ME, fr. L *scient-, sciens*, pres. part. of *scire* to know] : KNOWING, SKILLFUL

[1]**sci·en·ter** \sī'entə(r)\ *adv* [L, fr. *scient-, sciens*, pres. part. of *scire* to know] : KNOWINGLY, WILLFULLY

[2]**scienter** \"\ *n* -s **1** : a degree of knowledge that makes an individual legally responsible for the consequences of his act — compare MISTAKE **2** : an allegation in a legal pleading of such knowledge on the part of the accused or defendant as is necessary to constitute his act a crime or tort

sci·en·tia \skē'entēə, sī'enchēə\ *n, pl* **scienti·ae** \-tē,ī, -chē,ē\ [L] : KNOWLEDGE, SCIENCE; *esp* : knowledge based on demonstrable and reproducible data

sci·en·tial \(')sī¦enchəl\ *adj* [ME *sciencial*, fr. ML *scientialis*, fr. L *scientia* knowledge + *-alis* -al] **1** : relating to or producing knowledge or science **2** : having efficient knowledge : CAPABLE

sci·en·tia sci·en·ti·a·rum \skē¦entēəskē,entē'ärəm\ *n* [L, science of sciences] : PHILOSOPHY

[1]**sci·en·tif·ic** \,sīən-¦tifik, -fēk, *in rapid speech often* (')sīn-\ *adj* [ML *scientificus*, fr. L *scient-, sciens* (pres. part. of *scire* to know) + *-i-* + *-ficus* -fic — more at SCIENCE] **1** *obs* : yielding knowledge deductively **2** : concerned with or treating of science : devoted to the study or practice of science ⟨a ~ treatise⟩ ⟨~ training⟩ ⟨~ in his interests⟩ **3** : of, relating to, or used in science or a branch of science ⟨~ apparatus⟩ ⟨a ~ formula⟩ **4** : agreeing with or conducted or prepared strictly according to the principles and practice of or for the furtherance of exact science : skilled in the methods of exact science : characteristic or typical of a true scientist esp. in perfect disinterestedness and absolute accuracy ⟨~ research⟩ ⟨a ~ experiment⟩ ⟨the ~ spirit⟩ **5** : conducted or systematized after the manner of science or according to results of investigation by science : practicing thoroughness or systematic methods approximating those of scientists or devised by scientists : applying expert knowledge or technical skill (as in sports, warfare, management) ⟨~ advertising⟩ ⟨~ baby care⟩ ⟨a ~ boxer⟩

[2]**scientific** \"\ *n* -s : SCIENTIST

sci·en·tif·i·cal \-fəkəl, -fēk-\ *adj* [ML *scientificus* + E *-al*] **1** *archaic* : SCIENTIFIC **2** *obs* : intended to propagate knowledge

sci·en·tif·i·cal·ly \-k(ə)lē, -li\ *adv* : in a scientific manner : according to the rules or principles of science ⟨a scholar ~ trained in methods of accurate analysis⟩

sci·en·tif·i·cal·ness \-kəlnəs\ *n* -ES : scientific quality or nature

scientific empiricism *n* **1** : a philosophical movement that denies the existence of any ultimate differences in the sciences, strives for unified science through a synthesis of scientific methodologies, comprises in addition to logical positivists thinkers with similar objectives, and is distinguished from earlier empiricism mainly by emphasis upon the analysis of language — called also *unity of science movement* **2** : the point of view or the theories advocated by scientific empiricism

scientific management *n* : planned management of production or other industrial or business activity that is based on the use of codified and verified knowledge of the knowable factors and directed toward the drawing up and carrying out of an overall plan accompanied by detailed instructions for each operation as established from time and motion study standards and research, and that in practice provides for full and effective use of equipment and an incentive system giving adequate compensation to workers

scientific method *n* : the principles and procedures used in the systematic pursuit of intersubjectively accessible knowledge and involving as necessary conditions the recognition and formulation of a problem, the collection of data through observation and if possible experiment, the formulation of hypotheses, and the testing and confirmation of the hypotheses formulated

scientific name *n* : a taxonomic name : TAXON

scientific notation *n* : a method of expressing a number by giving only the significant figures within particular limits of accuracy and indicating multiplication by the proper power of 10 (as in 1.591 (10)⁻²⁶) — *written as* $1.591 (10)^{-26}$

sci·en·tif·i·co \ˌsīən-ˈtif₂ˌkō\ *n, pl* **scientificoes** *or* **scientificos** [*scientist* + *-fico* (as in *magnifico*)] : a practitioner in some branch of science

scientifico- *comb form* [*¹scientific* + *-o-*] : scientific and ⟨*scientifico*romantic⟩ ⟨*scientifico*philosophic⟩

scientific perspective *n* : LINEAR PERSPECTIVE

scientific skepticism *n* : an impartial attitude of the mind previous to investigation

scientific socialism *n* : socialism associated chiefly with Marxians and based principally upon a belief that historical forces (as economic determinism and the class struggle) determine usu. by violent means the achievement of socialist goals — compare UTOPIAN SOCIALISM

scientific stone *n* : a synthetic or imitation gemstone (as a ruby or sapphire artificially made of corundum)

sci·en·ti·fic·tion \ˌsīˌentə+\ *n* [blend of *¹scientific* and *fiction*] : SCIENCE FICTION

sci·en·tism \ˈsīən-ˌtizəm\ *n -s* [*scientist* + *-ism*] **1** : the methods, mental attitude, doctrines, or modes of expression characteristic or held to be characteristic of scientists **2** : a thesis that the methods of the natural sciences should be used in all areas of investigation including philosophy, the humanities, and the social sciences : a belief that only such methods can fruitfully be used in the pursuit of knowledge

sci·en·tist \ˈsīəntə̇st, *rapid often* ˈsīn-\ *n -s* [L *scientia* science + E *-ist* — more at SCIENCE] **1** : one learned in science and esp. natural science : a scientific investigator ⟨what distinguishes the ~ is his ability to state problems, to frame questions, so that the technicians can make the machines yield facts that are significant —W.A.L.Johnson⟩ ⟨the social ~ is somewhat more handicapped than is the physical or biological ~ in holding extraneous influences constant —A.M.Rose⟩ ⟨put him in the front rank of linguistic ~s —Kemp Malone⟩ **2** *usu cap* : CHRISTIAN SCIENTIST ⟨the lesson-sermon of the Sunday service is prepared by a committee of *Scientists* —F.S.Mead⟩

sci·en·tis·tic \ˌsīən-ˈtistik\ *adj* **1** : devoted or pretending to the methods of scientists : professedly scientific **2** : of, relating to, or characterized by scientism — **sci·en·tis·ti·cal·ly** \-tək(ə)lē\ *adv*

sci·en·tize \ˈsīən-ˌtīz\ *vt* **-ED/-ING/-S** [L *scientia* science + E *-ize*] : to apply scientific methods and principles to : SYSTEMATIZE ⟨~ a business⟩

sci fa *abbr* scire facias

¹scili·cet \ˈsilə̇ˌset, ˈsīlə̇ˌset, ˈskēlə̇ˌket\ *adv* [ME, fr. L, fr. *scire* to know + *licet* it is permitted, 3d pers. sing. pres. indic. of *licēre* to be permitted — more at SCIENCE, LICENSE] : to wit : NAMELY, VIDELICET — used before a word that is to be supplied or understood (as in completing a text felt to be obscure)

²scilicet \"\ *n -s* : an instance of the use of scilicet or something (as a clause) introduced by it ⟨a text full of ~s⟩

scil·la \ˈs(k)ilə\ *n* [NL, fr. L, squill — more at SQUILL] **1 a** *cap* : a large genus of Old World bulbous herbs (family Liliaceae) comprising the squills, having narrow basal leaves, pink, blue, or white racemose flowers borne on a naked scape, and a globose 3-lobed capsule, and including several that are cultivated chiefly as ornamentals — see CUBAN LILY, SPANISH JACINTH, WOOD HYACINTH **b** *-s* : any plant, bulb, or flower of the genus *Scilla* **2** *-s* : the sliced bulb of squill

scil·li·ro·side \-lərōˌsīd\ *n -s* [NL *Scilla* + *-i-* + *-roside* (as in *heteroside*)] : a crystalline steroid cardiac glucoside $C_{32}H_{44}O_{12}$ from red squill

scil·li·tan \ˈsilətən\ *adj, usu cap* [prob. fr. (assumed) LL *scillitanus*, fr. L *Scillium*, ancient town in Byzacium, Roman province of Africa + LL *-itanus* (as in *metropolitanus* metropolitan)] : of or relating to the ancient town of Scillium in Roman Africa

¹scil·lo·ni·an \sə̇ˈlōnēən\ *adj, usu cap* [*Scilly* Isles, group of small islands in southwest England + E *-onian* (as in *Devonian*)] : of or relating to the Scilly Isles or their inhabitants

²scillonian \"\ *n -s cap* : a native or inhabitant of the Scilly Isles

scim·i·tar \ˈsimədə(r), -mətə(r)\ *also* **scim·i·ter** \-əd-, -ə-, -ətə-\ *or* **scim·e·tar** *like* SCIMITAR\ *or* **cim·e·ter** *like* SCIMITER\ *n -s* [MF *cimeterre*, fr. OIt *scimitarra*, perh. fr. Per *shimshīr*] : a saber having a curved blade with the edge on the convex side that is used chiefly by Arabs and Turks **2** : something felt to resemble a scimitar (as in sharpness or shape) ⟨~ blasts⟩; *esp* : a long-handled billhook

scimitar 1

scim·i·tared \-ə(r)d, -ärd, -ȧd\ *adj* : armed with or shaped like a scimitar

¹scin·cid \ˈskin̂kə̇d, ˈsinsə̇d\ *adj* [NL *Scincidae*] : of or relating to the Scincidae

²scincid \"\ *n -s* : a lizard of the family Scincidae

scin·ci·dae \ˈskin̂kəˌdē, ˈsinsə-\ *n pl, cap* [NL, fr. *Scincus*, type genus (fr. L, skink) + *-idae* — more at SKINK] : a cosmopolitan family of pleurodont lizards (section Scincomorpha) comprising the skinks

scin·ci·doid \-ˌdȯid\ *adj* [NL *Scincidae* + E *-oid*] : resembling or related to the Scincidae

scin·coid \ˈs(k)in̂ˌkȯid\ *also* **scin·coi·di·an** \(ˈ)ˌkȯidēən\ *adj* [*scincoid* prob. fr. (assumed) NL *scincoides* lizard of the family Scincidae, fr. *Scincus*, genus of skinks + L *-oīdes* -oid; *scincoidian* prob. fr. (assumed) NL *scincoīdes* + E *-an*] : of, relating to, or resembling skink

scin·co·mor·pha \ˌs(k)in̂kəˈmȯrfə\ *n pl, cap* [NL, fr. *Scincus*, genus of skinks + *-morpha*] : a section of the saurian division Autarchoglossa comprising the Scincidae and related families in which the clavicles when present are dilated, the tongue scaly or obliquely plicate, the teeth often perforate and rarely conical or recurved, and the hemipenes usu. laminate

scin·dap·sus \sin̂ˈdapsəs\ *n, cap* [NL, fr. Gk *skindapsos*, an ivylike tree] : a genus of climbing vines (family Araceae) chiefly of eastern Asia and Australasia, having ovate often variegated leaves, sometimes replaced by phyllodia and flowers in a short spadix subtended by a green spathe — compare ANTHURIUM; see IVY-ARUM

scin·iph \ˈsinə̇f\ *n -s* [LL *sciniphes*, pl., *sciniphs*, fr. Gk *skniphes*, pl. of *sknips* small woodworm; akin to Gk *knips*, an insect — more at NIP] : a stinging or biting insect in Exod 8:17 (DV) or a gnat (RSV)

scin·ti·gram \ˈsintəˌgram\ *n* [*scintillation* + *-gram*] : a picture produced by scintigraphy

scin·tig·ra·phy \sin̂ˈtigrəfē\ *n -ES* [*scintillation* + *-graphy*; fr. the scintillation counter used to record gamma radiation on the scintigram] : a diagnostic technique in which a two-dimensional picture of a bodily radiation source is obtained by the use of radioisotopes

scin·til \ˈsin̂t²l\ *n -s* [L *scintilla*] *archaic* : SCINTILLA

scin·til·la \sin̂ˈtilə\ *n, pl* **scintillas** \-ləz\ *also* **scintil·lae** \-ˌ(,)lē\ [L] **1** : a barely perceptible manifestation : the slightest particle or trace ⟨not a ~ of evidence⟩ **2** : a glittering particle

scin·til·lance \ˈsin̂t²lən(t)s\ *n -s* : a scintillant condition or emission

scin·til·lant \-nt\ *adj* [L *scintillant-, scintillans*, pres. part. of *scintillare* to sparkle] : emitting sparks or fine igneous particles : SCINTILLATING — **scin·til·lant·ly** *adv*

scin·til·lan·te \ˌshen·tə̇ˈlän-, (ˌ)tä\ *adj* (*or adv*) [It, fr. pres. part. of *scintillare* to sparkle, fr. L] : in a sparkling manner — used as a direction in music

scin·til·late \ˈsin̂t²lˌāt, *usu* -ād-+V\ *vb* **-ED/-ING/-S** [L *scintillatus*, past part. of *scintillare* to sparkle, fr. *scintilla* spark, scintilla] *vi* **1** : to emit sparks : SPARK **2** : to gleam or emit quick flashes as if throwing off sparks ⟨eyes that ~ with fury⟩ ⟨genius that ~s⟩; *also* : SPARKLE, TWINKLE ⟨fixed stars that ~ in the sky⟩ ~ *vt* : to throw off as a spark or as sparking flashes ⟨~ witticisms⟩

scin·til·lat·ing·ly *adv* : in a scintillating manner : so as to scintillate

scin·til·la·tion \ˌsin̂t²lˈāshən\ *n -s* [L *scintillaton-, scintillatio*, fr. *scintillatus* (past part.) + *-ion-, -io* -ion] **1** : an act or instance of scintillating; *esp* : rapid changes in the brightness of a celestial body caused by turbulence in the earth's atmosphere : TWINKLING **2 a** (1) : a spark or flash emitted in scintillating (as from iron exposed to the oxyhydrogen flame) (2) : a flash of light produced in a phosphor by an ionizing event (as impingement of an alpha particle) **b** : a scintillating or brilliant outburst (as of thought or genius) **c** : a flash of the eye (as in anger or merriment) **3** : SCINTILLA

scintillation counter *n* : a device for detecting and registering individual scintillations (as due to radioactive emission or cosmic rays)

scintillation spectrometer *n* : an apparatus in which mass or energy spectra are observed and their frequency distribution determined by means of a scintillation counter

scin·til·la·tor \ˌ²ˌlād·ə(r), -ätə-\ *n -s* : one that scintillates: as **a** : a scintillating star **b** : a phosphor in which scintillations occur (as in a scintillation counter) **c** : a person that scintillates (as in conversation) **d** (1) : a device for sending out scintillations of light (2) : SCINTILLATION COUNTER

scin·til·les·cent \ˌ²ˌesᵊnt\ *adj* [L *scintillare* to sparkle + E *-escent*] : scintillating or twinkling somewhat faintly

scin·til·lom·e·ter \ˌ²ˈäməd₂(r), ²\ *n* [ISV *scintill-* (fr. L *scintilla* spark, scintilla) + *-meter*] **1** : an attachment to a telescope by which the image of a star is made to revolve in a circle to measure the scintillation **2** : SCINTILLATION COUNTER

scin·til·lo·scope *also* **scin·til·li·scope** \sin̂ˈtilə̇ˌskōp\ *n* [*scintillo-, scintilli-* (fr. L *scintilla*) + *-scope*] : a small instrument similar to the spinthariscope for exhibiting scintillations (as of a radioactive substance) on a sensitive screen

scintle *var of* SKINTLE

scio- — see SCI-

sci·o·lism \ˈsīə̇ˌlizəm\ *n -s* [LL *sciolus* sciolist + E *-ism*] : superficial knowledge : a show of learning without substantial foundation

sci·o·list \-lə̇st\ *n -s* [LL *sciolus* + E *-ist*] : one whose knowledge or learning is superficial : a pretender to scholarship

sci·o·lis·tic \ˌsīə̇ˈlistik\ *adj* [*sciolist* + *-ic*] : of or relating to sciolism or a sciolist : partaking of sciolism : being or suited to a sciolist ⟨~ arguments⟩ — **sci·o·lis·ti·cal·ly** \-tək(ə)lē\ *adv*

sci·o·lous \ˈsīələs\ *adj* [LL *sciolus* sciolist, one having little knowledge, dim. of *scius* knowing, fr. *scire* to know — more at SCIENCE] : knowing superficially or imperfectly : SCIOLISTIC

sciol·to \ˈshȯl(ˌ)tō\ *adv* (*or adj*) [It (past part. of *sciogliere* to loosen), fr. L *exsolutus*, past part. of *exsolvere* to loosen, untie release — more at EXSOLVE] **1** : with freedom and without strictness — used as a direction in music **2** : with detachment and without legato in musical performance

sci·o·man·cy \ˈsīəˌman(t)sē\ *n -ES* [LL *sciomantia*, fr. LGk *skiomanteia*, fr. Gk *ski-* sci- + *manteia* -mancy] : divination by consulting the shades of the dead

sci·o·man·tic \ˌsīəˈmantik\ *adj* [LL *sciomantia* + E *-ic*] : of, relating to, or obtained by means of sciomancy

sci·on *also* **ci·on** \ˈsīən *sometimes* -ī₂ˌän\ *n -s* [ME *scion, sioun, ciun*, fr. MF *cion, sion*, of Gmc origin; akin to OHG *kīnan, chīnan* to sprout, OE *cīth* sprout, shoot — more at CHINE] **1** : a detached living portion (as a year-old shoot) of a plant designed or prepared for union with a stock in grafting and usu. supplying solely or predominantly aerial parts to a graft **2** : DESCENDANT, CHILD ⟨twelve-year-old ... ~ of the famous circus family —Henry La Cossitt⟩

scion-rooting \ˈ²²ˌ²²\ *adj* : developing roots at the point where a scion is inserted into a stock

sci·oph·i·lous \(ˈ)sīˈäfələs\ *or* **sci·aph·i·lous** \-ˌiaf-\ *adj* [*sci-* + *-philous*] of a plant : thriving in shade

scio·phyte \ˈsīəˌfīt\ *n -s* [*sci-* + *-phyte*] : a plant that endures or thrives best at lowered light intensity

sci·op·tic \(ˈ)sīˈäptik\ *adj* [*sci-* + *optic*] : of or relating to the formation of images in a darkened room (as in a camera obscura)

sci·op·tics \-ks\ *n pl but usu sing in constr* : the art or process of exhibiting luminous images (as of external objects) in a darkened room by arrangements of lenses or mirrors

sci·os·o·phist \ˈsīˈäsəfə̇st\ *n -s* : an accepter or propounder of sciosophy

sci·os·o·phy \-fē\ *n -ES* [*sci-* + *-sophy*] : pretended knowledge of natural or supernatural forces systematized by tradition or imaginative invention

¹sci·ot \ˈshē₂ˌät\ *or* **chi·ot** \ˈkī₂t, ˈkē₂t, -ē₂ˌät\ *adj, usu cap* [*sciot* modif. (influenced by It *Scio* Chios, island in the Aegean sea) of NGk *Chiōtēs* of Chios, fr. Gk *Chios* Chios + *-ōtēs* *-ote*; *chiot* fr. NGk *Chiōtēs*] : of or relating to the island of Chios

²sciot \"\ *or* **chiot** \"\ *n -s cap* : a native or inhabitant of Chios

sci·re fa·ci·as \ˌsīrē̇ˈfāsh(ē)əs, ˈske̱ˌrȧˈfäkēˌäs\ *n* [ME, fr. ML, you should cause to know] : a judicial writ founded upon some matter of record and requiring the party proceeded against to show cause why the record should not be enforced, annulled, or vacated **2** : a legal proceeding instituted by a scire facias

sci·ren·ga \sə̇ˈren̂gə\ *n -s* [origin unknown] : a West Indian and Mediterranean grouper (*Parepinephelus acutirostris*)

scirocco *var of* SIROCCO

scir·pus \ˈs(k)ərpəs, ˈskir-\ *n, cap* [NL, fr. L, rush, bulrush] : a large genus of widely distributed annual or perennial sedges (family Cyperaceae) that bear solitary or much-clustered spikelets containing perfect flowers with a perianth of six bristles — see BULRUSH, TULE

scirrhe *obs var of* SCIRRHUS

scir·rhoid \ˈs(k)iˌrȯid\ *adj* [NL *scirrhus* + E *-oid*] : resembling a scirrhus

scir·rhous \-irəs\ *adj* [NL *scirrhosus*, fr. *scirrhus* + L *-osus* *-ose*] **1** : of, relating to, or constituting a scirrhus ⟨~ infiltration⟩ **2** : resembling a scirrhus esp. in being hard or indurated with or as if with fibrous tissue ⟨a ~ carcinoma⟩

scirrhous cord *n* : a chronic fibrous enlargement of the cut end of the spermatic cord in a castrated animal caused by bacterial infection

scir·rhus *also* **schir·rhus** \ˈs(k)irəs, *n*, *scir·rhi* \ˈs(k)iˌrī, ˈski₂ˌrē\ *also* **scirrhus·es** \ˈs(k)irəsə̇z\ [NL, fr. Gk *skirrhos, skiros* hard tumor, fr. *skiros* hard] **1 a** *obs* : an indurated organ or part; *esp* : an indurated gland **b** : a hard cancerous tumor; *specif* : one in which the hardness is due to preponderance of fibrous tissue in the growth **2** : an abnormal condition : the process of becoming scirrhous or the process of scirrhi

scis·sel \ˈsisəl, -izəl\ *n -s* [F *cisailles*, pl., scissels, fr. *cisailler* to clip with shears, fr. *cisailles* shears, fr. (assumed) VL *caesaculum*, fr. L *caesus*, past part. of *caedere* to cut, hew] : metal scrap clippings left over in various mechanical operations; *esp* : the remnants of fillets from which coin blanks have been punched

scis·sile \"\ *adj* [F, fr. L *scissilis*, fr. *scissus* (past part. of *scindere* to split) + *-ilis* -ile — more at SHED] : capable of being cut smoothly or split easily ⟨a configuration ~ by the enzyme —Experiment Station Record⟩

scis·sion \ˈsizhən, *n*, -ish-\ *n -s* [F, fr. LL *scission-, scissio*, fr. *scissus* (past part. of *scindere* to split) + *-ion-, -io* -ion] **1** : a division or split in a group or union **2** : a state of dissension : SCHISM **2 a** : an act of cutting, dividing, or splitting or the state of being cut, divided, or split : DIVISION : CLEAVAGE **5** ⟨cracking or carbon-carbon ~⟩

scis·si·par·i·ty \ˌsisəˈparəd₂ē, ˌsizə-\ *n* [L *scissus* (past part.) + E *-i-* + *-parity* (porous condition)] : SCHIZOGENESIS

¹scis·sor \ˈsizə(r)\ *n -s often attrib* [ME *scissoure, cisoure*, fr. MF *cisoire*, sing. of *cisoires* scissors] : SCISSORS ⟨wore a ~ on her belt⟩

²scis·sor \"\ *vb* **scissored; scissored; scissoring** \-z(ə)rin̂\ **scissors** *vt* **1 a** : to cut, cut up, or cut off with scissors or shears **b** *archaic* : to trim (as the beard) with scissors **2** : to cut out in the form of clippings; *broadly* : MINIMIZE, REDUCE, ELIMINATE ⟨items ~ed from the budget⟩ **3 a** : to hold or hinge together in a crossed position suggestive of scissors **b** : to move (as one's legs) in a manner suggestive of the snipping of scissors ~ *vi* : to move in a manner suggestive of the snipping of scissors ⟨long legs ~ing down the street⟩

scissorbill \ˈ²²ˌ²\ *n* [trans. of F *bec-en-ciseaux*] **1** : SKIMMER 3 **2** *chiefly West* : an inferior or stupid person: as **a** : a worker indifferent to the interests of the laboring class (as one unwilling to join a union) **b** : a worker learning to be a railway brakeman

scissorbird \ˈ²²ˌ²\ *n* : SCISSORTAIL

scis·sor·er \-zərə(r)\ *n -s* : one that scissors; *also* : COMPILER

scissor jack *n* : a powerful lifting jack operated by a screw in horizontal position that lengthens or shortens the horizontal diagonal of a parallelogram consisting of the linkages of the jack

scissorlike \ˈ²²ˌ²\ *adj* : resembling a scissors esp. in having crossing parts or motion involving crossing of parts

scis·sors \ˈsizə(r)z\ *n pl but sometimes sing in constr, often attrib* [ME *sisoures, sisours*, fr. MF *cisoires*, fr. (assumed) VL *caesorium* cutting instrument (pl. *caesoria*) — more at CHISEL] **1** : a cutting instrument consisting of two bevel-edged cutting blades with handles that are movable past one another in the center by which they are held together : a small shears ⟨the ~ are sharp⟩ ⟨took a ~, cut the bedspread, a table scarf, and a plant —Croswell Bowen⟩ ⟨a pair of ~⟩ **2** : something felt to resemble a pair of scissors (as in movement, form, or cutting ability): as **a** : something that cuts short or makes excisions ⟨use the ~ vigorously on your report⟩ **b** : a gripping contrivance (as a tongs) **c** *usu sing in constr* (1) : any of several gymnastic feats (as on the horse and parallel bars) in which the legs are moved in an antero-posterior plane in a manner suggesting the opening and closing of a pair of scissors (2) : a wrestling hold in which a contestant locks his legs around the head or body of the opponent (3) : a technique of high jumping in which the jumper lifts the leg nearest the bar first so that the body passes over the bar with the buttocks to the bar and the jumper lands first on the leading leg — compare WESTERN ROLL

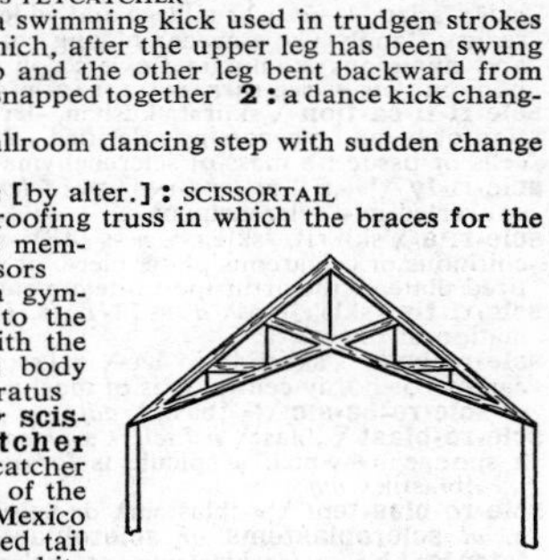

scissors 1: *1* buttonhole, *2* embroidery, *3* manicure, *4* bandage

scissors-and-paste \ˌ²²²²ˈ²\ *adj* : based on or prepared by compilation : lacking in originality or independent thought and investigation ⟨scissors-and-paste studies⟩ ⟨a scissors-and-paste method⟩

scissorsbill \ˈ²²ˌ²\ *n* [by alter.] : SCISSORBILL 2

scissorsbird \ˈ²²ˌ²\ *n* : SCISSORTAIL

scissors bridge *or* **scissors-type bridge** *n* : a folding light metal bridge that is carried and put in position by a tank

scissors chair *n* : SAVONAROLA CHAIR

scissors fault *n* : a geological fault in which there is increasing displacement along the strike from an initial point of no displacement

scissors-grinder \ˈ²²ˌ²²\ *n* **1** : the common European nightjar **2** : RESTLESS FLYCATCHER

scissors kick *n* **1** : a swimming kick used in trudgen strokes and sidestrokes in which, after the upper leg has been swung forward from the hip and the other leg bent backward from the knee, the legs are snapped together **2** : a dance kick changing legs in the air

scissors step *n* : a ballroom dancing step with sudden change of direction

scissorstail \ˈ²²ˌ²\ *n* [by alter.] : SCISSORTAIL

scissors truss *n* : a roofing truss in which the braces for the rafters cross like the members of a pair of scissors

scissors vault *n* : a gymnastic vault similar to the straddle vault but with the legs crossing as the body passes over the apparatus

scissortail \ˈ²²ˌ²\ *or* **scissor-tailed flycatcher** \ˈ²²ˌ²\ *n* : a flycatcher (*Muscivora forficata*) of the southern U.S. and Mexico having a deeply forked tail and being gray above, white beneath, salmon on the sides, and scarlet at the base of the crown feathers

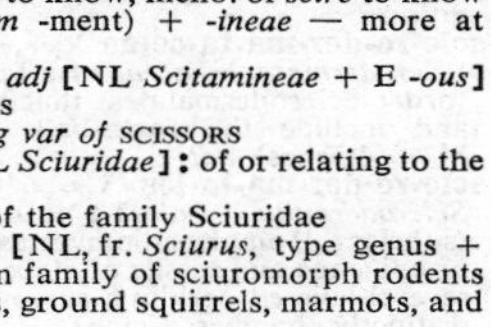

scissors truss

scissor-tailed \ˈ²²ˌ²\ *adj* : having a deeply forked tail ⟨scissor-tailed birds⟩

scissor tooth *n* : a cutting tooth : CARNASSIAL

scissor truss *n* : SCISSORS TRUSS

scis·sure \ˈsizhə(r), -ish-\ *n -s* [ME, fr. L *scissura*, fr. *scissus* (past part. of *scindere* to split) + *-ura* -ure — more at SHED] **1** *archaic* : a cleft or elongated opening in a body or surface made by or as if by cutting : a cleft separating bodily parts or opening into the body **2** *obs* : a split or division in a group or union : SCHISM

scis·su·rel·la \ˌsizhəˈrelə, -ish-\ *n, cap* [NL, fr. L *scissura* scissure + *-ella*] : a genus of small marine snails (suborder Rhipidoglossa) having several long ciliated tentacles on each side of the body and a small spiral shell the last whorl of which has a broad fissure or sinus

scit·a·mi·na·les \ˌsid₂əmə̇ˈnā(ˌ)lēz\ [NL, fr. *Scitamineae* + *-ales*] *syn of* MUSALES

scit·a·min·e·ae \ˌsid₂əˈmin₂ē, -ˈmin̂ˌē\ *n pl* [NL, fr. L *scitamenta* delicacies, dainties (fr. *scitus* delicate, dainty — fr. past part. of *sciscere* to approve, accept, inquire, seek to know, incho. of *scire* to know — + *-menta*, pl. of *-mentum* -ment) + *-ineae*] *syn of* MUSALES

scit·a·min·e·ous \ˈ²²²ˈnēəs\ *adj* [NL *Scitamineae* + E *-ous*] : of or relating to the Musales

scith·ers \ˈsith̯ə(r)z\ *dial Eng var of* SCISSORS

¹sci·urid \ˈsī(y)ṳrə̇d\ *adj* [NL *Sciuridae*] : of or relating to the Sciuridae

²sciurid \"\ *n -s* : a rodent of the family Sciuridae

sci·uri·dae \-rəˌdē\ *n pl, cap* [NL, fr. *Sciurus*, type genus + *-idae*] : a nearly cosmopolitan family of sciuromorph rodents consisting of the true squirrels, ground squirrels, marmots, and related forms

sci·uroid \ˈsī(y)ə̇ˌrȯid, sīˈ(y)ṳˌr-\ *adj* [L *sciurus* squirrel + E *-oid*] **1 a** : resembling a squirrel **b** : resembling the tail of a squirrel — used of the spike of grasses (as barley) **2** [NL *Sciurus* + E *-oid*] : related to the Sciuridae

sci·uroi·dea \ˌsī(y)ə̇ˈrȯidēə\ *n pl, cap* [NL, fr. *Sciurus* + *-oidea*] in some classifications : a superfamily coextensive with the family Sciuridae

¹sci·uro·morph \ˈsī(y)ṳrəˌmȯrf\ *also* **sci·uro·mor·phic** \ˌsī(y)ṳrəˈmȯrfik\ *or* **sci·uro·mor·phous** \-fəs\ *adj* [*sciuromorph* fr. NL *Sciuromorpha; sciuromorphic, sciuromorphous* fr. NL *Sciuromorpha* + *-ic* or *-ous*] : of or relating to the Sciuromorpha

²sciuromorph \"\ *n* : a sciuromorph rodent

sci·uro·mor·pha \ˌ²²²ˈmȯrfə\ *n pl, cap* [NL, fr. Gk *skiouros* squirrel + NL *-morpha* — more at SQUIRREL] : a suborder or formerly a subfamily of Rodentia comprising relatively large more or less primitive forms (as the squirrels, marmots,

gophers, beavers, and related rodents) — compare HYSTRICOMORPHA, MYOMORPHA

sci·urop·ter·us \ˌsī(y)əˈräptərəs\ *n, cap* [NL, fr. Gk *skiouros* squirrel + NL *-pterus*] **:** a genus of flying squirrels including only the polatouche of northern Europe and Asia and occurring in several geographic races but formerly including all the smaller Old and New World flying squirrels — compare GLAUCOMYS, PETAURISTA

sci·urus \ˈsī(y)ürəs\ *n, cap* [NL, fr. L, squirrel — more at SQUIRREL] **:** the type genus of Sciuridae formerly including all the squirrels but now restricted to a cosmopolitan group of typical moderate sized arboreal squirrels

scive *var of* SKIVE

scivvy *var of* SKIVVY

scl *abbr* scale

SCL *abbr* student of the civil law

¹sclaff \ˈsklaf, -aa(ə)-, -ai-, -ä-\ *n* -S [prob. imit.] **1** *Scot* **:** a slight blow **:** SLAP **2 :** a golf stroke in which the club head strikes the ground behind the ball before contacting the ball

²sclaff \ʺ\ *vb* -ED/-ING/-S *vi* **1** *Scot* **:** to scuff or shuffle along **2 :** to make a sclaff in golf ~ *vt* **1** *Scot* **:** to strike with something flat **:** SLAP **2 a :** to cause (a golf club) to make a sclaff **b :** to strike (the ground) in making a sclaff

sclar·e·ol \ˈsklə(a)rēˌōl, -ˌȯl\ *n* -S [NL *sclarea* (specific epithet of the clary *Salvia sclarea*) + E *-ol*] **:** a liquid bicyclic diterpenoid alcohol $C_{20}H_{34}(OH)_2$ occurring in the leaves of a clary (*Salvia sclarea*)

sclav \ˈskl-\ *cap, archaic var of* SLAV

sclaw \ˈskl-\ *dial Eng var of* CLAW

scler- *or* **sclero-** *also* **sclera-** *comb form* [NL, fr. Gk *sklēr-*, *sklēro-*, fr. *sklēros* hard — more at SKELETON] **1 a :** hard **:** dry ⟨*scler*ite⟩ ⟨*sclero*blast⟩ **b :** sclerotic ⟨*sclero*derma⟩ **2 :** relating to or affecting the sclera ⟨*scler*oiritis⟩ ⟨*scler*ectomy⟩

scle·ra \ˈsklirə\ *n, pl* **scleras** \-rəz\ *or* **scle·rae** \-ˌirē, -ˌrī\ [NL, fr. Gk *sklēros* hard] **:** the dense fibrous opaque white outer coat enclosing the eyeball except the part covered by the cornea and being in some cases reinforced with cartilage and sometimes (as in most birds and in the extinct ichthyosaurs) supported in front by a ring of bony plates — see EYE illustration

scle·ral \-irəl\ *adj* [*scler-* *-al*] **:** SCLEROTIC

scle·ran·thus \skləˈran(t)thəs\ *n, cap* [NL, fr. *scler-* + *-anthus*] **:** a small Old World genus of annual weedy prostrate herbs (family Caryophyllaceae) having opposite subulate leaves, small cymose perfect apetalous flowers, and tiny one-seeded utricles — see KNAWEL

sclere \ˈskli(ə)r\ *n* -S [Gk *sklēros* hard] **:** a minute skeletal element (as a spicule of a sponge)

scle·rec·to·my \skləˈrektəmē\ *n* -ES [ISV *scler-* + *-ectomy*] **:** surgical removal of a part of the sclera

scle·re·id \ˈsklirēəd\ *n* -S [ISV *sclere-* (as in *sclerenchyma*) + *-id*] **:** a sclerenchymatous cell of a higher plant distinguished chiefly by having its diameters essentially alike — compare FIBER, STEREID

scle·re·ma ad·ul·to·rum \skləˈrēmə,adᵊlˈtōrəm, -ˌa,dəl-\ *n* [NL, lit. hardening of the tissues of adults] **:** SCLERODERMA

sclerema neo·na·to·rum \-ˌnēənəˈtōrəm\ *n* [NL, lit., hardening of the tissues of the newborn] **:** hardening of the cutaneous and subcutaneous tissues in newborn infants

scle·ren·chy·ma \skləˈreŋkəmə\ *n, pl* **sclerenchymas** \-məz\ *or* **scle·ren·chym·a·ta** \ˌskli,renˈkimədə, ˌskle,r-, -ˌrən-\ [NL, fr. *scler-* + *-enchyma*] **1 :** a protective or supporting tissue in higher plants composed of cells with walls thickened and lignified and often mineralized — compare COLLENCHYMA, FIBER, SCLEREID **2 :** SCLERODERM 2

scle·ren·chy·ma·tous \ˌskli,renˈkimədəs, ˌskle,r-, -ˌrən-\ *adj* [NL *sclerenchymat-*, *sclerenchyma* + E *-ous*] **:** constituting or consisting of sclerenchyma

scle·ren·chyme \ˈsklirən,kīm, ˈskler-\ *n* -S [NL *sclerenchyma*] **:** SCLERENCHYMA

scler·erythrin \skləˈrerəthrən; ˌsklirəˈrith-, -ler-\ *n* -S [*scler-* + *erythrine*] **:** a red or violet coloring matter of ergot

scle·ret·i·nite \skləˈretᵊnˌīt\ *n* -S [*scler-* + Gk *rhētinē* resin + E *-ite*] **:** a mineral resin found in the coal measures of Wigan, England, in the form of reddish-brown to black pellets

scle·ria \ˈsklirēə\ *n, cap* [NL, fr. Gk *sklēria* hardness, fr. *sklēr-* scler- + *-ia* -y] **:** a large and widely distributed genus of sedges (family Cyperaceae) having solitary pistillate flowers and numerous staminate flowers followed by hard shining bony nutlets — see NUT GRASS, RAZOR GRASS

scle·ri·fi·ca·tion \ˌsklirəfəˈkāshən, -ler-\ *n* -S **1 :** the condition of being or becoming sclerified **2 :** an area of sclerified cells or tissue **:** a mass of sclerenchyma

scle·ri·fy \ˈ==,fī\ *vt* -ED/-ING/-ES [*scler-* + *-ify*] **:** to become converted into sclerenchyma

scle·rite \ˈskli,rīt, ˈskle,r-\ *n* -S [ISV *scler-* + *-ite*] **:** a hard chitinous or calcareous plate, piece, or spicule; *esp* **:** a sclerotized plate of the arthropod integument

scle·ri·tis \skləˈrīdəs\ *n* -ES [NL, fr. *scler-* + *-itis*] **:** inflammation of the sclera

scle·ro·base \ˈsklirō,bās, -ler-\ *n* [*scler-* + *base*] **:** the calcareous or horny central axis of most compound alcyonarians — **scle·ro·ba·sic** \ˌ==ˈbāsik\ *adj*

scle·ro·blast \-,blast\ *n* [*scler-* + *-blast*] **:** one of the cells of a sponge by which a spicule is formed — **scle·ro·blas·tic** \ˌ==ˈblastik\ *adj*

scle·ro·blas·tem \ˌ==ˈblastəm\ *or* **scle·ro·blastema** \ˌ==+\ *n, pl* **scleroblastems** *or* **scleroblastemas** *or* **scleroblastemata** [NL *scleroblastema*, fr. *scler-* + *blastema*] **:** the mesodermal tissue forming bone — **scle·ro·blastemic** \ˌ==+\ *adj*

scle·ro·cau·ly \ˈ==,kȯlē\ *n* -ES [*scler-* + *caul-* + *-y*] **:** exceptional development of sclerenchyma in a stem (as of various desert plants) — compare SCLEROPHYLLY

scle·ro·corneal \ˌ==+\ *adj* [*scler-* + *corneal*] **:** of or involving both sclera and cornea

scle·ro·dac·tyl·ia \ˌ==,dakˈtilēə\ *or* **scle·ro·dac·ty·ly** \ˌ==ˈ=təlē\ *n, pl* **sclerodactylias** *or* **sclerodactylies** [*sclerodactylia* fr. NL, fr. *scler-* + *-dactylia; sclerodactyly* fr. *scler-* + *-dactyly*] **:** scleroderma of the fingers and toes

¹scle·ro·derm \ˈ==,dərm\ *n* -S [ISV *scler-* + *-derm*] **1 :** TRIGGERFISH, FILEFISH **2 :** the hard tissue of the skeleton of ordinary stony or madreporarian corals

²scleroderm \ʺ\ *adj* **:** SCLERODERMATOUS

scle·ro·der·ma \ˌ==ˈdərmə\ *n* [NL, fr. *scler-* + *-derma*] **1** *cap* **:** a genus of fungi (family Sclerodermataceae) having hard-skinned fruiting bodies that open irregularly and having a single-layered peridium — compare FALSE TRUFFLE **2** *pl* **sclerodermas** \-məz\ *or* **scleroderma·ta** \-mədə\ **:** a disease of the skin characterized by thickening and hardening of the subcutaneous tissues and resulting in a rigid hidebound condition

scle·ro·der·ma·ta·ce·ae \ˌ==,=məˈtāsē,ē\ *n pl, cap* [NL, fr. *Sclerodermata* + *-aceae*] **:** a family of basidiomycetous fungi (order Sclerodermatales) that have a single-layered peridium and include the earth-balls — **scle·ro·der·ma·ta·ceous** \ˌ==ˌ=ˈtāshəs\ *adj*

scle·ro·der·ma·ta·les \ˌ==,=ˈtā(,)lēz\ *n pl, cap* [NL, fr. *Sclerodermata* + *-ales*] **:** an order of basidiomycetous fungi (subclass Homobasidiomycetes) having closed subterranean or epigeous and sessile or stalked sporocarps with a simple or several-layered peridium surrounding an unchambered or indistinctly chambered gleba — compare LYCOPERDALES

scle·ro·der·ma·tous \ˌ==ˈdərmədəs\ *adj* [*scler-* + *-dermatous*] **1 a :** having a hard external covering (as of bony plates or horny scales) **b :** having a skeleton of scleroderm **2** [NL *sclerodermat-*, *scleroderma* + E *-ous*] **:** of, relating to, or affected with scleroderma

scle·ro·der·mi \ˌ==ˈdər,mī\ *n pl, cap* [NL, fr. *scler-* + Gk *derma* skin — more at DERM-] *zool, in some classifications* **:** a suborder or other division of Plectognathi, comprising the triggerfishes and filefishes

scle·ro·der·mia \-rmēə\ *n* -S [NL, fr. *scler-* + *-dermia*] **:** SCLERODERMA 2

scle·ro·der·mic \ˌ==ˈ=mik\ *adj* [NL *scleroderma* + E *-ic*] **:** SCLERODERMATOUS 2

scle·ro·der·mite \ˌ==ˈ=,mīt\ *n* -S [*scler-* + *derm-* + *-ite*] **:** the hard integument of a segment of an arthropod — **scle·ro·der·mit·ic** \ˌ==,dərˈmidik\ *adj*

scle·ro·der·mous \ˌ==ˈdərməs\ *adj* [ISV *scler-* + *derm-* + *-ous*] **1 :** SCLERODERMATOUS **2** [NL *Scleroderma* + E *-ous*] **:** of or relating to fungi of the genus *Scleroderma*

scle·ro·gen \ˈsklirəjən, -ler-, -ˌjen\ *n* -S [*scler-* + *-gen*] **:** the lignified and mineralized material of the walls of a brachysclereid

scle·rog·e·nous \skləˈräjənəs, (ˈ)skliˈr-, (ˈ)skleˈr-\ *also* **scle·ro·gen·ic** \ˌsklirəˈjenik, -ler-\ *adj* [ISV *scler-* + *-genous* or *-genic*] **:** making or secreting hard tissue

scle·roid \ˈskli,rȯid, -le,r-\ *adj* [ISV *scler-* + *-oid*] **:** HARD, INDURATED ⟨~ tissue cells⟩

scle·ro·ma \skləˈrōmə\ *n, pl* **scleromas** \-məz\ *or* **scle·roma·ta** \-mədə\ [NL, fr. Gk *sklērōma*, fr. *sklēroun* to harden (fr. *sklēros* hard) + *-ōma* -oma — more at SKELETON] **:** hardening of tissues; *specif* **:** RHINOSCLEROMA

scle·ro·meninx \ˌsklirō, -lerō+\ *n* [NL, fr. *scler-* + *meninx*] **:** DURA MATER

scle·ro·mere \ˈsklirə,mi(ə)r, -ler-\ *n* -S [*scler-* + *-mere*] **:** a metamere of the skeleton

scle·rom·e·ter \skləˈrämәd·ə(r)\ *n* [ISV *scler-* + *-meter*] **:** any of various instruments for determining the relative hardnesses of materials usu. by measuring the pressure necessary to make a scratch or the amount of penetration of a stylus under a given pressure

scle·rop·a·ges \skləˈräpə,jēz\ *n, cap* [NL, fr. Gk *sklēropagēs* firmly put together, fr. *sklēr-* scler- + *-pagēs* (fr. *pagos* fixed, fastened, fr. *pēgnynai* to fix, fasten together) — more at PACT] **:** a genus of large fishes (family Osteoglossidae) of Australia and Borneo including the barramunda

scle·ro·pa·rei \ˌsklirōpəˈrē,ī, -ler-\ *n pl, cap* [NL, fr. *scler-* + Gk *pareia* cheek] **:** a large and economically important order of spiny-finned fishes comprising the scorpion fishes, greenlings, sculpins, gurnards, and related forms that are distinguished by a process of the third suborbital plate extending backward to or toward the preopercle — compare MAIL-CHEEKED

¹scle·ro·phyll \ˈ=rə,fil\ *or* **scle·ro·phyl·lous** \ˌ==ˈfiləs\ *adj* [ISV *scler-* + *-phyll* or *-phyllous*] **1 :** of, relating to, or exhibiting sclerophylly ⟨~ plants⟩ ⟨~ characteristics⟩ **2 :** made up of sclerophyll plants ⟨a ~ scrub⟩

²sclerophyll \ʺ\ *n* -S **:** a sclerophyll plant

scle·ro·phyl·ly \ˈ==,filē\ *n* -ES [*scler-* + *phyll-* + *-y*] **:** exceptional development of sclerenchyma in leaves (as in many desert plants) resulting in thickened hardened foliage resistant to water loss — compare SCLEROCAULY

scle·ro·phyte \-,fīt\ *n* -S [*scler-* + *-phyte*] **:** SCLEROPHYLL

scle·ro·protein \ˌsklirō+\ *n* [ISV *scler-* + *protein*] **:** any of a class of fibrous proteins (as collagen, keratin, fibroin) that are usu. insoluble in aqueous solvents and are resistant to chemical reagents — called also *albuminoid*

scle·ro·scope \ˈsklirə,skōp, -ler-\ *n* [fr. *Scleroscope*, a trademark] **:** a sclerometer devised esp. for use with metals in which the height of rebound of a small standard object dropped from a fixed height onto the surface of a specimen is used as a measure of the hardness of the specimen

scle·rose \skləˈrōs, ˈskli,r-, ˈskle,r-, -ōz\ *vb* -ED/-ING/-S [back-formation fr. *sclerosed*] *vt* **:** to cause sclerosis in ⟨chronic infections may ~ kidneys⟩ ~ *vi* **:** to undergo or become affected with sclerosis **:** become sclerotic ⟨arteries of older people often tend to ~⟩

scle·rosed \-ōst,-ōzd\ *adj* [NL *sclerosis* (fr. ML *sclirosis*) + E *-ed*] **1 :** affected with sclerosis **:** HARDENED, INDURATED **2 :** LIGNIFIED; *esp* **:** having thickened pitted walls ⟨sclereids may be interpreted as ~ parenchyma cells⟩

scle·ro·sep·tum \ˌsklirō, -lerō+\ *n* [NL, fr. *scler-* + *septum*] **:** a calcareous radial septum of a coral

scle·ro·sis \skləˈrōsəs\ *n, pl* **sclero·ses** \-ō,sēz\ [ME *sclirosis*, fr. ML, fr. Gk *sklērōsis*, fr. *sklēroun* to harden (fr. *sklēros* hard) + *-sis* — more at SKELETON] **1 a :** pathological hardening of tissue produced by overgrowth of fibrous tissue and other changes (as in arteriosclerosis) or by increase in interstitial tissue and other changes (as in multiple sclerosis) **b :** any of various diseases characterized by sclerosis — usu. used in combination; see ARTERIOSCLEROSIS, MULTIPLE SCLEROSIS **2 :** hardening of plant cell walls by thickening or by deposition of lignin

scle·ro·skeleton \ˌsklirō, -lerō+\ *n* [*scler-* + *skeleton*] **:** the part of the skeleton that is formed by ossifications in tendons, ligaments, and aponeuroses

scle·ros·po·ra *n, cap* [NL, fr. *scler-* + *-spora*] **:** a genus of downy mildews (family Peronosporaceae) parasitic on various grasses and having thick-walled resting spores that are united with the walls of the oogonia

scle·ro·stome \ˈsklirə,stōm, -ler-\ *n* -S [NL *Sclerostoma*, genus of nematode worms in former classifications, fr. *scler-* + *-stoma*] **:** PALISADE WORM

scle·ro·tal \skləˈrōdᵊl\ *n* -S [NL *sclerotica* + E *-al*] **:** any of the bony plates in the sclerotic of various vertebrates

scle·rote \ˈskli,rōt, -le,r-, skləˈrōt\ *n* -S [NL *sclerotium*] **:** SCLEROTIUM

scle·ro·tial \skləˈrōsh(ē)əl\ *adj* [NL *sclerotium* + E *-al*] **1 :** of or relating to a sclerotium **:** bearing sclerotia **2** [NL *Sclerotium* + E *-al*] **:** of or relating to the form genus *Sclerotium*

¹scle·rot·ic \-rädik\ *adj* [in sense 1, fr. *scler-* + *-otic*; in other senses, prob. fr. (assumed) ML *scleroticus*, fr. *scler-* + *-oticus* (as in L *exoticus* exotic) — more at EXOTIC] **1 :** HARD, INDURATED: as **a :** being or relating to the sclera **b :** SCLEROSED ⟨a ~ cell wall⟩ ⟨~ patients⟩ ⟨~ arteries⟩ **2 :** of or relating to sclerosis

²sclerotic \ʺ\ *n* -S [ML *sclerotica*] **:** SCLERA

scle·rot·i·ca \-dəkə\ *n* -S [ML, prob. fr. fem. of (assumed) ML *scleroticus* sclerotic] **:** SCLERA

sclerotic cell *n* **:** SCLEREID

sclerotic coat *n* **:** SCLERA

scle·ro·tin \ˈsklirətən, -ler-\ *n* -S [ISV *sclerot-* (fr. Gk *sklērotēs* hardness) + *-in*] **:** an insoluble tanned protein permeating and stiffening the chitin of the cuticle of arthropods

scle·ro·tin·ia \ˌ==ˈtinēə\ *n* [NL, fr. *sclerotin-* (irreg. fr. *sclerotium*) + *-ia*] **1** *cap* **:** a large genus of ascomycetous fungi (order Helotiales) having apothecia that arise from a sclerotium and including various destructive plant pathogens — see BROWN ROT **2** -S **:** any fungus of the genus *Sclerotinia* ⟨~ rots⟩ — **scle·ro·tin·i·al** \ˌ==ˈtinēəl\ *adj*

scle·ro·tin·i·ose \-nē,ōs *also* -ōz\ *n* -S [NL *Sclerotinia* + *-ose*] **:** a plant disease caused by a sclerotinia

scle·ro·ti·oid \skləˈrōshē,ȯid\ *also* **scle·ro·toid** \ˈsklirə,tȯid, -ler-\ *adj* [NL *sclerotium* + E *-oid*] **:** resembling a sclerotium

scle·ro·ti·tis \ˌsklirəˈtīdəs, -ler-\ *n* -ES [NL, fr. ML *sclerotica* sclerotic + NL *-itis*] **:** SCLERITIS

scle·ro·tium \skləˈrōsh(ē)əm\ *n* [NL, fr. Gk *sklērotēs* hardness (fr. *sklēros* hard) + NL *-ium* — more at SKELETON] **1** *pl* **sclero·tia** \-)ə\ **a :** a compact mass of hardened mycelium stored with reserve food material in various true fungi that is usu. dark-colored, often has cells which are short and stout or irregular in shape, and when mature becomes detached and remains dormant until a favorable opportunity for growth when it either sends out hyphae or produces spore fruits ⟨the ergot of rye is a ~⟩ **b :** a waxy mass of protoplasm into which the plasmodium of a myxomycete is transformed during dry seasons **2** *cap* **:** a form genus of sterile fungi (order Mycelia Sterilia) including many that form sclerotia and some that cause blights or rots of plants

sclerotium disease *or* **sclerotium rot** *n* **:** a plant disease caused by fungi of the genus *Sclerotium; also* **:** one in which sclerotia are formed

scle·ro·ti·za·tion \ˌsklirətəˈzāshən, -ler-, -ˌtīˈz-\ *n* -S [*sclerotized* + *-ation*] **:** the quality or state of being sclerotized

scle·ro·tized \ˈ==,tīzd\ *adj* [¹*sclerotic* + *-ize* + *-ed*] **:** SCLEROSED; *esp* **:** hardened by substances other than chitin — used chiefly of the cuticle of an insect

scle·ro·tome \-,tōm\ *n* -S [*scler-* + *-tome*] **1 :** a fibrous partition separating two myotomes **2 :** the ventromesial portion of a somite that proliferates mesenchyme which migrates about the notochord to form the axial skeleton and ribs — **scle·ro·tomic** \ˌ==ˈtōmik, -ˈtäm-\ *adj*

scle·rot·o·my \skləˈrädəmē\ *n* -ES [*scler-* + *-tomy*] **:** surgical cutting of the sclera

scle·rous \ˈsklirəs, -ler-\ *adj* [Gk *sklēros*] **:** HARD, INDURATED

sclimb \ˈsklim\ *chiefly Scot var of* CLIMB

ScM *abbr or n* -S [NL *scientiae magister*] Master of Science

SCM *abbr* **1** state certified midwife **2** summary court-martial

scob \ˈskäb\ *n* -S [origin unknown] *dial Brit* **:** a rod or splint of wood esp. a thatch peg

scob·by \ˈskäbi\ *n* -ES [origin unknown] *dial Brit* **:** CHAFFINCH

sco·bic·u·lar \skōˈbikyələ(r)\ *adj* [L *scobis* sawdust, filings + E *-icular* (as in *reticular*); akin to L *scabere* to scratch, scrape — more at SHAVE] **:** SCOBIFORM

scob·i·form \ˈskäbə,fȯrm, ˈskōb-\ *adj* [L *scobis* + E *-form*] **:** resembling sawdust or raspings

scob·i·nate \ˈskäbənət, -ˌnāt\ *adj* [L *scobina* rasp + E *-ate*; akin to L *scabere* to scratch, scrape] **:** NODULATED

scodgy \ˈskäjē\ *n* -ES [origin unknown] *Scot* **:** DRUDGE

¹scoff \ˈskäf, ˈskȯf\ *n* -S [ME *scof*, prob. of Scand origin; akin to obs. Dan *skuf*, *skof* jest, mockery, deceit, *skuffe* to jest; akin to OFris *skof* mockery, and perh. to OE *scop* poet — more at SCOP] **1 :** SCOFFING, MOCKERY **2 :** a mocking expression of scorn, derision, or contempt **:** GIBE ⟨subject to the ~s and guffaws of his fellows —C.M.Dudley⟩ **3 :** an object of scorn, mockery, or derision ⟨turn the whole matter into a ~ and call it a trifle —*Encore*⟩

²scoff \ʺ\ *vb* -ED/-ING/-S [ME *scoffen*, fr. *scof*, n.] *vi* **:** to show contempt by derisive acts or language **:** speak contemptuously or with ridicule or mockery ⟨one of those attending the lecture . . . had come to ~, but was converted —Lucile E. Hoyme⟩ — often used with *at* ⟨we may ~ at him in health, but we send for him in pain —B.N.Cardozo⟩ ~ *vt* **:** to treat or address with derision **:** mock at ⟨how I have ~*ed* them in my heart —A.C.Gunter⟩

syn SCOFF, JEER, GIBE, FLEER, GIRD, SNEER, and FLOUT can all mean to show one's contempt in derision or mockery. SCOFF stresses insolence, lack of respect, or incredulity as motivating the derision ⟨in consequence of this illiteracy, he *scoffed* at education and considered the professional scrivener an object of ridicule —L.C.Douglas⟩ ⟨*scoffed* at the idea that modern man might have developed before Neanderthal —L.C.Eiseley⟩ JEER stresses a coarse derisive laughter ⟨before she had yanked me halfway across the floor, men and women were *jeering* at her, calling her a cradle robber —Conrad Richter⟩ ⟨they would laugh at his warning. They would *jeer* him, and, if practicable, pelt him with missiles —Stephen Crane⟩ GIBE stresses taunting whether derisive or good-natured ⟨*gibe* and catcall at a speaker for his political sentiments⟩ ⟨hoot and *gibe* at her —Carl Jonas⟩ FLEER emphasizes derisive grins, grimaces, and laughter rather than utterances ⟨listened with a *fleering* mouth —Joseph Hergesheimer⟩ ⟨saying nothing but *fleering* unpleasantly at any and all remarks⟩ GIRD stresses an attack marked by scoffing, gibing, or jeering ⟨warned us, instead of *girding* at general prejudices, to employ our sagacity in discovering the latent wisdom that commonly exists in them —Walter Moberly⟩ SNEER, of all these terms, carries the strongest implication of ill-natured or caustic contempt, usu. connoting the use of irony or satire augmented by an insultingly contemptuous facial expression, tone of voice, or general manner ⟨his attitude . . . has been often unduly critical, occasionally to the point of *sneering* denunciation —F.E.Hirsch⟩ ⟨they used to *sneer* and to jibe at the Redskin Fife and Drum Ensemble —W.B.Ready⟩ ⟨too many teachers just *sneer* at TV and refuse to look at it —S.H.Horton⟩ FLOUT stresses a contempt of something shown by refusal to heed it or by denial of its truth or force ⟨scorn or neglect of institutions, and characteristic *flouting* or reversing of convention —F.J.Hoffman⟩ ⟨the law of supply and demand cannot be *flouted* indefinitely —C.T. Lanham⟩ ⟨believes that our present immigration laws *flout* fundamental American traditions and ideals —*President's Commission on Immigration & Naturalization*⟩

³scoff \ʺ\ *vb* -ED/-ING/-S [alter. of earlier *scaff*, of unknown origin] *vt* **1 :** to eat greedily **:** EAT **2 :** PLUNDER, STEAL ~ *vi* **:** to eat greedily **:** EAT ⟨clothes' moth starts ~*ing* the moment she hatches —*Monsanto Mag.*⟩

⁴scoff \ʺ\ *n* -S **:** FOOD, MEAL

scoff·er \-fə(r)\ *n* -S [ME, fr. *scoffen* to scoff + *-er*] **:** one that scoffs; *esp* **:** one that scoffs at religion

¹scoffing *n* -S [ME, fr. gerund of *scoffen* to scoff] **:** the act of one who scoffs

²scoffing *adj* [fr. pres. part. of ²*scoff*] **:** DERISIVE, CONTEMPTUOUS — **scoff·ing·ly** *adv*

scofflaw \ˈ=,=\ *n* [²*scoff* + *law*] **:** one who scoffs at or violates the law ⟨a traffic ~⟩

scoffs *pl of* SCOFF, *pres 3d sing of* SCOFF

scog \ˈskäg\ *var of* SCUG

scoggin *n* -S [after John (Thomas?) *Scoggin* (Scogan) *fl* 1480–1500 jester at the court of King Edward IV of England] **:** a coarse or scurrilous jester

scoin·son arch \ˈskȯin(t)sən-\ *n* [*scoinson* alter. (influenced by MF *escoinsson* sconcheon) of *sconcheon*] **:** an arch carrying a part of the thickness of a wall

scoke \ˈskōk\ *n* -S [Massachuset *m'skok*, lit., that which is red] **:** POKEWEED

¹scold \ˈskōld\ *n* -S [ME *scald*, *scold*, prob. of Scand origin; akin to ON *skald*, *skāld* poet, skald, Icel *skālda* to make scurrilous or libelous verse; perh. akin to OIr *scēl* story, W *chwedl*] **1 :** one addicted to abusive ribald speech ⟨really was a ~, in the strong old Saxon acceptation of the word . . . had fought life singlehanded, tooth and nail, with all the ferocity of outraged sensibilities, and had come out of the fight scratched and disheveled, with few womanly graces —Harriet B. Stowe⟩ **:** one who scolds ⟨afraid of going down to posterity as the despised ~ in her husband's life —E.J.Simmons⟩ ⟨as editor . . . became the country's No. 1 crusader and ~, as well as its conscience —*New Yorker*⟩ ⟨only the squirrels, those born ~*s*, to reprove our indolence —*New Yorker*⟩; *specif* **:** COMMON SCOLD **2 :** SCOLDING ⟨a writing that is a ~⟩

²scold \ʺ\ *vb* -ED/-ING/-S [ME *scalden*, *scolden*, fr. *scald*, *scold*, n.] *vi* **1** *obs* **:** to quarrel noisily **:** use harsh or vituperative language **2 :** to find fault usu. noisily or rudely **:** utter harsh rebuke **:** chide sharply and severely — often used with *at* ⟨could come to terms if they came truly to grips instead of ~*ing* at each other over a barrier of misunderstanding —Edward Sapir⟩ ⟨farmers . . stood up in their wagons and ~*ed* at the horses —Sherwood Anderson⟩ ~ *vt* **1 :** to force by scolding — used esp. with *out of* **2 :** to chide loudly or rudely **:** rebuke or reprove with severity **:** censure severely or angrily ⟨~*ed* the . . . press, not only for undue emphasis on sex and crime but for failure to guess the outcome of elections —*Newsweek*⟩ ⟨~*ed* for attaching too much importance to phonetic similarity —C.E.Bazell⟩ ⟨the . . . investor for unwillingness to assume risks —J.F.Rippy⟩ ⟨~ the younger generation of writers severely for their sins —C.I.Glicksberg⟩

syn SCOLD, UPBRAID, RATE, BERATE, TONGUE-LASH, JAW, BAWL (*out*), WIG, RAIL, REVILE, and VITUPERATE mean, in common, to reproach or censure angrily and more or less abusively. SCOLD suggests the censure of a disobedient child by a mother, or implies irritation or ill temper ⟨*scold* a child for getting home late⟩ ⟨one officer who had *scolded* his subordinates for picking apples from trees alongside a road while on a march —Hanama Tasaki⟩ ⟨a catbird . . . flew up on a lilac limb to *scold* us —John Moore⟩ UPBRAID usu. suggests a more or less justifiable anger ⟨the Queen *upbraided* Henry for the scandal he was giving —Francis Hackett⟩ ⟨the scene in which Lincoln *upbraids* his schoolfellows for maltreating a turtle —*Reporter*⟩ RATE and BERATE suggest a more prolonged angry censure and, generally, abusiveness ⟨*rated* himself most severely for this feeling of vengefulness —Howard Nemerov⟩ ⟨*rated* him for his want of tact —Adrian Bell⟩ ⟨*berate* the agent for his ill management of the estates —Pearl Buck⟩ ⟨heatedly *berated* the government's . . . attitude —*Time*⟩ TONGUE-LASH stresses the effect of severe unrestrained censure or berating upon the person berated ⟨*tongue-lashed* them in a way that could be heard blocks off —Howard Fast⟩ ⟨*tongue-lashes* him about the exploitation of the workers —*Time*⟩ The terms JAW, BAWL (*out*), and WIG (chiefly British) emphasize the energetic or noisy harangue that usu. characterizes a berating ⟨when we went home late for chores, we got *jawed* some —C.T.Jackson⟩ ⟨a tall, red-headed foreman whose chief asset was *bawling out* his men —H.A.Overstreet⟩ ⟨got a sound *wigging* in the current issue from one of their own and from a pair of practitioners in other fields —*Time*⟩ RAIL, usu. with *at* or *against*, is a strong, more abusive, usu. contemptuous berating ⟨*rail* against humanity for not being abstract perfection —T.L.Peacock⟩ ⟨physicians time and again *rail* at the courts for applying a test of mental responsibility so narrow and inadequate —B.N.

Cardozo) ⟨had called his people lazy louts . . . *railed* against his inclination to dreams —Sherwood Anderson⟩ REVILE puts emphasis upon abusiveness more strongly than any of the others, and usu. implies vilification ⟨had to hear themselves *reviled* as traitors by lesser Americans —Kenneth Roberts⟩ VITUPERATE is interchangeable with REVILE though suggesting even more violence of censure or attack ⟨with his angry face and his trembling hands *vituperating* him —Archibald Marshall⟩ ⟨how the sage reviled and *vituperated* the horrors of city life —A.C.Benson⟩

scol·de·nore \ˈskōldə,nō(ə)r\ *n* -s [origin unknown] **:** OLDSQUAW

scold·er \ˈskōldə(r)\ *n* -s [ME, fr. *scolden* to scold + *-er*] **:** one who scolds

scolding *n* -s [ME, fr. gerund of *scolden* to scold] **1 :** the action of one who scolds **2 :** harsh or severe reproof ⟨he issued a circular . . . that evoked a ~ —F.L.Paxson⟩

scolding locks *n pl, dial* **:** locks of hair usu. curled that do not stay in place

scold·ing·ly *adv* **:** in a scolding manner

scolds *pl of* SCOLD, *pres 3d sing of* SCOLD

scold's bridle *n* **:** BRANK 1a

scolec- *or* **scoleco-** *comb form* [Gk *skōlēk-, skōlēko-*, fr. *skōlēk-, skōlēx* worm, grub — more at SCOLEX] **:** worm ⟨*scoleco*logy⟩ ⟨*scoleco*spore⟩ **:** scolex ⟨*scolec*oid⟩

sco·lec·i·da \skōˈlesədə\ *n pl, cap* [NL, fr. *scolec-* + *-ida*] *in some classifications* **:** a phylum or other major division of Metazoa that comprises triploblastic bilaterally symmetrical invertebrate animals lacking a true coelom and having nonstriated musculature, a nonmetameric nervous system, and a primitive or no circulatory system and that includes Platyhelminthes, Nemertea, Acanthocephala, Gastrotricha, Rotifera, Nematoda, Nematomorpha, Kinorhyncha, and Entoprocta — compare ASCHELMINTHES

sco·lec·i·dan \-d°n\ *adj* [NL *Scolecida* + E *-an*] **:** of or relating to the Scolecida

scol·e·cite \ˈskälə,sīt, ˈskōl-\ *n* -s [G *skolezit*, fr. *skolez-* scolec- + *-it* -ite] **:** a mineral $CaAl_2Si_3O_{10}·3H_2O$ that is a hydrous calcium aluminum silicate, is a zeolite, occurs in delicate radiating groups of white crystals, in fibrous masses, and in nodules, and in some forms shows a wormlike motion when heated

sco·le·co·dont \skōˈlēkə,dänt\ *n* -s [*scolec-* + Gk *odont-, odōn* tooth — more at TOOTH] **:** a fossil worm jaw

sco·le·coid \skōˈlē,kȯid, ˈskōlə,-\ *adj* [*scolec-* + *-oid*] **:** resembling a scolex or worm

sco·le·co·spore \skōˈlēkə,spō(ə)r\ *n* [*scolec-* + *spore*] **:** a slender threadlike spore; *specif* **:** such a spore distinguished from one of another type but both produced by the same fungus (as in the genus *Phomopsis*)

sco·lex \ˈskō,leks\ *n, pl* **scoli·ces** \ˈskōlə,sēz\ *also* **scol·e·ces** \ˈskälə,sēz, ˈskōl-\ *or* **scolexes** [NL, fr. Gk *skōlēx* worm, grub; akin to Gk *skelos* leg — more at CYLINDER] **:** the head of a tapeworm either in the larva or adult stage from which the proglottids are produced by budding

-sco·lex \ˈskō,leks\ *n comb form* [NL, fr. Gk *skōlēx* worm, grub] **:** worm — in generic names ⟨*Desmoscolex*⟩

sco·lia \ˈskōlēə\ *n, cap* [NL] **:** a genus (the type of the family Scoliidae) of wasps that build or dig no nest but lay their eggs on the bodies of the burrowing larvae of various beetles

¹sco·li·id \-ēəd\ *adj* [NL *Scoliidae*] **:** of or relating to the genus *Scolia* or family Scoliidae

²scoliid \"\ *n* -s **:** a wasp of the genus *Scolia* or family Scoliidae

sco·li·on *also* **sko·li·on** \ˈskōlē,än\ *n, pl* **sco·lia** \-ēə\ [Gk *skolion*, fr. neut. of *skolios* crooked — more at CYLINDER] **:** an ancient Greek song sung in turn by guests at a banquet and possibly improvised

sco·li·o·sis *also* **sko·li·o·sis** \,skōlēˈōsəs, ,skäl-\ *n, pl* **scolio·ses** \-ˈō,sēz\ [NL, fr. Gk *skoliōsis* crookedness, fr. *skolios* + *-ōsis*] **:** a lateral curvature of the spine — **sco·li·ot·ic** \;==ˈäd·ik\ *adj*

sco·lite \ˈskō,līt\ *n* -s [Gk *skōlēx* worm, grub + E *-lite* — more at SCOLEX] **:** any of various tubular structures found in rocks and believed to be fossil burrows of marine worms

sco·li·thus \ˈskōləthəs\ *n* -ES [NL, fr. Gk *skōlēx* + NL *-lithus* -lite] **:** SCOLITE

scollop *var of* SCALLOP

scol·o·pa·ceous \;skäləˈpāshəs\ *adj* [LL *scolopac-, scolopax* snipe, woodcock + E *-eous*] **:** resembling a snipe

scol·o·pac·i·dae \,skäləˈpasə,dē\ *n pl, cap* [NL, fr. *Scolopac-, Scolopax*, type genus + *-idae*] **:** a family of birds (suborder Charadrii) including the woodcocks, snipes, sandpipers, tattlers, curlews, and godwits — see CHARADRIIDAE

¹scol·o·pa·cine \;==ˈpā,sīn, -s°n\ *adj* [NL *Scolopac-, Scolopax* + E *-ine*] **:** of or relating to the Scolopacidae

²scolopacine \"\ *n* -s **:** a bird of the family Scolopacidae

scol·o·pax \ˈ==,paks\ *n, cap* [NL, fr. LL, woodcock, snipe, fr. Gk] **:** the type genus of Scolopacidae comprising the European woodcock and a few obscure East Indian birds but formerly including several other birds

scol·o·pen·dra \,skäləˈpendrə\ *n* [NL, fr. L, a kind of millipede, fr. Gk *skolopendra*] **1** *cap* **:** a widely distributed genus of centipedes that contains some of the largest tropical forms (as the giant red and black centipede, *S. galapagensis* of the Galapagos islands which may reach a foot in length) **2** -s **:** CENTIPEDE

scol·o·pen·drel·la \,==penˈdrelə\ *n, cap* [NL, dim. of L *scolopendra*] **:** a genus (the type of the family Scolopendrellidae) of terrestrial arthropods resembling small centipedes with 15 to 24 dorsal scutes and 12 pairs of short legs

scol·o·pen·drel·li·dae \-lə,dē\ *n pl, cap* [NL, fr. *Scolopendrella*, type genus + *-idae*] **:** a family of minute terrestrial arthropods (class Symphyla) with the first pair of legs usu. reduced or imperfect — see SCOLOPENDRELLA

scol·o·pen·drel·loid \;==ˈdre,lȯid\ *adj* [NL *Scolopendrella* + E *-oid*] **:** resembling or related to the genus *Scolopendrella*

scol·o·pen·dri·dae \,==ˈpendrə,dē\ *n pl, cap* [NL, fr. *Scolopendra*, type genus + *-idae*] **:** a large cosmopolitan family of centipedes of which *Scolopendra* is the type — **scol·o·pen·drine** \;==ˈpen,drīn, -drən\ *adj*

scol·o·pen·dri·form \-endrə,fȯrm\ *adj* [NL *Scolopendra* + E *-iform*] **:** resembling a centipede ⟨a ~ beetle larva⟩

scol·o·pen·dri·um \,skäləˈpendrēəm\ *n* [NL, fr. LL *scolopendrion*, a kind of fern thought to resemble a millipede, fr. Gk *skolopendrion*, dim. of *skolopendra*] *syn of* PHYLLITIS

scol·o·pid·i·um \,skäləˈpidēəm\ *n, pl* **scolopid·ia** \-ēə\ [NL, fr. Gk *skolop-, skolops* stake, pale, anything pointed + NL *-idium*; akin to Gk *skalops* mole (animal) — more at HALF] **:** a chordotonal organ

sco·lop·o·phore \skəˈläpə,fō(ə)r\ *also* **scol·o·phore** \ˈskälə,-\ *n* -s [*scolopophore* fr. Gk *skolopo-* (fr. *skolop-, skolops*) + E *-phore*; *scolophore* contr. of *scolopophore*] **:** an integumentary sense organ in insects believed to be auditory in function — **sco·loph·o·rous** \skəˈläf(ə)rəs\ *adj* — **scol·o·poph·o·rous** \;skälə,päˈ-\ *adj*

scol·y·mus \ˈskäləməs\ *n, cap* [NL, fr. L *scolymos*, a kind of thistle, fr. Gk *skolymos*] **:** a small genus of thistlelike herbs (family Compositae) of the Mediterranean region having flower heads with only ray flowers — see GOLDEN THISTLE

¹sco·lyt·id \skəˈlid·əd\ *adj* [NL *Scolytidae*] **:** of or relating to the Scolytidae

²scolytid \"\ *n* -s **:** a beetle of the family Scolytidae

sco·lyt·i·dae \-d·ə,dē\ *n pl, cap* [NL, fr. *Scolytus*, type genus + *-idae*] **:** a large family of bark-boring or wood-boring rhynchophorous beetles having a very short beak and clubbed antennae and being small but very destructive to forest trees and fruit trees — see BARK BEETLE

scol·y·toid \ˈskälə,tȯid\ *adj* [NL *Scolytus* + E *-oid*] **1 :** resembling or related to the family Scolytidae **2 :** being or passing through the stage next before the pupa in hypermetamorphic beetles of the family Meloidae

scol·y·tus \-ləd·əs\ *n, cap* [NL, irreg. fr. Gk *skolyptein* to cut short; akin to Gk *kolos* docked, hornless — more at HALT (lame)] **:** the type genus of Scolytidae comprising numerous small bark beetles of which some are destructive to economically important plants and one (*S. multistriatus*) is a vector of the fungus that causes Dutch elm disease

scom·ber \ˈskämbə(r)\ *n, cap* [NL, fr. L, mackerel, fr. Gk *skombros*] **:** the type genus of Scombridae containing the common Atlantic mackerel

scom·ber·om·o·rus \,skämbəˈrämərəs\ *n, cap* [NL, fr. L *scomber* mackerel + Gk *homoros* closely resembling, fr. *homos* same — more at SAME] **:** a genus of elongated compressed fishes (family Scombridae) having the snout long and pointed, the mouth large, and the scales few and rudimentary and including a number of important food and sport fishes

scom·bre·soc·i·dae \,skämbrəˈsäsə,dē\ *n pl, cap* [NL, fr. *Sombresoc-, Sombresox*, type genus + *-idae*] **:** a family of slender elongate thin-scaled fishes including only the sauries and with the needlefishes (family Belonidae) forming a distinct suborder of the order Synentognathi

scom·bre·sox \ˈ==,säks\ *n, cap* [NL, fr. L *scombr-, scomber* mackerel + *esox* pike — more at ESOX] **:** the type genus of Scombresocidae

¹scom·brid \ˈskämbrəd\ *adj* [NL *Scombridae*] **:** of or relating to the Scombridae

²scombrid \"\ *n* -s **:** a fish of the family Scombridae

scom·bri·dae \-rə,dē\ *n pl, cap* [NL, fr. *Scombr-, Scomber*, type genus + *-idae*] **:** a family of fishes (suborder Scombroidea) comprising the typical mackerels, the chub mackerels, and a few related forms but formerly including all or nearly all the scombroids

scom·bri·form \-,fȯrm\ *adj* [NL *Scombriformes*] **1 :** of or relating to the Scombriformes **2** [L *scombr-, scomber* mackerel + E *-iform*] **:** resembling mackerel

scom·bri·for·mes \,==ˈfȯr,mēz\ [NL, fr. L *scombr-, scomber* mackerel + NL *-iformes*] *syn of* SCOMBROIDEA

scom·brine \ˈskäm,brēn, -,brən\ *n* -s [ISV *scombr-* (fr. L *scombr-, scomber* mackerel) + *-ine*] **:** a protamine obtained from the mackerel

¹scom·broid \ˈskäm,brȯid\ *adj* [NL *Scombroidea*] **:** resembling or related to the Scombridae **:** of or relating to the Scombroidea

²scombroid \"\ *n* -s **:** a fish of the suborder Scombroidea

scom·broi·dea \skämˈbrȯidēə\ *n pl, cap* [NL, fr. *Scombr-, Scomber* + *-oidea*] **:** a suborder of Percomorphi that comprises active streamlined marine fishes having a narrow caudal peduncle, scales absent or small and sometimes spiny, a usu. long dorsal fin without projecting spines but sometimes with finlets, a lunate or forked caudal fin and including numerous oily-fleshed fishes (as mackerels, tunas, albacores, bonitos, and swordfishes) and that are of great economic importance as food fishes

scom·broi·dei \-ē,ī\ [NL, fr. *Scombr-, Scomber* + *-oidei*] *syn of* SCOMBROIDEA

¹sconce \ˈskän(t)s\ *n* -s [ME *sconse, sconce*, fr. MF *esconse* hiding place, screened lantern with a handle, fr. OF, fr. fem. of *escons*, past part. of *escondre* to hide, fr. L *abscondere* — more at ABSCOND] **1 a** *obs* **:** a screened lantern or candlestick with a handle **b :** a flat candlestick with a handle **2 a :** a bracket candlestick or group of candlesticks projecting or hanging from a plaque and usu. forming an ornamental object secured to a wall **b :** an ornamental electric light fixture for a wall that resembles a bracket candlestick or group of candlesticks **c :** the circular socket of a candlestick into which a candle is inserted esp. when the socket has a brim **3 a :** HEAD, SKULL ⟨knock him about the ~ with a dirty shovel —Shak.⟩ **b :** BRAINS, SENSE

sconce 2a

²sconce \"\ *n* -s [D *schans*, fr. G *schanze*, fr. MHG, fagot, fascine, sconce] **1 :** a detached or isolated defensive work; *specif* **:** a counterfort or redoubt built to defend a particular point **2 :** a protecting cover or screen **:** PROTECTION, SHELTER

³sconce *vt* -ED/-ING/-S *obs* **:** to provide with a sconce **:** ENTRENCH, SHELTER

⁴sconce \ˈskän(t)s\ *vt* -ED/-ING/-S [origin unknown] **:** FINE

⁵sconce \"\ *n* -s **:** a fine imposed at an English university for a breach of rules or customs

scon·cheon \ˈskänchən\ *or* **scun·cheon** \ˈskən-\ *n* -s [ME *scouchon, skonchon, sconcheon*, fr. MF *escoinsson, escouchon, escochon*, fr. *coing, coin* wedge, stamp, corner — more at COIN] **:** the part of the side of an opening from the back of the reveal to the inside face of the wall usu. forming in the masonry a rabbet in which the wooden frame is set

scone *or* **scon** \ˈskōn, ˈskän, ˈskən\ *n* -s [perh. fr. D *schoonbrood* fine white bread, fr. MD *schoonbroot*, fr. *schone* bright, clean, beautiful + *broot* bread — more at SHEEN] **1 a :** a quick bread made of oatmeal or barley flour, rolled into a round shape, cut into quarters, and baked on a griddle **b :** a quick bread made of a baking powder dough sometimes enriched with eggs, sugar, and currants, cut into various shapes (as rounds, diamonds, wedges) and usu. baked in an oven **2** *or* **scone cap :** a broad flat bonnet worn by the Lowland Scots

scooch \ˈsküch\ *vi* -ED/-ING/-ES [origin unknown] *chiefly dial* **:** to crouch esp. in hiding

¹scoop \ˈsküp\ *n* -s [ME *scope*, fr. MD *schope, schoepe*; akin to MLG *schōpe* scoop, MHG *schuobe* scoop, OHG *skepfen* to form, shape, create, draw up water — more at SHAPE] **1 :** any of various containers or utensils for holding or removing liquid or loose materials: as **a :** a large ladle **:** a vessel with a long handle used for dipping or skimming liquids ⟨a ~ for bailing a rowboat⟩ **b :** a deep shovel or similar but smaller and handheld implement for digging out and dipping or for shoveling ⟨a coal ~⟩ ⟨a flour ~⟩ ⟨a grain ~⟩ ⟨a measuring ~⟩ **c :** a hemispherical utensil with a handle for dipping out soft food (as ice cream or mashed potatoes) **d :** a small utensil often with a spoon-shaped blade for cutting or gouging; *specif* **:** a spoon-shaped surgical instrument used in extracting various materials (as debris, pus, foreign bodies) **e :** a receptacle with high curved sides for holding a loose bulk commodity on a weighing scale **f :** the bucket of a dredging machine or an earth-moving vehicle; *also* **:** an earth-moving vehicle having a bucket **g :** CRANBERRY RAKE **2 a :** the amount contained in a scoop ⟨a ~ of ice cream⟩ **b :** an amount of something obtained in large quantity as if with a scoop (as a large profit in speculation) ⟨had made a huge ~ on the stock exchange —Max Beerbohm⟩ **3 :** SCOOP NET **4 a :** the action of taking with a scoop or ladle **:** a motion with or like that made with a scoop ⟨off these volcanic islands another ~ is made for bait —*Time*⟩ **b :** the act of scooping or the musical effect achieved by it **:** PORTAMENTO ⟨with an occasional hoot and a more than occasional ~ to betray the toll time has taken of her voice —Irving Kolodin⟩ **c** (1) **:** the taking in of all the cards on the table in one play in casino (2) **:** SCOPA **d :** a field hockey stroke executed with the hands apart and the blade of the stick laid back to lift the ball **5 a :** a place hollowed out **:** a basin-shaped cavity **:** HOLLOW ⟨small city rests on a ~ between rocky hills —*Springfield (Mass.) Union*⟩ **b :** a shallow depression in the earth prepared by various birds as a foundation for their nest **c :** a funnel-shaped opening for channeling a fluid (as air or oil) into a desired path — compare AIR SCOOP **d :** a usu. multiple unit and floodlight with a more or less shovel-shaped reflector used esp. in movie and television studios **6 a :** information esp. of immediate interest or significance ⟨you heard the hot ~ —J.A.Michener⟩ ⟨give him the ~ on the identification —J.K.Harris⟩ **b :** an exclusive news report **:** BEAT 10b ⟨the story was a ~ by just a few hours —Stephen Watts⟩ ⟨men whose self-restraint will give way before their desire for a ~ —*Time*⟩ **7 :** a rounded and usu. low-cut neckline on a woman's garment

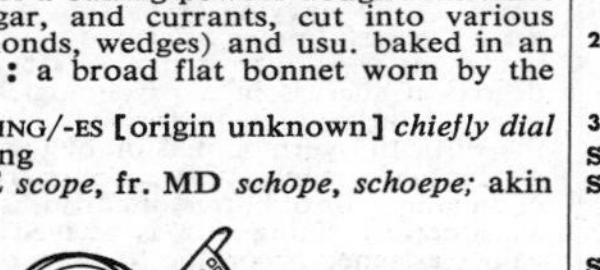

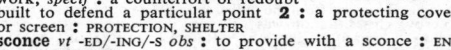

scoop 1c

²scoop \"\ *vb* -ED/-ING/-S [ME *scopen*, fr. *scope*, n.] *vt* **1 a :** to take out or up with or as if with a scoop **:** DIP ⟨~ sugar out of a barrel⟩ ⟨~ the center out of a melon⟩ ⟨~*ed* up another mug of flip —Kenneth Roberts⟩ ⟨every time she rolled to leeward, she would ~ up the South Atlantic Ocean —H.A.Chippendale⟩ ⟨~*ed* up a handful of the salty earth —Marion Wilhelm⟩ **b :** to gather, take, or get sometimes surreptitiously in a more or less wholesale manner as if with a scoop **:** pick up ⟨~*ed* up a couple of cakes of soap from the hotel —Gilbert Millstein⟩ ⟨~*ing* his books up off the ground —Grace Metalious⟩ **c :** to lift (the ball) into the air with the stick without taking a preliminary swing in field hockey **2 :** to empty by ladling ⟨to ~ a boat dry⟩ **3 :** to make hollow **:** dig out **:** EXCAVATE ⟨the earth had been ~*ed* away —Willa Cather⟩ **4 a :** to make or shape by or as if by scooping — often used with *out* ⟨water that by slow attrition had ~*ed* out this wide channel —P.E. More⟩ **b :** to cut (material) away along a curved line; *specif* **:** to make (a garment) with a scoop neck or neckline ⟨a ~*ed* dress⟩ **5 a :** BEAT 4j ⟨let the radio stations consistently ~ the press, or vice versa —Daniel Melcher & Nancy Larrick⟩ **b :** to obtain (a news story) as a beat **c :** to win against **:** BEAT 4d ⟨next film . . . intended to ~ the screen adaptation of the year's biggest stage hit —Lewis Jacobs⟩ **6 :** to glide from (one tone) to another tone esp. in singing so as to sound the intermediate pitches or to begin (a tone) with a slide to the correct pitch ~ *vi* **1 :** to do lading, hollowing, or gathering with or as if with a scoop **2 :** to scoop a tone ⟨the habit of sliding or ~*ing* is another undesirable feature of singing —Sergius Kagen⟩ ⟨she ~*s*, strains for notes —Robert Evett⟩

scoop bonnet *n* **:** a bonnet with a long narrow front shaped somewhat like a scoop and formerly much worn by women

scoop car *n* **:** a railroad car with a scoop for removing obstructions (as snow, rocks, earth slides) from the track

scoop·er \-pə(r)\ *n* -s **1 :** one that uses or works with a scoop (as on a grain unloader or on a centrifugal machine charger) **2 a :** one that scoops **b :** SCORPER **3 a :** AVOCET **b :** SHOVELER 2

scoop·ful \-p,fu̇l\ *n, pl* **scoopfuls** \-lz\ *or* **scoops·ful** \-ps,fu̇l\ **:** SCOOP 2a

scoop net *n* **:** a shallow dip net on a handle used in fishing; *also* **:** a net for sweeping the bottom of a river

scoor \ˈsku̇(ə)r\ *chiefly Scot var of* SCOUR

¹scoot \ˈsküt, *usu* -üd·+V\ *vb* -ED/-ING/-S [prob. of Scand origin; akin to ON *skjōta* to shoot — more at SHOOT] *vi* **1 a :** to go suddenly and swiftly **:** DART, SCUD ⟨cracked the whip over the mare like a rifle shot and she ~*ed* by —H.B.Altuler⟩ ⟨trucks of one of the evening papers ~*ing* around town to deliver the latest editions —Mollie Panter-Downes⟩ ⟨farm prices usu. ~ up and down much faster than the prices of what the farmer buys —*Time*⟩ ⟨~*ed* up the stairs —Richard Burke⟩ **:** go away in haste **:** DECAMP ⟨took his collections and ~*ed* —N.M.Clark⟩ ⟨~*ed* out of the courtroom like the Devil was after her —Eudora Welty⟩ ⟨~ or you will be late⟩ **b :** to slide suddenly or swiftly ⟨~*ed* down a little in his chair —William Brinkley⟩ ⟨placed one hand on his shoulder; the other on the craft's gunwale, raised his feet and ~*ed* overside —K.M. Dodson⟩ **2** *dial chiefly Brit* **:** to shoot or squirt forth ⟨water ~*s* from a hose⟩ ~ *vt* **1 :** to cause to scoot ⟨~*ing* their shoe toes up their calves to restore the shine —Darrell Berrigan⟩ ⟨~*ed* his chair a bit closer —H.O.Yardley⟩ ⟨~*ed* his glass around in large circles —H.D.Skidmore⟩ **2** *chiefly Scot* **:** SQUIRT ⟨~*ing* each other with the hose —Carson McCullers⟩

²scoot \"\ *n* -s **1** *chiefly Scot* **:** a sudden flow (as of water from a hose) **2 :** an act of scooting ⟨its a quick ~ down the sailboat-filled harbor —Pete Barrett⟩ **3 :** a single logging sled **:** DRAY **4 :** a trapshooting game for four-man teams in which the first releases a target with a handtrap, the second man tries to break the target, the third covers for the second and scores if he breaks the target missed by the second, and a fourth acts as scorekeeper, players rotating positions until 20 targets have been thrown **5** *dial* **:** SCOTER

³scoot \"\ *n* -s [origin unknown] **1 :** a piece of hardwood lumber that is inferior to any recognized grade **2 :** a piece of lumber that is very defective and practically worthless

¹scoot·er \ˈsküd·ə(r), -ütə-\ *n* -s [¹*scoot* + *-er*] **1 :** one that scoots: as **a :** a strongly built sailboat having a flat bottom shod with steel runners and a sharply rising stem for sailing through water or over ice as either is met with **b :** GLIDER 1b **c :** a child's vehicle that consists typically of a narrow footboard mounted between two wheels tandem with an upright handle attached to the front wheel and that is operated by the child placing one foot on the footboard, pushing with the other foot, and steering with the handle **d :** MOTOR SCOOTER **2 :** a plow with a single handle and single shovel used for marking furrows, opening furrows for seed, and breaking up soil between crop rows

scooter 1c

²scooter \"\ *vi* -ED/-ING/-S **:** to go on a scooter esp. with a motor ⟨~*ing* in this country was pretty much started by eggheads, as a hobby or sport —Gene Pavey⟩

³scooter *var of* SCOTER

scoot·er·ist \-ərəst\ *n* -s **:** one that operates a motor scooter

scoot·ers \ˈsküd·ə(r)z\ *or* **scoots** \ˈsküts\ *n pl but sing or pl in constr* **:** the barracuda (*Sphyraena argentea*) of the Pacific coast of No. America

scop \ˈskäp, ˈskōp\ *n* -s [OE; akin to OS *skop* poet, OHG *schof* poet, ON *skop, skaup* mockery, and prob. to OE *scūfan, scēofan* to shove — more at SHOVE] **:** an Old English bard or poet ⟨a long way now from the times of oral epic, ~*s*, and ballad singers —Richard Wilbur⟩

scopa \ˈskōpə\ *n, pl* **sco·pae** \-ō,pē\ *or* **scopas** [NL, fr. L, broom — more at SHAFT] **1 :** a group or arrangement of short stiff hairs on the body surface of an insect that usu. functions like a brush in collecting something (as pollen); *usu* **:** POLLEN BRUSH **2** *pl* **scopas** [It, lit., broom, fr. L] **:** a card game similar to casino

sco·pa·rin \ˈskōpərən\ *n* -s [ISV *scopar-* (fr. NL *scoparius*, specific epithet of *Cytisus scoparius*) + *-in*] **:** the yellow crystalline coloring matter $C_{22}O_{22}O_{11}$ of the flowers of broom (*Cytisus scoparius*)

sco·par·i·us \skōˈpa(a)rēəs\ *n* -ES [NL, fr. *scoparius*, specific epithet of *Cytisus scoparius*, fr. LL, sweeper, fr. L *scopa* broom + *-arius* -ary] **:** the dried tops of the common broom (*Cytisus scoparius*) containing the alkaloid sparteine and formerly used as a diuretic

sco·pate \ˈskō,pāt\ *adj* [L *scopa* broom + E *-ate*] **:** resembling a brush

¹scope \ˈskōp\ *n* -s [It *scopo* aim, goal, purpose, object, fr. L *scopus*, fr. Gk *skopos* watcher, goal, purpose, object; akin to Gk *skopein* to view, contemplate, inspect — more at SPY] **1 :** space or opportunity for free and unhampered motion, activity, intention, thought, or vision **:** BREADTH, COMPREHENSIVENESS ⟨full ~ for the exercise of such ability as I had —R.M.Lovett⟩ ⟨a mind remarkable both for its ~ and its mastery over details —John Buchan⟩ **2 a :** an intention in speaking or writing **:** PURPOSE ⟨the author's ~ or aim⟩ **b :** something aimed at or desired **:** OBJECT, END ⟨making religion the main ~ of his life⟩ **c** *obs* **:** a mark aimed at **:** GOAL ⟨arrows speeding to the ~⟩ **3** *chiefly dial* **:** a tract of land esp. when extensive **4 a :** the general range or extent of cognizance, consideration, activity, or influence ⟨the synopsis is a very brief indication of the ~ of the whole argument —Norman Angell⟩ ⟨the ~ of this view — more than 100 miles in all directions —*Amer. Guide Series: Vt.*⟩ ⟨humility . . . a sense of infinite powers beyond our ~ —M.R.Cohen⟩ **b :** the limited field or subject under consideration **:** the range of the matter being treated **:** the marked off area of relevancy ⟨the period of his public career . . . lies outside the ~ of this book —R.W.Southern⟩ ⟨with the extension of the ~ of government to include a wide array of public services —W.J.Shepard⟩ **c :** length of cable or hawser on which a ship rides ⟨pay out more ~, stand by to make sail —S.E.Morison⟩ **5 :** DOMAIN 7 **6 :** the range of operation of a logical operator **:** the part of a statement in the functional calculus that is governed by a quantifier **syn** see RANGE

²scope \"\ *n* -s [*-scope*] **1 :** any of various instruments for viewing or observing: as **a :** BRONCHOSCOPE **b :** GASTROSCOPE **c :** MICROSCOPE **d :** TELESCOPE **e :** TELESCOPE SIGHT **f :** OSCILLOSCOPE **g :** RADARSCOPE **2 :** HOROSCOPE

-scope \ˌskōp\ *n comb form* -s [NL *-scopium*, fr. Gk *-skopion*, fr. *skopein*] **:** a means (as an instrument) for viewing with the eye or observing in any way ⟨micro*scope*⟩
scope·less \ˈskōpləs\ *adj* **:** having or affording no scope
sco·pel·i·dae \skəˈpeləˌdē\ [NL, fr. *Scopelus*, type genus (fr. Gk *skopelos* lookout place, promontory, fr. *skopein* to view) + *-idae*] *syn of* MYCTOPHIDAE
scophony \ˈskäfənē\ *n* -ES [prob. blend of Gk *skopein* to view and E *-phony*] **:** a television system in which the scanning is accomplished by the use of mechanical and optical devices rather than a scanning disk or electronic methods
scopi- *comb form* [L *scopa* broom — more at SHAFT] **:** brush ⟨*scopi*form⟩
scop·ic \ˈskäpik\ *adj* [Gk *skopein* + E *-ic*] **1 :** VISUAL ⟨a ~ method of illustrating a scientific principle⟩ **2 :** having a wide scope **:** COMPREHENSIVE ⟨a ~ subject as the theory of photography —L.E.Varden⟩
-scop·ic \¦skäpik, -pēk\ *adj comb form* [Gk *skopein* + E *-ic*] **1 :** looking in a (specified) direction ⟨basi*scopic*⟩ **2 :** viewing or observing ⟨ortho*scopic*⟩ ⟨noo*scopic*⟩
scop·i·dae \ˈskäpəˌdē\ *n pl, cap* [NL, fr. *Scopus*, type genus + *-idae*] **:** a family of African wading birds (suborder Ciconiae) consisting of the hammerkop
sco·pine \ˈskōˌpēn, -ˌpən\ *n* -s [ISV *scop*olamine + *-ine*] **:** a crystalline heterocyclic amino alcohol $C_8H_{13}NO_2$ that is obtained by hydrolysis of scopolamine and that is an epoxy derivative of tropine
sco·pi·ous \ˈskōpēəs\ *adj* [1*scope* + *-ious*] **:** having a wide scope **:** SPACIOUS ⟨a theme ~ enough to include a wide variety of characters and incidents —*Times Lit. Supp.*⟩
sco·po·la \ˈskōpələ\ *also* **sco·po·lia** \skəˈpōlēə\ *n* -s [NL *Scopolia*, genus name of *Scopolia carniolica*] **:** the dried rhizome of an herb (*Scopolia carniolica*) of the family Solanaceae that contains the alkaloids scopolamine, atropine, and hyoscyamine and is used as a hypnotic and analgesic
sco·pol·a·mine \skəˈpäləˌmēn, -ˌmən, ˌskōpəˈlamən\ *n* [G *scopolamin*, fr. NL *Scopolia* genus of plants of the family Solanaceae (fr. Giovanni A. *Scopoli* †1788 It. naturalist + NL *-ia*) + G *amin* amine] **:** a poisonous alkaloid $C_{17}H_{21}NO_4$ that is known in three optically isomeric forms of which the syrupy liquid levorotatory isomer occurs in plants of the genus *Scopolia* and other solanaceous plants and is used chiefly in the form of its crystalline hydrobromide as a sedative in connection with morphine or other analgesics in surgery and obstetrics, in the prevention of motion sickness, and as the truth serum in lie detector tests and that is the ester of scopine and tropic acid — called also *hyoscine*
sco·po·le·tin \ˌskōpəˈlētᵊn, skəˈpäləd·ən\ *n* -s [ISV *scopol-* (fr. NL *Scopolia*) + *-et-* + *-in*] **:** a crystalline lactone $C_{10}H_8O$ that is found in various solanaceous plants (as members of the genus *Scopolia* or belladonna) and that is a methyl ether of esculetin
sco·po·line \ˈskōpəˌlēn, -ˌlən\ *n* -s [ISV *scopol*amine + *-ine*] **:** a crystalline heterocyclic amino alcohol $C_8H_{13}NO_2$ formed intramolecularly from scopine esp. with an acid or alkali as catalyst and thus usu. formed by hydrolysis of scopolamine
sco·po·ne \skəˈpōnā\ *n* -s [It, aug. of *scopa* — more at SCOPA] **:** a variety of scopa usu. played by four players in two partnerships
sco·po·phil·ia \ˌskōpəˈfilēə\ *or* **scop·to·phil·ia** \ˌskäptəˈ-\ *n* -s [*scopophilia*, NL, fr. Gk *skopein* to view + NL *-o-* + *-philia; scoptophilia*, NL, fr. (assumed) Gk *skoptos* (verbal of Gk *skopein*) + NL -philia — more at SPY] **:** a desire to look at sexually stimulating scenes esp. as a substitute for actual sexual participation that constitutes a partial or component instinct often sublimated (as in a desire for learning) — **sco·po·phil·i·ac** \¦==¦filēˌak\ *or* **scop·to·phil·i·ac** \¦==¦filēˌak\ *n or adj* — **sco·po·phil·ic** \¦==¦filik\ *or* **scop·to·phil·ic** \¦==¦filik\ *adj*
scop·per·il \ˈskäpərəl\ *n* -s [ME *scoprelle*, *scoperelle*, perh. of Gmc origin; akin to Icel *skoppara*kringla top (toy), *skoppa* to run, jump, spin, OSw *skuppa*, *skoppa* to run, jump; perh. akin to OE *scūfan*, *scēofan* to shove — more at SHOVE] **1** *dial chiefly Eng* **:** a spinning top **2** *dial chiefly Eng* **:** a restless active creature
scops *pl of* SCOP
scops owl \ˈskäps-\ *n* [*scops* fr. NL *Scops*, genus of owls, fr. Gk *skōps*, a kind of owl] **:** a small eared owl of *Otus* or a related genus
scoptical *adj* [Gk *skōptikos* scoptical (fr. *skōptein* to mock — prob. fr. *skōps*, a kind of owl — + *-ikos* -ic) + E *-al*] *obs* **:** JESTING, JEERING, SCOFFING — **scoptically** *adv*
scop·u·la \ˈskäpyələ\ *n, pl* **scopulas** \-ləz\ *or* **scopu·lae** \-yəˌlē\ [NL, fr. LL, small broom, dim. of L *scopa* broom — more at SHAFT] **1 a :** a bushy tuft of hairs **:** SCOPA **b :** a tuft of hairs on the feet and chelicerae of spiders that is used in making the web **2 :** an ornamented rhabdus
scop·u·late \-yələt, -yəˌlāt\ *adj* [NL *scopula* + E *-ate*] **:** having scopulae; *also* **:** SCOPATE
scop·u·lite \ˈskäpyəˌlīt\ *n* -s [LL *scopula* small broom + E *-ite*] **:** a crystallite in the form of a stem with a radiating terminal brush or a number of lateral brushes
sco·pus \ˈskōpəs\ *n, cap* [NL, prob. fr. Gk *skopos* watcher — more at SCOPE] **:** the type genus of Scopidae consisting of the umbrette
-sco·pus \skəpəs\ *n comb form* [NL, fr. Gk *skopos*] **:** one that watches — in generic names
-sco·py \skəpē, -pi\ *n comb form* -ES [Gk *-skopia*, fr. *skopein* to view + *-ia* -y — more at SPY] **:** viewing, examination, scrutiny, observation ⟨fluoro*scopy*⟩ ⟨micro*scopy*⟩ ⟨spectro*scopy*⟩
scorbute *n* [MF *scorbut*, fr. NL *scorbutus*] *obs* **:** SCURVY
scor·bu·tic \(ˈ)skȯ(r)¦byüd·¦ik, -üt¦, ¦ēk\ *also* **scor·bu·ti·cal** \¦əkəl, ¦ēk-\ *adj* [NL *scorbuticus*, fr. *scorbutus* scurvy (prob. of Gmc origin; akin to OE *scurf*, *sceorf* scurf) + L *-icus* -ic, -ical — more at SCURF] **1 :** of or relating to scurvy **:** having the nature of scurvy **:** diseased with scurvy **2** *obs* **:** ANTISCORBUTIC — **scor·bu·ti·cal·ly** \¦ək(ə)lē\ *adv*
scor·bu·ti·gen·ic \skȯ(r)ˈbyüd·əˌjenik\ *adj* [NL *scorbut*us + E *-i-* + *-genic*] **:** causing scurvy ⟨~ diet⟩
scor·bu·tus \skȯ(r)ˈbyüd·əs\ *n* -ES [NL] **:** SCURVY
1**scorch** \ˈskȯ(ə)rch, -ȯ(ə)ch\ *vb* -ED/-ING/-ES [ME *scorchen*, alter. of *scorcnen*, prob. of Scand origin; akin to ON *skorpna* to shrivel up (as from heat); akin to OE *scrimman* to dry up — more at SHRIMP] *vt* **1 :** to burn an exposed surface or portion of typically so as to change color and texture or flavor without consuming ⟨a shirt ~*ed* by a careless laundress⟩ ⟨the bottom of the roast ~*ed* by the cook⟩ **2 a :** to burn and shrivel or parch with or as if with unrelieved intense heat ⟨the long drought had ~*ed* the leaves of the trees —Ellen Glasgow⟩ **b :** to burn, excoriate, or otherwise painfully afflict often with or as if with censure or sarcasm ⟨devils in Dante — tearing, mangling . . . ~*ing* demons —Charles Lamb⟩ ⟨~*ed* the court . . . with his acid portrayals of spendthrift profligates —*Time*⟩ **3 a :** to destroy by or as if by fire **:** BURN **b :** to devastate completely esp. before abandoning to the enemy ⟨~*ing* whatever other facilities there were of military value —*Newsweek*⟩ ⟨~*ed* by two wars in a generation —*U.N. World*⟩ — used in the phrase *scorched earth* esp. of property of possible use to an enemy ⟨will resort to mass demolitions — even to a ~*ed* earth policy —P.W.Thompson⟩ ⟨practiced the ~*ed* earth policy by flooding mines, felling fruit trees —Paul Alpert⟩ **4 :** to dry (a newly molded stereotype matrix) in a scorcher **5 :** to cause (a rubber compound) to scorch ~ *vi* **1 a :** to become scorched ⟨cotton and linens may ~ at high temperatures —*Modern Home Laundering*⟩ **b** *of a rubber compound* **:** to undergo vulcanization prematurely (as during mixing or calendering or on standing) **2 :** to burn its way ⟨the scarlet letter, which forthwith seemed to ~ into Hester's breast, as if it had been red hot —Nathaniel Hawthorne⟩ **3 a :** to ride or drive at great usu. excessive speed ⟨~*ing* off on his bicycle —Anne Parrish⟩ ⟨~*ing* by on a motorcycle —Alan Moorehead⟩ **b :** to travel fast ⟨a missile that could . . . ~ off toward a land target —M.G.Miles⟩ ⟨something ~*es* past your face —Fred Majdalany⟩ **syn** see BURN
2**scorch** \"\ *n* -ES **1 :** a result of scorching **:** a surface burn; *also* **:** heat that scorches **2 :** a browning or scorched appearance of plant tissues that is symptomatic of some diseases or is caused by heat or parasites — called also *scorching;* see BARK SCORCH, LEAF SCORCH **3 :** an act of scorching ⟨a play that is all ~ —*Time*⟩ **4 :** a run at high speed (as in a motor vehicle)
3**scorch** \"\ *vt* [alter. (influenced by 1*scorch*) of 2*score*] *dial chiefly Eng* **:** CUT, SLASH, SCRATCH
scorched \-cht\ *adj* **:** parched or discolored by or as if by scorching
scorch·er \-chə(r)\ *n* -s **1 a :** something very hot ⟨the day was a ~⟩ **b :** a heating device used for drying newly molded stereotype matrices — called also *roaster* **2 :** something withering or caustic ⟨the rebuke was a ~⟩ **3 a :** one that drives or rides at an excessive rate of speed **b :** a stroke or shot imparting great speed to an object (as a ball or puck) **4 :** one that creates a sensation **:** one that is startling
1**scorching** *adj* [fr. pres. part. of 1*scorch*] **1 :** that scorches **:** BURNING ⟨several days of ~ heat —Allison Danzig & Joe King⟩ **2 :** BLISTERING, SCATHING, STINGING, WITHERING ⟨capable of making ~ retorts when provoked —F.L.Paxson⟩ ⟨~ indictment of the foreign policies —Reinhold Niebuhr⟩ ⟨a ~ message to congress blasting the idle rich —W.A.White⟩ — **scorch·ing·ly** *adv*
2**scorching** *adv* **:** to a scorching degree ⟨the day was ~ hot —Winston Churchill⟩
3**scorching** *n* -s [fr. gerund of 1*scorch*] **1 :** an act of one that scorches **2 :** SCORCH 2
scorchy \-chē\ *adj* -ER/-EST **:** increasing the tendency of a rubber compound to scorch ⟨stronger but less ~ accelerators⟩
scor·da·tu·ra \ˌskȯ(r)dəˈtu̇rə\ *n, pl* **scordatu·re** \-u̇rā\ *or* **scordaturas** [It, fr. *scordato* (past part. of *scordare* to be out of tune, fr. L *discordare* to disagree, be out of tune) + *-ura* -ure (fr. L) — more at DISCORD] **:** an unusual tuning of a stringed musical instrument for some special effect
scor·di·um \ˈskȯ(r)dēəm\ *n* -s [NL, alter. of L *scordion*, fr. Gk *skordion*, dim. of *skorodon*, *skordon* garlic; akin to Alb *hurdhë* garlic] *archaic* **:** WATER GERMANDER
1**score** \ˈskō(ə)r, ˈskȯ(ə)r, -ōə, -ȯ(ə)\ *n* -s *see sense 1a* [ME *scor*, fr. ON *skor* notch, tally, twenty; akin to ON *skera* to cut, carve — more at SHEAR] **1 a** *or pl* **score** (1) **:** a sum of twenty **:** TWENTY ⟨more than a ~ of cities⟩ ⟨his paintings have . . . appeared in over a ~ of smaller exhibitions —*Think*⟩ (2) **:** a group of 20 things ⟨a few ~ . . . will be authorized to write and speak —O.T.Mallery⟩ ⟨the flock numbers about two ~⟩ ⟨his years were four ~⟩ (3) **:** a unit of weight esp. for pigs or oxen equal to 20 or 21 pounds (4) *obs* **:** a unit of distance equal to 20 yards **b scores** *pl* **:** a group containing an indefinitely large number ⟨~*s* of lakes⟩ ⟨~*s* of people made homeless by a storm⟩ **2 a :** a line made with or as if with a sharp instrument **:** NOTCH, INCISION, SCRATCH ⟨the ~ should run with the grain whenever possible —*Book Production*⟩ ⟨~*s*, although they do not pass entirely through the skin, are almost as bad as cuts, because they weaken the leather —*Crops in Peace & War*⟩ ⟨a ~ made by a piston on a cylinder wall⟩; *esp* **:** one made as a tally mark **b** (1) **:** a notch (as made in timber) in which another part is fitted (2) **:** the groove cut at the ends and sides of a block to admit the strap **c :** an indented line or partial cut in paper, metal, or other material to aid in folding or tearing **3 a :** a mark used as a starting point or a goal **:** TAW — see CURLING illustration **b :** a mark made on the surface of a pavement by traffic **c :** a mark or line made for the purpose of keeping account **4 a :** an account or reckoning kept by making marks on a tally **b :** ACCOUNT ⟨I keep . . . some sort of log or ~ of what occupies me —Gilbert Ryle⟩ ⟨bade them call at the inn on their way home and drink a pint on his ~ —Adrian Bell⟩ **c :** amount due **:** INDEBTEDNESS ⟨leaving others to pay the ~ —Edith Wharton⟩ **5 :** an obligation or injury kept in mind for requital **:** GRUDGE ⟨took advantage of the meeting to settle old ~*s* —*Amer. Guide Series: La.*⟩ **6 a :** ACCOUNT, REASON, MOTIVE, GROUND ⟨the first airplane was not perfect but it was not chopped up and abandoned on that ~ —H.C.Lodge⟩ ⟨excused himself from the bullring on the ~ of fatigue —Frank Yerby⟩ ⟨his situation was still very desperate; on that ~ he allowed himself no illusions —Rafael Sabatini⟩ **b :** BEHALF, SAKE ⟨ideas on the ~ of feminine loveliness were bounded on all four sides by the golden vision —T.B.Costain⟩ ⟨the droning on that ~ I had to listen to —Learned Hand⟩ **7 a :** the original and entire draft or its transcript of a musical composition or an arrangement with the parts for the different instruments or voices written on staffs one above another — compare REDUCTION, SHORT SCORE ⟨orchestral ~⟩ ⟨piano ~⟩ **b :** a musical composition having parts for different instruments or voices **c :** a complete description of a dance composition in choreographic notation — compare LABAN SYSTEM **8 a :** the number of points gained by contestants in a game or other contest **b :** an account of points made and other specific items in a game or contest; *broadly* **:** total count, SUMMARY ⟨had a ~ of 21 killings —W.J.Ghent⟩ ⟨holds low ~ on reading best sellers —*Current Biog.*⟩ **c :** an act or instance of scoring in a game or contest; *also* **:** a winning point ⟨~*s* are made by carrying or passing the ball over the goal line⟩ **d :** a successful move or stroke **:** HIT ⟨the remark was not intended as a ~ against him⟩ **9 :** a number expressing the degree of success in a psychological or educational test in terms of the amount performed or of the time required or of the difficulty surmounted or of the accuracy and excellence of the performance **10 :** a numerical rating of quality (as of an animal or of butter) that usu. is made on the basis of 100 as a perfect rating and is arrived at by adding numerical values assigned according to some definite scheme to specific significant characteristics (as conformation, condition of coat, aroma) ⟨93 ~ butter⟩ ⟨no animal had a ~ above 80⟩ **11** *slang* **:** a successful theft or its proceeds **12 :** the stark inescapable facts or often the unglossed prospects of a situation ⟨know the ~ on unemployment⟩ ⟨many victims of communism know what the ~ is —*Armed Forces Talk*⟩ — **go off at score 1 a :** to go briskly from the starting mark (as in a walking contest) **b :** to start off briskly **:** proceed without hesitancy or break **2 :** to lose command or control of oneself — **in score :** having all the musical parts arranged and placed one over the other
2**score** \"\ *vb* -ED/-ING/-S [ME *scoren*, fr. ON *skora*, fr. *skor*, n.] *vt* **1 a :** to keep record or account of by or as if by notches on a tally **:** set down **:** RECORD, CHARGE **b :** to enter a record of the indebtedness of — often used with *up* ⟨*scoring* up the customers⟩ **c :** to enumerate in a record **:** COUNT, LIST, RECKON — often used with *up* ⟨men who would observe and ~ up each point and counterpoint —Osbert Sitwell⟩ ⟨asked to ~ a high rating —*Book Production*⟩ ⟨~*s* him right —J.D.Morris⟩ **2 :** to mark with a line ⟨jet planes ~ the heavens with their vapor trails —Phil Stong⟩: as **a** *obs* **:** to indicate by or as if by lines — used with *out* ⟨to ~ out a path⟩ **b :** to mark with significant lines or notches (as in keeping account of something) ⟨to ~ a tally⟩ ⟨pavements . . . were *scored* with chalk marks for hopscotch —Rebecca West⟩ **c :** to cancel by drawing a line through — often used with *off* or *out* ⟨~*s* through a figure that is wrong —*Seven to Eleven*⟩ ⟨he introduced into his reckoning sets of fixed exceptions, amendments on amendments; then he *scored* them all off —Van Wyck Brooks⟩ **3 :** to cut so as to mark with lines, scratches, or notches **:** NOTCH, SCRATCH, FURROW ⟨~ timber⟩ ⟨the brakedrum surface becomes *scored* when it is worn by braking action —*Principles of Automotive Vehicles*⟩ ⟨the flood has *scored* out a deep channel in the middle of the lane —C.S.Jarvis⟩: as **a :** to cut deeply into in more or less parallel lines ⟨~ the flounder diagonally into a diamond pattern nearly to the backbone of the fleshy side —Jan Sebastian⟩ ⟨peels . . . cucumbers, ~*s* them with the tines of a fork —Jane Nickerson⟩ **b :** to abrade in parallel scratches ⟨rock *scored* by a moving glacier⟩ **c :** to crease (as paper or paperboard) so that it will fold easily at a desired line ⟨each form is *scored* without ink in two places across the face to provide a guide and aid for folding —L.B.Gatchell⟩ **d :** to record by cuts or notches — used with *on* or *upon* **4 a :** to lash so as to mark with welts **b :** BERATE, EXCORIATE, SCOLD, CASTIGATE ⟨my predecessors were equally *scored* for expressing personal opinions at variance with the criticism in the magazine —Norman Cousins⟩ ⟨magistrate . . . *scored* the youths, calling them "rough, tough show-offs" —*N.Y. Times*⟩ ⟨much more interesting conversation than the itch to ~ people off —J.C.Powys⟩ **5 a :** to gain (as points or runs in a game) for addition to the score ⟨*scored* a home run⟩ **b :** to make an entry of the score of (a game or contest) **:** keep score in **c :** to have as a value in a game or contest **:** COUNT ⟨a touchdown ~*s* six⟩ **d :** to add to one's score (as in a game or contest) **e :** to cause (a teammate) to make a score ⟨*scored* the man on second⟩ **f :** GAIN, ACHIEVE, WIN ⟨the enemy *scored* a local gain⟩ ⟨~ a victory⟩ ⟨~ a theatrical success⟩ ⟨a reporter *scored* a scoop⟩ ⟨a bomb that ~*s* a direct hit⟩ **6 a :** to determine the merit of **:** GRADE, MARK ⟨~ a test or examination⟩ ⟨~ candidates for a job on the basis of their skill or knowledge⟩ **b :** to determine or judge the score of ⟨butter was *scored* weekly —G.H.Wilster⟩ ⟨dogs were *scored* according to their merits —W.F.Brown b.1903⟩ **7 a :** to orchestrate or arrange (a musical composition) for performance ⟨one refrain takes two and a half hours to ~ and copy —R.R.Bennett⟩ ⟨was originally *scored* for four orchestras —Ralph Hill⟩ **b** (1) **:** to compose a score for (a motion picture) (2) **:** to add music to a motion picture that already has sound effects **8 a :** to bring (as a horse) up to the starting line **b :** to warm up (a trotter or pacer) down the stretch immediately prior to a race ~ *vi* **1** *obs* **:** to run up an account of indebtedness **2 a :** to make marks **b :** to mark lines (as by incision) **c :** CUT **3 :** to keep score in a game or contest **4 :** to make or count a point in or as if in a game or contest **:** TALLY ⟨*scored* in the 7th inning⟩ ⟨a bad throw from the catcher is almost sure to allow the runner to ~ —W.L.Myers⟩ **5 a :** to gain or have the advantage **:** WIN ⟨enjoyed *scoring* over an opponent —Béla Menczer⟩ ⟨nylon also ~*s* over cotton and wool in being resistant to moths —Desmond Reilly⟩ **b :** to make a success ⟨an actor who ~*s* in a play⟩ **c :** RATE ⟨poinsettias have *scored* high, especially at Christmastime —Anne Dorrance⟩ **6 a :** to approach the starting line ready for the start ⟨a horse ~*s* for a race⟩ **b** *of a pack of hounds* **:** to give tongue as a group on finding the scent **7** *slang* **:** to purchase narcotics ⟨told his stories of *scoring* in such places —Clellon Holmes⟩
scoreboard \ˈ=ˌ=\ *n* **:** a large usu. elevated and often electrically operated board for displaying the score of a game or match and sometimes other pertinent information (as playing time)
scorecard \ˈ=ˌ=\ *n* **1 :** a card upon which scores are recorded ⟨a golfer's ~⟩ ⟨the judge's ~ at a dog show⟩ **2 :** a card identifying players or contestants, showing their numbers and giving other information about them (as their positions) ⟨a baseball ~⟩
scored *adj* [fr. past part. of 1*score*] **:** marked with lines or grooves ⟨his face was ~ with laughing wrinkles —Elinor Wylie⟩ ⟨~ cylinders may be caused . . . by dirt in oil —A.L. Dyke⟩ ⟨a drug marketed in ~ tablets⟩
scorekeeper \ˈ=ˌ==\ *n* **:** an official who records the score during the progress of a game or contest
score·less \ˈ=ləs\ *adj* **:** having no score; *specif* **:** involving no points ⟨a game that ended in a ~ tie⟩
score off *vt* **:** to get the better of **:** triumph over (as in an argument) ⟨the sissy who ends by *scoring off* the world which has been making fun of him —Edmund Wilson⟩ ⟨*scoring off* an old opponent⟩
scorepad \ˈ=ˌ=\ *n* **:** a pad of paper printed so that the score of a card or other game may be conveniently recorded
scor·er \ˈskōrə(r), ˈskȯr-\ *n* -s [ME, fr. *scoren* to score + *-er* — more at SCORE] **:** one that scores: as **a :** a logger who marks trees to be felled **b :** an instrument (as a creasing machine or a nib on a woodworking bit) used for scoring **c :** a worker who marks paper for creasing or feeds a creasing machine **d** (1) **:** SCOREKEEPER (2) **:** one that makes a score (as in a game or contest)
scores *pl of* SCORE, *pres 3d sing of* SCORE
sco·ria \ˈskōrēə, ˈskȯr-\ *n, pl* **scori·ae** \-ēˌē\ [ME, fr. L, fr. Gk *skōria*, fr. *skōr* excrement + *-ia* -y — more at SCAT-] **1 a :** the refuse from melting of metals or reduction of ores **:** DROSS, SLAG **b :** a burned clay or clinker deposit characteristic of burned-out coal beds on the western Great Plains **2 :** rough vesicular cindery usu. dark lava developed by the expansion of the enclosed gases in basaltic magma; *also* **:** a piece of such lava
sco·ri·ac \-ēˌak\ *adj* [*scoria* + *-ac* (as in *ammoniac*)] **:** SCORIACEOUS
sco·ri·a·ceous \¦==¦āshəs\ *adj* [*scoria* + *-aceous*] **:** having the nature of scoria ⟨~ lava⟩ ⟨~ rock⟩
sco·ri·fi·ca·tion \ˌskōrəfəˈkāshən, ˌskȯr-\ *n* -s [*scoria* + *-fication*] **:** the act, process, or result of scorifying; *specif* **:** a process in assaying that involves the use of a scorifier and consists either of an oxidizing fusion of the ore or other product with lead and borax to produce a slag and leave the gold and silver in a lead button or of such a fusion of the lead button obtained either as above or by fusion in a crucible to reduce its size or purify it for cupellation
sco·ri·fi·er \ˈskōrəˌfī(ə)r, ˈskȯr-, -īə\ *n* -s **1 :** one that scorifies **2 :** a furnace in which sweepings containing waste gold or silver are burnt preparatory to extracting the gold and silver **3 :** a crucible (as of clay) for scorifying a metal

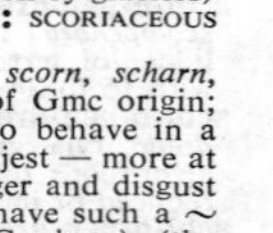

scorifier 3

sco·ri·form \-ˌfȯrm\ *adj* [*scoria* + *form*] **:** having the form of scoria
sco·ri·fy \-ˌfī\ *vt* -ED/-ING/-ES [*scoria* + *-fy*] **:** to reduce to scoria **:** to subject to scorification
scoring *n* -s [fr. gerund of 2*score*] **1 :** the act or process of making a score **2 a :** SCORE ⟨not likely to allow the conductor to alter his ~ —Edward Sackville-West & Desmond Shawe-Taylor⟩ ⟨many pencil-*scorings* against passages he especially hated —H.J.Laski⟩ **b :** SCORES ⟨~ made on rock by glaciers⟩
sco·ri·ous \ˈskōrēəs\ *adj* [*scoria* + *-ous*] **1 :** SCORIACEOUS **2 :** containing scoria
1**scorn** \ˈskȯ(ə)rn, -ȯ(ə)n\ *n* -s [ME *scarn*, *scorn*, *scharn*, *schorn*, fr. OF *escarn*, *escharn*, *escar*, *eschar*, of Gmc origin; akin to OHG *scern* jest, joke, trick, *scerōn* to behave in a rowdy manner, MHG *scherzen* to leap for joy, jest — more at CARDINAL] **1 :** an emotion involving both anger and disgust **:** passionate contempt **:** DISDAIN ⟨most of us have such a ~ and loathing of robbery or forgery —B.N.Cardozo⟩ ⟨the public's attitude toward his work changing from ~ to veneration during his lifetime —R.M.Coates⟩ **2 :** an expression of extreme contempt **:** GIBE, FLOUT, TAUNT **3 :** an object of extreme disdain, contempt, or derision ⟨the unfair fighter was the ~ of the spectators⟩
2**scorn** \"\ *vb* -ED/-ING/-S [ME *scarnen*, *scornen*, *schornen*, fr. OF *escarnir*, *escharnir*, of Gmc origin like *escarn*, *escharn* — more at 1SCORN] *vt* **1** *archaic* **:** to treat with extreme contempt **:** make the object of insult **:** scoff at **:** MOCK, DERIDE **2 a :** to hold in or reject with extreme contempt **:** CONTEMN ⟨if one does not work and contribute to the general welfare, he is ~*ed* as a drone —*Amer. Guide Series: Ariz.*⟩ ⟨~*ed* the committee's report⟩ **b :** to be unwilling because of scorn **:** DISDAIN — used with a following infinitive ⟨accepted advertisements which other publishers ~*ed* to print —W.A.Swanberg⟩ ⟨~*ed* to reply in any way —Arnold Bennett⟩ ⟨textbooks . . . published by business men who do not ~ to be educators as well —V.M. Rogers⟩ ~ *vi* **:** to show contumely or derision **:** act disdainfully **:** SCOFF, MOCK ⟨you have ~*ed* at my gifts —Charles Kingsley⟩ ⟨end all patient love with ribald ~*ing* —Donagh MacDonagh⟩ **syn** see DESPISE
scorn·er \-nə(r)\ *n* -s [ME, fr. *scornen* to scorn + *-er*] **:** one that scorns **:** MOCKER
scorn·ful \-nfəl\ *adj* [ME, fr. *scorn* + *-ful*] **1 :** full of scorn **:** contemptuous, disdainful — often used with *of* ⟨a ~ attitude⟩ ⟨a ~ smile⟩ ⟨~ of the conventions that he esteemed —Ellen Glasgow⟩ **2** *obs* **:** treated with scorn **:** exciting scorn — **scorn·ful·ly** \-lē, -li\ *adv* — **scorn·ful·ness** *n* -ES
scor·o·dite \ˈskȯrəˌdīt, ˈskär-\ *n* -s [G *skorodit*, fr. Gk *skorodon*, *skordon* garlic + G *-it* -ite; fr. its odor when heated — more at SCORDIUM] **:** a leek green or brownish mineral $FeAsO_4.2H_2O$ that is a hydrous ferric arsenate and that is isomorphous with mansfieldite and isostructural and prob. isomorphous with variscite and strengite (hardness 3.5–4, sp. gr. 3.1–3.3)
scor·paena \skȯ(r)ˈpēnə\ *n, cap* [NL, fr. L, a kind of fish, fr. Gk *skorpaina*] **:** the type genus of the family Scorpaenidae
1**scor·pae·nid** \-ēnəd\ *or* **scor·pae·noid** \-ēˌnȯid\ *adj* [*scorpaenid* fr. NL *Scorpaenidae; scorpaenoid* fr. NL *Scorpaenoidea*] **:** of or relating to the Scorpaenidae
2**scorpaenid** \"\ *or* **scorpaenoid** \"\ *n* -s **:** a fish of the family Scorpaenidae
scor·pae·ni·dae \-ēnəˌdē\ *n pl, cap* [NL, fr. *Scorpaena*, type genus + *-idae*] **:** a large family of carnivorous usu. bottom-dwelling marine spiny-finned fishes (suborder Scorpaenoidea)

having a large head with usu. one or more pairs of spiniferous ridges above, wide gill openings, usu. ctenoid scales, a dorsal fin that is typically supported by strong spines which in some forms have poison glands and inflict severe wounds, occurring in all seas but most abundant in the Pacific, and including numerous forms that are used for food — see ROCKFISH, SCORPION FISH

scor·pae·noi·dea \ˌskȯ(r)pēˈnȯidēə\ *n pl, cap* [NL, fr. *Scorpaena* + *-oidea*] **:** a large suborder of Scleroparei comprising the mail-cheeked fishes (as the scorpion fishes and gurnards) — see SCORPAENIDAE

scor·per \ˈskȯrpər\ *n* -s [alter. of ²*scalper*] **:** a graver with a sharpened square or U-shaped working end: as **1** *or* **scau·per** \ˈskȯpə(r)\ **a :** a flat tool used in wood engraving to clear away the spaces between the lines **b :** a gouge used in line engraving **c :** a tool for leveling the insides of barrel staves **2 :** a jeweler's chisel for engraving, cutting, or piercing metal

scor·pi·dae \ˈskȯ(r)pəˌdē\ [NL, irreg. fr. *Scorpis* + *-idae*] *syn of* SCORPIDIDAE

scor·pid·i·dae \skȯ(r)ˈpidəˌdē\ *n pl, cap* [NL, fr. *Scorpid-, Scorpis*, type genus (fr. Gk *skorpid-, skorpis*, a kind of seafish) + *-idae*] **:** a small family of scaly-finned percoid fishes of the Pacific ocean including the half-moon that have a deep compressed body, well-developed teeth, and a single dorsal fin

scor·pio \ˈskȯ(r)pēˌō\ *n* [L, lit., scorpion — more at SCORPION] **1** -s *usu cap* **:** the 8th sign of the zodiac — see SIGN table, ZODIAC illustration **2** *cap* [NL, fr. L, scorpion] **:** a genus of scorpions formerly including all known forms but now restricted to a few obscure African species

¹**scor·pi·oid** \-ˌōid\ *adj* [Gk *skorpioeidēs*, fr. *skorpios* scorpion + *-eidēs* -oid — more at SCORPION] **1 a :** resembling a scorpion **b :** of or relating to the Scorpionida **2 :** having a circinate arrangement of parts — used chiefly of inflorescences

²**scorpioid** \"\ *n* -s **:** SCORPION

scorpioid cyme *n* **:** a cyme in which the axis is curved and the flowers arise two-ranked and on alternate sides of the axis (as in the forget-me-not)

scor·pi·oi·dea \ˌ==ˈȯidēə\ [NL, fr. *Scorpio* + *-oidea*] *syn of* SCORPIONIDA

scor·pi·on \ˈskȯ(r)pēən\ *n* -s [ME *scorpioun*, fr. OF *scorpion*, fr. L *scorpion-, scorpio*, fr. Gk *skorpios*, akin to OE *scearfian* to cut off, scrape, OHG *scarbōn* to cut into small pieces, ON *skarfr* scarf (of a board), *skera* to cut — more at SHEAR] **1 a :** any of numerous arachnids of most warm and tropical regions that constitute the order Scorpionida, that have an elongated body divided into a cephalothorax and a segmented abdomen whose posterior part forms a narrow segmented tail generally carried curled up over the back and carrying a venomous sting at the tip, that has four pairs of walking legs and in front a pair of limbs with large pinchers and a pair of chelicerae, that breathe by lungs, are viviparous and nocturnal, prey esp. on insects and spiders, sometimes enter houses, sometimes become four or five or even eight or more inches long, and that have a severe sting which is rarely fatal to man — see BOOK SCORPION, WHIP SCORPION **b :** any of various lizards: as (1) **:** BLUE-TAILED SKINK (2) **:** PINE LIZARD **c :** SCORPION FISH; *esp* **:** FORTESCUE **d :** a toadfish (*Opsanus tau*) **2 a :** a scourge prob. studded with metal ⟨my father chastised you with whips, but I will chastise you with ~*s* —1 Kings 12:11 (RSV)⟩ **3 :** an ancient military engine for throwing missiles (as stones) **:** CATAPULT, ONAGER **4 :** something that incites to action like the severe sting of a scorpion ⟨the ~*s* of absolute necessity —Arnold Bennett⟩

scorpion bug *n* **:** WATER SCORPION

scor·pi·o·nes \ˌ==ˈōˌnēz\ [NL, fr. pl. of L *scorpion-, scorpio*] *syn of* SCORPIONIDA

scorpion fish *n* **1 :** a fish of the family Scorpaenidae; *esp* **:** one having a venomous spine or spines on the dorsal fin **2 :** the common toadfish (*Opsanus tau*)

scorpion fly *n* **:** an insect of the family Panorpidae; *broadly* **:** any insect of the order Mecoptera

scorpion grass *n* **:** FORGET-ME-NOT 1a

scor·pi·on·ic \ˌskȯ(r)pēˈänik\ *adj* **:** relating to or resembling the scorpion

¹**scor·pi·o·nid** \ˈskȯ(r)pēənəd\ *adj* [NL *Scorpionida*] **:** of or relating to the Scorpionida

²**scorpionid** \"\ *n* -s **:** an arachnid of the order Scorpionida

scor·pi·on·i·da \ˌskȯ(r)pēˈänədə\ *n pl, cap* [NL, fr. *Scorpion-, Scorpio* + *-ida*] **:** an order of Arachnida constituted by the true scorpions

scor·pi·o·nid·ea \ˌskȯ(r)pēəˈnidēə\ [NL, fr. *Scorpion-, Scorpio* + *-idea*] *syn of* SCORPIONIDA

scorpion lobster *n* **:** a slender burrowing crustacean of the subtribe Thalassinidea

scorpion mouse *n* **:** GRASSHOPPER MOUSE

scorpion senna *n* **:** a yellow-flowered shrub (*Coronilla emerus*) of southern Europe having a slender jointed pod that resembles a scorpion's tail

scorpion shell *n* **:** any of numerous tropical marine snails (genus *Lambis*) that as adults have the outer lip of the aperture produced into a series of long curved spines

scorpion spider *n* **:** WHIP SCORPION

scorpion's-tail \ˈ===ˌ=\ *n, pl* **scorpion's-tails :** a plant of the genus *Scorpiurus*

scorpionweed \ˈ===ˌ=\ *n* **:** a plant of the genus *Phacelia*

scorpios *pl of* SCORPIO

scor·pi·u·rus \ˌskȯ(r)pēˈyu̇rəs\ *n, cap* [NL, fr. LL, a kind of heliotrope, fr. L *scorpiuron*, fr. Gk *skorpiouron*, fr. neut. of *skorpiouros* having a tail like that of a scorpion, fr. *skorpios* scorpion + *-ouros* -urous — more at SCORPION] **:** a genus of herbs (family Leguminosae) of the Mediterranean region and the Canary islands having simple leaves, small yellow flowers on naked peduncles, and twisted pods

scorse \ˈskȯ(ə)rs\ *vb* [prob. alter. of ²*corse*] *dial Eng* **:** EXCHANGE, TRADE

scor·za·lite \ˈskȯ(r)zəˌlīt\ *n* -s [Evaristo P. *Scorza* Brazilian mineralogist + E *-lite*] **:** a mineral $FeAl_2(PO_4)_2(OH)_2$ consisting of basic phosphate of iron and aluminum, isomorphous with lazulite

scor·zo·ne·ra \ˌskȯ(r)zəˈnirə\ *n* [NL, fr. Sp *escorzonera* black salsify, fr. Catal *escurçonera*, fr. *escurçó* viper, fr. (assumed) VL *excurtion-, excurtio*, fr. L *ex-* + LL *curtion-, curtio* viper, fr. L *curtus* short + *-ion-, -io* -ion — more at SHEAR] **1** *cap* **:** a large genus of European herbs (family Compositae) having narrow leaves and solitary heads of yellow flowers on long peduncles with plumose pappus and ribbed achenes — see BLACK SALSIFY **2** -s **:** any plant or root of the genus *Scorzonera*

¹**scot** \ˈskät, *usu* -äd·+V\ *n* -s *cap* [ME *Scottes* (pl.) Scotchmen, fr. OE *Scottas* Irishmen, Scotchmen, fr. LL *Scotus, Scottus* Irishman] **1 :** one of a Gaelic people of northern Ireland settling in Scotland about A.D.500 and giving it their name **2 a :** a native or inhabitant of Scotland **b :** one that is of Scotch descent

²**scot** \"\ *n* -s [ME, fr. ON *skot* shot, contribution — more at SHOT] **:** an amount of money assessed or paid

³**scot** \"\ *vt* **scotted; scotted; scotting; scots :** to assess for tax

scot and lot *n* [ME] **1 :** a parish assessment formerly laid on subjects in Great Britain according to their ability to pay **2 :** obligations of all kinds taken as a whole ⟨experienced men of the world know very well that it is best to pay *scot and lot* as they go along —R.W.Emerson⟩

¹**scotch** \ˈskäch\ *vt* -ED/-ING/-ES [ME *scocchen*, prob. fr. AF *escocher* to make an incision, fr. MF *es-* ex- + *coche* notch] **1** *archaic* **:** CUT, GASH, SCORE ⟨he ~*ed* him and notched him like a carbonado —Shak.⟩ **2 :** to injure so as to make temporarily harmless ⟨~*ed* the snake, not killed it —Shak.⟩ ⟨what seemed crushed had only been ~*ed* —*Times Lit. Supp.*⟩ **3 a :** to put a stop to **:** stamp out **:** CRUSH ⟨luckily the mischief was as quickly ~*ed* —Mrs. Humphry Ward⟩ **b :** to end decisively by demonstrating the falsity of ⟨the newspapers ~*ed* reports that four ministers . . . had resigned by publishing a photograph —*N.Y.Times*⟩ ⟨statistics of some accuracy were made available and the depopulation theory was finally ~*ed* —J.H.Plumb⟩

²**scotch** \"\ *n* -ES **1 :** a slight cut **:** SCORE **2 :** one of the lines marked on the ground for hopscotch

³**scotch** \"\ *adj, usu cap* [contr. of ¹*scottish*] **1 a :** of, relating to, or characteristic of Scotland **b :** of, relating to, or characteristic of the inhabitants of Scotland **2 :** of, relating to, or characteristic of the English language of Scotland **3 :** FRUGAL

syn SCOTCH, SCOTTISH, and SCOTS can all apply to what constitutes, belongs to, or derives from the people of Scotland. SCOTCH is most widely used outside Scotland, esp. in the spoken language ⟨the entire *Scotch* people⟩ ⟨the inconvenience of having nothing in England like the *Scotch* one-pound note —J.A.Todd⟩ ⟨a schism in the *Scotch* Church —O.W Holmes †1935⟩ ⟨the overwhelming proportion being English, *Scotch*, or Irish in descent —*Carnegie Mag.*⟩ ⟨a *Scotch* painter⟩ ⟨not all the Scottish names that survive today are truly *Scotch* in origin —H.L.Mencken⟩ SCOTTISH has a more literary, less colloquial flavor and use ⟨the zest, courage, and good humor of the nineteenth-century *Scottish* author are infectious —E.A. Bloom⟩ ⟨she left for Edinburgh the following year to assume the *Scottish* crown —Geoffrey Bruun & H.S.Commager⟩ ⟨the *Scottish* Universities —J.G.Winant⟩ ⟨*Scottish* literature⟩ SCOTS is used in the same way as SCOTTISH ⟨the names of *Scots* and English shipowners —Joseph Conrad⟩ ⟨a *Scots* writer —Howard M. Jones⟩ except that SCOTS is sometimes preferred to SCOTTISH in reference to law and in historical references to money ⟨a pound *Scots*⟩ In Scotland itself SCOTTISH and SCOTS are often preferred to SCOTCH ⟨a delegation of *Scottish* editors —*Scotsman*⟩ ⟨*Scottish* cricket —*Scotsman*⟩ ⟨the *Scots* community in New York —*Scotsman*⟩ ⟨new *Scots* air link —*Scotsman*⟩ but SCOTCH also is used ⟨the signs confirmed my recollection that the *Scotch* Scotch are not ashamed of the word *Scotch* and do not go about protesting that *Scottish* and *Scots* are preferable forms —A.J.Liebling⟩ esp. with regard to the products of Scotland ⟨wool jersey . . . and *Scotch* tweeds are favorite fabrics —*Women's Wear Daily*⟩

⁴**scotch** \"\ *n* -ES *see sense 2* **1** *cap* **:** SCOTS **2** *pl in constr, cap* **:** the people of Scotland **3** *often cap* **a :** SCOTCH WHISKY **b :** a drink of Scotch whisky

⁵**scotch** \"\ *n* -ES [origin unknown] **1 :** a chock placed under a wheel or other curved object to prevent rolling or slipping **2 :** IMPEDIMENT ⟨now there was a ~ in his running with her —D.H.Lawrence⟩

⁶**scotch** \"\ *vb* -ED/-ING/-ES *vi, dial chiefly Eng* **:** to exercise self-control or hesitate before acting ~ *vt* **1 :** to block with a chock to prevent rolling or slipping ⟨~*ed* the back wheels of the wagon with two pieces of wood⟩ **2 :** to put an obstacle in the way of **:** HINDER, THWART ⟨sensible and limited proposals for the reform of spelling and grammar have been ~*ed* —C.P. Barbier⟩ **3 :** to wedge into place ⟨~*ed* a flat stone behind each wheel —E.L.Thomas⟩ ⟨tried to break the slat by ~*ing* it against the wall and hitting it with her foot —H.E.Bates⟩

⁷**scotch** *var of* SCUTCH

Scotch \"\ *trademark* — used for any of numerous adhesive tapes that typically have a tacky coating of a pressure-sensitive adhesive on paper, cloth, or film and can be sealed under slight pressure without heating or moistening: as **a :** a transparent tape with a cellophane or cellulose acetate backing used chiefly for sealing, mending, or attaching **b :** a tape with an impregnated paper backing used as a masking tape (as in painting)

scotch baptist *n, usu cap S&B* [³*scotch*] **:** a member of a Baptist denomination composed chiefly of immigrants from Scotland to northern England uniting with the English Disciples of Christ to form the Churches of Christ

scotch barley *n, usu cap S* **:** HULLED BARLEY

scotch blue *n, often cap S* **:** a dark purplish blue that is slightly stronger and very slightly lighter than homage blue and slightly lighter than national flag blue — called also *infernal blue*

scotch brier *n, usu cap S* **:** any of a race or class of roses developed from the Scotch rose

scotch broom *n, usu cap S* **:** a deciduous erect, spreading, or occas. prostrate broom (*Cytisus scoparius*) that is native to western Europe, is widely cultivated for its bright yellow or sometimes partly red flowers, and has escaped in several areas to become a destructive pest

scotch broth *n, usu cap S* **:** a soup made from beef or mutton and vegetables and thickened with barley

scotch cap *n, usu cap S* **1 :** BONNET 1a **2 :** GLENGARRY

scotch carpet *n, usu cap S* [so called fr. being made largely in Scotland] **:** KIDDERMINSTER

scotch cart *n, usu cap S* **:** a small two-wheeled cart of southern Africa with a detachable or slanting panel at the back

scotch catch *n, usu cap S* **:** SCOTCH SNAP

scotch collie *n, usu cap S* **:** COLLIE 1

scotch comb *n, usu cap S* **:** a steel comb used to dress the coat of an animal

scotch crocus *n, usu cap S* **:** any of various early-flowering white to lilac or white and lilac cultivated crocuses derived from a species (*Crocus biflorus*) that is native from Italy eastward to Persia

scotch deerhound *n, usu cap S* **:** DEERHOUND

scotch douche *n, usu cap S* **:** a douche with alternate spraying of hot and cold water

scotched *past of* SCOTCH

scotch edge *n, usu cap S* **:** an extension of the outside edge of the outsole of a shoe — called also *spade edge*

scotch elm *n, usu cap S* **:** WYCH ELM

¹**scotch·er** \ˈskächə(r)\ *n* -S **:** one that scotches

²**scotcher** *var of* SCUTCHER

scotches *pres 3d sing of* SCOTCH, *pl of* SCOTCH

scotch fiddle *n, usu cap S* [³*scotch*] **:** ITCH

scotch fingering *n, usu cap S* **:** a loose woolen yarn used in knitting

scotch fir *n, usu cap S* **:** Scotch pine or its wood

scotch foursome *n, usu cap S* **:** FOURSOME 2b

scotch gaelic *n, cap S&G* **:** SCOTTISH GAELIC

scotch gale *n, usu cap S* **:** SWEET GALE

scotch grain *or* **scotch grain leather** *n, usu cap S* **:** a heavy leather marked by a coarse pebbled grain, made usu. of chrome-tanned cowhide, and used esp. for men's shoes

scotch grass *n, usu cap S* **:** PARA GRASS

scotch gray *n, often cap S* **:** a grayish yellow green that is yellower and paler than average sage green or palmetto and greener and duller than mermaid

scotch hands *n pl, usu cap S* **:** a pair of small paddles for working butter

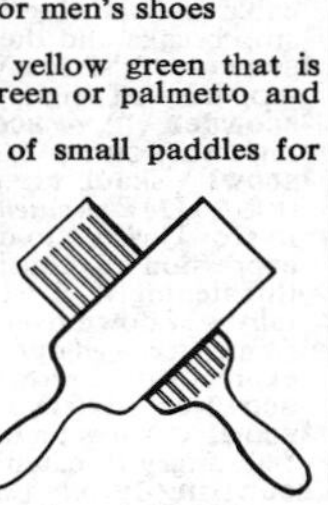
Scotch hands

scotch heath *n, usu cap S* **1 :** SCOTCH HEATHER **2 :** TWISTED HEATH

scotch heather *n, usu cap S* **:** a heather (*Calluna vulgaris*)

scotch-hoppers \ˈ=ˌ==\ *n pl but sing in constr, usu cap S* [²*scotch*] **:** HOPSCOTCH

scotch·i·fy \ˈskächəˌfī\ *vt* -ED/-ING/-ES *often cap* **:** to make Scotch

scotch·i·ness \-chēnəs\ *n* -ES *usu cap* **:** the quality or state of being Scotchy

scotching *n* -s [fr. gerund of ¹*scotch*] **:** the act or process of dressing stone with a pointed instrument (as a pick)

scotch-irish \ˈ=ˈ==\ *adj, usu cap S&I* [³*scotch*] **1 :** of, relating to, or characteristic of the population of northern Ireland that is descended from Scotch settlers **2 :** of, relating to, or characteristic of the people of Scotch descent emigrating from northern Ireland to the U.S. before 1846 or their descendants

scotch kale *n, usu cap S* **:** any of various kales with light green tightly curled leaves

scotch laburnum *n, usu cap S* **:** an ornamental European shrub or tree (*Laburnum alpinum*) having the pod with the upper suture winged

scotch lovage *n, usu cap S* **:** LOVAGE b

scotch·man \ˈskächmən\ *n, pl* **scotchmen 1** *cap* **a :** a man who is a native or inhabitant of Scotland **b :** a man of Scotch descent **2** *sometimes cap* **:** a piece of metal, wood, leather, or canvas used (as over a rope) to prevent chafing **3** *usu cap* **:** a professional golfer **4 :** SCOTSMAN 2

scotch marigold *n, usu cap S* **:** POT MARIGOLD

scotch marriage *n, usu cap S* **:** COMMON-LAW MARRIAGE

scotch mist *n, usu cap S* **1 :** a dense mist mixed with drizzle **2 :** WOOD BEDSTRAW — **scotch-misty** \ˈ=ˈ==\ *adj, usu cap S*

scotch·ness \ˈskächnəs\ *n* -ES *usu cap* **:** the quality or state of being Scotch

scotch nightingale *n, usu cap S* **:** SEDGE WARBLER

scotch pebble *n, usu cap S* **:** a pebble of cryptocrystalline quartz (as agate or chalcedony) found in Scotland and used for ornament after being cut and polished

scotch pine *n, usu cap S* **:** a pine (*Pinus sylvestris*) of northern Europe and Asia with spreading or pendulous branches, short rigid twisted needles, and hard yellow wood that provides valuable timber

scotch rose *n, usu cap S* **:** a thorny Eurasian rose (*Rosa spinosissima*) with small leaflets, pink, white, or yellow flowers, and globose black fruit

scotch snap *n, usu cap S* **:** a rhythmic figure that consists of a sixteenth note on the beat followed by a dotted eighth note

scotch stone *n, usu cap 1st S* **:** AYR STONE

scotch-tape \ˈ=ˈ=\ *vt* **:** to fasten with or apply Scotch tape to ⟨cracked window had been neatly *scotch-taped* —Richard Wormser⟩

scotch terrier *n, usu cap S* **:** SCOTTISH TERRIER

scotch thistle *n, usu cap S* **1 :** any of several European thistles **2** [so called fr. its use as the national emblem of Scotland] **:** COTTON THISTLE

scotch topaz *n, usu cap S* **:** a cairngorm that resembles yellow topaz

scotch verdict *n, usu cap S* **1 :** a verdict of not proven that is allowed by Scottish criminal law in some cases instead of a verdict of not guilty **2 :** an inconclusive decision or pronouncement

scotch whisky *n, usu cap S* **:** whiskey distilled in Scotland in a patent still or a pot still

scotch whist *n, usu cap S* **:** CATCH THE TEN

scotchwoman \ˈ=ˌ==\ *n, pl* **scotchwomen** *cap* **:** a woman of Scotch birth, nationality, or origin

scotch woodcock *n, usu cap S* **:** toast spread with anchovy paste and topped with soft scrambled egg

scotchy \ˈskächē\ *adj* -ER/-EST *usu cap* [³*scotch* + *-y*] **:** having Scotch characteristics

scotch yoke *n, usu cap S* **:** a slotted crosshead used (as in a donkey engine or steam fire engine) in place of a connecting rod

sco·ter \ˈskōd·ə(r), \|tə-\ *also* **scoo·ter** \ˈskü\|\ *n, pl* **scoters** *or* **scoter** *also* **scooters** [origin unknown] **:** any of several sea ducks constituting the genera *Oidemia* and *Melanitta* that inhabit the northern coasts of Europe and No. America and some larger inland waters

scot-free \ˈ=ˈ=\ *adj* [²*scot* + *free*] **1 :** free from obligation to pay (as a tax, tribute, or bill) ⟨a mere handful may be owners of land and be taxed while many may own their own houses and escape *scot-free* —Brian Chapman⟩ **2 :** completely free of harm ⟨some soul walking *scot-free* in the place of torment —Joseph Conrad⟩ **3 :** completely free of penalty ⟨all his clients were guilty and all of them got off *scot-free* —Norman Douglas⟩

sco·tia \ˈskōsh(ē)ə\ *n* -s [L, fr. Gk, *skotia*, darkness, fr. *skotos* darkness; fr. the deep shadow which it casts — more at SHADE] **:** a concave molding used esp. in classical architecture in the bases of columns — see BASE illustration, MOLDING illustration

scot·ic \ˈskäd·ik\ *adj, usu cap* [LL *scoticus, scotticus*, fr. *Scotus, Scottus* Scot + L *-icus* -ic] **:** of or relating to the ancient Scots

scoticism *usu cap, var of* SCOTTICISM

sco·tism \ˈskōˌtizəm\ *n* -s *usu cap* [John Duns *Scotus* †*ab*1308 Scot. scholastic theologian + E *-ism*] **:** the doctrines of the Scholastic Duns Scotus who in his criticism of Thomism proposes a separation of philosophy and theology approaching the conception of twofold truth and is known esp. for his voluntarism, logical realism, and principles of haecceity and the plurality of substantial forms

sco·tist \-ōd·əst\ *n* -s *usu cap* [John Duns *Scotus* + E *-ist*] **:** an adherent of Scotism

sco·tis·tic \skəˈtistik, skōˈ-\ *also* **scotist** *adj, usu cap* **:** of, relating to, or characteristic of Scotism or Scotists

scot·land \ˈskätlənd\ *adj, usu cap* [fr. *Scotland*, northern part of the island of Great Britain] **:** of or from Scotland **:** of the kind or style prevalent in Scotland **:** SCOTCH, SCOTTISH

scoto- *comb form, usu cap* [NL, fr. LL *Scotus* Scot] **1 :** Scotch ⟨*Scoto*-Celtic⟩ **2 :** Scotch and ⟨*Scoto*-Irish⟩

scot·o·din·ia \ˌskäd·əˈdinēə, ˌskōd-·-\ *n* -s [NL, fr. Gk *skotos* darkness + *dinos* whirling; dizziness + NL *-ia* — more at SHADE, DINO-] **:** dizziness with headache and impairment of sight

scot·o·graph \ˈskäd·əˌgraf, ˈskōd·-, -räf\ *n* [Gk *skotos* darkness + E *-graph*] **:** RADIOGRAPH

sco·to·ma \skəˈtōmə, skōˈ-\ *n, pl* **scotomas** \-məz\ *or* **scotomata** \-məd·ə\ [NL *scotomat-, scotoma*, fr. ML, dimness of vision, fr. Gk *skotōmat-, skotōma*, fr. *skotoun* to darken, blind, fr. *skotos* darkness — more at SHADE] **:** a blind or dark spot in the visual field

sco·tom·a·tous \-ˈtäməd·əs\ *adj* [NL *scotomat-, scotoma* + E *-ous*] **:** of, relating to, or affected with scotoma

scotomy *n* -ES [ML *scotomia*, alter. of *scotoma*] *obs* **:** dizziness with dimness of sight

scot·o·pe·lia \ˌskäd·əˈpēlēə, ˌskōd·əˈ- *n, cap* [NL, fr. Gk *skotos* darkness + *pelios* livid; akin to Gk *polios* gray — more at SHADOW, FALLOW] **:** a genus of African owls (family Bubonidae) comprising the fish owls

sco·to·pia \skəˈtōpēə, skōˈ-\ *n* -s [NL, fr. Gk *skotos* darkness + NL *-opia*] **:** vision in dim light with dark-adapted eyes believed to be mediated by the rods of the retina — opposed to *photopia* — **sco·top·ic** \-ˈtäpik\ *adj*

¹**scots** \ˈskäts\ *adj, usu cap* [ME *scottis*, alter. of *scottish*] **:** ³SCOTCH 1, 2 **syn** see SCOTCH

²**scots** \"\ *n* -ES *cap* **:** the English language of Scotland

³**scots** *pl of* SCOT, *pres 3d sing of* SCOT

scots broom *n, usu cap S* **:** SCOTCH BROOM

scots elm *n, usu cap S* **:** WYCH ELM

scots grey *n, usu cap S&G* **:** YELLOW-FEVER MOSQUITO

scots·man \ˈskätsmən\ *n, pl* **scotsmen** *see sense 2* [ME *Scottisman*, fr. *scottis* Scots + *man*] **1** *cap* **:** SCOTCHMAN 1 **2** *or pl* **scotsman :** a brilliantly colored southern African marine percoid food fish (*Polysteganus praeorbitalis*)

scots pine *n, usu cap S* **:** SCOTCH PINE

scots pint *n, usu cap S* **:** an old unit of capacity equivalent to about three imperial pints

scotswoman \ˈ=ˌ==\ *n, pl* **scotswomen** *cap* **:** SCOTCHWOMAN

scott connection *n, usu cap S* [fr. the proper name *Scott*] **:** T CONNECTION

scotted *past of* SCOT

scot·ti·cism \ˈskäd·əˌsizəm, -ätə-,\ *n* -s *usu cap* [LL *scotticus* Scotic + E *-ism*] **1 :** a characteristic feature of Scottish English esp. as contrasted with the standard English of England **2** *or* **scot·i·cism** \"\ **:** predilection for what is Scottish

scot·ti·cize \-ˌsīz\ *vt* -ED/-ING/-S *see -ize in Explan Notes, often cap* [LL *scotticus* + E *-ize*] **1 :** SCOTCHIFY **2 :** to cause to conform with the characteristics of Scottish English ⟨*scotticized* the Latin words without any scruple⟩

scot·tie \ˈskäd·\|ē, -ät\|, \|i\ *n* -s [¹*scot* + *-ie*] **1** *cap* **:** SCOTCHMAN 1 **2** *also* **scot·ty** -ES *often cap* \"\ **:** SCOTTISH TERRIER

scot·ti·fi·ca·tion \ˌskäd·əfəˈkāshən\ *n* -s *often cap* [LL *Scottus* Scot + E *-i-* + *-fication*] **:** the act, action, or product of scotticizing

scot·ti·fy \ˈskäd·əˌfī\ *vt* -ED/-ING/-ES *often cap* [LL *Scottus* Scot + E *-ify*] **:** SCOTTICIZE

scotting *pres part of* SCOT

¹**scot·tish** \ˈskäd·\|ish, -ät\|, \|ēsh\ *adj, usu cap* [ME *scottisc, scottish*, fr. *Scottes* Scotchmen + *-isc, -ish* -ish — more at SCOT] **:** SCOTCH 1, 2 **syn** see SCOTCH

²**scottish** \"\ *n* -ES *cap* **:** SCOTS

scottish asphodel *n, usu cap S* **:** an herb (*Tofieldia palustris*) of the north temperate zone that has a dense raceme of small greenish flowers

scottish blackface *n* **1** *usu cap S&B* **:** a Scottish breed of hardy black-faced long-wooled mutton sheep used esp. in crossbreeding for better meat production **2** *usu cap S & often cap B* **:** a sheep of the Scottish Blackface breed

scottish deerhound *n, usu cap S* **:** DEERHOUND

scottish gaelic *n, cap S&G* **:** the Gaelic language of Scotland — see INDO-EUROPEAN LANGUAGES table

scottish-gaelic *adj, usu cap S&G* [*Scottish Gaelic*] **:** of, relating to, or characteristic of the Gaelic language of Scotland

scot·tish·ly *adv, usu cap* **:** in a Scottish manner
scot·tish·man \'ˌ=·mən\ *n, pl* **scottishmen** *cap* **:** SCOTCHMAN 1
scot·tish·ness *n* -ES *usu cap* **:** SCOTCHNESS
scottish philosophy *n, usu cap S* **:** the natural realism developed by the Scottish school principally in reaction to Berkeleian idealism and Humean skepticism
scottish rite *n, usu cap S & often cap R* **1 :** a ceremonial observed by one of the Masonic systems **2 :** a system or organization that observes the Scottish rite and confers 33 degrees — compare YORK RITE
scottish terrier *n* **1** *usu cap S&T* **:** an old Scottish breed of terrier that has short legs, a large head with small prick ears and a powerful muzzle, a broad deep chest, and a very hard coat of wiry hair about two inches long **2** *usu cap S & often cap T* **:** a dog of the Scottish Terrier breed
scott's spleenwort \'skäts-\ *n, usu cap 1st S* [prob. after D. H. *Scott* †1934 Eng. botanist] **:** EBONY SPLEENWORT
scouch \'skauch\ *var of* SCOOCH
[1]**scoun·drel** \'skaundrəl\ *n* -S [origin unknown] **1 :** a bold selfish man that has very low ethical standards **2 :** RASCAL **syn** see VILLAIN
[2]**scoundrel** \"\ *adj* **:** SCOUNDRELLY ⟨all sorts of coarse artifices and ~ flatteries —W.M.Thackeray⟩
scoun·drel·dom \-ldəm\ *n* -S [[1]*scoundrel* + *-dom*] **:** scoundrels as a class or as a body
scoun·drel·ism \-rəˌlizəm\ *n* -S **:** the character or behavior of a scoundrel
scoun·drel·ly \-rəlē\ *adj* [[1]*scoundrel* + *-ly*] **:** of, relating to, or having the characteristics of a scoundrel ⟨I will none of his ~ money —Thomas Carlyle⟩ ⟨the tyranny of a ~ aristocracy —W.M.Thackeray⟩
scoup \'sküp\ *vi* [ME *scoupen*, of Scand origin; akin to ON *skopa* to take or run — more at SKIP] *chiefly Scot* **:** to run with skips and leaps
[1]**scour** \'skaù(ə)r, -aùə\ *vb* -ED/-ING/-S [ME *scuren, scouren*, prob. of Scand origin; akin to Sw *skura* to rush] *vi* **1 a :** to hurry about in search of something ⟨~*ed* over the hillside for kindling⟩ **b :** to move rapidly **:** RUSH ⟨wild as a hare . . . ~*ed* thro' the heather —Hilary Corke⟩ ⟨~*ed* on my way with more speed than before —George Borrow⟩ **2** *obs* **:** to roister violently through the streets ~ *vt* **1 a :** to move rapidly through (a region or area) ⟨each bishop was a missionary . . . ~*ing* the surrounding districts —G.G.Coulton⟩ **b :** to range usu. rapidly through (a region or area) in search of something ⟨~*ed* the town in vain for more yellow roses —Edith Wharton⟩ ⟨~*ed* Europe in search of cheap labor —*Amer. Guide Series: Mass.*⟩ **c :** to make a thorough examination or search of ⟨~*ed* all the official documents and wrote his novel⟩ **2** *obs* **:** to subject to rough treatment while roistering **syn** see SEEK
[2]**scour** \"\ *n* -S **:** rapid motion **:** RUSH ⟨the white-hot ~ of racing gases —J.N.Leonard⟩
[3]**scour** \"\ *vb* -ED/-ING/-S [ME *scouren*, prob. fr. MD *schuren*, fr. OF *escurer*, fr. LL *excurare* to clean off, fr. L *ex-* + *curare* to care for, cleanse — more at CURE] *vt* **1 a :** to rub hard esp. with a rough material for the purpose of cleansing **:** make clean and bright by friction and washing ⟨~*ed* the pans until they gleamed⟩ **b :** to remove by rubbing hard and washing ⟨~*ed* the stains off with strong soap⟩ **c :** to take the flesh from (a hide) by rubbing **2** *archaic* **:** to make (a region or area) free (as from undesired occupants) **:** RID ⟨~ me this famous realm of enemies —Francis Beaumont & John Fletcher⟩ **3 :** to clean by purging **:** PURGE **4** *obs* **:** BEAT, PUNISH ⟨I will pay the dog, I will ~ him —Henry Fielding⟩ **5 :** to clear (as a pipe or ditch) by removing dirt and debris **6 :** to cleanse from natural impurities or processing liquids; *esp* **:** to cleanse (raw wool) by washing **7** *archaic* **:** to rake with gunfire **8 :** to remove as if by rubbing or cleaning; *esp* **:** to carry off (as by a flood) ⟨the tide enters far up each channel ~*ing* out mud and sand —Charles Lyell⟩ **9 a :** to clear or dig by a powerful current of water ⟨at time of flood the stream may break across and ~ out a channel through the narrow neck between adjacent meanders —C.A.Cotton⟩ **b :** to wear away (as by water, ice, or wind) **:** ERODE ⟨was born of lean land but raised on newer better soils before they were wracked and ~*ed* —Russell Lord⟩ ⟨the tops of hills and level places where there was only a small amount of mantlerock were ~*ed* by the continental glaciers —E.B. Branson & W.A.Tarr⟩ **10 :** to free (grain) from dust, loose bran, and other wastes by blowing while rubbing against a rough surface ~ *vi* **1 :** to perform a process of scouring ⟨~*ed* at rusted spots —*Monsanto Mag.*⟩ **2 :** to suffer from diarrhea or dysentery **:** PURGE **3 a :** to pass through the ground in soil tillage without any soil clinging to the smooth blade of the cultivating implement ⟨this plow ~*s* well⟩ **b :** to become polished when in contact with the soil
[4]**scour** \"\ *n* -S **1 :** a place scoured by running water **2 a :** the scouring action of a current of water or a glacier **b (1) :** an artificial current of water that is used to remove mud or other deposit from the bed of a stream **(2) :** an engineering structure built to produce such a current **3** *Scot* **:** a hearty swig **4 :** DIARRHEA, DYSENTERY — usu. used in pl. but sing. or pl. in constr. **5 :** SCOURING
[1]**scour·er** \-aùrə(r)\ *n* -S [[1]*scour* + *-er*] **:** one that scours: as **a** *archaic* **:** one who roisters violently through the streets **b :** one who ranges far and wide ⟨the relentless boy ~ of Patagonian seas —Bret Harte⟩
[2]**scourer** \"\ *n* -S [[3]*scour* + *-er*] **1 :** one whose work consists of scouring: as **a :** one who cleans drains **b :** one who polishes or cleanses by scouring **c :** one who smooths and stretches hides by scraping **d :** one who scours shoe lasts to shape on an abrasive wheel **2 :** a machine that scours; *specif* **:** a machine that scours wheat
[1]**scourge** \'skərj, 'skəj, 'skəij *sometimes* 'skō(ə)rj *or* 'skȯ(ə)rj *or* -ōəj *or* -ȯ(ə)j\ *n* -S [ME, fr. AF *escorge*, fr. (assumed) OF *escorgiée* to whip, drive out with a whip (whence OF *escorgiée* whip), fr. OF *es-* ex- (fr. L *ex-*) + L *corrigia* shoelace, strap, whip — more at CORRIGIOLA] **1 :** WHIP; *esp* **:** a whip that is used to inflict pain or punishment **2 a :** one that is an instrument of punishment or severe criticism ⟨can safely ignore it and talk as if he had always been the ~ of reaction —R.H. Rovere⟩ **b :** a cause of widespread or great affliction: as **(1) :** a person who brings misery ⟨made himself the special ~ of the region —C.L.Jones⟩ **(2) :** a wasting disease that affects a large area ⟨smallpox finally ceased to be a ~ —*Amer. Guide Series: Mass.*⟩ **(3) :** a large destructive swarm ⟨a ~ of grasshoppers descended and devoured every sprig of vegetation —*Amer. Guide Series: Texas*⟩ **(4) :** a social evil ⟨the ~ of recurrent unemployment —Archibald MacLeish⟩
[2]**scourge** \"\ *vt* -ED/-ING/-S [ME *scourgen*, fr. [1]*scourge*] **1 :** to whip severely **:** LASH, FLOG **2 a :** to punish severely ⟨God had not yet sufficiently *scourged* the city —Daniel Defoe⟩ **b :** to subject to a great affliction **:** DEVASTATE ⟨barbarians *scourged* the land and destroyed all civilization⟩ ⟨dust storms *scourged* the prairie states —*Newsweek*⟩ **c :** to force into a position as if by the blows of a whip ⟨television . . . is going to ~ the phonies out of politics —Stuart Chase⟩ **d :** to subject to severe criticism or satire ⟨~*s* the schools for their low standards⟩ **3** *Scot* **:** to cause (as soil) to become exhausted
scourg·er \-jə(r)\ *n* -S **:** one that scourges; *specif* **:** a public official charged with scourging
scour·ing \'skaùriŋ, -rēŋ\ *n* -S [ME, fr. *scouren* to scour + *-ing*] **1 :** the act or action of one that scours **2 :** the process of cleaning raw stock, yarns, or cloth; *specif* **:** the removal of impurities (as natural grease and foreign substances) from raw wool usu. by a series of washings in soap, alkalies, or chemical solvents **3 a :** material removed by scouring or cleaning **:** REFUSE ⟨the patients in the pump room don't swallow the ~*s* of the bathers —Tobias Smollett⟩ **b :** the lowest rank of society **:** SCUM — usu. used in pl. ⟨the associate of the ~*s* of the jail and hulks —Charles Dickens⟩ **4 :** the erosion of earth or rock by the action of flowing water or of a glacier
scouring barrel *n* **:** TUMBLING BARREL
scouring cinder *n* **:** a basic slag that is produced in an iron blast furnace, is rich in ferrous oxide, and attacks the furnace lining by taking silica from it
scouring rush *n* **:** a plant of the order Equisetales; *esp* **:** a widely distributed plant (*Equisetum hyemale*) with strongly siliceous stems formerly used for scouring utensils
scours *pres 3d sing of* SCOUR, *pl of* SCOUR
scourway \'ˌ=ˌ=\ *n* [[3]*scour* + *way*] **:** a channel formed by a strong current; *esp* **:** one of the channels of temporary streams associated with margins of Pleistocene ice sheets
scouse \'skaùs\ *n* -S [by shortening] **:** LOBSCOUSE
[1]**scout** \'skaùt, *usu* -aùd.+V\ *vb* -ED/-ING/-S [ME *scouten*, fr. MF *escouter* to listen, attend to, fr. OF *ascouter*, fr. L *auscultare* to listen — more at AUSCULTATION] *vi* **1 :** to explore an area to obtain information (as about an enemy) ⟨~ far and wide into the realm of night —John Milton⟩ **2 a :** to make a search ⟨descended into the basement to ~ around for available lumber —H.A.Overstreet⟩ ⟨began to ~ for a better way to do this —*Linotype News*⟩ **b :** to act as an athletic scout ⟨the jobs of coaching the freshman football team and ~*ing* for the varsity team —*Current Biog.*⟩ **3** *archaic* **:** to act as a fielder in cricket ~ *vt* **1 a :** to observe in order to obtain information ⟨rode back through the little basin once more carefully ~*ing* the cabin —P.E.Lehman⟩ **b :** to observe (as an athlete or an actor) in order to evaluate ⟨whispered phony rumors to the cast telling them that producers were out front to ~ them —June Allyson⟩ **2 :** to explore in order to obtain information **:** RECONNOITER ⟨had his dragoons to ~ the territory ahead of him —F.V.W.Mason⟩ **3 :** to find by making a search ⟨launched the artists he had ~*ed*⟩ ⟨~*s* his own material —Roger Angell⟩ ⟨could ~ up clients and talk up lawsuits —Jackson Burgess⟩
[2]**scout** \"\ *n* -S [MF *escoute* act of listening, listener, sentry, fr. *escouter* to listen] **1 a :** the act of scouting ⟨set myself upon the ~ as often as possible —Daniel Defoe⟩ **b :** a scouting expedition **:** RECONNAISSANCE ⟨set out on foot for a week's rapid ~ in the hope of finding just the right place for a permanent camp —D.C.Worcester⟩ **2 a :** one sent out to obtain and bring back information (as about the position and movements of an enemy) **b (1) :** WATCHMAN, LOOKOUT **(2)** *archaic* **:** SPY, SNEAK **c** *archaic* **:** a reconnoitering party **d :** one employed by a petroleum company to obtain information about prospective oil well locations and operations **3 a :** a ship sent out in war to reconnoiter and obtain information about the position, movements, and strength of the enemy **b :** AIR SCOUT **1 4 :** a servant to a student at Oxford University **5 :** a person whose occupation is searching for something rare or difficult to find ⟨the very prince of ~*s* for searching blind alleys, cellars, and stalls for rare volumes —Sir Walter Scott⟩ **6** *archaic* **a :** a fielder in cricket **b :** a boy who chases and returns hit balls in baseball batting practice **7 a :** BOY SCOUT **b :** GIRL SCOUT **8 :** FELLOW, GUY — usu. used in the phrase *good scout* **9 a (1) :** a person sent out to secure firsthand information about the style of play, tactics, and strength of a rival in sports **(2) :** a person sent out by a professional club or by a college to obtain information about players by watching them in action with a view to making recommendations about the acquisition of players **b :** a person sent out to search for talented newcomers to a profession ⟨a ~ for the motion-picture industry⟩
[3]**scout** \"\ *n* -S [ME, fr. MD *schute*; akin to ON *skūta* small ship, OE *scēotan* to shoot — more at SHOOT] **:** SCHUYT
[4]**scout** \"\ *n* -S [origin unknown] **1 :** GUILLEMOT **2 :** RAZORBILL
[5]**scout** \"\ *vb* -ED/-ING/-S [of Scand origin; akin to ON *skūta*, *skūti* taunt — more at SHOUT] *vt* **1 :** to make fun of **:** MOCK, DERIDE ⟨~*ed* the stories as he told them⟩ **2 :** to reject scornfully **:** dismiss as absurd ⟨economists still ~ the idea that the new wave of price hikes spells inflation —*Newsweek*⟩ ~ *vi* **:** SCOFF — usu. used with *at* ⟨~*ed* at the greenness of the cit who would build his sole piazza to the north —Herman Melville⟩ **syn** see DESPISE
scout car *n* [[1]*scout*] **1 :** a fast armored military reconnaissance vehicle with a four-wheel drive and an open top **2 :** a police patrol car
scoutcraft \'ˌ=ˌ=\ *n* [[2]*scout* + *craft*] **:** the craft, skill, or practice of a scout
scout·er \'skaùd·ə(r), -aùtə-\ *n* -S **1 :** one that scouts **2 :** a member of the Boy Scouts of America over 18 years of age
scouth \'sküth\ *n* [origin unknown] **1** *Scot* **:** ROOM, RANGE, SCOPE **2** *Scot* **:** PLENTY
scou·ther \'sküthər\ *n* [origin unknown] **1** *dial Scot* **:** a light shower **2** *dial Scot* **:** a light fall of snow
scouting *n* -S [in sense 1 fr. *gerund of* [1]*scout;* in other senses prob. fr. [2]*scout* + *-ing*] **1 :** the action of one that scouts **2 :** the organization, program, activities, and leadership of the various worldwide Boy Scout and Girl Scout movements **3 :** SCOUTCRAFT
scout·ing·ly *adv* [*scouting* (fr. pres. part. of [5]*scout*) + *-ly*] **:** in a scornful manner
scouting plane *n* [*scouting* (fr. pres. part. of [1]*scout*) + *plane*] **:** AIR SCOUT
scoutmaster \'ˌ=ˌ=ˌ=\ *n* [[2]*scout* + *master*] **:** the leader of a band of scouts; *specif* **:** the adult leader of a troop of boy scouts
scouts *pres 3d sing of* SCOUT, *pl of* SCOUT
scove \'skōv\ *vt* -ED/-ING/-S [prob. of Scand origin; akin to ON *skōf* crust on the bottom of a pan, *skafa* to scrape — more at SHAVE] **:** to cover (the outside exposed surfaces of bricks in a kiln) with a mask of clay in order to save heat
scove kiln *n* **:** a kiln in which green bricks are stacked, enclosed with burned bricks that are then daubed with clay to reduce the loss of heat, and burned
scov·y \'skōvē\ *adj* [perh. fr. *scove* + *-y*] *dial Eng* **:** BLOTCHY, SMEARED
[1]**scow** \'skaù\ *n* -S [D *schouw*, fr. MD *schouwe, schoude;* akin to OHG *scalta* cutoff pole, punt pole, *scaltan* to push, shove off, ON *skālda* pole, boat, and prob. to OE *scild, sceld* shield — more at SHIELD] **1 :** a large flat-bottomed boat with broad square ends that is used chiefly for transporting sand, gravel, or refuse **2 :** a sailboat of very light draft, broad beam, blunt bow, and long overhangs that is used chiefly for racing
[2]**scow** \"\ *vt* -ED/-ING/-S **:** to transport in a scow
[3]**scow** \"\ *vt* -ED/-ING/-S [origin unknown] **:** to fasten (an anchor) by the crown to the end of a cable with a stop on the cable and the ring in such a way that if the anchor fouls the stop breaks and the anchor can be lifted clear by the crown
[1]**scow·der** \'skōdər\ *or* **scou·ther** *or* **scow·ther** \-ōthər\ *vb* -ED/-ING/-S [origin unknown] *chiefly Scot* **:** SCORCH
[2]**scowder** \"\ *or* **scouther** \"\ *n, chiefly Scot* **:** a slight burning **:** SCORCHING
[1]**scowl** \'skaùl, *esp before pause or consonant* -aùəl\ *vb* -ED/-ING/-S [ME *skoulen*, prob. of Scand origin; akin to Dan *skule* to scowl] *vi* **1 :** to draw down the forehead and make a face in expression of considerable displeasure **:** frown angrily and threateningly **2 :** to exhibit a threatening aspect ⟨the mountain ~*ed* down over the valley⟩ **3 :** to express itself in a scowl ⟨a menace ~*ed* upon the brow —Washington Irving⟩ ~ *vt* **:** to express with a scowl ⟨~*ed* his disappointment at his father⟩ — **scowl·er** \-lə(r)\ *n* -S
[2]**scowl** \"\ *n* -S **:** a facial expression of considerable displeasure **:** an angry threatening frown
scowl·ing·ly *adv* [*scowling* (fr. pres. part. of [1]*scowl*) + *-ly*] **:** with a scowl
scow·man \'skaùmən\ *n, pl* **scowmen** [[1]*scow* + *man*] **:** one who works on a scow
scp *abbr* **1** scrip **2** script
SCP *abbr, often not cap* spherical candlepower
scr *abbr* **1** screen **2** screw; screwed **3** scrip **4** script **5** scruple
SCR *abbr* senior common room
scrab \'skrab\ *vb* **scrabbed; scrabbed; scrabbing; scrabs** [perh. fr. D *schrabben*, fr. MD] **:** SCRATCH
[1]**scrab·ble** \'skrabəl\ *vb* **scrabbled; scrabbled; scrabbling** \-b(ə)liŋ\ **scrabbles** [D *schrabbelen* to scratch, paw the ground, fr. MD, freq. of *schrabben* to scratch, perh. alter. of *schrapen* to scrape — more at SCRAPE] *vi* **1 :** SCRAWL, SCRIBBLE ⟨*scrabbled* on the doors of the gate —1 Sam 21:13 (AV)⟩ **2 a :** to scratch or claw about clumsily or frantically ⟨fell *scrabbling* in the dirt . . . crying "have mercy" —Rudyard Kipling⟩ **b :** to grope or search hastily or blindly ⟨began to ~ in her handbag for a handkerchief⟩ **3 a :** to struggle for a foothold **:** SCRAMBLE, CLAMBER ⟨six mules, by hard *scrabbling*, managed to pull the car out of the river —F.B.Gipson⟩ **b :** to struggle by or as if by scraping or scratching ⟨~ for a living on a mountain farm⟩ ~ *vt* **1 :** to gather or make hastily by clutching or scraping ⟨*scrabbled* up a supper out of leftovers⟩ ⟨*scrabbled* a living as a part-time teacher and mechanic —*Time*⟩ **2 :** to make scratching movements on ⟨hens *scrabbling* the muddy cobbles —Dylan Thomas⟩ or with ⟨heard the dog *scrabbling* his nails on the door⟩ **3 :** to mark with irregular lines or letters **:** SCRIBBLE
[2]**scrabble** \"\ *n* -S **1 :** something scribbled or scrawled **:** SCRIBBLE **2 :** a repeated scratching or clawing ⟨a ~ of squirrels on the roof⟩ **3 :** SCRAMBLE ⟨a ~ for tickets to the game⟩ ⟨a mad ~ up the cliff⟩
Scrabble \"\ *trademark* — used for a board game in which players take turns placing letter tiles each with a count value on squares some of which are marked for extra count to form words with as high a count as possible
scrab·bler \-b(ə)lə(r)\ *n* -S **:** one that scrabbles
scrab·bly \-lē\ *adj* **1 :** SCRATCHY, RASPY ⟨a ~ little scratching sound came out of her throat —Alma Stone⟩ **2 :** SPARSE, SCRUBBY ⟨owned a ~ potato patch in Maine —Bennett Cerf⟩
scrabe \'skrāb\ *or* **scra·ber** \-bə(r)\ *n* -S [Dan & Faeroese; Dan *skrabe*, fr. Faeroese *skrāpur;* prob. akin to ON *skrapa* to scrape — more at SCRAPE] **1 :** MANX SHEARWATER **2 :** BLACK GUILLEMOT
[1]**scrae** \'skrā\ *n* -S [prob. of Scand origin; akin to ON *skrā* dry skin, scroll; akin to OHG *scraz, screz* goblin, ON *skratti* monster, wizard, Lith *skręsti* to become covered with a dry crust] **1** *Scot* **:** an old worn-out shoe **2** *Scot* **:** a thin wizened person
[2]**scrae** \"\ *dial var of* SCREE
scraf·fle \'skrafəl\ *vb* -ED/-ING/-S [perh. alter. of [1]*scrabble*] *dial Eng* **:** SCRAMBLE
[1]**scrag** \'skrag, -raa(ə)g, -raig\ *n* -S [perh. alter. of [2]*crag*] **1 a :** a rawboned or scrawny person or animal **b** *or* **scrag end :** the lean end of a neck of mutton or veal **c :** NECK **2** *Brit* **:** a rough crooked tree or branch **3** *or* **scrag whale :** any of various small whales with no dorsal fin but with protuberances on the dorsal ridge near the tail usu. regarded as young or abnormal examples of the right whale
[2]**scrag** \"\ *vt* **scragged; scragged; scragging; scrags** **1 a :** to execute by hanging or garroting **b :** to wring the neck of ⟨~ a turkey⟩ **2 a :** to seize roughly by the neck **:** CHOKE, MANHANDLE ⟨*scragged* by the angry mob⟩ ⟨before they *scragged* me and trussed me up —Rose Macaulay⟩ **b :** KILL, MURDER **3 :** to bend (as spring steel) for testing
[1]**scragged** *adj* [perh. alter. of *cragged*] *obs* **:** ROUGH, RUGGED
[2]**scrag·ged** \-gəd\ *adj* [[1]*scrag* + *-ed*] **:** LEAN, SCRAWNY ⟨~ neck⟩ — **scrag·ged·ly** *adv* — **scrag·ged·ness** *n* -ES
scrag·ger \-gə(r)\ *n* -S **:** one that scrags; *esp* **:** HANGMAN
scrag·gi·ness \-gēnəs, -gin-\ *n* -ES **:** the quality of being scraggy
scrag·gle \'skragəl, -raig-\ *n* -S [prob. back-formation fr. *scraggled, scraggling, scraggly*] **:** sparse or ragged growth ⟨~*s* of grass⟩ ⟨~ of fresh beard —Conrad Richter⟩
scrag·gled \-ld\ *adj* [fr. *scraggling*, after such pairs as E *dangling* (pres. part. of [1]*dangle*): *dangled* (past part. of [1]*dangle*)] **:** SCRAGGLY
scrag·gling \-g(ə)liŋ\ *adj* [[1]*scrag* + *-le* + *-ing*] **:** SCRAGGLY
scrag·gly \-lē, -li\ *adj* [*scraggl-* (as in *scraggling*) + *-y*] **:** of rough or irregular outline **:** RAGGED, UNKEMPT ⟨~ little path to his door —R.M.Coates⟩ **:** of sparse growth **:** STRAGGLY ⟨~ beard⟩ ⟨~, frost-heaved lawn —Roger Angell⟩ ⟨two years of ~ border warfare —A.J.Liebling⟩
scrag·gy \'skragē, -raag-, -raig-, -gi\ *adj* -ER/-EST [[1]*scrag* + *-y*] **1 :** rough with irregular points **:** RUGGED, JAGGED, KNOTTED ⟨~ cliffs⟩ **2 :** lean and thin in body **:** BONY, MEAGER, SCRAWNY ⟨his sinewy, ~ neck —Sir Walter Scott⟩
scraich \'skrāk\ *Scot var of* SCREECH
[1]**scram** \'skram\ *vt* **scrammed; scrammed; scramming; scrams** [ME *-skramen*] *dial chiefly Eng* **:** BENUMB, PARALYZE
[2]**scram** \"\ *adj, dial Eng* **:** WITHERED ⟨~ hand⟩
[3]**scram** \"\ *dial Eng var of* CRAM
[4]**scram** \'skram, -aa(ə)m\ *vi* **scrammed; scrammed; scramming; scrams** [short for [1]*scramble*] **:** to go away at once **:** get out **:** run away ⟨you're not wanted here, so ~⟩
[5]**scram** \"\ *n* -S **:** a sudden or emergency shutting down of a nuclear reactor ⟨leaped for the ~ button⟩
scram·a·sax \'skramәˌsaks\ *n* -ES [LL *scramasaxus*, fr. (assumed) OFrk *skramasax*, fr. *skrama-* (akin to MHG *schram* gash) + *sax* knife (akin to OE *seax* knife, short sword) — more at CREAM, SAX] **:** a large knife used by the early Saxons and Franks as a weapon or hunting knife
[1]**scram·ble** \'skrambəl, -aam-\ *vb* **scrambled; scrambled; scrambling** \-b(ə)liŋ\ **scrambles** [perh. alter. of [1]*scrabble*] *vi* **1 a :** to move or climb hastily on all fours ⟨~ over rocks⟩ ⟨~ up a steep bank⟩ **b :** to move with the urgency of or as if of anxiety or panic ⟨*scrambled* into his clothes⟩ ⟨*scrambled* to his feet⟩ **2 a :** to struggle eagerly with others for something on the ground ⟨~ for coins⟩ **b :** to struggle or strive unceremoniously for possession of something ⟨~ for front seats⟩ ⟨all the networks *scrambled* gleefully for the film —*Newsweek*⟩ **c :** to get or gather something with difficulty or in irregular ways ⟨~ for a living⟩ ⟨had to do considerable *scrambling* to get up the tax money —*Newsweek*⟩ **3 a :** to spread or grow irregularly **:** SPRAWL, RAMBLE, STRAGGLE ⟨*scrambling* frontier town⟩ **b** *of a plant* **:** to climb upon or over a support — distinguished from *twine* **4** *of an air squadron* **:** to take off with all speed at the reported approach of hostile or unidentified aircraft ~ *vt* **1 :** to collect by scrambling — used with *up* or *together* ⟨~ up a hasty dinner⟩ **2 :** to scale or traverse by scrambling ⟨~ a cliff⟩ **3 a :** to toss or mix together in confusion **:** throw into disorder **:** JUMBLE ⟨bad weather *scrambled* the air schedules⟩ ⟨trying to collect his *scrambled* wits⟩ ⟨~ the pages of a manuscript⟩ **b :** to prepare (eggs) by stirring during frying **c :** to make (a telephonic or radio message) unintelligible to interceptors by disarranging the frequencies of the transmission **d :** to effect an interdependent combination of (government-owned and privately owned industrial property) ⟨shipyard facilities have been *scrambled* through government building on private land⟩ **4 :** to cause or order (a fighter-interceptor group) to take off quickly in response to an alert
[2]**scramble** \"\ *n* -S **1 :** an act of moving or climbing on all fours ⟨near the top of the hill the climb became a ~⟩ **2 a :** a jostling and pushing for possession ⟨a ~ for places at the rail⟩ **b :** an eager and unceremonious or unscrupulous struggle for possession ⟨unseemly ~ for invitations⟩ ⟨a ~ for scarce raw materials⟩ ⟨the ~ for Africa⟩ **c :** a disorderly or confused progress, race, contest, or proceeding ⟨careful to keep the rapid finale of the symphony from becoming a ~⟩ **3 :** a disorderly or jumbled mass ⟨a ~ of tents and huts spread out all over the rocks —*Skyways*⟩ ⟨his plot, which is an improbable ~ of killings —H.A.L.Craig⟩ ⟨when you get your wits working on that crazy ~ of letters . . . sense appears in nonsense —*Cryptogram Bk.*⟩ **4 a** *chiefly Brit* **:** an engagement with enemy aircraft **:** DOGFIGHT **b :** an emergency takeoff of fighter-interceptor airplanes in the shortest possible time
scrambled eggs *n pl* **1 a :** eggs whose whites and yolks are stirred together while cooking **b :** eggs beaten slightly usu. with a little milk and stirred while cooking **2 a :** embroidery worn on the cap visors of military officers of the rank of colonel or above or commander or above **b :** officers having such rank
scrambled mitchell *n, usu cap M* [*scrambled* (past part. of [1]*scramble*) + *mitchell* (as in *Mitchell movement*)] **:** a Mitchell movement in which the north-south and east-west pairs exchange compass directions halfway through a bridge game
scramble net *n* **:** a rope net hung over the side of ship for men to climb up or down
scram·bler \-b(ə)lə(r)\ *n* -S **:** one that scrambles: as **a :** a plant that scrambles with or without hooks **b :** a device that disarranges the elements of telephone, teletype, facsimile, or television transmissions in order to make them unintelligible to interception
scram·bly \-lē\ *adj* **:** IRREGULAR, HAPHAZARD
scran \'skran\ *n* -S [origin unknown] **:** scraps of food **:** LEFTOVERS; *also* **:** GRUB, PROVISIONS
scran bag *n* **1 :** a bag for leftover food ⟨a beggar's *scran bag*⟩ **2 :** a receptacle for articles found lying about on a ship
scranch \'skranch\ *archaic var of* SCRAUNCH
scran·nel \'skranᵊl\ *adj* [origin unknown] **1 :** thin and grating on the ears **:** UNMELODIOUS ⟨their lean and flashy songs grate on their ~ pipes of wretched straw —John Milton⟩ **2** *chiefly dial* **:** POOR ⟨a ~ crop of winter wheat —Adrian Bell⟩
scran·ton \'skrantᵊn, -aan-\ *adj, usu cap* [*Scranton*, city in northeast Pennsylvania] **:** of or from the city of Scranton, Pa. ⟨a *Scranton* textile mill⟩ **:** of the kind or style prevalent in Scranton

scran·to·ni·an \skran·ˈtōnēən\ *n* -s *cap* [*Scranton* + E *-an*] **:** a native or resident of Scranton, Pennsylvania

¹scrap \ˈskrap\ *n* -s [ME, fr. ON *skrap* scraps, trifles; akin to ON *skrapa* to scrape] **1 scraps** *pl* **:** fragments of discarded or leftover food ⟨fed the dog on ~*s*⟩ **2 a :** a small detached piece **:** BIT ⟨~ of paper⟩ **b :** a fragment of something written or printed **:** a brief excerpt ⟨read ~*s* of a letter⟩ **:** a picture cut out or detached from a book or magazine or newspaper for saving in a scrapbook **c :** the least piece ⟨not a ~ of evidence for it⟩ **3 scraps** *pl* **:** the crisp substance that remains after trying out animal fat (as of a whale or fish) **:** CRACKLINGS ⟨pork ~*s*⟩ **4 a :** small pieces, cuttings, or chips of stock removed in the process of making any product **b :** manufactured articles or parts rejected for imperfection or discarded because of excessive wear or lack of demand and useful only as raw material for reprocessing ⟨metal ~⟩ ⟨rubber ~⟩ **c :** CULLET **5 :** coarsely ground animal waste used as a fertilizer or feed ⟨fish ~⟩ ⟨meat ~⟩ **6 a :** a by-product of the handling of tobacco consisting of loose tangled pieces of leaves, floor sweepings, but no stems **b scraps** *pl* **:** coarsely broken or cut tobacco used for chewing and smoking

²scrap \"\ *vt* **scrapped; scrapped; scrapping; scraps 1 :** to make into scrap **:** dispose of as scrap often for salvage ⟨~ a battleship⟩ **2 :** to abandon or get rid of as no longer of enough worth, merit, use, or effectiveness to retain ⟨by the year 1500 Western civilization was already adapting or trying to ~ its medieval heritage —Stringfellow Barr⟩ **syn** see DISCARD

³scrap \"\ *adj* **1 :** being in the form of scraps or fragments **:** valuable only as raw material ⟨~ metal⟩ **2 :** made up of odds and ends **:** consisting of scraps ⟨~ dinner⟩

⁴scrap \"\ *n* -s [origin unknown] **:** FIGHT, QUARREL ⟨got into a ~ in a barroom⟩ **:** PRIZEFIGHT ⟨the smaller fighter put up a good ~⟩ **syn** see BRAWL

⁵scrap \"\ *vi* **scrapped; scrapped; scrapping; scraps :** SQUABBLE, QUARREL ⟨continually *scrapping* with her sister⟩ **:** FIGHT

scrap basket *n* **:** WASTEBASKET

scrapbook \ˈ=,=\ *n* **1 :** a blank book in which miscellaneous items (as newspaper clippings or pictures) may be pasted or inserted **2 :** a book of miscellaneous contents

¹scrape \ˈskrāp\ *vb* -ED/-ING/-S [ME *scrapen* to scrape, erase, fr. ON *skrapa* to scrape; akin to OE *scrapian* to scrape, MD *schrapen* to scrape, MHG *schreffen* to scratch, L *scrobis* trench, Russ *skorb'* sorrow, grief, Gk *keirein* to cut — more at SHEAR] *vt* **1 :** ERASE, EXPUNGE ⟨~ out a word⟩ **2** *obs* **:** to scratch or dig with the nails **3 a :** to remove (adhering or excrescent matter) from a surface by usu. repeated strokes of an edged instrument drawn or pushed firmly across nearly at right angles to the surface ⟨~ paint off a chair⟩ ⟨~ scales off a fish⟩ ⟨~ mud off shoes⟩ **b** (1) **:** to make (a surface) smooth or clean with strokes of an edged instrument or an abrasive — often used with *down* ⟨*scraped* down and refinished a pine chest⟩ (2) **:** to draw a road grader over **4 a :** to grate harshly over or against ⟨the keel *scraped* the stony bottom⟩ **b :** to damage or injure the surface of by sliding contact with a rough surface ⟨*scraped* his knee on the pavement⟩ ⟨*scraped* a fender in a near collision⟩ **c :** to draw roughly or noisily over a surface ⟨stop *scraping* your feet⟩ ⟨broke the silence by *scraping* a chair on the floor⟩ **5 :** to collect by or as if by scraping **:** gather in small portions by laborious effort — used with *up* or *together* ⟨~ up money for the rent⟩ **6 :** to produce (an engraving) by scraping the previously prepared surface of the plate — compare MEZZOTINT **7 :** to prepare (raw pelts) by removing the flesh and fat and breaking or loosening the fibers to make more flexible by rubbing with a dull-edged instrument — compare FLESH **8 :** to collect scrape from (trees) ~ *vi* **1** *obs* **:** SCRATCH **2 :** to move in sliding contact with a rough surface ⟨*scraped* against the gateposts⟩ **3 :** to accumulate money by small economies ⟨*scraping* and saving to educate their children⟩ **4 :** to bow a stringed instrument; *esp* **:** to play with a rough unmusical tone **5 :** to draw back the foot along the ground in making a bow ⟨bowing and *scraping*⟩ **6 :** to manage to make one's way with difficulty or succeed by a narrow margin ⟨*scraping* along on a small income⟩ ⟨~ through a final examination⟩ — **scrape acquaintance :** to make acquaintance by making advances esp. without an introduction — **scrape a leg :** to make a low bow

²scrape \"\ *n* -s [ME, fr. *scrapen*, v.] **1 a :** the act of scraping ⟨rocks worn by the ~ of glaciers⟩ ⟨took up the remaining mortar with a ~ of his trowel⟩ **b :** a sound made by scraping ⟨rumble and ~ of the wheels of guns and limbers —H.N.Cole⟩ ⟨~ of footsteps up the stairs⟩ **2 a :** SCRAPER; *esp* **:** a dredge for taking crabs or oysters **b :** a bare place, hollow, or heap made by scraping ⟨the tern's nest is a ~ in the sand —C.L. Barrett⟩ **c** *also* **scrape of the pen** *chiefly Scot* **:** a scrap of writing **:** a hasty note ⟨not a ~ from you since your card at Christmas —Michael McLaverty⟩ **3 :** a bow made by drawing back the foot **4 :** a disagreeable predicament **:** an awkward or distressing situation ⟨his brother was continually helping him out of ~*s* at school⟩; *often* **:** CONFLICT, FIGHT ⟨got into a shooting ~ with a political opponent⟩ **5 :** crude turpentine that collects and hardens on the trunks of turpentined trees and is gathered usu. at the end of the season — compare DIP 6d **syn** see PREDICAMENT

scrape down *vt, chiefly Brit* **:** to silence (a speaker) by scraping the feet ⟨another was coughed and *scraped down* —T.B. Macaulay⟩

scrape–finished \ˈ=ˈ==\ *adj* **:** finished to a smooth level surface with a scraper ⟨*scrape-finished* lathe bed⟩

scrap·er \ˈskrāpə(r)\ *n* -s **1 :** a tool for scraping **:** an instrument with which something is scraped: as **a :** an edged blade fixed upright near an entrance for scraping mud off shoes **b :** any of various instruments or

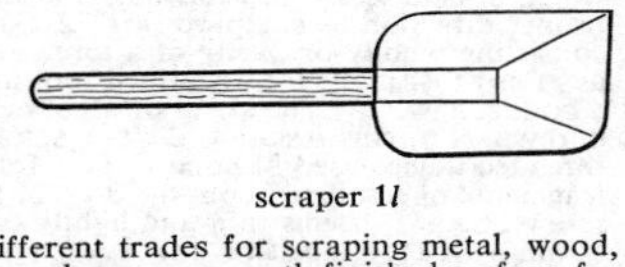

scraper 1*l*

tools used esp. in different trades for scraping metal, wood, leather for producing a clean or a smooth finished surface, for cutting grooves, or for shaping objects by scraping away superfluous material **c :** any of various appliances for removing an extraneous coating or layer from something: as (1) **:** a broad hoe for cleaning roads or stables (2) **:** a device for scraping up snow from ice (3) **:** a hoe-shaped implement for raking out ashes **d :** a device armed with curved knives and forced through a pipeline or a flue to clear out obstructions **e :** a curved wooden or metal device for removing the sweat from horses **f :** a 3-sided tool used by engravers to remove lines or burrs **g :** a board or blade whose edge rubs over a tympan sheet to make an impression in an old type of lithographic printing press **h :** ROAD GRADER **i :** a metal scoop with a bail to which motive power is attached for excavating or moving loose or soft material short distances **j :** a contrivance for cleaning out the detritus from a borehole **k :** a power-drawn wheeled self-loading conveyor used to move earth in grading and filling operations **l :** a kitchen tool made of a blade of hard rubber on a wood handle and used to scrape food from dishes or remove batter from mixing bowls **2 a :** one that scrapes money **:** MISER, SKINFLINT **b :** FIDDLER **c :** BARBER **d :** one that cleans, trims, or shapes by scraping **3 :** a bird that scratches the soil **4** *slang* **:** COCKED HAT **5 :** a roughened area on the legs or wings of an insect used in producing sounds

scraperboard \ˈ==,=\ *n* **1 :** a scratchboard with a smooth finish used to produce drawings usu. in white lines that are incised in a blackened surface **2 a :** the art or practice of using a scraperboard **b :** a product of such art or practice

scraper conveyor *n* **:** DRAG CONVEYOR

scraper ring *n* **:** a piston ring designed to scrape excess oil from the cylinder wall to prevent its entrance into the combustion chamber

scrapes *pres 3d sing of* SCRAPE, *pl of* SCRAPE

scrap heap *n* **1 :** a pile of discarded metal (as iron) **2 :** the place to which useless things are relegated **:** DISCARD, OBLIVION

scrap·i·ana \,skrapēˈanə\ *n pl* [¹*scrap* + *-ana*] **:** miscellaneous literary scraps

scrap·ie \ˈskrāpē\ *n* -s [¹*scrape* + *-ie*] **:** a virus disease of sheep characterized by twitching, excitability, intense itching, excessive thirst, emaciation, weakness, and finally paralysis

¹scraping *n* -s [ME *scrapinge* action of one that scrapes, fr. gerund of *scrapen* to scrape] **:** something scraped off, up, or together — usu. used in pl. ⟨street ~*s*⟩ ⟨fed on pot ~*s*⟩

²scraping *adj* [fr. pres. part. of ¹*scrape*] **:** that scrapes; *specif* **:** MISERLY — **scrap·ing·ly** *adv*

scrap·ler *or* **scrap·pler** \ˈskrapl(ə)r\ *n* -s [by alter. (influence of ¹*scrap*)] **:** SCABBLER

scrap·man \ˈskrap,man, -,maa(ə)n, -mən\ *n, pl* **scrapmen 1 :** a man dealing in scrap **:** JUNKMAN **2 a :** one who works at disposing of or salvaging scrap **b :** CHIPMAN 1 **3 :** a tobacco worker who blends cigar-filler scrap

scrap·page \ˈskrapij\ *n* -s **1 :** scrapped material **2 :** the rate of taking articles, buildings, or machinery out of use ⟨prosperity required the ~ and replacement of 4 million cars a year —S.H.Slichter⟩

scrapped *past of* SCRAP

¹scrap·per \ˈskrapə(r)\ *n* -s [⁵*scrap* + *-er*] **:** QUARRELER, FIGHTER ⟨strong-willed, persistent, and a ~ through and through —*advt.*⟩; *esp* **:** PRIZEFIGHTER

²scrapper \"\ *n* -s [²*scrap* + *-er*] **1 :** one that disposes of scraps **2 :** a worker who knocks off or pulls out the waste parts of scored cardboard box blanks — called also *breaker*

scrap·pi·ly \-pəlē, -li\ *adv* **:** in a scrappy manner

scrap·pi·ness \-pēnəs, -pin-\ *n* -ES **:** the quality or state of being scrappy **:** fragmentary nature **:** DISCONNECTEDNESS

scrapping *pres part of* SCRAP

¹scrap·ple \ˈskrapəl\ *n* -s [ME *scrapill*, fr. *scrapen* to scrape] *dial Eng* **:** a tool for scraping

²scrapple \"\ *n* -s [dim. of ¹*scrap*] **:** mush containing meat scraps made by boiling cornmeal in the liquor in which bones and meats (as pork) for headcheese and other products have been boiled, seasoned with condiments and herbs, poured into a mold to cool, and served sliced and fried

¹scrap·py \ˈskrapē, -pi\ *adj* -ER/-EST [¹*scrap* + *-y*] **:** consisting of scraps **:** lacking unity or consistency **:** FRAGMENTARY ⟨~ dinner⟩ ⟨~ narrative⟩ ⟨~ education⟩

²scrappy \"\ *adj* -ER/-EST [⁴*scrap* + *-y*] **1 :** QUARRELSOME **2 :** showing sharp and vigorous attacking qualities and an aggressive and determined spirit ⟨~ football team⟩ ⟨~ admiral⟩

scraps *pl of* SCRAP, *pres 3d sing of* SCRAP

scrap value *n* **:** the value of an item at the time it is discarded **:** the value which it is estimated an item will have at the time it is discarded

scrapy \ˈskrāpē\ *adj* -ER/-EST [¹*scrape* + *-y*] **:** sounding like scraping **:** produced by scraping ⟨made a small ~ sound in her throat⟩ ⟨~ violin playing⟩

scrapyard \ˈ=,=\ *n* **:** a place for receiving or handling scrap **:** JUNKYARD; *broadly* **:** SCRAP HEAP ⟨demanding that every vessel . . . be sent to the ~ —*No. Amer. Rev.*⟩

¹scrat \ˈskrat\ *vb* **scratted; scratted** *or* **scrat; scratting; scrats** [ME *scratten*] *dial Brit* **:** SCRATCH

²scrat \"\ *n* -s *dial chiefly Eng* **:** a small insignificant thing or amount

³scrat \"\ *n* -s [ME *skratt, scrate*, prob. fr. ON *skratti* monster — more at SCRAE] *chiefly dial* **:** HERMAPHRODITE

¹scratch \ˈskrach\ *vb* -ED/-ING/-ES [blend of ¹*scrat* and obs. E *cratch* to scratch; obs. E *cratch* fr. ME *cracchen*, prob. fr. MD *cratsen* to scratch, scrape; akin to OHG *krazzōn* to scratch, OSw *kratta* to scratch, Alb *gërrüej* I scratch] *vt* **1 :** to scrape with the claws or nails ⟨~*ed* out the eyes of the owl —Ben Jonson⟩ **2 :** to rub and tear or mark the surface of with something sharp or jagged **:** scrape, roughen, or wound slightly by drawing something pointed or rough across ⟨hard enough to ~ glass⟩ ⟨legs ~*ed* by the briers⟩ **3 :** to scrape or rub lightly with something pointed or rough in order to relieve itching ⟨took turns ~*ing* each other's backs⟩ or as a gesture indicating perplexity or hesitation ⟨thoughtfully ~*ing* his jaw⟩ ⟨~*ed* his head in bewilderment⟩ **4 a :** to dig or heap with the claws **b :** to scrape (as money) together **5 a :** to make shallow cuts on the surface of ⟨~*ed* his boot soles to prevent slipping⟩ — often used with *up* ⟨the table was all ~*ed* up by the movers⟩ **b :** to write or draw (as letters, figures) on a surface by such cuts ⟨~*ed* a map on the wet sand⟩ ⟨~*ed* his initials on the silver cover⟩ **c :** to cultivate lightly **:** make shallow furrows in **6 a :** to cancel by drawing a line through **b :** to obliterate with repeated strokes of the pen — used with *out* **c** *obs* **:** to expel or bar from a club **d :** to withdraw (an entry) from competition ⟨his horse was ~*ed* in the third race⟩ **e :** to mark (a ballot) so as to vote for most of the candidates of one party but for some belonging to another party **7 :** to write or draw hastily or roughly **:** SCRIBBLE ⟨~*ed* a note⟩ ⟨~*ed* his signature⟩ **8 :** SCRATCHBRUSH ⟨~ a casting⟩ **9 :** to scrape along a rough surface ⟨~ a match⟩ **10 :** to spur (a horse) by keeping the feet moving in a kicking motion alternately forward and backward ~ *vi* **1 a :** to use the claws in digging, tearing, or wounding ⟨that cat will ~⟩ **b :** to find or make one's way or one's living ⟨turned out at an early age to ~ for themselves⟩ **2 :** to rub oneself with something pointed or rough to relieve itching **3 :** to gather money or get a living by hard work and saving **4 :** to make a thin grating sound ⟨this pen ~*es*⟩ ⟨the dog was ~*ing* lightly at the door⟩ **5 a :** to withdraw from a contest after one's name is listed **b :** to fail to keep a social engagement **6 :** to scratch the name of a candidate on the ticket of one's party or faction **:** split the ticket **7 a :** to make a scratch in billiards or pool **b :** to score by a scratch — **scratch one's back :** to gratify one by favors or flattery esp. in expectation of favors in return ⟨you ~ my back and I'll ~ yours⟩ — **scratch the surface :** to make a beginning on a project, progress, a solution of a problem, a field of inquiry or investigation

²scratch \"\ *n* -ES **1 :** a mark or injury produced by scratching **:** a slight wound ⟨came through the battle without a ~⟩ **2 scratches** *pl but sing or pl in constr* **:** grease heel in its early stages **3 :** a line or furrow that is made in a surface by rasping or rubbing with a pointed or jagged object ⟨her ring left a ~ on the polished table top⟩ ⟨a million years, a mere ~ on the surface of earth's time —W.E.Swinton⟩ **4 :** a written scrawl **:** SCRIBBLE **5 :** a short wig **6 :** the sound made by scratching ⟨~ of a pencil⟩; *esp* **:** noise caused by the friction of a phonograph needle on the surface of a record **7 a :** the line from which contestants start in a race **b :** NOTHING, ZERO ⟨two whole towns have had to be built almost from ~ —Kent Strong⟩ ⟨task of organizing a major institution of learning almost from ~ —William DuBois⟩ **8 a :** a line formerly drawn across a prize ring that a contestant had to approach to begin or continue the fight **b :** a trial or test of courage ⟨imagine myself wanting at the ~ —Henry James †1916⟩ **c :** satisfactory physical condition or standard of performance ⟨bulls . . . that are not up to ~ as to size —*Farmer's Weekly (So. Africa)*⟩ ⟨her acting was right up to ~⟩ ⟨bringing him up to fighting ~ —H.J.Laski⟩ **9 :** the starting time or station or initial score of a competitor who neither is allowed odds nor receives a penalty **10 :** a contestant (as a horse or dog) whose name has been withdrawn from a race in which it was entered ⟨a list of late ~*es*⟩ **11** *also* **scratch feed :** a poultry feed (as mixed grains) scattered on the litter or ground esp. to induce birds to exercise **12 a :** a shot in billiards or pool that fails to comply with some requirement of the game and involves a penalty of loss of one or more balls or points; *specif* **:** a pocketing of the cue ball without touching the object ball **b :** a shot that scores by accident **:** FLUKE **c :** SCRATCH HIT **13** *slang* **:** MONEY

³scratch \"\ *adj* **1 :** made as or used for a tentative effort ⟨~ map⟩ **2 :** made or done by chance and not in the way intended ⟨~ shot⟩ **3 :** arranged or put together with little selection of material **:** HAPHAZARD ⟨~ meal⟩ ⟨~ team⟩ **4 :** made up of heterogeneous elements insufficient to be representative ⟨~ vote⟩ **5** *of a contest or a contestant* **:** being without handicap or allowance ⟨~ golfer⟩ ⟨one of the ~ boats in a handicap race⟩ **6 :** CANCELED

scratch·able \-chəbəl\ *adj* **:** capable of being scratched

scratch awl *n* **:** an awl with a sharp point for scratching guidelines on wood or metal **:** SCRIBER

scratchback \ˈ=,=\ *n* **:** BACK SCRATCHER

scratchboard *also* **scratchcard** \ˈ=,=\ *n* **:** a chalk-covered cardboard often with line or stipple pattern on which an effect resembling block printing or engraving may be achieved by scratching away desired portions (as highlights, shadings, white lines) with a steel tool; *also* **:** the art or practice of using scratchboard

¹scratchbrush \ˈ=,=\ *n* [¹*scratch* + *brush*] **:** a stiff wire brush for cleaning metal (as iron castings)

²scratchbrush \"\ *vt* **:** to clean or finish with or as if with a scratchbrush

scratch·brush·er \"+ə(r)\ *n* [²*scratchbrush* + *-er*] **1 :** a machine equipped with scratchbrushes **2 :** a worker who uses a scratchbrush or scratchbrusher

scratch carving *n* **:** furniture carving in which the design is outlined by narrow scratched or incised lines

scratch coat *n* **:** the first coat applied in plastering having lines scratched on its surface to improve the bond with the next coat — called also *first coat*

scratch comma *n* **:** a diagonal formerly used as a comma

scratch dial *n* **:** an early simple sundial formed by lines cut usu. on a church wall

scratch division *n* **:** an old method of division in which the partial products are not set down at all but only the remainders so that it is necessary to scratch out each figure of the dividend from which subtraction is made and place the remainder each time above it — called also *galley method*

scratched *adj* [fr. past part. of ¹*scratch*] **:** CANCELED ⟨8̸ and 9̸ are ~ figures⟩

scratch·er \ˈskrachə(r)\ *n* -s **1 :** one that scratches: **a :** a workman who uses a tool in scratching or tends a machine which does this work **b :** SCRATCHBRUSHER **c :** one who hand-finishes metal castings to be used as patterns **d :** a rasorial bird **2 a :** a tool used to roughen or scratch the scratch coat of plaster to improve the adhesion between the scratch coat and the brown coat **b :** a tool for corrugating the ends of sewer pipe so that cement will adhere when they are joined **c :** a tool for blazing trees **3** *slang* **:** FORGER 1c

scratches *pres 3d sing of* SCRATCH, *pl of* SCRATCH

scratch–farming \ˈ=,==\ *n* **:** the growing of crops on land after shallow or indifferent tillage

scratch feed *n* **:** SCRATCH 11

scratch gauge *n* **:** a metalworker's scriber or gauge resembling the carpenter's marking gauge

scratch grass *n* **1 :** TEARTHUMB **2 :** CLEAVERS

scratch hit *n* **:** a batted ball not solidly hit or cleanly fielded yet credited to the batter as a base hit

scratch·i·ly \ˈskrachəlē\ *adv* **:** in a scratchy manner

scratch·i·ness \-chēnəs\ *n* -ES **:** the quality or state of being scratchy

scratching *pres part of* SCRATCH

scratching post *n* **:** a sturdy wood post or block often covered with carpeting for a cat to scratch its claws on

scratch·ings \ˈskrachənz, -chiŋz\ *n pl* [pl. of *scratching*, gerund of ¹*scratch*] *dial Eng* **:** CRACKLINGS

scratch·less \ˈskrachləs\ *adj* **1 :** not marred or wounded **2 :** not likely to scratch ⟨~ vise⟩

scratch line *n* **1 :** a starting line for a race **2 :** a line that marks the extreme limit of the takeoff for a broad jump **3 :** a line from which the javelin is thrown and which must not be overstepped by the thrower

scratch pad *n* **:** a pad of scratch paper

scratch paper *n* **:** any paper that may be used for jottings, memoranda, or other casual writing

scratchproof \ˈ=ˈ=\ *adj* **:** resistant to scratches

scratch sheet *n* **:** a racing publication listing horses scratched from races and giving the handicapper's grading of the horses in order of winning chances

scratch test *n* **1 :** a test to discover the amount of abrasive material present (as in a paste or powder detergent) or to discover the relative resistance of a surface to abrasive material **2 :** a test for allergy in which scratches are made in the epithelial layer of the skin and the suspected allergen rubbed into the area and which determines a positive reaction by development of redness or a wheal around the scratched part — compare INTRACUTANEOUS TEST, PATCH TEST

scratchweed \ˈ=,=\ *n* **:** CLEAVERS

scratch wig *n* **:** a short wig

scratchwork \ˈ=,=\ *n* **1 :** SCRATCH COAT **2 :** SGRAFFITO

scratchy \ˈskrachē, -chi\ *adj* -ER/-EST **1 :** affected with the scratches ⟨horse with ~ feet⟩ **2 :** making a scratching noise ⟨~ tune came from the phonograph⟩ ⟨~ pen⟩ **3 :** marked or made with scratches ⟨~ drawing⟩ ⟨~ handwriting⟩ **4 a :** of sparse or straggly growth ⟨~ mane⟩ **b :** SCANT, MEAGER ⟨made only three hits, two of them ~⟩ **:** RAGGED ⟨played ~ golf through the first nine⟩ **5 :** causing tingling or itching **:** IRRITATING, PRICKLY ⟨~ wool sweater⟩ ⟨~ gas⟩

scrats *pres 3d sing of* SCRAT, *pl of* SCRAT

scratted *past of* SCRAT

scratting *pres part of* SCRAT

scrat·tle \ˈskratᵊl\ *vi* -ED/-ING/-S [¹*scrat* + *-le*] *dial Eng* **:** SCRATCH, SCRAMBLE

scrat·tling \ˈskratliŋ\ *adj* **:** BEGGARLY, SCANTY

scraunch \ˈskrönch\ *vb* -ED/-ING/-ES [imit.] *chiefly dial* **:** CRUNCH

scraw \ˈskrȯ\ *n* -s [IrGael *scraith* & ScGael *sgrath*] *Scot & Irish* **:** a piece of turf **:** SOD ⟨not fit to lift ~*s* from off the field —Augusta Gregory⟩

scrawk \ˈskrȯk\ *vi* -ED/-ING/-S [imit.] **1** *dial* **:** SCREECH **2** *dial* **:** SQUAWK

¹scrawl \ˈskrȯl\ *vb* -ED/-ING/-S [perh. by alter.] *archaic* **:** ¹CRAWL

²scrawl \"\ *vb* -ED/-ING/-S [origin unknown] *vt* **1 :** to write or draw awkwardly and irregularly **:** write hastily and carelessly **:** SCRIBBLE ⟨~ a brief note⟩ ⟨painfully ~*ed* his name⟩ **2 :** to mark or write on with irregular or hasty characters ⟨papers . . . ~*ed* with hieroglyphics —George Borrow⟩ ~ *vi* **:** to write awkwardly or carelessly

³scrawl \"\ *n* -s **1 :** careless, hasty, or irregular writing ⟨eventually deciphered the ~ —Francis King⟩ **2 :** SPRAWL ⟨saw the bright cabins and the ~ of a hidden stream —Bryan MacMahon⟩

scrawl·er \-lə(r)\ *n* -s **1 :** one that scrawls **2 :** a device for marking out fields preparatory to the planting of ridged row crops

scrawl·i·ness \-lēnəs\ *n* -ES **:** the quality of being scrawly

scrawly \-lē, -li\ *adj* -ER/-EST **:** awkwardly or carelessly irregular **:** SPRAWLING ⟨pages covered with ~ figures⟩

scrawm \ˈskrȯm\ *vi* -ED/-ING/-S [perh. by shortening & alter. fr. ¹SCRAMBLE] *dial Eng* **:** SCRAMBLE, CLAMBER

scrawn·i·ness \ˈskrȯ|nēnəs, -rä|, |nin-\ *n* -ES **:** the quality or state of being scrawny

scrawny \|nē, |ni\ *adj* -ER/-EST [origin unknown] **:** LEAN, THIN, RAWBONED **:** ill-nourished ⟨~ cattle⟩ ⟨~ bent-over pines⟩ ⟨a ~ ill-favored little girl —Margaret Mead⟩ **syn** see LEAN

¹scray \ˈskrā\ *n* -s [prob. modif. of D *schraag* trestle, fr. MD *schrage*; akin to MHG *schrage* trestle, Gk *kirkos* ring — more at CIRCLE] **:** a simple container or similar part on a machine where piece goods collect in folds after passing through a machine process

²scray *or* **scraye** \"\ *n* -s [origin unknown] **:** TERN

¹screak *also* **screek** \ˈskrēk\ *vi* -ED/-ING/-S [of Scand origin; akin to ON *skrækja* to screech — more at SCREAM] **1 :** to emit suddenly a sharp shrill sound **:** SCREECH ⟨~*ed* when she saw the mouse⟩ **2 :** to make a harsh rasping noise **:** GRATE, SQUEAL ⟨that gate ~*s* when it is opened⟩

²screak *also* **screek** \"\ *n* -s **:** a sound of screaking **:** a harsh rasping noise ⟨the moaning ~ of brakes, and racing, starting motors —Thomas Wolfe⟩ ⟨can remember the ~ on stones of his hoe —Richard Wilbur⟩

screaky \-kē\ *adj* **:** of, making, or resembling a screak **:** very shrill or raspy ⟨bats . . . making their ~ sounds —Eric Knight⟩

¹scream \ˈskrēm\ *vb* -ED/-ING/-S [ME *scremen*; akin to MD *schreem* screech, Flem *schreemen* to scream, OS *skrikon* to screech, OS & OHG *scrian* to scream, yell, ON *skrækja* to shriek, screech, *skraumi* screamer, and perh. to OE *hrǣfn* raven — more at RAVEN] *vi* **1 a** (1) **:** to voice a sudden sharp loud cry ⟨~*ed* and fainted —Louis Bromfield⟩ ⟨~*ed* with amusement —Marcia Davenport⟩ ⟨children fight and ~ . . . in the streets —Sherwood Anderson⟩ (2) **:** to produce harsh and unpleasant high-pitched musical tones ⟨even a prima donna has been known to ~⟩ ⟨horns ~*ed*, and flutes wailed —John Blofeld⟩ **b :** to make an outburst of noise

resembling a scream : move with a screaming sound ⟨the wind rose and ~*ed* through the streets —H.E.Rieseberg⟩ ⟨brilliant blue kingfishers ~ at intruders —*Amer. Guide Series: La.*⟩ ⟨a jet ~*ed* out of the cushion of the gray cotton sky —*Saturday Rev.*⟩ **2** : to speak or write with expressions of intense hysterical emotion : make violent protestations or demands ⟨growing industries . . . are ~*ing* for water —*Time*⟩ ⟨travelers . . . ~*ed* loud and long at the shipping lines —*N. Y. Times*⟩ ⟨papers ~ to the heavens about . . . troops along their borders —*Atlantic*⟩ **3** : to produce a vivid, blatant, or startling effect like a scream ⟨framed in garish red, a bold black headline ~*ed* —Paul Hofmann⟩ ⟨the obviousness . . . fairly ~*s* at the reader who is surely ready by now for profounder insights —*New Republic*⟩ ~ *vt* **1 a** : to utter with or as if with a scream ⟨a newsboy in the street below began to ~ an extra —F.V.W. Mason⟩ ⟨~*ed* that she was drowning —George Meredith⟩ **b** : to sing harshly and unpleasantly esp. at high pitch ⟨vocally delivered . . . although some of the second-act music was ~*ed* —*Musical Digest*⟩ **2** : to demand or protest as if in a screaming voice : blare forth ⟨artists . . . write letters to the newspapers ~*ing* that they are being snubbed —Francis Steegmuller⟩ ⟨headlines ~*ed* the news all over the Union —*Atlantic*⟩ ⟨been ~*ing* to go into show business —Myles MacSweeney⟩

[2]**scream** \"\ *n* -s **1 a** : a sudden loud sharp penetrating cry usu. expressing anger, terror, pain, or sometimes hysterical merriment ⟨her ~*s* filled the air as she turned and fled⟩ **b** : a sound resembling or having the effect of a scream ⟨the crows come flapping with their ~*s* —Thomas Vance⟩ ⟨the shrill ~ of . . . saws and the odor of fresh cedar wood —*Amer. Guide Series: Oregon*⟩ **2** : one that provokes screams of mirth ⟨the instructions are a ~ from start to finish —Margaret Lane⟩ ⟨what a ~ he was on a party —Ring Lardner⟩

scream·er \-mə(r)\ *n* -s **1** : one that screams; *esp* : one that sings in a loud harsh penetrating manner **2** : any of several So. American birds constituting the family Anhimidae — see CRESTED SCREAMER, HORNED SCREAMER **3** *slang* : one that shows remarkable excellence **4** : one (as a play, a comedian) that causes screams usu. either of excitement or mirth **5** : a sensationally large or startling headline **6** *slang* : EXCLAMATION POINT **7** : one engaged to provoke excitement by screaming ⟨began as a publicity stunt with the first swooners and ~*s* —Bruce Bliven b. 1889⟩

screamer bomb *n* : a bomb that has an attachment emitting a penetrating whistle as the bomb falls and that is used to terrify the enemy

[1]**screaming** *n* -s [ME *skremyng*, fr. gerund of *skremen, scremen* to scream — more at SCREAM] : the act of or sound made by one that screams ⟨a ~ of brakes generally heralded the arrival —Benedict Thielen⟩ ⟨the fog siren began its ~ —John Steinbeck⟩ ⟨distortion of action, harsh ~*s* of the voice . . . are not admissible in the theatric art —Joshua Reynolds⟩

[2]**screaming** *adj* [fr. pres. part. of [1]*scream*] **1** : uttering screams : emitting or producing sounds resembling screams ⟨snows driven by ~ sea winds —Ann F. Wolfe⟩ ⟨a car rounded the corner with ~ tires —Erle Stanley Gardner⟩ ⟨a ~ jet plane flew overhead —Sam Pollock⟩ ⟨~ hordes of movie fans —Peter Ustinov⟩ **2** : having characteristics similar to a scream : resembling a scream in effect : blatantly arresting : STARTLING ⟨rugs in harsh colors and ~ designs —R.W.Murray⟩ ⟨the papers carried ~ headlines —R.M.Lovett⟩ **3** : evoking screams usu. of raucous mirth ⟨fetched along the book with all those ~ snapshots —Dearing Ward⟩ **4** : EXCELLENT, SPLENDID ⟨within the tradition of the dramatic fiction film, it balances a great weight with ~ finesse —Cecile Starr⟩

scream·ing·ly *adv* : to an extreme degree ⟨thought the whole effort so ~ funny —Joseph Millard⟩

screaming meemies *n pl but sing in constr* [origin unknown] : extreme and intolerable terror or nervous hysteria : JITTERS ⟨about two jumps ahead of the *screaming meemies* —*Time*⟩

screamy \-mē\ *adj* : given to or suggestive of screaming

scree \ˈskrē\ *n* -s [of Scand origin; akin to ON *skritha* landslide, debris from a landslide, fr. *skritha* to creep, glide — more at CRISSUM] a heap of stones or rocky debris lying on a slope or at the base of a cliff : TALUS ⟨the steep *scree*-strewn lower slopes of the mountains —Alistair MacLean⟩

[1]**screech** \ˈskrēch\ *vb* -ED/-ING/-ES [alter. of earlier *scritch*, fr. ME *scrichen*; akin to ON *skrækja* to screech — more at SCREAM] *vi* **1** : to utter a high shrill piercing cry : make an outcry usu. in terror or pain **2** : to make a sound resembling a screech ⟨the driver applied his brakes . . . and the car ~*ed* to a standstill —Bruce Marshall⟩ ⟨the gate ~*ed* behind him —Nadine Gordimer⟩ ~ *vt* : to utter with or as if with a screech ⟨their voices ~*ing* out the battle cries —T.B.Costain⟩

[2]**screech** \"\ *n* -ES **1** : a high very shrill piercing cry usu. expressing extreme pain or terror ⟨the voice was a strident ~ torn from the lungs —Marcia Davenport⟩ **2** : a sound resembling or having the effect of a screech ⟨an earsplitting ~ of brakes —Donald Windham⟩ ⟨the ~ of fire sirens —H.A. Chippendale⟩

screechbird \ˈ⸗,⸗\ *also* **screech cock** *or* **screech thrush** *n* : FIELDFARE 1

screech·er \-chə(r)\ *n* -s **1** : one that screeches **2 a** : SWIFT **b** : MISTLE THRUSH

[1]**screeching** *n* -s [fr. gerund of [1]*screech*] : the act of or sound made by one that screeches ⟨greeted as usual by the . . . ~ of her parrot —Moray Firth⟩ ⟨the chugging of locomotives, the ~ of whistles —*Amer. Guide Series: Pa.*⟩

[2]**screeching** *adj* [fr. pres. part. of [1]*screech*] : uttering screeches : emitting or producing sounds resembling screeches ⟨a large red cab came to a ~ stop —Reginald Bretnor⟩ ⟨~ seagulls⟩ — **screech·ing·ly** *adv*

screech martin *n* : the common European swift

screech owl *n* **1** : BARN OWL **2** : any of numerous small owls of the genus *Otus* that range from southern Canada to Brazil, are closely related to the Old World scops owls, and have erectile ear tufts and plumage with blackish streaks and vermiculation; *esp* : an eastern No. American owl (*O. asio*) that is represented by several geographical varieties in the west and southwest and that exhibits two distinct phases of coloration consisting of a reddish brown and a gray

screechy \-chē\ *adj* -ER/-EST : given to or suggestive of screeching

[1]**screed** \ˈskrēd\ *n* -s [ME *screde*, fr. OE *scrēade* — more at SHRED] **1 a** *dial Brit* : FRAGMENT; *esp* : one torn off a piece of cloth : SHRED **b** *dial Brit* : a strip of land **c** *dial Eng* : a strip or band esp. around the border of a cap **2** *Scot* : RENT, TEAR **3 a** : a lengthy discourse : DIATRIBE **b** : a piece of writing: as (1) : a friendly letter ⟨send me a ~ . . . as often as you can —T.B.Aldrich⟩ (2) : an informal essay, story, or dissertation ⟨wrote a long ~ . . . for the Edinburgh professor —John Buchan⟩ **4 a** *or* **screed strip** : FLOATING SCREED **b** : a strike board usu. used to level up or strike off concrete pavement slabs or to cushion courses for block pavements **5** *Scot* : a drinking bout

[2]**screed** \"\ *vt* -ED/-ING/-S [ME *screden*, fr. OE *scrēadian* — more at SHRED] **1** *chiefly Scot* : REND, TEAR **2** : to smooth off with a screed ⟨the plaster was laid on very evenly and then ~*ed off* —Katharine S. Woods⟩

screed coat *n* : a layer of plaster laid level with screeds

screek *var of* SCREAK

scree·man \ˈskrēmən\ *n, pl* **screemen** [alter. of *screenman*] : a coal screener

[1]**screen** \ˈskrēn\ *n* -s [ME *screne*, fr. MF *escren, escran*, fr. MD *scherm* screen, shield, protection; akin to OHG *skirm, skerm* shield, screen, MLG *scerm* shield, screen, L *corium* skin, hide — more at CUIRASS] **1** : a device used as a protection from the heat of a fireplace or from drafts or as an ornamental piece: as **a** : a folding temporary partition consisting of hinged leaves usu. made of wood or metal framework covered with cloth, leather, or paper — see FIRE SCREEN **b** : a cloth, paper, or wooden implement with a handle to hold between oneself and the fire **c** : a high-backed settle **2 a** : a nonbearing partition that may be solid or pierced, is often ornamental, and is carried up to a height necessary for separation and protection **b** : a passage screened or partitioned off from the lower end of the hall of a Tudor or Elizabethan house and used to connect the buttery and the kitchen **c** (1) : CHOIR SCREEN (2) : ROOD SCREEN **3** : something that shelters, protects esp. from injury or danger, or conceals from view: as **a** *Scot* : a large head scarf **b** : a natural or cultivated growth of plants ⟨a ~ of ivy across the window⟩ ⟨a ~ of tall pines sheltered the orchard from winter storms⟩ **c** (1) : a body of troops thrown out toward the enemy to protect a command or an area (2) : a formation of light naval vessels (as destroyers or cruisers) about a formation of heavier ships to protect the heavier formation from attack esp. by submarines or aircraft (3) : air patrolling by fighter-interceptors to protect from air attack specific targets (as slower aircraft or surface forces) : air patrolling to defend the entire friendly territory from air incursion (4) : smoke, camouflage, or a natural factor that protects an armed force from observation ⟨misty clouds . . . made such a perfect ~ that the Confederate batteries on top of the mountain could render no effective help —*Amer. Guide Series: Tenn.*⟩ **4 a** : something that guards : a security from possible inconvenience, censorious judgment, or harm ⟨adult care interposes a ~ between the small child and . . . society —Ralph Linton⟩ **b** : a shield for secret sometimes nefarious practices ⟨geniality . . . in our initial sessions was only a ~ —A.H.Vandenberg †1951⟩ ⟨petty larceny . . . only a ~ for something bigger —Claud Cockburn⟩ **5 a** (1) : a perforated plate, cylinder, or similar device or a meshed wire or cloth fabric usu. mounted on a frame and used to separate coarser from finer parts or to allow the passage of smaller portions while preventing that of larger (2) : a continuously operating mechanical straining device for removing knots and coarse foreign matter from paper stock in suspension in water (3) : a device for separating the grain husks from the liquid portion of whole stillage (4) : SILK SCREEN **b** : something that resembles a screen for sifting physical materials; *esp* : a system for examining in order to make a separation into different groups ⟨the new battalion passes through the ~ of officer and instructor observation —*Scientific American*⟩ **6 a** (1) : a flat surface afforded usu. by a curtain, sheet, or wall upon which an image (as a picture) is projected by a lantern, solar microscope, or motion-picture projector (2) : the motion-picture industry **b** : something that resembles a motion-picture screen ⟨a collection of poems . . . provides the reader with that larger ~ on which the poet's essential qualities are thrown —Sara H. Hay⟩ ⟨engrave its picture on the ~ of our mind —Walter Sorell⟩ **7 a** : a part of an instrument or piece of apparatus designed to prevent agencies in one part from affecting other parts ⟨optical ~⟩ ⟨electric ~⟩ ⟨magnetic ~⟩ **b** : a device to prevent radio waves or magnetic or electric fields from crossing a particular area **8** : an erection of white canvas or wood placed near the boundary at both ends of a cricket field in line with the wickets to enable the batsmen to see the ball better **9** : a three-color mosaic of regular pattern used in making the negative and viewing the transparency in the separate screen processes of additive color photography — compare SCREEN PLATE **10 a** : a glass plate ruled with crossing opaque lines through which an image is photographed onto a plate in making a halftone and on which the latticework of the crossed lines produces a dot formation **b** : a unit of measure of the textural fineness of a halftone being the number of dots per linear inch ⟨a coarse 65-*screen* newspaper cut⟩ ⟨a fine 200-*screen* engraving⟩ **11 a** : a frame holding a metallic or textile netting used esp. in a window or door to exclude insects **b** : SCREEN CLOTH **12** : the surface upon which an image or pattern is produced in a television or radar receiver or in a similar apparatus **13** : an act or instance of screening in athletic contests

screen 1a

[2]**screen** \"\ *vb* -ED/-ING/-S [ME *screanen*, fr. *screne*, n.] *vt* **1 a** : to guard from injury or danger : shield from harm or punishment ⟨the whole village was in a conspiracy to ~ the bandits⟩ **b** : to protect from the attack of an enemy by means of an advance guard (as of fighter aircraft) **2 a** : to give shelter or protection (as from light or wind) to ⟨~*ed* his eyes with his hand⟩ **b** : to shut off by interposing something that resembles a screen ⟨will perhaps try whether the magnetic power is not to be ~*ed* off —John Tyndall⟩ ⟨was ~*ed* by army regulations which forbid his making political speeches —*Time*⟩ **c** : to separate (an opponent in a game) as if with a screen: as (1) : to prevent (an opponent in basketball) from reaching a desired position without causing bodily contact (2) : to prevent (an opponent in soccer) from having a clear view of the ball by standing or moving so as to conceal it (3) : to cover (one's own server) in order to conceal the direction of the serve from opponents in volleyball **3** : to conceal from view or knowledge : HIDE ⟨20 paces of thick falling snow ~*ed* the man from him —Morley Callaghan⟩ ⟨works in a bookshop, her identity ~*ed* from the customers —*Newsweek*⟩ **4 a** (1) : to pass through a screen; *esp* : to pass (as coal, gravel, or paper stock) through a screen in order to separate one part from another (2) : to remove by or as if by a screen — usu. used with *out* ⟨moisture in the air ~*s* out much of the solar heat radiation —Marston Bates⟩ **b** (1) : to examine usu. methodically in order to make a separation into different groups ⟨the students were ~*ed* before leaving their home countries, insuring that no one with false opinions or dangerous attitudes would get through —W.C.Booth⟩ ⟨carefully ~*s* all visa applications —Ralph de Toledano⟩ ⟨industry will be ~*ed* again for the young, healthy, and dispensable —*Newsweek*⟩ ⟨several antibiotics . . . have been ~*ed* for antituberculosis activity —J.F.Bohmfalk⟩ (2) : to examine (an area) in order to remove whatever is undesirable ⟨preceded the diplomats and ~*ed*, made sanitary and reasonably murderproof the area of the conference —H.S.Canby⟩ (3) : to select by a screening process ⟨the colonel had invited 5000 carefully ~*ed* leading citizens to sip punch —*Time*⟩ (4) : to eliminate by or as if by a screening process ⟨the committee should ~ from the material received any items it deems unsuitable —*Accounting Rev.*⟩ — usu. used with *out* ⟨even the best educated . . . are ~*ed* out socially by the policy of white supremacy —Margaret Mackay⟩ (5) : to examine as a censor : CENSOR ⟨passed an ordinance creating a board of review to ~ literature sold in the city —James Rorty⟩ **5** *Brit* : to post on a bulletin board **6 a** : to provide with a screen to keep out insects **b** : to provide (as an electronic device) with a screen to prevent agencies in one part of an apparatus from affecting other parts **7 a** : to project (as a motion-picture film) on a screen ⟨exhibitors were required by law to ~ a short with every feature —Helen Grayson⟩ **b** : to present in a motion picture ⟨~*ed* an abbreviated version of the book⟩ ⟨was ~*ed* in the male leads of several westerns⟩ **8** : SILK-SCREEN ~ *vi* : to appear on a motion-picture screen ⟨he ~*s* well⟩ ⟨sounds a bit more silly and maudlin than it ~*s* —*Newsweek*⟩ **syn** see CONCEAL

[3]**screen** \"\ *adj* [[1]*screen*] **1** : having a screen to keep out insects ⟨~ door⟩ ⟨~ porch⟩ **2** : of or relating to motion pictures ⟨an actor who became famous as a ~ star⟩ ⟨the novel's ~ potentialities —*Publishers' Weekly*⟩ **3** : SILK-SCREEN

screen·able \-nəbəl\ *adj* : capable of being screened esp. for a motion picture ⟨old-time romances while seldom ~ still furnish plot examples —Louella Parsons⟩

screen analysis *n* : examination of grain meal by passing the particles through screens whose openings gradually decrease in size and by measuring the amount retained on each screen

screen bulkhead *n* : a bulkhead that is dust-tight but not watertight

screen cloth *n* : material for screens; *specif* : a metal or plastic mesh for window and door screens

screen·er \-nə(r)\ *n* -s : one that screens: as **a** : one that puts in screens (as in windows or doors) **b** : SCREENMAN

screen facade *n* : a facade that conceals the form or dimensions of the building to which it is attached (as by exceeding the building in height or width)

screen gate *n* : a screen over the outlet of a drain that blocks entrance but is hinged so as to permit the escape of debris

screen grid *n* : a grid placed between the plate and the control grid of an electron or vacuum tube to eliminate the effect of plate-potential variations on the control grid

screenhouse \ˈ⸗,⸗\ *n* : a structure in which berries or other fruits are screened or sorted

screenier *comparative of* SCREENY

screeniest *superlative of* SCREENY

screening *n* -s **1** : the act or action of one that screens: as **a** : the work of a screener **b** : a showing of a motion picture ⟨requested a ~ of his picture —A.D.Roe⟩ **c** : the act of examining in order to make a separation into different groups ⟨sends newly offered finishes through his laboratory for a thorough ~ —R.E.Ellsworth⟩ **2 screenings** *pl but sing or pl in constr* **a** : material that has been passed through a screen: as (1) : the small imperfect grains, weed seeds, and other foreign material having feeding value that are separated in cleaning grain by a screen (2) : fine coal separated from the larger lumps by a screen having holes usu. from slightly more than ½ inch to two inches in diameter — compare SLACK **b** : material retained by a screen: as (1) : the coarse material retained by a screen in the treatment of wood pulp or paper stock (2) : the material removed from sewage by a screen **c** : a coarse wrapping paper made from pulp screenings **3** : a process of stripping a halftone tint film on a transparent area of another negative **4** : SCREEN CLOTH

screenland \ˈ⸗,⸗\ *n* : FILMDOM

screen·less \-nləs\ *adj* : having no screen

screenlike \ˈ⸗,⸗\ *adj* : resembling a screen

screenman \ˈskrēnmən\ *n, pl* **screenmen** : a worker who uses or operates screens to clean or size, to sift, to separate, or to strain — called also *screener*

screen memory *n* : an imagined or real recollection of early childhood that is recalled with magnification of importance or other distortion and that aids in the repression of another memory of deep emotional significance

screeno \ˈskrē(ˌ)nō\ *n* -s *sometimes cap* [*screen* + *-o*] : bingo designed for play by audiences in motion-picture theaters

screen pass *n* : a forward pass play in football in which the receiver is protected by a screen of blockers

screen plate *n* : a photographic plate on which one of the coatings consists of the minute color filters usu. red, green, and blue violet that are necessary for taking and projecting a color image

screenplay \ˈ⸗,⸗\ *n* : the written form of a story prepared for motion-picture production including description of characters, details of scenes and settings, dialogue, and stage directions

screen print *n* : a silk-screen print

screen printing *n* : silk-screen printing

screen process *n* **1** : an additive three-color process in which a mosaic screen composed of minute color elements distributed either in an irregular fashion (as in the autochrome) or in a regular order (as in the Finlay process) is so placed that the light during exposure must pass through the screen before it affects a panchromatic emulsion behind it **2** : SILK-SCREEN PROCESS

screens *pl of* SCREEN, *pres 3d sing of* SCREEN

screens·man \ˈskrēnzmən\ *n, pl* **screensmen** : a tender of a grain-cleaning machine

screen test *n* **1** : a photographic test for estimating the ability of a prospective motion-picture actor **2** : a short film sequence made in order to estimate the ability of a prospective motion-picture actor

screen-test \ˈ⸗,⸗\ *vt* [*screen test*] : to subject to a screen test

screen tree *n* : a tree that is left standing in a woodlot to provide shade

screen-wall \ˈ⸗,⸗\ *n* : a wall that is erected to conceal or break a view and that supports no vertical weight other than its own weight

screenwell \ˈ⸗,⸗\ *n* : a vertical recess for the traveling screen imposed on the cooling-water intake of a steam power plant

screen wiper *n, Brit* : WINDSHIELD WIPER

screenwork \ˈ⸗,⸗\ *n* : work that constitutes a screen which sets off or protects : GRILLWORK

screenwriter \ˈ⸗,⸗⸗\ *n* : a writer of screenplays

screeny \ˈskrēnē\ *adj* -ER/-EST : suggestive of a screen

screes *pl of* SCREE

[1]**screeve** \ˈskrēv\ *vi* [ME *scryven*, fr. MF *escrever* (3d sing. pres., *escrive, escrieve*), lit., to burst open, fr. OF, fr. *es-* (fr. L *ex-*) + *crever* to burst, fr. L *crepare* to crack — more at RAVEN] *dial Brit* : to exude moisture : OOZE, LEAK

[2]**screeve** \"\ *n* -s [prob. fr. It *scrivere* to write, fr. L *scribere* — more at SCRIBE] *chiefly Brit* : a piece of writing; *esp* : a begging letter

[3]**screeve** \"\ *vb* -ED/-ING/-S [prob. fr. It *scrivere* to write] *vt, chiefly Brit* : to write (as a letter) in order to beg ~ *vi, chiefly Brit* : to draw pictures on a sidewalk in order to attract passersby and obtain charity

screev·er \-və(r)\ *n* -s *chiefly Brit* : one who makes a living by drawing pictures on sidewalks in order to obtain charity from passersby : SIDEWALK ARTIST

[1]**screw** \ˈskrü\ *n* -s [ME *skrewe*, fr. MF *escroe, escroue* female screw, nut, fr. ML *scrofa*, fr. L, sow] **1 a** : a simple machine of the inclined plane type consisting of a spirally grooved solid cylinder and a correspondingly grooved hollow cylinder of equal dimensions in which the applied force acts in a spiral path along the grooves while the resisting force acts along the axis of the cylinder — compare JACKSCREW **b** : a cylinder with a helical cut groove on the outer surface or a cone with a conical spiral groove used variously (as to fasten, apply pressure, transmit motion, or make adjustments) esp. where a large mechanical advantage and irreversible motion are desired; *specif* : a cylindrical fastener that is usu. pointed, that has a head with a slot or recess, that is helically or spirally threaded, and that is designed for insertion into material by rotating (as with a screwdriver) — compare ARCHIMEDES' SCREW, DIFFERENTIAL SCREW, HINDLEY'S SCREW, INTERRUPTED SCREW, LEFT-HAND SCREW THREAD, MACHINE SCREW, RIGHT-HANDED SCREW, WOOD SCREW, WORM **c** : a hollow cylinder or cone with a spiral groove upon its inner surface into which a male screw may advance and fit when rotated in the proper direction — compare NUT **2** : any of various devices consisting wholly or partly of a screw or possessing a worm: as **a** *obs* : GIMLET **b** : a wormed tool used for pulling; *specif* : CORKSCREW **c** : the worm of a corkscrew or gimlet **d** *usu* **screws** *pl* : THUMBSCREW 2 **e** : SCREW PROPELLER **f** : a threaded device used in bone surgery for fixation of parts (as fragments of fractured bones) **3 a** (1) : a form resembling a screw : SPIRAL ⟨stems thin and lightly twisted — the ~ being communicated to the surface —Albert Hartshorne⟩ (2) : something having a spiral form ⟨scarcely the ~ of his tail to be seen —R.D.Blackmore⟩ (3) : a twisting out of shape : CONTORTION ⟨a kind of ~ in her face and carriage, expressive of suppressed emotion —Charles Dickens⟩ **b** : a spiral twisting motion : a screwing motion ⟨the barber pole rested its stripes from their daily ~ —Herbert Gold⟩ **c** : spiral threading or grooving **d** (1) *Brit* : spin imparted to a cue ball by screwing it (2) *Brit* : a shot made by screwing the cue ball (3) : a similar spin imparted to the ball in various other games (as ping-pong) **4** : a means of applying painful physical, mental, or moral pressure (as for coercion or extortion) ⟨the bookie turns on the ~*s* for his money —*Newsweek*⟩ ⟨they feel the ~: they dread exposure —Henry James †1916⟩ — usu. used in pl. **5 a** : an act of copulation — usu. considered vulgar **b** : a partner in sexual intercourse — usu. considered vulgar **6** : KEY **7** : a worn-out, broken-down, or otherwise unsound horse **8 a** (1) : a prison guard (2) : TURNKEY (3) : POLICEMAN **b** : an extortionate person : a sharp bargainer : SKINFLINT **c** *slang* : FOOL ⟨why, the old ~ took that for a compliment —Joseph Hergesheimer⟩ **d** : COWBOY **9** *chiefly Brit* : a small paper packet wrapped by twisting both ends and often used for small quantities (as of tobacco, salt, pepper) for ready use **10** : SCREW-SHIP **11** *Brit* : SALARY, PAY **12** *Brit* : LOOK, GLANCE ⟨had a ~ at his self in the glass —Richard Llewellyn⟩

[2]**screw** \"\ *vb* -ED/-ING/-S *vt* **1 a** (1) : to attach or fasten by means of a screw ⟨~ a lock on a door⟩ (2) : to close and seal shut by means of a screw ⟨~*ed* the box top tight⟩ (3) : to unite or separate by means of a screw or a twisting motion ⟨~ the two pieces together⟩ (4) : to press tightly in a vise or other device operated by a screw (5) : to operate, tighten, or adjust by means of a screw; *specif* : to tighten or raise the pitch of (a musical string) by turning a screw or key (6) : to torture by means of a thumbscrew (7) : to lace very tight (8) : to cap or uncap by twisting a cover ⟨so clumsy with sleepiness that he could hardly ~ open the toothpaste —Clemence Dane⟩ ⟨~ the jar tight⟩ **b** (1) : to insert (as a spirally grooved object) into a usu. spirally grooved receptacle with a twisting motion ⟨~ one piece of the fishing rod into the other⟩ (2) : to cause

to rotate spirally about an axis ⟨the level may be adjusted by ~ing the bolt up or down⟩ (3) : to rotate ⟨a receptacle with internal spiral grooves⟩ about a male screw ⟨~ on a nut⟩ **2 a** (1) : to twist ⟨as the face⟩ into strained or contorted configurations ⟨their tanned faces ~ed into painful and unaccustomed lines of concentration —E.A.McCourt⟩ ⟨their shoulders ~ed up with the cold —Willa Cather⟩ (2) : to partially close or otherwise alter the shape of ⟨an eye⟩ : SQUINT ⟨~ed her eyes tight and tried to read the lettering —Mavis Gallant⟩ ⟨~ up one eye into an imaginary monocle —J.P. O'Donnell⟩ (3) : to roll and twist into a shapeless mass : CRUMPLE ⟨with disgust he ~ed the sheet up and threw it across the hut —R.E.Robinson⟩ **b** (1) : to cause to move in a spiral, twisting, or tortuous manner ⟨as into or through a narrow opening⟩ ⟨capable of rotating ... and thus ~ing themselves through the water —K.A.Bisset⟩ (2) : to cause ⟨a scrimmage in rugby⟩ to twist round (3) : to cause ⟨a ball⟩ to swerve; specif, Brit : to hit ⟨a cue ball⟩ low down and slightly to the side so that it will be deflected in a curve after striking an object ball **c** : to furnish with a spiral groove or ridge : THREAD **3** : to increase the intensity, quantity, or capability of — usu. used with up ⟨the speed ~ed up exhilaration to a point almost beyond bearing —P.H.Scott⟩ ⟨... himself up to the talking point —Aldous Huxley⟩ ⟨trying to ~ up courage to confess —Will Scott⟩ **4 a** obs : to root deeply ⟨an idea or habit⟩ by insinuation **b** archaic : to insinuate ⟨oneself⟩ gradually ⟨~ himself into the partial confidence of the Laird —Sir Walter Scott⟩ **5** : to alter the sense of to suit one's purpose ⟨by jurisprudential construction, ~ up misdemeanors into felonies —Jeremy Bentham⟩ **6 a** : to practice extortion upon : oppress or dispossess by unreasonable or extortionate exactions or conditions ⟨quarrelled with his agents and ~ed his tenants —W.M.Thackeray⟩ **b** : to extract by pressure or threat ⟨landlords were ~ing the last penny from their poor tenants —Hugh McVeigh⟩ ⟨stayed on for over two months, in order to ~ out of the ... prime minister a promise —Reader Bullard⟩ **c** : to induce to a reduction in price or rent ⟨~ed the landlady down to a shilling —Harry Lauder⟩ **d** slang : to deprive of something due : CHEAT ⟨split up the dirty jobs among the deckhands, so nobody got ~ed —Richard Bissell⟩ **7** : to copulate with — usu. considered vulgar **8** : to enter for burglary by means of a skeleton key **9** slang : to spoil by meddling or incompetence — usu. used with up ⟨somebody's ~ed things up, we're nowhere near our objective —Infantry Jour.⟩ ~ vi **1 a** : to rotate or have the ability to rotate like a screw ⟨the nut ~s on here⟩ ⟨this piece ~s into the other⟩ **b** : to function as a screw **2** : to turn or move with a twisting or writhing motion ⟨~ing about to catch a glimpse of that little beauty —Geoff Bingham⟩ **3** : to cause a ball to swerve **4** : to be parsimonious : SCRIMP ⟨must ~ and save in order to pay off the money —W.M.Thackeray⟩ **5** : to move by means of a screw propeller **6** : COPULATE — usu. considered vulgar **7** slang : to leave quickly : hurry away ⟨come on, let's ~ out of here —Robert Lowry⟩

³**screw** or ²**scrow** \skrō\ n -s [prob. modif. of obs. F escrouelle (now écrouelle)] : an amphipod crustacean — compare SAND SCREW

screw·able \'skrüəbəl\ adj : capable of being screwed
screw anchor n **1** : an anchor in the form of a sharp-pointed screw with broad flanges used principally for moorings **2** : an expanding metal shell that wedges itself into a drilled hole upon insertion and is used to retain a screw in material ⟨as concrete, brick, or tile⟩ otherwise unsuitable
screw arbor n : an arbor to which a cutter is attached by means of a screw thread
screw around vi, slang : to waste or pass time : LOITER ⟨got all night to screw around here —Richard Bissell⟩
screw auger n **1** : AUGER 1 **2** : a widely distributed ladies' tresses (Spiranthes cernua) having creamy white vanilla-scented flowers and growing esp. in low damp places through much of eastern and central No. America
screw back vt, Brit : DRAW 1l
¹**screwball** \'s₌,₌\ n [¹screw + ball] **1** : a baseball pitch having reverse spin and a break in opposite direction to a curve **2** : one whose ideas, expressions, or actions are considered whimsical, eccentric, dizzily fantastic, or insane
²**screwball** \"\ adj : crazily eccentric or nonsensical : ZANY ⟨carry on a ~ campaign in their editorial columns ... to undo the work ... done by their headlines —Canadian Forum⟩ ⟨a fantastic ménage characterized by dabbling in the arts, ~ acquaintances drifting in and out, terrible tantrums, and soul-searching —N.Y. Herald Tribune Bk. Rev.⟩ **2** : characterized by eccentric or whimsical responses to speech or action upon a pattern of otherwise normal behavior ⟨~ comedy⟩ ⟨~ heroine⟩
screw bean n **1** : a shrub or small tree (Prosopis pubescens) of the southwestern U.S. — called also tornillo **2** : a spirally twisted sweet pod that is the fruit of the screw bean and is used for fodder or ground into meal for use as feed
screw bell n : an internally threaded bell-shaped device for recovering tools dropped down a borehole
screw bolt n : a bolt having a screw thread on it
screw box n **1** : a socket for a screw **2** : a screw plate for cutting wooden screws
screw cap n : a cap that screws onto a threaded container finish ⟨as on a bottle or jar⟩
screw conveyor n : CONVEYER 2a(8)
screw coupling n : an internally threaded sleeve nut that usu. has right-and-left threads and is used for coupling ⟨as rods or pipes⟩
screw-cutting lathe \'s₌,₌-₌\ n : a slide-rest lathe having a lead screw with a pitch suitable for cutting threads
screw·drive \'skrü,drīv\ vt [back-formation fr. screwdriver] : to drive in with or as if with a screwdriver
screw·driv·er \-və(r)\ n **1** : a tool for turning screws so as to

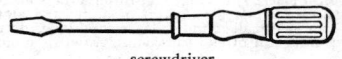

screwdriver

drive them into their place having usu. a thin wedge-shaped end that enters the slot or recess in the head of a screw **2** : a mixture of vodka and orange juice served with ice
screwdriver bit n : a brace bit shank with a screwdriver tip
screwed adj [fr. past part. of ²screw] Brit : INTOXICATED, DRUNK
screwed tail var of SCREW TAIL
screw·er \'skrüə(r)\ n -s : one that screws
screw eye n **1** : a wood screw with a head in the form of a closed eye **2** : a long screw with a handle used esp. by stage carpenters
screw fern n : EBONY SPLEENWORT
screwfly \'s₌,₌\ n : the adult of a screwworm
screw gear or **screw gearing** n **1** : SCREW WHEEL **2** : gearing composed of or having as a chief essential a worm and worm wheel
screwhead \'s₌,₌\ n : the head of a screw
screw hook n : a small hook with a threaded shank for screwing into woodwork or masonry
screwier comparative of SCREWY
screwiest superlative of SCREWY
screw jack n : JACKSCREW
screw joint n : a joint formed by screwing together mating male and female screws
screw key n **1** : a wrench or spanner for turning a screw or nut **2** : a threaded key
screw·less \'skrüləs\ adj : having no screw
screw machine n : a form of turret lathe usu. having a hollow spindle through which a bar can be fed to be machined into bolts, studs, and other screws or any small repetition work ⟨as handles or spindles⟩
screw machinery n : machinery for making screws; esp : semiautomatic machinery for turning out screws in large quantities
screw·man \-ᵻmən\ n, pl **screwmen 1** : one who passes metal through a rolling mill and reduces it to desired thickness

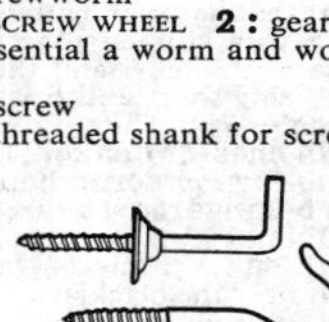

by adjusting screws that regulate roller clearance **2** : one who helps to prepare the way for and to set up power shovels and cranes — called also jackman **3** : one who loads bales of cotton onto a riverboat
screwnail \'s₌,₌\ n **1 a** : WOOD SCREW **b** : DRIVESCREW **2** : a nail with a screw thread to increase its holding power
screw nut n : NUT 3
screw peg n : a small screw without a head used esp. for fastening screw and shoe soles
screw pile n : a usu. hollow and cast iron pile that has a screw flange of usu. from one to two turns and is used in soft mud or other location requiring a large supporting surface at the end of the pile
screw-pile or **screw-piled** \'s₌,₌\ adj [screw pile] : built on screw piles
screw pine n : a plant of the genus Pandanus including several that are cultivated for their ornamental foliage — see TEXTILE SCREW PINE
screw-pine family n : PANDANACEAE
screw-pitch gage n : THREAD GAGE
screw plate n : a flat metal plate with one or more holes drilled, tapped, and filed with a cutting edge for threading screws, pipes, or rods by hand
screw pod or **screw-pod mesquite** n : SCREW BEAN
screw press or **screw punch** n : a press having a ram that is forced downward by the turning of a spindle with a steep-pitched thread
screw propeller n : a device consisting of a central hub with two, three, or more similar radiating blades symmetrically placed and twisted so that each forms part of a helical surface like that of a screw thread and used to propel a vehicle ⟨as a steamship, motorboat, or airplane⟩
screw pump n : a pump in which the working pressure is created by means of screw-shaped impellers in the vertical water column
screw rivet n : a short bolt threaded throughout its length and riveted over on its ends when in place
screws pl of SCREW, pres 3d sing of SCREW
screw shell n : a long slender spiral gastropod shell ⟨as of a gastropod of Turritella or related genera⟩
screw-ship n : a ship driven by a screw propeller
screw spike n : a railroad spike with a screw thread on the upper part of the shank so that the spike can be screwed home after being driven part way in
screw stay n : STAY BOLT
screwstem \'s₌,₌\ n : a plant of the genus Bartonia
screw stud n : STUD BOLT
screw surface n : a surface resembling a screw in form
screw tail or **screwed tail** n : a short knotty twisted tail characteristic of the bulldog but abnormal in most other animals
screw tap n : TAP 5a
screw thread n **1** : the projecting helical rib of a screw **2** : one complete turn of a screw thread — compare PITCH 2b(2); BUTTRESS THREAD, MULTIPLE THREAD, SQUARE THREAD
screw tree n : a shrub or tree of the genus Helicteres; esp : an East Indian shrub (H. isora) sometimes cultivated for its hairy leaves and orange-red flowers
screw up vt **1** : to tighten, fasten, or lock by or as by turning a screw **2** : to raise ⟨as a rent⟩ extortionately
screw vault n : a vault in gymnastics in which the body is raised sideward to clear the apparatus while making a ¾ turn in the opposite direction around its long axis
screw wheel n : a gear wheel with teeth intersecting the pitch surface in helical lines and thus forming parts of the threads of a many-threaded screw : HELICAL GEAR — called also screw gear
screwworm \'s₌,₌\ n : a grub that is the larva of a two-winged fly (Callitroga hominivorax) occurring in the warmer parts of America and sometimes laying its eggs in sores or wounds or in the nostrils of mammals including man, that is armed with rings of small spines, and that bores into the flesh and causes serious or sometimes fatal results; broadly : a calliphorid larva that parasitizes the flesh of mammals
screwworm fly n : SCREWFLY
screw wrench or **screw spanner** n : a wrench that has a jaw adjusted by a screw : ADJUSTABLE WRENCH
screwy \'skrüē, -ùi\ adj -ER/-EST **1** Brit : somewhat intoxicated **2** : hard and exacting in selling or renting : NIGGARDLY, MEAN **3** : involuted like a screw : WINDING, TWISTED, SPIRAL ⟨a big-eared head with glasses and ~ hair —Josephine Johnson⟩ **4 a** : crazily absurd, eccentric, or unusual : oddly and often disturbingly different and unfamiliar ⟨unusual chords and odd slips in the tune and ~ rhythms —Leonard Bernstein⟩ ⟨something is haywire, ~, and badly disrupted —F.A.Johnson⟩ **b** : CRAZY, INSANE ⟨she must have been ~ —Leslie Charteris⟩
scrib·al \'skrībəl\ adj [scribe + -al] : of, relating to, or due to scribes ⟨a ~ error⟩
scrib·bla·tive \'skrībləd·iv\ adj [¹scribble + -ative] : of, relating to, or given to verbose and hastily written writing ⟨the arts babblative and ~ —Robert Southey⟩
¹**scrib·ble** \'skribəl\ vb scribbled; scribbled; scribbling \-b(ə)liŋ\ scribbles [ME scriblen, fr. ML scribillare, fr. L scribere to write — more at SCRIBE] vt **1** : to write hastily or carelessly without regard to legibility, correctness, or considered thought ⟨had to ~ the very first ideas that tinkled in his head —Earle Birney⟩ ⟨just enough time to ~ their own name —H.A.Smith⟩ **2** : to fill or cover with careless or worthless writings ⟨a scribbled envelope⟩ ⟨papers ... scribbled over with clues —English Digest⟩ ~ vi : to write or draw in haste without care as to legibility or value : make indecipherable or meaningless marks
²**scribble** \"\ n -s : a writing of little value; esp : a note written without thought **2** : hasty or careless writing or drawing : illegible or random marks written or drawn ⟨these ~s are the fragmentary meanings I contrive to disengage from the ~s —Aldous Huxley⟩
³**scribble** \"\ vt -ED/-ING/-S [alter. of earlier scruble, prob. fr. D schrobbelen to card, freq. of schrobben to scrub] : to card ⟨wool fibers⟩ coarsely; specif : to perform the preliminary operation of tearing apart
scrib·ble·ment \-bəlmənt\ n -s [¹scribble + -ment] : a scribbled writing : SCRIBBLING
¹**scrib·bler** \-b(ə)lə(r)\ n -s [¹scribble + -er] : one that scribbles: as **a** : an unknown, minor, or amateur writer ⟨an unimportant ~ whose name does not deserve to be dignified by mention —W.M.Payne⟩ **b** : one that writes rapidly, voluminously, or energetically ⟨I am generally supposed to be a determined and energetic ~ —J.B.Priestley⟩
²**scribbler** \"\ n -s [³scribble + -er] : a machine that scribbles wool fibers
scrib·bling·ly adv [scribbling (fr. pres. part. of ¹scribble) + -ly] : in a scribbling manner
scrib·bly \-b(ə)lē, -li\ adj [²scribble + -y] : covered with or consisting of scribbles
scribbly gum n : so-called fr. marks on its bark made by insects] : any of several Australian white ashes (esp. Eucalyptus rossii or E. haemastoma)
¹**scribe** \'skrīb\ n -s [ME, fr. L scriba official writer, fr. scribere to write; akin to Gk skariphasthai to scratch an outline, sketch, skariphos stylus, sketch, keirein to cut — more at SHEAR] **1** : one of a class of men devoted to the study and exposition of the law during the Persian and early Greek periods of Jewish history and serving orig. as copyists, editors, and interpreters of Scripture and esp. of the law and in New Testament times mainly as jurists — called also sopher; compare RABBI **2 a** : an official or public writer acting usu. as a clerk or keeper of accounts **b** : one who writes at dictation **c** : one having secretarial duties; specif : the secretary of a girl scout troop **d** : a skilled penman **e** : one who writes : AUTHOR, WRITER; specif : JOURNALIST **f** : a political writer or journalist
²**scribe** \"\ vb -ED/-ING/-S vi : to work as a scribe : WRITE ~ vt : to write down : INSCRIBE
³**scribe** \"\ vt -ED/-ING/-S [prob. short for describe] **1 a** : to mark ⟨as wood, metal, or brick⟩ by cutting or scratching a line with a pointed instrument ⟨as a scriber or a pair of compasses⟩ **b** : to make ⟨as a line⟩ by cutting or scratching **2** : to cut ⟨an object⟩ to fit closely to a somewhat irregular surface ⟨as a board to the curves of a molding⟩
⁴**scribe** \"\ n -s **1** dial Brit : a written mark **b** : a short

piece of writing **2 a** : SCRIBER **b** : a tool used ⟨as in marking survey lines⟩ for cutting marks into wood or bark **c** also **scribe saw** : a saw-toothed tool for cutting up beef carcasses
scribe saw n : a slaughterhouse worker using a scribe saw
scrib·er \-bə(r)\ n -s [³scribe + -er] **1** : one that scribes; specif : a sharp-pointed tool for marking off material ⟨as wood or metal⟩ to be cut — called also scratch awl

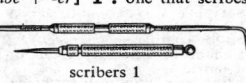

scribers 1

2 [⁴scribe + -er] : a slaughterhouse worker using a scribe saw
scribing n -s [fr. gerund of ³scribe] : an incised or written marking : INSCRIPTION
scribing block n : SURFACE GAUGE 1
scribing iron n : an iron-pointed instrument used for scribing ⟨as on a cask or log⟩
scrib·ism \'skrīᵻbizəm\ n -s [¹scribe + -ism] **1** : the doctrines and activities of the Jewish scribes in the time of Christ **2** : internal authoritarianism and literalistic legalism ⟨as in religion⟩
scried past of SCRY
scries pl of SCRY, pres 3d sing of SCRY
¹**scrieve** \'skrēv\ vi [of Scand origin; akin to ON skrefa to stride] Scot : to move along swiftly and smoothly
²**scrieve** \"\ var of SCRIVE
scriev·er \'skrēvər\ Scot var of SCRIVER 1
¹**scrig·gle** \'skrigəl\ n -s [blend of squirm & wriggle] : WRIGGLE, TWIST, SQUIRM
²**scriggle** \"\ vi -ED/-ING/-S : the act of wriggling **2** : SQUIGGLE
scrike \'skrīk\ vi -ED/-ING/-S [ME scriken, of Scand origin; akin to Norw skrike to shriek, Dan skrige] : SHRIEK
scrim \'skrim\ n -s [origin unknown] **1** : a durable plain-woven fabric usu. of cotton woven loosely with fine to coarse meshes and given various finishes for use in clothing, curtains, building trades, and industry **2** : thin canvas glued on the inside of a panel to prevent distortion ⟨as by shrinking or checking⟩ **3** : a transparent theater drop or a transparent section in a drop **4** : a gauze or mesh panel placed outside of the range of a camera to diffuse harsh light
¹**scrim·mage** \'skrimij, -mēj\ n -s [alter. of ¹skirmish] **1 a** : a minor battle between small forces of armed men : SKIRMISH **b** : a confused scrambling fight between two or more parties : SCUFFLE, BRAWL ⟨escaped from the ~ minus his hat and with his garments woefully torn —Rachel Henning⟩ **2 a** : SCRUMMAGE **b** : the interplay between two teams in American football that begins with the snap of the ball and continues until the ball is dead **c** : practice play between a team's various squads ⟨as in football⟩ **d** : the first line of scrimmage formed after a kickoff in football ⟨first play from ~⟩
²**scrimmage** \"\ vb -ED/-ING/-S vi **1** : to search busily **2** : to take part in a scrimmage ~ vt **1** : to throw ⟨a ball⟩ into a scrimmage **2** : to compete against ⟨an opposing team⟩ in a practice football game ⟨the junior varsity⟩
scrimmage line n : LINE OF SCRIMMAGE
scrim·mag·er \-jə(r)\ n -s [²scrimmage + -er] : a participant in a scrimmage
¹**scrimp** \'skrimp\ adj [perh. of Scand origin; akin to Sw skrympa to shrink — more at SHRIMP] : SCANTY, MEAGER
²**scrimp** \"\ vb -ED/-ING/-S vt **1** : to be niggardly in providing for : put on short allowance ⟨~s his family⟩ **2** : to make too small, short, or scanty : be sparing or niggardly in or with : limit too closely ⟨~ the pattern of a coat⟩ ⟨~ food⟩ **3** : to save slowly and with difficulty by minor economies ⟨here's five bob I've been ~ing from the house money —Ruth Park⟩ ~ vi : to be frugal or niggardly in economizing ⟨office girls who ~ all year to pay for their vacations —Tibor Koeves⟩ ⟨in restoring the place they ~ed on plumbing —W.A.White⟩
scrimp·tion \-m(p)shən\ n -s [²scrimp + -tion] chiefly dial : a small amount ⟨chiefly dial⟩ : PITTANCE
scrimpy \-mpē,-mpi\ adj -ER/-EST [scrimp + -y] **1** : small or barely sufficient in size or quantity : MEAGER, SCANTY ⟨her ~ and short white petticoat —Elizabeth C. Gaskell⟩ **2** : given to scrimping : PARSIMONIOUS syn see MEAGER
scrimshander or **scrimshandy** var of SKRIMSHANDER
scrim·shank \'skrim,shaŋk\ vi -ED/-ING/-S [origin unknown] Brit : to shirk one's work or obligations
scrim·shank·er \-ᵻŋkə(r)\ n -s [scrimshank + -er] Brit : SHIRKER
¹**scrim·shaw** \'skrim,shȯ\ n -s [prob. alter. of skrimshander] **1** : any of various carved or engraved useful or decorative articles ⟨as canes, cribbage boards, corset stays, snuff boxes, or small pieces of statuary⟩ sometimes colored by brushing ink into the engraved lines and made esp. by American whalemen esp. from whalebone or whale ivory **2** : scrimshawed work ⟨a large collection of ~⟩ **3** : the art, practice, or technique of producing scrimshaw
²**scrimshaw** \"\ vb -ED/-ING/-S vt : to carve or engrave ⟨as a whale's tooth or jawbone⟩ into scrimshaw ~ vi : to produce scrimshaw
scri·my \'skrīmē\ adj -ER/-EST [origin unknown] **1** : STINGY, NIGGARDLY **2** : DIRTY, DISGUSTING ⟨worry about the gossip, secretiveness, and other ~ sides —Al Hine⟩
scrin \'skrin\ n -s [prob. akin to OHG scrunta split, crack, scrintan to split] dial Eng : a small ore vein
scrinch \'skrinch\ vt -ES [origin unknown] dial Eng : a tiny bit : PINCH
¹**scringe** \'skrinj\ vi -ED/-ING/-S [alter. (perh. influenced by shrink) of ¹cringe] dial : CRINGE, FLINCH
²**scringe** \"\ vt [origin unknown] dial : to flog the water in fishing
³**scringe** \"\ n -s : a small seine net used in scringing
¹**scrip** \'skrip\ n -s [ME scrippe, fr. ML scrippum pilgrim's knapsack, perh. fr. L scirpus bulrush, reed] archaic : a small bag or wallet carried esp. by a pilgrim or shepherd
²**scrip** \"\ n -s [in senses 1 & 2 short for ¹script; in senses 3 & 4 prob. short for subscription receipt] **1** : a short writing ⟨as a certificate, memorandum, schedule, or list⟩ ⟨call them generally, man by man, according to the ~ —Shak.⟩ **2** : a small piece or scrap ⟨as of paper⟩ **3** : any of various documents used as evidence that the holder or bearer is entitled to receive something either absolutely or conditionally: as **a** : a preliminary certificate issued after an allotment usu. on payment of the first installment to one who has subscribed for stock of a bank, railroad, or other company, for a share of other joint property, or for a loan stating the amount subscribed for, the amount already paid, and the dates when the installments are due ⟨insurance ~⟩ ⟨consol ~⟩ and when all installments are paid exchanged for a bond or share certificate **b** : a certificate for a fractional part of a share of stock or of a bond often issued to bondholders upon reorganization or to a stockholder in lieu of a cash dividend and usu. convertible when presented in an amount equal to the face value of a share or bond **c** : a paper currency or token issued for temporary use in an emergency **d** : a certificate of indebtedness in the form of a promise to pay or a certification good for money or goods receivable from a concern that needs funds or pays wages partly in orders on a company store **e** : a certificate ⟨as issued by a federal or state government⟩ that the holder is entitled to take up or receive an allotment of land **4** : documents issued as scrip
scrip abbr scriptural; scripture
scrip dividend n [²scrip] : a dividend payable in promissory notes instead of cash
scrip·less \'skripləs\ adj [¹scrip + -less] : having no wallet
scrip·page \'skripij\ n -s [¹scrip + -age] : the contents of a scrip
¹**script** \'skript\ n -s [L scriptum thing written, fr. neut. of scriptus, past part. of scribere to write — more at SCRIBE] **1 a** : something written : TEXT ⟨ancient philosophers whose ~s they had diligently studied —Erwin Schrödinger⟩ **b** : an original or principal instrument or document ⟨as a will or codicil⟩ when executed with copies or a copy when the original is lost **c** (1) : MANUSCRIPT 2 (2) : the written text of a stage play, screenplay, or radio or television broadcast; specif : the typescript or mimeographed or published text of a stage play, screenplay, or radio or television broadcast **2 a** : a printed letter similar to a handwritten letter — sometimes used of letters that join each other and thereby distinguished from cursive **b** : written characters : HANDWRITING ⟨drew a sheet of paper to him and began to cover it with his thin irritable ~

—Ngaio Marsh⟩ ⟨some of the letters were printed capitals, others were in ~ —E.D.Radin⟩ **c** : a set of characters used in writing one or more languages : ALPHABET ⟨written in a ~ which consists entirely of consonants —T.H.Gaster⟩

²script \"\ vt -ED/-ING/-S **1** : to prepare a script for ⟨has his program ~ed, though eventually he plans to work into an ad-lib routine —*Newsweek*⟩ **2** : to prepare a script from : adapt for the stage, screen, or broadcasting ⟨~ a novel into a movie⟩

script abbr scriptural; scripture

script editor or **script reader** n [¹script] : one that edits radio and television scripts, continuities, and commercials to assure conformity with government regulations and company policy — compare CONTINUITY ACCEPTANCE

script·er \'skriptə(r)\ n -s [²script + -er] : SCRIPTWRITER

script girl n [¹script] : a secretary to a motion-picture director who records information about the photographing of each scene, prompts actors, and writes a synopsis for advertising the movie

scrip·tio de·fec·ti·va \'skriptē,ō,dā,fek'tēvə\ n [NL, lit., defective writing] : a writing in a Semitic alphabet that contains no vowel points

scrip·tion \'skripshən\ n -s [L scription-, scriptio act of writing, fr. scriptus (past part. of scribere to write) + -ion, -io -ion — more at SCRIBE] **1** obs : INSCRIPTION **2** : style of handwriting : HANDWRITING

scrip·tio ple·na \,skriptē,ō'plānə\ n [NL, lit., full writing] : a writing in a Semitic alphabet that contains vowel points

script lichen n [¹script] : a letter lichen (*Graphis scripta*)

scriptore n -s [alter. (influenced by scriptory) of obs. E scritore escritoire, modif. of F escritoire] obs : WRITING DESK

scrip·to·ri·al \(')skrip¦tōrēəl\ adj [L scriptorius of writing + E -al] : of, relating to, or resembling script

scrip·to·ri·um \skrip'tōrēəm\ also **scrip·to·ry** \'skriptərē\ n, pl **scripto·ria** \skrip'tōrēə\ also **scriptories** \'skriptərēz\ [ML scriptorium, fr. L scriptus + -orium -ory] : a writing room; specif : a copying room in a medieval monastery set apart for the scribes

scrip·to·ry \'skriptərē\ adj [L scriptorius, fr. scriptus (past part. of scribere to write) + -orius -ory — more at SCRIBE] : of, relating to, expressed in, or used in writing

script-scene \'=,=\ n : a division of a shooting script or screenplay corresponding to a single shot in a motion picture

scrip·tur·al \'skripchərəl, -psh(ə)rəl\ adj [scripture + -al] **1** sometimes cap : of, relating to, contained in, or according to a sacred writing; specif : of or relating to the Bible : BIBLICAL **2** : done in or relating to writing

scrip·tur·al·ism \-ə,lizəm\ n -s [scriptural + -ism] : literal adherence to a body of scripture

scrip·tur·al·ist \-ələst\ n -s often cap [scriptural + -ist] **1** : one who derives his religious beliefs and general philosophy of life from a body of scripture teaching a single harmonious system of doctrine **2** : one learned in or a devoted student of a body of scripture **3** : KITABI

scrip·tu·ral·i·ty \,skripchə'ralədē, -pshə-, -lətē, -i\ n -ES sometimes cap [scriptural + -ity] **1** : the quality of being scriptural **2** : a thing that is scriptural

scrip·tur·al·ly \'skripchərəlē, -psh(ə)r-, -li\ adv [scriptural + -ly] : in accordance with scripture

scrip·tur·al·ness \-rəlnəs\ n -ES : the quality or state of being scriptural

scrip·ture \'skripchə(r), -psh-\ n -s [ME, fr. LL scriptura, fr. L, act or product of writing, fr. scriptus (past part. of scribere to write) + -ura -ure — more at SCRIBE] **1 a (1)** usu cap : the books of the Old and New Testament or of either of them : BIBLE ⟨a collection . . . from the various parts of the *Scripture* —J.C.Swaim⟩ — often used in pl. ⟨the demand for the *Scriptures* in a familiar tongue has found expression in a great activity of Bible translation —L.A.Weigle⟩ (2) usu cap : a passage or text from the Bible ⟨in their case was the *Scripture* fulfilled that the first shall be last and the last first —E.C. Colwell⟩ **b** : sacred writing of a religion ⟨Buddhist ~⟩ **c** : a body of writings considered as authoritative ⟨his critical essays provide the ~ of the movement⟩ or as classically embodying the essence of a way of life, movement, era, or nation — often used in pl. ⟨the American ~s, the great books of the eighteen-fifties —Van Wyck Brooks⟩ **2** : something written : a writing or portion of a writing ⟨the primitive man's awe for any ~ —George Santayana⟩

scripturient adj [LL scripturient-, scripturiens, pres. part. of scripturire to desire to write, desiderative of L scribere] obs : having a strong urge to write

scrip·tur·ism \'skripchə,rizəm, -psh-\ n -s [scripture + -ism] **1** sometimes cap : SCRIPTURALISM **2** : a phrase originating in Scripture

scrip·tur·ist \-pchərəst, -psh(ə)r-\ n -s sometimes cap [scripture + -ist] : SCRIPTURALIST

scriptwriter \'=,==\ n [¹script + writer] : one that writes screenplays or radio or television programs

scritch \'skrich\ chiefly dial var of SCREECH

scri·vaille \skrə'vī\ n -s [by alter.] : SCRIVELLO

scrivan or **scrivano** n, pl **scrivans** or **scrivani** [It scrivano, fr. (assumed) VL scriban-, scriba — more at SCRIVENER] : SCRIBE

¹scrive \'skrīv, -rēv\ vt -ED/-ING/-S [ME scriven, prob. fr. MF escrivre, fr. L scribere — more at SCRIBE] chiefly Scot : WRITE, INSCRIBE

²scrive \"\ n -s **1** chiefly Scot : written matter **2** chiefly Scot : HANDWRITING

scrive board n : a platform of well-seasoned boards on which are drawn full-size the lines of the body of a ship to be built — compare BODY PLAN

scri·vel·lo \skrə'vel(,)lō\ n -ES [origin unknown] : an elephant's tusk of a small size commonly used for making billiard balls

scriv·en \'skrivən\ vt **scrivened; scrivened; scrivening** \-v(ə)niŋ\ **scrivens** [back-formation fr. scrivener] archaic : to put in writing : WRITE ⟨this is the thesis ~ed in delight —Wallace Stevens⟩

scriv·en·er \'skriv(ə)nə(r)\ n -s [ME scriveiner, fr. scrivein copyist, professional writer (fr. MF escrivein, escrivain, fr. — assumed — VL scriban-, scriba, fr. L scriba scribe) + -er — more at SCRIBE] **1 a** : a professional or public copyist or writer : SCRIBE **b** : a usu. minor or unknown author ⟨never before had mere ~s received weekly salaries in the four-figure bracket —Roger Butterfield & Roland Gelatt⟩ **2** : one whose occupation is to draw contracts or prepare writings : NOTARY **3** : a former agent receiving money for investment at interest and performing duties now usu. performed by a banker, broker, or lawyer

scrivener's palsy n : WRITER'S CRAMP

scriv·en·ery \-v(ə)nərē\ n -ES [scrivener + -ry] : a scrivener's occupation, writing, or place of work

scrivening n -s [fr. gerund of scriven] : the occupation or product of a scrivener : WRITING ⟨editorials and the ~s of columnists —R.E.Wolseley⟩

scriv·er \'skrīvər, -rēv-\ n -s [¹scrive + -er] **1** chiefly Scot : WRITER **2** : PARTING TOOL

scrn abbr screen

scrobe \'skrōb\ n -s [L scrobis ditch, trench — more at SCRAPE] : a small groove (as at the base of the antenna of a weevil or on the outer surface of a mandible)

scro·bic·u·la \skrō'bikyələ\ also **scrobi·cule** \'skrōbə,kyül, -räb-\ n, pl **scro·bi·cu·lae** \skrō'bikyə,lē, -,lī\ also **scrobicules** [NL scrobicula, alter. of L scrobiculus little trench, dim. of scrobis] : a shallow trench (as one of the smooth depressions surrounding the tubercles of a sea urchin) — **scro·bic·u·lar** \skrō'bikyələ(r)\ adj

scro·bic·u·late \skrō'bikyələt, -,lāt\ adj [L scrobiculus + E -ate] : having numerous shallow grooves or depressions : PITTED

scro·bic·u·lus \-ləs\ n, pl **scrobicu·li** \-,lī\ [NL, fr. L, small trench] : SCROBICULA

¹scrod \'skräd\ or **es·crod** \ə'skräd\ n -s [perh. fr. obs. D schrood piece cut off, shred, fr. MD schrode — more at SHRED] **1 a** : a young cod (*Gadus morrhua*) **b** : the young of any of several other fishes (as the haddock) **2 a** : a small cod split and boned for cooking **b** : a fillet taken from the thick meat just ahead of the tail of a fish (as a cod, haddock, pollack)

²scrod \"\ vt **scrodded; scrodded; scrodding; scrods** : to split or fillet (a fish) for cooking

scroful- or **scrofulo-** comb form [NL, fr. ML scrofula] **1** : scrofula ⟨*scrofulosis*⟩ **2** : scrofulous and ⟨*scrofulotuberculous*⟩

scrof·u·la \'skrȯfyələ also -räf-\ n -s [ML, fr. LL scrofulae (pl.) swellings of the lymph glands of the neck, lit., little sows, pl. of scrofula, dim of L scrofa breeding sow] : tuberculosis of lymph glands esp. in the neck

scrofularoot \'===,=\ n [scrofula + root; fr. its supposed efficacy in the treatment of scrofula] : DOGTOOTH VIOLET

scrofulaweed \'===,=\ n [scrofula + weed; fr. its supposed efficacy in the treatment of scrofula] : a rattlesnake plantain (*Goodyera pubescens*)

scrof·u·lo·der·ma \,==lō'dərmə\ n -s [NL, fr. scroful- + -derma] : a disease of the skin of tuberculous origin (as an inflammation of the neck from draining tuberculous lymph glands) — **scrof·u·lo·der·mic** \¦===¦dərmik\ adj

scrof·u·lo·sis \,==='lōsəs\ n, pl **scrofulo·ses** \-ō,sēz\ [NL, fr. scroful- + -osis] : the condition of being scrofulous : scrofular diathesis

scrof·u·lous \'skrȯfyələs also -räf-\ adj [scrofula + -ous] **1** archaic **a** : of, relating to, or characteristic of scrofula ⟨a child, full of ~ ulcers —Tobias Smollett⟩ **b** : afflicted with scrofula ⟨handled a ~ Quaker, and made him a healthy man —T.B.Macaulay⟩ **2 a** : having a diseased appearance ⟨our canoe . . . lay with her ~ sides on the shore —Farley Mowat⟩ **b** : morally contaminated ⟨denounce the ~ wealth of the times —J.D.Hart⟩

scrog \'skräg\ n -s [ME skrogge, scroge] **1** dial Brit : a stunted shrub, bush, or branch : SCRUB **2** dial Brit : scrubby land — usu. used in pl.

¹scroll \'skrōl\ n -s often attrib [ME scrowle, alter. (influenced by rolle roll) of scrowe, fr. MF escroe, escroue scrap, strip of parchment, scroll, of Gmc origin; akin to MD schrode piece cut off, shred — more at SHRED] **1 a** : a long strip (as of papyrus, leather, or parchment) used as the body of a written document and often having a rod with handles at one or both ends for convenience in rolling and storing it ⟨when parchment became available . . . its greater strength permitted the transcription of the entire book on to one long ~ —A.P. Davies⟩ **b** archaic : a written message (as a letter) ⟨do not exceed the prescript of this ~ —Shak.⟩ **c** : a roster of names : LIST ⟨his name was placed high upon the ~ of the world's great —J.C.Fitzpatrick⟩ **d** : an ornamental riband with rolled ends often inscribed with a motto; specif : ESCROL **e** : a formal testimonial usu. engraved or hand illuminated on special paper (as parchment or vellum) ⟨the guest of honor received a framed ~ —*Springfield (Mass.) Union*⟩ **2 a** : something that is likened to a scroll ⟨a great glissando, a ~ from the wind instruments —Sacheverell Sitwell⟩ ⟨history which forms the running ~ of his . . . experience —S.H. Adams⟩ **b** : a crescentic deposit of a meandering stream on a floodplain **3** : a part or ornament more or less resembling a scroll in shape: as **a** : any of various spiral or convoluted forms in ornamental design derived from the curves of a loosely or partly rolled parchment scroll ⟨an oval mat with a row of ~s forming the center —Mabel Roffey & Charlotte Cross⟩ **b (1)** : a volute of an Ionic, Corinthian, or composite capital (2) : a curved molding common in medieval work **c** : a spiral formation or ornament of furniture — see FLEMISH SCROLL; LEG illustration **d** : the curved head of a bowed stringed musical instrument — see VIOLIN illustration **e** : SCROLLHEAD **f (1)** : a spiral-shaped rib or slot for gearing with a slot on a radially moving part (as the jaw of a scroll chuck) (2) : a casing for a turbine wheel having a spiral waterway of converging aperture (3) : a similar casing on a centrifugal pump or blower (4) : a curved portion at the end of a leaf spring (5) : a loop or coil of copper tubing inside a still

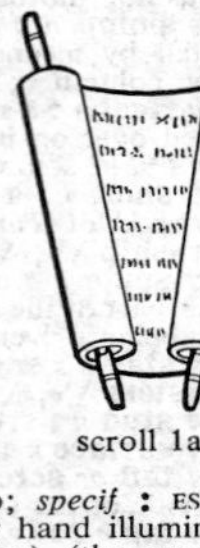

scroll 1a

²scroll \"\ vb -ED/-ING/-S vt **1** : to inscribe on or as if on a scroll ⟨the panel on which 38B was delicately ~ed —Kay Boyle⟩ **2** : to form into or adorn with scrolls ⟨the river is ~ed in shining bends across the flatlands⟩ ~ vi : to curl up or roll out like a scroll ⟨bright yellow material, with ~ing scarlet roses —H.E.Bates⟩ ⟨the long hourly routine ~ed ahead of me —Nathaniel Burt⟩

scroll chuck n : a universal chuck having jaws moved by a metal scroll that engages slots or threads in the jaws

scroll creeper n : CROCKET 1

scroll-cut \'=¦=\ adj : cut in the form of a scroll or with a scroll saw

scrolled \'skrōld\ adj [¹scroll + -ed] **1** : formed into or adorned with scrolls ⟨the dark ~ iron of balustrades —Jack Kerouac⟩ ⟨a boldly ~ tie —Katharine T. Kinkead⟩ **2** : CURVED, SERPENTINE ⟨the ~ earthworks of the mound builders⟩

scroll·ery \-l(ə)rē, -ri\ n -ES [¹scroll + -ery] : SCROLLWORK

scroll foot n : the foot of a piece of furniture terminating in a downward turning scroll — see FOOT illustration

scroll front n : the serpentine face of a piece of furniture characteristic esp. of the late Empire style

scroll gear also **scroll wheel** n : a variable gear in the form of a flat scroll having the teeth showing on one face

scrollhead \'=,=\ n : an ornamental curved timber at the prow of a ship

scroll lathe n : a special wood-turning lathe for cutting scrolls and spirals

scroll pediment n : a broken pediment with raking cornices in the form of reverse curves

scroll saw n **1** : a thin handsaw for cutting curves or irregular designs **2** : FRETSAW, JIGSAW

scroll-shaped \'=¦=\ adj : formed in a compound curve

scroll step n, archit : a curtail step

scrollwork \'=,=\ n : ornamentation characterized by scrolls ⟨gilt ~ on hand-painted china⟩; esp : fancy designs in wood often made with a scroll saw ⟨a wide veranda with ~ along the edge of its roof —Raymond Chandler⟩

scrolly \'skrōlē\ adj, sometimes -ER/-EST [¹scroll + -y] : full of scrolls or curlicues ⟨fine ~ script⟩ ⟨~ Victorian furniture⟩

scrooch \'skrüch also -ü·\ vi -ED/-ING/-ES [by alter.] : CROUCH, HUDDLE — often used with down ⟨~ed down in the seat and tried to hide —H.E.Giles⟩ ⟨she ~ed down in under all the covers —Richard Bissell⟩

scrooge \'skrüj\ n -s often cap [fr. Ebenezer Scrooge, chief character in *A Christmas Carol* (1843), story by Charles Dickens †1870 Eng. author] : a miserly person ⟨Scrooges in the pursuit of the almighty dollar —Warner Olivier⟩

scroonch var of SCRUNCH

scroop \'skrüp\ n -s [imit.] : a rasping sound : CREAK, SCRAPE; specif : the crisp rustle of silk or similar cloth that has been treated with dilute acid

scroph·u·lar·ia \,skräfyə'la(a)rēə, -rȯf-\ n [NL, fr. ML scrofula, scrophula scrofula + NL -aria; fr. the supposed efficacy of such plants in the treatment of scrofula] **1** cap : a large genus (the type of the family Scrophulariaceae) of coarse often strong-smelling perennial herbs that are native to temperate regions and have terminal clusters of small flowers with a gibbous corolla consisting of four erect lobes and one spreading lip, four anthers, and one staminodium **2** -s : any plant or flower of the genus *Scrophularia*

scroph·u·lar·i·a·ce·ae \,==,=='āsē,ē\ n pl, cap [NL, fr. Scrophularia, type genus + -aceae] : a widely distributed family of herbs, shrubs, or rarely trees (order Polemoniales) having exstipulate leaves, a more or less irregular bilabiate corolla with four didynamous stamens, and a 2-celled ovary — see FIGWORT — **scroph·u·lar·i·a·ceous** \¦==,==¦āshəs\ adj

scrot- or **scroti-** or **scroto-** comb form [NL scrotum] **1** : scrotum ⟨*scrotiform*⟩ **2** : scrotal and ⟨*scrotofemoral*⟩

scro·tal \'skrōd·ᵊl, -ōtᵊl\ adj [NL scrotalis, fr. L scrotum + -alis -al] **1 a** : of or relating to the scrotum : lying in or having descended into the scrotum ⟨~ testes⟩ **b** : grooved, furrowed, or fissured like a scrotum ⟨~ tongue⟩ **2** : having a scrotum ⟨~ mammals⟩

scro·ti·form \¦ə,fȯrm\ adj [scrot- + -iform] : shaped like a pouch

scro·to·cele \¦ə,sēl\ n -s [scrot- + -cele] : a scrotal hernia

scro·tum \'skrōd·|əm, -ōt|\ n, pl **scro·ta** \|ə\ or **scrotums** [L; akin to L scrupus sharp stone — more at SHRED] : the external pouch that in most mammals contains the testes

scrouge \'skrüj, -raùj\ or **scrooge** \-rüj\ vb -ED/-ING/-S [alter. of scruze] chiefly dial : to squeeze together : CROWD, PRESS

¹scrounge \'skraùnj\ vb -ED/-ING/-S [alter. of E dial. scrunge to wander about idly] vt **1 a** : to collect by foraging : round up : FIND, SALVAGE ⟨~ wood from bombed-out areas —A.W. Bromage⟩ — often used with up ⟨manpower might be summoned . . . and feed material scrounged up —R.E.Lapp⟩ **b** : to acquire by other expedient means (as by borrowing, stealing, or swapping) ⟨got a shave and a haircut from a fellow prisoner who had scrounged a pair of clippers somewhere —E.J.Kahn⟩ ⟨had to ~ water from the engine for their tea —Jack Wadsworth⟩ **2** : to obtain by persuasion : CADGE, WHEEDLE ⟨the more money they can ~ out of local communities, the more projects they can build —*New Republic*⟩ **3** chiefly dial : SCROUGE ⟨a number of his colleagues . . . are scrounged down into two columns under the cartoon —A.J.Liebling⟩ ~ vi **1** : to make a search : poke around : FORAGE, HUNT ⟨scrounged for food in a burned field —*Look*⟩ — often used with around ⟨~ around and persuade someone to run off mimeographed copies for you —*Infantry Jour.*⟩ ⟨not ashamed to ~ around at night, picking up useful things —Richard Harrington⟩ **2** : WHEEDLE ⟨on relief and scrounging for more of the city's money than they were entitled to —Harrison Smith⟩

²scrounge \"\ n -s **1** : material acquired by scrounging ⟨decided to improve our surroundings with ~ from neighboring houses —*Infantry Jour.*⟩ **2** : an act of scrounging

scroung·er \-jə(r)\ n -s : one that scrounges

scrounging n -s [fr. gerund of ¹scrounge] : the acquisition of goods or services other than by direct purchase ⟨did a little ~ when he was British ambassador to the Porte in 1801, and . . . our possession of these sculptures is due to a mixture of luck and audacity —Elizabeth Montizambert⟩

scrow var of SCREW

scroyle \'skrȯi(ə)l\ n -s [origin unknown] archaic : GOOD-FOR-NOTHING, SCOUNDREL

¹scrub \'skrəb\ n -s often attrib [ME, alter. of schrobbe, shrobbe shrub — more at SHRUB] **1 a** : a stunted tree or shrub ⟨tundra vegetation . . . consists of moss, lichen, dwarf ~s and peat moor —W.G.East⟩ **b** : vegetation consisting chiefly of dwarf or stunted trees and shrubs that is often thick and impenetrable and grows in poor soil or in sand ⟨mallee ~⟩ ⟨pine ~⟩ **c** : a tract of country covered with such vegetation (as a palmetto barren of the southern U.S.) **2 a** : a domestic animal of mixed or unknown parentage and usu. without definite type or markings **b** : MONGREL **3 a** : a person of insignificant size or social standing : NOBODY, RUNT ⟨some pimpled dirty little ~ in sandals —Virginia Woolf⟩ **b (1)** : a person of secondary rank : SUBORDINATE ⟨represented in the Far East . . . by incompetents and ~s —Richard Watts⟩ (2) : a hotel or restaurant worker who substitutes for or assumes part of the responsibility of his superior **4 a** : a sports contest involving random individuals or teams having fewer than the regular number of players; specif : a softball or baseball game in which players participate as individuals rather than as team members and rotate to new positions as each out is made **b (1)** : a player not belonging to the first string (2) : a team composed of such players

²scrub \"\ vb **scrubbed; scrubbed; scrubbing; scrubs** [of LG or Scand origin; akin to MLG & MD schrobben, schrubben to scrub, Sw skrubba, Dan skrubbe] vt **1 a** : to clean with abrasive action (as by using a washboard or a stiff brush) : SCOUR ⟨~ clothes⟩ ⟨~ a floor⟩ ⟨we scrubbed her with lye and swabbed her down with seawater —Kenneth Roberts⟩ **b** : to subject to friction : RUB, SCRATCH ⟨scrubbed his eyes in disbelief —*Time*⟩ ⟨rubber tires scrubbed the runway —Horace Sutton⟩ **c** : to cleanse and disinfect (the hands and forearms) before participating in surgery **2 a** : to wash (a gas or vapor) with water, a light hydrocarbon oil, or other liquid to remove impurities or recover desired components **b** : to separate from a gas — often with out ⟨the light oil scrubbed from carbureted water gas⟩ ⟨~ out acetone from tank acetylene⟩ **3** : to wipe out : CANCEL, ELIMINATE ⟨under the tight moon-shooting timetable, a brief delay . . . can ~ the shoot —*Newsweek*⟩ ⟨200 housing units blueprinted for construction there had been scrubbed when the . . . budget was reduced —*N.Y.Times*⟩ ~ vi **1** : to do washing and scouring ⟨must ~ and clean for you the rest of my life —W.M.Gallichan⟩ **2** : to get ready for surgery by scrubbing ⟨the surgeon was preparing to ~ —H.F. & Katharine Pringle⟩

³scrub \"\ n -s **1** : an act or instance of scrubbing; specif : a surgical scrub-up **2 a** : an implement used for scrubbing : BRUSH ⟨churn brushes, deck ~s . . . and sundry others —*Country Life*⟩ **b** : something that resembles a scrub brush ⟨a square military ~ of a moustache —William Sansom⟩ **3** : one that scrubs : DRUDGE ⟨hotel ~s and chambermaids⟩

scrub·ba·ble \'skrəbəbəl\ adj : capable of being scrubbed

scrubbed adj [fr. past part. of ²scrub] **1** archaic : SCRUBBY ⟨a little ~ boy —Shak.⟩ **2** : made clean by or as if by scrubbing ⟨an immaculate, ~ Scotsman —Eamonn Andrews⟩ ⟨stroll . . . in the ~ Sunday twilight —Alan Schneider⟩

¹scrub·ber \'skrəbə(r)\ n -s [²scrub + -er] : one that scrubs: as **a** : one that cleans (as floors, clothes, pelts) by scrubbing **b** : ABRASIVE, BRUSH **c** : an apparatus for removing impurities esp. from gases ⟨large exhaust ~s . . . filter the exhaust of harmful gases —*Sperryscope*⟩ ⟨ammonia tower ~s⟩ ⟨spray ~s⟩

²scrubber \"\ n -s [¹scrub + -er] **1 a** : one that inhabits the scrub **b** Austral : a domestic animal that has run wild **2** Austral : ¹SCRUB 2

scrubbing n -s [fr. gerund of ²scrub] : a removal of dirt or impurities : SCOURING, WASHING ⟨repeated ~s have given the wood a silvery sheen —*Amer. Guide Series: Mich.*⟩ ⟨passage of steam through the spray falling from this baffle furnishes additional ~ —*advt*⟩

scrub birch n [¹scrub] : a flat mat-forming or sometimes ascending shrub (*Betula glandulosa*) of arctic and alpine No. America that has small roundish leaves and twigs dotted with resinous glands and often forms dense growths on mountaintops

scrubbird \'=,=\ n : a bird living in or frequenting brush or scrub; esp : a small Australian passerine bird (*Atrichornis rufescens*) related to the lyrebirds, inhabiting dense forests, and having only two pairs of syringeal muscles and rudimentary clavicles

scrubboard \'=,=\ n [²scrub + board] : BASEBOARD

scrub brush or **scrubbing brush** n : a brush with hard bristles for heavy cleaning (as scrubbing floors)

scrub·by \'skrəbē, -bi\ adj -ER/-EST [¹scrub + -y] **1 a** : stunted in size : meager in quality : RUNTY, POOR ⟨jack oak and . . . ~ cut-over pine —W.F.Davis⟩ ⟨stretches of forests, broken . . . by small ~ farms —*Amer. Guide Series: Maine*⟩ **b** : lacking distinction in rank or appearance : INFERIOR, SHABBY ⟨~ little shipping clerks —Marguerite Steen⟩ ⟨wears a ~ old tweed coat that has seen better days⟩ **2** : consisting of scrub : covered with stunted vegetation ⟨open ~ forests —P.E.James⟩ ⟨the ~, blotchy land through which he rides —Curtis Dahl⟩ **3** : being short and bristly ⟨a sandy, ~, wayward little mustache —W.A.White⟩

scrub chestnut oak n [¹scrub] : CHINQUAPIN OAK b

scrub fowl or **scrub hen** n : MEGAPODE

scrub kangaroo n : GIANT KANGAROO

scrubland \'=,=\ n : land covered with scrub

scrub oak n : any of various chiefly American oaks (as the bear oak, the blackjack, or a chinquapin oak) of small size and usu. shrubby habit that are often a dominant life form on thin dry soils and sometimes form dense thickets of great extent

scrub palmetto n : any of several low-growing palmettos; esp : SAW PALMETTO

scrub pine n **1** : a pine of dwarf, straggly, or scrubby growth usu. by reason of environmental conditions : a pine tree unsuitable for lumber by reason of inferior or defective growth ⟨much eastern *scrub pine* is Jersey pine while in some western areas it is lodgepole pine⟩ **2** : BLACK CYPRESS PINE

scrub plane n : a narrow carpenter's plane with a rounded cutting edge used for the removal of an excessive amount of stock

scrub robin n : an Australian singing bird of the genus *Drymodes*

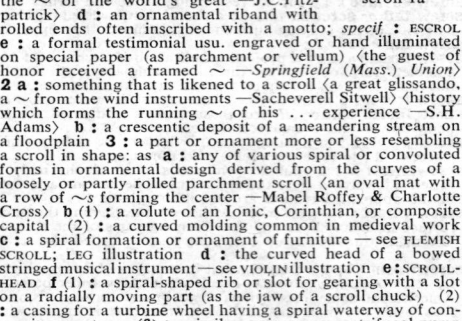

scrubs *pl of* SCRUB, *pres 3d sing of* SCRUB
scrub sandalwood *n* **1 :** a small Australian timber tree (*Exocarpus latifolius*) of the family Santalaceae **2 :** the wood of the scrub sandalwood tree
scrub tick *n* **:** an Australian tick (*Ixodes holocyclus*) that attacks mammals and poultry
scrub turkey *n* **:** MEGAPODE; *esp* **:** BRUSH TURKEY
scrub typhus *n* **:** TSUTSUGAMUSHI DISEASE
scrub–up \ˈ=,=\ *n* -S [³*scrub* + *up*] **:** an act or process of scrubbing ⟨the bathroom is equipped with both shower and tub, for quick *scrub-ups* —*Better Homes & Gardens*⟩; *specif* **:** aseptic preparation for surgery
scrub vine *n* [¹*scrub*] **:** a leafless woody vine (*Cassytha melantha*) of Australia
scrub wallaby *n* **:** PADEMELON; *esp* **:** DAMA PADEMELON
scrubwoman \ˈ=,=\ *n, pl* **scrubwomen** [²*scrub* + *woman*] **:** CLEANING WOMAN, CHARWOMAN
scrubwood \ˈ=,=\ *n* [¹*scrub*] **1 :** SCRUB 1b **2 :** GUMWOOD 2
scrub wren *n* **:** a small Australian singing bird of the genus *Sericornis*
¹**scruff** \ˈskrəf, -rüf-\ *n* -S [alter. of *scurf*] **1** *dial chiefly Eng* **:** DANDRUFF, SCURF **2 :** one that is worthless or contemptible **3 a** *dial chiefly Eng* **:** a thin coating **:** CRUST, FILM **b :** skimmings from tinning pots
²**scruff** *vt* -ED/-ING/-S *obs* **:** to treat lightly **:** slur over
³**scruff** \ˈskrəf\ *n* -S [alter. (perh. influenced by ¹*scruff*) of ³*scuff*] **1 :** the back of the neck **:** NAPE **2 :** a loose part of the clothing (as a coat collar or the seat of the pants)
scruf·fle \ˈskrəfəl, -rüf-\ *dial Eng var of* SCUFFLE
scruff·man \ˈskrəfmən\ *n, pl* **scruffmen** [¹*scruff* + *man*] **:** a smelter who melts tin for use in galvanizing steel in a reverberatory furnace
scruffy \ˈskrəfē\ *adj* -ER/-EST [¹*scruff* + -*y*] **:** of a worthless or slovenly character **:** SHABBY, MISERABLE ⟨a surge of ragged ~ children —Bruce Marshall⟩ ⟨moved to a ~ little coffee bar . . . and sat at a smeared table —Martha Gellhorn⟩ ⟨that ~, sandy waste —Osbert Lancaster⟩
scrum \ˈskrəm\ *or* **scrum·mage** \-mij\ *n* -S [*scrum* short for *scrummage*; *scrummage*, alter. of *scrimmage*] **:** a rugby play in which the forwards of each side crouch side by side typically in 3-2-3 formation and with locked arms, the two front lines meet shoulder to shoulder, and play starts by the placing of the ball between the front lines for the two sides to compete for possession of — called also *tight scrummage*; compare LOOSE SCRUM
scrum half *n* **:** the rugby halfback who places the ball in the scrum
scrum·mage \ˈskrəmij\ *vi* -ED/-ING/-S [*scrummage*, n.] **:** to form a rugby scrum
scrum·mag·er \-jə(r)\ *n* -S **:** one that scrummages
¹**scrump** \ˈskrəmp, -ü-\ *n* -S [prob. of Scand origin; akin to Sw & Dan *skrumpen* shriveled] *dial Eng* **:** something that is shriveled or cooked to a crisp
²**scrump** \ˈ"\ *vb* -ED/-ING/-S [prob. of Scand origin; akin to Dan *skrumpe* to shrivel] *dial Eng* **:** SHRIVEL, SHRINK
scrump·tious \ˈskrəm(p)shəs\ *adj* [prob. alter. of *sumptuous*] **:** affording keen pleasure **:** exceptionally rich or fine **:** DELIGHTFUL, EXCELLENT ⟨after a ~ lunch they went to a matinee —John Dos Passos⟩ ⟨a brown alligator traveling bag, quite ~ —W.A.White⟩ — **scrump·tious·ly** *adv*
¹**scrunch** \ˈskrənch, -ü-\ *vb* -ED/-ING/-ES [alter. (perh. influenced by *squeeze*) of ¹*crunch*] *vt* **1 :** CRUNCH, CRUSH ⟨a young fox . . . ~*ing* the insects up hungrily as he unearthed them —Gerald Durrell⟩ ⟨dropped her half-smoked cigarette to the floor, ~*ed* it out with a precise toe —Boyce Eakin⟩ **2 a** *also* **scroonch** \-ü-\ **:** to squeeze together **:** make into a compact mass **:** CONTRACT, HUNCH ⟨~*ed* his eyebrows down again —A.J.Liebling⟩ **b :** CRUMPLE, RUMPLE ⟨~ a paper plate and throw it on the fire⟩ ⟨don't ~ my dress —Lillian Smith⟩ ~ *vi* **1 a :** to make a crunching sound ⟨walked on tiptoe . . . in order that the pebbles might not ~ under my feet —Dwight MacDonald⟩ **b :** to move with a crunching sound ⟨ice ~*ed* along the vessel's sides —Frank Hurley⟩ **2** *also* **scroonch :** CROUCH, SQUEEZE ⟨~*ed* behind the boxwood hedge and reconnoitered —Al Hine⟩ ⟨we ~*ed* together like bulls in a horse trailer —A.J.Liebling⟩ ⟨my bigger brothers had to ~ down to pass for under six —Mary McCarthy⟩
²**scrunch** \ˈ"\ *n* -ES **:** a crunching sound ⟨a ~ of wheels on the gravel outside —Agatha Christie⟩
scrunchy \-chē\ *adj* -ER/-EST [¹*scrunch* + -*y*] **:** CRUNCHY
scrunty \ˈskrəntē\ *adj* [E dial. *scrunt* stunted object or person (prob. blend of ¹*scrump* & *runt*) + -*y*] *chiefly dial* **:** STUNTED, RUNTY
¹**scru·ple** \ˈskrüpəl\ *n* -S [ME *scriple*, fr. L *scrupulus*, *scripulum*, a unit of weight equal to one twenty-fourth of an ounce, fr. *scrupulus* small sharp stone — more at ²SCRUPLE] **1 a :** a unit of apothecaries' weight equal to 20 grains or ⅓ dram — abbr. *sc*; see MEASURE table **b :** a minute particle or quantity **:** IOTA, JOT ⟨indignant if the old ugly routine . . . is altered by so much as one poor ~ —Margery Bailey⟩ **2** *obs* **:** any of several small units of measure (as a minute of arc or a minute of time) **3 :** a British unit of liquid capacity equal to 20 minims or 0.04166 fluid ounce
²**scruple** \ˈ"\ *n* -S [MF *scrupule*, fr. L *scrupulus* small sharp stone, cause of mental or moral discomfort, scruple, dim. of *scrupus* sharp stone — more at SHRED] **1 a :** an ethical consideration **:** a moral principle that inhibits action ⟨a religious ~ . . . jeopardized his academic career —W.H.Salter⟩ ⟨was not overburdened with constitutional ~*s* where measures he favored were concerned —A.H.Meneely⟩ **b :** SCRUPULOUSNESS ⟨the want of ~ or humanity in jockeying for diplomatic advantage —*Times Lit. Supp.*⟩ **c** *archaic* **:** a conscientious excuse or protest **:** APOLOGY, DEMUR ⟨small ~ is made by the authorities in opening private letters —Richard Ford⟩ ⟨made no ~ at taking these goods —Daniel Defoe⟩ **d :** a twinge of conscience **:** mental reservation **:** QUALM ⟨had forgotten his ~*s* about accepting lavish hospitalities —Willa Cather⟩ **2** *obs* **:** a lack of certainty **:** DOUBT ⟨hope my innocency will appear beyond a ~ —William Penn⟩
syn COMPUNCTION, QUALM, DEMUR agree with SCRUPLE in denoting restraint upon intended action, usu. self-imposed and arising from a nice sense of what is right or proper; but SCRUPLE is distinguished by the implication that a principle rather than a personal feeling is involved ⟨moral *scruples*⟩ ⟨religious *scruples*⟩ ⟨began to have *scruples*, to feel obligations, to find that veracity and honor were . . . compelling principles —G.B. Shaw⟩ SCRUPLE may sometimes imply undue fastidiousness ⟨overconscientiousness . . . has wrecked many a promising career; I honor *scruples*, but they . . . have their place and should be kept there —Elinor Wylie⟩ COMPUNCTION denotes a spontaneous feeling of personal responsibility often accompanied by compassion for a potential victim ⟨Lady Macbeth . . . had the *compunction* which he lacked — she could not kill . . . the king —S.L.Gulick b.1902⟩ but is now also used of a passing or superficial concern ⟨social *compunction* about occupying so exclusively the attention of the room —Mary Deasy⟩ DEMUR usu. suggests resistance to or protest against an outside influence ⟨fashion is accepted by average people with little *demur* —Edward Sapir⟩ QUALM emphasizes personal aversion to an act offensive to taste or morals ⟨few little girls can squash insects and kill rabbits without a *qualm* —Rose Macaulay⟩ ⟨serious *qualms* were felt by the respectable citizenry . . . at the idea of . . . young women walking unescorted through the town —*Amer. Guide Series: Mass.*⟩
³**scruple** \ˈ"\ *vb* **scrupled; scrupled; scrupling** \-p(ə)liŋ\ **scruples** *vt* **1** *archaic* **a :** to have or raise scruples about **:** boggle at ⟨*scrupled* no means to obtain his ends —Earl of Chesterfield⟩ **b :** to have doubts about **:** QUESTION **2** *obs* **:** to cause to feel scruples **:** TROUBLE ~ *vi* **1 :** to have or raise scruples **:** become worried **:** FRET ⟨knew it was not so, and did not ~ about lying —Irwin Edman⟩ **2 :** to be reluctant on grounds of conscience **:** HESITATE ⟨conspirators will often readily perjure themselves and take the oath, while some conscientious men may ~ to do so —Will Herberg⟩ ⟨when any financial advantage can accrue to us . . . we do not ~ to destroy —Farley Mowat⟩ **syn** see DEMUR
scru·pler \-p(ə)lə(r)\ *n* -S *archaic* **:** one that scruples
scru·pu·list \ˈskrüpyəlәst\ *n* -S [L *scrupulus* scruple + E -*ist*] *archaic* **:** SCRUPLER
scru·pu·los·i·ty \,=ˈläsəd·ē\ *n* -ES [MF *scrupulosité*, fr. L *scrupulositat-*, *scrupulositas* scrupulousness, fr. *scrupulosus* scrupulous + -*itat-*, -*itas* -ity] **1 :** the quality or state of being scrupulous ⟨the classical unities are observed with a ~ rare in modern writers —Oliver Evans⟩ **2 :** SCRUPLE ⟨tied hand and foot by senseless *scrupulosities* —*Reader's Digest*⟩
scru·pu·lous \ˈskrüpyələs\ *adj* [ME, fr. L *scrupulosus*, fr. *scrupulus* scruple + -*osus* -ous] **1 a :** characterized by scruple **:** having moral integrity **:** PRINCIPLED ⟨less ~ producers sent bundles that were deceptive in appearance —*Amer. Guide Series: Md.*⟩ ⟨a more ~ court would disqualify itself —H.L. Ickes⟩ **b :** correct to the smallest detail **:** punctiliously exact **:** PAINSTAKING, PRECISE ⟨the orchestral score . . . was articulated with ~ precision and clarity —*Musical America*⟩ ⟨endeavored to follow the originals with ~ care, even to . . . reproducing mistakes in spelling —M.M.Mathews⟩ ⟨her recoil from her husband's inefficiency was in the direction of a ~ neatness —Ellen Glasgow⟩ **c :** carefully adhering to ethical standards **:** CONSCIENTIOUS, STRICT ⟨it is this ~ honesty toward herself and others that is the redeeming side of her character —Malcolm Cowley⟩ ⟨distinguished for ~ fairness, he was notoriously insusceptible to any political influence —S.H.Adams⟩ **2** *obs* **:** open to question on moral grounds ⟨the justice of that cause ought to be evident; not obscure, not ~ —Francis Bacon⟩ **3 a** *obs* **:** excessively careful **:** CAUTIOUS, WARY ⟨so curious and ~ in many of their cities . . . that they will admit no stranger within the walls —Thomas Coryat⟩ **b** *archaic* **:** hesitant esp. for ethical reasons **:** DOUBTFUL, RELUCTANT ⟨primitive Christians were very ~ of calling the emperors *Dominus* —Edward Stillingfleet⟩ **syn** see CAREFUL, UPRIGHT
scru·pu·lous·ly *adv* **:** in a scrupulous manner **:** CONSCIENTIOUSLY, PAINSTAKINGLY
scru·pu·lous·ness *n* -ES [*scrupulous* + -*ness*] **:** conformity to high standards of ethics or excellence **:** INTEGRITY, PUNCTILIOUSNESS
scrush \ˈskrəsh\ *dial var of* CRUSH
scru·ta·ble \ˈskrüd·əbəl, -ütə-\ *adj* [LL *scrutabilis* searchable, fr. L *scrutari* to search, investigate, examine + -*abilis* -able — more at SCRUTINY] **:** capable of being deciphered **:** COMPREHENSIBLE, LEGIBLE
scru·ta·tor \ˈskrü,tād·ə(r), =ˈ==\ *n* -S [L, fr. *scrutatus* (past part. of *scrutari* to search, examine) + -*or*] **:** OBSERVER, EXAMINER
scru·ti·neer \,skrüt°nˈi(ə)r, -iə\ *n* -S [*scrutiny* + -*eer*] **1 :** one that examines **2** *Brit* **:** CANVASSER a
scru·ti·nize *also* **scru·ti·nise** \ˈskrüt°n,īz *also* -üd·ə,nīz *or* -ütə,nīz\ *vb* -ED/-ING/-S [*scrutiny* + -*ize*] *vt* **:** to subject to scrutiny **:** examine closely **:** INSPECT ⟨*scrutinized* the inscription as if it were stubbornly withholding from them some information that they ought to possess —J.B.Benefield⟩ ⟨*scrutinized* herself eagerly and long in her mirror —Robert Grant †1940⟩ ⟨knowledge of one other culture should sharpen our ability to ~ . . . our own —Margaret Mead⟩ ~ *vi* **:** to make a scrutiny ⟨come . . . to perceive and apprehend, or, as critics, to ~ and evaluate —R.W.Stallman⟩
syn SCRUTINIZE, SCAN, INSPECT, EXAMINE, and AUDIT can mean, in common, to look at or look over critically and searchingly. SCRUTINIZE implies close observation and attention to minute detail ⟨the immigration officials carefully *scrutinized* the passengers' entry permits —Robert Sherrod⟩ ⟨manufacturers must *scrutinize* every possible way to lower production costs —*Steel*⟩ SCAN implies a survey from point to point, often suggesting a cursory overall observation ⟨stooping over as he went, his eyes *scanning* every foot of the ground —O.E. Rölvaag⟩ ⟨took his duties seriously, attending meetings and *scanning* reports from every corporation minutely —A.F. Harlow⟩ ⟨had drawn out their telescopes and were *scanning* the mountain above us —H.D.Quillin⟩ ⟨a scheme whereby all journals would be *scanned* and indexed on receipt —*Amer. Documentation*⟩ ⟨to *scan* the headlines over breakfast⟩ INSPECT in general use implies little more than careful observation, but in legal, military, governmental, or industrial use implies a searching scrutiny for errors, defects, or shortcomings ⟨ruefully *inspected* himself after trying on his first white tie and tails —Flora Lewis⟩ ⟨extension of credit is by installments, and projects financed are *inspected* by members of the bank's staff —E.L.Smith⟩ ⟨freshly picked grapes are *inspected* and cleansed before delivery —*Amer. Guide Series: Pa.*⟩ EXAMINE implies a close scrutiny or investigation to determine the facts about or real nature or condition of a thing or to test the thing's quality, truth, validity, and so on ⟨ever bothered to *examine* the serial number on a bank note —*Irish Digest*⟩ ⟨when personality is *examined* as closely and candidly as it has been in the twentieth-century novel —Robert Humphrey⟩ ⟨undying trivialities which the public find romantic without seeking to *examine* them for truth —J.F.Gore⟩ ⟨speakers *examined* great world religions to discover to what extent faith in them encouraged their adherents to escape from life, to exploit life, or to redeem it —Christmas Humphreys⟩ AUDIT applies to a searching examination of accounts to determine their correctness, sometimes extending to any accounting examination ⟨each bank is *audited* annually by a certified public accountant —*Safety for Your Savings*⟩ ⟨*audit* a company's books⟩ ⟨the scandal manages to shake up the other people into *auditing* their close-to-bankrupt lives —*Time*⟩
scru·ti·niz·er *also* **scru·ti·nis·er** \-zə(r)\ *n* -S **:** one that scrutinizes
scru·ti·niz·ing·ly *adv* [*scrutinizing* (fr. pres. part. of *scrutinize*) + -*ly*] **:** in a scrutinizing way **:** ATTENTIVELY
scru·ti·nous \ˈskrüt(°)nəs\ *adj* [*scrutiny* + -*ous*] *archaic* **:** disposed to examine closely **:** INQUISITIVE, SEARCHING — **scrutinously** *adv*
scru·ti·ny \ˈskrüt(°)nē, -ni *also* -üd·ən- *or* -ütən-\ *n* -ES [L *scrutinium* search, investigation, fr. *scrutari* to search, investigate, examine, fr. *scruta* trash, rags; perh. akin to OHG *scrōt* piece cut off — more at SHRED] **1** *archaic* **a :** an act or instance of taking a formal vote by roll call or by secret ballot ⟨the people went to a ~ and began to give their voices —Philemon Holland⟩ **b :** an official examination (as by a committee) of the votes or ballots cast in a parliamentary election **2 a :** a searching study or inquiry **:** close inspection **:** EXAMINATION, INVESTIGATION ⟨fine old houses . . . stand open to the ~ of the tourists —*Monsanto Mag.*⟩ ⟨survived the cold ~ and judicious pruning of the committee —R.S.Churchill⟩ ⟨are . . . diplomats to be terrified by the prospect of future public *scrutinies* staged by politicians —C.L.Sulzberger⟩ **b :** a searching look ⟨the lynxlike ~ of counsel —L.P.Stryker⟩ **c :** a close watch **:** SURVEILLANCE ⟨keeps public officials under constant public ~ —*Amer. Guide Series: Mass.*⟩ **3 a :** a public examination of catechumens before baptism consisting of catechizings and exorcisms that form a part of the rite of baptism in the Roman Catholic Church **b :** an inquiry and examination preceding elevation to orders **c :** an ecclesiastical method of election by secret written ballot (as in a conclave)
scru·toire \(ˈ)skrü·ˌtwär\ *n* -S [modif. of F *escritoire*] **:** ESCRITOIRE
scruze \ˈskrüz\ *vt* -ED/-ING/-S [perh. alter. (influenced by ²*screw*) of ¹*squeeze*] *chiefly dial* **:** SQUEEZE, CRUSH
¹**scry** \ˈskrī\ *n* -ES [ME *scrye*, short for *ascrye*, fr. *ascryen* to call out, fr. MF *escrier*, fr. OF, fr. *es-* ex- (fr. L *ex-*) + *crier* to cry — more at CRY] *chiefly dial* **:** OUTCRY, SHOUT
²**scry** \ˈ"\ *vb* **scried; scried; scrying; scries** [by shortening] *vt, archaic* **:** DESCRY ~ *vi* **:** to practice crystal gazing
scry·er *also* **skry·er** \-ī(ə)r, -īə\ *n* -S [²*scry* + -*er*] **:** CRYSTAL GAZER, SEER
scrying *n* -S [fr. gerund of ²*scry*] **:** CRYSTAL GAZING, DIVINATION
SCS *abbr* superintendent of car service
sct *abbr* scout
sctd *abbr* scattered
sctr *abbr* sector
scu·ba \ˈsk(y)übə\ *n* -S [*self-contained underwater breathing apparatus*] **:** an apparatus used for breathing while swimming under water
¹**scud** \ˈskəd\ *vb* **scudded; scudded; scudding; scuds** [prob. of Scand origin; akin to Norw *skudda* to push, thrust; akin to OE *hūdenian* to shake — more at QUASH] *vi* **1 a :** to move or run swiftly esp. as if driven forward ⟨a brisk wind sending small white clouds *scudding* across the . . . sky —Osbert Lancaster⟩ ⟨freezing weather that sent the delegates and their briefcases *scudding* —Mollie Panter-Downes⟩ **b :** to run before a gale **2** *of an arrow* **:** to fly too high and off the proper course ~ *vt* **1** *archaic* **:** to pass over quickly ⟨the startled red deer ~*s* the plain —Sir Walter Scott⟩ **2 :** to cause to scud ⟨*scudded* the jeep back on the paving —S.L.Rubinstein⟩ **3 :** to shake (herring) from a net
²**scud** \ˈ"\ *n* -S **1 :** the act of scudding **:** a driving along **:** RUSH ⟨following her in a ~ came the servants and helpers —Virginia Woolf⟩ **2 a :** loose vapory clouds or fragments of cloud driven swiftly by the wind **b :** something resembling scud: as (1) **:** a slight sudden shower (2) **:** a gust of wind (3) **:** mist, rain, snow, or spray driven by the wind ⟨a strong easterly gale was driving ~*s* of rain and torn leaves across the . . . lawns —Margaret Irwin⟩ ⟨a strong wind . . . whipping up a ~ of whitecaps on the bay —Wright Morris⟩ ⟨the air was flecked with a ~ of white specks —Hugh MacLennan⟩ **3 :** an amphipod crustacean (as a beach flea)
³**scud** \ˈ"\ *vt* **scudded; scudded; scudding; scuds** [obs. E *scud* dirt, refuse, prob. blend of E ¹*scum* and ¹*mud*] **:** to scrape (a depilated and trimmed hide or skin) in order to remove undesirable matter (as remaining hairs or lime)
⁴**scud** \ˈ"\ *n* -S **:** the matter that is worked out of hides or skins in scudding
scud·der \-də(r)\ *n* -S [³*scud* + -*er*] **:** a beamer who scrapes skins by hand or machine
scud·dle \ˈskəd°l\ *vi* [freq. of ¹*scud*] **:** HURRY, SCUTTLE
scud·dy \ˈskədi\ *adj* -ER/-EST [origin unknown] *Scot* **:** NAKED
scu·do \ˈskü(,)dō\ *n, pl* **scu·di** \-dē\ [It, lit., shield, fr. L *scutum* shield — more at ESQUIRE] **1 a :** a gold coin first issued in the 15th century or a silver coin first issued in the 16th century and used in Italy to the 19th century approximately equivalent to a dollar **b :** a unit of value equivalent to a scudo **2** [modif. of Sp *escudo* — more at ESCUDO] **:** ESCUDO
¹**scuff** \ˈskəf\ *vb* -ED/-ING/-S [prob. of Scand origin; akin to Sw *skuffa* to push and perh. to ON *skūfa*, *skȳfa* to shove — more at SHOVE] *vi* **1 a :** to walk without lifting the feet **:** proceed with a scraping or dragging movement **:** SHUFFLE ⟨peasant girls with . . . their bare feet ~*ing* on the flags —Gerald Durrell⟩ **b :** to poke or shuffle a foot in exploration or embarrassment ⟨farmers ~*ed* at the powder-dry earth —*Time*⟩ **2 :** to become scratched, chipped, or roughened by wear ⟨a sleek, hard surface that won't dent, crack, or ~ —*advt*⟩ ~ *vt* **1 a** *Scot* **:** to touch lightly in passing **:** GRAZE **b** *Scot* **:** to brush aside **:** wipe off **2 :** to attack or injure with or as if with the fists **:** CUFF, BUFFET ⟨nursing a ~*ed* eyelid . . . after the match —*Time*⟩ ⟨a play that has been brutally ~*ed* by the critics —Philip Hamburger⟩ **3 a :** to scrape (as the feet) along a surface while walking or back and forth while standing ⟨~*ed* my shoes on a mat —Joseph Wechsberg⟩ **b :** to scatter, tread, or toss aside by or as if by shuffling with the feet ⟨~*ing* the leaves and sniffing the dusty smell of them —John Moore⟩ ⟨the world ~*s* them underfoot like dirty snow —*Time*⟩ **c :** to poke at with the toe ⟨mountain people ~ rocks on unpaved Main Street while discussing the weather —Bob Koonce⟩ **4 :** to scratch, gouge, wear away the surface of, or otherwise injure through abrasion or use ⟨a plain pine floor that was very much ~*ed* —R.M.Coates⟩ ⟨his cuffs were frayed, his shoes were ~*ed* —*New Yorker*⟩
²**scuff** \ˈ"\ *n* -S **1** *Scot* **:** a light glancing blow **:** CUFF **2 :** a noise of or as if of scuffing ⟨the soft ~ of his own footsteps —Leslie Charteris⟩ **3 a :** the act or an instance of scuffing **:** a wearing away or injuring by use or abrasion **b :** a mark, gouge, roughness, or other injury caused by scuffing ⟨shoe leather that resists ~*s*⟩ **4 :** a usu. flat-soled house slipper without quarter or counter — compare MULE **5 :** a brush with the heel forward in tap dancing

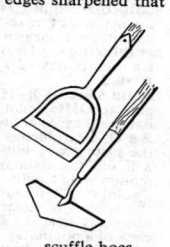

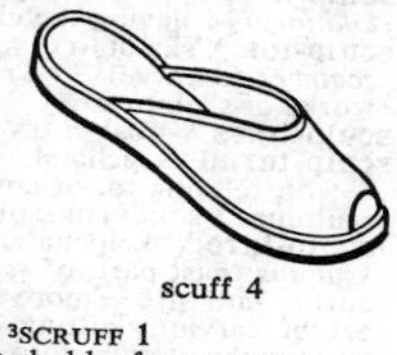
scuff 4

³**scuff** \ˈ"\ *n* -S [origin unknown] **:** ³SCRUFF 1
scuffed *adj* [fr. past part. of ¹*scuff*] **:** shabby from wear
scuff·er \ˈskəfə(r)\ *n* -S [²*scuff* + -*er*] **1 :** SCUFF 4 **2** [by alter.] **:** SCUFFLER
¹**scuf·fle** \ˈskəfəl\ *vb* **scuffled; scuffled; scuffling** \-f(ə)liŋ\ **scuffles** [prob. of Scand origin; akin to Sw *skuffa* to push — more at SCUFF] *vi* **1 :** to contend with vigor and resolution **2 :** to strive or struggle at close quarters with disorder and confusion **3 a :** to accomplish a task hurriedly, superficially, or haphazardly **b** (1) **:** to make one's way in or as if in a scuffle **:** go in hurry and confusion (2) **:** to move with a quick shuffling gait or sound **:** SCURRY ⟨a mouse ran *scuffling* behind the wainscoting —Oscar Wilde⟩ (3) **:** to move with a shuffling plodding gait ⟨*scuffled* through the four-inch layer of dust —Ben Riker⟩ ~ *vt* **1 :** to poke at or disturb **:** SCUFF ⟨brushed through branches of yew and *scuffled* the gravel —Elizabeth Taylor⟩ ⟨*scuffling* up the dust with long bare feet —Marjorie K. Rawlings⟩ **2 :** to cause to scuff, shuffle, or otherwise move in a confused manner **syn** see WRESTLE
²**scuffle** \ˈ"\ *n* -S **1 a :** a rough haphazard struggle with scrambling and confusion ⟨during the ~ several GI shoes trample his camera underfoot —Ray Duncan⟩ **b :** a verbal conflict usu. involving several sides and with confused claims ⟨without a strong executive the presidential form of government declines into a ~ of local interests —*Times Lit. Supp.*⟩ **2 :** a soft confused shuffling sound ⟨listened to the ~ of children's feet on the great stone floor —Irwin Shaw⟩ **3 :** a brush forward and back in tap dancing
³**scuffle** \ˈ"\ *vt* -ED/-ING/-S [modif. of D *schoffelen* to hoe, scuffle, fr. MD, to shovel, fr. *schoffel*, *schuffel* shovel] **:** to use a scuffle hoe upon
⁴**scuffle** \ˈ"\ *n* -S [modif. of D *schoffel*, fr. MD *schoffel*, *schuffel* shovel — more at SHOVEL] **:** SCUFFLE HOE
scuffle hoe *n* **:** a garden hoe with both edges sharpened that can be pushed forward or drawn back — called also *Dutch hoe*, *push hoe*, *thrust hoe*
scuf·fler \ˈskəf(ə)lə(r)\ *n* -S [³*scuffle* + -*er*] **:** CULTIVATOR 2; *esp* **:** one drawn by hand or horse and used principally for weed eradication
scuf·fling·ly *adv* **:** in a scuffling manner
scuff plate *n* [¹*scuff*] **:** a protective metal plate; *specif* **:** one fitting over the threshold of the door of an automotive vehicle to cover the flanges of the side body panels

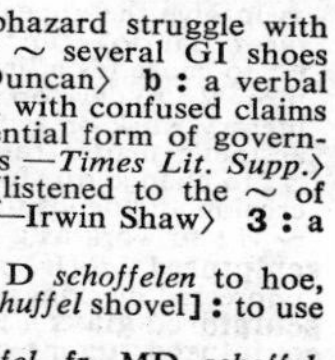
scuffle hoes

scuffs *pres 3d sing of* SCUFF, *pl of* SCUFF
¹**scug** \ˈskəg\ *n* -S [ON *skuggi* — more at SKY] **1** *Scot* **:** SHADE, SHADOW **2** *Scot* **a :** SHELTER **b :** a sheltered place; *esp* **:** the side of a hill
²**scug** \ˈ"\ *vt* **scugged; scugged; scugging; scugs** **1** *Scot* **:** to screen from view or danger **2** *Scot* **:** to conceal (a sin or wrongdoing) from discovery
³**scug** \ˈ"\ *n* -S [origin unknown] *Brit* **:** a schoolboy without academic or athletic distinction, social grace, or personal attraction; *broadly* **:** an unattractive meanspirited person
sculch \ˈskəlch, -lsh\ *n* -ES [prob. alter. of *culch*] *chiefly dial* **:** TRASH, JUNK, RUBBISH
scul·dud·dery \ˌskəl,dəd(ə)rē, ˌ=ˈ=(=)=\ *n* -ES [origin unknown] *chiefly dial* **:** shockingly gross or lewd conduct
sculduggery *or* **sculdduggery** *var of* SKULDUGGERY
sculk *var of* SKULK
¹**scull** *also* **skull** \ˈskəl\ *n* -S [ME *sculle*, *skulle*] **1 a :** an oar used at the stern of a boat to propel it forward with a thwartwise motion **b :** one of a pair of oars usu. less than 10 feet in length and operated by one person **2 :** a boat usu. for racing propelled by one or sometimes two persons using sculls **3 sculls** *pl* **:** a sculling race **4 :** the act of sculling
²**scull** *also* **skull** \ˈ"\ *vb* -ED/-ING/-S *vt* **1 a :** to propel (a boat) by means of one or more pairs of sculls **b :** to propel (a boat) by means of a large oar resting in a notch in the transom and worked thwartwise with a turning motion **2 :** to convey by sculling ⟨had all he could do to ~ us through the breakers —J.E.H.Nolan⟩ ~ *vi* **1 a :** to scull a boat **b** *of a boat* **:** to admit of being sculled **2 :** to move forward in water by the slow sideways motion of the tail ⟨the sinuous power of the dolphins, whose easy ~*ing* imparts such astounding impetus —William Beebe⟩ **3 :** to draw a canoe broadside in the direction

of the paddle by moving the blade in feathered position in the pattern of a figure-eight parallel to the canoe always drawing the blade against the water **4 a :** to propel oneself through the water esp. on the back by moving the hands in figure-eight rotations and pressing the palms always away from the direction of movement **b :** to maintain the body at the surface of the water by moving the hands in a similar pattern with the palms pressing downward

³scull \"\ *n* -s [ScGael or ON; ScGael *sgulan* large wicker basket, fr. ON *skjóla* bucket; akin to ON *skjōl* hiding place, refuge — more at CULET] *Scot* **:** a large shallow wicker basket often used for produce or fishing tackle

⁴scull *n* -s [by shortening] *obs* **:** SCULLION

⁵scull *Scot var of* SKULL

¹scull·er \ˈskələ(r)\ *n* -s [¹*scull* + *-er*] **1 :** one that sculls **2 :** a boat rowed by one man with two sculls

²scull·er \"\ *n* -s [*scull* (alter. of *skull*) + *-er*] **:** a metallurgical workman who removes skull

scul·lery \ˈskəl(ə)rē, -ri\ *n* -ES [ME, fr. MF *escuelerie*, fr. *escuele, escuelle* bowl, dish (fr. L *scutella* drinking bowl) + *-erie* -ery — more at SCUTTLE] **1** *obs* **:** a department of a household having charge of the dishes and kitchen utensils **2 :** a room near a kitchen for cleaning and storing dishes and culinary utensils, washing vegetables, and similar work

¹scul·lion \ˈskəlyən\ *n* -s [ME *sculion*, fr. MF *escouillon* dishcloth, alter. of *escouvillon*, fr. *escouve* broom, fr. L *scopa* broom, twig; akin to L *scapus* shaft, stalk — more at SHAFT] **:** a kitchen helper whose chief task is washing

²scullion \"\ *adj* **:** BASE, MENIAL

³scullion *var of* SCALLION

¹sculp \ˈskəlp\ *vt* -ED/-ING/-S [L *sculpere* — more at SCULPTURE] **1** *obs* **:** CARVE, ENGRAVE **2 :** SCULPTURE

²sculp \"\ *vt* -ED/-ING/-S [by alter.] **:** SCALP

³sculp \"\ *n* -s [prob. alter. of ¹*scalp*] **:** the skin or pelt of a seal and esp. of a young seal with the adherent blubber

⁴sculp \"\ *vt* -ED/-ING/-S **:** to remove the skin or the skin and blubber of (a seal)

⁵sculp \"\ *vt* -ED/-ING/-S [alter. of obs. E *scalp*, alter. of E *scapple* — more at SCABBLE] **:** to break (slate) into slabs suitable for splitting

sculp *abbr* **1** [L *sculpsit*] he or she carved or engraved it **2** sculptor **3** sculptural; sculpture

sculp·er \ˈskəlpə(r)\ *n* -s [alter. of ²*scalper*] **:** SCORPER 1

scul·pin \ˈskəlpən\ *n, pl* **sculpins** *also* **sculpin** [origin unknown] **1 a :** any of numerous spiny large-headed broad-mouthed fishes of Cottidae and closely related scorpaenoid families that usu. are scaleless and have scanty and bony flesh **b :** a dragonet (*Callionymus lyra*) **c :** a scorpion fish (*Scorpaena guttata*) of the southern California coast esteemed for food and sport **2 :** a worthless creature

sculpt \ˈskəlpt\ *vb* **sculpted** \-ptəd\ **sculpted; sculpting; sculpts** [F *sculpter*, alter. (influenced by *sculpteur* sculptor, fr. L *sculptor*) of obs. F *sculper* to sculp, fr. L *sculpere*] **:** CARVE, SCULPTURE

sculpt *abbr* **1** [L *sculpsit*] he or she carved or engraved it **2** sculptor **3** sculptural; sculpture **4** [L *sculptus*] carved or engraved

sculp·ti·to·ry \ˈskəlptəˌtōrē\ *adj* [¹*sculpture* + *-itory* (as in *auditory*)] **:** having the characteristics of sculpture

sculp·tor \ˈskəlptə(r)\ *n* -s [L, fr. *sculptus* (past part. of *sculpere* to carve) + *-or*] **:** one that sculptures or produces works of sculpture

sculp·tress \-trəs\ *n* -ES [*sculptor* + *-ess*] **:** a female sculptor

sculp·tur·al \-pchərəl, -psh(ə)rəl\ *adj* [¹*sculpture* + *-al*] **1 :** of, relating to, or consisting of sculpture **2 :** resembling sculpture **:** SCULPTURESQUE — **sculp·tur·al·ly** \-rəlē, -li\ *adv*

¹sculp·ture \ˈskəlpchə(r), -psh-\ *n* -s [ME, fr. L *sculptura*, fr. *sculptus* (past part. of *sculpere* to carve, fr. *scalpere* to carve, cut) + *-ura* -ure — more at SHELF] **1 a** (1) **:** the act, process, or art of carving, cutting, hewing, molding, welding, or constructing materials into statues, ornaments, or figures (2) **:** the act, process, or art of producing figures or groups in plastic or hard materials **b** (1) **:** work produced by sculpture **:** the body of primarily three-dimensional works of art ⟨an exhibit of painting and ~⟩ (2) **:** a carved or molded statue or figure; *broadly* **:** a nonfunctional work of art whose aesthetic effect depends primarily on three-dimensional relationships ⟨a snow ~⟩ ⟨a forged steel ~⟩ **2** *archaic* **:** an engraved figure or design ⟨published his play with ~s and a preface —Samuel Johnson⟩ **3 :** impressed or raised markings or the pattern of such markings on the surface of a plant or animal part **4 :** a modification of the forms of the earth's surface by sculpturing

²sculpture \"\ *vb* **sculptured; sculptured; sculpturing** \-pchəriŋ, -psh(ə)r-\ **sculptures** *vt* **1 a** (1) **:** to form an image or representation of with a chisel or other tool from wood, stone, metal, or other material (2) **:** to carve, engrave, mold, weld, or construct (plastic or hard materials) into a primarily three-dimensional work of art (3) **:** to cover or adorn with sculpture or carved work **b :** to mold or form so as to give the appearance of sculpture or bas relief ⟨a *sculptured* hairdo⟩ ⟨an automobile body of *sculptured* metal⟩ **c :** to cause (as a line) to flow in the manner of classic sculpture **2 :** to develop sculpturesque qualities in (as a musical or literary work or a painting); *specif* **:** to mold from the basic aesthetic matter rather than adorn by extraneous ornament **3 :** to change (the form of the earth's surface) by erosion or by erosion and deposition ⟨the *sculpturing* of a canyon by a river⟩ ~ *vi* **:** to work as a sculptor

sculptured *adj* [fr. past part. of ²*sculpture*] **:** having raised or impressed markings on the surface ⟨a ~ conch⟩

sculptured glass *n* **:** CAMEO GLASS

sculptured rug *n* **:** CARVED RUG

sculptured tortoise *or* **sculptured turtle** *n* **:** WOOD TORTOISE

sculp·tur·er \-pchərə(r), -psha-\ *n* -s **:** one that sculptures

sculp·tur·esque \ˌ==ˈresk\ *adj* [¹*sculpture* + *-esque*] **:** done in the manner of or resembling sculpture **:** resembling a statue in amplitude or clearness of outline — **sculp·tur·esque·ly** *adv*

sculpturing *n* -s [fr. gerund of ²*sculpture*] **1 :** the action of one who sculptures **2 :** the occupation of a sculptor **3 :** SCULPTURE 3

¹scum \ˈskəm\ *n* -s [ME *scum, scume*, fr. MD *schum, schume*; akin to OHG *scūm* foam, froth and prob. to ON *skūmi* twilight, *skuggi* shadow — more at SKY] **1** *obs* **:** FOAM, FROTH **2 a** (1) **:** extraneous matter or impurities risen to or formed on the surface of a liquid (2) **:** a foul filmy covering floating on a liquid (as a stagnant pool) **b :** the scoria of metals in a molten state **:** DROSS **c :** a slimy film formed on the surface of a solid or gelatinous object **d :** the impurities precipitated in the process of sugar refining **3 a :** vile, worthless, or rotten objects **:** REFUSE **b** (1) **:** the lowest and most undesirable class of a population ⟨the social ~, the passively rotting people who lie at the bottom of the social scale —M.D.Geismar⟩ (2) **:** a rabble made up of low or evil people (3) **:** a low, evil, or worthless person ⟨he's not a ~⟩

²scum \"\ *vb* **scummed; scummed; scumming; scums** [ME *scumen*, fr. *scum, scume* scum] *vt* **1** *archaic* **:** to take the scum from **:** SKIM **2** *obs* **:** to range over **:** SCOUR **3 :** to cover with or as if with scum ~ *vi* **:** to become covered with or as if with scum

¹scum·ble \ˈskəmbəl\ *vt* **scumbled; scumbled; scumbling** \-b(ə)liŋ\ **scumbles** [freq. of ²*scum*] **1 a :** to make (color or a painting) less brilliant by covering with a thin coat of opaque or semiopaque color applied with a nearly dry brush **b :** to apply (a color) in this manner **2 :** to soften the lines or colors of (a drawing) by rubbing lightly (as with a stump or a finger) **3 :** to paint, draw, or produce by scumbling

²scumble \"\ *n* -s **1 :** the act of scumbling **2 :** a softened effect produced by scumbling **3 :** a material (as paint) used for scumbling

scumbling *n* -s [fr. gerund of ¹*scumble*] **:** the effect produced by or the color applied in or as if in a scumble

scumboard \ˈ==ˌ=\ *n* **:** a device for the removal of scum in sewage-treatment plants

scum·fish \ˈskəmˌfish\ *vt* [by shortening & alter. fr. ¹*discomfit*] *dial Brit* **:** to overpower esp. by suffocation

scum·less \-mləs\ *adj* **:** lacking scum

scum·mer \-mə(r)\ *n* -s [ME, fr. ¹*scum* + *-er*] **:** a utensil for removing scum

scumming *n* -s [fr. gerund of ²*scum*] **1 :** the removal of scum **2 :** scum formed on the surface of an object: as **a :** an imperfection resulting when matter being printed takes ink from a nonprinting area of a printing surface (as a lithographic plate) **b** (1) **:** a white or light-colored stain on brick caused by salts in the clay (2) **:** a defect in enamel characterized by areas of poor gloss

scum·my \ˈskəmē, -mi\ *adj* -ER/-EST [¹*scum* + *-y*] **1 a :** covered with scum **b :** of the nature of or resembling scum **2 :** CONTEMPTIBLE, MEAN, SCURVY

scuncheon *var of* SCONCHEON

scun·gil·li *also* **scun·gi·li** \skünˈjēlē, -jilē\ *n* -s [modif. of It dial. *scunciglio* conch, seashell, prob. alter. of It *conchiglia* seashell, shellfish, fr. L *conchylium* shellfish — more at CONCHYLIUM] **1 :** alimentary paste in the shape of conch shells **2 :** the meat of a conch cooked and served with a highly seasoned sauce

¹scun·ner \ˈskənər\ *vi* -ED/-ING/-S [ME (Sc dial.) *skoneren, skunniren*] *chiefly Scot* **:** to be in a state of disgusted irritation — usu. used with *at* or *with*

²scun·ner \-nə(r)\ *n* -s **1 :** an unreasonable or extremely subjective dislike ⟨took a ~ at his daughter's newest boyfriend⟩ **2 :** a unfavorable prejudice ⟨will be accused of having a ~ against the English —J.R.Chamberlain⟩

scup \ˈskəp\ *n, pl* **scup** *also* **scups** [Narraganset *mishcùp*, fr. *mishe* big + *kuppe* close together; fr. its large, close scales] **:** either of two sparid fishes (genus *Stenostomus*) of the Atlantic coast of the U.S.: **a :** a fish (*S. chrysops*) occurring from So. Carolina to Maine and esteemed as a panfish — called also *northern porgy, northern scup* **b :** a related fish (*S. aculeatus*) of more southerly distribution — called also *southern porgy, southern scup*

scup·paug \(ˌ)skəˈpȯg\ *n* -s [Narraganset *mishcùppaûog*, pl. of *mishcup*] **:** SCUP a

¹scup·per \ˈskəpə(r)\ *n* -s [ME *skopper*] **1 a :** a drainage opening cut through the side of a ship flush with the deck **b :** a drain set in the deck of a ship **c scuppers** *pl* **:** WATERWAYS **2 a :** an opening in the wall of a building to permit water to drain off a floor or flat roof **b :** a device placed in an opening to facilitate drainage

²scupper \"\ *vt* -ED/-ING/-S [origin unknown] **1** *Brit* **:** to put or leave in danger or difficulty **2** *Brit* **:** AMBUSH

scup·per·nong \ˈskəpə(r)ˌnȯŋ, -näŋ\ *n* -s [fr. *Scuppernong*, small river and lake in Tyrrel county, No. Carolina] **1 a :** MUSCADINE 2 **b :** any of various cultivated muscadines that are derived from wild muscadines, may constitute a natural variety, and have yellowish green fruits suggesting a plum in flavor **2 :** a white aromatic table wine that is light amber in color, is sweeter and heavier than the average table wine, and is made from the scuppernong

scupper pipe *or* **scupper shoot** *n* [¹*scupper*] **:** a drainpipe from a deckhouse roof to the scuppers or from the deck to an opening in the side

scup·pit \ˈskəpət, -kůp-\ *n* -s [ME *scopette*, prob. fr. *scope* scoop + *-ette* — more at SCOOP] *dial Eng* **:** a small shovel

¹scur \ˈskər(·)\ *var of* SKIRR

²scur \"\ *n* -s [E dial. *scur* scab, scurf, perh. alter. of ¹*scurf*] **:** a small rounded portion of horn tissue attached to the skin of the horn pit of a polled animal

¹scurf \ˈskərf, -kəf, -kəif\ *n* -s [ME, of Scand origin; akin to Icel *skurfa* scurf, Dan *skurv*; akin to OE *sceorf* scurf, OHG *scorf* scurf, OE *sceorfan* to gnaw, L *carpere* to pluck — more at HARVEST] **1 :** material like bran that becomes detached from the epidermis in thin dry scales esp. in an abnormal skin condition **2 a :** anything like flakes or scales adhering to a surface **b :** the foul remains of anything adherent **3 :** the off-scourings of society **:** SCUM **4 :** the deposit or covering resembling scales or bran found on some plant parts **5 a :** a localized or general darkening and roughening of a smooth plant surface that is usu. more pronounced than russeting **b :** any of several plant diseases characterized by scurf: as (1) **:** a disease of sweet potatoes caused by an imperfect fungus (*Moniliochaetes infuscans*) (2) **:** SILVER SCURF

²scurf \"\ *vt* -ED/-ING/-S **1 a :** to whiten like scurf **b :** to cover with or as if with scurf **2 :** to remove (as scurf) by scraping, rubbing, or wiping ⟨~*ing* a patch away from the glazed window —Thomas Wolfe⟩; *esp* **:** to remove deposits of carbon from (as the inner surfaces of coal gas retorts or coke ovens)

scurf·er \-fə(r)\ *n* -s **:** a wooden tool coated with coarse emery for smoothing a surface (as of leather) after scraping

scurfy \-fē, -fi\ *adj* -ER/-EST [ME, fr. ¹*scurf* + *-y*] **1 :** having or producing scurf **:** covered with or as if with scurf **2 :** resembling or consisting of scurf — compare LEPIDOTE

scurfy bark louse *n* **:** SCURFY SCALE

scurfy pea *also* **scurf pea** *or* **scurvy pea** *n* **:** any of several plants of the genus *Psoralea*; *esp* **:** a bushy branched herb (*P. tenuiflora floribunda*) of central No. America with white canescent foliage and purplish flowers in oblong spikes

scurfy scale *n* **:** a scale (*Chionaspis furfura*) injurious to trees (as apple or pear)

scurred \ˈskərd\ *adj* **:** having scurs

scur·rile \ˈskər·əl, -əˌrəl, -ər,ˌīl, -əˌrīl\ *or* **scur·ril** \-ər·əl, -əˌrəl\ *adj* [MF *scurrile*, fr. L *scurrilis*, fr. *scurra* buffoon, jester + *-ilis* -ile] **:** SCURRILOUS

scur·ril·i·ty \skəˈriləd·ē, -lətē, -i\ *n* -ES [MF & LL; MF *scurrilité*, fr. LL *scurrilitat-, scurrilitas*, fr. L *scurrilis* scurrilous + *-itat-, -itas* -ity] **1 :** the quality or state of being scurrilous **2 a :** scurrilous or abusive language usu. marked by coarse or indecent wording or innuendo, unjust denigration, or clownish jesting ⟨this was the day of journalistic ~ —*Amer. Guide Series: Pa.*⟩ **b :** an instance of scurrility **:** a rude or abusive remark **syn** see ABUSE

scur·ri·lous \ˈskər·ələs, -kə·rə-\ *adj* [L *scurrilis* jeering, scurrilous + E *-ous*] **1 :** using or given to using the language of low buffoonery; *broadly* **:** vulgar and evil in habit or demeanor ⟨~ imposters who used a religious exterior to rob poor people —Edwin Benson⟩ **2 :** containing low obscenities or coarse abuse ⟨a ~ collection of highly obscene verses —R. A.Hall b.1911⟩ ⟨a pamphleteering campaign filled with ~ charges and countercharges —A.D.Graeff⟩ — **scur·ri·lous·ly** *adv* — **scur·ri·lous·ness** *n* -ES

¹scur·ry \ˈskər·|ē, ˈskə·r|, |i\ *vb* -ED/-ING/-ES [short for *hurry-scurry*] *vi* **1 :** to move in or as if in a brisk rapidly alternating step ⟨~ for miles through inky tunnels —Claudia Cassidy⟩ ⟨*scurried* to a rock for shelter —Audrey Barker⟩ **2 :** to circulate in an agitated, confused, or fluttering manner ⟨~*ing* snow whirls —F.V.W.Mason⟩ ⟨a great deal of ~*ing* around, grabbing for slippers or bumping into each other —Gilbert Millstein⟩ ~ *vt* **:** to cause to scurry ⟨such a thought might ~ any recalcitrant patient into paying the fee due —W.T.Corlett⟩ ⟨gusty winds *scurried* the crisped and fallen leaves —H.B.Alexander⟩

²scurry \"\ *n* -ES **1 :** the act or an instance of scurrying **:** a hurried or confused movement ⟨the ~ of men mounting in haste —*Blackwood's*⟩ ⟨a little ~ now and then when one cow bumped another —Nancy Hale⟩ **2 :** a short run or race **3 :** a jumping race in equitation over a series of obstacles with a penalty of one second for each fault **4 :** FLURRY ⟨huge snow *scurries* —Robert Payne⟩

S curve *n, cap S* **:** a curve resembling the letter S

scur·vi·ly \ˈskər·vəlē, -kəv-, -kəiv-, -li\ *adv* **:** in a scurvy manner

scur·vi·ness \-vēnəs, -vin-\ *n* -ES **:** the quality or state of being scurvy

scur·vish \-vish\ *n* -ES [alter. of *scabish*] **:** an evening primrose (*Oenothera biennis*)

¹scur·vy \ˈskərvē, -kəv-, -kəiv-, -vi\ *adj* -ER/-EST [¹*scurf* + *-y*] **1 :** covered or affected with scurf **:** SCURFY **2 :** characterized by meanness and despicableness **:** CONTEMPTIBLE ⟨went to sea with his ~ crew —C.B.Driscoll⟩ ⟨weather played some ~ tricks⟩ **syn** see CONTEMPTIBLE

²scurvy \"\ *n* -ES **:** a disease characterized by spongy gums, loosening of the teeth, and a tendency to bleed into the skin and mucous membranes and caused by a dietary deficiency of ascorbic acid ⟨suggested that the anemia of ~ is due to iron deficiency —*Therapeutic Notes*⟩

scurvy grass *n* **1 :** any of several cresses reputed to have value in the treatment or prevention of scurvy: as **a :** WINTER CRESS **b :** a widely distributed arctic cress (*Cochlearia officinalis*) **2** *Austral* **:** DAYFLOWER a

scuse *n* ˈskyüs, *v* -üz\ *n or vb* [by shortening] **:** EXCUSE

scus·in \ˈskyüzᵊn\ *prep* [alter. of *excusing*] *chiefly South & Midland* **:** EXCEPT

¹scut \ˈskət\ *n* -s [origin unknown] **:** the short erect tail of an animal, esp. of a hare or rabbit

²scut \"\ *n* -s [prob. alter. of obs. E *scout*, fr. ME, prob. of Scand origin; akin to ON *skūta, skúti* taunt — more at SCOUT] **:** a contemptible fellow

scut- *or* **scuti-** *comb form* [NL, fr. L *scutum* shield] **1 :** shield ⟨*scutal*⟩ ⟨*scutella*⟩ ⟨*Scuti*branchia⟩ **2 :** scute **:** scutum ⟨*scuta*tion⟩ ⟨*scuti*ped⟩

scuta *pl of* SCUTUM

scu·tage \ˈskyüd·ij\ *n* -s [ME, fr. ML *scutagium*, fr. L *scutum* shield (i.e., military) + *-agium* -age (fr. OF *-age*) — more at ESQUIRE] **:** an impost tax or fine levied upon a tenant of a knight's fee in commutation for or for default in the render of the military service attached to the fee

scu·tal \ˈskyüd·ᵊl\ *adj* [*scut-* + *-al*] **:** of or relating to a shield, scute, or scutum

scu·tate \ˈskyüˌtāt\ *or* **scu·tat·ed** \-ˌād·əd\ *adj* [*scutate* fr. NL *scutatus*, fr. L, armed with a shield, fr. *scutum* shield + *-atus* -ate; *scutated* fr. NL *scutatus* + E *-ed*] **1 :** shaped like a buckler **:** PELTATE **2 :** covered by bony or horny plates or large scales

scu·ta·tion \skyüˈtāshən\ *n* -s [*scut-* + *-ation*] **:** the arrangement of scutes

¹scutch \ˈskəch\ *vt* -ED/-ING/-ES [obs. F *escoucher* (now *écoucher*), fr. (assumed) VL *excuticare* to beat out, fr. L *excutere* to shake out, beat out, fr. *ex-* ¹ex- + *quatere* to shake, strike — more at QUASH] **1** *dial* **:** WHIP, BEAT **2** *or* **skutch :** to separate the woody fiber from (flax or hemp) by beating **3** *chiefly Brit* **:** to open (cotton fiber) by beating and form into a lap **4 a :** to open (cloth) full width **b :** DISENTANGLE ⟨~ skeins of yarn⟩

²scutch \"\ *or* **scotch** \ˈskäch\ *n* -ES [obs. F *escouche* (now *écouche*) scutcher, fr. *escoucher* to scutch] **1 :** SCUTCHER **2 :** a bricklayer's hammer for cutting, trimming, and dressing bricks

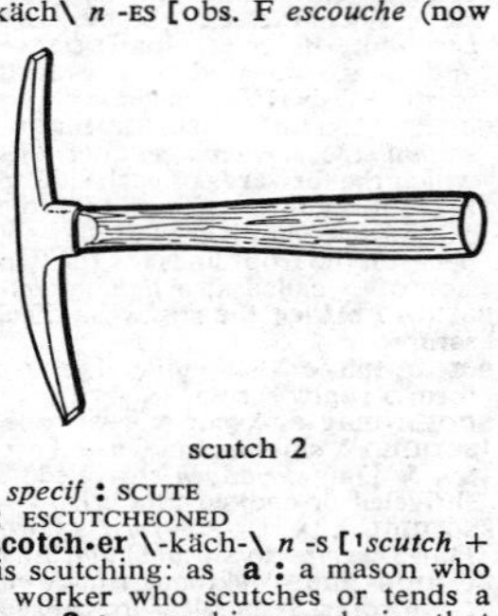

scutch 2

³scutch \"\ *or* **scutch grass** *n* -ES [*scutch* short for *scutch grass*; *scutch grass* alter. of *couch grass*] **1 :** COUCH GRASS 1a **2 :** BERMUDA GRASS

scutch·eon \ˈskəchən\ *n* -s [ME *scochon*, fr. MF *escuchon* — more at ESCUTCHEON] **1 :** ESCUTCHEON **2 :** something shaped like an escutcheon; *specif* **:** SCUTE

scutch·eoned \-nd\ *adj* **:** ESCUTCHEONED

scutch·er \ˈskəchə(r)\ *or* **scotch·er** \-käch-\ *n* -s [¹*scutch* + *-er*] **1 :** one whose work is scutching: as **a :** a mason who cuts with a scutch **b :** a worker who scutches or tends a machine that does scutching **2 :** a machine or device that scutches; *specif* **:** an implement or machine for scutching flax, cotton, or cloth

scute \ˈsk(y)üt\ *n* -s [ME, fr. L *scutum* shield; trans. of MF *ecu* ecu, shield — more at ESQUIRE] **1** *archaic* **:** a coin of small value **2** [NL *scutum*] **:** an external bony or horny plate **:** a large scale **:** SCUTUM: as **a :** one of the large scales on the head of a snake or other reptile **b :** one of the broad transverse scales on the belly of a snake **c :** one of the tergal plates of a myriapod **d :** ELYTRON 2

scu·tel \(ˈ)skyüˈtel\ *n* -s [NL *scutellum*] **:** SCUTELLUM

¹scu·tel·la \sk(y)üˈtelə\ *n, pl* **scutel·lae** \-e(ˌ)lē, -eˌlī\ [NL, fr. *scut-* + *-ella*] **1 :** SCUTELLUM 2b **2 :** a very small dermal bone or ossicle **:** a small scute

²scutella *pl of* SCUTELLUM

scu·tel·lar \(ˈ)=ˈ;telə(r)\ *adj* [NL *scutellum* + E *-ar*] **1 :** of or relating to a scutellum **2 :** having scutella

scu·tel·lar·ia \ˌsk(y)üd·ᵊlˈa(a)rēə\ *n, cap* [NL, fr. L *scutella* drinking bowl + NL *-aria* — more at SCUTTLE] **1 :** a very large widely distributed genus of herbs (family Labiatae) having purple, blue, pink, red, yellow, or white, flowers either axillary or in a terminal raceme and a bilabiate calyx with a scale or a helmetlike appendage above — see SKULLCAP **2** -s **:** the dried overground portion of the mad-dog skullcap used esp. formerly as a bitter tonic, antispasmodic, and stomachic

scu·tel·larin \sk(y)üˈtelərən, ˌsk(y)üd·ᵊlˈa(a)rən\ *n* -s [ISV *scutellar-* (fr. NL *Scutellaria*) + *-in*] **1 :** a resinoid prepared from the root of the mad-dog skullcap and related mints of the genus *Scutellaria* and used esp. formerly as a tonic and nerve sedative **2 :** a yellow crystalline compound $C_{21}H_{18}O_{12}$ obtained from the root of the mad-dog skullcap

scu·tel·late \ˈsk(y)üˈtelət, ˈsk(y)üd·ᵊlˌāt\ *adj* [prob. fr. (assumed) NL *scutellatus*, fr. NL *scutellum* + L *-atus* -ate] **1 a :** rather flat with a distinct rim and a rounded to oval outline ⟨a fungus with a ~ fruiting body⟩ **b :** of or resembling a scutellum **2** *or* **scu·tel·lat·ed** \ˈsk(y)üd·ᵊlˌād·əd\ [*scutellated* fr. (assumed) NL *scutellatus* + E *-ed*] **a :** covered with scales, small plates, or scutella **b :** faced with a series of broad usu. imbricated plates — used of the tarsus of a bird **3** *or* **scutellated :** having a scutellum — used of an insect (as a beetle)

scu·tel·la·tion \ˌsk(y)üd·ᵊlˈāshən\ *n* -s [*scutellate* + *-ion*] **:** LEPIDOSIS 2

¹scu·tel·ler·id \sk(y)üˈtelərəd\ *adj* [NL *Scutelleridae*] **:** of or relating to the Scutelleridae

²scutellerid \"\ *n* -s **:** an insect of the family Scutelleridae

scu·tel·ler·i·dae \ˌsk(y)üd·ᵊlˈerəˌdē\ *n pl, cap* [NL, fr. *Scutellera*, type genus (fr. *scutella*) + *-idae*] **:** a family of broadly oval flattened terrestrial insects (order Hemiptera) having the antennae five-jointed, the legs spineless, and a large scutellum that almost entirely covers the abdomen

scu·tel·li·form \sk(y)üˈteləˌfȯrm\ *adj* [NL *scutellum* + E *-iform*] **:** shaped like a scutellum

scu·tel·lig·er·ous \ˌsk(y)üd·ᵊlˈijərəs\ *adj* [NL *scutellum* + E *-igerous*] **:** having scutella **:** SCUTELLATE

scu·tel·li·plantar \sk(y)üˈtelə+\ *adj* [*scutellate* + connective *-i-* + *plantar*] **:** having the tarsi scutellate in front and behind (as some birds) — opposed to *laminiplantar* — **scu·tel·li·plantation** \"+\ *n*

scu·tel·lum \sk(y)üˈteləm\ *n, pl* **scutel·la** \-lə\ [NL, fr. *scut-* + *-ellum* (neut. of *-ellus* -el)] **1 a :** a rounded apothecium occurring in lichens and having an elevated rim formed of the thallus proper **b :** the shield-shaped cotyledon of a monocotyledon (as a grass) **c :** the conical cap of the endosperm in a cycad **2 a :** the third of the four pieces forming the upper part of a thoracic segment of an insect situated between the scutum and the postnotum; *specif* **:** the scutellum of the mesothorax **b :** one of the transverse scales on the tarsi and toes of birds

scutellum rot *n* **:** a molding and rotting seedling disease of germinating maize characterized by and caused by various fungi (esp. of the genera *Rhizopus, Mucor, Penicillium*, and *Fusarium*)

scutes *pl of* SCUTE

scuti- — *see* SCUT-

scu·ti·branch \ˈsk(y)üd·əˌbraŋk\ *n* -s [NL *Scutibranchia*] **:** a gastropod of the group Scutibranchia

scu·ti·bran·chia \ˌ==ˈbraŋkēə\ *n, pl, cap* [NL *scut-* + *-branchia*] *in some classifications* **:** a heterogeneous group of gastropods distinguished by possession of a simple shield-shaped shell and more or less exactly equivalent to Aspidobranchia esp. in modern usage — **scu·ti·bran·chi·an** \ˌ==ˈbraŋkēən\ *adj or n* — **scu·ti·bran·chi·ate** \-ēət, -ēˌāt\ *adj or n*

scu·ti·bran·chi·a·ta \ˌ==,==ˈäd·ə, -ˈād·ə\ [NL *scut-* + *branchiata*] *syn of* SCUTIBRANCHIA

scu·tif·er·ous \(ˈ)sk(y)üˈtif(ə)rəs\ *adj* [*scut-* + *-ferous*] **:** bearing scutes

scu·ti·form \ˈsk(y)üd·əˌfȯrm\ *adj* [NL *scutiformis*, fr. L *scutum* shield + *-iformis* -iform — more at ESQUIRE] **:** having the shape of a shield **:** SCUTATE

scu·ti·ger \ˈsk(y)üd·əjə(r)\ *n* -s [NL *Scutigera*] **:** a centipede of the genus *Scutigera* — **scu·tig·er·al** \(ˈ)sküˈtijərəl\ *adj*

scu·tig·era \sk(y)üˈtijərə\ *n, cap* [NL *scut-* + *-gera* (fr. L

gerere to bear) — more at CAST] : a genus (the type of the family Scutigeridae) of centipedes including the house centipede

scu·tig·er·el·la \(,)sk(y)ü,tijə'relə\ *n, cap* [NL, fr. *Scutigera* + *-ella*] : a genus of symphilids that includes the widely distributed garden centipede

scu·tig·er·ous \(')sk(y)ü¦tijərəs\ *adj* [*scut-* + *-gerous*] : SCUTIFEROUS

scu·ti·ped \'sk(y)üd·ə,ped\ *adj* [*scut-* + *-ped*] *of a bird* : having scutellate tarsi

scuts *pl of* SCUT

¹scut·ter \'skəd·ə(r)\ *vb* -ED/-ING/-S [alter. (prob. influenced by *scatter*) of ²*scuttle*] : SCURRY, SCUTTLE

²scutter \"\ *n* -S **1** *chiefly Scot* : SCURRY, SCRAMBLE **2** *dial* : someone remarkable (as for rascality or excellence)

¹scut·tle \'skəd·ᵊl, -ət³l\ *n* -S [ME *scutel*, fr. L *scutella* drinking bowl, tray, dim. of *scutra* flat plate, platter; perh. akin to L *scutum* shield — more at ESQUIRE] **1** : a shallow open basket of wood or wickerwork for carrying something (as grain or garden produce) **2** : COAL SCUTTLE **3** *Brit* : COWL 3c **4** : a large glass for beer or ale ⟨~ of suds⟩

²scuttle \"\ *n* -S [ME *skottell*, prob. fr. OSp *escotilla*] **1** : a small opening in an outside wall or covering furnished with a lid: as **a** : a small opening or hatchway in the deck of a ship large enough to admit a man and with a lid for covering it **b** : a small hole in the side or bottom of a ship furnished with a lid or glazed **c** : an opening in the roof or a floor of a house fitted with a lid **2** : a lid that covers or closes a scuttle

³scuttle \"\ *vt* **scuttled; scuttled; scuttling** \-d·ᵊliŋ, -t(ᵊ)liŋ\ **scuttles 1** : to cut a hole through the bottom, deck, or sides of (a ship); *specif* : to sink or attempt to sink by making holes through the bottom of **2 a** : to damage severely or destroy completely ⟨war was in full swing, and this effectually *scuttled* my family's travel plans —Polly Adler⟩ **b** : ABANDON ⟨the overtime provisions of the old contract were *scuttled* in the new agreement —*N.Y. Times*⟩

⁴scuttle \"\ *n* -S [alter. of ¹*cuttle*] **1** : CUTTLEFISH **2** : OCTOPUS

⁵scuttle \"\ *vi* -ED/-ING/-S [prob. blend of ¹*scud* and *shuttle* v.] **1** : to move with or as if with short rapidly alternating steps : SCURRY ⟨a tiny man came *scuttling* in by another door —Gordon Merrick⟩ ⟨armies of brown fiddler crabs ~ across the road —*Amer. Guide Series: Fla.*⟩ ⟨a little motorcar so small that it *scuttled* up the road . . . with the abruptness of a wound-up toy —Thomas Wolfe⟩ **2** : to withdraw from or abandon a possession or country once occupied or a policy or obligation in a hasty manner ⟨*scuttling* out of our responsibilities in the Middle East —*New Statesman & Nation*⟩

⁶scuttle \"\ *n* -S **1 a** : a quick shuffling pace ⟨a chimpanzee can easily run away and escape from a man with its half-quadrupedal, half-bipedal ~ —Weston LaBarre⟩ **b** : a short swift run ⟨suddenly made a last frantic ~ —A.J.Cronin⟩ **2** : hurried withdrawal from occupation or control of a country or area ⟨follow up . . . an electoral reversal by an Imperial ~ —*New Statesman & Nation*⟩

scut·tle·butt \'skəd·ᵊl,bət, -kət³l-, *usu* -bəd·+V\ *n* [²*scuttle* + *butt* (cask)] **1 a** : a cask on shipboard to contain fresh water for a day's use **b** : a drinking fountain on a ship or at a naval or marine installation **2** : RUMOR, GOSSIP ⟨started a round of ~ to the effect that the regiment would arrive soon —H.L. Merillat⟩

scut·tler \'skəd·ᵊlə(r), -kət³l-\ *n* -S [⁵*scuttle* + *-er*] **1** : one that scuttles **2** : RACE RUNNER

scu·tu·late \'sk(y)üchə,lāt, -üd·ᵊl,āt\ *also* **scu·tu·lat·ed** \-,ād·əd\ *adj* [*scutulate* prob. fr. (assumed) NL *scutulatus*, fr. L *scutulum* small shield + *-atus* -ate; *scutulated* fr. (assumed) NL *scutulatus* + E *-ed*] : SCUTELLATE

scu·tu·lum \-chələm, -d·ᵊl\ *n, pl* **scutu·la** \|ə\ [NL, fr. L, small shield, dim. of *scutum* shield] : one of the yellow cup-shaped crusts occurring over hair follicles in favus

scu·tum \'sk(y)üd·əm\ *n, pl* **scu·ta** \-ə\ [NL, fr. L, shield — more at ESQUIRE] **1** : a bony, horny, or chitinous plate : SCUTE: as **a** : the second and largest of the four parts forming the upper surface of a thoracic segment of an insect between the prescutum and the scutellum **b** : one of the two lower valves of the operculum of a barnacle

scyb·a·lous \'sibələs\ *adj* [NL *scybalum* + E *-ous*] : formed of hardened feces

scyb·a·lum \-ləm\ *n, pl* **scyba·la** \-lə\ [NL, fr. LL, dung, fr. Gk *skybalon*] : a hardened fecal mass

scyd·mae·ni·dae \sid'mēnə,dē\ *n pl, cap* [NL, fr. *Scydmaenus*, type genus (fr. Gk *skydmainein* to be angry with) + *-idae*] : a widely distributed family of very small beetles

scye \'sī\ *n* -S [origin unknown] : ARMSCYE

¹scyl·io·rhi·nid \¦silēō¦rīnəd\ *adj* [NL *Scyliorhinidae*] : of or relating to the Scyliorhinidae

²scyliorhinid \"\ *n* -S : a cat shark of the family Scyliorhinidae

scyl·io·rhin·i·dae \,==ə'rinə,dē\ *n pl, cap* [NL, fr. *Scyliorhinus*, type genus (fr. Gk *skylion* dogfish + NL *-rhinus*) + *-idae*] : a family of galeoid sharks including the typical cat sharks

scyl·la \'silə\ *n* -S *usu cap* [fr. *Scylla* (now *Scilla*), headland on the Italian coast projecting into the Strait of Messina opposite the whirlpool Charybdis on the Sicilian coast, fr. L, fr. Gk *Skylla*] : a destructive peril — usu. used as the alternative to *Charybdis* ⟨the *Scylla* of incomprehensibility and the Charybdis of inaccuracy have both been avoided —*Times Lit. Supp.*⟩

scyl·laea \sə'lēə\ *n, cap* [NL, fr. *Scylla*, in Greco-Roman mythology a female monster who inhabited the rock Scylla on the Italian coast and was a menace to seafarers, fr. L, fr. Gk *Skylla*] : a genus (coextensive with the family Scyllaeidae) of pelagic nudibranch mollusks that have small branched gills situated on the upper side of four fleshy lateral lobes and on a median crest on the posterior part of the back and that live among and mimic sargassum and other floating seaweeds

¹scyl·lar·i·an \sə'la(a)rēən\ *adj* [NL *Scyllarus*, genus of crustaceans + E *-an*] : of or relating to the Scyllaridae

²scyllarian \"\ *n* -S : a crustacean of the family Scyllaridae

scyl·lar·i·dae \sə'larə,dē\ *n pl, cap* [NL, fr. *Scyllarus*, type genus (fr. Gk *skyllaros*, *kyllaros* hermit crab) + *-idae*] : a family of marine decapod crustaceans (tribe Palinura) having the body broad and flat, the antennae short and scalelike, and the eyes in sockets in the carapace and living in shallow water buried in mud or sand

scyl·lio·rhin·i·dae [NL] *syn of* SCYLIORHINIDAE

scyl·li·tol \'silə,tōl, -tȯl\ *n* -S [NL *Scyllium*, genus name of the dogfish *Scyllium canicula* (fr. Gk *skylion* dogfish) + ISV *-itol*] : an optically inactive sweet crystalline polyhydroxy alcohol $C_6H_6(OH)_6$ that is found esp. in the dogfish, in the leaves of the coconut palm, in flowering dogwood, and in acorns

scyph- *or* **scypho-** *also* **scyphi-** *comb form* [NL, fr. L *scyphus* cup, scyphus — more at SCYPHUS] : cup : can : scyphus ⟨*scyphi*form⟩ ⟨*Scypho*zoa⟩ ⟨*scypho*se⟩

¹scy·pha \'sīfə\ *n, pl* **scyphae** [NL, fr. L *scyphus* cup] : SCYPHUS 2

²scypha \"\ *n, cap* [NL, fr. L *scyphus* cup] *in some classifications* : a genus equivalent to *Sycon* that is often considered invalid since it was described as a genus of plants

scy·phate \-,fāt\ *adj* [*scyph-* + *-ate*] : shaped like a cup

scy·phis·to·ma \sī'fistəmə\ *n, pl* **scyphisto·mae** \-(,)mē\ *also* **scyphistomas** [NL, fr. *scyph-* + *-stoma*] : a sexually produced polypoid larva of many scyphozoans that is attached to the substrate, may produce other scyphistomae by budding, but ultimately repeatedly constricts transversely and abscises ephyrae which develop into free-swimming medusae — see STROBILA

scy·pho·medusae \¦sī(,)fō+\ [NL, fr. *scyph-* + *medusae*, pl. of *medusa*] *syn of* SCYPHOZOA

scy·pho·polyp \¦sīfō+\ *n* [*scyph-* + *polyp*] : SCYPHISTOMA

scy·phose \'sī,fōs\ *adj* [*scyph-* + *-ose*] : having scyphi

scy·pho·zoa \,sīfə'zōə\ *n pl, cap* [NL, fr. *scyph-* + *-zoa*] : a class of Coelenterata comprising jellyfishes that have endodermal gastric tentacles, endodermal gonads which discharge their products into the digestive cavity, and usu. tentaculocysts, that lack a true hydroid and have the asexual generation represented by a scyphistoma, and that usu. lack a velum — see CORONATAE, CUBOMEDUSAE, RHIZOSTOMAE, SEMAEOSTOMEAE, STAUROMEDUSAE — **scy·pho·zo·an** \¦sīfə¦zōən\ *adj or n*

scyphu·la \'sīfyələ, 'sif-\ *n, pl* **scyphu·lae** \-,lē\ [NL, fr. *scyph-* + *-ula*] **1** : SCYPHISTOMA **2** : a hypothetical ancestral scyphozoan

scyphu·lus \-ləs\ *n, pl* **scyphu·li** \-,lī\ [NL, fr. LL, little cup, dim. of L *scyphus* cup] : the vaginula of a liverwort

scy·phus \'sīfəs\ *n, pl* **scy·phi** \-,fī\ [L, fr. Gk *skyphos*] **1** *or* **sky·phos** \'skī,fäs\ *pl* **sky·phoi** \-,fȯi\ : a drinking vessel with a deep body, flat bottom, and two small horizontal handles near the rim and used esp. in ancient Greece **2** [NL, fr. L, cup] : a cup-shaped enlargement of the podetium in lichens — called also *scypha*

scyt- *or* **scyto-** *comb form* [NL, fr. Gk *skyto-*, fr. *skytos* skin, leather — more at HIDE] : skin : integument ⟨*scyt*itis⟩ ⟨*scyto*blastema⟩

scyt·a·le \'sid·ᵊl(,)ē\ *n* -S [L *scytale*, *scytala*, *scutula*, fr. Gk *skytalē* staff, cylinder, message] **1** : a method of cipher writing used esp. by the Spartans in which a narrow strip of parchment was wound on a rod and the message written across the adjoining edges **2 a** : a message written in the scytale cipher **b** : a parchment bearing such a message

scyth \'sith\ *n* -S *usu cap* [ME *Sith*, fr. L *Scytha*, *Scythes*, fr. Gk *Skythēs*] : SCYTHIAN

¹scythe \'sīth, ÷'sī, *esp before a voiceless consonant (as in "scythestone")* 'sīth; *absence of* th *or* th *is more common in the plural than in the singular*\ *n* -S [ME *sithe*, fr. OE *sithe*, *sigthe*; akin to MLG *segede*, *sigde* scythe, MD *sichte*, ON *sigthr* scythe, sickle, OE *sagu*, *sage* saw — more at SAW] : an implement used for mowing grass, grain, or other crops and composed of a long curving blade fastened at an angle to a long handle

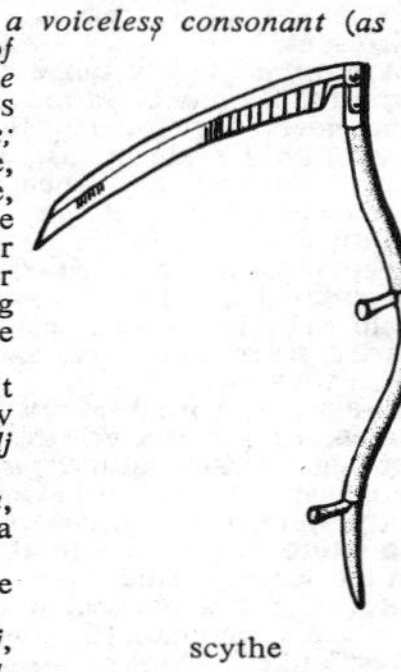

scythe

²scythe \"\ *vt* -ED/-ING/-S : to cut with or as if with a scythe : MOW

scythe·less \'sīthləs, ÷'sīl-\ *adj* : lacking a scythe

scythe·man \-īthmən, ÷-īm-\ *n, pl* **scythemen** : one who uses a scythe : MOWER

scythestone \'=,=\ *n* : a whetstone for sharpening a scythe

¹scyth·i·an \'sithēən, -th-\ *adj, usu cap* [L *Scythia* (fr. Gk *Skythia*, fr. *Skythēs* Scythian + *-ia* -y) + E *-an*] **1 a** : of, relating to, or characteristic of Scythia, an ancient country lying partly north and northeast of the Black sea and partly east of the Aral sea **b** : of, relating to, or characteristic of the people of Scythia **2** : of, relating to, or characteristic of the Scythian language

²scythian \"\ *n* -S *usu cap* [L *Scythes*, *Scytha* Scythian + E *-an*] **1** : one of an ancient nomadic people inhabiting Scythia **2** : the Iranian language of the Scythian people

scythian antelope *n, usu cap S* : SAIGA

scythian lamb *n, usu cap S* **1** : an Asiatic tree fern (*Cibotium barometz*) the dense matted hairs of which are sometimes used as a styptic **2** : COTTON 2

¹scyth·ic \-thik, -th-\ *adj, usu cap* [L *Scythicus*, fr. Gk *Skythikos*, fr. *Skythēs* Scythian + *-ikos* -ic] : SCYTHIAN

²scythic \"\ *n* -S : SCYTHIAN 2

scyth·ism \-,thizəm, -th-\ *n* -S *usu cap* [LGk *skythismos*, fr. Gk *Skythēs* Scythian + *-ismos* -ism] *archaic* : the paganism developed by the Scythians

scytho- *comb form, usu cap* [L *Scytha* Scythian + E *-o-*] : Scythian and ⟨*Scytho*-Aryan⟩ ⟨*Scytho*-Greek⟩

scytho-dravidian \¦si(,)thō, -thō+\ *adj, usu cap S&D* : of, relating to, or constituting a mixed racial type found chiefly in Bombay Province, India, and characterized by brachycephaly, medium stature, fair complexion, scanty beard, and well-formed nose

scy·to·dep·sic \¦sīd·ō¦depsik\ *adj* [F *scytodepsique*, fr. Gk *skytodepsikos*, fr. *skytodepsein* to dress leather (fr. *skytos* leather, skin + *depsein* to knead) + *-ikos* -ic — more at HIDE, DIPHTHERIA] : of or relating to a tanner or tanning

scy·to·ne·ma·ce·ae \,sīd·ōnə'māsē,ē\ *n pl, cap* [NL, fr. *Scytonema*, type genus (fr. *scyt-* + *-nema*) + *-aceae*] *syn of* SCYTONEMATACEAE

scy·to·nema·ta·ce·ae \,sīd·ō,nēmə'tāsē,ē, -nem-\ *n pl, cap* [NL, fr. *Scytonemat-*, *Scytonema*, type genus (fr. *scyt-* + *-nemat-*, *-nema*) + *-aceae*] : a family of filamentous blue-green algae (order Hormogonales) that differ from the Rivulariaceae in having no differentiation in the tips of the filaments and in exhibiting false branching of the filaments — **scy·to·nema·ta·ceous** \¦==,==¦tāshəs\ *adj* — **scy·to·nema·toid** \¦==¦==,tȯid\ *adj* — **scy·to·nema·tous** \¦==¦==məd·əs\ *adj*

scy·to·pet·a·la·ce·ae \,sīd·ō,ped·ᵊl'āsē,ē\ *n pl, cap* [NL, fr. *Scytopetalum*, type genus (fr. *scyt-* + *petalum* petal) + *-aceae* — more at PETAL] : a tropical African family of shrubs and trees (order Malvales) having coriaceous leaves, small clustered flowers with numerous stamens, and woody or drupaceous one-seeded fruits

sd *abbr* **1** said **2** sand **3** seasoned **4** seed **5** sewed **6** signed **7** sound

SD *abbr or n* -S [NL *scientiae doctor*] : a doctor of science

SD *abbr* **1** same day **2** sash door **3** saturation deficit **4** sea damage **5** semidiameter **6** senior deacon **7** service dress **8** several dates **9** short delay **10** short delivery **11** sight draft **12** *often not cap* [L *sine dato*] without date **13** *often not cap* [L *sine die*] without day **14** single deck **15** soft drawn **16** solid drawn **17** special delivery **18** special duty **19** specially denatured **20** stage direction **21** standard deviation **22** straight duty **23** supply department; supply depot **24** survival dose

SDA *abbr* specific dynamic action

sdain *or* **sdeign** *vb* -ED/-ING/-S [It *sdegnare*, fr. (assumed) VL *disdignare* — more at DISDAIN] *obs* : DISDAIN

SDBL *abbr* sight draft, bill of lading attached

SDD *abbr* store door delivery

sdeignful *adj, obs* : DISDAINFUL

sdg *abbr* siding

sdl *abbr* **1** saddle **2** seedling

sdr *abbr* sender

sdruc·cio·la \'zdrüchə,lä\ *adj* [It, fem. of *sdrucciolo* slipping, sliding, having the accent on the antepenult, fr. *sdrucciolare* to slip, slide] : being or exhibiting triple rhyme in which the last accent falls on the antepenultimate syllable (as in *femina*, *semina*)

SDT *abbr* shell-destroying tracer

SE *abbr* **1** sanitary engineering **2** *often not cap* second entrance **3** single entry **4** southeast; southeastern **5** standard error **6** starch equivalent **7** stock exchange

Se *symbol* selenium

'se *var of* 's

¹sea \'sē\ *n* -S [ME *see*, fr. OE *sǣ*; akin to OFris *sē* sea, OS & OHG *sē*, *sēo*, ON *sær*, *sjōr*, *sjār*, Goth *saiws*] **1 a** : the great body of salty water that covers much of the earth's surface : the oceans of the world with their dependent saline waters; *broadly* : the waters of the earth as distinguished from the land and air **b** : a particular part of the sea ⟨southern ~s⟩ ⟨the fair ~ of England⟩ **c** : one of the bodies of salt water of the earth that are secondary in size to oceans : a body of salt water of second rank more or less landlocked and generally forming part of, or connecting with an ocean or a larger sea ⟨the Mediterranean ~⟩ **d** : OCEAN — compare HIGH SEA **e** : an inland body of water esp. if large or if salt or brackish ⟨the Caspian ~⟩ ⟨the *Sea* of Aral⟩; *sometimes* : a small freshwater lake ⟨the *Sea* of Galilee⟩ **2 a** : surface motion on a large body of water or its direction ⟨the ~ sits southward⟩; *also* : rough water : a heavy swell or wave ⟨a ~ struck us⟩ ⟨heavy ~s nearly swamped the boat⟩ **b** : the disturbance of the ocean or other body of water due to the wind blowing at the time and place of observation ⟨mild breezes and little ~⟩ **3** : something (as a vast expanse, an overwhelming flood, or an agitated surface) felt to resemble a sea ⟨saw only an endless ~ of sandy plain⟩ ⟨a ~ of folly⟩ ⟨lost in the ~s of time⟩ **4** : the expanse of the high seas as a field of life, business, or naval operations : voyaging as a livelihood ⟨follow the ~⟩ ⟨retired from the ~⟩ **5** : SEASHORE, SEASIDE ⟨spent the summer at the ~⟩ **6** : SEAWATER **7** : ³MARE — **at sea 1** : on the sea; *specif* : on a sea voyage including for legal purposes the time from the beginning of the voyage till the arrival of the ship at its port of destination or until the intention of proceeding on the voyage is abandoned **2** : without landmarks for guidance : LOST, BEWILDERED — often used with *all* ⟨we were all *at sea* and didn't know what to do next⟩ ⟨*at sea* as to where to turn for help⟩ — **beyond seas** *or* **beyond sea** *or* **beyond the sea** *or* **beyond the seas 1** : on the farther side of or over the sea **2** : out of the territory, realm, or jurisdiction of a state — **to sea** *adv* : to or upon the open waters of the sea ⟨put *to sea* for a six months cruise⟩

²sea \"\ *adj* **1** : of, relating to, or characteristic of the sea or a sea ⟨~ arm⟩ ⟨~ smells⟩ **2** : of or relating to a ship, ship personnel, equipment or related matters : of or used by seamen or passengers on a ship ⟨~ discipline⟩ **3 a** : occurring on, upon, or over the waters of the sea or a sea ⟨~ traffic⟩ ⟨~ routes⟩ **b** : of or relating to navigation, shipping, or similar matters ⟨~ charts⟩ ⟨~ terms⟩ **c** : fit for use on the high seas : SEAGOING ⟨a ~ yacht⟩ **4** : of or relating to the navy : NAVAL ⟨a ~ engagement⟩ ⟨~ bases⟩ **5** : having the sea or part of the sea for field, territory, subject, object (as of activity, interest, concern) ⟨~ robber⟩ ⟨a ~ painter⟩ ⟨~ poem⟩ ⟨~ stories⟩ ⟨~ dominion⟩ **6** : inhabiting the sea or seashore ⟨~ nymphs⟩ ⟨~ dwellers⟩ **7** : deposited by the sea ⟨~ gravel⟩ **8** : of, occurring on, or belonging to the seacoast or seashore ⟨~ forts⟩ ⟨~ dunes⟩ **9** : coming from or showing over the sea or occurring at sea ⟨~ clouds⟩ ⟨the deep ~ roar⟩ **10** : made, formed, or shaped by the sea or the action of the sea ⟨a ~ frontier⟩ ⟨~ cobbles⟩

sea *abbr* seaman

sea acorn *n* : ACORN BARNACLE

sea adder *n* **1** : a European 15-spined stickleback (*Spinachia spinachia*) **2** : any of several European pipefishes of the genus *Nerophis*

sea air *n* : air (as over the sea and neighboring regions) markedly affected by the evaporation of salt water

sea-air \'=¦=\ *adj* [¹*sea* + *air*] **1** : concerned with both sea and air ⟨a *sea-air* naval operation⟩ **2** : occurring between or at the interface of sea and air ⟨a *sea-air* temperature differential⟩

sea anchor *n* : a drag typically in the form of an open canvas cone that is thrown overboard to retard the drifting of a ship and to keep its head to the wind : DROGUE; *also* : a similar device to restrain a seaplane resting on the water

sea anemone *n* : any of numerous almost invariably solitary and often large and brilliantly colored polyps of the order Actiniaria that in form, bright and varied colors, and cluster of tentacles surrounding the mouth superficially resemble a flower, that develop no skeleton, that reproduce sexually or rarely by budding or fission, and that prey on small animals which they catch with tentacles armed with stinging cells

sea arrow *n* : a squid of the genus *Ommastrephes* or family Ommastrephidae : FLYING SQUID

sea arrow grass *n* : an arrow grass (*Triglochin maritima*)

sea ash *n* : PRICKLY ASH 1

sea aster *n* : SEA STARWORT

seabag \'=,=\ *n* : a cylindrical canvas bag used esp. by a sailor for clothes and other gear

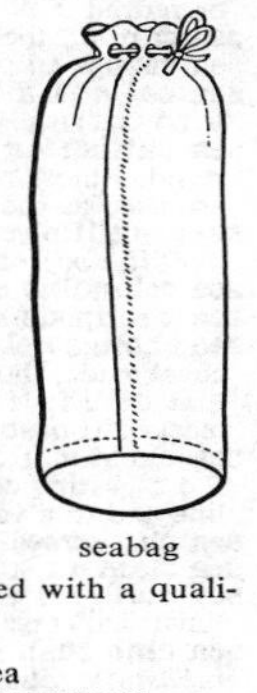

seabag

sea ball *n* : a spherical mass of living or fossil vegetation (as algae) produced by the compacting effect of moving shallow waters

sea bamboo *n* : a brown alga (*Ecklonia maxima*) that resembles those of the genus *Laminaria* when young but later develops lateral pinnae

sea bank *n* [ME *see bank*] **1 a** : the margin of the sea : SEASHORE **b** : a sandbank or dune adjacent to the sea **2** : SEAWALL

sea barley *n* : a European annual coastal squirrel grass (*Hordeum marinum*) that is highly tolerant of saline soil and is sometimes used for pasture

sea basket *n* : BASKET STAR

sea bass *n* **1** : any of numerous marine fishes of the family Serranidae that includes usu. the smaller more active members of the family as distinguished from the groupers; *esp* : BLACK SEA BASS 1 **2** : any of numerous croakers (as the weakfish or the channel bass) — often used with a qualifying term

sea bat *n* **1** : BATFISH a **2** : DEVILFISH 1

seabeach \'=,=\ *n* : a beach lying along the sea

seabeach morning-glory *n* : GOATSFOOT CONVOLVULUS

seabeach sandwort *n* : a perennial succulent herb (*Arenaria peploides*) having decussate leaves and small solitary axillary or terminal flowers

sea bean *n* **1 a** : any of various beans or showy seeds of tropical origin that are frequently carried by ocean currents to remote shores and often used as ornaments: as (1) : the large chocolate-colored seed of a snuffbox bean used in poultices and as an emetic (2) : OXEYE BEAN (3) : NICKER NUT **b** : a plant producing sea beans **2** : the hard flat rounded calcareous operculum of any of various mollusks (as those of the family Turbinidae)

sea bear *n* **1** : FUR SEAL **2** : POLAR BEAR

seabeard \'=,=\ *n* : a marine green alga (*Cladophora rupestris*) that grows in dense tufts

sea-beaten \'=,==\ *also* **sea-beat** \'=,=\ *adj* : battered or lashed by the sea; *also* : worn by life at sea

sea beaver *n* : SEA OTTER

seabed \'=,=\ *n* : the floor of a sea or ocean : land underlying the sea

sea·bee \'sē,bē\ *n* -S *usu cap* [alter. of *cee* + *bee* (letter); fr. the initials of *construction battalion*] : a member of one of the construction battalions organized as a volunteer branch of the Civil Engineer Corps of the U.S. Navy for building aviation facilities and naval installations and defending them

sea beef *n* **1** : beef corned for use at sea **2** : the flesh of a porpoise or whale used as food **3** *chiefly West Indies* : a chiton used as food

sea beet *n* **1** : a wild Old World beet (*Beta maritima* or *B. vulgaris maritima*) lacking a conspicuously swollen root that is prob. the ancestor of the common garden beets **2** : SEA LAVENDER

sea bells *n pl but sing or pl in constr* : a coastal bindweed (*Convolvulus soldanella*) having pink campanulate flowers

sea belt *n* : SEA GIRDLE

sea bent *n* **1** : BEACH GRASS **2** : SAND SEDGE

sea-berry \'sē- — *see* BERRY\ *n* **1** : REDBERRY 1 **2** : either of two Australasian plants of the genus *Haloragis* (*H. alata* and *H. tetragyna*)

sea bindweed *n* : SEA BELLS

seabird \'=,=\ *n* : any of various birds (as gulls, petrels, shearwaters, albatrosses) frequenting the open ocean

sea biscuit *n* **1** : hard biscuit or loaf bread prepared for use on shipboard : HARDTACK **2** : HEART URCHIN

sea bladder *n* : PORTUGUESE MAN-OF-WAR

sea blite *n* : any of various halophile herbs or shrubs of the genus *Suaeda* with fleshy alternate more or less terete leaves; *esp* : a plant (*Suaeda maritima*) that grows in salt marshes and has pale green leaves sometimes used as a potherb

sea bloom *or* **sea blossom** *n* : a free-floating marine blue-green alga (*Trichodesmium erythraeum*) that has a red pigment in addition to the phycocyanin and sometimes occurs so abundantly in the warmer seas as to color the water red — compare WATER BLOOM

sea blubber *n* : JELLYFISH

sea blue *n* : a moderate bluish green that is bluer and deeper than porcelain green and greener and deeper than Bremen blue

¹seaboard \'=,=\ *n* [ME *seebord*, fr. *see* sea + *bord* board — more at SEA, BOARD] **1** *obs* : the side of a ship toward the sea — used with *a*, *at*, *on*, or *to* **2** : SEACOAST; *also* : the country bordering a seacoast

²seaboard \"\ *adj* : bordering on or being near the sea

sea boat *n* **1** : a boat adapted to the open sea: as **a** : a ship having the power, size, and equipment for maintaining itself on the high seas ⟨these lighter craft cannot be considered *sea boats*⟩ : a ship that handles well in heavy seas ⟨the best *sea*

boat we ever owned⟩ **b** : a ship's boat adapted for use at sea **2** : CHITON 2

sea bob *n* [by folk etymology fr. AmerF *six barbes*, lit., six beards; fr. the appearance of the first long pair of legs together with the antennae and antennules] : a small shrimp (*Xiphopenaeus kroyeri*) that has the first pair of legs much elongated and is usu. used dried

sea book *n, archaic* : a nautical map

seaboot \ˈsē‚büt\ *n* : a very high waterproof boot used esp. by sailors and fishermen

sea-born \ˈsē‚bȯrn\ *adj* **1** : born of or in the sea ⟨*sea-born* nymphs⟩ **2** : originating in or rising from the sea ⟨a *sea-born* isle⟩ ⟨*sea-born* rocks⟩

seaborne \ˈsē‚bȯrn\ *adj* **1** : borne over or upon the sea : transported by ship ⟨~ supplies⟩ ⟨a ~ invasion⟩ **2** : engaged in or carried on by overseas shipping ⟨~ trade⟩

sea bottle *n* **1** : a marine green alga (*Valonia ventricosa*), whose thallus is a single inflated cell **2 a** : an alga of the genus *Fucus* — usu. used in pl. **b** : one of the swollen vesicles on the thallus of such an alga

seabound \ˈsē‚baund\ *adj* **1** : bounded by the sea **2** : bound for the sea

sea boy *n* **1** : SHIP BOY **2** : a very young sailor

sea brant *n* **1** : a common brant (*Branta bernicla*) of Europe and eastern No. America **2** : WHITE-WINGED SCOTER

sea breach *n* **1** : a breaking or overflow (as of a bank or dike) by the sea **b** *obs* : SEABEACH **2** : a destructive breaker or series of breakers

sea bread *n* **1** : HARDTACK **2** : CRUMB-OF-BREAD SPONGE

sea bream *n* : any of numerous marine percoid fishes: as **a** : a fish of the family Sparidae **b** : POMFRET 1; *broadly* : a fish of the family Bramidae **c** : any of several grunts (as the pinfish or the pompon)

sea breeze *n* : a cooling breeze blowing inland from the sea generally in the daytime

sea brief *n* : SEA LETTER

sea buckthorn *n* : a Eurasian maritime shrub (*Hippophaë rhamnoides*) of the family Eleagnaceae having silvery leaves and orange-red edible berries and yielding a yellow dye

sea-bull \ˈsē‚bul\ *n* [ME *see-bule*, fr. *see* sea + *bule* bull — more at SEA, BULL] : a male sea cow

sea bun *n* : HEART URCHIN

sea buoy *n* : the first buoy at the channel entrance to a harbor from the sea

sea burdock *n* : a halophile cocklebur (*Xanthium echinatum*) native to coastal areas of eastern No. America but widely distributed by commerce

sea bush or **sea club** *n* : GORGONIAN

sea butterfly *n* : PTEROPOD

sea cabbage *n* **1** : SEA KALE **2** : a European maritime plant (*Brassica oleracea*) from which the cabbage, cauliflower and broccoli have been derived in cultivation

sea cabin *n* : an emergency cabin near a ship's bridge for the use of captain and officers

sea calf *n* [ME *see calf*, fr. *see* sea + *calf*] : HARBOR SEAL

sea campion *n* : a European maritime perennial herb (*Silene maritima*) with bluish gray foliage and showy trusses of usu. white single or double flowers

sea captain *n* : the master of a merchant vessel whether active or retired

sea card *n* : the card of a mariner's compass

sea cat *n* **1 a** : FUR SEAL **b** : HARBOR SEAL **2 a** : WEEVER a **b** : WOLFFISH **c** : SEA CATFISH **3** *chiefly Africa* : OCTOPUS

sea catfish *n* : any of numerous marine fishes of the family Ariidae most of which are mouthbreeders and few of which are used as food

sea cauliflower *n* : a multilobed alcyonarian (*Alcyonium multiflorum*) of the No. Atlantic fishing banks

sea celandine *n* : HORNED POPPY

sea centipede *n, Austral* : any of several marine isopods

sea change *n* **1** : a change wrought by the sea ⟨of his bones are coral made, those are pearls that were his eyes; nothing of him that doth fade but doth suffer a *sea change* —Shak.⟩ **2** : a marked transformation (as to something richer or finer)

sea chest *n* **1** : a sailor's storage chest for personal property **2** : a casting connected to the side of a ship below the water line and to a valve for obtaining seawater (as for condensers)

sea chickweed *n* : SEABEACH SANDWORT

sea clam *n* : SURF CLAM

sea cloth *n* : a painted cloth representing waves for use on a theatrical stage

sea club rush *n* : a common No. American bulrush (*Scirpus robustus*); *also* : a closely related Old World bulrush (*S. lacustris*)

sea coal *n* [ME *seecole*, fr. *see* sea + *cole* coal — more at SEA, COAL] **1** *archaic* : mineral coal **2** : pulverized bituminous coal used as a foundry facing

seacoast \ˈsē‚kōst\ *n* [ME *seecost*, fr. *see* sea + *cost* coast — more at COAST] : the shore or border of the land adjacent to the sea

seacoast angelica *n* : a stout perennial herb (*Coelopleurum lucidum*) of the family Umbelliferae common in northeastern coastal No. America and having compound leaves on inflated stalks, compound umbels of greenish flowers, and prominently ribbed fruits

seacoast bluestem *n* : a bluestem (*Andropogon littoralis*) of beaches and dunes of eastern No. America that is very similar to and often considered a variety of the little bluestem and that is locally valued as a palatable forage grass and as an arrester of wind erosion of sandy soil

seacoast laburnum *n, Austral* : LABURNUM 2

sea cock *n* **1** : a cock or valve close to a ship's hull for opening or closing a pipe which communicates with the sea **2** : BLACK-BELLIED PLOVER

sea coconut *n* **1** *also* **sea coco a** : a lofty fan palm (*Lodoicea seychellarum*) of the Seychelle islands having leaves that are used for thatching **b** : the fruit of the sea coconut which often weighs 50 pounds and in which are 3 or 4 bilobed nuts with a smooth rind — called also *double coconut* **2** : the fruit of the bussu

sea cole *n* : SEA KALE

sea compass *n* : MARINER'S COMPASS

sea coot *n* **1** : SCOTER **2** : GUILLEMOT

sea corn *n* : the yellow mass of egg capsules produced by some marine snails (as whelks)

sea cow *n* **1** : SIRENIAN, MANATEE, DUGONG; *esp* : STELLER'S SEA COW **2** : WALRUS **3** : HIPPOPOTAMUS

sea cradle *n* : CHITON 2

seacraft \ˈsē‚kraft\ *n* **1** : sea-going ships **2** : skill in navigation

seacrafty \ˈsē‚kraftē\ *adj* : skilled in matters relating to the sea

sea crawfish or **sea crayfish** *n* : SPINY LOBSTER

sea cress *n* : GLASSWORT 1

seacross *n* : JELLYFISH; *esp* : a jellyfish in which four radial canals appear in the form of a cross

sea crow *n* **1** : a chough (*Pyrrhocorax pyrrhocorax*) **2** : CORMORANT **3** : BLACK-HEADED GULL **4** : a skua (*Catharacta skua*) **5** *Brit* : RAZORBILL **6** : a coot (*Fulica americana*) **7** : BLACK SKIMMER **8** : OYSTER CATCHER

sea cucumber *n* : HOLOTHURIAN; *esp* : any holothurian whose contracted body suggests a cucumber in form

sea cudweed *n* : a hoary European cottonweed (*Diotis maritima*) of the family Compositae

seaculture \ˈsē‚kəlchər\ *n* : the cultivation of marine life forms (as plankton or fishes) for food

sea-cun-ny \ˈsē‚kŏnē\ *n* -ES [by folk etymology fr. Per *sukkānī*, fr. *sukkān* rudder, helm, fr. Ar] *India* : STEERSMAN, QUARTERMASTER

sea cushion or **sea daisy** *n* : a thrift (*Armeria maritima*)

sea-cut \ˈsē‚kət\ *adj* : formed by the erosive action of sea waves : WAVE-CUT ⟨a *sea-cut* terrace⟩

sea-daddy *n, Brit* : a skilled seaman who is detailed to instruct young or green hands

sea daffodil *n* **1** : a white-flowered bulbous herb (*Pancratium maritimum*) common along the Mediterranean **2** : a bulbous herb (*Hymenocallis calathina*) of Peru and Bolivia that resembles the Mediterranean sea daffodil

sea dahlia *n* : a plant of the genus *Coreopsis* of the Pacific coast of the U.S. with flowers resembling yellow dahlias

sea date *n* : any of various bivalves of the genus *Lithophagus* somewhat resembling dates in shape : DATE MUSSEL

that often causes fouling of the bottoms of ships **3** : a cirrus cloud of wavy hairlike elements

sea day *n* : a period of 24 mean solar hours beginning at local mean noon

sea dayak or **sea dyak** *n, usu cap S&D* : IBAN 1

sea devil *n* **1** : DEVILFISH 1 **2** : MONKFISH 1 **3** : BLACK SEA DEVIL **4** : STONEFISH

sea dock *n* : a bear's-breech (*Acanthus mollis*)

sea dog *n* **1 a** (1) : HARBOR SEAL (2) : CAPE SEAL (3) : a small sea lion (*Zalophus californianus*) of the California coast **b** : a heraldic representation of a seal with a beaver tail, long back fin, webbed feet, and scaly legs and body **2** : DOGFISH **3 a** : an experienced sailor : one long at sea **b** : PRIVATEER, PIRATE

seadog \ˈsē‚dȯg\ *n* : FOGBOW

sea dotterel *n* **1** *dial Eng* : TURNSTONE **2** *dial Eng* : the common European ring plover (*Charadrius hiaticula*)

sea dove *n* **1** : DOVEKIE **2** : BLACK GUILLEMOT

sea dragon *n* **1** : DRAGONET **2** : SEA MOTH **3** : any of several beautifully colored Australian fishes (family Syngnathidae) intermediate between the pipefishes and the sea horses and having many large leaflike appendages on the plates of the body that simulate the seaweed among which they live

sea drake *n* **1** : CORMORANT **2** : a male eider

sea-drome \ˈsē‚drōm\ *n* [¹sea + -drome] : a floating airdrome serving as an intermediate or emergency landing place for airplanes

sea drum *n* : BLACK DRUM

sea duck *n* : any of various ducks (as the scoters, mergansers, and eiders) that frequent the sea; *esp* : EIDER

sea dust *n* **1** : fine and usu. reddish dust blown to sea by winds from arid lands and when caught in falling raindrops giving rise to blood rain **2** *slang* : SAND

sea duty *n* : duty in the U.S. Navy performed outside the continental U.S. or specified dependencies thereof

sea eagle *n* **1 a** : any of various eagles that are related to the bald eagle and feed largely on fish — see KAMCHATKAN SEA EAGLE, WHITE-TAILED SEA EAGLE **b** : FISHING EAGLE **c** : OSPREY **2** : EAGLE RAY

sea-ear \ˈsē‚ir\ *n* : ABALONE

sea eel *n* : a marine eel (as the conger eel); *also* : SEA LAMPREY

sea egg *n* : SEA URCHIN; *specif* : the bare test of a sea urchin from which the spines have fallen

sea elephant *n* : ELEPHANT SEAL

sea explorer *n* : a youth at least 14 years old who is enrolled in the sea exploring program of the Boy Scouts of America

sea fan *n* : a gorgonian that branches in a fanlike form; *esp* : a gorgonian (*Gorgonia flabellum*) of Florida and the West Indies

seafarer \ˈsē‚farər\ *n* -s : one occupied in or given to seafaring; *specif* : MARINER

¹**seafaring** \ˈsē‚farin\ *adj* [¹sea + *faring*, pres. part. of *fare*] : of, given to, or engaged in seafaring ⟨~ days⟩ : occurring in the course of or concerned with seafaring ⟨a ~ adventure⟩ ⟨~ yarns⟩

²**seafaring** \"\ *n* -s [¹sea + *faring*, gerund of *fare*] : traveling over the sea as a pursuit or recreation; *esp* : the mariner's calling

sea feather *n* : a gorgonian that branches in a plumelike form; *esp* : SEA PEN

sea fennel *n* : SAMPHIRE 1

sea fern *n* **1** : a gorgonian that branches like a fern **2** : finely branched and often brightly dyed material resembling a growth of algae, used as an aquarium ornament, and prob. the remains of a marine colonial bryozoan

sea fig *n* : BEACH APPLE

sea fight *n* : an engagement between ships at sea

sea fir *n* : a sertularian hydroid; *esp* : a hydroid (*Abietinaria abietina*) common on the British coast that branches like a miniature fir

sea fire *n* : marine bioluminescence

sea fisherman *also* **sea fisher** *n* : one who fishes esp. as an occupation out in the open sea

sea flea *n* : BEACH FLEA

seaflower *n* **1** : a sea anemone or similar actinozoan

sea-foam \ˈsē‚fōm\ *n* [ME *seefome*, fr. *see* sea + *fome, fom* foam — more at SEA, FOAM] **1** : froth on the sea **2** [trans. of G *meerschaum*] : MEERSCHAUM 1

seafoam \"\ *n* [sea-foam] : a brilliant to light green that is very slightly lighter than chrysoprase

seafoam green *n* : a pale yellow green that is yellower, lighter, and stronger than smoke gray, yellower and slightly lighter and stronger than oyster gray, and yellower and paler than average Nile

seafoam yellow *n* : a pale yellow green that is yellower, lighter, and stronger than smoke gray, yellower, lighter, and slightly stronger than oyster gray, and yellower and paler than average Nile

sea fog *n* : a fog drifted onshore or condensed from relatively warm onshore winds

seafolk \ˈsē‚fōk\ *n* : seafaring people : MARINERS

seafood \ˈsē‚füd\ *n* : marine fish and shellfish used as food or of kinds suitable for food

sea-for-thia \sē'fȯrthēə\ *n* [NL, fr. Francis Mackenzie Humbertson, Lord Seaforth †1815 Eng. nobleman + NL -ia] syn of PTYCHOSPERMA

seafowl \ˈsē‚faul\ *n* : a bird (as an auk, gannet, gull, tern, or petrel) that frequents the sea

sea fox *n* **1** : THRESHER SHARK **2 a** : a lanky long-muzzled long-eared more or less rufous jackal (*Canis variegatus*) of the northeastern African seacoast

sea fret *n* [²fret] : SEA FOG

seafront \ˈsē‚frənt\ *n* : the waterfront of a seaside place; *also* : a built-up zone (as of buildings and promenades) along such a front

sea frontage *n* : frontage on the sea : an extent of seafront

sea frontier *n* : a large nonadministrative sea and land area command (as in the U.S. Navy) organized under a district commandant

sea froth *n* : SEA-FOAM

sea furbelow *n* : a sea tangle (*Laminaria bulbosa*)

sea garfish *n* : an Australian pelagic halfbeak (*Hyporhamphus intermedius*)

sea gasket *n* : a fixed furling line such as is used at sea

sea-gate \ˈsē‚gāt\ *n* [³gate] **1** : a long rolling swell of the sea **2** : a way (as a gate, beach, or channel) that gives access to the sea **2** : a gate that serves as a protection against seas

sea gherkin *n* : a small sea cucumber of *Cucumaria* or related genera

sea ginger *n* : a hydrocoral (*Millepora alcicornis*) with branching fingerlike processes that much resembles dried gingerroot

sea girdle *n* **1** *or* **sea hanger** : VENUS'S-GIRDLE **2** : any of various kelps of the genus *Laminaria* (esp. *L. digitata*) with palmately cleft fronds

seagirt \ˈsē‚gərt\ *adj* : surrounded or enclosed by the sea

sea-god \ˈsē‚gäd\ *n* : a deity (as Neptune) held to live in or rule the sea or a part of the sea ⟨the *sea-gods* ride upon the sounding waves —William Hazlitt⟩

seagoer \ˈsē‚gō(ə)r\ *n* : one that travels by sea : SEAFARER

¹**seagoing** \ˈsē‚gōin\ *n* : travel by sea : SEAFARING

²**seagoing** \"\ *adj* **1 a** : designed or adapted for sailing the open sea in distinction from rivers or harbors ⟨a ~ tug⟩ **b** : fitted to be used on a seagoing vessel ⟨a ~ chronometer⟩

sea goose *n* **1** : PHALAROPE **2** : DOLPHIN

sea gooseberry *n* : a ctenophore of *Pleurobrachia* or a related genus : a typical ctenophore

sea gown *n* **1** : a garment for use at sea ⟨my *sea gown* scarf't about me —Shak.⟩

sea grape *n* **1 a** : GULFWEED **b** : a tree or shrub of the genus *Coccoloba*; *esp* : a variable plant (*C. uvifera*) of sandy shores of Florida and tropical America having rounded leaves with cordate bases and bearing clusters of bluish edible berries **c** : a leafless shrub (*Ephedra distachya*) of southeastern Europe **d** : GLASSWORT **2 sea grapes** *pl* : the clusters of gelatinous egg capsules of squids (as those of the genus *Loligo*)

sea grass *n* **1 a** : a tassel grass (*Ruppia maritima*) **b** : a plant of the genus *Salicornia* (esp. *S. europaea*) **c** : THRIFT 6 **d** *or* **sea hay** : EELGRASS 1; *also* : its dried stems widely used for stuffing furniture and in making coarse fabrics **2** : any of several seaweeds (esp. a green alga (genus *Enteromorpha*

sea green *n* **1 a** : a moderate green that is bluer and paler than myrtle (sense 3a) and bluer, lighter, and stronger than laurel green (sense 1) — called also *spruce green* **b** : a moderate yellow green that is greener, lighter, and stronger than average moss green, lighter, stronger, and very slightly yellower than average pea green, and stronger than apple green (sense 1) — called also *sea-water green* **c** : SEA BLUE **2** : land overflowed by the sea in spring tides

sea-green \ˈsē‚grēn\ *adj* **1** : green like seawater esp. in waters fathomable with a hand sounding line **2** : of the color sea green

sea-green incorruptible *n* : one utterly, disinterestedly, and rigidly devoted to some ideal or objective esp. in the world of political thought or action

sea gudgeon *n* : any of various marine gobies

sea gull *n* **1** : a gull frequenting the sea; *broadly* : GULL **2** *slang* : a waterfront prostitute or one chiefly catering to sailors

sea gypsy *n* : BAJAU

sea-hair coralline *n* : a delicate sertularian hydroid (*Sertularia operculata*)

sea hare *n* : any of various large naked mollusks constituting the genus *Tethys*, having arched backs and anterior tentacles that project like ears, and being reputed to attain a length of nearly 2 feet and a weight of over 15 pounds

sea hawk *n* : JAEGER, SKUA

sea heath *n* : a plant of the genus *Frankenia*

sea-heath family *n* : FRANKENIACEAE

sea hedgehog *n* **1** : SEA URCHIN **2** : GLOBEFISH

sea hen *n* **1** : any of several sea birds: as **a** : SKUA **b** *Brit* : a common guillemot (*Uria aalge*) **2** : a lumpsucker (*Cyclopterus lumpus*)

sea hog *n* : PORPOISE

sea holly *n* **1** : a European evergreen herb (*Eryngium maritimum*) formerly used as an aphrodisiac **2** : a bear's-breech (*Acanthus mollis*)

sea hollyhock *n* : a rose mallow (*Hibiscus moscheutos*)

sea horse *n* [ME *sehors*, fr. *se, see* sea + *hors* horse — more at SEA, HORSE] **1 a** : WALRUS 1 **b** *obs* : HIPPOPOTAMUS **2** : a fabulous creature half horse and half fish; *also* : a heraldic representation of a monster with the foreparts of a horse joined to the tail of a fish and with webbed feet **3 a** : any of numerous small fishes (family Syngnathidae) mostly of the genus *Hippocampus* that are related to the pipefishes but of stockier build, have the head and forepart of the body sharply flexed and suggestive of the head and neck of a horse, are covered with rough bony plates and equipped with a prehensile tail and in the male a short broad pouch immediately behind the vent in which the eggs hatch, and occur in most warm and warm-temperate seas **b** : HORSEFISH 1d **4** : a large whitecap on a wave **5** : a short-handled clam rake with long prongs

sea horse 3a

seahound \ˈsē‚haund\ *n* [ME *seehound*, fr. *see* sea + *hound*] : DOGFISH

sea ice *n* : ice formed by the freezing of seawater : masses of floating ice that have drifted to sea

sea island cotton *also* **sea island** *n, often cap S&I* [fr. Sea islands, chain of islands in the Atlantic off the coast of So. Carolina, Georgia, and Florida] : a cotton (*Gossypium barbadense*) with unusually long and silky fiber grown esp. in the West Indies and along the coast region of the southeastern U.S. — called also *tree cotton*; see EGYPTIAN COTTON

sea island myrtle *n* : GROUNDSEL BUSH

sea jelly *n* : JELLYFISH

sea kale *n* : a European perennial herb (*Crambe maritima*) that has a fleshy branching rootstalk and is sometimes cultivated for its large ovate long-stalked leaves which are used as a potherb — called also *sea cole*

seakale beet \ˈsē‚kāl-\ *n* : a garden beet grown for its edible foliage and usu. lacking an enlarged root

seakeeping \ˈsē‚kēpin\ *adj* : remaining or capable of remaining at sea during severe storms ⟨a ~ ship⟩ ⟨the ~ qualities of a ship design⟩

sea kemp *n* : SEA PLANTAIN — usu. used in pl.

sea kidney *n* : SEA PANSY

sea-kindliness \ˈsē‚kīndlēnəs\ *n* : the quality or state of being sea-kindly

sea-kindly \ˈsē‚kīndlē\ *adj* : well adapted to handling at sea ⟨a *sea-kindly* ship⟩

sea king *n* **1** [trans. of ON *sækonungr*] : a Norse pirate chief — compare VIKING **2** : a prehistoric king in Crete

sea kit-tie \ˈsē‚kiti\ *n* [*kittie*, short for *kittiwake*] *Brit* : KITTIWAKE

¹**seal** \ˈsēl, *esp before pause or consonant* -ēəl\ *n, pl* **seals** *or* **seal** *often attrib* [ME *selch, sele*, fr. OE *seolc-, seolh*; akin to MLG *sel* seal, OHG *selah* seal, ON *selr* seal, and perh. to OE *sulh* furrow — more at SULCUS] **1** : any of numerous marine aquatic carnivorous mammals that constitute the families Phocidae and Otariidae, live chiefly near cool seacoasts or on ice floes but crawl ashore to bear young and to breed, feed on fish and other marine animals, have the limbs modified into webbed flippers adapted primarily to swimming, and have been extensively hunted for fur, hides, and oil : any pinniped other than a walrus — see EARED SEAL, EARLESS SEAL, ELEPHANT SEAL, FUR SEAL, HAIR SEAL, SEA LION **2 a** : the pelt of a fur seal usu. plucked and dyed for use in garments and often imitated by shearing and dyeing rabbit or muskrat ⟨a ~ coat⟩ **b** : leather made from the skin of a seal — see PIN SEAL **3** *or* **seal brown** : a dark grayish yellowish brown that is less strong and slightly redder than sepia brown and slightly redder and paler than otter

²**seal** \"\ *vi* -ED/-ING/-s : to hunt seals

³**seal** \"\ *n* -s [ME *seel*, fr. OF, fr. L *sigillum* small figure, small image, seal, dim. of *signum* sign, mark, figure, image — more at SIGN] **1 a** : something that confirms, ratifies, or makes secure : GUARANTEE, ASSURANCE **b** (1) : a device (as an emblem, symbol, or word) used to identify or replace the signature of an individual or organization and to authenticate (as under common law) written matter purportedly emanating from such individual or organization (2) : a surface (as of a medallion or the face of a ring) bearing such a device incised so as to be reproducible in plastic material (as wax or moist clay); *also* : an object (as a ring) bearing such a seal (3) : an impression of such a device (as on or attached to a document) in plastic material; *also* : a piece of wax, a wafer, or other substance bearing such an impression **c** : an impression, device, sign, or mark given the effect of a common-law seal by statute law or by American local custom recognized by judicial decision ⟨the word "seal" or the letters "L.S." written or printed, or a scroll made with the pen may constitute a ~ within the meaning of the law⟩ **d** : an adhesive stamp bearing a symbolic or pictorial design suggestive of a particular cause and usu. distributed as an appeal for or acknowledgment of a contribution to that cause **2** : something that firmly closes or secures: as **a** : a piece of material (as sealing wax) placed in such a manner (as on an envelope or a folded document) as to prevent opening without breaking it; *also* : any of various closures or fastenings (as on a door, container, or railway car) that cannot be opened without rupture and that serve as a check against tampering or unauthorized opening **b** : something (as a vow) that obliges one to maintain silence **c** (1) : a tight and perfect closure (as against the passage of gas or water) ⟨turn the jars upside down to be sure the ~ is tight⟩ ⟨the flashing must make a ~ with the roofing⟩ (2) : a device to prevent the passage or return of gas or air into a pipe or container (as by submerging the open end of a pipe in a liquid, by keeping filled with liquid a deep bend in a pipe, or by projecting a partition or gland into a liquid-filled space) ⟨a water ~⟩ ⟨a gland ~⟩ (3) : a tight joint formed by the lap or bearing of a valve or similar member beyond the opening or space which the valve closes (4) : a cemented stone cover of an altar sepulcher **d** : a sealing coat applied in the finishing of wood **3** *chiefly Brit* : an official seal (as of a chancellor or secretary of state) esp. as a symbol

of official status : an indication or mark of office — usu. used in pl. and with *the* ⟨his majesty ordered the immediate surrender of the ~*s*⟩ **4** *obs* : a ceremony of affixing the great seal to documents **5 a** : something that gives a character to a person such that he may be recognized as belonging to an indicated agent ⟨the Holy Spirit: the ~ of God⟩ **b** : an indication of status and esp. of approved, superior, or desirable status ⟨gave the party the ~ of her approval⟩ — **under seal** *adv* : with an authenticating seal affixed; *esp* : with both signature and seal

⁴seal \"\ *vb* -ED/-ING/-S [ME *selen*, fr. OF *seeler*, fr. *seel*, n.] *vt* **1** : to confirm or make secure by or as if by a seal : confirm in a particular association — often used in allusion to Rev 7:2–8 (RSV) ⟨God ~*s* His own⟩: as **a** : to give a character to (a person) such that he may be recognized as belonging to an agent — used esp. of God in relation to the faithful **b** : to solemnize for eternity (as a marriage or an adoption of a child) — used by Mormons **2 a** : to set or affix an authenticating seal to; *also* : to formally authenticate : RATIFY **b** : to mark with a stamp usu. as an evidence of standard exactness, legal size, weight, or capacity, or merchantable quality **c** : to give under or as if under seal : grant authentically ⟨now must your conscience my acquittance ~ —Shak.⟩ **d** : to give authenticity to : serve as the seal of ⟨their pleasure ~*s* our satisfaction⟩ **3 a** : to fasten with or as if with a seal to prevent tampering ⟨~ a letter⟩ ⟨the coroner ~*ed* the premises⟩ **b** : to keep shut, enclosed, or confined ⟨lips ~*ed* by a promise⟩ ⟨ice may ~ in the boats as early as September⟩ **c** : to close or fasten by a coating or other fastening that prevents access or leakage ⟨~*ed* the patch in place with strong pitch⟩ ⟨~ each jampot with hot wax⟩; *often* : to make gas or fluid tight by a process of sealing ⟨~*ed* the leak with a blowout patch⟩ ⟨the jars must be perfectly ~*ed* if the food is to keep⟩ **d** : to make fast (as a piece of iron in a wall or a wire in a bulb) with cement, plaster, fusible glass, or other filling : close up chinks, crevices, or breaks in with or as if with plaster ⟨~ a leaky wall⟩; *also* : to close the pores of (a wooden or other porous surface) with a sealer **e** : to complete the movement of (as an electric contactor, switch, or relay) after the contacting parts touch each other **4 a** : to mark or fasten when applied — used esp. of a seal ⟨the new seal ~*ed* it cleanly and without blurring⟩ **b** : to fix firmly or steadily as if fastened **5** : to determine irrevocably or indisputably ⟨this answer ~*ed* our fate⟩ ~ *vi* **1 a** : to affix one's seal or a seal **b** *obs* : to give an assent by or as if by affixing a seal **2** : to perform the act of closing by sealing — **seal a move** : to file a sealed statement of a move to be made on resumption of an adjourned chess game

⁵seal \"\ *n* -S [ME *sele*, fr. (assumed) ME *selen* to tie up cattle (whence E dial. *seal*), fr. OE *sǣlan* to tie, bind, fr. *sāl* rope — more at SOLE] *chiefly Scot* : a rope or chain used to tie cattle

seal·able \-ləbəl\ *adj* : capable of sealing or being sealed

sea lace *n* : a seaweed (*Chorda filum*) having blackish fronds resembling cords — usu. used in pl. — called also *sea twine*

sea ladder *n* **1** : a rope ladder or set of steps to be lowered over a ship's side for use in coming aboard (as at sea) **2** : SEA STEPS, JACOB'S LADDER

sea lamprey *n* : an anadromous lamprey (*Petromyzon marinus*) of the Atlantic coasts of No. America and Europe that attains a length of about three feet, is sometimes used as food, at maturity ascends streams to breed and then dies, and has recently become a serious pest destructive of native fish fauna in the Great Lakes

sea–lane \'=,=\ *n* : an established sea route : TRADE ROUTE

sea language *n* : sailors' cant

seal·ant \'sēlənt\ *n* -S [⁴*seal* + -*ant*] : a sealing agent ⟨radiator ~⟩

sea lark *n* **1** : ROCK PIPIT **2** *Brit* : any of several small shore birds (as a ringed plover, turnstone, red-backed sandpiper, or sanderling)

sea laurel *n* : a coarse American commercial sponge (*Euspongia dura*)

sea lavender *n* **1** : a plant of the genus *Limonium* **2** : SEA LUNGWORT **3** : a maritime shrub (*Mallotonia gnaphalodes*) of the family Boraginaceae found in subtropical and tropical coastal No. America and having fleshy hairy leaves and white flowers in scorpioid racemes or spikes

sea law *n* : MARITIME LAW; *specif* : any of various compilations of customary maritime laws made in medieval times

sea lawyer *n* **1 a** : GRAY SNAPPER **b** : SHARK **2** : an argumentative captious sailor; *broadly* : a person skilled in the use of red tape and minutiae esp. to avoid unwanted tasks or responsibilities — compare PHILADELPHIA LAWYER

seal brown *n* [¹*seal*] : SEAL 3

sealch \'selk, -lk\ *n* [ME (Sc dial.) *selghe*, fr. OE *seolh* — more at SEAL] *chiefly Scot* : ¹SEAL 1

seal character *n* [³*seal*] : Chinese writing of an early type that is still employed on seals and inscriptions

seal coat *n* [³*seal*] : a final coat of bituminous material applied during construction to a bituminous macadam or concrete for sealing the surface of the pavement

seal cylinder *n* [³*seal*] : CYLINDER SEAL

sea league *n* : MARINE LEAGUE

sealed *adj* [fr. past part. of ⁴*seal*] **1** : unknown or unknowable like a sealed book ⟨a ~ language⟩ **2** : undisclosed at the start like sealed orders ⟨~ handicaps in a race⟩ ⟨a ~ bid⟩

sealed bank bill *n* : BANK BILL 1

sealed–beam \'=,=\ *adj* : of, relating to, or being an electric light with prefocussed reflector and lens sealed in the lamp vacuum ⟨*sealed-beam* automobile headlights⟩

sealed book *n* : something as inaccessible to the understanding as a book that cannot be opened

sealed orders *n pl* : sealed written directions not to be opened until a specified time; *esp* : such directions given to the captain of a ship whose destination is not to be known until it is at sea

sealed verdict *n* : a written verdict sealed up by the jury prior to leaving their place of confinement and deliberation, delivered to a proper office of the court in the absence of the judge or of the defendant in a criminal case, and not final until read in court with judge, jury and defendant in a criminal case present and then approved by the jury

sealed will *n* : MYSTIC WILL

sea legs *n pl* **1** : adjustment to or ability to move normally in the presence of the rolling or pitching of a ship at sea **2** : freedom from seasickness

sea lemon *n* : any of several nudibranchiate mollusks of the family Dorididae having a smooth convex yellow body

sea lentil *n* : GULFWEED

sea leopard *n* **1 a** : LEOPARD SEAL **b** : WEDDELL SEAL **c** : HARBOR SEAL **2** : leather prepared from the skin of the wolffish

¹seal·er \'sēlə(r)\ *n* -S [ME *seler*, fr. *selen* to seal + -*er* — more at SEAL] **1** : one that seals: as **a** : an official who attests or certifies conformity to a standard of correctness or quality ⟨a ~ of weights and measures⟩ ⟨a ~ of leather⟩ **b** : one whose work is sealing containers (as jars, bags, boxes) or articles (as storage batteries, radio tubes); *also* : an operator of a sealing machine **c** : a device or machine that seals ⟨a can ~⟩ **d** : a coat (as of size) applied to prevent subsequent coats of paint or varnish from sinking in **2** : CAPPER 5

²sealer \"\ *n* -S [²*seal* + -*er*] : a mariner or a ship engaged in hunting seals

sealer's finger *n* : SEAL FINGER

seal·ery \'sēlərē\ *n* -ES [¹*seal* + -*ery*] : SEAL FISHERY

sea·less \'sēləs\ *adj* [¹*sea* + -*less*] : having no sea

sea letter *n* : a ship's passport issued in time of war to a neutral vessel on leaving a port, entitling the master to sail under the flag and pass of the nation to which it belongs, and specifying its cargo and crew, the names of its captain and owners, place of lading, port of registry, and destination — called also *sea brief*, *sea pass*

sea lettuce *n* : any of various seaweeds (genus *Ulva*) having flat expanded crinkly green fronds sometimes eaten as salad

sea level *n* **1** : the level of the surface of the sea **2** : sea level at its mean position midway between mean high and low water adopted as a standard for the measurement of heights — called also *mean sea level*

seal finger *n* [¹*seal*] : a finger rendered swollen and painful by erysipeloid or a similar infection and occurring esp. in seamen

seal fishery *n* **1** : the act, process, or occupation of taking seals for their oil, skin, or fur **2** : a place (as a rookery) where seals are hunted

sealflower \'=,=\ *n* [³*seal* + *flower*] : BLEEDING HEART 1

seal hole *n* : a breathing hole made in the ice by a seal

sea light *n* **1** : a light (as a beacon) for guiding ships at sea **2** : the light over or peculiar to the sea

¹sealike \'=,=\ *adj* [¹*sea* + *like*] : resembling the sea

²sealike \"\ *adv* : in the manner of the sea

sea lily *n* : CRINOID; *esp* : a stalked crinoid

sea line *n* **1** : a sea outline (as the horizon or coastline) **2** : a line used in the sea (as for sounding or deepwater fishing)

seal·ine \(')sē¦lēn\ *n* [¹*seal* + -*ine*] : rabbit fur from Australia and New Zealand sheared and dyed to simulate seal

¹sealing *n* -S [fr. gerund of ⁴*seal*] **1 a** : an impression made by a seal **b** : a small piece of clay or other malleable material on which an intaglio seal has been imprinted **2 a** : a thin machine-glazed paper used as a parcel wrapper **b** : a heavy wrapping paper used in covering ream packages of book or writing paper

²sealing *n* -S [fr. gerund of ²*seal*] : the hunting or catching of seals

sealing nut *n* : a nut used in making a seal; *specif* : a nut for sealing the terminal post of a battery at the point where the post leaves the cover of the case

sealing tape *n* : a gummed paper tape used in securing wrapped or boxed packages

sealing wax *n* : a composition that is plastic when warm and is used for sealing (as letters, documents, dry cells, cans) and that in medieval times contained beeswax but now is a resinous composition made usu. by fusing shellac with Venice turpentine and coloring matter

sea lion *n* **1** : any of several large eared seals native to the Pacific ocean related to the fur seals but lacking their valuable coat and including several largely coastal members of the genera *Zalophus* (as the Australian *Z. lobatus* and the Californian *Z. californianus*) and *Otaria* (as the So. American *O. byronia* or *O. jubata*) — see STELLER'S SEA LION **2** : a heraldic representation of a monster having the forepart of a lion with web feet and the tail of a fish

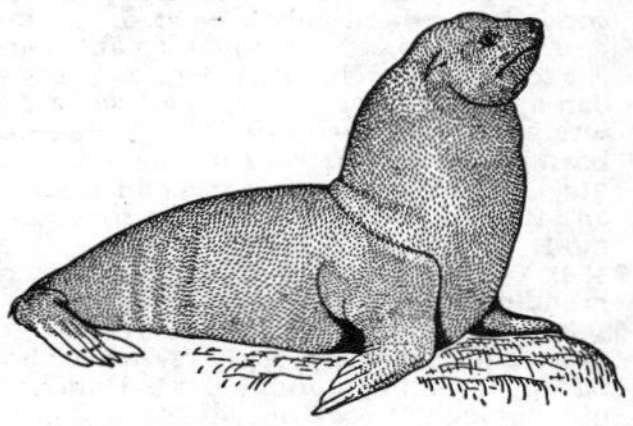
sea lion

sea lizard *n* **1** : an amphibious lizard (*Amblyrhynchus cristatus*) of the Galápagos islands **2** : any of various pelagic nudibranchs that constitute the genus *Glaucus*, are widely distributed in warm seas, and are blue or sometimes white in color

seallike \'=,=\ *adj* [¹*seal* + *like*] : resembling a marine seal esp. in grace of movement, sleekness, or streamlined form

seal lock *n* [³*seal*] : a lock having a seal (as of glass) that must be broken for the lock to be unlocked

seal maker *n* [³*seal*] : one that makes seals esp. as an occupation

sea–lock \'=,=\ *n* : an elongated narrow arm of the sea projected into the adjacent land mass

seal off *vt* [⁴*seal*] : to close tightly so as to eliminate ingress or egress ⟨a glass tube *sealed off* by fusing the material together⟩ ⟨*sealed* the airport *off* with a cordon of police⟩

seal oil *n* : a colorless or pale yellow to red-brown unsaturated fatty oil obtained from seal blubber and used chiefly in making soap, in dressing leather and fur, as a lubricant, and formerly as a burning oil

sea lord *n* : one of those lords commissioners of admiralty having direct charge of naval matters under the first lord of the admiralty and including the chief of naval staff with his deputy and assistant, the chief of naval personnel, the controller, and the chief of supplies and transport

sea louse *n* **1** : any of various marine isopods — compare WOOD LOUSE **2** : FISH LOUSE

sea lovage *n* : LOVAGE

seal point *n* : a Siamese cat with cream or fawn-colored body and seal brown points

seal press *n* [³*seal*] : any of various presses having an engraved die in one jaw and used for embossing (as in impressing crests or making seals)

seal record *n* : a record of information about freight car seals made from examinations of the seals at various points en route

seal ring *n* : a ring engraved with a seal emblem or monogram or set with a similarly engraved stone : SIGNET RING

seals *pl of* SEAL, *pres 3d sing of* SEAL

sealskin \'=,=\ *n, often attrib* [ME *seleskin*, fr. *sele* seal + *skin*] **1** : the skin of a seal and esp. of a fur seal **2** : a garment (as a jacket, coat, cape) of sealskin **3** : a strip of sealskin or a coarser fur attachable to the bottom of a ski for preventing slipping backward in uphill climbing — usu. used in pl.

sealstone \'=,=\ *n* [³*seal* + *stone*] : a stone engraved with a seal and commonly dating from prehistoric times

seal–top spoon *n* [³*seal*] : a silver spoon having a handle with its end in the form of a circular seal and popular in England in the later 16th and 17th centuries

sea lungs *n pl but sing or pl in constr* [trans. of L *pulmo marinus*] *archaic* : JELLYFISH, CTENOPHORE

sea lungwort *n* : a fleshy perennial herb (*Mertensia maritima*) of the northern coasts of both hemispheres with ovate to spatulate leaves and usu. long-stalked rose-pink flowers fading to pale blue or almost white

sealwort \'=,=\ *n* [³*seal* + *wort*; fr. the markings on the rootstock] **1** : SOLOMON'S SEAL 1 **2** : a pearlwort (*Sagina procumbens*)

sea·ly·ham terrier \'sēlē,ham-, -lēəm-\ *n* [fr. *Sealyham*, Pembrokeshire, Wales, where it was developed] **1** *usu cap S&T* : a Welsh breed of long-headed heavy-boned chiefly white terriers with short legs, strong jaws, and long supple body that give it an advantage in tackling the badger underground though it is also used in bolting the fox and the otter **2** *or* **sealyham** -S *usu cap S* : a dog of the Sealyham Terrier breed

sea lyme grass *n* : a grass (*Elymus arenarius*) of the Pacific seacoast that is useful as a sand binder

¹seam \'sēm\ *n* -S [ME *sem*, *seem*, fr. OE *sēam*; akin to MD *soom* load of a pack animal, MLG *sōm*, OHG *soum*; all fr. a prehistoric WGmc word borrowed fr. (assumed) VL *sauma* packsaddle (whence ML *sauma*), fr. LL *sagma* — more at SUMPTER] **1** *dial chiefly Eng* : the amount borne by a beast of burden; *esp* : a suitable or standard load for a packhorse **2** *dial chiefly Eng* : any of various units of weight or capacity based on a standard load for a packhorse ⟨a ~ of grain is usu. eight bushels⟩

²seam \"\ *n* -S [ME *sem*, *seem*, fr. OE *sēam*; akin to OFris *sām* hem, seam, MD *sōm*, OHG *soum*, ON *saumr* seam, OE *sīwian* to sew — more at SEW] **1 a** : a joining by a line of stitching of two pieces of cloth, leather, or other material usu. near the edge ⟨you must sew more evenly, your ~ is all bumpy⟩ — see FLAT-FELL SEAM, FRENCH SEAM **b** : the line of stitching used in making such a joining **c** : material between the line of stitching and the outer edges of the cloth that is usu. turned to the inside of an article **d** : the slightly-indented line on the outside of an article formed when the joining is pressed open or flat **e** : an imitation joining; *esp* : one made in a single piece of material by a full-length tuck on the wrong side or a line of purl or pattern stitches in a knit garment **2** : a crevice or interstice where edges (as of planks or plates) abut; *esp* : the space between adjacent planks or strakes of a ship — usu. used in pl. ⟨the heavy seas opened her ~*s*⟩ **3** : a line of junction (as between metals or plastics) : a line, groove, ridge, or other mark formed by the abutment of edges ⟨~*s* in brickwork⟩: as **a** : SUTURE **b** : a thin layer or stratum (as of rock) between distinctive layers; *also* : a bed of coal or other valuable mineral of any thickness **c** : a line left by a cut or wound; *also* : WRINKLE **4** : a surface defect of limited length in iron or steel caused by a blowhole made visible by working

³seam \"\ *vb* -ED/-ING/-S *vt* **1 a** (1) : to join (pieces of cloth or other material) by stitching ⟨~ two lengths of carpet together⟩ (2) : to make the seams of (as a garment) ⟨~ up a dress⟩ (3) : to decorate or finish (an article) at the seam or seams or with ornamental seams ⟨~ a slip with faggoting⟩ ⟨stitched and ~*ed* the shoes⟩ **b** : to join as if by sewing (as by the use of welding, riveting, or heat-sealing) **2** : to mark (a surface) with lines suggesting seams : LINE, FURROW, SCAR ⟨a face ~*ed* with saber cuts⟩ ⟨creeks ~ the valley⟩ ~ *vi* : to become fissured or ridgy : crack open ⟨land drying and ~*ing* in the heat⟩

⁴seam \"\ *var of* SAIM

sea magpie *n, Brit* : OYSTER CATCHER

sea–maid \'=,=\ *also* **sea–maiden** \'=,==\ *n* : MERMAID; *also* : a goddess or nymph of the sea

sea mail *n* **1** : mail carried over the sea by ship **2** : postal service carrying mail by ship

sea mallow *n* : TREE MALLOW

sea·man \'sēmən\ *n, pl* **seamen** [ME *seeman*, fr. *see* sea + *man* — more at SEA, MAN] **1 a** : a man whose occupation is concerned with the handling, working, or navigating of ships at sea : a man who follows the sea as a way of life : SAILOR — distinguished from *landsman* **b** : a person other than a master, pilot, or duly indentured and registered apprentice employed or engaged in any capacity on board any ship of the English merchant shipping **c** : a person other than an apprentice employed or engaged in any capacity aboard a U.S. ship : a member of a ship's company; *sometimes* : a worker specifically concerned with the working of a ship as distinguished from either an officer or a worker concerned with the ship's engines and power supply **d** : a naval enlistee or draftee who starts as a seaman recruit, becomes a seaman apprentice upon finishing recruit training, and is then promoted to a rating just below petty officer **2** : MERMAN

seaman apprentice *n* : a naval enlistee or draftee who has completed recruit training and has qualified for the rating of seaman

seaman gunner *n, archaic* : an enlisted man (as in the U.S. Navy) passing through courses of instruction in such matters as the construction and handling or ordnance, torpedoes, explosives, or electricity

sea·man·ite \'sēmə,nīt\ *n* -S [Arthur E. *Seaman* †1937 Am. geologist + E -*ite*] : a rare mineral $Mn_3(PO_4)(BO_3).3H_2O$ that is a phosphate and borate of manganese and that occurs in pale yellow orthorhombic crystals

seamanlike \'=,=,=\ *adj* : characteristic of or befitting a seaman : indicating competent seamanship

sea·man·ly *adj* : SEAMANLIKE

seaman recruit *n* : an enlistee or draftee of the lowest grade in the navy

sea·man·ship \'sēmən,ship\ *n* : the art or skill in the art of handling, working, and navigating a ship; *esp* : the principles and practices of ship operation and maintenance within the province of the deck department

sea mantis *n* : SQUILLA

sea marigold *n* : SEA OXEYE

seamark \'=,=\ *n* [ME *see marke*] **1** : a line on a coast marking the tidal limit; *specif* : FULL SEAMARK **2** : an elevated object discernible at or from sea and serving to guide or warn mariners : BEACON, LANDMARK; *also* : a sign of danger

sea marker *n* : a patch of dye deposited on the sea (as to catch the attention of an airplane's crew)

sea mat *n* : BRYOZOAN; *esp* : an encrusting bryozoan (as of the genus *Flustra*)

sea matweed *n* : BEACH GRASS

seam·berry palm \'sēm- . . . -— *see* BERRY\ *n* [so called fr. the seamy albumen in the fruit] : a palm of the genus *Coccothrinax*

seam binding *n* : a covering or reinforcement for a seam; *esp* : a narrow strip of fabric in plain weave used (as in garments) to strengthen seams, finish hems, or cover raw edges

seam blasting *n* : the act or process of shattering a boulder by packing a charge of dynamite into a crack or seam in it, tamping clay on top of the charge, and exploding

sea meadow *n* **1** : SALT MARSH **2 sea meadows** *pl* : the upper layers of the open sea that by reason of the abundance of the phytoplankton furnish food for marine animal life

seamed *adj* [fr. past part. of ³*seam*] **1 a** : having a seam **b** : joined by seams **2** : WRINKLED, FURROWED ⟨a ~ face⟩

seam·er \'sēmə(r)\ *n* -S [³*seam* + -*er*] : one that seams or makes seams: as **a** : an operator of a seaming machine; *also* : SEAMSTRESS **b** : a worker who removes seams **c** : one whose work is to seam a specified thing or in a specified way — usu. used in combination ⟨a saddle ~⟩ **d** : a machine for sewing seams **e** : a handtool or machine for making joints (as in sheet metal)

seamer man *n* : an operator of a double seamer

sea mew *n* [ME *see mew*, fr. *see* sea + *mew* — more at SEA, MEW] : SEA GULL; *esp* : a European gull (*Larus canus*) resembling the herring gull but smaller

seam face *n* : a face on a building stone formed by a natural seam in the rock

seamier *comparative of* SEAMY

seamiest *superlative of* SEAMY

sea mile *n* : NAUTICAL MILE

sea milkwort *n* : a small fleshy herb (*Glaux maritima*) that is common along northern seashores — called also *sea trifoly*

seam·i·ness \'sēmēnəs\ *n* -ES : seamy condition

seam·ing \'sēmiŋ, -mēŋ\ *n* -S [ME *semyng*, fr. *sem*, *seem* seam + -*ing* — more at SEAM] **1 a** : the act or process of forming a seam (as by stitching or welding) **b** : a product of seaming **2** *also* **seaming lace** : narrow insertion used for decoration esp. between or over seams

seaming dies *n pl* : a set of shaping dies that press against folded sheet-metal edges and by squeezing the folds together make a seam

sea mink *n* **1** : KING WHITING **2** : NORTHERN WHITING

sea mist *n* **1** : mist from the sea **b** : ART GRAY

seam·less \'sēmləs\ *adj* [ME *semlesse*, fr. *sem*, *seem* seam + -*lesse* -less] : having no seam: as **a** : woven full width ⟨a ~ rug⟩ **b** *of a tubular fabric* : woven as a double cloth ⟨~ bagging⟩ **c** : CIRCULAR-KNIT — **seam·less·ly** *adv* — **seam·less·ness** *n* -ES

seamlike \'=,=\ *adj* : resembling a seam esp. in forming a linear joint or differentiated line

sea·mo·bile \'sēmō,bēl\ *n* [¹*sea* + -*mobile*] : a small shallow draft cargo ship driven by automobile-type engines

sea monk *n* : MONK SEAL

sea monster *n* **1** : a large or extraordinary sea animal **2** : a fabulous monster of the sea often represented as man-devouring

sea moss *n* **1** : SEAWEED; *esp* : any of various red algae (as carrageen or dulse) with rose to violet or purple gracefully elaborate fronds **2** : a branched marine bryozoan resembling moss **3 a** : AUCUBA GREEN **b** : PERSIAN GREEN

sea·most \'sē,mōst, *esp Brit also* -,məst\ *adj* : situated nearest the sea

sea moth *n* : a fish of the family Pegasidae — called also *sea dragon*

seamount \'=,=\ *n* : a submarine mountain rising above the deep sea floor commonly from 3000 to 10,000 feet and having the summit 1000 to 6000 feet below sea level — compare GUYOT

sea mouse *n* **1** : a large broad marine polychaete worm of *Aphrodite* or a related genus having a thick coat of long slender hairlike setae **2 a** *dial Eng* : RED-BACKED SANDPIPER **b** : HARLEQUIN DUCK **3** : a flattened sea urchin (suborder Spatangina) with relatively long spines; *esp* : one belonging to the genus *Lovenia*

seam–rent \'=,=\ *adj* **1** *archaic* : ripped out at the seams **2** *archaic* : wearing garments that are ripped ⟨poor ~ fellows —Ben Jonson⟩

seam roller *n* : a tool used by a paperhanger to make a seam flat and tight

seams *pl of* SEAM, *pres 3d sing of* SEAM

seam set *n* : any of various tools for flattening seams (as of metal sheets or leatherwork)

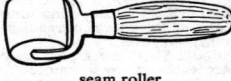

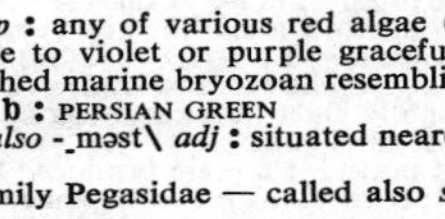
seam roller

seam squirrel *n* : BODY LOUSE

seam·ster \'sēmztə(r), -m(p)st-, *chiefly Brit* 'sem-\ *also* **semp-**

ster \'sem(p)st-\ *n* -s [ME *semester, semster*, fr. OE *sēamestre* seamstress, tailor, fr. *sēam* seam + *-estre* -ster] : a person that is employed at sewing; *usu* : a man so employed : TAILOR — compare SEAMSTRESS

seam·ster·ing \-t(ə)riŋ\ *n* -s : the art or occupation of a seamster

seam strap *also* **seam strip** *n* : EDGE STRIP

seam·stress *also* **semp·stress** \-trə̇s\ *n* -ES [¹*seamster, sempster* + *-ess*] : a woman who sews by hand or machine; *esp* : one whose occupation is making, altering, or repairing garments, curtains, household linens, or industrial articles of cloth (as airplane covers)

sea mud *or* **sea ooze** *n* : mud from the sea; *specif* : a slimy deposit along the seashore sometimes used as a manure

sea mugwort *n* : SEA RAGWEED

sea mule *n* : a boxy steel tug driven by a diesel engine and used esp. for handling pontoons and barges

sea mullet *n* **1 a** : a common bluish green food fish (*Mugil dobula*) of the Australian coasts **b** : a related smaller fish (*Agonostomus forsteri*) often landlocked in Australian lakes **2** : any of several whitings

seam weld *n* : a joint made by seam welding

seam-weld \'=,=\ *vt* [*seam weld*] : to unite by a seam weld

seam welding *n* : resistance welding in which the weld is made linearly (as between two rollers, a roller and a bar)

seamy \'sēmē, -mi\ *adj* -ER/-EST [²*seam* + *-y*] **1 a** *archaic* : having the rough side of the seam showing **b** : less pleasing, less worthy, or less presentable ⟨the ~ side of urban life⟩ **2** : forming or resembling a seam ⟨a ~ scar⟩; *also* : marked by seams : SEAMED ⟨an ancient ~ face⟩

sea myrtle *n* : GROUNDSEL BUSH

sé·ance \'sā,än(t)s *sometimes* (ˈ)sā¦äⁿs\ *n* -s [F, lit., sitting, fr. *seoir* to sit (fr. L *sedēre*) + *-ance* — more at SIT] : SITTING: as **a** : a coming together or session (as of a public body, a learned society, a class) for a particular purpose (as deliberation, discussion, recitation) **b** : a meeting for the purpose of receiving spirit communications ⟨the ancestral . . . ghost talked at a ~ —*Times Lit. Supp.*⟩ **c** : a sitting for a portrait

sea necklace *n* : a string of disk-shaped egg cases of any of various large whelks of the genus *Busycon* — called also *sea ruffle*

sea nettle *n* : a stinging jellyfish (as a siphonophore)

sea oak *n* **1** : any of various rockweeds (esp. *Fucus vesiculosus* and *F. serratus*) **2** *Brit* : a sertularian hydroid (*Dynamena punila*) that forms a small much-branched arborescent colony with a tough horny skeleton into which the polyps can contract

sea oat *n* **1** : a tall grass (*Uniola paniculata*) that has panicles resembling those of the oat, grows on the coast of the southern U.S., and is useful as a sand binder — usu. used in pl. **2 sea oats** *pl* : a cluster of yellowish vase-shaped egg cases of a whelk of the genus *Thais* : SEA CORN

sea onion *n* **1** : a squill (*Urginea maritima*) **2** : a small delicate European herb (*Scilla verna*) with fragrant blue flowers in clusters that resemble corymbs

sea orach *n* : an orach (*Atriplex hastata*) that grows on wasteland esp. near the sea and is used in Europe as a substitute for spinach — compare GARDEN ORACH

sea orange *n* : a large American holothurian (*Psolus fabricii*) having an orange-colored convex body

sea otter *n* **1** : a rare large marine otter (*Enhydra lutris*) of the northern Pacific coasts that attains a maximum length of nearly six feet, has short legs, a blunt cylindrical tail, and larged webbed hind feet, feeds largely on shellfish which it crushes with its broad flat-crowned molars, and produces a pelt which furnishes the most valuable of all fur and consists of rich dark brown underfur with an outer coat of gray-tipped coarser hairs **2** : the fur or pelt of the sea otter

sea-otter's-cabbage \'=,==\ *n, pl* **sea-otter's-cabbages** : a gigantic kelp (*Nereocystis lütkeana*) of the northern Pacific in beds of which the sea otter makes its home — called also *bladder kelp*

sea oxeye *n* : a plant of the genus *Borrichia*; *esp* : either of two shrubby coastal plants (*B. frutescens* and *B. arborescens*) of the southern U.S. and tropical America with thick fleshy leaves — called also *sea marigold*

sea painter *n* : a long strong rope for use on a ship's lifeboat

sea palm *n* : an olive-brown kelp (*Postelsia palmaeformis*) of the Pacific coast having an erect stalk resembling a trunk and palmately divided fronds at the apex

sea pansy *n* : a showy purple alcyonarian (genus *Renilla*) — called also *sea kidney*

sea parrot *n* : PUFFIN

sea parsley *n* : LOVAGE a, b

sea parsnip *n* : a European plant of the genus *Echinophora* (family Umbelliferae); *esp* : a white-flowered prickly-foliaged herb (*E. spinosa*)

sea-partridge \'=,==\ *n* : a small variably-colored wrasse (*Ctenolabrus melops*) common along weedy shores of Britain and western Europe

sea pass *n* : SEA LETTER

sea pay *n* : pay for service on a ship in commission

sea pea *n* : BEACH PEA

sea peach *n* : an ascidian (*Tethyum pyriformis*) of the coasts of northeastern No. America having the velvety surface and color of a ripe peach

sea pear *n* : a stalked ascidian of *Boltenia* or a related genus

sea peat *n* : peat formed from seaweeds

sea pen *n* **1** : any of numerous alcyonarians belonging to *Pennatula* and related genera in which the colony has a feathery form and the stem or shaft of the colony contains a calcareous or horny axis embedded at the lower end in the mud of the sea bottom **2 a** : PEN SHELL **b** : SQUID

sea perch *n* **1** : any of various sea basses (family Serranidae) **2** : TRIPLETAIL

sea perils *n pl* : PERILS OF THE SEA

sea pheasant *n* **1** : PINTAIL **2** : OLD-SQUAW

sea pie *n, chiefly Brit* : OYSTER CATCHER

seapiece \'=,=\ *n* : a representation of the sea (as in a painting) : SEASCAPE

sea pig *n* **1 a** : PORPOISE, DOLPHIN **b** : DUGONG **2** : a buoy or spar towed by a ship in a fog to guide a following ship

sea pigeon *n* **1** : a small guillemot of the genus *Cepphus* : BLACK GUILLEMOT, PIGEON GUILLEMOT **2** *chiefly Scot* : ROCK PIGEON

sea pike *n* : any of various marine fishes resembling the true pike in their elongate form and voracity (as garfish or hake); *esp* : BARRACUDA

sea pimpernel *n* : SEABEACH SANDWORT

sea pine *n* : a maritime pine; *esp* : CLUSTER PINE

sea pink *n* **1 a** : THRIFT 6 **b** : MARSH PINK **2** : a strong pink that is yellower and duller than carnation rose, duller and slightly bluer than coral (sense 3b), and bluer and duller than rose d'Althaea

sea plain *n* : a plain produced by marine erosion

seaplane \'=,=\ *n* : an airplane designed to rise from and alight on the water — see FLYING BOAT, FLOATPLANE

sea plantain *n* : either of two plantains that grow near the sea: **a** : a perennial usu. glabrous Eurasian plantain (*Plantago maritima*) that thrives along shore and in alpine areas **b** : a perennial plantain (*P. decipiens*) having fleshy leaves and found along the cooler coasts of No. America

sea plume *n* : a gorgonian of plumose form (as *Gorgonia acerosa* or *G. setosa*)

sea poacher *also* **sea poker** *n* : a fish of the family Agonidae — see POGGE

sea·poose \'sē,püs\ *n* -s [by folk etymology fr. a word of Algonquian origin; akin to Delaware *sepoŭs*, *sepus* small brook, Natick *sepuēse* brook, *sepu* river, Narragansett *sepoêse* little river, *sepe* river] **1** : a shallow inlet or tidal stream along the Long Island shore **2** : SEA PUSS

sea poppy *n* : HORNED POPPY

sea porcupine *n* **1** : PORCUPINE FISH **2** : SEA URCHIN

sea pork *n* : a compound tunicate (genus *Amaroucium*) often forming thick slabs of reddish or whitish growth on pilings or other supports

seaport \'=,=\ *n* : a port, harbor, or town on the seacoast or accessible (as by a connecting river) to seagoing ships and active in shipping or other marine activities ⟨a ~ with waterfront saloons catering to sailors⟩

seapost \'=,=\ *n* : SEA MAIL

sea post office *n* : a post office maintained on a steamer or packet boat for letters mailed at sea

sea potato *n* : an ascidian (*Boltenia rubra*) of the northeastern coast of No. America the body of which is borne on a long stalk and in form resembles a potato

sea power *n* **1** : a nation having formidable naval strength **2** : naval strength including those weapons, installations national resources, and geographical circumstances that enable a country to control the sea and the air above it

sea pumpkin *n* : HOLOTHURIAN

sea purse *n* **1** : the horny egg case of skates and of some sharks that is usu. of quadrangular outline with the angles produced into filaments by which it becomes attached (as to seaweeds) and that commonly contains but one egg or embryo **2** : a coenocytic marine green alga of the genus *Codium* resembling a sponge

sea purslane *n* **1** : SEABEACH SANDWORT **2** : any of several plants of the genus *Atriplex* (esp. *A. hastata*) **3** : a plant of the genus *Sesuvium*

sea puss *or* **sea purse** *n* [by folk etymology fr. the source of *seapoose* — more at SEAPOOSE] : a dangerous swirling of undertow due to the combined effect of several breakers; *also* : an undertow setting along shore

sea quail *n* **1** : TURNSTONE **2** : CASSIN'S AUKLET

sea·quake \'sē,kwāk\ *n* [¹*sea* + *-quake* (as in *earthquake*)] : a submarine earthquake; *also* : a seismic disturbance appreciable at sea

¹**sear** *var of* SERE

²**sear** \'si(ə)r, 'siə\ *vb* -ED/-ING/-S [ME *seren*, fr. OE *sēarian*, fr. *sēar* dry, withered, sere — more at SERE] *vi* **1** *obs* : to wither away : become sere **2** : to cause withering or drying ⟨harsh winds that ~ and burn⟩ ~ *vt* **1** : to make withered and dry : DESICCATE, PARCH, SHRIVEL ⟨plants ~*ed* by frost and wind⟩ **2** : to burn, scorch, or harden (as flesh) with or as if with sudden application of intense heat: as **a** : CAUTERIZE **b** : to injure with or as if with fire ⟨the bullet ~*ed* his leg⟩ ⟨had a bad burn where he was ~*ed* by the soldering iron⟩ **c** : to cook quickly the surface of (a piece of meat) usu. to develop color and flavor : brown quickly as a first stage in cooking **syn** see BURN

³**sear** \"\ *n* -s : a mark or scar left by searing or by a cautery or branding iron

⁴**sear** \"\ *n* -s [prob. fr. MF *serre* grip, grasp, clip, fr. *serrer* to press, squeeze, grasp, fr. LL *serare* to bolt (a door), fr. L *sera* bar for fastening a door] **1** : the catch that holds the hammer of a gunlock at cock or half cock **2** *obs* : a releasing or yielding point or stage ⟨the clown shall make those laugh whose lungs are tickle o' the ~ —Shak.⟩

sea radish *n* : a European wild radish (*Raphanus maritimus*)

sea ragweed *n* : a European mostly seaside ragweed (*Ambrosia maritima*) with small heads of green flowers — called also *sea mugwort*

sea ragwort *n* : DUSTY MILLER 1a

sea raider *n* : one (as a pirate or submarine) that roams the sea preying upon merchant shipping

sea raven *n* : a sculpin (*Hemitripterus americanus*) of the northern Atlantic coast of America

¹**searce** \'sərs\ *also* **search** \-rch\ *n, pl* **searces** *also* **searches** [ME *saarce, sarche*, fr. MF *saas* small sieve made of horsehair or bristles, fr. ML *setaceum*, fr. L *seta, saeta* bristle — more at SETA] *archaic* : a fine sieve : STRAINER

²**searce** \"\ *vt* -ED/-ING/-S [ME, fr. *saarce, sarche*, n.] *archaic* : SIFT, BOLT

searc·er \-sər\ *also* **search·er** \-chə(r)\ *n* -s *archaic* : SIEVE

¹**search** \'sərch, 'sə̄ch, 'səich\ *vb* -ED/-ING/-ES [ME *cerchen, serchen*, fr. MF *cerchier* to travel through, traverse, survey, search, fr. LL *circare* to travel through, traverse, fr. L *circum* round about — more at CIRCUM-] *vt* **1** : to look into or over carefully or thoroughly in an effort to find or discover: as **a** : to go about or traverse in careful quest ⟨~*ed* the northerly slope of the hill . . . his eyes scanning every foot of the ground —O.E. Rölvaag⟩ ⟨~*ing* the woods for the lost child⟩ **b** : to look into with thorough scrutiny and rigorous objective examination ⟨~ me, O God, and know my heart —Ps. 139: 23(AV)⟩ ⟨~*ing* my conscience while I was compiling these criticisms of others —Elmer Davis⟩ **c** : to look through or explore thoroughly esp. by checking on possible places of concealment or investigating circumstances possibly leading to something being overlooked ⟨~*ing* the apartment building for the suspect⟩ ⟨his hand ~*ing* his pocket for a match —William Faulkner⟩ — often used with *through* ⟨~*ed* through her handbag for a dime⟩ **d** : to peruse thoroughly and usu. with a particular objective : subject to a careful check ⟨~ the records of the case⟩ ⟨~*ing* those works for a clue to their authorship⟩ ⟨let him ~ the scriptures for consolation⟩; *esp* : to examine a public record or register for information about ⟨~*ing* titles in the courthouse⟩ **e** : to examine (a person) thoroughly to check on whatever articles are carried or concealed ⟨the police ~*ed* the suspect⟩ **f** : to look at fixedly in order to or as if in order to discover true intention, meaning, nature ⟨~*ed* him with a glance —George Meredith⟩ **2** : to uncover, find, or come to know by diligent persevering inquiry or scrutiny ⟨as if to ~ and value every element in the conflict —Thomas De Quincey⟩ — usu. used with *out* ⟨the broad principle of toleration . . . ~*es* out and lays bare every insincerity —V.L.Parrington⟩ **3** : to probe or explore with a surgical instrument ⟨doctors ~*ing* the wound⟩ **4 a** : to play upon or surge against or over a particular area as though looking for a weak, vulnerable, or vital point : pierce or penetrate at an unprotected point ⟨waves ~ the bases of the cliffs⟩ **b** : to distribute (gunnery fire) over an area; *specif* : to distribute (fire) by changes in elevation in gunnery with automatic weapons — compare TRAVERSE ~ *vi* **1** : to look or inquire diligently and carefully — usu. used with *for* ⟨~*ed* long for the missing papers⟩ **2** : to examine, investigate, or explore usu. with challenging or rejecting of a superficial or popularly accepted impression ⟨I am a student . . . and ~ into all matters —Edna S. V. Millay⟩ **syn** see SEEK — **search me** — used as a disclaimer of knowledge in response to a question

²**search** \"\ *n* -ES [ME *serche*, fr. MF *cerche*, fr. OF, fr. *cerchier*] **1 a** : an act or the action of searching : an endeavor to find, ascertain, recover, or bring into view ⟨a prolonged ~ for a lost will⟩ **b** : pursuit with a view to finding ⟨went south in ~ of health⟩ **c** : a critical scrutiny or survey (as of a ship's cargo or baggage) ⟨a customs ~⟩; *esp* : an act of boarding and inspecting a vessel on the high seas in exercise of right of search **d** *obs* : an examination of conscience **e** *obs* : RESEARCH, INVESTIGATION **2** : a person or party that searches **3** : power or range of searching and esp. of penetrating; *also* : a penetrating effect

search·able \-chəbəl\ *adj* : capable of being searched or of being found by searching

search coil *n* : FLIP COIL

search ephemeris *n* : an approximate ephemeris for use in locating a returning comet, asteroid, or planet suspected but not yet discovered

search·er \-chə(r)\ *n* -s [ME *serchere*, fr. *serchen* to search + *-ere* -er — more at SEARCH] **1** : one that searches ⟨a ~ after knowledge⟩ **2** : a person (as an inspector, looker, tracer) employed to search: as **a** : a guild official formerly functioning as an inspector to maintain standards of workmanship and quality **b** : an officer of the customs who examines (as ships, merchandise, luggage) for dutiable goods or contraband **c** *archaic Brit* : CORONER **d** (1) *archaic* : a civil officer appointed to observe and report objectionable conduct (2) : a minor police officer appointed to search persons arrested **e** : a person employed (as by a title insurance company) to search public records **f** : a kosher examiner who looks for evidence of contamination in freshly killed animals **3** : an implement (as a probe) used in searching : SEEKER **4** : a large metallic blue-green No. American ground beetle (*Calosoma scrutator*) that feeds on caterpillars

search·ful \-chfəl\ *adj* : full of searching : INQUIRING; *also* : interested or active in searching

search·ing·ly *adv* : in a searching manner : with searching

search·ing·ness *n* -ES : searching quality or state

search lamp *n* : SEARCHLIGHT 1a

search·less \-chlə̇s\ *adj* : impossible to be searched : INSCRUTABLE

searchlight \'=,=\ *n* **1 a** : an apparatus for projecting a powerful beam of light of approximately parallel rays usu. devised so that it can be swiveled about **b** : a beam of light projected by such an apparatus **c** : FLASHLIGHT d **2** : something that reveals the obscure or concealed in the manner of a searchlight

searchlight lantern *n* : a lantern backed by a metal reflector

search warrant *n* : a legally issued warrant authorizing an examination or search of a house or other place orig. chiefly for stolen goods but in modern practice under statutory provisions for intoxicating liquors, gambling implements, counterfeiters' or burglars' tools, obscene literature, smuggled goods, or other articles kept or concealed in violation of the law and in some instances for the discovery of persons

sea reach *n* : the straight course of a river where it reaches or approaches the sea

seared *past of* SEAR

seared green *n* : a moderate yellow green that is paler than average moss green, yellower and less strong than average pea green, and yellower and duller than apple green (sense 1) — called also *glowworm*

¹**searer** *comparative of* SEAR

²**sear·er** \'sirə(r)\ *n* -s [²*sear* + *-er*] : one that sears

³**searer** \"\ *n* -s [modif. of Sp *sierra* saw, sawfish, cero — more at SIERRA] : CERO

searest *superlative of* SEAR

sea return *n* : a radar echo reflected by waves and tending to obscure target indication

sea rim *n* : the horizon as seen over the sea

searing *pres part of* SEAR

sear·ing·ly *adv* : in a searing manner : so as to sear

sea risks *n pl* : PERILS OF THE SEA

searles·ite \'sərl,zīt\ *n* -s [John W. *Searles*, 19th cent. Am. settler in California + E *-ite*] : a mineral $NaB(SiO_3)_2.H_2O$ consisting of a hydrous sodium borosilicate occurring in small white spherulites

sea road *n* **1** : a sea route **2** : ROAD 2

sea robber *n* **1** : a robber at sea; *specif* : PIRATE **2** : JAEGER

sea robin *n* **1** : any of several gurnards; *esp* : an American gurnard of the genus *Prionotus* having more or less red or brown on the body and fins and the first three rays of the pectoral fin separate from the others and used in walking about over the sea bottom **2** : RED-BREASTED MERGANSER

sea rocket *n* : a plant of the genus *Cakile*

sea rod *n* **1** : a gorgonian with long round branches **2** : VIRGULARIAN

sea room *n* **1** : room or space at sea to maneuver without peril of running aground or of collision **2** : opportunity for freedom (as of action or movement)

sea rover *n* : one that roves the sea; *specif* : PIRATE

sears *pres 3d sing of* SEAR, *pl of* SEAR

sea ruffle *n* : SEA NECKLACE

sea-run \'=,=\ *also* **sea-running** \'=,==\ *adj* : having ascended or having the habit of ascending a river from the sea : ANADROMOUS ⟨caught a *sea-run* salmon⟩ ⟨*sea-run* races of brook trout⟩

sear up *vt* : to close by or as if by searing

sea rush *n* : a tall erect perennial rush (*Juncus maritimus*) that is nearly cosmopolitan and often a floral dominant in salt marshes and other moist saline environments

seas *pl of* SEA

sea salt *n* : salt resulting from the evaporation of seawater and containing chiefly sodium chloride with small amounts of magnesium chloride, magnesium sulfate, and calcium sulfate

sea-salt \'=,=\ *adj* : salty with seawater : like sea salt

sea sand *n* [ME *see sond*, fr. *see* sea + *sond* sand — more at SEA, SAND] **1** : sand of the sea floor or seashore **2 sea sands** *pl* : a sandy seabeach

sea sandpiper *n* : PURPLE SANDPIPER

sea sand reed *also* **sea sand grass** *n* : BEACH GRASS

sea sandwort *n* : SEABEACH SANDWORT

sea scallop *n* : GIANT SCALLOP

sea·scape \'sē,skāp\ *n* -s [¹*sea* + *-scape*] **1** : a view of or over the sea **2** : a picture representing a scene at sea — compare LANDSCAPE

sea·scap·ist \-pə̇st\ *n* -s : a maker of seascapes

sea scorpion *n* **1** : SCULPIN; *esp* : a common father-lasher (*Cottus scorpius*) **2** : EURYPTERID

sea sedge *n* : any of several maritime sedges; *esp* : SAND SEDGE

sea serpent *n* **1** : a large marine animal more or less resembling a serpent that is often reported to have been seen at sea but is not identifiable with any known animal and that is prob. based on faulty observation of schools of porpoises, various cetaceans, oarfishes, or other large marine animals or on pure fiction **2** : SEA SNAKE 1 **3** : OARFISH

sea service *n* : service at sea or aboard a seagoing vessel; *sometimes* : naval as distinguished from military service

seashell \'=,=\ *n* : the shell of a marine animal and esp. of a mollusk (as a whelk, clam, oyster, or scallop)

seashell pink *n* : a light to moderate yellowish pink that is less strong and much yellower than Chatenay pink — called also *tussore*

seashine \'=,=\ *n* : the shine of the sea; *esp* : light reflected off the sea

seashore \'=,=\ *n* **1** : land adjacent to the sea : SEACOAST, SEABEACH **2** : all the ground between the ordinary high-water and low-water marks : FORESHORE

seashore heliotrope *n* : SEASIDE HELIOTROPE

seashore lupine *n* : a hairy decumbent lupine (*Lupinus littoralis*) that is common on coastal sands of the Pacific coast of No. America and has strong bright yellow roots and blue flowers

sea shrub *n* : a shrubby gorgonian

seasick \'=,=\ *adj, sometimes* -ER/-EST [¹*sea* + *sick*] **1** : affected with or suggestive of seasickness **2** : sick of the sea ⟨thy ~, weary bark —Shak.⟩

sea·sick·ness *n* : motion sickness experienced on the water

seaside \'=,=\ *n, often attrib* [ME *seeside*, fr. *see* sea + *side*] **1** : the district or land bordering the sea : country adjacent to the sea : SEASHORE **2** : the side (as of a town) facing the sea

seaside alder *n* : a small tree (*Alnus maritima*) of the southeastern U. S. with soft light brown wood

seaside arrowgrass *n* : a grassy perennial herb (*Triglochin maritima*) found in salt marshes throughout cooler regions in the north temperate zone and having an erect slender spike of small greenish white flowers

seaside balsam *n* : CASCARILLA 2

seaside bean *n* : a jack bean (*Canavalia ensiformis*)

seaside bent *n* : a coarse seashore grass (*Agrostis maritima*) found along the Atlantic coasts of No. America and northern Europe

seaside crowfoot *n* : a widely distributed perennial herb (*Ranunculus cymbalaria*) that is common in saline situations and has mostly basal nearly round or reniform leaves, yellow solitary flowers, and tightly compressed heads of small achenes

seaside daisy *n* : a perennial maritime herb (*Erigeron glaucus*) of the Pacific coast with solitary heads of lilac or violet flowers — called also *beach aster*

seaside gerardia *n* : a slender annual herb (*Gerardia maritima*) found along the Atlantic coast of the U. S. and having narrow leaves and purple nearly regular flowers

seaside goldenrod *n* : a vigorous showy goldenrod (*Solidago sempervirens*) that is common along the eastern and gulf coast of No. America — called also *beach goldenrod*

seaside grape *n* : SEA GRAPE 1b

seaside heliotrope *n* : a widely distributed tropical annual weed (*Heliotropium curassavicum*) found mostly in saline situations and having one-sided spikes of small white yellow-eyed flowers that become blue on aging — called also *Chinese pusley*

seaside laurel *n* : a West Indian plant (*Xylophylla speciosa*) of the family Euphorbiaceae with flattened evergreen branches resembling leaves and whitish flowers

seaside mahoe *n* : PORTIA TREE

seaside millet *n* : a joint grass (*Paspalum distichum*) used for forage in Australia

seaside morning-glory *n* : GOATSFOOT CONVOLVULUS

seaside oat *n* : SEA OAT

seaside pea *n* : BEACH PEA

seaside pimpernel *n* : SEABEACH SANDWORT

seaside pine *n* : CLUSTER PINE

seaside plantain *n* : SEA PLANTAIN

seaside plum *n* **1** : MOUNTAIN PLUM **2** : SEA GRAPE 1b

sea·sid·er \'sē,sīdə(r)\ *n* **:** a seaside resident or frequenter
seaside sandwort *n* **:** a common sand spurry (*Spergularia marina*) found in salt marshes throughout the north temperate zone
seaside sparrow *also* **seaside finch** *n* **:** a salt-marsh sparrow (*Ammospiza maritima*) of the Atlantic and Gulf coasts
seaside spurge *n* **:** a prostrate annual weedy herb (*Euphorbia polygonifolia*) with opposite small linear-oblong leaves and small axillary solitary flowers that is found along the Atlantic coast and shores of the Great Lakes
sea silk *n* **1 :** silky usu. golden yellow fiber obtained from the byssus of mollusks of the genus *Pinna* **2 :** any of various fibers derived from marine algae
Sea Sled *trademark* — used for a gliding shallow-draft high-powered motorboat
sea slope *n* **:** a slope (as of land) toward the sea
sea slug *n* **1 :** HOLOTHURIAN **2 :** a naked marine gastropod; *specif* **:** NUDIBRANCH
sea smoke *n* **:** a fog in arctic regions produced in below-freezing air that lies over a warm sea surface
sea snail *n* **1 :** a creeping marine gastropod mollusk with a spiral shell (as a whelk, triton, or moonshell) **2 :** any of numerous small tadpole-shaped mail-cheeked fishes (family Liparididae) found in cold seas, covered with very lax skin, and usu. having the pelvic fins modified to form a sucker
sea snake *n* **1 :** any of numerous venomous aquatic snakes constituting the family Hydrophidae, having the tail compressed and with small scales on the ventral surface, being usu. viviparous, and with few exceptions living in warm littoral seas and feeding on fish **2 :** SEA SERPENT 1
sea snipe *n* **1 :** PHALAROPE; *broadly* **:** any of various shore birds **2 :** BELLOWS FISH 1
sea soldier *n* **:** MARINE 3
¹sea·son \'sēzᵊn\ *n* -S [ME *sesoun, seisoun*, fr. OF *saison, seson*, fr. L *sation-, satio* action of sowing, fr. *satus* (past part. of *serere* to sow) + *-ion-, -io* -ion — more at SOW] **1 a :** a time or period of time characterized or made significant by a particular feature, circumstance, or event ⟨during this ~ of sorrow⟩ **b :** a suitable, fitting, or natural time or occasion **:** a proper conjuncture ⟨this is not the ~ for such arguments⟩ ⟨in due ~ you will understand⟩ **c :** a period not specifically limited but usu. of short or moderate duration ⟨agreed to wait for a ~⟩ **d :** a particular point in a period of time or the course of events ⟨at that ~ I could reach no decision⟩ ⟨visitors and interruptions at all ~*s*⟩ **2 :** a particular period of the year: as **a (1) :** the annual period during which a plant produces its fruit, flower, or other economic part ⟨the too brief strawberry ~⟩ **(2) :** the annual period in which an animal engages in some activity (as mating or migrating) or is available for hunting or food ⟨during the mating ~ old bucks may be vicious⟩ ⟨the ~ for oysters⟩; *also* **:** ESTRUS, HEAT ⟨a single annual ~⟩ — usu. used with *in* ⟨as heifers come in ~⟩ **b :** the period normally characterized by a particular kind of weather ⟨a long rainy ~⟩ ⟨during the cold ~⟩; *sometimes* **:** inclement weather **:** a spell of damp or rainy weather **c :** the period during which a particular agricultural activity is commonly performed ⟨the planting ~⟩ **d** *archaic* **:** the period in which an organized body (as a court or university) is in session **e :** one of the divisions of the year marked by alterations in the length of day and night or by distinct conditions of temperature and moisture caused mainly by the relation of the earth's axis with respect to the sun **f :** a period of the year set off or conceived of as set off by a particular and usu. high level of activity in some field (as social, cultural, or business) ⟨a good theatrical ~⟩ ⟨the height of the social ~⟩ ⟨the dull ~ that follows the holidays⟩; *also* **:** the annual period when a place is most frequented for social activities or amusement ⟨the London ~ lasts from May to July⟩ **g (1) :** a brief annual period in which a particular holiday occurs; *esp* **:** a period extending from shortly before Christmas through New Year's Day ⟨sent out ~'*s* greeting⟩ ⟨the busy rush of the holiday ~⟩ **(2) :** any of various periods in the Christian year commemorative chiefly of Christ's life (as Advent, Christmastide, Epiphany, Lent, Eastertide, Ascensiontide, Whitsuntide, Trinity) **3** [ME *sesoun*, fr. *sesounen*, v.] *obs* **:** something that gives relish **:** SEASONING **4** *archaic* **:** a recurrent period in the course of heavenly bodies **5 seasons** *pl* **:** YEARS — used in reckoning age ⟨a boy of seven ~*s*⟩ **6 :** one of eight tiles whose use is optional in a Mah-Jongg game — called also *flower* **7 :** the total schedule of games played or to be played by a sports team during a playing season; *also* **:** the results of such a series of games ⟨an unbeaten ~⟩ — **in season** *adv* **1 :** at the right or fitting time **:** OPPORTUNELY ⟨you will know *in season*⟩; *also* **:** in good time **:** EARLY ⟨arrived *in season*⟩ **2 :** in a state or at the stage of greatest fitness (as for use, marketing, eating) ⟨peaches are *in season*⟩ **3 :** in condition to be hunted or taken and esp. as dictated by law ⟨trout is *in season* for another month⟩ — **in season and out of season :** at all times without regard to season **:** CONTINUOUSLY — **out of season :** not in season; *esp* **:** available or marketed at other than the usual local season ⟨*out of season* fruits⟩ ⟨get tomatoes *out of season*⟩
²season \"\ *vb* **seasoned; seasoned; seasoning** \-z(ᵊ)niŋ\ **seasons** [ME *sesounen*, fr. MF *assaisoner* to ripen, make palatable by adding a seasoning, fr. OF, fr. *a-* (fr. L *ad-*) + *saison, seson* season] *vt* **1 a :** to render palatable by adding a tasty ingredient (as a condiment or flavoring) **:** give zest or relish to **:** SPICE ⟨~ a dish too highly⟩ **b :** to render more agreeable (as by an addition of something) ⟨~*ing* our thoughts with laughter⟩; *also* **:** to adapt to taste **c** *archaic* **(1) :** to qualify by admixture **:** MODERATE, TEMPER ⟨when mercy ~*s* justice —Shak.⟩ **(2) :** IMBUE, TINGE **2 :** to treat in such a manner or by such a process as will fit best to some end or use ⟨~ a pipe by careful smoking⟩: as **a** *obs* **:** EMBALM **b :** to fit or prepare by time or habit **:** HABITUATE, ACCLIMATIZE **c** *obs* **:** DISCIPLINE, TRAIN **d :** to prepare (lumber) for use by drying in the open air or in a kiln ~ *vi* **1 :** to become seasoned; *esp* **:** to become dry and hard by escape of the natural juices or by being penetrated with other substance ⟨timber that ~*s* well in the open air⟩ **syn** see HARDEN
sea·son·able \'sēz(ᵊ)nəbəl\ *adj* [ME *sesounable*, fr. *sesoun* season + *-able* — more at SEASON] **1 :** occurring in good or proper time **:** OPPORTUNE ⟨~ advice⟩ ⟨a ~ time for discussion⟩ **2 :** suitable to or in keeping with the season or circumstances **:** TIMELY ⟨a hard but ~ frost⟩ ⟨~ care⟩
syn TIMELY, WELL-TIMED, OPPORTUNE, PAT: SEASONABLE describes what is peculiarly fit or appropriate to the season, occasion, or situation ⟨*seasonable* weather⟩ ⟨*seasonable* clothes⟩ ⟨*seasonable* consolation during his time of trouble⟩ TIMELY refers to whatever occurs or appears at the moment when it is of most use, benefit, or assistance ⟨a *timely* book⟩ ⟨a similar fate for the column on the left bank of the stream was averted by the *timely* arrival of . . . the main army —R.A.Billington⟩ ⟨unfortunate if absorption in affairs at home should cause us to forget that *timely*, well-considered aid now to countries teetering on the verge of economic breakdown and political anarchy would go far to avert the danger of another costly conflict —Vera M. Dean⟩ WELL-TIMED suggests care, forethought, precision, or design in achieving timeliness ⟨the *well-timed* and splendidly executed offensive . . . was a part of the same major strategy —F.D.Roosevelt⟩ OPPORTUNE may describe that which comes at the best possible time, perhaps by accident, and invites being capitalized on ⟨as if this was an encounter which was something more than convenient, something really *opportune* —Rebecca West⟩ ⟨the literary scene was too full of chaotic and short-lived movements to make the launching of a large work *opportune* —J.M.Barzun⟩ PAT applies to that which has happened at the most fit moment or which shows characteristics completely fit or apt for the occasion or often so seemingly apt that it is suspect ⟨one, whose eyes dwelt in a distant void, with spell and omen *pat* upon his lips, and a purse for any crystal prophet ripe —John Drinkwater⟩ ⟨had assuredly the air of a miracle, of something dreamed in a dream, of something pathetically and impossibly appropriate — *pat*, as they say —Arnold Bennett⟩
sea·son·able·ness *n* -ES **:** the quality or state of being seasonable
sea·son·ably \-blē, -li\ *adv* [ME *sesounably*, fr. *sesounable* + *-ly*] **:** in a seasonable manner **:** so as to be seasonable
sea·son·al \'sēz(ᵊ)nəl\ *adj* [¹*season* + *-al*] **1 :** of, relating to, or occurring at a particular season ⟨~ rates⟩ ⟨a ~ opportunity⟩ ⟨~ bloom⟩ **2 :** characterized by or being affected by seasons **:** not continuous (as in activity or availability) ⟨~ industries⟩ ⟨~ employment⟩ ⟨a ~ resort⟩ — **sea·son·al·ly** \-əlē, -əli\ *adv*
sea·son·al·i·ty \,sēzᵊn'alədē\ *n* -ES **:** the quality or state of being seasonal
season check *n* **:** a longitudinal crack in timber or lumber caused by rapid or uneven seasoning — compare FROST CRACK
season crack *n* **1 :** a crack sometimes occurring in brass or other metal that has been severely strained in rolling or other process of manufacture and left in a condition of internal stress **2 :** SEASON CHECK
season cracking *n* **:** the condition of having season cracks
seasoned *adj* [ME *sesouned*, fr. past part. of *sesounen* to season — more at SEASON] **1 :** made savory with or as if with condiments **2 a :** made fit for use by a process of curing (as by suitable drying and hardening) **b** *of paper* **:** having a moisture content that is uniform and in equilibrium with that of the surrounding atmosphere — compare GREEN **3 a :** made fit by habitude or use ⟨smoking a ~ pipe⟩ **:** HABITUATED, EXPERIENCED ⟨a ~ traveler⟩ **b :** outstanding for a long time and proven in quality by experience — used of securities
sea·soned·ly *adv* **:** in a seasoned manner
sea·son·er \'sēz(ᵊ)nə(r)\ *n* -S **:** one that seasons: as **a :** a user of seasonings ⟨a heavy ~⟩ **b :** SEASONING **c :** a worker that seasons hides or leather (as with oil, grease, or tallow) — called also *surfacer*
seasoning *n* -S [fr. gerund of ²*season*] **1 :** something that serves to season: as **a :** an ingredient (as a condiment, spice, or flavoring) added to food primarily for the savor that it imparts **b :** a brightening, stimulating, or enlivening element ⟨wit is the ~ of good conversation⟩ **c :** the diamond dust with which a lapidary's mill is charged **2 :** the process of becoming or making seasoned ⟨the ~ of an executive by responsibility⟩
sea·son·less \'sēzᵊnləs\ *adj* **:** exhibiting no seasonal changes ⟨the ~ world of the deep sea⟩
seasons *pl of* SEASON, *pres 3d sing of* SEASON
season ticket *n* **:** a ticket giving its holder a privilege (as entrance to all games at an athletic field or daily transportation between two places) for a specified season
sea spider *n* **1 a :** SPIDER CRAB **b :** any of various small marine arthropods constituting the class Pycnogonida **2 :** OCTOPUS **3 :** BASKET STAR
sea squab *n* **:** the tail of a puffer fish when served as food
sea squirt *n* [so called fr. its habit of contracting and squirting out water when disturbed] **:** a simple ascidian
sea staff *n* **:** SEA WAND
sea star *n* **1 :** STARFISH **2 :** MARSH PINK
sea starwort *n* **:** a common European salt-marsh aster (*Aster tripolium*) — called also *sea aster*
sea steps *n pl* **:** projecting metal plates or bars attached to the side of a ship by which it may be boarded — called also *sea ladder*
sea stickleback *n* **:** FIFTEEN-SPINED STICKLEBACK
sea stock *n* **:** provisions for use at sea **:** ship's stores **:** SEA STORES
sea stores *n pl* **:** supplies (as of foodstuffs) laid in before starting on a sea voyage
seastrand \'=,=\ *n* [ME *seestrond, seestrand*, fr. OE *sǣstrand*, fr. *sǣ* sea + *strand* — more at SEA, STRAND] **:** SEASHORE
sea swallow *n* **1 :** TERN; *esp* **:** a common medium-sized tern (*Sterna hirundo*) that is closely related to and much resembles the arctic tern **2 :** STORM PETREL
sea swine *n* [ME *see swine*, fr. *see* sea + *swin, swine* swine] **1 :** PORPOISE **2 :** BALLAN
¹seat \'sēt, *usu* -ēd.+V\ *n* -S [ME *sete*, fr. ON *sæti*, fr. the stem of *sitja* to sit — more at SIT] **1 a :** a special chair (as of a throne) of one in eminence; *also* **:** the status of which such chair is an emblem **b :** something (as a chair, stool, bench) intended to be sat in or on **c :** the particular part of something on which one rests in sitting ⟨the ~ of a chair⟩ ⟨a worn trouser ~⟩; *also* **:** the part of the body that bears the weight in sitting **:** the gluteal region **:** BUTTOCKS **d :** FORM 6a **2 a :** the place on or at which one sits or which is available for sitting ⟨rented a block of ~*s* for the season⟩ ⟨a ~ by the fire⟩; *esp* **:** an assigned or regularly assumed sitting place ⟨had a ~ on the aisle⟩ ⟨father's ~ at table⟩ **b :** a right of sitting (as in a deliberative body) ⟨held a ~ in congress for over 20 years⟩ **c :** membership on an exchange **3 :** a place occupied by something **:** a resting place **:** ABODE ⟨starry ~*s* of bliss⟩: as **a :** the see of a bishop **b :** a place (as a city) from which authority is exercised **:** CAPITAL **c :** a bodily part in which some function or condition is centered ⟨the ~ of the pain⟩ ⟨the intestine is the chief ~ of digestion⟩ **d :** the status of an area in respect to factors (as climate) that determine its desirability for a purpose (as habitation) ⟨a home with a charming ~ among gentle wooded slopes⟩ **e :** a place where something specified is prevalent **:** CENTER ⟨the ~ of shoe manufacture in New England⟩ ⟨a ~ of learning⟩ ⟨has long been a ~ of war⟩ **f :** a superior rural residence **:** COUNTRYSEAT **g** *obs* **:** location in space or on the earth's surface **:** geographic location **4** *Scot* **:** COURT OF SESSION **5 :** posture in or way of sitting (as on horseback) ⟨a rider with excellent ~ and hands⟩ **6 a** *obs* **:** a place prepared for the erection of something (as a building) **b :** the part at or forming the base of something ⟨the ~ of a pillar⟩ **c :** a part or surface on which another part or surface rests **:** SEATING ⟨the surface of a bridge abutment on which an end of the bridge rests is the ~⟩ ⟨a rubber-cushioned engine ~⟩ ⟨formed a new ~ for the valve⟩ **d :** FLOOR 8 **e :** the part of a shoe sole to which the heel is secured
²seat \"\ *vb* -ED/-ING/-S *vt* **1 a :** to establish or install in a seat of special dignity or office ⟨the queen was ~*ed* the same year⟩ **b (1) :** to cause to sit **:** assist in sitting down **:** find a seat for ⟨~*ed* the guests at small tables⟩ ⟨ushers ~ strangers in vacant pews⟩ ⟨my son will ~ you⟩ **(2) :** to provide seats or seating for ⟨a theater ~*ing* 1000 persons⟩; *also* **:** to provide with seats ⟨~ a church⟩ **c :** to sit (oneself) down ⟨~ yourself by the window and watch the rain⟩ **d :** to put (as oneself) in a sitting position **2 a :** to establish in a place of residence **:** SETTLE **b** *archaic* **:** to provide (as a country) with inhabitants **3 :** to repair the seat of **:** provide a new seat for ⟨~*ed* the chairs with strong cane⟩ **4 :** to adjust on or in relation to a seat **:** fit to or with a seat ⟨~ a valve⟩ ~ *vi* **1** *archaic* **:** to take one's seat or place **2 :** to fit correctly on a seat ⟨the lid must ~ accurately⟩ ⟨this valve does not ~ well⟩
seatang \'=,=\ *n* [¹*sea* + *tang*] **:** ³TANG
sea tangle *n* **:** any of various kelps esp. of the genus *Laminaria* **:** TANG
seat belt *n* **:** an arrangement of straps or webbing designed to hold a person steady in a seat (as during the takeoff of an airplane or in an automobile collision)
seat board *n* **1 :** a board supporting or serving as a seat **2 :** a shelf that supports the movement in a timepiece (as in a long case clock)
seat bone *n* **:** ISCHIUM
seat clip *n* **:** SPRING CLIP 1
seat cut *n* **:** a cut at the outer end of a rafter that adapts it to fit the plate and normally has the form of a right-angled notch — compare PLUMB CUT
seat drop *n* **:** a fundamental trampoline stunt in which the performer drops to a sitting position with his legs straight then rebounds to a standing position
seat·ed \'sēd·əd, -ētəd\ *adj* **1 :** having or equipped with a seat esp. of a specified kind — often used in combination ⟨double-*seated* trousers⟩ ⟨a soft-*seated* chair⟩ **2 :** settled or established in or as if in a seat **:** SITUATED, LOCATED ⟨deeply ~ disease⟩ ⟨a well-*seated* hatred⟩ **3** *of a horseshoe* **:** having the bearing surface hollowed
seat·er \'sēd·ə(r), -ētə-\ *n* -S **1 a :** one that puts in seats ⟨a chair ~⟩ **b :** a tool or implement for adjusting or fitting something (as a valve) into its seat **2** *archaic* **:** one (as an usher) who apportions seats or assigns persons to seats **3 :** something (as a vehicle) provided with seats esp. of a specified number — usu. used in combination ⟨toured the countryside in a four-*seater*⟩
sea term *n* **:** a seaman's term **:** a nautical word or phrase
sea thief *n* [ME *seethef*, fr. OE *sǣthēof*, fr. *sǣ* sea + *thēof* thief — more at SEA, THIEF] *archaic* **:** SEA ROBBER 1
sea thong *n* **1 :** a brown seaweed (*Himanthalia lorea*) found on the northern coasts of the Atlantic and having a long slender thallus that rises from a top-shaped holdfast **2 :** any of several seaweeds having corded fronds: as **a :** a sea lace (*Chorda filum*) **b :** a member of the genus *Laminaria*
sea thrift *n* **1 :** a thrift (*Armeria maritima*) **2 :** SEA LAVENDER
sea tiger *n* **:** GREAT BARRACUDA
sea time *n* **1 :** time spent at sea **2 :** time as reckoned at sea from noon to noon
seating *n* -S [partly fr. gerund of ²*seat*; partly fr. ¹*seat* + *-ing*] **1 :** the act of providing with seats ⟨the ~ of the crowd took a long time⟩ ⟨in charge of ~⟩ **2 a :** material for covering or upholstering seats ⟨strong cotton ~⟩ **b :** a seat in which something rests ⟨a valve ~⟩
sea titling *n, Brit* **:** ROCK PIPIT
seat·less \'sētləs\ *adj* **:** having or requiring no seat ⟨a ~ valve⟩
seat·mate \'=,=\ *n* **:** one with whom one shares a seat (as in a vehicle equipped with double or paired seats)
seat mile *n* **:** PASSENGER-MILE
sea toad *n* **1 :** any of various fishes of heavy or grotesque form: as **a :** SCULPIN **b :** TOADFISH **c :** ANGLER **2 :** an Australian spider crab (*Gonatorhynchus tumidus*) with a rough carapace suggesting the skin of a toad
seat-of-the-pants \'===='=\ *adj* **:** based on personal experience and appraisal rather than on the use of mechanical aids ⟨*seat-of-the-pants* navigation⟩
sea town *n* **:** a seaside town **:** SEAPORT
seat-pack parachute *n* **:** a parachute that is attached to the harness in such a manner that it may be used by the wearer as a seat cushion
seat-rail \'=,=\ *n* **:** a horizontal member at the front of a seat (as of a chair or sitter)
sea train \'=,=\ *n* **1 :** a seagoing ship equipped for carrying a train of railroad cars **2 :** several army or navy transports forming a convoy at sea
sea tree *n* **:** an arborescent seaweed (as of the genus *Lessonia*)
sea trifoly *n* **:** SEA MILKWORT
seat ring *n* **:** a replaceable ring that forms the seat of a valve
sea·tron \'sē·trən\ *n* -S [blend of *sea* and *citron*] **:** a confection or conserve made from a bladder kelp (*Nereocystis lütkeana*) usu. in syrup
sea trout *n* **1 :** any of various trouts or chars that as adults inhabit the sea but ascend rivers to spawn; *esp* **:** a European fish (*Salmo trutta*) that resembles the salmon but is smaller, weaker, and with smaller scales, that occurs in numerous subspecies in different regions which are sometimes considered separate species, and that may often become landlocked **2 :** any of various marine fishes that more or less resemble trouts: as **a :** WEAKFISH 1 **b :** GREENLING 1 **c :** the queenfish of California
se·at·tle \(')sē¦ad·ᵊl, -¦atᵊl\ *adj, usu cap* [fr. *Seattle*, Washington] **:** of or from the city of Seattle, Wash. ⟨a *Seattle* shipyard⟩ **:** of the kind or style prevalent in Seattle
se·at·tle·ite \-ᵊl,īt\ *n* -S *cap* [*Seattle*, Wash. + E *-ite*] **:** a native or resident of Seattle
sea turn *n* **:** a breeze or gale from the sea that often brings mist
sea turnip *n* **:** SEA-OTTER'S-CABBAGE
sea turtle *or* **sea tortoise** *n* **:** any of various large turtles having the feet modified into paddles, including the recent leatherback, hawksbill, loggerhead, and green turtles and numerous extinct forms, and being widely distributed in warm seas
sea twine *n* **:** SEA LACE
seatwork \'=,=\ *n* **:** work done at one's seat (as in school)
seat worm *n* **:** the human pinworm
seau \'sō\ *n, pl* **seaux** \'sō(z)\ [F, pail, fr. (assumed) VL *sitellus*, alter. of L *sitella*, a kind of urn, dim. of *situla* bucket, pail, voting urn] **:** a pottery pail that forms a part of the typical 18th century dinner service
sea unicorn *n* **:** NARWHAL
sea urchin *n* **1 :** an echinoderm of the class Echinoidea; *esp* **:** one of somewhat flattened globular form having a thin brittle shell or test of calcareous plates covered with well-developed and often very sharp movable spines as distinguished from the disk-shaped sand dollars or cake urchins and the heart urchins which also belong to the Echinoidea **2** *Austral* **:** CUSHIONFLOWER
sea urchin cactus *n* **:** any of several cacti (as of the genus *Echinopsis*) that are shaped like a sea urchin
seavalley \'=,==\ *n* **:** a submarine depression having the form of a valley and lacking the steep walls of a submarine canyon
sea valve *n* **:** a valve in the bottom or side of a ship communicating with the sea
sea vampire *n* **:** DEVILFISH 1
seave \'sēv\ *n* -S [ME *seve*, of Scand origin; akin to ON *sef* rush — more at SIEVE] *dial Eng* **:** RUSH
seawall \'=,=\ *n* [ME *seewall*, fr. *see* sea + *wall*] **:** a wall or embankment to resist encroachments of the sea
sea-walled \'=,=\ *adj* **:** provided with or protected by a seawall
sea walnut *n* **:** CTENOPHORE
seawan *or* **seawant** *var of* SEWAN
sea wand *n* **:** a kelp (*Laminaria digitata*) — called also *sea staff*
sea·wan·ha·ka boat \sə'wänəkə-\ *n, usu cap S* [fr. the *Seawanhaka* yacht club, Oyster Bay, Long Island, N.Y.] **:** a flat broad sailboat with centerboard widely used in the U. S.
¹sea·ward \'sēwə(r)d\ *also* **sea·wards** \-dz\ *adv* [*seaward* fr. ME *seeward*, fr. *see* sea + *-ward*; *seawards* fr. *seaward* + *-s*] **:** toward the sea
²seaward \"\ *n* -S **1 :** the direction or side away from land and toward the open sea; *also* **:** a location in this direction ⟨to fly to the ~⟩ **2 :** a service under old English feudal law consisting in guarding or watching against enemies from the sea
³seaward \"\ *adj* **1 :** directed or situated toward the sea **2 :** coming from the sea ⟨a ~ wind⟩
sea·ward·ly *adj* **:** accustomed to looking seaward or traveling at sea ⟨~ eyes⟩
seaware \'=,=\ *n* **:** sea wrack for use as manure
sea-washed \'=,=\ *adj* **:** wet by sea waves
sea wasp *n* **:** any of various cubomedusan jellyfishes that sting virulently
sea watch *n* **:** WATCH 6a(1)
seawater \'=,==\ *n* [ME *seewater*, fr. OE *sǣwæter*, fr. *sǣ* sea + *wæter* water — more at SEA, WATER] **:** water in or from the sea **:** SALT WATER
sea-water green *n* **:** SEA GREEN 1b
sea wax *n* **:** MALTHA
seaway \'=,=\ *n* **1 :** a moderate or rough sea ⟨caught in a ~⟩ **2 :** a ship's headway **3 :** the sea as a route for travel; *also* **:** an ocean traffic lane **4 :** a deep inland waterway that admits ocean shipping
sea-weary \'=,==\ *adj* **:** worn out or wearied by sea voyaging **:** tired by or of the sea
seaweed \'=,=\ *n* **1 :** a mass or growth of marine plants (as algae) **2 :** a plant growing in the sea; *esp* **:** a marine alga (as a kelp, dulse, rockweed, sea lettuce) widely distributed in the ocean, occurring from tide level to considerable depths, floating free or being anchored by specialized holdfasts of the thallus, and including many that are of economic importance (as for food, fertilizer, agar, fiber, potash, or iodine)
seaweed crab *n* **:** any of several common shallow-water Australian spider crabs (genus *Naxia*) that cover the carapace with seaweed
seaweed fern *n* **:** HART'S-TONGUE 1
seaweed glue *n* **:** FUNORI 2
seaweed green *n* **:** a grayish yellow green that is yellower and paler than average sage green and yellower and lighter than palmetto
seaweed marquetry *n* **:** marquetry of Italian origin in the form of conventionalized small-scale foliated or twining forms somewhat resembling seaweed and used esp. in late 17th century England
seaweedy \'=,==\ *adj* **:** characterized by or abounding in seaweeds
sea whip *n* **:** a gorgonian with an elongated flexible unbranched or little-branched axis
sea widgeon *n* **1 :** SCAUP DUCK **2 :** PINTAIL
seawife \'=,=\ *n, pl* **seawives :** either of two European wrasses (*Labrus vetula* and *Acantholabrus yarrelli*) related to the tautog
sea willow *n* **:** a gorgonian with long flexible branches

seawise \'=,=\ *adj* : schooled in ways and problems of the sea

sea wolf *n* **1 a** *obs* : a fabulous sea beast **b** : any of several voracious marine fishes; *esp* : WOLFFISH **c** *archaic* (1) : ELEPHANT SEAL (2) : SEA LION **2** : PIRATE, PRIVATEER; *also* : SUBMARINE

sea woodcock *n, Brit* : BAR-TAILED GODWIT

sea worm *n* **1** : a marine annelid **2** : SEA SERPENT 1 **3** : SHIPWORM

sea wormwood *n* : an aromatic somewhat woody chiefly coastal Eurasiatic perennial herb (*Artemisia maritima*) with woolly leaves and racemose panicles of tiny heads of yellowish to reddish hermaphroditic flowers

seaworn \'=,=\ *adj* **1** : impaired or eaten away by the sea ⟨~ shores⟩ **2** : SEA-WEARY

sea·wor·thi·ness \'sē,wərthēnəs\ *n* : the quality or state of being seaworthy; *specif* : the fitness of a ship for a particular voyage with reference to the condition of its hull and machinery, the extent of its fuel and provisions supply, the quality of its officers and crew, and its adaptability for the type of voyage proposed

seaworthy \'=,==\ *adj* [1*sea* + *worthy*] : fit for a sea voyage : able to stand stormy weather in safety ⟨a ~ ship⟩

sea wrack *n* **1 a** : a growth of seaweed esp. of the large forms (as rockweeds and kelps) **b** : a plant (as the bladder wrack) that tends to form large sea wracks **2** : EELGRASS 1

seax \'saks\ *var of* SAX

seb·a·cate \'sebə,kāt, sə'ba,kāt\ *n* -s [ISV *sebac*ic (in *sebacic acid*) + *-ate*] : a salt or ester of sebacic acid

se·ba·ceous \sə'bāshəs\ *adj* [L *sebaceus* made of tallow, fr. *sebum* tallow, grease + *-aceus* -aceous — more at SOAP] **1** : relating to, secreting, or composed of fatty matter ⟨the ~ glands of the skin⟩ **2** : resembling fat in appearance : FATTY ⟨~ secretions of some plants⟩

sebaceous cyst *n* : a cyst filled with sebaceous matter and formed by distention of a sebaceous gland as a result of obstruction of its excretory duct : WEN

sebaceous gland *n* : any of the small sacculated glands lodged in the substance of the derma, usu. opening into the hair follicles, and secreting an oily or greasy material composed in great part of fat which softens and lubricates the hair and skin

se·bac·ic acid \sə'basik-, -bās-\ *n* [*sebacic* ISV *sebac-* (fr. L *sebaceus*) + *-ic*] : a crystalline dicarboxylic acid $HOOC(CH_2)_8COOH$ that is made by destructive distillation of a mixture of sodium ricinoleate from castor oil and sodium hydroxide or is obtained as a component of isosebacic acid; decane-dioic acid

se·ba·go salmon \sə'bā(,)gō-\ *n, usu cap 1st S* [*Sebago* Lake, southwestern Maine] : LANDLOCKED SALMON 1

se·bala cat \sə'balə-\ *n* [prob. fr. the name *Sebala*] : BLACK-FOOTED CAT

se–baptism \'sē¦=,=\ *n* [fr. *se-baptist*, after E *baptist: baptism*] : the doctrine or practice of baptizing oneself

se–baptist \'=¦==\ *n* [L *se* oneself + E *baptist* — more at SUICIDE] : one that baptizes himself

se·bas·to·des \sə'bastə(,)dēz\ *n, cap* [NL, fr. *Sebastes*, genus of scorpaenid fish (fr. Gk *sebastos* august, worthy of reverence, fr. *sebesthai* to revere, feel awe) + *-odes;* akin to Skt *tyajati* he leaves, renounces, *tyajate* he shuns] : the chief genus of rockfishes (family Scorpaenidae)

se·bas·to·pol goose \sə'vastə,pōl, -aas- *also* ='==,pȯl *sometimes* ='==,pəl *or* ¦sevə¦stȯpəl *or* ¦==¦stōpəl\ *n, usu cap S* [*Sebastopol* (*Sevastopol*), city in southwestern U.S.S.R.] : a domestic goose having many of its feathers fantastically curled and twisted

sebat *usu cap, var of* SHEBAT

se·bes·ten \sə'bestən\ *n* -s [ME, fr. Ar *sibistān*, fr. Per *segpistān*] **1 a** : an East Indian tree (*Cordia myxa*) with white flowers in loose terminal panicles — called also *Assyrian plum* **b** *or* **sebesten plum** : the fruit of the sebesten used in India for pickles and dried as a demulcent **2 a** : GEIGER TREE **b** : the white edible fruit of the geiger tree

sebi- *or* **sebo-** *comb form* [NL, fr. L *sebum* tallow, grease — more at SOAP] : fat : grease : sebum ⟨*sebi*fic⟩ ⟨*sebo*rrhea⟩

se·bif·ic \sə'bifik\ *adj* [*sebi-* + *-fic*] : fat-producing : FATTY

se·bil·ian \sə'bilyən\ *adj, usu cap* [ISV *sebil-* (fr. *Sebil*, locality in southeastern Egypt) + *-an*] : of or relating to a Mesolithic culture of Upper Egypt characterized by microlithic flint tools and composite weapons using microliths

se·bil·la \sə'bilə\ *n* -s [modif. of F *sébile*, prob. fr. Ar *zabīl* date basket, sack] : a wooden receptacle used by stonecutters and ore assayers

seb·kha *also* **seb·ka** \'sebkə\ *or* **sab·a·kha** \'sabəkə\ *or* **sab·kha** \'sabkə\ *n* -s [Ar *sabkhah* saline infiltration, shallow lagoon] : a smooth flat often saline plain in northern Africa sometimes occupied after a rain by a shallow lake

seb·or·rhea *or* **seb·or·rhoea** \,sebə'rēə\ *n* -s [NL, fr. *sebi-* + *-rrhea*] : a functional disturbance of the sebaceous glands characterized by increased secretion and discharge of sebum that produces an oily appearance of the skin and the formation of greasy scales — **seb·or·rhe·ic** *or* **seb·or·rhoe·ic** \¦==¦rēik\ *adj*

se·bright \'sē,brīt\ *n* [after Sir John S. *Sebright* †1846 Eng. agriculturist] **1** *usu cap* : an old British breed of rose-comb bantam fowls with dark-laced silvery or golden feathers **2** -s *often cap* : any bird of the Sebright breed

se·bum \'sēbəm\ *n* -s [L, tallow, grease] : the material secreted by the sebaceous glands

seb·un·doy \¦sebən¦dȯi\ *n, pl* **sebundoy** *or* **sebundoys** *usu cap* **1 a** : a people of southern Colombia **b** : a member of such people **2** : the language of the Sebundoy people

se·bun·dy *also* **se·bun·dee** \sə'bəndē\ *n, pl* **sebundy** *or* **sebundies** [Hindi *sibandī*, fr. Per] : irregular native soldiery of the British in India

sec \'sek\ *adj* [F, lit., dry — more at SACK] *of champagne* : containing three to five percent sugar by volume : slightly sweet : drier than demi-sec and sweeter than extra sec : DRY

sec- *comb form, usu ital* [*secondary*] : secondary (sense 2e) — esp. in names of organic chemical radicals ⟨*sec*-butyl⟩

sec *abbr* **1** secant **2** second; secondary **3** secretary; secretariat **4** section **5** sector **6** [L *secundum*] according to **7** secured **8** security

se·ca·le \sə'kā(,)lē\ *n, cap* [NL, fr. L, rye] : a genus of cereal grasses having the 2-flowered spikelets in a dense spike, the lemma tipped with a long awn, and the empty glumes one-nerved — see RYE 1

sec·a·lin \'sekələn\ *n* -s [ISV *secal-* (fr. NL *Secale*) + *-in*] **1** : a prolamin obtained from rye **2** : SECALOSE

sec·a·lose \-,lōs\ *n* -s [NL *Secale* + E *-ose*] : a polysaccharide made up of fructose units obtained from green rye and oats or from rye flour

sec·a·mo·ne \,sekə'mō(,)nē\ *n, cap* [NL, modif. of L *scammonia* scammony] : a genus of Old World tropical woody vines (family Asclepiadaceae) bearing flowers with rotate corollas and scales of the crown with distinct tips

1se·cant \'sē,kant, -,kaa(ə)nt, -,kənt\ *adj* [L *secant-*, *secans*, pres. part. of *secare* to cut — more at SAW] : CUTTING ⟨a ~ line⟩

2secant \"\ *n* -s [NL *secant-*, *secans*, fr. L, pres. part. of *secare*] **1** : a straight line cutting a curve at two or more points **2 a** : a right line drawn from the center of a circle through one end of a circular arc to a tangent drawn from the other end of the arc **b** : the ratio of this line to the radius of the circle : the reciprocal of the cosine — abbr. *sec*

sec art *abbr* [L *secundum artem*] according to art

sec·a·teur \'sekə,tə̄(r *also* -,tə(r\ *n* -s [F *sécateur*, fr. L *secare* to cut + F *-ateur* -ator (fr. OF *-atour*)] *chiefly Brit* : SCISSORS, SHEARS — usu. used in pl. ⟨roses and other tough flowers are cut with a pair of ~*s* —*Punch*⟩

1sec·co \'se(,)kō\ *n* -s [It, fr. *secco*, adj., dry, fr. L *siccus* — more at SACK] : the art of painting on dry plaster with pigments suspended in a water-thinned binding vehicle — called also *fresco secco;* compare FRESCO 1a(1)

2secco \"\ *adj* (*or adv*) [It, lit., dry] **1** : short and very staccato — used as a direction in music **2** *of a recitative* : accompanied only by the instrument or instruments (as the harpsichord) playing the continuo

Sec·co·tine \'sekə,tēn, ,=='=\ *trademark* — used for an adhesive cement

se·cede \sə'sēd, sē'-\ *vi* -ED/-ING/-S [L *secedere*, fr. *sed-*, *se-* apart (fr. *sed*, *se* without) + *cedere* to go — more at IDIOT, CEDE] : to withdraw into isolation : leave a group : QUIT; *esp* : to withdraw from an organization, communion, or federation (as a church or political party) ⟨*seceded* from the conversation —Elizabeth Bowen⟩ ⟨about 10 more deputies have *seceded* from the government majority —*Atlantic*⟩

se·ced·er \-də(r)\ *n* -s **1** : one that secedes **2** *usu cap* : a member of the Secession Church of Scotland or any of its daughter churches

se·cern \sə'sərn,sē'-\ *vb* -ED/-ING/-S [L *secernere* to separate, distinguish — more at SECRET] *vt* **1** : SEPARATE; *esp* : to discriminate in thought : DISTINGUISH **2** *also* **se·cer·nate** \-,nāt\ [*secernate* fr. *secern* + *-ate*] : SECRETE ~ *vi* : SEPARATE

se·cern·ent \-,nənt\ *n* -s [*secern* + *-ent*] : something that secretes or promotes secretion

se·cern·ment \-nmənt\ *n* -s : the act or process of secerning

1se·cesh \sə'sesh, sē'-\ *n, pl* **secesh** [by shortening & alter. fr. *secession* & *secessionist*] : a U. S. secessionist

2secesh \"\ *adj* : of or relating to U. S. secessionists or secessionism

secess *n* -ES [L *secessus*, fr. *secessus*, past part. of *secedere*] *obs* : RETIREMENT, SECESSION

se·ces·sion \sə'seshən, sē'-\ *n* -s [L *secession-*, *secessio* withdrawal, secession, fr. *secessus* (past part. of *secedere* to withdraw, secede) + *-ion-*, *-io* -ion — more at SECEDE] **1** : withdrawal into privacy or solitude : RETIREMENT ⟨secret ~ from the trials of the status system —D.B.Meyer⟩ **2** : formal withdrawal from an organization (as a religious communion or political party or federation) **3** [trans. of G *sezession*] : an Austrian style in art and architecture parallel with French art nouveau and approximately contemporary with it

se·ces·sion·al \-shən°l, -shnəl\ *adj* : of or relating to secession or to the Secession Church of Scotland

se·ces·sion·ism \-shə,nizəm\ *n* -s : the doctrine or policy of secession : the tenets of secessionists

se·ces·sion·ist \-sh(ə)nəst\ *n* -s : one who joins in a secession or maintains that secession is a right

sech *abbr* hyperbolic secant

sechelt *usu cap, var of* SEECHELT

se·chi·um \'sēkēəm\ *n, cap* [NL, perh. irreg. fr. Gk *sikyos* cucumber — more at CUCUMBER] : a genus of herbaceous vines (family Cucurbitaceae) having fruit with a single seed and yellow racemose flowers — see CHAYOTE

se·chua·na \,sechə'wänə, sech'w-\ *n, pl* **sechuana** *or* **sechuanas** *usu cap* : TSWANA

seck \'sek\ *dial var of* SACK

se·cle \'sekəl\ *n* -s [L *saeculum* generation, age, century — more at SECULAR] *archaic* : CENTURY, CYCLE, AGE

sec leg *abbr* [L *secundum legem*] according to law

se·clude \sə'klüd, sē'-\ *vt* -ED/-ING/-S [ME *secluden* to keep away, forbid to enter, fr. L *secludere* to confine, separate, seclude, fr. *sed-*, *se-* apart (fr. *sed*, *se* without) + *-cludere* (fr. *claudere* to shut, close) — more at IDIOT, CLOSE] **1 a** : to shut up apart : confine in a place hard to reach or enter : make inaccessible : SECRETE, HIDE **b** : to remove or separate (oneself or another) from intercourse or outside influence : withdraw into solitude : ISOLATE ⟨was accused . . . of an intention to ~ himself in magnificent isolation —Robert Grant †1940⟩ **2** *obs* **a** : to exclude or debar from a privilege, rank, or dignity : expel or bar from a membership or office ⟨22 of the old *secluded* members having been at the House door the last week to demand entrance —Samuel Pepys⟩ **b** : to exclude from consideration **c** : to keep out from a place or society **3** : to shut off : PROTECT, SCREEN ⟨a *secluded* spot frequented by those interested in fishing and tramping —*Amer. Guide Series: N.H.*⟩ **4** *obs* : to separate by or as if by a barrier : keep apart or distinct ⟨nothing but clergy could us two ~ —Andrew Marvell⟩

secluded *adj* **1** : screened or hidden from view : SEQUESTERED ⟨a ~ valley⟩ **2** : living in seclusion : SOLITARY ⟨~ monks⟩ — **se·clud·ed·ly** *adv* — **se·clud·ed·ness** *n* -ES

se·cluse \sə'klüs, sē'-\ *adj* [L *seclusus*, past part. of *secludere*] : SECLUDED, RETIRED, WITHDRAWN

se·clu·sion \sə'klüzhən, sē'-\ *n* -s [ML *seclusion-*, *seclusio*, fr. L *seclusus* (past part. of *secludere*) + *-ion-*, *-io* -ion] **1** : the act of secluding ⟨the ~ of prisoners in cells⟩ **2** : the condition of being secluded ⟨yellow violets are common . . . in the ~ of damp woods —*Amer. Guide Series: N.H.*⟩ **3** : a secluded or isolated place **4** *Scots law* : the act of keeping out : EXCEPTION, EXCLUSION

se·clu·sion·ist \-zh(ə)nəst\ *n* -s : one favoring seclusion: as **a** : an advocate of monasticism **b** : one favoring exclusion of immigrants of specified races from his country

se·clu·sive \sə'klüs|iv, sē'-, -üz|, |ēv *also* |əv\ *adj* [fr. *seclusion*, after such pairs as E *inclusion: inclusive*] : tending or serving to seclude; *esp* : inclined to seclude oneself : disposed to seek retirement or solitude — **se·clu·sive·ly** \|əvlē, -li\ *adv* — **se·clu·sive·ness** \|ivnəs, |ēv- *also* |əv-\ *n* -ES

sec nat *abbr* [L *secundum naturam*] naturally

seco- *comb form* [L *sec*are to cut + E *-o-*] : having an opened ring — in names of organic chemical compounds ⟨2,3-*seco*cholestane⟩

sec·o·barbital \,se(,)kō+\ *n* [*seco*nal + *barbital*] : a barbiturate $C_{12}H_{18}N_2O_3$ used chiefly in the form of its bitter hygroscopic powdery sodium salt as a hypnotic and sedative; 5-allyl-5-(1-methyl-butyl)-barbituric acid

sec·odont \'sekə,dänt\ *adj* [ISV *sec-* (fr. L *secare* to cut) + *-odont* — more at SAW] : of, relating to, or having teeth adapted for cutting

Sec·o·nal \'sekə,nȯl, -,nal, -,n°l\ *trademark* — used for secobarbital

1sec·ond \'sekənd, -ənt, *before a consonant often* -kən *sometimes* -k°ŋ\ *adj* [ME *second*, *secound*, fr. OF *second*, fr. L *secundus* second, following, favorable, fr. *sequi* to follow — more at SUE] **1 a** (1) : being number two in a countable series ⟨the ~ day⟩ — abbr. *2d*, *2nd;* see NUMBER table (2) : being a type of grammatical declension or conjugation conventionally placed second in a standard arrangement of the types (3) : being the next to the lowest forward gear or speed in an automotive vehicle **b** : next to the first in place or time ⟨~ in line for promotion⟩ **c** (1) : next to the first in value, power, excellence, dignity, or degree ⟨her husband was the ~ man in the nation —Martha T. Stephenson⟩ ⟨a ~ car⟩ ⟨the teaching of English as a ~ language —L.L. Rockwell⟩ ⟨production facilities ~ to none —*Punch*⟩ (2) : INFERIOR, SUBORDINATE **d** : ranking next below the top of a grade or degree in authority or precedence — used in titles ⟨~ mate⟩ **e** : ALTERNATE, OTHER ⟨every ~ Englishman calls himself shy —*Time*⟩ ⟨elects a mayor every ~ year⟩ **f** : resembling, suggesting, or behaving like a prototype : ANOTHER ⟨a ~ Cato⟩ **g** : ingrained by discipline, training, or effort : ACQUIRED ⟨~ nature⟩ **2** : of or relating to a part in concerted or ensemble music typically lower in pitch than the first or to the player or singer performing this part ⟨~ violin⟩ ⟨~ bass⟩ **3** : being between 1.51 and 2.50 on the magnitude scale — used of the magnitude of a star

2second \"\ *n* -s **1 a** : number two in a countable series ⟨the ~ of the month⟩ **b** : one that is next after the first in rank, position, or any other serial order ⟨the ~ in line⟩ **2** : one who assists or supports another; *esp* : the supporter of a duelist or pugilist ⟨his ~*s* have to pick him up and yet he's the winner —Charles Oldfather⟩ — compare PRINCIPAL **3 a** : the musical interval embracing two diatonic degrees **b** : a tone at this interval; *specif* : the second note or tone of a scale : SUPERTONIC **c** : the harmonic combination of two tones a second apart **4 a** : an article of merchandise that is of a grade inferior to the best or that does not conform to a standard grade — usu. used in pl. **b seconds** *pl* : tobacco leaves of an inferior quality — compare LEAF 1c(4) **5 a** : SECOND-IN-COMMAND **b** : one having authority or precedence next below that of a person (as a mate or lieutenant) ranking first in a grade or degree ⟨sent the mate ashore to see if he could hire a ~⟩ **6** : the act or declaration by which a parliamentary motion is seconded ⟨do I hear a ~⟩ **7 a** : a place rated as secondary or inferior to the first (as in an examination, competition, or contest) : SECOND CLASS **b** : one obtaining such a place **8** : SECONDE **9** : SECOND BASE **10** : the second gear or speed in an automotive vehicle ⟨the gears locked in ~ —Herbert Passin⟩ **11** : a playing card that is next under or only a few cards removed from the top card of a pack being dealt and is dealt instead of the top card by card-sharpers or in card tricks — used esp. in the phrase *to deal seconds;* compare BOTTOM DEALER, SECOND DEALER **12 seconds** *pl* : a second helping of food ⟨hungry farmhands who called for ~*s*⟩

3second \"\ *adv* [ME *secounde*, fr. *second*, *secound*, adj.] **1** : in the second place : SECONDLY **2** : with one exception ⟨the nation's ~ largest city⟩

4second \"\ *n* -s [ME *seconde*, *secunde*, fr. ML *secunda*, fr. L, fem. of *secundus*, adj., second; fr. its being the second sexagesimal division of a unit, as a minute is the first] **1** : the 60th part of a minute of angular measure ⟨5 minutes and 10 ~*s* north of this place⟩ — symbol ″ **2** : the 60th part of a minute of time; *specif* : the cgs unit of time : $\frac{1}{86,400}$ part of the mean solar day — compare SIDEREAL SECOND **3** : an instant of time : MOMENT ⟨said he'd be back in a ~⟩ **4** : a second of time considered as a unit of measurement of the viscosity of fluids

5second \", *in sense 5* sə'känd\ *vt* -ED/-ING/-S [MF or L; MF *seconder*, fr. L *secundare*, fr. *secundus* favorable — more at 1SECOND] **1 a** : to give support or encouragement to (a person or his efforts) : back up : ASSIST ⟨warmly ~*ed* his daughter's efforts toward an education —W.J.Ghent⟩ **b** *obs* : to serve as follower or retainer of : ATTEND, ACCOMPANY **c** (1) : to support (a fighting man or group) in combat : bring up reinforcements for : act as second to (2) *obs* : to take the place of (a fallen fighter) : SUCCEED **2 a** : to support or assist (a speaker or a cause) in contention or debate ⟨was ~*ed* in this by the other members of the delegation —Jane Nickerson⟩ **b** : to endorse (a motion or a nomination) so that it may be debated or voted on under parliamentary procedure **c** *obs* : to act in support of (an opinion or its holder) : CONFIRM, CORROBORATE **3** [1*second*] **a** : to be second to : FOLLOW ⟨lumbering is the leading industry, ~*ed* by agriculture —*Amer. Guide Series: Texas*⟩ **b** *archaic* : REPEAT — used esp. of a blow **4** [1*second*] *obs* : to parallel (something) with an equivalent : bring forward the equal of **5** [F *second*, n., second position (in the phrase *en second* in second position, subordinate), fr. *second*, adj.] *Brit* : to remove (a military officer) temporarily from a regiment or corps for employment on the staff or in some appointment outside a regiment : attach temporarily : LEND ⟨holds the rank of captain in the Royal Engineers, ~*ed* for special duties —Nevil Shute⟩

second advent *n, usu cap S&A* : ADVENT 2b

second adventist *n, usu cap S&A* [*second advent* + *-ist*] : ADVENTIST

second angle *n* : an angle of the Great Triangle formed on the palm by the intersection of the lines of Life and Mercury that when acute is usu. held by palmists to indicate a weak constitution — called also *lower angle;* compare FIRST ANGLE, THIRD ANGLE

secondar *var of* SECONDER

sec·ond·ar·i·ly \¦sekən¦derəlē, -li *sometimes* -k°ŋ¦-\ *adv* [ME *secundarily*, fr. *secundarie*, *secundarie* secondary + *-ly*] **1** *obs* **a** (1) : for the second time (2) : next in time after the first **b** : as a second consideration : SECONDLY **2** : as an indirect result : in consequence of intermediate agents or causes **3** : in a secondary place, manner, degree, or sense : INCIDENTALLY

sec·ond·ar·i·ness \-rēnəs, -rin-\ *n* -ES : the quality or state of being secondary

1sec·ond·ary \'sekən,derē, -ri *sometimes* -k°ŋ,d-\ *adj* [ME *secundarie*, *secondarie*, fr. L *secundarius*, fr. *secundus* second + *-arius* -ary — more at SECOND] **1 a** : of second rank, importance, or value : next below the first in grade or class ⟨~ streets⟩ **b** : of less than first value or importance : INFERIOR, SUBORDINATE ⟨everything was ~ to the will to survive —Frank Rounds⟩ **c** : serving to assist or supplement : AUXILIARY, SUBSIDIARY ⟨~ boycott⟩ **d** : of, relating to, or constituting the second strongest of the three or four degrees of stress recognized by most linguists ⟨the third syllable of *basketball* carries the ~ stress⟩ ⟨the fourth syllable of *basketball floor* carries the ~ stress⟩ **e** : expressive of past time — used of a grammatical tense ⟨the imperfect, aorist, and pluperfect indicative are the Greek ~ tenses⟩ **2 a** : immediately derived from something original, primary, or basic : dependent on or following something fundamental or first : having derivative rank, position, or consequence ⟨a ~ producer, manufacturing aluminum alloys into nonfabricated forms from scrap aluminum —*New Republic*⟩; *esp* : being a derivative source for scholars ⟨a ~ history or analysis written after study of original material⟩ **b** : derivative from primary qualities — see SECONDARY QUALITY **c** : formed later than and often from the substance of earlier mineral deposits (as by weathering or by groundwater action) **d** : of or relating to the induced current or its circuit in an induction coil or transformer ⟨a ~ coil⟩ ⟨~ voltage⟩ **e** : characterized by replacement in the second degree : resulting from the substitution of two atoms or groups in a molecule ⟨a ~ salt⟩ ⟨~ phosphates⟩; *esp* : being or characterized by a carbon atom united by two valences to chain or ring members ⟨~ butyl $CH_3CH_2CH(CH_3)-$⟩ — compare PRIMARY 5, TERTIARY **f** (1) : not first in order of occurrence or development : relating to or derived from a later stage of differentiation or growth (2) : produced by activity of formative tissue and esp. cambium other than that at a growing point **g** (1) : dependent or consequent on another disease ⟨Bright's disease is often ~ to scarlet fever⟩ (2) : occurring or being in the second stage ⟨~ symptoms of syphilis⟩ (3) : occurring some time after the original injury ⟨a ~ hemorrhage⟩ **h** : produced by a second process (as by treatment of old metal and alloys, sweepings, or drosses) : not obtained directly from ore **3 a** : of or relating to the second order or stage in a series ⟨the stone will be hauled . . . to a ~ and tertiary crusher —*Wall Street Jour.*⟩ **b** *obs* (1) : MESOZOIC (2) : PALEOZOIC **c** : of, relating to, or being the second segment of the wing of a bird or the quills of this segment **d** : of or relating to a school intermediate between elementary school and college **e** : more advanced than a primary stage : next above the first in grade or class

2secondary \"\ *n* -ES [ME *secundarie*, fr. *secundarie*, *secondarie*, adj.] **1** : one occupying a subordinate or auxiliary position rather than that of a principal: as **a** : DELEGATE, DEPUTY **b** : a former officer of the corporation of the City of London **c** : a clergyman of second rank on the staff of an English cathedral **2** : a defensive football backfield — contrasted with *line* **3 a** : the star of lesser mass or brightness in a double-star system : COMPANION 4d **b** : SATELLITE **4** : a secondary electrical circuit or coil **5 a** : a cyclone relatively small in extent but often intense within the outer isobars of an older and larger storm **b** : a small area of low barometric pressure associated with a larger primary one **6 a** : any of the quill feathers arising from the forearm of a bird — see BIRD illustration **b** : one of the hind wings of an insect (as a butterfly or moth) **c** : one of the tubercles on the test of a sea urchin that is noticeably larger than a miliary tubercle but much smaller than a primary; *also* : a spine borne by such a tubercle

secondary accent *n* : an accent in compound musical measures other than that on the first beat (as on the third beat in 4/4 or on the fourth in 6/8 time)

secondary alcohol *n* : an alcohol that is characterized by the group >CHOH consisting of a carbon atom holding the hydroxyl group and one hydrogen atom and attached by its other two valences to other carbon atoms in a chain or ring and that can be oxidized to a ketone

secondary amine *n* : an amine (as dimethylamine or piperidine) having two organic substituents attached to the nitrogen atom

secondary axis *n* : a line through the center of a thin lens or through the center of curvature of a concave or convex mirror other than the principal axis of the lens or mirror

secondary battery *n* **1** : STORAGE CELL **2** : the guns of lesser caliber in a man-of-war having more than one caliber of guns exclusive of antiaircraft guns

secondary body *n* : the part of a plant developed from cambial layers — compare PRIMARY BODY

secondary boycott *n* : the boycott of an employer by his unionized employees at the instance of another employer's unionized employees in order to induce the first employer to help the cause of the second's employees in a labor dispute usu. by bringing pressure to bear on the second employer

secondary bud *n* : ACCESSORY BUD

secondary burial n : the reburial of human remains or the reburied remains — contrasted with *primary burial*

secondary cambium n : any of several formative layers that arise after the initial cambial layer in some roots (as of the beet) and produce a ring of tissue

secondary capitulum n : one of the six small cells surmounting each of the capitula in the antheridium of Characeae

secondary cell n : STORAGE CELL — compare PRIMARY CELL

secondary circle n : a great circle through the poles of another great circle and perpendicular to its plane

secondary color n : a color formed by mixing primary colors in equal or equivalent quantities : BINARY COLOR

secondary cortex n : a phelloderm developed in the cortex

secondary covert n : a wing covert covering the base of a secondary of a bird

secondary distribution n : the sale of a large block of an already outstanding stock through dealers but off the floor of an exchange

secondary dormancy n : dormancy induced in seeds capable of germinating immediately after ripening by the presence of one or more conditions unfavorable to germination

secondary electron n : an electron belonging to a beam of secondary radiation or emission (as an electron emitted from a metal surface when the surface is bombarded by high speed electrons)

secondary emission n : the emission of electrons from a surface that is bombarded by electrons or ions from a primary source

secondary enrichment n : ENRICHMENT 2

secondary evidence n : legal evidence admitted upon failure to obtain primary evidence (as a copy of a contract when the original is lost)

secondary fermentation n : the fermentation initiated by the addition of sugar or a sweet syrup to wine (as champagne and other sparkling wines) to induce natural carbonation — see CUVÉE; compare DOSAGE

secondary gain n : pleasure derived from a neurosis primarily necessary to the individual for other reasons

secondary group n : a social group characterized by conscious collective interest and formal association — contrasted with *primary group*; compare GESELLSCHAFT

secondary growth n : growth in plants that results from the activity of a cambium producing increase esp. in diameter, is mainly responsible for the bulk of the plant body, and supplies protective, supporting, and conducting tissue — compare PRIMARY GROWTH

secondary host n : INTERMEDIATE HOST 1

secondary infection n : infection initiated by spores or other infective bodies produced in a primary infection or another secondary infection

secondary meaning n : a close and prolonged identification in the public mind of a name, description, or designation of goods, services, or a product that is not in itself susceptible of being a technical trademark with a particular manufacturer or producer who under the law becomes entitled to exclusive use (evidence was insufficient to show that the word had acquired a *secondary meaning* entitling it to protection)

secondary meristem n : a meristem that develops from cells that have differentiated and functioned as part of a mature tissue system and then become meristematic again — compare PRIMARY MERISTEM

secondary minimum n : a sometimes very slight depression in the light curve of an eclipsing variable that occurs when the fainter of the two stars is eclipsed by the brighter — compare PRIMARY MINIMUM

secondary modern school n : a British secondary school of a type established since World War I providing a general education — called also *modern school*; compare SECONDARY TECHNICAL SCHOOL

secondary mycelium n : a dikaryotic mycelium

secondary nucleus n : PRIMARY ENDOSPERM NUCLEUS

secondary periderm n : a periderm layer other than the first and outermost layer

secondary phloem n : phloem produced by the cambium — compare PRIMARY PHLOEM

secondary port n : a port for which tide tables list differentials from the predictions for a standard port

secondary quality n : a mode of perception induced by some character of an object that does not coincide with the perception itself (such qualities, which in truth are nothing in the objects themselves, but powers to produce various sensations in us by their primary qualities, i.e. by the bulk, figure, texture, and motion of their insensible parts, as colors, sounds, tastes, etc., these I call *secondary qualities* —John Locke) — contrasted with *primary quality* and *tertiary quality*

secondary radiation or **secondary rays** n : rays (as X rays or beta rays) emitted by molecules or atoms as the result of the incidence of a primary radiation and of the same general nature as the latter

secondary rainbow n : a rainbow that is concentric with and near but somewhat larger and fainter than a primary rainbow and that differs from it in formation in that there are two internal reflections and the red is seen on the inside edge of the bow

secondary ray n : a vascular ray formed in the cambium — compare PRIMARY RAY

secondary reserve n : bank assets (as government securities and bank acceptances) readily convertible into cash to replenish primary reserves

secondary road n 1 : a road not of primary importance whose classification and maintenance vary according to township, county, and state regulations 2 : FEEDER ROAD

secondary root n 1 : one of the branches of a primary root 2 : ADVENTITIOUS ROOT

secondary school n : a school more advanced in grade than an elementary school and offering general, technical, vocational, or college-preparatory courses — compare GYMNASIUM 2, LYCÉE, PUBLIC SCHOOL 1

secondary screwworm n : a screwworm (*Callitroga Macellaria*)

secondary seventh n : a seventh chord based on some other tone than the dominant of the key

secondary sex characteristic or **secondary sex character** n : a morphological or psychological peculiarity (as the breasts of a female mammal or the nuptial plumage of a male bird) that becomes differentiated at puberty or in seasonal breeders at the breeding season in members of one sex and that is not directly concerned with reproduction

secondary spectrum n 1 : the spectrum of an element in the molecular state as distinct from its atomic line spectrum 2 : residual dispersion by a lens that has been corrected as far as possible for chromatic aberration 3 : the fainter of the two superimposed spectra of a spectroscopic binary star

secondary spermatocyte n : a spermatocyte that gives rise to spermatids : a spermatocyte of the last generation before the spermatozoon — compare PRIMARY SPERMATOCYTE

secondary spore n : a spore of a basidiomycete other than a basidiospore

secondary substance n, Aristotelianism : GENUS 2

secondary syphilis n : the second stage of syphilis appearing from 2 to 6 months after primary infection, marked by lesions esp. in the skin but also in other organs and tissues, and lasting from 3 to 12 weeks

secondary technical school n : a British secondary school emphasizing technical studies — compare SECONDARY MODERN SCHOOL

secondary triad n : a musical triad not based on the tonic, dominant, or subdominant of the key — compare PRIMARY TRIAD

secondary twinning n : the externally caused twinning of crystals (as by pressure in a rock mass after formation of the mineral)

secondary tympanic membrane n : a membrane closing the cochlear fenestra and separating the scala tympani from the middle ear

secondary use n, chiefly Eng law : SHIFTING USE

secondary wall n : the portion of a plant-cell wall formed internal to and subsequent to deposition of the primary wall after the cell has attained its final size and shape usu. constituting most of the cell wall, often being very complex and consisting of several anisotropic layers, and frequently being

buttressed internally by or consisting almost entirely of prominent rings, spirals, bars, or reticulations

secondary word n : a word whose immediate constituents are free forms (as the compound *catfish*) or a free form and a bound form (as the secondary derivative *fisher*)

se·con·da vol·ta \sə̇ˌkōndəˈvōltə\ n [It, second time] : a second ending of a musical section performed only at the repetition of the section and with omission of the first ending

second ballot n : an electoral system in which the voters choose between the two candidates with the greatest number of votes in an earlier election that fails to produce a majority for any one candidate

second base n 1 : the base that must be touched second by a base runner in baseball 2 : the player position for defending the area of the baseball infield on the first-base side of second base

second baseman n : the baseball player stationed at the second-base position — see BASEBALL illustration

second-best \ˈꞏ=ꞏ\ adj [ME secunde best, fr. second, secound, secunde second + best] : next to the best (give unto my wife my *second-best* bed with the furniture —Shak.)

¹second best n [second-best] : one that is below or after the best (look upon the president's proposal as a *second best* —New Republic)

²second best adv [second-best] : in second place — often used in the phrase *come off second best*

second birth n : REGENERATION 2

second blessing n : an experience of sanctification coming sometime after conversion as a second gift (as in holiness churches) of the Holy Spirit and adding to justification the power to live a holy life

second bottom n : the first terrace above a floodplain

second breath n : SECOND WIND

second cause n : a cause caused by something else (a *second cause* through which God, the First Cause, works)

second chamber n : the house in a bicameral legislature that is inferior in status and powers on the ground of constitutional prescription, of custom, or of the locus of responsibility of the ministry, is often orig. designed as a check on the other house, and is often constituted on a different basis (as heredity) from election

second childhood n : DOTAGE

second class n 1 a : the second and usu. next to highest group in a classification; specif : the group of persons who have obtained next to highest distinction in an honors course at a British university b : a place in or a member of such a group 2 : a class of accommodations (as on a railroad train) superior to third or tourist class and inferior to first class — compare CABIN CLASS 3 : a class of U.S. or Canadian mail comprising newspapers and periodicals sent to regular subscribers — see TRANSIENT SECOND CLASS 4 : the second rank in the rising scale of ranks in the Boy Scouts of America or the Girl Scouts of America — compare FIRST CLASS, TENDERFOOT

¹second-class \ˈꞏ=ꞏ\ adj [second class] 1 : of or relating to the next to the highest grade in a series (a *second-class* railway carriage) (a *second-class* honors degree) 2 : INFERIOR, MEDIOCRE (maybe that is the way to conduct *second-class* works —Virgil Thomson); esp : socially or economically deprived, suppressed, or limited (racism and its attendant theory of the *second-class* citizen —S.H.Sowell)

²second-class \ˈꞏ\ adv : by a second-class conveyance : with second-class accommodations (travel *second-class*)

second classman n : a third-year cadet or midshipman (as at a military or naval academy) — compare FIRST CLASSMAN, PLEBE

second coming n, usu cap S&C : ADVENT 2b

second cranial nerve n : OPTIC NERVE

second crop n 1 : a second harvest from the regrowth or second growth of a crop (as broomcorn) after harvesting earlier in the season 2 : a crop planted after harvesting another crop on the same land earlier in the season

second crown bud n : a flower bud (as on the chrysanthemum) that may develop after the first crown bud has been removed

second curvature n : TORSION 2

second-cut file \ˈꞏ=ꞏ\ n : a file of a fineness between bastard and smooth

second day n, usu cap S : MONDAY — used chiefly by the Friends

second dealer n : one skilled in dealing the second card from the top of a deck as if it were the first — compare BOTTOM DEALER

second death n : condemnation to eternal separation from God : punishment of the souls of the lost after bodily death

second deck n 1 : the first complete deck of a ship below the main deck 2 : the main deck on a typical merchant ship — see DECK

second-degree \ˈꞏ=ꞏ\ adj [fr. the phrase second degree] : of a degree next to the first; specif : of a degree of criminal culpability or seriousness next to first-degree (*second-degree* murder)

second-degree burn n : a burn characterized by pain, blistering, and superficial destruction of the dermis accompanied by edema and hyperemia of the tissues beneath the burn

second derivative n : the derivative of the derivative of a function

second-drawer \ˈꞏ=ꞏ(ꞏ)\ adj [fr. the phrase second drawer] : of a grade next to the top : less than primary or first-rate : INFERIOR, MEDIOCRE (preoccupied with money and with quick, *second-drawer* ways of making it —Budd Schulberg)

se·conde \sə̇ˈkänd, -ˈgä-\ n -s [F, fr. fem. of second, adj. — more at SECOND] : a parry or guard fencing position defending the lower outside right target in which the hand is in a position of pronation, the arm slightly bent, and the tip of the blade directed at the opponent's knee — compare OCTAVE 4

seconded past of SECOND

second empire n, usu cap S&E [fr. the noun phrase Second Empire (the French empire of 1852–1871 under Napoleon III †1873 emperor of the French), trans. of F second Empire] : of or relating to a style in furniture and architecture developed in France under Napoleon III and marked by heavy ornate modification of Empire styles

¹sec·ond·er \ˈsekəndə(r)\ n -s [²second + -er] : one who seconds what another attempts, affirms, moves, or proposes (a most efficient ~ of the department when the House and Administration were harmonious —Allan Nevins)

²seconder or **sec·ond·ar** \ˈꞏ=ꞏ\ n -s [seconder modif. (influenced by ¹second and -er) of L secundarius, adj., secondary : secondar modif. (influenced by ¹second) of L secundarius, adj. — more at SECONDARY] : a university student formerly second in social rank to a son of a nobleman — compare TERNAR

second fiddle n : one who fills a subordinate or secondary role or function — usu. used in the phrase *to play second fiddle* (played *second fiddle* in her own home to her own sister —V.S.Pritchett)

second filial generation n : the second generation from a cross produced by random interbreeding of the first filial generation and resulting in recombination and segregation of the various characters in which the members of the parental generation differ — compare MENDEL'S LAW

second-first \ˈꞏ=ꞏ\ adj : of, relating to, or being the sabbath second between Passover and Pentecost and first after the beginning of the Paschal week

second floor n : SECOND STORY

second-foot \ˈꞏ=ꞏ\ n : a unit of flow used esp. in connection with the flow of streams that is equal to one cubic foot per second

second-generation \ˈꞏ=ꞏꞏ=ꞏ\ adj [fr. the phrase second generation] 1 : being a member of the second generation of a family to be born in the U.S. 2 : native-born of foreign or mixed parentage (the *second-generation* girl avoids . . . the feminine alliances that typify the girl of American-born parents —S.G.Dulsky)

second growth n : a growth developing after another growth or on land devoted primarily to some other crop; specif : forest trees that come up naturally after removal of the first growth by cutting or by fire

second-guess \ˈꞏ=ꞏ\ vt [fr. the phrase second guess] 1 : to apply hindsight to or to criticize the course of action of 2 a : OUTGUESS b : PREDICT — **second-guesser** n

¹second hand n [ME seconde honde, fr. seconde, second,

secound, adj., second + honde, hand hand] 1 : an intermediate person or means : INTERMEDIARY — usu. used in the phrase *at second hand* (even this historical fact I had only at *second hand*, from my aunt —Ben Riker) 2 : an assistant foreman esp. in textile industries 3 : an assistant hand : a manual laborer's helper 4 : the second player to have the right to bid or the second player to play to any trick in bridge

²second hand n [⁴second + hand] : the hand marking seconds on a watch or clock — compare HOUR HAND, MINUTE HAND

¹secondhand \ˈꞏ=ꞏ\ adj [¹second hand] 1 : received from or through an intermediary rather than directly from the source : BORROWED, DERIVED (this is a ~ account of a memory of something once read, shaky evidence indeed —Ruth P. Randall) 2 a : used or worn by a previous owner : bought or acquired after being used by another : not new (~ books) (~ clothing) (a ~ car) b : dealing in secondhand merchandise (a ~ bookstore)

²secondhand \ˈꞏ\ adv : at second hand : INDIRECTLY (a region that, like the stars, man must know for the most part ~ —T.A.Manar)

secondhanded \ˈꞏ=ꞏ\ adj [second hand + -ed] chiefly dial : SECONDHAND

sec·ond·hand·ed·ness n -ES [secondhanded + -ness] : the quality or state of being secondhand : JEUNENESS (actually to have read it all through must remove most *second-handedness* from one's mind —Cyril Connolly)

second head n : broken rice consisting of pieces one-third to three-fourths the size of the rice grains

second-in-command \ˈꞏ=ꞏꞏ=ꞏ\ n, pl seconds-in-command : the person ranking next to the head : the military officer ranking next below the commanding officer

secondines var of SECUNDINES

seconding pres part of SECOND

second-in-hand \ˈꞏ=ꞏꞏ=ꞏ\ n : ¹SECOND HAND 4

second injury fund n : a fund maintained by assessments collected from insurers out of which a worker injured a second time is paid an amount that when added to workmen's compensation benefits brings the total to the amount payable under workmen's compensation for the combined injuries

second intention n 1 : a conception (as species, genus, whiteness) generalized from or formed by reflection on first intention 2 : the healing of an incised wound by granulations that bridge the gap between skin edges — compare FIRST INTENTION

second inversion n : a musical chord with its fifth in the bass — see SEVENTH CHORD illustration

second joint n : the thigh segment of a fowl's leg — compare DRUMSTICK

second law of thermodynamics : LAW OF THERMODYNAMICS 2

second lieutenant n 1 : an army, marine, or air force officer of the lowest commissioned rank 2 : a Salvation Army officer ranking above a probationary lieutenant and below a first lieutenant

sec·ond·ly adv [ME secoundly, fr. second, secound second + -ly] : in the second place (firstly it isn't true and ~ it isn't important)

second maxilla n : one of the paired appendages immediately behind the first maxillae of an arthropod that in an insect together form the labium

se·cond·ment \sə̇ˈkän(d)mənt\ n -s [²second + -ment] : the detachment of a person (as a military officer) from his regular organization for temporary assignment elsewhere

second mile n [so called fr. the precept of Jesus in Mt 5:41 (RSV) "if any one forces you to go one mile, go with him two miles"] : a deed of charity or kindness beyond the demands of duty — used chiefly in the phrase *go the second mile* (employee benefits which go the *second mile* in human relations of this type —Think)

second mortgage n : a mortgage the lien of which is subordinate to that of a first mortgage — compare JUNIOR MORTGAGE

second mourning n : mourning dress of black relieved by white or of dark gray worn for a time after the period of strict mourning

second nature n : acquired ingrained habits or traits as distinguished from innate or instinctive ones (conformity to the discipline of a small society had become almost his *second nature* —Edith Wharton)

second nerve n : OPTIC NERVE

sec·ond·ness n -ES : a fundamental category in Peircean philosophy comprising actual facts and expressive of necessity, force, and determination — compare FIRSTNESS, THIRDNESS

se·con·do \sə̇ˈkōn(ˌ)dō, -kōn-, -kīn-\ n, pl secon·di \-dē\ [It, fr. secondo, adj., second, fr. L secundus — more at SECOND] : the second part in a concerted piece; esp : the lower part (as in a piano duet) — compare PRIMO

second officer n : a second mate in the merchant service

second-order reaction \ˈꞏꞏ=ꞏꞏ=ꞏ\ n : a chemical reaction in which the rate of reaction is proportional to the concentration of each of two reacting molecules — compare ORDER OF A REACTION

second papers n pl : a petition for citizenship that an alien seeking naturalization must file from two to seven years after his first papers

second person n 1 a : a set of linguistic forms (as verb forms, pronouns, and inflectional affixes) referring to the person or thing addressed in the utterance in which they occur (Latin *videtis* "you see" is in the *second person* plural) (English *you* is a pronoun of the *second person*) b : a linguistic form belonging to such a set (Latin *vides* "you see" and *is* "you go" are *second persons*) 2 : reference of a linguistic form to the person or thing addressed in the utterance in which it occurs (the Latin verb ending -s that marks the *second person*)

second personal adj : of or relating to the second person (a *second personal* pronoun)

second philosophy n, Aristotelianism : the special sciences or branches of science (as physics) — distinguished from *First Philosophy*; compare METAPHYSICS

second pointed adj : DECORATED 7

second public examination n : the final examination for the B.A. degree (as at Oxford University)

second-rate \ˈꞏ=ꞏ\ adj [fr. the phrase second rate] : of second or inferior quality or value : lacking excellence : MEDIOCRE (will reject this slate of *second-rate* candidates)

sec·ond-rate·ness n -ES

second-rater \ˈꞏ=ꞏꞏ=ꞏ\ n : one that is second-rate (a team made up of aging *second-raters*)

second reader n, usu cap S&R : a member of a Christian Science church or society chosen for a term of office to assist the First Reader in conducting services by reading aloud selections from the Bible

second reading n 1 : the stage in the British legislative process following the first reading and usu. providing for debate on the principal features of a bill before its submission to a committee for consideration of details 2 : the stage in the U.S. legislative process that occurs when a bill has been reported back from committee and that provides an opportunity for full debate and amendment before a vote is taken on the question of a third reading of the bill — compare LEGISLATION 1

second run n : the run of a motion picture under a second release

seconds pl of SECOND, pres 3d sing of SECOND

second sacker n : SECOND BASEMAN

second service n [so called fr. the fact that it follows Morning Prayer] Church of England : COMMUNION 2

second sheet n 1 : an often blank sheet of writing paper used for the second and subsequent pages of a letter of which the first sheet bears a letterhead 2 : sheet of manifold paper

second sight n : the capacity to see remote or future objects or events : CLAIRVOYANCE, PRECOGNITION

second-sighted \ˈꞏ=ꞏ\ adj : having second sight — **second-sight·ed·ness** n -ES

second slip n : a fielding position in cricket near to and on the off side of first slip; also : a player fielding in this position — see CRICKET illustration

second sound n : transfer of heat which is much faster than conduction or convection, which is observed only in helium II, and in which waves of temperature resembling sound waves travel at speeds of about 20 meters per second

seconds pendulum *n* **:** a pendulum requiring exactly one second for each swing in either direction or two seconds for a complete vibration and having a length between centers of suspension and oscillation of 99.353 centimeters at sea level in latitude 45 degrees

second story *n* **1 :** the story just above the ground floor **2** *Brit* **:** the second story above the ground floor

second-story man *n* **:** a burglar who enters a house by an upstairs window **:** CAT BURGLAR

second-string \ˈ=ˈ=\ *adj* [fr. the phrase *second string*] **1 :** being a substitute as distinguished from a regular (as on a football team) ⟨went so far as to have his *second-string* catcher . . . play second base in the eighth inning —Roscoe McGowen⟩ ⟨short road tours with *second-string* casts —*Current Biog.*⟩ — compare FIRST-STRING **2 :** being of the second or an inferior order of quality or importance ⟨reporters and *second-string* strategists —R.H.Rovere⟩

second table *n* **1 :** a position of inferiority **2 :** a second setting of tables at a meal partaken of by more persons than can be served at once

second team *n* **:** the members of a squad (as in football or basketball) used chiefly as substitute players

second thigh *n* **:** the part of the hind leg of a quadruped that lies between the stifle joint and the hock

second thought *n* **:** reconsideration after a decision subsequently regarded as impulsive, premature, or otherwise ill-taken ⟨*second thought* became more sober as the days advanced —F.L.Paxson⟩

second touch *n* **:** the second point to which pipe-organ keys or pistons may be moved in a double-touch action

second water *n* **:** the quality or luster next below first water — used of a gem (as a diamond or pearl)

second wind *n* **1 :** recovered full power of respiration after the first exhaustion during exertion due to improved action of the heart **2 :** renewed energy or capacity for effort and endurance ⟨the *second wind* of creative energy which would have carried their early brilliance into ripe maturity —De Lancey Ferguson⟩

se·cours \səˈkü(ə)r\ *n, pl* **secours** \"\ [MF, fr. OF *secors, sucors* — more at SUCCOR] **:** AID, ASSISTANCE, SUCCOR

se·cre·cy \ˈsēkrəsē, -si\ *n* -ES [alter. (influenced by *-cy*) of earlier *secretie*, fr. ME *secretee*, fr. *secre* secret (fr. MF *secré*, fr. L *secretus*) + *-tee, -te* -ty] **1 a :** the habit or practice of keeping secrets or maintaining privacy or concealment **:** SECRETIVENESS ⟨~ is an inherent feature of all governmental administration —C.J.Friedrich⟩ ⟨readily assured her of his ~ —Jane Austen⟩ **b :** the condition of being hidden or concealed ⟨complete ~ surrounded the meeting —*Current History*⟩ **2 :** something concealed or concealing **:** MYSTERY, SECRET ⟨the footsteps . . . sounded peculiarly dim and harmless in the gentle ~ of dusk —Elinor Wylie⟩ **3** *obs* **a :** confidential relationship **:** intimate confidence **:** TRUST **b :** PRIVACY, SECLUSION

sec reg *abbr* [L *secundum regulam*] according to rule

¹se·cret \ˈsēkrət, *usu* - əd·+V\ *adj, sometimes* -ER/-EST [ME, fr. MF, fr. L *secretus*, past part. of *secernere* to separate, distinguish, fr. *sed-, se-* apart (fr. *sed, se* without) + *cernere* to sift — more at IDIOT, CERTAIN] **1 a :** kept from knowledge or view **:** CONCEALED, HIDDEN ⟨advised him, against his own judgment, to keep his mission ~ for a time —W.C.Ford⟩ ⟨the baronage had plunged almost to a man into ~ conspiracies —J.R.Green⟩ **b :** marked by the habit of discretion or faithful concealment **:** loyal to a confidence **:** trustworthy in preserving secrecy **:** CONFIDENTIAL, CLOSEMOUTHED, RETICENT **c :** working with hidden aims or methods **:** UNDERCOVER ⟨a ~ agent⟩ **d :** UNACKNOWLEDGED, UNAVOWED, UNDECLARED ⟨a ~ enemy⟩ ⟨a ~ bride⟩ **2 :** remote from human frequentation or notice **:** RETIRED, SECLUDED ⟨~ harbors —R.W.Hatch⟩ **3 :** known or felt inwardly without avowal ⟨~ alarm⟩ ⟨~ exultation⟩ **:** INMOST ⟨his ~ soul⟩ **4 a :** revealed only to the initiated **:** ESOTERIC, MYSTIC ⟨the ~ learning of the cabalists⟩ **b :** lying beyond ordinary comprehension **:** relating to or dealing with mysteries or occult matters **:** ABSTRUSE, RECONDITE ⟨you ~, black, and midnight hags —Shak.⟩ **5 :** done or undertaken with evident purpose of concealment ⟨we must stand together . . . in ~ alliance —Jack London⟩ **6 :** GENITAL ⟨~ parts⟩ **7 :** constructed so as to elude observation or detection ⟨a ~ panel⟩ ⟨a ~ passage⟩ or to conceal means or mechanics ⟨~ nailing⟩ ⟨a ~ dovetail⟩ **8 :** INVISIBLE, UNSEEN **9 :** classified below top secret but above confidential in a scale rating the value of information to a nation's security — compare CLASSIFICATION 1f

syn COVERT, CLANDESTINE, STEALTHY, SURREPTITIOUS, FURTIVE, UNDERHAND, UNDERHANDED: SECRET is a general term applicable to anything hidden, concealed, known, or known about by a limited few. ⟨seized a lamp . . . and hurried towards the *secret* passage —Horace Walpole⟩ COVERT is the antonym of *overt* or *open;* it stresses the fact of being concealed or veiled ⟨some form of coercion, overt or *covert* —John Dewey⟩ ⟨the meaning of the *covert* addresses of a villain —W.M. Thackeray⟩ CLANDESTINE refers to a situation obtaining, a practice adhered to, a thing made or used in wary or timorous secrecy, often against usage, sanction, or authority ⟨she proposed a *clandestine* marriage, but he swore that when afterwards detected, it would cause his dismissal —Anthony Trollope⟩ ⟨hunted by the gestapo for his anti-Nazi pamphlets and *clandestine* magazine *La Pensée Libre* —*Time*⟩ STEALTHY may suggest slow, wary, sly avoidance of being observed as one proceeds in doing something evil, sinister, or reprehensible ⟨a valet, of *stealthy* step, thence conducted me, in silence, through many dark and intricate passages —E.A.Poe⟩ ⟨comparable to . . . the suffocation of the York princes in the Tower. I'll admit the setting is consonant with that sort of *stealthy*, romantic crime —W.H.Wright⟩ SURREPTITIOUS refers to actions done, emotions cherished, things held or enjoyed secretly, often with opportune cleverness, against usage or authority ⟨enjoying a *surreptitious* cigarette —P.G.Wodehouse⟩ ⟨over the paling of the garden we might obtain an oblique and *surreptitious* view —Henry James †1916⟩ FURTIVE implies sly, wary, slinking caution to escape being perceived, recognized, or apprehended ⟨asked the man, in a *furtive* frightened way —Charles Dickens⟩ ⟨*furtive* shortcuts across the fields of persons who might easily have bawled at me if they had caught sight of me —Siegfried Sassoon⟩ UNDERHAND and UNDERHANDED stress dishonest deception rather than merely the fact of secrecy in itself ⟨whatever scrape he may have been in, I'll warrant there was nothing mean or *underhanded* in his share of it . . . he hasn't a tricky or a dishonest bone in his body —C.B.Nordhoff & J.N.Hall⟩

²secret \"\ *n* -S [ME, fr. MF & L; MF *secret*, fr. L *secretum*, fr. neut. of *secretus*, past part. of *secernere* to separate, distinguish — more at ¹SECRET] **1 a :** something kept hidden **:** an unexplained or inscrutable process or fact (as an operation of God or of nature) **:** MYSTERY ⟨an intimation of the ~ of mysticism —Havelock Ellis⟩ **b :** something kept from the knowledge of others, concealed as one's private knowledge, or shared only confidentially with a few persons **:** information entrusted to one in confidence ⟨a man who knew the ~*s* of one's innermost soul —H.J.Laski⟩ — see TRADE SECRET **c :** a method, formula, or process used in an art or a manufacturing operation and divulged only to those of one's own company or craft ⟨~*s* long cherished by monkish wine makers⟩ **d secrets** *pl* **:** the practices or knowledge making up the shared discipline or culture of an esoteric society ⟨the ~*s* of the ancient Essenes⟩ **2** [ML *secreta*, fr. L, fem. of *secretus*, past part. of *secernere*] **:** a prayer said in a low or inaudible voice by the celebrant just before the preface in the mass **3 :** something taken to be a specific or key to some desired end ⟨called discreet and steady use of whiskey the ~ of his living to the age of a hundred⟩ **4 secrets** *pl* **:** PART 1d(3) **5 :** a coat of mail worn concealed under one's clothing — **in secret** *adv* **:** in a private manner or place **:** in secrecy ⟨already there existed *in secret* . . . a considerable opposition party —J.G.Lockhart⟩

³secret \"\ *adv* [¹*secret*] *archaic* **:** SECRETLY

⁴secret *vt* -ED/-ING/-S [¹*secret*] *obs* **:** ²SECRETE

secret- *or* **secreto-** *comb form* [*secretion*] **:** secretion ⟨*secretin*⟩ ⟨*secretomotor*⟩

¹se·cre·ta \səˈkrā(ˌ)tä\ *n, pl* **secre·tae** \-āˌtä\ [ML, fr. L, fem. of *secretus*, past part. of *secernere*] **:** SECRET 2

²secreta *pl of* SECRETUM

³se·cre·ta \səˈkrēd·ə, sēˈ-, -ētə\ *n pl* [NL, fr. L, neut. pl. of *secretus*, past part. of *secernere*] **:** products of secretion

se·cret·age \ˈsēkrəd·ij\ *n* -S [F *secrétage*, fr. *secréter* to carrot + *-age* — more at SECRETE] **:** the carroting of fur

se·cre·ta·gogue *also* **se·cre·to·gogue** \səˈkrēd·əˌgäg, sēˈ-, *sometimes* -gȯg\ *n* -S [*secretagogue* fr. *secret-* + *-agogue; secretogogue* irreg. (influenced by *-o-*) fr. *secret-* + *-agogue*] **:** a substance that stimulates secretion (as of the stomach or pancreas)

se·cre·taire \ˌsekrəˈta(a)(ə)r, -te|, |ə\ *n* -S [F *secrétaire* escritoire, secretary (person), fr. MF *secretaire* secretary (person), confidant, fr. OF, confidant, fr. ML *secretarius*] **:** ESCRITOIRE, SECRETARY

sec·re·tar·i·al \ˌsekrəˈterēəl, -ta(a)r-, *in rapid speech* ÷ -kəˈt-\ *adj* **:** of or relating to a secretary or the work of a secretary

sec·re·tar·i·at *also* **sec·re·tar·i·ate** \ˌ==ˈterēət *sometimes* -ta(a)r- *or* -ēˌat\ *n* -S [*secretariat* fr. F *secrétariat*, fr. ML *secretariatus*, fr. *secretarius* secretary, confidant + L *-atus* -ate; *secretariate* alter. (influenced by *-ate*) of *secretariat*] **1 :** the office or position of a secretary **2 :** a secretarial corps (as in a business office) **:** the working force of secretaries or the clerical staff of an organization **3 a :** the government administrative department presided over by a secretary-general or a cabinet secretary ⟨the ~ of state⟩ ⟨the United Nations ~⟩ **b :** the quarters occupied by a government secretariat **c :** the staff of a secretariat

sec·re·tary \ˈsekrəˌterē, *in rapid speech* ÷-k(ə)ˌt-\ *n* -ES [ME *secretarie*, fr. ML *secretarius* secretary, confidant, fr. L *secretum* secret + *-arius* -ary — more at SECRET] **1** *obs* **a :** one entrusted with the secrets or confidences of a superior **:** ADVISER, CONFIDANT **b :** one considered to understand the secrets of God or of nature or to have penetrated other mysteries **2 :** one employed to handle correspondence and manage routine and detail work for a superior **3 a :** an officer of a business concern who may issue notices and keep records of directors' and stockholders' meetings, oversee and preserve records of stock ownership and transfer and of other company affairs, and cooperate with counsel in supervision of the company's legal interests **b :** an officer of an organization or society responsible for its records and correspondence **4 :** an officer of state who superintends a government administrative department and is usu. a member of the chief executive's cabinet or advisory council ⟨the ~ of the treasury⟩ ⟨the ~ of labor⟩ ⟨foreign ~⟩ **5** [trans. of F *secrétaire*] **a :** WRITING DESK, ESCRITOIRE **b** *or* **secretary bookcase :** a writing desk with a top section for books **6 :** SECRETARY BIRD

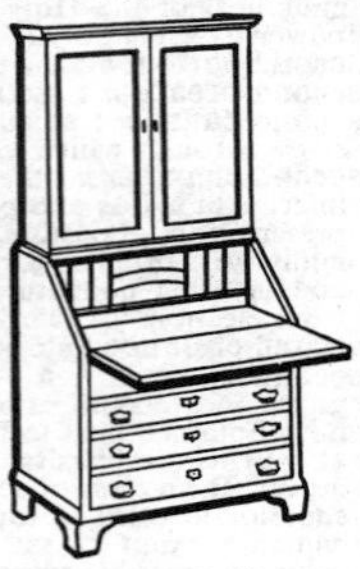

secretary 5b

secretary at war : the representative of the army in the British Parliament until 1855

secretary bird *n* [prob. so called fr. the resemblance of the crest to a bunch of quill pens stuck behind the ear] **:** a large long-legged raptorial bird (*Sagittarius serpentarius*) of southern Africa that has a powerful hooked beak, a crest of long feathers, and a long tail, is predominantly blue-gray with black wing quills, thighs, abdomen, and bars on the tail, feeds largely on reptiles, and is often tamed to rid premises of them

secretary–general \ˈ==ˌ==ˈ=(=)=\ *n, pl* **secretaries–general :** a principal administrative officer ⟨the *secretary-general* of the United Nations⟩ ⟨the *secretary-general* of a political party⟩ ⟨the *secretary-general* to a colonial governor⟩

secretary hand *n* **:** a handwriting style formerly used in engrossing — compare SECRETARY TYPE

secretary of state : the chief officer of a government administrative department: as **a :** any of several British ministers ⟨the *secretary of state* for home affairs⟩ **b :** the head of the U.S. department of state **c :** the head of a department of the government of a U.S. state whose miscellaneous duties include the making and keeping of records

sec·re·tary·ship \-ˌship\ *n* **:** the duties or office of a secretary

secretary type *n* **:** a former black-letter type made to imitate engrossing script — compare SECRETARY HAND

secret ballot *n* **:** AUSTRALIAN BALLOT

¹se·crete \səˈkrēt, sēˈ-, *usu* -ēd·+V\ *vb* -ED/-ING/-S [back-formation fr. *secretion*] *vt* **1 :** to produce and emit (a secretion) from a gland **2 :** to produce or generate in the manner of a gland ⟨to trust . . . to the facts to ~ a purpose of their own —Archibald MacLeish⟩ ~ *vi* **:** to produce and emit a secretion ⟨the mucosa was *secreting* normally⟩

²se·crete \səˈkrē|t, sēˈ-, ˈsēkrə|, *usu* |d·+V\ *vt* -ED/-ING/-S [alter. (influenced by L *secretus*, past part. of *secernere* to separate, distinguish) of ⁴*secret*] **1 :** to deposit or conceal in a hiding place **:** HIDE ⟨he will ~ a small piece of iron about his person —J.G.Frazer⟩ **2 :** to appropriate (another's possessions) secretly **:** ABSTRACT **syn** see CONCEAL

³se·crete \səˈkrēt, sēˈ-, *usu* -rēd·+V\ *vt* -ED/-ING/-S [F *secréter*, fr. *secret*, n.; prob. fr. the fact that the process was originally a trade secret — more at SECRET] **:** ²CARROT

secreter *comparative of* SECRET

secretest *superlative of* SECRET

se·cre·tin \səˈkrēd·ən\ *n* -S [*secret-* + *-in*] **:** a hormone of polypeptide structure that is found in the mucous membrane of the upper intestine and is capable of stimulating the pancreas to secrete its juice and the liver to secrete bile

secret ink *n* **:** a fluid for invisible writing to be made visible afterwards: as **a :** a colorless plant juice that can be made visible by subjecting to heat **b :** one of a pair of water solutions of chemicals that are colorless or nearly so and that when combined form a strongly colored compound **c :** a water solution of a fluorescent substance that is colorless in visible light but leaves characters on paper that fluoresce when exposed to ultraviolet light

se·cre·tion \səˈkrēshən, sēˈ-\ *n* -S [F *sécrétion*, fr. L *secretion-, secretio* separation, fr. *secretus* (past part. of *secernere* to separate, distinguish) + *-ion-, -io* -ion — more at SECRET] **1 a :** the act or process of segregating, elaborating, and releasing some material that is either specialized to perform some function in the organism (as saliva) or is isolated for excretion from the body (as urine) **b :** a product of such secretion formed in the animal or plant body (as the cellulose wall of a plant cell or the pancreatic juice of an animal); *sometimes* **:** any such product that performs a specific useful function in the organism — distinguished from *excretion* **2** [²*secrete* + *-ion*] **:** the act of hiding something **:** CONCEALMENT ⟨thwarted his attempt at ~ of some costly gemstones about his person⟩

se·cre·tion·ary \-shəˌnerē, -ri\ *adj* **:** of or relating to secretion **:** formed by secretion

se·cre·tive *in senses 1 & 2:* ˈsēkrəd·iv, -ətiv; səˈkrēd·|iv, sēˈ-, -ˈkrēt|, |ēv *also* |əv; *in sense 3:* =ˈ=+\ *adj* [back-formation fr. *secretiveness*] **1 :** disposed to secrecy **:** given to concealment of one's activities or purposes **:** preferring privacy ⟨the king was a ~ child, and showed little of his mind —Edith Sitwell⟩ **2 :** indicating or betokening a disposition to secrecy ⟨his blue eyes were guarded and ~ —Katherine A. Porter⟩ **3** [*secret-* + *-ive*] **:** SECRETORY **syn** see SILENT

se·cre·tive·ly \-əvlē, -li\ *adv* **:** in a secretive manner

se·cre·tive·ness \-ivnəs, -ēv- *also* -əv-\ *n* -ES [part trans. of F *secrétivité*, fr. *secrétiv-* (fr. *secret*, n. + *-if* -ive) + *-ité* -ity — more at SECRET] **:** the quality or state of being secretive

se·cret·ly *adv* [ME, fr. ¹*secret* + *-ly*] **1 :** in secret **:** in secrecy **:** not openly **2 :** in a low voice **:** INAUDIBLY — used esp. of liturgical prayer

secret mark *n* **:** a minute mark on a stamp or currency note introduced in the die or plate as a distinguishing mark of a particular engraver or of a particular plate or printer rather than as part of the design

se·cret·ness *n* -ES [ME *secretnesse*, fr. ¹*secret* + *-nesse* -ness] **:** the quality or state of being secret

secreto- — see SECRET-

secretogogue *var of* SECRETAGOGUE

se·cre·to·inhibitory \səˈkrēd·ō+\ *adj* [*secret-* + *inhibitory*] **:** checking secretion

se·cre·to·motor \"+\ *adj* [*secret-* + *motor*] **1 :** promoting secretion **2** *of nerves* **:** inducing secretion when stimulated

se·cre·tor \səˈkrēd·ə(r), sēˈ-\ *n* -S [¹*secrete* + *-or*] **:** an individual freely producing and excreting water-soluble group-specific substances in body fluids (as saliva, tears, urine) — compare NONSECRETOR

se·cre·to·ry \səˈkrēd·ərē, sēˈ-, -ētə-, -ri *sometimes* ˈsēkrəˌtōr- *or* -ˌtȯr-\ *adj* [*secret-* + *-ory*] **:** connected with or promoting secretion **:** produced by secretion

secretory duct *n* **:** any of the small ducts within a glandular organ that collect the secretion and convey it to a main duct that carries it from the organ

secret partner *n* **:** a partner whose membership in a partnership is kept secret from the public — called also *silent partner;* compare GENERAL PARTNER, LIMITED PARTNER

secret police *n* **:** a police organization operating for the most part in secrecy and esp. for the political purposes of its government often with terroristic methods — compare POLICE STATE

secret process *n* **:** a process that is a trade secret that would be valuable to competitors but is often protected by rule of court from compulsory disclosure although not protected by patent

secret reserve *n* **:** an amount by which stated net worth is reduced by understatement of asset values or overstatement of liabilities — called also *hidden reserve*

secrets *pl of* SECRET, *pres 3d sing of* SECRET

secret service *n* **1** *archaic* **:** confidential and publicly unacknowledged service to a government **2 :** a government detective or intelligence department ⟨*secret service* men begin to guard a U. S. president as soon as he is known to be elected⟩

secret society *n* **1 :** a society of a kind common among primitive peoples that often exercises magical or religious functions or administers punitive justice **2** *or* **secret order :** any of various modern oath-bound societies usu. devoted to purposes of brotherhood, moral discipline, and mutual assistance

se·cre·tum \səˈkrēd·əm, sēˈ-, -ētəm\ *n, pl* **secre·ta** \-ēd·ə, -ētə\ [ML, fr. L, neut. of *secretus*, past part. of *secernere* to separate, distinguish — more at SECRET] **:** a private seal

sect \ˈsekt\ *n* -S [ME *secte*, fr. MF & LL & L; MF, group, sect, fr. LL *secta* organized ecclesiastical body, fr. L, way of life, school of thought, class of persons, fr. *sequi* to follow — more at SUE] **1 a :** a dissenting religious body; *esp* **:** one that is heretical in the eyes of other members within the same communion **b :** a group within an organized religion whose adherents recognize a special set of teachings or practices ⟨the Pharisees have been called a ~ within Judaism⟩ **c :** an organized ecclesiastical body; *specif* **:** one outside one's own communion ⟨offered religious freedom to all ~*s* except the Roman Catholics⟩ **d :** a comparatively small recently organized exclusive religious body; *esp* **:** one that has parted company with a longer-established communion **2 a** *obs* **:** a class, order, or kind of persons **b** *archaic* **:** a religious order **c** *archaic* **:** SEX ⟨so is all her ~ —Shak.⟩ **3 a :** a separate group adhering to a distinctive doctrine or way of thinking or to a particular leader ⟨fashionable . . . among many different ~*s* of writers —L.S.Woolf⟩ **b :** a school of philosophy or of philosophic opinion ⟨the ~ Epicurean —John Milton⟩ **c :** a group holding similar political, economic, or other views: as (1) **:** PARTY (2) **:** an opinionated faction (as of a party) ⟨Trotskyism . . . and other independent communist ~*s* —Jim Cork⟩ (3) **:** a school of opinion (as in science or medicine) ⟨medical ~*s* in ancient Greece⟩ **4** *obs* **:** a body of followers **:** FOLLOWING **syn** see RELIGION

¹-sect \ˌsekt\ *adj comb form* [L *sectus*, past part. of *secare* to cut, divide — more at SAW] **:** cut **:** divided ⟨pinnati*sect*⟩

²-sect \"\ *vb comb form* -ED/-ING/-S [L *sectus*, past part. of *secare*] **:** cut **:** divide ⟨bi*sect*⟩ ⟨quadri*sect*⟩

sect *abbr* section; sectional

sec·ta \ˈsektə\ *n pl* [ML, fr. L, way of life, school of thought, class of persons] **1 :** the followers or witnesses brought by the plaintiff to support his case in Anglo-Saxon law **2 :** a lawsuit in Anglo-Saxon law

sec·tar·i·al \(ˈ)sekˈta(a)rēəl\ *adj* [¹*sectary* + *-al*] **:** of, relating to, or distinguishing a religious sect in India ⟨a ~ mark⟩

¹sec·tar·i·an \-rēən\ *adj* [¹*sectary* + *-an*] **1 :** of or relating to one or more sectaries; *specif* **:** of or relating to the Independents or another Protestant nonconformist sect (as in 17th century England) **2 :** of, relating to, or having the characteristics of one or more sects esp. of a religious character ⟨~ differences⟩ **3 a :** confined to the limits of one religious group, one school, or one party **:** DENOMINATIONAL, PARTISAN ⟨~ religious training⟩ ⟨the negations of ~ ideology —Sidney Hook⟩ ⟨~ squabbles in psychology —*Times Lit. Supp.*⟩ **b :** limited in character or scope **:** of narrow interests **:** characterized by bigotry **:** PAROCHIAL ⟨a ~ mind⟩ ⟨wishing to avoid a ~ presentation of the matter⟩

²sectarian \"\ *n* -S **1 a :** an adherent of a particular religious sect **b :** DISSENTER 2 **2 :** one characterized by a narrow and bigoted adherence to a sect **:** one limited to narrow and partisan views, interests, or sympathies

sec·tar·i·an·ism \-əˌnizəm\ *n* -S **:** sectarian spirit or beliefs **:** exclusive or narrow-minded attachment to a sect, denomination, party, or school ⟨religious ~⟩ ⟨socialist ~⟩

sec·tar·i·an·ize \-ˌnīz\ *vb* -ED/-ING/-S *vi* **:** to act as sectarians **:** become divided into sects ~ *vt* **:** to make sectarian **:** imbue with sectarian principles or feelings **:** subject to the control of a sect ⟨~ public education⟩

sec·ta·rism \ˈsektəˌrizəm\ *n* -S [¹*sectary* + *-ism*] **:** the spirit, practices, or principles of a religious sect **:** SECTARIANISM

sec·ta·rist \-ˌrəst\ *n* -S [¹*sectary* + *-ist*] *archaic* **:** SECTARY

¹sec·ta·ry \-rē, -ri\ *n* -ES [prob. fr. NL *sectarius*, fr. LL *secta* organized ecclesiastical body + L *-arius* -ary — more at SECT] **1 a :** an adherent of a religious sect held to be heretical or schismatic **b** *sometimes cap* **:** a dissenter from the Church of England; *specif* **:** an Independent or other Protestant nonconformist **2 :** a usu. zealous adherent of a sect ⟨religious or political *sectaries*⟩ **3 a :** a zealous follower, disciple, or partisan (as of a leader, teacher, party, or school) ⟨each old town . . . has its cult of *sectaries*, devotees of its history —Lucien Price⟩ **b :** a votary of a particular study or pursuit ⟨been a ~ astronomical —Shak.⟩ **4** *archaic* **:** SECT

²sectary \"\ *adj, archaic* **:** SECTARIAN

sec·ta·tor \sekˈtād·ə(r)\ *n* -S [MF *sectateur*, fr. L *sectator*, fr. *sectatus* (past part. of *sectari* to follow, accompany, freq. of *sequi* to follow) + *-or* — more at SUE] **:** a usu. devoted follower (as of a teacher or leader) **:** DISCIPLE

sec·tile \ˈsekt°l, -ˌtīl, -(ˌ)til\ *adj* [L *sectilis*, fr. *sectus* (past part. of *secare* to cut) + *-ilis* -ile] **1 a :** capable of being severed by a knife with a smooth cut but yet pulverizable **b :** cut into small divisions **2 :** constituting a type of mosaic formed of relatively large pieces of marble shaped to fit one another

sec·til·i·ty \sekˈtilәd·ē, -ətē, -i\ *n* -ES **:** the property or condition of being sectile ⟨the ~ of chalcocite⟩

¹sec·tion \ˈsekshən\ *n* -S *often attrib* [L *section-, sectio*, fr. *sectus* (past part. of *secare* to cut) + *-ion-, -io* -ion — more at SAW] **1 a :** the action of cutting or separating by cutting; *esp* **:** the action of dividing (as tissues) surgically ⟨nerve ~⟩ ⟨abdominal ~⟩ ⟨cesarean ~⟩ **b :** an instance of such cutting **2 :** a distinct part or portion of a writing: as **a :** a subdivision of a chapter (as a paragraph or a series of paragraphs not separated by a heading) **b :** a division of a law, statute, or legislative act **c :** a distinct component part of a newspaper ⟨the sports ~⟩ **3 a :** the description or representation of something (as a building, piece of machinery, segment of the earth's crust) as it would appear if cut through by an intersecting plane **:** depiction of what is beyond a plane passing or supposed to pass through an object **:** PROFILE **b :** a diagram showing rock units and structures along a usu. vertical plane below the surface **4 a :** a natural subdivision of a taxonomic group and esp. of a genus but sometimes of a higher group **b :** a tribal segment or a group of segments usu. based on descent, function, or territorial occupancy **5 :** the plane figure resulting from the cutting of a solid by a plane **6 :** the character § commonly used in printing to mark a section or the beginning of a section (as of a statute) and as the fourth in series of the reference marks **7 :** a piece of land one square mile or 640 acres in area forming one of the 36 subdivisions of a township in a U. S. public-land survey **8 a :** a distinct part of a terri-

torial area (as a country or continent) set apart by geographic, economic, cultural, or other distinctive characteristics ⟨the West, the South, and other ~s of the U. S.⟩ ⟨the only important grape-growing ~ of Pennsylvania —*Amer. Guide Series: Pa.*⟩ **b** : a usu. distinctive quarter or district (as of a city or town) ⟨the business ~ of the city⟩ **9 a** : a part that is, may be, or is held to be separated : DIVISION, PORTION, SLICE ⟨the southern ~ of the route⟩ ⟨chop the stalks into ~s —*Amer. Guide Series: La.*⟩ ⟨an important ~ of the milling industry —*Amer. Guide Series: Minn.*⟩ ⟨a ~ of the task⟩ **b** : one segment of a fruit (as an orange or grapefruit) : CARPEL **c** : one of the parts into which the warp threads are divided during weaving preparation (as warping, beaming, and slashing) **10 a** : a portion of a group of people having or held to have a distinct and separate status usu. by virtue of one or more distinctive characteristics ⟨a cheering ~⟩ ⟨royally entertained by all ~s of the local community —Guthrie Moir⟩ ⟨the strongest ~ of the European population —Patrick Smith⟩ **b** : one of the classes formed by dividing a group of students taking a particular course ⟨ten ~s of English I⟩ **c** : one of the groups into which a conference of teachers, scholars, or specialists in a given field is divided for discussion purposes **11 a** : a military unit composed of two or more squads **b** : a military unit constituting the basic unit of a larger unit **12 a** : a very thin slice (as of tissue or rock) suitable for microscopic examination **b** : an exposed surface revealing successive geological strata **13 a** : a division of a railroad sleeping car including both an upper and a lower berth or when these are not made up two double seats facing each other **b** : a portion of a permanent railroad way under the care of a particular set of men **c** : one of two or more trains, planes, buses, or similar vehicles which run on the same schedule and for which special signals are usu. shown **14** : one of several component parts that may be assembled or reassembled ⟨a cutter bar with 15 ~s⟩ ⟨a bookcase in ~s⟩ **15** : one of the frames each made about four inches square, designed to hold about a pound when full, and placed in the super of a hive for bees to store surplus honey in **16** : a profile on a plane perpendicular to the plane of the principal line or trace in fortification **17** : a division of an orchestra composed of one class of instruments ⟨brass ~⟩ ⟨string ~⟩ **18** : SIGNATURE 5b **19** : a subdivision of an office, staff, department, bureau, or other organization ⟨the political ~ of an embassy⟩ ⟨a Communist party ~⟩ ⟨the U. S. ~ of the British Foreign Office⟩ **20** : the sequence of rock units in a given locality or region **syn** see PART — **in section** *adv* : in the view revealed by a section ⟨show a blood vessel *in section*⟩

²**section** \"\ *vb* **sectioned; sectioned; sectioning** \-sh(ə)niŋ\ **sections** *vt* **1 a** : to cut or separate into sections : make a section of ⟨~ a history class by ability ratings⟩ ⟨~ a rock for examination⟩ **b (1)** : to divide (a body part or organ) surgically ⟨~ a nerve⟩ **(2)** : to cut (fixed tissue) into thin slices for microscopic examination **2** : to shade (as a part of a mechanical drawing) with crosshatching to indicate a section : to represent in sections ~ *vi* : to form sections : become cut or separated into parts

¹**sec·tion·al** \-shən³l, -shnəl\ *adj* **1 a** : of, relating to, or based upon a section ⟨~ repair of a tire⟩ ⟨a ~ view⟩ ⟨~ drawings⟩ **b** : belonging to a distinct part of a larger body (as a society or population) or territory : local or regional rather than general in character ⟨~ interests⟩ ⟨~ jealousies⟩ ⟨a ~ dialect⟩ — compare PROVINCIAL 2 **2 a** : consisting of or divided into sections ⟨a ~ wire⟩ ⟨~ furniture⟩ **b** : designed for construction by assembling a series of component parts ⟨a ~ garage⟩ — see SECTIONAL BOILER **c** : made up of sections to be added or reduced at will ⟨a ~ bookcase⟩ ⟨a ~ dictionary⟩ ⟨a ~ sofa⟩

²**sectional** \"\ *n* -s : a piece of furniture made up of modular

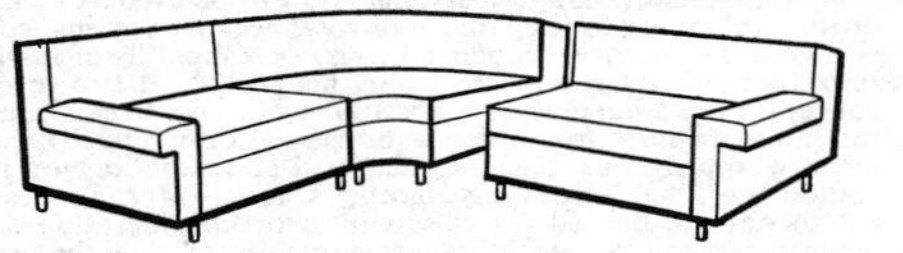

sectional

units capable of use separately or in various combinations (as a sectional sofa whose parts may be used as chairs)

sectional boiler *n* : a boiler whose parts are fabricated and shipped in sections and erected in suitable supporting frames and brickwork settings

sectional density *n* : the ratio of the weight of a projectile to the square of its diameter

sec·tion·al·ism \-sh(ə)nə,lizəm\ *n* -s : disproportionate devotion to the interests peculiar to one section (as of a country) : sectional feeling, spirit, or prejudice : consciousness by the people of a section of a common and peculiar set of identifying characteristics (as customs, interests, or social traits) ⟨when ~ exists within a state . . . it may be an upstate versus downstate division —D.D.McKean⟩

sec·tion·al·ist \-ləst\ *n* -s : one characterized by sectionalism : one that advocates sectional interests or aims : one having usu. excessive sectional feeling

sec·tion·al·iza·tion \,seksh(ə)nələ'zāshən, -,lī'z-\ *n* -s : the action of sectionalizing or of becoming sectionalized : the state of being sectionalized

sec·tion·al·ize \'seksh(ə)nə,līz\ *vt* -ED/-ING/-S **1** : to divide into sections : make in sections esp. for later assembly **2** : to divide according to geographical sections or local interests : cause to become characterized by sectionalism

sectional leaf cutting *n* : a section of a leaf (as of a begonia) on which with the proper environment adventitious buds and roots will develop

sec·tion·al·ly \-³lē, -əlē, lī\ *adv* : in a sectional manner : along sectional lines : from a sectional point of view

¹**sec·tion·ary** \'sekshə,nerē\ *adj* : of or relating to a section : SECTIONAL 1 ⟨~ leaders⟩

²**sectionary** \"\ *n* -ES : a member or partisan of a sectional group

section bar *n* : a bar of iron or steel rolled so as to have a definite cross section

section boss *n* **1** *or* **section foreman** : the foreman of a section gang **2** : a third hand in a textile mill

section eight *n, pl* **section eights** *usu cap S&E* [*Section VIII*, Army Regulation 615-360, in effect from December 1922 to July 1944] **1** : a discharge from the U. S. Army for military inaptitude or undesirable habits or traits of character **2** : a soldier discharged for military inaptitude or undesirable habits or traits of character ⟨where the *Section Eights* wandered around whimpering all the time —R.O.Bowen⟩

section-eight \"=\ *vt* -ED/-ING/-S *often cap S&E* [*section eight*] : to discharge (a soldier) from the U. S. Army for military inaptitude or undesirable habits or traits of character ⟨until you . . . go crazy and get *section-eighted* —Ernest Hemingway⟩

section gang *also* **section crew** *n* : a gang or crew of trackmen employed to maintain a railroad section

section hand *n* : a laborer belonging to a section gang

section house *n* **1** : a small building for storing tools and equipment needed to maintain a railroad section **2** : a railroad-owned dwelling at or near a railroad section for housing a section boss and his family or the members of a section gang

sec·tion·ize \'sekshə,nīz\ *vt* -ED/-ING/-S : to divide into sections ⟨~ land for disposal to settlers⟩

section line *n* **1** : the boundary line of a section in surveying or land distribution ⟨in eastern Ohio . . . roads followed *section lines* —R.H.Brown⟩ **2** : one of a series of thin parallel lines placed on the cut surfaces of section views (as in an architectural drawing)

section man *n* **1** : SECTION HAND **2** : SECTION BOSS 2

section manager *n* : FLOORWALKER 1

section paper *n, Brit* : GRAPH PAPER

section plane *n* **1** : a surface seen in section (as in cross section) **2** : a hypothetical plane cutting a section

sections *pl of* SECTION, *pres 3d sing of* SECTION

sect·ism \'sek,tizəm\ *n* -s : SECTARIANISM

sect·ist \-,təst\ *n* -s *obs* : SECTARIAN 1

¹**sec·tor** \'sektə(r) *also* -,tō(ə)r *or* -ō(ə)\ *n* -s [LL (trans. of Gk *tomeus*), fr. L, cutter, fr. *sectus* (past part. of *secare* to cut) + *-or* — more at SAW] **1 a** : the geometrical figure bounded by two radii and the included arc of a circle **b (1)** : a subdivision of a defensive military position assigned to a commander as an area of responsibility, bounded by arbitrary lines on the sides and rear, and in front extending to the maximum range of the weapons of the garrison — compare ZONE OF ACTION **(2)** : a portion of a front in military operations **c** : something (as an area or a portion or part of something) resembling or held to resemble a sector : DIVISION, QUARTER, SECTION ⟨the Soviet ~ of Berlin⟩ ⟨a reforested ~ of cutover land —*Amer. Guide Series: Oregon*⟩ **d** : a sociological, economic, or political subdivision of society ⟨maintenance of public order is primarily the responsibility of the public ~ —*Kerner Report*⟩ **2** : a mathematical instrument consisting of two rulers connected at one end by a joint and marked with several scales (as of equal parts chords, sines, or tangents) **3 a** : an astronomical instrument whose limb embraces only a part of a circle and which is used for measuring angles too great for the compass of a micrometer **b** : an arc-shaped attachment to an equatorial mounting often used for communicating slow-motion control of the driving clock to the polar axis **4** : a part of an apparatus whose principal kinematic lines form a sector ⟨an index ~⟩ **syn** see PART

²**sector** \-tə(r)\ *vb* **sectored; sectored; sectoring** \-t(ə)riŋ\ **sectors** *vt* : to divide into or furnish with sectors ~ *vi* : to form colonies made up of visibly different sectors — used chiefly of bacteria and fungi that form mutant strains early in the colony history

sec·tor·al \'sekt(ə)rəl\ *adj* : of or relating to a sector ⟨~ line⟩

sec·tored disk \'sektə(r)d-\ *also* **sector disk** *or* **sector wheel** *n* : a disk with alternate opaque and open sectors used in photometers to vary the brightness in a known manner

sector gate *n* : a roller gate in part-circle or sector form for a dam crest

sector gear *n* **1** *or* **sector wheel** : a toothed device resembling a portion of a gear wheel containing the center bearing and a part of the rim with its teeth **2** : a gear having a sector gear as its chief essential feature

¹**sec·to·ri·al** \(')sek¦tōrēəl, -tȯr-\ *adj* [¹*sector* + *-ial*] **1** : of, relating to, or having the shape of a sector ⟨a ~ box⟩ **2** *of a chimera* : made up of a sector of variant growth involving more than one type of tissue interposed in an otherwise normal body of tissue — compare PERICLINAL

²**sectorial** \"\ *adj* [NL *sectorius* sectorial (fr. L *sectus* — past part. of *secare* to cut — + *-orius* -ory) + E *-al*] : adapted for cutting : CARNASSIAL ⟨a ~ tooth⟩

sector of a sphere : the solid generated by the revolution of the sector of a circle about one of its radii

sects *pl of* SECT

-sects *pres 3d sing of* -SECT

sectuary *n* -ES [by alter. (influence of such words as *actuary*)] *obs* : SECTARY

secty *abbr* secretary

¹**sec·u·lar** *also* **saec·u·lar** \'sekyələ(r)\ *adj* [ME, alter. (influenced by LL *saecularis*) of *seculer*, fr. OF, fr. LL *saecularis* secular, worldly, pagan, fr. L, coming or observed once in an age, fr. *saeculum* breed, generation, age + *-aris* -ar; akin to W *hoedl* lifetime, Lith *sėkla* seed, L *serere* to sow — more at SOW] **1 a** : of or relating to the worldly or temporal as distinguished from the spiritual or eternal : not sacred : MUNDANE ⟨~ affairs⟩ ⟨~ occupations⟩ **b** : not overtly or especially religious ⟨~ rites⟩ ⟨~ music⟩ ⟨~ drama⟩ **c** : of or relating to the state as distinguished from the church : CIVIL ⟨~ courts⟩ ⟨~ jurisdiction⟩ ⟨the champion of the ~ power —A.J.Toynbee⟩ **d** : of or relating to the laity as distinguished from the clergy : NONCLERICAL, LAY ⟨the ~ landowners⟩ ⟨~ benefactors⟩ **e** : not formally related to or controlled by a religious body ⟨the greater number of ~ than denominational schools in the country⟩ **f** : rationally organized around impersonal and utilitarian values and patterns and receptive to new traits ⟨our modern industrialized ~ society⟩ — contrasted with *sacred* **g** : of, relating to, or advocating secularism : SECULARIST ⟨an enlightened ~ humanism —H.N.Fairchild⟩ ⟨the disenchantment of absolute faiths which expresses itself in the ~ outlook of modern man —Louis Wirth⟩ **2 a** : living in the world : not living in a monastery or religious community : not bound by monastic vows or rules ⟨a ~ priest⟩ ⟨the ~ clergy⟩ — opposed to *regular;* compare MONK 1 **b** : of or relating to clergy not bound by monastic vows ⟨~ vestments⟩ **3** [L *saecularis*] **a** : coming or observed once in an age or a century ⟨~ phenomena⟩ **b** : existing or continuing through ages or centuries : AGELONG, CENTURIED, DIUTURNAL ⟨~ oaks⟩ ⟨~ enmities⟩ **c** : of or relating to a long-enduring process ⟨~ change⟩ ⟨regions of the earth's surface where . . . slow ~ movements of the crust are still in progress —*Endeavour*⟩ **d** : taking place within a century ⟨~ fluctuation⟩ ⟨the ~ variation in an astronomical position⟩ **e** : requiring or taking ages (as for operation or completion) ⟨~ forces⟩ ⟨the improvement of man is ~ —John Tyndall⟩ **f** : of or relating to a long term of indefinite duration ⟨the ~ trend of prices⟩ ⟨a ~ increase in the quantity of money is required in a growing economy —Milton Friedman⟩ — compare CYCLICAL 2 **g** : recurring at intervals greater than one year ⟨~ cycles in population pressure⟩ **syn** see PROFANE

²**secular** \"\ *n* -s [ME *seculer*, fr. OF, fr. *seculer*, adj.] **1** : a secular ecclesiastic (as a parish priest) **2** : LAYMAN

secular arm *n* [ME *seculer arm*, trans. of ML *bracchium saeculare*] : the secular or civil power as distinguished from that of the church

secular canoness *n* : a canoness who is allowed to hold private property and is bound only by vows of celibacy and obedience

secular games *n pl* [trans. of L *ludi saeculares*] : games honoring the gods of ancient Rome, lasting for three days and nights, and celebrated at long irregular intervals with sacrifices, theatrical shows, feasting, and singing of hymns composed for or appropriate to the occasion

secular hymns *n pl* [trans. of L *carmina saecularia*] : hymns composed for or sung at the secular games of ancient Rome

sec·u·lar·ism \'sekyələ,rizəm\ *n* -s : a view of life or of any particular matter based on the premise that religion and religious considerations should be ignored or purposely excluded ⟨a policy of strict ~ in government⟩; *specif* : a system of social ethics based upon a doctrine that ethical standards and conduct should be determined exclusively with reference to the present life and social well-being without reference to religion

sec·u·lar·ist \-rəst\ *n* -s : one who advocates secularism ⟨the overemphasis by ~s on the scientific —J.L.Teller⟩

²**secularist** \"\ *or* **sec·u·lar·is·tic** \¦==¦ristik, -tēk\ *adj* : of, relating to, or advocating secularism ⟨every philosophy of life is either religious or ~ —Walter Moberly⟩ ⟨the ~ basis of humanism⟩ ⟨that we not transfer our loyalties to hidden ~ presuppositions —J.A.Pike⟩

sec·u·lar·i·ty \,sekyə'larəd·ē, -rətē, -i *also* -'ler-\ *n* -ES [ML *saecularitat-, saecularitas*, fr. LL *saecularis* secular, worldly, pagan + L *-tat-, -tas* -ty — more at SECULAR] **1** : something secular ⟨shunning all *secularities* on the Sabbath⟩ **2** : the quality or state of being secular ⟨prompts them to stress a denominational catholicity if not a candid ~ —W.L.Sperry⟩

sec·u·lar·iza·tion \,sekyələrə'zāshən, -,rī'z-\ *n* -s [F *sécularisation*, fr. MF *secularisation*, fr. *seculariser* + *-ation*] : the act or process of secularizing : the condition of being secularized ⟨demands for ~ of the schools⟩ ⟨the increasing ~ of our culture⟩ — contrasted with *sanctification*

sec·u·lar·ize \'sekyələ,rīz\ *vt* -ED/-ING/-S [F *séculariser*, fr. MF *seculariser*, fr. LL *saecularis* secular, worldly, pagan + MF *-iser* -ize] **1** : to make secular ⟨those centuries *secularized* our belief —Max Lerner⟩ **2** : to transfer from ecclesiastical to civil or lay use, possession, or control ⟨the abbey . . . was *secularized* in 1535 —*Times Lit. Supp.*⟩ **3** : to convert to or imbue with secularism ⟨European civilization became *secularized* —Stringfellow Barr⟩

sec·u·lar·ly *adv* [ME *secularelie*, alter. (influenced by LL *saecularis* secular) of *seculerli*, fr. *seculer*, adj., secular + *-li* -ly] : in a secular manner

secular vicar *n* : CLERK VICAR

secund \'sē,kənd, 'se,-\ *adj* [L *secundus* following] : having some part or element arranged on one side only : UNILATERAL ⟨~ racemes⟩

se·cun·der·a·bad \sə'kəndərə¦bad, -bäd\ *adj, usu cap* [fr. *Secunderabad*, city in south central India] : of or from the city of Secunderabad, India : of the kind or style prevalent in Secunderabad

se·cun·di·grav·id \sə¦kəndē¦gravəd\ *adj* [NL *secundigravida*] : pregnant for the second time

se·cun·di·grav·i·da \=,==ʹ=vədə\ *n* -s [NL, fr. *secundi-* (fr. L *secundus* second, following) + L *gravida* pregnant woman — more at SECOND, GRAVIDA] : a woman in her second pregnancy

secun·dines *or* **secon·dines** \'sekən,dīnz, -,dēnz, sə'kəndənz\ *n pl* [pl. of obs. E *secundine, secondine* afterbirth, fr. ME *secundine*, fr. LL *secundinae* (pl.), fr. L *secundus* second, following + *-inae*, fem. pl. of *-inus* -ine] : AFTERBIRTH

se·cun·dip·a·ra \,sekən'dipərə\ *n* -s [NL, fr. *secundi-* (fr. L *secundus*) + *-para*] : a woman who has borne children in two separate pregnancies

sec·un·dip·a·rous \¦==¦dipərəs\ *adj* [*secundipara* + *-ous*] : of or relating to a secundipara

secund·ly *adv* : in a secund manner : UNILATERALLY

se·cun·do·gen·i·ture \sə,kən(,)dō'jenəchə(r)\ *n* [*secundo-* (fr. L *secundus* second, following) + *geniture*] **1** : the right or system by which inheritance belongs to the second son **2** : a property or possession inherited by secundogeniture

se·cun·dum le·gem \sə'kəndəm 'lē,jem\ *adv* [L] : according to law

se·cur·able \sə'kyu̇rəbəl, sē'-\ *adj* : capable of being secured : OBTAINABLE ⟨fellowships ~ by promising college graduates⟩

se·cur·ance \-rən(t)s\ *n* -s : the act of making secure or of assuring : ASSURANCE ⟨guaranties . . . which are the ~ of freedom —Elisha Mulford⟩

¹**se·cure** \-kyu̇(ə)r, -u̇ə\ *adj, sometimes* -ER/-EST [L *securus* free from care, safe, secure, fr. *sed, se* without + *cura* care — more at IDIOT, CURE] **1 a** *archaic* : unwisely free from fear or distrust : CARELESS, OVERCONFIDENT ⟨went up . . . and smote the host: for the host was ~ —Judg 8:11 (AV)⟩ **b** : free from fear, care, or anxiety : easy in mind : CONFIDENT ⟨~ himself . . . he went out of his way to help others —Vance Palmer⟩ ⟨~ in the knowledge that a nurse is there to take over if necessary —Dorothy Barclay⟩ **c** : assured in opinion or expectation : having no doubt ⟨~ in a belief⟩ ⟨grow to feel too ~ in their power —F.L.Mott⟩ **d** *archaic* : confident of a sure or safe prospect : CERTAIN ⟨~ to be as blest as thou canst bear —Alexander Pope⟩ ⟨when she is ~ of him, there will be leisure for falling in love —Jane Austen⟩ **2 a** : free from danger ⟨the feudal lord and his people were no longer ~ behind their fortifications —Tom Wintringham⟩ — often used with *from* or *against* ⟨~ *from* harm⟩ ⟨~ *against* attack⟩ **b** : free from risk of loss ⟨no man's life or fortune was ~ —F.D.Roosevelt⟩ **c** : affording safety : INVIOLABLE ⟨a ~ hideaway⟩ ⟨a ~ telephone line⟩ **d** : TRUSTWORTHY, DEPENDABLE ⟨his judgment on them is not so ~ —Roy Lewis & Angus Maude⟩ ⟨voice under ~ control —John Briggs⟩ **e** : strong, stable, or firm enough to ensure safety : SOLID, UNASSAILABLE ⟨a ~ foundation⟩ ⟨a ~ lock⟩ ⟨made a ~ place for himself in criticism —T.S.Eliot⟩ **3** : capable of being expected or counted on with confidence : ASSURED, SURE ⟨a ~ victory⟩ ⟨~ of an audience that shared his views —C.H.Rickword⟩ **syn** see SAFE

²**secure** \"\ *vb* -ED/-ING/-S *vt* **1** *obs* : to free (as a person) from care, fear, or anxiety ⟨I came *secured* by her promises —Thomas Fuller⟩ **2 a** : to relieve from exposure to danger : make safe : GUARD ⟨labor's efforts to ~ itself —*New Republic*⟩ — often used with *from* or *against* ⟨~ the country from a repetition of the experience —*Irish Digest*⟩ ⟨~ your own countrymen against brutality —Kenneth Roberts⟩ **b** : to shield or make secure (as a military position or movement) from capture, destruction, or hostile interference ⟨for the time being, the beach was *secured* —Irwin Shaw⟩ **3 a** *archaic* : to give certitude to : ASSURE ⟨finds a way . . . to ~ himself of a powerful advocate —William Broome⟩ **b** : to put beyond hazard of losing or of not receiving : GUARANTEE ⟨~ the blessings of liberty to ourselves and our posterity —*U.S. Constitution*⟩ ⟨*securing* that there are no unfilled gaps —*Lancet*⟩ **c (1)** : to give pledge of payment to (a creditor) **(2)** : to give pledge or payment of (an obligation) ⟨~ a note by a pledge of collateral security⟩ **4 a** : to seize and confine (a person) : hold fast : PINION ⟨~ a prisoner with handcuffs⟩ ⟨two redcoats quickly *secured* him —Rex Ingamells⟩ **b** : to make fast : tie down : SEAL ⟨~ a door⟩ ⟨~ the hatches of a ship⟩ ⟨~ a letter with a wax seal⟩ **5** *archaic* **a** : to safeguard against (as an evil or danger) : PREVENT ⟨*securing* false and illegal trade —W.S. Perry⟩ **b** : to divert (a person) from a dangerous course ⟨so I may ~ you from acting with . . . rashness —Sir Walter Scott⟩ **6 a** : to come into secure possession of; *esp* : to acquire as the result of effort : PROCURE ⟨~ employment⟩ ⟨~ cooperation⟩ ⟨~ a confession⟩ ⟨the good and rare things, in most countries *secured* and held by the few —Russell Lord⟩ ⟨*secured* an inside room on one of the largest steamers —David Fairchild⟩ **b** : to bring about : EFFECT, PRODUCE ⟨*secured* his ignominious dismissal —T.J.P.Lever⟩ ⟨we *secured* that they remain for some months —Herbert Hoover⟩ ⟨perfect technique will always ~ a finer performance —Warwick Braithwaite⟩ **7** : to release (naval personnel) from work or duty : DISMISS, EXCUSE ⟨~ unnecessary personnel, partly to make it easier on those who still must stay on duty —E.L. Beach⟩ ~ *vi* **1** *of naval personnel* : to stop work : go off duty : knock off ⟨you may ~ now . . . get yourself some eggs and coffee —Herman Wouk⟩ **2** *of a ship* : to tie up : BERTH ⟨she *secured* alongside —Alan Villiers⟩ **syn** see ENSURE, GET

³**secure** \"\ *n* -s [²*secure*] : a naval signal announcing time to secure

se·cure·ly *adv* : in a secure manner: as **a** *archaic* : without care : TRUSTINGLY ⟨devise not evil against thy neighbor seeing he dwelleth ~ by thee —Prov 3:29 (AV)⟩ **b** : with assurance : SAFELY ⟨she was ~ happy —Ellen Glasgow⟩ ⟨it may ~ be denied —Hilaire Belloc⟩ **c** : without question : CERTAINLY ⟨the shadows of poverty . . . had been ~ dispelled —Osbert Sitwell⟩ **d** : FIRMLY ⟨~ corked⟩ ⟨~ clamped in place⟩ ⟨authority . . . ~ established —B.K.Sandwell⟩

se·cure·ment \-mənt\ *n* -s : the act or process of making secure or of securing: as **a** *obs* : PROTECTION, RELIEF ⟨grew afraid thereof and obtained a ~ from it —Sir Thomas Browne⟩ **b** : ASSURANCE, CERTAINTY ⟨the ~ of maximal clinical control of the . . . infection —*Ciba Clinical Symposia*⟩ **c** : PROCUREMENT ⟨the ~ of an efficient body of public servants —F.W. Taussig⟩

se·cure·ness *n* -ES *archaic* : carefree lack of fear or distrust : TRUSTFULNESS ⟨you think all well; this may be not assurance but ~ —Thomas Adams⟩

se·cu·rif·era \,sekyə'rifərə\ [NL, fr. L *securis* ax, hatchet (fr. *secare* to cut) + *-fera*, neut. pl. of *-fer* -ferous — more at SAW] *syn of* SERRIFERA

¹**se·cu·ri·ty** \sə'kyu̇rəd·ē, sē'-, -rətē, -i\ *n* -ES *often attrib* [ME *securite*, fr. L *securitat-, securitas*, fr. *securus* free from care, safe, secure + *-itat-, -itas* -ity] **1** : the quality or state of being secure: as **a** : freedom from danger : SAFETY ⟨~ from famine⟩ ⟨~ against aggression⟩ ⟨everyone has the right to life, liberty and ~ of person —*U.N. Declaration of Human Rights*⟩ ⟨seeking after the illusion of certainty . . . in the form of a quest for absolute ~ —E.N.Griswold⟩ **b** *archaic* : carefree or cocky overconfidence ⟨~ is mortals' chiefest enemy —Shak.⟩ **c** : freedom from fear, anxiety, or care ⟨this need for ~ dates back into infancy —K.C.Garrison⟩ ⟨~. . . thought of as a harmony between internal needs and the social availability of the means for their satisfaction —W.C.Olson⟩ ⟨my one chance of ~ lies in fixing attention solely on the first chapter —Arnold Bennett⟩ **d (1)** : freedom from uncertainty or doubt : CONFIDENCE, ASSURANCE ⟨knowing she still had the ~ of his faithful devotion —Morley Callaghan⟩ ⟨distinguished by a certain ~ of judgment —J.R.Lowell⟩ **(2)** : sureness of technique ⟨the cellist plays with great ~ but overlooks opportunities to let the sunlight in —Arthur Berger⟩ **e** : basis for confidence : GUARANTEE ⟨the only plan gives us no ~ that we shall get the steam engine —G.B.Shaw⟩ **f** : FIRMNESS ⟨~ of attachment⟩ : DEPENDABILITY, STABILITY ⟨the ~ of a knot⟩ ⟨a moral poise, a ~ of values that is very rare in our age —Irving Howe & Eliezer Greenberg⟩ **2 a** : something given,

deposited, or pledged to make certain the fulfillment of an obligation (as the payment of a debt) **:** property given or serving to make secure the enjoyment or enforcement of a right **:** GUARANTY, PLEDGE ⟨the ~ is poor⟩ **b :** one who becomes surety for another or engages himself for the performance of another's obligation **:** SURETY ⟨was willing to go ~ for his friend⟩ ⟨fined and ordered to find *securities* for good behavior —Edward Jenks⟩ **3 :** a written obligation, evidence, or document of ownership or creditorship (as a stock, bond, note, debenture, or certificate) giving the holder the right to demand and receive property not in his possession ⟨a government ~⟩ ⟨negotiable *securities*⟩; *specif* **:** one issued to investors to finance a business enterprise **4 :** something that secures **:** DEFENSE, PROTECTION, GUARD ⟨their one source of ~ in a glowering alien climate —A.R.Marcus⟩: as **a :** measures taken (as by a military unit) to ensure against surprise attack ⟨the battalion . . . set up ~ —Walter Bernstein⟩ **b :** measures taken (as by a national government or a governmental unit) to guard against espionage, observation, sabotage, and surprise ⟨~ prevents the reporting of actual production figures —*New Republic*⟩ **c :** protection against economic vicissitudes ⟨government guarantees for old age ~ —T.W.Arnold⟩ ⟨the very heavy emphasis that younger men are now placing on . . . ~ —*Fortune*⟩ **d :** penal custody ⟨the new prison system . . . provides for the care of offenders on the basis of classification as to custody (maximum, medium, and minimum ~) —C.E.Johnson⟩ **5 :** the resistance of a cryptogram to cryptanalysis measured usu. by the time and effort needed to solve it

²security \"\ — an international radiotelephone signal word introducing a safety message

security analysis *n* **:** the work or procedures of the security analyst

security analyst *n* **:** one that studies elements of value and factors affecting future value of securities to appraise their worth in relation to their price

security for costs : an undertaking often required by a court of a nonresident plaintiff to pay the costs of litigation in event of an adverse result

se·cus \ˈsēkəs\ *adv* [L; akin to L *sequi* to follow — more at SUE] *law* **:** to the contrary **:** not so **:** OTHERWISE

secy *abbr* secretary

SED *abbr* skin erythema dose

se·dan \səˈdan, sēˈ-, -aa(ə)n\ *n* -s [origin unknown] **1** *or* **sedan chair a :** a portable chair or covered vehicle for carrying a single person usu. borne on poles by two men **b :** a conveyance borne like a sedan (as a litter or palanquin) **2 a :** an automobile having four or two doors and an enclosed body with permanent top of one compartment seating four to seven persons including the driver **b :** a powerboat having one passenger compartment

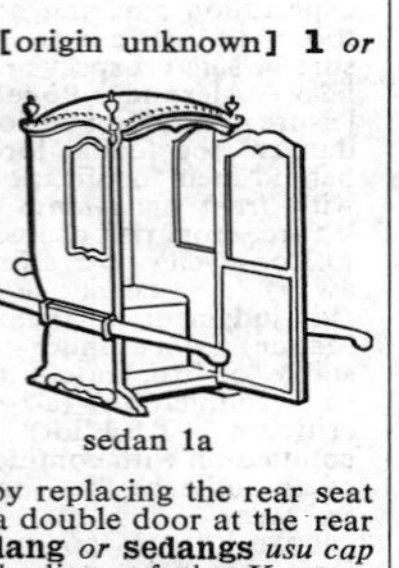

sedan 1a

sedan delivery truck *n* **:** a sedan modified for delivery service by replacing the rear seat and tail section with panel sides and a double door at the rear

se·dang \səˈdaŋ, (ˈ)säˈdäŋ\ *n, pl* **sedang** *or* **sedangs** *usu cap* **1 a :** a people related to the Cambodians of the Kontum plateau in central Vietnam **b :** a member of the Sedang people **2 :** the Mon-Khmer language of the Sedang people

sedan landaulet *n* **:** an automobile body similar to the sedan except that the top behind the rear doors is collapsible

sedan limousine *n* **:** a sedan with an adjustable partition behind the front seat

sedarim *pl of* SEDER

¹se·date \səˈdāt, sēˈ-, *usu* -ād.+V\ *adj, usu* -ER/-EST [L *sedatus*, fr. past part. of *sedare* to settle, calm, soothe, appease, caus. of *sedēre* to sit — more at SIT] **1 a :** uninfluenced or not liable to influence by disturbing elements **:** QUIET, DISPASSIONATE ⟨a balance so calm and ~ as to exclude rapture —John Dewey⟩ **b :** of a staid, sober, or grave nature or constitution ⟨the more ~ winter settlers who find antic youth somewhat less attractive than their rocking-chair companions —C.L. Biemiller⟩ **2 :** characteristic of or suitable to sedate persons **:** placid or unobtrusive in appearance or nature ⟨in their ~ beauty of ruby and brown, the trees stretched ahead —T.B. Costain⟩ ⟨a sober brown cover, broken only by a ~ listing of its table of contents —J.D.Adams⟩ **syn** see SERIOUS

²sedate \"\ *vt* -ED/-ING/-S [back-formation fr. *sedative*] **:** to put (a patient) under the influence of a sedative drug

se·date·ly *adv* **:** in a sedate manner

se·date·ness *n* -ES **:** the quality or state of being sedate

se·da·tion \sēˈdāshən, səˈ-\ *n* -s [MF or L; MF *sedation*, fr. L *sedation-, sedatio*, fr. *sedatus* (past part. of *sedare* to calm) + *-ion-, -io* -ion] **1 :** the inducing of a relaxed easy state esp. by the use of sedatives **2 :** a state resulting from or like that resulting from sedation

¹sed·a·tive \ˈsedəd·iv, -ətiv\ *adj* [F or ML; F *sédatif*, fr. ML *sedativus*, fr. L *sedatus* (past part. of *sedare* to calm) + *-ivus* -ive — more at SEDATE] **:** tending to calm, moderate, or tranquilize; *specif* **:** allaying irritability, nervousness, or excitement

²sedative \"\ *n* -s **:** a sedative agent; *specif* **:** a drug that allays irritability, nervousness, or excitement

sedative salt *n* **:** BORIC ACID

se·dens \ˈsē,denz\ *n, pl* **se·den·tes** \səˈden,tēz\ [NL *sedent-, sedens*, fr. L, pres. part. of *sedēre* to sit] **:** a person who remains a resident of the place or region of his birth — compare NOMAD, MIGRANT

se·dent \ˈsēdᵊnt\ *adj* [L *sedent-, sedens*, pres. part. of *sedēre* to sit — more at SIT] **:** SITTING — used esp. of a statue

sed·en·tar·ia \,sedᵊnˈta(a)rēə\ *n pl, cap* [NL, fr. L, neut. pl. of *sedentarius* sedentary] *in some classifications* **:** a division of Polychaeta comprising sedentary usu. tube-dwelling worms with reduced parapodia and sense organs and typically with highly developed filamentous anterior respiratory organs or gills — compare ERRANTIA, SABELLARIA

sed·en·tar·i·ae \-ē,ē\ *n pl, cap* [NL, fr. L, fem. pl. of *sedentarius* sedentary] *in former classifications* **:** a group including sedentary web-spinning spiders that wait for their prey to become entangled in their snares

sed·en·tar·i·ly \ˌsedᵊnˈterəlē\ *adv* **:** in a sedentary manner

sed·en·tar·i·ness \ˈ==,terēnəs\ *n* -ES **:** the quality or state of being sedentary

sed·en·tary \-rē, -ri\ *adj* [MF *sedentaire*, fr. L *sedentarius* of one that sits, sedentary, fr. *sedent-, sedens* (pres. part. of *sedēre* to sit) + *-arius* -ary — more at SIT] **1 a :** staying in one or the same place **:** not migratory **:** STATIONARY, SETTLED ⟨~ birds⟩ ⟨a ~ tribe⟩ **b :** of, relating to, or characteristic of sedentes ⟨~ culture⟩ **c** *usu cap* **:** of or belonging to a period of development of the Hohokam culture about A.D. 900 to 1000 that precedes the Classic and is characterized by settled villages **2 a :** characterized by or requiring sitting or slight activity ⟨for ~ relaxation he is likely to listen to music —*Current Biog.*⟩ **b :** accustomed to sit much or long ⟨we think of the lawyer, teacher, and bookkeeper as ~ —L.A.Sylvester⟩ **c** *obs* **:** LAZY, INACTIVE **3 :** permanently attached ⟨the ~ oyster⟩ ⟨~ barnacles⟩

sedentary soil *n* **:** soil remaining on the rock from which it has developed

sed·en·ta·tion \,sedᵊnˈtāshən\ *n* -s [L or NL *sedent-, sedens* + E *-ation*] **:** the adoption of a sedentary mode of life or practices of sedentes

se·der \ˈsādə(r)\ *n, pl* **se·da·rim** \səˈdärəm\ *or* **seders** *often cap* [Heb *sēdher* order, division] **:** a Jewish home or community service and ceremonial dinner held on the first evening of the Passover and repeated on the second by Orthodox Jews except in Israel commemorating chiefly the exodus from Egypt

se·de·runt \səˈdirənt\ *n* -s [L, there sat (the following), 3d pl. perf. indic. of *sedēre* to sit, word used to introduce list of those attending a session — more at SIT] **1 a :** a session of an ecclesiastical assembly or other official body **b :** the persons or a list of persons present at a sederunt **2 :** a prolonged sitting (as for relaxation, reading, or discussion) ⟨the seat under the vine trellis where they had been having their evening ~ —John Buchan⟩

¹sedge \ˈsej\ *n* -s [ME *segge*, fr. OE *secg*; akin to MHG *segge* sedge, OE *sagu, sage* saw — more at SAW] **1 a :** a plant of the family Cyperaceae and esp. of the genus *Carex* **b :** SWEET FLAG **c :** YELLOW IRIS **2 a :** any of the caddis flies common along trout streams **b :** an artificial fly imitating a caddis fly **3 :** a grayish brown that is lighter than chestnut, lighter and slightly redder than coconut, and redder and slightly lighter than new cocoa — called also *beach tan, cashew nut, winter leaf*

²sedge *var of* SIEGE

sedge family *n* **:** CYPERACEAE

sedge fly *n* **:** any of several mayflies or caddis flies

sedge grass *n* **1 :** SWEET FLAG **2 :** a broom sedge (*Andropogon virginicus*)

sedge hen *n* **:** CLAPPER RAIL

sedgelike \ˈ=,=\ *adj* **:** resembling or suggesting sedge

sedge root *n* **:** an edible-rooted sedge; *esp* **:** CHUFA

sedge warbler *also* **sedge bird** *or* **sedge wren** *n* **:** a small warbler (*Acrocephalus schoenobaenus*) that breeds among reeds and sedges in Europe and Asia and winters in Africa, is rusty brownish above with dark centers to the feathers and buffy white below, and has a loud sweet song

sedgy \ˈsejē\ *adj* -ER/-EST [¹*sedge* + *-y*] **1 :** of, relating to, or like sedge **2 :** overgrown or bordered with sedge ⟨drainage and steam power have turned ~ marshes into farm and meadow —J.R.Green⟩

se·di·le \səˈdīlē\ *n, pl* **sedil·ia** \-ˈdilēə\ [L, seat, fr. *sedēre* to sit] **:** one of usu. three seats in the chancel of a church near the altar used by officiating clergy during intervals of a service and in an English church usu. placed in a recess in the south wall

¹sed·i·ment \ˈsedəmənt\ *n* -s [MF, fr. L *sedimentum* settling, subsidence, fr. *sedēre* to sit, sink down + *-mentum* -ment — more at SIT] **1 :** the matter that settles to the bottom of a liquid **:** SETTLINGS, LEES, DREGS, FOOTS **2 :** material or a mass of material deposited (as by water, wind, or glaciers)

²sediment \"\ *vb* -ED/-ING/-S *vt* **:** to deposit as sediment ~ *vi* **1 :** to settle to the bottom in a liquid **2 :** to deposit sediment

sed·i·men·tal \ˌsedəˈmentᵊl\ *adj* [¹*sediment* + *-al*] **:** formed of or from sediment

sed·i·men·tar·i·ly \ˌsedəmən·ˈterəlē\ *adv* **:** in a sedimentary manner

¹sed·i·men·ta·ry \ˌsedəˈmentərē, -ntrē, -ri\ *adj* [¹*sediment* + *-ary*] **1 :** of, relating to, or containing sediment ⟨~ deposits⟩ **2 :** formed by or from deposits of sediment ⟨~ clay⟩

²sedimentary \"\ *n* -ES **:** a sedimentary deposit, rock, or formation

sedimentary rock *n* **:** rock formed of mechanical, chemical, or organic sediment: as **a :** clastic rock (as conglomerate, sandstone, or shale) formed of fragments of other rock transported from its source and deposited in water **b :** rock (as rock salt or gypsum) formed by precipitation from solution **c :** rock (as limestone) formed from secretions of organisms

sed·i·men·tate \ˈsedəmən·,tāt, ,sedəˈmen-\ *vt* -ED/-ING/-S [back-formation fr. *sedimentation*] **:** to cause (as sewage) to deposit sediment

sed·i·men·ta·tion \,sedəmən·ˈtāshən\ *n* -s [¹*sediment* + *-ation*] **:** the action or process of depositing sediment **:** SETTLING; *also* **:** the depositing esp. by mechanical means of matter suspended in a liquid ⟨the ~ of a water supply⟩; *broadly* **:** the movement in any direction of solid particles through a fluid as a result of gravitational or other force — compare CREAMING

sed·i·men·ta·tion·ist \-sh(ə)nəst\ *n* -s **:** one who investigates sedimentation or studies sedimentary processes

sedimentation rate *n* **:** the speed at which red blood cells settle to the bottom of a column of citrated blood and which is used esp. in diagnosing the progress of various abnormal conditions (as chronic infections)

sediment bulb *n* **:** a bulb retaining sediment separated by gravity from liquid in a tank

sed·i·men·to·log·i·cal \ˌsedəˌmentᵊlˈäjəkəl\ *adj* **:** of or relating to sedimentology

sed·i·men·tol·o·gist \,sedəmən·ˈtäləjəst\ *n* -s [*sedimentology* + *-ist*] **:** SEDIMENTATIONIST

sed·i·men·tol·o·gy \-jē\ *n* -ES [¹*sediment* + *-o-* + *-logy*] **:** the description, classification, and interpretation of sediments

se·di·tion \səˈdishən, sēˈ-\ *n* -s [ME, fr. MF, fr. L *sedition-, seditio* civil discord, faction, lit., separation, fr. *sed-, se-* apart (fr. *sed, se* without) + *ition-, itio* act of going, fr. *itus* (past part. of *ire* to go) + *-ion-, -io* -ion — more at IDIOT, ISSUE] **1 :** an insurrection against constituted authority **:** a tumult caused by dissension, partisan hatred, or discontent ⟨by reason of inequalities, cities are filled with ~ —Benjamin Jowett⟩ **2 :** conduct consisting of speaking, writing, or acting against an established government or seeking to overthrow it by unlawful means **:** resistance to lawful authority **:** conduct tending to treason but without an overt act

se·di·tion·ary \-shə,nerē\ *n* -ES [LL *seditionarius* rebel, revolutionary, fr. L *sedition-, seditio* sedition + *-arius* -ary] **:** an inciter or promoter of sedition

se·di·tion·ist \-sh(ə)nəst\ *n* -s [*sedition* + *-ist*] **:** SEDITIONARY

se·di·tious \-shəs\ *adj* [ME, fr. MF *seditieux*, fr. L *seditiosus*, fr. *seditio* sedition + *-osus* -ous] **1 :** disposed to arouse or take part in or guilty of sedition **:** FACTIOUS, TURBULENT ⟨a ~ agitator⟩ **2 :** of, relating to, of the nature of, or tending to excite sedition ⟨the punishment of ~ utterances —J.L.O'Brian⟩ **syn** see INSUBORDINATE

se·dja·deh \səˈjädə\ *n* -s [Turk *seccade*, fr. Ar *sajjādah*, fr. *sajada* to kneel] **:** a small Oriental rug about four feet by six feet

se·do·heptose \ˌsēdō+\ *n* [NL *Sedum* + *-o-* + E *heptose*] **:** SEDOHEPTULOSE

se·do·heptulose \"+\ *n* [NL *Sedum* + *-o-* + E *heptulose*] **:** an amorphous ketose sugar $HOCH_2(CHOH)_4COCH_2OH$ of the heptose class that is obtained esp. from the leaves and stems of various stonecrops (as *Sedum spectabile*), that plays a role in carbohydrate metabolism but is not fermented by yeast, and that is a laboratory source of D-altrose and D-ribose — called also *altro-heptulose*

sedra *var of* SIDRA

se·duce \səˈd(y)üs, sēˈ-\ *vt* -ED/-ING/-S [L *seducere* to lead aside, lead away, fr. *se-* apart (fr. *sed, se* without) + *ducere* to lead — more at IDIOT, TOW] **1 :** to persuade into disobedience, disloyalty, or desertion ⟨pleaded guilty . . . to the charge of endeavoring to ~ a member of his Majesty's forces from his duty of allegiance —*Manchester Guardian Weekly*⟩ **2 :** to persuade or entice astray in action or belief ⟨employers have tried to ~ union leaders with rewards of money or advancement —Ed Marciniak⟩ ⟨abstract thoughts . . . ~ his mind away from essential experience —J.W.Aldridge⟩ **3 :** to persuade or entice into partnership in sexual intercourse **:** practice seduction upon; *specif* **:** to persuade (a female) to have sexual intercourse for the first time **4 :** to induce or force to come or go ⟨staircases which ~ us upwards to no successful result —Nathaniel Hawthorne⟩ **5 :** to attract or gain by or as if by quiet subtle charm **:** COAX ⟨trying to ~ her back to health with their futile offerings of plums and tangerines —Jean Stafford⟩ ⟨knew how to ~ the interest of his pupils; he did not drive, he led —L.K.Anspacher⟩ ⟨a composer who *seduced* new sounds out of the piano —*Time*⟩ **syn** see LURE

se·duc·ee \səˌd(y)üˈsē\ *n* -s [*seduce* + *-ee*] **:** one who is seduced

se·duce·ment \səˈd(y)üsmənt, sēˈ-\ *n* -s [*seduce* + *-ment*] **1 :** SEDUCTION **2** *obs* **:** the quality or state of being seduced **3 :** something that serves to seduce **:** a seductive temptation **:** ENTICEMENT

se·duc·er \-sə(r)\ *n* -s **:** one that seduces; *specif* **:** one that induces a female to surrender her chastity

se·duc·i·ble *also* **se·duce·able** \-səbəl\ *adj* [*seducible* fr. LL *seducibilis*, fr. *seducere* to seduce (fr. L, to lead aside, lead away) + L *-ibilis* -ible; *seduceable* fr. *seduce* + *-able*] **:** capable of being seduced

se·duc·ing·ly *adv* [*seducing* (fr. pres. part. of *seduce*) + *-ly*] **:** in a seductive manner

se·duc·tion \səˈdəkshən, sēˈ-\ *n* -s [MF, fr. LL *seduction-, seductio*, fr. L, act of leading aside, fr. *seductus* (past part. of *seducere* to lead aside) + *-ion-, -io* -ion] **1 :** the act of seducing esp. to wrong acts or beliefs ⟨the effect of social ~ by public spectacles on an immature mind —Fredric Wertham⟩; *specif* **:** the enticement of a female by some statutes required to be then chaste to unlawful sexual intercourse by promise of marriage or other means of persuasion without use of force **2 :** that which seduces or is adapted to seduce **:** a means of corrupting **3 :** something that entices or influences by attraction or charm ⟨the irresistible ~ of eloquence and literary pursuits —Norman Douglas⟩ ⟨the home carpenter usually succumbs to the ~*s* of the tool catalogs and buys an assortment of power tools —M.I.Zisowitz⟩

se·duc·tive \-ktiv, -tēv *also* -təv\ *adj* [ML, fr. *seductus* (past part. of *seducere* to seduce, fr. L, to lead aside) + L *-ivus* -ive — more at SEDUCE] **:** tending or having the qualities to seduce **:** ALLURING, TEMPTING, ATTRACTIVE ⟨an exceptionally beautiful and ~ woman —*N.Y. Times Bk. Rev.*⟩ ⟨the ~ temptations of a policy of opposition for the sake of opposition —J.G.Colton⟩ — **se·duc·tive·ly** \-təvlē, -li\ *adv* — **se·duc·tive·ness** \-tivnəs, -tēv- *also* -təv-\ *n* -ES

se·duc·tress \-ktrəs\ *n* -ES [fem. of obs. *seductor* male seducer, fr. LL, fr. *seductus* (past part. of *seducere* to seduce, fr. L, to lead aside) + L *-or*] **:** a female seducer

se·du·li·ty \səˈd(y)üləd·ē\ *n* -ES [L *sedulitat-, sedulitas*, fr. *sedulus* sedulous + *-itat-, -itas* -ity] **:** sedulous activity **:** DILIGENCE, INDUSTRY

sed·u·lous \ˈsejələs\ *adj* [L *sedulus* diligent, fr. *sedulo* sincerely, on purpose, diligently, fr. *se* without + *dolus* guile, fraud, deceit — more at IDIOT, TALE] **1 :** marked by or accomplished with care and perseverance ⟨his products had . . . the mark of a ~ craftsmanship —H.E.Clurman⟩ ⟨the ~ evasion of racial issues —Oscar Handlin⟩ **2 :** diligent in application or pursuit **:** persevering in endeavors to effect an object **:** steadily industrious ⟨the notes of the great man are gathered together by a ~ devotee —Irwin Edman⟩ **syn** see BUSY

sed·u·lous·ly *adv* **:** in a sedulous manner

sed·u·lous·ness *n* -ES **:** the quality or state of being sedulous

se·dum \ˈsēdəm\ *n* [NL, fr. L, houseleek] **1** *cap* **:** a genus of fleshy widely distributed herbs (family Crassulaceae) having cymose yellow, white, or pink flowers, pellicular fruit, and often tufted stems — see ORPINE, STONECROP **2** -s **:** any plant of the genus *Sedum*

¹see \ˈsē\ *vb* **saw** \ˈsȯ\ *or substand* **seed** \ˈsēd\ *or* **seen** \ˈsēn\ **seen** *or substand* **seed** *or* **saw**; **seeing**; **sees** \ˈsēz\ [ME *seen, sen*, fr. OE *sēon*; akin to OHG *sehan* to see, ON *sjā*, Goth *saihwan*, OE *secgan* to say — more at SAY] *vt* **1 a :** to perceive by the eye **:** apprehend through sight ⟨opens his eyes to ~ the sunlight coming in through the window⟩ **b :** to perceive as if by sight ⟨it was wonderful what that boy *saw* who was blind —Stuart Cloete⟩ **c :** to detect the presence of ⟨the supersonic streamlining of this vehicle makes it difficult to ~ by radar —L.N.Ridenour⟩ **2 a :** to have experience of **:** UNDERGO ⟨*saw* sea duty on a minesweeper —*Current Biog.*⟩ ⟨if anyone keeps my word, he will never ~ death —Jn 8:51 (RSV)⟩ ⟨opening for keen, practical, final year student to ~ dairy cattle and small-animal practice —*Veterinary Record*⟩ ⟨*seen* better days⟩ ⟨~ life⟩ **b :** to learn or find by observation or experience **:** come to know **:** DISCOVER ⟨a point of view which I have since *seen* cause to modify —John Buchan⟩ **c :** to find out by investigation **:** ASCERTAIN ⟨~ if the hat fits⟩ ⟨~ if the car needs oil⟩ ⟨~ who's at the door⟩ **d :** to give rise to **:** be marked by ⟨the late glacial times *saw* the complete triumph of our ancestral stock —Jacquetta & Christopher Hawkes⟩ **e :** to serve as the setting for **:** be the scene of **:** WITNESS ⟨that house *saw* more worry and unhappiness —Virginia D. Dawson & Betty D. Wilson⟩ **3 a :** to form a mental picture of **:** VISUALIZE ⟨can still ~ her as she was twenty years ago⟩ ⟨*saw* her in his dreams⟩ **b :** to perceive the meaning or importance of **:** COMPREHEND, UNDERSTAND ⟨because the frontier gives shape and life to our national myth, we have preferred to ~ its story in romantic outline —Dayton Kohler⟩ **c :** to be aware of **:** RECOGNIZE ⟨planning to fire you tomorrow, because you just can't ~ a good news story —Sinclair Lewis⟩ ⟨~*s* the folly of further resistance —T.B.Costain⟩ ⟨~*s* only his faults⟩ **d :** to form a conception of **:** imagine as a possibility **:** SUPPOSE ⟨can you ~ me knowing how to furnish a house —Edith Sitwell⟩ ⟨was never whipped . . . she was so dignified and superior you just couldn't ~ her across my mother's lap —Myron Brinig⟩ **e :** to have presented for observation or consideration **:** be made aware of ⟨we *saw*, in the previous lecture, how the problem arose⟩ **f :** to look at from a particular point of view ⟨~ ourselves as others see us —Robert Burns⟩ **g :** to look ahead to **:** FORESEE ⟨can ~ the day when a college will not try to cover the whole field of liberal arts —*Time*⟩ **4 a :** to direct one's attention to **:** put under observation **:** EXAMINE, SCRUTINIZE ⟨want to ~ how he handles the problem⟩ **b** (1) **:** to inspect or read understandingly (something written or printed) ⟨have you *seen* the story of yesterday's game⟩ ⟨let me ~ your pass, soldier⟩ ⟨*seen* and allowed⟩ (2) **:** to read of ⟨I *saw* your appointment in the newspapers⟩ **c :** to refer to ⟨for further information, ~ the documents printed in the appendix⟩ ⟨~ the explanatory notes at the beginning of the book⟩ **d :** to attend or visit as an observer or spectator ⟨~ a parade⟩ ⟨~ a play⟩ ⟨~ the sights of the city⟩ **5 a :** to take care of **:** provide for ⟨would like him to have enough to ~ him easily to the end of his days —T.B.Costain⟩ **b :** to take care or heed **:** make sure ⟨~ thou say nothing to any man —Mk 1:44 (AV)⟩ ⟨~ that your wet umbrella is not placed between your seat and the next —Agnes M. Miall⟩ ⟨will ~ that he is brought up properly⟩ **6 a :** to regard as **:** CONSIDER, JUDGE ⟨the electorate did not ~ fit to ratify the new frame of government —B.W.Bond⟩ ⟨did not ~ it right to ask for special favors⟩ **b :** to prefer to have **:** allow to happen **:** WELCOME ⟨would probably ~ himself shot before he told a deliberate falsehood —J.G.Cozzens⟩ ⟨I'll ~ you dead before I accept your terms⟩ **c :** to regard with approval or liking **:** find acceptable or attractive ⟨still can't ~ the portholes but this is our only complaint in an otherwise clean design —Walt Woron⟩ ⟨hope you'll be able to make her ~ it —W.S.Maugham⟩ ⟨can't understand what he ~*s* in her⟩ **7 a** (1) **:** to make a call upon **:** VISIT ⟨stopped off at the office to ~ his former employer⟩ (2) **:** to call upon or meet with in order to obtain help or advice ⟨~ a doctor⟩ ⟨~ a lawyer⟩ **b** (1) **:** to be in the company of regularly or frequently esp. in courtship or dating ⟨had been ~*ing* each other for a year before they became engaged⟩ (2) **:** to grant an interview to or accept the visit of **:** meet with **:** RECEIVE ⟨the president of the bank will ~ you in a few minutes⟩ ⟨~*s* only a few old friends these days⟩ (3) **:** to meet with for the purpose of influencing esp. by bribery or pressure ⟨charged that the witness had been *seen* by the defense⟩ **8 a :** ACCOMPANY, ESCORT ⟨young men would wait to ~ the young ladies home —Agnes S. Turnbull⟩ **b :** to wait upon **:** be present with ⟨*saw* her onto the plane⟩ ⟨*saw* him off at the station⟩ **c :** to give continued attention, assistance, or guidance to — used with *through* ⟨*saw* a new edition of his book through the press⟩ ⟨the sympathy of his friends *saw* him through this period of grief⟩ **9 :** to meet (a bet) in poker or to equal the bet of (a player) **:** CALL ~ *vi* **1 a :** to give or pay attention ⟨~, the train is coming⟩ **b :** to look about ⟨stood up and fired his pistol in the air, and the naked Indians came out on the shore to ~ —Meridel Le Sueur⟩ **2 a :** to have the power of sight **:** have vision ⟨whereas I was blind, now I ~ —Jn 9:25 (AV)⟩ ⟨he ~*s* poorly with his left eye⟩ **b :** to apprehend objects by sight ⟨it was so foggy that he could hardly ~⟩ **c :** to perceive objects as if by sight ⟨the butterfly lightness that was teaching his fingers to ~ —Marcia Davenport⟩ **3 a :** to grasp something mentally **:** have insight **:** UNDERSTAND ⟨this fundamental bias of all thinking . . . is what enables us to ~, gives thought its real use —H.J.Muller⟩ **b :** to take note ⟨these aren't ordinary trout, you ~ —Corey Ford⟩ **c :** CONSIDER, THINK ⟨when can I finish this — let me ~⟩ **4 a :** to make investigation or inquiry ⟨you'll ~ about the rates, won't you —Agnes S. Turnbull⟩ **b :** to arrive at a conclusion through observation and experience ⟨I can't give you an answer yet, but we shall ~⟩

syn BEHOLD, DESCRY, ESPY, VIEW, SURVEY, OBSERVE, NOTICE, REMARK, NOTE, PERCEIVE, DISCERN: SEE is broad and general and may stand for any of the other words here ⟨I *see* you⟩ ⟨I *see* it⟩ BEHOLD may be used in situations involving awe, grandeur, or dignity, with suggestions of observant, complete vision ⟨it was on a dreary night of November that I *beheld* the accomplishment of my toils —Mary W. Shelley⟩ ⟨Grecian spectators . . . when they *beheld* the innumerable Persian host

crossing the Hellespont —George Grote⟩ DESCRY may suggest watchful, careful scanning and observation of the distant or the difficult to view ⟨on a superb day he can *descry* Greenwich, 28 miles away —*New Yorker*⟩ ESPY is similar in suggestion to DESCRY but is more likely to be used to refer to the obscure or covert ⟨flowers we *espy* beside the torrent growing, flowers that peep forth from many a cleft and chink —William Wordsworth⟩ ⟨on these analogies it is not altogether fantastic to *espy* . . . the ghost of a Minoan universal church —A.J. Toynbee⟩ VIEW may designate an overall or comprehensive looking at a subject, often from a specific or particular position or in a specific or peculiar way ⟨the little chapel . . . the white dove . . . green tufted islands . . . the youth had long been *viewing* these pleasant things —John Keats⟩ ⟨the effort is an interesting one if you *view* it in terms of the techniques of political symbolism —Max Lerner⟩ SURVEY, in this sense, may be used in reference to a broad view from a high point or may designate a comprehensive examination of a subject with careful consideration of its salient points ⟨am monarch of all I *survey* —William Cowper⟩ ⟨had plenty of leisure now, day in, day out, to *survey* her life as a tract of country traversed —Victoria Sackville-West⟩ OBSERVE may suggest careful, heedful attention directed and sustained ⟨a genuine scientific process — the play of intellect and imagination around a few fragments of *observed* fact —Havelock Ellis⟩ ⟨the Navy is *observing* the new programs in the Army and Air Force with interest —*Atlantic*⟩ NOTICE may suggest careful observation and intention to record or remember ⟨if we tried to *notice* all the ways in which the idea of beauty has been corrupted —Irving Babbitt⟩ REMARK and NOTE mean to see or sense and to record or make a mental note ⟨I *remarked* their English accents —James Joyce⟩ ⟨believed that the artist should not number the streaks of the tulip but should *remark* general properties and large appearances —F.W.Hilles⟩ ⟨in these brilliant and gifted inhabitants . . . one may *note* a number of characteristics —Geoffrey Bruun⟩ ⟨writers are perhaps the best of travelers, since their sharpened senses seize and *note* impressions —F.B.Millett⟩ PERCEIVE may combine the notions of seeing or sensing and of recognizing and realizing ⟨his lightning dashes from image to image, so quick that we are unable at first to *perceive* the points of contact —C.D.Lewis⟩ ⟨what a great novelist at his best *perceives* in human nature —Bernard De Voto⟩ DISCERN may apply to seeing or perceiving identities or differences which are not immediately obvious ⟨never for a moment *discerned* that there was in him anything out of the ordinary —W.S.Maugham⟩

syn SEE, LOOK, and WATCH can all mean to perceive something by means of the eyes. SEE stresses the reception of the visual impression ⟨*see* clearly with a telescope⟩ ⟨have the power of *seeing*⟩ LOOK stresses the directing of the eyes to something in order to see ⟨*look* and see the man leave⟩ ⟨turn suddenly to *look* at the man⟩ WATCH implies a persistent observing or the following of something with the eyes in order to observe fully ⟨*watch* what a child is up to⟩ ⟨a cat *watching* a mouse⟩ — **see about 1 :** to attend to ⟨I'll *see about* parking if you buy the tickets⟩ **2 :** to think over before deciding ⟨we can't give you an answer now, but we'll *see about* it⟩ — **see after :** to attend to or care for ⟨*see after* the baggage⟩ ⟨*see after* the baby⟩ — **see daylight 1 :** to get over the initial difficulties of a problem or undertaking ⟨after five years of trying, he began to *see daylight*⟩ **2** *slang, of a bronco rider* **:** to bounce high in the saddle so that daylight can be seen between the rider and the saddle — **see for** *dial chiefly Eng* **:** to look for — **see one's way :** to find a course of action possible or reasonable ⟨think I can *see my way* to lending you 10 dollars⟩ — **see red :** to become enraged **:** lose control of oneself ⟨has an insulting manner that makes others *see red*⟩ — **see the elephant** *slang* **:** to gain experience of the world — **see through :** to see the true meaning, nature, or character of ⟨pride themselves on *seeing through* the motives of politicians —*Times Lit. Supp.*⟩ ⟨we have *seen through* the environment theory as we *saw through* the race theory —A.J.Toynbee⟩ — **see to :** to take care of **:** attend to ⟨*saw to* the education of the children —Nancy Mitford⟩ — **see to it :** to make certain by taking necessary or appropriate action ⟨*saw to it* that the men in the armed services received higher pay —*Current Biog.*⟩

²see \"\ *n* -s [ME *se, see,* fr. OF *se, sed, sie* seat, throne, see, fr. L *sedes* seat; akin to L *sedēre* to sit — more at SIT] **1 a** *archaic* **:** CATHEDRA **b :** a church containing a cathedra **:** CATHEDRAL **c :** a seat or center of the power or authority of a bishop **:** a diocesan center **2 a :** the rank, office, power, or authority of a bishop ⟨the ~ of Rome⟩ **b :** the jurisdiction (as a diocese or province) of a bishop

see·able \'sēəbəl\ *adj* [ME *seable,* fr. *seen, sen* to see + *-able*] **:** capable of being seen

see·beck effect \zā,bek-, 'sē,bek-\ *n, usu cap S* [after Thomas J. *Seebeck* †1831 Ger. physicist] **:** the thermoelectromotive force generated in a circuit composed of different metals in successive contact when the junctions are not all at the same temperature; *also* **:** the current resulting from such force when the circuit is closed

see·catch \'sē,kach\ *n, pl* **see·catch·ie** \-chē\ [Russ *sekach*] **:** a grown male Alaskan fur seal

see·chelt *also* **se·chelt** \'sē,shelt\ *n, pl* **seechelt** *or* **seechelts** *usu cap* **1 a :** a Salishan people of southwestern British Columbia **b :** a member of such people **2 :** the language of the Seechelt people

¹seed \'sēd\ *n, pl* **seed** *or* **seeds** [ME *seed, sed,* fr. OE *sǣd;* akin to OHG *sāt* seed, ON *sāth,* Goth *manaseths* seed of men, world, OE *sāwan* to sow — more at SOW] **1 a :** something that is sown or to be sown ⟨as he sowed, some ~ fell along the path and the birds came and devoured it —Mk 4:4 (RSV)⟩ **b :** the fertilized and ripened ovule of a seed plant comprising a miniature plant usu. accompanied by a supply of food (as endosperm or perisperm), enclosed in a protective seed coat, often accompanied by auxiliary structures (as an aril or caruncle), and capable under suitable conditions of independent development into a plant similar to the one that produced it — see ENDOCARP illustration **c :** a propagative portion of a plant: as (1) **:** SPORE (2) **:** a dry seedlike fruit (as a caryopsis or seedball) (3) **:** a vegetative reproductive structure (as a bulb, corm, or tuber) **d** (1) **:** MILT, SEMEN, SPERM (2) **:** any of various eggs esp. of insects or other arthropods (3) **:** any of various developmental stages of lower animals suitable for transplanting; *specif* **:** SPAT **e :** the condition or stage of bearing seed ⟨in ~⟩ **2 :** PROGENY ⟨the green turban which proclaimed him to be of the ~ of the Prophet —Lawrence Durrell⟩ **3 :** something from which development or growth takes place **:** a beginning or source **:** GERM ⟨planted a ~ of suspicion in me, which by now has grown to a conviction —Thomas Wood †1950⟩ ⟨the bill had had a far-reaching effect and was the ~ of reform —Roger Burlingame⟩ **4 :** something that resembles a seed in shape or size: as **a :** a small bubble in glass **b :** a small usu. glass and gold or platinum capsule used as a container for a radioactive substance (as radium or radon) to be applied usu. interstitially in the treatment of cancer **5 a** *cap* **:** INNER LIGHT **b :** HOMOEOMERY 1 **6 :** a nucleus in seeding; *esp* **:** a crystal added to a liquid to cause crystallization **7 :** a player who has been seeded in competition — **go to seed** *or* **run to seed 1 :** to develop seed **2 :** to lose vitality or effectiveness **:** DECAY ⟨it is the picture of the idealist *gone to seed,* the sensitive man turned sour —H.E.Clurman⟩ ⟨the eighteenth century upper-class culture was *running to seed* —Roy Lewis & Angus Maude⟩

²seed \"\ *vb* -ED/-ING/-S [ME *seden,* fr. *sed* seed] *vi* **1 :** to go to seed **:** grow to maturity and produce seed **2 :** to sow seed **:** PLANT **3 :** to crystallize or form a precipitate or aggregate as the result of seeding **:** GRAIN ~ *vt* **1 a :** to sprinkle with seed **:** plant seeds in **:** SOW ⟨~ a plot with barley⟩ **b :** to cause to be filled or furnished with something that grows or stimulates growth or development ⟨a breeder reactor ~*ed* with plutonium —*Time*⟩ **c** (1) **:** to inoculate with microorganisms (2) **:** to inoculate (neighboring or distant tissues) by dispersion from the parent focus — used of bacteria or cancer cells **d :** to supply with nuclei (as of crystallization or condensation) ⟨~ a saturated solution with solid particles of solute⟩; *esp* **:** to treat (a cloud) with solid particles (as silver iodide crystals) for the purpose of converting supercooled water droplets into ice crystals in an attempt to produce precipitation artificially or to dissipate a supercooled cloud **e :** to allow or cause (as lard or syrup) to form granules or crystals by cooling **2 a :** to plant by scattering on or in the soil ⟨~ another crop in the field⟩ ⟨~ beets in the spring⟩ **b :** to distribute at random **:** SCATTER ⟨several hundred bright young intellectuals who were ~*ed* into overseas aid and information programs —Daniel Bell⟩ **3 a :** to extract the seeds from (stone fruit) **b :** ¹RIPPLE 1 **4 :** to give rise to **:** stimulate the development of ⟨although the theory is still not finally proved, it ~*ed* a whole generation of fruitful study —George Gamow⟩ **5 a :** to arrange (the draw in a sports event) so that certain contestants (as those of superior ability or of the same team) will not meet in the early rounds of competition; *also* **:** to arrange the order of competition of (contestants) by seeding **b :** to rank (a contestant) relative to others in a tournament on the basis of previous record

³seed \"\ *adj* [¹*seed*] **1 a :** grown or retained for the production of seed ⟨a ~ crop⟩ **b :** selected or used for planting or cultivation to produce a new crop or stock ⟨~ corn⟩ ⟨~ flax⟩ ⟨~ potato⟩ ⟨~ virus⟩ **c :** left or saved for breeding ⟨a ~ population⟩ **2 :** incompletely developed **:** SMALL ⟨the ovaries full of ~ eggs⟩

⁴seed *substand past of* SEE

seed·age \-dij\ *n* -s [²*seed* + *-age*] **:** the practice or method of propagating plants by means of seeds or spores

seedball \ˈ⸗ˌ⸗\ *n* [¹*seed* + *ball*] **1 :** a rounded and usu. dry or capsular fruit (as of a potato) **2 :** the collection of one-seeded fruits (as utricles) found in various plants (as the beet)

seedbed \ˈ⸗ˌ⸗\ *n* **1 :** the soil or forest floor upon which seed becomes bedded: as **a :** the surface soil of cultivated land prepared by tillage for the seeding of a crop **b :** a bed usu. of fine soil for growth of plants from seeds preparatory to transplantation **c :** a subdivision of a tree nursery for raising seedlings **2 :** a place or source of growth or development ⟨must protect and extend our basic research as the ~ of new advances —J.R.Killian⟩

seed beetle *n* **:** a beetle (as a bean weevil or pea weevil) that feeds on the seeds of plants

seedbird \ˈ⸗ˌ⸗\ *n* **1 :** ¹MEW **2 :** PIED WAGTAIL

seedbox \ˈ⸗ˌ⸗\ *n* **1 :** CAPSULE **2 :** any of various plants of the genus *Ludwigia; esp* **:** a No. American swamp herb (*L. alternifolia*) with yellow flowers and a loosely seeded angled capsule

seedcake \ˈ⸗ˌ⸗\ *n* **1 :** a cake or cookie containing aromatic seeds (as sesame or caraway) **2 :** OIL CAKE

seedcase \ˈ⸗ˌ⸗\ *n* **:** ²POD 1

seed coat *n* **:** the outer protective covering of a seed that is developed from one or more integuments often in combination with other adherent parts of the ovary (as in a caryopsis)

seed–corn beetle *n* **:** a carabid beetle (*Agonoderus lecontei*) that often feeds on corn seed in the ground

seed–corn maggot *n* **:** a small yellowish grub with a pointed head that is the larva of a grayish brown two-winged fly (*Hylemya platura*), is native to Europe but now widely distributed in No. America, and is typically a destructive borer in seeds and seedlings (as of Indian corn, beans, or melons) but sometimes attacks stems or roots of older plants — called also *corn maggot*

seed cotton *n* **:** the unginned cottonseed with the attached lint

seed down *vt* [²*seed* + *down*] **:** to sow with grass or forage legume seed

seedeater \ˈ⸗ˌ⸗⸗\ *n* [¹*seed* + *eater*] **:** any of various birds and esp. finches whose diet consists basically of seeds **:** HARD-BILL: as **a :** any of several southern African finches that resemble and were formerly classified with the canaries **b :** any of numerous tropical American finches of the genus *Sporophila* **c :** GRASSQUIT

seeded *adj* [fr. past part. of ²*seed*] **1 a :** supplied or sprinkled with seed **:** SOWN ⟨a ~ field⟩ **b :** having seeds ⟨a ~ breadfruit⟩; *esp* **:** having a specified kind, number, or quantity of seeds — usu. used in combination ⟨round-*seeded*⟩ ⟨one-*seeded*⟩ ⟨many-*seeded*⟩ **c :** INOCULATED **2 :** run to seed **:** FULL-GROWN, MATURE **3 :** having seeds or seed vessels of specified tincture — used of a heraldic flower **4 :** having the seeds extracted ⟨~ raisins⟩ **5** *of textiles* **:** having flecks or knops ⟨~ yarn⟩

seeded plum *n* **:** PERSIMMON 1a

seedee *var of* SIDI

seed·er \'sēdə(r)\ *n* -s [²*seed* + *-er*] **1 :** an implement used for planting or sowing seeds **2 :** one that seeds fruit ⟨a raisin ~⟩ **3 a :** a plant that produces seed freely **b :** a plant that abnormally produces seed the first season **4 :** one that seeds clouds

seedfall \ˈ⸗ˌ⸗\ *n* [¹*seed* + *fall*] **:** the natural dispersal of seed from a plant and esp. from a tree

seed feed cup *n* **:** the seed feed attachment of a cup drill

seed fern *n* **:** a plant or fossil of the order Cycadofilicales **:** PTERIDOSPERM

seed fish *n* **:** a fish full of ripe spawn

seed·ful \'sēdfəl\ *adj* **:** full of seed **:** GENERATIVE ⟨his critical essays are as fruitful — or one might rather call them ~ ~ as any written in our time —Malcolm Cowley⟩

seedgall \ˈ⸗ˌ⸗\ *n* **:** a gall that resembles a seed; *esp* **:** one caused by a phylloxera

seed hair *n* **1 :** KAPOK **2** *or* **seed crown** *or* **seed down :** ²COMA 1c

seedier *comparative of* SEEDY

seediest *superlative of* SEEDY

seed·i·ly \'sēd°lē, -d°li, -dəl-\ *adv* **:** in a seedy manner

seed·i·ness \-dēnəs, -din-\ *n* -ES **:** the quality or state of being seedy

seeding *n* -s [ME *seding,* fr. gerund of *seden* to seed] **1 a** *archaic* **:** the act or an instance of producing seed **b :** the act or an instance of sowing seed **2 :** SPAWNING ⟨the ~ of spring salmon was fairly satisfactory —*Report: Canadian Fisheries Dept.*⟩ **3 :** the act or an instance of treating a cloud with solid particles **4 :** the act or practice of placing some players in such a position in the draw that they will not meet in the earlier rounds of a tournament; *also* **:** the posted list of such an arrangement

seeding lath *or* **seeding trough** *n* **:** a device used to distribute tree seeds evenly in drills in the seedbed

seeding plow *var of* SEED PLOW

seed lac *n* [¹*seed*] **:** a granular resinous material obtained from stick lac by crushing, cleaning, and washing and further processed to yield shellac

seed leaf *n* **:** COTYLEDON 2

seedleaf \ˈ⸗ˌ⸗\ *n* **:** a broadleaf tobacco used in cigars

seed·less \'sēdləs\ *adj* **:** lacking seeds ⟨~ grapefruit⟩ — **seed·less·ness** *n* -ES

seedless orange *n* **:** NAVEL ORANGE

seed·let \-lət\ *n* -s **:** a small seed

seedlike \ˈ⸗ˌ⸗\ *adj* **:** resembling a seed

¹seed·ling \'sēdliŋ, -lēŋ\ *n* -s [¹*seed* + *-ling*] **1 a :** a plant grown from seed as distinguished from one propagated by a vegetative part (as a cutting or layer) **b** (1) **:** a tree grown from seed as distinguished from one developed as a stump sucker (2) **:** a young tree smaller than a sapling **c :** a nursery plant (as a tree) that has not been transplanted **2 :** a small seed **3 :** a young sponge

²seedling \"\ *adj* **1 :** grown or developed from seed **2 :** resembling a small seed **:** existing in an undeveloped form ⟨the poor, rare, struggling, ~ counterpart —A.L.Kroeber⟩

seedling-rooted \ˈ⸗⸗ˌ⸗⸗\ *adj, of a tree* **:** developed from grafting or budding on a seedling stock — compare OWN-ROOT

seed·lip \'sēd,lip\ *n* [ME *sedelip,* fr. OE *sǣdlēap,* fr. *sǣd* seed + *lēap* basket — more at SEED, LEAP] *dial chiefly Eng* **:** a basket or other container in which seed to be sowed broadcast is carried

seed·man \'sēdmən\ *n, pl* **seedmen** [¹*seed* + *man*] **:** SEEDSMAN

seedness *n* -ES [¹*seed* + *-ness*] *obs* **:** the act of sowing or the state of being sown ⟨blossoming time that from the ~ the bare fallow brings to teeming foison —Shak.⟩

seed oyster *n* **:** a young oyster after settling and becoming attached to the substrate; *esp* **:** one of a size suitable for transplantation

seed pan *n* **:** a shallow flowerpot used esp. for germinating seeds

seed parent *n* **:** the pistillate parent in plant breeding

seed pearl *n* [³*seed*] **1 a :** a very small and often irregular pearl **b :** minute pearls imbedded in some binding material **2 :** a pale to grayish yellow that is redder and less strong than wine yellow and less strong and slightly redder than Naples yellow — called also *cartridge buff, Spanish flesh*

seed piece *n* **:** any of various parts used in plant propagation: as **a :** a cutting of sugar cane **b :** a piece of a potato tuber including at least one eye

seed plant *n* [¹*seed*] **:** a plant that bears seeds; *specif* **:** a plant of the Spermatophyta

seed planter *n* **:** SEEDER 1

seed plate *n* **:** a round perforated metal plate in the bottom of the hopper of a corn or cotton planter that sorts out and releases the correct amount of seed to be dropped at regular intervals

seed-plot \ˈ⸗ˌ⸗\ *n* **:** SEEDBED ⟨its local and national prestige as a *seed-plot* of scholarship —*Dial*⟩

seed plow *or* **seeding plow** *n* **:** a plow equipped with an automatic seeding device

seedpod \ˈ⸗ˌ⸗\ *n* **:** ²POD 1

seeds *pl of* SEED, *pres 3d sing of* SEED

seeds hay *n, Brit* **:** hay cut from a temporary or rotation meadow sown not more than 2 to 6 years previously

seeds·man \'sēdzmən\ *n, pl* **seedsmen 1 :** one who sows seed **2 :** one who deals in or handles seed

seed snipe *n* **:** any of several So. American charadriiform birds constituting the family Thinocoridae, related to the sheathbill but resembling quail in general appearance, and mainly frequenting dry inland regions

seedstalk \ˈ⸗ˌ⸗\ *n* **:** the fruiting stalk of a flowering plant

seed stitch *n* **1 :** a short straight stitch used for background filling in embroidery **2 :** MOSS STITCH

seed stock *n* **1 :** a supply of seed, tubers, or roots reserved for planting **2 :** the residual population of an animal needed to restock a range (as after hunting); *also* **:** a small population introduced to stock a new or disused range

seed tick *n* **:** the six-legged larva of a tick

seedtime \ˈ⸗ˌ⸗\ *n* [ME, fr. ¹*seed* + *time*] **1 :** the season of sowing seeds **2 :** a period of development or preparation

seed treatment *n* **:** the act or process of applying a pesticide to seed

seed tree *n* **:** a tree that bears seed; *specif* **:** a tree left uncut to provide seed for forest reproduction

seed vessel *n* **:** PERICARP

seed weevil *n* **:** any of numerous small weevils that live in seeds

seedy \'sēdē, -di\ *adj,* *usu* -ER/-EST [¹*seed* + *-y*] **1 a** (1) **:** abounding in seeds **:** bearing or containing seeds (2) **:** run to seed **b** *of a fish* **:** full of spawn **c** *of glass* **:** containing many small bubbles **d** *of bacon* **:** containing granules of melanin **2 a :** shabby or unprepossessing in dress or appearance ⟨a tall ~ man dressed in a frock coat that shone in the sun and looked greenish in the shade —J.B.Priestley⟩ **b :** being in a run-down uncared-for condition **:** DECAYED ⟨a ~ village of long huts with galvanized-iron roofs —John Dos Passos⟩ ⟨an area of ~ houses, industrial plants, and warehouses —*Amer. Guide Series: N.Y. City*⟩ **c :** MEAN, SQUALID ⟨the change in his character from an affluent good fellow to a ~ miser —C.C.Walcutt⟩ **3 :** lacking in vitality or strength **:** under the weather **:** DEBILITATED, SPIRITLESS ⟨have been rather ~ . . . with another cold and coughing at night —O.W.Holmes †1935⟩

seedy buckberry *n* **:** PRIVET ANDROMEDA

seedy toe *n* **:** an abnormality of a horse's foot marked by separation of the wall from the sole in the white line

see-er \'sēə(r)\ *n* -s **:** one who sees ⟨the painter is the *see-er,* he whose trained eye is sensitive —*Scientific Monthly*⟩

see·gar \'sē,gär, ⸗'⸗\ *n* -s [Sp *cigarro*] *chiefly dial* **:** CIGAR ⟨with a hitch and sway . . . in the shoulders, and his ~ at a more declarative angle —R.P.Warren⟩

see-ho \sē'hō\ *v imper* [prob. alter. (influenced by *see,* imper. of ¹*see*) of *soho*] — a call to indicate the first sighting of the hare in a hunt

¹seeing *n* -s [ME, fr. gerund of *seen, sen* to see] **1 a :** the act of using one's sense of sight ⟨~ is believing⟩ ⟨a sight worth ~⟩ ⟨recounts his ~*s* and doings —Virginia Woolf⟩ **b :** the faculty or power of sight or insight **:** VISION ⟨gain the gift of deeper ~ —Amy Lowell⟩ **2 :** the quality of the images of celestial bodies observed telescopically as determined by the state of turbulence of the parts of the atmosphere through which the light has passed and usu. rated on a scale from 0 for very poor quality to 10 for perfect quality

²seeing *adj* [ME, fr. pres. part. of *seen, sen* to see] **:** having the power of sight or insight ⟨if not a blind force but a ~ force runs things —William James⟩ — **see·ing·ly** *adv*

³seeing *conj* **:** in view of the fact that **:** inasmuch as **:** CONSIDERING — often used with *that* or *as*

Seeing Eye *trademark* — used for a guide dog trained to lead the blind

seeing glass *n* [¹*seeing*] *dial chiefly Eng* **:** MIRROR

¹seek \'sēk\ *vb* **sought** \'sȯt, *usu* -ȯd·+V\ **sought; seeking; seeks** [ME *sechen, seken* (past *soughte,* past part. *sought*), fr. OE *sēcan* (past *sōhte,* past part. *gesōht*); akin to OHG *suohhen* to seek (past *suohta,* past part. *gisuohhit*), ON *sœkja* (past *sōtti,* past part. *sōttr*), Goth *sokjan* to seek (past *sokida,* past part. *sokiths*), *sakan* to quarrel, L *sagire* to perceive keenly, Gk *hēgeisthai* to go ahead, lead] *vt* **1** *obs* **:** to follow or advance against in order to attack **:** PURSUE ⟨of us must Pompey presently be *sought,* or else he ~*s* out us —Shak.⟩ **2 :** to resort to **:** go to ⟨for an hour everyone ~*s* the shade to rest —Richard Roche⟩ ⟨departed for Rome which at that time was *sought* by American painters and sculptors —Charles de Kay⟩ **3 a** (1) **:** to go in search of **:** look for **:** search for ⟨if management does decide to ~ the man within the ranks of the company —Bruce Payne⟩ ⟨~*ing* out keymen and awarding them fellowships —*Bull. of Meharry Med. Coll.*⟩ (2) **:** to move or act so as to reach or arrive at ⟨water ~*s* its own level⟩ ⟨rockets designed to ~ out and destroy with uncanny accuracy enemy bombers —H.W. Baldwin⟩ **b :** to try to discover ⟨not all research is confined to ~*ing* new chemicals —*Monsanto Chemical Co. Annual Report*⟩ ⟨~ the truth⟩ **4 :** to inquire for **:** ask for **:** ENTREAT, REQUEST ⟨his advice was *sought* by many of the party's leaders —H.J.Howland⟩ **5 :** to try to acquire or gain **:** aim at ⟨never held public office, nor did he ever ~ it —W.C.Ford⟩ ⟨teach the child to ~ the good and to avoid the bad —*Better Homes & Gardens*⟩ ⟨~ fame and fortune⟩ **6 :** to make an attempt **:** TRY — used with an infinitive ⟨all governments, of course, ~ to keep the bulk of their people contented —D.M.Potter⟩ **7** *archaic* **:** to look through **:** EXPLORE ⟨have I *sought* every country far and near —Shak.⟩ ~ *vi* **1 :** to make a search or inquiry ⟨~*ing* along the shelf for a volume —G.B.Shaw⟩ **2** *archaic* **:** to pay a visit **:** GO, RESORT ⟨wisdom's self oft ~*s* to sweet retired solitude —John Milton⟩ **3** *archaic* **:** to have recourse **:** make request **:** APPLY ⟨to whom I ~ for my medicine —Geoffrey Chaucer⟩ **4 a :** to be sought or looked for ⟨the connection between dress and war is not far to ~ —Virginia Woolf⟩ **b** *archaic* **:** to be at a loss to know or act ⟨for the details of our itinerary, I am all to ~ —R.L.Stevenson⟩ **c** *archaic* **:** to be at a disadvantage ⟨leave us wholly to ~ in the art of political wagering —Jonathan Swift⟩ **5 :** to retrieve killed game — used chiefly as a command to dogs

syn SEARCH, HUNT, RUMMAGE, RANSACK, SCOUR, COMB, FERRET (*out*): SEEK is a general term meaning to look for; it lacks special connotation but may occas. have a somewhat archaic suggestion ⟨poor health compelled Webb to *seek* some more healthful climate —C.W.Mitman⟩ ⟨the Poles have always *sought* the centers of heavy industry —*Amer. Guide Series: N.Y. State*⟩ ⟨gaze *sought* the horizon —Ellen Glasgow⟩ ⟨those who *seek* the harvest of the sea —Stuart Cloete⟩ ⟨marched out to *seek* battle —C.H.Lanza⟩ SEARCH usu. implies a thorough, careful, sustained seeking or examining of a person, place, or thing ⟨detectives *search* the arrested suspect⟩ ⟨the summer was spent *searching* the Ozark region for the fabled seven cities —R.A.Billington⟩ ⟨*search* the house from top to bottom for a lost ring⟩ HUNT implies a searching or questing after something elusive or well hidden and quite hard to find ⟨*hunt* for a lost collar button⟩ ⟨land speculators . . . reaped a quick fortune, and *hunted* for new bonanzas —*Amer. Guide Series: Minn.*⟩ ⟨the strength to *hunt* out logical difficulties, antinomies, or paradoxes in our own views —M.R.Cohen⟩ RUMMAGE implies the making of a usu. sustained or thorough search or investigation in which things are disarranged, dislodged, or moved around ⟨*rummaged* among the papers that cluttered up the high, old-fashioned desk —Hartley Howard⟩ ⟨*rummaged* in the packs and announced gleefully that their contents were quite dry

—John Buchan⟩ RANSACK suggests a thorough search, esp. of a container, room, or building, often done forcefully and with resulting disorder and sometimes for something stolen or for something to be pillaged or looted ⟨each man *ransacked* his chest or seabag and unearthed trinkets of various kinds —H.A.Chippendale⟩ ⟨St. John's Church . . . was ill-attended in the reaction following the Revolution, and was *ransacked* during the War of 1812 —*Amer. Guide Series: Va.*⟩ SCOUR means to make a very diligent search of (an area) omitting no part or section ⟨*scoured* the coppices and woods and old quarries, so long as a blackberry was to be found —D.H. Lawrence⟩ ⟨while *scouring* the countryside for fresh mounts —*Amer. Guide Series: Ind.*⟩ COMB implies an examination, usu. of territory, as thoroughgoing as the action of a fine comb passing through hair ⟨state policemen *combing* the county for the escaped prisoners⟩ ⟨*comb* London's teeming millions for him —Dorothy Sayers⟩ ⟨*comb* the literature of mythology carefully —Martin Gardner⟩ FERRET (*out*) suggests searching out with keen crafty or shrewd, relentless determination ⟨did remove the bulk of the tribe, but they could not *ferret out* every Indian —A.W.Long⟩ ⟨spent hours trying to *ferret out* the true reasons for the crime⟩

— seek after 1 : to attempt to find, take, or make use of ⟨these marsh buffaloes are much *sought after* —Wilfred Thesiger⟩ **2 :** to desire the presence or companionship of **:** COURT, PURSUE ⟨was much *sought after* on account of his wide reading, charm of manner, and brilliant conversational powers —J.F.Fulton⟩

²seek *n* -s *obs* **:** a hunting signal sounded on a horn

seek·er \-kə(r)\ *n* -s [ME *secher, seker,* fr. *sechen, seken* to seek + *-er*] **:** one that seeks or is used in seeking ⟨a tone more suggestive of the scientific ~ for the truth —B.N.Cardozo⟩: as **a** *usu cap* **:** one of a small group of the English Independents who claimed religious liberty, who professed to seek further revelation as to the true church, ministry, and sacraments, and many of whom joined the Friends **b :** a slender instrument that has a smooth rounded end and is used in dissecting to follow up delicate tubular structures **:** a slender probe **c :** a device in a missile that is attracted to some form of emission (as light, heat, sound, or radio waves); *also* **:** a missile equipped with such a device

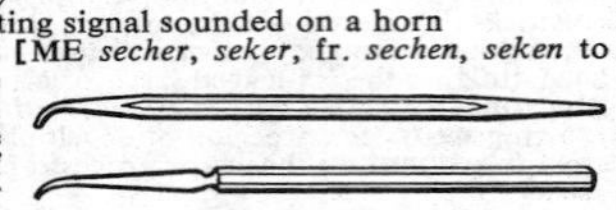

seekers b

seek·er·ism \-ə,rizəm\ *n* -s *usu cap* **:** the doctrine or practice of the Seekers

seeking *n* -s [ME *seking,* fr. gerund of *seken* to seek] **:** the act of one who seeks; *specif* **:** one's invitation, search, or choice of action ⟨a misfortune of his own ~⟩

seek·ing·ly *adv* [*seeking* (fr. ME *seking,* fr. pres. part. of *seken* to seek) + *-ly*] **:** in a seeking manner **:** SEARCHINGLY

¹seel \ˈsē(ə)l, ˈsā(-\ *var of* SELE

²seel \ˈsē(ə)l\ *vt* -ED/-ING/-S [alter. of ME *silen,* fr. MF *siller, ciller,* fr. ML *ciliare,* fr. L *cilium* eyelid — more at CILIA] **1 :** to close the eyes of (as a hawk) by drawing threads through the eyelids **2** *archaic* **:** to close up (one's eyes) **:** deprive of sight **:** BLIND ⟨when we in our viciousness grow hard . . . the wise gods ~ our eyes —Shak.⟩

see-low \ˈsē,lō\ *n* [modif. of Chin (Cant) *sz-ng-lûk,* fr. *sz* four + *ng* five + *lûk* six] **:** FOUR-FIVE-SIX

see·ly \ˈsēlē\ *adj* [ME *sely* — more at SILLY] **1** *archaic* **a :** blissfully happy **b :** BLESSED **2** *archaic* **:** GOOD **3** *archaic* **a :** INNOCENT **b :** SIMPLE-MINDED **c :** FOOLISH, SILLY **4** *archaic* **a :** pitiable esp. because of weak physical or mental condition **b :** FRAIL

seem \ˈsēm\ *vi* -ED/-ING/-S [ME *semen,* of Scand origin; akin to ON *sōma* to beseem, befit, *sæmr* becoming, *sæma* to honor, conform, OE *sēman* to reconcile, pacify, Goth *samjan* to please, ON *samr* same — more at SAME] **1** *obs* **:** to be suitable **:** BEFIT **2 a** (1) **:** to be in appearance **:** give the impression of being **:** look to be **:** APPEAR ⟨this officer, who ~*ed* a reasonable human being —Glenway Wescott⟩ ⟨the project had begun to ~ a waste of time —J.G.Cozzens⟩ (2) **:** to pretend to be **:** FEIGN ⟨either you are ignorant, or ~ so craftily —Shak.⟩ **b :** to appear to the observation or understanding ⟨~*ed* to know all of them and to be able to call each one by name —W.A.Slade⟩ ⟨a tiny pebble in the middle of your back ~*s* to grow all night, and by the crack of dawn has grown to boulder size —*Boy Scout Handbook*⟩ **c :** to appear to one's own mind or opinion ⟨~*ed* to leave the café with one or two germs of ideas —Arnold Bennett⟩ ⟨~ to feel no pain⟩ ⟨can't ~ to solve this problem⟩ **d :** to appear according to the known facts ⟨~*s* not to have studied in Europe or to have taken a doctorate —Louise Pound⟩ ⟨~*s* that he began as a painter —Hollis Alpert⟩ ⟨the merger will not take place, it ~*s*⟩ **3 :** to present all the signs of being the case **:** be evidently true **:** be obvious ⟨~*s* to me that he has given up more than he has gained⟩ ⟨would ~ to be a good investment⟩ **4 :** to give evidence of existing or being present ⟨police indicated there ~*ed* nothing in his background that could spawn the brutal attack —*Springfield (Mass.) Daily News*⟩

seem·er \-mə(r)\ *n* -s **:** one who seems; *esp* **:** one who makes a pretense **:** PRETENDER

¹seeming *n* -s [ME *seming,* fr. gerund of *semen* to seem] **1 a :** the manner of appearing to sight or mind **:** outward appearance ⟨to all ~ his pious gift was irrevocable —Frederick Pollock & F.W.Maitland⟩ **b :** external appearance as distinguished from true being or character **:** SEMBLANCE ⟨his combination of honest ~ with devilish actuality —F.R. Leavis⟩ **2 :** the form or condition in which a person or thing presents itself **:** LOOK ⟨in the ~ of a rather modest canal —J.B.Cabell & A.J.Hanna⟩

²seeming *adj* [fr. pres. part. of *seem*] **:** apparent on superficial view or examination **:** OSTENSIBLE ⟨the geographic fact of the nation's ~ continental security —Reinhold Niebuhr⟩ **syn** see APPARENT

³seeming *adv* **:** SEEMINGLY ⟨that ~ marble heart —Lord Byron⟩

seem·ing·ly *adv* [*²seeming* + *-ly*] **1** *archaic* **:** BECOMINGLY, SEEMLY **2 a :** so far as can be seen or judged **:** EVIDENTLY ⟨had a marked influence on him and ~ led him into his loved occupation of surveying —C.W.Mitman⟩ **b :** to outward appearance only ⟨~ spontaneous yet carefully devised movements —*Current Biog.*⟩ ⟨two ~ contrasting but naturally allied forces —A.C.Cole⟩

seem·ing·ness *n* -ES [*²seeming* + *-ness*] **:** the quality or state of seeming **:** SEMBLANCE

seem·less \ˈsēmləs\ *adj* [*seem* + *-less*] *archaic* **:** UNSEEMLY

seem·li·head \ˈsēmlē,hed\ *n* [ME *semelihed,* fr. *semely* seemly + *-hed* -hood (akin to ME *-hod* -had -hood)] *archaic* **:** SEEMLINESS

seem·li·ness \ˈsēmlēnəs, -lin-\ *n* -ES [ME *semelinesse,* fr. *semely* seemly + *-nesse* -ness] **:** the quality or state of being seemly **:** FITNESS, PROPRIETY

¹seem·ly \-lē, -li\ *adj, usu* -ER/-EST [ME *semelich, semely,* fr. ON *sæmiligr,* fr. *sæmr* becoming + *-ligr* -ly — more at SEEM] **1 a :** GOOD-LOOKING, HANDSOME ⟨endowed with a delicate physique, a ~ appearance, and a subtle intelligence —Harry Levin⟩ **b :** having properties pleasing to the eye **:** agreeably fashioned or proportioned ⟨the redeveloped city may well be beautiful, but the planners are determined that it shall at least be ~ —S.P.B.Mais⟩ **2 :** conforming to accepted standards of good form or taste **:** PROPER ⟨the company of those whose morals and behavior are less ~ than his own —E.M.Lustgarten⟩ **3 :** suited to the occasion, purpose, or person **:** FIT ⟨a ~ military escort drew near from the direction of the post —Owen Wister⟩ **syn** see DECOROUS

²seemly \"\ *adv, usu* -ER/-EST [ME *semely,* fr. ON *sæmiliga* becomingly, fr. *sæmiligr* becoming] **1** *archaic* **:** in an attractive manner **:** PLEASINGLY **2** *archaic* **:** in a fitting manner **:** APPROPRIATELY, BECOMINGLY

¹seen \ˈsēn\ *adj* [ME *seyn,* fr. past part. of *seen, sen* to see] **1 :** perceived or verified by sight **:** VISIBLE ⟨~ beauty⟩ **2** *archaic* **:** learned in a particular field **:** VERSED ⟨a schoolmaster well ~ in music —Shak.⟩

²seen \"\ [ME *sene, seyn* (past part.), fr. OE *gesegen*] *past part & substand past of* SEE

see·nie bean \ˈsēnē-\ *n* [alter. of *senvy*] **:** the seed of a yellow-flowered shrub (*Sesbania longiflora*) of southern U.S. and northern Mexico formerly used as a substitute for coffee

see out *vt* [*¹see*] **1 :** to continue with to the end ⟨went back to school determined to *see* his education *out*⟩ **2** *Scot* **:** OUTLIVE

¹seep \ˈsēp\ *vi* -ED/-ING/-S [alter. of *sipe,* fr. ME *sipen,* fr. OE *sipian;* akin to MLG *sipen* to seep] **1 :** to flow or pass slowly through fine pores or small openings **:** OOZE ⟨water had ~*ed* in through a crack in the ceiling⟩ **2 a :** to enter or penetrate slowly ⟨some change gradually ~*ed* into these regions —G.R. Willey⟩ **b :** to become diffused or spread **:** PERMEATE ⟨a sadness ~*ed* through his being —Agnes S. Turnbull⟩ ⟨fear of the plague ~*s* like a miasma through the very air of this story —Jean S. Untermeyer⟩ **3 :** to become lost or dissipated by a gradual process **:** LEAK ⟨speeches and other tokens of immediate vitality ~ away into a colorless feeling of merely belonging —Edward Sapir⟩

²seep \"\ *n* -s **1 a :** a spot where a fluid (as water, oil, or gas) contained in the ground oozes slowly to the surface and often forms a pool **b :** a small spring **2 :** SEEPAGE

³seep \"\ *n* -s [blend of *sea* and *jeep*] **:** an amphibious jeep

seep·age \-pij, -pēj\ *n* -s [*¹seep* + *-age*] **1 a :** the act or process of seeping **:** OOZING ⟨many streams lose water by ~ in certain stretches —A.N.Sayre⟩ **b :** a quantity of a fluid that has seeped through porous material (as soil) ⟨~*s* of oil and gas are widely distributed throughout the world —C.G.Lalicker⟩ ⟨families stood barefoot in cellars bailing out ~ —*N.Y. Times*⟩ **2 a :** a draining off by gradual leakage ⟨the unfathomable ~ of all excitement, meaning and potency from so many of our long-cherished values —John Hurkan⟩ **b :** a gradual penetration **:** INFILTRATION ⟨the increasing ~ of gold into certain areas⟩

seepweed \ˈ=,=\ *n* [*²seep* + *weed*] **:** a glabrous undershrub (*Suaeda intermedia*) of alkali plains of western U.S. with narrowly linear leaves that is held to indicate the proximity of groundwater

seepy \ˈsēpē\ *adj* -ER/-EST [*¹seep* + *-y*] **:** full of moisture **:** poorly drained **:** OOZY

¹seer \ˈsi(ə)r, ˈsiə, *esp in sense 1* ˈsēə(r)\ *n* -s [ME, fr. *seen, sen* to see + *-er*] **1 :** one who sees ⟨the ~ of visions makes the attempt to humanize —*Times Lit. Supp.*⟩ ⟨she stared and started like a ghost-*seer* —George Eliot⟩ **2 a :** one who predicts events or developments **:** PROPHET ⟨he was the ~ of coming steam engines —Havelock Ellis⟩ ⟨a series of secular ~*s* warned civilized men that civilization was dying —*Time*⟩ **b :** one who has or is thought to have extraordinary intuitive and spiritual insight ⟨the ~'*s* hour of vision is short and rare —R.W.Emerson⟩ **3 :** one who practices divination; *specif* **:** CRYSTAL GAZER

²seer *also* **ser** *or* **sir** \ˈsi(ə)r, ˈse(ə)r, ˈsər(·)\ *n, pl* **seers** *or* **seer** [Hindi *ser;* perh. akin to Per *sīr*] **1 :** any of various Indian units of weight; *esp* **:** a unit equal to 2.057 pounds **2 :** an Afghan unit of weight equal to 15.6 pounds

³seer \ˈsi(ə)r\ *or* **seerfish** \ˈ=,=\ *also* **seir** \ˈsi(ə)r\ *or* **seirfish** \ˈ=,=\ *n, pl* **seers** *or* **seerfish** *or* **seerfishes** [Pg *serra,* lit., saw, fr. L] **1 :** any of several large fishes (genus *Cybium*) resembling the related mackerels and widely distributed in the tropical Indo-Pacific area and sought for sport and food **2 :** an Indian threadfin (*Polynemus indicus*)

seercraft \ˈ=,=\ *n* [*¹seer* + *craft*] **:** the skill or practice of a seer

seer·ess \ˈsirəs\ *n* -ES [*¹seer* + *-ess*] **:** a female seer **:** PROPHETESS

seer·paw \ˈsir,pȯ\ *n* -s [Hindi *sar-ā-pā* head to foot, fr. Per] **:** KHALAT

seer·ship \ˈsi(ə)r,ship\ *n* [*¹seer* + *-ship*] **:** the attributes or function of a seer

seer·suck·er \ˈsir,səkər, ˈsiə,səkə(r\ *n* -s [Hindi *śīrśakar,* fr. Per *shīr-o-shakar,* lit., milk and sugar] **:** a durable plainwoven fabric orig. of linen or cotton and now usu. of cotton or rayon, having stripes alternately flat and puckered that are produced by varying the tension in the warp threads, and used for clothing, curtains, bedspreads

sees *pres 3d sing of* SEE, *pl of* SEE

¹see·saw \ˈsē,sȯ\ *n* [prob. redupl. of *³saw*] **1 :** an alternating up-and-down or backward-and-forward motion or movement; *specif* **:** a contest or struggle in which now one side now the other has the lead ⟨warfare . . . has been a continuing ~ between the offensive and the defensive —S.L.A.Marshall⟩ **2 a :** a game in which two children or groups of children ride on opposite ends of a plank or similar piece balanced in the middle so that one end goes up as the other goes down **b :** an apparatus (as a long plank or piece set on a center mount) improvised or manufactured for use in the game of seesaw — called also *teeter-totter*

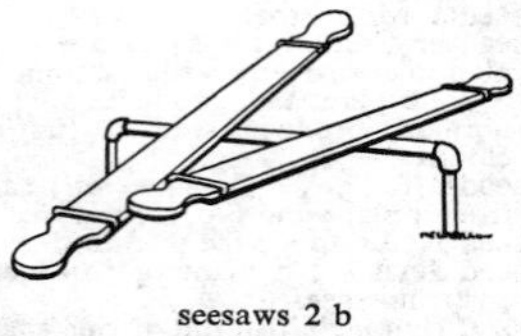

seesaws 2 b

²seesaw \"\ *vi* **1 a :** to move backward and forward or up and down ⟨planes could not land on the ~*ing* box-top flight deck at night —Wirt Williams⟩ **b :** to play at seesaw **2 :** ALTERNATE ⟨it ~*s* between biography and criticism —J.L.Davis⟩ ⟨the lead ~*ed* between the two runners right up to the finish line⟩ **~** *vt* **:** to cause to move in seesaw fashion ⟨~*ed* her skywards —Israel Zangwill⟩

³seesaw \"\ *adj* **:** moving up and down or to and fro **:** having a reciprocating motion **:** RECIPROCAL ⟨the ~ nature of the war during the early stages —Greg MacGregor⟩

see·see \ˈsē,sē\ *or* **seesee partridge** *n* -s [perh. imit.] **:** a small Asiatic sand partridge (*Ammoperdix griseogularis*)

seet \ˈsēt\ *chiefly dial var of* SIGHT

¹seethe \ˈsēth\ *vb* **seethed** \-thd\ *or archaic* **sod** \ˈsäd\ **seethed** \-thd\ *or archaic* **sod·den** \-dᵊn\ **seething; seethes** [ME *sethen,* fr. OE *sēothan;* akin to OHG *siodan* to seethe, ON *sjōtha,* Lith *siausti* to rage, Av *hāvayeiti* he stews] *vt* **1 :** to cook in a boiling or simmering liquid **:** BOIL, STEW ⟨allowed to eat anything that is roasted or *seethed* —William Chomsky⟩ ⟨thou shalt not ~ a kid in his mother's milk —Exod: 23:19 (AV)⟩ **2 a :** to soak or saturate in a liquid **:** reduce by soaking or boiling to a flabby lifeless condition **b :** to dull (as the brain or blood) by heat or intoxicating liquor **~** *vi* **1** *archaic* **:** to be cooked by boiling **:** come to a boil **2 a :** to be in a state of rapid and agitated movement ⟨a dark mass in which *seethed* houses, freight cars, trees, and animals —V.G.Heiser⟩ ⟨swarms of flies *seethed* everywhere —Francis Birtles⟩ **b :** to bubble or foam as if boiling **:** BOIL, CHURN ⟨when the surge was *seething* free —Alfred Tennyson⟩ **3 :** to suffer violent internal excitement or commotion **:** be in a state of agitation or turmoil **:** FERMENT ⟨his brain *seethed* with answers, with retorts, with crushing arguments —Francis Hackett⟩ ⟨when the colonies were beginning to ~ with the spirit of revolt —*Nation's Business*⟩

²seethe \"\ *n* -s **:** the act or state of seething **:** EBULLITION ⟨a white ~ of foaming water —F.W.Crofts⟩ ⟨give some outlet to a ~ of violence in his muscles —Leslie Charteris⟩

¹seething *adj* [ME *sething,* fr. pres. part. of *sethen* to seethe] **1 :** intensely hot **:** BOILING ⟨a lamp drawn up into the scenery started a blaze, which soon became a ~ inferno —*Amer. Guide Series: Va.*⟩ **2 a :** in constant motion or activity **:** AGITATED ⟨the ~ life that goes on in those brown bamboo and mat huts —Robert Payne⟩ ⟨lovers and madmen have such ~ brains —Shak.⟩ **b :** INTENSE, VIOLENT ⟨had a ~ contempt for mankind —Gordon Merrick⟩ **— seeth·ing·ly** *adv*

²seething *adv* **:** BOILING ⟨~ hot⟩

seewee bean *var of* SIEVA BEAN

sefer torah *usu cap S&T, var of* SEPHER TORAH

¹seg *or* **segg** \ˈseg\ *n* -s [prob. of Scand origin; akin to Dan dial. *seeg, sæg* pig castrated at maturity] *dial Brit* **:** an animal (as a bull or boar) when castrated as a mature adult

²seg \"\ *n* -s [of Scand origin; akin to ON *sigg* callus] *dial Eng* **:** CALLUS

seg *abbr* segment

se·gar *var of* CIGAR

se·ger cone \ˈzāgə(r)-, ˈsāgə(r)-\ *n, usu cap S* [after Hermann August *Seger* †1893 Ger. ceramist] **:** PYROMETRIC CONE

seg·e·tal \ˈsejədᵊl\ *adj* [LL *segetalis,* fr. L *seget-, seges* field of grain, crop] **:** growing in fields of grain

seg·gy \ˈsegi\ *dial Eng var of* SEDGY

¹seg·ment \ˈsegmənt\ *n* -s *often attrib* [L *segmentum,* fr. *secare* to cut + *-mentum* -ment — more at SAW] **1 a :** a piece or separate fragment of something **:** PORTION ⟨chopped off the ~ of the line closest to the open hatch —Wirt Williams⟩ ⟨surgeon must remove the affected ~ of the bowel —Greer Williams⟩ ⟨ores of commercial value . . . are found in ~*s* of varying length —*Amer. Guide Series: Nev.*⟩ **b** (1) **:** a portion cut off from a geometrical figure by a line or plane; *esp* **:** the part of a circular area bounded by a chord and an arc of that circle or so much of the area as is cut off by the chord (2) **:** the part of a sphere cut off by a plane or included between two parallel planes (3) **:** the finite part of a line between two points in the line **c :** a portion of an act of speech; *esp* **:** a minimal portion consisting of an item of spoken language that is known as a vowel or a consonant — compare SUPRASEGMENTAL **2 a :** one of the constituent parts into which a body, entity, or quantity is or may be divided **:** SECTION, DIVISION ⟨the canning of juices and ~*s* —*Newsweek*⟩ ⟨calyx of five ~*s*, very deeply cleft —F.E.Hulme⟩ ⟨the concept of fairness toward every ~ of the economy —*Nation's Business*⟩ ⟨the natural gas industry is split into three major ~*s*: producers, pipeliners, and distributors —Walter Goodman⟩ ⟨the ~*s* of a tribe have the same characteristics as a tribe —Audrey Butt⟩ **b :** LOOP 4a **3 a :** a piece or casting (as of a sectional flywheel) in the form of the segment or sometimes the sector of a circle or part of a ring **b :** SEGMENT GEAR **c :** a segmental arch **syn** see PART

²seg·ment \ˈseg,ment\ *vt* -ED/-ING/-S **1 :** to cause to undergo segmentation by division or multiplication of cells ⟨the new cells which are successively ~*ed* off from the terminal cell —T.H.Huxley & H.N.Martin⟩ **2 :** to separate into segments ⟨the first criteria are linguistic and are used to ~ the poem into manageable units —W.E.Bull⟩ ⟨provides a thoroughness and consistency of instruction lacking in a ~*ed* course of study —J.R.Butler⟩ ⟨the clams are ~*ed* into lineages —Audrey Butt⟩ ⟨the strategy of the police . . . was to keep the demonstration ~*ed* and disorganized —*N.Y. Times*⟩

seg·men·tal \(ˈ)segˈmentᵊl\ *adj* [*¹segment* + *-al*] **1 a :** of, relating to, or having the form of the segment or sector of a circle ⟨removable ~ bushings extend across the entire width of the chain —*Modern Industry*⟩ ⟨~ sewer blocks⟩ ⟨~ fanlight⟩ ⟨~ pediment⟩ **b** *of an arch* (1) **:** centered below the springing and having an intrados which forms the segment of a circle (2) **:** drawn from two centers below the springing and having a low pointed intrados **2 a :** of, relating to, or composed of the somites or metameres of a segmented animal; *specif* **:** repeated in successive segments of such an animal **b :** of or relating to the segmental organs **3 :** of or relating to segmentation **:** individualized or isolated in organization or experience **:** SUBSIDIARY ⟨a method of synthesis of ~ data whereby the facts of anthropology, psychology, physiology, biology . . . would be related —*Quarterly Rev. of Biol.*⟩ ⟨religion becomes a ~ experience of no greater value in integrating their lives —Ruth Cavan⟩ ⟨many advertising campaigns, moreover, involve only ~ and not central responses —L.W.Doob⟩ ⟨sets of relationships which . . . will prove to be discontinuous and ~, spanning only part of the way —Oliver Garceau⟩

segmental apparatus *n* [so called fr. the segmental arrangement of the cranial nerves] **:** the brainstem in which the primitive chordate metameric pattern is still perceptible (as by the emergence of cranial nerves) — compare ARCHIPALLIUM, SUPRASEGMENTAL

segmental duct *n* **:** the duct of a segmental organ of a vertebrate embryo; *esp* **:** the duct of the pronephros that persists after the degeneration of the pronephros, receives the tubules of the mesonephros, becomes the mesonephric duct, and in lower vertebrates gives rise to the müllerian duct

segmental interchange *n* **:** RECIPROCAL TRANSLOCATION

seg·men·tal·iza·tion \seg,mentᵊlə̇ˈzāshən\ *n* -s **:** the act or process of segmentalizing or the state of being segmentalized

seg·men·tal·ize \segˈmentᵊl,īz\ *vt* -ED/-ING/-S [*segmental* + *-ize*] **:** to divide or separate into segments ⟨our larger *segmentalized* and confused mass society —Kimball Young⟩ ⟨introduces experimentally the concept of wholes in place of *segmentalized* thinking and acting —H.A.Dobbs⟩

seg·men·tal·ly \(ˈ)segˈmentᵊlē\ *adv* **:** in a segmental manner ⟨~ arranged organs⟩ ⟨a detective can identify only casually and ~ with his occupational role —R.N.Denney⟩

segmental organ *n* **1 :** NEPHRIDIUM **2 :** an embryonic excretory organ of a vertebrate whether a pronephros, mesonephros, or metanephros

segmental phoneme *n* **:** one of the phonemes (as \k, a, t\ in *cat, tack, act*) of a language that can be assigned to a relative sequential order of minimal segments — compare SUPRASEGMENTAL PHONEME

segmental resection *n* **:** excision of a segment of an organ; *specif* **:** excision of a portion of a lobe of a lung — compare PNEUMONECTOMY

seg·men·tary \ˈsegmən,terē, -ri\ *adj* [*¹segment* + *-ary*] **:** SEGMENTAL

seg·men·tate \-,tāt\ *adj* [*¹segment* + *-ate*] **:** composed of segments

seg·men·ta·tion \,segmənˈtāshən, -g,men-\ *n* -s [*²segment* + *-ation*] **1 :** the act or process of dividing into segments; *esp* **:** the formation of many cells from a single cell (as in a developing egg) — compare CLEAVAGE **2 :** annular contraction of smooth muscle (as of the intestine) that seems to cut the part affected into segments — compare PERISTALSIS

segmentation cavity *n* **:** BLASTOCOEL

seg·men·tec·to·my \,segmənˈtektəmē\ *n* -ES [ISV *¹segment* + *-ectomy*] **:** SEGMENTAL RESECTION

segmented seed *n* [fr. past part. of *²segment*] **:** a cut or sheared section of a beet seed ball usu. containing a single seed for planting

seg·ment·er \ˈseg,mentə(r)\ *n* -s [*²segment* + *-er*] **:** SCHIZONT

segment gear *n* [*¹segment*] **1 :** SEGMENT RACK **2 :** SECTOR GEAR

segment-headed \ˈ=,=,==\ *adj* **:** topped by a segmental arch ⟨a *segment-headed* window⟩

seg·men·ti·na \,segmənˈtīnə\ *n, cap* [NL, fr. L *segmentum* segment + NL *-ina*] **:** a genus of Asiatic freshwater snails (family Planorbidae) of medical importance as intermediate hosts of the intestinal fluke (*Fasciolopsis buski*)

seg·ment·ize \ˈsegmən,tīz\ *vt* -ED/-ING/-S [*¹segment* + *-ize*] **:** SEGMENTALIZE ⟨~ production into unit tasks —Jackson Martindell⟩ ⟨sectarian programs ~ the community —H.J. Whiting⟩ ⟨has been so *segmentized* that he has lost the concept of life as a basic unity —Harry Schacter⟩

segment rack *n* **:** a curved rack

segments *pl of* SEGMENT, *pres 3d sing of* SEGMENT

segment saw *n* **:** a saw that consists of a tapered metal flange with several steel segments fastened along its periphery and that is designed for cutting veneer with a small kerf

se·gno \ˈsā(,)nyō\ *n* -s [It, sign, fr. L *signum* — more at SIGN] **:** a notational sign; *specif* **:** the sign that marks the beginning or end of a musical repeat

se·go lily \ˈsē(,)gō-\ *also* **sego** *n* -s [Paiute *sego*] **:** a perennial herb (*Calochortus nuttallii*) of western No. America with bell-shaped flowers that are white within and yellowish green without

seg·re·ant \ˈsegrēənt\ *adj* [origin unknown] *heraldry* **:** having the wings expanded — used of a griffin or wyvern which is assumed to be rampant unless preceded by an adjective denoting a different position ⟨a griffin ~⟩ ⟨a griffin passant ~⟩

seg·re·ga·ble \ˈsegrəgəbəl\ *adj* [L *segregare* to segregate + E *-able*] **:** capable of being segregated ⟨these principles involve the concept of two units of heredity —H.H.Laughlin⟩

seg·re·gant \-əgənt\ *n* -s [*³segregate* + *-ant*] **:** SEGREGATE

¹seg·re·gate \ˈsegrə\|gət, -rē|, |,gāt, *usu* -d.+V\ *adj* [ME, fr. L *segregatus,* past part. of *segregare* to segregate] **:** SEGREGATED ⟨the human animals were immovably ~ —G.B.Shaw⟩

²segregate \"\ *n* -s **1 :** an individual or class of individuals differing in one or more genetic characters from the parental line usu. because of segregation of genes ⟨attempts to develop tomato ~*s* resistant to early blight⟩ **2 :** a taxonomic unit separated out from another of the same rank ⟨~*s* from the old genus *Polygonum*⟩

³seg·re·gate \|,gāt, *usu* -ād.+V\ *vb* -ED/-ING/-S [L *segregatus,*

past part. of *segregare* to set apart, segregate, fr. *se-* apart (fr. *sed, se* without) + *greg-, grex* flock, herd — more at IDIOT, GREGARIOUS] *vt* **1 :** to separate or set apart from others or from the general mass or main body **:** ISOLATE ⟨the scheme . . . to ~ in the foreign-aid bill all capital funds for neutrals —Haldore Hanson⟩ ⟨resumed his research in *segregating* the pure vitamin —*Current Biog.*⟩ ⟨suggestions . . . for tracing and *segregating* the impact of various causal and accentuating factors —Clark Warburton⟩ **2 :** to cause or force the separation of (as races or social classes) from the rest of society or from a larger group ⟨municipal ordinances meant to ~ races were declared void —Paul Hartmann & Morton Puner⟩ ⟨objections were raised to these schools on the ground that they tended to ~ Jewish children —Shlomo Katz⟩ **3 :** to remove nonfringing components from (a fatty oil) by winterizing or other methods **~** *vi* **1 :** to separate or withdraw (as from others or from a main body) ⟨observations were made . . . as to whether the solids and the liquid had segregated —R.A.Heindl & W.L.Pendergast⟩ ⟨a community of a million inevitably ~*s* somewhat into classes . . . or castes —A.L. Kroeber⟩ **2 :** to practice or enforce a policy of segregation ⟨railroads admit that they ~—*Issue*⟩ ⟨unwillingness of prison officials to . . . ~ on an intelligent basis —C.R.Minor⟩ **3 :** to separate during meiosis — used esp. of allelic genes ⟨the two genes at a given locus ~ from one another at meiosis —H.P. Riley⟩

segregated *adj* [fr. past part. of ³*segregate*] **1 a :** set apart or separated from others of the same kind or group ⟨a ~ account in a bank⟩ ⟨consists of a ~ area for absolute beginners —Priscilla Shirley⟩ **b :** divided in facilities or administered separately for members of different groups or esp. races ⟨~ education is . . . provided in the state constitution —*Time*⟩ ⟨the process by which ~ education has come to be accepted doctrine —L.W.Levy⟩ **c :** restricted to members of one group or esp. one race by a policy of segregation ⟨a Negro passenger . . . is placed in a ~ coach —*New Republic*⟩ ⟨~ drinking fountains, rest rooms and restaurants —*Jet*⟩ ⟨state laws requiring ~ schools for Negroes and whites —J.B.Robison⟩ **2 :** practicing or maintaining segregation esp. of races ⟨the inequalities inherent in a ~ economy and status system —M.C. Hill & B.C.McCall⟩ ⟨three . . . were from ~ states —*N.Y. Times*⟩

seg·re·ga·tion \ˌsegrəˈgāshən, -rēˈ-\ *n* -s *often attrib* [LL *segregation-, segregatio,* fr. L *segregatus* (past part. of *segregare* to segregate) + *-ion-, -io* -ion] **1 a :** the act or process of segregating or the state of being segregated ⟨the attempted ~ of the elements of truth from the picture of an idealized past⟩ ⟨that ~ of the order of grace and the order of nature which . . . others accepted —Douglas Bush⟩ **b** *obs* **:** DISPERSION ⟨a ~ of the Turkish fleet —Shak.⟩ **2 :** the separation or isolation of individuals or groups from a larger group or from society: as **a :** the separation or isolation of a race, class, or ethnic group by enforced or voluntary residence in a restricted area, barriers to social intercourse, divided educational facilities, or other discriminatory means ⟨in only four . . . states where there is educational ~ is a Negro permitted to study law —Henry Wallace⟩ ⟨city-dwelling Southerners have been assured . . . that residential ~ will preserve the separate schools —H.C.Fleming⟩ — see APARTHEID **b :** the separation for special treatment or observation of individuals or items from a larger group ⟨large-scale ~ of gifted children into special classes —H.J.Baker⟩ ⟨~ of extraordinary expenses in the municipal budget⟩ **c :** the separate confinement of individuals or groups (as hardened criminals, perverts, or the mentally deficient) from the rest of the inmate population in an institution ⟨the ~ of the small fraction of incorrigible . . . prisoners —H.E.Barnes⟩ **3 :** the tendency of individuals or units to separate from a larger group or society and associate together on a basis of similar characteristics ⟨industrial areas . . . and financial districts are some examples of industrial and commercial ~ —C.A.Dawson & W.E.Gettys⟩ ⟨~ according to lot size is often a feature of upper-class residential districts⟩ **4 :** a special cell or cellblock for the confinement of persons separated from the rest of the inmate population in an institution ⟨typical action of the adjustment committee includes counseling the offender . . . or placing him in ~—*Jour. of Social Work Process*⟩ **5 :** the separation of allelic genes that occurs typically during meiosis — see MENDEL'S LAW **6 :** a nonuniform distribution of particles of aggregate throughout a quantity of concrete, mortar, or plaster **7 :** the concentration of alloying elements in specific parts of a metallic alloy

seg·re·ga·tion·ist \-sh(ə)nəst\ *n* -s **:** one that believes in, advocates, or practices segregation ⟨~*s* formed battle lines . . . to preserve the South's traditional color barriers —*United Press*⟩

seg·re·ga·tive \ˈ==ˌgād·|iv, -ät|, |ēv *also* |əv\ *adj* [ML *segregativus,* fr. L *segregatus* + *-ivus* -ive] **1 :** tending to segregate; *esp* **:** inclined to isolate oneself ⟨one man was as ~ as the other was sociable⟩ **2 :** of, relating to, or implementing segregation ⟨restrictive and ~ color policies —John Hughes⟩

segs *pl of* SEG

¹**se·gue** \ˈsā(ˌ)gwā, ˈse(-\ *v imper* [It, there follows, 3d sing. pres. indic. of *seguire* to follow, fr. L *sequi* — more at SUE] **1 :** perform the music that follows at once — compare ATTACCA **2 :** perform the music that follows like that which has preceded

²**segue** \"\ *vi* **segued; segued; segueing; segues :** to proceed without pause from one musical number or theme to another ⟨*segued* into a hot wild . . . chorus —Frederic Wakeman⟩ ⟨~*ing* from one number to the next —Lane Kauffmann⟩

³**segue** \"\ *n* -s **:** a transition from one musical number or sound effect to another

se·gui·di·lla \ˌsāgēˈdē(y)ə, ˌseg-, -ēlyə\ *n* -s [Sp, dim. of *seguida,* a dance, lit., sequence, fr. fem. of *seguido,* past part. of *seguir* to follow, fr. L *sequi* — more at SUE] **1 :** a Spanish stanza of four or seven short verses partly assonant **2 a :** a Spanish dance having many regional variations in mood and tempo **b :** music for such a dance in its triple measure usu. performed with guitar and castanets

sehna *usu cap, var of* SENNA

sehna knot *or* **senna knot** *n, usu cap S* **:** a knot used in making carpets and rugs in which the yarn ends appear at the surface with one on each side of the adjacent yarns of warp around which they are twisted — compare GHIORDES KNOT

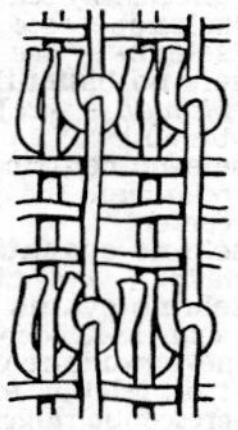

Sehna knot

sei \ˈsā\ *also* **sei whale** *n* -s [*sei,* short for *sei whale; sei whale,* part trans. of Norw *seihval,* fr. *sei* coalfish (akin to ON *seidhr* coalfish) + *hval* whale; fr. its habit of following the coalfish in search of food — more at SAITHE] **:** a common and widely distributed small white-spotted rorqual (*Balaenopterus borealis*)

sei·cen·to \sāˈchen(ˌ)tō\ *n, sometimes cap* [It, lit., six hundred (abbr. of sixteen hundred), fr. *sei* six (fr. L *sex*) + *cento* hundred, fr. L *centum* — more at SIX, HUNDRED] **:** the 17th century; *specif* **:** the 17th century period in Italian literature and art of Italy

seiche \ˈsāsh\ *n* -s [F] **:** an oscillation of the surface of a lake or landlocked sea that varies in period from a few minutes to several hours and is thought to be initiated chiefly by local variations in atmospheric pressure aided in some instances by winds and tidal currents and that continues for a time after the inequalities of atmospheric pressure have disappeared

se·id \ˈsāəd\ *n, pl* **seid** *or* **seids** *usu cap* [Ar *sayyid,* lit., lord, prince] **:** a member of a Turkoman people in the Turkmen Soviet Socialist Republic claiming Arab descent

sei·del \ˈsīdᵊl, ˈzīdᵊl\ *n* -s [G, fr. MHG *sīdel,* fr. L *situla* bucket, pail, voting urn] **:** a large glass for beer

seid·litz powders \ˈsedləts- *sometimes* ˈsīdləts-\ *n pl, usu cap S* [fr. *Sedlitz, Sedlice,* town of southwestern Bohemia, Czechoslovakia; fr. the similarity of their effects to those of the water of the town] **:** effervescing salts that consist of two separate powders with one of 40 grains of sodium bicarbonate mixed with 2 drams of Rochelle salt and the other of 35 grains of tartaric acid and that are mixed in water and drunk while effervescing as a mild cathartic — called also *Rochelle powders*

seif *or* **saif** \ˈsāf, ˈsīf\ *n* -s [Ar *saif* sword] **:** a long narrow sand dune or chain of dunes extending in a direction parallel to the wind responsible for its construction

sei·gnette salt *or* **seignette's salt** \(ˈ)senˈyet-\ *n, usu cap 1st S* [after Pierre *Seignette* †1719 Fr. apothecary] **:** ROCHELLE SALT

sei·gneur \sānˈyər(·)\ *n* -s *often cap* [MF, fr. ML *senior* superior, magnate, lord, fr. L, adj., elder — more at SENIOR] **:** a lord or gentleman: as **a :** a feudal lord ⟨now ~ of the feudal island of Sark —*N.Y. Times*⟩ **b :** a member of the landed gentry of Canada

sei·gneu·ri·al \-ˈyu̇rēəl\ *adj* [F, fr. MF, fr. *seigneur* + *-ial*] **:** of, relating to, or befitting a seigneur

sei·gneury \ˈsānyərē\ *n* -ES *sometimes cap* [F *seigneurie,* fr. OF, lit., lordship, fr. *seigneur* + *-ie* -y] **1 a :** the territory under the government of a feudal lord **b :** a landed estate held in Canada by feudal tenure until 1854 **2 :** the manor house of a Canadian seigneur

sei·gnior \ˈsēnyə(r)\ *n* -s [ME *seignour,* fr. MF *seigneur*] **:** a man of rank or authority; *esp* **:** the feudal lord of a manor

sei·gnior·age *or* **sei·gnor·age** *also* **sei·gneur·age** \-rij, -rēj\ *n* -s [ME *seigneurage,* fr. MF, right of the lord, esp. to coin money, fr. *seigneur* + *-age*] **1 :** a government revenue derived from the manufacture of coins that is calculated in the U. S. as the difference between the monetary and the bullion value of the silver contained in silver coins disregarding any alloy metal, all the metals contained in minor coins (as the nickel and the cent), or the silver bullion that is held as backing for silver certificates — compare BRASSAGE **2** *archaic* **:** DOMINION, POWER

sei·gniory *or* **sei·gnory** \ˈsēnyərē, -ri\ *n* -ES [ME, fr. OF *seigneurie* — more at SEIGNEURY] **1 a :** LORDSHIP, DOMINION; *specif* **:** the power or authority of a feudal lord **b** *also* **seigniory in gross :** a right of feudal superiority annexed to land apart from its ownership and including the rent or services attached thereto **2 :** the territory over which a lord holds jurisdiction **:** MANOR, DOMAIN ⟨their ~ had been broken up during the . . . nineteenth century —Hugh MacLennan⟩ **3 :** SIGNORY

sei·gno·ri·al \sēnˈyōrēəl, -ˈyȯr-\ *also* **sei·gnior·al** \ˈsēnyərəl\ *or* **sei·gnior·i·al** \sēnˈyōrēəl, -ˈyȯr-\ *or* **sei·gnor·al** \ˈsēnyərəl\ *adj* [obs. E *seignor* seignior (fr. ME *seignour*) or E *seignior* + *-ial* or *-al*] **:** of, relating to, or befitting a seignior **:** MANORIAL

¹**seine** \ˈsān\ *also* **seine net** *n* -s *often attrib* [ME, fr. OE *segne;* akin to OHG *segina* seine; both fr. a prehistoric WGmc word borrowed fr. L *sagena* seine, fr. Gk *sagēnē* — more at SUMPTER] **:** a large net having one edge provided with sinkers and the other with floats that hangs vertically in the water and encloses fish when its ends are brought together or drawn ashore — compare POUND NET, PURSE SEINE

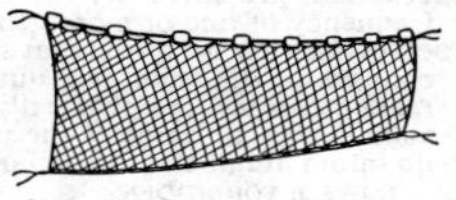

seine

²**seine** \"\ *vb* -ED/-ING/-S *vi* **:** to fish with or catch fish with a seine ⟨going to the creek to ~ —Elizabeth M. Roberts⟩ ⟨*seining* for alligators . . . at the edge of the river —Don Brown⟩ **~** *vt* **1 :** to seek or catch with a seine ⟨schooners out *seining* mackerel⟩ **2 :** to fish or seek in (something) with or as if with a seine ⟨the fleet ~*s* the lower river daily⟩ ⟨*seined* such old tomes . . . for obscure facts —*Time*⟩

sein·er \-nə(r)\ *also* **seine-netter** \ˈ=ˌ==\ *n* -s **:** a person or boat that fishes with a seine

seir *or* **seirfish** *var of* SEER

seis *pl of* SEI

seise *var of* SEIZE

sei·sin *or* **sei·zin** \ˈsēzᵊn\ *n* -s [ME *seisine, sesin,* fr. OF *saisine,* fr. *saisir* to seize — more at SEIZE] **1 :** the possession of land or chattels **:** possession with quiet enjoyment ⟨take ~ of the land⟩ **2 :** the possession of or status with relation to land arising from the completion of feudal investiture by livery of seisin **3 :** the possession of a freehold estate in land by one having title thereto

seism \ˈsīzəm\ *n* -s [Gk *seismos* — more at SEISMIC] **:** EARTHQUAKE

-seism \ˌsīzəm\ *n comb form* -s [Gk *seismos* earthquake] **:** seismic movement ⟨tachy*seism*⟩

seis·mal \ˈsīzməl\ *adj* [Gk *seismos* earthquake + E *-al*] **:** SEISMIC

seis·mat·i·cal \sīzˈmad·əkəl\ *adj* [Gk *seismat-, seisma* act of shaking (fr. *seiein* to shake) + E *-ical* — more at SEISMIC] **:** of or relating to the study of seismic phenomena

seis·met·ic \-ˈmed·ik\ *adj* [Gk *seismos* + E *-etic*] **:** SEISMIC

seis·mic \ˈsī|zmik, -mēk *also* |sm- *sometimes* ˈse| *or* ˈsā| *or* ˈsē|\ *also* **seis·mi·cal** \-məkəl, -mēk-\ *adj* [Gk *seismos* shock, earthquake (fr. *seiein* to shake, quake) + E *-ic, -ical;* akin to Skt *tveṣati* he is violently moved] **:** of, subject to, or caused by an earthquake or an earth vibration produced artificially (as by an explosion in geophysical prospecting) — **seis·mi·cal·ly** \-mək(ə)lē, -mēk-, -li\ *adv*

seis·mic·i·ty \=ˈmisəd·ē, -ətē, -i\ *n* -ES [ISV *seismic* + *-ity*] **:** the quality or state of being seismic; *specif* **:** the relative frequency and distribution of earthquakes ⟨progress has been made in determining the ~ in a given area —Beno Gutenberg⟩

seismic sea wave *n* **:** one of many gravitational water waves propagated outward in all directions from the epicenter of a submarine earthquake **:** TSUNAMI — compare TIDAL WAVE

seismic vertical *n* **:** the point on the surface of the earth vertically over the focus from which the impulse of an earthquake proceeds; *also* **:** the vertical line joining these two points

seis·mism \ˈ=ˌmizəm\ *n* -s [Gk *seismos* earthquake + E *-ism*] **:** earthquake phenomena **:** seismic activity

seismo- *comb form* [Gk, fr. *seismos* — more at SEISMIC] **:** earthquake **:** vibration ⟨*seismo*meter⟩ ⟨*seismo*tropism⟩

seis·mo·chronograph \¦=mə+\ *n* [*seismo-* + *chronograph*] **:** a chronograph adapted to determining the exact time of earthquake shocks

seis·mo·gram \ˈsī|zməˌgram, -aa(ə)m *also* |sm- *sometimes* ˈse| *or* ˈsā| *or* ˈsē|\ *n* [ISV *seismo-* + *-gram*] **:** the record of an earth tremor made by a seismograph

seis·mo·graph \-raf, -raa(ə)f, -raif, -räf\ *n* [ISV *seismo-* + *-graph*] **:** an apparatus of varying type and structure designed to measure and record vibrations within the earth and of the ground (as produced during an earthquake or by artificial explosions or atmospheric conditions)

seis·mog·ra·pher \=ˈmägrəfə(r)\ *n* -s [*seismography* + *-er*] **:** a specialist in seismography **:** SEISMOLOGIST

seis·mo·graph·ic \¦sī|zmə¦grafik, -fēk *also* |sm- *sometimes* ˈse| *or* ˈsā| *or* ˈsē|\ *also* **seis·mo·graph·i·cal** \-fəkəl, -fēk-\ *adj* [ISV *seismograph* + *-ic*] **:** of, relating to, or indicated by a seismograph or seismography

seis·mog·ra·phy \=ˈmägrəfē, -fi\ *n* -ES [ISV *seismo-* + *-graphy*] **1 :** the description of earthquakes; *specif* **:** the art of registering the shocks and undulatory movements of earthquakes **2 :** SEISMOLOGY

seis·mo·log·i·cal \¦sī|zmə¦läjəkəl, -jek- *also* |sm- *sometimes* ¦se| *or* ¦sā| *or* ¦sē|\ *also* **seis·mo·log·ic** \-jik, -jēk\ *adj* **:** of or relating to seismology — **seis·mo·log·i·cal·ly** \-jək(ə)lē, -jēk-, -li\ *adv*

seis·mol·o·gist \=ˈmäləjəst\ *n* -s **:** a geophysicist who specializes in seismology **:** SEISMOGRAPHER

seis·mo·logue \ˈ=məˌlȯg\ *n* -s [*seismo-* + *catalogue*] **:** a description or catalog of earthquakes

seis·mol·o·gy \sīzˈmäləjē, -ji *also* |sˈ- *sometimes* se| *or* sā| *or* sē|\ *n* -ES [ISV *seismo-* + *-logy*] **:** a science that deals with earthquakes and attendant phenomena including the study of artificially produced elastic waves in earth materials

seis·mom·e·ter \-ˈmäməd·ə(r), -mətə-\ *n* [*seismo-* + *-meter*] **:** a seismograph that furnishes data for measuring the actual movements of the ground; *specif* **:** the part of a seismograph assembly that detects the ground movement

seis·mo·met·ric \¦sī|zmə¦me·trik, -rēk *also* |sm- *sometimes* |se| *or* ¦sā| *or* ¦sē|\ *or* **seis·mo·met·ri·cal** \-rəkəl, -rēk-\ *adj* **:** of or relating to a seismometry or a seismometer

seis·mom·e·try \=ˈmämə·trē, -ri\ *n* -ES [ISV *seismo-* + *-metry*] **:** the scientific study of earthquake phenomena esp. by means of the seismometer

seis·mo·nas·tic \¦=mə¦nastik, -aas-, -tēk\ *adj* [ISV *seismonasty* + *-ic*] **:** of or relating to seismonasty

seis·mo·nas·ty \ˈ==ˌnastē, -aas-, -ti\ *n* -ES [ISV *seismo-* + *-nasty*] **:** a nastic movement in plants caused by mechanical shock

seis·mo·scope \ˈ==ˌskōp\ *n* [ISV *seismo-* + *-scope*] **:** an instrument for recording only the time or fact of occurrence of earthquakes — compare SEISMOMETER — **seis·mo·scop·ic** \¦==¦skäpik, -pēk\ *adj*

seis·mo·tectonic \¦==+\ *adj* [*seismo-* + *tectonic*] **:** of, relating to, or designating structural features of the earth which are associated with or revealed by earthquakes

seis·mot·ic \=ˈmäd·|ik, -ät|, |ēk\ *adj* [Gk *seismos* earthquake + E *-otic* — more at SEISMIC] **:** SEISMIC

seisms *pl of* SEISM

-seisms *pl of* -SEISM

sei·so·na·cea \ˌsīsəˈnāshēə\ *n pl, cap* [NL, fr. *Seison,* genus of rotifers + *-acea*] **:** a small order of Rotifera comprising elongated rotifers with weakly developed trochal disks that are epizoic on marine crustaceans

sei·so·nid·ea \-ˈnidēə\ *or* **sei·so·nia** \sīˈsōnēə\ [NL, fr. *Seison,* genus of rotifers + *-idea* or *-ia*] *syn of* SEISONACEA

se·i·ty \ˈsēəd·ē\ *n* -ES [ML *seitat-, seitas,* fr. L *se* oneself + *-itat-, -itas* -ity — more at SUICIDE] **:** a quality peculiar to oneself **:** SELFHOOD, INDIVIDUALITY

Seitz \ˈzīts\ *trademark* — used for a filter of asbestos fibers compressed into a disk used esp. for sterilizing liquids that cannot be subjected to heat and for other bacteriological proceedings

sei·u·rus \sīˈyu̇rəs\ *n, cap* [NL, fr. Gk *seiein* to shake + NL *-urus* — more at SEISMIC] **:** a genus of warblers consisting of the No. American ovenbird and the water thrushes

sei whale *var of* SEI

seize \ˈsēz\ *vb* -ED/-ING/-S [ME *saisen, seisen, sesen,* fr. OF *saisir,* fr. ML *sacire* to effect legal possession, to assign, of Gmc origin; akin to Goth *satjan* to set — more at SET] *vt* **1 a** *usu* **seise** \"\ **:** to vest ownership of a freehold estate in with or without actual possession ⟨the lord of the manor *seises* his heir in land holdings⟩ ⟨the widow should have the third part of a fief of which her husband was *seised* at the time of their marriage —C.H.McIlwain⟩ **b** (1) *often* **seise :** to put in legal possession of estate or property ⟨we were landowners now, duly *seised* and possessed —Mark Twain⟩ ⟨entitled to inherit the estate of which said deceased died *seized* —*Detroit Law Jour.*⟩ ⟨signed to clear the title to other properties of which her father had died *seized* —G.L.Fake⟩ (2) *often* **seise :** to put in possession of something ⟨temperate men are *seized* of . . . wisdom and knowledge —Richard Carew⟩ ⟨the biographer will be *seized* of all pertinent papers and correspondence⟩ (3) **:** to endow (a governmental agency or deliberative body) with the responsibility for action on a matter by placing it on an agenda ⟨the House when *seized* of the matter either gave its decision forthwith after debate or referred the matter to a select committee —T.E.May⟩ ⟨points out that the Council is still officially *seized* with the dispute eight years after it was settled —*Hadassah Newsletter*⟩ ⟨the Committee may not, however, consider any matter of which the Security Council is *seized* and which the Council has not submitted to the Assembly —*U.N. Dept. of Public Information*⟩ **2 a :** to take possession of **:** CONFISCATE ⟨government *seized* the entire foreign-owned oil industry —R.W. Van Alstyne⟩ ⟨any authorized officer has power to ~ any article of food which appears to him unfit —C.R.A.Martin⟩ **b :** to take possession of (something) after or by a court order, legislative enactment, or other legal process ⟨*seized* control of steel plants to prevent the scheduled walkout —Mary K. Hammond⟩ ⟨ten of the exhibiting artists have had their paintings *seized* —*N.Y. Times*⟩ ⟨authority to ~ and impound the agency's funds⟩ **3 a :** to possess or take by force **:** CAPTURE ⟨the wind ready to ~ the hat off my head —Mary Deasy⟩ ⟨the tremendous riches *seized* in swift attacks on land and water —H.E.Rieseberg⟩ ⟨the military regime which had *seized* power —*Americana Annual*⟩ **b :** to take prisoner **:** ARREST ⟨the three men were *seized* by a large body of Sioux —I.B.Richman⟩ ⟨the determination of the Allied Powers to ~ and punish war criminals —R.G.Neumann⟩ **4 a** (1) **:** to take hold of **:** CLUTCH ⟨ordered his soldiers to shave off their beards so that their enemies might not ~ them —F.J. Haskin⟩ ⟨*seizing* between his teeth the cartilage —G.B.Shaw⟩ (2) **:** to take hold of quickly or eagerly ⟨the hero *seized* her in unaccustomed arms —G.W.Brace⟩ ⟨*seized* pen and paper —John Irwin⟩ **b :** to possess oneself of **:** GRASP ⟨and rise to ~ the everlasting prize —W.W.Walford⟩ ⟨~ the leadership of social reform —*Current Biog.*⟩ ⟨*seized* for the committee the right to report on . . . national finances —Allan Nevins⟩ **c :** to take or use eagerly or quickly often as a rationalization or last resort ⟨*seized* the opportunity to calculate a number of fresh latitudes —Benjamin Farrington⟩ ⟨they'll ~ any excuse to stop work and cut down a tree —Ellen Glasgow⟩ **d :** to understand fully and distinctly **:** APPREHEND ⟨we can only try to ~ the meaning of serfdom —R.W.Southern⟩ ⟨the artist . . . possesses the power of surely and frequently *seizing* reality —Clive Bell⟩ ⟨there's no one now to grasp my half-*seized* thought —Donagh MacDonagh⟩ **5** *obs* **:** to fix or establish in a place ⟨the gentleman was *seized* in my country —Thomas Stafford⟩ **6 a :** to attack or overwhelm physically **:** AFFLICT ⟨suddenly *seized* with an acute illness —H.G. Armstrong⟩ ⟨the arthritis which had *seized* him during the summer —Virginia D. Dawson & Betty D. Wilson⟩ **b :** to possess (one's mind) completely or overwhelmingly ⟨he was early *seized* with the idea of building cars —A.F.Harlow⟩ ⟨a kind of panic *seized* her —Mary Austin⟩ ⟨*seized* the popular imagination —Basil Davenport⟩ ⟨conviction *seized* him —Henry Miller⟩ **7 :** to bind or fasten together with a lashing of small stuff (as yarn, marline, or fine wire) **~** *vi* **1 a :** to take possession — usu. used with *on* or *upon* ⟨amassed fortunes, either by *seizing* on their property, or by selling their persons —G.G.Coulton⟩ **b :** to make use often as a last resort — usu. used with *on* or *upon* ⟨*seized* upon business as their sacrificial goat —B.F.Fairless⟩ ⟨~ on any plan, despite its imperfections, hoping for relief —*Dance Observer*⟩ ⟨~ upon the drug as a cure for their real or imaginary ailments —*Irish Digest*⟩ **2 :** to cohere or stick fast to a relatively moving part (as a bearing, a gas-engine piston, or a slide valve) through excessive pressure, temperature, or friction **3** *chiefly Brit* **:** to slow down or proceed with awkwardness or difficulty — usu. used with *up* ⟨the verse *seized* up, sometimes by sheer surfeit of imagery —C.D.Lewis⟩ ⟨compositions for wind alone often *seize* up in the middle parts —Edward Sackville-West⟩ **syn** see TAKE

seiz·er \-zə(r)\ *n* -s **:** one that seizes: as **a :** SEIZOR **b :** a dog trained to seize game

seizin *var of* SEISIN

seizing *n* -s [ME *seising,* fr. gerund of *seisen* to seize] **1 :** the operation of fastening together or lashing with small stuff that is usu. tarred **2 a :** the cord or lashing used in seizing — compare FOX **b :** the fastening so made

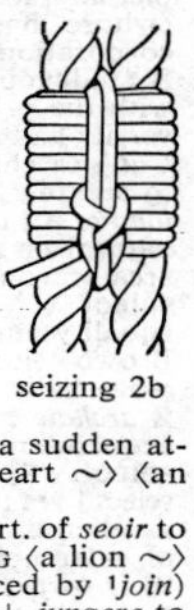

seizing 2b

sei·zor \ˈsēzər, -ēˌzȯ(ə)r\ *n* -s [*seize* + *-or*] **:** one that seizes or takes possession esp. of a freehold estate

sei·zure \ˈsēzhə(r)\ *n* -s [ME *seisure,* fr. *seisen* to seize + *-ure*] **1 a :** the act or process of seizing or the state of being seized ⟨need to guard against the private ~ of power over a free market —T.W.Arnold⟩ ⟨tanks of the division crossed the bridge immediately after its ~ —P.W.Thompson⟩ **b :** the act of taking possession of person or property by virtue of a warrant or by legal authority **2** *obs* **a :** POSSESSION, OWNERSHIP **b :** HOLD, GRIP **3 :** a sudden attack (as of a disease or sickness) ⟨died of a heart ~⟩ ⟨an epileptic ~⟩

se·jant \ˈsējənt\ *adj* [modif. of MF *seant,* pres. part. of *seoir* to sit, fr. L *sedēre* — more at SIT] *heraldry* **:** SITTING ⟨a lion ~⟩

se·join \səˈjȯin\ *vt* -ED/-ING/-S [modif. (influenced by ¹*join*) of L *sejungere,* fr. *se-* apart (fr. *sed, se* without) + *jungere* to join — more at IDIOT, YOKE] *archaic* **:** SEPARATE

se·junc·tion \səˈjəŋ(k)shən\ *n* [L *sejunction-, sejunctio,* fr. *sejunctus* (past part. of *sejungere* to sejoin) + *-ion-, -io* -ion] **:** SEPARATION

se·ka·ni \səˈkänē\ *n, pl* **sekani** *or* **sekanis** *usu cap* **1 a :** an Athapaskan people of the upper Peace river drainage, British

Columbia **b** : a member of such people **2** : the language of the Sekani people — called also *Montagnard*

sek·hwan \'sĕ̄ˌkwän\ *n, pl* **sekhwan** *or* **sekhwans** *usu cap* [Chin (Amoy dial.)] : one of the distinct aboriginal and agricultural peoples of Formosa

se·kos \'sē̆ˌkäs\ *n* -ES [Gk sēkos pen, sacred enclosure] : a sacred enclosure or inner sanctuary of an Egyptian temple

sel \'sel\ *chiefly Scot var of* SELF

sel *abbr* **1** select **2** selected **3** selection **4** selector

se·la \'sēlə\ *n* -S [native name in Burma] : rice that is heated before milling

1se·la·chi·an \sə̇'lākēən\ *n* -S [NL Selachii + E -an (n. suffix)] : a fish (as a shark or ray) of the group Selachii

2selachian \"\ *adj* [NL Selachii + E -an (adj. suffix)] : of or relating to the Selachii

se·la·chii \-ˌkē̄ˌī\ *n pl, cap* [NL, irreg. fr. selachos cartilaginous fish; akin to Gk selas light, brightness — more at SELEN-] *in some classifications* : a variously delimited group of elasmobranch fishes : **a** : a primary division of Pisces that includes all the elasmobranchs and is equivalent to Chondrichthyes **b** : a class or subclass that includes all the elasmobranchs except the chimaeras **c** : a subclass or order that includes the existing sharks and rays as distinguished from the extinct Pleuropterygii and Ichthyotomi **d** : a suborder that includes the existing sharks as distinguished from the rays and is equivalent to Pleurotremata

1sel·a·choid \'selə̇ˌkȯid\ *adj* [NL Selachoidei] : of or relating to the Pleurotremata

2selachoid \"\ *n* -S : one of the Pleurotremata

sel·a·choi·dei \ˌselə̇'kȯidēˌī\ [NL, fr. Selachii + -oidei] *syn of* PLEUROTREMATA

sel·a·cho·le·ic acid \ˌselə(ˌ)kō̄'lēik-, -ˌsɛˈkō̄ˌlēik-\ *n* [selacholeic fr. Gk selachos cartilaginous fish + oleic; fr. its being found in some fish-liver oils] : NERVONIC ACID

sel·a·cho·stome \'selə̇kəˌstōm, sə̇'lak-\ *n* -S [NL Selachostomi] : PADDLEFISH

sel·a·chos·to·mi \ˌselə̇'kä̀stəˌmī\ *n pl, cap* [NL, fr. Gk selachos cartilaginous fish + NL -stomi] *in some classifications* : an order of ganoid fishes comprising the paddlefishes

sel·a·chos·to·mous \ˌselə̇'kästəməs\ *adj* [NL Selachostomi + E -ous] : of or relating to the Selachostomi

sel·a·chyl alcohol \'selə̇ˌkil-\ *n* [selachyl ISV selach- (fr. NL Selachii) + -yl] : a liquid unsaturated alcohol C₁₈H₃₅-CH(OH)CH₂OH found in the unsaponifiable portion of fish oils (as shark-liver oil); glycerol x-9-octa-decen-yl ether

se·la·dang *or* **sa·la·dang** \sə̇'lä̀ˌdäŋ\ *or* **sla·dang** \'slä̀d-\ *n* -S [Malay sĕladang] : the gaur of the Malay archipelago

seladon green *var of* CELADON GREEN

se·lag·i·na·ce·ae \sə̇ˌlajə̇'nāsēˌē\ *n pl, cap* [NL, fr. Selago + -aceae] *syn of* SCROPHULARIACEAE

se·lag·i·nel·la \sə̇ˌlajə̇'nelə\ *n* [NL, fr. L selagin-, selago, a plant resembling the savin + -ella] **1** *cap* : the type and usu. sole genus of the family Selaginellaceae — compare ISOETES **2** -S : any plant of the genus Selaginella

se·lag·i·nel·la·ce·ae \ˌ=ˌ==ˌnə̇'lāsē̆ˌē\ *n pl, cap* [NL, fr. Selaginella, type genus + -aceae] : a family of terrestrial chiefly tropical plants (order Lycopodiales) that resemble mosses, have branching stems and scalelike leaves which are many-ranked and uniform or 4-ranked and of 2 kinds spreading in 2 planes, and produce 1-celled sporangia which contain both megaspores and microspores — see SELAGINELLA

se·lag·i·nel·la·ceous \ˌ=ˌ===ˈlāshəs\ *adj*

se·lag·i·nel·la·les \ˌ=ˌ==ˌnə̇'lā(ˌ)lēz\ *n pl, cap* [NL, fr. Selaginella + -ales] : an order of lower vascular plants (subclass Lycopodineae) that are sometimes included among the Lycopodiales from which they differ chiefly in having ligulate leaves, four-sided strobiles, and heterosporous reproduction and that are all placed in the single recent genus Selaginella

se·lag·i·nel·li·tes \-'lī̄d-(ˌ)ēz\ *n, cap* [NL, fr. Selaginella + -ites] : a form genus of Paleozoic heterosporous herbaceous plants that suggest and are probably closely related to members of the genus Selaginella

se·la·go \sə̇'lä̀(ˌ)gō̄\ *n, cap* [NL, fr. L, a plant resembling the savin] : a genus of low African shrubs (family Scrophulariaceae) resembling the heath and having spicate flowers with a nearly regular corolla, four didynamous stamens, a two-celled ovary, and drupaceous or capsular fruit

se·lah \'selə, -ˌlä, sə̇'lä̀\ *interj* [Heb selāh] — used 71 times in the Psalms and 3 times in Habakkuk probably as an exclamation (as amen or hallelujah) or possibly as a direction to temple musicians or chorus to lift up music or voices ⟨God will . . . uproot you from the land of the living. Selah —Ps 52:5 (RSV)⟩

selas *pl of* SELA

sel·couth \'selˌkǖth\ *adj* [ME, fr. OE selcū̆th, fr. seld- (fr. seldan seldom) + cū̆th familiar, known — more at COUTH] *archaic* : UNUSUAL, STRANGE, MARVELOUS ⟨this ~ girl, so rarely fashioned in mind and body —Llewelyn Powys⟩

seld \'seld\ *adv (or adj)* [ME selde, back-formation fr. seldere (compar. of selden seldom) & seldeste (superl. of selden seldom), fr. OE seldor (compar. of seldan seldom) & seldost (superl. of seldan seldom)] *archaic* : SELDOM

1sel·dom \'seldəm\ *adv* [ME selden, selden, fr. OE seldan, seldon, seldun, seldun; akin to OFris selden seldom, OHG seltan, ON sjaldan, Goth silda-; akin to L sed, se without, suus one's own — more at SUICIDE] : in few instances : RARELY, INFREQUENTLY — opposed to often ⟨he ~ changed a conclusion he had formed —A.H.Tuttle⟩

2seldom \"\ *adj* [ME, fr. seldom, adv.] : RARE, INFREQUENT ⟨silence was such a ~ thing —R.O.Bowen⟩ ⟨one of those ~ people whom you can love unashamedly —Loudie Claar⟩ ⟨with her small ~ smile —Ethel Wilson⟩

sel·dom·ly \ˌseldəm + -lȳ\ *archaic* : SELDOM

sel·dom·ness *n* -ES : INFREQUENCY, RARENESS

sele \'sē̄(ə)l, 'sā̄(-\ *n* [ME, fr. OE sǣl happiness, good fortune, sele — more at SILLY] **1** *dial chiefly Brit* : good fortune — usu. used in greetings and proverbial expressions **2** *dial chiefly Brit* : TIME, OCCASION — used esp. of opportune or favorable times

1se·lect \sə̇'lekt\ *adj* [L selectus, past part. of seligere to separate by, picking out, select, fr. sed-, se- apart (fr. sed, se without) + legere to gather, select — more at IDIOT, LEGEND] **1** : chosen from a number or group by fitness or preference ⟨the valuable ~ bibliography covers 30 pages —R.L.Morton⟩ ⟨with the Bible and Shakespeare in the ~ library to be taken to the proverbial desert island —J.K.M.Rothenstein⟩ **2 a** : of signal value or excellence : SUPERIOR, CHOICE ⟨a workshop for a ~ group of young players —Current Biog.⟩ ⟨a ~ group of blue-chip shares —Paul Heffernan⟩ ⟨a ~ group of 30 voices which sings for . . . services —Bull. of Bates Coll.⟩ **b** : exclusively or fastidiously chosen often with regard to social, economic, or cultural characteristics ⟨formed literary, charitable, and social clubs with ~ memberships —Oscar Handlin⟩ ⟨whoso has passed the system, then, is . . . one of a close corporation, of a ~ and individual few —G.D.Brown⟩ **3** : judicious or restrictive in choice : DISCRIMINATING ⟨pleased with the ~ appreciation of his books —Osbert Sitwell⟩ ⟨university had its beginnings in a pioneer ~ school —Alfred Univ. Cat.⟩ ⟨a change in emphasis . . . from being exclusive and ~ to seeking for all means of outreach —Janet Whitney⟩ **4** of lumber : of a generally clear grain : of a quality suitable for natural or paint finish **b** : having a large proportion of its area or volume suitable for use in manufacture

2select \"\ *n* -S **1** : one that is select — often used in pl. ⟨quality lumber, notably the ~s and clear grades —N.C. Brown⟩ ⟨it is possible to buy ware that is composed wholly of ~s —Sally Taylor⟩ ⟨the oysters he chooses are only the ~s⟩ **2** *archaic* : a select class or group ⟨had his ~ of friends and acquaintance —Roger North⟩

3select \"\ *vb* -ED/-ING/-S [L selectus, past part. of seligere to select] *vt* : to choose from a number or group usu. by fitness, excellence, or other distinguishing feature ⟨the difficult task of ~ing a presidential candidate —H.D.Jordan⟩ ⟨farmers ~ their own tracts of ground —Amer. Guide Series: Fla.⟩ ⟨content to know only those ~ed and fitted to meet him —H.J.Laski⟩ ~ vi : to choose something from a number or group : to make a selection ⟨has ~ed and edited well —Alan Devoe⟩ ⟨whatever the basis, ~ with care and foresight⟩

se·lect·ance \sə̇'lektən(t)s\ *n* -ES [3select + -ance] : the selectivity or discrimination in response to signals of slightly different frequency (as in radio reception)

select committee *n* : a legislative committee appointed to inquire into or to consider a particular matter or bill

selected *adj* [fr. past part. of 3select] : SELECT; *specif* : of a higher grade or quality than the ordinary ⟨prefers ~ steel to the mill-run steel⟩

se·lect·ee \sə̇ˌlek'tē̄\ *n* -S [3select + -ee] : one inducted into military service under selective service : DRAFTEE

se·lec·tion \sə̇'lekshən\ *n* -S [L selection-, selectio, fr. selectus (past part. of seligere to select) + -ion-, -io -ion] **1** : the act or process of selecting : the state of being selected ⟨the ~ of the school he should attend —Sidney Lovett⟩ ⟨pilot ~ in this country . . . is not perfect —H.G.Armstrong⟩ ⟨friends applauding his ~ as president⟩ **2 a** : one that is selected : CHOICE ⟨each has been a ~ of one of the major book clubs —Current Biog.⟩ ⟨discussed with some of his cabinet ~s the ways of increasing pressure —Nation's Business⟩ **b** : a composition or passage selected for reading or performance (included . . . musical comedy ~s —Current Biog.⟩ ⟨culled and copied ~s suitable for coming obituaries —Agnes S. Turnball⟩ ⟨~s from the best writers of the era⟩ **c** : a horse, dog, or other contestant selected usu. by a specialist for betting purposes ⟨the trackman's ~s often run in the money⟩ **3 a** : a natural or artificial biological process that results or tends to result in preventing some individuals or groups of organisms from surviving and propagating and in allowing others to do so with the result that particular traits of the latter are given pronounced expression — compare DARWINISM, NATURAL SELECTION **b** : the removal at relatively short intervals of mature timber so that continuous natural reproduction of a forest is encouraged and a stand of uneven age maintained — compare SUSTAINED YIELD **4 a** : the act of selecting land **b** : a piece of land taken up in Australian processes of land settlement ⟨~s on which . . . women and children helped to grub the land —E.H.Collis⟩ **5** : the process by which an insurance company accepts or rejects risks **syn** see CHOICE

selection coefficient *n* : a measure of the survival value of a given gene or mutation by comparison of the growth rate of the experimental form with that of the wild type

selection forest *n* : a forest in which trees of all age classes are represented

se·lec·tion·ism \-shə̇ˌnizəm\ *n* -S [ISV selection + -ism] : a system or theory based on the doctrine of natural, artificial, or social selection

se·lec·tion·ist \-sh(ə̇)nə̇st\ *n* -S : one who considers natural selection a fundamental factor in evolution

selection pressure *n* : the effect of selection on the relative frequency of one or more genes within a population

selection rule *n* : a rule that states which of all the conceivable changes in the state of a quantized system (atoms, nuclei, or related entities) are physically possible under specified circumstances usu. in terms of the possible numerical changes in the quantum numbers that characterize the system — compare ALLOWED, FORBIDDEN

selection value *n* : the presumed value of a trait or characteristic for the effective operation of the processes of natural selection

se·lec·tive \sə̇'lektiv, -tēv also -təv\ *adj* [L selectus (past part. of seligere to select) + E -ive — more at SELECT] **1** : of, relating to, or characterized by selection : selecting or tending to select ⟨buyers for retail stores have become more and more ~ —Glenn Fowler⟩ ⟨some dyes were highly ~ in their action —S.F.Mason⟩ ⟨monetary controls may be either general or ~ —Jules Backman⟩ ⟨an exceptionally quick and ~ reader —John Mason Brown⟩ **2** : of, relating to, or constituting the ability of an electrical circuit or apparatus to respond to a specific frequency without interference

selective absorption *n* : the absorption by a substance of only certain wavelengths of radiation with the coincident exclusion or transmission of others ⟨selective absorption of green⟩

selective assembly *n* : the selection from two or more stocks of the particular parts of a mechanism that will fit with the desired degree of clearance when assembled

selective cutting *or* **selective logging** *n* : the cutting out of trees that are mature or defective, or of inferior kinds to encourage the growth of the remaining trees in a forest or wood

selective flotation *n* : the form of flotation in which only one mineral is floated from an ore pulp containing two or more floatable minerals

se·lec·tive·ly \-tə̇vlē, -li\ *adv* : in a selective manner : by selection

se·lec·tive·ness \-tivnə̇s, -tēv- also -təv-\ *n* -ES : the act or process of being selective

selective radiation *n* : the radiation emitted by a surface whose emissivity is distinctly varied for different wavelengths

selective reflection *n* : the reflection emitted by a surface that reflects waves of different lengths with varying intensity

selective service *n* : the service of a person in the armed forces consequent to induction under a governmental act or decree : DRAFT

selective transmission *n* : a transmission for automobiles and similar powered vehicles by which the gear can be changed directly from one speed to any other by a single lever

se·lec·tiv·i·ty \sə̇ˌlek'tivəd-ē̄, -vətē̄, -i also (ˌ)sēˌl-\ *n* -ES **1** : the quality or state of being selective ⟨circulation policy which stressed ~ as opposed to mass sales —Current Biog.⟩ ⟨the ~ of students in the technical institute —C.V.Newsom⟩ ⟨newer insecticides . . . are tending toward a high degree of ~ —Industrial & Engineering Chemistry⟩ **2 a** : the state of possessing or exhibiting selective reflection **b** : a quantitative or qualitative measurement of the degree to which an electrical circuit or apparatus responds to a desired signal and rejects others

se·lect·ly \sə̇'lektlē, -tli\ *adv* [1select + -ly] : in a select manner : with selectivity

se·lect·man \sə̇'lek(t)ˌman, sē̄'le-, 'sle-, -maa(ə)n, (ˌ)ˌ=ˌ)ˌ=ˈ= also (=)ˈ=ˌmən; 'sē̄ˌlek(t)ˌman, -ˌlȯk-, -maa(ə)n, (ˌ)ˌ=ˈ= sometimes 'si(ˌ)ˌ=ˈ= or ˌsi(ˌ)ˈ= or 'se(ˌ)ˌ=ˈ= or ˌse(ˌ)ˈ=ˈ=\ *n, pl* **select·men** \-men for -man or -maa(ə)n in singular, -mən for -mon in singular\ [1select + man] : a person chosen to exercise special powers in a system of government; esp : one of a board of officers chosen usu. in staggered three-year terms in towns of all the New England states except Rhode Island to transact and administer the general public business of the town

select meeting *n* : a meeting of ministers and elders in the Society of Friends

select mortality table *n* : a mortality table based on medically selected lives

se·lect·ness \sə̇'lek(t)nə̇s\ *n* -ES : the quality or state of being select

se·lec·tor \-ktə(r)\ *n* -S [LL, fr. L selectus (past part. of seligere to select) + -or] : one that selects: as **a** : a person who selects ⟨~ of All-America teams —Current Biog.⟩ ⟨the ~ . . . knows good-looking merchandise —Women's Wear Daily⟩ ⟨edited by an expert librarian —Saturday Rev.⟩ **b** (1) : a person who selects Australian public land to settle on (2) : a small farmer of Australia **c** : a mechanical or electrical device for automatically selecting predetermined shapes, sizes, or materials or chosen or actuated for starting or stopping (as an elevator) **d** (1) : the element in a transmission gearshift of an automotive vehicle that is guided by the gearshift lever so that the desired gearshift bar is actuated (2) : the lever in an automatic gearshift operated by the driver to select the desired speed **e** : a converter with horizontal tuyeres to produce bottoms and a purified copper in one operation **f** : an electric switch mechanism designed to move over a number of terminals and to select a particular one or group in accordance with the signal received **g** : STATION SELECTOR **h** : an apparatus for operating either or any of two or more railroad signals by a single lever so as automatically to connect the particular signal controlling the route or track for which a switch has been set

selector coil *n* : an electric coil that when energized will attract and hold in place an armature to permit a predetermined movement of a mechanism

selector switch *n* : an electric switch that selects a particular circuit or group of circuits (as on a telephone switchboard)

selects *pl of* SELECT, *pres 3d sing of* SELECT

select school *n* : a privately supported and administered elementary or secondary school whose student body is selectively chosen usu. on a sectarian, social, or economic basis ⟨the business of instruction in our universities, colleges, acad-

emies, boarding schools, select schools, and common schools —Universal Traveller⟩

1selen- *or* **seleno-** also **seleni-** *comb form* [L selen-, fr. Gk selēn-, fr. selēnē moon; akin to Gk selas light, brightness, L sol sun — more at SOLAR] : moon : crescent-shaped ⟨selenomorphic⟩ ⟨Selenicerous⟩ ⟨Selenarctos⟩

2selen- *or* **seleni-** *or* **seleno-** *comb form* [Sw, fr. NL selenium] **1** : selenium ⟨selenic⟩ ⟨seleniferous⟩ ⟨selenobismuthite⟩ **2** *usu seleno-* : containing bivalent selenium usu. in place of oxygen ⟨selenocyanic⟩ — compare THI-

selena- *or* **selen-** *comb form* [ISV, fr. NL selenium] : containing selenium in place of carbon or regarded as in place of carbon usu. in place of the methylene group —CH₂— ⟨selenacyclopentadiene⟩ ⟨selenazole⟩ — compare OXA-, THIA-

sel·en·arc·tos \ˌselə̇'närktəs, -ˌtäs\ *n, cap* [NL, fr. 1selen- + Gk arktos bear — more at ARCTIC] : a genus of mammals (family Ursidae) that includes the Asiatic black bear and is often regarded as indistinguishable from Ursus

sel·e·nate \'selə̇ˌnāt\ *n* -S [Sw selenat, fr. selen selenic (fr. NL selenium) + -at -ate] : a salt or ester of selenic acid

se·le·ni·an \sə̇'lēnēən\ *adj* [1selen- + -an] : of, relating to, or designating the moon

se·le·ni·ate \-ē̄ˌāt\ *n* -S [Sw seleniat, fr. seleni- (fr. NL selenium) + -at -ate] : SELENATE

1se·len·ic \sə̇'lenik, -lēn-\ *adj* [1selen- + -ic] : of, relating to, or like the moon

2selenic \"\ *adj* [Sw selen selenic (fr. NL selenium) + E -ic] : of, relating to, or containing selenium — used esp. of compounds in which this element has a higher valence than in selenious compounds

selenic acid *n* : a strong acid H₂SeO₄ that is crystalline when pure, that resembles sulfuric acid but is a more powerful oxidizing agent since in hot concentrated form it oxidizes hydrogen chloride and attacks gold and platinum, and that is made by oxidation usu. of selenious acid or selenium dioxide

se·le·ni·cer·eus \sə̇ˈlēnə̇+\ *n, cap* [NL, fr. 1selen- + Cereus] : a genus of mostly epiphytic climbing cacti ranging from southern Texas to Argentina and having ribbed or angled and not very spiny stems and immense white night-blooming flowers that are much prized in northern greenhouses

sel·e·nide \'selə̇ˌnīd, -nə̇d\ *n* -S [ISV 2selen- + -ide] : a binary compound of selenium usu. with a more electropositive element or radical

sel·e·nif·er·ous \ˌselə̇'nif(ə)rəs\ *adj* [ISV 2selen- + -ferous] : containing or yielding selenium ⟨~ vegetation⟩

seleniferous plant *n* : a plant that absorbs large quantities of selenium from the soil and retains it within the plant tissues

sel·e·nin·ic acid \ˌselə̇'ninik-\ *n* [ISV 2selen- + -in + -ic] : any of a series of organic acids having the general formula RSeO₂H analogous to the sulfinic acids and obtainable by oxidizing diselenides with nitric acid

se·le·ni·ous \sə̇'lēnēəs\ *also* **sele·nous** \sə̇'lēnəs, 'selən-\ *adj* [ISV selen- + -ious or -ous] : of, relating to, or containing selenium — used esp. of compounds in which this element has a lower valence than in selenic compounds

selenious acid *n* : a poisonous hygroscopic crystalline acid H₂SeO₃ that is a weaker acid than sulfurous acid, that is an oxidizing agent yielding selenium as it is reduced and that is made by oxidizing selenium with nitric acid or by dissolving selenium dioxide in water

se·le·ni·pe·di·um \sə̇ˌlēnə̇'pēdēəm\ *n, cap* [NL, fr. 1selen- + Gk pedion plain, flat surface — more at PEDION] : a genus of large reedlike tropical American orchids that is closely related to Cypripedium and includes forms with pods used locally as a substitute for vanilla

1sel·e·nite \'selə̇ˌnīt\ *n* -S [L selenites, fr. Gk selēnitēs (lithos), lit., (stone) of the moon, fr. selēnitēs of the moon, fr. selēnē moon + -itēs -ite) + lithos stone; fr. the belief that it waxed and waned with the moon — more at SELEN-] : a variety of gypsum occurring in transparent crystals or crystalline masses

2selenite \"\ *n* -S [ISV selenious + -ite] : a salt or ester of selenious acid

1sel·e·nit·ic \ˌselə̇'nid-ik\ *also* **sel·e·nit·i·cal** \-də̇kəl\ *adj* [1selenite + -ic or -ical] : of, resembling, or containing selenite

2selenitic \"\ *adj* [Gk selēnitēs of the moon + E -ic] : of, relating to, or influenced by the moon

se·le·ni·um \sə̇'lēnēəm\ *n* -S [NL, fr. 1selen- + -ium; fr. the fact that it is related to an earlier the name of which (tellurium) derives from the Latin word for the planet earth (tellus)] : a nonmetallic toxic element that is related to sulfur and tellurium and resembles them chemically, that occurs in allotropic forms including an amorphous red powder or black vitreous form, a red crystalline form, and a stable gray metallike form conducting electricity much more readily in the light than in the dark, that is found to a small extent in native sulfur and combined in native sulfides, in a few selenides (as clausthalite), and in various soils and plants, that is obtained usu. as a by-product in the electrolytic refining of copper, and that is used chiefly in photoelectric cells, rectifiers, and other electronic devices, in decolorizing glass, and as a pigment esp. for ruby glass and ceramic glazes and enamels — symbol Se; see ELEMENT table

selenium cell *n* : an insulated strip of selenium suitably mounted with electrodes, designed for use as a photoconductive element, and commonly used in photometric work

selenium dioxide *n* : a poisonous white crystalline compound SeO₂ that sublimes to a yellow-green vapor, that is made by oxidation of selenium with nitric acid or air or by dehydration of selenious acid, and that is used chiefly as a catalyst and an oxidizing agent in organic chemistry (as for oxidizing a methylene group next to a carbonyl group to a second carbonyl group)

selenium oxychloride *n* : a vesicant liquid compound SeOCl₂ that is made usu. by reaction of selenium dioxide and hydrogen chloride or by chlorination of a mixture of selenium and selenium dioxide, that has a high dielectric constant, and that is used chiefly as a solvent

selenium rectifier *n* : a rectifier employing the asymmetrical conductivity characteristic of selenium

selenium red *n* : CADMIUM RED 1

sel·e·nized \'selə̇ˌnīzd\ *adj* [2selen- + -ize + -ed] : containing selenium ⟨~ plants from seleniferous soil⟩ ⟨a ~ animal affected by selenosis⟩

1seleno- — see 1SELEN-

2seleno- — see 2SELEN-

sele·no·bis·muth·ite \sə̇ˌlē(ˌ)nō̄, ˌselə̇(ˌ)nō̄+\ *n* [2selen- + bismuth + -ite] : a compound containing both selenium and bismuth

sele·no·cen·tric \"+\ *adj* [ISV 1selen- + -centric] : of or relating to the center of the moon : referred to the moon as a center

sele·no·cy·anate \"+\ *n* [ISV selenocyan- (in selenocyanic acid) + -ate] : a salt or ester of selenocyanic acid

sele·no·cy·an·ic acid \"+...-\ *n* [ISV 2selen- + cyanic] : an acid HSeCN containing selenium analogous to thiocyanic acid

1se·len·odont \sə̇'lēnəˌdänt, -len-\ *adj* [ISV 1selen- + -odont] : of, relating to, characteristic of, or being molar teeth with crescentic ridges on the crown ⟨~ artiodactyls⟩

2selenodont \"\ *n* -S : a mammal with selenodont teeth

se·len·o·don·ta \ˌ=ˌ=ˈdäntə\ *n pl, cap* [NL, fr. 1selen- + -odonta] *in some classifications* : a group of artiodactyls comprising mammals with selenodont teeth and including the Tylopoda and Pecora

se·len·o·don·ty \sə̇ˌlēnə̇'däntē\ *n* -ES [1selen- + -odonty] : the quality or state of being selenodont

sel·e·nog·ra·pher \ˌselə̇'nägrəfə(r)\ *n* -S [selenography + -er] : a specialist in selenography

se·le·no·graph·ic \sə̇ˌlēnə̇'grafik\ *also* **se·le·no·graph·i·cal** \-fə̇kəl\ *adj* [selenography + -ic or -ical] : of or relating to selenography — **selenographically** *adv*

selenographic chart *n* : a map representing the surface of the moon

sel·e·nog·ra·phy \ˌselə̇'nägrəfē\ *n* -ES [1selen- + -graphy] **1** : the science of the physical features of the moon ⟨attention of astronomers was directed to other fields, and . . . made no further progress +R.B.Baldwin⟩ **2** : the physical geography of the moon ⟨the first major treatise on descriptive ~ to appear in English for a quarter-century —Joseph Ashbrook⟩

se·le·no·lite \sə̇'lēnⁿlˌīt\ *n* -ES [2selen- + -lite] : a mineral SeO₂ consisting of native selenium dioxide

se·le·no·log·i·cal \sə̇ˌlēnəˈläjəkəl\ *adj* [ISV *selenology* + *-ical*] : of or relating to selenology — **se·le·no·log·i·cal·ly** \-k(ə)lē\ *adv*

sel·e·nol·o·gist \ˌseləˈnäləjəst\ *n* -s [*selenology* + *-ist*] : a specialist in selenology

sel·e·nol·o·gy \-jē\ *n* -ES [¹*selen-* + *-logy*] : a branch of astronomy that deals with the moon

sel·e·no·ni·um \ˌseləˈnōnēəm\ *n* -s [NL, fr. ²*selen-* + *-onium*] : a univalent cation SeH_3^+ or radical SeH_3 analogous to sulfonium with selenium in place of sulfur

se·le·no·phile \sə̇ˈlēnəˌfīl\ *n* -s [²*selen-* + *-phile*] : a plant that when growing in a seleniferous soil tends to take up selenium in quantities greater than can be explained on a basis of chance — **se·le·no·phil·ic** \=ˌ==ˈfilik\ *adj*

sel·e·no·sis \ˌseləˈnōsə̇s\ *n* -ES [NL, fr. ²*selen-* + *-osis*] : poisoning of livestock by selenium due to ingestion of plants grown in seleniferous soils characterized in the acute phase by diffuse necrosis and hemorrhage resulting from capillary damage and in chronic poisoning by degenerative and fibrotic changes esp. of the liver and of the skin and its derivatives — called also *alkali disease, blind staggers*

selenous *var of* SELENIOUS

sel·en·sulfur \ˈselən+\ *n* [²*selen-* + *sulfur*] : a vitreous brownish red mixture of selenium and sulfur

¹**se·leu·cid** \sə̇ˈlüsə̇d, sə̇lˈyü-\ *n* -s *usu cap* [NL *seleucides*, fr. *Seleucus I* †280 B.C. Macedonian general and founder of the Seleucid dynasty + L *-ides*, masc. patronymic suffix — more at -ID] : a member of a Greek dynasty ruling Syria and at various times other Asian territories from 312 B.C. to 64 B.C.

²**seleucid** \"\ *adj, usu cap* : of or relating to the Seleucids or their era

¹**self** \ˈself, ˈseu̇f, *South often* ˈse(ə)f\ *pron* [ME, fr. OE *self, seolf, sylf*; akin to OFris & OS *self*, OHG *selb*, ON *sjālfr*, Goth *silba*; akin to L *se* oneself — more at SUICIDE] **1** : MYSELF ⟨he died when we — ~, two brothers, one sister — were very young —*Current Biog.*⟩ **2** : HIMSELF, HERSELF ⟨his family, living in a four-roomed house, consisted of ~, wife, and six —I.J.C.Brown⟩

²**self** \"\ *adj* [ME, fr. OE *self, seolf, sylf*] **1** *obs* : belonging to oneself : OWN ⟨by ~ and violent hands took off her life —Shak.⟩ **2** *obs* : IDENTICAL, SAME ⟨that ~ chain about his neck which he forswore most monstrously to have —Shak.⟩ **3 a** : having a single character or quality throughout : UNIFORM, UNMIXED; *specif* : having one color only : SELF-COLORED ⟨a ~ flower⟩ **b** *of an archer's bow* : made of a single piece of wood — contrasted with *backed* **c** : of the same kind (as in color, material, or pattern) as something with which it is used ⟨a ~ belt⟩ ⟨a ~ trimming⟩

³**self** \"\ *n, pl* **selves** *see sense 6* \ˈselvz, ˈseu̇vz, *South often* ˈse(ə)vz\ [ME, fr. *self*, pron.] **1 a** : the entire person of an individual ⟨his fair daughter's ~ . . . is my object —Robert Browning⟩ **b** : the realization or embodiment of an abstract quality ⟨she was beauty's ~ —James Thomson †1748⟩ **2 a** : a personality or mode of behavior regarded as typical of a particular individual ⟨his true ~ was at last revealed⟩ **b** : an aspect of one's personality predominant at a certain time or under certain conditions ⟨his better ~⟩ ⟨his weaker ~⟩ ⟨his reckless ~⟩ ⟨my clothes keep my various *selves* buttoned up together —L.P.Smith⟩ **c** : a person in his normal state of health or best physical or mental condition ⟨feel like my old ~ today⟩ ⟨looked like his old ~ in the ring⟩ **3 a** : the integrated unity of subjective experience specif. including those characteristics and attributes of the experiencing organism of which it is reflexively aware **b** : the internal regulatory system of response and activity tendencies within the organism : the source of social adaptation and growth of the individual personality **c** : the dynamic organization of patterns of behavior acquired through social frustration **4** : personal interest or advantage : SELF-INTEREST ⟨the really successful people in it are those who put service before ~ —*Farmer's Weekly (So. Africa)*⟩ **5 a** *usu cap, objective idealism* : the supreme self : ABSOLUTE **b** (1) *often cap, Hinduism* : ATMAN (2) *Buddhism* : a dynamic unstable agglomerate of skandhas that in itself possesses no inherent substantiality or enduring quality and that continues in constant flux until final dissolution at death **6** *pl* **selfs** \-fs\ **a** : an individual produced by self-fertilization — distinguished from *crossbred* **b** : a self-colored individual

⁴**self** \"\ *vb* -ED/-ING/-S *vt* **1** : to cause (individuals of the same race or strain) to breed together : INBREED **2** : to pollinate with pollen from the same flower or plant : SELF-FERTILIZE : SELF-POLLINATE ~ *vi* : to engage in self-pollinating : undergo self-pollination ⟨try to prevent test strains from ~*ing*⟩

self- *comb form* [ME, fr. OE *self-, seolf-, sylf-*, fr. *self, seolf, sylf*, pron. & adj.] **1 a** : oneself or itself ⟨*self*-asserting⟩ ⟨*self*-loving⟩ **b** : of oneself or itself ⟨*self*-abandonment⟩ ⟨*self*-congratulation⟩ **c** : by oneself or itself : independent : automatic ⟨*self*-rule⟩ ⟨*self*-propelled⟩ ⟨*self*-feeder⟩ ⟨*self*-action⟩ **2 a** : to, with, for, or toward oneself or itself ⟨*self*-consistent⟩ ⟨*self*-concerned⟩ ⟨*self*-addressed⟩ ⟨*self*-love⟩ **b** : of or in oneself or itself inherently ⟨*self*-evident⟩ ⟨*self*-existent⟩ **c** : from or by means of oneself or itself ⟨*self*-fertile⟩ ⟨*self*-fruitful⟩

self-abandoned \ˌ=ˌ=ˈ=\ *adj* : abandoned by oneself; *esp* : given up to one's impulses : free from moral restraint : ABANDONED

self-abandonment \ˌ=ˌ=ˈ==\ *n* **1** : a surrender of one's selfish interests or desires ⟨the earnest prayer and the complete *self-abandonment* which arise from wise reading and true meditation —Phyllis Hodgson⟩ **2** : a lack of self-restraint ⟨has in its relaxed *self-abandonment* something underbred and ignoble —Matthew Arnold⟩

self-abasement \ˌ=ˌ=ˈ==\ *n* : a humiliation of oneself based on feelings of inferiority, guilt, or shame ⟨continual ups and downs of rapture and depression, arrogance and *self-abasement* —Edith Wharton⟩

self-abnegating \(ˈ)=ˈ==ˌ==\ *adj* : SELF-DENYING

self-abnegation \ˌ=ˌ==ˈ==\ *n* : SELF-DENIAL, SELF-SACRIFICE

self-absorbed \ˌ=(ˌ)=ˈ=\ *adj* : absorbed in one's own thoughts, activities, or interests

self-absorption \ˌ=(ˌ)=ˈ==\ *n* **1** : absorption in oneself : preoccupation with oneself **2** : resonance absorption of part of the radiation emitted by a substance in the outer layers of the emitter itself and esp. noticeable in flame spectra

self-abuse \ˌ=ˌ=ˈ=\ *n* **1** *obs* : SELF-DECEPTION ⟨my strange and *self-abuse* is the initiate fear that wants hard use —Shak.⟩ **2** : reproach of oneself ⟨the *self-abuse* for throwing away his future on the movement for independence —Edward Ryerson⟩ **3** : MASTURBATION

self-accusation \ˌ=ˌ==ˈ==\ *n* : the act or an instance of accusing oneself

self-accusatory \ˌ=ˌ=ˈ==ˌ==\ *adj* : SELF-ACCUSING

self-accusing \ˌ=ˌ=ˈ==\ *adj* : acting or serving to accuse oneself

self-acquired \ˌ=ˌ=ˈ=\ *adj* : acquired by oneself or for one's own use and benefit

self-acting \ˌ=ˈ==\ *adj* : acting or capable of acting of or by itself : AUTOMATIC

self-action \ˈ=ˈ==\ *n* : action not dependent on an external agency or force : independent action

self-active \ˌ=ˈ==\ *adj* : acting of itself without dependence on an external agency or force

self-activity \ˌ=ˌ=ˈ===\ *n* : SELF-ACTION

self-actor \ˈ=ˈ==\ *n* : a self-acting machine; *esp* : a self-acting mule

self-addressed \ˌ=ˌ=ˈ=, ˈ=ˌ=ˈ=\ *adj* : addressed for return to the sender and enclosed or to be enclosed in a communication for the convenience of one making a reply ⟨*self-addressed* envelope⟩

self-adjusting \ˌ=ˌ=ˈ==\ *adj* : adjusting by itself ⟨a *self-adjusting* wrench⟩

self-adjustment \ˌ=ˌ=ˈ==\ *n* : adjustment to oneself or one's environment

self-administered plan \ˌ=ˌ=ˈ===-\ *n* : a pension or retirement plan administered by the employer or by the employer and a trustee jointly — compare INSURED PLAN

self-admiration \ˌ=ˌ==ˈ==\ *n* : SELF-CONCEIT

self-affected \ˌ=ˌ=ˈ==\ *adj* : being in love with oneself : CONCEITED

self-affirmation \ˌ=ˌ==ˈ==\ *n* **1** : recognition and judgment of the existence of the conscious self **2** *logic* : the character of a truth or proposition that makes it undeniable without inconsistency

self-aggrandizement \ˌ=ˌ=ˈ=(ˌ)==, (ˌ)=ˈ===ˈ==\ *n* : the act or process of making oneself greater (as in power or influence)

self-aggrandizing \ˌ=ˌ=ˈ==ˌ==, (ˈ)=ˈ==ˌ==\ *adj* : acting or seeking to make oneself greater

self-analysis \ˌ=ˌ=ˈ===\ *n* : a systematic attempt by an individual to understand his own personality dynamics without the aid of another person; *specif* : psychoanalysis without transference

self-analytical \ˌ=ˌ==ˈ===\ *adj* : using self-analysis

self-annihilation \ˌ=ˌ=ˌ==ˈ==\ *n* : annihilation of the self (as in mystical contemplation of God)

self-applauding \ˌ=ˌ=ˈ=\ *adj* : applauding oneself : marked by self-applause

self-applause \ˌ=ˌ=ˈ=\ *n* : an expression or feeling of approval of oneself

self-appointed \ˌ=ˌ=ˈ==\ *adj* : appointed or chosen (as to a function or position) by oneself usu. without warrant or qualifications ⟨a *self-appointed* guardian of public morals⟩

self-approbation \ˌ=ˌ==ˈ==\ *n* : satisfaction with one's actions and achievements

self-asserting \ˌ=ˌ=ˈ==\ *adj* **1** : asserting oneself or one's own rights or claims **2** : putting oneself forward in a confident or arrogant manner — **self-assert·ing·ly** \ˌ=ˌ=ˈ===\ *adv*

self-assertion \ˌ=ˌ=ˈ==\ *n* **1** : the act of asserting oneself or one's own rights or claims **2** : the act of asserting one's superiority over others esp. by aggressive or inconsiderate behavior

self-assertive \ˌ=ˌ=ˈ==\ *adj* : given to or characterized by self-assertion **syn** see AGGRESSIVE

self-assertively \ˌ=ˌ=ˈ===\ *adv* : in a self-assertive manner

self-assertiveness \ˌ=ˌ=ˈ===\ *n* : the quality or state of being self-assertive

self-assigned \ˌ=ˌ=ˈ=\ *adj* : assigned by oneself

self-assumption \ˌ=ˌ=ˈ==\ *n* : SELF-CONCEIT

self-assurance \ˌ=ˌ=ˈ==\ *n* : assured self-confidence

self-assured \ˌ=ˌ=ˈ=\ *adj* : sure of oneself : SELF-CONFIDENT **syn** see CONFIDENT

self-assuredness \ˌ=ˌ=ˈ===\ *n* : the quality or state of being self-assured

self-awareness \ˌ=ˌ=ˈ===\ *n* : an awareness of one's own personality or individuality

self-baptizer \ˌ=ˌ=ˈ==, ˈ=ˈ=ˌ==\ *n, sometimes cap S&B* : SE-BAPTIST

self-betrayal \ˌ=ˌ=ˈ(=)\ *n* : SELF-REVELATION

self-binder \ˈ=ˈ=\ *n* : BINDER 4b

self-blimped \ˈ=ˌ=\ *or* **self-blimping** \ˈ=ˌ==\ *adj, of a motion-picture camera* : sound-insulated by its own housing

self blue *n* : a paper that is derived from blue rag pulp made from indigo-dyed rags and that has a bluish color which is fast to light

self-born \ˈ=ˈ=\ *adj* : arising within the self ⟨*self-born* sorrows⟩ : springing from a prior self ⟨phoenix rising *self-born* from the fire⟩

self-bounty \ˈ=ˈ==\ *n, obs* : inherent kindness and benevolence ⟨would not have your free and noble nature, out of *self-bounty*, be abused —Shak.⟩

self-break \ˈ=ˈ=\ *n* : break of tulips in which the flower turns a darker color or develops darker stripes of the basic color

self-buried \ˈ=ˈberēd\ *adj* : buried by natural forces rather than by an intentional act of man ⟨uncovered *self-buried* implements that had sunk into the earth long ago⟩

self-care \ˈ=ˈ=\ *n* : care for oneself

self-castigation \ˌ=ˌ==ˈ==\ *n* : SELF-PUNISHMENT

self-catalysis \ˌ=ˌ=ˈ===\ *n* : catalysis of a chemical reaction without the addition of a special catalyst : AUTOCATALYSIS

self-caused \ˈ=ˈ=\ *adj* : SELF-CREATED

self-centered \ˈ=ˈ==\ *adj* **1** : STATIONARY, UNMOVING **2** : not dependent on outside force or influence : SELF-SUFFICIENT ⟨in a world plagued by desperate insecurity, there are still tiny cases of interest that are private, intimate, intensely personal, *self-centered* —J.T.Winterich⟩ **3** : concerned solely with one's own desires, needs, or interests : SELFISH ⟨a *self-centered*, arrogant boy who can't have his own way with life —Jay Williams⟩ — **self-centered·ly** *adv* — **self-centered·ness** *n* -ES

self-centering \ˈ=ˈ=(=)=\ *adj* **1** : centering in or of oneself **2** *of a chuck* : having jaws or dogs that can be made to move with gripping faces always equidistant from the chuck axis

self-charity \(ˈ)=ˈ===\ *n, obs* : charity toward oneself ⟨unless *self-charity* be sometimes a vice —Shak.⟩

self-closing \ˈ=ˈ==\ *adj* : closing or shutting automatically after being opened

self-cocker \ˈ=ˈ==\ *n* : a self-cocking revolver

self-cocking \ˈ=ˈ==\ *adj* : cocked by the operation of some part of the action ⟨*self-cocking* on closing the bolt⟩

self-collected \ˌ=ˌ=ˈ==\ *adj* : SELF-POSSESSED

self-colored \ˈ=ˈ==\ *adj* : of a single color — used esp. of a flower, an animal, or textile fabric

self-command \ˌ=ˌ=ˈ=\ *n* : command of oneself : SELF-CONTROL

self-compatible \ˌ=ˌ=ˈ===\ *adj* : capable of effective self-pollination that results in the production of seeds and fruits

self-complacency \ˌ=ˌ=ˈ===\ *n* : SELF-SATISFACTION

self-complacent \ˌ=ˌ=ˈ==\ *adj* : SELF-SATISFIED **syn** see COMPLACENT

self-composed \ˌ=ˌ=ˈ=\ *adj* : having control over one's emotions : CALM, COLLECTED — **self-composedly** \ˌ=ˌ=ˈ===\ *adv* — **self-composedness** \ˌ=ˌ=ˈ(=)==\ *n* -ES

self-conceit \ˌ=ˌ=ˈ=\ *n* : an exaggerated opinion of one's own qualities or abilities

self-conceited \ˌ=ˌ=ˈ==\ *adj* : marked by self-conceit : VAIN

self-concentered \ˌ=ˌ=ˈ==\ *adj* : concentrated in oneself or itself

self-concern \ˌ=ˌ=ˈ=\ *n* : a selfish or morbid concern for oneself

self-concerned \ˌ=ˌ=ˈ=\ *adj* : marked by self-concern

self-condemnation \ˌ=ˌ(ˌ)==ˈ==\ *n* : condemnation of one's own character or actions

self-condemned \ˌ=ˌ=ˈ=\ *adj* : condemned by oneself

self-conduct \ˈ=ˈ(ˌ)=\ *n* : regulation and control of oneself

self-confessed \ˌ=ˌ=ˈ=\ *adj* : openly acknowledged : AVOWED ⟨a *self-confessed* intellectual⟩ ⟨a *self-confessed* gambler⟩

self-confession \ˌ=ˌ=ˈ==\ *n* : AVOWAL

self-confidence \(ˈ)=ˈ===\ *n* **1** : arrogant or excessive reliance on oneself : COCKINESS, OVERCONFIDENCE ⟨swaggering *self-confidence* and exaggerated efforts to keep up a good front —*Christian Science Monitor*⟩ **2** : confidence in oneself : ASSURANCE ⟨a normal adult manly *self-confidence* —Weston La Barre⟩

self-confident \(ˈ)=ˈ===\ *adj* **1** : arrogantly overconfident ⟨unruly, impatient of discipline, and too aggressively *self-confident* —Allan Nevins & H.S.Commager⟩ **2** : confident of one's own strength or ability : SELF-RELIANT ⟨looked to be hardly more than a boy, but firm-knit and *self-confident* —S.H.Adams⟩ **syn** see CONFIDENT

self-confidently \(ˈ)=ˈ====\ *adv* : in a self-confident manner

self-confiding \ˌ=ˌ=ˈ==\ *adj, archaic* : showing self-confidence ⟨free, and fearless, and *self-confiding* —Sir Walter Scott⟩

self-congratulation \ˌ=ˌ=ˌ==ˈ==\ *n* : congratulation of oneself; *esp* : a complacent acknowledgment of one's own superiority or good fortune

self-congratulatory \ˌ=ˌ=ˈ===ˌ==\ *adj* : indulging in self-congratulation

self-conscious \ˈ=ˈ==\ *adj* **1 a** : conscious of one's own acts or states as belonging to or originating in oneself : aware of oneself as an individual that experiences, desires, and acts ⟨not only thinks, but he knows himself as thinking . . . is not only conscious, but he is *self-conscious* —Rufus Jones⟩ **b** : intensely aware of oneself or itself : CONSCIOUS : DELIBERATE ⟨have been very *self-conscious* about their roles as guardians of the social values —D.M.Potter⟩ ⟨this highly *self-conscious* poetical prose —*Times Lit. Supp.*⟩ **2** : uncomfortably conscious of oneself as an object of the observation of others : ill at ease ⟨wondered if there would ever be a time in his life when he could be untidy without being *self-conscious* about it —Jean Stafford⟩ — **self-consciously** \(ˈ)=ˈ===\ *adv*

self-conscious·ness \ˈ=ˈ===\ *n* : the quality or state of being self-conscious

self-consequence \(ˈ)=ˈ=(ˌ)=\ *n* : SELF-IMPORTANCE

self-consistency \ˌ=ˌ=ˈ===\ *n* : the quality or state of being self-consistent

self-consistent \ˌ=ˌ=ˈ==\ *adj* : consistent with oneself or itself : logically consistent throughout : having each part consistent with the rest

self-constituted \(ˈ)=ˈ===\ *adj* : constituted by oneself or itself

self-contained \ˌ=ˌ=ˈ=\ *adj* **1 a** : sufficient in itself : INDEPENDENT ⟨the world of technics is not isolated and *self-contained* —Lewis Mumford⟩ **b** : showing self-command : SELF-CONTROLLED ⟨taller than most of the early frontiersmen . . . more *self-contained* and more dependable —Mari Sandoz⟩ **c** : formal and reserved in manner ⟨cool, composed, indulgent, *self-contained* . . . she watched with sympathy the liberal manners of the new century —Ellen Glasgow⟩ **2 a** : having none of its parts in common with anything surrounding it or adjacent to it : complete in itself ⟨a *self-contained* machine⟩ ⟨small *self-contained* houses, with each its own hedged garden —Mary Baum⟩ **b** *Brit* : including all necessary living facilities and restricted to the use of one family ⟨a *self-contained* house⟩ **c** : having a self-cover — **self-contained·ly** \ˌ=ˌ=ˈ===\ *adv* — **self-contained·ness** \ˌ=ˌ=ˈnə̇dnə̇s\ *n* -ES

self-contained ornament *n* : ornament in which the design is a single complete whole intended to fill a space without being repeated

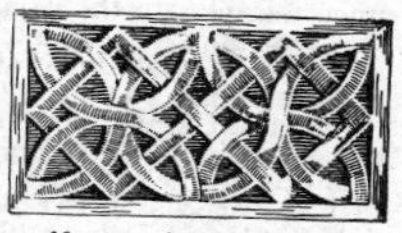
self-contained ornament

self-containment \ˌ=ˌ=ˈ==\ *n* : a self-contained condition or state

self-contamination \ˌ=ˌ=ˌ==ˈ==\ *n* : contamination by oneself or itself : contamination from within

self-contempt \ˌ=ˌ=ˈ=\ *n* : contempt for oneself

self-content \ˌ=ˌ=ˈ=\ *n* : SELF-SATISFACTION ⟨lived in eminent *self-content*, as one lying on a soft cloud —George Meredith⟩

self-contented \ˌ=ˌ=ˈ==\ *adj* : SELF-SATISFIED — **self-contentedly** \ˌ=ˌ=ˈ===\ *adv* — **self-contentedness** \ˌ=ˌ=ˈ===\ *n* -ES

self-contentment \ˌ=ˌ=ˈ==\ *n* : SELF-SATISFACTION

self-contradiction \ˌ=ˌ==ˈ==\ *n* **1** : contradiction of oneself or itself ⟨a person with a poor memory and changeable mind who is given to frequent *self-contradiction*⟩ **2** : a self-contradictory statement or proposition

self-contradictory \ˌ=ˌ==ˈ=(=)=\ *adj* : consisting of two members or parts one of which contradicts the other ⟨to be and not to be at the same time is a *self-contradictory* statement⟩

self-control \ˌ=ˌ=ˈ=\ *n* : control of oneself : restraint exercised over one's own impulses, emotions, or desires ⟨his anger blazed out and burned up his *self-control* —H.E.Scudder⟩ ⟨passionate and rebellious, she never learned *self-control* —E.C.Wagenknecht⟩

self-controlled \ˌ=ˌ=ˈ=\ *adj* : manifesting self-control

self-copulation \ˌ=ˌ==ˈ==\ *n* : copulation with itself : AUTOCOPULATION

self-correcting \ˌ=ˌ=ˈ==\ *adj* : acting automatically to correct or compensate for (as errors, weaknesses, or imbalances)

self-corrective \ˌ=ˌ=ˈ==\ *adj* : SELF-CORRECTING

self-cover \ˈ=ˈ==\ *n* : a cover (as of a pamphlet) of the same paper as the inside leaves; *also* : a publication having such a cover — called also *integral cover*

self-created \ˌ=ˌ=ˈ==\ *adj* : created or appointed by oneself

self-critical \(ˈ)=ˈ===\ *adj* : critical of oneself

self-criticism \(ˈ)=ˈ===\ *n* : the act of or capacity for criticizing one's own faults or shortcomings

self-culture \ˈ=ˈ==\ *n* : the development of one's mind or capacities through one's own efforts

self-deceit \ˌ=ˌ=ˈ=\ *n* : SELF-DECEPTION

self-deceived \ˌ=ˌ=ˈ=\ *adj* : deceived or misled esp. respecting oneself by one's own mistake

self-deceiver \ˌ=ˌ=ˈ==\ *n* : one who practices self-deception

self-deceiving \ˌ=ˌ=ˈ==\ *adj* : given to self-deception or serving to deceive oneself ⟨a *self-deceiving* hypocrite⟩ ⟨*self-deceiving* excuses⟩

self-deception \ˌ=ˌ=ˈ==\ *n* : the act of deceiving oneself or the state of being deceived by oneself ⟨to presume agreement where none exists is the most dangerous form of *self-deception* —Agnes Repplier⟩

self-deceptive \ˌ=ˌ=ˈ==\ *adj* : SELF-DECEIVING

self-dedication \ˌ=ˌ==ˈ==\ *n* : dedication of oneself to a cause or ideal

self-defeating \ˌ=ˌ=ˈ==\ *adj* : acting to defeat its own purpose

self-defense \ˌ=ˌ=ˈ=\ *n* : the act of defending oneself or something that belongs or relates to oneself ⟨the manly art of *self-defense*⟩ ⟨issued a statement in *self-defense* after the newspaper's attack on him⟩; *esp* : a plea of justification for assaulting or killing a human being sustained under very technical rules of law after examining the surrounding circumstances and considering such factors as whether the defendant was the initial aggressor or free from fault, whether he had a reasonable opportunity to retreat to a place of safety, and whether the force used by him was reasonable and used to protect himself or those under his protection

self-defensive \ˌ=ˌ=ˈ==\ *adj* : given to or involving self-defense ⟨a *self-defensive* person⟩ ⟨a *self-defensive* attitude⟩

self-delight \ˌ=ˌ=ˈ=\ *n* : delight in or gratification of oneself

self-deluded \ˌ=ˌ=ˈ==\ *adj* : SELF-DECEIVED

self-delusion \ˌ=ˌ=ˈ==\ *n* : SELF-DECEPTION

self-denial \ˌ=ˌ=ˈ(=)=\ *n* : denial of oneself : a restraint or limitation of one's own desires or interests ⟨mouth closed tight from . . . disillusion and *self-denial* —D.H.Lawrence⟩

self-denied \ˌ=ˌ=ˈ=\ *adj* : marked by self-denial

self-denier \ˌ=ˌ=ˈ(=)=\ *n* : one who practices self-denial

self-denying \ˌ=ˌ=ˈ==\ *adj* : forbearing to gratify oneself or advance one's interests : involving or showing self-denial — **self-denyingly** \ˌ=ˌ=ˈ===\ *adv*

self-dependence \ˌ=ˌ=ˈ==\ *n* : dependence on one's own resources or exertions : SELF-RELIANCE

self-dependent \ˌ=ˌ=ˈ==\ *adj* : marked by self-dependence ⟨encourage voluntary *self-dependent* education throughout life —*Amer. Guide Series: Vt.*⟩

self-deprecating \(ˈ)=ˈ===ˌ==\ *adj* : given to self-depreciation

self-depreciation \ˌ=ˌ=ˌ==ˈ==\ *n* : disparagement or undervaluation of oneself

self-despair \ˌ=ˌ=ˈ=\ *n* : despair of oneself : HOPELESSNESS

self-destroyer \ˌ=ˌ=ˈ(=)=\ *n* : one who destroys himself

self-destroying \ˌ=ˌ=ˈ==\ *adj* : SELF-DESTRUCTIVE

self-destruction \ˌ=ˌ=ˈ==\ *n* : destruction of oneself or itself; *esp* : SUICIDE

self-destructive \ˌ=ˌ=ˈ==\ *adj* : acting or tending to destroy oneself or itself : SUICIDAL ⟨postulated an innate death instinct to account for aggression and *self-destructive* urges —G.S.Blum⟩ — **self-destructively** \ˌ=ˌ=ˈ===\ *adv*

self-determination \ˌ=ˌ=ˌ==ˈ==\ *n* **1** : determination of one's acts or states by oneself without external compulsion **2** : the right of a people to decide its future political status (as with respect to form of government or independence) or its action in so deciding usu. by plebiscite

self-determined \ˌ=ˌ=ˈ==\ *adj* : determined by oneself or itself

self-determining \ˌ=ˌ=ˈ===\ *adj* : capable of determining one's or its own acts ⟨a *self-determining* organism⟩

self-determinism \ˌ=ˌ=ˈ===\ *n* : a doctrine that the actions of a self are determined by itself — compare DETERMINISM 1a, INDETERMINISM 1

self-development \ˌ=ˌ=ˈ===\ *n* : development of the capabilities or possibilities of oneself or itself

self-devoted \ˌ=ˌ=ˈ==\ *adj* : characterized by self-devotion — **self-devotedly** \ˌ=ˌ=ˈ===\ *adv* — **self-devotedness** \ˌ=-

self-devoting \ˌ=ˌ=ˈ==\ *adj* : SELF-DEVOTED

self-devotion \ˌ=ˌ=ˈ==\ *n* : devotion of oneself esp. in service or sacrifice ⟨his *self-devotion* to science cost him his life⟩

self-devouring \ˌ=ˌ=ˈ==\ *adj* : devouring itself : AUTOPHAGOUS ⟨*self-devouring* cruelty —Philip Sidney⟩

self-differentiation \ˌ=ˌ==ˌ==ˈ==\ *n* : differentiation of a structure or tissue due to factors existent in itself and essentially independent of other parts of the developing organism

self-digestion \ˌ=(ˌ)=ˈ==\ *n* : the decomposition of plant or animal tissue by internal process : AUTOLYSIS

self-directed \ˌ=(ˌ)=ˈ==\ *adj* : directed by oneself or itself : not guided or impelled by an outside force or agency ⟨a *self-directed* personality⟩

self–directing \¦=(ˌ)=¦==\ *adj* **:** directing oneself or itself

self–direction \¦=¦==\ *n* **:** guidance by oneself or itself

self–discharging \¦=¦==, (ˈ)=¦=ˌ==\ *adj* **:** discharging by itself

self–discipline \(ˈ)=¦=(=)=\ *n* **:** the correction or regulation of oneself for the sake of improvement

self–disciplined \(ˈ)=¦=(=)=\ *adj* **:** capable of or subject to self-discipline

self–discovery \¦==¦=(=)=\ *n* **:** the act or process of achieving self-knowledge ⟨sport leads to the most remarkable *self-discovery* of our limitations as well as our abilities —Roger Bannister⟩

self–discrepant \¦=¦==\ *adj* **:** incompatible with self or selfhood

self–distributing \¦=¦===\ *adj* **:** distributing itself automatically

self–distrust \¦==¦=\ *n* **:** a lack of confidence in oneself **:** DIFFIDENCE ⟨he taught self-reliance and felt *self-distrust* —S.E.Whicher⟩

self–distrustful \¦=¦==\ *adj* **:** lacking in self-confidence

self–division \¦==¦==\ *n* **:** division of itself by its own action or process of growth

self·dom *pronunc at* ¹SELF+dəm\ *n* -s [³*self-* + *-dom*] **:** the essence of one's self **:** INDIVIDUALITY

self–doubt \ˈ=¦=\ *n* **:** a lack of faith in oneself **:** a feeling of uncertainty as to the value of one's actions or way of life ⟨all my yearning to live a creative life rushed up and all my characteristic *self-doubt* also —Elise Jerard⟩

self–doubting \ˈ=¦==\ *adj* **:** given to self-doubt

self–dramatizing \(ˈ)=¦==ˌ==\ *adj* **:** seeing and presenting oneself as an actor in a drama **:** giving a false dignity and nobility to one's actions and words ⟨*self-dramatizing*, fraternizing, weak and irresponsible, longing for a literary life —*N.Y. Herald Tribune Bk. Rev.*⟩

self–drive \ˈ=¦=\ *adj, Brit* **:** DRIVE-YOURSELF

self–driven \¦=¦==\ *adj* **:** driven by itself **:** AUTOMOTIVE

self–duplicating \(ˈ)=¦==ˌ==\ *adj* **:** reproducing itself **:** passing on its characteristics

self–ease \ˈ=¦=\ *n* **:** bodily comfort

selfed *past of* SELF

self–educated \(ˈ)=¦==ˌ==\ *adj* **:** educated by one's own efforts without formal instruction

self–education \¦==¦==\ *n* **:** education achieved by one's own efforts esp. through reading and informal study

self–effacement \¦==¦==\ *n* **:** effacement of oneself; *specif* **:** the placing or keeping of oneself in the background ⟨Christianity . . . its terms of value all derive from a law of *self-effacement* and of consideration for others —R.M.Weaver⟩

self–effacing \¦==¦==\ *adj* **:** RETIRING ⟨essentially humble, modest, and *self-effacing* —B.K.Malinowski⟩ — **self–effacingly** \¦==¦===\ *adv*

self–elect \¦==¦=\ *or* **self–elected** \¦==¦==\ *adj* **:** chosen or elected by oneself **:** SELF-APPOINTED

self–employed \¦==¦=\ *adj* **:** earning income directly from one's own business, trade, or profession rather than as a specified salary or wages from an employer

self–employment \¦==¦==\ *n* **:** the state of being self-employed

self–endeared \¦==¦=\ *adj* **:** SELF-LOVING ⟨she cannot love . . . she is so *self-endeared* —Shak.⟩

self–energizing brake \(ˈ)=¦==ˌ==-\ *n* **:** a brake that contains within itself some means (as the wrapping action in a band brake) for augmenting the power imparted to it by the pressure on the brake pedal

self–energy \(ˈ)=¦===\ *n* **:** energy that is generated in or by itself

self–enforcing \¦==¦==\ *adj* **:** containing in itself the authority or means to guarantee its enforcement ⟨a *self-enforcing* order⟩ ⟨a *self-enforcing* treaty⟩

self–enrichment \¦==¦==\ *n* **:** the act or process of increasing one's intellectual or spiritual resources

self–esteem \¦==¦=\ *n* **1 :** a confidence and satisfaction in oneself **:** SELF-RESPECT ⟨worth while to remind ourselves of the reasons that we have for national *self-esteem* —Bertrand Russell⟩ **2 :** one's good opinion of oneself **:** AMOUR PROPRE **:** SELF-CONCEIT ⟨an unfortunate peculiarity of an otherwise admirable personality was his inordinate *self-esteem* —H.W.H. Knott⟩ **syn** see CONCEIT

self–esterification \¦=ˌ===¦==\ *n* **:** the reaction of a compound (as lactic acid or other hydroxy organic acid) with itself to form one or more esters

self–evidence \(ˈ)=¦===\ *n* **1 :** evidence given by itself of its own truth **2 :** the quality or state of being self-evident

self–evidencing \(ˈ)=¦==(ˌ)==\ *adj* **:** giving evidence of its own truth — **self–evidencingly** \(ˈ)=¦=¦===\ *adv*

self–evident \(ˈ)=¦==(ˌ)=\ *adj* **:** evident without proof or argument **:** producing conviction on a bare presentation or statement ⟨we hold these truths to be *self-evident* —*U.S. Declaration of Independence*⟩ — **self–evidently** \(ˈ)=¦==(ˌ)==\ *adv*

self–evolution \¦=ˌ==¦==\ *n* **:** development by inherent quality or power

self–exaltation \¦=ˌ=(ˌ)=¦=\ *n* **:** exaltation of oneself **:** VAINGLORY

self–exalting \¦==¦==\ *adj* **:** VAINGLORIOUS — **self–exaltingly** \¦==¦===\ *adv*

self–examination \¦=ˌ=ˌ==¦=\ *n* **:** INTROSPECTION

self–excite \¦==¦=\ *vt* **:** to excite (the field magnets of a dynamo) by a current produced by the dynamo itself

self–exciter \¦==¦=\ *n* **:** a dynamo whose field magnets are self-excited

self–executing \(ˈ)=¦==ˌ==\ *adj* **:** providing for its own execution **:** containing a clause giving effect to its provisions by operation of law on the occurrence of a contemplated event or contingency ⟨a *self-executing* law⟩

self–exiled \ˈ=¦=ˌ=\ *adj* **:** exiled by one's own wish or decision

self–existence \¦==¦==\ *n* **:** the quality or state of being self-existent

self–existent \¦==¦==\ *adj* **:** existing of or by oneself or itself **:** independent of any other being or cause

self–experience \¦==¦===\ *n* **:** one's own experience

self–explaining \¦==¦==\ *adj* **:** SELF-EXPLANATORY

self–explanatory \¦==¦==ˌ==\ *adj* **:** explaining itself **:** capable of being understood without explanation

self–expression \¦==¦==\ *n* **:** the expression of one's own personality **:** the assertion of one's individual traits ⟨*self-expression* is dynamic and ever-changing according to the child's mental and emotional level —W.M.Ivey⟩

self–expressive \¦==¦==\ *adj* **:** given to self-expression or serving as a means of self-expression ⟨a *self-expressive* painter⟩ ⟨*self-expressive* behavior⟩

self–faced \ˈ=¦=\ *adj, of stone* **:** having a natural, broken, or undressed face

self–feed \ˈ=¦=\ *vt* **:** to provide rations to (animals) in bulk so as to permit each animal to select the kind and quantity of food that it wants — compare HAND-FEED

self–feeder \¦=¦==\ *n* **:** one that feeds itself automatically; *specif* **:** a device for feeding livestock that is equipped with a feed hopper that automatically supplies a trough below

self–feeling \¦=¦==\ *n* **:** self-centered emotion

self–fertile \ˈ=¦=(ˌ)=\ *adj* **:** fertile by means of its own pollen or sperm — used of either a plant or animal; opposed to *self-sterile*

self–fertility \¦==¦===\ *n* **:** the quality or state of being self-fertile

self–fertilization \¦=ˌ==(ˌ)=¦==\ *n* **:** fertilization effected by pollen or sperm from the same individual

self–fertilized \(ˈ)=¦==ˌ=\ *adj* **:** fertilized by means of one's own pollen or sperm ⟨a *self-fertilized* flower⟩

self–flattering \(ˈ)=¦=(=)=\ *adj* **:** given to self-flattery

self–flattery \(ˈ)=¦=(=)=\ *n* **:** flattery of oneself **:** the glossing over of one's own weaknesses or mistakes or the exaggeration of one's own qualities and achievements

self–forgetful \¦==¦==\ *adj* **:** forgetful of one's own self or selfish interests or marked by forgetfulness of self ⟨absorbed in work of contemplation, *self-forgetful* and lost to consciousness of his surroundings —Laurence Binyon⟩ — **self–forgetfully** \¦==¦===\ *adv* — **self–forgetfulness** \¦==¦===\ *n*

self–forgetting \¦==¦==\ *adj* **:** SELF-FORGETFUL — **self–forgettingly** \¦==¦===\ *adv*

self–formed \ˈ=¦=\ *adj* **:** formed or developed by one's own efforts

self–fruitful \ˈ=¦==\ *adj* **:** capable of setting a crop of self-pollinated fruit without regard to the fertility of the seeds — **self–fruitfulness** \(ˈ)=¦===\ *n*

self–fulfilling \¦==¦==\ *adj* **:** SELF-REALIZING

self–fulfillment \¦==¦==\ *n* **:** fulfillment of oneself

self–generated \(ˈ)=¦==ˌ==\ *adj* **:** generated by itself **:** produced by self-generation **:** AUTOGENETIC, AUTOGENOUS

self–generation \¦=ˌ==¦==\ *n* **:** generation independent of external force or agency — called also *autogeny*

self–given \ˈ=¦==\ *adj* **1 :** derived from itself **:** INDEPENDENT ⟨a *self-given* entity⟩ **2 :** given by oneself ⟨the *self-given* role of elder statesman —T.H.White b.1915⟩

self–giving \ˈ=¦==\ *adj* **:** SELF-SACRIFICING, UNSELFISH ⟨*self-giving* creative work without thought of financial compensation —*Key Reporter*⟩

self–glorification \¦=ˌ===¦==\ *n* **:** a feeling or expression of one's superiority to others

self–glorifying \(ˈ)=¦==ˌ==\ *adj* **:** BOASTFUL

self–glorious \(ˈ)=¦===\ *adj, obs* **:** BOASTFUL, VAIN

self–glory \ˈ=¦==\ *n* **:** personal vanity **:** PRIDE

self–good \ˈ=¦=\ *n* **:** personal advantage

self–governed \¦=¦==\ *adj* **1 :** not influenced or controlled by others **2 :** exercising self-control

self–governing \(ˈ)=¦===\ *adj* **:** having control or rule over oneself or itself **:** not subject to outside authority **:** AUTONOMOUS, INDEPENDENT ⟨set up an independent church on a local, *self-governing* basis —V.L.Parrington⟩

self–government \(ˈ)=¦=(=)=\ *n* **1 :** SELF-COMMAND, SELF-CONTROL **2 a :** control of one's or its own affairs **:** AUTONOMY 2a, INDEPENDENCE **b :** government by the joint action of the mass of people constituting a civil body **:** democratic government **:** DEMOCRACY

self–gratification \¦=ˌ===¦==\ *n* **:** the act of pleasing oneself or of satisfying one's desires ⟨the raw human being has unconscious forces that push him crudely toward *self-gratification* —Priscilla Robertson⟩

self–gratulation \¦=ˌ==¦==\ *n* **:** SELF-CONGRATULATION

self–gratulatory \(ˈ)=¦===ˌ==\ *adj* **:** SELF-CONGRATULATORY

self–hardening \(ˈ)=¦=(=)=\ *adj* **:** hardening by itself ⟨*self-hardening* clay⟩

self–hardening steel *n* **:** AIR-HARDENING STEEL

self–hate \ˈ=¦=\ *or* **self–hatred** \ˈ=¦==\ *n* **:** hatred redirected toward one's self rather than toward others

self–hating \ˈ=¦==\ *adj* **:** given to self-hate

self–heal \ˈ=ˌ=\ *n* [ME *selfhele*, fr. *self-* + *hele*, back-formation fr. *helen* to heal — more at HEAL] **:** any of several plants thought to possess healing properties; *esp* **:** a blue-flowered Eurasian mint (*Prunella vulgaris*) naturalized throughout No. America

self–help \ˈ=¦=\ *n* **1 a :** the act or an instance of providing for or helping oneself without dependence on others ⟨the differences between a good refugee camp and a bad refugee camp, particularly from the point of view of *self-help* —Gardner Murphy⟩ **b :** a program of part time usu. domestic or clerical work permitted or made available by a school or college to students to help them defray their expenses **2 :** the act or right of redressing or preventing wrongs by one's own action (as in self-defense, distress, or abatement of a nuisance) without recourse to legal proceedings

self–heterodyne \(ˈ)=¦=(=)=ˌ=\ *n* **:** AUTODYNE

self·hood \ˈself¦hu̇d, ¦f,hu̇d, ˈseu̇l, ˈse(ə)l — *see* ¹SELF\ *n* -s [³*self* + *-hood*; intended as trans. of G *meinheit* (syn. of G *selbheit* selfhood)] **1 a :** the state of possessing an individual identity or the individuality so possessed **:** IPSEITY ⟨the intrinsic ~ of each individual thing in nature —Walker Gibson⟩ **b :** one's own character or personality ⟨the struggle of the partially emancipated woman for ~ —G.J.Becker⟩ **2 :** SELF-CENTEREDNESS, SELFISHNESS ⟨expose the quivering uncleanliness of a festering ~ —Perry Miller⟩

self–humbling \(ˈ)=¦=(=)=\ *adj* **:** acting or serving to humble oneself

self–hunter \ˈ=¦==\ *n* **1 :** a hunting dog who ignores the directions of his master and hunts to suit himself **2 :** a dog who habitually hunts without his master

self–hypnosis \¦=(ˌ)=¦==\ *n* **:** hypnosis of oneself

self–identical \¦=(ˌ)=¦===\ *adj* **:** having self-identity

self–identification \¦=(ˌ)=ˌ==¦==\ *n* **:** identification with someone or something outside oneself ⟨blasphemous in a man's *self-identification* with the deity —H.J.Morgenthau⟩

self–identity \¦=(ˌ)=¦===\ *n* **1 :** the identity of a thing with itself **:** substantial sameness **2 :** identity of subject and object in life and consciousness

self–ignite \¦==¦=\ *vi* **:** to become ignited without flame or spark (as under high compression)

self–ignition \¦==¦==\ *n* **:** ignition without flame or spark

self–image \ˈ=¦==\ *n* **:** one's conception of oneself or of one's role ⟨changing the *self-image* which many petty offenders have —Irwin Deutscher⟩

self–immolation \¦=ˌ==¦==\ *n* **:** a deliberate and willing sacrifice of oneself ⟨welcoming *self-immolation* to an overwhelming force —Charles Anderson⟩

self–importance \¦==¦==\ *n* **1 :** an exaggerated estimate of one's own importance or merit **:** SELF-CONCEIT **2 :** arrogant or pompous bearing or behavior

self–important \¦==¦==\ *adj* **:** having or showing self-importance **:** arrogant or pompous — **self–importantly** \¦==¦===\ *adv*

self–imposed \¦==¦=\ *adj* **:** imposed by oneself or itself **:** voluntarily assumed ⟨a pity that it should labor under a *self-imposed* handicap —J.L.Lowes⟩

self–impotent \(ˈ)=¦===\ *adj* **:** SELF-STERILE

self–improvement \¦==¦==\ *n* **:** improvement of oneself by one's own actions

self–improving \¦==¦==\ *adj* **:** achieving or aiming at self-improvement

self–inclusive \¦==¦==\ *adj* **:** enclosing itself **:** complete in itself ⟨a *self-inclusive* system⟩

self–incompatibility \¦=ˌ==ˌ==¦===\ *n* **:** the quality or state of being self-incompatible

self–incompatible \(ˈ)=¦=¦===\ *adj* **:** incapable of effective self-pollination — compare SELF-COMPATIBLE

self–incriminating \¦==¦==ˌ==\ *adj* **:** serving or tending to incriminate oneself

self–incrimination \¦=ˌ==¦==\ *n* **:** incrimination of oneself; *specif* **:** the giving of evidence or answering questions the tendency of which would be to subject one to a criminal prosecution

self–induced \¦==¦=\ *adj* **:** induced by oneself or itself ⟨would wallow in a *self-induced* gloom —Norman Mailer⟩; *specif* **:** existing in a circuit by reason of variation of current in the circuit itself ⟨a *self-induced* voltage⟩

self–inductance \¦==¦==\ *n* **:** INDUCTANCE 1(1)

self–induction \¦==¦==\ *n* **:** induction of an electromotive force in a circuit by a varying current in the same circuit

self–indulged \¦==¦=\ *adj* **:** pampered by oneself

self–indulgence \¦==¦==\ *n* **:** excessive or unrestrained gratification of one's own appetites, desires, or whims **:** irresponsible self-gratification ⟨always fond of the good things of life, he had found . . . increasing opportunity for *self-indulgence* —A.C.Cole⟩

self–indulgent \¦==¦==\ *adj* **:** indulging oneself or marked by self-indulgence ⟨a mild, *self-indulgent* bachelor —G.K. Chesterton⟩ ⟨an easy, *self-indulgent*, dilettante way of looking at life —Havelock Ellis⟩ — **self–indulgently** \¦==¦===\ *adv*

self–inflicted \¦==¦==\ *adj* **1 :** SELF-IMPOSED ⟨*self-inflicted* penance —Lord Byron⟩ **2 :** inflicted by one's own hand ⟨a *self-inflicted* wound⟩

selfing *pres part of* SELF

self–insurance \¦==ˌ==, ˌ=ˈ=ˌ==\ *n* **:** insurance of oneself or of one's own interests by the setting aside of money at regular intervals to provide a fund to cover possible losses (as in the event of fire)

self–insured \¦==¦=\ *adj* **:** insured by oneself

self–insurer \¦==¦==\ *n* **:** one who practices self-insurance

self–interest \(ˈ)=¦=(=)(ˌ)=\ *n* **1 :** one's own interest or advantage ⟨our *self-interest* . . . requires that we do everything in our power to guarantee that the children of Europe grow up strong —George Kent⟩ **2 :** a concern for one's own advantage and material well-being ⟨*self-interest* is regarded as the most, if not the only, reliable motivating force in economic behavior —A.F.Chalk⟩

self–interested \(ˈ)=¦=(=)(ˌ)==\ *adj* **:** characterized or motivated by self-interest — **self–interestedness** \(ˈ)=¦=(=)(ˌ)===\ *n*

self–involution \¦=ˌ==¦==\ *n* **:** SELF-ABSORPTION

self–involved \¦==¦=\ *adj* **:** SELF-ABSORBED

self·ish *pronunc at* ¹SELF + ish *or* ēsh\ *adj* [³*self* + *-ish*] **1 a :** concerned excessively or exclusively with oneself **:** seeking or concentrating on one's own advantage, pleasure, or well-being without regard for others ⟨if he could be proud and patriotic, so too he could be ~ and mean —Francis Parkman⟩ ⟨a formal, greedy, ~ old gentleman —L.P.Smith⟩ ⟨~ ambition⟩ **b :** SELF-CENTERED ⟨the sympathy of children with those who weep is innocently ~ —G.D.Brown⟩ **2 a :** believing or teaching that the chief motives of human action are derived from love of self ⟨the ~ school of philosophers —William Fleming⟩ **b :** performed to benefit oneself esp. in disregard of the welfare of others ⟨a ~ act⟩ — **self·ish·ly** \-əshlē, -li\ *adv*

self·ish·ness \-ishnəs, -ēsh-\ *n* -ES **:** the quality or state of being selfish **:** a concern for one's own welfare or advantage at the expense of or in disregard of others ⟨he was the personification of ~; and as he loved and cared for no one, so did no one love or care for him —George Borrow⟩

self·ism \-ˌfizəm\ *n* -s [³*self* + *-ism*] **1 :** concentration on self-interest **2 :** a system of selfish ethics

self·ist \-fəst\ *n* -s [³*self* + *-ist*] **:** a selfish person

self–justification \¦=ˌ===¦==\ *n* **:** the act or an instance of making excuses for oneself

self–justifying \(ˈ)=¦==ˌ==\ *adj* **1 :** seeking to excuse oneself **2 :** automatically justifying itself ⟨a *self-justifying* typewriter⟩

self–killed \ˈ=¦=\ *adj, obs* **:** killed by oneself ⟨liest victorious among thy slain *self-killed* —John Milton⟩

self–knowing \ˈ=¦==\ *adj* **:** knowing oneself **:** having self-knowledge

self–knowledge \ˈ=¦==\ *n* **:** knowledge of oneself or of one's capabilities **:** understanding of one's own character, feelings, or motivations **:** AUTOGNOSIS ⟨having *self-knowledge* impelled him to start writing —William Saroyan⟩

self–laceration \¦=ˌ=¦==\ *n* **:** laceration of oneself

self–legislating \(ˈ)=¦==ˌ==\ *adj* **:** making rules or laws for oneself

self·less *pronunc at* ¹SELF + ləs\ *adj* [³*self* + *-less*] **:** having no concern for self **:** UNSELFISH ⟨~ service to community, state, and nation —*Current Biog.*⟩ — **selflessly** *adv* — **selflessness** *n* -ES

self–life \ˈ=ˌ=\ *n* **1** *obs* **:** SELF-EXISTENCE ⟨who sees God's face, that is *self-life*, must die —John Donne⟩ **2 :** selfish living

self–limitation \¦=ˌ==¦==\ *n* **:** the quality or state of being self-limiting

self–limited \(ˈ)=¦===\ *adj* **:** limited by one's or its own nature; *specif* **:** running a definite and limited course ⟨the disease is *self-limited*, and the prognosis is good —*Science*⟩

self–limiting \(ˈ)=¦===\ *adj* **:** limiting oneself or itself **:** SELF-LIMITED

self–linkage \ˈ=¦==\ *n* **:** linkage of a substance to itself or to others of the same type **:** CATENATION b

self–liquidating \(ˈ)=¦==ˌ==\ *adj* **1 :** of or relating to a commercial transaction in which goods are converted into cash in a short time **2 :** generating funds from its own operations to repay the original investment made to create it ⟨a *self-liquidating* housing project⟩

self–liquidating loan *n* **:** a loan having a term approximately equal to the period in which the borrower can complete the transaction financed and use the proceeds to repay the loan

self–loader \ˈ=¦==\ *n* **:** a semiautomatic firearm

self–loading \ˈ=¦==\ *adj, of a firearm* **:** SEMIAUTOMATIC

self–locking \ˈ=¦==\ *adj* **:** locking by its own action

self–lost \ˈ=¦=\ *adj* **:** lost by one's own fault

self–love \ˈ=¦=\ *n* **1 a :** love of oneself **:** AMOUR PROPRE ⟨peevish, proud, idle, made of *self-love* —Shak.⟩ **b :** love redirected toward one's self rather than toward others ⟨return to *self-love* as a consequence of failure to make satisfactory attachments to others —G.S.Blum⟩ **2 :** regard for one's own happiness or advantage **syn** see CONCEIT

self–loved \ˈ=¦=\ *adj, archaic* **:** SELF-LOVING

self–loving \ˈ=¦==\ *adj* **:** characterized by self-love

self–lubricating \(ˈ)=¦==ˌ==\ *adj* **:** lubricating itself

self–luminous \(ˈ)=¦===\ *adj* **:** having in itself the property of emitting light

self–made \ˈ=¦=\ *adj* **1 :** made by oneself or itself **2 :** raised from poverty or obscurity by one's own efforts ⟨a *self-made* man⟩

self–mailer \ˈ=¦==\ *n* **:** a folder or broadside that can be sent by mail without enclosure in an envelope by use of a gummed sticker or a precanceled stamp to hold the leaves together

self–mailing \ˈ=¦==\ *adj* **:** capable of being mailed without being enclosed in an envelope

self–mastery \(ˈ)=¦=(=)=\ *n* **:** SELF-COMMAND, SELF-CONTROL

self–mate \ˈ=¦=\ *n* **:** SUIMATE

self–mortification \¦=ˌ===¦==\ *n* **:** the infliction of pain or discomfort on oneself

self–motion \ˈ=¦==\ *n* **:** spontaneous or voluntary motion

self–motive \ˈ=¦==\ *adj* **:** having self-motion

self–moved \ˈ=¦=\ *adj* **:** moved by inherent power

self–movement \ˈ=¦==\ *n* **:** SELF-MOTION

self–mover \ˈ=¦==\ *n* **:** one that moves itself **:** AUTOMATON

self–moving \ˈ=¦==\ *adj* **:** capable of moving by itself

self–murder \ˈ=¦==\ *n* **:** SELF-DESTRUCTION, SUICIDE

self–naughting \ˈ=¦==\ *n* **:** SELF-EFFACEMENT

self·ness *n* -ES [³*self* + *-ness*] **1 :** EGOISM, SELFISHNESS **2 :** PERSONALITY, SELFHOOD

self–observation \¦=ˌ==¦==\ *n* **1 :** observation of one's own appearance **2 :** INTROSPECTION, SELF-EXAMINATION

self–operating \(ˈ)=¦=(=)ˌ==\ *or* **self–operative** \(ˈ)=¦=(=)ˌ==\ *adj* **:** SELF-ACTING

self–opinion \¦==¦==\ *n* **:** high or exaggerated estimate of oneself **:** SELF-CONCEIT ⟨if I should ever attain to the degree of *self-opinion* requisite to such an undertaking —William Cowper⟩

self–opinionated \¦==¦==ˌ==\ *adj* **1 :** having a high or exaggerated opinion of oneself or one's own views **2 :** stubbornly holding to one's own opinion **:** OPINIONATED — **self–opinionatedness** *n* -ES \¦==¦==ˌ===\

self–opinionative \¦==¦==ˌ==\ *adj* **:** SELF-OPINIONATED — **self–opinionativeness** \¦==¦==ˌ===\ *n*

self–opinioned \¦==¦==\ *adj* **:** SELF-OPINIONATED — **self–opinionedness** \¦==¦===\ *n*

self–organization \¦=ˌ==(ˌ)=¦==\ *n* **:** organization of oneself; *specif* **:** the act or process of forming or joining a labor union

self–originated \¦==¦==ˌ==\ *adj* **:** originated by oneself or itself

self–originating \¦==¦==ˌ==\ *adj* **:** originating by or from oneself or itself

self–partiality \¦=ˌ=(=)¦===\ *n* **1 :** an excessive estimate of oneself as compared with others **2 :** a prejudice in favor of one's own claims or interests

self–perpetuating \¦==¦==ˌ==\ *adj* **:** capable of continuing or renewing oneself or itself indefinitely ⟨the theoretical fear of a *self-perpetuating* president —J.C.Fitzpatrick⟩ ⟨administered by its own *self-perpetuating* board of trustees —*Current Biog.*⟩

self–perpetuation \¦=ˌ==ˌ=¦==\ *n* **:** perpetuation of oneself or itself ⟨concerned with *self-perpetuation* in office they too often ignore the public welfare —E.M.Eriksson⟩

self–picture \ˈ=¦==\ *n* **:** SELF-IMAGE

self–pity \ˈ=¦==\ *n* **:** pity for oneself; *esp* **:** a self-indulgent lingering on one's own sorrows or misfortunes ⟨the immensity of her self-love and *self-pity* . . . steeped her pages in an ignoble emotionalism —Agnes Repplier⟩

self–pitying \(ˈ)=¦===\ *adj* **:** given to self-pity — **self–pityingly** \(ˈ)=¦====\ *adv*

self–pleased \ˈ=¦=\ *adj* **:** SELF-COMPLACENT

self–pleasing \ˈ=¦==\ *adj* **:** pleasing to oneself

self–poise \ˈ=¦=\ *n* **:** the quality or state of being self-poised

self–poised \ˈ=¦=\ *adj* **1 :** balanced without support **2 :** having poise by self-command ⟨sturdy moral habit and *self-poised* temperament made him perhaps unduly optimistic —Gamaliel Bradford⟩

self–pollinated \(ˈ)=¦==ˌ==\ *adj* **:** subjected to or produced by self-pollination

self–pollination \¦=ˌ==¦==\ *n* **:** the transfer of pollen from the anther of a flower to the stigma of the same flower or sometimes to that of another flower of the same plant or of another plant of the same clone — compare CROSS-POLLINATION

self–portrait \ˈ=¦=(ˌ)=\ *n* **1 :** a portrait of an artist done by him-

self 2 : a picture of one's character or personality created by oneself ⟨a pleasing *self-portrait* emerges from the letters —Douglas Stewart⟩

self-possessed \ʾ:ʾ:ʾ\ *adj* : having or showing self-possession : composed in mind or manner : CALM ⟨remains strong and *self-possessed* in the face of trouble and strain —James Hewitt⟩ — **self-possessedly** \ʾ:ʾ:ʾ\ *adv*

self-possession \ʾ:ʾ:ʾ\ *n* : control of one's emotions or reactions : presence of mind : SELF-COMMAND, COMPOSURE ⟨that carefully cultivated air of quiet self-emotions of *self-possession*, suggesting inner repose and serenity —Harold Strauss⟩

self-potential method \ʾ:ʾ:ʾ\ *n* : a method of electrical prospecting in which the electromotive forces existing in and around an ore body are measured at the surface

self-powered \ʾ:ʾ:ʾ\ *adj* : having its own power or propelling force

self-praise \ʾ:ʾ:ʾ\ *n* : praise of oneself

self-preservation \ʾ:ʾ:ʾ\ *n* 1 : preservation of oneself from destruction or harm ⟨*self-preservation* demands a certain amount of public spirit —S.M.Crothers⟩ 2 : a natural or instinctive tendency to act so as to preserve one's own existence ⟨man has not only the impulse of *self-preservation*, but also a social impulse —Frank Thilly⟩

self-preservative \ʾ:ʾ:ʾ\ *adj* : tending to self-preservation ⟨*self-preservative* behavior⟩

self-preserving \ʾ:ʾ:ʾ\ *adj* : acting or tending to preserve oneself or itself

self-pride \ʾ:ʾ:ʾ\ *n* : pride in oneself or in something that belongs or relates to oneself

self-proclaimed \ʾ:ʾ:ʾ\ *adj* : based on one's own say-so ⟨a *self-proclaimed* genius⟩

self-produced \ʾ:ʾ:ʾ\ *adj* : produced by oneself or itself : arising from oneself or itself

self-propelled \ʾ:ʾ:ʾ\ *adj* 1 a (1) : propelled by its own motor ⟨a *self-propelled* vehicle⟩ (2) : propelled by its own fuel ⟨a *self-propelled* missile⟩ b : moved forward by one's or its own force or momentum ⟨a thundering *self-propelled* egotist —Winthrop Sargeant⟩ ⟨the arms program is now *self-propelled* —Time⟩ 2 a : mounted on or fired from a moving vehicle ⟨a *self-propelled* gun⟩ b : serving as a moving carrier for a weapon ⟨a *self-propelled* mount⟩

self-propelling \ʾ:ʾ:ʾ\ *adj* : SELF-PROPELLED

self-propulsion \ʾ:ʾ:ʾ\ *n* : propulsion by one's or its own power

self-protection \ʾ:ʾ:ʾ\ *n* : protection of oneself : SELF-DEFENSE ⟨as a measure of *self-protection* against the lawless element —Blue Bk.⟩

self-protective \ʾ:ʾ:ʾ\ *adj* : serving or tending to protect oneself

self-pruning \ʾ:ʾ:ʾ\ *n* : NATURAL PRUNING

self-punishment \(ʾ)ʾ:ʾ:ʾ\ *n* : punishment of oneself

self-purification \ʾ:ʾ:ʾ\ *n* 1 : purification by natural process ⟨*self-purification* of water⟩ 2 : purification of oneself ⟨moral *self-purification*⟩

self-quadder \ʾ:ʾ:ʾ\ *n* : QUADDER

self-question \ʾ:ʾ:ʾ\ *n* : a question put to a person by himself ⟨from the *self-questions* came the self-doubts —Mark Schorer⟩

self-questioning \ʾ:ʾ:ʾ\ *n* : the act or process of questioning oneself : the examination of one's own actions and motives : SELF-SEARCHING ⟨entering a world of imponderables, and at every stage occasions for *self-questioning* arise —Sir Winston Churchill⟩

self-raised \ʾ:ʾ:ʾ\ *adj* : raised by one's or its own power or effort

self-rake \ʾ:ʾ:ʾ\ *n* : a reaper with a rake attachment for sweeping off gavels from the platform

self-rating \ʾ:ʾ:ʾ\ *n* : determination of one's own rating with reference to a standard educational scale or other rating device

self-reacting \ʾ:ʾ:ʾ\ *adj* : automatically compensating or adjusting to changed conditions

self-reading \ʾ:ʾ:ʾ\ *adj* : capable of being easily read

self-reading rod \ʾ:ʾ:ʾ\ *n* : a leveling rod with graduations designed to be read directly by the observer

self-realization \ʾ:ʾ:ʾ(ʾ)ʾ\ *n* 1 : fulfillment by oneself of the possibilities of one's character or personality ⟨has no resource except his impulses and only in improvised and violent action can he attain even an illusion of *self-realization* —A.M. Mizener⟩

self-realizationism \ʾ:ʾ:ʾ(ʾ)ʾ\ *n* -s : the ethical theory that the highest good for man consists in realizing or fulfilling himself usu. on the assumption that he has certain inborn abilities constituting his real or ideal self

self-realizationist \ʾ:ʾ:ʾ(ʾ)ʾ\ *n* -s : an advocate of self-realizationism

self-realizing \(ʾ)ʾ:ʾ:ʾ\ *adj* : marked by or achieving self-realization

self-recording \ʾ:ʾ:ʾ\ *adj* : making an automatic record : AUTOGRAPHIC ⟨a *self-recording* flowmeter⟩

self-recrimination \ʾ:ʾ:ʾ\ *n* : the act of accusing or blaming oneself

self-rectifying \(ʾ)ʾ:ʾ:ʾ\ *adj* : capable of accomplishing rectification by itself

self-reflection \ʾ:ʾ:ʾ\ *n* : INTROSPECTION

self-reflective \ʾ:ʾ:ʾ\ *adj* : INTROSPECTIVE

self-reflexive \ʾ:ʾ:ʾ\ *adj* : reflecting itself : giving back an image of itself — **self-reflexiveness** \ʾ:ʾ:ʾ\ *n*

self-reform \ʾ:ʾ:ʾ\ *n* : reform of oneself

self-regard \ʾ:ʾ:ʾ\ *n* 1 : consideration of oneself or one's own interests 2 : SELF-RESPECT

self-regarding \ʾ:ʾ:ʾ\ *adj* : concerned with oneself or one's own interests ⟨the new generation . . . is iconoclastic, undisciplined, *self-regarding*, violent —Dial⟩

self-registering \(ʾ)ʾ:ʾ:ʾ\ *adj* : registering automatically ⟨a *self-registering* barometer⟩

self-regulating \ʾ:ʾ:ʾ\ *adj* : regulating oneself or itself ⟨a *self-regulating* community⟩; *specif* : AUTOMATIC ⟨a *self-regulating* mechanism⟩

self-regulating currency *n* : AUTOMATIC CURRENCY

self-regulation \ʾ:ʾ:ʾ\ *n* : regulation of or by oneself or itself : control or supervision from within ⟨*self-regulation* of business⟩

self-regulative \(ʾ)ʾ:ʾ:ʾ\ *or* **self-regulatory** \(ʾ)ʾ:ʾ:ʾ\ *adj* : serving or tending to regulate oneself or itself

self-relation \ʾ:ʾ:ʾ\ *n* : SELF-IDENTITY

self-reliance \ʾ:ʾ:ʾ\ *n* : reliance upon one's own efforts, judgment, or ability : SELF-CONFIDENCE ⟨the people are weathered and bronzed, possessed of a sturdy independence and *self-reliance* —Amer. Guide Series: N.C.⟩

self-reliant \ʾ:ʾ:ʾ\ *adj* : not dependent on others : having confidence in and exercising one's own powers or judgment ⟨a mood of fighting men, venturesome, *self-reliant*, proud —J.R. Green⟩

self-renouncing \ʾ:ʾ:ʾ\ *adj* : marked by self-renunciation

self-renunciation \ʾ:ʾ:ʾ\ *n* : renunciation of one's own wishes, desires, or ambitions

self-repression \ʾ:ʾ:ʾ\ *n* : the keeping to oneself of one's thoughts, wishes, or feelings ⟨habit of absolute *self-repression*, and of concealment of emotion again prevailed —S.W.Mitchell⟩

self-reproach \ʾ:ʾ:ʾ\ *n* : the act or an instance of reproaching oneself : SELF-ACCUSATION ⟨felt both *self-reproach* and considerable grief concerning the loss of his friends —Elizabeth Rosenberg⟩

self-reproachful \ʾ:ʾ:ʾ\ *adj* : reproachful of oneself

self-reproaching \ʾ:ʾ:ʾ\ *adj* : reproaching oneself — **self-reproachingly** \ʾ:ʾ:ʾ\ *adv* — **self-reproachingness** \ʾ:ʾ:ʾ\ *n* -ES

self-reproof \ʾ:ʾ:ʾ\ *n* : the act or an instance of reproving oneself : censure of oneself

self-reproving \ʾ:ʾ:ʾ\ *adj* : feeling or expressing self-reproof — **self-reprovingly** \ʾ:ʾ:ʾ\ *adv*

self-repugnant \ʾ:ʾ:ʾ\ *adj* : INCONSISTENT, SELF-CONTRADICTORY

self-rescuer \(ʾ)ʾ:ʾ:ʾ\ *n* : a pocket-size respirator for emergency use that protects the wearer for a period of about one-half hour against atmospheres containing carbon monoxide gas (as in a contaminated mine)

self-respect \ʾ:ʾ:ʾ\ *n* 1 : an appropriate respect for oneself : a confidence in one's own worth as a human being and a concern to maintain it ⟨to cause him to lose his *self-respect*, to

---

make him feel diminished as a person —A.W.Hummel⟩ 2 : regard for one's or its own standing or position ⟨national *self-respect* demands a high level of education⟩

self-respectful \ʾ:ʾ:ʾ\ *adj* : SELF-RESPECTING

self-respecting \ʾ:ʾ:ʾ\ *adj* : having respect for oneself or itself : marked by self-respect ⟨every *self-respecting* library should have a copy —M.G.Bishop⟩ ⟨such bargaining seemed unworthy of a *self-respecting* nation —S.E.Morison & H.S. Commager⟩

self-restraining \ʾ:ʾ:ʾ\ *adj* : marked by self-restraint

self-restraint \ʾ:ʾ:ʾ\ *n* : restraint imposed on oneself : SELF-CONTROL ⟨enough to tax the *self-restraint* of an exceedingly hot-tempered foster sister —H.G.Wells⟩

self-revealing \ʾ:ʾ:ʾ\ *adj* : marked by self-revelation : serving to reveal oneself ⟨pruned her letters of all that was *self-revealing* —Spectator⟩

self-revelation \ʾ:ʾ:ʾ\ *n* : revelation of one's own thoughts, feelings, and attitudes esp. without deliberate intent ⟨his letters compare more than favorably with any . . . in their *self-revelation*, spontaneity, mother wit —Emily Skeel⟩

self-revelative \ʾ:ʾ:ʾ\ *or* **self-revelatory** \ʾ:ʾ:ʾ\ *adj* : SELF-REVEALING

self-reversal \ʾ:ʾ:ʾ\ *n* : transformation due to self-absorption of what should be a brighter spectrum line into a dark one

self-rewarding \ʾ:ʾ:ʾ\ *adj* : rewarding oneself : being its own reward ⟨a *self-rewarding* virtue⟩

self-righteous \ʾ:ʾ:ʾ\ *adj* : convinced of one's own righteousness esp. in contrast with the actions and beliefs of others : narrowly moralistic and intolerant : PHARISAICAL ⟨were altogether very superior, if not stuffy, very much like some smug, *self-righteous* moralists —Edison Marshall⟩ ⟨all the *self-righteous* cruelty of a woman whose happiness has been given up for others —Time⟩ — **self-righteously** \ʾ:ʾ:ʾ\ *adv*

self-righteousness \ʾ:ʾ:ʾ\ *n*

self-righting \ʾ:ʾ:ʾ\ *adj* : capable of righting itself when capsized ⟨a *self-righting* boat⟩

self-rising \ʾ:ʾ:ʾ\ *adj* : rising or capable of rising by itself

self-rising flour *n* : a commercially prepared mixture of flour, salt, and a leavening agent — compare MIX 2a

self-rolled \ʾ:ʾ:ʾ\ *adj* : rolled or coiled upon itself

self-rule \ʾ:ʾ:ʾ\ *n* : independent rule : SELF-GOVERNMENT

self-ruling \ʾ:ʾ:ʾ\ *adj* : ruling oneself : SELF-GOVERNING

selfs *pl of* SELF, *pres 3d sing of* SELF

self-sacrifice \(ʾ)ʾ:ʾ:(ʾ)ʾ\ *n* : sacrifice of oneself or one's interests for others or for some cause or ideal ⟨an act of *self-sacrifice* in giving up a lucrative business career for public service⟩

self-sacrificer \(ʾ)ʾ:ʾ:ʾ\ *n* : one that practices self-sacrifice

self-sacrificing \(ʾ)ʾ:ʾ:ʾ\ *adj* : sacrificing oneself for others or marked by self-sacrifice ⟨a *self-sacrificing* parent⟩ ⟨*self-sacrificing* love⟩ — **self-sacrificingly** \ʾ:ʾ:ʾ\ *adv* — **self-sacrificingness** \(ʾ)ʾ:ʾ:ʾ\ *n*

selfsame \ʾ:ʾ\ *adj* [ME *selve same*, fr. *selve* (var. of 2*self*) + *same*] : precisely the same : IDENTICAL ⟨more useful to date by authors than to express the *selfsame* ideas in terms of centuries and part centuries —T.E.Hope⟩ *syn* see SAME

self-same-ness \ʾ:ʾ:ʾ\ *n* [*selfsame* + *-ness*] : IDENTICALNESS, IDENTITY

self-satisfaction \ʾ:ʾ:ʾ\ *n* : a usu. smug and complacent satisfaction with oneself or one's position or achievements : SELF-COMPLACENCY ⟨have the *self-satisfaction* of courage without the inconvenience of danger —W.S.Maugham⟩

self-satisfied \ʾ:ʾ:ʾ\ *adj* : marked by self-satisfaction : SELF-COMPLACENT ⟨an air of *self-satisfied* dignity⟩ *syn* see COMPLACENT

self-satisfying \(ʾ)ʾ:ʾ:ʾ\ *adj* : giving satisfaction to oneself

self-scrutiny \(ʾ)ʾ:ʾ:ʾ\ *n* : INTROSPECTION, SELF-EXAMINATION

self-sealing \ʾ:ʾ:ʾ\ *adj* : capable of sealing itself after puncture ⟨a *self-sealing* tire⟩ ⟨a *self-sealing* fuel tank⟩

self-searching \ʾ:ʾ:ʾ\ *adj* : SELF-QUESTIONING

self-secure \ʾ:ʾ:ʾ\ *adj* : secure of oneself or one's position

self-security \ʾ:ʾ:ʾ\ *n* : security with respect to oneself or one's position

self-seed \ʾ:ʾ\ *vi* : SELF-SOW

self-seeker \ʾ:ʾ:ʾ\ *n* : one that seeks only or mainly his own advantage or pleasure ⟨one that tries to get the most out of government for himself ⟨got into politics, and was victimized by *self-seekers* —Amer. Guide Series: Minn.⟩

¹self-seeking \ʾ:ʾ:ʾ\ *n* : the act or practice of seeking to advance one's own ends : SELFISHNESS

²self-seeking \"\ *adj* [¹*self-seeking*] : seeking primarily to further one's own interests : SELFISH ⟨was no *self-seeking* politician, but a man of vision —V.L.Parrington⟩ — **self-seeking-ness** \(ʾ)ʾ:ʾ:ʾ\ *n* -ES

self-selection \ʾ:ʾ:ʾ\ *n* : selection of goods by retail customers from display racks or counters in a store or department having salespeople available to advise and help the customers in such selection

self-service \ʾ:ʾ:ʾ\ *n* : service of customers or patrons by themselves (as in a restaurant, retail food market, or store) with payment usu. made at a designated check-out counter

self-serving \ʾ:ʾ:ʾ\ *adj* : serving one's own interests often in disregard of the truth or the reasonable interests of others ⟨a reckless, *self-serving* distortion of facts —M.E.Pew⟩

self-serving declaration *n* : a statement made to serve one's own interests; *specif* : such a statement made out of court by a party to a legal action and usu. not admissible as evidence

self-slain \ʾ:ʾ\ *adj* : killed by oneself

self-slaughter \ʾ:ʾ:ʾ\ *n* : SELF-MURDER, SUICIDE ⟨that the Everlasting had not fixed his canon 'gainst *self-slaughter* —Shak.⟩

self-slaughtered \ʾ:ʾ:ʾ\ *adj* : killed by oneself

self-slayer \ʾ:ʾ:ʾ\ *n* : one that kills himself

self-sounding \ʾ:ʾ:ʾ\ *adj* : sounding by itself : creating its own sound : IDIOPHONIC

self-sow \ʾ:ʾ\ *vi* : to sow itself by dropping seeds : produce a new generation without human intervention ⟨grasses that *self-sow* and build a firm turf⟩

self-sown *also* **self-sowed** \ʾ:ʾ:\ *adj* : sown autonomically or by an inanimate agency ⟨by wind or water current⟩

self-starter \ʾ:ʾ:ʾ\ *n* 1 : something that actuates itself : PERPETUUM MOBILE 2 a : any of various more or less automatic attachments for starting an internal combustion engine other than the simple starting crank or an auxiliary turning engine b : a machine or vehicle equipped with such an attachment 3 : one that has initiative ⟨the officials associated with its further progress have to be *self-starters* if that progress is to take place —Atlantic⟩

self-starting \ʾ:ʾ:ʾ\ *adj* : capable of starting by oneself or itself

self-sterile \ʾ:ʾ:(ʾ)ʾ\ *adj* : sterile to its own pollen or sperm — used of either a plant or animal; opposed to *self-fertile*

self-sterility \ʾ:ʾ:ʾ\ *n* : the quality or state of being self-sterile

self-study \ʾ:ʾ:ʾ\ *n* : study of oneself or itself; *also* : a record of observations from such study ⟨recently completed a community *self-study* —Harry Serotkin⟩

self-styled \ʾ:ʾ:ʾ\ *adj* : given a specified designation or title by oneself : SOI-DISANT ⟨*self-styled* experts⟩ ⟨the *self-styled* champion⟩

self-subdued \ʾ:ʾ:ʾ\ *adj* : subdued by oneself

self-subsistence \ʾ:ʾ:ʾ\ *or* **self-subsistency** \ʾ:ʾ:ʾ\ *n* : the quality or state of being self-subsistent

self-subsistent \ʾ:ʾ:ʾ\ *adj* : subsisting independently of anything external to itself

self-subsisting \ʾ:ʾ:ʾ\ *adj* : SELF-SUBSISTENT

self-substantial \ʾ:ʾ:ʾ\ *adj* : of or derived from one's own substance

self-sufficiency \ʾ:ʾ:ʾ\ *also* **self-sufficience** \ʾ:ʾ:ʾ\ *n* : the quality or state of being self-sufficient

self-sufficient \ʾ:ʾ:ʾ\ *adj* [trans. of Gk *autarkēs*] 1 a (1) : able to maintain oneself or itself without outside aid : capable of providing for one's or its own needs : SELF-SUPPORTING ⟨organisms are not *self-sufficient*, closed systems —Weston LaBarre⟩ ⟨a rich town, prosperous, clean, self-contained and *self-sufficient* —Arnold Bennett⟩ (2) : economically independent : not dependent on imports from other countries or regions : AUTARKIC 2 b : sufficient in or to itself : SELF-CONTAINED ⟨these are not essays, it seems, independent and *self*-

---

sufficient, but fragments broken off from some larger book —Virginia Woolf⟩ 2 : having an extreme confidence in one's own ability or worth : HAUGHTY, OVERBEARING ⟨felt *self-sufficient* . . . he acted superior and everyone around the place could hardly stand him —W.J.Reilly⟩ — **self-sufficientness** \"\ *n*

self-sufficing \ʾ:ʾ:ʾ\ *adj* : SELF-SUFFICIENT — **self-sufficingly** \"\ *adv* — **self-sufficingness** \ʾ:ʾ:ʾ\ *n* -ES

self-suggestion \ʾ:ʾ:ʾ\ *n* : AUTOSUGGESTION

self-suggestive \ʾ:ʾ:ʾ\ *adj* : AUTOSUGGESTIVE

self-support \ʾ:ʾ:ʾ\ *n* : independent support of oneself or itself

self-supported \ʾ:ʾ:ʾ\ *adj* : supported by oneself or itself

self-supporting \ʾ:ʾ:ʾ\ *adj* : supporting oneself or itself

self-sure \ʾ:ʾ\ *adj* : sure of oneself — **self-sureness** \ʾ:ʾ:ʾ\ *n*

self-surrender \ʾ:ʾ:ʾ\ *n* : the giving up of one's or one's will to some feeling or influence ⟨absorption, *self-surrender*, a passing into another world —Charles Morgan⟩

self-sustained \ʾ:ʾ:ʾ\ *adj* : sustained by oneself or itself : needing no outside support

self-sustaining \ʾ:ʾ:ʾ\ *adj* : maintaining or capable of maintaining oneself or itself by one's or its independent efforts : SELF-SUPPORTING ⟨the individual ranchos had to be *self-sustaining*, for the arrival of the supply ship was uncertain —Amer. Guide Series: Calif.⟩ — **self-sustainingly** \ʾ:ʾ:ʾ\ *adv*

self-tapping screw \ʾ:ʾ:ʾ\ *n* : TAPPING SCREW

self-taught \ʾ:ʾ\ *adj* 1 : having knowledge or skills acquired by one's own efforts without formal instruction or training ⟨a *self-taught* painter⟩ 2 : learned or worked out by oneself ⟨*self-taught* instrumentation⟩ ⟨*self-taught* perspective⟩

self-tightening \(ʾ)ʾ:ʾ:ʾ\ *adj* : tightening by itself

self-timer \ʾ:ʾ:ʾ\ *n* : a delayed-action shutter-tripping device often built into a camera that permits the photographer to be included in a picture

self-toning paper \ʾ:ʾ:ʾ\ *n* : a printing-out paper in which a gold salt incorporated in the emulsion tones the image during fixing

self-torment \ʾ:ʾ:ʾ\ *n* : the act or an instance of tormenting oneself — **self-tormentor** \ʾ:ʾ:(ʾ)ʾ\ *n*

self-tormenting \ʾ:ʾ:(ʾ)ʾ\ *adj* : tormenting oneself or marked by self-torment

self-transcendence \ʾ:ʾ:ʾ\ *n* : the capacity to transcend oneself

self-treatment \ʾ:ʾ:ʾ\ *n* : AUTOTHERAPY

self-trust \ʾ:ʾ\ *n* : SELF-CONFIDENCE

self-understanding \ʾ:ʾ:ʾ\ *n* : understanding of oneself : SELF-KNOWLEDGE

self-unfruitful \ʾ:ʾ:ʾ\ *adj* : deficient in self-fertility : setting no fruits or a greatly reduced crop of fruits in the absence of cross-pollination ⟨sweet cherries are *self-unfruitful*⟩ — **self-unfruitfulness** \ʾ:ʾ:ʾ\ *n*

self-unloader \ʾ:ʾ:ʾ\ *n* : a bulk cargo ship used on the Great Lakes that specializes in the hauling of limestone, sand, aggregates, coal, and sometimes grain and that is equipped with swinging booms and endless belt or chain devices permitting independence of harbor facilities

self-validating \(ʾ)ʾ:ʾ:ʾ\ *adj* : validating itself : needing no guarantee or judgment of its validity outside of itself

self-violence \ʾ:ʾ:ʾ\ *n* : violence inflicted on oneself; *specif* : SELF-MURDER

¹self-ward *pronunc at* ¹SELF + wə(r)d\ *or* **self-wards** \-dz\ *adv* [³*self* + *-ward*, *-wards*] : toward oneself

²selfward \"\ *adj* : directed or turned toward oneself — **self-ward-ness** \ʾ:ʾ\ *n* -ES

self-will \ʾ:ʾ\ *n* [ME *selfwil*, *self-will*, fr. OE *selfwill*, fr. *self*, *pron.* & *adj.* + *will* — more at SELF, WILL] : stubborn adherence to one's own desires or ideas esp. in opposition to others : OBSTINACY ⟨each of us has his psychopathic streak of *self-will* and rebellion —Weston La Barre⟩

self-willed \ʾ:ʾ\ *adj* [ME, fr. *self-will*, n. + *-ed*] : governed by one's own will : not yielding to the wishes or opinions of others : OBSTINATE ⟨human beings . . . have a way of remaining annoyingly individualistic and *self-willed* —A.M.Schlesinger b.1888⟩ — **self-willed-ly** \ʾ:ʾ:ʾ\ *adv* — **self-willed-ness** \ʾ:ʾ:ʾ\ *n*

self-winding \ʾ:ʾ:ʾ\ *adj* : winding itself : not needing to be wound by hand ⟨a *self-winding* watch⟩

self-wisdom \ʾ:ʾ:ʾ\ *n* : the quality or state of being self-wise

self-wise \ʾ:ʾ\ *adj* : wise in one's own estimation

self-worship \ʾ:ʾ:ʾ\ *n* : worship of oneself : AUTOTHEISM — **self-worshiper** \(ʾ)ʾ:ʾ:ʾ\ *n*

self-wrong \ʾ:ʾ\ *n* : wrong done to oneself

sel-ig-mann-ite \ʾseləgmən,nīt\ *n* -s [G *seligmannit*, fr. Gustav *Seligmann* †1920 Ger. banker and mineral collector + G *-it* *-ite*] : a mineral PbCuAsS₃ consisting of a lead and copper arsenic sulfide and occurring in metallic lead-gray orthorhombic crystals

se-li-hoth *or* **se-li-hot** *also* **se-li-choth** *or* **se-li-chot** \sə-ʾlē̇,kō̇t(h), -ō̇s\ *n pl, sometimes cap* [Heb *səlīhōth*, pl. of *səlīhāh* pardon] : liturgical poems recited as prayers of repentance and forgiveness on Jewish fast days and on the days preceding the high holy days

sel-ion \ʾselyən\ *n* -s [ME *sellion*, fr. MF *seillon*, a measure of land, fr. OF *sillon* ridge, furrow] : one of the strips or ridges of land allotted for cultivation in the open-field system

¹sel-juk \ʾsel,jük, -jük, ʾ:ʾ\ *or* **sel-ju-ki-an** \ʾ:ʾ;ʾ:ʾ\ *adj*, *usu cap* [*seljuk* fr. Turk *Selçuk*, eponymous ancestor of the dynasties; *seljukian* fr. Turk *selçuki* Seljukian, fr. *Selçuk*] 1 : of or relating to any of several Turkish dynasties that ruled over a great part of western Asia in the 11th, 12th, and 13th centuries 2 : of, relating to, or characteristic of a Turkish people ruled over by a Seljuk dynasty

²seljuk \"\ *or* **seljukian** \"\ *n* -s *usu cap* 1 : a member of a Seljuk dynasty 2 : a Turk subject to a Seljuk ruler

sel-kirk-shire \ʾsel(ʾ)kə̇rk,shi(ə)r, -,shər\ *or* **selkirk** *adj, usu cap* [fr. *Selkirkshire or Selkirk*, Scotland] : of or from the county of Selkirk, Scotland : of the kind or style prevalent in Selkirk

sel-kirk's violet \ʾsel,kə̇rks-\ *n, usu cap S* [perh. fr. *Selkirk*, range of the Rocky mountains in British Columbia, Canada] : an acaulescent violet (*Viola selkirkii*) found in the cooler parts of No. America and in Greenland that has large-spurred flowers of a pale violet color

sel-kup \ʾsel(ʾ)kəp\ *n -s usu cap* : OSTYAK SAMOYED

¹sell \ʾsel\ *vb* **sold** \ʾsōld\ **sold; selling; sells** [ME *sellen*, fr. OE *sellan*; akin to OHG *sellen* to sell, ON *selja* to deliver, sell, Goth *saljan* to offer, present; causative-denominative fr. a prehistoric noun represented by OE *salu* sale, OHG *sala* delivery of goods, ON *sal* payment, OSlav *sŭlŭ* deliverer, messenger; akin to Gk *helein* to take, OIr *selb* possession, property] *vt* 1 : to deliver or give up in violation of duty, trust, or loyalty : BETRAY ⟨the puppet who had no compunction over *~ing* his country —Times Lit. Supp.⟩ — often used with *out* ⟨won their confidence to *~* them out⟩ 2 a (1) : to give up (property) to another for money or other valuable consideration : hand over or transfer title to (as goods or real estate) for a price ⟨*sold* his books⟩ ⟨*sold* his house⟩ ⟨*sold* his stock⟩ — opposed to *buy* (2) : to offer for sale : deal in as an article of sale ⟨*~s* home appliances⟩ ⟨*~s* insurance⟩ b : to give up in return for something else ⟨*~* my title for a glorious grave —Shak.⟩; *esp* : to exchange foolishly or dishonorably ⟨*sold* his birthright for a mess of pottage⟩ ⟨*sold* his Puritan heritage for southern trade profits —V.L.Parrington⟩ c *Brit* : to give up (a military commission or command) by sale under the purchase system formerly in effect d : to exact a price for ⟨put up a fierce resistance in his determination to *~* his life dearly⟩ 3 a : to deliver into slavery for money ⟨*sold* their captives to slave traders⟩ b : to give into the power of another ⟨*~* his soul to the devil⟩ c : to deliver the personal services of for money ⟨noblemen still continued to *~* themselves and their soldiers to foreign war lords —J.S.Roucek⟩ ⟨had *sold* her to other rich men —F.M.Ford⟩ d : to transfer the contract of for money or other consideration ⟨*sold* their star shortstop for an undisclosed sum⟩ 4 : to dispose of or manage for profit instead of in accordance with conscience, justice, or duty ⟨even the juries were flagrantly in the business of *~ing* their verdicts —Amer. Guide Series: Nev.⟩ ⟨*sold* his vote to the highest bidder⟩ 5 a : to develop a belief in the truth, value, or desirability of : gain acceptance for ⟨*sold* their

candidate as a true frontiersman and military hero —C.R. Adrian⟩ ⟨trying to ~ his program to Congress —*Kiplinger Washington Letter*⟩ **b :** to persuade or influence to a course of action or to the acceptance of something (as a doctrine, belief, or activity) ⟨after you'd been *sold*, you were to pull the chestnuts out of the fire —Erle Stanley Gardner⟩ ⟨had a tough time ~*ing* her dad on the idea —A.A.Fenton⟩ ⟨~ children on reading⟩ **6 :** to impose upon : CHEAT, DECEIVE, TRICK ⟨the belief was profound that America was *sold* in 1917–19 —*New Republic*⟩ ⟨after all my hurry I was *sold*, for the doctor had been called away —Henry Lapham⟩ **7 a :** to cause or promote the sale of ⟨comics ~ newspapers —Coulton Waugh⟩ ⟨his name on the cover ~*s* the book⟩ **b :** to make or attempt to make a sale to ⟨~*s* gift shops⟩ ⟨~*s* druggists⟩ ⟨gives a big dinner party for a prospective customer so he can ~ him —James Jones⟩ **c :** to influence or induce to make a purchase ⟨here are the coats that ~ the whole family —*Women's Wear Daily*⟩ ⟨your product, effectively displayed, will ~ the shopper —*Phoenix Flame*⟩ **~ vi 1 a :** to dispose of something by sale : make a sale ⟨not allowed to ~ to minors⟩ ⟨must use these next four years to ~, to merchandise our competitive enterprise system —*Printers' Ink*⟩ **b :** to promote sales ⟨the basic purpose of any window or interior display is to ~ —M.S. Hutchins⟩ **2 a :** to achieve a sale : find a buyer ⟨fall suits are ~*ing* briskly⟩ **b :** to admit of being sold ⟨the tickets would not ~ —*Amer. Guide Series: N.H.*⟩ ⟨an item that doesn't ~⟩ **3 :** to have a specified price — used with *at* or *for* ⟨~ at three for a dollar⟩ ⟨~ for ten dollars each⟩ — **sell a bill of goods 1 :** to get the better of esp. by fraud : DUPE, STICK ⟨a poor sucker who was *sold a bill of goods*⟩ **2 :** to saddle with something disadvantageous ⟨*sold* him *a bill of goods* and got him to buy the tax-ridden property⟩ — **sell short 1 :** to sell something one doesn't own : make a short sale ⟨made a fortune on the stock exchange by *selling short*⟩ **2 :** to fail to value properly : UNDERESTIMATE ⟨are more inclined to see our world simple and *sell* it *short* —H.J.Muller⟩ ⟨made the mistake of *selling* his rival *short*⟩ — **sell the dummy to :** to deceive (an opponent in rugby) by faking a pass

²sell \"\ *or* **selle** \"\ *n* -s [ME *selle*, fr. MF, fr. L *sella* seat, chair, saddle — more at SETTLE] *archaic* : SADDLE

³sell \"\ *chiefly Scot var of* SELF

⁴sell \"\ *n* -s [¹*sell*] **1 :** a deliberate deception : CHEAT, HOAX, IMPOSITION ⟨the suspicion is aroused . . . that the principles are fake; and that, in fact, they have been the victims of a ~ —G.E.G.Catlin⟩ **2 a :** the act or an instance of selling : SALESMANSHIP ⟨thanks to its chief announcer it was solid ~ for thirty minutes —Goodman Ace⟩ **b :** sales appeal ⟨needed a package with plenty of ~ —*Newsweek*⟩

sel·la \ˈselə\ *n, pl* **sellas** \-ləz\ *or* **sellae** \-e(ˌ)lē, -eˌlī\ [NL, fr. L, seat, saddle] : SELLA TURCICA

sell·able \ˈseləbəl\ *adj* [ME, fr. *sellen* to sell + *-able*] : SALABLE

sel·la·ite \ˈseləˌīt\ *n* -s [It *sellaite*, fr. Quintino *Sella* †1884 Ital. mineralogist + It *-ite*] : a mineral MgF_2 consisting of magnesium fluoride and occurring in colorless tetragonal prismatic crystals (hardness 5, sp. gr. 3)

sel·lar \ˈselər, -ˌlär\ *adj* [ISV *sell-* (fr. NL *sella*) + *-ar*] : of, relating to, or involving the sella turcica

sel·late \ˈseˌlāt\ *adj* [L *sella* saddle + E *-ate*] : having a saddle — used of the suture of certain cephalopod shells

sel·la tur·ci·ca \ˌseləˈtərkikə, -rsōkə\ *n, pl* **sel·lae tur·ci·cae** \ˌseˌlīˈtərkiˌkī, ˌse(ˌ)lēˈtərsəˌsē\ [NL, lit., Turkish saddle; fr. its shape] : a depression in the middle line of the upper surface of the sphenoid bone in which the pituitary body is lodged

sellenders *var of* SALLENDERS

sel·len·ger's round \ˈselənjə(r)z-\ *n, usu cap S* [*sellenger* prob. alter. of the name *St. Leger*] : an English country-dance performed as a round esp. popular in the late 16th century; *also* : the music for this dance

sell·er \ˈselə(r)\ *n* -s [ME, fr. *sellen* to sell + *-er* — more at SELL] **1 :** one that offers for sale ⟨when goods are scarce, the ~ has an advantage over the buyer⟩; *specif* : SALESMAN ⟨he is too shy and too reserved to make a real ~ —*English Digest*⟩ **2 :** a product offered for sale and purchased readily or to a specified extent ⟨a poor ~⟩ ⟨a heavy ~⟩ ⟨a popular ~⟩

sel·lers hob \(ˈ)selə(r)z-\ *n, usu cap S* [after William *Sellers* †1905 Am. engineer and inventor] : a hob designed to be run on centers with the work held against it and fed to it by the motion of the lathe carriage

sellers' market *n* : a market in which goods are relatively scarce, buyers have a limited range of choice, and prices are prevailingly high — contrasted with *buyers' market*

seller's option *n* : an option allowed to one who contracts to sell stocks to make delivery within a specified period usu. not less than five business days nor more than 60 days after the date of the contract

sellers' thread \ˌselə(r)z-\ *n, usu cap S* [after William *Sellers* †1905 Am. engineer and inventor] : an American standard screw thread with an angle of 60 degrees and flat crests and roots

¹selling *n* -s [ME, fr. gerund of *sellen* to sell] **1 :** the act or occupation of one who sells ⟨has been in ~ since he left school⟩ **2 :** the act, process, or art of offering goods for sale : SALESMANSHIP ⟨competitive ~⟩ ⟨high-pressure ~⟩ ⟨industrial ~⟩

²selling *adj* [fr. pres. part. of ¹*sell*] **1 :** readily finding buyers : SALABLE ⟨a fast ~ book⟩ **2 :** engaged in selling : making a business of selling ⟨maintains at least five ~ crews —*Fortune*⟩ **3 :** of or relating to sale ⟨the ~ price is one dollar⟩

selling agent *n* : an agent who sells for a commission the entire output of his principals on a continuing contractual basis, provides them with market information, and often also furnishes financial assistance

selling plate *n* : SELLING RACE

selling-plater \ˈ==ˌplād·ə(r)\ *n* : a horse that runs in selling races

selling race *n* : a claiming race in which the winning horse is put up for auction

sell off *vt* : to dispose of by selling esp. completely ⟨what business firm would seek to improve its position by *selling off* its soundest assets —Bradford Smith⟩ ⟨scraped together all of its assets and *sold* them *off*⟩ **~ vi :** to suffer a drop in selling prices : FALL ⟨the market has been *selling off* for six months —*N.Y. Herald Tribune*⟩

sell-off \ˈ=ˌ=\ *n* -s [*sell off*] : a decline in prices of stocks or bonds

sell out *vt* **1 :** to part with by sale : dispose of entirely ⟨*sold out* their stock within an hour⟩ **2 :** to sell the goods of (a debtor) in order to pay off debts from the proceeds **3 a :** to sell in open market (stocks or commodities) to satisfy an uncovered margin or other unpaid obligation **b :** to sell the stocks or commodities of in such manner **~ vi 1 :** to dispose of one's goods by sale ⟨had to *sell out* at a loss⟩ **2 :** to betray one's cause or associates ⟨accused him of *selling out*⟩

sellout \ˈ=ˌ=\ *n* -s [*sell out*] **1 :** the act or an instance of betraying one's cause or associates ⟨the cynical ~ of the League's principles by all concerned was the mortal blow to the peace —*New Yorker*⟩ **2 :** a show, exhibition, or contest for which the seats are all sold ⟨every home game has been a ~⟩ **3 :** the exhaustion of the supply of an article of merchandise because of an unusual demand ⟨two stores report ~*s* on lots of snow suits —*Women's Wear Daily*⟩

sells *pres 3d sing of* SELL, *pl of* SELL

sell up *vt* [ME *sellen up*, fr. *sellen* to sell + *up* — more at SELL] *Brit* : to sell out ⟨when the hunting box . . . was *sold up* to pay her accumulated feed, farrier, and tack bills —James Reynolds⟩

selsyn \ˈselˌsin\ *n* -s [*self-synchronous*] : a system comprising a generator and a motor connected by a multiple wire circuit of appreciable length, transmitting currents that turn the motor simultaneously to the same relative position as existing or established for the generator, and repeating instrument indications and valve settings remotely — called also *synchro*

selt·zer \ˈseltsə(r)- *sometimes* -lzə-\ *or* **seltzer water** *or* **sel·ter** \-ltə(r)\ *or* **sel·ters water** \-ltə(r)z-\ *n* -s *sometimes cap S* [modif. of G *selterser (wasser)* water of Nieder Selters, fr. *selterser* of (Nieder) Selters + *wasser* water, fr. OHG *wazzar* — more at WATER] **1 :** a mineral water from Nieder Selters in the district of Wiesbaden, Germany, containing much free carbon dioxide **2 :** SODA WATER 2a

se·lung \səˈlüŋ\ *n* -s *usu cap* [prob. Burmese] **1 a :** a seagypsy people inhabiting the Mergui archipelago and parts of the Malay peninsula **b :** a member of such people **2 :** the Austronesian language of the Selung people

¹sel·va \ˈselvə\ *n* -s [Sp & Pg, forest, fr. L *silva* wood, grove] : tropical rain forest

²selva \"\ *n* -s [origin unknown] : OPOSSUM RAT

¹sel·vage *or* **sel·vedge** \ˈselvij, -vēj\ *n* -s [ME *selvage*, prob. fr. MFlem *selvage*, *selvegge*, fr. *selv-* self- + *egge* edge; akin to OE *self-* and to OHG *ecka* edge — more at SELF-, EDGE] **1 a** (1) **:** the edge on either side of a woven or flat-knitted fabric so finished as to prevent raveling; *specif* : a narrow border often woven of different or heavier threads than the fabric and sometimes in a different weave — see SPLIT 2e (2) **:** the margin of a sheet or booklet pane of stamps having an outside straight edge as contrasted with the perforated edge of the margin of a single stamp **b :** an edge (as of fabric or paper) meant to be cut off and discarded : a waste cutting ⟨begging people to use the ~*s* and scraps of their time —Sinclair Lewis⟩ **2 :** BORDER, EDGE ⟨actually believes it up to the ~ of his consciousness —Rex Stout⟩ ⟨his nondescript, worsted, uncreased trousers, mud-spattered at the ~ —A.J. Cronin⟩ **3 :** a rope or wire selvagee **4 :** GOUGE 4 **5 :** the edge plate of a lock through which the bolt is projected

²selvage *or* **selvedge** \"\ *vt* -ED/-ING/-S : to form a border to ⟨all the tiny settlements *selvaging* the desert —*All-Story Weekly*⟩

sel·vaged *or* **sel·vedged** \-jd\ *adj* [fr. past part. of ²*selvage* or *selvedge*] : having a selvage

sel·va·gee \ˌselvəˈjē\ *n* -s [prob. fr. ¹*selvage* + *-ee*] **1 :** a skein of rope yarns wound round with yarns or marline (as for stoppers or straps) **2 :** a number of parallel wires bound together with a fine wire serving

selves *pl of* SELF

sem *abbr* **1** semble **2** semicolon **3** semimobile **4** seminar; seminary

se·ma \ˈsēmə\ *n, pl* **sema** *or* **semas** *usu cap* **1 :** a Naga people of Assam related to the Angami **2 :** a member of the Sema people

se·mae·o·sto·ma·ta \səˌmēəˈstōməd·ə\ [NL, fr. Gk *sēmaia*, *sēmeia* standard, token (fr. *sēma* sign) + NL *-stomata*] *syn of* SEMAEOSTOMEAE

¹se·mae·o·stome \=ˈ==ˌstōm\ *adj* [NL *Semaeostomeae*] : of or relating to the Semaeostomeae

²semaeostome \"\ *n* -s : a jellyfish of the order Semaeostomeae

se·mae·o·sto·me·ae \=ˌ=ˈstōmēˌē\ *n pl, cap* [NL, fr. Gk *sēmaia*, *sēmeia* standard, token + NL *-stomeae* (fr. *-stoma*)] : an order of Scyphozoa comprising jellyfishes that have large mouths with four lips and large tentacles at the margin of the umbrella

se·main·ean *or* **se·main·ian** \səˈmānēən, -nyən\ *adj, usu cap* [fr. *Semain*, village in Upper Egypt where remains of the culture were found + E *-an*] : of or relating to an Aeneolithic culture of Upper and Middle Egypt forming a branch of Gerzean culture or a survival thereof into early dynastic times

se·mai·nier \səˈmen(ˌ)yā\ *n* -s [F, fr. *semaine* week (fr. LL *septimana*, fr. fem. of L *septimanus* of seven, fr. *septem* seven) + *-ier* -er — more at SEVEN] : a tall chest with seven drawers for use in a bedroom or dressing room

se·mang \səˈmäŋ\ *n, pl* **semang** *or* **semangs** *usu cap* **1 a :** a Negrito people of Malaya **b :** a member of such people **2 :** the Mon-Khmer language of the Semang people

se·man·teme \səˈmanˌtēm\ *n* -s [F *sémantème*, fr. *sémant-* (fr. *sémantique* semantic, semantics) + *-ème* -eme] : a word (as the noun *dog*, the verb *run*, the adjective *new*, the concrete adverb *fast*) or a base (as Latin *can-* in *canis* "dog", *curr-* in *currere* "to run", *nov-* in *novus* "new") that expresses a definite image or idea — distinguished from *morpheme*

¹se·man·tic \səˈmantik, sēˈ-, -maan-, -tēk\ *also* **se·man·ti·cal** \-təkəl, -tēk-\ *adj* [*semantic* fr. Gk *sēmantikos* significant; *semantical* fr. Gk *sēmantikos* + E *-al*] **1 :** of or relating to meaning in language ⟨English *soon* has undergone ~ change from the Old English meaning of *sōna* "immediately"⟩ — compare FORMAL 1b(2) **2 :** of or relating to differing connotations of words of similar denotative meaning **3 :** of or relating to semantics ⟨a ~ approach to criticism⟩ — **se·man·ti·cal·ly** \-tək(ə)lē, -tēk-, -lī\ *adv*

²semantic \"\ *n* -s [F *sémantique*] : a system or theory of meaning

semantic aphasia *n* : the loss of recognition of the meaning of words and phrases

semantic conception *or* **semantic theory** *n* : a rule of translation by which a statement (as "the sentence 'grass is green' is true") in a metalanguage is logically equivalent to a corresponding statement (as "grass is green") in an object language; *also* : a theory that defines truth as a logical conjunction of the infinite number of such equivalences

semantic definition *n* : DEFINITION 4b(2)

semantic field *n* : FIELD 8c

se·man·ti·cian \səˌmanˈtishən, -maan-\ *n* -s [*semantics* + *-an*] : SEMANTICIST

se·man·ti·cist \səˈmantəsəst, sēˈ-, -maan-\ *n* -s [*semantics* + *-ist*] : a specialist in semantics

se·man·ti·cize \-ˌsīz\ *vt* -ED/-ING/-S [¹*semantic* + *-ize*] **1 :** to give a meaning to **2 :** to subject to semantic analysis ⟨~ this difference between knowledge by poetry and knowledge by abstraction out of existence —Archibald MacLeish⟩

se·man·tics \səˈmantiks, sēˈ-, -maan-, -tēks\ *n pl but usu sing in constr* [F *sémantique*, fr. Gk *sēmantikos* significant, fr. *sēmainein* to signify, show by a sign, indicate, mean, fr. *sēma* sign; akin to Alb *ditme* wisdom, knowledge, Skt *dhyāti* he thinks] **1 :** the study of meanings: **a :** the historical and psychological study and the classification of changes in the signification of words or forms viewed as factors in linguistic development and including such phenomena as specialization and expansion of meaning, meliorative and pejorative tendencies, metaphor, and adaptation **b :** the study dealing with the relations between signs and what they refer to, the relations between the signs of a system, and human behavior in reaction to signs including unconscious attitudes, influences of social institutions, and epistemological and linguistic assumptions : SEMIOTIC **c :** a branch of semiotic dealing with the relations between signs and what they refer to and including theories of denotation, extension, naming, and truth — compare PRAGMATICS **d :** the study of the relations of a sign to its referent and to other signs within a system **e :** the study of the connotations and ambiguities of words and their function in communication and propaganda **2 :** GENERAL SEMANTICS **3 a :** the meaning or relationship of meanings of a sign or set of signs ⟨one of the few words in our list to have received close attention as to its ~ —A.H.Schutz⟩ ⟨this lack of understanding has resulted from different terminologies, but the problem is not merely one of ~ —E.L.Kelly⟩; *esp* : connotative meaning **b :** the management or exploitation of connotation and ambiguity (as in propaganda) ⟨the dubious ~ of the racist fanatics⟩

se·man·to·gen·ic \səˌmantəˈjenik\ *adj* [*semantics* + connective *-o-* + *-genic*] : arising from impairment in the use of language

se·man·tron \səˈmanˌträn\ *n* -s [LGk *sēmantron* sign, signal, semantron, fr. Gk, seal, sign, fr. *sēmainein* to signify] : a wooden plank or an iron bar that gives a sound like a gong when struck with a mallet and that takes the place of a bell in Eastern Orthodox churches

¹sem·a·phore \ˈseməˌfō(ə)r, -fȯ(ə)r, -ōə, -ȯ(ə)\ *n* -s *often attrib* [ISV *sema-* (fr. Gk *sēma* sign) + *-phore*; perh. orig. formed as F *sémaphore*] **1 :** an apparatus for visual signaling (as by the position of one or more movable arms): as **a** *or* **semaphore telegraph :** one of a series of apparatuses on towers used formerly for rapid visual communication by means of code combinations of the positions of orig. movable shutters and later of two movable arms **b :** a mechanical signal for railway traffic consisting of an upright post with an arm moving in a vertical plane for day signals and colored lights for night signals **2 :** a system of visual signaling (as between ships) in which the sender holds a flag in each hand and moves his arms to different positions according to a code alphabet — compare WIGWAG

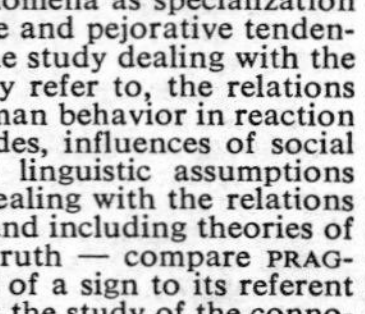

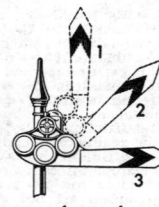

arms of semaphore 1b indicating: *1* clear, *2* caution, *3* stop

²semaphore \"\ *vb* -ED/-ING/-S : to signal by or as if by semaphore

semaphore plant *n* : TELEGRAPH PLANT

sem·a·phor·ic \ˌ==ˈfȯrik\ *also* **sem·a·phor·i·cal** \-rəkəl\ *adj* [Gk *sēma* sign + E *-phoric*] : of, relating to, or suggesting a semaphore — **sem·a·phor·i·cal·ly** \-rək(ə)lē\ *adv*

sem·a·phor·ist \ˈ==ˌfōrəst, -fȯr-\ *n* -s [¹*semaphore* + *-ist*] : one who operates a semaphore or signals by semaphore

se·ma·rang *or* **sa·ma·rang** \səˈmäˌräŋ\ *adj, usu cap* [fr. *Semarang, Samarang*, Java] : of or from the city of Semarang on the island of Java, Indonesia : of the kind or style prevalent in Semarang

se·ma·si·o·log·i·cal \səˌmāsēəˈläjəkəl, sēˌ-, -māˌ, ˌzē-, -jēk-\ *adj* [ISV *semasiology* + *-ical*] : SEMANTIC — **se·ma·si·o·log·i·cal·ly** \-jək(ə)lē, -jēk-, -lī\ *adv*

se·ma·si·ol·o·gist \=ˌ==ˈäləjəst\ *n* -s [*semasiology* + *-ist*] : SEMANTICIST

se·ma·si·ol·o·gy \-jē, -ji\ *n* -ES [ISV *semasi-* (fr. Gk *sēmasia* meaning, fr. *sēmainein* to mean) + *-o-* + *-logy*; orig. formed as G *semasiologie*] : SEMANTICS 1a, 1b

se·mat·ic \səˈmad·ik\ *adj* [Gk *sēmat-*, *sēma* sign + E *-ic*] : serving as a warning of danger — used of conspicuous colors of a poisonous or noxious animal

sem·a·tol·o·gy \ˌseməˈtäləjē\ *n* -ES [Gk *sēmat-*, *sēma* sign + *-o-* + *-logy* — more at SEMANTICS] : SEMANTICS

¹sem·bla·ble \ˈsembləbəl\ *adj* [ME, fr. MF, fr. OF, fr. *sembler* to be like, seem + *-able*] **1 :** SIMILAR **2 :** CONFORMABLE, SUITABLE **3 :** APPARENT, OSTENSIBLE, SEEMING — **sem·bla·bly** \-blē\ *adv*

²semblable \"\ *n* -s [ME, fr. MF, fr. *semblable*, adj.] **1** *archaic* : something similar : the like **2 :** one's fellow — usu. used with a possessive ⟨her ~, . . . like her a seeker after hidden faces —Virginia Woolf⟩

sem·blance \ˈsemblən(t)s\ *n* -s [ME *semblaunce*, fr. MF *semblance*, fr. OF *sembler* to be like, seem + *-ance* — more at RESEMBLE] **1 :** the appearance of a person or thing : outward show : FORM **2 :** COUNTENANCE, FACE, ASPECT **3 a :** phantasmal form : APPARITION **b :** one that resembles another : IMAGE, LIKENESS **4 :** actual or apparent resemblance : SIMILARITY **5 :** specious appearance : mere show ⟨a somewhat different form of protectorate which has the ~ of a pact between equals —*Atlantic*⟩ **6 :** slightest appearance ⟨without the ~ of an excuse⟩ **syn** see APPEARANCE

¹semblant *n* -s [ME, fr. OF, fr. pres. part. of *sembler* to be like] *obs* : SEMBLANCE; *also* : POMP, PRETENSE

²sem·blant \ˈsemblənt\ *adj* [ME, fr. MF, fr. OF, fr. pres. part. of *sembler* to be like] **1** *obs* : LIKE, RESEMBLING **2 :** SEEMING, APPARENT

sem·bla·tive \ˈsembləd·iv\ *adj* [obs. E *semble* to resemble (fr. ME *semblen*, fr. MF *sembler* to be like) + *-ative* (as in *ablative*)] : tending to or characterized by semblance

¹sem·ble \ˈsembəl\ *vt* -ED/-ING/-S [F *sembler* to seem, fr. OF] **1 :** SIMULATE **2 :** to make a representation or likeness of : PICTURE

²semble \"\ *vb* -ED/-ING/-S [F, 3d pers. sing. pres. indic. of *sembler* to seem] ; it seems — used chiefly impersonally in legal reports and judgments to express an obiter dictum

sem·bra·do·ras \ˌsembrəˈdōrəz, -rəs\ *n* -ES [MexSp, fr. Sp, fem. of *sembradores* sowers, pl. of *sembrador* sower, fr. L *seminator*, fr. *seminatus* (past part. of *seminare* to sow, plant) + *-or*] : an agricultural dance of Michoacan, Mexico, performed on Candlemas Day by a group of Indian men and women with mime of sowing and harvesting

¹se·mé \səˈmā, ˈse(ˌ)mā\ *adj* [MF, past part. of *semer* to sow, fr. L *seminare* to sow, plant, fr. *semin-*, *semen* seed — more at SEMEN] **1** *also* **se·méed** \-ād\ [*seméed* fr. F *semée* (fem. of *semé*) + E *-ed*] : having an ornamental pattern consisting of usu. regularly disposed separate objects or groups of small figures (as flowers or stars) : SOWN, DOTTED ⟨porcelain demitasses . . . ~ with rows of graduated turquoise blue enamel jewels on a gilded ground —*Parke-Bernet Galleries Cat.*⟩ **2** *or* **se·mee** \-ā\ [*semee* fr. F *semée*, fem. of *semé*] *of a heraldic field* : having a pattern of small charges : POWDERED ⟨azure ~ of five crosslets —Allan Marquand⟩

²semé *also* **semée** \"\ *n* -s : a semé pattern ⟨the ~ of slipped trefoils symmetrically disposed around the shield —W. de G. Birch⟩

seme·car·pus \ˌseməˈkärpəs, ˌsēm-\ *n, cap* [NL, prob. fr. Gk *sēmeion* mark (fr. *sēma* sign) + NL *-carpus*] : a genus of Indo-Malayan trees (family Anacardiaceae) that have coriaceous leaves and small panicled flowers with five petals, five stamens, and three styles followed by a hard nut with a thick black-juiced rind — see ITCHWOOD TREE, MARKING NUT

se·mée-de-lis \səˌmādˈlēs *sometimes* -ēs\ *adj* [F *semée de (fleurs de) lis*] *heraldry* : sprinkled with fleur-de-lis

semei·og·ra·phy *also* **semi·og·ra·phy** \ˌsēˌmīˈägrəfē, ˌsel, ˌmē-\ *n* -ES [ISV *semeio-*, *semio-* (fr. Gk *sēmeion* sign) + *-graphy*] : a description of the symptoms of disease

semei·o·log·ic \səˌmīəˈläjik; ˈsēl, ˌmīə-, ˈsel, ˌmēə-\ *or* **semei·o·log·i·cal** \-jəkəl\ *adj* : of or relating to semeiology

se·mei·ol·o·gist \ˌsēlˌmīˈäləjəst, ˌsel, ˌmē-\ *n* -s : a specialist in semeiology

se·mei·ol·o·gy *also* **semi·ol·o·gy** \-jē, -ji\ *n* -ES [NL *semaeologia*, fr. Gk *sēmeion* sign + NL *-logia* -logy] : the study or art of signs: **a :** SEMANTICS 1b **b :** SYMPTOMATOLOGY

se·mei·on \səˈmīˌän\ *n, pl* **semeia** \-īə\ [LGk *sēmeion*, fr. Gk, mark, sign, note, fr. *sēma* sign — more at SEMANTICS] **1 :** MORA **2 :** either of the two divisions of a foot; *also* : a corresponding division of a measure or colon in Greek and Latin prosody

semei·ot·ic \ˈsēlˌmīˈäd·ik, ˈsel, ˌmē-\ *also* **semei·ot·i·cal** \-d·əkəl\ *adj* [*semeiotic* fr. Gk *sēmeiōtikos* observant of signs; *semeiotical* fr. Gk *sēmeiōtikos* + E *-al* — more at SEMIOTIC] : of or relating to symptoms of disease

semei·ot·ics \-d·iks, -d·ēks\ *n pl but sing or pl in constr* : SYMPTOMATOLOGY

sem·e·le \ˈseməˌlē\ *n* [NL, prob. fr. *Semele*, Greek goddess, fr. L, fr. Gk *Semelē*] **1** *cap* : a widely distributed genus of small bivalve mollusks (suborder Tellinacea) with long separate siphons and a thin oval or oblong shell that gapes at the posterior end and is usu. finely striated **2** -s : any mollusk of the genus *Semele*

sem·el·fac·tive \ˌseməlˈfaktiv\ *adj* [L *semel* once (akin to L *simul* together, at the same time) + E *factive* — more at SAME] *of a verb form or aspect* : expressing action as single in its occurrence without repetition or continuation : INSTANTANEOUS, MOMENTARY

sem·eme \ˈseˌmēm\ *n* -s [ISV *sem-* (fr. Gk *sēmainein* to mean) + *-eme* — more at SEMANTICS] : the meaning of a morpheme (sense 2)

se·men \ˈsēmən\ *n, pl* **semi·na** \ˈsemənə *sometimes* ˈsēm-\ *or* **semens** [L; akin to OHG & OS *sāmo* seed, OSlav *sěme* semen, L *serere* to sow — more at SOW] **1 :** SEED 1b — used chiefly in pharmacy and usu. in combination ⟨~ pedicularis, the seed of *Delphinium staphysagra*⟩ **2 a :** a viscid whitish usu. neutral to slightly alkaline fluid produced in the male reproductive tract, consisting of spermatozoa suspended in secretions of accessory glands (as prostate and Cowper's glands), usu. released from the body by ejaculation (as in coitus), and serving as the vehicle in which sperm are maintained in the male genital tract and transferred to that of the female — used esp. of the fluid as characteristically developed in mammals and birds **b :** spermatozoa as released by a male animal together with any accompanying fluid : SPERM ⟨fish ~⟩ ⟨worms breaking into a cloud of ~ and eggs⟩

semen con·tra \ˈ==ˈkän·trə\ *or* **semen ci·nae** \-ˈsī(ˌ)nē\ *n* [*semen contra* fr. NL, short for L *semen contra vermes* seed against worms; fr. its vermicidal action; *semen cinae* fr. NL, lit., santonica seed] : SANTONICA

se·men·te·ra \ˌsāmənˈtārə\ *n* -s [Sp, fr. *sementar* to sow, fr. *simiente* seed, fr. L *sementis* sowing, cultivation, fr. *semen* seed] *Philippines* : a cultivated field

se·me·os·to·ma \ˌsēmēˈästəmə\ [NL, fr. Gk *sēmeia* standard, token (fr. *sēma* sign) + NL *-stoma*] *syn of* SEMAEOSTOMEAE

se·mes·ter \sə'mestə(r)\ *n* -s [G, fr. L *semestris* half-yearly, fr. *sex* six + *mensis* month — more at SIX, MOON] **1 :** a half a year **:** a period of six months **2 :** either of the two periods of instruction commonly 18 weeks in length into which an academic year is usu. divided — compare QUARTER 4b **3 :** any term of instruction **:** SESSION ⟨the second ~ of summer school⟩
semester hour *n* **:** a unit of academic credit or load representing an hour a week for an academic semester devoted to class meetings ⟨a course awarding three *semester hours*⟩ — abbr. *SH;* compare QUARTER HOUR
se·mes·tral \-strəl\ *or* **se·mes·tri·al** \-,trēəl\ *adj* [L *semestris* half-yearly + E *-al* or *-ial*] **:** occurring every six months or within a period of six months **:** of or relating to a six-month period
¹semi \'semē, -mī\ *n* -ES [NL, short for *semi bejanus* semibejan, fr. L *semi-* + NL *bejanus* bejan] **:** SEMIBEJAN
²semi \"\ *n* -s [short for *²semidetached*] *chiefly Brit* **:** one of a pair of semidetached residences
³semi \", 'se,mī\ *n* -s [by shortening] **:** SEMITRAILER
⁴semi \"\ *n* -s [by shortening] **:** SEMIFINAL — usu. used in pl.
semi- *in pronunciations below,* ¦≠(,)≠ = ¦semē *or* ¦se,mī *or* ¦semi *or (usu not before vowels)* ¦semə\ *prefix* [ME, fr. L; akin to OE *sam-* half, OHG *sāmi-*, Gk *hēmi-*, Skt *sāmi-*] **1 a :** precisely half of: (1) **:** forming a bisection of ⟨*semi*ellipse⟩ ⟨*semi*chord⟩ ⟨*semi*cylinder⟩ (2) **:** being a usu. vertically bisected form of (a specified architectural feature) ⟨*semi*arch⟩ ⟨*semi*bay⟩ ⟨*semi*dome⟩ **b :** half in quantity or value **:** half of or occurring halfway through (a specified period of time) ⟨*semi*revolution⟩ ⟨*semi*annual⟩ ⟨*semi*centenary⟩ ⟨*semi*phase⟩ — compare BI- **2 a :** to some extent **:** partly **:** incompletely ⟨*semi*-independent⟩ ⟨*semi*dry⟩ ⟨*semi*plastic⟩ ⟨*semi*acid⟩ ⟨*semi*quantitatively⟩ — compare DEMI-, HEMI- **b :** having (a specified characteristic) for half the length or on one side ⟨*semi*pinnate⟩ ⟨*semi*adherent⟩ **3 a :** partial **:** incomplete ⟨*semi*positivism⟩ ⟨*semi*education⟩ ⟨*semi*adherent⟩ ⟨*semi*-Augustinianism⟩ ⟨*semi*wig⟩ **b :** having some of the characteristics of (a specified class or object) ⟨*semi*luxury⟩ ⟨*semi*campus⟩ ⟨*semi*benzene⟩ ⟨*semi*porcelain⟩ ⟨*semi*citizen⟩ **c :** QUASI- ⟨*semi*governmental⟩ ⟨*semi*judicial⟩ ⟨*semi*monastic⟩ ⟨*semi*ubiquitous⟩
semi·abstract \¦≠(,)≠ *at* SEMI- +\ *adj* [*semi-* + *abstract*] **:** having the character of a semiabstraction
semi·abstraction \"+\ *n* [*semi-* + *abstraction*] **:** a composition or creation (as in painting or sculpture) in which the subject matter is easily recognizable though the form is stylized according to an abstract system or device
semi·aerial \"+\ *adj* [*semi-* + *aerial*] **:** occurring partially or part of the time in the air
semi·amphibious \"+\ *adj* [*semi-* + *amphibious*] **:** partially amphibious
semi·annual \"+\ *adj* [*semi-* + *annual*] **:** occurring, appearing, or being made, done, or acted upon every six months or twice a year
semi·annually \"+\ *adv* **:** twice a year **:** every six months
semi·anthracite \"+\ *n* [*semi-* + *anthracite*] **:** a coal intermediate between anthracite and bituminous coal; *esp* **:** coal approaching anthracite in nonvolatile character
semi·ape \"+\ *n* [*semi-* + *ape*] **:** LEMUR
semi·aquatic \"+\ *adj* [*semi-* + *aquatic*] **:** chiefly aquatic: as **a :** growing indifferently in or adjacent to water (as in moist lowlands) **b :** frequenting but not living wholly in water ⟨mink and other ~ mammals⟩
semi·arboreal \"+\ *adj* [*semi-* + *arboreal*] **:** often inhabiting or frequenting trees **:** incompletely arboreal
semi·arch \"+\ *n* [*semi-* + *arch*] **:** an arch having only one springer and terminating at its highest point **:** half arch
semi·arian \"+\ *n, usu cap S&A* **:** one of the Homoiousians led by Basil, 4th-century A.D. bishop of Ancyra
semi·arianism \"+\ *n, usu cap S&A* **:** the doctrines of the Semi-Arians
semi·arid \"+\ *adj* [*semi-* + *arid*] **:** characterized by light rainfall and high evaporation, the growth of short grasses, and dry farming of limited yield; *specif* **:** having from about 10 to 20 inches of annual precipitation
semi·auto \"+\ *adj* [short for *¹semiautomatic*] **:** SEMIAUTOMATIC b
¹semi·automatic \"+\ *adj* [*semi-* + *automatic*] **:** not fully automatic: as **a :** operated partly automatically and partly by hand ⟨a lathe that operates automatically after insertion of the rough piece by the operator is ~⟩ **b** *of a firearm* **:** that employs gas pressure or force of recoil and mechanical spring action in ejecting the empty cartridge case after the first shot and in loading the next cartridge from the magazine but that requires release and another pressure of the trigger for firing each successive shot — compare AUTOMATIC 5 — **semi·automatically** \"+\ *adv*
²semiautomatic \"\ *n* **:** a semiautomatic device or machine; *esp* **:** a semiautomatic firearm
semi·autonomous \¦≠(,)≠ *at* SEMI- +\ *adj* [*semi-* + *autonomous*] **:** largely self-governing (as with respect to local affairs) within a larger political or organizational entity ⟨a federation of ~ states⟩ ⟨a ~ unit within the police agency —D.E.J. MacNamara⟩
semi–bantu \"+\ *n, usu cap S&B* **:** a group of African languages sharing certain characteristics of the Bantu languages but excluded from them — used sometimes of the Central Branch of the Niger-Congo family exclusive of Bantu and sometimes of all west African languages with noun classes marked by prefixes
semi·basement \"+\ *n* [*semi-* + *basement*] **:** a basement that is below ground level for only part of its depth
semi·beam \¦≠(,)≠+,-\ *n* [*semi-* + *beam*] **:** CANTILEVER
semi·bejan \¦≠(,)≠ *at* SEMI-+\ *n* [NL *semi bejanus*, lit., half a bejan] **:** a second-year student at some Scottish universities
semi·bituminous \"+\ *adj* [*semi-* + *bituminous*] *of coal* **:** intermediate between bituminous coal and anthracite and averaging from 10 to 20 percent of volatile matter
semi·breve \¦≠(,)≠ *at* SEMI- +,-\ *n* [*semi-* + *breve*] *chiefly Brit* **:** WHOLE NOTE — compare CROTCHET, MINIM, QUAVER
-se·mic \¦sēmik\ *adj comb form* [LL *-semus* (fr. Gk *-sēmos*, fr. *sēmeion* unit of time, note, mark, sign) + E *-ic* — more at SEMEION] **:** having (a specified number of) units of prosodic time ⟨deca*semic*⟩ ⟨icosa*semic*⟩
semi·cadence \¦≠(,)≠ *at* SEMI- +\ *n* [*semi-* + *cadence*] **:** HALF CADENCE
semi·carbazide \"+\ *n* [ISV *semi-* + *carbazide*] **:** a crystalline compound $NH_2CONHNH_2$ that is made from hydrazine by reaction with either urea or cyanic acid or from the nitro derivative of urea by reduction and that is used chiefly as a reagent for aldehydes and ketones by the formation of semicarbazones; the hydrazide of carbamic acid
semi·car·ba·zone \"+'kärbə,zōn\ *n* -s [ISV *semicarbazide* + *-one*] **:** any of a class of usu. well-crystallized compounds having the general formula $RR'C{=}NNHCONH_2$ and formed by the action of semicarbazide on an aldehyde or ketone — compare HYDRAZONE, OXIME
semi·castrate \¦≠(,)≠ *at* SEMI- +\ *vt* [*semi-* + *castrate*] **1 :** to deprive of one testis **2 :** to emasculate partially (as with hormone sprays that do not destroy all pollen) — **semi·castration** \"+\ *n*
semi·cell \¦≠(,)≠+,-\ *n* [*semi-* + *cell*] **:** either of the halves of a desmid cell
semi·centenary \¦≠(,)≠ *at* SEMI- +\ *n or adj* [*semi-* + *centenary*] **:** SEMICENTENNIAL
¹semi·centennial \"+\ *adj* [*semi-* + *centennial,* adj.] **:** of or relating to a 50th anniversary **:** occurring in a 50th year
²semicentennial \"\ *n* [*semi-* + *centennial,* n.] **:** a 50th anniversary or its celebration
semi·ceremonial \¦≠(,)≠ *at* SEMI- +\ *adj* [*semi-* + *ceremonial*] **:** having some of the characteristics of a ceremony
semicha *also* **semichah** *var of* SEMIKAH
semi·chemical \¦≠(,)≠ *at* SEMI- +\ *adj* [*semi-* + *chemical*] *of wood pulp* **:** cooked very lightly by any of the chemical processes to give increased yield but less pure fiber
semi·china \"+\ *n* [*semi-* + *china*] **:** china fired at a low temperature
semi·choric \"+\ *adj* [*semichorus* + *-ic*] **1 :** of or relating to a semichorus **2** [*semi-* + *choric*] **:** half choral in character; *specif* **:** half sung and half spoken
semi·chorus \"+\ *n* [*semi-* + *chorus*] **:** a musical passage to be sung by a selected portion of the voices (as by a few from each part or by either the male or female voices only) in contrast with the full chorus; *also* **:** the portion of voices or singers that sing such a passage
¹semi·circle \¦≠(,)≠+,-\ *n* [L *semicirculus*, fr. *semi-* + *circulus* circle — more at CIRCLE] **1 a :** the part of a circle from one end of a diameter to the other **:** an arc equal to one half of a circumference **:** half circle — called also *semicircumference* **b :** either half of a circular area divided diametrically **2 a :** body, formation, or arrangement of objects in the form of half of a circle or half of a circumference **3 :** an instrument of semicircular form used esp. for measuring angles
²semicircle \"\ *vt* **:** to form or throw into a semicircle **:** surround with a semicircle ⟨the port ~*s* a blue bay —Sylvia Martin⟩ ~ *vi* **:** to become a semicircle **:** move in a semicircle
semi·circular \¦≠(,)≠ *at* SEMI- +\ *adj* [ML *semicircularis*, fr. L *semicirculus* semicircle + *-aris* -ar] **1 :** having the form of a semicircle **2 :** ROUND 1d — **semi·circularly** \"+\ *adv* — **semi·circularness** \"+\ *n*
semicircular canal *n* **:** any one of the loop-shaped tubular parts of the membranous labyrinth of the ear that together constitute a sensory organ associated with the maintenance of bodily equilibrium, each canal communicating by either end with the utriculus, having near one end an expanded ampulla that contains an area of sensory epithelium, being enclosed in a corresponding canal of the bony labyrinth, and in all vertebrates above cyclostomes forming one of a group of three in each ear usu. in planes nearly at right angles with one another
semicircular dome *n* **:** a dome consisting of a half sphere
semicircular vault *n* **:** BARREL VAULT
semi·circumference \¦≠(,)≠ *at* SEMI- +\ *n* [*semi-* + *circumference*] **:** SEMICIRCLE 1a
semi·circumferentor \"+\ *n* [*semi-* + *circumferentor*] **:** a surveyor's instrument used for setting out land or buildings to any angle and in preliminary survey work generally and made up of a horizontal graduated semicircle that surrounds a compass and is attached to a base with fixed vertical sights at each end and of a movable arm with vertical sights at each end that pivots on the center of the base
semi·cirque \¦≠(,)≠+,-\ *n* [*semi-* + *cirque*] **:** something (as a hollow among hills) having the shape of a half circle
semi·classic \¦≠(,)≠ *at* SEMI- +\ *n* [*semi-* + *classic*] **:** a semiclassical work (as of music or literature)
semi·classical \"+\ *or* **semi·classic** \"+\ *adj* [*semi-* + *classical* or *classic*] **1 :** having some of the characteristics (as of traditional style) of the classical: as **a :** of or being a musical composition that acts as a bridge between classical and popular music or jazz **:** LIGHT **b :** of or being a classical composition that through repeated performance or extraneous association has developed popular appeal **2 :** inferior to the classical in importance or quality **:** of second rank ⟨a ~ theory in physics⟩
semi·climber \"+\ *n* [*semi-* + *climber*] **:** a plant that tends to climb or assume a vining habit of growth
semi·climbing \"+\ *adj* [*semi-* + *climbing*] *of a plant* **:** inclined to climb
semi·coke \"+\ *n* [*semi-* + *coke*] **:** the solid residue obtained by carbonization esp. of coal at a relatively low temperature (as below 700° C) that is in general softer and more friable than coke from carbonization at higher temperatures, that gives a hot smokeless fire, and that can be used as a domestic fuel
semi·co·lon \'semə,kōlən, -mē,k-\ *n* [*semi-* + *colon*] **:** a punctuation mark ; that is usu. used to separate the independent clauses of a compound sentence when the clauses are joined by no connective, when the clauses are joined by a conjunctive adverb, or when the clauses are joined by a coordinating conjunction but are long and contain internal punctuation and that is often used to separate long items in a series
semicolon butterfly *n* **:** VIOLET TIP
semi·colonial \¦≠(,)≠ *at* SEMI- +\ *adj* [*semi-* + *colonial*] **1 :** nominally independent but actually under foreign domination **2 :** dependent on foreign nations to supply manufactured goods needed and to purchase raw materials produced ⟨a ~ economy⟩
semi·colonialism \"+\ *n* [*semi-* + *colonialism*] **:** the quality or state of being semicolonial
semi·column \"+\ *n* **:** a half-engaged column
semi·coma \"+\ *n* [*semi-* + *coma*] **:** a coma from which a person can be aroused
semi·commercial \"+\ *adj* [*semi-* + *commercial*] **:** of or adapted to limited marketing of an experimental product
semi·compreg \"+\ *n* [*semi-* + *compreg*] **:** wood that has been impregnated with resin and compressed to a density of less than 1.25
semi·conducting \"+\ *also* **semi·conductive** \"+\ *adj* [*semi-* + *conducting* or *conductive*] **:** of, relating to, or having the characteristics of a semiconductor
semi·conduction \"+\ *n* [*semi-* + *conduction*] **:** conduction occurring in a semiconductor
semi·conductor \"+\ *n* [*semi-* + *conductor*] **:** one of a class of solids (as germanium, silicon) whose feeble electrical conductivity is neither metallic nor electrolytic — compare CONDUCTION
semi·conscious \"+\ *adj* [*semi-* + *conscious*] **:** half conscious **:** imperfectly conscious — **semi·consciously** \"+\ *adv* — **semi·consciousness** \"+\ *n*
semi·consonant \"+\ *n* [*semi-* + *consonant*] **:** SEMIVOWEL — **semi·consonantal** \"+\ *adj*
semi·continuous \"+\ *adj* [*semi-* + *continuous*] **:** not fully continuous
semi·crisp \"+\ *adj* [*semi-* + *crisp*] **:** slightly stiff in texture
semi·crustaceous \"+\ *adj* [*semi-* + *crustaceous*] **:** tending to form a somewhat crisp or brittle layer **:** imperfectly crustaceous
semi·crystalline \"+\ *adj* [*semi-* + *crystalline*] **:** HEMICRYSTALLINE
semi·cubical \"+\ *adj* [*semi-* + *cubical*] **:** characterized by the square root of the cube of a quantity ⟨a ~ parabola⟩
semi·cursive \"+\ *n* [*semi-* + *cursive*] **:** a Roman minuscule cursive with the principal strokes thickened used as a book hand from about the 5th to the 9th centuries — called also *old Italian book hand*
semi·cyclic \"+\ *adj* [*semi-* + *cyclic*] **:** half or partly cyclic ⟨a ~ compound containing both a ring and a chain⟩ ⟨a ~ double bond attached to a ring but not a part of it⟩ — **semi·cyclically** \"+\ *adv*
semi·cylinder \"+\ *n* [*semi-* + *cylinder*] **:** a half of a cylinder divided longitudinally — **semi·cylindrical** \"+\ *adj*
semi·darkness \"+\ *n* [*semi-* + *darkness*] **:** partial darkness
semi·dehydrated \"+\ *adj* [*semi-* + *dehydrated*] **:** partially dehydrated
¹semi·desert \"+\ *n* [*semi-* + *desert*] **:** an area having some of the characteristics of a desert and often lying between a desert and grassland or woodland
²semidesert \"\ *adj* **:** of or characteristic of a semidesert
¹semi·detached \"+\ *adj* [*semi-* + *detached*] **1 :** intermediate between legato and staccato **2** *of a house* **:** built with one wall in common with another residence as part of a single building; *specif* **:** forming one of a pair of residences joined into one building by a common side wall
²semidetached \"\ *n* -s *chiefly Brit* **:** ²SEMI
semi·diameter \¦≠(,)≠ *at* SEMI- +\ *n* [*semi-* + *diameter*] **:** the apparent radius of a generally spherical heavenly body ⟨the ~ of the sun is about half a degree⟩
semi·diesel engine \"+...\ *n* **:** an internal-combustion engine usu. of the two-stroke cycle type and below 50 horsepower that resembles a diesel engine: **a :** an internal-combustion engine of a type resembling the diesel engine in using heavy oil as fuel but employing a lower compression pressure of 100 to 350 pounds per square inch and igniting the charge by spraying it under pressure against an uncooled portion of the combustion chamber, by spraying it into a separate chamber kept above the ignition temperature of the charge by the heat of compression, or by the preignition or supercompression of a portion of the charge in a separate member or uncooled portion of the combustion chamber **b :** a true diesel engine using other means of fuel injections than compressed air **c :** a mixed-cycle engine closely resembling a diesel engine
semi·dine \'semə,dīn, -,dən\ *n* -s [ISV *semi-* + *benzidine*] **:** any of a group of bases that are ortho and para amino derivatives of diphenylamine and are usu. formed by a molecular rearrangement of hydrazo compounds (as $p\text{-}RC_6H_4NHNHC_6H_5 \rightarrow p,p'\text{-}RC_6H_4NHC_6H_4NH_2$)
semi·diurnal \¦≠(,)≠ *at* SEMI- +\ *adj* [*semi-* + *diurnal*] **1 :** relating to or accomplished in half a day **2 :** occurring twice a day **3 :** occurring approximately every half day ⟨the ~ tides⟩
semidiurnal arc *n* **:** the arc described by a heavenly body (as the sun) between its meridian and its rising or setting
semi·divine \"+\ *adj* [*semi-* + *divine*] **:** more than mortal but not fully divine **:** possessing a degree of divine awesomeness or authority
¹semi·documentary \"+\ *n* [*semi-* + *documentary*] **:** a motion picture that sets a fictional story in a factual background or tells a story true to the type of an actual story or true in outline but not literally true
²semidocumentary \"\ *adj* **:** of or characteristic of a semidocumentary
semi·dome \¦≠(,)≠+,-\ *n* [*semi-* + *dome*] **:** a roof or ceiling covering a semicircular or nearly semicircular room or recess and being approximately the quarter of a hollow sphere — compare CUL-DE-FOUR — **semi·domed** \¦≠(,)≠+\ *adj*
semi·domesticated \"+\ *or* **semi·domestic** \"+\ *adj* [*semi-* + *domesticated* or *domestic*] **:** of or living in semidomestication ⟨varieties found only in a ~ state⟩ ⟨~ circus animals⟩
semi·domestication \¦≠(,)≠ *at* SEMI- +\ *n* [*semi-* + *domestication*] **:** a captive state (as on a fur or game farm or in a zoo) of a wild animal in which its living conditions and often its breeding are controlled and its products or services used by man
semi·dominant \"+\ *n* [*semi-* + *dominant*] **:** a gene that has a different effect when heterozygous than when homozygous ⟨the yellow lethal gene of mice which mediates yellow coat color when heterozygous but causes death of the embryo when homozygous is a typical ~⟩
semi·dormancy \"+\ *n* **:** a decrease in rate of growth of a plant that may be seasonal or associated with usu. transitory unfavorable environmental conditions
semi·double \"+\ *adj, of a flower* **:** having more than the normal number of petals or disk florets though retaining some pollen-bearing stamens or some perfect disk florets
semi–double \"\ *n* [trans. of ML *semiduplex*] **:** a feast of the Roman Catholic Church marked by omission of part of the antiphon before each psalm in the sacred office and formerly ranked above a simple and below a double but now reduced to the rank of simple
semi·dress \¦≠(,)≠ *at* SEMI-+\ *n* [*semi-* + *dress*] **:** semiformal dress — **semi·dressy** \"+\ *adj*
semi·dry \"+\ *adj* [*semi-* + *dry*] **:** moderately dry
semi·drying \"+\ *adj* [*semi-* + *drying*] **:** that dries imperfectly or slowly — used of fatty oils (as cottonseed oil) intermediate between drying oils like linseed oil and nondrying oils
semi·durables \"+\ *or* **semi·durable goods** \"+-\ *n pl* [*semi-* + *durables, durable goods*] **:** nondurables (as clothing or house furnishings) whose usefulness diminishes gradually
semi·early \"+\ *adj, of a plant* **:** intermediate in bloom or maturity between an early and a later variety **:** MIDSEASON
semi·effigy \"+\ *n* [*semi-* + *effigy*] **:** a half-length effigy
semi·elastic \"+\ *adj* [*semi-* + *elastic*] **1 :** slightly elastic **2 :** that stretches in only one direction
semi·ellipse \"+\ *n* [*semi-* + *ellipse*] **:** the part of an ellipse from one end of usu. the transverse diameter to the other **:** half ellipse
semi·elliptic \"+\ *or* **semi·elliptical** \"+\ *adj* **:** of, relating to, or forming a semiellipse
semi·erect \"+\ *adj* [*semi-* + *erect*] **:** imperfectly erect; *specif* **:** erect for half the length
semies *pl of* SEMI
semi·evergreen \¦≠(,)≠ *at* SEMI-+\ *adj* **:** HALF-EVERGREEN
¹semi·final \"+\ *adj* [*semi-* + *final*] **1 :** next to the last **2 :** of or participating in a semifinal
²semifinal \"\ *n* **:** a semifinal round, match, heat, or game: **a :** the next to the last round in an elimination tournament in which four players or teams are paired off in two matches and the winner of each moves on to the final match **b :** a series of contests (as in track and field events) designed to eliminate all but the number designated to participate in the final event
semi·finalist \"+\ *n* [*¹semifinal* + *-ist*] **:** any of the contestants who meet in the semifinal round or heat of an elimination contest
semi·finished \"+\ *adj* [*semi-* + *finished*] **1 :** partially finished ⟨a ~ nut⟩ **2 :** of or being a material manufactured for use in fabricating finished articles; *specif* **:** rolled from raw ingots into shapes (as bars, billets, blooms, plates, and rods) ready for further processes ⟨~ steel⟩
semi·fixed \"+\ *adj* [*semi-* + *fixed*] **:** fixed in some respect or temporarily
semifixed ammunition *n* [*semi-* + *fixed*] **:** ammunition consisting of complete rounds that can be loaded as a unit but have a cartridge case which is not fixed to the projectile and can be removed in order to remove increments of the propelling charge
semi·flexible \"+\ *adj* [*semi-* + *flexible*] **1 :** somewhat flexible **2** *of a book cover* **:** consisting of a heavy flexible board under the covering material
semi·floating axle \"+...-\ *n* [*semi-* + *floating*] **:** a live axle for a self-propelled vehicle in which an inner revolving shaft turns the wheels and the weight of the vehicle is carried on the ends of a fixed axle housing attached to the shaft at each end by bearings
semifloating hitch *n* **:** a hitch allowing limited independent vertical movement of tractor and implement
¹semi·fluid \"+\ *adj* [*semi-* + *fluid*] **:** having the qualities of both a fluid and a solid but being more closely related to a fluid **:** imperfectly fluid **:** VISCOUS ⟨fluid and ~ greases⟩
²semifluid \"\ *n* **:** a semifluid substance
semi·form \¦≠(,)≠+,-\ *n* [*semi-* + *form*] **:** a half or imperfect form
semi·formal \¦≠(,)≠ *at* SEMI-+\ *adj* [*semi-* + *formal*] **:** being or suitable for an occasion of moderate formality or solemnity ⟨a ~ dinner⟩ **:** formal in some features ⟨a ~ gown for a small wedding⟩
semi·fossil \"+\ *adj* [*semi-* + *fossil*] **:** incompletely fossilized ⟨~ resins⟩
semi·freestone \"+\ *n* **:** a peach that is neither completely freestone nor clingstone
semi·girder \"+\ *n* [*semi-* + *girder*] **:** CANTILEVER
semi·glaze \¦≠(,)≠+,-\ *n* [*semi-* + *glaze*] **:** a slight glaze
semi·globular \¦≠(,)≠ *at* SEMI- +\ *adj* [*semi-* + *globular*] **:** having the form of half a sphere
semi·gloss \¦≠(,)≠ *at* SEMI-+\ *adj* **:** having a low luster; *specif* **:** having a reflectivity between flat and gloss on a dried surface — used esp. of enamel or paint
semi·governmental \"+\ *adj* [*semi-* + *governmental*] **:** having some governmental functions and powers ⟨a ~ bank⟩
semi·gregarious \"+\ *adj* [*semi-* + *gregarious*] **:** partially gregarious **:** occurring or living usu. in greater proximity than seems likely on the basis of chance ⟨~ predators⟩
semi·hard \"+\ *adj* [*semi-* + *hard*] **:** moderately hard; *specif* **:** that can be cut with little difficulty
semi·hardy \"+\ *adj* [*semi-* + *hardy*] **:** capable of withstanding a moderately low temperature **:** HALF-HARDY
semi·hexagonal \"+\ *adj* [*semi-* + *hexagonal*] **:** forming half of a hexagon
semi·holiday \"+\ *n* [*semi-* + *holiday*] **:** a weekday during a religious festival (as the Passover) on which ceremonial observances continue but activities prohibited on full festival days are permitted though discouraged
semi·hydrate \"+\ *n* [*semi-* + *hydrate*] **:** HEMIHYDRATE
semi–independent \"+\ *adj* **:** partially independent; *specif* **:** SEMIAUTONOMOUS
semi·indirect \"+\ *adj* **:** using a translucent reflector that transmits some primary light (as to the floor) while reflecting most of it (as to the ceiling) ⟨a *semi-indirect* lamp⟩
semi–infinite \"+\ *adj* **1 :** extending to infinity in one direction or dimension ⟨the propagation of a temperature wave along a *semi-infinite* rod⟩ **2 :** limited only by an infinite plane ⟨a *semi-infinite* metal with a constant flux of heat into its surface —M.L.Storm⟩

semi-ionic \"+\ *adj* : SEMIPOLAR

semi-jobber \"+\ *n* : a merchant doing both wholesale and retail business

se·mi·kah *or* **se·mi·cha** *also* **se·mi·chah** \sə'mikə\ *n, pl* **semikahs** *or* **semi·koth** \-ˌkōt(h),-ōs\ *or* **semichas** \-ˌkəz\ *or* **semi·choth** \-ˌkōt(h),-ōs\ [LHeb *sĕmīkhāh*, fr. Heb, laying on of hands, leaning on, fr. *sāmōkh* to lean on] : rabbinical ordination : the traditional rabbinical degree conferred by Orthodox rabbis

semi-late \ˈ;ᵊ(ˌ)⹁ at SEMI-+\ *adj, of a plant* : intermediate in season between midseason and late forms

semi-legal \"+\ *adj* [*semi-* + *legal*] : having a broader application than the technical use in law

semi-legendary \"+\ *adj* [*semi-* + *legendary*] : known in legend but historically dubious or unverifiable ⟨~ king⟩

1semi-liquid \"+\ *adj* [*semi-* + *liquid*] : having the qualities of both a liquid and a solid but being more closely related to a liquid : partially liquid : SEMIFLUID ⟨~ peat⟩

2semiliquid \"\ *n* : a semiliquid substance

semi-literate \"+\ *adj* [*semi-* + *literate*] **1** : able to read and write on an elementary level but deficient in learning **2** : able to read but not to write

semi-live skid \ˈ;ᵊ⹁\ *n* : a platform skid with two fixed feet and two wheels to facilitate movement

semi-logarithmic \ˈ;⹁ᵊ+\ *also* **semi-log** \"+\ *adj* [*semi-* + *logarithmic* or log (short for *logarithmic*)] **1** : having one scale logarithmic and the other arithmetic or of uniform spacing — used of graph paper or of a chart or plot made on such paper **2** : being or relating to the relationship of things plotted on semilogarithmic graph paper

semilive skid

semi-looper \ˈ;⹁ᵊ+\ *n* [*semi-* + *looper*] : a caterpillar that is the larva of any of various plusiid moths and that moves like a geometrid larva

1semi-lunar \"+\ *adj* [NL *semilunaris*, fr. L *semi-* + *lunaris* lunar — more at LUNAR] : shaped like a crescent : CRESCENTIC

2semilunar \"\ *n* : **semilunar bone** *n* : LUNATUM 1

semilunar fibrocartilage *or* **semilunar cartilage** *n* : one of the crescentic lamellae of fibrocartilage that border and partly cover the articulating surfaces on the head of the tibia : the medial or lateral meniscus

semilunar ganglion *n* **1** : GASSERIAN GANGLION **2** : COELIAC GANGLION

semilunar lobe *n* : either of a pair of rather large crescent-shaped lobes situated one on each side in the posterior and ventral part of the cerebellum

semilunar notch *n* : the deep depression by which the ulna articulates with the humerus at the elbow

semilunar valve *n* : any of the crescentic cusps that occur as a set of three between the heart and the aorta and another of three between the heart and the pulmonary artery, are forced apart by pressure in the ventricles during systole and pushed together by pressure in the arteries during diastole, and prevent regurgitation of blood into the ventricles; *also* : either set of three cusps : an aortic or pulmonary valve

semi-lune \ˈ;ᵊ(ˌ)⹁+ ⹁\ *n* [*semi-* + *lune*] : something having the shape of a crescent

semi-lustrous \ˈ;ᵊ;ᵊ+\ *adj* [*semi-* + *lustrous*] : slightly lustrous

semi-machine \"+\ *vt* [*semi-* + *machine*] : to machine partly

semi-magnetic controller \ˈ;⹁ᵊ-\ *n* : a controller of electric power (as on a motor) that has part of its functions performed by electromagnets and part by other means

semi-major axis \"+\ *n* [*semi-* + *major*] : half the major axis of the elliptical orbit of a celestial body representing the mean or average distance of the body from its primary

semi-manufactures \"+\ *n pl* [*semi-* + *manufactures*] : products (as steel, rubber, newsprint) made from raw materials and used to manufacture finished goods

semi-mat *or* **semi-matt** *or* **semi-matte** \"+\ *adj* [*semi-* + *mat, matt, matte*] : halfway between glossy and mat : having a slight luster ⟨~ photographic paper⟩ ⟨a ~ black glaze⟩

semi-member \"+\ *n* [*semi-* + *member*] : a tie or strut in a frame or truss that ceases to act as such when the stress in it tends to be reversed by variation in the load

semi-mem·bra·no·sus \ˌseměˌmembrə'nōsəs\ *n, pl* **semi-membrano·si** \-ˌō-ˌsī\ [NL, fr. L *semi-* + LL *membranosus* membranous, fr. L *membrana* membrane + *-osus* -ose — more at MEMBRANE] : a large muscle of the inner part and back of the thigh arising by a thick tendon from the back part of the tuberosity of the ischium and inserted into the medial condyle of the tibia

semi-metal \ˈ;ᵊ;⹁ at SEMI-+\ *n* [*semi-* + *metal*] : an element (as arsenic, antimony, tellurium) possessing metallic properties in an inferior degree and not malleable — compare METALLOID **2c** — **semi-metallic** \"+\ *adj*

semi-micro \"+\ *adj* [*semimicro-*] : intermediate in size between micro and macro quantities on a scale intermediate between microchemical and macrochemical

semimicro- *comb form* [*semi-* + *micr-*] : of, involving, or for quantities intermediate in size between micro and macro quantities : on a scale intermediate between microchemical and macrochemical ⟨*semimicrodetermination*⟩

semi-microanalysis \ˈ;ᵊ(ˌ)⹁ᵊ+\ *n* [*semimicro-* + *analysis*] : chemical analysis (as of quantities of the order of centigrams) on a scale intermediate between macroanalysis and microanalysis

semi-microdetermination \"+\ *n* [*semimicro-* + *determination*] : determination by semimicroanalysis

semi-minim \ˈ;ᵊ(ˌ)⹁ at SEMI-+\ *n* [*semi-* + *minim*] **1** *also* **semi-minima** \"+\-s [*semiminima* fr. NL, fr. L *semi-* + ML *minima* minim — more at MINIM] : a note in mensural notation corresponding to the quarter note **2** : QUARTER NOTE

semi-minor axis \"+-\ *n* [*semi-* + *minor*] : half the minor axis of the elliptical orbit of a celestial body

semi-mobile \"+\ *adj* [*semi-* + *mobile*] **1** : partly equipped with vehicles ⟨a ~ unit⟩ **2** : mobile when partially disassembled ⟨~ artillery⟩

semi-moist \"+\ *adj* [*semi-* + *moist*] : slightly moist

semi-monastic \"+\ *adj* [*semi-* + *monastic*] : having some features like those of a monastic order

semi-monocoque \"+\ *n* [*semi-* + *monocoque*] : a stressed shell structure for airplane fuselages that differs from the monocoque in being reinforced with longitudinal stringers

1semi-monthly \"+\ *adj* [*semi-* + *monthly*] **1** : occurring, appearing, or being made, done, or acted upon twice a month — compare BIMONTHLY

2semimonthly \"\ *n* : a semimonthly publication

3semimonthly \"\ *adv* : twice a month ⟨paid ~ on the 15th and last days of the month⟩

semi-mystical \ˈ;ᵊ⹁ at SEMI-+\ *adj* [*semi-* + *mystical*] : having some of the qualities of mysticism : somewhat mystical

semi-nal \ˈsemən²l\ *adj* [ME, fr. MF, fr. L *seminalis*, fr. *semin-, semen* seed + *-alis* -al — more at SEMEN] **1** : of, derived from, containing, or consisting of seed or semen ⟨~ vessels⟩ **2** : having the character of an originative power, principle, or source : containing or contributing the seeds of later development : GERMINATIVE, ORIGINAL ⟨existentialism . . . has at least acted as a ~ force, inducing other and perhaps contradictory ideas —Philip Toynbee⟩ ⟨fruitful dialectical interplay between literary history and literary criticism, the ~ ideas of one discipline influencing the growth of the other —C.I.Glicksberg⟩ ⟨one of the great ~ minds of our age, . . . a thinker whose insights have become a ~ part of our cultural heritage —Sidney Ratner⟩

seminal animalcule *or* **seminal filament** *n, archaic* : SPERMATOZOON

seminal duct *n* : a tube or passage serving esp. or exclusively as an efferent duct of the testis and in man being made up of the tubules of the epididymis, the vas deferens, and ejaculatory duct

seminal fluid *n* **1** : SEMEN **2** : the part of semen that is produced by various accessory glands : semen excepting the spermatozoa

sem·i·nal·i·ty \ˌseməˈnalədˌē,-lətē,-i\ *n* -ES **1** : the quality or state of being seminal **2** : a seminal property or particle

semi·nal·ly \ˈsemən²lē *also* ˈsēm- *or* -i\ *adv* : in a seminal manner

seminal receptacle *n* : SPERMATHECA — see ECHINOCOCCUS illustration

seminal root *n* : a root that develops from the radicle — compare ADVENTITIOUS ROOT, CORONAL ROOT

seminal vesicle *n* : a pouch on either side of the male reproductive tract that is variously formed in different animals, is connected with the seminal duct, and serves for temporary storage of the semen

sem·i·nar \ˈseməˌnär⹁-ˌnä(r,ˌ⹁ᵊᵊ⹁ at \ *n* -s [G, fr. L *seminarium* seminary] **1** : a group of advanced students studying a subject under a professor, each doing some original research, and all exchanging results by informal lectures, reports, and discussions **2 a** : a course of study pursued by a seminar; *broadly* : an advanced or graduate course **b** : a scheduled meeting of a seminar **c** : a room for such meetings **3** : a meeting for giving and discussing information : a briefing session ⟨CONFERENCE (periodic ~s . . . of the top sales team serves the same end as the summary report —J.K.Blake⟩

sem·i·nar·i·an \ˌseməˈnerēən,-na(ə)r-,-när-\ *or* **sem·i·nar·ist** \ˈ⹁ᵊᵊ⹁nerəst,-nar-\ *n* -s [*seminary* + *-an* or *-ist*] **1 a** : a clergyman educated in a seminary **b** : SEMINARY PRIEST **2 a** : a seminary student

sem·i·nary \ˈseməˌnerē,-ri\ *n* -ES *often attrib* [ME, fr. L *seminarium*, fr. neut. of *seminarius* of seed, fr. *semin-, semen* seed + *-arius* -ary — more at SEMEN] **1 a** *archaic* : a plot where plants for transplantation are raised from seed **b** *obs* : a stock or breeding place of animals **c** : an environment in which something originates and from which it is propagated : a seed bed producing an often specified class of persons or things ⟨many holy monks from Ireland and Scotland, then *seminaries* of saints —Alban Butler⟩ ⟨the prisons were . . . *seminaries* of every crime and every disease —T.B.Macaulay⟩ **2 a** : an institution of secondary or higher education ⟨by affording aids to *seminaries* of learning already established, by the institution of a national university, or by other expedients —H.L.Wells⟩ *specif* : an academy for girls ⟨the female ~ common in the 19th century⟩ ⟨young English ladies who are being "finished off" in suitable *seminaries* —Cecil Beaton⟩ **b** : an institution for the training of candidates for the priesthood, ministry, or rabbinate: as (1) : a Roman Catholic institution preparing young men for diocesan priesthood or for membership in a religious order and having a course of study comprising typically 12 years of secondary, collegiate, and theological training (2) : a similar Roman Catholic institution having only the final 6-year course of senior college and theological studies — called also *major seminary* (3) : PREPARATORY SEMINARY (4) : a professional school giving training in religion esp. for men preparing for ordination as church pastors, usu. associated with a Protestant denomination, requiring a college degree for entry, and having a three-year course of study leading to a bachelor's degree in theology or divinity **3** *obs* : SEMINARY PRIEST **4** : SEMINAR 1

2seminary \"\ *adj* [L *seminarius*] **1** *obs* : SEMINAL 1 **2** : SEMINAL 2

3seminary priest *n* -ES *obs* : GERM

seminary priest *n* : a Roman Catholic priest trained and ordained at Douay, France, or some other continental seminary in the 16th and 17th centuries for mission work in England and distinguished in English penal law from a priest ordained in England during the Marian period

sem·i·nate \ˈseməˌnāt\ *vb* -ED/-ING/-s [L *seminatus*, past part. of *seminare* to sow, plant, fr. *semin-, semen* seed] : INSEMINATE

sem·i·na·tion \ˌseməˈnāshən\ *n* -s

sem·i·na·tive \ˈseməˌnādiv\ *adj* [L *seminatus* (past part. of *seminare* to sow) + E *-ive*] : propagative by or as if by seed

sem·i·nif·er·ous \ˌseməˈnifˌ(ə)rəs\ *also* **sem·i·nif·er·al** \-rəl\ *adj* [*seminiferus* fr. L *semin-, semen* seed + E *-iferous*; *seminiferal* fr. L *semin-, semen* + *-ifer* -fer + E *-al*] **1** : producing or bearing seed **2** : bearing or producing semen ⟨~ epithelium⟩

seminiferous tubule *n* : any of the coiled threadlike tubules that make up the bulk of a testis and are lined with a germinal epithelium from which the spermatozoa are produced

sem·i·nif·ic \ˌseməˈnifik\ *also* **sem·i·nif·i·cal** \-fəkəl\ *adj* [L *semin-, semen* + E *-i-* + *-fic* or *-fical* (fr. *-fic* + *-al*)] : forming or producing seed or semen

sem·i·nist \ˈsemənəst\ *n* -s [L *semin-, semen* + E *-ist*] : an adherent of the old theory that the offspring is formed by admixture of the seed of the male with the supposed seed of the female — compare OVISM, SPERMISM

sem·i·niv·o·rous \ˌseməˈnivərəs, -vrəs\ *adj* [prob. fr. (assumed) NL *seminivorus*, fr. L *semin-, semen* + *-i-* + *-vorus* -vorous] : feeding on seeds

sem·i·nole \ˈseməˌnōl\ *or* **seminole** *or* **seminoles** *usu cap* *n, pl* **seminole** *or* **seminoles** *usu cap* [Creek *simanō·li, simalō·ni* wild, runaway, escape, Seminole, fr. AmerSp *cimarron* wild, savage — more at MAROON] **1 a** : a member of the Creek Muskogean people formed from the portions of the Creek Confederacy that separated from the main body and moved into Florida — see MIKASUKI **b** : a member of such people **2** : MUSKOGEE 2

sem·i·no·ma \ˌseməˈnōmə\ *n, pl* **seminomas** *or* **seminoma·ta** \-ˌmədə\ [NL, fr. L *semin-, semen* seed, semen + *-oma*] : a malignant tumor of the testis

semi·nomad \ˈ;ᵊ(ˌ)⹁ at SEMI-+\ *n* [*semi-* + *nomad*] : a member of a people living usu. in portable or temporary dwellings and practicing seasonal migration but having a base camp at which some crops are cultivated — **semi-nomadic** \"+\ *adj*

semi-occasional \"+\ *adj* [*semi-* + *occasional*] : rather rare : occurring once in a while — **semi-occasionally** \"+\ *adv*

semi-occlusive \"+\ *n* [*semi-* + *occlusive*] : AFFRICATE

semi-official \"+\ *adj* [*semi-* + *official*] : having some official authority or importance : half official ⟨a ~ statement⟩ ⟨~ status⟩ — **semi-officially** \"+\ *adv*

semiofficial stamp *n* : a postage stamp authorized by but not issued by a government

semiography *var of* SEMEIOGRAPHY

semiology *var of* SEMEIOLOGY

1sem·i·o·no·tid \ˌsemēə'nōdˌəd\ *adj* [NL *Semionotidae*] : of or relating to the Semionotidae

2semionotid \"\ *n* -s : a fish of the family Semionotidae

sem·i·o·noti·dae \ˌsemēə'nōdˌə,dē,-'näd-\ *n pl, cap* [NL, fr. *Semionotus*, type genus + *-idae*] : a family of extinct Triassic ganoid fishes from America, Europe, and Africa that have a deep body, small mouth with teeth adapted chiefly to grinding or crushing, and rhomboid scales and that are often considered ancestral to the present-day freshwater gars

sem·i·o·no·tus \-ˈnōdˌəs\ *n, cap* [NL, fr. Gk *sēmeion* sign + *-NL-notus*] : the type genus of the family Semionotidae

semi-opal \ˈ;ᵊ(ˌ)⹁ at SEMI-+\ *n* [*semi-* + *opal*; trans. of G *halbopal*] : an impure opal

semi-opaque \"+\ *adj* [*semi-* + *opaque*] : nearly opaque

semi-organized \"+\ *adj* [*semi-* + *organized*] : partially organized; *specif* : acting under the direction of a leader

semi-oriental \"+\ *adj* [*semi-* + *oriental*] : somewhat oriental

semi·o·sis \ˌsē⹁mī'ōsəs,ˌse\, ⹁ˌmē'-\ *n, pl* **semio·ses** \-ō,sēz\ [NL, fr. Gk *sēmeiōsis* observation of signs, examination, fr. *sēmeioun* to observe signs + *-ōsis* -osis] : the process in which something functions as a sign to an organism

1sem·i·ot·i·cal \ˌsemē'äd·ik\ *also* **sem·i·ot·i·cal** \-d·əkəl\ *adj* [*semiotic* fr. Gk *sēmeiōtikos* observant of signs, fr. *sēmeiousthai* to note or interpret signs, fr. *sēmeion* sign, fr. *sēma* sign; *semiotical* fr. Gk *sēmeiōtikos* + E *-al* — more at SEMANTICS] **1** : SEMEIOTIC **2** : of or relating to semiotic

2semiotic \"\ *n, pl* **semiotics** *but sing or pl in constr* : a general philosophical theory of signs and symbols that deals esp. with their function in both artificially constructed and natural languages and comprises the three branches of syntactics, semantics, and pragmatics — **sem·i·o·ti·cian** \sə⹁miə'tishən,ˌsē-,ˌsel⹁mīə-,ˌse⹁\ *n*

semi-oval \ˈ;ᵊ(ˌ)⹁ at SEMI-+\ *adj* [*semi-* + *oval*] : having the form of a half oval

semi-oviparous \"+\ *adj* [*semi-* + *oviparous*] : bearing imperfectly developed young ⟨a ~ marsupial⟩

semi-pa·la·tinsk \ˌsempə'lädˌinzk,ˌse-,-in(t)sk\ *adj, usu cap* [fr. *Semipalatinsk*, U.S.S.R.] **1** : of or from Semipalatinsk, U.S.S.R. **2** : of the kind or style prevalent in Semipalatinsk

semi-palmate \ˈ;ᵊ(ˌ)⹁ at SEMI-+\ *or* **semi-palmated** \"+\ *adj*

[*semi-* + *palmate, palmated*] : having the anterior toes joined only part way down with a web

semipalmated plover *n* : a small ring plover (*Charadrius hiaticula semipalmatus*) breeding in arctic America and migrating to So. America that is similar to the common ring plover of Europe but has semipalmate feet

semipalmated sandpiper *n* : a small widely distributed American sandpiper (*Ereunetes pusillus*) slightly larger than the least sandpiper and having semipalmate feet

semipalmated snipe *or* **semipalmated tattler** *n* : WILLET

semi-palmation \"+\ *n* [*semi-* + *palmation*] : the quality or state of being semipalmate : partial webbing

semi-parasite \"+\ *n* [*semi-* + *parasite*] : HEMIPARASITE — **semi-parasitic** \"+\ *adj*

semi-ped \ˈseməˌped\ *n* -s [L *semiped-, semipes*, fr. *semi-* + *ped-, pes* foot — more at FOOT] : a metrical half foot — **semi-pedal** \ˈ⹁ᵊᵊ'ped³l, -pēd-; sə'mipəd-, se'm-\ *adj*

1semi-pelagian \ˈ;ᵊ(ˌ)⹁ at SEMI-+\ *n* [*semi-* + *pelagian*] : a person (as a theologian of a 5th or 6th century monastery in Gaul) holding that man requires special help and not merely general guidance from God to overcome original sin, that such help is offered freely to all men, that each man must of his own initiative accept or reject this special divine help, that the individual and not God takes the first step leading to his salvation, and that God's grace toward him is conditioned by his own attitude of acceptance or rejection

2semi-pelagian \"\ *adj, often cap S & usu cap P* : of or relating to semi-Pelagians or semi-Pelagianism

semi-pelagianism \"+\ *often cap S & usu cap P* : the doctrines of semi-Pelagians that were condemned by a synod at Orange in A.D. 529

semi-permanent \"+\ *adj* [*semi-* + *permanent*] **1** : permanent in some respects : partly permanent ⟨a ~ mounting⟩ **2** : lasting for an indefinite time : virtually permanent ⟨a ~ low⟩

semi-permeability \"+\ *n* [*semipermeable* + *-ity*] : the quality or state of being semipermeable

semi-permeable \"+\ *adj* [*semi-* + *permeable*] : partially but not freely or wholly permeable : of or constituting a natural or artificial membrane that is permeable to some usu. small molecules (as of water or inorganic salts) but bars the passage of other usu. larger particles (as protein molecules) ⟨the living cell is enclosed in a ~ membrane and often a rigid permeable cell wall⟩

1semi-plant \"+\ *n* [*semi-* + *plant*] : SEMIWORKS

2semiplant \"\ *adj* : larger than that of a laboratory or pilot plant but smaller than that of a plant in commercial production ⟨preparation of the new product on a ~ scale⟩

semi-plumaceous \ˈ;ᵊ(ˌ)⹁ at SEMI-+\ *adj* [*semi-* + *plumaceous*] : having the character of a semiplume

semi-plume \ˈ;ᵊ;ᵊ+⹁\ *n* [*semi-* + *plume*] : a feather having a plumy or downy web with the shaft of an ordinary feather

semi-pneumatic tire \ˈ;ᵊ(ˌ)⹁ at SEMI-+-\ *n* : a rubber tire (as for a hand truck, lawnmower, wheelbarrow) having thick completely tubular walls enclosing air not under pressure and having no inner tube and no valve

semi-polar \"+\ *adj* [*semi-* + *polar*] : partly polar — used esp. of chemical bonds and structures regarded as possessing polarity associated with nonpolar covalence (as in an amine oxide $R_3N^+{-}O^-$)

semipolar bond *or* **semipolar double bond** *n* : COORDINATE BOND

semi-political \"+\ *adj* [*semi-* + *political*] : having some association with politics or involving some political features or activity : slightly political ⟨the work is largely routine and ~, involving the passage of inspection laws and the asking for appropriations —Science⟩

semi-porcelain \"+\ *n* [*semi-* + *porcelain*] : any of several ceramic wares resembling or imitative of porcelain: as **a** : a porcelanous stoneware **b** : IRONSTONE CHINA **c** : a relatively high-fired and hard-glazed white earthenware widely used for tablewares

semi-portable \"+\ *adj* [*semi-* + *portable*] : capable of being comparatively easily moved but not designed for ready transportation; *specif* : constituting a steam engine having an attached boiler but not mounted on wheels

1semi-postal \"+\ *or* **semipostal stamp** *n* [*semi-* + *postal*] : a postage stamp the price of which goes partly to pay postage and partly to the support of some public expense project (as a charity, a monument, or the restoration of a ruined building) ⟨~s have not been issued in the U.S.⟩

semi-precious \"+\ *adj* [*semi-* + *precious*] : of a gemstone : of less commercial value than those called precious (such ~ stones as the amethyst, garnet, jade, and tourmaline); *specif* : less than 8 in hardness

semi-privacy \"+\ *n* [*semi-* + *privacy*] : partial privacy

semi-private \"+\ *adj* : of, receiving, or associated with hospital service in which the patient has more privileges than a ward patient but fewer than a private patient (as in having his own doctor, sharing a room with only one other patient)

1semi-professional \"+\ *or* **semi-pro** \"+\ *adj* [*semipro-fessional* fr. *semi-* + *professional*; *semipro* short for *semiprofessional*] **1 a** : engaging in an activity (as a sport) for pay or gain but not as a full-time occupation ⟨amateur and ~ ballplayers⟩ ⟨a ~ actor⟩ **b** : engaged in by semiprofessional players ⟨~ baseball⟩ **2** : being or engaged in work resembling professional work in relating to a broad field of science, learning, or art, but requiring less theoretical knowledge or less creative skill and often less exercise of originality and judgment and typically restricted to the application of technical or mechanical details — **semi-professionally** \"+\ *adv*

2semiprofessional \"\ *or* **semipro** \"\ *n* : a person engaging in an activity (as a sport) semiprofessionally

semi-proof \ˈ;ᵊ(ˌ)⹁ at SEMI-+\ *n* [*semi-* + *proof*] : evidence from the testimony of a single witness

semi-prostrate \"+\ *adj* [*semi-* + *prostrate*] : imperfectly prostrate ⟨the creeping oxeye, a ~ herb⟩; *specif* : prostrate for half the length

semi-public \"+\ *adj* [*semi-* + *public*] **1** : having some of the features of a public institution; *specif* : maintained as a public service by a private nonprofit organization ⟨a ~ institution⟩ **2** : open to some persons (as the families and guests of members) outside the regular constituency but not to the general public ⟨a ~ meeting⟩

semi-pupa \"+\ *n* [NL, fr. *semi-* + *pupa*] **1** : any of various insects in a developmental stage between the larva and pupa **2** : PSEUDOPUPA — **semi-pupal** \"+\ *adj*

semi-pyramidal \"+\ *adj* [*semi-* + *pyramidal*] : having the form of a half pyramid vertically divided

semi-quantitative \"+\ *adj* [*semi-* + *quantitative*] : approaching or designed to approach the quantitative in precision ⟨a ~ relationship⟩

semi-quaver \"+\ *n* [*semi-* + *quaver*] : SIXTEENTH NOTE

semi-quietism \"+\ *n* [*semi-* + *quietism*] : a moderate form of quietism practiced in France toward the end of the 17th century having none of the antinomianism of pure quietism but placing the essence of the spiritual life in complete surrender to love of God without thought of reward or punishment

semi-quinone \"+\ *n* [*semi-* + *quinone*] : any of a class of free radicals derived from quinones or quinone imines by the addition of a single hydrogen atom to a molecule — compare MERIQUINONE

semi-recondite \"+\ *adj* [*semi-* + *recondite*] : partly concealed; *specif* : half covered by the thorax ⟨an insect with a ~ head⟩

semi-religious \"+\ *adj* [*semi-* + *religious*] : having some association with religion or involving some religious features or activity : somewhat religious in character

semi-respectable \"+\ *adj* [*semi-* + *respectable*] : half respectable

semi-responsible \"+\ *adj* [*semi-* + *responsible*] : having or providing for an executive responsible except in reserved matters to the legislature ⟨a ~ colonial government⟩

semi-rigid \"+\ *adj* [*semi-* + *rigid*] **1** : rigid to some degree or in some parts ⟨of an airship⟩ : having a flexible cylindrical gas container with an attached stiffening keel that carries the load

semi-rimmed \"+\ *adj, of a cartridge case* : having a rim that is only slightly greater in diameter than the body of the case

and having a groove immediately forward of the rim for the extractor to engage — compare RIMLESS

semi·ring \ˈ=(,)=+,-\ *n* [*semi-* + *ring*] **:** a partial or incomplete ring; *esp* **:** HALF RING

semi·rotary \ˈ=(,)= *at* SEMI- +\ *or* **semi·rotative** \"+\ *or* **semi·rotatory** \"+\ *adj* [*semi-* + *rotary* or *rotative* or *rotatory*] **:** capable of turning or rocking about halfway round ⟨a ~ valve⟩

semi·round \"+\ *adj* [*semi-* + *round*] **:** round on one side and flat on the other

¹se·mis \ˈsāməs, ˈsēm-\ *n* -ES [L, fr. *semi-* + *as*, a copper coin — more at ACE] **:** any of three coins of ancient Rome: **a :** a half as of Republican Rome **b :** a half aureus of Imperial Rome **c :** a half solidus under Constantine and later

²se·mis \səˈmē\ *n* -ES [F, act or instance of sowing, fr. *semer* to sow, fr. MF — more at SEMÉ] **:** a scattering repetition of small design motifs to produce an overall pattern

³sem·is \ˈsemēz, -ˌmīz, -ˌmiz\ *n pl* [by shortening] **1 :** SEMIMANUFACTURES **2 :** semifinished metal

⁴semis *pl of* SEMI

semi·sacred \ˈ=(,)= *at* SEMI- +\ *adj* [*semi-* + *sacred*] **:** SEMIRELIGIOUS

¹semi·scald \"+\ *vt* [*semi-* + *scald*] **:** to dip (fowl) for less than a minute in water heated to just below the boiling point

²semiscald \"\ *n* **:** an act of semiscalding

semi·sedentary \ˈ=(,)= *at* SEMI- +\ *adj* [*semi-* + *sedentary*] **:** sedentary during part of the year and nomadic otherwise ⟨~ tribespeople⟩

semi·serious \"+\ *adj* [*semi-* + *serious*] **:** of a light nature but having a possible serious implication or interpretation **:** partly serious — **semi·seriously** \"+\ *adv* — **semi·seriousness** \"+\ *n*

semi·servile \"+\ *adj* [*semi-* + *servile*] **:** half servile; *esp* **:** of or being a class of men (as the Roman colonus or the Welsh aillt) having many rights of freemen but not free in other respects

semi·shrub \"+\ *n* [*semi-* + *shrub*] **:** SUBSHRUB, UNDERSHRUB — **semi·shrubby** \"+\ *adj*

semi·skilled \"+\ *adj* [*semi-* + *skilled*] **:** having or requiring less training (as for a few weeks) and the exercise of less independent judgment than skilled labor and more than unskilled labor ⟨while the ~ worker may lack specific experience, he is often used to factory discipline —R.L.Raimon⟩ ⟨machine attendants are typical ~ laborers —J.B.Horton⟩

semi·soft \"+\ *adj* [*semi-* + *soft*] **:** moderately soft; *specif* **:** firm but easily cut ⟨a ~ cheese⟩

¹semi·solid \"+\ *adj* [*semi-* + *solid*] **:** having the qualities of both a solid and a liquid but being more closely related to a solid **:** partly solid **:** highly viscous ⟨jelly and paste are ~⟩ ⟨the ~ mass becomes semifluid —Morris Fishbein⟩

²semisolid \"\ *n* **:** a semisolid substance

semi·span \ˈ=(,)= *at* SEMI- +\ *adj* [*semi-* + *span*] **:** consisting of or incorporating only half of the complete wing or tail of an airplane

semi·sphere \ˈsemə,sfi(ə)r, -iə\ *n* [ML *semisphaera*, fr. L *semi-* + *sphaera* sphere — more at SPHERE] **:** HEMISPHERE — **semi·spher·ic** \ˈ==ˈsfirik, -fer-, -rēk\ *or* **semi·spher·i·cal** \-rəkəl, -rēk-\ *adj*

semi·spi·na·lis \,semə,spīˈnāləs, -nal-\ *n, pl* **semispina·les** \-a(,)lēz, -ā(,)lēz\ [NL, fr. *semispinalis*, adj., fr. L *semi-* + LL *spinalis* spinal — more at SPINAL] **:** a deep layer of muscle of the back on each side of the spinal column extending from the lower dorsal region to the second cervical vertebra, consisting of a number of long slender fasciculi that arise each from the transverse process of one of the lower vertebrae, pass obliquely upward across several vertebrae, and are inserted into the spinous process of a vertebra farther up, and being divided into lower, middle, and upper segments — called also respectively *semispinalis dor·si* \-ˈdȯr,sī\, *semispinalis cer·vi·cis* \-ˈsərvəsəs\, and *semispinalis ca·pi·tis* \-ˈkapəd·əs\

semi·square \ˈ=(,)= *at* SEMI- +\ *adj* [*semi-* + *square*] **:** forming half of a square

semi·steel \"+\ *n* [*semi-* + *steel*] **:** cast iron of low carbon content made by replacing part (as one fourth) of the pig iron in the cupola charge by steel scrap

semi·stock \"+\ *n* [*semi-* + *stock*] **:** a part or machine that is not carried in stock but can be made up of parts that are carried in stock

semi·subterranean \"+\ *adj* [*semi-* + *subterranean*] **:** half underground ⟨small, rectangular, single-unit, ~ houses of pole, brush and adobe —R.W.Murray⟩

semi·sul·co·spi·ra \,semə,səlkəˈspīrə\ *n, cap* [NL, fr. *semi-* + L *sulcus* furrow + NL *-spira* (fr. *spirare* to breathe) — more at SPIRIT] **:** a genus of freshwater snails (family Thiaridae) of eastern Asia and the Pacific islands where they are sometimes used as food and are of prime medical importance as intermediate hosts of pathogenic trematode worms

semi·sweet \ˈ=(,)= *at* SEMI- +\ *adj* [*semi-* + *sweet*] **:** slightly sweetened **:** not very sweet ⟨a ~ cake⟩ ⟨~ chocolate⟩

semi·synthetic \"+\ *adj* [*semi-* + *synthetic*] **:** partly synthetic **:** relating to or produced by synthesis from natural starting materials (as cellulose)

sem·ite \ˈse,mīt, *usu* -īd.+V; *chiefly Brit* ˈsē,m-\ *n* -s *cap* [F *sémite*, fr. *Sem*, son of Noah, eponymous ancestor of the Semites (Gen 10: 22-31) (fr. LL, fr. Gk *Sēm*, fr. Heb *Shēm*) + F *-ite*] **1 :** a member of one of the peoples listed in the Scriptures as descended from Shem, a son of Noah **2 :** a member of one of a group of peoples of southwestern Asia speaking Semitic languages and chiefly represented now by the Jews and Arabs but in ancient times also by the Babylonians, Assyrians, Aramaeans, Canaanites, and Phoenicians

sem·i·ten·di·no·sus \,semē,tendəˈnōsəs\ *n, pl* **semitendi·no·si** \-ō,sī\ [NL, fr. *semitendinosus*, adj., fr. L *semi-* + NL *tendinosus* tendinous — more at TENDINOUS] **:** a fusiform muscle of the posterior and inner part of the thigh that arises from the tuberosity of the ischium along with the biceps femoris and is inserted by a remarkably long round tendon which forms part of the inner hamstring into the inner surface of the upper part of the shaft of the tibia

semi·terrestrial \ˈ=(,)= *at* SEMI- +\ *adj* [*semi-* + *terrestrial*] **:** chiefly terrestrial: as **a :** growing on boggy ground ⟨~ peats⟩ **b :** frequenting but not living wholly on land ⟨~ amphipod⟩

¹se·mit·ic \səˈmid·ik, -mit|, |ēk *also* seˈm-\ *adj, usu cap* [G *semitisch*, fr. *semit, semite* Semite (prob. fr. NL *semita*, fr. LL *Sem*, son of Noah + L *-ita* -ite) + *-isch* -ic] **:** of, relating to, characteristic of, or constituting the Semites or the Semitic languages ⟨*Semitic* peoples⟩ ⟨*Semitic* dialects⟩; *specif* **:** JEWISH

²semitic \"\ *n* -s *cap* **1 a :** the Semitic languages as a group ⟨discrepancies between structure and function are actually greater in Indo-European than in *Semitic* —*Language*⟩ **b :** one of the Semitic languages ⟨the Babylonians and Assyrians spoke *Semitic* —C.S.Coon⟩ **2 :** SEMITE

semitic languages *n pl, cap S* **:** a branch of the Afro-Asiatic language family including Hebrew, Aramaic, Arabic, Ethiopic — see AFRO-ASIATIC LANGUAGES table

se·mit·ics \-ks\ *n pl but sing in constr, usu cap* [¹*Semitic* + *-s*] **:** the study of the language, literature, and history of Semitic peoples; *specif* **:** Semitic philology

sem·i·tism \ˈsemə,tizəm\ *n* -s *usu cap* [*Semite* + *-ism*] **1 a :** Semitic character or qualities **b :** a Semitic idiom or expression (as in Jewish or Christian Greek literature or in versions of the Bible) **2 :** policy (as political policy) favorable to Jews **:** predisposition in favor of Jews

sem·i·tist \-təst\ *also* **se·mit·i·cist** \səˈmid·əsəst, sēˈ-\ *n* -s [*semitist* fr. *Semite* + *-ist*; *semiticist* fr. ¹*Semitic* + *-ist*] **1** *usu cap* **:** a scholar of the Semitic languages, cultures, or histories **2 :** a person favoring or disposed to favor the Jews

sem·i·tize \ˈsemə,tīz\ *also* **se·mit·i·cize** \səˈmid·ə,sīz\ *vt* -ED/-ING/-s *often cap* [*semitize* fr. F *sémite* Semite + E *-ize*; *semiticize* fr. ¹*Semitic* + *-ize*] **:** to make Semitic (as in language)

semito- *comb form, usu cap* [¹*Semitic*] **:** Semite **:** Semitic ⟨*Semito*-Hamite⟩ ⟨*Semito*-Hamitic⟩

semi·tonal \ˈ=(,)=+\ *adj* [*semitone* + *-al*] **:** CHROMATIC 3b, SEMITONIC ⟨the ~ scale implies . . . the negation of scale —Gerald Abraham⟩ — **semi·tonally** \"+\ *adv*

semi·tone \ˈ=(,)=+,-\ *n* [*semi-* + *tone*] **:** the tone at a half step; *also* **:** HALF STEP

semi·tonic \ˈ=(,)=+\ *adj* [*semitone* + *-ic*] **:** of, relating to, or consisting of semitones — **semi·tonically** \"+\ *adv*

semi·trailer \"+\ *n* [*semi-* + *trailer*] **1 :** a freight trailer that when attached is supported at its forward end by the fifth wheel device of the truck tractor — compare FULL TRAILER **2 :** a trucking rig made up of a tractor and a semitrailer — called also *semi*

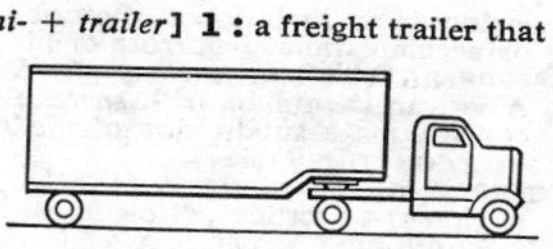

semitrailer 1

semi·trailing \"+\ *adj* [*semi-* + *trailing*] **:** imperfectly trailing: *specif* **:** trailing for half the length

semi·transparency \"+\ *n* -ES [*semi-* + *transparency*] **:** the quality or state of being semitransparent

semi·transparent \"+\ *adj* [*semi-* + *transparent*] **:** imperfectly transparent

semi·tropic \"+\ *or* **semi·tropical** \"+\ *adj* [*semi-* + *tropic* or *tropical*] **:** SUBTROPICAL

semi·tropics \"+\ *n pl* [*semi-* + *tropics*] **:** SUBTROPICS

¹semi·uncial \"+\ *adj* [*semi-* + *uncial*] **:** written in or being half uncial characters

²semiuncial \"\ *n* **1 :** HALF UNCIAL **2 :** a letter or writing in half uncial

semi·underground \ˈ=(,)= *at* SEMI- +\ *adj* [*semi-* + *underground*] **:** partially underground

semi·vitreous \"+\ *adj, ceramics* **:** having not enough glassy phase to reduce porosity below 0.2 percent

semi·vitrification \"+\ *n* [*semi-* + *vitrification*] **:** half or imperfect vitrification; *also* **:** a semivitrified substance

semi·vitrified \"+\ *adj* [*semi-* + *vitrified*] **:** partially vitrified

semi·vocalic \"+\ *adj* [*semi-* + *vocalic*] **:** of or relating to a semivowel

semi·vowel \"+\ *n* [*semi-* + *vowel*] **1 :** any speech sound not a stop, aspirate, or vowel, and not at any stage of the language having a stop as a component — used esp. of ancient Greek ⟨λ, μ, ν, γ nasal, ρ, and σ were ~s⟩ **2 :** one of the glides \y\, \w\, \r\ **3 :** a letter representing one of these sounds

semi·water gas \"+-\ *n* [*semi-* + *water*] **:** a producer gas intermediate in composition between water gas and air gas (sense 2) made by blowing a mixture of steam and air into a producer

¹semi·weekly \"+\ *adj* [*semi-* + *weekly*] **:** occurring, appearing, or being made, done, or acted upon twice a week — compare BIWEEKLY

²semiweekly \"\ *n* -ES **:** a publication issued twice weekly

³semiweekly \"\ *adv* **:** twice a week

semi·wildcat \ˈ=(,)= *at* SEMI- +\ *n* [*semi-* + *wildcat*] **:** an oil well drilled near but not in an established field

semi·woody \"+\ *adj* [*semi-* + *woody*] **:** somewhat woody **:** partially lignified ⟨the ~ stem of the milkweed⟩

semi·works \ˈ=(,)=+,-\ *n pl, often attrib* [*semi-* + *works*] **:** a manufacturing plant operating on a limited commercial scale to provide final tests of a new product or process and to supply market samples

sem·mel \ˈseməl, ˈze-\ *n, pl* **semmels** *or* **semmel** [G, fr. OHG *semala, simila* fine wheat flour, fr. L *simila* finest wheat flour — more at SIMNEL] **:** a bread roll with a crisp crust and a variously shaped top

sem·mit \ˈsemət\ *n* -s [origin unknown] *Scot* **:** UNDERSHIRT

sem·no·pi·the·cus \,sem(,)nōpəˈthēkəs, -ˈpithəkəs\ [NL, fr. Gk *semnos* revered, sacred (akin to Gk *sebesthai* to revere, feel awe) + NL *-pithecus* — more at SEBASTODES] *syn of* PRESBYTIS

sem·no·pi·theque \-pəˈthek\ *n* -s [F *semno-pithèque*, fr. *semno-* (fr. Gk *semnos* revered) + *pithèque* monkey, ape, fr. Gk *pithēkos* — more at BEBUNG] **:** LANGUR

sem·o·li·na \,seməˈlēnə\ *n* -s [modif. of It *semolino*, dim. of *semola* bran, modif. of L *simila* finest wheat flour — more at SIMNEL] **1 :** the purified middlings of durum or other hard wheat used for macaroni and other alimentary pastes **2 :** coarse middlings used for breakfast cereal, puddings, or polenta

se·mol·o·gy \səˈmäləjē\ *n* -ES [Gk *sēma* sign + E *-o-* + *-logy* — more at SEMANTICS] **:** SEMANTICS 1a, 1b

se·mos·to·mae \səˈmästə,mē\ [NL, fr. Gk *sēma* sign + NL *-o-* + *-stomae* (fr. *-stoma*)] *syn of* SEMAEOSTOMEAE

semp *abbr* sempre

sem·per pa·ra·tus \,sempə(r)pəˈrädəs, -räd-\ *n* [L, always ready] **:** a plea at law by which a defendant in an action of assumpsit alleges that he has always been ready to comply with the demand

sem·per·vi·rent \ˈ==ˈvīrənt\ *adj* [NL *sempervirent-, sempervirens*, fr. L *semper* always + *virent-, virens*, pres. part. of *virere* to be green] **:** EVERGREEN

sem·per·vi·rine \,==ˈvī,rēn, -rən\ *n* -s [ISV *sempervir-* (fr. NL *sempervirens* — specific epithet of the woody vine *Gelsemium sempervirens* —, fr. *sempervirent-, sempervirens* evergreen) + *-ine*] **:** a crystalline alkaloid $C_{19}H_{16}N_2$ obtained from the yellow jessamine shrub

sem·per·vi·vum \,==ˈvīvəm\ *n* [NL, fr. L, neut. of *sempervivus* ever-living, fr. *semper* ever, always + *vivus* alive — more at QUICK] **1** *cap* **:** a large genus of Old World fleshy often acaulescent herbs (family Crassulaceae) many of which have cymose variously colored flowers with numerous sepals and petals and are cultivated as ornamentals **2** -s **:** any plant or flower of the genus *Sempervivum*

sem·pi·ter·nal \ˈsempəˈtərnᵊl\ *also* **sem·pi·tern** \ˈ==,tərn\ *adj* [*sempiternal* fr. ME, fr. LL *sempiternalis*, fr. L *sempiternus* eternal (fr. *semper* always, fr. *sem-* one + *per* through) + *-alis* -al; *sempitern* fr. ME *sempiterne*, fr. MF, fr. L *sempiternus* — more at SAME, FOR] **:** of never-ending duration **:** EVERLASTING, ETERNAL ⟨as they are ubiquitous and ~, war against them must be everlasting —G.W.Johnson⟩ — **sem·pi·ter·nal·ly** \ˈ==ˈtərnᵊlē\ *adv*

sem·pi·ter·ni·ty \,==ˈtərnəd·ē\ *n* -ES [LL *sempiternitas*, fr. L *sempiternus* eternal + *-itas* -ity] **:** ETERNITY

sem·ple \ˈsempəl\ *adj* [alter. of *simple*] *Scot* **:** of humble birth **:** SIMPLE ⟨whether ye be gentle or ~ —Sir Walter Scott⟩

sem·pli·ce \ˈsemplə,chā\ *adj (or adv)* [It, fr. L *simplic-, simplex* simple — more at SIMPLE] **:** SIMPLE, UNAFFECTED — used as a direction in music

sem·pre \ˈsem(,)prā\ *adv* [It, fr. L *semper*] **:** ALWAYS — used as a direction in music ⟨~ legato⟩

sempster *var of* SEAMSTER

sempstress *var of* SEAMSTRESS

sems \ˈsemz\ *n, pl* **sems** [prob. fr. *sem* (short for *assembly*) + *-s*] **:** a fastener assembly consisting of a screw with a washer put on before the threading is cut

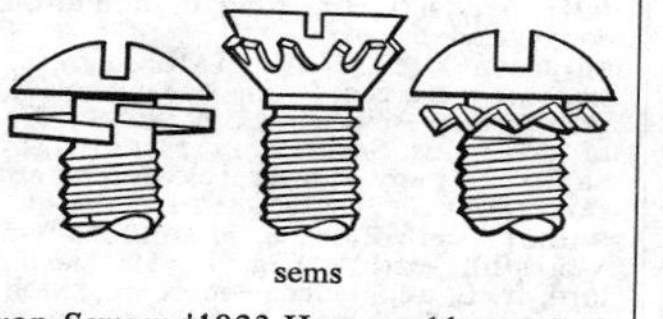

sems

sem·sem \ˈsem-,sem\ *n* -s [Ar *simsim* — more at SESAME] **:** SESAME

sem·sey·ite \ˈsem-zē,īt\ *n* -s [G *semseyit*, fr. Andor von *Semsey* †1923 Hung. nobleman + G *-it* -ite] **:** a mineral $Pb_9Sb_8S_{21}$ consisting of a lead antimony sulfide similar in appearance to jamesonite

semul \ˈsēməl, ˈsem-\ *n* -s [Hindi *semal*] **:** SILK-COTTON TREE

semy \ˈsemē\ *adj* [F *semée*, fem. of *semé* — more at SEMÉ] **:** SEMÉ 2

¹sen \ˈsen\ *n, pl* **sen** [Jap, fr. Chin *ch'ien²* coin, cash, money] **1 :** a Japanese monetary unit equal to ¹⁄₁₀₀ yen — see MONEY table **2 :** a coin representing one sen

²sen \"\ *n, pl* **sen** [native name in Indonesia] **1 :** an Indonesian monetary unit equal to ¹⁄₁₀₀ rupiah — see MONEY table **2 :** a coin representing one sen

³sen \"\ *n, pl* **sen** [native name in Cambodia] **:** a subsidiary unit of value of Cambodia from 1954 equal to ¹⁄₁₀₀ riel

⁴sen \"\ *dial Eng var of* SELF

sen *abbr* **1** senate; senator **2** senior **3** [It *senza*] without

sena·ite \ˈsenə,īt, ˈsān-\ *n* -s [Joachim da Costa *Sena*, 19th cent. Brazilian mineralogist + E *-ite*] **:** a mineral (Fe,Mn,Pb)TiO_3 consisting of an oxide of iron, manganese, lead, and titanium occurring in black rounded crystals and fragments in the diamond-bearing sands of Minas Geraes, Brazil

se·nam \səˈnäm\ *n* -s [Ar *sanām* hump, mound] **:** one of a type of dolmen in Algiers and Tripoli formerly regarded as belonging to the megalithic period but now recognized as the remains of oil presses of the Roman period

se·nar·ius \səˈna(a)rēəs, sēˈ-, -ˈnär-\ *also* **se·nar·i·an** \-rēən\ *n, pl* **se·nar·ii** \-rē,ī\ *also* **senarians** [*senarius* fr. L, fr. *senarius* consisting of six each, fr. *seni* six each (fr. *sex* six) + *-arius* -ary; *senarian* fr. L *senarius* + E *-an* — more at SIX] **:** a verse of six feet in Latin prosody; *esp* **:** the classical iambic trimeter

sen·ar·mon·tite \,senə(r)ˈmän,tīt\ *n* -s [Henri de *Sénarmont* †1862 Fr. mineralogist + E *-ite*] **:** a colorless or grayish mineral Sb_2O_3 consisting of native antimony trioxide and occurring in octahedral crystals or in masses

¹senary *n* -ES [L *senarius* consisting of six each] *obs* **:** six or a group of six **:** something that is constituted of six figures, things, or parts ⟨four *senaries* of hours —Paschall⟩

²sena·ry \ˈsēnərē, ˈsen-, -ri\ *adj* [L *senarius*] **:** of, based upon or characterized by six **:** compounded of six things **:** consisting of six parts **:** SEXTUPLE ⟨~ scale⟩ ⟨~ division⟩

senat *var of* SENIT

sen·ate \ˈsenət, *usu* -əd.+V\ *n* -s [ME *senat*, fr. OF, fr. L *senatus*, lit., council of elders, fr. *sen-, senex* old, old man + *-atus* -ate — more at SENIOR] **1 a :** an assembly or council usu. possessing high deliberative and legislative functions: as (1) **:** the supreme council of the ancient Roman republic and empire (2) **:** the governing body in various European free cities ⟨the *Senate* of Frankfort⟩ (3) **:** the second chamber in the bicameral legislature of a major political unit (as a nation, state, or province) ⟨the *Senate* of the United States shall be composed of two senators from each state —*U.S.Constitution*⟩ ⟨the life-appointed Canadian *Senate* —Alexander Brady⟩ ⟨the New York State Legislature consists of an assembly and a ~ —Robert Rienow⟩ **b :** a governing or legislative assembly held to resemble such a senate **2 :** the hall or chamber in which a senate meets ⟨on the floor of the ~⟩ **3 a :** a governing body of a British university charged with maintaining academic standards and regulations and usu. composed of the principal or representative members of the faculty — compare COUNCIL 4c, COURT **b :** a similar body at an American university

sen·a·tor \ˈsenəd·ə(r), -nətə-, *in rapid speech esp before a surname* -ntə- *or* -ndə-; *sometimes* -nə,tō(ə)r *or* -ō(ə)\ *n* -s [ME *senatour*, fr. OF *senateur*, fr. L *senator*, fr. *senatus* senate + *-or*] **1 a :** a member of a senate ⟨a Roman ~⟩ ⟨the duke and ~s of Venice greet you —Shak.⟩ ⟨U. S. *Senator* from Connecticut⟩ ⟨Canadian ~s are appointed⟩ **b :** a member of a legislative body resembling or held to resemble a senate ⟨most accomplished ~ . . . in either House of Parliament —William King⟩ **2** *or* **senator of the college of justice :** LORD OF COUNCIL AND SESSION **3 :** the civil head of the government of the city of Rome under papal administration

sen·a·to·ri·al \,senəˈtōrēəl, -tȯr-\ *adj* [L *senatorius* of a senator (fr. *senator* + *-ius* -y) + E *-al*] **1 a :** of, relating to, or befitting a senator or a senate ⟨~ office⟩ ⟨~ voice⟩ ⟨~ dignity⟩ ⟨~ rank⟩ **b :** composed of senators ⟨the Roman ~ order⟩ **2 :** administered by the Roman senate rather than by the emperor ⟨a ~ province⟩

senatorial courtesy *n* **:** a custom of the U. S. Senate of refusing to confirm a presidential appointment of an official in or from a state whose senators or senior senator of the president's party are opposed to the appointment

senatorial district *n* **:** a territorial division from which a senator is elected — compare CONGRESSIONAL DISTRICT

sen·a·to·ri·an \-rēən\ *adj* [L *senatorius* senatorial + E *-an*] **:** SENATORIAL; *specif* **:** of or relating to the ancient Roman senate ⟨the ~ order⟩

sen·a·tor·ship \ˈ===,ship\ *n* [*senator* + *-ship*] **:** the office or position of senator ⟨the Democratic candidate for the ~ —*Nation*⟩

¹senatory *adj* [L *senatorius* — more at SENATORIAL] *obs* **:** SENATORIAN

²sen·a·to·ry \ˈsenə,tōrē, -tȯr-, -ri\ *n* -ES [F *sénatorerie*, fr. L *senator* + F *-erie* -ery] **:** an estate granted to a senator in early 19th century France

se·na·tus aca·de·mi·cus \səˈnād·ə,sakəˈdeməkəs\ *or* **senatus** *n, pl* **senatus academi·ci** \-mə,sī\ *or* **senatus** [NL, academic senate] **:** the senate in some Scottish universities

senatus con·sul·tum \-,ənkənˈsəltəm\ *or* **senatus con·sult** \-ˈkän,səlt, -,kənˈs-\ *n, pl* **senatus consul·ta** \-tə\ *or* **senatus consults** [L *senatus consultum* decree of the senate] **1 :** a decree of the ancient Roman senate **2 :** a decree of the senate in Napoleonic France

¹send \ˈsend\ *vb* **sent** \ˈsent\ **sent; sending; sends** [ME *senden*, fr. OE *sendan*; akin to OHG *senten, sendan* to send, ON *senda*, Goth *sandjan*, OE *sīth* journey, road, OHG *sind*, ON *sinni*, Goth *sinths* going, time OI *sēt* road] *vt* **1 :** to cause to go by physical means or direct volition: as **a :** to propel or discharge with an aim **:** throw or direct in a particular direction ⟨~ an arrow⟩ ⟨~ a bullet⟩ ⟨~ a rocket to another planet⟩ ⟨*sent* an empty pickle jar whizzing after them —Thomas Hughes⟩ **b** *obs* **:** THRUST **c :** DELIVER ⟨*sent* a blow straight to his chin⟩ **d :** DRIVE ⟨*sent* the ball between the goalposts⟩ **2 a :** to cause to happen or come into existence **:** bestow or grant as a blessing **:** ordain or inflict as a punishment ⟨God ~s not ill —Alexander Pope⟩ **b :** to grant (as the fulfillment of a hope or a request) to a person ⟨heaven . . . ~ me just thoughts —Charles Dickens⟩ ⟨God ~ your mission may bring back peace —Sir Walter Scott⟩ ⟨God . . . ~ your sleep is light —*N.Y. Times*⟩ **3 :** to dispatch by a means of communication (as the post or telegraph) ⟨~ him a letter of appreciation⟩ ⟨~ our compliments⟩ **4 a :** to commission, direct, order, or request (as a person) to go **:** dispatch on an errand or as a messenger **b** (1) **:** to dispatch to a specified destination for a course or term (as of residence or employment) ⟨~ a son to college⟩ ⟨~ as a representative to Congress⟩ (2) **:** to permit (a person) to attend a college, school, or other educational institution by paying all or part of the expenses involved ⟨able to ~ both his children to boarding school⟩ **c :** to direct by advice or reference **:** refer to some person or authority **:** advise to go to some place or in some direction ⟨*sent* him to the dictionary⟩ ⟨*sent* him to the information desk⟩ **d :** to describe (a person) in narrative as going to a specified place ⟨next he ~s him to Paris⟩ **e :** to cause to enter the world as a gift or on a mission from God ⟨never ceased to hope that they would be *sent* a child⟩ ⟨sincerely believed he had been *sent* to save his people⟩ **f :** to bid to go **:** cause or order to depart from one **:** DISMISS ⟨~ him home with a reprimand⟩ ⟨~ him from me⟩ **5 a :** to force or compel to go **:** DRIVE, IMPEL ⟨~ the rebels flying⟩ ⟨*sent* all the townspeople scuttling out of their houses —Laurence Critchell⟩ **b :** to cause to enter or assume a specified state **:** drive into a specified condition ⟨~ one mad⟩ ⟨*sent* the household into a frenzy of excitement⟩ **6 :** to cause to issue **:** give forth as a source — usu. used with *forth* or *out*: as **a :** to pour out or discharge (as a liquid) ⟨clouds ~*ing* forth long-needed rain⟩ **b :** to cause to issue in sound **:** UTTER ⟨~ forth a cry⟩ ⟨*sent* out a bitter bleating⟩ ⟨the steeples *sent* forth a joyous peal —T.B.Macaulay⟩ **c :** to give off or out (as heat or light) **:** EMIT ⟨tropical flowers *sent* out clouds of warm perfume —Eve Langley⟩ **d :** to throw out (as nerves or stems) in the course of development ⟨each branch and twig began to ~ out clusters of small buds —William Beebe⟩ ⟨an ice cap which . . . ~s out steep glacier tongues to the south —Valter Schytt⟩ **7 :** to cause (as a person) to be carried or conducted to a destination; *esp* **:** to consign or commit to death or a place of punishment ⟨~ a convict to the gallows⟩ **8 a :** to cause (something) to be conveyed or transmitted by an agent to a destination (as a person or place) ⟨~ flowers by wire⟩ **b :** to cause (as food or drink) to be brought or served ⟨~ in dinner⟩ **c :** to cause (as a boat or vehicle) to be made available or ready (as at a designated place or time) ⟨asked us to ~ a taxi for him⟩ **9 :** to transmit by directing the eyes or the attention **:** DIRECT ⟨*sent* an inquiring glance at his wife —Laura Krey⟩ **10 :** to cause (as music or a cry) to sound through the air ⟨visiting choirs . . . ~ their music through the pine forest —Oscar Schisgall⟩ **11 :** to dispatch (a person) in a specified capacity ⟨*sent* him as ambassador to France⟩ **12 :** to use force or influence so as to impel **:** cause to go up or down ⟨~ up a rocket⟩ ⟨*sent* prices down⟩ **13 :** to transmit by pulsation ⟨~ a current⟩ ⟨~ blood to the lungs⟩ **14 :** to strike or thrust so as to

impel violently ⟨~ him sprawling⟩ **15 :** to cause to move, travel, or operate usu. in a specified manner ⟨~ the engines full speed ahead⟩ **16 :** TRANSMIT **17 :** to enthrall, delight, or excite esp. by one's performance or personality ⟨trumpet never failed to ~ his listeners⟩ **~** *vi* **1 :** to dispatch an agent or messenger to convey a message or to do an errand **:** dispatch a messenger or missive ⟨~ to one to come⟩ ⟨*sent* to invite her to supper —C.C.Clarke⟩ — often used with *away, off, out* ⟨~ away to the manufacturer for instructions⟩ ⟨*sent* off for a replacement⟩ ⟨~ out and order some coffee and doughnuts⟩ **2 a :** to become carried forward by the impulse of a wave ⟨the ship ~*s* violently⟩ **b :** SCEND **3 :** TRANSMIT **4 :** to perform esp. in jazz improvisation in an inspired or admirable way

syn DISPATCH, FORWARD, TRANSMIT, REMIT, ROUTE, SHIP: SEND is a general term meaning to cause to go toward or to reach a given destination; its varying suggestions are indicated by contexts ⟨*send* an order for the supplies⟩ ⟨*send* gifts to the children⟩ ⟨*send* a letter by special delivery⟩ ⟨*send* a murderer to the electric chair⟩ ⟨he *sent* all his children to college⟩ DISPATCH may suggest speed in sending and heighten notions of specific destination or cause ⟨an ambulance and doctor can be *dispatched* within thirty seconds after a call for aid has been received —*Amer. Guide Series: N.Y. City*⟩ ⟨a messenger was *dispatched* with a reprieve but failed to arrive before the soldier had been shot —*Amer. Guide Series: Conn.*⟩ FORWARD indicates a sending on or forward, usu. of something stopped, delayed, or missent ⟨*forward* a letter⟩ ⟨if sent in a commercial code the censor, before passing it, decodes the message and if he considers that the message might contain a hidden meaning, the cable is never *forwarded* —H.O.Yardley⟩ TRANSMIT is likely to be accompanied by an indication of the force or medium involved in sending ⟨a disease *transmitted* by body lice⟩ ⟨a message *transmitted* by shortwave radio⟩ REMIT may mean a sending back, although this is not its most common meaning today ⟨your account is overdue; please *remit*⟩ ⟨the case was *remitted* to the lower court⟩ ⟨to find himself awakened at the small inn to which he had been *remitted* until morning —Charles Dickens⟩ ROUTE suggests a sending along a determined route, course, or itinerary ⟨heavy trucks being *routed* over a detour avoiding the bridge⟩ ⟨when the four railroads to the Pacific coast were completed, all freight from the West was *routed* through what was called the Minnesota Transfer —*Amer. Guide Series: Minn.*⟩ ⟨mail *routed* to the accounting departments⟩ SHIP is sometimes interchangeable with SEND but is likely to suggest carriage in some specific means of transport, as a ship, train, truck, or plane ⟨she was being *shipped* by her father and her mother to marry the youth across the sea —Francis Hackett⟩ ⟨*ship* freight by rail⟩ ⟨orchids *shipped* by plane⟩

— **send about one's business :** to dismiss summarily or peremptorily — **send for 1 :** to request by message to come or be brought **:** SUMMON ⟨*sent for* the child's mother⟩ ⟨*send for* the doctor⟩ **:** ORDER ⟨*sent for* some stamps on approval⟩ **2 :** to summon (a political leader) to the presence of the sovereign as for the purpose of offering the office of prime minister — **send in one's papers :** RESIGN — **send packing :** to send off roughly or in disgrace **:** DISMISS; *esp* **:** to dismiss unceremoniously ⟨she that she *sends* this young whippersnapper *packing* —Louis Auchincloss⟩ — **send to the rightabout 1 :** to cause (as enemy soldiers) to turn and retreat or flee **2 :** to dismiss or turn away unceremoniously — **send word :** to dispatch (to a person) a message or notification of information ⟨*sent* me *word* to stay within —Shak.⟩

2send \"\ *n* -s **1 a :** the impulse of a wave by which a vessel is carried bodily ⟨borne on the ~ of the sea —H.W.Longfellow⟩ **b :** SCEND 1 **2** *archaic* **:** MESSAGE **3 :** an impetus or accelerating impulse

sen·dai \(ˈ)sen¦dī\ *adj, usu cap* [fr. *Sendai*, Japan] **:** of or from the city of Sendai, Japan **:** of the kind or style prevalent in Sendai

sen·dal *or* **cen·dal** \ˈsendᵊl\ *n* -s [ME, fr. OF *cendal*, fr. ML *sendallum, cendalum*] **:** a thin medieval silk of oriental origin used for fine clothing and church vestments

send away *vt* **1 :** DISPATCH ⟨*send away* a messenger⟩ ⟨*sent* his application *away* in the evening mail⟩ **2 :** to banish from a place ⟨*sent* him *away* for misconduct⟩

send back *vt* **:** to put out (a batsman in cricket)

send down *vt* [ME *senden doun*, fr. *senden* to send + *doun* down] **1 :** to dispatch to a person, body, or place held to be lower (as in rank or status) **2** *Brit* **:** to suspend or expel (a student) from a university

send·ee \(ˈ)sen¦dē\ *n* -s [¹*send* + *-ee*] **:** the person to whom something is sent

send·er \ˈsendə(r)\ *n* -s **:** one that sends ⟨this space for ~'*s* name and address⟩; *esp* **:** a telegraph, telephone, or radio transmitter

send forth *vt* **1 :** to yield as produce **2 :** EXPORT **3 :** PUBLISH

send in *vt* **1 :** to cause to be delivered (as to some central place) ⟨*sent* his contest entry *in* early⟩ ⟨*send in* a letter of complaint⟩; *specif* **:** render (a bill) for payment **2 :** to give (one's name or card) to a servant when making a call **3 :** to send (a player) into an athletic contest ⟨coach *sent* several substitutes *in*⟩

send·ing \ˈsendiŋ, -dēŋ\ *n* -s [ME, fr. gerund of *senden* to send] **1 :** the action of one that sends; *esp* **:** transmission by telegraph or radio **2 :** something sent (as a message or a visitation of a supernatural power)

sending set *n* **:** TRANSMITTING SET

sending station *n* **:** TRANSMITTING STATION

send off *vt* **:** to cause (as a message or a messenger) to go from one **:** DISPATCH ⟨they were late in *sending* their Christmas packages *off*⟩ ⟨hastily *sent off* two ships laden with coin —Sidney Warren⟩

send-off \ˈ=,=\ *n* -s [*send off*] **1 :** a sending off or start given to contestants (as in a race) **2 :** a usu. organized demonstration of goodwill and enthusiasm for the beginning of a new venture (as a trip or a new business) ⟨a crowd of friends gave them a fine *send-off*⟩

send on *vt* **:** to dispatch in advance or from one place to another **:** FORWARD ⟨readdress a letter and *send it on*⟩ ⟨had his baggage *sent on* ahead⟩

send out *vt* [ME *senden out*, fr. *senden* to send + *out*] **1 :** ISSUE ⟨had *sent* the wedding invitations *out*⟩ ⟨*sent out* their final decision on all applications⟩ **2 :** to dispatch (as an order or shipment) from a store or similar establishment

sendout \ˈ=,=\ *n* -s [*send out*] **:** the amount sent out or distributed (as by a dealer) ⟨the daily ~ of gas to these cities varies —*Iron Trade*⟩

send over *vt* [ME *senden over*, fr. *senden* to send + *over*] **:** to dispatch across the sea, through the air, or from one place to another

send round *vt* **1 :** CIRCULATE ⟨a circular is being *sent round* to all the members —E.B.Pusey⟩ **2 :** to dispatch (as a message or a messenger) for some object or purpose

sends *pres 3d sing of* SEND, *pl of* SEND

send up *vt* **1 :** to shoot out or upward **:** give off **:** EMIT, VENT ⟨sparks *sent up* by a fire⟩ ⟨the timbers of the drawbridge *sent up* a booming sound —Rafael Sabatini⟩ **2 a :** to dispatch to a person, body, or place regarded as higher ⟨the master of the inn . . . *sent up* the bill by the waiter —Frederick Marryat⟩ ⟨a bill . . . having been passed by the Commons and *sent up* to the Lords —Herbert Morrison⟩ ⟨not a single appropriations bill has been *sent up* to the president —*N.Y. Times*⟩ **b :** to send (as a schoolboy) to the headmaster for punishment or reward **3 :** to hoist (as a yard) into place ⟨the night pennant is *sent up* at once —C.D.Lane⟩ **4 :** to sentence to imprisonment **:** send to jail ⟨take his revenge on the marshal . . . who *sent* him *up* —*Time*⟩

1sen·e·ca \ˈsenəkə\ *n, pl* **seneca** *or* **senecas** *usu cap* [D *Sennecaas* (pl.), collective name for the Seneca, Oneida, Onondaga, and Cayuga, fr. Mahican *A'sinnika* Oneida, trans. of Iroquois *Onēyóde'*, lit., standing rock] **1 a :** an Iroquoian people of western New York, one of the Five Nations **b :** a member of such people **2 :** the language of the Seneca people

2seneca \"\ *var of* SENEGA

seneca grass *n, usu cap S* [¹*Seneca*] **:** SWEET GRASS 1 b

1sen·e·can \ˈsenəkən\ *adj, usu cap* [Lucius Annaeus *Seneca* †65 A.D. Roman philosopher + E *-an*] **:** of, relating to, or resembling Seneca, his Stoic philosophy, or the characteristics of his writings (as the sententiousness of his prose style or the melodrama, high-flown rhetoric, supernatural machinery, or accumulation of horrors of his tragedies)

2senecan \"\ *adj, usu cap* [fr. *Senecan*, subdivision of the American Devonian, fr. ¹*Seneca* + E *-an*] **:** of, relating to, or constituting a subdivision of the American Devonian — see GEOLOGIC TIME table

seneca oil *n, usu cap S* [¹*Seneca;* fr. its discovery in their territory] **:** a crude petroleum formerly in medicinal use

se·ne·cic acid \sə̇ˈnēsik-\ *n* [NL *Senecio* + E *-ic*] **:** an unsaturated hydroxy dicarboxylic acid $HOC_8H_{13}(COOH)_2$ that occurs combined in alkaloids of plants of the genus *Senecio*

se·ne·cio \sə̇ˈnēs(h)ē,ō\ *n* [NL, fr. L *senecion-, senecio* old man, groundsel (fr. its hoary pappus), fr. *sen-, senic-, senex* old, old man — more at SENIOR] **1** *cap* **:** a genus of very widely distributed herbs, shrubs, and trees (family Compositae) that have alternate or basal leaves and heads composed of both tubular and radiate or only tubular flowers, have the rays mostly yellow and pistillate, and have terete achenes crowned by a pappus of soft white hairs — see CINERARIA, ¹GROUNDSEL **2** -s **:** any plant of the genus *Senecio*

se·ne·ci·o·ic acid \=,==ˈōik-\ *n* [NL *Senecio* + E *-ic*] **:** a crystalline unsaturated fatty acid $(CH_3)_2C{=}CHCOOH$ found esp. in rhizomes of various plants of the genus *Ligularia* but usu. made from isovaleric acid by bromination and treatment with base; β-methyl-crotonic acid or β, β-dimethyl-acrylic acid

se·ne·ci·oid \=ˈ==,ȯid\ *adj* [NL *Senecio* + E *-oid*] **:** of, relating to, or resembling plants of the genus *Senecio*

se·ne·ci·o·nine \=ˈ== ə,nēn, -,nən\ *n* -s [L *senecion-, senecio* groundsel + ISV *-ine*] **:** a poisonous crystalline alkaloid $C_{18}H_{25}NO_5$ in various plants of the genus *Senecio*

se·ne·ci·o·sis \=,==ˈōsə̇s\ *n, pl* **senecio·ses** \-,sēz\ [NL, fr. *Senecio* + *-osis*] **:** a frequently fatal intoxication of livestock feeding on ragworts that is marked by intense acute or chronic necrosis and cirrhosis of the liver

se·nec·ti·tude \sə̇ˈnektə,tüd, -ə,tyüd\ *n* -s [ML *senectitudin-, senectitudo*, irreg. fr. L *senectus* old age (fr. *sen-, senic-, senex* old, old man) + L *-tudin-, -tudo* -tude — more at SENIOR] **:** OLD AGE 1 ⟨the mental changes of senescence and ~ —*Science*⟩

sen·e·cu \ˈsenə,kü\ *n, pl* **senecu** *or* **senecus** *usu cap* **1 :** a Tanoan people occupying a pueblo in New Mexico **2 :** a member of the Senecu people

senecu del sur \-,delˈsü(ə)r\ *n, pl* **senecu del sur** *or* **senecus del sur** *usu cap both Ss* [AmerSp, lit., Senecu of the south] **1 :** a Tanoan people occupying a pueblo in Chihuahua state, Mexico **2 :** a member of the Senecu del Sur people

sen·e·ga \ˈsenə̇gə\ *or* **sen·e·ca** \-ə̇kə\ *n* -s [*senega root*] **1 :** SENEGA ROOT 1 **2 a :** the dried root of senega root containing an irritating saponin **b :** the dried root of a related plant (*Polygala alba*) of the central and southern U.S.

sen·e·gal \¦senə̇¦gȯl, -nē¦g-\ *adj, usu cap* [fr. *Senegal*, state in West Africa] **:** of or from Senegal **:** of the kind or style prevalent in Senegal **:** SENEGALESE

senegal ebony *n, usu cap S* **:** AFRICAN BLACKWOOD

1sen·e·gal·ese \¦senə̇gə¦lēz, -,gȯ¦-, -lēs\ *adj, usu cap* [F *sénégalais*, fr. *Sénégal* Senegal, state in West Africa + F *-ais* -ese] **1 :** of, relating to, or characteristic of Senegal **2 :** of, relating to, or characteristic of the Senegalese

2senegalese \"\ *n, pl* **senegalese** *usu cap* **:** a native or inhabitant of Senegal

senegal gum *n, usu cap S* **:** gum arabic from the vicinity of the Senegal river

senegal mahogany *n, usu cap S* **:** MAHOGANY 1b(1)

1sen·e·gam·bi·an \¦senə̇¦gambēən\ *adj, usu cap* [*Senegambia*, region of the Senegal and Gambia rivers, West Africa + E *-an*] **1 :** of, relating to, or characteristic of Senegambia **2 :** of, relating to, or characteristic of the Senegambians

2senegambian \"\ *n* -s *cap* **:** a native or inhabitant of the region of Senegambia in West Africa

sen·e·ga root \ˈsenə̇gə-\ *or* **senega snakeroot** *or* **sen·e·ka root** \-nəkə-\ *or* **seneka snakeroot** *n* [alter. of ¹*Seneca;* fr. its use by the Seneca as a remedy against snakebite] **1 :** a No. American milkwort (*Polygala senega*) having tufted leafy stems terminated by small white flowers **2 :** SENEGA 2a

sen·e·gin \ˈsenə̇jə̇n\ *n* -s [G, fr. NL *senega* (specific epithet of *Polygala senega* senega root, fr. E *senega*) + G *-in*] **:** a saponin obtained from senega root as an amorphous yellow powder

se·nesce \sə̇ˈnes\ *vi* -ED/-ING/-S [L *senescere*, incho. of *senēre* to be old, fr. *sen-, senex* old, old man — more at SENIOR] **:** to grow old **:** WITHER ⟨growing and *senescing* leaves —J.J.Kennedy⟩

se·nes·cence \sə̇ˈnesᵊn(t)s\ *n* -s [fr. *senescent*, after such pairs as E *benevolent: benevolence*] **1 :** the quality or state of being senescent ⟨clinical problems of later maturity, ~, and senility —*Therapeutic Notes*⟩ ⟨racial ~⟩ **2 :** the phase of plant growth that extends from full maturity to actual death and is characterized by an accumulation of metabolic products, increase in respiratory rate, and a loss in dry weight esp. in leaves and fruits

se·nes·cent \-sᵊnt\ *adj* [L *senescent-, senescens*, pres. part. of *senescere* to grow old] **1 :** growing old **:** AGING ⟨~ persons⟩ ⟨a ~ animal⟩ **2 :** of, relating to, or characteristic of one that is aging or obsolescent ⟨~ arthritis⟩ ⟨~ mannerisms⟩ ⟨~ tools⟩ ⟨a ~ industrial system⟩

sen·e·schal \ˈsenə̇shəl\ *n* -s [ME, fr. MF, of Gmc origin; akin to OHG *senescalh* eldest servant, fr. *sene-* old (akin to Goth *sineigs* old) + *scalh, scalc* servant — more at SENIOR, MARSHAL] **1 :** a bailiff, steward, or majordomo of a great medieval lord or king representing the lord (as in the feudal courts, in the management of his estate, and in the superintendence of feasts and domestic ceremonies) and in a royal household often becoming a high officer of state or military commander **2 a :** an administrative or judicial officer (as a governor) in a city or province **b :** a minor judicial officer in Sark

sen·e·schal·ship \-,ship\ *n* [*seneschal* + *-ship*] **:** SENESCHALSY

sen·e·schal·sy \-,sē, -si\ *n* -ES [ME *seneschalcie*, fr. MF, fr. ML *senescalcia*, fr. *senescalcus* seneschal (fr. OHG *senescalh*) + L *-ia* -y] **1 :** a district under a seneschal ⟨the old royal administrative divisions of bailliages and seneschalsies —D.W.S.Lidderdale⟩ **2 :** the office of a seneschal

sen·et *or* **sen·net** \ˈsenə̇t\ *n* -s [origin unknown] **:** any of several barracudas

seng·i·er·ite \ˈseŋēə,rīt\ *n* -s [Edgard *Sengier*, 20th cent. Belgian mine official + E *-ite*] **:** a mineral $Cu(UO_2)(VO_4)(OH).4H_2O(?)$ consisting of a hydrous basic vanadate of copper and uranyl

sen·green \ˈsen,grēn\ *n* [ME *singrene*, fr. OE *singrēne*, fr. *singrēne* evergreen, fr. *sin-* one, always (akin to L *sem-* one) + *grēne* green — more at SAME, GREEN] **1 :** any of several plants of the genus *Sedum; esp* **:** HOUSELEEK **2** *also* **sengreen saxifrage :** any of several saxifrages; *esp* **:** YELLOW MOUNTAIN SAXIFRAGE **3 :** ¹PERIWINKLE 1a

se·nhor \sə̇nˈyō(ə)r\ *n, pl* **senhors** \-ō(ə)rz\ *or* **senho·res** \-ōrēs(h), -ēz(h)\ [Pg, fr. ML *senior* superior, magnate, lord, fr. L, adj., elder — more at SENIOR] **1 :** MISTER — used as a title of courtesy prefixed to the name of a Portuguese or Brazilian man **2 :** a Portuguese or Brazilian man

se·nho·ra \-ˈrə\ *n* -s [Pg, fem. of *senhor*] **1 :** MISTRESS — used as a title prefixed to the name of a married Portuguese or Brazilian woman **2 :** a married Portuguese or Brazilian woman

se·nho·ri·ta \,senyəˈrēd·ə\ *n* -s [Pg, dim. of *senhora*] **1 :** MISS — used as a title prefixed to the name of an unmarried Portuguese or Brazilian woman **2 :** an unmarried Portuguese or Brazilian woman

sen·i·jex·tee \¦senə,jek¦stē\ *n, pl* **senijextee** *or* **senijextees** *usu cap* **1 a :** a Salishan people of the Columbia river valley in Washington and British Columbia **b :** a member of such people **2 :** a dialect of Okanagon

1senile \ˈsē,nīl *also* ˈse,- *sometimes* -nᵊl *or* -(,)nil\ *adj* [L *senilis*, fr. *sen-, senex* old, old man + *-ilis* -ile — more at SENIOR] **1 :** of, relating to, or characteristic of old age ⟨~ weakness⟩ ⟨~ decay⟩ ⟨~ wisdom⟩ **2 a :** showing the characteristics of old age **:** AGED ⟨a ~ porter still handling baggage⟩ ⟨shoes that looked positively ~⟩ **b :** marked by the weakness of old age **:** DECREPIT ⟨a ~ person⟩ ⟨a ~ empire⟩; *esp* **:** exhibiting a loss of mental faculties associated with old age **:** DODDERING ⟨the oldest man and woman of the group are regarded as the ultimate authority, if they are not ~ —E.H. Spicer⟩ **3 :** approaching the end of a geological cycle of erosion ⟨a ~ topography⟩ ⟨a ~ river⟩

2senile \"\ *n* -s **:** a senile person **:** DOTARD 1b

senile atrophy *n* **:** the atrophy occurring with old age

senile cataract *n* **:** a cataract of a type that occurs in the aged and is characterized by an initial opacity in the lens, subsequent swelling of the lens, and final shrinkage with complete loss of transparency

senile dementia *n* **:** SENILE PSYCHOSIS

senile deterioration *n* **:** SENILE PSYCHOSIS

senile gangrene *n* **:** gangrene due to lack of blood supply resulting from sclerosis of blood vessels

senile·ly \-(l)lē, -li\ *adv* **:** in a senile manner ⟨chatters ~ —Rudyard Kipling⟩

senile psychosis *n* **:** a severe mental disorder of the aged that is manifested by loss of memory, judgment, and moral and aesthetic values, is often accompanied by confusion, irrational ideas, and disturbed emotionality, and commonly results from organic changes in the brain

se·nil·i·ty \sə̇ˈniləd·ē, seˈn-, -lətē, -i *also* seˈn-\ *n* -ES [¹*senile* + *-ity*] **:** the quality or state of being senile: as **a :** OLD AGE **b :** DOTAGE 1a, SENILE PSYCHOSIS

1sen·ior \ˈsēnyə(r)\ *n* -s [ME, fr. L, *senior* older, elder] **1 a :** an elderly or old person ⟨know how to make us ~*s* very unnecessary —R.W.Emerson⟩ ⟨the ~*s* were active in the local affairs —Roy Lewis & Angus Maude⟩ **b :** a person accorded distinction or deference in respect for his age **:** ³ELDER 3 **c :** one who is older than another ⟨throwt among his ~*s* in the upper grades of the school⟩ **d** *Brit* **:** a student in a senior school **2 a :** a person holding a position of higher standing in a hierarchy of ranks ⟨as his ~ he would of course command the entire force —H.E.Scudder⟩ **b :** a senior fellow of a college at an English university; *specif* **:** a member of a governing council of a college (as at Trinity College, Cambridge) **c :** HEAD BOY **d :** a student in his last year before graduating from an educational institution of secondary or higher level ⟨a high school ~⟩ ⟨college ~*s*⟩ ⟨a ~ in law school⟩ **3 :** a sexually mature animal **4 :** ELDEST HAND; *specif* **:** the player at the left of the declarer in bridge

2senior \"\ *adj* [ME, fr. L, compar. of *sen-, senex* old; akin to Goth *sineigs* old, *sinista* eldest, ON *sina* old grass, Gk *henos* old, Skt *sana*] **1 a :** more advanced in age than another **:** OLDER ⟨~ to her classmate by a full year⟩ ⟨having to support . . . human creatures ~ and junior to themselves —F.L.Allen⟩ — abbr. *Sr* or *sr;* used chiefly and often cap. to distinguish a father with the same given name as his son; opposed to *junior* **b :** advanced in age **:** ELDERLY ⟨too ~ to begin to try for Cabinet office —John Buchan⟩ ⟨furnish our ~ citizens . . . the cost of a decent standard of living —L.H.Keyserling⟩ **c :** earliest in date of origin or founding ⟨piracy, one of the ~ sins of the human race —George Woodbury⟩ ⟨the ~ organization of its kind —Thurston Dart⟩ **d :** ranking above another in length of service ⟨the ~ senator of the state⟩ ⟨the ~ members of the committee⟩; *specif* **:** having more seniority than another ⟨the most ~ airline pilots flying on the more desirable assignments —H.R.Northrup⟩ **2 a :** higher in standing or rank esp. in a hierarchy of ranks **:** SUPERIOR ⟨the ~ scholars of the university⟩ ⟨lieutenant ~ grade⟩ ⟨~ scientists⟩ ⟨the more ~ the officer, the more time he has —G.S.Patton⟩ ⟨young for so ~ a post —William Ridsdale⟩ **b :** associated with one or more others in a leading or primary role ⟨~ partner⟩ ⟨~ member of a law firm⟩; *specif* **:** mentioned first and given major credit among collaborating authors (as of a scientific paper) ⟨the name of the ~ author will be widely recognized —Paul Woodring⟩ **3 :** of or relating to seniors in an educational institution ⟨the ~ class⟩ ⟨the ~ prom⟩ **4 a** *of a bond* **:** having a lien preference prior to other bonds **b** *of a preferred stock* **:** having a dividend preference prior to other stocks ⟨a ~ security⟩

senior captain *n* [²*senior*] **:** a Salvationist officer ranking above a captain and below a major

senior chief petty officer *n* **:** a noncommissioned naval officer rating just below a master chief petty officer and above a chief petty officer

senior classic *n* **:** a man obtaining the highest honors in the classical tripos at Cambridge University — compare SENIOR MORALIST, SENIOR WRANGLER

senior college *n* [¹*senior*] **1 :** a college offering the regular four-year course traditionally required for a bachelor's degree — contrasted with *junior college* **2 :** the upper division or last two years of a 4-year college

senior common room *n* **:** a common room at a British college reserved for the use of fellows and members of the teaching staff

senior girl scout *or* **senior scout** *n* **:** a girl scout in the age group ranging approximately from 14 through 17 years

senior high school *also* **senior high** *n* **:** a secondary school usu. public-supported that is organized on a 3-year basis to comprise grades 10 through 12 and usu. includes several divisions (as college preparatory, commercial, general) — contrasted with *junior high school*

se·nior·i·ty \sēnˈyȯrəd·ē, -ˈyär-, -rətē, -i\ *n* -ES *often attrib* [ML *senioritat-, senioritas*, fr. L *senior* + *-itat-, -itas* -ity] **1 :** the quality or state of being senior **:** priority esp. of birth, office, or service ⟨next in ~ of age —Philip O'Connor⟩ ⟨the historical ~ of the experimental field —B.F.Skinner⟩; *specif* **:** a status attained by length of continuous service (as in a company, institution, or organization or in a department, job, rank, or occupational group) to which are attached by custom or prior collective agreement various rights or privileges (as preference in tenure, priority in promotion, and choice of work or shift) on the basis of ranking relative to others ⟨arguments over the relative weight to be given to ~ and ability —Dale Yoder⟩ ⟨~ system⟩ ⟨~ list⟩ ⟨~ rights⟩ **2** *often cap* **:** the body of senior fellows of a British college ⟨a matter brought before the ~⟩

seniority rule *n* **1 :** a rule in the U.S. Congress by which members have their choice of committee assignments in order of rank based solely on length of service **2 :** a rule in the U.S. Congress by which the member of the majority party who has served longest on a committee receives the chairmanship

seniority unit *n* **:** the unit (as department, plant, company) within which an employee may exercise his seniority rights

senior major *n* [²*senior*] **:** a Salvationist officer ranking above a major and below a brigadier

senior master sergeant *n* **:** a noncommissioned officer in the air force rating just below a chief master sergeant and above a master sergeant

senior matriculation *n* [¹*senior*] **:** a certificate awarded to a high school graduate in Canada for successfully completing at a high school a year of additional studies chiefly of college grade — compare JUNIOR MATRICULATION

senior moralist *n* [²*senior*] **:** a student obtaining the highest honors in the moral sciences tripos at Cambridge University — compare SENIOR CLASSIC, SENIOR WRANGLER

senior optime *n* **:** a man in the optime class at Cambridge University

senior school *n* [¹*senior*] **:** a part of the British school system serving children from 14 to 17 years of age — compare INTERMEDIATE SCHOOL, JUNIOR SCHOOL

senior security *n* [²*senior*] **:** a security having priority over another ⟨mortgage bonds and preferred stocks are *senior securities* compared to debentures and common stocks respectively⟩

senior soldier *n* **:** an enrolled member of the Salvation Army aged 14 years or older

senior sophister *n* [¹*senior*] *archaic* **:** a university student in his last undergraduate year — compare SENIOR 2d

senior wrangler *n* [²*senior*] **:** a man obtaining the highest honors in the mathematical tripos at Cambridge University and ranking first among the wranglers — compare SENIOR CLASSIC, SENIOR MORALIST

senior yearling *n* **:** an animal of an age between 18 and 24 months on a specified date of the year (as Aug. 1) established by rules for livestock exhibits of the season

sen·it *also* **sen't** *or* **sen·at** \ˈsenə̇t\ *n* -s [Egypt *snjt*] **:** a game of ancient Egyptian origin that resembles backgammon

se·ni·um \ˈsēnēəm\ *n* -s [L, fr. *sen-, senex* old, old man — more at SENIOR] **:** OLD AGE 1

[1]sen·na \'senə\ *n* -s [NL, fr. Ar *sanā*] **1 :** a plant of the genus *Cassia; esp* **:** a plant of this genus having medical use **2 :** the dried leaflets of various sennas (esp. *Cassia acutifolia* and *C. angustifolia*) used in medicine as a purgative — see ALEXANDRIA SENNA, TINNEVELLY SENNA

[2]senna *also* **seh·na** \"\ *n* -s *usu cap* [fr. *Sinneh*, town of northwest Iran] **:** a usu. small Persian rug having a very fine weave with short pile harsh and sandy to the touch and small allover patterns and subdued colors

sennachie *var of* SHANACHIE

senna knot *usu cap S, var of* SEHNA KNOT

senna tree *n* [[1]*senna*] **:** a tropical American tree (*Cassia emarginata*) with showy axillary clusters of yellow flowers

sen·ne·grass *also* **saen·ne·grass** \'senə+,-\ *n* [part trans. of Norw *sennegress*] **:** a widely distributed sedge (*Carex vesicaria*) with grasslike leaves that is used by arctic and antarctic explorers as insulating material

[1]sen·net \'senət\ *or* **sin·net** \'sin-\ *n* -s [prob. alter. of *signet*] **:** a signal call on a trumpet or cornet for entrance or exit on the stage

[2]sennet *var of* SENNIT

sen·nett's oriole \'senəts-\ *or* **sennett's hooded oriole** *n, usu cap S* [after George B. *Sennett* †1900 Am. ornithologist] **:** HOODED ORIOLE

sen·night *also* **se'n·night** \'se,nīt, -,nət\ *n* [ME *sevenight, sennight*, fr. OE *seofon nihta* seven nights] *archaic* **:** the space of seven nights and days **:** WEEK ⟨the rest . . . were to be heard this day *se'nnight* —Samuel Pepys⟩ ⟨on Sunday *se'nnight* . . . died by a fall —Thomas Gray⟩

sen·nit *also* **sen·at** \'senət\ *usu* -əd·+V\ *or* **sin·net** \'sin-\ *n* -s [perh. fr. F *coussinet* pad, mat, dim. of *coussin* cushion; fr. its use to protect cables from fraying — more at CUSHION] **1 :** a braided cord or fabric of plaited rope yarns or other small stuff **2 :** a straw or grass braid for hats; *esp* **:** a rice straw braid for men's stiff straw hats

se·no·nian \sə'nōnēən, -nyən\ *adj, usu cap* [F *sénonien*, fr. L *Senones*, ancient people of central Gaul + F *-ien* -ian] **:** of or relating to a subdivision of the European Cretaceous — see GEOLOGIC TIME table

se·nor *or* **se·ñor** \(')sān'yō(ə)r, sēn'y-\ *n, pl* **senors** \-ō(ə)rz\ *or* **señores** \-yō(,)rās, -yō(-\ [Sp, fr. ML *senior* superior, magnate, lord, fr. L, adj., elder — more at SENIOR] **1 :** MISTER — used as a title of courtesy prefixed to the name of a Spanish or Spanish-speaking man **2 :** a Spanish or Spanish-speaking man

se·no·ra *or* **se·ño·ra** \sān'yōrə, sēn-, -yȯrə\ *n* -s [Sp, fem. of *señor*] **1 :** MISTRESS — used as a title prefixed to the name of a married Spanish or Spanish-speaking woman **2 :** a married Spanish or Spanish-speaking woman

se·no·ri·ta *or* **se·ño·ri·ta** \,sānyə'rēd·ə, ,sēn-, -ētə\ *n* -s [Sp, dim. of *señora*] **1 a :** MISS — used as a title prefixed to the name of an unmarried Spanish or Spanish-speaking woman **b :** an unmarried Spanish or Spanish-speaking woman **2 :** a slender compressed cream and brown wrasse (*Oxyjulis californica*) of the California coast

senr *abbr* senior

sensa *pl of* SENSUM

[1]sensate *adj* [LL *sensatus*, fr. L *sensus* sense + *-atus* -ate] **:** endowed with sense or sensation

[2]sen·sate \'sen,sāt\ *vt* -ED/-ING/-S [back-formation fr. *sensation*] **:** to feel or apprehend through a sense or the senses

[3]sensate \", *usu* -ād·+V\ *adj* [ML *sensatus* perceived by sense, fr. L, endowed with sense] **1 :** felt or apprehended through a sense or the senses **2 :** preoccupied with or exclusively directed toward that which can be experienced through a sense modality **:** MATERIALISTIC — **sen·sate·ly** *adv*

sen·sa·tion \sen'sāshən, sən'-\ *n* -s [ML *sensation-, sensatio*, fr. LL *sensatus* endowed with sense + L *-ion-, -io* -ion] **1 a :** a state of consciousness produced by impingement of an external object or condition upon the body **b :** a mode of mental functioning referable to immediate stimulation of the body from without; *often* **:** such a mode of mental functioning as distinguished from the conscious awareness of the process **c :** the direct, immediate, and not further analyzable awareness (as of heat or pain) resulting from adequate stimulation of a receptor organ in a living organism **d** (1) **:** awareness endopsychic in origin and not the immediate result of sensory stimulation (2) **:** a state of consciousness of a kind usu. caused by physical objects or internal bodily changes but having no physical source **2 a :** a more or less indefinite bodily feeling **b :** a particular emotional feeling **3 a :** an internal organic stimulus **b :** a physical object or something that provides awareness of a physical object **c :** an object (as an afterimage or hallucination) of an endopsychic process of sensation **4 a** (1) **:** a state of excited interest or feeling ⟨his death created quite a ~⟩ (2) **:** the cause of such a state ⟨the new soprano was the ~ of the season⟩ **b :** a vivid emotion or experience attended by excitement **5 :** the use of sensational matter or the evoking of sensational reactions as an effect in art

syn SENSE, FEELING, SENSIBILITY: SENSATION, as here discussed, may center attention on perception through or as if through the sense organs, with or without comprehension, cognition, or other intellectual or emotional reaction ⟨now that he was by her side, she felt his nearness intimately, like a touch. She tried to disregard this *sensation* —Joseph Conrad⟩ ⟨the sweet *sensations* of returning health made me happy for a time; but such *sensations* seldom outlast convalescence —W.H. Hudson †1922⟩ ⟨still he would drink, only instead of port it must be brandy to lash his flagging palate into *sensation* —Virginia Woolf⟩ SENSE may indicate only a sensation or sensory perception; it may indicate a more intellectual cognition marked by full awareness or consciousness ⟨his first consciousness was a *sense* of the light dry wind blowing in through the windows —Willa Cather⟩ ⟨never since the age of seven had he been able to look on feminine beauty without a *sense* of warmth and faint excitement —John Galsworthy⟩ ⟨solaced, even in your chagrin, by a *sense* of injured innocence —B.N.Cardozo⟩ FEELING may indicate the sense of touch, along with awareness to pressure and temperature; it may indicate a complex of sensation, emotion, and thought experienced as a reaction to a situation ⟨some people itch more easily than others because their threshold for *feeling* in the skin is lower than that of other people —Morris Fishbein⟩ ⟨a deep sensation of cold, compounded with deep pressure — in short, a numb *feeling* — persisted even when the skin itself had ceased to deliver the sensation of cold —R.S. Woodworth⟩ ⟨it wasn't raining but there was the *feeling* of its being a rainy night —R.H.Newman⟩ ⟨serious danger that a *feeling* of futility and despair would spread over the continent like a creeping paralysis —Vera M. Dean⟩ SENSIBILITY may suggest power to respond, often a capacity for delicate appreciation or a lively responsiveness to impression, sometimes sentimental, forced, or affected ⟨the extreme *sensibility* to physical suffering which characterizes modern civilization —W.R.Inge⟩ ⟨she was a creature of palpitating *sensibility*, with feelings so delicate that they responded to every breath —S.M.Crothers⟩

sen·sa·tion·al \-shənᵊl, -shnəl\ *adj* **1 :** of or relating to sensation or the senses **:** having or characterized by sensation **:** involving, depending on, or inducing sensations **2 a :** arousing or suited or designed to arouse a quick, intense, and usu. superficial emotional response ⟨a ~ news report⟩ ⟨a ~ play⟩ ⟨~ crime reporting⟩ **b :** capturing attention or interest **:** ARRESTING, SPECTACULAR ⟨her ~ private life kept her continually before the public —*Amer. Guide Series: La.*⟩ ⟨fantastically ~, simply beautiful and good stonecutting —Willa Cather⟩ **c :** EXTRAORDINARY, PHENOMENAL ⟨a ~ rookie⟩ ⟨a ~ comeback from major to major general —*Time*⟩ **3 :** of or relating to sensationalism ⟨the ~ school⟩

sen·sa·tion·al·ism \-shənᵊl,izəm, -shnə,li-\ *n* -s [*sensational* + *-ism*] **1 a :** sensational subject matter or treatment of subject matter or the use of such matter or treatment (as in a literary or dramatic work) ⟨the story is told without swagger or ~ —Margaret Hexter⟩ ⟨the ~ of the daily press⟩ **b :** the effect of such subject matter or treatment ⟨the desire for ~ for its own sake, as sometimes fulfilled in news of sex and crime, must be placed very low in the scale —F.L Mott⟩ **2 :** a doctrine in ethics that postulates feeling as the sole criterion of good; SENSUALISM **3 :** a doctrine in philosophy that postulates the origin of all our knowledge in sensation or sense perceptions; *also* **:** the view that all knowledge is made up of sense elements — contrasted with *rationalism;* compare ASSOCIATIONISM, EMPIRICISM **4 :** SENSATIONISM 2

sen·sa·tion·al·ist \-ləst\ *n* -s [*sensational* + *-ist*] **1 a :** one who seeks to make sensations **b :** one who practices sensationalism (as in writing) **2 :** an advocate of or believer in ethical or philosophical sensationalism

sen·sa·tion·al·is·tic \=;=shənᵊl'istik, -shnə,l-\ *adj* **:** of or relating to sensationalists or sensationalism

sen·sa·tion·al·ize \=ˈ=shənᵊl,īz, -shnə,līz\ *vt* -ED/-ING/-S *see -ize in Explan Notes* [*sensational* + *-ize*] **:** to present in a sensational manner **:** give an effect of sensationalism to ⟨~ a problem⟩

sen·sa·tion·al·ly \-nᵊlē, -nəlē, -li\ *adv* **:** in a sensational manner

sen·sa·tion·ism \=ˈ=shə,nizəm\ *n* -s [*sensation* + *-ism*] **1 :** SENSATIONALISM 3 **2 :** a system of psychology based upon sensations as the constituent elements of all conscious experience

[1]sen·sa·tion·ist \-,nəst\ *n* -s [*sensation* + *-ist*] **:** SENSATIONALIST

[2]sensationist \"\ *also* **sen·sa·tion·is·tic** \=;=;=ˈnistik\ *adj* [*sensationist* fr. [1]*sensationist; sensationistic* fr. [1]*sensationist* + *-ic*] **:** SENSATIONALISTIC

sen·sa·tion·less \=ˈ=ləs\ *adj* **:** producing or responding to no sensation

sensation level *n* **:** the range of intensity of sound vibrations in which they are perceived as sound **:** the range between the threshold of audibility and that of feeling usu. expressed in decibels

sensation–monger \=ˈ=,=,=\ *n* **:** a purveyor of the sensational (as in literature)

sensations *pl of* SENSATION

sen·sa·to·ry \'sen(t)sə,tōrē, -tȯr-, -ri\ *adj* [[2]*sensate* + *-ory*] **:** SENSORY

[1]sense \'sen(t)s\ *n* -s [MF or L; MF *sens*, fr. L *sensus* sensation, feeling, understanding, signification, fr. *sensus*, past part. of *sentire* to perceive, feel, suppose: akin to OHG *sin* mind, sense, *sinnan* to travel, strive after, *sind* journey, road — more at SEND] **1 :** something to be grasped, comprehended, known **:** SIGNIFICATION: as **a :** one of the multifold (as literal, anagogic, allegorical, tropological) meanings considered present in the Bible or in allegorical writings (as the Divine Comedy) **b** (1) **:** the particular meaning intended (as by a writer or speaker) ⟨you miss my ~ —Shak.⟩ ⟨the addition corrupted the ~ of the passage⟩ (2) **:** the one of two or more literal meanings by which a word or passage may rationally be construed in context ⟨there can be but one ~ here⟩ ⟨the context will not admit of such a ~⟩ **c** (1) **:** an interpretation that may be given to a group of words forming a passage **:** the meaning of such a group as a functional unit ⟨I did not understand him in that ~⟩ ⟨learned the speech by heart and missed the ~ entirely⟩ (2) **:** general or essential meaning of an utterance **:** SUBSTANCE, GIST ⟨the ~ of the decision was presented in a summary⟩ ⟨give the ~ of his argument⟩ **d :** the meaning of a word or fixed phrase or one of the distinct meanings that it may bear in diverse situations; *esp* **:** a meaning of a word as segregated in a dictionary or glossary **e :** meaning that is rational or intelligible ⟨he speaks ~ —Shak.⟩ **f :** prose supplied to a student for expression in Greek or Latin verse **2 a :** a mechanism or faculty of perception **:** (1) **:** the faculty of receiving mental impressions through the action of sense organs of the body or of perceiving changes in the condition of the body — not often used technically (2) **:** any special faculty of sensation ⟨spiritual and occult ~*s*⟩ (3) **:** a specialized mechanism or function by virtue of which an animal is receptive and responsive to a particular stimulus or class of stimuli either arising externally (as in the case of the senses of sight, hearing, smell, taste, touch, temperature, or pain) or internally (as in the case of the kinesthetic and organic senses) (4) **:** the total function comprising the several sensory mechanisms regarded as a unit distinct from other functions (as of movement or thought) ⟨knowledge derived from ~⟩ ⟨~ experience⟩ **b** *obs* **:** SENSE ORGAN **c :** power or means of perception **:** capacity to perceive and interpret stimuli **:** CONSCIOUSNESS, SANITY — usu. used in pl. ⟨lose her ~*s*⟩ ⟨his ~*s* were clear to the last⟩ **d** (1) **:** power of interpolating or deducing from observations or unnoted stimuli in respect to a particular field or relation ⟨a ~ of time⟩ ⟨a good ~ of location⟩ (2) **:** instinctive comprehension (as of fine points) and acuteness or resourcefulness in gaining mastery or success in respect to a particular thing (as an art or a game or medium) ⟨keen musical ~⟩ ⟨a natural language ~⟩ ⟨a born flier with a real air ~⟩ (3) **:** a faculty for intellectual and aesthetic grasp and appreciation ⟨a ~ of beauty⟩ **3 :** awareness or perception arrived at through or as if through interpretation of sensory stimuli: as **a :** perception by means of the intellect **:** understanding or discerning awareness or comprehension **:** APPRECIATION ⟨a good ~ of values⟩ **b** (1) **:** an awareness or feeling of a particular nature resulting from a particular stimulus ⟨a ~ of well-being⟩ ⟨a sudden ~ of warmth on entering the house⟩ (2) **:** a vague and unanalyzable but persistent awareness or feeling ⟨had a ~ that the child was in danger⟩ ⟨a ~ of insecurity⟩ (3) **:** a sensitive and usu. sympathetic or grateful recognition ⟨a ~ of God's mercies⟩ (4) **:** a self-conscious motivating awareness or conviction ⟨a ~ of shame⟩ ⟨tried to control his ~ of injury⟩ (5) **:** a moral awareness or appreciation **:** recognition based on established usage or in accordance with normal behavior ⟨utterly careless and lacking any ~ of responsibility⟩ **c** (1) **:** perception by means of the senses and esp. when aesthetic or emotional in content or orientation ⟨shall reason yield to mere ~⟩ (2) **:** an avenue of sensory perception — usu. used in pl. ⟨feast the ~*s* on that scene of delight⟩ **4 :** something that is felt or held as a sentiment, view, or opinion — used chiefly of groups of persons ⟨the ~ of the meeting⟩ **5 a :** MIND, SENTIENCE, INTELLIGENCE ⟨as if the steel had ~ —Edmund Spenser⟩ **b :** sound mental capacity often marked by shrewd practical understanding ⟨a man of ~⟩ ⟨had ~ enough to win⟩; *also* **:** something that is based on or typical of such sense **:** a logical, sensible, or practical thing, act, or way of doing ⟨no ~ in waiting⟩ ⟨your decision makes ~⟩ **6** [F *sens*, of Gmc origin; akin to OHG *sinnan* to travel, strive after] **a :** a direction in which something (as motion) takes place or is visualized as taking place **:** TREND, COURSE **b :** one of two opposite directions in which a line, surface, or region may be supposed to be described by the motion of a point, line, or surface — symbolically denoted respectively by + and —

syn COMMON SENSE, GOOD SENSE, HORSE SENSE, JUDGMENT, WISDOM, GUMPTION: SENSE, as herein treated, indicates an accustomed steady ability to judge and decide between possible courses with intelligence and soundness ⟨the only one that has any *sense* in that family —Margaret Deland⟩ ⟨whose practical *sense* equaled his intuitive genius —Henry Adams⟩ COMMON SENSE, GOOD SENSE, and HORSE SENSE add only slight additional suggestions to SENSE, COMMON SENSE suggesting ordinary good judgment and prudence without sophistication, learning, or special knowledge, GOOD SENSE implying an especial perception of circumstances and soundness in analysis, HORSE SENSE connoting a blending of sense with hard, plain, uncultured shrewdness or depth of observation ⟨freedom with *common-sense* regulations that any sensible man may be expected to observe —H.S.Commager⟩ ⟨the main attribute required is a certain balance of experience, prudence and sympathy which is generally called *common sense* —*Economist*⟩ ⟨the tall young king went through the long, intricate, and exhausting service with dignity and *good sense*, and added meaning to much of the symbolism by his understanding of it —*Manchester Guardian Weekly*⟩ ⟨possessed . . . good *horse sense*, which was at times more valuable than the complex conceptions put forth by the party and its leading theoreticians —D.J.Dallin⟩ JUDGMENT involves notions of sense refined and tempered by experience, maturity, training, or discipline to discern coolly and judge soundly in difficult matters ⟨the ultimate test of true worth . . . is the trained *judgment* of the good and sensible man —G. L.Dickinson⟩ ⟨that all shrewdness of speculation had given place to shrewdness of practical *judgment* based on very definite experience —John Galsworthy⟩ WISDOM, of these synonyms the one indicating highest praise, suggests great soundness, sagacity, and insight, the result of blending together common sense, wit, experience, maturity, learning, and understanding ⟨*wisdom*, she saw at last, was knowledge plus vision —Helen Howe⟩ ⟨*wisdom* is a kind of knowledge. It is knowledge of the nature, career and consequences of human values. Since these cannot be separated from the human organism and the social scene, the moral ways of man cannot be understood without knowledge of the ways of things and institutions —Sidney Hook⟩ GUMPTION, like HORSE SENSE in being informal in suggestion, may connote a combination of clever common sense and initiative or drive, especially the latter in today's English ⟨a man's common sense means his good judgment, his freedom from eccentricity, his *gumption* —William James⟩ **syn** see in addition SENSATION

— **in a sense** *adv* **:** according to an interpretation other than the most natural or obvious though possibly admissible under particular circumstances ⟨it was true *in a sense*⟩

[2]sense \"\ *vt* -ED/-ING/-S **1 a :** to perceive by the senses **b :** to have consciousness of **:** feel the imminence or presence of **:** ANTICIPATE ⟨~ danger⟩ ⟨*sensed* a flaw in the reasoning⟩ **2** *obs* **a :** to give the sense or meaning of **:** EXPOUND **b :** TEST, EXAMINE, ANALYZE **3 :** to get the meaning of **:** GRASP, COMPREHEND, REALIZE ⟨did not ~ his meaning⟩ **4 :** to become aware of without express communication ⟨*sensed* her dislike⟩ **5 :** to estimate the position of burst of (a round or a shot) with reference to a target **6 :** to detect (a symbol) automatically or mechanically ⟨computing machines that ~ the holes in tabulating cards with appropriately spaced steel pins⟩

sense cell *n* **:** a receptor cell of a sense organ; *esp* **:** an isolated cell constituting the receptor mechanism of a sense organ

sensed \'sen(t)st\ *adj* [[1]*sense* + *-ed*] **:** invested with sense of a specified kind — usu. used in combination ⟨a keen-*sensed* observer⟩

sense–datum \'=ˈ=,=\ *n, pl* **sense–data :** an immediate unanalyzable private object of sensation ⟨a sharp pain, an afterimage, or a round coin experienced as an ellipse is a *sense-datum*⟩

sense–datum language *n* **:** a language whose terms refer exclusively to sense-data and their properties or relations — contrasted with *thing-language*

sense finder *n* **:** a portion of a radio direction finder by which the sense of the direction is determined

sense·ful \'=fəl\ *adj* **:** full of sense **:** SIGNIFICANT, JUDICIOUS

sense impression *n* **:** a psychical and physiological effect resulting directly from the excitation of a sense organ **:** SENSATION

[1]sense·less \'=ləs\ *adj* **:** destitute of, deficient in, or contrary to sense: as **a :** lacking sensibility or feeling **:** INSENSIBLE, UNCONSCIOUS; *also* **:** incapable of sensation or perception **b** *archaic* **:** having no consciousness **c :** deficient in knowledge, appreciation, or reasoning power **:** STUPID **d :** lacking good sense **:** UNWISE, UNREASONABLE, NONSENSICAL **e :** proceeding from or characterized by lack of intelligence or meaning **:** FOOLISH, PURPOSELESS, MEANINGLESS ⟨a ~ custom⟩ — **sense·less·ly** *adv* — **sense·less·ness** *n* -ES

[2]senseless *adv, obs* **:** SENSELESSLY

sensemaking \'=;=,=\ *adj* **:** that makes sense **:** SENSIBLE, REASONABLE, PRACTICABLE ⟨a ~ proposal⟩

sense of humor : the faculty of perceiving and appreciating the humorous; *sometimes* **:** addiction to buffoonery and witticisms ⟨has a great *sense of humor* — always kidding⟩

sense organ *or* **sensory organ** *n* **:** a bodily structure that is affected by a stimulus (as heat or sound waves) in such a manner as to initiate a wave of excitation in associated sensory nerve fibers which conveys specific impulses to the central nervous system where they are interpreted as corresponding sensations (as of warmth or sound) **:** RECEPTOR

sense perception *n* **:** perception by the senses as distinguished from intellectual perception

sense pore *n* **:** a sense organ contained in a cuticular pit of an arthropod

sens·er \'sen(t)sə(r)\ *n* -s **:** one that senses something

sense rod *n* **:** a terminal filament on the sense cell of some insect sense organs

senses *pl of* SENSE, *pres 3d sing of* SENSE

sense stress *n* **:** SENTENCE STRESS

sense–world \'=;=\ *n* **:** the world as known through the physical senses

sen·si·bil·ia \,sen(t)sə'bilēə, -lyə\ *n pl* [LL, fr. neut. pl. of *sensibilis* capable of being perceived — more at SENSIBLE] **:** what is sensed

sen·si·bil·i·sin \-ləsən\ *n* -s [prob. fr. G, fr. *sensibilisieren* to sensibilize (fr. F *sensibiliser*) + *-in*] **:** ANAPHYLACTIN

sen·si·bil·i·tist \-ləd·əst\ *n* -s [*sensibility* + *-ist*] **:** one having acute sensibility

sen·si·bil·i·ty \-ləd·ē, -ətē, -i\ *n* -ES [ME *sensibilite*, fr. MF *sensibilité*, fr. LL *sensibilitat-, sensibilitas*, fr. *sensibilis* sensible + L *-itat-, -itas* -ity] **1 :** the ability to receive sensation **:** responsiveness to stimuli **:** SENSITIVENESS ⟨tactile ~⟩ **2 :** SENSITIVITY **a** **3 a :** capacity of emotion or feeling as distinguished from intellect and will **:** peculiar or excessive susceptibility to pleasurable or painful impression **:** acuteness of feeling ⟨great ~ to pain⟩ ⟨~ to praise⟩ — often used in pl. ⟨a man of strong *sensibilities*⟩ **b :** a manifestation of such a capacity ⟨answered the charge with marked ~⟩ **4 :** awareness of and responsive feeling toward something (as emotion in another); *also* **:** an instance or token of this ⟨our ~ of your distress⟩ **5 :** refined sensitiveness in emotion and taste with especial responsiveness to the pathetic ⟨excessive ~ of late 18th century poetry⟩ **6 :** susceptibility to slight or unkindness **syn** see SENSATION

sen·si·bi·lize \'sen(t)səbə,līz\ *vt* -ED/-ING/-S [F *sensibiliser*, fr. *sensible* + *-iser* -ize] **:** SENSITIZE

sen·si·bi·liz·er \-zə(r)\ *n* -s [*sensibilize* + *-er*] **:** SENSITIZER

[1]sen·si·ble \'sen(t)səbəl\ *adj, sometimes* -ER/-EST [ME, fr. MF, fr. LL *sensibilis* capable of perceiving or being perceived, fr. L, capable of being perceived, fr. *sensus* (past part. of *sentire* to feel, perceive) + *-ibilis* -ible — more at SENSE] **1 a** (1) **:** capable of being perceived by the senses **:** apprehensible through the sense organs ⟨a ~ contact⟩ ⟨~ impressions⟩ (2) **:** perceptible to the mind **:** making an impression upon the sense, reason, or understanding ⟨a warm and clearly ~ affection⟩ ⟨his distress was ~ from his manner⟩ **b :** perceptibly large **:** of a significant size, amount, or degree **:** CONSIDERABLE ⟨a ~ error⟩ **c** (1) **:** readily perceptible by the senses **:** affecting the senses acutely ⟨a ~ odor⟩ (2) *obs* **:** producing a strong impression on the mind (3) *archaic* **:** tending to produce an acute emotional response either positive or negative (4) **:** MATERIAL ⟨waiting to receive more ~ marks of his uncle's approval⟩ **d :** SENSUOUS 1 **2 a :** capable of receiving impressions from external objects through the sense organs **:** liable to be affected by stimuli ⟨the more ~ parts of the skin⟩ ⟨~ to pain⟩ **b :** liable to impression from without **:** easily affected **:** having or exhibiting nice perception or acute feeling ⟨disturbed in the most ~ reaches of his spirit⟩ ⟨with affection wondrous ~ —Shak.⟩ **c** *archaic* **:** capable of reacting readily to an activating force ⟨~ instruments⟩ **3 a :** perceiving or having perception either through the senses or the mind **:** COGNIZANT ⟨made ~ of his mistake⟩ ⟨~ of the gathering storm⟩; *also* **:** perceiving so clearly as to be convinced **:** PERSUADED, SATISFIED ⟨~ of the error in our decision⟩ **b :** perceiving and responding emotionally ⟨~ of his faults⟩ ⟨very ~ of your distress⟩ **4 :** having or containing sense or reason **:** characterized by or resulting from sober serious examination and study **:** INTELLIGENT, REASONABLE ⟨a ~ man⟩ ⟨~ plans⟩ ⟨a ~ answer⟩ **syn** see AWARE, MATERIAL, PERCEPTIBLE, WISE

[2]sensible \"\ *n* -s **:** something that impresses the senses **:** something perceptible

sensible heat *n* **:** thermal energy whose transfer to or from a substance results in a change of temperature — compare LATENT HEAT

sensible horizon *n* **:** HORIZON 1b(3)

sen·si·ble·ness *n* -ES **:** the quality or state of being sensible

sensible note *or* **sensible tone** *n* [trans. of F *note sensible*] **:** LEADING TONE

sensible species *n, Thomism* **:** an object as apprehended through an act of sensual cognition — contrasted with *intelligible species*

sen·si·bly \'sen(t)səblē, -li\ *adv* [ME, fr. *sensible* + *-ly*] **:** in a sensible manner: as **a :** so as to be perceptible usu. to the senses ⟨became ~ warmer⟩ **b :** APPRECIABLY, SIGNIFICANTLY ⟨~ nearer their goal⟩ **c :** INTELLIGENTLY, DISCREETLY, JUDICIOUSLY ⟨acted ~ in the crisis⟩

sen·sif·ics \sen'sifiks\ *n pl but sing or pl in constr* [¹*sense* + *-ifics* (as in *significs*)] : SIGNIFICS

sen·si·fy \'sen(t)sə,fī\ *vt* -ED/-ING/-ES [¹*sense* + *-ify*] : to make (a stimulus) perceptible as sensation

sen·sile \'sen,sīl, -n(t)səl\ *adj* [L *sensilis*, fr. *sensus* (past part. of *sentire* to feel, perceive) + *-ilis* -ile — more at SENSE] **1** : capable of sensation : SENTIENT **2** : felt or sensed but not registered by an ordinary dry-bulb thermometer ⟨~ temperature changes⟩

sen·sil·lum \sen'siləm\ *n, pl* **sensil·la** \-lə\ [NL, dim. of L *sensus* sense] : a simple epithelial sense organ composed of one or a few cells with a nerve connection and usu. taking the form of a spine, plate, rod, cone, or peg

sensimotor *var of* SENSORIMOTOR

sensing *n* -S [fr. gerund of ²*sense*] : the determination by observation of the location of a gunnery burst or center of impact in relation to a target; *also* : an announcement of such location — often qualified by an indication of direction and amount of deviation from target ⟨~ 200 yards over⟩

sens·ism \'sen,sizəm\ *n* -S [¹*sense* + *-ism*] **1 a** : the philosophic doctrine that sense perceptions furnish the sole data of knowledge **b** : SENSATIONALISM — usu. used disparagingly **2** : hedonistic resort to the sensuous

¹**sen·si·tive** \'sen(t)səd·iv, -n(t)s(ə)tiv *also* -n(t)stəv\ *adj* [ME, fr. MF *sensitif*, fr. ML *sensitivus*, of sensation, receiving sense impressions, irreg. (influenced by LL *intellectivus* intellective) fr. *sensus*, past part. of *sentire* to feel, perceive — more at SENSE] **1** : conveying or receiving sense impressions ⟨~ nerves⟩ **2 a** *obs* : serving to affect the senses : functioning as a sensory stimulus **b** : experienced by means of the senses : SENSUOUS ⟨a ~ pleasure⟩ ⟨~ experience⟩ **3 a** : possessing a capacity for sensation or feeling : receptive to external stimuli **b** *obs* : having capacity to react to stimuli but lacking power to reason **c** : capable of being stimulated or excited by external agents (as light, gravity, contact) functioning as stimuli ⟨~ protoplasm⟩ ⟨~ cells⟩ **d** : exhibiting irritomotility ⟨a ~ compound leaf⟩ **4** : having quick and acute sensibility either to the action of external objects or to impressions upon the mind and feelings : highly susceptible : easily and acutely affected ⟨was too ~ to abuse and calumny —T.B.Macaulay⟩: as **a** : peculiarly or excessively susceptible to the action or effect of a usu. specified factor (as drought, drugs, hypnotism) : HYPERSENSITIVE — usu. used with *to* ⟨~ to moisture⟩ ⟨~ to allergenic pollens⟩ **b** : fluctuating or liable to fluctuation; *esp* : subject to unusual or excessive fluctuations in price and demand ⟨a ~ security⟩ ⟨a ~ market⟩ **c** : abnormally susceptible often because of a specific sensitization ⟨~ to eggs⟩ **d** : having a capacity of being easily affected or moved : capable of indicating minute differences : DELICATE ⟨a ~ thermometer⟩ ⟨~ weighing scales⟩ **e** : readily affected or changed by various agents ⟨photographic paper is ~ to actinic rays⟩ ⟨a ~ explosive is easily exploded by a shock⟩ ⟨a ~ colloid is readily coagulated⟩ — compare PHOTOSENSITIVE **f** : having a higher octane number when tested at specified slower speeds than when tested at specified higher speeds ⟨~ gasolines⟩ **g** : high in radiosensitivity **5** : of or relating to sensation and the senses : SENSORY **6** : indicating by a relatively large angular change any slight movement of the observer toward or away from its center — used esp. in nautical surveying and of a circle passing through two fixed objects and the observer's station so that the angle subtended by the chord joins the objects **7** *of a tree or forest* : marked by unevenness and irregularity in the growth of annual rings that is associated with variations in growing conditions in different years — opposed to *complacent* **8** : concerned with or held vital to the national security by reason of dealing with highly restricted information and materials : demanding or intended to be treated with a high degree of discretion and unquestioned loyalty **syn** see LIABLE

²**sensitive** \"\ *n* -S **1** *obs* : an individual capable of sensory perception **2** : a person having or reputed to have occult or supernormal abilities (as for crystal gazing, clairvoyance, clairaudience, telepathy) **3** : a sensitive person

sensitive brier *n* : any of various trailing prickly perennial herbs constituting the genus *Schrankia* (family Leguminosae) and having twice pinnate leaves which exhibit irritomotility and are divided into numerous leaflets, procumbent stems, and small rosy flowers in round axillary heads

sensitive drill *n* : a drilling machine that responds to delicate adjustments

sensitive fern *n* : a No. American fern (*Onoclea sensibilis*) the leaves of which are notably susceptible to early frosts and when plucked show a slight tendency to fold together

sensitive frog *n* : the plantar cushion of a hoof

sensitive joint vetch *n* : an annual herb (*Aeschynomene virginica*) of the southeastern U. S. and tropical America having foliage sensitive to the touch and jointed pods — called also *curly indigo*

sensitive lamina *n* : LAMINA 2c

sen·si·tive·ly \-əvlē, -li\ *adv* : in a sensitive manner : with sensitivity

sen·si·tive·ness \-ivnəs *also* -əv-\ *n* -ES : the quality or state of being sensitive

sensitive paper *n* : paper prepared for photographic purposes by coating or impregnating it with a substance sensitive to light

sensitive pea *n* : any of several herbs of the genus *Cassia* having leaflets somewhat sensitive to the touch; *esp* : either of two No. American plants (*C. fasciculata* and *C. nictitans*)

sensitive plant *n* **1** : any of several plants of the genus *Mimosa* with leaves sensitive to tactile stimulation; *esp* : a tropical American herb (*M. pudica*) that is often cultivated in greenhouses and has palmate leaves the divisions of which are pinnate with many small leaflets and whose leafstalk droops and pinnae and leaflets close tightly when the plant is touched **2** : any of various plants (as a sensitive brier or the sensitive pea) showing motions after irritation

sensitive rose *n* : SENSITIVE BRIER

sensitive shrub *n* : SENSITIVE PLANT 1

sen·si·tiv·i·ty \,sen(t)sə'tivəd·ē, -vətē, -i\ *n* -ES [¹*sensitive* + *-ity*] : the quality or state of being sensitive: as **a** : the rate of displacement of the indicating element with respect to change of the measured quantity — chiefly in technical use ⟨the ~ of a photographic film to light⟩ ⟨a galvanometer of extreme ~⟩ **b** (1) : the capacity of an organism or of a sense organ to respond to stimulation : IRRITABILITY; *also* : the degree of such responsiveness measured inversely by the weakest stimulus that awakens sensation or other response (2) : the capacity of a person to respond emotionally to changes in his interpersonal or social relationships; *also* : excessive capacity to respond thus **c** : abnormal responsiveness (as to an allergen or parasite) : HYPERSENSITIVITY **d** : the degree to which a radio receiving set responds to incoming waves; *esp* : the quotient of the power or other function of output of the set divided by the power or other function of its input

sensitivity center *n* : a region of a silver halide crystal that increases the photographic sensitivity of the crystal : a region at which latent image material forms or is concentrated

sensitivity speck *n* : a sensitivity center that is considered to constitute a region of impurity (as of silver sulfide) in the silver halide crystal

sen·si·tiza·tion \,sen(t)səd·ə'zāshən, -ə,tī'z-\ *n* -S **1** : the quality or state of being sensitized (as to an antigen) **2** : the act or process of sensitizing

sen·si·tize \'sen(t)sə,tīz\ *vb* -ED/-ING/-S *see -ize in Explan Notes* [¹*sensitive* + *-ize*] *vt* : to cause to become sensitive ~ *vi* : to become sensitive

sen·si·tiz·er \-zə(r)\ *n* -S : one that sensitizes: as **a** : a sensitizing antibody (as a lysin or amboceptor) **b** : an agent that will make a material sensitive to radiation or will increase its sensitivity to radiation **c** : an operator of a machine for sensitizing photographic or blueprint paper

sen·si·tom·e·ter \,sen(t)sə'tämәd·ə(r)\ *n* [ISV *sensito-* (fr. *sensitive* + *-o-*) + *-meter*] : an instrument used in the measurement of sensitivity (as of photographic material or of the human eye) by producing upon the sensitive surface a series of known exposures

sen·si·to·metric \;sen(t)səd·ō+\ *adj* : relating to or used in sensitometry — **sen·si·to·metrically** \"+\ *adv*

sensitometric curve *n* : CHARACTERISTIC CURVE a

sen·si·tom·e·try \,sen(t)sə'tämə·trē\ *n* -ES [ISV *sensito-* (fr. *sensitive* + *-o-*) + *-metry*] : the science, art, or act of measuring sensitivity (as of photographic material or of the human eye)

sen·sive \'sen(t)siv\ *adj* [MF, fr. ML *sensivus*, fr. L *sensus* (past part. of *sentire* to feel, perceive) + *-ivus* -ive — more at SENSE] *archaic* : SENTIENT

sen·so \'sen;sō\ *n* -S [perh. fr. Chin *shên*[4] kidneys, testes + *su*[4] essence] : a Chinese medicine for dropsy consisting essentially of the dried skin secretion of a native toad and apparently containing appreciable quantities of bufagin

sen·sor \'sen(t)sə(r)\ *n* -S [L *sensus* (past part. of *sentire* to feel, perceive) + E *-or*] : a device designed to respond to a physical stimulus (as heat or cold, light, a particular motion) and transmit a resulting impulse for interpretation or measurement or for operating a control

sensori- *also* **senso-** *comb form* [*sensori-* fr. ²*sensory; senso-* fr. L *sensus* sense] : sensory : sensory and ⟨*senso*paralysis⟩ ⟨*sensori*motor⟩

sen·so·ri·al \(')sen'sōrēəl, -sȯr-\ *adj* [²*sensory* + *-al*] **1** : relating to or concerned in sensation : SENSORY **2** : preoccupied with or primarily responsive to sensations — **sen·so·ri·al·ly** \-ēəlē, -li\ *adv*

sen·so·ri·motor \;sen(t)sərē+\ *also* **sen·si·motor** \;sen(t)sə+\ *or* **sen·so·motor** \;sen(t)sə+\ *adj* [*sensorimotor, sensomotor*, fr. *sensori-, senso-* + *motor; sensimotor* fr. L *sensus* sense + E *-i-* + *motor*] : of, relating to, concerned with, or functioning in both sensory and motor aspects of bodily activity ⟨~ disturbances⟩ ⟨~ area⟩

sen·so·ri·um \sen'sōrēəm\ *n, pl* **sensoriums** \-ēəmz\ *or* **senso·ria** \-ēə\ [LL, seat or organ of sensation, fr. L *sensus* (past part. of *sentire* to feel, perceive) + *-orium* — more at SENSE] **1 a** *obs* : the brain or a part of the brain regarded as the seat of the mind **b** : BRAIN, MIND — not used technically **2** : the parts of the brain that are concerned with the reception and interpretation of sensory stimuli; *broadly* : the sensory apparatus including receptors, nerves, and central components **3** : a percipient apparatus ⟨existed . . . only as a mechanical ~ and active apparatus —George Santayana⟩ ⟨a social ~ which would serve as the equivalent of the central nervous system —Louis Wirth⟩

¹**sen·so·ry** \'sen(t)sərē, -ri\ *n* -ES [LL *sensorium*] **1** *obs* : SENSE ORGAN **2** *archaic* : SENSORIUM

²**sensory** \"\ *adj* [L *sensus* (past part. of *sentire* to feel, perceive) + E *-ory* — more at SENSE] **1** : of or relating to sensation or to the senses ⟨~ psychology⟩ ⟨~ data⟩ **2** : conveying nerve impulses from the sense organs to the nerve centers : AFFERENT ⟨~ nerve fibers⟩

sensory aphasia *n* [²*sensory*] : inability to understand spoken, written, or tactile speech symbols that results from a brain lesion

sensory area *n* **1** : an area of the cerebral cortex that receives afferent projection fibers **2** : DERMATOME 2b

sensory cell *n* **1** : a peripheral nerve cell (as an olfactory cell) located at a sensory receiving surface and being the primary receptor of a sensory impulse **2** : a cell of the cerebrospinal nervous system (as a spinal ganglion cell) transmitting sensory impulses

sensory hair *n* : a hair in an arthropod connected basally with a nerve, extending outward through the cuticle, and held to be a receptor of tactile sensation

sensory organ *var of* SENSE ORGAN

sen·su \'sen(,)sü\ *prep* [NL, fr. L, abl. of *sensus* sense] : in the sense of : as understood or defined by — used esp. in technical taxonomic references ⟨*Cortinarius claricolor* ~ Ricken⟩

sen·su·al \'sench(ə)wəl\ *adj* [ME, fr. LL *sensualis*, fr. L *sensus* sense + *-alis* -al] **1** : of, relating to, or affecting the sense organs or senses : perceptible or perceived through the sensory apparatus : SENSORY ⟨~ objects⟩ ⟨~ perception⟩ **2** : relating to or consisting in the gratification of the senses or the indulgence of appetite : CARNAL, FLESHLY **3 a** : devoted to or preoccupied with the senses or appetites ⟨a ~ enjoyment of bodily strength⟩ ⟨the ~ content of a pampered cat⟩ **b** : involving or oriented to the voluptuous or lewd ⟨~ excesses⟩ ⟨a very ~ man⟩ **c** : deficient in moral, spiritual, or intellectual interests : WORLDLY; *esp* : IRRELIGIOUS **4** : MATERIALISTIC ⟨a ~ doctrine⟩ ⟨~ approaches to a problem⟩ **5** : relating to the doctrine of sensationalism **6** : indicative of or affected by sensuality ⟨a ~ age⟩ ⟨~ faces⟩ **syn** see CARNAL, SENSUOUS

sen·su·al·ism \-ə,lizəm\ *n* -S [*sensual* + *-ism*] **1 a** : SENSATIONALISM, SENSISM **b** : stress on the sensuous qualities of an object or on the sensuous as the chief element of beauty as distinguished from ideal and formal qualities and elements **c** : the view in ethics that gratification of the senses is the highest good **2** : preoccupation with sensual matters : persistent or excessive pursuit of sensual pleasures and interests

sen·su·al·ist \-ləst\ *n* -S [*sensual* + *-ist*] : a practicer or adherent of some form of sensualism

sen·su·al·is·tic \;⸗⸗⸗listik, -tēk\ *adj* [*sensualist* + *-ic*] : relating to or characterized by sensualism

sen·su·al·i·ty \,senchə'waləd·ē, -lətē, -i\ *n* -ES [ME *sensualite*, fr. MF *sensualité*, fr. LL *sensualitat-, sensualitas* capacity for sensation, fr. *sensualis* sensual + L *-itat-, -itas* -ity] **1 a** : the purely animal or physical part of human nature **b** *obs* : the lusts of the flesh **2** : the quality or state of being sensual : devotedness to the gratification of the bodily appetites : free indulgence in carnal or sensual pleasures

sen·su·al·iza·tion \,senchəwələ'zāshən, -ə,lī'z-\ *n* -S : the act of sensualizing or state of being sensualized

sen·su·al·ize \'senchəwə,līz\ *vt* -ED/-ING/-S [*sensual* + *-ize*] : to make sensual: as **a** : to subject to the love of sensual pleasure : debase by carnal gratifications **b** : to represent materialistically **c** : to ascribe to an origin in sensation

sen·su·al·ly \'senchəwəlē, -li\ *adv* : in a sensual manner : so as to be sensual

sen·su·al·ness *n* -ES : the quality or state of being sensual

sensu la·to \-'lād·(,)ō\ *adv* [NL] : in a broad sense — used esp. with names of taxa to indicate that the name is used more inclusively than sanctioned by current practice ⟨*Pyrus sensu lato* includes pear, apple, quince, mountain ash and related forms⟩; compare SENSU STRICTO

sen·sum \'sen(t)səm\ *n, pl* **sen·sa** \-sə\ [NL, fr. L, neut. of *sensus*, past part. of *sentire* to feel, perceive — more at SENSE] : an object of sense or content of sense perception : SENSE-DATUM

sensum theory *n* : a theory in philosophy: sensa are real entities intermediate between the content of perception as such and the ultimate physical reality

sen·su·os·i·ty \,senchə'wäsəd·ē, -sətē, -i\ *n* -ES [fr. *sensuous*, after such pairs as E *pompous: pomposity*] : SENSUOUSNESS

sen·su·ous \'senchəwəs\ *adj* [L *sensus* + E *-ous*] **1** : of or relating to the senses or sensible objects : addressing the senses : suggesting pictures or images of sense ⟨to this poetry would be made precedent, as being less subtle and fine, but more simple, ~, and passionate —John Milton⟩ **2** : characterized by sense impressions or imagery addressing the senses ⟨~ description⟩ ⟨a purely ~ satisfaction⟩ **3** : producing an agreeable effect on the senses : conducive to physical comfort or content ⟨mild ~ breezes⟩ **4** : highly susceptible to influence through the senses

syn SENSUOUS, SENSUAL, LUXURIOUS, VOLUPTUOUS, SYBARITIC, and EPICUREAN can mean, in common, having to do with or providing gratification of the senses. SENSUOUS and SENSUAL, though interchangeable in applying to things of the senses as opposed to spirit or intellect, are often used to carry a distinction: SENSUAL in such case usu. implies gratification in the sense of indulgence of appetite ⟨acute sensitivity to the *sensual* and intellectual pleasures that make life so abundantly worth living —Anthony West⟩ ⟨the richer tobacco enthusiasts want not merely the *sensual* pleasure their pipe brings —*Irish Digest*⟩ ⟨a *sensual* person given to lying on soft couches and overeating⟩ SENSUOUS can imply less an indulgence of appetite than an aesthetic gratification or delight as in beauty of color, sound, or artistic form and usu. carries a weaker overtone of carnality than does SENSUAL ⟨some philosophers insist that most of the arts are *sensuous* and hence that beauty is *sensuous*, but W. T. Stace maintains that . . . beauty must be admitted to display itself in internal percepts —D.H.Rankin⟩ ⟨a *sensuous* love of food and drink and gaiety —William Soskin⟩ ⟨the cat . . . lolling before the fire, stretched in a paroxysm of *sensuous* happiness upon the hearth rug —F.A.Swinnerton⟩ ⟨poetry took on a new and bizarre intricacy of *sensuous* decoration and symbolic metaphor —Douglas Bush⟩ ⟨he eyed the fresh linen laid upon a yellow-painted chair with *sensuous* delight —Elinor Wylie⟩ LUXURIOUS implies indulgence in or provision of either sensual or sensuous pleasures esp. of a kind inducing a pleasant languor, a delightful ease esp. of body, or a grateful peace of mind ⟨in her *luxurious* bed, beneath the satin coverlet, which was scented with lavender —Ellen Glasgow⟩ ⟨sat down to a long, *luxurious* smoke —Rudyard Kipling⟩ ⟨turned his head upon the high cushioned back of his chair and closed his eyes for one *luxurious* instant —Elinor Wylie⟩ VOLUPTUOUS implies a stronger abandonment to sense pleasure esp. for its own sake than does LUXURIOUS ⟨the core of [his] genius is *voluptuous*, surcharged with indolence and passion —Cyril Connolly⟩ ⟨a sullen *voluptuous* mouth —Edmund Wilson⟩ ⟨Cleopatra — fierce, *voluptuous*, passionate, tender, wicked, terrible, and full of poisonous and rapturous enchantment —Nathaniel Hawthorne⟩ SYBARITIC implies luxuriousness and voluptuousness of an extreme, often overrefined sort and esp. indulgence in rare and choice foods and in surroundings calculated to provide a maximum of bodily gratification ⟨a life of pleasure, folly, misfortune, vice, and *sybaritic* elegance —Philip Sherrard⟩ ⟨imagining the feel of the long silky fleece against bare toes makes one shiver with *sybaritic* pleasure —*New Yorker*⟩ ⟨a *sybaritic* banquet of seven courses, each with its own wine or liqueur⟩ EPICUREAN in this context can commonly imply sensuality or voluptuousness or, when nearer to an original sense, a sensuous, often fastidious delight in refined physical pleasures, often of eating or drinking but sometimes in intellectual pleasures ⟨out-of-season delicacies, wines of rare vintage, *epicurean* specialties of a ten-thousand-dollar-a-year chef —J.J.Floherty⟩ ⟨drinking his tea with *epicurean* satisfaction —J.C.Powys⟩

sen·su·ous·ly *adv* : in a sensuous manner : so as to be sensuous ⟨loved ~ the feel of the silk clothes she pressed and folded —Attia S. Hosain⟩

sen·su·ous·ness *n* -ES : the quality or state of being sensuous

sen·sus com·mu·nis \;sen(t)səskə'myünəs\ *n* [L] : a sense held to unite the sensations of all senses in a general sensation or perception

sensu stric·to \-'strik,tō\ *adv* [NL] : in a narrow sense — used esp. with names of taxa to indicate that the name is used in a restricted manner ⟨*Pyrus sensu stricto* includes only the pears⟩; compare SENSU LATO

¹**sent** *past of* SEND

²**sent** \'sent\ *n, pl* **sen·ti** \-(,)tē\ *or* **sents** [Estonian *senti*, prob. fr. Finn *sentti*, fr. L *centum* hundred — more at HUNDRED] **1** : a unit of monetary value in Estonia from 1928–40 equal to 1/100 kroon **2** : a coin representing one sent

sent *abbr* sentence

sen't *var of* SENIT

sentd *abbr* sentenced

¹**sen·tence** \'sent°n(t)s, -tən-, -nz\ *n* -S *often attrib* [ME, fr. OF, fr. L *sententia* feeling, opinion, expression of opinion, judgment, maxim, fr. (assumed) *sentent-, sentens* (irreg. pres. part. of *sentire* to feel) + *-ia* -y — more at SENSE] **1 a** *obs* : a stated opinion, decision, or judgment; *esp* : a conclusion given on request or reached after deliberation ⟨such applause was heard as Mammon ended, and his ~ pleased, advising peace —John Milton⟩ **b** : a decision or judicial determination of a court or tribunal : DECREE: as (1) : the judgment of a court pronounced in a cause in civil and admiralty law (2) : the judgment passed by a court or judge on a person on trial as a criminal or offender (3) : the order by which a court or judge imposes punishment or penalty upon a person found guilty; *esp* : the punishment or penalty so imposed ⟨the ~ was 10 years and a large fine⟩ **2** : a brief spoken or written passage: as **a** : a short or pithy saying usu. conveying moral instruction : AXIOM, MAXIM, SAW **b** *usu cap* : one of the verses of Scripture with which morning and evening prayers and the burial service commence in churches of the Anglican communion **3** : a grammatically self-contained unit consisting of a word or a syntactically related group of words that expresses an assertion, a question, a command, a wish, or an exclamation, that in writing usu. begins with a capital letter and concludes with appropriate end punctuation, and that in speech is phonetically distinguished by various patterns of stress, pitch, and pauses — compare MINOR SENTENCE, PREDICATION **4** : a complete musical idea usu. consisting of two phrases : PERIOD **5** : a declarative sentence or statement in logic : PROPOSITION

²**sentence** \"\ *vb* -ED/-ING/-S [ME *sentencen*, fr. MF *sentencier*, fr. LL *sententiare*, fr. L *sententia* sentence] *vt* **1** *obs* : to decree, decide, or announce judicially **2 a** : to pronounce sentence on : to condemn to penalty or punishment ⟨the defendant was *sentenced* at the conclusion of the trial⟩ **b** : to prescribe the penalty or punishment of : DOOM — usu. used with *to* ⟨was tried on the charge of inciting to riot and *sentenced* to thirty days in jail —E.S.Bates⟩ **3** : to judge the merits of (as a person or thing) ⟨let us not ~ the play before seeing it⟩ **4** : to cause to suffer or undergo something : DESTINE ⟨elopement *sentenced* her to exile —Ann F. Wolfe⟩ ⟨forces would be *sentenced* to an indefinite and costly stalemate —*Time*⟩ ⟨sat down his reactions to the quiet desperation of life they are *sentenced* to endure —W.F.Albright⟩ ~ *vi* **1** *obs* : to give judgment **2** : to pronounce sentence ⟨the judges assemble for *sentencing*⟩

sentence adverb *n* : an adverb that qualifies a sentence as a whole (as *surely* in "surely goodness and mercy shall follow me all the days of my life")

sentence fragment *n* : a word, phrase, or clause usu. having in speech the intonation characteristic of a sentence but lacking the grammatical completeness and independence of a full sentence

sentence sense *n* : the ability to recognize a group of words that forms a written complete sentence as distinguished from a minor sentence or adjacent sentences

sentence stress *also* **sentence accent** *n* : the manner in which stresses are distributed on the syllables of words assembled into sentences — called also *sense stress;* compare WORD STRESS

sen·ten·tia \sen'tenchēə\ *n, pl* **sententi·ae** \-ē,ē\ [L — more at SENTENCE] : an aphorism, maxim, or brief comment on life or living — usu. used in pl. ⟨in 1895 the following *sententiae* on daily life were worth setting forth: . . . never allow yourself to be hurried; do not drink with your mouth full —E.V.Lucas⟩

sen·ten·tial \(')sen¦tenchəl\ *adj* [ME, fr. LL *sententialis*, fr. L *sententia* opinion, judgment, maxim + *-alis* -al] **1** : containing or made up of sentences or maxims ⟨a ~ book⟩ ⟨a collection of ~ sayings⟩ **2** *obs* : of the nature of a judicial sentence **3 a** : of or relating to a sentence or a syntactical sequence ⟨and the sense of the poem as a whole, and of the ~ parts of it —V.C.Aldrich⟩ **b** : PROPOSITIONAL

sentential calculus *n* [trans. of G *satzkalkül*] : PROPOSITIONAL CALCULUS

sentential connective *n* : BICONDITIONAL 2

sentential function *n* : an expression that contains one or more free variables and becomes a declarative sentence when constants are substituted for the variables (as in *x is green, x is taller than y*) — compare PROPOSITION 3a

sen·ten·tial·ly \-əlē, -li\ *adv* [ME, fr. *sentential* + *-ly*] : in a sentential manner

sentential variable *n* : a variable that may be replaced by a declarative sentence

sen·ten·tiary \sen'tenchē,erē\ *n* -ES [ML *sententiarius* theological candidate studying the *Sentences* of Peter Lombard 12th cent. theologian, fr. L *sententiae* sentences] : APHORIST

sen·ten·tious \(')sen¦tenchəs\ *adj* [ME, fr. L *sententiosus*, fr. *sententia* opinion, maxim + *-osus* -ous — more at SENTENCE] **1** *obs* : full of meaning or wisdom ⟨your reasons at dinner have been sharp and ~ —Shak.⟩ **2 a** : terse, aphoristic, or moralistic in expression : PITHY, EPIGRAMMATIC ⟨"contentment is a proposition with which every one can agree, that it breeds happiness" . . . is a proposition with which we can hardly quarrel; ~, sedate, obviously true —A.T.Quiller-Couch⟩ ⟨that ~ brevity which, using not a word to spare, leaves not a moment for inattention —Adrienne Koch⟩ ⟨to push home her ideas on social injustice by ~ precept —Leslie Rees⟩ **b** (1) : given to or abounding in aphoristic expression ⟨"young people often feel they're caged," I said . . . with a

feeling that I was being ~ —Edmund Wilson⟩ ⟨the ~ expression of the middle period of a life that came to late maturity —V.L.Parrington⟩ ⟨there is the type magisterial or imperative; the type laconic or ~ —B.N.Cardozo⟩ (2) : given to or abounding in excessive moralizing ⟨they were verbose, ~, circumlocutious, and grandiloquent —Harold Rosen & H.E. Kiene⟩ ⟨too often the significant episode deteriorates into ~ conversation —Kathleen Barnes⟩ **syn** see EXPRESSIVE

sen·ten·tious·ly adv : in a sententious manner

sen·ten·tious·ness n -ES : the quality or state of being sententious

senti pl of SENT

sen·tience \'sench(ē)ən(t)s\ also **sen·tien·cy** \-ənsē, -si\ n, pl **sentiences** also **sentiencies** [sentience fr. ¹sentient; sentiency fr. ¹sentient, after such pairs as E intelligent: intelligence; sentiency fr. ¹sentient + -cy] 1 : the readiness to receive sensation, idea, or image : unstructured available consciousness ⟨then I shall see light . . . and I shall hear the notes of birds; and this ~, this negation of death, will be in itself for me an Easter sermon —Harry Lang⟩ 2 : a state of elementary or undifferentiated consciousness : feeling as contrasted with sensation, perception, or ideation ⟨gave ~ to slugs and newts —Richard Eberhart⟩

sen·ti·en·dum \ˌsentēˈendəm, ˌsenchē-\ n, pl **sentien·da** \-də\ [NL, fr. L, neut. of sentiendus, gerundive of sentire] : SENSE-DATUM

¹sen·ti·ent \'sench(ē)ənt\ adj [L sentient-, sentiens, pres. part. of sentire to feel, perceive — more at SENSE] 1 : capable of sensation and of at least rudimentary consciousness ⟨a ~ being⟩ ⟨the conception . . . of impulsive, instinctive, and ~ life —Susanne K. Langer⟩ ⟨these highly ~, motile, instinctive, and often intelligent creatures —D.C.Peattie⟩ 2 a : consciously perceiving : AWARE — used with of ⟨he alone is ~ of the intolerable load —Elinor Wylie⟩ ⟨a boy so ~ of his surroundings —W.A.White⟩ b : conscious or capable of fine distinctions or perceptions : SENSITIVE ⟨at its best democracy breeds the ~ person —Elizabeth Bowen⟩ ⟨the problems which confront us all as ~ responsible beings —Randall Stewart⟩ 3 : capable of receiving and reacting to sensory stimuli ⟨the ~ cells of the brain⟩ 4 : marked by the stimulation or exercise of the senses or of conscious perception ⟨the highly ~ quality in the experiences —G.A.Woods⟩ ⟨her . . . conviction of the tragedy of the ~ life —Hudson Strode⟩

²sentient \"\ n -s : a sentient being; also : the conscious mind

sen·tient·ly adv : with feeling, consciousness, or perception ⟨had ~ been an artist —Janet Flanner⟩

sen·ti·ment \'sentəmənt\ n -s [F or ML; F sentiment fr. ML sentimentum, fr. L sentire to feel, perceive + -mentum -ment — more at SENSE] 1 a : an attitude, thought, or judgment permeated or prompted by feeling : a complex of emotion and idea : PREDILECTION ⟨rising ~ for broadening the tax base —N. Y. Times⟩ ⟨public ~ for good roads greatly increased —Amer. Guide Series: N. C.⟩ ⟨his own antislavery ~s were sincere —Helen C. Boatfield⟩ b : a specific view or notion : OPINION ⟨am obliged to differ from nearly every ~ expressed —Gilbert Parker⟩ ⟨share their . . . ~s . . . on school problems —Julius May⟩ 2 a : FEELING, EMOTION ⟨generated within him a ~ of good will and cooperation —A.L.Funk⟩ ⟨stimulating to the ~s and occasionally interesting to the mind —Virgil Thomson⟩ b : refined feeling : keen or delicate sensibility esp. as expressed in a work of art or evinced in conduct ⟨a strong, frank, and positive character, of keen wit and generous ~ —E.V.Wilcox⟩ ⟨poems of ~ and reflection —Matthew Arnold⟩ ⟨an almost religious ~ of the dignity of art —Meyer Schapiro⟩ c : emotional idealism ⟨community life in those days was a requisite of survival rather than a matter of ~ —Dana Burnet⟩ ⟨making ~ a substitute for action⟩ d : a romantic or nostalgic feeling verging on sentimentality ⟨still keeps a bartender to preside over its ornate old bar, mostly for ~'s sake —Green Peyton⟩ ⟨so much slush and ~ —Jack London⟩ ⟨just the difference between passion and silly ~ —A.T.Quiller-Couch⟩ 3 a : an emotional idea as set forth in literature or art ⟨the book expresses the noblest ~s⟩ b : the emotional significance of a passage or expression as distinguished from its verbal context ⟨a diplomatic statement is a statement about which everything is true except the ~ which prompts it —Joseph Conrad⟩ ⟨to my thinking the ~s of the pledge, properly interpreted, are unexceptionable —W.T. Hastings⟩ c : an emotionally tinged thought or wish expressed as a maxim, axiom, or epigram ⟨cards . . . with appropriate verses and ~s —Bks. of Jewish Interest⟩ ⟨I'll give you a ~; here's Success to usury —R.B.Sheridan⟩ **syn** see FEELING, OPINION

¹sen·ti·men·tal \ˌsentəˈment³l\ adj 1 a : of, relating to, or characterized by sentiment ⟨a scientific as opposed to a ~ appraisal of the situation —Times Lit. Supp.⟩; esp : marked or governed by feeling, sensibility, or emotional idealism ⟨his sincerely ~ love for children —Sir Winston Churchill⟩ ⟨was profoundly ~; his warm, expansive heart yearned for sympathy —G.S.Haight⟩ ⟨in his earlier days was a ~ liberal —J.T.Farrell⟩ b : expressive of sentiment or feelings : addressed or appealing to the emotions : stimulating an emotional response ⟨the ~ or sensuous appeal of an art —André Malraux⟩ ⟨was a ~ comedy of love in the modern equivalent of a cottage —Current Biog.⟩ c : resulting from or motivated chiefly by feeling rather than reason or thought ⟨many of our old notions . . . are more ~ than accurate —W.H. Whyte⟩ ⟨working-class unity, both for ~ and realistic reasons, has remained an obsession —J.G.Colton⟩ 2 a : having an excess of sentiment or sensibility : indulging in feeling to an unwarranted extent : affectedly or mawkishly emotional ⟨are incurably ~, and take immoderate pleasure in the contemplation of domestic bliss —Eric Linklater⟩ ⟨pity without values is as ~ as if applied to insects —Accent⟩ ⟨an age in which the most natural feeling of tenderness, happiness, or sorrow was likely to be called ~ —Randall Jarrell⟩ b : expressing or stimulating an excessive, affected, or unwarranted emotional indulgence ⟨much that is hackneyed, shoddy, and falsely ~ is foisted upon the public under the guise of the Biblical novel —Edmund Fuller⟩ ⟨rant and bombast and ~ cant of politics —Florence Converse⟩ ⟨works of art which have ~ subjects (partings, deaths, waiting for a lover's return, children . . . praying or crying over a hurt pet) —Hunter Mead⟩

syn SENTIMENTAL, ROMANTIC, MAWKISH, MAUDLIN, SOPPY, MUSHY, and SLUSHY can mean unduly or affectedly emotional. SENTIMENTAL can apply to anyone strongly and esp. unduly, habitually, or promiscuously affected by the softer, pleasanter, more feminine emotions, or it can apply to anything marked by such an affection, but usu. it suggests a lack of complete genuineness or naturalness, implying that the emotion arises from a factitious situation or out of hyperesthesia, or is purposely evoked for the thrill, as an affectation, or a given even though often obscure purpose ⟨a sentimental mother cherishing every memento of the babyhood of her children⟩ ⟨whisky made him somewhat sentimental —Sherwood Anderson⟩ ⟨sentimental popular songs⟩ ⟨the advertising agent . . . must wax as sentimental over one man's soap as over another's laxative —Roger Burlingame⟩ ⟨theological discussion of any kind, as distinct from a loosely sentimental religiosity —C.A. Lejeune⟩ ⟨sentimental and cheap novels —J.T.Farrell⟩ ⟨compassionate without being sentimental —Gertrude Buckman⟩ ROMANTIC implies emotion that derives from things not so much as they actually or generally are but as they may be or are imaginatively or ideally conceived, as in literature, drama, or one's waking dreams ⟨a romantic story of love and adventure in the South Seas⟩ ⟨I am filled with a sense of the French romantic spirit. It soars, it expands, it engulfs you with a sweet kind of poetry that is charming, but very unreal —Irving Kolodin⟩ ⟨his idealism — reflected in his romantic love of country, hatred of materialism, and concept of the general interest —A.S.Link⟩ ⟨a romantic young lady waiting for her Prince Charming to come along⟩ MAWKISH suggests a sickening sentimentality marked by gross insincerity or objectionable emotional excess ⟨stories simpering with delight and mawkish with pathos —J.D.Hart⟩ ⟨his mixture of harshness and mawkish sentimentality —Peter Quennell⟩ ⟨murder was punished without mawkish concern or delay —C.M.Webster⟩ MAUDLIN suggests an excess of emotion or feeling marked by an unwarranted weeping or an inappropriately gushing expression of love, grief, or the like ⟨silly maudlin ballads of the suicide of young lovers⟩ ⟨the death of a famous actress is the signal, as

a rule, for a great deal of maudlin excitement —Ben Hecht⟩ SOPPY, MUSHY, and SLUSHY are all informal equivalents of MAWKISH, SOPPY, chiefly Brit., often carrying the suggestion of silliness ⟨a novel . . . soppy with manufactured emotionalism —John Cournos⟩ ⟨a naturally sad but never soppy poet —G.S. Fraser⟩, MUSHY suggesting a driveling sentimentality ⟨the language is mushy with sentiment and turgid with rhetoric —C.J.Rolo⟩ ⟨he croons with mushy sentimentality over his heroes —Anthony West⟩ ⟨writing mushy letters to women admirers —Stanley Walker⟩, and SLUSHY applying chiefly to utterances and like MUSHY, suggesting a sentimental or emotional drivel esp. about love ⟨slushy letters from an adolescent admirer⟩ ⟨slushy and woebegone songs⟩

²sentimental \"\ n -s : a sentimental person

sentimental comedy n : comedy that addresses itself to the spectator's love of goodness rather than to his sense of humor and emphasizes the moral aspects of its situations and the virtues of its characters

sen·ti·men·tal·ism \ˌ�ˈ ̷ ̷t³l,izəm\ n -s [¹sentimental + -ism] 1 a : the quality or state of being sentimental : the disposition to favor or indulge in sentiment ⟨there was . . . a normal adolescent ~, but none of the turbulence, the storm and stress —H.S.Commager⟩ ⟨rise above the level of gushy ~ —John Dewey⟩ ⟨~ in 19th century art arose . . . largely from the belief that art was a moral agent —Bernard Smith⟩ b : ROMANTICISM ⟨degenerated into a superficial ~, dominated by ~ wishes which were taken for facts —Time⟩ ⟨scientific writing that is not accurate . . . can become a kind of sloppy ~ —C.E. Kellogg⟩ ⟨his doctrine was a ~ which tended to present all human instincts as naturally good —L.J.A.Mercier⟩ ⟨the ~ of making our own paltry woes glorious in their bitterness —W.L.Sullivan⟩ 2 : a conception or statement marked by or expressive of sentimentality ⟨in this program he was handicapped by various ~s —Carl Van Doren⟩

sen·ti·men·tal·ist \ˌ ̷ ̷t³ləst\ n -s [¹sentimental + -ist] : one disposed to indulge in sensibility or sentimentality : ROMANTICIST ⟨was essentially a ~ with feelings close to the surface and stirred by the lightest touch —G.S.Haight⟩ ⟨the ~, who lives by illusions, is let down more gently in English fiction than in French —Harry Levin⟩ ⟨the nerveless ~ and dreamer, who spends his life in a weltering sea of sensibility and emotion —William James⟩

sen·ti·men·tal·i·ty \ˌ ̷ ̷men·talədē, - ̷ ̷man-, -lətē, -i\ n -ES [¹sentimental + -ity] 1 : the quality or state of being sentimental esp. to excess or in affectation ⟨what was respected as honest sentiment is branded as ~, and mocked at, when the emotion which sustained it no longer exists —John Mason Brown⟩ ⟨the indulgence in sentiment that sometimes passes into ~ —N.F.Adkins⟩ ⟨the same objectivity, ruthlessness, and lack of any ~ —Harrison Smith⟩ ⟨culminated in the vapid ~ of a good deal of English romanticism and its steadily more mawkish offshoots —Joseph Frank⟩ 2 : a sentimental idea or its expression ⟨is a regular American with sentimentalities that are supposed to be sentiments —J.T.Farrell⟩

sen·ti·men·tal·i·za·tion \ˌ ̷ ̷ˌment³lˈzāshən, - ̷ ̷ˌī ̷z-\ n -s : the act or process of sentimentalizing : the state of being sentimentalized

sen·ti·men·tal·ize \ˌ ̷ ̷ˈment³l,īz\ vb -ED/-ING/-s [¹sentimental + -ize] vi 1 : to indulge in sentiment : ROMANTICIZE ⟨it's a waste of breath to go back over the past and ~ —Agatha Christie⟩ ⟨analyzed lust in its crudest form . . . and grieved without sentimentalizing over it —Monica Stirling⟩ ~ vt : to look upon or imbue (as a person or thing) with sentiment : ROMANTICIZE ⟨denounced as a sentimentalized Christianity that religious attitude which prefers slavery to war —Current Biog.⟩ ⟨the mistake of sentimentalizing the politician as a poor abused fellow —John Lodge⟩ ⟨the most insidious vices are those that began as virtues, and have been sentimentalized long after they became ugly —Katharine F. Gerould⟩

sen·ti·men·tal·ly \ˌsentəˈment³lē, -li\ adv : in a sentimental manner : with sentiment or sentimentality

sen·ti·ment·less \ˌ ̷ ̷ ̷ ̷ləs\ adj : that is without sentiment

sentiments pl of SENTIMENT

¹sen·ti·nel \'sent(ə)nəl, - tənəl\ n -s [MF sentinelle, fr. OIt sentinella, fr. sentina vigilance, fr. sentire to perceive, fr. L — more at SENSE] 1 : one that watches or guards : SENTRY 2 a obs : WATCH, GUARD ⟨keep ~⟩ b obs : WATCHTOWER c : SOLDIER 3 : an officer of a secret society who is stationed outside the door of a meeting place to prevent unauthorized entry — compare WARDER

²sentinel \"\ vt sentineled or sentinelled; sentineled or sentineling; sentineling or sentinelling; sentinels 1 : to watch over as a sentinel ⟨long lines of shivering poplars that sentinelled the meadows —Willa Cather⟩ 2 : to furnish with a sentinel : place under the guard of a sentinel or sentinels 3 : to post as sentinel

sentinel crab n : a crab (Podophthalmus vigil) of the Indian ocean with very long eyestalks

¹sen·try \'sen·trē, -tri\ n -ES [alter. of ME seintuarie — more at SANCTUARY] archaic : SANCTUARY

²sentry \"\ n -ES [perh. fr. ¹sentry] 1 obs : SENTINEL 2b 2 : a soldier standing guard (as at a passing point) 3 : one that guards as a sentry ⟨rooks . . . always left a ~ posted on a tree —Adrian Bell⟩ 4 : KITE 7a

³sentry \"\ vb -ED/-ING/-s vt : to guard as a sentry ⟨its marble entrance hall sandbagged and sentried —R.M.Ingersoll⟩ ~ vi : to stand guard : act as a sentry ⟨herons had begun ~ing up and down, stalking minnows —Edwin Granberry⟩

sentry board n [²sentry] 1 : a platform for a sentry outside the gangway 2 : a board hung near a sentry post for posting instructions and orders

sentry box n : a hut or box to shelter a sentry on his post

sentry go n [fr. the phrase sentry, go] 1 : a call for the changing of the guard 2 : duty as a sentry

sents pl of SENT

se·nu·fo \səˈnüfō\ n, pl **senufo** or **senufos** usu cap 1 : a people of the interior of the Ivory Coast Republic and the Republic of Mali widely known for their wood carving and masks 2 : a member of such people 3 : a Gur language of the Senufo people

senussi usu cap, var of SANUSI

sen·vy \'senvē\ n -ES [ME senevey, senvey, fr. MF senevé, fr. L sinapi, sinapis — more at SINAPIS] 1 : the mustard plant 2 : MUSTARD SEED

sen·za rep·li·ca \ˌsentsəˈrepləkə, ˌsenzə-\ adv [It, lit., without repetition] : without the (normally indicated) repeat — used as a direction in music

seoul \'sōl sometimes 'sül or 'saúl or se'ül\ adj, usu cap [fr. Seoul, So. Korea] : of or from Seoul, the capital of So. Korea : of the kind or style prevalent in Seoul

sep abbr 1 sepal 2 separate; separated

sep·al \'sēpəl also 'sep-\ n -s [NL sepalum, fr. sepa (modif. of Gk skepas, skepē covering) + -lum (as in petalum); akin to Lith kepurè head covering] : one of the modified leaves comprising a calyx — compare PETAL; see CARPEL illustration

sep·aled also **sepalled** \-ld\ adj [NL sepalum + E -ed] : having sepals

sep·al·ine \'sepəˌlīn, 'sēp-, - ̷ ̷lən\ adj [NL sepalinus, fr. sepalum + L -inus -ine] : SEPALOID

sep·a·lo·dy \'sepəˌlōdē, 'sēp-\ n -ES [ISV sepal + -ody] : metamorphosis of other floral organs into sepals

sep·al·oid \-ˌlȯid\ adj [NL sepaloideus, fr. sepalum + -oideus (fr. L -oides -oid + -eus -ous)] : resembling or having the nature of a sepal

-sep·al·ous \ˌsepələs\ adj comb form [sepal + -ous] : having sepals ⟨gamosepalous⟩ ⟨tetrasepalous⟩

sep·a·ra·bil·i·ty \ˌsep(ə)rəˈbiləd·ē, -lətē, -i\ n [ML separabilitas, fr. L separabilis separable + -itas -ity] : the quality or state of being separable ⟨of the nuclear motion from the electronic motion in molecules —L.M.Branscomb⟩ ⟨consider the ~ of the provision from the remainder of the statute —R.W.Ginnane⟩

separability clause n : a clause included in a legal document (as a contract) stating that invalidation of some sections or clauses in the document will not affect the validity of the remainder

sep·a·ra·ble \'sep(ə)rəbəl\ adj [ME seperable, fr. L separabilis, fr. separare to separate + -abilis -able] 1 : capable of being separated or dissociated : DISTINGUISHABLE, SEVERABLE 2 obs : causing separation ⟨a ~ spite . . . doth steal sweet

hours from love's delight —Shak.⟩ — **sep·a·ra·bly** \-blē,-bli\ adv

separable attachment plug n : an attachment plug having a removable cap

sep·a·ra·ble·ness n -ES : SEPARABILITY

separata pl of SEPARATUM

¹sep·a·rate \'sepəˌrāt also -əˌprāt; usu -ād+V\ vb -ED/-ING/-s [ME separaten, fr. L separatus, past part. of separare, fr. se- apart (fr. sed, se without) + parare to prepare, procure — more at IDIOT, PARE] vt 1 a : to set or keep apart : DETACH ⟨two longitudinal valleys ~ the mountains into three high ranges —Samuel Van Valkenburg & Ellsworth Huntington⟩ ⟨a pull on the tab . . . ~s seal just below cap —Modern Packaging⟩ ⟨~ the white from the yolk of an egg⟩ b : to make a distinction between : DISCRIMINATE, DISTINGUISH ⟨how difficult it is to ~ religion from magic in the beliefs . . . of savages —W.R.Inge⟩ ⟨there is usually not much difficulty in ~ a butterfly from a moth —A.D.Imms⟩ c : SORT ⟨~ mail⟩ ⟨cards into suits⟩ ⟨parcels fly . . . as clerks ~ them by regions and states —A.C.Fisher⟩ d : to disperse in space or time : SCATTER ⟨theaters in Canada are so widely separated that the costs of travelling are prohibitive —Report: (Canadian) Royal Commission on Nat'l Development⟩ e slang : to cause to divest oneself : STRIP — used with from ⟨tricks for separating country bumpkins from their bankrolls⟩ ⟨~ them from . . . money to back ventures that never were produced —E.D.Radin⟩ 2 archaic : to set aside for a special purpose : CHOOSE, DEDICATE ⟨came into existence with the sense of being a ''separated'' nation, which God was using to make a new beginning for mankind —Reinhold Niebuhr⟩ 3 : to part by or as if by a legal separation: a : sever conjugal ties with ⟨cause to live apart ⟨payments made to a divorced or legally separated wife —W.C.Warren&S.S.Surrey⟩ b : to sever contractual relations with : DISCHARGE ⟨he was separated from the service with the rank of captain —E.J.Kahn⟩ ⟨more than 100 employees have been separated from the firm in the past six months⟩ ⟨any student who does not remove his probationary status . . . may be separated from the institution —Bull. of Meharry Med. Coll.⟩ 4 : to block off : BAR, SEGREGATE ⟨a . . . rood screen ~s the nave from the chancel —Amer. Guide Series: N. Y.⟩ ⟨the rural worker . . . is not separated from the landed aristocracy by racial difference —P.E.James⟩ 5 a : to isolate from a mixture : single out : EXTRACT ⟨~ cream from milk by putting it through a separator⟩ ⟨~ gold from an alloy⟩ — often used with out ⟨by whatever method the smaller organisms are separated out —R.E.Coker⟩ ⟨static episodes . . . separated out of a larger and more complex historical situation —M.D. Geismar⟩ b archaic : to give off : SECRETE ⟨glands, which ~ a substance that has the smell of musk —Jedidiah Morse⟩ ~ vi 1 : to become divided ⟨the airflow over the trailing edge of the flap has begun to ~ —Skyways⟩ ⟨the Uralian languages . . . ~ into three branches —W.K.Matthews⟩ 2 a : to sever an association : become estranged : WITHDRAW ⟨Puritans . . . unwilling to ~ from the Established Church —Amer. Guide Series: Mass.⟩ b : to cease to live together as man and wife ⟨after two stormy years of married life the couple separated by mutual consent⟩ 3 : to go in different directions : part company : DISPERSE ⟨after dinner we separated, the women to the library —Lucien Price⟩ ⟨thought the House would like to know, before it separated —Sir Winston Churchill⟩ 4 : to become isolated from a mixture ⟨oil . . . ~s readily from water —B.G.A.Skrotzki & W.A.Vopat⟩

syn SEPARATE, PART, DIVIDE, SEVER, SUNDER, and DIVORCE can all mean to become or cause to become disunited or disjoined. SEPARATE implies a putting or keeping apart ⟨separate the sheep from the goats⟩ ⟨the political boundary separating this country from Mexico —R.S.Thoman⟩ ⟨the ten centuries which separated the reign of Charlemagne and the reign of Napoleon —T.B.Macaulay⟩ or a scattering or dispersion of units ⟨the war separated many families⟩ or a removal of one thing from another ⟨separate a troublesome boy from a group⟩ PART suggests the separation, often complete, of two persons or things in close union or association, or of two parts of one thing ⟨the two friends had not part until they had reached the station⟩ ⟨a man and wife parted only by death⟩ ⟨the cable parted under the strain⟩ DIVIDE commonly stresses the idea of parts, groups, or sections resulting from cutting, breaking, partitioning, or branching ⟨divide a cake into two pieces⟩ ⟨the land is divided by natural boundaries such as streams⟩ ⟨the auditorium proper divided into a pit, one or more galleries —C.F.Wittke⟩ ⟨it can also be used in the sense of SEPARATE, esp. when mutual antagonism or wide separation is suggested ⟨the war divided many families⟩ ⟨no religious difference arose to divide the old inhabitants from the English —G.M.Trevelyan⟩ ⟨the suspicion which the Citizens' Committee predicted would divide neighbor from neighbor —David Clinton⟩ SEVER often adds the idea of violence, suggesting forced separation, esp. of part from whole or of persons joined in affection, close association, and so on ⟨with one stroke he severed the head from the body⟩ ⟨man's ancestors later became severed from this separate line of evolution —R.W.Murray⟩ ⟨an immense peninsula slightly severed from the main mass —Forrest Morgan⟩ ⟨severs relations with a hostile nation⟩ ⟨severed friend from friend⟩ SUNDER implies a violent rending or wrenching apart ⟨the sundered atom —M.C.Faught⟩ ⟨the dearest ties of friendship and of blood were sundered —T.B. Macaulay⟩ DIVORCE, in implying the legal dissolution of a marriage, usu. suggests the separation of things so closely associated that they interact, are often regarded as inseparable, or commonly work, often work best, only in union ⟨an institution concerned with general education . . . divorced from research and education for the professions is admittedly not a university but a college —J.B.Conant⟩ ⟨form in art divorced from matter⟩ ⟨divorce the worker's income from any dependence on the efforts he makes —Time⟩ ⟨his gaiety was as divorced from scorn or cynicism as it was wedded to melancholy —John Mason Brown⟩

²sep·a·rate \'sep(ə)rət sometimes -pərt; usu |d-+V\ adj [L separatus, past part. of separare to separate] 1 a archaic : characterized by segregation from other people : SOLITARY, SECLUDED ⟨the tendency of prolonged ~ confinement is to affect the mind —Edinburgh Rev.⟩ ⟨the plan of my bungalow, with all convenience for being ~ and sulky when I please —Sir Walter Scott⟩ b : having an incorporeal existence : DISEMBODIED, IMMATERIAL ⟨being . . . is now seen as the nature which constitutes ~ entity —Alan Gewirth⟩ c : set or kept apart : standing alone : DETACHED, ISOLATED ⟨the more perfect the artist, the more completely ~ in him will be the man who suffers and the mind which creates —T.S.Eliot⟩ ⟨ceremonial chambers . . . were built as ~ units in the central courtyards —Amer. Guide Series: Ariz.⟩ 2 a : not shared with another : INDIVIDUAL, SINGLE ⟨group consciousness . . . makes the individual think lightly of his own ~ interests —M.R.Cohen⟩ ⟨the world's largest city deserves ~ consideration —L.D. Stamp⟩ b often cap : estranged from a parent body ⟨there were 90 Separate churches, with 6,490 members —F.S.Mead⟩ 3 a : existing by itself : AUTONOMOUS, INDEPENDENT ⟨the partitioning of India created two ~ jute economies —F.F.George⟩ ⟨reorganization of schools into ~ primary and postprimary units —H.C.Dent⟩ b : dissimilar in nature or identity : DISTINCT, DIFFERENT ⟨my most recent works, in their ~ ways, embody this tendency —Aaron Copland⟩ ⟨the full bibliography . . . lists 2204 ~ publications —Geog. Jour.⟩ ⟨built-in facilities . . . permit cooking in seven ~ ways without the use of additional utensils —Report of General Motors Corp.⟩ **syn** see DISTINCT, SINGLE

³separate \"\ n -s 1 usu cap : NEW LIGHT 3; esp : SEPARATE BAPTIST 2 : OFFPRINT ⟨sent out ~s and reprints of his major monographs —J.C.Burnham⟩ 3 : a group of soil particles of a definite size or grade obtained in separation (as in mechanical analysis) 4 **separates** pl : articles of dress designed to be worn interchangeably with others to form various costume combinations

separate baptist n, usu cap S&B : a member of a Baptist sect organized in 1662 as the English Puritan Separate Baptist Church and migrating to America in 1695, being congregational in polity, and observing open communion, baptism by immersion, and foot washing

separate but equal adj : of, relating to, or constituting a doctrine of segregation whereby Negroes and whites have equal

facilities (as for education or transportation) ⟨the *separate but equal* doctrine has been directly challenged and the Supreme Court has consented to review three cases involving it —Charles Thompson⟩
separated *past of* SEPARATE
separated aggregate *n* [*separated* fr. past part. of ¹*separate*] **:** aggregate for use in concrete that has been separated by the producer into fine and coarse aggregates
separated milk *n* **:** milk left after extraction of the cream
sep·a·ra·tee \ˌsep(ə)rəˈtē\ *n* -s [¹*separate* + *-ee*] **:** an individual in process of separation from active military service
separate estate *n* **:** an estate the ownership and control of which is enjoyed by a person free from any rights or control of others; *esp* **:** an estate enjoyed by a married woman independent of her husband
separate-loading ammunition \ˈ=(=)=ˌ==-\ *n* **:** ammunition in which the projectile, propelling charge, and primer are loaded separately rather than as a unit
sep·a·rate·ly \ˈsep(ə)rətlē, -pərt-, -li\ *adv* **:** in a separate manner **:** INDIVIDUALLY, INDEPENDENTLY
separately excited *adj* **:** having the field magnets excited by a current from a separate source — used of a machine
separate maintenance *n* **:** an allowance made to a wife by her husband under deed of separation or under a court order or decree
sep·a·rate·ness *n* -ES **1 a :** the quality or state of being isolated **:** DETACHMENT, LONELINESS ⟨writing letters . . . to fellow artists in order to counteract the soul-destroying ~ that he felt had caused the poet's death —*New Republic*⟩ **b :** the quality or state of being exclusive or excluded **:** ALOOFNESS, SEGREGATION ⟨the ~ of classes entrenched . . . by the force of law and custom —Oscar Handlin⟩ ⟨~ which denies each group enriching contact with others —C.H.Nichols⟩ **2 :** distinctive character **:** INDIVIDUALITY ⟨it is the ~ of the films that gives the program its strength —Cecile Starr⟩ **3 :** AUTONOMY, INDEPENDENCE ⟨seeking complete political ~ for Lower Canada —B.K.Sandwell⟩
separates *pres 3d sing of* SEPARATE, *pl of* SEPARATE
separate school *n, Canad* **:** a state-supported sectarian school operated outside a local public school system under either Protestant or Catholic control ⟨public, private, and ~ schools⟩
separating *adj* [fr. pres. part. of *separate*] **:** designed or used for or capable of separation
separating funnel *n* **:** SEPARATORY FUNNEL
separating power *n* **:** RESOLVING POWER
sep·a·ra·tio bo·no·rum \ˌsepəˈrädēˌōbəˈnōrəm\ *n* [LL, lit., separation of goods] **1** *Roman law* **:** the keeping separate of the estate of a deceased person from that of his heirs or the right of the creditors of the estate to insist on such a separation **2** *Roman law* **:** the estate of an individual at the time of his death together with any subsequent increment
sep·a·ra·tion \ˌsepəˈrāshən\ *n* -s [ME *separacion*, fr. MF *separation*, fr. L *separation-*, *separatio*, fr. *separatus* (past part. of *separare* to separate) + *-ion-*, *-io* -ion — more at SEPARATE] **1 a :** an act or instance of dividing **:** DETACHMENT, DISPERSAL ⟨~ of church and state⟩ ⟨shipment of fragile or delicate articles . . . requires ~ and cushioning of items —*Export Packing*⟩ ⟨families . . . would face ~ if they should avail themselves of the provisions of the Refugee Relief Act —D.D.Eisenhower⟩ **b :** arrangement of mail according to destination **:** SORTING ⟨after cancellation . . . trundled the letters on wheeled trays to the next process, ~ —*Nat'l Geographic*⟩ **c :** BURBLE 3 **d :** SEPARATENESS, SEGREGATION ⟨courts and legislature work in ~ and aloofness —B.N.Cardozo⟩ ⟨we can no longer risk letting any large section of the human race live in ~, cut off from . . . the rest —I.A.Richards⟩ **e :** dissimilarity of character **:** DIFFERENCE, DISTINCTION ⟨should not give the impression that there is . . . no great ~ between the ends of Communism and those of the West —D.H.Gillis⟩ **2 a :** an act or instance of parting company ⟨after the ~ of the three boats . . . in the storm —W.J.Ghent⟩ **b** (1) **:** withdrawal from a parent body **:** SECESSION, SCHISM ⟨personally loyal though he was . . . believed that ~ was inevitable —T.M.Spaulding⟩ (2) *usu cap* **:** a body of dissenters esp. from an established church **:** SEPARATISTS ⟨one of the greatest of the early leaders of the *Separation* —George Willison⟩ **3 :** isolation from a mixture **:** EXTRACTION ⟨~ of flour from bran by bolting⟩ **4 a** (1) **:** cessation of cohabitation between husband and wife by mutual agreement; *esp* **:** JUDICIAL SEPARATION (2) *canon law* **:** ANNULMENT **b :** termination of a contractual relationship **:** RESIGNATION, DISCHARGE ⟨~ from the service⟩ ⟨~ from employment⟩ ⟨a serious breach of accepted standards of deportment . . . may be punished by loss of social privileges, probation, or ~ —*College of William & Mary Cat.*⟩ **5 a :** a point or line of division **:** DEMARCATION ⟨recommend that there be a clear line of ~ —J.P.Colbert⟩ **b :** a cause or means of dividing **:** BARRIER, PARTITION; *specif* **:** a compartment in a mail-sorting case ⟨sorted 100 cards to 53 ~*s* at the rate of 50 per minute —*Postal Service News*⟩ **c :** an intervening space **:** GAP, INTERVAL ⟨the ~ between the spokes of a wheel⟩ **d :** the distance between the two parts of an orig. continuous surface (as the top of a stratum) after dislocation by faulting — compare NORMAL HORIZONTAL SEPARATION, PERPENDICULAR SEPARATION **6 a :** a method or result of dividing: as **a :** the propagation of plants by parts which are naturally or easily removed from the parent plant (as gladiolus corms, lily bulbels) — compare DIVISION 20 **b :** COLOR SEPARATION **c :** a batch of sorted mail
separation disk *n* **:** a biconcave gelatinous layer found between two adjoining vegetative cells in some blue-green algae and associated with hormogonium formation
sep·a·ra·tion·ist \ˌsepəˈrāsh(ə)nəst\ *n* -s **:** one that advocates secession or schism
separation layer *n* **:** a distinct layer within an abscission zone of a plant varying in thickness and composed of cells that are smaller and different in shape from those above and below and contain abundant starch and dense cytoplasm by the disorganization of which abscission is effected — called also *abscission layer*
separation negative *n* **:** a monochrome negative obtained by photographing a subject through a filter and used as one of the component negatives in color printing
separation of powers : the allocation of executive, legislative, and judicial powers to branches of government independent of each other
separation of variables : a regrouping of the terms of a differential equation so that each differential has as a factor a function of the corresponding independent variable
separation point *n* **:** BURBLE POINT
sep·a·rat·ism \ˈsep(ə)rəd·ˌizəm, -ə,ti-\ *n* -s [²*separate* + *-ism*] **1 a :** a disposition toward secession or schism ⟨arrest the wave of ~ among the nationalities —Julian Towster⟩; *esp* **:** advocacy of withdrawal from a parent group (as a church) ⟨though a militant Puritan . . . was still opposed to *Separatism* —George Willison⟩ — compare INDIVIDUALISM, ISOLATIONISM **b :** the principles and practices of a separatist ⟨promoters of secession . . . who swept the South into the adventure in ~ —J.G.Randall⟩; *esp, cap* **:** the principles and practices of the Separatists **2 :** social separation **:** EXCLUSIVENESS, SEGREGATION ⟨centuries of class ~ —E.B.George⟩ ⟨various forms and degrees of racial ~ —Sophia McDowell⟩
¹sep·a·rat·ist \ˈsep(ə)rə|d·əst, -pə,ral, |tə-\ *n* -s [²*separate* + *-ist*] **1 :** a dissenter from an established church: as **a** *usu cap* **:** a Congregationalist or English Independent of the 16th and 17th centuries; *esp* **:** one separating from the Church of England **:** NONCONFORMIST ⟨those *Separatists* who founded the Plymouth colony in America⟩ **b :** a member of a congregation of no generally recognized denomination **c :** ZOARITE **2** *archaic, often cap* **:** one that observes strict piety and morality **:** PHARISEE **3** *often cap* **:** an advocate of political autonomy or independence **:** REVOLUTIONARY, SECESSIONIST ⟨sided with Quebec ~*s* in their struggles against . . . federal usurpation of power —M.S.Stewart⟩ **4 :** an advocate of segregation ⟨~*s* in the matter of church and state —F.J.B. Flynn⟩ — **sep·a·ra·tis·tic** \ˌsep(ə)rəˈtistik\ *adj*
²separatist \"\ *adj, often cap* **1 :** of, relating to, or characteristic of separatists **2 :** advocating separatism
sep·a·ra·tive \ˈsepəˌrād·iv, -p(ə)rəd-·\ *adj* [LL *separativus*, fr. L *separatus* (past part. of *separare* to separate) + *-ivus* -ive — more at SEPARATE] **1 :** tending toward or causing separation ⟨the uniting influence was stronger than the ~ —J.A.Froude⟩ **2 a :** DISTRIBUTIVE 2 **b :** expressive of separation or removal ⟨the ~ genitive⟩ **c :** DISJUNCTIVE 4
sep·a·ra·tor \ˈsepəˌrād·ə(r), -ātə- *also* -eˌprā-\ *n* -s *often attrib* [LL, one that separates, fr. L *separatus* (past part.) + *-or*] **1** *often cap* **:** SEPARATIST **2 :** one that separates a mixture into its constituent elements: as **a :** THRESHING MACHINE **b :** a device for extracting water from steam before it enters a steam engine **c :** a device for separating liquids of different specific gravities (as cream from milk) or liquids from solids; *esp* **:** CENTRIFUGE **d :** a revolving screen or a machine containing a revolving perforated cylinder with beater arms for separating cottonseed meats from the hulls **e** (1) **:** any of various machines for dressing ore or removing slate from coal (2) **:** an electromagnetic apparatus to separate magnetic ores from rock, sand, or other impurities **3 :** one that divides or serves as a barrier: as **a** (1) **:** RADDLE 3 (2) **:** a spindle guard that controls the ballooning of yarn — called also *antiballooner* **b :** a device (as of wood or perforated hard-rubber sheets) for preventing metallic contact between the electrodes of opposite polarity within a voltaic cell **c :** a casting for separating the sections of a built-up girder **d :** a dental appliance for separating adjoining teeth to give access to their surfaces **e :** a traffic barrier to discourage or prevent the passage of vehicles from one lane to another **4 :** a worker who separates by hand or machine: as **a :** an operator of a centrifugal machine for reclaiming lubricating oil **b :** one who cuts individual garment parts (as collars, sleeves) from a roll **c :** a classifier of laundry
separator man *n* **:** an operator of a separating apparatus (as a cream separator, a threshing machine)
separator pulp *n* **:** solids remaining after macerated fruit pulp has been centrifuged
sep·a·ra·to·ry \ˈsep(ə)rəˌtōrē\ *adj* [L *separatus* (past part. of *separare* to separate) + E *-ory*] **:** serving to separate **:** used in separating
separatory funnel *n* **:** a funnel usu. in the shape of a globe or cylinder provided with a stopcock for drawing off the lower layer of a mixture of immiscible liquids

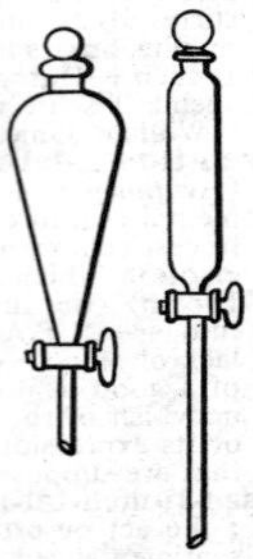

separatory funnels

sep·a·ra·trix \ˌsepəˈrāˌtriks\ *n, pl* **sepa·ratri·ces** \ˌsepəˈrā·trəˌsēz, -ˌrəˈtrī(ˌ)sēz\ *also* **separatrixes** [NL, fr. LL, fem. of *separator*] **1 :** a diagonal or upright stroke used to separate one marginal proof correction from another in the same line **2 :** DIAGONAL 4
sep·a·ra·tum \ˌsepəˈrād·əm\ *n, pl* **sepa·ra·ta** \-d·ə\ [NL, fr. L, neut. of *separatus*, past part. of *separare* to separate] **:** OFFPRINT
sepd *abbr* separated
sepg *abbr* separating
se·phar·di \səˈfärdē, -ˌfärˈdē\ *n, pl* **se·phardim** \-ˈfärdəm, -ˌfärˈdēm\ *also* **sephardi** *usu cap* [LHeb *sĕphāradhī*, fr. *Sĕphāradh* Spain, fr. Heb, region prob. in northern Asia Minor where Jews were once held in captivity (Obad 20)] **:** a member of the occidental branch of European Jews early settling in Spain and Portugal and later spreading to Greece, the Levant, England, the Netherlands, and the Americas — compare ASHKENAZI
¹se·phar·dic \səˈfärdik\ *also* **se·phar·di** \səˈfärdē, -ˌfärˈdē\ *adj, usu cap* [*sephardic* fr. *sephardi*, n. + *-ic*; *sephardi* fr. LHeb *sĕphāradhī*, n. & adj., *sephardi*, *sephardic*] **:** of, relating to, or characteristic of the Sephardim — compare ASHKENAZIC
²sephardic \"\ *n* -s *cap* [*sephardi*, n. + *-ic*] **:** Hebrew as spoken by the Sephardim
se·pher torah *or* **se·fer torah** \ˈsāfər-\ *n, pl* **si·phrei torah** *or* **si·frei torah** \ˈsiˌfrā-\ *or* **sepher torahs** *or* **sefer torahs** *usu cap S&T* [Heb *sēpher tōrāh*, lit., book of law] **:** a leather or parchment scroll of the Pentateuch used in a synagogue for liturgical purposes
se·phi·rah \səˈfērə\ *adj* [Heb *sĕphīrāh* counting, fr. *sĕphōr* to count; fr. the custom of formally counting the 49 days according to the Commandment in Lev 23:15–16] **:** of, relating to or constituting one of the 49 days of Omer ⟨during the ~ days . . . no marriages may take place —H.E.Goldin⟩
¹se·pia \ˈsēpēə\ *n* [NL, fr. L, cuttlefish, fr. Gk *sēpia*; akin to Gk *sēpein* to make putrid, *sapros* rotten, putrid; fr. its inky secretion — more at SAPR-] **1 a** *cap* **:** a genus (the type of the family Sepiidae) of oval-bodied cephalopods comprising the cuttlefishes and having narrow fins as long as the body, a large calcareous internal shell, and an ink sac containing a dark fluid used in the preparation of drawing inks and watercolor bister **b** -s **:** the inky secretion of a cuttlefish **2** -s **:** a pigment of rich brown color containing melanin, prepared from the ink of various cuttlefishes, and used in watercolor painting and in ink **3** -s **a :** a drawing executed in sepia or a print or photograph of a brown color resembling sepia **b :** SEPIA PAPER **4** -s **:** a brownish gray to dark olive brown
²sepia \"\ *adj* **1 a :** of the color sepia **b :** made of or done in sepia ⟨~ print⟩ **2 :** having brown skin; *specif* **:** NEGRO ⟨the ~ lady with the glittering eyes and mellow singing voice —Brooks Atkinson⟩
sepia brown *n* **:** a dark grayish yellowish brown that is stronger and slightly yellower than seal and stronger and slightly yellower and lighter than otter
sepia paper *n* **:** photographic paper sensitized by a process analogous to kallitype and used esp. for plan copying
se·pi·idae \səˈpīəˌdē\ *n pl, cap* [NL, fr. *Sepia*, type genus + *-idae*] **:** a family of Decapoda comprising the true cuttlefishes
sep·i·ment \ˈsepəmənt\ *n* -s [L *saepimentum*, fr. *saepire* to fence, enclose with a hedge (fr. *saepes* hedge, fence); prob. akin to Gk *haimos* thicket, *haimasia* stone wall] **:** something (as a hedge or fence) that encloses
se·pi·o·la \ˌsēpēˈōlə\ *n, cap* [NL, dim. of *Sepia*] **:** a genus (the type of the family Sepiolidae) of short thick-bodied usu. small squids with a rudimentary internal chitinous shell or none and large rounded lobular fins
se·pi·o·lite \ˈsēpēəˌlīt\ *n* -s [G *sepiolith*, fr. Gk *sēpion* cuttlebone + G *-lith* -lite] **:** MEERSCHAUM 1
se·pi·oph·o·ra \ˌsēpēˈäpərə\ *n pl, cap* [NL, fr. *Sepia* + *-o-* + *-phora*] *in some classifications* **:** a suborder of Decapoda coextensive with the family Sepiidae and comprising the cuttlefishes
se·pi·um \ˈsēpēəm\ *n, pl* **se·pia** \-pēə\ [NL, fr. Gk *sēpion*, fr. *sēpia* cuttlefish] **:** CUTTLEBONE
sepn *abbr* separation
sepose *vt* -ED/-ING/-S [modif. (influenced by ¹*pose* & ¹*suppose*) of L *sepositus*, past part. of *seponere* to set apart, fr. *sed-*, *se-* apart (fr. *sed*, *se* without) + *ponere* to place — more at IDIOT, POSITION] *obs* **:** to set aside **:** RESERVE ⟨God *seposed* a seventh of our time for his exterior worship —John Donne⟩
se·poy \ˈsēˌpȯi\ *n* -s [modif. of Pg *sipai*, *sipaio*, fr. Hindi *sipāhī*, fr. Per, horseman, soldier of the cavalry, fr. *sipāh* army] **:** a native of India employed as a soldier in the service of a European power; *esp* **:** one serving in the British army
sep·pu·ku \seˈpü(ˌ)kü\ *n* -s [Jap, fr. Chin (Pek) *ch'ieh*⁴ to cut + *fu*³ bowels] **:** HARA-KIRI 1
seps \ˈseps\ *n, pl* **seps** [L, fr. Gk *sēps*; akin to Gk *sēpein* to decay] **:** a lizard of an Old World genus (*Chalcides* syn. *Seps*) of the family Scincidae having a snakelike body, very small legs, and smooth overlapping scales, and regarded as poisonous by the ancients
¹sep·sid \ˈsepsəd\ *adj* [NL *Sepsidae*] **:** of or relating to the Sepsidae
²sepsid \"\ *n* -s **:** a fly of the family Sepsidae
sep·si·dae \ˈsepsəˌdē\ *n pl, cap* [NL, fr. Gk *sēpsis* decay + NL *-idae*] **:** a family of acalyptrate usu. shiny black flies (superfamily Muscoidea) that develop in decaying organic matter or excrement
sep·sis \ˈsepsəs\ *n, pl* **sep·ses** \-pˌsēz\ [NL, fr. Gk *sēpsis* decay; akin to Gk *sēpein* to make putrid — more at SEPIA] **:** a toxic condition resulting from the multiplication of pathogenic bacteria and their products in a region of infection and their absorption into the blood stream; *esp* **:** SEPTICEMIA
¹sept \ˈsept\ *n* -s [prob. alter. of *sect*] **:** a branch of a family; *esp* **:** one in which all members are believed to have descended from a single ancestor **:** CLAN, SIB — used esp. of the dependents of a flaith in ancient Ireland
²sept \"\ *n* -s [L *septum* — more at SEPTUM] **1** *archaic* **:** an enclosed area (as of a building) set apart for a special purpose **2 :** a partition (as a screen or railing) that marks off a sept
¹sept- *or* **septi-** *comb form* [L, fr. *septem* — more at SEVEN] **:** seven ⟨*sept*insular⟩ ⟨*septi*folious⟩ ⟨*sept*illion⟩
²sept- *or* **septo-** *also* **septi-** *comb form* [NL, fr. *septum* — more at SEPTUM] **:** septum ⟨*sept*al⟩ ⟨*septi*fragal⟩ ⟨*septo*costa⟩
septa *pl of* SEPTUM
sep·tal \ˈseptəl\ *adj* [²*sept-* + *-al*] **:** of, relating to, or being a part of a septum
septal cartilage *n* **:** the cartilage of the nasal septum
septal cell *n* **:** a small histiocyte characteristic of the lung
septal neck *n* **:** a short tubular prolongation of a septum in a cephalopod shell where it is perforated for the siphon
sep·tan·y·chus \sepˈtanəkəs\ *n, cap* [NL, prob. alter. of *Septonychus*, fr. ¹*sept-* + *-onychus* (fr. Gk *onych-*, *onyx* nail, claw); fr. the mites being seven-jointed — more at NAIL] **:** a genus of plant-feeding mites
sep·tarch \ˈsepˌtärk\ *adj* [¹*sept-* + *-arch*] **:** having seven protoxylem groups — used of a plant stem
sep·tar·i·an \(ˈ)sepˈta(a)rēən\ *adj* [NL *septarium* + E *-an*] **:** of, relating to, or being a septarium
septarium \=ˈ==əm\ *n, pl* **septar·ia** \-ə\ [NL, fr. ²*sept-* + L *-arium*] **:** a concretionary nodule usu. of limestone or clay ironstone intersected within by cracks filled with calcite, barite, or other minerals — compare GEODE
sep·tate \ˈsepˌtāt\ *also* **sep·tat·ed** \-ād·əd\ *adj* [*septate* fr. ²*sept-* + *-ate*; *septated* fr. ²*sept-* + *-ate* + *-ed*] **:** divided by or having a septum
sep·ta·tion \sepˈtāshən\ *n* -s [²*sept-* + *-ation*] **1 :** division into parts by a septum **:** the condition of being septate **2 :** SEPTUM
septavalent *var of* SEPTIVALENT
sep·tem·ber \(ˈ)sepˈtembə(r), səpˈt-\ *n* -s *usu cap* [ME *septembre*, fr. OF, fr. L *september* (seventh month), fr. *septem* seven — more at SEVEN] **:** the ninth month of the Gregorian calendar — abbr. *Sept.*; see MONTH table
september elm *n, usu cap S* **:** a tree (*Ulmus serotina*) of the southeastern U.S. that flowers in the autumn — called also *red elm*
sep·tem·brist \=ˈ=brəst\ *n* -s *often cap* [Pg *Setembrista* supporter of the successful revolution of September 1836 in Portugal, fr. *setembro* September (fr. L *september*) + *-ista* -ist] **:** REVOLUTIONARY
septemfluous *adj* [L *septemfluus*, fr. *septem* seven + *-fluus* (fr. *fluere* to flow) — more at FLUID] *obs* **:** flowing in seven streams
sep·tem·vir \sepˈtemvə(r)\ *n, pl* **septemvirs** \-və(r)z\ *also* **septemvi·ri** \-vəˌrī, -vəˌrē\ [L, back-formation fr. *septemviri*, pl., fr. *septem viri* seven men, fr. *septem* seven + *viri*, pl. of *vir* man — more at VIRILE] **:** a member of a ruling body of seven men; *specif* **:** one of seven officiating priests in ancient Rome — compare EPULO
sep·tem·vi·ral \(ˈ)sepˈtemvərəl\ *adj* [L *septemviralis*, fr. *septemvir* + *-alis* -al] **:** of or relating to septemvirs or a septemvirate
sep·tem·vi·rate \=ˈ=vərət, -ˌrāt\ *n* -s [L *septemviratus*, fr. *septemvir* + *-atus* -ate] **1 :** the office or government of septemvirs **2 :** a body of septemvirs
sep·te·nar \sepˈtēnər, ˈseptəˌnär\ *n* -s [L *septenarius*] **:** SEPTENARY 2
sep·te·nar·i·us \ˌseptəˈna(a)rēəs\ *n, pl* **septenar·ii** \-ēˌī\ [L, fr. *septenarius* of or relating to seven] **:** SEPTENARY 2
¹sep·tenary \sepˈtenərē, ˈseptəˌnerē, sepˈtēnərē\ *n* -ES [L *septenarius*, fr. *septenarius* of or relating to seven] **1** *archaic* **:** a group or set of seven; *specif* **:** SEPTENNIUM **2 :** a fourteener (as the trochaic tetrameter catalectic in medieval Latin verse, the iambic verse of seven and a half feet of Middle English poetry) often printed in two lines — called also *septenar*, *septenarius*
²sep·tenary \(ˈ)sepˈtenərē, ˈseptəˌnerē, (ˈ)sepˈtēnərē\ *adj* [L *septenarius*, fr. *septeni* seven each, seven (fr. *septem* seven) + *-arius* -ary] **1 :** of or relating to the number seven or to a septenary **2 :** SEPTUPLE
sep·ten·decillion \ˌsepˌten+\ *n often attrib* [L *septendecim* seventeen + E *-illion* (as in *million*)] — see NUMBER table
sep·ten·decimal \"+\ *adj* [L *septendecim* seventeen (fr. *septem* seven + *decem* ten) + E *-al* — more at SEVEN, TEN] **:** relating to the number 17 **:** based on the number 17
sep·te·nate \sepˈteˌnāt, -ˌnət; ˈseptəˌnāt\ *n* -s [F *septennat*, fr. *septennal* septennial (fr. LL *septennalis*, fr. L *septennis* of seven years + *-alis* -al) + *-at* -ate] **:** a period of seven years; *esp* **:** a seven-year term of office
sep·ten·nial \(ˈ)sepˈtenēəl, -nyəl\ *adj* [L *septennium* period of seven years (fr. *septennis* of seven years, fr. *septem* seven + *annus* year) + E *-al* — more at ANNUAL] **1 :** occurring, appearing, or being made, done, or acted upon every seven years **2 :** continuing or lasting for seven years ⟨~ parliaments⟩
sep·ten·nial·ly \-ēlē, -əli\ *adv* **:** every seven years
sep·ten·ni·um \sepˈtenēəm\ *n, pl* **septenniums** \-ēəmz\ *or* **septen·nia** \-ēə\ [L] **:** a period of seven years
sep·ten·tri·on \sepˈten·trēˌän, -ēən\ *n, pl* **septentrions** \-nz\ *also* **septentrio·nes** \(ˌ)sepˌten·trēˈō(ˌ)nēz\ *often cap* [ME *septemtrioun*, fr. MF *septentrion*, fr. L *septentriones*, pl., the seven stars near the north pole, the northern regions (sing. *septentrio*), fr. *septem* seven + *Triones* Great Bear, Little Bear, fr. *triones* plow oxen, pl. of *trio* plow ox; akin to L *terere* to rub, grind, thresh — more at THROW] *obs* **:** the northern regions **:** NORTH ⟨thou art as opposite to every good . . . as the South to the *Septentrion* —Shak.⟩
sep·ten·tri·o·nal \(ˈ)sepˈten·trēənᵊl\ *adj* [ME, fr. L *septentrionalis*, fr. *septentriones* the northern regions + *-alis* -al] **:** NORTHERN ⟨coldest stretch of ~ weather —Janet Flanner⟩
sep·tet *or* **sep·tette** \(ˈ)sepˈtet\ *n* -s [G *septet*, fr. ¹*sept-* + *-et*] **1 :** a group of seven persons or objects ⟨a ~ of husky linemen⟩ **2 a :** a composition for seven instruments or voices **b :** a performance of such a composition **c :** seven musicians performing such a composition **3 :** a stanza or poem having seven lines — compare RHYME ROYAL
sept·foil \ˈsep(t)ˌfȯil\ *n* [LL *septifolium*, fr. L *sept-* ¹sept- + *folium* leaf — more at BLADE] **1 :** TORMENTIL **2 :** an ornamental foliation having seven lobes
septi- — see SEPT-
sep·ti·bran·chia \ˌseptəˈbraŋkēə\ *n pl, cap* [NL, fr. ²*sept-* + *-branchia*] **:** a small order of Lamellibranchia comprising marine bivalves with gills reduced to a horizontal symmetrically fenestrated muscular partition
sep·ti·branchiata \ˌseptə+\ [NL, fr. ²*sept-* + *branchiata*] *syn of* SEPTIBRANCHIA
sep·tic \ˈseptik, -tēk\ *adj* [L *septicus*, fr. Gk *sēptikos*, fr. *sēptos* putrified (verbal of *sēpein* to make putrid) + *-ikos* -ic — more at SEPIA] **1 a :** characterized by or producing bacterial decomposition **:** PUTREFACTIVE ⟨~ sewage⟩ ⟨~ action takes place at the bottom of the tank⟩ **b :** of, relating to, or characteristic of septicemia **:** HECTIC ⟨a ~ temperature curve⟩ **2 :** of an odious or contaminated nature **:** CORRUPT, OBNOXIOUS ⟨a ~ pool of guilt —*Time*⟩ ⟨suffering . . . from a ~ economy —*New Republic*⟩
sep·ti·ce·mia *or* **sep·ti·cae·mia** \ˌseptəˈsēmēə\ *n* -s [NL, fr. L *septicus* septic + NL *-emia*, *-aemia*] **:** invasion of the blood stream by virulent microorganisms from a focus of infection marked by chills, fever, and prostration and often by the formation of secondary abscesses in various organs — called also *blood poisoning*; compare PYEMIA — **sep·ti·ce·mic** *or* **sep·ti·cae·mic** \ˌseptəˈsēmik\ *adj*
sep·ti·centennial \ˌseptə+\ *n* [¹*sept-* + *centennial*] **:** a 700th anniversary or its celebration
sep·ti·ci·dal \ˌseptəˈsīdᵊl\ *adj* [²*sept-* + *-cidal*] *of a capsular fruit* **:** dehiscent longitudinally at or along a septum — compare LOCULICIDAL; see FRUIT illustration — **sep·ti·ci·dal·ly** \-ᵊlē\ *adv*
sep·ti·ci·za·tion \ˌseptəsəˈzāshən, -ˌsīˈz-\ *n* -s [*septic* + *-ization*] **:** treatment of sewage by septic action
sep·ti·colored \ˈseptə+ˌ-\ *adj* [¹*sept-* + *colored*] **:** having seven colors
sep·ti·co·pyemia \ˌseptə(ˌ)kō+\ *n* [NL, fr. *septico-* (fr. L *septicus* septic) + *pyemia*] **:** PYEMIA — **sep·ti·co·pyemic** \"+\ *adj*

septic pneumonia *n* : hemorrhagic septicemia marked by pneumonia esp. in young animals (as calves)

septic sore throat *n* : sore throat characterized by inflammation of the throat and pharynx with associated fever, marked prostration, and other evidences of toxemia and caused by infection with hemolytic streptococci

septic tank *n* : a tank in which the organic solid matter of continuously flowing sewage is deposited and retained until it has been disintegrated by anaerobic bacteria

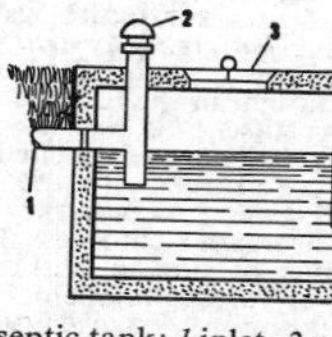

septic tank: *l* inlet, 2 vent cap, 3 manhole, 4 outlet

sep·tième \(')se.'tyem\ *n* -s [F, lit., seventh, fr. L *septimus*, fr. *septem* seven — more at SEVEN] : a mutation stop of 2⅔ and 1⅓ foot pitch on the manuals and 4⁴⁄₇ foot pitch on the pedals

sep·tier \sə.'tyā\ *n* -s [F, alter. of *setier* — more at SETIER] : SETIER

sep·tif·ra·gal \(')sep'tifrəgəl\ *adj* [²sept- + L *frag-* (stem of *frangere* to break) + E *-al* — more at BREAK] : breaking from the partitions — used of dehiscence in which the valves of a capsule or pod break away from the dissepiments — **sep·tif·ra·gal·ly** \-əlē\ *adv*

sep·tile \'sep.tīl, -.təl\ *adj* [ISV ²sept- + *-ile*; prob. orig. formed in F] : of or relating to septa

sep·til·lion \(')sep'tilyən\ *n* -s *often attrib* [F, fr. ¹sept- + *-illion* (as in *million*)] — see NUMBER table

sep·ti·mal \'septəməl\ *adj* [L *septimus* seventh (fr. *septem* seven) + E *-al* — more at SEVEN] : based on the number seven

sep·time \'septəm, -.tēm\ *n* [L *septima*, fem. of *septimus* seventh; fr. its being the seventh parrying position] : a parry or guard position in fencing that defends the lower inside target with the hand to the left in a position of supination and the top of the blade directed at the opponent's knee — compare QUINTE

sep·ti·mole \'septə.mōl\ *also* **sep·tole** \-.tōl\ *n* -s [*septimole* fr. L *septimus* seventh + E *-ole*; *septole* fr. ¹sept- + *-ole*] : SEPTUPLET

sept·insular \(')sept+\ *adj, usu cap* [¹sept- + *insular*] : of, relating to, or consisting of the seven Ionian islands ⟨*Septinsular* Republic⟩

sep·ti·syllabic \'septə+\ *adj* [¹sept- + *syllabic*] : consisting of seven syllables

sep·ti·syllable \"+\ *n* [¹sept- + *syllable*] : a word of seven syllables

sep·ti·valent *also* **sep·ta·valent** \'septə+\ *adj* [¹sept- + *valent*] : HEPTAVALENT

septleva \n [F *sept-et-le-va*, lit., seven and the first stake] : a sum equal to seven times the amount of the first stake in a game of basset

septo- — see SEPT-

sep·to·basidium \'sep(.)tō+\ *n, cap* [NL, fr. ²sept- + *basidium*] : a genus (the type of the family Septobasidiaceae) of smooth shelf fungi usu. having a well-developed sometimes thick-walled hypobasidium

sep·to·costa \'septə+\ *n* [NL, fr. ²sept- + *costa*] : an external costa on the calyx of a coral that marks the position of or is a continuation of a radial septum

sep·to·cylindrical \'sep(.)tō+\ *adj* [²sept- + *cylindrical*] : cylindrical with one or more cross septa ⟨the ~ conidia of some fungi⟩

sep·to·gloe·um \'septə'glēəm\ *n, cap* [NL, fr. ²sept- + *-gloeum* (fr. Gk *gloios* gum) — more at GLOEO-] : a form genus of fungi (order Melanconiales) having hyaline two-septate to several-septate and oblong conidia and including one member (*S. profusum*) that causes a leaf spot of elm and hazel

septole *var of* SEPTIMOLE

sep·to·let \'septə.let\ *n* -s [alter. (influenced by *-et* as in *septuplet*) of *septole*] : SEPTUPLET

sep·to·marginal \'sep(.)tō+\ *adj* [²sept- + *marginal*] : of or relating to the margin of a septum

¹sep·to·maxillary \"+\ *adj* [²sept- + *maxillary*] : of, relating to, or situated in the region of the nasal septum and the maxilla

²septomaxillary \"\ *n* -ES : a small bone lying between the nasal septum and the maxilla in many amphibians and reptiles and in some birds

sep·to·nasal \'sep(.)tō+\ *adj* [²sept- + *nasal*] : of, relating to, or situated in the region of the nasal septum

sep·to·ria \sep'tōrēə\ *n, cap* [NL, fr. ²sept- + L *-oria* (fem. of *-orius* -ory)] : a form genus of imperfect fungi (family Sphaeropsidaceae) having hyaline elongate to threadlike septate spores formed in pycnidia on the leaves of the host and being known in many cases to be the imperfect stages of ascomycetous fungi of the genus *Mycosphaerella* — see HARD ROT

septs *pl of* SEPT

¹sep·tu·age·nar·i·an \(')sep.t(y)üəjə'nerēən, .sepchəwaj-, .septə.waj-, .sepchə,waj-, -na(ə)r-, -när-\ *adj* [L *septuagenarius* septuagenary + E *-an*] : SEPTUAGENARY

²septuagenarian \"\ *n* -s : a person who is 70 or more but less than 80 years old

sep·tu·agenary \.septyə'wajə,jenərē, -pchəw-, -'jēn-; ,wajə,nerē\ *adj* [L *septuagenarius*, fr. *septuageni* seventy each (fr. *septuaginta* seventy) + *-arius* -ary] : based on the number 70 ⟨2 : 70 or between 70 and 80 years old⟩

sep·tu·a·ges·i·ma \.septəwə'jesəmə, -pchəw-, -jäzəmə\ *n* -s [ME *septuagesime*, fr. LL & ML; MF *septuagesime*, fr. LL *septuagesima*, fr. L, fem. of *septuagesimus* seventieth, fr. *septuaginta* seventy] **1** *obs* : the period of 70 days extending from the third Sunday before Lent to the Saturday after Easter **2** *or* **septuagesima sunday** *usu cap both Ss* : the third Sunday before Lent or the ninth before Easter in the church year observed by various branches of the Christian church

sep·tu·a·gint \'sep't(y)üəjənt; 'septəwə,jint, -pchəw-\ *n* -s [L *septuaginta* seventy, fr. *septem* seven + *-ginta* (akin to L *-ginti* in *viginti* twenty) — more at SEVEN, VICENARY] **1** *usu cap* **a** : the 70 or 72 Jewish scholars at Alexandria held to have translated the Old Testament into Greek [b LL *Septuaginta*, fr. L *septuaginta* seventy] : a copy or edition of the Greek translation of the Old Testament including the Apocrypha prepared in the 3d and 2d centuries B.C., constituting the first vernacular translation of the Bible, designed to meet the needs of Greek-speaking Jews of Egypt unable to read their Scriptures in Hebrew, and still used in the Eastern Orthodox Church — symbol *LXX* **2** *sometimes cap* : a group of 70

sep·tu·a·gin·tal \(')sep't(y)üə,jint'l, .septəwə'-, .sepchəwə-\ *adj, usu cap* : of or relating to the Septuagint

sep·tu·la \'septələ, -pchə-\ *n, pl* **septu·lae** \-,lē, -,lī\ [NL, fr. ²sept- + *-ula*] : one of the small perforations in the walls of the cells between adjacent bryozoan polyps

sep·tu·late \-.lət, -.lāt\ *adj* [NL *septulum* + E *-ate*] *bot* : having imperfect or spurious septa

sep·tu·lum \-.'əm\ *n, pl* **septu·la** \-lə\ [NL, dim. of *septum*] : a small septum

sep·tum \'septəm\ *n, pl* **sep·ta** \-tə\ *or* **septums** [NL, fr. L *septum, saeptum* enclosure, fence, fr. *sepire, saepire* to hedge in, enclose, fr. *sepes, saepes* fence, hedge; akin to Gk *haimos* coagulum, thicket, *haimasia* stone wall] **1** : a dividing wall or membrane: as **a** : a wall separating two plant cells or two cavities or masses (as in a compound ovary or fruit) — called also *dissepiment* **b** : NASAL SEPTUM **c** : CRURAL SEPTUM **d** : a narrow dividing layer of rock material separating larger features of the rock fabric **e** : one of the transverse partitions dividing the shell of a cephalopod or a rhizopod into chambers **f** : one of the transverse partitions between the segments of an annelid **2** : one of the radial calcareous plates projecting from a calyculus of a coral

septum pel·lu·ci·dum \-pə'lüsədəm\ *n, pl* **septa pelluci·da** \-də\ [NL, transparent septum] : the thin double partition extending vertically from the lower surface of the corpus callosum to the fornix and neighboring parts, separating the lateral ventricles of the brain, and enclosing the fifth ventricle

septum transversum *n, pl* **septa transversa** [NL, transverse septum] : the diaphragm or the embryonic structure from which it in part develops

¹sep·tu·ple \'septəpəl, (')sep't(y)üp-\ *adj* [LL *septuplus*, fr. L

septem seven + *-uplus* (as in *quadruplus* quadruple) — more at SEVEN] **1** : consisting of seven : being seven times as great or as many : SEVENFOLD **2** : taken by sevens or in groups of seven sevenfold amount : the seventh multiple

²septuple \"\ *n* -s : a sum seven times as great as another : a sevenfold amount : the seventh multiple

³septuple \"\ *vb* **septupled; septupled; septupling** \-p(ə)liŋ\ **septuples** *vt* : to make seven times as much or as many ~ *vi* : to become seven times as much or as many

sep·tup·let \(')sep'təplət, -.'t(y)üp- *sometimes* '.sep.təp-\ *n* -s

septuplet 3

[¹*septuple* + *-et*] **1** : a combination of seven of a kind **2 a** : one of seven offspring born at one birth **b septuplets** *pl* : a group of seven such offspring **3** : a group of seven musical notes to be played in the time of four or six of the same value — called also *septimole, septolet*

¹sep·tu·pli·cate \(')sep't(y)üpləkət, -lēk- *sometimes* -lə,kāt\ *adj* [ML *septuplicatus*, past part. of *septuplicare* to multiply by seven, fr. LL *septuplus* septuple, after such pairs as L *quadruplus* quadruple: *quadruplicare* to quadruple] : made in seven identical copies : SEVENFOLD

²septuplicate \"\ *n* -s [¹] **1** : a seventh thing like six others of the same kind **2** : seven copies all alike — used with *in* (typed in ~)

³sep·tu·pli·cate \-lə,kāt\ *vt* -ED/-ING/-s : to multiply by seven : reproduce six times : SEPTUPLE; *specif* : to make at one time an original and six carbon copies

sep·ul·cher *or* **sep·ul·chre** \'sepəlkə(r) *archaic* sə'p-\ *n* -s [ME *sepulcre*, fr. OF, fr. L *sepulcrum, sepulchrum*, fr. *sepelire* to bury; akin to Gk *hepein* to care for, prepare, Skt *sapati* he seeks after, courts, honors, *saparyati* he pays homage, worships] **1 a** : a place for the interment of a dead body : GRAVE, TOMB **b** : a final or resting place ⟨my heart . . . shall be thy ~ —Shak.⟩ ⟨the ~ of all . . . French hopes —F.L.Schuman⟩ **c** : REPOSITORY, TERMINUS ⟨my heart . . . shall be thy ~ —Shak.⟩ **2 a** : a receptacle for religious relics esp. in an altar **b** : EASTER SEPULCHER 1

²sepulcher *or* **sepulchre** \"\ *vt* -ED/-ING/-s : to place or receive in a sepulcher : BURY, ENTOMB

se·pul·chral \sə'pəlkrəl, se'p-\ *adj* [L *sepulcralis*, fr. *sepulcrum* sepulcher + *-alis* -al] **1** : of, relating to, or serving as a sepulcher or a memorial to the dead : MORTUARY ⟨~ inscriptions⟩ ⟨the ~ darkness of the catacombs —Nathaniel Hawthorne⟩ ⟨erect ~ monuments in the church —Nikolaus Pevsner⟩ **2 a** : suited to or suggestive of burial rites : having a funereal quality ⟨a ~ whisper⟩ ⟨rows of empty benches in the dusk gave the room a somewhat ~ aspect —Hanns Sachs⟩ **b** : emanating from or as if from the tomb ⟨the hollow, ~ tone of editorial comment —G.W.Johnson⟩ — **se·pul·chral·ly** \-ōlē\ *adv*

se·pul·tural \sə'pəlch(ə)rəl, 'sepəl,chúrəl\ *adj* [¹*sepulture* + *-al*] *archaic* : SEPULCHRAL

¹sep·ul·ture \'sepəlchər, -.chú(ə)r\ *n* -s [ME, fr. OF, fr. L *sepultura*, fr. *sepultus* (past part. of *sepelire* to bury) + *-ura* -ure] **1** : BURIAL **2** : SEPULCHER

²sepulture \"\ *vt* -ED/-ING/-s : to place in or as if in a grave : BURY

seq *abbr* **1** sequel **2** sequence **3** [L *sequens, sequentes, sequentia*] the following **4** [L *sequitur*] it follows

seqq *abbr* **1** [L *sequentes, sequentia*] the following **2** [L *sequentibus*] in the following places

sequ *abbr* [L *sequitur*] it follows

se·qua·cious \sə'kwāshəs, sē'k-\ *adj* [L *sequac-, sequax* sequacious (fr. *sequi* to follow) + E *-ious*] **1 a** *archaic* : inservile : IMITATIVE, OBSEQUIOUS **2** *obs* : characterized by malleability : DUCTILE, PLIABLE **3** : logically sequent

se·qua·ci·ty \-wasəd-ē\ *n* -ES [LL *sequacitas*, fr. L *sequac-, sequax* inclined to follow, sequacious + *-itas* -ity] : the quality or state of being sequacious : disposition to follow

Se·qua·ni \'sekwə,nī, -,nē; 'sākwə,nē\ *n pl, cap* [L] : a Celtic people of ancient Gaul inhabiting a region around the sources of the Seine

se·quel \'sēkwəl\ *n* -s [ME *sequel, sequele*, fr. MF *sequelle*, fr. L *sequela, sequela*, fr. *sequi* to follow — more at SUE] **1** *obs* **a** : a member of a retinue : FOLLOWER, RETAINER — usu. used in pl. ⟨friends, adherents, and ~s, should be comprehended in the truce —John Speed⟩ **b** : SUCCESSION, SERIES ⟨his daughter first; and in ~, all —Shak.⟩ ⟨a ~ of four —Lancelot Andrewes⟩ **2 a** : something that follows naturally from an antecedent cause : CONSEQUENCE, RESULT ⟨higher prices as a ~ to rising production costs⟩ *b obs* : a logical inference ⟨so fareth it with the bodies and by ~ with the souls —Thomas Walkington⟩ **c** : SEQUELA 1 ⟨gangrene is a ~ of wounds⟩ **3 a** : the next in an unfolding series (as of events) : subsequent development ⟨powered flight as the evolutionary ~ to gliding⟩ **b** : the next installment (as of a speech or narrative) : CONTINUATION; *esp* : a literary work continuing the course of a narrative begun in a preceding one ⟨the hero performs even more astonishing feats in the ~⟩ **4** : an allowance of meal or other small perquisite made in thirlage to the servants of the dominant mill for actual or nominal services in grinding — usu. used in pl. **syn** see EFFECT

se·que·la \sə'kwēlə, sē'k-\ *n, pl* **sequelae** \-(.)lē\ [NL, fr. L, sequel] **1** : an aftereffect of disease or injury ⟨enteritis . . . as a ~ of indigestion —F.B.Hadley⟩ ⟨the necessity for frequent blood counts to avoid serious sequelae —G.F.Dick⟩ **2 a** : a secondary result : CONSEQUENCE ⟨the poisonous sequelae of war —R.M.MacIver⟩

¹se·quence \'sēkwən(t)s, -,kwen-\ *n* -s [ME, fr. ML *sequentia*, fr. LL, succession, state or fact of following, fr. L *sequent-, sequens* (pres. part. of *sequi* to follow) + *-ia* -y] **1** : a hymn or rhythm having no regular meter read or sung between the gradual and the Gospel on certain occasions as part of a Christian liturgical service (as in Roman Catholic and Anglican churches) — called also *prose* **2** : a continuous or connected series: as **a** : a group of similar or related elements ⟨a ~ of market fluctuations⟩ ⟨a photo ~⟩ ⟨bringing . . . a ~ of low hills —*Amer. Guide Series: Texas*⟩; *specif* : an extended series of poems united by a single theme ⟨sonnet ~⟩ **b** : three or more playing cards usu. of the same suit in consecutive order of rank (as jack, ten, nine, eight, seven) **c** : a succession of repetitions of a musical phrase each in a new position ⟨rising chromatic ~⟩ — compare ROSALIA **d** : a mathematical aggregate ordered in the same manner as the positive integers — compare SERIES 2 **e** : a planned program of courses ⟨a four-year ~ in social studies —J.B.Conant⟩ **f** *archaeol* (1) : a set of components occurring in successive strata, preferably in one site ⟨a local ~⟩ (2) : a group of local sequences consolidated into one of larger scope ⟨a cultural ~⟩ **g** (1) : a section of a motion picture consisting of a succession of related shots or scenes in which a single subject or a single phase of a story is developed ⟨the . . . roller-coaster ~ in *Cinerama* —Lloyd Shearer⟩ (2) : a self-sufficient combination of dance movements permitting of further development, or a movement series with repetition of a theme on an ever lowered or heightened plane of space or dynamic intensity **3** (1) : EPISODE ⟨the ~ from which the book takes its title —*Times Lit. Supp.*⟩ ⟨the ~ of the hearsals of each ~ in the coronation ceremony —Blake Ehrlich⟩ **h** (1) : an agreed or keyed succession in cryptography (2) : KEYING SEQUENCE (3) : an arrangement of the alphabet in cryptology **3 a** (1) : a chronological succession ⟨birds have no prevision . . . of the ~ of the seasons —E.A.Armstrong⟩ (2) : a succession of geologic events, processes, or formations in chronologic order; *esp* : STRATIGRAPHIC SEQUENCE **b** (1) : a methodical arrangement or consecutive order ⟨a . . . ~ whereby he gets the apartment three days a week, she gets it twice —Lewis Nichols⟩ ⟨the ~ in which one word follows another —Stuart Chase⟩ ⟨paints each little square in ~ —Harland Manchester⟩ **c** : a dimensional ordering of elements or terms in logic (3) : an arrangement of the tenses of successive verbs in a sentence designed to express a coherent interrelationship esp. between main and

subordinate verbs (as in indirect discourse, conditional sentences) (4) : the order in which portions of a recording are placed on a series of phonograph records — compare AUTOMATIC SEQUENCE **4 a** : a natural result or logical inference : SEQUEL ⟨action in ~ is . . . sincere idealism —*Times Lit. Supp.*⟩ ⟨the order of successional stages . . . has been reconstructed by the methods of inference and ~ —*Ecology*⟩ **b** : a subsequent development ⟨everybody was caught up in a succession of ~s —*Time*⟩ **c** : the order in which events are connected or related in time : simple succession; *esp* : the connection of antecedent and consequent in a temporal series apart from any causal necessity ⟨the reactions of chemical agents may be conceived as merely invariable ~s⟩ **5** : the quality or state of being sequent : continuity between parts : CONSECUTIVENESS, PROGRESSION ⟨narrative ~⟩ ⟨formal ~ is useful in the architecture of public buildings because it helps to direct the visitor⟩ ⟨~ in learning depends upon continuity of growth in the learner —Dora Smith⟩

²sequence \"\ *vt* : to arrange in a sequence

se·quenc·er \-ənsə(r), -en(t)s-\ *n* -s [¹*sequence* + *-er*] **1** : a book of liturgical sequences **2** : one that determines a sequence ⟨an electronic ~ will control the rocket's functions —A.C.Fisher⟩

sequenciary *or* **sequentiary** *n* -ES [ML *sequentiarius*, fr. *sequentia* sequence (sense 1) + L *-arius* -ary] : SEQUENCER 1

se·quen·cy \'sēkwənsē\ *n* -ES [LL *sequentia*] : SEQUENCE

¹se·quent \'sēkwənt\ *adj* [L *sequent-, sequens*, pres. part. of *sequi* to follow — more at SUE] **1** : occurring in sequence : ENSUING, CONSECUTIVE **2** : following as a result : CONSEQUENT

²sequent \"\ *n* -s **1** *obs* : one of a sequence; *esp* : a member of a retinue ⟨a letter to a ~ of the stranger queen's —Shak.⟩ **2** : CONSEQUENCE, SEQUEL ⟨I adopt the mode of action; and the expected . . . ~ actually follows —C.I.Lewis⟩

se·quen·tial \sə'kwenchəl, (')sē'k-\ *adj* [LL *sequentia* sequence + E *-al*] **1 a** : occurring as a sequela of disease or injury **b** : of, relating to, or forming a sequence : CONSECUTIVE, SERIAL ⟨combination of two courses into one —S.L.Pressey⟩ ⟨set forth the essential facts . . . in a well ordered, ~ manner —*N.Y.Herald Tribune*⟩ ⟨the . . . Neolithic setting for which ~ stages have been most fully revealed —H.B.Collins⟩ **c** : having the form or character of a musical sequence ⟨~ arpeggio⟩ **2 a** : occurring without interruption : CONTINUOUS **b** : based on an undetermined number of samples or observations analyzed as they are accumulated to the point where a sufficiently precise result (as of an experiment) can be determined without further analysis ⟨~ analysis⟩ ⟨~ sampling⟩ **3** : occurring as a result : CONSEQUENT — **se·quen·tial·ly** \-ōlē,əli\ *adv*

sequential system *n* : a system of color television based on the successive showing of the three primary colors as dots, lines, or rapidly succeeding whole pictures so that through persistence of vision the colors appear in their proper proportions

¹se·ques·ter \sə'kwestə(r), sē'k-\ *vb* -ED/-ING/-s [ME *sequestren*, fr. MF *sequestrer*, fr. LL *sequestrare* to set aside for safekeeping, surrender, remove, separate, fr. L *sequester* depositary, trustee; akin to L *sequi* to follow — more at SUE] *vt* **1 a** : to set apart : separate for a special purpose : REMOVE, SEGREGATE ⟨the dentist must ~ with a rubber dam the tooth he is working on —*New Yorker*⟩ ⟨a quarry ~ed for hearthstones and flaggings —C.M.Webster⟩ *b obs* : to deprive of membership (as in a church) or of public office or station ⟨was ~ed from parliament —David Hume †1776⟩ **c** : to hide from public view : withdraw from circulation : SECLUDE, SECRETE ⟨old houses . . . ~ed under leafy boughs —*Amer. Guide Series: Vt.*⟩ ⟨no crusading idealist . . . ever thought it right to ~ himself in an estate —Norman Thomas⟩ **2 a** : to seize esp. by public authority : CONFISCATE ⟨police continued to uncover and . . . arms and ammunition —R.G.Woolbert⟩ **b** (1) : to take (property) from the possession of one or more parties to a controversy and put into the possession of a third party until profits have paid an obligation or until the owner has performed a decree of court or clears himself of contempt (2) *international law* : to appropriate under the right of preemption **3** : to bind (as a metal or metal ion) in the form of a soluble complex or chelate by adding a suitable reagent for the purpose of preventing precipitation in water solution by chemical agents that would normally bring it about, of solubilizing precipitates already formed, or of otherwise suppressing undesired chemical or biological activity ⟨~ calcium and magnesium ions in the softening of hard water⟩ ~ *vi* **1** *archaic* : to withdraw into seclusion : RETIRE **2** : to disclaim legal responsibility

²sequester \"\ *n* -s [L] **1** *Roman & civil law* : a depositary of property pending the settlement of a dispute as to its ownership : a receiver appointed by the court [²F *séquestre*, fr. L *sequestrum* sequestration, deposit, fr. *sequester* depositary] *obs* : SEPARATION ⟨this hand of yours requires a ~ from liberty —Shak.⟩ **3** [NL *sequestrum*] : SEQUESTRUM

sequestered *adj* [fr. past part. of ¹*sequester*] **1** *obs* : cut off from companionship or congenial surroundings : ISOLATED, SEGREGATED ⟨a poor ~ stag that from the hunters . . . had taken a hurt —Shak.⟩ **2 a** : CONFISCATED, IMPOUNDED ⟨when the royal officers in Philadelphia seized fifty pipes of Madeira . . . a mob assaulted them and stole the ~ goods —C.A. & Mary Beard⟩ *b archaic* : deprived of privilege or property : DISPOSSESSED **3 a** : withdrawn from public view : SHELTERED, SECLUDED ⟨sat close together . . . in the ~ pergola —L.C. Douglas⟩ **b** : living the life of a recluse : SOLITARY

sequestra *pl of* SEQUESTRUM

se·ques·tra·ble \-trəbəl\ *adj* [¹*sequester* + *-able*] *archaic* : liable to exclusion or seizure

se·ques·trant \-trənt\ *n* -s [¹*sequester* + *-ant*] : a sequestering agent (as a sodium phosphate glass, a salt of ethylenediamine-tetraacetic acid, or citric acid)

¹se·ques·trate \sə'kwe,strāt, sē'k-; 'sēkwə,s-, 'sekwə,s-; 'sekwə,s-; *usu* -,ād-+V\ *adj* [ME, fr. LL *sequestratus*, past part. of *sequestrare* to remove, separate] *archaic* : SEQUESTERED

²sequestrate \"\ *vb* -ED/-ING/-s [LL *sequestratus*, past part. of *sequestrare*] *vt* **1** : SEQUESTER **2** : to form a sequestrum in ~ *vi* : to form a sequestrum

seques·tra·tion \.sēkwə'strāshən, (.)sē,kwe's-, sə,kwe's-, .sekwə's-\ *n* -s [ME *sequestracion*, fr. LL *sequestration-, sequestratio*, fr. *sequestratus* (past part. of *sequestrare* to remove, separate) + *-ion-, -io* -ion — more at SEQUESTER] **1 a** : an act or instance of cutting off : EXCLUSION, SEPARATION ⟨forced into retirement by parliamentary ~ —Douglas Bush⟩ **b** : the quality or state of being sequestered : ISOLATION, SECLUSION ⟨lonely ~ on an island —*Time*⟩ **2** : the separation or removal of property from a person in possession of it in order that the property or the proceeds thereof may be dealt with as a court or other competent authority may direct: as **a** : the authorization of a sheriff or commissioners to take into custody the property of a defendant who is in contempt or its rents and profits until he complies with the orders of a court **b** *English eccl law* : an attachment of a vacant benefice usu. granted by a bishop to church wardens for the management of its offices during the vacancy **c** *civil law* : a deposit whereby a neutral depositary agrees to hold property in litigation and to restore it to the party to whom it is adjudged to belong **d** *Scots law* : the appropriation of the property of a bankrupt in order to divide it among his creditors **e** *international law* : the seizure of the property of an individual for use by the state; *esp* : the seizure by a belligerent power of debts due from its subjects to the enemy or of property subject to the right of preemption **f** *probate law* : the subjection of a renounced interest to judicial management for distribution as the testator would have desired if he had had in mind the renunciation of the interest he tried to create **3** : a seizure of property esp. by public authority : CONFISCATION ⟨the taxation and ~ suffered during and after the Civil War . . . brought him into debt —J.B.Leishman⟩ **4** : the formation of a sequestrum **5** : the process of sequestering or result of being sequestered ⟨in soils various minor elements such as copper, zinc, and manganese are applied in organic complex ~ form so as to be kept from the normal precipitation reaction in soils —M.L. Jackson⟩

seques·tra·tor \'prounc at SEQUESTRATE +ə(r)\ *n* -s [ML, fr. LL *sequestratus* (past part.) + L *-or*] *law* : one that is ap-

pointed to receive property in sequestration or to execute a sequestration writ

seques·tra·trix \,sēkwə'strā·triks, ,sē,kwe's-, ,sekwə's-\ *n, pl* **sequestratri·ces** \,=(,)='strā·trə,sēz; sə,kwestrə·'trī(,)sēz, sē,k-\ [NL, fem. of ML *sequestrator* — more at -TRIX] **:** a female sequestrator

se·ques·trec·to·my \,sē,kwe'strektəmē\ *n* -ES [ISV *sequestr-* (fr. NL *sequestrum*) + *-ectomy*] **:** the surgical removal of a sequestrum

se·ques·tree \,sē,kwe¦strē, sə'kwe,s-\ *n* -S [¹*sequester* + *-ee*] *archaic* **:** SEQUESTRATOR

se·ques·trum \sə'kwestrəm, sē'k-\ *n, pl* **sequestrums** \-rəmz\ *also* **seques·tra** \-rə\ [NL, fr. L, sequestration, deposit, fr. *sequester* depositary — more at SEQUESTER] **:** a fragment of dead bone that becomes detached from the sound portion ⟨necrotic fragments of teeth and bone ~s —L.R. Cahn⟩ ⟨an involucrum forms about a ~ in osteomyelitis —C.E.Dunlap⟩ — compare ³SLOUGH 2a

se·quin \'sēkwən\ *n* -S [F, fr. It *zecchino*, fr. *zecca* mint, fr. Ar *sikkah* die, stamp, stamped coin] **1 :** an old gold coin of Italy and Turkey first struck at Venice about the end of the 13th century — called also *chequeen, zecchino, zechin, zequin* **2 a :** a small ornament (as a flat disk, star, or other shape) usu. of shiny metal or plastic pierced with a hole for sewing onto cloth in decorative designs **:** SPANGLE

se·quined *or* **se·quinned** \-ənd\ *adj* **:** ornamented with or as if with sequins ⟨separate skirts, ~ and quilted and otherwise bedizened —Lois Long⟩ ⟨petals ~ with dew⟩

sequitur *n* -S [L, it follows, 3d pers. sing. pres. indic. of *sequi* to follow — more at SUE] **:** an inference that follows from a premise ⟨state certain basic postulates and . . . several useful ~s —J.B.McMillan⟩ — compare NON SEQUITUR

se·quoia \sə'kwȯi(y)ə, sē'k- *also* -wȯyə\ *n* [NL, after *Sequoya* (George Guess) †1843 Am. Indian scholar] **1** *cap* **:** a genus of coniferous trees (family Taxodiaceae) distinguished by having both linear and awl-shaped decurrent leaves and the winter buds with imbricated scales — see REDWOOD; compare SEQUOIADENDRON **2** -S **:** any tree of the genus *Sequoia* or of the related genus *Sequoiadendron*: *specif* **:** BIG TREE 1

se·quoia·den·dron \=¦==¦dendrən\ *n, cap* [NL, fr. *Sequoia* + *-dendron*] **:** a genus of coniferous trees (family Taxodiaceae) sometimes included in the genus *Sequoia* but distinguished by having all the leaves scalelike or awl-shaped and appressed and the winter buds naked — compare SEQUOIA 1

sequoia pitch moth *n* **:** a small clearwing moth (*Vespamima sequoiae*) whose larvae are esp. destructive to lodgepole pine and western yellow pine

ser *var of* SEER

ser *abbr* **1** serial **2** series **3** sermon **4** serve; service; serving

sera *pl of* SERUM

se·rac \sə'rak, (')sā¦rak\ *n* -S [F *sérac* a solid white cheese, serac, fr. ML *seracium* whey, fr. L *serum* whey — more at SERUM] **:** a jagged pinnacle, sharp ridge, or block of ice among the crevasses of a glacier (as in an icefall) — compare NIEVE PENITENTE

se·ra·glio \sə'ral(,)yō, -räl-,-ral-\ *n, pl* **seraglios** *also* **sera·gli** \-)yē\ [It *serraglio* enclosure, cage, sultan's palace, harem, partly fr. OIt, fr. ML *serraculum* bar of a door, bolt, fr. (assumed) VL *serrare* to lock up, bolt, fr. LL *serare*; partly fr. Turk *saray* palace — more at SEAR, SERAI] **1 a :** HAREM 1a **b :** a place of licentious pleasure; *esp* **:** BROTHEL **2 :** a palace or residence of a sultan **3** *obs* **a :** CARAVANSARY **b :** WAREHOUSE

se·rai \sə'rī\ *n* -S [Turk & Per; Turk *saray* palace, mansion, fr. Per *sarāī* palace, mansion, inn — more at CARAVANSARY] **1 :** CARAVANSARY **2 :** SERAGLIO 2

se·rail \sə'rī, -rī(ə)l, -rā(ə)l\ *n* -S [MF, fr. OIt *serraglio*] **:** SERAGLIO

serajevo *usu cap, var of* SARAJEVO

ser·al \'sirəl\ *adj* [⁵*sere* + *-al*] **:** of, relating to, or characteristic of an ecological sere ⟨a ~ community of mixed shrubs and trees⟩ ⟨~ stages in climax development⟩

ser·and·ite \'serən,dīt\ *n* -S [F *sérandite*, fr. J. M. *Sérand*, 20th cent. West African mineral collector + F *-ite*] **:** a mineral consisting of hydrous silicate of manganese, lime, soda, and potash and occurring in rose-red monoclinic crystals

se·rang \sə'raŋ\ *n* -S [Per *sarhang* commander, boatswain, fr. *sar* chief + *hang* authority] **1 :** BOATSWAIN **2 :** the skipper of a small boat

serape *var of* SARAPE

ser·a·pe·um \,serə'pēəm\ *n, pl* **serapeums** \-ēəmz\ *or* **sera·pea** \-ēə\ *usu cap* [LL, fr. Gk *sarapeion, serapeion*, fr. *Sarapis, Serapis*, Egyptian god] **:** a place or building or group of buildings sacred to Serapis

¹**ser·aph** \'serəf\ *also* **ser·a·phim** \-,fim *also* -,fēm *sometimes* ,=='=\ *n, pl* **seraphim** *or* **seraphs** *also* **seraphims** [LL *seraphim, seraphin* seraphs, fr. Heb *śĕrāphīm*] **1 :** one of an order of fiery six-winged angels who guard God's throne — see CELESTIAL HIERARCHY **2 :** a representation of a seraph often in red symbolizing sacred ardor **3 :** one that is seraphic in character

²**seraph** \"\ *adj* **:** relating to or being a seraph **:** SERAPHIC ⟨the ~ way of those above —Lord Byron⟩ ⟨a ~ wind —G.W. Russell⟩

se·raph·ic \sə'rafik, -fēk\ *also* **se·raph·i·cal** \-fəkəl, -fēk-\ *adj* [*seraphic* fr. ML *seraphicus*, fr. LL *seraphim, seraphin*, seraphs + L *-icus* -ic; *seraphical* fr. ML *seraphicus* + E *-al*] **1 :** of, relating to, or befitting a seraph **:** ANGELIC, SUBLIME, PURE ⟨~ arms and trophies —John Milton⟩ ⟨could have imagined a ~ presence in the room —George Meredith⟩ ⟨his ~ church-offertory style —*N.Y.Times*⟩ **2 :** resembling a seraph esp. in beauty or ecstatic adoration ⟨~ smile⟩ ⟨in appearance he was ~ —E.J.Kahn⟩ — **se·raph·i·cal·ly** \-fək(ə)lē,-fēk-, -li\ *adv* — **se·raph·i·cal·ness** \-kəlnəs\ *n* -ES

ser·a·phim \'serə,fim *also* -,fēm *sometimes* ,=='=\ *n, pl* **seraphim** [NL, fr. LL, seraphs] **:** a fossil eurypterid (genus *Pterygotus*)

ser·a·phin \-fin, -fēn\ *n* -S [LL, seraphs] *archaic* **:** SERAPH

ser·a·phine \'serə,fēn, ,=='=\ *also* **ser·a·phi·na** \,=='fēnə\ *n* -S [*seraph* + *-ina*] **:** a 19th century English keyboard reed instrument similar to the American organ

seraphlike \'==,=\ *adj* **:** resembling a seraph **:** SERAPHIC

se·ra·pi·as \sə'rāpēəs\ [NL, fr. L, an orchid, fr. Gk, fr. *Serapis, Sarapis*, Egyptian god] *syn of* EPIPACTIS

se·raya \sə'rīə\ *n* -S [native name in Borneo] **:** any of several trees of the genus *Shorea*

¹**serb** \'sər|b, 'sō|, 'səi|\ *n* -S *cap* [Serb *Srb*] **1 :** a native or inhabitant of the former kingdom of Serbia or of the federal republic of Serbia in Yugoslavia **2 :** SERBIAN 2

²**serb** \"\ *adj, usu cap* **:** SERBIAN

¹**ser·bi·an** \|bēən\ *or* **ser·vi·an** \|vē-\ *n* -S *cap* [*Serbia* (formerly *Servia*), former Balkan kingdom (now a republic of Yugoslavia) + E *-an*] **1 :** SERB 1 **2 a :** the Serbo-Croatian language as spoken in Serbia **b :** a literary form of Serbo-Croatian using the Cyrillic alphabet

²**serbian** \"\ *or* **servian** \"\ *adj, usu cap* [*Serbia, Servia* + E *-an*] **1 a :** of, relating to, or characteristic of Serbia **b :** of, relating to, or characteristic of the Serbs **2 a :** of, relating to, or characteristic of the Serbo-Croatian language as spoken in Serbia **b :** of, relating to, or characteristic of a literary form of Serbo-Croatian using the Cyrillic alphabet

serbian spruce *n, usu cap 1st S* **:** a pyramidal evergreen tree (*Picea omorika*) of southeastern Europe that is widely planted for its rich dark green foliage and brown oblong cones

serbo- *comb form, usu cap* [*serb*] **1 :** Serbian ⟨*Serbo*phile⟩ **2 :** Serbian and ⟨*Serbo*-Bulgarian⟩

serbo-croat \¦=(,)bō+\ *n or adj, usu cap S&C* [*serbo-* + *croat*] **:** SERBO-CROATIAN

¹**serbo-croatian** \"+\ *n, cap S&C* [*serbo-* + *croatian*] **1 :** the Slavic language of the Serbs and Croats consisting of Serbian written in the Cyrillic alphabet and Croatian written in the Roman alphabet **2 :** one whose native language is Serbo-Croatian

²**serbo-croatian** \"\ *adj, usu cap S&C* **1 :** of, relating to, or characteristic of the Serbo-Croatian language **2 :** of, relating to, or characteristic of the Serbo-Croatians

ser·cial \¦sersē¦al, (')sers¦yal\ *n* -S *usu cap* [F] **:** a dry Madeira wine

ser·dab \sə(r)'däb\ *n* -S [Ar *sirdāb* cellar, underground vault, fr. Per *sardāb* ice cellar, fr. *sard* cold + *āb* water] **1 :** a narrow chamber of the ancient Egyptian mastaba either concealed or accessible only by a narrow passage and containing a statue of the deceased **2 :** a living room in the basement of a house in the Near East that provides coolness during the summer months

serdar *var of* SIRDAR

¹**sere** *also* **sear** \'si(ə)r, -iə\ *adj* -ER/-EST [ME, fr. OE *sēar*; akin to MLG *sōr* dry, OHG *sōrēn* to wither, L *sudus* dry (of weather), Gk *hauos* dry, *hauein* to parch, dry, Skt *śuṣyati* it dries up, withers] **1 :** dried up **:** WITHERED ⟨rank summer vegetation turns ~ —Marjorie K. Rawlings⟩ ⟨~, cracked mud flats —*Amer. Guide Series: Calif.*⟩ **2** *archaic* **:** worn thin **:** THREADBARE ⟨sails that were so thin and ~ —S.T. Coleridge⟩

²**sere** \"\ *n* -S **1 :** a sere period or condition ⟨the ~ and autumn of the moss animals' year —William Beebe⟩ **2 :** sere vegetation ⟨flame was so swift that it barely singed the green grass among the winter ~ —John Onslow⟩

³**sere** \"\ *n* -S [MF *serre* grip, grasp, clip — more at SEAR (catch of a gunlock)] *archaic* **:** CLAW, TALON

⁴**se·re** \'(t)sā(,)rā\ *n* -S [Heb *ṣērē, ṣērī*, lit., perh. a split, opening] **:** a vowel point .. written below its consonant indicating Hebrew close *e* pronounced \ā\

⁵**sere** \'si(ə)r, -iə\ *n* -S [L *series* series] **:** a series of ecological communities that follow one another in the course of the biotic development of an area or formation from pioneer stage to climax — see HYDROSERE, LITHOSERE, PSAMMOSERE, XEROSERE

serebend *var of* SARABAND

¹**se·reh** \sə'rā\ *n* -S [Malay *sērē, sērai*] **:** CITRONELLA GRASS

²**sereh** \"\ *n* -S [¹*sereh*] **:** a destructive East Indian virus disease of sugarcane characterized by necrosis of the phloem, fanlike tops, and general degeneration

se·rein \sə'raⁿ, -ran\ *n* -S [F, fr. MF *serain* evening, nightfall, fr. L *sero* late — more at SOIREE] **1** *archaic* **:** the supposed fall of dew from a clear sky just after sunset **2 :** mist or fine rain falling from an apparently clear sky

se·re·na \sə'rānə\ *n* -S [Prov, poem expressing a lover's longing for evening, fr. *ser* evening, fr. L *sero* late — more at SOIREE] **:** an evening love song — compare ¹ALBA

¹**ser·e·nade** \¦serə¦nād\ *n* -S [F *sérénade*, fr. It *serenata* (influenced in meaning by *sera* evening, fr. L, fr. fem. of *serus* late), fr. *sereno* clear, calm (of weather), fr. L *serenus* — more at SINCE, SERENE] **1 a :** music sung or played esp. for gallantry in the open air at night **b :** a musical composition suitable for a serenade **c :** the performance of a serenade ⟨a lover's ~ beneath his lady's window⟩ **2 :** SERENATA 2 **3 :** an instrumental composition in several movements, written for a small ensemble and midway in style between the suite and the symphony **4** *dial* **:** SHIVAREE 1 **5 a :** the performance of any music esp. in the open air in compliment to a person or group **b :** the music played at such a performance

²**serenade** \"\ *vb* -ED/-ING/-S *vt* **:** to entertain with or perform a serenade in honor of ⟨singers still gather around your car and ~ you —Green Peyton⟩ ~ *vi* **:** to play a serenade

ser·e·nad·er \-də(r)\ *n* -S **:** one that serenades

ser·e·na·ta \,serə'nädə\ *n, pl* **serenatas** \-ädəz\ *also* **serena·te** \-ä(,)tā\ [It, serenade — more at SERENADE] **1 a :** SERENA **b :** SERENADE **2 :** a cantata or secular ode of a pastoral or dramatic character usu. composed in honor of an individual or event

seren·dib·ite \,serən¦di,bīt, sə'rendə,b-\ *n* -S [fr. *Serendib, Serendip*, former name for Ceylon (fr. Ar *Sarandīb*) + E *-ite*] **:** a mineral $(Ca,Mg)_5Al_5B_2Si_2O_{10}$ consisting of a silicate and borate of calcium, magnesium, and aluminum and occurring in irregular blue grains in Ceylon

ser·en·dip·i·tist \,serən'dipəd·əst, -pətə-\ *n* -S [*serendipity* + *-ist*] **:** one who finds valuable or agreeable things not sought for

ser·en·dip·i·tous \¦==¦=pəd·əs, -pətəs\ *adj* [*serendipity* + *-ous*] **:** obtained or characterized by serendipity ⟨~ discoveries⟩

ser·en·dip·i·ty \,serən'dipəd·ē, -pətē, -i\ *n* -ES [*Serendip, Serendib*, former name for Ceylon (fr. Ar *Sarandīb*) + E *-ity*; fr. the possession of the gift by the heroes of the Persian fairy tale *The Three Princes of Serendip*] **:** an assumed gift for finding valuable or agreeable things not sought for

¹**se·rene** \sə'rēn\ *adj, often* -ER/-EST [L *serenus* clear, fair, calm (of weather), peaceful, cheerful; akin to OHG *serawēn* to become dry, Gk *xeron* dry land, *xēros* dry] **1 a :** completely clear, fine, or balmy **:** suggesting or conducive to calm peacefulness free of storms or unpleasant change ⟨~ weather⟩ ⟨~ skies⟩ ⟨~ will be our days and bright —William Wordsworth⟩ **b :** shining bright and steady and unobscured ⟨elegant contrasts between . . . the ~ shining of the planets and our hot feverish lives —L.P.Smith⟩ **2 :** marked by or suggestive of utter calm and unruffled repose or quietude without suggestions of agitation, trouble, fitful activity, or sudden change ⟨to the end his mind remained ~ and undisturbed —W.S. Maugham⟩ ⟨a ~ expression upon her face —Samuel Butler †1902⟩ ⟨genuine intellectual certainty is generally ~ —Gilbert Murray⟩ ⟨myself sitting all ~ in the rest house —Arthur Grimble⟩ ⟨a ~ lake⟩ **3 :** most high — used as part of a royal style ⟨His *Serene* Highness⟩ **syn** see CALM

²**serene** \"\ *vt* -ED/-ING/-S [L *serenare*, fr. *serenus* serene] *archaic* **:** to make serene **:** TRANQUILIZE

³**serene** \"\ *n* -S [L *serenum*, fr. neut. of *serenus* serene] **1 :** a serene condition or expanse (as of sky, sea, or light) ⟨the blue deep's ~ —Lord Byron⟩ ⟨the day's intense ~ —P.B.Shelley⟩ **2 :** SERENITY, TRANQUILLITY, CALMNESS

⁴**serene** *n* -S [MF *serein* serein, fr. earlier *serain* evening, nightfall — more at SEREIN] *obs* **:** the cool or damp of evening air

se·rene·ly *adv* **:** in a serene manner ⟨~ beautiful⟩

se·rene·ness *n* -ES [¹*serene* + *-ness*] **:** SERENITY

sere·ness *n* -ES [ME *sernesse*, fr. ¹*sere* + *-nesse* -ness] **:** the quality or state of being sere

se·ren·i·ty \sə'renəd·ē, -nətē, -i\ *n* -ES [MF *serenité*, fr. L *serenitat-, serenitas*, fr. *serenus* serene + *-itat-, -itas* -ity] **1 :** the quality or state of being serene **:** CALM, PEACEFULNESS, REPOSE ⟨the ~ of a mind at ease with itself and kindly disposed towards everyone —Jane Austen⟩ **2** *usu cap* **:** a person of honor ⟨Highnesses, *Serenities*, and Excellencies . . . arrived from all quarters—W.M.Thackeray⟩ — used as a title of honor given to reigning princes and other dignitaries ⟨your *Serenity*⟩

sere·noa \sə'rēnəwə, ,serə'nōə\ *n, cap* [NL, after *Sereno* Watson †1892 Am. botanist] **:** a small genus of nearly stemless fan palms of the southern U.S. having spiny-toothed petioles, nearly round leaves, and ovoid or globose drupes — see SAW PALMETTO

¹**serer** *comparative of* SERE

²**se·rer** \sə're(ə)r\ *n, pl* **serer** *or* **serers** *usu cap* **1 :** a Negro of a people who dwell about Cape Vert, Senegal, and who are among the tallest of Negro peoples **2 :** a West-Atlantic language of the Serer people

¹**se·res** \'si(,)rēz, 'sē(-\ *n pl, usu cap* [L, fr. Gk *Sēres*] **:** a people of eastern Asia mentioned by Greeks and Romans as making silk fabrics and now usu. identified with the Chinese

²**seres** *pl of* SERE

serest *superlative of* SERE

serf \'sərf, 'səf, 'səif\ *n* -S [F, fr. L *servus* slave, servant, serf — more at SERVE] **1 :** THEOW **2 :** a person (as the English villein of the 12th or 13th century) belonging to any of various grades of the lower class esp. in different feudal systems, bound to the soil and more or less subject to the will of the owner of the soil, and separable from the lord's land by manumission only **3 :** VILLEIN 3 **4 :** any of various unemancipated classes of tillers of the soil (as in Germany, Poland, and Russia) esp. of the 17th and 18th centuries **5 :** SLAVE

serf·age \-fij, -fēj\ *n* -S [*serf* + *-age*] **:** SERFDOM

serf·dom \-fdəm\ *n* -S [*serf* + *-dom*] **:** the quality, state, or fact of being a serf **:** SLAVERY — compare HELOTRY, PEONAGE

serf·hood \-,fůd, -f,hůd\ *n* [*serf* + *-hood*] **:** SERFDOM

serf·ish \-,fish,-fēsh\ *adj* **:** characteristic of a serf — **serf·ish·ness** *n* -ES

serf·ism \-,fizəm\ *n* -S [*serf* + *-ism*] **:** social polity in which serfdom exists

serf·ship \-,f,ship\ *n* [*serf* + *-ship*] **:** SERFDOM

serg *abbr, often cap* sergeant

¹**serge** \'sərj, 'səj, 'səij\ *n* -S [ME *sarge*, fr. MF, fr. (assumed) VL *sarica*, fr. L *serica*, fem. of *sericus* of silk — more at SERICEOUS] **:** a durable twilled fabric having a smooth clear face and a pronounced diagonal rib on the front and the back, made in various weights from worsted, wool, cotton, silk, or rayon, and used esp. for suits, coats, and dresses

²**serge** \"\ *vt* -ED/-ING/-S **:** to overcast (raw edges of fabric) usu. with a three-needle machine that forms V-shaped stitches

ser·gean·cy *also* **ser·jean·cy** *or* **ser·geant·cy** *or* **ser·jeant·cy** \'särjən(t)sē, 'sáj-, -)si\ *n* -ES [*sergeant* + *-cy*] **:** the function, office, rank, or commission of a sergeant

ser·geant *also* **ser·jeant** \'särjənt, 'sáj-\ *n* -S [ME, fr. OF *sergent, serjant*, fr. L *servient-, serviens*, pres. part. of *servire* to serve — more at SERVE] **1 a** *obs* **:** SERVANT **b** *obs* **:** an attendant upon a knight in the field **c** *obs* **:** a common soldier **d :** SERGEANT AT ARMS 1 **e** — used with various designations of office (as to indicate appointment by and attendance upon a royal person) ⟨~ surgeon to the king⟩ ⟨~ painter to the court⟩ **2** *usu serjeant* **:** BARRISTER; *esp* **:** SERJEANT-AT-LAW **3 a** *obs* **:** an officer who enforces the judgments of a court or the commands of one in authority **b :** SERGEANT AT ARMS 2 **c :** any of various municipal officers of lower rank (as in the City of London) — see SERGEANT-AT-MACE **d :** an officer in a police force ranking in the U.S. just below captain or sometimes lieutenant and in England just below inspector **4 :** a noncommissioned officer in the army and marine corps rating just below a staff sergeant and above a corporal — see CHEVRON illustration **5 :** SERGEANT FISH **6 a :** a local Salvation Army officer appointed for specific duty **b :** a Salvation Army cadet appointed to assist in the training of officer candidates **7 :** a fire-department officer ranking just below a lieutenant

sergeant at arms [ME] **1 a :** a tenant holding a sergeanty of service as an armed personal attendant for protection of a feudal lord and enforcement of his commands; *esp* **:** such an attendant upon the king or on the king's lord high steward in court to arrest traitors and other offenders **b :** one of two officers who nominally by allowance of the sovereign attend on the houses of Parliament to execute their commands; *also* **:** an officer similarly attending on the Court of Chancery **2 :** an officer of a legislative body, a deliberative or judicial assembly, or other organization (as a fraternal lodge) who attends upon it to execute commands or orders (as in preserving order or arresting offenders)

sergeant-at-law *var of* SERJEANT-AT-LAW

sergeant-at-mace *n, pl* **sergeants-at-mace** \¦==¦=¦=\ **:** a minor official carrying a mace as his insignia

sergeant ba·ker \,=='bākə(r)\ *n, usu cap S&B* [prob. fr. the name *Sergeant Baker*] **:** a brightly colored fish (*Aulopus purpurissatus*) related to the lantern fishes of the Australian coasts and becoming about two feet long

sergeant first class *n* **:** PLATOON SERGEANT

sergeant fish *n* [so called fr. the stripes on the fins] **1 :** COBIA **2 :** SNOOK 1a

sergeant major *n, pl* **sergeants major** *or* **sergeant majors** **1** *obs* **:** a regimental field officer serving either as a major or adjutant **2** *obs* **:** a general officer commanding large bodies of troops **3 a :** a noncommissioned officer in the marine corps ranking above a first sergeant — see RANK table **b :** a noncommissioned officer in the army, air force, or marine corps serving as chief administrative assistant in a headquarters **4 a :** a small deep-bodied compressed damselfish (*Abudefduf marginatus*) bluish green to yellow with black vertical stripes on the sides that is widely distributed in warm seas on both coasts of the Americas **b :** a related fish (*A. saxatilis*) of the western tropical Atlantic **5 :** the chief local officer in a Salvation Army corps who assists the corps officer

sergeant major of the army : a noncommissioned officer of the highest enlisted rank in the army — see RANK table

sergeant major of the marine corps : a noncommissioned officer of the highest enlisted rank in the marine corps — see RANK table

sergeant of the guard : the senior noncommissioned officer of an interior guard

ser·geant·ry *or* **ser·jeant·ry** \'=jəntrē, -ri\ *n* -ES [ME *serjauntrye*, fr. MF *sergenterie*, fr. *sergent* sergeant + *-erie* -ery] **:** SERGEANTY

ser·geant·ship *also* **ser·jeant·ship** \-jənt,ship\ *n* [*sergeant* + *-ship*] **:** the office of a sergeant

ser·geanty *or* **ser·jeanty** \-ntē\ *n* -ES [ME *sergeantie*, fr. MF *sergentie*, fr. *sergent* sergeant + *-ie* -y] **:** any of numerous feudal services of a somewhat personal or menial nature by which an estate is held of the king or other lord distinct from military tenure though it might involve service in war and from socage tenure and varying greatly with different holdings (as steward, marshal, constable, chamberlain, or esquire) — see GRAND SERGEANTY, PETIT SERGEANTY

serg·er \'sərjər\ *n* -S **:** one that serges

serges *pl of* SERGE, *pres 3d sing of* SERGE

serging *n* -S [fr. gerund of ²*serge*] **:** stitching made by serging

sergt *abbr, often cap* sergeant

se·ri \'serē, 'sārē\ *n, pl* **seri** *or* **seris** *usu cap* **1 a :** an Indian people of the state of Sonora, Mexico **b :** a member of such people **2 :** the Serian language of the Seri people **3 :** SERIAN

¹**se·ri·al** \'sirēəl, 'sēr-\ *adj* [*series* + *-al*] **1 :** of, relating to, consisting of, or arranged in a series, rank, or row ⟨~ pictures⟩ ⟨~ observations⟩ ⟨a ~ act like walking —A.T.Weaver⟩ **2 :** occurring in regular succession ⟨~ concerts⟩ **3 :** appearing in successive parts or numbers ⟨a ~ story⟩ ⟨a ~ play⟩ ⟨wrote her a ~ account of his adventures —J.W.Krutch⟩ **4 :** belonging to a series; *specif* **:** belonging to a series maturing in installments periodically rather than on a single maturity date ⟨~ bonds⟩ ⟨~ equipment trust certificates⟩ **5 :** causing or producing a series ⟨~ production of a new-model boat⟩ ⟨denies that he is the pursued ~ murderer —Siegfried Kracauer⟩ **6 :** STICHIC **7 :** of or relating to music based on a series of tones in a fixed order without regard to traditional tonality; *esp* **:** TWELVE-TONE

²**serial** \"\ *n* -S **1 a :** a novel or other literary or pictorial work published in sections in successive issues of a publication **b :** a section of such a serial appearing in a single issue of a publication ⟨a cartoon ~ . . . in a boys' magazine —Malcolm Lowry⟩ **2 :** a publication (as a newspaper, journal, yearbook, or bulletin) issued as one of a consecutively numbered and indefinitely continued series **3 a :** a motion picture or radio or television play presented in a number of successive installments or continued indefinitely ⟨soap-opera ~s⟩ **b :** a single installment of such a serial ⟨sit through six complete showings of the western and the ~ —William Humphrey⟩ — compare EPISODE 1d **4 :** a subdivision (as of a military force) for movement by marching, by water (as in amphibious operations), or by air ⟨could see shells exploding along the rear of the ~ —*Combat Forces Jour.*⟩ ⟨battalion . . . moving as an independent ~ —P.W.Thompson⟩

serial bond *n* [¹*serial*] **:** one of a series of bonds maturing periodically rather than on a single maturity date

serial homology *n* **:** the resemblance between different members of a single series of structures (as vertebrae) in an organism

se·ri·al·ist \-ələst\ *n* -S [²*serial* + *-ist*] **1 :** a writer of serials **2 :** a composer of serial music

se·ri·al·i·ty \,sirē'aləd·ē\ *n* -ES [¹*serial* + *-ity*] **:** serial quality or state

se·ri·al·iza·tion \,sirēələ'zāshən, ,sēr-, -,lī'z-\ *n* -S **:** the act or process of serializing; *esp* **:** arrangement and publication in the form of a serial ⟨~ rights to a book⟩

se·ri·al·ize \'===,līz\ *vt* -ED/-ING/-S *see -ize in Explan Notes* [¹*serial* + *-ize*] **1 :** to arrange in serial form ⟨*serialized* questions save time —S.L.Payne⟩ ⟨some system of concepts mentally classified, *serialized* —William James⟩ **2:** to publish in serial form ⟨~ a novel⟩

se·ri·al·ly \-ēəlē, -li\ *adv* **:** in serial form **:** in sequence ⟨~ numbered brass tags —W.E.Shinn⟩ ⟨school bonds, maturing ~ —*N.Y.Times*⟩

serial number *n* **:** a number indicating place in a series and used as a means of identification ⟨a soldier's *serial number*⟩

se·ri·al·o·graph \,=='alə,graf, -räf\ *or* **se·rio·graph** \'== ə,g-\ *n* [*serialograph* fr. ¹*serial* + *-o-* + *-graph*; *seriograph* fr. *series* + *-o-* + *-graph*] **:** a device for making a number of radiographs in rapid sequence

serial radiography *n* [¹*serial*] **:** the technique of making radiographs in rapid sequence for the study of high-speed phenomena (as of the flow of blood through an artery)

serial rights *n pl* [²*serial*] **:** a right created by a copyright to

publish a manuscript or artistic work or production separately as a serial in a periodical

serial tap *n* [¹*serial*] **:** one of a set of three taps used in succession for forming an internal screw thread first by making a roughing cut, second by cutting the thread a little fuller, and third by smoothing the thread and making it exact

seri·an \ˈsirēən, ˈsär-\ *n* -s *usu cap* [*Seri* + E *-an*] **:** a language family of the Hokan stock in Mexico comprising only the Seri language

se·ri·ary \ˈsirē͵erē\ *adj* [*series* + *-ary*] **:** of or relating to a series

¹**se·ri·ate** \ˈsirē͵ā|t, ˈsēr-, -ēə|, *usu* |d.+V\ *adj* [(assumed) NL *seriatus*, fr. L *series* + *-atus* -ate] **1 :** arranged in a series or succession **2 :** characterized by crystals that vary gradually or in a continuous series ⟨granitized rocks have a haphazard, uneven ~ texture —G.E.Goodspeed⟩ — **se·ri·ate·ly** *adv*

²**se·ri·ate** \-ē͵āt, *usu* -ād.+V\ *vt* -ED/-ING/-S [back-formation fr. *seriation*] **:** to arrange in a series ⟨measurements and indices of adults were *seriated* —F.M.Setzler⟩ ⟨rates for all the years covered were *seriated* —P.A.Sorokin⟩

¹**se·ri·atim** \͵==ˈād·əm *also* -ˈad-\ *adv* [ML, fr. L *series*] **:** in a series **:** SERIALLY ⟨the judges delivered their opinions ~ —*Harvard Law Rev.*⟩ ⟨setting forth ~ the terms of the offer —J.E.Davies⟩

²**seriatim** \ˈ==͵==\ *adj* **:** following seriatim ⟨elaborate ~ opinions —*Harvard Law Rev.*⟩ ⟨turn to the ~ discussion of these six needs —Carlos Baker⟩

se·ri·a·tion \͵==ˈāshən\ *n* -s [L *series* + E *-ation*] **1 :** formation, arrangement, succession, or position in a series or orderly sequence **2 :** a method of determining a chronology (as for archaeological material) by a detailed study of a particular style or type (as of potsherds) that reveals an increase or decrease in the popularity of the style giving a tentative scale from early to late

seric \ˈsirik, ˈser-\ *adj*, *usu cap* [L *sericus* — more at SERICEOUS] **:** of, relating to, or characteristic of the Seres

sericea lespedeza \səˈrish(ē)ə-\ *or* **sericea** *n* -s [NL *Lespedeza sericea*, fr. *Lespedeza* + *sericea*, fr. LL, fem. of *sericeus* sericeous] **:** a perennial herbaceous lespedeza (*Lespedeza cuneata* syn. *L. sericea*) that is widely planted as a leguminous forage and hay crop esp. on poor soils

sericeo- *comb form* [LL *sericeus* sericeous] **:** sericeous and ⟨*sericeo*tomentose⟩

se·ri·ceous \səˈrishəs\ *adj* [LL *sericeus*, fr. L *sericum* silk, silk garment, fr. neut. of *sericus* of the Seres, silken, fr. Gk *sērikos*, fr. *Sēres* Seres + *-ikos* -ic] **1 :** of or relating to silk **:** consisting of silk **:** SILKY **2 :** PUBESCENT ⟨~ leaf⟩

se·rici·culture \səˈrisə͵kəlchə(r), ˈserəsə-\ *n* [F *sériciculture*, fr. L *sericum* silk + F *culture*, fr. MF — more at SERICEOUS] **:** SERICULTURE

ser·i·cin \ˈserəsən\ *n* -s [ISV *seric-* (fr. L *sericum* silk) + *-in*] **:** a gelatinous protein that cements the two fibroin filaments in a silk fiber and that can be removed by degumming — called also *silk gum*

ser·i·cite \ˈserə͵sīt\ *n* -s [G *sericit*, fr. L *sericus* silken + G *-it* -ite — more at SERICEOUS] **:** a scaly variety of muscovite having a silky luster and occurring in various metamorphic rocks — **ser·i·cit·ic** \͵==ˈsid·ik\ *adj*

ser·i·cit·iza·tion \͵serə͵sīd·əˈzāshən\ *n* -s [*sericite* + *-ization*] **:** the process or state of alteration by which minerals (as feldspar) are converted into sericite

ser·i·cit·ize \ˈserə͵sīd͵īz\ *vt* -ED/-ING/-S [back-formation fr. *sericitization*] **:** to alter to sericite

ser·i·co·car·pus \͵serəkōˈkärpəs\ *n*, *cap* [NL, fr. Gk *sērikos* silken + NL *-carpus* — more at SERICEOUS] **:** a small genus of herbs (family Compositae) of the eastern U.S. having corymbose white-rayed flower heads with an ovoid involucre, squamous bracts, and silky achenes

ser·i·cor·nis \͵serəˈkȯrnəs\ *n*, *cap* [NL, fr. Gk *sērikos* + NL *-ornis*] **:** a genus of small noisy semiterrestrial insectivorous warblers (family Sylviidae) of Australia and New Guinea

ser·i·co·sto·mat·i·dae \͵serəkōstōˈmad·ə͵dē\ *n pl*, *cap* [NL, fr. *Sericostomat-*, *Sericostoma*, type genus (fr. Gk *sērikos* + NL *-stomat-*, *-stoma*) + *-idae*] **:** a large and widely distributed family of caddis flies

ser·ic·te·ri·um \͵se(͵)rikˈtirēəm\ *n*, *pl* **sericte·ria** \-ēə\ [NL, fr. Gk *sērikon* silk, fr. neut. of *sērikos* silken] **:** SERICTERY

se·ric·tery \səˈriktərē\ *n* -ES [NL *sericterium*] **:** the silk-producing gland of a caterpillar or other insect larva — compare SILK GLAND

seri·cultural \ˈserə+\ *adj* **:** of or relating to sericulture

seri·culture \ˈserə+͵-\ *n* [L *sericum* silk + E *culture* — more at SERICEOUS] **:** the production of raw silk by raising silkworms — **seri·cul·tur·ist** \͵serəˈkəlch(ə)rəst\ *n*

ser·i·ema \͵serēˈēmə, -ˈāmə\ *n* -s [Tupi *çariama*, *seriema*, lit., crested] **:** CARIAMA 2

¹**se·ries** \ˈsi(͵)rēz, ˈsē(-, -͵riz\ *n*, *pl* **series** [L, fr. *serere* to join, bind together, entwine, link; akin to Gk *eirein* to fasten in rows, string together, *hormos* chain, necklace] **1 :** a group of usu. three or more things or events standing or succeeding in order and having a like relationship to each other **:** a spatial or temporal succession of persons or things **:** a group that has or admits an order of arrangement exhibiting progression ⟨a concert ~⟩ ⟨a TV ~⟩ ⟨a ~ of talks⟩ ⟨a ~ of governors⟩ ⟨a ~ of three European maps —*Nat'l Geographic*⟩ **2 :** the expression obtained from a mathematical sequence by connecting its terms with plus signs **3 a :** the coins or currency of a particular country and period, denomination, or ruler or for a particular purpose considered as a unit for study or collection ⟨ancient Greek ~⟩ ⟨U.S. half-dollar ~⟩ ⟨a commemorative ~⟩ **b :** a group of postage or semipostal stamps in different denominations and for different postal uses issued for a single commemorative or fund-raising purpose or having a common design theme **4 a :** a number of volumes by the same author connected by similarity of subject, grouped usu. under a collective title, and distinguished from his other works **b :** a number of volumes connected by similarity of subject and issued in succession by a single publisher usu. with a collective title and in uniform style **c :** a number of successive parts or volumes of a periodical publication or of writings similar in character or by the same author numbered separately to distinguish them from other similar sequences ⟨second ~⟩ **d :** a number of volumes put out by a single publisher and similar in format and price ⟨a dime-novel ~⟩ ⟨some so-called ~ are nothing more than miscellaneous collections of books published at the same price and in the same style —L.R. McColvin⟩ **5 a :** a succession of sedimentary or igneous rocks either continuously deposited or related in the history of their accumulation **b :** a division of sedimentary formations that are usu. larger than a stage and smaller than a system and are deposited during an epoch ⟨the Niagara ~⟩ ⟨the salt ~ of the Permian basin —H.I.Smith⟩ **6 a :** a group of specimens or types progressively differing from each other in some morphological or physiological attribute ⟨a ~ of fossils⟩ ⟨a ~ of plants⟩ ⟨a ~ of antitoxins⟩ **b :** a category of classification to which various taxonomic ranks have been assigned by different authors **7 a :** a group of chemical compounds related in composition and structure ⟨a homologous ~⟩ **b :** a sequence of chemical elements of increasing atomic numbers (as a period or part of a period in the periodic table) **c :** RADIOACTIVE SERIES **8 :** an arrangement of the parts of or elements in an electric circuit whereby the whole current passes through each part or element without dividing or branching — contrasted with *parallel* **9 :** a set of vowels connected by ablaut (as *i*, *a*, *u* in *ring*, *rang*, *rung*) — compare GRADE 4 **10 :** a range of printing types of the same name and face but in different sizes ⟨Caslon Old Style ~⟩ ⟨Caslon Old Style italic ~⟩ — compare FAMILY **11 a :** a number of baseball games (as 3 or 4) played on successive days between two league teams **b :** WORLD SERIES **12 :** a group of successive coordinate sentence elements joined together in one or another degree of distinctness represented by separation by commas, separation by commas and connection by *and*'s or *or*'s, separation by commas and connection by *and* or *or* between the last two members, or connection by *and*'s or *or*'s ⟨an a, b, and c ~⟩ **13 :** a rhythmic sequence ordered by continuous repetition of a rhythmic or metrical unit without further organization of the sequence as a whole into some pattern or system based not upon continuous repetition alone but upon other relations and correspondences of elements — compare SYSTEM, STROPHE **14 :** SOIL SERIES **15 :** three consecutive games in bowling **16 :** a classificatory grouping of pottery by similarity of some feature (as shape or design) — **in series :** in a serial arrangement **:** in sequence ⟨water could be raised from great depths by placing several pumps *in series* —S.F.Mason⟩

²**series** \"\ *adj* **:** of or relating to a series; *specif* **:** having its parts arranged or connected in series ⟨a ~ circuit⟩ **:** being in series with other units **:** SERIES-WOUND ⟨~ motor⟩

series dynamo *n* **1 :** a series-wound generator or motor **2 :** a dynamo running in series with another or others

series limit *n* **:** the position (as of a wavelength, wave number, or frequency) in an atomic line spectrum toward which the series progresses in the ultraviolet direction and which though there is no line at this point corresponds to the limiting value of photon energy characteristic of the series

series parallel *also* **series multiple** *n* **:** an arrangement of cells or circuit elements in which groups of two or more in parallel are connected in series

series resonance *n* **:** electrical resonance accomplished with a capacitance and an inductance in series — **series-resonant** \ˈ=(͵)=ˈ=(=)=\ *adj*

series turn *n* **:** one of the turns in a series winding

series winding *n* **1 :** a winding in which the armature coil and the field-magnet coil are in series with the external circuit — opposed to *shunt winding* **2 :** WAVE WINDING

series-wound \ˈ=(͵)=ˈ=\ *adj* **:** having the armature coil and the field-magnet coil in series with the external circuit ⟨*series-wound* dynamo⟩

ser·if *also* **ser·iph** *or* **cer·iph** \ˈserəf\ *n* -s [prob. fr. D *schreef* stroke, line, fr. MD, fr. *schriven* to write, fr. L *scribere* — more at SCRIBE] **:** any of the short lines stemming from and at an angle to the upper and lower ends of the strokes of a letter — see TYPE illustration

seri·graph \ˈserə͵graf, -ráf\ *n* [L *sericum* silk + Gk *graphein* to write, draw — more at SERICEOUS, CARVE] **:** an original print produced by serigraphy ⟨there were some 60 ~*s* and other prints on view —*Newsweek*⟩

Serigraph \"\ *trademark* — used for an instrument for testing the breaking strength of materials (as silk)

se·rig·ra·pher \səˈrigrəfə(r)\ *n* -s [*serigraph* + *-er*] **:** one that produces prints by serigraphy

se·rig·ra·phy \-fē\ *n* -ES [L *sericum* + E *-graphy*] **:** the silk-screen process performed by an artist in producing an original print from his own design with color stencils of his own execution

se·rim·pi \səˈrimpē\ *n*, *pl* **serimpi** *or* **serimpis** [Malay *sĕrimpi*] **1 :** a female choric dancer at a Javanese court **2 :** a court dance performed by four serimpi

se·rin \səˈraⁿ, -an\ *n* -s [F, fr. MF, perh. fr. OProv *serena* bee-eater, fr. L *siren*, *sirena* siren] **:** a small European finch (*Serinus canarius*) related to the canary

ser·ine \ˈse͵rēn, ˈsi͵-, -͵rən\ *n* -s [ISV *sericin* + *-ine*; prob. orig. formed in G] **:** a crystalline amino acid $HOCH_2CH(NH_2)COOH$ known in three optically isomeric forms; *esp* **:** the levorotatory L-form obtained by hydrolysis of many proteins (as sericin, fibroin, or casein) or of various cephalins; β-hydroxy-alanine

ser·i·nette \͵serəˈnet\ *n* -s [F, fr. *serin*] **:** a small hand organ used in training songbirds

serin finch *n* [NL *Serinus*] **:** a finch of the Old World genus *Serinus*

se·rin·ga \səˈriŋgə\ *n* -s [Pg, syringe, rubber latex (fr. the use of rubber by the Brazilian Indians to make syringes), fr. ML *siringa* syringe] **1 :** MOCK ORANGE 1 **2 :** any of several Brazilian plants of the genus *Hevea* yielding rubber (as *H. brasiliensis*)

ser·in·gal \͵serənˈgal\ *n* -s [Pg, fr. *seringa* rubber latex] **:** a grove or collection of trees (*Hevea brasiliensis* and possibly other species) yielding rubber

seringe *n* -s [by alter.] *archaic* **:** SYRINGE

ser·in·guei·ro \͵serənˈgā(͵)rü, -͵rō\ *n* -s [Pg, fr. *seringa* rubber latex + *-eiro* -er, fr. L *-arius*] **:** a Brazilian rubber gatherer

se·ri·nus \səˈrīnəs, -rēn-\ *n*, *cap* [NL, fr. F *serin* serin] **:** an Old World genus of finches including the canary, the serin, and related forms

se·rio \ˈsirē͵ō\ *n* -s [by shortening] **:** SERIOCOMIC

serio- *comb form* [*serious*] **1 :** serious ⟨*serio*comedy⟩ **2 :** serious and ⟨*serio*ludicrous⟩

se·rio·comedy \ˈsirē(͵)ō+\ *n* [*serio-* + *comedy*] **:** a comedy with serious elements or overtones **:** TRAGICOMEDY

¹**se·rio·comic** *also* **se·rio·comical** \"+\ *adj* [*serio-* + *comic*, *comical*] **1 :** having a mixture of seriousness and sport **:** serious and comic ⟨a ~ novel⟩ ⟨conducting a ~ feud with certain advertising and network executives —Clifton Fadiman⟩ **2 :** mock serious ⟨a ~ vocalist⟩ — **se·rio·comically** \"+\ *adv*

²**seriocomic** \"\ *n* **:** a seriocomic performer

seriograph *var of* SERIALOGRAPH

se·ri·o·la \səˈrīələ, -rēə-\ *n* [NL, fr. L, small jar, dim. of *seria* jar] **:** a genus of fishes containing the typical amberfishes and sometimes made type of a separate family but usu. included among the Carangidae — **se·ri·o·line** \-ə͵līn, -ə͵lēn, -lən\ *adj*

se·ri·os·i·ty \͵sirēˈäsəd·ē\ *n* -ES [ML *seriositat-*, *seriositas*, fr. LL *seriosus* serious + L *-itat-*, *-itas* -ity] **:** SERIOUSNESS

se·ri·o·so \͵sirēˈō(͵)sō, ͵ser-, -)zō\ *adj* [It, fr. LL *seriosus*] **:** SERIOUS, GRAVE — used as a direction in music

se·ri·ous \ˈsirēəs, ˈsēr-\ *adj* [ME *seryows*, fr. MF or LL; MF *serieux*, fr. LL *seriosus*, alter. (influenced by L *-osus* -ous) of L *serius*; prob. akin to OE *swǣr* heavy, sad, OHG *swār*, *swāri*, ON *svārr*, Goth *swers* respected, Lith *sváras* heavy] **1 :** grave in disposition, appearance, or manner **:** not light, not gay, nor volatile ⟨we were ~ to the point of solemnity —James Joyce⟩ ⟨her habitual expression was sedate and ~ —Eric Linklater⟩ ⟨such a stern and ~ face —Charles Kingsley⟩ ⟨will say facetious things in a most ~ way —Harvey Breit⟩ **2 a :** demanding earnest application **:** requiring considerable care ⟨work which has prevented me from any ~ correspondence —H.J. Laski⟩ ⟨settled down to the ~ study of music —J.T.Howard⟩ **b :** addressed to grave moods — used esp. of literature, drama, and music ⟨~ books⟩ ⟨a ~ play⟩ **c :** demanding or intended to be accepted as sincerely and earnestly motivated ⟨not a good work of art, but it is a ~ work of art —Arnold Bennett⟩ ⟨~ novelists⟩ ⟨~ candidates⟩ **3 a :** being in earnest **:** not jesting, trifling, or deceiving ⟨this observation was not ~. It was merely a trifle of affectionate malicious embroidery —Arnold Bennett⟩ ⟨no ~ antiquarian researches have been carried out —Norman Douglas⟩ ⟨~ conversation⟩ ⟨a ~ question⟩ **b** *archaic* **:** earnest about religious matters **c :** deeply interested **:** DEVOTED ⟨if there are ~ fishermen in your party —Jackson Rivers⟩ ⟨a ~ checker player⟩ ⟨~ drinkers⟩ **4 a :** IMPORTANT, SIGNIFICANT, EMPHATIC ⟨morning was sacred to ~ tasks like sewing —Virginia Woolf⟩ ⟨a drama — on which a ~ amount of care has been spent by many —A.T.Quiller-Couch⟩ ⟨take all the meals that would require any ~ cooking in the nearest restaurant —G.B.Shaw⟩ ⟨took ~ exception to the theory —Irving Babbitt⟩ ⟨the book is a ~ disappointment —*Geog. Jour.*⟩ **b** (1) **:** not easily answered or solved **:** WEIGHTY, DIFFICULT ⟨leaders began to raise ~ objections —C.E.Black & E.C.Helmreich⟩ ⟨a ~ problem⟩ (2) **:** such as to call forth strong measures for combatting or rectifying ⟨most of these systems are in a ~ financial position —*Economist*⟩ ⟨so ~ a lack of knowledge —C.D.Forde⟩ ⟨commodities which are not in ~ competition with our dynamic home industry —R.S.Thoman⟩ **c :** such as to cause considerable distress, anxiety, or inconvenience **:** attended with danger ⟨a ~ injury⟩ ⟨a ~ accident⟩ ⟨~ warfare broke out —R.A.Billington⟩

syn GRAVE, SOLEMN, SOMBER, SEDATE, STAID, SOBER, EARNEST: SERIOUS suggests absorption in, concern about, or inclination to purposive or important work, deep thought, or earnest care rather than frivolity or levity ⟨a *serious* book is one which holds before us some image of society to consider and condemn —Lionel Trilling⟩ ⟨a *serious* student intent on learning⟩ GRAVE may imply both seriousness and dignity, often accompanied by suggestions of weighty interest and responsibilities ⟨the slow, *grave*, simple, convinced tones with which she uttered the things that seemed to her the most worth while in life were more impressive than any arts of the orator —Havelock Ellis⟩ ⟨his *gravest* tone, the one he reserved for his rare appearances in the federal appellate courts —Louis Auchincloss⟩ SOLEMN may indicate deep, serious impressiveness or awesomeness with utter lack of levity ⟨holding the attorney's letter in his hand, and with so *solemn* and important an air that his wife, always ingeniously on the watch for calamity, thought the worst was about to befall —W.M.Thackeray⟩ ⟨Sabbath was made a *solemn* day, meet only for preaching, praying, and Bible reading —C.A. & Mary Beard⟩ SOMBER applies to a melancholy or depressing gravity completely lacking in color, light, or cheer ⟨the Scots, famed for *somber* Calvinism and its intellectual theologizing, did not expect to warm to the enthusiastic kind of religion —P.D.Whitney⟩ ⟨slowly she swept into the *somber* rhythms . . . beginning so softly that the music was scarcely audible, climbing steadily toward a climax —Louis Bromfield⟩ SEDATE implies accustomed, decorous seriousness and studied absence of insouciance or lightness ⟨a professional army man is as *sedate* as a lawyer —Green Peyton⟩ ⟨her habitual expression was *sedate* and serious, a permanent reproof, as it were, to those who were first attracted by the voluptuous quality of her admirable figure —Eric Linklater⟩ STAID indicates a settled, accustomed sedateness and self-restraint ⟨most of the other cults had their public festivals, when the *staid* Roman citizen was repelled by the wild dances and the frenzied paeans —John Buchan⟩ ⟨the older city of *staid* residences, spotless streets, and a homogeneous population, all overhung with a quickly felt aura of contentment and satisfaction —*Amer. Guide Series: Pa.*⟩ SOBER may apply to grave controlling or subduing of emotion or to serious concentrating on purpose ⟨this work is certainly of more *sober* mien than most of its author's others. It is very long and very serious, and both these qualities are certainly deliberate observances —Virgil Thomson⟩ ⟨I never saw a *soberer* holiday crowd . . . it was almost sabbatarian in its decorousness —Robert Lynd⟩ EARNEST suggests steady sincerity and intentness of purpose ⟨an *earnest* student⟩ ⟨many of the *padres* were scholars, and all were *earnest* in their endeavor to convert and civilize the natives —*Amer. Guide Series: Fla.*⟩

se·ri·ous·ly *adv* **:** in a serious manner or vein **:** to a serious extent **:** EARNESTLY, SEVERELY ⟨most of the land . . . is ~ overgrazed —W.W.Beatty⟩ ⟨if we consider his works at all ~ —George Woodcock⟩ ⟨the ~ retarded readers —E.W.Kinne⟩ ⟨could see he was ~ an invalid —Kenneth Roberts⟩

serious-minded \ˈ==͵==ˈ=\ *adj* **:** having a serious disposition or trend of thought — **serious-minded·ly** *adv* — **serious-minded·ness** *n* -ES

se·ri·ous·ness *n* -ES **:** the quality or state of being serious ⟨a lack of solemnity is not necessarily a lack of ~ —Robert Rice⟩ ⟨consider the ~ of the charges⟩

seriph *var of* SERIF

se·rir \səˈri(ə)r\ *n*, *pl* **serir :** a pebble-strewn desert in the Libyan Sahara

seris *pl of* SERI

serj *abbr*, *often cap* serjeant

ser·ja·nia \sə(r)ˈjānyə, -nēə\ *n*, *cap* [NL, irreg. fr. Philippe *Serjeant*, 17th cent. Fr. botanist + NL *-ia*] **:** a genus of tropical American woody tendril-bearing vines (family Sapindaceae) having compound leaves, irregular yellow racemose flowers with four petals and five concave sepals, and fruit that is wing-margined

serjeant *var of* SERGEANT

serjeant-at-law \ˈ==͵=ˈ=\ *also* **sergeant-at-law** *n*, *pl* **serjeants-at-law** *also* **sergeants-at-law :** a barrister of the highest rank answering to the doctor of the civil law, outranking king's counsel socially but in professional rank inferior to them, and until 1846 having the exclusive right to be heard in the Court of Common Pleas

serjt *abbr*, *often cap* serjeant

ser·mo \ˈse(ə)r(͵)mō\ *n*, *pl* **sermo·nes** \serˈmō(͵)nās\ **:** SERMO GENERALIS

sermocination *n* -s [L *sermocination-*, *sermocinatio* conversation, fr. *sermocinatus* (past part. of *sermocinari* to converse, fr. *sermo* speech, conversation) + *-ion-*, *-io* -ion — more at SERMON] **1** *obs* **:** DISCOURSE, SERMON **2** *obs* **:** a form of prosopopoeia in which the speaker answers his own question or remark immediately

sermo co·ti·di·a·nus \-kō͵tēdēˈänəs\ *n* [ML, fr. L, everyday speech] **:** Vulgar Latin spoken by the educated class — distinguished from *sermo plebeius*

sermo ge·ne·ra·lis \-͵genəˈräləs\ *n*, *pl* **sermones genera·les** \-ä(͵)lās\ [ML, lit., general sermon] **:** AUTO-DA-FÉ

¹**ser·mon** \ˈsərmən, ˈsə̄m-, ˈsəim-, *dial* ˈsärm-, ˈsám-\ *vb* -ED/-ING/-S [ME *sermonen*, fr. OF *sermoner*, fr. *sermon*] *vt*, *archaic* **:** to preach to ~ *vi*, *archaic* **:** PREACH

²**sermon** \"\ *n* -s [ME, fr. OF, fr. ML *sermon-*, *sermo* speech, conversation, religious discourse, fr. L, speech, conversation, fr. *serere* to join, link together — more at SERIES] **1** *obs* **:** DISCOURSE, TALK **2 a :** a religious discourse delivered in public usu. by a clergyman as a part of a worship service ⟨preached his maiden ~ last Sunday⟩ **b :** a written discourse delivered or intended for delivery as a sermon ⟨a book of ~*s*⟩ **3 a :** a serious address **:** a lecture on conduct or duty **:** HOMILY ⟨going around the country preaching ~*s* on the need of defending the freedom of the mind —Elmer Davis⟩ ⟨the usual ~ by the teacher . . . on "why you should like to go to school" —H.C.McKown⟩ ⟨such little ~*s* on intelligent marketing are part of the instruction —*New Yorker*⟩ **b :** an annoying harangue ⟨didn't ask for a ~ on the subject⟩ **4 :** a person or thing whose nature suggests edifying thoughts ⟨~*s* in stones —Shak.⟩ ⟨her story is a ~ warning men against a devotion to lust —F.N.Magill⟩

ser·mon·ary \-mə͵nerē\ *n* -ES [¹*sermon* + *-ary*] **:** a collection of sermons

ser·mon·ette \͵=ˈnet\ *n* -s [¹*sermon* + *-ette*] **:** a short sermon ⟨dial a . . . telephone number and receive a two-minute ~ spoken by a minister —Freling Foster⟩

ser·mon·ic \(ˈ)=ˈmanik\ *also* **ser·mon·i·cal** \-nəkəl\ *adj* [¹*sermon* + *-ic*, *-ical*] **1 :** of, relating to, resembling, or appropriate to a sermon ⟨devotional and ~ books⟩ ⟨four ~ addresses⟩ ⟨a long ~ essay —Roger Hazelton⟩ **2 :** given to sermonizing **:** DIDACTIC ⟨teachers . . . who are ~ —*Christian Century*⟩ ⟨the *sermonical* turn which I now feel I must take —*Yale Rev.*⟩

ser·mon·ish \ˈ=-mənish\ *adj* [¹*sermon* + *-ish*] **1 :** suggestive of a sermon **2 :** disposed to hear or deliver a sermon

ser·mon·ism \-͵nizəm\ *n* -s [L *sermon-*, *sermo* speech, conversation + E *-ism* — more at SERMON] **:** the conceptualism of Abelard

ser·mon·ist \-nəst\ *n* -s [¹*sermon* + *-ist*] **:** one who writes or delivers sermons

ser·mon·ize \-͵nīz\ *vb* -ED/-ING/-S *see -ize in Explan Notes* [¹*sermon* + *-ize*] *vi* **1 a :** to compose, write, or deliver a sermon ⟨listen attentively to the *sermonizing* of the bishop —H.E.Rollins⟩ **b :** to discourse didactically or dogmatically ⟨cannot even enjoy a sunny day without *sermonizing* —*Times Lit. Supp.*⟩ **2 :** to inculcate rigid rules **:** LECTURE, ADMONISH ⟨the film attempts neither to dramatize nor ~ —Arthur Knight⟩ ~ *vt* **1 :** to preach or discourse to or on **:** address at length in a didactic and solemn manner ⟨tries to ~ the government —Isaac Deutscher⟩ ⟨happily does not ~ the gospel of work —Herbert Feinstein⟩ **2 :** to force or put by preaching ⟨to ~ one into energy⟩

ser·mon·iz·er \-zə(r)\ *n* -s **:** one that sermonizes **:** PREACHER

ser·mon·less \-mənləs\ *adj* **:** lacking a sermon

ser·mon·ol·o·gy \͵=məˈnäləjē\ *n* -ES [¹*sermon* + *-o-* + *-logy*] **1 :** knowledge or study of sermons **2 :** the preaching of sermons **3 :** SERMONS

sermo ple·be·ius \ˈ=(͵)=plēˈbā(y)əs\ *n* [ML, fr. L, speech of the lower classes] **:** Vulgar Latin spoken by the common people — distinguished from *sermo cotidianus*

sero- *comb form* [L *serum* — more at SERUM] **1 :** serum **:** connection with or relation to serum ⟨*sero*diagnosis⟩ **2 :** serous and ⟨*sero*fibrinous⟩

se·ro·diagnosis \ˈsi(͵)rō *sometimes* ˈse(-+\ *n* [NL, fr. *sero-* + *diagnosis*] **:** diagnosis by the use of serum (as in the Wassermann and Widal's tests) typically involving either the testing of serum from a patient for its behavior with a known germ or the testing of a germ isolated from a patient against serum from a patient with a known disease

se·ro·diagnostic \"+\ *adj* [*sero-* + *diagnostic*] **:** of or relating to serodiagnosis

se·ro·fibrinous \"+\ *adj* [ISV *sero-* + *fibrinous*] **:** composed of or characterized by serum and fibrin ⟨~ pleurisy⟩

se·ro·log·ic \ˌsirəˈläjik, ˌser-\ *or* **se·ro·log·i·cal** \-jəkəl\ *adj* **:** of, relating to, or employing the methods of serology — **se·ro·log·i·cal·ly** \-jək(ə)lē\ *adv*

se·rol·o·gist \səˈräləjəst, seˈr-\ *n* -s **:** a specialist in serology

se·rol·o·gy \-jē\ *n* -ES [ISV *sero-* + *-logy*] **1 :** a science that treats of serums and their reactions and properties esp. concerned with antibodies, antigens, haptens, and complement — compare IMMUNOLOGY **2 a :** serological knowledge in respect to a particular state or disease ⟨the ~ of syphilis⟩ **b :** a serological test ⟨blood ~ was negative⟩

se·ro·mucoid \ˌsi(ˌ)rō *sometimes* ˌse(-+\ *n* [*sero-* + *mucoid*] **:** a glycoprotein of serum that is not coagulated by heat

se·ro·muscular \"+\ *adj* [NL *serosa* + *muscularis*] **:** of combined serosa and muscularis ⟨the ~ layer of the stomach⟩

se·ron \səˈrōn, -rōn\ *n* -s [MexSp *cerón*] **:** a rather small tropical American tree (*Phyllostylon brasiliensis*) of the family Ulmaceae that yields Santo Domingan boxwood

se·ro·negative \ˌsi(ˌ)rō *sometimes* ˌse(-+\ *adj* [ISV *sero-* + *negative*] **:** having a negative serum reaction ⟨early ~ syphilis⟩

se·ro·negativity \"+\ *n* **:** the state of being seronegative often used as a criterion of the elimination of an infection ⟨after six months' medication complete ~ was attained⟩

se·roon *also* **ce·roon** \səˈrün\ *or* **se·ron** \səˈrōn, -rōn\ *n* -s [Sp *serón* hamper, crate, aug. of *sera* basket] **:** a bale or package (as of indigo) covered with hide or wood bound with hide

se·root *also* **seroot fly** *or* **se·rut** \səˈrüt(-)\ *n* -s [perh. fr. Ar *surāṭ* sharp like a sword, voracious] **:** a bloodsucking tabanid fly (genus *Pangonia*) that is remarkable for its very long proboscis and is very troublesome to men and animals in southern Egypt and the Republic of the Sudan

se·ro·positive \ˌsi(ˌ)rō *sometimes* ˌse(-+\ *adj* [ISV *sero-* + *positive*] **:** having a positive serum reaction

se·ro·purulent \"+\ *adj* [*sero-* + *purulent*] **:** consisting of a mixture of serum and pus ⟨a ~ exudate⟩

se·ro·reaction \"+\ *n* [ISV *sero-* + *reaction*] **:** a serological reaction

se·ro·resistance \"+\ *n* [*sero-* + *resistance*] **:** failure to attain seronegativity after intensive or prolonged treatment that results in subsidence of clinical symptoms — used chiefly of advanced or congenital syphilis — **se·ro·resistant** \"+\ *adj*

se·ro·sa \səˈrōsə, -ōzə\ *n, pl* **serosas** \-əz\ *also* **sero·sae** \-ˌsē, -ˌzē\ [NL, fr. fem. of *serosus* serous, fr. L *serum* + *-osus* -ous] **1 a :** CHORION 1 **b :** a comparable membrane of blastodermic origin that encloses the embryo of many insects and other arthropods **2 :** a serous membrane; *specif* **:** the outermost delicate layer of serous connective tissue and mesothelial cells that encloses an organ or lines a bodily cavity

se·ro·sal \-ōsəl,-ōzəl\ *adj* [NL *serosa* + E *-al*] **:** of, relating to, or made up of serosa ⟨the ~ surface of the bowel⟩ ⟨a ~ cyst on the ovary⟩

se·ro·sanguinous *or* **se·ro·sanguineous** \ˌsi(ˌ)rō *sometimes* ˌse(-+\ *adj* [*sero-* + *sanguinous* or *sanguineous*] **:** containing both blood and serous fluid ⟨a ~ discharge⟩

se·ro·si·tis \ˌsirōˈsīdəs, ˌser-, -ˈzī-\ *n* -ES [NL, fr. *serosa* + *-itis*] **:** inflammation of one or more serous membranes (as the pleura and pericardium)

se·ros·i·ty \səˈräsədē\ *n* -ES [F *sérosité*, fr. MF, fr. *sereux* serous + *-ité* -ity] **:** the quality or state of being serous

se·ro·therapy \ˌsi(ˌ)rō *sometimes* ˌse(-+\ *n* [ISV *sero-* + *therapy*] **:** the treatment of a disease with specific immune serum

se·rot·i·nal \səˈrätᵊnəl, seˈr-; ˌserəˈtīnᵊl\ *adj* [L *serotinus* coming late + E *-al* — more at SEROTINE] **:** of or relating to the latter and usu. drier part of summer **:** occurring in the latter half of summer ⟨a ~ generation of aphids⟩ ⟨ponds . . . drying up about the beginning of the ~ season —*Ecology*⟩

¹se·ro·tine \ˈserəˌtīn, -ˌtən, -ˌtēn\ *adj* [L *serotinus* coming late, fr. *sero* late — more at SOIREE] **:** late esp. in developing or flowering

²se·ro·tine \-ˌtēn\ *n* -s [F *sérotine*, fr. L *serotina*, fem. of *serotinus* coming late] **:** a common European brown bat (*Eptesicus serotinus*)

se·rot·i·nous \səˈrätᵊnəs, seˈr-\ *adj* [L *serotinus* coming late] **:** SEROTINAL

se·ro·to·nin \ˌsirəˈtōnən, -tän-\ *n* -s [*sero-* + *tonic* + *-in*; fr. its constrictive effect] **:** a crystalline phenolic amine $HOC_8H_5NCH_2CH_2NH_2$ derived from indole that is a powerful vasoconstrictor, that occurs esp. in the blood serum and gastric mucosa of mammals, in small amounts in the brain, and in the secretions of various amphibians and that is formed in animal tissues from tryptophan — called also *5-hydroxytryptamine*

se·ro·type \ˈsirəˌtīp, ˈser-\ *n* [*sero-* + *type*] **:** a group of intimately related microorganisms distinguished by the possession of a common set of antigens; *also* **:** the antigen set characteristic of such a group

se·rous \ˈsirəs, *sometimes* ˈsēr- *or* ˈser-\ *adj* [MF *sereux*, fr. *serum* (fr. L) + *-eux* -ous] **1 :** resembling serum esp. in thin watery constitution ⟨a ~ exudate⟩ ⟨~ fluid⟩ **2 :** of or relating to serum ⟨the ~ fraction of blood⟩

serous gland *n* **:** a gland secreting a serous fluid

serous membrane *n* **:** any of various thin membranes (as the peritoneum, pericardium, or pleurae) that consist of a single layer of thin flat mesothelial cells resting on a connective-tissue stroma, secrete a serous fluid, and usu. line bodily cavities or enclose the organs contained in such cavities

se·row \səˈrō\ *n* -s [Lepcha *să-ro* long-haired Tibetan goat] **:** any of several Asiatic goat antelopes of a widely distributed genus (*Capricornis*) related to the gorals and including a large thin-coated maned southern type (*C. sumatraensis*) and a much smaller maneless woolly-coated northern type (*C. crispus*) of Japan and Formosa

serozem *var of* SIEROZEM

se·ro·zyme \ˈsirəˌzīm, ˈser-\ *n* -s [ISV *sero-* + *-zyme*] **:** PROTHROMBIN

¹ser·pent \ˈsərpənt, ˈsə̄p-, ˈsəip-, *dial* ˈsärp- *or* ˈsăp-\ *n* -s *often attrib* [ME, fr. MF, fr. L *serpent-, serpens*, fr. pres. part. of *serpere* to creep; akin to Gk *herpein* to creep, Skt *sarpati* he creeps, *sarpa* serpent] **1 a** *archaic* **:** a noxious creature (as a snake, crocodile, spider, or toad) that creeps, hisses, or stings **b :** SNAKE; *esp* **:** a large snake **c :** SEA SERPENT **2 :** DEVIL 1 ⟨the great dragon was cast out, that old ~ —Rev 12:9 (AV)⟩ **3 :** a representation of a serpent esp. in the form of an ornament **4 :** a subtle treacherous malicious person or personified quality ⟨a ~ that has betrayed your brother —Liam O'Flaherty⟩ **5 :** a large cannon of the 15th to 17th centuries — compare BOMBARD, ⁵SERPENTINE **6 a :** a firework having a serpentine motion through the air or along the ground **b :** PHARAOH'S SERPENT **7 a :** a bass wind instrument of the trumpet type having a cupped mouthpiece, a long serpentine-twisted conical wooden tube pierced with finger holes, and a strong but coarse tone — compare CORNET 1a **b :** a pipe-organ reed stop with a trombone tone **8 :** a pale green that is bluer and stronger than celadon gray and yellower and darker than spray green

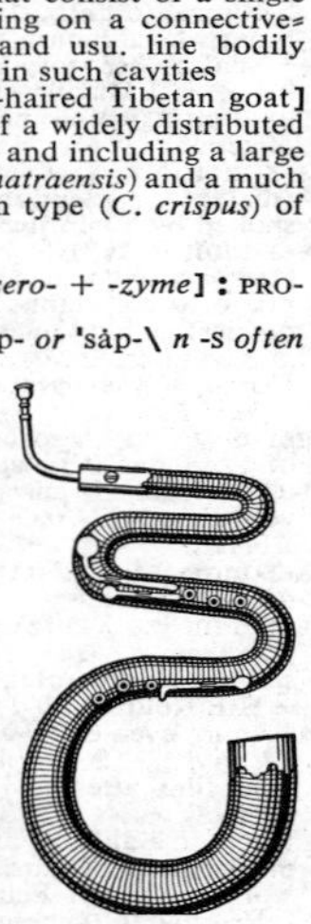
serpent 7a

²serpent \"\ *vi* -ED/-ING/-S [F *serpenter*, fr. MF, fr. *serpent*] **:** to wind or turn like a serpent **:** MEANDER ⟨old rocks want monstrous roots to ~ among them —Robinson Jeffers⟩

ser·pen·tar·ia \ˌsərpənˈta(a)rēə\ *n* -s [LL, snakeroot, fr. L *serpent-, serpens* serpent, snake + *-aria* -ary] **1 :** the dried rhizome and roots of a birthwort (*Aristolochia serpentaria*) **2 :** the dried rhizome and roots of the Texas snakeroot

ser·pen·tar·i·um \-ēəm\ *n, pl* **serpentariums** \-ēəmz\ *or* **serpentar·ia** \-ēə\ [NL, fr. L *serpent-, serpens* + *-arium*] **:** an enclosure in which snakes are kept

ser·pen·tary *also* **serpentary root** \ˈ==,terē\ *n* -ES [LL *serpentaria*] **:** SERPENTARIA

ser·pent·cleide \ˈ=pənt,klīd\ *n* -s [¹*serpent* + *ophicleide*] **:** a large ophicleide with a wooden tube

serpent cucumber *n* **:** SNAKE MELON

ser·pent d'é·glise \ˌser,pänˈdāˈglēz\ *n, pl* **serpents d'église** \"\ [F, lit., church serpent; fr. its being used to accompany the voice in plainchant] **:** SERPENT 7a

serpent eagle *n* **1 :** any of several raptorial birds of the genus *Spilornis* that prey on snakes and inhabit southern Asia and the East Indies **2 :** HARRIER EAGLE

serpent eater *n* **1 :** SECRETARY BIRD **2 :** MARKHOR

serpent eel *n* **:** SNAKE EEL

ser·pen·tes \(ˌ)sərˈpen·(ˌ)tēz\ *n pl, cap* [NL, fr. L, pl. of *serpent-, serpens* serpent] **:** a suborder or other division of Squamata comprising the snakes

serpent fern *n* **:** a tropical often epiphytic American fern (*Phlebodium aureum*) with brown scaly rhizomes often cultivated for its large simple deeply lobed fronds

serpent gourd *n* **:** SNAKE GOURD 2a

serpent grass *n* **:** ALPINE BISTORT

serpenti- *comb form* [L, fr. *serpent-, serpens*] **:** serpent ⟨*serpentivorous*⟩

ser·pen·ti·form \(ˌ)sərˈpentəˌfȯrm\ *adj* [LL *serpentiformis*, fr. L *serpenti-* + *-formis* -form] **:** having the form of a snake

ser·pen·tile \ˈsərpənˌtīl, -ˌtəl, -(ˌ)til, -ˌtēl\ *adj* [¹*serpent* + *-ile*] **:** resembling a serpent (as in nature or appearance)

¹ser·pen·tine \ˈsərpənˌtēn, -tīn\ *adj* [ME, fr. MF *serpentin*, fr. LL *serpentinus*, fr. L *serpent-, serpens* serpent + *-inus* -ine] **1 :** relating to a serpent **:** resembling a serpent (as in form or movement) ⟨the muscular line moved and swayed in a ~ rhythm —Margaret Long⟩ **2 :** relating to or like the serpent as typifying Satan **:** subtly wily or tempting **:** GUILEFUL, DIABOLIC ⟨the ~ will to power —J.C.Powys⟩ ⟨an inescapable fascination of a ~ kind —Richard Watts⟩ ⟨that ~ plotter —R.B.Morris⟩ **3 :** winding or turning one way and another **:** MEANDERING, SINUOUS ⟨a ~ road⟩ ⟨a ~ wall⟩ ⟨~ braid⟩ ⟨these essays . . . in their intricate and ~ manner —R.W.B. Lewis⟩ **4 :** having a compound curve whose central curve is convex — used esp. of the front of a piece of cabinet furniture; opposed to *oxbow*

²serpentine \"\ *vb* -ED/-ING/-S *vi* **:** to move like a serpent **:** wind along ⟨the trail *serpentining* down —Carl Jonas⟩ ⟨behind them *serpentined* the long line of yoked couples —C.S. Forester⟩ ~ *vt* **:** to take by a serpentine course or serpentine methods **:** INSINUATE

³serpentine \"\ *n* -s **1 :** something (as a line, a wall, or a section of road) that winds sinuously ⟨the cart wheeled round the steep ~s —Marcia Davenport⟩; *specif* **:** a file (as of people) moving in a sinuous or winding line ⟨a few minor processions along with any number of spontaneous ~s —Ray Duncan⟩ — compare CROCODILE **2 a** *or* **serpentine dance :** a mixed group dance in single file with a leader guiding a wavering snakelike course along the ground — compare FARANDOLE, SNAKE DANCE **2 b :** a show dance with sinuous manipulation of streamers **3 :** a skating figure in which the skater executes a series of usu. three circles requiring changes of edge **4 :** a light green that is deeper and very slightly bluer than average mint green and bluer and deeper than variscite green — compare SERPENTINE GREEN

⁴serpentine \"\ *n* -s [ME, fr. the rock serpentine, fr. ML *serpentina, serpentinum*, fr. LL, fem. & neut. of *serpentinus* resembling a serpent] **1 :** CHRYSOTILE **2 :** ANTIGORITE **3 :** a rock composed of chrysotile and antigorite often in layers with or without other minerals having usu. a dull green color often with a spotted or mottled appearance or a red or brownish hue due to the presence of iron, occurring in masses (as antigorite) or in fibrous form (as chrysotile), resulting from the alteration of other magnesian minerals (as olivine, amphibole, and pyroxene), and used as an ornamental stone — compare ASBESTOS **4** *or* **serpentine soil :** soil formed by the weathering of serpentine rock

⁵serpentine \"\ *n* -s [ME, fr. MF *serpentin*, fr. *serpentin* resembling a serpent, fr. LL *serpentinus*] **1 :** a cannon of the 15th to 17th centuries of various calibers usu. longer and lighter than a bombard **2 :** a serpentine attachment of a harquebus lock to hold the match

⁶ser·pen·tine \-tēn\ *also* **ser·pen·tin** \-tan\ *n* -s [F *serpentin*, fr. *serpentin* resembling a serpent, fr. MF] **1 :** long narrow strips of rolled colored paper thrown (as at a carnival or party) so as to unroll as streamers ⟨everyone throws ~ and confetti —Bess A. Garner⟩ **2 :** a piece of serpentine ⟨various kinds of noisemakers and ~s at each place —*Los Angeles (Calif.) Examiner*⟩

serpentine green *n* [¹*serpentine*] **:** a light olive color that is greener and paler than citrine, redder and deeper than grape green, and redder and paler than old moss green — compare ³SERPENTINE 4

serpentine jade *n* **:** a serpentine that resembles jade

serpentine layerage *n* **:** a method of layering which is used chiefly with woody vines and in which the stem to be propagated is laid on the ground and covered with earth at intervals to induce rooting of the buried sections which are later separated to form new plants

serpentine leaf miner *n* **:** a grub that is the larva of a small fly (*Liriomyza brassicae*) and that eats out slender white winding burrows in the leaves of cabbage and related plants

ser·pen·tine·ly *adv* **:** in a serpentine manner

serpentine roulette *n* **:** a wavy-line stamp roulette that produces scallops on the edge of a detached stamp

serpentine verse *n* [¹*serpentine*; fr. the frequent depiction of serpents with their tails in their mouths] **:** a line of verse beginning and ending with the same word

serpentine ware *n* [⁴*serpentine*] **:** a hard green-spotted or green-veined pottery suggestive of serpentine

ser·pen·tin·ing·ly *adv* [*serpentining* (fr. pres. part. of ²*serpentine*) + *-ly*] **:** in a serpentining manner **:** WINDINGLY

ser·pen·tin·ite \ˈsərpən‚tēˌnīt, -tī,nīt, -tī,n-\ *n* -s [ISV ⁴*serpentine* + *-ite*] **:** a rock consisting chiefly of serpentine

ser·pen·tin·iza·tion \ˌ==,nəˈzāshən, -ˌnīˈz-\ *n* -s [ISV ⁴*serpentine* + *-ization*] **:** the process or state of alteration by which minerals (as olivine) are converted into serpentine

ser·pen·tin·ize \-ˌnīz\ *vt* -ED/-ING/-S [prob. back-formation fr. *serpentinization*] **:** to convert (a magnesian silicate) into serpentine ⟨*serpentinized* dunite⟩

ser·pen·tin·oid \-ˌnȯid\ *adj* [⁴*serpentine* + *-oid*] **:** SERPENTINOUS

ser·pen·ti·nous \-ˌnəs\ *adj* [ISV ⁴*serpentine* + *-ous*] **:** relating to, consisting of, or resembling serpentine ⟨~ rocks⟩ ⟨~ gangue mineral⟩

ser·pent·ize \ˈ=pən,tīz, -nt,īz\ *vb* -ED/-ING/-S [¹*serpent* + *-ize*] **:** SERPENTINE ⟨the river . . . ~s more than you can conceive in the vale —Horace Walpole⟩

serpentlike \ˈ==,=\ *adj* **:** resembling or felt to resemble a serpent **:** SERPENTINE, SNAKELIKE, TREACHEROUS

ser·pent·ly *adv* [ME, fr. ¹*serpent* + *-ly*] *archaic* **:** in the manner of a serpent

serpent melon *n* **:** SNAKE MELON

serpent radish *n* **:** RAT-TAILED RADISH

ser·pent·ry \ˈsərpəntrē\ *n* -ES [¹*serpent* + *-ry*] **:** SERPENTS

serpents *pl of* SERPENT, *pres 3d sing of* SERPENT

serpent star *n* **:** OPHIUROID

serpent stone *n* **:** ADDER STONE

serpent's–tongue \ˈ==,=\ *n* **1 :** ADDER'S-TONGUE 1 **2 :** the fossil tooth of a shark

serpentwood \ˈ==,=\ *n* **1 :** an East Indian shrub (*Rauwolfia serpentina*) the root of which is used as a source of reserpine **2 :** NUX VOMICA 2

serpent worm *n* **:** GUINEA WORM

¹ser·phid \ˈsərfəd\ *adj* [NL *Serphidae*] **:** of or relating to the Serphidae

²serphid \"\ *n* -s **:** a wasp of the family Serphidae

ser·phi·dae \-fəˌdē\ *n pl, cap* [NL, fr. *Serphus*, type genus (fr. Gk *serphos* a small winged insect) + *-idae*] **:** a family of small serphoid wasps having a tubular retractile ovipositor and being parasitic in the eggs and larvae of other insects

¹ser·phoid \-ˌfȯid\ *adj* [NL *Serphoidea*] **:** of or relating to the Serphoidea

²serphoid \"\ *n* -s **:** a wasp of the superfamily Serphoidea

ser·phoi·dea \(ˌ)sərˈfȯidēə\ *n pl, cap* [NL, fr. *Serphus* + *-oidea*] **:** a superfamily of minute wasps that as larvae are parasites of other insects and sometimes spiders and have females with the usu. tubular ovipositor emerging from the extreme end of the body

ser·pie·rite \ˈsərpēəˌrīt, sərˈpiˌr-\ *n* -s [F *serpiérite*, fr. J. B. *Serpieri* 19th cent. It. engineer, explorer of the ancient silver mines at Laurium + F *-ite*] **:** a mineral $(Cu,Zn,Ca)_5(SO_4)_2(OH)_6.3H_2O$ consisting of a hydrous basic sulfate of copper, calcium, and zinc occurring in small tabular bluish green crystals and tufts

ser·pig·i·nous \(ˌ)sərˈpijənəs\ *adj* [ML *serpigin-, serpigo* + E *-ous*] **:** CREEPING, SPREADING ⟨~ ringworm⟩; *broadly* **:** healing over in one portion while continuing to advance in another ⟨~ ulcer⟩ — **ser·pig·i·nous·ly** *adv*

ser·pi·go \(ˌ)sərˈpī(ˌ)gō, -pē(-\ *n, pl* **ser·pig·i·nes** \-pijəˌnēz\ *or* **serpigoes** [ME, fr. ML *serpigin-, serpigo*, fr. L *serpere* to creep — more at SERPENT] *archaic* **:** a creeping or spreading skin disease (as ringworm)

ser·po·let \ˌsərpəˈlet\ *n* -s [F, fr. Prov *serpolet*, dim. of *serpol* wild thyme, fr. L *serpyllum, serpullum*, modif. (influenced by *serpere* to creep) of Gk *herpyllon*, fr. *herpein* to creep — more at SERPENT] **:** WILD THYME

ser·pu·la \ˈsərpyələ\ *n* [NL, fr. L, little snake, fr. *serpere* to creep] **1** *cap* **:** a genus (the type of the family Serpulidae) of small marine polychaete worms having brightly colored gills and constructing and living in contorted calcareous tubes that may be closed with horny opercula **2** *pl* **serpulas** \-ləz\ *or* **serpulae** \-ˌlē, -ˌlī\ **:** any worm of the genus *Serpula* or family Serpulidae

ser·pu·lan \-lən\ *n* [NL *Serpula* + E *-an*] **:** SERPULA 2

¹ser·pu·lid \-ləd\ *adj* [NL *Serpulidae*] **:** of or relating to the Serpulidae

²serpulid \"\ *n* -s **:** a worm of the family Serpulidae

ser·pu·li·dae \(ˌ)sərˈpyüləˌdē\ *n pl, cap* [NL, fr. *Serpula*, type genus + *-idae*] **:** a large family of marine polychaete worms including various cosmopolitan genera — see SERPULA — **ser·pu·li·dan** \-dən\ *adj or n*

ser·pu·line \ˈsərpyəˌlīn, -lən, -ˌlēn\ *adj* [NL *Serpula* + E *-ine*] **:** of or relating to the Serpulidae **:** formed by or composed of the tubes of serpulae

ser·pu·lite \-ˌlīt\ *n* -s [ISV *serpula* + *-ite*] **:** a fossil worm tube — **ser·pu·lit·ic** \ˌ==ˈlid·ik\ *adj*

ser·pu·loid \ˈ==,lȯid\ *adj* [NL *Serpula* + E *-oid*] **:** resembling or related to the Serpulidae

¹ser·ra \ˈserə\ *n, pl* **ser·rae** \-ˌrē, -ˌrī\ [NL, fr. L, saw, sawfish] **1 :** a sawlike organ or part (as the saw of a sawfish or of a sawfly) **2 :** SERRATION

²serra \"\ *n* -s [Pg, saw, serra, fr. L, saw] **:** SIERRA 1a

ser·ra·del·la \ˌserəˈdelə\ *also* **ser·ra·dil·la** \-dilə\ *n* -s [Pg *serradela*, fr. L *serratula* betony, fr. *serratus* serrate] **:** a Eurasian annual herb (*Ornithopus sativus*) of the family Leguminosae with pinnate leaves and long-stalked honey-producing flowers that is used for forage and green manure — called also *bird's-foot*

¹ser·ranid \səˈranəd, -ran-,-rän-\ *adj* [NL *Serranidae*] **:** of or relating to the Serranidae

²serranid \"\ *n* -s **:** a fish of the family Serranidae

ser·ran·i·dae \-ranəˌdē\ *n pl, cap* [NL, fr. *Serranus*, type genus + *-idae*] **:** a large and widely distributed family of carnivorous marine percoid fishes having an oblong and more or less compressed body covered with ctenoid scales and including many important food and sport fishes esp. of warm seas — see SEA BASS

ser·ra·no \səˈrä(ˌ)nō\ *n, pl* **serrano** *or* **serranos** *usu cap* [AmerSp, fr. Sp, mountaineer, fr. *sierra* saw, jagged mountain range + *-ano* -an — more at SIERRA] **1 :** a Shoshonean people of southern California **2 :** a member of the Serrano people

¹ser·ranoid \ˈserəˌnȯid, -raˌ-, -rä,-\ *adj* [NL *Serranus* + E *-oid*] **:** resembling or related to the Serranidae

²serranoid \"\ *n* -s **:** a serranoid fish

ser·ra·nus \-rānəs, -rän-\ *n, cap* [NL, fr. L *serra* saw + *-anus* -an] **:** a genus (the type of the family Serranidae) of fishes including numerous small Pacific sea basses some of which are regarded as highly toxic

¹ser·ra·sal·mo \ˌserəˈsal(ˌ)mō\ [NL, fr. L *serra* saw + *salmo* salmon] *syn of* SERRASALMUS

²serrasalmo \ˌ==ˈ=(ˌ)=\ *n* -s **:** CARIBE

ser·ra·sal·mus \ˌ==ˈ=məs\ *n, cap* [NL, fr. L *serra* saw + *salmo* salmon] **:** a genus of So. American characin fishes comprising the caribe

¹ser·rate \ˈseˌrāt, *usu* -ād.+V\ *vt* -ED/-ING/-S [LL *serratus*, past part. of *serrare* to saw, fr. L *serra* saw] **:** to notch or form sawlike teeth on the edge or surface of **:** mark with a serration ⟨~ the ends of a steel shaft⟩ ⟨firs that ~ the long ridge —A.T. Quiller-Couch⟩ ⟨peaks . . . ~ the skyline —*Amer. Guide Series: N.H.*⟩

²ser·rate \-ˌrā|t, -rə|, *usu* |d.+V\ *adj* [L *serratus*, fr. *serra* saw + *-atus* -ate] **1 :** notched or toothed on the edge **:** SAW-TOOTHED, SAW-EDGED, DENTICULATE ⟨jagged peaks and ~ ridges —R.F.Flint⟩ — see ANTENNA illustration **2 :** having marginal teeth pointing forward or toward the apex ⟨a ~ leaf⟩

serrate-ciliate \ˌ=(ˌ)=+\ *adj* [trans. of NL *serrato-ciliatus*] **:** having fine hairs like eyelashes on the serrations ⟨*serrate-ciliate* leaves⟩

ser·rat·ed \-ˌrād·əd, -ātəd\ *adj* [fr. past part. of *serrate*] **:** SERRATE ⟨a ~ wall of high buildings —A.J.Liebling⟩ ⟨a low fence of ~ green —Richard Jefferies⟩ ⟨the lanceolate leaves have a ~ margin —Walter Bally⟩

serrate-dentate \ˌ=(ˌ)=+\ *adj* [trans. of NL *serrato-dentatus*] **:** having the margins of the serrations toothed **:** doubly serrate — used of leaves

serrated impulse *n* **:** electronic output chopped into toothlike pulses (as for frame synchronization in television reception)

ser·ra·tia \səˈrāsh(ē)ə, -rād·ēə\ *n, cap* [NL, fr. Serafino *Serrati*, 19th cent. Ital. entrepreneur + NL *-ia*] **:** a genus of small aerobic saprophytic bacteria (family Enterobacteriaceae) that commonly produce bright red pigments

ser·ra·tion \seˈrāshən\ *n* -s [²*serrate* + *-ion*] **1 :** the condition of being serrate ⟨the continual ~ of the pine forest —John Ruskin⟩ **2 a :** a formation resembling the toothed edge of a saw ⟨mountains receding in ~s to the west⟩ **b serrations** *pl* **:** the fine scales projecting from the surface of wool fiber **3 :** one of the teeth in a serrate margin ⟨a dial with two hundred ~s⟩

serrato- *comb form* [NL, fr. L *serratus* serrate] **:** serrate and ⟨*serrato*crenate⟩ ⟨*serrato*dentate⟩

ser·rat·u·la \seˈrachələ\ *n, cap* [NL, fr. L, betony, fr. *serratus* serrate + *-ula*] **:** a genus of Old World perennial herbs (family Compositae) with spirally arranged leaves that are not spiny and solitary or corymbose heads of tubular flowers — compare SANDWORT

ser·ra·ture \ˈserəˌchu̇(ə)r, -ˌchər\ *n* -s [LL *serratura* act of sawing, fr. *serratus* (past part. of *serrare* to saw) + L *-ura* -ure] **:** SERRATION

ser·ra·tus \seˈrād·əs, -rād·əs\ *n, pl* **serra·ti** \-ˌā,tī, -ä,tē\ [NL, fr. L, serrate] **:** any of several muscles of the trunk having complex origins but chiefly from the ribs or vertebrae that give them a notched appearance and comprising in man (1) a large muscle arising chiefly from the eight upper ribs and inserted into the vertebral border of the scapula, (2) another arising chiefly from the spinous processes of the last two thoracic and two or three upper lumbar vertebrae and inserted into the four lower ribs, and (3) a muscle arising chiefly from the spinous processes of the last cervical and first and two or three additional thoracic vertebrae and inserted into the second, third, fourth, and fifth ribs — called also respectively (1) *serratus mag·nus* \-ˈmagnəs\, *serratus anterior*, (2) *serratus posterior inferior*, (3) *serratus posterior superior*

serred *past of* SERR

serre·fine \ˈserəˌfēn, (ˈ)serˈf-\ *n* -s [F *serre-fine*, lit., fine clamp, fr. *serre* grip, clamp + *fine*, fem. of *fin* fine, fr. OF — more at SEAR (catch of a gunlock), FINE] **:** a small forceps for clamping a blood vessel

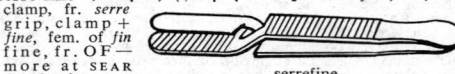

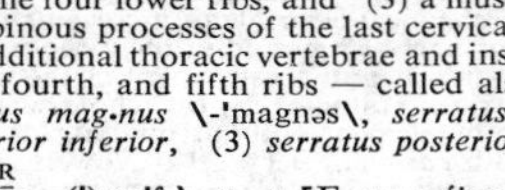
serrefine

serri- *comb form* **:** saw ⟨*serri*ferous⟩

¹ser·ri·corn \ˈserəˌkȯrn\ *adj* [NL *Serricornia*] **:** of or relating to the Serricornia

²serricorn \"\ *n* -s **:** a beetle of the division Serricornia

ser·ri·cor·nia \ˌ==ˈkȯrnēə\ *n pl, cap* [NL, fr. *serri-* + L *cornu* horn + NL *-ia*] **:** a division of beetles including the Elateridae, Buprestidae, Lampyridae, and related forms in which the antennae are usu. serrate along their inner margin, all the

tarsi are usu. pentamerous, and the first ventral abdominal segment is exposed for its entire breadth

ser·ried \ˈserēd, -rid\ *adj* [fr. past part. of *serry*] **1 :** crowded or pressed together **:** COMPACT, DENSE ⟨parents are all seated there in ~ rows —Harold Nicolson⟩ ⟨the crowd collected in a ~ mass —W.S.Maugham⟩ ⟨a ~ phalanx of reeds —William Beebe⟩ ⟨squat houses huddle, meanly ~ —Laurence Binyon⟩ **2 :** precisely coherent and concise — used of discourse ⟨perorations, but not ~ argument —H.J.Laski⟩ ⟨the reader wading through these solid, ~ pages —*Times Lit. Supp.*⟩ **3** [alter. of ²*serrate*] **:** marked by ridges or serrations **:** SERRATE ⟨his brow ~ in an inquisitive frown —Harris Downey⟩ ⟨to the south rise the ~ contours of the . . . mountains —*Amer. Guide Series: Oregon*⟩ ⟨to the east headland after headland of the north coast . . . stood out in ~ rank —John Wymer⟩ — **ser·ried·ly** *adv* — **ser·ried·ness** *n* -ES

ser·rif·era \səˈrif(ə)rə, səˈr-\ *n pl, cap* [NL, fr. *serri-* + L *-fera*, neut. pl. of *-fer* -ferous] *in some classifications* **:** a division of Hymenoptera including the sawflies and horntails and related forms and being essentially equivalent to Chalastogastra

ser·rif·er·ous \-f(ə)rəs\ *adj* [*serri-* + *-ferous*] **:** having a sawlike organ

ser·ru·la \ˈser(y)ələ\ *n* -s [NL, fr. L, small saw, dim. of *serra* saw] **:** a toothed keel; *esp* **:** one on the endite of most spiders that assists in the maceration of prey

ser·ru·late \ˈser(y)ələt, -ˌlāt\ *also* **ser·ru·lat·ed** \-ˌlād·əd\ *adj* [NL *serrulatus*, fr. L *serrula* small saw + *-atus* -ate] **:** finely serrate **:** DENTICULATE

ser·ru·la·tion \ˌ==ˈlāshən\ *n* -s [*serrulate* + *-ion*] **1 :** the state of being serrulate **2 :** a serrulate formation

ser·ry \ˈserē, -ri\ *vb* -ED/-ING/-ES [MF *serré*, past part. of *serrer* to press, crowd — more at SEAR (catch of a gunlock)] *vi, archaic* **:** to press together esp. in ranks **:** CROWD ~ *vt* **:** to close up **:** crowd together

ser·ta \(ˈ)serˌtä\ *also* **ser·to** \-tō\ *n* -s [Syriac *sertā*, lit., line, writing] **:** the Syriac cursive script characterized by horizontal lines or ligatures uniting the lower portions of the letters

ser·to·li cell \ˈserd·əlē-, serˈtōlē-\ *also* **sertoli's cell** *n, usu cap S* [after Enrico *Sertoli* †1910 Ital. histologist] **:** one of the elongated striated cells in the tubules of the testis to which the spermatids become attached and from which they apparently derive nourishment

ser·tu·lar·ia \ˌsərchəˈla(a)rēə\ *n, cap* [NL, fr. L *sertula* (*campana*) melilot (dim. of *serta*, garland, melilot, fr. fem. of *sertus*, past part. of *serere* to entwine, bind together) + NL *-aria* — more at SERIES] **:** a genus (the type of the family Sertulariidae) of delicate branching calyptoblastic hydroids having small sessile hydrothecae arranged bilaterally along the sides of the branches

¹**ser·tu·lar·i·an** \ˌ==ˈ==ən\ *adj* [NL *Sertularia* + E *-an*] **:** of or relating to the genus *Sertularia* or to the family Sertulariidae

²**sertularian** \"\ *n* -s **:** a sertularian hydroid

ser·tu·lar·i·oid \ˌ==ˈ==ˌȯid\ *or* **ser·tu·la·roid** \ˈ==ləˌrȯid\ *adj* [NL *Sertularia* + E *-oid*] **:** resembling or related to the sertularians

ser·tule \ˈsər(ˌ)chül\ *n* -s [NL *sertulum*] **:** SERTULUM

ser·tu·lum \ˈsərchələm\ *n, pl* **sertu·la** \-lə\ [NL, dim. of L *sertum* garland, fr. neut. of *sertus*, past part. of *serere* to entwine, bind together — more at SERIES] **1 :** UMBEL **2** [NL, dim. of *sertum*] **:** a collection of scientifically studied plants

ser·tum \ˈsərd·əm\ *n, pl* **ser·ta** \-d·ə\ [NL, fr. L, garland] **:** a scientific treatise upon a collection of plants

ser·ule \ˈser(ˌ)yül, -e(ˌ)rül\ *n* -s [⁵*sere* + *-ule*] **:** the brief and small sere of a microhabitat

se·rum \ˈsirəm, *sometimes* ˈsēr- *or* ˈser-\ *n, pl* **serums** \-rəmz\ *or* **se·ra** \-rə\ *often attrib* [L, whey, watery fluid, serum; akin to Gk *oros* whey, serum, *hormē* rush, onset, assault, Skt *sarati* it runs, flows] **1 :** the watery portion of an animal fluid remaining after coagulation: **a :** BLOOD SERUM; *esp* **:** immune blood serum that contains specific immune bodies (as antitoxins or agglutinins) ⟨antitoxin ~⟩ — compare VACCINE **b :** WHEY **c :** a normal or pathological serous fluid (as in a blister) **2 :** the watery part of a vegetable fluid; *specif* **:** the watery part of rubber latex on which the rubber floats after coagulation

serum accident *n* **:** an allergic reaction to the injection of a serum to which an individual is hypersensitive

se·rum·al \-rəməl\ *adj* [*serum* + *-al*] **:** belonging to or derived from serum or serous exudations ⟨a ~ calculus at the root of a tooth⟩

serum albumin *n* **:** a crystallizable albumin or mixture of albumins that normally constitutes more than half of the protein in blood serum, blood plasma, and other serous fluids, that can be isolated after precipitation of the globulins or by electrophoresis, that is synthesized in the liver, and that serves to maintain the osmotic pressure of the blood and is used in transfusions for the treatment of shock and other medical and surgical conditions — called also *blood albumin*

serum anaphylaxis *n* **:** anaphylaxis to a foreign serum to which a patient is sensitive (as in the second injection of an antitoxin)

serum globulin *n* **:** a globulin or mixture of globulins occurring with albumin in blood serum, blood plasma, and other serous fluids from which it can be separated by precipitation or by electrophoresis — compare ALPHA GLOBULIN, BETA GLOBULIN, GAMMA GLOBULIN

serum hepatitis *or* **serum jaundice** *n* **:** INFECTIOUS HEPATITIS

serum sickness *or* **serum disease** *n* **:** an allergic reaction to the injection of foreign serum (as in serotherapy) manifested by swelling, urticaria, eruption, arthritis, and fever

serum therapy *n* **:** SEROTHERAPY

serut *var of* SEROOT

serv *abbr* **1** [L *serva*] preserve **2** servant **3** service

ser·val \ˈsərvəl, (ˌ)sərˈval\ *n* -s [F, fr. Pg *lobo cerval* lynx, fr. ML *lupus cervalis*, fr. L *lupus* wolf + LL *cervalis* cervine, fr. L *cervus* deer, stag + *-alis* -al — more at WOLF, HART] **1 :** a wildcat (*Felis capensis* or *F. serval*) common in Africa having long legs, large untufted ears, and a tawny coat with black spots and rings **2 :** the pelt of the serval

¹**ser·va·line** \ˈsərvəˌlīn, -ˌlən, -ˌlēn\ *adj* [*serval* + *-ine*] **:** of, relating to, or resembling the serval

²**servaline** \"\ *also* **servaline cat** *n* -s [NL *servalina* (specific epithet of *Felis servalina*) fr. F *serval* + NL *-ina*] **:** a wildcat (*Felis servalina*) of western Africa resembling the serval but with a more densely spotted coat

¹**ser·vant** \ˈsərvənt, ˈsə̄v-, ˈsəiv-, *dial* ˈsärv- *or* ˈsȧv-\ *n* -s [ME, fr. OF, fr. pres. part. of *servir* to serve — more at SERVE] **1 a :** a person bound to do the bidding of a master or superior **:** one that must work for another and obey him: as **a :** one that performs duties about the person or home of a master or employer **:** a personal or domestic attendant **b :** a person in the employ and subject to the direction of an individual or company **:** a wage-earning employee **c :** something (as an animal, tool, or machine) that serves the purposes of another **:** an object or device used as an instrument ⟨organization and machinery, which should be our ~*s* and not our masters, demand we should adapt ourselves to them —J.B.Priestley⟩ ⟨electricity, this marvelous ~ that turns factory wheels —Leonard Engel⟩ ⟨make atomic energy a ~ of man⟩ **2 :** an adherent or agent of a god or of the Deity **3** *obs* **:** an avowed suitor for a woman's affections **:** one that pays court to her or dances attendance on her; *also* **:** PARAMOUR **4 servants** *pl, obs* **:** a troupe of actors under the patronage of an English king or nobleman ⟨his majesty's ~*s*⟩ **5 :** a government official considered as the servant of his sovereign or of the public ⟨a ~ of her majesty the queen⟩ **:** PUBLIC SERVANT — compare CIVIL SERVANT **6 :** SLAVE **7 :** a member of Jehovah's Witnesses who functions in capacities like those of a clergyman

²**servant** *vt* -ED/-ING/-S **1** *obs* **:** to make subject **:** SUBORDINATE **2** *obs* **:** to furnish with a servant **3** *obs* **:** to act as servant — used in the phrase *to servant it*

ser·vant·less \-ləs\ *adj* **:** having no servant ⟨baby's playpen . . . one of the drearier manifestations of the ~ age —*New Yorker*⟩

ser·vant·ry \-ntrē\ *n* -ES [¹*servant* + *-ry*] **:** all the servants of one master or house ⟨all the ~ of the dairy were standing in the red-brick entry —Thomas Hardy⟩

ser·vant·ship \nt,ship\ *n* [¹*servant* + *-ship*] **:** the place or condition of a servant

¹**serve** \ˈsərv, ˈsə̄v, ˈsəiv, *dial* ˈsärv *or* ˈsȧv\ *vb* -ED/-ING/-S [ME *serven*, fr. OF *servir*, fr. L *servire* to be a slave, serve, be of use, fr. *servus* slave, servant, perh. of Etruscan origin] *vi* **1 a :** to be a servant **:** become employed in domestic service, at manual labor, or upon another's business **:** do menial service ⟨*served* on the staffs of various wealthy households⟩ ⟨so they made the people of Israel ~ with rigor, and made their lives bitter with hard service —Exod 1:13, 14 (RSV)⟩ **b** *obs* **:** to do service (as to God or a feudal superior) — used with *to* ⟨blessed angels he sends to and fro to ~ to wicked man —Edmund Spenser⟩ **c :** to do military or naval service **:** be a soldier or sailor ⟨two of his great-grandfathers *served* in the Revolutionary War —Edna Yost⟩ **2 a :** to perform the duties of a priest or clergyman **:** officiate in a clerical capacity **b :** to assist a celebrant as server at mass **3 a :** to be of use **:** answer a purpose **:** have a function ⟨in a day when few people could write, seals *served* as signatures —Elizabeth W. King⟩ ⟨nothing he had ever experienced *served* to quiet him so much as these end-of-the-week concerts —Edward Bok⟩ ⟨a disused fire station *served* for a clubhouse⟩ **b :** to be favorable, opportune, or convenient ⟨met a tide that *served* for an immediate departure⟩ ⟨told and retold the story wherever occasion *served*⟩ **c :** to be worthy of reliance or trust ⟨it was in the last year of his life, if memory ~*s*⟩ **d :** to hold an office **:** discharge a duty or function **:** act in a capacity ⟨*served* on a jury⟩ ⟨*served* as mayor for several years⟩ **4 a :** to prove adequate or satisfactory **:** SATISFY, SUFFICE ⟨nothing would ~ but she must pack a box for me to take back —John Buchan⟩ **b :** to prove out **:** hold good **:** pass as valid ⟨a safe-conduct that *served* not only for him but for the entire party⟩ **5 :** to help persons to food: as **a :** to wait at table **b :** to set out portions of food or drink **6 :** to wait on customers ⟨~*s* in a grocery store⟩ **7 :** to put the ball in play in any of various games (as tennis or handball) **8** *of a male animal* **:** COPULATE ~ *vt* **1 a :** to be a servant to **:** work for (a master or employer) **:** do tasks set by (a superior) **:** minister to **:** ATTEND ⟨his master shall bore his ear through with an awl; and he shall ~ him for life —Exod 21:6 (RSV)⟩ ⟨*served* several actresses as personal maid⟩ **b :** to give the service and respect due to (a lord, sovereign, or other superior) ⟨several times *served* the queen as prime minister⟩ **c :** to comply with the commands or demands of ⟨*served* the will of venal men⟩ **:** satisfy the needs or wants of **:** GRATIFY **d :** to render military or naval service to **:** fight for **:** be a soldier or sailor of ⟨*served* the nation as a commander in three wars⟩ **e :** to perform the duties of (an office or post) **:** discharge the requirements of **2 :** to offer habitual worship and obedience to (a god or devil) ⟨God whom I ~ with a clear conscience —2 Tim 1:3 (RSV)⟩ **3 a :** to assist (a priest) at mass as server **b :** to act as server at (mass) ⟨*served* mass on Sunday⟩ **c :** to act as pastor to ⟨*served* several large parishes⟩ **4** *archaic* **:** to pay a lover's or suitor's court to (a lady) **5 a :** to work through or perform a term of service ⟨had *served* his time as a mate in the merchant marine⟩ ⟨*served* out an apprenticeship⟩ **b :** to put in (a term of imprisonment) **:** SPEND, UNDERGO ⟨felt that anyone who had *served* time was a marked man⟩ ⟨*served* seven years for armed assault⟩ **6 a :** to wait on (one) at table **b :** to bring (food) to a diner — often used with *up* ⟨*served* him up a hearty dinner⟩ **c :** to place food on (the table) **d** *archaic* **:** to put out food for (an animal) **:** FEED **7 a :** to furnish or supply (one) with something needed or desired ⟨a consolidated school *served* the children who had attended the several former one-room schools⟩ **b :** to wait on (a customer) in a store **c :** to provide merchandise serviceable or desirable to (a buyer) ⟨that task has been and continues to be to ~ the American customer well —H.H.Curtice⟩ **d :** to furnish professional service to ⟨a physician who had *served* his community with distinction for nearly half a century⟩ **8 a :** to be of use to or answer the needs of **:** provide for **:** AVAIL ⟨private reservoirs and canals . . . ~ each separate estate —P.E.James⟩ **b :** to be enough for **:** SUFFICE, LAST ⟨the slightest smile would ~ him for encouragement⟩ **c :** to be of help in bringing about **:** contribute to **:** PROMOTE ⟨engaged . . . in *serving* the purposes of the Revolution —Van Wyck Brooks⟩ **9** *obs* **:** ENCOURAGE, PROMPT, PERMIT ⟨certainly my conscience will ~ me to run from this Jew my master —Shak.⟩ **10 :** to treat or act toward in a specified way **:** deal with **:** REQUITE ⟨he *served* me ill⟩ **11 a :** to bring to notice, deliver, or execute actually or constructively as required by law **:** put into effect ⟨to ~ a summons or process is to deliver it, or to read it so as to give due notice, or both⟩ ⟨to ~ an attachment or execution is to levy it by seizure or taking possession⟩ **b :** to make legal service upon (a person named in a writ) **c** *Scots law* **:** to declare (someone) heir to an estate after formal adjudication **12** *archaic* **:** FIT, SUIT **13** *obs* **:** to avail (oneself) of someone or something **:** make use of **14** *archaic* **:** to make convenient opportunity for (one) **:** provide occasion or means for (a person) **:** FAVOR **15 :** to put up or flush game before (a hawk) — used of either the falconer or the dog **16** *of an animal* **:** to copulate with **:** COVER — distinguished from *settle* **17 :** to do (one) a good or bad turn **:** play (one) a trick **:** deal (one) a blow **18 :** to wind spun yarn, canvas, or wire tightly around (a rope or stay) to protect from chafing or from the weather **:** wrap serving around (a bowstring) **19 :** to stand by (one) **:** prove worthy of trust by — used esp. of the memory ⟨that was his last appearance, if memory ~*s* me⟩ **20 :** to provide services that benefit or help ⟨the most distinctive characteristic of a profession — its obligation to ~ society —H.A.Wagner⟩ **21 :** to put (the ball) in play in any of various games (as tennis or handball) **22 :** to keep (artillery or naval guns) in action **:** FIRE **23** *Scot* **a :** to give satisfaction to ⟨heirs were *served*⟩ **b :** prove enough or too much for — **serve one right :** to deal with one as he deserves **:** be the just or fitting return for what one is or does ⟨they *served him right* for his thieving⟩ ⟨felt that his disgrace *served him right*⟩ ⟨it *serves you right* for trying to get ahead of everyone else in line⟩ — **serve the time** *or* **serve the hour :** to be a timeserver **:** TEMPORIZE

²**serve** \"\ *n* -s **:** the act of putting the ball in play in any of various net or court games (as tennis) ⟨won many games with his powerful and accurate ~*s*⟩

served *past of* SERVE

ser·ven·tism \sərˈventˌizəm, -nˌti-\ *or* **ser·ven·te·ism** \-ntēˌizəm\ *n* -s [(*cavalier*) *servente* + *-ism*] **:** the social convention countenancing the cavalier servente

serve out *vt* **:** to revenge oneself on **:** pay back **:** retaliate against ⟨*served* them out royally for their many acts of cruelty and oppression⟩

serv·er \ˈsərvər, ˈsə̄və(r, ˈsəivə(r\ *n* -s [ME, fr. *serven* to serve + *-er*] **1 a :** one that brings food and drink to persons at table **b :** one that dishes up food (as in a cafeteria) **2 :** the player who puts the ball in play in any of various net or court games (as tennis) **3 :** one that assists the celebrant in the Mass, Divine Liturgy, or Holy Communion **:** ACOLYTE **4 :** something used in serving: as **a :** any of various articles of furniture (as a buffet or a wheeled table) from which food may be served **:** CREDENZA, SIDEBOARD, TEA WAGON **b :** a tea or coffee service usu. consisting of pot, sugar bowl, cream pitcher, and tray **c :** a tray, salver, or covered plate used as a serving utensil **d :** any of various special-purpose implements (as salad tongs or a pie lifter) used to serve a particular food **e :** an insulated often decorative vessel for keeping foods hot or cold until served

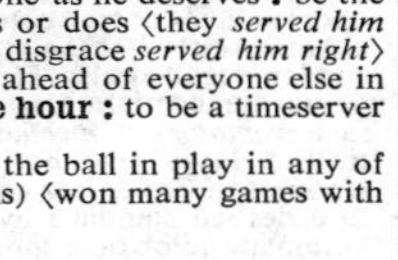

server 4b

serv·ery \-vərē\ *n* -ES [¹*serve* + *-ery*] **1 :** BUTLER'S PANTRY **2 :** a service alcove with counter or buffet between dining room and kitchen

serves *pres 3d sing of* SERVE, *pl of* SERVE

ser·ve·tian \ˌsərˈvēshən, ˌsərˈv-\ *n* -s *usu cap* [Michael *Servetus* †1553 Spanish theologian and physician + E *-ian*] **:** a follower of Michael Servetus who was burned at the stake in Geneva in 1553 for anti-Trinitarianism and antipedobaptism

ser·vette \ˌsərˈvet\ *n* -s [¹*serve*] **:** a small folding table

¹**servian** *usu cap, var of* SERBIAN

²**ser·vi·an** \ˈsərvēən\ *adj, usu cap* [*Servi*us Tullius + E *-an*] **:** of or relating to Servius Tullius who was the sixth of the legendary kings of Rome 578–534 B.C. ⟨the *Servian* wall⟩

¹**ser·vice** \ˈsərvəs, ˈsə̄v-, ˈsəiv- *dial* ˈsärv- *or* ˈsȧv-\ *n* -s [ME *servise, service*, fr. OF, fr. L *servitium* condition of a slave, servitude, body of slaves or servants, fr. *servus* slave + *-itium* -ice — more at SERVE] **1 :** the condition or occupation of a servant **:** the serving of a master: as **a :** the position of a domestic servant ⟨the daughters of yeoman and peasant alike could take ~ with the wife of a squire who had known them all their lives —Roy Lewis & Angus Maude⟩ **b :** the domestic employment of a particular master ⟨entered the ~ of a wealthy townsman⟩ **2 :** the performance of work commanded or paid for by another **:** a servant's duty **:** attendance on a superior ⟨most true, I have lost my teeth in your ~ —Shak.⟩ **3 a :** the employment of a public servant ⟨distinguished himself in his country's ~⟩ **b :** a specified branch or department of government employment or the staff of persons working in it ⟨consular ~⟩ ⟨intelligence ~⟩ **c :** the duties, work, or business performed or discharged by a government official **4 a :** one of a nation's organized fighting forces (as the army, navy, or air force) **b :** the performance of military duty esp. in war **:** COMBAT ⟨saw active ~ in several campaigns⟩ **c :** a particular military operation **:** CAMPAIGN, ENGAGEMENT, EXPEDITION **d :** the profession or career of arms **:** the occupation of a soldier, sailor, or military flier **5 a :** an act done for the benefit or at the command of another ⟨impose some ~ on me for thy love —Shak.⟩ ⟨felt that to avenge his friend's death was the only ~ he could still do him⟩ **b :** the constancy, attentions, or devotion of a lover for his lady **6 a :** the habit or practice of serving God or the acts done with that intention ⟨devoted himself altogether to the ~ of God⟩ **b :** a form or ritual of worship (as public worship) established for customary use, celebration, or observance **c :** the performance of religious worship esp. according to settled public forms or conventions **d :** an assembly or meeting for worship **e :** rites (as religious rites) appropriate to a particular event ⟨a burial ~⟩ ⟨a marriage ~⟩ **f :** a liturgical office set to music **:** a set of such settings esp. of the choral canticles and chants **7 a :** the bringing of food and drink to diners seated at table **:** the work or activity of waiting at table ⟨it was a small place but the ~ was excellent⟩ **b** (1) **:** the food and drink apportioned to one person (2) *obs* **:** COURSE **c :** the dishes, implements, or utensils needed to serve a meal, a specified number of persons, or a particular food or drink ⟨a silver ~ for 12⟩ ⟨a coffee ~⟩ **d :** a set of vessels used at the altar in celebrating communion ⟨the silver Eucharistic ~ . . . was saved by being hidden in a cistern —*Amer. Guide Series: La.*⟩ **e :** a set of implements and vessels for use in the toilet **:** DRESSER SET **8 :** the return in money, in kind, or in labor owed by a feudal tenant to his lord for the enjoyment of his tenancy **:** RENDER **9 a :** action or use that furthers some end or purpose **:** conduct or performance that assists or benefits someone or something **:** deeds useful or instrumental toward some object ⟨the pioneer-baiters do the country a ~ —Russell Lord⟩ ⟨did me a valuable ~⟩ **b :** professional or other useful ministrations ⟨legal ~*s*⟩ ⟨a bill collection ~⟩ **c :** supply of needs ⟨a vending machine set up for the ~ of casual passersby⟩; *also* **:** UTILITY **10** *archaic* **:** a profession of respect or duty — used in various expressions of courtesy (as in greetings or in toasts) **11 :** the act of putting the ball in play in any of various net or court games (as tennis) **12 :** an act of administering or applying something **13 :** the wrapping or covering of a rope (as with spun yarn, small lines, or canvas) to prevent chafing; *also* **:** the materials used for this purpose **14 a :** useful labor that does not produce a tangible commodity — usu. used in pl. ⟨railroads, telephone companies, and physicians perform ~*s* although they produce no goods⟩ **b :** DEBT SERVICE **c :** a facility or provision for maintenance and repair (as of houses or manufactured articles) ⟨property ~⟩ ⟨radio and television ~⟩ ⟨automobile repair ~⟩ **d :** the provision, organization, or apparatus for conducting a public utility or meeting a general demand ⟨telephone ~⟩ ⟨air freight ~⟩ **15 a :** the act of bringing a legal writ, process, or summons to notice actually or constructively as prescribed by law ⟨accepted ~ of a subpoena⟩ **b :** the carrying into effect or execution of a writ or process (as an attachment by seizing the goods or person attached or an execution by levying it upon the goods or person of the defendant) — compare PERSONAL SERVICE 1, SUBSTITUTED SERVICE **16 :** the act of serving or covering the female — used of a male animal **17 :** a regularly scheduled trip over a public transportation route ⟨three airline ~*s* daily between island and mainland⟩ **18 :** a branch of a hospital medical staff devoted to a particular specialty ⟨obstetrical ~⟩ ⟨pediatric ~⟩ **19 a :** a pipe branching from a gas or water main to serve the premises of a user **b :** the lead-in conductors from an electric power or telephone line to a user's premises **20 :** effort inspired by philanthropic motives or directed to human welfare or betterment **syn** see USE — **at one's service :** ready to do one's bidding **:** available for use ⟨assured her that he was entirely *at her service*⟩ ⟨placed a car *at his service*⟩ — **of service :** of use **:** SERVICEABLE, HELPFUL, USEFUL ⟨protested that he was happy to be *of service*⟩

²**service** \"\ *adj* **1 a :** of or relating to the armed services or one of them **:** belonging to or used in the army, navy, or air force ⟨a ~ newspaper⟩ **b :** of, relating to, or constituting a branch of an army (as an ordnance department) that exists to serve or supply the army's fighting men **2 :** of or relating to domestic service **:** used in serving or by servants ⟨a ~ hatch⟩ **3 :** worn in or intended for everyday use **:** DURABLE ⟨service-weight stockings⟩ **4 a :** providing services rather than tangible goods ⟨transportation and entertainment are ~ industries⟩ **b :** offering a product useful only in making another product or in performing associated tasks or services ⟨diemakers and allied ~ industries —*New Englander*⟩ **c :** offering repair, maintenance, or incidental services

³**service** \"\ *vt* -ED/-ING/-S **:** to perform services for **:** meet the needs of **:** SERVE: as **a :** to repair or provide maintenance for ⟨I've had some dealings with them in the *servicing* of my English car —Richard Joseph⟩ **b :** to meet interest and sinking fund payments on (as government debt) **c :** to perform any of the business functions auxiliary to production or distribution of ⟨the accounting department ~*s* the manufacturing and sales programs⟩ **d :** to provide information or other assistance to ⟨for many years the Department of State has *serviced* the press and the scholars interested in foreign affairs —F.H.Russell⟩ **e :** to provide (a philatelic cover) with first-day cancellation or cachet **f :** to copulate with (a female animal) ⟨deer are polygamous and one buck may claim and ~ several does —Lyle St. Amant & Carrol Perkins⟩

⁴**service** \"\ *n* -s [ME *serves*, pl. of *serve* service tree, fruit of the service, fr. OE *syrfe*, fr. (assumed) VL *sorbea*, fr. L *sorbus* service tree, sorb tree] **1 :** SERVICE TREE 1 **2 :** the fruit of a service tree

ser·vice·abil·i·ty \ˌ==əˈbiləd·ē, -lətē, -i\ *n* [*serviceable* + *-ity*] **:** fitness to give service **:** usefulness for a purpose **:** wearing quality **:** DURABILITY, SERVICEABLENESS ⟨~ is an essential characteristic of all assets —R.B.Kester⟩

ser·vice·able \ˈ==əbəl\ *adj* [ME *servisable*, fr. MF, fr. OF, fr. *servise, service* service + *-able*] **1 :** ready or willing to help **:** disposed to give good offices **:** HELPFUL, USEFUL ⟨a ~ friend⟩ **2 :** fit for use **:** suited for a purpose **:** usable to advantage **:** wearing well in use ⟨a ~ design⟩ ⟨a ~ knife⟩ ⟨~ shoes⟩ ⟨some of the Mound Builders mined copper for ornamental purposes and made ~ pottery —R.W.Murray⟩

ser·vice·able·ness *n* -ES **:** the quality or state of being serviceable

ser·vice·ably \-blē,-bli\ *adv* **:** in a serviceable manner

serviceage *n* -s [¹*service* + *-age*] *obs* **:** SERVITUDE

ser·vice·ber·ry \ˈsär|vəs-, ˈsȧ|, ˈsər|, ˈsə̄|, ˈsəi| — *see* BERRY\ *n* [⁴*service* + *berry*] **:** JUNEBERRY

service book *n* [¹*service* + *book*] **:** a book setting forth forms of worship used in religious services

service box *n* [²*service*] **1 :** a casing or box let in flush with the pavement for access to a corporation cock **2 :** a metal box installed where the electric service wires enter a building to house the main switch with its fuses **3 :** the area in which a player stands while serving in various wall and net games

service brake *n* **:** an automobile brake usu. foot-operated that is used in ordinary driving — compare EMERGENCY BRAKE

service cap *n* : a flat-topped visor cap about 3½ inches high worn by officers and men with a military service uniform — compare DRESS CAP

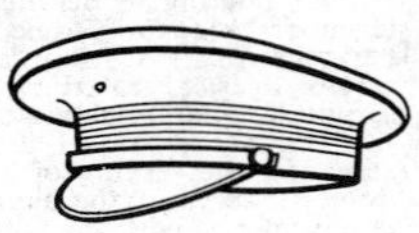

service ceiling *n* : the height above sea level at which under standard air conditions a particular airplane can no longer rise at a rate greater than a small designated rate (as 100 feet per minute in the U.S. and England) — called also *ceiling*; compare ABSOLUTE CEILING

service cap

service charge *n* : a fee (as an extra fare, a cover charge, or a bank's fee for maintaining an unprofitable checking account) charged for a particular service often in addition to a standard or basic fee

service club *n* 1 : a club of business and professional men and women concerned esp. with community welfare and usu. forming part of a national or international organization 2 : a social and recreational club for enlisted men provided by one of the armed services at one of its posts or installations

service company or **service battery** *n* : an administrative military unit concerned mainly with transportation and supply

service court *n* : a part of the court into which the ball or shuttlecock must be served in any of various court games — see TENNIS illustration

serviced *past of* SERVICE

service door *n* [²*service*] : a door intended for the use of servants or to facilitate service (as delivery of goods or removal of waste)

service flag *n* : a flag displayed in wartime to show that a member of a family or organization is in active military service or has died in such service

service flat *n, Brit* : a flat in which the rental includes housekeeping care and to which prepared meals will be sent if ordered

service hatch *n* : an opening in a wall (as between kitchen and dining room) through which dishes may be passed

service life *n* : the time during which something can be used economically or the time during which it is used by one owner

service line *n* [¹*service*] **1 a** : a line 21 feet from the net in tennis and parallel to it that marks the rear of a service court — compare FOOT FAULT **b** : a line that is perpendicular to the rear service line and bisects the service court **2** : a line drawn parallel to a front wall or board in wall games (as handball) to mark a boundary which must not be overstepped in serving

ser·vice·man \'¤¤₁man, -₁mən, -₁maa(ə)n\ *n, pl* **servicemen** [²*service + man*] **1** : a male member of the armed forces **2** : a man employed to repair or maintain equipment

service mark *n* : a mark or device used to identify a service (as transportation, dry cleaning, or insurance) offered to customers — compare TRADEMARK

service medal *n* : a medal awarded to an individual who does military service in a specified war or campaign — compare DECORATION

service of an heir [¹*service*] *Scots law* : a proceeding by inquest of a jury or by publication and proof before a competent officer without a jury to determine the heir of a person deceased

service pipe *n* [²*service*] : a pipe connecting a main pipe (as a gas or water main or an electrical conduit) with a building

service plate *n* : a large elaborate plate used to indicate a place at table and to serve as an under plate during the first courses

service road *n* : FRONTAGE ROAD

services *pl of* SERVICE, *pres 3d sing of* SERVICE

service side *n* [¹*service*] : the side of a court-tennis court from which service is made — compare HAZARD SIDE

service speed *n* [²*service*] : the average speed maintained by a ship under normal load and weather conditions

service stamp *n* : OFFICIAL STAMP

service star *n* : a five-pointed gold star worn on a boy scout's uniform and bearing a numeral to indicate years of membership

service state *n* : WELFARE STATE ⟨the *service state* . . . takes the whole domain of human welfare for its province and would solve all economic and social ills through its administrative activities —Roscoe Pound⟩

service station *n* 1 : FILLING STATION 2 : a depot or place at which some service is offered

service stripe *n* : a stripe worn on an enlisted man's left sleeve to indicate three years of service in the army or air force or four years in the navy — compare CHEVRON, HASH MARK

service switch *n* : a building's main electric switch usu. located in the service box

service tree *n* [⁴*service*] **1** or **service** *n* -s : MOUNTAIN ASH 1: **a** : a medium-sized Old World tree (*Sorbus domestica*) that resembles the common rowan tree but has larger flowers and larger edible fruits containing grit cells **b** : a similar Old World tree (*S. torminalis*) with simple broad ovate and usu. somewhat cordate leaves and small speckled brown fruits — called also *wild service tree* **2** : JUNEBERRY 1

service uniform *n* [²*service*] : a military uniform for routine service — compare DRESS UNIFORM, FULL-DRESS UNIFORM

service wall *n* [¹*service*] : the front wall of a court-tennis court

ser·vice·wom·an \'¤¤₁wümən\ *n, pl* **servicewomen** [²*service + woman*] : a female member of the armed forces

servicing *n* -s [fr. gerund of ³*service*] : the act of providing service

ser·vi·ent \'sərvēənt\ *adj* [L *servient-, serviens*, pres. part. of *servire* to serve] **1 a** : doing service : SERVING **b** : characteristic of a servant or subordinate : INSTRUMENTAL, SERVILE **2** : subject to some person or thing that dominates, rules, or controls : subject to a servant, agreement, or servitude

ser·vi·ette \¹sərvē₁et\ *n* -s [F, fr. MF, fr. *servir* to serve] *chiefly Brit* : a table napkin

ser·vi·grous \sə(r)'vīgrəs\ *adj* [alter. (perh. influenced by *vigorous*) of *savagerous*] *South* : SAVAGEROUS

¹ser·vile \'sərvəl, 'sǝ̄l, 'səi, ₁₁vīl, ₁(₁)vil\ *adj* [ME, fr. L *servilis*, fr. *servus* slave, servant + *-ilis* -ile — more at SERVE] **1 a** : of, relating to, or appropriate to slaves ⟨the stigmata . . . of his ~ antecedents —Oscar Handlin⟩ **b** : befitting a slave or servant : unsuitable for a free man ⟨the machine increased the servitude of ~ personalities —Lewis Mumford⟩ **c** : held in servitude : subject to a master or owner ⟨manors . . . within which both independent farmers and ~ tenants lived —R.B. Morris⟩ **d** : held by or relating to base services or a base as opposed to a free tenure of land under feudal law **2** *Roman Catholicism* : of, relating to, or constituting physical or manual as distinguished from mental labor ⟨in their first day shall be most solemn unto you, and holy: you shall do no ~ work therein —Lev 23:7 (DV)⟩ **3** : subject to despotic or tyrannical rule : politically oppressed or subjugated ⟨doomed . . . to be destroyed or reduced to a ~ station —Sir Winston Churchill⟩ **4 a** : behaving like a slave : lacking spirit or independence : ABJECT, SUBMISSIVE ⟨the ~ attitude which he always maintained towards authority in intellectual and religious matters —R.A.Hall b.1911⟩ ⟨leaves a ~ old man in the clutches of his daughter —Times Lit. Supp.⟩ ⟨too ~ to the authority of older dictionaries —Louise Pound⟩ **b** : lacking moral worth or dignity : IGNOBLE ⟨~ fear⟩ **5** : CONTROLLED, SUBJECT, SUBORDINATE — used with *to* **5** : slavishly imitative of a model esp. in literature or art : lacking independence or originality ⟨could draw inspiration from the past without stooping to ~ imitation —Amer. Guide Series: N.Y.⟩ **6** : of, relating to, or engaged in the work of a servant or menial ⟨if it is used by a ~ class it is avoided by the educated —A.N. Whitehead⟩ **7 a** : of or relating to a derivational, inflectional, or relational element of speech : not belonging to the root ⟨~ sounds or letters⟩ ⟨S in English *sits, man's, dogs* is ~⟩ **b** : not itself sounded but serving to indicate a long preceding vowel ⟨the *e* in *stone* is ~⟩ **c** : subject to assimilation **8** : constituting a means rather than an end : INSTRUMENTAL ⟨in philosophy itself investigation and reasoning are only preparatory and ~ parts, means to an end —George Santayana⟩ *syn* see SUBSERVIENT

²servile \'¤\ *n* -s **1** : a servile person **2** : a servile linguistic element or particle

ser·vile·ly \-əl(l)ē, -¹lē∥, -il(l)\ ∥i\ *adv* : in a servile manner, state, or spirit

---

ser·vil·ism \-₁lizəm, -₁l-, -il\ *n* -s [¹*servile + -ism*] **1** : a base or abject servility or obsequiousness **2** : a doctrine advocating slavery or a system based on slavery

ser·vil·i·ty \(₁)sər'viləd-ē, sǝ̄'v-, sǝi'v-, -lǝtē, -i\ *n* -es [¹*servile + -ity*] **1** : a slave's condition : the state of slavery : SERVITUDE **2 a** : a mean or cringing submissiveness : OBSEQUIOUSNESS ⟨his political advisers flattered him with grotesque ~ —Times Lit. Supp.⟩ **b** : lack of independence or spirit : undue dependence or deference **3** : slavish imitation in following a model : want of originality, inspiration, or invention

¹serving *n* -s [ME, fr. gerund of *serven* to serve] **1** : the act or function of one that serves ⟨the ~ of a meal⟩ **2** : a helping of food or drink **3** : the thread or cord wrapped around the middle of a bowstring to protect it from the nock of the arrow — called also *whipping* **4** : a layer of protective material (as jute yarn) put on the exterior of an armored or lead-covered electric cable **5** : SERVICE 13

²serving *adj* [ME, fr. pres. part. of *serven* to serve] **1** : employed or used to serve ⟨a low ~ bench on which are placed four or five pots containing food —Norman Mailer⟩ ⟨~ wench⟩ **2** : belonging to a military service ⟨a ~ officer in the British army —M.C.A.Henniker⟩

serving board *n* [¹*serving*] : a spoon-shaped wooden tool used in putting on service esp. on eye splices

serving mallet *n* : a wooden device shaped like a mallet, grooved on the bottom, and used in serving stuff or service ropes

serving stuff *n* [¹*serving*] : small lines for serving ropes

serving table *n* : a side table used in serving food : a small sideboard

serv·ing·man \'¤¤₁viŋ₁man\ *n, pl* **servingmen** [ME, fr. ²*serving + man*] : a male servant

a serving mallet;
b mallet in use

servingwoman \'¤¤₁¤¤\ *n, pl* **servingwomen** [ME, fr. ²*serving + woman*] : a female servant

ser·vite \'sər₁vīt\ *n* -s *cap* [ML *Servitae* (pl.), fr. L *servus* slave + *-itae*, pl. of *-ita* -ite] : a member of a mendicant order of friars founded at Florence in 1233

ser·vi·tial \sər'vishəl\ *adj* [ML *servitialis*, fr. LL *servitium* service + L *-alis* -al] : of or relating to servitium

ser·vi·ti·um \-shēəm\ *n, pl* **servi·tia** \-shēə\ [LL, fr. L, condition of a slave — more at SERVICE] : SERVICE

ser·vi·tor \'sərvəd·ər, -və₁tō(ə)r\ *n* -s [ME *servitour*, fr. MF, fr. LL *servitor*, fr. L *servitus* (past part. of *servire* to serve) + L *-or*] **1** : a male servant : MENIAL; *esp* : a table waiter **2** *archaic* : one that serves a king esp. as a soldier **3** : an undergraduate (as at Oxford) acting as servant to the fellows in return for his college expenses under a system now disused — compare EXHIBITIONER, SIZAR **4** : a member of a chair of glassworkers who shapes the body of the product being made — compare FOOTMAKER, GAFFER

ser·vi·to·ri·al \¹sərvə¹tōrēəl\ *adj* [*servitor + -ial*] : of, relating to, or resembling a servitor

ser·vi·tor·ship \'sərvəd·ər₁ship, -və₁tòr₁sh-\ *n* [*servitor + -ship*] : the position or work of a servitor

ser·vi·tress \-və₁trəs\ *n* -es [*servitor + -ess*] : a woman servant

ser·vi·tude \'sərvə₁tüd, 'sǝ̄v-, 'sǝiv-, -və₁tyüd\ *n* -s [ME, fr. MF, fr. L *servitudin-, servitudo*, fr. *servus* slave, servant + *-tudin-, -tudo* -tude — more at SERVE] **1** : the condition of a slave or serf : a state of subjection to an owner or master : BONDAGE, SERFDOM, SLAVERY ⟨neither slavery nor involuntary ~, except as a punishment for crime whereof the party shall have been duly convicted, shall exist within the United States —U.S.Constitution⟩ **2 a** : subjection to foreign overlordship or political oppression : subjugation by a conqueror or tyrant ⟨society may be expected to disintegrate and fall into ~ when men deny . . . these realities and transcendent obligations —Michael Polanyi⟩ **b** : a particular imposition or term imposed on a defeated or subject people ⟨meant the overthrow of many of the ~s placed upon them by the peace treaties —C.E. Black & E.C.Helmreich⟩ **3** : a subjection likened to that of slavery : an unworthy subservience ⟨by criticizing religion they would attempt to free the religious spirit from its present ~ —Virginia Woolf⟩ **4** *archaic* : the state of being a servant (as a domestic servant or an indentured servant) **5** *archaic* : the service of an apprentice : APPRENTICESHIP **6** *penal* SERVITUDE **7** : a right in respect of an object (as land owned by one person) in virtue of which the object is subject to a specified use or enjoyment by another person or for the benefit of another thing (the common-law easement is a species of ~) — compare NEGATIVE EASEMENT, POSITIVE EASEMENT

ser·vi·tus \'sərvə₁tüs\ *n, pl* **servitu·tes** \¹¤¤¹tii₁tās\ [L *servitus, servitus*, fr. *servus* slave] **1** *Roman law* : SERVITUDE, SLAVERY, SUBJECTION **2** *Roman law* : EASEMENT

ser·vo \'sər(₁)vō *sometimes* 'ser-\ *n* -s *often attrib* [by shortening] **1** : SERVOMOTOR **2** : SERVOMECHANISM

servo- *comb form, usu cap* [*servian*] : SERBO-

servo amplifier *n* : a torque-amplifying component of a servomechanism

servo brake *n* **1** : a multiple-shoe automobile brake in which the action of one part upon another as a result of the forward motion of the vehicle increases the pressure between the second shoe and the brake drum and so increases the brake's effectiveness **2** : a brake in which pedal or lever power is augmented (as by a servomotor) : POWER BRAKE

servo control *n* : an auxiliary aeronautical device to reinforce by an aerodynamic or mechanical relay a pilot's effort in operating a control commonly consisting of a small hinged auxiliary airfoil at the trailing edge of an aileron, elevator, or rudder — called also *Flettner control*

ser·vo·mech·a·nism \'sər(₁)vō₁mek-₁ iz- + \ *n* [*servo- (in servomotor) + mechanism*] : an automatic device for controlling large amounts of power by means of very small amounts of power and correcting performance of a mechanism to a desired standard by an error-sensing feedback (as in an automatic pilot or a gun-aiming apparatus)

ser·vo·mo·tor \'¤¤₁(₁)vō, ¤¤va+₁\ *n* [*servo-moteur*, fr. L *servus* slave, servant + F *moteur* motor, fr. L *motor* one that moves — more at SERVE, MOTOR] : a power-driven mechanism that supplements a primary control operated by a comparatively feeble force (as in a servomechanism)

servo system *n* : SERVOMECHANISM

ser·vo·tab \'¤¤₁+₁, -₁\ *n* [*servo + tab*] : SERVO CONTROL

servt *abbr* servant

ses·a·me \'sesəmē, -mi *also* -₁mē *sometimes* 'sezə-\ *n* -s [alter. (influenced by F *sésame*, fr. L *sesamum*) of earlier *sesam, sesama*, fr. L *sesamum, sesama*, fr. Gk *sēsamon, sēsamē*, of Sem origin; akin to Assyr *šamaššamu* sesame, Aram *shŭmshē-mā*, Ar *simsim*] **1** : an East Indian annual erect herb (*Sesamum indicum*) having chiefly rosy or white flowers **2** or **sesame seed** : the small obovate flattish seeds of sesame that yield an oil and are used as a flavoring agent — called also *benniseed* **3** : OPEN SESAME ⟨recognition that wealth, power, fame are not the ~ to happiness —Israel Goldstein⟩

sesame grass *n* : GAMA

sesame oil *n* : a pale yellow bland semidrying fatty oil obtained from sesame seeds and used chiefly as an edible oil (as in margarine), as a vehicle for various pharmaceuticals, and in cosmetics and soaps — called also *gingelly oil, teel oil* **2** : CAMELINE OIL

se·sa·mia \sə'sāmēə, se's-\ *n, cap* [NL, fr. L *sesamum* sesame + NL *-ia*] : a genus of noctuid moths many of which have larvae that are destructive to maize, sugarcane, rice, and other grasses

ses·a·min \'sesəmən *sometimes* -ez-\ *n* -s [L *sesamum* sesame + ISV *-in*] : a crystalline cyclic ether $C_{20}H_{18}O_6$ that is obtained esp. from sesame oil and is a powerful synergist for pyrethrum insecticides

¹ses·a·moid \-₁mȯid\ *adj* [Gk *sēsamoeidēs*, lit., resembling sesame seed, fr. *sēsamon* sesame seed] **1** : of, relating to, or being a nodular mass of bone or cartilage in a tendon esp. where the tendon passes over a joint or some bony prominence

²sesamoid \'¤\ *n* -s : a sesamoid bone or cartilage

---

ses·a·moid·itis \-₁₁mȯi'dīd·əs\ *n* -es [NL, fr. E ²*sesamoid* + NL *-itis*] : inflammation of the navicular bone and adjacent structures in the horse

ses·a·mol \'¤¤₁mȯl, -mȯl\ *n* -s [ISV *sesame + -ol*] : a crystalline phenolic ether $HOC_6H_3O_2CH_2$ that occurs both free and combined in sesame oil and is an antioxidant for fats and oils; 3,4-methylenedioxy-phenol

ses·a·mo·lin \'sesəmə₁lin, se'samə₁lǝn\ *n* -s [*sesamol + -in*] : a crystalline cyclic ether $C_{20}H_{18}O_7$ that is obtained from sesame oil, is closely related chemically to sesamin, and is an equally powerful synergist for pyrethrum insecticides

ses·a·mum \'sesəməm\ *n* [NL, fr. L, sesame] **1** *cap* : a genus of tropical African and Indian herbs (family Pedaliaceae) having entire or divided leaves and irregular campanulate flowers with a curved tube dilated above the 4-angled unarmed capsule — see SESAME **2** -s : SESAME

¹ses·ban \'ses₁ban\ *n* -s [F, fr. Ar *saisabān*, fr. Per *sīsabān*] : either of two East Indian plants of the genus Sesbania (*S. aculeata* and *S. aegyptiaca*) — compare DAINCHA

²sesban \'¤\ [NL, fr. F *sesban*] *syn of* SESBANIA

ses·ba·nia \ses'bānēə\ *n, cap* [NL, fr. F *sesban* + NL *-ia*] **1** *cap* : a small genus of chiefly tropical pinnate-leaved herbs, shrubs, or trees (family Leguminosae) usu. having large showy pealike flowers — see COLORADO RIVER HEMP **2** -s : any plant of the genus Sesbania

ses·cu·ple \¹₁se'skyüpəl, 'seskyəp-\ *adj* [L *sescuplus* one and a half times as great, fr. *sesqui- + -plus* (as in *duplus* double) — more at DOUBLE] : HEMIOLIC

ses·e·li \'sesəlē\ *n* [NL, fr. L *seselis* seseli, fr. Gk *seselis, seseli*, perh. of Egypt origin] **1** *cap* : a large genus of smooth perennial herbs (family Umbelliferae) that are natives of temperate regions of the Old World and have ternately compound leaves, white flowers, and fruit with solitary oil tubes **2** -s : any plant of the genus Seseli

se·si·idae \sə'sīə₁dē\ *n, pl cap* [NL, fr. *Sesia* (syn. of *Aegeria*), fr. Gk *sēs* moth + NL *-ia* + *-idae*] *syn of* AEGERIIDAE

ses·qui \'seskwē\ *n* -s [by shortening] : SESQUICENTENNIAL

sesqui- *comb form* [L, one and a half, half again, lit., and a half, fr. *semis* half (fr. *semi-*) + *-que* and (enclitic); akin to Gk *te* and, Skt *ca*, Goth *-h*, *-uh* — more at SEMI-] **1** : one and a half times of the type : SUPER-, ULTRA- ⟨*sesqui*heretic⟩ **2** *archaic* : more than the norm or half times ⟨*sesqui*centennial⟩ **3** : one and a half times the degree of a (specified) aspect in astrology ⟨*sesqui*quadrate⟩ **4 a** : a compound containing three atoms or equivalents of a (specified) element or radical esp. when combined with two of another ⟨*sesqui*oxide⟩ **b** : a compound intermediate between two others or a mixture or combination of two others — not used systematically ⟨*sesqui*carbonate⟩ ⟨*sesqui*silicate⟩ **c** : a compound containing half again as many atoms as another ⟨*sesqui*terpene⟩

¹ses·qui·al·ter \₁seskwē'ȯltə(r), -₁ȯl-\ *adj* [L] : SESQUIALTERAL

²sesquialter \'¤\ *n* -s : SESQUIALTERA

ses·qui·al·te·ra \¹¤¤ə'¤ltərə\ *n* -s [NL, fr. L, fem. of *sesquialter*] **1** : a musical triplet of three minims in the time of two preceding — compare HEMIOLA **2** : a mixture pipe-organ stop containing usu. two ranks of pipes that reinforce some high harmonics of ground tone and make the sound more brilliant

ses·qui·al·ter·al \¹¤¤ə'¤ltərəl\ *adj* [L *sesquialter* one and a half times as great (fr. *sesqui- + alter* other of two, second) + E *-al* — more at ALTER] : one and a half times as great as another : having the ratio of one and a half to one

ses·qui·car·bon·ate \¹seskwə+\ *n* [*sesqui- + carbonate*] : a salt that is neither a simple normal carbonate nor a simple bicarbonate but in some cases (as sodium sesquicarbonate) a combination of the two — not used systematically

ses·qui·cen·ten·a·ry \₁¤¤+\ *adj or n* [*sesqui- + centenary*] : SESQUICENTENNIAL

¹ses·qui·cen·ten·ni·al \¹¤¤+\ *n* [*sesqui- + centennial*] : a 150th anniversary

²sesquicentennial \¹¤¤+\ *adj* : of or relating to a 150th anniversary

¹ses·qui·dip·loid \¹¤¤+\ *n* [*sesqui- + diploid*] : a triploid produced by a cross between tetraploid and diploid parents

²sesquidiploid \¹¤¤+\ *adj* : of, relating to, or being a sesquidiploid

sesquih *abbr* [L *sesquihora*] an hour and a half

ses·qui·ox·ide \¹seskwē+\ *n* [*sesqui- + oxide*] : an oxide containing three atoms of oxygen combined with two of the other constituent in the molecule (ferric oxide is a ~)

ses·quip·e·dal \se'skwipəd³l, ¤¤s+\ *adj* [L *sesquipedalis*] : SESQUIPEDALIAN

ses·qui·pe·da·lia \¹¤¤kwə₁pə'dālyə\ *n pl* [L *sesquipedalia (verba)*, lit., (words) a foot and a half long] : very long words

¹ses·qui·pe·da·lian \¹¤¤₁dālyən\ *adj* [L *sesquipedalis* a foot and a half long (fr. *sesqui- + ped-, pes* foot + *-alis* -al) + E -an — more at FOOT] **1** : having many syllables : LONG ⟨simplest language, without any ~ technical terms —J.H.Göttmer⟩ **2** : given to or characterized by the use of long words ⟨~ orators⟩ ⟨~ style⟩ ⟨this ~ way of saying one has no money —W.F.De Morgan⟩

²sesquipedalian \'¤\ *n* -s : a very long word

ses·qui·pe·da·lian·ism \¹¤¤¤'dālyə₁nizəm\ *also* **ses·quip·e·dal·ism** \se'skwipəd³l₁izəm, sǝ̄'s-\ *n* -s [*sesquipedalian, sesquipedal + -ism*] : SESQUIPEDALITY

ses·qui·pe·dal·i·ty \¹¤¤¤₁(₁)skwipə'daləd-ē\ *n* -es [*sesquipedal + -ity*] **1** : the quality or condition of being sesquipedal **2 a** : the use of sesquipedalian words **b** : a style characterized by the use of sesquipedalian words

ses·qui·plane \'seskwə+₁,-\ *n* [*sesqui- + plane*] : a biplane having one wing of less than half the area of the other

ses·qui·quad·rate \¹¤¤+\ *n* [fr. (assumed) NL *sesquiquadratus*, fr. L *sesqui- + quadrant-, quadrans* quadrant + *-atus* -ate] : the astrological aspect of two heavenly bodies when separated by 1½ quadrants

ses·qui·sil·i·cate \¹¤¤+\ *n* [*sesqui- + silicate*] : a silicate (as sodium sesquisilicate) that is intermediate between two silicates **2** : a mixture of an orthosilicate or metasilicate and a disilicate used esp. in smelting

ses·qui·sul·fide \¹¤¤+\ *n* [*sesqui- + sulfide*] : a sulfide that contains three atoms of sulfur in the molecule and that may or may not be analogous to a sesquioxide — compare PHOSPHORUS SESQUISULFIDE

ses·qui·ter·pene \¹¤¤+\ *n* [ISV *sesqui- + terpene*] : any of a class of terpenes $C_{15}H_{24}$ containing half again as many atoms in the molecule as monoterpenes; *also* : a derivative of such a terpene

¹ses·qui·ter·pe·noid \¹seskwə¹tərpə₁nȯid\ *n* [*sesquiterpene + -oid*] : a sesquiterpene or sesquiterpene derivative (as farnesol or santonin)

²sesquiterpenoid \'¤\ *adj* [*sesquiterpene + -oid*] : resembling a sesquiterpene in molecular structure

sess *Brit var of* ¹CESS, ²CESS 1a, 1b

sess *abbr* session

ses·sile \'sesəl, -e₁sīl, -e(,)sil\ *adj* [L *sessilis* of or fit for sitting, low, dwarf (of plants), fr. *sessus* (past part. of *sedēre* to sit) + *-ilis* -ile — more at SIT] **1 a** : attached directly by the base : not raised upon a peduncle ⟨~ bubble⟩ ⟨sessile-eyed⟩; *specif* : resting on a main stem or branch without an intervening stalk ⟨sessile-fruited⟩ ⟨sessile-leaved⟩ **b** : attached not free to move about : SEDENTARY ⟨~ marine animals and plants —R.E.Coker⟩ ⟨~ employment⟩ ⟨~ population units⟩ : a removable wealth —C.D.Forde⟩ — compare VAGILE

sessile barnacle *n* : a barnacle (as the acorn barnacle) of which the calcareous shell is attached directly to the substrate — compare PEDUNCULATE BARNACLE

sessile gonophore *n* : a gonophore that never becomes detached

sessile hydatid *n* : HYDATID OF MORGAGNI 2

sessile oak *n* : DURMAST

ses·sil·i·ty \se'siləd-ē\ *n* -es [*sessile + -ity*] : the state of being sessile

ses·si·li·ven·tres \₁sesəli'ven-(₁)trēz\ *n pl* [NL, fr. *sessilis* sessile (fr. L, of or fit for sitting) + L *ventr-, venter* belly — more at VENTER] *syn of* CHALASTOGASTRA

ses·sion \'seshən\ *n* -s [ME, fr. MF, fr. L *session-, sessio* act of sitting, session, fr. *sessus* (past part. of *sedēre* to sit) + *-ion-, -io* -ion — more at SIT] **1** : an actual or constructive sitting of a body (as a court, council, or legislature); *also*

: the actual or constructive assembly of the members of such a body for the transaction of business ⟨morning ~⟩ ⟨evening ~⟩ ⟨read the letters to the House in secret ~ —C.L.Becker⟩ **2 sessions** *pl* **a** *Eng law* (1) : a sitting of justices of the peace in the exercise of the powers conferred by their commissions — see GENERAL SESSIONS, PETTY SESSIONS, SPECIAL SESSION (2) : an English court holding such sessions **b** : any of various courts answering more or less to the English sessions **3** *usu cap, Scots law* : COURT OF SESSION **4** : the time, period, or term during which a body (as a court, council, or legislature) meets regularly for business : the space of time between the first meeting and the prorogation or final adjournment ⟨biennial legislative ~s⟩ — see SPECIAL SESSION **5 a** : Jesus Christ's sitting at the right hand of God **b** *archaic* : the action of sitting : a being seated **6** : the ruling body of a Presbyterian congregation consisting of the elders in active service moderated by the pastor and exercising the government and discipline of the church and often also direct control of its temporal affairs — compare CONSISTORY, PRESBYTERY **7 a** *chiefly Scot* : ACADEMIC YEAR **b** : TERM 4 ⟨summer ~⟩ **c** : the part of the day during which a public school conducts classes ⟨many overcrowded schools have double ~s⟩ **d** : PERIOD 11a **8** : a group of students in a Salvation Army officers' training school having the same year of graduation **9** : a period usu. in a series devoted to a particular activity esp. by a group of persons ⟨recording ~⟩ ⟨briefing ~⟩ ⟨were in for a ~ of mental improvement —S.H.Adams⟩ ⟨square dance ~s will be held weekly —Walter Terry⟩ ⟨neglected his tennis ~s —George Sklar⟩ ⟨one ~ with a mop —A.W.Baum⟩ — see BULL SESSION, JAM SESSION

ses·sion·al \ˈseshənᵊl, -shnəl\ *adj* : of, relating to, or restricted to a session : recurring or renewed at each session ⟨~ program⟩ ⟨~ resolution⟩ ⟨~ allowance⟩

sessional order *or* **sessional rule** *n* : an order or rule framed to continue only during the session (as of Parliament) — distinguished from *standing order*

ses·sion·ary \ˈseshə,nerē\ *adj* [*session* + *-ary*] : SESSIONAL

sessioner *n* -s [*session* + *-er*] **1** *obs* : a member of a court of session **2** *obs* : a member of a kirk session

session laws *n pl* : a publication in bound-volume form of all enactments and resolutions of a legislature passed at a particular session, indexed, and numbered usu. in chronological order — distinguished from *code*

session of the peace : a sitting of justices of the peace for the trial of cases or the exercise of other assigned powers — usu. used in pl.

ses·so·blast \ˈsesə,blast\ *n* [*sessile* + *-o-* + *statoblast*] : a bryozoan statoblast that remains fixed to the zooecial wall

sessor *n* -s *obs* : one that assesses a tax

ses·terce \ˈse(,)stərs\ *n* -s [L *sestertius*, fr. *sestertius* two and a half times as great (fr. its being equal orig. to two and a half asses), fr. *semis* a half (fr. *semi-*) + *tertius* third — more at SEMI-, THIRD] **1 a** : an ancient Roman coin equal to ¼ denarius **b** : a corresponding unit of value **2** : SESTERTIUM

ses·ter·tium \-sh(ē)əm\ *n, pl* **sester·tia** \-sh(ē)ə\ [L, orig. gen. pl. of *sestertius* in the phrase *milia sestertium* thousands of sesterces] : a unit of value in ancient Rome equal to one thousand sesterces

ses·ter·tius \seˈstərsh(ē)əs, səˈs-\ *n, pl* **sester·tii** \-shē,ī\ [L] : SESTERCE 1

ses·tet \(ˈ)seˈstet\ *n* -s [It *sestetto*, fr. *sesto* sixth (fr. OIt, fr. L *sextus*) + *-etto* (as in *duetto* duet) — more at SEXT] **1** : SEXTET 1 **2** : a stanza or a poem of six lines; *specif* : the last six lines of a sonnet of the Italian type — compare OCTAVE 2b

ses·tet·to \seˈsted·(,)ō\ *n* -s [It] : SEXTET 1

ses·ti·na \seˈstēnə\ *n* -s [It, fr. OIt, fr. *sesto* sixth] : a lyrical form developed before 1200 by Provençal troubadours and now fixed in the form of six 6-line stanzas orig. unrhymed, six end words repeated in different order in each stanza, and a 3-line envoi in which three of these six words occur in the middle and three at the end of the lines

ses·tine \(ˈ)seˈstēn\ *n* -s [MF, fr. OIt *sestina*] : SESTINA

ses·tole \ˈse,stōl\ *or* **ses·to·let** \ˈsestə¦let\ *n* -s [alter. (influenced by It *sesto* sixth) of *sextole, sextolet*] : SEXTUPLET 3

ses·ton \ˈse,stän\ *n* -s [G, fr. Gk *sēston*, neut. of *sēstos*, verbal of *sēthein* to strain, filter] : minute material moving in water and including both living organisms (as plankton and nekton) and nonliving matter (as plant debris or suspended soil particles) — see BIOSESTON; compare TRIPTON — **ses·ton·ic** \(ˈ)se¦stänik\ *adj*

sesunc *abbr* [L *sesuncia*] an ounce and a half

se·su·to \səˈsüd·(,)ō\ *n* -s *usu cap* : SOTHO

se·su·vi·um \səˈsüvēəm\ *n, cap* [NL] : a small genus of fleshy maritime herbs (family Aizoaceae) widely distributed esp. in tropical regions and having opposite leaves and reddish flowers with a 5-lobed calyx and five stamens — see SEA PURSLANE

¹**set** \ˈset, *usu* -ed·+V\ *vb* **set; set; setting; sets** [ME *setten*, fr. OE *settan*; akin to OHG *sezzen* to set, ON *setja*, Goth *satjan*; causative fr. the root of E *sit*] *vt* **1 a** : to cause to sit : make assume a sitting position or attitude **b** : to place in or on a seat ⟨~ a man on horseback⟩ ⟨~ a king on a throne⟩ **c** *archaic* : to seat in readiness for an activity ⟨were ~ to cards —W.M.Thackeray⟩ ⟨when he was ~, his disciples came unto him —Mt 5:1 (AV)⟩ **2 a** : to put (a fowl) on eggs to hatch them **b** : to put (eggs) into a nest for a fowl to hatch or into an incubator **3** : to place (oneself) in a position to start running in a race **4** *chiefly Scot* : to be becoming to : SUIT ⟨this bonnet ~s me —J.M.Barrie⟩ **5 a** : to put to stay in place : place with care or deliberate purpose ⟨~ a lamp on the table⟩ ⟨~ a ladder against the wall⟩ ⟨~ a stone on a grave⟩ ⟨~ a figure on a pedestal⟩ **b** : to fix (a plant) in the ground ⟨~ fruit trees⟩ — often used with *out* ⟨~ out seedlings⟩ **c** (1) : to put (as a trap or snare) in a proper condition or position to catch prey (2) : to force point and barb of (a hook) into the jaw of a fish **d** (1) : to put aside (as dough) to rise (2) : to fill (a fermenter or yeast tub) with mash, yeast, and other ingredients for distilling and to adjust the contents to the proper temperature for fermentation **e** : to place so as to have relation to something or someone ⟨dainty dish to ~ before a king⟩ ⟨~ a light at each window⟩ **6** : to direct with fixed attention and preoccupation ⟨had ~ his heart on going with us⟩ ⟨you can solve this problem if you ~ your mind to it⟩ **7 a** *archaic* : to fix in writing : PHRASE **b** : to place in a particular location or relation in a writing : put down : ENTER — used with *down* ⟨~ down all the items in one column⟩ ⟨all the happenings ~ down in his diary⟩ **8** : to cause to assume a specified condition, relation, or occupation ⟨when the slaves were ~ free⟩ ⟨made a raft and ~ it afloat⟩ ⟨~ him over the rest as a foreman⟩ **9** : to appoint or assign to an office or duty : POST, STATION ⟨~ pickets around the camp⟩ ⟨the order to ~ the first watch came at 8 o'clock⟩ **10** : to cause to assume a specified posture or position ⟨~ the chair back on its feet⟩ ⟨~ the door ajar⟩ ⟨his age ~s him apart from the others⟩ ⟨~ him astride a horse and led him away⟩ **11 a** : to fix as a distinguishing imprint, sign, or appearance ⟨the years have ~ their mark on him⟩ ⟨I do ~ my bow in the cloud —Gen 9:13 (AV)⟩ **b** *archaic* : ATTACH ⟨~ feathers to thy heels —Shak.⟩ **c** : AFFIX ⟨my will to which I ~ my hand and seal⟩ **d** : APPLY ⟨~ pen to paper⟩ ⟨~ the horn to his lips⟩ ⟨~ spurs to his horse⟩ ⟨~ a match to the pile of leaves⟩ **12** : to play (a domino) to begin a game **13 a** : to fix or decide upon as a time, limit, or regulation : PRESCRIBE ⟨~ a wedding day⟩ ⟨~ certain conditions as part of the bargain⟩ ⟨~ bounds to ambition⟩ **b** : to lay or mark off (a line) in surveying or drafting **c** : to take the bearings of (as a landfall) ⟨~ a landmark⟩ **d** *obs* : to inflict as a burden or penalty : IMPOSE **e** : to establish by authority : DECREE ⟨once the rules had been ~ there was no changing them⟩ **14** *dial Brit* : RENT, LEASE **15** *obs* : to put in order : SETTLE **16 a** : to establish as the highest level or best performance ⟨~ a record for the half mile⟩ ⟨~s a new record for government spending⟩ **b** : to furnish as a pattern or model ⟨~ an example of generosity⟩ ⟨let another runner ~ the pace⟩ ⟨~ the fashion for epic poems⟩ ⟨preferred to work on lines ~ by his predecessors⟩ **c** : to give a pitch to (a melody) for singing : start by fixing the keynote ⟨~ a psalm⟩ **d** : to allot or appoint as a task or portion of work ⟨three books were ~ to be read by the class during the term⟩ ⟨he was ~ the task of finding a way to balance the budget⟩ ⟨the home team was ~ 75 runs to win the cricket match⟩ **17 a** : to put into a desired position, adjustment, or condition ⟨~ a thermostat at 70⟩ ⟨~ the camera lens for a long range shot⟩ ⟨brought the car to a stop and ~ the brake⟩ **b** : to pull (a bell) into the position of standing inverted ready for a full stroke **c** : to fix (a combination of pipe-organ stops) so that the pushing of a piston will throw an entire combination **d** : to restore to normal position or connection when dislocated or fractured ⟨~ a broken bone⟩ **e** *obs* : to set up : ERECT, RAISE **f** : to spread to the wind ⟨~ the sails of a ship⟩ **g** *obs* : to dispose tactically for battle **18 a** : to put in order for immediate use ⟨the table was ~ for three⟩ ⟨~ a place for a guest⟩ ⟨~ a lathe for screw cutting⟩ **b** : to provide (as words, verses) with melody and instrumental accompaniment ⟨~ a sonnet to music⟩; *also* : to adapt (a melody) to a text ⟨the same prevailing tunes . . . were customarily ~ to native American folksongs —S.P.Bayard⟩ **c** : to make scenically ready for a performance ⟨~ the scene⟩ ⟨~ the stage⟩ **d** : to compose (type) for printing : put (copy) into type ⟨~ a page⟩ ⟨~ a book by hand⟩ — often used with *up* ⟨the copy is already ~ up in pages⟩ **e** : to position (an insert) when tipping into the sections of a book usu. so as to correct bad margins **19** *also* **sett** \"\ : to determine the fineness of texture of (a fabric) before weaving **20 a** : to put a fine edge on (a cutting blade) by grinding or honing ⟨~ a razor⟩ **b** : to shape (metal) with a set hammer **c** : to bend slightly the tooth points of (a saw) alternately in opposite directions to widen the kerf and so prevent sticking **d** : to adjust (a measuring instrument) to a desired position ⟨~ a pair of calipers to size on a rule⟩ **e** : to fix the iron of (a carpenter's plane) in position so as to take off the desired thickness of shaving **f** : to sink (a nailhead) below the surface **21** : to dispose (a specimen) for preservation and examination ⟨~ an insect⟩ **22** : to make (a dye or color) fast **23** : to put the finishing coat on ⟨plaster, float, and ~ a wall⟩ **24** : to wave, curl, or arrange (hair) by wetting (as with a wave solution) and drying (as with heat) **25 a** : to cover or border or surround with plants ⟨~ the grounds with trees and bushes⟩ ⟨a parkway ~ with sycamores⟩ **b** : to adorn with something affixed or infixed : STUD, DOT ⟨the house was ~ about with fir trees⟩ ⟨clear sky ~ with stars⟩ **c** (1) : to fix (as a precious stone) in a border of metal : place in a setting ⟨~ a diamond in a ring⟩ (2) : to place in or amid something that serves as a setting ⟨~ glass in a sash⟩ (3) : to arrange (artificial teeth) upon a plate **26** *obs* : to fix upon or watch with a view to theft **27 a** : to hold something in regard or esteem at the rate of — used with *by* ⟨~s a great deal by daily exercise⟩ **b** *obs* : ASSUME, SUPPOSE **c** : to place in a relative rank or category ⟨~ duty before pleasure⟩ ⟨justly ~ the gem above the flower —Alexander Pope⟩ **d** : to fix at or adjust to a certain amount ⟨~ bail at $500⟩ ⟨~ the price higher⟩ **e** : WAGER, STAKE ⟨I have ~ my life upon a cast —Shak.⟩ **f** : VALUE, RATE — used with *at* ⟨I do not ~ my life at a pin's fee —Shak.⟩ ⟨his promises were ~ at naught after so many betrayals⟩ **g** *archaic* : to rate for assessment ⟨blamed for *setting* so wealthy a man at so low a rate —T.B.Macaulay⟩ **h** : to place as an estimate of something's worth ⟨~ a high value on every man's life⟩ **i** : ESTIMATE ⟨fire losses were ~ at a million dollars⟩ **28** : to place in relation for comparison or balance ⟨when theory is ~ against practice⟩ ⟨after *setting* our gains against our losses⟩ **29 a** : to direct to action : put into activity ⟨~ the children to raking leaves⟩ ⟨~ a thief to catch a thief⟩ ⟨wind the clock and ~ it running⟩ **b** : to incite to attack ⟨~ the dogs on an intruder⟩ or antagonism ⟨war that ~s brother against brother⟩ **30 a** : to place by transporting ⟨~ ashore on the island⟩ ⟨a ferry ~ them across the river⟩ **b** : to put in motion ⟨~ the tongues a-wagging⟩ ⟨~ the bells a-ringing⟩ **c** : to bring by imparting motion ⟨a current ~ us to the northward⟩ ⟨stern started to swing with the tide, *setting* the vessel toward a submerged wreck —*All Hands*⟩ **d** : to put and fix in a direction ⟨~ our faces toward home once more⟩ **e** *of a dog* : to point out the seat or position of (as a bird) by holding a fixed attitude **31** : to adjust in conformity with some standard ⟨~ his watch by the radio time signal⟩ **32** : to propel (a boat) by poling **33** : to defeat (an opponent or his contract) in bridge : cause to go down **34 a** : to fix firmly : make immobile : give rigid form or condition to ⟨~ his jaw in renewed determination to win⟩ ⟨~ her lips firmly and shook her head⟩ **b** : to make unyielding or obstinate ⟨~ his mind against all appeals⟩ **35 a** *archaic* : to cause or allow to get stuck **b** *dial* : to put into a confusing or embarrassing position : CHECK, STUMP **36** : to cause to settle or convert into a solid form ⟨~ milk for cheese⟩ ⟨~ jelly by adding pectin⟩ **37** : to cause (fruit or seed) to develop ⟨the peaches failed to ~ fruit⟩ ⟨some varieties do not ~ seed under cultivation⟩ **38 a** : to straighten (a bow or arrow) by heating, correcting the deformity, and quickly cooling **b** : to fix (leather) by stretching **39** : to treat (viscose) so as to cause precipitation of cellulose **40** : to fix the form or shape of (a synthetic fabric) as with heat or chemicals ~ *vi* **1** *chiefly dial* : SIT **2** : to be becoming : be suitable : FIT ⟨his behavior does not ~ well with his years⟩ **3** *of a fowl* : to cover and warm eggs to hatch them : BROOD **4** : to become lodged or fixed — used with *on* or *upon* ⟨the pudding ~ heavily on his stomach⟩ **5** *of a blossom, fruit, or seed* : to adhere to a parent plant and initiate growth or normal development as a result of a stimulus (as pollination) **6** : to settle and become attached ⟨spawning and *setting* of oysters⟩ **7 a** *of a heavenly body* : to pass below the horizon : go down : DECLINE ⟨the sun ~s later now⟩ — opposed to *rise* **b** : to sink out of sight : come to an end : pass away **8** : to place plants or shoots in the ground : PLANT ⟨in some cases *setting* is preferable to sowing⟩ **9 a** *obs* : to make a stake or wager : BET **b** : to make the first play in a game of dominoes **10 a** *chiefly dial* : to begin to move : set out : set forth **b** : to apply oneself to some activity ⟨~ to work to finish the job⟩ **11 a** : to have a specified direction in motion : FLOW, TEND ⟨the current ~s to the north⟩ ⟨the wind was *setting* from Pine Hill to the farm —Esther Forbes⟩ **b** : to have a trend : gather headway in a definite direction ⟨art is *setting* against modernism⟩ **12** *of a dog* : to indicate the position of game by crouching or pointing **13** : to dance face to face with another in a square dance — used usu. with *to* ⟨~ to your partner and turn⟩ **14 a** : to become fixed or rigid; *specif* : to become more solid or hardened (as by chemical action or by cooling or drying) ⟨use up the cement before it ~s⟩ ⟨this ink ~s rapidly⟩ **b** *of cream* : to rise and settle at the top **c** *of milk* : CURDLE **d** *of a dye or color* : to become fast or permanent **15 a** *of a bone* : to become whole by knitting **b** *of metal* : to acquire a permanent twist or bend from strain **16** *of a balance wheel* : to stop swinging

syn PUT, PLACE, LAY, DISPOSE, STOW, DEPOSIT: SET suggests the putting of a person or thing firmly in a specified place, condition, or relationship ⟨bring these fellows into the country, or *set* them aboard ship —R.L.Stevenson⟩ ⟨*set* all her hopes in the son, particularly in her oldest —Franz Alexander⟩ ⟨some new apprentice . . . may turn out in the end to be either a bungler or an enemy, and *set* the whole appliance out of gear —B.N.Cardozo⟩ PUT applies to a motion or action placing a person or thing in an indicated situation or condition ⟨*putting* somebody else in a comfortable chair and making him listen to their efforts —Barrett Wendell⟩ ⟨proceedings in the lower courts were *put* on the same footing as proceedings in the higher ones —B.N.Cardozo⟩ ⟨the Gospels, especially the apocryphal, were *put* into Old French —H.O.Taylor⟩ PLACE may suggest a preciseness or considered intent lacking in PUT ⟨church buildings along Main Street are *placed* some distance back, but the commercial buildings abut the sidewalks —*Amer. Guide Series: N.H.*⟩ ⟨efforts were directed to *placing* his young friend where his talents could find a steady market —H.S.Canby⟩ LAY may convey the notion that the thing moved has been put into a flat position, one compatible with reclining rather than standing ⟨the lacquered services are *laid* upon the matting before them by maidens whose bare feet make no sound —Lafcadio Hearn⟩ ⟨Apollo has not *laid* aside his bow, nor Neptune his trident —William Hazlitt⟩ DISPOSE is likely to suggest considered or calculated placing and arranging ⟨orchids had been conspicuously *disposed* in various receptacles —Edith Wharton⟩ ⟨numerous auxiliary regiments, foot and horse, which were *disposed* over the hill-country —Jacquetta & Christopher Hawkes⟩ STOW is likely to suggest compact or neat and convenient placing, storing, packing ⟨air out the cabin and *stow* away our winter supplies —Willa Cather⟩ ⟨roomy enough for a skillful packer to *stow* a two-week supply of clothes in —*New Yorker*⟩ DEPOSIT may suggest either careful and attentive placing or putting away as in a cache or, in the natural sciences, letting fall to accumulate ⟨two copies of each measure are printed on special vellum . . . to be *deposited* in the Public Record Office —F.A.Ogg & Harold Zink⟩ ⟨took off the silk hat . . . and *deposited* it on the front seat of the cab —Joseph Conrad⟩ ⟨*deposits* more or less of the matter which it holds in suspension —T.H.Huxley⟩

syn FIX, SETTLE, ESTABLISH: SET suggests to put in place, maybe as a definite and final placing, forming, or making ⟨the patristic system of dogma with the antique philosophy *set* the forms of medieval expression —H.O.Taylor⟩ FIX is likely to suggest stability and permanence ⟨his character, his tastes and his private way of life also are during these years pretty well *fixed* —J.W.Krutch⟩ ⟨slowly his place in the McCoy household had been *fixed* —Sherwood Anderson⟩ SETTLE implies finality and permanence ⟨both English and French have been *settled* in their present form roughly since the eighteenth century —*Times Lit. Supp.*⟩ ESTABLISH on the other hand is likely to connote a combination first of placing and forming and second of furthering and fostering until the thing in question is stable and permanent ⟨by distinguishing what the author assumes from what he *establishes* through arguments —M.J.Adler⟩ ⟨enlarging our personality by *establishing* new affinities and sympathies with our fellowmen, with nature, and with God —W.R.Inge⟩

— **set about 1** : to begin to do or accomplish ⟨had soon *set about* changing the flat tire⟩ ⟨*set about* finding a track into the mountains —Francis Kingdon-Ward⟩ ⟨Arab population suddenly *set about* smashing French shop windows —Claire Sterling⟩ **2** : to aim at doing : ATTEMPT ⟨*sets about* moving the listeners to that position —R.M.Weaver⟩ **3** : ATTACK — **set abroad** *archaic* : to set (a rumor) going : put in circulation — **set apart 1** : to reserve to a particular use **2** : to make noticeable or outstanding ⟨his enormous strength *set* him *apart* from ordinary men⟩ — **set aside 1** : to put to one side : DISCARD **2** : to set apart for a purpose : RESERVE, SAVE ⟨*set aside* part of the weekly income⟩ ⟨*set* the yolks *aside* to be used later in the sauce⟩ **3** : to reject from consideration ⟨objections were *set aside* as trivial⟩ **4** : ANNUL, OVERRULE ⟨the verdict was *set aside* by a higher court⟩ **5** : EXCLUDE, EXCEPT ⟨*setting aside* the question of financing the project⟩ — **set a sponge** : to make a thin yeast batter which when risen and added to the full amount of flour for bread dough will facilitate fermentation — **set at** : ATTACK, ASSAIL ⟨*set at* the invaders with knives and pitchforks⟩ — **set at defiance** : DEFY — **set at naught** : to treat as of no account : DISREGARD, DESPISE — **set by the ears** : to cause to quarrel — **set cock a hoop** : to become reckless : act with jubilant abandon : CAROUSE — **set eyes on** : to catch sight of : BEHOLD, SEE ⟨fell in love the first time he *set eyes on* her⟩ — **set flying** : to set (a sail) without support by spar or stay by hoisting by a halyard until the luff is taut — **set foot in** : ENTER — **set forth 1** *obs* : to fit out : EQUIP **2** *obs* : PUBLISH **3** : to give an account or statement of : present fully and clearly : EXPLAIN, DESCRIBE ⟨this ideal . . . is *set forth* with very detailed and precise description —R.A.Hall b. 1911⟩ **4** : to start on a journey : set out : START — **set forward 1** : to cause or help to advance : FURTHER **2** : to cause (a timepiece) to indicate a later time **3** : to set out on a journey : START — **set home** : to drive (as caulking) into final position — **set light by** : to treat lightly : UNDERVALUE, SLIGHT — **set naught by** : to set at naught — **set one back** : COST ⟨a new suit *set him back* $65⟩ — **set one's cap for** : to try to catch (a man) in marriage — **set one's face against** : to show opposition toward : OPPOSE — **set one's hand to** : to set about doing : UNDERTAKE — **set on foot** : to begin the development or progress of : set in motion ⟨plans were *set on foot* for a very much larger set of negotiations⟩ ⟨sinister rumors were *set on foot* by interested parties⟩ — **set sail** : to begin a voyage : start out ⟨we are *setting sail* for England next week⟩ — **set store by** : to consider valuable or trustworthy or worthwhile ⟨*set store by* dieting as a means to health⟩ ⟨convinced that the poorest people *set* the most *store by* family ties —*Irish Digest*⟩ — **set taut** : to take up the slack in running gear preliminary to heaving in on it — **set the palette** : to lay on the palette the required pigments in a special order according to the intended use of them — **set the temperament** : to tune a single octave of a keyboard instrument according to a desired temperament as a standard by which to tune the rest of its scale — **set upon** : to attack with violence : ASSAULT ⟨soldiers were *set upon* by thugs loafing around barracks . . . who knocked down their victims and rifled wallets —Dixon Wecter⟩

²**set** \"\ *adj* [ME *sett*, fr. past part. of *setten* to set — more at ¹SET] **1 a** : SITUATED, LOCATED ⟨a house ~ on a hilltop⟩ **b** : fixed in place ⟨eyes ~ deep in his head⟩ **2** : INTENT, DETERMINED — used with *on* or *upon* ⟨~ upon going⟩ ⟨~ on becoming a doctor⟩ **3** : PITCHED ⟨~ battle⟩ **4** : fixed by authority or appointment ⟨work at a ~ wage⟩ : PRESCRIBED, SPECIFIED ⟨~ forms of worship⟩ ⟨~ hours of study⟩ ⟨~ rules of procedure⟩ **5** *of a style of handwriting* : precise, clear, and even ⟨the indictment . . . which in a ~ hand fairly is engrossed —Shak.⟩ **6** : deliberately conceived, composed, or expressed : INTENTIONAL, PREMEDITATED ⟨did it of ~ purpose⟩ ⟨dislike of ~ speeches⟩ ⟨railed on Lady Fortune . . . in good ~ terms —Shak.⟩ **7** : ASSIGNED, REQUIRED ⟨asked to prepare a talk on a ~ subject⟩ ⟨reading ~ books in preparation for examinations⟩ **8 a** : not open to persuasion or argument : reluctant to change : OBSTINATE ⟨an old man very ~ in his ways⟩ **b** *chiefly dial* : disposed or resolved either by natural inclination or act of will ⟨~ to lead a virgin's life to my death —Philip Sidney⟩ **9 a** : fixed in position or attitude : IMMOVABLE, RIGID ⟨~ line of his jaw⟩ ⟨~ frown⟩ ⟨read in measured, ~ tones⟩ **b** : BUILT-IN **10** : remaining unchanged : SETTLED, PERSISTENT ⟨~ defiance⟩ ⟨~ rains⟩ **11 a** : PREPARED, READY ⟨all ~ for an early morning start⟩ ⟨the storm broke before we could get ~ for it⟩ **b** : securely balanced for delivering a blow ⟨continual jabbing kept his opponent from getting ~ for a good punch⟩ ⟨change of pace keeps the batter from getting ~⟩ **c** : poised to start running or to dive in at the instant the signal is given ⟨ready, ~, go⟩

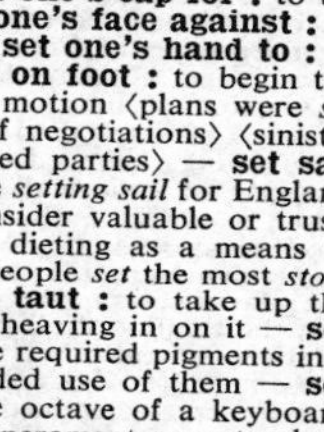

set 31b

³**set** \"\ *n* -s [ME *sett, sette*, partly fr. *sett*, past part. of *setten* to set; partly fr. *setten* to set; in some senses, fr. or influenced in meaning by obs. *sette* religious body, sect, fr. MF, fr. L *secta* — more at ¹SET, SECT] **1** : the descent of a heavenly body below the horizon ⟨that will be ere the ~ of sun —Shak.⟩ **2** *or* **sett** \ˈset\ *Scots law* : the constitution of a burgh **3** *obs* : state of being stopped : STANDSTILL, CHECK **4 a** : the first play in the game of dominoes **b** : the first domino played **5** : an instance of being defeated at a contract in bridge ⟨tried for an overtrick at the risk of a ~⟩ **6** : DEAD SET **7 a** : the hardening or solidifying of a plastic or liquid substance by chemical action (as of mortar, concrete, cement) or by cooling and drying (as of glue) **b** : the chemical and physical action causing a paint or varnish to become dry and firm **c** : the property of an enamel slip that enables it to form an adherent layer on a metal surface **8 a** : mental inclination, tendency, or habit : BENT ⟨a definite ~ toward mathematical reasoning⟩ **b** : a state of preparedness usu. of limited duration for action in response to an anticipated stimulus or situation ⟨mental ~ which functions in blocking all responses except those suited to the occasion —Arthur Weider⟩ ⟨motor ~ produced by lifting a weight⟩ **9** : direction of flow ⟨against the ~ of the current⟩ ⟨the ~ of public opinion was now strongly toward peace⟩ ⟨the current had a northeasterly ~⟩ **10** : form or carriage of the body or of its parts ⟨formidable ~ of his shoulders⟩ ⟨graceful ~ of her head⟩ **11** : the manner of fitting or of being placed or suspended ⟨carefully adjusting the ~ of her hat⟩ **12 a** : amount of deflection from a straight

line ⟨~ of an axle⟩ ⟨~ of a saw's teeth⟩ or level position ⟨~ of a gun aimed for distance⟩ **b :** the camber of a curved roofing tile **c :** the camber of a leaf spring **13 :** fixed direction of growth ⟨rubbing against the ~ of the fur⟩ **14 a :** a permanent bend or loss in elasticity ⟨~ in a bow⟩ ⟨~ of a permanent fishing rod⟩ **b :** permanent change of form (as of metal) due to repeated or excessive stress — compare FATIGUE, PERMANENT SET **15 a :** the act of arranging hair by curling or waving when wet with water or wave solution **b :** the result of such arranging **16 :** the act or position of a dog in setting game **17** *also* **sett a :** a young plant or rooted cutting ready for setting out ⟨a ~ of a strawberry⟩ **b :** a small tuber or section of tuber, bulb, or corm ⟨an onion ~⟩ ⟨potato ~⟩ **c :** the amount of bloom produced on a plant **d :** the blossoms of a plant (as a fruit tree) that have set fruit as a result of fertilization of the flowers ⟨heavy ~ of apples⟩ **e :** the attachment of young mollusks (as oysters) to the substrate; *also* **:** the crop set at a particular time **18** *obs* **:** a pleat in a ruff; *also* **:** the manner in which a ruff is pleated **19 :** the burrow of a badger **20 :** a trap or snare placed to catch game ⟨visit each ~ daily⟩ **21** *also* **sett :** SHOT 1d, 4 **22 :** the width of the shank of a piece of type; *also* **:** the overall width of a letter — compare POINT-SET, UNIT-SET; see TYPE illustration **23** *also* **sett a :** a piece placed temporarily upon the head of a pile that cannot be reached directly by the weight or hammer **b :** SET HAMMER **c :** ³PUNCH 1a(3) **d :** SNAP 11a **24 :** the artificially constructed setting in which a stage or television play or motion picture is enacted including decor, properties, and furniture **25** *also* **sett :** a rectangular block of granite or sandstone used for paving streets and truck highways **26 :** SET IRON **27 :** the finishing coat of plaster **28 a :** the contents of a fermenting vat just after all ingredients have been added **b :** the *p*H value of a freshly filled fermenter **29 :** SET SHOT **30 :** SETUP 6g **31 a :** a unit in a tennis match consisting of a group of games of which one side wins six to opponent's four or less or in case of a deuced score wins two consecutive games **b :** a combination of three or more playing cards of the same rank or of the same suit in sequence **:** MELD **32 :** a number of things naturally connected by location ⟨~ of muscles⟩ ⟨~ of footprints⟩ or formation ⟨~ of teeth⟩ or order in time ⟨~ of temperature readings⟩ **33 :** a collection of books forming a unit: as **a :** the works of one author issued in volumes in uniform style **b :** a file of issues of a periodical **c :** a group of related works on a particular subject or of unrelated volumes printed uniformly and intended to be sold as a group **34 :** a number of associated buildings or rooms ⟨~ of farm buildings⟩ **35 :** the eggs laid by a bird for a single incubation or brood **:** CLUTCH **36 a :** the number of persons necessary for a square dance **b :** the formation assumed by a group of dancers to start a square dance **c :** a balancing step in country-dance usu. done by partners face to face **d :** the music played for a single turn of square, country, or ballroom dancing ⟨between ~s . . . balladeer sings folk songs —*New Yorker*⟩ **37 :** a group of musical compositions forming a whole ⟨~ of dances⟩ **38 :** a team of matched horses **39 a :** a group of articles of uniform design ⟨~ of dining room furniture⟩ ⟨~ of dishes⟩ **b :** the complete apparatus or equipment used in a particular process (as gas manufacture) **c :** an assortment of tools or instruments of identical kind ⟨~ of drill bits in graded sizes⟩ or complementary relationship ⟨~ of drafting tools⟩ ⟨~ of carpenter's tools⟩ ⟨~ of golf clubs⟩ **d :** a complete collection of articles necessary for playing a game ⟨croquet ~⟩ ⟨chess ~⟩ **e** *Brit* **:** a string of railway cars of the same exterior style **f :** a group of pumps that are used for lifting water from one level to another **g :** a group comprising breaker, intermediate, and finisher cards used in wool carding **40 :** a heavy timber frame for supporting the sides of an excavation, shaft, or tunnel **41** *also* **sett :** a standard measurement of the fineness of cloth usu. determined by the number of threads in one inch and the number of threads in each dent of the reed **42 a :** a number of persons associated by custom, occupation, social activity, or age; *collectively* **:** the persons of a specified social type ⟨belonged to the horsy ~⟩ ⟨the younger married ~⟩ **b :** a number of associated workers **:** GANG **c :** a small breeding group of domestic animals; *esp* **:** a gander and one or more geese **43 a :** a series of postage stamps **b :** a group of postage stamps including the lower denominations of a single series **44 a :** a group formed by classification ⟨~ of ideas⟩ ⟨~ of grammatical forms⟩ **b :** the totality of all points or numbers that satisfy a mathematical condition **:** a well-defined collection of objects **:** AGGREGATE **45 :** an apparatus of electrical or electronic components assembled so as to function as a unit ⟨radio ~⟩ ⟨television ~⟩ ⟨amplifying ~⟩ ⟨sending ~⟩ **46 :** the chromosome complement of a gamete **47 :** TWELVE-TONE-ROW

se·ta \ˈsēd·ə\ *n, pl* **se·tae** \-ˈsēd·(ˌ)ē, ˈsēˌtē\ [NL, fr. L *seta, saeta* bristle — more at SINEW] **:** any of numerous slender typically rigid or bristly and springy organs or parts of animals or plants: as **a :** one of the hairs of a caterpillar **b :** a slender spine on the carapace of a crustacean **c :** one of the organelles in the form of processes of fused cilia that function in the movement of various ciliated protozoans **d :** the slender stalk of the sporogonium of a bryophyte **e :** one of the stalked glands on plants of the genus *Rubus* **f :** the bristle in the utricle of some plants of the genus *Carex* **g :** one of the chitinous often complex bristles that project from the body wall or from parapodia of chaetopod annelid worms and assist in locomotion **h :** one of the spiny feathers about the base of the bill of various birds **:** rictal bristle **i :** the slender maxilla of various insects with piercing or sucking mouthparts

se·ta·ceous \səˈtāshəs, sēˈ-\ *adj* [L *seta, saeta* bristle + E *-aceous*] **1 :** set with or consisting of bristles **:** BRISTLY **2 :** resembling a bristle in form or texture — see ANTENNA illustration — **se·ta·ceous·ly** *adv*

set acid *n* **:** the titratable acidity of a freshly filled fermenter

se·tal \ˈsēd·ᵊl\ *adj* [NL *seta* + E *-al*] **:** relating to a seta

se·tar·ia \səˈta(a)rēə\ *n* [NL, fr. *seta* + *-aria*] **1 a** *cap* **:** a large and widely distributed genus of annual and perennial grasses having a dense or open cylindrical inflorescence in which the individual spikelets are subtended by one or more bristles that persist after the spikelets fall and including several grasses that yield forage or hay — see FOXTAIL 2a, FOXTAIL MILLET **b -s :** any grass of the genus *Setaria* **2** *cap* **:** a genus of filarial worms parasitic as adults in the body cavity of various ungulate mammals and producing larvae that wander in the tissues and occas. invade the eye

se·tar·id \-rəd\ *n* -s [NL *Setaria* + E *-id*] **:** a worm of the genus *Setaria*

se·tar·i·ous \-rēəs\ *adj* [NL *setarius*, fr. L *seta* + *-arius* -ary] **:** resembling a bristle **:** ARISTATE

set-aside \ˈ≈,≈\ *n* -s [*set aside*] **:** a required reserving and earmarking of a food or other commodity up to a specified quantity or percentage of production for a particular purpose esp. by governmental order for the use of the military, for housing, or for veterans; *also* **:** a quantity so set aside

se·ta·tion \səˈtāshən\ *n* -s [NL *seta* + E *-ation*] **:** a covering or growth of setae ⟨the ~ of the hind tarsi⟩

set back *vt* **1 :** HINDER, CHECK, DELAY ⟨the harvest was *set back* by bad weather⟩ **2 :** to cause (a timepiece) to indicate an earlier time ⟨forgot to *set* his watch *back* on his trip west⟩ **3 :** to defeat (an opponent) with the effect that points are subtracted from the opposing score (as in a card game)

setback \ˈ≈,≈\ *n* -s [*set back*] **1 :** a checking of progress ⟨~ in steel production occurred this week⟩ ⟨union organization received a ~⟩ **:** a putting in a position less advanced than before ⟨~ in prices⟩ **2 :** DEFEAT, REVERSE ⟨military ~⟩ ⟨diplomatic ~⟩ ⟨baseball team's first ~ of the season⟩ **3 :** BACKSET 2 **4 :** a card game in which points are deducted from a player's score during the play; *esp* **:** AUCTION PITCH **5 a :** OFFSET 3a **b :** a withdrawal of the face of a building to a line some distance to the rear of the building line or to the rear of the wall below in order to reduce the obstruction the upper stories offer to sunlight reaching the streets and the lower stories of adjacent buildings **6 :** the reaction of a mass (as a projectile) to a force producing or tending to produce acceleration (as in ballistics) **7 :** a device for moving over the needles in an annunciator to the normal position after a call

set bar *n* **:** SET IRON

set by *vt* **1** *obs* **:** give up **:** REJECT, DISMISS **2 :** to set apart for future use

set down *vt* **1 :** to cause to sit down **:** SEAT **2 :** to place at rest on a surface or on the ground ⟨I *set* it *down* in this room somewhere and now it's lost⟩ **3** *obs* **:** to place or encamp (an army) so as to besiege **4 :** to suspend (a jockey) from racing because of an offense **5 :** to cause or allow to get off a vehicle ⟨the bus *set* him *down* right before his house⟩ **6 :** to land (an airplane) on the ground or water **7 a :** to lay down **:** ORDAIN, ESTABLISH **b :** to write down **:** record or relate in writing ⟨tried to *set* his thoughts *down* in an orderly way⟩ or in painting ⟨always *set down* exactly what he saw⟩ **8 a :** REGARD, CONSIDER, ESTIMATE ⟨soon *set* him *down* as a liar and a faker⟩ **b :** ATTRIBUTE ⟨let it be *set down* to his credit that he did not retreat⟩ ⟨*set* his success *down* to sheer perseverance⟩ **9 :** to lower the spirit or pride of **:** SNUB, DEFLATE, HUMILIATE **10 a :** to defeat (an opponent) in a game or contest **b :** to prevent (a batter) from reaching base **:** RETIRE ⟨*set* them *down* in order in the last inning⟩ **~** *vi* **1** *archaic* **:** to make up one's mind **:** RESOLVE **2** *archaic* **:** to discharge passengers or occupants ⟨watched the carriages *setting down* for a reception —Osbert Lancaster⟩ **3 :** LAND ⟨time to *set down* and gas up —*Fortune*⟩

setdown \ˈ≈,≈\ *n* -s [*set down*] **1** *archaic* **:** a drive in a vehicle **:** TRIP; *also* **:** a lift in a passing vehicle **2 :** an act of humbling or deflating **:** REPROOF, SNUB

se te·nant \sətəˈnäⁿ\ *adj* [F, holding together] *of postage stamps* **:** joined together as in the original sheet **:** not separated

seter *var of* SAETER

set-fair \ˈ≈,≈\ *n* -s [fr. the phrase *set fair*] **:** a good troweled surface of plaster; *esp* **:** the coat after roughing-in leveled with the float

setfast *var of* SITFAST

set gage *n* **:** a gage for determining the set of sawteeth

set gun *n* **:** a firearm set as a trap to fire on an intruder or on game when a wire attached to its trigger is disturbed

seth *or* **sett** \ˈsāt\ *n* -s [Hindi *seṭh*, fr. Skt *śreṣṭha* chief or best person; akin to Gk *kreiōn* noble, master, Skt *śrī* beauty, majesty, power, Av *srī-* beauty] *India* **:** a rich merchant **:** BANKER

set hammer *n* **1 :** a hammer used as a swage or flatter in blacksmithing **2 :** a hammer with a hollowed-out face used as a swage in riveting

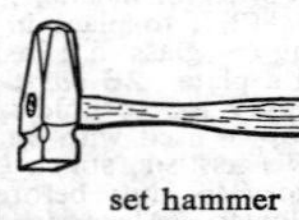
set hammer

set-hands dial *n* **:** a small auxiliary dial observable by a person when setting a turret clock or other large clock

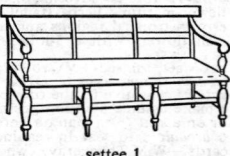

sethead \ˈ≈,≈\ *n* **:** HEADCAP

set-hedge \ˈ≈,≈\ *n* **:** a planted hedge

seth·ite \ˈseˌthīt\ *or* **seth·i·an** \ˈsethēən\ *n* -s *usu cap* [*Sethite* fr. *Seth*, a son of Adam in the Bible + E *-ite*; *Sethian* fr. ML *Sethianus*, fr. LGk *Sēthianos*, fr. *Sēth* Seth + Gk *-ianos* -ian] **:** a member of a Gnostic school of serpent worshipers

set hook *n* **:** a hook on a setline

seti- *comb form* [L *seti-, saeti-*, fr. *seta, saeta* — more at SINEW] **:** bristle ⟨*setiferous*⟩

se·tier \səˈtyā\ *n* -s [MF *sestier, setier*, fr. L *sextarius*, a liquid measure, fr. *sextus* sixth + *-arius* -ary — more at SEXT] **:** any of various old French units of capacity or land area

se·ti·fi·ca·tion \ˌsēd·əfəˈkāshən\ *n* -s [*seti-* + *-fication*] **:** the development of setation

se·ti·form \ˈsēd·əˌfȯrm\ *adj* [*seti-* + *-form*] **:** like a bristle

se·ti·ger \ˈsēd·əjə(r)\ *n* -s [NL, fr. L *setiger, saetiger* setigerous] **:** a segment or process bearing bristles

se·tig·er·ous \səˈtijərəs\ *adj* [L *setiger, saetiger* setigerous (fr. *seti-* + *-ger* -gerous) + E *-ous*] **:** bearing or producing setae

set in *vt* **1 :** to put in **:** INSERT; *esp* **:** to stitch (a small part) within a large article ⟨*set in* a sleeve of a dress⟩ ⟨*set in* a belt at the waistline⟩ **2 :** to direct (a ship) towards shore **~** *vi* **1 :** to enter upon a particular state **:** become prevalent or settled ⟨cold weather *set in* before the British could take the forts —E.P.Alexander⟩ **2 :** to set to work **:** begin to function **3 :** to blow or flow toward shore ⟨the wind was beginning to *set in*⟩

¹set-in \ˈ≈,≈\ *adj* [fr. *set in*, past part. of *set in*] **1 :** placed, located, or built as a part of some other construction ⟨*set-in* bookcase⟩ ⟨*set-in* wash basin⟩ **2 :** cut separately and stitched in ⟨*set-in* sleeves⟩ ⟨*set-in* pocket⟩

²set-in \ˈ≈,≈\ *n* -s [*set in*] **1 :** an instance or time of something setting in ⟨early *set-in* of frosty nights⟩ **2 :** something that is set in **:** INSERT

set iron *n* **:** a flat plate bar of soft iron used in ship construction to transfer the curvature of the frames from the scrive board to the bending slab — called also *set bar*

set kettle *n* **:** SET POT

setline \ˈ≈,≈\ *n* **1 :** a long heavy fishline consisting of one or more skates of gear that is anchored at either end and marked with buoys and used chiefly for bottom fishing — called also *groundline* **2 :** TROTLINE

set mark *n* **:** a defect in cloth; *esp* **:** a crosswise streak caused by a loom stoppage or improper setting

set·ness *n* -ES [²*set* + *-ness*] **:** the quality or state of being set **:** FIXITY, RIGIDITY ⟨~ of his gaze showed his fear⟩ ⟨~ of his habits⟩

setnet \ˈ≈,≈\ *n* **:** a fishnet that is anchored in position rather than drifted, trawled, or manipulated by hand

set nut *n* **:** LOCK NUT 1

set off *vt* **1** *obs* **:** REMOVE **2 a :** to put in relief **:** show up or intensify by contrast ⟨bright with flowers . . . a sinister brightness . . . *set off* by the blackness of the shadows —William Beebe⟩ **b :** ADORN, EMBELLISH ⟨ribbons and laces to *set off* the faces of pretty young sweethearts —W.S.Gilbert⟩ **c** *obs* **:** to give a flattering description of **d :** to set apart **:** make distinct or outstanding ⟨dramatic fire that generally *sets off* the leaders among men —C.B.Forcey⟩ **3 a :** OFFSET, COUNTERBALANCE, COMPENSATE ⟨more variety in the Lancashire weather to *set off* its most disagreeable phases —*Geog. Jour.*⟩ — often used with *against* ⟨strength of the middle classes . . . has been their ability to *set off*, within themselves, intellect against money —Roy Lewis & Angus Maude⟩ **b :** to make a setoff of **:** plead as a setoff **4 a :** to set in motion **:** cause to begin ⟨speculation in stocks often *sets off* speculation in commodities —*Kiplinger Washington Letter*⟩ ⟨sensations of thirst can be shown to be *set off* by dryness of the mouth —F.A.Geldard⟩ **b :** to cause to explode **:** touch off ⟨lightning may *set off* nitroglycerin —Stanley Frank⟩ **5 :** to measure or mark off on a surface **:** lay off **~** *vi* **1 :** to start out on a course or a journey ⟨*set off* for home⟩ ⟨saddled up and *set off* in pursuit⟩ **2 :** to smear the next sheet with ink **:** OFFSET

setoff \ˈ≈,≈\ *n* -s [*set off*] **1 :** something that is set off against another thing: **a :** something used to improve the appearance of anything **:** DECORATION, ORNAMENT **b :** COMPENSATION, COUNTERBALANCE **2 :** OFFSET 3a **3 :** the discharge of a debt by setting against it a distinct claim in favor of the debtor; *also* **:** the claim itself — compare COUNTERCLAIM, CROSS CLAIM, RECOUPMENT **4 :** OFFSET 8a **5 :** a railroad car removed from a train to a siding between yards or terminals

set-off man \ˈ≈,≈-\ *n* **:** FLOORMAN 1b

setoff sheet *n, Brit* **:** SLIP SHEET

set on *vt* **1 :** to set upon **:** ATTACK **2 a** *obs* **:** to set on foot **:** PROMOTE **b :** to urge (as a dog) to attack or pursue **:** UNLEASH **c :** to incite to action **:** INSTIGATE ⟨*set on* to rebellion by their leaders⟩ **d :** to set to work **:** set about ⟨an extra gang was *set on* to the job⟩ **~** *vi* **:** to go on **:** ADVANCE

¹se·ton \ˈsētᵊn\ *n* -s [ME, fr. ML *seton-, seto*, fr. *seta* silk, fr. L, bristle — more at SINEW] **1 :** one or more threads or horsehairs or a strip of linen introduced beneath the skin by a knife or needle to form an issue — compare ROWEL **2 :** SUTURE

²seton \ˈ"\ *vt* -ED/-ING/-S **:** to use a seton on

se·toph·a·ga \səˈtäfəgə\ *n, cap* [NL, fr. Gk *sēt-* (fr. *sēs* moth, prob. fr. Syr *sāsā*) + NL *-phaga*] **:** a genus of fly-catching warblers consisting of the American redstart and numerous related species of Central and So. America — **se·toph·a·gine** \-fəˌjīn, -jən\ *adj*

se·tose \ˈsēˌtōs\ *also* **se·tous** \ˈsēd·əs\ *adj* [L *setosus, saetosus*, fr. *seta, saeta* bristle + *-osus* -ose, -ous — more at SINEW] **:** BRISTLY, SETACEOUS

set out *vt* **1** *obs* **:** to equip and send out **2 a :** ISSUE, PROMULGATE ⟨this act *sets out* the personnel of a tribunal as follows —F.D.Smith & Barbara Wilcox⟩ **b :** to recite, describe, or state at large ⟨distributed copies of a pamphlet *setting out* his ideas in full —S.F.Mason⟩ **3** *obs* **:** to place in relief **:** set off **4 a :** to arrange and present graphically or systematically ⟨the grammar is well *set out*⟩ ⟨in fig. 67 you will see *set out* the semaphore code —Peter Heaton⟩ **b :** to mark out (as a design) **:** lay out the plan of ⟨*sets out* the wood with square and marking knife, shapes and joints it —*Choice of Careers: Furniture Manufacturing*⟩ **c :** to smooth or flatten (a wet hide or skin) when dressing **5 :** to separate (a railroad car) from a train and place on a siding **6 :** to begin with the purpose of achieving **:** INTEND, ENGAGE, UNDERTAKE ⟨given up the attempt to read poets who *set out* deliberately to mystify him —Douglas Stewart⟩ ⟨necessary for the effect he *set out* to produce —Bernard De Voto⟩ **~** *vi* **:** to start out on a course, a journey, or a career ⟨*set out* across the sea⟩ ⟨*set out* early from his cabin⟩ ⟨the engineering course he had originally *set out* on⟩

setout \ˈ≈,≈\ *n* -s [*set out*] **1 a** (1) **:** ARRAY, DISPLAY ⟨complete ~ of dinnerware and glassware⟩ (2) **:** ARRANGEMENT, LAYOUT ⟨in ~ the catalog had the appearance of an ode —Adrian Bell⟩ **b :** BUFFET, SPREAD **c :** TURNOUT 6a **d :** COSTUME, GETUP **e :** OUTFIT, EQUIPMENT ⟨a gambling ~⟩ **2 :** PARTY, ENTERTAINMENT, AFFAIR **3 :** BEGINNING, OUTSET **4 :** the act of taking a car out of a train ⟨average number of ~s for hot boxes per car-mile⟩

setover \ˈ≈,≈≈\ *n* -s [fr. *set over*, v.] **1 :** distance or amount set over **2 :** a device by which a lathe headstock or tailstock can be moved perpendicular to the ways for taper turning

set piece *n* **1 :** a composition of formal pattern in painting, sculpture, music, or literature ⟨an autobiographical *set piece*⟩ ⟨thrilling effect of . . . any of Shakespeare's great *set pieces* —W.S.Maugham⟩ ⟨the *set pieces*, too — the cathedrals and galleries and parks and palaces . . . come alive —Mitchell Goodman⟩ **2 a :** a flat cut to the silhouette of a building, tree, mountain, or some other object required in a stage setting **b :** a piece of constructed scenery **3 :** a framework on which fireworks are so arranged as to form a design on burning ⟨the *set piece* of our flag unfurled —R.S.Hillyer⟩ **4 :** a precisely planned and conducted military operation

set pin *n* **:** DOWEL

set point *n* **1 :** a point that decides a tennis set if won by the side having an advantage in the score **2 :** a point at which it is desired to have a control system maintain the variable quantity (as of pressure, temperature, relative humidity) **:** SETTING

set pot *n* **:** a vessel usu. of stainless steel heated either directly or indirectly in a fixed location for manufacturing synthetic resins and varnishes — called also *set kettle*

sets *pres 3d sing of* SET, *pl of* SET

set sample *n* **:** a sample taken from a freshly filled fermenter for chemical analyses

setscrew \ˈ≈,≈\ *n* **1 :** a machine screw designed to be screwed through a metal part (as a collar) and to jam tightly upon another part (as a shaft) so as to prevent relative movement — compare CLAMP SCREW **2 :** a screw for regulating a valve opening or a spring tension

setscrew wrench *n* **:** ALLEN WRENCH

set shot *n* **:** a two-handed floor shot in basketball from a stationary position

sets·man \ˈsetsmən\ *n, pl* **setsmen :** a workman in a stone quarry who cuts stone paving blocks

set square *n* **1 :** TRIANGLE 3e **2 :** a drafting instrument having a straightedge that may be set at any desired angle with an edge of the drawing board **3 :** a try square with an adjustable sliding head

set-stitched \ˈ≈ˌ≈\ *adj* **:** embroidered on tapestry

¹sett *var of* SET

²sett *var of* SETH

³sett \ˈset\ *n* -s [prob. fr. obs. var. of ³*set*] **:** a pattern of a Scottish tartan

set·te·cen·tist \ˌsed·əˈchentəst\ *n, pl* **settecentists** \-sts\ *or* **settecentis·ti** \-ˌchenˈtēstē\ [It *settecentista*, fr. *settecento* seven hundred, 18th century (fr. *sette* seven — fr. L *septem* — + *cento* hundred, fr. L *centum*) + *-ista* -ist — more at SEVEN, HUNDRED] **:** an artist, poet, or student of the 18th century period in Italian literature and art

¹set·tee \seˈtē\ *n* -s [modif. of It *saettia*, fr. ML *sagittea*, fr. L *sagitta* arrow] **:** a boat with a long sharp prow and single deck fitted with two or three masts with lateen sails and formerly used in the Mediterranean

²settee \ˈ"\ *n* -s [alter. (influenced by *-ee*) of ¹*settle*] **1 :** a long seat having a back and made to accommodate several at once **2 :** a medium-sized sofa with arms and a back

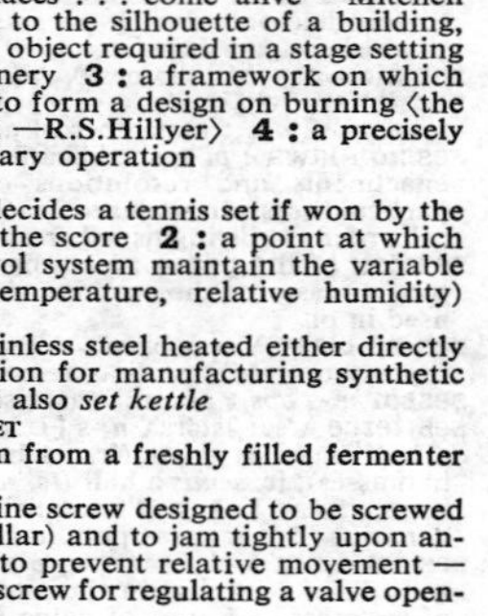
settee 1

settee bed *n* **:** a settee convertible into a bed by turning down or pulling out the seat

settee sail [¹*settee*] *n* **:** a quadrilateral sail on a lanteen yard hung obliquely to the mast

set·ter \ˈsed·ə(r), -etə-\ *n* -s [ME, fr. *setten* to set + *-er* — more at SET] **1 :** one that sets ⟨~ of traps⟩ ⟨an accurate ~ of type⟩ ⟨good ~ of fruit⟩ ⟨~ of fashions⟩ — used often in combination ⟨*bricksetter*⟩ ⟨*tilesetter*⟩ **2 :** a worker who sets something esp. by putting it in readiness for some operation or process or by placing it at a permanent location: as **a :** a sawmill worker who rides on the log carriage of the head saw and adjusts the position of logs so that planks are cut to desired thickness **b :** a textile worker who prepares harnesses for drawing-in **c :** one that places stacks of brick or tile in kilns **d :** one that adjusts paper-cutting machines **e** (1) **:** one that erects stone monuments (2) **:** one that sets stone blocks in a masonry wall **f :** BED SETTER **g :** one that sets stones or seals in jewelry **h :** a leather worker who smooths wrinkles from oiled hides with a dull scraper or by machine — called also *putter-out, setter-out, striker-out* **3 :** one of those who place the cocks beak to beak in a cockfight **4 :** one that sets out plants ⟨tobacco ~⟩ **5** *Scots law* **:** LESSOR **6 :** something used in setting: as **a :** a stone for setting an edge on a tool **b :** a fireclay container to hold a single piece (as a plate or saucer) in the kiln **c :** a low short sawhorse that is placed under the axle of a vehicle after it is raised with a jack and that leaves the wheels free to turn **d :** SAW SET **e :** a device for setting a combination of stops in a pipe organ **7 a :** one that finds and decoys victims for sharpers or thieves **b :** a police spy **:** INFORMER **c :** one employed to run up prices at auctions **8 :** a large bird dog of a type formerly trained to set on finding game but now expected to point — see ENGLISH SETTER, GORDON SETTER, IRISH SETTER; compare POINTER **9 setters** *pl* **:** WOMEN — distinguished from *pointers*

settergrass \ˈ≈≈,≈\ *n* **:** BEAR'S-FOOT

setter-in \ˈ≈≈ˈ≈\ *n, pl* **setters-in** [*set in* + *-er*] **:** a pottery worker who packs ware in saggers and places them in kilns

setter-on \ˈ≈≈ˈ≈\ *n, pl* **setters-on** [*set on* + *-er*] **1 :** one that sets on or attacks **:** ATTACKER **2 :** one that instigates or incites ⟨*setter-on* to treason⟩

setter-out \ˈ≈≈ˈ≈\ *n, pl* **setters-out** [*set out* + *-er*] **1 :** SETTER 2h **2 :** a carpenter or metalworker who lines out the details of the work

setter-to \ˈ≈≈ˈ≈\ *n, pl* **setters-to** [*set to* + *-er*] **:** SETTER 3

setter-up \ˈ≈≈ˈ≈\ *n, pl* **setters-up** [*set up* + *-er*] **:** one that sets something up: as **a :** RAISER 4 **b :** a worker who inserts linings into leather products **c :** a worker who assembles cardboard boxes **d :** one that sets up and sets off fireworks displays **e :** SETTER 2h

setterwort \ˈ≈≈,≈\ *n* [*setter-* (of unknown origin) + *wort*] **:** BEAR'S-FOOT

set theory *n* **:** a branch of mathematical or symbolic logic that deals with the nature and relations of aggregates

setting *n* -s [ME, fr. gerund of *setten* to set — more at SET] **1 a :** the manner, position, or direction in which something is set ⟨change the ~ of a thermostat⟩ **b :** the numerical reading of a graduated circle or other scale (as in right ascension or declination) by which an instrument is pointed at a celestial body **c :** the placing of a micrometer wire centrally on the

image of an object whose position is being measured **d :** the arrangement of spools of colored face yarn for axminster weaving **2** *chiefly Scot* **:** LEASE **3 a :** the frame or bed in which a gem is set; *also* **:** style of mounting ⟨marquise ~⟩ **b :** a station, bed, or resting place for a machine **4 a :** the temporal and spatial environment of the action of a narrative ⟨an old plot in a modern ~⟩ **b :** the scenic environment indoors or out including all the physical surroundings (as properties, furniture, buildings) within which a scene of a play or motion picture is enacted **5 :** the music composed for a poem, psalm, or other text **6 :** the articles of tableware required for setting a table or a place at table ⟨a dining room with ~s for 26 —*Time*⟩ ⟨a ~ of sterling flatware⟩ **7 :** the mechanism in a timepiece that permits the hands to be manually moved to the correct time **8 :** a group of retorts for gas manufacture **9 a :** the area from which logs are skidded by the rigging attached to one spar tree **b :** a site to which grain is hauled for threshing or at which the grain is stacked before the arrival of the thresher **10 a :** the eggs incubated by a fowl at one time **b :** a batch of eggs for incubation **11 a :** the arrangement of individual clichés in a plate or of stamps in a sheet **b :** the arrangement of an overprint on a stamp

setting block *or* **setting board** *n* **:** a grooved block or board usu. of cork used by entomologists in setting the wings and other parts of insects in the position for drying

setting circle *n* **1 :** a graduated scale or wheel on the mounting of an equatorial telescope for indicating right ascension or declination **2 :** coordinate scales on any optical pointing instrument (as a surveyor's transit)

setting coat *n* **:** a finishing coat of plaster

setting dog *n, archaic* **:** SETTER 8

setting gage *n* **:** a definite gage used as a standard for testing a limit gage or for setting an adjustable limit gage in size

setting hen *n* **:** BROODY HEN

setting-out \ˈ⸗⸗ˈ⸗\ *n, pl* **settings-out** [fr. gerund of *set out*] **1 :** beginning of a course or journey **:** DEPARTURE **2 :** a bride's trousseau and furniture

setting-out machine *n* **:** STRIKING-OUT MACHINE

setting point *n* **1 :** the temperature at which a liquid changes to a solid or semisolid **:** FREEZING POINT **2 :** a place in a mechanism where adjustments may be made

setting pole *n* **:** a pole usu. having a steel tip and used for pushing boats along in shallow water

setting punch *n* **:** a punch used esp. for closing a rivet (as in leatherwork) over a washer — called also *rivet set*

setting room *n, chiefly Midland* **:** SITTING ROOM

setting rule *n* **:** COMPOSING RULE

setting stake *n* **:** a device for setting circular saws that has an adjustable cone center and a hardened revolvable steel anvil beveled at various angles around the edge of its face

setting stick *n* **1 :** POKING STICK **2 :** DIBBLE **3 :** COMPOSING STICK

setting-up exercise \ˈ⸗⸗ˈ⸗-\ *n* **:** any of a series of gymnastic exercises used to give an erect carriage, supple muscles, and easy control of the limbs

¹set·tle \ˈsed·ᵊl, -etᵊl\ *n* -s [ME *setle, settil, settle,* fr. OE *setl;* akin to OHG *sezzal* seat, chair, Goth *sitls* seat, L *sella* seat, chair, saddle, Gaulish *sedlon* seat, OE *sittan* to sit — more at SIT] **1** *obs* **:** a place for sitting; *also* **:** chief place of abode **:** SEAT **2 a :** a wooden bench with arms, a high solid back sometimes extending to the floor, and often an enclosed foundation serving as a chest whose cover is the seat — see BOX SETTLE, TABLE SETTLE **b :** SETTEE **3 :** a raised platform, shelf, or frame; *specif* **:** a ledge about the lower part of an altar **4** [²*settle*] **a :** action or result of settling or sinking ⟨sand boils, bubbles, slides, and ~s . . . threaten to wipe out all efforts —*Time*⟩ **b :** the shrinkage measured in height of a kiln of brick when burning

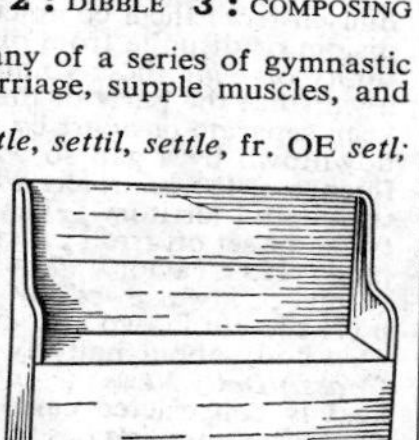

settle 2a

²settle \ˈ"\ *vb* **settled; settled; settling** \-d·ᵊliŋ, -t(ᵊ)liŋ\ **settles** [ME *setlen, settlen,* fr. OE *setlan,* fr. *setl,* n.] *vt* **1 a** *obs* **:** to cause to sit **:** SEAT **b :** to place so as to remain or to be comfortable ⟨*settled* himself in an armchair⟩ ⟨~ a child in its crib⟩ **c :** to direct or apply the attention, will, or effort of (oneself) ⟨the class *settled* itself to work⟩ **2 a :** to establish in residence ⟨~ refugees on farmland⟩ **b :** to furnish with inhabitants **:** COLONIZE, PLANT ⟨the colony was first *settled* by the Dutch⟩ ⟨a region *settled* by recent emigrants⟩ **c :** to establish (as residence) permanently **d :** to establish in married life ⟨managed to ~ all his daughters⟩ **e** *obs* **:** to set up (as a business) in a particular place **f** *archaic* **:** to establish in a pastoral office **3 a :** to make (loose material) compact **:** CONSOLIDATE ⟨~ the contents of a bag by shaking it⟩ ⟨watering the soil to ~ it as the hole was filled in⟩ **b :** to restore (a road or lawn) or bring to a smooth, dry, or passable condition **c :** to reduce in height or to a lower level ⟨~ a deck⟩ ⟨~ a sail⟩ **d :** to cause (land) to appear lower — opposed to *raise* **e :** to clear of dregs and impurities by causing them to sink **:** render pure or clear ⟨put eggshells in the coffee to ~ it⟩ **4 a :** to stop by killing or stunning ⟨*settled* his enemy with a single blow⟩ **b :** to reduce to order or to good behavior **:** SILENCE ⟨a word from his father was enough to ~ him⟩ **5 :** to change from disturbance and agitation to repose and tranquillity ⟨a drink to ~ his nerves⟩ ⟨she gave them ten seconds to ~ their faces —Virginia Woolf⟩ ⟨the bump on the head must have *settled* my brain —S.H.Adams⟩ **6 a :** to put in a fixed or permanent state ⟨~ the order of royal succession⟩ **:** make firm or stable ⟨~ the government on a parliamentary basis⟩ ⟨both English and French have been *settled* in their present form roughly since the eighteenth century —*Times Lit. Supp.*⟩ **b :** to resolve or judge finally **:** remove from uncertainty, unclarity or dispute ⟨time has *settled* few or none of the essential points of dispute —Henry Adams⟩ **c :** to put in order **:** ADJUST ⟨*settled* her patient's pillows⟩ ⟨always removed or *settled* their hats with both hands —E.A.Poe⟩ **7 a :** to fix (as a price) by mutual agreement **b :** to conclude (a lawsuit) by agreement between the parties usu. out of court **c :** to close (as an account) by payment **:** LIQUIDATE; *often* **:** to close by compromise and payment of less than full amount claimed or due **8 :** to secure (a right or an estate) to someone by legal form ⟨*settled* her whole fortune on her nephew⟩ ⟨the family estate is usually *settled* on the eldest son⟩ — compare SETTLEMENT **9 a :** to arrange for proper disposal of on death ⟨~ an estate⟩ **b :** to put in order ⟨*settled* his affairs before entering the army⟩ **10** *of an animal* **:** to impregnate or to cause to conceive — distinguished from *serve* **~** *vi* **1 a :** to come to rest from flight **:** ALIGHT ⟨the flock *settled* on the meadow⟩ ⟨a fly *settled* on the ceiling⟩ **b :** to descend usu. slowly and stay down or over ⟨mists *settling* in the valley⟩ ⟨dust had *settled* on the furniture⟩ ⟨a pall of silence *settled* over the room⟩ **2 a :** to fall slowly to the bottom ⟨waiting for the coffee grounds to ~⟩ — often used with *out* ⟨suspended pigment . . . is allowed to ~ out —H.J. Wolfe⟩ **b :** to become clear after being turbid or roiled **:** clarify by depositing sediment or scum ⟨let the wine ~ for a while before pouring⟩ **c** *of ground* **:** to become firm, dry, and hard after the effects of rain or frost have disappeared **3 :** to separate in the soapmaking process into layers of neat soap, nigre, and lye on standing after fitting **4 a :** to sink gradually to a lower level **:** SUBSIDE ⟨cracks appeared in the walls as the foundations *settled*⟩ **b** *of a ship* **:** to become steadily more submerged ⟨*settling* fast by the stern⟩ **5 a :** to become established in a fixed location or direction ⟨the wind has *settled* in the east⟩ ⟨a cold *settled* in her chest⟩ **b :** to become fixed or permanent **:** assume a lasting form or condition ⟨*settling* gracefully into old age⟩ ⟨his mood had *settled* into a dull apathy⟩ ⟨his expression *settled* into a permanent frown⟩ ⟨it is *settling* in to rain now⟩ **6 a :** to establish one's residence — often used with *down* ⟨his sons had married and *settled* down nearby⟩ **b :** to establish an abode or colony abroad ⟨the Germans who *settled* in Pennsylvania⟩ **7 a :** to direct successfully the attention, will, or effort **:** apply oneself — usu. used with *down* ⟨*settled* down to study⟩ ⟨*settled* down to a steady canter⟩ **b** *of a hunting dog* **:** to become fixed on a scent **8 a :** to become calm **:** cease from agitation ⟨~ into a relaxed attitude⟩ ⟨~ into sleep⟩ **b :** to take up an ordered way of life; *esp* **:** to assume the duties and restrictions of the married state — usu. used with *down* ⟨time to marry and ~ down⟩ **9 a :** to adjust differences or accounts **:** come to an agreement **:** COMPOUND ⟨~ with creditors⟩ — often used with *up* ⟨~ up after a poker game⟩ **b :** RESOLVE — used with *on* or *upon* ⟨after much discussion *settled* on the plan originally proposed⟩ ⟨unable to *settle* on which hat to buy⟩ **10 :** to become pastor of a church **:** take over a parish, church, or congregation **11** *of a female animal* **:** to become pregnant **:** CONCEIVE **syn** see CALM, DECIDE, SET — **settle accounts :** to make up a quarrel or breach by requital or by agreeing to terms — **settle for :** to content oneself with **:** be content with ⟨asked an endowment of two million but had to *settle for* one⟩ ⟨would *settle for* a tie score⟩ — **settle halyards :** to slack away on halyards to lower a yard — **settle one's hash :** to give a quietus to **:** dispose of **:** SUBDUE, SILENCE — **settle order :** to agree upon or determine a matter (as a court judgment) previously uncertain or in dispute ⟨*settle order* on notice to counsel of the parties⟩ — **settle the stomach :** to remove or relieve the distress or nausea of indigestion in the stomach

set·tle·abil·i·ty \ˌsed·ᵊlə'biləd·ē\ *n* **:** the quality or state of being settleable

set·tle·able \ˈsed·ᵊləbəl\ *adj* **:** capable of removal by settling ⟨~ solids in sewage⟩

settle bed *n* **:** SETTEE BED

settled *adj* **1 a :** unlikely to change or be changed **:** FIXED, STABLE, STEADFAST ⟨~ opinion⟩ ⟨~ purpose⟩ ⟨~ habits⟩ **b :** not moving about or wandering ⟨nomads were from time to time absorbed among the ~ people —Owen & Eleanor Lattimore⟩ **2 :** established or decided beyond dispute or doubt ⟨~ principles⟩ **3** *of weather* **:** fair and calm **4 :** peopled with settlers **:** BUILT-UP **5 :** secured or held by legal settlement ⟨~ income⟩ — **set·tled·ly** *adv* — **set·tled·ness** *n* -ES

settled charge *n* **:** an ecclesiastical charge into which a minister is regularly inducted

settle down *vi* **1 :** to become established in a dwelling place or in a permanent job, profession, or business **:** begin to live a normal life **2 :** to become inactive or sluggish ⟨liked to *settle down* with the evening paper after dinner⟩ **3 :** to make oneself comfortable for rest or sleep ⟨*settled down* for the night⟩

settled production *n* **:** the production from an oil well after the first abnormally heavy production has steadied down and the flow is not subject to rapid diminution

set·tle·ment \ˈsed·ᵊlmənt, -etᵊl-\ *n* -s [²*settle* + *-ment*] **1 :** the act of settling or state of being settled **2 a :** fixation in position **b :** a fixed position **c :** establishment in life, in business, in office **d :** ordination or installation as pastor **3 a :** establishment of order **:** REGULATION **b :** an established order **4 a :** an act of bestowing or giving possession under legal sanction **:** a formal and permanent grant or conveyance **b :** something that is bestowed formally and permanently **:** the sum, estate, or income secured to one by a settlement **c :** a disposition of property usu. through the medium of trustees for the benefit of some person or of persons in succession — compare JOINTURE **2 d :** a provision in addition to salary (as by gift of land or house) made by a congregation for its minister on his installation to help him set up house **5 a :** an act of settling oneself in a position or location ⟨~ of small industries . . . was encouraged —G.W.Hoffman⟩ **b :** legal residence of a person in a particular parish or town that entitles him to maintenance if a pauper and subjects the parish or town to his support **6 a :** occupation by settlers **:** COLONIZATION ⟨~ preceded survey instead of following it —Arthur Geddes⟩ **b :** a colony newly established **:** a place or region newly settled **c :** a small village in a sparsely settled region ⟨site of a once prosperous crofting ~ —L.D.Stamp⟩ **d :** an area set apart in eastern countries for the residence of foreigners **e :** a community formed by members of a religious body or faith ⟨Mennonite ~⟩ **f :** a small cluster of houses or huts; *esp* **:** slave quarters on a plantation **g :** an institution founded and maintained among a congested city population often under the auspices of a church, college, or similar organization to supply various educational, recreational, medical, and other services to the community ⟨social ~⟩ ⟨art ~⟩ — called also *neighborhood house* **7 a :** clarification by deposition of sediment or separation of scum **b :** subsidence of sand or loose earth **c** (1) **:** the gradual sinking of a structure either by the yielding of the ground under the foundation or by the compression of the joints or the material (2) **settlements** *pl* **:** fractures or dislocations caused by unequal sinking of a structure **d :** TRANQUILIZATION **8 a :** composure of doubts or differences **:** ADJUSTMENT ⟨~ of a controversy⟩ ⟨~ of a strike⟩ **b** *India* **:** the act of arranging between the government and the cultivators the terms and incidence of the land revenue demand over specific areas **9 :** payment or adjustment of an account **:** satisfaction of a claim by agreement often with less than full payment ⟨~ of tax arrears⟩ **10 :** the administrative determination pursuant to statute of the amount due under a public contract with the government or a subdivision thereof **11 :** an act or process by or the period during which transactions for the account on the London stock exchange are settled by arranging to carry them over or by completing the bargains by payment and delivery

settlement day *n* **:** the day of settling an account; *specif* **:** the last day of the settlement upon which payment must be made on any account on a stock exchange except such as are to be carried over to the next settlement — called also *account day, payday, settling day*

settlement house *n* **:** SETTLEMENT 6g

settlement option *n* **1 :** an option giving to an insured or his beneficiary a choice as to how the liability of an insurance company under its policy is to be discharged **2 :** an option of an insurer (as in fire insurance) to repair or rebuild instead of paying the loss in cash

settlement sheet *n* **:** the statement of a bank teller or department summarizing the day's transactions

set·tler \ˈsed·lə(r), -et(ᵊ)l-\ *n* -s **1 :** one that settles ⟨~ of disputes⟩ **2 :** a vessel or receptacle in which something is allowed to settle **:** settling tank **:** SEPARATOR; *specif* **:** a forehearth in which the molten furnace products are allowed to settle to separate the lighter from the heavier **3 :** one that settles esp. in a new region or a colony **:** COLONIST ⟨the first ~s of New England⟩ **4 :** SETTER 3

settler's-clock \ˈ⸗(⸗)⸗ˌ⸗\ *n, pl* **settler's-clocks :** KOOKABURRA

settler's twine *n* **:** an Australian aroid (*Gymnostachys anceps*); *also* **:** its coarse fiber

settles *pl of* SETTLE, *pres 3d sing of* SETTLE

¹settling *n* -s [fr. gerund of ²*settle*] **1 :** SUBSIDENCE, SEDIMENTATION **2 settlings** *pl* **:** matter that settles at the bottom of a liquid **:** LEES, DREGS

²settling *adj* [fr. pres. part. of ²*settle*] **:** used for holding fluids so that suspended matter may settle out ⟨~ basin⟩ ⟨~ chamber⟩ ⟨~ pond⟩ ⟨~ tank⟩

settling day *n* **:** a day for settling accounts; *specif* **:** SETTLEMENT DAY

settling price *n* **:** an arbitrary price used as the basis for the settlement of contracts through a clearinghouse

settling reservoir *n* **:** a reservoir consisting of a series of shallow basins arranged in steps with long weirs between so that only the clear upper layer of each will be drawn off

set·tlor \ˈsed·ᵊlə(r), -et(ᵊ)l-\ *n* -s [alter. (influenced by *-or*) of *settler*] **:** one that makes a settlement or creates a trust of property; *specif* **:** one that makes a marriage settlement

set to *vi* **1 :** to begin actively and earnestly **:** make an eager or determined start on a job or activity ⟨seized a broom and *set to*⟩ ⟨*set to* with a will on the dinner⟩ **2 :** to begin fighting ⟨in the third round stopped sparring and *set to* in earnest⟩

set-to \ˈ⸗,⸗\ *n* -s [*set to*] **:** a bout of boxing or fighting or arguing **:** a usu. brief and vigorous contest

set trigger *n* **1 :** a trigger on a rifle that may be adjusted for the amount of pressure required to pull it **2 :** one of a pair of triggers on some rifles that sets the action so that a very light pull on the second trigger will fire the piece

setts *pl of* SETT

setts·man *or* **sets·man** \ˈsetsmən\ *n, pl* **settsmen** *or* **setsmen :** a maker of paving sets

set tub \ˈ⸗,⸗ *sometimes* (ˈ)⸗ˈ⸗\ *n* **:** LAUNDRY TRAY

set·u·la \ˈsechələ\ *n, pl* **setu·lae** \-ˌlē\ [LL *setula, saetula,* dim. of L *seta, saeta* bristle — more at SINEW] **:** a small short hair, seta, or bristle

set·ule \ˈseˌchül\ *n* -s [LL *setula, saetula*] **:** SETULA

set·u·lose \ˈsechəˌlōs\ *or* **set·u·lous** \-ələs\ *adj* [*setula* or *setule* + *-ose* or *-ous*] **:** having or covered with small hairs or bristles

set up *vt* **1 a :** to raise to and place in a high position ⟨*set up* a mark to shoot at⟩ ⟨*set up* a sail⟩ ⟨*set up* a flag⟩ **b :** to place in view **:** POST ⟨*set up* a sign⟩ **c :** to put forward (as a plan, a theory) for acceptance **d** *obs* **:** to put up (as for sale or auction) **2 a :** to make (a loud noise) with the voice ⟨*set up* a fearful bawling⟩ **b :** to cause (a condition) to come into effect ⟨the wind *sets up* a humming in the wires⟩ ⟨the added sugar *sets up* a fermentation⟩ ⟨the splinter *set up* an inflammation⟩ **3 a :** to make taut (a stay, shroud, hawser) **b :** to raise the pitch of (a string) by tightening **c :** to transpose to a higher key ⟨a baritone aria *set up* for a tenor⟩ **d** *obs* **:** to heighten the brilliance of (a color) **e :** to tighten firmly (as a nut or a pipe joint) **4 a :** to place in power or in office ⟨plotting to *set* him *up* on the throne⟩ ⟨a rival pope was *set up*⟩ **b :** to place in a position of hostility or opposition **:** OPPOSE ⟨degree of presumption . . . to *set* himself *up* against the authority of so many great men —T.L.Peacock⟩ **c :** to raise from depression **:** ELATE, GRATIFY ⟨*set up* by unexpected praise from her husband⟩ **d :** to make proud or vain ⟨much *set up* by flattery⟩ **e :** to put forward or extol as a model **f :** to claim (oneself) to be ⟨*sets* himself *up* as an authority on art⟩ or to be capable of ⟨literary journalist . . . seldom *setting up* to pass judgment on major writers —*Brit. Bk. News*⟩ **5 a :** to place upright **:** ERECT ⟨*set up* a building⟩ ⟨*set up* a post⟩ ⟨*set up* a roadblock⟩ ⟨*set up* a tent⟩ ⟨*set up* a card table⟩ **b :** to assemble the parts of and erect in position for use or operation ⟨*set up* a printing press⟩ **c :** to put (a machine) in readiness or adjustment for a tooling operation **6 a** *archaic* **:** to put aside and save for future use **b :** to erect (a perpendicular or a figure) on a base in a drawing or diagram **7 a :** FOUND, INSTITUTE, INAUGURATE ⟨*set up* a religious order⟩ ⟨*set up* rules and bylaws for a club⟩ ⟨*set up* a school⟩ ⟨*set up* a regulating committee⟩ **b :** to put (as a way of living or a means of livelihood) in operation esp. for oneself ⟨*set up* housekeeping⟩ ⟨*set up* shop in a new neighborhood⟩ **c :** ESTABLISH 11 **d :** to clear (a route) for the free passage of a train **8 a :** to provide with means or opportunity of making a living ⟨*set* his son-in-law *up* in business⟩ **b :** to place in or restore to comparative prosperity or a chance of success **c :** to bring or restore to normal health and strength **d :** to cause (one) to take on a soldierly or athletic appearance esp. through drill ⟨*set up* recruits⟩ **9 a :** to make carefully worked out plans for ⟨*set up* a bank robbery⟩ **:** PREARRANGE **b :** to execute one or more plays in preparation for scoring (a goal or touchdown) **10 :** to pole (a boat) in hunting waterfowl **11 a :** to pay for (drinks) **b :** to treat (someone) to something ⟨*set* him *up* to a meal and new suit⟩ **~** *vi* **1 :** to come into active operation or use **2 :** to begin business ⟨saved enough to *set up* for himself as a contractor⟩ **3 :** to make pretensions **:** claim to be or be capable ⟨are you *setting up* for a wit now⟩ **4 :** to solidify too rapidly ⟨ways to avoid *setting up* in the cement mixer⟩ — **set up one's staff :** to take up residence **:** settle down ⟨appeared in London and there *set up their staff* —Anthony Trollope⟩

setup \ˈ⸗,⸗\ *n* -s [*set up*] **1 a :** carriage of the body; *esp* **:** erect and soldierly bearing **b :** CONSTITUTION, MAKEUP ⟨expert . . . in the determination of the physical and mental ~ required for the combat aviator —H.H.Arnold & I.C.Eaker⟩ **2 a :** the assembly and arrangement of the tools and apparatus required for the performance of an operation **b :** the portion of an operation devoted to preparatory work; *esp* **:** the preparation and adjustment of machines for an assigned task **3 a :** a restaurant table setting or place setting often including bread and butter **b :** glass, ice, and mixer served to patrons who supply their own liquor in unlicensed premises **4 a :** a camera position from which a scene is filmed; *also* **:** the footage taken from one camera position **b :** the final arrangement of the set and properties for the filming of a scene **c :** the arrangement of performers, musicians, and broadcasting equipment for a radio or television program **5 a :** the difference in level between the windward and leeward edges of a body of water **b :** the ratio between the strength of the black and the white television signal measured from the blanking signal and usu. expressed as a percent **6 a :** a position of the balls in billiards or pool from which it is easy to score or to make one's play **b :** a task or contest purposely made easy **c :** something easy to get or accomplish **d :** a game or match arranged with an opponent who can easily be defeated **e :** a boxer who engages in a match which he has no chance to win **f :** a ball so played (as in tennis) as to give one's opponent an opportunity for a scoring shot (as a smash return) **g :** a shot in which a volleyball is sent high into the air and close to the net in preparation for a spike by a teammate; *also* **:** the player who makes such a shot **7 a :** the manner in which the elements or components of a machine, apparatus, or mechanical, electrical, or hydraulic system are arranged, designed, or assembled **b :** the relatively unchanging or dominating patterns within which political, social, or administrative forces operate **:** customary or established practice **c :** the structure of an organization **d :** facilities and material existing or specially created for a particular goal, service, or task **8 :** PROJECT, PLAN, SCHEME

setup box *n* **:** a rigid container of wood or paperboard that cannot be flattened or folded for shipment to the packers

setup man *n* **:** one who makes the adjustments for machine tool operations to be performed by one or more routine operators

set·wall \ˈset,wȯl\ *n* -s [ME *sedewale, cetewale, setewale* zedoary, fr. OF *citoual, citoal, citouar,* fr. Per *zadwār*] **:** GARDEN HELIOTROPE 1

set·wise \ˈset,wīz\ *adv* [³*set* + *-wise*] **:** in the direction of the set — used of printing type ⟨a letter measured ~⟩

setwork \ˈ⸗,⸗\ *n* **1 :** embroidery used on tapestry **2 :** two⸗coat plastering on lath **3 :** boatbuilding in which abutting strakes are battened inside **4 setworks** *pl* **:** the mechanism on a sawmill carriage by means of which a log is advanced towards the saw after each cut

seu·dah \ˈsüdə\ *n, pl* **seu·doth** *or* **seu·dot** *or* **seu·dos** \ˈsü,dōt(h), -ōs\ *or* **seudahs** [Heb *sĕʽūdhāh*] **:** a Jewish feast or banquet; *esp* **:** a festive Purim meal

seugh *or* **seuch** \ˈshük\ *n* -s [ME *sough* — more at SOUGH] *chiefly Scot* **:** an open trench or drainage ditch

sev *abbr* several

se·vas·to·pol \səˈvastə,pōl, -aas- *also* ⸗ˈ⸗⸗,pōl *sometimes* ⸗ˈ⸗⸗,pəl *or* ˌsevəˈstōpəl *or* ˌ⸗⸗ˈstōpəl\ *adj, usu cap* [fr. *Sevastopol,* U.S.S.R.] **:** of or from the city of Sevastopol, U.S.S.R. **:** of the kind or style prevalent in Sevastopol

¹sev·en \ˈsevən, ˈsevᵊm, ˈsebᵊm\ *adj* [ME, adj. & pron., fr. OE *seofon;* akin to OHG & Goth *sibun* seven, ON *sjau,* L *septem,* Gk *hepta,* Skt *sapta*] **:** being one more than six in number ⟨~ years⟩ — see NUMBER table

²seven \ˈ"\ *pron, pl in constr* [ME] **:** seven countable persons or things not specified but under consideration and being enumerated ⟨~ are here⟩ ⟨~ were found⟩

³seven \ˈ"\ *n* -s [ME, fr. *seven,* adj. & pron.] **1 :** one more than six **2 a :** seven units or objects ⟨a total of ~⟩ **b :** a group or set of seven ⟨arranged by ~s⟩ **3 a :** the numerable quantity symbolized by the arabic numeral 7 **b :** the figure 7 **4 :** seven o'clock — compare BELL table, TIME illustration **5 :** a score in a dice game made by throwing with usu. two dice any combination of numbers that totals seven (as 4 and 3, 5 and 2, 6 and 1) ⟨has great luck throwing ~s⟩ — see CRAPS **6 :** the seventh in a set or series: as **a :** a playing card marked to show that it is seventh in a suit **b :** an article of clothing of the seventh size ⟨wears a ~⟩ **c :** the rower behind the stroke in an 8-oared boat ⟨is a strong ~ on the crew⟩ **7 :** something having as an essential feature seven units or members; *esp* **:** an English trochaic meter with seven syllables

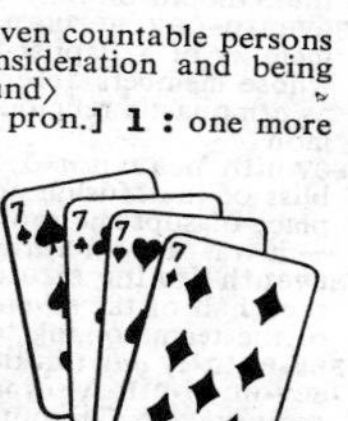

sevens 6a

to the line and typically four lines to the stanza — usu. used in pl. ⟨a poem in ~s⟩

4**seven** \"\ *vi* -ED/-ING/-S : to cast a seven in craps ⟨the man ~ed —A.B.Guthrie⟩ — often used with *out* ⟨has just ~ed out with the dice —Florabel Muir⟩

seven and a half *n* : a card game resembling twenty-one in which face cards count ½ point each and the object is to get a count up to but not exceeding 7½

seven arts *n pl* [trans. of ML *septem artes*] : LIBERAL ARTS 1

sevenbark \'==,=\ *n* **1** : WILD HYDRANGEA 1 **2** : NINEBARK

seven–card stud *n* : stud poker in which each player receives seven cards dealt two facedown and one faceup on the first round, one faceup on each of the next three rounds, and one facedown on the last round with betting following each round and a final showdown in which a player selects five of his cards as his poker hand — called also *seven-toed Pete*

sev·en·er \'sevənə(r)\ *n* -S *usu cap* [3*seven* + *-er*] : a member of an Islamic Shi'ite sect that maintains that the seventh imam went into deathless concealment and is to return as the Mahdi — compare TWELVER

seven–eyes *or* **seven–holes** \'==,=\ *n pl but sing in constr* [so called fr. the seven gill holes on each side of the neck] : LAMPERN

1**sev·en·fold** \'=='fōld\ *adj* [ME, fr. OE *seofonfeald*, fr. *seofon* seven + *-feald* -fold] **1** : having seven parts or aspects **2** : being seven times as large, as great, or as many as some understood size, degree, or amount ⟨a ~ increase⟩

2**sevenfold** \"\ *adv* [ME, fr. *sevenfold*, adj.] : to seven times as great or as many : by seven times ⟨increased ~⟩

sev·en·fold·ed \'=='fōldəd\ *adj* : made of seven parts ⟨~ shield⟩

seven–gilled shark \'==,=-\ *or* **seven–gill shark** *n* : a shark of the genera *Notorynchus* and *Heptranchias*

seven–league \'=='=\ *adj* : traversing seven leagues at a stride ⟨*seven-league* boots⟩ ⟨a *seven-league* step in the right direction —*Newsweek*⟩

sevens *n pl but sing in constr* : FAN-TAN

seven seas *n pl* : all the waters or oceans of the world ⟨sails the *seven seas*⟩

seven sisters *also* **seven sisters rose** *n, pl* **seven sisters** *also* **seven sisters roses** : a hybrid climbing rose (*Rosa multiflora platyphylla*) that is related to the crimson rambler and has rather large leaves and deep pink flowers in clusters

seven sleeper *n* : FAT DORMOUSE

1**sev·en·teen** \¦sevən¦tēn, -evᵊm¦-, -ebᵊm¦-\ *adj* [ME *seventene*, adj. & pron., fr. OE *seofontiene, seofontȳne, seofontēne* (akin to ON *sjautjān, sjautān* seventeen), fr. *seofon* seven + *-tīene, -tȳne, -tēne* (fr. *tien, tȳn, tēn* ten) — more at SEVEN, TEN] : being one more than 16 in number ⟨~ years⟩ — used prepositively to designate various years of the 18th century ⟨the *seventeen*-eighties⟩ ⟨the early *seventeen*-hundreds⟩; see NUMBER table

2**seventeen** \"\ *pron, pl in constr* [ME *seventene*] : 17 countable persons or things not specified but under consideration and being enumerated ⟨~ are here⟩ ⟨~ were found⟩

3**seventeen** \"\ *n* -S **1** : 10 and seven **2 a** : 17 units or objects ⟨a total of ~⟩ **b** : a group or set of 17 **3** : the numerable quantity symbolized by the arabic numerals 17 **4** : the 17th in a set or series; *esp* : an article of clothing of the 17th size ⟨wears a ~⟩

1**sev·en·teenth** \-ēn(t)th\ *adj* [ME *sevententhe*, alter. (influenced by *seventene*) of *seventethe*, fr. OE *seofontēotha* (akin to ON *sjautjāndi, sjautāndi* seventeenth), fr. *seofontīene, seofontȳne, seofontēne* seventeen + *-otha, -tha* -th] **1** : being number 17 in a countable series ⟨the ~ day⟩ — see NUMBER table **2** : being one of 17 equal parts into which something is divisible ⟨a ~ share of the money⟩

2**seventeenth** \"\ *n, pl* **seventeenths** **1** : number 17 in a countable series ⟨the ~ of the month⟩ **2** : the quotient of a unit divided by 17 : one of 17 equal parts of something ⟨one ~ of the total⟩ **3 a** : an interval of two octaves and a third **b** : a pipe-organ stop sounding two octaves and a major third above the normal

seventeen–year locust *n* : a cicada (*Magicicada septendecim*) common in eastern parts of the U. S. that has in the north a life of seventeen years and in the south of thirteen years, remains nearly the whole of this time underground in the nymphal condition, and after emerging quickly attains the adult condition in which it lives only a few weeks while it lays its eggs in slits made in the twigs of trees

1**sev·enth** \'sevən(t)th, 'sevᵊmth, 'sebᵊm-\ *adj* [ME *seventhe*, alter. (influenced by *seven*) of *sevethe*, fr. OE *seofotha* (akin to OHG *sibunto* seventh, ON *sjaundi, sjundi*), fr. *seofon* seven + *-tha* -th — more at SEVEN] **1** : being number seven in a countable series ⟨the ~ day⟩ — see NUMBER table **2** : being one of seven equal parts into which something is divisible ⟨a ~ share of the money⟩

2**seventh** \"\ *n, pl* **sevenths** **1** : number seven in a countable series ⟨the ~ of the month⟩ **2** : the quotient of a unit divided by seven : one of seven equal parts of something ⟨one ~ of the total⟩ **3 a** : a musical interval embracing seven diatonic degrees **b** : a tone at this interval; *specif* : the seventh tone of a scale : LEADING TONE **c** : the harmonic combination of two tones a seventh apart **4** : SEPTIME

3**seventh** \"\ *adv* **1** : in the seventh place **2** : with six exceptions ⟨the nation's ~ largest city⟩

seventh chord *n* : a chord comprising a fundamental musical

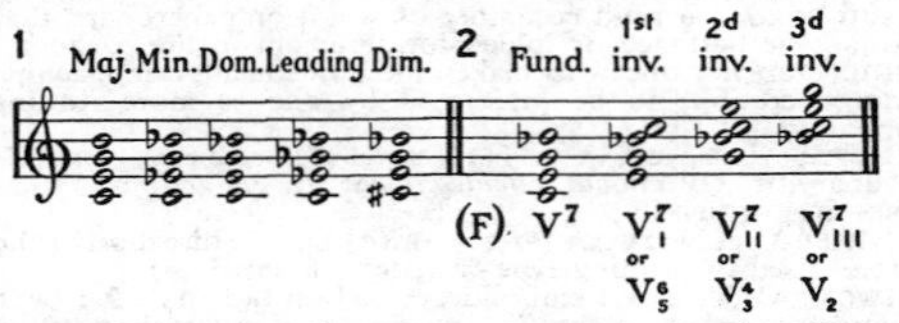

seventh chords: *1* five kinds of seventh chord, *2* dominant seventh chord of key of F and its inversions

note or tone with its third, fifth, and seventh and usu. designated by adding a small 7 to the numerals for triads

seventh cranial nerve *or* **seventh nerve** *n* : FACIAL NERVE

seventh day *n, usu cap S* **1** : SATURDAY — used chiefly by the Friends **2** : the Sabbath of the Jews and some Christian bodies

seventh–day \'=='=\ *adj* [*seventh day*] **1** : of, relating to, or occurring on the seventh day **2** : advocating or practicing observance of Saturday as the Sabbath

seventh–day adventist *n, usu cap S&A & often cap D* : ADVENTIST

seventh–day baptist *n, usu cap S&D&B* **1** : a member of a Baptist body organized in Rhode Island in 1671 and observing the Sabbath on Saturday **2** : SEVENTH-DAY GERMAN BAPTIST

seventh–day german baptist *n, usu cap S&D&G&B* : a member of a Baptist body founded in Pennsylvania in 1728 whose members observe the seventh day as the Sabbath, live as a monastic religious community, and share goods in common

seventh heaven *n* **1** : the last and highest of the abodes of bliss of the Muslim and of the cabalist systems : the abiding place of supreme rapture **2** : HEAVEN 4a ⟨when I was a kid — it was *seventh heaven* to have my feet wet —Audrey Barker⟩

seventh–inning stretch *n* : a brief period at the beginning of each half of the seventh inning of a baseball game when fans of the team coming to bat customarily stand or move about

sev·enth·ly *adv* : in the seventh place (as in a series of topics)

1**sev·en·ti·eth** \'sevəntēəth, -vᵊm|, 'sebᵊm|, |dē-\ *adj* [ME *seventithe*, fr. OE *hundseofontigotha*, fr. *hundseofontig* seventy + *-otha, -tha* -th — more at SEVENTY] **1** : being number 70 in a countable series ⟨the ~ day⟩ — see NUMBER table **2** : being one of 70 equal parts into which something is divisible ⟨a ~ share of the money⟩

2**seventieth** \"\ *n* -S **1** : number 70 in a countable series **2** : the quotient of a unit divided by 70 : one of 70 equal parts of something ⟨one ~ of the total⟩

seven–toed pete \'=,=-\ *n, usu cap P* [*pete* fr. *Pete*, nickname for *Peter*] : SEVEN-CARD STUD

seven–top turnip \'==,=-\ *also* **seventop** \'==,=\ *n* : a stout biennial herb (*Brassica septiceps*) prob. of European origin that produces numerous stems from a woody taproot bearing leaves that are used for greens or in salads — called also *Italian kale*

1**sev·en·ty** \'sevən|tē, -vᵊm|, 'sebᵊm|, |dē, |ī\ *adj* [ME, fr. OE *seofontig*, short for *hundseofontig*, fr. *hundseofontig*, n., group of 70, fr. *hund* 100 + *seofon* seven + *-tig* group of ten — more at HUNDRED, SEVEN, EIGHTY] : being one more than 69 in number ⟨~ years⟩ — see NUMBER table

2**seventy** \"\ *pron, pl in constr* [ME, fr. *seventy*, adj.] : 70 countable persons or things not specified but under consideration and being enumerated ⟨~ are here⟩ ⟨~ were found⟩

3**seventy** \"\ *n* -ES **1** : seven tens : twice 35 : five times 14 **2 a** : 70 units or objects ⟨a total of ~⟩ **b** : a group or set of 70 **3** : the numerable quantity symbolized by the arabic numerals 70 **4** : the 70th in a set or series **5** : something having as an essential feature 70 units or members **6 a** *usu cap* : a group of the traveling elders of the Mormon church who are esp. commissioned by ordination for missionary service and serve under the direction of the apostles **b** : a member of this group ⟨appointed a *Seventy*⟩ **7 seventies** *pl* **a** : the numbers 70 to 79 inclusive ⟨a golf score in the *seventies*⟩ ⟨all his grades in that subject are in the *seventies*⟩ **b** : the members of a series or set of successive numbers that end in 70 to 79 inclusive ⟨the *seventies* of the preceding century⟩ ⟨lives in the *seventies* in the next block⟩ **c** : the portion of a continuum lying between 70 and 80 on a scale of measurement or segmentation ⟨temperatures in the high *seventies* tomorrow⟩ ⟨a man in his *seventies*⟩ ⟨overcoats selling in the *seventies*⟩

1**seventy–eight** \¦==¦=¦=\ *adj* : being one more than 77 in number ⟨*seventy-eight* years⟩ — see NUMBER table

2**seventy–eight** \"\ *pron, pl in constr* : 78 countable persons or things not specified but under consideration and being enumerated ⟨*seventy-eight* are here⟩ ⟨*seventy-eight* were found⟩

3**seventy–eight** \"\ *n* **1** : eight and 70 : three times 26 : six times 13 **2 a** : 78 units or objects ⟨a total of *seventy-eight*⟩ **b** : a group or set of 78 **3** : the numerable quantity symbolized by the arabic numerals 78 **4** : the 78th in a set or series **5** : a phonograph record designed to be played at 78 revolutions per minute — usu. written 78

1**seventy–eighth** \¦==¦=¦=\ *adj* **1** : being number 78 in a countable series ⟨the *seventy-eighth* day⟩ — see NUMBER table **2** : being one of 78 equal parts into which something is divisible ⟨a *seventy-eighth* share of the money⟩

2**seventy–eighth** \"\ *n* **1** : number 78 in a countable series **2** : the quotient of a unit divided by 78 : one of 78 equal parts of something ⟨one *seventy-eighth* of the total⟩

1**seventy–fifth** \¦==¦=¦=\ *adj* **1** : being number 75 in a countable series ⟨the *seventy-fifth* day⟩ — see NUMBER table **2** : being one of 75 equal parts into which something is divisible ⟨a *seventy-fifth* share of the money⟩

2**seventy–fifth** \"\ *n* **1** : number 75 in a countable series **2** : the quotient of a unit divided by 75 : one of 75 equal parts of something ⟨one *seventy-fifth* of the total⟩

1**seventy–first** \¦==¦=¦=\ *adj* **1** : being number 71 in a countable series ⟨the *seventy-first* day⟩ — see NUMBER table **2** : being one of 71 equal parts into which something is divisible ⟨a *seventy-first* share of the money⟩

2**seventy–first** \"\ *n* **1** : number 71 in a countable series **2** : the quotient of a unit divided by 71 : one of 71 equal parts of something ⟨one *seventy-first* of the total⟩

1**seventy–five** \¦==¦=¦=\ *adj* : being one more than 74 in number ⟨*seventy-five* years⟩ — see NUMBER table

2**seventy–five** \"\ *pron, pl in constr* : 75 countable persons or things not specified but under consideration and being enumerated ⟨*seventy-five* are here⟩ ⟨*seventy-five* were found⟩

3**seventy–five** \"\ *n* **1** : five and 70 : three times 25 : five fifteens **2 a** : 75 units or objects ⟨a total of *seventy-five*⟩ **b** : a group or set of 75 **3** : the numerable quantity symbolized by the arabic numerals 75 **4** : the 75th in a set or series **5** : a 75 millimeter gun; *esp* : the fieldpiece of this caliber used in the armies of France and of the U. S. in World War I — often written *75*

1**seventy–four** \¦==¦=¦=\ *adj* : being one more than 73 in number ⟨*seventy-four* years⟩ — see NUMBER table

2**seventy–four** \"\ *pron, pl in constr* : 74 countable persons or things not specified but under consideration and being enumerated ⟨*seventy-four* are here⟩ ⟨*seventy-four* were found⟩

3**seventy–four** \"\ *n* **1** : four and 70 : two times 37 **2 a** : 74 units or objects ⟨a total of *seventy-four*⟩ **b** : a group or set of 74 **3** : the numerable quantity symbolized by the arabic numerals 74 **4** : the 74th in a set or series **5** : an old-time warship rated as carrying 74 guns **6** : a highly regarded southern African sparid food fish (*Polysteganus undulosus*) having a rosy red color above shading to white below with several wavy longitudinal blue streaks along the sides

1**seventy–fourth** \¦==¦=¦=\ *adj* **1** : being number 74 in a countable series ⟨the *seventy-fourth* day⟩ — see NUMBER table **2** : being one of 74 equal parts into which something is divisible ⟨a *seventy-fourth* share of the money⟩

2**seventy–fourth** \"\ *n* **1** : number 74 in a countable series **2** : the quotient of a unit divided by 74 : one of 74 equal parts of something ⟨one *seventy-fourth* of the total⟩

1**seventy–nine** \¦==¦=¦=\ *adj* : being one more than 78 in number ⟨*seventy-nine* years⟩ — see NUMBER table

2**seventy–nine** \"\ *pron, pl in constr* : 79 countable persons or things not specified but under consideration and being enumerated ⟨*seventy-nine* are here⟩ ⟨*seventy-nine* were found⟩

3**seventy–nine** \"\ *n* **1** : nine and 70 **2 a** : 79 units or objects ⟨a total of *seventy-nine*⟩ **b** : a group or set of 79 **3** : the numerable quantity symbolized by the arabic numerals 79 **4** : the 79th in a set or series

1**seventy–ninth** \¦==¦=¦=\ *adj* **1** : being number 79 in a countable series ⟨the *seventy-ninth* day⟩ — see NUMBER table **2** : being one of 79 equal parts into which something is divisible ⟨a *seventy-ninth* share of the money⟩

2**seventy–ninth** \"\ *n* **1** : number 79 in a countable series **2** : the quotient of a unit divided by 79 : one of 79 equal parts of something ⟨one *seventy-ninth* of the total⟩

1**seventy–one** \¦==¦=¦=\ *adj* : being one more than 70 in number ⟨*seventy-one* years⟩ — see NUMBER table

2**seventy–one** \"\ *pron, pl in constr* : 71 countable persons or things not specified but under consideration and being enumerated ⟨*seventy-one* are here⟩ ⟨*seventy-one* were found⟩

3**seventy–one** \"\ *n* **1** : one and 70 **2 a** : 71 units or objects ⟨a total of *seventy-one*⟩ **b** : a group or set of 71 **3** : the numerable quantity symbolized by the arabic numerals 71 **4** : the 71st in a set or series

1**seventy–second** \¦==¦=¦=\ *adj* **1** : being number 72 in a countable series ⟨the *seventy-second* day⟩ — see NUMBER table **2** : being one of 72 equal parts into which something is divisible ⟨a *seventy-second* share of the money⟩

2**seventy–second** \"\ *n* **1** : number 72 in a countable series **2** : the quotient of a unit divided by 72 : one of 72 equal parts of something ⟨one *seventy-second* of the total⟩

1**seventy–seven** \¦==¦=¦=\ *adj* : being one more than 76 in number ⟨*seventy-seven* years⟩ — see NUMBER table

2**seventy–seven** \"\ *pron, pl in constr* : 77 countable persons or things not specified but under consideration and being enumerated ⟨*seventy-seven* are here⟩ ⟨*seventy-seven* were found⟩

3**seventy–seven** \"\ *n* **1** : seven and 70 : seven times 11 **2 a** : 77 units or objects ⟨a total of *seventy-seven*⟩ **b** : a group or set of 77 **3** : the numerable quantity symbolized by the arabic numerals 77 **4** : the 77th in a set or series

1**seventy–seventh** \¦==¦=¦=\ *adj* **1** : being number 77 in a countable series ⟨the *seventy-seventh* day⟩ — see NUMBER table **2** : being one of 77 equal parts into which something is divisible ⟨a *seventy-seventh* share of the money⟩

2**seventy–seventh** \"\ *n* **1** : number 77 in a countable series **2** : the quotient of a unit divided by 77 : one of 77 equal parts of something ⟨one *seventy-seventh* of the total⟩

1**seventy–six** \¦==¦=¦=\ *adj* : being one more than 75 in number ⟨*seventy-six* years⟩ — see NUMBER table

2**seventy–six** \"\ *pron, pl in constr* : 76 countable persons or things not specified but under consideration and being enumerated ⟨*seventy-six* are here⟩ ⟨*seventy-six* were found⟩

3**seventy–six** \"\ *n* **1** : six and 70 : four times 19 **2 a** : 76 units or objects ⟨a total of *seventy-six*⟩ **b** : a group or set of 76 **3** : the numerable quantity symbolized by the arabic numerals 76 **4** : the 76th in a set or series

1**seventy–sixth** \¦==¦=¦=\ *adj* **1** : being number 76 in a countable series ⟨the *seventy-sixth* day⟩ — see NUMBER table **2** : being one of 76 equal parts into which something is divisible ⟨a *seventy-sixth* share of the money⟩

2**seventy–sixth** \"\ *n* **1** : number 76 in a countable series **2** : the quotient of a unit divided by 76 : one of 76 equal parts of something ⟨one *seventy-sixth* of the total⟩

1**seventy–third** \¦==¦=¦=\ *adj* **1** : being number 73 in a countable series ⟨the *seventy-third* day⟩ — see NUMBER table **2** : being one of 73 equal parts into which something is divisible ⟨a *seventy-third* share of the money⟩

2**seventy–third** \"\ *n* **1** : number 73 in a countable series **2** : the quotient of a unit divided by 73 : one of 73 equal parts of something ⟨one *seventy-third* of the total⟩

1**seventy–three** \¦==¦=¦=\ *adj* : being one more than 72 in number ⟨*seventy-three* years⟩ — see NUMBER table

2**seventy–three** \"\ *pron, pl in constr* : 73 countable persons or things not specified but under consideration and being enumerated ⟨*seventy-three* are here⟩ ⟨*seventy-three* were found⟩

3**seventy–three** \"\ *n* **1** : three and 70 **2 a** : 73 units or objects ⟨a total of *seventy-three*⟩ **b** : a group or set of 73 **3** : the numerable quantity symbolized by the arabic numerals 73 **4** : the 73d in a set or series

1**seventy–two** \¦==¦=¦=\ *adj* : being one more than 71 in number ⟨*seventy-two* years⟩ — see NUMBER table

2**seventy–two** \"\ *pron, pl in constr* : 72 countable persons or things not specified but under consideration and being enumerated ⟨*seventy-two* are here⟩ ⟨*seventy-two* were found⟩

3**seventy–two** \"\ *n* **1** : two and 70 : three times 24 : four times 18 : six times 12 : six dozen **2 a** : 72 units or objects ⟨a total of *seventy-two*⟩ **b** : a group or set of 72 **3** : the numerable quantity symbolized by the arabic numerals 72 **4** : the 72d in a set or series

seven–up \'=='=\ *n* -S : an American variety of all fours in which a turned-up card becomes trump and in which one point is scored in each deal for holding the highest and lowest trumps and the jack of trumps if it is dealt and for winning in tricks the greatest number of high cards or in some variants the ten of trumps with a total of seven points being necessary to win a game — called also *all fours, high-low-jack, old sledge*

seven–year apple *n* **1** : a shrub (*Casasia clusiaefolia*) of Florida and the West Indies having coriaceous leaves, fragrant white flowers, and a fruit similar to the apple **2** : the fruit of the seven-year apple

sev·er \'sevə(r)\ *vb* **severed; severed; severing** \-v(ə)riŋ\ **severs** [ME *severen*, fr. MF *severer, sevrer*, fr. L *separare* — more at SEPARATE] *vt* **1 a** : to put asunder : PART ⟨had been ~ed from the case because of illness —Paul Harris⟩ ⟨should ~ himself from them completely —Samuel Butler †1902⟩ **b** : to disjoin or disunite from one another ⟨will . . . take an opportunity of ~ing these young men —Sir Walter Scott⟩ ⟨fighting a war that the parts of the nation might not be ~ed⟩ **2** : to keep separate or apart by intervening ⟨a world ~ed from . . . downtown by a gap so wide —Louis Auchincloss⟩ ⟨the confluence of the . . . rivers which virtually ~s it from the rest of the capital territory —H.W.H.King⟩ **3** : to discriminate between or set off from : DISTINGUISH ⟨~ theology from philosophy —H.O.Taylor⟩ **4 a** : to divide or break up into parts ⟨army . . . was ~ed by inroads —Sir Winston Churchill⟩ **b** (1) : to cut in two : SUNDER, CLEAVE ⟨came to a stop with the ~ed body about halfway under the locomotive —*Springfield (Mass.) Daily News*⟩ ⟨~ing the cable and releasing the flaming, heavily constructed car —*Amer. Guide Series: Minn.*⟩ ⟨~ed their last remaining ties to the Old World —Oscar Handlin⟩ ⟨~ connections⟩ ⟨~ diplomatic relations⟩ (2) : to separate (from a whole) with suddenness or force ⟨the guillotine ~s the head from the body⟩ **c** : to scatter into parts : DISPERSE ⟨as wild geese that . . . ~ themselves and madly sweep the sky —Shak.⟩ **5** : to disunite, disconnect, or divide into independent parts, rights, liabilities, or provisions (as an estate in joint tenancy or a contract or statute) ~ *vi* **1** : to go apart or asunder : to become parted or separated ⟨if from me thou ~ not —John Milton⟩ ⟨in all their lives not to ~⟩ **2** : to become divided or separated into parts ⟨the army must ~ in three parts —Edward Hall⟩ **3** : to act independently or separately in a court of law ⟨claimed the right of ~ing in their challenge —T.B. Macaulay⟩ **syn** see SEPARATE

sev·er·abil·i·ty \,sev(ə)rə'bilədē\ *n* : the quality or state of being severable

sev·er·able \'sev(ə)rəbəl\ *adj* [*sever* + *-able*] : capable of being severed ⟨grew as a song, never unsung or conceived of as ~ from its melody —H.O.Taylor⟩; *esp* : capable of being divided into legally independent rights or obligations — used of a statute or contract of which the part to be performed consists of distinct items to which the consideration may be apportioned so that the invalidity or failure of performance as to one item does not necessarily affect the others

1**sev·er·al** \'sev(ə)rəl, *esp before a vowel* -vərl\ *adj* [ME, fr. AF, fr. ML *separalis*, fr. L *separ* separate (fr. *separare* to separate) + *-alis* -al — more at SEPARATE] **1 a** *archaic* : having a separate existence : SEPARATE, APART ⟨must do it . . . as a person ~ from them —John Milton⟩ **b** (1) *obs* : privately or individually owned or controlled ⟨a ~ plot —Shak.⟩ — opposed to *common* (2) : possessed by or attributed to specified individuals : RESPECTIVE ⟨having thirteen children which somewhat reduced their ~ inheritances —Lucien Price⟩ ⟨will call the members for their ~ opinions —T.R.Ybarra⟩ **c** : being a separate member of a group, class, or series : individually different within a type ⟨elegance of diction was . . . the result of her knowledge of three ~ tongues —Elinor Wylie⟩ **d** (1) : being of different kinds : DIVERSE, VARIOUS ⟨one of the ~ effects of the postwar changes —Taylor Cole⟩ ⟨threw his ~ mercantile ventures into the hands of creditors —Frank Monaghan⟩ (2) *obs* : made up of different elements : diversely composed **e** : of or relating separately to each individual of two or more tenants, persons, or parties involved (as in a contract or a suit) : SEVERABLE ⟨a ~ judgment may be had on a counterclaim . . . when judgment may be rendered for the plaintiff, or all of the plaintiffs, if more than one, or for the defendant, or all of the defendants, if more than one —S.J. Ervin⟩; *specif* : enforceable separately against each party ⟨the contractual liability of each company to insured is ~ and not joint —R.E.Keeton⟩ — compare JOINT 2b(3), JOINT AND SEVERAL **2 a** : more than one **b** : consisting of an indefinite number more than two and fewer than many usu. of the same class or group ⟨were around 75 . . . men present but only ~ women —Linda Braidwood⟩ ⟨a sojourn of ~ months in England —G.H.Genzmer⟩ ⟨have had ~ children —W.J. Ghent⟩ **c** *chiefly dial* : being a good many : MANY ⟨~ young men . . . run into a worse extreme —Jonathan Swift⟩ **syn** see DISTINCT

2**several** \"\ *n* -S [ME, fr. AF, fr. *several*, adj.] **1 a** *archaic* : land that is privately owned or controlled; *specif* : an enclosed plot of such land **b** *obs* : private property or ownership **2** *obs* **a** : something that is particular : an individual part : PARTICULAR, DETAIL — usu. used in pl. ⟨the ~s and unhidden passages of his true titles —Shak.⟩ **b severals** *pl* : individual persons or things **3 severals** *pl, chiefly dial* : several persons or things — **in several** *adv, archaic* : SEPARATELY, INDIVIDUALLY ⟨compare respectively the greatness of each part of the world *in several* —Philemon Holland⟩

3**several** \"\ *adv* ['*several*] *archaic* : by itself : SEVERALLY, SEPARATELY

4**several** \"\ *pron, pl in constr* ['*several*] **1** : an indefinite number more than two and fewer than many ⟨~ of the alumni have served on the board of trustees —*Bull. of Meharry Med. Coll.*⟩ ⟨goes to the store for oranges and purchases ~⟩ **2** *chiefly dial* : a good many : MANY

several fishery *n* : a private fishery founded upon ownership of the underlying soil

1**sev·er·al·fold** \¦=(=)=¦fōld\ *adj* ['*several* + *-fold*] **1** : having several parts or aspects **2** : being several times as large, as great, or as many as some understood size, degree, or amount

2**severalfold** \"\ *adv* : to several times as much or as many : by several times ⟨increased ~⟩

sev·er·al·i·ty \,sevə'ralədē\ *n* -ES [alter. of *severalty*] **1** *archaic* : something separate : QUALITY, DETAIL, PART **2** *obs* : the quality or state of being several

sev·er·al·ize \'sev(ə)rə,līz\ *vt* -ED/-ING/-S : DISTINGUISH, SEPARATE

sev·er·al·ly \'sev(ə)rəlē, -li\ *adv* [ME, fr. *several* + *-ly*] **1** : one at a time : each by itself : SEPARATELY ⟨people would point to . . . herself and Henry, ~, as the perfect wife and husband —Victoria Sackville-West⟩ ⟨premises which are ~ clear, distinct, and certain —A.N.Whitehead⟩ ⟨the strips or lands were not ~ enclosed —G.M.Trevelyan⟩ ⟨the beneficiary to be identified by any of us four jointly or ~ —Geoffrey Household⟩ **2** : apart from others : INDEPENDENTLY ⟨when they are hung ~, they came out . . . smooth and unwrinkled —R.K.Johnson⟩ **3** : RESPECTIVELY **4** *obs* : VARIOUSLY

sev·er·al·ty \'sev(ə)rəltē, -ti\ *n* -ES [ME *severalte*, fr. AF *severalté*, fr. *several* + *-té* -ty] **1** : the quality or state of being several : DISTINCTNESS, SEPARATENESS ⟨things combined may lose their ~⟩ **2 a** : a sole, separate, and exclusive possession, dominion, or ownership : one's own right without a joint interest in any other person — usu. used with *in* ⟨holds an estate in ~⟩ ⟨has tenants in ~⟩; distinguished from *coparcenary, joint tenancy*; opposed to *common* **b** : the quality or state of being individual or particular — usu. used with *in* ⟨treat of each great department of our social life in ~ —H.D. Traill⟩ **3 a** : land owned by individual right ⟨broke up the commons into *severalties*⟩ **b** : the quality or state of being held by individuals ⟨by unanimous vote of the town meeting the common field was converted into ~⟩ **4** *obs* : something separate : QUALITY, DETAIL, PART

sev·er·ance \'sev(ə)rən(t)s, -vərn-\ *n* -S [ME *severaunce*, fr. MF *sevrance*, *severance*, fr. *sevrer*, *severer* to sever + *-ance* — more at SEVER] **1 a** : the act or process of severing : the state of being severed ⟨control over native affairs and ~ of the territory —Manfred Nathan⟩ ⟨~ from the authority of traditional organs of government —H.D.Gunn⟩ ⟨the unhappy ~ of the scholar and the man of letters —F.B.Millett⟩ ⟨~ of diplomatic relations —David Lawrence⟩ ⟨~ of the leg below the knee⟩ **b** : DISTINCTION, DIFFERENCE — usu. used with *between* ⟨lines of ~ between truth and falsehood —W.E. Gladstone⟩ **2** : the division of the provisions, rights, liabilities, or similar legal considerations arising under or in something: as **a** : the destruction of the unity of interest in a joint estate **b** : the separation of two or more parties joined in an action so that one may proceed on the other being nonsuited **c** : the separation of two or more codefendants in a criminal prosecution for separate trial **d** : the detachment of fixtures from realty or of crops, fruits, timber, minerals, or related products from the soil **e** : the termination of a contractual association (as employment)

severance contract *n* : an agreement for employment that stipulates certain benefits for the employee at the time of severance

severance pay *n* : an allowance usu. based on length of service that is payable to an employee on severance except usu. in case of disciplinary discharge ⟨provide *severance pay* for officers and enlisted men released from active duty —*Military Rev.*⟩ ⟨reasonable *severance pay* . . . to mitigate technological unemployment —H.R.Northrup⟩

severance tax *n* : a tax on the taking and use of natural resources imposed at the time the mineral or other product is extracted or severed from the earth

sev·er·a·tion \,sevə'rāshən\ *n* -S [*sever* + *-ation*] : SEVERANCE

se·vere \sə'vi(ə)r, sē'-, -viə\ *adj* -ER/-EST [MF or L; MF, fr. L *severus*, perh. fr. *sed*, *se* without + *-verus* kindliness, friendliness; akin to L *verus* true — more at IDIOT, VERY] **1 a** : strict or uncompromising in judgment, discipline, or government ⟨parent ~ to the pitch of hostility —H.G.Wells⟩ ⟨the king's temper was arbitrary and ~ —T.B.Macaulay⟩ ⟨did perfect work and was a more ~ taskmistress than the teacher who had sight —Marie A. Kasten⟩ **b** : of a strict or stern bearing or demeanor ⟨her face was composed but not ~ —Archibald Marshall⟩ ⟨her matronly expression became more ~ —Ellen Glasgow⟩ ⟨a hefty six-footer with a rather ~ mien —*Current Biog.*⟩ **2** : absolute or rigorous in restraint, punishment, or requirement : INFLEXIBLE, STRINGENT, RESTRICTIVE ⟨martial law is very ~ in this matter —C.B.Nordhoff & J.N.Hall⟩ ⟨the ~ discipline of military life —John Lodge⟩ ⟨the penalties become more ~ as the bottom is approached —R.A.Hall b.1911⟩ ⟨in connection with phantom circuits, *severer* cross talk requirements have necessitated more precise balances —*Bell System Technical Jour.*⟩ **3** : strongly critical or condemnatory : CENSORIOUS ⟨some voluntary societies have been very ~ about certain films . . . which they consider vague, incoherent, and technically poor —*Report: (Canadian) Royal Commission on Nat'l Development*⟩ ⟨very ~ on the dangers and disease of intoxication —George du Maurier⟩ ⟨delivers ~ remarks against his enemies⟩ **4 a** : establishing or maintaining a scrupulously exacting standard of behavior or self-discipline ⟨there appeared a sounder logic in the ~ decorum and ironbound theology of her youth —Ellen Glasgow⟩ ⟨faults that must seem so black to her, with her simple ~ notions —George Eliot⟩ ⟨one of the *severest* moralists of his times⟩ **b** : establishing or exhibiting scrupulously exacting standards of accuracy and integrity in intellectual processes ⟨models of exact research and ~ scholarship —D.M.Robinson⟩ ⟨the kind of truth demanded by ~ logicians —H.J. Muller⟩ **5** : sober or restrained in decoration or manner : conservatively adorned : AUSTERE, PLAIN ⟨the only decoration to an otherwise ~ facade —*Amer. Guide Series: La.*⟩ ⟨in his ~ black garb —*Amer. Guide Series: Del.*⟩ ⟨in cool, ~ prose —*Amer. Guide Series: Fla.*⟩ **6 a** : inflicting physical discomfort or hardship : INCLEMENT, HARSH ⟨the snows of a ~ New England winter —*Amer. Guide Series: Maine*⟩ ⟨conditions too ~ to effect a rescue either by surf boats or by a breeches buoy —J.P.Baxter b.1893⟩ ⟨growing under ~ alpine conditions —G.R.Stewart⟩ **b** : inflicting pain or distress : AFFLICTIVE, GRIEVOUS ⟨disturbance which may be mild and benign or ~ and malign —*Diseases of the Nervous System*⟩ ⟨the ~ aches connected with muscles —F.A.Geldard⟩ ⟨a ~ wound which . . . cost him a leg —Mary A. Hamilton⟩ ⟨the pain of a badly fitting or too ~ bit is a constant cause of trouble —Beauvoir de Lisle⟩ **7** : requiring great effort : ARDUOUS, DIFFICULT ⟨pathetic suggestion, which makes no ~ call upon either the will or the intellect —W.R.Inge⟩ ⟨faces a ~ test of his capacity —*New Statesman & Nation*⟩ ⟨showing, in a ~ physical contest . . . that his bodily strength is not decayed —J.G.Frazer⟩ **8** *chiefly dial* : extremely strong, powerful, or effective ⟨takes a big ~ dog to do that —Horace Kephart⟩ **9** : of a great degree or an undesirable or harmful extent : MARKED, SERIOUS ⟨a ~ economic depression —B.K. Sandwell⟩ ⟨the fight was not ~ for there was only one fatality —*Amer. Guide Series: Calif.*⟩ ⟨~ shortages⟩ ⟨~ difficulties⟩

syn STERN, AUSTERE, ASCETIC: SEVERE implies unsparing adherence to rigorous standards, often those prescribing the hard or plain, enforced without indulgence and sometimes with harshness ⟨a *severe* code of Spartan living⟩ ⟨has high and *severe* standards —C.L.R.James⟩ ⟨was unyielding in his understandable insistence on discipline, was apt to be *severe* —Arthur Berger⟩ STERN may imply inflexible or inexorable severity, often along with a harsh, forbidding, or cold disposition ⟨during 21 *stern* years in the courtroom, Parker sentenced 151 men to the gallows —*Amer. Guide Series: Ark.*⟩ ⟨love indeed they did give, but it was a *stern* and passionless affection —E.T.Thurston⟩ ⟨on its surrender the *stern* justice of Hubert hung the twenty-four knights and their retainers who formed the garrison —J.R.Green⟩ AUSTERE may describe cold, barren, or dispassionate lack of feeling, warmth, color, or animation; it may apply to rigorous and stark restraint, simplicity, or self-denial ⟨*austere*, chill, precise, and dignified, his demeanor made familiarity impossible —Allan Nevins⟩ ⟨banks have sometimes cultivated a cold, *austere* atmosphere, symbolized by hard, cold marble and polished brass —*Banking*⟩ ASCETIC may refer to self-denying abstention, monastic or reminiscent of monasticism, from the pleasurable, easy, or indulgent, or even a courting of the disagreeable and hard in spiritual or intellectual discipline ⟨knowing the *ascetic* measure of his appetites, he was doubly certain that she would not let him starve; crisp drops of spring water and spare and wholesome crusts could never be denied him —Elinor Wylie⟩ ⟨his crabbed style and *ascetic* reasoning —V.L.Parrington⟩ ⟨this intermeddling with worldly business, which the *ascetic* reformer looked upon as the curse that robbed prelates and churchmen of that spiritual authority which could alone meet the vice and suffering of the time —J.R.Green⟩

se·vere·ly *adv* : in a severe manner : with severity

se·vere·ness *n* -ES : SEVERITY

severer *comparative of* SEVERE

severest *superlative of* SEVERE

¹se·ve·ri·an \sə'virēən\ *n* -S *usu cap* [ML *Severianus*, fr. *Severus*, 2d cent. Gnostic + L *-ianus* -ian] : one of a sect of Encratite Gnostics of the 2d century

²severian \"\ *n* -S *usu cap* [*Severus* †538 Pisidian ecclesiastic, bishop of Antioch + E *-ian*] : a follower of the Monophysite patriarch Severus who taught that the body of Christ was subject to corruption prior to his resurrection

severing *pres part of* SEVER

se·ver·i·ty \sə'verəd·ē, sē'-, -ətē, -i *sometimes* -'vir-\ *n* -ES [MF or L; MF *severité*, fr. L *severitat-*, *severitas*, fr. *severus* severe + *-itat-*, *-itas* -ity — more at SEVERE] : quality or state of being severe ⟨the ~ of the winter⟩ ⟨the naked *severities* of science —Thomas De Quincey⟩

severity rate *n* : the time lost through injuries as calculated in total days lost per 1000 hours worked

severs *pres 3d sing of* SEVER

sev·ery \'sev(ə)rē\ *n* -ES [ME *severie*, fr. MF *civoire*, *ciboire* ciborium, severy, fr. ML *ciborium* — more at CIBORIUM] : a section or compartment of a vaulted roof; *esp* : a bay of a Gothic vaulted ceiling

se·vi·lla·na \,sāvē(l)'yänə\ *n* -S [Sp, fr. fem. of *sevillano* of Seville] : SEGUIDILLA; *esp* : the seguidilla as danced or played in Seville — often used in pl. ⟨all women of Sevilla . . . dance the ~s, a graceful dance —Luis Marden⟩

se·vi·lla·no \-ä(,)nō\ *n* -S *cap* [Sp — more at SEVILLIAN] : SEVILLIAN

se·ville \sə'vil, *chiefly Brit* 'sevəl\ *adj, usu cap* [fr. *Seville*, Spain] : of or from the city of Seville, Spain : of the kind or style prevalent in Seville

seville orange *n* [fr. *Seville*, Spain] **1** *usu cap S* : SOUR ORANGE **2** *often cap S* : a moderate orange that is darker and slightly yellower and less strong than honeydew and redder and duller than Persian orange

¹se·vil·lian \sə'vilyən\ *adj, usu cap* [Sp *sevillano*, adj. & n., fr. *Sevilla* Seville + Sp *-ano* -an] **1** : of, relating to, or characteristic of Seville, Spain **2** : of, relating to, or characteristic of the people of Seville

²sevillian \"\ *n* -S *cap* [Sp *sevillano*] : a native or resident of Seville, Spain

sevl *abbr* several

sè·vres \'sevrə\ *n, pl* **sè·vreses** [fr. *Sèvres*, France] **1** *usu cap* : a fine often elaborately decorated French porcelain made at the national factory at Sèvres **2** *or* **sèvres blue a** *often cap S* : a strong blue that is redder and less strong than cerulean blue (sense 1b), redder and paler than cyanine blue (sense 1a), and greener, lighter, and stronger than Victoria blue **b** *usu cap S* (1) : the lighter blue of the Sèvres porcelain esp. of pieces antedating the French Revolution (2) : the darker blue of the Sèvres porcelain — called also *bleu de roi*

se·vum \'sēvəm\ *n* -S [L *sebum*, *sevum* tallow, grease — more at SOAP] : TALLOW

¹sew \'sō\ *vb* **sewed**; **sewn** \'sōn\ *or* **sewed**; **sewing**; **sews** [ME *sowen*, *sewen*, fr. OE *sīwian*, *sēowian*, *sīwan*, *sēowan*; akin to OHG *siuwen* to sew, ON *sȳja*, Goth *siujan*, L *suere* to sew, Skt *sīvyati* he sews] *vt* **1 a** : to unite, attach, or fasten by stitches made with a flexible thread or filament ⟨~*ed* and embroidered the clothes and moccasins for the family —Weston La Barre⟩ ⟨long swatches of fur . . . are *sewn* together to make a coat —*Time*⟩ ⟨stand still while mother ~*s* on the button⟩ **b** : to close or enclose by sewing ⟨~ the money in a bag⟩ ⟨with his money ~*ed* into the lining of his coat⟩ — often used with *up* ⟨~*ing* up the tear in his trousers⟩ ⟨to cut out this dangerously weakened area and ~ up the aorta again —Ben & Marie Pearse⟩ ⟨orders to ~ up the body in a canvas for the rites at sea⟩ **2** : to secure together (the sections of an assembled book) with thread or wire — distinguished from *stitch* ~ *vi* : to practice or engage in sewing ⟨is learning to ~ in her home science course⟩; *specif* : to work with needle and thread ⟨~*s* to earn extra money⟩

²sew \'sü\ *vb* -ED/-ING/-S [MF *essever*, *essewer*, *sewer* to drain — more at SEWER] *vt, chiefly dial* : to drain the water from ~ *vi* **1** *chiefly dial* : to ooze out **2** *or* **sue** *of a ship* : to become grounded

sew·age \'süij, -üēj\ *n* -S [³*sewer* + *-age*] : the contents of a sewer or household drain : refuse liquids or waste matter carried off by sewers

sewage disposal *n* : the process of removing and destroying or converting the noxious substances of sewage esp. by ammonification and nitrification through bacterial action

sewage farm *n* : a farm fertilized and irrigated with raw sewage or sewage liquids

sewage fly *n* : any of several flies of the genus *Psychoda* that breed in sewage or sink drains

sew·all wright effect \'süəl'rīt-\ *n, usu cap S&W* [after *Sewall Wright* b1889 Am. geneticist] : differentiation within a group arising from chance fixation of nonadaptive characters in small isolated populations

se·wan *also* **sea·wan** \'sē,wän\ *or* **sea·want** \-nt\ *n* -S [D (New Amsterdam) *sewan*, *zeewan*, *zeewant*, of Algonquian origin; akin to Narraganset *siwān* sewan, Natick *seawan*, *sewan* loose beads, *seāhham* he scatters] : WAMPUM

sewed shoe *n* [*sewed* fr. past part. of ¹*sew*] : a shoe in which the upper is attached to the sole by stitching

se·wee \'sē,wē\ *n, pl* **sewee** *or* **sewees** *usu cap* **1** : a people on the So. Carolina coast between the Santee and Ashley rivers usu. regarded as Siouan but sometimes considered to be Muskogean **2** : a member of the Sewee people

sewee bean *var of* SIEVA BEAN

se·wel·lel \sə'weləl\ *n* -S [Chinook *šᵊulal* blanket of sewellel skins (taken as the name of the animal), fr. dual of *ugwulal* sewellel] : MOUNTAIN BEAVER

sew·en *also* **sew·in** \'süən\ *or* **si·win** \'sēwən\ *n* -S [origin unknown] : the sea trout as found along the west coast of England and Wales and the coasts of Ireland whence it is sometimes regarded as constituting a distinct variety (*Salmo trutta cambricus*)

¹sew·er \'süə(r), 'sü(ə)r, 'süə\ *n* -S [ME, fr. AF *asseour*, fr. OF *asseoir* to seat + AF *-our* -or — more at ASSIZE] : a medieval servant or household officer often of high rank in charge of serving the dishes at table and sometimes of seating and tasting

²sew·er \'sō(ə)r, 'sōə\ *n* -S [ME *sower*, *sewer*, fr. *sowen*, *sewen* to sew + *-er* — more at SEW] **1** : one that sews ⟨became an expert textile finishing ~⟩ ⟨fastest shank button ~ ever made —*advt*⟩ **2** : LEAF SEWER

³sew·er \'süə(r), 'sü(ə)r, 'süə\ *n* -S [ME, fr. MF *esseveur*, *esseweur*, *seweur*, fr. *essever*, *essewer*, *sewer* to drain (fr. — assumed — VL *exaquare*, fr. *ex-* + *aqua* water) + *-eur* -or — more at ISLAND] **1** : a ditch or surface drain **2** : an artificial usu. subterranean conduit to carry off water and waste matter (as surface water from rainfall, household waste from sinks or baths, or waste water from industrial works)

⁴sewer \"\ *vt* -ED/-ING/-S : to furnish with a system of sewers : drain by sewers ⟨a small proportion of the streets were ~*ed* —*Amer. Jour. of Pub. Health*⟩

sew·er·age \-rij, -rēj\ *n* -S [³*sewer* + *-age*] **1** : SEWAGE **2** : the systematic removal and disposal of sewage and general surface water by sewers **3** *or* **sewerage system** : the system of sewers in a city, town, or locality **4** : unclean thought or language ⟨shocked even his fellow partisans by the ~ he poured forth in an . . . address —C.G.Bowers⟩

sewer brick *n* : a brick made from shale or clay, burned to a greenish blue color in a flame of low oxygen in a kiln, and used in drainage structures for the conveyance of sewage, industrial wastes, and storm water — called also *blue brick*

sewg *abbr* sewing

sew·ing \'sōiŋ, -ōēŋ\ *n* -S [ME *sowing*, *sewing*, fr. gerund of *sowen*, *sewen* to sew — more at SEW] **1** : the action or method of one that sews by hand or machine; *also* : the action of a machine that sews **2** : work in progress or products made by a person or machine that sews **3** : the occupation of operating a machine that sews

sewing awl *n* : an awl used (as by a shoemaker) for piercing holes for stitches in leather — see AWL illustration

sewing bird *n* : a clamp usu. fastened to a table edge and having a birdlike beak to hold work to be sewed by hand

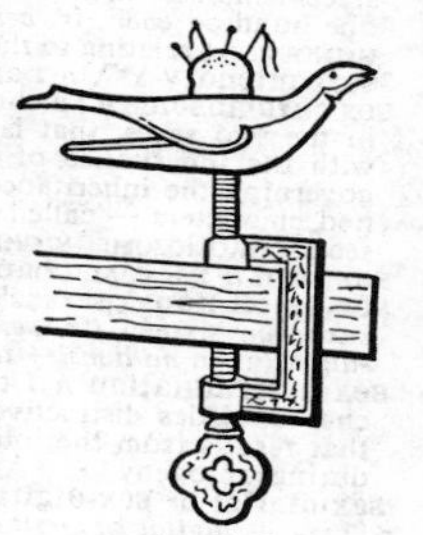

sewing bird

sewing cord *n* : material (as hemp) to which book sections are sewn with thread and which is later laced into boards

sewing cotton *n* : hard-twisted cotton thread usu. of three or six plies spooled for home and industrial sewing

sewing machine *n* : any of various machines for stitching material (as cloth, leather, or paper) usu. having a needle and shuttle to carry thread and powered by a foot treadle or electricity

sewing press *or* **sewing bench** *or* **sewing frame** *n* : a wooden device for bookbinding having a baseboard and two screw-threaded uprights supporting a crossbar from which cords used in hand sewing are stretched to the baseboard

sewing silk *n* : silk thread having two or three yarns tightly twisted together for sewing or loosely twisted together for embroidery

sewn *past part of* SEW

sewround \'sō,raund\ *n* [fr. the phrase *sew round*] : STITCHDOWN

sews *pres 3d sing of* SEW

sew·ster \'sōstə(r)\ *n* -S [ME *sowestre*, *sewestre*, fr. *sowen*, *sewen* to sow + *-estre* -ster] *archaic* : SEAMSTRESS

sew up *vt* **1** *Brit* : to wear out : FATIGUE ⟨reclining hopelessly on a settee, already dazed, *sewn up*, exhausted, and knocked out —Herbert Read⟩ **2 a** : to secure or assure exclusive control of (as a business proposition or arrangement) usu. by verbal agreement or contract : MONOPOLIZE ⟨the guilds had *sewed up* such primitive trade and industry as there were —D. C.Coyle⟩ ⟨in a position to *sew up* the preferred time spots —Goodman Ace⟩ **b** : to arrange for exclusive control or use of the services of (a person) : to place under contract ⟨the stars were already *sewed up* in three-year deals by the established hotels —*Time*⟩ ⟨hopes to *sew up* the champion for a 15-round battle⟩ **c** : to obtain or make certain of the support or cooperation of (a person or group) ⟨*sew up* as many . . . delegates as possible —*Newsweek*⟩ ⟨we *sewed up* the women's vote with this one —*Time*⟩ **d** *slang* : to gain exclusive hold on the affection or attention of (a person) ⟨the girl who asked him hadn't been able to *sew up* the captain of the . . . football team —Scott Fitzgerald⟩ **3** : to settle or determine (as the outcome or development) ⟨backstage negotiations have *sewed up* the results in advance —*Newsweek*⟩ ⟨need only one more victory to *sew up* their third straight . . . championship —*Time*⟩ ⟨when he confessed before he died, that *sewed* the whole thing *up* —Hartley Howard⟩

¹sex \'seks\ *n* -ES *often attrib* [ME, fr. L *sexus*; prob. akin to L *secare* to cut — more at SAW] **1** : one of the two divisions of organic esp. human beings respectively designated male or female ⟨a member of the opposite ~⟩ **2** : the sum of the morphological, physiological, and behavioral peculiarities of living beings that subserves biparental reproduction with its concomitant genetic segregation and recombination which underlie most evolutionary change, that in its typical dichotomous occurrence is usu. genetically controlled and associated with special sex chromosomes, and that is typically manifested as maleness and femaleness with one or the other of these being present in most higher animals though both may occur in the same individual in many plants and some invertebrates and though no such distinction can be made in many lower forms (as some fungi, protozoans, and possibly bacteria and viruses) either because males and females are replaced by mating types or because the participants in sexual reproduction are indistinguishable — compare HETEROTHALLIC, HOMOTHALLIC; FERTILIZATION, MEIOSIS, MENDEL'S LAW; FREEMARTIN, HERMAPHRODITE, INTERSEX **3** : the sphere of interpersonal behavior esp. between male and female most directly associated with, leading up to, substituting for, or resulting from genital union ⟨agree that the Christian's attitude toward ~ should not be considered apart from love, marriage, family —M.M.Forney⟩ **4** : the phenomena of sexual instincts and their manifestations ⟨with his customary combination of philosophy, insight, good will toward the world, and entertaining interest in ~ —Allen Drury⟩ ⟨studying and assembling what modern scientists have discovered about ~ —*Time*⟩; *specif* : SEXUAL INTERCOURSE ⟨an old law imposing death for ~ outside marriage —William Empson⟩

²sex \"\ *vt* -ED/-ING/-ES **1** : to determine the sex of (an organic being) ⟨it is difficult to ~ the animals at a distance —E.A.Hooton⟩ — compare AUTOSEXING **2 a** : to increase the sexual appeal or attraction of — usu. used with *up* ⟨titles must be ~*ed* up to attract 56 million customers —*Time*⟩ **b** : to arouse the sexual instincts or desires of — usu. used with *up* ⟨watching you ~*ing* up that bar kitten —Oakley Hall⟩

sex- *or* **sexi-** *comb form* [L *sex* — more at SIX] : six ⟨*sex*annulate⟩ ⟨*sexi*syllable⟩

sex act *n* : SEXUAL INTERCOURSE

¹sexa·decimal \,seksə+\ *adj* [*sexa-* (as in *sexagesimal*) + *decimal*] : of or relating to sixteen or sixteenths : proceeding in computation by sixteens : expressed in the scale of sixteens

²sexadecimal \"\ *n* : a sixteenth part

¹sex·a·ge·nar·i·an \,seksəjə'na(a)rēən, -'ner-, -'nār-\ *n* -S [L *sexagenarius* containing or consisting of sixty + E *-an*, n. suffix] : a person 60 or more and less than 70 years old

²sexagenarian \"\ *adj* **1** : 60 or more and less than 70 years old **2** : of or relating to a sexagenarian

sex·a·ge·nar·i·an·ism \,==='==,nizəm\ *n* -S : the state of being a sexagenarian

¹sex·a·ge·nary \(')sek'sajənerē, -ri\ *adj* [L *sexagenarius* containing or consisting of sixty, fr. *sexageni* sixty each (fr. *sexaginta* sixty, irreg. — influence of *quadraginta* forty — fr. *sex* six + *-ginta* — akin to L *-ginti* in *viginti* twenty) + *-arius* -ary — more at QUADRAGESIMAL, SIX, VICENARY] **1** : of, relating to, or based on the number 60 **2** : SEXAGENARIAN

²sexagenary \"\ *n* -ES **1** : SEXAGESIMAL **2** : SEXAGENARIAN

sex·a·ges·i·ma \,seksə'jesəmə, -jāzəmə\ *also* **sexagesima sunday** *n* -S *usu cap both Ss* [LL *sexagesima*, fr. L, fem. of *sexagesimus* sixtieth] : the second Sunday before Lent and the eighth before Easter in the church year as observed by various branches of the Christian church

¹sex·a·ges·i·mal \;==;==məl\ *adj* [L *sexagesimus* sixtieth (fr. *sexaginta* sixty) + E *-al*] : SEXAGENARY

²sexagesimal \"\ *n* -S : a sexagesimal fraction

sexagesimal arithmetic *n* : arithmetic in which computation proceeds by sixties

sexagesimal fraction *or* **sexagesimal number** *n* : a fraction whose denominator is some power of 60 (as $\frac{1}{60}$, $\frac{1}{3600}$, $\frac{1}{216000}$)

sex·a·ges·i·mal·ly \-məlē\ *adv* : into or by sixtieths

sexagesimal scale *n* : a scale of numbers that proceeds by sixties (as in degrees or hours, minutes, and seconds)

sex·a·ges·i·mo-quarto \,seksə;jesə(,)mō+\ *n* [L *sexagesimo quarto*, abl. of *sexagesimus quartus* sixty-fourth, fr. *sexagesimus* sixtieth + *quartus* fourth — more at QUART] : SIXTY-FOURMO — see BOOK tables

sex·ag·o·nal \(')sek'sagənᵊl\ *adj* [*sex-* + *-agonal* (as in *hexagonal*)] : HEXAGONAL

sexangled \(')=;==\ *adj* [*sex-* + *angled*] : HEXAGONAL

sex·an·gu·lar \(')sek'saŋgyələ(r)\ *adj* [L *sexangulus* hexagonal (fr. *sex* six + *angulus* angle) + E *-ar* — more at SIX, ANGLE] : HEXAGONAL

sex appeal *n* **1** : personal appeal or physical attractiveness for members of the opposite sex ⟨a girl with *sex appeal*⟩ ⟨set the new standard for masculine *sex appeal* —Lloyd Morris⟩ **2** : general appeal or attractiveness ⟨neither of these rates of return has much *sex appeal* —George Shea⟩ ⟨old hands in the Senate knew there was no political *sex appeal* in reorganization —William Benton⟩

sexa·valent \,seksə+\ *adj* [*sexa-* (as in *sexagesimal*) + *valent*] : HEXAVALENT

sex cell *n* : EGG CELL, SPERM CELL

¹sex·cen·te·nary \ˈsek,sen·ˈtenərē, (ˈ)sekˈsent³n,erē\ *adj* [L *sescenteni, sexcenteni* six hundred each (fr. *sex* six + *centeni* one hundred each, fr. *centum* hundred) + E *-ary* — more at HUNDRED] **:** relating to the number 600 or a 600th anniversary
²sexcentenary \"\ *n* **:** a 600th anniversary or its celebration
sex chromosome *n* **:** a chromosome that is inherited differently in the two sexes, that is or is held to be concerned directly with the inheritance of sex, and that is the seat of factors governing the inheritance of various sex-linked and sex-limited characters — called also *idiosome;* opposed to *autosome;* see X CHROMOSOME, Y CHROMOSOME
sex cord *n* **:** SEXUAL CORD
sex·de·cil·lion \,seksdəˈsilyən\ *n, often attrib* [L *sesdecim, sexdecim* sixteen (fr. *sex* six + *-decim,* fr. *decem* ten) + E *-illion* (as in *million*) — more at SIX, TEN] — see NUMBER table
sex determination *n* **:** the process of imparting sex and the characteristics distinctive of a sex to a developing organism that results from the interaction of genetic and other factors during ontogeny
sex·digital *or* **sex·digitated** \(ˈ)seks+\ *adj* [*sex-* + *digital* or *digitate, digitated*] **:** having six fingers or six toes
sex·dig·it·ism \seksˈdijə,tizəm\ *n* -s **:** the state of being sexdigital
sexed \ˈsekst\ *adj* [in sense 1, fr. ¹*sex* + *-ed;* in sense 2, fr. past part. of ²*sex*] **1 :** having sex or sexual instincts ⟨is so urgently ~ as to strain the confines of formal monogamous marriage —Weston La Barre⟩ **2 :** marked by qualities that arouse the sexual instincts **:** having sex appeal ⟨the actual dancing is highly ~ and uninhibited —John Martin⟩
sex·en·ni·al \(ˈ)sekˈsenēəl\ *adj* [L *sexennium* period of six years (fr. *sex* six + *-ennium,* fr. *annus* year) + E *-al* — more at SIX, ANNUAL] **1 :** continuing or lasting six years ⟨a ~ period⟩ **2 :** occurring, appearing, or being made, done, or acted upon every six years — **sex·en·ni·al·ly** \-ēəlē, -li\ *adv*
sex·er \ˈseksə(r)\ *n* -s [²*sex* + *-er*] **:** one that identifies the sex of an animal or other organism; *specif* **:** one that determines the sex of newly hatched chicks by examining the structures associated with the vent
sexes *pl of* SEX, *pres 3d sing of* SEX
sex·foil \ˈseks+,-\ *n* [*sex-* + *foil*] **1 a :** a flower with six perianth segments **b :** a leaf with six leaflets **c :** a group of six leaves **2 :** a figure enclosed by six joined foils; *specif* **:** a 6-lobed foliation in Gothic tracery **3 :** a conventionalized heraldic flower showing six lobe-shaped petals

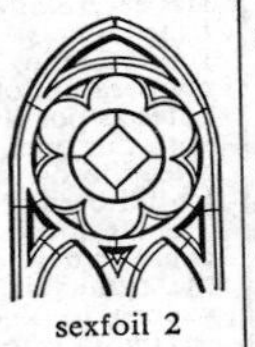
sexfoil 2

sex gland *n* **:** TESTIS, OVARY
sex·hood \ˈseks,hu̇d\ *n* **:** the quality or state of being of one sex or the other
sex hormone *n* **:** a hormone having an effect that is usu. stimulatory on the growth or function of the reproductive organs or on the development of secondary sex characters; *esp* **:** one produced in the ovaries or testes ⟨the *sex hormones,* like the adrenal cortical hormones, are all steroids —H.B. MacPhillamy⟩—compare ANDROGEN, ESTROGEN, PROGESTERONE
sexi- — see SEX-
sexier *comparative of* SEXY
sexiest *superlative of* SEXY
sex·i·ness \ˈseksēnəs\ *n* -ES **:** the quality or state of being sexy
sex–influenced \ˈ=,==\ *adj* **:** acting or occurring as a dominant in one sex and a recessive in the other ⟨*sex-influenced* genes⟩ — compare SEX-LIMITED, SEX-LINKED
sexing *pres part of* SEX
sex–intergrade \ˈ=ˈ==,=\ *n* **:** an individual intermediate in sexual characters **:** INTERSEX
sexi·valent \ˈseksə+\ *adj* [*sex-* + *valent*] **:** HEXAVALENT
sex·less \ˈsekslǝs\ *adj* **:** lacking sex **:** NEUTER — **sex·less·ly** *adv*
sex·less·ness *n* -ES **:** the quality or state of being sexless
sex–limited \ˈ=ˈ===\ *adj* **:** completely lacking penetrance in one sex ⟨a *sex-limited* character⟩ ⟨*sex-limited* gene⟩ — compare SEX-INFLUENCED, SEX-LINKED
sex–link \ˈ=,=\ *n* **:** an individual having one or more sex-linked characters; *specif* **:** a crossbred fowl having a sex-linked difference in color pattern that makes the hybrid autosexing
sex–linkage \ˈ=ˈ==\ *n* **:** the quality or state of being sex-linked
sex–linked \ˈ=ˈ=\ *adj* **1 :** located in a sex chromosome; *specif* **:** heterozygous in one sex and homozygous in the other ⟨a *sex-linked* gene⟩ **2** *of a heritable character* **:** mediated by a sex-linked gene — compare SEX-INFLUENCED, SEX-LIMITED
sex·o·log·i·cal \,seksəˈläjəkəl\ *adj* **:** of or relating to sexology
sex·ol·o·gist \sekˈsäləjəst\ *n* -s **:** a specialist in sexology
sex·ol·o·gy \-jē, -ji\ *n* -ES [¹*sex* + *-o-* + *-logy*] **:** the study of sex or of the interaction of the sexes esp. among human beings
sex·os·ti·a·tae \,sek,säsˈtēˈäd·(,)ē\ *n pl, cap* [NL, fr. *sex-* + *ostium* + L *-atae,* fem. pl. of *-atus* -ate] *in some classifications* **:** a group of spiders distinguished by the presence of six cardiac ostia
sex·os·ti·ate \(ˈ)sekˈsästēət, -ē,āt\ *adj* [*sex-* + NL *ostium* + E *-ate*] **1 :** having six ostia **2** [NL *Sexostiatae*] **:** of or relating to the Sexostiatae
sex·partite \(ˈ)seks+\ *adj* [*sex-* + *partite*] **:** divided into or made up of a combination of six parts **2 :** of or relating to an architectural system (as in the earliest Gothic) in which a vaulting square has two arched subdivisions on each side and one at each end
sex pervert *n* **:** SEXUAL PERVERT
sex play *n* **:** PLAY 1c(2)
sex·pot \ˈsek,spät\ *n* **:** a conspicuously sexy woman ⟨no lush store beauty she . . . no dished-up ~ —H.E.Clurman⟩
sex ratio *n* **:** the proportion of males to females in a population as expressed by the number of males per hundred females
sex skin *n* **:** areas of skin adjacent to the female external genitals of various lower primates that undergo marked alteration in turgidity and often in color during estrus
sext \ˈsekst\ *n* -s [ME *sexte,* fr. LL *sexta,* fr. L, fem. of *sextus* sixth, fr. *sex* six + *-tus,* adj. suffix used esp. to form ordinal numbers and past participles — more at SIX, -TH] **1** *often cap* **:** the fourth of the seven canonical hours or the sixth hour of the day according to the ancient Roman reckoning **:** 12 o'clock noon; *also* **:** an office recited at this time or in the Roman Catholic Church often somewhat earlier **2** [L *sexta,* fem. of *sextus*] **a :** a musical interval of a sixth **b :** a pipe-organ mixture stop with two ranks of pipes consisting of a twelfth and a seventeenth that sound a sixth apart
sex·tain \ˈsek,stān\ *n* -s [modif. (influenced by *sex-* and *quatrain*) of obs. F *sestine* — more at SESTINE] **1 :** SESTINA **2 :** a stanza of six lines
sex·tans \ˈsek,stanz\ *n, pl* **sextans** [L, sixth part of anything, sextans] **:** a bronze coin of the Roman Republic constituting the sixth part of an as
sex·tant \ˈsekstənt\ *n* -s [NL *sextant-, sextans,* fr. L, sixth part of anything, fr. *sextus* sixth + *-ant-, -ans* -ant — more at SEXT] **1 :** the sixth part of a circle **2 :** an instrument for measuring altitudes of celestial bodies from a moving ship or airplane with a maximum angle of 60 degrees between its two reflecting mirrors — compare OCTANT
sex·tet *or* **sex·tette** \(ˈ)sekˈstet, *usu* -ed·+V\ *n* -s [alter. of *sestet*] **1 a :** a musical composition in six voice parts or for six voices or instruments **b :** the musicians that perform a sextet **2 :** a 6-line stanza or poem **:** SESTET **3 :** a group or set containing six persons or things; *specif* **:** a team (as a hockey team) composed of six players
sexti- *comb form* [L *sextus* sixth — more at SEXT] **:** six ⟨*sextipara*⟩ ⟨*sextipolar*⟩
¹sex·tile \ˈsekstəl\ *adj* [L *sextilus* sixth, fr. *sextus* sixth + *-ilis* -ile] **:** of, relating to, or measured by 60 degrees
²sextile \"\ *n* -s **:** the aspect of two heavenly bodies when 60 degrees distant from each other
sex·til·lion \sekˈstilyən\ *n* -s *often attrib* [F, irreg. (influence of *septillion, octillion*) fr. *sex-* + *-illion* (as in *million*)] — see NUMBER table
sex·tip·a·ra \sekˈstipərə\ *n* -s [NL, fr. *sexti-* + *-para*] **:** a woman who has borne children in six pregnancies
sex·ti·polar \ˈsekstə+\ *adj* [*sexti-* + *polar*] **:** having six poles
sex·to \ˈsek(,)stō\ *n* -s [L (*in*) *sexto* in a sixth, fr. abl. of *sextus* sixth — more at SEXT] **:** SIXMO — see BOOK tables
sex·to·dec·i·mo \,sekstəˈdesə,mō\ *n* -s [L, abl. of *sextusdecimus* sixteenth, fr. *sextus* sixth + *decimus* tenth — more at DECIMATE] **:** SIXTEENMO — see BOOK tables
sex·tole \ˈsek,stōl\ *or* **sex·to·let** \-kstə,let\ *n* -s [*sextole* fr. G, fr. L *sextus* sixth + G *-ole* (as in *quintole*); *sextolet* fr. *sextole* + *-et*] **:** SEXTUPLET
sex·ton \ˈsekstən\ *n* -s [ME *secresteyn, sekesteyn, sexteyn, sexten,* fr. MF *secrestain,* fr. ML *sacristanus* — more at SACRISTAN] **:** a church custodian charged with keeping the church and parish buildings prepared for meetings, caring for church equipment, and performing related minor duties
sexton beetle *n* **:** BURYING BEETLE
sex·ton·ess \-nəs\ *n* -ES [ME *sexteynesse, sextenesse,* fr. *secresteyn, sekesteyn, sexteyn, sexten* sexton + *-esse* -ess] **:** a female sexton
sex·ton·ship \-n,ship\ *n* **:** the office or position of a sexton
sextry *n* -ES [ME *sextrie,* prob. fr. MF *secresterie,* modif. of ML *sacristia* — more at SACRISTY] *obs* **:** SACRISTY
sextupl *abbr* sextuplicate
¹sex·tu·ple \(ˈ)sekˈst(y)üpəl *also* -təp- *or* ˈsekstəp-\ *adj* [prob. fr. ML *sextuplus,* fr. L *sextus* sixth + *-plus* (as in *duplus* double) — more at DOUBLE] **1 :** consisting of six **:** being six times as great or as many **:** SIXFOLD **2 :** taken by sixes or in groups of six; *specif* **:** having six beats per musical measure **3 :** SEXTUPLEX 2
²sextuple \"\ *vb* -ED/-ING/-s *vt* **:** to make six times as much or as many ~ *vi* **:** to become six times as much or as many
³sextuple \"\ *n* -s **:** a sum six times as great as another **:** a sixfold amount **:** the sixth multiple
sex·tup·let \(ˈ)sekˈstəplət, -t(y)üp- *sometimes* ˈsekstəp-\ *n* -s [¹*sextuple* + *-et*] **1 :** a combination of six of a kind **2 a :** one of six offspring born at one birth **b sextuplets** *pl* **:** a group of six such offspring **3 a :** a group of six equal musical notes to be performed in the time ordinarily given to four of the same value and written in three groups of two **b :** a double triplet with accents on the first and fourth notes

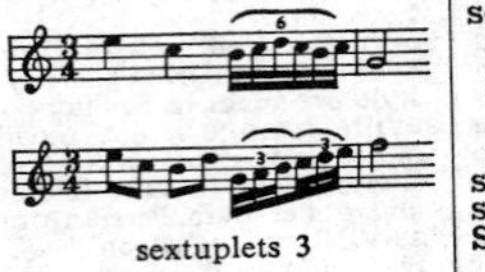
sextuplets 3

sex·tu·plex \ˈsekstə,pleks\ *adj* [NL, blend of ML *sextuplus* sextuple and L *-plex* (as in *duplex*)] **1 :** SIXFOLD **2 :** of, relating to, or consisting of a system of telegraphy in which six messages with three going each way can be sent simultaneously over one wire
¹sex·tu·pli·cate \(ˈ)sekˈst(y)üpləkət, -lə,kāt\ *adj* [blend of ¹*sextuple* and *-plicate* (as in *duplicate*)] **:** made in six identical copies **:** SIXFOLD
²sextuplicate \"\ *n* -s **1 :** a sixth thing like five others of the same kind **2 :** six copies all alike — used with *in* ⟨typed in ~⟩
³sex·tu·pli·cate \-lə,kāt\ *vt* -ED/-ING/-s **:** to multiply by six **:** SEXTUPLE **:** reproduce five times; *specif* **:** to make at one time an original and five carbon copies
sex·tur \ˈsek,stü(ə)r\ *n* -s [Dan *sekstur,* fr. *seks* six (fr. ON *sex*) + *tur* figure in a dance, fr. F *tour,* lit., turn — more at SIX, TOUR] **:** a Danish clockwise figure dance for six couples
sex type *n* **:** MATING TYPE
sex·u·al \ˈseksh(əw)əl\ *adj* [LL *sexualis,* fr. L *sexus* sex + *-alis* -al — more at SEX] **1 :** of, relating to, or associated with sex as a characteristic of an organic being ⟨~ differentiation⟩ ⟨~ distinctions⟩: **a :** having sex ⟨spores may be ~ or asexual⟩ **b :** involving sex ⟨the conception that bacteria have no ~ mode of reproduction —*Jour. of Bacteriology*⟩ **2 a :** of or relating to the male or female sexes or their distinctive organs or functions ⟨some biologists and anthropologists believe that the origins of art can be discovered in ~ display and ornamentation —Hunter Mead⟩ ⟨~ excitement⟩ ⟨~ compatibility⟩ **b :** of or relating to the sphere of behavior associated with libidinal gratification ⟨decided that the basis of almost all personality conflicts is ~ —*Time*⟩
sexual cell *n* **:** EGG CELL, SPERM CELL
sexual cord *n* **:** one of the cylindrical or band-form masses of mesothelial cells that contain the primitive sexual cells in the developing ovaries and testes of vertebrate embryos and that in the male develop into the seminiferous tubules
sexual cycle *n* **:** a cycle of bodily functional and structural changes associated with sex: **a :** ESTROUS CYCLE **b :** MENSTRUAL CYCLE **c :** a cycle in many males marked by the occurrence of seasonal or annual periods of virility with intervening periods of impotence in which neither sexual impulses nor secretions occur
sexual dimorphism *n* **1 :** a condition of having one of the sexes existing in two forms or varieties **2 :** a condition of having the two sexes markedly dissimilar in appearance (as in various birds)
sex·u·a·le \,sekshəˈwālē\ *n* -s [NL, fr. LL, neut. of *sexualis*] **:** a member of the bisexual generation in aphids
sexual generation *n* **:** the generation that reproduces by a sexual process in animals or plants which exhibit alternation of generations — compare ALTERNATION OF GENERATIONS, GAMETOPHYTE
sexual intercourse *n* **:** sexual connection esp. between humans **:** COITUS, COPULATION
sex·u·al·ism \ˈseksh(əw)ə,lizəm\ *n* -s **:** emphasis upon sex or sexuality as a major concern
sexual isolation *n* **:** biological isolation in which the isolating mechanism is a psychological inhibition of interbreeding
sex·u·al·ist \-ləst\ *n* -s [NL *sexualista,* fr. LL *sexualis* sexual + L *-ista* -ist — more at SEXUAL] **1 :** one who explains phenomena by sexuality **2 :** one who follows the sexual or artificial system of Linnaeus
sex·u·al·i·ty \,sekshəˈwaləd·ē, -lətē, -i\ *n* -ES **:** the quality or state of being sexual: **a :** the condition of having sex **b :** the condition of having reproductive functions dictated by the union of male and female — compare SEX 2 **c :** the expression of the sex instinct **:** sexual activity ⟨considered ~ as a dissipation of vital forces —Anthony West⟩ **d :** the condition, potential, or state of readiness of the organism with regard to sexual activity ⟨signs of excitation . . . and sometimes increased ~ —H.M.Parshley⟩
sex·u·al·iza·tion \,seksh(əw)ələˈzāshən\ *n* -s **:** the act or process of sexualizing **:** the state of being sexualized ⟨~ may not reach its prepubertal peak until about the ninth or tenth year —L.E.Hinsie⟩
sex·u·al·ize \ˈseksh(əw)ə,līz\ *vt* -ED/-ING/-s [*sexual* + *-ize*] **1 :** to make sexual **:** to endow with sex ⟨gender does not become *sexualized* until about the fifth or sixth year —L.E. Hinsie⟩ **2 :** to invest with sexual characteristics ⟨love of the child for his mother becomes contaminated with *sexualized* love —Weston La Barre⟩
sex·u·al·ly \-lē, -li\ *adv* **:** in a sexual manner **:** with regard to or by means of sex
sexual organ *n* **:** an organ of the reproductive system; *esp* **:** an external generative organ — often used in pl.; compare GENITALIA
sexual perversion *n* **:** activity (as sodomy, fellatio, bestiality) leading to complete sexual gratification that is preferred by an adult to heterosexual coitus
sexual pervert *or* **sexual deviate** *n* **:** one that practices a sexual perversion
sexual psychopathy *n* **:** the condition of a psychopathic or sociopathic personality manifested by the commission of sexual crimes
sexual relations *n pl* **:** COITUS
sexual selection *n* **:** the choice of a mate on a basis of various attractive characters (as color or bird song)
sexual skin *n* **:** SEX SKIN
sexual spore *n* **:** a spore formed as a result of conjugation of gametes or nuclei (as zygospore, ascospore, basidiospore) of opposite sex
sex·u·pa·ra \sekˈsüpərə\ *also* **sex·u·pare** \ˈseksə,pa(ə)(ə)r\ *n, pl* **sexupa·rae** \-üpə,rē\ *also* **sexupares** [NL *sexupara,* fr. L *sexus* sex + NL *-para*] **1 :** a parthenogenetic female producing eggs that give rise to males and to females which lay eggs requiring fertilization **2 :** a sexuparous insect
sex·u·pa·rous \-üpərəs\ *adj* [L *sexus* + E *-parous*] **:** producing eggs from which true males and females are hatched — used of various female aphids and phylloxeras
sexy \ˈseksē, -si\ *adj, usu* -ER/-EST **1 :** spicy or racy with references to or portrayals of sexually stimulating matter ⟨gay, charming, occasionally ~ tale of farm life —*Time*⟩ ⟨the *sexiest,* bawdiest and most outspoken comedy drama —*Ottawa (Canada) Jour.*⟩ ⟨read nothing more than the newspaper or perhaps a sadistic or ~ thriller —Eric Partridge⟩ **2 :** sexually suggestive **:** erotically stimulating ⟨struck ~ poses and smiled for advertising photographs —*Springfield (Mass.) Daily News*⟩ ⟨had a face angelic and ~ —Goodman Ace⟩
sey \ˈsī\ *n* -s [origin unknown] *Scot* **:** a cut of beef — compare BACKSEY, FORESEY
sey·bert·ite \ˈsībə(r)d·,īt\ *n* -s [F, fr. Henry *Seybert* †1883 Am. mineralogist + F *-ite*] **:** a basic aluminosilicate $Ca(Mg,Al)_3(Al,Si)_4(O,OH)_{12}$ of the clintonite group consisting of calcium, magnesium, and aluminum, occurring in monoclinic crystals and foliated masses and having a reddish brown, copper red, or yellowish color and submetallic luster (hardness 4–5, sp. gr.3–3.1)
sey·chel·lois \,sāshəlˈwä, -,shel-\ *n, pl* **seychellois** \-ä(z)\ [(assumed) F, fr. *Seychelles,* group of islands in the Indian ocean + F *-ois* -ese, fr. L *-ensis*] *cap* **:** a native or inhabitant of the Seychelles islands — **seychellois** *adj, usu cap*
sey·me·ria \sēˈmirēə\ *n, cap* [NL, fr. Henry *Seymer,* 19th cent. Eng. naturalist + NL *-ia*] **:** a genus of widely distributed herbs (family Scrophulariaceae) with pinnate leaves and solitary slightly irregular yellow flowers — see MULLEIN FOXGLOVE
¹sey·mour·i·a·morph \sēˈmōrēə,mȯrf\ *adj* [NL *Seymouriamorpha*] **:** of or relating to the Seymouriamorpha
²seymouriamorph \"\ *n* -s **:** an amphibian or fossil of the order Seymouriamorpha
sey·mour·i·a·mor·pha \=,===ˈmȯrfə\ *n pl, cap* [NL, fr. *Seymouria,* genus of Permian Labyrinthodontia + *-morpha*] **:** an order of Permian Labyrinthodontia comprising generalized forms exhibiting a mixture of amphibian and reptilian characters and possibly on the ancestral line of the true reptiles
seyyid *or* **seyid** *var of* SAYYID
sf *abbr* sforzando
SF *abbr* **1** *often not cap* science fiction **2** semifinished **3** senior fellow **4** shipfitter **5** signal-frequency **6** sinking fund **7** spot-faced **8** square foot **9** *often not cap* [L *sub finem*] toward the end **10** *often not cap* surface foot
Sf *symbol* sexagesimo-quarto
SFC *abbr* sergeant first class
sfer·ics *or* **spher·ics** \ˈsfiriks, -fer-, -rēks\ *n pl* [*sferics* by shortening & alter. fr. *atmospherics; spherics* short for *atmospherics*] **1 :** ATMOSPHERICS 1 **2** *sing in constr* **:** an electronic detector of storms using devices for plotting electrical discharges
SFM *abbr, often not cap* surface feet per minute
sfo·ga·to \sfōˈgäd·(,)ō\ *adj* [It, past part. of *sfogare* to exhale, give vent to, fr. *s-* (fr. L *ex-*) + *-fogare* (fr. L *fugare* to put to flight, fr. *fuga* act of running away, flight) — more at FUGUE] **1 :** light and airy in performance — used as a direction in music **2 :** high and thin in tone — used chiefly of a voice in the phrase *soprano sfogato*
¹sfor·zan·do \sfȯ(r)tˈsän(,)dō\ *adj (or adv)* [It, verbal of *sforzare* to force, fr. *s-* (fr. L *ex-*) + *forzare* to force, fr. (assumed) VL *fortiare* to attack, compel — more at FORCE] **:** ACCENTED — used as a direction in music to indicate that a single tone or chord is to be sounded more loudly than the rest of a passage — abbr. *sf, sfz;* symbol >
²sforzando \"\ *n, pl* **sforzandos** \-dōz\ *or* **sforzan·di** \-dē\ **:** an accented tone or chord
sfor·za·to \-äd·(,)ō\ *adj (or adv)* [It, past part. of *sforzare*] **:** SFORZANDO
SFPM *abbr, often not cap* surface feet per minute
sft *abbr* **1** shaft **2** soft
sftwd *abbr* softwood
sfu·ma·to \sfüˈmä(,)tō\ *n* -s [It, fr. *sfumato,* past part. of *sfumare* to evaporate, shade off into another color, fr. *s-* (fr. L *ex-*) + *fumare* to smoke, fr. L — more at FUME] **:** the definition of form without abrupt outline by delicate gradation from light to shadow producing an atmospheric effect (as in the painting of Leonardo da Vinci) — compare CHIAROSCURO
sfz *abbr* sforzando
sg *abbr* **1** signed **2** singular **3** surgeon
SG *abbr* **1** screen grid **2** secretary-general **3** *often not cap* senior grade **4** solicitor general **5** *often not cap* specific gravity **6** surgeon general
sga·bel·lo \zgäˈbe(,)lō, skä-\ *n* -s [It, fr. L *scabellum* low stool, dim. of *scamnum* bench, stool — more at SHAMBLES] **:** an Italian-Renaissance wooden side chair consisting of a stool or similar form with a simple upright back
sgaw *also* **sgau** \ˈskō\ *n, pl* **sgaw** *or* **sgaws** *also* **sgau** *or* **sgaus** *usu cap* **1 a :** a Karen people of Lower Burma **b :** a member of such people **2 :** the language of the Sgaw people
sgd *abbr* signed
sgg *abbr* signatures
sgl *abbr* single
SGO *abbr* **1** squadron gunnery officer **2** surgeon general's office
sgraf·fi·to \zgräˈfē(,)tō, skr-\ *also* **sgraf·fi·a·to** \,zgräfēˈä(,)tō, ,skr-\ *n, pl* **sgraffi·ti** \=ˈfē(,)tē\ [*sgraffito* fr. It, fr. *sgraffito,* past part. of *sgraffire* to scratch, produce sgraffito, fr. *sgraffio* scratch, sgraffito, fr. *sgraffiare* to scratch, produce sgraffito, fr. *s-* (fr. L *ex-*) + *graffiare* to scratch; *sgraffiato* fr. It, past part. of *sgraffiare* — more at GRAFFITO] **1 :** decoration by cutting away parts of a surface layer (as of clay or plaster) to expose a different colored ground — compare GRAFFITO **2 :** something (as traditional Pennsylvania Dutch pottery) decorated with sgraffito
sgt *abbr, often cap* sergeant
sh \sh *often prolonged*\ *interj* [origin unknown] — often used in a reduplicated form to enjoin silence or urge moderation of sound
sh *abbr* **1** sash **2** shall **3** share **4** sheep **5** sheet **6** shell **7** shilling **8** shipping **9** shipwright **10** shock **11** shop **12** short **13** show **14** shower **15** shunt
SH *abbr* **1** sacrifice hit **2** schoolhouse **3** *often not cap* semester hour **4** serum hepatitis **5** ship's heading **6** specified hours **7** scrum half
sha \ˈshä, ˈshō\ *n* -s [prob. native name in Ladakh] **:** URIAL
SHA *abbr* sidereal hour angle
sha'ban *also* **shaa·ban** \shəˈbän, shäˈb-,shōˈb-\ *n* -s *usu cap* [Ar *sha'bān*] **:** the 8th month of the Muhammadan year — see MONTH table
shab·bas goy *or* **shab·bos goy** \ˈshäbəs,-\ *n, usu cap S* [Yiddish *shabes goy,* fr. *shabes* Sabbath (fr. Heb *shabbāth*) + *goy* gentile, fr. Heb *gōy* people, nation] **:** a non-Jew employed by Orthodox Jews to tend fire, turn on and extinguish lights, or perform other similar services on the sabbath which Jews are forbidden to do on that day
shab·bat *or* **shab·bath** \shəˈbät, ˈshäbəs\ *or* **shab·bos** *or* **shab·bas** \ˈshäbəs\ *n, pl* **shab·bat·im** *or* **shabba·thim** \shəˈbätəm\ *or* **shabba·sim** \shəˈbōsəm\ *or* **shabbo·sim** \shəˈbōsəm, -ˈbōsəm\ [Heb *shabbāth* — more at SABBATH] **:** the Jewish Sabbath
shabbathaian *or* **shabbethaian** *usu cap, var of* SABBATIAN
shab·bat shu·bah *or* **shab·bath shu·bah** *or* **shab·bat shu·vah** *or* **shab·bath shu·vah** \,shäbəs(h)ˈshüvə\ *n, usu cap both Ss* [LHeb *shabbāth shūbhāh,* lit., Sabbath of return; fr. the fact that Heb *shūbhāh* (return) is the first word of the haftarah read on that day] **:** the Jewish Sabbath that falls between Rosh Hashanah and Yom Kippur
shab·bi·fy \ˈshabə,fī\ *vt* -ED/-ING/-s **:** to make shabby
shab·bi·ly \-bəlē, -li\ *adv* **:** in a shabby manner
shab·bi·ness \-bēnəs, -bin-\ *n* -ES **:** the quality or state of being shabby
shab·by \-bē,-bi\ *adj* -ER/-EST [obs. E *shab* scab + E *-y*] **1 a :** threadbare and faded from wear **:** appearing outworn ⟨~ finery⟩ ⟨saved fragments of lace from her dresses when they became too ~ for use —*Amer. Guide Series: Md.*⟩ **b :** ill kept and worn out **:** POOR, DECAYING, DILAPIDATED, NEGLECTED ⟨~, unpainted shacks, dropping with decay —Van Wyck Brooks⟩ ⟨~ wallpaper⟩ ⟨a ~ neighborhood⟩ **2 :** clothed with worn or seedy garments ⟨an uncommonly comic doctor, ~ alike in dress and ethics —Brooks Atkinson⟩ ⟨when he . . . saw the smartly dressed clerks standing before the stores, he looked at his own ~ person and was ashamed to enter —Sherwood Anderson⟩ **3 a :** MEAN, PALTRY, DESPICABLE ⟨the Nazis,

for all the terrible damage they have done, may turn out to be the *shabbiest* villains in history —*N. Y. Herald Tribune Bk. Rev.*⟩ ⟨all the efforts of propagandists . . . could not make the war anything but ~ in its origin —D.W.Brogan⟩ **b** : UN-GENEROUS, UNFAIR, DISHONORABLE ⟨laments the ~ way in which this country often treated a poet so deeply devoted to it —Paul Engle⟩ ⟨concerned both with the dearth of teachers and with the ~ scale on which they are paid —*Pleasures of Publishing*⟩ ⟨the opinions of the man on the street . . . are a motley of hand-me-downs, baggy generalities, and ~ preju-dices —H.J.Muller⟩ ⟨both parties played furious and some-times ~ politics⟩ ⟨she drifts into a ~ and then a *shabbier* love —Carl Van Doren⟩ ⟨the explorer's mistress shows up with the ~ truth of the man's life —Henry Hewes⟩ **c** : evincing scant liberality or generosity ⟨a ~ allowance ⟨a ~ gift⟩ ⟨had paid a very ~ dividend —W.M.Thackeray⟩ **d** : inferior in quality : SLOVENLY ⟨a ~ lot of fighting men, as their captured officers contemptuously admitted —*New Yorker*⟩ ⟨a member of a ~ theatrical troupe which tours the provinces —Donald Heiney⟩ ⟨his reasoning is weak, even ~ —J.T.Farrell⟩ **syn** see CONTEMPTIBLE
shab·rack *also* **shab·raque** \'sha,brak\ *n* -s [G & F: F *schabraque*, fr. G *schabracke*, fr. Hung *csáprág*, fr. Turk *çaprak*] : a saddlecloth often of goatskin formerly used by European light cavalry
sha·bun·der *also* **sha·ban·dar** \shä'bəndə(r)\ *n* -s [Per *shähbandar*, fr. *shäh* King + *bandar* city, harbor — more at CHECK] : a harbor master formerly the chief official to deal with foreign traders in the East Indies
sha·bu·oth *or* **sha·bu·ot** *or* **sha·vu·ot** *or* **sha·vu·os** *or* **she·vu·oth** *or* **she·vu·os** \shə'vü,ōt(h), -,ōs, -,əs\, *pl* **shabuoths** *or* **shabuots** *or* **shavuoths** *or* **shavuots** \-,ōt(h)s, -,ōs, -,əs\ *or* **shavuos·es** \-,ōsəz, -,əs-\ *or* **shevuoths** \-,ōt(h)s, -,ōs, -,əs\ *or* **shevuos·es** \-,ōsəz, -,əs-\ *usu cap* [Heb *shābhū'ōth*, pl. of *shābhūa'* week] : a Jewish holi-day observed on the 6th and 7th of Sivan and commemorating the revelation of the Law at Mt. Sinai and the wheat festival celebrated in biblical times 7 weeks or 50 days after the 16th of Nisan — called also *Feast of Weeks*, *Pentecost*
shacharit *or* **shacharith** *var of* SHAHARITH
shach·le *also* **shack·le** \'shakəl, 'shäk-\ *vb* -ED/-ING/-s [perh. imit.] **1** *vi, Scot* : to walk in a shuffling gate : SHAMBLE ~ *vt* **1** *Scot* : to wear (shoes) out of shape **2** *Scot* : to distort esp. by improper use
¹**shack** \'shak\ *n* -s [E dial. *shack* to shake, alter. of ¹*shake*] **1** *dial chiefly Eng* : grain and stubble left on the field after harvest **2** : liberty or right of turning pigs or poultry into fields after harvest to feed on the shack; *also* : the land so used **3** : a catch of miscellaneous fish mostly of cheap kinds
²**shack** \"\ *n* -s [perh. by shortening & alter. fr. *shakerag*] **1** *chiefly dial* : a shiftless fellow : BUM, TRAMP **2** *slang* : a rail-road brakeman
³**shack** \"\ *vi* -ED/-ING/-s : to go sluggishly or with a lumber-ing gait ⟨the old horse ~*ed* along⟩
⁴**shack** \"\ *n* -s [prob. back-formation fr. *shackly*] **1** : a small roughly built and often crudely furnished house : HUT, SHANTY ⟨a ~ made of old boards and tar paper —C.M.Webster⟩ ⟨found inadequate shelter in a grass ~ —E.E.Shipton⟩ ⟨the camps, with their close-serried ~s of tarpaulin, plywood, oil-cloth strips, cardboard —Han Suyin⟩ **2** : a room or similar enclosed structure for a particular person or thing ⟨an am-munition ~⟩ ⟨a cook's ~⟩ ⟨a guard's ~⟩ ⟨the operator's ~ on a crane⟩ ⟨a radio ~⟩
⁵**shack** \"\ *vi* : LIVE, DWELL ⟨the schoolhouse had been originally put up for the sawmill hands to ~ in —Clifton Johnson⟩ **2** *slang* : SHACK UP
⁶**shack** \"\ *vt* [perh. alter. of ⁷*shag*] : CHASE, RETRIEVE ⟨he'd ~ us away a half-dozen times a night —*Springfield (Mass.) Union*⟩ ⟨~ a baseball⟩
⁷**shack** \"\ *dial var of* SHUCK
shack·bolt \'shak,bōlt\ *n* [prob. short for *shackle bolt*] : a shackle used as a heraldic charge
shack·el *also* **shack·le** \'shakəl\ *n* -s [¹*shackle*] : a section of gill net
¹**shack·le** \'shakəl\ *n* -s [ME *schakel*, *schakle*, fr. OE *sceacul*; akin to MD *schakel* link of a chain, ON *skökull* pole of a cart] **1** : something that confines the legs or arms so as to prevent their free motion: as **a** : a ring or band en-closing ankle or wrist and fastened to something else (as its mate) by a chain or a strap : MANACLE, FETTER ⟨a ~ hobble for a horse⟩ **2** : something that acts like fetters to check or prevent free action — usu. used in pl. ⟨throw off the party ~s and do what was best for their country —Elie Abel⟩ ⟨the subtle, intimate, soul-gripping ~s of memory and usage that held her by the roots —Timothy Wharton⟩ ⟨free enterprise without the ~s of government control —W.M.Blair⟩ ⟨those who have tossed off the ~s of illiteracy —Ben Bradford⟩ ⟨must release ourselves from the ~s of yesterday's traditions and let our minds be bold —Hubert Humphrey⟩ ⟨want no ~s on the mind or the spirit —A.E.Stevenson b.1900⟩ **3** : any of various devices for making something fast: as **a** : a U-shaped metal fitting with a pin through the ends : CLEVIS, COUPLING — compare *anchor shackle* **b** : one of the U-shaped parts that join a spring in a vehicle to its hanger **c** : the link that engages with the staple in a padlock **d** : one of the rope handles for a sea chest **4** : a length of cable or anchor chain usu. 15 feet

shackle 3a

²**shackle** \"\ *vb* **shackled**; **shackled**; **shackling** \-k(ə)liŋ\ *vt* **1 a** : to confine the limbs of so as to prevent free motion : bind with or as if with shackles : FETTER, CHAIN **b** : to make fast with a shackle : JOIN, COUPLE ⟨each end of a spring to the axle ~s ⟨got in the port anchor and *shackled* it on the cable —H.A. Chippendale⟩ ⟨*shackled* the policemen together with their own handcuffs —Jan Valtin⟩ **2 a** : to deprive of freedom esp. of action by means of restrictions or handicaps : IMPEDE, HAMPER ⟨the illiterate, often with heavy physical and mental handicaps, *shackled* by habits of irritability and poor family background —Dixon Wecter⟩ ⟨*shackled* with precedents⟩ ⟨*shackled* with inherited conventions⟩ ⟨*shackled* by superstition⟩ ⟨people *shackled* by poor leadership⟩ **b** : to tie (a person or thing) to something that is detrimental ⟨the vast resources of the film industry remain predominantly *shackled* to its entertainment deities —E.D.Canham⟩ **syn** see HAMPER
³**shackle** \"\ *vi* [prob. fr. E dial. *shack* to idle, loaf (fr. E ²*shack*) ⟨E dial.] : to wander around idly : LOAF
shackle bar *n* **1** : a link coupling formerly used between rail-road cars **2** : a device consisting of an ordinary pinch bar with a hinged shackle near the point for pulling out something (as a driftbolt or railroad spikes)
shackle bolt *n* **1** : the bolt of a shackle **2** : a bolt with a shackle
shacklebone \'≈≠,≈\ *n, Scot* : WRIST
shackle joint *n* **1** : a joint consisting of a shackle fitted through a ring **2** : a joint formed by a bony ring passing through a hole in a bone (as at the base of the spine in some fishes)
shack·ler \'shak(ə)lə(r)\ *n* -s : one that shackles : COUPLER
shack·ly \'≈\ *adj* [prob. fr. E dial. *shackle* to shake, rattle (fr. E dial. *shack* to shake + E -*le*) + E -*y* — more at SHACK] **1** *chiefly dial* : RICKETY, RAMSHACKLE **2** *chiefly dial* : LOOSE-JOINTED, SHAMBLING
shacks *pl of* SHACK, *pres 3d sing of* SHACK
shacktown \'≈≠\ *n* : a group of shacks serving as dwellings ⟨migrant workers have settled by the hundreds and thousands in a gigantic ~ that has grown up in the vicinity —R.H.Fitz-gibbon⟩
shack up *vi, slang* : to become established in a dwelling or shelter esp. when involving cohabitation : spend the night : COHABIT — often used with *with* ⟨he *shacked* up with another girl he knew —Wenzell Brown⟩ ~ *vt, slang* : to establish in a dwelling or shelter esp. when involving cohabitation ⟨were *shacked* up comfortably inside bamboo huts —*Infantry Jour.*⟩ ⟨the girls get boyfriends who *shack* them up for a time —Marya Mannes⟩
shackup \'≈≈,≈\ *n* -s [*shack up*] *slang* : the act of shacking up : COHABITATION
shacky \'shake\ *adj* : characterized by the presence or sem-blance of a shack ⟨a ~ settlement near the town dump⟩

---

shad \'shad, -aa(ə)-\ *n, pl* **shad** *or* **shads** [fr. (assumed) ME *shad*, fr. OE *sceadd*; akin to L *scatēre* to bubble, gush, be abundant, Lith *suskàsti* to leap up] **1 a** : any of several clupeid fishes (genus *Alosa*) that differ from the typical her-rings in having a relatively deep body and in being anadromous **b** : a common food fish (*A. sapidissima*) of the Atlantic coast of No. America that is naturalized along the Pacific coast and is bluish green above with silvery sides and undersurface — see ALLICE SHAD, RIVER SHAD, TWAITE SHAD **b** : any of several other clupeid fishes (as a menhaden) — usu. used with a qualifying term; see GIZZARD SHAD **2** : any of various fishes of families other than Clupeidae: as **a** : BROAD SHAD; *also* : any of several similar mojarras **b** *southern Africa* : BLUE-FISH 1
shad-bellied \'≈,≈-\ *adj* **1** : constituting or resembling a man's coat similar to a cutaway and having the front edges cut on a gradual slant from the front to the tails **2** : having a thin or flat belly ⟨a *shad-bellied* old man⟩
shadbelly \'≈,≈\ *n, pl* **shadbellies 1** *also* **shadbelly coat** : a shad-bellied coat **2** : a wearer of a shad-bellied coat; *esp* : FRIEND 6
shad·ber·ry \'shad, -aa(ə)d-\ *n* — *see* BERRY *n* **1** : the fruit of the shadbush **2** : SHADBUSH
shadbird \'≈,≈\ *n* **1** *dial Eng* : the common sandpiper **2** *dial* : WILSON'S SNIPE
shadblow \'≈,≈\ *n* **1** *also* **shadblow serviceberry** : JUNE-BERRY 1; WHITLOW GRASS a
shadbush \'≈,≈\ *n* : JUNEBERRY 1
shad·chan *or* **schat·chen** *or* **shad·chen** \'shätkən, -ädk-\ *n, pl* **shad·cho·nim** \-'kónəm, -nêm⟩ *or* **shadchans** *or* **schat·chens** *or* **shadchens** [Yiddish & MHeb; Yiddish *shadkhn*, fr. MHeb *shadhkhān*, fr. LHeb *shidděkh* to arrange a marriage] : a Jewish marriage broker or a matchmaker
shad·dock \'shadək\ *n* -s [after Captain *Shaddock*, 17th cent. Eng. ship commander who brought the seed from the East Indies to Barbados in 1696] **1 a** : a very large thick-rinded typically pear-shaped citrus fruit closely related to the grape-fruit but differing esp. in its loose rind and often rather coarse dry pulp — called also *pomelo* **2** *also* **shaddock tree** : a small round-headed citrus tree (*Citrus grandis*) that produces shad-docks and is probably native to southeastern Asia or the Pacific islands but is widespread in warm regions as an escape though largely replaced in cultivation by the grapefruit
¹**shade** \'shād\ *n* -s *often attrib* [ME, fr. OE *sceadu*; akin to OHG *scato* shadow, Goth *skadus*, OIr *scáth* shadow, Gk *skótos* dark-ness] **1 a** : comparative darkness or obscurity owing to interception of the rays of light : partial or relative dark-ness caused by the intervention of an opaque body between the space con-templated and the source of light **b** : absence of complete illumination ⟨the ~ of the convent⟩ **2 a** : cover provided by the intervention of an opaque body be-tween the space contemplated and the source of heat or light; *esp* : shelter from the sun provided by tree foliage **b** (1) : protective foliage (2) : PRO-

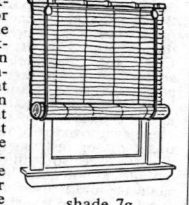

shade 7g

TECTION **3 a** : a spot not exposed to sunlight : a place shel-tered from the sun : ground overshadowed by foliage ⟨having come . . . to a pleasant ~ near a brook —Cedomilj Mijatovic⟩ **b** : a secluded retreat : a retired spot : a quiet habitation : an abode sheltered from the world ⟨let us seek out some desolate ~ —Shak.⟩ **4 a** *chiefly dial* : the figure appearing on the part of a surface from which light is cut off : SHADOW **b** : an evanescent or unreal appearance : a lingering image of some-thing passing away : something that has become reduced al-most to nothing **5 shades** *pl a* : the shadows which gather as darkness comes on : the growing darkness after sunset ⟨the ~s of night were falling fast —H.W.Longfellow⟩ **b** : the abode of the dead or of disembodied spirits : NETHERWORLD, HADES **6 a** : the soul after its separation from the body : the form of a dead person usu. held to be perceptible to the sight although not to the touch : a disembodied spirit : GHOST ⟨fol-lowed . . . by the ~ of their dead relative —J.G.Frazer⟩ **b** : the spirit of a dead or fictional person who would prob. have been startled or horrified by a particular action or situation **7** : something that shades: as **a** : something that intercepts or shelters from light or the direct rays of the sun : something that protects from heat or currents of air : SCREEN, SHELTER **b** : a protective cover of glass (as for a clock) **c** : a woman's head scarf or veil usu. of lace or fashionable during the 18th and 19th centuries **d** (1) : an ap-pliance of more or less translucent material (as glass, silk, or paper) used chiefly to diminish or to interrupt the flux of a lamp in directions where it is not wanted — compare REFLECTOR (2) : an appliance (as a globe) for protecting a flame or arc lamp from air currents **e** : a device or covering designed to protect the eyes from light — see EYESHADE, SUNSHADE **f** : a protective colored or smoked glass interposed between the eye and a bright light (as of the sun) **g** : a flexible screen usu. mounted on a roller and used to obstruct or regulate light pass-ing through a window or to obstruct the view through a window from within or without **h** : a usu. temporary struc-ture open at the sides and providing shelter esp. from the sun **8 a** : the reproduction of the effect of shade in painting or drawing (as by closely repeated lines or by adding a darker or lighter pigment to a given hue or tint) : absence of complete illumination as represented pictorially **b** : the part of a picture in which shade is represented **c** : the darker color expressing quality (as of a work of art) — often used in pl. ⟨lights and ~s of the work were captured by the pianist⟩ (2) : a defect of character ⟨implacable resentment is a ~ in a character —Jane Austen⟩ **9 a** : a color produced by a pigment or dye mixture having some black pigment or dye in it — compare TINT **b** : a color slightly different from the one under consideration **c** : a dye color different from the color under consideration or in some way not attributable to variation in strength of the dye used to produce that color **10 a** : a minute difference or variation (as of thought, belief, or expression) : NUANCE ⟨leaders of varying ~s of political opinion —Drew Middleton⟩ ⟨quibble over ~s of meaning —Lewis Nichols⟩ **b** : the quality or degree of something which is distinguished from others of like kind by slight differences **c** : a minute degree or quantity : a faint adumbration : a minute qualifying infusion : TINGE ⟨dropped her voice a ~ —Walter O'Meara⟩ ⟨sung a ~ too loud —Ann M.Lingg⟩ ⟨societies only a ~ less complicated than our own —Ralph Linton⟩ **11** *archaic* : SILHOUETTE **12** : a facial ex-pression of sadness or displeasure : CLOUD ⟨a ~ of displeasure on his brow —Sir Walter Scott⟩ ⟨a ~ of disappointment seemed to cross his face —*Yankee*⟩ **13** : a shutter in the swell box of a pipe organ **syn** see COLOR — **in the shade 1** : in a shaded place **2** : in a position screened from a source of heat or light (as the sun's rays) **2 a** : in retirement or com-parative obscurity **b** : in a state of comparative insignificance
²**shade** \"\ *vb* -ED/-ING/-s [ME *shaden*, fr. *shade*, n.] *vt* **1** : to shelter or screen by intercepting radiated light or heat : keep off illumination from : protect from glare or heat ⟨deep porches *shaded* with bright awnings —*Amer. Guide Series: Ark.*⟩ ⟨he *shaded* his eyes with his hand⟩ **b** : to place in the shade : shelter from light or heat ⟨the cattle . . . lie and themselves under their boughs —William Ellis⟩ **c** : to cover with a shade ⟨a lamp⟩ **2** : to hide partly or as if by a shadow : conceal with a shadow ⟨DISGUISE, SCREEN, VEIL **3** : to darken with or as if with a shadow ⟨a melancholy smile *shaded* his face —Sir Walter Scott⟩ **4 a** : to cast into the shade (as by some ex-hibition of superiority) : surpass by a shade : ECLIPSE, OVER-SHADOW ⟨a port which its attractive to liners . . . tends to ~ neighboring ports —F.W.Morgan⟩ **b** : to dim the brightness or luster of (as good qualities) : OBSCURE **5 a** : to represent the effect of shade or shadow on (an object) **b** : to add mark-ing to (as a drawing or painting) : COLOR so that the shades pass gradually from one to another **c** : to change by gradual transition or qualification **6** : to mark with grada-tions of light or color **d** : to change by gradual transition or qualification **7** : to reduce slightly (as the price of anything)

---

8 : to lower the pitch of (an open organ pipe) by an octave by closing its top **9** : to make (a bid, double, or redouble) in a card game on slightly less than the strength usu. required ~ *vi* **1** : to pass by slight changes or imperceptible degrees into something else ⟨work and play ~ into each other —H.E. Scudder⟩ ⟨the level . . . cast ~s off into the mountains —G.G. Coulton⟩ **2** : to undergo or exhibit minute difference or variation (as of color, value, meaning, or expression)
³**shade** \"\ *vt* -ED/-ING/-s [ME (northern dial.) *schaden* to distinguish, fr. OE *sceadan*, *scādan* to divide, separate — more at SHED] *chiefly Scot* : to make a part in (as the hair)
shaded *adj* **1 a** : protected from heat or light (as with shade or shadow) ⟨avenues⟩ **b** : having a shade (a ~ lamp) **2** : cov-ered with shadow ⟨o'er the ~ billows rushed the night —Alex-ander Pope⟩ **3** : having colors that shade : drawn or painted with shading
shaded-pole motor \'≈≈,≈-\ *n* : a single-phase induction motor in small ratings made self-starting by flux displacement derived by means of a permanently short-circuited, high-re-sistance winding or loop encircling a fraction of the pole piece or pole piece
shade-grown \'≈,≈\ *adj* : grown in the shade; *specif* : grown under cloth ⟨*shade-grown* tobacco⟩ — compare SUN-GROWN
shade grown *n, sometimes cap S&G* [*shade-grown*] : a tobacco grown under cloth in northern Florida and the Connecticut valley for cigar wrappers
shade·less \'shādləs\ *adj* : lacking shade : being without shelter from heat or light
shade pine *n* : SUGAR PINE
shade plant *n* **1** : a plant grown to provide shade to various crops (as coffee or vanilla) that require it **2** : a plant that grows normally in a shaded habitat where it receives only light of low intensity — compare SUN PLANT
shad·er \'shādə(r)\ *n* -s **1** : one that shades **2** : one that makes, tests, or colors with shades (as in dyeing and painting) **3** : one whose work is matching colors or sorting according to colors; *esp* : one that selects, grades, or classifies cigars ac-cording to their color **4** : a person who sorts brick as they are taken from a kiln
shade-ripened \'≈,≈-\ *adj* : ripened in the shade rather than in the sunlight ⟨*shade-ripened* berries⟩
shade roller pin *n* : a small metal pin which serves as the axle for the free end of a window shade roller
shades *pl of* SHADE, *pres 3d sing of* SHADE
shadetail \'≈,≈\ *n, South* : SQUIRREL
shade-tolerant \'≈,≈-\ *adj* : able to grow under shady condi-tions ⟨a *shade-tolerant* plant⟩
shade tree *n* : a tree (as the American elm) grown primarily to produce shade with the flowers being of secondary importance
shadflower \'≈,≈\ *n* **1** : ARBUTUS 1 **2** : JUNEBERRY 1 **3** : WHIT-LOW GRASS a
shad fly *n* : any of several insects (as the mayfly) that appear when shad enter the rivers
shad frog *n* : LEOPARD FROG
shadier *comparative of* SHADY
shadiest *superlative of* SHADY
shad·i·ly \'shādəlē, -li\ *adv* **1** : in a shady manner
shad·i·ness \-dēnəs, -din-\ *n* -ES : the quality or state of being shady ⟨the ~ of a deal⟩ ⟨the ~ of a woodland grove⟩
shading *n* -s **1** : a covering or sheltering with shade : protec-tion from heat or light **2** : the filling up within outlines that represents the effect of more or less darkness in a picture or a drawing **3** : a slight variation (as in color, quality, or class) : QUALIFICATION **4** : a musical effect gained by subtle changes in dynamics as effected by the player **5** : a process of com-pensating for unwanted signals in a television picture caused by the scanning process esp. during the trace interval or by inherent characteristics of the picture tube
shading coil *n* : a short-circuited coil surrounding part of the pole of an alternating-current magnet to reduce the magnetic flux in that part by currents induced in the coil and used to make single-phase motors self-starting
sha·doof *also* **sha·duf** \shə'düf, (')shä-\, (')sha'd-, -düf\ *n* -s [Ar *shādūf*] : a counterpoised sweep used in Egypt and nearby countries for raising water usu. for irrigation purposes
¹**shad·ow** \'sha(,)dō, -də; -,daw, -,dō+V\ *n* -s [ME *shadwe*, fr. OE *sceaduwe*, *sceadwe*, oblique case form of *sceadu* shade, shadow — more at SHADE] **1** : comparative darkness or shade within defined bounds : partial darkness or obscurity within a part of space from which rays from a source of light are cut off by an interposed opaque body (turned into the ~ of woods —John Buchan⟩ ⟨under the gathering ~ of the dim, purple sky —O.E.Rölvaag⟩ ⟨the grey sagebrush and the blue-grey rock . . . were already in ~ —Willa Cather⟩ **2 a** : a reflected image (as in a mirror or in water) **b** : a colorless or scantily pigmented or stained body (as a degenerate cell or empty membrane) only faintly visible under the microscope **3** : pro-tecting cover of wings) : protection from danger : shelter from observation ⟨under the ~ of the flag⟩ **4 a** : an imperfect and faint representation : an indistinct image : a dim or mystical bodying forth : ADUMBRATION **b** : an unreal appear-ance or image : an imaginary or delusive vision : a vain and unsubstantial object of pursuit **c** : an obscure indication : FORESHADOWING, PREFIGURATION, SYMBOL, TYPE **d** *obs* : a representation in painting or drama in distinction from the reality portrayed **e** : an imitation of something : COPY, COUNTERPART **5 a** : the image made by an obscured space on a surface that cuts across it usu. representing in silhouette the form of the interposed body : the dark figure cast upon a surface by a body intercepting the rays from a source of light ⟨the ~ of a man⟩ ⟨the ~ of a tree⟩ **b** : an acoustical phenome-non similar to the optical shadow produced by an obstructing of sound waves or electric waves ⟨the acoustic ~ of an object contains the low-frequency components of the sound —G.A. Miller⟩ **6** : a spiritual apparition : a spectral form : PHANTOM ⟨hence, horrible! —Shak.⟩ **7 shadows** *pl* : shaded parts of sky and landscape merging so as to bring on darkness ⟨night's sable ~s from the ocean rise —John Denham⟩ **8 a** : a shaded or darker portion of a picture usu. representing the less illuminated portions of the original **b** : the darkest areas of a photograph corresponding to the lightest areas of a negative of the same subject **9 a** : an attenuated form : a vestigial remnant : a form from which the substance has departed ⟨rep-tiles of today are but the veriest of a mighty dynasty —W.E. Swinton⟩ **b** : a person held to resemble a shadow as a result of extreme emaciation or feebleness **10 a** : one that follows or attends like a shadow : an inseparable companion or follower ⟨sin and her ~ death —John Milton⟩ **b** : one that shadows as a spy or detective : one that follows a person in order to keep watch on his movements **11** : a small degree or portion : a slight or faint appearance : TRACE ⟨a meaning . . . for which there is no ~ of justification —Reginald Reynolds⟩ ⟨hasn't really the ~ of a claim on us —Ellen Glasgow⟩ **12** : a pent-house or roof over the stage of an Elizabethan theater **13** *obs* : SHADE (as a veil or canopy) designed to afford shade or protection from light, heat, or observation **14 a** : influence casting a spell, gloom, or unhappiness ⟨love is sunshine, hate is ~ —H.W.Longfellow⟩ **b** : something qualifying adversely a usu. specified state or condition (as happiness, friendship, or fame) **15 a** : an area that is or is held to be within the shade cast by an object : PROXIMITY, VICINITY ⟨the Alamo . . . stands in the ~ of a modern skyscraper —*Amer. Guide Series: Texas*⟩ **b** : the pervasive and dominant influence, power, or reputation of someone or something ⟨reared under the ~ of absolutism —V.L.Parrington⟩ ⟨fallen within the ~ of Roman power —Benjamin Farrington⟩ ⟨a president . . . living in the ~ of his predecessor —H.J.Laski⟩
²**shadow** \"\ *vb* -ED/-ING/-s [ME *shadwen*, fr. OE *sceadwian*; akin to OHG *biscatwen* to overshadow, Goth *ufarskadwjan*; denominative fr. the root of OE *sceadu* shade, shadow — more at SHADE] *vt* **1** *archaic* : to shelter or protect as with covering wings : enfold with a beneficent and protecting influence **2 a** : to cast a shadow upon : cover or obscure with a shadow : overspread with obscurity : DARKEN, DIM ⟨the mountains . . . heavily ~*ed* by a storm cloud —G.R.Stewart⟩ ⟨a period of . . . history that is still thickly ~*ed* —*Amer. Guide Series: Ark.*⟩ **b** : to cast a gloom over : CLOUD ⟨a joy ~*ed* of his eyes —Hamilton Basso⟩ ⟨his cheerful face was suddenly ~*ed* —Katharine N. Burt⟩ **3** *obs* : to protect or shelter from the sun **4** *obs* : to conceal from view or knowledge : keep dark

: HIDE ⟨thereby shall we ~ the numbers of our host —Shak.⟩ **5** *obs* **a** : to serve as protection or security for : take under one's protection or patronage ⟨I saw thou wert a coward and ~*ed* thee —John Fletcher⟩ **b** : to screen from blame, punishment, or wrong **6** : to represent faintly, mystically, or figuratively : indicate obscurely or in slight outline : ADUMBRATE, BETOKEN, PREFIGURE, SYMBOLIZE, TYPIFY ⟨a statement could be delicately ~*ed* by an illusion —A.L.Guérard⟩ — often used with *forth* or *out* ⟨my theory of right conduct which these pages ~ forth —Herbert Spencer⟩ ⟨~ forth the doubts that men may have —Sonya Rudikoff⟩ **7** *obs* : to paint the likeness of : DEPICT, PAINT, PORTRAY **8** : to follow like a shadow : attend or follow and watch closely esp. in a secret manner : keep under surveillance : TRAIL ⟨a detective ~*ed* the suspect⟩ ⟨the cruiser was ~*ed* by a submarine⟩ **9** *archaic* : SHADE 5 ⟨no grays, no tones or softness to ~ the angular blacks —E.L. Wallant⟩ **10** : to produce a shadow of ⟨the light ~*ed* him against the side of the tent⟩ **11** : to prevent uniform deposition upon in electroplating — used of an object which by its position interferes with normal current distribution ~ *vi* **1** *archaic* : to cast a shadow ⟨the house ~*ed* over them —Richard Llewellyn⟩ **2** *obs* : to become closely alike or verge in color **3** : to pass gradually or by degrees : shade off ⟨the mountains . . . were ~*ing* into blackness —Lonnie Coleman⟩ ⟨smooth opal . . . ~*ing* to deep jade beneath the rocks —Rose Macaulay⟩ **4** : to become overcast with or as if with shadows : grow dark or gloomy ⟨his eyes ~*ed* with doubts —B.A. Williams⟩

3**shadow** \"\ *adj* [1*shadow*] **1** : SHADY **2** : having form without substance : DUMMY ⟨a ~ garrison⟩ ⟨the ~ government in exile⟩ **3 a** : having an indistinct pattern; *esp* : having patterns printed on the warp threads before weaving or having the warp threads twisted to produce faint stripes when woven ⟨~ prints⟩ **b** : having a darker section of design usu. in contrast to a sheer background — used esp. of needlework ⟨~ lace⟩ **4** : formulated or constructed in outline so as to be capable of quick completion when needed : inactive but ready to function immediately when the need arises ⟨a ~ factory⟩ ⟨~ army⟩

shadow band *n* : one of a series of darkish narrow parallel bands seen to rush swiftly across the landscape just before or after totality in a solar eclipse probably due to optical effects of the earth's atmosphere

shadow bird *n* : HAMMERKOP

shadow blue *n* : a variable color averaging a grayish blue that is redder and paler than electric, greener and duller than copenhagen, redder and deeper than Gobelin, and greener and deeper than old china

shadow box *n* **1** *or* **shadow box frame** : a shallow enclosing case usu. with a glass front in which something (as a painting, relief, or article of merchandise) is set for protection and display **2 a** : a device built in front of a screen used for daylight projection of motion pictures to shield it from the sun **b** : a partial enclosure on top and side of a screen of a microfilm reader protecting it from extraneous light

shadowbox \'==,=\ *vi* **1** : to box with an imaginary opponent esp. as a form of training **2** : to deal with an opponent cautiously usu. in order to avoid taking positive or decisive action

shadow cabinet *n* : a group of leaders of the parliamentary opposition who constitute the probable membership of the cabinet when their party is returned to power and who usu. are responsible for formulating party policy and for leading the opposition in parliamentary debate in the fields of their special competence ⟨resigned from Labour's *shadow cabinet*⟩

shadow–casting \'==,==\ *n* : the production of exaggerated contrast in electron microscopy by irradiating the specimen obliquely with a beam of gold atoms which makes opaque films on the slide in exact imitation of shadows

shadow cone *n* : UMBRA 3a ⟨the *shadow cone* of the moon⟩

shadow dance *n* : a dance shown by throwing the shadows of invisible performers or puppets on a screen

shad·ow·er \'shadəwə(r), -dōə-\ *n* -s : one that shadows

shadow figure *n* : SILHOUETTE

shad·ow·gram \'==,gram\ *n* : SKIAGRAM 2

shad·ow·graph \-,graf, -rȧf\ *n* **1** : SHADOW PLAY **2** : a photographic image resembling a shadow; *esp* : one made by means of X rays

shad·ow·graph·ic \¦==¦grafik\ *adj* : of or relating to shadowgraphs

shad·ow·graph·ist \'==,grafəst, -rȧf-\ *n* -s : an expert in or practitioner of shadowgraphy

shad·ow·graphy \-rafē\ *n* -ES : the making of shadowgraphs

shadow gray *n* : a brownish gray that is lighter and slightly redder than taupe, paler than chocolate, and redder and lighter than castor

shadow green *n* : a moderate yellow green that is paler than average moss green, yellower and paler than average pea green, and yellower and duller than apple green (sense 1)

shad·ow·i·ly \'shadəwəlē, dōə-, -li\ *adv* : in a shadowy manner : like a shadow ⟨~ visible through the murk⟩

shad·ow·i·ness \-dəw|ēnəs, -dō|, |in-\ *n* -ES : the quality or state of being shadowy ⟨the ~ of night⟩ ⟨that ~ . . . you find in people whose lives are part of the social organism —W.S. Maugham⟩

shadowing *n* -s **1** : the placing or distribution of shadow (as in a scene or painting) : SHADING **2** : a faint, obscure, or mystical representation ⟨in savage theology ~*s* . . . of the conception of a Supreme Deity —E.B.Tylor⟩

shadowland \'==,=\ *n* : the realm peopled by shadows or submerged in shadow: as **a** : the abode of spirits or phantoms **b** : OBSCURITY **c** : the domain of the unconscious

shad·ow·less \'shadōləs, -dəl-\ *adj* : having or casting no shadow

shadowlike \'==,=\ *adj* : SHADOWY

shadow line *n* **1** : the edge of the shadow of the gnomon of a sundial **2** : a thickened line in a linear drawing of an object supposed to be illuminated by parallel rays of light indicating the edges farthest from the source of light

shad·ow·ly \-dōlē, -dəl-, -li\ *adv* [1*shadow* + *-ly*] : as a shadow : OBSCURELY ⟨~ lit with indirect lighting —Chandler Brossard⟩

shadow of death [ME *shadwe of deeth*, trans. of LL *umbra mortis*, trans. of Heb *ṣalmāweth*] : deep darkness : GLOOM

shadow play *also* **shadow pantomime** *or* **shadow show** *n* : a drama exhibited by throwing the shadows of invisible puppets or sometimes of living actors on a screen

shadow roll *n* : a thick roll of sheepskin placed across the face of a pacing horse between eyes and nostrils so that he will not look down and be confused by shadows caused by his own movements

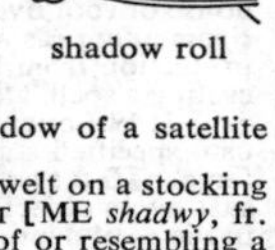

shadow roll

shadows *pl of* SHADOW, *pres 3d sing of* SHADOW

shadow stop *n* : the smallest aperture for use in making a halftone negative

shadow striping *n* : obscure striping that gives the effect of shadowing bolder stripes with which it is associated ⟨*shadow striping* in the pattern of a zebra⟩

shadow transit *n* : the passage of the shadow of a satellite across the disk of its primary

shadow welt *n* : a lightweight section of the welt on a stocking

1**shad·owy** \'shadəw|ē, -dō|, |i\ *adj* -ER/-EST [ME *shadwy*, fr. *shadwe* shadow + *-y*] **1 a** : of the nature of or resembling a shadow : FLEETING, IMAGINARY, UNSUBSTANTIAL ⟨dim, ~ forms —Bram Stoker⟩ ⟨strange fancies of unreal and ~ worlds —W.A.Butler †1848⟩ ⟨a ~ honor⟩ **b** *obs* : faintly representative : dimly embodying, representing, or foreboding : SYMBOLIC **c** : of or relating to the spirits of the dead : GHOSTLY, SPECTRAL ⟨from the river of death he recalls ~ ghosts —C.S.C. Bowen⟩ **d** : dim as a shadow : faintly perceptible : INDISTINCT VAGUE ⟨the ~ boundaries of a complex government —Edmund Burke⟩ ⟨her tender ~ voice —Elinor Wylie⟩ ⟨the ~ line between reason and faith —H.O.Taylor⟩ ⟨a ~ claim⟩ **2** : full of shade : protected from the sun : in or obscured by shadow ⟨deep ~ interiors⟩ ⟨~ cypress swamps —*Amer. Guide Series: N. C.*⟩ ⟨the wide nave and ~ aisles —Dorothy Sayers⟩ **3** : casting a shadow and affording shade ⟨a broad and ~ hat —Sir Walter Scott⟩

2**shadowy** \"\ *adv* : as a shadow : DIMLY ⟨in silver mail all ~ pale —Olive Custance⟩

shad porgy *n* : GRASS PORGY

shadrach \'sha,drak *sometimes* 'shā,d-\ *n* -s [after *Shadrach*, one of three loyal Hebrews who according to Dan 3:13–27 were unharmed when cast into a blazing furnace by order of King Nebuchadnezzar] : SALAMANDER 5

shads *pl of* SHAD

shad scale *n* : a scurfy grayish shrub (*Atriplex canescens*) of the western U. S. having a dense cluster of minute greenish flowers

shad tree *n* : JUNEBERRY 1

shad trout *n* : the common weakfish

shaduf *var of* SHADOOF

shady \'shādē, -di\ *adj* -ER/-EST [1*shade* + *-y*] **1** : producing or affording shade ⟨a ~ hat of natural straw —*Sydney (Australia) Bull.*⟩ ⟨naked trees whose ~ leaves are lost —Edmund Spenser⟩ **2** : sheltered from the glare or heat of the sun's rays : protected by shade : shaded from a source of heat or light : abounding in shade ⟨~ lawns and gardens —*Amer. Guide Series: N. C.*⟩ ⟨~ places⟩ **3** : DARK ⟨the ~ night —A.E.Housman⟩ ⟨her ~ hair —Thomas Hardy⟩ **4** : quiet so as to escape notice or detection — usu. used in the phrase *keep shady* ⟨keep ~ till we want you —Edward Eggleston⟩ **5 a** : equivocal in terms of merit or morality : of questionable merit : UNCERTAIN, UNRELIABLE ⟨what looks very well one way may look very ~ the other —R.S.Surtees⟩ **b** : better kept in darkness : unable to bear investigation : having a disreputable nature or character ⟨politician of large influence but ~ reputation —B.J.Hendrick⟩ ⟨the victim of various ~ speculations —Elinor Wylie⟩ — **on the shady side of** : on the afternoon side of : older than ⟨*on the shady side of* thirty —Washington Irving⟩

shaf·fle \'shafəl\ *vi* -ED/-ING/-S [perh. alter. of *shuffle*] **1** *dial Eng* : SHUFFLE **2** *dial Eng* : LOITER

sha·fi'i \'shafē,ē, 'shäf-\ *n* -s [after al-*Shafi'i* †A.D. 820 Arab scholar and religious leader] *usu cap* **1** : an orthodox school of Muslim jurisprudence predominating in southern Arabia and Indonesia — compare HANAFI, HANBALI, MALIKI **2** *or* **sha·fi·'ite** \-fē,īt\ [*shafi'ite* fr. al-*Shafi'i* + E *-ite*] : a follower of the Shafi'i school

1**shaft** \'shaft, -aa(ə)|, -ai|, -ȧ|\ *n, pl* **shafts** *see sense 1b* \|f(t)s *or, esp in sense 1b*, |vz\ [ME, fr. OE *sceaft*; akin to OHG *scaft* shaft, spear, ON *skapt* shaft, handle, L *scapus* shaft, stalk, *scopa* broom, Gk *skēptron* staff, Russ *shchepat'* to split — more at CAPON] **1 a** (1) : the long handle of a spear or similar weapon (2) : SPEAR, LANCE **b** *or pl* **shaves** \|vz\ : POLE; *specif* : either of two long pieces of wood between which a horse is hitched to a vehicle **c** (1) : an arrow esp. for a longbow — compare BOLT 1a (2) : the body or stem of an arrow extending from the nock to the head — see ARROW illustration **2 a** : a sharply delineated beam shining through an opening (as a window or a break in a cloud) ⟨~*s* of sunlight pouring through the 75-foot windows —*Amer. Guide Series: N. Y. City*⟩ **b** : a lightning bolt **3** : something suggestive of the shaft of a spear or arrow : a long slender esp. cylindrical part: as **a** : the stem of a tree : TRUNK ⟨straight pine ~*s*⟩ **b** : the body of a column : the cylindrical pillar between the capital and the base — see COLUMN illustration **c** : the part of a chimney above the roof **d** : the handle or helve of any of various tools or instruments (as a hammer, whip, pick, or golf club) — see GOLF illustration **e** : a bar that is commonly cylindrical and solid but sometimes hollow esp. when of large diameter and is used to support rotating pieces (as pulleys or flywheels) or to transmit power or motion by rotation — compare AXLE, FLEXIBLE SHAFT, SPINDLE **f** : the stem or midrib of a feather **g** : the narrowed basal part of any stalked structure **h** : the upright member of a cross; *esp* : the portion below the arms **i** : a rod at the end of the heddle of a loom; *also* : one of the series of harness frames on a loom — often used with a prefixed numeral in designating construction of cloth ⟨a 4-*shaft* twill⟩ **j** : the cylindrical part of a long bone between the enlarged ends **k** : a small architectural column (as one attached to a pier to support a vault rib or around a doorway or window) **l** : a column, obelisk, or other spire-shaped or columnar monument ⟨a marble ~ commemorates the battle —*Amer. Guide Series: Tenn.*⟩ **m** : the stem of a match **4** : any of various long hollow structures: as **a** (1) : a vertical or inclined opening of uniform and limited cross section made for finding or mining ore, raising water, or ventilating underground workings — compare ADIT (2) : a passage resembling a mine shaft in structure or function (as in a cave or a pyramid) **b** : the chamber of a blast furnace above the bosh **c** : a vertical opening or passage through the floors of a building ⟨air ~⟩ ⟨elevator ~⟩ **5 a** : a projectile (as a dart) thrown like a spear or shot like an arrow **b** : a scornful, satirical, or pithily critical remark : BARB ⟨directs ~*s* of ridicule against those who would keep the artist in isolation —L.L.Snyder⟩

2**shaft** *vb* -ED/-ING/-S *vt* **1** : to fit with a shaft **2** *slang* : to surprise by unfair or unexpectedly harsh treatment ⟨was really ~*ed* on that deal⟩ ~ *vi* : to emit or become emitted as a beam of light : BEAM ⟨sunlight ~*ed* through the dust —Donald Windham⟩

shaft eye *n* : a transverse hole in a shaft for a bolt or pin

shaft feather *n* : one of the two vanes of an arrow that run on the bow — compare COCK FEATHER

shaft furnace *n* : a furnace of upright form that is charged at the top and tapped at the bottom

shaft grave *or* **shaft tomb** *n* : PIT TOMB

shaft horsepower *n* : horsepower transmitted by an engine shaft : BRAKE HORSEPOWER

shaft house *n* : a structure erected at the top of a shaft to house hoisting machinery

shaft·ing \|ftiŋ, -tēŋ\ *n* -s **1 a** : shafts or material for shafts **b** : a system of connected shafts for communicating motion **2** : a lighter or darker coloring of the shaft of a feather (as of a domestic fowl) compared with that of the web

shaft key *n* : a key fitting in a shaft to secure an operating part fastened in or to the shaft

shaft kiln *n* : a kiln consisting of a steel shell with a vertical axis and a lining of firebrick

shaft·less \|f(t)ləs\ *adj* : having no shaft

shaft louse *n* : a biting louse (*Menopon gallinae*) that commonly infests domestic fowls

shaft·man \|f(t)mən\ *n, pl* **shaftmen** : one who sinks, inspects, or repairs mine shafts

1**shaft·ment** \|(t)mənt\ *n* -s [alter. (prob. influenced by *-ment*) of ME *shaftmond*, fr. OE *sceaftmund*, fr. *sceaft* shaft + *mund* hand — more at SHAFT, MANUAL] *archaic* : the distance from the tip of the extended thumb across the breadth of the palm used as a measure equivalent to about six inches : FISTMELE

2**shaftment** \"\ *n* -s [1*shaft* + *-ment*] : the part of an arrow on which the crest and feathers are placed

shaft–ring \'=,=\ *n* : a decorative annulet on the shaft of a column

shafts *pl of* SHAFT, *pres 3d sing of* SHAFT

shaft–straightener \'=,=(=)=\ *n* : ARROW STRAIGHTENER

shaft tunnel *or* **shaft alley** *n* : a narrow watertight compartment through which the propeller shaft of a ship passes from the after engine-room bulkhead to the stern tube

shaftway \'=,=\ *n* : SHAFT 4c

shafty \|ftē\ *adj* -ER/-EST **1** *of wool* : having a close compact free long strong staple **2** *of a feather* : having the shaft lighter or darker than the web

1**shag** \'shag, -aa(ə)-,-ai-\ *n* -s [fr. (assumed) ME *shagge*, fr. OE *sceacga*; akin to OE *scēon* to go quickly, happen, OHG *skehan* to befall, happen, ON *skegg* beard, *skaga* to project, OIr *scuchim* I depart, OSlav *skokŭ* leap; basic meaning: to jump, project] **1 a** : coarse matted wool, hair, or fiber ⟨the ~ of a woolly dog⟩ **b** : a matted or tangled mass of hair or fiber ⟨his great ~ of eyebrow —Eugene Walter⟩ **c** : long nap on cloth or felt ⟨~ rug⟩ **d** : a tangled or matted mass of bushes, trees, or foliage : THICKET **2 a** *archaic* : a worsted or silk cloth with a nap **b** : a shaggy garment or mat **3** : a strong coarse tobacco cut into fine shreds **4** : CORMORANT; *esp* : a European cormorant (*Phalacrocorax aristotelis*) that breeds in Great Britain — called also *green cormorant*

2**shag** \"\ *adj* : SHAGGY ⟨~ pony⟩

3**shag** \"\ *vb* **shagged; shagged; shagging; shags** *vi* : to fall or hang in shaggy masses ⟨a mean horse . . . with his head down a little and the mane *shagged* forward between the ears —R.P.Warren⟩ ~ *vt* : to make rough, jagged, or shaggy esp. by covering with shag or shaggy matter ⟨junipers *shagged* with ice —Wallace Stevens⟩ ⟨the long low wagons . . . returning in the evening *shagged* with hay —Virginia Woolf⟩

4**shag** \"\ *vt* [ME *shaggen* to toss about, prob. alter. of *shoggen* to jolt, shake — more at SHOG] *chiefly dial* : TOSS, PEG ⟨~ a stone across a pond⟩

5**shag** \"\ *n* -s [prob. short for 1*shagrag*] : RASCAL, BLACKGUARD

6**shag** \"\ *n* -s [prob. alter. of 1*shack*] : refuse barley or other grains

7**shag** \"\ *vt* **shagged; shagged; shagging; shags** [origin unknown] **1 a** : to chase after : chase away ⟨if another dog came in the yard he got *shagged* in a terrible hurry —P.D. Boles⟩ ⟨fields, where you *shagged* flies and slid home with the winning run —Irwin Shaw⟩ **b** : to run an errand after : FETCH **c** : FOLLOW; *specif* : to follow closely and push forward with harassment ⟨~ your crew in here —Allan Bruce⟩ **2** *slang* : to run after with intent to copulate

8**shag** \"\ *vi* **shagged; shagged; shagging; shags** [perh. alter. of 3*shack*] : to move along in a steady easy usu. slow gait : LOPE

9**shag** \"\ *n* -s [prob. fr. 8*shag*] : a dance step consisting of a lively hopping on each foot in turn

10**shag** \"\ *vi* **shagged; shagged; shagging; shags** : to dance the shag

shag·a·nap·pi \'shagə,napē, ,==¦==\ *n* -s [modif. of Cree *pishaganâbiy*, fr. *pishagan* what is flayed, hide + *âbii* cord] : a thread, cord, or thong of rawhide

shagbark \'=,=\ *n* [2*shag* + *bark*] **1 a** : SHAGBARK HICKORY **b** : a West Indian tree (*Pithecolobium micradenium*) having a contorted pod **2** : 1THRUSH 4

shagbark hickory *n* **1** : a tall straight erect forest tree (*Carya ovata*) that grows throughout the eastern and central U. S. chiefly in rich moist lowlands, is distinguished by a thick light gray bark which often curls back in large plates from the underlying structure, and yields a sweet edible somewhat aromatic nut — see TREE illustration **2** : a tough strong straight-grained light-colored wood yielded by the shagbark hickory and used esp. for implement handles

shag·gi·ly \'shagəlē, -aag-,-aig-, -li\ *adv* : in a shaggy manner

shag·gi·ness \-gēnəs, -gin-\ *n* -ES : the quality or state of being shaggy

shag·gy \-gē, -gi\ *adj* -ER/-EST [1*shag* + *-y*] **1 a** : covered with, possessing, or consisting of usu. long, coarse, or matted hair ⟨his face was ~ with a sprouting black beard —G.R.Stewart⟩ ⟨an extraordinary growth of ~ hair on his chest —Frank Sargeson⟩ **b** : covered with or consisting of thick, tangled, or unkempt vegetation ⟨cedar, spruce, pine, and balsam find a precarious foothold on the ~ cliffs —*Amer. Guide Series: Minn.*⟩ ⟨~ garden hedges —F.G.Turnbull⟩ **c** : having a rough nap, texture, or surface ⟨a ~, cream-colored sports coat —Raymond Chandler⟩ ⟨twisted, ~ tamarisk trees —Phyllis Pearsall⟩ **d** : having hairlike processes ⟨~ tongue⟩ **2 a** : unkempt or casual in appearance or action ⟨a sad, shabby, *shaggy*-looking lot —Peter Taylor⟩ **b** : RUDE, UNPOLISHED ⟨the rough ~ boy who had lived so much in the woods —S.V. Benét⟩ **c** : casually eccentric, vague, and individualistic **3** : confused and unclear in outline, conception, or thinking ⟨a young novelist . . . under the spell of . . . the *shaggier* manuals of psychoanalysis —Sinclair Lewis⟩ ⟨thoughts without words are vague and ~ —Carl Van Doren⟩

shaggy cap *n* : SHAGGYMANE

shaggy–dog story \'==¦=-\ *n* **1 a** : a long-drawn-out circumstantial story concerning an inconsequential happening that impresses the teller as humorous but the hearer as boresome and pointless **b** : a similar humorous story whose humor lies in the pointlessness or irrelevance of the punch line **2** : a humorous anecdote involving a talking animal (as a horse or dog)

shaggymane \'==,=\ *or* **shaggymane mushroom** *n* : a common edible mushroom (*Coprinus comatus*) having an elongated shaggy white pileus and black spores

shag hair *n* : a branched and often arborescent hair on a plant

sha·gia \shə'gēə\ *n, pl* **shagia** *or* **shagias** *usu cap* : a nomadic people of mixed Semitic origin inhabiting both sides of the Nile near the Third Cataract, speaking Arabic, and prob. descended from invaders from Arabia about the 7th century

shag·let \'shaglət\ *n* -s : a young cormorant

1**shag·rag** \'sha,grag, 'shaa,graa(ə)g, 'shai,graig\ *n* [alter. (prob. influenced by 2*shag*) of *shakerag*] **1** : a ragged or contemptible person **2** : RAGTAG 1 — used in the phrase *shagrag and bobtail*

2**shagrag** \"\ *adj, archaic* : SHAGGY, RAGGED, UNKEMPT

1**sha·green** \(')sha¦grēn, -aa¦g-, -ai¦g-, shə'g-\ *n* -s [by folk etymology (influence of 1*shag* and *green*) fr. F *chagrin*, fr. Turk *çagri*] **1** : an untanned leather prepared from the skins of horses, asses, camels, and other animals, covered with small round granulations by pressing small seeds into the grain or hair side when moist, scraping off the roughness when dry, and soaking to cause the compressed or indented portions of the skin to swell up into relief, and dyed a bright color usu. green **2** : the rough skin of various sharks and rays when covered with small close-set tubercles

2**shagreen** \"\ *or* **sha·greened** \-nd\ *adj* [*shagreen* fr. 1*shagreen*; *shagreened* fr. 1*shagreen* + *-ed*] : made of, covered with, or resembling the surface of shagreen

shags *pl of* SHAG, *pres 3d sing of* SHAG

shah \'shä, 'shō, 'shȧ\ *n* -s *often cap* [Per *shāh* king — more at CHECK] : the sovereign of Iran

sha·hap·ti·an \shə'haptēən\ *or* **sa·hap·tin** \sə'haptən\ *or* **sa·hap·ti·an** \-tēən\ *n, pl* **shahaptian** *or* **shahaptians** *or* **sahaptin** *or* **sahaptins** *or* **sahaptian** *or* **sahaptians** *usu cap* **1 a** : an Indian people of a large territory along the Columbia river and its tributaries in Oregon, Washington, and northern Idaho **b** : a member of such people **2** : the language of the Shahaptian people including Nez Percé and Yakima

sha·hara \shə'ha(a)rə, -härə\ *n, pl* **shahara** *or* **shaharas** *usu cap* **1** : a non-Arabic-speaking people inhabiting the region between Hadhramaut and Oman **2** : a member of the Shahara people

sha·ha·rith *or* **sha·ha·rit** *or* **sha·cha·rit** *or* **sha·cha·rith** \'shäkris\ *n* -s [Heb *shaḥărīth*] : the daily morning liturgy of the Jews — compare MAARIB, MINHAH, MUSAF

shah·dom \'shädəm, 'shȯd-, 'shȧd-\ *n* -s **1** : the state or territory ruled by a shah **2** : the rank or dignity of a shah

sha·hi *also* **sha·hee** *or* **cha·hi** \(')shä¦hē, (')shȯ¦-, (')shȧ¦-\ *n* -s [Per *shāhī*, fr. *shāhī* royal, fr. *shāh* king] : a former Persian unit of value equal to 1/20 silver kran; *also* : a corresponding coin of silver or copper or nickel

sha·hi·di \shä hēdē\ *n* -s *usu cap* [Hindi *shāhidī*, fr. Per, witness, testimony, fr. *shāhid* one who bears witness, fr. Ar] : AKALI

sha·hin *or* **sha·heen** \shä'hēn\ *n* -s [Per *shāhīn*, fr. *shāh* king] : an Indian falcon (*Falco peregrinus peregrinator*) having the underparts of a plain unbarred ferruginous color, being related to the peregrine falcon, and used in falconry

shah·ja·han·pur \¦shäjə¦hän,pu̇(ə)r\ *adj, usu cap* [fr. *Shahjahanpur*, city in northern India] : of or from the city of Shahjahanpur India : of the kind or style prevalent in Shahjahanpur

shah·za·da *or* **shah·za·dah** \¦shäzä¦dä\ *n* -s *often cap* [Hindi *shāh-zāda*, fr. Per, fr. *shāh* king + *zāda* son] : the son of a shah

shaikh *var of* SHEIKH

shaikh al–islam \¦shā,kalə¦släm, ¦shī,k-\ *or* **sheikh ul islam** \-kül-\ *n, usu cap S&I* [Ar *shaykh al-islām*] : the chief judge of any of various large Muslim cities; *esp* : the grand mufti of Constantinople

shai·khi *or* **shay·khi** \(')shī¦kē, (')shī¦-\ *n* -s *cap* [Ar *shaykhī*, fr. Shaikh Ahmad †1826 Shi'ite religious teacher] **1** : a Shi'ite sect emphasizing the mystical doctrine of a hidden imam as a living channel of communication **2** : a member of the Shaikhi sect

shai·tan *also* **shei·tan** \(')shā¦tän, (')shī¦-\ *n* -s [Ar *shayṭān*] : an evil spirit; *specif* : one of the rebellious jinn that lead men astray

shaiva *usu cap, var of* SAIVA

shakable *or* **shakeable** \'shākəbəl\ *adj* : capable of being shaken

sha·kal·sha \shə'kalshə\ *n, pl* **shakalsha** *or* **shakalshas** *usu cap* **1** : a people emigrating from Phrygia and colonizing Sicily in early times **2** : a member of the Shakalsha people

¹shake \ˈshāk\ *vb* **shook** \ˈshu̇k, *dial* ˈshək\ *or chiefly dial* **shaked** \ˈshākt\ *or dial* **shaken**; **shak·en** \ˈshākən\ *or chiefly dial* **shaked** *or* **shook**; **shaking**; **shakes** [ME *shaken,* fr. OE *sceacan;* akin to ON *skaka* to depart, ON *skaka* to shake, Skt *khajati* he churns, agitates, and prob. to ON *skaga* to project — more at SHAG] *vi* **1 :** to move to and fro : QUIVER, FLUTTER ⟨the long light ~*s* across the lakes —Alfred Tennyson⟩ ⟨sails *shaking* in the wind⟩ **2 :** to undergo vibration esp. as the result of a blow or shock ⟨the earth itself seemed to ~ beneath my feet —W.H.Hudson †1922⟩ ⟨felt the ship ~ and toss⟩ **3 a :** to tremble as a result of physical or emotional disturbance ⟨felt his heart *shaking* within him —Marguerite Young⟩ ⟨his voice *shook* and became shrill —Kenneth Roberts⟩ ⟨were *shaking* in their shoes⟩ **b :** to become convulsed with laughter **4 :** to experience a state of instability ⟨the economy was still *shaking* from the inflationary impact of the minimum wage decree —*Time*⟩ **5 :** to move something to and fro, up and down, or from side to side in a brisk manner esp. in order to bring about mixing ⟨~ well before using⟩ **6 :** to clasp hands ⟨agreed to ~ and be friends⟩ **7 :** TRILL **8 :** to form a crack by a separation between growth rings : SPLIT **9** *dial chiefly Brit* **:** FALL — usu. used of grain or fruit ~ *vt* **1 a :** to brandish, wave, or flourish often in a threatening manner ⟨people passing by . . . ~ their fists and curse —A.E. Housman⟩ ⟨the lightly clenched hand and fist *shaken* vigorously in the direction of the players concerned —Warwick Braithwaite⟩ **b :** to wave in farewell ⟨*shaking* her fingers playfully in the direction of the vehicle —W.M.Thackeray⟩ **2 a :** to cause to move in a quick jerky manner ⟨~ their heads like angry bulls —Goddard Lieberson⟩ ⟨rattling and *shaking* the latch —Dorothy C. Fisher⟩ **b :** to cause to be moved briskly in order to remove what adheres or is contained ⟨*shook* the dustcloth out the window⟩ ⟨*shook* the tree to get some apples⟩ **c :** to cause to be moved to and fro, up and down, or from side to side esp. in order to bring about mixing ⟨the vial is half filled and *shaken* vigorously —*Jour. of Economic Entomology*⟩ — often used with *up* **d :** to move (a part of the body) rhythmically in dancing ⟨resolved to ~ their heels . . . in jigs and Highland reels —David Grant⟩ **3 a :** to cause to quake, quiver, or vibrate ⟨the earthquake . . . *shook* all that coast —James Courage⟩ ⟨thunder that *shook* the tropical foliage —Allen Churchill⟩ ⟨the boom of a football rally ~*s* the night air —Corey Ford⟩ **b :** to cause to tremble ⟨a shudder *shook* the long emaciated frame —T.B.Costain⟩ ⟨toward afternoon another chill began to ~ her —Laura Krey⟩ **c :** to cause to become convulsed with laughter **4 a :** to take hold and move vigorously to and fro ⟨*shook* the boy until his teeth chattered⟩ ⟨*shook* him by the shoulder to wake him up⟩ **b :** WORRY 2 **5 a :** to free oneself from : cast off ⟨had *shaken* his bad habits and was firmly launched on his career —*Quick*⟩ ⟨have been disappointed so often that they cannot ~ their despair —M.H.Rubin⟩ — often used with *off* ⟨find it hard to ~ off these tentacles of organized crime —R.E.Merriam⟩ **b :** to get away from : get rid of ⟨can you ~ your friend? I want to talk to you alone —Elmer Davis⟩ ⟨the enemy gunboat has far too good a contact to be *shaken* so easily —E.L. Beach⟩ — often used with *off* ⟨there was no *shaking* off the press —Polly Adler⟩ **6 a :** to lessen the stability of : cause to waver : WEAKEN ⟨ignored any book that could ~ your faith —Virginia Woolf⟩ ⟨nothing that the emperor said or did could ~ him —Douglas Stewart⟩ **b :** to bring about an impairment of ⟨her mind had been *shaken* . . . by the cruelty of her husband —Mary H. Vorse⟩ **7 a :** to bring to a specified condition by or as if by repeated quick jerky movements ⟨the roads are so bad that we nearly get *shaken* to pieces —Rachel Henning⟩ ⟨*shook* his coat into place as he bent forward —Marguerite Steen⟩ **b :** to bring (oneself) to a specified state by or as if by a shake ⟨*shook* himself loose from the man's grasp⟩ **c :** to arouse (oneself) to or as if to activity ⟨~ thyself from the dust; arise —Isa 52:2 (AV)⟩ **8 a :** to distribute with or as if with a shake : SPRINKLE ⟨*shook* salt and pepper over the potatoes⟩ **b** *obs* **:** to cast down : SCATTER ⟨confounds thy fame as whirlwinds ~ fair buds —Shak.⟩ **9** *chiefly Austral* **:** ROB, STEAL **10 :** to dislodge or eject by or as if by quick jerky movements of the support or container ⟨~ the quarry from the limb —*Amer. Guide Series: Tenn.*⟩ ⟨*shook* the sand from his shoes⟩ **11 a :** to clasp (hands) in greeting or farewell or as a sign of good will or agreement **b :** GRASP ⟨*shook* him by the hand at parting —Joseph Addison⟩ **12 :** to stir the feelings of : UPSET ⟨the appalling nature of the disaster . . . *shook* her very much —Nevil Shute⟩ — often used with *up* ⟨you were all *shaken* up inside —R.H.Newman⟩ **13 :** TRILL ⟨~ a note in music⟩ **14 :** to cause a shake in (lumber) **15 a :** to separate the staves of (a cask) **b :** to disassemble (a cask) and bind into a shook

syn AGITATE, ROCK, CONVULSE: SHAKE means to move up and down or to and fro, usu. with sharp violence, or occas. to strike with jarring, unsettling impact ⟨as there is a high wind blowing nearly all the time, the nests are continually *shaken* to and fro —John Seago⟩ ⟨this social upheaval is *shaking* the underdeveloped parts of the world —A.H.Hansen⟩ AGITATE may suggest continued strong tossing or violent stirring or stirring up with commotion and disturbance ⟨the leaves on the trees were *agitated* as if by a high wind —W.H.Hudson †1922⟩ ⟨the water became *agitated* with the flapping of countless fins —Tom Marvel⟩ ⟨the physician interposes, frightens the family, *agitates* the patient to the utmost —H.A.Overstreet⟩ ROCK suggests a swinging back and forth, a violent swaying, or a violent impact bringing about or threatening a fall or collapse ⟨*rock* a child to sleep⟩ ⟨the road was rough and twisting, and the ambulance *rocked* a great deal —Fred Majdalany⟩ ⟨family life *rocked* with the rise in the divorce rate and the new liberty in sexual matters —Oscar Handlin⟩ CONVULSE suggests the violent, disturbed, wild motion of a spasm or paroxysm ⟨*convulsed* on the carpet in the paroxysms of an epileptic seizure —Thomas Hardy⟩ ⟨earthquakes *convulsing* the island⟩ ⟨*convulsed* with terror of hellfire —*Amer. Guide Series: Mass.*⟩ **syn** see in addition SWING

— **be shook on** *chiefly Austral* **:** to be infatuated with ⟨*was shook on* a big canecutter with more hair on his chest than a goat —D'Arcy Niland⟩ — **shake a leg 1 :** DANCE ⟨*shaking a leg* at junketings and fairs —Siegfried Sassoon⟩ **2 :** to hurry up : move quickly ⟨if you *shake a leg* and somebody doesn't get in ahead of you —John Dos Passos⟩ — **shake one's head :** to move the head from side to side esp. as an expression of disagreement, disapproval, or doubt

²shake \"\ *n* -S **1 :** an act of shaking: as **a :** an act of shaking hands ⟨welcomed the visitor with a hearty ~⟩ **b :** an act of shaking oneself ⟨now lapdogs give themselves the rousing ~ —Alexander Pope⟩ **2 a :** a blow or shock that upsets the equilibrium or disturbs the balance of something ⟨the rude ~*s* which science has given to . . . their cherished convictions —Herbert Spencer⟩ **b :** EARTHQUAKE **3 a :** nervous agitation resulting esp. from fear — usu. used in pl. ⟨I don't think I got over the ~*s* for two hours —Brad Sebstad⟩ **b :** a condition or disease accompanied by marked trembling — usu. used in pl. ⟨nobody has a hangover and . . . nobody has the ~*s* —Mary McCarthy⟩ **c shakes** *pl* **:** MALARIA 2a ⟨the ~*s* . . . supposed to be the result of a miasma emanating from the spring plowing of wild ground —Edna Ferber⟩ **d :** an attack of the shakes **4 :** something produced by or as if by shaking: as **a (1) :** a fissure or crack between and parallel to the annual rings of growth in timber usu. caused by wind or frost — compare CHECK 14a(1) **(2) :** a longitudinal crack in an archery bow **b :** a fissure in strata : a cleft in rock **c :** MILK SHAKE ⟨a chocolate ~⟩ **5 :** a wavering, quivering, or alternating motion caused by or as if by a blow or shock **6 :** TRILL **7 a :** a very brief period of time : INSTANT ⟨for a ~ they had stood there and looked at each other —Conrad Richter⟩ **b :** a unit of time used in nuclear physics and related fields that constitutes one hundredth of a microsecond **8 shakes** *pl* **:** one of importance or ability — usu. used in the phrase *no great shakes* ⟨no great ~*s* as a philosopher —Wanda Neff⟩ **9a (1) :** STAVE 2a **(2) :** SHOOK 1a **b :** a shingle split from a piece of log usu. three or four feet long **10 :** ³DEAL 2b ⟨the honest merchants who gave baffled marines a square ~ —L. M.Uris⟩ **11 :** DISMISSAL ⟨they all give him the cold ~ —Mark Twain⟩ **12 :** the mechanism that shakes the wet end of a fourdrinier paper machine sideways and thereby causes the fibers to felt together as they settle through the water **13** *Brit* **:** a slur or mackle in printing **14 :** BACKLASH **15 :** SHAKE CULTURE **16 a :** the distance between the fork and a roller in a watch while at the lock position **b :** the space between the lets off of an escape-wheel tooth and pallet stone in a watch while at the lock position **c :** the end play of arbors in a watch

shake·able *var of* SHAKABLE

shake–bag \ˈ=,=\ *n* **1** *archaic* **:** a cock turned out of a bag to fight **2** *archaic* **:** a rascally or roguish person

shake–bolt \ˈ=,=\ *n* **:** a bolt of timber used in making shakes

shake–cabin \ˈ=,==\ *n* [²*shake* (shingle) + *cabin*] **:** a cabin for temporary lodging

shake culture *n* **:** a deep culture of agar or gelatin through which the inoculum is evenly distributed by shaking before the medium is solidified and which is used chiefly for the demonstration of anaerobic colonies

shaked *chiefly dial past of* SHAKE

¹shakedown \ˈ=,=\ *n* -S [partly fr. the phrase *shake down;* partly fr. *shake down,* v.] **1 :** an improvised bed; *specif* **:** one made up on the floor **2 :** a boisterous dance **3 :** an act or instance of obtaining money in a dishonest or illegal manner; *esp* **:** EXTORTION ⟨an unparalleled opportunity for ~ and blackmail —Morris Ploscowe⟩ **4 :** a thorough search ⟨a ~ that didn't leave a tent fold unexplored —F.B.Gipson⟩ **5 :** an act or process of bringing to a more satisfactory state : ADJUSTMENT ⟨the economic ~ which the industry has experienced —*Financial World*⟩

²shakedown \"\ *adj* **:** designed to test a new ship or airplane under operating conditions and to familiarize the crew with it ⟨a ~ cruise⟩ ⟨~ flight⟩

shake down *vb* [¹*shake* + *down,* adv.] *vi* **1 a :** to take up temporary quarters ⟨a good plan for me to *shake down* in New York alone . . . before you join me —Margaret A. Barnes⟩ **b :** to occupy an improvised or hastily prepared bed ⟨had to be content to *shake down* with blankets in the inn parlor —B.L.K. Henderson⟩ **2 a :** to become accustomed or conditioned esp. to new surroundings or new duties ⟨four months . . . was long enough for a new man to *shake down* —Edwards Park⟩ **b :** to undergo a period of adjustment : settle down ⟨until the whole entertainment business *shakes down* and new patterns have been established —*Publishers' Weekly*⟩ **3 :** to become reduced ⟨the fighting *shook down* to a straight infantry battle —*Newsweek*⟩ ~ *vt* **1 :** to obtain money from in a dishonest or illegal manner (as under pretense of official authority or under promise of protection) ⟨impostors . . . *shook down* soldiers by pretending to arrest them —Dixon Wecter⟩ **2 :** to make a thorough search of ⟨decided to *shake down* the inmates to make sure nothing had been smuggled into the jail —*Police Detective*⟩ **3 :** to bring about a reduction of ⟨ordered . . . to *shake down* the hundreds of duplicating and overlapping service boards —*Time*⟩ **4 :** to test on a shakedown cruise ⟨the work . . . included training men and *shaking down* the ships for the Pacific theater —Walter Karig⟩

shake flask *n* **:** a culture flask (as for molds) in which the medium is kept uniform by constant agitation during incubation

shakefork \ˈ=,=\ *n* [ME *schakforke,* fr. *schaken, shaken* to shake + *forke* fork] **1** *chiefly dial* **:** a fork for shaking hay or straw **2 :** a heraldic ordinary or charge having the form of a Y with couped and pointed ends — compare PAIRLE

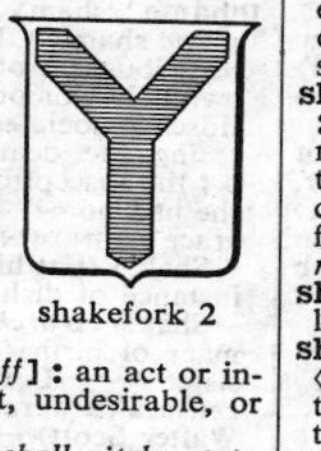
shakefork 2

shake–hand \ˈ=,=, =ˈ=\ *n* **:** a token payment consisting of goods or money given an African tribal landowner for the use of his land

shake–hands \ˈ=,=, =ˈ=\ *n pl but usu sing in constr* **:** HANDSHAKE

shaken [ME, fr. OE *scacen*] *dial past of* SHAKE, *past part of* SHAKE

shake–off \ˈ=,=\ *n* -S [fr. the phrase *shake off*] **:** an act or instance of getting rid of what is unpleasant, undesirable, or unwanted

shake off *vt* [¹*shake* + *off,* adv.] *of a baseball pitcher* **:** to express disagreement with (as a catcher's sign) by a negative gesture

shake out *vt* [ME *shaken out* to remove with or as if with a shake, fr. *shaken* to shake + *out,* adv.] **1 :** to let out with or as if with a shake ⟨took that whip from his saddle horn and *shook it out* —H.G.Evarts⟩ **2 :** to drive (weak speculators) from the market by increasing margin requirements or causing prices to move adversely

shake–out \ˈ=,=\ *n* -S [*shake out*] **1 :** an act or process of shaking out **2 a :** severe liquidation in a market at declining prices usu. with much forced or frightened selling **b :** a moderate slowing down of commercial and industrial activity and decrease in prices and employment after a protracted period of inflation **3 :** the removal of metal castings from a mold

shakeproof \ˈ=,=\ *adj* **:** capable of withstanding vibration

shak·er \ˈshākə(r)\ *n* -S [ME *schakare,* fr. *schaken, shaken* to shake + ME *-er, -ere, -are* -er] **1 a :** one that shakes ⟨thou mighty ~ of the earth —George Chapman⟩; *specif* **:** a worker who shakes things by hand or by machine to clean, separate, size, settle, loosen, or dry them **b :** any of various utensils or machines used in shaking: as **(1) :** a conveyor on which materials (as coal) are shaken to and fro by an eccentric or similar action **(2) :** a reciprocating rack in a thresher or combine that sifts grain and chaff from the straw **(3) :** a vibrating screen used in a distillery to clean grain; *also* **:** a similar screen used to separate spent beer into thick stillage and thin stillage **(4) :** a container with perforated top from which something (as salt) is shaken **(5) :** a utensil in which the ingredients of a mixed drink are prepared by shaking or stirring **2** *usu cap* **:** a member of any of several religious groups: as **a** [so called fr. a former practice of performing a dance with shaking movements as a part of worship] **:** a member of a communal and celibate religious body originating in England in the mid 18th century and brought to the U.S. in 1774, holding that God is both male and female, and stressing the obligation of living a simple and strict life under the guidance of the Holy Spirit **b :** a member of a Northwest Indian religious group founded in the late 19th century that combines traditional Christian beliefs with indigenous elements **3** *archaic* **:** FANTAIL 2a

shaker 1b(5)

shakerag \ˈ=,=\ *n* [¹*shake* + *rag,* n.] *archaic* **:** an unkempt disreputable person

shak·er·ess \ˈshākərəs\ *n* -ES *usu cap* **:** a Shaker woman

shak·er·ful \ˈshākə(r),fu̇l\ *n* -S **:** as much as a shaker will hold ⟨a ~ of salt⟩

shaker furniture *n, usu cap S* **:** wooden furniture made in the U. S. in the late 18th and early 19th centuries by the Shakers and characterized by simplicity and purity of design, sound construction, and complete practicality

shak·er·ism \ˈshākə,rizəm\ *n* -S *usu cap* **:** the beliefs and practices of the Shakers

shaker knit *adj* **:** coarse flat-knit

shaker tumbler *n* **:** a machine for untangling damp flat pieces of laundry and preparing them for ironing

shakes *pres 3d sing of* SHAKE, *pl of* SHAKE

¹shake·spear·ean *or* **shake·spear·ian** *also* **shak·sper·ean** *or* **shak·sper·ian** \(ˈ)shāk¦spirēən\ *adj, usu cap* [William *Shakespeare* (or *Shakspere*) †1616 Eng. dramatist and poet + E *-an*] **:** of, relating to, or having the characteristics of Shakespeare or his writings

²shakespearean *or* **shakespearian** *also* **shaksperean** *or* **shaksperian** \"\ *n* -S *usu cap* **:** an authority on or devotee of Shakespeare; *specif* **:** a specialist in the works of Shakespeare

shake·spear·eana *or* **shake·spear·iana** \(,)shāk,spirēˈanə, -ˈänə,-ˈānə *also* -ˈänə\ *n pl, usu cap* [William *Shakespeare* + E *-ana*] **:** collected items by, about, or relating to Shakespeare

shake·spear·ean·ize \ˈ=ˈ==ə,nīz\ *vt* -ED/-ING/-S *often cap* **:** to treat in the manner of Shakespeare

shakespearean sonnet *n, usu cap 1st S* **:** ENGLISH SONNET

shake up *vt* **1** *obs* **:** to denounce or chide vehemently ⟨go apart . . . and thou shalt hear how he will *shake* me *up* —Shak.⟩ **2 a :** to loosen with or as if with a shake ⟨*shook up* and arranged my pillows —Anne Marsh⟩ **b :** to arouse with or as if with a shake ⟨headed for the chart house to *shake up* the radar crew —K.M.Dodson⟩ **3 :** to jar by or as if by a physical shock ⟨the collision *shook up* the drivers of the two cars⟩ **4 :** HURRY — usu. used in the phrase *shake it up* ⟨*shake it up,* you fellows . . . we don't have all day —Ralph Ellison⟩ **5 :** to effect an extensive and often drastic rearrangement or reorganization of ⟨a trend that has *shaken up* the marketing notions of manufacturers —*Monsanto Mag.*⟩ ⟨the detective force was *shaken up* —Allan Nevins⟩

shake–up \ˈ=,=\ *n* -S [*shake up*] **1 :** MAKESHIFT; *specif* **:** a hastily constructed building **2 :** an act or instance of shaking up; *specif* **:** an extensive and often drastic rearrangement or reorganization ⟨is expected to result in personnel ~*s* in Soviet embassies —*N.Y.Times*⟩

shake wave *n* **:** a seismic disturbance in which the motion of particles is perpendicular to the direction of the wave's propagation — compare LOVE WAVE

shakh·ty \ˈshäktē\ *adj, usu cap* [fr. *Shakhty,* city in southwest U.S.S.R.] **:** of or from the city of Shakhty, U.S.S.R. **:** of the kind or style prevalent in Shakhty

shak·i·ly \ˈshākəlē, -li\ *adv* **:** in a shaky manner

shak·i·ness \-kēnəs, -kin-\ *n* -ES **:** the quality or state of being shaky

shaking *n* -S [ME, fr. gerund of *shaken* to shake] **1 :** something that is shaken down, out, or off — usu. used in pl. **2 shakings** *pl* **:** odds and ends of waste rope, canvas, and small stuff used esp. in making oakum

shaking chill *n* **:** a chill of severe degree

shaking grate *n* **:** a grate that can be shaken to drop ashes accumulated at the base of the bed of coals

shak·ing·ly *adv* **:** in a shaking manner

shaking palsy *n* **:** PARALYSIS AGITANS

shaking prairie *n* **:** a plain of delta land (as in Louisiana) with a soil of matted vegetable mold resting upon water, peat, or quicksands and vibrating to the tread

shaking quaker *n, usu cap S&Q* **:** SHAKER 2a

shaking table *n* **:** a table used for concentrating ores — compare WILFLEY TABLE

shako \ˈsha(,)kō, ˈshā(-, ˈshä(-\ *n, pl* **shakos** *or* **shakoes** [F *shako, schako,* fr. Hung *csákó,* prob. fr. G *zacke, zacken* peak, point, fr. MHG *zacke,* modif. of MLG *tacke* pointed instrument, sharp point — more at TACK] **:** a stiff military headdress with a metal plate in front, a high crown, and a plume

shako

shaksperean *or* **shaksperian** *usu cap, var of* SHAKESPEAREAN

shak·ta *or* **sak·ta** \ˈshäktə\ *n* -S *usu cap* [Skt *śākta* related to Shakti, fr. *Śakti*] **:** a worshiper of Shakti as a goddess

shak·ti *or* **sak·ti** \-tē\ *n* -S [Skt *śakti, Śakti,* fr. *śaknoti* he is strong, is able; akin to OIr *cēcht* power, Toch A *kākmart* lordship] **1 :** the creative energy of nature : life force **2** *usu cap* **:** the dynamic energy of a Hindu god (as Siva) personified as his female consort

shak·tism *or* **sak·tism** \-,tizəm\ *n* -S *usu cap* **:** a sect comprising the worshipers of Shakti under various names (as Kali, Durga) divided into a mother cult of devotion through contemplation and pure humble activity and a tantric cult with magical orgiastic rites involving the use of wine, meat, fish, grain, and sexual intercourse — called also respectively *right-hand Shaktism, left-hand Shaktism*

sha·ku \ˈshä(,)kü\ *n, pl* **shaku** [Jap] **:** a Japanese unit of length equal to 11.93 inches

shaky \ˈshākē, -ki\ *adj* -ER/-EST **1 :** characterized by shakes ⟨~ timber⟩ **2 a :** marked by insecurity or instability : likely to fall or be overthrown : PRECARIOUS ⟨extremism will wreck the present ~ center government —A.E.Stevenson b.1900⟩ ⟨the ~ market for cars and other durable goods —George Soule⟩ **b :** lacking in firmness of beliefs, principles, or allegiance : UNSETTLED ⟨this loyalty . . . does not become ~ or dubious as the years pass —D.F.Miller⟩ ⟨came to college with ~ religious foundations —W.J.Whalen⟩ **c :** lacking in authority, correctness, or reliability : QUESTIONABLE, UNTRUSTWORTHY ⟨studies . . . based on extremely ~ experimental methods —Martin Gardner⟩ ⟨was still ~ in English grammar —John Buchan⟩ ⟨in making such judgments . . . I am on ~ ground —S.L.Payne⟩ **3 a :** somewhat unsound in health ⟨am rather ~ just now —Charles Dickens⟩ **b :** characterized by shaking : TREMBLING, TREMULOUS ⟨lit a cigarette with ~ fingers —J.C.Powys⟩ ⟨a hoarse and ~ voice —Sinclair Lewis⟩ **4 :** easily shaken : likely to give way or break down : RICKETY ⟨a ~ chair⟩ **5 :** marked by or giving rise to jolting : BUMPY ⟨a ~ ride through the fields in a cart⟩

sha·lach mo·nos *or* **shalach ma·noth** \,shä,läkˈmō,nōs, -,nōs\ *n* [*shalach monos* fr. Yiddish *shlakh mones,* fr. Heb *mishlōaḥ mānōth* sending of portions; *shalach manoth* fr. NHeb *shālaḥ mānōth,* alter. of Heb *mishlōaḥ mānōth*] **1 :** the exchange of gifts or the sending of gifts to the poor at the time of the Purim festival **2 :** a Purim gift consisting typically of cakes, confections, fruit, wine, or money

sha·la·ko \shəˈlä(,)kō\ *n* -S *usu cap* [Zuñi] **1** *or* **shalako dancer :** one of the dancers impersonating a Zuñi mythical being of extraordinary stature **2 :** a Zuñi ceremony in which Shalakos play a central role and which celebrates the advent or departure of the kachinas

¹shale \ˈshāl, *esp before pause or consonant* -āəl\ *n* -S *often attrib* [ME, fr. OE *scalu, scealu* — more at SCALE] **1** *obs* **:** SHELL, HUSK **2** *dial chiefly Eng* **:** SCALE **3** *dial chiefly Eng* **:** a mesh of a net **4 :** a fissile rock that is formed by the consolidation of clay, mud, or silt, has a finely stratified or laminated structure parallel to the bedding, and is composed of minerals that have been essentially unaltered since deposition

²shale *vt* -ED/-ING/-S [ME *shalen,* fr. *shale,* n.] *obs* **:** to remove the shell from

³shale *same as* ¹SHALE\ *vi* -ED/-ING/-S [ME *schaylen*] *chiefly dial* **:** SHUFFLE

shale clay *n* **:** a clay produced by grinding shale and used for brick, tile, and pottery

shale green *n* **:** MALACHITE GREEN 3

shale naphtha *or* **shale spirit** *n* **:** naphtha obtained by refining shale oil

shale oil *n* **:** an oil obtained from oil shale by heating usu. in retorts **:** the crude dark green to brown oil from the first distillation that on refining yields liquid fuels and other useful products

shaley *var of* SHALY

shalier *comparative of* SHALY

shaliest *superlative of* SHALY

shall \shəl, (ˈ)shal\ *vb, past* **should** \shəd, (ˈ)shu̇d\ *or archaic 2d sing* **shouldst** \shəldzt, (ˈ)shu̇l, ldst, ltst\ *or* **should·est** \ˈshu̇dəst\ *pres sing & pl* **shall** *or archaic 2d sing* **shalt** \shəlt, (ˈ)shalt\ [ME *shal* owe, owes, ought to, must, am going to, is going to (1st & 3d sing. pres. indic., past *sholde*), fr. OE *sceal* owe, owes, ought to, must (past *sceolde*); akin to OHG *scal* owe, owes, ought to, must (infin. *scolan*), ON *skal* must (infin. *skulu*), Goth *skal* owe, owes, ought to, must, OE *scyld* debt, obligation, OHG *sculd,* ON *skuld,* Lith *skolà* debt] *verbal auxiliary* **1** *archaic* **a :** will have to : MUST ⟨he that parts us ~ bring a brand from heaven —Shak.⟩ **b :** will be able to : CAN ⟨how with this rage ~ beauty hold a plea —Shak.⟩ **2 a :** used to express a command or exhortation ⟨you ~ not kill —Exod 20:13 (RSV)⟩ ⟨ye ~ pray for the president of these United States —*Bk. of Com. Prayer*⟩ ⟨thou *shalt* let her go whither she will —Deut 21:14 (AV)⟩ **b —** used in laws, regulations, or directives to express what is mandatory ⟨a vessel when under way ~ carry at her stern a white light —*U.S.Code*⟩ ⟨it ~ be unlawful for any person to keep any wild animal in captivity —*Maine Hunting & Trapping Laws*⟩ **3 a —** used to express what is inevitable or what seems to be fated or decreed or likely to happen in the future ⟨cherubim and seraphim falling down before Thee, which wert and art and evermore ~ be —Reginald Heber⟩ ⟨those who can best bear taxation ~ have to do it —Francis Downing⟩ ⟨what-e'er be, don't let anyone bomb me —John Betjeman⟩ **b —** used to express simple futurity ⟨when ~ we three meet again —Shak.⟩ ⟨I ~ just put these papers together . . . and send them off by

the morning mail —A.J.Coutts⟩ ⟨even if you are too stingy to buy a guide book you ~ not remain uninstructed —Douglas Goldring⟩ ⟨~ you want to see me often —Arnold Bennett⟩ ⟨no young man believes he ~ ever die —William Hazlitt⟩ ⟨again ~ pleasure overflow thy cup with sweetness —Robert Bridges †1930⟩ ⟨~ he chat in an amiable way about things in general —Walter Goodman⟩ ⟨a brief story ~ suffice —C.H.Grandgent⟩ ⟨in the following chapter . . . the reader ~ be presented with examples —W.H.Mallock⟩ ⟨we have . . . agreed that they ~ publish their document and we ours —Sir Winston Churchill⟩ ⟨and all ~ come out right —John Galsworthy⟩ **4** — used to express determination ⟨one of the principal reasons why I have been against commercial gambling . . . and why I always ~ be —*New Republic*⟩ ⟨I came through and I ~ return —Douglas MacArthur⟩ ⟨the stone belongs to Scotland . . . we ~ get it back —Wendy Wood⟩ ⟨say what ye will I ~ deny no more —P.B.Shelley⟩ ⟨it ~ never break my heart I promise you —R.B.Sheridan⟩ **~ *vi*** : will go ⟨he to England ~ along with you —Shak.⟩

shal·lon \ˈshalən\ *n* -S [of AmerInd origin; akin to Chinook *-klkwšala* salal] **1** : SALAL **2** : the fruit of the salal

shal·loon \shəˈlün\ *n* -S [*Châlons*-sur-Marne, northeast France] : a lightweight twilled fabric of wool or worsted used chiefly for linings of coats and uniforms

shal·lop \ˈshaləp\ *n* -S [MF *chaloupe* — more at CHALOUPE] **1** : a usu. 2-masted ship with lugsails **2** : a small open boat propelled by oars or sails and used chiefly in shallow waters

shal·lot \shəˈlät, *usu* -äd.+V\ *n* -S [modif. of F *échalote*, fr. MF *eschalotte*, alter. of *eschaloigne*, fr. (assumed) VL *escalonia* — more at SCALLION] **1 a** : a bulbous perennial herb (*Allium ascalonicum*) that resembles an onion and produces small clustered bulbs used in seasoning **b** : GREEN ONION **2** : a thin metal tube in an organ reed pipe against which the reed or tongue is placed

¹shal·low \ˈsha(,)lō, -lə; -law, -lō+V\ *adj* -ER/-EST [ME *schalowe*; prob. akin to OE *sceald* shallow, Gk *skellein* to dry up — more at SKELETON] **1 a** : having little depth : not deep ⟨~ water⟩ ⟨a ~ dish⟩ ⟨~ wells⟩ ⟨a ~ grave⟩ ⟨~ valleys⟩ **b** *of soil* : forming a thin layer over rock **c** : departing from the horizontal by only a few degrees — used of an airplane dive, glide, or climb **2 a** : having little extension inward or backward ⟨the broad flight of ~ steps —Charles Dickens⟩ ⟨office buildings have taken the form of ~ slabs —Lewis Mumford⟩ ⟨a ~ bridgehead had been established —P.W. Thompson⟩ **b** *of a lens* : slightly convex or concave **3 a** : not penetrating farther than the easily or quickly apprehended : markedly obvious or apparent ⟨will not bare my soul to their ~ prying eyes —Oscar Wilde⟩ ⟨his short book is repetitious, untidy in form, ~ in characterization —Charles Lee⟩ ⟨offhand sayings, flippant judgments, and ~ generalizations —J.H.Newman⟩ **b** : lacking in depth of knowledge, thought, or feeling : SUPERFICIAL ⟨the general rule that specialists must be narrow and generalists ~ —W.B.Fagg⟩ ⟨a ~ demagogue who incited the mob —V.L.Parrington⟩ **4** *of musical tone* : lacking resonance : THIN **5** *of breathing* : displacing comparatively little air : WEAK

²shallow \"\ *vb* -ED/-ING/-S *vt* : to make shallow ⟨the slow current of the silt-laden water ~*ed* the canal —E.L.Sabin⟩ ~ *vi* : to become shallow ⟨the creek gully ~*ed* and widened —H.L.Davis⟩

³shallow \"\ *n* -S **1** : a shallow place or area in a body of water — usu. used in pl. but sometimes sing. in constr. ⟨wading in the rocky ~*s* of the river —Marcia Davenport⟩ ⟨the sloop . . . skimming a clear glass-green ~*s* —Nelson Hayes⟩ **2** : a low-crowned hat worn by men in the late 18th and early 19th centuries **3** *Brit* : a basket, tray, or cart used by street peddlers

⁴shallow \"\ *adv* : to or at a slight depth

shal·low·ish \ˈshaləwish, -lōi-\ *adj* : somewhat shallow

shal·low·ly *adv* : in a shallow manner

shal·low·ness *n* -ES : the quality or state of being shallow

shallow-pate \ˈ=(,)=,=\ *n, archaic* : a person of superficial intellectual achievements or abilities

sha·lu \ˈsha,lü\ *n* -S [Marathi *śāḷū*] : any of various grain sorghums usu. held to constitute a distinct variety (*Sorghum vulgare roxburghii*), introduced into the U.S. from India, and having slender dry stalks, large open pale yellow heads, and small hard seeds that are exposed at maturity

shalm *var of* SHAWM

sha·lom *or* **sho·lom** \shäˈlōm\ *interj* [Heb *shālōm* well-being, peace] — used as a Jewish greeting and farewell

shalom ale·chem *or* **shalom alei·chem** *or* **sholom alei·chem** \ˈshōləməˈläkəm\ *interj* [Heb *shālōm ʿalēkhem* peace unto you] — used as a traditional Jewish greeting

sha·losh seu·doth *or* **shalosh seu·dos** \ˈshä,lō(sh)ˈsü,dōt, -,dōs, ˈshälə(sh)ˈsüdəs\ *n* [Yiddish & LHeb; Yiddish *shalesh seudes*, fr. LHeb *shālōsh sĕʿūdhōth* 3 meals] : the 3d meal eaten on the Sabbath as ordained in the Talmud and usu. served as light refreshments accompanied by songs and ceremonies late in the afternoon following the minhah service in the synagogue

shalt *archaic pres 2d sing of* SHALL

shaltie \ˈshaltī, ˈshäl-\ *Scot var of* SHELTY

shaly *or* **shaley** \ˈshālē, -li\ *adj* **shalier; shaliest** [¹*shale* + *-y*] : of, containing, or resembling shale

¹sham \ˈsham, -aa(ə)m\ *n* -S [perh. fr. E dial. *sham* shame, alter. of E ¹*shame*] **1** : a trick that deludes : HOAX ⟨the so-called sale of stocks was a mere ~⟩ **2** : cheap falseness : HYPOCRISY, DECEITFULNESS ⟨saw through the hollowness, the ~, the silliness of the empty pageant —Oscar Wilde⟩ **3** : a decorative piece of cloth that is made to simulate an article of personal or household linen and is used in place of it or over it; *specif* : PILLOW SHAM **4** : a fraudulent imitation : a counterfeit purporting to be genuine ⟨has reduced national sovereignty to a ~ although it has left its outward symbols intact —Isaac Deutscher⟩ **5** : a person who shams **syn** see IMPOSTURE

²sham \"\ *vb* **shammed; shammed; shamming; shams** *vt* **1** *archaic* : TRICK, DECEIVE, CHEAT **2** : to put (as into a desirable position) by fraud ⟨*shammed* herself into favor at court⟩ **3** *obs* : to get rid of by fraud : pass off **4** : to go through the external motions necessary to counterfeit ⟨have *shammed* headache and have the garden all to myself —G.B.Shaw⟩ ~ *vi* **1** : to act intentionally so as to give a false impression : FAKE ⟨decided she was not sick but only *shamming*⟩ **2** : to pretend to be ⟨if you want me for a friend you must not ~ stupid —George Meredith⟩ **syn** see ASSUME — **sham abraham** *usu cap A* [*Abraham*, Biblical patriarch of the Jews; prob. fr. the use of the term *abraham-man* to denote a beggar feigning lunacy] : to feign sickness : MALINGER

³sham \"\ *adj* : marked by falseness: as **a** : not genuine ⟨the reaction of a terribly sincere spirit to something he believes to be ~ and sophisticated —Herbert Read⟩ ⟨fought ~ battles while waiting for the real thing⟩ ⟨~ pearls⟩ **b** : having such poor quality as to seem false : ADULTERATED ⟨~ tea, ~ jam, processed butter, gray bread scorched into toast —Wyndham Lewis⟩ **syn** see COUNTERFEIT

sha·ma \ˈshämə\ *n* -S [Hindi *śāmā*] : an Indian thrush (*Copsychus malabaricus*) that is noted for its song

sha·mal *or* **shi·mal** \shəˈmäl\ *n* -S [Ar *shamāl, shimāl*] : a northwesterly wind of Iraq and the Persian gulf

sha·ma millet \ˈshämə-\ *n* [Hindi *sāmā*, *sāmā*, fr. Skt *śyāmāka* millet] : a tropical Asiatic grass (*Echinochloa colona*) whose seeds are used as food in India

¹sha·man \ˈshämən, ˈshā-, ˈsha-, ˈshȧ-, shəˈmän, -əˈmȧn\ *n* -S [Russ or Tungus; Russ, fr. Tungus *šaman* shaman, Buddhist monk, fr. Pali *samana* Buddhist monk, fr. Skt *śramaṇa* Buddhist monk, ascetic, fr. *śrama* fatigue, exertion, religious exercise — more at ASHRAM] : a priest-doctor who uses magic to cure the sick, to divine the hidden, and to control events that affect the welfare of the people

²shaman \"\ *adj* : SHAMANISTIC

sha·man·ic \shəˈmanik, -män-, -mȧn\ *adj* : SHAMANISTIC

sha·man·ism \ˈshämə,nizəm, ˈshā-, ˈsha-\ *n* -S **1** : a religion of the Ural-Altaic peoples of northern Asia and Europe that is characterized by the belief that the unseen world of gods, demons, and ancestral spirits is responsive only to the shamans **2** : religious practices similar to the shamanism of the Ural-Altaic peoples of northern Asia and Europe followed esp. among Indians of No. America and characterized by use of the mediumistic trance

sha·man·ist \-nəst\ *n* -S : one who believes in or practices shamanism

sha·man·is·tic \ˌ==ˈristik, -tēk\ *or* **shamanist** *adj* : of, relating to, or characteristic of shamanism or shamanists

shamanistic dance *n* : a frenzied trance dance that is the climax of a shaman's ritual for cure or divination

sha·man·ize \ˈ==,nīz\ *vi* -ED/-ING/-S : to perform the functions of a shaman

shamas *or* **shamash** *var of* SHAMMASH

sham·ba \ˈshämbə\ *n* -S [Swahili, plantation] **1** *Africa* : a piece of ground under cultivation : GARDEN **2** *Africa* : PLANTATION

sham·ba·la \shämˈbälə\ *n, pl* **shambala** *or* **shambalas** *usu cap* **1 a** : a Bantu people of eastern Tanganyika **b** : a member of such people **2** : the language of the Shambala people

¹sham·ble \ˈshambəl, -aam-\ *vt* -ED/-ING/-S [fr. *shambles*] : SLAUGHTER

²shamble \"\ *adj* [fr. obs. E *shamble* table for the exhibition of meat for sale, fr. ME *shamel*; fr. the use of the expression *shamble legs* to refer to a person's legs resembling those of such a table] : BOWED, MALFORMED ⟨hobbled along on his ~ legs⟩

³shamble \"\ *vi* **shambled; shambled; shambling** \-b(ə)liŋ\ **shambles** **1** : to walk awkwardly with dragging feet : SHUFFLE **2** : to move awkwardly ⟨a crab *shambled* across the uneven bottom of the pool⟩ ⟨exercised a style that *shambled* and wobbled self-consciously in a welter of qualifications —Van Wyck Brooks⟩

⁴shamble \"\ *n* -S [³*shamble*] : a shambling gait

sham·bles \-lz\ *n pl but usu sing in constr, also* **shamble** [*shambles* fr. pl. of *shamble* meat market (also obs. E *shamble* table for the exhibition of meat for sale), fr. ME *shamel* table for the exhibition of meat for sale, shop counter, footstool, fr. OE *scamul, sceamul* money changer's table, stool; akin to MD *schamel* footstool, OHG *scamal*; all fr. a prehistoric WGmc word borrowed fr. (assumed) VL *scamellus* small bench, dim. of L *scamnum* bench, stool; akin to Skt *skabhnoti* he supports] **1** *archaic* : a meat market **2** : SLAUGHTERHOUSE **3 a** : a place of mass slaughter or bloodshed ⟨the bridge instantly became a ~, every officer and man on that key position being either killed or wounded —Russell Grenfell⟩ **b** (1) : a scene of great destruction ⟨the imposing entrance . . . is a ~ and inside the quadrangle the great aula is demolished from a direct bomb hit —J.G.Gray⟩ (2) : the result of great destruction : WRECKAGE, WRECK ⟨have not cleaned up the ~ of bombing —Ruth Benedict⟩ ⟨this buxom ball of fire makes a ~ of decorum —Irving Kolodin⟩ (3) : the state of being wrecked ⟨the bombers left the city in ~⟩ **c** (1) : a scene of great disorder ⟨the apartment became a ~ —S.J.Perelman⟩ ⟨conference this year was an utter ~ chaired by an elderly lawyer who apparently could neither speak nor hear —A.F.Buchan⟩ (2) : great confusion : MESS ⟨their ideals are vanity and illusion and their pretended moralities a ~ —Irwin Edman⟩

shambling *adj* [fr. pres. part. of ³*shamble*] : characterized by slow awkward movement ⟨a ~ village in which little happened⟩

sham·bling·ly *adv* : in a shambling manner

¹shame \ˈshām\ *n* -S [ME, fr. OE *scamu, sceamu*; akin to OHG *scama* shame, ON *skömm*] **1 a** : a painful emotion caused by consciousness of guilt, shortcoming, or impropriety in one's own behavior or position or in the behavior or position of a closely associated person or group ⟨she felt no ~, no remorse, seeing the death as purely accidental —Arnold Bennett⟩ **b** : the susceptibility to such emotion ⟨was not upset because she had no ~⟩ **2 a** (1) : the condition of one that is in disgrace : IGNOMINY ⟨free from these slanders and this open ~ —Shak.⟩ ⟨put his father to ~ by his dishonest acts⟩ (2) : an instance of dishonor ⟨let his ~*s* quickly drive him to Rome —Shak.⟩ **b** *archaic* : dishonor from loss of chastity or illegitimacy of birth ⟨every woe a tear can claim except an erring sister's ~ —Lord Byron⟩ **3 a** : something worthy of strong censure ⟨it were ~ to our profession were we to suffer it —Sir Walter Scott⟩ — often used interjectionally ⟨interrupted the speech by calling out ~⟩ **b** : a cause of feeling shame ⟨put out of human reach to be a warning and a ~ —Sacheverell Sitwell⟩ **c** *archaic* : the external genitalia **syn** see DISHONOR — **in shame of** *prep, obs* : in order to bring shame upon ⟨the gods do this in *shame of* cowardice —Shak.⟩

²shame \"\ *vb* -ED/-ING/-S [ME *shamen*, fr. OE *scamian*; akin to MD *schamen* to feel shame, be ashamed, OHG *scamōn*; denominative fr. the root of OE *scamu, sceamu*, n.] *vi, chiefly dial* : to feel shame ⟨I do ~ to think of it —Shak.⟩ ~ *vt* **1** : to bring shame to : cover with contempt : DISHONOR, DISGRACE ⟨public opinion tolerant to a degree which ~*s* the prejudice of other peoples —W.C.Brownell⟩ **2** *archaic* : to shun from shame ⟨she *shamed* his fond embrace —Robert Bridges †1930⟩ **3** : to put to shame by outrivaling ⟨the urge to self-preservation among politicians ~*s* that among the beasts of jungle and tundra —R.L.Neuberger⟩ **4** : to cause to feel shame : make ashamed ⟨his father had *shamed* him for playing with dolls —John Dollard⟩ **5** : to force by shame ⟨*shamed* him into action by running the gauntlet of the forts in his own small vessel —*Amer. Guide Series: La.*⟩ — **shame the devil** : to tell the truth

shamed *adj* **1** : ASHAMED ⟨was rather ~ to be traveling first-class in front of them all —Bruce Marshall⟩ **2** : marked by shame ⟨made a ~ supplicating gesture —Harriet La Barre⟩

shamed·ly \ˈshām(ə)dlē, -li\ *adv* : in a shamed manner

shameface \ˈ=,=\ *n* [back-formation fr. *shamefaced*] **1** : a shamefaced aspect **2** : a wild geranium (*Geranium maculatum*) of eastern No. America

shame·faced \ˈshām¦fāst\ *adj* [alter. (influenced by *faced*) of *shamefast*] **1** : marked by modesty : BASHFUL ⟨cheerfully bearing reproaches but ~ at praise —H.O.Taylor⟩ **2** : marked by shame : ASHAMED ⟨the weary, hangdog, and ~ air of the retreating enemy —Eric Linklater⟩ — **shame·faced·ly** \-¦fāsədlē, -fāstlē, -li\ *adv* — **shame·faced·ness** \-nəs\ *n* -ES

shamefaced crab *n* : BOX CRAB

shame·fast \ˈ=,fast\ *adj* [ME, fr. OE *scamfæst*, fr. *scamu, sceamu* shame + *fæst* firmly fixed — more at SHAME, FAST] : SHAMEFACED — **shame·fast·ly** *adv* — **shame·fast·ness** *n* -ES

shame·ful \ˈshāmfəl\ *adj* [ME, bringing shame, modest, fr. OE *scamful* modest, fr. *scamu, sceamu* shame + *-ful*] **1 a** : bringing shame : injurious to reputation : DISGRACEFUL ⟨the wicked rascally ~ conduct of the bankrupt —W.M.Thackeray⟩ **b** : arousing the feeling of shame : INDECENT ⟨that indecent exposure of teeth that became even more ~ when one realized the teeth were his own —Douglas Woolf⟩ **2** *archaic* : full of the feeling of shame : ASHAMED ⟨one of the most penitent and ~ offenders —John Keble⟩ — **shame·ful·ly** \-fəlē, -li\ *adv* — **shame·ful·ness** \-fəlnəs\ *n* -ES

shame·less \ˈ=ləs\ *adj* [ME *shameles*, fr. OE *scamlēas*, fr. *scamu, sceamu* shame + *-lēas* -less] **1** : devoid of shame : insensible to disgrace : UNSCRUPULOUS ⟨fiend and ~ courtesan —Shak.⟩ ⟨a ~ exploiter of the native workmen⟩ **2** : showing lack of shame on the part of the agent : DISGRACEFUL ⟨a ~ betrayal of principle —Rebecca West⟩ ⟨there was something ~ and indecent about not singing true —Willa Cather⟩

syn SHAMELESS, BRAZEN, BAREFACED, BRASH, and IMPUDENT, applying in common to persons or acts that defy the accepted moral of social code, mean, in this application, bold or lacking a sense of shame. SHAMELESS implies a lack in modesty, decency, respect for others, or so on ⟨makes such *shameless* use of patriotic feelings to advertise his product —Virgil Thomson⟩ ⟨a *shameless* display of arrogance⟩ ⟨a *shameless* and brutal treatment of relatives⟩ BRAZEN adds to *shameless* the idea of hardness and insolence ⟨hip movements and more or less *brazen* imitations of the sexual embrace —Samuel Putnam⟩ ⟨solicited praise and power with the *brazen*, businesslike air of a streetwalker on the prowl for clients —R.H.Rovere⟩ BAREFACED suggests an extreme and brazen effrontery ⟨the whole deal was a *barefaced* double cross —*Time*⟩ ⟨as *barefaced* a swindle —Arnold Bennett⟩ ⟨a *barefaced* lie⟩ BRASH stresses rather a heedlessness, implying a shamelessness that is largely callowness ⟨not like the other girls who were boisterous and *brash*, liking to walk loudly in their high heels across the drug store's tiled floor —Jean Stafford⟩ ⟨an all-too-intimate revue, it bawls out *brash* ditties, features loud-colored, low-cut skits, winks its eye and wiggles its hips —*Time*⟩ ⟨*brash* college graduates of recent vintage who claimed to know almost everything —R.F.Schols⟩ IMPUDENT, now rare in this sense, implies bold and cocky defiance of modesty or decency ⟨conduct so sordidly unladylike that even the most *impudent* woman would not dare do it openly —G.B.Shaw⟩

shame·less·ly *adv* : in a shameless manner

shame·less·ness *n* -ES : the quality or state of being shameless

¹shames *pl of* SHAME, *pres 3d sing of* SHAME

²shames *var of* SHAMMASH

shame vine *or* **shame brier** *n* : SENSITIVE BRIER

sham-feed \ˈ=,=\ *vt* : to give food to (an experimental animal) and recover it (as from a gastric fistula) before it has been wholly altered by digestive processes

sha·mi·a·na *or* **sha·mi·a·nah** \,shämēˈänə\ *n* -S [Hindi *shāmiyāna*, fr. Per *shāmyānah*] *India* : a cloth canopy

sham·ing·ly *adv* [*shaming* (pres. part. of ²*shame*) + *-ly*] : in a shameful or disgraceful manner

sha·mir \shəˈmi(ə)r, ˈshä,m-\ *n* -S [Heb *shāmīr*] **1** : a very hard precious stone believed to have been used in building Solomon's temple **2** : a tiny worm believed capable of splitting the hardest stone

shamisen *var of* SAMISEN

sham·ma·ite \ˈshamə,īt\ *n* -S *usu cap* [*Shammai*, 1st cent. B.C. Jewish teacher + E *-ite*] : an adherent of the rigorous and often literal interpretation of the Jewish law taught by Shammai as opposed to the more liberal interpretation of the contemporary Hillelites

sham·mar \ˈshämär\ *n, pl* **shammar** *or* **shammars** *usu cap* **1** : a bedouin nomadic people of Arabia **2** : a member of the Shammar people

sham·mash *or* **sha·mash** *or* **sham·mas** *or* **sha·mas** *or* **sham·mes** *or* **sha·mes** *or* **sham·mos** *or* **sha·mus** \ˈshäməs\ *n, pl* **sham·ma·shim** *or* **sha·ma·shim** *or* **sham·ma·sim** *or* **sha·ma·sim** *or* **sham·mo·sim** *or* **sha·mo·sim** \shäˈmōsəm, -sēm\ [Yiddish & MHeb; Yiddish *shames*, fr. MHeb *shammāsh*, fr. Aram *shĕmmāsh* to serve] **1** : the sexton of a synagogue **2** : the candle or taper used to light the other candles in a Hanukkah menorah

shammed *past of* SHAM

sham·mer \ˈshamə(r)\ *n* -S : one that shams

shamming *pres part of* SHAM

sham·mock \ˈshamək\ *vi* -ED/-ING/-S [perh. alter. of ³*shamble*] *chiefly dial* : to go around idly : LOAF, DAWDLE, SLOUCH

¹shammy *or* **shamoy** *var of* CHAMOIS

²sham·my \ˈshamē, -mi\ *n* -ES : a chamois bag used by Australian miners as a container for gold dust

¹sham·poo \(ˈ)sham¦pü\ *vt* -ED/-ING/-S [Hindi *cāpo*, imper. of *cāpnā* to press, knead, shampoo] **1** *archaic* : MASSAGE **2 a** : to wash (the hair and scalp) with soap and water or a specially prepared shampoo **b** : to wash the hair of (a person) **c** : to wash or clean (as a rug or upholstery) with soap and water or with a dry-cleaning preparation

²shampoo \"\ *n* -S **1** : an act or instance of shampooing **2** : a preparation (as a soap solution, dry powder, or chemical solvent) used in shampooing

sham·poo·er \-üə(r)\ *n* -S : one that shampoos; *specif* : a hairdresser who washes hair

sham·rock \ˈsham,räk *sometimes* -,rək\ *n* -S [IrGael *seamrōg*, dim. of *seamar* trefoil, clover, honeysuckle] **1** : any of several trifoliolate plants used as a floral emblem of the Irish: as **a** : a hop clover (*Trifolium dubium*) occurring naturally in Ireland and often regarded as the true or original shamrock **b** : a wood sorrel (*Oxalis acetosella*) **c** : WHITE CLOVER **a d** : BLACK MEDIC **2** *or* **shamrock green** : a strong yellowish green that is greener and darker than Cyprus green and lighter, stronger, and slightly yellower than emerald (sense 2b)

shamrock pea *n* : a trailing trifoliolate Asiatic and African herb (*Parochetus communis*) of the family Leguminosae having inconspicuous pale purple cleistogamous flowers

shams *pl of* SHAM, *pres 3d sing of* SHAM

¹shamus *var of* SHAMMASH

²sha·mus \ˈshäməs, ˈshā-\ *n* -ES [prob. fr. ¹*shamus*; prob. fr. a jocular suggestion of similarity between the duties of a sexton and those of a house detective in a department store] **1** *slang* : POLICEMAN **2** *slang* : PRIVATE DETECTIVE

shan \ˈshän, ˈshan\ *n, pl* **shan** *or* **shans** *usu cap* **1 a** : a group of Mongoloid peoples of the Tai stock of southern China, Assam, Burma, and Thailand who vary in civilization from savagery to a Buddhistic culture equal to that of the Thai **b** : a member of such people **2** : the Thai language of the Shan people

shan·a·chie \ˈshanə¦kē\ *n* -S [IrGael *seanchaidhe* antiquary, historian] *Irish* : a teller of old tales or legends

¹shan·de·an *also* **shan·de·ian** \ˈshandēən, =ˈ==\ *or* **shan·dy·an** \ˈshandēən\ *adj, usu cap* [*shandean, shandyan* fr. *Tristram Shandy* (1760–67), novel by Laurence Sterne †1768 Brit. novelist + E *-an*; *shandeian* irreg. fr. *Tristram Shandy* + E *-an*] : of, relating to, or characteristic of *Tristram Shandy* by Laurence Sterne

²shandean *also* **shandeian** \"\ *or* **shandyan** \"\ *n* -S *usu cap* : one who has the spirit of *Tristram Shandy*

shan·de·ism *also* **shan·dy·ism** \ˈshandē,izəm\ *n* -S *usu cap* [*shandeism* irreg. fr. *Tristram Shandy* + E *-ism*; *shandyism* fr. *Tristram Shandy* + E *-ism*] : the philosophy of *Tristram Shandy*

shand·ite \ˈshan,dīt\ *n* -S [James S. *Shand* †1957 Brit. geologist + E *-ite*] : a mineral $Ni_3Pb_2S_2$ consisting of sulfide of nickel and lead and occurring in rhombohedral crystals near Trial Harbour, Tasmania

shan·dry \ˈshandrē\ *n* -ES [origin unknown] : a light carriage on springs

shan·dry·dan \-drē,dan\ *also* **shan·dra·dan** \-drə,-\ *n* -S [origin unknown] **1** : a chaise with a hood **2** : a rickety vehicle ⟨saw a car moving up the road, not a decayed ~ like the other, but a new and powerful car —John Buchan⟩

¹shan·dy \ˈshandē\ *adj* [origin unknown] *dial chiefly Eng* : wild and inclined to irresponsible ideas

²shandy \"\ *n* -ES [short for *shandygaff*] **1** : SHANDYGAFF **2** : a drink consisting of lemonade and light ale

shan·dy·gaff \-,gaf\ *n* -S [origin unknown] : a drink consisting of beer and ginger beer or ginger ale

shang \ˈshäŋ\ *adj, usu cap* [*Shang*, Chin. dynasty (1766–1122 B.C.)] : of, relating to, or having the characteristics of the period of the Shang dynasty

shan·gal·la \shäŋˈgälə\ *or* **shan·kal·la** \-ˈkälə\ *n, pl* **shangalla** *or* **shangallas** *or* **shankalla** *or* **shankallas** *usu cap* [Amharic *khāngellā* Negro] **1** : any of the peoples living in western Ethiopia and in the eastern part of the Republic of the Sudan that are not of Ethiopian or of Arab origin **2** : a member of any of the Shangalla peoples

shan·gan \ˈshaŋən\ *n* -S [ScGael *seangan*] *chiefly Scot* : a cleft stick to fasten to the tail of a dog

¹shang·hai \(ˈ)shaŋ¦hī, -aiŋ(¦)-\ *adj, usu cap* [fr. *Shanghai*, China] : of or from the city of Shanghai, China : of the kind or style prevalent in Shanghai

²shanghai \"\ *n* -S *usu cap* : a tall long-legged red and black domestic fowl held to have been imported from the Orient

³shanghai \"\ *vt* **shanghaied; shanghaied; shanghaiing; shanghais** [fr. *Shanghai*, China; fr. the formerly widespread use of unscrupulous means to procure sailors for voyages to the Orient] **1 a** : to put aboard a ship by force often with the help of liquor or a drug ⟨was notorious as a hell ship whose sailors were usually ~*ed* —*Amer. Guide Series: Wash.*⟩ **b** : to put by force or a threat of force into or as if into a place of detention ⟨prisoners of war, ~*ed* laborers, forcibly displaced people and other uprooted men —*Jour. Amer. Med. Assoc.*⟩ ⟨~*ed* by a white slaver while on her way home from choir practice —Polly Adler⟩ **2** : to put by trickery into an undesirable position ⟨no other agent in this patriotic traffic has ~*ed* more unwary industrialists —E.J.Kahn⟩ — **shanghai·er** \-hī(ə)r, -īə\ *n* -S

⁴shanghai \"\ *n* -S [perh. alter. (influenced by *Shanghai*, China) of *shangan*] *Austral* : SLINGSHOT

shang·hai·land·er \=ˈ=ləndə(r)\ *n* -S *cap* [*Shanghai*, China + E *-lander* (as in *highlander*)] : a native or resident of Shanghai, China

shan·go \shäŋˈgō\ *adj, often cap* [fr. *Shango*, Yoruba god of thunder and fertility] : of or relating to the worship of Shango by the Yoruba people and by Negroes in Brazil and Trinidad

shan·gri-la \ˈshaŋgrē¦lä, -aiŋ-, -rə¦-, -lȧ\ *n* -S *usu cap S & often cap L* [fr. *Shangri-La*, imaginary mountain land depicted as a utopia in the novel *Lost Horizon* (1933) by James Hilton †1954 Eng. novelist] **1** : a remote beautiful imaginary place

where life approaches perfection : UTOPIA **2 a** : a remote usu. beautiful and delightful place ⟨by those familiar with these *Shangri-las* of the Atlantic coast its locale is readily identifiable —J.D.Adams⟩ **b** : a place whose name is not known or not given ⟨will fly in huge flocks from 100 unnameable *Shangri-las* to destinations which the Axis wishes it could guess —*Science News Letter*⟩

shan-jen \ˈshänˈrən\ *n, pl* **shan-jen** *or* **shan-jens** *usu cap* S&J [Chin (Pek) *shan*[1] *jen*[2], fr. *shan*[1] mountain, hill + *jen*[2] man, person, people] : any of several hill tribes (as the Lisu, the Chingpaw, or the Lashi) generally of Tibeto-Burman stock of the west Yunnan frontier region

¹shank \ˈshaŋk, -aiŋk-\ *n* -s [ME *shanke*, fr. OE *scanca*; akin to MLG *schenke* leg, shank, Sw *skank* leg, shank, ON *skakkr* crooked, askew, Gk *skazein* to limp, and perh. Skt *sakthi* thigh] **1 a** : the lower part of the leg: (1) : the part between the knee and the ankle in man (2) : the corresponding part in various other vertebrates; *specif* : the part between the fetlock and the joint above (3) : TARSOMETATARSUS (4) : TIBIA **b** : the entire leg in man ⟨sat down to rest his weary ~s⟩ **c** : a cut of beef, veal, mutton, or lamb from the upper or the lower part of the leg : SHIN — see BEEF illustration, LAMB illustration **d** : the part of a hide that comes from the leg of an animal **2 a** : a straight narrow usu. essential part of an object: as **a** : the straight part of a nail or pin **b** : a straight part of a plant : STEM, STALK; *specif* : the stalk to which an ear of Indian corn is attached **c** : the part of an anchor that is between the ring and the crown — see ANCHOR illustration **d** : the stem of a goblet or other glass with a stem **e** : the part of a fishhook that is between the eye and the bend **f** : the smooth part of a screw between the thread and the head **g** : the part of a key that is between the handle and the bit **h** (1) : the stem of a tobacco pipe (2) : the part of a tobacco pipe that is between the stem and the bowl **i** : the tang of a hoe, rake, knife, or other instrument with a handle **j** : each of the two parts of a pair of scissors between the joint and the bows **k** (1) : the narrow part of the sole of a shoe beneath the instep — see SHOE illustration (2) : SHANKPIECE **3 a** *Scot* : STOCKING **b** **shanks** *pl, dial* : LEGGINGS **4** *chiefly Scot* : a ridge joining a hill to the plain **5** : a part of an object by which it can be attached: as **a** (1) : a projection (as a loop or an eye) on the back of a solid button by which it is attached to the cloth (2) : a short bar of thread that holds a sewn button away from the cloth so that it can be buttoned and unbuttoned easily **b** : the projecting part of a knob handle that contains the spindle socket **c** : the end (as of a drill, milling cutter, or lathe center) that is gripped in a chuck **6** : ⟨¹BODY 10a⟩ **7** : the part of a finger ring that encircles the finger excluding the bezel and engraving **8 a** : a short rope or chain **b** : a tie strap of a halter **9** : the space between two channels of the Doric triglyph **10 a** : the latter part of a period of time ⟨along in the ~ of the afternoon —J.F.Dobie⟩ **b** : the early or main part of a period of time ⟨don't go yet; it is just the ~ of the evening —J.B.Weston⟩ **11 a** : a long-handled ladle for molten metal for use by two or more men **b** : a handle by which a ladle of molten metal can be carried by one or more men **12** : the curved iron bar that connects a cultivator shovel to the beam **13** : a device for locking inserted teeth in a circular saw **14** ⟨²shank⟩ : an act or instance of shanking a golf ball **15** *slang* : KNIFE

shank 5a(1)

²shank \"\ *vb* -ED/-ING/-s *vi* **1** *chiefly Scot* : to go on foot : WALK **2** : to decay at the footstalk; *specif* : to suffer from shanking ~ *vt* **1** *chiefly Scot* : to cause to go on foot **b** : to traverse on foot **2** : to form a shank on **3** : to hit (a golf ball) with the extreme heel of the club so that the ball goes sharply to the right **4** : to cut (a person) deeply with a knife

shankalla *usu cap, var of* SHANGALLA
shank bone *n* [ME *shanke bon*, fr. *shanke* shank + *boon, bon* bone] : TIBIA 1a
shank cutter *n* **1** : END MILL **2** : a device for trimming the edges of outsoles in the shank of a shoe
shanked \ˈshaŋkt, -aiŋ-\ *adj* **1** : having a shank **2** : having such or so many shanks — usu. used in combination ⟨long-shanked⟩ ⟨two-shanked⟩
shank-er \ˈshaŋkə(r), -aiŋ-\ *n* -s **1** : one whose work consists of making or fastening on shanks **2** : SHAFTMAN
shanking *also* **shanking disease** *n* -s [*shanking* fr. gerund of ²*shank*] **1** : a disease of tulips caused by a fungus (*Phytophthora erythroseptica*) and characterized by rot of the flower stalk base **2** : a disease of onions and shallots caused by a fungus (of the genus *Phytophthora*
shank mill *n* : an end mill that is formed solid with the shank
shank painter *n* [ME *shankpayntor*, fr. *shank*, *shanke* shank + *payntor, paynter* painter] : a short rope or chain that holds the shank of an anchor near the flukes against the vessel esp. on the billboard to a toe of the fumber arm
shankpiece \ˈ≠ˌ≠\ *n* : a piece of metal or other material inserted in the shank of a shoe to support the arch of the foot
shanks *pl of* SHANK, *pres 3d sing of* SHANK
shanks-man \ˈshaŋksmən, -aiŋ-\ *n, pl* **shanksmen** [*shank's* (gen. of ¹*shank*) + *man*] : SHAFTMAN
shanks' mare *also* **shank's mare** *or* **shanks' pony** *or* **shank's pony** *n* : one's own legs (just moseyed along mostly traveling by *shanks' mare* —Helen Eustis)
shan-na \ˈshänə\ [Sc *shan-* (fr. E *shall*) + *na*] *Scot* : shall not
¹shan-ny \ˈshani\ *adj* [prob. alter. of ¹*shandy*] *dial Eng* **1** : SILLY, GIDDY **2** : SHY
²shan-ny \ˈshanē\ *n* -ES [origin unknown] : a small European blenny (*Blennius pholis*) that is olive green with irregular dark spots and has no appendages on the head
shans *usu cap, var of* SHAN
shant \ˈshant, -aa)nt, -aint\ *n* -s [origin unknown] *slang* : a large stein : POT
shan't \ˈshant, -aa(ə)-, -ai-, -ä-, -ii-\ [by contr.] : shall not
shantey *or* **shanty** *var of* CHANTEY
shan-tung \(ˈ)shanˈtəŋ\ *n* -s *sometimes cap* [fr. *Shantung*, province in northeast China] : a fabric in plain weave characterized by a slightly irregular surface that is due to the uneven slubbed filling yarns of wild silk or other fibers
shantung straw *also* **shantung** *n* -s *sometimes cap* *Shantung* : a fine smooth hat straw woven from bantal
¹shan-ty \ˈshantē, -aan-, -ain-, -än-, -in\ *n* -ES [CanF *chantier* hut in a lumber camp, shack, fr. F, lumberyard, shipyard, gantry, fr. OF, gantry, fr. L *cantherius* trellis, rafter, gelding — more at GANTRY] **1** : a small poorly built dwelling usu. made of wood : SHACK **2** : a small crude building for temporary use **3** *Austral* : BAR, PUB
²shanty \"\ *vi* -ED/-ING/-ES : to live in a shanty
³shanty \"\ *adj* **1** : constituting a shanty ⟨rough ~ roadside restaurants —A.L.Himbert⟩ **b** : consisting of shanties ⟨a ~ native village⟩ **2** : living or having lived in a shanty ⟨a low social class ⟨the lower-lower class, the ~ Irish, not the lace-curtain Irish —J.P.Marquand⟩
shantyboat \ˈ≠≠ˌ≠\ *n* : a small crude houseboat
shantyboater \ˈ≠≠ˌ≠≠\ *n* : one who lives on a shantyboat
shanty boss *n* : BULL COOK
shantyboy \ˈ≠≠ˌ≠\ *n* : LOGGER
¹shan-ty-man \ˈ≠≠ˌmən\ *n, pl* **shantymen 1** : one who lives in a shanty; *specif* : SHANTYBOATER
²shantyman *also* **shanteyman** *var of* CHANTEYMAN
shantytown \ˈ≠≠ˌ≠\ *n* **1** : a section of a city or town in which the houses are shanties **2** : an entire town consisting mostly of shanties; *esp* : a poor suburb inhabited by Negroes in South Africa
shao-hing \(ˈ)shaúˈshiŋ\ *adj, usu cap* [fr. *Shaohing*, city in eastern China] : of or from the city of Shaohing, China : of the kind or style prevalent in Shaohing
shap-able *or* **shape-able** \ˈshāpəbəl\ *adj* **1** *usu* **shapeable** : capable of being shaped **2** *usu* **shapable** : SHAPELY
¹shape \ˈshāp\ *vb* **shaped; shaped** *or archaic* **shap-en** \-pən\ **shaping; shapes** [ME *shapen*, alter. of OE *sceppan, scyppan*; akin to OHG *skepfen* to shape, form, create, ON *skepja*, Goth *gaskapjan* to create, and perh. to L *scabere* to scratch, scrape — more at SHAVE] *vt* **1** : FORM, CREATE; *esp* : to give a particular or proper form to by or as if by molding or modeling from an undifferentiated mass **2** : to give definite or finished form to esp. by altering a prior shape ⟨*shaping* rolls

from dough⟩ ⟨*shaped* a sturdy mortar from the log⟩ **3** *obs* : ORDAIN, DECREE, DESTINE, APPOINT ⟨there's a divinity that ~s our ends, roughhew them how we will —Shak.⟩ **4** : to alter or manipulate so as to give a particular form or produce a particular object — usu. used with *into* ⟨*shaping* the seasoned lumber into a sturdy frame⟩ ⟨~s the clay into bricks⟩ ⟨heat and the iron⟩ *b obs* : to cut out and fashion (as a garment) : METAMORPHOSE **c** *archaic* : to adapt in shape usu. so as to fit neatly and closely — usu. used with *to* ⟨a dress *shaped* to her figure⟩ **e** : to fashion (a knitted garment) by decreasing or increasing according to pattern **f** : to style (hair) by thinning and tapering esp. to the contour of the head **5 a** : to marshal facts and present them by way of (answer) ⟨~s an earnest answer to the accusation⟩ **b** : to give a particular form or direction to : DEVISE, PLAN ⟨together *shaped* a dark conspiracy⟩ **c** : to embody in definite or definitive form ⟨*shaping* a folktale into an epic⟩ — used with *up* ⟨*shaping* up a set of notes for publication⟩ **6** *archaic* : to bring about : CONTRIVE **7 a** : to make fit for (as a particular use or purpose) : ADAPT, REGULATE, ADJUST ⟨*shaping* a character to future responsibilities⟩ **b** : to determine or direct the course of (as conduct, life, history) ⟨*shaping* our plans for a happy holiday⟩ **8** : to produce a plane surface on (work) by means of a tool that moves to and fro — compare MILL, PLANE ~ *vi* **1** : to come to pass usu. in a particular way : HAPPEN, BEFALL (if things ~ right) **2** *archaic* : to cut out and fashion clothing **3** *obs* : SUIT, CONFORM **4 a** : to take on or approach a mature form — often used with *up* **b** : to develop to or toward a definitive form (as in character, proficiency, or excellence) : show promise — often used with *up* **syn** see FORM — **shape one's course** : to direct one's way

²shape \"\ *n* -s [ME *shap*, fr. OE *gesceap* form, condition, fate, genitals, creature, fr. ge- (perfective, associative, and collective prefix) + -*sceap* (akin to OE *sceppan, scyppan* to shape, form, create) — more at CO-] **1 a** : the visible makeup characteristic of a particular item or kind of item : characteristic appearance or visible form ⟨a demon appearing in the ~ of a man⟩ **b** (1) : spatial form or contour that is usu. fixed by a relatively constant spatial relation between the parts of the periphery or surface ⟨water takes the ~ of its container⟩ ⟨a common ~ of glass⟩ ⟨the ~ of a jellyfish⟩ (2) : any of numerous standardized or universally recognized and usu. basically geometric spatial forms or contours ⟨squares, diamonds, and other ~s⟩ ⟨a hill of perfect cone ~⟩ **c** : phonetic composition or structure or a representation thereof ⟨emphatic *of* has the ~ \ˈov\ or \ˈäv\, unemphatic *of* usually has the ~ \əv\⟩ **2** : the appearance of the body usu. as distinguished from that of the face : bodily contour esp. with respect to beauty : FIGURE ⟨bathing beauties showing their ~s⟩ ⟨your whole ~ shows when you stand against the light⟩ **3** : ⟨ME *shap* male or female sex organ, fr. OE *sceap*; akin to OE *sceppan, scyppan*⟩ *dial chiefly Eng* : the female pudenda **4 a** *dial chiefly Eng* : a represented form (as a painting or photograph) **b** : PHANTOM, APPARITION **c** : assumed appearance : GUISE, LIKENESS ⟨our troubles started in the ~ of a helpful neighbor⟩ **d** (1) *obs* : a theatrical role or its makeup (2) : a stage costume **5** : form of embodiment (as in words) : form (as of thought) that is relatively definite and organized ⟨a plan was beginning to take ~ as they argued⟩ ⟨whipping his speech into ~⟩ **6** : a mode of existence or form of being having identifying or individuating features ⟨the first ~ of an essay⟩ ⟨the final ~ of a society⟩ **7** : something having a particular form ⟨a hatter's ~⟩ ⟨a metal ~ for holding flowers⟩: as **a** : a mold for imparting a shape to a food (as a jelly or blancmange); *also* : a dish molded in a shape **b** (1) : a length of metal (as a bar or beam) having a constant cross section; *also* : one with a cross section other than square, rectangular, round, or hexagonal (2) : a piece roughly forged to approximately the final form ⟨a cone, ball, or drum of light metal or canvas hoisted in making signals on a ship **c** : a gaming die with one or more faces rounded so that it is more likely to fall one way than another **e** : the bend of a fishhook **8** *dial chiefly Eng* : bodily posture : ATTITUDE **9 a** : condition in which someone or something exists at a particular time usu. as compared with a more general state or that of the same item at other occasions or on the average ⟨in excellent ~ for his age⟩ ⟨the market has been in poor ~ lately⟩ **b** : good condition (as for sports) **syn** see FORM — **in no shape** *adv* : NOWISE — **in shape** *adv* : in the original, normal, or fit condition ⟨exercises to keep *in shape*⟩ : in the best condition possible under the circumstances ⟨getting the property *in shape* for sale⟩
shapeable *var of* SHAPABLE
shaped \ˈshāpt\ *adj* **1 a** : having or fashioned to a particular form — often used in combination ⟨a V-shaped notch⟩ **b** : designed to conform to the contours of something ⟨a ~ coat⟩ **2** : formed by or as if by altering the shape of a plastic or pliable mass ⟨~ steel plates⟩ **3** : given direction or plan ⟨a carefully ~ course⟩
shaped charge *n* : an explosive charge the energy of which is focused in one direction; *esp* : a charge in a projectile so packed that an empty cone is left in the nose in which the force of the explosion on impact is directed largely to the front with armor-penetrating effect
shaped note *n* : SHAPE NOTE
shape forth *vt* : to picture or outline in visible or understandable form ⟨*shaping forth* his plan for their approval⟩
shape-ful \ˈshāpfəl\ *adj* : SHAPELY
shape-knife *n* : a knife in which shapes for heels are cut out
shape-less \ˈ≠-ləs\ *adj* [ME *scapless*, fr. *scap*, *shap* shape + -*less*, -*les* -less] **1** : destitute of regularity or fixity of shape ⟨a ~ blob of protoplasm⟩ **2** : deprived of usual or normal shape : MISSHAPEN ⟨a ~ old hat⟩ **3** : lacking the structural qualities that impart elegance and grace ⟨straight ~ garments⟩ ⟨a ~ young girl⟩ **3** : lacking direction or purpose — **shape-less-ly** *adv* — **shape-less-ness** *n* -ES
shape-li-ness \ˈshāplēnəs, -lin-\ *n* -ES [ME *shaplynesse*, fr. *shaply* shapely + -*nesse* -ness] : the quality or state of being shapely
shape-ly *adj* -ER/-EST [ME *shaply*, fr. *shap* shape + -*ly*] **1** : having a regular or pleasing shape : well formed : SYMMETRICAL **2** : having definiteness of form : orderly in arrangement or plan ⟨a ~ conception⟩
shap-en \ˈshāpən\ *adj* [ME, fr. past part. of SHAPE] : fashioned in or provided with a definite shape — usu. used in combination ⟨an ill-*shapen* body⟩
shape note *n* : one of a system of seven notes showing the

shape notes: **1** do, **2** re, **3** mi, **4** fa, **5** sol, **6** la, **7** ti, **8** do
musical scale degree by the shape of the note head — called also *buckwheat note, character note, patent note*
shap-er \ˈshāpə(r)\ *n* -s [ME, fr. *shapen* to shape + -*er*] : one that shapes: as **a** : one whose work is the shaping of articles (as of wood, metal, or cloth) either by hand or machine **b** : POET; *esp* : a bard who reworks old matter in fresh language **c** (1) : a machine tool for shaping metal or sometimes other materials (2) : a woodworking machine with one or two cutters mounted on vertical revolving spindles and projecting above a flat table for cutting irregular outlines (as of moldings) (3) : any of various tools or machines (as a swage for shaping saw teeth, for stamping or pressing sheet metal) (4) : a machine for blocking hats
shapes *pres 3d sing of* SHAPE, *pl of* SHAPE
shapeshifter \ˈ≠≠ˌ≠≠\ *n* : an individual (as a werewolf) able or held to be able to change form esp. at will
shape-shifting \ˈ≠≠ˌ≠≠\ *n* [*shifting* fr. gerund of *shift*] : a

change of physical form brought about by or as if by supernatural means
shape target *n* : a railroad target conveying meaning by shape
shape-up \ˈ≠ˌ≠\ *n* -s [*shape up*] : a system of hiring longshoremen by having applicants gather usu. in a semicircle at least once a day for selection by a union-appointed hiring boss of those to work on that day or shift; *also* : an instance of such hiring practice — compare HIRING HALL
¹shap-ing \ˈshāpiŋ\ *n* -s [ME *shapinge*, fr. gerund of *shapen* to shape] **1** : the act of one that shapes **2** : a thing created or shaped : CREATURE, CREATION
²shaping \"\ *adj* [ME *shapinge*, fr. pres. part. of *shapen* to shape] : that shapes or is designed to shape — **shap-ing-ly** *adv*
shaping dies *n pl* : a set of dies that bends, presses, draws, or hammers a material to a required form in a press or hammer — compare COINING DIE, SEAMING DIES, SPLIT DIE, WIRING DIES
shaping planer *n* : a planer (as a crank planer) with a shaper drive
sha-po \ˈshä(ˌ)pō\ *or* **sha-poo** \-ˌpü\ *n* -s [Tibetan *shabo*] : a wild sheep of Kashmir and Tibet that is a variety of the urial
shap-om-e-ter \shaˈpäməd-ə(r)\ *n* [²*shape* + -*o*- + -*meter*] : a device for measuring the shapes of pebbles
shaps *var of* CHAPS
shap-wai-lu-tan \ˌshap,wiˈlüt'n\ *n, usu cap* [*shahaptian* + *wailatpuan* + *lutuamian* + -*an*] : a language stock of Washington, Oregon, and Idaho comprising Shahaptian, Waiilatpuan, and Lutuamian
shar *or* **shar** *often cap, var of* SHARI'A
sharable *var of* SHAREABLE
¹shard \ˈshärd, ˈshåd\ *also* **sherd** \ˈshərd, -ȧd, -əid\ *n* -s [ME, fr. OE *sceard*; akin to MHG *scharte* notch, nick, ON *skarth* notch, mountain pass, OE *sceran, scieran* to cut, shear — more at SHEAR] **1 a** : a piece or fragment of a brittle substance (as of an earthen vessel) : *broadly* : a small piece : RESIDUE, REMAINS **b** : SHELL, SCALE; *esp* : an elytron of a beetle **c** *usu* **sherd** : fragments of pottery vessels found on sites and in refuse deposits where pottery-making peoples have lived and regarded as one of the best indexes of time differences in culture — compare STRATIGRAPHY **d** : highly angular curved glass fragments of tuffaceous sediments **2 a** : a notch or gap (as in a hedge or bank) **b** *obs* : a separating body of water
²shard \"\ *vb* -ED/-ING/-s *vt* : to break shards from : break into shards ~ *vi* : to shed bark in shards
³shard \"\ *n* -s [prob. alter. (influenced by ¹*shard*) of *sharn*] *chiefly dial* : a dropping of cow dung
⁴shard \"\ *archaic var of* CHARD
shar-da-na \shärˈdänə\ *n, pl* **shardana** *usu cap* : one of a group of early mercenary warriors from the eastern Mediterranean and prob. from Lydia and first fighting for Egypt then against it
shard beetle *n* [³*shard*] : a dung beetle of the genus *Geotrupes*
shard-born \ˈ≠ˌ≠\ *adj* [³*shard*] *archaic, of a beetle* : born in dung
shard-borne \ˈ≠ˌ≠\ *adj* [¹*shard*] *archaic* : borne on scaly wing cases ⟨*shard-borne* beetles⟩
¹sharded *adj* [³*shard* + -*ed*] *obs, of a beetle* : dwelling in dung
²shard-ed \ˈshärdəd, ˈshåd-\ *adj* [¹*shard* + -*ed*] *obs* : having elytra or scales
¹share \ˈshe(ə)r, ˈsha(ə), |ə\ *n* -s [ME, pubic region, due portion, share, fr. OE *scearu* tonsure, pubic region; akin to OHG *skara* troop, ON *skör* hair, rim, OE *sceran, scieran* to cut, shear — more at SHEAR] **1** *obs* **a** : the bony pubis or the pubic region **b** (1) : the fork of the human body (2) : PRIVATE **3 2 a** : a portion belonging to, due to, or contributed by an individual ⟨his ~ in his father's estate⟩ ⟨put up his ~ of the cost⟩ **b** : one's full or fair portion ⟨had his ~ of luck⟩ **c** (1) : the part allotted or belonging to one of a number owning together any property or interest : the undivided interest of any one of a number owning jointly or in common : an apportioned lot : ALLOTMENT, DIVIDEND (2) : any of the equal portions into which any property or invested capital is divided ⟨a ship owned in 64 ~s⟩; *usu* : any of the equal interests or rights into which the entire capital stock of a corporation is divided : any of a number of equal indivisible rights or interests in the management, profits, and ultimate assets of a corporation constituting the property of those who own it and being regularly evidenced by one or more certificates — compare PREFERRED STOCK (3) **shares** *pl, chiefly Brit* : STOCK 28a **3** *archaic* : SEGMENT, PIECE, DIVISION: as **a** *obs* : a portion of land assigned to a particular holder **b** *obs* : a part cut off : CUT, SECTION — **for one's share** : for one's part — **on shares** : on the basis of sharing in the risks and profits (as in fishery or farming)
²share \"\ *vb* -ED/-ING/-s *vt* **1** : to divide and distribute in portions : APPORTION, DIVIDE ⟨~ one's estate between one's heirs⟩ — usu. followed by *out* or *with* ⟨*shared* out the proceeds of the sale⟩ **2** : to partake of, use, experience, or enjoy with others : have a portion of ⟨~ a room⟩ **3** : to grant or be granted a share in ⟨~ one's gains with another⟩ ⟨*shared* their crops in season⟩ **4** : to participate in, take, possess, or undergo in common ⟨~ danger⟩ ⟨*sharing* a common responsibility⟩ **5** *archaic* : to allot as one's share **6** *obs* : to receive, take, or possess as one's share ~ *vi* **1** : to have a share : take part — used with *in* ⟨all may ~ in these pleasures ⟨willing to ~ in the work⟩ **2** : to apportion and take shares of something ⟨the robbers *shared* and fled separately⟩ — **share and share alike 1** : to be held in equal shares as tenants in common rather than in joint tenancy with a per capita rather than a per stirpes distribution or ownership **2** : to be distributed in severalty in equal shares

syn SHARE, PARTICIPATE, and PARTAKE can mean to have, use, exercise, experience, or engage in something in common with another or others. SHARE implies that one as original owner or holder grants to another the partial use, enjoyment, or possession of a thing ⟨*share* your lunch with a friend⟩ ⟨*share* one's enjoyment with another⟩ ⟨none has *shared* so generously with the reader her personal passion for the stuffs, jewels and decorations that made the palace a wonder —*Time*⟩ ⟨to *share* surpluses is not really to *share* at all —H.S. Truman⟩ or, often with *in*, that one as receiver accepts the partial use, enjoyment, or possession of something belonging to or held by another ⟨ask a neighbor to *share* in a Thanksgiving dinner⟩ ⟨*share* in another's joy⟩ ⟨*share* another's disgust at losing an important golf game⟩ ⟨those who do not *share* his faith in the sufficiency of empirical science —J.E. Smith⟩ or it can merely imply a mutual use, enjoyment, or possession of something ⟨the few artists or writers who have *shared* the tastes of the average man —Roger Fry⟩ ⟨diseases which man *shares* with animals —*Time*⟩ PARTICIPATE implies a having or taking of a part or of a share in a thing, as an experience, work, or an enterprise ⟨the citizens refused to *participate* in any further elections under this law —*Amer. Guide Series: Mich.*⟩ ⟨she did not *participate* in the inheritance of the husband after she were married —Ralph Linton⟩ ⟨a citizen of one state has no right to *participate* in the government of another —L.M.Goodrich⟩ ⟨invited to *participate* in the discussion —R.B.Taney⟩ PARTAKE, often used with *of* and sometimes with *in*, implies an accepting, taking, or acquiring a share of something, esp. food, drink, or a pleasure, often in extension signifying then to consume ⟨he had *partaken* of as much as a pint daily of alcohol for years —*Jour. Amer. Med. Assoc.*⟩ ⟨the story itself ceases to be merely melodramatic, and *partakes* of true drama —T.S.Eliot⟩ ⟨they unconsciously *partake* in his imagery —E.H.Erikson⟩
³share \"\ *n* -s [ME *shaar*, fr. OE *scear*; akin to MLG *schār, schāre* plowshare, OHG *scaro* plowshare, OE *sceran, scieran* to cut, shear] : PLOWSHARE — see PLOW illustration
⁴share *vt* [alter. of ¹*shear*] *obs* : CUT, SHEAR, CLEAVE, DIVIDE; *also* : to form by cutting
share-abil-i-ty \ˌshe(ə)rəˈbiləd-ē, ˌsha(ə)r-, -lətē, -i-\ *n* : the quality or state of being shareable
share-able *or* **shar-able** \ˈ≠≠ˌbəl\ *adj* : capable of being shared ⟨~ experience⟩
sharebone \ˈ≠ˌ≠\ *n, archaic* : PUBIS
sharebroker \ˈ≠ˌ≠≠\ *n, chiefly Brit* : STOCKBROKER
sharecrop \ˈ≠ˌ≠\ *vb* [back-formation fr. *sharecropper*] *vi* : to farm as a sharecropper ~ *vt* : to farm (land) or produce (a

particular crop) as a sharecropper ⟨*sharecropped* 100 acres⟩ ⟨*sharecropping* tobacco⟩

share·crop·per \'═,═\ n [*share-crop* (in the phrase *share= crop system*, fr. earlier *share of the crop system*) + -*er*] : a tenant farmer esp. in the southern U.S. who works the land, receives from the landlord seed, tools, stock, and usu. living quarters and credit for food and other necessities consumed prior to harvesting, and is paid a specified share of the crop from which deductions to cover advances (as for drainage and fencing) or for credit advanced may be made — compare SHAREMAN

shared *past of* SHARE

shareef *var of* SHARIF

share·hold·er \'═,═\ n : one that holds or owns a share in a joint fund or property; *esp* : STOCKHOLDER

share·man \'═,mən\ n, pl **sharemen** 1 : SHARESMAN 2 : a farmer who farms on shares in respect to both expenses and product and usu. has his own farming equipment — compare SHARECROPPER

share out vt 1 : to divide and assign in portions ⟨the executor *shared out* the estate⟩ ~ vi : to earn or produce shares (as of profits) ⟨some small cooperative enterprises *share out* very well⟩

share-out \'═,═\ n -s [*share out*] : an act or instance of distributing in shares

share·own·er \'═,═,═\ n : an owner of a share or shares; *esp* : STOCKHOLDER

share·push·er \'═,═\ n, Brit : a high-pressure salesman of often inferior securities

shar·er \'shera(r), 'sha(a)r-\ n -s : one that shares: as **a** obs : a member of a theatrical company who shares in the expenses and profits **b** obs : SHAREHOLDER **c** : PARTICIPATOR, PARTAKER **d** : DIVIDER, DISTRIBUTOR

share rent n : a rent for farm land in the form of an agreed or customary fractional part of a crop grown thereon — compare SHARE-TENANT

shares pl of SHARE, pres 3d sing of SHARE

shares·man \'sherzmən, 'sha(a)rz-\ n, pl **sharesmen** [*share's* (gen. of *¹share*) + *man*] : a member of a fishing crew who shares the risk and profits of a voyage or season

share-ten·ant \'═,═\ also **share-rent·er** \'═,═\ n : one who operates a farm owned by another, pays a share of the crop as rent, and provides labor, power and implements, and usu. his share of seed and fertilizer — compare SHARECROPPER

share warrant n, Brit : a freely transferable certificate indicating that the bearer is entitled to specified shares of stock

shar·gar also **shar·ger** \'shärgər\ n -s [ScGael *seargaire*] Scot : a lean, faded, or stunted person or animal : STARVELING, RUNT

sha·ri·fa or **sha·ria** \shə'rēə\ also **sha·ri·at** \-ēət\ or **shar** or **shar** \'shär\ or **she·ri** \shə'rē\ or **she·ria** \shə'rēə\ or **she·ri·at** \-ēət\ n -s often cap [Ar *sharī'ah*] : the body of formally established sacred law in Islam based primarily on Allah's commandments found in the Koran and revealed through the sunna of Muhammad, governing in theory not only religious matters but regulating as well political, economic, civil, criminal, ethical, social, and domestic affairs in Muslim countries, and commonly in practice being supplemented by the customary law of a region — compare ADAT

sha·rif or **she·rif** also **sha·reef** or **sha·rif** \-rēf\ n, pl **sharifs** or **sherifs** \-fs\ also **ash·raf** \'ash'räf\ [Ar *sharif* (pl. *ashrāf*), lit., noble, illustrious] : a descendant of the prophet Muhammad through his daughter Fatima; *broadly* : one of noble ancestry or religious preeminence in Islam — used chiefly as a title

sha·ri·fa or **she·ri·fa** \-'rēfə\ n [Ar *sharifah*, fem. of *sharif*] : the wife of a sharif

sha·rif·ian or **she·rif·ian** \shə'rēfēən\ adj : of or relating to a sharif

sharing n -s [fr. gerund of ²share] : mutual confession practiced in group meetings by the Oxford Group movement

¹shark \'shärk, 'shäk\ n -s [origin unknown] 1 **a** : any of numerous elasmobranch fishes that conform more or less nearly to the ordinary fishes in the fusiform shape of the body and lateral position of the gill clefts as distinguished from the greatly flattened rays and the grotesquely shaped chimaeras, that are mostly marine and though widely distributed most abundant in warm seas, that are usu. of medium or large size including the largest existing fishes, that have a tough, usu. dull gray, and sometimes conspicuously spotted skin which is roughened by minute tubercles, strongly heterocercal tail, and a snout produced beyond the mouth, that may be active, voracious, and rapacious predators including some which are dangerous to man or sluggish bottom dwellers feeding chiefly on mollusks, and that are of economic importance for their flesh which is in some cases used as food, for their large livers which are a source of oil, and for their hides from which leather is made — see BASKING SHARK, BLUE SHARK, DOGFISH, HAMMERHEAD, MAN-EATER, PORBEAGLE; compare CHONDRICHTHYES, SELACHII **b** : a living or extinct elasmobranch other than a skate or ray 2 : any of several large voracious fishes (as the goonch) 3 : a synchronized swimming stunt in which the body while lying on one side parallel to the surface with the back arched and the top arm extended overhead in line with the body is propelled in a circle headfirst by the action of the bottom arm

²shark \"\ vi -ED/-ING/-S 1 : to fish for sharks 2 : to prey or swim like a shark

³shark \"\ n -s [prob. modif. (influenced in form and meaning by *¹shark*) of G *schurke* scoundrel] 1 obs : PARASITE, SPONGE, SHARPER 2 : a rapacious crafty person who gains by usury, extortion, swindling, or trickery ⟨a mortgage ~⟩ ⟨~s of the poolroom and racetrack⟩ 3 slang Brit : a customs officer 4 : one who excels greatly esp. in a particular line : an exceptionally capable or brilliant person

⁴shark \"\ vb [*¹shark* & *³shark*] vt, archaic : to get or gather together rapaciously or by fraud, trickery, or other irregular means : get by playing the shark ~ vi 1 : to play the sharper : practice fraud or trickery 2 : to live by shifts and stratagems — **shark on** or **shark upon** obs : to sponge upon : SWINDLE

sharker n, obs : one that lives by sharking others : SHARPER

shar·ki \'shorkē\ n -s [Ar *sharqiy*, lit., eastern, fr. *sharq* east] : a southeasterly wind of the Persian gulf

shark·ish \'shärkish, 'shāk-, -kēsh\ adj : resembling or suggestive of a shark esp. in appearance, habits, rapacity, or fierceness

shark·let \-lət\ n -s : a small or young shark

shark·like \-,līk\ adj : resembling a shark; *esp* : having the streamlined elongate form of a typical shark

shark-liver oil \'═,═\ also **shark oil** n : a yellow to red-brown fatty oil obtained from the livers of various sharks (as the soupfin shark or various dogfishes) and used chiefly as a source of vitamin A and as a leather dressing

shark moth n : any of various noctuid moths (genus *Cucullia*) with larvae that feed mainly on flowers

shark pilot or **shark's pilot** \'═,═\ n 1 **a** : PILOT FISH 1 **b** : BANDED RUDDERFISH 2 : REMORA

shark ray n : MONKFISH

shark·skin \'═,═\ n 1 : the hide of a shark or leather made from it — compare SHAGREEN 2 **2 a** : a smooth durable woolen or worsted suiting made in twill or basket weave with small woven designs in two tones or colors **b** : a smooth crisp fabric with a dull finish made usu. of rayon in basket weave and used esp. for dresses or sportswear

shark's mouth n : an opening in a boat awning in the wake of a mast, stay, or other rigging

shark's-tooth \'═,═\ or **shark's-teeth** \'═,═\ adj : of, resembling, or armed with the teeth of sharks ⟨a *shark's-tooth* sword⟩

shark sucker n : REMORA 1a

shark·y \'shärkē, 'shāk-, -ki\ adj -ER/-EST [*¹shark* + -*y*] : infested with sharks

sharn \'shärn, 'shän\ n -s [ME, fr. OE *scearn* — more at SCAT-] *dial chiefly Eng* : DUNG

sharn·y \'shärni, 'shän-\ adj, chiefly Scot : befouled with dung

¹sharp \'shärp, 'shäp\ adj -ER/-EST [ME, fr. OE *scearp*; akin to OHG *scarf* sharp, ON *skarpr*, MIr *cerb* sharp, Russ *shcherba* notch, Gk *keirein* to cut — more at SHEAR] 1 : adapted to cutting or piercing: as **a** (1) : having a thin keen edge ⟨a ~

sword⟩ (2) : of such thinness and keenness as to facilitate cutting ⟨an axe with a ~ edge⟩ **b** (1) : tapering to a fine point ⟨a ~ needle⟩ (2) : of such tapered fineness as to facilitate piercing ⟨a pin with a ~ point⟩ **c** : beset with prickles : PRICKLY ⟨~ brambles and thorns⟩ **d** : briskly or bitingly cold : NIPPING, RAW ⟨~ wind⟩ ⟨several ~ frosts⟩ **e** : composed of hard angular particles : GRITTY ⟨~ sand⟩ 2 **a** : keen in intellect : mentally alert and able : QUICK-WITTED **b** : keen in perception : efficient in sensory function ⟨a ~ ear⟩ ⟨kept a ~ watch on the market⟩ **d** (1) obs : DISCRIMINATING, SAGACIOUS (2) : cleverly biting : aptly witty ⟨~ bits of whimsy⟩ **e** : keen in attention : VIGILANT ⟨a ~ lookout⟩ ⟨kept a ~ watch on the market⟩ **d** (1) obs : DISCRIMINATING, SAGACIOUS (2) : cleverly biting : aptly witty ⟨~ bits of whimsy⟩ **e** : keen in attention to one's own interest : unduly smart or shrewd in practical matters sometimes to the point of being unethical ⟨a ~ trader⟩ ⟨sometimes the customer may be ~*er* than the dealer⟩ 3 : keen in spirit or action : VIOLENT, IMPETUOUS: as **a** : conducted with eagerness or fierceness : FIERY, FURIOUS ⟨a ~ military engagement⟩ **b** : closely or keenly contested ⟨a ~ run⟩; *also* : full of activity or energy : BRISK ⟨~ blows⟩ ⟨a ~ young runner⟩ ⟨hounds in ~ condition⟩ **c** (1) of a hawk : urgent for prey or food (2) : impatient for gratification : demanding or requiring to be sated ⟨a ~ appetite⟩ **d** : capable of acting or reacting strongly : very active in some particular way; *esp* : CAUSTIC ⟨a ~ lime liquor for removing hair from hides⟩ ⟨a ~ soap rich in free alkali⟩ 4 : SEVERE, HARSH, MERCILESS: as **a** : inclined to or marked by intense irritability or anger : IRASCIBLE ⟨a ~ temper⟩ **b** : very trying to the feelings or spirit : causing intense mental or physical distress ⟨a ~ pain⟩ ⟨in ~*est* distress⟩ **c** : cutting in language or import : conveying or intended to convey rebuke, anger, or satire ⟨~ words⟩ ⟨a ~ rebuke⟩ **d** obs : AUSTERE **e** (1) archaic : flowing rapidly or turbulently — used of a stream of water (2) : marked by sudden brusque distention of the artery : JERKY ⟨a ~ pulse⟩ 5 : affecting the senses or sense organs intensely: as **a** (1) : having a characteristic strong and usu. pungent or acid odor or flavor ⟨~ cheese⟩ (2) : ACRID ⟨a ~ odor⟩ **b** : having a characteristic strong and usu. piercing or shrill sound ⟨a ~ whistle⟩ ⟨a ~ clap of thunder⟩ **c** : having the effect of or involving a sudden brilliant display of light ⟨a ~ flash⟩ 6 **a** : terminating in a point or edge : not smoothly obtuse or rounded : PEAKED, RIDGED, ANGULAR ⟨~ features⟩ ⟨a ~ hill⟩ **b** : at an angle : ACUTE (2) : requiring or involving an abrupt change of direction : formed about an acute angle ⟨a ~ turn⟩ (3) : involving marked change and usu. increase of gradient ⟨a ~ climb⟩ ⟨a ~ dip in the road⟩ **c** : appearing as if cut off clean : clear in outline or detail : DISTINCT ⟨figures standing out ~ against the sky⟩ ⟨a ~ photographic negative⟩ **d** : set forth with clarity and distinctness and usu. with marked contrast between elements : free from shading or transition ⟨a ~ line of demarcation⟩ ⟨in ~ contrast with modern methods⟩ **e** : FINE, NARROW ⟨used esp. of the bows of a ship⟩ 7 **a** : having a high pitch ⟨a *sharp*-toned musical instrument⟩ **b** of a musical note or tone : raised a half step in pitch ⟨a ~ fourth⟩ **c** : higher than the true pitch of a musical tone ⟨sang ~ all evening⟩ **d** : MAJOR, AUGMENTED — used of an interval in music **e** : having a sharp in the signature ⟨played in the key of F ~⟩ 8 : STYLISH, ELEGANT, DRESSY ⟨a ~ suit⟩ 9 of a radio circuit : having a rapidly varying response to different frequencies — opposed to *broad*

syn KEEN, ACUTE: SHARP, in reference to things, may refer either to fine edges making cutting easy or to fine points facilitating piercing ⟨a *sharp* knife⟩ ⟨*sharp* as a needle⟩ and in reference to persons may indicate quick accurate perception or analysis, general cleverness and resourcefulness, or tricky, sometimes questionable cunning ⟨a cold and analytical mind, as *sharp* in criticism and often as bitter as has appeared — *Irish Digest*⟩ ⟨lying was not half diplomacy, nor *sharp* practices good commerce —Haldane Macfall⟩ KEEN may describe quite sharp cutting edges ⟨a *keen* knife⟩ In reference to persons it implies perceptiveness, clear-sightedness, skill in quick analysis, and overall mental readiness ⟨skillfully and pleasantly written, it was in effect a *keen* attack upon the English Church and its clergy —H.E.Starr⟩ ⟨his teaching was remarkable for a variety of qualities: swift and *keen* generalization, ready control of the background of ideas —C.N. Greenough⟩ ACUTE is likely to refer to angles; in reference to people it may suggest discrimination and analytical penetration equipping one to solve more knotty problems ⟨it was very *acute* ... to put such a deep game —Joseph Conrad⟩ ⟨as the *acute* reader will not have failed to note —Havelock Ellis⟩

²sharp \"\ vb -ED/-ING/-S [ME *sharpen*, fr. OE *scerpan*, *scyrpan*; akin to MHG *scherpfen* to sharpen, Icel *skerpa*; causative fr. the root of E *¹sharp*] vt 1 dial : SHARPEN 2 : to raise (as a musical tone) in pitch; *esp* : to raise in pitch by a half step 3 archaic : to obtain by trickery or swindling : PILFER ~ vi 1 : to sing or play above the true pitch 2 archaic : to act the sharper

³sharp \"\ adv -ER/-EST [ME *sharpe*, fr. OE *scearpe*, fr. *scearp*, adj. — more at *¹SHARP*] 1 : in a sharp manner : SHARPLY: as **a** obs : SHRILLY **b** : to a point or edge **c** : close to the wind ⟨a ship braced ~ up⟩ **d** : higher than the true or accepted musical pitch ⟨sang ~⟩ **e** : ABRUPTLY, QUICKLY, BRISKLY **f** : PRECISELY, EXACTLY ⟨an appointment at one o'clock ~⟩ **g** : ACUTELY — often used in combination ⟨*sharp*-angled⟩ **h** : in a trim well-turned-out manner or style : so as to be notable for style or dressiness ⟨looking ~ in a new tweed⟩

⁴sharp \"\ n -s [ME, fr. *sharp*, adj. — more at *¹SHARP*] : one that is sharp: as **a** : a sharp edge or point **b** archaic : a sharp weapon **c** (1) : a musical note or tone one half step higher than a note or tone named ⟨C *sharp* is the ~ of C⟩ (2) : a character # on a line or space of the musical staff indicating a pitch a half step higher than the degree would indicate without it (3) : the keyboard, on musical staff, B key next to the right of any given key on a keyboard musical instrument ⟨sharp c(3), c(2): F sharp: *1* on a keyboard, on musical staff, *B* ⟩ **d** sharps pl, chiefly Brit : MIDDLING 1b **e** : a long needle with sharp point for general sewing ⟨a ~ real or self-styled expert; *also* : SHARPER **g** : a thin sharp piece of diamond used esp. for cutting, for cleaving, or for engraving gems

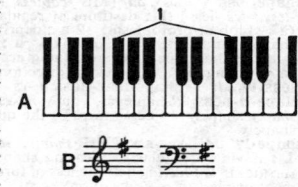

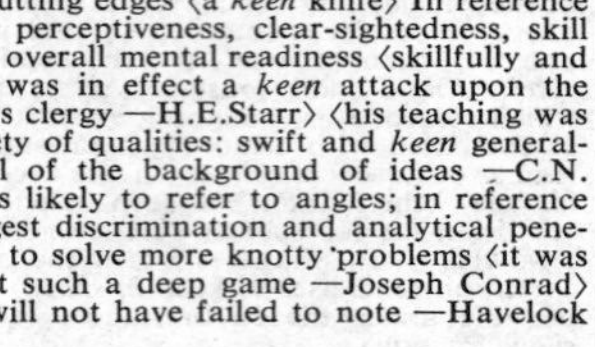

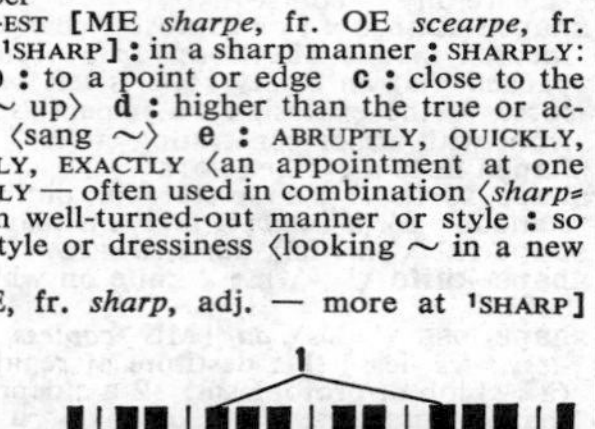

sharp-beaked \'═,═\ adj : having a pointed elongate beak or bill

sharp cedar n : ⁴CADE

sharp-cut \'═,═\ adj : cut so as to be sharp or make a clear well-defined impression ⟨an engraved plate with *sharp-cut* lines⟩

sharp dock n : ¹DOCK 1

sharp·en \'shärpən, 'shäp-\ vb **sharpened**; **sharpened**; **sharp·en·ing** \-p(ə)niŋ\ **sharpens** [ME *sharpenen*, fr. *¹sharp* + -*enen*, -*nen* -*en*] vt 1 : to make sharp : give a keen edge or fine point to ⟨~ an ax⟩ 2 : to make sharper: as **a** : to make quicker or more acute in perception or ready in action **b** : to make more eager **c** : to make (as a law) more severe **d** : to make more intense ⟨~ a pain⟩ **e** : to make (one's speech) biting, sarcastic, or harsh : to make shriller or more piercing **g** : to make more tart or pungent ⟨the rays of the sun ~ vinegar⟩ ⟨cheese ~ed by ripening⟩ **h** : to make thin or emaciated 1 : to make distinct in outline **j** : to increase the activity of ⟨lime liquors used in removing hair from hides⟩ usu. by adding sodium sulfide ⟨SHARP vt 2⟩ 3 chiefly Brit : SHARP vt 2 **4** : to brace up sharp ~ vi 1 : to grow or become sharp 2 chiefly Brit : SHARP vi 1 — **sharpen one's knife** : to get ready or preparing to punish or attack — usu. used with *for* ⟨*sharpening my knife* for the fellow that told that lie⟩

sharp·en·er \'shärp(ə)nər, 'shäp(ə)nər\ n -s : one that sharpens something (as tools or gears): as **a** : PENCIL SHARPENER **b** : one that sharpens the saws of linter machines

sharpening stone n : a hand sharpening device (as a whetstone)

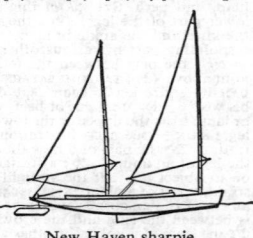

New Haven sharpie

sharp·er \'shärpər, 'shäpə(r)\ n -s [*¹sharp* + -*er*] 1 : an unduly sharp or canny person: as **a** : a cheater in bargains **b** : SWINDLER **c** : a cheating gamester : CARDSHARPER 2 chiefly South : an oyster having a thin sharp edge

sharpest superlative of SHARP

sharp-eyed \'═,═\ adj : having keen sight; *also* : keen in observing or penetrating

shar·pey's fiber \'shärpēz-, 'shäp-\ n, usu cap S : FIBER OF SHARPEY

sharp-fanged \'═,═\ adj : having sharp teeth : BITING, SARCASTIC

sharp-freeze \'═,═\ vt : QUICK-FREEZE

sharp-heeled \'═,═\ adj : having a sharp or pointed heel; *specif* : armed with spurs — used chiefly of a gamecock

sharp·ie or **sharpy** \'shärpē, 'shäpē, -pi\ n, pl **sharpies** [*¹sharp* + -*ie*] 1 **a** : a long rather narrow shallow-draft boat with flat or slightly V-shaped bottom and one or two masts that bear a triangular sail 2 **a** : SHARPER 1 **b** : an exceptionally keen alert person

sharping pres part of SHARP

sharp iron n [trans. of G *scharfeisen*] : a tool for opening seams (as in a wooden ship) into which caulking material is to be thrust

sharp·ish \'shärpish, 'shäp-, -pēsh\ adj : somewhat sharp

sharp·ite \-,pīt\ n -s [F, fr. R.R.*Sharp*, 20th cent. Brit. army officer + F -*ite*] : a mineral ($(UO_2)_6(SO_4)_3(OH)_2$-$6H_2O$(?) consisting of a hydrous basic carbonate of uranyl found with other uranium minerals

sharp·ly adv [ME, fr. OE *scearplice*, adv. of *scearplic* sharp, severe, fr. *scearp* sharp + -*lic* -ly] 1 : in a sharp manner : so as to be or appear sharp — often used as an intensifier ⟨distribution is to be ~ limited⟩

sharp mixture n : ACUTE MIXTURE

sharp·ness n -ES [ME *sharpnesse*, fr. OE *scearpnes*, fr. *scearp* sharp + -*nes* -ness] : the quality or state of being sharp

sharp-nosed \'═,'nōzd\ adj 1 : having a pointed nose or snout ⟨a *sharp-nosed* beetle⟩ 2 : keen of scent ⟨*sharp-nosed* still-hunting hounds⟩ — **sharp-nosed·ly** \-nōz(ə)dlē, -li\ adv — **sharp-nosed·ness** \-nəs\ n -ES

sharp-nosed crab n : a rough pear-shaped shallow-water spider crab (*Scyra acutifrons*) having the rostrum prolonged in two hornlike points and being common along the Pacific coast of No. America

sharp-nosed shark or **sharpnose shark** \'═,═\ n : a small gray or brown shark (*Scoliodon terrae-novae*) of both coasts of the Atlantic and esp. abundant in the Caribbean area; *also* : a closely related slaty or bluish gray shark (*S. longurio*) of the Pacific coast of Mexico and southern California

sharp practice n : dealing in which advantage is taken or sought unscrupulously; *also* : a particular piece of or custom involving such dealing ⟨determined to put down *sharp* practices in his department⟩

sharps pl of SHARP, pres 3d sing of SHARP

sharp sand n : sand with angular grains that is nearly or wholly free from foreign particles (as of clay or loam)

sharps and flats n pl 1 : keys of a keyboard musical instrument other than the ones in the natural scale of C major 2 : ACCIDENTALS ⟨the piece is full of *sharps and flats*⟩

sharp-set \'═,═\ adj 1 : set at a sharp angle : set so as to present a sharp edge 2 : eager in appetite or desire of gratification; *usu* : very hungry : RAVENOUS — **sharp-set·ness** n -ES

sharp·shin \'═,═\ n, archaic : a piece of cut money

sharp-shinned hawk \'═,═\ also **sharpshin** \[*sharp-shinned* fr. *¹sharp* + -*shinned* (fr. *shin*, n. + -*ed*)\] : a common widely distributed No. American hawk (*Accipiter striatus velox*) having the upper parts ashy gray, the underparts white barred with rufous, and the rather long tail barred with blackish and tipped with white, being scarcely larger than the American sparrow hawk, noted for its dash and spirit, and often attacking poultry

sharp·shod \'═,═\ adj, of a horse : shod with sharp calks

sharp·shoot·er \'═,═\ n -s [trans. of G *scharfschütze*] 1 **a** : one skilled in shooting : a good marksman: as (1) : a member of a military unit employed primarily in skirmishing or on outposts (2) : a member of an armed force who has formally qualified in marksmanship according to a prescribed standard and with a rating below expert but above marksman; *also* : the rating of such a qualified person **b** : a player in a sport whose aim is consistently accurate ⟨a basketball ~⟩ **c** : a person whose aim is to win without regard to equity or scruples : one who seeks to make an inordinate immediate profit without thought of building up a continuing business relationship 2 : any of numerous leafhoppers that have sharply conical heads and include various economically important pests some of which puncture and damage young cotton bolls 3 : the person in charge of explosives in an oil-well drilling operation 4 : a sailboat common around the Bahamas islands and having the form of a rather deep sharp-keeled catboat 5 : a usu. narrow-bladed spade

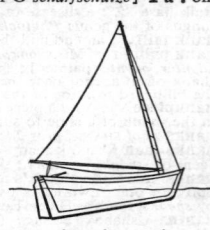

sharpshooter 4

sharp·shoot·ing \'═,═\ n -s [fr. *sharpshooter*, after E *shooter*: *shooting*] 1 : shooting with great precision 2 : accurate and usu. unexpected attack (as in words) : SNIPING

sharp-shot \'═,═\ n : BALL CARTRIDGE

sharp-sight·ed \'═,═\ adj 1 : having quick or acute sight 2 : mentally keen or alert — **sharp-sight·ed·ly** adv — **sharp-sight·ed·ness** n -ES

sharp·ster \'shärpstər, 'shäpstə(r)\ n -s : SHARPER

sharp·tail \'═,═\ n : any of several birds with a pointed tail (as a sharp-tailed grouse, duck, or sparrow)

sharp-tailed \'═,═\ adj [ME *sharpe tayled*, fr. *sharpe*, *sharp*, adj., *sharp* + *tayled*, *tailed* tailed] 1 : having a pointed tail 2 : having acuminate tail feathers

sharp-tailed duck n 1 chiefly Brit : OLD-SQUAW 2 : PINTAILED DUCK

sharp-tailed grouse n : a large grouse (*Pedioecetes phasianellus*) of the western U.S. and Canada that inhabits open prairies and foothills mostly farther west than the true prairie chicken that is often confused, that is light buff in color and barred and mottled with blackish, and that has the head slightly crested and the middle tail feathers somewhat elongated

sharp-tailed sandpiper n : a sandpiper (*Erolia acuminata*) similar to the pectoral sandpiper that breeds in eastern Siberia and winters as far south as Australia and New Zealand

sharp-tailed sparrow or **sharp-tailed finch** n : a No. American sparrow (*Ammospiza caudacuta*) having narrow pointed tail feathers and inhabiting salt marshes

sharp-tongued \'═,═\ adj : having a sharp tongue : harsh or bitter of speech

sharp-toothed \'═,═\ adj : having sharp teeth : ready to use the teeth (as in rending or tearing)

sharp tuning n : radio tuning such that the current in the receiving apparatus is changed materially by a slight change in the frequency of the received waves — compare FLAT TUNING

sharp·ware \'═,═\ n -s : EDGE TOOLS

sharp-wit·ted \'═,═\ adj : having an acute or quickly or nicely discerning mind — **sharp-wit·ted·ly** adv — **sharp-wit·ted·ness** n -ES

shar·py var of SHARPIE

shar·ra \'shärə\ n, pl **sharra** usu cap 1 : one of a Mongol people of Outer Mongolia who with the Kalmucks are the

most typical of the Mongols **2** : the dialect of Mongolian spoken by the Sharra people
shas *pl of* SHA
shash·lik *also* **shash·lick** *or* **shas·lik** \(')shäs(h)'lik\ *n* -s [Russ *shashlyk*, of Turkic origin; akin to Kazan Tatar *šyšlyk* kabob] : KABOB
sha·si \'shä;'sē\ *adj, usu cap* [fr. *Shasi*, city in east central China] : of or from the city of Shasi, China : of the kind or style prevalent in Shasi
shas·ta \'shastə\ *n, pl* **shasta** *or* **shastas** *usu cap* **1 a** : an Indian people of northern California and southern Oregon **b** : a member of such people **2 a** : a Shastan language of the Shasta people **3** : SHASTAN
shasta cypress *n, usu cap S* [fr. Mt. *Shasta*, northern California] : MACNAB CYPRESS
shasta daisy *n, usu cap S* : a large-flowered garden daisy that is a variety of a Pyrenean perennial herb (*Chrysanthemum maximum*) and resembles the common oxeye daisy
¹shas·tan \'shastən\ *n -s usu cap* [*Shasta* + *-an*, n. suffix] : a language family of the Hokan stock in northern California and southern Oregon comprising Achomawi, Atsugewi, and Shasta
²shastan \"\ *adj, usu cap* [*Shasta* + *-an*, adj. suffix] : of or relating to the Shasta people or their language
shasta red fir *also* **shasta fir** *n, usu cap S* [fr. Mt. *Shasta*] : an immense evergreen tree (*Abies magnifica shastensis*) of the Pacific coast of No. America closely related to the California red fir but less hardy in cultivation
shasta sam *n, usu cap both Ss* [fr. *Sam*, nickname fr. the name *Samuel*] : a card game like California Jack except that the pack drawn from is turned face down
shas·tra *or* **sas·tra** \'shästrə\ *n -s often cap* [Skt *śāstra*, lit., instruction, fr. *śāsti* he punishes, instructs; akin to Av *sāsti* he teaches] : the sacred scriptures of Hinduism consisting of four categories of text, the sruti, smriti, purana, and tantra — **shas·tra·ic** \(')shä'strāik, shä-\ *adj*
shat \'shat, *usu* -ad+V\ *also* **shat·ter** \-ad·ə(r), -atə\ *n -s chiefly Midland* [shat prob. alter. of ¹*chat; shatter* prob. alter. of ¹*chat*] (influenced by ²*shatter*) or ²*chat*] : PINE NEEDLE — usu. used in pl.
shath·mont \'shath,mänt\ *Scot var of* SHAFTMENT
¹shat·ter \'shad·ə(r), -atə-\ *vb* -ED/-ING/-s [ME *schateren*; perh. akin to MLG *schäteren* to explode, *schalmen* to scatter, Lith *skedervà* splinter] *vt* **1** : to cause to drop or be dispersed : SCATTER (with a measured tap of his forefinger he ~ed the ash from his cigar —Hamilton Basso) (the slightest jar ~s the petals of a full-blown rose) (wind could ~ out wheat —A.B.Guthrie) **2 a** : to splinter with or as if with a blow : reduce to fragments : FRACTURE, SMASH (fifty windowpanes were ~ed by the missiles —*Amer. Guide Series: Conn.*) (amethysts caught the light, ~ing it and sending it forth again in a thousand fragments —Louis Bromfield) **b** : to damage badly : RUIN, WRECK (men whose faces had been ~ed on the Italian fronts —James Stern) (rough weather . . . ~ed the mainmast —C.O.Paullin) **3 a** : to cause the disruption or annihilation of : DISINTEGRATE, DEMOLISH (riflemen . . . ~ed each wave of attackers before it could come within volleying distance —*Amer. Guide Series: Tenn.*) (one cold puff of piety . . . ~ed the warm colorful world of romance —Osbert Lancaster) (the legend of Rome's invincibility had been ~ed —John Buchan) **b** : to cause to break down : IMPAIR, DESTROY (his health was ~ed . . . by the war —V.H.Paltsits) (people collide with harsh experience and are ~ed —Paul Engle) (nothing but death was strong enough to ~ that inherited restraint —Ellen Glasgow) **4** : to separate (a flower) into clusters of petals which are then wired or taped (her wrist corsage was of ~ed yellow carnations —*Springfield (Mass.) Daily News*) ~ *vi* **1** : to make a rattling sound : CLATTER (rain . . . ~s at the windowpane —Maurice Hewlett) **2** : to break apart : become shattered —Maurice Hewlett) (the ~ing of . . . ~s at the windowpane —Maurice Hewlett) **2** : to break apart : become shattered (turned back . . . to see the laboratory window —W.N. Marsh) (the Empire of the Incas . . . ~ed at Pizarro's touch —Bernard De Voto) **3** : to drop or scatter leaves, petals, fruit (as kernels of ripe grain or the berries of grapes) (the wheat ~ed in the field before harvest) *syn see* BREAK
²shatter *n* **1** : FRAGMENT, SHRED — usu. used in pl. (the plate was in ~s on the floor) **2** : an act of shattering or state of being shattered; *specif* : a plant disease characterized by premature dropping or dehiscence (studies on the ~ of grapes —L.P.Miller) **3** : a result of shattering : SHOWER, SPATTER (sunlight broke . . . painfully in his eyes like a ~ of gold glass —David Beaty)
shat·ter·able \-rəbəl\ *adj* : capable of being shattered
shatterbrain \'=,=\ *n* : SCATTERBRAIN — **shatterbrained** \'=',=\ *adj, archaic*
shatter crack *n* : a minute crack which sometimes develops in the head of a rail usu. half an inch or more beneath the surface owing to defective forging
shat·ter·er \'shad·ərə(r), -atərə-\ *n -s* : one that shatters
¹shattering *adj* [fr. pres. part. of ¹*shatter*] **1** : causing deterioration or breakdown : DESTRUCTIVE, DEMORALIZING (the ~ action of frost —R.F.Flint) (somehow we staggered through that ~ heat —A.E.Stevenson b. 1900) (the economic collapse of the thirties was a ~ thing, a nightmare that still haunts us —Lester Markel) **2** : having tremendous impact : TERRIFIC, OVERPOWERING (the giants of our past, their ~ words, their stunning achievements —Jerome Weidman) (a ~ display of technical knowledge —Lennox Robinson) (the ~ tones of an enormous carillon reverberating through a tower room —Arthur Knight) — **shat·ter·ing·ly** *adv*
²shattering *n -s* [fr. gerund of ¹*shatter*] **1** : an act or result of breaking down **2** *dial Eng* : a small quantity : SPRINKLING
shatterpated \'=,=\ *adj* : SCATTERBRAINED
shatterproof \'=,=\ *adj* : proof against shattering (transparent, ~ acrylic plastic —W.A.Hamor)
shatterproof glass *n* : LAMINATED GLASS
shatters *pres 3d sing of* SHATTER, *pl of* SHATTER
shat·tery \'shad·ərē, -atərē, -ri\ *adj* : easily shattered
shat·tuck·ite \'shad·ə,kit\ *n -s* [*Shattuck* Denn Mine, near Douglas, Arizona + E *-ite*] : a mineral 2CuSiO₃·H₂O consisting of a massive fibrous blue hydrous copper silicate (sp. gr. 3.8)
shauch·le \'shäkəl\ *var of* SHACHLE
shaugh \'shäg\ *var of* SHOCH
shaugh·nes·sy playoff \'shönə,sē-, -si-\ *n, usu cap S* [after Frank J. *Shaughnessy*, 20th cent. Canadian baseball official] : a playoff among the top four teams of a league (as in minor league baseball and ice hockey) in which team one usu. plays team three, team two plays team four, and the two winners play each other
sha·van·té \shə'vantē\ *n, pl* **shavanté** *or* **shavantés** *usu cap* **2** : a member of any of the Shavanté peoples
¹shave \'shāv\ *vb* **shaved; shaved** *or* **shav·en** \'shāvən\ **shaving; shaves** [ME *shaven*, fr. OE *scafan*; akin to OHG *skaban* to scrape, shave, Goth *skaban* to shave, shear, L *scabere* to scratch, scrape, Russ *skobel'* plane, Gk *skaptein* to dig — more at CAPON] *vt* **1 a** : to remove a thin layer from : PARE, SCRAPE (showed him how to trim, ~ and properly soften a new and playable reed —Harold Sinclair) (the rims are delicately *shaved* by steam power —Lois I. Woodville) **b** : to cut off in thin layers or shreds : SLICE, SLIVER (a red-hot mass which a steel cutting machine was *shaving*, as though it were cheese —W.J.Locke) (maple sugar . . . in a bricklike cake which can be readily grated or *shaved* —*House Beautiful*); *specif* : to trim slightly (as the edge of a book page) (the paper of the MS has been *shaved* at the bottom —Sydney Race) **c** : to reduce or make uniform the thickness of (a hide) by cutting away a portion from the flesh side — compare SKIVE **d** : to cut off closely : CROP, DENUDE (a smooth *shaven* lawn) (a frontier he had *shaved* of all trees and shrubbery —Claire Sterling) **2 a** : to sever the hair from (the head or another part of the body) close to the roots (*shaving* . . . part of the scalp on aesthetic grounds or to denote a certain rank —A.G.Petitpierre) *specif* : TONSURE (~ the crown of a monk) **b** : to remove beard (from the face or neck) with a razor (hire a ballplayer to ~ himself on a TV commercial) **c** : to cut off (hair or beard) close to the skin (the hair off her legs) (got him to ~ off his beard) **3 a** *chiefly dial* : FLEECE 2 **b** : to discount

(a note) at an exorbitant rate — compare NOTE SHAVER **c** : to subtract or make smaller : DEDUCT, REDUCE (new procedures ~ . . . minutes from the unloading process —*N.Y. Times*) (imports must be cut, armed forces *shaved*, food rations trimmed —Arthur Hepner) **4** : to come close to or touch lightly in passing : CLIP, GRAZE (set the buoy rocking . . . as she *shaved* it close —Llewellyn Howland) ~ *vi* **1** : to cut off hair or beard close to the skin ~s with an electric razor (borrowed a friend's room so that he could ~ that morning —Russell Lord) **2** : to proceed with difficulty : SCRAPE (*shaved* through the gap with inches to spare —C.S.Forester)
²shave \"\ *n -s often attrib* [in sense 1, fr. ME *shave*, fr. OE *scafa*; in other senses, fr. ¹*shave*; OE *scafa* akin to OHG *scaba* scraper, plane, Icel *skafa*; derivative fr. the root of ¹*shave*] **1** *SHAVE 3*: as **a** : SPOKESHAVE **b** : DRAWKNIFE **c** : a tool through which basketwork splits are drawn to remove the pith and make them uniform in width **2** : SHAVING (took real pride in cutting delicate ~s of cold beef —Katherine Mansfield) **3 a** : an act or process of shaving (felt fresh from his ~ and shower —Hamilton Basso) **b** : a result of shaving (got a ~ and a haircut) **4** : CLOSE SHAVE (it was a ~ but we made it) (all-around sportsman — had gone after big game all over the world and had had a good many narrow ~s —Max Beerbohm) **5** *archaic* : SWINDLE
shaved *adj* **1** : finely sliced or shredded : CHIPPED (~ beef) (~ ice) **2 a** : having the hair or beard cut off close to the root (a clean-*shaved* man); *specif* : TONSURED (monk with a ~ head) **b** : TRIMMED, CROPPED (a ~ hide)
shave grass *also* **shave rush** *n* [*shave grass* fr. ME *schavegres*, fr. *schaven, shaven* to shave + *gres, gras* grass; *shave rush* fr. ¹*shave* + *rush*] : SCOURING RUSH
shave hook *n* [ME *shave hok*, fr. *shaven* to shave + *hok* hook] : a tool consisting of a sharp-edged steel plate set transversely at the end of a shank fixed in a handle and used esp. by plumbers and metalworkers for scraping metals

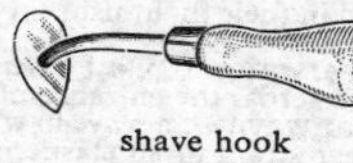

shave hook

shave·ling \'shāvliŋ, -lēŋ\ *n -s* **1** : a tonsured clergyman : PRIEST — usu. used disparagingly **2** : STRIPLING
shav·en \'shāvən\ *adj* [ME *shaven*, fr. past part. of *shaven* to shave] : SHAVED
shav·er \'shāvə(r)\ *n -s* [ME, fr. *shaven* to shave + *-er*] **1 a** : one that shaves with a razor; *specif* : BARBER **b** : one that slices, trims, or crops: as **(1)** : an operator of a machine for shaving fur from skins **(2)** : a workman who shaves hides to reduce them to even thickness or to remove rough spots **(3)** : one who trims the edges of granite blocks with a circular saw **(4)** : an operator of a machine for shaving split rattan to proper thickness and width for basketry **2 a** *archaic* : SWINDLER, EXTORTIONER **b** : NOTE SHAVER **3** : a tool or machine for shaving (took off the rough corners of the plank with a ~) (pull an ice ~ over the rink after each of the many skating sessions —Melvin Beck) (the transcribing machine; and the ~ —H.D.Fasnacht); *specif* : an electric-powered razor for removing a beard (a ~ is simpler to use than the old-fashioned hand razor) **4** : a little child : BOY, YOUNGSTER (a little ~ . . . wanted to be a doctor just like his daddy —*My Baby*) (tried to remember those ragged days when he was only a ~ —J.T.Farrell)
shaves *pl of* SHAVE *or of* SHAFT, *pres 3d sing of* SHAVE
shavetail \'=,=\ *n* [¹*shave* + *tail*; fr. the custom of shaving the tails of mules when they are broken in so that they can be easily distinguished from the untrained ones] **1** : a pack mule esp. when newly broken in **2** : a newly commissioned officer : SECOND LIEUTENANT — usu. used disparagingly (hell hath no fury like a ~ scorned —Harold Fleming)
¹sha·vi·an \'shāvēən, -vyən\ *n -s usu cap* [*Shavius* (latinized form of the name of George Bernard *Shaw* †1950 Brit. playwright, novelist, and critic) + E *-an*, n. suffix] : an admirer or devotee of G. B. Shaw, his writings, or his theory of social and political organization
²shavian \"\ *adj, usu cap* [*Shavius* + E *-an*, adj. suffix] : of, relating to, or characteristic of G. B. Shaw or his writings (*Shavian* wit) (this gem of *Shavian* perspicacity —*Newsweek*) (a fresh setting, a *Shavian* philosophy and a modern meaning —Hesketh Pearson)
sha·vi·ana \,shāvē'anə, -'änə,-ə,änə *also* -'änə\ *n pl, usu cap* [*Shavius* + E *-ana*] : memorabilia concerning G. B. Shaw (has just given Yale University his entire collection of *Shaviana* —*N.Y.Times*)
sha·vi·an·ism \'shāvēə,nizəm, -vyə,-\ *n -s usu cap* **1** : an attitude or utterance of or characteristic of G. B. Shaw **2** : devotion to the writings or social theories of G. B. Shaw
shav·ie \'shāvē\ *n -s* [perh. fr. ²*shave* + *-ie*] *Scot* : a practical joke : PRANK
shav·ing \'shāviŋ, -vēŋ\ *n -s* [ME, fr. gerund of *shaven* to shave] **1** : an act or process of trimming or cutting closely: as **a** : the removal of hair or beard with a razor (~ with an electric razor takes him about five minutes) **b** : the removal of excess material with a cutting tool (~ is now the most widely used productive method of finishing . . . gear teeth —R.S. Kegg) **c** : the scraping of old material from the surface of a recording medium (as a cylinder) to obtain a new recording surface **2 a** : a slice or fragment produced by a shaver: as **a** : a thin strip of wood pared off by a plane — usu. used in pl. (fragrant boards and ~s —G.W.Brace) **b** *shavings pl* : the strips trimmed from either side of a paper web or from a pile of sheets **c** : FLAKE, CHIP (the roll is then dusted with cocoa and decorated with ~s of bitter chocolate —*New Yorker*) **3 a** : the discounting of a note at an exorbitant rate **b** : a reduction in amount (some price ~s were announced —*Dun's Rev.*)
shaving board *n* : a small slanted beam on which barrel hoops are shaved
shaving brush *n* : a brush used to lather the face preparatory to shaving — see BRUSH illustration
shaving cream *n* : an emollient paste made usu. of soap and free fatty acid (as stearic acid) that forms a mild firm lather for softening the beard before shaving
shaving die *n* : a cutting die for shaving a thin finishing cut from work previously blanked or pierced nearly to size
shaving horse *n* **1** : a bench astride which a workman sits while shaving down work (as with a drawknife) **2** : a sloping frame having two wooden clamps to hold material being shaved
shaving machine *n* : a machine with a high speed revolving spiral knife for smoothing off the flesh side of a hide
shav·ings \'shāviŋz, -vēŋz\ *n pl but sing or pl in constr* : FRINGE TREE
shaving soap *n* : a soap made from either a soda or potash base to which is added a relatively large amount of free fatty acid (as palmitic acid or stearic acid) to decrease the customary alkalinity of the soap and produce a thick lather for shaving
shavuoth *or* **shavuot** *or* **shavuos** *usu cap var of* SHABUOTH
¹shaw \'shö\ *n -s* [ME *shaw*, fr. OE *scaga, sceaga*; akin to ON *skagi* promontory, *skaga* to project — more at SHAG] *dial* : a grove of trees : COPSE, THICKET (scattered through the ~ —C.S.Coon); *esp* : a strip of woods forming the boundary of a field
²shaw \'shö\ *chiefly dial var of* SHOW
³shaw \"\ *n -s* [prob. fr. ²*shaw*] *chiefly Brit* : the tops and stalks of a cultivated crop (as potatoes or turnips) (heavy-yielding ~s, with great ~s that protected the tubers from the hot sun —Paul de Kruif)
shawabti *var of* USHABTI
shaw·a·nese salad \'shö(w)ə'nēz-, -ēs-\ *n, usu cap 1st S* [*Shawanese* fr. obs. E *Shawanese* Shawnee, Shawanese, Shawnees, Shawnees, fr. Shawnee] : VIRGINIA WATERLEAF
shawfowl \'=,=\ *n* [perh. fr. ²*shaw* + *fowl*] *obs* : SCARECROW
¹shawl \'shöl\ *n -s often attrib* [Per *shāl*] **1** : a simple garment or wrapper usu. made of a square or oblong piece of fabric (as wool) and used esp. as a covering for the head or shoulders or as a light blanket **2** : something that resembles a shawl; *specif* : a section of window glass cut from a glass cylinder split lengthwise preparatory to flattening
²shawl \"\ *vt* -ED/-ING/-s : to wrap in or as if in a shawl (little convoys of overloaded donkeys and gaily ~ed women —John Masters) (eucalypt forests ~ed the quiet earth —June Hartnett) (hostility . . . carefully ~ed under her function as hostess —Elizabeth M. Roberts)

shawl collar *n* : an attached collar rolled back in a continuous tapering line that follows the surplice neckline of a garment
shawl goat *n* [so called fr. the use of its fur in weaving shawls] : KASHMIR GOAT
shawl·less \'shöllás\ *adj* : lacking a shawl
shawl pattern *n* : a pattern copied from a cashmere shawl and usu. made with bright-colored leaf or petal motifs — compare CASHMERE 2a
shawl strap *n* : a holder made of two or more straps attached to a handle and used for compactly carrying a shawl, steamer rug, or baggage roll
shawl tongue *n* : a long tongue of a shoe, slashed at the loose end and folded over at the instep to conceal the lacing of the shoe **2** : KILTIE 2a

shawl collar

shawm *also* **shalm** \'shöm\ *n -s* [ME *schalme, shalmye*, fr. MF *chalemie*, fr. OF, alter. of *chalemel, chalumel*, fr. LL *calamellus* small reed, dim. of L *calamus* reed, fr. Gk *kalamos* — more at HAULM] : one of a family of early double-reed straight-bodied woodwind instruments preceding the oboe family — compare BOMBARD, BOMBARDON
shaw·nee \(')shö'nē, (')shä;-\ *also* **shaw·a·nee** \'shö(w)ə'nē\ *or* **shaw·a·no** \-'nō\ *n, pl* **shawnee** *or* **shawnees** *usu cap* [*Shawnee*, Shawanese back-formation fr. obs. E *Shawnese*, Shawanese Shawnee, Shawnees, fr. Shawnee *Shaawanwaaki*, pl., lit., those in the south (fr. shaawanwa south) + E *-ese*: Shawano modif. of Shawnee *Shaawanwaaki*] **1 a** : an Indian people of the Cumberland river valley, Tenn., but ranging through most of the states east of the Mississippi and south of the Great Lakes **b** : a member of such people **2** : an Algonquian language of the Shawnee people
shawnee salad *n, usu cap 1st S* : VIRGINIA WATERLEAF
shawneewood \'=,=\ *n* : WESTERN CATALPA
shaw·ny \'shönē, shän-, -ni\ *n -ES* [alter. of *shawnee salad*] : VIRGINIA WATERLEAF
shaws *pl of* SHAW
shaw·wal \shə'wäl\ *n -s usu cap* [Ar *shawwāl*] : the 10th month of the Muhammadan year — see MONTH table
shay \'shā\ *n -s* [back-formation fr. *chaise*, taken as pl.] **1** *chiefly dial* : CHAISE 1 **2** : a slow wood-burning geared locomotive used esp. for hauling logs to a mill
shaykh *var of* SHEIKH
shaykhi *cap, var of* SHAIKHI
shays·ite \'shā,zīt\ *n -s usu cap* [Daniel *Shays* †1825 Am. Revolutionary officer and insurrectionist leader + E *-ite*] : a sympathizer with or participant in Shays' Rebellion of 1786–87 in Massachusetts brought on by business depression and heavy taxes
shcher·ba·kov \,shcherbə;'köf\ *adj, usu cap* [fr. *Shcherbakov*, city in north central European part of U.S.S.R.] : of or from the city of Shcherbakov, U.S.S.R. : of the kind or style prevalent in Shcherbakov
shd *abbr* should
¹she \(')shē, shi\ *pron* [ME *she, sho*, prob. alter. of *hve, hyo*, alter. of OE *hie, hio, hēo* — more at HE] **1** : that female one (~ is the wife of Marcus Antonius —Shak.) : that one regarded as feminine (as by personification) (if Nature . . . refused to reproduce the effect he wanted, he would patiently return, evening after evening, until ~ did —Hesketh Pearson) (I bought a motorcycle . . . and ~ was a dandy —Burl Ives) — used as nominative feminine pronoun of the third person singular usu. in reference to a previously specified subject or to someone identified by an accompanying relative clause or prepositional phrase; usu. considered impolite when used in reference to a woman or girl who has not previously been mentioned by name or referred to by means of an identifying noun; sometimes in poetry and in substandard speech used pleonastically together with a noun as subject of a verb (the Liner ~'s a lady —Rudyard Kipling); see ¹HER, ³HER, ¹HERS; compare HE, IT, THEY **2** *Scot* : I, YOU, HE — used esp. in literary representations of the English spoken by Scottish Highlanders **3** : YOU (did ~ bump her little head) — compare ¹HE **4 4 a** *substand* : HER — used in a compound object (between the boy and ~) **b** *dial chiefly Brit* : HER — used emphatically as object of a verb or preposition (the earth hath swallow'd all my hopes but ~ —Shak.) (no fit place for ~ —James Spilling)
²she \'shē\ *n -s often attrib* [ME, fr. ¹*she*, pron.] **1** : a female person or animal (you are the cruelest ~ alive —Shak.) — often used in compounds (*she*-cat) (*she*-cousin) **2 a** : one that is feminine in composition or characteristics — used in compounds (*she*-poetry) (*she*-society) **b** : a plant that resembles one of a different species that is regarded as better — used in compounds (*she*-balsam) (*she*-oak)
³she \"\ *n, pl* **she** *or* **shes** *usu cap* **1** : a people inhabiting the mountains in the interior borderland between Chekiang and Fukien provinces of China **2** : a member of the She people
shea butter \'shē-, 'shā-\ *n* : a solid grayish, yellowish, or whitish fat obtained from the seeds of the shea tree and used chiefly as a food, in soap, and in candles
shea butter tree *or* **shea** *var of* SHEA TREE
shead·ing \'shēdiŋ\ *n -s* [ME *sheding* separation, division — more at SHEDDING] : any of the six divisions into which the Isle of Man is divided for the purposes of civil jurisdiction and over which there is a coroner or chief constable appointed by the governor
¹sheaf \'shēf\ *n, pl* **sheaves** \-ēvz\ *also* **sheafs** [ME *sheef*, fr. OE *scēaf*; akin to OHG *scoub* sheaf, ON *skauf* fox's tail, Russ *chub* forelock] **1 a** : a quantity of the stalks and ears of wheat, rye, or other grain bound together **a** : a bundle of grain or straw **b** : a bundle of other plant stalks or flowers bound together (the altar banked with *sheaves* of lilies) **2** : something resembling or likened to a sheaf of grain: as **a** : a collection of things bound together : BUNDLE **b** : a quantity of arrows sufficient to fill a quiver; *also* : the allowance of arrows (as 24) allotted to each archer **c** : a cluster of similar items associated but not bound together (a ~ of letters in her hand) **d** : a representation of a sheaf (as of arrows) used as a crest **e** : planes of gunnery fire of two or more pieces of a battery as a group (a converged ~) (parallel ~) **3** *sheaves pl* : a large number or quantity
²sheaf *var of* SHEAVE
³sheaf \'shēf\ *n, pl* **sheaves** \-ēvz\ [by alter.] : SHEATH (had another knife with a blade better than this, a leather ~ to keep it in —Donald Windham)

sheaf 1a

sheaf arrow *n* [ME *shefe arow*, fr. *shefe, sheaf* sheaf + *arow, arewe* arrow] : an ancient English military arrow having a long and heavy stele, full fletching, and a narrow head with or without barbs
sheaf catalog *n* : a loose-leaf catalog
sheaflike \'=,=\ *adj* : resembling a bundle of sheaved grain
sheafy \'shēfē\ *adj* : of, resembling, or forming a sheaf (~ crystalline needles)
¹sheal \'shēl\ *var of* SHIEL
²sheal \"\ *vt* [ME *schelen, schyllen*; akin to OE *scealu* shell, husk — more at SHELL] *dial chiefly Eng* : SHELL
¹sheal·ing *or* **sheel·ing** \'shēliŋ\ *also* **shil·ling** \'shiliŋ\ *n -s* [ME *schylinge* action of removing shells, fr. gerund of *schelen, schyllen*] : husked grain — usu. used in pl.
²shealing \'shēliŋ\ *var of* SHIELING
shea nut *n* : the seed of the shea tree
shea-nut oil *n* : SHEA BUTTER
shea-oak *var of* SHE-OAK
¹shear \'shi(ə)r, -iə\ *vb* **sheared** \-i(ə)rd, -iəd\ *or chiefly dial* **shore** \'shō(ə)r, 'shó(ə)r, -ōə, -ó(ə)\ **sheared** \'shi(ə)rd, -iəd\ *or* **shorn** \'shō(ə)rn, -ōən, -ó(ə)rn\ **shearing; shears** [ME *sheren*, fr. OE *sceran, scieran*; akin to OHG *skeran* to shear,

ON *skera* to cut, L *cernere* to separate, sift, *curtus* shortened, Gk *keirein* to cut, Skt *kartati* he cuts] *vt* **1 a** (1) **:** to cut off the hair from ⟨with crown *shorn*⟩; *also* **:** to cut off or cut short (hair) by or as if by the use of shears ⟨~*ed* the baby curls away⟩ (2) *obs* **:** TONSURE **b :** to cut, clip, or sever from something (as wool from sheep or superfluous nap from cloth) with or as if with shears ⟨~*ed* 100 bales of wool⟩ ⟨a hidden rock ~*ed* the keel from the ship⟩; *also* **:** to cut something from ⟨*shorn* sheep⟩ ⟨a ~*ed* velvet⟩ ⟨~ a lawn⟩ **c** *chiefly Scot* **:** to reap (as hay or grain) with a sickle **d :** to cut superfluous material from (a woody plant); *esp* **:** to prune (a hedge) with shears or other implement that cuts to a smooth even contour **e :** to cut (as metal or glass) with shears or a similar instrument **2 a :** to cut with something sharp ⟨~*ing* the hawser asunder⟩ **b** *obs* **:** to injure or separate into pieces by or as if by cutting **3 :** to traverse by or as if by cleaving ⟨a ship ~*ing* the sea⟩ ⟨a swallow that ~*s* the summer sky⟩ **4 :** to deprive of something as if by cutting **:** STRIP, DIVEST ⟨his recent ill-health had *shorn* him of strength⟩ ⟨has been *shorn* of his authority⟩ **5 a :** to subject to a shear (sense 5a) **b :** to cause (as a rockface) to move along a surface of shear ~ *vi* **1 :** to cut through something with or as if with a sharp instrument or shears **:** cleave a way ⟨birds ~*ing* through the air⟩ **2** *chiefly Scot* **:** to reap crops with a sickle **:** use a sickle in reaping **3** *chiefly Scot* **:** to split and then continue in different directions — used chiefly in the phrase *where wind and water shears* **4 :** to become more or less completely divided under the action of a shear ⟨the bolt may ~ off⟩ **5 :** to cut a vertical groove in a face in mining coal

²shear \"\ *n* -s *often attrib* [in sense 1, fr. ME *shere*, fr. OE *scēara* (pl.); in other senses, fr. ¹*shear;* OE *scēara* akin to OHG *skār* blade, ON *skæri* pair of shears, OE *sceran, scieran* to shear] **1 a** (1) **:** a cutting implement similar or identical to a pair of scissors but typically larger ⟨a ~ blade⟩ — usu. used in pl. ⟨trim a hedge with ~*s*⟩ (2) **:** one element or one blade of a pair of shears **b :** an instrument whose blades are connected at one end by a curved spring and which is used esp. for shearing sheep or skins — usu. used in pl. **c :** any of various cutting tools or machines operating by the action of opposed cutting edges of metal: as (1) **:** a machine for shearing metal and esp. in sheets; *esp* **:** ROTARY SHEARS — usu. used in pl. (2) **shears** *pl* **:** a power or hand-operated machine that cuts by means of a blade or a set of blades working against a resisting edge with the material to be sheared being between the two — see GUILLOTINE SHEARS, LEVER SHEARS (3) **:** a tool for cutting a gob of glass from the punty or a feeder (4) **:** SHEARING MACHINE 2 **d :** something felt to resemble a shear or a pair of shears: as (1) *obs* **:** WING (2) **:** a hoisting apparatus consisting of two or sometimes more spars fastened together at their upper ends, resting on their spread heels, secured or steadied by a guy or guys, and provided with tackle for masting or dismasting ships or lifting guns or other heavy loads — usu. used in pl. but sing. or pl. in constr. ⟨rigged a ~*s* to handle the timbers⟩; called also *hoisting shears, shear legs* **e :** the bed piece of a machine tool on which a table or slide rest is secured **:** WAY — often used in pl. **2** *chiefly Brit* **:** SHEARING — used in combination to indicate the approximate age of sheep in terms of shearings undergone ⟨a flock of healthy three-*shears*⟩ **3** *chiefly dial* **:** a crop that has been mowed or harvested **4 :** something (as an animal, a fleece, or an edge) that is shorn **5 a :** a strain resulting from applied forces that cause or tend to cause contiguous parts of a body to slide relatively to each other in a direction parallel to their plane of contact; *specif* **:** the ratio of the relative displacement of these parts to the distance between them **b :** the stress giving rise to this strain — see SHEARING STRESS **6 :** the sliding of a part of a rock body past another part along a fracture **syn** see STRESS — **off shears** *Austral, of a sheep* **:** recently shorn

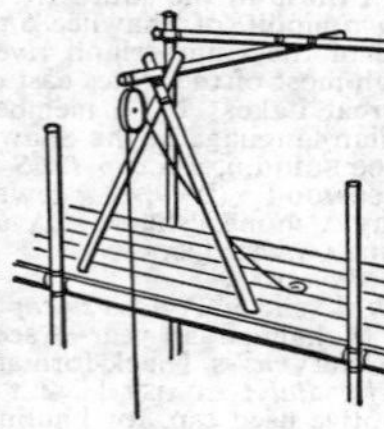
shear 1d(2)

³shear \"\ *dial var of* SHARE

shear·bill \'shi(ə)r,bil\ *n* [trans. of F *bec-en-ciseaux*] **:** BLACK SKIMMER

shear boom *n* [alter. (influenced by ²*shear*) of *sheer boom*] **:** a boom designed to guide floating logs in a desired direction

shear boy *n* **:** a worker in the glass industry who oils cutting shears and the funnels through which molten glass passes

sheard \'shärd\ *chiefly dial var of* SHARD

sheared *adj* **:** formed or finished by shearing ⟨a ~ border⟩; *esp* **:** cut to uniform length esp. to improve the appearance ⟨~ beaver⟩ ⟨~ raccoon⟩ ⟨a ~ hedge⟩

shear·er \'shirə(r)\ *n* -s [ME *sherer*, fr. *sheren* to shear + *-er*] **1 :** one that shears: as **a :** one that shears sheep **b :** a worker who uses shears on metal, textiles, leather, or other materials **c :** a machine that shears **d :** an operator of a machine for shearing out a channel down the working face of coal prior to blasting **2 :** one (as an animal) that is fit or ready for shearing or that yields a product (as fleece) to shearing ⟨sheep that are good ~*s*⟩

shear fracture *n* **:** a fracture produced in rocks by shear — compare GASH FRACTURE

sheargrass \'ˌ,ˌ\ *n* [ME *scheregresse*, fr. *scheren, sheren* to shear + *gresse, gras* grass] **:** any of various grasses or sedges with sharp-edged leaves: as **a :** SAW GRASS **b :** a plant of the genus *Leersia* **c :** COUCH GRASS 1a

shear·hog \'shi(ə),räg\ *n, dial Eng* **:** a sheep after the first shearing

shear hulk *n* **:** a ship unfit for other service that is fitted with shears for hoisting masts and other heavy articles

shearier *comparative of* SHEARY

sheariest *superlative of* SHEARY

shearing *pres part of* SHEAR

shearing deformation *n* **:** detrusion or deformation by which a small rectangle is changed into a parallelogram and in which deformation is measured as the total angular change in radians at each corner

shearing die *n* **:** a cutting die having a matrix and shearing punch for cutting off work from stock

shearing force *n* **:** either of a pair of equal opposed forces causing shear

shearing machine *n* **1 :** a machine with blades or rotary disks for cutting sheets, plates, or bars (as of metal) **2 :** a machine for shearing cloth usu. consisting of a roller with cutters operating against a ledger blade **3 :** a machine for shearing sheep

shearing punch *n* **:** a mechanical punch designed to act by shearing with little or no crushing

shearing strain *n* **:** SHEAR 5a

shearing stress *n* **:** a stress that results from the shear of an elastic solid and is measured by the force per unit area exerted by adjacent mutually displaced layers upon each other in the plane common to both

shearing tool *n* **:** a cutting tool (as a lathe tool) ground with considerable top rake

shear joint *n* **:** a crack produced in a rock body by compression **:** an incipient shear plane

shear legs *n pl but sing or pl in constr* **:** SHEAR 1d(2)

shear·less \'shi(ə)rləs\ *adj* **:** free from shear **:** having no shears

shear·ling \'shi(ə)rliŋ\ *n* -s [ME *scherling*, fr. *scheren, sheren* to shear + *-ling*] **1** *chiefly Brit* **:** a sheep that has produced one crop of wool **:** a one-year-old sheep **2 a :** sheepskin or lambskin taken from recently sheared sheep; *esp* **:** such skin tanned and dressed with the wool on **b shearlings** *pl* **:** short wool obtained by plucking from shearling skins

shear·man \'shi(ə)rmən\ *n, pl* **shearmen** [ME *sherman, shereman*, fr. *sheren* to shear + *man*] **:** one whose occupation is to shear something (as wool, cloth, or metal)

shear mark *n* **:** a mark or crease in pressed glass resulting from the local chilling action of the shears in cutting off the piece of glass for pressing

shear modulus *n* **:** the ratio of the shearing stress in a body to the corresponding shearing strain

shear·mouse \'shi(ə)r,maůs\ *n, pl* **shear·mice** \-mīs\ *dial chiefly Eng* **:** FIELD MOUSE

shear pin *n* **:** an easily replaceable pin (as the pin fixing the propeller to an outboard motor shaft) inserted at a critical point in a machine and designed to shear when subjected to excess stress — called also *break pin*

shear plane *or* **shearing plane** *n* **:** a plane or other surface along which rocks are ruptured by compressive stress

shears *pl of* SHEAR, *pres 3d sing of* SHEAR

shear skid *n* **:** FENDER SKID

shears·man \'shi(ə)rzmən\ *n, pl* **shearsmen** [by alter. (influence of *shears*)] **:** SHEARMAN

shear steel *n* **:** a steel produced by heating blister steel sheared into short lengths to a high heat, welding by hammering or rolling or both, and finally finishing under the hammer at the same or a slightly greater heat — called also *single-shear steel;* compare DOUBLE-SHEAR STEEL

shear strength *n* **:** capacity of a material or a union to resist shear

shear stress *n* **:** SHEARING STRESS

shear structure *n* **:** a local geologic structure resulting from the relief of earth stresses by the formation of a multitude of minute closely spaced fractures with slight slipping or faulting along each

sheartail \'ˌ,ˌ\ *n* **:** any of various hummingbirds with long forked tails

¹shearwater \'ˌ,ˌˌ\ *n* [¹*shear* + *water*, n.] **1 :** any of numerous oceanic birds chiefly of the genus *Puffinus* varying in size from that of a pigeon to that of a large gull, having like the related petrels and albatrosses tubular nostrils and long wings, and in their flight usu. skimming close to the waves **2 :** SKIMMER 3

²shearwater \"\ *n* [¹*shear* + *water*, n.] **:** a line of chained logs across the entrance of a bay or inlet to keep logs out

shear wave *n* **:** a wave in which the propagated disturbance is a shear strain in an elastic medium

sheary \'shirē\ *adj* -ER/-EST [perh. blend of *shiny* and *smeary*] **:** having a gloss that lacks uniformity ⟨a ~ painted surface⟩

shear zone *n* **:** a zone of shear structure or of closely spaced approximately parallel faults that often becomes a channel for underground solutions and the seat of ore deposition

she–ass \'ˌ,ˌ\ *n* [ME *she asse*, fr. ²*she* + *asse* ass] **:** a female donkey **:** JENNIE

sheat·fish \'shēt,fish\ *n* [alter. (perh. influenced by G *schaid* sheatfish, fr. OHG *sceida* sheatfish, sheath) of *sheathfish*] **:** a large elongated catfish (*Silurus glanis*) of central and eastern European rivers that may attain a length of 10 feet and a weight of 400 pounds and that lacks an adipose fin and has the long anal nearly confluent with the caudal; *broadly* **:** any of several large catfishes

sheath \'shēth\ *n, pl* **sheaths** \-ē*th*z, -ēths\ [ME *shethe*, fr. OE *scēath, scǣth;* akin to OHG *sceida* sheath, separation, ON *skeithir* sheath, OE *scēadan, scādan* to divide, separate — more at SHED] **1 :** a case for the blade of a sword, hunting knife, or other instrument to which it fits closely — compare SCABBARD **2 :** an investing cover or case of a plant or animal body or body part: as **a** (1) **:** the tubular fold of skin into which the penis of many mammals is retracted (2) **:** the connective tissue of an organ or part that binds together its component elements and holds it in place (3) **:** the lorica of a protozoan or rotifer **b** (1) **:** the lower part of a leaf (as of a grass) that more or less completely surrounds the stem (2) **:** an ensheathing spathe (3) **:** OCREA **3 :** any of various covering or supporting structures that are applied like or felt to resemble the sheath of a blade: as **a** *dial Brit* **:** a covering for holding and supporting a needle while knitting **b :** SHEATHING 2 **c :** a bar connecting the beam and sole in front in an old-time plow **d :** a thin metal plate having its edges bent over to hold a sheet of photographic film or a plate during exposure **e :** CONDOM **f :** a woman's close-fitting dress having narrow straight unbroken lines and usu. worn without a belt **g :** a portion of an electric discharge through a gas in which the positive and negative ion densities differ so much as to result in an appreciable space charge — compare PLASMA

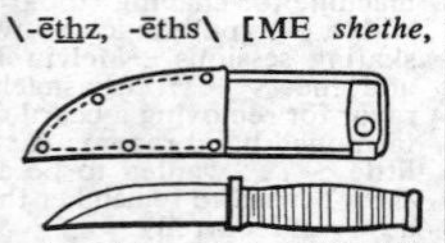
sheath 1 and sheath knife

sheathbill \'ˌ,ˌ\ *n* **:** any of several white shorebirds constituting the family Chionididae that are confined to the colder parts of the southern hemisphere, have a saddle-shaped horny sheath over the base of the upper mandible and a blunt carpal spur on the wing, and are in many characters intermediate between the gulls and plovers but suggest the pigeons in general appearance

sheathe \'shē*th*\ *also* **sheath** \-ēth\ *vt* **sheathed; sheathed; sheathing; sheathes** *also* **sheaths** [ME *shethen*, fr. *shethe* sheath] **1 :** to put into a sheath **:** enclose or cover with or as if with a sheath **2 a :** to plunge or bury (as a sword or tusk) in flesh **b :** to withdraw (a claw) into a sheath **3 :** to fit or furnish with or as if with a sheath **4 :** to case or cover with something (as thin boards or sheets of metal) that protects **:** cover with sheathing ⟨~ a ship's bottom with copper⟩ ⟨~ in the frame of a house⟩ **5 :** to make less noticeable: as **a** *archaic* **:** to render less acrid or pungent **b :** BLUNT, DULL

¹sheath·er \'shēthə(r)\ *n* -s [ME *shether*, fr. *shethe* sheath + *-er*] **:** a maker of sheaths

²sheath·er \'shē*th*ə(r), -ēthə-\ *n* -s [*sheathe* + *-er*] **:** one that sheathes; *esp* **:** a worker who applies sheathing

sheathfish \'ˌ,ˌ\ *n* [*sheath* + *fish;* prob. intended as approximate trans. of G *schaid*] **:** SHEATFISH

¹sheathing *n* -s [fr. gerund of *sheathe*] **1 :** the action of one that sheathes something **2 :** material used to sheathe something ⟨no. 1 tongue-and-groove ~⟩ **:** a protective or ornamental cover ⟨~ of copper⟩ ⟨waterproof ~⟩; *esp* **:** the first covering of boards or of waterproof material on the outside wall of a frame house or on a timber roof

²sheathing *adj* [fr. pres. part. of *sheathe*] **:** enclosing or investing as or with a sheath

sheathing board *n* **:** a composition board (as fiber board or gypsum plaster board) used to take the place of wood sheathing for buildings

sheathing paper *n* **:** a building paper of a heavier and better than usual grade

sheath knife \'shēth\ *n* **:** a knife having a fixed blade and designed to be carried in a sheath — see SHEATH illustration

sheath·less \'shēthləs\ *adj* **:** lacking a sheath **:** UNSHEATHED

sheathlike \'ˌ,ˌ\ *adj* **:** resembling or functioning like a sheath

sheath moth *n* **:** any of several moths whose larvae eat the sheaths of sugarcane and corn

sheath of hen·le \-'henlē, -lə\ *usu cap H* [after Friedrich Gustav Jacob *Henle* †1885 Ger. anatomist] **:** the attenuated extremely delicate prolongation of the perineurium at the peripheral ends of a nerve fiber

sheath of schwann \-'shwän, -'shvän\ *usu cap 2d S* [after Theodor *Schwann* †1882 Ger. naturalist] **:** NEURILEMMA 1

sheaths *pl of* SHEATH, *pres 3d sing of* SHEATHE

sheath–tailed bat \'ˌ,ˌ-\ *n* **:** any of numerous chiefly tropical bats (family Emballonuridae) distinguished by rather long slender tails free of the uropatagium

sheath–winged \'ˌ!ˌ\ *adj* **:** having the wings covered by sheaths **:** having elytra or wing cases ⟨beetles are *sheath-winged* insects⟩

sheathy \'shēthē, -e*th*ē\ *adj* -ER/-EST **:** resembling or having the form of a sheath ⟨a ~ skirt⟩ ⟨the ~ silhouette registers strongly in the sportswear market —*Women's Wear Daily*⟩

shea tree \'shē-, 'shā-\ *or* **shea butter tree** *or* **shea** *n* -s [*shea* fr. Bambara *si*] **:** a rough-barked tropical African tree (*Butyrospermum parkii*) of the family Sapotaceae having round to elongate fruits that usu. contain a single fatty nut and very hard heavy dark red wood used locally for fuel and construction — see SHEA BUTTER

¹sheave \'shiv, 'shēv\ *n* -s [ME *sheve, shive* sheave, slice; akin to OHG *scība* disk, Icel *skīfa* disk, L *scipio* staff, Gk *skipōn* staff, OE *scēadan, scādan* to divide, separate — more at SHED] **1** *also* **sheeve** \"\ **a :** the grooved wheel or pulley of a pulley block or any of several such wheels **b :** any grooved wheel or pulley **c :** the eccentric disk of an eccentric **2** *archaic* **:** SLICE

²sheave \'shēv\ *or* **sheaf** \-ēf\ *vt* -ED/-ING/-S [*sheave* fr. ¹*sheaf*, after such pairs as E *grief: grieve; sheaf* fr. ¹*sheaf*] **:** to gather and bind into a sheaf

³sheave \'shēv\ *vi* -ED/-ING/-S [perh. fr. ME *scheven* to shove, fr. OE *scēofan*, alter. of *scūfan* — more at SHOVE] **:** to reverse the action of the oars in rowing a boat **:** BACKWATER

sheaved \'shivd, 'shēvd\ *adj* **:** having a specified number or kind of sheaves ⟨a double-*sheaved* pulley block⟩ ⟨a thin-*sheaved* block⟩

sheave·less *adj* **:** having no sheave

sheave·man \'ˌmən\ *n, pl* **sheavemen :** a worker who greases and repairs sheaves

sheaves *pl of* SHEAF *or of* SHEAVE, *pres 3d sing of* SHEAVE

she·ba \'shēbə\ *n* -s [*Sheba*, ancient country in southern Arabia; fr. the Biblical account (1 Kings 10:1–13) of the Queen of Sheba's visit to Solomon] **:** an attractive and often flirtatious or giddy young woman

she–balsam \'ˌ,ˌˌ\ *n* [²*she* (plant) + *balsam*] **:** FRASER FIR

she·bang \shə'baŋ, shē'-, -aiŋ\ *n* -s [perh. alter. of *shebeen*] **1 :** a crude or primitive dwelling **:** HUT **2 :** ESTABLISHMENT, CONTRIVANCE, AFFAIR, CONCERN, THING ⟨put on a stylish ~⟩ — usu. used with *whole* ⟨blew up the whole ~⟩

she·bat *or* **se·bat** *also* **she·vat** \shə'bät, -'vät\ *or* **shvat** \'shvät\ *n* -s *usu cap* [Heb *shĕbhāṭ*, fr. Assyr-Bab *shabāṭu*] **:** the 5th month of the civil year or the 11th month of the ecclesiastical year in the Jewish calendar — see MONTH table

she–beech \'ˌ,ˌ\ *n* [²*she* (plant) + *beech*] **1 :** an Australian timber tree (*Cryptocarya obovata*) with close-grained aromatic wood **2 :** BOLLY GUM

she·been \shə'bēn\ *n* -s [IrGael *sībīn* bad ale] *chiefly Irish* **:** an unlicensed or illegally operated drinking establishment **:** SPEAKEASY

she·bek \(')shā¦bek\ *n, pl* **shebek** *or* **shebeks** *usu cap* **1 :** a people inhabiting the Mosul region of Iraq **2 :** a member of the Shebek people

she·chem·ite \'shēkə,mīt\ *n* -s *cap* [*Shechem*, ancient city in north central Palestine + E *-ite*] **:** a native or inhabitant of the ancient city of Shechem, Palestine

shechina *or* **schechinah** *usu cap, var of* SHEKINAH

shechita *or* **shechitah** *var of* SHEHITAH

¹shed \'shed\ *vb* **shed; shed; shedding; sheds** [ME *sheden* to divide, separate, shed, fr. OE *scēadan, scādan* to divide, separate; akin to OHG *skeidan* to separate, Goth *skaidan* to separate, L *scindere* to cut, split, Gk *schizein* to split, Skt *chinatti* he splits] *vt* **1 a** *chiefly dial* **:** to cause to separate from something **:** divide or draft off usu. from a larger group or body **:** set apart **:** SEGREGATE ⟨*shedding* off the best lambs for market⟩ ⟨~ the cattle into two groups⟩ **b** *archaic* **:** to divide (as hair or wool) by a part **:** PART **c :** to divide (the warp) in weaving so as to form a shed **2 a** *obs* **:** to distribute (as seed) abroad **:** SOW **b** *obs* **:** to cause (as mist) to break up or dissipate **c :** to cause to be dispersed without penetrating **:** throw off by repelling ⟨the duck's oily plumage ~*s* water⟩ **3 a :** to cause (blood) to flow by cutting or wounding **b :** to pour forth or down in drops ⟨*shedding* tears of remorse⟩ **c :** to give off in or as if in a stream **:** pour forth ⟨fishes *shedding* their eggs in spawning⟩; *also* **:** to give off or out **:** IMPART, RELEASE, DIFFUSE ⟨*shedding* kindness on all she met⟩ ⟨to ~ abroad such power may be dangerous⟩ ⟨the sun ~*s* warmth over the earth⟩ **4 :** to make disposal of or separate from (some natural part) in the normal course of life: as **a :** to cast off (as a hairy, chitinous, or other body covering) **:** MOLT ⟨caterpillars ~ their skins repeatedly⟩ ⟨the cat ~ hair over his trousers⟩ **b :** to be affected by a dropping of (as leaves or other parts) **c :** to eject (as seed or spores) from a natural receptacle ⟨a puffball *shedding* its spores⟩ ~ *vi* **1** *obs* **:** to become separated or divided **:** come apart **:** DIVIDE, DEPART **2** *dial chiefly Brit* **a :** FALL, DROP, DESCEND **b :** to pour out **:** SPILL **c :** to be dispersed **:** SCATTER **3 :** to separate off some natural covering (as of hair or skin) or part (as leaves or twigs) usu. in the normal course of life ⟨the dog is *shedding* badly⟩ ⟨some oats shatter and ~ more readily than others⟩ **syn** see DISCARD — **shed blood :** to cause death by bloodshed or violence

²shed \"\ *n* -s [ME *shed*, fr. OE *gescēad, gescād*, fr. *ge-* (perfective, associative, and collective prefix) + *-scēad, -scād* (fr. *scēadan, scādan* to divide, separate) — more at CO-] **1** *obs* **:** a separation of one thing from another; *also* **:** DISTINCTION, DIFFERENCE **2 a** *chiefly dial* **:** the part of one's hair **b :** a similar parting in the wool of a sheep **3 a** *obs* **:** a part broken away **:** FRAGMENT, CLOT **b :** something (as a cocoon or the skin of a snake) that is discarded in shedding **4 :** a divide of land — compare WATERSHED **5 :** a passageway between the threads of a warp which is made by raising and lowering the alternate or selected ends to form a narrow diamond-shaped opening and through which the shuttle is thrown in weaving

³shed \"\ *adj* [ME *sched* separated, fr. past part. of *scheden, sheden* to divide, separate, shed] **1 :** fallen off or out **:** let fall **:** SPILLED ⟨~ blood⟩ ⟨a mass of ~ hair⟩ **2** [prob. alter. (influenced by ³*shed*) of ³*shut*] *dial* **:** FREE, RID — usu. used with *of* ⟨couldn't get ~ of the old cat⟩

⁴shed \"\ *n* -s [alter. of earlier *shadde*, prob. fr. ME *shad, shade* shade — more at SHADE] **1 a :** a slight structure (as a penthouse, lean-to, or partially open separate building) built primarily for shelter or storage **:** OUTBUILDING; *esp* **:** a single-storied building with one or more sides unenclosed **b :** any of various buildings felt to resemble a shed (as in openness of structure, in use, or in having a pent roof): as (1) **:** WOODSHED (2) **:** a covered structure for housing aerostats **2** *archaic* **:** a place of shelter: **a :** an inferior dwelling or humble domicile **:** HUT **b :** the hiding or resting place of an animal **:** DEN, LAIR, NEST

⁵shed \"\ *vt* **shedded; shedded; shedding; sheds :** to put or house in a shed ⟨~ tobacco for curing⟩ ⟨the added cost of *shedding* cattle in cold weather⟩

⁶shed \"\ *Scot var of* SHADE

shed–builder ant *n* **:** any of various ants (as of the genus *Cremastogaster*) that build carton nests attached to trees or bushes

shed burn *n* **:** POLE ROT

shed·der \'shedə(r)\ *n* -s [ME *scheder*, fr. *scheden, sheden* to shed + *-er*] **1 :** one that sheds something ⟨a ~ of blood⟩: as **a** (1) **:** a crab or lobster about to begin to molt its shell **:** PEELER (2) **:** a crab that has just shed its shell **b :** a female salmon after spawning **c :** a spring device to eject a blank from a die **d :** an individual that sheds agents of infection (as through feces or other body discharges) — compare CARRIER **2 :** a fruit that has fallen from a tree

¹shed·ding \'shediŋ, -dēŋ\ *n* -s [ME *sheding*, fr. gerund of *sheden* to shed] **1 :** an act or the process by which things are shed **:** PARTING, DIVISION, SEPARATION **2 :** something that is shed off — usu. used in pl. **3 :** a nutritional disturbance in cotton resulting in the premature dropping of bolls

²shedding \"\ *adj* [fr. pres. part. of ¹*shed*] **:** that sheds or is shed ⟨~ rose petals⟩

³shedding \"\ *n* -s [⁴*shed* + *-ing*] **:** SHEDS; *esp* **:** storage or other facilities provided in the form of sheds

shedding box *or* **shedding float** *n* **:** a crab float in which crabs are held until they shed and emerge as marketable soft-shelled crabs

shed dormer *n* **:** a dormer window with a horizontal eave line as distinguished from a gabled dormer

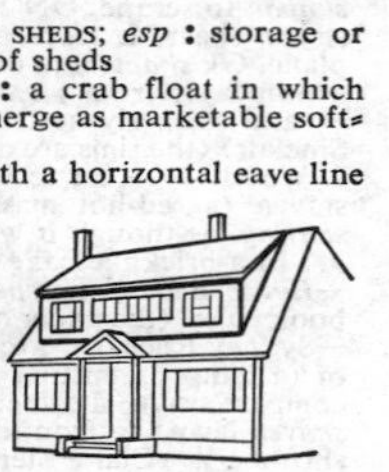
shed dormer

she·der \'shēdə(r)\ *n* -s [prob. fr. ²*she* + *deer* (animal)] *dial Eng* **:** a female sheep; *specif* **:** one past eight or nine months that has not yet been sheared

she–devil \'ˌ!ˌˌ\ *n* **:** a woman that is like a devil (as in harshness toward or torment of others)

shedhand \'ˌ,ˌ\ *n* **:** a workman employed in an Australian woolshed

shedlike \'ˌ,ˌ\ *adj* **:** resembling a shed

shed·man \'ˌmən\ *n, pl* **shedmen :** one who works in a shed: as **a :** one who stacks lumber in a shed **b :** a cannery worker who sorts food products according to size or grade and removes defective ones

shed roof *n* **:** PENT ROOF

sheds *pres 3d sing of* SHED, *pl of* SHED

she·du \ˈshā(ˌ)dü\ *n, pl* **she·dim** \-ādəm\ [Assyr-Bab *shēdu*] **1** *usu cap* **:** one of various semidivine beings represented by ancient Assyrian sculptors as colossal human-headed bulls or lions **2** [Heb *shēdh*, fr. Assyr-Bab *shēdu*] **:** a traditional Jewish evil demon

shee *var of* SIDHE

shee·fish \ˈshē,fish\ *n* [*shee* (prob. native name in Alaska or northwest Canada) + *fish*] **:** INCONNU

sheel \ˈshē(ə)l\ *var of* SHEAL

¹sheeling *var of* SHEALING

²sheel·ing \ˈshēliŋ\ *var of* SHIELING

¹sheen \ˈshēn\ *adj* [ME *shene*, fr. OE *scēne, sciene;* akin to MD *schone* bright, clean, beautiful, OHG *skōni* bright, beautiful, Goth *skauns* beautiful, OE *scēawian* to look — more at SHOW] **:** BEAUTIFUL, SPLENDID, RESPLENDENT, BRIGHT, GLITTERING, RADIANT

²sheen \"\ *adv* [ME *shene*, fr. *shene*, adj.] *archaic* **:** BEAUTIFULLY, BRIGHTLY

³sheen \"\ *vi* -ED/-ING/-S [ME (northern dial.) *shenen* to shine, fr. ME *shene*, adj.] **:** to be bright **:** show a sheen **:** SHINE

⁴sheen \"\ *n* -S [¹*sheen*] **1 a :** a bright or shining condition **:** BRIGHTNESS **b :** a subdued and often iridescent or metallic glitter that approaches but is just short of optical reflection **:** a surface luster (as of a mineral cleavage surface or of a dark feather) **c :** a lustrous surface ranging from dull to brilliant imparted to textiles through finishing processes or use of shiny yarns (as rayon) **2 :** something marked by surface brilliance: as **a :** bright or showy clothing **:** splendid raiment **b** *slang* **:** counterfeit coin **c :** a textile exhibiting notable sheen

⁵sheen \"\ *archaic pl of* SHOE

sheen·ful \-nfəl\ *adj* **:** exhibiting or characterized by sheen

sheen·less \-nləs\ *adj* **:** lacking sheen **:** having no surface luster or glitter **:** DULL

sheen·ly *adv* [ME *scheenely*, fr. *scheene, shene*, adj., sheen + *-ly*] **:** BRIGHTLY

¹sheeny \ˈshēnē, -ni\ *adj* -ER/-EST [⁴*sheen* + *-y*] **:** lustrous with sheen **:** SHINING, RADIANT

²shee·ny *or* **shee·nie** *also* **shee·ney** \"\ *n, pl* **sheenies** *also* **sheeneys** [origin unknown] **:** JEW — usu. taken to be offensive

¹sheep \ˈshēp\ *n, pl* **sheep** *often attrib* [ME, fr. OE *scēap, scēp;* akin to MD *schaep* sheep, OHG *scāf*] **1 :** any of numerous ruminant mammals (genus *Ovis*) native to upland regions of the northern hemisphere and related to the goats from which they may usu. be distinguished by a stockier build, absence of a beard in the male, and horns that when present are more divergent and in older males often coiled into flattened lateral spirals; *specif* **:** a mammal (*O. aries*) long domesticated for its flesh, specialized hair or wool, and other products and differentiated through continued selection into many breeds some of which are notable for meat production, others for wool, and a few for fur or milk — see EWE, LAMB, RAM; MUTTON; KARAKUL **2 :** one that is like a sheep (as in being a defenseless innocent creature or in being readily preyed upon or shorn): as **a :** mankind or a group of people under the shepherding care of God or Christ; *also* **:** a group under the charge of a pastor or similar director **b :** a stupid docile person **:** a silly bashful fellow **c** *obs* **:** a biddable kindly woman — often opposed to *shrew* **3 :** leather prepared from the skins of sheep **:** SHEEPSKIN

²sheep \"\ *vt* -ED/-ING/-S **:** to graze or pasture (as land or crops) by sheep — often used with *off* or *down* ⟨~*ing* off the grass⟩

sheepback \ˈ=,=\ *n* **:** ROCHE MOUTONNÉE

sheep·berry \ˈshēp- — *see* BERRY\ *n* **1 a :** a No. American shrub or small tree (*Viburnum lentago*) having white flowers in flat cymes **b :** the black edible berrylike drupe of this plant **2 :** BLACK HAW 1

sheepbine \ˈ=,=\ *n* **:** FIELD BINDWEED

sheepbiter *n* **1** *obs* **:** one that practices petty thefts **2** *obs* **:** PHILANDERER

sheep biting louse *n* **:** SHEEP LOUSE 1

sheep blowfly *n* **:** any of several blowflies that attack sheep

sheep bot *n* **:** the larva of the sheep botfly

sheep botfly *or* **sheep gadfly** *n* **:** a botfly (*Oestrus ovis*) whose larvae parasitize sheep and lodge esp. in the nasal passages, frontal sinuses, and throat

sheep bur *n* **:** any of several plants whose fruits or seeds tend to lodge in sheep's wool: as **a :** an annual composite weed (*Acanthospermum australe*) of the southern U.S. and tropical regions with a prickly fruit shaped like a starfish **b :** COCKLEBUR **c :** STICKSEED

sheep·cote \ˈshēp,kōt\ *also* **sheep·cot** \-kät\ *n* -S [ME *shepcote, schepcott*, fr. *shep, schep, sheep* sheep + *cote* shed for small domestic animals, small house & *cot* small house — more at COTE, COT] *chiefly Brit* **:** SHEEPFOLD, SHEEPHOUSE

sheep crab *n* **:** a large rough spider crab (*Loxorhynchus grandis*) living in shallow water along the California coast

sheepcrook \ˈ=,=\ *n* [ME *shepe-crook*, fr. *shepe, sheep* sheep + *crook, crok* crook] **:** a shepherd's crook

sheep–dip \ˈ=,=\ *n* **1 :** a liquid preparation of toxic chemicals into which sheep are plunged esp. to destroy parasitic arthropods (as lice, mites, keds, ticks) **2 :** a coal-tar disinfectant for use about farms or on animals' wounds

sheep dog *n* **:** a dog used to tend, drive, or guard sheep — compare OLD ENGLISH SHEEPDOG

sheep eater *n, usu cap S&E* **:** one of a band of Shoshone Indians in the neighborhood of Yellowstone Park

sheep·faced \ˈshēp,fāst\ *adj* **:** BASHFUL, SHY, SHEEPISH — **sheep·faced·ly** \-sədlē, -stlē, -li\ *adv* — **sheep·faced·ness** \-sədnəs, -s(t)nəs\ *n* -ES

sheep fescue *or* **sheep's fescue** *n* **:** a hardy European perennial fescue grass (*Festuca ovina*) that is widely cultivated for sheep pasturage in upland situations, is used as a lawn grass, and has densely tufted erect stems and very fine foliage

sheep flake *n, dial Brit* **:** a rack or open wicker cage for carrying fodder to sheep in winter

sheep fly *n* **:** any of several flies (superfamily Muscoidea) having larvae that live in the wool of sheep and feed on the flesh beneath and are particularly destructive in arid regions

sheepfold \ˈ=,=\ *n* [ME *sheep fold*, fr. ¹*sheep* + *fold*] **1 :** a pen or shelter for sheep **2 :** a source or center of security (as a church or sanctuary)

sheepfoot \ˈ=,=\ *n, pl* **sheepfoots :** BIRD'S-FOOT TREFOIL 1a

¹sheepgate \ˈ=,=\ *n* [¹*sheep* + *gate* (opening)] **:** a gate for the passage of sheep **:** a hurdle for enclosing sheep

²sheepgate \"\ *n* [¹*sheep* + *gate* (pasturage)] **:** pasturage for sheep; *also* **:** the cost of such pasturage

sheep grass *n* **:** BERMUDA GRASS

sheephead *var of* SHEEPSHEAD

sheepheaded \ˈ=,==\ *adj* **:** SILLY, SIMPLEMINDED, STUPID

sheepherder \ˈ=,==\ *n* **:** a worker in charge of a band of sheep esp. on open range **:** SHEPHERD

sheepherding \ˈ=,==\ *n* **:** the business of a sheepherder

sheephook \ˈ=,=\ *n* [ME *shephoke*, fr. *shep, sheep* sheep + *hoke, hok* hook] **:** a shepherd's crook

sheephouse \ˈ=,=\ *n* [ME *shephous*, fr. *shep, sheep* sheep + *hous* house] **:** a covered enclosure for housing sheep

sheepier *comparative of* SHEEPY

sheepiest *superlative of* SHEEPY

sheeping *pres part of* SHEEP

sheep·ish \ˈshēpish, -pēsh\ *adj* [ME *shepish*, fr. *shep, sheep* sheep + *-ish*] **1** *archaic* **:** of or relating to sheep **2 :** like a sheep in some quality (as meekness, stupidity, timidity): as **a :** meanly or foolishly diffident **:** timorous to excess **:** BASHFUL **b :** embarrassed by consciousness of a fault — **sheep·ish·ly** *adv* — **sheep·ish·ness** *n* -ES

sheep ked *n* **:** a wingless bloodsucking hippoboscid fly (*Melophagus ovinus*) that feeds chiefly on sheep and is a vector of sheep trypanosomiasis — called also *sheep tick*

sheepkill \ˈ=,=\ *n* **:** SHEEP LAUREL

sheep–kneed \ˈ=,=\ *adj* **:** having knees like those of a sheep — used of a horse when the foreleg below the knee deviates slightly forward

sheep laurel *n* **:** a No. American dwarf shrub (*Kalmia angustifolia*) that is poisonous to young stock and that resembles mountain laurel but has narrower leaves and smaller bright red flowers

sheep·less \ˈshēpləs\ *adj* **:** having no sheep

sheep–lice \ˈ=,=\ *n pl but sing or pl in constr* **:** HOUND'S-TONGUE 1

sheeplike \ˈ=,=\ *adj (or adv)* **:** like a sheep esp. in meekness, docility, or stupidity

sheep loco *n* **:** LOCOWEED; *esp* **:** any plant of the genus *Astragalus*

sheep louse *n* [ME *scheplows*, fr. *schep, sheep* sheep + *lows, lous* louse] **1 :** a biting louse (*Bovicola ovis*) that infests sheep and feeds on the wool **2 :** SHEEP KED

sheep maggot *n* **:** the larva of a sheep fly

sheep·man \ˈshēpmən, -,man, -,maa(ə)n\ *n, pl* **sheepmen :** a man engaged in the handling, raising, or breeding of sheep: as **a** *obs* **:** SHEPHERD, SHEEPHERDER **b :** an owner or rancher of sheep esp. when specializing in sheep to the exclusion of other activities

sheepmaster \ˈ=,==\ *n, chiefly Brit* **:** SHEEPMAN b

sheep measles *n pl but sing or pl in constr* **:** infestation of the muscles of sheep with cysticerci of a dog tapeworm (*Taenia ovis*)

sheepmint \ˈ=,=\ *n* **:** FIELD BALM 1

sheep nasal fly *or* **sheep nostril fly** *n* **:** any of several oestrid flies having larvae that live as parasites in the nasal cavities of sheep and occas. goats; *esp* **:** SHEEP BOTFLY

sheepnose \ˈ=,=\ *n* **:** any of several apples that have rather long fruit with four decided prominences at the blossom end

sheepnut \ˈ=,=\ *n* **:** JOJOBA

sheep plant *n* **:** any of several New Zealand plants of the genus *Raoulia* (as *R. eximia, R. lutescens*, and *R. mammillaris*) with white woolly tufted foliage that when viewed from a distance suggests the form of a sheep — called also *vegetable sheep*

sheep–pod \ˈ=,=\ *n* **:** any of several western No. American locoweeds of the genus *Astragalus*

sheep poison *n* **1 :** SHEEP LAUREL **2 :** a California lupine (*Lupinus densiflorus*) **3 :** a common yellow-flowered wood sorrel (*Oxalis stricta*)

sheep pox *n* **:** a virus disease of sheep and possibly goats that is related to smallpox and was formerly epizootic in warmer Old World areas, is marked by formation of vesicles or pocks esp. on the bare or thinly wooled areas of the body, and is frequently complicated by secondary septic infection

sheep rack *n* **:** a rack for feed for sheep

sheep rot *n* **1** *dial Eng* **a :** MARSH PENNYWORT **b :** BUTTERWORT **2 :** liver rot of sheep

sheeps *pres 3d sing of* SHEEP

sheep saffron *n* **:** SHEEP SORREL 1

sheep's–bane \ˈ=,=\ *n, pl* **sheep's–banes :** MARSH PENNYWORT

sheep's–bit \ˈ=,=\ *n, pl* **sheep's–bits :** a European herb (*Jasione montana*) that is adventive in the eastern U. S. and has blue flowers somewhat resembling those of scabious

sheep scab *n* **:** mange (as psoroptic mange) of sheep — compare HEAD SCAB

sheep's eye *n* **:** a shy longing and usu. amorous glance — usu. used in pl. ⟨cast *sheep's eyes* at someone⟩

sheep's fescue *var of* SHEEP FESCUE

sheep's–foot \ˈ=,=\ *n, pl* **sheep's–foots :** a metal bar formed into a hammer head at one end and a claw at the other and used as a lever and hammer esp. by printers

sheepsfoot roller \ˈ=,=-\ *or* **sheepsfoot tamper** *also* **sheeps-foot** *n, pl* **sheepsfoots :** a roller for earth or pavement with spikes inserted to compact, perforate, or scarify the rolled surface

sheep's–gowan \ˈ=,=\ *n, pl* **sheep's–gowans :** WHITE CLOVER a

sheepshank \ˈ=,=\ *n* **1 :** a knot for shortening a line **2** *Scot* **:** something of no worth or importance

sheepshead *or* **sheephead** \ˈ=,=\ *n* **1** *archaic* **:** a silly or stupid person **2 a :** a sparid food fish (*Archosargus probatocephalus*) of the Atlantic and Gulf coasts of the U. S. with broad incisor teeth suggesting those of a sheep and a compressed black-banded body **b :** FRESHWATER DRUM **c :** a common California wrasse (*Pimelometopon pulcher*) that in the males is black more or less marked with crimson and in the females and young uniformly rose-colored **3** [trans. of G *schafskopf, schajkopf*] **:** a simple form of skat — called also *schafskopf*

sheep's–head clock \ˈ=,=-\ *or* **sheep's–head** *n, pl* **sheep's–heads :** a lantern clock with one hand and a crown escapement and large dials that overlap the movement

sheepshead porgy *n* **:** a small fish (*Calamus penna*) of the family Sparidae found from Florida to Brazil

sheepshearer \ˈ=,==\ *n* **1 :** a person that shears sheep by hand or machine **2 :** a machine for shearing sheep

sheepshearing \ˈ=,==\ *n* **1 :** the act of shearing sheep **2 :** the time or season at which sheep are sheared; *also* **:** a festival held at or about this time

sheep shears *n pl but sing or pl in constr* **:** a shears with broad flat blades forming the two ends of an elastic steel bow by means of which they open automatically when released from the closing pressure of the hand

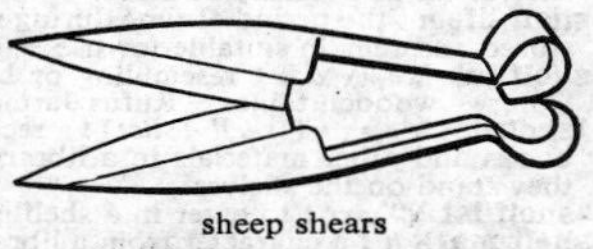

sheep shears

sheep–sick \ˈ=,=\ *adj, of soil or pasture* **:** heavily infested with parasitic worm eggs following prolonged or excessive pasturage of sheep; *broadly* **:** incapable of supporting sheep

sheepskin \ˈ=,=\ *n* [ME *shepskyn*, fr. *shep, sheep* sheep + *skyn, skin* skin] **1 a :** the skin of a sheep; *also* **:** leather prepared from it **b :** PARCHMENT **c :** a garment (as a jacket) made of or lined with sheepskin and usu. having the wool on the inside **2 :** DIPLOMA **3 :** MOTH GRAY

sheep sorrel *n* **1** *also* **sheep's sorrel :** a small herb (*Rumex acetosella*) common esp. in dry places and having pleasantly acid-tasting auricled leaves **2 :** SORREL b

sheep's–parsley \ˈ=,=\ *n, pl* **sheep's–parsleys** *dial Eng* **:** WILD CHERVIL 1; *also* **:** a related annual weedy herb (*Chaerophyllum temulum*)

sheepsplit \ˈ=,=\ *n* **:** a split of a sheepskin **:** a thin section made by splitting a sheepskin with a cutting knife or machine

sheepswool \ˈ=,=\ *also* **sheepswool sponge** *n* **:** WOOL SPONGE

sheep tansy *n* **:** FIDDLE-NECK 1

sheep tick *n* [ME *scheptyke*, fr. *schep, sheep* sheep + *tyke* tick] **1 :** SHEEP KED **2 :** CASTOR-BEAN TICK

sheep vault *n* **:** a gymnastic vault similar to a squat vault executed with the back arched and the knees flexed but with the thighs extended

sheep wagon *n* **:** an enclosed covered wagon fitted up as living accommodations for a sheepherder on the range

sheepwalk \ˈ=,=\ *n, chiefly Brit* **:** a pasture or range for sheep; *also* **:** a property devoted solely or primarily to sheep culture

sheep wash *n* **1 :** a place where sheep are washed **2** *chiefly Brit* **:** SHEEP-DIP

sheepweed \ˈ=,=\ *n* **1 :** SOAPWORT 1 **2 :** an Indian mallow (*Abutilon theophrasti*) **3 :** a butterwort (*Pinguicula vulgaris*)

sheepy \ˈshēpē\ *adj* -ER/-EST [ME *shepy*, fr. *shep, sheep* sheep + *-y*] **:** of, relating to, or suggestive of sheep ⟨a ~ odor⟩

sheepyard \ˈ=,=\ *n, Austral* **:** a place where sheep are yarded — compare STOCKYARD

¹sheer \ˈshi(ə)r, -iə\ *adj* -ER/-EST [ME *schere* acquitted, purged of sin or guilt, prob. alter. (influenced by ME *shire, shir* bright, pure, unmixed, fr. OE *scīr*) of *skere* purged of sin or guilt, unharmed, fr. ON *skærr* bright, pure; akin to OE *scīr* bright, pure, unmixed, MHG *schīr*, ON *skīrr* bright, pure, Goth *skeirs* clear, OE *scīnan* to shine — more at SHINE] **1** *obs* **:** BRIGHT, FAIR, SHINING **2 :** of very thin or transparent texture **:** fine and light in weight **:** DIAPHANOUS ⟨~ woolens⟩ ⟨a ~ summer dress⟩ **3 a :** being wholly as indicated or implied **:** belonging to such a kind or category and no other **:** unqualifiedly such **:** UTTER, ABSOLUTE ⟨frightened by the ~ immensity of the place⟩ ⟨~ folly⟩ **b :** being free from any adulterant or diluent **:** PURE, UNMIXED ⟨a layer of ~ sand provided drainage⟩ ⟨~ ale⟩ **c :** viewed or acting in dissociation from other matters **:** stressed or functioning to the exclusion of other factors ⟨the power of ~ mind⟩ ⟨won through by ~ determination⟩ **4 :** marked by great and unrelieved steepness **:** PRECIPITOUS ⟨a ~ drop⟩ **syn** see PURE, STEEP

²sheer \"\ *adv* **1 :** ALTOGETHER, COMPLETELY, DIRECTLY, QUITE ⟨fell ~ into the water⟩ **2 :** straight up or down without a break **:** PERPENDICULARLY

³sheer \"\ *n* -S **1 :** a sheer fabric (as chiffon, organdy, ninon); *also* **:** an article (as a dress) of such a fabric **2 :** PRECIPICE

⁴sheer \"\ *chiefly dial var of* SHEAR

⁵sheer \"\ *dial Eng var of* SHIRE

⁶sheer \"\ *vb* -ED/-ING/-S [perh. alter. of ¹*shear*] *vi* **:** to deviate from a course **:** turn aside to or as if to avoid collision **:** SWERVE — usu. used with an adverb of direction (as *off, away, up, in*) ~ *vt* **:** to cause to sheer ⟨~ a car around a puddle⟩ ⟨~ away the brunt of wind-driven tides —Walter Fountain⟩ **syn** see TURN

⁷sheer \"\ *n* -S **1 :** a turn, deviation, or change in a course (as of a ship) **:** SWERVE **2 :** the position of a ship riding to a single anchor and heading toward it

⁸sheer \"\ *n* [perh. alter. of ²*shear*] **1 :** the fore-and-aft curvature from bow to stern of a ship's deck as shown in side elevation **2 :** SHEER STRAKE

sheer batten *n* **:** a long strip of wood to guide carpenters in following the sheer plan in shipbuilding; *also* **:** SHEER POLE

sheer boom *n* [⁷*sheer*] **:** SHEAR BOOM

sheer draft *n, archaic* **:** SHEER PLAN

sheered \ˈshi(ə)rd\ *adj* [⁸*sheer* + *-ed*] *of a ship* **:** built with a specified sheer

sheer hook *n* [ME *sherhok*, fr. *sheren* to shear + *hok* hook] **:** an arrangement of heavy hooks usu. on a pole and with the inner surfaces sharpened formerly used to seize and cut an enemy ship's rigging

sheer leg *n* **:** one of two spars secured together at the head to form shears

sheerlegs \ˈ=,=\ *n pl but sing or pl in constr* **:** SHEAR 1d(2)

sheer line *n* [⁷*sheer*] **:** the stretched rope of a trail bridge to which a boat or raft is attached and along which it passes

sheer·ly *adv* **1 :** PURELY, SOLELY; *also* **:** ABSOLUTELY, QUITE, UTTERLY **2 :** SHARPLY, DIRECTLY **3 :** PERPENDICULARLY, VERTICALLY, PRECIPITOUSLY

sheer·ness *n* -ES **:** the quality or state of being sheer

sheer–off \ˈ=,=\ *n* -S [fr. the phrase *sheer off*] **:** an act or instance of sheering off

sheer plan *n* **:** a drawing of the profile or side elevation of a ship's form

¹sheer pole *n* [⁴*sheer* + *pole*] **:** SHEAR 1d(2)

²sheer pole *n* [⁸*sheer* + *pole;* fr. its position parallel to the sheer of the ship] **:** a pole seized to the shrouds of a ship just above the deadeyes and forming the first ratline — see SHIP illustration

sheer ratline *n* [⁸*sheer*] **:** every fifth ratline of the rigging of a ship extending to the swifters, after shrouds, and backstays

sheers *pl of* SHEER, *pres 3d sing of* SHEER

sheer strake *n* **:** the upper strake of shell plating at the main deck in a steel ship or the top line of planking in a wooden ship — see SHIP illustration

sheer thursday *n, usu cap S&T* [ME *scherethursday*, fr. *schere* purged of sin or guilt + *thursday;* prob. fr. the practice of confessing one's sins on Maundy Thursday — more at SHEER] **:** MAUNDY THURSDAY

¹sheet \ˈshēt, *usu* -ēd·+V\ *n* -S [ME *shete*, fr. OE *scēte, scȳte;* akin to OE *scēat* corner, region, napkin, fold, lap, OHG *scōz* coattail, lap, bosom, ON *skaut* corner, coattail, bosom, sheet (rope regulating a sail), Goth *skaut* edge (of a garment), OE *scēotan* to shoot — more at SHOOT] **1 a :** a piece of cloth (as a towel or napkin) — obs. except in specific applications **b :** WINDING-SHEET **c :** an oblong of usu. linen or cotton cloth used in pairs as an article of bedding and placed one immediately under and one immediately over the person ⟨fresh ~*s* each week⟩ **d :** a piece of cloth used as a covering or wrapping (as for a horse); *esp* **:** DUST COVER 1 **e :** SAIL 1 **2 :** a usu. oblong or square piece of paper esp. in one of the various sizes in which paper is made according to the uses to which it is to be put ⟨brown wrapping paper in separate ~*s*⟩ ⟨box of writing paper containing 24 ~*s* and 12 envelopes⟩ ⟨500-*sheet* roll of toilet paper⟩: as **a :** a piece of paper of a size suitable for printing esp. of books or other matter of which the page is a subdivision of a larger area — often distinguished from *reel* and *web;* compare SIGNATURE **b :** a printed signature for a book esp. before it has been folded, cut, or bound — usu. used in pl. ⟨a book in ~*s*⟩ **c :** a piece of paper comprising one unit of a larger printed whole ⟨a poster in 24 ~*s*⟩ **d :** a newspaper, periodical, or occasional publication; *often* **:** one of a scandalous or scurrilous nature ⟨a hate ~⟩ ⟨a scandal ~⟩ **e :** printed or duplicated matter for reference or instruction (as in an office, shop, or factory) and often in pamphlet form ⟨an 8vo style ~ of 64 pages⟩ **f** (1) **:** the unseparated postage stamps printed by one impression of a plate on a single piece of paper (2) **:** a quarter or half section of a sheet of stamps **:** PANE — called also *post-office sheet* (3) **:** one of the primary sections into which a reel of stamps printed by a rotary press is cut for shipment to post offices **:** MINIATURE SHEET, SOUVENIR SHEET **3 a :** a broad stretch or surface of something that is usu. thin in comparison to its length and breadth or that presents a white, bright, or glistening surface ⟨hills covered with a ~ of ice⟩ ⟨whole ~*s* of daisies deck the meadows⟩ ⟨a broad ~ of hardened lava⟩ **b :** the expanse of ice on which a curling match is played **4 a :** a suspended or moving expanse (as of fire, lightning, rain, or mist) ⟨rain came down in ~*s*⟩ ⟨~*s* of flame and smoke were driven by the wind⟩ ⟨a ~ of fog rolled in from the sea⟩ **b :** a thin flat current of compressed air striking the lip of a flue pipe in a pipe organ **5 :** a broad thinly expanded portion of metal or other substance: as **a :** a plate forming part of a tank or boiler regardless of thickness **b :** a portion of metal less than about a quarter or sometimes an eighth of an inch in thickness — distinguished from *plate;* compare LEAF 2d(2) **c :** SHEET RUBBER **d** (1) **:** a large shallow baking pan; *esp* **:** a flat baking utensil of tinned metal usu. with a lip on the front edge for handling — see COOKIE SHEET (2) **:** cake or bread baked in one piece in a large shallow pan ⟨a ~ of gingerbread⟩ **6 :** all of a surface so connected that it is possible to pass from any one point of it to any other without leaving the surface — **between the sheets :** in bed

²sheet \"\ *vb* -ED/-ING/-S *vt* **1 a :** to wrap in a sheet **:** cover with or as if with a sheet **:** SHROUD ⟨floors ~*ed* with dust⟩ **b :** to cover in a sheet or layer ⟨mist ~*s* the valleys⟩ **2 :** to furnish (as a bed) with sheets ⟨a freshly-*sheeted* couch⟩ **3 :** to form into sheets: as **a :** to convert rubber to sheet form by calendering **b** (1) **:** to cut (a roll of paper) into sheets (2) **:** to run (pulp) into a sheet (as on a paper machine) **4 :** SLIP-SHEET ~ *vi* **1 :** to fall, spread, or flow in or as if in a sheet ⟨fog ~*ing* in from the sea⟩ **2 :** to partially set and slip from a spoon in a sheet when poured after slight cooling — used of a test sample of jelly taken from a boiling mass ⟨bottle the jelly as soon as it ~*s*⟩

³sheet \"\ *adj* **1 :** rolled or spread out in a sheet ⟨~ copper⟩ **2 :** of, relating to, or concerned with the making of sheet metal ⟨a ~ mill⟩ ⟨~ rollers⟩

⁴sheet \"\ *n* -S [ME *shete*, fr. OE *scēata* corner, lap, lower corner of a sail; akin to MLG *schōte* sheet (rope regulating a sail), OE *scēat* corner, lap — more at ¹SHEET] **1 :** a rope or chain that regulates the angle at which a sail is set in relation to the wind — see MAINSHEET, WEATHER SHEET; compare TACK; see SAIL illustration **2 sheets** *pl* **:** the spaces at either end of an open boat not occupied by thwarts **:** foresheets and stern sheets together — **sheet in the wind** *or* **sheet to the wind :** a disordered state caused by drinking **:** INTOXICATION — used with *have* or *be* and often qualified quantitatively ⟨he was three *sheets in the wind* by then⟩ ⟨already had a *sheet in the wind*⟩

⁵sheet \"\ *vt* -ED/-ING/-S **:** SHEET HOME 1

⁶sheet \"\ *n* -S [by shortening] **:** SHEET ANCHOR

sheet·age \ˈshēd·ij\ *n* -S **:** the total surface area of a paperboard esp. as contrasted with its weight ⟨a high-*sheetage* boxboard high in bulk and low in weight⟩

sheet anchor *n* [alter. (prob. influenced by ⁴*sheet*) of earlier *shoot anchor*, fr. ME *shute anker*, perh. fr. *shute, shutte* sheet (rope regulating a sail) (fr. MLG *schōte*) + *anker* anchor] **1 :** a large strong anchor carried in the waist of a ship — called also *waist anchor* **2 :** something that constitutes a main support or dependence in danger **:** the best or surest hope, reliance, or refuge

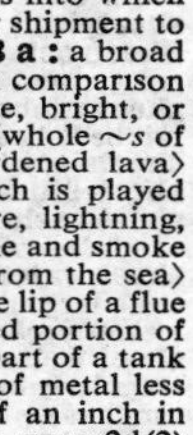

sheet bend

sheet bend *n* **:** a bend or hitch used for temporarily fastening a rope to the bight of another rope or to an eye — called also *becket bend, mesh knot, netting knot, swab hitch, weaver's knot*

sheet–block \ˈ=,=\ *n* **:** one of the blocks used to sheet sails home
sheet cable *n* **:** the cable of a sheet anchor
sheet chain *n* **:** a sheet cable of chain
sheet composting *n* **:** the incorporation (as by plowing under) of large quantities of organic residue in the soil usu. accompanied by the addition of extra nitrogen to speed decomposition
sheet deposit *n* **:** a mineral deposit (as a lode or bed) that is extended in length and breadth, has relatively small thickness, and is typically approximately horizontal
sheet·ed \ˌshēd·əd\ *adj* [¹*sheet* + *-ed*] **1 :** covered with or wrapped in a sheet or sheets **2 :** moving or driving in sheets ⟨~ rain⟩ **3** *dial Eng* **:** belted with white ⟨a ~ cow⟩ **4 :** consisting of so many sheets — usu. used in combination ⟨a 2-*sheeted* hyperboloid⟩
sheet·er \ˈshēd·ə(r)\ *n* -s **1 :** a worker that prepares or attends to sheets (as in metallurgy or papermaking) **2 :** a machine that makes sheets
sheet erosion *n* **:** erosion that removes surface material more or less evenly from an extensive area as contrasted with erosion along well-defined drainage lines that produces or enlarges gullies or ravines
sheet–fed \ˈ=,=\ *adj* [*fed* fr. past part. of *feed*] **1 :** designed to print sheets — used of a printing press; compare WEB-FED **2 :** printed by a sheet-fed press ⟨*sheet-fed* gravure⟩
sheet film *n* **:** photographic film cut into sheets of various sizes for individual exposure when held in suitable holders in a camera
sheetflood \ˈ=,=\ *n* **:** an expanse of moving water into which the transient streams of arid regions spread out as they issue from the mountains upon the plains
sheet·ful \ˈshēt,fu̇l\ *n* -s **:** a quantity sufficient to fill a sheet ⟨a ~ of equations⟩ ⟨carried home a ~ of nuts and apples⟩
sheet glass *n* **:** glass made in large sheets by the drawing process or esp. formerly by the cylinder glass process
sheet home *vb* [⁵*sheet* + *home*, adv.] *vt* **1 :** to extend (a sail) by hauling upon the sheets until it is set as flat as possible ⟨*sheeted* the topsail *home*⟩ **2 :** to fix the responsibility for **:** bring home to one ~ *vi* **:** to extend a sail by sheeting it home
sheet ice *n* **:** ice formed by the freezing of the surface layer of the sea or other water body
sheet imposition *n* **:** a process of imposition used when the front of a sheet is to be printed from one form and the back from another form — compare HALF SHEET, WORK AND TURN
¹**sheet·ing** \ˈshēd·iŋ, -ēt|, |ēŋ\ *n* -s [¹*sheet* + *-ing*] **1 :** material in the form of sheets or suitable for forming into sheets: as **a :** a sturdy cloth usu. plainwoven of cotton or linen, made full width on a broad loom, and used esp. for bed sheets **b :** material (as a plastic) in the form of a continuous film ⟨some beautiful ~*s* that are resistant to moisture, oils, greases and chemicals —*Steelways*⟩ **2 a :** a lining of planks or boards used for supporting an embankment, trench, or cofferdam and usu. placed vertically and supported by horizontal wales that are in turn supported by braces or piles **b :** a structure produced in rock by the formation of numerous closely spaced parallel fractures that divide the rock into plates or sheets
²**sheeting** \"\ *n* -s [fr. gerund of ²*sheet*] **:** the act or process of forming into, disposing in, or covering with sheets
sheeting pile *n* **:** SHEET PILE
sheet·less \ˈshētləs\ *adj* **:** lacking a sheet
sheet·let \-lət\ *n* -s **:** a small sheet; *esp* **:** a tabloid publication
sheet lightning *n* **:** lightning in diffused or sheet form due to reflection and diffusion by the clouds and sky
sheetlike \ˈ=,=\ *adj* **:** resembling a sheet esp. in flatness and broad expansion
sheet line *n* **:** the edge of a longitudinal seam of shell plating visible from inside of a ship
sheet metal *n* **:** metal in the form of a sheet
sheet metal screw *n* **:** TAPPING SCREW
sheet mill *n* **:** a mill in which metal sheets esp. of steel are rolled
sheet mold *n* **:** a mold (as *Fusarium javanicum* or any of several penicillia) growing on sheet rubber
sheet music *n* **:** music printed on large unbound sheets of paper
sheet pavement *n* **:** an asphalt pavement
sheet pile *n* **:** any of various thick boards or planks that are wedge-shaped at the lower end and sometimes tongued on one edge and grooved on the other and are driven into the ground close together between gauged piles to form walls (as of a cofferdam); *also* **:** a rolled steel member used for the same purpose and so designed that each pile interlocks along its edges with the adjacent piles
sheetpiling \ˈ=,==\ *n* **:** a row or wall of sheet piles
Sheetrock \ˈ=,=\ *trademark* — used for a plasterboard formed of gypsum between two surfaces of tough paper
sheet rubber *n* **:** freshly coagulated latex rolled into smooth or ribbed sheets — compare SMOKED SHEET
sheets *pl of* SHEET, *pres 3d sing of* SHEET
sheet–silicate \ˈ=,==(,)=\ *n* **:** PHYLLOSILICATE
sheetwash \ˈ=,=\ *n* **1 :** SHEETFLOOD **2 :** detritus transported and deposited by the water of a sheetflood
sheet watermark *n* **:** a watermark on a stamp that is a portion of a large design covering the entire sheet — called also *overall watermark*
sheet web *n* **:** a more or less extended tissue of web woven irregularly but largely in a single plane by various arachnomorph spiders — compare ORB WEB
sheetwise \ˈ=,=\ *adv (or adj)* **:** by sheet imposition ⟨a signature run ~⟩ ⟨printed by the ~ method⟩
sheetwork \ˈ=,=\ *n* **1 :** printing done by sheet imposition **2 :** bookbinders' work including all of the operations from handling flat printed sheets, inserts, and maps to sewing the sections together — compare ³CASE *vt* 1d, FORWARD *vt* 3
sheet writer *n* **:** a bookmaker's clerk who records odds and other racing information (as on sheets affixed to walls or on blackboards) and cashes winning tickets
sheety \ˈshēd·ē\ *adj* -ER/-EST [¹*sheet* + *-y*] **1 :** resembling a sheet esp. in forming a broad expanse **2 :** having a sheeting structure ⟨~ rock formations⟩
sheeve *var of* SHEAVE
shef·fer's stroke \ˈshefə(r)z-\ *n, usu cap 1st S* [after Henry M. Sheffer *b*1883 Am. philosopher] **1 :** JOINT DENIAL **2 :** ALTERNATIVE DENIAL
shef·field \ˈshe,fēld\ *adj, usu cap* [fr. *Sheffield*, city in northern England] **:** of or from the city of Sheffield, England ⟨*Sheffield* cutlery⟩ **:** of the kind or style prevalent in Sheffield
sheffield plate *n, usu cap S* **:** a clad plate made by rolling and fusing a thin covering of silver on either side of a copper sheet
she·getz \ˈshāgəts\ *n, pl* **shkotz·im** \ˈshkȯtsəm\ [Yiddish *sheygets*, *sheyget*s, fr. Heb *sheqeṣ* blemish, abomination] **1 :** a non-Jewish boy or youth — often used disparagingly **2 :** a Jewish boy who does not observe Jewish precepts — used esp. by Jews
she·he·he·ya·nu *or* **she·he·che·ya·nu** \ˌshe(he)kəˈyä(,)nü\ *n* -s [Heb *sheheḥeyānū*, lit., who has kept us alive; fr. the seventh word of the blessing] **:** a blessing pronounced by Jews on joyful occasions (as on the first night of a festival, at the first eating of a new fruit, on donning new clothes)
she·hi·tah *or* **she·hi·ta** *or* **she·chi·tah** *or* **she·chi·ta** \shəˈkētə\ *n* [Heb *shĕḥīṭāh* slaughter] **:** the slaughtering of animals for food in accordance with rabbinic law
sheikh *or* **sheik** *also* **sheykh** *or* **shaikh** *or* **shaykh** \ˈshēk, ˈshāk, ˈshīk, *in sense 2* ˈshēk\ *n* -s [Ar *shaykh*] **1 a :** the head of an Arab family or of a clan, tribe, or village **:** an Arab chief — often used as a title or form of respectful address **b :** a governor or prince among peoples of Arabian or Muslim descent **c :** a Muslim religious leader or scholar **2** *usu* **sheik :** a man supposed to be endowed with an irresistible fascination in the eyes of romantic young women
sheikh·dom *or* **sheik·dom** \-kdəm\ *n* -s **:** a region under the governance of a sheikh
sheikh·ly *or* **sheik·ly** *adj* **:** of, relating to, or suggestive of a sheikh
sheikh ul islam *usu cap S&I*, *var of* SHAIKH AL-ISLAM
shei·la \ˈshēlə\ *n* -s [alter. (influenced by the name *Sheila*) of E (slang) *shaler*] *Austral* **:** a young woman **:** GIRL
sheil·ing \ˈshēliŋ\ *var of* SHIELING
she–ironbark \ˈ=ˈ==\ *n* [²*she* (plant) + *ironbark*] **:** any of several Australian eucalypts (esp. *Eucalyptus boormani*)
sheitan *var of* SHAITAN
shei·tel \ˈshāt³l\ *n* -s [Yiddish *sheytl*, fr. MHG *scheitel* crown of the head, fr. OHG *skeitila*; akin to MLG *schēdele* crown of the head, OE *scēadan*, *scādan* to divide, separate — more at SHED] **:** a wig worn by some Orthodox Jewish matrons in accordance with the tradition of covering the hair as a sign of modesty
she·kar \shəˈkär\ *var of* SHIKAR
shek·el \ˈshekəl\ *n, pl* **shekels** \-lz\ *or* **she·ka·lim** \shəˈkäləm\ [Heb *sheqel* (pl. *sheqālīm*)] **1 a :** any of various ancient units of weight (as of the Babylonians, Hebrews, Syrians) equivalent to a small fraction (as 1/50 or 1/60) of a mina; *esp* **:** a Hebrew unit equal to about 252 grains troy **b :** a unit of value based on the value of a shekel weight of gold or silver **2 a :** a coin weighing one shekel (as a Tyrian or Phoenician coin or a Hebrew coin of the period between the 2d century B.C. and the 2d century A.D.) **b** *shekels pl* **:** MONEY, CASH **3 :** a small annual fee payable by a Zionist into the general fund of the World Zionist Organization entitling the payer to vote for delegates to the Zionist congress
she·ki·nah *also* **she·ki·na** *or* **she·chi·nah** *or* **sche·chi·na** \shəˈkēnə, -ˈkēnə, -ˈkīnə\ *n, usu cap* [Heb *shĕkhīnāh*] **:** the presence of God in the world conceived by Jewish and later by Christian theologians as manifested in natural and esp. supernatural phenomena (as the burning bush or the cloud on Sinai's summit) or as manifested in history through a mystical as opposed to revelational intervention in human affairs or as manifested in a sense of mystic personal communion with God felt by man
sheld·fowl \ˈshel(d),=\ *n* [*sheld-* (as in *sheldrake*) + *fowl*] *dial Eng* **:** SHELDRAKE
shel·drake \ˈshel,drāk\ *n, pl* **sheldrakes** *also* **sheldrake** [ME *sheldedrake*, *sheldrake*, fr. *shelde-*, *sheld-* (akin to MD *schillede* particolored, variegated, piebald) + *drake*; akin to G *schillern* to be iridescent, and perh. to MHG *schilhen* to wink, squint, OE *sceol* wry, squinting — more at CYLINDER] **1 :** a duck of the Old World genus *Tadorna*; *esp* **:** a common European duck (*T. tadorna*) that is slightly larger than the mallard, frequents coast regions and nests in burrows, and is chiefly black and white with the head and neck greenish, the lower breast broadly chestnut, the speculum green, and the bill with its frontal knob red **2 :** MERGANSER
shel·duck \ˈshel,dək\ *n* [*sheld-* (as in *sheldrake*) + *duck*] **1 :** SHELDRAKE **2 :** the female of the sheldrake
¹**shelf** \ˈshelf, ˈsheu̇f\ *n, pl* **shelves** \|vz\ *often attrib* [ME *shelfe*, *shelf*, prob. fr. OE *scylfe* deck of a ship, shelf; akin to OE *scylf* pinnacle, crag, ledge, MLG *schelf* frame, rack, MD *schelve* hayrick, haystack, ON *skjölf* bench (in *Hlithskjölf*, Odin's throne), L *scalpere*, *sculpere* to dig, scratch, carve, cut, Gk *skalops* mole (animal), OE *sciell* shell — more at SHELL] **1 a :** a thin flat usu. long and narrow piece of wood or other material fastened horizontally at a distance from the floor (as on a wall or in a frame) to hold objects **b :** one of several similar pieces in a closet, bookcase, cabinet or similar structure **c :** the books or other contents of a shelf **:** a number of items constituting or held to constitute the contents of a shelf **2 :** something resembling a shelf in form or position: as **a :** a sandbank in a river or the sea **:** a rock or ledge of rocks usu. partially submerged **:** REEF, SHOAL **b :** a stratum with a shelf-like surface **:** bedrock under alluvial soil **c :** a flat projecting layer of rock **d :** the submerged border of a continent or of an island extending from the shoreline to the depth at which the sea floor begins to descend steeply toward the bottom of the ocean basin — see CONTINENTAL SHELF **3 :** a longitudinal member of a wooden vessel extending the entire length immediately below the deck beams which rest on and are fastened to it **4 :** the upper edge of the bow hand on which an arrow rests when the bow is drawn — **on the shelf** *adv (or adj)* **1 :** in a state of inactivity or uselessness **:** out of the way ⟨a querulous old man who refuses to be put *on the shelf* —James Kelly⟩ **2 :** without matrimonial prospects — used of a woman
²**shelf** \"\ *vt* -ED/-ING/-S **:** to put on the shelf **:** SHELVE 3a ⟨brigadiers ~*ed* as principals of colleges —Charles Kingsley⟩
shelf angle *n* **:** an angle iron attached to an I beam to provide support for the ends of joists
shelfback \ˈ=,=\ *n* **:** BACKBONE 3
shelf·ful \ˈshelf,fu̇l, -eu̇f,f-\ *n* -s **:** a quantity sufficient to fill a shelf **:** the contents of a shelf
shelf fungus *n* **:** BRACKET FUNGUS — compare POLYPORACEAE
shelf ice *n* **:** an extensive ice sheet originating on land but continuing out to sea beyond the depths at which it rests on the sea bottom **:** BARRIER ICE
shelf ladder *n* **:** a tall ladder run on wheels for access to high shelves (as in a library or store)
shelf life *n* **:** the period of time during which a material may be stored and remain suitable for use — called also *storage life*
shelflike \ˈ=,=\ *adj* **:** resembling or held to resemble a shelf ⟨long ~ wooden tables —Rufus Jarman⟩
¹**shelflist** \ˈ=,=\ *n* [¹*shelf* + *list*] **:** a record kept on cards of the books and other materials in a library in the order in which they stand on the shelves
²**shelflist** \"\ *vt* **:** to enter in a shelflist
shelf mark *n* **:** a character from a library's system of book arrangement usu. appearing at the base of the spine of a book and used to indicate the shelf in a fixed location or the relative position of the book to others of its class in an expansive classification
shelfpiece \ˈ=,=\ *n* **:** SHELF 3 — see SHIP illustration
shelf register *n, Brit* **:** SHELFLIST
shelf rest *n* **:** an angle bracket for supporting adjustable-height cabinet shelves and having a plug extension on the side angle that is inserted in a hole in the side of the cabinet

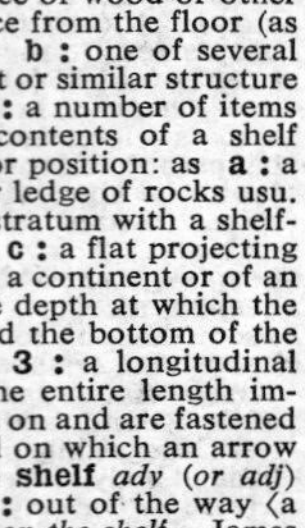

shelf rest

shelf sea *n* **:** the part of a sea or ocean which is on a continental or insular shelf **:** an epicontinental sea
shelfy \ˈshelfē, -eu̇f-, -fi\ *adj* -ER/-EST **:** abounding in shelves: **a :** full of sandbanks or dangerous shallows **b :** full of ledges or flat projecting layers of rock
¹**shell** \ˈshel\ *n* -s [ME *schell*, *shell*, fr. OE *sciell*; akin to OE *scealu* shell, husk, MLG *schelle* shell, scale on a fish, OHG *scala* shell, husk, ON *skel* shell, Goth *skalja* tile, L *silex* pebble, flint, *siliqua* pod, Gk *skallein* to hoe, Lith *skelti* to split, Skt *kalā* small part; basic meaning: to cut] **1 a :** a hard rigid covering of an animal that is commonly largely calcareous but in some cases is chiefly or partly chitinous, horny, or siliceous — see CLAM illustration **b :** the hard or tough outer covering of an egg esp. of a bird — see EGG illustration **c** *obs* **:** a scale of a fish or reptile **2 a :** the covering or outside part of a fruit or seed esp. when hard or fibrous **:** NUTSHELL, POD, HUSK ⟨the hazelnut ~⟩ ⟨the fiber-covered ~ of the coconut⟩ — compare PERICARP **b** *usu pl* **:** COCOA SHELLS **3 :** a seashell used for some purpose (as for a target or for drinking or sounding) **:** CONCH **4** *archaic* **:** OSTRACON **5 :** shell material or a quantity of shells esp. of mollusks, turtles, or tortoises **6 :** something that resembles or is held to resemble a shell: as **a :** a hollow structure usu. of a spherical, hemispherical, or domed shape **b :** a slight hollow structure **:** a framework or exterior structure that is frail in construction or has had its interior removed or destroyed or is regarded as not complete or filled in ⟨the ~ of a house⟩ **c :** a semicircular or nearly semicircular guard plate sometimes of openwork attached to the cross guard on either side of a European sword of the 15th century and later **:** COQUILLE **d** *archaic* **:** LYRE **e :** the external case or outside covering of something **:** HUSK ⟨the ~ of a ship⟩ ⟨the ~ of religion⟩ **f :** the outer frame or case of a pulley block **g** (1) **:** a rough or temporary wooden coffin (2) **:** a thin interior coffin enclosed in a more substantial one **h :** CONCHA 2b(1) **i** (1) **:** something shaped like a scallop shell; *esp* **:** a household utensil for cooking or serving (2) **:** an edible case for holding a filling **j :** a hollow cabochon **k :** a reinforced concrete arched or domed roof that is used primarily over large unpartitioned areas, is comparatively thin esp. at the crown of the arch, and carries no loads other than its own weight **l :** a prepared and usu. hollow counterpart of an object that is secretly substituted by a magician for the article itself **m :** an unlined article of outerwear; *esp* **:** a coat or jacket with a detachable lining **n :** a woman's small hat with a shell shape **o :** a needlework stitch forming a rounded edge similar to that of a shell **p :** a small beer glass **q :** the outer wall of a mold used in metallurgy **r :** the part in a loom in which the reed is fitted **s shells** *pl* **:** tinted glasses for protection of the eyes **t :** a tool used in grinding glass to exact curvatures **u :** the thin layer of copper or nickel deposited on a mold to form the face of an electrotype **v :** the outer wall of a hollow tile **w :** the metal frame around the core and tanks of the radiator and body of a motor vehicle **x :** an engraved copper roller used in calico printing **7 a :** the crust of the earth or of any of the continuous layers within the earth **b :** a thin hard layer of rock **8 :** an intermediate form at an English public school **9 :** unslaked limestone — usu. used in pl. **10 a :** a shell-bearing mollusk **b :** any of various other shell-bearing creatures — usu. used in combination **11 :** a building or similar structure without interior partitions and usu. without furnishings or decorations **12 :** an impersonal attitude or manner that conceals the presence or absence of feeling ⟨come out of one's ~⟩; *esp* **:** a forbidding and uncommunicative manner **13 :** a narrow light racing boat equipped with outriggers and sliding seats and propelled by one or more oarsmen: **a :** one used in sculling that has no rudder and is propelled by one, two, or four oarsmen who sit in single file each pulling a pair of oars **b :** one used in crew racing that is usu. steered with a rudder by a coxswain and is propelled by two, four, six, or eight oarsmen who sit in single file and pull a single oar placed alternately on the port or starboard side **14 :** the butt of a horsehide — compare CORDOVAN **15 :** a pale orange yellow that is paler and slightly yellower than sunset and paler and slightly redder than freestone **16 a :** a thin hollow cylinder (as the barrel of a cylindrical boiler or the knurled outer piece of a drill chuck) **b :** a concave grinding wheel **c :** a cupped usu. semifinished piece of sheet metal **d :** SHELL BIT **17 :** the part of a short loin of beef that contains no tenderloin **:** CLUB STEAK **18 a :** any of the spaces occupied by the orbits of a group of electrons of approximately equal energy surrounding the nucleus of an atom — see K-SHELL, L-SHELL, M-SHELL **b :** a group of nucleons of like type and approximately equal energy **19 :** a metal matrix from which phonograph records may be produced **20 a** *archaic* **:** a usu. metal casing filled with powder and shot and used primarily as a hand grenade **b :** a hollow projectile for cannon containing an explosive bursting charge, chemical, or other material which is ignited by a fuze at some point of its flight, upon impact, or after penetration with its effect being produced by the force of explosion or by the impact of its scattered fragments — compare COMMON SHELL **c :** a metal or paper case which holds the charge of powder and shot or bullet used with breech-loading small arms **:** CARTRIDGE — see BULLET illustration **d :** a firework consisting of a spherical case or a cartridge containing a charge of explosive material (as a garniture of stars) that bursts after having been projected high into the air often by a mortar — compare ³ROCKET 1 **e :** TORPEDO 4b **21 :** an unprinted paperboard carton to be overwrapped with a printed adhering paper covering **22 :** a casing without substance ⟨mere effigies and ~*s* of men —Thomas Carlyle⟩ — **in the shell 1 :** in an undeveloped or immature stage **2 :** being not yet hatched or removed from the shell
²**shell** \"\ *vb* -ED/-ING/-S *vt* **1 a :** to take out of a natural enclosing cover (as a shell, husk, pod, capsule) **:** strip, break off, or remove the shell of **:** SHUCK ⟨~ nuts or peas⟩ ⟨~ oysters⟩ **b :** to separate the kernels of (as an ear of Indian corn, wheat, or oats) from the cob, ear, or husk **2 :** to encase in or as if in a shell **3 :** to throw shells at, upon, or into **:** BOMBARD ⟨~ a town⟩ ⟨~ an enemy position or fortification⟩ **4 :** to cover (a surface) with shells ⟨~ an oyster bed⟩ ~ *vi* **1 :** to fall or scale off in the manner of a shell, crust, or outer coat **:** come off in thin pieces **2 :** to cast the shell or exterior covering **:** fall out of the pod or husk ⟨nuts ~ in falling⟩ **:** become disengaged from the ear or husk ⟨wheat or rye ~*s* in reaping⟩ **3 :** to gather shells (as from a beach) **:** collect shells **4 :** to form a shell of a solution (as on the inner surface of the container in freeze-drying)
³**shell** \"\ *adj* **1 :** having a shell ⟨a ~ animal or fruit⟩ **2 :** consisting of or containing shells and esp. seashells ⟨a ~ bluff⟩ ⟨~ marl⟩ ⟨~ concrete⟩ **3 a :** made from or ornamented with shells ⟨~ earrings⟩ ⟨a ~ belt⟩ ⟨~ workbox⟩ **b :** made of tortoise shell ⟨~ comb⟩ **4 :** resembling a shell in shape or pattern ⟨a ~ roof⟩ — used esp. of a carved decoration on furniture of the period 1720–80 ⟨a ~ chair⟩ ⟨~ trimmings⟩ **5 :** having a through longitudinal hole to receive a bar which is pushed through it and fastened in position — used of a tool ⟨a ~ end mill⟩
¹**shel·lac** *also* **shel·lack** \shəˈlak\ *n* -s [¹*shell* + *lac*, *lack*; trans. of F *laque en écailles*] **1 :** purified lac resin that is prepared in the form of thin orange or yellow flakes usu. by heating and filtering seed lac and is often bleached white and that is used chiefly in varnishes, polishing and sealing waxes, binding agents, stiffening agents (as for felt hats), electric insulators, phonograph records, and other molded products **2 :** a preparation of lac dissolved usu. in alcohol and used chiefly in filling wood and as a varnish — compare LACQUER 1a **3 a :** a composition containing shellac used for pressing phonograph records **b :** an old 78 rpm phonograph record ⟨a ~ containing only two songs —Thomas Lask⟩
²**shellac** \"\ *vt* **shellacked** *also* **shellaced** \-kt\ **shellacked** *also* **shellaced**; **shellacking** *also* **shellacing** \-kiŋ\ **shellacs** **1 :** to coat or otherwise treat with shellac or a shellac varnish **2 :** to defeat decisively or ignominiously **:** administer a beating to **:** DRUB ⟨played truant and got soundly ~*ed* for it when he was found out —William Irish⟩
shel·lack·ing \shəˈlakiŋ\ *n* -s [fr. gerund of ²*shellac*] **:** a sound drubbing **:** a decisive or ignominious defeat **:** BEATING ⟨a ~ he received that made him hors de combat after nine rounds —Nat Fleischer⟩ ⟨took a ~ in the fall election⟩ ⟨worst ~ in their military history —Richard Joseph⟩
shellac wax *n* **:** a hard wax separated from shellac (as by its insolubility in alcohol) and used chiefly in polishes and insulating materials
shell·ap·ple \ˈshe,lapəl\ *n* [alter. of earlier *sheldapple*, prob. fr. obs. E *sheld* particolored, variegated + *dapple*; akin to MD *schillede* particolored, variegated — more at SHELDRAKE] **1** *dial Eng* **:** CHAFFINCH **2** *dial Eng* **:** CROSSBILL
shellback \ˈ=,=\ *n* **1 :** an old or veteran sailor **:** OLD SALT **2 :** one who has crossed the equator and been initiated in the traditional ceremony — compare POLLIWOG 2
shellbark \ˈ=,=\ *or* **shellbark hickory** *n* **1 :** SHAGBARK HICKORY **2 :** BIG SHELLBARK
shell bark *n* **1 :** a disease of lemon trees caused by a fungus (*Phomopsis californica*) and characterized by scaling or sloughing of the bark — called also *decorticosis*; see DRY BARK **2 :** RHYTIDOME
shell–barked \ˈ=,bärkt\ *adj* **:** having a rhytidome
shell bean *n* **1 :** a bean grown primarily for its edible seeds — compare SNAP BEAN **2 :** the edible seed of any bean and esp. of a shell bean
shell bit *n* **:** a boring tool shaped like a gouge and used with a brace
shell cooling *n* **:** a method of storing potatoes in bins having tight sides and floors with air circulated around and under the bins by gravity or by power-operated blowers
shellcracker \ˈ=,==\ *n* **:** REDEAR
shell crest *n* **:** a rounded crest on the head (as of various pigeons) — distinguished from *peak crest*
shell dove *n* **:** SCALED DOVE
shell·drake *n, pl* **shelldrake** *or* **shelldrakes** [by alter.] **:** SHELDRAKE
shell drill *n* **:** a short 4-fluted drill mounted on an arbor and used for rough reaming — compare AUGER, ¹BIT 3a, CROSS BIT
shell·duck *n* [by alter.] **:** SHELDUCK
shelleater \ˈ=,==\ *n* **:** OPENBILL
shelled \ˈsheld\ *adj* [in sense 1, fr. ¹*shell* + *-ed*; in sense 2, fr. past part. of ²*shell*] **1 a :** having a shell **b :** covered or paved with shells ⟨a ~ road⟩ **c :** encased in a shell **2 a :** taken from the shell ⟨~ nuts⟩ ⟨~ oysters⟩ **b :** removed from the cob ⟨~ corn⟩
shell egg *n* **:** an egg in the shell as distinguished from a dried or powdered egg

shell·er \'shelə(r)\ *n* -s **:** one that shells: **a :** a worker who shells (as peas, nuts, grain, or bivalves) **:** an operator of a shelling machine **b :** a machine or device that shells ⟨a nut ~⟩

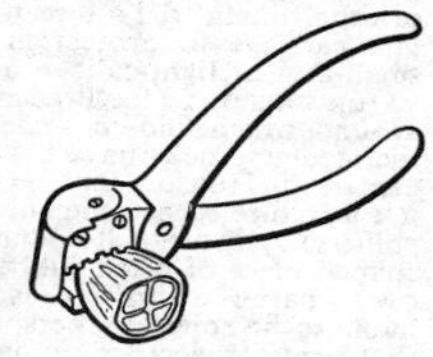

sheller b

shell expansion *n* **:** a drawing showing the shell plating of a ship and giving the size, shape, and weight of the plates and their connections

¹shel·ley·an *also* **shel·le·ian** \'shelēən, ='==\ *adj, usu cap* [Percy Bysshe *Shelley* †1822 Eng. poet + E *-an*] **:** of, relating to, or having the characteristics of the poet Shelley or his writings

²shelleyan \"\ *n* -s *usu cap* **:** a follower or admirer of the poet Shelley

shell eye *n* **:** any of numerous pigmented spots in the shell of chitons that are sensitive to light and to disturbances in the water and that sometimes develop a retina

shel·ley·esque \¦shelē¦esk\ *adj, usu cap* [Percy Bysshe *Shelley* + E *-esque*] **:** of, relating to, or characteristic of the poet Shelley or his writings ⟨such romantic and *Shelleyesque* claims for him —Kimon Friar⟩

shell fire *n, dial Eng* **:** phosphorescence from decaying matter

shellfire \'=,=\ *n* **:** firing or shooting of shells **:** the explosions from shells

shellfish \'=,=\ *n* [ME, fr. OE *scielfisc,* fr. *sciell* shell + *fisc* fish — more at SHELL, FISH] **1 :** an aquatic invertebrate animal having a shell: **a :** an oyster, clam, or other mollusk **b :** a lobster or other crustacean **2 :** BOXFISH

shell·fish·ery \'=,fish(ə)rē\ *n* **1 :** the production or catching of shellfish **2 :** the study of shellfish from the economic point of view

shellflower \'=,=\ *n* **1 :** MOLUCCA BALM **2 :** TURTLEHEAD **3 :** a showy East Indian herb (*Languas speciosa*) of the family Zingiberaceae commonly cultivated for its shining oblong leaves, bracted white flowers with shell-pink shading, and crisped yellow magenta-variegated lip

shell game *n* **:** a gambling game derived from the earlier thimblerig and in which a person by sleight-of-hand manipulates a pea or similar pellet and three half walnut shells or similar cuplike objects so that a spectator can seldom know surely under which shell the pea rests and then invites bets on the location of the pea ⟨the *shell game* is so often played dishonestly that its name has become symbolic of chicanery⟩ — compare THREE-CARD MONTE

shell ginger *n* **:** a large ornamental herb (*Alpinia speciosa*) from eastern Asia having clusters of irregularly bell-shaped flowers that are white marked with red and yellow and that bend downward from the tip of leafy arching stems which are 5 to 12 feet high

shell gland *n* **1 :** a looped tubular excretory organ of an entomostracan or the young of many other crustaceans that ends blindly at one extremity and opens to the exterior on or near the second maxilla **2 :** a glandular organ in the embryo of many mollusks that secretes the embryonic shell **3 :** a specialized glandular part of the oviduct of many animals that forms the egg's shell

shell gray *n* **:** a yellowish gray to light slightly yellowish gray that is duller than sand or natural — called also *plaza gray*

shell heap *or* **shell midden** *or* **shell mound** *n* **:** KITCHEN MIDDEN

shell hole *n* **:** the cavity made by the explosion of an artillery shell

shell ibis *n* **:** OPENBILL

shell ice *n* **:** ice orig. formed on a sheet of water but no longer resting on it because the water has been withdrawn — called also *cat ice*

shellier *comparative of* SHELLY

shelliest *superlative of* SHELLY

shel·ligs \'sheligz\ *n, pl* **shelligs** [origin unknown] **:** a large green crab (*Callinectes ornatus*) brightly marked with yellow, white, and red living in moderately deep water from New Jersey to Brazil

shelling *n* -s [fr. gerund of ²*shell*] **1 a :** hulled oats or other grain **b :** the husks or chaff from such grain **2 :** the action of one that shells: as **a :** the removal of the shell (as from nuts, peas, or oysters) **b :** the action of fertilizing with shells **c :** bombardment with shells **d :** the action of collecting shells esp. along the sea **3 :** a disease of the grape of uncertain origin causing the immature fruit to drop

shell jacket *n* **1 :** a short tight military jacket worn buttoned up the front **2 :** MESS JACKET

shell landings *n pl* **:** marks made on a ship's frames to show the location of the edges of the shell plates

shell–less \'shelləs\ *adj* **:** having no shell **:** lacking shells

shell–like \'shel,līk\ *adj* **:** resembling a shell (as in form or composition)

shell·man \'shelmən, -,man\ *n, pl* **shellmen :** JACKMAN 1

shell membrane *n* **:** the tough membraneous covering of an egg immediately within the shell

shell money *n* **:** a medium of exchange consisting of shells — compare COWRIE, WAMPUM

¹shell out *vb* [²*shell* + *out*] *vt* **1 :** to hand out or over (as money) demanded or needed **:** pay out **:** CONTRIBUTE, DISBURSE, PRODUCE ⟨known for his reluctance to *shell out* money —Barry Bingham⟩ **2 :** to remove entire by separation from its environment (as by the use of blunt instruments) ⟨*shell out* a tumor⟩ ~ *vi* **:** to furnish the money needed or called for **:** pay up ⟨makes it unnecessary to *shell out* to . . . racketeers —J.F.McDonald⟩

²shell out *n* **:** a pocket billiards game played with 15 object balls by three or more players with a stake being received by a player from his opponents each time a red ball is pocketed

shell parrakeet *or* **shell parrot** *n* **:** BUDGERIGAR

shell pink *n* **1 :** a variable color averaging a light yellowish pink that is yellower and slightly stronger than petal pink and slightly lighter and stronger than opera pink **2** *of textiles* **:** a strong yellowish pink

shell plating *n* **:** the plates covering over the frames of a steel ship and corresponding to the planking of a wooden ship

shellproof \'=¦=\ *adj* **:** capable of resisting shells or bombs **:** BOMBPROOF

shell pump *n* **:** a simple form of sand pump or sludger consisting of a hollow cylinder with a ball or clack valve at the bottom and used with a flush of water to remove detritus

shell quail *n* **:** SCALED QUAIL

shell reamer *n* **:** a hollow reamer that when used is fitted to a suitable shank made usu. of less expensive metal

shell reducer *n* **:** a thin metal shell or liner inserted into the force-feed shell of a grain drill to decrease the rate of planting of small seeds (as flaxseed)

shell road *n* **:** a road having a surface built of marine shells

shell roof *n* **:** a roof of relatively large expanse (as of a hangar or arena) composed of concrete panels curved cylindrically or spherically for strength

shells *pl of* SHELL, *pres 3d sing of* SHELL

shellshake \'=,=\ *n* **:** RING SHAKE

shell shock *n* **:** any of numerous psychoneurotic conditions akin to hysteria and anxiety neurosis appearing in soldiers exposed to modern warfare — compare COMBAT FATIGUE

shell–shock \'=,=\ *vt* [*shell shock*] **:** to affect with shell shock ⟨were gassed and wounded and *shell-shocked*⟩

shell socket *n* **:** TAPER REDUCER SLEEVE

shell strake *n* **:** a strake running the length of the hull of a ship

shell tint *n* **:** a variable color averaging a yellowish white that is stronger and slightly redder and darker than milk white — called also *pearl*

shell turtle *n* **:** HAWKSBILL TURTLE

shell–vault \'=,=\ *n* **:** a structure of thin material gaining its rigidity through its calculated shape rather than through bulk and strength

shellwork \'=,=\ *n* **:** work composed of a pattern of shells or adorned with shells

shelly \'shelē, -li\ *adj* -ER/-EST **1 a :** abounding in or covered with shells, esp. seashells ⟨a ~ shore⟩ ⟨~ ground⟩ **b :** consisting of shells or of a shell ⟨the hermit crab in his ~ cave⟩ **2 a :** of, relating to, or of the nature of a shell **:** CHITINOUS, SILICEOUS, TESTACEOUS **b :** of, relating to, or constituting fractured coal that breaks up easily into small pieces **3 :** having a shell **4 :** like a shell esp. in being hollow, frail, or easily breakable: as **a** *of a dog* **:** having a narrow weedy body **b** *of market livestock* **:** thin, gaunt, and ill-nourished (as from age) **c** *of a hoof* **:** thin and brittle and with the horny matter ridged

shellycoat \'==,=\ *n* [*shelly* + *coat*] *Scot* **:** a water sprite wearing a coat made of shells

shelly rail *n* **:** a rail in which small shell-like pieces have become detached from the top surface or side of the railhead

shel·ta \'sheltə\ *n* -s *usu cap* [origin still unknown] **:** a secret jargon of the tinkers and kindred groups still spoken to some extent in Great Britain and Ireland and consisting chiefly of a systematic deformation of Irish Gaelic and Scottish Gaelic

¹shel·ter \'sheltə(r)\ *n* -s *often attrib* [origin unknown] **1 a :** something that covers or affords protection esp. from the elements **:** something that provides refuge or defense (as from injury, exposure, observation, attack, pursuit, danger, or annoyance) **:** a means or place of protection **:** an area of safety **:** REFUGE, SCREEN **b :** a structure (as a small building in a park) used as a refuge in bad weather **c :** a structure or dugout affording protection to troops in the field **d :** an area or a specially constructed structure for refuge and protection from bombs, radiation, and other features of air attack ⟨an air raid ~⟩ ⟨bomb ~s⟩ **e :** HOUSING 3; *esp* **:** temporary housing **f :** a covering (as a box or cage) used to protect an object ⟨instrument ~⟩ **g :** an establishment to shelter the homeless: as (1) **:** a Salvationist institution operated for the homeless (2) **:** an institutional home (as for delinquent or neglected children or unmarried mothers) **h :** protection from bad weather (as by trees or walls) ⟨the trees afforded shade and ~ —Willa Cather⟩ **2 :** the state of being covered and protected (as from the elements) **:** PROTECTION ⟨I took ~ under a shed —Nora Waln⟩ ⟨the witness refuses to answer under the ~ of the Fifth Amendment —E.N.Griswold⟩

²shelter \"\ *vb* **sheltered; sheltered; sheltering** \-lt(ə)riŋ\ **-ltr-\ shelters** *vt* **1 :** to constitute or provide a shelter for: as **a :** to screen or protect from the elements ⟨the pedimented facade ~s a niched figure —*Amer. Guide Series: Md.*⟩ ⟨a light awning . . . to ~ the observer from the wind —*Topographic Surveying*⟩ **b :** to afford protection from something held to resemble unfavorable weather **:** shield from injury, attack, pursuit, annoyance, censure, punishment, or notice ⟨the defenders were . . . ~*ed* by the walls —Tom Wintringham⟩ ⟨women are ~*ed* . . . by the men of their families —Lois Long⟩ ⟨a ~*ed* life⟩ **c :** to provide with a home, security, refuge, temporary accommodation, or protection **:** HARBOR ⟨building that ~s the rare and extensive . . . collection —*Amer. Guide Series: Oregon*⟩ ⟨no other small community . . . has ~*ed* so many noteworthy American writers —*Amer. Guide Series: N.H.*⟩ **2 :** to place under shelter or protection **:** betake to cover or refuge **:** take to a safe place ⟨~ myself in the crannies of the rocks —Margaret A. Barnes⟩ ⟨every American political party . . . has ~*ed* itself behind the Supreme Court —Felix Frankfurter⟩ ~ *vi* **:** to take shelter **:** find refuge or cover ⟨if you must ~ under a tree —G.H.T.Kimble⟩ ⟨refugees . . . came here to ~ from trouble —Han Suyin⟩ ⟨a long annex . . . in which the animals ~ at night —Wilfred Thesiger⟩

shelterbelt \'==,=\ *n* **:** a natural or planted barrier of trees or shrubs primarily for protection of soil and crop fields from wind and storm and for lessening erosion — compare WINDBREAK

shelter deck *n* **:** a continuous deck of light construction above the principal deck of a ship and usu. covering a full-length superstructure or space not permanently closed against the weather — see DECK illustration

sheltered *adj* **1 :** protected from competition esp. from abroad ⟨~ trades⟩ ⟨a ~ industry⟩ ⟨~ domestic markets⟩ **2 :** protected from risks or from burdens (as taxes) ⟨a tax-sheltered investment in municipal bonds⟩ **3 :** providing a noncompetitive environment for the useful occupation and training of persons (as the physically disabled, the aged, or emotionally disturbed or handicapped children) in order to promote their adjustment and rehabilitation ⟨~ workshop⟩ ⟨~ employment⟩

shel·ter·er \-ltərə(r)\ *n* -s **1 :** one that takes shelter **2 :** one that provides shelter

shelter foot *n* **:** immersion foot from long exposure to cold and damp without actual immersion in water

shelter half *n* **:** one of the interchangeable halves of a two-man shelter tent

shelter leg *n* **:** SHELTER FOOT

shel·ter·less \'sheltə(r)ləs\ *adj* **1 :** destitute of shelter or protection **:** having no covering **2 :** affording no shelter

shelter tent *n* **1 :** a small tent usu. composed of two or more pieces of waterproof cotton duck fixed for buttoning or tying with accessory cords and poles and in military service divided into usu. interchangeable parts some of which will be carried by each soldier as part of his field equipment **2 :** a tent erected with two poles and a ridge rope with the roof sloping to the rear only often with a perpendicular drop, the sides perpendicular, and the front closed by a hanging flap that can be raised as an awning

shelter trench *n* **:** a trench hastily constructed to secure shelter from direct fire that is usu. first dug as a shallow excavation with the dirt thrown up as a parapet in front to shelter a man lying down and then if time permits is deepened as rapidly as possible until it will shelter a man standing

shelterwood method \'==,=-\ *n* [¹*shelter* + *wood*] **:** a method of securing natural tree reproduction under the shelter of old trees which are removed by successive cuttings to admit to the seedlings a gradually increasing amount of light

shel·tery \'sheltərē, -ltrē\ *adj* **:** affording shelter ⟨sitting in a ~ nook —Patrick Kennedy⟩

sheltopusic *or* **sheltopusik** *var of* SCHELTOPUSIK

shel·ty *or* **shel·tie** \'sheltē\ *n, pl* **shelties** [prob. of Scand origin; akin to ON *Hjalti* Shetlander] **1 :** SHETLAND PONY **2 :** SHETLAND SHEEPDOG

¹shelve \'shelv, -euv\ *vb* -ED/-ING/-S [fr. *shelves,* pl. of ¹*shelf*] *vt* **1 :** to furnish with shelves ⟨~ a closet⟩ ⟨~ a library⟩ ⟨a *shelved* table⟩ **2 :** to place on a shelf **:** arrange or store upon shelves ⟨~ books⟩ ⟨many libraries ~ recent fiction by itself —W.H.Jesse⟩ **3 :** to put on the shelf: as **a :** remove from active service **:** DISMISS ⟨~ an army officer⟩ **b :** to put aside (as from consideration) **:** put off indefinitely ⟨the dangerous inclination of . . . politicans to ~ thorny problems —Henri Peyre⟩ ⟨~ a project⟩ ⟨~ a bill⟩ ~ *vi* **:** to slope in a formation like a shelf **:** INCLINE — often used with an adverb of direction ⟨the mountains ~ off into the mesa country —*Amer. Guide Series: Colo.*⟩ ⟨the ground ~s steeply toward the north —James Whyle⟩ ⟨a grassy plain . . . ~s out into a clean white beach —George Tichenor⟩

²shelve \"\ *n* -s [back-formation fr. *shelves,* pl. of ¹*shelf*] **1** *archaic* **:** SHELF 2a **2 :** SHELF 2c

shelv·er \və(r)\ *n* -s **:** one that shelves (as books in a library)

shelves *pl of* SHELF *or of* SHELVE, *pres 3d sing of* SHELVE

¹shelv·ing \-viŋ\ *n* -s [fr. gerund of ¹*shelve*] **1 :** the state or degree of sloping **2 :** a sloping surface or place

²shelving \"\ *n* -s [²*shelve* + *-ing*] **1 :** material for shelves **2 :** a number or quantity of shelves; *esp* **:** the shelves inside a closet or fitted to a wall

shelvy \'shelvē, -euvē\ *adj* -ER/-EST [²*shelve* + *-y*] **:** sloping or inclining in the manner of a geologic shelf ⟨the shore was ~ and shallow —Shak.⟩

she·mi·ni a·tze·reth *or* **shemini a·tze·ret** *or* **shemini a·ze·ret** \shə'mē,nēät'tse(,)ret(h), -res\ *n, usu cap S&A* [LHeb *shĕmīnī 'ăṣereth,* fr. Heb *shĕmīnī* eighth + *'ăṣereth* assembly, convocation] **:** a Jewish festival observed on the 22d day of Tishri, following the 7th day of Sukkoth proper, and marked by a memorial service and a special prayer for seasonal rain

shem·ite \'she,mīt\ *n* -s *usu cap* [*Shem* (Sem), son of Noah and eponymous ancestor of the Semites (Gen 10:22–31) + E *-ite*] **:** SEMITE

she·mit·ic \shə'mid·ik, she'm-\ *adj, usu cap* **:** SEMITIC

shem·it·ish \'she,mīd·ish\ *adj, usu cap* **:** SEMITIC

she·mit·tah \shə'mētə\ *n, pl* **shemit·tot** *or* **shemi·toth** \-,tōt(h), -ōs\ [Heb *shĕmiṭṭāh,* lit., remission, release] **:** SABBATICAL YEAR

she·moz·zle *var of* SCHEMOZZLE

shen·a·chie \'shenə¦kē\ *var of* SHANACHIE

she·nan·go \shə'naŋ(,)gō\ *n, pl* **shenangoes** *also* **shenangos** [prob. fr. the *Chenango* river and *Chenango* canal in south-central N. Y. state] **:** a casually employed dock worker

she·nan·i·gan \shə'nanəgən, -anēg-\ *n* -s [origin unknown] **1 a :** an often devious trick used esp. to divert attention for an underhand purpose **:** DECEPTION, STRATAGEM, FAST ONE ⟨a scamp who had pinched pennies out of the teacups of the poor by various ~s —W.A.White⟩ **b :** any act that is high-spirited, daring, or mischievous **:** PRANK, ESCAPADE ⟨boys up to some ~ or other⟩ **2 a :** tricky or questionable practices or conduct **:** HUMBUG, FAKERY ⟨febrile prosperity . . . founded on ~ —*Yale Rev.*⟩ ⟨the simplest business transaction today is enveloped in such a mantle of idiotic ~ —*Amer. Mercury*⟩ ⟨revealed certain indications of ~ on the part of these judges —*N.Y.Sun*⟩ — usu. used in pl. ⟨symbol of all the fraud and force and ~s and duress —W.A.White⟩ ⟨unfair ~s by a competitor —M.T.Bloom⟩ **b :** any high-spirited, daring, or mischievous activity **:** GOINGS-ON, HIGH JINKS, MONKEY BUSINESS — usu. used in pl. ⟨the ~s attending a supercolossal film production —Ilka Chase⟩ ⟨as soon as the usual parade ~s were over —Saul Bellow⟩ ⟨the raiders, after an hour or two of highly diverting ~s . . . during which they drew the wildest kind of inaccurate fire, retired —Walter Karig⟩

¹shend \'shend\ *vt* **shent** \-nt\ **shent; shending; shends** [ME *shenden,* fr. OE *scendan;* akin to OFris *skenda* to shame, disgrace, OS *skendian,* OHG *scenten;* causative-denominative fr. the root of OE *scand* shame, disgrace, OFris *skande,* OHG *scanta,* Goth *skanda;* akin to OE *scamu* shame — more at SHAME] **1** *archaic* **a :** to confuse, confound, or put to shame esp. by superiority ⟨Cynthia doth ~ the lesser stars —Edmund Spenser⟩ **b :** to get the better of (as in battle or argument) **:** DISCOMFIT **2** *archaic* **:** to subject to reproach **:** REPROVE, REVILE ⟨I am *shent* for speaking to you —Shak.⟩ **3** *chiefly dial* **a :** INJURE, MAR, HARM **b :** RUIN, DESTROY ⟨the withered crown will soon slide down a skull all bleached and *shent* —G.M.Hopkins⟩

²shend *vt* [perh. alter. (influenced by ¹*shend*) of ²*shield*] *obs* **:** PROTECT, SHIELD, DEFEND

sheng *also* **shing** *or* **cheng** \'s(h)|eŋ, 'ch|, |iŋ\ *n, pl* **sheng** *or* **shengs** [Chin (Pek) *sheng¹*] **:** a Chinese unit of liquid capacity equal to 1.094 quarts or 1.035 liters according to the 1914 standard or 1.057 quarts or 1 liter according to the 1929 standard

shen·zi \'shen(,)zē\ *n, pl* **shenzi** *or* **shenzis** [Swahili] **:** an uncivilized African tribesman

she–oak \'=,=\ *n* [²*she* (plant) + *oak*] **1 :** any of several Australian trees of the genus *Casuarina* — compare BEEFWOOD 2a **2** [so called fr. its having been first applied to a kind of cheap beer regarded as inferior to good beer as the she-oak is inferior to the oak] *slang Austral* **:** BEER

she·ol \shē'ōl, shə'ōl, 'shē,ōl\ *n, usu cap* [Heb *Shĕ'ōl*] **:** the subterranean world of darkness that in early Hebrew thought resembled the Greek Hades in being an underworld abode where all spirits of the dead were assumed to live a shadowy existence involving neither punishment nor joy, was later conceived of as the intermediate realm of departed spirits where the wicked were punished and the good awaited resurrection to a blessed reward, and was still later conceived of as a place where the wicked were tortured and tormented — compare GEHENNA, HELL, NETHERWORLD

¹shep·herd \'shepə(r)d\ *n* -s [ME *sheephirde, sheepherde, shephirde, shepherde,* fr. OE *scēaphyrde,* fr. *scēap* sheep + *hyrde* herdsman — more at SHEEP, HERD] **1 :** a man employed in tending, feeding, and guarding sheep, esp. in a flock that is grazing **2 :** one charged with the religious care and guidance of others **:** PASTOR **3 :** a dog used as or considered suitable for use as a sheep dog; *esp* **:** one of any of several breeds having *shepherd* as part of their name ⟨toy ~⟩ — see GERMAN SHEPHERD **4 :** SHEPHERD KING

²shepherd \"\ *vt* -ED/-ING/-S **1 :** to tend as a shepherd **2 :** to gather, guard, herd, lead, or drive in the manner of a shepherd **:** ESCORT, CONDUCT ⟨a lawyer friend ~*ed* her into investment in two houses —Rex Ingamells⟩ ⟨gray ships, ~*ed* by sleek naval craft, off-loaded —A.H.Brown⟩ ⟨officers started ~*ing* the wounded aboard the hospital train —Fred Majdalany⟩ ⟨parents . . . ~*ing* a good-sized group of youngsters on an excursion —Dorothy Barclay⟩ **3 :** to give spiritual guidance to ⟨four missionaries . . . hurried back to bury the dead and ~ the living —W.C.Fairfield⟩

shepherd dog *or* **shepherd's dog** *n* [ME *scheperd dog, scheperds dogge*] **:** SHEEP DOG

shep·herd·ess \-dəs\ *n* -ES [ME *shepherdesse,* fr. *shepherde* + *-esse* -ess] **1 :** a woman or girl who tends sheep **:** a female shepherd **2 :** a rural lass

shep·her·dia \she'pərdēə, -ep'hə-\ *n, cap* [NL, fr. John *Shepherd* †1836 Eng. botanist + NL *-ia*] **:** a genus of American shrubs (family Elaeagnaceae) with silvery or scurfy opposite leaves, small dioecious flowers with eight stamens and baccate fruit — see BUFFALO BERRY

shepherd king *n, usu cap S* [trans. of Gk *basileus poimēn;* trans. of Egypt *ḥḳ¹ šsw*] **:** one of the Hyksos kings

shep·herd·less \'shepə(r)dləs\ *adj* **:** lacking a shepherd or guide

shepherdlike \'==,=\ *adj* **:** resembling or characteristic of a shepherd ⟨~ care of the needy —*Atlantic*⟩

shep·herd·ly \-pə(r)dlē\ *adj* **:** of, relating to, or having the characteristics of a shepherd **:** PASTORAL

shepherd's bag *n* [ME *schepherdes bagge*] **:** SHEPHERD'S PURSE

shepherd's check *or* **shepherd check** *or* **shepherd's plaid** *or* **shepherd plaid** *n* **1 :** a pattern of small even black-and-white checks **2 :** a fabric woven in shepherd's check pattern

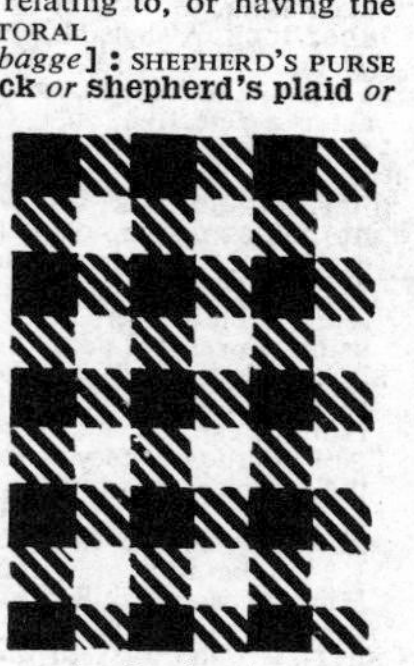

shepherd's check

shepherd's clock *n* **1** *or* **shepherd's weatherglass :** SCARLET PIMPERNEL **2 :** SALSIFY

shepherd's club *n* **:** a common mullein (*Verbascum thapsus*)

shepherd's coffin *n* **:** RATTLE 3a

shepherd's companion *n* **:** a fantail flycatcher (*Rhipidura leucophrys*) of Australia

shepherd's cress *n* **:** a small European annual herb (*Teesdalia nudicaulis*) of the family Cruciferae having a rosette of pinnatifid leaves and small white flowers in racemes

shep·herd·ship \'shepə(r)d,ship\ *n* **:** the position, duty, or occupation of a shepherd

shepherd's hourglass *n* **:** WOOD PIMPERNEL

shepherd's needle *n* **:** LADY'S-COMB

shepherd spider *n* **:** HARVESTMAN 2

shepherd's pie *n* **:** a savory mixture of leftover meat baked in a crust of mashed potatoes

shepherd's pipe *n* [ME *scheperdys pype*] **1 :** FLAGEOLET 1 **2 :** MUSETTE

shepherd's pouch *n* **:** SHEPHERD'S PURSE

shepherd's purse *n* [ME *shepherdys purs*] **:** a white-flowered annual European herb (*Capsella bursa-pastoris*) that is nearly cosmopolitan as an introduced weed and bears triangular notched pods

shepherd's thyme *n* **:** WILD THYME

shepherdy *n* -ES [¹*shepherd* + *-y*] *obs* **:** the position or occupation of a shepherd

she–pine \'=,=\ *n* [²*she* (plant) + *pine*] **1 :** an Australian timber tree (*Podocarpus elata*) the yellow durable wood of which is used for spars and masts **2** *also* **she pitch pine :** CARIBBEAN PINE

shep·pey argentine \'shepē-\ *n, usu cap S* [*Sheppey,* island at the mouth of the Thames, Eng. + *argentine*] **:** PEARLSIDES

shep·stare \'shepstər, -sta(ə)r, -ste(ə)r\ *or* **shep·star·ling** \'shep-,==\ *or* **shep·ster** \'shepstər\ *n* -s [*shep-* (as in *shepherd*) + *stare* (starling) *or starling*] *dial Eng* **:** the common starling

she·ra·ni *or* **shi·ra·ni** \shə'rānē\ *n, pl* **sherani** *or* **sheranis** *or* **shirani** *or* **shiranis** *usu cap* **1 a :** a chiefly agricultural people of northwestern Pakistan belonging to the Pathan

group and being short in stature and slim in body **2 :** a member of the Sherani people
sherard·ize \shəˈrär,dīz, ˈsherər,d-\ *vt* -ED/-ING/-S *see -ize in Explan Notes* [*Sherard* O. Cowper-Coles †1936 Eng. inventor + E *-ize*] **:** to coat (an article of iron or steel) with zinc by covering with commercial zinc dust in a tightly closed drum and heating for several hours at 300° to 420° C so that a zinc-iron alloy is formed at the surface through the action of zinc vapor — **sherard·iz·er** \-zə(r)\ *n* -s
sher·a·ton \ˈsherət°n, -rəd·ən,nətən\ *adj, usu cap* [after Thomas *Sheraton* †1806 Eng. furniture maker and designer, its inventor] **:** of, relating to, or closely imitating a style of furniture originating around 1800 in England and marked by straight lines and graceful proportions, delicate and often ingenious construction, much inlay esp. of satinwood, and as a rule sparing use of carving except in the characteristic reeding of tapering legs
sher·bet \ˈshərbət, ˈshəb-,ˈshəib-, *usu* -əd·+V\ *also* **sher·bert** \-bə(r)t, *usu* -)d·+V\ *n* -s [Turk & Per; Turk *şerbet*, fr. Per *sharbat*, fr. Ar *sharbah* drink, fr. *shariba* to drink] **1 :** a cooling drink made of sweetened and diluted fruit juice **2** *or* **sherbet powder :** a variously flavored preparation esp. of sodium bicarbonate, tartaric acid, and sugar for making an effervescent drink **3 :** a water ice to which milk, egg white, or gelatin is added before freezing **4** *or* **sherbet glass :** a footed glass cup for serving frozen or unfrozen desserts

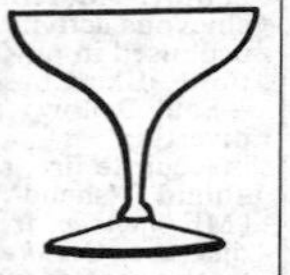
sherbet 4

sherd *var of* SHARD
shereef *var of* SHARIF
sheri *or* **sheria** *or* **sheriat** *often cap, var of* SHARI'A
sher·i·dan·ite \ˈsherəd°n,īt\ *n* -s [*Sheridan* county, Wyo., its locality + E *-ite*] **:** a mineral $(Mg_8Al_3)(Al_3Si_5)O_{20}(OH)_{16}$ of the chlorite group consisting of pale greenish colorless basic silicate of magnesium and aluminum
sherif *var of* SHARIF
sherifa *var of* SHARIFA
sher·iff \ˈsherəf, *dial or in rapid speech* ˈsherf, *dial* ˈshər(·ə)f\ *n* -s [ME *shirreve, sherreve, shiref, sheref, shreve*, fr. OE *scīrgerēfa*, fr. *scīr* district, shire + *gerēfa* reeve — more at SHIRE, REEVE] **1 :** the chief executive officer of a shire or county in Britain holding office usu. by royal appointment but sometimes formerly by inheritance and having duties and powers varying from time to time and from place to place (as in England, Scotland, Ireland) but typically being charged with the duty of superintending parliamentary elections, returning juries in criminal cases, attending the judges, holding certain courts, and executing the orders and processes of the courts and judges — see DEPUTY SHERIFF, POCKET SHERIFF, UNDERSHERIFF **2 :** an important county officer in the U. S. who is usu. elected by the people of the county as the chief executive officer of the courts of superior jurisdiction therein and is charged with the duty of attending these courts and executing their orders and processes through deputies appointed by him, has charge of the county jail and other penal institutions and the prisoners therein awaiting trial or under sentence, has the duty of preserving the peace and quelling riots with the power to deputize posses to apprehend criminals, has the duty of transferring prisoners sentenced to state prisons and patients committed to state institutions, and often has the power to summon jurors as well as other powers granted by statute **3 :** any officer (as a deputy sheriff or constable) performing duties relating to the office of sheriff
sher·iff·al·ty \-fəlte\ *n* -ES [by alter. (influence of *sheriff*)] **:** SHRIEVALTY
sher·iff·cy \-fsē\ *n* -ES [*sheriff* + *-cy*] **:** SHRIEVALTY
sheriff depute *n, Scots law* **:** a lawyer designated to perform the judicial duties of a sheriff
sher·iff·dom \-fdəm\ *n* -s [ME *shirrevedom, sherrevedom, shirefdom, sherefdom*, fr. *shirreve, sherreve, shiref, sheref* sheriff + *-dom*] **:** SHRIEVALTY
sheriff-pink \ˈ⸗(⸗),⸗ˈ\ *n* **:** DAISY 1b
sheriff's court *n* **1** *Eng law* **:** a court held by a sheriff or an undersheriff with a jury and authorized to assess damages in undefended and in compulsory taking-of-land cases, to find the value of defendants' lands taken on executions, and formerly to try other issues of fact sent to it by courts of superior jurisdiction **2** *Scots law* **:** a court presided over by a sheriff depute or a sheriff substitute trained in law that is the ordinary and the small debt court and a criminal court and since 1913 has jurisdiction in practically all civil actions with the principal exceptions of actions involving the status of marriage, divorce, or legitimacy, reductions, winding-up of companies where paid-up capital exceeds £10,000, and actions to prove the text of lost documents but cannot sentence to more than two years' imprisonment
sheriff substitute *n, Scots law* **:** an undersheriff who usu. hears cases in the first instance
sheriffwick \ˈ⸗⸗,⸗\ *n* [ME *shirrefwyke*, fr. *shirref, shirreve* sheriff + *wyke, wik* wick — more at WICK] **:** SHRIEVALTY
¹sherifian *var of* SHARIFIAN
²she·rif·ian \shəˈrēfēən\ *adj, usu cap* **:** of or relating to the Sherifian Empire
she·ris·ta·dar \shəˈristə,där\ *n* -s [Hindi *sarrishtadār*, fr. Per *sarrishta* record office + *dār* having] *India* **:** RECORDER, REGISTRAR, SECRETARY
¹sher·lock \ˈshər,läk, ˈshə,l-, ˈshəi,l-, *sometimes* ˈsher,l- *or* ˈsheə,l- *or* -,lək\ *vb* -ED/-ING/-S [after *Sherlock* Holmes] *vt* **:** to observe and infer in the manner of Sherlock Holmes ~ *vi* **:** to act as a detective
²sherlock \ˈ"\ *n* -s *often cap* [after *Sherlock* Holmes] **:** SHERLOCK HOLMES
sherlock holmes \,⸗(,)⸗ˈhōmz *also* -ōlmz\ *n, pl* **sherlock holmeses** *usu cap S&H* [after *Sherlock Holmes*, detective par excellence in short stories and novels by Sir Arthur Conan Doyle †1930 Brit. writer] **1 :** DETECTIVE; *esp* **:** one having remarkable powers of deduction **2 :** a person exhibiting unusual powers of deduction in solving any problem
sher·lock·ian \(ˈ;)⸗ˈläkēən\ *adj, usu cap* [*Sherlock* Holmes + E *-ian*] **:** of or resembling the fictional detective Sherlock Holmes esp. in the exercise of unusual powers of deduction ⟨solved the mystery with *Sherlockian* ease⟩ ⟨could almost see the *Sherlockian* glitter in the doctor's eyes —Philip Wheelwright⟩
sher·pa \ˈsherpə, ˈshər-\ *n, pl* **sherpa** *or* **sherpas** *usu cap* **1 :** a Tibetan people living on the high southern slopes of the Himalayas and skilled in mountain climbing **2 :** a member of the Sherpa people
sher·ra \ˈshərə\ *Scot var of* SHERIFF
sher·ra·moor \ˈsherə,mu̇(ə)r, ˈshər-\ *n* -s *usu cap* [alter. of *Sheriffmuir*, site of the battlefield in Perth county, Scotland, where on Nov. 13, 1715 the Jacobites were defeated by the Royalists and their rebellion checked] *Scot* **:** TUMULT, ROW
sher·ried \ˈsherēd, -rid\ *adj* [*sherry* + *-ed*] **:** flavored with sherry wine ⟨~ trifle⟩ ⟨~ lobster⟩
sher·ris \ˈsherəs\ *archaic var of* SHERRY
sherris-sack *n, obs* **:** sack imported into England from Jerez, Spain
sher·ry \ˈsherē, -ri\ *n* -ES [alter. of earlier *sherris* (taken as pl.), fr. *Xeres* (now *Jerez*), town near Cádiz, Spain] **1 a :** a fortified wine of Spanish origin ranging from pale to dark amber in color and from very dry to sweet in taste with typically a distinctive nutty flavor — see AMONTILLADO, FINO, OLOROSO **b :** a wine with characteristics similar to those of true Spanish sherry but produced elsewhere (as in the U. S. in New York and California) **2** *or* **sherry brown :** a moderate brown that is yellower and lighter than bay, yellower and duller than toast brown, and lighter, stronger, and slightly yellower than chestnut brown — called also *clove, Manchu, manganese brown, mineral bister, Rangoon*
sher·ry·val·lies \ˌsherēˈvalēz\ *n pl* [modif. of Pol *szarawary*, fr. Russ *sharavary*, fr. Gk *sarabara* loose trousers, prob. of Iranian origin; akin to Per *shalwār, shulwār* loose trousers] **:** overalls or protective leggings of thick cloth or leather formerly worn for riding on horseback
sher·wa·ni \shə(r)ˈwänē\ *n* -s [Hindi *śerwānī*] **:** a long-sleeved close-fitting knee-length coat with a stand-up collar worn by men of India and Pakistan

shes *pl of* SHE
shetadlan *var of* SHTADLAN
she teak *n* [²*she* (plant)] **:** NATIVE TEAK a
sheth \ˈsheth\ *n* -s [ME; akin to OE *scēath* sheath — more at SHEATH] **1 :** a number of rows (as of galleries in a mine or furrows in a field) at right angles to similar rows which they intersect or adjoin **2 :** one of the bars forming a framework (as of a wagon) **3 :** SHEATH 2a(2), 3c
sheth of boards : a group of cross workings in a mine
¹shet·land \ˈshetlənd\ *adj, usu cap* [fr. the *Shetland* islands, archipelago off northern Scotland] **:** of or from the Shetland islands constituting the county of Shetland, officially Zetland, in Scotland **:** of the kind or style prevalent in Shetland **:** SHETLANDIC
²shetland \ˈ"\ *n* -s **1** *usu cap* **:** an animal of a breed or type native to or developed in the Shetland islands: as **a :** SHETLAND PONY **b :** SHETLAND SHEEPDOG **2** *sometimes cap* **a :** a lightweight loosely twisted yarn of Shetland wool used for knitting and weaving **b :** a soft napped fabric loosely woven of Shetland wool
shetland argus *n, usu cap S&A* **:** a basket star (*Gorgonocephalus Linckii*)
shet·land·er \ˈshetləndə(r)\ *n* -s [*Shetland* islands + E *-er*] **1** *cap* **:** a native or inhabitant of Shetland **2** *usu cap* **:** SHETLAND PONY
shet·lan·dic \(ˈ)shetˈlandik\ *adj, usu cap* [*Shetland* islands + E *-ic*] **:** of, relating to, or characteristic of Shetland
shetland pony *n* **1** *usu cap S&P* **:** a breed of small, stocky, hardy ponies with a long rough coat and long mane and tail that originated in the Shetland islands **2** *usu cap S* **:** a pony of the Shetland pony breed
shetland sheepdog *n* **1** *usu cap both Ss* **:** a breed of small dogs resembling miniature collies with profuse double coats and developed in the Shetland islands presumably by interbreeding collies with smaller long-haired dogs native to the area and possibly with Pomeranians **2** *usu cap 1st S* **:** a dog of the Shetland sheep dog breed
shetland wool *n, usu cap S* **1 :** the fine undercoat hand-plucked from sheep raised in the Shetland islands **2 :** yarn hand-spun from Shetland wool
¹sheugh *also* **sheuch** \ˈshu̇k\ *n* -s [ME *sough* — more at SOUGH] **1** *chiefly Scot* **:** a small ravine or gully; *sometimes* **:** one with water running through it **2** *chiefly Scot* **:** a man-made ditch or trench
²sheugh \ˈ"\ *vt* -ED/-ING/-S **1** *chiefly Scot* **:** to make ditches or drains in ⟨~ a marsh⟩ **2** *chiefly Scot* **:** to cover over **:** heel in
she·va *n* -s [Heb *shĕwāʼ*] **:** SCHWA
shevat *usu cap, var of* SHEBAT
shev·eled *or* **shev·elled** \ˈshevəld\ *adj* [by shortening] **:** DISHEVELED
shevuoth *or* **shevuos** *usu cap, var of* SHABUOTH
shew \ˈshō\ *archaic var of* SHOW
she·wa *n* -s [Heb *shĕwāʼ*] **:** SCHWA
shewbread *or* **showbread** \ˈ⸗,⸗\ *n, pl* **shewbread** *also* **shewbreads** *or* **showbread** *also* **showbreads** [trans. of G *schaubrot*] **:** any of the 12 loaves of consecrated unleavened bread ritually placed by the Jewish priests on a table in the sanctuary of the Tabernacle on the Sabbath as an expression of the belief that Yahweh is the source of every material blessing and as an expression of gratitude
shew·el \ˈshüəl\ *n* -s [back-formation fr. ME *sheules, seweles*; akin to MLG *schūwelse* scarecrow, MHG *schiusel* scarecrow, OHG *sciuhen* to scare off, OE *scēoh* shy — more at SHY] *archaic* **:** SCARECROW; *esp* **:** one made of feathers tied to a string
shew·er \ˈshō(ə)r\ *archaic var of* SHOWER
she-woman \ˈ⸗,⸗⸗\ *n, pl* **she-women :** a woman abundantly endowed with obviously or pronouncedly feminine qualities
sheykh *var of* SHEIKH
sheyle \ˈshā(ə)l\ *vi* -ED/-ING/-S [akin to MHG *schilhen* to wink, squint, OE *sceol* wry, squinting — more at CYLINDER] *chiefly Scot* **:** to look cross-eyed **:** SQUINT
SHF *abbr, often not cap* superhigh frequency
shg *abbr* shipping
shi'a *or* **shia** *or* **shiah** \ˈshē(,)ä, -ēə\ *n* -s *usu cap* [Ar *shīʻah* following, sect — more at SHI'ITE] **1 :** the Muslims comprising one of the two major branches of Islam originating as a legitimist party rejecting the first three caliphs and holding Ali the son-in-law of Muhammad as the legitimate successor of the Prophet, established as the national faith of Persia since 1500, and comprising many diverse sects — compare SUNNI **2 :** SHI'ITE **3 :** the branch of Islam formed by the Shi'a
shi·bah *or* **shi·vah** *or* **shi·va** \ˈshivə\ *n* -s [Heb *shibh'āh* seven (days)] **:** a traditional 7-day period of mourning that follows the funeral of a close relative and is observed in the home by Jews ⟨the family will sit ~ until Friday⟩
shib·bo·leth \ˈshibələth *sometimes* -,leth\ *n* -s [Heb *shibbōleth* ear of grain, stream, flood; fr. the use of this word as a test to distinguish Gileadites from Ephraimites, who pronounced it *sibbōleth* (Judges 12:6)] **1 a :** a sound or a word containing a sound whose proper articulation is difficult for and whose mispronunciation is regarded as reliably indicating or betraying a speaker who is not native or whose speech has been influenced by early acquaintance with another language **b :** a custom or usage regarded as a criterion for distinguishing members of one group (as a social class) from those of another ⟨for most of the well-to-do in the town, dinner was a ~, its hour dividing mankind —Osbert Sitwell⟩ **2 a :** a word or saying characteristically used by the adherents of a party, sect, or belief and usu. regarded as empty of real meaning **:** CATCHWORD, SLOGAN ⟨the criticism of liberal and radical thought wherever it deteriorated to ~ and dogma —Lionel Trilling⟩ **b :** a use of language regarded as distinctive of a particular class, profession, or group of persons ⟨our listeners type us — stereotype us — according to the impression they gain from our verbal habits . . . every word we speak is a ~ —G.A.Miller⟩ **c :** a commonplace saying or idea **:** PLATITUDE, TRUISM ⟨some truth in the ~ that crime does not pay —Lee Rogow⟩
¹shib·i·lant \ˈshibələnt\ *adj* [alter. (influenced by the digraph *sh*, representing the sound \sh\) of *sibilant*] **:** pronounced or containing the sound \sh\ or \zh\ (\ch\ (=t+sh) and \j\ (=d+zh) are ~ affricates)
²shibilant \ˈ"\ *n* -s **:** a shibilant sound
shi·bu·ichi \ˌshēbəwəˈchē, ⸗⸗ˈwēchē\ *n* -s [Jap, fr. *shi* four + *bu* part, parts + *ichi* one] **:** an orig. Japanese alloy that consists of one part of silver to three parts of copper and that assumes a silvery gray patina when properly treated
shi·cer \ˈshīsə(r)\ *n* -s [G *scheisser* one that defecates, contemptible person, fr. *scheissen* to defecate (fr. OHG *scīzan*) + *-er* — more at SHIT] *Austral* **:** an unproductive mine
shick \ˈshik\ *adj* [Yiddish *shiker*] *Austral* **:** DRUNK
¹shick·er \ˈshikə(r)\ *or* **shick·ered** \-)d\ *adj* [*shicker* fr. Yiddish *shiker*, fr. Heb *shikkōr*, fr. *shikhar* to be drunk; *shickered* fr. Yiddish *shiker* + E *-ed*] *slang* **:** DRUNK
²shicker \ˈ"\ *n* -s [Yiddish *shiker*, fr. Heb *shikkōr*, adj.] *slang* **:** DRUNKARD
shicksa *var of* SHIKSA
shied *past of* SHY
shiel \ˈshē(ə)l\ *n* -s [ME (northern dial.) *schele, shale*; prob. akin to OFris *skūl* hiding place, *skiāle* stable, MLG *schūle* hiding place, ON *skjōl* shelter, cover, *skāli* hut, room, OE *hȳd* hide, skin — more at HIDE] *chiefly Scot* **:** SHIELING
¹shield \ˈshēld\ *n* -s [ME *sheld, shild*, fr. OE *scield, sceld, scyld, scild*; akin to OHG *scilt* shield, ON *skjöldr*, Goth *skildus* shield, OE *sciell* shell — more at SHELL] **1 a :** a broad piece of defensive armor (as of metal, wood, or leather) carried on the arm or held in the hand by a handle and formerly in general use for the protection of the body (as from spears, arrows, or sword thrusts) in battle or individual combat **b :** a means or method of defense ⟨a fighter ~ for their war industries —*Manchester Guardian Weekly*⟩ ⟨understanding . . . that the haughtiness was a ~ —Anne D. Sedgwick⟩ **c :** the field on which the bearings in coats of arms are placed **:** ESCUTCHEON **2 :** a structure, device, or part that serves as a protective cover or barrier: as **a :** the hard horny skin of a boar's flank or neck **b :** a protective structure on an animal (as a large scale, carapace, or lorica); *usu* **:** any of the large scales on the head of a snake or lizard or the horny plates of a turtle's shell **c :** an iron or steel framework moved forward

at the end of a tunnel or adit in process of excavation to support the ground ahead of the concrete, cast iron, brickwork, or other lining **d :** a screen of armor plate usu. attached to a gun carriage to protect an otherwise exposed gun against small-arm or light-caliber projectiles or shrapnel **e :** CULTIVATOR SHIELD **f :** the Precambrian nuclear mass of a continent around which and to some extent upon which the younger sedimentary rocks have been deposited ⟨the Canadian ~ . . . centers in Hudson Bay —C.O.Dunbar⟩ — compare CRATON **g :** a fixture or attachment placed over moving parts of machinery to protect attendants or others from injury **h :** a shaped piece of often rubberized cloth that is worn inside or over a part of a garment (as the underarm of a dress or blouse) liable to be soiled by perspiration **i (1) :** a screen or device that protects electrical apparatus from being affected by outside electrostatic or magnetic influences **(2) :** a wall, screen, housing, or other device that protects against radiation ⟨a lead ~⟩ **3 :** something that has the shape of a shield or is thought to resemble a shield: as **a (1) :** APOTHECIUM **(2) :** one of the eight wall cells of the antheridium of a stonewort **b :** a bodily marking or otherwise differentiated area of an animal resembling a shield **c :** a policeman's badge ⟨turned in his ~ and applied for retirement⟩ **d :** a decorative or identifying emblem (as of a state, club, or organization) ⟨these cars will carry no state ~ —*Springfield (Mass.) Daily News*⟩
²shield \ˈ"\ *vb* -ED/-ING/-S [ME *shelden, shilden*, fr. OE *scieldan, scildan, scyldan*, fr. *scield, sceld, scyld, scild*, n.] *vt* **1 a :** to protect with or as if with a shield **:** give cover to **:** DEFEND ⟨~*ing* his eyes from the light —John Seago⟩ ⟨have your work to retire into, your ideas to ~ you —Aldous Huxley⟩ **b :** to cut off from observation **:** CONCEAL, HIDE ⟨usually work in gangs, clustering about exhibits in such a manner as to ~ their activities —*Irish Digest*⟩ ⟨the act of concealment and the reasons for it are themselves ~*ed* from public observation —J.G.Palfrey⟩ **2** *obs* **:** AVERT, FORBID — used in the phrase *God shield* ⟨God ~ I should disturb devotion —Shak.⟩ **3 :** to ward off **:** keep off or out — often used with *off* ⟨their own messes and own company to ~ off loneliness —*Time*⟩ ~ *vi* **:** to serve as a shield **:** DEFEND, PROTECT ⟨a desire to ~ and save —Lord Byron⟩ **syn** see DEFEND
shield-back chair \ˈ⸗,⸗-\ *n* **:** a Hepplewhite chair that has a back whose short side posts support a shield-shaped framework
shield-backed bug \ˈ⸗,⸗-\ *n* **:** SHIELD BUG
shield bearer *n* **1 :** an attendant who carries a warrior's shield — compare SQUIRE **2 :** any of various small moths constituting a genus (*Coptodisca*) and having larvae that cut out an oval bit of leaf to form a case
shield budding *n* **:** plant budding in which an oval to shield-shaped piece of bark bearing a scion bud is fitted into an approximately T-shaped opening in the bark of the stock
shield bug *n* **:** a bug of the family Pentatomidae characterized by a very large scutellum suggesting a shield **:** STINKBUG
shield cell *n* **:** SHIELD 3a(2)
shield cone *or* **shield dome** *n* **:** a conical or domical shield volcano
shield·er \-ēldə(r)\ *n* -s **:** one that shields
shield fern *n* **:** any of various ferns (as of the genera *Dryopteris* and *Polystichum*) having more or less shield-shaped indusia — called also BUCKLER FERN
shield fungus *n* **:** a fungus of the family Microthyriaceae
shield graft *n* **:** a side graft in which a scion with a wedge-shaped base is inserted in a T-shaped cut in the side of the stock
shielding *n* -s **1 :** the act or process of protecting or supplying with a protective device or screen ⟨the problems the engineers solve in their bunker are complex exercises in ~ —*Newsweek*⟩ **2 :** something that protects; *specif* **:** a device or screen that protects against radiation ⟨the radioactive metals must be treated behind heavy ~ by remote control —Leon Svirsky⟩
shield·less \-ē(ə)ldləs\ *adj* **:** having no shield
shield-maid \ˈ⸗,⸗\ *or* **shield-maiden** \ˈ⸗,⸗⸗\ *n* [trans. of ON *skjaldmær*] **:** a woman warrior **:** VALKYRIE
shieldmay \ˈ⸗,⸗\ *n* [¹*shield* + *may* (maiden); trans. of ON *skjaldmær*] **:** SHIELD-MAID
shield of arms : a coat of arms carried or displayed on a shield or shield-shaped object or design
shield of brawn : a piece of a boar's shield stuffed with meat and cooked
shield of da·vid \-ˈdāvəd\ *usu cap S&D* [trans. of Heb *māghēn Dāwīdh*] **:** MAGEN DAVID
shield of pretense : a small shield of arms carried within another shield of arms
shields *pl of* SHIELD, *pres 3d sing of* SHIELD
shield scale *or* **shield louse** *n* **:** ARMORED SCALE
shield-shaped \ˈ⸗,⸗\ *adj* **:** having the shape of a shield; *specif* **:** PELTATE
shieldtail \ˈ⸗,⸗\ *n* **:** a small Oriental burrowing snake of the family Uropeltidae having a large scute on the tail
shield volcano *n* **:** a volcano built up by successive outpourings of lava with little or no fragmental material and consequently having a diameter at its base many times as great as its height — contrasted with *stratovolcano*; compare BASALT DOME
shiel·ing \ˈshēliŋ\ *n* -s [*shiel* + *-ing*] **1** *dial Brit* **:** a hut or small cottage in the hills or mountains that is used as a shelter by shepherds **2** *dial Brit* **:** a summer pasture in the mountains
¹shi·er \ˈshī(ə)r, -īə\ *comparative of* SHY
²shier \ˈ"\ *also* **shy·er** \ˈ"\ *n* -s [²*shy* + *-er*] **:** a horse given to shying
³shier \ˈ"\ *n* -s [⁴*shy* + *-er*] **:** one that shies a missile
shies *pres 3d sing of* SHY, *pl of* SHY
shiest *superlative of* SHY
¹shift \ˈshift\ *vb* -ED/-ING/-S [ME *shiften* (also, to arrange, order), fr. OE *sciftan*; akin to OFris *skifta, skiffa* to decide, determine, test, MLG *schiften, schichten* to divide, separate, arrange, order, MD *schichten* to arrange, order, ON *skipta* to divide, change, be of importance, OE *scēadan* to divide, separate — more at SHED] *vt* **1** *chiefly dial* **:** to apportion into shares **:** DISTRIBUTE, DIVIDE **2 a :** to exchange for or replace by another of the same category **:** CHANGE ⟨~ tasks to vary the monotony —Stuart Chase⟩ ⟨the clouds . . . were actually beginning to form very rapidly, and to ~ shape from moment to moment —G.R.Stewart⟩ ⟨~ his clothes⟩ ⟨~ the scenery⟩ **b** *chiefly dial* **:** to change the clothes of **3 a (1) :** to change the place, position, or direction of **:** MOVE, TRANSFER ⟨most everything on deck had to be ~*ed* to put the bow down —D.B. Putnam⟩ ⟨~*ed* his head round again to glance at her —Walter de la Mare⟩ ⟨the weight of the mammoth building was ~*ed* to new foundations —*Amer. Guide Series: Pa.*⟩ ⟨went forward to ~ the jib —Peter Heaton⟩ **(2) :** TRANSPLANT **(3) :** to cause (the printing position of a typewriter character) to be changed so that the character on the upper half of the key will print **b :** to make a change in (position or place) ⟨the shortstop ~*ed* his position as the next batter came up⟩ ⟨unto Southampton do we ~ our scene —Shak.⟩ **4 a :** to change the form or condition of **:** TRANSFORM ⟨different curtains and chairs — we can ~ the house all around —Marcia Davenport⟩ **b :** to change phonetically esp. in accordance with Grimm's law **5** *archaic* **:** AVOID, ESCAPE **6 :** to get rid of **:** DISLODGE ⟨nothing less than a hot shower will ~ the dirt that has caked on my skin —O.E.Middleton⟩ **7 :** to put away (food or drink) **:** CONSUME ⟨I've ~*ed* a lot in the last twenty years . . . not real heavy drinking —Geoffrey Household⟩ ~ *vi* **1 a :** to change place, location, or residence ⟨actual farm migrants, up against it, ~ from one place to another —Russell Lord⟩ **b :** to change position **:** move about ⟨interrupted her by ~*ing* heavily in his chair —Scott Fitzgerald⟩ **c :** to change direction ⟨the trail twisted and ~*ed* —Philip Rooney⟩ ⟨the wind ~*ed* to the east⟩ **d :** to make a shift on a stringed musical instrument **e :** to raise the carriage or lower the typebar segment of a typewriter by pressing a special key so that the character on the upper half of any typeface will print **f :** to shift gears **2 a (1) :** to manage by or for oneself **:** get along ⟨left the cadets to ~ for their own maintenance on their monthly pay of ten dollars —Herman Beukema⟩ ⟨his uncle died a year later so he was obliged to ~ for himself —W.R.Steiner⟩ **(2) :** to get along badly or with difficulty **:** make shift ⟨go around looking for worries to take up from other people, while their own house ~*s* along the best way it can —Mary Deasy⟩ **b :** to resort to evasions or fraud **:** make use of ex-

pedients ⟨prompts him to ~ and dissimulate —H.L.Mencken⟩ **3** *archaic* **:** to go away **:** DEPART, WITHDRAW ⟨let us not be dainty of leave-taking, but ~ away —Shak.⟩ **4 a :** to go through a change (as in form, character, or condition) **:** become transformed ⟨a voice deep, yet ~*ing* easily to falsetto quavers —William Beebe⟩ ⟨the situation ~*ed*⟩ **b :** to change one's clothes ⟨taught me to ~ into a madman's rags —Shak.⟩ **c :** to become changed phonetically esp. in accordance with Grimm's law **syn** see MOVE — **shift gears 1 :** to change the gear rotating the transmission shaft of an automobile **2 :** to make a change from one method, tempo, or approach to another ⟨*shifted gears* in the middle of his speech⟩ — **shift the helm :** to put the tiller of a boat from starboard to port or vice versa and usu. from hard over one way to hard over the other

²shift \"\ *n* -s **1 a :** a means or device for effecting an end ⟨an index may or may not be a trustworthy ~ for finding something —Joshua Whatmough⟩ — compare MAKESHIFT **b** *archaic* **:** ability to contrive **:** RESOURCEFULNESS **c** (1) **:** a deceitful or underhand scheme **:** DODGE, FRAUD, TRICK ⟨not amused by her ~*s* and her shameful deceit —C.B.Tinker⟩ (2) **:** an effort or expedient exerted or tried in difficult circumstances **:** EXTREMITY — usu. used in pl. ⟨during the air raids the staff were put to extraordinary ~*s* to keep the programs on the air at all —T.O.Beachcroft⟩ **2 :** the act of putting one thing in place of another **:** something put in place of another **:** SUBSTITUTION: as **a** (1) *chiefly dial* **:** a change of clothes (2) *chiefly dial* **:** SHIRT; *specif* **:** a long undershirt (3) **:** a woman's slip or chemise **b** (1) **:** a group of people who work or occupy themselves in turn with other groups ⟨three ~*s* of little citizens go to school in the same classroom each day —W.E.Goslin⟩ (2) **:** a change of one group of people (as workers or students) for another in regular alternation **:** a scheduled period of work or duty ⟨in a department working on ~*s*, the morning ~ started at 6:00 A.M. —B.B.Gardner⟩ ⟨nurses leaving their ~*s* at night —J.P.Browne⟩ **c :** one of the land units or successive crops in a crop rotation **d :** a change in emphasis, judgment, or attitude ⟨small or larger ~*s* in fashion are a commonplace of the literary scene —Bernard De Voto⟩ ⟨a sudden ~ in values⟩ **e :** CONSONANT SHIFT **f :** a bid in bridge in a suit other than the suit one's partner has bid **g :** the transposition of two portions of a pack of cards in a manner designed to escape detection by an observer **h :** the character on the upper half of a typewriter type bar ⟨the underscore is the ~ of the 6⟩ **3 :** a change in direction ⟨a ~ in the wind⟩ **4 :** a change in place or position ⟨he hesitated and I heard the slight sound of his ~ of weight —R.P.Warren⟩: as **a** (1) **:** a change in the position of the hand on the fingerboard in playing the violin or a similar musical instrument (2) **:** a change in position of the movable slide of a trombone (3) **:** the movement of the entire key action in a grand piano by the operation of the soft pedal so that the hammers strike only one or two strings instead of two or three **b** (1) **:** a dislocation of a mine vein or seam **:** FAULT (2) **:** the relative displacement of rock masses on opposite sides of a fault or fault zone and far enough away to be unaffected by bending or other local distortion along the zone of dislocation — compare SLIP **c :** the disposition of members in a structure (as a building or boat) so as to separate the joints and secure strength by overlapping **d** *dial Eng* **:** a change of residence **e** (1) **:** a simultaneous change of position in football esp. from one side of the line to the other made by two or more players of the side in possession of the ball just before the ball is snapped (2) **:** a change in position (as to the right or left) by one or more players on a baseball field for better defense against a particular hitter **f :** a change in frequency resulting in a change in position of a spectral line or band — see DOPPLER SHIFT, RED SHIFT **5 :** a removal from one person or thing to another **:** TRANSFER ⟨a ~ of responsibility⟩ ⟨a ~ of interest from natural philosophy to politics and ethics —Benjamin Farrington⟩ **6 :** GEARSHIFT **syn** see RESOURCE

shift·abil·i·ty \ˌshiftəˈbilədē\ *n* **:** the quality or state of being shiftable

shift·able \ˈshiftəbəl\ *adj* **:** capable of being shifted; *esp* **:** capable of being transferred from one holder or owner to another ⟨a ~ asset⟩

shift bid *n* **1 :** a deliberately unsound bid in bridge from which the bidder expects to rescue himself if he is doubled **2 :** SHIFT 2g

shift boss *n* **1 :** a foreman in charge of the workers of a particular shift **2 :** a foreman in charge of workers in a particular section of a metal mine — compare PIT BOSS

shifted *past of* SHIFT

shift·er \ˈshiftə(r)\ *n* -s **1 :** one that resorts to evasion in reasoning **2 :** one that shifts; *esp* **:** a worker whose job is to shift a specified thing ⟨bobbin ~⟩ ⟨stone ~⟩ **3 a :** a shift boss in a metal mine **b :** one that works in a coal mine assisting workers other than those who do the actual mining **4 :** any of various devices for shifting something: as **a :** BELT SHIFTER **b :** a wire for changing a loop from one needle to another (as in narrowing)

shifter fork *n* **:** a belt-shifter fork between whose prongs a belt runs and moves laterally (as from a loose to a tight pulley) in response to pressure from either prong

shift·ful \ˈshiftfəl\ *adj* **:** TRICKY

shiftier *comparative of* SHIFTY

shiftiest *superlative of* SHIFTY

shift·i·ly \ˈshiftəlē, -li\ *adv* **:** in a shifty manner

shift·i·ness \-tēnəs, -tin-\ *n* -ES **:** the quality or state of being shifty **:** TRICKINESS ⟨a look of ~ and hardness, a mixture of prison and the boxing ring —John Masefield⟩

shifting *pres part of* SHIFT

shifting accent *n* **:** SHIFTING STRESS

shifting backstay *n* **:** a permanent stay so rigged as to be set up or cast off as the working of a ship requires

shifting boards *n pl* **:** boards placed fore-and-aft in the hold of a ship to prevent bulk cargoes (as grain) from shifting

shifting executory devise *n* **:** a shifting use created by will

shifting pedal *n* **:** SOFT PEDAL 1

shifting stress *n* **:** stress that is not the same for a particular speech item with all speakers or in all occurrences or environments

shifting use *n* **:** a use that takes effect in derogation of some other estate and is expressly limited by the deed or may be created on a certain contingency by a person named in the deed

shift joint *n* **:** a vertical building joint so placed as to come above a solid member of the course below; *also* **:** the process of forming such a joint

shift key *n* **:** a typewriter key used for shifting

shift·less \ˈshiftləs, *in rapid speech* -fl-\ *adj* **1 a :** lacking in ability or resourcefulness **:** INEFFICIENT ⟨is not being backward or ~ when he clears a patch, burns the trees, cultivates it for a few years, and then abandons the area —W.H.Camp⟩ **b :** lacking in ambition or incentive **:** IDLE, LAZY ⟨caused many who were once proud, industrious, property-owning people to become indifferent, ~, languid and sickly —A.C. Chandler⟩ **2 :** marked by lack of ambition, energy, or purpose ⟨living there in a ~ way, without any serious purpose —Ellen Glasgow⟩ ⟨flabby, ~ writing —Whitney Balliett⟩ — **shift·less·ly** *adv* — **shift·less·ness** *n* -ES

shift lock *n* **:** a typewriter key that when depressed locks the carriage or typebars into shifted position

shift·man \ˈ=mən, -ˌman\ *n, pl* **shiftmen :** SHIFT BOSS

shift of butts : an arrangement of butts of planks or plates in a ship

shifts *pres 3d sing of* SHIFT, *pl of* SHIFT

shift to the left : alteration of an Arneth index by an increase of immature leukocytes in the circulating blood

shift to the right : alteration of an Arneth index by an increase in mature or overaged leukocytes in the circulating blood

shifty \ˈshiftē, -ti\ *adj, usu* -ER/-EST **1 :** full of expedients **:** capable of meeting situations **:** RESOURCEFUL ⟨the exigencies of a new country made them quick-witted and ~ —Edward Eggleston⟩ **2 a :** given to deception, evasion, or fraud **:** SLIPPERY, TRICKY ⟨the ~ little men whose craftiness for once would fail them —A.P.Davies⟩ **b :** capable of evasive movement **:** ELUSIVE ⟨a small, ~ back who's tough to nail with a low tackle —Eugene Hopper⟩ **3 :** indicative or characteristic of a deceitful or untrustworthy person **:** FURTIVE ⟨the ~ eyes above the lying mouth would peer and probe —G.D.Brown⟩ **4 :** not fixed **:** CHANGEABLE, UNSTABLE ⟨grammatical phenomena are extremely numerous, extremely varied, and bafflingly ~ —Charlton Laird⟩ **5 :** shifting or tending to shift in position or direction ⟨if the ~ election-year winds should blow the nomination into his lap —*Newsweek*⟩

shi·ga bacillus \ˈshēgə-, -(ˌ)gä-\ *also* **shiga dysentery bacillus** *n, usu cap S* [after Kiyoshi *Shiga*] **:** a widely distributed but chiefly tropical bacillus (*Shigella dysenteriae*) that causes dysentery in man and monkeys

shi·gel·la \shəˈgelə\ *n* [NL, fr. Kiyoshi *Shiga* †1957 Jap. bacteriologist + NL *-ella*] **1** *cap* **:** a genus of nonmotile aerobic bacteria (family Enterobacteriaceae) that form acid but no gas on many carbohydrates and do not form acetylmethylcarbinol and that cause dysenteries in man and other animals **2** *pl* **shigel·lae** \-(ˌ)lē, -ˌlī\ *also* **shigellas** *sometimes cap* **:** any bacterium of the genus *Shigella*

shig·el·lo·sis \ˌshigəˈlōsəs\ *n, pl* **shigello·ses** \-ōˌsēz\ [NL, fr. *Shigella* + *-osis*] **:** infection with or dysentery caused by bacteria of the genus *Shigella*

shi'i \ˈshēˌē, ˈ=ˌ=\ *n* -s *usu cap* [Ar *shīyaʻīy*] **:** SHI'ITE

shi'·ism *or* **shi·ism** \ˈshēˌizəm\ *n* -s *usu cap* [*shiʻa* + *-ism*] **:** the religious system or distinctive tenets of the Shiʻa

shi'·ite *or* **shi·ite** \-ˌīt\ *n* -s *usu cap* [Ar *shīyaʻīy* partisan, Shiʻite, fr. *shīʻah* following, sect, fr. *shāʻa* to accompany] **:** a Muslim belonging to the Shiʻa branch of Islam

shik \ˈshik\ *n, pl* **shik** *or* **shiks** *usu cap* **1 :** a people of the Turkmen Soviet Socialist Republic that is regarded as of Arabian origin but has become assimilated to the Turkoman people **2 :** a member of the Shik people

¹shi·kar \shəˈkär\ *n* -s [Hindi *śikār*, fr. Per *shikār*, MPer *shkār*] *India* **:** HUNTING, SPORT

²shikar \"\ *vb* **shikarred; shikarred; shikarring; shikars** *vi, India* **:** to hunt game ~ *vt, India* **:** to hunt (animals) for sport

shi·ka·ra \ˈshikərə\ *or* **sik·ar** \ˈsikə(r)\ *or* **si·kha·ra** \-kərə\ *n* -s [Skt *śikhara*] **1 :** the tower or spire of a medieval Indian temple; *esp* **:** a curvilinear spire in the northern style surmounted by an amalaka **2 :** a Kashmirian boat resembling a gondola

shi·kar·gah \shəˈkär(ˌ)gä\ *n* -s [Hindi *śikārgāh*, fr. Per *shikārgāh*, fr. *shikār* hunting + *-gāh* place — more at IDGAH] *India* **:** a game preserve

shi·ka·ri *also* **shi·ka·ree** \shəˈkarē, -karē\ *n* -s [Hindi *śikārī*, fr. Per *shikārī*, fr. *shikār* hunting] *India* **:** a big game hunter; *esp* **:** a professional hunter or guide

shi·kas·ta \shəˈkastə\ *n* -s [Per *shikasta* broken, fr. *shikastan* to break, fr. MPer *shkastan*] **:** the broken or current Persian hand in which correspondence and sometimes manuscripts are written

shike·poke \ˈshīkˌpōk\ *n* [euphemism] **:** SHITEPOKE

shik·ii \ˈshi(ˌ)kē\ *n* -s [Jap] **1 :** coarse rough silk filling **2 :** a heavy silk or rayon fabric with a texture similar to that of shantung

shi·kim·ic acid \shəˈkimik-\ *n* [Jap *shikimi* star anise + E *-ic*] **:** a crystalline acid $C_6H_6(OH)_3COOH$ that is obtained esp. from the fruit of the Japanese star anise and is formed as a precursor in the biosynthesis of aromatic amino acids and of lignin; 2,3,4,5-tetrahydro-gallic acid

shik·ken \(ˈ)shiˌken\ *n* -s [Jap] **:** a chief executive officer and later a virtual regent under the Japanese shoguns during the period from 1192 to 1333

shikker *var of* SHICKER

¹shi·ko \shiˈkō, ˈ=(ˌ)=\ *vi* -ED/-ING/-S [Burmese *śikhō* (written *hrikhō*)] **:** to assume the shiko ⟨she ~*ed* to him as though he had been royalty —F. Tennyson Jesse⟩

²shiko \"\ *n* -s **:** a Burmese posture of kneeling with joined hands and bowed head before a superior ⟨bowing, touching the floor with her forehead in the full ~ of utter abasement —George Orwell⟩

shik·ra \ˈshikrə\ *n* -s [Hindi *śikra*, fr. Per *shikara* bird trained to hunt, fr. *shikār* hunting] **:** a small Indian hawk (*Accipiter badius*) sometimes used in falconry

shik·sa *or* **shik·se** *or* **shick·sa** \ˈshiksə\ *n* -s [Yiddish *shikse*, fem. of *sheygets*, *sheygets* shegetz — more at SHEGETZ] **1 :** a non-Jewish girl — often used disparagingly ⟨goy and ~ were not words for such as her —Stanley Sultan⟩ **2 :** a Jewish girl who does not observe Jewish precepts — used esp. by Jews

shil·fa \ˈshilˌfä\ *n* -s [origin unknown] *chiefly Scot* **:** CHAFFINCH

shilha *usu cap, var of* SHLUH

shilingol *usu cap, var of* SILINGAL

¹shill \ˈshil\ *adj* [ME, fr. OE *sciell, scyl;* akin to OE *sciellan, scyllan* to resound, sound loudly, D *schel* shrill, strident, OHG *scellan* to resound, sound, ring, ON *skjallr* loud, shrill, *skjalla* to clash, clatter, Lith *skalyti* to bark for a long period of time, and perh. to OE *hlōwan* to low (like a cow) — more at LOW] *archaic chiefly Scot* **:** SHRILL, SONOROUS

²shill \"\ *var of* SHEAL

³shill \"\ *n* -s [prob. short for *shillaber*] **:** one who acts as a decoy or steerer: as **a :** one who is employed by an amusement enterprise (as a circus or carnival) to get the sale of tickets started after the barker has finished his spiel **b :** one who is employed by a pitchman to pose as a member of the audience and make the first purchase **c :** one who is employed by a gambling house to pose as a customer and keep action going **d :** one who poses as an innocent bystander to help a confidence man win over a prospective victim

⁴shill \"\ *vi* -ED/-ING/-S **:** to act as a shill

shil·la·ber \ˈshiləbə(r)\ *n* -s [origin unknown] **:** SHILL

shil·le·lagh *also* **shil·la·lah** \shəˈlālē, -āli *sometimes* -ālə\ *n* -s [fr. *Shillelagh*, town in County Wicklow, Ireland] *chiefly Irish* **:** CUDGEL; *specif* **:** one cut from an oak or blackthorn sapling

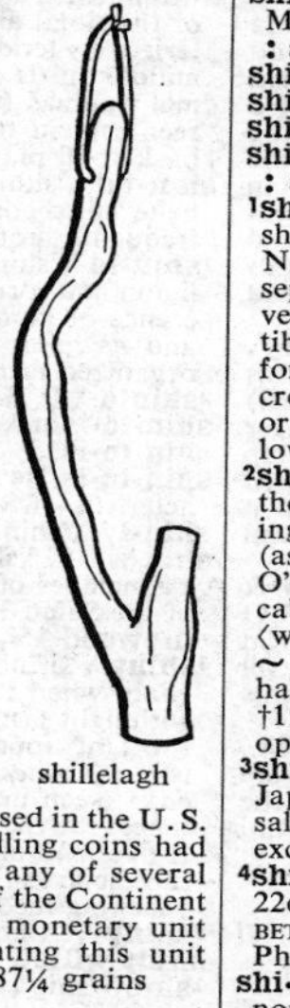

shillelagh

shil·let \ˈshilət, ˈshil-\ *n* -s [prob. fr. ²*shill* + *-et*] *dial Eng* **:** SHALE

shil·li·beer \ˈshiləˌbi(ə)r\ *n* -s [after George *Shillibeer* †1866 Eng. coach proprietor] **1 :** a horse-drawn omnibus **2 :** a horse-drawn hearse with seats for mourners

¹shil·ling \ˈshiliŋ, -lēŋ\ *n* -s *often attrib* [ME, fr. OE *scilling;* akin to OHG *skilling*, a gold coin, ON *skillingr*, Goth *skillings;* all fr. a prehistoric Gmc compound whose first constituent is represented by E ¹*shield* and whose second is represented by E *-ling*] **1 a :** a British monetary unit since the Norman conquest equal to twelve pence or 1/20 pound — see MONEY table **b :** a coin representing one shilling first issued under Henry VII and coined in silver until 1946 when it was changed to cupronickel **2 a :** a unit of value and corresponding coin of Scotland before 1707 that by the 17th century had depreciated to the value of one English penny **b** (1) **:** a unit of value equal to 1/20 pound in any of several countries in or formerly in the British Commonwealth (as Australia, New Zealand, Union of South Africa, Ireland) — see MONEY table (2) **:** a coin representing this unit **3 a :** any of several early American coins or tokens (as of Maryland or Massachusetts) **b :** any of numerous fluctuating units of value used in the U. S. in colonial times and later after the use of shilling coins had ceased ⟨New York ~⟩ ⟨Connecticut ~⟩ **c :** any of several units or coins (as the schilling or the skilling) of the Continent related to the English shilling **4 a :** the basic monetary unit of British East Africa **b :** a coin representing this unit **5 :** a measure of weight for arrows equal to 87¼ grains

²shilling *var of* SHEALING

shil·ling·less \-ŋləs\ *adj* **:** being without a shilling

shilling shocker *n* **1 :** a novel of crime or violence esp. popular in late Victorian England and costing orig. one shilling — compare DIME NOVEL, PENNY DREADFUL **2 :** a usu. short novel that is characterized by sensational incidents and lurid writing

shil·lings·worth \-ŋzˌ=\ *n* **:** the worth of a shilling **:** the amount that a shilling buys

shilluh *usu cap, var of* SHLUH

shil·luk \shəˈlük\ *n, pl* **shilluk** *or* **shilluks** *usu cap* **1 a :** a Nilotic Negro people of the Sudan dwelling mainly on the west bank of the White Nile **b :** a member of such people **2 :** a Nilotic language of the Shilluk people

¹shilly-shally \ˈshilēˌshalē, -iliˌshali\ *adv* [redupl. of *shall I*] **:** in an irresolute, undecided, or hesitating manner

²shilly-shally \"\ *adj* **:** showing or marked by indecisiveness **:** IRRESOLUTE, VACILLATING ⟨a *shilly-shally* person⟩ ⟨this man's *shilly-shally* temporizing —*Atlantic*⟩

³shilly-shally \"\ *n* -ES **1 :** INDECISION, IRRESOLUTION, VACILLATION ⟨one can hardly say suddenly after four years of *shilly-shally* —Janet Flanner⟩ **2 :** SHILLYSHALLYER

⁴shilly-shally \"\ *vi* **shilly-shallied; shilly-shallied; shilly-shallying; shilly-shallies 1 :** to fail to act **:** show hesitation or lack of resolution ⟨having reached a decision, I did not *shilly-shally* about the affair —*Harper's*⟩ **2 :** to alternate between two attitudes or courses of action **:** back and fill ⟨never took a stand but *shilly-shallied* on all sides of it —C.W.M.Hart⟩ **3 :** to waste time **:** DAWDLE ⟨twenty people for supper . . . and thee *shilly-shallying* in thy shirttail at six in the morning —Jessamyn West⟩

shilly·shally·er \-ə(r)\ *n* -s **:** one that shilly-shallies ⟨a ~ who can't make up her mind —John McCarten⟩

shi·lo·nite \ˈshī(ˌ)lōˌnīt\ *n* -s *cap* [irreg. (influence of LL *Silonita* Shilonite) fr. *Shiloh*, town of ancient Palestine + E *-ite*] **:** a native or inhabitant of the town of Shiloh in ancient Palestine

shil·pit \ˈshilpət\ *adj* [origin unknown] **1** *Scot* **:** having a pinched and starved appearance **:** PUNY **2** *Scot* **:** WEAK, INSIPID, FLAT ⟨pronounced the claret ~ —Sir Walter Scott⟩

shily *var of* SHYLY

¹shim \ˈshim\ *n* -s [prob. akin to OE *scīma* twilight, gloom, *scīma* ray, light, brightness, OS *skimo* shadow, OS & OHG *skīmo* brightness, ON *skimi* brightness, Goth *skeima* lantern, OE *scīnan* to shine — more at SHINE] **1** *dial Eng* **:** a white streak on a horse's face **2** *dial Eng* **:** a fleeting glimpse

²shim \"\ *n* -s [origin unknown] **1 :** a horizontal knife attachment to a cultivator used for surface scraping between crop rows and for weed removal **2 :** a thin piece or slip usu. of wood, metal, or stone that is often tapered, is used to fill in (as in leveling a stone in building or a railroad tie or rail), or is designed to be removed to take up wear (as in a bearing) **3 :** a shingle with sides not equally thick **4 :** a thin strip usu. of brass used to separate parts in making a piece mold

³shim \"\ *vt* **shimmed; shimmed; shimming; shims 1 :** to hoe or weed with a shim **2 a :** to fill out or level up to a desired height or a true surface by the use of a shim **b :** to fill up (cracks or joints) usu. with putty

shimal *var of* SHAMAL

¹shim·mer \ˈshimə(r)\ *vb* **shimmered; shimmered; shimmering** \-m(ə)riŋ\ **shimmers** [ME *schimeren, schemeren*, fr. OE *scimerian;* akin to MLG *schēmeren* to get dark, G *schimmern* to glimmer, OE *scimian* to shine, grow dark, *scīma* ray, light, brightness — more at SHIM] *vi* **1 :** to shine with a tremulous or fitful light **:** gleam faintly **:** GLIMMER ⟨the street lights ~*ed* behind the veil of snow —Morley Callaghan⟩ ⟨by moonlight its powdery sands ~ like snow —D.L.Graham⟩ **2 :** to reflect a wavering sometimes distorted visual image ⟨heat waves ~*ed* before our eyes —F.P. Conant⟩ ~ *vt* **1 :** to cause to shimmer ⟨the night breeze . . . stirred the leaves on trees, ~*ing* them in the moonlight —Stuart Cloete⟩

²shimmer \"\ *n* -s **1 :** a fitful, tremulous light **:** GLIMMER **:** a subdued sparkle or sheen **:** a scintillating effect ⟨the faint ~ of heat lightning —R.P.Warren⟩ ⟨the ~ of young foliage —L.P.Smith⟩ ⟨enough to give a ~ of danger to the atmosphere —Ellery Sedgwick⟩ **2 :** a wavering sometimes distorted visual image usu. produced by a reflection from heat waves ⟨the slate roofs sent ~*s* up . . . in the glare —Elizabeth Bowen⟩ ⟨a constant ~ of heat over wide concrete highways —S.W.Matthews⟩

³shimmer \"\ *vt* -ED/-ING/-S [²*shim* + *-er* (freq. suffix)] **1 :** SHIM 1 **2 :** to fit a shim between surfaces of (work)

⁴shimmer \"\ *n* -s [³*shim* + *-er* (n. suffix)] **1 a :** one that shims **b :** SHIM **2 :** one that inserts shims

¹shimmering *adj* [ME *schimering*, fr. pres. part. of *schimeren* to shimmer] **:** tremulously shining **:** having a subdued but often tantalizing sparkle or sheen **:** producing a scintillating effect ⟨~ chandeliers and deep carpets —Catherine Paul⟩ ⟨low emerald islands in a ~ painted sea —*Amer. Guide Series: Fla.*⟩ ⟨wore a gown of ~ satin⟩ ⟨~ sounds and sights and delights —Vicki Baum⟩ ⟨an easy style, a ~ humor —James Kelly⟩ — **shim·mer·ing·ly** *adv*

²shimmering *n* -s [ME *schimering, schemering*, fr. gerund of *schimeren, schemeren* to shimmer] **:** SHIMMER

shim·mery \ˈshim(ə)rē\ *adj* [¹*shimmer* + *-y*] **:** SHIMMERING ⟨black ~ velvet curtains —Rudyard Kipling⟩

¹shim·my \ˈshimē, -mi\ *n* -s [alter. of *chemise*] **1 :** CHEMISE **2** [short for *shimmy-shake* & *shimmy shiver*] **:** a jazz dance popular after World War I and similar in form and function to the cooch but probably of Negro origin and characterized by a shaking of the body from the shoulders down **3 :** an abnormal oscillation esp. in the front wheels of a motor vehicle reinforced by resonance at critical speeds

²shimmy \"\ *vi* -ED/-ING/-S **1 :** to shake, quiver, or tremble in or as if in dancing a shimmy **2 :** to oscillate abnormally — used esp. of automobiles

³shimmy \"\ *n* -ES [by folk etymology] *slang* **:** CHEMIN DE FER

shimmy shirt *n* **:** SHIMMY 1

shim·o·no·se·ki \ˌshimənōˈsākē, -ˈsekē; -ˈnōsəkē\ *adj, usu cap* [fr. *Shimonoseki*, Japan] **:** of or from the city of Shimonoseki, Japan **:** of the kind or style prevalent in Shimonoseki

shi·mo·se \shəˈmōsə\ *also* **shimose powder** *n* -s [after Masachika *Shimose* †1911 Jap. naval engineer, its inventor] **:** a Japanese explosive composed chiefly of picric acid

shim·per \ˈshimpə(r)\ *vi* -ED/-ING/-S [by alter.] **:** SHIMMER

shim plow *n* [²*shim*] **:** ²SHIM 1

shims *pl of* SHIM, *pres 3d sing of* SHIM

shim-sham shimmy \ˈshimˌsham-\ *n* [redupl. of ¹*shimmy*] **:** a swing step with stamps, heel-beats, and runs

¹shin \ˈshin\ *n* -s [ME *shine*, fr. OE *scinu;* akin to MD *schene* shin, OHG *scina* shin, needle, Sw dial. *skener* iceskate, Norw dial. *skina* thin plate or disk, OE *scēadan* to divide, separate — more at SHED] **1 a** (1) **:** the front part of the vertebrate leg below the knee (2) **:** the front edge of the tibia (3) **:** the lower part of the leg **b :** the lower part of the foreleg in beef cattle; *specif* **:** a cut of meat consisting of a cross section of lower-leg bone and muscle used for boiling or braising **c :** TIBIA 1b **2** *archaic* **:** the ridge of a hill **3 :** the lower forward corner of a plow moldboard

²shin \"\ *vb* **shinned; shinned; shinning; shins** *vi* **1 :** to use the shins in climbing **:** climb (as a mast, tree, rope) by embracing alternately with the arms or hands and legs without help (as of steps or spurs) ⟨*shinned* down a drainpipe —Frank O'Connor⟩ ⟨still building bridges, but was not *shinning* up cables —Allan Seager⟩ **2 :** to move forward rapidly on foot ⟨was up in a second and *shinning* down the hill —Mark Twain⟩ ~ *vt* **1 :** to kick or strike on the shins ⟨been well *shinned* half a dozen times in scrimmages at football —Samuel Butler †1902⟩ **2 :** to climb up or down by shinning ⟨reached the open window by *shinning* the tree⟩

³shin \", ˈshēn\ *n* -s *cap* [Jap, lit., belief, faith] **:** a major Japanese Buddhist sect growing out of Jodo that emphasizes salvation by faith alone, has a married clergy, and holds to the exclusive worship of Amida Buddha — called also *Shin-shu*

⁴shin \ˈshēn *also* ˈshin\ *n* -s [Heb *shīn*, lit., tooth] **1 :** the 22d letter of the Hebrew alphabet — symbol ש; see ALPHABET table **2 :** the letter corresponding to Hebrew shin in the Phoenician or in any of various other Semitic alphabets

shi·na \ˈshēnə\ *n* -s *usu cap* **:** the Dard language of Gilgit in northern Kashmir

shi·nar·ump \shəˈnarəmp\ *n* -s [origin unknown] *Southwest* **:** agatized wood

shinbone \ˈ=ˌ=\ *n* [ME *shinbon*, fr. OE *scinbān*, fr. *scinu* shin + *bān* bone — more at SHIN, BONE] **:** the anterior bone of the lower leg **:** TIBIA 1a

shin·dig \ˈshinˌdig\ *n* -s [prob. alter. (influenced by *shin* & *dig*) of *shindy*] **1 :** a festive occasion: as **a :** a social gathering often with dancing ⟨every community has its weekly ~ in some farm home —*Amer. Guide Series: Okla.*⟩ **b :** a usu. large often overly lavish party ⟨coming-out party . . . was the

gaudiest ~ since the war —*Time*⟩ **c :** an elaborate celebration often commemorating some special event and involving extensive planning ⟨to mark the day with the largest peacetime parade . . . I had drawn the assignment of assembling and staging this enormous ~ —Frank Zachary⟩ **2 :** SHINDY 2 ⟨touched off the whole bloody ~ that raged for years —Alan Devoe⟩

shin·dy \ˈshindē, -di\ *n, pl* **shindys** *or* **shindies** [prob. alter. of *shinny*] **1 :** SHINDIG 1 ⟨the summer tourist season . . . is marked by galas, festivals, and other ~*s* —*Holiday*⟩ **2 :** a general commotion **:** noisy row **:** FRACAS, UPROAR ⟨created a ~, saying that they were already an oppressed class —F.A.Swinnerton⟩ ⟨it must look bad after that ~ I had with the director —C.D.Lewis⟩

¹shine \ˈshīn\ *vb* **shone** \ˈshōn *also* ˈshän *sometimes* ˈshən *or* ˈshòn\ *or* **shined; shone** *or* **shined; shining; shines** [ME *shinen*, fr. OE *scīnan*; akin to OHG *skīnan* to shine, ON *skīna*, Goth *skeinan* to shine, Gk *skia* shadow, *skēnē* tent, stage, Skt *chāyā* shadow, reflection, OSlav *sijati* to shine, get bright] *vi* **1 :** to emit rays of light **:** give light **:** beam with steady radiance ⟨the stars ~ with a brilliance never seen down in valleys —G.W.Gray b.1886⟩ ⟨the points of light were . . . *shining* with a greenish luster —Ambrose Bierce⟩ **2 :** to be bright by reflection of light **:** GLEAM, GLISTEN **:** be glossy ⟨the berries . . . decorated with sunlight and dew *shone* like black-purple glass —G.S.Perry⟩ ⟨the air was bright and the water *shone* like dark silk —G.A.Wagner⟩ **3 :** to be eminent, conspicuous, or distinguished **:** exhibit brilliant talent or intellectual powers ⟨restrained any inclination to ~ or push himself forward —H.R.Warfel⟩ ⟨acquiring those graces which would enable him to ~ at dinner parties —E.J. Simmons⟩ **4 :** to have a bright glowing appearance **:** give the effect of radiance **:** display or show beauty or splendor ⟨as he talked his eyes began to ~ —Sherwood Anderson⟩ ⟨his withered face *shone* with a spiritual power —Liam O'Flaherty⟩ **5 :** to be conspicuously evident **:** be clearly apparent ⟨the courage and ability which ~ brightly in adversity —A.M.Young⟩ ⟨the glory of Greece ~*s* not only in her antiquity —Sir Winston Churchill⟩ ⟨human feeling ~*s* through all her books —S.T.Williams⟩ **6** *archaic* **:** to be sunny **:** DAWN **7 :** to cast an auspicious or favoring light ⟨the light which *shined* to him was the single divine light —V.L.Parrington⟩ — often used with *upon* **8 :** to sparkle or glow with cleanliness ⟨though the furnishings may be modest . . . her home fairly ~*s* —*Amer. Guide Series: La.*⟩ ~ *vt* **1 a** (1) **:** to cause to emit light (2) **:** to send forth like light ⟨the hardest thing . . . for one human being to ~ into another human being the glow that burned within himself —Bruce Marshall⟩ **b :** to throw or flash the light of ⟨stood there and *shined* our flashlights on the deck —Richard Bissell⟩ **2 :** to make bright by polishing ⟨was not going to ~ shoes longer than he had to —H.A.Sinclair⟩ ⟨*shined* his brass buttons —Robert Hazel⟩ **3 :** to throw light into (as the eyes of an animal) while hunting for the purpose of attracting the attention of and getting an opportunity to kill the prey

²shine \"\ *n* -s **1 a** (1) **:** brightness caused by the emission of light **:** ILLUMINATION, RADIANCE ⟨the ~ of a lantern signaled the approach of a sentry⟩ ⟨the windows gleamed gold in the ~ of the setting sun⟩ (2) *obs* **:** a beam of light **:** NIMBUS **b** (1) **:** a brilliance of quality or appearance **:** SPLENDOR ⟨a magazine with a high literary ~ —Norman Cousins⟩ ⟨grand opera . . . that has kept its ~ for 200 years —*Time*⟩ (2) **:** an ostentatious display **:** SHOW ⟨celebrate the nuptials with due ~ and celebration —Thomas Carlyle⟩ **2 a :** brightness caused by the reflection of light **:** LUSTER, SHEEN ⟨on the black ~ of boulevard the buses plowed up and down —Bruce Marshall⟩ **b :** brightness usu. of countenance reflected from an inner quality of spirit ⟨the sort of ~ you want . . . does come from the heart that is gay —Constance Foster⟩ ⟨exuding modesty, humility and the ~ of honesty —*Time*⟩ **3 :** fair weather **:** SUNSHINE ⟨will go rain or ~⟩ **4 a :** a stupid trick **:** silly caper **:** PRANK — usu. used in pl. ⟨figured you never would try to pull any ~*s* —R.P.Warren⟩ **b** *dial chiefly Eng* **:** a meeting or gathering that is noisy and disorderly **5 :** a sudden fancy **:** LIKING ⟨if she takes a ~ to you she'll treat you all right —H.A.Sinclair⟩ **6 a :** a polish or gloss given to shoes **b :** a single polishing of a pair of shoes **7 :** NEGRO — usu. taken to be offensive **8 :** MOONSHINE 3

³shine *adj* [alter. (influenced by ¹*shine*) of ¹*sheen*] *obs* **:** SHINING

shine ball *n* **1 :** a baseball polished on one side against the pitcher's uniform and rubbed with dirt or powder on the other side to obtain more curve when pitched **2 :** the pitch of a shine ball

shin·er \ˈshīnə(r)\ *n* -s **1 :** one that shines: as **a :** STAR **b :** DIAMOND **2 :** a bright piece of money **3** *slang* **:** a cardsharper's mirror used to reflect the cards in his opponent's hand **4 :** any of numerous small silvery freshwater American cyprinid fishes of *Notropis* and closely related genera: as **a :** a small blunt-nosed fish (*Notropis atherinoides*) of the Great Lakes region and Mississippi valley with a metallic greenish luster — called also *emerald shiner* **b :** GOLDEN SHINER **c :** SPOTTAIL SHINER **d :** REDFIN a,b **5 :** any of various silvery fishes: as **a :** DOLLARFISH **b :** MENHADEN **c :** SILVERFISH **6 a :** a shiny streak in a fabric (as rayon) produced by overstretched yarns **b :** a shiny spot in paper caused by calendering a lump of fiber, filler, or starch **c :** a gloss spot appearing on a flat or semigloss paint finish **7 :** BLACK EYE 1a **8 :** MOONSHINER

shine up *vi* **:** to pay marked attention esp. to one of the opposite sex — usu. used with *to* ⟨*shined up* to all the pretty girls⟩

shing *var of* SHENG

¹shin·gle \ˈshiŋgəl\ *n* -s [ME *scincle, schingel*, prob. fr. L *scindula*, alter. of *scandula*; akin to ON *skinn* skin — more at SKIN] **1 a :** a small thin piece of building material (as wood or asbestos) often with one end thicker than the other laid in overlapping rows as a covering for the roof or sides of a building **b :** a piece of wood similar in shape to a roofing shingle but larger and usu. from ⅞ to 1¼ inches thick at the butt and applied to the ordinarily flat bottom of a racing motorboat to form a series of small steps **2 :** a small signboard — usu. used with *hang out* ⟨hung out a ~ and worked up a nice medical practice —R.L.Taylor⟩ **3 :** a woman's haircut with the hair trimmed short from the back of the head to the nape

²shingle \"\ *vt* **shingled; shingled; shingling** \ g(ə)liŋ\ **shingles 1 :** to cover with or as if with shingles ⟨helped his neighbor to ~ his roof⟩ **2 :** to bob and shape (the hair) by cutting close at the nape of the neck and gradually longer up the back of the head **3 :** to lay or dispose so as to overlap ⟨bacon for this package is stacked rather than *shingled* —*Meat Mag.*⟩ **4 a :** to overlap or duplicate one's own claims on land **b :** to encroach knowingly upon the lawful claims of others

³shingle \"\ *n* -s [prob. of Scand origin; akin to Norw & Sw *singel* coarse gravel (esp. on the seashore); akin to MLG *singele* gravelly bank] **1 :** coarse rounded detritus or alluvial material esp. on the seashore differing from ordinary gravel only in the size of the stones which may be as large as a man's head **2 :** a place (as a beach) strewn with shingle

⁴shingle \"\ *vt* -ED/-ING/-s [F dial. (Picardy) *chingler*, lit., to whip, fr. MF dial., fr. *chingle* strap, belt, fr. L *cingula* — more at CINGLE] **:** to subject (as a mass of iron from the puddling furnace) to the process of expelling cinder and impurities by hammering and squeezing

shingle-back \ˈ=,=\ *n* [¹*shingle*] **:** STUMP-TAIL

shingle bolt *n* [¹*shingle*] **:** ¹BOLT 7a

¹shin·gled \-gəld\ *adj* [ME *schyngled*, fr. *scincle, schingel* shingle + *-ed*] **1 :** covered, roofed, or sheathed with shingles **2** *of hair* **:** cut in a shingle

²shingled \"\ *adj* [³*shingle* + *-ed*] **:** covered with shingle or coarse rounded detritus

shingle lap *n* [¹*shingle*] **:** a lap joint (as for a sheet-metal stack) in which the sections joined are tapered so that the bottom of each section fits over the top of the section below it

shingle nail *n* [ME *schingelneil*, fr. *schingel* shingle + *neil* nail] **:** a usu. galvanized nail used in applying shingles to a house

shingle oak *n* [¹*shingle*] **1 :** an American oak (*Quercus imbricaria*) with shining leaves resembling laurel and wood that is used in western states for shingles **2 :** SHE-OAK

shin·gler \-g(ə)lə(r)\ *n* -s [ME *shyngeler*, fr. *shyngel, schingel* shingle + *-er*] **:** one that shingles: as **a :** one who shingles esp. roofs **b :** a man or a machine that makes shingles **c :** a workman who tends a shingling machine or hammer **d :** a machine for shingling puddled iron

shin·gles \ˈshiŋgəlz\ *n pl but sing in constr* [ME *schingles*, by folk etymology fr. ML *cingulus*, fr. L *cingulum* girdle; trans. of Gk *zōnē* girdle, shingles — more at CINGULUM, ZONE] **:** HERPES ZOSTER

shingle tow *n* [¹*shingle*] **:** shredded wood resulting from the manufacture of shingles; *broadly* **:** wood shavings

shingle tree *n* [¹*shingle*] **:** an East Indian timber tree (*Acrocarpus fraxinifolius*) of the family Leguminosae with hard durable wood used esp. for tea boxes

shingle weaver *n* [¹*shingle*] **:** one that makes, trims, or packs shingles

shin·gling \ˈshiŋg(ə)liŋ\ *n* -s [³*shingle* + *-ing*] **:** the arrangement of pebbles by currents so that they slope in the same direction and overlap like shingles on a roof

shingling hatchet *n* **:** a hatchet usu. with a notch in the blade for extracting nails and a hammerhead opposite the cutting edge

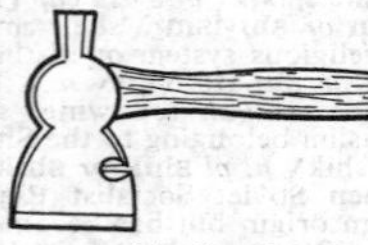

shingling hatchet

shin·gly \ˈshiŋg(ə)lē\ *adj* [³*shingle* + *-y*] **:** composed of or abounding in shingle ⟨landed at a ~ little beach —D.B.Putnam⟩

shin·gon \ˈshin,gän\ *n* -s *cap* [Jap, lit., true word] **:** a Japanese Buddhist sect that emphasizes a mystical symbolism of mantras and mudras together with an esoteric doctrine centered around the Buddha's ideal which is held to be essentially inexpressible

shin guard *n* **:** a protective covering for the shin that is usu. of stiffened canvas or leather and is used in various sports

shinier *comparative of* SHINY

shiniest *superlative of* SHINY

shin·i·ness \ˈshīnēnəs, -īnin-\ *n* -ES **:** the quality or state of being shiny ⟨hard days . . . have taken off the ~ of youth —Mary Deasy⟩

shining *adj* [ME, fr. pres. part. of *shinen* to shine — more at SHINE] **1 :** emitting light **:** shedding radiance **:** GLOWING ⟨one ~ morning —John Muir †1914⟩ ⟨gazed up at the ~ heavens⟩ **2 a :** reflecting light **:** GLEAMING, LUSTROUS ⟨its ~ white church and background of fir and spruce —*Amer. Guide Series: Maine*⟩ ⟨covered with ~ enamel —*Victorian Naturalist*⟩ **b :** reflecting an inner spirit often of radiance or joy ⟨essentially unsophisticated . . . with ~ eyes —Donald Foley⟩ **3 :** bright often splendid in appearance or aspect **:** RESPLENDENT ⟨its shape was destroyed, its ~ newness a bruised memory —Henry LaCossitt⟩ ⟨a warm and ~ company of friends —*Newsweek*⟩ **4 :** possessing a distinguished quality **:** marked by illustrious eminence or exceptional merit ⟨her sharp and ~ prose —Carl Van Doren⟩ ⟨had ~ virtues and few faults —Richard Garnett †1906⟩ ⟨singled out . . . as the ~ example of his tribe —C.R.Anderson⟩ **5 :** full of sunshine ⟨a wiser . . . way to improve the ~ hours —L.P.Smith⟩ ⟨have had my fair share of ~ hours —R.F.Wagner⟩ **6 :** unusually clean and bright ⟨the men and boys with ~ faces and in Sunday suits —Flora Thompson⟩

shining flycatcher *n* **1 :** SATIN FLYCATCHER **2 :** PHAINOPEPLA

shining gum *n* **:** an Australian gum tree (*Eucalyptus nitens*) with shiny often ribbony bark

shin·ing·ly *adv* [ME, fr. *shining* + *-ly*] **:** in a shining manner ⟨genius manifests itself most ~ —C.J.Rolo⟩

shin·ing·ness *n* -ES **:** a shining quality **:** BRILLIANCE ⟨the medals . . . in their rich ~ seemed to belong there —F.K.Kelly⟩

shining sumac *n* **:** DWARF SUMAC

shining willow *n* **:** a common No. American shrub (*Salix lucida*) with lanceolate shiny leaves

shinleaf \ˈ=,=\ *n, pl* **shinleafs** [prob. so called fr. its use in plasters to treat sore legs] **:** an American wintergreen of the genus *Pyrola*; *esp* **:** WILD LILY OF THE VALLEY 3

shinned *past of* SHIN

shin·nery \ˈshinərē, -ri\ *n* -ES [modif. of AmerF (La.) *chênière* chenier — more at CHENIER] **:** a dense growth of small trees; *esp* **:** a thick interlacing growth of scrub oak in the West and Southwest

shinnery oak *n* **:** any of several small shrubby oaks that tend to form thickets; *esp* **:** a low shrub (*Quercus havardii*) that spreads by underground suckers to form dense thickets, produces large sweet acorns, and grows on dry sandy land of the southwestern U.S.

shinning *pres part of* SHIN

¹shin·ny *also* **shin·ney** \ˈshinē, -ni\ *n* -ES [perh. fr. ¹*shin* + *-y*; fr. the damage done to shins by the sticks] **1 a :** the game of hockey as informally played with a curved stick and usu. a ball or block of wood by schoolboys **b :** the curved stick used in the game **2 :** ice hockey poorly played and usu. without benefit of proper equipment or officials

²shinny \"\ *vi* -ED/-ING/-s [alter. of ²*shin*] **:** SHIN 1

shin oak \ˈshin;=\ *n* [prob. alter. of *shinnery oak*] **:** any of various scrub oaks (esp. *Quercus mohriana* and *Q. undulata*) chiefly of the southern and western U.S.

shinplaster \ˈ=,==\ *n* [fr. obs. *shinplaster*, a plaster used to treat sore legs, fr. ¹*shin* + *plaster*] **1 :** a piece of privately= issued paper currency; *esp* **:** one poorly secured and depreciated in value **2 :** FRACTIONAL NOTE

shins *pl of* SHIN, *pres 3d sing of* SHIN

shin-shu *n, cap 1st S* [Jap *shinshū*] **:** ³SHIN

shin splints *n pl but sing in constr* **:** injury to and inflammation of the tibial and toe extensor muscles or their fasciae characterized by tenderness over the anterior surface of the lower and middle thirds of the tibia and fibula, caused by repeated minimal traumas (as by running on a wood or cement floor), and seen esp. in track athletes but sometimes also in football or basketball players

shin·tai \ˈshin·,tī\ *n, pl* **shintai** *or* **shintais** [Jap] **:** an object believed to contain the spirit of a kami **:** a Shinto fetish most frequently housed in a shrine

¹shin·to \ˈshin·,tō\ *n* -s *cap* [Jap *shintō*] **:** the indigenous religion and former ethnic cult of Japan characterized by the reverence of kami, deified nature spirits, and spirits of ancestors and its great antiquity but lack of an historical founder or organized teachings

²shinto \"\ *adj, usu cap* **:** SHINTOISTIC

shin·to·ism \-ō,izəm\ *n* -s *cap* **:** SHINTO

shin·to·ist \-ōəst\ *n* -s *usu cap* **:** an adherent of Shinto

shin·to·is·tic \;=;=ˈistik\ *adj, usu cap* **:** of, relating to, or characteristic of Shinto

shin·ty \ˈshinti\ *n* -ES [by alter.] *Brit* **:** SHINNY 1a

shin·wa·ri \shinˈwärē\ *n, pl* **shinwari** *or* **shinwaris** *usu cap* **:** a member of a nomadic Afghan people inhabiting the valleys of the Safed Koh range and south of Jalalabad

shinwood \ˈ=,=\ *n* **:** a ground hemlock (*Taxus canadensis*)

¹shiny \ˈshīnē, -ni\ *adj* -ER/-EST [¹*shine* + *-y*] **1 a :** SUNSHINY ⟨only when it is warm and ~ —Andrew Young⟩ **b :** filled with light **:** GLISTENING ⟨a ~ night —*Blackwood's*⟩ **2 :** having a bright appearance, aspect, or exterior **:** GLITTERING, POLISHED ⟨*shiniest* show place on the whole summer coast —*Holiday*⟩ ⟨seen in the ~ magazines —*Times Lit. Supp.*⟩ ⟨the taxi takes you past the rich ~ buildings —Bernard Gutteridge⟩ **3 :** rubbed or worn smooth ⟨clad in ~ rags that were in their time smart suits —C.P.Rodocanachi⟩ **4 :** scrubbed clean; *esp* **:** lacking face powder ⟨none likes a ~ nose⟩

²shiny \"\ *adv* **:** with a shiny surface or appearance

shiny willow *n* **:** SHINING WILLOW

¹ship \ˈship\ *n* -s *often attrib* [ME *schip, ship*, fr. OE *scip*; akin to OHG *skif* ship, boat, vessel for liquids, ON & Goth *skip* ship, boat, OE *scēadan* to divide, separate — more at SHED] **1 a :** any large seagoing boat **b :** a sailing boat having a bowsprit and usu. a square-rigged foremast, mainmast, and mizzenmast each composed of a lower mast, a topmast, a topgallant mast, and sometimes higher masts **2 a :** a boat intended or used for navigation and propelled by power or sail **b :** a boat or structure used for purposes of navigation or intended or used for transportation on a river, sea, ocean, or other navigable water without regard to its form or means of propulsion **3 :** a ship's company or crew ⟨the whole ~ cheering the captain⟩ **4 :** an incense vessel or boat **5 :** one's affairs or good fortune ⟨when his ~ comes in he will pay his debts⟩ **6 :** AIRSHIP, AIRPLANE **7 :** a part used to move something from one place to another ⟨the ~*s* of scissors⟩ **8 a :** a unit of at least five sea explorers of the Boy Scouts of America under the leadership of a skipper **b :** a senior girl scout mariner troop

²ship \"\ *vb* **shipped; shipped; shipping; ships** [ME *schippen, shippen*, fr. *schip, ship*, n.] *vt* **1 a :** to place or receive on board of a ship for transportation by water **:** cause to embark ⟨kept busy . . . *shipping* mackerel and cod —Cid R. Sumner⟩ **b** (1) **:** to cause to be transported ⟨~*s* hundreds of carloads annually —*Amer. Guide Series: Md.*⟩ ⟨was *shipped* off to do five months in jail —H.D.Quillin⟩ (2) **:** to transport or cause to be transported under military orders ⟨was *shipped* overseas as an infantry replacement —Gordon Harrison⟩ — often used with *out* ⟨recruits are *shipped* out as soon as they can be processed⟩ **2** *obs* **:** to provide with a ship **3 :** to put in place for use ⟨~ the tiller⟩ ⟨~ the mast⟩ ⟨lights should be *shipped* and in working order —*Manual of Seamanship*⟩ **4 :** to take into a ship or boat ⟨*shipped* his dripping paddle into the rented canoe —Erle Stanley Gardner⟩ ⟨when the oars are *shipped* they should be laid in the boat —H.A.Calahan⟩ **5 :** to engage or secure for service on a ship ⟨*shipping* 10 extra hands for the voyage⟩ **6 :** to take (as water) over the side ⟨had *shipped* a good amount of water —Alexander MacDonald⟩ ⟨~*s* up to 500 tons of ice topside —*Time*⟩ **7 :** to put or take on (as clothing or a burden) ⟨*shipped* the pack onto his back⟩ **8 :** to move (something) from one place or position to another **:** SHIFT ⟨*shipped* the gun to his shoulder and . . . fired both barrels —Gerald Durrell⟩ ~ *vi* **1 :** to embark on a ship **:** BOARD ⟨travelers to the Pacific ~ at a western port⟩ **2 a :** to go or travel by ship ⟨*shipped* to America in 1819 —W.A. Swanberg⟩ — often used with *out* ⟨might even ~ out on a tramp . . . and go to Mexico —James Jones⟩ **b :** to proceed by ship or other means under military orders ⟨had a letter . . . with a San Francisco A.P.O. number, and knew that Dennis had *shipped* overseas —C.O.Gorham⟩ — often used with *out* ⟨is now on a nine day leave before *shipping* out for overseas duty —*Manteca (Calif.) Bull.*⟩ **3 a :** to engage to serve on board of a vessel ⟨ran away from home and *shipped* before the mast —H.O.Brundidge⟩ **b :** to reenlist for navy or marine service — usu. used with *over* ⟨I mean when I finish this last hitch, not to ~ over —Martin Dibner⟩ **4 :** to rest or have its position when ready for use — used with *in* ⟨the lower end of a sprit ~*s* in a grommet⟩ **syn** see SEND — **ship a sea :** to have a wave come over the side

³ship \"\ *chiefly dial var of* SHEEP

⁴ship \"\ *n* -s [by shortening] *Brit* **:** COMPANIONSHIP

ship *abbr* **1** shipment **2** shipping

-ship \,ship\ *n suffix* -s [ME *-schipe, -shipe, -ship*, fr. OE *-scipe*; akin to OFris *-skip, -skipi* -ship, OS *-skap, -skepi, -skipi*, OHG *-scaf, -scaft*, ON *-skapr*; all fr. a prehistoric Gmc word represented by OHG *scaf* nature, condition, quality; akin to OE *sceppan, scyppan* to shape — more at SHAPE] **1 :** state **:** condition **:** quality ⟨son*ship*⟩ ⟨friend*ship*⟩ ⟨scholar*ship*⟩ **2 :** office **:** dignity **:** profession ⟨clerk*ship*⟩ ⟨chancellor*ship*⟩ ⟨lord*ship*⟩ ⟨author*ship*⟩ **3 :** art **:** skill ⟨horseman*ship*⟩ ⟨marksman*ship*⟩ ⟨seaman*ship*⟩ **4 :** something showing, exhibiting, or embodying a quality or state ⟨town*ship*⟩ ⟨fellow*ship*⟩ ⟨court*ship*⟩ **5 :** one entitled to a (specified) rank, title, or appellation — used with possessive pronouns ⟨his Lord*ship*⟩

ship auger *n* **:** an auger having a simple spiral body and a single cutting edge with or without a screw on the end of it and without a spur at the outer end of the cutting edge

shi·pau·lo·vi \shəˈpòləvē, -paùl-\ *n, pl* **shipaulovi** *or* **shipaulovis** *usu cap* **1 :** a Shoshonean people occupying a pueblo in northeastern Arizona **2 :** a member of the Shipaulovi people

ship biscuit *also* **ship bread** *n* **:** HARDTACK

shipboard \ˈ=,=\ *n* [ME *schipbord, shipbord*, fr. *schip, ship* + *bord* board — more at BOARD] **1 :** the side of a ship **2 :** SHIP — used chiefly in adverbial phrases ⟨prepared for storage on ~⟩ ⟨tipped a shilling simply because it was on ~ —Richard Joseph⟩

ship borer *n* **:** SHIPWORM

shipborne \ˈ=,=\ *adj* **:** transported or designed to be transported by ship ⟨~ expeditions prowled among the antarctic icebergs —*Time*⟩ ⟨~ aircraft⟩

shipbound \ˈ=,=\ *adj* **:** confined to a ship

shipboy *also* **ship's boy** \ˈ=,=\ *n* **:** a boy who serves in a ship usu. as a cabin attendant

ship–breaker \ˈ=,==\ *n* **:** one who breaks up vessels unfit for further use and deals in their materials

shipbreaking \ˈ=,==\ *n* **1 :** the occupation or business of a ship-breaker **2 :** the offense of breaking into a ship to commit there a criminal offense

shipbroken \ˈ=,==\ *adj* [ME *schipbroken*, fr. *schip* ship + *broken*] **:** destitute because of shipwreck **:** SHIPWRECKED

ship broker *n* **1 :** a mercantile agent employed in buying and selling ships **2 :** a representative acting in behalf of the ship owner in obtaining cargo and often in arranging such port activities of a vessel as the discharge and loading of cargo, clearance, and insurance

shipbuilding \ˈ=,==\ *n* **:** the occupation or business of constructing ships

ship canal *n* **:** a canal large enough for seagoing ships

ship carpenter *n* **:** SHIPWRIGHT

ship chandler *n* **:** a dealer in supplies and equipment for ships

ship·en·tine \ˈshipən·,tēn\ *n* -s [¹*ship* + *-entine* (as in *barkentine*)] **:** FOUR-MASTED BARK

ship fever *n* **:** TYPHUS 1a

shipfitter \ˈ=,==\ *n* **1 :** one that fits together the structural members of ships and puts them into position for riveting or welding **2 :** a naval enlisted man who works in sheet metal and performs the work of a plumber aboard ship

ship–holder \ˈ=,==\ *n* **:** REMORA

shi·pi·bo \shəˈpē(,)bō\ *n, pl* **shipibo** *or* **shipibos** *usu cap* **1 a :** a Panoan people dwelling in the middle Ucayali river valley of Peru **b :** a member of such people **2 :** the language of the Shipibo people

ship joiner *n* **:** a joiner who constructs the woodwork in a ship

shipkeeper \ˈ=,==\ *n* **1 :** a watchman in charge of a ship in the absence of officers and crew **2 :** the one left in charge of a whaling ship when the captain's boat is lowered

¹shiplap \ˈ=,=\ *n* [¹*ship* + *lap*] **1 a** (1) **:** wooden sheathing in which the boards are rabbeted so that the lower edge of each board overlaps the upper edge of the next (2) **:** boards rabbeted for such sheathing **b :** a shiplapped joint **2 :** the lapping of two steel plates (as in the hull plating of a ship)

²shiplap \"\ *vt* **1 a :** to work (as lumber) to a shiplap pattern **b :** to furnish with shiplap sheathing ⟨the house is *shiplapped*⟩ **2 :** to install in the manner of shiplap (as steel plates or planks on the side or deck of a ship)

ship·less \ˈshipləs\ *adj* **:** lacking a ship

ship letter *n* **1 :** a letter conveyed by a ship that is not a mail ship **2 :** a letter sent by a person on shipboard

shipload \ˈ=,=\ *n* **1 :** the load or cargo of a ship **2 :** as much as will fill or load a ship; *specif* **:** an indefinitely large amount ⟨~*s* of excellent gentlemen were driven from their firesides —V.L. Parrington⟩ ⟨~*s* of merchandise —H.R.Warfel⟩

ship·man \ˈshipmən\ *n, pl* **shipmen** [ME *schipman, shipman*, fr. OE *scipman*, fr. *scip* ship + *man*] **1 :** SEAMAN, SAILOR **2 :** SHIPMASTER

shipman's card *n* **:** COMPASS CARD

shipmaster \ˈ=,==\ *n* [ME *schipmaster*, fr. *schip* + *master*] **1** *obs* **:** STEERSMAN, PILOT **2 :** the master or commander of a ship other than a warship

shipmast locust \ˈ=,=-\ *n* **:** a locust that forms a variety (*Robinia pseudoacacia rectissima*) of the black locust, is native to Long Island, and has an erect stem and wood of great strength and durability

shipmate \ˈ=,=\ *n* **:** one who serves on board the same ship with another **:** a fellow sailor

ship·ment \ˈshipmənt\ *n* -s [²*ship* + *-ment*] **1 :** the act or process of shipping **:** the delivery of goods to a carrier for transportation **2 :** a commodity, consignment, or cargo shipped — compare UNLOAD

ship money *n* **:** an impost levied at various times on the ports, towns, or shires of England to provide ships for the national defense

ship: principal ropes, spars, parts of hull

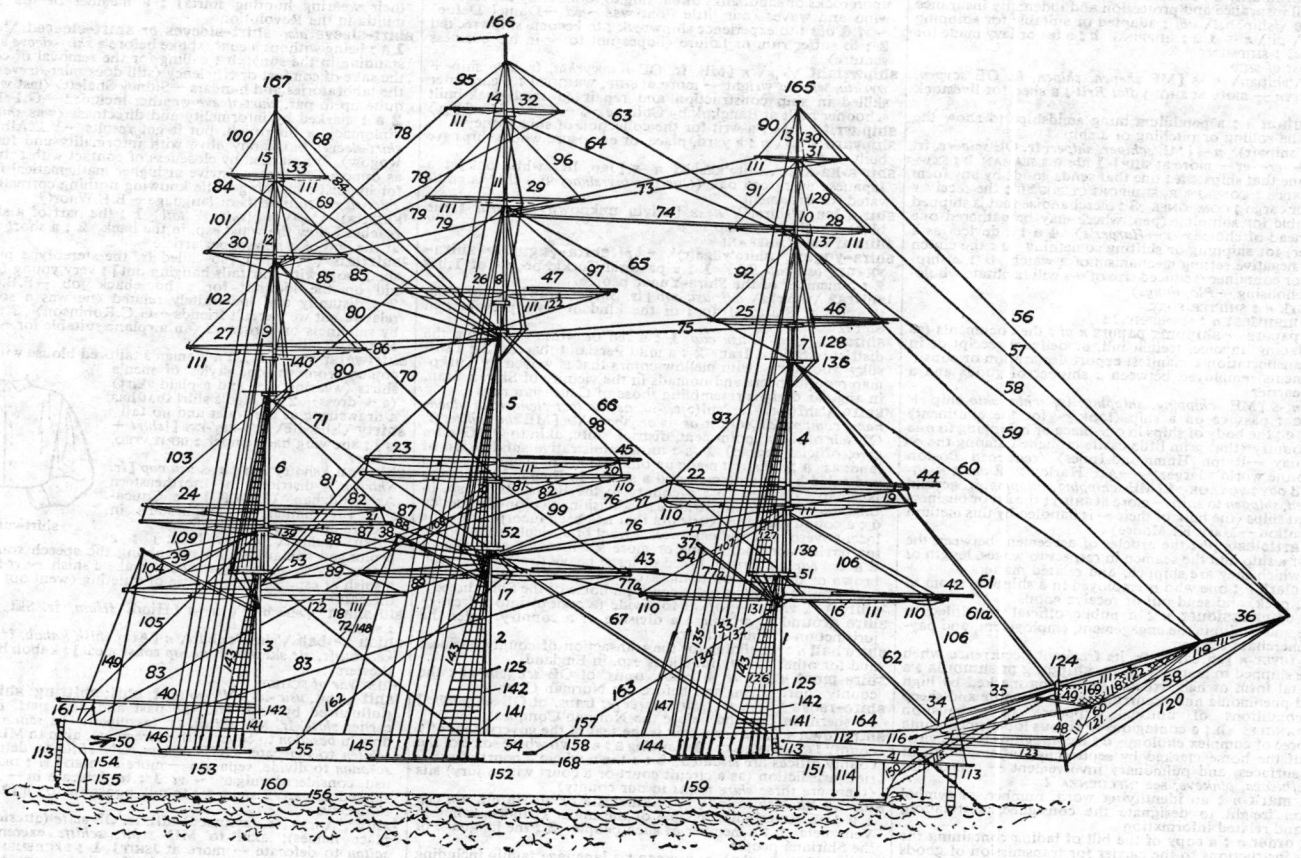

SHIP: PRINCIPAL ROPES, SPARS

1 foremast, 2 mainmast, 3 mizzenmast, 4 fore-topmast, 5 main-topmast, 6 mizzen-topmast, 7 fore-topgallant mast (at the doubling), 8 main-topgallant mast, 9 mizzen-topgallant mast, 10 fore-royal mast (sometimes not a part of the topgallant mast), 11 main-royal mast, 12 mizzen-royal mast, 13 fore-skysail pole, 14 main-skysail pole, 15 mizzen-skysail pole, 16 foreyard (at the quarter), 17 main yard (at the slings), 18 crossjack yard, 19 lower fore-topsail yard (at yardarm), 20 lower main-topsail yard, 21 lower mizzen-topsail yard, 22 upper fore-topsail yard, 23 upper main-topsail yard, 24 upper mizzen-topsail yard, 25 fore-topgallant yard, 26 main-topgallant yard, 27 mizzen-topgallant yard, 28 forroyal yard, 29 main-royal yard, 30 mizzen-royal yard, 31 fore-skysail yard, 32 main-skysail yard, 33 mizzen-skysail yard, 34 bowsprit, 35 jibboom, 36 flying jibboom (sometimes in a separate piece), 37 fore-trysail gaff, 38 main-trysail gaff, 39 spanker gaff, 40 spanker boom, 41 lower boom, 42 fore-topmast-studding-sail boom, 43 main-topmast-studding-sail boom, 44 mizzen-topmast-studding-sail boom, 45 main-topgallant-studding-sail boom, 46 fore-royal-studding-sail boom, 47 main-royal-studding-sail boom, 48 dolphin striker, 49 whisker boom, 50 main-brace bumpkin, 51 foretop, 52 maintop, 53 mizzen top, 54 foresheet sheave hole, 55 mainsheet sheave hole, 56 fore-skysail stay, 57 foreroyal stay, 58 flying-jib stay, 59 flying-jib stay, 60 jibstay, 61 fore-topmast stay, 61a fore-topmast staysail-stay, 62 forestays, 63 main-skysail stay, 64 main-royal stay, 65 main-topgallant stay, 66 main-topmast stay, 67 mainstays, 68 mizzen-skysail stay, 69 mizzen-royal stay, 70 mizzen-topgallant stay, 71 mizzen-topmast stay, 72 mizzen stay, 73 fore-skysail braces, 74 fore-royal braces, 75 fore-topgallant braces, 76 upper fore-topsail braces, 77 lower fore-topsail braces, 77a forebraces, 78 main-skysail braces, 79 main-royal braces, 80 main-topgallant braces, 81 upper main-topsail braces, 82 lower main-topsail braces, 83 main braces, 84 mizzen-skysail braces, 85 mizzen-royal braces, 86 mizzen-topgallant braces, 87 upper mizzen-topsail braces, 88 lower mizzen-topsail braces, 89 cross-jack braces, 90 fore-skysail lift, 91 port foreroyal lift, 92 port fore-topgallant lift, 93 port fore-topsail lift, 94 port fore lift, 95 port main-skysail lift, 96 starboard main-royal lift, 97 starboard main-topgallant lift, 98 starboard main-topsail lift, 99 starboard main lift, 100 port mizzen-skysail lift, 101 mizzen-royal lift, 102 port mizzen-topgallant lift, 103 port mizzen-topsail lift, 104 port crossjack lift, 105 spanker-boom topping lift, 106 lower-boom topping lift, 107 fore-trysail peak halyards, 108 main-trysail peak halyards, 109 spanker peak halyards, 110 Flemish horses, 111 footropes, 112 lifeline, 113 Jacob's ladders, 114 mooring pendants, 115 bobstays, 116 bowsprit shrouds, 117 whisker jumper, 118 jib guy, 119 flying jib guy, 120 flying jib martingale, 121 jib martingale, 122 stirrups, 123 backropes, 124 bowsprit cap, 125 ratlines, 126 fore rigging, 127 fore-topmast rigging, 128 fore-topgallant shrouds, 129 fore-royal shrouds, 130 fore-skysail shroud, 131 futtock shrouds, 132 fore-topmast backstays, 133 fore-topgallant backstays, 134 fore-royal backstay, 135 fore-skysail backstay, 136 fore-topmast crosstrees, 137 fore jack, 138 doubling of the masts, 139 mizzen cap (lower), 140 mizzen-topmast cap, 141 sheer poles, 142 swifters, 143 after shrouds, 144 fore-chains, 145 main chains, 146 mizzen chains, 147 foretrysail vangs, 148 main-trysail vangs, 149 spanker vangs, 150 cutwater, 151 starboard bow, 152 starboard beam, 153 starboard quarter, 154 starboard counter, 155 rudder, 156 waterline, 157 rail, 158 bulwarks, 159 entrance, 160 run, 161 spanker sheets, 162 starboard mainsheet, 163 starboard foresheet, 164 nameboard, 165 fore truck, 166 main truck and pennant, 167 mizzen truck, 168 sheer strake, 169 jib netting

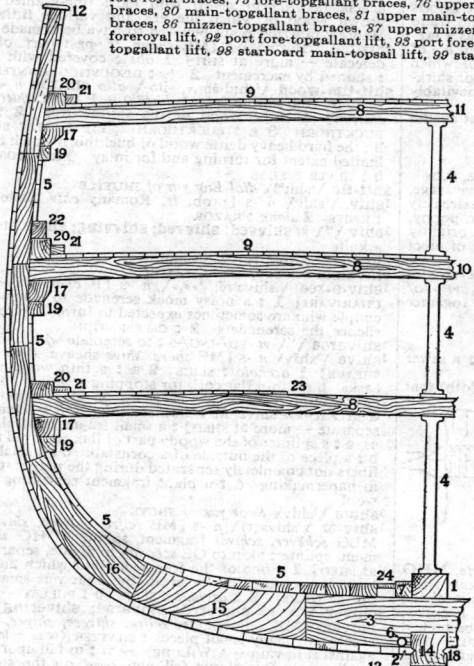

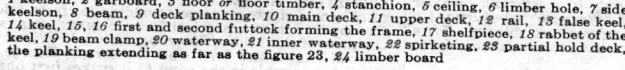

WOODEN SHIP: PRINCIPAL PARTS OF THE HULL

1 keelson, 2 garboard, 3 floor or floor timber, 4 stanchion, 5 ceiling, 6 limber hole, 7 side keelson, 8 beam, 9 deck planking, 10 main deck, 11 upper deck, 12 rail, 13 false keel, 14 keel, 15, 16 first and second futtock forming the frame, 17 shelfpiece, 18 rabbet of the keel, 19 beam clamp, 20 waterway, 21 inner waterway, 22 spirketing, 23 partial hold deck, the planking extending as far as the figure 23, 24 limber board

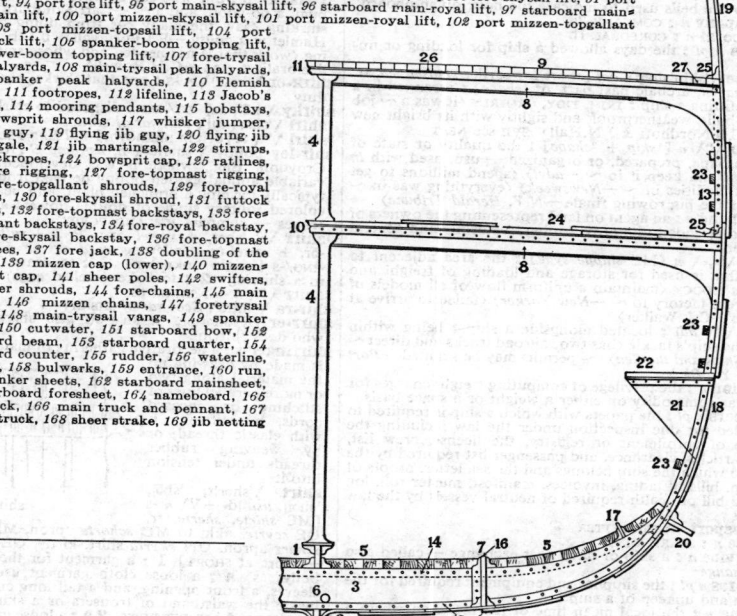

STEEL SHIP: PRINCIPAL PARTS OF THE HULL

1 keelson, 2 garboard, 3 floor or floor plate, 4 stanchion, 5 ceiling, 6 limber hole, 7 side keelson, 8 beam, 9 deck planking, 10 main deck, 11 upper deck, 12 rail, 13 frame angle iron, 14 reverse-frame angle iron, 15 bar keel, 16 intercostal plate of first longitudinal or side keelson, 17 bilge keelson or hold stringer, 18, 19 plating, 20 bilge keel, 21 bracket plate, 22 stringer, 23 batten, 24 steel deck, 25 stringer angle irons, 26 tie plate, 27 stringer plate

ship of state : the affairs of a state symbolized as a ship on a course

ship of the line : a ship of war large enough to have a place in the line of battle **:** a ship superior to a frigate and usu. a 74-gun or three-decker ship — called also *line-of-battle ship*

ship of war [ME *schep of war*] **:** WARSHIP

shipowner \ˈ=,==\ *n* **:** an owner of a ship or of a share in a ship

shipowner's club *n* **:** a mutual association of shipowners operating ordinarily on an assessment basis and organized for writing hull insurance and protection and indemnity insurance

ship·pa·ble \ˈshipəbəl\ *adj* **:** adapted or suitable for shipping

ship·page \-pij\ *n* -s **1 a :** SHIPPING **b :** a fee or levy made for shipping **2 :** SHIPMENT

shipped *past of* SHIP

ship·pen \ˈshipən\ *n* -s [ME *shepen, shipen*, fr. OE *scypen, scipen, scepen* — more at SHOP] *dial Brit* **:** a shed for livestock (as cows)

ship pendulum *n* **:** a pendulum hung amidships to show the extent of the rolling or pitching of a ship

ship·per \ˈshipə(r)\ *n* -s [ME *schiper, shiper*, fr. OE *scipere*, fr. *scip* ship + *-ere* -er — more at SHIP] **1** *obs* **a :** SEAMAN **b :** SKIPPER **2 :** one that ships: **a :** one that sends goods by any form of conveyance **:** CONSIGNOR, SHIPPING CLERK **b :** the receiver of goods or cargo **:** CONSIGNEE **3 :** merchandise that is shipped or is suitable for shipping ⟨pen, where may be gathered one hundred head of choice ~*s* —*Harper's*⟩ **4 a :** a device (as a belt shifter) for shipping or shifting something **b :** the clutch lever in a negative setting mechanism of a watch **5 :** a shipping case or container ⟨reduced size of ~*s* will facilitate wholesaler warehousing —*Playthings*⟩

shipper fork *n* **:** SHIFTER FORK

shipper's manifest *n* **:** MANIFEST 3a

shipper's papers *or* **shipping papers** *n pl* **:** the documents (as a bill of lading, invoice, freight bill, or delivery receipt or in marine transportation a manifest export declaration or consular documents) employed between a shipper of goods and a common carrier

shipping *n* -s [ME *schipping, shipping*, fr. *schip, ship* ship + *-ing*] **1 a :** passage on a ship ⟨took ~ for the continent⟩ **b :** SHIPS **c :** the body of ships in one place or belonging to one port or country ⟨that grim little castle crouched among the ~ at the quay —Ralph Hammond-Innes⟩ ⟨reopened Boston harbor to the world's larger ~ —A.F.Harlow⟩ **2** *obs* **:** NAVIGATION **3** *obs* **:** VOYAGE **4** [ME *schipping, shipping*, fr. gerund of *schippen, shippen* to ship — more at SHIP] **:** the act or business of one that ships ⟨the bulk of their ~ is handled by this method of distribution —Mary K. Moore⟩

shipping articles *n pl* **:** the articles of agreement between the captain of a ship and the seamen in respect to wages, length of time for which they are shipped, and related matters

shipping clerk *n* **:** one who is employed in a shipping room to assemble, pack, and send out or receive goods

shipping commissioner *n* **:** a public official appointed to supervise and facilitate the engagement, employment, and payment of merchant seamen

shipping fever *n* [so called fr. its frequent occurrence when cattle are shipped to market] **1** *also* **shipping pneumonia :** a highly fatal form of hemorrhagic septicemia marked by high fever and pneumonia and occurring chiefly in cattle and sheep under conditions of unusual exposure or exhaustion **2 a :** STRANGLES **b :** a contagious fibrinous lobar pneumonia of the horse of complex etiology **c :** a contagious febrile virus disease of the horse marked by septicemia, inflammation of mucous surfaces, and pulmonary involvement — called also *equine influenza, pinkeye;* see INFLUENZA 2

shipping mark *n* **:** an identifying word, number, or symbol placed on freight to designate the consignee, destination, weight, and related information

shipping order *n* **:** a copy of the bill of lading containing the shipper's instructions to the carrier for transmission of goods

ship·pon \ˈshipən\ *var of* SHIPPEN

ship railway *n* **1 :** an inclined railway running into the water with a car on which a ship may be drawn out on land for repairs or storage **2 :** a railway on which to transport ships overland between bodies of water

ship rat *n* **:** the common brown rat or the roof rat that frequently infests ships

ship–rigged \ˈ=,=\ *adj* **:** SQUARE-RIGGED

ship rigger *n* **:** a worker who takes care of a ship and its rigging while in port

ships *pl of* SHIP, *pres 3d sing of* SHIP

ship's articles *n pl* **:** SHIPPING ARTICLES

ship's bell *n* **1 :** a bell used on shipboard to strike each half hour of a watch **2 :** SHIP'S CLOCK

ship's boy *var of* SHIPBOY

ship's clerk *n* **1 :** CLERK 3b(2) **2 :** a warrant officer in the U. S. Navy whose specialty is the supervision of records, reports, correspondence and related matters

ship's clock *n* **:** a clock so constructed that its strokes correspond to the bells used to indicate the hour on shipboard

ship's company *n* **:** COMPANY 2d

ship's corporal *n* **:** CORPORAL 1b

ship's days *n pl* **:** the days allowed a ship for loading or unloading

¹**ship·shape** \ˈship¦shāp\ *adj* [short for earlier *shipshapen*, fr. ¹*ship* + *shapen*, archaic past part. of ¹*shape*] **:** arranged in a manner befitting a ship **:** TRIM, TIDY, ORDERLY ⟨it was a ~ job — stoutly built, weatherproof, and sightly with its bright new thatch —C.B.Nordhoff & J.N.Hall⟩ **syn** see NEAT

²**shipshape** \"\ *n* [¹*ship* + ²*shape*] **:** the quality or state of being shipshape, prepared, or organized — usu. used with *in* ⟨sail a boat and keep it in ~ —*advt*⟩ ⟨spend millions to get their dock facilities in ~ —*Newsweek*⟩ ⟨everything was in ~ tonight for the big rowing finale —*N.Y. Herald Tribune*⟩

ship's husband *n* **:** an agent on land representing the owners of a ship who attends to its provisioning, repairing, and general management

¹**shipside** \ˈ=,=\ *n* [ME *shippe syde*] **:** the area adjacent to shipping that is used for storage and loading of freight and passengers **:** DOCK ⟨maintain a uniform flow of all models of vehicles from factory to ~ —*New Yorker*⟩ ⟨failed to arrive at ~ on time —C.L.Walker⟩

²**shipside** \"\ *adj* **:** located alongside a ship **:** being within reach of the ship's tackle ⟨has two railroad tracks and direct ~ access —*Ships and the Sea*⟩ ⟨~ permits may be granted —*Port of Manila Yr. Bk.*⟩

ship's option *n* **:** the privilege of computing freight charges for a particular commodity on either a weight or a space basis

ship's papers *n pl* **:** the papers with which a ship is required to be provided for due inspection under the law including the certificate of enrollment or registry, the license, crew list, shipping articles, clearance, and passenger list required by the country to which the ship belongs and the sea letter, proofs of ownership, bills of lading, invoices, manifest, muster roll, log book, and bill of health required of neutral vessels by the law of nations

ship's passport *n* **:** SEA LETTER

ship splice *n* **:** SCARF JOINT

ship's service *n* **:** a ship or navy post exchange — called also *navy exchange*

ship's stores *n pl* **:** the supplies and equipment required for the operation and upkeep of a ship

ship's time *n* **:** the local mean time of the meridian where a ship is located

ship stuff *n* **1 :** a low-grade wheat flour with high bran content **2 :** wheat offals that are used as a stock feed

shipt *abbr* shipment

shipway \ˈ=,=\ *n* **1 :** the ways on which a ship is built **2 :** the supports used under a ship in dry dock **3 :** a channel for ships **:** a ship canal

shipworm \ˈ=,=\ *n* **:** any of various elongated marine clams mostly of the family Teredinidae that resemble worms, burrow in submerged wood, and are very destructive to piles of wharves or wooden ships — compare BANKIA

¹**ship·wreck** \ˈshi,prek\ *n* [alter. (influenced by *wreck*) of earlier *shipwrack*, fr. ME *schipwrak*, fr. OE *scipwræc*, fr. *scip* ship + *wræc* something driven by the sea — more at SHIP, WRACK] **1 :** a wrecked ship or its parts **:** WRECKAGE **2 :** the destruction or loss (as by sinking or being cast ashore or driven against rocks or shoals) of a ship **3 :** an irretrievable loss or failure **:** RUIN, DESTRUCTION ⟨the conference nearly ended in ~ —*New Statesman & Nation*⟩ ⟨the ~ of her marriage —Judith Heller⟩ ⟨the ~ of our hopes —Harrison Smith⟩

²**shipwreck** \"\ *vt* **1 a :** to cause (as sailors or passengers) to experience shipwreck ⟨they too were ~*ed* in another great mystery of the sea —W.E.Swinton⟩ **b :** to inflict with disaster or loss **:** RUIN ⟨~*ed* his career —C.L.Jones⟩ ⟨the human animal, nearly ~*ed*, will turn toward some means to save itself —J.S.Collis⟩ **2 :** to destroy (a ship) by driving ashore or upon rocks or sandbanks or causing to founder by the force of wind and waves ⟨our little float was ~*ed* —Daniel Defoe⟩ ~ *vi* **1** *obs* **:** to experience shipwreck **:** to become shipwrecked **2 :** to suffer ruin or failure ⟨hopes not to ~ in his business venture⟩

shipwright \ˈ=,=\ *n* [ME, fr. OE *scipwyrhta*, fr. *scip* ship + *wyrhta, wryhta* wright — more at SHIP, WRIGHT] **:** a carpenter skilled in ship construction and repair ⟨a small teak-built schooner built at Bangkok by Chinese ~*s* —*Times Lit. Supp.*⟩

ship writ *n, obs* **:** a writ for the collection of ship money

shipyard \ˈ=,=\ *n* **:** a yard, place, or enclosure where ships are built or repaired

shir·a·ka·shi \,shirəˈkäshē\ *n* -s [Jap, lit., white oak] **:** a Japanese evergreen oak (*Quercus myrsinaefolia*) that is cultivated for ornament

shir·a·lee \ˈshirəlē\ *n* -s [origin unknown] *Austral* **:** the blanket roll of a tramp

shirani *var of* SHERANI

shira–yugur \,shirəˈyügə(r)\ *n, pl* **shira–yugur** *or* **shira–yugurs** *usu cap S&Y* **1 :** a pastoral Turkic people of Tibet **2 :** a member of the Shira-Yugur people

¹**shi·raz** \shəˈräz\ *adj, usu cap* [fr. *Shiraz*, Iran] **:** of or from the city of Shiraz, Iran **:** of the kind or style prevalent in Shiraz

²**shiraz** \"\ *n* -ES *usu cap* **1 :** a red or white wine from the district of Shiraz, Iran **2 :** a mild Persian tobacco **3 :** a soft silky woolen rug with mellow colors that is woven by Turkoman mountaineers and nomads in the vicinity of Shiraz, Iran, in angular designs resembling those of Caucasian rugs

¹**shire** \ˈshī(ə)r, -īə, ˈshi(ə)r, -iə, *as the last element in place-name compounds* ,shi(ə)r *or* -iə *or* shə(r)\ *n* [ME *shir, shire*, fr. OE *scīr* office, appointment, district, shire; akin to OHG *scīra* care, official charge] **1** -s **:** an administrative subdivision of land: as **a :** a district made up of a number of smaller districts and ruled by an alderman and a sheriff in England before the Norman Conquest **b :** a county in the British Isles esp. in England **c :** an administrative subdivision of colonial America **d :** a country area in Australia that has been incorporated for local government and embraces a tract of agricultural or grazing territory including one or more small towns and villages **2 a** *usu cap* **:** a British breed of large heavy draft horses usu. brown or bay with white markings and heavily feathered legs **b** *also* **shire horse** -s *often cap S* **:** a horse of the Shire breed

²**shire** \"\ *vt* -ED/-ING/-S **:** to divide (a region) into shires

shire ground *n, archaic* **:** a division of a country under the jurisdiction of shire officers

shire hall *n* **:** a building for the transaction of county business and for other county functions esp. in England

shire moot *n* [¹*shire* + *moot;* trans. of OE *scīrgemōt*] **:** the county court in England before the Norman Conquest

shire–reeve \ˈ=,=\ *n* [¹*shire* + *reeve;* trans. of OE *scīrgerēfa*] **:** a sheriff in England before the Norman Conquest

shire town *n* **1 :** a town that is the seat of the government of a county **:** COUNTY SEAT **2** *NewEng* **a :** a town where some of the county offices are situated **b :** a town where a court of superior jurisdiction (as a circuit court or a court with a jury) sits ⟨there are three *shire towns* in our county⟩

shir·i·a·ná \,shirēəˈnä\ *n, pl* **shirianá** *or* **shirianás** *usu cap* **1 a :** an Amerindian people of the upper Orinoco valley in Venezuela **b :** a member of such people **2 :** the language of the Shirianá people

shir·i·a·nan \-ˈnän\ *n, usu cap* **:** a language family including Shirianá and Guaharibo

¹**shirk** \ˈshərk, ˈshə̄k, ˈshəik\ *vb* -ED/-ING/-S [origin unknown] *vi* **1 a** *obs* **:** to live by trickery and fraud **:** SHARK, SPONGE **b :** to take care of oneself under somewhat difficult circumstances **:** FEND, SHIFT ⟨turned the calves out into the fields to ~ for themselves⟩ **2 :** to go stealthily **:** SNEAK ⟨obliged to ~ on board by night to escape from their wives —W.M.Thackeray⟩ **3 a :** to withdraw because of lack of courage ⟨one of the cities ~*ed* from the league —Lord Byron⟩ **b :** to evade the performance of an obligation because of laziness or fear ⟨the timid flee, the lazy ~ —H.A.Overstreet⟩ ~ *vt* **1 a :** to avoid (as a disagreeable task) because of laziness, lack of courage, or distaste ⟨~*ed* telling her that no marriage would occur that day —Arnold Bennett⟩ **b :** to evade meeting (as a person) **:** DODGE ⟨~*ed* his gaze and stared at the floor⟩ **2 :** to shift (as a responsibility) elsewhere ⟨if he could ~ off the work upon the others he would —Nathaniel Hawthorne⟩ **syn** see DODGE

²**shirk** \"\ *n* -s **1** *obs* **:** one who lives by trickery and fraud **:** SHARK **2 :** one who shirks work or obligations ⟨was a lazy bum, a no-good, and a ~ —Carl Sandburg⟩ **3 a :** an act of shirking ⟨saw the many ~*s* from doing his duty of which Hamlet was guilty —F.J.Furnivall⟩ **b :** the practice of shirking ⟨work that is not needed and whose spirit of ~ inevitably demoralizes men —C.H.Rowell⟩

shirk·er \-kə(r)\ *n* -s **:** one that shirks; *esp* **:** one that evades duty

shirky \-kē\ *adj* -ER/-EST **:** disposed to shirk

¹**shirl** \ˈshər(·ə)l\ *dial var of* SHRILL

²**shirl** \"\ *vi* [origin unknown] *dial Eng* **:** SLIDE, GLIDE, SLIP

shir·ley poppy \ˈshərlē-\ *n, usu cap S* [fr. *Shirley* vicarage, Croydon, Eng., where it was developed] **:** an extremely variable annual garden poppy derived from the corn poppy, typically forming a branched plant, and bearing usu. brightly colored solitary single or double flowers at the end of erect scapes — compare ICELAND POPPY

¹**shirr** *R* ˈshər, + *vowel* -ər·; *–R* -ə̄, + *suffixal vowel* -ər· *also* -ə̄r, + *vowel in a following word* -ər· *or* -ə̄ *also* -ə̄r\ *vt* -ED/-ING/-S [origin unknown] **1 :** to draw (as cloth) together in a shirring **2 :** to bake (shelled eggs) until set

²**shirr** \"\ *n* -s **:** SHIRRING

shir·ra \ˈshirə\ *Scot var of* SHERIFF

shirr·er *R* ˈshər·ər, *–R* ˈshər·ə(r *also* ˈshə̄rə(r\ *n* -s **:** a sewer who does shirring

shirring *n* -s **:** a decorative gathering of material (as cloth) that is made by drawing up the material along two or more parallel lines of stitching or encased cords, by stitching it with elastic thread, or by weaving rubber threads under tension into it

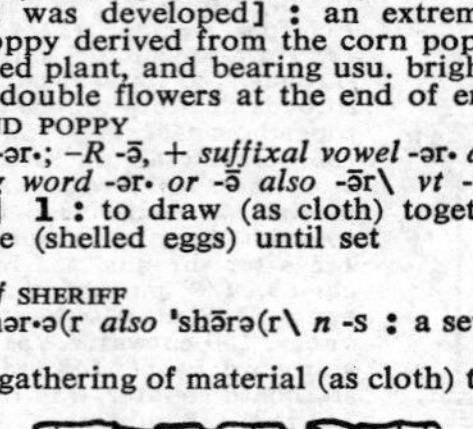

shirring

¹**shirt** \ˈshər|t, ˈshə̄|, ˈshəi|, *usu* |d· + V\ *n* -s [ME *shirte, sherte*, fr. OE *scyrte;* akin to MD *schorte* apron, MLG *schörte*, MHG *schurz* apron, ON *skyrta* shirt, kirtle, OE *scort, sceort* short — more at SHORT] **1 :** a garment for the upper part of the body: as **a :** a loose cloth garment usu. having a collar, sleeves, a front opening, and a tail long enough to be tucked inside the waistband of trousers or a skirt **b :** POLO SHIRT **c :** JERSEY **d :** UNDERSHIRT **2 a :** a loose garment that reaches to the thighs or lower ⟨a white ~ reached almost to his ankles —Humayun Kabir⟩ **b :** NIGHTSHIRT **3 :** all or a large part of one's possessions ⟨lost her ~ in the war —T.H.Fielding⟩ ⟨put his ~ on the favorite only to see a rank outsider about to nip him at the post —F.J.Warburg⟩ **4** *Austral* **:** a thin calico bag in which frozen carcasses are shipped **5 :** a member of a political organization that uses a colored shirt as its badge

²**shirt** \"\ *vt* -ED/-ING/-S **:** to clothe with a shirt

shirtband \ˈ=,=\ *n* **:** the neckband of a shirt

shirtfront \ˈ=,=\ *n* **1 :** the front of a shirt: as **a :** the part of a man's shirt that is not covered by his coat or vest **b :** the usu. starched, pleated, or ruffled front of a man's dress shirt **2 :** DICKEY

shirtfront wicket *n* **:** a cricket wicket esp. of turf that is in perfect condition

shirt·ing \ˈshər|d·|iŋ, -ə̄|, -əi|, |t|, |ēŋ\ *n* -s [¹*shirt* + *-ing*] **:** any of various fabrics (as fine lightweight cotton) suitable for men's shirts

shirt·less \-|t|ləs\ *adj* **:** being without a shirt — **shirt·less·ness** *n* -ES

shirtlike \ˈ=,=\ *adj* **:** resembling a shirt

shirtmaker \ˈ=,==\ *n* **1 :** one that makes shirts **2 :** a woman's tailored garment (as a dress or blouse) with details copied from a man's shirt

shirt·man \ˈshərtmən, -,man\ *n, pl* **shirtmen** [so called fr. their wearing hunting shirts] **:** a member of the Virginia militia in the Revolution

shirt–sleeve *also* **shirt–sleeves** *or* **shirt–sleeved** \ˈ=¦=\ *adj* **1 a :** being without a coat ⟨spoke before a *shirt-sleeve* audience standing in the sun⟩ **b :** calling for the removal of coats for the sake of comfort or efficiency ⟨still does *shirt-sleeve* work in the laboratories and hangars —Sidney Shalett⟩ ⟨last week was quite up to par, *shirt-sleeve* weather included —G.F.T.Ryall⟩ **2 a :** marked by informality and directness ⟨was *shirt-sleeve* diplomacy, a bit rough, but it got results —V.L.Albjerg⟩ ⟨a *shirt-sleeves* biography alive with informality and fun —Lee Rogow⟩ **b :** marked by closeness of contact with actual facts as opposed to theory ⟨strive at higher mathematical formulas for linguistic meaning while knowing nothing correctly of the *shirt-sleeve* rudiments of language —B.L.Whorf⟩

¹**shirttail** \ˈ=,=\ *n* [¹*shirt* + *tail*] **1 :** the part of a shirt that reaches below the waist esp. in the back **2 :** a short addition at the end of a newspaper article

²**shirttail** \"\ *adj* **1** [so called fr. the stereotype picture of small boys with shirttails hanging out] **:** very young ⟨just a ~ kid on the lookout for a horseback job —F.B.Gipson⟩ **2 :** distantly and indefinitely related ⟨he was a sort of ~ relative but we weren't friends —G.C.Robinson⟩ **3 :** marked by smallness or shortness ⟨an airplane suitable for ~ runs of 50 to 100 miles⟩

shirtwaist \ˈ=,=\ *n* **1 :** a woman's tailored blouse with details copied from various styles of men's shirts ⟨wearing a ~ and a plaid skirt⟩ ⟨a ~ dress⟩ **2 :** a man's shirt that has a drawstring at the waist and no tail

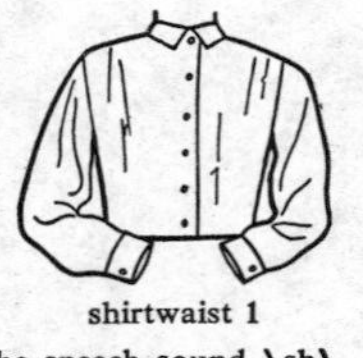

shirtwaist 1

shirty \ˈshərd·ē\ *adj* -ER/-EST [¹*shirt* + *-y*] **:** showing bad temper **:** IRRITATED, ANGRY

shir·van \shə(r)ˈvän\ *n* -s *usu cap* [fr. *Shirvan*, district in northeastern Azerbaidzhan, U.S.S.R.] **:** a Caucasian rug similar to Daghestans in texture and in geometric design

¹**shish** \ˈshish\ *n* -ES [imit.] **:** a prolonged sibilant sound resembling the speech sound \sh\

²**shish** \"\ *vb* -ED/-ING/-ES *vi* **:** to make a shish ~ *vt* **:** to make a shish at esp. for the purpose of quieting ⟨~*ed* the cats⟩

shi·sham \ˈshēshəm\ *n* -s [Hindi *śīśam*, fr. Skt *śiṁśapā*] **:** SISSOO

shish ke·bab \ˈshishkə,bäb\ *n* [Arm *shish kabab*, fr. Turk *şiş kebabı*, fr. *şiş* skewer + *kebap* roast meat] **:** kabob broiled on skewers

shist *var of* SCHIST

¹**shit** \ˈshit, *usu* -id·+V\ *vb* **shit; shit; shitting; shits** [alter. (influenced by ²*shit* and the past and past part. forms) of earlier *shite*, fr. ME *shiten*, fr. (assumed) OE *scītan* (attested only in *bescītan* to cover with excrement); akin to MLG & MD *schiten* to defecate, OHG *scīzan*, ON *skīta* to defecate, OE *scēadan* to divide, separate — more at SHED] *vi* **:** DEFECATE — usu. considered vulgar ~ *vt* **1 :** to defecate in — usu. considered vulgar **2** *slang* **a :** to talk nonsense to **b :** to attempt to deceive

²**shit** \"\ *n* -s [fr. (assumed) ME, fr. OE *scite* (attested only in place names); akin to MD *schit, schitte* excrement, OE *scītan* to defecate — more at ¹SHIT] **1 :** EXCREMENT — usu. considered vulgar **2 :** an act of defecation — usu. considered vulgar **3** *slang* **a :** NONSENSE, FOOLISHNESS **b :** something of little value ⟨didn't give a ~⟩ ⟨not worth a ~⟩ **c :** trivial and usu. boastful or inaccurate talk **4** *slang* **:** a contemptible person **5 shits** *pl but sing or pl in constr* [ME *schyt*, fr. OE *scitte;* akin to OE *scītan* to defecate] **:** DIARRHEA — used with *the;* usu. considered vulgar

shite \ˈshīt\ *obs var of* SHIT

shite·poke \ˈshīt,pōk, -īd,p-, -īk,p-\ *n* [*shite* + *poke;* fr. its traditional habit of defecating when flushed] **:** any of various herons: as **a :** GREEN HERON **b :** NIGHT HERON

shith·er \ˈshit͟hə(r)\ *vi* [perh. alter. of *shudder*] *dial Eng* **:** SHIVER

shit·tah \ˈshid·ə, -itə\ *or* **shittah tree** *n, pl* **shittahs** *or* **shit·tim** \-id·əm, -itəm\ *or* **shittah trees** [Heb *shiṭṭāh*, fr. Egypt *šanga, šangat*] **:** a tree of uncertain identity but prob. an acacia (as *Acacia seyal*) with hard fine-grained yellowish brown wood of which the ark and various fittings of the Hebrew tabernacle are believed to have been made

shit·ten \ˈshitᵊn\ *adj* [ME *shiten*, fr. past part. of *shiten* to defecate — more at SHIT] **1** *obs* **:** covered with excrement **:** stained by excrement **2** *obs* **:** DISGUSTING, CONTEMPTIBLE

shit·tim·wood \ˈshid·əm,=, -itə-\ *also* **shittim** *n* [*shittim-wood* fr. Heb *shiṭṭīm* (pl. of *shiṭṭāh*) + E *wood; shittim* fr. Heb *shiṭṭīm*] **1 :** the wood of the shittah tree **2 :** CASCARA BUCKTHORN **3 a :** BUCKTHORN 2; *esp* **:** FALSE BUCKTHORN **b :** the hard heavy dense wood of buckthorn which is used to a limited extent for turning and for inlay **4 a :** OPOSSUM WOOD **b :** SILVER BELL

shit·tle \ˈshitᵊl\ *dial Eng var of* SHUTTLE

¹**shiv** \ˈshiv\ *n* -s [prob. fr. Romany *chiv* blade] **1** *slang* **:** KNIFE **2** *slang* **:** RAZOR

²**shiv** \"\ *vt* **shivved; shivved; shivving; shivs :** to stab with a knife

shivah *or* **shiva** *var of* SHIBAH

shivaism *usu cap, var of* SIVAISM

¹**shiv·a·ree** \,shivəˈrē, ˈ==,=\ *n* -s [F *charivari* — more at CHARIVARI] **1 :** a noisy mock serenade to a newly married couple who are sometimes expected to furnish refreshments to silence the serenaders **2 :** CELEBRATION

²**shivaree** \"\ *vt* -ED/-ING/-S **:** to serenade with a shivaree

¹**shive** \ˈshīv\ *n* -s [ME *sheve, shive* sheave, slice — more at SHEAVE] **1** *archaic* **:** SLICE **2 a :** a thin wooden bung for casks **b :** a thin flat cork for stopping a wide-mouthed bottle

²**shive** \ˈshiv, ˈshīv\ *n* -s [ME *schyfe, schyffe;* akin to MLG & MD *schēve* shive, MHG *schebe* shive, OE *scēadan* to divide, separate — more at SHED] **:** a small fragment of plant matter: as **a :** a splinter of the woody part of flax removed in breaking **b :** a piece of the outside of a cornstalk **c :** a small bundle of fibers not completely separated during the preparation of pulp in papermaking **d :** a plant fragment remaining in scoured wool

³**shive** \ˈshiv\ *Scot var of* SHOVE

¹**shiv·er** \ˈshivə(r)\ *n* -s [ME *scifre, shivere, shiver;* akin to MLG *schēver, schiver* fragment, splinter, OHG *scivaro* fragment, splinter; akin to OE *scēadan* to divide, separate — more at SHED] **1 :** one of the fragments into which an object has been broken usu. by violence ⟨the boat was smashed to ~*s* on the rocks⟩ **2 a** *archaic* **:** SLICE **b :** PULLEY

²**shiver** \"\ *vb* **shivered; shivered; shivering** \-v(ə)riŋ\ **shivers** [ME *shiveren*, fr. *scifre, shivere, shiver*, n.] *vt* **:** to break into many small pieces **:** SHATTER ⟨was ~*ing* his lance against it in vain —A.W.Long⟩ ~ *vi* **:** to fall apart into many small pieces ⟨his statue fell and ~*ed* on the stones —J.A. Froude⟩ **syn** see BREAK

³**shiver** \"\ *vb* **shivered; shivered; shivering** \-v(ə)riŋ\ **shivers** [ME *shiveren*, alter. (influenced by ²*shiveren* to shatter) of *chiveren*] *vi* **:** to undergo trembling (as from cold, fear, or the application of a physical force) **:** SHAKE, QUIVER, VIBRATE ⟨in spite of the heat of the room he ~*ed* —Victor Canning⟩ ⟨crystal chandeliers ~*ed* when he sang —George Jellinek⟩; *specif* **:** to tremble in the wind as it strikes first one and then the other side — used of a sail ~ *vt* **1 :** to cause to shiver ⟨another jerk ~*ed* her body —Olive H. Prouty⟩; *specif* **:** to cause (a sail) to shiver by steering close to the wind **2 :** to produce with or as if with a shiver ⟨the sweet heaven-bird ~*ed* out his song above him —George Meredith⟩

⁴**shiver** \"\ *n* -s **1 :** an instance of shivering **:** TREMBLE ⟨a ~ ran down my spine —Helen Eustis⟩ ⟨a momentary ~ of leaves

drew our eyes to the left —William Beebe⟩ **2 shivers** *pl* **:** an attack of shivering; *specif* **:** AGUE — usu. used with preceding *the*

shiv·er·eens \ˌshivəˈrēnz\ *n pl* [¹*shiver* + *-eens* (as in *smithereens*)] *dial Brit* **:** SMITHEREENS

shiv·er·er \ˈshivərə(r)\ *n* -s **:** one that shivers

¹**shivering** *n* -s [ME, fr. gerund of *shiveren* to shiver (tremble) — more at SHIVER] **1 :** an act or action of one that trembles **2 :** a constant abnormal twitching of various muscles in the horse that is prob. due to sensory nerve derangement

²**shivering** *n* -s [ME, fr. gerund of *shiveren* to shiver (shatter) — more at SHIVER] **1 :** an act or action of one that breaks into fragments **2 :** the cracking and scaling of a glaze on pottery caused by unequal contractions between the materials as they cool

shiv·er·ing·ly *adv* **:** in a shivering manner

shivering owl *n* **:** SCREECH OWL

shiv·er·some \ˈshivə(r)səm\ *adj* **:** productive of shivers

shiver spar *n* [¹*shiver;* intended as trans. of G *schieferspar,* fr. *schiefer* slate + *spar*] **:** a calcite with a slaty structure

shiverweed \ˈ=,=\ *n* [³*shiver* + *weed*] *Austral* **:** CORN WOUNDWORT

¹**shiv·ery** \ˈshiv(ə)rē\ *adj* [²*shiver* + *-y*] **:** inclined to break into flakes **:** BRITTLE, FLAKY

²**shivery** \ˈ"\ *adj* [³*shiver* + *-y*] **1 :** characterized by shivers **:** TREMULOUS ⟨awoke sweating, cold, and ~ —Richard Sale⟩ ⟨thatched with ~ grasses —Ethel Anderson⟩ **2 :** causing shivers: as **a :** CHILLING, COLD ⟨a ~ January day⟩ **b :** frightening enough to cause trembling ⟨had the right uninhibited reactions to all the ~ threats —John Mason Brown⟩

shives *pl of* SHIVE

shivite *usu cap, var of* SAIVITE

shi·voo \shəˈvü\ *n* -s [origin unknown] *Austral* **:** a boisterous social gathering

shivs *pl of* SHIV, *pres 3d sing of* SHIV

shivved *past of* SHIV

shivving *pres part of* SHIV

shiv·wits \ˈshiv,wits\ *n, pl* **shivwits** *or* **shivwitses** *usu cap* **1 :** a band of Paiute Indians of southern Utah **2 :** a member of the Shivwits band

shivy *or* **shiv·ey** \ˈshivē, -īvē\ *adj* [²*shive* + *-y*] **:** containing shives ⟨~ wool⟩ ⟨~ paper⟩

shi·zo·ku \ˈshēzō,kü, shēˈzō(,)kü\ *n, pl* **shizoku** [Jap] **:** the Japanese social class consisting of the old samurai and their families and descendants as distinguished from the heimin and the kwazoku

shi·zu·o·ka \shēˈzüə,kä\ *adj, usu cap* [fr. *Shizuoka,* Japan] **:** of or from the city of Shizuoka, Japan **:** of the kind or style prevalent in Shizuoka

shkotzim *pl of* SHEGETZ

shl *abbr* **1** shell **2** shoal

shld *abbr* **1** shield **2** shoulder

shlemiel *var of* SCHLEMIEL

shlimazel *or* **shlimazl** *var of* SCHLIMAZEL

shlp *abbr* shiplap

shltr *abbr* shelter

shluh \shəˈlü, ˈshlü\ *or* **shil·ha** \-lä\ *or* **shil·luh** \-lü\ *n, pl* **shluh** *or* **shluhs** *or* **shilha** *or* **shilhas** *or* **shilluh** *or* **shilluhs** *usu cap* **1 a :** a Berber people of southern Morocco **b :** a member of the Shluh people **2 :** a Berber language of the Shluh people

shlw *abbr* shallow

SHM *abbr* simple harmonic motion

shmo *var of* SCHMO

shmoos *var of* SCHMOOZE

shnook *var of* SCHNOOK

shoad \ˈshōd\ *n* -s [origin unknown] *dial Eng* **:** a fragment of vein material removed by natural agencies from an outcrop and lying in the surface soil or debris; *specif* **:** ¹FLOAT 7a

¹**shoal** \ˈshōl\ *adj* -ER/-EST [alter. of earlier *shold, shoald,* fr. ME *sheld, shald, shold,* fr. OE *sceald* — more at SHALLOW] **:** having little depth **:** SHALLOW

²**shoal** \ˈ"\ *n* -s [alter. of earlier *shold, shoald,* fr. ME *sheld, shald, shold,* fr. *sheld, shald, shold,* adj.] **1 :** a place where a sea, river, or other body of water is shallow **:** SHALLOW **2 a :** a sandbank or sandbar which makes the water shoal; *specif* **:** an elevation or knoll which is not rocky and on which there is a depth of water of six fathoms or less — compare BANK, REEF **3 :** a rocky area on the sea bottom within soundings esp. where fish abound

³**shoal** \ˈ"\ *vb* -ED/-ING/-S [alter. of earlier *shold, shoald,* fr. *shold, shoald,* adj.] *vi* **:** to become shallow ⟨the loch ~s badly within three cables of its outer points —C.K.Finlay⟩ **~** *vt* **1 a :** to come to a shallow or less deep part of ⟨the ship ~s her water⟩ **b :** to cause to become shallow or less deep **c :** to fill up or block off with a shoal ⟨the inlet is continually ~*ed*⟩ **2 :** to drive (an otter) to shallow water

⁴**shoal** \ˈ"\ *adv* [¹*shoal*] **:** to or at a shallow depth

⁵**shoal** \ˈ"\ *n* -s [fr. (assumed) ME *shole,* fr. OE *scolu* multitude, troop — more at SCHOOL] **:** a great number thronged together or considered as a group ⟨herring ~s⟩ ⟨the ~ of congratulatory letters he received —*Times Lit. Supp.*⟩ ⟨students left in ~s to answer the call to arms —A.W.Long⟩

⁶**shoal** \ˈ"\ *vi* -ED/-ING/-S **:** to assemble in a large group **:** THRONG, SCHOOL ⟨why the shrimp ~ furiously off the ocean inlets is a mystery —V.O.Williams⟩

shoal duck *n* [²*shoal*] *NewEng* **:** EIDER DUCK

shoalgrass \ˈ=,=\ *n* [²*shoal* + *grass*] **:** a submerged herb (*Halodule wrightii*) of the family Potamogetonaceae that is native to the southeastern coastal U. S., has flat linear leaves and flowers with anthers unequally attached to the filament, and is an important food for wild fowl

shoal·i·ness \ˈshōlēnəs\ *n* -ES **1 :** the state of being shoal **2 :** the condition of being filled with shoals

shoal·ness *n* -ES **:** the state of being shallow **:** SHALLOWNESS

shoaly \-lē\ *adj* -ER/-EST [²*shoal* + *-y*] **:** full of shoals

shoat *also* **shote** \ˈshōt\ *or* **shott** \ˈshät\ *n* -s [ME *schoyth, shote;* akin to Flem *schote* shoat] **:** a young hog of either sex and esp. less than one year old — compare BARROW, GILT

shoch \ˈshäk\ *n* -s [IrGael *seach* (*tobac*), fr. *seach* turn, quantity taken at a time + *tobac* tobacco] *Irish* **:** a draw at a pipe of tobacco

shochet *var of* SHOHET

¹**shock** \ˈshäk\ *n* -s [ME; akin to MD *schoc, schocke* heap, pile, group of sixty, MLG *schok* shock, group of sixty, OS *scok* group of sixty, MHG *schoc* heap, pile, group of sixty, *schoche* haystack, G dial. (Switzerland) *hock* heap, pile, OE *hēah* high — more at HIGH] **1 a :** a pile or assemblage of usu. 8 to 16 sheaves of grain (as wheat) set up in a field with the butt ends down and one or two of the sheaves often broken to serve as a cap to protect the tops from weather — called also *stook* **b :** a somewhat conical stack of separate stalks of corn **c** *chiefly dial* **:** a pile of hay **:** HAYCOCK **2** [prob. fr. MD *schoc, schocke* or MLG *schok*] *archaic* **:** a group or lot of 60 pieces

²**shock** \ˈ"\ *vb* -ED/-ING/-S [ME *schocken,* fr. *schock,* n.] *vt* **:** to collect or make up into a shock ⟨on vacations he ~*ed* wheat and had other jobs —*Current Biog.*⟩ **~** *vi* **:** to build shocks

³**shock** \ˈ"\ *n* -s *often attrib* [MF *choc,* fr. *choquer* to strike against, shock — more at ⁴SHOCK] **1 a :** the impact or encounter of individuals or groups in a battle, charge, or joust **b :** the concentration of effort upon the force of impact in a battle (as in an armored or cavalry attack or close personal contact in an assault) ⟨the lack of tanks deprives the airborne force of one of its major means of ~ action —H.A.Jordan⟩ ⟨the defenders created small ~ . . . groups for the house-to-house fighting required there —*Infantry Jour.*⟩ **c :** the bringing to bear of concentrated effort upon a special objective ⟨~ workers whose output is very high and who develop new speed production methods —T.P.Whitney⟩ **2 a** (1) **:** a violent shake or jar **:** BLOW, COLLISION, CONCUSSION ⟨the ~ of tides that fall upon a crumbling shore —Francis Stuart⟩ ⟨banging the door with a ~ that made the house rattle —Arnold Bennett⟩ (2) **:** an oscillation, loss of equilibrium, or other effect of such violence **b** (1) **:** EARTHQUAKE (2) **:** the impact of an earth vibration (as an earthquake) **3 a** (1) **:** a disturbance in the equilibrium or permanence of an institution or organized entity ⟨the transition from the roles of childhood to those of adult life is accomplished with little ~ to the personality —Ralph Linton⟩ (2) **:** a sudden or violent disturbance in the mental or emotional faculties ⟨the ~ and elation of victory and defeat —Oscar Handlin⟩ ⟨fresh ~s of wonder at the unaccountable apparition —George Meredith⟩ (3) **:** a sense of outrage to one's convictions esp. of morality or propriety ⟨terms that in better districts would have caused disgust and ~ —Ruth Park⟩ **b :** something that causes outrage, horror, stupefaction, or disturbance or agitation in an institution, person, or organized system ⟨the further ~ of weaning —Henry Wynmalen⟩ ⟨he was liable not only to the ~ of outward circumstance but of inward impulses —Havelock Ellis⟩ ⟨ready the nation for that economic ~ —*New Republic*⟩ **4 a :** a state of profound depression of the vital processes of the body characterized by pallor, rapid but weak pulse, rapid and shallow respiration, restlessness, anxiety or mental dullness, nausea or vomiting associated with reduced total blood volume and low blood pressure and subnormal temperature resulting from severe esp. crushing injuries, hemorrhage, burns, major surgery, or other causes ⟨the patient was admitted to the hospital in ~⟩ **b :** a state induced for therapeutic purposes (as by the injection of a drug) ⟨insulin ~⟩ — compare SHOCK THERAPY **5 :** sudden stimulation of the nerves or convulsive contraction of the muscles accompanied by a feeling of concussion that is caused by the discharge through the animal body of electricity from a charged body — compare ELECTROSHOCK THERAPY **6 a :** a stroke of paralysis **:** APOPLEXY **b :** a condition resulting from or associated with myocardial infarction; *specif* **:** CORONARY THROMBOSIS **7 :** an acute disturbance of the physiology of a plant caused by extremes of temperature or moisture or by parasitic organisms or viruses and often marked or followed by reduction of yield or loss of leaves and fruit **8 :** SHOCK ABSORBER **syn** see IMPACT

⁴**shock** \ˈ"\ *vb* -ED/-ING/-S [MF *choquer,* fr. OF *choquier, chuquier,* prob. of Gmc origin; akin to MD *schocken* to shake, jolt, *schocke* swing, OS *skogka,* MHG *schoc, schocke*] *vt* **1 a** *obs* **:** to disorganize or cause to waver by a sudden violent attack **b** *obs* **:** to charge or assault suddenly and violently **:** ASSAIL **2 a :** to strike with surprise, terror, horror, or disgust **:** strongly affect **:** OFFEND, ASTONISH, SCANDALIZE ⟨the individual who may be ~*ed* by the expression of an unfamiliar or unpopular opinion —*Saturday Rev.*⟩ ⟨many audiences are ~*ed* by the sounds of new compositions —Goddard Lieberson⟩ **b :** to cause to undergo a physical or nervous shock **c :** to subject (the body or a body part) to the action of an electrical discharge so as to cause a more or less violent nervous and muscular response **3 a :** to cause to disappear or depart by or as if by a shock ⟨his sense of humor was ~*ed* out of him for the moment —Archibald Marshall⟩ **b :** to drive by or as if by a shock ⟨a way of ~*ing* the reader into realizing that both sides . . . have gone all-out in their savagery —Bruce Bliven b. 1916⟩ **~** *vi* **1 :** to meet with a shock **:** come together in violent encounter **:** COLLIDE ⟨her teeth ~*ed* against each other —Dorothy Baker⟩ **2 :** to cause or arouse astonishment, offense, horror, or fear ⟨the subject is meant to ~ rather than attract —Herbert Read⟩

⁵**shock** \ˈ"\ *n* -s [perh. fr. ¹*shock*] **1** *or* **shock dog :** a dog with long coarse hair **2 :** a thick bushy mass ⟨an untidy ~ of thick gray hair —Hamilton Basso⟩

⁶**shock** \ˈ"\ *adj* **:** BUSHY, SHAGGY ⟨the ~ headdress of hair besmeared with mutton fat —C.G.Seligman⟩

⁷**shock** \ˈ"\ *chiefly dial var of* SHUCK

⁸**shock** \ˈ"\ *n* -s [origin unknown] **:** a silvered pane of window glass ⟨~ mirror⟩

shock absorbent watch *n* [³*shock*] **:** a wristwatch having the balance pivot jewel bearings set into resilient housings to decrease the possibility of breakage due to a fall or shock

shock absorber *n* **1 :** any of several devices for absorbing the energy of sudden impulses or shocks: as **a :** a spring, pneumatic, or hydraulic device used on an automobile in addition to the regular springs to lessen the shocks from unevenness of the road **b :** a spring or damped elastic device interposed between the wheels, floats, or tail skid and the rest of an airplane to secure resiliency in landing and taxiing **2 :** something that acts as a buffer esp. against disturbing economic forces ⟨the private consumption sector and especially agriculture serve as *shock absorbers* with reference to labor —Naum Jasny⟩

shock bump *n* **:** an earth tremor resulting from the sudden collapse of rock over a subsidence cavity and usu. causing a heavy blow to a mine roof

shock cord *n* **:** a cord made of rubber strands bound in woven casing and used as landing shock absorbers on small airplanes, as supports for rotor blades, and as a tow for launching gliders

shock damper *n, Brit* **:** SHOCK ABSORBER

shock disease *n* [³*shock*] **:** an acute fatal hypoglycemia of wild hares and rabbits associated with degenerative changes of the liver and believed to be a factor in cyclic decline of the animals

shocked *past of* SHOCK

¹**shock·er** \ˈshäkə(r)\ *n* -s [⁴*shock* + *-er*] **1 a :** one that shocks **:** something horrifying, startling, astonishing, frightening, or offensive ⟨our verbal taboos are being shattered by the hundred, with the resulting ~s sometimes disguised by giving only initials —D.W.Maurer⟩ **b :** a work of fiction or drama designed to shock the moral sensibilities esp. by the use of sordid detail or to hold interest by the use of a high proportion of suspense, intrigue or sensational matter (as crime or violence) ⟨classy ~s of the hard-boiled school —C.J.Rolo⟩ — compare DREADFUL **2 :** an instrument for producing an electric shock

²**shocker** \ˈ"\ *n* -s [²*shock* + *-er*] **:** one that puts grain into shocks

shock excitation *n* [³*shock*] **:** IMPULSE EXCITATION

shock–head \ˈ=,=\ *n* [⁶*shock*] **:** a head with a shock of hair

¹**shocking** *adj* [fr. pres. part. of ⁴*shock*] **1 :** causing to shake or tremble **:** STUNNING ⟨repeated ~ blows to the head —W.A.D. Anderson⟩ **2 :** extremely startling and offensive **:** novel and distasteful through being or appearing immoral, horrifying, immoderate, reprehensible ⟨persons of old-fashioned views might regard this as a very ~ admission —Rebecca West⟩ ⟨solecism of this kind . . . would have seemed a ~ thing to so accurate a scholar —L.P.Smith⟩ **3 :** having a color tone that is striking, vivid, bright, or intense ⟨~ pink⟩ **syn** see FEARFUL

²**shocking** \ˈ"\ *adv* **:** SHOCKINGLY ⟨a ~ bad orator and altogether deficient in humanity —Norman Douglas⟩

shock·ing·ly *adv* **:** in a shocking manner

shock·ing·ness *n* -ES **:** the quality or state of being shocking

shock mount *n* [³*shock*] **:** a resilient mounting as for delicate instruments to absorb shock

shocks *pl of* SHOCK, *pres 3d sing of* SHOCK

shock stall *n* **:** a stall induced by separation of flow caused by pressure changes resulting from shock waves

shock therapy *or* **shock treatment** *n* **:** the treatment of mental disorder by the artificial induction of coma or convulsions through use of drugs or electricity

shock troops *n pl* **:** troops esp. suited and chosen for offensive work because of their high morale, training, and discipline

shock tube *n* **:** a long closed tube of uniform cross section used for studying the transient effects of a shock wave usu. produced when a diaphragm dividing the tube into two chambers containing gas at different pressures is ruptured

shock wave *n* **1 :** BLAST 5b **2 :** a compressional wave formed whenever the speed of a body relative to a medium exceeds that at which the medium can transmit sound and characterized by a disturbed region of small but finite thickness within which very abrupt changes occur in the pressure, density, and velocity of the medium ⟨passage of a *shock wave* (from an explosion . . . or from the leading wing edge of a supersonic airplane) through a compressible fluid such as air —*Fortune*⟩

shod \ˈshäd\ *adj* [ME, fr. past part. of *shoen* to shoe — more at SHOE] **1 a :** wearing shoes **b :** equipped with tires **2 :** furnished or equipped with a shoe (as of metal) — often used in combination

shodden *adj* [fr. past part. of ²*shoe*] *dial* **:** SHOD

shod·di·ly \ˈshädˀlē, -dəlē\ *adv* **:** in a shoddy manner

shod·di·ness \-dēnəs\ *n* -ES **:** the quality or state of being shoddy

¹**shod·dy** \ˈshädē, -di\ *n* -ES [origin unknown] **1 a :** wool of better quality and longer staple than mungo reclaimed from unfelted materials, rags, or waste and usu. mixed with new wool before reusing **b :** a fabric often of inferior quality manufactured in whole or in part from reclaimed wool (as shoddy) **2 a :** refuse, inferior, imitation, or pretentiously vulgar articles or matter ⟨cheap ~ for oak and mahogany —H.J.Massingham⟩ ⟨show up a younger generation of writers as the blunted manufacturers of ~ they are —*Times Lit. Supp.*⟩ **b :** a pretentious vulgarity in way of life esp. from the exploitation of newly or underhandedly acquired wealth ⟨preserved itself inviolate from respectability and ~ and the invasions of twentieth-century commonplaceness —Robert Lynd⟩ **3 :** reclaimed rubber

²**shoddy** \ˈ"\ *adj* -ER/-EST **1 :** made wholly or in part of shoddy ⟨~ cloth⟩ ⟨a ~ uniform⟩ **2 a :** falsely claiming moral worth and social status ⟨~ aristocracy⟩ **b :** cheaply imitative or vulgarly pretentious ⟨antique metalware is sold here as well as the *shoddiest* machine-made articles —*Amer. Guide Series: N.Y. City*⟩ ⟨a great deal of distinctly ~ veneered furniture was turned out —S.F.Horn⟩ **c :** employing, consisting of, or made by hasty, scamping, or unsound methods ⟨had done as cheap and ~ a job as he could do —Thomas Wolfe⟩ ⟨the construction of the shattered dam had been ~ —Louis Bromfield⟩ **d :** appearing sordid or squalid esp. through wear or use **:** SHABBY, RUN-DOWN ⟨sitting on a couch in the ~ hotel lobby —Knox Burger⟩ ⟨~ second-hand clothes⟩ **e :** vaguely reprehensible **:** DISREPUTABLE ⟨a ~ military adventurer had plunged his country into civil war —Anthony West⟩ ⟨the whole ~ fraud was disclosed —R.L.Riggs⟩

shode *var of* SHOAD

sho·der \ˈshōdə(r)\ *n* -s [modif. of F *chauderet, chaudret,* alter. of *chaucheret,* fr. obs. *chaucher* to press, fr. L *calcare* to tread on, trample, press, fr. *calc-, calx* heel — more at CALK] **:** a package of goldbeater's skins in which gold leaf is beaten the second time — compare ²CUTCH

¹**shoe** \ˈshü\ *n, pl* **shoes** \-üz\ *often attrib* [ME *sho, shoo,* fr. OE *scōh;* akin to OHG *scuoh* shoe, ON *skōr,* Goth *skohs* shoe, OE *hȳd* hide, skin — more at HIDE] **1 a :** an outer covering for the human foot usu. made of leather, with a thick or stiff sole and an attached heel: as (1) **:** an outer foot covering reaching to the ankle or thereabouts (2) **:** a low-cut outer foot covering — compare BOOT, OXFORD (3) **:** a foot covering with a leather sole and heel and an upper covering at least the instep for wear outdoors — compare OVERSHOE, SLIPPER **b :** a metal plate or rim usu. made of iron and nailed to the hoof of an animal to protect it from injury or to assist it in obtaining a foothold; *specif* **:** HORSESHOE **2 :** an object or device placed at the bottom, foot, or end of or beneath an object: as **a :** a socket or ferrule of iron or other material to protect the point of a wooden pile, pole, cane, or staff **b :** a metal socket or plate to take a thrust (as of a strut, rafter, or jack) **c :** a band of iron or steel or a slip of wood fastened to the bottom of the runner of a vehicle (as a sleigh) that slides on the snow or ice **d :** the removable iron or steel tip of a stamp in a set of stamps for crushing ore **e :** a steel cutting edge attached to the bottom of a caisson or lining in sinking a drop shaft **f :** the part of a bridge supporting the superstructure and bearing on a bearing plate or roller nest upon the supporting pier or abutment **g :** a small molding or strip placed in the angle between a baseboard and the floor of a room **h** (1) **:** an often disk-shaped turned or shaped termination on furniture legs used esp. during the 17th and early 18th centuries (2) **:** a metal, glass, or rubber cap or cup placed upon or under a furniture leg for protection or ornament **i :** a strong piece of paper or paperboard upon which standing type matter is sometimes placed for storage **j :** a wooden block or other device placed under an object to steady or support it or provide traction ⟨ladder ~⟩ **k :** a ground plate that forms or is attached to a link of a traction belt on a caterpillar tractor **3 shoes** *pl* **:** economic, social, or hierarchical status or position or a vantage point for regarding events or circumstances in a particular perspective ⟨next in line of succession for my boss's ~s —F.S.Mitchell⟩ — usu. used in such phrases as *in another's shoes* ⟨had never taken even two minutes to try to put himself in a woman's ~s —Louis Auchincloss⟩ **4 a :** a device serving as a trough or spout: as **a :** a trough or spout for conveying grain from a hopper to the eye of a millstone **b :** a trough-shaped or spout-shaped member at the foot of a water leader that directs the water outward **c :** an inclined trough in an ore-crushing mill to secure steady feeding **5 :** a device covering or jacketing an object (as for protection) ⟨propeller ~s for ice protection —*Flying*⟩: as **a :** a steel strip on the bottom of the keel of a boat **b :** TIRE **6 :** a gold or usu. silver ingot suggestive of a Chinese shoe in shape formerly used in China as money **:** a piece of sycee **7 :** a device that retards, stops, or controls the motion of an object ⟨the friction ~s engage the inner surface of the flywheel —*Mech. Engineering*⟩ ⟨clutch ~⟩: as **a :** DRAG 3a(2) **b :** the part of a brake that presses on the wheel of a wagon or other vehicle to retard its motion **c :** one of usu. two metal pieces lined with a frictional material that press upon a brake drum to retard its motion — see HYDRAULIC BRAKE illustration **8 :** any of various devices, members, or attachments that are inserted in or run along a track, channel, or groove to guide a movement, provide a contact or friction grip, or protect against wear, damage, or slippage: as **a :** a runner in the sash channel of a window or at the base of a door (as a metal fire door) **b :** the sliding contact member of a current collector ⟨a third-rail ~ of a subway car⟩ **c :** GIB 1 **d :** a track or pad that positions or otherwise influences (as by friction) the movement of a strip of photographic film or paper in its passage through a projector (as a camera or printer) **9 :** a wedge-shaped furrow opener used on some grain drills and on corn and cotton planters **10 :** the end of a dynamo pole usu. curved to conform to the arc of the armature and shaped to distribute the flux peripherally **11 :** a flat metal plate in a pressing machine or a concave metal plate in a mangle that is usu. heated by electricity and pressed against the buck or roller **12 :** a case designed to hold three or more packs of cards so that the top card may be pulled out singly and used in baccarat or chemin de fer

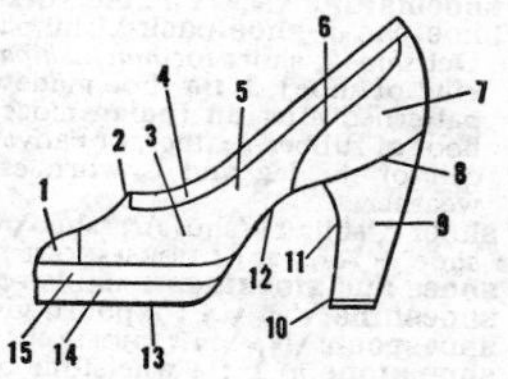

parts of shoe 1a: *1* tip, *2* throat, *3* vamp, *4* collar, *5* arch, *6* foxing, *7* quarter, *8* heel seat, *9* heel, *10* top lift, *11* breasting, *12* shank, *13* sole, *14* platform, *15* mudguard

²**shoe** \ˈ"\ *vt* **shod** \ˈshäd\ *also* **shoed; shod** \ˈshäd\ *also* **shoed** \ˈshüd\ *or* **shod·den** \ˈshädˀn\ **shoeing; shoes** [ME *shoen, shooen,* fr. OE *scōgian, scōgan, scōan,* fr. *scōh,* n.] **1 :** to put a shoe on **:** furnish with a shoe ⟨who will ~ your pretty little foot⟩ ⟨mules were much easier *shod* —W.F.Harris⟩ **2 :** to cover for protection, strength, or ornament with harder or handsomer material ⟨a pole *shod* with an iron tip —K.A. Henderson⟩ **3 :** to cover with or as if with a shoe ⟨fragments of hard rock with which the glacier was *shod* —W.J.Miller⟩ **4 :** to fit a tire to (a wheel of a vehicle)

shoebill *also* **shoebird** \ˈ=,=\ *n* **:** a large wading bird (*Balaeniceps rex*) that is related to the storks and herons, inhabits the valley of the White Nile, is chiefly ashy gray with blackish wings and tail, and has a much widened bill

shoeblack \ˈ=,=\ *n* [¹*shoe* + *black* (v.)] **:** BOOTBLACK

shoeblack plant *n* **:** CHINA ROSE 2

shoe block *n* **:** a block with two sheaves one above the other and at right angles to each other

shoe board *n* **:** a hard board of highly compressed wood pulp and leather clippings used in making soles and heels of shoes

shoe boil *n* **:** a soft swelling on the elbow of a horse caused by irritation (as from bruising in lying or by clipping with a heel calk)

shoe bolt *n* **:** a bolt with a long unslotted countersunk head for fastening a shoe on a sleigh runner

shoe button *n* **:** an often black, glossy, and globe-shaped button used in fastening a shoe

shoe–button spider *n* **:** BLACK WIDOW

shoecraft \ˈ=,=\ *n* **:** the art of designing and making shoes

shoe drill *n* **:** a grain drill with shoe furrow openers

shoeflower \ˈ=,=\ *n* **:** CHINA ROSE 2

¹shoehorn \'· \ n ['shoe + horn] : a curved piece (as of horn, wood, or metal) to aid in slipping on a shoe

²shoehorn \"\ vt 1 : to force (something unwanted) to be accepted or admitted : FOIST ⟨tried to ~ the cooperative societies . . . into the international alliance —Time⟩ 2 : to force into a small, narrow, or insufficient space : SQUEEZE ⟨papa, mama and children . . . would be ~ed into the family car —Rafe Gibbs⟩

shoe-ing \'shüiŋ, -üⁱŋ\ n -s [ME shoing; partly fr. gerund of shoen, shooen to shoe; partly fr. sho, shoo shoe + -ing — more at SHOE] 1 : the act of one who shoes 2 a : covering for the feet : SHOES b : a protective or supporting covering or band ⟨the ~ on the runner —J.S.Mutch⟩

shoeing-horn \'··ˌ·\ n [ME schoynge horne] 1 : SHOEHORN 2 archaic : APPETIZER 3 a : something that facilitates a transaction or passage ⟨the best shoeing-horn for drawing on a sound sleep —Sir Walter Scott⟩ b archaic : someone that acts for another (as a go-between or decoy)

shoeingsmith \'··ˌ·\ n : FARRIER

shoelace \'·ˌ·\ n : a thin cord or strip of material (as of fabric) used for lacing together the sides of a shoe upper over the arch

shoe-less \'shüləs\ adj : having no shoe

shoemake \'·ˌ·\ n -s [by folk etymology fr. sumac] : SUMAC; esp : SMOOTH SUMAC

shoemaker \'·ˌ··\ n [ME shomaker, fr. sho shoe + maker] 1 a : one that makes shoes 2 : a shopkeeper whose business is selling or repairing shoes 2 a : THREADFISH b : RAINBOW RUNNER

shoemaker's wax n : WAX 2d

shoemaking \'·ˌ··\ n : the work or occupation of a shoemaker

shoe-pac or **shoe-pack** \'shüˌpak\ n -s [by folk etymology fr. Del shipak, short for machtshipak, fr. machtshi bad + paku, a kind of shoe] 1 : a shoe made usu. of oil-tanned leather and patterned after an Indian moccasin 2 : a waterproof laced boot of rubber, leather, or canvas that usu. extends well up the calf of the leg and is worn esp. over heavy socks in cold weather

shoer \'shü(ə)r, 'shü(ə)r, 'shüə\ n -s [ME schoere, fr. shoen to shoe + -ere -er] : HORSESHOER

shoes and stockings : BIRD'S-FOOT TREFOIL 1a

shoeshine \'·ˌ·\ n : a polish given to shoes

shoespoon \'·ˌ·\ n : SHOEHORN

shoe stone n 1 : a whetstone used by shoemakers and other workers in leather 2 : a sharp-gritted sandstone used esp. for making shoe stones

¹shoestring \'·ˌ·\ n ['shoe + string] 1 : SHOELACE 2 [so called fr. shoestrings being a typical item sold by itinerant venders] : a small sum of money : capital inadequate or barely adequate to the needs of a transaction ⟨many eminently successful men started business on a ~ —J.R.Sprague⟩ 3 a : TRUMPET CREEPER b : the long slender tough root of a leadplant (Amorpha canescens) 4 also **shoestring disease** : a plant disease that is characterized by slender growth of leaves; esp : a disease of tomatoes caused by the cucumber mosaic virus 5 : SHOESTRING FUNGUS

²shoestring \"\ adj 1 : narrow and elongated as a shoestring ⟨~ tie⟩ 2 a : operating on, accomplished with, or consisting of little or no capital or backing ⟨efforts of a ~ producer to raise money for a theatrical venture —Henry Hewes⟩ ⟨~ financing —H.E.Hoagland⟩ b : small in conception, operation, or scope : MINOR, PETTY ⟨in amphibious warfare . . . the first landings of a ~ character compared with the power the enemy might assemble —W.V.Pratt⟩

shoestring catch n : a catch in baseball made while running and with the hands held close to the ground

shoestring district n : an election district gerrymandered into a long narrow strip

shoestringer \'·ˌ··\ n : a person that operates on a shoestring ⟨couldn't afford the performers and studios needed for . . . standard recorded fare, but he was a resourceful ~ —Daniel Lang⟩

shoestring fern n : GRASS FERN

shoestring fungus n : a fungus (esp. Armillaria mellea) that forms brown stringy rhizomorphs and causes destructive rot of the roots of trees (as apples or maples)

shoestring potato n : a long slender strip cut from a raw potato and fried in deep fat — usu. used in pl.

shoestring root rot n : root rot disease of trees caused by the shoestring fungus

shoestring sand or **shoestring sandstone** n : a very long narrow body of sand or sandstone in the midst of mud or shale

shoestring tackle n : a football tackle made at or near the ankles

shoe tree n 1 : a foot-shaped form over which a completed shoe is placed for finishing and dressing the upper 2 : a foot-shaped device for inserting in a shoe to preserve its shape

sho-far also **sho-phar** \'shōˌfär, -ō̇fär\ n, pl **shof-roth** also **shoph-roth** \shō̇'frō(t)h\ [Heb shōphār] : a ram's horn blown as a trumpet by the ancient Hebrews as a signal in battle and in high religious observances and used at present in synagogues before and during Rosh Hashanah and at the conclusion of Yom Kippur

shoe trees 2

¹shog \'shäg\ vb **shogged; shogged; shogging; shogs** [ME shoggen; prob. akin to MD schocken to shake, jolt — more at SHOCK (disorganize)] vt 1 chiefly dial : JOLT, SHAKE, JOSTLE 2 chiefly dial : to push aside : SHOVE 3 chiefly dial : RACK 6 ~ vi, chiefly dial : to move along

²shog \"\ n -s chiefly dial : SHAKE, JOG

sho-ga-ol \'shōgəˌ̇ȯl, -ˌōl\ n -s [ISV shoga- (fr. Jap shōga ginger) + -ol] : a liquid unsaturated phenolic ketone $C_{17}H_{24}O_3$ that constitutes one of the pungent principles of ginger and is synthesized by condensation of zingerone and hexanal

shog-gie \'shägi\ vb ['shog + Sc -ie, freq. suffix] chiefly Scot : SWAY, SWING

shog-gle \'shägəl\ vb -ED/-ING/-S [freq. of 'shog] 1 dial Eng : JOGGLE 2 dial Eng : DANGLE

shog-gly \-g(ə)lē\ adj [shoggle + -y] chiefly dial : LOOSE, SHAKY

sho-gi \'shōgē\ n -s [Jap shōgi] : Japanese chess played on a board of 81 squares with 20 pieces to the set

sho-gun \'shō(ˌ)gən\ n -s [Jap shōgun general, fr. Chin (Pek) chiang⁴ chün¹] : a military governor of Japan before the mid-19th century revolution with power exceeding the emperor's — called also tycoon

sho-gun-ate \'shōgənˌāt, -nət\ n -s : the office, dignity, or government of a shogun

sho-het also **sho-chet** \'shō̇ˌhet or -ˌchet\ n, pl **sho-he-tim** or **sho-che-tim** \-kə̇tēm\ or **sho-ha-tim** \-kə̇tēm\ also **shohets** or **shochets** \-kəts\ or **sho-ha-tim** \-kə̇tēm\ [Heb shōḥēṭ slaughterer] : a person officially licensed by rabbinical authority as slaughterer of animals and poultry for use as food in accordance with Jewish laws

sho-ji \'shōjē\ or **shoji screen** n, pl **shoji** also **shojis** [Jap shōji] : a paper screen serving as a wall, partition, or sliding door

sho-la-pur \'shōlə̇ˌpu̇(ə)r\ adj, usu cap [fr. Sholapur, India] : of or from the city of Sholapur, India : of the kind or style prevalent in Sholapur

shole \'shōl\ n -s [origin unknown] : a plank or plate placed beneath an object (as a shore) to give increased bearing surface or to act as a protection

sholom var of SHALOM

sho-mer \'shō̇ˌmer\ n, pl **shom-rim** \-ōmrēm\ [Heb shōmēr, fr. shēmōr to watch] : GUARDIAN, WATCHMAN; specif : a mounted guard of the Palestinian Jewish colonies

shom pen \'shämˌpen\ n, pl **shom pen** usu cap S&P 1 : a subdivision of the Nicobarese of Great Nicobar Island 2 : a member of the Shom Pen people

sho-na \'shōnə\ n, pl **shona** or **shonas** usu cap 1 a : a group of Bantu peoples of eastern Rhodesia south of the Zambesi river 2 : a member of any of the Shona peoples 2 : a Bantu language or group of closely related languages used by the Shona peoples 3 : a written language, designed consciously to serve as a literary medium for the whole Shona group — called also Union Shona

shone ME shoon, fr. OE scān past of SHINE

sho-neen \shō̇'nēn, '··\ n -s [IrGael seoinīn, dim. of Seon John, fr. E John] Irish : a would-be gentleman who puts on pretentious airs

shon-gop-o-vi \(ˌ)shäŋ'gäpəˌvē\ n, pl **shongopovi** or **shongopovis** usu cap 1 : a Shoshonean people occupying a pueblo in northeastern Arizona 2 : a member of the Shongopovi people

shon-kin-ite \'shäŋkəˌnīt\ n -s [Shonkin (Highwood mountains, Montana), its locality + E -ite] : a dark granular igneous rock consisting of augite with subordinate orthoclase and smaller amounts of olivine, biotite, nephelite, sodalite, and plagioclase

¹shoo \'shü\ interj [ME schowe] — used in frightening away an animal (as a hen)

²shoo \"\ vb -ED/-ING/-S vt 1 : to scare or drive away (as birds) by or in the manner of one crying shoo ⟨~ing out a parcel of hens —Ida Treat⟩ ⟨like a fly . . . settling whenever the hand ceased to ~ it away —Robert DeVries⟩ 2 a : to send or cause to move away or along esp. by urging gently with words or gestures suggestive of the shooing of fowls ⟨~ing the passengers off a country bus —Mollie Panter-Downes⟩ ⟨photographers were ~ed away from the building —Frontier⟩ ⟨~ed them off for their walk —Ann Bridge⟩ b : to drive out : chase away ⟨DISPEL ⟨softened her, ~ing away the madness —Adria L. Langley⟩ ⟨~ away the memory —D.B.Chidsey⟩ ~ vi 1 : to make the sounds or gestures of one shooing fowls ⟨~ing at them with her umbrella —Elizabeth Taylor⟩ 2 : to go away or along at or as if at the cry of shoo ⟨the fly ~ed —Danforth Ross⟩

shood or **shude** \'shüd\ n -s [akin to MLG schōde covering, pod, OHG scōta, OE hȳd skin, hide — more at HIDE] 1 dial Eng : the husk of oats after threshing 2 : rice husks or similar refuse used in adulterating linseed cake

shoofly \'·ˌ·\ n ['shoo + fly] 1 a : a child's rocker having the seat built on or usu. between supports representing an animal figure (as of a duck or swan) ⟨a swan ~⟩ ⟨a hobby horse⟩ 2 a : a wild indigo (Baptisia tinctoria) b : FLOWER-OF-AN-HOUR c : APPLE OF PERU 2 : a temporary track laid on the ground or on cribwork at one side of a railroad line to permit trains to pass an obstruction in that line b : a temporary road (as an access road) used during completion of a construction project 4 a : a policeman usu. in plain clothes detailed to watch or investigate other policemen ⟨~ squad⟩ b : a foreman in the postal service who checks on carriers and drivers 5 : a long-fingered device in some cylinder presses for freeing the printed sheet from the cylinder for delivery

shoofly pie also **shoofly cake** n ['shoo + fly] : a sticky dessert made by pouring a mixture of molasses, hot water, and soda into a pastry-lined pan, adding crumbs made by mixing flour, butter, and sugar, and baking till the molasses bubbles up through the layer of crumbs in dark syrupy veins

shoog-le \'shügəl\ var of SHOGGLE

shoo-in \'·ˌ·\ n -s [fr. shoo in, v.] : one that is a certain and easy winner (as among candidates for an office or contestants in a race) : one that is bound to be successful : SURE THING ⟨figures as a shoo-in again⟩ ⟨seems to be a shoo-in for a second term —Newsweek⟩ ⟨ants, another supposed shoo-in to supplant mankind —New Yorker⟩

¹shook [ME shook (past), fr. OE scōc] past or chiefly dial past part of SHAKE

²shook \'shu̇k\ n -s [origin unknown] 1 a : a set of staves and headings for one hogshead, cask or barrel trimmed and bound together compactly b (1) : a bundle or set of tops, bottoms, sides, and ends of boxes ready to be put together (2) : a veneer of wood out of which boxes (as wire-bound boxes) are made c : the parts of a piece of house furniture (as a bedstead) packed together 2 : a shock of sheaves ⟨broad fields covered with wheat in ~s —F.M.Ford⟩ ⟨rows of wigwam-shaped ~s —John Dos Passos⟩

³shook \"\ vt -ED/-ING/-S : to pack (as staves) in a shook

shook-up \'·ˌ·\ also **shook up** adj [shook-up fr. shook up, chiefly dial. past part. of shake up; shook fr. chiefly dial. past part. of shake] : SHAKEN; esp : suffering under or showing the effects of great emotional disturbance or disorganization : UNNERVED ⟨a shook-up generation⟩ ⟨had had it ~ he was shook-up⟩

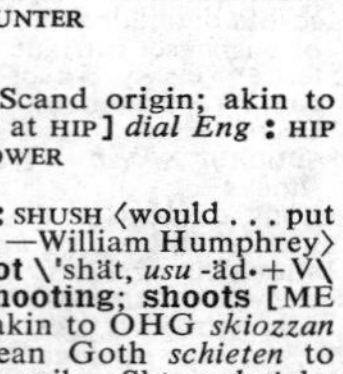

¹shool \'shül\ vi -ED/-ING/-S [origin unknown] 1 chiefly dial : to drag or scrape along : SHAMBLE, SHUFFLE 2 : to loaf or idle about begging : LOITER, SAUNTER

²shool \"\ dial var of SHOVEL

shoop \'shüp\ n -s [ME schowpe, of Scand origin; akin to Norw dial. hjupa hip of a rose — more at HIP] dial Eng : HIP

shoor \'shu̇(ə)r\ chiefly Scot var of SHOWER

shoos pres 3d sing of SHOO

shoosh \'shu̇sh\ vb -ED/-ING/-ES [imit.] : SHUSH ⟨would . . . put his finger to his lips and ~ her right back —William Humphrey⟩

¹shoot \'shüt, usu -üd-+V\ vb **shot** \'shät, usu -äd-+V\ also chiefly dial **shot-ten** \'shät°n\ **shooting; shoots** [ME sheten, shoten, shuten, fr. OE scēotan; akin to OHG skiozzan to shoot, ON skjóta to shoot, Crimean Goth schieten to shoot an arrow, Lith skudrus quick, agile, Skt codati he incites, skundate he hurries] vt 1 a (1) : to let fly or cause to be driven forward with force (as an arrow, bolt, stone, bullet) from a bow, sling, or similar device or from a firearm ⟨~ an arrow into the air⟩ ⟨~ six bullets after a fleeing burglar⟩ ⟨were ~ing off live ammunition⟩ (2) : of a device : to send forth or be capable of sending forth ⟨automatically ~s one bullet per second⟩ ⟨~ a line to a ship for hauling in a breeches buoy⟩; use or accommodate as its proper charge or missile ⟨a target pistol that ~s lead pellets⟩ ⟨this bow ~s standard arrows⟩ (3) : to cause a missile to be driven forth from ⟨as a bow, sling, gun⟩ : DISCHARGE ⟨expert at ~ing a pistol⟩ — often used with off ⟨was a grown man when he first shot off a gun⟩ ⟨the sound of rifles being shot off⟩; also : to set off the explosive charge in ⟨a gun⟩ ⟨~ing pistols loaded with blank cartridges⟩ b : to send forth in a manner suggestive esp. in suddenness or intensity of one discharging a missile from a bow or gun : DART ⟨the porcupine . . . does not, as commonly supposed, ~ his spines at an enemy —Amer. Guide Series: Minn.⟩ ⟨shot uneasy glances over their shoulders —Kenneth Roberts⟩ ⟨shot a long-toothed smile —Earle Birney⟩ ⟨shot at him a look of amazement⟩ c : to let fly or send forth in a manner suggestive esp. in the course taken of the flight of something shot: as (1) : to let fly (as a marble, a pellet) by propelling from the forefinger with the thumb ⟨shot a spitball across the room⟩ (2) : to send forth or drive along by a finger-tip flicked across the thumb ⟨shot a crumb off his sleeve⟩ ⟨~ a jack across a table⟩ (3) : to send forth (as a ball or puck) in a game esp. toward or at a particular objective : a goal, net, pocket, another player) by propelling with the hands or feet or with an implement ⟨~ing fouls with his left hand —Stanley Frank⟩ ⟨swung his mallet and shot the ball into the goal⟩ ⟨~ the eight ball into the side pocket ⟨scooped up the ball and shot it to second⟩; also : to score by so doing ⟨shot a basket⟩ ⟨~ the winning goal⟩ ⟨~ a hole in one⟩ ⟨~s an 80 on the home links⟩ 2 a : to strike with something shot : hit with a missile esp. from a bow or gun; esp : to wound or kill with a missile discharged from a firearm ⟨~ a rabbit⟩ ⟨~ a fleeing burglar⟩ ⟨was accidentally shot⟩; esp ⟨shot . . . dead⟩ ⟨shot him through the heart⟩ ⟨shot himself in the leg⟩ b (1) : to remove or destroy by means of something shot or by shooting ⟨set about ~ing it to bits⟩ ⟨had every building into rubble⟩ — often used with away, off, out ⟨shot away her masts⟩ ⟨had his hand shot off⟩ ⟨shot out the lock⟩ ⟨~ every

¹shoot window in the building out⟩ ⟨shot out the light⟩ (2) : to destroy as completely as something shot to pieces : RUIN, WRECK ⟨an occasional ~ing of the mood is a minor complaint of modern U.S. poets —Reporter⟩ ⟨a delicate mechanism shot by prolonged misuse⟩ : EXPLODE ⟨seems to ~ the theory that she was specially detailed to work on me —L.C.Stevens⟩ c : to put to death by a missile discharged from a firearm esp. as a penalty ⟨was sentenced to be shot as a spy⟩ ⟨that scoundrel ought to be taken out and shot⟩ ⟨we don't . . . traitors, we hang them⟩ d (1) : to engage in the practice of killing (as birds, game) with firearms esp. as a sport ⟨goes south every year to ~ quail⟩ ⟨preferred ~ing small game⟩ (2) : to do shooting for game in or on ⟨hunt over ⟨had shot the surrounding country many times⟩ ⟨~ a tract of woodland⟩ ⟨allowed no one to ~ his land⟩ 3 a : to push or slide (as the bolt of a door or a lock) into or out of a fastening ⟨slammed the iron door and shot the bolts —R.M.Stern⟩ ⟨a few minutes manipulation with a bunch of skeleton keys sufficed to ~ back the bolt —F.W.Crofts⟩ b : to pass (a shuttle or filling thread) through the warp threads in weaving 4 a : to throw or cast suddenly esp. with force : FLING, PRECIPITATE ⟨shot his rider over his head⟩ ⟨the pilot must be shot from his cockpit to clear the tail —Time⟩ ⟨grabbed the troublemakers and shot them out the door⟩ b : to discharge, dump, or empty esp. by overturning, upending, or directing into a slide ⟨the flour into the box; shot 10 tons of coal through the cellar window⟩ ⟨a pit into which the dead carts had nightly shot corpses by scores —T.B. Macaulay⟩ c : to deal with or dispose of as if throwing away or casting aside: as (1) : to toss or thrust hurriedly or carelessly ⟨~ the dishes into the sink⟩ ⟨shot the letter under the blotter as the door opened⟩ ⟨shot his hat and coat into the closet and dashed upstairs⟩ (2) slang : to get rid of : give up : DISCARD, QUIT (3) : to spend esp. extravagantly ⟨~ 1000 francs on a dinner for four —Sat. Eve. Post⟩ : use up : EXHAUST ⟨had shot his roll⟩ d : to throw out (dice) for inspection esp. in craps : CAST; also : to place or offer (a bet) on the result of such casting ⟨~ five dollars⟩ e of a crab or lobster : to drop or cast off (a limb) 5 a : to push or thrust forward : stick out : PROJECT, PROTRUDE ⟨shot his finger at my father's nose —Alan Harrington⟩ — usu. used with out ⟨out a hand in greeting⟩ ⟨tiny lizards ~ing out their tongues⟩ ⟨weather had warped and separated some of the clapboards, ~ing the nails —Thomas Williams⟩ b : to put forth (a growth) : send out ⟨~ EXTRUDE — usu. used with out or forth ⟨plants ~ing out buds⟩ ⟨out long thin hairs that act not only as organs of defense but as anchors —W.E.Swinton⟩ ⟨shot forth a thick growth of new branches⟩ 6 a (1) : to utter (as words, sounds) rapidly or suddenly or with force ⟨his stomach tightened as he heard . . . ~ the next question —Erle Stanley Gardner⟩ ⟨shot some angry words —J.D.Hart⟩ ⟨shot everything out in one sentence⟩ ⟨shot out a snort of disbelief⟩ (2) : to engage in (aimless talk) often as a means of passing the time ⟨sit around ~ing the bull⟩ b : to emit (as light, flame, fumes) suddenly or rapidly ⟨the clanking tractor monster . . . ~ing smoke and fumes out of its belly —A.R.Williams⟩ ⟨a small window shot an oblique square of whiter light —Stephen Crane⟩ c : to eject or discharge from within the body ⟨spitting snakes that are popularly supposed to ~ their venom⟩ ⟨the archerfish can ~ a drop of water six feet or more —Bill Beatty⟩ ⟨stepped to the rail and shot a stream of tobacco juice down into the water —Erle Stanley Gardner⟩: (1) obs : to discharge (excreta) from the bowels; also : to empty (as the bowels, the body) of wastes (2) of a fish : to make a deposit of (spawn) (3) of a spider : to spin out (thread) (4) : VOMIT ⟨shot his lunch⟩ 7 a : to place or bring in position by sudden motion (as in launching, casting anchor, seining) ⟨when the net is about the wind is brought abeam —G.S.L. Clowes⟩ ⟨shot the trawl over the starboard side —Robert Gibbings⟩; specif : to release (a fishing line) in casting b (1) : to cause (as a boat) to move suddenly or swiftly forward (2) : to urge (as a horse) swiftly forward c : to send or carry in haste or swiftly (as on an errand or to a destination) : DISPATCH ⟨elevators ~s to appointments on the fiftieth floor —Katharine F. Gerould⟩ ⟨a giant air bubble that shot him to the surface —Newsweek⟩ ⟨~ him over to that Tactical Air Force —J.G.Cozzens⟩ d slang : PASS ⟨~ the salt⟩ 8 a : to variegate by or as if by sprinkling or intermingling color in streaks, flecks, or patches — usu. used with with and often with through ⟨hair was shot with gray —Will Cook⟩ ⟨the Holy War had shot her earliest landscapes with a valiant blood-red —Francis Hackett⟩ ⟨descending through clouds shot with sunlight —Rex Ingamells⟩ ⟨like night, ~ through with star beams —Esther Carlson⟩ ⟨a most accomplished work . . . shot through with the reflections of a thoughtful man of action —William Clark⟩ ⟨level tones . . . faintly shot with irony —E.M.Lustgarten⟩ b : to subject to admixture in excessive amounts or of an undesirable kind — usu. used with through ⟨interpretation . . . shot through with partisan feeling —V.L.Parrington⟩ ⟨is shot through with restraints of trade —T.W. Arnold⟩ 9 a : to pass swiftly along or by going down ⟨~ing terrific rapids⟩ or by or past ⟨the London cabdriver will not ~ the traffic lights —Charles Roetter⟩ or under ⟨shot bridge after bridge —C.S.Forester⟩ or over ⟨have shot this reef many times —Ernest Beaglehole⟩ b : to dash by (a competitor) in a race 10 : to form by crystallization or similar physical change ⟨rock shot into figures⟩ 11 : to plane (as the edge of a board) straight or true : fit by planing 12 : to engage in a game of ⟨PLAY ⟨~ craps⟩ ⟨~ marbles⟩ ⟨~ a round of golf⟩ ⟨~ a little pool with some of the boys⟩ 13 a : to cause (as a blast) to explode : DETONATE, IGNITE : set off ⟨~ a charge of dynamite⟩ ⟨~ing off firecrackers⟩ b : to effect by blasting: (1) : to mine (coal) by blasting without previous undercutting or shearing ⟨~ off the solid⟩ (2) : to break up oil-retaining rock formation in (an oil well) by exploding nitroglycerin (3) : to remove (as a tree stump) by blasting 14 : to expose to or make the subject of an operation employing a device suggestive of a bow or gun (as in being trained on a distant object by aiming or sighting or in propelling a charge): as a : to take the altitude of ⟨I pick up my sextant and ~ the star Arcturus —C.F.Blair⟩ ⟨the optical, hand-held sextant which has shot the sun for mariners for centuries —Think⟩ b : to photograph with a motion-picture camera or with a still camera : take a picture of : FILM ⟨were ~ing a western⟩ ⟨shot her from various angles⟩ ⟨had to ~ several scenes over again⟩ ⟨techniques for ~ing sports⟩ c : to give an injection to esp. for inoculation against disease ⟨had the children shot for diphtheria⟩ ⟨all calves TB and Bang tested and shot for shipment fever — Nat'l Live Stock Producer⟩ ~ vi 1 a : to go or pass with the sudden swiftness of something shot : move rapidly and precipitately (or dart as if propelled or driven forcefully : precipitate oneself or be precipitated ⟨hoping to see a star ~⟩ — usu. used with an adverb or an adverbial phrase esp. of direction ⟨the bow twanged and the arrow shot across the narrow space —T.B.Costain⟩ ⟨far, far below him . . . shot upward⟩ ⟨felt his feet ~ out from under him⟩ ⟨into the stream of traffic —Paul Bowles⟩ ⟨great fists, left and right, shot into his face —Arthur Morrison⟩ ⟨dragonflies shot at tangents through our rigging —H.M.Tomlinson⟩ ⟨bundles of sawn lumber should begin to ~ down the flume —S.E.White⟩ ⟨steam ~s from a high-pressure nozzle —Waldemar Kaempffert⟩ ⟨a wild idea shot into new prominence —F.L. Allen⟩ ⟨~ out the door⟩ ⟨shot from his chair with a yell⟩ ⟨soon shot ahead of his classmates⟩ ⟨~ing to the surface to breathe⟩ ⟨shot back into the living room again —Irish Digest⟩ ⟨his horse, covered with foam, shot down the road over a bridge —H.E.Scudder⟩ ⟨shot a breathless towheaded twelve-year-old —Blanche E. Baughan⟩ ⟨shot along with a shriek that meant business —E.K.Brown⟩ ⟨with the thought of that lifeless immobility shot through my joy with a feeling of benumbing dread —P.E.More⟩ ⟨lifted his hand in parting and shot away —Marjorie K. Rawlings⟩ ⟨river ~s over the cliffs in a dazzling waterfall —Amer. Guide Series: Minn.⟩ b (1) : to move ahead by force of momentum ⟨a sailboat ~s when the helm is put hard alee⟩ ⟨a heavy boat will ~ much further than a light one —C.D.Lane⟩ (2) of a bowled ball in cricket : to travel fast and close to or along the ground after pitching

c : to stream out suddenly : SPURT ⟨blood *shot* from the wound at a frightening rate⟩ ⟨felt the tears —*ing* from his eyes⟩ **d** : to dart in or as if in rays : appear suddenly from or as if from a source of light ⟨the clouds split and a ray of pure sunlight *shot* through the clear air —William Beebe⟩ ⟨from her black eyes there *shot* a magnificent look of disdain —Winston Churchill⟩ ⟨a glint of humor *shot* into his eyes —Laura Krey⟩ **2 a** : to dart with a piercing sensation ⟨pain *shot* through the Negro bullfighter —F.B.Gipson⟩ **b** : to throb in pain ⟨waiting for the tooth to ~ again⟩ **3 a** : to cause an engine or weapon to discharge a missile ⟨they *shot* at a target⟩ ⟨tripped and fell just as he turned to ~⟩ **b** : to practice the sport of hunting or of target firing with a gun ⟨~s better than he rides⟩ ⟨has *shot* from childhood⟩ **c** : to practice archery **d** (1) : to become discharged : go off ⟨~s at the touch of a trigger⟩ (2) : to propel a missile ⟨guns that ~ many miles⟩ ⟨a rifle that ~s accurately⟩ **4** : PROTRUDE, PROJECT, EXTEND ⟨trees —*ing* up against the sky⟩ ⟨Broadway, coming in from the south, ~s north and east from Union Square —*Amer. Guide Series: N.Y. City*⟩ **5 a** (1) : GROW, SPROUT ⟨grass beginning to ~⟩ ⟨plant life —*ing* up on all sides⟩ (2) : to put forth shoots : BUD, GERMINATE **b** : to put out limbs — used of an animal **b** : DEVELOP, MATURE ⟨teach the young idea how to ~ —James Thomson †1748⟩ **6** : to spring up or grow rapidly : advance to maturity — usu. used with *up* ⟨~s up to twice its length⟩ ⟨now he was —*ing* up with the promise of attaining a man's proper stature after all —T.B.Costain⟩ ⟨*shot* up to be a tall lad for his slender fourteen years —Waldo Frank⟩ **7** : to solidify so as to form spicules or crystals **8** : to play by propelling a ball or other object esp. in a particular way: **a** : to kick the ball at goal in soccer **b** : to throw the ball at a basket in basketball **c** : to propel a ball to make a hit in croquet **d** : to drive the ball at goal in hockey or lacrosse **e** : to propel a golf ball toward a green or a cup **f** : to cast dice **9** : to slide into or out of a fastening ⟨something wrong with the way this bolt ~s⟩ ⟨a bolt that ~s in either direction⟩ **10** : to begin to speak : speak out : say what one has to say — usu. used as an imperative ⟨all right, ~⟩ ⟨and ~ quick. What's happened —J.M.Cain⟩ **11 a** : to photograph a scene esp. of a moving picture **b** : to operate a camera or set cameras in operation : take a photograph **12** : to explode a charge of dynamite to produce vibrations in the ground esp. in seismic prospecting : explore a region by means of portable seismographs **syn** see RUSH — **shoot at** or **shoot for** : to have in mind or in view as a goal : aim at : strive for ⟨when it is achieved there will be other goals for them to *shoot* at —Bernard De Voto⟩ ⟨all stores are *shooting for* sales gains —*Women's Wear Daily*⟩ ⟨a definite plan to *shoot at* —*N.Y.Times*⟩ ⟨*shot* for immortality —Barnaby Conrad⟩ — **shoot off one's mouth** or **shoot off one's face** : to talk freely often abusively regardless of the effect — **shoot one's bolt** : to do all within one's power : exhaust one's capabilities and resources ⟨had *shot his bolt* and had no more to say⟩ — **shoot one's cuffs** also **shoot one's linen** : to pull one's shirt cuffs below those of one's coat esp. as a gesture of self-importance or uneasiness — **shoot one's way** : to gain (an objective) by war or threat of war or by resort to other forms of force or intimidation — **shoot straight** also **shoot square** : to speak and deal honestly — **shoot the chutes** : to slide down a steep incline on a special type of toboggan or boat — **shoot the moon** *slang Brit* : to move one's goods by night to avoid foreclosure or seizure for overdue rent — **shoot the red** *Brit, of a young turkey* : to develop adult plumage and the red carunculated skin about head and neck that is characteristic of adulthood — **shoot the works** **1** : to play for the highest stake permitted : venture all one's capital on one play **2** : to put forth all one's efforts : to do something without restraint

²shoot \"\ *n* -s [ME *schoyte*, fr. *shoten* to shoot] **1** : a sending out of new growth (as by sprouting, budding) or the new growth or amount of new growth sent out: as **a** (1) : the aerial part of a plant : a stem with its leaves and other appendages in contrast to the root (2) : a branch or portion of plant growth developed from a bud and not yet mature **b** : a growth from a main stem or stock : OFFSHOOT ⟨was an easily identifiable ~ on such a family tree —Helen Howe⟩ ⟨turnpike ... may someday send ~s south to the Dayton-Columbus area —Richard Thruelsen⟩ **c** : a budding horn or antler **d** : a similar formation of crystal **e** : the part of an oyster shell between two yearly rings **2 a** : an act of shooting (as with a bow or a firearm) : discharge of a missile: (1) : SHOT ⟨hoped to get a ~ at a deer⟩ ⟨a wild ~ into the treetops⟩ (2) : the firing of a missile or a group of missiles during a limited period of time esp. by artillery ⟨a tremendous predawn artillery ~ —*Time*⟩ ⟨many of our ~s have been wild —H.W.Baldwin⟩ **b** *obs* : the reach of a shot : shooting distance : RANGE **c** (1) : a hunting trip ⟨a duck ~⟩ ⟨autumn ~s over the rough bogs —James Reynolds⟩ ⟨invited some of his friends down for a winter ~ —*Newsweek*⟩ (2) : the game shot on a hunting trip (3) : the right to shoot game in a particular area (4) : a piece of usu. privately owned land used and often reserved and specially kept up for shooting game ⟨a 5000-acre ~⟩ ⟨a walk around the ~ with dogs at heel —*Bk. of the Dog*⟩ (5) : a group of persons taking part in a hunting trip : shooting party ⟨was invited to be one of a small ~⟩ **d** (1) : SHOOTING MATCH ⟨horseshoe pitching and bow-and-arrow and gun ~s —*Amer. Guide Series: Tenn.*⟩ ⟨a tournament ~⟩ ⟨a skeet ~⟩ ⟨celebration will get into action again with a muzzle-loading rifle ~ —Warren Weaver⟩; *specif* : a prescribed form of competition at archery ⟨a wand ~⟩ ⟨a clout ~⟩ (2) : a round of shots in a shooting match **e** : any of various acts or actions suggestive of the discharge of a missile from a bow or firearm: as (1) : a cast of a fishnet (2) : the action of shooting (as a scene, a subject) with a camera (3) : a launching of a rocket device or a guided missile esp. experimentally ⟨shooting timetable averaging one big ~ a month —Edwin Diamond⟩ ⟨has been ... to Las Cruces to see a rocket ~ —Bruce Bliven b.1916⟩ ⟨a moon ~⟩ **3 a** : a motion or movement resembling or suggesting that of something shot : a movement of rapid thrusting ⟨a quick outward ~ of his arms⟩ or the space or distance traversed by such a movement: as (1) : a sudden or rapid advance ⟨the lift, ~, and swing of the seas —W.H.Taylor⟩ ⟨a ~ of lightning crossed the horizon —Theodora Keogh⟩ (2) [perh. by folk etymology fr. F *chute* — more at CHUTE] : a rush of water down a steep incline ⟨a ~ of water down a sheer incline down which toboggans or flatbottomed boats slide usu. to continue across a body of water at the bottom⟩

shoot off **1** : to participate in a shoot-off **2** : to talk too freely or unwisely : shoot off one's mouth ⟨shot off in Spain about atomic bombs —Drew Pearson⟩

shoot-off \'=,=\ *n* -s [*shoot off*] : a final shoot (as in a trapshooting or rifle-shooting contest) to determine the winner among two or more competitors that have tied in prior contests

shoot out vt : to settle by shooting ⟨to talk things out, no matter how inconclusively, rather than to *shoot them out* —A.H.Vandenberg †1951⟩ — often used with *it* ⟨tried to *shoot it out* with the cops —Mickey Spillane⟩

shoot-out \'=,=\ *n* -s [*shoot out*] : an exchange of shots resorted to as a means of settling a dispute or determining superiority; *esp* : a fight to the finish between gunfighters

shoot-root ratio *n* : the quotient of the dry weight of the shoots produced during a given growth period divided by the dry weight of the roots esp. for crop plants

shoots *pres 3d sing of* SHOOT, *pl of* SHOOT

shoot-the-chutes \'=-'=\ *n pl but sing or pl in constr* : an amusement ride consisting of a steep incline down which toboggans or flatbottomed boats slide usu. to continue across a body of water at the bottom

shoot up vi **1** : to rise sharply ⟨*shoots up* forty-one stories unrelieved and formidable —*Amer. Guide Series: N.Y.City*⟩ ⟨prices *shot up*⟩ ⟨corn *shot up* to seventy-three cents a bushel — John Bird⟩ ⟨hope *shot up* within me —Kenneth Roberts⟩ ⟨*shot up* to colonel —Green Peyton⟩ **2** *slang* : to take an injection of a narcotic ~ *vt* : to shoot or shoot at esp. promiscuously ⟨*shot up* a crowd of striking miners —*Atlantic*⟩ ⟨met a Russian patrol and *shot them up* —R.H.Newman⟩; *esp* : to pass through (as a town) shooting recklessly in all directions ⟨one of the factional leaders ... *shot up* the town —F.L.Paxson⟩ ⟨*shoots up* the countryside periodically —Henry Cavendish⟩

¹shop \'shäp\ *n* -s *often attrib* [ME *shoppe*, fr. OE *sceoppa*; akin to MD *schoppe* booth, OHG *scopf* shed, OE *scypen, scepen, scipen* cowshed, and prob. to OE *scēaf* sheaf — more at SHEAF] **1 a** : a handicraft establishment : ATELIER, STUDIO ⟨three ~s exclusively devoted to the hand-hammering of gold leaf —*Amer. Guide Series: N.J.*⟩ **b** : a team of glassworkers usu. consisting of a gatherer, blower, and servitor : CHAIR ⟨one ... ~ of men worked at each glory hole — Freda Diamond⟩ **2 a** : a building or room stocked with merchandise for sale : STORE ⟨he ~s offer plenty of food and consumers' goods —Drew Middleton⟩ ⟨in a ~ or shoppe \"\ (1) : a small retail establishment or a department in a large one offering a specified line of goods or services ⟨gift ~⟩ ⟨sport ~⟩ ⟨beauty ~⟩ (2) : a small retail establishment concentrating on exclusive or top quality merchandise : a specialty shop **c** : something that resembles a shop ⟨Paris University was the great thinking-*shop*, the main European market of theologico-philosophical ideas —G.G.Coulton⟩ **d** (1) : a center of operations ⟨sets up ~ on the tailboard of a station wagon — J.S.Redding⟩ ⟨set up ~ in the area ... and handled over half a million refugees before the exodus was stopped —*New Yorker*⟩ (2) : functional activity ⟨sets up ~ as the local commissar —*Time*⟩ ⟨the city shuts up ~ for a week —Ray Duncan⟩ **e** : a source of supply ⟨he's come to the wrong ~ for that —Charles Dickens⟩ **3 a** : a commercial establishment for the making or repairing of goods or machinery ⟨blacksmith's ~⟩ ⟨machine ~⟩ ⟨casting ~s and rolling mills —*Amer. Guide Series: Conn.*⟩ ⟨at the San Francisco yard ... one steel ~ covers almost five acres —*All Hands*⟩ **b** *obs* : something that resembles a workshop ⟨the liver ... the ~ and source of the blood —James Howell⟩ **c** : a home workshop ⟨spends every spare minute in his ~ making model airplanes⟩ **d** (1) : a laboratory in an elementary or secondary school equipped for instruction in manual arts ⟨the general ~ may provide facilities for work in metals, electricity, and transportation —L.V.Newkirk⟩ (2) : the art or science of working with tools and machinery ⟨there will be one exception, perhaps ... one boy out of twenty who does badly in English and well in ~ —C.D.Green⟩ ⟨made bookends for his mother as a project in ~⟩ **4 a** : a business establishment : place of employment ⟨print ~⟩; *esp* : OFFICE ⟨it had been a battle to get them into the ~ and behind their typewriters or drawing boards before 9:30 —*Advertising Age*⟩ — compare UNION SHOP **b** : a gathering place : center of activity ⟨farmers filled the front of the ~, waiting against the bar —Sigerson Clifford⟩ **c** : JOB; *esp* : a theatrical engagement ⟨now he would be out of a ~ all through the autumn —Leonard Merrick⟩ **d** : SHOPTALK ⟨safety-conscious young men who could talk intelligent ~ with any engineer in Detroit —*Time*⟩ ⟨summarized a good deal of dead musical ~ in smaller type —*New Statesman & Nation*⟩ ⟨talk golf-shop over a weekend out of season —Andrew Lang⟩

²shop \"\ *vb* **shopped; shopping; shops** *vt* **1** *dial* **a** : ARREST, IMPRISON **b** : to inform on : BETRAY ⟨she had *shopped* him to the police —*Manchester Guardian Weekly*⟩ **2** *archaic* : to take to market : put on sale **3 a** (1) : to look over (available goods or services) with an eye to purchase ⟨~ our quality collection of ... mink capes —*advt*⟩ (2) : to examine the stock of (get back in time to ~ the curio stores along the bay front —*Holiday*⟩ (3) : BUY ⟨~ me a couple of those little ... figurines —Lawrence Durrell⟩ **b** : to scan (as a newspaper) for information about available goods or services ⟨make a habit of *shopping* the catalogs —F.F.Rockwell⟩ **4** : to send to a repair shop ⟨~ a railroad car for periodic maintenance⟩ ~ *vi* **1** : to examine goods and services with intent to buy ⟨~ for groceries⟩ ⟨~ for clothes⟩ — compare WINDOW-SHOP **b** : to probe a market in search of the best buy ⟨exhibitors were kept busy ... booking orders, despite the tendency to ~ on opening day —*Women's Wear Daily*⟩ — usu. used with *around* ⟨after you've decided on a brand, ~ around — there is more than one dealer for each make of car —*Motor Trend*⟩ **c** : to look something over ⟨went to his sage panel and *shopped* over it with his eyes —Joseph Whitehill⟩ **2** : to make a search : HUNT ⟨two very similar parties each *shopping* for winning ideas —F.L.Allen⟩ — often used with *around* ⟨students ... *shopping* around for something consoling to believe —Sidney Hook⟩

shop assistant *n, Brit* : a clerk in a retail store

shopboard \'=,=\ *n* **1** *archaic* : a counter or table for the display of merchandise **2** *archaic* : a table or platform on which a tailor sits to sew

shopbreaker \'=,==\ *n* : one that breaks into a shop or breaks out after having committed a crime therein

shopbreaking \'=,==\ *n* : the act of a shopbreaker

shop card *n* : a card posted by a union as evidence that the shop in which it is displayed is operating under a union contract

shop coat *n* : a priming coat applied in a manufacturing plant

shop committee *n* : a committee elected by workers in a plant to represent them in discussing grievances with the management

shop drawing *n* : WORKING DRAWING

shope papilloma \'shōp-\ also **shope's papilloma** *n, usu cap S* [after Richard E. *Shope* †1966 Am. physician] : a transmissible fibrous tumor of cottontail rabbits of which the transmitting agent is believed to be a specific nucleoprotein that behaves as a pathogenic virus in wild rabbits but an innocuous plasmagene in domestic ones — compare TUMOR VIRUS

shop-ful \'shäp,fùl\ *n* -s : as many as a shop will contain ⟨a ~ of customers⟩ ⟨pick your way through ~s of ... trinkets — *Mademoiselle*⟩

shopgirl \'=,=\ *n* : SALESWOMAN

shophar \'=,=\ *n* : var of SHOFAR

shopkeeper \'=,==\ *n* : the proprietor of a retail store : STOREKEEPER

shopkeeping \'=,==\ *n* -s : the occupation of a shopkeeper

shop-lift \'shäp,lift\ *vb* [back-formation fr. *shoplifter* and *shoplifting*] *vt* : to steal (goods that are on display) from a store ⟨bought a nickel sack of tobacco and ~ed a bag of flour —Russell Lord⟩ ~ *vi* : to steal displayed merchandise from a store ⟨diagnosis of the mental quirk that led them to ~ — Dwight Macdonald⟩

shop-lift-er \-tə(r)\ *n* [*shop* + *lifter*] : a thief that steals merchandise on display in stores

shop-lift-ing \-tiŋ, -tēŋ\ *n* -s [*shop* + *lifting*] : the stealing of goods on display in stores

shop lumber *n* : FACTORY LUMBER

shop-man \'shäpmən\ *n, pl* **shopmen 1** *chiefly Brit* : a clerk in a retail store **2** : a workman in a shop : a mechanic who assists with repairs

shopmark \'=,=\ *n* : HALLMARK 1c

shop mileage *n* : the mileage potentiality of a steam locomotive after undergoing general repairs

shop paper *n* : thin wrapping paper

shoppe *var of* SHOP

shopped *past of* SHOP

shop-per \'shäpə(r)\ *n* -s **1** : one that shops for goods or services esp. in a store : CUSTOMER, PURCHASER ⟨~s were three deep at the bargain counter⟩ ⟨~s, going from one community agency to another —H.A.Rusk⟩ **2** : one whose occupation is shopping as an agent for customers or for an employer — see COMPARISON SHOPPER, PERSONAL SHOPPER

shopping *n* -s [fr. gerund of ²shop] **1** : searching for, inspecting, or buying available goods or services ⟨~ not only was keener ... but selling was more satisfactory —*Retailing Daily*⟩ ⟨does her weekly ~ at the supermarket⟩ **2** : overhauling in a repair shop ⟨modern steam locomotives require ~ after 200,000 to 275,000 miles —*Scientific American*⟩

shopping center *n* : a concentration of retail stores and service establishments in a suburban area usu. with generous parking space and usu. planned to serve a community or neighborhood

shopping goods *n pl* : consumer goods that are usu. purchased only after the customer has compared price, quality, and style in more than one store — compare CONVENIENCE GOODS, SPECIALTY 2a(4)

shop right *n* : the right of an employer to use without payment of any royalty his employee's invention developed in the course of his employment

shop rivet *n* : a rivet driven in place in a shop — opposed to *field rivet*

shops *pl of* SHOP, *pres 3d sing of* SHOP

shop steward or **shop chairman** *n* : a union member elected by the employees in a shop, department, or plant to serve as the representative of the union and charged mainly with negotiating adjustment of grievances of employees with the employer usu. through the foreman — called also *committeeman*

shoptalk \'=,=\ *n* : the jargon or subject matter peculiar to an occupation or a special area of interest ⟨graduate students ... talking their highly specialized ~ —Dorothy Baker⟩

shopwalker \'=,==\ *n, Brit* : FLOORWALKER

shopwindow \'=,=-(,)=\ *n* [ME] **1** : a display window of a store ⟨new spring⟩ prints brighten winter ~s⟩ **2** : something that serves as a showcase ⟨film festivals ... recognized in recent years as a sort of international ~ —Arthur Knight⟩

shopwork \'=,=\ *n* : mechanical work (as carpentry, patternmaking, molding, machining, forging) done in a shop

shopworker \'=,==\ *n* : one who works in a shop

shopworn \'=,=\ *adj* **1** : faded, soiled, or otherwise impaired by remaining too long on display in a store ⟨sell ~ merchandise at a sizeable discount⟩ **2** : deprived of freshness or effectiveness by continuous use or exposure to detrimental influences : BEDRAGGLED, JADED ⟨half-melted glaciers of a

---

(center column)

b : to cause (as an airplane) to fall to earth by shooting ⟨four of our planes were *shot down* in flames⟩ ⟨shot his first plane *down* at the age of eighteen⟩

shoot-ee \(')shùd-'ē\ *n* -s [¹*shoot* + -*ee*] : one that is shot or shot at

shoot-er \'shùd-ə(r), -ütə-\ *n* -s [ME *sheter, shoter, shuter*, fr. *sheten, shoten, shuten* to shoot + -*er* — more at SHOOT] **1 a** : a person (as an archer, gunner, sharpshooter, hunter) that shoots a missile-discharging device esp. for sport ⟨a well-known skeet ~⟩ **b** *archaic* : a guard on a horse-drawn coach **c** : a person that sets off explosives esp. as an occupation : BLASTER; *specif* : one that sets off explosives in oil wells to start the flow of oil **2** : something that shoots: as **a** : SHOOTING STAR **b** : a plant of very rapid growth **c** : a cricket ball that on bouncing keeps very close to the ground **3** : something that is shot or is used in shooting: as **a** : a marble shot from the hand : TAW **b** : FIREARM; *esp* : a repeating pistol — used chiefly in combination ⟨six-shooter⟩ ⟨five-shooter⟩ **4** : one that casts or launches: as **a** : one that casts the net in seining **b** : one that moves or transfers something (as a commodity) by directing into or through a chute **c** : the player who is shooting the dice in a crap game **5** : a printer's shooting stick

shoo-ther \'shùth-ə(r)\ *dial Brit var of* SHOULDER

shoot-ing \'shùd-iŋ, -ùt-, -ēŋ\ *n* -s [ME *sheting, shoting, shuting*, fr. gerund of *sheten, shoten, shuten* to shoot] **1 a** : the act or practice or a performance of one that shoots ⟨expert rifle ~⟩ ⟨best in the league at foul ~⟩ **b** : a wounding or killing with a firearm ⟨a mysterious ~ at a summer resort⟩; *specif* : the killing of game with a gun : HUNTING **c** *chiefly Brit* (1) : the right to shoot game in a given area (2) : the area designated **2** : a sensation of darting pain **3 a** : sprouting or rapid growth (as of a plant); *also* : a shoot or cluster of shoots **b** : the period in the growth of various plants (as grasses and cereal grains) when the flowering and fruiting stem develops **4** : the issue of spicules in crystallization **5** : BLASTING

shooting board *n* **1** : a fixture used as a guide in planing or shooting the edge of a board when greater accuracy is required than can be obtained with the miter box — called also *miter shooting board* **2** : a metal table equipped with a plane for trimming, squaring, and sometimes beveling metal printing plates (as electrotypes)

shooting box or **shooting lodge** *n, chiefly Brit* : a cabin or small house in the country for use in the shooting season

shooting brake *n, Brit* : STATION WAGON

shooting fields *n* : a group of adjoining archery fields containing rovers at ranges of 140 to 360 yards

shooting fish *n* : ARCHERFISH

shooting gallery *n* **1** : a range usu. covered and equipped with targets for practice or competition with firearms **2** *slang* : a place where an injection of a narcotic can be bought

shooting glove *n* : an archer's glove for protecting the fingers in drawing the bow

shooting iron *n* : FIREARM; *esp* : HANDGUN

shooting line *n* : a line that an archer must straddle when shooting at a target

shooting match *n* **1** : a competitive test in shooting : competition in marksmanship **2** : a collection or aggregate of persons or things : LOT; *also* : the entire affair or matter : CONCERN, BUSINESS — used chiefly in the phrase *the whole shooting match* ⟨sick and tired of the whole *shooting match*⟩ ⟨rich enough to buy the whole *shooting match*⟩

shooting script *n* **1** : the final completely detailed version of a motion picture script in which scenes are grouped in the order most convenient for shooting and without regard to plot sequence **2** : the final version of a television script used in the production of a program

shooting star *n* **1** : a visual meteor appearing as a temporary streak of light in the night sky : FIREBALL **2** : a plant of the genus *Dodecatheon; esp* : a No. American perennial herb (*D. meadia*) with entire oblong leaves and showy umbellate, purple, pink or white flowers — called also *American cowslip, bird bills, cowslip*

shooting stick *n* **1** : a spiked stick with a top that opens into a seat typically used at a hunting stand or at races **2** : a short wooden or iron bar often with a notched end used by printers for loosening and tightening wooden quoins

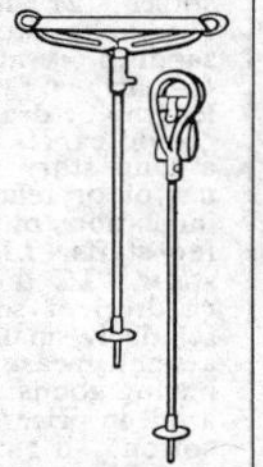

shooting tab *n* : a flat piece of leather worn on the fingers used in shooting a bow

shooting time *n* : the period of elongation of the flower stem of a plant (as a hardy bulb) that is being forced

shooting war *n* : a war or warfare involving military operations and actual conflict between armed forces — compare COLD WAR, WAR OF NERVES

shoot-ist \'shùd-əst\ *n* -s [¹*shoot* + -*ist*] : one who shoots; *esp* : MARKSMAN

shoot-man \'shùtmən\ *n, pl* **shootmen** [²*shoot* (chute) + *man*] **1** *Austral* : a workman who stacks sawn timber **2** *Brit* : a coal teemer

shoot moth *n* : any of several moths of the family Olethreutidae whose larvae burrow in developing shoots of conifers

shooting stick
1, open and closed

rather ~ kind, looking like . . . dirty corn snow —Christopher Rand⟩ ⟨this figure astonishes even a ~ newspaperman —G.W. Johnson⟩ ⟨the tendency to use ~ clichés —Helen Mustard⟩ **syn** see TRITE

shor \'shō(ə)r\ *n* -s [Russ, of Altaic origin; akin to Kalmuck & Mongolian *šor* salt, Turk *şûre* brackish soil] **:** a salt lake in Turkestan **:** SALINA

sho·ran \'shōr,an, 'lȯ,ran, ≈'≈\ *n* -s [*short range navigation*] **:** a system of short-range navigation in which two radar signals transmitted by an airplane are intercepted and rebroadcast to the airplane by two ground stations of known position with the time that the signals take for their round trips indicating the distance to each station and thus the position of the airplane

¹shore [alter. (influenced by *shorn*) of *sheared*] *chiefly dial past of* SHEAR

²shore \'shō(ə)r, 'shȯ(ə)r, -ōə, -ȯ(ə)\ *n* -s *often attrib* [ME *shor, shore,* fr. (assumed) OE *scor, scora* (attested only in place names); akin to Fris *skoarre* shoal, alluvial land outside a dike, MD *schor, schore, schorre* shoal, alluvial land, MLG *schōr* foreland, foreshore, *schār* shore, OHG *scorra* steep cliff, OE *sceran, scieran* to cut — more at SHEAR] **1 a :** the land bordering a usu. large body of water; *specif* **:** the land bordering the sea **:** COAST **b :** FORESHORE 2 **2 :** a boundary or the country or place that it bounds ⟨hold him accountable for difficulties beyond our ~s that he could do nothing about —Dorothy Fosdick⟩ **3 :** land as distinguished from the sea

³shore \"\ *vt* -ED/-ING/-S **1 :** to set ashore **:** LAND **2 :** to serve as a shore to **:** BORDER ⟨a sand river, half a mile wide, of golden-colored sand, *shored* by green trees —Ernest Hemingway⟩

⁴shore \'shäər, 'shō(ə)r\ *vt* -ED/-ING/-S [ME *schoren*] **1** *chiefly Scot* **:** to scold with a warning of punishment **:** THREATEN **2** *chiefly Scot* **:** OFFER

⁵shore \'shō(ə)r, 'shȯ(ə)r, -ōə, -ȯ(ə)\ *vt* -ED/-ING/-S [ME *shoren;* akin to Fris *skoarje* to support, brace up, MD *schooren,* ON *skortha* to support, brace up, ME *shore,* n. — more at ⁶SHORE] **1 :** to support by a shore **:** PROP — often used with *up* ⟨dug into hedgerows, which they *shored* up with timbers —*Infantry Jour.*⟩ **2 :** to give support to **:** BRACE ⟨a tunnel which is electrically lit and *shored* with concrete —Ralph Hammond-Innes⟩ — often used with *up* ⟨*shoring* up farm prices —W.S.White⟩

⁶shore \"\ *n* -s [ME; akin to Fris *skoarre* prop, stay, support, MD *schore, schoor,* MLG *schōre, schāre,* ON *skortha* prop, stay, support, and prob. to OE *sceran, scieran* to cut — more at SHEAR] **:** a prop (as a timber) placed against the side of a structure **:** a prop (as a beam) placed beneath something to prevent sinking or sagging

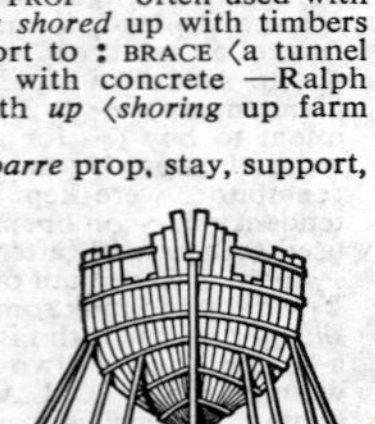
shores supporting a ship

⁷shore \'shäər, 'shō(ə)r\ *n* -s [prob. alter. of ³*sewer*] *dial chiefly Brit* **:** an open sewer or drainage ditch

sho·rea \'shōrēə\ *n, cap* [NL, after John *Shore,* Lord Teignmouth †1834 governor general of India] **:** a genus of Indo-Malayan timber trees (family Dipterocarpaceae) that are rich in resin, have flowers with twisted petals, a very short calyx tube, and sepals which become enlarged and winglike in fruit, and that include forms yielding valuable lumber — see RED LAUAN, SAL

shorebird \'≈,≈\ *n* **:** a bird of the suborder Charadrii (as a plover, snipe, or sandpiper) chiefly found along the seashore

shore boat *n* **:** a boat plying from shore to ship

shore cod *n* **:** cod caught off the New England coast — called also *native cod*

shore cover *n* **:** an extension of the coverage under a marine insurance policy to include risks to goods while in the custody of land transportation companies or while located at docks, wharves, or piers

shore crab *n* **:** any of numerous crabs living between the tide-marks: as **a :** GREEN CRAB **b :** a spider crab of the genus *Libinia* common along the eastern coast of the U.S. **c :** any of several grapsoid crabs of the western coast of No. America — usu. used with a qualifying term; see PURPLE SHORE CRAB, STRIPED SHORE CRAB, YELLOW SHORE CRAB **d :** a common So. Australian grapsoid crab (*Leptograpsus variegatus*)

shore current *n* **:** a current in water adjacent to a shoreline and often moving in a direction more or less parallel to it

shored *past of* SHORE

shore dinner *n* **:** a usu. full course dinner consisting mainly of seafood

shore drift *n* **:** material moving in or deposited by waves and currents along a shore

shoreface \'≈,≈\ *n* **:** the narrow zone seaward or lakeward from the low watermark in which sand and gravel are moved by waves and currents

shore fast *n* **:** any of the lines securing a vessel to a pier or the shore

shorefish \'≈,≈\ *n* **:** a sea fish living near shore; *broadly* **:** any marine fish not living in the depths of the ocean

shore fly *n* **:** a fly of the family Ephydridae

shoregoing \'≈,≈≈\ *adj* **1 :** living on shore **2 :** used for or suitable for going ashore

shore grape *n* **:** SEA GRAPE

shore grass *n* **:** SHOREWEED

shore hardness \'shō(ə)r-, 'shȯ(ə)r-\ *n, usu cap S* [after Albert F. *Shore,* 20th cent. Am. manufacturer] **:** hardness of metal or other material as measured by a Shore scleroscope

shore juniper *n* **:** a low mat-forming Japanese shrub (*Juniperus conferta*) used as an ornamental and having needlelike leaves in whorls of three

shoreland \'≈,≈\ *n* **:** land along a shore

shore lark *n* **:** HORNED LARK

shore leave *n* **:** a leave of absence to go on shore granted to a sailor or naval officer

shore·less \'≈ləs\ *adj* **1 :** having no shore ⟨the sea beats against a ~ cliff⟩ **2 :** of indefinite or unlimited extent **:** BOUNDLESS ⟨a great expanse of ~ water —H.L.Bridgman⟩

shoreline \'≈,≈\ *n* **:** the outline of the shore **:** the zone of contact of a body of water with the land

shore·man \'≈mən\ *n, pl* **shoremen 1 :** one who dwells on a shore or on shore **2 :** SHORESMAN

shore onion *n* **:** CHIVE

shore party *n* **:** a task organization formed to provide logistic support for a landing force during early phases of an amphibious military operation ⟨detailed a *shore party* to stockpile gasoline drums on the beachhead⟩

shore patrol *n* **1 :** an organized naval unit that has duties similar to those of the military police **2 :** a member of a shore patrol — abbr. *SP*

shore pine *n* **:** LODGEPOLE PINE a

shore pipit *n* **:** ROCK PIPIT

shore plate *n* **:** a blue plate consisting mainly of seafood

shor·er \'shōrə(r), 'shȯr-\ *n* -s [ME, fr. *shoren* to shore + *-er* — more at SHORE (to prop)] **:** one that shores up; *specif* **:** one that builds cribbing which will serve as a retaining wall to support the sides of an open excavation — called also *bracer, cribber*

shores *pl of* SHORE, *pres 3d sing of* SHORE

shore scleroscope *n, usu cap 1st S* [after Albert F. *Shore,* 20th cent. Am. manufacturer] **:** SCLEROSCOPE

¹shoreside \'≈,≈\ *n* [²*shore* + *side*] **:** the margin of the shore

²shoreside \"\ *adj* **:** ONSHORE

shores·man \'≈mən\ *n, pl* **shoresmen :** one who works on shore in connection with a maritime business or enterprise (as a fishery)

shore snipe *n* **1 :** SANDPIPER **2 :** SHOREBIRD

shore spurge *n* **:** SEASIDE SPURGE

shore terrace *n* **:** a coastal terrace that is cut in rock or built up of gravel or sand

¹shore·ward \'shō(ə)r,ward, 'shȯ(ə)-\ *or* **shore·wards** \-dz\ *adv* [²*shore* + *-ward, -wards*] **:** toward the shore

²shoreward \"\ *adj* **:** facing or moving toward the shore

shoreweed \'≈,≈\ *n* **:** an aquatic weed (*Littorella uniflora*) of the family Plantaginaceae that has few flowered scapes and flowers with a one-celled ovary — called also *plantain shoreweed*

shor·ey·er \'shō,rī(ə)r\ *n* -s [perh. fr. ²*shore* + *eyer,* alter. of *eider*] **:** EIDER

shoring *n* -s [fr. gerund of ⁵*shore*] **1 :** the act of supporting or strengthening with or as if with a prop **2 :** a system or group of shores

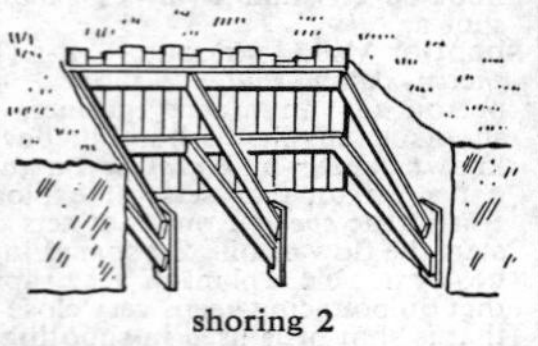
shoring 2

shorl *var of* SCHORL

¹shorn *past part of* SHEAR

²shorn *n* -s [¹*shorn*] **:** a market sheep offered for sale after shearing

shors *pl of* SHOR

¹short \'shȯ(ə)r|t, -ȯ(ə)|, *usu* |d.+V\ *adj* -ER/-EST [ME *short, shert,* fr. OE *scort, sceort;* akin to OHG *scurz* short, ON *skort, skortr* lack, *skorta* to be lacking, *skera* to cut — more at SHEAR] **1 a :** having little length **:** not extending far from end to end ⟨the big guns pointed ~, ugly snouts seaward —Bill Davidson⟩ ⟨~ pouting lips —William Empson⟩ **b :** having little height **:** not tall **:** LOW ⟨a ~ man⟩ ⟨of ~ stature⟩ ⟨a ~ smokestack⟩ **2 a :** not extended in time **:** of brief duration **:** lasting a little while only ⟨a diversion which brought him ~ periods of physical peace —Louis Bromfield⟩ ⟨a ~ life⟩ ⟨a ~ season⟩ **b :** not retentive for more than a brief period ⟨a ~ memory⟩ **c :** EXPEDITIOUS, QUICK ⟨wished to make ~ work of the business —H.E. Scudder⟩ **d :** seeming to pass quickly ⟨in the space of a few ~ years made terrifying headway —R.K.Carr⟩ **e :** allowing or requiring little time for preparation or action ⟨~ notice⟩ **3 a** *of a speech sound* **:** having a relatively short duration ⟨the vowel of *dock* is ~*er* than the vowel of *dark* when the *r* is not pronounced⟩ **b :** indicating the member of a pair of similarly spelled vowel or partly vowel sounds that is descended from a durationally short vowel but that now is not durationally short or does not have duration as its chief distinguishing feature ⟨~ *a* in *fat*⟩ ⟨~ *e* in *equity*⟩ ⟨~ *i* in *sin*⟩ ⟨~ *o* in *odd*⟩ ⟨~ *u* in *fuss*⟩ **c** (1) *of a syllable in Greek or Latin verse* **:** of relatively brief duration (2) *of a syllable in English verse* **:** UNSTRESSED **4 a :** limited in vision or range ⟨the windows on to the outer world were few, and the view from them was ~ and uninviting —R.W.Southern⟩ **b :** limited in distance **:** not covering much ground or space ⟨a ~ walk⟩ ⟨a ~ trip⟩ ⟨a ~ flight⟩ **c** *archaic* **:** traveling only a few miles — used of a train or train passenger **5 a :** not coming up to a measure, standard, or requirement ⟨eliminate adulteration, ~ weights and measures —V.S.Alanne⟩ **:** not sufficient in quantity **:** INADEQUATE, INSUFFICIENT, SCANTY ⟨stockpile critical materials in ~ supply —J.M.Minifie⟩ ⟨on ~ rations then, trying to live on a dollar a day —R.B. Gehman⟩ **b :** not extending, reaching, or traveling far enough ⟨the coat is ~ on him⟩ ⟨the page is two lines ~⟩ ⟨his throw was ~⟩ **c :** having an insufficient supply **:** lacking a needed article or amount — usu. used with *of* or *in* ⟨~ of cash at the end of the month⟩ ⟨five dollars ~ in his accounts⟩ ⟨somebody might marry her and leave him ~ a cook —H.G.Evarts⟩ **d :** enduring privation **:** doing without ⟨local settler families . . . who may be temporarily ~ as a result of a poor harvest or bad planning —J.B.Watson⟩ **e :** inherently or basically weak in — used with *on* ⟨long on ambition but ~ on brains⟩ ⟨long on ideas but ~ on knowledge⟩ **6 a :** ABRUPT, CURT, UNCEREMONIOUS ⟨the service is rendered in a blunt, impersonal, irritated, or ~ manner —Lou Smyth⟩ ⟨was less ~ with her at such moments than usual —David Walden⟩ **b :** quick to respond to provocation **:** easily aroused ⟨tempers are ~ in the morning —W.S.Gilbert⟩ **7 a :** recurring quickly in succession — used of recurrent bodily phenomena (as breaths or pulse beats) **b :** having waves that break in quick succession **:** CHOPPY ⟨their swift currents and steep, ~ seas —*Amer. Guide Series: Mass.*⟩ **8 a** *archaic* **:** not distant in time **:** near at hand **b :** payable at an early date **9 a :** easily broken **:** crumbling readily (as from shortening content) **:** CRISP, FRIABLE ⟨~ pastry⟩ **b** (1) *of metal* **:** brittle under certain conditions — compare COLD-SHORT, HOT-SHORT, RED-SHORT (2) **:** lacking tensile strength (as through desiccation) ⟨~ lumber stock⟩ (3) **:** difficult to spread because of excess sanding ⟨~ mortar⟩ (4) **:** defective in tenacity or plasticity ⟨~ clay⟩ **c :** not flowing readily **:** STICKY ⟨~ ink⟩ **10 a :** not lengthy or drawn out in content or style **:** CONCISE, SUCCINCT ⟨could express my faith in ~*er* terms —John Adams⟩ ⟨make a long story ~⟩ **b :** ABBREVIATED ⟨*doc* is ~ for *doctor*⟩ **c :** of or relating to a musical score having the notes and indications of essential parts of a full score condensed onto a few staffs **11 :** consisting of or containing chopped or cut straw **12 a :** consisting of undiluted liquor **:** STRAIGHT ⟨a drop of something ~⟩ **b** *of a beverage* **:** served in a relatively small glass usu. of five ounces or less **:** constituting a small measure ⟨a ~ beer⟩ ⟨a ~ rum punch⟩ **13 a :** not having goods or property that one has sold in anticipation of a fall in prices — usu. used with *of* or *in* ⟨~ of wheat⟩ ⟨~ in cotton⟩ **b :** consisting of, relating to or involving a sale of securities, commodities, or foreign exchange that the seller does not possess or has not contracted for at the time of the sale ⟨a ~ sale⟩ ⟨~ contracts⟩ **14 :** having or containing fewer than the average number of cards in a particular suit; *specif* **:** having or containing fewer than three cards in a particular suit in bridge **15 a :** pitched at a spot too near the bowling end to be considered of good length — used of a bowled ball in cricket **b :** placed relatively close to the batsman's wicket — used of a fielder or fielding position ⟨~ slip⟩ ⟨~ mid on⟩ **syn** see BRIEF — **in short order** *adv* **:** with dispatch **:** EXPEDITIOUSLY ⟨disposed of the piles of correspondence *in short order*⟩

²short \"\ *adv* -ER/-EST [ME, fr. *short,* adj.] **1 :** in a curt manner ⟨always going about in his apron and talking ~ with everyone —W.D.Steele⟩ **2 :** for or during a brief time — used in combination ⟨*short-lasting*⟩ ⟨*short-living*⟩ **3 :** TIGHTLY ⟨caught him up ~ by his coat lapels —Barnaby Conrad⟩ **4 :** at a disadvantage **:** ABACK, UNAWARES ⟨caught ~⟩ ⟨taken ~⟩ **5 :** so as to interrupt ⟨took him up ~ before he could continue⟩ **6 :** ABRUPTLY, SUDDENLY ⟨would halt ~, order everybody to be still, and insist that she had heard something —H.L.Davis⟩ **7 :** at some point or distance before a goal or limit aimed at or approached ⟨his throw fell five yards ~⟩ ⟨the shells dropped ~⟩ **8 :** clean across ⟨the axle was snapped ~⟩ **9 :** by or as if by a short sale — compare SELL SHORT

³short \"\ *n* -s [¹*short*] **1 :** the sum and substance **:** UPSHOT — usu. used with *the* ⟨the ~ of it is, in my judgment —A.E. Stevenson b.1900⟩ **2 a :** a short musical note **b :** a short syllable **c :** a short sound or signal (as in Morse code) ⟨the buzzer sounded in the hall: three longs and a ~ —Harold Brodkey⟩ **3 shorts** *pl* **a :** a by-product of wheat milling that includes the germ, fine bran, and a small amount of flour **b :** refuse, clippings, or trimmings, discarded in various manufacturing processes **4 :** straight liquor **5 shorts** *pl* **a :** SMALLCLOTHES 1 **b :** knee-length or less than knee-length trousers made in various styles for informal wear or sportswear **c :** short drawers **6 a :** one who purchases or operates on the short side of the market — compare ¹BEAR 3b **b shorts** *pl* **:** short-term bonds **7 shorts** *pl* **:** items that are lacking to make up a quantity or total **:** DEFICIENCIES; *specif* **:** the copies of different printed sheets needed to complete an imperfect edition **8 :** something of less than a full or required length: as **a shorts** *pl* **:** lumber of less than standard length **b :** a fish or lobster of less than the length required for legal catching **c :** a clothing size for short men **d :** one of the smaller standard firearm cartridges **e :** a short often documentary or educational film shown with a full-length feature or as part of a program of short films **f :** a brief news story or feature item in a newspaper or periodical **9 :** something that falls short; *specif* **:** a shot that strikes or bursts short of the target **10 :** SHORT CIRCUIT **11 a :** SHORTSTOP ⟨plays a fine ~⟩ **b :** SHORT FIELD ⟨hit the ball to deep ~⟩ — **for short** *adv* **:** by way of abbreviation — **in short** *adv* **1 :** by way of summary **:** in brief **:** BRIEFLY **2 :** in an inner column in a statement of figures in accounting — **the short and long** *or* **the short and the long :** the whole story **:** the long and short **:** GIST

⁴short \"\ *vt* -ED/-ING/-S [¹*short*] **1 :** to supply with less than is customary, needed, or expected ⟨~*ed* him on his favorite hog jowl and turnip greens —*Time*⟩ **2 :** SHORTCHANGE, CHEAT ⟨slugged a . . . weighman who was ~*ing* him at the scales —*Irish Digest*⟩ **3 :** SHORT-CIRCUIT

short account *n* **1 :** the account of a short seller **2 :** the total of open short sales in a given subject of trade or in the market as a whole

short·age \'shȯr|d·|ij, -ȯ(ə)|, |t|, |ēj\ *n* -s **:** a deficiency in an amount required **:** DEFICIT ⟨a ~ in petty cash⟩ ⟨a ~ of trained teachers⟩ ⟨a ~ of oil⟩ — opposed to *overage*

short and *n* **:** AMPERSAND

short and sweet *adj* **:** brief and to the point

short appoggiatura *n* **:** a grace note performed very quickly, played either on the beat or before the beat, and symbolized by a small note with a stroke through the stem — see APPOGGIATURA illustration

short arm *n* **:** HANDGUN

short arm inspection *also* **short arm** *n* **:** an examination of the penis for venereal disease or other abnormal condition

short ballot *n* **:** a ballot limiting the number of elective offices to the most important legislative and executive posts and leaving minor positions to be filled by appointment — compare BLANKET BALLOT

short bill *n* **:** a bill of exchange maturing in 30 days or less and sometimes in ten days or less — compare LONG BILL

short-billed marsh wren \'≈,≈-\ *n* **:** a marsh wren (*Cistothorus stellaris*) of No. America that resembles the long-billed marsh wren but is smaller, has a bill much shorter than its head, and has fine whitish streaks along its upper parts

shortbread \'≈,≈\ *n* **:** a thick cookie traditionally made of flour, a small amount of sugar, and a proportionately large amount of butter or other shortening

short-breathed \'≈'≈\ *adj* **1 :** breathing with quick shallow respirations **2 :** of brief duration or limited breadth ⟨the poems of the later years being obviously more fragmentary and *short-breathed* —Irving Howe⟩

shortcake \'≈,≈\ *n* **1 :** a cake rich in shortening; *specif* **:** a crisp and often unsweetened biscuit, cookie, or teacake with the texture of pastry **2 a :** a dessert made of very short baking-powder-biscuit dough typically cooked in a large cake and served hot after being split, buttered, and spread with sweetened esp. fresh fruit (as strawberries or peaches) **b :** a sweet but not necessarily short cake spread with fruit and served cold **3 :** a luncheon dish consisting of a rich biscuit split and covered with a meat mixture (as chicken or turkey)

short change *n* **:** an amount of change less than the amount due

shortchange \(')≈'≈\ *vt* [*short change*] **1 :** to give less than the correct amount of change to ⟨charged that the cashier had *shortchanged* him⟩ **2 :** to deprive of something due or to give less than the due amount of to **:** CHEAT ⟨most people ~ themselves on the good things of life —*House Beautiful*⟩

short-change \'≈'≈\ *adj* [*short change*] **:** of or relating to cheating ⟨a *short-change* artist⟩ ⟨a *short-change* racket⟩

shortchanger \(')≈'≈≈\ *n* **:** one that shortchanges

short circuit *n* **1 :** a conductor of comparatively low resistance that is accidentally or intentionally connected between points on a circuit between which the resistance is normally much greater; *also* **:** direct contact between such points that makes the resistance zero **2 :** something that interrupts, cuts off, or bypasses ⟨the extent to which *short circuits* may be developing in the system of internal check —*Jour. of Accountancy*⟩; *specif* **:** an artificial communication established surgically between two parts (as of the alimentary canal) to enable the contents to pass around an intervening obstruction

short-circuit \(')≈'≈≈\ *vt* [*short circuit*] **1 :** to apply a short circuit to or establish a short circuit in **2 a :** to jump over or detour around **:** BYPASS ⟨had to *short-circuit* the amending procedure and work through ordinary legislative enactment —C.H.Driver⟩ ⟨*short-circuiting* the judgment and appealing directly to the emotions —Louise Young⟩ **b :** to create (a short circuit) by surgery **3 :** to interfere with or put out of action **:** FRUSTRATE, IMPEDE ⟨nothing can more quickly *short-circuit* friendly feelings —F.M.Keesing⟩ ⟨would *short-circuit* the country's rapid development —Welles Hangen⟩ **~** *vi* **:** to become shunted by a short circuit

short-circuit·er \"+ə(r)\ *n* **:** something that short-circuits; *specif* **:** a device operated by centrifugal force that actuates the mechanism which short-circuits the commutator bars or raises the brushes from the commutator in some forms of single-phase motors

shortclothes \'≈,≈\ *n pl* **:** SMALLCLOTHES 1

shortcoat \'≈,≈\ *vt* [fr. the phrase *short coat*] **:** to put (a child) into its first smallclothes ⟨think o' that boy, ~*ed* but yesterday —Eden Phillpotts⟩

shortcoming \(')≈'≈≈\ *n* [¹*short* + *coming* (after the phrase *come short*)] **:** the condition or fact of failing to reach an expected or required standard of character or performance **:** DEFECT, IMPERFECTION ⟨guilt feeling may exist from a sense of personal ~ —R.L.Jenkins⟩ ⟨management ~s in one form or another cause most business failures —*Nation's Business*⟩

short corner *n* **:** PENALTY CORNER

short count *n, often cap S&C* **:** a system of dating in the Maya calendar according to the current katun or series of katuns — compare LONG COUNT

short covering *n* **:** buying in securities or other property to terminate or close out a short sale

¹shortcut \'≈,≈\ *n* [¹*short* + *cut* (easy passage)] **1 :** a route more direct or more quickly traveled than the one ordinarily taken **2 :** a method of doing or achieving something more directly and quickly than by ordinary procedure ⟨the ~s which we have worked out to make the work simple and easy —Tom Marvel⟩ ⟨no panaceas or ~s to peace or stability —S.K.Padover⟩ **3** *usu* **short cut :** something cut into short parts; *specif* **:** tobacco cut in short bits instead of in long shreds

²shortcut \"\ *adj* [²*short* + *cut,* past part. of *cut*] **1** *usu* **short-cut** \'≈'≈\ **:** cut so as to be short **2 :** affording or constituting a shortcut

short-cut \'≈,≈\ *vb* [¹*shortcut*] *vt* **:** to shorten by use of a short-cut **~** *vi* **:** to take or use a shortcut

short-cycled *also* **short-cycle** \'≈'≈≈\ *adj* **:** lacking an aecial or uredinial stage or both and sometimes also a pycnial ⟨*short-cycled* rusts⟩ — opposed to *long-cycled*

short-dated \'≈'≈≈\ *adj* **:** having little time to run after date — used of a bill or note

short-day \'≈'≈\ *adj* **:** responding to a short photoperiod — used of a plant

short deck *n* **:** a pack of cards having fewer than the prescribed number

short-eared hare \'≈,≈-\ *n* **:** a hare (*Nesolagus netscheri*) of Sumatra that has short ears and fur and whose color shades from grayish yellow on the forparts to mahogany-brown on the haunches with black bands on back, sides, face, and hind feet

short-eared harvest mouse *n* **:** a common harvest mouse (*Reithrodontomys humilis*) of eastern U. S.

short-eared owl *n* **:** a medium-sized nearly cosmopolitan owl (*Asio flammeus*) that frequents seacoasts and grassy marshes, commonly nests on the ground, is dark brown above and buff below streaked with brown, and has very short ear tufts

shorted *past of* SHORT

short·en \'shȯrtᵊn, -ȯ(ə)tᵊn\ *vb* **shortened; shortened; shortening** \-t(ə)niŋ\ **shortens** [¹*short* + *-en*] *vt* **1 a :** to make short or shorter **:** reduce the length or duration of ⟨~ the roads that lead to a profession —J.B.Conant⟩ ⟨voted to ~ the firm name —*Wall Street Jour.*⟩ ⟨~ a dangerous and costly war —D.H.McLachlan⟩ **b :** to cause to seem short ⟨have tried to ~ or to enliven the tedium of waiting —C.E. Montague⟩ ⟨many a long night he ~*ed* for us with his stories and songs —Michael O'Reilly⟩ **c :** to cut down in amount or extent **:** LESSEN ⟨found their pleasures ~*ed* by emptiness of purse —J.A.Froude⟩ **d :** to cut back (a shoot) in pruning **2 a :** to reduce in power or efficiency ⟨is my hand ~*ed,* that it cannot redeem —Isa 50:2 (RSV)⟩ **b** *obs* **:** to deprive of effect ⟨to be known ~*s* my made intent —Shak.⟩ **c :** to prevent from securing **3 :** to get a closer grip on **:** grasp nearer the middle ⟨~*ed* his bat⟩ **4 :** to put into smallclothes **5 :** to make crumbly ⟨~ pastry with butter⟩ **~** *vi* **1 :** to become short or shorter ⟨when lazy summer days begin to cool and ~ —Hugh Cave⟩ **2** *of betting odds* **:** DECREASE, LOWER

⟨looked quickly at the betting . . . six to one, ~ing to eleven to two —Robert Westerby⟩
syn CURTAIL, ABBREVIATE, ABRIDGE, RETRENCH: these verbs have in common the sense of to reduce in extent, esp. by cutting. SHORTEN commonly implies reduction in length or duration ⟨*shorten* a rope⟩ ⟨*shorten* a war⟩ ⟨*shorten* the pain by administering drugs⟩ ⟨*shorten* a life⟩ CURTAIL generally adds to SHORTEN the idea of docking, a cutting that in some way deprives of completeness ⟨emergency orders drastically *curtailing* the use of fuel —*Current Biog.*⟩ ⟨the country editor *curtailed* his contributions on large issues —*Amer. Guide Series: Minn.*⟩ ABBREVIATE implies a making shorter usually by omitting some part or cutting off some normally following part; thus, one *abbreviates* a word or phrase by cutting out or cutting off letters in such a way that the remaining part stands for the whole ⟨*abbreviate* the name *Shakespeare* to *Shak.*⟩ ⟨a . . . man of great physical strength and energy, though of *abbreviated* intelligence —W.L.Shirer⟩ ABRIDGE, sometimes interchangeable with SHORTEN and CURTAIL ⟨*abridge* visiting hours at the hospital during the epidemic⟩ ⟨*abridge* freedom of speech⟩ generally suggests reduction in extent, compass, or scope but usu. implies the retention of the essential elements and a relative completeness in the result ⟨so fearful of being detected . . . that I must *abridge* this narrative —Charles Dickens⟩ ⟨*abridge* the large volume so that it can be read in one evening⟩ RETRENCH puts stress upon reduction in extent or costs of something felt to be in excess ⟨must *retrench* on the expenses of her household —Edith Sitwell⟩ ⟨in keeping with the austerity drive the school administration *retrenched* on our coal supply —Maria Yen⟩ — **shorten sail** : to reduce the extent of sail (as by reefing or furling)

short end *n* **1** : the inferior or losing end **2** : the side receiving odds in a bet
shorten down *vi* : to shorten sail ⟨the wind came ripping out of the west, and for the first time we *shortened down* to less than working canvas —A.F.Loomis⟩
short·en·er \-t(ᵊ)nə(r)\ *n* -s : one that shortens
shorten in *vt* **1** : to take in the slack of (a rope) **2** : to heave in (a cable)
shortening *n* -s [fr. gerund of *shorten*] **1** : the action or process of making or becoming short; *specif* : the dropping of the latter part of a word so as to produce a new and shorter word of the same meaning **2** : an edible fat used to shorten baked goods (as pastry or cookies)
shorter *comparative of* SHORT
short ess *var of* SHORT S
shortest *superlative of* SHORT
shortfall \'⸗,⸗\ *n* [¹*short* + *fall* (after the phrase *fall short*)] : the act or an instance of falling short or the amount by which something falls short : DEFICIT, SHORTAGE ⟨standing useless because of a ~ in traversing mechanisms —*Time*⟩ ⟨the ~ will amount to $4 to $5 billion —*Newsweek*⟩
short-fed \'⸗'⸗\ *adj, of cattle* : kept on a fattening ration for a period of three months or less — compare LONG-FED
short field *n* : the area of a baseball infield to the left of second base
short-focus lens \'⸗,⸗⸗-\ *n* : a camera lens having a focal length substantially less than that of the lens normally supplied with a particular type of camera
short game *n* **1** : the phase of golf in which accuracy of direction and control of limited distance (as in approach play or putting) are factors of first importance — compare LONG GAME **2** : a card game in which not all the cards are dealt
short gown *n* [ME *short goun*] **1** : NIGHTGOWN **2** : a short-skirted dress
short grain *adj* : having the machine direction running the short way of the sheet ⟨*short grain* paper⟩
short-grained \'⸗'⸗\ *adj* : having a short fiber — used chiefly of wood and bone
shortgrass \'⸗,⸗\ *n* : any of various grasses that are characterized by short stature and marked drought tolerance, form the dominant feature of dry upland plains (as those just east of the Rocky mountains), and include important range grasses of such lands — compare MIDGRASS, TALLGRASS
shorthair \'⸗,⸗\ *also* **short-haired cat** \'⸗,⸗-\ *n* : a domestic cat with a relatively short close coat in which the guard hairs are not notably elongated — compare LONG HAIR
¹**shorthand** \'⸗,⸗\ *n* [¹*short* + *hand*] **1** : a method of writing rapidly by substituting characters, abbreviations, or symbols for letters, words, or phrases : STENOGRAPHY — compare LONGHAND **2** : a system or instance of rapid or abbreviated communication or notation ⟨could converse in a joking verbal ~, which meant little to anyone else —Robert Graves⟩ ⟨a master of visual ~ . . . could capture in a few light strokes the elusive passing moment —*Fortnight*⟩
²**shorthand** \"\ *adj* **1 a** : using shorthand ⟨a ~ reporter⟩ **b** : written in shorthand ⟨a ~ report⟩ **2** : of, relating to, or involving an abbreviated or symbolic method of communication or expression ⟨one of those rare watercolorists who work from nature in quick ~ notes —L.S.Reiss⟩ ⟨this ~ historical chronicle —Nancy Ross⟩ **3** : resembling shorthand : ABRIDGED, CONDENSED ⟨the committee majority type of ~ mathematics —R.M.Blough⟩
shorthanded \'⸗'⸗⸗\ *adj* **1** : short of the regular or necessary number of people : inadequately staffed : UNDERMANNED ⟨passed shells to the ~ mortar crew —*Time*⟩ **2** : having short hands — **short·hand·ed·ness** *n* -ES
short haul *n* **1** : transportation of goods or passengers for a short distance **2** : a comparatively brief period of time — used with *the* ⟨to achieve this, Americans must work for the long pull — not the *short haul* —Earl Bunting⟩
short-haul \'⸗'⸗\ *adj* [*short haul*] **1** : traveling or involving a short distance ⟨a *short-haul* bus⟩ ⟨*short-haul* flights⟩ **2** : of, relating to, or lasting for a short period ⟨*short-haul* attractions such as the glitter of a fraternity —C.E.Lovejoy⟩
shorthead \'⸗,⸗\ *n* : a brachycephalic individual : ROUNDHEAD
short head *n, Brit* : a margin of victory in a horse race of less than the length of a horse's head
short-headed \'⸗'⸗⸗\ *adj* : BRACHYCEPHALIC — **short-head·ed·ness** *n* -ES
shorthorn \'⸗,⸗\ *n* **1** *usu cap* : a breed of red, roan, or white beef cattle originating in the north of England and including good milk-producing strains from which the Milking Shorthorn breed has been evolved — called also *Durham* **2** -s *often cap* **a** : an animal of the Shorthorn breed **b** : any of various small African cattle with short horns and a high resistance to trypanosome infections **3** -s *slang* : TENDERFOOT
short-horned buffalo \'⸗,⸗-\ *n* : a small reddish or blackish West African buffalo that is a variety of the Cape buffalo distinguished by short upwardly curved horns and fringed ears
short-horned grasshopper *n* : a grasshopper of the family Acrididae
short hundredweight *n* : HUNDREDWEIGHT a — see MEASURE table
shor·tia \'shȯ(r)d·ēə\ *n* [NL, fr. Charles Wilkins *Short* †1863 Am. physician and botanist + NL *-ia*] **1** *cap* : a genus of perennial herbs (family Diapensiaceae) having smooth coriaceous basal leaves and long-stalked showy white and solitary flowers with campanulate corollas — see OCONEE BELLS **2** -s : any plant of the genus *Shortia*
shortie *var of* SHORTY
shorting *pres part of* SHORT
short interest *n* : the sum of securities or commodities sold short as of a given date — called also *short position*
short iron *n* **1** : a golf iron (as a No. 7, No. 8, or No. 9 iron) that has a short shaft and relatively great loft and is used for hitting a ball near the green **2** : a shot or stroke made with a short iron — compare LONG IRON
short·ish \'shȯrd·ish\ *adj* : somewhat short
short·ite \'shȯrd·,īt\ *n* -s [Maxwell N. *Short* †1952 Am. mineralogist + E *-ite*] : a mineral $Na_2Ca_2(CO_3)_3$ consisting of a carbonate of sodium and calcium
short jenny *n* : a losing hazard in English billiards in which the ball is played in a middle pocket of the table — compare LONG JENNY
short-jointed \'⸗'⸗⸗\ *adj* : having short intervals between the joints
short-laid \'⸗'⸗\ *adj* : HARD-LAID
shortleaf pine \'⸗,⸗-\ *n* **1** *also* **shortleaf yellow pine** **a** : a pine (*Pinus echinata*) of the southern U. S. that has short flexible leaves and cinnamon-colored bark **b** : the yellow wood of the shortleaf pine **2** : LOBLOLLY PINE 1
short-leaved pine \'⸗,⸗-\ *n* : SHORTLEAF PINE
short leet *n, Scot* : a select list; *esp* : a limited list of candidates submitted to an elective or appointive authority
short leg *n* : a fielding position in cricket on the leg side relatively close to the batsman; *also* : a player fielding in this position — compare LONG LEG; see CRICKET illustration
short line *n* **1** : the railroad or combination of railroads having the shortest mileage between two points **2** : a transportation system (as a railroad or bus line) operating over a relatively short distance
short-lived \'⸗'līvd, -livd\ *adj* [²*short* + *lived*] **1** : having a short life or a relatively short life ⟨a *short-lived* individual⟩ ⟨men are *short-lived* in comparison with women⟩ **2** : lasting only a short time ⟨*short-lived* joy⟩ ⟨short-lived interest⟩ **syn** see TRANSIENT
short-lived·ness *n* -ES : the quality or state of being short-lived
short loin *n* : the portion of a hindquarter of beef which starts behind the ribs and from which club, T-bone, and porterhouse steaks are cut — see BEEF illustration
short·ly *adv* [ME, fr. OE *scortlīce*, fr. *scortlic* brief, fr. *scort* short + *-lic* -ly — more at SHORT] **1 a** : in a few words : BRIEFLY ⟨may be described ~⟩ ⟨to put it ~⟩ **b** : in an abrupt manner : CURTLY, HARSHLY ⟨said ~ that they looked all right, his antagonism beginning to rise —Archibald Marshall⟩ **2 a** : in a short time : PRESENTLY, SOON ⟨the two concluding volumes which will appear ~ —P.H.Douglas⟩ **b** : at a short interval of time ⟨the glacial action which ~ preceded man's arrival in America —R.W.Murray⟩ ⟨~ before⟩ ⟨~ after⟩ **c** : for a short time **3** : at or for no great distance : not far ⟨~ beyond this site —*Amer. Guide Series: Vt.*⟩ ⟨an apron that fell from her waist to ~ below her knees —*Newsweek*⟩
short mark *n* : BREVE 2a
short meter *n* **1** *also* **short measure** : a quatrain of which the first, second, and fourth lines are in iambic trimeter and the third in iambic tetrameter : a poulter's measure written as a quatrain — abbr. *S.M.* **2 a** : quick work ⟨make *short meter* of the job⟩ **b** : a short time ⟨finished the job in *short meter*⟩
short-natured \'⸗'⸗⸗\ *adj, of glass* : having a short temperature range during which easy working or shaping is possible : setting quickly — contrasted with *good-natured*
short·ness *n* -ES [ME *shortnesse*, fr. *short* + *-nesse* -ness] **1** : the quality or state of being short in length, distance, or duration : BREVITY ⟨the ~ of his fingers⟩ ⟨the ~ of the trip⟩ ⟨the ~ of the days in winter⟩ **2 a** *obs* : CONCISENESS ⟨your plainness and your ~ please me well —Shak.⟩ **b** : ABRUPTNESS, CURTNESS ⟨our anger changed to glumness and ~ with each other —A.R.Matthews⟩ **3** : defectiveness of range or vision ⟨the ~ of his sight⟩ **4** *of metals* : BRITTLENESS **5** : DEFICIENCY, SCANTINESS ⟨the ~ of provisions⟩ ⟨hampered by a ~ of money⟩
short-nosed cattle louse \'⸗,⸗-\ *n* : a large bluish broad-bodied and short-headed sucking louse (*Haematopinus eurysternus*) that attacks domestic cattle
shortnose gar *also* **short-nosed gar** *or* **short-nosed garfish** \'⸗,⸗-\ *n* : a gar of the family Lepisosteidae
short oat *n* : an oat (*Avena brevis*) cultivated in mountainous parts of Europe for its grain
short octave *n* : an incomplete lowest octave in an organ or keyboard musical instrument having certain seldom used tones omitted and tuned according to those tones most frequently used — called also *broken octave*
short of *prep* **1** : not reaching to : on this side of : up to ⟨possesses a meticulous memory just *short of* total recall —Robert Cantwell⟩ ⟨took all measures *short of* war⟩ ⟨a talent little *short of* genius⟩ **2** : with the exclusion or exception of : except for ⟨*short of* a new fight by the senators on the patent or power provisions, the bill may soon be law —*New Republic*⟩
short-oil \'⸗'⸗\ *adj* : containing a relatively low proportion of drying oil to resin ⟨*short-oil* varnishes are very hard, brittle and glossy⟩ — compare OIL LENGTH
short·om·e·ter \shȯ(r)d·'ämǝd·ǝ(r)\ *n* [*shortening* + *-o-* + *-meter*] : a device used by commercial bakers for testing the shortening power of various fats in dough
short order *n* : an order for food that can be quickly cooked
short-paid \'⸗'⸗\ *adj* **1** : bearing less than the required amount of stamps : having insufficient postage ⟨*short-paid* airmail letter⟩ **2** : paid short of the legal requirement ⟨*short-paid* postage⟩
short paint *n* : a stiff paint that has poor flowing properties
short pair *n* : a pair short of opening requirements in poker jackpots : a pair ranking lower than a pair of jacks
short particular meter *n* : a six-line hymn stanza of which the first, second, and fifth lines are iambic trimeter and the third, fourth, and sixth are iambic tetrameter
shortpath distillation \'⸗,⸗-\ *n* : MOLECULAR DISTILLATION
short-period comet *n* : one of numerous periodic comets whose times of revolution around the sun range from 3.3 years (as for Encke's comet) to a few dozen years
short-period variable *n* : a variable star whose regular cycle of light fluctuations has a length of a few hours, days, or weeks
short plate *n* : the shortest leaf of a leaf spring
short position *n* : SHORT INTEREST
short-range \'⸗'⸗\ *adj* : having a short range : of or relating to a short distance or a short period of time ⟨*short-range* navigation⟩ ⟨a *short-range* policy⟩
short rate *n* : an insurance premium charge for less than a year of coverage that is more than a pro rata part of the annual premium
short ribs *n pl* : a cut of beef consisting of rib ends between the ribroast and the plate — see BEEF illustration
short run *n* **1** : a period during which the factors in a situation remain relatively stable **2** : a run in cricket that is invalidated by the failure of a batsman to touch the ground inside the popping crease at one end before he starts to run to the other end; *also* : a run made from a hit that sends the ball a very short distance
short-run \'⸗'⸗\ *adj* [*short run*] **1** : of or relating to a relatively brief period of time ⟨*short-run* planning⟩ ⟨*short-run* thinking⟩ **2** : only partially filled with molten metal — used of a mold or casting
shorts *pl of* SHORT, *pres 3d sing of* SHORT
short s *or* **short ess** *n* : the ordinary written or printed lowercase form of the letter s — compare LONG S
short·schat \'shȯrt,shat\ *or* **shortschat pine** *also* **short·shat** \"\ *or* **shortshat pine** *n* -s [¹*short* + *shat*] **1** : SHORTLEAF PINE 1 **2** : a scrub pine (*Pinus virginiana*)
short score *n* : a condensed orchestral score with the less important parts omitted — called also *compressed score*
short-sea \'⸗'⸗\ *adj* : moving or carried on between ports relatively close to each other ⟨*short-sea* traffic⟩ ⟨*short-sea* trade⟩ — compare COASTWISE
short seller *n* [¹*short* + *seller* (after *sell short*)] : one who makes a short sale
short selling *n* [¹*short* + *selling* (after *sell short*)] : the act or practice of making a short sale
short service line *n* : a line 6½ feet behind the net that marks the point beyond which a serve in badminton must travel
short session *n* : a session of a U. S. Congress before 1934 beginning in December of an even-numbered year following an election and terminating on March 3 of the next year — compare LAME DUCK
short sheet *n* : a sheet leading from the inner clew of a topmast studding sail into the top
short-sheet \'⸗'⸗\ *vt* : to make up (a bed) in such a way that a person cannot get in under the covers
short-short \'⸗'⸗\ *n* : an extremely brief short story usu. seeking an effect of shock or surprise
short shrift *n* **1** : a brief respite from death ⟨a man condemned to a *short shrift* by his doctor —Joseph Conrad⟩ **2 a** : summary treatment : little consideration ⟨this kind of talk, however good, gets *short shrift* from me —M.D.Armstrong⟩ ⟨unfortunately, culture is given *short shrift* —R.K.Beardsley⟩ **b** : quick work ⟨of this breed we can make *short shrift* —Lucius Garvin⟩
short-shucks \'shȯrt,shǝks\ *n pl but sing or pl in constr* : SHORTSCHAT 2
short sight *n* : MYOPIA
shortsighted \'⸗'⸗⸗\ *adj* **1** : not able to see far : NEARSIGHTED, MYOPIC **2 a** (1) : not looking ahead : not anticipating or planning for the future : lacking foresight ⟨became the object of widespread derision by ~ critics —*Amer. Guide Series: Minn.*⟩ (2) : characterized by lack of foresight ⟨~ policies⟩ ⟨~ investments⟩ **b** : concerned with immediate advantage only ⟨a ~ rush for quick profits —P.E.James⟩ — **short·sight·ed·ly** *adv*
short·sight·ed·ness *n* -ES : the quality or state of being shortsighted
short snorter *n* [*short snort* quick drink + *-er*] **1** : a member of an informal club for which a pilot, crew member, or passenger who has made a transoceanic flight is eligible **2** : a piece of paper money (as a dollar bill) endorsed by short snorters as a membership certificate for a new member
short·some \'shärtsǝm\ *adj* [¹*short* + *-some*] *Scot* : making time seem short : DIVERTING, ENTERTAINING
short splice *n* : a splice using less material than the long splice but increasing the circumference

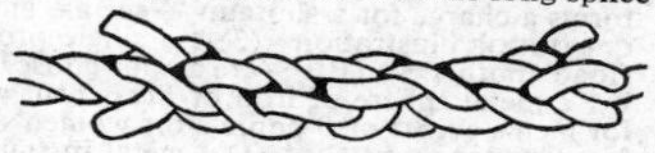

short splice

short-spoken \'⸗'⸗⸗\ *adj* : not given to wasting words : CURT
short-staple \'⸗'⸗⸗\ *adj* : having relatively short fibers
¹**shortstop** \'⸗,⸗\ *n* [¹*short* + *stop* (after the phrase *stop short*)] **1** : a workman at a rod mill who diverts the rod for winding in a coil **2 a** : the player position in baseball for defending the infield area to the third-base side of second base — see BASEBALL illustration **b** : the player stationed in the shortstop position **3** : an agent that interrupts at some desired stage a polymerization reaction proceeding by way of radicals
²**shortstop** \"\ *vt* : to cause (a polymerization reaction) to stop by adding a suitable chemical
short-stop \'⸗,⸗\ *or* **short-stop bath** *n* [¹*short* + *stop* (after the phrase *stop short*)] : STOP BATH
short story *n* **1** : a relatively brief invented prose narrative that typically deals with a limited group of characters involved in a single action, usu. aims at unity of effect, and often concentrates on the creation of mood rather than the telling of a story **2** *slang* : a forged check
short-story writer *n, slang* : a check forger
short subject *n* : a short film
short sweetening *n, South & Midland* : SUGAR — compare LONG SWEETENING
short-swing \'⸗,⸗\ *adj* : tending to close out commitments quickly ⟨*short-swing* traders⟩; *also* : SHORT-TERM 2b
shortswing \'⸗,⸗\ *n* [trans. of G *kurzschwung*] : a skiing technique developed for maximum speed esp. in slalom racing and based on sideslipping, heel thrusting, and keeping the ski edges parallel
shorttail \'⸗,⸗\ *n* : a snake of the family Aniliidae
short-tailed albatross \'⸗,⸗-\ *n* : a large and chiefly white albatross (*Diomedea albatrus*) found in the northern Pacific ocean
short-tailed mealybug *n* : a mealybug having short terminal filaments
short-tailed shrew *n* : any of several No. American shrews of *Blarina* or a related genus with dense usu. gray or dark brown fur, a tail less than half the body length, often a toxic saliva, and in some cases scent glands on the sides which release a noxious secretion
short-tailed wallaby *n* : QUOKKA
shortt clock \'shȯ(ǝ)rt-\ *n, usu cap S* [after William H. *Shortt*, 20th cent. Eng. inventor] : an accurate clock having an improved free pendulum
short-tempered \'⸗'⸗⸗\ *adj* : having a quick temper
short-term \'⸗'⸗\ *adj* **1** : occurring over or involving a relatively short period of time — opposed to *long-term* **2 a** : of or relating to a financial transaction based on a term usu. of less than a year **b** : of or relating to capital assets held for less than six months
short-term·er \"+ǝ(r)\ *n* [fr. the phrase *short term* + *-er*] : a person serving a short prison sentence
short-term note *n* : a financial obligation that generally runs for less than two years
short-term paper *n* : a negotiable paper (as a note or bill) that matures within a three to six months period
short time *n* : a reduced working period
short-time \'⸗'⸗\ *adj* [fr. the phrase *short time*] : of, relating to, or limited to a short period of time
short-tim·er \"+ǝ(r)\ *n* [fr. the phrase *short time* + *-er*] : one that serves for a short time; *esp* : SHORT-TERMER
short title *n* : an abbreviated form of entry for a book in a list or catalog that usu. gives only the author's name, the title in brief, the date and place of publication, and the publisher's or printer's name
short-toed eagle \'⸗,⸗-\ *n* : HARRIER EAGLE
short ton *n* : TON 1b — see MEASURE table
¹**shortwave** \'⸗,⸗\ *n, often attrib* [¹*short* + *wave*] **1** : an electromagnetic or radio wave of 60-meter wavelength or less **2** : a radio transmitter using shortwaves
²**shortwave** \'⸗,⸗\ *vt* : to transmit by radio using shortwaves
shortwave therapy *n* : medical diathermy in which wavelengths of about 11 meters are employed
short weight *n* : weight less than the stated weight : UNDERWEIGHT
short-weight \'⸗'⸗\ *vt* [*short weight*] : to defraud with short weight
short whist *n* : whist played under the rule that five points constitute a game
short-winded \'⸗'⸗⸗\ *adj* [ME, fr. *short* + *winded*] **1** : affected with or characterized by shortness of breath : easily put out of breath **2 a** : BRIEF ⟨the most sensible, sympathetic, scholarly, and *short-winded* exposition —*Times Lit. Supp.*⟩ **b** : broken up into short units : DISCONNECTED ⟨an especially bumpy kind of *short-winded* prose —S.E.Fitzgerald⟩
¹**short-wool** *or* **short-wooled** \'⸗'⸗\ *adj* [¹*short* + *wool* or *wooled*, fr. *wool* + *-ed*] : of, relating to, or being domestic sheep that have short but fine wool ⟨Southdown, Shropshire, and Suffolk are breeds of *short-wooled* sheep⟩
²**short-wool** \'⸗,⸗\ *n* : a short-wool sheep
shorty *or* **short·ie** \'shȯrd·ē, -ō(ǝ)|, |t|, |i\ *n, pl* **short·ies** : one that is short: as **a** : a person of less than average height **b** : a garment of less than average length
short yard rope *n* : a rope hooked to the slings of a topgallant or royal yard and used with a purchase whose fall leads to the deck to hoist the yard
short yearling *n* : a young beef animal approaching one year in age; *esp* : one between 9 and 12 months old
shor·tzy \'shȯrtsē\ *n, pl* **shortzy** *or* **shortzies** *usu cap* **1** : a mixed nomadic Tatar people of western Siberia **2** : a member of the Shortzy people
sho·sho·ko \shǝ'shō(,)kō, shō'-\ *n, pl* **shoshokoes** *or* **shoshokos** *usu cap* [Shoshoni, lit., walker] **1** : a Shoshonean people of southern Utah and neighboring states **2** : a member of the Shoshoko people
sho·sho·ne·an \shǝ'shōnēǝn, shō'-, ˌshōshǝˈnēǝn\ *n, pl* **shoshonean** *or* **shoshoneans** *usu cap* [*Shoshone* + *-an*] **1** : a language family of the Uto-Aztecan phylum comprising the languages of most of the Uto-Aztecan peoples in the U. S. **2 a** : any of the Indian peoples whose language is Shoshonean **b** : a member of any such peoples
sho·sho·ni *also* **sho·sho·ne** *or* **sho·sho·nee** \shǝ'shōnē, shō'-, -ni\ *n, pl* **shoshoni** *or* **shoshonis** *also* **shoshone** *or* **shoshones** *or* **shoshonee** *or* **shoshonees** *usu cap* **1 a** : a group of Shoshonean peoples in California, Colorado, Idaho, Nevada, Utah, and Wyoming **b** : a member of such group of peoples **2** : the language of the Shoshoni people
¹**shot** \'shät, *usu* -äd.+V\ *n* -s [ME, fr. OE *scot, sceot*; akin to OFris & ON *skot* action of throwing, missile, shot, OHG *scoz* missile, *scuz* shot, *skiozzan* to shoot — more at SHOOT] **1 a** : an act of shooting : RUSH, FLASH ⟨a ~ of lightning⟩ ⟨heard the ~ of the bolt on the front door⟩ **b** : a directed propelling of a missile (as an arrow, stone, rocket) ⟨took a ~ at the hat with his snowball⟩ ⟨fired a second rocket ~ at the

moon); *specif* : a directed discharge of a firearm ⟨heard three ~s fired in rapid succession⟩ ⟨exchanged ~s but no one was hit⟩ ⟨a bad ~ that missed by a mile⟩ **c** (1) : a stroke in a game (as billiards, golf, or tennis) (2) : a scoring stroke or throw (as in cricket, curling) (3) : a try for goal (as in basketball, hockey, lacrosse, soccer) **d** : a single cast and haul of a fishing net or set of nets **e** : one throw of the shuttle in weaving **⁵**PICK 2a **f** : the act of estimating distance or altitude by means of an instrument (as a sextant, transit) **g** : a setting off of a charge of explosives : BLAST ⟨the fifth ~ of the 1955 nuclear test series —*N. Y. Times*⟩ **h** : an injection of a drug, immunizing substance, nutrient, or medicament ⟨got a ~ for the pain⟩ ⟨gave himself a second ~ of the narcotic⟩ **2 a** *pl* **shot** : material propelled by shooting: as (1) : large solid or nearly solid projectiles (as for a cannon) with no bursting charge ⟨heaps of shells, scrap iron, and solid ~ were placed on top of the gunpowder —C.S.Forester⟩ ⟨granite ~ was used for guns ... in the sixteenth century —E.E.Evans⟩ ⟨the ~ and shell of an election year —*Time*⟩ (2) : small lead or steel pellets of any of various sizes for ammunition of which a quantity usu. loaded in a cartridge forms a charge for a shotgun — see BB, BIRD SHOT, BUCKSHOT; CARTRIDGE illustration (3) : a single projectile of such shot ⟨load another~⟩ ⟨BB ~ are a poor goose load —Elmer Keith⟩ **b** : a metal sphere of iron or brass usu. weighing 16 pounds for men's events or 8 pounds for women's events which is put for distance **c** *pl* **shot** (1) : metal in small pellets for use as an abrasive (as for blast cleaning of castings, core drilling, and sawing, grinding, and polishing stone), for peening, and for other industrial or craft use — compare GRIT (2) : a single pellet of such shot ⟨a cracked ~⟩ ⟨~ are soldered to metal parts —A.F.Rose & Antonio Cirino⟩ **3** : one of the forged lengths of chain usu. 15 fathoms long and joined by shackles to form an anchor cable **4 a** : a place or spot for setting nets **b** : a single catch of fish **5 a** : the distance that a missile is or can be thrown ⟨lying a cannon ~ apart⟩ **b** : the distance within which something is effective : RANGE, REACH ⟨out of the ~ and danger of desire —Shak.⟩ **6** : a charge to be paid (as at a tavern) : SCOT, BILL **7** *dial Eng* : FURLONG 2a **8** : one that shoots: **a** *obs* : a soldier with a firearm; *also* : a group of such soldiers **b** : MARKSMAN ⟨policemen who are all good ~s with a pistol⟩ **9 a** (1) : an effort designed to accomplish a definite end : ATTEMPT, TRY, GO ⟨his first ~ at saying anything —P.G.Wodehouse⟩ — often used in the phrase *have a shot at* ⟨sent for the village priest to have a ~ at reforming him —*Calgary (Canada) Herald*⟩ (2) : an exchange in checkers that is advantageous to the side that forces it **b** : GUESS, CONJECTURE ⟨made rather random ~s in identifying the men ... cantering up and down —William Black⟩ ⟨dating on stylistic grounds alone is but a ~ in the dark because too often we lack the proper elements of comparison —Maurice Vieyra⟩ **c** : a chance at odds ⟨a horse that left the gate as a 12 to 1 ~⟩ ⟨it's a 10 to 1 ~ that he'll be on time⟩ **d** : a chance to do something : OPPORTUNITY ⟨give you a ~ at the property first —Sinclair Lewis⟩ **e** : a single appearance as an entertainer ⟨was offered a guest ~ on a television program⟩ **10** *dial Brit* : a creature of little value ⟨as an animal culled from a herd or a young or stunted animal⟩ **11** : a remark so directed as to have telling effect ⟨"you're finished in New York ..." was his parting ~ —Polly Adler⟩ **12 a** : a single photographic exposure; *esp* : SNAPSHOT **b** : a single sequence of a motion picture or a television program shot by one camera without interruption : a continuous view produced from one camera angle or by panning or dollying ⟨a moving ~⟩ ⟨a head-on ~⟩ ⟨an action ~⟩ — see CLOSE SHOT, LONG SHOT, MEDIUM SHOT, PROCESS SHOT, TRAVEL SHOT **13 a** : a weft thread shot through the shed in one throw of a weaving shuttle : **⁵**PICK 2b **b** : the number of filling yarns to each row of tufts in carpet manufacture ⟨two-*shot* carpet⟩ **14 a** : a charge of explosives ⟨a ~ of nitroglycerine⟩ **15 a** : a quantity (as of a drug) for injection **b** : a single drink of liquor : a serving (as of whiskey) that can be drunk in one swallow; *esp* : a jigger of spirits taken undiluted **c** : a small amount applied at one time : DOSE ⟨sometimes, in flight, the pilot may want a momentary ~ of oxygen —*Popular Science Monthly*⟩ ⟨a dramatist could inject a ~ of colloquialism into a tragic aria —Kenneth Tynan⟩ **16** : the quantity (as of plastic) injected into a mold at one time — **like a shot** *adv* **1** : QUICKLY, INSTANTANEOUSLY ⟨the dog lunged against the opening, came through *like a shot* ... and tore out of the house —Erle Stanley Gardner⟩ **2** : without hesitation : WILLINGLY ⟨if we could do anything in return, then we would *like a shot* —D.G. Mackail⟩ — **shot in the arm** : STIMULUS, BOOST ⟨possible for such inspirational or emotional *shots in the arm* to hop us up and give us temporary relief —W.J.Reilly⟩ ⟨machine tool industry will get a 500 million *shot in the arm* —*Time*⟩ — **shot in the locker 1** : a shot left in a war vessel's shot locker **2** : a remnant or reserve of money or supplies : a last resource

²shot \ˈ\ *adj* [partly fr. **¹**shot, partly fr. *shot* (past part. of *shoot*), fr. ME *shoten, shotten* — more at SHOTTEN] **1** : of, relating to, or used with ordnance or firearms shot ⟨~ hoist⟩ **2 a** : of contrasting and changeable color effects in fabrics produced by weaving warp and weft threads of different colors or by dyeing a fabric made of two fibers (as cotton and nylon) that react to dyes in varying manner : IRIDESCENT ⟨~ silk⟩ : VARIEGATED ⟨black cloth ~ with silver thread⟩ **b** : suffused or streaked with a color ⟨the sky was a cold gray, ~ over with a coppery light —T.B.Costain⟩ ⟨his hair was ~ with gray —Erle Stanley Gardner⟩ **c** : interpenetrated with an often contrasting quality or element : INFUSED, PERMEATED ⟨full of robust satire, ~ with gleams of tenderness —John Squire⟩ ⟨an outdated, feudalistic upper class, ~ through with quislings and collaborators —Bernard Seeman⟩ **3** : having the form of pellets resembling shot ⟨~ clay soil⟩ ⟨~ copper⟩ ⟨~ ore⟩ **4** : WELDED ⟨the birds scissors⟩ **5 a** (1) : hit by a discharged missile ⟨the birds swallow lead pellets picked up ... in heavily ~ areas —*Texas Game & Fish*⟩ (2) : reduced to a state of ruin, prostration, or uselessness ⟨went to a doctor because his nerves were ~ : washed up : FINISHED ⟨a strike that left the bus line's business all ~⟩ : worn out ⟨replace the faucets that are pretty well ~ with some of the new type⟩ **b** *slang* : INTOXICATED ⟨killed the bottle and got ~⟩ **c** : used up ⟨my stock of adjectives is really ~, though, this late in the game —Richard Joseph⟩ **6** : bleached ~, though, this late in the game —Richard Joseph⟩ **6** : bleached ~, or otherwise injured by excessive moisture ⟨~ wheat⟩

³shot \ˈ\ *vb* **shotted; shotted; shotting; shots** [**¹**shot] *vt* **1** : to subject to or form by the shotting process **2** : to form into small round particles (as by spraying) ~ *vi* : to form into granules

⁴shot \ˈ\ *chiefly dial var of* SHUT

shot bag *n* : a bag designed for carrying pellets of shot for a gun ⟨keeps his money in a *shot bag*⟩

shot berry *n* : a small imperfectly developed berry in a grape cluster

shot blade *n* [**²**shot] : the part of a grain stalk that encloses the developing head

¹shotblast \ˈ₋₋₋\ *n* [**¹**shot + *blast*] : a stream of shot forcibly projected against a surface by air or steam (as for removing scale from oxidized metal)

²shotblast \ˈ\ *vt* : to clean or descale with a shotblast

shotblaster \ˈ₋₋₋\ *n* : one that does the work of a sandblaster using fine steel shot instead of sand

shot borer *n* : SHOT-HOLE BORER

shotbush \ˈ₋₋\ *n* [**²**shot; fr. the shape of the fruit] **1** : HERCULES'-CLUB **3 2** : WILD SARSAPARILLA 1

shot cartridge *n* : a cartridge loaded with a charge of shot rather than a solid projectile

shot-clog *also* **shot-log** *n, obs* : a bore tolerated only because he pays the shot

¹shotcrete \ˈ₋₋₋\ *n* [**²**shot + *concrete*] : a Gunite mixture

²shotcrete \ˈ\ *vb* -ED/-ING/-S : GUNITE

shot drill *n* : a rotary rock drill using chilled steel shot as an abradant — compare CORE DRILL

shote *var of* SHOAT

shot effect *n* [trans. of G *schroteffekt*] : random fluctuations in the number of thermions per second emitted from the filament of a valve (as a vacuum tube) that give rise to sputtering or popping noises in the amplifier — compare THERMAL NOISE

shot-firer \ˈ₋₋₋\ *n* : a miner who loads and fires drill holes

shot-free \ˈ₋₋\ *adj* [**¹**shot + *free*] **1** *archaic* : safe from being shot **2** : SCOT-FREE

shot glass *n* : a glass holding one shot (as of whiskey)

¹shotgun \ˈ₋₋\ *n* [**¹**shot + *gun*] **1** : an often double-barreled smoothbore shoulder weapon for firing shot at short ranges — see GAUGE table; compare PUMP GUN **2** : a variety of draw poker in which there is betting after each round of cards is dealt (as in stud poker)

²shotgun \ˈ\ *adj* **1** : of, relating to, or using a shotgun ⟨a ~ shell⟩ ⟨~ hunting⟩ **2** : involving coercion (as by the threat of arms) : obtained, enforced, or marked by duress ⟨a ~ title⟩ ⟨a ~ quarantine⟩ ⟨a ~ agreement⟩ ⟨a ~ merger⟩ **3 a** : containing many ingredients or features of which one is expected to prove efficacious ⟨a ~ prescription⟩ ⟨~ therapy⟩ **b** : applied to a whole group or class without consideration of individual circumstances : covering a wide field with hit-or-miss effectiveness : inclusive but random ⟨~ propaganda mailed to all boxholders —*New Republic*⟩ ⟨rely on direct controls, and ... use a rifle not a ~ technique —*Fortune*⟩ **4** *South & Midland* : of or being a shotgun house ⟨a shack of ~ construction⟩

³shotgun \ˈ\ *vt* **1** : to shoot with a shotgun ⟨an enemy who *shotgunned* him from ambush⟩ **2** : to compel as if with a shotgun : force by duress ⟨~ western Europe into federal unity —Andrew Roth⟩

shotgun can *n* : a tall narrow milk can holding about four gallons (as for setting)

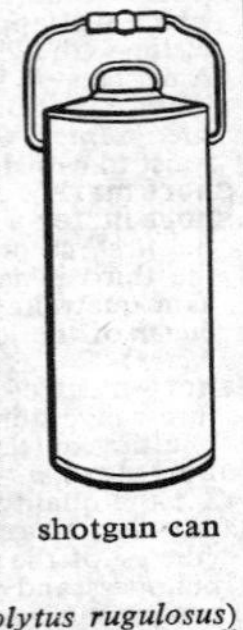

shotgun feed *n* : a steam-driven feed for the log carriage of a sawmill

shotgun house *n, South & Midland* : a house in which all the rooms are in direct line with each other usu. front to back

shotgun marriage *or* **shotgun wedding** *n* **1** : a marriage forced or required because of pregnancy **2** : a forced union or accord because of two groups or elements

shotgun messenger *n* : an armed guard on a stagecoach

shot hole *n* **1** : a drilled hole in which a charge of dynamite is exploded in mining or to produce artificial earth vibrations in seismic prospecting for oil **2** : a hole made in wood by a boring insect **3 a** *also* **shot-holing** \ˈ₋₋₋\ : the dropping out of small rounded fragments of leaves because of parasitic action or other causes with a resultant shot-riddled appearance — compare CHERRY LEAF SPOT **b** : one of the perforations so formed

shot-hole borer *n* : a small bark beetle (*Scolytus rugulosus*) that attacks orchard fruit trees and kills the bark of small branches and twigs; *broadly* : any of several other beetles of the family Scolytidae attacking trees or shrubs (as the beetle *Xyleborus fornicatus* that attacks the tea plant)

shot-less \ˈshätləs\ *adj* : having no shot

shot lighter *n* : BLASTER

shotlike \ˈ₋₋\ *adj* : resembling pellets of shot in shape or size

shot line *n* : a light line attached to a projectile and used with a Lyle or other line-throwing gun (as to pass a cable to a wrecked vessel)

shotmaker \ˈ₋₋₋\ *n* : one that makes shots ⟨a left-handed ~ who because of his ability to shoot from any angle plays right wing —*Newsweek*⟩

shot-man \ˈshätmən\ *also* **shots-man** \-tsm-\ *n, pl* **shotmen** *also* **shotsmen** : BLASTER

shot metal *n* : an alloy of 98 percent lead and 2 percent arsenic for making small shot

shot noise *n* : a sputtering or popping produced (as in a radio) by shot effect

shot plant *n* : an Indian shot (*Canna indica*)

shot point *n* : the place at which an explosion generates vibrations in the ground (as in seismic prospecting)

shot put *n* [**¹**shot + *put* (after the phrase *put the shot*)] **1** : a field event consisting in putting the shot for distance from a circle 7 feet in diameter **2** : a throw of the shot in the shot put

shot-putter \ˈ₋₋₋\ *n* [**¹**shot + *putter* (after the phrase *put the shot*)] : one who puts the shot in a field event

shot-putting \ˈ₋₋₋\ *n* [**¹**shot + *putting* (after the phrase *put the shot*)] : the act or practice of putting the shot in a field event

shot rock *n* : the stone that is nearest the center of the rings in curling

shot rope *n* : a guide rope used in deep-sea diving that is attached to the ship near the ladder and has a sinker on the lower end

shots *pl of* SHOT, *pres 3d sing of* SHOT

shot samples *n* : samples taken for assay from molten metal by pouring a portion into water to granulate it

shotshell \ˈ₋₋\ *n* : a shotgun cartridge loaded with shot — compare RIFLED SLUG

shotstar \ˈ₋₋\ *n* [**²**shot + *star*] **1** *archaic* : METEOR **2** : an alga (*Nostoc commune*)

¹shott \ˈshät\ *dial Brit var of* **¹**SHOT 10

²shott *var of* CHOTT

³shott *var of* SHOAT

shot-ted \ˈshäd·əd\ *adj* [**¹**shot + -ed] **1** : loaded with a shot — used esp. of a cannon not loaded with a blank charge (as for saluting, giving warning) **2** : weighted down with shot ⟨a ~ tennis skirt⟩

shot-ten \ˈshät³n\ *adj* [ME *shotyn*, fr. *shoten, shotyn* (past part. of *sheten, shoten, shuten* to shoot), fr. OE *gescoten*] **1 a** : having ejected the spawn and so of inferior food value ⟨full or ~ herrings⟩ ⟨lean as a ~ herring⟩ **b** *dial* (1) : WEAKENED, DISPIRITED (2) : GOOD-FOR-NOTHING **2** *obs* : shot out of its socket ⟨swayed in the back and shoulder ~ —Shak.⟩

shotting -s [fr. gerund of **³**shot] **1** : a process for producing metal shot or powders by dropping molten metal (as lead) through small openings from a height (as in a shot tower) so that the metal forms spherical drops in the descent that are received in water or other liquid **2** : an operation in a process of producing wrought iron in which molten pig iron is poured into a ladle of molten slag at a temperature below the freezing point of the iron so that small globules of iron are formed, the slag absorbs the gases, and on cooling a porous ball of wrought iron forms — compare PUDDLING

shot to pieces *adj* : **²**SHOT 5a2

shot tower *n* : a tower about 200 feet high for making shot by the shotting process

shot-ty \ˈshäd·ē\ *adj* -ER/-EST [**¹**shot + -y] : hard and round like a pellet of shot ⟨~ lymph nodes⟩

shot window *n* [ME *shotwyndoue*, fr. *shot* + *wyndowe, windowe* window] : a small casement window often with little or no glass formerly common in Scotland

shou \ˈshō\ *n* [Chin (Pek) *shou*³] : a Chinese character signifying longevity and often used in decoration

¹shough *n* -s [origin unknown] *obs* : a curly-haired lapdog believed to come orig. from Iceland

²shough \ˈshük\ *var of* SHEUGH

should [ME *sholde*, fr. OE *scolde, scolde*; akin to OHG *scolta* owed, was obliged to, had to, ON *skylda* had to, Goth *skulda* owed, was obliged to, had to — more at SHALL] *past of* SHALL **1** — used in auxiliary function to express condition ⟨if he ~ call, I'm out⟩ ⟨for if he ~ leave his father, his father would die —Rupert Brooke⟩ ⟨Naples be captured ... we shall have a first-rate port —Sir Winston Churchill⟩ ⟨as if the atom bomb ~ find a benevolent use —Herbert Kupferberg⟩ ⟨I ~ not allow anyone to inconvenience me if I could hinder it —Emily Brontë⟩ ⟨they can very easily be ennobled ~ they wish it —Nancy Mitford⟩ **2** — used in auxiliary function to express duty, obligation, necessity, propriety, or expediency ⟨for 'tis commanded I ~ do so —Shak.⟩ ⟨but now he is dead, why ~ I fast —2 Sam 12:23 (RSV)⟩ ⟨the law was then passed ... that every senator ~ take an oath —J.A.Froude⟩ ⟨in such cases the officer ~ first give notice to those in the house —Paul Wilson⟩ ⟨and this is as it ~ be —H.L.Savage⟩ ⟨was determined that his son ~ have a good education⟩ ⟨you ~ brush your teeth after each meal⟩ **3** — used in auxiliary function to express futurity from a point of

view in the past ⟨she realized that she ~ have to do most of her farm work before sunrise —Ellen Glasgow⟩ ⟨had expected that he ~ be able to press forward —T.B.Macaulay⟩ **4** *archaic* : MIGHT, COULD ⟨may have wondered what this present distress ~ mean —John Keble⟩ **5** — used in auxiliary function to express what is probable or expected ⟨this year's treasury deficit ~ be $6 billion or more —T.R.Ybarra⟩ ⟨effects of the trends cited above ~ not be felt ... for another decade —A.W.Griswold⟩ ⟨recordings which ~ confuse even the most ingenuous listener —Robert Evett⟩ ⟨with an early start, they ~ be here by noon⟩ **6** — used in auxiliary function to express a desire or request in a polite or unemphatic manner or to tone down a direct or blunt statement ⟨one aspect of his critical work to which I ~ like to call attention —Malcolm Cowley⟩ ⟨I ~ suggest that a guide to available materials is the first essential —L.D.Reddick⟩ ⟨you ~ wish to look at it —O.Henry⟩ ⟨in general I ~ say that the salaries ... make up very nearly two thirds of the budget —Deems Taylor⟩ *syn* see OUGHT

should-be \ˈ₋₋\ *adj* [fr. the phrase *should be*] : that ought to be ⟨looking out for his *should-be* guardian⟩

¹shoul-der \ˈshōld·ə(r)\ *n* -s *often attrib* [ME *shulder, sholder*, fr. OE *sculdor*; akin to OFris *skuldere* shoulder, MLG *schulder*, MD *schouder*, OHG *scultra, sculterra* shoulder, OE *sciell* shell — more at SHELL] **1 a** : the laterally projecting part of the human body on each side of the base of the neck that is formed of the bones and joints by which the arm is connected with the trunk and the muscles covering them **b** : the corresponding but usu. less projecting region of the body of a lower vertebrate : the structures connecting the forelimb with the trunk **c** : the bend of the wing of a bird — not used technically, see GOOSE illustration **2 a** : the two shoulders and the upper part of the back forming together the part of the human frame on which it is most easy to carry a heavy burden — usu. used in pl. ⟨his ~s bowed with age⟩ **b shoulders** *pl* : capacity for bearing a task or blame : the seat of responsibility ⟨the task of conservation farming rested squarely on the ~s of the farmer —*Farmer's Weekly (So. Africa)*⟩ ⟨placed the guilt on the ~s of the planters —*Amer. Guide Series: Fla.*⟩ **3 a** : the upper joint of the foreleg and adjacent parts of an animal dressed for market including more or less of the neck and chest ⟨~ of mutton⟩ — see LAMB illustration **b** : the part of a leather hide between the butt and the cheeks and head — see HIDE illustration **4** : the part of a garment at the wearer's shoulder **5** : a part suggesting a human shoulder in shape, position, or function: as **a** : an angle or curve in the outline of an object (as between the body and the neck of a bottle) and often also the parts adjacent to it ⟨overloading causes ... excessive strain of the fabric of the sidewalls and ~s of the tire —L.W.Mason⟩ ⟨a bolt threaded up to the ~⟩ ⟨the northwest ~ of Europe⟩ **b** : an abrupt projection that forms an abutment on an object or limits motion (as the projection around a tenon, the ring next to the wheel on an axle) ⟨~ on an abutting projection between a blade and a tang (as of a knife or chisel)⟩ **d** : the flat top of the body of a piece of printing type from which the bevel rises to join the face; *sometimes* : the part of this area at the belly and back ends — compare SIDE BEARING; see TYPE illustration **e** (1) : the part of a hill or mountain near the top : the slope below the summit ⟨a road along the ~ of the mountain⟩ (2) : a lateral protrusion or extension of a hill or mountain ⟨from valley to intermediate ~s and crags, to a secondary and thence to the highest point —W.O.Douglas⟩ **f** (1) : the part of a railroad ballast between the end of the tie and the edge of the ballast slope (2) : the part of the railroad subgrade between the edge of the ballast and the top of ditch in cuts or between the edge of the ballast and the top of a slope on an embankment (3) : either edge of a roadway; *specif* : the part of a roadway outside of the traveled way on which vehicles may be parked in an emergency **g** (1) : a rough edge or ridge left beside a line or dot on a photoengraved plate (2) : a beveled edge around a printing plate by which the plate can be fastened to a base **h** : RIDGE 6 **i** : the section of a finger ring on either side of the central ornament or bezel **j** : the part of a flat key between the bow and the blade **6** : HALF SOLE — **from the shoulder** *adv* : in a direct or outspoken manner of telling : without holding anything back ⟨let them straight *from the shoulder* ... that we intend to stay until someone kicks us out —O.E.Rölvaag⟩ — **shoulder to shoulder** *adv* **1** : in close proximity : side by side ⟨soldiers fighting *shoulder to shoulder*⟩ ⟨old brick houses standing *shoulder to shoulder* against the sidewalk⟩ **2** : in close cooperation ⟨work *shoulder to shoulder* in the common cause⟩

²shoulder \ˈ\ *vb* **shouldered; shouldered; shouldering** \-d(ə)riŋ\ **shoulders** [ME *shulderen, sholderen*, fr. *shulder, sholder*, n.] *vt* **1** : to push or thrust with or as if with the shoulder : JOSTLE ⟨~s his way through the crowd⟩ ⟨in China ... the Dutch ~ed other European competitors aside — Stringfellow Barr⟩ **2 a** : to provide with a shoulder : form a shoulder on (as a casting) **b** : to fill or pad out as a shoulder (as ballast on the sides of a railroad track or mortar under the edge of a roofing slate) **3 a** : to place or bear on the shoulder ⟨~ a basket⟩; *specif* : to place (as a rifle) aslant on the shoulder **b** : to assume the burden or responsibility of ⟨~ing the burden of preparing these two books for publication —Geog. Jour.⟩ ⟨called to ~ the great responsibilities of high office —Clement Attlee⟩ ⟨~ the blame⟩ ⟨the costs of the war⟩ **4** : to stand close beside ⟨old frame buildings ~ modern masonry structures in the business center —*Amer. Guide Series: Oreg.*⟩ ~ *vi* **1** : to push with or as if with the shoulders : make one's way (as through a crowd) in an aggressive manner ⟨the mules ~ up to the trough —Christopher Rand⟩ ⟨the Scandinavians ... who are trying to ~ into their sacred, ancient Yankee caste —Sinclair Lewis⟩ **2** : to rise or protrude in a manner suggesting a shoulder ⟨the ridge that ~ed trude in a manner suggesting a shoulder ⟨the ridge that ~ed to the sky —J.H.Stuart⟩ ⟨a particularly dilapidated building that ~ed alarmingly out to one side —W.O.Mitchell⟩ **3** : to move side by side ⟨a yoke of the great sulky white bullocks ... came ~ing along together —Rudyard Kipling⟩

shoulder arm *n* : SHOULDER WEAPON

shoulder bag *n* : a woman's handbag that can be worn suspended by a shoulder strap

shoulder belt *n* : a belt passing over the shoulder — compare BANDOLIER

shoulder blade *n* [ME *shulder blade*] : SCAPULA 1a

shoulder block *n* : a block with a projection near the upper end so that it can rest against a spar without jamming the rope

shoulder board *n* : one of a pair of broad pieces of stiffened cloth worn on the shoulders of a military uniform and carrying insignia of rank; *specif* : SHOULDER MARK

shoulder bone *n* [ME *shulderbon, sholderbon*] : SCAPULA 1a

shoulder-clapper \ˈ₋₋₋\ *n, archaic* : BAILIFF

shoulder arch *n* : a spanning member consisting of a straight lintel carried on corbels projecting into the opening and usu. cut into hollow curves under their projecting ends

should-er-ette \ˌshōldəˈret\ *n* -s [*shoulder* + -ette] : a woman's light shawl with ends formed into sleeves

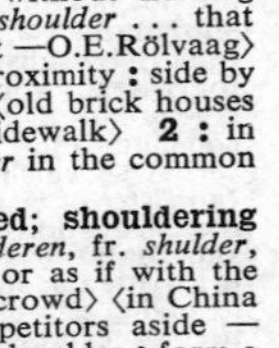

shoulder girdle *n* : PECTORAL GIRDLE; *esp* : a pectoral girdle that is complex and highly developed (as in most quadrupeds or in man)

shoulder-hand syndrome *n* : pain in and stiffening of the shoulder followed by stiffening of the hand and fingers often associated with or following myocardial infarction

shoulder head *n* : a printed head or subhead set flush with the left margin

shoulder-high \ˈ₋₋\ *adv* (*or adj*) : as high as or up to one's shoulder ⟨carried him *shoulder-high*⟩ ⟨a *shoulder-high* shelf⟩

shoulder-hitter \ˈ₋₋₋\ *n* : ROWDY

shoul-der-ing \ˈshōld(ə)riŋ\ *n* [**¹**shoulder + -ing] : a projecting or supporting part: as **a** : the mortar under the edge of roofing slates **b** : SHOULDER 5f

shoulder knot *n* : an ornamental knot of ribbon or lace worn on the shoulder in the 17th and 18th centuries (as by

men of fashion, liveried servants) **2 :** a detachable ornament consisting of braided wire cord and worn on the shoulders of a uniform of ceremony by a commissioned officer

shoulder loop *n* **:** a flap on each shoulder of a service uniform

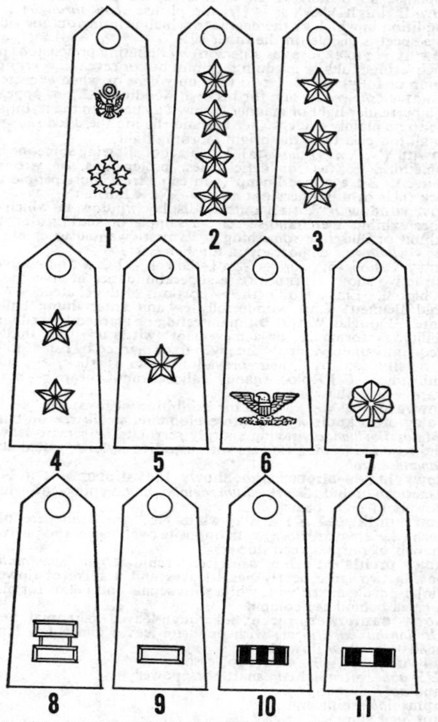

shoulder loops of United States Army: *1* general of the army, *2* general, *3* lieutenant general, *4* major general, *5* brigadier general, *6* colonel, *7* lieutenant colonel (silver oak leaf) and major (gold oak leaf) *8* captain, *9* first lieutenant (silver bar) and second lieutenant (gold bar) *10* chief warrant officer, grade IV (silver bar) and chief warrant officer, grade II (gold bar) *11* chief warrant officer, grade III (silver bar) and warrant officer (gold bar)

(as of the U.S. Air Force, Army, or Marine Corps) which extends inward from the sleeve seam and fastens by a button at the edge of the collar and on which an officer wears metal insignia of rank

shoulder mark *n* **:** one of a pair of nearly rectangular pieces

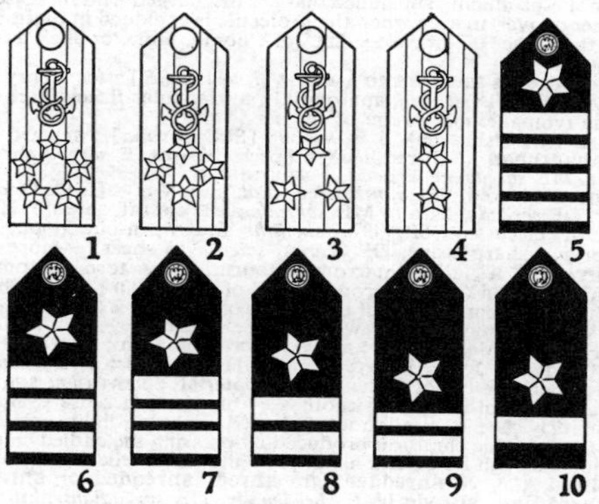

shoulder marks of United States Navy: *1* fleet admiral, *2* admiral, *3* vice-admiral, *4* rear admiral, *5* captain, *6* commander, *7* lieutenant commander, *8* lieutenant, *9* lieutenant junior grade, *10* ensign

of stiffened cloth worn parallel to the shoulder seam of some uniforms of U.S. Navy officers, bearing embroidered or gold lace or black braid insignia of rank and line or corps devices, and secured at the inner triangular end by a gilt button — called also *shoulder board*

shoulder note *n, printing* **:** a note at the top outer corner of a page

shoulder-of-mutton sail \ˈ≈≈≈ˈ≈≈-\ *n* **:** LEG-OF-MUTTON SAIL

shoulder patch *n* **:** a cloth patch bearing an identifying mark and worn on one sleeve of a uniform below the shoulder; *specif* **:** SHOULDER SLEEVE INSIGNIA

shoulder pitch *or* **shoulder point** *n, archaic* **:** ACROMION

shoulders *pl of* SHOULDER, *pres 3d sing of* SHOULDER

shoulder screw *n* **:** a screw having an unthreaded shoulder below the head to act as a fulcrum for a lever pivoted on it

shoulder sleeve insignia *n* **:** a distinctive cloth patch worn on the left sleeve of a uniform just below the shoulder seam by individuals assigned to Army divisions, corps, and armies, to Air Force wings, and to other specifically authorized organizations and also worn on the right sleeve by individuals to indicate overseas service with certain units during periods of active operations — called also *shoulder patch*

shoulder strap *n* **1 :** a strap or one of two straps that pass across the shoulder or shoulders and hold up an article or garment **2 a :** one of a pair of narrow rectangular pieces of cloth worn parallel to the shoulder seams of a military dress uniform, bearing the wearer's insignia of rank embroidered in gold or silver, being of the color of his branch (as dark blue for a general officer, red for an artillery officer), bordered with gold bullion, and now replaced in the U.S. Navy by shoulder marks and worn in the U.S. Army only on the blue dress coat **b :** SHOULDER LOOP

shoulder-striker \ˈ≈≈,≈≈\ *n* **:** ROWDY

shoulder tuft *n* **:** TEGULA

shoulder weapon *or* **shoulder gun** *n* **:** a firearm that is normally fired while held in the hands and braced against or upon the shoulder — called also *shoulder arm*

should·na \ˈshu̇dnə\ *Scot* **:** should not

shouldn't \ˈshu̇dᵊnt\ [by contr.] **:** should not

shouldst *or* **shouldest** *archaic past 2d sing of* SHALL

shous *pl of* SHOU

[1]**shout** \ˈshau̇t, *usu* -au̇d·+V\ *vb* -ED/-ING/-S [ME *shouten;* prob. akin to ON *skūta, skūti* taunt, *skjōta* to shoot — more at SHOOT] *vi* **1 a :** to utter a sudden loud cry (as to express joy or triumph or to attract attention) ⟨the crowd . . . ~*ed* with delight —Sherwood Anderson⟩ ⟨like any grief-stricken peasant, ~*ing* against the misery of death —Robert Payne⟩ ⟨a crowd quickly gathered and ~*ed* for a speech —*Amer. Guide Series: Md.*⟩ **b :** to speak in a loud voice ⟨can't hear even when people ~ in her ear⟩ ⟨became angry and began ~*ing* at each other⟩ **c** *of a bird* **:** to utter a cry or song ⟨the cuckoo ~*s* all day at nothing —A.E.Housman⟩ **2 a :** to command attention as if by shouting **:** be conspicuous (as in appearance) ⟨girls whose lips ~*ed* with red⟩ ⟨~*ing* needs⟩ **b :** to issue publicity (as in praise or protest) **:** make a great to-do ⟨natural beauties that give the chamber of commerce plenty to ~ about⟩ **3** *Austral* **:** to treat a person to a drink, refreshments, or entertainment **:** stand treat ⟨now I'm going to stand treat; you've ~*ed* for us already —Henry Lapham⟩ **4 :** to give expression to religious ecstasy often in vigorous rhythmic movements (as shuffling, jumping, jerking); *specif* **:** to take part in a ring shout **5 :** to render the words of a song (as a blues song) in a vigorous rhythmic recitative manner ~ *vt* **1 a :** to utter in a loud voice ⟨~*ed* insults at each other across the street⟩ ⟨~*ed* out the names on the list⟩ ⟨~*ed* "Hallelujah!" and "Amen!" throughout the preacher's exhortation⟩ **b** *archaic* **:** to acclaim with a shout **c :** to make public announcement of in a loud voice ⟨the peddlers . . . ~ their wares with a cry which is like the howl of a wolf —Erle Stanley Gardner⟩ ⟨listened for the conductor to ~ the stations⟩ **d :** to cause to be, come, or go by or as if by shouting ⟨~ himself hoarse⟩ ⟨had to ~ up a clerk from the back room to wait on him⟩ ⟨~ the runners on to the finish line⟩ ⟨a number of newspapers, all strident in upholding their own views and in ~*ing* down rival opinion —H.L.Smith b.1906⟩ **2** *Austral* **a :** to treat a person to (as a drink) ⟨I had to go in and have a drink with them, and ~ one in return —Nevil Shute⟩ **b :** to treat (a person) to a drink or some other refreshment ⟨came in considerably the worse for Saint Patrick's Day, for he had been ~*ed* by more than one of his friends —Ruth Park⟩

[2]**shout** \"\ *n* -S [ME; akin to ME, *shouten* to shout] **1 :** a loud burst of voice **:** a vehement and sudden outcry (as to attract attention); *esp* **:** the outcry of a crowd expressing joy, triumph, rage, or other strong emotion ⟨~ of welcome⟩ ⟨drew a loud ~ of laughter from the audience⟩ **2** *Austral* **a :** a free drink **:** TREAT **b :** one's turn to order (as a round of drinks) **3 a :** RING SHOUT **b :** a religious gathering (as in a praise house) marked by a ring shout **c :** SHOUT SONG **4** *slang* **:** EXCLAMATION POINT

shout·er \ˈshau̇d·ə(r), -au̇tə-\ *n* -S **1 :** one that shouts **2** *usu cap* **:** a member of a religious sect found among Negroes in the West Indies and marked by the use of ceremonies resembling African rituals

shou·ther \ˈshüt͟hə(r)\ *chiefly Scot var of* SHOULDER

shouting distance *n* **:** easy reach — usu. used with *within* ⟨a barber's shop within *shouting distance* of the Cotton Exchange —Constance Foley⟩ ⟨from just under $200,000,000 in 1939 to within *shouting distance* of the billion mark —*Monsanto Mag.*⟩

shout·ing·ly *adv* **:** in a shouting manner

shout song *n* **1 :** a strongly rhythmic religious song used by Negroes in the South, associated with a ring shout, and characterized by responsive singing or shouting between a leader and the congregation **2 :** any song delivered in a responsive or shouting manner

[1]**shove** \ˈshəv\ *vb* -ED/-ING/-S [ME *shuven, shouven, shoven,* fr. OE *scūfan;* akin to OHG *scioban* to push, shove, ON *skūfa, skȳfa* to push, shove, Goth *afskiuban* to reject, cast off, Lith *skùbti* to hurry, OSlav *skubati* to pluck, tear] *vt* **1** *archaic* **:** to thrust or cast violently away **2 :** to cause to go by the application of force: as **a :** to move forcibly by the direct and continuous application of strength **:** DRIVE ⟨more than forty steamboats . . . , piece by piece, had been *shoved* and pulled from the lower river on makeshift rollers —Tom Marvel⟩ **b :** to push or put in a rough, careless, or hasty manner **:** THRUST ⟨~ the smaller children out of the way and take over the swings⟩ ⟨*shoved* the papers into his bag and ran for the bus⟩ **c :** to force by other than physical means **:** COMPEL ⟨the vigilance committee . . . may ~ aside police and courts —B.N.Cardozo⟩ ⟨~ the bill through the legislature⟩ ⟨a surplus that will ~ the price down from a dollar to 60 cents⟩ ⟨felt he was being *shoved* around by his boss and should show his independence⟩ **3 a :** to dispose of to advantage by passing ⟨*shoving* the boring jobs off onto other people —Ann Bridge⟩ ⟨~ counterfeit money⟩ **b :** engage in the sale of (narcotics) **:** PEDDLE ⟨~ dope⟩ ~ *vi* **1 :** to move by forcing a way ⟨glaciers that ~ seaward⟩ ⟨bargain hunters ~ up to the counter⟩ **2 a :** to move something by exerting force ⟨boarded the boat and *shoved* off from the dock⟩ **b :** to go away from a place **:** LEAVE ⟨put on his hat and *shoved* off for home⟩ ⟨let's have one for the road and ~ out of this rathole —Maritta Wolff⟩ ⟨saw the cops coming and said it was time to ~⟩ **3** *of bituminous paving* **:** to form surface waves under traffic when softened by heat **syn** see PUSH

[2]**shove** \"\ *n* -S [ME *shov,* fr. *shuven, shouven, shoven,* v.] **1 :** an act or instance of shoving **:** a forcible push ⟨gave him a ~ that sent him reeling⟩ ⟨gave the project the ~ it needed to succeed⟩ **2 :** STRIKE SLIP

[3]**shove** \ˈshōv\ *n* -S [by alter.] **:** SHIVE a,b

shoved joint *also* **shove joint** *n* **:** PUSH JOINT

shovegroat \ˈ≈,≈\ *n* [ME *shove grote,* fr. *shoven* to shove + *grote* groat] **:** SHOVE-HALFPENNY

shove–halfpenny *or* **shove–ha'penny** \ˈ≈ˈ≈(≈)≈\ *n* [[1]*shove* + *halfpenny* or *ha'penny*] **:** a game played on a special board in which players drive coins or other disks with the thumb or palm from the edge of the board into scoring beds at the other end

[1]**shov·el** \ˈshəvəl\ *n* -S *often attrib* [ME, fr. OE *scofl;* akin to MLG *schūfle, schuffele* shovel, OHG *scūfla, scūvala,* OSw *skofl* shovel, OE *scūfan* to shove — more at SHOVE] **1 a :** a hand implement consisting of a broad scoop or a more or less hollowed out blade with a handle used to lift and throw material (as earth, coal, grain) **b :** a working part in an implement or machine resembling a shovel in shape or use: as (1) **:** a working point in a cultivator (2) **:** the share of a shovel plow — compare TWISTED SHOVEL (3) **:** SPADE **c :** an excavating machine **2 :** SHOVEL HAT **3 :** SHOVELFUL **4 :** a cue used in shuffleboard (sense 2a) **5 :** a small abrasive or polishing hand lap used in conjunction with a watchmaker's lathe to finish cylindrical surfaces **6 :** the upcurved forward tip of a ski

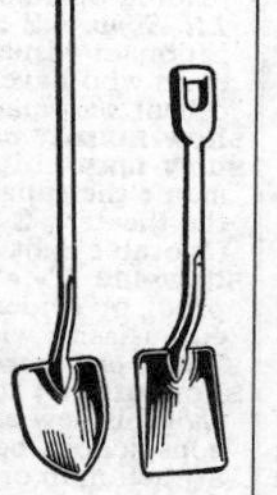

shovels 1a

[2]**shovel** \"\ *vb* **shoveled** *or* **shovelled; shoveled** *or* **shovelled; shoveling** *or* **shovelling** \-v(ə)liŋ\ **shovels** [ME *shovelen,* fr. *shovel,* n.] *vt* **1 :** to take up and throw with a shovel **:** turn with a shovel **2 :** to dig or clean out (as a ditch) with a shovel **3 :** to throw or convey roughly or in the mass as if with a shovel ⟨*shoveled* his food into his mouth⟩ ~ *vi* **:** to take up and cast something with a shovel

[3]**shovel** \"\ *vi* -ED/-ING/-S [ME *shovelen,* freq. of *shuven, shoven* to shove — more at SHOVE] **:** SHUFFLE

shovelbill \ˈ≈≈,≈\ *n* **:** SHOVELER 2

shovelboard \ˈ≈≈,≈\ *n* [alter. (influenced by [1]*shovel*) of obs. E *shove-board,* fr. [1]*shove* + *board*] **1** *archaic* **:** SHOVE-HALFPENNY, *also* **:** a coin or table used in playing shove-halfpenny **2 :** SHUFFLEBOARD 2

shovel cultivator *n* **:** a mechanical cultivator with flat triangular blades for use with row crops

shov·el·er *or* **shov·el·ler** \ˈshəv(ə)lə(r)\ *n* -S [ME *shoveler;* in sense 1, fr. *shovelen* to shovel + *-er;* in sense 2, fr. *shovel,* n. + *-er*] **1 :** one that shovels; *esp* **:** SHOVELMAN **2 :** any of several river ducks (genus *Anas*) having a large and very broad bill; *esp* **:** a widely distributed duck (*A. clypeata*) that in the male has the head and neck blackish green and the abdomen chestnut

shovelfish \ˈ≈≈,≈\ *n* [so called fr. the shape of its head] **:** PADDLEFISH

shov·el·ful \ˈshəvəl,fu̇l\ *n, pl* **shovelfuls** *or* **shovelsful :** the quantity that a shovel contains

shovel hat *n* **:** a shallow-crowned hat with a wide brim curved up at the sides that is worn by some clergymen

shovelhead \ˈ≈≈,≈\ *n* **1** *or* **shovelhead shark :** BONNETHEAD **2** *also* **shovelhead cat** *or* **shovelhead catfish :** FLATHEAD CATFISH

shovellike \ˈ≈≈,≈\ *adj* **:** resembling a shovel (as in being broad and flat in the forward part or in curving up at the sides)

shov·el·man \ˈshəvəl,man, -lmən\ *n, pl* **shovelmen :** one who works with a hand or power shovel

shovelnose \ˈ≈≈,≈\ *n* **:** any of various shovel-nosed animals: as **a :** SHOVELER 2 **b :** SHOVEL-NOSED RAY **c :** SHOVELNOSE SHARK **d :** SHOVELNOSE STURGEON **e :** GUITARFISH

shovel–nosed \ˈ≈≈ˈ≈\ *adj* **:** having a broad flat head, nose, or beak

shovel–nosed duck *n* **:** SHOVELER 2

shovel–nosed ray *n* **:** an Australian guitarfish (*Rhinobatos banksii*) that reaches a length of about four feet

shovelnose shark *or* **shovel–nosed shark** *n* **1 :** COW SHARK; *esp* **:** a large dark cow shark (*Hexanchus corinus*) of the Pacific coast of No. America **2 :** GUITARFISH **3 :** a hammerhead shark or a closely related shark

shovelnose sturgeon *n* **1 :** a small sturgeon (*Scaphirhynchus platorhynchus*) of the Mississippi valley that has a broad flattened snout — called also *hackleback* **2 :** a light-colored sturgeon (*Parascaphirhynchus albus*) of the Mississippi river

shovel pass *n* **:** a short forward pass thrown underhand

shovel plow *n* **:** a plow having a triangular share and used for cultivating

shovel–tusker \ˈ≈≈,≈≈\ *n* **:** any of several Miocene and Pliocene mastodons with the lower tusks broadened and flattened into a large structure suggesting a shovel

shovelweed \ˈ≈≈,≈\ *n* [so called fr. the shape of the pods] **:** SHEPHERD'S PURSE

shove net *n* [ME *shofnet,* fr. *shuven, shoven* to shove + *net* — more at SHOVE, NET] **:** a fishing net attached to a hoop on a handle

[1]**shov·er** \ˈshəvə(r)\ *n* -S [[1]*shove* + *-er*] **:** one that shoves: as **a :** an aggressive person **b :** a passer of counterfeit money **c :** a slaughterhouse worker who pushes carcasses and cuts from place to place on an overhead conveyor

[2]**shov·er** \ˈshəvə(r\ *n* -S [by alter.] *slang Brit* **:** CHAUFFEUR

shoves *pres 3d sing of* SHOVE, *pl of* SHOVE

shoving *pres part of* SHOVE

[1]**show** \ˈshō\ *vb* **showed; shown** \ˈshōn *sometimes* ˈshōən\ *or* **showed; showing; shows** [ME *shewen, showen* (also, to look at), fr. OE *scēawian* to look, see, look at; akin to OFris *skāwia, skōwia* to look, see, look at, OS *skauwon,* OHG *scouwōn* to look, see, look at, L *cavēre* to be on one's guard — more at HEAR] *vt* **1 :** to cause or permit to be seen: as **a :** to put on view ⟨would have ~*ed* us their sacristy —Thomas Gray⟩ ⟨had *shown* his strength, the power of reason over panic —Victor Canning⟩ **b :** to present (as oneself) to public notice in a personal appearance ⟨~*ed* himself in public places to quiet rumors that he was ill⟩ **c :** to hold (a light) in the dark or as a signal **d :** to present (as a sign or indication) to view or observation ⟨~*ed* every mark of extreme agitation⟩ **2 a :** to offer for inspection ⟨~*ed* his ticket at the gate⟩ ⟨had to ~ their passports⟩ **b :** to set out for sale **:** place on view for customers **:** OFFER ⟨stores were ~*ing* luxury goods of every kind⟩ ⟨~*ing* new spring suits⟩ **3 :** to make evident or apparent **:** serve as the means to reveal or make visible ⟨a style that ~*ed* a lovely figure to perfection⟩ ⟨a basement window ~*ed* him just the feet of passersby⟩ **4 :** to wear (colors) in indication of loyalty **:** hang out or carry (a flag) ⟨openly ~*ed* royalist colors⟩ **5 :** to present as a public spectacle **:** PERFORM ⟨a play that had been *shown* in every town hall and opera house⟩ **6 :** to make deliberate or conscious display of for the notice or admiration of others ⟨~*ed* the trimmest of well-turned ankles and the demurest of pert smiles⟩ **7 :** to present (a part or aspect) to view **:** make (a particular appearance) noticeable ⟨trees were ~*ing* the first light shimmer of green⟩ ⟨a rundown house ~*ed* a blind and vacant face to the street⟩ **8 :** to offer to the sight of eye or mind **:** present for consideration or reflection ⟨lies in a valley as beautiful as France can ~ —A.B.Osborne⟩ ⟨attractions for tourists such as only a metropolis can ~⟩ **9 :** to reveal (something) by one's condition or nature **:** make conspicuous ⟨a light-colored overcoat that ~*ed* soil readily⟩ **10 a :** to give a reading of **:** INDICATE ⟨a lighted tower clock ~*ed* the time to be 2:15⟩ ⟨speedometer ~*ed* 70⟩ **b :** to exhibit when counted, recorded, or reported ⟨utilities ~*ed* slight gains in generally erratic trading⟩ ⟨major crops continued to ~ a surplus⟩ ⟨~*ed* a loss for the first time in several years⟩ **11 a :** to point out (as an object, a place) to someone **:** conduct (as a person, a group) to or about a place or thing **:** act as cicerone or conductor in guiding or exhibiting ⟨~*ed* him the house and grounds⟩ ⟨~*ed* the view of the distant mountaintops to his companion⟩ ⟨~*ed* them around the city⟩ **b :** ESCORT, USHER ⟨~*ed* me to an aisle seat⟩ ⟨~*ed* him to his room⟩ ⟨~*ed* him over the property⟩ **12 a :** to reveal or display (an inward disposition, feeling, or trait) by appearance or behavior ⟨his speech and bearing ~*ed* a mind at ease⟩ ⟨~*ed* the generosity and freedom of gentle breeding⟩ **b :** to prove (oneself) to be of a particular disposition or kidney ⟨~*ed* himself kind no less than brave⟩ **c :** to make (itself) evident, apparent, or manifest — used of a condition or trait ⟨a strange deviousness ~*ed* itself in everything he did⟩ **13 :** to accord (favor) to **:** do (kindness) to **:** exhibit (a disposition) toward ⟨render true judgments, ~ kindness and mercy each to his brother —Zech 7:9 (RSV)⟩ **14 a :** to set forth in a statement, account, or description **:** make evident or clear **:** ASSERT, DECLARE ⟨presented a carefully worked out report ~*ing* the benefits to be expected from a system of expressways⟩ ⟨a composition that ~*s* predominantly classical influences⟩ **b** *archaic* **:** ANNOUNCE, COMMUNICATE, TELL **c :** ALLEGE, PLEAD, PRESENT — used esp. in law ⟨~ cause why judgment should not be entered⟩ **15 a :** to demonstrate or establish by argument or reasoning **:** PROVE ⟨~ . . . that the method of knowledge-by-definition is and long has been in standard use —Vilhjalmur Stefansson⟩ ⟨~*s* the futility of many accepted inferences⟩ ⟨this is *shown* by every test of reason and tradition⟩ **b :** to constitute evidence of **:** amount to proof of **:** establish by inference ⟨uneven inking ~*s* carelessness in the pressroom⟩ ⟨this habit ~*s* that discipline has been long continued⟩ **c :** to give an explanation of **:** TEACH, INFORM, INSTRUCT ⟨~*ed* me how to solve the problem⟩ **16 :** to present the image or likeness of ⟨a photograph ~*ing* his whole family⟩ ⟨a painting that ~*s* the author as a young man⟩ **17 :** to claim (points won) in cribbage ⟨~*ed* eight and won the game⟩ ~ *vi* **1 a :** to be or come in view **:** be visible ⟨the lovely peaks . . . ~*ed* for a while as spectral shapes above the tree tops —E.E.Shipton⟩ **b :** to put in an appearance **:** join a gathering **:** appear in company ⟨the guest of honor failed to ~ —*Newsweek*⟩ **c :** to come as expected **:** be on hand **:** turn up ⟨I'm glad you ~*ed,* kid —H.A.Sinclair⟩ ⟨shad have begun to ~ at the dam⟩ **2 a :** to give a particular appearance **:** have a particular look or quality ⟨his nature ~*ed* strong in adversity⟩ **b :** to appear in a particular way or manner — used with an adverb ⟨slackness among civilians . . . ~*ed* plainly in public life —Dixon Wecter⟩ **c** *obs* **:** to have an appearance implying or suggesting something not actually so or not known to be so — used with *as if* **3 :** to give a theatrical performance ⟨a tough town to ~ in⟩ **4 :** to appear as a contestant (as in entering a prize ring) **5 :** to finish third or at least third esp. in a horse race **6 :** to indicate and claim cribbage points for the combinations in one's hand and crib after the play

syn EVINCE, MANIFEST, EVIDENCE, DEMONSTRATE: in this series SHOW is a general term, usu. interchangeable with any of the others, for indicating, revealing, displaying ⟨in this decision he *showed* his capacity for extreme boldness —John Buchan⟩ EVINCE in today's English may designate revealing, or making perceptible, for inspection or consideration ⟨the two phases seem to draw apart, or at least to *evince* themselves in distinct expression —H.O.Taylor⟩ ⟨proposal *evinces* a change of attitude —*New Republic*⟩ MANIFEST may designate fuller, plainer, or more obvious revelation or indication requiring no examination or attention for perception ⟨a wealth of creative design as is *manifested* in these prints —Laurence Binyon⟩ ⟨the power the Western democracies can wield is greater than that which Soviet Communism can *manifest* in aggression —Sumner Welles⟩ EVIDENCE may occas. suggest indication or display which on consideration could serve as valid evidence ⟨she was a good business woman, as is *evidenced* by the success

of her petition, November 4, 1779, to the General Assembly —R.W.Thorp⟩ ⟨retains a strong appreciation of its history, *evidenced* in the collections of antiquities —*Amer. Guide Series: N. H.*⟩ DEMONSTRATE may indicate most obvious revelation or indication, either full and orderly or marked and palpable ⟨undertook both to *demonstrate* and popularize the Copernican hypothesis —Stringfellow Barr⟩ ⟨one whose entire life had *demonstrated* an inability to grapple successfully with business and financial problems —Edna Yost⟩

syn EXHIBIT, DISPLAY, PARADE, FLAUNT, EXPOSE: SHOW is the general term for presenting in such way as to invite notice. EXHIBIT applies to putting forward prominently, openly, or conspicuously to attract rather than merely permit attention and inspection ⟨he *exhibited* with peculiar pride two cream-colored mules —Willa Cather⟩ ⟨we are sure that she would like to hurl the prayer book, *exhibited* so ostentatiously before the dowagers, in the face of the congregation —E.K.Brown⟩ ⟨can *exhibit* a contempt of death because of the exaltation of her faith —F.R.Leavis⟩ DISPLAY may indicate an unfolding, stretching out, spreading out, or otherwise showing in full detail or to best advantage ⟨*displaying* the new fabrics to the buyers⟩ ⟨certain events considered important were *displayed* under six-column headlines —Jacques Kayser⟩ PARADE suggests sustained ostentatious, arrogant, or defiant display ⟨he did not *parade* his knowledge. Indeed he seemed honestly apologetic because he knew so little —L.C.Douglas⟩ ⟨they could not *parade* their virtue. They had lost, and that was the end —Irving Stone⟩ FLAUNT, a close synonym of PARADE, may suggest ostentatious challenging, boasting, or mocking ⟨ladies of the bluest blood and the highest social rating flippantly *flaunted* their lovers and their husbands made no secret of their mistresses —C.G.Bowers⟩ ⟨the grandees no longer *flaunted* their wealth in exotic entertainments, for most were dead or bankrupt —John Buchan⟩ ⟨and ye vaunted your fathomless power, and ye *flaunted* your iron pride —Rudyard Kipling⟩ EXPOSE may indicate a displaying after being brought out of concealment or from under cover or being discovered or unmasked ⟨he . . . looked me over as though I had been *exposed* for sale —Joseph Conrad⟩ ⟨he shrinks from *exposing* his mind. He is bashful, constrained, often resentful —H.A.Overstreet⟩ ⟨a vitriolic joy in *exposing* their pretentions and their hypocrisy —Van Wyck Brooks⟩ — **show one's hand 1 :** to display one's cards faceup **2 :** to declare one's intentions or reveal one's resources — **show one's heels to :** OUTRUN, OUTSTRIP — **show the door :** to tell (a person) to get out (as from a house or a room) : turn out : send packing

²show \"\ *n* -s *often attrib* [ME *shewe*, fr. *shewen, showen*, v.] **1 :** an exhibition or display intended as a demonstration of strength (as of military power) ⟨sent a squadron to make a ~ of force⟩ **2 a** *archaic* **:** outward appearance ⟨command him in ~ at least —Robert Burton⟩ **b :** a vain or empty semblance or pretense or one intended to deceive ⟨made a plausible ~ of being a man of means and position⟩ **c :** an appearance or semblance more or less consonant with reality, fact, or substance ⟨seemed to be acting with some ~ of reason⟩ **d :** an appearance or suggestion of a particular kind ⟨the place made a poor ~ of domestic comfort and warmth⟩ ⟨carefully tended shrubs and flowers made a striking ~⟩ **e :** a display meant to impress others **:** OSTENTATION, PARADE ⟨in moments of introspection, when there is no longer a necessity of putting off with a ~ of wisdom the uninitiated interlocutor —B.N. Cardozo⟩ **3 :** a favorable opportunity (as to prove oneself) **:** CHANCE, PROBABILITY ⟨his background was irregular but they gave him a ~⟩ ⟨do you see any ~ of discovering who fired the gun⟩ **4 :** something or someone exhibited or proposed for regard of any kind (as wonder or ridicule) **:** CYNOSURE, SPECTACLE ⟨she was a boast, a marvel, and a ~ —Lord Byron⟩ ⟨between the cliffs it booms, a mighty ~, then softly laps the shore —P.A.Cole⟩ **5** *obs* **:** the apparition either of beings held to be supernatural or of visions seeming to present such beings **6 :** a large display arranged or organized to arouse interest or enthusiasm or to stimulate sales **:** EXPOSITION ⟨a state flower ~⟩ ⟨the national motorboat ~⟩ **7 a :** a theatrical presentation (as a play or motion picture) ⟨significant steps forward in the development of the musical ~ in this country from . . . operetta —H.W.Wind⟩ ⟨~ people are a hardy and resilient lot⟩ **b :** a dramatic or other radio or television program ⟨hundreds of cowboy movies and television ~s are watched . . . by millions of Americans —D.B.Davis⟩ ⟨top-drawer radio ~s began to be presented from recordings⟩ **c :** an act by singers, dancers, instrumentalists, or other performers presented as entertainment in a nightclub or cabaret or the entire program of such acts given at one time **d :** a pageant, contest, or other large spectacular presentation intended to amuse or inform large numbers of people ⟨the Romans had some success in low comedy . . . but their instinct turned to ~s and circuses —T.S. Eliot⟩ ⟨you get more free ~s in Britain than anywhere else on earth —Anthony Day⟩ **e :** a circus or carnival or any of its acts or sideshows — compare RIDE **8 :** a public art exhibition (as of paintings or sculpture) in a museum or gallery intended to display an artist's work or promote its sale ⟨a sidewalk ~ of watercolors⟩ **9 a :** a military operation or engagement **:** ACTION ⟨pilots . . . who had not gone out with us were pretty peeved to think that they had missed the ~ —*McGill News*⟩ ⟨that battle was the fleet's big ~⟩ **b :** a unit or group engaged in a military operation or mission ⟨the other member of my ~ rode at my wing tip, a big black shape, sinister in the half-light —J.L.Rhys⟩ **10 a :** an event or performance regarded as carried off well or esp. as visually or theatrically satisfying ⟨the first stake race of the season was a good ~ —G.F.T.Ryall⟩ **b :** personal or group conduct regarded as meeting or falling short of some test or standard or as meriting praise or blame ⟨good ~, his flying that old crate to get here when you were ill⟩ ⟨the department had been drained of morale and pride and was putting on a pretty poor ~⟩ **11 :** an effort or operation (as a business enterprise) taken as a whole or regarded as to its success or prospects ⟨a new president who tried at first to run the whole ~ in all its details himself⟩ ⟨logging proved a poor ~ that winter⟩ **12 :** a trace or indication showing that a mine contains metal or a well gas or oil ⟨widely used to test cores, samples, and drilling mud for oil ~s —C.G.Lalicker⟩ **13 a :** a discharge of mucus streaked with blood from the vagina at the onset of labor **b :** the first appearance of blood in a menstrual period **14 :** ¹CAP 9 **15 :** third place at the finish of a horse race ⟨paid $2.60 for ~⟩ — compare WIN, PLACE

show·able \'shōəbəl\ *adj* **:** capable of being shown

show bill *n* **:** an advertising poster

show biz \-ˈbiz\ *n* [by shortening & alter.] **:** SHOW BUSINESS

showboard \'ˌ=,=\ *n* **:** a small billboard for outdoor advertising

showboat \'ˌ=,=\ *n* **:** a river steamship containing a theater and carrying a troupe of actors to give plays at river communities

show box *n* **:** a box for a peep show

showbread *var of* SHEWBREAD

show business *n* **:** the amusement arts, occupations, and businesses (as theater, motion pictures, circus, radio, and television)

show card *n* **:** an advertising placard or display card

show card color *n* **:** POSTER COLOR

¹showcase \'ˌ=,=\ *n* [²*show* + *case*] **1 :** a glazed case, box, or cabinet to display and protect wares in a store or articles in a museum **2 a :** a setting or framework for exhibiting something esp. at its best ⟨after the run . . . a proud ~ of the legitimate theater will close its doors —*N.Y.Times*⟩ **b :** a medium or vehicle for exhibiting a tentative offering or tryout of something ⟨a program that has consistently been a ~ for rising talent⟩

²showcase \"\ *vt* **:** EXHIBIT ⟨network radio alone programs some six hours a week of regularly scheduled shows that ~ the candidates —*Newsweek*⟩

show cause order *n, law* **:** an order from a court or judge to a litigant ordering him to appear at a stated time to give a good reason why a conditional order should not be made absolute or why something should not be permitted or done in the case

show dahlia *n* **:** any of various dahlias having much doubled flower heads with closely packed ray florets

showdown \'ˌ=,=\ *n* [fr. *show down* to display one's hand at poker] **1 a :** the placing of poker hands faceup on the table to determine the winner of a pot **b :** COLD HANDS **2 :** the final settlement of a contested issue or the test of strength by which it is settled ⟨emerged on the winning end of a 257–26 ~ in the House of Commons —*Wall Street Jour.*⟩

showdown inspection *n* **:** a detailed inspection of the clothing and equipment of each individual in a military unit for completeness and serviceability

showed *past of* SHOW

¹show·er \'shau̇(ə)r, -au̇ə, *esp in the southern US* -au̇wə(r\ *n* -s [ME *shur, shour, showre*, fr. OE *scūr*; akin to OHG *scūr* shower, storm, ON *skūr* shower, Goth *skūra* (*windis*) windstorm, L *caurus, corus* northwest wind, Lith *šiaurys* northwind, OSlav *sěverŭ* north, Arm *curt* cold, shower; basic meaning: north, northwind] **1 a :** a fall of rain that is of short duration or rapidly varying intensity over a limited area with drops usu. about $^1/_{25}$ inch in diameter and a velocity of from 10 to 25 feet per second — compare DRIZZLE **b :** a like fall of sleet, hail, or snow **c :** a shower of meteors **d :** COSMIC-RAY SHOWER **2 :** something likened to a rain shower: as **a :** a spray of water (as from a hose or waterfall) **b :** a rain of sparks **c :** a dense fall of bullets or other missiles ⟨the whole target area was left ablaze and cratered with huge bomb holes from a ~ of incendiary and high-explosive missiles —*Springfield (Mass.) Union*⟩ **d :** a firework for producing a brilliant shower (as of slow-burning stars) **3 :** something that comes in large and concentrated numbers or quantity ⟨walked down from the aircraft in a ~ of applause —*N.Y.Times*⟩ ⟨brought down on his head a ~ of reproaches —A.P.Ryan⟩ ⟨organized a postcard ~ to cheer him up after the accident⟩ **4 :** a party given by friends or well-wishers who bring gifts often of a particular kind ⟨the bride was given linen and kitchen ~s⟩ ⟨got up a stork ~ for her when her baby was expected⟩ **5 :** SHOWER BATH ⟨felt fresh from his shave and ~ —Hamilton Basso⟩ **6 a :** one of the individual flowers or small bouquets that hang by ribbons from a shower bouquet **b :** a ribbon used in a shower bouquet

²shower \"\ *vb* -ED/-ING/-S *vi* **1 :** to rain or fall in or as if in a shower ⟨it had ~ed off and on all day⟩ ⟨letters ~ed on him in praise and in protest⟩ **2 :** to bathe in a shower bath ⟨~ed and changed to clean clothes —James Jones⟩ ~ *vt* **1 a :** to pour down on in or as if in showers (as of rain, spray, or drops) **b :** to wet with rain showers, water spray, or other liquid **c :** to spray or bedew **:** pour on like a shower ⟨the wind veered and ~ed a fishing boat with radioactive ash⟩ ⟨factory chimneys ~ the district with soot⟩ ⟨gusts were ~ing dust and bits of paper and other small debris on our yard⟩ **2 :** to bestow liberally **:** give in abundance **:** RAIN ⟨~ed invitations on him⟩; *also* **:** to cover as if with a shower of rain ⟨~ed him with honors⟩

³show·er \'shō(ə)r, -ōə\ *n* -s [ME *shewer, shoer*, fr. *shewen, showen* to show + *-er* — more at SHOW] **:** one that shows **:** EXHIBITOR

shower bath *n* **1 :** a bath in which water is showered on the person **2 :** the apparatus including a finely perforated nozzle that provides a shower bath

shower bouquet *n* **:** a large bouquet from which many small bouquets or individual flowers hang by ribbons of various lengths ⟨the maid of honor and flower girl carried *shower bouquets* of pink sweetheart roses and ivy —*New Orleans (La.) Times-Picayune*⟩

shower of gold : YELLOW ELDER

showerproof \'ˌ=,=\ *adj* **:** treated so as to shed or resist slight wetting (as from a shower) — used of a fabric; compare RAINPROOF, WATERPROOF

show·ery \'shau̇(ə)rē, -ri, *esp in the southern US* -au̇wər-\ *adj* **1 :** raining in showers **:** abounding with frequent showers of rain **2 :** of, relating to, or resembling a shower **3 :** producing, produced by, or falling in showers

show fever *n* **:** PANLEUCOPENIA

showfolk \'ˌ=,=\ *n pl* **:** the performers in any kind of show business

show geranium *n* **:** MARTHA WASHINGTON GERANIUM

show girl *n* **:** a chorus girl in a musical comedy or nightclub show; *esp* **:** one who performs or poses in elaborate costumes

show glass *n, Brit* **:** SHOWCASE

showgoer \'ˌ=,==\ *n* **:** one who habitually attends shows

showground \'ˌ=,=\ *n* **:** the site of a circus, fair, or exposition

showhouse \'ˌ=,=\ *n* **1 :** THEATER **2 :** a greenhouse (as in a park, a botanical garden, or on a private estate) used primarily for display

show-how \'ˌ=,=\ *n* -s [fr. the phrase *show how*] **:** a demonstration esp. of technical method or procedure — compare KNOW-HOW

show·i·ly \'shōəlē, -li\ *adv* **:** in a showy manner

show·i·ness \'shōēnəs, -ōin-\ *n* -ES **:** the quality or state of being showy

show·ing \'shōiŋ, -ōēŋ\ *n* -s [ME *shewing*, fr. gerund of *shewen* to show — more at SHOW] **1 :** an act of putting something on view (as a play or motion picture, the work of an artist, new merchandise) **:** DISPLAY, EXHIBITION ⟨a ~ of new-model cars⟩ **2 :** performance in a test of skill or power or of comparative effectiveness **:** RECORD ⟨made a good ~ in competition with acknowledged front-runners⟩ **3 a :** a statement or presentation of a case or an interpretation of a set of facts ⟨it is, on the treasury's own ~, impossible . . . to sustain a boom on this basis —*New Statesman & Nation*⟩ **b :** APPEARANCE, EVIDENCE ⟨on present ~, this industry seems to have little future⟩ **4 :** ²SHOW 12 ⟨a number of wells . . . had reported ~s of oil and gas —A.I.Levorsen⟩ **5 :** proof or prima facie proof of a matter of fact or law **6 a :** an advertising poster **:** BILLBOARD **b showings** *pl* **:** a group of posters or billboards sold as a unit designed to provide adequate coverage of a market

showish *adj, obs* **:** SHOWY

show·man \'shōmən\ *n, pl* **showmen 1 :** the producer of a play or other theatrical show ⟨one of the great *showmen* whose reading of human nature has passed the test of time —*Times Lit. Supp.*⟩ **2 :** a person having a sense or knack for dramatization or visual effectiveness ⟨some young American musicians who have established themselves in the first rank are excellent *showmen* —Robert Evett⟩

show·man·ly *adj* **:** characteristic of or befitting a showman

show·man·ship \-n,ship\ *n* **1 :** the art or skill of a showman **:** the capacity for effective or spectacular display esp. in the theater **2 :** the ability to present a person or thing in a favorable light (as to win support or favor or to promote sales)

show-me \'ˌ=,=\ *adj* [fr. the phrase *show me*] **:** insistent on proof or evidence **:** SKEPTICAL, INCREDULOUS ⟨faced popular enthusiasms with a questioning, *show-me* attitude⟩

shown *past part of* SHOW

show off *vt* **:** to display with ostentation or pride ⟨wanted to *show* his new car *off*⟩ ~ *vi* **1 :** to seek to attract attention by conspicuous behavior **:** display strength, adroitness, or other attraction in order to be noticed ⟨was *showing off* for the girls⟩ **2 :** to begin sparring in a round of boxing

show-off \'ˌ=,=\ *n* -s [*show off*] **1 :** the act of showing off **:** conspicuous or ostentatious display **2 :** one that shows off **:** EXHIBITIONIST ⟨some nasty little high-I.Q. *show-off* —J.D. Salinger⟩

show of hands : a display of raised hands expressing the vote of a group ⟨voted overwhelmingly by a *show of hands* to have a picnic⟩

showpiece \'ˌ=,=\ *n* **:** a prime or outstanding example used for exhibition ⟨the ship was a ~ of advanced nautical design —James Dugan⟩

show pipe *n* **:** a pipe that forms part of the case of a pipe organ

showplace \'ˌ=,=\ *n* **1 :** a place where plays or theatrical or other spectacles are shown or where exhibitions are held ⟨New York . . . is the ~ of change —*Time*⟩ **2 :** a place (as an estate or building) that is frequently exhibited or is regarded as an example of beauty or excellence ⟨the rambling stone mansion . . . is one of the ~s of the state —*Amer. Guide Series: Md.*⟩

show-ring \'ˌ=,=\ *n* **:** a ring (as at a cattle show) where animals are displayed

showroom \'ˌ=,=\ *n* **1 :** a room where merchandise is exposed for sale or where samples are displayed **2 :** a room where a show is exhibited

shows *pres 3d sing of* SHOW, *pl of* SHOW

showshop \'ˌ=,=\ *n* **1 :** a shop where salable wares are displayed **2 :** THEATER ⟨the realm of the ~s . . . where a hummable melody . . . is apt to be the highest musical expectation —John Mason Brown⟩ ⟨a fairly clever farce-melodrama . . . not without its entertaining moments, its ~ shrewdness —*New Republic*⟩

show stone *n* **:** a crystal gazer's glass

showstopper \'ˌ=,==\ *n* **:** an act, song, or performer that wins applause so prolonged as to interrupt a performance

show-through \'ˌ=,=\ *n* -s [fr. the phrase *show through*] **:** a condition in which or the degree to which printing on one side of a sheet is visible on the other side

show up *vt* **:** to expose (as a person) by deflating pretensions or uncovering faults or misdoings **:** point out or reveal (as wrongdoing or folly) ~ *vi* **1 :** to turn up where or when expected **:** ARRIVE ⟨*showed up* late for his own wedding⟩ **2 :** to appear in a particular light or manner ⟨*showed up* badly in the tryouts⟩ **3 :** to be plainly evident ⟨her age and the life she'd led *showed up* all too clearly in the bright morning light⟩

showup \'ˌ=,=\ *n* -s [*show up*] **1 :** an act of showing someone or something up (as for deficiencies, pretensions, or wrongdoings) **2 :** a police lineup ⟨you can't trust most people to pick their own mothers out at a ~ —W.R.Burnett⟩

show window *n* **1 :** an outside display window in which a store exhibits merchandise **2 :** a sample or setting used to exhibit or illustrate something at its best ⟨wanted to create a *show window* of democracy in the Far East⟩

showy \'shōē, -ōi\ *adj* -ER/-EST [²*show* + *-y*] **1 a :** making an attractive show **:** STRIKING ⟨a superabundance of splendidly ~ bloom —Emily Holt⟩ ⟨the ~ portions of the chateau —Arnold Bennett⟩ ⟨this wonderfully ~ and entertaining ballet suite —Douglas Watt⟩ **b :** manifesting or marked by brilliant ability, performance, or achievement ⟨wit is a ~ gift that is frequently undervalued⟩ **2 :** given to or marked by ostentation **:** FLASHY, GAUDY ⟨their prevailing note is slick, ~, and Philistine —C.J.Rolo⟩ ⟨gaudy calicoes and cheap ~ brass ware —G.B.Shaw⟩

showyard \'ˌ=,=\ *n* **:** a yard for exhibition of livestock

showy crab apple *n* **:** a profuse-blooming small tree or bush (*Malus floribunda*) having sharply serrulate or serrate leaves and rose-red to pink flowers with usu. five styles — called also *Japanese crab*

showy lady's-slipper *also* **showy ladyslipper** *n* **:** a No. American orchid (*Cypripedium reginae*) having pink-and-white flowers of great beauty

showy milkweed *n* **:** a silky-white No. American perennial herb (*Asclepias speciosa*) with opposite oval leaves and profuse umbels of purple-green flowers

showy orchis *n* **:** a No. American orchid (*Orchis spectabilis*) having two large nearly basal leaves and a spike of flowers violet-purple mixed with white with sepals and petals forming a galea behind the column

showy sunflower *n* **:** a tall rough-leaved perennial herb (*Helianthus laetiflorus*) with opposite leaves and a few large heads of yellow flowers

sho·yu \'shō(,)yü\ *n* -s [Jap] **:** SOY

SHP *abbr, often not cap* shaft horsepower

shpg *abbr* shipping

shpmt *abbr* shipment

shpt *abbr* shipment

SHQ *abbr* station headquarters

shr *abbr* share

shrab \'shräb, -rȯb\ *n* -s [Hindi *sharāb*, fr. Ar — more at SYRUP] *India & Pakistan* **:** any plain or mixed drink containing alcohol

shraddha *var of* SRADDHA

shrammed \'s(h)ramd, -aa(ə)md\ *adj* [prob. alter. of *scrammed*, past part. of ¹*scram*] *dial Eng* **:** shriveled and benumbed with cold

shrank [ME *schrank*, fr. OE *scranc*] *past of* SHRINK

shrap·nel \'shrapnəl, *esp South* 'sra-, *dial* 'swa-\ *n, pl* **shrapnel** [after Henry *Shrapnel* †1842 Eng. artillery officer] **1 :** a projectile consisting of a case provided with a powder charge and a large number of usu. lead balls packed in resin or a smoke-producing substance that are discharged with increased energy over an area when the projectile is exploded in flight by a time fuse — compare SHELL **2 :** bomb, mine, or shell fragments

shrap·nell's membrane \-nəlz-\ *n, usu cap S* [after Henry J. *Shrapnell fl*1832 Eng. anatomist] **:** a triangular flaccid part of the tympanic membrane of the ear

shra·van \'shrävən\ *n* -s *usu cap* [Skt *śrāvaṇa*] **:** SAWAN

shread·head \'s(h)red,hed\ *n* [perh. fr. obs. E *shread* shred (fr. ME *shrede*) + E *head*] **:** JERKINHEAD

¹shred \'shred, *esp South* 'sred, *dial* 'swed\ *n* -s [ME *shrede*, fr. OE *scrēade*; akin to MD *schrode* piece cut off, shred, OHG *scrōt* piece cut off, ON *skrjōthr* old worn-out book, L *scrupus* sharp stone, OE *sceran, scieran* to shear — more at SHEAR] **1 a :** a long narrow piece usu. cut or torn off something **:** STRIP ⟨a ~ of ground⟩ ⟨~s of paper⟩ **b :** a very thin shaving or paring ⟨~s of bark⟩ ⟨~s of celery⟩ **2 a :** a thread-like or stringy piece **:** WISP ⟨whole wheat ~s⟩ ⟨~s of fog —Herman Melville⟩ **b :** a ragged scrap of cloth **:** TATTER ⟨~s of canvas —John Hunt & Edmund Hillary⟩ **3 :** a very small fragment or bit of something immaterial **:** PARTICLE, SCRAP ⟨a successful novelist without a ~ of common sense —H.A. Smith⟩ **4 :** a small nodule-shaped piece of light-sensitive photographic emulsion produced by pressing the chilled emulsion through holes in a metal plate in a hydraulic press

²shred \"\ *vb* **shredded** *also* **shred; shredded** *or* **shred; shredding; shreds** [ME *shreden*, fr. OE *scrēadian*; akin to MD *schroden* to cut up, grind into coarse meal, OHG *scrōtan* to cut, OE *scrēade*, n., shred] *vt* **1** *archaic* **a :** to cut or lop (as a branch, bodily part, or lock of hair) ⟨scythe blades which ~ off the unwary passenger's limb —Sir Walter Scott⟩ **b :** PRUNE **2 :** to cut or tear into shreds **:** rip up ⟨*shredded* streamers hung . . . from the roof —D.C.Loughlin⟩ ⟨sharks . . . *shredded* the great fish —J.D.Adams⟩; *specif* **:** to cut (food) into shreds ⟨sugarcane *shredded* by machine⟩ ⟨a dish of *shredded* cabbage⟩ ⟨a frosting with *shredded* coconut⟩ **3 :** to press and break up (photographic emulsion) into shreds ⟨the emulsion . . . is *shredded* and thoroughly washed to remove water-soluble salts —*Complete Photographer*⟩ ~ *vi* **:** to come apart in or break up into shreds ⟨one of the yellow tearoses had *shredded* —Stephen Longstreet⟩ — **shred out :** to subdivide (a project) usu. for handling by persons not fully trained

shred·cock \'s(h)red,käk\ *n, dial Eng* **:** FIELDFARE

shred·der \'shredə(r), *esp South* 'sre-, *dial* 'swe-\ *n* -s **:** one that shreds: as **a :** any of various utensils, implements, or machines for cutting, scraping, or tearing something (as corn, sugarcane, wheat, vegetables, wastepaper) into shreds **b :** HUSKER-SHREDDER **c :** an operator of a machine for flaking scrap metal for use in polishing powder — called also *schrother*

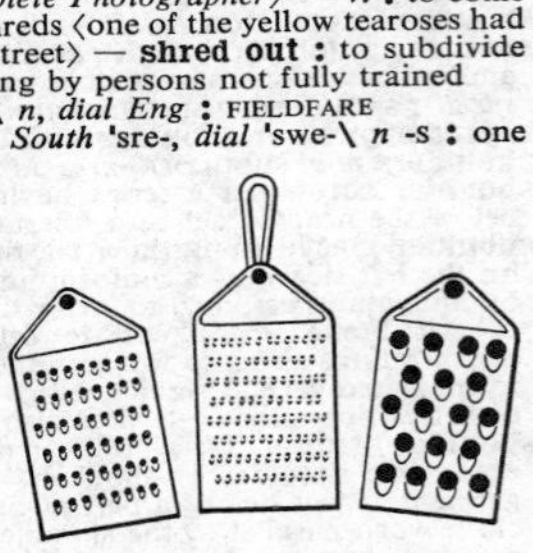

shredders for vegetables

shred·ding \-diŋ, -dēŋ\ *n* -s [ME *schredynge* action of pruning, fr. OE *scrēadung* action of pruning, shred, fr. *scrēadian* to lop off + *-ung* -ing] **:** a strip or piece shredded off something **:** SHRED ⟨sewn together . . . with ~s of warmed saplings —J.M.Cooper⟩

shred·dy \-dē, -di\ *adj* -ER/-EST **:** consisting of or resembling shreds **:** RAGGED ⟨a ~ garment⟩

shredout \'ˌ=,=\ *n* -s [fr. the phrase *shred out*] **:** a division or analysis of a project (as a job, piece of work, course of study) into subunits usu. so that it can be carried out by persons not fully trained — compare BREAKDOWN 7a

shreeve \'s(h)rēv\ *archaic var of* SHERIFF

shrend \'s(h)rend\ *vi* -ED/-ING/-S [prob. fr. G dial. *schrinden*, fr. OHG *scrintan* to crack open — more at BERGSCHRUND] **:** to break into shivers as a result of internal stresses — used of glass not properly tempered or annealed

shreve·port \'shrēv,pō(ə)rt, -ō(ə)rt, -ōət, -ō(ə)l, *usu* |d.+V; *esp South* 'srē-, *dial* 'swē-\ *adj, usu cap* [fr. *Shreveport*, city in northwest Louisiana] **:** of or from the city of Shreveport, La. **:** of the kind or style prevalent in Shreveport

shreve·port·er \|də(r)\ *n* -s *cap* **:** a native or resident of Shreveport, Louisiana

¹shrew \ˈshrü, *esp South* ˈsrü, *dial* ˈswü\ *n* -S [ME *shrewe* evil person, scolding person, scolding woman, fr. OE *scrēawa* shrew (small mammal)] **1 :** any of numerous small mouselike chiefly nocturnal mammals of the family Soricidae which are most closely related to the moles, have a long pointed snout, very small eyes, and velvety fur, feed mainly on worms and insects, and of which most U. S. forms belong in two genera (*Sorex* and *Blarina*) — see ELEPHANT SHREW, LONG-TAILED SHREW, SHORT-TAILED SHREW, TREE SHREW, WATER SHREW **2** *obs* **:** a wicked or evil person **:** SCOUNDREL **3 :** a vexatious, scolding, or brawling woman **:** SCOLD, TERMAGANT ⟨a ~, a woman with the temper of a fiend —C.S.Forester⟩ ⟨~ berating her unemployed husband for not supporting her —John McCarten⟩ — often opposed to *sheep*

²shrew \"\ *vt* -ED/-ING/-S [ME *shrewen*, fr. *shrewe*, n.] **1** *obs* **:** CURSE ⟨~ me if I would lose it —Shak.⟩ **2 :** to treat with shrewish abuse ⟨a wicked woman to ~ his splendid features out of shape —Randall Jarrell⟩

shrewd \ˈshrüd, *esp South* ˈsrüd, *dial* ˈswüd\ *adj* -ER/-EST [ME *shrewed*, fr. *shrewe* + *-ed*] **1 a** *archaic* **:** causing trouble **:** MISCHIEVOUS, NAUGHTY ⟨a ~ and knavish spirit called Robin Goodfellow —Shak.⟩ **b** *obs* **:** causing injury **:** HURTFUL ⟨an ant . . . is a ~ thing in an orchard —Francis Bacon⟩ **2** *obs* **:** marked by bad temper **:** SHREWISH, ABUSIVE ⟨~ words . . . improved into smart blows —Thomas Fuller⟩ ⟨thou wilt never get thee a husband if thou be so ~ of thy tongue —Shak.⟩ **3 a** *obs* **:** tending to disadvantage **:** OMINOUS, UNFORTUNATE **b :** beset with hardships or difficulties **:** DANGEROUS, DISTRESSING ⟨the ordeal of a situation ~ as any that can happen to her sex in civilized life —George Meredith⟩ **4 a :** SEVERE, HARD ⟨a ~ knock⟩ ⟨gives out ~ galvanic shocks —R.L.Stevenson⟩ ⟨give you a ~ kick in the wind —*Punch*⟩ **b :** BITING, PIERCING ⟨a ~ wind⟩ ⟨the first ~ gust of a storm —S.H.Adams⟩ **5 a :** marked by cleverness, discernment, or sagacity **:** ASTUTE, KEEN ⟨~ observer⟩ ⟨~ design⟩ ⟨~ reply⟩ ⟨~ business sense⟩ ⟨~ appraisal of political maneuvers —W.A.Swanberg⟩ **b :** marked by artfulness or trickiness **:** WILY ⟨a ~ operator —Irving Bacheller⟩ **c :** penetrating near the truth **:** KNOWING ⟨~ guess⟩ ⟨~ suspicion⟩ ⟨had a very ~ idea where to look for her —Margery Allingham⟩ **d :** sharp and searching ⟨a ~ eye⟩ ⟨an inspection of the ~*est* sort —Sarah O. Jewett⟩

syn SAGACIOUS, PERSPICACIOUS, ASTUTE: SHREWD may describe a blended practical, hardheaded cleverness, judgment, and acute perception ⟨could on occasions be surprisingly *shrewd* — she had a habit of seeing through people's words right down into their motives —Victoria Sackville-West⟩ ⟨he is *shrewd*, sharp, hard and acute, and he is, one believes, the greatest master of the art of publicity and propaganda to arise in this generation —Sidney Hyman⟩ SAGACIOUS may connote wisdom, penetration, discernment, farsightedness and, above all, keen mature judgment ⟨his strength was in his *sagacious* sifting of practical ideas from the mass of suggestions proffered by his contemporaries —T.D.McCormick⟩ ⟨a strategical withdrawal might have been *sagacious* here —C.H.Sykes⟩ PERSPICACIOUS may indicate unusual power to perceive or understand what is obscure or mysterious ⟨these were the fundamental difficulties, but few men were *perspicacious* enough to appreciate them —Allan Nevins & H.S.Commager⟩ ⟨those blind spots which are found in the most *perspicacious* mortals —L.P.Smith⟩ ASTUTE may indicate mature shrewd perspicacity with esp. careful discretion, wise diplomacy, and calculated discernment ⟨a masterpiece of calculated cajolery from an *astute* adventuress —J.C.Powys⟩ ⟨*astute* financiers who see in the large organization an easier mechanism for their manipulations of credit, for their inflation of capital values, for their monopolistic controls —Lewis Mumford⟩

shrewd·ly *adv* [ME *shrewedly*, fr. *shrewed* shrewd + *-ly*] **:** in a shrewd manner: as **a :** HURTFULLY, SEVERELY ⟨gore him ~ in the exposed flank —James Stevenson-Hamilton⟩ **b :** INTENSELY ⟨hated each other ~ —H.O.Taylor⟩ **c :** ASTUTELY, KNOWINGLY ⟨~ estimating his son as a man of very mediocre parts —Herman Wouk⟩ ⟨her eyes followed him ~ —Liam O'Flaherty⟩

shrewd·ness *n* -ES [ME *shrewednesse*, fr. *shrewed* shrewd + *-nesse* -ness] **:** the quality or state of being shrewd: as **a :** sagacity in practical affairs ⟨the political ~ that characterized his later career —Carol L. Thompson⟩ **b :** keenness of discernment **:** ACUMEN ⟨the tradition of rural ~ —Malcolm Cowley⟩

shrewdy \-dē, -di\ *n* -ES *slang* **:** a shrewd person

shrew·ish \ˈshrüish, -üēsh, *esp South* ˈsrü-, *dial* ˈswü-\ *adj* **:** resembling or having the characteristics of a shrew **:** ILL-TEMPERED, INTRACTABLE ⟨a small, ~ woman with . . . eyes which boded temper —Dorothy Sayers⟩ ⟨her ~ tongue —Peggy Durdin⟩ ⟨the ~ river —Murray Schumach⟩

shrew·ish·ly *adv* **:** in a shrewish manner

shrew·ish·ness *n* -ES **:** the quality or state of being shrewish

shrewlike \ˈ=,=\ *adj* **:** resembling a shrew

shrew·ly *adv* [obs. E *shrew*, adj., evil, malicious (fr. ME *shrewe*, fr. *shrewe*, n., evil person) + E *-ly* — more at SHREW] **:** SHREWDLY

shrew mole *n* **:** any of numerous relatively slender moles that somewhat resemble shrews: as **a :** a mole of an Asiatic genus (*Uropsilus*) **b :** one of a No. American genus (*Neurotrichus*)

shrewmouse \ˈ=,=\ *n, pl* **shrewmice :** SHREW 1

shrews *pl of* SHREW, *pres 3d sing of* SHREW

shrews·bury cake \ˈsh(r)ü|zb(ə)rē-, ˈsh(r)ō|, -,berē-, -ri- *sometimes by* r-*dissimilation* ˈshü| *or* |ˈshō|\ *n, usu cap S* [fr. *Shrewsbury*, city in western England] **:** a short sweet biscuit baked in wafers

shri *var of* SRI

¹shriek \ˈshrēk, *esp South* ˈsrēk, *dial* ˈswēk\ *vb* -ED/-ING/-S [prob. irreg. fr. ME *shriken* to shriek; akin to ON *skrækja* to screech — more at SCREAM] *vi* **1 a :** to utter a sharp shrill sound (as of some birds and animals) ⟨hear . . . an old hare ~ —G.G.Carter⟩ **b :** to cry out in a high-pitched voice **:** SCREECH ⟨the ladies ~*ed* at the sight of the skull —T.L.Peacock⟩ ⟨a tangle of hysterical girls . . . sweeping down the main street, ~*ing* —Jean Stafford⟩ **2 a :** to make a sound resembling a shriek ⟨keep the siren ~*ing* —*Amer. Guide Series: Minn.*⟩ ⟨the wind . . . ~*ing* like ten thousand devils —P.B.Cronk⟩ **b :** to suggest such a sound (as by vividness of expression) ⟨yellow landscape print that ~*ed* from the flowered wallpaper —Margaret Long⟩ ~ *vt* **1 :** to utter or sound forth with a shriek or sharply and shrilly ⟨~ an alarm⟩ ⟨the sirens ~*ed* their warning —*Rotarian*⟩ **2 :** to express in a manner suggestive of a shriek ⟨headlines ~*ing* their sensational news of the murder⟩

²shriek \"\ *n* -S **1 :** a shrill usu. wild or involuntary cry (as of sudden or extreme terror or pain or of violent laughter) ⟨a starling . . . gave a piercing ~ —*Time*⟩ ⟨the agonizing ~*s* of the wounded —Charles Lever⟩ ⟨~*s* of mirth —R.B.D. French⟩ **2 :** a sound resembling a shriek ⟨the sudden ~ of chalk on a blackboard —Earle Birney⟩

shriek·ing·ly *adv* **:** with a shriek ⟨~ the timber cracks —George Meredith⟩

shriek owl *n* **1 a** *archaic* **:** SCREECH OWL **b** *dial Eng* **:** BARN OWL **2** *dial Eng* **:** SWIFT

shrieky \-kē, -ki\ *adj* -ER/-EST **:** resembling a shriek **:** HIGH-PITCHED, HYSTERICAL ⟨a ~ voice⟩

shriev·al \ˈshrēvəl, *esp South* ˈsrē-, *dial* ˈswē-\ *adj* [shrieve + *-al*] **:** of or relating to a sheriff ⟨~ badge⟩ ⟨the functions of his ~ office⟩

shriev·al·ty \-ltē, -ti\ *n* -ES [*shrieve* + *-alty* (as in *royalty*)] *chiefly Brit* **1 :** the office of a sheriff ⟨the honor of the ~⟩ **2 :** the term of office of a sheriff ⟨the events of his ~⟩ **3 :** the jurisdiction of a sheriff ⟨the sheriff has publicly admitted that there are . . . milk bars in his ~ —H.F.Ellis⟩

¹shrieve \ˈs(h)rēv\ *archaic var of* SHERIFF

²shrieve \"\ *archaic var of* SHRIVE

¹shrift \ˈshrift, *esp South* ˈsri-, *dial* ˈswi-\ *n* -S [ME *shrift*, *shrifte*, fr. OE *scrift*, fr. *scrīfan* to shrive — more at SHRIVE] **1** *archaic* **a :** the act of shriving **:** confession of one's sins esp. to a priest in the sacrament of penance **b :** ABSOLUTION 3a **2 :** acknowledgment or disclosure (as of guilt, wrongdoing, something secret) to someone ⟨those . . . who have made ~ of love —Sebastian Evans⟩ **3** *obs* **:** CONFESSIONAL ⟨his bed shall seem a school, his board a ~ —Shak.⟩

²shrift \"\ *vt* -ED/-ING/-S *archaic* **:** SHRIVE

shriftfather \ˈ=,==\ *n* [ME *shriftfader*, fr. *shrift*, *shrifte* shrift + *fader* father] *archaic* **:** FATHER CONFESSOR

¹shrike \ˈshrīk, *esp South* ˈsrīk, *dial* ˈswīk\ *chiefly dial var of* SHRIEK

²shrike \"\ *n* -S [perh. fr. (assumed) ME *shrik*, fr. OE *scrīc* thrush; akin to ME *shriken* to shriek — more at SHRIEK] **1 :** any of numerous oscine birds of the family Laniidae and esp. of the genus *Lanius* that have a strong notched bill hooked at the tip, feed chiefly on insects and often impale their prey on thorns, and generally have the plumage predominantly gray or brownish with the wings and tail black marked with white — see BUTCHER-BIRD, LOGGERHEAD SHRIKE, MIGRANT SHRIKE, NORTHERN SHRIKE, RED-BACKED SHRIKE, WHITE-RUMPED SHRIKE **2 :** any of various birds felt to resemble or formerly classified with the Laniidae (as an antbird or drongo) — usu. used with a qualifying term; see ANTSHRIKE, CUCKOO SHRIKE, WOOD SHRIKE

shrike thrush *n* **1 :** an Indian timaliine bird of the genus *Gampsorhynchus* **2 :** any of several Australian singing birds of the genus *Colluricincla* that resemble the shrike

shrike tit *n* **1 :** any of several species of Australian birds of the genus *Falcunculus* that have a strong toothed bill and sharp claws and that creep over the bark of trees like titmice in search of insects **2 :** HILL TIT **3 :** FALCONET 3

¹shrill \ˈshril, *esp South* ˈsril, *dial* ˈswil\ *vb* -ED/-ING/-S [ME *shrillen*; prob. akin to OE *scrallettan* to resound loudly, OSw *skrælla* to rattle, bang] *vi* **:** to utter or emit an acute, piercing sound **:** produce a sharp shrill sound **:** SCREECH, SCREAM ⟨in the trees outside the cicadas were ~*ing* —Lucien Price⟩ ⟨the loudspeaker ~*ed* with the noise —C.S.Forester⟩ ~ *vt* **:** to utter or express (as a sound or words) in a shrill tone ⟨~*ed* orders and then fell with a scream —F.V.W.Mason⟩ ⟨headlines have ~*ed* disquieting news —Dorothy Barclay⟩

²shrill \"\ *adj* -ER/-EST [ME *shrille*, fr. *shrillen*, v.] **1 a :** having or emitting a sharp high-pitched tone or sound **:** PIERCING, PENETRATING ⟨a ~ whistle⟩ ⟨the ~ music of the calliope —*Amer. Guide Series: Tenn.*⟩ **b :** accompanied by sharp high-pitched sounds or cries ⟨make ~, hysterical little sorties around the shops after lunch —C.G.Glover⟩ **2 :** having an intense, sharp, or vivid effect on the senses **:** KEEN, PUNGENT ⟨arc lamps bathed the occasion in ~ blue light —Noel Coward⟩ ⟨everything looked different: the outlines were ~*er* —Elizabeth Pollet⟩ **3 a :** marked by a sharp insistence on being heard **:** ILL-TEMPERED, STRIDENT ⟨criticism . . . so ~ and partisan that it has provoked resistance and resentment —R.K. Carr⟩ **b :** marked by a lack of restraint or emotional control **:** INTEMPERATE, EXTRAVAGANT ⟨with every look his wrath became ~er, narrower, more personal —Max Lerner⟩

³shrill \"\ *adv* [ME *shrille*, fr. *shrille*, adj.] *archaic* **:** SHRILLY ⟨through the high wood echoing ~ —John Milton⟩

⁴shrill \"\ *n* -S [¹*shrill*] **:** a shrill sound ⟨the ~ of a ship's whistle⟩ ⟨the ~ of crickets —F.D.Ommanney⟩

shrilling *n* -S [fr. gerund of ¹*shrill*] **:** a more or less continued shrill noise or cry ⟨the clash of swords and ~ of trumpets —P.J.Searles⟩; *esp* **:** STRIDULATION ⟨the slow ~ of the field cricket in the grass —Sidney Lanier⟩

shrill·ness *n* -ES **:** the quality or state of being shrill ⟨the voice of woman . . . stretched into unnatural ~ by anger and impatience —T.L.Peacock⟩ ⟨the ~ of the . . . electoral campaign —*Foreign Affairs*⟩

¹shril·ly \-il(l)ē, -)li\ *adv* [²*shrill* + *-ly*] **:** in a shrill manner: as **a :** in a high-pitched voice or tone ⟨the medics were whistling ~ —R.O.Bowen⟩ **b :** in a high-strung, sharply insistent manner ⟨protests a little too ~ —Robert Payne⟩

²shrilly \-ilē, -li\ *adj* [²*shrill* + *-y*] **:** somewhat shrill ⟨a ~ sound⟩ ⟨parrots of ~ green —W.W.Gibson⟩

¹shrimp \ˈshrimp, *esp South* ˈsri-, *dial* ˈswi-\ *n, pl* **shrimps** *also* **shrimp** [ME *shrimpe* shrimp (crustacean), puny person; akin to MHG *schrimpf* scratch, slight wound, *schrimpfen* to wrinkle, Sw *skrympa* to shrink, L *curvus* curved — more at CROWN] **1 a :** any of numerous relatively small mostly marine decapod crustaceans (suborder Natantia) having a slender elongated body with a laterally compressed abdomen, long legs, and a long, more or less spiny rostrum **b :** any of various small crustaceans (as mysids, euphausids, amphipods, and branchiopods) that resemble the true shrimps — often used with a qualifying term — see BRINE SHRIMP, FAIRY SHRIMP; compare PRAWN **2 :** a very small or puny person or thing — usu. used disparagingly ⟨an unimposing little ~ of a man —*Living Age*⟩ **3** *or* **shrimp pink** *or* **shrimp red :** a variable color averaging a deep pink that is bluer, lighter, and stronger than average coral and stronger and slightly yellower and lighter than fiesta

²shrimp \"\ *vi* -ED/-ING/-S **:** to fish for or catch shrimps ⟨~*ing* further offshore —*Fishing Gazette*⟩

shrimp·er \-pə(r)\ *n* -S **:** one that shrimps: **a :** a shrimp fisherman **b :** a boat engaged in shrimping

shrimpfish \ˈ=,=\ *n* **:** any of numerous small compressed East Indian marine fishes of the family Centriscidae that are related to the bellows fish and have a tubular snout and the body covered with an armor of transparent bony plates which is fused with the endoskeleton, extends over and beyond the down-turned dorsal and caudal fins, and terminates in a long spine

shrimp·ish \-pish, -pēsh\ *adj* **:** somewhat diminutive **:** PUNY ⟨tied the apron around his ~ person —Christopher Morley⟩

shrimp plant *n* **:** a widely cultivated tropical American shrubby plant (*Beloperone guttata*) of the family Acanthaceae having whitish flowers borne in spikes and protruding from overlapping broadly ovate reddish brown bracts

shrimpy \-pē, -pi\ *adj* -ER/-EST **1 :** full of shrimp ⟨a ~ bay⟩ **2 :** DIMINUTIVE ⟨a ~ child —Doris Peel⟩ ⟨~ rosebuds —*Harper's*⟩

¹shrine \ˈshrīn, *esp South* ˈsrīn, *dial* ˈswīn\ *n* -S [ME *shrin*, *shrine*, fr. OE *scrīn*, fr. L *scrinium* case, chest, box; perh. akin to Russ *krivoĭ* crooked, L *curvus* curved — more at CROWN] **1 :** a case, box, or receptacle; *esp* **:** one in which sacred relics (as the bones of a saint) are deposited **:** RELIQUARY **2 :** a receptacle (as a casket or tomb) for the dead; *esp* **:** the tomb of one considered holy or of hallowed memory **3 a :** a place or object hallowed or honored from its history or associations ⟨a small country township . . . famous to tourists as the ~ of a late-Victorian novelist —*Sydney (Australia) Bull.*⟩ **b :** an object, structure, or place that is considered sacred by a religious group and that serves as the focus of the performance of some ritual **:** SANCTUARY

²shrine \"\ *vt* -ED/-ING/-S [ME *shrinen*, fr. *shrin*, *shrine*, n.] **1** *archaic* **:** to place in or provide with a shrine ⟨a goddess *shrined* in every tree —Alexander Pope⟩ **2 :** to enclose as if in a shrine **:** ENSHRINE ⟨has the feeling of truth already *shrined* in his own breast —William Hazlitt⟩

shrin·er \-nə(r)\ *n* -S *usu cap* [*Shrine* (in the name *Order of the Mystic Shrine*) + *-er*] **:** a member of a secret fraternal society called the Order of the Mystic Shrine that is non-Masonic but admits only Knights Templars and 32d-degree Masons to membership

¹shrink \ˈshr|iŋk, *esp South* ˈsr|, *dial* ˈsw|\ *vb* **shrank** \|aŋk, |aiŋk\ *also* **shrunk** \|əŋk\ **shrunk** *or esp in adjectival use* **shrunk·en** \-kən *sometimes* -kᵊŋ\ **shrinking; shrinks** [ME *shrinken*, fr. OE *scrincan*; akin to MD *schrinken* to draw back, shrink back, OSw *skrunkin* shrunken, L *curvus* curved — more at CROWN] *vi* **1 :** to contract or curl up the body or part of it usu. because of physical stress, fear, or revulsion **:** HUDDLE, COWER ⟨~ with cold⟩ ⟨~ in horror⟩ ⟨seemed to ~ into himself —Gordon Merrick⟩ ⟨found the atmosphere . . . so gusty that he was glad to ~ out of sight —Samuel Butler †1902⟩ **2 a :** to contract to a less extent or compass ⟨the black peaty earth *shrank* as soon as it was dry —G.M.Trevelyan⟩ **b :** to become smaller or more compacted (as from heat or wetting) ⟨*shrank* over 30% after five launderings —*For Instance*⟩ **c :** to contract after the release of tension ⟨nylon yarn, when wound off a package into skein form, ~*s* . . . as much as 2.8% —W.E. Shinn⟩ **d :** to lose substance or weight (as in cooking) ⟨meat ~*s* in cooking by losing water and fat⟩ **e :** to lessen in value **:** DWINDLE ⟨seeing their earnings ~ as overtime gave way to shorter work weeks —J.A.Lack⟩ **3 a :** to draw back **:** retire to shelter ⟨*shrank* toward a doorway some few yards on —Arthur Morrison⟩ **b** (1) **:** to withdraw to avoid encounter **:** slink away ⟨turns and ~*s* from the room —Sidney Howard⟩ (2) **:** FLINCH ⟨refused to ~ from a . . . thrusting knife —Ward Moore⟩ **c :** to hold back (as from an action or responsibility) esp. because of fear or distaste **:** RECOIL ⟨a very formidable deed, but he was determined not to ~ from it —Eden Phillpotts⟩ ~ *vt* **1** *obs* **:** to draw back or in (as a horn) **:** RETRACT ⟨make the Sun ~ in his beam —Edward Young⟩ **2 a** *archaic* **:** to reduce (as by the body) to smaller compass ⟨her body huge she *shrank* —William Morris⟩ **b :** to cause to contract or shrink ⟨human heads *shrunk* to orange-size —J.H.Cutler⟩ **c :** to compact (cloth) by causing to contract when subjected to washing, boiling, steaming, or other processes **d :** to make smaller or less significant ⟨~*ing* the office to the holder's ability⟩ **3 a** *archaic* **:** to draw or move out of the way (a part of the body) ⟨she *shrank* her hand back —George Meredith⟩ **b** *obs* **:** SHRUG ⟨he *shrunk* up his shoulders at it —Daniel Defoe⟩ **syn** see CONTRACT, RECOIL — **shrink on :** to cause (as a metal ring or hoop) to become fixed tightly around another object by heating sufficiently to slip into place while expanded and then allowing to cool and contract — **shrink out :** to remove (fullness) in tailoring esp. woolen fabrics by steam pressing

²shrink \"\ *n* -S **1 :** the act of shrinking **:** WITHDRAWAL, RECOIL ⟨the shiver and ~ with which the sitter caught sight of him —Lew Wallace⟩ **2 :** SHRINKAGE

shrink·able \-kəbəl\ *adj* **:** capable of being shrunk ⟨a ~ fabric⟩

shrink·age \-kij, -kēj\ *n* -S **1 :** the act or process of shrinking: as **a :** the contraction of metal when cooled **b :** the reduction in volume of excavated earth when compacted in the fill **c :** the loss in weight of livestock during shipment and in the process of preparing the meat for consumption **d :** the loss in weight of meat during cooking **e :** DRY SHRINKAGE **f :** reduction in number or value ⟨a deplorable ~ in the number of qualified teachers —Douglas Bush⟩ ⟨a ~ in the public budget will depress . . . economic activity —R.A.Musgrave⟩ **2 :** the amount of contraction, reduction or depreciation ⟨suffered a 10% ~ in transit⟩

shrinkage rule *or* **shrink rule** *n* **:** CONTRACTION RULE

shrinkage stope *n* **:** an overhand stope without timbering in which the broken ore is stored as a filling to support the workings and form a working floor

shrink·er \-kə(r)\ *n* -S **:** one that shrinks: as **a :** one that puts articles (as textiles) through a shrinking process **b :** one that shrinks on a metal part **c :** a device for reducing the diameter of a metal tire while hot

shrinkhead \ˈ=,=\ *also* **shrinking head** *n* **:** FEEDHEAD

shrinking *pres part of* SHRINK

shrink·ing·ly *adv* **:** in a frightened or withdrawing manner **:** SHYLY ⟨staring ~ at you as you pass —G.W.Cable⟩

shrinking violet *n* **:** a bashful or retiring person ⟨no *shrinking violet* when it comes to telling the umpires off —*Springfield (Mass.) Daily News*⟩; *esp* **:** one who shrinks from public recognition of his merit

shrink link *n* **:** PRISONER 2b

shrink-mixed concrete \ˈ=,=-\ *n* **:** concrete that is partially mixed in a stationary mixer before being finally mixed in a truck mixer

shrink ring *n* **:** a ring shrunk on in order to hold assembled parts (as the commutator bars of a dynamo) in fixed relative position

shrinks *pres 3d sing of* SHRINK, *pl of* SHRINK

shrite \ˈs(h)rīt\ *n* -S [prob. alter. of ²*shrike*] *dial Eng* **:** MISTLE THRUSH

shrive \ˈshr|īv, *esp South* ˈsr|, *dial* ˈsw|\ *vb* **shrived** \|īvd\ *or* **shrove** \|ōv\ **shriv·en** \|ivən *also* ivᵊm *or* ibᵊm\ *or* **shrived; shriving; shrives** [ME *shriven*, fr. OE *scrīfan* to shrive, prescribe; akin to OFris *skrīva* to shrive, write, OHG *scrīban* to write; all fr. a prehistoric WGmc word borrowed fr. L *scribere* to write — more at SCRIBE] *vt* **1 :** to hear the confession of, impose penance on, and give absolution to (a person) in the sacrament of penance ⟨the resident parson . . . would sing his daily Mass and come in to ~ the sick —G.G.Coulton⟩ **2 :** to free from guilt **:** PARDON, PURGE ⟨~*s* his burdened mind —Robert Trumbull⟩ ~ *vi* **1** *archaic* **:** to hear confessions, to impose penance, and to give absolution in performance of the ecclesiastical office of confessor ⟨priests were praying, preaching, *shriving* —T.B.Macaulay⟩ **2 :** to confess one's sins esp. to a priest ⟨mocked at the priest when he called her to ~ —Elizabeth B. Browning⟩

¹shriv·el \ˈshrivəl, *esp South* ˈsri-, *dial* ˈswi-\ *vb* **shriveled** *or* **shrivelled; shriveled** *or* **shrivelled; shriveling** *or* **shrivelling** \-v(ə)liŋ\ **shrivels** [origin unknown] *vi* **1 :** to draw or be drawn into wrinkles **:** shrink and form corrugations ⟨the skin ~*s* with age⟩ ⟨the expanding economy would ~ like a pricked balloon —*Lamp*⟩ — often used with *up* ⟨a leaf ~*s* up in the hot sun⟩ **2 :** to become reduced to inanition, helplessness, or inefficiency ⟨all their vain terrors ~*ing* up like ghosts at sunrise —Edith Wharton⟩ ~ *vt* **:** to cause to shrivel **:** SHRINK, WITHER ⟨one blazing weekend can ~ the receipts for the stoutest hit —Richard Maney⟩ ⟨filmy clouds which do not always disperse until the sun has risen and *shrivelled* them —Mary S. Broome⟩

²shrivel \"\ *n* -S **:** something (as a withered nut or fruit) that is shriveled

¹shroff \ˈshräf\ *n* -S [Hindi *ṣarrāf*, fr. Ar] **:** a banker or money changer in the Far East; *esp* **:** one who tests and determines the worth of coin

²shroff \"\ *vb* -ED/-ING/-S *vt* **:** to inspect and sort (coins) and separate out bad pieces ~ *vi* **:** to act as a shroff

shroff·age \-fij, -fēj\ *n* -S [¹*shroff* + *-age*] **:** the commission charged for shroffing

shrogs \ˈs(h)rägz\ *n pl* [ME *shrogys*, pl. of *shrog*, perh. alter. of *skrogge* stunted shrub or branch] *dial Eng* **:** BRUSHWOOD

¹shrop·shire \ˈs(h)räp,shi(ə)r, -iə, -pshə(r)\ *adj, usu cap* [fr. *Shropshire*, county in western England] **:** of or from Shropshire, England **:** of the kind or style prevalent in Shropshire **:** SALOPIAN

²shropshire \"\ *n, usu cap* **:** a widely distributed English breed of dark-faced hornless mutton-type sheep that are similar to the Southdown but larger and that produce a heavy well-crimped fleece of medium fineness and length

¹shroud \ˈshraůd, *esp South* ˈsraůd, *dial* ˈswaůd\ *n* -S [ME, fr. OE *scrūd*; akin to ON *skrūth* shrouds of a ship, cloth, OE *scrēade* shred — more at SHRED] **1 a** *obs* **:** a covering for the body **:** GARMENT **b :** burial garment **:** WINDING-SHEET, CEREMENT **2 a** *obs* **:** a covered place (as a cave or den) used as a retreat or shelter **b shrouds** *pl, archaic* **:** an underground chapel (as the chapel of St. Faith's under St. Paul's Cathedral in London) **c** *obs* **:** PROTECTION ⟨put yourself under his ~, the universal landlord —Shak.⟩ **d** *archaic* **:** the overspreading foliage of a tree ⟨a cedar . . . with fair branches, and with a shadowing ~ —Ezek 31:3 (AV)⟩ **3 :** something that covers, screens, or guards ⟨a ~ of secrecy⟩ ⟨a ~ of dust hanging over the city⟩: as **a :** the metal piece between the hood and the cowl on an automobile body **b** *or* **shroud plate :** one of the two annular plates at either side at the periphery of a water-wheel that form the sides of the buckets **c :** one of two similarly placed flanges forming part of the wheel casting to strengthen the teeth of a gear wheel or peripheral support to turbine or fan bedding **d :** the disk ends of lantern clock pinions into which the pins are set **e :** the muslin cloth put on dressed beef for protection and cleanliness **f :** a sheet-metal guard protecting an airplane fuselage from exhaust heat **4 a :** one of the ropes of hemp or wire leading usu. in pairs from a ship's mastheads to give lateral support to the masts — see SHIP illustration **b** *also* **shroud line :** one of the cords that suspend the harness of a parachute from the canopy

²shroud \"\ *vb* -ED/-ING/-S [ME *shrouden*, fr. *shroud*, n.] *vt* **1 a** *archaic* **:** to cover (as a person) for protection **:** SHELTER ⟨~ these weaklings from blows —Nathaniel Fairfax⟩ **b** *obs* **:** to conceal (as a person) in a secret or hidden place ⟨I have been closely ~*ed* in this bush —Shak.⟩ **2 a :** to cut off from view **:** SCREEN ⟨trees ~*ed* in a heavy mist⟩ **b :** to veil under another appearance (as by obscuring or disguising) ⟨~*ed* in cipher⟩ ⟨uncertainty . . . ~*s* the identity of the early peoples —*Amer. Guide Series: Ind.*⟩ **3 :** to cover with a shroud; *esp* **:** to enclose in a winding sheet **:** dress for burial **4 :** to cover (sides of beef) with muslin **5 :** TRIM, LOP ⟨climb up . . . and ~ off the lower boughs —Thomas Hardy⟩ ~ *vi, archaic* **:** to take or seek shelter ⟨wilt thou ~ in haunted cell —William Collins †1759⟩

shrouding *n* -S **:** the shrouds on a water wheel, gear wheel, fan wheel, or propeller

shroud knot *n* **:** a knot for fastening together a parted ship's shroud

shroud–laid \ˈ=ˌ=\ *adj, of a rope* **:** composed of four strands and laid right-handed with a heart or core

shroud·less \ˈ=ləs\ *adj* **:** having no shroud or winding-sheet ⟨~ dead on their rocky beds —Jane Wilde⟩

shroud·man \ˈ=mən\ *n, pl* **shroudmen :** a worker who assembles the sheet-metal guards that protect airplane fuselages from exhaust heat

shroud plate *n* **1 :** a chain plate to which a ship's shrouds are fastened **2 :** SHROUD 3b

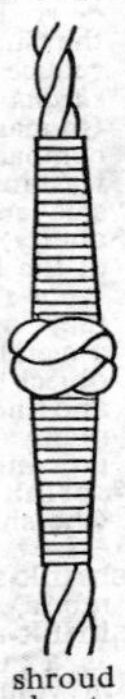

shroud knot

¹shrove [ME *shroof*, fr. OE *scrāf*] *past of* SHRIVE

²shrove *vi* -ED/-ING/-S [fr. *shrove-* (in *shrovetide*)] *obs* **:** to make merry ⟨went a-*shroving* through the city —John Fletcher⟩; *esp* **:** to join in the festivities of Shrovetide

³shrove \ˈshrōv, *esp South* ˈsrōv, *dial* ˈswōv\ *n* -S *usu cap* **:** SHROVETIDE

shrove monday *n, usu cap S&M* [ME *shrovemonday*, fr. *shrove-*, *schrof-* (as in *schroftyde* Shrovetide) + *monday*] **:** the Monday before Ash Wednesday

shrove sunday *n, usu cap both Ss* [ME *shrofsunday*, fr. *shrof-*, *schrof-* (as in *schroftyde* Shrovetide) + *sunday*] **:** the Sunday before Ash Wednesday **:** QUINQUAGESIMA

shrovetide \ˈ=ˌ=\ *n, usu cap* [ME *schroftyde*, fr. *schrof-* (fr. *shriven* to shrive) + *tyde, tide* time — more at SHRIVE, TIDE] **:** the period usu. of three days immediately preceding Ash Wednesday

shrove tuesday *n, usu cap S&T* [ME *chroftetewesday*, fr. *chrofte-*, *schrof-* (as in *schroftyde* Shrovetide) + *tewesday*, *tuesday* Tuesday] **:** the Tuesday immediately before Ash Wednesday — called also *Pancake Day*

¹shrub \ˈshrəb, *esp South* ˈsrəb, *dial* ˈswəb\ *n* -S [ME *schrubbe*, *schrobbe*, *shrobbe*, fr. OE *scrybb* brushwood; akin to Norw *skrubbebær* dwarf cornel] **1 :** a low usu. several-stemmed woody plant — compare HERB, TREE **2 :** CAROLINA ALLSPICE

²shrub \"\ *vt* **shrubbed; shrubbed; shrubbing; shrubs 1 :** to clear (ground) of shrubs **2 :** LOP, PRUNE ⟨~ a tree⟩ ⟨~ a branch⟩ **3 :** to plant (as a lawn) with shrubs

³shrub \"\ *n* -S [Ar *sharāb* alcoholic drink, beverage — more at SYRUP] **1 :** a beverage that consists of an alcoholic liquor, fruit juice, fruit rind, and sugar aged in crockery, glass, or wood and then strained and that is usu. served iced and diluted with water and soda ⟨rum ~⟩ **2 :** a beverage made by adding acidulated fruit juice to iced water ⟨raspberry ~⟩

shrubbed \-bd\ *adj* [¹*shrub* + -*ed*] **:** SHRUBBY

shrub·ber·ied \-b(ə)rēd, -rid\ *adj* **:** bordered with shrubbery

shrub·bery \-b(ə)rē, -ri\ *n* -ES **1 :** a plantation of shrubs **:** HEDGE ⟨driving her opponent's croquet ball into a ~ —C.D. Lewis⟩ ⟨a huge gaunt house . . . asleep in its *shrubberies* —H.V.Morton⟩ **2 :** a growth or group of shrubs ⟨planned to trim the ~ after lunch⟩ ⟨hills covered only with kunai grass or an occasional grove of ~ —Norman Mailer⟩

shrub·bi·ness \-bēnəs, -bē'n-\ *n* -ES **:** the quality or state of being shrubby

shrub·by \-bē, -bi\ *adj* -ER/-EST [¹*shrub* + -*y*] **1 :** consisting of or covered with shrubs ⟨every ~ field was alive with butterflies —William Beebe⟩ **2 :** resembling a shrub (as in size, habit, or growth) **:** SCRUBBY ⟨a subalpine species, usually ~ or prostrate in habit —William Dallimore & A.B.Jackson⟩

shrubby althaea *or* **shrubby althea** *also* **shrub althaea** *or* **shrub althea** *n* **:** ROSE OF SHARON 3

shrubby bittersweet *n* **:** BITTERSWEET 2b

shrubby cinquefoil *n* **:** a much-branched low shrub (*Potentilla fruticosa*) with pinnately compound leaves and yellow solitary or cymose flowers — called also *golden hardhack, hardhack*

shrubby fern *n* **:** SWEET FERN 2

shrubby horsetail *n* **:** any joint fir of the genus *Ephedra*

shrubby st.–john's–wort *n, usu cap 2d S&J* **:** a stiff shrub or woody herb (*Hypericum spathulatum*) having oblong entire leaves and dense cymes of yellow flowers with numerous stamens

shrubby trefoil *n* **:** HOP TREE

shrub garden *n* **:** a planting of shrubs in garden style

shrub layer *or* **shrub stratum** *n* **:** the undergrowth of a forest consisting usu. of plants from 3 to about 15 feet in height and including both shrubby vegetation and seedling trees

shrub·let \ˈshrəblət, *esp South* ˈsrə-, *dial* ˈswə-\ *n* -S **:** a small shrub

shrub mallow *n* **:** ROSE OF SHARON 3

shrub oak *n* **:** SCRUB OAK

shrubs *pl of* SHRUB, *pres 3d sing of* SHRUB

shrubwood \ˈ=ˌ=\ *n* **:** a woodland in which shrubs predominate

shrub yellowroot *n* **:** a half-shrubby plant (*Xanthorhiza apiifolia*) of the family Ranunculaceae with large pinnate or bipinnate leaves and small brownish racemose flowers

shruff \ˈs(h)rəf\ *n* -S [perh. fr. ME *schroff* rubbish; prob. akin to OE *sceorf* scurf — more at SCURF] **:** dross of metals

¹shrug \ˈshrəg, *esp South* ˈsrəg, *dial* ˈswəg\ *vb* **shrugged; shrugged; shrugging; shrugs** [ME *schruggen* to shiver, shrug] *vi* **1** *obs* **:** to shudder with cold or nervousness **:** SHIVER ⟨it makes me ~ when I call to mind the agonies which he suffered —Samuel Parker †1730⟩ **2 :** to raise or draw in the shoulders esp. as an expression of indifference, aloofness, or aversion ⟨the ordinary citizen has no defense against incredible and unwelcome statements other than to ~, turn the page, forget it —Russell Lord⟩ **3** *obs* **a :** to move the body sidewise as in expressing uneasiness or complacency **:** FIDGET **b :** SHRINK, COWER ~ *vt* **1 :** to lift or contract (the shoulders) esp. by way of expressing lack of interest, aloofness, or dislike **2 :** to express by a shrug ⟨*shrugged* his low opinion of the occupant of the room —T.B.Costain⟩ **3 a :** to draw together or bunch up (as the body) in putting on a garment ⟨took out her own serviceable blue coat . . . *shrugged* herself into it —Shirley Jackson⟩ **b :** to pull or work (as a garment or covering) into place ⟨*shrugging* the clothes together upon his body —Pearl Buck⟩

²shrug \"\ *n* -S **1 :** a drawing up of the shoulders usu. to express indifference **2 :** a woman's small waistlength or shorter jacket that is easily slipped on and off and often has a one-button closing

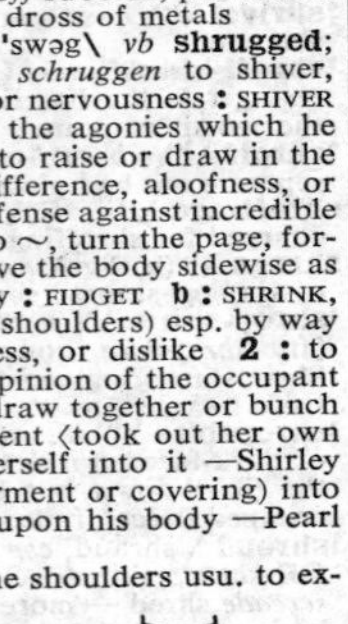

shrug 2

shrug away *vt* **:** to get rid of **:** throw off **:** DISREGARD ⟨*shrugged away* her annoyance —Mary Jane Rolfs⟩

shrug·ging·ly *adv* **:** with a shrug **:** INDIFFERENTLY

shrug off *vt* **1 :** to brush aside **:** MINIMIZE, EVADE ⟨*shrug off* this whole problem —C.D.Lewis⟩ **2 :** to shake off ⟨the continent, which is *shrugging off* the sleep of centuries —*Atlantic*⟩ **3 :** to remove (a garment) by wriggling out of it ⟨she *shrugged* it *off*, draped it over the electric jigsaw —John Updike⟩

shrunk [ME *shronk* (past), *shronken* (past part.), fr. OE *scruncon* (past pl.), *gescruncen* (past part.)] *past of* SHRINK

shrunken [ME *shronken*, fr. OE *gescruncen*] *past part of* SHRINK

shruti *var of* SRUTI

sht *abbr* sheet

shtad·lan *also* **she·tad·lan** \ˈshtäd(ˌ)län\ *n, pl* **shtad·la·nim** *also* **she·tad·la·nim** \=ˈlōnəm, -nēm\ [Yiddish & MHeb; Yiddish *shtadlen*, fr. MHeb *shtădlān*] **:** a person appointed by a Jewish community to represent Jewish interests (as before a government or ruler)

shtetl *also* **shtet·el** \ˈshtetᵊl\ *n, pl* **shtet·lach** \-tläk, -lək\ [Yiddish *shtetl*, fr. MHG *stetel* small place, small town, dim. of *stat* place, town, city, fr. OHG, place — more at STEAD] **:** a Jewish small town or small-town community in Eastern Europe

shtg *abbr* shortage

shthg *abbr* sheathing

shu \ˈshü\ *n* -S [Chin (Pek) *shu*⁴] *Confucianism* **:** reciprocity or mutual considerateness in all actions

shua *usu cap, var of* SHUWA

shu·ba \ˈshübə\ *n* -S [Russ, fr. MHG *schūbe* outer garment, fr. OIt *giubba* jacket, fr. Ar *jubbah*] **:** a Russian fur or fur-lined overcoat or cloak

shu·bun·kin \ˈshübən,kin, shüˈbuŋkən\ *n* -S [Jap] **:** a goldfish of a breed having transparent scales covering a mottled skin and slightly lengthened fins

¹shuck *vi* -ED/-ING/-S [origin unknown] *obs* **:** to shrink back **:** RECOIL ⟨bitter pills, at which we so wince and ~ —John Bunyan⟩

²shuck \ˈshək\ *n* -S [origin unknown] **1 :** an outer covering **:** HUSK, SHELL, POD: as **a :** the husk of Indian corn **b :** the outer covering of a nut (as the walnut, peanut, chestnut) **c :** the shell of an oyster or clam **d :** the dried calyx of the peach flower usu. pushed off by the expanding fruit **e :** the nymphal cuticle cast off by a subimago mayfly **2 :** a cigarette or cigar rolled in corn shucks **3 :** something of little value — usu. used in the pl. often interjectionally ⟨not worth ~*s*⟩ ⟨don't care ~*s* about it⟩ ⟨can't sing for ~*s*⟩ ⟨no great ~*s* for looks⟩ ⟨~*s*, that's not worth talking about⟩

³shuck \"\ *vb* -ED/-ING/-S *vt* **1 :** to strip the shucks or husks from ⟨~ corn⟩ ⟨~ peas⟩ **2 :** to remove (oysters) from the shell **3 a :** to peel off or remove (as clothing) — often used with *off* ⟨~*ed* off his clothes and slid between the sheets —Clements Ripley⟩ **b :** to lay aside **:** slough off **:** DISCARD — usu. used with *off* ⟨some of the bad habits are being ~*ed off* —A.W.Smith⟩ ~ *vi* **:** to take off or slip out of a covering (as clothes) — usu. used with *out of* ⟨went to my room and ~*ed* out of my soaked clothes —J.R.Phillips⟩

⁴shuck \"\ *n* -S [origin unknown] *dial Eng* **:** a spectral hound whose appearance is held to presage a calamity

shuck–bottom \ˈ=ˌ=\ *or* **shuck–bottomed** \ˈ=ˌ=\ *adj* [*shuck-bottom* fr. ²*shuck* + *bottom*, n.; *shuck-bottomed* fr. ²*shuck* + *bottomed* (past part. of *bottom*, v.)] **:** having a seat of interwoven maize husks ⟨a *shuck-bottom* chair⟩

shuck bottom *n* [²*shuck* + *bottom*, n.] **:** a shuck-bottom chair

shuck·er \ˈshəkə(r)\ *n* -S **:** one that shucks: as **a :** a worker who shucks something (as oysters) for a livelihood **b :** a shucking machine

shucking *n* -S **:** CORNHUSKING, HUSKING BEE

shuck–split \ˈ=ˌ=\ *adj* **:** of or relating to the growth stage when the dry calyxes of peach flowers split

shuck spray *n* **:** CALYX SPRAY

shuckworm \ˈ=ˌ=\ *n* **:** HICKORY SHUCKWORM

shucky bean \ˈshəkē-, -ki-\ *n* [*shucky* fr. ²*shuck* + -*y*] **:** a shell bean dried in the pod

¹shud·der \ˈshədə(r)\ *vb* **shuddered; shuddered; shuddering** \-d(ə)riŋ\ **shudders** [ME *shoddren*; akin to MLG *schodderen* to shudder, OFris *skedda* to shake, OHG *skutten* to shake, Lith *kutėti* to shake up, arouse] *vi* **1 :** to tremble convulsively **:** shake with fear, horror, or aversion **:** shiver with cold **:** QUAKE ⟨~*ed* constantly in the chill air⟩ ⟨~ at the thought of contamination with persons . . . lower in the social scale —L.C.Douglas⟩ **2 :** to move as if with a shudder **:** QUIVER ⟨a rumbling roar . . . the windows rattle and the floor ~*s* sickeningly —Michael Allen⟩ ⟨the train slowed, ~*ed*, halted, the air brakes panting —Marc Brandel⟩ ~ *vt* **:** to cause to shudder **:** SHAKE ⟨the chill of an age-old recognition ~*ed* my spine —Arthur Miller⟩

²shudder \"\ *n* -S **1 :** an act or instance of shuddering **:** TREMOR ⟨a ~ of alarm ran . . . through the senate house —J.A.Froude⟩ ⟨the . . . ~ of the ship as her screw comes above the surface —F.A.Swinnerton⟩ **2 a :** an involuntary tremor of the body (as from fear, horror, or cold) ⟨shrank back with a strong ~ —Zane Grey⟩ **b shudders** *pl* **:** a fit of shuddering — usu. used with *the*

shuddering *adj* **1 :** moving with a shudder **:** FEARFUL, TREMBLING ⟨delicate ~ introverts —J.B.Priestley⟩ **2 :** marked by or producing a shudder ⟨a ~ sense of chill and desolation —Alfred Buchanan⟩ ⟨~ slums —J.P.O'Donnell⟩

shud·der·ing·ly *adv* **:** with a shudder or in such a manner as to produce a shudder ⟨~ sensational plots —Carl Van Doren⟩

shud·der·some \ˈshədə(r)səm\ *adj* **:** marked by or producing shudders ⟨the crime story and the unexpected and ~ ending —*Encore*⟩

shud·dery \ˈshəd(ə)rē, -ri\ *adj* **:** SHUDDERSOME ⟨the most terrible and ~ of all tales of murder and revenge —John Mason Brown⟩

shude *var of* SHOOD

shudra *usu cap, var of* SUDRA

¹shuf·fle \ˈshəfəl\ *vb* **shuffled; shuffled; shuffling** \-f(ə)liŋ\ **shuffles** [perh. irreg. fr. ¹*shove* + -*le*] *vt* **1 a :** to mix in a mass confusedly **:** throw into disorder **:** JUMBLE ⟨war has . . . *shuffled* our population —Lucien Price⟩ **b :** to cause to mingle indiscriminately — usu. used with *among* or *with* ⟨*shuffled* first offenders in with hardened criminals⟩ **2 a :** to introduce into trickily **:** smuggle in ⟨contrived by your enemies and *shuffled* into the papers that were seized —John Dryden⟩ **b :** to put or thrust aside or under cover ⟨*shuffled* the whole matter out of his mind⟩ ⟨*shuffling* the letter out of sight as someone entered⟩ **3 a :** to manipulate (as a group of playing cards, dominoes, tiles) with the real or ostensible purpose of causing a later appearance in random (as in dealing or drawing) **b :** to push or move about, back and forth, or from one place to another **:** SHIFT ⟨~ funds among various accounts⟩ ⟨pulled all the drawers open to ~ his belongings more handily —Josephine Pinckney⟩ ⟨dispatchers had godlike . . . power to ~ us to and fro —Christopher Morley⟩ **4 a :** to move (as the feet) by sliding along or back and forth without lifting ⟨*shuffled* his feet nervously as he waited⟩ ⟨*shuffled* his slippers over the floor⟩ **b :** to perform (as a dance) with a dragging, sliding step ⟨~ a saraband⟩ ~ *vi* **1 :** to work into or out of trickily **:** WORM — usu. used with *in, into,* or *out of* ⟨managed to ~ in with his betters⟩ ⟨*shuffled* out of the difficulty somehow⟩ **2 :** to act or speak in a shifty or evasive manner **:** EQUIVOCATE ⟨the more the cardinals *shuffled*, the more furiously the mob raged —G.G.Coulton⟩ ⟨without *shuffling* for a moment about his past errors —J.M.Barzun⟩ **3 a :** to move or walk in a sliding, dragging manner without lifting the feet **:** SCUFF, SCUFFLE ⟨saw a bear *shuffling* along⟩ ⟨boxers *shuffling* around in the ring⟩ ⟨saw him *shuffling* through the streets in his battered carpet slippers —Van Wyck Brooks⟩ **b :** to dance in a lazy nonchalant manner with sliding and tapping motions of the feet **c :** to execute in a perfunctory or clumsy manner — usu. used with *through* ⟨allowed to ~ through his lessons —George Eliot⟩ **d :** to get into or out of shoes or clothing awkwardly or fumblingly — usu. used with *into, off, on,* or *out of* ⟨began to ~ on his fur jacket and his moccasins —Willa Cather⟩ ⟨watched him ~ gloomily into his overcoat —William DuBois⟩ **4 :** to mix playing cards or counters (as dominoes or tiles) by shuffling **5 :** to attack with the spurs in cock fighting

²shuffle \"\ *n* -S **1 :** an evasion of the issue **:** EQUIVOCATION ⟨answer it now, yes or no, plain word and no ~ —Max Pemberton⟩ **2 a :** an act of shuffling (as of cards or playing counters) ⟨after the ~ the players select tiles in turn⟩ **b :** a right or turn to shuffle ⟨reminded sharply that it was his ~⟩ **c :** a confused mass **:** JUMBLE ⟨a desk with a ~ of papers on it —Adrian Bell⟩ ⟨the goal of training good teachers had been lost in the ~ of educational trappings —Benjamin Fine⟩ **3 a :** a dragging sliding walk **:** SCUFFLE ⟨the . . . ~ of the man's feet across the dusty floor —Victor Canning⟩ **b** (1) **:** a sliding or scraping step in dancing (2) **:** a dance characterized by such a step ⟨dancing a sailor's ~⟩ ⟨the double ~⟩

shuffleboard \ˈ=ˌ=\ *n* [alter. (influenced by ¹*shuffle*) of obs. E

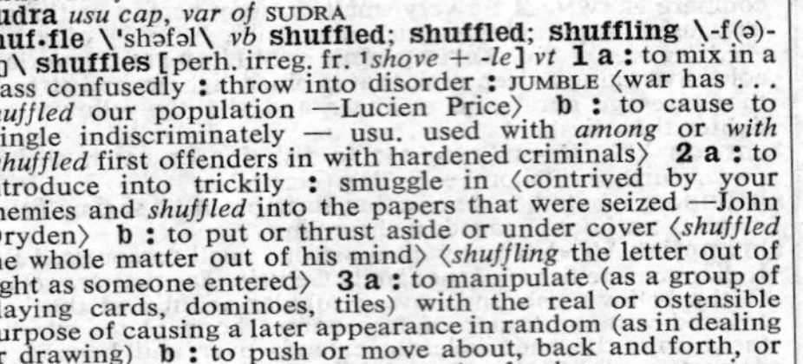

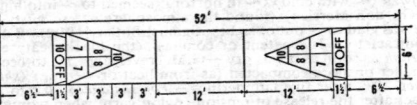

shuffleboard 2b

shove-board, fr. E ¹*shove* + *board*] **1 :** SHOVELBOARD 1 **2 a :** a game in which players use long-handled cues to shove wooden disks into scoring beds of a diagram marked on a smooth surface **b :** the diagram on which this game is played

shufflecap \ˈ=ˌ=\ *n* **:** a game in which the stake is money shaken in a hat or cap

shuffle dance *n* **:** an Iroquois women's round dance marked by a gliding sideward twist of the foot

shuffle off *vt* **:** to get rid of **:** push away **:** SHIRK ⟨when we have *shuffled off* this mortal coil —Shak.⟩ ⟨*shuffle off* the heavy burden of our guilt —Richard Chase⟩ ⟨teachers cannot . . . *shuffle off* their responsibility —C.I.Glicksberg⟩ ~ *vi* **:** to be on one's way **:** mosey along ⟨let him *shuffle off* to the wilderness —J.B.Priestley⟩

shuf·fler \ˈshəf(ə)lə(r)\ *n* -S **1 :** one that shuffles; *esp* **:** one that shuffles cards or whose turn it is to do so **2 :** SCAUP DUCK

shuffle walk *n* **:** a step-drag used in square dancing

shufflewing \ˈ=ˌ=\ *n, dial Brit* **:** HEDGE SPARROW

shuffling *adj* **:** disposed to shuffle: as **a :** moving with a shuffle ⟨a ~ dancer⟩ **b :** EVASIVE, OPPORTUNISTIC ⟨a ~ politician⟩ — **shuf·fling·ly** *adv*

shug \ˈshəg, ˈshu̇g\ *var of* SHOG

shug·ni \ˈshu̇gnē\ *n, pl* **shugni** *or* **shugnis** *usu cap* **1 :** an Iranian people of the western Pamirs **2 :** a member of the Shugni people

shu·kria \shüˈkrēə\ *n, pl* **shukria** *or* **shukrias** *usu cap* **1 :** a nomadic Arabic-speaking people of the region between the Blue Nile and the Atbara river in northeastern Africa **2 :** a member of the Shukria people

shul *also* **schul** \ˈshu̇l *sometimes* ˈshül\ *n* -S [Yiddish *shul*, fr. MHG *schuol*, *schuole*, lit., school, fr. OHG *scuola*, fr. L *schola* — more at SCHOOL] **:** SYNAGOGUE

shumac *var of* SUMAC

shu·mard oak \(ˈ)shüˈmärd-\ *also* **shumard red oak** *n, usu cap S* [after Benjamin F. *Shumard* †1869 Am. geologist] **:** a large red oak (*Quercus shumardii*) of the southern and eastern U.S. that grows chiefly over limestone and has dark shiny elliptical leaves divided into 7 to 9 lobes, medium to very large acorns, and coarse-grained wood of medium hardness and weight

shummick *South & Midland var of* SHAMMOCK

shun \ˈshən\ *vt* **shunned; shunned; shunning; shuns** [ME *shunnen*, *shunen*, fr. OE *scunian*] **1 :** to avoid deliberately and esp. habitually **:** keep clear of **:** shy away from **:** ESCHEW ⟨~ temptation⟩ ⟨~ publicity⟩ ⟨was *shunned* by his former friends⟩ ⟨lived alone, *shunning* all community activities⟩ ⟨~*s* pure theory and sticks to ascertainable facts —J.H.Powers⟩ **2** *archaic* **:** to escape from **:** EVADE ⟨no man of woman born . . . can ~ his destiny —W.C.Bryant⟩ **3** *archaic* **:** PREVENT ⟨wish you may be able to ~ for us this war —Thomas Jefferson⟩ **syn** see ESCAPE

shu·nam·mite \ˈshünə,mīt\ *n* -S *cap* [modif. (influenced by -*ite*) of Heb *shūnammīth*, fr. *Shūnēm* Shunem, town in ancient Palestine] **:** a native or inhabitant of the town of Shunem north of Mt. Gilboa in ancient Palestine

shune \ˈshün\ *chiefly dial pl of* SHOE

shun·less \ˈshənləs\ *adj* **:** UNAVOIDABLE ⟨with ~ destiny —Shak.⟩

shunning *n* -S [fr. gerund of *shun*] **:** a Mennonite practice of excluding from any social interaction with other members of a congregation a church member who has been censured for some serious infraction

shunpike \ˈ=ˌ=\ *n* **:** a side road used to avoid toll on a turnpike

¹shunt \ˈshənt\ *vb* -ED/-ING/-S [ME *shunten* to flinch, shy, run away, perh. fr. *shunen* to shun] *vt* **1 :** to shove or put aside or out of the way **:** SIDETRACK ⟨didn't want to feel ~*ed* —Peggy Bennett⟩ ⟨the manufacturer had been ~*ed* aside —*Advertising Age*⟩ **2 :** to turn off to one side **:** SHIFT ⟨~ cattle into a corral⟩; *specif* **:** to turn off (as a car or train) from one track to another **:** SWITCH ⟨the train was ~*ed* to a siding⟩ **3 a :** to provide with or divert by means of a shunt **b :** to interrupt (the flow of an electrical circuit in a railroad track) and so cause the signals in the block affected to change their aspect automatically ⟨the circuit is ~*ed* by the wheels of a train, the opening of a switch, or the breaking of a rail⟩ **c :** to divert (blood) from one part to another by surgical creation of a shunt ~ *vi* **1 :** to move to the side **:** turn off from a course being followed ⟨~*ed* from his main interest to a profitable sideline⟩; *specif* **:** to move onto a sidetrack ⟨one of the standard goods engines . . . was ~*ing* at the time —O.S.Nock⟩ **2 :** to travel back and forth **:** SHUTTLE ⟨~*s* between the two towns⟩

²shunt \"\ *n* -S **:** a means or mechanism for turning or thrusting aside: as **a** *chiefly Brit* **:** a railroad switch **b** (1) **:** a conductor joining two points in an electrical circuit so as to form a parallel or alternative path through which a portion of the current may pass (as for the purpose of regulating the amount passing in the main circuit) (2) **:** a conductor providing a low-resistance path for the flow of current ⟨a brush ~⟩ (3) **:** DIVERTOR **c :** a vascular passage by which blood is diverted from its usual or normal circulatory path ⟨an arteriovenous ~⟩; *esp* **:** a surgical passage created between two blood vessels to divert blood from one part to another ⟨portacaval ~⟩

shunt dynamo *or* **shunt motor** *n* **:** a shunt-wound generator or motor

shunt·er \ˈshəntə(r)\ *n* -S **1 :** one that shunts: as **a** *Brit* **:** SWITCHMAN **b** *Brit* **:** a locomotive used in a railroad yard for switching **2** *Brit* **:** ARBITRAGER

shunt excitation *n* **:** excitation by shunt winding

shunting *n* -S [fr. gerund of ¹*shunt*] *Brit* **:** arbitrage conducted between certain local markets without the necessity of the exchange involved in foreign arbitrage

shunt valve *n* **:** a valve permitting a fluid under pressure an easier avenue of escape than normally; *specif* **:** a valve actuated by the governor and used in one system of marine-engine governing to connect both ends of the low-pressure cylinder as a supplementary control

shunt winding *n* **:** a winding so arranged as to divide the armature current and lead a portion of it around the field-magnet coils — opposed to *series winding*

shunt–wound \ˈ=ˌ=\ *adj* **:** wound so that the armature winding and field winding are in parallel ⟨a *shunt-wound* direct-current generator⟩

shus *pl of* SHU

¹shush \ˈshəsh\ *n* -ES [imit.] **:** a sibilant sound uttered to enjoin silence ⟨listeners who break into a spontaneous handclap or two are immediately shamed with pious ~*es* —Winthrop Sargeant⟩

²shush \"\ *vb* -ED/-ING/-ES *vt* **1 :** to urge quiet upon (as by making the sound "sh" and holding an index finger before the lips) **:** repress the agitation or clamor of **:** HUSH, SILENCE ⟨made animal noises until he was ~*ed* —John McDonald⟩ ⟨applauded happily but was ~*ed* by my neighbors —Hyman Toldberg⟩ ⟨the policeman ~*ed* him with his hand —Claud Cockburn⟩ **2 :** to restrain from a desired course or action **:** SUPPRESS ⟨those . . . who demurred and privately pressed for a changed policy were ~*ed* by the functionaries —Frank Tollman⟩ ~ *vi* **:** to become silent **:** grow still **:** HUSH — used in the imperative to urge cessation of talk or moderation of sound ⟨~ now, let's be quiet enough to hear a pin drop⟩

shu·swap \ˈshü,swäp\ *n, pl* **shuswap** *or* **shuswaps** *usu cap* **1 a :** a Salishan people of the Fraser and Columbia river valleys in British Columbia **b :** a member of such people **2 :** a language of the Shuswap people

¹shut \ˈshət, *dial* ˈshet; *usu* |d.+V\ *vb* **shut; shut; shutting; shuts** [ME *shutten*, *shetten*, *shitten*, fr. OE *scyttan*; akin to MD *schutten* to shut in, hinder, OE *scēotan* to shoot — more at SHOOT] *vt* **1** *obs* **:** to move (as a bolt) so as to fasten something (as a door, window) **2 a :** to move (as a door, window, gate) into position to close an opening ⟨~ the lid⟩ ⟨leads us to ~ the gates of mercy —M.R.Cohen⟩ ⟨~ his door against his enemies⟩ — often used with *up* ⟨~ up his windows and closed the shop⟩ or *down* ⟨~ all the windows down⟩ ⟨~*s* the top down and locks it⟩ **b :** to prevent passage to or from by closing doors or openings **:** CLOSE ⟨~ the cottage for the winter⟩ — often used with *up* ⟨~ up the house and set off for Europe⟩ **c :** to close (as an opening, a passage) by an obstacle or barrier ⟨the enemy ~ every pass through the mountains⟩ — often used with *up* or *in* ⟨another upland valley ~ in by the easy slope of wooded hills —*Amer. Guide Series: Vt.*⟩ **d :** to close (as the mind) to ideas and other influences from without ⟨prejudice ~*s* the mind tighter than illiteracy —Bice Clemow⟩ — often used with *up* **3 :** to confine by or as if by enclosure or by closing a means of escape ⟨~ him in the closet⟩ ⟨was ~ in prison⟩ — usu. used with *up* ⟨~ up with him in the . . . chill smoky carriage —Anne D. Sedgwick⟩ ⟨food and muskets and gunpowder to stand by their own army ~ up in Boston —Dorothy C. Fisher⟩ ⟨~ up in an acquired intellectual pride —V.S.Pritchett⟩ **4 :** to fasten with a lock or bolt ⟨buys a lock to ~ his chest⟩ **5 :** to close by bringing enclosing or covering

parts together ⟨~ the eyes⟩ ⟨~ the mouth⟩ ⟨~ the fist⟩ ⟨~ a book⟩ ⟨~ a locket⟩ — often used with *up* ⟨~ up the piano⟩ **6 :** to cause to cease or suspend operation or business — often used with *down* ⟨obliged the administration to ~ down the university for the remainder of the spring term —R.G.Woolbert⟩ **7 :** WELD **~ vi 1 :** to close itself or become closed ⟨door ~ with a slam⟩ ⟨flowers ~ at night⟩ ⟨the seams worked . . . opening and *shutting* as the ship strained on the waves —C.S. Forester⟩ — often used with *down* ⟨the lid ~*s* down to keep the dust out⟩ **2 :** to become visually continuous without a perceptible break ⟨earth and the sky and the sky and the sea, seem *shutting* together as a book that is read —Joaquin Miller⟩ **3 :** to close in ⟨and soon evening will ~ —A.E.Housman⟩ — often used with *in* ⟨observing the sunshine beginning to ~ in —Samuel Richardson⟩ **4 :** to cease or suspend an operation or business : CLOSE ⟨cafés and bars which never seemed to ~ while I was there —James Reach⟩ — often used with *up* ⟨all my kids . . . were reporting for the parade, so I thought we'd ~ up early —J.G.Cozzens⟩ or *down* ⟨plants cut down the number of their employees and in many cases ~ down entirely —*Amer. Guide Series: N.H.*⟩ ⟨force newspapers to accept censorship or ~ down —*Time*⟩ — **shut one's eyes :** to pretend not to see : IGNORE ⟨*shut their eyes* to crime in which they did not themselves participate —George Horne b.1902⟩ — **shut one's face** *or* **shut one's head** *slang* **:** to shut one's mouth ⟨when, she asked herself angrily, would she learn to *shut her face* —Margaret Long⟩ — **shut one's mouth :** to stop or refrain from speaking ⟨our first barbaric impulse is to *shut* the *mouth* of any man or woman who says anything that might offend . . . tribal customs —Manus O'Neill⟩ ⟨if you *shut your mouth*, you have your choice —Scott Fitzgerald⟩ — **shut the door :** to exclude from participation or consideration : cut off ⟨cannot afford to *shut the door* on any honest speculator —Elmer Davis⟩ ⟨it *shut the door* upon all democratic aspiration —V.L.Parrington⟩ — **shut up shop :** to cease or suspend an operation or activity ⟨the committee decided to *shut up shop*, at least for the present —*Atlantic*⟩ ⟨even the city's criminals seem to have *shut up shop* for the occasion —S.E.Hyman⟩

[2]**shut** \"\ *n* -s [ME *schett*, fr. *shutten, shetten, shitten*, v. — more at [1]SHUT] **1 :** a device used in shutting or closing: **a** *archaic* **:** BOLT, BAR **b** *chiefly dial* **:** SHUTTER **c :** a door or plate used to close an opening **2 :** the act or time of shutting ⟨at ~ of evening⟩ **3 :** the line or place of union at a welded joint **4 :** COLD SHUT

[3]**shut** \"\ *adj* [fr. past part. of [1]*shut*] **1 :** closed, fastened, or folded together ⟨the ~ door was blank against the summer sunlight —Elizabeth M. Roberts⟩ ⟨listened with ~ eyes⟩ ⟨has her mind ~ against all other civilizations —Nora Waln⟩ ⟨a terrible, white ~ face —S.V.Benét⟩ **2 :** RID, CLEAR, FREE — usu. used with *of* ⟨I thought I'd never get ~ of him⟩ ⟨would soon be ~ of them all —Hervey Allen⟩

[4]**shut** \'shət, 'shu̇t, 'shet\ *chiefly dial var of* SHOOT

shut away *vt* **:** to remove or isolate from others ⟨in order to escape from the prison where society *shut* her *away* —H.M. Parshley⟩ ⟨I *shut* myself *away* for two hours —R.G.G.Price⟩

shut down *vi* **:** to settle so as to obscure vision : close in ⟨the rain mists *shut down* like stained rolls of wool —Marjory S. Douglas⟩ ⟨the night *shut down* early⟩

shutdown \'ˌ=ˌ=\ *n* -s [*shut down*] **:** the cessation or suspension of an activity or function: as **a :** a usu. temporary stoppage of work in a factory, mine, or other business enterprise (as because of a strike, lockout, installation or repair of equipment, vacation, or lack of orders or materials) ⟨workers were threatening a total ~ —Ida A.R. Wylie⟩ ⟨increasing the efficiency . . . and decreasing maintenance ~*s* —H.W.Iversen⟩ ⟨trains . . . resumed operating this morning after a 24-hour ~ —*N.Y.Times*⟩ **b :** the stopping of a machine or engine that activates itself ⟨the ~ . . . of generating equipment in 17 industrial plants —*Ohio Edison Co. Report*⟩ ⟨permitting escape of neutrons and causing a ~ of the chain reaction —J.L. Collins⟩ **c :** the discontinuance of a physical function (as of an organ) ⟨to prevent kidney ~ —*Anesthesia Digest*⟩

[1]**shute** *var of* SHOOT

[2]**shute** *var of* CHUTE

shut-eye \'ˌ=ˌ=\ *n* [[3]*shut* + *eye*] *slang* **:** SLEEP ⟨when he awakes . . . he makes no attempt to fall back on the pillow and catch a little more *shut-eye* —Philip Hamburger⟩

shut in *vt* [ME *shetten in*, fr. *shutten, shetten, shitten* to shut + *in*, adv.] **1 :** CONFINE, ENCLOSE ⟨*shut* himself *in* for days on end⟩ ⟨had been *shut in* by illness during much of the winter⟩ **2 :** to prevent production of (oil) by closing down a well

[1]**shut-in** \'ˌ=ˌ=\ *adj* [fr. past part. of *shut in*] **1 :** confined to one's home or an institution by illness or incapacity ⟨made more than 7000 home visits to *shut-in* boys and girls —Dorothy Barclay⟩ **2 :** so encompassed as to be confined or cut off ⟨thickly wooded foothills, broken knob country, and narrow valleys have made it . . . the most *shut-in* section of the state —*Amer. Guide Series: Tenn.*⟩ **3 a :** closed in : BROODING, SECRETIVE ⟨twisted, sad, with a bitter, *shut-in* face —Claudia Cassidy⟩ ⟨assumed the proud, *shut-in* look with which he guarded himself from doubt —Gordon Merrick⟩ **b :** tending to avoid social contact : WITHDRAWN ⟨diagnostic and prognostic significance of the *shut-in* personality type —S.K. Weinberg⟩

[2]**shut-in** \'ˌ=ˌ=\ *n* -s **1 :** an invalid or incapacitated person who is confined to his home, a room, or his bed ⟨through your love of music and your skill you can bring happiness to *shut-ins* —*Girl Scout Handbk.*⟩ **2 :** a narrow gorge-shaped part of an otherwise wide valley **3 :** available oil or gas which is not being produced from an existing well

shut-mouthed \'ˌ=ˌ=\ *adj* **:** CLOSEMOUTHED, SECRETIVE ⟨didn't want people to know about it . . . decided to keep *shut-mouthed* —F.B.Gipson⟩

shut·ness *n* -ES **:** the quality or state of being shut ⟨against the Spanish ~ . . . I lacked energy to battle —Rose Macaulay⟩

shut off *vt* **1 a :** to cut off (as a flow or passage or something flowing or passing) : STOP ⟨*shut* the steam *off*⟩ ⟨would require *shutting off* the patient's circulation during part of the operation —Ben & Marie Pearse⟩ ⟨*shut off* the flow of visitors —*Amer. Guide Series: Ark.*⟩ **b :** to stop the operation of (as a machine) ⟨*shuts off* his motor —P.B.Kyne⟩ ⟨*shuts* the machine *off* when a full package of yarn is completed —V.A.Schiffer⟩ ⟨*shut* the radiator *off*⟩ **c :** to block or terminate the operation or activity of ⟨*shut off* the supply of new three percent savings bonds —Harold Wincott⟩ ⟨*shut off* its high-powered . . . recruiting campaign —*Newsweek*⟩ ⟨*shut off* this racket by scowling at him —L.C.Douglas⟩ **2 :** to close off : SEPARATE — usu. used with *from* ⟨would have *shut* Guatemala *off* from the Atlantic coast —C.L.Jones⟩ ⟨long arms of the ridge *shut* us *off* from the world —Elyne Mitchell⟩ ⟨*shut off* from most of the activities and pleasures of normal children —W.E.Clark⟩ **~ vi :** to cease operating : STOP ⟨the generator *shuts off* automatically⟩

shutoff \'ˌ=ˌ=\ *n* -s [*shut off*] **1 a :** something that shuts off : VALVE, STOPPER ⟨must build a cement ~ to plug the leaking well casing⟩ ⟨~ is located in the cellar⟩ **b** *or* **shutoff nozzle :** a fire hose nozzle designed to control the flow of water as it leaves the hose **2 :** the act of shutting off ⟨a ~ of blood flow to the brain would be required for the type of operation —Ben & Marie Pearse⟩ **3 :** a closed season for game

shut out *vt* [ME *shetten out*, fr. *shutten, shetten, shitten* to shut + *out*, adv.] **1 :** to keep or force out ⟨branches meet . . . *shutting out* the sunlight —*Amer. Guide Series: Mich.*⟩ ⟨his nostrils clenched as if to *shut out* the evil and moldy smell of the room —Marcia Davenport⟩ ⟨not to know . . . was to be *shut out* of his life completely —Morley Callaghan⟩ — sometimes used with *from* ⟨began to talk French, *shutting out* the mulatto woman from their conversation —Louis Bromfield⟩ ⟨*shutting out* from his thoughts any thought that disturbs him —Morris Fishbein⟩ **2 :** to hide from sight ⟨clouds *shut* the sun *out*⟩ ⟨as we rounded the point the peninsula *shut out* the bay⟩ **3 a :** to prevent (an opponent) from scoring in a game or contest ⟨*shut* them *out* with two hits⟩ ⟨*shut* them *out* 1–0⟩ ⟨a fisherman . . . was *shut out* the first two days and boated only two on the lush last day —*Newsweek*⟩ **b :** to forestall the bidding of (one's opponents in bridge) by making a high or preemptive bid ⟨*shut* the opposition *out* with a bid of five hearts⟩ **syn** see EXCLUDE

shutout \'ˌ=ˌ=\ *n* -s [in sense 1, fr. *shut out;* in sense 2, fr. past part. of *shut out*] **1 a :** a game or contest in which one side fails to score ⟨punched out a three-touchdown ~ 20–0 —*Newsweek*⟩ ⟨had a six-hit ~ going into the 9th inning —Roscoe McGowen⟩ **b :** a preemptive bid in bridge **c :** the presence of sufficient men on a player's inner table in backgammon to prevent entrance to the table by the opponent's men **2 :** one that is shut out ⟨was a shut-in within a paralyzed body and a *shutout* from the world outside —*Jour. Amer. Med. Assoc.*⟩

shuts *pres 3d sing of* SHUT, *pl of* SHUT

shut·tance \'shət°n(t)s, 'shu̇t-\ *n* [[1]*shut* + *-ance*] *dial Eng* **:** RIDDANCE

shut·ten \'shət°n, 'shu̇t-\ *dial past part of* SHUT

[1]**shut·ter** \'shəd-ə(r), -ətə-\ *n* -s *often attrib* **1 :** one that shuts **2 a :** a usu. movable cover or screen for a window or door (as to shut out the light or obstruct the view) — compare BLIND, JALOUSIE, LOUVER **b :** such a cover or screen for a picture or altarpiece **3 a :** a mechanical device of various forms (as the rotary, iris diaphragm, or focal-plane shutter) attached to a camera to expose the film or plate by opening and closing an aperture **b :** a usu. rotating element that obscures the light in the optical path of a motion-picture mechanism at a predetermined interval **4 :** a removable cover, lid, or gate for closing an aperture (as the passageway through which molten iron flows from a ladle) **5 :** the movable louvers in a pipe organ by which the swell box is opened and which are manipulated by means of the swell pedal

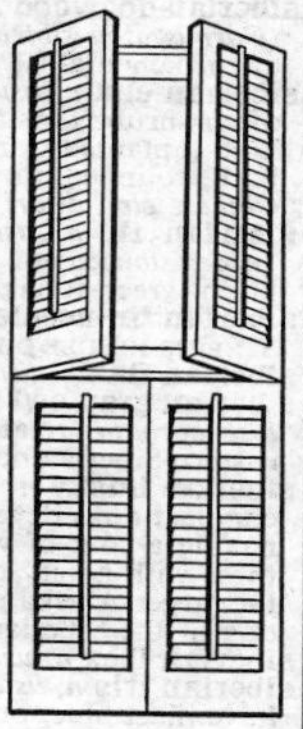

shutters 2a

[2]**shutter** \"\ *vb* **shuttered; shuttered; shuttering** \-d-əriŋ, -ətər-, -ə-tr-\ **shutters** *vt* **1 :** to close with or by shutters ⟨saw us looking out the windows and came up and ~*ed* them —Rumer Godden⟩ ⟨the gate was ~*ed* —Anne Green⟩ ⟨during the heat of the day, houses are ~*ed* —*Amer. Guide Series: Fla.*⟩ **2 :** to close (an establishment) to business by or as if by closing shutters ⟨suppressed their dances, banned movies, ~*ed* nightclubs —*Time*⟩ ⟨a ~*ed* butcher's shop —Lionel Shapiro⟩ **3 :** to close (the eyes) as if with shutters ⟨death in his ~*ed* eyes —Dorothy Hewett⟩ **~ vi 1 :** to close to business by or as if by closing shutters ⟨the bars in the village ~ at midnight —Leslie Waller⟩ ⟨many operators will ~ rather than take continuous gambles —*Billboard*⟩ **2 :** to close as if with shutters ⟨eyes that ~ too quick — when someone speaks —Jennette Yeotman⟩

shutter box *n* **:** a recess at the side of a window to receive an inside shutter when opened

shutterbug \'ˌ=ˌ=\ *n* **:** a photography enthusiast ⟨you will find other ~*s* if you are a camera fiend —Christina Kirk⟩

shutter dam *or* **shutter weir** *n* **:** a dam formerly consisting of one or more simple shutters or gates turning on a horizontal axis near the top and now consisting of a series of short pieces that revolve on their horizontal axes and are lowered to rest flatwise on the sill

shut·tered \'shəd-ə(r)d, -ətə-\ *adj* [[1]*shutter* + *-ed*] **:** provided with shutters ⟨a church with a ~ belfry and spire⟩

shut·ter·ing \-d-əriŋ, -ətər-, -ə-tr-, -riŋ\ *n* -s [[1]*shutter* + *-ing*] **1 a :** material for making shutters **b :** SHUTTERS **2 :** FORMWORK

shut·ter·less \'ˌ=ˌləs\ *adj* **:** without shutters

shut·ting \'shəd-|iŋ, 'shət|, |ēŋ\ *n* -s [ME *shutyng, schettyng, shitting*, fr. gerund of *shutten, shetten, shitten* to shut] **:** the act or process of one that shuts; *specif* **:** WELDING

shutting post *n* **:** GATEPOST

shutting stile *n* **:** the stile of a hinged door which strikes the rabbet of the jamb when the door is shut and on which the fastenings are secured — compare HANGING STILE

[1]**shut·tle** \'shəd-°l, -ət°l\ *n* -s *often attrib* [ME *schutylle, schetyll, shittle*, prob. fr. OE *scytel, scytels* bar, bolt; akin to ON *skutill* bar, bolt, Dan *skyttel* shuttle, OE *scēotan* to shoot — more at SHOOT] **1 a :** any of various types of slender pointed wooden devices used in weaving for passing or shooting the thread of the woof between the threads of the warp from one side of the cloth to the other **b :** a spindle-shaped device holding the thread that one manipulates in tatting, knotting, or netting **c** (1) **:** any of various sliding thread holders for the lower thread of a sewing machine that carry the lower thread through a loop of the upper thread to make a stitch (2) **:** a sewing-machine bobbin **2 :** SHUTTLECOCK **3 :** a sliding shutter (as for a sluiceway) **4** *dial chiefly Brit* **:** a small drawer (as for odds and ends); *sometimes* **:** a drawer for money **5** [[3]*shuttle*] **a :** a going back and forth over a specified route or path at regular intervals; *esp* **:** such a plying by any of various vehicles (as planes, automobiles, trains, ships) ⟨in addition to planes that fly direct to Bermuda and return in a ~, some flights continue to England —*Skyways*⟩ ⟨kept up a round-the-clock ~ delivering a truckload of coral every 40 seconds —*Time*⟩ **b :** an established or specified route used in a shuttle ⟨carted paratroopers across the short ~ from Denmark to Norway —Richard Thruelsen & Elliott Arnold⟩ **c :** a vehicle used in a shuttle ⟨took the ~ across the city⟩ **6 :** CLAW 4f

[2]**shut·tle** \'shə|d-°l, 'shu̇|, |t°l\ *adj* [ME *schyttyl*, fr. *schutylle, schetyll, shittle*, n.] *chiefly dial* **:** WAVERING, UNSETTLED

[3]**shut·tle** \'shəd-°l, -ət°l\ *vb* **shuttled; shuttled; shuttling** \-d-°liŋ, -t(°)liŋ\ **shuttles** [[1]*shuttle*] *vt* **1 :** to cause to move around or back and forth frequently ⟨was *shuttled* from one unsympathetic relative to another —Ruth & Edward Brecher⟩ ⟨reserves to be *shuttled* between branches to meet varying . . . needs —*Investor's Reader*⟩ **2 :** to move or transport in, by, or as if by a shuttle ⟨crews were to be *shuttled* from their ships to the gun-carrying ships before landing —*Coast Artillery Jour.*⟩ ⟨dual drive tractors ~ eight 35-foot insulated trailers between the eastern and western terminals —*Motor Transportation in the West*⟩ ⟨keeps *shuttling* substitutes in and out with instructions to run until they tire, then signal for relief —*Time*⟩ **~ vi 1 :** to move or travel around or back and forth frequently ⟨continued feverishly to ~ between sidewalk and stairs —H.J.Kaplan⟩ ⟨tangled with red tape, they have *shuttled* from bureau to bureau —*Newsweek*⟩ ⟨the book ~*s* from one locale to another —*Time*⟩ **2 :** to move or travel in, by, or as if by a shuttle ⟨every type of landing craft *shuttling* continuously between the tumultuous beaches and the scores of cargo vessels —E.L.Jones⟩ ⟨bombed it and *shuttled* to Africa —Tex McCrary & D.E.Scherman⟩ ⟨*shuttled* over to Milwaukee —L.E.Arndt⟩ ⟨has *shuttled* back and forth across the years —Pamela Taylor⟩

shuttle armature *n* **:** an armature shaped like an elongated shuttle with wires that run longitudinally in grooves

shuttle bone *n* **:** the navicular of the foot of a horse

shuttle box *n* **1 :** a case at either end of the lay of a loom to receive the shuttle after its passage through the shed **2 :** any of various compartments containing additional shuttles with different colored threads to be brought into action as the pattern requires

[1]**shuttlecock** \'ˌ=ˌ=\ *n* [[1]*shuttle* + *cock* (bird)] **1 a :** a feathered object with a rounded base that is volleyed back and forth with rackets in badminton and battledore and shuttlecock — called also *bird, shuttle* **b :** BATTLEDORE AND SHUTTLECOCK **2 :** GADWALL

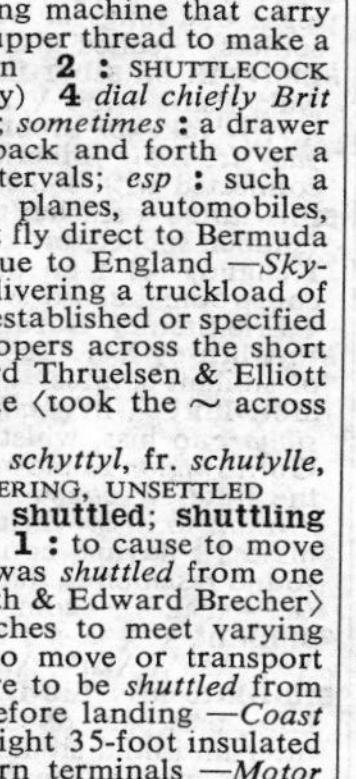

shuttlecock 1a

[2]**shuttlecock** \"\ *vt* **:** to send or toss to and fro : BANDY ⟨they just go on ~*ing* letters —Israel Zangwill⟩ ⟨I waver and am lost: ~*ed* between the opinions of others —*Good Housekeeping (London)*⟩ **~ vi :** to go to and fro ⟨was ~*ing* up and down behind the zinc counter dolloping out cups of coffee —Bruce Marshall⟩

[3]**shuttlecock** \"\ *adj* **:** bandied here and there or back and forth : VARIABLE

shut·tle·man \'ˌ=ˌmən\ *n, pl* **shuttlemen 1 :** a worker who inspects and repairs loom shuttles **2 :** an operator of a locomotive for shuttling supplies in a mine yard

shuttle mark *n* **:** a fabric defect resulting from injury of the warp threads by the shuttle

shut·tler \'shəd-°lə(r), -ət(°)l-\ *n* -s [[1]*shuttle* + *-er*] **:** a textile worker who replaces the empty shuttles

shuttle race *n* **1 :** a relay race which is run back and forth over a straight course with the first and third runners of a team running in one direction and the second and fourth runners running in the opposite direction **2 :** LAY RACE

shuttle shell *n* **:** any of several cowries having a smooth spindleshaped shell (as the egg cowry)

shuttle train *n* **:** a train running back and forth over a short route

shut up *vb* [ME *shutten up*, fr. *shutten, shetten, shitten* to shut + *up*, adv.] *vt* **1** *archaic* **:** to finish up : TERMINATE, CONCLUDE ⟨will *shut up* this melancholy subject with part of a letter —John Wesley⟩ **2 :** to cause or force (a person) to stop talking ⟨couldn't *shut* him *up* or keep him talking in a straight line —W.F.Davis⟩ **~ vi :** to cease writing or speaking ⟨want this to sail tomorrow . . . and so must *shut up* in a minute —O.W. Holmes †1935⟩ ⟨you would be wise to *shut up* —Marcia Davenport⟩ ⟨sit down and *shut up* —Erle Stanley Gardner⟩

shu·wa *also* **shua** \'shü(w)ə\ *n, pl* **shuwa** *or* **shuwas** *usu cap* **1 :** a negroid Arabic-speaking nomadic or seminomadic pastoral people of the Lake Chad region of western Africa **2 :** a member of the Shuwa people

SHV *abbr, often not cap* [L *sub hoc voce* or *sub hoc verbo*] under this word

shvat *usu cap, var of* SHEBAT

shwa *var of* SCHWA

shwr *abbr* shower

[1]**shy** \'shī\ *adj, usu* **shi·er** *or* **shy·er** \-ī(ə)r, -īə\ *usu* **shi·est** *or* **shy·est** \-īəst\ [ME *schey*, fr. OE *scēoh;* akin to MHG *schiech* shy, OHG *sciuhen* to frighten off, make timid, Sw *skygg* shy, OSlav *ščuti* to chase] **1 a :** easily frightened : SKITTISH, TIMID ⟨a diminutive mouse deer, *shiest* of them all —Virginia Hamilton⟩ **b :** expressive of fear or timidity ⟨fled down the forest glade with ~ and subtle steps —Elinor Wylie⟩ **2 :** disposed to avoid a person or thing : CAUTIOUS, DISTRUSTFUL, SUSPICIOUS ⟨the gorilla is sullen, untamable and ferocious, ~, wary, and slow-moving —Weston La Barre⟩ ⟨a boy is ~ of a girl who does not have these proofs of efficiency —Margaret Mead⟩ **3 a :** hesitant or chary in committing oneself in action or belief : RELUCTANT, CIRCUMSPECT ⟨not in the least ~ about disclosing the secrets of their craft to the uninstructed —*Listener*⟩ ⟨travellers were very ~ of being confidential on a short notice —Charles Dickens⟩ ⟨~ of assuming the moral attitude —W.S.Maugham⟩ **b :** disinclined to discuss or admit to consideration ⟨may well be rather ~ of reverting to topics that are not . . . yet exhausted —F.R.Leavis⟩ ⟨very ~ about the actual condition and number of the . . . navy —G.M.Dallas⟩ ⟨scholars had been ~ of these documents, for fear of their destroying the authority of the . . . text —Edmund Wilson⟩ **4 a :** sensitively diffident or retiring : RESERVED, BASHFUL ⟨~ in the presence of strangers and bold with people she knew well —Sherwood Anderson⟩ ⟨the boy ~ and sidelong with adolescence's indecisive shames and inferiorities —Ruth Park⟩ ⟨of a ~ modesty and excessive fear of intrusion which often obscured his real . . . worth —H.E.Starr⟩ **b :** expressive of such reticence or bashfulness ⟨spoke in a ~, delicate voice, hushed and bookish —Irwin Shaw⟩ ⟨remembered her childlike look . . . and ~ tremulous grace —Oscar Wilde⟩ **5 :** withdrawn from view or notice : HIDDEN, SECLUDED ⟨the ~ recesses of the woodland —George Meredith⟩ ⟨the ~, almost sly, processes of evolution —Holbrook Jackson⟩ ⟨some ~ intuition on the edge of consciousness that would disappear if looked at directly —F.R.Leavis⟩ **6 a :** meager in growth or reproduction : UNPRODUCTIVE ⟨sells off his ~ breeders annually⟩ ⟨is a ~ bloomer in the house —Bessie Buxton⟩ ⟨the greengage . . . is a ~ bearer —F.D.Smith & Barbara Wilcox⟩ **b** (1) **:** having less than the full or a specified amount or number : SCANT, LACKING, SHORT ⟨looks about 10 years ~ of his 62 —E.P.Snow⟩ ⟨could get $2000 on a GI loan but would still be $6000 ~ —N.M.Clark⟩ (2) having less money at stake than required in a game; *esp* **:** indebted to the pot (as in poker) **7 :** of a disreputable character or type ⟨gambling hells and ~ saloons —*Blackwood's*⟩

syn BASHFUL, DIFFIDENT, MODEST, COY: SHY applies to a reserved or timid tendency to be unobtrusive, to avoid familiarity or contact with others, or to shun participation in group activity ⟨a *shy* youth, uneasy with girls⟩ ⟨the young people seemed *shy*, almost apprehensive. None stepped forward to greet the stranger; they seemed rather to shrink from him, whispering together in little groups —C.B.Nordhoff & J.N. Hall⟩ BASHFUL implies a frightened or hesitant shyness, often characteristic of childhood or awkward adolescence ⟨he became increasingly *bashful*, and he never had a close friend of either sex —R.J.Donovan⟩ ⟨*bashful* children afraid of the guests⟩ DIFFIDENT may apply to a shyness arising from lack of confidence or distrust in one's ability or personality ⟨a small-town youth, unsure, *diffident*, reaching toward friendship with noble minds, and then drawing back with an unmannerly shrug —H.S.Canby⟩ ⟨too *diffident* a man to have much truck with girls —Nevil Shute⟩ MODEST may indicate absence of any undue self-confidence or conceit ⟨the board in its report cautions scientists to be *modest* and restrained when they step beyond their special fields in expression of opinions as citizens —Vannevar Bush⟩ ⟨the *modest* procedure is not to avow loudly, not to protest too much, our love of truth —G.W. Sherburn⟩ COY may suggest an artful or coquettish affectation of shyness and hesitation ⟨*coy*, like the no's of a woman who has decided in advance to yield —James Burnham⟩ ⟨the ladies of the chansons are not *coy*, and often make the first advances. Such natural lusty love is not romantic —H.O.Taylor⟩

[2]**shy** \"\ *vb* **shied; shied; shying; shies** *vi* **1 :** to develop or exhibit a sudden antipathy : SHRINK, RECOIL ⟨here an old liberal should begin to ~; to halt and wonder —Ernest Barker⟩ — often used with *at* or *from* ⟨*shied* at the publicity guns trained on him —Eloise Hazard⟩ ⟨the conservative court . . . had *shied* from the idea of encouraging revolutionaries —Oscar Handlin⟩ **2 :** to start suddenly aside through fright or alarm ⟨always *shied* at this particular spot —Laura Krey⟩ ⟨falls that thump the ~*ing* trout —Allen Tate⟩ ⟨seemed to ~, white-eyed, from the figure . . . on the kitchen floor —Kenneth Roberts⟩ **3 :** to move or dodge to evade a person or thing — usu. used with *away* or *off* ⟨does not come near to touching this point, but *shies* away into . . . misleading examples —*Times Lit. Supp.*⟩ ⟨candidates *shied* away as soon as they heard the old pastor had not been paid —R.C.Wood⟩ ⟨you ~ off me because I am not your sort —Elizabeth Bowen⟩ and sometimes with *clear* ⟨always *shied* clear of publicity —*Fortune*⟩ **~ vt :** to fight shy of : AVOID, SHUN ⟨in trade it is a dangerous thing to ~ danger —Isak Dinesen⟩ **syn** see DEMUR

[3]**shy** \"\ *n* -ES [[2]*shy*] **:** a sudden start aside (as from fright) ⟨thrown by the horse's unexpected ~⟩

[4]**shy** \"\ *vb* **shied; shied; shying; shies** [perh. fr. [1]*shy;* fr. the once popular amusement of throwing sticks or stones at cocks specially trained in wariness and ability to dodge] *vt* **:** to throw (an object) with a jerk : FLING ⟨boys who delighted in ~*ing* stones at her fowls —H.A.Overstreet⟩ **~ vi :** to make a sudden throw ⟨young men . . . ~*ing* for coconuts —Adrian Bell⟩

[5]**shy** \"\ *n* -ES **1 :** the act of shying : TOSS, THROW **2 :** a verbal fling ⟨took a few *shies* at the integrity of his opponent⟩ **3 :** an experimental attempt : TRY ⟨made a few *shies* at orchestral recording —Roland Gelatt⟩ **4 :** COCKSHY 1a, 2a

shy·ish \'shīish, -ēsh\ *adj* **:** rather shy : inclined to be shy

[1]**shy·lock** \'shī͵läk\ *n* -s *usu cap* [after *Shylock*, merciless moneylender portrayed in *The Merchant of Venice* (1596) by William Shakespeare †1616 Eng. dramatist and poet] **:** an extortionate creditor or moneylender ⟨an international spider web of *Shylocks* squeezing the heart of hungry multitudes —D.L.Molinari⟩

[2]**shylock** \"\ *vi* -ED/-ING/-S **:** to lend money at high rates of interest ⟨exposé of systematic thievery . . . ~*ing*, and murder —*Current Biog.*⟩

shy·ly *also* **shily** *adv* **:** in a shy manner ⟨blinking ~ before the press cameras —J.B.Boothroyd⟩ ⟨listened ~ to the stranger —H.A.Sinclair⟩ ⟨spring steals in ~ —D.C.Peattie⟩

shy·ness *n* -ES **:** the quality or state of being shy : TIMIDITY

[1]**shy·ster** \'shīstə(r)\ *n* -s [prob. after *Scheuster* *fl*1840 Am. attorney frequently rebuked in a New York court for pettifoggery] : one who is professionally unscrupulous esp. in the practice of law or politics : PETTIFOGGER ⟨has observed too many ~*s*, too many ambulance chasers, too many political confidence men, too many blackmailers —Stanley Walker⟩ ⟨there are tyrants and ~*s* in all positions, and especially those dressed in subordinate authority —Walt Whitman⟩

[2]**shyster** \"\ *vi* **shystered; shystered; shystering** \-t(ə)riŋ\ **shysters** : to deal as a shyster

si \'sē\ *n* -s [It] **1** : the tone *B* in the fixed-do system of solmization **2** : the seventh tone of the diatonic scale in solmization

si *abbr* silent

SI *abbr* **1** *often not cap* short interest **2** staff inspector

Si *symbol* silicon

sia \'sēə\ *or* **zia** \'zēə, '(t)sēə\ *n, pl* **sia** *or* **sias** *or* **zia** *or* **zias** *usu cap* **1 a** : a Keres people occupying a pueblo in northwestern New Mexico **b** : a member of such people **2** : the language of the Sia people

sia·fu \sē'ä(,)fü\ *n* -s [Swahili] : an African driver ant esp. of the genus *Anomma*

si·al \'sī,al\ *n* -s [G, fr. NL *si*licium + *al*uminium] **1** : siliceous or acid igneous rock whether solid or molten **2** : the lighter outer portion of the earth composed mainly of solid or molten rocks rich in silica and alumina — compare SIMA

sial- *or* **sialo-** *comb form* [NL, fr. Gk, fr. *sialon;* akin to L *spuere* to spit — more at SPEW] : saliva ⟨*sialo*lith⟩

si·al·a·gog·ic \(¦)sī¦alə¦gäjik, -gägik\ *adj* [*sialagogue* + *-ic*] : promoting the flow of saliva

si·al·a·gogue \sī'alə,gäg\ *n* -s [NL *sialagogum*, neut. of *sialagogus* inducing flow of saliva, fr. *sial-* + LL *-agogus* -agogue] : an agent which promotes the flow of saliva

si·a·lia \sī'ālēə\ *n, cap* [NL, fr. Gk *sialis*, a bird + NL *-ia*] : a genus of singing birds (family Turdidae) comprising the American bluebirds

[1]**si·al·ic** \(')sī¦alik\ *adj* [*sial-* + *-ic*] : of or relating to the saliva : SALIVARY

[2]**sialic** \"\ *adj* [ISV *sial* + *-ic*] : of or relating to the sial ⟨~ rocks⟩ ⟨the basic substratum, in which the ~ continents float —*Jour. of Geol.*⟩

sialic acid *n* : any of a group of crystalline reducing amido acids of carbohydrate character that are acyl (as acetyl or glycolyl) derivatives of neuraminic acid and that are found esp. as components of various gangliosides, blood glycoproteins and mucoproteins

[1]**si·a·lid** \'sīələd\ *also* **si·al·i·dan** \(')sī¦alədən\ *adj* [*sialid* fr. NL *Sialidae; sialidan* fr. NL *Sialidae* + E *-an*] : of or relating to the Sialidae

[2]**sialid** \"\ *also* **sialidan** \"\ *n* -s : an insect of the family Sialidae

si·al·i·dae \sī'alə,dē\ *n pl, cap* [NL, fr. *Sialis*, type genus + *-idae*] : a family of usu. large insects (order Megaloptera) including the hellgrammite, alderflies, and related forms and having the hind wings broad at the base with their anal angle folding in plaits

si·a·lis \'sīələs\ *n, cap* [NL, fr. Gk, a bird] : a genus (the type of the family Sialidae) of insects

si·al·kot \sē'äl,kōt\ *adj, usu cap* [fr. *Sialkot*, Pakistan] : of or from the city of Sialkot, Pakistan : of the kind or style prevalent in Sialkot

sialogogue *n* -s [by alter.] : SIALAGOGUE

si·al·o·gram \sī'alə,gram\ *n* [*sial-* + *-gram*] : a roentgenogram of the salivary tract made by sialography

si·a·log·ra·phy \,sīə'lägrəfē\ *n* -ES [*sial-* + *-graphy*] : roentgenography of the salivary tract after injection of a radiopaque substance

si·a·loid \'sīə,lȯid\ *adj* [*sial-* + *-oid*] : resembling saliva

si·al·o·lith \sī'alə,lith\ *n* -s [ISV *sial-* + *-lith*] : a salivary calculus

si·al·o·li·thi·a·sis \sī¦alə+\ *n* [NL, fr. *sial-* + *lithiasis*] : the condition of having one or more salivary calculi

si·al·or·rhea *also* **si·al·or·rhoea** \(,)sī,alə'rēə\ *n* -s [NL, fr. *sial-* + *-rrhea, -rrhoea*] : SALIVATION

si·am \(')sī¦am, -¦aa(ə)m\ *adj, usu cap* [fr. *Siam* (Thailand), country in southeastern Asia] : THAILAND

si·a·mang \'sēə,maŋ, -mäŋ\ *n* -s [Malay] : a black gibbon (*Symphalangus syndactylus*) of Sumatra that is the largest of the gibbons and has the second and third toes partially united by a web

[1]**si·a·mese** \¦sīə¦mēz, -ēs\ *adj* [*Siam* (Thailand) + E *-ese* (adj. suffix)] **1** *usu cap* : THAILAND **2** *usu cap* [fr. *siamese* (*twin*)] : exhibiting great resemblance : very like — compare SIAMESE TWIN **3** [fr. *siamese* (*twin*)] **a** : serving to connect two or more pipes or hose so as to permit discharge in a single stream ⟨~ connection⟩ ⟨~ joint⟩ **b** : having a siamese connection ⟨~ fire-hose lines⟩

[2]**siamese** \"\ *n, pl* **siamese** [*Siam* (Thailand), country in southeastern Asia + E *-ese* (n. suffix)] **1** *cap* : THAI 1 **2** *cap* : THAI 2 **3** *usu cap* [[1]*siamese*] : SIAMESE CAT **4** [[1]*siamese*] : a siamese connection or joint

[3]**siamese** \"\ *vt* -ED/-ING/-S *sometimes cap* [fr. *siamese* (*twin*)] : to unite in a manner suggestive of Siamese twins; *esp* : to unite (as pipes) by the use of a siamese connection

siamese cat *n, usu cap S* : a slender blue-eyed short-haired domestic cat of a breed of oriental origin having the body fawn or pale gray and the ears, paws, tail, and face darker brown or gray

siamese fighting fish *n, usu cap S* : BETTA 2

siamese twin *n, usu cap S* [so called after Chang †1874 and Eng †1874 congenitally united twins born in Meklong, Siam, of Chinese parentage] **1 a** : one of a pair of congenitally united twins in man or animals — compare CRANIOPAGUS, THORACOPAGUS, XIPHOPAGUS **b** : a double monster (as a conjoined fruit) **2** : one of two persons or things that are closely or indissolubly associated ⟨distribution (the *Siamese twin* of production) —Lewis Galantiere⟩

si·an \(')shē¦än\ *adj, usu cap* [fr. *Sian*, China] : of or from the city of Sian, China : of the kind or style prevalent in Sian

si·a·po \sē'ä(,)pō\ *n* -s [Samoan] *in Samoa* : TAPA

sias *pl of* SIA

[1]**sib** \'sib\ *n* -s [ME *sib*, *sibbe*, fr. OE *sibb;* akin to OHG *sippa*, *sippea* kinship, family, ON *sifjar*, pl., Goth *sibja* and prob. to Skt *sabhā* assembly; akin to L *suus* one's own — more at SUICIDE] : KINSHIP

[2]**sib** \"\ *adj* [ME *sib*, *sibbe*, fr. OE *sibb*, fr. *sibb*, n., kinship] **1** : related by blood : AKIN — usu. used with *to* ⟨owners of the neighborhood, ~ to English squire or Scots laird —Mary Johnston⟩ **2** *chiefly dial* : on good or intimate terms — usu. used with *to* ⟨~ to the ladies⟩ ⟨this ethereal quality of hers was always ~ to the earth —Llewelyn Powys⟩ **3** *dial* : WELL-DISPOSED, CONGENIAL — usu. used with *to*

[3]**sib** \"\ *n* -s [ME *sib*, *sibbe*, fr. OE *sibb*, fr. *sibb*, adj., related] **1 a** : KINDRED, RELATIVES **b** : a blood relation : KINSMAN **2 a** : a brother or sister considered irrespective of sex : SIBLING 1a **b** : a plant or animal having the same degree of relation to another as human siblings **3** : a group consisting of all persons unilaterally descended from a real or supposed ancestor

sib·bal·di·us \sə̇'baldēəs, -bȯl-\ [NL, fr. Sir Robert *Sibbald* †1722 Scot. scientist] *syn of* SIBBALDUS

sib·bald's rorqual \'sibəl(d)z-\ *n, usu cap S* [after Sir Robert *Sibbald* †1722] : BLUE WHALE

sib·bal·dus \sə̇'baldəs, -bȯl-\ *n, cap* [NL, fr. Sir Robert *Sibbald* †1722 Scot. scientist] : a genus of marine cetaceans including solely the blue whale and being often included in the genus *Balaenoptera*

sib·bing \'sibiŋ\ *n* -s [[3]*sib* + *-ing*] : the process of pollinating (as in corn breeding) an emasculated plant with pollen from a sister plant — compare SELF-POLLINATION

si·be·ria \(')sī¦birēə, -bēr-\ *adj, usu cap* [fr. *Siberia*, region of the U.S.S.R. in Asia] : of or from Siberia : of the kind or style prevalent in Siberia : SIBERIAN

[1]**si·be·ri·an** \-ēən\ *adj, usu cap* [*Siberia*, region of the U.S.S.R. extending from the Ural mountains to the Pacific ocean in northern Asia (fr. NL, fr. Russ *Sibir'* — fr. *Sibir'*, first Tatar fort in the region conquered by Cossacks in 1581 — + NL *-ia*) + E *-an* (adj. suffix)] **1** : of, relating to, or characteristic of Siberia **2** : of, relating to, or characteristic of the Siberians

[2]**siberian** \"\ *n* -s [*Siberia* + E *-an* (n. suffix)] **1** *cap* : a native or inhabitant of Siberia **2** *usu cap* [by shortening] : SIBERIAN HUSKY 2

siberian brown *n, often cap S* : a moderate olive brown that is stronger and very slightly darker than olive brown and redder and paler than average mustard brown (sense 1)

siberian cedar *n, usu cap S* : SWISS PINE

siberian chipmunk *n, usu cap S* : BARONDUKI

siberian crab *also* **siberian crab apple** *n, usu cap S* : an Asiatic wild crab apple (*Malus baccata*) that is an ancestor of cultivated forms and has small yellow or red very hard fruits — called also *cherry apple, cherry crab*

siberian cranesbill *n, usu cap S* : an Asiatic annual weed (*Geranium sibiricum*) that is adventive in the eastern U. S. and has deeply parted leaves and showy nearly white flowers

siberian dogwood *n, usu cap S* : a shrubby Siberian dogwood (*Cornus alba sibirica*) having brilliant red stems and used as an ornamental

siberian elm *n, usu cap S* : a rapid-growing small to medium often shrubby Asiatic tree (*Ulmus pumila*) naturalized in the U. S., planted for shelter or ornament, and having rough bark, rounded crown, and glabrous branchlets — called also *Chinese elm, dwarf elm*

siberian fir *n, usu cap S* : an ornamental evergreen tree (*Abies sibirica*) of eastern Asia that is often cultivated for its bright green foliage and handsome bluish cones

siberian fir–needle oil *or* **siberian pine–needle oil** *n, usu cap S* : PINE-NEEDLE OIL b

siberian flax *n, usu cap S* : FIREWEED b

siberian gray owl *n, usu cap S* : a large owl (*Scotiaptex nebulosa barbata*) related to the great gray owl and occurring in eastern Siberia and casually in Alaska

siberian husky *n* **1** *usu cap S&H* : a breed of medium-sized compact dogs developed as sled dogs in northeastern Siberia, having a coat of white, gray, black, or some combination of these with a very dense undercoat, and in general resembling the larger Alaskan malamute **2** *usu cap S & often cap H* : a dog of the Siberian Husky breed

siberian ibex *n, usu cap S* : a large-horned Siberian wild goat

siberian iris *n, usu cap S* : any of various beardless irises that have lilac, blue, or white rather small flowers borne on stiffly erect stalks and are mostly hybrids between two Old World species (*Iris sibirica* and *I. sanguinea*)

siberian larch *n, usu cap S* : a larch (*Larix sibirica*) of northeastern Russia and Siberia used in cultivation and having leaves two inches or more in length and cone scales slightly incurved at the apex

siberian millet *n, usu cap S* : a foxtail millet (*Setaria italica rubrofructa*) having orange to reddish fruits in long spikes beset with purple bristles — compare GERMAN MILLET

siberian oilseed *n, usu cap S* : GOLD-OF-PLEASURE

siberian pea tree *n, usu cap S* : a small spiny tree or shrub (*Caragana arborescens*) of eastern Asia with yellow flowers that is often cultivated in shelterbelts and hedges

siberian pine *n, usu cap S* : SWISS PINE

siberian sable *n, usu cap 1st S* : an Old World sable (*Martes zibellina*) or its fur — compare AMERICAN SABLE

siberian snow hare *n, usu cap 1st S* : any of several large active northern Asiatic hares that constitute distinct races of the common hare (*Lepus timidus*) and that turn white in winter

siberian spruce *n, usu cap 1st S* : a tall evergreen tree of northern Europe and Asia that is considered a variety of the Norway spruce or assigned to a separate species (*Picea obovata*) and that has brownish branchlets and bluish green leaves

siberian squill *n, usu cap 1st S* : a Eurasian blue-flowered herb (*Scilla sibirica*) cultivated as a spring-blooming bulb

siberian squirrel *n, usu cap 1st S* : any of several northern and eastern Old World squirrels which constitute varieties of the common squirrel (*Sciurus vulgaris*) and whose soft fur is used for linings and trimmings

siberian wallflower *n, usu cap S* : a showy erect biennial or short-lived perennial cruciferous herb (*Cheiranthus × allionii*) that is often cultivated for its terminal racemes of bright orange-yellow flowers with the claws of the petals exceeding the calyx in length

si·be·rite \sī'bi,rīt, 'sībə,r-\ *n* -s [F *sibérite*, fr. *Sibérie* Siberia + *-ite*] : rubellite from Siberia

si·ber·ski \sə̇'birskē, sī'b-\ *n, pl* **siberski** *or* **siberskis** *usu cap* [Russ *sibirskiĭ*, fr. *Sibir'* Siberia + *-skiĭ* (adj. & n. suffix denoting a person or thing originating from or connected with a specified place)] : a Siberian settler from European Russia; *esp* : one long settled in Siberia or born of earlier Siberian settlers — called also *Siberyak*

siber·yak *or* **siber·iak** *also* **sibir·yak** *or* **sibir·iak** \¦sībər¦yak, ¦sib-, -,bir-\ *n, pl* **siberyaks** \-ks\ *or* **siber·yaki** \,=(,)='yakē\ *or* **siberiaks** *or* **siber·iaki** *usu cap* [Russ *sibiryak*, fr. *Sibir'* Siberia + *-yak* (n. suffix denoting a person connected with something specified)] : SIBERSKI

sib·i·lance \'sibələn(t)s\ *n* -s **1** : an *s*-like or sibilant quality ⟨sudden silence, broken only by the ~ of mass sniffing —C.B. Kelland⟩ **2** : an utterance characterized by sibilance ⟨the courtroom buzzed with a sudden ~ of whispered comment —Erle Stanley Gardner⟩

sib·i·lan·cy \-nsē,-nsi\ *n* -ES **1** : SIBILANCE **2** : high content of sibilant sounds

[1]**sib·i·lant** \-nt\ *adj* [L *sibilant-*, *sibilans*, pres. part. of *sibilare* to hiss, whistle; of imit. origin like Gk *sizein* to hiss, Goth *swiglon* to blow the flute, whistle, OHG *sweglōn* to blow the flute, W *chwythu* to blow an instrument, OSlav *svistati*, *zvizdati* to hiss, whistle, Skt *kṣvedati* he whistles, roars, hums, hisses] : having, containing, or producing the sound of or a sound resembling that of the *s* or the *sh* in *sash* ⟨a ~ affricate⟩ ⟨a ~ snake⟩ — compare SHIBILANT — **sib·i·lant·ly** *adv*

[2]**sibilant** \"\ *n* -s : a sibilant speech sound (as English \s\, \z\, \sh\, \zh\, \ch(=tsh)\, or \j(=dzh)\)

sib·i·late *also* **sib·il·late** \'sıbə,lāt\ *vb* -ED/-ING/-S [L *sibilatus*, past part. of *sibilare* to hiss, whistle] *vi* **1** : HISS **2** : to utter an initial sibilant : prefix an \s\-sound ~ *vt* **1** : HISS **2** : to pronounce with an initial sibilant : prefix an \s\-sound to

sib·i·lat·ing·ly *adv* : in a sibilating manner

sib·i·la·tion \,sibə'lāshən\ *n* -s [LL *sibilation-*, *sibilatio*, fr. L *sibilatus* (past part.) + *-ion-*, *-io* -ion] **1** : the action of sibilating **2** : a sibilated utterance

sib·i·la·tor \-,lād·ə(r)\ *n* -s [*sibilate* + *-or*] : one that sibilates

sib·i·la·to·ry \'sibələ,tōrē\ *adj* [*sibilate* + *-ory*] : hissing or characterized by hissing : SIBILANT

sib·i·lous \'sibələs\ *adj* [L *sibilus*, fr. *sibilus* act of hissing, act of whistling, fr. *sibilare* to hiss, whistle] *archaic* : SIBILANT

si·bir·ic \(')sī¦birik, sə̇'b-\ *adj, usu cap* [Russ *Sibir'* Siberia + E *-ic*] : relating to or resembling the peoples of Siberia (as the Tungus, Mongols, and Tatars)

sib·ley stove \'siblē-\ *n, usu cap 1st S* [after Henry Hopkins *Sibley* †1886 Am. army officer] : a simple heating stove for a tent consisting of a sheet-iron cone with a small stovepipe attached extending outside the tent

sibley tent *n, usu cap S* [after Henry Hopkins *Sibley* †1886] : a light tent of conical shape erected on a tripod with a ventilating device at the top and sometimes with a vertical drop near the bottom

sib·ling \'sibliŋ, -lēŋ\ *n* -s [[3]*sib* + *-ling*] **1 a** : one of two or more persons who have the same parents but are not necessarily of the same birth; *sometimes* : one of two or more persons having one common parent ⟨~ rivalry⟩ **b** : SIB 2b **2** : a member of a sib

sibling species *n* [trans. of G *geschwisterarten*] : one of two or more physiologic races that are morphologically nearly or completely indistinguishable

[1]**sibmate** \'=,=\ *n* [[3]*sib* + *mate*] : one that belongs to the same sib as another

[2]**sibmate** \"\ *vi* : to interbreed sibs esp. in the production of inbred lines ~ *vt* : to produce by sibmating

sib·ness *n* -ES [ME *sibnesse*, prob. fr. OE *gesibness*, fr. *gesibb* akin, related (fr. *ge-*, perfective, associative, and collective prefix + *sibb* kinsman, sib) + *-ness* — more at CO-, SIB] *archaic* : KINSHIP, RELATIONSHIP, CONNECTION

siboney *usu cap, var of* CIBONEY

sib·ret *or* **sib·rit** \'sibrə̇t\ *n* -s [ME *sibred*, *sibrede*, fr. *sibred*, *sibrede* kinship, consanguinity, fr. OE *sibrǣden*, fr. *sibb*, adj., sib + *rǣden* condition: prob. fr. the mention in the banns of certain forms of kinship as impediments to marriage — more at SIB, KINDRED] *dial Eng* : BANNS 1 — often used in pl.

sibs *pl of* SIB

sib·ship \'sib,ship\ *n* [[3]*sib* + *-ship*] **1** : the quality or state of being a sib or a member of a sib **2 a** : SIB 3; *broadly* : KINDRED **b** : a group of sibs : KINSHIP ⟨of 16 ~ groups, 13 consisted of two and 3 of three siblings each —J.H.Conn & Leo Kanner⟩

sib test *n* : a test of the desirability of individuals as breeders based on the performance of their brothers or sisters and serving as an indirect test of prepotency — compare PROGENY TEST

si·bu·cao \¦sēbə¦kaủ\ *n* -s [Tag *sibukáw*] : SAPPANWOOD

sib·yl *also* **syb·il** \'sibə̇l\ *n* -s *often cap* [ME *sibile*, *Sybylle*, fr. MF *Sibile*, *Sebile*, fr. L *Sibylla*, fr. Gk] **1** : any of several prophetesses usu. accepted as 10 in number and credited to widely separate parts of the ancient world (as Babylonia, Egypt, Greece, and Italy) **2 a** : a female prophet **b** : FORTUNE-TELLER

si·byl·la \sə̇'bilə\ *n, pl* **sibyl·lae** \-i(,)lē, -i,lī\ *usu cap* [L] : SIBYL

si·byl·lic \-ilik\ *adj* [L *Sibylla* + E *-ic*] : SIBYLLINE

sib·yl·line *also* **syb·il·line** \'sibə,līn, -,lēn, -,lən\ *adj* [L *sibyllinus*, fr. *Sibylla* sibyl + *-inus* -ine] **1** *often cap* **a** : of, relating to, resembling, or characteristic of a sibyl : PROPHETIC ⟨the novelist . . . growing a little ~ in her success —Lionel Trilling⟩ **b** : uttered or written in or as if in prophecy ⟨a kind of *Sibylline* book in which ready and infallible answers will be found to problems —*Times Lit. Supp.*⟩ **2 a** : MYSTERIOUS, CRYPTIC, OCCULT ⟨thoroughly ~ in most of his pronouncements —John Gunther⟩ **b** : AMBIGUOUS, EQUIVOCAL ⟨utterances remained ~ —A.R.E.Pinchot⟩

sib·yl·list \-,lə̇st\ *n* -s *usu cap* [LGk *sibyllistēs* interpreter of the Sibylline Oracles, fr. Gk *Sibylla* sibyl + *-istēs* -ist] : one who believes in sibylline prophecies

[1]**sic** \(¦)sik\ *chiefly Scot var of* SUCH

[2]**sic** *or* **sick** \'sik\ *vt* **sicced** *or* **sicked** \-kt\ **sicced** *or* **sicked; siccing** *or* **sicking; sics** *or* **sicks** [alter. of [1]*seek*] **1** : SEEK, CHASE, ATTACK — usu. used as an imperative esp. to a dog ⟨~ 'em⟩ **2** : to incite or urge to an attack, to pursuit, or to harassment : SET ⟨tried to ~ his old feist dog on us —Walter Karig⟩ ⟨had to ~ her lawyer on him first —John Dos Passos⟩ **syn** see URGE

[3]**sic** \'sik, 'sēk\ *adv* [L, thus; akin to L *si* if, OL *soc* so, OE *swā* — more at SO] : intentionally so written — used after a printed word or passage to indicate that it is intended exactly as printed ⟨it is better to say . . . *Teusday* (~) than *Choosdy* — R.S.Bridges⟩ or to indicate that it exactly reproduces an original ⟨all that glisters [~] is not gold⟩

SIC *abbr, often not cap* specific inductive capacity

si·ca·na \sə̇'kānə\ *n, cap* [NL, fr. native name in Peru] : a genus of tendril-bearing herbaceous vines (family Cucurbitaceae) found in tropical America with angled stems, large roundish leaves, solitary yellow monoecious flowers, and bright-colored aromatic fruit

si·car·i·us \sə̇'ka(a)rēəs\ *n, pl* **sicar·ii** \-ē,ī\ *often cap* [L, assassin, murderer, fr. *sica* dagger; akin to L *secare* to cut — more at SAW] : one of a party of Zealots and terrorists resorting to murder in attempting to expel the Romans from Palestine A.D. 52–60

sic·car *chiefly Scot var of* [1]SICKER, [3]SICKER

sic·ca rupee \¦sikə-\ *n* [Hindi *sikkā rupīyā*, *sikka rūpaiya*, fr. Ar *sikkah* die, stamp, stamped coin + Hindi *rupīyā*, *rūpaia* rupee — more at RUPEE] **1** : a newly coined or unworn rupee **2** : a rupee issued in Bengal before 1836 weighing more than the rupee of the British East India Company

[1]**sic·ca·tive** \'sikəd·iv, -ətiv\ *adj* [LL *siccativus*, fr. L *siccatus* (past part. of *siccare* to dry, fr. *siccus* dry) + *-ivus* -ive — more at SACK] : causing to dry : promoting the action of drying

[2]**siccative** \"\ *n* -s : that which promotes drying; *esp* : DRIER 2

[1]**sice** \'sīs, 'sīz\ *n* -s [ME *sice*, *sis*, fr. MF *sis*, fr. L *sex* six — more at SIX] *archaic* : the number six on a die : a throw of six in dice

[2]**sice** *var of* SYCE

sic·el \'sikəl, -isəl\ *n, usu cap* [Gk *Sikelos*] **1** : one of the Siculi **2** : the Italic language of the Siculi

si·cel·i·ot \sə̇'kelēət, sə̇'se-, -ē,ät\ *or* **si·kel·i·ot** \sə̇'k-\ *n* -s *cap* [Gk *Sikeliōtēs*, fr. *Sikelia* Sicily + *-ōtēs* -ote] : one of the ancient Greeks colonized in Sicily

si·chom·o·vi \sə̇'chəməvē, -chäm-\ *n, pl* **sichomovi** *or* **sichomovis** *usu cap* **1** : a Shoshonean people occupying a pueblo in northeastern Arizona **2** : a member of the Sichomovi people

sicht \'sikt\ *Scot var of* SIGHT

[1]**si·cil·ian** \sə̇'silyən, -lēən\ *n* -s *cap* [L *Sicilia* Sicily, island in the Mediterranean sea west of the Italian peninsula (fr. Gk *Sikelia*, fr. *Sikelos* Sicel + *-ia* -y) + E *-an* (n. suffix)] **1** : a native or inhabitant of Sicily **2** : the Italian language as spoken in Sicily

[2]**sicilian** \"\ *adj, usu cap* [L *Sicilia* Sicily + E *-an* (adj. suffix)] **1 a** : of, relating to, or characteristic of Sicily **b** : of, relating to, or characteristic of the people of Sicily **2** : of, relating to, or characteristic of the Sicilian dialects of Italian

sicilian circle *n, usu cap S* : a blend of square and round dance with an indefinite number of couples who meet in figures and proceed to other vis-a-vis couples

si·cil·ian·ism \-ə,nizəm\ *n* -s *usu cap* [ISV *sicilian* + *-ism;* prob. orig. formed as It *sicilianismo*] : a word or phrase peculiar to the dialects of Sicily

si·cil·i·a·no \sə̇,silē'ä(,)nō, sə̇,chi-\ *or* **si·cil·i·a·na** \-,nə\ *or* **si·cil·i·enne** \sə̇¦silē¦en\ *n* -s [*siciliano* modif. (influenced by It *siciliano* Sicilian) of It *siciliana; siciliana* fr. It, fr. fem. of *siciliano* Sicilian, fr. *Sicilia* Sicily (fr. L) + *-ano* -an (fr. L *-anus*); *sicilienne* fr. F, fr. It *siciliana*] **1** : a graceful Sicilian rustic dance in which the partners are joined with handkerchiefs **2** : the music for the siciliano in 6/8 or 12/8 time characterized by a lyrical melody with dotted rhythm and similar to the pastorale

sicilian octave *n, usu cap S* : a stanza or poem having eight iambic pentameters rhyming *abababab*

sicilian sumac *n, usu cap S* : TANNER'S SUMAC

sicilian umber *n, usu cap S* : RAW UMBER

sicilo- *comb form, usu cap* [L *Sicilia* Sicily] : SICULO- ⟨*Sicilo*-Norman⟩ ⟨*Sicilo*-Muslim⟩

[1]**sick** \'sik\ *adj, usu* -ER/-EST [ME *sik*, *sek*, *seke*, fr. OE *sēoc;* akin to MD *siec* sick, OHG *siuh*, *sioh* sick, ON *sjūkr* sick, distressed, Goth *siuks* sick, MIr *socht* depression, silence] **1 a** (1) : affected with disease : not well or healthy : ILL, AILING, INDISPOSED ⟨lay ~ of a fever —Mk 1:30 (AV)⟩ ⟨fell ~ of an obscure depressing fever —Frank Outram & G.E.Fane⟩ ⟨took ~ this morning⟩ (2) : accompanying, indicating, or suggestive of sickness : SICKLY ⟨the ~ smell of age and medicine — Irwin Shaw⟩ (3) : designed for or put to the use or service of a sick person ⟨~ chair⟩ ⟨~ lamp⟩ ⟨~ ward⟩ (4) : relating to the sick ⟨~ benefit⟩ ⟨~ insurance⟩ ⟨~ pay⟩ **b** : affected with or attended by nausea : inclined to vomit or being in the act of vomiting : QUEASY — used with *stomach* with *at*, *to*, *in*, or *on* ⟨felt ~ at his stomach —Ernest Hemingway⟩; compare AIRSICK, CARSICK, SEASICK **c** *chiefly dial* : confined in childbed **d** : MENSTRUATING **2** : spiritually or morally unsound or corrupt ⟨and heal my soul diseased and ~ —John Wesley⟩ **3 a** : affected by some strong emotion (as shame, horror, fear, or envy) to the degree that one feels nauseated or faint ⟨~ with fear⟩ ⟨worried ~ by repeated failures⟩ **b** : having a strong distaste from surfeit : SATIATED — used with *of* ⟨~ of flattery⟩ ⟨~ of a task⟩ ⟨~ of the noise and the smoke —William Black⟩ **c** : DISGUSTED, CHAGRINED ⟨gossip that makes one ~⟩ **d** : depressed and longing for something ⟨~ for one's home⟩ **4 a** : mentally or emotionally unsound or disordered : MORBID, UNWHOLESOME ⟨a ~ personality⟩ ⟨~ thoughts⟩ **b** : dealing with unpleasant or macabre subjects ⟨~ jokes⟩ **5** : requiring repair or replacement : DEFECTIVE, FAULTY ⟨a ~ locomotive⟩ **6** : weak during molting — used of a bird's feathers **7 a** : pale or sickly in appearance or tone : SALLOW, WAN ⟨a ~ skin —John Updike⟩ ⟨light from my torch showed his heavy square face a ~ yellow —Marcia Davenport⟩ **b** (1) : lacking vigor : subnormal in growth or development ⟨a ~ tree⟩ (2) *of grain* : low in viability and deteriorated in milling quality due to slightly excessive moisture content at the time of storing ⟨~ wheat⟩ **c** : SICKLY 5a(2) ⟨said . . . finally, in a ~ whisper

—T.B.Costain⟩ **d :** badly outclassed **:** POOR — usu. used with *look* ⟨observers rated up 141 species, making their previous record of 113 look ~ —*Time*⟩ ⟨a girl won . . . and made the speedsters look very ~ —*Irish Digest*⟩ **8 :** SPAWNING; *broadly* **:** POOR, WATERY ⟨~ fish⟩ ⟨~ oysters⟩ **9 :** being in a declining or inactive state esp. after a period of excessive speculation ⟨a ~ market⟩ ⟨~ commodities⟩ ⟨a ~ economy⟩ **10 :** incapable of producing profitable yields of a crop because infested with disease organisms ⟨clover ~ soils⟩ ⟨ground that gets ~ to melons —*Market Growers Jour.*⟩ ⟨~ valleys across the land —R.G.Struble⟩ **11** *of glass* **:** having a cloudy appearance caused esp. by impurities — **sick to death :** extremely fatigued or bored — **sick unto death 1 :** mortally ill **2 :** sick to death ⟨*sick unto death* of the violent partisanship —Inez Robb⟩

²sick \"\ *n* -S [ME *sik, sek,* fr. OE *sēoc,* fr. *sēoc,* adj., sick] **1** *pl* **sick :** a sick person ⟨then saith he to the ~ of the palsy —Mt 9:6 (AV)⟩ — usu. used collectively ⟨the number of absentees and ~ has risen —*Time*⟩ **2** -S **a :** SICKNESS **b** *chiefly Brit* **:** VOMIT ⟨a room smelling rather of ~ —Elizabeth Taylor⟩

³sick *vb* -ED/-ING/-S [ME *siken, seken,* fr. *sik, sek,* adj., sick] *vi* **1** *obs* **:** to become ill **:** fall sick **2 :** VOMIT — often used with *up* ~ *vt, obs* **:** to cause to be ill **:** make sick

⁴sick \(ˈ)sik\ *dial Brit var of* SUCH

⁵sick *var of* SIC

¹sick–abed \ˈ=,=\ *adj* [fr. the phrase *sick abed*] **:** confined to bed by illness ⟨*sick-abed* youngsters —*Playthings*⟩

²sick–abed \"\ *n* -S **:** one confined to bed by illness ⟨an ideal gift for the *sick-abed* —Rosemary Benét⟩

sick and tired *adj* **:** thoroughly fatigued or bored ⟨*sick and tired* of so much idle talk⟩

sick bay *or* **sick berth** *n* **1 :** a compartment in a ship (as a warship or transport) used as a dispensary and hospital **2 :** a place (as a ward in a hospital or the infirmary of a school) restricted to the care of the sick or injured ⟨opened *sick bays* and dispensaries in the refugee camps —*Picture Post*⟩ ⟨got him back to the palm shack we used as *sick bay* —J.F.Regan⟩

sickbed \ˈ=,=\ *n* [ME *seke bed,* fr. *seke* sick + *bed* — more at SICK, BED] **:** the bed upon which one lies sick ⟨forced to direct operations from a ~ —*Current Biog.*⟩

sick book *n* **:** a book in which are entered the names of all individuals esp. in a military unit who require medical attention

sick call *n* **1 a :** a usu. daily formation at which individuals report as sick to the medical officer ⟨the attendance at *sick call* would vary —T.O.Heggen⟩ ⟨missed our duty formation and I thought I would cover up by going on *sick call* —Joseph Grant⟩ **b :** the period during which sick call is held **2 a :** a visit (as by clergyman or physician) to a sick person ⟨the doctor on his round of *sick calls*⟩

sicked *past of* SIC *or of* SICK

sick·en \ˈsikən\ *vb* **sickened; sickened; sickening** \-k(ə)niŋ\ **sickens** [ME *seknen,* fr. *sek,* adj., sick + *-nen* -en — more at SICK] *vt* **1 :** to make sick **:** DISEASE, NAUSEATE ⟨the fogs have settled . . . thousands of persons have been ~*ed* —*N.Y. Times*⟩ **2 a :** to cause revulsion as a result of weariness or satiety ⟨the growing pile of cakes on the scrubbed table ~*ed* him —John Morrison⟩ **b :** to make nauseated or faint from some strong feeling (as fear, disgust, envy) ⟨feel more ~*ed* than stimulated by the public admiration —T.E.Lawrence⟩ ⟨others, ~*ed* by conditions under which they lived —Sinclair Lewis⟩ ⟨~*ed* by the sight of blood⟩ **3 :** to make sickly **:** IMPAIR, WEAKEN, IMPOVERISH ⟨land ~*ed* by overgrazing⟩ ~ *vi* **1 :** to become sick **:** fall into disease ⟨a hummingbird which had apparently been hurt or had ~*ed* —B.A.Williams⟩ **2 a :** to become faint or nauseated as a result of being affected by some strong emotion (as fear, horror, or desire) ⟨his heart ~*ed* at the thought of this brutal indignity —F.V.W.Mason⟩ — often used with *of* ⟨when the expected excesses began he speedily ~*ed* of the spectacle —J.C.Fitzpatrick⟩ **b :** to become weary or satiated — often used with *of* ⟨voters might ~ of political bickering —W.J.Jorden⟩ **3 :** to become weak or faded **:** DECAY, DECLINE, DETERIORATE ⟨his self-esteem ~*ed* —Maurice Hewlett⟩ ⟨became plain my story was ~*ing* from surfeit of material —Catherine D. Bowen⟩ **4** *chiefly Brit* **:** to undergo the preliminary symptoms — used with *for* ⟨he was ~*ing* for mumps⟩ ⟨pig that looked as though it were ~*ing* for a disease —Pearl Buck⟩ **syn** see DISGUST

sick·en·er \-k(ə)nə(r)\ *n* -S **:** something that tends to sicken or disgust **:** a sickening blow **:** OVERDOSE

sick·en·ing·ly *adv* **:** in a manner or to a degree that sickens ⟨a ~ unctuous person⟩ ⟨a ~ sweet syrup⟩

¹sick·er \ˈsikər\ *adj* [ME *siker,* fr. OE *sicor;* akin to OFris *sikur* safe, secure, OS *sikor,* OHG *sichur, sichor;* all fr. a prehistoric WGmc word borrowed fr. L *securus* free from care — more at SECURE] **1** *chiefly Scot* **:** SECURE, SAFE ⟨a ~ road⟩ **2** *chiefly Scot* **:** TRUSTWORTHY, DEPENDABLE ⟨a ~ man⟩ **3** *chiefly Scot* **:** CONFIDENT, ASSURED **4** *chiefly Scot* **:** firm and well-established

²sicker \"\ *vi* -ED/-ING/-S [ME *sikeren,* fr. OE *sicerian;* akin to LG *sikern* to trickle, froth, drizzle, and prob. to OHG *sīhan* to filter — more at SACK] *chiefly dial* **:** TRICKLE, OOZE

³sicker \"\ *adv* [ME *siker,* fr. *siker,* adj., safe] **1** *chiefly Scot* **:** SECURELY, SAFELY **2** *chiefly Scot* **:** ASSUREDLY, CERTAINLY

⁴sicker \"\ *vt* -ED/-ING/-S [ME *sikeren,* fr. *siker* safe] *archaic* **:** ASSURE, SECURE, PLEDGE

⁵sicker *comparative of* SICK

sick·er·ly *adv* [ME *sikerly, sikerlich,* fr. *siker* safe + *-ly, -lich* -ly] *chiefly Scot* **:** SICKER

sickest *superlative of* SICK

sick flag *n* **:** QUARANTINE FLAG

sick headache *n* **:** MIGRAINE

sick house *n* [ME *sekehous,* fr. *seke* sick + *hous* house — more at SICK, HOUSE] **:** HOSPITAL, INFIRMARY ⟨convalescing after measles in the *sick house* —C.G.Chenevix-Trench⟩

sicking *pres part of* SIC *or of* SICK

sic·king·ia \siˈkiŋēə\ *n, cap* [NL, prob. fr. Franz von *Sickingen* †1523 Ger. knight + NL *-ia*] **:** a genus of small or medium-sized Central and So. American trees (family Rubiaceae) of which some yield usable timber and some are a source of red dyes and extracts of repute in local folk medicine esp. as febrifuges and purgatives — see ARARIBA

sick·ish \ˈsikish\ *adj* [¹*sick* + *-ish*] **1** *archaic* **:** somewhat ill **:** SICKLY **2 :** somewhat nauseated **:** somewhat qualmish ⟨made her feel ~ the way she felt from the ether —Josephine Pinckney⟩ **3 :** somewhat sickening ⟨a ~ odor⟩ ⟨a *sickish*-sweet taste⟩ ⟨disperse the ~ fog of sentimentality that has clouded man's knowledge of himself —J.L.Liebman⟩ — **sick·ish·ly** *adv* — **sick·ish·ness** *n* -ES

sicklaemia *var of* SICKLEMIA

¹sick·le \ˈsikəl\ *n* -S [ME *sikel,* fr. OE *sicol, sicel;* akin to OHG *sihhila* sickle, MD *sekele;* all fr. a prehistoric WGmc word borrowed fr. L *secula* sickle — more at SAW] **1 a :** an agricultural implement consisting of a hook-shaped metal blade with a short handle fitted on a tang **b** (1) **:** the cutting mechanism of a binder, reaper, combine, or header consisting of a flat bar to which are riveted a head and a series of sharp serrated 5-sided cutting blades (2) **:** the knife with smooth sections used on a mower **2 :** any of a series of sickle-shaped arms in a spinning mule to guide the thread **3 :** SICKLE FEATHER **4 :** something that is suggestive of a sickle in shape or use **:** CRESCENT ⟨this ~ of sand which encloses one of the finest harbors —Mary H. Vorse⟩

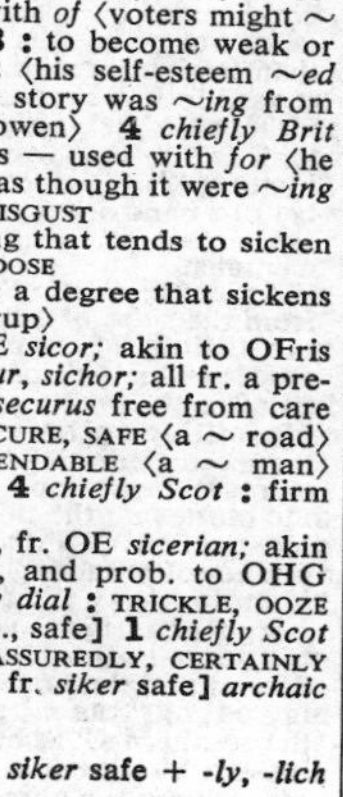
sickle 1a

²sickle \"\ *vb* **sickled; sickled; sickling** \-k(ə)liŋ\ **sickles** *vt* **1 :** to mow or reap with a sickle ⟨~ down the weeds along the wall —Rumer Godden⟩ **2 :** to form (a red blood cell) into a crescent ~ *vi* **1 :** to move in a curving line suggestive of that of a sickle ⟨children . . . would ~ quietly back like boomerangs along the soundless lawn —Ray Bradbury⟩ **2 :** to form into a crescent ⟨the ability of red blood cells to ~⟩

³sickle \"\ *adj* **:** having the form of a sickle blade **:** having a curve similar to that of a sickle blade ⟨the ~ moon⟩ ⟨a ~ beach⟩

sickle alfalfa *also* **sickle lucerne** *or* **sickle medick** *n* **:** a European medic (*Medicago falcata*) naturalized in No. America and having yellow flowers and falcate or nearly straight pods

sickle and hammer *n, sometimes cap S&H* **:** HAMMER AND SICKLE

sick leave *n* **1 :** a period of absence from duty due to illness or other disability ⟨the foreign secretary was on *sick leave* when the decisions were taken —*New Statesmen & Nation*⟩ ⟨ill health required several *sick leaves* —C.D.Rhodes⟩ **2 :** an allowance of paid leave specified in days or hours per month or year that is granted to employees or salaried personnel for absence due to illness or other disability ⟨entitled to 40 hours' *sick leave* each calendar year —*New South Wales Industrial Gazette*⟩ ⟨as a rule, *sick leave* accumulates at the same rate, namely eighteen days each year —*Employment Opportunities in the Civil Service* (*Canada*)⟩ **3 :** SICK PAY ⟨paid us *sick leave* for the six weeks Jack was in hospital —*Sat. Eve. Post*⟩

sickle bar *n* **1 :** CUTTER BAR **2 :** the complete cutting mechanism of any grain harvester consisting of the sickle, the guards and ledger plates, and the bar to which they are attached

sicklebill \ˈ==,=\ *n* [³*sickle* + *bill*] **:** any of various birds with a strongly curved bill: as **a :** CURLEW; *specif* **:** HEN CURLEW **b :** any of several thrashers; *esp* **:** CALIFORNIA THRASHER **c :** a bird of paradise of the genus *Drepanornis* **d :** a saberbill of the genus *Campylorhamphus* **e :** any of several Hawaiian birds of the family Drepanididae and esp. of the genus *Drepanis* **f :** a So. and Central American hummingbird of the genus *Eutoxeres*

sickle–billed \ˈ==ˌ=\ *adj* **:** having a bill curved like a sickle

sickle cell *n* **:** an abnormal red blood cell of crescent shape

sickle–cell anemia *or* **sickle–cell disease** *n* **:** a chronic familial anemia in which a large proportion or the majority of the red cells in the blood are sickle cells and which occurs mainly in persons of Negro blood

sickle–cell trait *n* **:** SICKLEMIA

sick·led \ˈsikəld\ *adj* [¹*sickle* + *-ed*] **:** furnished with a sickle or sickles ⟨the ~ tail of chanticleer⟩

sickle feather *n* **:** one of the long curved tail feathers of a cock; *esp* **:** one of the middle or upper pair — see COCK illustration

sickle–grass \ˈ==,=\ *n* **1 :** a stout 3-angled sedge (*Carex crinita*) of eastern No. America with dense drooping sickle-shaped spikes **2 :** a tearthumb (*Polygonum arifolium*)

sickle ham *n* **:** SICKLE HOCK — **sickle–hammed** \ˈ==ˌ=\ *adj*

sickle hock *n* **:** a hock (as of a horse) that is much flexed with the foot far under the body — **sickle–hocked** \ˈ==ˌ=\ *adj*

sicklelike \ˈ==,=\ *adj* **:** resembling or suggesting a sickle

sick·le·man \ˈsikəlmən\ *n, pl* **sicklemen :** one who uses a sickle **:** REAPER

sick·le·mia *also* **sick·lae·mia** \ˌsikəˈlēmēə, siˈklē-\ *n* -S [NL, fr. E ³*sickle* + NL *-emia*] **:** a familial condition characterized by the presence in the blood of red cells that are more or less crescentic in form occurring mainly in persons of Negro blood and rarely developing into sickle-cell anemia — called also *sickle-cell trait* — **sick·le·mic** \ˌsikəˈlēmik, (ˈ)siˌklē-\ *adj*

sicklepod \ˈ==,=\ *n* [³*sickle* + *pod*] **1 :** a No. American rock cress (*Arabis canadensis*) having very long curved pods **2 :** a cosmopolitan tropical weed (*Cassia tora*) with yellow flowers and slender curved pods

sick·ler \ˈsik(ə)lə(r)\ *n* -S [¹*sickle* + *-er*] **:** one that uses a sickle **:** SICKLEMAN

sick·ler·ite \ˈsikləˌrīt\ *n* -S [*Sickler* family of Pala, San Diego county, Calif. + E *-ite*] **:** a mineral $(Li,Mn)(PO_4)$ consisting of a hydrous lithium manganese phosphate and occurring in dark brown cleavable masses and isomorphous with ferrisicklerite (sp. gr. 3.4)

sickles *pl of* SICKLE, *pres 3d sing of* SICKLE

sickle senna *n* **:** SICKLEPOD 2

sickle tail *n* **:** a tail (as of a dog) that curves upward and over the back

sickle–tailed \ˈ==ˌ=\ *adj* **:** having a tail carried curved like a sickle

sicklewort \ˈ==,=\ *n* [ME *sikelwert,* fr. *sikel* sickle + *wert* wort — more at SICKLE, WORT] **:** a yellow-flowered European vetch (*Coronilla scorpioides*) with curved pods

sick·li·ly \ˈsikləlē, -əli\ *adv* **:** in a sickly manner

sick·li·ness \-klēnəs, -klin-\ *n* -ES **:** the quality or state of being sickly

sickling *pres part of* SICKLE

sick list *n* **:** a list containing the names of the sick — **on the sick list :** ILL, INDISPOSED

sick·lo·cyte \ˈsik(ə)ləˌsīt\ *n* -S [³*sickle* + *-o-* + *-cyte*] **:** SICKLE CELL

¹sick·ly \ˈsiklē, -li\ *adj* -ER/-EST [ME *siklich, sekly,* fr. *sik, sek* sick + *-lich, -ly* -ly — more at SICK] **1 :** somewhat sick **:** disposed to illness **:** habitually ailing ⟨a ~ body⟩ ⟨~ children⟩ **2 a :** produced by or associated with sickness ⟨a ~ complexion⟩ ⟨a ~ appetite⟩ **b** *archaic* **:** of or relating to a sick person or to sickness **3 :** characterized by the presence of sickness **:** attended with disease ⟨a ~ place⟩ ⟨a ~ season⟩ ⟨the ~ aims, the false ideals, of our age —Oscar Wilde⟩ **4 :** producing or tending to disease **:** UNHEALTHY ⟨a ~ climate⟩ **5 a** (1) **:** appearing as if sick **:** WEAK, LANGUID, PALE ⟨uneasy influence of that ~ moonlight —David Kidd⟩ ⟨lamp burning with a ~ flame⟩ (2) **:** WRETCHED, UNHAPPY, UNEASY ⟨a ~ smile⟩ ⟨a ~ attempt at humor⟩ ⟨shared their ~ social unease —Herbert Gold⟩ **b :** resembling in state a sickly person ⟨a ~ plant⟩ ⟨a ~ mind⟩ ⟨~ beer⟩ **6 a :** tending to produce nausea ⟨the air was ~ with the odor of locust beans —Norman Lewis⟩ **b :** disgusting or repelling by reason of being weak, silly, or sentimental **:** MAWKISH ⟨why do they want to play those ~ waltzes —Winifred Bambrick⟩ **syn** see UNWHOLESOME

²sickly \"\ *vt* -ED/-ING/-ES **:** to make sick or sickly (as in hue) — usu. used with *over* ⟨*sicklied* o'er with the pale cast of thought —Shak.⟩ ⟨an era which has been *sicklied* over with doubt —John Lodge⟩

³sickly \"\ *adv* [¹*sick* + *-ly*] **:** in a sick manner or condition **:** ILL ⟨heart lurched ~ as the footsteps attacked the stairs —Marcia Davenport⟩

sick·ness *n* -ES [ME *siknesse, seknesse,* fr. OE *sēocnesse,* fr. *sēoc* sick + *-nesse* -ness — more at SICK] **1 a :** the condition of being ill **:** ill health **:** ILLNESS **b :** a disordered, weakened, or unsound condition ⟨a ~ of judgment would seem to be easily recognizable —*Cross Currents*⟩ **2 a :** a form of disease **:** MALADY **b :** MENSES **3 a :** NAUSEA, QUEASINESS ⟨~ of stomach⟩ — see MOTION SICKNESS **b :** VOMIT

sick nurse *n* **:** a nurse who tends the sick

sick pay *n* **:** salary or wages paid to an employee while on sick leave

sickroom \ˈ=,=\ *n* [¹*sick* + *room*] **:** a room in which a person is confined by sickness

sicks *pres 3d sing of* SIC *or of* SICK, *pl of* SICK

siclike \ˈsiˌklīk\ *chiefly Scot var of* SUCHLIKE

sic passim \ˈsik-, ˈsēk-\ *adv* [L] **:** so throughout — used esp. to indicate that something (as a word or idea) is to be found at various places throughout a book or writer's work

sics *pres 3d sing of* SIC

si·cu *also* **si·ku** \ˈsē(ˌ)kü\ *n* -S [native name in Bolivia] **:** the Bolivian panpipe

sic·u·la \ˈsikyələ\ *n, pl* **sicu·lae** \-ˌlē\ [NL, fr. L, small dagger, dim. of *sica* dagger — more at SICARIUS] **:** the conical chitinous skeleton of the initial zooid of a colony of graptolites — **sic·u·lar** \-lə(r)\ *adj*

¹sic·u·lan \ˈsikyələn\ *adj, usu cap* [L *siculus* siculan (fr. *Siculus* Sicel, fr. Gk *Sikelos*) + E *-an* (adj. suffix)] **:** of, relating to, or characteristic of the Siculi

²siculan \"\ *n* -S *cap* [L *Siculus* Sicel + E *-an* (n. suffix)] **:** one of the Siculi

sic·u·li \ˈsikyəˌlī\ *n pl, cap* [L, fr. Gk *Sikeloi*] **:** an ancient people occupying part of the island of Sicily — **si·cu·li·an** \siˈkyülēən\ *adj or n, usu cap*

siculo- *comb form, usu cap* [L *siculus* siculan] **:** Sicilian and ⟨*Siculo*-Arabian⟩ ⟨*Siculo*-Norman⟩

¹sic·y·o·nian \ˌsisēˈōnyən, -ikē-, -ōnēən\ *adj, usu cap* [L *sicyonius* of Sicyon (fr. Gk *sikyōnios,* fr. *Sikyōn* Sicyon) + E *-an* (adj. suffix)] **1 :** of, relating to, or characteristic of the ancient city of Sicyon in the Peloponnesus or the surrounding district Sicyonia **2 :** of, relating to, or characteristic of the people of Sicyon or Sicyonia

²sicyonian \"\ *n* -S *cap* [L *Sicyonii,* pl., Syconians (fr. *sicyonius* of Sicyon) + E *-an* (n. suffix)] **:** a native or inhabitant of Sicyon or Sicyonia

sic·y·os \ˈsisēəs, -ikē-, -ē,äs\ *n, cap* [NL, fr. Gk *sikyos* cucumber — more at CUCUMBER] **:** a genus of annual herbaceous vines (family Cucurbitaceae) found in the New World and Australasia with branched tendrils, angled or lobed leaves, small greenish white monoecious flowers, and spiny indehiscent fruit

sid \ˈsid\ *n* -S [perh. alter. of ¹*seed*] *Brit* **:** an inner husk of a grain

si·da \ˈsīdə\ *n* [NL, fr. Gk *sidē,* a water plant] **1** *cap* **:** a very large genus of tropical herbs or shrubs (family Malvaceae) having usu. small white or yellow flowers followed by five or more schizocarps with solitary pendulous ovules and including forms that yield useful fibers or mucilaginous substances — see INDIAN MALLOW, QUEENSLAND HEMP **2** -S **:** any plant of the genus *Sida*

si·dal·cea \sīˈdalshēə, səˈd-\ *n, cap* [NL, fr. *Sida* + *Alcea,* genus of mallows, fr. L *alcea* mallow, fr. Gk *alkaia*] **:** a genus of often showy herbs (family Malvaceae) confined to western No. America and having palmately cleft leaves, variously colored spicate or racemose flowers, and 5 to 9 spiculate schizocarps

¹sid·dha \ˈsidə\ *n* -S *usu cap* [Skt, lit., successful, fr. *sidhyati* he goes straight to a goal, succeeds; akin to Skt *sādhati* he comes to his goal — more at ATHROGENIC] *Jainism & Hinduism* **:** one who has attained perfection esp. as shown by occult powers

²siddha \"\ *n* -S [native name in Bengal] **:** rice that is soaked in water and then boiled before milling

sid·dur \ˈsiˌdü(ə)r. -üə, -də(r)\ *n, pl* **sid·du·rim** \səˈdürəm\ *also* **siddurs** [MHeb *siddūr,* lit., order, arrangement, short for Heb *sēder tĕfillōth* order of prayers] **:** a Jewish prayer book containing both Hebrew and Aramaic prayers used chiefly in the daily liturgy — compare MAHZOR

¹side \ˈsīd\ *n* -S [ME, fr. OE *sīde;* akin to OS *sīda* side, OHG *sīta,* ON *sītha;* derivative fr. a prehistoric adj. represented by OFris *side* low, wide, OE *sīd* long, large, wide, OHG *sīto,* adv., weakly, loose, ON *sīthr* long, pendulous; akin to OE *sāwan* to sow — more at SOW] **1 a :** the right or left lateral part of the wall or trunk of the body ⟨a pain in the ~⟩ **b** *archaic* **:** the female seat of generation or birth **c :** the area in which is felt the exertion produced by speaking or by boisterous laughter ⟨split his ~*s* with laughing —Charles Dickens⟩ **2 :** a place, space, or direction with respect to a center or to a line of division (as of an aisle, river, or street) ⟨found on all ~*s*⟩ ⟨on this ~⟩ **3 :** one of the surfaces or surface parts of an object which are distinguished from the ends as being longer and from the front or back as being more or less perpendicular to the observer ⟨tacking . . . bunting to the front and ~*s* of the platform —John Updike⟩ — often used in combination ⟨be*side*⟩ ⟨fore*side*⟩ ⟨in*side*⟩ ⟨top*side*⟩ ⟨up*side*⟩ **4 a :** a bounding line of a geometrical figure ⟨the ~ of the road⟩ ⟨the ~ of a triangle⟩ **b :** one of the surfaces and esp. one of the longer surfaces that define or limit a solid **:** a part (as a wall of a room) connecting the extremities of the top and bottom **:** FACE ⟨the ~ of a box⟩ ⟨the ~ of a prism⟩ **c** (1) **:** either of the two surfaces of a thin object (as a sheet, disk, slice, or partition) ⟨the other ~ of the coin⟩ (2) **:** the inner or outer aspect of something **d :** one of the surfaces serving to enclose or bound a space ⟨the ~ of a pool⟩ ⟨~ of a valley⟩ ⟨~*s* of a cave⟩ **e :** a line joining two consecutive vertices of a polygon **f** (1) **:** one playing surface of a phonograph record (2) **:** a single recorded selection **5 :** the space immediately beside or in close proximity to someone ⟨never from thy ~ henceforth to stray —John Milton⟩ **6 a :** the outer surface of a ship on either side above the waterline **b :** the portion of the outer surface below the main deck — distinguished from *topside* **7 a :** an outer portion of something held to face in a particular direction ⟨the upper ~ of a sphere⟩ **b :** an aspect or part of something held to be contrasted with some other aspect or part ⟨the better ~ of his nature⟩ ⟨try to find the brighter ~ of the tragedy⟩ **8 a :** a slope or declivity (as of a hill or bank) considered as opposed to another slope over the ridge ⟨along the ~ of yon small hill —John Milton⟩ — often used in combination ⟨hill*side*⟩ ⟨mountain*side*⟩ **b** *obs* **:** the outskirts of a grove or city **c :** land bordering a body of water **:** BANK, SHORE — often used in combination ⟨lake*side*⟩ ⟨river*side*⟩ ⟨sea*side*⟩ **9 :** the attitude or action of one person or group with respect to another **:** PART **10 :** a position viewed as opposite to or contrasted with another ⟨balanced on both ~*s*⟩ ⟨there are two ~*s* to every question⟩ **11 a :** the position of a person or party regarded as opposed to another person or party whether as a rival or a foe ⟨God on our ~, doubt not of victory —Shak.⟩ **b :** the interest or cause which one maintains against another **:** a doctrine or cause opposed to another **12 a :** one of the halves of the body of an animal or man on either side of the mesial plane ⟨a ~ of beef⟩ **b :** a cut of meat including that about the ribs of one lateral half of the body — used chiefly of smoked pork products ⟨a well-cured ~⟩; see PORK illustration **13 a :** one of the parties in a transaction, battle, or debate **:** a body of advocates or partisans **:** a political party or faction ⟨a victory for neither ~⟩ **b :** one of the contesting parties in a game or sport **c :** a group of players in a card game who are partners **d** *Brit* **:** TEAM ⟨a soccer ~⟩ ⟨a match is played between two ~*s* of eleven players each —*Laws of Cricket*⟩ **14 :** a line of descent traced through one parent ⟨the grandfather on one's mother's ~⟩ ⟨of Irish ancestry on his father's ~ —*Current Biog.*⟩ **15 a :** a part (as of a place or thing) located in a particular direction from a center or line of division ⟨on one ~ of the church⟩ ⟨this ~ of the city⟩ **b** (1) **:** a geographical region or district (2) **:** the inhabitants of such a region — usu. used in combination ⟨country*side*⟩ **16 :** one page of a book or writing **:** one side of a sheet of paper ⟨a man might blur ten ~*s* of paper in attempting a defense —Charles Lamb⟩ **17 :** a position, movement, or inclination away from a central line or point ⟨to one ~⟩ ⟨on one ~⟩ **18 :** one half of a hide divided along the backbone for use in leather manufacturing **19 :** sideways spin imparted to a billiard ball — compare ENGLISH 5 **20 a :** a sheet containing the lines and cues for a single theatrical role and used in learning a role **b :** a speech in a play ⟨she knew all her ~*s* after only a few rehearsals⟩ **21 :** the front or back cover of a book **22 :** the aspect and the functioning of a court in some distinct portion of its general jurisdiction ⟨the criminal-law ~ of the English High Court of Justice⟩ ⟨the admiralty ~ of a U.S. district court⟩ ⟨the equity ~ of a state court⟩ **23 :** the surface of a screw thread that joins a crest with a root **24 :** the men and equipment engaged in the removal of a section of timber in logging **25 :** the area outside the center in craps or an imaginary area outside the layout in banking games where bets are held to be placed by players among themselves rather than against the shooter or house ⟨place a bet on the ~⟩ — see SIDE BET **syn** see PHASE — **at side :** running with its dam and nursing without restriction — used of a young domestic mammal ⟨a heifer with bull calf *at side*⟩ ⟨ewes with lambs *at side*⟩ — **on the side** *adv* **1 :** in addition to the regular or main portion ⟨a hamburger with onions *on the side*⟩ **2 :** in addition to a regular or principal occupation or pursuit ⟨took a night job *on the side*⟩ ⟨bet a dollar *on the side*⟩ — **over the side** *adv* **1 :** from outside a ship on to its deck (as in arriving on board) **2 :** from the deck of a ship to its outside (as in leaving) — **this side :** short of **:** not beyond ⟨that's all we may expect of man *this side* the grave —Robert Browning⟩ — **through one's sides** *archaic* **:** through one as if by transfixing **:** indirectly through one ⟨attacked him, *through my sides,* in a pamphlet —James Boswell⟩

²side \"\ *adj* [ME, fr. *side,* n.] **1 :** of, relating to, or used on the side (as of a person) ⟨~ armor⟩ ⟨a ~ sore⟩ **2 a :** directed toward or from the side ⟨a ~ blow⟩ ⟨~ thrust⟩ **b :** held to be directed toward or from the side **:** COLLATERAL, INCIDENTAL, INDIRECT ⟨a ~ issue⟩ ⟨a ~ view⟩ ⟨a ~ remark⟩ **c :** made on the side ⟨a ~ agreement between member A and member B may . . . prevent general agreement —Harold Stein⟩ ⟨~ money⟩ ⟨~ payment⟩ **d :** additional to the regular or main portion or order ⟨a ~ order of french fries⟩ **3 a :** located at or towards the side (as of a building, structure, or thoroughfare) ⟨~ window⟩ ⟨~ room⟩ ⟨~ path⟩ **b :** having the principal part (as the blade or head) located on one side rather than on the end ⟨~ chisel⟩ ⟨~ hammer⟩ ⟨~ plane⟩ — see SIDE TOOL **c :** used at the side ⟨~ screen⟩ ⟨~ hook⟩ **d :** of, relating to, or

used on the side of a boat ⟨~ guy⟩ ⟨~ plates⟩ **e :** growing to or from one side ⟨a ~ branch⟩ ⟨~ shoot⟩ **4 :** blowing at right angles to a line from the mark to an archer ⟨a ~ wind⟩

³side \"\ *adv* [ME, fr. *side*, n.] **:** to, at, by, or from one side ⟨~ launched them for use as cargo barges —K.M.Dodson⟩ — usu. used in combination ⟨*side*cast⟩ ⟨*side*-hanging⟩

⁴side \"\ *vb* -ED/-ING/-S [ME *siden*, fr. *side*, n.] *vt* **1** *archaic* **:** to cut or carve (as a haddock) into sides **2 :** to be or range oneself on the side with **:** agree with **:** SUPPORT ⟨not a fighting friend left to ~ him —F.B.Gipson⟩ **3 :** to range (as oneself) on or with one of two contesting sides **4 :** to be, go, or stand at the side of **:** come to the side of **:** walk by the side of **:** be side by side with **5 :** to work (as a timber or rib) to a specified thickness by trimming the sides **6** *dial* **a :** to put (as a room) in order **:** clean or tidy up (as a table) **:** ARRANGE — often used with *up* **b :** to place at one side **:** set or put aside **:** clear away **:** REMOVE ⟨~ dishes⟩ **7 :** to furnish with sides or siding ⟨~ a house⟩ **8 :** to draw (as a rope) toward the side **:** draw over or out **9 :** to apply covers of cloth or other material to the boards of (as a book or case) after the backbone and corners have been affixed — often used with *up* **~** *vi* **1 :** to embrace the opinions of one party or engage in its interest in opposition to another party **:** take sides **:** join or form sides ⟨all ~ in parties and begin the attack —Alexander Pope⟩ — usu. used with *with* or *against* ⟨the local justice of the peace *sided* with the squatters —*Amer. Guide Series: Pa.*⟩ ⟨*sided* against the Administration on most issues⟩ **2 :** to move, turn, or bend sideways **3** *chiefly dial* **:** to stand or move to one side

⁵side \"\ *adj* [ME, long, large, wide, fr. OE *sīd* — more at SIDE (n.)] *chiefly Scot* **:** WIDE, CAPACIOUS, FLOWING — used esp. of a garment

⁶side \"\ *n* -S [obs. E *side* proud, boastful, fr. ME, wide, capacious] **:** swaggering manner **:** arrogant behavior **:** CONCEIT, PRETENTIOUSNESS

side action *n* **:** SIDE EFFECT ⟨some *side actions* may be alleviated by symptomatic therapy —*Therapeutic Notes*⟩

side aisle *n* **:** one of the lateral aisles of a building (as a church, basilica, or theater) as distinguished from the central aisle or nave

side arm *n* **:** a weapon worn at the side or in the belt (as a sword, revolver, or bayonet)

¹sidearm \ˈ=ˌ=\ *adj* [¹*side* + *arm*] **1 :** of, relating to, or constituting a style of pitching or throwing (as in baseball) in which the arm is not raised above the shoulder and the ball is delivered with a sideways sweep of the arm across the body between the shoulder and the hip ⟨~ delivery⟩ **2 :** of, relating to, or constituting a device with outlet on the side (as a gas-fired heater for connection to a water tank)

²sidearm \"\ *adv* **:** in a sidearm manner or style **:** with a sidearm delivery ⟨he pitched ~⟩

side ax *n* **:** an ax having the handle bent to one side

side band *n* **:** the band of radio frequencies on either side of the carrier frequency produced by the process of modulation — compare SIDE FREQUENCY

side-band transmission *n* **:** CARRIER SUPPRESSION

sidebar \ˈ=ˌ=\ *n* [¹*side* + *bar*] **1 a :** either of a pair of longitudinal elastic wooden bars on which the bodies of buggies and other light vehicles are sometimes suspended **b :** either of two plates uniting the pommel and cantle of a saddle **c :** either of the outside plates located one on each side of the lower part of a side-bar keel **2 :** a short news story designed to accompany a major news story and present sidelights (as personalities or human interest aspects) of the major story ⟨a ~ on the crime investigation⟩

side-bar keel *n* **:** a bar keel formed in three thicknesses

side-bar rule *n* [so called fr. its being formerly moved for by the attorneys within a bar on the side of the court in Westminster Hall, former chief law court of England] **:** an English legal rule authorized by the court to be granted by the clerk of the rules upon a praecipe as a matter of course without formal application being made to the court

side beam *n* **:** a walking beam of a side-lever engine

side-beam engine *n* **:** SIDE-LEVER ENGINE

side bearing *n* **:** the part of the shoulder of a piece of printing type at the right and left sides of the face

side bench *n* **:** the seat along the side of a small boat; *esp* **:** the fore-and-aft planking over the air tanks in a small boat fitted with air tanks that is available as a seat

side bet *n* **1 :** a bet made with a player other than a house that customarily books all bets or other than with the shooter (as in craps) **2 :** a bet made by the shooter in craps on any event other than the outcome of his center bets **3 :** a bet (as on whose hand holds the highest spade) made on an event not integral to the game being played **4 :** a bet with another player in a game additional to the regular stakes for which the game (as in bridge or golf) is being played

sideboard \ˈ=ˌ=\ *n* [ME *side-bord*, fr. ¹*side* + *bord* board — more at BOARD] **1 :** a table at the side of the dining hall or room: as **a** *obs* **:** a side table as distinguished from the head table **b :** a heavy open cupboard or dresser (as of oak) for dishes or wines common in the 16th and 17th centuries **:** CREDENCE **c** (1) **:** a serving table with drawers and cupboards beneath its tabletop developed by Georgian designers (2) **:** a combination serving table and dresser often with a mirror developed in the 19th century — compare BUFFET **2 a :** a board forming a side or part of a side of a structure (as of a crib or hospital bed) **b :** an additional removable board fitted on the side of a vehicle (as a wagon or cart) to increase the carrying capacity **3 :** a piece of dining-room furniture having compartments and shelves for holding articles of table service **4 sideboards** *pl* **:** SIDE-WHISKERS

sideboard-table \ˈ=ˌ=ˌ==\ *n* **:** a serving table usu. with a marble top and often having one or two narrow drawers in the apron

sidebone \ˈ=ˌ=\ *n* **1 :** the lateral part of the hipbone of a fowl easily separable from the backbone in carving **2 a** *also* **sidebones** *pl but sing in constr* **:** abnormal ossification of the cartilages in the lateral posterior part of a horse's hoof (as of a forefoot) often causing lameness **b :** one of the bony structures so caused

side-box \ˈ=ˌ=\ *n* **:** a box or enclosed seat on the side of a theater

side boy *n* **:** one of from two to eight members of the crew of a ship who are detailed to stand at the gangway as a mark of respect to a person arriving or departing

side·burned \ˈsīdˌbərnd, -bənd, -bəind\ *adj* [*sideburns* + *-ed*] **:** having or characterized by sideburns ⟨lavishly ~ lotharios —G.A.Wagner⟩

side·burns \-nz\ *n pl* [anagram of *burnsides*] **1 :** SIDE-WHISKERS; *esp* **:** short side-whiskers worn with a smooth chin **2 :** continuations of the hairline in front of the ears whether the hair is long or clipped short

side by side *adv* [ME] **1 :** beside one another with bodies in line ⟨walked *side by side* down the aisle⟩ **2 :** in the same place, time, or circumstances ⟨lived peacefully *side by side* in the same villages —Philip Mason⟩

¹side-by-side \ˈ=ˌ=ˈ=\ *adj* **:** standing or situated next to one another

²side-by-side \"\ *n* **:** a double-barreled shotgun having the barrels mounted on the frame in a horizontally side-by-side position — compare OVER-AND-UNDER

sidecar \ˈ=ˌ=\ *n* [¹*side* + *car*] **1 :** JAUNTING CAR **2 :** a car attached to a motorcycle for the accommodation of a passenger seated abreast of the cyclist and usu. supported by a single third wheel **3 :** WING CAR **4 :** a cocktail consisting of an orange flavored liqueur, lemon juice, and brandy shaken in cracked ice and served strained and garnished with a twist of lemon peel

side card *n* **:** an unmatched card other than part of a pair or of three or four of a kind in a poker hand

side-centered \ˈ=ˈ==\ *adj* **:** centered on the side faces only — used of crystals

side chain *n* **1 :** one of the two chains passing over the pinions on the countershaft and the gears on the driving wheels in a chain final drive on automotive vehicles **2 :** a branched chain of atoms attached to the principal chain or to a ring in a molecule ⟨aromatic hydrocarbons with paraffinic *side chains*⟩

side-chain theory *n* **:** a largely displaced theory of the chemical basis of immunological phenomena: living organisms are complex aggregations of complex molecules capable of reacting with one another through some of their side chains when these side chains have a definite correspondence in structure exemplified by various outlying cell receptors that can combine with foreign molecules (as of food or toxins), and stimulate the cell to the production of other like receptors some of which may become detached from the cell and function as antibodies

side chair *n* **:** a chair without arms used esp. in the dining room — see WINDSOR CHAIR illustration

side chapel *n* **:** a small chapel within a church usu. at the side or back of the choir or chancel — compare LADY CHAPEL

sidecheck \ˈ=ˌ=\ *n* **:** a checkrein carried at the side of a horse's head — compare OVERCHECK

side clearance *n* **:** BACKLASH 1b

side-close \ˈ=ˌ=\ *n* -S **:** a ballroom step in which a dancer places one foot to the side and brings the other to it

side-coat \ˈ=ˌ=\ *n* [ME *side cote*, fr. *side*, adj., long, large, wide + *cote* coat — more at SIDE, COAT] *archaic* **:** GREATCOAT 1

side comb *n* **:** a short slightly-curved comb for holding a woman's hair in place esp. at the side of the head

side construction *n* **:** hollow structural blocks or tiles laid with the cells running horizontally — compare END CONSTRUCTION

side couple *n* **:** the couple at right angles to the head couple in a square dance set

side curtain *n* **1 :** a curtain attached or fitted so as to be attached at the side of something (as a vehicle, window, or building) ⟨the *side curtains* of an automobile⟩ ⟨canvas *side curtains* for a tent⟩ **2 a :** one of several canvas weather cloths rigged vertically between the deck or the bulwarks and the ridgerope of a ship **b :** one of several similar cloths used to close the openings between the hull and the canopy of a small boat

¹side cut *n* **:** an intersecting way (as a road, path, or canal) branching out from the main one

²side cut *n* **:** BREAKDOWN 5

side-cut \ˈ=ˌ=\ *adj* **:** containing no pith — used of pieces of timber and lumber

side-cut brick *n* **:** wire-cut brick having the bed surfaces wire cut — compare END-CUT BRICK

side cutting *n* **:** material excavated outside the established slopes required for a roadbed

sid·ed \ˈsīdəd\ *adj* [ME, fr. ¹*side* + *-ed*] **1 :** having or provided with sides ⟨a salad bowl ~ with fruit sections⟩ **2 :** having sides of a specified number or of a specified kind or quality — used in combination ⟨steep-*sided*, sharp-peaked mountains —Joaquin Noval⟩ ⟨an open-*sided* structure . . . resembling an airplane hangar —*Amer. Guide Series: La.*⟩ ⟨a shingle-*sided* house⟩ — see MANY-SIDED, ONE-SIDED **3 :** having a specified siding — used in shipbuilding

side degree *n* **:** one of various Masonic degrees conferred in the Cryptic rite

side-delivery rake *n* **:** a hay rake carrying teeth usu. on a reel that lift and push the hay to the side into a windrow at right angles to the forward path of the rake

side dish *n* **:** one of the foods subordinate to the main course of a meal

sid·ed·ness *n* -ES **1 :** the quality or state of being sided in a specified way — usu. used in combination ⟨one-*sidedness*⟩ **2 :** a tendency to functional dominance of complementary organs (as the hands or eyes) of one side of the body

side door *n* **1 :** a door in one side of a structure or of a main door ⟨the large *side doors* were thrown open towards the sun to admit a bountiful light —Thomas Hardy⟩ **2 :** an indirect or less conspicuous means of entrance ⟨trying to get religion back by the *side door* of the new physics —H.J.Laski⟩

side draft *n* **1 :** the tendency of a tillage implement (as a plow) to move or be forced in a direction at right angles to the direction of its forward motion **2 :** the amount of the force applied to overcome the direction of a side draft

side draw *n* **:** a ballroom step in which a dancer places one foot to the side and slides the other to it

side-dress \ˈ=ˌ=\ *vi* **:** to place plant nutrients on or in the soil near the roots of a growing crop usu. beside each row and often by means of a cultivator having a fertilizer-distributing attachment **~** *vt* **:** to place plant nutrients on or in the soil near the roots of ⟨*side-dress* a crop⟩

side-dressing \ˈ=ˌ==\ *n* **:** the plant nutrients (as fertilizer) used to side-dress a crop

side drum *n* **:** SNARE DRUM

side effect *n* **:** an effect of a drug other than the one it was administered to evoke ⟨a fall in blood pressure often is a *side effect* of spinal anesthesia⟩ ⟨a *side effect* of drowsiness caused by antihistamines⟩ ⟨a *side effect* of chloroform may be damage to the liver⟩

side-end lines \ˈ=ˌ=-\ *n pl* **:** the sidelines of a mining claim that are considered as end lines (as for determining extralateral rights)

side-eyed \ˈ=ˌ=\ *adj* **:** having the eyes placed well to the sides of the head — used of a mammal (as a deer or rabbit) that depends much on visual acuity to escape danger

side face *n* **:** a face or a representation of a face seen in profile

side fender *n* **:** a fender constituted by fore-and-aft timbers faced with steel fastened on the outside of a ship's hull for protection

sideflash \ˈ=ˌ=\ *n* [¹*side* + *flash*] **:** a disruptive discharge between a conductor traversed by an oscillatory current of high frequency (as lightning) and neighboring masses of metal or between different parts of the same conductor

side frame *n* **:** either of the longitudinal side members of the frame of an automotive vehicle

side frequency *n* **:** any of the frequencies in the side band

side-glance \ˈ=ˌ=\ *n* **1 :** a glance directed to the side ⟨she shot an impatient *side-glance* at him —S.H.Adams⟩ **2 :** a passing allusion **:** an indirect or slight reference **:** a cursory examination ⟨a rather suspicious *side-glance* at poetry —W.R.Benét⟩

side graft *n* **:** a plant graft in which the scion is inserted into the side of the stock and the aerial head of the stock permitted to grow until union is established between stock and scion — see PEG GRAFT

sidehall \ˈ=ˌ=\ *adj* [¹*side* + *hall*] **:** designed with an entrance to one side rather than at the center ⟨~ layout⟩ ⟨~ brick residence⟩

sidehead \ˈ=ˌ=\ *n* [¹*side* + *head*] **1 :** an additional slide rest on a planer **2 :** a subhead placed at or in the side of printed matter; *esp* **:** one placed in the left side of the first line of a paragraph in bookwork

¹sidehill \ˈ=ˌ=\ *n* [¹*side* + *hill*] **:** HILLSIDE ⟨horses grazing up the ~ —H.L.Davis⟩

²sidehill \"\ *adj* **1 :** used on or designed for sidehills ⟨a ~ attachment for farm machinery⟩ **2 :** located on a sidehill ⟨a ~ road⟩ ⟨~ village⟩ ⟨~ land⟩

sidehill plow *n* **:** a reversible or two-way plow for turning all furrows to the lower side of the slope

sidehold \ˈ=ˌ=\ *n* **1 :** a hold in mountain climbing in which the edge or point of a projecting rock is grasped with the hand turned sideways **2 :** a hold in wrestling in which each wrestler places his right arm around the opponent's waist and with the left hand grasps the opponent's right elbow

side horse *n* **:** a piece of apparatus made with a leather-covered cylindrical body having two pommels on top near the center, held parallel to the floor by two uprights attached to a steel frame and adjustable in height, and used in gymnastics esp. for vaulting — called also *horse;* compare LONG HORSE

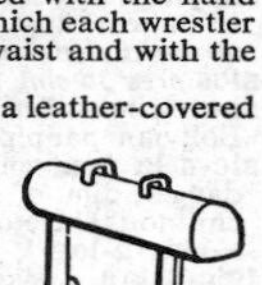

side horse

side issue *n* **:** an issue apart from the main point **:** something of subordinate or incidental importance

side judge *n* **:** a judge seated at the side of the chief or presiding judge **:** an associate judge of a court

side keelson *n* **:** a reinforcing keelson between the main keelson and the commencement of the bilge curvature — called also *sister keelson;* see SHIP illustration

sidekick \ˈ=ˌ=\ *also* **sidekicker** \ˈ=ˌ==\ *n* [¹*side* + *kick* or *kicker*] **:** a person closely associated with another esp. in a subordinate capacity **:** ASSISTANT, PAL, PARTNER

side lamp *n* **:** a lighting unit on either side of a vehicle to indicate its location

side leather *n* **:** leather used generally for shoe uppers and made from cattlehide divided in the tanning process into two sides

side·less \ˈsīdləs\ *adj* **:** having no sides **:** open at the sides

side lever *n* **:** SIDE BEAM

sidelight \ˈ=ˌ=\ *n* **1 a** *or* **side lighting :** light coming or produced from the side **b** (1) **:** incidental light or information upon a subject ⟨fragments of information and of ~ —Helen Macafee⟩ ⟨it throws so much ~ upon that rationalistic temper —William James⟩ (2) **:** a means of such incidental illustration or illumination ⟨curious ~*s* thrown upon the politics of appointments —*Saturday Rev.*⟩ ⟨throws many interesting ~*s* upon the Russian character —*Dial*⟩ ⟨giving humorous ~*s* on misadventures —*English Jour.*⟩ **2 :** a narrow window flanking a door or larger window ⟨the paneled doorway is flanked by fluted columns and ~*s* —*Amer. Guide Series: La.*⟩ **3 :** the red light on the port bow or the green light on the starboard bow carried by ships under way at night **4 :** SIDE LAMP **5 :** the thick glass covering of a ship's porthole

¹sideline \ˈ=ˌ=\ *n* **1 :** a line extending along or marking the side of something; *esp* **:** a line running usu. at right angles to a goal line or end line and marking a side of an area (as a court or field of play) used for sports — see FIELD HOCKEY illustration **2 a :** a line of goods sold in addition to one's principal articles of trade **b** (1) **:** a course of business or activity pursued aside from one's regular occupation ⟨a farmer who had taken to writing as a ~ —A.J.P.Taylor⟩ (2) **:** something subsidiary to the principal subject considered ⟨his pursuit . . . took him into many interesting ~*s* —*Current Biog.*⟩ **3 a :** the space immediately outside the lines along either side of an athletic field or court — usu. used in pl. **b :** the standpoint of persons not immediately participating (as in an athletic contest) — usu. used in pl. — **on the sidelines :** out of action **:** confined to or choosing the role of a spectator rather than a participant ⟨when he was forbidden to play . . . fretted through a winter *on the sidelines* —W.B.Furlong⟩

²sideline \"\ *vt* [¹*sideline*] **1** *West* **:** to restrain or hobble (an animal) by tying together the front and hind leg on the same side of the body **2 :** to prevent (as a player) from taking part in a game or other activity ⟨a sore shoulder *sidelined* him⟩ ⟨has been *sidelined* with a broken arm⟩

side·lin·er \"+ə(r)\ *n* **1 :** one that remains on the sidelines during an activity **:** one that does not participate **2 :** SIDEWINDER 2

¹side·ling *or* **sid·ling** \ˈsīdliŋ, -lēŋ\ *adv* [ME, fr. ¹*side* + *-ling*] **1 :** in a sidelong direction **:** with a sideward movement **:** OBLIQUELY, SIDEWAYS **2** *obs* **:** on a sidesaddle

²sideling *or* **sidling** \"\ *adj* **1 :** directed or moving toward one side **:** OBLIQUE ⟨with a ~ motion of the head —Hall Caine⟩ ⟨a ~ glance⟩ **2 :** having an inclination **:** inclining or sloping to one side **:** STEEP ⟨~ hill⟩ ⟨~ ground⟩

³sideling \"\ *n* -S *chiefly dial* **:** SLOPE

side·lings \ˈsīd·lənz, -liŋz\ *also* **side·lins** \-lənz\ *adv* [ME *sidelinges*, fr. ¹*side* + *-linges* -lings] **1** *dial Brit* **:** SIDEWAYS **2** *dial Brit* **:** ALONGSIDE **3** *dial Brit* **:** FURTIVELY, STEALTHILY

sidelock \ˈ=ˌ=\ *n* **:** a lock of hair falling at the side of the face and often worn as a distinguishing mark esp. by some Jews and by children in some cultures ⟨an old Jew . . . with a beard and ~*s* —Walter Sorell & Denver Lindley⟩ ⟨wearing the ~ of youth⟩

¹sidelong \ˈ=ˌ=\ *adv* [¹*side* + *long*] **1 :** in the direction of or along the side **:** LATERALLY, OBLIQUELY, SIDEWAYS ⟨darting eyes looking ~ out of a wizened face —*Irish Digest*⟩ ⟨glanced at them ~ —*Hearst's*⟩ **2 :** with the side toward someone or something ⟨seated . . . ~ to the window —Nathaniel Hawthorne⟩ **3 :** on the side **:** with one side to the ground or floor ⟨~ the plow beside the field-gate lay —William Morris⟩

²sidelong \"\ *adj* **1 :** having a slanting direction or a sloping position **:** lying on or inclining to one side ⟨moved downwards in a ~ way —Bram Stoker⟩ ⟨~ country⟩ **2 a :** directed to one side or sideways ⟨the bashful virgin's ~ looks of love —Oliver Goldsmith⟩ ⟨~ glances⟩ **b :** moving or extending sideways ⟨shot out ~ boughs —Alfred Tennyson⟩ **c :** indirect rather than straightforward or open ⟨a ~ hope that there will be . . . reward in it —Frances Keene⟩

side-look \ˈ=ˌ=\ *n* **:** a look or glance to one side **:** an oblique look ⟨a *side-look* from the girl was enough —Eden Phillpotts⟩

sideman \ˈ=ˌ=\ *n, pl* **sidemen 1** *obs* **:** SIDESMAN 1 **2 :** a member of a band or orchestra or of a section of a band or orchestra esp. a jazz or swing orchestra; *specif* **:** a supporting instrumentalist

side meat *n, chiefly South & Midland* **:** salt pork or bacon usu. from the sides of a hog

side milling *n* **:** the process of milling surfaces that are at right angles to the axis of rotation of the cutter with a side milling cutter

side milling cutter *n* **:** a cylindrical milling cutter with teeth on the circumferential surface and on both sides — see MILLING CUTTER illustration

side money *n* **:** the chips or money in a side pot in a poker game

side-necked \ˈ=ˌ=\ *adj* **:** capable of bending the neck sideways but not of retracting it — used of turtles; compare PLEURODIRA

sidenote \ˈ=ˌ=\ *n* **:** a note of reference that is set in the side margin of a page usu. in smaller type than the text

side oat *n* **:** an oat (*Avena orientalis*) in which the panicle usu. droops and the branches are on one side — usu. used in pl.

side oats grama *n* **:** a forage grass (*Bouteloua curtipendula*) of the southern U. S. having loosely flowered second racemes

side-on \ˈ=ˈ=\ *adv* **:** with one side facing in a given direction esp. toward the observer

side out *n* **:** the termination of a team's right to serve (as in volleyball)

side paper *n* **:** plain or patterned paper used on the front and back covers of books

side partner *n* **:** one that works closely with another

sidepiece \ˈ=ˌ=\ *n* **:** a piece forming or contained in the side of something ⟨the ~ of a window⟩ ⟨the ~ of a carriage⟩

side planer *n* **:** OPENSIDE PLANER

side play *n* **:** lateral freedom of motion in a moving machine part ⟨prevent *side play* in gears —*Motor Transportation*⟩

side pocket *n* **:** a pocket in or at one side (as of a garment or billiard table) ⟨hands in the *side pockets* of his . . . jacket —Rayne Kruger⟩ ⟨put the eight ball in the *side pocket*⟩

side porch *n* **:** a porch or the part of a porch at one side of a building

side port *n* **:** an opening in the side of a ship for handling cargo

side post *n* **1 :** DOORJAMB **2 :** a post supporting a roof at or near one side

side pot *n* **:** a second or subsequent pot in poker played with table stakes from which is excluded any player who has bet his entire table stake in a previous pot

¹sider *n* -S [⁴*side* + *-er*] *obs* **:** one that takes a side **:** an adherent of a person **:** a partisan of a cause

²sid·er \ˈsīdə(r)\ *n* -S [¹*side* + *-er*] **:** one placed or living in a usu. specified side (as an area or section of a city) — used in combination ⟨an east-*sider*⟩

sider- *or* **sidero-** *comb form* [MF, fr. L, fr. Gk *sidēr-, sidēro-*, fr. *sidēros*] **:** iron ⟨*sider*olite⟩ ⟨*sider*osis⟩

sideraerolite *var of* SIDEROLITE

side rail *n* **:** one of the long narrow members connecting the headboard and footboard of a bed

side rake *n* **:** the angle of deviation of a side of a cutting tool from a specified reference plane (as a plane normal to the surface of the work and parallel to the line of relative motion of tool and work)

sid·er·al \ˈsidərəl\ *adj* [MF, fr. L *sideralis*, fr. *sider-*, *sidus* star, constellation + *-alis* -al] **1 :** SIDEREAL **2** *archaic* **:** emanating from the stars and esp. from stars held to be malefic **:** BALEFUL

siderate *vt* -ED/-ING/-S [L *sideratus*, past part. of *siderari* to be struck by a star, be sunstruck, fr. *sider-*, *sidus* star] *obs* **:** to blast or strike down (as with lightning)

sid·er·az·ot *or* **sid·er·az·ote** \ˌsidəˈraˌzōt, -ərəˈzōt\ *n* -S [*sider-* + *azote*] **:** a mineral Fe_5N_2 consisting of a nitride of iron and found about Vesuvius and Etna volcanoes after various eruptions

side reaction *n* **1 :** a less important reaction of two or more chemical reactions occurring at the same time ⟨undesirable complex *side reactions*⟩ — compare SIMULTANEOUS REACTION **2 :** SIDE EFFECT

si·de·re·al \sīˈdirēəl\ *adj* [L *sidereus* sidereal (fr. *sider-*, *sidus* star, constellation + *-eus* -eous) + E *-al;* akin to Lith

svidus shining and prob. to OHG *swīdan* to burn, ON *svītha* to burn, OE *swathul* smoke] **1 :** of or relating to stars or constellations ⟨~ system⟩ ⟨~ bodies⟩ **2 :** expressed in relation to the heavens above — see SIDEREAL TIME
sidereal astronomy *n* **:** a branch of astronomy that treats of the origin, nature, and relationship of the stars including the nebulas
sidereal clock *n* **:** an astronomical clock regulated to sidereal time
sidereal day *n* **:** the interval between two successive transits of the March equinox over the upper meridian of a place that is equal to 23 hours, 56 minutes, 4.09 seconds of mean solar time — compare SIDEREAL MIDNIGHT
sidereal hour *n* **:** the twenty-fourth part of a sidereal day
sidereal hour angle *n* **:** a coordinate in the equator system of coordinates used by navigators in place of right ascension, measured westward from the March equinox, and expressed in degrees up to 360°
sidereal midnight *n* **:** the instant when the March equinox crosses the lower meridian of a place — compare SIDEREAL DAY
sidereal minute *n* **:** the sixtieth part of a sidereal hour
sidereal month *n* **:** the mean time of the moon's revolution in its orbit from a star back to the same star **:** 27 days, 7 hours, 43 minutes, 11.5 seconds of mean solar time
sidereal noon *n* **:** the instant when the March equinox crosses the upper meridian of a place
sidereal period *or* **sidereal revolution** *n* **:** the time in which a planet or satellite completes one revolution round its primary as referred to a star seen from the primary
sidereal second *n* **:** the sixtieth part of a sidereal minute — compare SECOND 2
sidereal time *n* **1 :** time based on the sidereal day consisting of 24 hours of sidereal minutes and seconds **2 :** the hour angle of the March equinox at a place
sidereal year *n* **:** the time in which the earth completes one revolution in its orbit around the sun measured with respect to the fixed stars **:** 365 days, 6 hours, 9 minutes, and 9.54 seconds of solar time
side relief angle *n* **:** the angle between the part of the flanks of a cutting tool below the cutting edge and a plane perpendicular to the base
sid·er·in yellow \ˈsidərən-\ *n* [*sider-* + *-in*] **1 :** a pale yellow pigment consisting of a basic iron chromate, used esp. mixed with water glass and giving a very durable paint **2 :** MARS YELLOW 2
sid·er·ism \ˈsidəˌrizəm\ *n* -s [NL *siderismus*, fr. *sider-* + L *-ismus* -ism] **:** a phenomenon similar to animal magnetism formerly supposed to result from the bringing of iron or other inorganic bodies into connection with the human body
¹sid·er·ite \ˈsidəˌrīt, *usu* -īd +V\ *n* -s [*sider-* + *-ite*] **1 a** *archaic* **:** PHARMACOSIDERITE **b** *archaic* **:** HORNBLENDE **c** *archaic* **:** SAPPHIRE QUARTZ **d** *obs* **:** LAZULITE **e :** HOLOSIDERITE **2 :** a nickel-iron meteorite
²siderite \"\ *n* -s [G *siderit*, fr. *sider-* + *-it* -ite] **:** a native ferrous carbonate $FeCO_3$ that occurs in rhombohedral crystals often with curved faces, in cleavable or granular masses, and in botryoid and globular forms, that may also contain manganese and magnesium, that is usu. light yellowish brown but is sometimes white or gray, that contains 48.2 percent of iron when pure, and that is a valuable iron ore — called also *chalybite, sparry iron, spathic iron*
sid·er·it·ic \ˌsidəˈridik\ *adj* [¹*siderite* + *-ic*] **:** of, relating to, or containing siderite ⟨~ limestone⟩
sid·er·i·tis \ˌsidəˈrīdəs\ *n, cap* [NL, fr. L, ironwort, fr. Gk *sidēritis*, fr. fem. of *sidēritēs* of iron, fr. *sidēr-* sider- + *-itēs* -ite] **:** a genus of European woolly mints having small flowers with the corolla included in the calyx
¹sidero- — see SIDER-
²sidero- *comb form* [L *sider-, sidus* star, constellation — more at SIDEREAL] **1 :** star ⟨*sideromancy*⟩ ⟨*siderostat*⟩ **2 :** sidereal ⟨*siderograph*⟩
side road *n* **:** a road off a main road **:** a feeder or branch road
sid·er·o·cyte \ˈsidərəˌsīt\ *n* -s [*sider-* + *-cyte*] **:** an atypical red blood cell containing iron not bound in hemoglobin
side rod *n* **1 :** either of the rods connecting the piston-rod crosshead with the side levers in a side-lever engine **2 :** a steel rod connecting the crankpins of any two adjoining driving wheels on the same side of a locomotive to distribute power from the main rod to each of the driving wheels **:** COUPLING ROD
sid·er·o·graph \ˈsidərəˌgraf, -rāf\ *n* [²*sidero-* + *-graph*] **:** a combination clock and navigation device that keeps the sidereal time of the Greenwich meridian of longitude
sid·er·og·ra·pher \ˌsidəˈrägrəfə(r)\ *n* -s [ISV *sider-* + *-grapher*] **:** one that makes steel plate engravings
sid·er·o·graph·ic \ˌsidərəˈgrafik\ *adj* [ISV *sider-* + *-graphic*] **:** of, relating to, or executed by siderography ⟨~ art⟩ ⟨~ impressions⟩
sid·er·og·ra·phy \ˌsidəˈrägrəfē\ *n* -ES [ISV *sider-* + *-graphy*] **:** the art of engraving steel; *esp* **:** a process of multiplying facsimiles of an engraved steel plate by rolling over it when hardened a soft steel cylinder and then rolling the cylinder when hardened over a soft steel plate
sid·er·o·lite \ˈsidərəˌlīt\ *or* **sid·er·aerolite** \ˌsidə(r)+\ *n* -s [*siderolite* fr. *sider-* + *-lite*; *sideraerolite* fr. *sider-* + *aerolite*] **:** a stony iron meteorite **:** one containing at least 25 percent of both metal and stone
sid·er·o·mel·ane \ˌsidərəˈmeˌlān\ *n* -s [G *sideromelan*, fr. *sider-* + *-melan* -melane] **:** OBSIDIAN
sid·er·o·na·trite \ˌsidərəˈnāˌtrīt\ *n* -s [It, fr. *sider-* + *natr-* + *-ite*] **:** a mineral $Na_2Fe(SO_4)_2(OH).3H_2O$ consisting of a basic hydrous sulfate of sodium and iron occurring in fibrous yellow masses
sid·er·o·phile \ˈsidərəˌfīl\ *adj* [ISV *sider-* + *-phile*] **:** having so little affinity for oxygen and sulfur that in a molten mass the greatest concentration (as of an element) would be found in the metallic phase (as in the iron of a blast furnace) — compare CHALCOPHILE, OXYPHILE
sid·er·oph·i·lin \ˌsidəˈräfələn\ *n* -s [*sider-* + *-phil* + *-in*] **:** TRANSFERRIN
sid·er·ose \ˈsidəˌrōs\ *adv* [ISV *sider-* + *-ose*] **:** full of or like iron
sid·er·o·sis \ˌsidəˈrōsəs\ *n* -ES [NL, fr. *sider-* + *-osis*] **1 :** pneumoconiosis occurring in iron workers from inhalation of particles of iron **2 :** deposit of iron pigment in a tissue
sid·er·o·stat \ˈsidərəˌstat\ *n* -s [ISV ²*sidero-* + *-stat*] **:** an equatorially mounted mirror moved by clockwork to reflect the rays of a celestial body observed in a constant usu. horizontal direction — compare HELIOSTAT
sid·er·o·stat·ic \ˌ≡≡ˈstadik\ *adj* **:** of, relating to, or consisting of a siderostat
sid·er·ot·ic \ˌsidəˈrädik\ *adj* [*sider-* + *-otic*] **:** of or relating to siderosis
sid·er·o·til \ˈsidərəˌtil\ *n* -s [G *siderotyl*, fr. *sider-* + *-tyl* (irreg. fr. Gk *tilos* anything plucked, fiber, fr. *tillein* to pluck)] **:** a mineral $FeSO_4.5H_2O$ consisting of hydrous ferrous sulfate
sid·er·ous \ˈsidərəs\ *adj* [*sider-* + *-ous*] **:** FERROUS
sid·er·ox·y·lon \ˌsidəˈräksəˌlän\ *n, cap* [NL, fr. *sider-* + *-xylon*] **:** a large genus of tropical trees (family Sapotaceae) having very hard wood and somewhat bell-shaped regular pentamerous flowers and round few-seeded berries — compare IRONWOOD
side run *n* **:** paper made to utilize the full width of the paper machine wire but differing in width from the main portion of the run
sides *pl of* SIDE, *pres 3d sing of* SIDE
¹sidesaddle \ˈ≡ˌ≡≡\ *n* [ME *sid saddil*, fr. *sid*, *side* side + *saddil*, *sadel* saddle — more at SIDE, SADDLE] **:** a saddle for women in which the rider sits with both legs on the same side of the horse

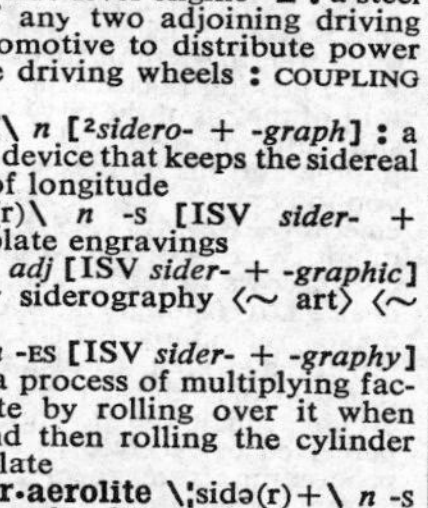
sidesaddle

²sidesaddle \"\ *adv* **:** on or as if on a sidesaddle ⟨the girl rode ~⟩
sidesaddle flower *also* **sidesaddle** *n* **1 :** a common pitcher plant (*Sarracenia purpurea*) **2 :** the flower of the sidesaddle flower
side scene *n* **1 a :** a wing in a theater **b :** a movable piece of stage scenery **2 :** a dramatic scene occurring to one side of the main action
sidescraper \ˈ≡ˌ≡≡\ *n* [¹*side* + *scraper*] **:** a prehistoric flint scraper having a curved scraping edge on one side
side-sew \ˈ≡ˌ≡\ *vt* **:** to fasten (as a book or magazine) with a side stitch usu. of thread
sideshake \ˈ≡ˌ≡\ *n* [¹*side* + *shake*] **1 :** a shake or play from side to side **2 a :** the free space between a timepiece pivot and the inside surface of its bearing **b :** the distance of this space
side shot *n* **:** a survey reading to locate a point off the traverse
sideshow \ˈ≡ˌ≡\ *n* **1 :** a subsidiary show accompanying or part of a main exhibition (as of a circus) **:** a minor attraction **2 :** an incidental diversion ⟨the constant danger of dispersing military strength on ~*s* —J.P.Marquand⟩ ⟨comedy admits of interludes and ~*s* —James Smith⟩ ⟨regarding student activities as a sort of educational ~ —D.D.Feder⟩
side shuffle *n* **:** an American Indian round dance step consisting of a sideward shuffling with flexible knees
¹sideslip \ˈ≡ˌ≡\ *vi* [³*side* + *slip*] **:** to slip or skid sideways: as **a :** to skid sideways — used esp. of an automobile or cycle **b :** to slide sideways through the air in a downward direction along an inclined lateral axis; *esp* **:** to slide in such a manner while turning — used of something (as an airplane) in flight **c :** to slide sideways in a downward direction in skiing (as by slightly advancing one ski and edging both skiis slightly for retardation)
²sideslip \"\ *n* **1 :** the action of sideslipping **2 :** an instance of sideslipping
sides·man \ˈsīdzmən\ *n, pl* **sidesmen** [*sides* (poss. of ¹*side*) + *man*] **1 :** an assistant to the churchwarden of a parish **2 :** one who directs shunting in collieries
sidespin \ˈ≡ˌ≡\ *n* [¹*side* + *spin*] **:** a rotary motion that causes a ball to revolve horizontally
sidesplitter \ˈ≡ˌ≡≡\ *n* **:** one that is sidesplitting; *specif* **:** an exceedingly funny story or joke
sidesplitting \ˈ≡ˌ≡≡\ *adj* **:** affecting the sides convulsively (as with laughter) ⟨a ~ yarn⟩
side sprig *n* **:** a lateral growth on the comb of a fowl that is considered a defect in an exhibition bird
side step *n* **1 a :** a step aside (as in boxing to avoid a blow) **b :** a step taken sideways (as when climbing on skis) **2 :** a step attached at the side of something ⟨climbed the *side steps* to the porch⟩
sidestep \ˈ≡ˌ≡\ *vb* [³*side* + *step*] *vi* **1 :** to take a side step **2 :** to avoid meeting an issue, taking a stand, or making a decision ⟨men who know how to dodge, trim, and ~ —C.M. Fassett⟩ ~ *vt* **1 :** to avoid (as a blow) esp. by moving to one side **2 :** to avoid as if by physical movement **:** EVADE ⟨~ issues⟩ ⟨~ responsibility⟩ ⟨~ a question⟩ **syn** see DODGE
sidestepper \ˈ≡ˌ≡≡\ *n* **:** one that sidesteps
sidestick \ˈ≡ˌ≡\ *n* **:** a wooden or metal strip that when wedged with quoins secures one side of a locked-up type page in printing
side stitch *or* **side-thread stitch** *n* **:** a stitch made by passing thread or wire from side to side through a complete book or magazine before covering — called also *side-wire stitch*
sidestitch \ˈ≡ˌ≡\ *vt* [*side stitch*] **:** to fasten by means of side stitches
side strap *n* **:** a strap attached to or fitted to be attached to the side of an object (as in harness)
side street *n* **:** a street joining and terminated by a main thoroughfare — compare BACK STREET, CROSS STREET
side stringer *n* **:** a structure similar to a keelson between the turn of the bilge and the lowest deck beams of a ship
side-striped jackal \ˈ≡ˌ≡-\ *n* **:** a common African jackal (*Canis adustus*)
¹sidestroke \ˈ≡ˌ≡\ *n* **:** a stroke made by a swimmer while lying on his side in which the arms are alternately worked forward and backward without breaking water, and the legs execute a scissors kick
²sidestroke \"\ *vi* [¹*sidestroke*] **:** to swim by using a sidestroke
side suit *n* **1 :** a suit other than the trump suit in a card game (as bridge) **2 :** a long suit held in addition to trumps
sidesway \ˈ≡ˌ≡\ *n* [¹*side* + *sway*] **:** the action of swaying from side to side — used esp. of an automotive vehicle ⟨a good car should . . . take curves without excessive ~ —*advt*⟩
sideswept \ˈ≡ˌ≡\ *adj* [¹*side* + *swept*] **:** pulled or arranged to one side — used esp. of an asymmetrical clothing design or a hairdo
¹sideswipe \ˈ≡ˌ≡\ *vt* [prob. fr. ³*side* + *swipe*] **1 :** to strike with a glancing blow along the side ⟨*sideswiped* a parked car⟩ ⟨the derailed cars were *sideswiped* by an express train⟩ **2 :** to block (an opponent in football) by throwing one's body across the legs from the side
²sideswipe \"\ *n* **1 a :** the action of sideswiping **b :** an instance of sideswiping **:** a glancing blow **2 :** a criticism made in passing **:** an incidental deprecatory remark, allusion, or reference ⟨the author takes some well-aimed ~*s* at our foreign policy —*New Yorker*⟩
side table *n* [ME] **1 :** a table (as a console table or pier table) designed to be placed against a wall **2 :** a table placed at the side of or apart from the main table **:** a table set at or toward one side of a room **3 :** a usu. large table used as a sideboard until near the 19th century
sidetone \ˈ≡ˌ≡\ *n* **1 :** the sound heard in a telephone receiver originating in signals being picked up by the associated transmitter **2 :** the sound of a speaker's voice as received at his own ears
side tool *n* **:** a tool with its principal cutting edge on one side rather than on the end
¹sidetrack \ˈ≡ˌ≡\ *n* [¹*side* + *track*] **1 :** SIDING **2 :** a position or condition of secondary importance to which one may be diverted
²sidetrack \"\ *vt* **1 :** to transfer to a railroad siding from a main line ⟨the president's special train was ~*ed* to clear the main line —*Spokane (Wash.) Spokesman-Rev.*⟩ **2 a :** to turn aside from a purpose **:** divert (as from the main subject or principal trend of action) into another and usu. less important channel ⟨~ a person⟩ **b :** to divert to a position that is relatively secondary (as in activity, importance, or effectiveness) **:** reduce to a subordinate condition **:** prevent action upon by diversionary tactics ⟨~ an issue⟩ ⟨~ a question⟩ ⟨~ a problem⟩
side trip *n* **:** an excursion incidental to a trip
side vault *n* **:** FLANK VAULT
side view *n* **1 :** a view from the side **:** a view apart from the main view **2 :** a view of a person or object presenting a side instead of a front toward the observer or camera **:** a profile view
sidewalk \ˈ≡ˌ≡\ *n* **:** a walk for foot passengers usu. at the side of a street or roadway **:** a foot pavement
sidewalk artist *n* **:** an artist who makes drawings usu. with chalk directly on the sidewalk to obtain money from passersby
sidewalk bike *n* **:** a child's bicycle having a usu. detachable extra wheel placed on either side of the rear wheel to serve as support and guidance for a child learning to ride a bicycle

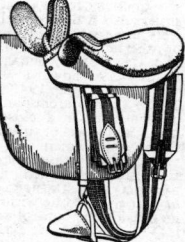

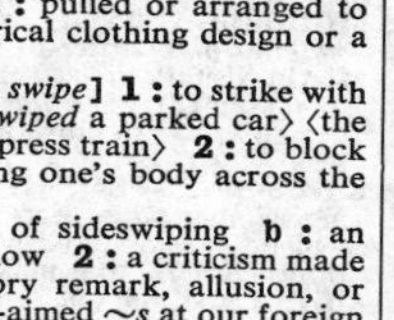
sidewalk bike

sidewalk bridge *n* **:** a temporary bridge over an excavation or obstruction in the area of a sidewalk
sidewalk door *n* **:** a cellar door opening out of a sidewalk and lying flush with the sidewalk when closed
sidewalk elevator *n* **:** an elevator or lift operating through a sidewalk esp. for the handling of goods or refuse
sidewalk superintendent *n* **:** one that watches demolition or construction work in progress
sidewall \ˈ≡ˌ≡\ *n* [ME *side-wall*, fr. ¹*side* + *wall*] **:** a wall forming the side of something: as **a :** FOURCHETTE 2 **b :** the side of an automotive tire between the tread shoulder and the rim bead
¹side·ward \ˈsīdwə(r)d\ *or* **side·wards** \-dz\ *adv* [*sideward* fr. ME *side-warde*, fr. ¹*side* + *-warde* -ward; *sidewards* fr. ¹*side* + *-wards*] **:** toward the side **:** to one side or the other ⟨turning a figure ~ —Kenneth Croft⟩ ⟨the craft can be flown . . . *sidewards* —S.A.Constantino⟩
²sideward \"\ *or* **sidewards** \"\ *adj* **:** moving, directed, or tending toward one side ⟨a soulful ~ glance —James Lord⟩ ⟨the extreme end of its *sidewards* journey —B.E.Ellis⟩
sidewash \ˈ≡ˌ≡\ *n* [¹*side* + *wash*] **:** the lateral flow of the air about an airfoil or airplane
¹sideway \ˈ≡ˌ≡\ *n* **1 :** a way (as a road or path) lying to the side of or diverging from a main road **:** BYWAY **2 :** a roadside path **:** SIDEWALK
²sideway \"\ *adv (or adj)* [¹*side* + *way*] **:** SIDEWAYS
¹side·ways \ˈsīdˌwāz\ *adv* [¹*side* + *-ways*] **1 :** from the side ⟨the scenes are viewed ~ —*Eastman Kodak Monthly Abstract Bull.*⟩ **2 :** with one side to the front or in advance **:** with the side rather than the face, front, or end presented to view **:** with the side foremost **:** in a position so as to offer one side ⟨lie ~⟩ ⟨turn ~⟩ **3 a :** to, toward, or at one side horizontally **:** in a lateral or sideward direction **:** OBLIQUELY ⟨slip ~⟩ ⟨glance ~⟩ ⟨swim ~⟩ **b :** downward on one side **:** with an inclination downward and to one side ⟨leaning ~⟩ **c :** with a slighting, scornful, or flirting glance ⟨look ~ at someone⟩
²sideways \"\ *adj* **:** moving, directed, or tending toward one side **:** INDIRECT ⟨~ glances⟩ ⟨a ~ movement⟩
side-wedge graft *n* **:** PEG GRAFT
side-wheel \ˈ≡ˌ≡\ *adj* **:** of, relating to, or constituting a steamer having a paddle wheel on each side
side-wheeler \ˈ≡ˌ≡≡\ *n* **1 :** a side-wheel steamer **2 :** PACER 1b **3 :** a left-handed baseball pitcher **:** SOUTHPAW
side whip graft *n* **:** a whip graft in which the scion is placed on the side of the stock
side-whiskered \ˈ≡ˌ≡≡\ *adj* [*side-whiskers* + *-ed*] **:** having or characterized by side-whiskers ⟨a *side-whiskered* old gentleman⟩
side-whiskers \ˈ≡ˌ≡≡\ *n pl* **:** whiskers on the side of the face usu. worn long
side wind *n* [ME] **1 :** a wind from or on one side **2 :** an indirect attack, means, method, or manner
side-wind \ˈ≡ˌ≡\ *adj* [*side wind*] **1 :** INDIRECT **2 :** ILLEGITIMATE
sidewinder \ˈ≡ˌ≡≡\ *n* [¹*side* + *winder*] **1 :** a heavy swinging blow from the side **2 :** a small pale-colored desert rattlesnake (*Crotalus cerastes*) of the southwestern U.S. that does not crawl but moves by throwing the body forward in a series of loops — called also *horned rattlesnake* **3 a :** a falling tree that upon hitting another tree rolls on its axis **b :** a tree knocked down by a falling tree
side-wire \ˈ≡ˌ≡\ *vt* **:** to fasten (as a book or magazine) with a side stitch
side-wire stitch *n* **:** SIDE STITCH
sidewise \ˈ≡ˌ≡\ *adv (or adj)* **:** SIDEWAYS
side yard *n* **:** an area adjoining one side of a house or other building
sidhe *also* **shee** \ˈshē\ *n, pl* **sidhe** *or* **sidhes** [partly fr. Ir *sīdh* fairy hill; partly fr. Ir *sidhe* fairy folk] **1** *pl* **sidhes :** an underground fort or palace in which fairies in Gaelic folklore are held to live **2 a** *sidhe pl* **:** the fairy folk of Ireland in Gaelic folklore **b :** a member of the sidhe **:** a fairy in Gaelic folklore — compare BANSHEE
¹si·di \ˈsēdē\ *n* -s [Ar (in India and Africa) *sīdī*, fr. *sayyidī* my lord, fr. *sayyid* lord] **1 :** an African Muslim holding a high position under a King of the Deccan — used as a title of respect **2** *India & East Africa* **a :** ETHIOPIAN **b :** NEGRO
²sidi *var of* SAYYID
siding *n* -s [fr. gerund of ⁴*side*] **1** *archaic* **:** the action of taking sides (as in a debate or conflict) **:** attachment to a party **:** PARTISANSHIP ⟨seriously religious without any taint of ~ or faction —Richard Baxter⟩ **2 :** the dimensions of a ship's timber measured parallel to the center line — opposed to *molding* **3** *or* **siding track a :** a short railroad track connected by switches or points at one or more places with the main track and used esp. to enable trains to pass each other or to provide a storage place for temporarily idle cars — called also *sidetrack* **b :** a short track connecting a railroad directly with the premises of a business concern **4 :** material (as boards or metal sections) of special design usu. nailed horizontally to vertical studs with or without intervening sheathing to form the exposed surface of outside walls of frame buildings — see BEVEL SIDING, DROP SIDING **5 :** a passing place for ships in a canal **6 :** a board cut from the outer portion of a log of which the central portion becomes a timber — compare SLAB
siding tool *n* **:** SIDE TOOL
¹si·dle \ˈsīdᵊl\ *vb* **sidled; sidled; sidling** \-d(ᵊ)liŋ\ **sidles** [prob. back-formation fr. ¹*sideling*] *vi* **1 :** to go or move with one side foremost **:** move sideways esp. in a furtive advance **:** advance obliquely in an unobtrusive manner ⟨when a seedy-looking man ~*s* up to you —T.H.Fielding⟩ ⟨edgewise I *sidled* through the narrow aperture —*Pall Mall Mag.*⟩ ⟨the little ship slowly *sidled* away from her sister craft —L.C. Douglas⟩ ~ *vt* **:** to cause to move or turn sideways **:** direct sideways ⟨*sidled* his horse back along the wagon —Jackson Burgess⟩ ⟨the pilot *sidled* the boat up to the dock⟩
²sidle \"\ *n* -s **:** the act or action of sidling
sidling *var of* SIDELING
¹si·do·ni·an \sīˈdōnēən\ *n* -s *cap* [LL *Sidonii*, pl., Sidonians (fr. L, fr. Gk *Sidōnioi*, fr. *Sidōn* Sidon, fr. Heb *Ṣīdōn*) + E *-an*] **:** a native or inhabitant of Sidon
²sidonian \"\ *adj, usu cap* [L *sidonius* (fr. Gk *sidōnios*, fr. *Ṣīdōn*) + E *-an*] **:** of or relating to the ancient seaport Sidon in Phoenicia
si·dot blende \sēˈdō-\ *n, usu cap S* [ISV, after T. *Sidot*, 19th cent. Fr. chemist] **:** a synthetic highly phosphorescent crystalline zinc sulfide
sid·ra \ˈsidrə\ *or* **sed·ra** \ˈsed-\ *n, pl* **sidras** \ˈsidrəz\ *or* **sid·roth** *or* **sid·rot** \ˈsiˌdrōt(h)\ *or* **sedras** \ˈsedrəz\ *or* **sed·roth** *or* **sed·rot** \ˈseˌdrōt(h)\ [LHeb *sidrāh*, lit., order, arrangement, fr. Heb *sēder* order] **:** a weekly portion of the Pentateuch read in the synagogue on the Sabbath
sids *pl of* SID
sie \ˈsī\ *vb* [ME *sien, syen* to strain, fr. OE *sīon, sēon* to strain, filter — more at SACK] *vt, chiefly Scot* **:** STRAIN ~ *vi, dial Brit* **:** DROP, DRIP
sieg·bahn unit \ˈsēgˌbän-\ *n, usu cap S* [after Karl Manne Georg *Siegbahn* b1886 Swed. physicist] **:** X UNIT
¹siege \ˈsēj\ *n* -s *often attrib* [ME *sege*, fr. OF, seat, act of sitting, act or instance of setting, siege, fr. (assumed) VL *sedicum*, fr. *sedicare* to sit, settle, fr. L *sedēre* to sit — more at SIT] **1** *obs* **a :** a seat usu. of distinction (as in a theater) for a knight **b :** THRONE **2** *obs* **:** a center of power or authority **:** SEE, SEAT **3 a :** the operations of an army around or before a fortified place for the purpose of compelling its surrender or of reducing it by assault after systematic blockade, advances, and bombardment; *broadly* **:** BESIEGING, BELEAGUERING ⟨the battlement on which 15 Americans were to withstand . . . an arm's length ~ by a force tenfold their strength —S.L.A.Marshall⟩ ⟨a weapon designed to conduct ~ operations —*Time*⟩ **b :** a persistent attack (as of illness or other misfortune) ⟨a ~ of typhoid fever⟩ ⟨the ~ of age-old fears —Francis Ratcliffe⟩ **c :** a period of time esp. when trying ⟨a ~ in the territorial prison and also a term in the insane asylum —D.D.Martin⟩ ⟨your ~ in the hospital —Louis Auchincloss⟩ **d :** a large amount **:** QUANTITY ⟨didn't get around much because of having such a ~ of work to be done —Eugene Walter⟩ ⟨after a ~ of persuasion agreed to visit the recruiting station —*Springfield (Mass.) Union*⟩ **4** *obs* **a :** PRIVY **b :** evacuation of the bowels **c :** fecal matter **d** (1) **:** ANUS (2) **:** RECTUM **5** *or* **sedge** \ˈsej\ **:** a flock or brood of birds (as herons or bitterns); *also* **:** the station of a heron on the lookout for prey **6 :** the floor of a glass furnace **7 :** a hewer's workbench — **lay siege to 1 :** to besiege militarily ⟨*laid siege to* the town⟩ **2 :** to pursue diligently or persistently **:** BESIEGE ⟨*lays siege to* Anastasie and is making excellent progress until he ventures a clumsy reference to her father —E.K.Brown⟩ ⟨*laid* diplomatic *siege to* the Greeks —Alexander Kendrick⟩
²siege \"\ *vt* -ED/-ING/-S [ME *segen*, fr. *sege*, n., siege] **:** BESIEGE ⟨mankind is sorely *sieged* by hate's black hordes —E.P.Fewster⟩
siege coin *or* **siege piece** *n* **:** a coin issued for use during a siege
sie·gen·ite \ˈsēgəˌnīt, ˈzē-\ *n* -s [*Siegen*, city in western Germany, its locality + E *-ite*] **:** a mineral $(Co,Ni)_3S_4$ con-

sisting of sulfide of nickel and cobalt isomorphous with linnaeite, violarite, carrollite, and polydymite

sieg·er \ˈsēgə(r)\ *n* -s [²siege + -er] : BESIEGER

siege tower *n* : TOWER 1d

sie·mens's law \ˈsēmənz(əz)-, ˈzē-\ *n, usu cap S* [after Werner von *Siemens* †1892 Ger. electrical engineer and inventor, its formulator] : a statement in electricity: the greater the ratio of counter electromotive force to impressed electromotive force in a motor, the greater is its efficiency

si·ena \sēˈenə\ *n* -s *often cap* [after *Siena*, city in central Italy] : VENETIAN RED 2a

¹**si·en·ese** *also* **si·en·nese** \ˌsēəˈnēz, -ˈnēs\ *n, pl* **sienese** *cap* [*sienese* fr. It, fr. *Siena*, city in central Italy + It *-ese*; *siennese* fr. *Sienna*, *Siena*, Italy + E *-ese*] : a native or resident of Siena

²**sienese** *also* **siennese** \"\ *adj, usu cap* [*sienese* fr. It, fr. *Siena*, Italy + It *-ese* (adj. & n. suffix); *siennese* fr. *Sienna*, *Siena*, Italy + E *-ese* (adj. & n. suffix)] **1** : of or relating to Siena, Italy; *also* : characteristic of Siena or the Sienese **2** : being in or following a style of art ascribed traditionally to Siena and marked by a decorative surface treatment, delicate painting, and a conservative approach to religious iconography — compare FLORENTINE

si·en·na \sēˈenə\ *n* -s [short for earlier *terra-sienna*, modif. of It *terra di Siena* earth of Siena, fr. *terra* earth (fr. L) + *di* of (fr. L *de* from, away) + *Siena*, Italy — more at DE-, TERRACE] : any of various earthy substances that are brownish yellow when raw and orange red to reddish brown when burnt, that in general are darker in color and more transparent in oils than ochers, that occur in limonites, and that are used as pigments for oil stains as well as paints — compare IRON OXIDE, UMBER

sienna brown *n* : a moderate brown that is deeper than auburn and redder and deeper than chestnut brown — called also *teak*

siennese drab *n, often cap S* : a light grayish brown to reddish brown that is duller than sandstone and paler than wood rose

sien-pi \ˈsyenˈpē\ *n, pl* **sien-pi** *or* **sien-pis** *usu cap* **1** : a Tartar people orig. of Mongolia and later of northern Korea **2** : a member of the Sien-pi people

si·er·o·zem \sēˈerəˌzem\ *or* **ser·o·zem** \ˈser-\ *n* -s [Russ *serozem*, fr. *seryĭ* gray + *zemlya* earth; akin to Lith *žemė* earth, L *humus* — more at HUMBLE] : any of a group of zonal soils that are brownish gray at the surface and lighter colored below, based in a carbonate layer or a hardpan layer, and characteristic of temperate to cool arid regions with mixed shrub vegetation

¹**si·er·ra** \sēˈerə\ *n* -s [Sp, lit., saw, fr. L *serra* saw] **1 a** : a range of mountains esp. with a serrated or irregular outline ⟨the wild ~ overhead, the desert's death below —J.G.Whittier⟩ — often used in pl. ⟨never lost sight of the towering *~s* —*Library of Congress Information Bull.*⟩ ⟨north of Lake Tahoe the *~s* are divided —W.W.Atwood †1949⟩ **b** : a mountainous region ⟨in the ~, the prevailing pattern among the Indian population is subsistence farming —*Internat'l Reference Service*⟩ ⟨the southern ~ fairly bristles with distinguished art —*Scientific Monthly*⟩ **2** : any of various large fishes (genus *Scomberomorus*) that resemble mackerel: as **a** : CERO **b** : either of two common Spanish mackerel (*S. maculatus* and *S. sierra*) **3** *often cap* : VENETIAN RED 2a

²**sierra** \"\ *usu cap* — a communications code word for the letter *s*

sierra brownbark pine *n* : PONDEROSA PINE

sierra juniper *n* : WESTERN CEDAR 1

sier·ra le·one \sēˈerəlēˈōn, *chiefly Brit* ˈsirə-\ *adj, usu cap S & L* [fr. *Sierra Leone*, West Africa] : of or from Sierra Leone : of the kind or style prevalent in Sierra Leone

¹**sier·ra le·on·e·an** \sēˈerəlēˈōnēən, ˈsirə-\ *adj, usu cap S&L* [*Sierra Leone*, West Africa + E *-an* (adj. suffix)] **1** : of, relating to, or characteristic of Sierra Leone, West Africa **2** : of, relating to, or characteristic of Sierra Leoneans

²**sierra leonean** \"\ *n, pl* **sierra leoneans** *cap S&L* [*Sierra Leone*, West Africa + E *-an* (n. suffix)] : a native or resident of Sierra Leone; *esp* : a native of Sierra Leone claiming no tribal affiliation

sierra leone peach *n, usu cap S&L* : COUNTRY FIG 1

¹**si·er·ran** \sēˈerən\ *adj* [¹*sierra* + *-an*] **1** : of or relating to a sierra, the region around it, or its inhabitants **2** *usu cap* : of or relating to the Sierra Nevada mountains of the western U.S. ⟨the Rocky and *Sierran* mountain systems —A.C.Kinsey⟩ ⟨darkness had accompanied a *Sierran* stagecoach toward the summit —Bret Harte⟩

²**sierran** \"\ *n* -s *cap* [*Sierra* Nevada, mountain range in eastern Calif. + E *-an*] : a native or inhabitant of the region around the Sierra Nevada mountains ⟨about one hundred . . . Appalachians and *Sierrans* were gathered around a campfire —*Out West*⟩

sierra plum *n* : a shrub or small tree (*Prunus subcordata*) of the Pacific coast of the U.S. with somewhat spinescent branches and small red insipid fruit

sierra redbark pine *n* : JEFFREY PINE

sierra shrew *n, usu cap 1st S* : a small upland shrew (*Sorex vagrans amoenus*) of the western U.S.

-sies *pl of* -SY

¹**si·es·ta** \sēˈestə\ *n* -s [Sp, fr. L *sexta (hora)* sixth (hour) (i.e., after sunrise), noon, fr. *sexta*, fem. of *sextus* sixth + *hora* hour — more at SEXT, HOUR] : an afternoon nap or rest in some usu. Latin countries and esp. formerly so customary that business is usu. suspended daily to allow for it ⟨when he slept his ~ (as the Spaniard calls it) —James Howell⟩ ⟨the honored Italian ~ —*Time*⟩; *also* : a short sleep or rest ⟨about nine or ten in the morning the sheep settle down to a ~⟩ ⟨take a ~ for twenty minutes or so —Anita Colby⟩ — sometimes used without the article ⟨the hour of ~⟩ ⟨roused the . . . museum guardian from ~ —Claudia Cassidy⟩

²**siesta** \"\ *vi* -ED/-ING/-S : to take a siesta : NAP ⟨could not ~ with the argument going on —Gerald Durrell⟩

sie·va bean \ˈsēvə-\ *also* **see·wee bean** *or* **se·wee bean** \ˈsēwē-\ *n* [*sieva, seewee, sewee* of unknown origin] **1** : any of several bush or weakly vining beans that are derived from a tropical American annual species (*Phaseolus lunatus*), are closely related to and sometimes classed as lima beans, and are cultivated esp. in the southern U.S. for their small flat edible seeds — compare JAVA BEAN **2** : the seed of a sieva bean — called also *butter bean*

¹**sieve** \ˈsiv\ *n* -s [ME *sive, seve*, fr. OE *sife*; akin to MD *seve* sieve, OHG *sib* sieve, ON *sef* rush (plant), Serb *sipiti* to drizzle; basic meaning: drip, trickle] **1 a** : a meshed or perforated device or utensil through which dry loose material (as flour or ashes) is winnowed or refined, material containing liquid is strained, and soft solids (as hard-boiled eggs) are comminuted by forcing (as with a pestle); *sometimes* : SIFTER **b** : material meshed or perforated like a sieve ⟨strips of ~⟩ **2** : a meshed or perforated sheet (as of metal or cloth) with apertures of uniform size used to separate powdered or granulated material according to the size of its particles as: **a** : one woven from wire cloth having square apertures and used chiefly in a chemistry laboratory **b** : a rectangular wooden frame covered with wire screen on one side and silk cloth on the other and used in a flour-milling sifter **3** : GOSSIP ⟨the ~ of a patron let it out —Lord Byron⟩ **4** *slang* : a body riddled by bullets ⟨made a mistake trying to kill his ex-wife's new husband — ending up a ~ —Bill O'Rourke⟩ **5** : SIEVE OF ERATOSTHENES — usu. used with *the* ⟨first proposed by the ancient Greek philosopher and mathematician Eratosthenes and . . . usually known as the ~ —George Gamow⟩

sieve 1a with pestle

²**sieve** \"\ *vb* -ED/-ING/-S *vt* **1 a** : to put through a sieve or sifter or meshed material ⟨*sieved* avocado⟩ ⟨~ the cocoa with the flour⟩ ⟨the oxide catalyst is . . . crushed and *sieved* to give granules of uniform size —E.R.Riegel⟩ **b** : to separate or separate out by putting through a sieve or sifter or meshed material ⟨~ the juice from the pulp⟩ — usu. used with *out* ⟨~ out the finer grains⟩ **2 a** : to study (a whole) carefully for the purpose of extracting a part : SCREEN ⟨a hundred candidates must be *sieved* to find one who knows the score —H.M. Silver⟩ **b** : to separate by a process of careful study or by trial : WINNOW — usu. used with *out* ⟨~ out inessentials⟩ ⟨the test *sieved* out several of the candidates⟩ ⟨in order to identify the essence of a national style one must ~ out the radical evidence —Harvey Breit⟩ **3** : PERFORATE ⟨the ceiling . . . *sieved* with millions of pinpoint holes for ventilation —*New Republic*⟩ ~ *vi* **1** : to use a sieve or sifter : do sieving **2** : to pass through or as if through a sieve or sifter or meshed material ⟨the dust from the ashes *sieved* through⟩ ⟨her mother's voice . . . *sieved* through the screen . . . out of the lighted kitchen —John Hermann⟩ — compare SIFT

sieve analysis *n* : a grading by size of particles of powdered or granulated material done with a sieve

sieve and shears *n pl but sing in constr* : divination (as for guilt or a marriage partner) by observation of the motion of a sieve suspended from the points of an open pair of shears : COSCINOMANCY — called also *riddle and shears*

sieve area *also* **sieve field** *n* : an area in the wall of a sieve-tube element, sieve cell, or parenchyma cell in which are clustered pores through which cytoplasmic connections pass to adjoining cells and which in sieve-tube elements are typically most highly developed on the end walls between adjacent elements where they constitute sieve plates

sieve cell *n* : an elongated tapering cell characteristic of the phloem of gymnosperms and lower vascular plants that is basically similar in form, function, and relationships to a sieve-tube element but distinguished by rather uniformly distinguished sieve areas which are not aggregated into sieve plates — compare TRACHEID

sieve element *n* : a transport element of phloem whether taking the form of a sieve cell or a sieve-tube element

sievelike \ˈ=ˌ=\ *adj* : resembling a sieve in appearance or function

sieve of er·a·tos·the·nes \-ˌerəˈtästhəˌnēz\ *usu cap E* [after *Eratosthenes* fl 3d cent. B.C. Greek astronomer and geographer] : a device for finding prime numbers consisting of the writing down of the odd numbers from 3 up in succession and of erasing every third number after 3, every fifth after 5, every seventh after 7, and so on, the numbers remaining being prime

sieve pit *n* : one of the fine perforations that occur in a sieve plate

sieve plate *or* **sieve disk** *n* : a wall or portion of a wall between sieve-tube elements containing one or more sieve areas — compare COMPOUND SIEVE PLATE, SIEVE TUBE

siev·er \ˈsivə(r)\ *n* -s [¹*sieve* + *-er*] **1** : one that makes sieves **2** : one that sieves : SIFTER

sie·ver·sia \sēˈvərsēə\ *n, cap* [NL, fr. J. *Sievers*, 18th cent. Ger. botanist + NL *-ia*] *in some classifications* : a genus of perennial herbs that includes the prairie smoke and is usu. made a subgenus of *Geum*

sieves *pl of* SIEVE, *pres 3d sing of* SIEVE

sieve tissue *n* : PHLOEM

sieve tube *n* : a tube consisting of an end to end series of thin-walled living cells characteristic of the phloem, having no nucleus when mature, and believed to function chiefly in translocation of organic solutes — compare COMPANION CELL, SIEVE CELL, SIEVE PLATE

sieve-tube element *or* **sieve-tube member** *n* : a thin-walled elongated living cell that has no nucleus at maturity, is continuous with other similar cells by protoplasmic strands which pass through the perforations of specialized sieve plates, prob. functions primarily in the translocation of organic solutes, and is the basic element of the sieve tube — compare SIEVE CELL

sieving *n* -s [fr. gerund of ²*sieve*] **1** : the act or process of sieving **2** : the work of a siever **3 sievings** *pl* : sieved material **4** : a turn through a sieve ⟨give the flour two *~s*⟩; *also* : the amount resulting from a turn through a sieve ⟨a shovelful and a ~⟩

si·faka \səˈfakə\ *also* **si·fac** \ˈsēˌfak\ *n* -s [Malagasy] : any of several diurnal lemurs of the genus *Propithecus* that have a long tail and silky fur and that are of a usu. black and white color

si·fat·ite \səˈfädˌīt\ *n* -s *usu cap* [Ar *Ṣifātī* (fr. *ṣifāt* attributes) + E *-ite*] : one of an early Muslim school holding to a literal interpretation of the Koran and to an anthropomorphic interpretation of the attributes of Allah

sife \ˈsīf\ *dial Eng var of* SIGH

sif·fi·late \ˈsifəˌlāt\ *vb* -ED/-ING/-S [modif. (influenced by *sibilate*) of F *siffler* to whistle, fr. MF] : WHISPER

sif·fle \ˈsifəl\ *vi* -ED/-ING/-S [ME *siflen*, fr. MF *siffler, sifler*, fr. (assumed) VL *sifilare*, fr. L *sibilare* to hiss, whistle — more at SIBILANT] : to blow or speak with a sibilant sound : WHISTLE, HISS

sif·fleur *R* sēˈflər, +V -lər-; -*R* -lə̄, + *vowel in a word following without pause* -lər- *or* -lə̄ *also* -lər\ *n* -s [F, fr. *siffler* to whistle + *-eur* -or] : WHISTLER; *esp* : an animal (as the whistling marmot) that makes a whistling noise

sif·flöt \ˈsifˌflət\ *n* -s [G, prob. modif. (influenced by *flöte* flute) of F *sifflet* whistle, fr. MF, fr. *siffler* to whistle + *-et* — more at BLOCKFLÖTE] **1** : a whistle flute **2** : a small flute organ stop with a whistling tone

sifrei torah *pl of* SEPHER TORAH

¹**sift** \ˈsift\ *vb* -ED/-ING/-S [ME *siften*, fr. OE *siftan*; akin to MLG *siften* to sift, OE *sife* sieve — more at SIEVE] *vt* **1 a** : to put through a sifter or sieve or meshed material ⟨~ flour⟩ ⟨*~ed* through coarse screens to remove matter larger than the wheat kernels —*Studies for Flour Salesmen*⟩ ⟨grinding granulated sugar and *~ing* through silk or nylon cloth —L.A.Wills⟩ **b** : to separate or separate out by putting through a sifter or sieve or meshed material ⟨~ the fine grains from the coarse⟩ — often used with *out* ⟨~ out the powdered portion⟩ **2 a** : to study or examine carefully and extract the good, essential, or desirable (as that which falls in a class) : SCREEN ⟨knowing where to get information is of little importance unless you know how to ~ and evaluate it —*Armed Forces Talk*⟩ ⟨offer, ~, and pass as many basic laws as came from the first two sessions —F.L.Paxson⟩ ⟨~ the men who enter the armed forces⟩ **b** : to separate or separate out by a process of careful study or examination or by trial : WINNOW ⟨~ propaganda from fact —Karl Baehr⟩ ⟨*~ing* Ph.D. candidates who are a drain on faculty time —S.E.Harris⟩ — often used with *out* ⟨~ out the fact from the theory —C.I.Glicksberg⟩ ⟨a training process which *~s* out . . . the students with a natural aptitude in our direction —H.D.Gideonse⟩ **c** : to study or investigate thoroughly : PROBE ⟨will ~ this matter to the uttermost —Sir Walter Scott⟩ ⟨~ a family pretty thoroughly before turning a . . . dog over to them —Arthur Mayse⟩ **d** : to subject to close questioning ⟨multiplied his questions and *~ed* me thoroughly —Jonathan Swift⟩ **3** : to scatter by or as if by passing through a sieve ⟨~ sugar on a cake⟩ **4** : to run one's fingers through ⟨the barber was lifting and *~ing* her tresses —P.H. Newby⟩ ~ *vi* **1** : to use a sifter or sieve : do sifting **2** : to pass through or as if through a sifter or sieve or meshed material : SIEVE : FILTER ⟨the flour *~ed* through⟩ ⟨snow *~ing* in around the sashes —Dixon Wecter⟩ ⟨men *~ed* in along the border —Oscar Handlin⟩ ⟨bags sewn with a close stitch to minimize *~ing*⟩ **3 a** : to study or examine something carefully and extract from it the good, essential, or desirable (as something that falls in a class) : SCREEN ⟨in working through the documents he was constantly *~ing*⟩ **b** : to separate something out by sifting : WINNOW : SELECT ⟨in all his people . . . he is *~ing* until he comes down to the infinitesimal deposit of humanity —V.S.Pritchett⟩ **c** : to study or investigate something thoroughly : PROBE ⟨the mind unwilling to be rushed to conclusions, the *~ing*, scientific mind —H.A.Overstreet⟩ — compare SIEVE — **sift through** : to work through by sifting ⟨has *sifted through* some of the material used in the monumental project —R.D.Gardner⟩ ⟨*sift through* them for the one that best suits his purpose —Shirley A. Briggs⟩

²**sift** \"\ *n* -s : that which is sifted ⟨acres . . . when their toughness is reduced by winter frosts to a rich ~, as of molehills —Adrian Bell⟩

sift·age \-tij\ *n* -s **1** : SIFT ⟨pulling asunder the fibrous clods, but not reducing them to ~ —R.D.Blackmore⟩ **2** : the action of sifting ⟨a small sleeve and large valve prevent ~ —*Modern Packaging*⟩

sift·er \-tə(r)\ *n* -s : one that sifts: as **a** : a device or utensil like a sieve but usu. of finer mesh for winnowing or refining powdered or granulated substances (as flour) and more often with a contrivance (as a rotator) to aid the action of sifting; *sometimes* : SIEVE **b** : SHAKER; *also* : the perforated top of a shaker **c** : a machine used in flour milling to separate particles of ground grain according to size by running them through sieves of increasing degrees of fineness arranged one above the other so that the coarsest is on top **d** : a worker who sifts cut tobacco on a riddle

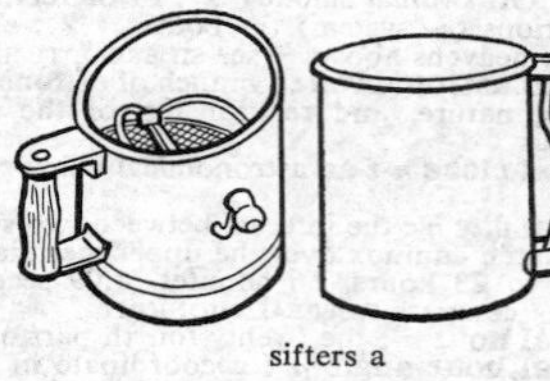

sifters a

sifting *n* -s [ME, fr. gerund of *siften* to sift] **1** : the act or process of sifting **2** : the work of a sifter **3** : **siftings** *pl* : sifted material ⟨bran mixed with *~s*⟩ **4** : a turn through a sifter ⟨give the flour a ~⟩; *also* : the amount resulting from a turn through a sifter ⟨the farmer has no time to weigh and measure; he speaks to his men of double handfuls, *~s*, forkfuls —Adrian Bell⟩

sig \ˈsig\ *n* -s [abbr. of *signature*] : SIGNATURE: as **a** : the logotype of a newspaper **b** : the identifying music that closes a broadcast program or commercial

sig *abbr* **1** signal; signaller; signalman **2** signature **3** signifying **4** *often cap* signor

si·ga·nid \səˈganəd, -gān-\ *adj* [NL *Siganidae*] : of or relating to the Siganidae

si·gan·i·dae \-ganəˌdē\ *n pl, cap* [NL, fr. *Siganus*, type genus + *-idae*] : a small family of compressed ovate-bodied herbivorous fishes having minute scales concealed in slippery skin and strong fin spines capable of inflicting painful wounds that is usu. isolated in a special suborder of the order Percomorphi and is widely distributed in the tropical Indo-Pacific

si·ga·nus \səˈgānəs\ *n, cap* [NL, fr. Ar *sijān* rabbitfish] : the type genus of Siganidae comprising the rabbitfishes

sig·a·to·ka \ˌsigəˈtōkə\ *n* -s [fr. *Sigatoka*, district and river in the Fiji islands] : a serious leaf spot disease of bananas occurring esp. in tropical America and caused by a sooty mold (*Cercospora musae*)

sigg *abbr* signatures

¹**sigh** \ˈsī\ *vb* -ED/-ING/-S [ME *sihen, sighen* (past *sihte, sighte*), prob. alter. (after such pairs as ME *techen* to teach: *tahte, taghte* taught) of *sichen*, fr. OE *sīcan*; akin to MD *versiken* to sigh] *vi* **1** : to let out slowly and audibly a deeply drawn breath esp. as the involuntary expression of weariness, dejection, grief, regret, longing, yearning, relief **2** : to make a sound like sighing ⟨wind *~ing* in the branches⟩ ⟨the sails did ~ like sedge —S.T.Coleridge⟩ **3** : LAMENT, GRIEVE, YEARN — used often with *for* ⟨*~ing* for the days of his youth⟩ ~ *vt* **1 a** : to express by sighs : utter in or with sighs ⟨*~ed* out her grief⟩ ⟨poor shawled woman *~ing* her prayers —Sean O'Faolain⟩ **b** : to breathe out in sighs ⟨drove his blade . . . to the bull's heart . . . as the wild life *~ed* itself out, and vanished —C.G.D. Roberts⟩ **2** *archaic* : to utter sighs over : MOURN ⟨shall bless her name, and ~ her fate —Matthew Prior⟩ **3** : to spend or waste in sighing ⟨*~ing* away his days⟩ **4** : to bring by sighs into a particular state ⟨*~ed* himself to sleep⟩

²**sigh** \"\ *n* -s [ME *sihe, sighe*, fr. *sihen, sighen*, v.] **1** : an act of sighing : a deep and prolonged audible inspiration and expiration of air esp. when involuntary and expressing some emotion or feeling (as grief, yearning, weariness, or relief) ⟨*~s* of parting⟩ **2** : the sound of gently moving or escaping air ⟨~ of the summer breeze⟩ ⟨the engine stopped with a ~⟩

sigh·er \ˈsī(ə)r, -īə\ *n* -s : one that sighs

sigh·ful \ˈsīfəl\ *adj* : full of sighs : MOURNFUL

sigh·ing·ly *adv* [ME, fr. *sihing, sighing* (pres. part. of *sihen, sighen* to sigh) + *-ly*] : in a sighing manner : with sighing

¹**sight** \ˈsīt, *usu* -īd·+V\ *n* -s [ME *sighth, sith, siht, sight*, fr. OE *sihth, gesihth, gesiht*; akin to MLG & MD *sicht* sight, OHG *siht*; derivative fr. the root of E *see*] **1 a** : something that is seen or beheld : SPECTACLE, SHOW ⟨a ~ more familiar to our forefathers than to us —Dana Burnet⟩ **b** *obs* : VISION 1 **2 a** : a thing regarded as worth seeing — used usu. in pl. ⟨a tour of the *~s* of the city⟩ **b** : something ludicrous, surprising, shocking, or disorderly in appearance ⟨he had fallen in a puddle and his clothes were a ~⟩ ⟨you must get some sleep, you look a ~⟩ **c** *obs* : ASPECT, APPEARANCE ⟨in ~ like unto an emerald —Rev 4:3 (AV)⟩ **3 a** *chiefly dial* : a great number or quantity ⟨a ~ of old women in decent shawls —Mary Webb⟩ ⟨~ of cows to feed —Jean Stafford⟩ **b** *chiefly dial* : a great deal : LOT ⟨thought a ~ of you all my life and . . . tried to make you happy —J.C.Lincoln⟩ **4** *dial* : a straight uninterrupted stretch (as of a road) **5 a** : the process, power, or function of seeing : the animal sense whose end organ is the eye by which the position, shape, and color of objects are perceived or received as stimuli through the medium of light proceeding from them : EYESIGHT, VISION **b** : faculty of mental or spiritual perception resembling vision ⟨truth as it appeared to his inward ~⟩ — compare SECOND SIGHT **c** : mental view : VIEWPOINT, OPINION, JUDGMENT ⟨abomination in the ~ of God —Lk 16:15 (AV)⟩ **d** : power of seeing exercised by a particular individual ⟨made my pledge in the cathedral in the ~ of God —Frank Yerby⟩ **6 a** : act of looking at or beholding ⟨always fainted at the ~ of blood⟩ ⟨I know him only by ~, not intimately⟩ **b** *archaic* : GLANCE, LOOK **c** : INSPECTION, PERUSAL ⟨this letter is intended for your ~ only⟩ **d** : VIEW, GLIMPSE ⟨window cartons giving a ~ of their contents —L.A.Lewinton⟩ **e** : an observation taken for determining direction or position ⟨when the . . . mate gets another ~ this afternoon that'll give us a good fix of the ship's position —N.D.Ford⟩ **7 a** : perception of an object by the eye : presence in the field of vision ⟨caught ~ of the fox⟩ ⟨lost ~ of the plane in the clouds⟩ **b** : the space through which the power of vision extends : range of view ⟨a ship came into ~ over the horizon⟩ **c** : position affording a view ⟨came within ~ of the mountains⟩ **d** : presentation of a note or draft to the maker or draftee : DEMAND 1b **8** : opportunity of seeing, examining or investigating: as **a** : the right to a showdown in a poker game **b** : a viewing of goods arranged for prospective buyers ⟨the diamond buyers of the world come to the monthly ~ —Russell Chappell & E.W.Griffiths⟩ **9** *dial* **a** : EYE **b** : the pupil of the eye **c sights** *pl* : SPECTACLES **10 a** *obs* : VISOR **b sights** *pl* : the eye slits in a helmet or in the visor of a helmet ⟨their eyes of fire, sparkling through *~s* of steel —Shak.⟩ **11 a** (1) : a device for guiding the eye in aiming a firearm that consists of a small often beaded projection (as a blade or a post) placed on top of the muzzle end of the barrel (2) : a transverse bar or leaf fixed near the breech and having a notch or a hole that allows alignment with a projection at the muzzle end and is often adjustable for changes in range or direction — usu. used in pl. and often with *pair* ⟨a pair of *~s*⟩; see OPEN SIGHT, PANORAMIC SIGHT, PEEP SIGHT, TELESCOPE SIGHT **b** : a device with a small aperture through which objects are to be seen and by which their direction is settled or ascertained ⟨the ~ of a quadrant⟩ **c** : BOW SIGHT **d sights** *pl* : AIM, GOAL, ASPIRATION ⟨plenty of time for adjusting the business *~s* upward —*Kiplinger Washington Letter*⟩ ⟨set its *~s* high for the 1949 March of Dimes —Basil O'Connor⟩ **12 a** : a transparent pane or window through which substances or processes in a closed chamber or flue can be observed **b** : a glass vessel or tube for exhibiting the flow of oil in a lubricating arrangement **13** : the opening in a picture frame; *also* : the part of a picture exposed to view within a frame — **at first sight** *adv* : without investigation or analysis : OFFHAND, IMMEDIATELY, SUPERFICIALLY ⟨though these problems appear, *at first sight*, to lie within the agricultural industry, they often lie outside the control of the individual farmer —G.P.Wibberley⟩ — **at sight** *adv* : as soon as seen or presented to view ⟨a draft payable *at sight*⟩ ⟨play a piece of music *at sight*⟩ ⟨translate a passage *at sight*⟩ ⟨vowed to shoot his enemy *at sight*⟩ — **in sight** : at or within a reasonable distance away in space or time ⟨able to keep the quarry *in sight*⟩ ⟨the end of our

troubles is now *in sight*⟩ ⟨victory is *in sight*⟩ ⟨a girl who hasn't a man *in sight* by the time she is 20 —Sidonie M. Gruenberg⟩ — **on sight** *adv* **:** at sight — **out of sight 1 :** beyond comparison ⟨*out of sight* the best thing he has written⟩ **2 :** beyond all expectation or reason; *esp* **:** excessively high ⟨butter . . . went almost *out of sight* when price ceilings . . . were removed —*New Republic*⟩ — **sight for sore eyes :** one whose appearance or arrival is an occasion for joy or relief **:** a gladdening or heartening sight

²**sight** \"\ *adj* **1 :** calling for or based on recognition or comprehension without previous study or recourse to notes, reference books, or other aid ⟨a ~ translation⟩ ⟨teachers should build up the ~ vocabulary of children⟩ **2 :** payable on presentation ⟨~ draft⟩ ⟨~ exchange⟩

³**sight** \"\ *vb* -ED/-ING/-S *vt* **1** *obs* **:** INSPECT, SCRUTINIZE **2 :** to get or catch sight of **:** see for the first time ⟨~ a star⟩ ⟨several whales were ~*ed*⟩ ⟨more than merely ~*ing* a familiar face in a crowd —Irving Kolodin⟩ ⟨~*ed* land soon after sunrise⟩ **3 :** to look at through or as if through a sight; *esp* **:** to test for straightness or trueness by looking along the length of ⟨~ a rifle⟩ **4 a :** to aim (a firearm) by means of sights **b :** to aim at (a target) **c :** to sight in **5 a :** to equip with sights **b :** to adjust the sights of ⟨the rifle was ~*ed* to 1000 yards⟩ **6 :** to present (as a bill) for payment ~ *vi* **1 :** to take aim ⟨hard to ~ for the center of the greatly narrowed channel —C.S.Forester⟩ **2 :** to look carefully in a certain direction ⟨~ along the edge of a board⟩ ⟨~ down a gun barrel⟩ — **sight the anchor :** to haul up an anchor enough to see whether it is fouled or clear

sight board *n* **:** SCREEN 8

sight draft *n* **:** a draft payable on presentation

sight·ed \ˈsīd·əd, -ītəd\ *adj* [¹*sight* + *-ed*] **1 :** having the use of one's sight **:** SEEING ⟨to the ~, loss of vision seems the most hopeless and pitiable . . . —P.A.Zahl⟩ ⟨son who was partially ~ —Alice Lake⟩ **2 :** having a specified kind of sight — usu. used in combination ⟨clear-*sighted*⟩ ⟨quick-*sighted*⟩

sight edge *n* **:** the edge of an overlapping or outer strake of the shell plating of a ship

sight·er \ˈsīd·ə(r), -ītə-\ *n* -S **1 :** one who tests the accuracy of sights on small arms — called also *aligner, targeteer* **2 :** SIGHTING SHOT

sight–feed \ˈ=,=\ *adj* **:** of or belonging to a feed-pipe fitting, device, or system arranged so that the flowing liquid may be observed through a transparent section of a tube or wall ⟨*sight-feed* oil cup⟩

sight gag *n* **:** a comic bit or episode achieved by pantomime or camera shot rather than words

sight glass *n* **:** a transparent section in a pipe or tank wall for giving visual indication of level or flow of liquids

sight in *vt* **:** to adjust the sights of (a gun) so that at a selected range the missile will strike the point aimed at

sighting *n* -S **:** an act of one who sights ⟨no further ~*s* of the enemy were made⟩

sighting angle *n* **:** RANGE ANGLE

sighting hood *n* **:** a raised hood with slits or peepholes in the sides mounted on top of a gun turret

sighting shot *n* **:** a shot made to test the adjustment of the sights of a firearm

sight·less \ˈsītləs\ *adj* [ME *sightles*, fr. *sight* + *-les* -less] **1 :** lacking sight **:** being without sight **:** BLIND **2 a :** INVISIBLE **b** *obs* **:** UNSIGHTLY **c :** UNSEEN — **sight·less·ly** *adv* — **sight·less·ness** *n* -ES

sight line *n* **:** a straight line extending from the eye of a spectator to an object or area (as of a stage) to be viewed **:** one of the lines that define an unimpeded field of vision ⟨the complications of providing good *sight lines* increase proportionately with the numbers to be seated —*Architect & Building News*⟩

sight·li·ness \ˈsītlēnəs, -lin-\ *n* -ES **:** the quality or state of being sightly

¹**sight·ly** \-lē,-li\ *adj* -ER/-EST [¹*sight* + *-ly*] **1** *obs* **:** CONSPICUOUS, VISIBLE **2 :** acceptable or pleasing to the sight **:** decent in appearance ⟨~ building⟩ ⟨~ typography⟩ **3 :** affording a fine view ⟨homes . . . enjoying a ~ location overlooking the river —*Springfield (Mass.) Union*⟩

²**sightly** \"\ *adv* **:** in a sightly manner

sight·me·ter \ˈsīt,mēd·ə(r)\ *n* **:** a light meter that indicates in foot-candles relative visibilities of illuminated surfaces or positions

sight picture *n* **:** the alignment of the sights of a firearm with the target as seen by the firer

sightproof \ˈ=,=\ *adj* **:** impenetrable to sight ⟨~ hedge six feet high⟩

sight radius *n* **:** the distance between the front and rear sights of a firearm

sight–read \ˈ=,=\ *vb* [back-formation fr. *sight reading* & *sight reader*] *vt* **:** to read (as a foreign language) or perform (music) without previous preparation or study ~ *vi* **:** to read something at sight; *esp* **:** to play or sing music at sight

sight reader *n* **:** one who reads at sight something that ordinarily requires previous study; *specif* **:** a musician who can read or perform music at first sight of the score

sight–reading \ˈ=,==\ *n* **1 a :** the action or an instance of reading at sight **b :** the ability to read at sight **2 :** material for reading at sight

sight rhyme *n* **:** EYE RHYME

sights *pl of* SIGHT, *pres 3d sing of* SIGHT

sight–see \ˈ=,=\ *vi* [back-formation fr. *sight-seeing*] **:** to go about seeing sights of interest

¹**sight–seeing** \ˈ=,==\ *adj* [¹*sight* + *seeing*, pres. part. of *see* (after the phrase *see the sights*)] **:** engaged in, devoted to, or used for seeing sights ⟨~ trip⟩ ⟨~ buses⟩

²**sight–seeing** \"\ *n* [¹*sight* + *seeing*, gerund of *see* (after the phrase *see the sights*)] **:** the act or pastime of seeing sights

sightseer \ˈ=,==\ *n* -S **:** one that visits places of interest **:** one that goes about in search of novelty or picturesque sights or scenery

sight–shot \ˈ=,=\ *n* **:** EYESHOT

sightsinging \ˈ=,==\ *n* **:** the sight reading of vocal music

sight tree *n* **:** LINE TREE

sight unseen *adv* **:** without inspection or opportunity of appraisal ⟨can't expect him to buy such an expensive place *sight unseen*⟩

sightworthy \ˈ=,==\ *adj* **:** worth seeing

sig·il \ˈsijəl\ *n* -S [L *sigillum* — more at SEAL] **1 :** SEAL, SIGNET **2 :** a sign, word, or device of supposed occult power in astrology or magic **3 :** a coded bibliographical reference consisting typically of letters and numerals representing respectively date, name of publication, volume, page, and article

sigill *abbr* [L *sigillum*] seal

sig·il·lar·ia \,sijəˈla(a)rēə\ *n, cap* [NL, fr. L *sigillum* seal + NL *-aria*; fr. the leaf scars that resemble seals] **:** a genus (the type of the family Sigillariaceae) of fossil arborescent club mosses of the Middle Carboniferous — **sig·il·lar·id** \,==ˈ=rəd\ *n or adj*

sig·il·lar·i·a·ce·ae \,==,=rēˈāsē,ē\ *n pl, cap* [NL, fr. *Sigillaria*, type genus + *-aceae*] **:** a family of arborescent Carboniferous club mosses (order Lepidodendrales) that have the trunks marked with vertical rows of leaf scars suggesting seals — **sig·il·lar·i·a·ce·ous** \,==,==ˈāshəs\ *adj*

sig·il·lar·i·os·tro·bus \,==,=rēˈästrəbəs\ *n, cap* [NL, fr. *Sigillaria* + *-o-* + Gk *strobos, strombos* top, ball; akin to Gk *strephein* to turn — more at STROPHE] **:** a form genus based on lepidodendrid cones believed to belong to plants of the genus *Sigillaria*

¹**sig·il·late** \ˈsijə,lāt\ *vt* -ED/-ING/-S [L *sigillatus*, past part. of *sigillare*, fr. *sigillum* seal — more at SEAL] **:** to close by or as if by a seal **:** SEAL

²**sigillate** \ˈsijə,lāt, səˈjilət\ *or* **sig·il·lat·ed** \ˈsijə,lād·əd\ *adj* [*sigillate* fr. L *sigillatus*, fr. *sigillum* + *-atus* -ate; *sigillated* fr. L *sigillatus* + E *-ed*] **1 :** decorated by means of stamped-on patterns or motifs — used esp. of ancient Roman ware **2 :** having markings like seals ⟨~ rootstock⟩

sig·il·la·tion \,sijəˈlāshən\ *n* -S [ML *sigillation-, sigillatio*, fr. L *sigillatus* (past part. of *sigillare* to seal) + *-ion-, -io* -ion] **1 :** impression of or by a seal **2 :** the mark of a cicatrix **3 :** decoration by means of stamped designs

sig·il·log·ra·phy \,==ˈlägrəfē\ *n* -ES [F *sigillographie*, fr. L *sigillum* seal + F *-o-* + *-graphie* -graphy] **:** the study of seals **:** SPHRAGISTICS

si·glar·i·an \siˈgla(a)rēən\ *adj* [*siglum* + *-ary* + *-an*] **:** of or relating to sigla

si·glos \ˈsi,gläs\ *n, pl* **si·gloi** \-lòi\ [Gk *siglos, siklos*, of Sem origin; akin to Heb *sheqel* shekel] **:** a silver coin of ancient Persia equal to 1/20 daric and weighing about 5.6 grams

sig·lum \ˈsigləm\ *n, pl* **sig·la** \-lə\ [L, dim. of *signum* sign, mark, figure, image — more at SIGN] **1 :** a sign, abbreviation, letter, or character standing for words in ancient manuscripts or on coins or medals **2 :** a letter used to indicate manuscript or other source of an edited text

sig·ma \ˈsigmə\ *n* -S [Gk, of Sem origin; akin to Heb *sāmekh* samekh] **1 :** the 18th letter of the Greek alphabet — symbol Σ or σ or ς; see ALPHABET tables; compare LUNAR SIGMA **2 :** the thousandth part of a second **:** MILLISECOND **3 a :** STANDARD DEVIATION — symbol σ **b :** the sum of — symbol Σ **4 :** a C-shaped sponge spicule

sig·ma·spire \-,spī(ə)r\ *n* [*sigma* + *spire*] **:** an S-shaped sponge spicule **:** a sigma twisted spirally

¹**sig·mate** \ˈsig,māt\ *vt* -ED/-ING/-S [*sigma* + *-ate* (v. suffix)] **:** to affix a sigma or *s* to (a root) in forming a tense or a plural

²**sigmate** \"\ *adj* [*sigma* + *-ate* (adj. suffix)] **1 :** having the shape or form of the Greek sigma or the letter S **2** *of a sponge spicule* **:** C-SHAPED

sig·mat·ic \(ˈ)sigˈmad·ik\ *adj* [ISV *sigmat-* (fr. Gk, fr. *sigma*) + *-ic*] *of a tense* **:** characterized by the addition of *s* to the root in forming the tense stem — used esp. of an aorist and a future in Greek and of corresponding forms in other Indo-European languages; opposed to *asigmatic*

sig·ma·tion \sigˈmāshən\ *n* -S **:** the addition of a sigma or *s* to a root

sig·ma·tism \ˈsigmə,tizəm\ *n* -S [ISV *sigmat-* (fr. Gk) + *-ism*] **:** faulty articulation of sibilants

sig·mo·don \ˈsigmə,dän\ *n, cap* [NL, fr. Gk *sigma* + NL *-odon*] **:** a genus of cricetid rodents including the American cotton rats

sig·mo·dont \-nt\ *adj* [*sigma* + *-odont*] **:** having bituberculate molars — used of a rodent

sig·mo·don·tes \,==ˈdän·(,)tēz\ *n pl, cap* [NL, fr. pl. of *Sigmodon*] *in former classifications* **:** a group of New World rodents approximately equal to the typical subfamily of Cricetidae

¹**sig·moid** \ˈsig,mòid\ *also* **sig·moi·dal** \(ˈ)sigˈmòidᵊl\ *adj* [*sigmoid* fr. Gk *sigmoeidēs*, fr. *sigma* + *-oeidēs* -oid; *sigmoidal* fr. Gk *sigmoeidēs* + E *-al*] **1 a :** curved like the letter C **b :** curved in two directions like the letter S **2 :** relating to the sigmoid flexure of the intestine ⟨the ~ artery branches from the inferior mesenteric⟩ — **sig·moi·dal·ly** \-ᵊlē\ *adv*

²**sigmoid** \"\ *n* -S **:** a sigmoid bodily part; *esp* **:** SIGMOID FLEXURE

sigmoid cavity *n* **:** either of two articulatory surfaces in the elbow: **a :** SEMILUNAR NOTCH — called also *greater sigmoid cavity* **b :** a surface on the inner side of the distal end of the radius for articulation with the ulna — called also *lesser sigmoid cavity*

sig·moid·ec·to·my \,sig,mòiˈdektəmē\ *n* -ES [²*sigmoid* + *-ectomy*] **:** surgical removal of part of the sigmoid flexure

sigmoid flexure *n* **1 :** an S-shaped curve (as in the neck of a bird or turtle) **2** *or* **sigmoid colon :** the contracted and crooked part of the intestine between the descending colon and the rectum terminating in the latter at the brim of the true pelvis — see DIGESTION illustration

sig·moid·itis \-ˈdīd·əs\ *n* -ES [NL, fr. ISV ²*sigmoid* + NL *-itis*] **:** inflammation of the sigmoid flexure of the colon

sigmoid notch *n* **:** a curved depression on the upper border of the lower jaw between the coronoid process and the articulatory condyle absent in lower primates and some extinct men

sig·moid·o·scope \sigˈmòidə,skōp\ *n* [²*sigmoid* + *-o-* + *-scope*] **:** a long hollow tubular instrument designed to be passed into the sigmoid colon through the anus and to permit inspection, diagnosis, treatment, and photography — **sig·moid·o·scop·ic** \=,=ˈ=ˈskäpik\ *adj* — **sig·moid·os·co·py** \,sig,mòiˈdäskəpē\ *n* -ES

sig·moid·os·to·my \,sig,mòiˈdästəmē\ *n* -ES [ISV ²*sigmoid* + *-o-* + *-stomy*] **:** transabdominal formation of an artificial anus in the sigmoid by means of surgery

sigmoid valve *n* **:** SEMILUNAR VALVE

¹**sign** \ˈsīn\ *n* -S *see sense 10b* [ME *signe*, fr. OF, fr. L *signum* sign, mark, figure, image; perh. akin to L *secare* to cut — more at SAW] **1 a :** a motion, gesture, or bodily action by which a thought is expressed or a command or a wish is made known **b :** SIGNAL 3a **c :** a unit of language (as a word) that means, stands for, designates, or denotes something to an interpreter — compare ICON, INDEX, SYMBOL **d :** one of the members of a methodical set of gestures used to represent language directly word by word or letter by letter — compare DACTYLOLOGY **2 a :** a conventional mark or device having a recognized particular meaning and used in place of words **b :** an ideographic mark, figure, or picture conventionally used in writing or printing to represent a usu. technical term or conception ⟨brackets are frequently used in bibliographical work as a ~ of inference —Fredson Bowers⟩ **c :** a character standing for a number or a contraction in braille or other system of writing for the blind **3 :** one of the 12 divisions of the zodiac that are marked by the positions of the 12 zodiacal constellations beginning at the point of intersection of the ecliptic and the equator and reckoning eastward each being now because of the precession of the equinoxes displaced 30 degrees to the west of the constellation bearing its name

THE SIGNS OF THE ZODIAC

NUMBER	NAME	SYMBOL	SUN ENTERS
1	Aries the Ram	♈	March 21
2	Taurus the Bull	♉	April 20
3	Gemini the Twins	♊	May 21
4	Cancer the Crab	♋	June 22
5	Leo the Lion	♌	July 23
6	Virgo the Virgin	♍	August 23
7	Libra the Balance	♎	September 23
8	Scorpio the Scorpion	♏	October 24
9	Sagittarius the Archer	♐	November 22
10	Capricorn the Goat	♑	December 22
11	Aquarius the Water Bearer	♒	January 20
12	Pisces the Fishes	♓	February 19

4 a : a character (as a flat, sharp) used in musical notation; *specif* **:** SEGNO **b :** a character indicating a relation between quantities (as + addition, = equality) or an operation performed (as the radical √, integral ∫, factorial !); *also* **:** a character that forms part of a representation of a number (as — in —4) **5** *archaic* **a :** a heraldic or military device (as on a banner or a shield) **b :** STANDARD, BANNER, ENSIGN **c signs** *pl, obs* **:** INSIGNIA **d** *obs* **:** an attesting mark (as on a seal) **e** *obs* **:** EFFIGY, IMAGE, IMPRINT **6 a :** a lettered board or other public display placed on or before a building, room, shop, or office to advertise the business there transacted or the name of the person or firm conducting it **b :** a conspicuously placed word or legend (as on a board or placard) of direction, warning, identification, or other information of general concern ⟨ignoring the Danger Keep Out ~ he opened the gate and entered⟩ ⟨looking for street ~*s*⟩ **c :** SIGNBOARD **7 a :** something material or external that stands for or signifies something spiritual — compare SACRAMENT 1 **b :** something that serves to indicate the presence or existence of a thing or quality or condition **:** TOKEN ⟨removed their hats as a ~ of respect⟩ ⟨all the ~*s* point to him as the guilty one⟩ ⟨~*s* of suffering in his drawn face and tightened mouth⟩ **c :** PRESAGE, PORTENT ⟨~*s* of an early spring⟩ ⟨the wind changed, a ~ of coming rain⟩ **d** (1) **:** an objective evidence of disease esp. as observed and interpreted by the physician rather than by the patient or lay observer ⟨narrow retinal vessels are a ~ of arteriosclerosis⟩ — contrasted with *symptom;* see PHYSICAL SIGN (2) **:** an indication of disease (as spores of the pathogen, gummy exudate) other than the reaction of the plant itself — contrasted with *symptom* **8 :** a remarkable event believed to indicate the will or power of a deity **:** MIRACLE, WONDER, PRODIGY, OMEN ⟨what things I have wrought in Egypt, and my ~*s* which I have done among them, that ye may know how that I am the Lord —Exod 10:2 (AV)⟩ **9 :** a grammatical inflection characteristic of a mood, tense or number ⟨*to* is traditionally the ~ of the infinitive in English⟩ ⟨*s* is the usual plural ~⟩ **10 a :** remaining evidence **:** VESTIGE — used chiefly in negative construction ⟨no ~ of human habitation⟩ ⟨no ~ of remorse⟩ ⟨not a sound, not a ~ of life anywhere⟩ **b** *pl usu* **sign :** traces (as footprints, droppings) left by a wild animal ⟨we found plenty of bear ~ about but never saw a bear⟩ **11** *obs* **:** SEMBLANCE, PRETENSE

syn MARK, TOKEN, BADGE, NOTE, SYMPTOM: SIGN is a very general term for any indication to be perceived by the senses or reason ⟨the *sign* of the cross⟩ ⟨suicide is a *sign* of failure, misery, and despair —Havelock Ellis⟩ ⟨the *signs* of her fate in a footprint here, a broken twig there, a trinket dropped by the way —Joseph Conrad⟩ ⟨a patient showing *signs* of improvement⟩ ⟨highway *signs*⟩ MARK may more strongly indicate some indication deeply impressed, inherently characteristic, or properly affixed ⟨the bitter experience left its *marks* on him⟩ ⟨the *mark* of a gentleman⟩ ⟨the *mark* of Cain on their foreheads, which sets them visibly apart from the rest of humanity before they have committed their crime —H.J.Morgenthau⟩ ⟨a flood's *marks*⟩ ⟨making his *mark* on the paper⟩ TOKEN may refer to a sign expressive of something intangible ⟨he wears a silver ring on his ankle as a *token* of his dignity —J.G. Frazer⟩ ⟨marriage if you do not regard it as a sacrament — as no doubt it ought to be regarded — was nothing more than a *token* that a couple intended to stick to each other —F.M. Ford⟩ BADGE designates a distinctive emblem or an accoutrement or a characteristic serving as an emblem to indicate a belonging or being part of ⟨a policeman's *badge*⟩ ⟨to wear a leopard's skin (the *badge* of royalty) —J.G.Frazer⟩ ⟨the diplomat wearing his *badge* of office, the Homburg hat —Tom Siler⟩ ⟨essentially we were taught to regard culture as a veneer, a *badge* of class distinction —Malcolm Cowley⟩ NOTE may indicate any distinguishing mark; it may suggest something that seems to emanate from a thing as an indication of its true, inherent nature ⟨tolerance, moderation, and pity are the abiding *notes* which help to keep Chaucer's poetry level with life —H.S.Bennett⟩ ⟨the genteel poverty which was the *note* of his grandfather's house —Archibald Marshall⟩ SYMPTOM may indicate a sign of some change, new development or old condition not thoroughly perceived ⟨the *symptoms* of disease⟩ ⟨the decadence of the walls was a *symptom* of the decline of that intense civic patriotism which had inspired medieval townsfolk —G.M.Trevelyan⟩ ⟨every *symptom* of being hopelessly in love —W.S.Gilbert⟩ **syn** see in addition CHARACTER — **at the sign of :** at the inn or tavern or shop having the sign specified ⟨an appointment to meet . . . *at the sign of* the griffin —Sir Walter Scott⟩

²**sign** \"\ *vb* -ED/-ING/-S [ME *signen*, fr. MF *signer*, fr. L *signare* to mark, seal, fr. *signum* sign, mark, figure, image — more at ¹SIGN] *vt* **1 a :** to place a sign upon **:** consecrate, bless, or mark esp. with the sign of the cross **b :** CROSS 3a **c :** to represent or indicate by a sign **2 a :** to affix a signature to **:** ratify or attest by hand or seal ⟨~ a legislative bill into law⟩ **:** subscribe in one's own handwriting ⟨confession was typed out and read to the prisoner, who then ~*ed* it⟩ **b :** to write down (one's name) ⟨~*ed* his name with a flourish⟩ **c :** to identify (a printed signature) with a symbol at the bottom of the first page **3 a :** to assign or convey formally ⟨~*ed* away his rights in the invention⟩ ⟨~*ed* over the property to his brother⟩ **b :** to accept as a professional obligation **:** agree to perform or carry out ⟨~*ed* to direct two plays for the newly formed company⟩ **4 :** to communicate by making a sign ⟨~*ed* that he was ready to leave, glancing toward the door⟩ **:** signify or express in signs or a sign language **5 :** to engage or hire by securing the signature of ⟨~*ed* to act in a movie⟩ ⟨the club has ~*ed* two new pitchers⟩ **6 :** to place signs on or along ⟨~ a street⟩ ⟨~ a highway intersection⟩ ~ *vi* **1 :** to write one's name esp. as a token of assent, responsibility, or obligation **2 :** to make a sign or signal **:** communicate or converse by signs or a sign language **3** *obs* **:** to be an omen or portent **:** BODE ⟨a mischief in the air . . . it ~*s* well, does it not —Shak.⟩ **4 :** to place signs (as along a highway)

signa *pl of* SIGNUM

sign·able \ˈsīnəbəl\ *adj* **1 :** suitable to be signed **2 :** requiring signature

¹**sig·nal** \ˈsignəl, -nᵊl\ *n* -S [ME, fr. MF *seignal, segnel, signal*, fr. ML *signale*, fr. LL, neut. of *signalis* of a sign, fr. L *signum* sign + *-alis* -al — more at SIGN] **1** *obs* **:** EMBLEM, SYMBOL **2** *archaic* **:** TOKEN, INDICATION ⟨in ~ of my love to thee —Shak.⟩ **3 a :** an act, event, or watchword that has been agreed upon as the occasion of concerted action ⟨~ fires of rebellion⟩ **b :** something that incites to action **:** an immediate cause or impulse ⟨his remark was the ~ for a storm of weeping⟩ **4 a :** a sound or gesture made to give warning or command ⟨~ that warns of an air raid⟩ ⟨waiting for the ~ to open fire⟩ **b :** an object placed to convey notice or warning: as (1) **:** a device (as a colored light) for regulating vehicular or pedestrian traffic (2) **:** a device used to warn trainmen or persons approaching a railroad of danger or to convey orders or information to a train crew **5 :** an object (as a flag on a pole) centered over a point so as to be observed from other positions in surveying **6 a :** an identifying tab (as of a thumb index) fastened to a book leaf at its fore edge **b :** a small projecting tab that attaches to the edge of a card or folder as an aid in filing or indexing **7 :** a play indicating to one's partner in a card game that one holds certain cards or desires a certain play **8 :** the beam of light reflected from the face of a crystal rotated into a particular position in a goniometer **9 a :** an object used to transmit or convey information beyond the range of human voice ⟨flying a flag as a distress ~⟩ **b :** the intelligence, message, sound, or image conveyed in telegraphy, telephony, radio, radar, or television **c :** a detectable physical quantity or impulse (as a voltage, current, magnetic field strength) by which messages or information can be transmitted **10 :** a speech sound or form or combination of sounds and forms that communicates a meaning or a difference in meaning — compare MORPHEME, PHONEME

²**signal** \"\ *vb* **signaled** *or* **signalled; signaled** *or* **signalled; signaling** *or* **signalling; signals** *vt* **1 :** to notify by a signal **:** make a signal to ⟨~*ed* his wife to leave the room⟩ ⟨~*ed* the fleet to turn back⟩ **2 a :** to communicate (a message) by signals ⟨~ orders to a field unit⟩ **b :** announce by signal ⟨the ship ~*ed* her departure with warning blasts on the whistle⟩ **c :** to determine or fix (meaning) in a speech utterance ⟨the kind of sentence . . . is ~*ed* by special contrastive patterns in the arrangement of . . . parts of speech —C.C.Fries⟩ **:** constitute a characteristic feature of (a meaningful linguistic form) ⟨plurality is usually ~*ed* by *s*⟩ **3 :** SIGNALIZE ⟨waiter with tray ~*s* a café —*Nat'l Geographic*⟩ ~ *vi* **:** to make or send a signal ⟨frantically ~*ing* with both arms⟩

³**signal** \"\ *adj* [modif. of F *signalé*, past part. of *signaler* to distinguish, fr. OIt *segnalare* to signal, distinguish, fr. *segnale* signal, fr. ML *signale*] **1 :** distinguished from what is ordinary **:** NOTICEABLE, OUTSTANDING ⟨~ achievement⟩ ⟨students of ~ promise⟩ ⟨~ experience⟩ **2 :** SIGNIFICATIVE, DISTINCTIVE ⟨~ markings⟩ **3 :** employed or used in signaling ⟨~ beacon⟩ ⟨~ flags⟩ ⟨~ corps⟩ **syn** see NOTICEABLE

signal board *n* **:** a board on which signals are recorded; *esp* **:** such a board with electrical connections for indicating the source of a signal **:** ANNUNCIATOR

signal box *n, Brit* **:** SIGNAL TOWER

signal bridge *n* **1 :** BRIDGE 3 l **2 :** an open platform near the navigating bridge of a warship for the use of signalmen

sig·nal·er *or* **sig·nal·ler** \-ə(r)\ *n* -S **1 :** one that signals **:** a signaling device or mechanism **2 :** SIGNALMAN

signal halyard *or* **signal halliard** *n* **:** a woven cotton line used for halyards on signal yards because free from kinking

sig·nal·i·ty \sigˈnaləd·ē\ *n* -ES [³*signal* + *-ity*] **:** the quality or state of being notable or outstanding **:** SIGNIFICANCE

sig·nal·iza·tion \,signələˈzāshən, -nᵊlə-, -nə,līˈz-, -nᵊl,īˈz-\ *n* -S **1 :** the act of signalizing **2 :** the act of equipping with signals ⟨parking restrictions . . . and improved ~ —Robert Moses⟩

sig·nal·ize \ˈ=nə,līz, -nᵊl,īz\ *vb* -ED/-ING/-S *see -ize in Explan Notes* [³*signal* + *-ize*] *vt* **1 :** to make conspicuous **:** make known **:** MARK, DISTINGUISH ⟨conform to some ceremonial prescribed to ~ loyalty —G.W.Johnson⟩ ⟨~ their product by a distinctive name or label —D.M.Potter⟩ **:** CELEBRATE ⟨~ an anniversary⟩ **2 :** to point out carefully or distinctly **:** draw attention to ⟨to ~ the extension of an idea, *moreover* is usually more appropriate than *also* —R.M.Weaver⟩ **3 a :** to make signals to **:** SIGNAL ⟨~ an approaching ship⟩ **b :** to announce or indicate by a signal ⟨stood up to ~ the departure of the ladies —J.W.Krutch⟩ **4 :** to place traffic signals at or on ⟨~ an intersection⟩ ~ *vi* **:** to send or exchange signals **:** converse by means of signals

sig·nal·ly \-nəl|ē, -nᵊl|, |i\ *adv* **1 :** in a signal manner **:** NOTABLY, UNMISTAKABLY, REMARKABLY ⟨~ undiplomatic methods of dealing with those . . . in a position to help them —R.D.Altick⟩ **2 :** by way of a signal ⟨a term which is used symbolically and not ~ —Susanne K. Langer⟩

sig·nal·man \|mən\ *n, pl* **signalmen 1 :** one who inspects and maintains railroad signals **2 a** *Brit* **:** one who sets railroad signals **b :** a logger who signals orders from the yard boss to the yarder engineer **c :** a member of a construction crew who signals operators of power hoisting equipment — called also *highballer* **3 :** a petty officer esp. qualified in visual-signal duties

sig·nal·ment \|mənt\ *n* -S [F *signalement*, fr. *signaler* to distinguish, mark out, describe + *-ment* — more at SIGNAL] **:** description by peculiar, appropriate, or characteristic marks; *specif* **:** the systematic description of a person for purposes of identification — compare BERTILLON SYSTEM; DACTYLOGRAPHY, DACTYLOSCOPY

signal noise ratio *n* **:** the ratio of radio field intensity to noise field intensity; *also* **:** the ratio of the signal transmitted through a piece of radio equipment to the noise generated within the equipment itself

signal number *n* **:** a naval officer's numerical order on the official seniority list

signal oil *n* **:** a petroleum distillate that burns slowly and cleanly and is used in signal lanterns

signal plate *n* **:** an element of a television camera tube from which the electrical signal is obtained for transmission into the television system

signal red *n* **:** CHINESE VERMILION

signals *pl of* SIGNAL, *pres 3d sing of* SIGNAL

signal tower *n* **:** an enclosed or armored elevated structure from which signals are displayed or controlled; *specif* **:** a switch tower for a system of railroad signals

sig·na·ry \ˈsignərē\ *n* -ES [L *signum* sign + E *-ary*] **:** a system or list of syllabic or alphabetic signs of a language or an ancient script ⟨hieroglyphic ~⟩

sig·na·tary \ˈsignə,terē\ *n* -ES [L *signatus* (past part. of *signare* to mark, seal) + E *-ary* — more at SIGN] **:** SIGNATORY

sig·nate \ˈsig,nāt, -,nət\ *adj* [L *signatus*, past part. of *signare* to mark, seal, designate — more at SIGN] **1 :** DESIGNATED, IDENTIFIED **2 :** having markings like letters

signate matter *n* **:** matter that is numerically distinct in different individuals but is the same in quality or character for cognition

sig·na·tion \sigˈnāshən\ *n* -S [LL *signation-*, *signatio*, fr. *signatus* (past part. of *signare* to make the sign of the cross, fr. L, to mark, seal) + L *-ion-*, *-io* -ion] **1 :** the act of making the sign of the cross **2** *obs* **:** a distinguishing mark

¹**sig·na·to·ry** \ˈsignə,tōrē, -tȯr-, -ri\ *adj* [L *signatorius* of sealing, fr. *signatus* + *-orius* -ory] **1** *obs* **:** relating to a seal **:** used in sealing **2 :** joining or sharing in a signature **:** bound by the terms of a signed agreement

²**signatory** \"\ *n* -ES **:** a signer with another; *specif* **:** a government bound with others to the terms of a signed convention

sig·na·tur·al \-nə,chu̇rəl\ *adj* **:** of or relating to a signature

¹**sig·na·ture** \ˈsignə,chu̇(ə)r, -u̇ə, -nəchə(r), -nēchə(r) *also* -nə,tu̇(ə)r *or* -nə,tyu̇- *or* -u̇ə\ *n* -S [MF or ML; MF, fr. ML *signatura*, fr. L *signatus* (past part. of *signare* to mark, seal) + *-ura* -ure — more at SIGN] **1** *Scots law* **:** a writing prepared to be signed or sealed as a warrant for a proposed royal grant or charter **2 a :** the name of a person written with his own hand to signify that the writing which precedes accords with his wishes or intentions **b :** the act of signing one's name ⟨letters waiting for his ~⟩ ⟨witnesses to the ~⟩ **3 :** a feature in the appearance or qualities of a natural object (as a plant) formerly held to indicate its utility in medicine either because of a fancied resemblance to a body part (as a heart-shaped leaf indicating utility in heart disease) or because of a presumed relation to some phase of a disease (as the prickly nature of thistle indicating utility in case of a stitch in the side) **4 a** *obs* **:** STAMP, IMPRESSION **b :** a distinguishing or identifying mark, feature, or quality ⟨a clear little eye in her center, the ~ of a hurricane —*Time*⟩ ⟨the ~ of the Church is legible enough on the houses and streets of Oxford —P.E.More⟩ **5 a :** a letter or figure placed usu. at the bottom of the first page on each sheet of printed pages (as of a book) as a direction to the binder in arranging and gathering the sheets **b :** the sheet itself which when folded becomes one unit of the book — compare GATHERING, QUIRE **6 a** *obs* **:** natural markings forming an image or figure **b** *obs* **:** BIRTHMARK **7 a :** KEY SIGNATURE **b :** TIME SIGNATURE **8 :** the part of a medical prescription which contains the directions to the patient — abbr. *s, Sig.* **9 :** a tune, sound effect, or pictorial device used to identify a program, entertainer, or orchestra

²**signature** \"\ *vt* -ED/-ING/-S **1** *obs* **:** DESIGNATE **2 :** to subscribe to or authenticate with one's signature

signature by mark : an indication usu. in the presence of witnesses by a distinctive sign or mark (as an X) of acquiescence in or assent to the content of a document by one unable to write

sig·na·ture·less \-ləs\ *adj* **:** lacking a signature **:** UNSIGNED

signature loan *n* **:** a loan granted without security

signature tune *n* **:** a melody, passage, or song chosen by an orchestra or musical entertainer as a means of identification and played at the opening or close or both of each program

sig·na·tur·ist \-u̇rəst, -chərə-\ *n* -S **:** one who holds to belief in signatures of healing agents

signboard \ˈ=,=\ *n* **1 :** a board bearing a notice or sign — compare BILLBOARD **2 :** a conspicuous indication or warning

signed *past of* SIGN

signed number *n* **:** one of a system of numbers represented by a sign + or — prefixed to a digit or other numeral such that the sum of two numbers with unlike signs and like numerical elements is 0

sign·ee \(ˈ)sīˈnē\ *n* -S [²*sign* + *-ee*] **:** SIGNATORY

sign·er \ˈsīnə(r)\ *n* -S **1 :** one that signs **:** SIGNATORY **2 :** one who uses sign language

¹**sig·net** \ˈsignət, *usu* -əd·+V\ *n* -S [ME, fr. MF, dim. of *signe* sign, seal — more at SIGN] **1 :** a seal used officially to give personal authority to a document in lieu of signature: **a :** the seal used formerly by the sovereign of England in sealing private letters and grants prior to the affixing of the great seal **b :** the seal used formerly in Scotland to authenticate royal warrants connected with administration of justice **2 a :** the impression made by or as if by a signet **b :** an identifying or authenticating mark or stamp **3 a :** a small intaglio seal (as in a finger ring) **b :** SIGNET RING

²**signet** \"\ *vt* -ED/-ING/-S [ME (Sc dial.) *signeten*, fr. *signet*, n.] **:** to stamp or authenticate with a signet

signet ring *n* **1 :** a finger ring having a bezel engraved with a signet, seal, or monogram or bearing a stone so engraved **:** SEAL RING **2 :** something shaped like a signet ring; *esp* **:** a malaria parasite in an intracellular developmental stage in which the nucleus is peripheral and the cytoplasm somewhat attenuated and annular

sig·ni·fer \ˈsignəfə(r)\ *n* -S [L, fr. *signifer*, adj., bearing a sign, bearing the heavenly signs, fr. *signum* sign + *-i-* + *-fer* -ferous — more at SIGN] **1** *obs* **:** ZODIAC **2 :** STANDARD-BEARER

sig·ni·fi·able \ˈsignə,fīəbəl, ˌ==ˈ===\ *adj* **:** capable of being represented by a sign or symbol

sig·ni·fi·ant \ˈ==,fīənt\ *n* -S [F, fr. pres. part. of *signifier* to signify — more at SIGNIFY] **:** SIGNIFICANT, SIGN

sig·nif·ic \(ˈ)sigˈnifik\ *adj* [*signify* + *-ic*] **:** acting as a sign or signal ⟨argues that the expression of ideas may be through a symbolic function, not a ~ function —L.W.Elder⟩

sig·nif·i·cance \sigˈnifəkən(t)s, -fēk-\ *n* -S [ME *significaunce*, fr. L *significantia*, fr. *significant-*, *significans* + *-ia* -y] **1 a :** something signified **:** IMPORT, MEANING, BEARING ⟨a familiar sight enough though it broke upon her now with a new ~ —Thomas Hardy⟩ ⟨having cosmic ~s, which I never suspected, extracted from my work —T.S.Eliot⟩ ⟨apt to read ~ into every casual remark⟩ **b :** the quality of conveying or implying **:** SUGGESTIVENESS ⟨the young gentleman uttered this exultant sound with mysterious ~ —Charles Dickens⟩ **2 a :** the quality of being important **:** CONSEQUENCE, MOMENT ⟨knack for discovering the ordinary and investing it with warmth and ~ —Arthur Knight⟩ ⟨the industrial ~ of coal⟩ **b :** the quality of being statistically significant **syn** see IMPORTANCE

sig·nif·i·can·cy \-kənsē, -si\ *n* -ES [L *significantia*] **1 :** the quality or state of being significant **:** EXPRESSIVENESS **2 :** SIGNIFICANCE

¹**sig·nif·i·cant** \-kənt\ *adj* [L *significant-*, *significans*, pres. part. of *significare* to signify — more at SIGNIFY] **1 :** having meaning; *esp* **:** full of import **:** SUGGESTIVE, EXPRESSIVE ⟨the painter's task to pick out the ~ details —Herbert Read⟩ ⟨~ anecdote⟩ **2 a :** suggesting or containing some concealed, disguised, or special meaning **:** standing as a sign or token ⟨perhaps her glance was ~⟩ **b :** INDICATIVE ⟨his actions were more ~ of his real purpose than were his words⟩ **3 a :** having or likely to have influence or effect **:** deserving to be considered **:** IMPORTANT, WEIGHTY, NOTABLE ⟨even though the individual results may seem small, the total of them is ~ —F.D.Roosevelt⟩ **b :** characterized by conveyance of an idea, thought, or feeling ⟨transform what would otherwise be meaningless juxtapositions or sequences of sensations into ~ entities —Vernon Lee⟩ **c :** probably caused by something other than mere chance ⟨~ decrease in average yearly growth⟩ ⟨statistically ~ correlation between vitamin deficiency and disease⟩ **d :** characteristic and essential to the determination of some larger element of a language **:** DISTINCTIVE ⟨a ~ grammatical form⟩ ⟨every language . . . moves within a clearly definable range of ~ speech sounds —R.A.Hall b.1911⟩ ⟨the difference between the initial sounds of *keel* and *cool* is not ~ in English⟩ **syn** see EXPRESSIVE

²**significant** \"\ *n* -S **:** something that has or conveys significance **:** SIGN, TOKEN, SYMBOL

significant figures *n pl* **:** figures of a number that begin with the first figure to the left that is not zero and that end with the last figure to the right that is not zero or is a zero that is considered to be correct

sig·nif·i·cant·ly *adv* **:** in a significant manner ⟨mentioned ~ that he was very short of money⟩ **:** to a significant degree ⟨~ large number of exceptions⟩ ⟨men made ~ higher scores than the women⟩

sig·nif·i·cate \-kət, -fə,kāt\ *n* -S [ME *significat*, fr. L *significatum*, fr. neut. of *significatus*, past part. of *significare*] **1 a :** thing that is signified or indicated **2 :** one of several characters or instances signified by a common term

sig·ni·fi·ca·tion \,signəfəˈkāshən\ *n* -S [ME *significacioun*, fr. OF *signification*, fr. L *signification-*, *significatio*, fr. *significatus* (past part. of *significare* to signify) + *-ion-*, *-io* -ion — more at SIGNIFY] **1 a :** the act of signifying **:** a making known (as a choice, intent, decision) by signs or other means **b :** a formal notification ⟨~ of a judicial decree⟩ **2 a :** IMPORT, SIGNIFICANCY ⟨few of our poets have responded to its beauty and ~ —Norman Douglas⟩ **b :** the meaning that a sign, character, or token is intended to convey **:** SENSE ⟨using the word in its ordinary ~⟩ **c** *obs* **:** TOKEN, INDICATION **3** *chiefly dial* **:** IMPORTANCE, CONSEQUENCE **4 a :** the connotation or comprehension of a term or the implications of a proposition **b :** the process of designating — compare DESIGNATION 6

¹**sig·nif·i·ca·tive** \sigˈnifə,kā|d·|iv, -,kə|, |t|, |ēv *also* |əv\ *adj* [ME, fr. MF *significatif*, fr. LL *significativus*, fr. L *significatus* + *-ivus* -ive] **1 :** pointing out or representing by an external sign **:** serving as a sign **:** INDICATIVE **2 :** having signification or meaning **:** expressive of a usu. concealed meaning **:** SIGNIFICANT, SUGGESTIVE **3 :** of or relating to signification (sense 4) **:** DESIGNATIVE ⟨in the proposition "she is a beauty" *beauty* is a ~ term⟩ — **sig·nif·i·ca·tive·ly** \|əvlē, -li\ *adv* — **sig·nif·i·ca·tive·ness** \|ivnəs, |ēv- *also* |əv-\ *n* -ES

²**significative** \"\ *n* -S **:** a significative thing or term

sig·nif·i·ca·tor \-,kād·ə(r), -ātə-\ *n* -S [LL, fr. L *significatus* + *-or*] **:** one that signifies or foreshows; *specif* **:** a planet that rules a house in a horoscope

significator of life : ASCENDANT 1

sig·nif·i·ca·to·ry \-,kə,tōrē\ *adj* [LL *significatorius*, fr. L *significatus* + *-orius* -ory] **:** SIGNIFICATIVE ⟨names of deities are often ~ of their special powers⟩

sig·nif·i·ca·tum \(,)sig,nifəˈkād·əm, -kād-\ *n, pl* **significa·ta** \-d·ə\ [L — more at SIGNIFICATE] **:** something that a sign intensionally signifies **:** SIGNIFICATION

sig·nif·i·ca·vit \-kāvət, -kāv-\ *n* -S [ME, fr. L, he has signified (the first word in the writ), 3d per. sing. perf. ind. of *significare*] **1 a :** a bishop's certificate that a person has been in a state of excommunication for 40 days **b :** a resulting chancery writ ordering the recalcitrant's imprisonment until submission to the church **2 :** a writ commanding a stay of a suit because of plaintiff's excommunication

sig·nif·ics \sigˈnifiks\ *n pl but sing or pl in constr* [*signify* + *-ics*] **:** SEMIOTIC, SEMANTICS

si·gni·fié \ˌsēnyəfˈyā\ *n* -S [F, fr. past part. of *signifier*] **:** SIGNIFICATUM

sig·ni·fi·er \ˈsignə,fī(ə)r, -īə\ *n* -S **:** one that signifies **:** SIGN

sig·ni·fy \-ī\ *vb* -ED/-ING/-ES [ME *signifien*, fr. OF *signifier*, fr. L *significare*, fr. *signum* sign, mark + *-i-* + *-ficare* -fy — more at SIGN] *vt* **1 a :** to be a sign of **:** MEAN, DENOTE ⟨a well-proportioned voice that *signified* a sense of justice and compassion —Osbert Sitwell⟩ ⟨sentences ~ propositions⟩ ⟨perfection . . . *signifies* the approaching end of an epoch —A.N. Whitehead⟩ ⟨the name is derived from the Celtic *alb*, which by some is made to ~ white, by others height —Marrion Wilcox⟩ **b :** to bear as an inference or logical consequence **:** IMPLY ⟨machinery *signifies* urgency —David Sylvester⟩ **2 a :** to show or make known esp. by a conventional token (as word, signal, gesture) ⟨*signified* his desire for another slice⟩ **b :** ANNOUNCE, INTIMATE ⟨*signified* his willingness to run for the office⟩ **3** *obs* **:** INFORM ~ *vi* **:** to have meaning or significance **:** be of consequence **:** MATTER ⟨according to this interpretation, only economic relations ~ —*Times Lit. Supp.*⟩ ⟨never mind, it doesn't ~⟩ ⟨married to Vulcan or married to Mars, what does it ~ —W.S.Gilbert⟩ **syn** see MEAN

sign in *vi* **:** to make a record of arrival by signing a register or punching a time clock ~ *vt* **:** to record arrival of (a person) or receipt of (an article) by signing

signing *pres part of* SIGN

sign·ist \ˈsīnəst\ *n* -S [¹*sign* + *-ist*] **1 :** SIGN PAINTER **2 :** one who believes in the exclusive use of signs for teaching the deaf

sign language *n* **1 :** a method of communicating by means of systematic conventionalized chiefly manual gestures used by the deaf or by people speaking different languages ⟨*sign language* of the American Plains Indians⟩ **2 :** DACTYLOLOGY

sign·less \ˈsīnləs\ *adj* **:** having no algebraic sign

sign·man \-mən\ *n, pl* **signmen :** SIGN PAINTER

sign manual *n, pl* **signs manual 1 a :** SIGNATURE; *specif* **:** the king's signature on a royal grant or charter placed at the top of the document **b :** an identifying mark or device **2 :** a hand gesture for conveying a command or message

sign of aggregation : any of various conventional devices used in mathematics to indicate that two or more terms are to be treated as one quantity — compare BRACE, BRACKET, PARENTHESIS, VINCULUM

sign off *vi* **1 :** to withdraw from an engagement or association **2 :** to make a sign-off bid ⟨partner *signed off* with four spades⟩ **3 a :** to announce the end of a message, program, or broadcast and discontinue transmitting **b :** to end a speech or a conversation **:** fall silent **c :** to cease or withdraw from an activity **:** QUIT

sign-off \ˈ=,=\ *n* -S [*sign off*] **:** the act of signing off; *specif* **:** a bid in contract conventionally urging one's partner to pass

sign of inequality : a sign (as ≠ or ≑) indicating that one quantity is not equal to another

sign of summation : the Greek character Σ placed before a general term to indicate the sum of all terms of which it is the type

sign of the cross : a gesture of the hand forming a cross; *esp* **:** such a motion from one's forehead to the breast and from the left to the right shoulder in the Roman Catholic Church or from the right to the left shoulder in the Eastern Orthodox Church

sign on *vi* **:** to engage oneself for duty by signature or agreement **:** ENLIST ⟨*signed on* as a member of the crew⟩ ⟨*signed on* for another six years⟩ ~ *vt* **:** to secure the signature of **:** sign up **:** EMPLOY

si·gnor *also* **si·gnior** \(ˈ)sēnˈyō(ə)r, -yō(-\ *n, pl* **signors** \-rz\ *or* **si·gno·ri** \ˌ=ˈyō(,)rē, -ȯ(,)rē\ [It *signor* (when followed by a name), *signore*, fr. ML *senior* superior, magnate, lord, fr. L, adj., elder — more at SENIOR] **1 :** a usu. Italian man of rank or gentility **2 :** MISTER — used as a title of courtesy prefixed to the name of an Italian man

si·gno·ra \(ˈ)sēnˈyōrə, -yȯrə\ *n, pl* **signoras** \-rəz\ *or* **si·gno·re** \-ōr(,)ā, -ȯ(,)rā\ [It, fem. of *signore*] **1 :** an Italian married woman usu. of rank or gentility **2 :** MISTRESS — used as a title prefixed to the name of an Italian married woman

si·gno·re \-ōr(,)ā, -ȯ(,)r|\ *n, pl* **signo·ri** \|ē\ [It] **:** SIGNOR 1

si·gno·ria \,sēnyəˈrēə\ *n* -S [It, fr. *signore* + *-ia* -y (fr. L)] **:** SIGNORY

si·gno·ri·al \(ˈ)sēnˈyōrēəl, -yȯr-; ˌsēnyəˈr-\ *adj* **:** relating or belonging to a signory or a lord ⟨~ privilege⟩ ⟨~ courts⟩

si·gno·ri·na \ˌsēnyəˈrēnə\ *n, pl* **signorinas** \-rēnəz\ *or* **signori·ne** \-rē(,)nā\ [It, dim. of *signora*] **1 :** an unmarried Italian woman **2 :** MISS — used as a title prefixed to the name of an unmarried Italian woman

¹**si·gno·ry** *or* **si·gnio·ry** \ˈsēnyərē\ *n* -ES [ME *signerie*, *signorie*, fr. MF *seigneurie*, *signerie*, *signorie* — more at SEIGNEURY] **:** SEIGNIORY

²**signory** \"\ *n* -ES [It *signoria*] **:** the chief executive body of a medieval Italian city (as Venice)

sign out *vi* **:** to indicate departure by signing a register ⟨*signed out* of her dormitory for the evening⟩ ⟨*sign out* of a hospital⟩ or by punching a time clock ~ *vt* **:** to record or approve the release or departure of ⟨*sign* books *out* of a library⟩

sign painter *n* **:** one who paints signs, notices, billboards, posters

¹**signpost** \ˈ=,=\ *n* [¹*sign* + *post*] **1 :** a post bearing a sign or signs; *specif* **:** a guidepost at a crossroad **2 :** GUIDE, BEACON ⟨~s which, in a well-regulated market, show the way along which savings ought to move —W.T.C.King⟩

²**signpost** \"\ *vt* **:** to provide with signposts or guides ⟨statistics and endpaper maps to ~ the reader —Grace Banyard⟩

signs *pl of* SIGN, *pres 3d sing of* SIGN

sig·num \ˈsignəm\ *n, pl* **sig·na** \-nə\ [L — more at SIGN] **1 :** something that marks or identifies or represents **:** SIGN, SIGNATURE **2** [ML, fr. LL, ringing of a bell, fr. L, sign] **:** a tower bell large enough to serve as a signal

sign up *vi* **:** to join a working force or an organization or scheme or accept an obligation by signing a contract **:** CONTRACT ⟨*sign up* for a set of reference volumes⟩ ~ *vt* **:** to induce to sign a contract **:** contract with ⟨*sign* a customer *up* for a new car⟩

sign vehicle *n* **:** a particular event (as a sound or gesture) or object (as a written character or word) that acts as a sign

signwriter \ˈ=,==\ *n* **:** one that letters signs (as for advertising)

sigs *pl of* SIG

si·gua \ˈsē(,)(g)wä\ *n, pl* **sigua** *or* **siguas** *usu cap* [Sp, of AmerInd origin] **1 :** a Nahuatlan people on the Atlantic coast of Panama **2 :** a member of the Sigua people

si·ha·sa·pa \səˈhäsəpə\ *n, pl* **sihasapa** *or* **sihasapas** *usu cap* **1 :** SIKSIKA **2 :** a people of the western plains constituting a division of the Teton Dakotas

¹**si·ka** \ˈsēkə\ *n* -S [Jap *shika*] **1 :** JAPANESE DEER **2 :** any of several deers of the eastern Asiatic mainland closely related to the Japanese deer

²**sika** \ˈsikə\ *n* -S [of Cariban origin; akin to Galibi *chico* chigoe] **:** CHIGOE

sikar *or* **sikhara** *var of* SHIKARA

sike \ˈsīk\ *n* -S [ME *syke*, *sike*, fr. OE *sīc*; akin to OHG *seih* urine, ON *sīk* small stream, ditch, OE *sicerian* to trickle — more at SICKER] **1** *dial chiefly Brit* **:** a small stream; *esp* **:** one that dries up in summer **:** BROOK, GUTTER **2** *dial chiefly Brit* **:** DITCH, TRENCH, DRAIN

si·kel·i·an \səˈkelēən\ *n* -S [Gk *sikeloi* Sicels + E *-ian*] **:** SICEL

sikeliot *cap, var of* SICELIOT

sik·er \ˈsikə(r)\ *chiefly Scot var of* ¹SICKER

¹**sikh** \ˈsēk\ *n* -S *usu cap* [Hindi, lit., disciple, fr. Skt *śikṣati* he studies, desiderative of *śaknoti* he is strong, is able — more at SHAKTI] **:** an adherent of Sikhism

²**sikh** \"\ *adj, usu cap* **1 :** of, relating to, or characteristic of Sikhism **2 :** of, relating to, or characteristic of the Sikhs

sikh·ism \ˈsē,kizəm\ *n* -S *cap* [¹*sikh* + *-ism*] **:** a radically monotheistic religion of India founded about 1500 in the Punjab and characterized by its worship of one deity, by its allegiance to sacred scriptures, and by its witness to a line of 10 personal gurus until the guruship was transferred in 1708 — compare KHALSA 2, NANAKPANTHI

si·kin·nis \səˈkinəs\ *n* -ES [Gk, of Thraco-Phrygian origin] **:** a grotesque orgiastic dance of ancient Greece associated with the satyric drama

sik·kim·ese \ˌsikəˈmēz, -ēs\ *n, pl* **sikkimese** *cap* [*Sikkim* + E *-ese*] **:** a native or inhabitant of the territory of Sikkim in northeastern India

sik·si·ka \ˈsiksəkə\ *n, pl* **siksika** *or* **siksikas** *usu cap* [Blackfoot, fr. *siksinam* black + *oqkatsh* foot] **1 a :** an Algonquian people of Montana and southern Alberta and Saskatchewan, Canada **b :** a member of such people **2 a :** ¹BLACKFOOT 1a **b :** ¹BLACKFOOT 1b

siku *var of* SICU

sil \ˈsil\ *n* -S [L] **:** YELLOW OCHER 1

sil- *comb form* [*silicon*] **:** containing or derived from silicon ⟨*silane*⟩ — compare SILIC-

sil *abbr* **1** silence **2** silver

sila- *or* **sil-** *comb form* [ISV, fr. *sil-* + *-a-*] **:** containing silicon esp. in place of carbon ⟨*sila*cyclohexane C_5SiH_{12}⟩

¹**si·lage** \ˈsīlij, -lēj\ *n* -S [short for ¹*ensilage*] **:** fodder (as of field corn, sorghum, grass, or clover) either green or mature converted into succulent winter feed for livestock through processes of fermentation usu. by being cut fine and blown into an airtight chamber (as a silo) where it is compressed to exclude air and where it undergoes an acid fermentation that retards spoiling — called also *ensilage*

²**silage** \"\ *vt* -ED/-ING/-S **:** ENSILE

silage cutter *n* **1 :** a stationary machine for chopping forage for silage and delivering it into the silo **2** *or* **silage harvester :** FIELD CHOPPER

sil·ane \ˈsi,lān\ *n* -S [ISV *sil-* + *methane*] **:** any of several silicon hydrides having the general formula Si_nH_{2n+2} analogous to that of hydrocarbons of the methane series; *esp* **:** MONOSILANE — compare CHLOROSILANE, DISILANE

sil·crete \ˈsil,krēt\ *n* -S [*silica* + ²*concrete*] **:** a superficial quartzite formed by the cementation of rock fragments (as soil, sand, or gravel) by silica

sild \ˈsil\ *n, pl* **sild** *or* **silds** [Norw, herring; akin to ON *sīld*, *síld* herring and perh. to ON *sā* to sow — more at SOW] **:** a young herring other than a brisling that is canned as a sardine in Norway

¹**sile** \ˈsī(ə)l\ *n* -S [ME, perh. fr. OE *sȳl* pillar, column; akin to OHG *sūl* pillar, ON *sūl*, *sūla*, Goth *sauls*] *Scot* **:** BEAM, RAFTER

²**sile** \"\ *vi* -ED/-ING/-S [ME] *dial chiefly Brit* **:** to move esp. downward with a flowing or gliding motion ⟨the rain *siled* down⟩

³**sile** \"\ *vt* -ED/-ING/-S [ME *silen*, of Scand origin; akin to Sw *sila* to strain, *sil* strainer, Norw *sile* to strain, *sil* strainer] *dial Brit* **:** STRAIN, FILTER ⟨~ milk⟩

⁴**sile** \"\ *n* -S [ME, of Scand origin; akin to Sw & Norw *sil* strainer] *dial Brit* **:** STRAINER, SIEVE

⁵**sile** \"\ *dial var of* SOIL

⁶**sile** \"\ *n* -S [of Scand origin; akin to ON *sīld* herring — more at SILD] *dial Brit* **:** spawn or fry of fish (as herring)

si·len \ˈsīlən\ *n* -S [L *silenus* — more at SILENUS] **:** SILENUS

¹**si·lence** \ˈsīlən(t)s\ *n* -S [ME, fr. OF, fr. L *silentium*, fr. *silent-*, *silens* silent] **1 :** the state of keeping or being silent **:** forbearance from speech or noise **:** MUTENESS ⟨that ~ in the kitchen when, on a drowsy afternoon, the ticking of the clock

would stop —Carson McCullers⟩ ⟨sat close together smoking contentedly and in ~ —Fred Majdalany⟩ ⟨complete radio ~ guarded whereabouts of the . . . powerful task force —K.M. Dodson⟩ — often used interjectionally **2 a :** absence of sound **:** absence of noise ⟨~ of midnight⟩ **b :** a general stillness **:** a relative stillness in which particular sounds may be distinctly heard ⟨rooster would crow lingeringly in the sunny ~ —Marjory S. Douglas⟩ ⟨starlings chattered in a rural ~ —Aldous Huxley⟩ **3 :** absence of mention: **a :** OBLIVION, OBSCURITY ⟨wrote it in the thirties of last century and after seventy years of ~ someone gave it forth again —H.J.Laski⟩ **b** (1) **:** failure to make something known **:** tacit omission ⟨in the ~ of any positive rule it would be presumed that foreign corporations were by comity permitted to make contracts —Charles Fairman⟩ ⟨took advantage of the fundamental law's ~ to twist it to their own purposes —F.A.Ogg & Harold Zink⟩ ⟨the studied ~s of the document as to the existence of God —W.L.Sperry⟩ (2) **:** SECRECY ⟨broke the ~ which has shrouded use of radar for aircraft navigation by the armed forces —David Mannheimer⟩ **c :** withholding from written communication ⟨a decade of ~ on the part of such a writer —M.D.Geismar⟩; *broadly* **:** cessation of any state of communicativeness or productivity ⟨producing sculptors of this authority after so long and heavy a ~ —J.T.Soby⟩ **4 a :** a period of being silent **:** a space of time marked by the cessation or absence of speech or of noises ⟨a movie of waiting and of ~s at the pithead and in the pit as the rescuers work their way toward the trapped men —*Time*⟩; *specif* **:** such a period observed in commemoration **b :** REST 5 ⟨elegiac meter of the poems (in which a ~ takes the place of the last foot of the distich) —Madeleine S. & J.L.Miller⟩ **5 a** *usu cap* **:** the state beyond death **b :** DEATH **6 :** lack of flavor or odor in distilled spirits **:** FLATNESS

²silence \"\ *vb* -ED/-ING/-S *vt* **1 :** to compel or reduce to silence **:** cause to be still **:** stop the noise of **:** STILL ⟨whatever specious arguments would ~ an opponent —John Dewey⟩ ⟨the air intake must be *silenced* to some degree —R.L.Boyer⟩ **2 a :** to restrain from the exercise of any function involving the expression of opinion; *esp* **:** to restrain from the act of preaching **b :** to put down **:** REPRESS, SUPPRESS ⟨violent means were used to ~ unwelcome opinions —R.P.Ludlum⟩ ⟨a nation that ~s or intimidates original minds —H.S. Commager⟩ **3 :** to cause to cease hostile firing by return fire or bombing ⟨~ the batteries of an enemy⟩ ⟨*silenced* the guns with hand grenades —P.W.Thompson⟩ ~ *vi* **1 :** to become silent **2 :** to cause silence ⟨the common denominator ~s and satisfies —B.N.Cardozo⟩

silence cloth *n* **:** a pad (as of flannel or felt) used under a tablecloth

silenced *adj* [fr. past part. of ²*silence*] **:** reduced to silence

si·lenc·er \-nsə(r)\ *n* -S **:** one that silences: as **a :** a device that when applied to exhaust or suction lines absorbs or silences the sound waves which produce undesirable noises **b** *chiefly Brit* **:** the muffler of an internal-combustion engine **c :** a silencing device for small arms that permits the exit of the projectile but reduces the noise without materially impeding the escape of the exploding gases **d :** a device for silencing or reducing noise ⟨door ~⟩

si·le·ne \sī'lēnē\ *n* [NL, prob. fr. L *silenus* silenus] **1** *cap* **:** a very large and widely distributed genus of plants (family Caryophyllaceae) having mostly showy flowers of various colors with a 10-nerved 5-toothed calyx and 3 styles and fruit with a capsule opening by 3 or 6 teeth — see BLADDER CAMPION, CATCHFLY, MOSS CAMPION, WILD PINK; compare LYCHNIS **2** -S **:** any plant of the genus *Silene*

si·le·nic \sī'lēnik\ *adj, sometimes cap* [*silenus* + *-ic*] **:** of, relating to, or characteristic of Silenus or the sileni

¹si·lent \'sīlənt\ *adj, often* -ER/-EST [L *silent-, silens,* fr. pres. part. of *silēre* to be silent; akin to Goth *anasilan* to subside, abate (of wind), L *sinere* to leave, let go, lay — more at SITE] **1 :** making no utterance: **a :** unable to speak **:** MUTE, TONGUE-TIED, AWESTRUCK ⟨stared at the Pacific . . . ~, upon a peak in Darien —John Keats⟩ **b :** unaccustomed or indisposed to speak **:** not conversing or answering **:** resolved not to speak ⟨he laughed and chattered, but she was ~, seeming to brood over something —D.H.Lawrence⟩ ⟨the ~ suspect, refusing to answer the police⟩ **2 :** free from sound or noise **:** making no sound or noise **:** perfectly quiet **:** NOISELESS, STILL ⟨a ~ room⟩ ⟨a ~ audience⟩ ⟨a ~ forest⟩ **3 a :** conducted, performed, enjoyed, or borne without spoken word or utterance **:** UNSPOKEN, TACIT ⟨the banquet, at first so ~, slowly changes to a merry tumult —Lafcadio Hearn⟩ ⟨~ protest must at length come to words —Thomas Carlyle⟩ ⟨~ reading⟩ ⟨~ prayer⟩ **b :** not expressed in words **:** felt or experienced without expression in words or vocal utterance ⟨suffering in ~ grief⟩ **4 a :** making no mention or account **:** omitting explanation and leaving questions unanswered ⟨on the crucial point of enforcement methods the assembly resolution is ~ —Ruth Lawson⟩ ⟨did not tell us that logic is to be ignored when experience is ~ —B.N.Cardozo⟩ ⟨remained ~ on the reasons for the change⟩ **b :** not recorded **:** not mentioned, explained, or referred to ⟨the secretary's ~ role in the conspiracy⟩ **c :** not known or not generally known **:** unnoticed and therefore not appreciated ⟨the railways might well be said to render a ~ service —O.S.Nock⟩ ⟨new ways of life developing under the ~ pressure of a freer environment —V.L.Parrington⟩ **d :** taking no active part in the conduct of a business ⟨a ~ member of a firm⟩ — compare SILENT PARTNER **e :** unresponsive esp. from lack of feeling or understanding ⟨this humbug of the judge as a soulless automaton whose mind and heart are ~ when he performs his operations —H.J.Laski⟩ **5 :** being an orthographic letter or letter combination which if removed from a word would still leave letters enough to account for the pronunciation of the word ⟨~ *b* in *doubt*⟩ ⟨~ *ph* in *phthisis*⟩ or which serves as a conventional indicator of the quality of another letter without itself being pronounced ⟨~ *e* in *pine* shows that the *i* has the value \ī\ rather than the value \i\ in *pin*⟩ **6 a :** maintaining a state of inactivity ⟨a ~ volcano⟩ **b** (1) **:** not exhibiting the usual evidences (as signs or symptoms) of presence ⟨a ~ bone fracture⟩ ⟨~ heat in cattle⟩ **:** causing no symptoms ⟨~ gallstones⟩ ⟨~ tuberculosis⟩ (2) **:** characterized by such a silent state ⟨the ~ phase of a tumor⟩ (3) **:** yielding no detectable response to stimulation — used esp. of an association area of the brain **7 :** FLAVORLESS, FLAT — used of distilled spirits esp. when rectified for use in the arts **8 a :** lacking spoken dialogue **b :** of or relating to silent motion pictures ⟨the ~ screen⟩ ⟨Hollywood in the great days of the ~ stars —Budd Schulberg⟩ **9 :** inaudible to the human ear because outside its frequency range ⟨a ~ dog whistle⟩

syn RETICENT, RESERVED, TACITURN, UNCOMMUNICATIVE, CLOSE, CLOSE-MOUTHED, CLOSE-LIPPED, TIGHT-LIPPED, SECRETIVE: as here discussed, SILENT may refer to a disposition to speak rather little or to a determination not to speak ⟨a *silent* man with a great sense of his personal worth which made his speeches guarded —Joseph Conrad⟩ ⟨was very *silent* during the speech and . . . had listened attentively —George Meredith⟩ RETICENT indicates reluctance to speak out induced either by cautious discreetness or by shy lack of assertiveness ⟨almost *reticent* in his stingy use of words exactly chiseled out of the moment's need —W.A.White⟩ ⟨about his own experiences . . . was inclined to be *reticent* . . . because he considered them, as he put it, uninteresting —Kenneth Roberts⟩ RESERVED describes speaking or acting under the restraining influence of caution or formality checking easy unguarded expression ⟨I wished that she had told me frankly . . . Jane was always so *reserved* —Rose Macaulay⟩ ⟨even the *reserved* Washington wrote caustically of their bad manners —Allan Nevins & H.S. Commager⟩ TACITURN suggests a deep and accustomed disinclination to talk much; it may connote the unsociable or the laconic ⟨he had become more and more gloomy and *taciturn.* Mills tried in vain to draw him into talk —C.B.Nordhoff & J.N.Hall⟩ ⟨always *taciturn,* he now hardly spoke at all —Stuart Cloete⟩ UNCOMMUNICATIVE indicates an unwillingness to impart information ⟨an atomic scientist quite *uncommunicative* about his work⟩ CLOSE indicates a general disposition to keep information from being revealed ⟨will confide in nobody . . . every one feels that he is emphatically *close* —J.H.Newman⟩ ⟨you're a *close* one, but you give yourself away sometimes —Willa Cather⟩ CLOSE-MOUTHED and CLOSE-LIPPED have about the same suggestions as CLOSE, although they are more likely to be used in reference to matters confidential or secret ⟨a millionaire's *close-mouthed* confidential secretary⟩ ⟨a duke's *close-lipped* adviser⟩ TIGHT-LIPPED may suggest resolute or determined silence about a specific matter ⟨company officials, all *tight-lipped* about the uranium thefts⟩ SECRETIVE suggests either a disposition towards carefully guarding secrets or undue caution or concealment about less important matters ⟨you're so excessively *secretive* that I can't help being curious —Dashiell Hammett⟩

²silent \"\ *n* -S **1** *obs* **:** a time of silence ⟨the ~ of the night —Shak.⟩ **2 silents** *pl* **:** motion pictures without spoken dialogue ⟨some primitive Western of the ~s, at which you were supposed to laugh —Edmund Wilson⟩ ⟨in the days of the ~s —Alfred Kazin⟩

silent area *n* [so called fr. the comparative absence of symptoms when it is injured] **:** an association area of the cerebral cortex

silent barter *or* **silent trade** *n* **:** DUMB BARTER

silent butler *n* **:** a small portable receptacle with projecting handle and hinged lid for gathering up table crumbs and the contents of ash trays

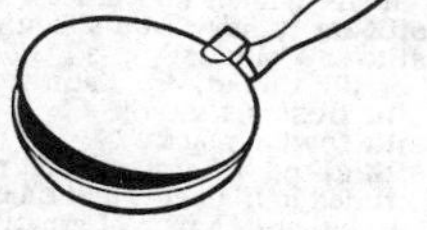

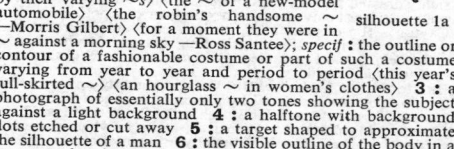

silent butler

silent cop *n* **:** a device usu. equipped with lights and signs and placed at the center of a crossroads to replace an officer directing traffic

silent gerrymander *n* **:** a gerrymander that has been developed through failure of a legislature to revise election district boundaries in accord with population shifts usu. with benefit to one political party over its opponents

si·len·tial \sī'lenchəl\ *adj* [L *silentium* silence + E *-al*] **:** conducted in silence **:** SILENT

si·len·ti·ary \sī'lenchē,erē\ *n* -ES [L *silentiarius* slave charged with maintaining silence among the domestic staff, fr. *silentium* silence + *-arius* -ary] **1 :** an advocate of silence esp. as a religious observance **2 :** one of various court officials of the later Roman Empire sworn not to divulge secrets of state **3 :** one appointed to keep silence and order (as in a court of law or a public assembly)

si·len·tious \sī'lenchəs\ *adj* [L *silentiosus,* fr. *silentium* + *-osus* -ous] **:** habitually silent **:** TACITURN, RETICENT

si·lent·ly *adv* **:** in a silent manner **:** in silence **:** without speaking **:** NOISELESSLY

si·lent·ness *n* -ES **:** the quality or state of being or keeping silent **:** NOISELESSNESS, SPEECHLESSNESS

silent partner *n* **1 :** a partner who has no voice in the firm business as between partners **2 :** SECRET PARTNER

silent service *n* **1 :** NAVY — used with *the* **2 :** the submarine service — used with *the*

silent system *n* **:** a system of penal discipline that forbids conversation among prisoners ⟨subjected to a *silent system* . . . for infraction of rules —L.E.Lawes⟩

silent treatment *n* **:** an act of completely ignoring a person or thing by resort to silence esp. as a means of expressing contempt or disapproval ⟨too often, the most forthright speakers were given the *silent treatment* —Saul Carson⟩

silent vote *n* **:** the vote of those whose choice is not publicly known ⟨it's feared the *silent vote* is going to go against the administration —*Newsweek*⟩

si·le·nus \sī'lēnəs\ *n, pl* **sile·ni** \-ē,nī\ *often cap* [L, fr. Gk *silēnos,* fr. *Silēnos* Silenus, foster father and companion of Dionysus] **:** a minor woodland deity of ancient Greek mythology having usu. human form but with a horse's ears and tail and occas. with the legs of a horse or goat and being one of the companions of Dionysus but usu. distinguished from a satyr by being always old, frequently bald, and always bearded

siles *pl of* SILE, *pres 3d sing of* SILE

si·le·sia \sī'lēzh(ē)ə, sə'-, -ēsh(ē)ə\ *n* -S [fr. *Silesia,* former Prussian province] **1** *archaic* **:** a linen cloth of Silesian origin **2 :** a soft sturdy lightweight cotton with a lustrous finish that is closely woven in twill weave and used esp. for linings and pockets

¹si·le·sian \-(ē)ən\ *adj, usu cap* [*Silesia,* region of central Europe formerly partly in Prussia & partly in Poland + E *-an*] **1 :** of, relating to, or characteristic of Silesia **2 :** of, relating to, or characteristic of the people of Silesia

²silesian \"\ *n* -S *cap* **:** a native or inhabitant of Silesia; *esp* **:** a German native of Silesia

si·letz \sī'lets, sə'-\ *n, pl* **siletz** *or* **siletzes** *usu cap* **1 a :** a Salishan people of the Oregon coast **b :** a member of such people **2 :** a language of the Siletz people

si·lex \'sī,leks\ *n* -ES [L *silic-, silex,* hard stone, flint, quartz — more at SHELL] **1 :** SILICA; *esp* **:** a pure form (as finely ground quartz or flint) for use as a filler in paints or wood or as a dental material **2 :** siliceous powders (as tripoli) for uses similar to those of silex

Silex \"\ *trademark* — used for a vacuum coffee maker

si·lex·ite \'sī,lek,sīt\ *n* -S [L *silex* + E *-ite*] **:** an igneous rock composed essentially of quartz, occurring in dikes, and representing the end members of the pegmatitic intrusions

¹sil·hou·ette \¦silə¦wet, usu -ed·+V\ *n* -S [F, after Étienne de *Silhouette* †1767 Fr. controller general of finances; fr. his parsimony and petty economies] **1 a :** a representation of the outlines of an object filled in with black or some other uniform color ⟨~s cut from paper⟩ ⟨a book illustrated with ~s⟩ **b :** a style of representation in which outlines are filled in with black or some other uniform color ⟨illustrations done in ~⟩ **2 :** the outline or a delineation of the outline of a person or thing esp. when used as a means of characterizing or identifying ⟨learn to identify ships or planes by their varying ~s⟩ ⟨the ~ of a new-model automobile⟩ ⟨the robin's handsome ~ —Morris Gilbert⟩ ⟨for a moment they were in ~ against a morning sky —Ross Santee⟩; *specif* **:** the outline or contour of a fashionable costume or part of such a costume varying from year to year and period to period ⟨this year's full-skirted ~⟩ ⟨an hourglass ~ in women's clothes⟩ **3 :** a photograph of essentially only two tones showing the subject against a light background **4 :** a halftone with background dots etched or cut away **5 :** a target shaped to approximate the silhouette of a man **6 :** the visible outline of the body in a motion of action in the dance **syn** see OUTLINE

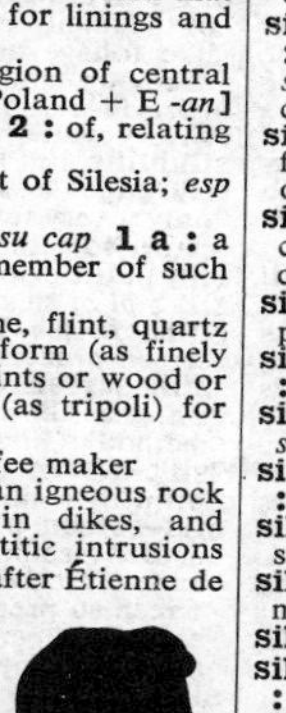

silhouette 1a

²silhouette \"\ *vb* **silhouetted**; **silhouetted**; **silhouetting**; **silhouettes** *vt* **1 :** to represent by a silhouette **:** project upon a background like a silhouette ⟨the line of the dune *silhouetted* against the sky —W.T.Scott⟩ ⟨deep off-white color which does not ~ the pictures like the more glaring whites —J.T.Soby⟩ ⟨attack with the moon *silhouetting* the targets —E.L.Beach⟩ ⟨a flock of roosting vultures, *silhouetted* on the sky —G.W. Cable⟩ **2 :** to etch or cut away background dots of (a halftone) ~ *vi* **:** to appear in profile like a silhouette

sil·hou·et·tist \-ed·əst\ *n* -S [¹*silhouette* + *-ist*] **:** one who makes silhouettes

silic- *or* **silico-** *comb form* [*silicon* or *silicium*] **1 :** relating to or containing silicon or its compounds ⟨*silicone*⟩ ⟨*silicofluoride*⟩ ⟨*silicochloroform*⟩ — compare SIL-, SILA- **2 :** silicic and ⟨*silicoalkaline*⟩ **3 :** silicosis and ⟨*silicotuberculosis*⟩

sil·i·ca \'siləkə, -lēkə\ *n* -S [NL, fr. L *silic-, silex* hard stone, flint, quartz — more at SHELL] **:** the chemically resistant dioxide SiO_2 of silicon that occurs naturally in the three crystalline modifications of quartz, tridymite, and cristobalite, in amorphous and hydrated forms (as opal), and in less pure forms (as sand, diatomite, tripoli) and combined in silicates, that can be prepared artificially as a fine white powder from water glass or other soluble silicates and also in colloidal form, and that is used chiefly in making glass, ceramic products, and refractories, in producing elemental silicon, its alloys, and compounds, and as an abrasive, adsorbent, and filler

silica aerogel *n* **:** colloidal silica in the form of a fine lightweight powder with grains having minute pores that is made from silica gel and used chiefly as thermal insulation esp. at low temperatures (as in refrigerators)

silica brick *n* **:** brick made from crushed quartzite bonded with milk of lime and used as a high-grade refractory

silica cement *n* **:** a refractory mortar suitable for laying silica brick

silica gel *n* **:** colloidal silica resembling coarse white sand in appearance but possessing many fine pores and therefore extremely adsorbent that is made by coagulation of hydrated silica and is used chiefly as a selective adsorbent and as a catalyst or catalyst carrier

silica glass *n* **:** VITREOUS SILICA

sil·i·cane \'silə,kān\ *n* -S [*silic-* + meth*ane*] **:** MONOSILANE

¹sil·i·cate \'silə,kāt\ *vt* -ED/-ING/-S [NL *silica* + E *-ate*] **:** to combine with silica or silicates **:** coat or impregnate with silica or silicates

²silicate \", -ləkət, *usu* -d·+V\ *n* -S [NL *silica* + E *-ate*] **1 :** a salt or ester derived from a silicic acid; *esp* **:** ORTHOSILICATE **2 :** any of numerous insoluble often complex metal salts that contain silicon and oxygen in the anion, that constitute the largest chemical group of minerals and with quartz make up the greater part of the earth's crust (as in rocks, soils, and clays) and building materials such as cement, concrete, bricks, and glass, and that have crystal structures characterized by fundamental units of SiO_4 tetrahedrons consisting of one silicon atom surrounded by four oxygen atoms either as independent groups (as in nesosilicates) or linked by sharing of one or more oxygen atoms — compare ALUMINOSILICATE, CYCLOSILICATE, INOSILICATE, PHYLLOSILICATE, SOROSILICATE, TECTOSILICATE

silicate bond *n* [²*silicate*] **:** a water-glass binder for abrasive particles (as in grinding wheels and sanding disks)

silicate cotton *n* **:** MINERAL WOOL

silicate of soda **:** SODIUM SILICATE — not used systematically

silicate paint *n* **:** a paint the vehicle of which consists chiefly of water glass and which is used esp. for painting on mortar

sil·i·ca·tion \,silə'kāshən\ *n* -S [¹*silicate* + *-ion*] **:** the act or process of silicating; *specif* **:** the development of silicates in rocks (as carbonates) orig. poor in them

sil·i·ca·ti·za·tion \,silə,kād·ə'zāshən\ *n* -S [²*silicate* + *-ization*] **:** SILICIFICATION

sil·i·ca·tor \'silə,kād·ə(r)\ *n* -S [¹*silicate* + *-or*] **:** one that puts a coat of sodium silicate on the inside of steel drums that are to be used for shipping caustic soda

silica ware *n* **:** ware consisting of silica usu. in the form of pure sand partly or wholly fused and shaped into tubes, dishes, and beakers for use as scientific apparatus

si·li·cea \sə'lishēə\ [NL, fr. L, neut. pl. of *siliceus* siliceous] *syn of* NONCALCAREA

siliceo- *comb form* [L *siliceus* siliceous] **:** siliceous and ⟨*siliceo*-calcareous⟩ ⟨*siliceo*feldspathic⟩

si·li·ceous *also* **si·li·cious** \sə'lishəs\ *adj* [L *siliceus* of flint, fr. *silic-, silex* flint, quartz — more at SHELL] **1 :** of, relating to, or derived from silica **:** containing or resembling silica or a silicate ⟨~ limestone⟩ **2 :** SILICICOLOUS

siliceous sinter *n* **:** sinter formed by evaporation of the water of hot siliceous springs or geysers

siliceous sponge *n* **:** a sponge having a siliceous skeleton

silici- *comb form* [NL *silica*] **1 :** silex **:** silica ⟨*silici*ferous⟩ **2 :** siliceous and ⟨*silici*calcareous⟩

si·lic·ic \sə'lisik, -sēk\ *adj* [*silica* or *silicium* + *-ic*] **:** of, relating to, or derived from silica or silicon ⟨highly ~ rocks, such as normal granite —A.M.Bateman⟩

silicic acid *n* **:** any of various weakly acid substances formed in dilute solution or as gelatinous masses by treating soluble silicates with acids or obtained in the form of salts or esters; *esp* **:** ORTHOSILICIC ACID — compare METASILICIC ACID, SILICA GEL

sil·i·cic·o·lous \¦silə¦sikələs\ *adj* [*silici-* + *-colous*] **:** growing or thriving in siliceous soil ⟨~ plants⟩

sil·i·cide \'silə,sīd, -,səd\ *n* -S [ISV *silic-* + *-ide*] **:** a binary compound of silicon usu. with a more electropositive element or radical

si·lic·i·dize \sə'lisə,dīz\ *vt* -ED/-ING/-S [*silicide* + *-ize*] **:** to convert into a silicide

sil·i·cif·er·ous \¦silə¦sif(ə)rəs\ *adj* [*silici-* + *-ferous*] **:** producing, containing, or united with silica

si·lic·i·fi·ca·tion \sə,lisəfə'kāshən\ *n* -S [*silici-* + *-fication*] **:** the act or process of silicifying **:** the state of being silicified; *specif* **:** the development of silica minerals (as quartz and chert) by metasomatic action

silicified wood *n* [fr. past part. of *silicify*] **:** chalcedony in the form of petrified wood often preserving even microscopic details of the replaced wood

si·lic·i·fy \sə'lisə,fī\ *vb* -ED/-ING/-ES [*silici-* + *-fy*] *vt* **:** to convert into or impregnate with silica or siliceous material commonly in the form of quartz ~ *vi* **:** to become silicified

si·lic·i·o·phite \sə'lisēə,fīt\ *n* [*silici-* + *ophite*] **:** serpentine penetrated by opal

sil·i·ci·sponge \'siləsə,spənj, sə'lisə,-\ *n* [NL *Silicispongiae*] **:** a sponge of the class Noncalcarea

sil·i·ci·spon·gi·ae \,siləsə'spənjə,ē, sə,lisə'-, -pän-\ [NL, fr. *silici-* + *-spongiae*] *syn of* NONCALCAREA

si·li·ci·um \sə'lishēəm, -isēəm\ *n* -S [NL, fr. *silica* + *-ium*] **:** SILICON

sil·i·cize \'silə,sīz\ *vt* -ED/-ING/-S [*silic-* + *-ize*] **:** to treat with silicon or silica

sil·i·cle \'siləkəl\ *n* -S [L *silicula,* dim. of *siliqua* pod, husk — more at SHELL] **:** a silique of nearly equal length and width

silico- — see SILIC-

sil·i·co·aluminate \¦silə(,)kō+\ *n* [*silic-* + *aluminate*] **:** ALUMINOSILICATE

sil·i·co·chloroform \"+\ *n* [*silic-* + *chloroform*] **:** TRICHLOROSILANE

sil·i·co·flagellata \"+\ *n pl, cap* [NL, fr. *silic-* + *flagellata,* neut. pl. of *flagellatus* flagellate] *in some classifications* **:** a group of marine flagellates formerly classified among the radiolarians but now usu. constituting a family of the order Chrysomonadina and having one or two flagella, a definite nucleus, and a spiny siliceous skeleton like that of a radiolarian — **sil·i·co·flagellate** \"+\ *n*

sil·i·co·flagellatae \"+\ [NL, fr. *silic-* + *flagellatae,* fem. pl. of *flagellatus*] *syn of* SILICOFLAGELLATA

sil·i·co·fluoride \"+\ *n* [*silic-* + *fluoride*] **:** FLUOSILICATE — not used systematically

sil·i·co·mag·ne·sio·flu·o·rite \,silə̇kōmag,nēshō'flü(ə),rīt\ *n* -S [*silic-* + *magnesio-* + *fluor-* + *-ite*] **:** a mineral $Ca_4Mg_3Si_2O_5(OH)_2F_{10}$ consisting of a basic fluoride and silicate of calcium and magnesium

sil·i·co·manganese \¦silə(,)kō+\ *n* [*silic-* + *manganese*] **:** a crude alloy of silicon and manganese and some iron used esp. in the manufacture of alloy steel

sil·i·con \'siləkən, -lēkən, -lə,kän\ *n* -S [*silica* + *-on* (as in *carbon*)] **:** a tetravalent nonmetallic element that occurs in combined form as the most abundant element next to oxygen in the earth's crust, that can be obtained as brittle hard lustrous gray crystals with the lattice structure of diamond, as a glistening black graphitic form, or as a dark brown powder, that is usu. prepared by reducing silica with carbon in an electric furnace, and that is used chiefly in the form of alloys (as ferrosilicon), in combination with ceramic materials in cermets, and as a semiconductor (as in transistors) and element in photovoltaic cells ⟨~ plays an important part in the inorganic world, similar to that played by carbon in the organic world —Linus Pauling⟩ — symbol *Si;* see ELEMENT table

silicon bronze *n* **:** an alloy of copper and usu. 1.5 or 3 percent silicon with small amounts of various third elements (as zinc, tin, or manganese)

silicon carbide *n* **:** a compound SiC of silicon and carbon that is obtained as brittle crystals next to diamond and boron carbide in hardness and often dark bluish black and iridescent, that is made by heating sand and coke together in an electric resistance furnace, and that is used chiefly in crushed form as an abrasive esp. for grinding hard materials of low tensile strength (as cast iron or marble) and materials needing sharp cutting (as fiber, rubber, or aluminum), as a refractory, and in electric resistors

silicon chloride *n* **:** a chloride of silicon; *esp* **:** SILICON TETRACHLORIDE

silicon copper *n* **:** an alloy of 80 to 70 percent copper and 20 to 30 percent silicon used as an ingredient to free molten copper or brass from oxygen

silicon dioxide *n* : SILICA
sil·i·cone \'siləˌkōn\ *n* -s [*silic-* + *-one*] **1 a** : an organic compound R_2SiO analogous to a ketone **b** : an organic siloxane; *esp* : any of a large group of polymerized organic siloxanes that are unusually stable over a wide temperature range, that are obtained as oily fluids, resins, and elastomers convertible into greases and other compounds, coatings, and rubbers, and that are used chiefly in waterproofing, lubrication, and electric insulation — see BOUNCING PUTTY **2** : an organosilicon compound in which silicon is attached directly to carbon — used chiefly commercially
silicone rubber *n* : rubber made from silicone elastomers and characterized by its retention of flexibility, resilience, and tensile strength over a wide temperature range (as from −100° to +500°F) and its resistance to weathering, the electric arc, and many chemicals
silicon fluoride *n* : a fluoride of silicon; *esp* : SILICON TETRAFLUORIDE
silicon hydride *n* : a compound of silicon with hydrogen — see SILANE
sil·i·con·iza·tion \ˌsiləkənə'zāshən\ *n* -s : the process of siliconizing
sil·i·con·ize \'siləkəˌnīz\ *vt* -ED/-ING/-S [*silicon* + *-ize*] **1** : to combine or impregnate with silicon; *specif* : to treat (a metal) with silicon or a silicon compound to form a protective surface alloy ⟨~ steel⟩ **2** : to treat or coat (as a lens) with a silicone
silicon oxide *n* : an oxide of silicon; *esp* : SILICA
silicon spiegel *n* : a spiegeleisen containing 15 to 20 percent of manganese and 8 to 15 percent of silicon and used in making certain special steels
silicon tetrachloride *n* : a colorless fuming corrosive liquid $SiCl_4$ made usu. by heating silicon or silicon carbide with chlorine and used chiefly for smoke screens and in making chlorosilanes, silicones, and other organic derivatives of silicon
silicon tetrafluoride *n* : a colorless fuming suffocating gas SiF_4 made by the action of fluorine on silicon or of hydrofluoric acid on silica or silicates (as glass) and used chiefly in making fluosilicic acid and fluosilicates
sil·i·co·sis \ˌsilə'kōsəs\ *n, pl* **silico·ses** \-ōˌsēz\ [NL, fr. *silic-* + *-osis*] : a condition of massive fibrosis of the lungs marked by shortness of breath and resulting from prolonged inhalation of silica dusts by those (as stonecutters, asbestos workers, miners) regularly exposed to such dusts — compare ¹³CON b
sil·i·co·thermic \ˌsilə(ˌ)kō+\ *adj* [*silic-* + *thermic*] : of or relating to a method of producing heat and chemical reduction by oxidizing finely crushed silicon or ferrosilicon with oxygen taken from another metal (as chromium)
¹sil·i·cot·ic \ˌsilə'kädik\ *adj* [*silic-* + *-otic*] : relating to, caused by, or affected with silicosis
²silicotic \"\ *n* -s : a person affected with silicosis
sil·i·co·titanate \ˌsilə(ˌ)kō+\ *n* [*silic-* + *titanate*] : a combined silicate and titanate
sil·i·co·tuberculosis \"+\ *n* [NL, fr. *silic-* + *tuberculosis*] : silicosis and tuberculosis in the same lung
sil·i·co·tungstate \"+\ *n* [*silic-* + *tungstate*] : a salt of a silicotungstic acid — called also *tungstosilicate*
sil·i·co·tungstic acid \"+ . . . -\ *n* [*silic-* + *tungstic*] : any of several heteropoly acids of silicon and tungsten; *esp* : a pale-yellow crystalline acid $H_4SiW_{12}O_{40}.xH_2O$ containing 12 atoms of tungsten in the molecule, obtainable by acid hydrolysis of a mixture of sodium tungstate and sodium silicate, and used chiefly as a precipitant for alkaloids — called also *tungstosilicic acid*
si·lic·u·la \sə'likyələ\ *n, pl* **silicu·lae** \-yəˌlē\ [NL, fr. L, dim. of *siliqua* pod, husk — more at SHELL] : SILICLE
si·lic·u·lar \-lə(r)\ *adj* [NL *silicula* + E *-ar*] : having the form or appearance of a silicle
sil·i·cule \'siləˌkyül\ *n* -s [NL *silicula*] : SILICLE
si·lic·u·lose \sə'likyəˌlōs\ *adj* [NL *siliculosus*, fr. *silicula* + L *-osus* -ose, -ous] **1** : bearing silicles **2** : of the form or appearance of a silicle : SILICULAR
si·lic·u·lous \-yələs\ *adj* [NL *siliculosus*] : SILICULOSE
siling *pres part of* SILE
silin·gal *or* **shilin·gol** \shə'-\ *n, pl* **silingal** *or* **silingals** *or* **shilingol** *or* **shilingols** *usu cap* **1** : a branch of the East Mongols living in Inner Mongolia **2** : a member of the Silingal people
sil·i·qua \'siləkwə\ *n, pl* **sili·quae** \-ləˌkwē\ [L, pod, husk, a small weight, coin worth ¹⁄₂₄ solidus — more at SHELL] **1** : SILIQUE **2** : a Roman silver coin first issued by Constantine the Great : the ¹⁄₂₄ solidus or later the half miliarensis — **sil·i·qua·ceous** \ˌsilə'kwāshəs\ *adj*
sil·i·qua·ria \ˌsilə'kwa(a)rēə\ *n, cap* [NL, fr. L *siliqua* pod, husk + NL *-aria*] : a genus of worm shells (family Vermetidae) sometimes placed in a separate family and comprising forms that differ from those of the genus *Vermetus* in having a continuous slit or row of clefts or pores throughout the whorls of the shell
si·lique \sə'lēk, 'silik\ *n* -s [F, fr. L *siliqua* pod, husk — more at SHELL] : a narrow elongated usu. many-seeded capsule that is characteristic of the family Cruciferae, consists of two valves with a false dissepiment, opens by sutures at either margin, and has the seeds attached to two parietal placentas
siliqui- *comb form* [NL *siliqua*] : siliqua ⟨*siliqui*ferous⟩ ⟨*siliqui*form⟩
sil·i·quose \'siləˌkwōs\ *or* **sil·i·quous** \-ˌkwəs\ *adj* [NL *siliquosus*, fr. *siliqua* + *-osus* -ose, -ous] : bearing or having the form of a silique
¹silk \'silk, 'siuk\ *n* -s [ME *selk, silk*, fr. OE *sioloc, seolc*, prob. of Baltic or Slav origin; akin to OPruss *silkas* silk, OSlav *shelkŭ*] **1** : a fine continuous protein fiber produced by various insect larvae usu. for cocoons; *esp* : the lustrous tough elastic hygroscopic fiber that is produced by silkworms by secreting from two glands viscous fluid in the form of two filaments consisting principally of fibroin cemented into a single strand by sericin and solidifying in air, that is capable of being reeled in a single strand from the cocoon, and that with or without boiling off the sericin is used for textiles **2 a** : thread, yarn, or fabric made from silk filaments — see SPUN SILK **b** : strands of silk thread of various thicknesses and plain or braided used as suture material in surgery ⟨surgical ~⟩ ⟨~ technique⟩ **3 a** : a garment (as a dress) of silk : silk apparel ⟨a crowd dressed in ~⟩ ⟨printed ~s on sale today⟩ ⟨wear ~⟩ **b** (1) : a gown worn by a King's or Queen's Counsel or barrister of high rank appointed by the lord chancellor (2) : a King's or Queen's Counsel (3) : the rank or persons entitled to such a gown — see SILK GOWN **c silks** *pl* : the colored cap and blouse of a jockey or harness horse driver made in the registered racing color of the stable for which he is riding or driving in a particular race **4 a** : a filament resembling silk but produced by some other organism: as (1) : the filament produced by various spiders esp. in building their webs and used for cloth and telescopic sights (2) : the byssal thread of a mollusk of the genus *Pinna* **b** : a thread of such material or of wire (as used in a sieve of a sifter in flour milling) **5 a** : CORN SILK **b** : a style of corn silk — compare ¹TASSEL 2a **6** : inclusions of minute crystals that impart a silky luster to a gem (as a ruby) **7** : SILK SPONGE **8** : PARACHUTE ⟨pack the ~⟩ ⟨the ~ opened⟩
²silk \"\ *adj* [ME, fr. ¹*silk*] **1** : relating to or made of silk : SILKEN ⟨a ~ ribbon⟩ **2** : resembling silk
³silk \"\ *vb* -ED/-ING/-S [¹*silk*] *vt* **1** : to fashion of or cover with silk **2** : to strip (an ear of corn) of silk ~ *vi* **1** : BLOSSOM — used of corn ⟨inbred lines were pollinated at successive intervals after ~*ing* —R.H.Andrew⟩ **2** : to develop a striated appearance and luster suggestive of silk cloth — used of varnish and enamels
silk·a·line *or* **silk·o·line** *also* **silk·o·lene** \ˌsilkə'lēn -iuk-\ *n* -s [*silkaline, silkolene*, fr. *silk* + *-aline, -olene*, alter. of *-oline* (as in *crinoline*); *silkoline* fr. *silk* + *-oline*] : a soft light cotton fabric in plain weave with a smooth lustrous finish similar to silk used plain or printed esp. for curtains and linings
silk cotton *n* : a cottony substance enveloping the seeds of any of various trees of the family Bombacaceae; *esp* : KAPOK — compare VEGETABLE SILK
silk-cotton family *n* [*silk cotton*] : BOMBACACEAE
silk-cotton tree *n* : a tree of the family Bombacaceae that produces silk cotton: as **a** : CEIBA 2a **b** : SIMAL
silk crab *n* : a mature female crab
silked \'silkt\ *adj* [¹*silk* + *-ed*] : dressed in or covered with silk
¹silk·en \'silkən, 'siuk-\ *adj* [ME, fr. OE *seolcen*, fr. *seolc* silk + *-en*] **1** : made of silk : consisting of silk ⟨~ threads⟩ ⟨a ~ veil⟩ ⟨in certain spiders the female carries the eggs about with her in a ~ case —H.M.Parshley⟩ **2** : resembling silk: as **a** : SOFT, LUSTROUS ⟨her ability to look gracefully ~ on occasion —Adrian Bell⟩ **b** (1) : agreeably smooth : HARMONIOUS ⟨~ voices⟩ ⟨the ~ sonority of the strings —Virgil Thomson⟩ ⟨doesn't hold with the ~ and the silver epithet —Josephine Miles⟩ (2) : INGRATIATING, INSINUATING ⟨said . . . in the ~ town voice —Paul Bowles⟩ **c** : DELICATE, TENDER, GENTLE ⟨~ slumbers⟩ ⟨a ~ touch⟩ **d** : LOW, EVEN ⟨a ~ sound⟩ **e** : extremely graceful : LITHE ⟨whirled upon him with the ~ savagery of a little panther —Elinor Wylie⟩ **3** : furnished with silk : producing silk ⟨from ~ Samarcand —John Keats⟩ ⟨~ chambers⟩ **4 a** : dressed in silk ⟨~ ankles⟩ **b** : LUXURIOUS ⟨~ young gallants —F.X.Braun⟩ ⟨reading public is preoccupied with murder, mayhem, and ~ dalliance —*Police Rev.*⟩ **c** : EFFEMINATE ⟨~ sons of pride —Van Wyck Brooks⟩
²silken \"\ *vt* -ED/-ING/-S **1** : to make silken or silklike ⟨a shampoo that ~s your hair —*advt*⟩ ⟨the new ~*ed* worsted —*N. Y. Times Mag.*⟩ **2** : to cover with or as if with silk : dress in silk ⟨smiles and graces of ~*ed* beauty —George Catlin⟩
silk·en·ly *adv* : in a silken manner
silk·er \'silkə(r)\ *n* -s [¹*silk* + *-er*] : one that works with silk or silk thread; *esp* : POINTER 1a(2)
silk floss *n* : KAPOK
silk fowl *n* : SILKY
silk gland *n* : a gland that produces a viscid fluid which is extruded in filaments and on exposure to air hardens into silk: as **a** : either of a pair of greatly enlarged modified salivary glands of an insect larva that extend backward along the sides of the body and produce a compound filament from which is spun a larval or pupal cover (as a cocoon) **b** : any of two or more abdominal glands of a spider that open through spinnerets and produce a filament used chiefly in the spinning of webs
silk gown *n* **1** : the distinctive robe of a King's or Queen's Counsel — compare STUFF GOWN **2** : a King's or Queen's Counsel
silk grass *n* **1 a** : a needlegrass (*Stipa comata*) **b** : a mountain rice (*Oryzopsis hymenoides*) with long awns **c** *Austral* : ROUGH BENT **2** : any of several fiber plants esp. of *Agave* or the related genus *Nidularium* (family Bromeliaceae) **3** : any of several commercial fibers from plants of the family Bromeliaceae: as **a** : a fine flexible lustrous strong fiber obtained from the pineapple and used for textiles **b** : a similar fiber from a karatas (*Karatas plumieri*)
silk green *n* : DEEP CHROME GREEN
silkgrower \'=ˌ==\ *n* [¹*silk* + *grower*] : one that raises silkworms for their silk
silk gum *or* **silk glue** *n* : SERICIN
silk gut *n* : a strong gut used for fishing tackle and surgery and made from the silk gland of the silkworm — called also *silkworm gut*
silk hat *n* : a hat with a tall cylindrical crown usu. made with a silk-plush finish and worn by men as a dress hat and sometimes by women as a riding hat

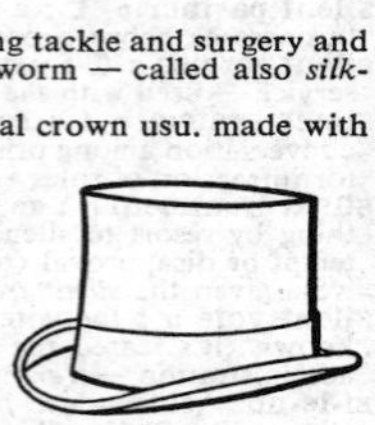
silk hat

silkie *var of* SILKY
silkier *comparative of* SILKY
silkiest *superlative of* SILKY
silk·i·ly \'silkəlē, 'siuk-, -li\ *adv* : in a silky manner ⟨the young wheat shone ~ —D.H.Lawrence⟩
silk·i·ness \-kēnəs, -kin-\ *n* -ES : the quality or state of being silky
silking *pres part of* SILK
silking machine *n* [fr. gerund of ³*silk*] : a machine for removing the silk from the ears of fresh sweet corn being processed
silklike \'=ˌ=\ *adj* : resembling silk in softness, fineness, or luster
silkman \'=mən\ *n, pl* **silkmen** [¹*silk* + *man*] **1** : one who makes silks **2** : one who sells silks
silk moth *n* : a silkworm moth
silk oak *or* **silky oak** *n* : any of various Australian timber trees of the family Proteaceae (as of the genus *Grevillea*) having fernlike foliage and attractively mottled wood that is used in cabinetry and veneering; *specif* : a medium to large tree (*Grevillea robusta*) with feathery bipinnate leaves that are silvery white below and orange-red flowers
silkoline *also* **silkolene** *var of* SILKALINE
silk paper *n* **1** : a paper similar to granite paper but having only a very few silk fibers scattered in the tissue **2** : a safety paper sometimes used in printing postage and revenue stamps
silk plant *or* **silk plantain** *n* : RUGEL'S PLANTAIN
silks *pl of* SILK, *pres 3d sing of* SILK
silk screen *n* **1** : a screen usu. of silk or organdy used in a silk-screen process **2** : SILK-SCREEN PROCESS
¹silk–screen \'=ˌ=\ *adj* [*silk screen*] : of, made or done by, or using a silk-screen process ⟨*silk-screen* printing⟩ ⟨*silk-screen* method⟩ ⟨*silk-screen* print⟩
²silk–screen \'=ˌ=\ *vt* [*silk screen*] : to produce, reproduce, or print by a silk-screen process
silk–screen process *n* : a stencil process in which coloring matter (as ink, paint, or dye) is forced with a squeegee onto the material to be printed through the meshes of a silk or organdy screen so prepared (as by blocking out with tusche and glue) as to have pervious printing areas and impervious nonprinting areas — compare SERIGRAPHY
silk snapper *n* : a medium-sized West Indian snapper (*Lutjanus vivanus*) similar to the red snapper
silk spider *n* : a large spider (*Nephila clavipes*) native to the southern U. S. and remarkable for its large webs composed of strong silk; *broadly* : any of several related spiders that produce unusually heavy silk
silk sponge *n* : a very fine-textured soft close-grained Old World commercial sponge
silk–stocking \'=ˌ==\ *adj* [²*silk* + *stocking*] **1** : elegantly or richly dressed : LUXURIOUS ⟨a *silk-stocking* audience⟩ **2** : ARISTOCRATIC, EXCLUSIVE, WEALTHY ⟨*silk-stocking* politicos —H.R. Cayton⟩ **3** : of or relating to the American Federalist party **4** : of or relating to the silk-stocking district of a city ⟨lost the *silk-stocking* and middle-class precincts —W.G.Carleton⟩ ⟨*silk-stocking* ward⟩
silk stocking *n* [*silk-stocking*] **1** : an elegantly dressed person **2** : an aristocratic or wealthy person ⟨they know who the *silk stockings* are —August Hollingshead⟩ **3** : FEDERALIST 2
silk–stocking district *n* : a part of a city in which the aristocratic or wealthy class is politically influential or active
silk–stockinged \'=ˌ==\ *adj* : SILK-STOCKING
silk system *n* : a warping system in which sections of the warp are wound separately on a reel and then simultaneously rewound on a loom beam
silktail \'=ˌ=\ *n* [²*silk* + *tail*] *dial Brit* : BOHEMIAN WAXWING
silk–tassel tree *also* **silk tassel** *n* : a plant of the genus *Garrya*; *esp* : an evergreen shrub or small tree (*G. elliptica*) of western Oregon and California with inconspicuous flowers in silky drooping racemes
silk throwster *or* **silk thrower** *n* : THROWSTER
silk tree *n* : an Asiatic tree (*Albizzia julibrissin*) having flowers with long silky stamens
silk vine *n* : a Eurasian woody nearly evergreen vine (*Periploca graeca*) with silky seeds
silkweed \'=ˌ=\ *n* **1** : MILKWEED **2** : any of several filamentous smooth algae
silk wire *n* : silk-covered wire
silkwoman \'=ˌ==\ *n, pl* **silkwomen** [ME, fr. ¹*silk* + *woman*] *archaic* : a woman who makes, sells, or sews silk
silkwood \'=ˌ=\ *n* : any of several trees with lustrous wood: as **a** : CALABUR TREE **b** : FLINDERSIA 2
silkworm \'=ˌ=\ *n* [ME, fr. OE *seolcwyrm*, fr. *seolc* silk + *wyrm* worm] : a moth larva that spins a large amount of strong silk in constructing its cocoon before changing to a pupa: as **a** : a rough wrinkled hairless whitish caterpillar that is the larva of a stocky creamy white Asiatic moth (*Bombyx mori*), feeds chiefly on the leaves of white and black mulberry, is found almost entirely under human care and has been reared in China since the dawn of recorded history, and matures in about 45 days to pupate in a thick oval white or yellowish cocoon which is the source of most of the silk of commerce **b** : the larva of any of various moths of the family Saturniidae (as the ailanthus silkworm, the pernyi silkworm, the tussah silkworm, and the yamamai silkworm) — called also *giant silkworm, wild silkworm*
silkworm gut *n* : SILK GUT
silkworm jaundice *n* : polyhedrosis of the silkworm
silkworm rot *n* : CALCINO
silkworm seed *n* : the eggs of the silkworm
¹silky \'silkē, 'siuk-, -ki\ *adj, usu* -ER/-EST [¹*silk* + *-y*] **1 a** : consisting of silk **b** (1) : like silk in appearance, feel, or sound : SOFT, SMOOTH, GLOSSY, SLEEK ⟨~ printed cottons —Lois Long⟩ ⟨velvet that feels almost as thick and ~ as fur —*New Yorker*⟩ ⟨commonest of these ~ quartzes is tigereye —*Jewelers' Circular-Keystone*⟩ ⟨faint, ~ cirrus wisps —John Muir †1914⟩ ⟨hear the ~ swish of a hurled spear —Charles Lee⟩ (2) : INGRATIATING ⟨~ insinuations⟩ ⟨a ~ voice⟩ ⟨names that have a ~ sound to them —John McNulty⟩ **2** : having or covered with fine soft hairs, plumes, or scales
²silky *or* **silk·ie** \"\ *n, pl* **silkies** [¹*silky*] **1** : a bird of a breed of small five-toed crested domestic fowls having soft white webless feathers and the ear lobes and the lumpy rose comb purple **2** : a mutation of the domestic fowl in which the barbs of the feathers are not linked together to form a web
silky anteater *n* : a squirrel-sized So. American arboreal anteater (*Cyclopes didactylus*) distinguished by very beautiful long silky golden fur — called also *two-toed anteater*
silky ash *n* : an Australian timber tree (*Ehretia acuminata*) with lustrous tough firm light wood that works well
silky beech *n* : an Australian evergreen tree (*Villaresia moorei*) of the family Icacinaceae with hard lustrous grayish wood that is used esp. for cabinetwork and interior joinery
silky bent grass *n* : a stout leafy European grass (*Agrostis spica-venti*) occas. naturalized in the eastern U. S.
silky camellia *n* : a shrub or small tree (*Stewartia malachodendron*) of the southeastern U.S. often cultivated as an ornamental and having white flowers with blue anthers and dark purple filaments
silky cornel *or* **silky dogwood** *n* : either of two No. American shrubs: **a** : a shrub (*Cornus amomum*) with purplish twigs, finely pubescent leaves, and blue fruit — called also *kinnikinnick* **b** : a closely related and very similar shrub (*C. obliqua*)
silky marmoset *n* **1** : a tawny Brazilian marmoset (*Callithrix chrysoleucos*) with long silky fur **2** : SILKY TAMARIN
silky oak *var of* SILK OAK
silky swallowwort *n* : a common milkweed (*Asclepias syriaca*)
silky tamarin *n* : a golden yellow So. American lion monkey (*Leontocebus rosalia*) having long soft hair forming a mane
silky wallaby *n* : NAIL-TAILED WALLABY
silky willow *n* **1** : WHITE WILLOW **2** : a No. American willow (*Salix sericea*) with silky-pubescent leaves that usu. blacken in drying **3** : SITKA WILLOW
silky wisteria *n* : a Chinese wisteria (*Wisteria venusta*) widely cultivated as an ornamental vine and having white flowers and leaves that are pubescent at maturity
¹sill *also* **cill** \'sil\ *n* -s [ME *sille, selle*, fr. OE *syll*; akin to OHG *swelli* beam, threshold, ON *svill, syll* sill, Gk *selis* crossbeam, rower's bench, *selma* deck, rower's bench] **1 a** : a horizontal piece (as a timber) that forms the lowest member or one of the lowest members of a framework or supporting structure (as of a house, a bridge, a loom, a mine set, or a truck body) — compare MUDSILL **b** : the horizontal member or structure (as of wood, stone, or brick) at the base of a window opening serving esp. to cover the wall at the base of the opening : WINDOWSILL **c** : the timber or stone at the foot of a door : THRESHOLD **d** : a piece of timber across the bottom of an entrance to a dock or a canal lock for the gates to shut against **e** (1) : the inner lower edge of an embrasure of a fortification (2) : one of the horizontal timbers forming the upper and lower boundaries of a gun port (as on an old warship) **2** : the floor of a coal seam **3** : a tabular body of igneous rock injected while molten between sedimentary or volcanic beds or along foliation planes of metamorphic rocks **4** : an elevation (as a low ridge between mountains) separating two valleys or basins; *esp* : a submerged ridge at relatively shallow depth separating the basins of two bodies of water **5** : the top surface of a usu. low or normally submerged dam
²sill \"\ *vt* -ED/-ING/-S : to provide with a sill
³sill \"\ *n* -s [by alter.] *archaic* : THILL
sillabub *var of* SYLLABUB
sil·la·gin·i·dae \ˌsilə'jinəˌdē\ *n pl, cap* [NL, fr. *Sillagin-, Sillago*, type genus + *-idae*] : a small family of elongate percoid fishes of the shallow waters of the tropical Indo-Pacific that though small are excellent food fishes
¹sil·lag·i·noid \sə'lajəˌnȯid\ *adj* [NL *Sillagin-, Sillago* + E *-oid*] : resembling or related to the Sillaginidae
²sillaginoid \"\ *n* -s : a sillaginoid fish
sil·la·go \sə'lā(ˌ)gō\ *n, cap* [NL *Sillagin-, Sillago*] : a genus (the type of the family Sillaginidae) of percoid fishes — see WHITING
sil·lar \sēl'yär\ *n, pl* **silla·res** \-äˌrās\ [Sp, ashlar, fr. *silla* seat, chair (fr. L *sella*) + *-ar* (fr. L *-aris*) — more at SETTLE] : building material consisting of large blocks cut from a natural deposit (as of lava, tuff, limestone, or compact clay)
sill cock *n* : a water faucet placed at about sill height on the outside of a building and usu. threaded for attaching a hose — called also *hose cock*
sill course *n* : a course at the level of a windowsill
sil·len·ite \'siləˌnīt\ *n* -s [L. G. *Sillén* 20th cent. Swed. mineralogist + E *-ite*] : a mineral Bi_2O_3 that consists of a native bismuth oxide in earthy masses and that is polymorphous with bismite
sil·ler \'silə(r)\ *chiefly dial var of* SILVER
sill floor *n* : the bottom floor of a stope in the square-set system of mining
sillibub *var of* SYLLABUB
sil·li·ly \'siləlē, -li\ *adv* : in a silly manner
sil·li·man·ite \'siləməˌnīt\ *n* -s [Benjamin *Silliman* †1864 Am. chemist and geologist + E *-ite*] : a brown, grayish, or pale green mineral Al_2SiO_5 that consists of an aluminum silicate in orthorhombic crystals often occurring in fibrous or columnar forms and that is polymorphous with cyanite and andalusite — called also *fibrolite*; see SILLIMANITE GROUP
sillimanite group *n* : the group of minerals comprising sillimanite, cyanite, andalusite, dumortierite, topaz, and mullite
sil·li·ness \'silēnəs, -lin-\ *n* -ES **1** : the quality or state of being silly **2** : a silly practice
silling *pres part of* SILL
sill man *n* : a worker who replaces rotten sills of lead-lined copper-refining tanks
sil·lock \'silək\ *n* -s [Sc *sill* young herring (of Scand origin; akin to Norw *sild* herring) + *-ock* — more at SILD] *Scot* : a young pollack
sil·log·ra·pher \sə'lägrəfə(r)\ *n* -s [Gk *sillographos*, fr. *sillos* satirical poem + *-graphos* writer, fr. *graphein* to write — more at CARVE] : a writer of satires
sills *pl of* SILL, *pres 3d sing of* SILL
¹sil·ly \'silē, -li\ *adj* -ER/-EST [ME *sely, silly* happy, blessed, innocent, pitiable, feeble, fr. (assumed) OE *sǣlig*, fr. *sǣl* happiness + *-ig* -y; akin to OHG *sālig* happy, ON *sæla* happiness, Goth *selei* kindness, L *solari* to console, comfort, Gk *hilaros* cheerful] **1 a** : needing compassion or sympathy : PATHETIC **b** : helpless against attack : DEFENSELESS — now usu. used of sheep **c** : WEAK, SICKLY **d** *obs* : MEAGER, PALTRY, SCANTY **2 a** : RUSTIC, SIMPLE, PLAIN ⟨~ buckets on the deck —S.T. Coleridge⟩ ⟨a sound peaceful and ~ as any cowbell heard in the Alps —Osbert Sitwell⟩ **b** *obs* : lowly in station : HUMBLE **3 a** : weak in intellect : destitute of ordinary strength of mind ⟨a child who was rather ~⟩ **b** : exhibiting a lack of judgment or intelligence : FOOLISH, INANE, VACUOUS ⟨although we maintained a blackout at night, we felt ~ about it —A.J.Liebling⟩ ⟨the ~ air of one who does not understand fear —Arnold Bennett⟩ **c** : contrary to reason : ABSURD, RIDICULOUS, IRRATIONAL ⟨the question is as ~ as it sounds —Telford Taylor⟩ ⟨always making ~ remarks⟩ **d** : lacking importance or serious meaning : TRIVIAL, TRIFLING, FRIVOLOUS ⟨written in a facetious strain that accords with the rather ~ title —*Times Lit. Supp.*⟩ ⟨if we tend to regard the pursuit of the new as necessarily ~ and modish —E.R.Bentley⟩ ⟨passed the time by telling ~ stories⟩ **4** : DAZED, STUNNED, STUPEFIED — used postpositively ⟨was knocked ~ by the blow⟩ ⟨would slap me ~ —J.H.Burns⟩

⟨bored ~ by the unwonted inactivity⟩ **5 :** very close to the batsman — used of a fielding position in cricket or the player in it ⟨~ point⟩ ⟨~ mid on⟩ ⟨~ leg⟩ **syn** see FOOLISH, SIMPLE

2silly \"\ *adv* **:** SILLILY ⟨behave ~⟩

3silly \"\ *n* -ES **:** one who is silly ⟨am very likely a ~ — meeting trouble half-way —D.H.Lawrence⟩ ⟨well then, ~, why not stay! —Edna Ferber⟩

4silly \"\ *vb* -ED/-ING/-ES *vt, chiefly dial* **:** to make silly **~** *vi, chiefly dial* **:** to be or act silly

silly billy *n, usu cap B* [1*silly* + *Billy*, nickname for William; prob. after William IV †1837, king of England] **:** a foolish person

sillyhow \ˈ==ˌ=\ *n* [1*silly* + *how* (caul)] *chiefly Scot* **:** a caul on a newborn infant

silly season *n* **:** a period (as late summer) when newspapers must resort to minor or fantastic matters for lack of major news stories

1si·lo \ˈsī(ˌ)lō\ *n* -S [Sp, perh. of Celtic origin; akin to OIr *sil* seed; akin to OE *sāwan* to sow — more at SOW] **1 :** a trench, pit, or typically cylindrical structure usu. sealed (as with earth, heavy paper, or plastic) when full to exclude air and used for storing silage **2** *chiefly Brit* **:** a tall usu. cylindrical bin for grain storage esp. as part of a grain elevator; *also* **:** ELEVATOR 1c **3 a :** a deep usu. cylindrical bin either aboveground or belowground for storing material (as cement or coal) **b :** an underground structure for storing a guided missile in readiness for firing

2silo \"\ *vt* -ED/-ING/-ES **:** to place (as fodder) in a silo **:** ENSILE

silo filler *n* **:** a machine for blowing, elevating or unloading chopped fodder into a silo **:** SILAGE CUTTER

si·lox·ane \səˈläkˌsān\ *n* -S [blend of *silane* and *oxygen*] **:** any of a class of compounds that contain alternate silicon and oxygen atoms in either a linear structure [as $H_3Si(OSiH_2)_n$-$OSiH_3$] or a cyclic structure [as $(H_2SiO)_n$] and that in many cases contain methyl, phenyl, or other organic radicals in place of some or all of the hydrogen atoms and that are made by hydrolysis of chlorosilanes or alkoxy-silanes — see SILICONE

sil·pha \ˈsilfə\ *n, cap* [NL, fr. Gk *silphē* cockroach, bookworm] **:** a genus (the type of the family Silphidae) of clavicorn beetles

1sil·phid \-fəd\ *adj* [NL *Silphidae*] **:** of or relating to the Silphidae

2silphid \"\ *n* -S **:** a beetle of the family Silphidae

sil·phi·dae \-fəˌdē\ *n pl, cap* [NL, fr. *Silpha*, type genus + *-idae*] **:** a widely distributed family of clavicorn beetles comprising the burying beetles, carrion beetles, and related forms

sil·phi·um \ˈsilfēəm\ *n* [L, fr. Gk *silphion*; of North African origin] **1** *pl* **sil·phia** \-ēə\ **:** an extinct umbelliferous plant of the genus *Ferula* not definitely identifiable as to species but well known to the ancient Greeks and used by them medicinally **2** *cap* [NL, fr. L] **:** a large genus of tall No. American perennial herbs (family Compositae) having coarse heads of yellow flowers with fertile rays and broad flat winged achenes — see CUP PLANT

sils *pl of* SIL

1silt \ˈsilt\ *n* -S [ME *cylte*, prob. of Scand origin; akin to Dan & Norw *sylt* salt marsh, Sw dial. *sylta*; akin to OHG *sulza* salt marsh, OE *sealt* salt — more at SALT] **1 a :** unconsolidated or loose sedimentary material whose constituent rock particles are finer than grains of sand and larger than clay particles; *specif* **:** material consisting of mineral soil particles ranging in diameter from 0.02 to 0.002 millimeters **b :** sedimentary material consisting esp. of mineral particles intermediate in size between those of sand and clay suspended in running or standing water **c :** a deposit of sediment (as by a river) **d :** a material that is similar to silt in particle size and consistency **:** FINES ⟨coal ~⟩ **2 :** SCUM, DREGS, RESIDUE ⟨chocolate . . . covered with tobacco grains from the ~ of his pockets —Norman Mailer⟩

2silt \"\ *vb* -ED/-ING/-S *vi* **1 :** to become choked or obstructed with silt — often used with *up* ⟨the channel ~*ed up*⟩ **2 :** to flow as silt **:** PERCOLATE, DRIFT ⟨sand ~*ed* over wheat fields —*Lamp*⟩ **~** *vt* **:** to choke, fill, cover, or obstruct with silt or mud ⟨the beaver had ~*ed* the creek —Hugh Fosburgh⟩ — often used with *up* ⟨its harbor is now entirely ~*ed* up —L.R. Colcord⟩

silt·age \-tij\ *n* -S [2*silt* + *-age*] **:** a mass of silt

sil·ta·tion \silˈtāshən\ *n* -S [2*silt* + *-ation*] **:** the deposition or accumulation of silt ⟨since ~ has been negligible, the lake is clear —W.H.Thompson & Don Hutson⟩

silting *n* -S [fr. gerund of 2*silt*] **1 :** the process by which a stream deposits silt behind a dam or other place of retarded flow **:** SILTATION **2 :** the act of filling old mine workings hydraulically with fine waste material

silt loam *n* [1*silt*] **:** soil containing not less than 70 percent silt and clay and not less than 20 percent sand

silt soil *n* **:** soil containing not less than 80 percent silt and not more than 12 percent sand

siltstone \ˈ=ˌ=\ *n* **:** a rock composed chiefly of indurated silt

silty \ˈsiltē, -ti\ *adj* -ER/-EST **:** full of silt **:** of, like, or suggestive of silt ⟨~ soil⟩

silty clay *n* **:** a clay soil containing from 50 to 70 percent silt

silty clay loam *n* **:** soil containing from 50 to 80 percent silt

si·lu·res \ˈsilyəˌrēz\ *n pl, usu cap* [L] **:** a people of ancient Britain described by Tacitus as occupying chiefly southern Wales

1si·lu·ri·an \səˈlu̇rēən, sīˈ-\ *adj, usu cap* [L *Silures* + E *-ian*] **1 :** of or relating to the Silures or their place of habitation **2 :** of or relating to the part of the Paleozoic era between the Ordovician and Devonian characterized by the flourishing of invertebrate marine life, the beginning of coral-reef building, and the appearance of some great crustaceans — see GEOLOGIC TIME table

2silurian \"\ *n* -S *usu cap* **1 :** one of the Silures **2 :** the Silurian period or system of rocks

silurian gray *n, often cap S* **:** a pale yellow green that is yellower, stronger, and slightly lighter than smoke gray, stronger than oyster gray, and yellower and slightly lighter than average Nile

1si·lu·rid \səˈlu̇rəd, sīˈ-\ *adj* [NL *Siluridae*] **:** of or relating to the Siluridae

2silurid \"\ *n* -S **:** a catfish of the family Siluridae

si·lu·ri·dae \-rəˌdē\ *n pl, cap* [NL, fr. *Silurus*, type genus + *-idae*] **:** a family of catfishes formerly comprising most of the catfishes but now usu. restricted to various freshwater fishes of Europe and Asia that differ from No. American catfishes in having the adipose dorsal fin rudimentary or lacking and in having the anal fin long and more or less confluent with the eellike caudal fin

sil·u·rist \ˈsilyərəst\ *n* -S *usu cap* [L *Silures* + E *-ist*] **:** a native of Brecknockshire in Wales

1si·lu·roid \-ˈu̇ˌrȯid\ *adj* [NL *Siluroidea*] **:** of or relating to the Siluroidea

2siluroid \"\ *n* -S **:** a fish of the suborder Siluroidea **:** CATFISH

sil·u·roi·dea \ˌsilyəˈrȯidēə\ *n pl, cap* [NL *Silurus* + *-oidea*] **:** a suborder of the order Ostariophysi comprising the catfishes

sil·u·roi·dei \-ēˌī\ [NL *Silurus* + *-oidei*] *syn of* SILUROIDEA

si·lu·rus \səˈlu̇rəs, sīˈ-\ *n* [NL, fr. L, a large river fish, fr. Gk *silouros*, fr. *sil-* (of unknown origin) + *oura* tail; akin to Gk *orrhos* buttocks — more at ASS] **1** *cap* **:** the type genus of Siluridae containing the sheatfish and several other Old World catfishes **2** -ES **:** any fish of the genus *Silurus*

sil·va \ˈsilvə\ *n, pl* **silvas** \-əz\ *or* **sil·vae** \-ˌlˌvē\ [NL, fr. L, wood, forest] **1 a :** the forest trees of a region or country **b :** a description of or treatise on the trees of a region **2 :** 1SELVA

1silvan *var of* SYLVAN

2sil·van *or* **syl·van** \ˈsilvən\ *adj* [NL *silva* + E *-an*] **:** of or relating to a silva

silvanite *var of* SYLVANITE

1sil·ver \ˈsilvə(r)\ *n* -S [ME, fr. OE *seolfor*; akin to OHG *silabar, silbar* silver, ON *silfr*, Goth *silubr*; all fr. a prehistoric Gmc word borrowed fr. an Asiatic source] **1 :** a white metallic element that is sonorous, ductile, very malleable, capable of a high degree of polish, and chiefly univalent in compounds, that has the highest thermal and electric conductivity of any substance, that is found native and also combined (as in stephanite, argentite, proustite, pyrargyrite, cerargyrite), that is obtained as the main product and as a by-product in copper and lead smelting, that is one of the noble metals in view of its resistance to oxidation or corrosion except tarnishing by combination with sulfur, that is usu. alloyed with copper to increase its hardness, and that is used for coinage, tableware, jewelry, plate, and a great variety of articles, in photography, in electrical contacts, and as a catalyst — symbol *Ag*; see COIN SILVER, ELEMENT table **2 :** silver as a commodity ⟨the value of ~ has risen⟩ **3 :** coin made of silver **:** silver money **:** MONEY ⟨cross my palm with ~⟩ ⟨customers . . . came now with cold hard ~ —Nelson Algren⟩ ⟨this I do for you and not for ~ —Pearl Buck⟩ **4 a :** flatware used at table and made of a variety of materials including sterling or plated silver ⟨her ~ is of stainless steel⟩ **b :** hollow ware made of silver or other metal and usu. used at table **5 :** 1ARGENT 3 **6 a :** something having the luster or appearance of silver: as (1) **:** SILVER FOX (2) **:** SILVER SALMON **b :** a nearly neutral slightly brownish medium gray — called also *argent*

2silver \"\ *adj* [ME, fr. 1*silver*] **1 :** made of silver ⟨polished ~ candlesticks⟩ **2 :** resembling silver: as **a :** having a white lustrous sheen **:** silvery in appearance ⟨a land of ~ rivers where the salmon leap —*Holiday*⟩ ⟨balloons waved slowly . . . looking like huge fat ~ sausages —Upton Sinclair⟩ ⟨her ~ head was held erect in spite of the years⟩ **b :** having or producing a clear resonant sound **:** dulcet in tone ⟨the ~ sound of the river over the pebbles —Winston Churchill⟩ **c :** eloquently persuasive ⟨whose . . . ~ tongue was heard in every movement of reform —Meridel Le Sueur⟩ **3** *obs* **:** sweetly gentle **:** PEACEFUL **4 a :** ARGENTIFEROUS **b :** partly composed of silver **5 :** of, relating to, or characteristic of silver ⟨the ~ legislation of 1873⟩ ⟨~ wagons headed down from the mines⟩ **6 :** of or relating to a silver age ⟨great periods of golden and ~ Latin —T. H. Savory⟩ **7 :** advocating the adoption of silver as a standard of currency **8 :** mounted, coated, or plated with silver **9 :** ARGENT 3 **10** [so called fr. the practice during the construction of the Panama canal of paying skilled white labor in gold and unskilled colored labor in silver] **:** of or for the Negro population in the Panama Canal Zone — compare GOLD 5

3silver \"\ *vb* **silvered; silvered; silvering** \-v(ə)riŋ\ **silvers** [ME *silveren*, fr. 1*silver*] *vt* **1 a :** to cover with silver (as by electroplating) **b :** to coat with a substance (as a metal) resembling silver ⟨~ a glass with an amalgam of tin and mercury⟩ **2 a :** to give a silvery luster to ⟨daylight fails and the moon ~*s* your way —Dorothy P. Richards⟩ **b :** to make white like silver ⟨time had ~*ed* her hair⟩ **~** *vi* **1 :** to move like a stream of silver **2 :** to acquire a silvery color ⟨light ~*ed* on windshields and fenders where cars were parked —Richard Llewellyn⟩

silver age *n* [2*silver*] **:** an historical period of successful achievement but falling short of the highest ideals and goals — compare GOLDEN AGE

silver anniversary *n* **:** a 25th anniversary

silver ash *n* **:** any of various trees of the genus *Flindersia*; *esp* **:** BUNJI-BUNJI

silver aster *n* **:** an aster (*Chrysopsis graminifolia*) with silvery pubescent leaves

silver award *n* **:** the highest of three ranks in the exploring program of the Boy Scouts of America

silverback \ˈ==ˌ=\ *n, NewEng* **:** 3KNOT b

silver-backed fox \ˈ==ˌ=-\ *n* **:** CAAMA 1

silver bal·li \-ˈbalē\ *n* [alter. of *siruaballi*] **1 :** any of several timber trees of the genera *Nectandra, Ocotea* and *Aniba* of northern So. America with yellowish or brown wood **2 :** the wood of a silver balli

silver bass *n* **1 :** WHITE PERCH 1 **2 :** FRESHWATER DRUM **3 :** WHITE BASS 1

silver bath *n* **:** a bath of dissolved silver salt

silver beard grass *n* **:** a tropical American grass (*Andropogon saccharoides*) established in No. America and having a dense panicle made up of several short clusters on an elongate axis with the pedicels and rachis joints being long-villous

silverbeater \ˈ==ˌ==\ *n* [1*silver* + *beater*] **:** one that beats silver into leaf or foil

silver beech *n* [2*silver*] **:** a New Zealand tree of the genus *Nothofagus* (esp. *N. Menziesii*)

silver beet *n, Austral & NewZeal* **:** CHARD

silver bell *also* **silver-bell tree** *n* **:** a medium sized tree (*Halesia carolina*) of the southeastern U.S. often cultivated for its showy bell-shaped white flowers — called also *opossum wood*

sil·ver·bel·ly \ˈsilvə(r)ˌbelē\ *also* **sil·ver·bid·dy** \-ˌbidē\ *n* [*silverbelly* fr. 2*silver* + *belly*; *silverbiddy*, alter. of *silverbelly*] *Austral & NewZeal* **:** a fish of the family Gerridae

sil·ver·berry \ˈsilvə(r)- — see BERRY\ *n* [2*silver* + *berry*] **:** a silvery No. American shrub (*Elaeagnus commutata*)

silverberry family *n* **:** ELAEAGNACEAE

silverbill \ˈ==ˌ=\ *n* [2*silver* + *bill*] **:** a weaverbird of the genus *Lonchura*

silver birch *n* **1 :** PAPER BIRCH **2 :** YELLOW BIRCH **3 :** a British birch (*Betula verrucosa*) having a trunk that is black and fissured below but silvery white above

silver-black fox *n* **:** SILVER FOX 1a

silver blight *n* **:** SILVERLEAF 2

sil·ver-blu \ˈsilvə(r)ˌblü\ *adj* [2*silver* + *blu*, alter. of *blue*] **:** a silvery gray-blue variety of mutation mink

silver bream *n* **:** any of several silvery fishes: as **a :** a large sea bream (*Rhabdosargus sarba*) of the tropical Indo-Pacific; *broadly* **:** any of several fishes of the genus *Rhabdosargus* (as the white stumpnose) **b :** TREVALLY 1

silver bromide *n* [1*silver*] **:** a compound AgBr that occurs naturally as bromyrite and is obtained synthetically as a white to yellowish curdy precipitate when aqueous solutions of a silver salt and a bromide are mixed and that is extremely sensitive to light and is much used in photography in the preparation of sensitive emulsion coatings for films, plates, and paper

silverbush \ˈ==ˌ=\ *n* [2*silver* + *bush*] **1 :** JUPITER'S-BEARD 2 **2 :** SILVERBERRY

silver button *n* **:** PEARLY EVERLASTING

silver cape *n, usu cap C* **:** a Cape diamond having a very slight yellow tint

silver carp *n* **1 :** the common carpsucker (*Carpiodes carpio*) **2 :** CARP 1a

silver cedar *n* **:** ROCKY MOUNTAIN JUNIPER

silver certificate *n* **:** a paper certificate issued by a government against silver deposited with it to a specified amount and payable to the bearer on demand; *specif* **:** a certificate issued against the deposit of silver coin that is legal tender for all public and private debts and for public charges, taxes, duties, and dues in the U.S. and its possessions — compare GOLD CERTIFICATE, TREASURY NOTE

silver chain *n* **:** LOCUST 3a(2)

silver chickweed *n* **:** a small silvery leaved perennial herb (*Paronychia argyrocoma*) of the southeastern U.S.

silver china grass *n* **:** RAMIE 1

silver chloride *n* [1*silver*] **:** a compound AgCl that occurs naturally as cerargyrite and is obtained synthetically as a white curdy precipitate when aqueous solutions of a silver salt and a chloride are mixed, that is sensitive to light becoming violet and finally black, and that is used chiefly in photography esp. for papers

silver cloth *n* [2*silver*] **1 :** CLOTH OF SILVER **2 :** LAMÉ

silver-copper glance *n* **:** STROMEYERITE

silver cord *n* **1 :** UMBILICAL CORD **2 :** the emotional tie between mother and child

silver cyanide *n* [1*silver*] **:** a poisonous compound AgCN or $Ag_x(CN)_x$ that is obtained as a white curdy precipitate when a soluble cyanide is added to aqueous solutions of a silver salt and that readily forms complex cyanides (as potassium argentocyanide $KAg(CN)_2$) used in silver plating

silver deposit *n* **:** silver electroplated often in intricate designs to glass

silvered *adj* [fr. past part. of 3*silver*] **1 a :** covered, adorned, or dressed with or as if with silver **b :** backed with quicksilver and tinfoil and thus made into a mirror **2 :** having a silvery sheen, luster, or color ⟨~ furs⟩ ⟨~ gray hair⟩ **3 :** affected with silverleaf

silvered glass *n* **:** MERCURY GLASS

silver eel *n* [2*silver*] **1** *South* **:** CUTLASS FISH **2 :** an eel just attained to sexual maturity, characterized by a silvery color, and about to return to the ocean to breed

sil·ver·er \ˈsilvərə(r)\ *n* -S **:** one that silvers: as **a :** ELECTROPLATER **b :** a worker who silvers mirror glass **c :** a device used for silvering

silvereye \ˈ==ˌ=\ *n* [2*silver* + *eye*] **:** any of several small Old World singing birds of *Zosterops* or related genera (as *Z. palpebroso* of India or *Z. lateralis* of Australia and New Zealand) having the eyes encircled by a ring of white feathers — called also *white-eye*

silver fern *n* **:** any of various ferns (as of the genera *Gleichenia, Notholaena*, and *Pityrogramma*) having the lower surface of the fronds silvery white

silverfin \ˈ==ˌ=\ *n* [2*silver* + *fin*] **1 :** SATINFIN **2 :** SPOTTAIL SHINER

silver fir *n* **:** any of various true firs having leaves white or silvery white beneath: as **a :** a valuable European timber tree (*Abies alba*) yielding Burgundy pitch and Strasbourg turpentine **b :** AMABILIS FIR **c :** WHITE FIR 1a (1) **d :** BALSAM FIR

silverfish \ˈ==ˌ=\ *n, pl* **silverfish** *or* **silverfishes** **1 :** any of various silvery fishes: as **a :** TARPON **b :** a white or silvery variety of the goldfish **c :** SILVERSIDES **d :** GOLDEN SHINER **e :** SILVER HAKE **f :** CUTLASS FISH **g :** any of several fishes of the family Denticidae; *esp* **:** an important So. African food fish (*Argyrozona*, or *Dentex, argyrozona*) **2** *pl silverfish* **:** any of various small wingless silvery insects of the order Thysanura; *esp* **:** an insect (*Lepisma saccharina*) found about houses and sometimes injurious to sized papers or starched clothes — called also *fish moth*

silver fizz *n* **:** a fizz made from lemon juice, gin, and white of egg

silver foil *n* [ME *silverfoile*, fr. 2*silver* + *foile* foil] **:** silver or other metal of a similar color (as aluminum) in very thin sheets

silver fox *n* **1 a :** a color phase of the red fox in which the pelt is black and more or less tipped with white and which apparently represents a genetic variant that can be induced to breed true under controlled conditions **b :** CAAMA 1 **c :** BLACK-BACKED JACKAL **2** *usu cap* **:** an American breed of rabbits with white hairs scattered among the jet black fur

silver fulminate *n* [1*silver*] **:** a white crystalline compound AgONC similar to mercury fulminate but more violently explosive

silver gar *n* [2*silver*] **:** NEEDLEFISH 1

silver gibbon *n* **:** an ashy gray gibbon (*Hylobates moloch*) of Java and Borneo

silver gilt *n* [ME, fr. 1*silver* + *gilt*, adj.] **:** gilded silver ⟨the coronets are of *silver gilt* —H.S.London⟩

silver glance *n* [2*silver*] **:** ARGENTITE

silver grain *n* **:** the lines or figures of the medullary rays on various woods (as oak or bird's-eye maple) in longitudinal or tangential sections

silver-grained \ˈ==ˌ=\ *adj* **:** QUARTER-SAWED

silver grass *n* **:** any of several grasses or grasslike plants having silvery pubescence: as **a :** RIBBON GRASS **b :** a plant of the genera *Danthonia, Deschampsia*, and *Festuca* of Australia and New Zealand **c :** a golden aster (*Chrysopsis graminifolia*) of southern U.S. with silvery grasslike foliage

silver gray *n* **:** a light brownish gray that is yellower, lighter, and slightly less strong than slate gray and yellower and lighter than ashes

silver-gray fox *n* **:** SILVER FOX

silver green *n* **:** a grayish yellow green that is yellower and paler than average sage green and yellower, lighter, and stronger than palmetto

silver-haired bat \ˈ==ˌ=-\ *n* **:** a No. American vespertilionid bat (*Lasionycteris noctivagans*) that is blackish brown with the hairs tipped with silvery white

silver hake *n* **:** a common hake (*Merluccius bilinearis*) of the northern New England coast that is important as a food fish

silver halide *n* [1*silver*] **:** a halide of silver; *esp* **:** one used in photography — see PHOTOHALIDE; compare SILVER BROMIDE, SILVER CHLORIDE, SILVER IODIDE

silverhead \ˈ==ˌ=\ *n* [2*silver* + *head*] **:** SILVER CHICKWEED

silver herring *n* **:** the menhaden esp. when processed and canned for food

sil·ver·i·ness \ˈsilv(ə)rēnəs\ *n* -ES **:** the quality or state of being silvery

silvering *n* -S [fr. gerund of 3*silver*] **1 a :** the silver or a film resembling silver on a silvered object **b :** the act or process of covering with silver **2 :** a silvery appearance **3 :** a sprinkling of white or light hairs in the coat of a mammal

silver iodide *n* [1*silver*] **:** a compound AgI occurring naturally as iodyrite and obtained synthetically as a yellow curdy precipitate when aqueous solutions of a silver salt and an iodide are mixed that darkens on exposure to light, and that is used chiefly in photography, in rainmaking, and in medicine in colloidal form in treatment of infections of mucous membranes

sil·ver·ite \ˈsilvəˌrīt\ *n* -S [1*silver* + *-ite*] **:** one favoring use or establishment of silver as a monetary standard

sil·ver·ize \-ˌīz\ *vt* -ED/-ING/-S [1*silver* + *-ize*] **:** to cover or treat with silver **:** make silvery

silver jackal *n* [2*silver*] **1 :** BLACK-BACKED JACKAL **2 :** CAAMA 1

silver jenny *n, pl* **silver jennies** **:** a small mojarra (*Eucinostomus gula*) of the Atlantic coast from Cape Cod to Rio de Janeiro

silver jubilee *n* **:** SILVER ANNIVERSARY

silver king *n* **:** TARPON

silver lace *n* **:** lace or braid formerly made of silver wire but now made of threads or cords with a silver color or with a covering of silver threads and used for uniforms or official robes as an indication of rank

silver-laced \ˈ==ˌ=\ *adj* [*silver lace* + *-ed*] **:** adorned with silver lace

silver-lace vine *n* **:** a twining perennial (*Polygonum aubertii*) of China having racemes of fragrant greenish flowers

silver-lead \ˈ==ˌ=\ *adj* [1*silver* + *lead*] **:** containing silver and lead ⟨*silver-lead* ore⟩

silver leaf *n* **:** very thin silver foil

silverleaf \ˈ==ˌ=\ *n* [2*silver* + *leaf*] **1 :** any of several plants having silvery leaves: as **a :** BUFFALO BERRY **b :** a hydrangea (*Hydrangea radiata*) with white tomentum on the lower leaf surfaces **c :** QUEEN'S-DELIGHT **d :** WHITE POPLAR 1a **e :** JEWELWEED **f :** HARDHACK 1 **g :** HONESTY 3 **h :** PEARLY EVERLASTING **2** *also* **silver leaf disease** **:** a disease of shrubs and trees caused by a basidiomycete (*Stereum purpureum*) and characterized by the peculiar silvery appearance of the leaves; *also* **:** a similar symptom of various other diseases — called also *silver blight*

silverleaf nightshade *also* **silver-leaved nightshade** \ˈ==ˌ=-\ *n* **:** TROMPILLO

silverleaf oak *n* **:** a small to medium-sized oak (*Quercus hypoleuca*) of the southwestern U.S. and adjacent Mexico having silvery white tomentum on the lower surfaces of the slender lanceolate leaves — called also *whiteleaf oak*

silver linden *n* **1 :** WHITE BASSWOOD **2 :** a basswood (*Tilia tomentosa*) that is native to eastern Europe and Asia Minor but widely cultivated as an ornamental and that has leaves with a white tomentum on their lower surfaces

silverline system \ˈ==ˌ=-\ *n* [2*silver* + *line*] **:** a series of superficial lines in many protozoans that stain intensely with silver impregnation techniques and are variously regarded as supporting or coordinating organelles or as surface striations and sculpturings

sil·ver·ling \ˈsilvə(r)liŋ\ *n* -S [G *silberling*, fr. OHG *silabarling*, fr. *silabar* silver + *-ing* — more at SILVER] **:** a small silver coin

silver lining *n* [2*silver*] **1 :** a white edge on a cloud **2 :** a consoling or hopeful prospect

silver lip *n* **:** a pearl oyster that is specif. identical with the gold lip but has the inner shell margin white or silvery

silver louse *n* **:** SILVERFISH 2

silver lunge *n* **:** LAKE TROUT b

silver lupine *n* **:** SILVERY LUPINE

sil·ver·ly *adv* [2*silver* + *-ly*] **:** with silvery appearance or sound ⟨Venus brooding ~ above a line of pale green sky —Edith Wharton⟩

silver-mail \ˈ==ˌ=\ *n* [2*silver* + *mail* (payment)] **:** WHITE RENT

silver maple *n* **1 :** a common No. American maple (*Acer saccharinum*) with deeply cut leaves that are light green above and silvery white beneath **2 :** the hard close-grained but brittle light brown wood of the silver maple

silver marlin *n* **:** a silvery blue marlin of the Pacific ocean sometimes recognized as a distinct variety (*Makaira nigricans tahitiensis*)
silver mite *n* **:** RUST MITE
silver moth *n* **:** SILVERFISH 2
sil·vern \ˈsilvə(r)n\ *adj* [ME *silveren, selvern,* fr. OE *seolfren, seolfern,* fr. *seolfor* silver + *-en*] **1 :** made of silver **2 :** resembling or characteristic of silver **:** SILVERY ⟨the soft ~ voice . . . quickened the place —W.A.White⟩
sil·ver·ness *n* -ES **:** the quality or state of being silver
silver nitrate *n* [¹*silver*] **:** a poisonous irritant crystalline soluble salt $AgNO_3$ obtained by the action of nitric acid on silver that blackens on contact with organic matter, that is used chiefly in making silver halides for photography, in silvering (as glass for mirrors), as a chemical reagent in indelible inks and hair dyes, and in medicine externally as an astringent, antiseptic, and germicide — see LUNAR CAUSTIC
silver oak *n* [²*silver*] **1 :** FLANNELBUSH **2 :** SILK OAK
silver owl *n* **:** BARN OWL
silver oxide *n* [¹*silver*] **:** an oxide of silver; *esp* **:** the compound Ag_2O obtained as a dark-brown amorphous precipitate when an aqueous solution of a silver salt is treated with a caustic alkali, that reacts as a hydroxide if moist, that dissolves in ammonia water, and that oxidizes aldehydes to acids
silver palm *n* [²*silver*] **:** a fan palm (*Coccothrinax argentata*) of Florida and the West Indies, with leaves brilliantly white on the underside — called also *silver thatch, silvertop*
silver paper *n* **1 :** a fine white tissue paper; *esp* **:** tissue paper free from acids and sulfur used as a wrapping for silverware — called also *silver tissue* **2 :** a metallic paper with a coating or lamination resembling silver — called also *tinfoil*
silver-penciled \ˈ==ˌ==\ *adj* **1 :** penciled in silver **2** *of feathers* **:** penciled with white
silver perch *n* **:** any of various somewhat silvery fishes that resemble perch: as **a :** a silvery brown-dotted Australian freshwater grunt (*Therapon bidyana*) or a related fish esteemed for food and sport **b :** a mademoiselle (*Bairdiella chrysura*) **c :** WHITE PERCH 1 **d :** CRAPPIE **e :** any of several mojarras
silver pheasant *n* **1 a :** a large long-tailed pheasant (*Lophura nycthemera* or *Gennaeus nycthemerus*) of southern China that is often reared in Europe and America, has in the male a naked red face, a flowing bluish black crest, white tail, upper parts lightly penciled with black, and bluish black underparts, and is in the female chiefly mottled brownish **b :** any of various other pheasants of the same genus **2 :** any of several of the eared pheasants
silver picrate *n* [¹*silver*] **:** a poisonous explosive yellow crystalline salt $(O_2N)_3C_6H_2OAg.H_2O$ used as an antiseptic esp. in vaginitis and urethritis
silver pine *n* [²*silver*] **1 :** WESTERN WHITE PINE 1 **2 :** PONDEROSA PINE 1 **3 :** BALSAM FIR 1 **4 :** any of several evergreen timber trees of the genus *Dacrydium* (esp. *D. colensoi*) having shiny white wood
silver plate *n* **1 :** a plating of silver **2 :** domestic flatware and hollow ware made of silver or of a silver-plated base metal
silver-plate \ˈ==ˌ=\ *vt* [*silver plate*] **:** to electroplate with silver
silver plover *n, Scot* **:** ³KNOT
silverpoint \ˈ==ˌ=\ *n* [²*silver* + *point*] **1 :** the process of drawing with a pencil of silver usu. on paper or parchment which has been specially prepared (as with a wash of Chinese white) **2 :** a drawing made by this process
silver point *n* [¹*silver*] **:** the melting point of silver that is 960.8°C and that is used as one of the fixed points of the international temperature scale
silver poplar *n* [²*silver*] **:** WHITE POPLAR 1a
silver print *n* **1 :** a photographic print on a surface sensitized with silver salts or formerly on albumen printing-out paper **2 :** a print made by silver printing
silver-print drawing *n* **:** a pen drawing that is made over the photographic image of a light-sensitive paper after which the silver print is bleached out leaving the traced drawing and that is used frequently for changing a photograph into a line drawing
silver printing *n* **:** printing in silver usu. by using size instead of ink and dusting over with silver bronze
silver protein *n* [¹*silver*] **:** any of several colloidal light-sensitive preparations of silver and protein used in aqueous solution on mucous membranes as antiseptics and classified by their efficacy and irritant properties: as **a :** a preparation containing 19 to 23 percent of silver and consisting of dark brown or almost black shining scales or granules — called also *mild silver protein* **b :** a more irritant preparation containing 7.5 to 8.5 percent of silver and consisting of a pale yellowish orange to brownish black powder — called also *strong silver protein*
silver quandong *n* [²*silver*] **:** BRISBANE QUANDONG
silverrod \ˈ==ˌ=\ *n* **1 :** a European asphodel (*Asphodelus ramosus*) with paniculate white flowers **2 :** a white-rayed goldenrod (as *Solidago bicolor*)
silvers *pl of* SILVER, *pres 3d sing of* SILVER
silver sage *n* **:** any of several sages having silvery foliage: as **a :** PURPLE SAGE **b :** SILVER SAGEBRUSH
silver sagebrush *n* **:** a usu. low and much-branched perennial sagebrush (*Artemisia cana*) of the western U.S. that has silvery entire leaves and is an important browse and shelter plant — called also *gray sage*
silver salmon *n* **1 :** a rather small salmon (*Oncorhynchus kisutch*) that has flesh which is very light-colored but of good flavor and that is a native of both coasts of the No. Pacific **2 :** KING SALMON
silver salt *n* [in sense 1, fr. ¹*silver;* in sense 2, fr. ²*silver*] **1 :** a salt of silver **2 :** a silvery crystalline salt $C_{14}H_7O_2SO_3Na$ used in dye manufacture **:** the sodium salt of anthraquinone-2-sulfonic acid
silverscale \ˈ==ˌ=\ *n* [²*silver* + *scale*] *n* **:** a bushy annual saltbush (*Atriplex argentea*) that has scurfy gray foliage and is widespread on alkaline soils of the western U.S.
silver screen *n* **1 :** a motion-picture screen **2 :** MOTION PICTURES ⟨my favorite heroine of the *silver screen* —Richard Bissell⟩
silver scurf *also* **silver scab** *n* **1 :** a disease of potato tubers caused by a fungus (*Spondylocladium atrovirens*) and characterized by silvery patches on the skin **2 :** a silvering of citrus fruits caused by thrips
silverside \ˈ==ˌ=\ *n* [²*silver* + *side*] *Brit* **:** top of a round of beef
silversides \ˈ==ˌsīdz\ *n pl but sing or pl in constr, also* **silverside** \-d\ [²*silver* + *sides, side*] **1 :** any of various small fishes of the family Atherinidae that have a silvery stripe along each side of the body and are related to the gray mullets; *esp* **:** a fish (*Menidia notata*) that is very abundant on the American Atlantic coast **2 :** any of various freshwater minnows of *Notropis* and related genera **3 :** SILVER SALMON
silverskin \ˈ==ˌ=\ *n* [²*silver* + *skin*] **:** a thin papery layer that surrounds a coffee bean immediately inside the parchment
silversmith \ˈ==ˌ=\ *n* [ME, fr. OE *seolforsmith,* fr. *seolfor* silver + *smith*] **1 :** an artisan who makes vessels, jewelry, or other articles of silver **2 :** a manufacturer of or dealer in silver or silverware
silversmith·ing \"+iŋ\ *n* [*silversmith* + *-ing*] **:** the work of a silversmith
silver snake *n* [²*silver*] **:** RUBBER BOA
silver solder *n* **:** any of various solders containing silver
silver spoon *n* **:** WEALTH; *esp* **:** inherited wealth ⟨whether . . . endowed with a *silver spoon* or burdened with poverty —P.A.Sorokin⟩ ⟨born with a *silver spoon* in his mouth⟩ ⟨social grace is acquired more easily by those who grow up with *silver spoons* in their mouths —C.J.Friedrich⟩
silver-spoon \ˈ==ˌ=\ *adj* [*silver spoon*] **:** having a prosperous background **:** of a well-to-do family environment ⟨you might from a hint of courtliness . . . think he's a *silver-spoon* man —Anita Brenner⟩
silverspot \ˈ==ˌ=\ *n* [²*silver* + *spot*] **:** a butterfly of *Speyeria* or a related genus having silvery spots on the underside of the hind wings
silver spruce *n* **:** any of several spruces of western No. America with pale or glaucous leaves: as **a :** COLORADO SPRUCE **b :** SITKA SPRUCE **c :** ENGELMANN SPRUCE
silver squeteague *n* **:** a common weakfish (*Cynoscion nothus*) of the Atlantic coast of No. America that is tan above and silvery below
silver stain *n* **:** a transparent yellow enamel used upon the glass of decorative windows and esp. prominent in windows of the sixteenth century
silver standard *n* [¹*silver*] **:** a monetary standard under which the basic unit of currency is defined by a stated quantity of silver and which is usu. characterized by the coinage and circulation of silver, unrestricted convertibility of other money into silver, and the free import and export of silver for the settlement of international obligations
silver stick *n* [²*silver*] **1 :** a silver-headed staff presented by the British sovereign to a field officer of the Life Guardsmen **2** *usu cap both Ss* **:** one entitled to carry the silver stick on state occasions
silversword \ˈ==ˌ=\ *n* [²*silver* + *sword*] **:** a low growing plant (*Argyroxiphium sandwichense*) of the family Compositae that is found only in craters in Hawaii and has narrow pointed silver green leaves in rosettes and clusters of purplish flower heads
silvertail \ˈ==ˌ=\ *n* [²*silver* + *tail*] **:** SILVERFISH 2
silver tea *n* [¹*silver*] **:** a tea at which voluntary contributions of money are given usu. for special fund-raising or charitable purposes
silver teal *n* [²*silver*] **:** CINNAMON TEAL
silver tetra *n* **:** a small silvery compressed So. American characin fish (*Ctenobrycon spilurus*) often kept in the tropical aquarium
silver thatch *n* **:** any of several thatch palms with silvery leaves: as **a :** SILVER PALM **b :** SILVERTOP 2a **c :** a palm (*Thrinax parviflora* syn. *T. keyensis*) of southern Florida and the West Indies that is closely related to and much resembles the common silvertop but has leaves somewhat bluish green at maturity
silver thaw *n* **1** *or* **silver storm :** a coating of ice on trees and other exposed objects **:** GLAZE **2 :** RIME
silver thistle *n* **:** COTTON THISTLE
silvertip \ˈ==ˌ=\ *n* [²*silver* + *tip*] **:** a grizzly bear having the hairs whitish at the tips
silver tissue *n* **:** SILVER PAPER 1
silver-tongue \ˈ==ˌ=\ *n* [²*silver* + *tongue*] **1 :** a silver-tongued person **2 :** SONG SPARROW
silver-tongued \ˈ==ˌ=\ *adj* **:** possessed of agreeable persuasive speech **:** ELOQUENT
silvertop \ˈ==ˌ=\ *n* -S **1 :** an abnormal condition of various plants marked by whitened patches on the leaves and distortion and dwarfing of growing parts and caused by the feeding of insects or mites: **a :** such a condition of cereal and other grasses caused usu. by a mite (*Sitopteres graminum*) **b :** a widespread condition of onions caused by the onion thrips **2** *or* **silvertop palmetto a :** a rather small stocky fan palm (*Thrinax microcarpa*) of southernmost Florida and Cuba that has broad fan-shaped long-petioled leaves pale green above and whitish and tomentose below — called also *silver thatch* **b :** any of various usu. low-growing and silvery-leaved palms (as a silver palm) of southern Florida or the West Indies that resemble or are related to the common silvertop **3 :** any of several eucalypts: as **a :** SHINING GUM **b :** SPOTTED GUM
silver torch *or* **silver torch cactus** *n* **:** a cylindrical cactus (*Cleistocactus strausii*) of the family Cactaceae having numerous hairlike white spines and red flowers
silver tree *n* **1 :** a So. African tree (*Leucadendron argenteum*) commonly cultivated for its long silvery silky leaves **2 :** an Australian timber tree (*Tarrietia argyrodendron*) of the family Sterculiaceae **3 :** SILVER BELL
silver tree fern *n* **:** a showy New Zealand tree fern (*Cyathea medullaris*) frequently cultivated for its handsome crown of much-pinnate fronds which are whitish on the underside
silver trout *n* **:** any of several silvery fishes: as **a :** a trout that is a silvery variety of the cutthroat trout and is native to Lake Tahoe and adjacent waters **b :** a salmon that is a small landlocked variety of the sockeye salmon **c :** a trout that is a silvery variety of the brook trout and is known only from Monadnock Lake
silver twig *n* **:** a diseased condition of smooth-barked twigs in which the epidermis is lifted up causing a silvery appearance
silvervine \ˈ==ˌ=\ *n* **1 :** a climbing Indo-Malayan aroid (*Scindapsus pictus argyraeus*) often cultivated for its white-mottled foliage **2 :** an ornamental dioecious woody vine (*Actinidia polygama*) of eastern Asia that has edible fruits and is very attractive to cats
silverware \ˈ==ˌ=\ *n* **:** SILVER PLATE; *esp* **:** table knives, forks, and spoons usu. of silver, a silver-plated base metal, or stainless steel
silver wattle *n* **:** any of several plants of the genus *Acacia:* as **a :** a shrub or small tree (*Acacia dealbata*) with white or silvery bark and young foliage **b :** LIGHTWOOD 2a
silver wedding *n* **:** a silver anniversary of a wedding
silverweed \ˈ==ˌ=\ *n* **:** any of various somewhat silvery plants: as **a** (1) **:** a European perennial cinquefoil (*Potentilla anserina*) with leaves silvery white beneath that is naturalized in the eastern U.S. (2) **:** a prostrate cinquefoil (*Potentilla argentea*) of the north temperate zone with 5-foliolate to many-foliolate leaves that are densely white-tomentose beneath and small yellow flowers **b :** an East Indian shrub of the genus *Argyreia* (family Convolvulaceae) **c :** JEWELWEED b **d :** TALL MEADOW RUE **e :** HARDHACK 1
silver white *n* **1 :** WHITE 1c **2 :** any of various white pigments (as flake white)
silver whiting *n* **:** a dull silvery whiting (*Menticirrhus littoralis*) marked with oblique dusky bars that is common along the south Atlantic and Gulf coasts of the U.S.
silver whitlowwort *n* **:** SILVER CHICKWEED
silver willow *n* **:** any of several willows having silvery leaves; *esp* **:** a pussy willow (*Salix discolor*)
silverwing \ˈ==ˌ=\ *n* **:** CINDER GRAY
silver witch *n* **:** SILVERFISH 2
silverwork \ˈ==ˌ=\ *n* **:** work in silver **:** a piece of work made of silver esp. when ornamental or decorative **:** the work of the silversmith
sil·very \ˈsilv(ə)rē, -ri\ *adj* [¹*silver* + *-y*] **1 :** having the clear musical tone of silver **:** RESONANT **:** soft and clear in sound ⟨the clarinet's . . . tone will be muted and ~ —Roland Gelatt⟩ ⟨the ~ tinkling of his spurs as he moved —Zane Grey⟩ **2 :** resembling or having the luster of silver **:** lustrous and of the color silver ⟨repeated scrubbings have given the wood a ~ sheen —*Amer. Guide Series: Mich.*⟩ ⟨a mop of ~ curls —Thomas Wood †1950⟩ **3 :** full of, containing, or made of silver or something resembling silver
silvery anchovy *n* **:** any of numerous small fishes of *Anchoviella* or related genera of the family Engraulidae having a silvery stripe along the side
silvery cinquefoil *n* **:** SILVERWEED a(2)
silvery gibbon *n* **:** SILVER GIBBON
silvery-haired bat \ˈ==(=)ˌ=-\ *n* **:** SILVER-HAIRED BAT
silvery hair grass *n* **:** a hair grass (*Aira caryophyllea*) with silvery shining panicles
silvery iron *n* **:** a peculiar light-gray fine-grained variety of cast iron of high silicon content
silvery lupine *n* **:** either of two silvery-pubescent herbs of the western U.S. with blue or purple flowers: **a :** an herb (*Lupinus argenteus*) that has foliage poisonous to sheep **b :** an herb (*L. caudatus*) that is common on well-drained land
silvery minnow *n* **:** a cyprinoid fish (*Hybognathus nuchalis*) that is common in the rivers of the eastern, central, and southern U.S., *also* **:** any of several related fishes
silver y moth *n, cap Y* [²*silver* + *y* + *moth*] **:** a moth of the genus *Plusia* having a silvery Y on the fore wings; *esp* **:** GAMMA MOTH
silvery sage *n* **:** SILVER SAGEBRUSH
silvery spleenwort *n* **:** a fern (*Athyrium thelypterioides*) with elongate silvery indusia
sil·ves·ter method \silˈvestə(r)-\ *n, usu cap S* [after Henry Robert *Silvester* †1908 Eng. physician] **:** a method of artificial respiration in which the subject is laid on his back and air is expelled from his lungs by pressing his arms over his chest and fresh air drawn in by pulling them above his head
sil·vi·cal \ˈsilvəkəl\ *adj* [*silvics* + *-al*] **:** of or relating to silvics
sil·vic·o·lous \silˈvikələs\ *adj* [L *silvicola* inhabitant of a wood (fr. *silva* wood + *-i-* + *-cola* — fr. *colere* to inhabit) + E *-ous* — more at WHEEL] **:** living in or inhabiting woodlands
sil·vics *or* **syl·vics** \ˈsilviks\ *n pl but sing in constr* [NL *silva, sylva* + E *-ics*] **:** the study of the life history and characteristics of forest trees esp. as they occur in stands and with particular reference to environmental influences
sil·vi·cul·tur·al \ˌsilvəˈkəlch(ə)rəl\ *adj* **:** of or relating to silviculture — **sil·vi·cul·tur·al·ly** \-rəlē\ *adv*
sil·vi·cul·ture *or* **syl·vi·cul·ture** \ˈ==ˌkelchə(r)\ *n* [F, fr. L *silva, sylva* wood, forest + *-i-* + F *culture,* fr. L *cultura*] **:** a phase of forestry that deals with the establishment, development, reproduction, and care of forest trees — compare ARBORICULTURE
sil·vi·cul·tur·ist \ˌ==ˈkəlch(ə)rəst\ *n* **:** a forester who specializes in silviculture
sil·yl \ˈsiləl\ *n* -S [*sil-* + *-yl*] **:** the univalent radical SiH_3 derived from monosilane by removal of one hydrogen atom
sim *abbr* **1** similar **2** simile
SIM *abbr* sergeant instructor of musketry
¹**si·ma** \ˈsīmə\ *var of* CYMA
²**sima** \"\ *n* -S [G, fr. *silicium* + *magnesium*] **:** basic igneous rock whether solid or molten — compare SIAL — **si·mat·ic** \(ˈ)sīˈmad·ik\ *adj*
si·ma·ba \səˈmäbə\ *n, cap* [NL, fr. native name in Guiana] **:** a genus of tropical So. American trees (family Simaroubaceae) having pinnate leaves and panicles of small flowers with 5 imbricated sepals, 5 petals, and 10 stamens — see CEDRON
si·mal \ˈsēməl\ *n* -S [Hindi *semal*] **1 :** an East Indian silk-cotton tree (*Bombax malabarica*) that yields a fiber inferior to kapok **2 :** the fiber of the simal tree — called also *red silk cotton*
si·mar *or* **sy·mar** \səˈmär\ *n* -S [F *simarre,* fr. It *zimarra,* fr. Sp *zamarra,* prob. fr. Basque *zamar* sheepskin] **1** *archaic* **a** *or* **si·marre** \"\ **:** a flowing coat dress with a full skirt and train worn by women during the Renaissance **b** *or* **cy·mar** \"\ **:** a light undergarment **:** SHIFT **2 :** ZIMARRA
sim·a·rou·ba \ˌsiməˈrübə\ *n, cap* [NL, fr. F, fr. Galibi *simaruba*] **:** a genus (the type of the family Simaroubaceae) of tropical American shrubs and trees with odd-pinnate leaves, pale light soft wood, bitter bark sometimes used medicinally, and clustered thin-fleshed drupes — see MARUPA, PARADISE TREE
sim·a·rou·ba·ce·ae \ˌ==(ˌ)=ˈbāsēˌē\ *n pl, cap* [NL, fr. *Simarouba,* type genus + *-aceae*] **:** a family of chiefly tropical trees and shrubs (order Geraniales) having bitter bark, mainly pinnate leaves, small 3-merous to 5-merous flowers with a prominent disk that are succeeded by a drupe, berry, or samara — see AILANTHUS, SIMAROUBA — **sim·a·rou·ba·ceous** \ˌ==(ˌ)=ˈbāshəs\ *adj*
sim·a·ru·ba \ˌsiməˈrübə\ [NL, fr. Galibi] *syn of* SIMAROUBA
sim·e·on·ism \ˈsimēəˌnizəm\ *n* -S *usu cap* [Charles *Simeon* †1836 Eng. evangelical preacher + E *-ism*] **:** the principles and practices of the Simeonites
¹**sim·e·on·ite** \-ˌnīt\ *n* -S *usu cap* [LL *Simeonitae* Simeonites, fr. *Simeon,* second son of the patriarch Jacob + L *-itae,* pl. of *-ita* -ite] **:** a member of the Hebrew tribe of Simeon
²**simeonite** \"\ *n* -S *usu cap* [Charles *Simeon* †1836 + E *-ite*] **1 :** a follower of the clerical leader Charles Simeon of the Evangelical Revival in the Church of England and founder of a trust for purchasing advowsons for Low Churchmen **2 :** LOW CHURCHMAN
sim·fer·o·pol \ˌsim(p)fəˈrōpəl, -rōp-\ *adj, usu cap* [fr. *Simferopol,* city of Crimea Region, U.S.S.R.] **:** of or from the city of Simferopol, U.S.S.R. **:** of the kind or style prevalent in Simferopol
sim·hah *or* **sim·cha** \ˈsimkə\ *n, pl* **sim·hoth** *or* **sim·hot** \-ˌkōt(h), -ōs\ *or* **sim·has** \-kəz\ *or* **sim·choth** *or* **sim·chot** \-ˌkōt(h), -ōs\ *or* **sim·chas** \-kəz\ [Heb *śimḥāh* rejoicing, mirth] **:** a happy occasion **:** a joyous celebration (as a bar mitzvah) ⟨the neighbors were guests at the family ~⟩
sim·hath to·rah *or* **sim·hat to·rah** *or* **sim·chas to·rah** *or* **sim·chath to·rah** *or* **sim·chat to·rah** \ˈsimkäˈstōrə\ *n, usu cap S&T* [Heb *śimḥath tōrāh* rejoicing of the Torah] **:** a festival observed on the 23d of Tishri in celebration of the completion of the Pentateuchal readings in the annual cycle
sim·ia \ˈsimēə\ *n, cap* [NL, fr. L, ape — more at SIMIAN] **:** a Linnaean genus of primates orig. including most of the apes and monkeys, subsequently restricted to the orang, later transferred to the chimpanzee and still later to the Barbary ape, and finally suppressed by international agreement to avoid confusion
sim·i·al \-ēəl\ *adj* [L *simia* ape + E *-al*] *archaic* **:** SIMIAN
¹**sim·i·an** \-mēən, -myən\ *adj* [L *simia* ape (fr. *simus* snub-nosed, fr. Gk *simos*) + E *-an;* prob. akin to OHG *swīnan* vanish, subside, ON *svina*] **:** of, relating to, characteristic of, or resembling monkeys or apes
²**simian** \"\ *n* -S **:** MONKEY, APE; *esp* **:** ANTHROPOID 2
sim·i·an·i·ty \ˌsimēˈanəd·ē\ *n* -ES **:** the quality or state of being simian
simian shelf *n* **:** a bony ledge on the inside of the mandible characteristic of the anthropoid apes
sim·i·as \ˈsimēəs\ *n, cap* [NL, fr. L *simia* ape] **:** a genus including solely the pig-tailed langur
¹**sim·i·id** \-ēəd\ *adj* [NL *Simiidae*] **:** of or relating to the Pongidae
²**simiid** \"\ *n* -S **:** an ape of the family Pongidae
si·mi·i·dae \səˈmīəˌdē\ [NL, fr. *Simia* + *-idae*] *syn of* PONGIDAE
¹**sim·i·lar** \ˈsim(ə)lə(r) *also* -ml-, *substand* -myəl-\ *adj* [F *similaire,* fr. MF, fr. L *similis* like, similar + OF *-aire* -ary — more at SAME] **1 :** having characteristics in common **:** very much alike **:** COMPARABLE ⟨for shaping slots, keyways . . . or ~ cuts —H.D.Burghardt & Aaron Axelrod⟩ ⟨instruction for children in daily ethics, religion . . . and ~ subjects —S.P.Chase & J.K.Snyder⟩ ⟨extremists of the right — so ~ in so many ways to the extremists of the left —J.B.Oakes⟩ **2 :** alike in substance or essentials **:** CORRESPONDING ⟨no two animal habitats are exactly ~ —W.H.Dowdeswell⟩ **3 a :** having the same shape **:** differing only in size and position — used of geometrical figures **b :** moving in the same direction in relation to pitch — used of the motion of two or more voice parts in a musical progression **syn** see LIKE
²**similar** \"\ *n* -S **:** one that resembles another **:** COUNTERPART, LIKE
sim·i·lar·i·ty \ˌsiməˈlarəd·ē, -myə-, -rətē, -i *also* -ler-\ *n* -ES **1 :** the quality or state of being similar **:** RESEMBLANCE, CONFORMITY ⟨the ~ between cougars and jaguars⟩ ⟨the dangerous ~ of a mushroom to a toadstool⟩ ⟨~ of tastes among teen-agers⟩ ⟨of association by contiguity, by ~ and by contrast —R.S.Woodworth⟩ **2 :** a comparable aspect **:** ANALOGY, CORRESPONDENCE ⟨has a better eye for *similarities* among cultures than for diversities —Raphael Demos⟩
sim·i·lar·ly *adv* [¹*similar* + *-ly*] **:** in the same or a comparable manner **:** CORRESPONDINGLY, LIKEWISE ⟨suffered less from declining . . . production than most ~ situated communities —*Amer. Guide Series: Texas*⟩ ⟨~, the political and economic background of the conspiracy is inadequately treated —Nathan Schachner⟩
similarly placed *adj* **:** having the corresponding sides parallel and directed in the same sense
¹**sim·i·la·tive** \ˈsiməˌlād·iv, -lәd·-\ *adj* [L *similis* similar + E *-ative*] **:** expressing similarity
²**similative** \"\ *n* -S **:** something expressing similarity
sim·i·le \ˈsimə(ˌ)lē, -li\ *n* -S [L, fr. neut. of *similis* like, similar] **1 :** a figure of speech comparing two essentially unlike things and often introduced by *like* or *as* (as in *cheeks like roses, a heart as hard as flint*) — compare METAPHOR **2 :** SIMILARITY ⟨a close ~ between the conditions of occurrence of the disease and those of certain other virus diseases —*Veterinary Record*⟩
²**si·mi·le** \ˈsēməˌlā\ *adv* [It, fr. L *similis*] **:** LIKE, SIMILAR — used as a direction in music to continue the same phrasing, use of pedals, or whatever has been previously directed
³**simile** \" *or* **simile mark** *n, pl* **simi·li** \(ˌ)lē\ [It *simile*] **:** a printed sign (as ' / / .) indicating that a musical figure or measure is to be repeated as often as the mark occurs
¹**si·mil·i·ter** \səˈmiləd·ə(r)\ *n* -S [L, in like manner, fr. *similis* like] **:** a reply by which the pleader in a common law pleading concurs with the other party in requesting trial by jury
²**similiter** \"\ *adv* [L] **:** in like manner
si·mil·i·tude \səˈmiləˌtüd, -əˌtyüd\ *n* -S [ME, fr. MF, likeness, resemblance, fr. L *similitudin-, similitudo,* fr. *similis* similar + *-tudin-, -tudo* -tude] **1 a :** COUNTERPART, DOUBLE ⟨met my own ~ —Agnes Repplier⟩ **b :** a visible likeness

: IMAGE, SEMBLANCE ⟨a spirit or devil in the ~ and proportion of a man —Margaret A. Murray⟩ **2** : an imaginative comparison : ALLEGORY, SIMILE ⟨London is often likened to Babylon; but the ~ is . . . unjust —Arthur Helps⟩ **3 a** : RESEMBLANCE, UNIFORMITY ⟨~ of specimens and test conditions was maintained —*Technical News Bull.*⟩ **b** : a point of comparison ⟨all medieval variances of thought show common ~s —H.O. Taylor⟩ **4** : maximal similarity of adjacent phonemes because of use of maximally similar allophones

sim·i·lize \ˈsiməˌlīz\ *vt* -ED/-ING/-S [*simile* + *-ize*] : LIKEN, COMPARE; *esp* : to express in simile

sim·i·ous \ˈsimēəs\ *adj* [L *simia* ape + E *-ous* — more at SIMIAN] : SIMIAN

sim·lin \ˈsimlən\ *also* **sim·ling** \-liŋ\ *n* -S [prob. alter. of *simnel*] *chiefly South & Midland* : CYMLING

sim·men·tal *also* **sim·men·thal** \ˈzimən.ˌtäl\ *or* **sim·men·tha·ler** \-lə(r)\ *n* [*Simmental, Simmenthal* fr. *Simmental*, valley of the Simme river in central Switzerland; *Simmenthaler* fr. G *Simmentaler* of Simmental, fr. *Simmental*] **1** *usu cap* : a Swiss breed of large buff or dull red and white cattle used widely in Europe for meat, milk, and draft **2** -S *sometimes cap* : an animal of the Simmental breed

[1]**sim·mer** \ˈsimə(r)\ *vb* **simmered; simmered; simmering** \-m(ə)riŋ\ **simmers** [alter. of ¹*simper*, fr. ME *simperen*, of imit. origin] *vi* **1** : to stew gently with a bubbling sound below or just at the boiling point ⟨cover with water and let ~ four hours⟩ ⟨an iron pot . . . ~*ing* in one corner —*Amer. Guide Series: Tenn.*⟩ **2 a** : to be in a state of incipient development : FERMENT ⟨manages to keep about four plots constantly ~*ing* —Martin Levin⟩ ⟨a crisis began to ~ a fortnight ago —*Time*⟩ **b** : to be in inward turmoil : SEETHE ⟨this family . . . ~s with hostilities —Brooks Atkinson⟩ ⟨underneath these well-mannered exchanges there will continue to ~ a deeply felt . . . irritation —H.G.Nicholas⟩ ~ *vt* : to cook slowly in a liquid at a uniform heat just below the boiling point ⟨~ the meat until tender⟩ ⟨fruits which are to be kept whole should be ~*ed* —Marjorie M. Heseltine & Ula M. Dow⟩

[2]**simmer** \ˈ"\ *n* -S **1** : a condition approaching a boil ⟨the bubble and ~ of a stew⟩ ⟨crowded tenement houses, always on the ~ with crime —*Fortnight*⟩ **2** : a degree of heat that produces simmering ⟨electric ranges now can be adjusted for . . . degrees of heat, from ~ to superhot —*House Beautiful*⟩ ⟨that ~ of sun —Ira Wolfert⟩

[3]**sim·mer** \ˈsimər\ *Scot var of* SUMMER

simmer down *vi* [¹*simmer*] **1** : to become reduced by or as if by simmering ⟨let the broth *simmer down* to a rich stock⟩ ⟨it . . . all *simmers down* to a matter of design —E.B.White⟩ **2** : to become calm or peaceful : QUIET, RELAX ⟨protests angrily but soon *simmers down*⟩ ⟨time would have elapsed for things to *simmer down* —Nevil Shute⟩ ⟨early May days find social activities *simmering down* a bit —Alice Dameron⟩

sim·mon \ˈsimən\ *n* -S [by shortening] : PERSIMMON

sim·monds' disease \ˈsimən(d)z-\ *n, usu cap S* [after Morris *Simmonds* †1925 Ger. physician] : a disease characterized by extreme and progressive emaciation with atrophy of internal organs, loss of body hair, evidences of premature aging and caused by atrophy or destruction of the anterior lobe of the pituitary gland

sim·nel \ˈsimnəl\ *n* -S [ME *simenel*, fr. OF, fr. L *simila* finest wheaten flour, prob. of Sem origin like Gk *semidalis* finest wheaten flour; akin to Assyr *samīdu* fine meal, Syr *sĕmīdā*] **1** *or* **simnel bread** : a bun or bread made of the finest wheat flour **2** *or* **simnel cake** *Brit* **a** : a fruited cake resembling a plum pudding that is covered with a flour paste and first boiled, then baked, and traditionally eaten on Mothering Sunday **b** : a rich fruit cake sometimes coated with almond paste and baked for mid-Lent, Easter, and Christmas

si·mo·leon \səˈmōlēən, -lyən\ *n* -S [perh. alter. (influenced by *napoleon*) of earlier *simon*, of unknown origin] *slang* : DOLLAR

[1]**si·mo·ni·ac** \sīˈmōnēˌak, səˈm-\ *n* -S [ME, fr. MF or ML; MF *simoniaque*, fr. ML *simoniacus*, fr. *simoniacus* of simony, fr. LL *simonia* simony] : one who practices simony

[2]**simoniac** \"\ *or* **si·mo·ni·a·cal** \ˌsīməˈnīəkəl, ˌsim-\ *adj* : of, relating to, or characterized by simony — **si·mo·ni·a·cal·ly** \-k(ə)lē, -li\ *adv*

[1]**si·mo·ni·an** \sīˈmōnēən\ *n* -S *usu cap* [LGk *simōnianoi* followers of Simon Magus, fr. pl. of *simōnianos* of Simon, fr. *Simōn*, personal name of Simon Magus, 1st cent. Samaritan sorcerer] : a follower of Simon Magus : a member of any of various early gnostic sects reputed to follow his teachings

[2]**simonian** \"\ *adj, usu cap* : of, relating to, or characteristic of Simon Magus or the Simonians

si·mo·nian·ism \-əˌnizəm\ *n* -S *usu cap* : the doctrines and practices of Simonians

si·mo·ni·ous \sīˈmōnēəs, səˈm-\ *adj* [*simony* + *-ous*] *archaic* : SIMONIAC

simo·nist \ˈsīmənəst, ˈsim-\ *n* -S : one who practices or defends simony

si·mo·nize \ˈsīməˌnīz\ *vt* -ED/-ING/-S [fr. *Simoniz*, a trademark] : to polish with or as if with wax ⟨the children had been bathed, brushed and scrubbed till they looked sullen but *simonized* —Peter De Vries⟩

si·mon le·gree \ˈsīmənlə'grē\ *n, pl* **simon legrees** *usu cap S&L* [after *Simon Legree*, cruel slave dealer in *Uncle Tom's Cabin* (1852), novel by Harriet Beecher Stowe †1896, Am. author] : a cruel taskmaster

[1]**simon-pure** \ˈ==ˈ=\ *adj* [fr. the phrase *the real Simon Pure*, alluding to a character impersonated by another in the play *A Bold Stroke for a Wife* (1718) by Susanna Centlivre †1723 Eng. dramatist and actress] **1** : of unqualified authenticity : GENUINE, UNADULTERATED ⟨remained during the thirties a *simon-pure*, uncompromising Marxist —C.I.Glicksberg⟩ **2** : untainted by bribery ⟨fight to make U.S. college football a *simon-pure* amateur game —*Time*⟩

[2]**simon-pure** \"\ *n* -S : a legitimate amateur ⟨was a professional until his reinstatement as a *simon-pure* —*Newsweek*⟩

simo·ny \ˈsīmənē, ˈsim-, -ni\ *n* -ES [LL *simonia*, fr. *Simon* Magus, 1st cent. Samaritan sorcerer rebuked by Peter for offering money to purchase the power of giving the Holy Ghost, Acts 8: 9–24 + L *-ia* -y] : the buying or selling of a church office or ecclesiastical preferment

si·moom \səˈmüm, sīˈmüm\ *also* **si·moon** \-ün\ *or* **sa·mum** \səˈmüm\ *n* -S [Ar *samūm*] : a hot dry violent wind laden with dust from Asian and African deserts — called also *samiel*

simorg *or* **simorgh** *var of* SIMURGH

simous *adj* [L *simus* snub-nosed — more at SIMIAN] *obs* : flat or curving in : CONCAVE, SNUB ⟨a ~ nose⟩ ⟨~ beak⟩

simp \ˈsimp\ *n* -S [by shortening] : SIMPLETON

sim·pai \ˈsimˌpī\ *n* -S [Malay] : a highly colored Sumatran langur (*Presbytis melalopha*) having a narrow blackish crest, the forehead, cheeks, and underparts yellowish, the upper parts brown and reddish — called also *black-crested monkey*

sim·pati·co \simˈpädiˌkō, -pad-\ *adj* [It *simpatico* (fr. *simpatia* sympathy, congeniality — fr. L *sympathia* sympathy — + *-ico* -ic, fr. L *-icus*) & Sp *simpático*, fr. *simpatía* (fr. L *sympathia*) + *-ico*, fr. L *-icus* — more at SYMPATHY] **1** : possessing attractive qualities : APPEALING, LIKABLE ⟨a bull I liked — a ~, noble animal —Barnaby Conrad⟩ **2** : exhibiting or inclined toward harmony : CONGENIAL, SYMPATHETIC ⟨buildings . . . ~ with the early Spanish and Indian motif —Conrad Richter⟩

[1]**sim·per** \ˈsimpə(r)\ *vi* **simpered; simpered; simpering** \-p(ə)riŋ\ **simpers** *dial Eng* : SIMMER

[2]**simper** \"\ *vb* -ED/-ING/-S [perh. of Scand origin; akin to Norw *semper* fine, smart, Dan dial. *semper, simper* affected, coy] *vi* **1** : to smile fatuously : SMIRK ⟨a two-fisted writer . . . does look out of place ~*ing* over a cup of tea —Jeann Beattie⟩ **2** *dial Eng* : WHIMPER ~ *vt* : to say with a simper

[3]**simper** \"\ *n* -S : an inane self-conscious smile : vacuous grin : SMIRK

sim·per·er \-p(ə)rə(r)\ *n* -S : one that simpers

simpering *adj* [fr. pres. part. of ²*simper*] : marked by insipidity : COY, PUSILLANIMOUS ⟨in a rather ~ voice —J.B.S.Haldane⟩ ⟨chocolate boxes flaunting their ~ inanity —Albert Dasnoy⟩ — **sim·per·ing·ly** *adv*

[1]**sim·ple** \ˈsimpəl\ *adj* **simpler** \-p(ə)lə(r)\ **simplest** \-p(ə)ləst\ [ME, fr. OF, plain, uncomplicated, artless, fr. L *simplus* or *simplex*; L *simplus* fr. *sem-*, *sim-* one + *-plus* multiplied by; L *simplic-*, *simplex* fr. *sem-*, *sim-* + *-plic-*, *-plex* -fold; akin to Gk *diplak-*, *diplax* twofold, double, and perh. to L *plaga* surface, region — more at SAME, DOUBLE, FLAKE] **1** : free from guile : INNOCENT, ARTLESS ⟨children grow up in ~ beauty around his table —*Irish Digest*⟩ **2 a** : free from vanity or conceit : MODEST, UNASSUMING ⟨his ~ manners and unaffected friendliness —A.W.Long⟩ **b** : free from ostentation or display : PLAIN, UNADORNED ⟨her black dress, ~ to austerity —W.S.Maugham⟩ ⟨a ~ rectangular brick building —*Amer. Guide Series: Va.*⟩ ⟨his home ~, his possessions few —P.E.James⟩ ⟨love of the ~ life, of trees and small animals —B.M.Woodbridge⟩ **3 a** : of humble origin : COMMON ⟨found it easier to proclaim himself a prophet than in his home city, where everyone had known him as a ~ camel driver —H.W. Van Loon⟩ **b** *archaic* : lacking special distinction : ORDINARY ⟨this change affected . . . only the ~ barons —William Stubbs⟩ **c** *archaic* : wanting in power or importance : FEEBLE, INSIGNIFICANT ⟨a ~ woman, much too weak to oppose your cunning —Shak.⟩ ⟨scoffed at . . . this high quest as at a ~ thing —Alfred Tennyson⟩ **4 a** : lacking in knowledge or scholarly finesse : UNEDUCATED, INEXPERT ⟨a ~ amateur . . . or a serious scholar —Denys Sutton⟩ ⟨show my mind, according to my shallow ~ skill —Shak.⟩ **b** (1) : mentally retarded : STUPID, HALF-WITTED ⟨one of the girls is ~, the other works as a domestic —J.M.Mogey⟩ (2) : easily deceived : CREDULOUS, GULLIBLE ⟨the whole town was baited with . . . trickery to catch the ~ cowhand and remove his cash —S.H.Holbrook⟩ **c** : being at a relatively low cultural level : NAÏVE, UNSOPHISTICATED ⟨the worldwide story of the conquest of ~ peoples and their homelands by the civilization, arms, and diseases of a more dominant race —*Amer. Guide Series: Minn.*⟩ **5 a** : lacking admixture or qualification : PURE, SHEER ⟨~ honesty requires us to admit that none of our creeds are entirely free from guesswork —M.R.Cohen⟩ ⟨a net rusher pure and ~ lacking a really powerful serve —*Sydney* (*Australia*) *Bull.*⟩ ⟨in no case may a warrant be issued for a ~ exploratory search —Paul Wilson⟩ ⟨ratification of treaties by a ~ majority —Vera M. Dean⟩ **b** (1) : free of secondary complications ⟨a ~ fracture⟩ (2) : containing or consisting of elementary ingredients ⟨her cures were ~ . . . usually very sensible —Mary Webb⟩ **c** : consisting of or constituting a basic element : FUNDAMENTAL, UNCOMPOUNDED ⟨one of those ~ and profound experiences . . . which people seem always to have known when it happens to them —Thomas Wolfe⟩ ⟨even under the most uniform laboratory conditions, a ~ color will be complex to the extent of having a bluish edge —John Dewey⟩; *specif* : ELEMENTAL 2a(2) **d** (1) : having a relatively small and uncomplicated molecule : not complex (2) : made up of essentially similar constituents ⟨a ~ compound⟩ : characterized by the same groups, radicals, or ions ⟨triacetin is a ~ glyceride⟩ — opposed to *mixed* **e** : admitting of no analysis into parts — opposed to *complex* **f** : having the least possible scoring value in its class **6 a** : grammatically uncomplicated: as (1) : having no subsidiary components (as suffixes or combining forms) : being a simplex ⟨a ~ word⟩ — contrasted with *complex, compound* (2) : having only one main clause and no subordinate clauses ⟨"let's go for a walk" is a ~ sentence⟩ — contrasted with *complex, compound* (3) : having no modifiers, complements, or objects ⟨in the sentence "birds fly" *birds* is the ~ subject and *fly* the ~ predicate⟩ — compare COMPLETE (4) : formed without the use of an auxiliary verb ⟨~ tense⟩ — opposed to *compound* **b** (1) : having two, three, or four basic rhythmic units to the musical measure (as 2/4, 3/2, 4/8) ⟨~ time⟩ ⟨~ meter⟩ — compare COMPOUND (2) : free from elaboration or figuration ⟨~ harmony⟩ ⟨~ counterpoint⟩ — contrasted with *figurate* (3) : not greater than the octave ⟨~ interval⟩ **c** : not complex or compound ⟨~ fractions⟩ ⟨~ magnitudes⟩ ⟨~ operations⟩ ⟨~ equations⟩ ⟨~ interest⟩ **d** (1) : not subdivided into branches ⟨~ stem⟩ (2) : MONOCARPELLARY (3) : consisting of cells of a similar structure and function ⟨~ tissue⟩ (4) : developing from a single ovary ⟨~ fruit⟩ **e** : uncomplicated in structure ⟨a ~ lens⟩ ⟨a ~ democracy in which the heads of families met fortnightly to consult about . . . matters —*Amer. Guide Series: R.I.*⟩ **f** : apparently dependent on the action of a single gene ⟨~ inherited characters⟩ **g** (1) : HOMOGENEOUS 2a ⟨a ~ mineral⟩ (2) : PRIMITIVE 1c — compare SPACE LATTICE **7 a** : oral or written but not under seal or of record ⟨~ contract⟩ **b** : unaccompanied by complicating factors (as violence) **c** : having no limitation or restrictions : ABSOLUTE, UNCONDITIONAL ⟨~ obligation⟩ — compare FEE SIMPLE **8** : readily understood or performed : causing little difficulty : EASY, STRAIGHTFORWARD ⟨our mother . . . was as complex as our father was ~ —L.C.Powys⟩ ⟨the causes . . . lie deep, and to explain them is not ~ —William Petersen⟩ ⟨nontechnical, clear-cut, easily understandable, ~ step-by-step . . . rules which could be used by the average person —W.J.Reilly⟩

syn FOOLISH, SILLY, FATUOUS, ASININE: SIMPLE in this sense may imply either a degree of intelligence inadequate to cope with anything complex, a more definite feeblemindedness, or, in relation to persons of normal capacity, a failure to use one's intelligence ⟨she's rather *simple*, poor dear, and she thinks we're all wonderful —W.S.Maugham⟩ ⟨you are fretting about General Tilucy, and that is very *simple* of you —Jane Austen⟩ FOOLISH may indicate a mere lack of judgment or discretion or capricious failure to employ good sense and seriousness ⟨virtuous or vicious, thrifty or careless, wise or *foolish* —G.B. Shaw⟩ ⟨but *foolish* man foregoes his proper bliss —William Cowper⟩ SILLY may describe gross lack of judgment; it may connote folly, inanity, or nonsense ⟨the cut of her chiffon dress hinted that she had a *silly* conception of romance —Rebecca West⟩ ⟨the vapid and *silly* chatter of ordinary sociability —J.C.Powys⟩ FATUOUS is likely to involve fond, delusive, obtuse foolishness and disregard of reality ⟨with *fatuous* beaming he described a night at Barney's; without any success whatever, he tried to be funny —Sinclair Lewis⟩ ⟨her haughtiness in the day of glory was simply *fatuous*, based on stupidity —Arnold Bennett⟩ ⟨a number of *fatuous* theories about the connection of Central American culture with that of the Old World have been broached —Edward Clodd⟩ ASININE describes utter failure to exercise normal intelligence, rationality, or perception ⟨his reply was simply contemptuous . . . "What an *asinine* question!" —Bram Stoker⟩ ⟨their cumulative efforts have resulted in the most *asinine* and inept movie that has come out of Hollywood in years —John McCarten⟩ **syn** see in addition EASY, NATURAL, PLAIN, PURE

[2]**simple** \"\ *n* -S [ME, fr. ¹*simple*] **1 a** : a person of humble birth : COMMONER ⟨thought very little of anybody, ~s or gentry —Virginia Woolf⟩ **b** (1) : an uneducated or unduly credulous person : IGNORAMUS, GULL ⟨universal education destroyed the advantage which the shrewd had over the ~ —Reinhold Niebuhr⟩ (2) : a mentally retarded person : SIMPLETON ⟨buffoons . . . were usually ~s or hunchbacks —J.S.Clarke⟩ **2 a** : a plant used for its supposed medicinal properties ⟨the herb garden and barn redolent with drying bunches of ~s —Lucy Embury⟩ **b** : a vegetable drug or medicinal preparation having only one ingredient ⟨herbs for their homely ~s —Flora Thompson⟩ **3** : a single element : one component of a complex; *specif* : an unanalyzable constituent **4 simples** *pl, dial chiefly Eng* : foolish behavior : SILLINESS ⟨you should be cut for the ~s this morning —Jonathan Swift⟩ **5** : a set of cords for raising the heddles of a drawloom **6** : a feast of the lowest liturgical order of precedence in the Roman Catholic Church — compare DOUBLE 1b

[3]**simple** \"\ *adv* **1** *obs* : in an unassuming manner : HUMBLY, MODESTLY ⟨as ~ as I stand here —Ben Jonson⟩ **2** *dial* : in a silly manner : FOOLISHLY

[4]**simple** \"\ *vb* **simpled; simpled; simpling** \-p(ə)liŋ\ **simples** *vi* [²*simple*] *obs* : to gather herbs for simples ~ *vt* [¹*simple*] : to cause (a compound steam engine) to work like a simple engine by admitting live steam directly from the boiler to the low-pressure cylinder ⟨~ the engine in starting a heavy freight train⟩

simple beam *n* [¹*simple*] : a structural beam that rests on a support at each end

simple bitters *n pl* : bitters containing practically no aromatic oils or tannin

simple bond *n* : a bond without conditions

simple bud *n* : a bud that produces either a vegetative leaf-bearing shoot or a flower but not both — compare MIXED BUD

simple consequence *n* : IMMEDIATE INFERENCE 1

simple contract *n* : PAROL CONTRACT

simple conversion *n* : the transposing of the subject and predicate of a proposition without altering the quantity or quality ⟨"no P is S" becomes "no S is P" by *simple conversion*⟩

simple curve *n* : a circular arc (as of railroad track) joining two tangents — compare COMPOUND CURVE

simple engine *n* **1** : an engine (as a steam engine) in which the expansion is completed in a single phase and exhausted to atmosphere or condenses after a single stroke of the piston — compare COMPOUND ENGINE **2** : a steam engine in which the live steam is fed directly to the cylinders and after a single use of its expansive force is allowed to escape through the exhaust — contrasted with *compound engine*

simple equation *n* : LINEAR EQUATION

simple eye *n* : an eye having a single lens — compare COMPOUND EYE; see INSECT illustration

simple-faced \ˈ==ˌ=\ *adj* [¹*simple* + *faced*] : having no nasal appendages — used of vespertilionid bats

simple fraction *n* : a fraction having whole numbers for the numerator and denominator — compare COMPLEX FRACTION

simple harmonic motion *n* : a harmonic motion of constant amplitude in which the acceleration is proportional and oppositely directed to the displacement of the body from a position of equilibrium : the projection on any diameter of a point in uniform motion around a circle

simplehearted \ˈ==ˈ==\ *adj* [¹*simple* + *hearted*] : having a simple nature : ARTLESS, UNSOPHISTICATED

simple honors *n pl* : three trump honors or three aces at a no-trump contract in bridge held by the same side

simple idea *n* : an idea of an unanalyzable quality : an immediate object of sensation or reflection

simple immersion *n* : immersion of a metal in an electroplating solution without the application of an external electromotive force

simple interest *n* : interest paid or computed on the original principal only of a loan or on the amount of an account often on the assumption that each day is 1/360 of a year — compare COMPOUND INTEREST

simple interval *n* : a musical interval of an octave or less — compare COMPOUND INTERVAL

simple knot *n* : OVERHAND KNOT

simple larceny *n* : larceny that is not accompanied by special aggravating circumstances

simple leaf *n* : a leaf whose blade is not divided to the midrib even though lobed — compare COMPOUND LEAF

simple machine *n* : any of various elementary mechanisms having the elements of which all machines are composed and including the lever, the wheel and axle, the pulley, the inclined plane, the wedge, and the screw

simpleminded \ˈ==ˈ==\ *adj* [¹*simple* + *minded*] **1** : characterized by simplicity : devoid of subtlety : CANDID, UNSOPHISTICATED ⟨~ in the fashion that only geniuses can be —Irving Kristol⟩ ⟨terrors which the religious belief in demons . . . aroused in the daily lives of ~ men and women —M.R.Cohen⟩ **2** : lacking in education or mental capacity : FEEBLEMINDED, SLOW ⟨palming off paper imitations of . . . valuables on the ~ ghosts and gods, who take them in all good faith for the genuine articles —J.G.Frazer⟩ **3** : marked by foolishness or frivolity : STUPID, NONSENSICAL ⟨a ~ mistake⟩ ⟨~ games, like scattering beans on the floor and handing out straws for the guests to draw them up —*Fortune*⟩ — **sim·ple·mind·ed·ly** *adv* — **sim·ple·mind·ed·ness** *n* -ES

simple mode *n, Lockeanism* : a mode resulting from the combination of simple ideas of the same kind (as a dozen or a score) — contrasted with *mixed mode*

simple motion *n* : a motion in a straight line, circle or circular arc, or helix ⟨*simple motion* of a clock pendulum⟩

sim·ple·ness *n* -ES [ME *simplenesse*, fr. ¹*simple* + *-nesse* -ness] **1** *archaic* : SIMPLICITY **2** *obs* : irresponsible behavior : FOOLISHNESS ⟨what ~ is this —Shak.⟩

simple ointment *n* : an ointment consisting of 5 percent white wax and 95 percent white petrolatum

simple ore *n* : an ore yielding only one metal

simple pendulum *n* : an ideal pendulum consisting of a point mass suspended by a weightless inextensible perfectly flexible thread and free to vibrate without friction — distinguished from *physical pendulum*

simple pit *n* : a plant cell pit lacking a prominent overarching margin — compare BORDERED PIT

simple prebend *n* : a prebend having no parish responsibility for cure of souls attached to it

simple proposition *n* **1** : CATEGORICAL PROPOSITION **2** : a proposition not resolvable into separate statements : an atomic proposition

simple protein *n* : a protein (as an albumin or globulin) that yields amino acids as the chief or only products of complete hydrolysis — distinguished from *conjugated protein*

[1]**simpler** *comparative of* SIMPLE

[2]**sim·pler** \ˈsimp(ə)lə(r)\ *n* -S [²*simple* + *-er*] *archaic* : HERBALIST 1a

simple reaction time *n* : the time required for a subject to initiate a prearranged response to a defined stimulus

simpler's-joy \ˈ==ˌ=\ *n* [²*simpler*] : BLUE VERVAIN

simples *pl of* SIMPLE, *pres 3d sing of* SIMPLE

simplest *superlative of* SIMPLE

simple stress *n* : stress consisting either of tension or compression but not both

simple substitution *n* : MONOALPHABETIC SUBSTITUTION

simple syllogism *n* **1** : CATEGORICAL SYLLOGISM **2** : a syllogism not resolvable into other syllogisms

simple tide *n* : a tide theoretically resulting from the influence of the sun and the moon if moving in circular orbits in the plane of the equator — see TIDAL CONSTANT

sim·ple·ton \ˈsimpəltən, -tən\ *n* -S [¹*simple* + *-ton*, as in *skimmington*] : a simpleminded person **syn** see FOOL

simple tone *n* : PURE TONE

simple vault *n* : a vault having a smooth intrados without ribs or cross arches

simple vow *n* : a public vow taken by a religious in the Roman Catholic Church under which retention of property by the individual is permitted and marriage though regarded as a sin is valid under canon law — compare SOLEMN VOW

simple watermark *n* : UNIT WATERMARK

[1]**sim·plex** \ˈsimˌpleks\ *adj* [L *simplic-*, *simplex* — more at SIMPLE] **1** : SIMPLE, SINGLE **2 a** : having one representative of a given dominant gene — used esp. of an autotetraploid; compare DUPLEX 2 **b** : having the gametic or haploid number of chromosomes **3** : allowing telecommunication in only one direction at a time ⟨~ system⟩ — compare DUPLEX 3

[2]**simplex** \"\ *n* -ES **1** *or pl* **sim·pli·ces** \-ˌplə,sēz\ *or* **sim·pli·cia** \simˈplish(ē)ə\ : a simple word — contrasted with *complex* **2** : a method of telecommunication employing only one direction of transmission at any one time **3** : a spatial configuration of *n*-dimensions determined by *n* + 1 points in a space of dimension equal to or greater than *n*

[3]**simplex** \"\ *vt* -ED/-ING/-ES : to make simplex

simplex machine *n* [¹*simplex*] : a warp knitting machine that resembles a tricot machine but has two sets of needles and produces a double fabric

simplex ob·li·ga·tio \-ˌäbləˈgād·ē,ō\ *n* [NL, lit., simple obligation] : an unconditional bond — compare ¹SIMPLE 7c

simplex pile *n* [¹*simplex*] : a bearing pile formed by driving a steel shell with a specially designed point into the ground and filling the hole with concrete as the shell is withdrawn

simplex pump *n* : a pump having one steam and one water cylinder

simplex winding *n* : an armature winding that has only two paths from a brush of one polarity to another of opposite polarity

sim·pli·cial \simˈplishəl\ *adj* [*simplicia* + *-al*] : of or relating to simplexes ⟨~ mapping⟩

sim·plici·den·ta·ta \simˌplisəˌdenˈtäd·ə, -tād·ə\ *n pl, cap* [NL, fr. L *simplic-*, *simplex* simple + *-i-* + *dentata*, neut. pl. of *dentatus* toothed — more at DENTATE] *in former classifications* : a suborder of Rodentia coextensive with the order as now limited — compare LAGOMORPHA

sim·pli·cist \ˈsimpləsəst\ *n* -S [L *simplic-*, *simplex* simple + E *-ist*] : an advocate or practitioner of simplism — **sim·pli·cis·tic** \ˌ==ˈ=sistik, -tēk\ *adj*

sim·pli·ci·ter \simˈplisəd·ə(r)\ *adv* [L, simply, fr. *simplic-*, *simplex* simple] **1** : in or by itself : SIMPLY **2** *chiefly Scots law* : of its own nature : UNQUALIFIEDLY, UNCONDITIONALLY

sim·plic·i·ty \sim'plisəd·ē, -sətē, -i\ *n* -ES [ME *simplicite*, fr. MF, fr. L *simplicitat-, simplicitas*, fr. *simplic-, simplex* simple + *-itat-, -itas* -ity] **1 a :** absence of complexity in form or structure ⟨the ~ of the circular zonation within the city —H.W.H.King⟩ **b :** an irreducible element ⟨people seeking the basic *simplicities* of life : FUNDAMENTAL —T.J.Panter⟩ **c :** organic unity ⟨the multiplicity . . . of our environment seems suddenly to attain clarification, ~, and homogeneity —Hunter Mead⟩ **2 :** lack of knowledge or good judgment : IGNORANCE, STUPIDITY ⟨because of his relative political ~ . . . can still be the prey of extremists —Ignazio Silone⟩ ⟨to save his contemptible life . . . dared to practice on our credulous ~ —W.S.Gilbert⟩ **3 a :** ingenuousness of spirit : freedom from vanity or guile : HUMILITY, CANDOR ⟨retained a great ~ and kindliness of character, was always easily approachable —Martha Gruening⟩ ⟨wish to appear all innocence and ~, and they full of malice and deceit all the time —George Borrow⟩ **b :** unaffected naturalness : freedom from artificiality or display : GENUINENESS, PLAINNESS ⟨the peace and ~ of natural surroundings —J.L.Phelan⟩ ⟨the almost bare ~ of life in his grandfather's house —Archibald Marshall⟩ **c :** INNOCENCE, NAÏVETÉ ⟨the combination of great intellect with childlike ~ —Bertrand Russell⟩ **4 a :** directness of expression : absence of ambiguity or overrefinement : CLARITY, INTELLIGIBILITY ⟨pleased the general reader by the smoothness and ~ of her verse —Bertha Stearns⟩ ⟨sang with feeling and ~ —T.L.Peacock⟩ **b :** limitation in the use of ornament : AUSTERITY, RESTRAINT ⟨all garments were white . . . and of the utmost ~ in cut and material —*Amer. Guide Series: Pa.*⟩ ⟨the dignity and ~ of colonial architecture⟩ **5 a :** a simple act, idea, or characteristic ⟨reverence for the *simplicities* of . . . rural and village America —Bernard De Voto⟩ ⟨the *simplicities* and certainties of 1914 had given way to . . . confusions —*Times Lit. Supp.*⟩ **b :** an instance or epitome of something simple ⟨the average transatlantic flight is ~ itself —Richard Joseph⟩

sim·pli·fi·ca·tion \ˌsimpləfə'kāshən\ *n* -S [ML *simplificatus* (past part. of *simplificare*) + E *-ion*] **:** an act, process, or result of simplifying: as **a :** the elimination of superfluous detail in art : ABSTRACTION, GENERALIZATION ⟨the public understands . . . his subtle and beautiful *~s* down to essential form as part of the great tradition of sculpture —Aline B. Saarinen⟩ **b :** the reduction or elimination of complexity or multiplicity : STREAMLINING ⟨~ of the control panel of an airplane⟩ ⟨product-line ~ is equally applicable to wholesale and retail businesses⟩ **c (1) :** the reduction of a double consonant to a single one (as in Latin *vacilo* for *vacillo*) **(2) :** the elision of silent letters (as in *gram* for *gramme*) — compare CONTRACTION 4 **d :** SIMPLISM

simplified *adj* [fr. past part. of *simplify*] **:** made simple : reduced in complexity

simplified spelling *n* **:** REFORMED SPELLING

sim·pli·fi·er \'simpləˌfī(ə)r, -īə\ *n* -S **:** one that simplifies

sim·pli·fy \-ˌfī\ *vt* -ED/-ING/-ES [F *simplifier*, fr. ML *simplificare*, fr. L *simplus* simple + *-ificare* -ify] **:** to make simple or simpler: as **a :** to reduce to basic essentials : divest of superfluous elements ⟨hooded fishermen whose forms are *simplified* to black silhouettes —Stewart Beach⟩ **b :** to diminish in scope or complexity : ABRIDGE, STREAMLINE ⟨~ an application form⟩ ⟨~ a manufacturing process⟩ **c :** to make more intelligible : CLARIFY, EXPLAIN ⟨*simplifies* the issue for his hearers⟩ **d :** OVERSIMPLIFY ⟨there are too many people in this country who go after a slogan, who ~ things down —F.D.Roosevelt⟩

simpling *pres part of* SIMPLE

sim·plism \'simˌplizəm\ *n* -S [F *simplisme*, fr. *simple* simple, single + *-isme* -ism] **:** OVERSIMPLIFICATION; *esp* **:** the tendency to concentrate on a single aspect (as of a problem) to the exclusion of all complicating factors ⟨division of mankind into workingmen and capitalists suffers from the fallacy of ~ —M.R.Cohen⟩

sim·plis·tic \(ˈ)sim¦plistik, -tēk\ *adj* **:** of, relating to, or characterized by simplism — **sim·plis·ti·cal·ly** \-tək(ə)lē, -tēk-, -li\ *adv*

sim·ply \'simplē, -li, *in senses 1 & 2 sometimes* -pəl-\ *adv* [ME *simplely, simply*, fr. ¹*simple* + *-ly*] **1 :** in a straightforward manner : MODESTLY, SINCERELY ⟨behaved so ~ and magnificently that even his enemies found themselves won over —C.L.Carmer⟩ **2 a :** without ambiguity : INTELLIGIBLY, CLEARLY ⟨let the narrative unfold ~ and objectively —R.A. Cordell⟩ **b :** without extravagance or embellishment : PLAINLY ⟨within the range of the ~ educated —J.H.Plumb⟩ ⟨a graceful structure, built ~ when simplicity was not considered a virtue —*Amer. Guide Series: Minn.*⟩ **c :** without complexity or subterfuge : DIRECTLY, CANDIDLY ⟨everything . . . came to happen as ~ and as naturally and as gradually as a season coming on —R.P.Warren⟩ ⟨this she said as ~ as a child recites a tale —Pearl Buck⟩ **3 a** *obs* **:** ABSOLUTELY, CATEGORICALLY ⟨that they have any being, purely and ~, I deny —R.G.Preston⟩ **b :** in or of itself : without augmentation : MERELY, SOLELY ⟨readers who read books ~ to finish them —James Thurber⟩ ⟨in this chapter . . . we ~ note the principal characteristics of the period —Tom Wintringham⟩ ⟨she was ~ and solely a beautiful woman —Jean Stafford⟩ **c :** in actual fact : LITERALLY, REALLY ⟨there ~ is not enough work to go around —Hamilton Basso⟩ — often used as an intensive ⟨you ~ must wear a British bowler —John McCaffrey⟩ **4** *archaic* **:** IGNORANTLY, FOOLISHLY ⟨got money from various ~ disposed persons, under pretence of getting them confidential appointments —W.M.Thackeray⟩

simps *pl of* SIMP

simp·son·ite \'sim(p)sᵊnˌīt\ *n* -S [Edward S. *Simpson* †1939 Australian mineralogist + E *-ite*] **:** a mineral $AlTaO_4$ consisting of an oxide of aluminum and tantalum in short hexagonal crystals

simp·son's honey-plant \'sim(p)sᵊnz-\ *n, usu cap S* [perh. after Sir George *Simpson* †1860 Canadian explorer] **:** a figwort (*Scrophularia marylandica*)

simpson's rule *n, usu cap S* [after Thomas *Simpson* †1761 Eng. mathematician] **:** a method used esp. by naval architects for computing the approximate area bounded by a curve by adding the areas of a series of figures formed from an odd number of equally spaced ordinates to the curve and parabolas drawn through the points where these ordinates cut the curve

sim·sim \'simˌsim\ *n* -S [Ar; akin to Assyr *šamaššamu* sesame — more at SESAME] **:** SESAME

sim·son \'sim(p)sᵊn\ *n* -S [alter. of earlier *sinsion*, fr. ME *synchon*, fr. MF *senechion*, fr. L *senecion-, senecio* — more at SENECIO] **:** GROUNDSEL

simson line *n, usu cap S* [after Robert *Simson* †1768 Scot. mathematician] **:** the line joining the feet of the perpendiculars let fall from any point on the circumcircle of a triangle upon the sides of the triangle

sims system \'simz-\ *n, usu cap 1st S* [after Philip H. *Sims* †1949 Amer. bridge expert] **:** a system of bidding at contract bridge characterized by notably strong opening bids by first or second hand, weaker opening bids by third or fourth hand, and very strong opening no-trump bids

sim·u·la·cre \'simyəˌlākə(r)\ *n* -S [ME, fr. MF, fr. L *simulacrum*] **:** SIMULACRUM

sim·u·la·crum \ˌ==ˈlākrəm, -ˈlak-\ *n, pl* **simula·cra** \-rə\ *also* **simulacrums** [L, fr. *simulare* to imitate, represent — more at SIMULATE] **1 :** a representation of something : IMAGE, EFFIGY ⟨after the doge's death, a wax figure, his ~, was laid out in the chamber —Mary McCarthy⟩ ⟨only . . . tireless interworking of sources could have produced this vibrant ~ of a period —Marianne Moore⟩ **2 a :** something having the form but not the substance of a material object : IMITATION, SHAM ⟨moved silently away in the night, . . . leaving an exact ~ of its tanks, where it had been, and proceeded to its points of attack —Sir Winston Churchill⟩ **b :** a superficial likeness : APPEARANCE, SEMBLANCE ⟨was glad to have his presence and that of his weapon justified by some ~ of fear and trouble —C.E.Craddock⟩ **syn** see IMPOSTURE

¹sim·u·lar \-lə(r)\ *n* -S [irreg. fr. L *simulare* + E *-ar*] *archaic* **:** DISSEMBLER

²simular \"\ *adj* [L *simulare* + E *-ar*] *archaic* **:** COUNTERFEIT, IMITATIVE

¹sim·u·late \-lət, -ˌlāt, *usu* -d·+V\ *adj* [ME, fr. L *simulatus*, past part. of *simulare*] *archaic* **:** SIMULATED

²sim·u·late \-ˌlāt, *usu* -ād·+V\ *vb* -ED/-ING/-S [L *simulatus*, past part. of *simulare* to imitate, represent, feign, fr. *similis* like, similar — more at SAME] *vt* **1 :** to give the appearance or effect of : FEIGN, IMITATE ⟨felt obliged to ~ reluctance, and the air of having had her hand forced —Edith Wharton⟩ ⟨to ~ real mink, the muskrat pelts are let out —Pete Barrett⟩ ⟨pegs in the oak flooring further ~ pioneer construction —*Amer. Guide Series: Ark.*⟩ **2 :** to have the characteristics of : RESEMBLE ⟨the raised forelegs of the praying mantis ~ the attitude of a man at prayer⟩ ⟨mycoses . . . which may involve the lungs and ~ tuberculosis —J.B.Amberson⟩ **~** *vi* **:** to make believe : PRETEND ⟨while the unseen musician plays, the actor *~s*⟩ **syn** see ASSUME

simulated *adj* [fr. past part. of ²*simulate*] **:** of a feigned or imitative character : MOCK, SHAM ⟨a large scale experimental parachute drop . . . under ~ combat conditions —J.G. Cozzens⟩ ⟨the handles are handsome, ~ stag or mother-of-pearl —*N.Y. Times*⟩

simulated pearl *n* **:** a bead made to resemble a pearl ⟨mock-jeweled trim of *simulated pearls* and glass beads —*Sears, Roebuck Cat.*⟩ — contrasted with *cultured pearl*

simulated rank *n* **:** a civilian status equated to a military rank ⟨the chief of research had the *simulated rank* of colonel⟩

sim·u·la·tion \ˌsimyə'lāshən\ *n* -S [ME *simulacion*, fr. MF, fr. L *simulation-, simulatio*, fr. *simulare* to simulate + *-ion-, -io* -ion] **1 a :** the act or process of simulating : IMITATION, PRETENSE ⟨the ~ of tigers by the rainmakers at the grave may be intended to intimidate the dead man —J.G.Frazer⟩ ⟨flung her arms around his neck with an almost perfect ~ of surprise and spontaneity —Louis Auchincloss⟩ **b :** a sham object : COUNTERFEIT ⟨bogus gilt dadoes . . . and other *~s* —Janet Flanner⟩ **2 :** willful deception : COLLUSION, MISREPRESENTATION **3 :** one that shows a superficial resemblance : ANALOGUE ⟨the ~ of a black mask on the face of a raccoon⟩ ⟨a shabby room that still gave a ~ of elegance⟩

sim·u·la·tor \'==ˌlād·ə(r), -ātə-\ *n* -S [L, fr. *simulatus* (past part. of *simulare*) + *-or*] **:** one that simulates; *specif* **:** a device in a laboratory that enables the operator to reproduce under test conditions phenomena likely to occur in actual performance

¹si·mul·cast \'siməlˌkast, -aa(ə)st, -aist, -ȧst\ *vb* [*simul*taneous + broad*cast*] **:** to broadcast by radio and television simultaneously

²simulcast \"\ *n* -S **:** a simultaneous transmission over radio and television

¹si·mu·li·id \sə'myülēəd\ *adj* [NL *Simuliidae*] **:** of or relating to the Simuliidae

²simuliid \"\ *n* -S **:** a fly of the family Simuliidae

sim·u·li·i·dae \ˌsimyə'līəˌdē\ *n pl, cap* [NL, fr. *Simulium*, type genus + *-idae*] **:** a family of small biting two-winged flies including the blackflies and related pests and having larvae that usu. live in rapidly flowing water — see SIMULIUM

si·mu·li·um \sə'myülēəm\ *n, cap* [NL, fr. L *simulare* to simulate] **:** the type genus of Simuliidae comprising dark-colored biting flies of which some are vectors of onchocerciasis or of protozoan diseases of birds

simul·ta·ne·i·ty \ˌsīməltə'nēəd·ē, ˌsim-, -ēətē, -i\ *n* -ES [ML *simultaneitas*, fr. (assumed) ML *simultaneus* + L *-itas* -ity] **:** the quality or state or an instance of being simultaneous ⟨the ~ of these events has been exaggerated —G.G.Simpson⟩; *specif* **:** the presentation of different views of the same object (as a profile and full view of a face) in one work of art ⟨~ . . . in Egyptian painting —Helen Gardner⟩

simul·ta·neous \ˌsīməl¦tānēəs, ˌsim-, -nyəs\ *adj* [fr. (assumed) ML *simultaneus* (whence *simultaneitas* simultaneity), fr. L *simul* at the same time (fr. *similis* same, similar) + ML *-taneus* (fr. LL *momentaneus* momentary) — more at SAME, MOMENTANEOUS] **1 :** existing or occurring at the same time : COINCIDENT, CONCURRENT ⟨~ fixing of prices of commodities affecting each other . . . as maize and dairy or pig products —*Farmer's Weekly (So. Africa)*⟩ ⟨just by twisting a dial, visitors to the U.N. General Assembly can hear ~ interpretations of what the speaker is saying in any of the five official languages⟩ **2 :** satisfied by the same values of the variables ⟨~ equations⟩ **syn** see CONTEMPORARY

simultaneous contrast *n* **:** the tendency of a color to induce its opposite in hue, value and intensity upon an adjacent color and be mutually affected in return ⟨by the law of *simultaneous contrast* a light, dull red will make an adjacent dark, bright yellow seem darker, brighter and greener; in turn, the former will appear lighter, duller and bluer⟩

simultaneous death act *n* **:** a statute prescribing the rules of inheritance applicable when two or more persons die at the same time or from the same accident or event, or within a specified short period

simul·ta·neous·ly *adv* **:** in a simultaneous manner : at the same time : CONCURRENTLY

simul·ta·neous·ness *n* -ES [*simultaneous* + *-ness*] **:** SIMULTANEITY

simultaneous reaction *n* **:** any of two or more chemical reactions occurring at the same time in the same system — compare SIDE REACTION

si·murgh *or* **si·murg** \sē'mü(ə)rg, '=ˌ=\ *also* **si·morg** *or* **si·morgh** \-mȯ(ə)rg\ *n* -S [Per *sīmurgh*, fr. MPer *sēnmurv*; akin to Av *mərəγhō saēnō*, fr. *mərəgha-* bird + *saēna-* eagle] **:** a huge ancient bird of Persian legend credited with possessing great wisdom — compare ROC

¹sin \'sin\ *n* -S [ME *sinne*, fr. OE *synn, syn;* akin to OFris *sende sin*, OS *sundia*, OHG *sunta, suntea* and perh. to L *sont-, sons* guilty; prob. akin to L *est* is —more at IS] **1 a :** a transgression of religious law : an offense against God ⟨making her dream . . . of the ~ which he resolved to allure her to commit —Daniel Defoe⟩ **b :** a serious offense : a violation of propriety ⟨colleges which glorify research and publication . . . are guilty of a grave and perhaps irreparable ~ against civilization —Millicent McIntosh⟩ ⟨the rhetorical ~ of the meaningless variation —Lewis Mumford⟩ **c :** a serious shortcoming : FAULT ⟨the English ~ has always been . . . a lack of social coherence —Herbert Read⟩ **2 :** violation of religious law : disregard of God's will ⟨thought about the nature of ~ in general —H.E.Fosdick⟩; *specif* **:** violation of proscription of fornication ⟨accused . . . of living in ~ with her fiancé —Leslie Rees⟩ — see ACTUAL SIN, DEADLY SIN, MORTAL SIN, ORIGINAL SIN, VENIAL SIN

²sin \"\ *vb* **sinned; sinned; sinning; sins** [ME *sinnen, singen*, fr. OE *syngian*; akin to MD *sondigen* to sin, ON *syndga*; denominative fr. the root of E ¹*sin*] *vi* **1 :** to violate religious law : commit an offense against God; *specif* **:** FORNICATE **2 :** to commit an offense ⟨critics often *sinned* against good critical sense —C.I.Glicksberg⟩ **~** *vt* **1 :** to perform sinfully ⟨there remains so much to be *sinned* and suffered in the world —Nathaniel Hawthorne⟩ **2** *archaic* **:** to drive by sinning ⟨we have *sinned* him hence —John Dryden⟩ — **sin one's mercies :** to show ingratitude

³sin *var of* SYNE

⁴sin \'sēn *also* 'sin\ *n* -S [Heb *šīn*] **1 :** the 21st letter of the Hebrew alphabet — symbol שׂ; see ALPHABET table **2 :** the letter corresponding to Hebrew sin in the Phoenician or in any of various other Semitic alphabets

sin *abbr* **1** sine **2** [L *sinistra*] left hand

si·na·gua \sə'nä(g)wə\ *adj, usu cap* [fr. *Sinagua*, village in northern Arizona where remains of the culture were found] **:** of or relating to a people living in northern Arizona from about A.D. 600 to about 1400 whose culture is characterized by rectangular pit houses entered through a hole in the roof, by pueblo structures on high land, by pottery shaped with paddle and anvil and fired in an oxidizing atmosphere, ball courts, and extended burial with offerings

si·na·ite \'sīnəˌīt\ *n* -S [F, fr. *Sinai*, peninsula in Egypt + F *-ite*; fr. its being the type of rock found in the Gebel Musa group of mountains in the Sinai peninsula] **:** SYENITE

si·na·it·ic \ˌ==¦id·ik\ *adj, usu cap* [NL *sinaiticus*, fr. *Sinai*, mountain prob. of the Gebel Musa group in So. Sinai peninsula from which according to Exod 19:20 God gave the Ten Commandments to the Israelites and *Sinai*, peninsula in northeastern Egypt at the north end of the Red sea (fr. LL, fr. Heb *Sīnai*) + L *-iticus* -itic] **1 :** of or relating to Mount Sinai **2 :** of or relating to the Sinai peninsula

sinaitic alphabet *n, usu cap S* **:** an alphabet found in inscriptions in Sinaitic mines that forms a link between the Egyptian hieroglyphs and the Phoenician alphabet

si·nal \'sīnᵊl\ *adj* [NL *sinus* + E *-al*] **:** of, relating to, or coming from a sinus ⟨a ~ discharge⟩

sinalagmatic *var of* SYNALLAGMATIC

sin·al·bin \sə'nalbən\ *n* -S [ISV *sin-* (fr. L *sinapis* mustard) + L *alba* (fem. of *albus* white) + ISV *-in* — more at ELF] **:** a bitter crystalline glucoside $C_{30}H_{42}N_2O_{15}S_2$ in white mustard seeds that on hydrolysis by myrosin yields glucose, sinapine hydrogen sulfate, and the yellow irritant mustard oil *para*-hydroxy-benzyl isothiocyanate

sina·may \ˌsēnə'mī, 'sinəˌmī\ *n* -S [Tag *sinamáy*] **:** a stiff coarse open textile woven in the Philippines chiefly from abaca

sin·an·thro·pus \sə'nan(t)thrəpəs, ˌsiˌnan'thrōpəs\ *n* [NL, fr. LL *Sinae*, pl., Chinese + NL *-anthropus* — more at SINOLOGUE] **1** *cap* **:** a genus of fossil primitive men that includes the Peking man and is often considered generically inseparable on the one hand from *Pithecanthropus* and on the other from *Homo* **2** -ES **:** PEKING MAN

sin·a·pate \'sinəˌpāt\ *n* -S [ISV *sinap-* (in *sinapic acid*) + *-ate*] **:** a salt or ester of sinapic acid

si·nap·ic acid \sə'napik-\ *n* [ISV *sinap-* (in *sinapine*) + *-ic*] **:** a yellow crystalline phenolic unsaturated acid $HO(CH_3O)_2$-$C_6H_2CH{=}CHCOOH$ that is related structurally both to cinnamic acid and to pyrogallol and obtained by hydrolysis of sinalbin

sin·a·pine \'sinəˌpīn, -ˌpən\ *n* -S [ISV *sinap-* (fr. L *sinapis* mustard) + *-ine*; orig. formed as G *sinapin*] **:** an alkaloid $C_{16}H_{25}NO_6$ in black mustard seeds that is an unstable ester of choline and sinapic acid — see SINALBIN

si·na·pis \sə'nāpəs\ *n* [NL, fr. L *sinapi, sinapis* mustard, fr. Gk] **1** *cap, in some classifications* **:** a genus comprising cruciferous herbs with a long beak on the tip of the seedpod and being now usu. included as a section in the genus *Brassica* **2** -ES **:** MUSTARD

sin·a·pism \'sinəˌpizəm\ *n* -S [LL *sinapismus*, fr. Gk *sinapismos* act of using mustard plaster, fr. *sinapizein* to apply mustard plaster, fr. *sinapi, sinapis* mustard] **:** MUSTARD PLASTER

sin·ar·quism \'siˌnärˌkizəm, sə'n-\ *or* **sin·ar·quis·mo** \ˌsiˌnär'kiz(ˌ)mō\ *also* **sin·ar·chism** *or* **syn·ar·chism** \'=ˌ=ˌkizəm\ *n* -S *usu cap* [MexSp *sinanarquismo*, fr. Sp *sin* without (fr. L *sine*) + *anarquismo*, fr. *anarquia* anarchy (fr. Gk *anarchia*) + *-ismo* -ism (fr. L *-ismus*) — more at SUNDER, ANARCHY] **:** a Mexican counterrevolutionary movement embracing chiefly peasants and workers under secret leaders that seeks restoration of an early Christian social order, favors hispanidad, and opposes communism, Pan-Americanism, labor unionism, and military conscription

¹sin·ar·quis·ta \ˌsiˌnär'kēstə\ *also* **sin·ar·quist** *or* **syn·ar·chist** \'=ˌ=ˌkəst\ *n* -S *usu cap* [MexSp *sinarquista*, fr. *sinarquismo*, after Sp *anarquismo* anarchism: *anarquista* anarchist] **:** an adherent of Sinarquism

²sinarquista \"\ *also* **sinarquist** *or* **sin·ar·chist** *or* **synarchist** \"\ *adj, usu cap* [MexSp *sinarquista*] **:** of, relating to, or characteristic of Sinarquism

si·nay bean \(ˈ)sē¦nī-\ *n* [Ilocano *sinay*] **:** RICE BEAN

sincamas *var of* SINGKAMAS

¹since \(¦)sin(t)s, -sən-, *chiefly dial* (¦)sen-\ *adv* [ME *sins, sinnes* afterwards, since, contr. of *sithens, sithenes*, adv. & prep., since, fr. *sithen* (fr. OE *siththan*, contr. of *sith tham* afterwards, since that, fr. *sith*, adv. & prep., since + *tham*, dat. of *thæt* that) + *-s, -es*; akin to OHG *sīd* since, ON *sith*, adv., late, Goth *seithu*, neut. adj., late, OIr *sīr* long-lasting, L *serus* late, *serere* to sow — more at THAT, SOW] **1 :** continuously from a time in the past until the present ⟨established in 1935 . . . it has ~ been the majority party —*Current Biog.*⟩ — often used with *ever* ⟨went abroad eight years ago and has stayed there ever ~⟩ **2 :** before the present time : AGO ⟨that wood fire he let out of hand some time ~ —J.H.Powers⟩ — often used with *long* ⟨a bachelor's degree has long ~ lost any meaning —J.B.Conant⟩ **3 :** after a time in the past : SUBSEQUENTLY ⟨in 1719 a brick wall, ~ removed, was ordered built around the churchyard — *Amer. Guide Series: Va.*⟩ ⟨settled in what has ~ become South Carolina —*Current Biog.*⟩

²since \(¦)sin(t)s, *chiefly dial* (¦)sen-\ *prep* **1 :** in the period after a specified time in the past ⟨a few improvements have been made ~ the beginning of the century⟩ **2 :** continuously from a specified time in the past ⟨~ that time the two groups have opposed each other —Cecil Hobbs⟩

³since \'sin(t)s, *chiefly dial* 'sen-\ *adj, archaic* **:** occurring or existing after ⟨my ~ experience of Sunday evenings —J.A. Froude⟩

⁴since \(¦)sin(t)s, *chiefly dial* (¦)sen-\ *conj* [ME *sinnes*, fr. *sins, sinnes*, adv.] **1 :** after the time in the past when ⟨the building has been razed ~ I visited the city⟩ ⟨it has been 20 years ~ he was first elected⟩ **2** *obs* **:** the time in the past when : WHEN ⟨thou remembrest ~ once I sat upon a promontory —Shak.⟩ **3 :** up to the present time from the time in the past when ⟨has known him ever ~ he was a child⟩ **4 :** for the reason that : because of the fact that ⟨~ it was raining he wore a hat⟩

sin·cere \(ˈ)sin¦si(ə)r, ˌsən's-, -iə\ *adj, usu* -ER/-EST [MF, fr. L *sincerus*, prob. fr. *sem-* one + *-cerus* (fr. *creare* to create) — more at SAME, CRESCENT] **1 :** marked by genuineness: as **a :** free of dissimulation : not hypocritical : REAL, TRUE, HONEST ⟨the missionaries were prompted by a ~ desire for good —Herman Melville⟩ ⟨was above all ~ and detested any form of pretense or affectation —Terry de Valera⟩ **b (1) :** free from adulteration : not mixed ⟨to find and isolate Nazism in its pure ~ form proved extremely difficult —J.C.Harsch⟩ **(2) :** not containing any foreign element : PURE ⟨wood is cheap and wine ~ outside the city gate —Robert Browning⟩ **c :** marked by truth : GENUINE ⟨the only ~ glimpse that we get of the living breathing word-compelling Dante —J.R.Lowell⟩ **d :** motivated by a desire for meaningful expression ⟨the emotional substratum which we feel to be inseparable from a truly great and ~ work of musical art —Edward Sapir⟩ **2** *archaic* **:** DEVOID ⟨air ~ of ceremonious haze —J.R.Lowell⟩ **3 :** characterized by firm belief in the validity of one's own opinions ⟨an entirely ~ and cruel tyrant⟩

syn WHOLEHEARTED, WHOLE-SOULED, HEARTFELT, HEARTY, UNFEIGNED: SINCERE suggests absence of hypocrisy, dissimulation, falsification, feigning, or embellishment and consequent honest genuineness ⟨too *sincere* for dissimulation —Ellen Glasgow⟩ ⟨individuals are considered *sincere* when there is little or no discrepancy between the goals they seek and those they claim to be seeking —L.W.Doob⟩ WHOLEHEARTED and WHOLE-SOULED stress lack of reservation or misgiving and may suggest devotion, zeal, and sincerity ⟨writes himself down a frank and *wholehearted* Tory —V.L.Parrington⟩ ⟨who could help liking her? her generous nature, her gift for appreciation, her *wholehearted*, fervid enthusiasm —L.P.Smith⟩ ⟨men whose dedication to their country was *whole-souled*, nevertheless, and for whom the supreme frustration of personal ambition never deflected them away from public services of a monumental nature —Eric Sevareid⟩ HEARTFELT suggests a genuine stirring of innermost feelings and usu. contrasts with formal, conventional, outwardly indicated, more or less factitious manifestation ⟨our sympathy for you therefore is *heartfelt*, for we are sharing the same sufferings —Sir Winston Churchill⟩ ⟨if ever men have offered *heartfelt* thanks to God for deliverance from the perils of the sea, surely we were those men —C.B.Nordhoff & J.N.Hall⟩ HEARTY may suggest vigorous manifestations like notable warmth and robust exuberance ⟨infuriated elderly traveling salesmen were backslapped all day long by *hearty* and powerful unknown persons —Sinclair Lewis⟩ ⟨a courtier's laugh, decorous, brief and not too *hearty* —J.H.Wheelwright⟩ UNFEIGNED may stress spontaneity and absence of simulation ⟨I confess to *unfeigned* delight in the insurgent propaganda —J.L.Lowes⟩

sin·cere·ly *adv* **:** in a sincere manner — often used as a complimentary close often followed by *yours*

sin·cere·ness *n* -ES **:** SINCERITY 1

sin·cer·i·ty \sən'serəd·ē, -'sir-, -rətē, -i\ *n* -ES [MF *sincerité*, fr. L *sinceritat-, sinceritas*, fr. *sincerus* sincere + *-itat-, -itas* -ity] **1 :** the quality or state of being sincere ⟨the passionate ~ of artists and other intellectuals may still be warped by wishful preferences —H.J.Muller⟩ **2 a :** a sincere feeling ⟨grounded not on garnitures and semblances but on realities and *sincerities* —Thomas Carlyle⟩ **b :** an expression of a sincere feeling ⟨his voice altered and ceased to sing its pleasantly tuned *sincerities* —Nancy Keesing⟩

sinch *var of* CINCH

sin·cip·i·tal \(ˈ)sin¦sipəd·ᵊl\ *adj* [L *sincipit-, sinciput* + E *-al*] **:** of or relating to the sinciput

sin·ci·put \ˈsin(t)sə(ˌ)pət, *usu* -əd.+V\ *n, pl* **sinciputs** \-ts\ *or* **sin·cip·i·ta** \sin'sipədə\ [L, fr. *semi-* + *caput* head — more at HEAD] **:** a part of the head: **a :** FOREHEAD **b :** the whole upper half of the skull **:** CALVA **c :** the forepart of the head of a bird from the base of the bill to the crown **d :** the part of the head of an insect and esp. of a beetle between the vertex and the clypeus

sin·cos·ite \ˈsiŋkə,sīt\ *n* -s [*Sincos*, Peru, where it was discovered + E *-ite*] **:** a mineral $Ca(VO)_2(PO_4)_2.5H_2O$ consisting of hydrous calcium vanadyl phosphate and occurring in thin tetragonal scales or plates

sind \ˈsin(d), ˈsīn\ *vt* [ME (Sc & northern dial.) *sinden*] *chiefly Scot* **1 :** to rinse out **2 :** to wash down (food)

sin·der \ˈsində(r), ˈsinə-\ *chiefly Scot var of* SUNDER

sin·dhi \ˈsindē\ *n* [Ar *Sindi*, fr. *Sind* Sind, Sindh, region in the northwestern part of the Indian subcontinent, fr. Hindi; akin to Skt *sindhu* river — more at INDIA] **1** *also* **sin·di** \"\ *pl* **sindhi** *or* **sindhis** *also* **sindi** *or* **sindis** *usu cap* **a :** a Scytho-Dravidian mostly Muslim people of Sind **b :** a member of such people **2** *pl* **sindhi** *or* **sindhis** *usu cap* **:** the Indic language of Sind **3 a** *usu cap* **:** an Indian breed of dark red short-horned humped dairy cattle that is widely distributed and much used for crossbreeding in warm regions **b** *pl* **sindhi** *or* **sindhis** *often cap* **:** an animal of the Sindhi breed

sind ibex \ˈsind-\ *n, usu cap S* [*sind* fr. *Sind*, region in the northwestern part of the Indian subcontinent] **:** a wild goat (*Capra hircus blythi*) of Sind and Baluchistan

sin·di·co \ˈsendə,kō\ *n* -s [Sp, fr. LL *syndicus* — more at SYNDIC] **:** SYNDIC

sin·don \ˈsindən\ *n* -s [ME, fr. L, fr. Gk *sindōn*] **1** *archaic* **:** a fine fabric esp. of linen **2** *archaic* **:** a covering made of sindon: as **a :** SHROUD ⟨Christ's ~⟩ **b :** ¹CORPORAL

sin·dry \ˈsindri\ *chiefly Scot var of* SUNDRY

sine \ˈsīn\ *n* -s [ML *sinus* (intended, under influence of Ar *jaib* curve, as trans. of Ar *jiba* sine, fr. Skt *jīva* bowstring, chord of an arc), fr. L, curve, fold — more at SINUS] **:** the *y* coordinate of any point except the vertex on the terminal side of an angle divided by the distance between the vertex and the point, the vertex coinciding with the origin of a plane rectangular coordinate system and the initial side of the angle coinciding with the positive x-axis

sin–eater \ˈ=,==\ *n* **:** a person formerly hired to assume the sins of a dead person by eating food placed near the corpse

sin–eating \ˈ=,==\ *n* **:** the act or practice of a sin-eater

sine bar *n* **:** a device that consists of a steel straightedge at whose extremities buttons are attached with their centers equidistant from the straightedge and that is used to locate work at desired angles on angle plates

¹**si·ne·cure** \ˈsīnə,kyu̇(ə)r, ˈsin-, -nē,-, -u̇ə\ *n* -s [ML (*beneficium*) *sine cura* (benefice) without cure of souls] **1 :** an ecclesiastical benefice without cure of souls **2 :** an office or position that requires little or no work and that usu. provides an income

²**sinecure** \"\ *adj* **:** having the characteristics of a sinecure ⟨a practically ~ office —Valentine Heywood⟩

sine·cur·ism \-,rizəm\ *n* -s **:** the practice of granting sinecures

sine·cur·ist \-rəst\ *n* -s **:** one who has a sinecure

sine curve *n* **:** the graph in rectangular coordinates of the equation $y = a \sin bx$ where *a* and *b* are constants that when $a = 1$ and $b = 1$ passes through the origin and all points on the x-axis where the abscissas are multiples of π radians, is concave towards the x-axis, and has maximum and minimum ordinate values of +1 and −1

¹**sine die** \ˌsīnēˈdīˌē, -nəˈd-, ÷ -dī *also* ˌsin-; ˌsi¦(ˌ)nāˈdēˌā, ˌsē¦, ǀnēˈd-, ǀnəˈd-, -di,ā\ *adv* [L] **:** without any future date being designated (as for resumption) **:** INDEFINITELY ⟨declared the House adjourned *sine die* —Hodding Carter⟩

²**sine die** \"\ *adj* **:** made without any future date being designated (as for resumption) **:** INDEFINITE ⟨favored an adjournment *sine die* of Congress⟩

sine law *n* **:** LAW OF SINES

sine plate *n* **:** a block or plate for holding parts for machining at desired angles

sine pro·le \ˌsīnēˈprō,lā, ˌsin-, -nəˈp-; ˌsi¦(ˌ)nāˈprō(ˌ)lā, ˌsē¦, ǀnēˈp-, ǀnəˈp-\ *adv* [L] **:** without issue ⟨died *sine prole* in his 80th year⟩

¹**sine qua non** \ˌsi¦(ˌ)nā,kwäˈnōn, ˌsē¦, ǀnēk-, ǀnək-, -ˈnän; ˌsīnē,kwāˈnän, -ǀnə,k- *also* ˌsin-\ *n, pl* **sine qua nons** [LL, lit., without which not] **1 :** the one thing that is absolutely essential ⟨the *sine qua non* . . . is that the star shall appear bright enough to give a measurable spectrum —Herbert Dingle⟩ **2 :** something that is considered essential ⟨this book is a *sine qua non* for Mill scholars —W.D.Templeman⟩

²**sine qua non** \"\ *adj* **:** absolutely necessary **:** ESSENTIAL, INDISPENSABLE ⟨wider spaced patterns are . . . *sine qua non* in men's wardrobes —*N.Y.Times*⟩ ⟨it's the *sine qua non* sense —Amy Lowell⟩

sinetic *usu cap, var of* SINITIC

¹**sin·ew** \ˈsi(ˌ)nyü *also* ÷ ˈsi(ˌ)nü\ *n* -s [ME *sinwe, senewe*, fr. OE *sinu, seonu*; akin to MD *senewe* sinew, OHG *senawa*, ON *sin* sinew, MIr *sin* chain, L *seta, saeta* bristle, Gk *himas* leather strap, thong, Skt *syati, sinati* he binds, straps] **1 :** TENDON; *esp* **:** one dressed for use as a cord or thread ⟨his linden cradle . . . safely bound with reindeer ~s —H.W.Longfellow⟩ **2** *obs* **:** NERVE **3 a :** solid resilient strength **:** POWER, FORCE ⟨to espouse democratic government demands intellectual and moral ~ as well as armies and good feeling —G.K.Chalmers⟩ ⟨a solidly constructed novel, a tale with thews and ~s —William McFee⟩ **b :** the chief supporting force **:** MAINSTAY — usu. used in pl. ⟨equipment . . . providing the ~s of better living —Sam Pollock⟩ **c :** financial or material resources — usu. used in the phrase *sinews of war*

²**sinew** \"\ *vt* -ED/-ING/-S **1 :** to run through as if with sinews in order to make strong ⟨no ordinary belt . . . because it is ~*ed* with finely stranded airplane-type steel cables —*Newsweek*⟩ **2 :** to give force or solidity to **:** STRENGTHEN ⟨serve to ~ the state in times of danger —Oliver Goldsmith⟩

sine wave *n* **:** a fundamental form of wave (as in one of the sound waves giving rise to a pure tone or in a wave of alternating current) that represents periodic oscillations in which the amplitude of displacement at each point is proportional to the sine of the phase angle of the displacement and that is visualized as a sine curve

sinew–backed bow \ˈ=(ˌ)=¦=-\ *n* **:** REINFORCED BOW

sin·ewed \ˈsi(ˌ)nyüd *also* ÷ ˈsi(ˌ)nüd\ *adj* [¹*sinew* + *-ed*] **:** having sinews **:** SINEWY

sin·ew·i·ness \ˈsin(y)əwēnəs, -win-\ *n* -ES **:** the state or quality of being sinewy

sin·ew·less \ˈ=(ˌ)=ləs\ *adj* **:** having no sinews

sin·ew·ous \ˈsin(y)əwəs\ *adj* **:** SINEWY

sin·ewy \-(y)əwē, -wi\ *adj* [ME *senewy*, fr. *senewe* sinew + *-y*] **1 :** having sinews: **a :** full of sinews **:** TENDINOUS ⟨the ~ parts of a cut of meat⟩ **b :** marked by strong or prominent sinews ⟨~ arms rising and falling in tireless unison —T.B. Costain⟩ **2 :** marked by the strength of sinews **:** strong and firm **:** TOUGH ⟨putting down the sum of his experience in his rich ~ prose —Cyril Connolly⟩ ⟨bitter and ~ intellectuality —Robert Halsband⟩

sin·fo·nia \ˌsinfəˈnēə, -imf-\ *n, pl* **sinfo·nie** \-ē,ā\ [It, symphony, sinfonia, fr. L *symphonia* — more at SYMPHONY] **1 :** an orchestral musical composition of Italian origin found in 18th century opera or other vocal composition **:** OVERTURE **2 :** SYMPHONY 2

sin·fo·nie \¦zinfə¦nē, ¦si-\ *n, pl* **sinfoni·en** \ˌ=·=ˈnēən\ *usu cap* [G, fr. It *sinfonia*] **:** SYMPHONY

sin·fo·niet·ta \ˌsinfənˈyed·ə, -fōn-, -etə\ *n* -s [It, dim. of *sinfonia* symphony] **1 :** a symphony of less than standard length or for fewer instruments **2 :** a small symphony orchestra; *esp* **:** an orchestra of strings only

sin·ful \ˈsinfəl\ *adj* [ME, fr. OE *synfull*, fr. *syn* sin + *-full* -ful — more at SIN] **1 :** tainted with or full of sin **:** WICKED, INIQUITOUS ⟨~ men⟩ **2 :** marked by or involving sin ⟨~ thoughts⟩ ⟨~ practices⟩ **3 :** highly culpable ⟨a ~ waste in a world that lacks a sufficiency of food —Lionel Trilling⟩

sin·ful·ly \-fəlē, -li\ *adv* [ME, fr. *sinful* + *-ly*] **1 :** in a sinful manner **:** WICKEDLY **2 :** CULPABLY, UNREASONABLY ⟨cars can be hired at a ~ high price —T.H.Fielding⟩

sin·ful·ness \-lnəs\ *n* -ES [ME *sinfulnesse*, fr. *sinful* + *-nesse* -ness] **:** the quality or state of being sinful ⟨man of moderate intelligence and normal ~ —R.H.Rovere⟩

¹**sing** \ˈsiŋ\ *vb* **sang** \ˈsaŋ, -aiŋ\ *or* **sung** \ˈsəŋ\ **sung** *also* **sang; singing; sings** [ME *singen*, fr. OE *singan*; akin to OHG *singan* to sing, ON *syngja*, Goth *singwan* to sing, MW *deongl* to explain, Gk *omphē* voice, oracle and prob. to Prakrit *saṃghai* to say, teach] *vi* **1 a :** to produce musical tones by means of the voice **b :** to utter words in musical tones and with musical inflections and modulations ⟨to ~ at one's work⟩ ⟨children that dance and ~⟩ **c :** to produce in a proper or skilled manner tones generated by vibrations of the vocal cords and resonated by the various oral cavities; *also* **:** to deliver songs, arias, or other compositions in the character of a trained or professional singer ⟨~ extremely well⟩ ⟨~ for charity or in opera⟩ **2 :** to make a shrill whining or whistling sound ⟨a kettle ~*ing* on the hearth —Elizabeth Goudge⟩ ⟨the high overtone of the saw . . . ~*ing* when it runs free —*Amer. Guide Series: Ark.*⟩ ⟨bullets hit the road surface and *sung* off —Ernest Hemingway⟩ **3 a :** to relate, describe, or celebrate something in verse ⟨~*s* of Arthur and his Knights of the Round Table⟩ ⟨poets *sang* of the natural man —*Amer. Guide Series: Minn.*⟩ ⟨gave substance and reality to the beauty of which he *sang* —H.M.Reynolds⟩ **b :** to compose poetry **:** make verse ⟨it was in blank verse that she *sang* —Virginia Woolf⟩ **c :** to convey in or through words a feeling or sense of rhythm ⟨writes a prose remarkable for its live and lyric qualities; she makes the language ~ —Charles Lee⟩ ⟨the second means of writing prose that ~*s* is to train yourself to feel the cadence of words —Grace Fletcher⟩ ⟨his lyrics ~ and flow, with simple, fresh imagery, with delicacy and often humor —Eleanor Sickels⟩ **4 a :** to produce musical or harmonious sounds ⟨grasshoppers chirping and birds ~*ing* —G.B.Shaw⟩ ⟨frogs and crickets *sang* —Rex Ingamells⟩ ⟨most mysterious thing about a pack of hounds is the way they ~ or . . . chime —Thurstan Holland-Hibbert⟩ **b :** to give forth such sounds when played ⟨when the violin *sang* —J.D.Carr⟩ ⟨to hear the heavy tuba ~ sweetly —Arthur Berger⟩ **5** *obs* **:** to chant or intone a religious observance ⟨sad and solemn priests still ~ for Richard's soul —Shak.⟩ **6 a :** to be filled with a humming or buzzing **:** RING ⟨next moment her ears were ~*ing* —Audrey Barker⟩ **b :** to be heard repetitively in the imagination **:** ECHO ⟨their murmured words of farewell *sang* in my ears —Eula Long⟩ ⟨voice saying, Remember my party, Remember my party, *sang* in his ears —Virginia Woolf⟩ **7 :** to be fit or apt for vocal rendition ⟨thinks *Medea* ~*s* as well as any concert work she knows —*Time*⟩ ⟨any translation would be something of a pity when it ~*s* so well in French —Douglas Watt⟩ **8 :** to make a cry **:** CALL — usu. used with *out* ⟨heard the captain of his escort ~ out to him in the darkness —Winston Churchill⟩ ⟨"You don't feel weak, or anything?" she *sung* out at me —Mary R. Rinehart⟩ **9 :** to give evidence or information ⟨is tough enough to have his goons dispatch anyone who dares to ~ to a crime commission —A.H.Weiler⟩ ⟨*sang* to a grand jury in return for a promise of leniency —*Time*⟩ ⟨don't let him know we *sung* on him —Priest Collins⟩ **~** *vt* **1 a :** to utter with musical inflections; *esp* **:** to interpret in musical tones produced by the voice ⟨~ a tune⟩ ⟨~ the tenor part⟩ **b :** to produce vocally the musical tones of ⟨~ G⟩ **2 a :** to relate, describe, or celebrate (something) in verse ⟨~*ing* the beauties of the garden and of simplicity —John Ciardi⟩ ⟨in antique style it ~*s* the loss of friends and fields —H.O.Taylor⟩ ⟨as men have loved their lovers . . . and *sung* their wit, their virtue, and their grace —Edna S. V. Millay⟩ **b :** to announce or proclaim in a clear or resonant manner ⟨stationmaster ~*ing* the stops to the west coast⟩ — often used with *out* ⟨the bell ~*ing* out the hour of midnight⟩ **3 :** CHANT, INTONE ⟨a high mass of requiem . . . will be *sung* —*N.Y.Times*⟩ **4 a :** to bring or accompany to a place or state by singing ⟨~*s* the child to sleep⟩ ⟨his blithe and cheerful verse *sang* itself into the memory —Brander Matthews⟩ **b :** to move or drive by singing ⟨hopes to ~ away his troubles⟩ — **sing one's praises :** to laud a person or thing vigorously and openly ⟨the west country thereafter is the richer for one more pen to *sing its praises* —*Times Lit. Supp.*⟩ ⟨parents *singing his praises* after the award⟩ — **sing the blues :** to express a pessimistic or discouraged attitude **:** COMPLAIN ⟨called me every now and then to *sing the blues* about her troubles —Polly Adler⟩

²**sing** \"\ *n* -s **:** the act of singing: as **a :** a singing esp. in company ⟨an all-night gospel ~ down South —Furman Bisher⟩ **b :** a ritualistic ceremony of a primitive society consisting largely of chanting ⟨without instruction the Navajo chorus at a ~ provides a moving choral performance —Joyce R. Muench⟩

sing *abbr* **1** single **2** singular **3** [L *singulorum*] of each

sing·able \ˈsiŋəbəl\ *adj* [ME *singabil* (part trans. of LL *cantabilis*) fr. *singen* to sing + L *-abilis* -able] **:** apt or suitable for singing ⟨every word is ~ and modestly poetic —Winthrop Sargeant⟩ ⟨agrees that ~ melody is the essence of music —Winthrop Sargeant⟩

singa·pore \ˈsiŋ(g)ə,pō(ə)r, -ó(ə)r, -ōə, -ó(ə), ˌ==ˈ=\ *adj, usu cap* [fr. *Singapore*, Asia] **:** of or from the city or the country of Singapore **:** of the kind or style prevalent in Singapore

¹**singa·po·re·an** \ˌ=·=¦pōrēən, -pór-\ *adj, usu cap* [*Singapore*, country and its capital off the south end of the Malay peninsula (fr. Malay *Singapora*, fr. Skt *Siṁhapura*, lit., lion city, fr. *siṁha* lion + *pura* city) + E *-an*] **1 :** of, relating to, or characteristic of Singapore, southeast Asia **2 :** of, relating to, or characteristic of the people of Singapore

²**singaporean** \"\ *n -s cap* **:** a native or resident of Singapore

singapore sling *n, usu cap 1st S* **:** a sling in which cherry brandy and sometimes Benedictine are added to the usual gin base

¹**singe** \ˈsinj\ *vt* **singed; singed; singeing; singes** [ME *sengen*, fr. OE *sengan*; akin to OHG *bisengan* to singe, OFris *ofsendza* to singe off, scorch, MD *sengen* to singe, MHG *senge* dryness, Sw dial. *sjängla* to singe, OSlav *isočiti* to dry] **1 :** to burn (something) superficially or lightly **:** SCORCH: as **a :** to remove the hair or down from (an animal or fowl) by passing over a flame **b :** to remove projecting fibers and fuzz from (thread, yarn, or cloth) by passing rapidly over a gas flame or heated rollers **2 :** to cause (a person) unexpected trouble, distress, or embarrassment (as for an injudicious interference or venture) ⟨after being *singed* once or twice, I gave up on direct haggling —C.W.Morton⟩ **syn** see BURN

²**singe** \"\ *n* -s **:** a slight burn **:** SCORCH

³**singe** *obs var of* SIGN

singed \ˈsinjd\ *adj* [ME *senged*, fr. past part. of *sengen* to singe] **1 :** that has undergone singeing **2** *of fur* **:** having dried or curled over guard hairs caused by an animal's rubbing or inferior processing

singed cat *n* **:** one that is of better quality than appearance indicates ⟨had an instinctive sympathy for underpups and *singed cats* and the courage to champion their causes —I.S. Cobb⟩

¹**sing·er** \ˈsiŋə(r)\ *n* -s [ME, fr. *singen* to sing + *-er* — more at SING] **:** one that sings: as **a :** one whose profession is to sing **:** vocal artist **b :** POET ⟨the sweet ~ of Avon⟩ **c :** a bird with a natural or acquired ability to sing **:** SONGBIRD **d :** one of an order of officials managing and taking part in the psalmody in the early Christian church **e :** a primitive medicine man who cures sickness and gets rid of evil influences by means of a chanted ritual

²**sing·er** \ˈsinjə(r)\ *n* -s [¹*singe* + *-er*] **:** one that singes: as **a :** a textile worker who singes cloth **b :** one that singes surplus threads from shoe uppers with a gas flame or torch **c :** a slaughterhouse worker who removes hair from hog carcasses with a singeing torch

sin·ge·rie \(ˈ)saⁿzh¦rē, ¦saⁿzhə¦rē\ *n* -s [F, fr. *singe* ape (fr. L *simius, simia*) + *-erie* -ery — more at SIMIAN] **:** a picture, decoration, or design in which monkeys are depicted

sing·er's node \ˈsiŋə(r)z-\ *n* **:** a thickening of tissue on a vocal cord resulting from excessive or incorrect use of the voice

singh \ˈsiŋ\ *n* -s [Hindi *siṅgh*, lit., lion, fr. Skt *siṁha*] **:** a member of one of the warrior castes of northern India; *specif* **:** a Sikh baptized into the Khalsa

singhalese *or* **singalese** *usu cap, var of* SINHALESE

singing *n* -s [ME, fr. gerund of *singen* to sing] **1 :** the act or sound of one that sings **2 :** SING a — often used in pl. ⟨Sunday night ~s for the young people —J.W.Frey⟩ **3 :** a whining, whistling, or humming sound made by something in vibration ⟨the ~ of crosscut saws —*Amer. Guide Series: Mich.*⟩ ⟨the strange high ~ of some aeroplane overhead —Virginia Woolf⟩; *specif* **:** a humming or ringing in one's ears

singing arc *n* **:** a direct current arc in parallel with which is a local circuit containing a condenser and inductance in series where oscillations take place according to the tuning and cause the arc to emit a musical note — compare POULSEN ARC

singing bird *n* **1 :** SONGBIRD **2 :** a passerine bird

singing canary *n* **:** BELUGA 2

singing falcon *or* **singing hawk** *n* **:** CHANTING FALCON

singing fish *n* **:** the midshipman (*Porichthys notatus*) or a related toadfish that makes a humming sound by vibration of the air bladder

singing flame *n* **:** MUSICAL FLAME

singing game *n* **:** a game (as *Farmer in the Dell* or *London Bridge*) in which the players accompany their actions with the singing of a narrative song **2 :** SWINGING PLAY

singing gibbon *n* **:** SILVER GIBBON

sing·ing·ly *adj* **:** in a singing manner **:** LYRICALLY

singing muscle *n* **:** an intrinsic syringeal muscle in a bird

sing·ka·mas *also* **sincamas** \ˌsēŋkäˈmäs\ *n* -ES [Tag, fr. MexSp *jicama*, fr. Nahuatl *xicama*] **:** YAM BEAN

¹**sin·gle** \ˈsiŋgəl\ *adj* [ME *single, sengle*, fr. MF, fr. L *singulus* one only, individual; akin to L *sem-* one — more at SAME] **1 a :** living in an unmarried state **:** CELIBATE ⟨take anything she can get in the way of a husband rather than face penury as a ~ woman —G.B.Shaw⟩ **b :** of or relating to celibacy ⟨prefers the ~ state⟩ **2 :** unattended or unaccompanied by others **:** SOLITARY ⟨he is left alone, ~ and unsupported, like a leafless trunk —*Mirror*⟩ **3 a** (1) **:** consisting of or having only one part, feature, or portion as opposed to or contrasted with double or complex ⟨double consonants are often used in place of ~ consonants⟩ ⟨binocular ~ vision was tested —H.G. Armstrong⟩ (2) **:** consisting of one as opposed to or in contrast with many **:** UNIFORM ⟨undertaking to justify a ~ scale of rates for the entire country —W.M.W.Splawn⟩ ⟨the states sought a ~ type of automobile plate⟩ (3) **:** consisting of only one in number ⟨a ~ anchor holds the boat⟩ ⟨holds to a ~ ideal⟩ — often used with *not* ⟨not a ~ opponent of statehood appeared before the committee —*Midwest Jour.*⟩ ⟨has not made one ~ concession to any other quarter —R.T.H.Fletcher⟩ **b :** having only the normal number of petals or rays **:** not double — used esp. of a horticultural plant ⟨a ~ rose⟩ **4 a :** of or relating to a particular member or part **:** INDIVIDUAL ⟨when nature is so careless of the ~ life, why should we coddle ourselves —R.L.Stevenson⟩ ⟨each ~ citizen is an important part of the community⟩ **b :** of, relating to, or involving only one person ⟨check his ~ judgments against a larger conception or in a perspective of the whole —Meyer Schapiro⟩ ⟨will try his ~ strength against all the world⟩ **5 a** *obs* **:** lacking qualification or addition **:** PLAIN **b** *archaic* **:** of poor quality **:** WEAK ⟨drank his ~ ale⟩ **6 :** taken by itself apart from its group or constituency **:** DISTINCT, SEPARATE ⟨every ~ minute I kept wishing —Agnes S. Turnbull⟩ ⟨the most important ~ resource —B.B.Jennings⟩ ⟨more than any other ~ influence of their period —*Amer. Guide Series: Texas*⟩ ⟨the largest ~ agency providing assistance —Shlomo Katz⟩ **7 a :** free from duplicity or insincerity **:** FRANK, HONEST, OPEN ⟨the willingness of the incumbent . . . to devote himself with a ~ mind to the public good —R.M.Dawson⟩ ⟨jealousy is the flaw in the ~ heart —Ellen Glasgow⟩ ⟨keep your eye ~ and your hands clean —Charles Kingsley⟩ **b :** exclusively concerned or attentive — usu. used of an eye ⟨lives with an eye ~ to his own advantage —*New Republic*⟩ ⟨everything in this line has been procured . . . with an eye ~ to the taste of his numerous patrons —D.D.Martin⟩ **8 :** consisting of a whole **:** UNBROKEN, UNDIVIDED ⟨science and speed have made our world into a ~ neighborhood —Barbara Ward⟩ ⟨the great cause was the same; the source of all the movements was elemental, natural, and ~ —J.L.Motley⟩ **9 :** having one on each side **:** man to man ⟨who now defies thee thrice to ~ fight —John Milton⟩ **10 :** having no equal or like **:** UNUSUAL, SINGULAR ⟨was that rare critic, perhaps even that unique and ~ critic —J.C.Ransom⟩ ⟨~ among his fellows⟩ **11 :** ONLY, SOLE ⟨his ~ speech, that of January 31, 1861, received high praise —W.C.Ford⟩ ⟨his ~ intent was to speak a word of sympathy —A.T.Quiller-Couch⟩ ⟨the ~ piece of evidence⟩ **12 :** having the added musical part lying uniformly above or below the cantus firmus in two-part counterpoint **13 :** designed for the use of one person or family only ⟨a ~ room⟩ ⟨a ~ house⟩

syn SOLE, UNIQUE, LONE, SOLITARY, SEPARATE, PARTICULAR: SINGLE applies to that consisting of one alone and not capable of being felt as accompanied by or joined with another ⟨a *single* instance⟩ ⟨a *single* currency system⟩ ⟨Maine . . . is the only one adjoined by but a single sister state —*Amer. Guide Series: Maine*⟩ ⟨the lover imagines but a *single* joy; to be master of his love in body and soul —George Santayana⟩ SOLE may intensify the notion that what is under consideration is the only one ⟨the *sole* lien to the estate⟩ ⟨the *sole* product of his factory⟩ ⟨invention is almost never the *sole* work of a single inventor —Lewis Mumford⟩ ⟨buy out his partners . . . and thus become *sole* stockholder —*Current Biog.*⟩ ⟨the *sole* casualty of the battle . . . was one cow —R.W.Hatch⟩ UNIQUE in reference to things like manuscripts and coins designates the only one extant; in other uses it indicates that which stands alone because of its unusual character ⟨the manuscript of Beowulf is *unique*⟩ ⟨the *unique* character of the English conquest of Britain needs special emphasis —Kemp Malone⟩ ⟨a *unique* combination of warm and relatively sunny winters, and a summer without excessively high temperatures —E.L.Ullman⟩ LONE and SOLITARY may suggest both single and isolated ⟨who in cells deep and *lone* have languished —P.B.Shelley⟩ ⟨the ambitious Aaron Burr who played a *lone* hand against the field —V.L.Parrington⟩ ⟨the *solitary* sin of an otherwise blameless character⟩ ⟨a sentry kept *solitary* vigil —J.H. Cutler⟩ SEPARATE stresses lack of connection with others; it indicates discreteness rather than singleness ⟨there was no *separate* church, in our sense of the term, as an independent organism within the state —G.L.Dickinson⟩ ⟨given in two *separate* and distinct sections of the constitution —John Marshall⟩ PARTICULAR in this sense stresses the fact of being regarded as distinct ⟨we shall venture beyond the *particular* book in search of qualities that group books together —Virginia Woolf⟩ ⟨some *particular* achievement of modern technology, like an electric shaver or the automobile —D.W. Brogan⟩

²**single** \"\ *n* -s [ME *sengle*, fr. *sengle*, adj., single] **1 a :** a claw of a hawk or falcon **b :** the tail of a deer **2 a :** a separate individual person ⟨the guests arrive in ~*s* and pairs⟩ **b :** a separate individual member of a large class of similar or identical objects: as (1) **:** a one-dollar bill ⟨flashing a big bankroll, generally a wad of ~*s* wrapped up in a hundred-dollar bill —*Police Gazette*⟩ (2) **:** a phonograph record usu. with not over five minutes of recording on each side ⟨will release the sides both as ~*s* and as an . . . LP record —*Down Beat*⟩ (3) **:** a piece or section of sheet metal over ¹⁄₃₂ of an inch in thickness — used in pl. **c :** a modification of the coursing order in change ringing consisting of holding one bell in place through several changes **3 singles** *pl* **:** change ringing as performed on four bells **4 a :** a continuous strand of reeled or spun silk **b :** a thread or yarn of any fiber that is twisted or thrown — often used in pl. **5 a :** a hit for one run in the game of cricket **b :** ONE-BASE HIT **6 singles** *pl* **a :** a tennis match or similar game with one player on each side ⟨we play ~*s* or doubles⟩ **b :** a golf match between two players — distinguished from *foursome* **7 :** a boat or shell propelled by one oarsman **8 a :** a performance or entertainment by only one person ⟨offers to do ~*s* on other shows and in some clubs —*Newsweek*⟩ **b :** a person who does a single ⟨started hiring out as a ~ at lodge dances —*Time*⟩ **9 :** a flower having the normal number of petals or ray florets typical of the species **10 :** a room, apartment, or house designed to accommodate one person or one family ⟨the apartment is a ~⟩ ⟨small ~*s* of five and six rooms —Brendon Shea⟩

³**single** \"\ *vb* **singled; singled; singling** \-g(ə)liŋ\ **singles** [¹*single*] *vt* **1 a** *archaic* **:** to move asunder **:** PART, SEPARATE **b :** to separate (an animal) from a herd in order to chase or

hunt separately ⟨~ out a young cow⟩ **2** *obs* **:** to lead aside **:** SEQUESTER, WITHDRAW ⟨I have ~*ed* thee alone —Shak.⟩ **3 a :** to select or distinguish (a person or thing) from a number or group ⟨walks up to the line and ~*s* every 10th man⟩ — usu. used with *out* ⟨~*s* out for special praise the guidebook to Wells cathedral —Pyke Johnson⟩ **b :** to select or distinguish (a person or thing) for especial attention or comment — usu. used with *out* ⟨something about his person that *singled* him out from the rest of the punctual moving crowd —E.V. Lucas⟩ ⟨had *singled* him out as his successor —John Buchan⟩ ⟨all I can do is to ~ out a few of the basic ideas —A.W. Hummel⟩ **4** *Brit* **:** to thin (seedlings) so as to leave space between the plants **5 a** *archaic* **:** to reduce to only one **:** CONCENTRATE **b :** to reduce (as a doubled rope) from a number of parts to one **6 a :** to advance (a base runner) by a one-base hit ⟨*singled* him to third base⟩ **b :** to bring about the scoring of (a run) by a one-base hit **~** *vi* **1** *archaic* **:** to separate oneself from others **:** proceed alone **2 :** to thin out seedlings **3 :** to take in all bights of mooring lines on a ship except single lines preparatory to getting under way — usu. used with *up* **4 :** to make a one-base hit ⟨*singled* to center and knocked in two more runs —James Thurber⟩ ⟨*singled* behind his catcher —John Drebinger⟩

⁴single \" \ *adv* **:** SINGLY

single–acting \ˈ==ˈ==\ *adj* **:** acting in one direction only ⟨a *single-acting* plunger⟩

single–action \ˈ==ˈ==\ *adj* **1 :** SINGLE-ACTING **2** *of a firearm* **:** that requires cocking before each shot

single–banked \ˈ==ˈbaŋkt, -aiŋ-\ *adj* **:** having a single bank or row: as **a :** having a single row of oarsmen or one on each thwart with the oars alternating on each side **b :** having but one tier of oarsmen (as a unireme) — compare DOUBLE-BANKED

singlebar \ˈ==,=\ *n* [¹*single* + *bar*] **:** SINGLETREE

single–barrel \ˈ==ˈ=\ *n* **:** a single-barreled gun

single–barreled \ˈ==ˈbarəld *also* -ber-\ *adj, of a gun* **:** having one barrel

single–base powder \ˈ==ˈ=-\ *n* **:** an explosive powder or propellant that contains nitrocellulose as the only essential component — compare DOUBLE-BASE POWDER

single bill *or* **single bond** *n* **1 :** a bill or bond for the future payment of money with no annexed condition **2 :** a bill on which a single party is to be heard in a judicial proceeding

single bond *n* **:** SIMPLE BOND

single–breasted \ˈ==ˈ==\ *adj, of a coat or jacket* **:** having a center closing with one row of buttons and no lap — compare DOUBLE-BREASTED

single brilliant *n* **:** a brilliant with 16 facets above the girdle and 12 or 16 facets below

single–chamber \ˈ==ˈ==\ *adj* **:** having a single chamber **:** UNICAMERAL ⟨a *single-chamber* legislature⟩

single–coat·ed \ˈ==ˈkōd·əd\ *adj, of paper or board* **:** coated only once on one or both sides

single comb *n* **:** a comb on a fowl having the form of an erect or pendant median serrated crest — see COMB illustration

single corner *n* **:** one of the two diagonally opposed corners of a checkerboard that have a single dark or playing square

single counterpoint *n* **:** counterpoint in which the added part lies uniformly above or below the cantus firmus

single–crop \ˈ==ˈ=\ *vi* **:** to practice one-crop farming **:** grow a single crop on the same land repeatedly **~** *vt* **:** to use (land) in a one-crop system ⟨*single-cropping* their lands with wheat —*Rev. of Reviews*⟩

single cross *n* **:** the heterotic first generation hybrid between two selected and usu. inbred lines ⟨many commercial hybrid seeds are *single crosses*⟩ — compare DOUBLE CROSS, HETEROSIS, TOPCROSS

single cut *n* **:** a simplified brilliant cut used on small stones — see CUT illustration

single–cut file \ˈ==ˈ=-\ *n* **:** a file having a single parallel series of diagonal cuts across its face

single doubler *n* **:** DOUBLER 2a

single–end·ed \ˈ==ˈendəd\ *adj* **:** having the principal or working portion at one end only ⟨a *single-ended* boiler⟩

single entry *n* **:** a method or system of bookkeeping that recognizes only one side of a business transaction and usu. consists only of a record of cash and personal accounts with debtors and creditors — compare DOUBLE ENTRY

single–entry table *n* **:** a mathematical table in which a tabulated function depends on but one independent variable

single escheat *n, Scots law* **:** escheat to the crown of one's movable estate

single–eye \ˈ==ˈ=\ *adj* **:** having only one bud ⟨a *single-eye* cutting⟩

single–eyed \ˈ==ˈ=\ *adj* **1 :** having a clear honest eye **:** SINGLE **2 :** having but one eye or the sight of one eye

¹single file *n* **:** a line of persons, animals, or things moving one behind another; *also* **:** a single row — called also *Indian file* ⟨marching in *single file*⟩

²single file *adv* **:** in a single line ⟨traffic is slowed by having to crawl *single file* through the doors in the . . . barricades —Mollie Panter-Downes⟩

single–file \ˈ==ˈ=-\ *vi* [fr. *single file*, n.] **:** to walk or move in single file ⟨all *single-filed* past the . . . bed —J.D.Salinger⟩ ⟨*single-filing* down the St. George's channel to Liverpool —Gordon Webber⟩

single fish *n* **:** a single fish joint

¹single–foot \ˈ==,=\ *n, pl* **single–foots :** ⁷RACK b

²single–foot \" \ *vi, of a horse* **:** to go at a rack ⟨has seen him *single-foot* up to a wall and go over clear —Allan Forbes & R.M.Eastman⟩ — **single–footer** \ˈ==,==\ *n*

single–framed roof \ˈ==ˈ=-\ *n* **:** a roof in which opposite rafters are tied together by the upper floor frame or by boards nailed across horizontally

single–gear \ˈ==ˈ=\ *vt* **:** to gear directly (as by belting or a single pair or train of gears) without the use of any additional speed-reducing mechanism

¹single–handed \ˈ==ˈ==\ *also* **single–hand** \ˈ==ˈ=\ *adj* **1 :** managed or done by one person or with one on a side ⟨account of his *single-handed* journeys in the sixties —*Brit. Bk. News*⟩ ⟨a cannon used . . . in his *single-handed* defense of the local coastline —*Amer. Guide Series: Conn.*⟩ ⟨fighting in *single-handed* combat⟩ **2 :** working alone or unassisted by others ⟨reference book . . . for the *single-handed* cook with a family to feed —Margaret Lane⟩ ⟨people who are *single-handed* or too old to manage holdings —A.D.Rees⟩ **3 :** used or adapted for using with one hand ⟨*single-handed* fishing rod⟩ **4 :** having or using only one hand ⟨a *single-handed* billiard player⟩ — **single–hand·ed·ness** *n* -ES

²single–handed \" \ *adv* **:** with or by oneself or without assistance ⟨fought his own cause in both war and politics *single-handed* —*advt*⟩ ⟨had to build his little log hut *single-handed* —A.F.Harlow⟩

single–hand·ed·ly *adv* **:** in a single-handed manner ⟨undertook the superhuman task of *single-handedly* creating a historical dictionary —Robert Pick⟩

single–hearted \ˈ==ˈ==\ *adj* **1 :** SINGLE 7a ⟨the perfect, *single-hearted*, crusading knight —H.O.Taylor⟩ **2 :** characterized by or resulting from sincerity and unity of purpose or dedication ⟨such a task requires an expenditure of time and energy, a *single-hearted* consecration —B.N.Cardozo⟩ ⟨the man who seizes on one deep-reaching idea . . . and with *single-hearted* fervor forces it upon the world —P.E.More⟩ ⟨her lifelong, *single-hearted*, and unshakable conviction —Albert Lynd⟩

single–heart·ed·ly *adv* **:** in a single-hearted manner ⟨works nobly and *single-heartedly*⟩

single–heart·ed·ness *n* -ES **:** the quality or state of being single-hearted ⟨fervent saint who sang because he suffered, and whose mysticism was tinged with kindly *single-heartedness* —Frances P. Keyes⟩

single jack *n* **:** a short-handled hammer weighing about four pounds and used in hand drilling

single jacker *n* **:** a miner using a single jack

single knot *n* **:** OVERHAND KNOT

single–leaf \ˈ==,=\ *or* **single–leaf pine** *or* **single–leaf pinyon** *n* **:** PIÑON

single–leaf ash *also* **single–leaved ash** *n* **:** a unifoliolate or rarely bifoliolate or trifoliolate ash (*Fraxinus anomala*) of the western U.S.

single–line \ˈ==ˈ=\ *adj* **:** confining commercial activity to one line of goods ⟨a *single-line* manufacturer⟩ ⟨a *single-line* representative⟩

single–loader \ˈ==ˈlōdə(r)\ *n* **:** a firearm in which each charge is inserted separately

single man *n* **:** a checker that may be moved only forward — compare KING

single–member district \ˈ==ˈ==-\ *also* **single–member constituency** *n* **:** an electoral district or constituency having a single representative in a legislative body rather than two or more — compare LIST SYSTEM, PROPORTIONAL REPRESENTATION

single–minded \ˈ==ˈ==\ *adj* **1 :** SINGLE 7a ⟨a dedicated, *single-minded* man —*Time*⟩ ⟨an honest, farsighted, *single-minded* and liberal statesman —J.F.Gore⟩ — opposed to *double-minded* **2 :** SINGLE-HEARTED 2 ⟨his *single-minded*, selfless devotion to the liberation of his country —H.H. Fisher⟩ ⟨had a *single-minded* love of God and a catholic love of humanity —W.L.Sperry⟩ **3 :** having one unifying purpose ⟨with all the emotional ferocity and energy of genius, was *single-minded* for victory —J.H.Plumb⟩ ⟨his *single-minded* concern with the political dimension —Martin Price⟩ ⟨affable manner covered a *single-minded* ruthlessness —*Time*⟩

single–mind·ed·ly *adv* **:** in a single-minded manner

single–mind·ed·ness *n* -ES **:** the quality or state of being single-minded ⟨had a passionate *single-mindedness* which their divided minds and loyalties lacked —W.L.Sperry⟩

single money *n, obs* **:** small currency **:** SMALL CHANGE

single–name paper \ˈ==ˈ=-\ *n* **:** a promissory note with no endorsement other than the signature of the maker

sin·gle·ness *n* -ES [¹*single* + *-ness*] **1 :** sincerity and honesty in design or intent **:** STRAIGHTFORWARDNESS ⟨a man the ~ of whose motives could not be questioned —Winston Churchill⟩ ⟨those who with ~ of mind try to do God's will —*Interpreter's Bible*⟩ **2 :** the state of being unmarried **:** CELIBACY ⟨traces the trends in nuptiality and ~ —*Population Index*⟩ **3 :** the fact of being single or one of a kind or group **:** ONENESS ⟨the ~ of a small operation . . . lost in the confusion of dozens of outfits —H.D.Skidmore⟩ **4 :** the condition of standing or remaining alone or apart ⟨the vulnerability of ~ will disappear before unity of effort —Douglas MacArthur⟩ **5 :** the quality of concentrating on one central objective ⟨the ~ of our aim generates a tremendous sense of solidarity —F.A. Perry⟩

single nickel salt *n* **:** NICKEL SULFATE

single–nose \ˈ==ˈ=\ *adj* **:** having only one growing point and usu. producing a single flower stalk ⟨a *single-nose* narcissus bulb⟩ — compare DOUBLE-NOSE

single–pass \ˈ==ˈ=\ *vt* **:** to pass (gases) once across the tubes of a boiler

single–phase \ˈ==ˈ=\ *adj* **:** of or relating to a circuit energized by a single alternating electromotive force with the currents in the two wires differing in phase by 180 degrees or a half cycle

single–phaser \ˈ==ˈ==\ *n* **:** a single-phase machine

single–phasing \ˈ==ˈ==\ *n* -S **:** the operation of a polyphase motor on single-phase supply

single–pole switch \ˈ==ˈ=-\ *n* **:** an electric switch having only one blade and one contact

single premium *n* **:** the sum that would meet in a single payment the cost of a life insurance policy for the entire policy term

single–punch \ˈ==ˈ=\ *vt* **:** to punch one hole at a time in

single–rail crane \ˈ==ˈ=-\ *n* **:** WALKING CRANE

single–rail track circuit *n* **:** a track circuit comprising two running rails with one divided into sections by insulated joints and the other used as a common return

single rhyme *n* **:** a monosyllabic rhyme

single–rivet \,==ˈ==\ *vt* **:** to secure (a joint) by a single row of rivets or by a single row on each side of the seam of a butt joint

singles *pl of* SINGLE, *pres 3d sing of* SINGLE

singles court *n* **:** a court (as for tennis) laid out for only two players

single–screw \ˈ==ˈ=\ *adj* **:** having one screw propeller ⟨a *single-screw* ship⟩ — compare TWIN-SCREW

single–seater \ˈ==ˈ==\ *n* **:** a vehicle (as an airplane) with a single seat

single–seed cucumber \ˈ==ˈ=-\ *n* **:** STAR CUCUMBER

single shear *n* **:** shear along one surface only

single–shear steel *n* **:** SHEAR STEEL

single–shot \ˈ==ˈ=\ *adj* **:** capable of firing only one shot without reloading

single–shot pistol *n* **:** a pistol that can be loaded with only one cartridge at a time and that is used chiefly in target practice — compare AUTOMATIC PISTOL

single–side–band modulation \ˈ==ˈ=ˈ=-\ *n* **:** a modulation used in a radio or telephone carrier in which the normal carrier signal is eliminated and one of the two modulation side bands is removed usu. by filtering

single–side–band transmission *n* **:** carrier suppression in which the power associated essentially with one side band is not transmitted

single–space \ˈ==ˈ=\ *vt* **:** to type (copy) leaving no blank line spaces ⟨*single-space* the list of services, but leave a double space both before and after —D.D.Lessenberry & T.J.Crawford⟩ **~** *vi* **:** to type on every line space

single spanish burton *n, usu cap 2d S* **:** a tackle with three single blocks

single spruce *n* **:** WHITE SPRUCE 1a

single–stage \ˈ==ˈ=\ *adj* **:** of one stage only **:** complete in one rather than in two or more operations ⟨*single-stage* turbine⟩ ⟨*single-stage* rocket⟩ ⟨*single-stage* trigger⟩

single standard *n* **1 :** MONOMETALLISM **2 :** a set of principles that apply equally to all members of a group; *specif* **:** a code of morals that applies the same standards of sexual behavior to both men and women — compare DOUBLE STANDARD

singlestick \ˈ==,=\ *n* [¹*single* + *stick*] **1 :** fighting or fencing with a one-handed wooden stick or sword ⟨the crisp click of sportsmen at ~ —Lawrence Durrell⟩ **2 :** the weapon used in singlestick fencing

singlesticker \ˈ==,==\ *n* [¹*single* + *stick* + *-er*] **:** a single-masted vessel **:** SLOOP, CUTTER

single stitch *n* **:** a bookbinder's stitch made by passing a single loop through the center of the matter to be secured and tying

single–surfaced \ˈ==ˈ==\ *adj* **:** having one finished surface ⟨*single-surfaced* airplane wing⟩

sin·glet \ˈsiŋglət, *usu* -əd.+V\ *n* -S [¹*single* + *-et*] **1 a** *dial chiefly Brit* **:** an unlined waistcoat **b** *chiefly Brit* **:** an undershirt or athletic jersey ⟨his copper-brown torso that was only partly covered by the torn ~ —Vance Palmer⟩ ⟨athletes, stripped to their ~*s* and shorts, raced, cycled and pole-jumped —H.V.Morton⟩ **2 a :** an atomic, molecular, or nuclear energy level with a spin of zero **b :** a spectrum line that is not resolved into components by even the highest dispersion

single–tap r \ˈ==ˈ=-\ *n* **:** a trilled *r* made by a single flip of the point of the tongue against the teethridge (as in the southern British pronunciation of *very* sometimes spelled *veddy*)

sin·gle·tary pea \ˈsiŋgəl,terē-\ *n* [*singletary* prob. fr. ¹*single* + *-tary* (as in *solitary*); fr. its being an escape] **:** a weak-stemmed and usu. decumbent winter annual legume (*Lathyrus hirsutus*) native to the Mediterranean region but long established as an escape in the southern U.S. and more recently cultivated as a cover and pasture crop — called also *Caley pea, rough pea, wild winterpea*

single tax *n* **:** a tax to be levied on a single object as the sole source of public revenue esp. by taxing the entire economic rent of land

single taxer *n* **:** an advocate of a single-tax system

single–throw switch \ˈ==ˈ=-\ *n* **:** a switch (as on an electrical switchboard) that by one operation engages a set of fixed contacts

sin·gle·ton \ˈsiŋgəltən, -tᵊn\ *n* -S [F, fr. E ¹*single* + F *-eton* (dim. suffix)] **1 :** a card (as in bridge) that is the only one of its suit orig. held in a hand — compare DOUBLETON **2 :** an individual member or thing distinct from others grouped with it ⟨a quatrain consisting of a triplet and a ~⟩ ⟨the birds scattered . . . and the ~*s* were easy to pick up one by one —Thomas Barbour⟩; *specif* **:** a single offspring ⟨in May or June the spotted fawns are born, usually ~*s*, but rarely twins —W.A.Weber⟩

single–tongue \ˈ==ˈ=\ *vi* [⁴*single* + *tongue*, v.] **:** to articulate notes on a wind instrument by repeated single articulations (as *t, t*) — compare DOUBLE-TONGUE

single–track \ˈ==ˈ=\ *adj* **1 :** having but one track ⟨a *single-track* railroad⟩ **2 :** lacking intellectual range, receptiveness, or flexibility **:** ONE-TRACK ⟨with a *single-track* mind devoted solely to his duty —Leo Crane⟩

single transferable vote *n* **:** a vote on a ballot that can be transferred from a candidate of first choice who has already obtained the necessary quota of votes for election to a candidate marked by the voter as second or third choice in order that every vote may count toward the election of a candidate — compare HARE SYSTEM

sin·gle·tree \ˈsiŋgəl(,)trē, -l·tri\ *n* [¹*single* + *tree*] **1 :** WHIFFLETREE **2 :** a heavy horizontal bar sometimes used to spread the loop of a hoisting chain to prevent crushing the load

single–valued \ˈ==ˈ(,)=\ *adj* **:** having only one value for any one value of the argument ⟨a *single-valued* function⟩

single vote *or* **single nontransferable vote** *n* **:** a simple form of proportional representation by which each voter casts his ballot for one candidate only

single whip *n* **:** a purchase consisting of a single block and a small rope for lifting light articles — compare DOUBLE WHIP

single wicket *n* **:** a variation of cricket that is played on a pitch with a single batting end having three stumps and a bowling end usu. marked by one stump with all bowling being done from the same end and but one batsman being in at a time

single wingback formation *or* **single wing** *n* **:** an offensive football formation to the left or right in which a back plays just outside of and a yard behind one of the ends, the blocking back is on the same side of the center and usu. a yard behind the guard, and the two other backs are four or five yards behind a balanced or unbalanced line and in a position to receive a direct snap from the center

singling *n* -S [fr. gerund of ³*single*] **1 :** the act or process of one that singles **2 singlings** *pl* **:** the crude product that first passes over in distilling **:** the low wine that is usu. redistilled at a lower temperature **3 :** a defect in the plying of yarns caused by the omission of one or more strands

sin·gly \ˈsiŋg(ə)lē, -li\ *adv* [ME *sengle*ly, fr. *sengle* single + *-ly* — more at SINGLE] **1 a :** by or with oneself **:** as an individual person or thing **:** SEPARATELY ⟨they come ~ or in scattered groups —*Amer. Guide Series: Pa.*⟩ ⟨the tree-living primate mother and her ~ born infant —Weston La Barre⟩ **b :** without the assistance or support of others **:** SINGLE-HANDEDLY ⟨either ~ or in cooperation, have carried on noteworthy educational activities —*Amer. Guide Series: Oregon*⟩ ⟨~ and successfully opposed the . . . proposal for a drastic shortening of hours in industry —*Current Biog.*⟩ **2** *archaic* **:** as or by a single unit **:** EXCLUSIVELY, SOLELY **3 :** STRAIGHTFORWARDLY, HONESTLY, SINCERELY ⟨having its accomplishment ~ in mind —F.J.Haskin⟩

sing·pho \ˈsiŋ,pō\ *n, pl* **singpho** *or* **singphos** *usu cap* **:** CHINGPAW

sings *pres 3d sing of* SING, *pl of* SING

¹sing–sing \ˈsiŋ,siŋ\ *n* -S [Malinke *si-nsing* antelope] **:** a West African waterbuck (*Kobus defassa unctuosus*) distinguished by rather long sandy brown distinctly greasy hair

²sing–sing \" \ *n* [redupl. of ¹*sing*] **:** an Oceanian ceremony of singing and dancing

¹singsong \ˈ=,=\ *n* [¹*sing* + *song*] **1 a :** a verse selection with marked and regular rhythm and rhyme **:** a jingling song or ballad **b :** verse of such characteristics ⟨the ~ of the epic, its repetitious phrases and familiar story —*College English*⟩ **2** *chiefly Brit* **:** SING 1a ⟨food, refreshments, entertainment, and a ~ combined to make it a highly enjoyable evening —*Crowsnest*⟩ **3 :** a voice delivery characterized by a narrow range of pitch or a mechanically repetitious pitch variation ⟨began in the ~ of a professional guide —Donn Byrne⟩ ⟨the ~ of . . . campaign oratory —Max Ascoli⟩ ⟨the auctioneer with his rapid ~ —*Amer. Guide Series: Tenn.*⟩ ⟨speaking English in a Welsh ~ —John Barkham⟩

²singsong \" \ *adj* **1 :** making or delivering singsong ⟨is known as a ~ poet⟩ **2 :** characterized by the light or trivial usu. monotonously expressed ⟨writes ~ verse⟩ ⟨cases of long-windedness, foggy meanings, clichés, and ~ phrases —Stuart Chase⟩ **3 :** having a monotonous cadence or rhythm **:** marked by a singsong ⟨story in a deliberately rhythmical, ~ prose —*New Yorker*⟩ ⟨cultivated a ~ manner of speaking —Thomas Pyles⟩ ⟨the ~ orchestration from a loud radio sawed the air —Kathryn Grondahl⟩

³singsong \" \ *vb* -ED/-ING/-S *vt* **1 :** to move by or as if by means of a singsong or chant ⟨watched coolies ~ a dismantled truck up the cliff —*Time*⟩ **2 :** to speak, chant, or declaim in singsong ⟨the class ~*ing* the number tables⟩ ⟨~*ed* her way through Shakespeare with a . . . native-born inflection —Joan Comay⟩ **~** *vi* **:** to speak, chant, or sing in a singsong manner ⟨droning on and on, his voice ~*ing* almost unrecognizably —Norman Mailer⟩ ⟨vendors ~*ed* up and down the platform —Jobo Nakamura⟩

singsong girl *n* **:** a Chinese girl engaged in professional entertainment similar to that performed by the geisha

sing·songy \ˈ=,sȯŋē, -ŋi *also* -,säŋ-\ *adj* [¹*singsong* + *-y*] **:** suggestive of singsong

sing·spiel \ˈsiŋ,spēl, ˈziŋ,shpēl\ *n, usu cap* [G, fr. *singen* to sing (fr. OHG *singan*) + *spiel* play, fr. OHG *spil* — more at SING, SPIEL] **:** a somewhat dramatic musical work popular in Germany esp. in the latter part of the 18th century, usu. comic in nature, and characterized by spoken dialogue interspersed with popular or folk songs — compare BALLAD OPERA

sing·spi·ra·tion \,siŋspəˈrāshən\ *n* -S [¹*sing* + *inspiration*] **:** a song service featuring the group singing of hymns conducted esp. by revivalistic churches and often followed by a sermon

¹sin·gu·lar \ˈsiŋgyələ(r)\ *adj* [ME *singuler*, fr. MF *singuler, singulier*, fr. L *singularis* single, solitary, singular, fr. *singulus* one only, individual + *-aris* -ar — more at SINGLE] **1 a :** of or relating to a separate person or thing **:** INDIVIDUAL ⟨every fact in the world might be ~, that is, unlike any other fact and sole of its kind —William James⟩ ⟨assumption that the ~ person can be understood apart from his culture —*Amer. Polit. Sci. Rev.*⟩ ⟨saw that each weed was a ~ knife —Stephen Crane⟩ ⟨to all and ~ to whom these presents shall come, greetings⟩ **b :** of, relating to, or being a word form denoting one person, thing, or instance ⟨one subject usually takes a ~ verb⟩ — opposed to *plural;* compare DUAL **c :** of or relating to a single instance or to something considered by itself **:** applied to only one individual ⟨a ~ term⟩ ⟨a ~ proposition⟩ — opposed to *general* **d** (1) **:** of or relating to a single or individual unit ⟨convey several parcels of land all and ~⟩ (2) **:** of, relating to, or affecting a particular property or one or more separate interests or rights in property as distinguished from the entire body of a decedent's estate or any interest or right in property acquired otherwise than by inheritance — compare SINGULAR SUCCESSION **2 a** *obs* **:** set apart or distinguished by superiority **:** EMINENT **b :** of considerable extent or worth **:** EXTRAORDINARY, EXCEPTIONAL ⟨achieved a ~ mechanical triumph that won him wide renown —Sherwood Anderson⟩ ⟨a ~ poetic achievement —H. W.Lange⟩ ⟨holds a ~ regard for his people⟩ ⟨his death is a ~ loss⟩ **c** *obs* **:** especially helpful or efficacious **:** BENEFICIAL **3** *archaic* **a :** consisting of one only **b :** having but one on each side ⟨those in his high place fight no ~ combats —Sir Walter Scott⟩ **4 a :** of unusual quality **:** UNCOMMON, UNIQUE ⟨various speculations put forward in explanation of the ~ phenomena of this remarkable place —Harry Luke⟩ ⟨a work of ~ originality and analytical power —*Economica*⟩ ⟨that woman of ~ mystery, the Mona Lisa —Elizabeth Janeway⟩ **b :** RARE, VALUABLE ⟨a man of ~ charm and sterling character —D.S. Muzzey⟩ ⟨an effect of ~ grace and delicacy —*Amer. Guide Series: Maine*⟩ ⟨of ~ and exquisite workmanship⟩ **5 a :** being at variance with others **:** DIFFERING, CONTRARY ⟨am not ~ in the opinion that much of the disease which does prevail might be avoided —Charles Dickens⟩ ⟨nor are we ~ in our judgment —Aldous Huxley⟩ **b :** departing from general usage or expectation **:** PECULIAR, ECCENTRIC ⟨a ~

dog . . . of the color of chocolate —Arnold Bennett⟩ ⟨~ to say, the one dangerous and objectionable feature in this little volume preserved it from limbo —George Meredith⟩ ⟨hit upon the ~ expedient of diminishing the quality of their justice in order to reduce the demand for it —T.F.T.Plucknett⟩ **c :** possessing various unique mathematical properties ⟨a ~ point or integral in a differential equation⟩ **syn** see STRANGE

²singular \"\ *n* -s [L *singularis*, fr. *singularis*, adj., single] **1 :** the singular number, the inflectional form denoting it, or a word in that form ⟨that the human mind has to think in terms of ~ and plural —Weston La Barre⟩ ⟨*he* is the ~ of *they*⟩ **2 a** *archaic* **:** a single person, instance, or thing **:** INDIVIDUAL ⟨eloquence would be but a poor thing, if we should converse only with ~*s* —Ben Jonson⟩ **b :** something that is considered by itself or as a single term; *also* **:** SINGULAR PROPOSITION — usu. used in pl. ⟨experiences might all have been ~*s*, no one of them occurring twice —William James⟩ ⟨an accepted principle in the middle ages that reason or intellect and science are of universals, whereas the senses are of ~*s* —G.P.Klubertanz⟩ **c** (1) *obs* **:** an adult wild boar (2) **:** a company of wild boars

singular integral *n* **:** SINGULAR SOLUTION

sin·gu·lar·ism \'siŋgyələ,rizəm\ *n* -s **:** any philosophy that derives the universe from a single principle — contrasted with *pluralism;* compare MONISM

sin·gu·lar·i·ty \,==ˈlarəd·ē, -rətē, -i *also* -ler-\ *n* -ES [ME *singularite*, fr. MF *singularité*, fr. LL *singularitat-, singularitas*, fr. L *singularis* single, singular + *-itat-, -itas* -ity — more at SINGULAR] **1 :** something that is separate or singular **:** UNIT ⟨for the Aristotelian, knowledge of universals proceeds from experience with *singularities*⟩ **2 a :** an unusual manifestation or eccentricity in manner or behavior ⟨*singularities* of dress and speech make life a burden for their unfortunate possessors —Sacheverell Sitwell⟩ ⟨even our faults have some attractiveness for us . . . as if they were pleasant *singularities* —F.A. Swinnerton⟩ **b :** a unique or remarkable characteristic or development ⟨some natural productions require such a ~ of soil and situation —Adam Smith⟩ **c :** an odd or peculiar feature or characteristic ⟨forgotten habits, uses that are now lost to memory, significances once powerful . . . all of these things and many more *singularities* are recalled to the student of plant names —*Notes & Queries*⟩ **3 :** the quality or state of being singular ⟨the amount of ~ one finds among the people of the country —*New Republic*⟩ ⟨personality . . . expresses its ~ even in handwriting —O.W.Holmes †1935⟩ ⟨as individuality approaches ~, it . . . isolates itself —J.L.Lowes⟩ ⟨the ~ of an analytic function⟩

sin·gu·lar·iza·tion \,==,lərəˈzāshən, -,rīˈz-\ *n* -s **:** the act or process of singularizing **:** the state of being singularized

sin·gu·lar·ize \ˈ==lə,rīz\ *vt* -ED/-ING/-S [¹*singular* + *-ize*] **:** to make singular: as **a :** DISTINGUISH, SIGNALIZE ⟨observes the rule that never by display of peculiarity, or even by a display of brave or noble behavior, must she ~ herself by standing out —Albert Hubbell⟩ **b :** to make single ⟨in this people that we place our confidence — in the specific and *singularized* vocation of each one of its members —*Commonweal*⟩

sin·gu·lar·ly *adv* [ME *singulerly*, fr. *singuler* singular + *-ly* — more at SINGULAR] **:** in a singular manner ⟨potash, a ~ effective component of these fertilizers —*advt*⟩ ⟨a woman of ~ frank temperament —Robert Hichens⟩ ⟨a ~ charming woman —Rudyard Kipling⟩ ⟨had first stood there so ~, and vanished at the approach of strangers —Thomas Hardy⟩ ⟨majority of these high altitude birds are ~ voiceless —Douglas Carruthers⟩

sin·gu·lar·ness *n* -ES **:** SINGULARITY

singular point *n* **:** a point of the curve f(x, y)=0 where both partial derivatives are zero

singular proposition *n* **:** a proposition having as its subject a proper name or a descriptive phrase which applies only to one individual

singular solution *n* **:** a mathematical solution that contains no arbitrary constant and is not a particular solution — called also *singular integral*

singular square matrix *n* **:** a square matrix whose determinant is zero

singular statement *n* **:** a statement that contains only constants and no variables — contrasted with *general statement*

singular succession *n, chiefly Scots law* **:** the succession to a particular object or property — distinguished from *universal succession*

singular syllogism *n* **:** a syllogism whose middle term is a singular term

singular universal *n* **:** CONCRETE UNIVERSAL

sin·gu·li in so·li·dum \,siŋgyə,līin'sälədəm, -gə,lēin-\ *adj* [L, singly for the whole] **:** singly liable for a whole amount due

sin·gult \'siŋ,gəlt\ *n* -s [L *singultus*] *archaic* **:** SOB ⟨heart= thrilling cries, with sobs and ~*s* sore —Gilbert West⟩ — usu. used in pl.

sin·gul·ti·ent \siŋ'gəltēənt\ *adj* [L *singultient-, singultiens*, pres. part. of *singultire* to sob, hiccup, fr. *singultus* sob, hiccup] *archaic* **:** SOBBING ⟨wakes with a deep-drawn ~ breath —Lewis Morris⟩

sin·gul·tus \-ltəs\ *n* -ES [L] **:** HICCUP

sinh *abbr* [*sine* + *hyperbolic*] hyperbolic sine

¹sin·ha·lese \,sin(h)ə'lēz, -ēs\ *also* **sin·gha·lese** \,siŋgə-, -iŋ(h)ə-\ *or* **sin·ga·lese** \-iŋ(g)ə-\ *or* **cin·ga·lese** \-iŋ(g)ə-\ *or* **cin·gha·lese** \-iŋgə-, -iŋ(h)ə-\ *adj, usu cap* [Skt *Siṁhala* Ceylon, island in the Indian ocean south of the Indian subcontinent + E *-ese* (adj. suffix)] **1 :** of, relating to, or characteristic of the Sinhalese **2 :** of, relating to, or characteristic of the Sinhalese language

²sinhalese \"\ *also* **singhalese** \"\ *or* **singalese** \"\ *or* **cingalese** \"\ *or* **cinghalese** \"\ *n, pl* **sinhalese** *cap* [Skt *Siṁhala* Ceylon + E *-ese* (n. suffix)] **1 a :** a people inhabiting the island of Ceylon and forming a major portion of its population **b :** a member of such people **2 :** the Indic language of the Sinhalese people which is the leading language of Ceylon

sin·ha·lite \'sin(h)ə,līt\ *n* -s [*sinhal-* (as in *sinhalese*) + *-ite;* fr. the fact that the gemstones identified as sinhalite came from Ceylon] **:** a mineral consisting of a magnesium aluminum borate that is structurally related to olivine and is occas. used as a gem

sin·ha·san \sin'hāsᵊn, -'həs-\ *n* -s [Skt *siṁhasana*, lit., lion's seat] **:** a throne often depicted in sculpture with legs in the shape of lions and designed as a seat for the figure of a deity

sin·ic \'sinik, -nēk\ *adj, usu cap* [ML *sinicus*, fr. LL *Sinae*, pl., Chinese + L *-icus* -ic — more at SINOLOGUE] **:** CHINESE, SINITIC

sin·i·cism \'sinə,sizəm\ *n* -s *usu cap* [*sinic* + *-ism*] **:** something (as a manner or custom) peculiar to the Chinese

sin·i·ci·za·tion \,==sə'zāshən, -,sī'z-\ *n* -s *usu cap* **:** the act or process of sinicizing **:** the state of being sinicized

sin·i·cize \'==,sīz\ *vt* -ED/-ING/-S *often cap* [*sinic* + *-ize*] **:** to modify by Chinese influence

sinico- *comb form, usu cap* [*sinic* + *-o-*] **:** Chinese and ⟨*Sinico*= Japanese⟩ ⟨*Sinico*=Russian⟩

sin·i·co-japanese \'sinə,kō-, -nē,kō-\ *n, cap S&J* **1 :** Chinese as adapted and used in Japanese **2 :** a style of writing in Japanese modeled on the Chinese classics and containing many Chinese words and idioms

sin·i·fi·ca·tion \,sinəfə'kāshən\ *n* -s *usu cap* [LL *Sinae* + E *-i-* + *-fication*] **:** SINICIZATION

sin·i·fy \'==,fī\ *vt* -ED/-ING/-ES *often cap* [LL *Sinae*, pl., Chinese + E *-ify*] **:** SINICIZE

sin·i·grin \'sinəgrən\ *n* -s [ISV *sinigr-* (fr. NL *Sinapis nigra*, genus of black mustard seed) + *-in*] **:** a crystalline glucoside $CH_2{=}CHCH_2C(SC_6H_{11}O_5){=}NOSO_3K$ found in the seeds of black mustard (*Brassica nigra*) and other brassicas that on enzymatic hydrolysis by myrosin yields glucose, potassium hydrogen sulfate, and allyl isothiocyanate by Lossen rearrangement — compare MUSTARD OIL

¹sin·is·ter \'sinəstə(r), *chiefly archaic* sə'nis-\ *adj* [ME *sinistre*, fr. L *sinister* left, on the left side, awkward, injurious, evil, unlucky, inauspicious; fr. the fact that omens observed from one's left were considered unlucky] **1** *archaic* **:** ominous of evil or wrongdoing **:** UNFAVORABLE, PREJUDICIAL **2** *obs* **:** conveying misleading or detrimental opinion or advice ⟨the ~ application of the malicious, ignorant, and base interpreter —Ben Jonson⟩ **3** *archaic* **:** dishonestly underhanded **:** FRAUDULENT ⟨nimble and ~ tricks and shifts —Francis Bacon⟩ **4 :** evil or productive of evil **:** BAD, CORRUPTIVE ⟨the ~ character of the early factory system —Walter Lippmann⟩ ⟨emotions long repressed sometimes find ~ outlets —V.L. Parrington⟩ ⟨the scheme of some ~ intelligence bent on punishing him —Thomas Hardy⟩ ⟨critics who . . . exaggerate the ~ influence of a kind of underworld of economic werewolves —F.L.Mott⟩ ⟨denouncing the ~ aims and wicked conduct of those in high places —C.L.Becker⟩ **5 a :** of, relating to, or situated to the left or on the left side of something ⟨was placed on . . . the ~ side of the church —J.A. Davison⟩ ⟨on a helmet, a wreath with the crest, a dexter and a ~ hand proper, grasping a two-handed sword argent —F.W.Steer⟩; *specif* **:** of or relating to the side of a heraldic shield or escutcheon at the left of the bearer ⟨a theory that the bearings of a person who fled . . . could be assumed and borne in a ~ quarter —F.P.Barnard⟩ **b :** of ill omen by reason of being on the left ⟨the victor eagle, whose ~ flight retards our host —Alexander Pope⟩ **6 :** presaging ill fortune or trouble **:** PORTENTOUS, OMINOUS ⟨everything in the room had a new significance, a ~ meaning —G.D. Brown⟩ ⟨something devilish and ~ about the whole business —Lewis Mumford⟩ ⟨or, more ~ still, the black fog full of birds —*Listener*⟩ ⟨a ~ brightness — a poisonous, threatening flash of pigment, set off by the blackness of the shadows —William Beebe⟩ ⟨with a somewhat ~ haircut, a unique black beard that would mark him as a dangerous man —Harrison Smith⟩ **7 :** accompanied by or leading to disaster or unfavorable developments ⟨expressed their alarm over the ~ results that had followed —W.H.Lawrence⟩ ⟨was a ~ idea from the beginning, a surefire recipe for civil war —Edmond Taylor⟩

²sinister \"\ *adv* **:** to or toward the left ⟨the flag was criticized because the eagle faced ~, that is, to its own left —Elizabeth W. King⟩

sinister base point *n* **:** the lower sinister part of the field of an escutcheon — see POINT illustration

sinister chief point *n* **:** the upper sinister part of the field of an escutcheon — see POINT illustration

sin·is·ter·i·ty \,sinə'sterəd·ē, -rətē, -i\ *n* -ES [L *sinisteritas*, fr. *sinister* left + *-itas* -ity] **:** SINISTERNESS

sin·is·ter·ly *adv* [ME *sinistrely*, fr. *sinistre* sinister + *-ly*] **:** in a sinister manner ⟨rolled his yellow eyes ~ —Earle Birney⟩ ⟨a ~ mature concealment of evil —R.B.Heilman⟩ ⟨its water . . . was ~ opaque —Anthony West⟩ ⟨vultures . . . coasted ~ away into the mist —Dan Wickenden⟩

sin·is·ter·ness *n* -ES **:** the quality or state of being sinister ⟨among the club names collected the predominant connotations are of power, speed, and aggressiveness, with ~ as a muted countermelody —Arthur Minton⟩

sinistr- *or* **sinistro-** *comb form* [ML, fr. L *sinistr-, sinister* left, on the left side] **1 a :** left ⟨*sinistr*ad⟩ **b :** better developed in or using preferentially the left ⟨*sinistro*cular⟩ **2 :** levorotatory ⟨*sinistr*in⟩

si·ni·stra \sə'nēstrə\ *n* -s [It, fr. L, fr. fem. of *sinister* left] **:** the left hand — used as a direction in music to play a note or passage with this hand

sinis·trad \'sinə,strad, sə'ni,s-\ *adv* [*sinistr-* + *-ad*] **:** toward the left side **:** SINISTRALLY

¹sinis·tral \'sinəstrəl, sə'nis-\ *adj* [ML *sinistralis*, fr. L *sinistr-, sinister* left + *-alis* -al] **:** of or relating to the left **:** inclined to the left: as **a :** LEFT-HANDED **b** *of a flatfish* **:** having the left side turned uppermost — opposed to *dextral* **c** *of a gastropod shell* **:** having the whorls turning from the right toward the left as viewed with the apex toward the observer or having the aperture open toward the observer to the left of the axis when held with the spire uppermost

²sinistral \"\ *n* -s **:** a person exhibiting dominance of the left hand and eye **:** a typical left-handed individual ⟨if you are left-handed and also definitely left-eyed . . . you are classified as a straight ~ and you, too, will be able to shoot with both eyes open with the greatest of ease —Bob Nichols⟩

sin·is·tral·i·ty \,sinə'stralǝd·ē, -lətē, -i\ *n* -ES **1 :** the quality or state of having the left side or one or more of its parts (as the hand or eye) different from and usu. less efficient than the right or its corresponding parts; *also* **:** LEFT-HANDEDNESS ⟨dental societies don't keep track of ~ among their members —*New Yorker*⟩ **2 :** the condition of being sinistral — used esp. of a mollusk shell

sinis·tral·ly \'sinəstrəlē, sə'nis-, -li\ *adv* **:** toward the left ⟨recross ~ his legs —V.V.Nabokov⟩

sin·is·tra·tion \,sinə'strāshən\ *n* -s [¹*sinistral* + *-ation*] **:** the quality or state of being sinistral

sinis·trin \'sinəstrən, sə'nis-\ *n* -s [ISV *sinistr-* + *-in*] **:** a levorotatory polysaccharide $(C_6H_{10}O_5)_x$ derived from squill and constituted of repeating fructose units

sin·is·troc·u·lar \,sinə'sträkyələ(r)\ *adj* [*sinistr-* + *ocular*] **:** using the left eye habitually or more effectively than the right — **sin·is·troc·u·lar·i·ty** \,==,==ˈlarəd·ē\ *n* -ES

sinis·trorse \'sinə,strō(ə)rs, sə'ni,s-\ *also* **sin·is·tror·sal** \,sinə'strȯrsəl\ *adj* [*sinistrorse* fr. NL *sinistrorsus*, fr. L *sinistrorsum, sinistrorsus* toward the left side, fr. *sinistr-, sinister* left, on the left side + *versus*, past part. of *vertere* to turn; *sinistrorsal* fr. NL *sinistrorsus* + E *-al* — more at WORTH] **1** *of a plant* **:** twining spirally upward around an axis from right to left: **a :** twining counterclockwise when the observer's point of view is within or above the spiral **b :** twining clockwise when the observer's point of view is outside the spiral — compare DEXTRORSE **2 :** SINISTRAL **c** — **sinis·trorse·ly** \-slē\ *also* **sinis·tror·sal·ly** \-səlē\ *adv*

sinis·trous \'sinəstrəs, sə'nis-\ *adj* [L *sinistr-, sinister* + E *-ous*] **:** SINISTER — **sin·is·trous·ly** *adv*

si·nit·ic \sə'nid·ik, (')sī¦n-\ *also* **si·net·ic** \-ned-\ *adj, usu cap* [LL *Sinae*, pl., Chinese + E *-itic* or *-etic* — more at SINOLOGUE] **:** of or relating to the Chinese or the Chinese language or culture

¹sink \'siŋk\ *vb* **sank** \-aŋk, -aiŋk\ *or* **sunk; sunk** \-əŋk\ *or* **sunk·en** \-kən\ **sinking; sinks** [ME *sinken*, fr. OE *sincan;* akin to OHG *sinkan* to sink, ON *sökkva*, Goth *sinqan* to sink, Gk *heaphthē* clung, sank, Arm *ankanim* I fall, yield] *vi* **1 a :** to become submerged **:** go to the bottom **:** SUBMERGE ⟨the Atago ~*s* in 19 minutes —H.W.Baldwin⟩ ⟨the overloaded raft *sank* below the surface⟩ **b :** to become partly buried or submerged (as in mud) ⟨~*ing* up to his hips in the snow⟩ ⟨must ~ deeper into the morass before we again emerge onto firm ground —Vannevar Bush⟩ **c :** to descend into or become engulfed by the earth ⟨whole towns ~*ing* as the earth opens great cracks⟩ **2 a** (1) **:** to fall or drop to a lower place or level ⟨letting his head ~ to his chest⟩ ⟨peeled off and *sank* into a cloud layer —W.F.Jenkins⟩ ⟨the hand opens out fully and . . . quietly ~*s* down below the waist —Warwick Braithwaite⟩ (2) **:** to flow at a lower depth or level ⟨water . . . ~*s* down in the sandstone and finds its way extremely slowly north —K.S.Sandford⟩ ⟨after the spring floods the brooks ~⟩ (3) **:** to burn with lower intensity **:** die down ⟨watching the flames ~ and the coals begin to glow⟩ (4) **:** to fall to a lower pitch or tone **:** become fainter ⟨in the general hush his voice *sank* to a whisper —Waldo Frank⟩ ⟨sounds of voices ~*ing* in the distance⟩ **b :** to subside gradually **:** SETTLE ⟨some parts of the mainland are slowly ~*ing* and some rising as time works its changes —*Amer. Guide Series: Texas*⟩ **c :** to move or go out of sight **:** disappear from view ⟨riding on, he looked back to see the workers ~ below the tops of the hedgerows⟩ **d :** to move down in the sky toward or at the horizon ⟨the sun *sank* below the western rim of the prairies —F.B.Gipson⟩ ⟨though sun is *sunk* and darkness near —R.P.Warren⟩ ⟨to follow knowledge like a ~*ing* star —Alfred Tennyson⟩ **e :** to decline or slope gradually **:** DIP ⟨a spur of hills ~*ing* into the opalescence of the far seas —Osbert Sitwell⟩ ⟨ahead of her the road *sank* between the autumn fields and the brilliant patches of woods —Ellen Glasgow⟩ **3 a :** to become lost or absorbed **:** PENETRATE ⟨the river seems literally to ~ into the earth before the hills on the horizon —Tom Marvel⟩ ⟨the ink quickly ~*s* in the blotting paper⟩ ⟨the kind of psychological poison which ~*s* so deeply into our system —H.A.Overstreet⟩ **b :** to become impressively known or felt or comprehended — usu. used with *in* or *into* ⟨the lesson of inflation had not *sunk* in —Roy Lewis & Angus Maude⟩ ⟨the gloomy truth has *sunk* in that the buffalo no longer fill the prairies —D.W.Brogan⟩ ⟨any abstract pattern . . . may in this way ~ into my mind —Herbert Read⟩ ⟨for any picture really to ~ into your imagination . . . it is necessary to carry the feeling of the picture away with you —J.C.Powys⟩ **4 :** to become deeply absorbed or immersed **:** FALL — usu. used with *in* or *into* ⟨drew thoughtfully at his pipe and *sank* into a reverie —Dorothy Sayers⟩ ⟨had *sunk* morosely into thought —Berton Roueché⟩ ⟨overcome by exhaustion she *sank* quietly into sleep —Louis Bromfield⟩ **5 a :** to go downward or deteriorate in quality, state, or condition **:** DEGENERATE, RETROGRESS — usu. used with *into* or *to* ⟨the old aristocracy *sank* in wealth and prestige —F.J.Mather⟩ ⟨architectural training and taste had *sunk* back into a period of chaos —J.E.Gloag⟩ ⟨should ~ back into another Dark Age —Lindsay Rogers⟩ ⟨~ into decay and eventual ruin —Ivor Bulmer-Thomas⟩ ⟨causes the world of custom to ~ into its deserved oblivion —C.S.Kilby⟩ ⟨if the writer of fiction turns from this task he will ~ deservedly to the level of formalistic entertainer —Elizabeth Janeway⟩ **b :** to grow less in amount **:** diminish in worth **:** DECLINE ⟨the population . . . *sank* from about 20 millions to about 9 —Herbert Agar⟩ ⟨support from public funds had *sunk* to the vanishing point —C.L.Jones⟩ ⟨real estate values *sank* to a new low —*Amer. Guide Series: N.Y.City*⟩ **c :** to fall in reputation or standing **:** lower oneself ⟨I had *sunk* considerably in her estimation —Norman Douglas⟩ ⟨no medieval artist ~*s* so low —G.G.Coulton⟩ ⟨she'd die rather than ~ to such a deed —Eden Phillpotts⟩ **6 a :** to fall or drop slowly for lack of strength **:** give way **:** COLLAPSE ⟨nearly *sank* to the ground through languor and extreme weakness —Mary W. Shelley⟩ ⟨rose and *sank* upon her seat . . . fainting, praying, raving, despairing —Thomas De Quincey⟩ ⟨his legs ~ beneath him⟩ **b :** to move oneself gradually to a lower position ⟨he *sank* down on the steps —Laura Krey⟩ ⟨his body crouched almost as if he were going to ~ upon all fours —Edith Sitwell⟩ ⟨widows, bachelors, and old folk would ~ back in their chairs with a nostalgic look —Charles Ruffing⟩ **7 a :** to become borne down by misfortune or the pressure of events or difficulties ⟨in imminent danger of ~*ing* under the tyranny of a succession of small men —T.B.Macaulay⟩ **b :** to become depressed, discouraged, or sorrowful ⟨studied this fresh proof of poverty with a ~*ing* heart —T.B.Costain⟩ ⟨sometimes his heart *sank* when he asked himself whether he and his family were withstanding it —Glenway Wescott⟩ ⟨his courage *sank*⟩ **c :** to fail in health or strength ⟨the frail system had been shattered, and all around saw that she was slowly ~*ing* —William Black⟩ ⟨his frame soon *sank* under the effects of study, toil, and persecution —T.B.Macaulay⟩ ⟨were chasing a ~*ing* fox and babbling for the kill —G.S.Patton⟩ ~ *vt* **1 a :** to cause or allow (something) to go or drop to a lower point or level ⟨could have *sunk* the gun down the after hatch —Nevil Shute⟩ ⟨*sank* his chin on his hands —Christine Weston⟩ **b :** to force or send down esp. below the earth's surface ⟨the iron clothes post Burton had *sunk* for her . . . near the fence —Minnie H. Moody⟩ ⟨framed their rude huts with pairs of light poles *sunk* in the ground —*Amer. Guide Series: N.Y.*⟩ ⟨he had been *sunken* into his grave —Marguerite Young⟩ **c :** to cause (something) to become embedded **:** DRIVE, THRUST ⟨saw the hideous creature . . . as it prepared to ~ its proboscis —William Beebe⟩ ⟨*sank* the dagger up to its hilt⟩ — often used with *into* ⟨*sank* her nails into the palms of her hands —John Dos Passos⟩ **2 a :** to cause (a ship or other object) to plunge or go under the water or to the bottom ⟨estuaries were cluttered with *sunken* shipping —*Current Biog.*⟩ ⟨*sank* his colors in the Rio Grande and led the remnant of his command into Mexico —B.I.Wiley⟩ **b :** to place or force beneath the water **:** SUBMERGE ⟨caissons had been *sunk* to keep out the water —*Amer. Guide Series: Vt.*⟩ ⟨men . . . *sunk* a grappling hook into position —Erle Stanley Gardner⟩ **c :** to engage deeply **:** engross the attention of **:** IMMERSE — usu. used with *in* or *into* ⟨a wish to ~ my mind into everything I saw and did and to absorb it all —Elyne Mitchell⟩ ⟨described the scientist aptly by saying . . . that he ~*s* himself in the object —H.A.Overstreet⟩ ⟨some producers can't bear the idea of ~*ing* their own individualities in that of a man perhaps long since dead —Warwick Braithwaite⟩ ⟨*sunk* in a sea of mystery —W.L.Sullivan⟩ **3 a :** to dig or bore (a well or shaft) in the earth **:** EXCAVATE ⟨this mine had been *sunk* to the tenth level —*Amer. Guide Series: Minn.*⟩ ⟨hopes . . . to ~ a shaft on the north side of the pyramid —Patrick Smith⟩ ⟨water wells are *sunk* in various ways —W.J.Miller⟩ ⟨*sank* a trial pit —O.M.Marashian⟩ **b** (1) **:** to form (a hole or depression) by cutting or excising ⟨~ words in stone⟩ (2) **:** to permit ingress or insertion of (something) by such sinking ⟨~ the screwhead level with the wood⟩ ⟨a new kind of pottery . . . with loop handles *sunk* in the body on either side —Jacquetta & Christopher Hawkes⟩ **4 :** to cast down or bring to a low condition or state **:** OVERWHELM, RUIN, DEFEAT ⟨fighting gallantly under odds which would ~ a less courageous . . . people —T.H.Fielding⟩ ⟨*sunk* to the hovels though he was, he had the rags of a finer past about him —Robert Lynd⟩ ⟨we've got to watch our step clear through . . . or we're *sunk* —Christopher Isherwood⟩ — sometimes used as an imprecation ⟨~ me, mister, but ye gave me a turn! I never heard ye open the door —Max Peacock⟩ **5 a :** to lower in standing or reputation **:** ABASE ⟨my motive . . . will not ~ me in your esteem —Jane Austen⟩ ⟨his prestige in society was *sunk* —Virginia Woolf⟩ **b** *archaic* **:** to set or consider as being at a low state or level **:** DEGRADE **6 a** *obs* **:** to cause (as water) to subside **:** LOWER **b :** to make (something) disappear by moving or sailing away ⟨the ship gradually *sank* the coast⟩ **7 a** *archaic* **:** to cause (a person) to become depressed or dejected **b** (1) **:** to weaken physically **:** DEBILITATE ⟨trouble enough to ~ a much younger man⟩ ⟨seemed too *sunken* under the heat to take any notice of who took their passports —Dan Jacobson⟩ (2) **:** to weaken or reduce the strength of (a bow) ⟨~ your bow with repeated flexings⟩ **8 a** *archaic* **:** to lessen in value or amount **:** cause (as prices) to decline **b :** to lower or soften (the voice) in speaking **:** MODULATE ⟨he went on, ~*ing* his voice —Hugh Walpole⟩ **9 a :** to stop using **:** ABANDON ⟨*sank* his old name when he got his title⟩ **b** (1) **:** to avoid mention of or reference to (a matter or fact) ⟨has a habit of ~*ing* unpleasant truths⟩ (2) **:** to conceal (a card or combination) by not melding (as in calling a trio when one holds quatorze at piquet) **c :** to subtract (the weight of the offal) when weighing meat **d** (1) **:** to set aside **:** RESTRAIN, SUPPRESS ⟨so to ~ our personality as to be ready to drift with every current of opinion —S.J.Brown⟩ ⟨men are able to ~ passions for the good of the race —Waldemar Kaempffert⟩ ⟨~*s* her pride and approaches the despised neighbor —Richard Harrison⟩ (2) **:** to exclude from consideration **:** SUBORDINATE ⟨induce rival groups to ~ their differences in the face of common danger —C.L.Jones⟩ ⟨was ready to ~ his republicanism so long as the nation was made —*Times Lit. Supp.*⟩ **10** *archaic* **:** to take or assume (as money) for personal use **:** APPROPRIATE **11 :** to pay off (as a debt) **:** LIQUIDATE **12 a :** to invest (capital or labor) in a holding or development with intent to gain income or other receipts ⟨no government could take land away from settlers who have *sunk* skill and capital in it for 50 years —Elspeth Huxley⟩ ⟨will ~ something over a million dollars into this plant just as a starter —Green Peyton⟩ **b :** to invest or spend (money) unprofitably or without hope of financial return ⟨were more inclined to hurry past a town where they had *sunk* money that would never come back —Willa Cather⟩ ⟨in undertaking to make this a sylvan retreat he *sunk* a large part of his patrimony —I.J.Cox⟩ **13 :** to place (as the heading of a section of a book) below the level of the top line of the full text page ⟨~ preface four picas⟩ **14 :** to cause (a ball or other object) to go in or through a receptacle or hole in a game ⟨~*s* foul shots consistently⟩ ⟨*sank* the eight ball in the corner pocket⟩ ⟨always ~*s* his putts⟩ **syn** see FALL — **sink one's teeth 1 :** BITE ⟨pleasure of *sinking one's teeth* into a succulent apple —W.F.Hambly⟩ **2 :** to deal directly with as a reality or a concrete matter explicitly set forth **:** to treat with as something substantial — usu. used with *into* ⟨stories such as a man can *sink his teeth* into —Richard Joseph⟩ ⟨approach that can change an ethereal abstraction into meat and potatoes that people can *sink their teeth* into —S.L.Payne⟩ — **sink or swim 1 :** to drown unless one swims ⟨if he fall in, good night, or *sink or swim* —Shak.⟩ **2 :** to fail or perish unless one exerts oneself ⟨sending him out on his own to *sink or swim*⟩

²sink \"\ *n* -s [ME *sinke*, fr. *sinken* to sink — more at ¹SINK] **1 a** (1) **:** a pool or sand-filled pit for the deposit of waste or sewage **:** CESSPOOL (2) **:** a container for foul matter or waste ⟨the sea is the ~ of the earth⟩ ⟨making ~s of our rivers⟩ **b :** a ditch, drainpipe, or vaulted tunnel for carrying off sewage **:** SEWER **c :** a stationary basin or a cabinet with a basin connected with a drain and usu. a water supply for washing and drainage **2 a :** a place where vice, corruption, or evil collects or gathers **:** DEN ⟨came to be a ~ of debauchery, vice, and crime —R.A.Hall b.1911⟩ ⟨will seem to him a ~ of mediocrity and human indecency —V.S. Pritchett⟩ ⟨known as a ~ of iniquity⟩ **b :** a place where such evil breeds and spreads ⟨from this ~ of sin and bawdy carousal issued murderers, theves, footpads, burglars, harlots, arsonites, and swindlers of every variety —Herbert Asbury⟩ **3** *obs* **:** the vicious, corrupt, or evil persons of a place **4 :** a preliminary excavation or pit to be enlarged until it is a full-sized shaft **:** SUMP **5 a :** a depression in the land surface; *esp* **:** one having a central playa or saline lake with no outlet **b :** a hollow in a limestone region communicating with a cavern or subterranean passage so that waters running into it disappear — called also *sinkhole, swallow* **6** *obs* **:** WELL 3a **7** *archaic* **:** a place where things disappear or are engulfed **8 :** a depression made in a flat surface (as in the face of a timepiece) **9 :** a part of the printing area of a plate (as an electrotype) that is too low to print properly **10 :** a body or substance used for the disposal of a fluid or heat in the course of a hydrodynamic or a thermodynamic process (as the condenser of a steam engine)

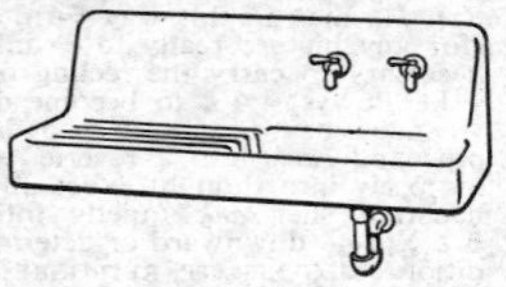

sink 1c

sink·able \ˈsiŋkəbəl\ *adj* **:** capable of being sunk

sink·age \-kij, -kēj\ *n* -s **1 :** the act, process, or degree of sinking ⟨important in view of ~, heel, and change of trim that might ensue after damage —E.L.Attwood⟩ ⟨the creek . . . disappeared through ~ and evaporation —Rex Ingamells⟩ **2 :** SINKING, DEPRESSION ⟨a square block on which was carved a rosette set in a small ~ —A.S.Whiton⟩ **3 :** the distance from the level of the top line of a full text page to the first line of sunk matter **4 :** SHRINKAGE

sinkapace *n* [by alter.] *obs* **:** CINQUEPACE

sinkbox \ˈ⸗,⸗\ *or* **sinkboat** \ˈ⸗,⸗\ *n* [²*sink* + *box* or *boat*] **:** a device used in hunting wild fowl consisting of a raft or broad low float having a rectangular depression in which a hunter may conceal himself — called also *battery*

sink·er \ˈsiŋkə(r)\ *n* -s [¹*sink* + *-er*] **1 :** one that sinks: as **a** (1) **:** one who sinks mine shafts and puts in supporting timber or concrete (2) **:** SINKER DRILL (3) **:** SINKING PUMP **b :** any of several devices in knitting machines for depressing the loops upon or between the needles **c** (1) **:** a weight (as a piece of lead or a stone) that is used to sink a fishline or sounding line below the surface or to the bottom (2) **:** a large weight of metal, concrete, or other material for sinking or holding in position the mooring line of a ship, mine, buoy, or other floating object **2** *slang* **a :** base coin **b :** a silver dollar **3 a :** doughy muffin; *also* **:** DOUGHNUT **4 a :** HAUSTORIUM **b :** DROPPER 3 **5 :** a slender wire nail **:** COOLER NAIL **6 a :** a ball pitched in baseball that sinks or drops when it reaches the batter **:** DROP 2a(3) **b :** a fly ball that sinks rapidly as it approaches a fielder **7 :** DEADHEAD 2 **8 :** a small square or rectangle in a woven design that usu. indicates where the warp passes under the filling — compare RISER 8

sinker bar *n* **:** a short bar or stem placed above the drill jars to give force to the upward jar in well drilling with cable tools

sinker drill *n* **:** a rock drill of the jackhammer type commonly used in shaft sinking — called also *sinker*

sink·er·less \ˈ⸗⸗ləs\ *adj* **:** having no sinker

sinker wood *n* **:** lumber sawed from deadheads or other heavy wet logs

sinkfield \ˈ⸗,⸗\ *n* [by folk etymology] **:** CINQUEFOIL 1

sinkhead \ˈ⸗,⸗\ *or* **sinking head** *n* **:** FEEDHEAD

sinkhole \ˈ⸗,⸗\ *n* [ME *sinke holl*, fr. *sinke* sink + *holl* hole] **1 a :** a hollow place or depression where drainage or waste collects or is deposited **:** CESSPOOL **b :** the outlet or drain of a sink **2 :** a place or center for the gathering, accumulation, or concentration of undesirable or evil things ⟨during the thirties it was a ~ of depression and unemployment —J.V.Kelleher⟩ ⟨surroundings he considered the ~ of culture —Harry Hansen⟩ ⟨a wild and pagan ~ —Harrison Smith⟩ ⟨that infamous ~ of fever and death —*Dial*⟩ **3 :** SINK 5 **4 :** an unprofitable enterprise in which money is repeatedly sunk

sinking *pres part of* SINK

sinking fund *n* **:** a fund set up and accumulated by usu. regular payments or interest-earning deposits for paying off the principal of a debt when it falls due — compare AMORTIZATION

sinking–fund bond *n* **:** a bond issued with a provision that a specified amount or percentage of the issuer's income will be paid annually into a sinking fund set up to retire the bond issue

sinking pump *n* **:** a pump esp. designed for use in shaft sinking — called also *sinker*

sinking speed *n* **:** the rate of vertical descent of an airplane in a steady glide

sinking spell *n* **:** a short-lived decline in prices ⟨stocks suffered a *sinking spell*⟩

sin·ki·use \siŋˈkī,(y)üs\ *n, pl* **sinkiuse** *or* **sinkiuses** *usu cap* **:** COLUMBIA

sinks *pres 3d sing of* SINK, *pl of* SINK

sin·ky·one \ˈsiŋkē,ōn\ *n, pl* **sinkyone** *or* **sinkyones** *usu cap* **1 :** an Athapaskan people of northwestern California **2 :** a member of the Sinkyone people

sin·less \ˈsinləs\ *adj* [ME *sinnelesse*, fr. OE *synlēas*, fr. *syn* sin + *-lēas* -less — more at SIN] **:** free from sin **:** IMPECCABLE, HOLY — **sin·less·ly** *adv* — **sin·less·ness** *n* -ES

sin money *n* [trans. of LL *pecunia pro peccatis*, trans. of Heb *keseph hakippūrim*] **:** money offered in expiation of sin

sinned *past of* SIN

sin·ner \ˈsinə(r)\ *n* -s [ME, fr. *sinne* sin + *-er* — more at SIN] **1 a :** one that sins; *esp* **:** one that sins without repenting **b :** a persistent and incorrigible transgressor **:** one condemned by the law of God **2 a :** OFFENDER, REPROBATE, SCAMP **b** *chiefly dial* **:** FELLOW, PERSON

sinnet *var of* SENNIT

sinn fein·ism \ˈshinˈfā,nizəm\ *n* -s *usu cap S&F* [*Sinn Fein*, national Irish society founded about 1905 (fr. Ir *sinn fēin* we ourselves) + E *-ism*] **1 :** the doctrines, policies, or practices of Sinn Fein **2 :** a movement based on the doctrines of Sinn Fein

sinning *pres part of* SIN

sin·nin·gia \səˈninjēə\ *n, cap* [NL, fr. Wilhelm *Sinning* †1874 Ger. horticulturist + NL *-ia*] **:** a genus of Brazilian tuberous herbs (family Gesneriaceae) having large petioled leaves and large flowers with a turbinate calyx and irregular bell-shaped 5-lobed corolla — see GLOXINIA 2

sin·ning·ly *adv* **:** in a sinning manner

sin·ning·ness *n* -ES **:** a tendency to sin

¹sino- *comb form, usu cap* [F, fr. LL *Sinae* — more at SINOLOGUE] **1 :** Chinese ⟨*Sino*gram⟩ **2 :** Chinese and ⟨*Sino*-American⟩ ⟨*Sino*-Japanese⟩ — compare ¹CHINO-

²sino- *or* **sinu-** *comb form* [NL *sinus*] **1 :** relating to the sinus and ⟨*sino*respiratory⟩ **2 :** relating to the sinus venosus and the ⟨*sinu*ventricular⟩

si·no·atrial \ˌsī(,)nō+\ *also* **si·nu·atrial** \ˌsī(,)n(y)ü+\ *adj* [²*sino-* + *atrial*] **1 :** of or relating to the sinus venosus and the right auricle of the heart **2 :** of, involving, or being the sinoatrial node

sinoatrial node *n* **:** a small mass of tissue made up of Purkinje fibers, ganglion cells, and nerve fibers, embedded in the musculature of the right auricle of higher vertebrates, representing the remains of the sinus venosus of lower forms, serving as a pacemaker to the heart, and transmitting the impulse to beat by way of the Purkinje's network to the auricles, the atrioventricular node and bundles, and the ventricles — called also *sinus node*

si·no·auricular \"+\ *or* **si·nu·auricular** \"+\ *adj* [²*sino-* + *auricular*] **:** SINOATRIAL

sin offering *n* [prob. trans. of G *sündopfer*, trans. of Heb *ḥaṭṭā'th*] **:** a sacrifice for sin **:** something offered as an expiation for sin; *specif* **:** an animal sacrifice in ancient Jewish religious ceremony in which the blood is smeared on the altar, the choice and fat parts are burned there, and the remainder is burned outside the sanctuary

sino·gram \ˈsīnō,gram *sometimes* ˈsinō *or* ˈsēnō-\ *n, usu cap* [¹*sino-* + *-gram*] **:** a Chinese phonogram or other written character

sino–japanese \ˌsī(,)nō *sometimes* ˌsi(,)nō *or* ˌsē(,)nō+\ *n, cap S&J* **:** the Japanese language as strongly affected by Chinese

sino·log·i·cal \ˌ⸗⸗ˈläjəkəl\ *also* **sino·log·ic** \-jik\ *adj, sometimes cap* [*sinological* fr. *sinologue* + *-ical; sinologic* prob. fr. F *sinologique*, fr. *sinologue* + *-ique* -ic] **:** of, relating to, or characteristic of the Chinese culture, language, or literature

si·nol·o·gist \sīˈnäləjəst, sə'-, sē'n-\ *n* -s *sometimes cap* [prob. fr. F *sinologie* sinology + E *-ist*] **:** SINOLOGUE

sino·logue *also* **sino·log** \ˈsīnə,lȯg, ˈsin-, ˈsēn- *also* -läg\ *n* -s [F *sinologue*, fr. *sino-* (fr. LL *Sinae*, pl., Chinese, fr. Gk *Sinai*, fr. Ar *Sīn* China, prob. fr. Chin *Ch'in²*, feudal state in China during 897–221 B.C. that established the Ch'in dynasty in the 3d century B.C.) + *-logue*] **:** a specialist in sinology

si·nol·o·gy \sīˈnäləjē, sə'n-, -ji\ *n* -ES *sometimes cap* [prob. fr. F *sinologie*, fr. *sino-* ¹sino- + *-logie* -logy] **:** the study of the Chinese esp. with reference to their language, literature, history, and culture

si·nom·e·nine \səˈnämə,nēn, -nən\ *n* -s [*sinomen-* (fr. NL *Sinomenium*, genus name of the woody vine *Sinomenium acutum*) + *-ine*] **:** a crystalline alkaloid $C_{19}H_{23}NO_4$ structurally related to thebaine but obtained from various eastern Asiatic plants (as *Sinomenium acutum*) of the family Menispermaceae

si·non \ˈsī,nän\ *n* -s *usu cap* [fr. *Sinon*, a relative of Odysseus described in the *Aeneid* (epic poem by Vergil †19 B.C. Roman poet) as the Greek who by a false tale induced the Trojans to drag the wooden horse into Troy, fr. L, fr. Gk *Sinōn*] **:** one who deceives and betrays by false tales **:** one guilty of perfidy

sin·o·per \ˈsinəpə(r)\ *n* -s [MF *sinopre, sinople* sinople] *archaic* **:** SINOPLE

¹sino·phile \ˈsīnə,fīl, ˈsin-, ˈsēn-\ *also* **sino·phil** \-,fil\ *adj, often cap* [¹*sino-* + *-phile, -phil*] **:** approving or favoring the Chinese or their policy or characteristics

²sinophile \"\ *also* **sinophil** \"\ *n* -s *sometimes cap* **:** one partial to or esp. fond of Chinese culture or characteristics

si·no·pia \səˈnōpēə\ *or* **si·no·pis** \-pəs\ *n, pl* **sinopias** *or* **sinopises** [*sinopia* fr. NL, fr. L *sinopis* sinopite + *-ia; sinopis* fr. NL, fr. L *sinopis*] **:** a red pigment made from sinopite

si·nop·ic \(ˈ)sīˈnōpik, səˈn-, -näp-\ *adj, usu cap* [L *sinopicus*, fr. Gk *sinōpikos*, fr. *Sinōpē* Sinope + Gk *-ikos* -ic] **1 :** of, relating to, or characteristic of the ancient city of Sinope in Asia Minor **2 :** of, relating to, or characteristic of the natives or inhabitants of Sinope

sin·o·pite \ˈsinə,pīt\ *n* -s [G *sinopit*, fr. L *sinopis* + G *-it* -ite] **:** a brick-red ferruginous clay used by the ancients as a paint

sin·o·ple \ˈsinəpəl\ *n* -s [MF *sinople, sinopre*, fr. L *sinopis* sinopite, fr. Gk *sinōpis*, fr. *Sinōpē*, ancient seaport on the Black sea in Asia Minor] **:** ferruginous quartz that is blood-red or brownish red sometimes with a tinge of yellow

si·no·respiratory \ˌsī(,)nō+\ *adj* [²*sino-* + *respiratory*] **:** of, relating to, or affecting both the sinuses and the respiratory tract ⟨~ symptoms⟩

sino–tibetan \ˌsī(,)nō *sometimes* ˌsi(,)nō *or* ˌsē(,)nō+\ *n, cap S&T* **:** a language group comprising Tibeto-Burman and Chinese and sometimes considered to include Thai

si·no·ventricular \ˌsī(,)nō+\ *also* **si·nu·ventricular** \ˌsī(,)n(y)ü+\ *adj* [²*sino-* + *ventricular*] **1 :** of or relating to the sinus venosus and the ventricles of the heart **2 :** of, involving, or being the sinoventricular system

sinoventricular system *n* **:** the system of modified muscle fibers that regulates the beat of the heart — compare PURKINJE'S NETWORK, SINOATRIAL NODE

sins *pl of* SIN, *pres 3d sing of* SIN

sins·ring \ˈsins,riŋ\ *n* -s [Jav] **:** TREE SHREW

sin·syne \ˈsin,sīn\ *adv* [ME (Sc) *sensyne*, fr. (Sc) *sen*, prep., from, since (contr. of *sethen, sithen*, adv. & prep., since) + (Sc) *syne*, adv., since — more at SINCE, SYNE] *chiefly Scot* **:** since that time **:** AGO

¹sin·ter \ˈsintə(r)\ *n* -s [G, fr. OHG *sintar* dross, slag — more at CINDER] **1 :** a deposit formed by the evaporation of spring or lake water — see SILICEOUS SINTER; compare GEYSERITE, TRAVERTINE **2 :** the product of sintering

²sinter \"\ *vb* **sintered; sintered; sintering** \-ntəriŋ, -n·triŋ\ **sinters** *vt* **:** to cause to become a coherent mass by heating without melting — used of powdered or earthy substances ~ *vi* **:** to become a coherent mass from heating without melting — **sin·ter·er** \-ntərə(r)\ *n* -s

sinu- — see SINO-

¹sin·u·ate \ˈsinyəwət, -,wāt, *usu* -d.+V\ *adj* [L *sinuatus*, past part. of *sinuare* to curve, bend, fr. *sinus* curve, fold — more at SINUS] **1 :** SINUOUS, WAVY, TORTUOUS **2 :** having the margin wavy with strong indentations ⟨~ leaves⟩ — compare UNDULATE — **sin·u·ate·ly** *adv*

²sinuate \-,wāt, *usu* -ād.+V\ *vi* -ED/-ING/-S [L *sinuatus*, past part. of *sinuare* to curve, bend] **:** to bend or curve in and out **:** be sinuous **:** WIND ⟨saw the river *sinuating* toward the sea —Anaïs Nin⟩

sin·u·at·ed \ˈsinyəˌwād.əd, -ātəd\ *adj* [L *sinuatus* (past part.) + E *-ed*] **:** SINUATE

sinuate–dentate \ˌ⸗⸗(,)⸗ˈ⸗,⸗\ *adj* **:** varying between sinuate and dentate

sin·u·a·tion \ˌsinyəˈwāshən\ *n* -s [LL *sinuation-, sinuatio*, fr. L *sinuatus* (past part. of *sinuare* to curve, bend) + *-ion-, -io* -ion] **:** a winding or bending in and out

sinuatrial *var of* SINOATRIAL

sinuauricular *var of* SINOAURICULAR

sin·u·ose \ˈsinyə,wōs\ *adj* [L *sinuosus*] **:** SINUOUS — **sin·u·ose·ly** *adv*

sin·u·os·i·ty \ˌ⸗⸗ˈwäsəd.ē, -sətē, -i\ *n* -ES [ML *sinuositas*, fr. L *sinuosus* sinuous + *-itas* -ity] **1 :** the quality or state of being sinuous ⟨the flexible ~ of a serpent —J.C.Powys⟩ **2 :** that which is sinuous: as **a :** BEND, WINDING, CURVE ⟨the *sinuosities* of the canyon —E.L.Ullman⟩ **b :** INTRICACY ⟨the *sinuosities* of a murder-mystery plot⟩ **c :** sinuous movement ⟨the dancer's *sinuosities*⟩

sin·u·ous \ˈsinyəwəs\ *adj* [L *sinuosus*, fr. *sinus* curve, fold + *-osus* -ose] **1 a :** bending in and out **:** of a serpentine or wavy form **:** WINDING ⟨the lava cascade glows as a ~ ribbon —*Endeavour*⟩ ⟨great ~ vines —Bill Beatty⟩ **b :** marked by strong lithe movements ⟨a ~ grace of movement —Francis King⟩ **2 a :** INTRICATE, COMPLEX ⟨a ~ system of canals —W.E. Rudolph⟩ **b :** deviating esp. morally ⟨~ arguments⟩ **3 :** SINUATE — **sin·u·ous·ly** *adv* — **sin·u·ous·ness** *n* -ES

si·nus \ˈsīnəs\ *n* -ES [NL, fr. L, curve, fold, hollow, bay; prob. akin to Alb *gíri* bosom, lap, Serb *zaošijati* to bend] **:** CAVITY, HOLLOW, RECESS: as **a :** a narrow elongated cavity or tract which extends from a focus of suppuration or other inflammatory softening to a free surface and through which pus discharges ⟨a tuberculous ~ leading to the skin surface from a tuberculous bone or abscess⟩ — compare FISTULA 2 **b :** a cavity, recess, or depression that forms part of an animal body: (1) **:** a cavity in the substance of a bone of the skull that usu. communicates with the nostrils and contains air ⟨the frontal ~⟩ (2) **:** one of the broad channels the outer coats of which are formed by the dura mater and which conduct blood from the brain (3) **:** one of the spaces among the muscles and viscera of various invertebrates through which blood returns to the heart (4) **:** a dilatation in a canal or vessel (as at the commencement of the internal jugular vein) (5) **:** PALLIAL SINUS (6) **:** a moderately deep indentation in the outer lip of the aperture of a univalve shell (as of a member of the genus *Scissurella*) that is progressively filled in as the shell grows and forms a distinct band **c** (1) *archaic* **:** a hole in the earth (2) **:** a bay of the sea ⟨the deep ~ of the Norwegian trench —A.H.W. Robinson⟩ **d :** a cleft or indentation between adjoining lobes (as of a leaf or corolla) **e :** the folds of the drapery of a toga covering the left arm and serving as a pocket

sinus gland *n* **:** a small glandular mass in the eyestalk of a crustacean having an endocrine function and being in some respects analogous to the neurohypophysis of the vertebrates

si·nus·i·tis \ˌsīnəˈsīd.əs, -ītəs\ *n* -ES [NL, fr. *sinus* + *-itis*] **:** inflammation of a sinus

sinus node *n* **:** SINOATRIAL NODE

sinus of mor·ga·gni \-mȯrˈgänyē\ *usu cap M* [after Giovanni B. *Morgagni* †1771 Ital. anatomist] **:** a space at the upper back part of each side of the pharynx where the walls are deficient in muscular fibers and closed by the aponeurosis only

sinus of val·sal·va \-välˈsälvə\ *usu cap V* [after Antonio M. *Valsalva* †1723 Ital. anatomist] **:** any one of the pouches of the aorta and pulmonary artery which are located behind the flaps of the semilunar valves and into which the blood in its regurgitation toward the heart enters and thereby closes the valves

si·nus·oid \ˈsīnə,sȯid\ *n* -s [ISV *sinus* + *-oid*] **1 :** the curve whose ordinates are proportional to the sines of the abscissas with the equation $y = a \sin x$ **2 :** a minute endothelium-lined space or passage for blood in the tissues of an organ (as the liver)

si·nus·oi·dal \ˌ⸗⸗ˈsȯidᵊl\ *adj* [ISV *sinusoid* + *-al;* orig. formed in F] **:** of or relating to a sinusoid — **si·nus·oi·dal·ly** \-dᵊlē, -dᵊli\ *adv*

sinusoidal projection *n* **:** an equal-area map projection capable of showing the entire surface of the earth with all parallels as straight lines evenly spaced, the central meridian as one half the length of the equator, and all other meridians as curved lines

sinus rhom·boi·da·lis \-,räm,bȯiˈdāləs\ *n* [NL, rhomboidal sinus] **:** the posterior expanded and for a long time incompletely closed part of the medullary canal of vertebrate embryos; *also* **:** an expansion of the central canal in the sacral region derived from it

sinus ve·no·sus \-vəˈnōsəs\ *n* [NL, venous sinus] **1 :** a distinct chamber of the heart formed by the union of the large systemic veins and opening into the auricle in lower vertebrates and the embryos of higher forms **2 :** the main cavity of either auricle esp. of the human heart **3 :** the part of the right auricle between the openings of the venae cavae

sinuventricular *var of* SINOVENTRICULAR

sin·ward \ˈsinwə(r)d\ *adv* **:** toward sin

sion *usu cap, var of* ZION

siou·an \ˈsüən\ *n, pl* **siouan** *or* **siouans** *usu cap* [*Sioux* + *-an*] **1 :** a language stock of central and eastern No. America including Crow, Hidatsa, Dakota, Chiwere, Winnebago, Dhegiha, Ofo, Biloxi, Tutelo, Catawba **2 a :** a group of peoples speaking Siouan languages — called also *Sioux* **b :** a member of such peoples — called also *Sioux*

sioux \ˈsü\ *n, pl* **sioux** *usu cap* [F, Dakota, short for *Nadowessioux*, fr. Chippewa *Nadoweisiw*, lit., little snake, enemy] **1 :** DAKOTA **2 :** SIOUAN

¹sip \ˈsip\ *vb* **sipped; sipped; sipping; sips** [ME *sippen*; akin to LG *sippen* to sip] *vi* **:** to drink a small quantity esp. repeatedly with the lips **:** take a sip of something ⟨*sipped* delicately at the bottle like effete bees —John Steinbeck⟩ ⟨*sipped* at the fragrant steaming liquid —*Chatelaine*⟩ ⟨listeners understood, after one fleeting hearing, what the composer intended for slow *sipping* —P.H.Lang⟩ ~ *vt* **1 :** to take into the mouth in small drafts ⟨~ tea⟩ **:** drink in small quantities ⟨she has *sipped* excitement experimentally, the way people ~ a drink —Sally Benson⟩ **2 :** to take sips from ⟨~ a flower⟩ **:** TASTE **3 :** to bring to a specified condition by sipping ⟨*sipped* the glass dry⟩

²sip \"\ *n* -s **1 :** the act of sipping **2 :** a small draft taken with the lips **:** a slight taste ⟨a ~ . . . from reservoirs of abstract philosophy —Thomas De Quincey⟩

SIP *abbr* **1** standard inspection procedure **2** step in place

si·pa·pu \ˈsē,pä(,)pü\ *n* -s [Hopi *sïpaapu*] **:** a hole in the floor of a Pueblo Indian kiva symbolizing the place where the mythical tribal ancestors first emerged from the primordial underworld regions into the earthly realm

¹sipe \ˈsēp, *Brit usu* ˈsīp\ *vi* [ME *sipen*, fr. OE *sipian* — more at SEEP] *chiefly dial* **:** SEEP, PERCOLATE

²sipe \"\ *n* -s [¹*sipe*; fr. its wiping the road surface dry] **:** any of the small often hook-shaped or bracket-shaped grooves in the tread of an automobile tire for providing extra traction and preventing skids

¹si·phon *also* **sy·phon** \ˈsīfən *sometimes* -,fän\ *n* -s [F *siphon*, fr. L *sipho, siphon* tube, pipe, siphon, fr. Gk *siphōn*; prob. akin to L *tibia* shinbone] **1 a :** a tube bent to form two branches of unequal effective length by which a liquid can be transferred to a lower level over an intermediate elevation by the pressure of the atmosphere in forcing the liquid up the shorter branch of the tube immersed in it while the excess of weight of the liquid in the longer branch when once filled causes a continuous flow that takes place only when the discharging extremity is lower than the liquid surface and when no part of the tube is higher above that surface than the same liquid will rise by atmospheric pressure **b :** a channel through which water passes as if in a siphon **c :** INVERTED SIPHON **d** *usu syphon* **:** a bottle for holding aerated water that is driven out through a bent tube in its neck by the pressure of the gas when a valve in the tube is opened ⟨a soda water *syphon*⟩ **e :** any of several small reservoirs placed at certain points in a gas main to drain off condensed water **2 a :** either of a pair of posteriorly extending tubes in many bivalve mollusks formed by the coalescence and extension of the edges of the mantle lobes of each side of the body and commonly more or less united externally though their passages are separate: (1) **:** a ventral tube that conducts water to the mouth and gills (2) **:** a dorsal tube that carries away waste water — see CLAM illustration **b :** an anterior channel-shaped prolongation of the mantle in many gastropods serving to conduct water to the gills and often being protected by a grooved extension of the margin of the shell — see SNAIL illustration **c :** the swimming funnel of a cephalopod **d :** the membranous siphuncle of a shelled cephalopod **e :** the sucking proboscis of various arthropods **f :** the cornicle of an aphid **g :** a tubular anal respiratory organ in a bug of the family Nepidae consisting of two grooved filaments **h :** the branchial or atrial orifice in an ascidian esp. when borne on a more or less produced tube

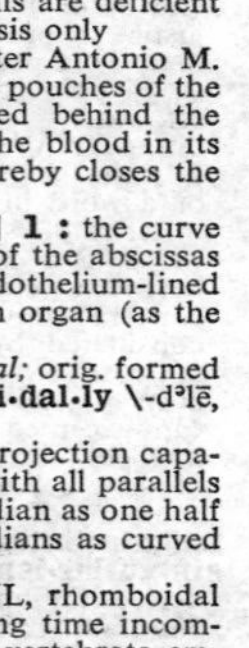

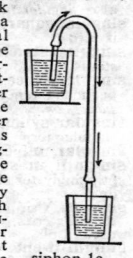

siphon 1a

²siphon *also* **syphon** \"\ *vb* **siphoned; siphoned; siphoning** \-f(ə)niŋ, -,fän-\ **siphons** *vt* **1 :** to convey, draw off, or empty by or as if by a siphon ⟨~ gasoline from a tank⟩ ⟨a dredge ~*ing* up bay bottom —George Bourke⟩ **2 :** to divert for a special purpose **:** WITHDRAW ⟨an expressway to ~ motor traffic from the crowded downtown area —J.H.Fenton⟩ ⟨irresponsible ~*ing* of skilled farm labor by the Selective Service —Louis Bromfield⟩ — often used with *off* ⟨the federal government is ~*ing* off their wealth to support itself —D.L.Hamilton⟩ ⟨heavy taxes ~ off the huge profits —*N.Y. Times*⟩ ~ *vi* **:** to pass or become conveyed by or as if by a siphon ⟨a fine spray of gasoline was still ~*ing* from three of the holes —E.K.Gann⟩

siphon- *or* **siphono-** *also* **siphoni-** *comb form* [NL, fr. Gk *siphōn-, siphōno-*, fr. *siphōn*] **1 :** siphon **:** tube **:** pipe ⟨*Siphon*aptera⟩ ⟨*Siphono*phora⟩ ⟨*Siphoni*ata⟩ ⟨*siphoni*ate⟩ **2 :** Siphonophora ⟨*siphono*some⟩ ⟨*siphono*zooid⟩

si·phon·aceous \ˌsīfəˈnāshəs\ *adj* [*siphon-* + *-aceous*] **1 :** resembling a siphon esp. in forming a continuous protoplasmic column or tube ⟨lower fungi with ~ mycelia⟩ **2 :** having a siphon or group of siphons ⟨~ mollusks⟩

si·phon·age \ˈsīf(ə)nij\ *n* -s [*siphon-* + *-age*] **:** the action or use of a siphon

si·phon·al \-fənᵊl\ *adj* [*siphon-* + *-al*] **:** of, relating to, or resembling a siphon

si·phon·ales \ˌsīfəˈnā(,)lēz\ *n pl, cap* [NL, fr. *siphon-* + *-ales*] **:** an order of marine and freshwater green algae (class Chlorophyceae) whose filaments consist essentially of a large multinucleate cell with cross walls rare and usu. only adjacent to reproductive organs — compare CODIUM, SIPHONOCLADALES

si·phon·anth \ˈsīfə,nan(t)th\ *n* -s [back-formation fr. obs. E *siphonanthous* of or belonging to the siphonophoran suborder Siphonanthae, fr. NL *Siphonanthae* (fr. *siphon-* + *-anthae* — fem. pl. of *-anthus*) + E *-ous*] **:** a feeding zooid of a compound siphonophore

si·phon·aptera \ˌsīfən+\ *n pl, cap* [NL, fr. *siphon-* + *Aptera;* fr. the piercing and sucking mouthparts] **:** an order of insects consisting of the fleas — **si·phon·apterous** \"+\ *adj*

si·phon·ap·ter·ol·o·gy \ˌsīfəˌnaptəˈräləjē\ *n* -ES [NL *Siphonaptera* + E *-logy*] : a branch of entomology concerned with the fleas

si·pho·nar·ia \ˌsīfəˈna(a)rēə\ *n, cap* [NL, fr. *siphon-* + *-aria*] : the type genus of Siphonariidae

si·pho·na·ri·idae \ˌsīfənəˈrīəˌdē\ *n pl, cap* [NL, fr. *Siphonaria*, type genus + *-idae*] : a family of littoral gastropod mollusks (order Opisthobranchia) that cling to rocks along seacoasts, resemble limpets, and have both gills and a pulmonary sac

si·pho·na·ta \ˌsīfəˈnād·ə, -nād·ə\ *n pl, cap* [NL, fr. *siphon-* + *-ata*] *in some classifications* : a division formerly ranked as a suborder of bivalve mollusks including all having siphons

si·phon·ate \ˈsīfənət, -ˌnāt\ *adj* [*siphon-* + *-ate*] : having a siphon ⟨the aperture of the shell is said to be entire or ~ —Nellie Eales⟩

siphon barometer *n* : a J-shaped mercury barometer having the longer leg closed at the top and the other exposed to the air

si·pho·ne·ae \sīˈfōnēˌē\ *n pl, cap* [NL, fr. fem. pl. of *siphoneus* siphoneous] *in some classifications* : a class of algae approximately equivalent to the Siphonales

siphoned *past of* SIPHON

si·pho·ne·ous \(ˈ)sīˈfōnēəs\ *adj* [NL *siphoneus*, fr. *siphon-* + L *-eus* -eous] : SIPHONACEOUS

si·phon·et \ˌsīfəˈnet\ *n* -S [*siphon-* + *-et*] : a honey tube of an aphid

siphoni- — see SIPHON-

si·pho·ni·a·ta \ˌ(ˌ)sīˌfōnēˈād·ə, -ˈäd·ə\ [NL, fr. *siphon-* + *-ata*] *syn of* SIPHONATA

si·phon·ic \(ˈ)sīˈfänik\ *adj* [*siphon-* + *-ic*] **1** : of or relating to a siphon **2** : characterized by siphonage

si·pho·nif·era \ˌsīfəˈnif(ə)rə\ [NL, fr. neut. pl. of *siphonifer* one of the Siphonifera, fr. *siphon-* + *-fer*] *syn of* TETRABRANCHIA

siphoning *pres part of* SIPHON

si·pho·ni·um \sīˈfōnēəm\ *n, pl* **si·pho·nia** \-ēə\ [NL, fr. Gk *siphōnion*, dim. of *siphōn* tube, siphon — more at SIPHON] : a bony tube in some birds connecting the tympanum with the air chambers of the articular piece of the mandible

si·phon·less \ˈsīfənləs\ *adj* [*siphon-* + *-less*] : having no siphon

siphono- — see SIPHON-

si·pho·no·branchiata \ˈsīfə(ˌ)nō+\ *n pl, cap* [NL, fr. *siphon-* + *branchiata*] *in former classifications* : a group of gastropods having the margin of the mantle produced into a siphon — **si·pho·no·branchiate** \"+\ *adj or n*

si·pho·noc·la·da·les \ˌsīfəˌnäkləˈdā(ˌ)lēz\ *n pl, cap* [NL, fr. *Siphonocladus*, type genus (fr. *siphon-* + Gk *klados* branch, sprout) + *-ales* — more at GLADIATOR] : an order of green algae (class Chlorophyceae) originally including all multinucleate members of the class capable of vegetative division but now usu. restricted to those that are apparently derived from the Siphonales and are nonseptate when young (as in the families Valoniaceae and Dasycladaceae)

si·pho·no·cla·di·a·les \ˌsīfəˌnō(ˌ)nōˌklādēˈā(ˌ)lēz\ [NL] *syn of* SIPHONOCLADALES

si·pho·nog·a·ma \ˌsīfəˈnägəmə\ [NL, fr. *siphon-* + Gk *gamos* marriage — more at BIGAMY] *syn of* SPERMATOPHYTA

si·pho·nog·a·mous \ˌsīfəˈnägəməs\ *adj* [*siphon-* + *-gamous*] : accomplishing fertilization by means of a pollen tube ⟨most seed plants are ~⟩ — **si·pho·nog·a·my** \ˌ=ˈ=ˌ=mē\ *n* -ES

si·phono·glyph \sīˈfänəˌglif, ˈsīfənōˌg-\ *also* **si·pho·nog·ly·phe** \ˌsīfəˈnägləˌ(ˌ)fē\ *n* -S [*siphon-* + Gk *glyphē* carved work — more at GLYPH] : a special groove leading down into the gullet from a corner of the mouth in many anthozoans

si·pho·noph·o·ra \ˌsīfəˈnäf(ə)rə\ *n pl, cap* [NL, fr. *siphon-* + *-phora*; prob. fr. the hollow float] : an order of Hydrozoa consisting of various free-swimming or floating pelagic mostly delicate transparent and often showily colored forms that are usu. regarded as compound animals composed of zooids modified to perform various functions for the colony (as feeding, defense, locomotion), that sometimes have two or more zooids in the form of a bell which by their contractions cause the colony to swim, and that often have a hollow float which keeps the colony afloat — compare DIPHYES, PORPITA, PORTUGUESE MAN-OF-WAR, VELELLA — **si·pho·noph·o·ran** \ˌ=ˈ=ˈ==rən\ *adj or n* — **si·phono·phore** \sīˈfänəˌfō(ə)r, ˈsīfənəˌf-\ *n* -S — **si·pho·noph·o·rous** \ˌsīfəˈnäfərəs\ *adj*

si·phono·plax \sīˈfänəˌplaks, ˈsīfənōˌp-\ *n* -ES [NL, fr. *siphon-* + Gk *plax* flat surface, tablet — more at PLEASE] : one of the calcareous plates that protect the siphon of various boring mollusks

si·pho·no·rhi·nal \ˌsīfənōˈrīnᵊl\ *or* **si·phono·rhine** \sīˈfänəˌrīn, ˈsīfənōˌr-\ *adj* [*siphon-* + *rhinal* or *-rhine*] : SIPHORHINAL

si·phono·some \sīˈfänəˌsōm, ˈsīfənəˌs-\ *n* -S [*siphon-* + *-some*] : the part of the stock of a siphonophore bearing the nutritive and reproductive zooids

si·phono·stele \sīˈfänəˌstēl, ˈsīfənōˌs- *also* ˌsīfənōˈstēlē\ *n* [*siphon-* + *stele*] : a stele consisting of vascular tissue surrounding a central core of pith parenchyma — compare PROTOSTELE — **si·phono·ste·lic** \ˌsīfənōˈstēlik, sīˌfänəˈs-\ *adj* — **si·phono·ste·ly** \ˈsīfənōˌstēlē, sīˈfänəˌs-\ *n* -ES

si·pho·no·sto·ma·ta \ˌsīfənōˈstōməd·ə\ *n pl, cap* [NL, fr. *siphon-* + *stomata*] **1** *in some classifications* : a tribe of parasitic copepod crustaceans including many parasites of fishes (as the lernaeans) that have a mouth adapted to suck blood **2** *in former classifications* : an artificial group of marine snails possessing a canal for the passage of the siphon at the base of the aperture — **si·phono·stome** \sīˈfänəˌstōm, ˈsīfən-\ *n* -S

si·pho·no·stoma·tous \ˌsīfənōˈstōməd·əs, -täm-\ *adj* [*siphon-* + *-stomatous*] **1** : having the front edge of the aperture of the shell prolonged in the shape of a channel for the protection of the siphon — used of various marine snails **2** : having a tubular mouth **3** [NL *Siphonostomata* + E *-ous*] : of or relating to the Siphonostomata

si·pho·no·zooid \ˈsīfənə+\ *n* [*siphon-* + *zooid*] : one of various degenerate zooids of some alcyonarians supposed to serve to regulate the water supply of the colony

siphon recorder *n* : a sensitive recorder which is used in submarine telegraphy and the record of which is an irregular line made by ink discharged from a small siphon

siphons *pl of* SIPHON, *pres 3d sing of* SIPHON

siphon spillway *n* : a spillway that siphons water from a reservoir when a predetermined head is reached

si·phon·u·la \sīˈfänyələ\ *n, pl* **siphonu·lae** \-ˌlē, -ˌlī\ [NL, fr. *siphon-* + *-ula*] : a bilaterally symmetrical larva of various siphonophores

si·pho·rhi·nal \ˌsīfəˈrīnᵊl\ *also* **si·pho·rhin·i·an** \-rinēən\ *adj* [L *sipho* siphon + E *rhinal* or *-rhinian* (fr. *-rhine* + *-ian*)] : having tubular nostrils ⟨petrels are ~⟩

si·pho·some \ˈsīfəˌsōm\ *n* -S [L *sipho* siphon + E *-some*] : SIPHONOSOME

siphrei torah *pl of* SEPHER TORAH

si·phun·cle \ˈsīˌfəŋkəl\ *n* -S [NL *siphunculus*, fr. L, little pipe, dim. of *sipho*, *siphon* siphon — more at SIPHON] **1 a** : a membranous tubular extension of the mantle which runs through the partitions of the chambers to the apex of a shelled cephalopod : SIPHON **b** : the shelly structures that are usu. funnel-shaped or tubular processes of the septa and that ensheathe and support the cephalopod siphuncle **2** : a cornicle of an aphid

si·phun·cled \-ld\ *adj* [*siphuncle* + *-ed*] : SIPHUNCULATE

si·phun·cu·lar \(ˈ)sīˈfəŋkyələ(r)\ *adj* [NL *siphunculus* + E *-ar*] : of, relating to, or of the nature of a siphuncle

si·phun·cu·la·ta \(ˌ)sīˌfəŋkyəˈlād·ə, -lād·ə\ [NL, fr. *siphunculus* siphuncle + *-ata*] *syn of* ANOPLURA

si·phun·cu·late \(ˈ)sīˈfəŋkyələt\ *or* **si·phun·cu·lat·ed** \-ˌlād·əd\ *adj* [NL *siphunculus* + E *-ate* or *-ated* (fr. *-ate* + *-ed*)] : having a siphuncle

sip·id \ˈsipəd\ *adj* [back-formation fr. ¹*insipid*] : SAPID — **si·pid·i·ty** \səˈpidəd·ē\ *n* -ES

si·po \ˈsē(ˌ)pō\ *also* **sipo mahogany** *n* -S [*sipo* native name in the Cameroons] : a very large African mahogany (*Entandrophragma utile*) that occurs chiefly in the Cameroons and Ivory Coast and that yields an attractively banded moderately hard and heavy light to dark red or reddish brown scented wood which is sometimes exported in quantity

sipped *past of* SIP

sip·per \ˈsipə(r)\ *n* -S [¹*sip* + *-er*] **1** : one that sips **2** : BIBBER, TOPER **3** [fr. *Sipper*, a trademark] : a device (as a straw or a paper or plastic cylinder) adapted for sipping liquid

sip·pet \ˈsipət\ *n* -S [*sip* (alter. — influenced by ¹*sip* — of ¹*sop*) + *-et*] **1** : a small bit or piece of toast soaked in milk or broth : a small piece of toasted or fried bread for garnishing **2** : a small piece : tiny bit : FRAGMENT

sipping *pres part of* SIP

sip·pio \ˈsipēˌō\ *n* -S [origin unknown] : a game of the bagatelle kind played with eight object balls and a cue ball on a table having fifteen numbered holes into which the balls are driven

sip·ple \ˈsipəl\ *vb* [¹*sip* + *-le*] *Scot* : TIPPLE

sip·py diet \ˈsipē-\ *or* **sippy regimen** *n, usu cap S* [after Bertram W. *Sippy* †1924 Am. physician] : a bland diet for the treatment of peptic ulcer consisting mainly of measured amounts of milk and cream, farina, and egg taken at regular hourly intervals for a specified period of time

sips *pres 3d sing of* SIP, *pl of* SIP

si·pun·cu·la·cea \(ˌ)sīˌpəŋkyəˈlāshēə\ [NL, fr. *Sipunculus*, genus of marine worms + *-acea*] *syn of* SIPUNCULOIDEA

¹si·pun·cu·lid \(ˈ)sīˈpəŋkyələd\ *or* **si·pun·cu·loid** \-ˌlȯid\ *adj* [*sipunculid* fr. NL *Sipunculida*; *sipunculoid* fr. NL *Sipunculoidea*] : of or relating to the Sipunculoidea

²sipunculid \"\ *or* **sipunculoid** \"\ *n* -S : a sipunculid worm

si·pun·cu·li·da \ˌsīˌpəŋˈkyüləd·ə\ [NL, fr. *Sipunculus*, genus of marine worms + *-ida*] *syn of* SIPUNCULOIDEA

si·pun·cu·loi·dea \(ˌ)sīˌpəŋkyəˈlȯidēə\ *n pl, cap* [NL, fr. *Sipunculus*, genus of marine worms (fr. L *sipunculus*, *siphunculus* little pipe) + *-oidea* — more at SIPHUNCLE] **1** : a group of marine worms of obscure systematic position that are commonly classed as a division of Gephyrea and that lack setae and have the mouth at the end of a retractile introvert similar to a proboscis and usu. provided with tentacles and the anus anterior and dorsal **2** *in some classifications* **a** : a group coextensive with Gephyrea **b** : a class or other group comprising Sipunculoidea (sense 1) and Priapuloidea

¹sir *R* ˌsər, ˈsər, + *vowel* ˈsər·; –*R* sə, (ˌ)sə, *South often* ˈsə + *suffixal vowel* ˈsər· *also* ˈsər, + *vowel in a following word* ˌsə(r) *or* ˈsər· *or* (ˌ)sə *or* sə *also* (ˌ)sər\ *n* -S *often cap* [ME, fr. *sire* — more at SIRE] **1 a** : a man of rank or position : GENTLEMAN, LORD ⟨some ~ of note —*Shak.*⟩ ⟨a very . . . petulant hot little ~ —*Saturday Rev.*⟩ **b** : a man entitled to be addressed as *sir* : KNIGHT ⟨the proprietor was now a ~ —Max Beerbohm⟩ — used as a title of honor before the given name of a knight or baronet ⟨*Sir* Charles⟩ ⟨*Sir* William Smith, Bart.⟩; formerly sometimes used as a title of honor before the names of historical or legendary figures ⟨*Sir* Pandarus of Troy⟩ and as a title of respect before the given name of a priest ⟨*Sir* Robert, the parish priest⟩ ⟨the medieval custom of calling any priest *Sir* John⟩ **2** *obs* — used often disparagingly as a form of address before a common noun (as of rank or occupation) ⟨I am *Sir* Oracle —*Shak.*⟩ **3** *obs* — used in a British university before the surname of a bachelor of arts **4** — used as a usu. respectful form of address (as to an older person, a superior, or the presiding officer of a legislative assembly) ⟨your car is ready, ~⟩ ⟨I'd be very grateful, ~, for your advice⟩ ⟨I rise, ~, to a point of personal privilege⟩ **5** — used as a conventional form of address in the salutation of a letter ⟨Dear *Sir*⟩

²sir *stressed forms at* ¹SIR\ *vt* **sirred**; **sirred**; **sirring**; **sirs** : to address as *sir* ⟨thinks good discipline means *sirring* officers —A.C.Fields⟩

³sir *var of* SEER

si·rat \sēˈrät\ *n* -S *usu cap* [Ar *sirāṭ* road] : a bridge in Muslim eschatology which spans the chasm of hell and connects this world with paradise and over which according to tradition only the righteous can cross while the unrighteous fall to a flaming punishment — called also *al sirat*

sir·car *or* **sir·kar** *also* **cir·car** \ˈsərˌkär, (ˌ)sərˈk-\ *n* -S *often cap* [Hindi *sarkār*, fr. Per] **1** : a district or province in India under the Mogul empire **2** *India* **a** : the supreme authority : GOVERNMENT **b** : MASTER — used also as a title of respect **3** *Bengal* **a** : a domestic servant having the functions of a steward **b** : PURCHASING AGENT, ACCOUNTANT

sir·dar \ˈsərˌdär, (ˌ)sərˈd-\ *or* **sar·dar** *or* **ser·dar** *n* -S [Hindi *sardār*, fr. Per] **1 a** : a person of high rank (as an hereditary noble, a chieftain, or a high military officer) in India, Pakistan, or Afghanistan **b** : a commander in chief esp. in Turkey or Egypt **2** : one holding a position of some responsibility in India: as **a** *or* **sirdar bearer** : a head palanquin bearer **b** : VALET **c** : FOREMAN, STEWARD **d** : TENANT FARMER

¹sire \ˈsī(ə)r, -īə\ *n* -S [ME, fr. OF, fr. L *senior* older, elder — more at SENIOR] **1 a** : a male parent : FATHER ⟨carried almost as many business burdens as his ~ —R.J.Purcell⟩ **b** *archaic* : male ancestor : FOREFATHER ⟨we are wiser than our ~*s* —Alfred Tennyson⟩ **c** : one that produces or originates something; *specif* : AUTHOR ⟨the ~ of an immortal strain —P.B.Shelley⟩ **2 a** *archaic* : a man of rank, station, or authority; *esp* : one who holds the lordship of a domain or realm : LORD, MASTER — used formerly as a form of address and as a title (as of the king of France) **b** *obs* : an elderly man : SENIOR ⟨an aged ~, all hoary gray —Edmund Spenser⟩ **3 a** : the male parent of an animal and esp. of a domesticated mammal or bird — compare DAM **b** : a stallion having at least one colt who has won a race

²sire \"\ *vt* -ED/-ING/-S **1** : to make oneself the father of : FATHER, BEGET, PROCREATE ⟨*sired* seven children —Green Peyton⟩ — used esp. of domestic animals ⟨was mated with 25 ewes and *sired* 18 lambs —*Fla. Agric. Experimental Station Bull.*⟩ **2 a** : to bring into being : GENERATE, ORIGINATE ⟨motion picture industry, *sired* and nourished by private enterprise —W.H.Hays⟩ **b** : to be the author of (a literary work) ⟨*sired* another play —E.L.Wallant⟩

si·re·don \sīˈrēˌdän, -ēdᵊn\ *n, cap* [NL, fr. Gk *seirēdōn* siren] *in some classifications* : a genus of salamanders comprising members of the genus *Ambystoma* that normally continue as axolotls throughout life

siree *var of* SIRREE

sire index *n* : a measure of the prepotency and quality of a sire in terms of the production of his offspring and esp. in respect to characteristics (as egg or milk production) that he cannot himself exhibit — compare PROGENY TEST

sire·less \ˈsī(ə)rləs, -īəl-\ *adj* [¹*sire* + *-less*] : FATHERLESS

¹si·ren \ˈsīrən *sometimes* ˈsī(ə)rn, *in sense 3* " *or* +(ˈ)sīˈrēn\ *n* [ME *serein, siren*, fr. MF *sereine* & L *siren*; MF *sereine*, fr. LL *sirena*, fr. L *siren*, fr. Gk *seirēn*, *seirēdōn*] **1** -S *often cap* **a** : one of a group of creatures in Greek mythology having the heads and sometimes the breasts and arms of women but otherwise the forms of birds that were believed to lure mariners to destruction by their singing **b** *obs* : MERMAID **2** -S **a** : a woman who sings with bewitching sweetness : SONGBIRD **b** : an alluringly beautiful woman ⟨so young and delicious a ~ —Ben Hecht⟩; *esp* : one who is usu. insidiously or deceptively enticing or seductive to men : TEMPTRESS, FEMME FATALE ⟨the slinky ~ of the silent screen⟩ ⟨while constantly emanating sex, she lacked the graceful presence, the subtlety of manner, the mysterious reticence of a real ~ —Carey McWilliams⟩ **3** -S [F *sirène*, lit., siren (sense 1), fr. MF *sereine*; fr. its property of producing sounds in water] **a** : an apparatus producing musical tones esp. in acoustical studies by the rapid interruption of a current of air, steam, or fluid by a perforated rotating disk **b** : a similar device often electrically operated for producing a penetrating warning sound ⟨fire ~⟩ ⟨ambulance ~⟩ ⟨the three-minute warbling sound of the air-raid ~*s* —*N.Y. Times*⟩ **4 a** *cap* [NL, fr. L] : a genus of elongated amphibians (family Sirenidae) having small forelimbs but lacking hind legs and pelvis and having permanent external gills as well as lungs **b** -S : any amphibian of the genus *Siren* or of the family Sirenidae **5** -S : SIRENOMELUS **6** -S : SEA COW 1

²si·ren \ˈsīrən *sometimes* ˈsī(ə)rn\ *adj* : of or relating to a siren : ENTICING, BEWITCHING, BEGUILING ⟨a ~ song⟩ ⟨listening intently to the ~ voice⟩ ⟨the ~ call of modern materialism —George Thomas⟩

³siren *like* ¹SIREN\ *vi* -ED/-ING/-S : to proceed with siren sounding to clear the way ⟨fire trucks ~*ed* to the scene from two miles away —*Time*⟩

si·re·nia \sīˈrēnēə\ *n pl, cap* [NL, fr. L *siren* + NL *-ia*] : an order of large aquatic herbivorous mammals including the manatee, dugong, Steller's sea cow, and several fossil forms that have the tail horizontally flattened and expanded into a broad rounded or bilobed fin, the hind limbs rudimentary or wanting and the front ones paddle-shaped, and jaws with horny plates on the front part and usu. numerous flat-crowned molar teeth

¹si·re·ni·an \(ˈ)sīˈrēnēən\ *adj* [NL *Sirenia* + E *-an* (adj. suffix)] : of or relating to the Sirenia

²sirenian \"\ *n* -S [NL *Sirenia* + E *-an* (n. suffix)] : a mammal of the order Sirenia

si·ren·ic \(ˈ)sīˈrenik\ *or* **si·ren·i·cal** \-nəkəl\ *adj* [¹*siren* + *-ic* or *-ical*] : of, resembling, or suited to a siren : MELODIOUS, ALLURING, DECEPTIVE ⟨~ song⟩ ⟨~ enchantments⟩ — **si·ren·i·cal·ly** \-nək(ə)lē\ *adv*

si·ren·i·dae \sīˈrenəˌdē\ *n pl, cap* [NL, fr. *Siren*, type genus + *-idae*] : a family of eel-shaped amphibians comprising the sirens (genera *Siren* and *Pseudobranchus*) of the southern U. S.

¹si·ren·oid \ˈsīrəˌnȯid\ *adj* [NL *Sirenoidei*] **1** : resembling or related to the Sirenoidei **2** [¹*siren* + *-oid*] : of, relating to, or resembling a siren or sirenomelus

²sirenoid \"\ *n* -S **1** : a lungfish of the group Sirenoidei **2** : SIRENOMELUS

si·ren·oi·dei \ˌsīrəˈnȯidēˌī\ *also* **si·ren·oi·dea** \-ēə\ *n pl, cap* [NL, fr. L *siren* + NL *-oidei*, *-oidea*] *in some classifications* : a group of lungfishes containing the genera *Neoceratodus* and *Lepidosiren* and some extinct forms from the Mesozoic

si·re·nom·e·lus \ˌsīrəˈnämələs\ *n, pl* **sirenome·li** \-ˌlī\ [NL, fr. *siren* mermaid (fr. L *siren*) + *-o-* + *-melus*] : a congenital malformation in which the lower limbs are fused

siren song *n* : an alluring utterance or appeal; *esp* : one that is seductive or deceptive ⟨the *siren song* of the metropolis⟩ ⟨the *siren song* of the advertising man —H.H.Martin⟩ ⟨follow the *siren song* of printing more money —W.M.Martin b.1906⟩

sires *pl of* SIRE, *pres 3d sing of* SIRE

si·rex \ˈsīˌreks\ *n* [NL, irreg. fr. L *siren* — more at SIREN] **1** *cap* : the type genus of the family Siricidae including various horntails that are destructive pests of unseasoned lumber from coniferous trees **2** -ES : any horntail of the genus *Sirex*

sir galahad *n, usu cap S&G* : GALAHAD

sir·gang \ˈsərˌgaŋ\ *n* -S [prob. fr. native name in Ceylon and Sumatra] : a predominantly pale green crested cissa (*Kitta chinensis*) that has largely maroon-red wings and black markings from bill to nape, on the wings, and across the tail and that occurs from the Himalayas through southeastern Asia and into the Pacific islands

siri *or* **sir·ih** \ˈsirē\ *n* -S [Malay *sireh*] : BETEL

sir·i·an \ˈsirēən\ *adj, usu cap* [*Sirius*, star of the constellation Canis Major that is the brightest in the sky (fr. ME, fr. L, fr. Gk *Seirios*, fr. *seirios* glowing, burning) + E *-an*] : of, relating to, or resembling (as in spectrum) the star Sirius

si·ri·a·sis \səˈrīəsəs\ *n, pl* **siria·ses** \-əˌsēz\ [L, fr. Gk *seiriasis*, fr. *seirian* to be hot, be scorching (fr. *seirios* glowing, burning) + *-sis*; akin to Gk *seiein* to shake, quake — more at SEISMIC] : SUNSTROKE

¹si·ric·id \səˈrisəd, ˈsīrəsəd\ *adj* [NL *Siricidae*] : of or relating to the Siricidae

²siricid \"\ *n* -S : a wasp of the family Siricidae

si·ric·i·dae \səˈrisəˌdē\ *n pl, cap* [NL, fr. *Siric-*, *Sirex*, type genus + *-idae*] : a family of hymenopterous insects comprising the horntails and having larvae that are wood borers and female adults with a stout hornlike ovipositor for inserting the eggs in wood

siring *pres part of* SIRE

sir·i·o·no \ˌsirēəˈnō\ *or* **sir·i·o·ne** \-ˈnā\ *n, pl* **siriono** *or* **sirionos** *or* **sirione** *or* **siriones** *usu cap* **1 a** : a Guaranian people of eastern Bolivia **b** : a member of such people **2** : the language of the Siriono people

si·ris \səˈrēs\ *n* -ES [Hindi *siris*, fr. Skt *śirīṣa*, prob. of Dravidian origin; akin to Tamil *uṛiñcil*, Kanarese *sirsala*] : any of several trees of the genus *Albizzia*: as **a** : LEBBEK **b** : SILK TREE

sirkar *var of* SIRCAR

sir·keer \ˈsərˌki(ə)r, sərˈk-\ *n* -S [perh. fr. Hindi *sarkīr*, fr. *sar* head + *kīr* parrot] : a large Indian cuckoo (*Taccocua leschenaultii*)

sir·ki \ˈsirkē, sirˈkē\ *also* **sir·ky** \ˈsirkē\ *n, pl* **sirkis** *or* **sirkies** [Hindi *sirkī*] **1** : the culms of munj **2** : a matting or thatch made of the upper part of the flower stalks of munj

sir knight \ˈ=ˌ=\ *n* : a member of a fraternal society styling itself an order of knighthood (as the Knights Templar)

sir·loin \ˈsərˌlȯin, ˈsəˌl-, ˈsəiˌl-\ *n* [alter. (influenced by ¹*sir*) of earlier *surloin*, modif. (influenced by *loin*) of MF *surlonge*, fr. *sur* over, above (fr. L *super*) + *longe*, alter. of *loigne* loin — more at OVER, LOIN] : a cut of meat and esp. of beef taken from the hindquarter usu. from between the porterhouse and the round — see BEEF illustration, LAMB illustration

sirmark *var of* SURMARK

sir·mi·an \ˈsərmēən\ *adj, usu cap* [*Sirmium* + E *-an*] : of or relating to the city of Sirmium in the eastern and now Yugoslav part of the Roman province of Pannonia; *esp* : of or relating to any of four councils held there in the fourth century or to the Arian creeds issued by them

sir·muel·lera \(ˌ)sərˈmyülərə, -mil-\ [NL, after Sir Ferdinand von *Müller* †1896 Australian naturalist born in Germany] *syn of* BANKSIA

siro·ba·sid·i·a·ce·ae \ˌsī(ˌ)rōbəˌsidēˈāsēˌē, ˌsī(-\ *n pl, cap* [NL, fr. *Sirobasidium*, type genus (fr. Gk *seira* cord, rope + NL *basidium*) + *-aceae* — more at QUARTZ] : a family of jelly fungi (order Tremellales) with the basidia borne in chains

si·roc \ˈsīˌräk, səˈr-\ *n* -S [obs. F *siroch* (now *siroc*, *sirocco*), fr. It *sirocco*, *scirocco*] : SIROCCO

si·roc·co \səˈrä(ˌ)kō\ *also* **sci·roc·co** \shə-\ *n* -S [It *sirocco*, *scirocco*, fr. Ar *sharq* east] **1 a** : a hot oppressive dust-laden wind from the Libyan deserts that blows on the northern Mediterranean coast chiefly in Italy, Malta, and Sicily **b** : a warm moist oppressive southeast wind in the same regions **2** : a hot or warm wind of cyclonic origin (as the harmattan of the west coast of Africa, the hot winds of Kansas and Texas, the khamsin of Egypt) blowing from an arid or heated region

s–iron \ˈ=ˌ=(=)\ *n, cap S* : an S-shaped iron driven into and across the end of a railroad tie to prevent splitting

si·rop \sēˈrō\ *n* -S [F, syrup, fr. MF — more at SYRUP] : a syrup of concentrated fruit juice, sugar, and water ⟨a kiosk that sold ices and ~*s* —Rumer Godden⟩

sir·rah *also* **sir·ra** \ˈsirə\ *n* -S [alter. of ¹*sir*] *obs* — used as a form of address implying inferiority and often used in anger, contempt, or disrespectful familiarity ⟨go to, ~! leave your jesting and tell us where he is —Christopher Marlowe⟩

sirred *past of* SIR

sir·ree *also* **sir·ee** \səˈrē, ˌsərˈē *also* sōˈrē\ *n* -S [by alter.] : SIR 4 — used as an emphatic form usu. after *yes* or *no* ⟨no, ~, you'll never see me there⟩

sir–reverence \ˈ=ˈ=(=)=\ *n* [prob. alter. (influenced by ¹*sir*) of *sa-reverence*, contr. of *save-reverence*, trans. of L *salva reverentia* saving (your) reverence] **1** *obs* — used as an expression of apology before a statement that might be taken as presumptuous or offensive ⟨such a one as a man may not speak of without he say *sir-reverence* —*Shak.*⟩ — compare ²SAVING 2 **2** *archaic* **a** : human excrement : FECES 2 ⟨a pan of *sir-reverence* —Tobias Smollett⟩ **b** : a lump of human excrement ⟨a ponderous *sir-reverence* —J.H.Frere⟩

sirring *pres part of* SIR

sir rog·er de cov·er·ley \-ˌräjə(r)dəˈkəvə(r)lē\ *or* **sir roger** *n, usu cap S&R&C* [*sir roger de coverley* alter. (influenced by *Sir Roger de Coverley*, fictitious country gentleman appearing in many of the *Spectator* papers by Joseph Addison †1719 and Sir Richard Steele †1729 Eng. essayists, fr. *roger of coverley*) of *roger of coverley*, prob. fr. *Roger* (the name) + *of* + *Coverley* (a fictitious place name); *sir roger* short for *sir roger de coverley*] : an English country-dance in compound triple measure performed longways by an indefinite number — compare VIRGINIA REEL

sirs *pl of* SIR, *pres 3d sing of* SIR

sir·ua·bal·li \ˌs(h)irəwəˈbalē\ *n* -S [Arawak, fr. *sirua*, a tree of the genus *Nectandra* + *balli* similar] : SILVER BALLI

sirup *var of* SYRUP

sir·vente \(ˌ)sərˈvent, sirˈvänt\ *or* **sir·ven·tes** \sərˈventəs\ *also* **sir·vent** \(ˌ)sərˈvent, sirˈvänt\ *n, pl* **sir·ventes** \-t(ə)s\ *also* **sir·vents** \-ts\ [F *sirvente*, fr. Prov *sirventes*, lit., servant's song, fr. *sirvent*, *servent* servant (fr. L *servient-*,

serviens, pres. part. of *servire* to serve) + *-es* -ese (prob. fr. L *-ensis*) — more at SERVE] **:** a usu. moral or religious song of the Provençal troubadours satirizing social vices

[1]**sis** *pl of* SI

[2]**sis** \ˈsis\ *n* -ES [by shortening] **:** SISTER

-sis \səs\ *n suffix, pl* **-ses** [L, fr. Gk, fem. suffix of action] **1 :** process **:** action **:** -ING ⟨analy*sis*⟩ ⟨peristal*sis*⟩ ⟨ar*sis*⟩ **2 :** diseased state **:** disease produced by ⟨stephanofilaria*sis*⟩

si·sal \ˈsīsəl, ˈsīzəl *also* səˈsäl *or* ˈsēsəl *or* ˈsēzəl *or* ˈsisəl\ *n* -s [MexSp, fr. *Sisal*, Yucatán, Mexico] **1 a** *also* **sisal hemp :** a strong durable white fiber that is three to five feet long and is used for hard fiber cordage and for binder twine **b :** a West Indian agave (*Agave sisalana*) whose leaves yield sisal for which it is widely cultivated (as in Java, East Africa, the Bahama islands, and Mexico) **2 :** a fiber derived from any of various plants (as henequen, false sisal) related to sisal

si·sa·la·na \ˌsīsəˈlänə, ˌsīzə-, ˌsēs-, ˌsēz-, -lanə, -lānə\ *n* -s [NL (specific epithet of *Agave sisalana*), fr. MexSp *sisal* + NL *-ana* (fr. L, neut. pl. of *-anus* -an)] **:** SISAL 1a

sisal rug *n* **:** a summer rug of sisal yarn

sis·co·wet \ˈsiskəˌwet\ *n* -s [CanF *ciscoette*, fr. Ojibway *pemitewiskawet* fish with oily flesh] **:** a large lake trout (*Cristivomer namaycush siscowet*) found in the deeper parts of Lake Superior and some of the other Great Lakes

sisel \ˈsisəl, ˈsēs-\ *n* -s [G *ziesel*, fr. MHG *zisel*, of Slav origin; akin to Czech *sysel* suslik, Pol *susel*, Russ *suslik*] **:** SUSLIK

sis·er·ara \ˌsisəˈra(a)rə\ *or* **sis·er·ary** \-rē\ *n, pl* **siseraras** *or* **siseraries** [obs. E *siserari, sasarara* certiorari, fr. ME *sesserary*, modif. of L *certiorari* — more at CERTIORARI] **1** *chiefly dial* **:** a severe blow or attack **2** *chiefly dial* **:** a violent scolding — **with a siserary** *adv, chiefly dial* **:** with a vengeance

siser·skite \ˈsisərˌskīt, səˈsər-\ *n* -s [G *sisserskit*, fr. *Syssertsk*, Sverdlovsk region, U.S.S.R. + G *-it* -ite] **:** a mineral consisting of a natural alloy of osmium and iridium with the latter ranging from 20 to 50 percent — compare IRIDOSMINE

sish \ˈsish\ *n* -ES [prob. alter. of *slush*] **:** fine slushy ice **:** new and thin ice

si·si \səˈsē\ *n* -s [AmerSp *sesí*] **:** PORKFISH

sisith *var of* ZIZITH

sis·kin \ˈsiskən\ *n* -s [G dial. *sisschen*, dim. of MHG *zīse, zīsic* siskin, of Slav origin; akin to Czech *čiž, čížek* siskin, Pol *czyż*, Russ *chizh*; all of imit. origin] **1 :** a small sharp-billed chiefly greenish and yellowish finch (*Spinus spinus*) of temperate Europe and Asia related to the goldfinch **2 :** any of various small birds resembling the siskin — usu. used in combination; see RED SISKIN

siss \ˈsis\ *vi* -ED/-ING/-ES [ME *sissen, cissen*, of imit. origin] **:** HISS

sis·se·ton \ˈsisətᵊn\ *n, pl* **sisseton** *or* **sissetons** *usu cap* [Dakota *sisitoṅwaṅ*, fr. *sisiṅ, siṅsiṅ* besmeared, slimy + *toṅwaṅyaṅ* to make a village, dwell at a place] **:** a member of a Dakota people of the northern Mississippi valley

sis·si·fied \ˈsisəˌfīd\ *adj* [ˡ*sissy* + *-fy* + *-ed*] **:** SISSY

sis·si·ness \ˈsisēnəs, -isin-\ *n* -ES **:** the quality or state of being sissy

sis·sle \ˈsisəl\ *dial Eng var of* SIZZLE

sis·sonne *or* **sis·sone** \səˈsän, -ˈsȯn, -ˈsōn\ *n* -s [after François César de Roussy, count of *Sissonne*, 17th cent. Fr. nobleman credited with the invention of the step] **:** a ballet step in which the legs are spread in the air and closed on the descent

sis·soo *also* **sis·su** \ˈsi(ˌ)sü\ *n* -s [Hindi *sīso*, fr. Skt *śiṁśapā*] **1 :** any of several trees of the genus *Dalbergia*; *esp* **:** an East Indian tree (*D. sissoo*) whose leaves are used as fodder **2 :** the dark brown compact and durable timber of the sissoo tree used esp. in shipbuilding and for making railroad ties

[1]**sis·sy** \ˈsisē, -isi\ *n* -ES [*sis* + *-y*] **1 :** SISTER **2 a :** an effeminate man or boy **b :** a timid or cowardly person ⟨one old lady . . . didn't want to be a ~ —Robert Rice⟩

[2]**sissy** \"\ *adj* -ER/-EST **:** of, relating to, or having the characteristics of a sissy ⟨no longer think it ~ to give or carry flowers —*Amer. Quarterly*⟩ ⟨a ~ boy with nastily damp hands and white eyelashes —Jean Stafford⟩

sissy-pants \ˈ==,=\ *or* **sissy-britches** \ˈ==,==\ *n pl but sing or pl in constr* **:** SISSY 2

[1]**sist** \ˈsist\ *vt* [L *sistere* to cause to stand, stop; akin to L *stare* to stand — more at STAND] **1** *chiefly Scot* **:** to bring into court **:** SUMMON **2** *chiefly Scot* **:** to stay by judicial decree

[2]**sist** \"\ *n* -s *chiefly Scot* **:** a stay or suspension of legal proceedings; *also* **:** an order for a stay of proceedings

sist *abbr* sister

sis·ta·ni \səˈstänē\ *n, pl* **sistani** *or* **sistanis** *usu cap* **1 :** a people of southwestern Afghanistan **2 :** a member of the Sistani people

sis·ten \ˈsiˌsten\ *or* **sistens** \-nz\ *n, pl* **sistens** \-nz\ *or* **sisten·tes** \səˈstentˌ(ˌ)ēz\ [NL *sistent-, sistens*, fr. L, pres. part. of *sistere* to stand still, cause to stand] **:** a wingless parthenogenetic form of a plant louse

[1]**sis·ter** \ˈsistə(r)\ *n* -s *often attrib* [ME *sister, suster, soster*, partly fr. OE *sweostor* and partly of Scand origin; akin to ON *systir* sister; akin to OHG *swester* sister, Goth *swistar*, L *soror*, OSlav *sestra*, Skt *svasṛ*] **1 a** (1) **:** a female human being related to another person having the same parents (2) **:** HALF SISTER (3) **:** SISTER-IN-LAW **b** (1) **:** a kinswoman by blood (2) **:** a female member of the same family, clan, or line **c :** a girl or woman felt to be a sister ⟨she was a ~ to the homeless child⟩ **d :** a female of a lower animal in relation to another having a common parent **2** *often cap* **a :** a member of a religious sisterhood **b :** a female member of a Christian church — often used with a surname or given name **3 a :** a woman related or linked to another by a common tie or interest ⟨she has ~s in graciousness over all the world —William Beebe⟩; *esp* **:** a female human being sharing a common national or racial origin with another ⟨the brightness . . . of their Irish, Danish, and French ~s —T.H.Fielding⟩ **b :** one having similar characteristics to another ⟨the sonata is a thing . . . without ~s in more familiar musical literature —David Hebb⟩ **4** *chiefly Brit* **:** a head nurse in a hospital ward or clinic; *broadly* **:** NURSE **5** *slang* **a :** GIRL, WOMAN — often used in direct address ⟨get going, ~, while you're able —Erskine Caldwell⟩ **b :** PERSON — usu. used in the phrase *weak sister* ⟨a subject introduced into the curriculum for the benefit of the weaker ~s —Kemp Malone⟩

[2]**sister** \"\ *vt* **sistered; sistered; sistering** \-t(ə)riŋ\ **sisters 1 :** to stand in the relationship of a sister to **:** treat in the manner of a sister ⟨her art ~s the natural roses —Shak.⟩ **2 :** to address by the name of sister

sister block *n* **:** a tackle block having two sheaves of the same size one above the other

sister-german \ˈ==ˈ==\ *n, pl* **sisters-german** [ME *sister germain*, part. trans. of MF *sœur germaine*, fr. *sœur* sister + *germaine*, fem. of *germain* having the same parents — more at GERMAN] **:** a sister through both father and mother **:** a full sister — compare HALF SISTER

sis·ter·hood \ˈsistə(r)ˌhu̇d\ *n* [ME *sosterhode*, fr. *soster* sister + *-hode* -hood] **1 a :** the state of being a sister **b :** sisterly relationship ⟨the dark shades of her ~ —Virginia Woolf⟩ **2 :** a community or society of sisters; *specif* **:** a community or society of women religious **3 :** a group associated by common characteristics ⟨joined the ~ of nations⟩ ⟨resists the Hollywood ~'s best efforts —*Time*⟩

sister hook *n* **:** either of a pair of hooks fitted together so that the shank of each forms a mousing for the other; *also* **:** a pair of such hooks — called also *clip hook, clove hook*

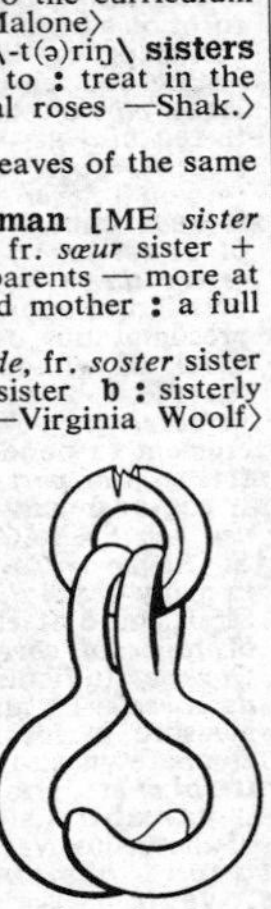
sister hooks

sistering *adj* [fr. pres. part. of [2]*sister*] **:** close by **:** CONTIGUOUS

sister-in-law \ˈsistə(r)ənˌlȯ, -trən-, -tə(r)n-\ *n, pl* **sisters-in-law** \-tə(r)z-ən-\ [ME *suster-in-lawe*; prob. fr. the fact that the canon law forbids marriage with one's spouse's sister or brother] **1 :** the sister of one's spouse **2 a :** the wife of one's brother **b :** the wife of one's spouse's brother

sister keelson *n* **:** SIDE KEELSON

sis·ter·less \ˈsistə(r)ləs\ *adj* **:** having no sister

[1]**sisterlike** \ˈ==,=\ *adv* [ˡ*sister* + *like*] **:** in the manner of sisters

[2]**sisterlike** \"\ *adj* **:** SISTERLY

sister line *n* **:** a line on the palm running parallel to another and more important line and usu. held by palmists to add strength to it

sis·ter·li·ness \ˈsistə(r)lēnəs, -lin-\ *n* -ES **:** the quality or state of being sisterly

[1]**sis·ter·ly** \-lē,-li\ *adj* [ˡ*sister* + *-ly* (adj. suffix)] **:** of, relating to, or having the characteristics of a sister; *specif* **:** AFFECTIONATE ⟨~ kindness⟩

[2]**sisterly** \"\ *adv* [ˡ*sister* + *-ly* (adv. suffix)] **:** in a sisterly manner ⟨a kiss sagely and ~ administered —Robert Browning⟩

sis·tern \-tə(r)n\ *chiefly dial pl of* SISTER

sister of charity *usu cap S&C* [trans. of F *sœur de charité*] **:** a member of a Roman Catholic sisterhood founded in France by St. Vincent de Paul in 1634 for nursing the sick

sister of charity of montreal *usu cap S&C&M* **:** a nun of a Roman Catholic community established in Montreal in 1745 and devoted esp. to the service of the suffering

sister of lo·ret·to \-ləˈred·(ˌ)ō\ *usu cap S&L* **:** a member of a Roman Catholic community of nuns founded in 1812 at Loretto, Kentucky, and devoted to educational work and the care of orphans

sister of mercy *usu cap S&M* **:** a member of a Roman Catholic congregation founded in 1827 by Catherine McAuley in Dublin and devoted to works of charity and education

sister of no·tre dame de na·mur \-ˌnōd·ərˈdämdənäˈmu̇(ə)r, -ō·trəˈd-, -dənəˈm- *also* -däm- *or* -dȧm- *sometimes* -dam- *or* -daam-\ *usu cap S & both Ns & 1st D* [part. trans. of F *sœur de Notre Dame de Namur*, after *Notre Dame de Namur* Our Lady of Namur, patron saint of Namur, province in southern Belgium] **:** a member of a Roman Catholic community founded in 1803 and devoted chiefly to teaching

sister of providence *usu cap S&P* [part. trans. of F *sœur de providence*] **1 :** a member of a Roman Catholic teaching order founded in France in 1806 **2 :** a member of a Roman Catholic congregation founded in Montreal in 1843 and devoted to teaching and charitable works

sister of st. jo·seph \-sāntˈjōzəf, -sənt- *also* -ōsəf\ *usu cap both Ss&J* [trans. of F *sœur de Saint-Joseph (du Puy)*, after *Joseph*, husband of Mary, mother of Jesus] **:** a member of a Roman Catholic congregation established in Le Puy, France, in 1650 and devoted to teaching and charitable works

sister of saint vin·cent \-ˈvin(t)sənt\ *usu cap both Ss&V* [trans. of F *sœur de Saint-Vincent (de-Paul)*, after *Saint Vincent de Paul* †1660 Fr. Roman Catholic priest who founded the sisterhood] **:** SISTER OF CHARITY

sister of the good shepherd *usu cap both Ss&G* [trans. of F *sœur du Bon Pasteur*] **:** a member of a cloistered Roman Catholic order established at Caen, France, in 1641 and devoted esp. to the shelter and rehabilitation of girls and women

sister of the holy cross *usu cap S&H&C* [trans. of F *sœur de la Sainte Croix*] **:** a member of a Roman Catholic sisterhood founded at Le Mans, France, in 1841 and devoted to teaching and charitable works

sister of the holy names of jesus and mary *usu cap S&H &N&J&M* [after *Jesus* Christ and *Mary*, mother of Jesus] **:** a member of a Roman Catholic congregation founded in Canada in 1843 and devoted to teaching

sister of the immaculate heart of mary *usu cap S&I&H&M* [after *Mary*, mother of Jesus] **:** a member of a Roman Catholic teaching sisterhood founded at Monroe, Michigan, in 1845

sisters *pl of* SISTER, *pres 3d sing of* SISTER

sis·ter·ship \ˈsistə(r)ˌship\ *n* **:** SISTERHOOD

sister ship *n* **:** one of two or more essentially similar ships usu. built from the same general plans

sister superior *n, pl* **sister superiors** *also* **sisters superior :** MOTHER SUPERIOR

[1]**sis·tine** \ˈsiˌstēn *sometimes* səˈstēn, *chiefly Brit* ˈsiˌstīn\ *or* **six·tine** \ˈsikˌstīn, -ˌstēn, -ˌstən\ *adj, usu cap* [*sistine* fr. It *sistino*, fr. NL *sixtinus*, fr. L *sextus* sixth + *-inus* -ine; *sixtine* fr. NL *sixtinus* — more at SEXT] **1 :** of or relating to any of the popes named Sixtus ⟨the *Sistine* edition of the Vulgate⟩ **2** [so called fr. its having been built by Pope Sixtus IV †1484] **:** of or relating to the Sistine chapel in the Vatican ⟨the *Sistine* choir⟩

[2]**sistine** \"\ *n, often cap* [after the *Sistine* chapel in the Vatican, noted for its famous paintings esp. the frescoes on its ceilings painted by Michelangelo Buonarroti †1564 Ital. sculptor, painter, architect, and poet of the High Renaissance] **:** a pale blue that is redder and deeper than average powder blue, greener and stronger than average cadet gray, redder and stronger than old blue, and greener and darker than average Wedgwood (sense 2a)

sis·tren \ˈsistrən, -tə(r)n\ *chiefly dial pl of* SISTER

sis·trum \ˈsistrəm\ *n, pl* **sistrums** \-rəmz\ *or* **sis·tra** \-rə\ [ME, fr. L, fr. Gk *seistron*, fr. *seiein* to shake — more at SEISMIC] **1 :** an ancient Egyptian percussion instrument consisting of a thin metal frame with numerous metal rods or loops that jingle when shaken **2 :** any of various musical instruments played like a rattle

sis·tru·rus \səˈstrürəs\ *n, cap* [NL, fr. L *sistrum* rattling instrument, sistrum + NL *-urus*] **:** a genus of small rattlesnakes (family Crotalidae) having the top of the head covered with plates — see MASSASAUGA

sists *pl of* SIST

si·sym·bri·um \səˈsimbrēəm\ *n* [L, a fragrant herb, perh. mint, fr. Gk *sisymbrion* bergamot, watercress] **1** *cap* **:** a genus of annual or biennial herbs (family Cruciferae) having a pubescence of simple unbranched hairs, lyrate pinnatifid leaves, and terete stems and comprising the hedge mustards — see DESCURAINIA **2** -s **:** any plant of the genus *Sisymbrium*

sis·y·phe·an \ˌsisəˈfēən\ *or* **si·syph·i·an** \səˈsifēən\ *adj, usu cap* [L *sisypheius, sisyphius* sisyphean (fr. Gk *sisypheios, sisyphios*, fr. *Sisyphos* Sisyphus, in Greco-Roman mythology the cruel king of Corinth whose punishment in Hades was to roll up a hill a heavy stone that constantly rolled down again) + E *-an*] **:** of, relating to, or suggestive of the labors of Sisyphus; *specif* **:** requiring continual and often ineffective effort ⟨would go back to the National Assembly for rereading and repassage, a *Sisyphean* task —Janet Flanner⟩

si·syr·i·dae \səˈsirəˌdē\ *n pl, cap* [NL, fr. Gk *sisyra* fur, goat's hair + NL *-idae*; fr. the hairy covering of the body and wings] **:** a family of neuropterous insects having larvae that feed on freshwater sponges

sis·y·rin·chi·um \ˌsisəˈriŋkēəm\ *n* [NL, fr. Gk *sisyrinchion* sisyrinchium] **1** *cap* **:** a genus of chiefly No. American grass-like mostly blue-flowered herbs (family Iridaceae) having mostly basal leaves and several 6-parted flowers usu. from a single spathe **2** -s **:** any plant of the genus *Sisyrinchium*

[1]**sit** \(ˈ)sit, *usu* -id·+V; *before a vowel-initial adverb with primary stress often* ˌsəd· *or* ˌsət; *before "down" often* (ˈ)sa\ *also* (ˈ)si\ *vb* **sat** \(ˈ)sat, -ad·, *before "down" often* (ˈ)sa\ *also chiefly dial* **sot** \(ˈ)sät|, |d·\ *or archaic* **sate** \(ˈ)sāt|, |t·\ *or chiefly dial* **sot** \(ˈ)sät|, |d·\ *or archaic* **sit·ten** \ˈsitᵊn\ **sitting; sits** [ME *sitten*, fr. OE *sittan*; akin to OHG *sizzen* to sit, ON *sitja*, Goth *sitan*, L *sedēre*, Gk *hezesthai* to sit, *hedra* seat, Skt *sīdati* he sits] *vi* **1 :** to rest in a position in which the body is essentially vertical and supported or balanced chiefly on the buttocks or thighs or both ⟨~ on a stool⟩ ⟨~ in a chair⟩ ⟨~ cross-legged⟩ **2 a** *obs* **:** KNEEL **b** *of an animal* **:** to assume a position with the hindquarters at rest on a supporting surface ⟨a dog trained to stand and ~ at command⟩ **c** *of a bird* **:** to perch or rest esp. with the feet drawn up close or with the body touching the ground **3 :** to occupy a place as a member of an official body ⟨~ in Congress⟩ ⟨~ on the board of directors⟩ ⟨~ as a member of a committee⟩ **4 :** to hold a session **:** be in session for official business ⟨magistrate . . . may ~ in any place convenient —F.T.Giles⟩ ⟨the legislature is still *sitting*⟩ ⟨official committee . . . *sitting* on the question of the ultimate size and organization —Roy Lewis & Angus Maude⟩ **5 :** to have or continue in an occupation or function ⟨gamblers held *sat* lookout with their sombreros on —W.N.Burns⟩ **6** *of a hen* **:** to cover eggs for hatching **:** BROOD, SET **7 a :** to take a position for having one's portrait painted or for being photographed ⟨~ for a painter⟩ **b :** to serve as the original of a painted or sculptured figure or of a fictional character **8 a** *archaic* **:** to have one's dwelling place **:** DWELL **b** *obs* **:** to remain as a tenant **9 :** to lie in wait ⟨anyone *sitting* at the entrance to the pass, they'll see us if we go through the field —Norman Mailer⟩ **10 a** *of clothing* **:** to lie or hang relative to the wearer ⟨the collar *sits* awkwardly at the back⟩ ⟨trying to see how the new coat ~s behind⟩ **b :** LIE, REST — used with *on* or *upon* ⟨author's assumed regionalism ~s uneasily on his verse —W.M.Maidment⟩ ⟨great triumvirate of Edwardian novelists . . . that label ~s comfortably on these three —P.M.Fulcher⟩ **c :** to affect one with or as if with a certain weight **:** PRESS, WEIGH ⟨her years *sat* lightly upon her⟩ ⟨the pie *sat* heavily on his stomach⟩ **11 :** to float in a specified manner ⟨load so that the ship ~s several feet deeper in the water aft⟩ ⟨the boat ~s practically on top of the water⟩ **12 a :** to have a location ⟨thy rapt soul *sitting* in thine eyes —John Milton⟩ ⟨cottage *sitting* on the edge of a cliff⟩ ⟨house ~s well back from the road⟩ **b** *of wind* **:** to blow from a certain direction ⟨when the wind ~s one way I can hear the steam train —Christopher Morley⟩ ⟨always rains when the wind ~s in the west⟩ **13 :** to please or agree with one — used with *with* and an adverb ⟨setting an example that may not ~ well with the more obedient Communist leaders —*N.Y. Times*⟩ **14 :** to remain in the same state ⟨left the dishes *sitting* on the table⟩ **:** remain inactive or quiescent ⟨the car ~s in the garage unused all week⟩ ⟨do something, don't just ~ there⟩ ⟨*sitting* behind prison bars⟩ **15 :** to be a candidate for a degree, certificate, or award **:** take or prepare to take an examination — used with *for* ⟨was *sitting* for a scholarship at Newton College —Angela Thirkell⟩ ⟨*sat* for his examinations . . . as a river pilot —*N.Y. Herald Tribune*⟩ **16 :** to act as a relief for a parent or nurse in watching over a child or an invalid ⟨~ with a friend's baby⟩ ~ *vt* **1 :** to cause (oneself) to be seated — usu. used with *down* ⟨*sat* him down to write a letter⟩ **2 :** to cause to be seated **:** place on or in a seat **:** put in a sitting position ⟨let me ~ you on the sofa . . . and talk over small matters —F.D.Roosevelt⟩ ⟨a story that *sat* me up straight —S.H.Holbrook⟩ **3** *of a hen* **:** to sit upon (eggs) **4 a :** to keep one's seat upon ⟨~ a horse⟩ **b :** to trim (a boat) by the poise of the body or by the use of oars **5** *chiefly dial* **:** SUIT, BECOME, BEFIT **6 :** to provide seats or seating room for ⟨the car will ~ six people comfortably⟩ **7** *Brit* **:** to answer the questions of (an examination) in writing — **sit at one's feet :** to listen to or follow as a pupil, disciple, or admirer — **sit at table :** to be at table for eating **:** DINE — **sit loose :** to be heedless or indifferent ⟨scholars . . . who *sit loose* to the obligations and responsibilities of church membership —Alan Richardson⟩ — **sit on 1 :** to hold deliberations concerning ⟨several judges have *sat on* this case⟩ **2 :** REPRESS, SQUELCH **3 :** to delay action or decision concerning **:** keep quiet or out of sight **:** SUPPRESS ⟨he had *sat on* stories before, like some other newsmen — *Time*⟩ ⟨*sat on* appropriations plans until they were certain which way winds . . . were blowing —*Newsweek*⟩ — **sit on one's hands 1 :** to withhold applause **:** fail to show approval or enthusiasm **2 :** fail to take expected or appropriate action **:** sit by — **sit on the lid :** to keep down agitation **:** hold in check forces of protest or rebellion — **sit on the splice** *cricket* **:** STONEWALL — contrasted with *lay on the wood* — **sit on the throne :** REIGN — **sit pretty :** to be in a highly favorable situation ⟨*sitting pretty* with a full house against a flush and a straight⟩ ⟨Americans . . . had a virtual monopoly of piston-engined air transports, and they were *sitting pretty* —Charles Gardner⟩ — **sit tight 1 :** to maintain one's position without change ⟨preferred to *sit tight* with his present investments⟩ ⟨colonel decided to *sit tight* and send out patrols —Walter Bernstein⟩ **2 :** to remain quiet in or as if in hiding — **sit under :** to attend religious service under the instruction or ministrations of; *also* **:** to attend the classes or lectures of (a teacher)

[2]**sit** \ˈsit, *usu* -id·+V\ *n* -s **1 :** an act or period of sitting ⟨a long ~ at the station between trains⟩ **2 :** the manner in which a garment fits ⟨~ of a coat around the shoulders⟩ **3 :** a settling or falling of the roof of a mine — usu. used in pl. **4 :** an entire mature celery plant

sit *abbr* situation

SIT *abbr* **1** spontaneous ignition temperature **2** stopping or storage in transit

si·tao \səˈtaů\ *n* -s [Tag *sitaw*] **:** a long-podded cowpea of the Philippines

si·tar *also* **si·tār** \səˈtär\ *n* -s [Hindi *sitār*] **:** a Hindu guitar with a long neck and a varying number of strings

sit around *vi* **:** to be idle **:** LOAF ⟨had to *sit around* until they got orders —Ira Wolfert⟩

sit·a·tun·ga *or* **sit·u·tun·ga** \ˌsid·əˈtu̇ŋgə\ *n, pl* **sitatungas** *or* **sitatunga** *or* **situtungas** *or* **situtunga** [Subiya & Tonga] **:** an antelope (*Strepsiceros spekei*) of the central African swampland that is nearly related to the harnessed antelope but shows white striping only when young

sit back *vi* **:** to rest or withdraw from work or active participation ⟨the man in the street . . . can *sit back* in indifference or in helpless bewilderment —*advt*⟩

sit by *vi* **:** to assume an attitude of indifference or passivity or restraint ⟨we see nothing . . . that compels the government to *sit by* while a food supply is cut off —O.W.Holmes †1935⟩

sit down *see* ˡSIT\ *vi* [ME *sitten doun*, fr. *sitten* to sit + *down* down — more at SIT, DOWN] **1 a :** to lower oneself to a sitting position **:** take a seat **b :** to fall on the buttocks ⟨suddenly *sat down* on the ice⟩ **c :** to pause from activity through fatigue or complacency **d :** to establish a residence **:** settle down **2 :** to begin a siege **:** ENCAMP **3 :** to enter into conference, negotiation, or consultation ⟨if we could *sit down* together and straighten out our differences peaceably⟩ **4 :** ALIGHT, LAND ⟨a field big enough for a bomber to *sit down* on safely⟩ — **sit down on :** REPRIMAND, SQUELCH

[1]**sit-down** \ˈ=,=\ — *see* ˡSIT\ *n* -s [fr. *sit down*, v.] **1 a :** act or place of sitting down ⟨a nice quiet *sit-down* by the fire —Elizabeth Taylor⟩ **b** *or* **sit-down strike :** a cessation of work by employees while maintaining continuous occupation of shop, plant, or like place of employment as a protest and means toward forcing compliance with demands — called also *sit-in*; compare STAY-IN STRIKE **2 :** a meal taken sitting down — compare BUFFET, HANDOUT

[2]**sit-down** \"\ *adj* **:** that one sits or settles down to ⟨a *sit-down* lunch⟩ **:** performed in a sitting position ⟨*sit-down* dance⟩

sit-down·er \ˈ=,=ə(r)\ *n* -s **:** a worker engaged in a sit-down strike

[1]**site** \ˈsīt, *usu* -īd·+V\ *n* -s [ME, fr. MF or L; MF *site*, fr. L *situs* position, place, site, fr. *situs*, past part. of *sinere* to leave, let go, lay, place; akin to L *serere* to plant, sow — more at SOW] **1 a** *obs* **:** the original or fixed position of a thing ⟨wisdom of God in the ~ and motion of the sun —Sir Thomas Browne⟩ **b** *obs* **:** ATTITUDE, POSTURE ⟨fixed in melancholy ~, with head declined —James Thomson †1748⟩ **2 a :** the local position of building, town, monument, or similar work either constructed or to be constructed esp. in connection with its surroundings ⟨how Oxford and Cambridge in particular came to be chosen for ~s —A.T.Quiller-Couch⟩ ⟨suitable ~ for a factory⟩ ⟨his structural solutions and his great sense of ~ —Lincoln Kirstein⟩ **b :** a space of ground occupied or to be occupied by a building ⟨offered the city a library . . . if the city would provide a ~ —*Amer. Guide Series: Md.*⟩ **c :** land made suitable for building purposes by dividing into lots, laying out streets, and providing facilities (as water, sewers, power supply) ⟨desirable corner ~s are available⟩ ⟨waterfront ~s for summer cottages⟩ **3 :** the scene of an action ⟨battle ~⟩ ⟨~ of the murder⟩ ⟨~ of an auto collision⟩ or specified activity ⟨mining ~⟩ ⟨picnic ~⟩ ⟨launching ~ for a rocket⟩ ⟨choosing a ~ for a convention⟩ ⟨~ of a bone fracture⟩ **4 :** a place where a group of remains of prehistoric human occupation is or has been located ⟨a burial ~⟩ ⟨a village ~⟩ ⟨excavations at a ~⟩ **5 :** the situation of a growing plant with respect to all the environmental factors (as climate, soil, drainage, other plant and animal life) affecting growth **6 :** the angle between the horizontal and a line joining the base of a target and a firing piece

[2]**site** \"\ *vt* -ED/-ING/-S **1 :** to provide with a site **:** LOCATE ⟨hotel magnificently *sited* on a headland —Mitchell Goodman⟩ ⟨the camp kitchen should be *sited* so that the breeze will not blow smoke into the cook's face —R.H.Graves⟩ **2 :** to put

(artillery) in position so as to be able to perform a specific mission ⟨~ a machine gun⟩
site index *n* : a measure of the worth of a particular area as a habitat for forest usu. given as the average height in feet of the dominant or codominant trees at a given age (as 50 or 100 years)
¹sitfast *or* **setfast** \ˈ=,=\ *n* -s [¹*sit* or ¹*set* + *fast* (after the phrase *sit fast, set fast*)] : a callosity with inflamed edges formed on a horse's back by the chafing of the saddle — compare SADDLE SORE
²sitfast \"\ *adj* [¹*sit* + *fast* (after *sit fast*, v.)] *chiefly dial* : FIXED, STATIONARY, IMMOVABLE
sith \(ˈ)sith\ *or* **sith·ence** \ˈsithən(t)s\ *or* **sith·ens** \-nz\ *archaic var of* SINCE
sith·cund \ˈsēth,ku̇nd\ *n* -s [by shortening] : GESITHCUND
sithe \ˈsīth, -t͟h\ *dial var of* SIGH
sit in *vi* **1** : to take a hand in a card game **2** : to take part in or be present at a session (of music, discussion) as a visitor ⟨*sit in* with a dance band⟩ — usu. used with *on* ⟨invited to *sit in* on a rehearsal⟩ ⟨*sat in* on some of the board's policy-making meetings⟩ **3** *Brit* : BABY-SIT **4** *Brit* : to sit down at table
sit–in \ˈ=,=\ *n* -s **1** : SIT-DOWN 1b **2 a** : an act of occupying seats in a racially segregated establishment as an organized protest against discrimination **b** : an act of sitting in the seats or on the floor of an establishment as a means of organized protest
si·tio \ˈsēd·ē,ō\ *n* -s [Sp, place, prob. modif. of L *situs* site — more at SITE] : a hamlet or subdivision of a barrio in the Philippines
sit·ka \ˈsitkə\ *n, pl* **sitka** *or* **sitkas** *usu cap* [Tlingit, lit., behind on Shi (native name of Baranof Island)] **1** : a Tlingit people on Baranof and Chichagof Islands, Alaska **2** : a member of the Sitka people
sitka alder \ˈ==-\ *n, usu cap S* [fr. *Sitka*, town in Baranof Island, prob. fr. Tlingit *Sitka*] : a shrub or small tree (*Alnus sinuata*) ranging from Alaska to California and having oval bright green leaves and clustered catkins
sitka crab *n, usu cap S* : a small anomuran crustacean (*Cryptolithodes sitchensis*) that resembles a crab with a domed carapace bright red in the male, rosy gray in the female and lives among rocks near the tide line from Alaska to California
sitka cypress *n, usu cap S* : YELLOW CEDAR 1a
sit·kan \ˈsitkən\ *n* -s *cap* [*Sitka*, Baranof Island, Alaska + E *-an*] : a native or resident of Sitka, Alaska
sitka spruce *n, usu cap 1st S* : a tall spruce (*Picea sitchensis*) of the northern Pacific coast having loosely scaled thin reddish brown bark and flat needles
sitka spruce beetle *n, usu cap 1st S* : a bark beetle (*Dendroctonus obesus*) the larva of which is a serious pest on Sitka spruce in northwestern No. America
sitka spruce weevil *n, usu cap 1st S* : a curculionid weevil (*Pissodes sitchensis*) that is very destructive to Sitka spruce
sitka willow *n, usu cap S* : a tree (*Salix sitchensis*) ranging from Alaska to Oregon and having oblong leaves often with glandular-toothed margins
sito- *comb form* [Gk, fr. *sitos*] **1** : grain ⟨*Sito*philus⟩ ⟨*sito*sterol⟩ **2** : food ⟨*sitology*⟩
si·tol·o·gy \sīˈtäləjē, səˈt-\ *n* -ES [ISV *sito-* + *-logy*] : the science of nutrition and dietetics
si·to·na \səˈtōnə\ *n, cap* [NL, prob. fr. LL, grain buyer, fr. Gk *sitōnes*, fr. *sitos* grain] : a genus of weevils including some that are injurious to various crop plants — see SWEETCLOVER WEEVIL
si·toph·i·lus \sīˈtäfələs, səˈt-\ *n, cap* [NL, fr. *sito-* + *-philus*] : a widely distributed genus of weevils containing two (*S. granarius* and *S. oryzae*) that are highly destructive to grain
si·to·sterol \sīˈd·ō(,)ō+\ *n* [*sito-* + *sterol*] : any of several widely occurring sterols or a mixture of such sterols useful as a starting material for the synthesis of steroid hormones: as **a** : a crystalline secondary alcohol $C_{29}H_{49}OH$ obtained esp. from cottonseed oil, tall oil, wheat-germ oil, or cinchona bark or synthetically from stigmasterol by hydrogenation — called also *beta-sitosterol* **b** : a crystalline alcohol $C_{29}H_{49}OH$ that is stereoisomeric with beta-sitosterol, that is the principal sterol of soybean oil, and that is also found in several invertebrates — called also *gamma-sitosterol*
sit out *vt* **1** : to remain to the end of ⟨*sit out* a dull speech⟩ **2** : to outstay in a social call ⟨determined to *sit* his rival *out*⟩ **3 a** : to remain seated during (a dance) **b** : to fail to take part in : stay aloof from ⟨believe we would find it impossible to *sit out* any war in Europe —Elmo Roper⟩ **4** : to stretch the back of (a skirt) by wearing while sitting
sit over *vi* : to move sideways on a seat or along a row of seats to make room
sit·rep \ˈsit·,rep\ *n* -s [*situation report*] : a periodic report of the current military situation
sits *pres 3d sing of* SIT, *pl of* SIT
sit spin *n* : a spin in figure skating executed on one foot in a sitting position with the other leg extended forward — called also *Jackson Haines*
sit·ta \ˈsid·ə\ *n, cap* [NL, fr. Gk *sittē* nuthatch] : the type genus of Sittidae comprising various typical nuthatches
sit·ta·ble \ˈsid·əbəl\ *adj* [¹*sit* + *-able*] : suitable for sitting on ⟨~ chairs⟩ or sitting through ⟨a movie of ~ length⟩
sittar *var of* SITAR
sit·tee \(ˈ)sidˈē\ *n* -s [¹*sit* + *-ee*] : one occupying a seat
sitten *archaic past part of* SIT
sit·ter \ˈsid·ə(r), -itə-\ *n* -s [ME, fr. *sitten* to sit + *-er* — more at SIT] **1** : one that sits: as **a** *obs* : RIDER **b** : a broody hen **c** : one who sits for a portrait or a bust **d** : one who has a seance with a psychic **e** [by shortening] : BABY-SITTER **f** : B-GIRL **2 a** : an easy target ⟨~ for enemy submarines⟩ **b** : an easy scoring or fielding chance : SETUP **3** *Brit* : SITTING ROOM
sitter–by \ˈ==ˈ=\ *n, pl* **sitters–by** : one who sits near or apart
sitter–in \ˈ==ˈ=\ *n, pl* **sitters–in** *chiefly Brit* : BABY-SITTER
sit through *vt* : to watch or listen to without enjoyment : sit out ⟨conscientiously *sitting through* the movies which it is one of his official duties to censor —Edmund Wilson⟩
sit·ti·dae \ˈsid·ə,dē\ *n pl, cap* [NL, fr. *Sitta*, type genus + *-idae*] : a family of passerine birds consisting of the nuthatches and formerly regarded as a subfamily of Paridae or of Certhiidae
sit·tine \ˈsi,tīn\ *adj* [NL *Sitta* + E *-ine*] : of or relating to the nuthatches
¹sitting *n* -s [ME, fr. gerund of *sitten* to sit] **1** : an act of one that sits; *esp* : a single occasion of continuous sitting ⟨read a book at one ~⟩ ⟨finished the portrait in three ~*s*⟩ ⟨turkey supper at the church . . . with ~*s* at 5:30 and 6:30 —*Springfield (Mass.) Daily News*⟩ **2 a** : a brooding over eggs or time or season for brooding over eggs for hatching **b** : SETTING 10 **3** : the actual presence or meeting of a body of persons in their seats with authority to transact business : SESSION ⟨a ~ of a court⟩ ⟨~ of the legislature⟩ — often used in pl. **4** : a space occupied by or allotted for one person (as in a church or theater) ⟨a space of 18 in. in the length of the pew is considered a ~ —J.H.Frank⟩ **5** : SÉANCE b
²sitting *adj* [ME, fr. pres. part. of *sitten* to sit] **1** : that is setting ⟨~ hen⟩ **2** : occupying a judicial or legislative seat : being in office ⟨the first business of any ~ politician is, naturally, to be reelected —W.S.White⟩ **3** *Brit* : being in occupancy : holding tenancy ⟨prices to ~ tenants are often very favorable —*advt*⟩ **4** : easily hit or played ⟨~ target⟩ ⟨~ game in spades⟩
sitting duck *n* : an easy or defenseless target for attack ⟨the tanks ran out of gas and became *sitting ducks* for enemy artillery⟩ or criticism or sharp practice ⟨Eliot's intellectual and mystic snobbishness put him in the unfortunate position of a *sitting duck* —C.B.Davis⟩ ⟨an alien may be a *sitting duck* for extortioners —*New Republic*⟩
sitting height *n* : the distance from the vertex of the head to the supporting surface on which a person is sitting erect
sitting room *n* **1** : a room for sitting in; *esp* : a room provided in addition to the bedroom of a private suite ⟨had a bedroom and *sitting room* on the same floor of a small private hotel —Nevil Shute⟩ **2** : LIVING ROOM 1
sitting shot *n* : a shot made while in a sitting position
sitting trot *n* : a slow trot in which a rider does not post
sit·trin·gee \səˈtrinjē\ *n* -s [Per *shatranjī*, lit., checkered, fr. *shatranj, shatrang* chessboard, chess, fr. Skt *caturaṅga*, lit., four limbs, fr. *catur* four + *aṅga* limb — more at FOUR, ANKLE] *India* : a carpet of striped or checkered cotton
sit·u·al \ˈsichəwəl\ *adj* [ML *situalis*, fr. L *situs* site, position + *-alis* -al] : POSITIONAL — **sit·u·al·ly** \-wəlē\ *adv*
¹sit·u·ate \ˈsichəwə̇t, -,wāt, *usu* |d.+V\ *adj* [ML *situatus*, past part. of *situare* to place] : having its site : LOCATED ⟨parcel of land ~ in the village of Riverview —*Detroit Law Jour.*⟩
²sit·u·ate \-,wāt, *usu* -ād.+V\ *vt* -ED/-ING/-S [ML *situatus*, past part. of *situare* to place, fr. *situs* place, position, site — more at SITE] **1** : to place in a site : LOCATE **2** : to place in a situation : give a place to ⟨~ the reader in the main currents of the life of a dynamic society —*New Republic*⟩ **3** : to assign to a category or particular set of associations : LOCALIZE ⟨study that tries to ~ the particular thinker and his thought in their proper place in man's ever growing consciousness —J.W. Evans⟩ ⟨liberalism alone does not create . . . it does not ~ truth —H.E.Clurman⟩
situated *adj* [fr. past part. of ²*situate*] **1** : having a site, situation, or location : LOCATED ⟨a town ~ on a hill⟩ **2** : CIRCUMSTANCED ⟨his family, while not rich, were comfortably ~⟩
sit·u·a·tion \,sichəˈwāshən\ *n* -s [MF or ML; MF, fr. ML *situation-, situatio*, fr. *situatus* (past part. of *situare* to place) + L *-ion-, -io* -ion] **1 a** : the way in which something is placed in relation to its surroundings ⟨its insular ~ made it readily accessible —Kemp Malone⟩ ⟨in some spelling ~*s* letters represent no sounds —*ABC Language Arts Bull.*⟩ **b** : SITE ⟨so uneasy . . . that we thought of removing our ~ —Daniel Defoe⟩ **c** *archaic* : LOCALITY, SPOT ⟨small rancho in a lonely spot . . . the ~ was also wild and solitary —W.H.Hudson †1922⟩ **2** *obs* : act of situating, settling, or occupying **3 a** *archaic* : state of health ⟨the flesh of the bear in this ~ . . . is inferior —E.H.Criswell⟩ **b** : state of pregnancy ⟨the woman should have concealed her ~ —Sir Walter Scott⟩ **4 a** : position or place of employment : POST, JOB ⟨rise in help, ~ wanted ads —*Nation's Business*⟩ **b** : position in life : STATUS ⟨striving to better his ~⟩ **5 a** : position with respect to conditions and circumstances ⟨the rebels' military ~ appeared to be hopeless⟩ ⟨in the unpleasant ~ of having to choose between two evils⟩ **b** : the sum total of internal and external stimuli that act upon an organism within a given time interval **c** : the total set of physical, social, and psychocultural factors that act upon an individual in orienting and conditioning his behavior **6 a** : relative position or combination of circumstances at a given moment ⟨how to behave in unexpected ~*s*⟩ ⟨daily reports on the ~ at each stage of the campaign⟩ ⟨the ~ seemed to call for a general retreat⟩ ⟨a ~ map attached to the report⟩ **b** : a critical, trying, or unusual state of affairs ⟨in the event of a recession . . . to arouse the people to the need of using their own ingenuity to meet the ~ —Paul Wooton⟩; *often* : PROBLEM ⟨no human ~ is simple, has one cause and one cure —D.W.Brogan⟩ **c** : a particular or striking complex of affairs at a stage in the action of a narrative or drama : CRISIS, CLIMAX ⟨highly contrived and implausible ~*s*⟩
syn see STATE
sit·u·a·tion·al \ˌ==ˈwāshənᵊl, -shnəl\ *adj* **1** : relating to or caused by a situation ⟨elaborate ~ plot of a novel⟩ ⟨~ testing of officer candidates⟩ **2 a** : produced or conditioned by a specific set of social or interpersonal circumstances ⟨delinquency due to family ~ factors⟩ ⟨~ drinker⟩ **b** : dealing with the total situation as determining the individual's behavior ⟨a ~ analysis of prejudice⟩ — **sit·u·a·tion·al·ly** \-ᵊlē, -əl|, |ī\ *adv*
situational neurosis *n* : a reactive neurosis
sit·u·a·tion·ism \,==ˈwāshə,nizəm\ *n* -s : a theory viewing human personality as a function of response to situations
sit·u·a·tion·ist \-sh(ə)nəst\ *n* -s : one who holds a theory of situationism
sit·u·la \ˈsichələ, -id·ᵊlə\ *n, pl* **situ·lae** \-chə,lē, -d·ᵊl,ī\ [L] : an ancient vessel shaped like a bucket usu. of decorated bronze and found in Italy and other parts of Europe
sit up *vi* [ME *sitten up*, fr. *sitten* to sit + *up* — more at SIT, UP] **1** : to rise from a lying to a sitting position : sit with the body erect ⟨able to *sit up* and take nourishment⟩ **2** : to show interest or alertness or surprise ⟨we *sit up* with pleasure when he suddenly lashes out at some literary stuffed shirt —Alfred Kazin⟩ **3** : to stay up after the usual time for going to bed ⟨*sit up* with a sick child⟩ ⟨a late movie not worth *sitting up* for⟩ — **sit up and take notice** : to show a lively interest or apprehension
sit–up \ˈ=,=\ *n* -s [*sit up*] : a conditioning exercise consisting of raising the trunk to a sitting position from a supine position with the legs remaining straight
sit–upon \ˈ==,=\ *n* -s [fr. *sit upon*, v.] **1** : BUTTOCKS **2** : a square of waterproof cloth carried by hikers and campers for sitting on wet ground
si·tus \ˈsīd·əs, ˈsēd\ *n* -ES [L, place, site — more at SITE] **1** : the place where something exists or originates ⟨~ of a bodily function⟩ ⟨~ of an inflammation⟩ ⟨~ and quantity of the local water supplies —P.A.Rollins⟩ ⟨Palestine as . . . the ~ of their Semitic ancestry —B.A.Javits⟩ **2** : the place to which an intangible right or property is deemed to belong for purposes of taxation or legal jurisdiction ⟨~ of a corporation⟩ ⟨a taxpayer's ~ of income⟩
situs in·ver·sus \-inˈvərsəs\ *n* [NL, lit., inverted position] : a congenital abnormality characterized by lateral transposition of the viscera (as of the heart or the liver)
situtunga *var of* SITATUNGA
sitz bath \ˈsits-\ *n* [part trans. of G *sitzbad*, fr. *sitz* act of sitting (fr. MHG *siz*, fr. *sitzen* to sit, fr. OHG *sizzen*) + *bad* bath — more at SIT] **1** : a tub in which one bathes in a sitting posture **2** : a bath used esp. in postoperative cases in which the hips and thighs of the patient are immersed in hot water for the therapeutic effect of the moist heat in the perineal and anal regions

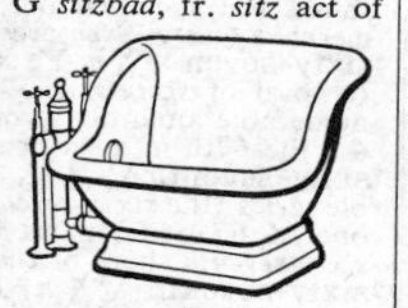

sitz bath 2

sitz·krieg \ˈsits,krēg, ˈzi-\ *n* -s [G *sitz* act of sitting + *krieg* war] : static warfare — contrasted with *blitzkrieg*
sitz·mark \-t,smärk\ *n* [part trans. of G *sitzmarke*, fr. *sitz* act of sitting + *marke* mark, sign] : a depression left in the snow by a skier falling backward
si·u·ai \sēˈ(y)ü,ī\ *n, pl* **siuai** *or* **siuais** *usu cap* **1** : a Papuan people inhabiting a section of southwestern Bougainville Island **2** : a member of the Siuai people
si·um \ˈsīəm\ *n, cap* [NL, fr. Gk *sion*, a marsh plant, perh. the water parsnip or marshwort] : a small genus of herbs (family Umbelliferae) that are natives of the north temperate zone and of southern Africa and have pinnate leaves, white flowers, and fruit with prominent ribs bearing oil tubes in the intervals
si·u·si \sēˈ(y)üsē\ *n, pl* **siusi** *or* **siusis** *usu cap* **1 a** : an Arawakan people of the Içana river valley in northwestern Brazil **b** : a member of such people **2** : the language of the Siusi people
si·u·slaw \sēˈ(y)ü(,)slȯ\ *n, pl* **siuslaw** *or* **siuslaws** *usu cap* [Siuslaw *šayušta*] **1 a** : an Indian people of the Pacific coast of Oregon **b** : a member of such people **2** : a Yakonan language of the Siuslaw and Kuitsh peoples
si·va \ˈsēvə\ *n* -s [Samoan] **1** : a western Polynesian gesture dance with vocal accompaniment **2** : a gathering at which the siva is danced
si·va·ism \ˈsēvə,izəm\ *or* **shi·va·ism** \ˈshē-\ *n* -s *usu cap* [*Siva, Shiva*, supreme god of many Hindu sects (fr. Skt *Śiva*, lit., friendly, auspicious) + E *-ism*; akin to OE *hīwan*, pl., members of a household — more at HOME] : a sect comprising the worshipers of the god Siva
si·va·ite *or* **shi·va·ite** \-və,īt\ *n* -s *usu cap* [*Siva, Shiva*, supreme god of many Hindu sects + E *-ite*] : SAIVA
si·van *or* **si·wan** \ˈsivən\ *n* -s *usu cap* [Heb *Sīwān*, fr. Assyr-Bab *Simānu*] : the 9th month of the civil year or the 3d month of the ecclesiastical year in the Jewish calendar — see MONTH table
si·va·pithe·cus \,sēvəpəˈthēkəs, -ˈpithək-\ *n, cap* [NL, fr. *Siva* (fr. Skt *Śiva*) + *-pithecus*] : a genus of generalized Lower Pliocene Indian apes related to *Dryopithecus* and exhibiting resemblances to the orangutan
siva snake *n* : KING COBRA
¹si·va·there \ˈsēvə,thi(ə)r\ *adj* [NL *Sivatherium*] : of or relating to *Sivatherium*
²sivathere \"\ *n* -s [NL *Sivatherium*] : a mammal or fossil of the genus *Sivatherium*
si·va·the·ri·oid \ˌ==ˈthirē,ȯid\ *adj* [NL *Sivatherium* + E *-oid*] : resembling or related to the genus *Sivatherium*
si·va·the·ri·um \ˌ==ˈ==ēəm\ *n, cap* [NL, fr. *Siva*, supreme god of many Hindu sects (fr. Skt *Śiva*) + *-therium*] : a genus that comprises very large mammals from the Pliocene of India with two pairs of horns of which the posterior are large and somewhat palmated and a muzzle probably fleshy or dilated like that of the saiga antelope and that is placed in the same family as the giraffe or sometimes made the type of a distinct family
si·va·ti \səˈväd·ē\ *n, pl* **sivati** *or* **sivatis** *usu cap* **1** : a Pathan people of the Afghan-Pakistan frontier **2** : a member of the Sivati people
siv·vy bean \ˈsivē-, -vi-\ *n* [by alter.] *chiefly South* : SIEVA BEAN
SIW *abbr* self-inflicted wound
si·wan \ˈsēwən\ *adj, usu cap* [*Siwa*, oasis in northwestern Egypt + E *-an*] **1** : of, relating to, or characteristic of the Egyptian oasis Siwa **2** : of, relating to, or characteristic of the people of Siwa
¹si·wash \ˈsī,wȯsh, -wäsh\ *n* -ES *usu cap* [Chinook Jargon, fr. F *sauvage* savage, fr. MF — more at SAVAGE] **1** *Northwest* : AMERICAN INDIAN — usu. used disparagingly **2** : the jargon used by and in talking with Siwashes
²siwash \"\ *vb* -ED/-ING/-ES *sometimes cap, vi* **1** *Northwest* : to live or do things like a Siwash — often used with *it* ⟨~ it in some cabin up on the flats⟩ **2** *Northwest* : to camp or travel with little or no equipment : rough it ⟨~*ing* up there by the head of the ravine —*Alaska Sportsman*⟩ — often used with *it* ~ *vt* : to do (something) in a slipshod manner; *esp* : to haul (logs) so as to sideswipe trees and stumps
³siwash \"\ *n* -ES *usu cap* [fr. *Siwash*, fictional college in stories by George Fitch †1915 Am. author] : a small usu. inland college that is notably provincial in outlook
siwin *var of* SEWEN
¹six \ˈsiks\ *adj* [ME *six, sex*, adj. & pron., fr. OE *six, siex, seox*; akin to OHG *sehs* six, ON *sex*, Goth *saihs*, L *sex*, Gk *hex*, Skt *ṣaṣ*] : being one more than five in number ⟨~ years⟩ — see NUMBER table
²six \"\ *pron, pl in constr* [ME] : six countable persons or things not specified but under consideration and being enumerated ⟨~ are here⟩ ⟨~ were found⟩
³six \"\ *n* -ES [ME, fr. *six*, adj. & pron.] **1** : twice three : three times two **2 a** : six units or objects ⟨a total of ~⟩ **b** : a group or set of six ⟨arranged by ~*es*⟩ **3 a** : the numerable quantity symbolized by the arabic numeral 6 **b** : the figure 6 **4** : six o'clock — compare BELL table, TIME illustration **5 a** : a playing card marked to show that it is sixth in a suit **b** : a domino with six spots on one of its halves **c** : a die with six spots on the uppermost side **d** : an article of clothing of the sixth size ⟨wears a ~⟩ **6** *cricket* : a hit that counts six runs (as by crossing the boundary before touching the ground); *also* : one from which six runs are scored **7 a** : a playing team of six members (as in ice hockey) **b** (1) : a boat rowed by six oars (2) : a crew of six oarsmen (3) **sixes** *pl* : races for 6-oared boats **8 a** : an internal-combustion engine having six cylinders **b** : an automobile powered with a six-cylinder engine **9** : the subdivision of six girls in a brownie scout pack in the Girl Guide movement in Britain, Canada, and various other countries — **at sixes and sevens** *also* **at six and seven** : in disorder : CONFUSED ⟨the house is rather *at sixes and sevens* —Arnold Bennett⟩ ⟨far from being the only authorities who are *at sixes and sevens* on this problem —R.S.Churchill⟩
six–ace flats *n pl* : a pair of dice so shaped as to produce a disproportionate frequency of appearance of the numbers 6, 2, and 12, and so to increase the likelihood of the shooter's losing in craps
six·ain \səˈzān, (ˈ)sikˈsān\ *n* -s [F, fr. OF *sisain*, fr. *sis* six, fr. L *sex*] : a stanza of six lines : SEXTAIN
six–banded armadillo \ˈ=,==-\ *n* : PELUDO 1
six–bid solo *n* : a card game resembling frog
six–by–six \ˈ=ˌbəˈ=\ *n* : a six-wheeled motor vehicle with six driving wheels
six–coupled locomotive \ˈ=,==-\ *n* : a locomotive with three pairs of driving wheels connected together by coupling rods
six–day bicycle race *n* : an endurance race usu. held on an indoor track between teams of two cyclists who ride alternately for a total of 144 hours
six–day disease *n* : a highly fatal nutritional deficiency disease of very young chicks marked by extreme thirst, incoordination, collapse, and death
six–eared barley \ˈ=,==-\ *n* : SIX-ROWED BARLEY
six·er \ˈsiksə(r)\ *n* -s : a leader of a six in a pack of brownie scouts in the Girl Guide movement in Britain, Canada, and various other countries
six·ern \ˈsiksərn\ *n* -s [Norw *seksæring, seksring*, fr. ON *sexæringr*, fr. *sex* six + *ār* oar + *-ingr* -ing; akin to OE *ār* oar — more at SIX] : a long Scottish fishing boat propelled by six oars and used esp. in the Shetland islands
six·foil \ˈsik,sfȯil\ *n* [by alter.] : SEXFOIL
¹six·fold \ˈsikˈsfōld\ *adj* [ME *sexfold*, fr. OE *sixfeald*, fr. *six* + *-feald* -fold] **1** : having six parts or aspects **2** : being six times as large, as great, or as many as some understood size, degree, or amount ⟨a ~ increase⟩
²sixfold \"\ *adv* : to six times as much or as many : by six times ⟨increased ~⟩
six–gilled shark *also* **sixgill shark** \ˈ=,=-\ *n* : a cowshark (genus *Hexanchus*) having six gill slits; *esp* : a common dusky Pacific shark (*H. griseus*) — compare HEXANCHIDAE
six–gun \ˈ=,=\ *n* : a 6-chambered revolver
six–man football *n* : football retaining the basic features of the American game and played on a modified field between six-man teams
six–mast·er \ˈ=ˈ=ə(r)\ *n* : a 6-masted ship
six·mo \ˈsik(,)smō\ *n* -s [*six* + *-mo*] : the size of a piece of paper cut six from a sheet; *also* : paper or a page of this size — abbr. *6mo*; symbol *6°*; see BOOK tables
six–o–six *or* **606** \ˌsik,sōˈsiks\ *n* [so called fr. its having been the 606th compound tested and introduced by Paul Ehrlich †1915 Ger. bacteriologist] : ARSPHENAMINE
six–pack \ˈ=,=\ *n* **1** : a container for six bottles or cans purchased together **2** : the contents of a six-pack

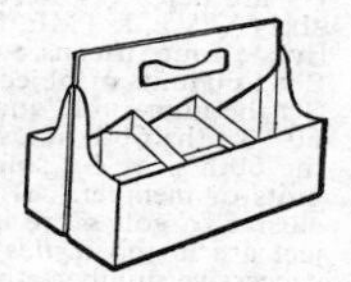

six-pack

six–pack bezique *n* : rubicon bezique played with six packs of cards shuffled together — called also *Chinese bezique*
six·pence \ˈsikspən(t)s *or* -k,spen-; *Brit* ˈsikspən(t)s\ *n, pl* **sixpence** *or* **sixpences** [ME *sexe pans*, fr. *sex* six + *pans* pence, pl. of *peny* penny — more at SIX, PENNY] **1 a** : the sum of six usu. British pennies **b** : a coin representing six pennies or half a shilling **2** : FIPPENNY BIT
six·pen·ny \-nē, -ni\ *adj* [ME *sixpeny*, fr. ¹*six* + *peny* penny] **1** : of the value of or costing sixpence ⟨a ~ thriller⟩ **2** : of trifling worth : CHEAP, TRASHY
sixpenny bit *n* : SIXPENCE
sixpenny nail *n* [ME *sixpeny nail* nail costing sixpence per hundred, fr. *sixpeny* sixpenny + *nail*] : a nail about 2 inches long
six·pen·ny·worth \(ˈ)sikˈspeni,wərth, (ˈ)sikˈspenəth, ˈsikspəni,wərth\ *n* [ME *sixe peny worthe*] : amount purchasable with or valued at sixpence
six–principle baptist *n, usu cap S&P&B* : a member of a Baptist denomination organized in Providence, R.I., in 1653 and distinguished generally by the acceptance of six foundational principles of repentance, baptism, faith, laying on of hands, resurrection of the dead, and eternal judgment drawn from Hebrews 6:1–2
six–rowed barley \ˈ=,=-\ *n* : a barley having the three spikelets of each cluster fertile so that the spike is six-rowed — compare FOUR-ROWED BARLEY
six–shafted bird of paradise \ˈ=,==-\ *n* : a bird of paradise (*Parotia sefilata*) having three long spatulate feathers on each side of the head
six–shooter \ˈ=ˈ==\ *n* : SIX-GUN

six·some \'siksəm\ *n* -s : a group of six persons or things esp. when playing together

six-spotted leafhopper \'⸗,⸗⸗-\ *n* : a leafhopper (*Macrosteles fascifrons*) that feeds on various crop plants and transmits several virus diseases of plants

six-spotted mite \'⸗,⸗⸗-\ *n* : a plant-feeding mite (*Eotetranychus sexmaculatus*) that causes injury to citrus and other fruit trees

six-square \'⸗,⸗\ *adj* : HEXAGONAL 2 : CUBICAL

sixte \'sikst\ *n* -s [F, lit., sixth, fr. L *sextus*; fr. its being the sixth parrying position — more at SEXT] : a fencing parry or guard position defending the upper outside right target in which the hand is to the right at breast height in a position of supination and the tip of the blade is directed at the opponent's eyes — compare TIERCE

¹six·teen \(')sik'stēn\ *adj* [ME *sixtene*, adj. & n., fr. OE *sixtȳne* (akin to OHG *sehszehan*, ON *sextān*), fr. *six* + -*tȳne* (fr. *tȳn* ten) — more at SIX, TEN] : being one more than 15 in number ⟨~ years⟩ — see NUMBER table; used prepositively to designate specified years of the 17th century ⟨the *sixteen*-eighties⟩ ⟨the early *sixteen*-hundreds⟩

²sixteen \"\ *pron, pl in constr* [ME *sixtene*, fr. *sixtene*, n. & adj.] : 16 countable persons or things not specified but under consideration and being enumerated ⟨~ are here⟩ ⟨~ were found⟩

³sixteen \"\ *n* -s [ME *sixtene*, fr. OE *sixtȳne*] 1 : 10 and six twice eight : eight times two : four fours : the square of four 2 a : 16 units or objects ⟨a total of ~⟩ b : a group or set of 16 3 : the numerable quantity symbolized by the arabic numerals 16 4 : the 16th in a set or series; *esp* : an article of clothing of the 16th size ⟨wears a ~⟩ 5 *sixteens pl* : SIXTEENMO

sixteen-foot octave *n* : CONTRAOCTAVE

sixteen-foot pitch *n* : the pitch of a 16-foot stop on a pipe organ

sixteen-foot stop *n* : a pipe-organ stop sounding pitches an octave lower than the notes indicate — compare EIGHT-FOOT STOP

six·teen·mo \⸗'⸗⸗,mō\ *n* -s [*sixteen* + -*mo*] : the size of a piece of paper cut 16 from a sheet; *also* : paper or a page of this size — abbr. *16mo*; symbol *16°*; see BOOK tables

sixteen-penny nail \⸗'⸗⸗,penē-\ *n* : a nail about 3½ inches long

six·teenth \(')sik'stēn(t)th\ *adj* [ME *sixtenthe*, alter. (influenced by *sixtene* sixteen) of *sixtethe*, fr. OE *sixtēotha* (akin to MHG *sehzehende*, ON *sextāndi*) fr. *sixtȳne* sixteen + -*otha*, -*tha* -th] 1 : being number 16 in a countable series ⟨the ~ day⟩ — see NUMBER table 2 : being one of 16 equal parts into which something is divisible ⟨a ~ share of the money⟩

²sixteenth \"\ *n, pl* **sixteenths** \-n(t)s, -n(t)ths\ 1 : number 16 in a countable series ⟨the ~ of the month⟩ 2 : the quotient of a unit divided by 16 : one of 16 equal parts of something ⟨one ~ of the total⟩ 3 a : a musical interval comprising two octaves and a second b : SIXTEENTH NOTE

sixteenth note *n* : a musical note with the time value of one sixteenth of a whole note — called also *semiquaver*

sixteenth rest *n* : a musical rest corresponding in time value to the sixteenth note

¹sixth \'siks(t)th, -kst\ *adj* [ME *sixte*, *sexte*, fr. OE *sixta*, *siexta* (akin to OHG *sehto*, *sehsto*, ON *sētti*, Goth *saihsta*), fr. *six*, *sex* six + -*ta* (fr. -*otha*, -*tha* -th)] 1 : being number six in a countable series ⟨the ~ day⟩ — see NUMBER table 2 : being one of six equal parts into which something is divisible ⟨a ~ share of the money⟩

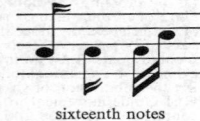

sixteenth notes

²sixth \"\ *n, pl* **sixths** \-ks(ts), -ks(t)ths\ 1 : number six in a countable series ⟨the ~ of the month⟩ 2 : the quotient of a unit divided by six : one of six equal parts of something ⟨one ~ of the total⟩ 3 a : a musical interval embracing six diatonic degrees b : a tone at this interval; *specif* : the sixth note or tone of a scale : SUBMEDIANT c : the harmonic combination of two tones a sixth apart 4 : SIXTE

³sixth \"\ *adv* 1 : in the sixth place 2 : with five exceptions ⟨the nation's ~ largest city⟩

sixth chord *n* : a musical chord consisting of a tone with its third and sixth above and usu. being the first inversion of a triad

sixth column *n* 1 : the aggregate of persons in a country at war who assist the subversive activities of the fifth column by defeatist talk, the spreading of rumors, and other activities that weaken resistance or appease the enemy 2 : a group organized to combat the fifth column

sixth columnist *n* : a member of a sixth column

sixth cranial nerve *or* **sixth nerve** *n* : ABDUCENS NERVE

sixth day *n, usu cap* S : FRIDAY — used chiefly by the Friends

sixth form *n* : the highest form of a British secondary school traditionally representing the moral and intellectual leadership of the school

sixth·ly *adv* : in the sixth place

six-three-three \'⸗'⸗'⸗\ *adj* : of or relating to a plan of school organization with six grades for the elementary school and three each for the junior and senior high schools — compare EIGHT-FOUR

sixth sense *n* : a power of perception like but not one of the five senses : a special ability to perceive or comprehend : a keen intuitive power ⟨journalists who have a *sixth sense* of news —R.S.Simpson⟩

six·ti·eth \'sikstēith, -tiə\ *adj* [ME *sixtithe*, fr. OE *sixtigotha* (akin to ON *sextugandi*), fr. *sixtig* sixty + -*otha*, -*tha* -th] 1 : being number 60 in a countable series ⟨the ~⟩ — see NUMBER table 2 : being one of 60 equal parts into which something is divisible ⟨a ~ share of the money⟩

²sixtieth \"\ *n* -s 1 : number 60 in a countable series 2 : the quotient of a unit divided by 60 : one of 60 equal parts of something ⟨one ~ of the total⟩

sixtine *usu cap, var of* SISTINE

¹six·ty \'sikstē\ *adj* [ME, fr. OE *sixtig*, *siextig*, n., group of 60, fr. *six*, *siex* six + -*tig* group of ten — more at SIX, EIGHTY] : being one more than 59 in number ⟨~ years⟩ — see NUMBER table

²sixty \"\ *pron, pl in constr* : 60 countable persons or things not specified but under consideration and being enumerated ⟨~ are here⟩ ⟨~ were found⟩

³sixty \"\ *n* -ES [ME, fr. *sixty*, adj.] 1 : six tens : twice 30 : 12 fives : four fifteens : three twenties : three score : five dozen 2 a : 60 units or objects ⟨a total of ~⟩ b : a group or set of 60 3 : the numerable quantity symbolized by the arabic numerals 60 4 : the 60th in a set or series; *esp* : an article of clothing of the 60th size 5 : something having as an essential feature 60 units or members 6 **sixties** *pl* a : the numbers 60 to 69 inclusive ⟨a golf score in the *sixties*⟩ ⟨all his grades in that subject are in the *sixties*⟩ b : the members of a series or set of successive numbers that end in 60 to 69 inclusive ⟨the *sixties* of the preceding century⟩ ⟨lives in the *sixties* in the next block⟩ c : the portion of a continuum lying between 60 and 70 on a scale of measure or segmentation ⟨temperatures in the high *sixties* tomorrow⟩ ⟨a man in his *sixties*⟩ ⟨overcoats selling in the *sixties*⟩ — **like sixty** : with great speed, ease, or force ⟨run *like sixty*⟩ ⟨reading a book and chewing gum *like sixty* —Jean Stafford⟩ ⟨it was raining *like sixty* —Mark Twain⟩

¹sixty-eight \⸗'⸗\ *adj* : being one more than 67 in number ⟨*sixty-eight* years⟩ — see NUMBER table

²sixty-eight \⸗'⸗\ *pron, pl in constr* : 68 countable persons or things not specified but under consideration and being enumerated ⟨*sixty-eight* are here⟩ ⟨*sixty-eight* were found⟩

³sixty-eight \"\ *n* 1 : eight and 60 : four times 17 2 a : 68 units or objects ⟨a total of *sixty-eight*⟩ b : a group or set of 68 3 : the numerable quantity symbolized by the arabic numerals 68 4 : the 68th in a set or series

¹sixty-eighth \⸗'⸗\ *adj* 1 : being number 68 in a countable series ⟨the *sixty-eighth* day⟩ — see NUMBER table 2 : being one of 68 equal parts into which something is divisible ⟨a *sixty-eighth* share of the money⟩

²sixty-eighth \"\ *n* 1 : number 68 in a countable series 2 : the quotient of a unit divided by 68 : one of 68 equal parts of something ⟨one *sixty-eighth* of the total⟩

¹sixty-fifth \⸗'⸗\ *adj* 1 : being number 65 in a countable series ⟨the *sixty-fifth* day⟩ — see NUMBER table 2 : being one of 65 equal parts into which something is divisible ⟨a *sixty-fifth* share of the money⟩

²sixty-fifth \"\ *n* 1 : number 65 in a countable series 2 : the quotient of a unit divided by 65 : one of 65 equal parts of something ⟨one *sixty-fifth* of the total⟩

¹sixty-first \⸗'⸗\ *adj* 1 : being number 61 in a countable series ⟨the *sixty-first* day⟩ — see NUMBER table 2 : being one of 61 equal parts into which something is divisible ⟨a *sixty-first* share of the money⟩

²sixty-first \"\ *n* 1 : number 61 in a countable series 2 : the quotient of a unit divided by 61 : one of 61 equal parts of something ⟨one *sixty-first* of the total⟩

¹sixty-five \⸗'⸗\ *adj* : being one more than 64 in number ⟨*sixty-five* years⟩ — see NUMBER table

²sixty-five \"\ *pron, pl in constr* : 65 countable persons or things not specified but under consideration and being enumerated ⟨*sixty-five* are here⟩ ⟨*sixty-five* were found⟩

³sixty-five \"\ *n* 1 : five and 60 : five times 13 2 a : 65 units or objects ⟨a total of *sixty-five*⟩ b : a group or set of 65 3 : the numerable quantity symbolized by the arabic numerals 65 4 : the 65th in a set or series

¹six·ty·fold \'sikstē'fōld\ *adj* [ME, fr. OE *sixtigfeald*, fr. *sixtig* sixty + -*feald* -fold — more at SIXTY] 1 : having 60 parts or aspects 2 : being 60 times as large, as great, or as many as some understood size, degree, or amount ⟨a ~ increase⟩

²sixtyfold \"\ *adv* : to 60 times as much or as many : by 60 times ⟨brought forth fruit, some an hundredfold, some ~, some thirtyfold —Mt 13: 8 (AV)⟩

¹sixty-four \⸗'⸗\ *adj* : being one more than 63 in number ⟨*sixty-four* years⟩ — see NUMBER table

²sixty-four \"\ *pron, pl in constr* : 64 countable persons or things not specified but under consideration and being enumerated ⟨*sixty-four* are here⟩ ⟨*sixty-four* were found⟩

³sixty-four \"\ *n* 1 : four and 60 : four times 16 : the square of 8 : the cube of 4 2 a : 64 units or objects ⟨a total of *sixty-four*⟩ b : a group or set of 64 3 : the numerable quantity symbolized by the arabic numerals 64 4 : the 64th in a set or series

sixty-four–dollar question *n* [so called fr. the fact that $64 was the highest award in the CBS radio quiz show "Take It or Leave It" (1941–48)] : a crucial question expressing the basic issue on a problematical subject

sixty-four-mo \⸗'⸗'⸗,mō\ *n* -s [*sixty-four* + -*mo*] : the size of a piece of paper cut 64 from a sheet; *also* : paper or a page of this size — abbr. *64mo*; symbol *64°*; see BOOK tables

¹sixty-fourth \⸗'⸗\ *adj* 1 : being number 64 in a countable series ⟨the *sixty-fourth* day⟩ — see NUMBER table 2 : being one of 64 equal parts into which something is divisible ⟨a *sixty-fourth* share of the money⟩

²sixty-fourth \"\ *n* 1 : number 64 in a countable series 2 : the quotient of a unit divided by 64 : one of 64 equal parts of something ⟨one *sixty-fourth* of the total⟩

sixty-fourth note *n* : a musical note with half the time value of a thirty-second note

sixty-fourth rest *n* : a musical rest corresponding in time value to the sixty-fourth note

six·ty·ish \'sikstēish, -ti·ish\ *adj* : approaching or being about 60 years old ⟨a tall thin ~ man⟩

sixty-fourth notes

¹sixty-nine \⸗'⸗\ *adj* : being one more than 68 in number ⟨*sixty-nine* years⟩ — see NUMBER table

²sixty-nine \"\ *pron, pl in constr* : 69 countable persons or things not specified but under consideration and being enumerated ⟨*sixty-nine* are here⟩ ⟨*sixty-nine* were found⟩

³sixty-nine \"\ *n* 1 : nine and 60 : three times 23 2 a : 69 units or objects ⟨a total of *sixty-nine*⟩ b : a group or set of 69 3 : the numerable quantity symbolized by the arabic numerals 69 4 : the 69th in a set or series 5 : SOIXANTE-NEUF

¹sixty-ninth \⸗'⸗\ *adj* 1 : being number 69 in a countable series ⟨the *sixty-ninth* day⟩ — see NUMBER table 2 : being one of 69 equal parts into which something is divisible ⟨a *sixty-ninth* share of the money⟩

²sixty-ninth \"\ *n* 1 : number 69 in a countable series 2 : the quotient of a unit divided by 69 : one of 69 equal parts of something ⟨one *sixty-ninth* of the total⟩

¹sixty-one \⸗'⸗\ *adj* : being one more than 60 in number ⟨*sixty-one* years⟩ — see NUMBER table

²sixty-one \"\ *pron, pl in constr* : 61 countable persons or things not specified but under consideration and being enumerated ⟨*sixty-one* are here⟩ ⟨*sixty-one* were found⟩

³sixty-one \"\ *n* 1 : one and 60 2 a : 61 units or objects ⟨a total of *sixty-one*⟩ b : a group or set of 61 3 : the numerable quantity symbolized by the arabic numerals 61 4 : the 61st in a set or series

six·ty-pen·ny nail \'⸗⸗,penē-\ *n* : a nail about 6 inches long

¹sixty-second \⸗'⸗\ *adj* 1 : being number 62 in a countable series ⟨the *sixty-second* day⟩ — see NUMBER table 2 : being one of 62 equal parts into which something is divisible ⟨a *sixty-second* share of the money⟩

²sixty-second \"\ *n* 1 : number 62 in a countable series 2 : the quotient of a unit divided by 62 : one of 62 equal parts of something ⟨one *sixty-second* of the total⟩

¹sixty-seven \⸗'⸗\ *adj* : being one more than 66 in number ⟨*sixty-seven* years⟩ — see NUMBER table

²sixty-seven \"\ *pron, pl in constr* : 67 countable persons or things not specified but under consideration and being enumerated ⟨*sixty-seven* are here⟩ ⟨*sixty-seven* were found⟩

³sixty-seven \"\ *n* 1 : seven and 60 2 a : 67 units or objects ⟨a total of *sixty-seven*⟩ b : a group or set of 67 3 : the numerable quantity symbolized by the arabic numerals 67 4 : the 67th in a set or series

¹sixty-seventh \⸗'⸗\ *adj* 1 : being number 67 in a countable series ⟨the *sixty-seventh* day⟩ — see NUMBER table 2 : being one of 67 equal parts into which something is divisible ⟨a *sixty-seventh* share of the money⟩

²sixty-seventh \"\ *n* 1 : number 67 in a countable series 2 : the quotient of a unit divided by 67 : one of 67 equal parts of something ⟨one *sixty-seventh* of the total⟩

¹sixty-six \⸗'⸗\ *adj* : being one more than 65 in number ⟨*sixty-six* years⟩ — see NUMBER table

²sixty-six \"\ *pron, pl in constr* : 66 countable persons or things not specified but under consideration and being enumerated ⟨*sixty-six* are here⟩ ⟨*sixty-six* were found⟩

³sixty-six \"\ *n* 1 : six and 60 : three times 22 : six times 11 2 a : 66 units or objects ⟨a total of *sixty-six*⟩ b : a group or set of 66 3 : the numerable quantity symbolized by the arabic numerals 66 4 : the 66th in a set or series 5 : a two-hand card game played with a 24-card pack in which the object is to score 66 of a possible 130 points

¹sixty-sixth \⸗'⸗\ *adj* 1 : being number 66 in a countable series ⟨the *sixty-sixth* day⟩ — see NUMBER table 2 : being one of 66 equal parts into which something is divisible ⟨a *sixty-sixth* share of the money⟩

²sixty-sixth \"\ *n* 1 : number 66 in a countable series 2 : the quotient of a unit divided by 66 : one of 66 equal parts of something ⟨one *sixty-sixth* of the total⟩

¹sixty-third \⸗'⸗\ *adj* 1 : being number 63 in a countable series ⟨the *sixty-third* day⟩ — see NUMBER table 2 : being one of 63 equal parts into which something is divisible ⟨a *sixty-third* share of the money⟩

²sixty-third \"\ *n* 1 : number 63 in a countable series 2 : the quotient of a unit divided by 63 : one of 63 equal parts of something ⟨one *sixty-third* of the total⟩

¹sixty-three \⸗'⸗\ *adj* : being one more than 62 in number ⟨*sixty-three* years⟩ — see NUMBER table

²sixty-three \"\ *pron, pl in constr* : 63 countable persons or things not specified but under consideration and being enumerated ⟨*sixty-three* are here⟩ ⟨*sixty-three* were found⟩

³sixty-three \"\ *n* 1 : three and 60 : three times 21 : seven times nine 2 a : 63 units or objects ⟨a total of *sixty-three*⟩ b : a group or set of 63 3 : the numerable quantity symbolized by the arabic numerals 63 4 : the 63d in a set or series

¹sixty-two \⸗'⸗\ *adj* : being one more than 61 in number ⟨*sixty-two* years⟩ — see NUMBER table

²sixty-two \"\ *pron, pl in constr* : 62 countable persons or things not specified but under consideration and being enumerated ⟨*sixty-two* are here⟩ ⟨*sixty-two* were found⟩

³sixty-two \"\ *n* 1 : two and 60 : 31 times two 2 a : 62 units or objects ⟨a total of *sixty-two*⟩ b : a group or set of 62 3 : the numerable quantity symbolized by the arabic numerals 62 4 : the 62d in a set or series

six-weeks grama *or* **six week grama** *n* [so called fr. its rapid growth] : any of various grama grasses (as *Bouteloua barbata*) of the western and southwestern U.S.

six-weeks grass *n* : any of several low quick-growing annual grasses (as *Poa annua*)

six-wheel·er \'⸗,⸗⸗(r)\ *n* : a vehicle (as a motor truck) with six wheels

si·yakh·push \sē'(y)ŭk,push\ *n, pl* **siyakhpush** *or* **siyakhpushes** *usu cap* : one of an early people of the southwestern Pamir region of Central Asia

siz·able *or* **size·able** \'sīzəbəl\ *adj* [²*size* + -*able*] 1 : of reasonable or suitable size or bulk : fairly large : CONSIDERABLE ⟨the settlement soon grew into a ~ community —Ray Millholland⟩ ⟨a ~ mud puddle —Ring Lardner⟩ 2 : LARGE ⟨a ~ man⟩ ⟨a pretty ~ chunk of votes —*Emporia* (Kans.) *Gazette*⟩

siz·able·ness *n* -ES : the quality or state of being sizable

siz·ably \-blē,-bli\ *adv* [*sizable* + -*ly*] : in a sizable manner : to a sizable degree

si·zal \'sīzəl\ *n* -s [alter. of *sisal*] : SISAL HEMP

siz·ar *also* **siz·er** \'sīzə(r)\ *n* -s [*sizar* alter. of *sizer; sizer* fr. ¹*size* (sense 2) + -*er*] : a student (as in the universities of Cambridge and Dublin) who receives orig. in return for acting as a servant to other students an allowance toward his college expenses — compare SERVITOR

siz·ar·ship \-,ship\ *n* : the position or standing of a sizar

¹size \'sīz\ *n* -s [ME *sise*, fr. MF, fr. OF, short for *assise* — more at ASSIZE] 1 *dial Brit* : ASSIZE 5a — usu. used in pl. 2 a *obs* : ASSIZE 3 b : a fixed portion of food or drink allowed esp. to a university student 3 a (1) : physical magnitude, extent, or bulk : the actual, characteristic, normal, or relative proportion of a thing : relative or proportionate dimensions ⟨measure the ~ of a box⟩ ⟨trees of all ~s⟩ ⟨attain full ~⟩ (2) : equal magnitude ⟨boys all of a ~⟩ b : relative aggregate amount ⟨the ~ of an order⟩ ⟨the ~ of her bank account⟩ c : considerable amount, proportions, volume, character, or importance : BIGNESS ⟨few of the fish attain any ~⟩ ⟨we saw no inhabited place of any ~ —Heinrich Harrer⟩ ⟨every town of ~ in the Balkans —*Christian Science Monitor*⟩ 4 a : one of a series of graduated measures esp. of manufactured articles (as of clothing) conventionally identified by numbers or letters each representing a particular dimension or set of dimensions ⟨a ~ 7 hat⟩ ⟨a shoe of ~ 4A⟩ ⟨~ B pajamas⟩ ⟨khaki breeches about two ~s too big —Danforth Ross⟩ ⟨book —~s⟩ ⟨rope —~s⟩ b (1) : an article of a particular size ⟨just fills this ~ of glass⟩ ⟨I prefer this ~⟩ (2) : one of a series of articles of graduated size ⟨shoe manufacturers make 72 —~s —*Women's Wear Daily*⟩ c : ²COUNT 8a 5 : character, quality, or status of a person or thing esp. with reference to importance, relative merit, or correspondence to needs ⟨the office demands a man of larger ~⟩ 6 a : actual state of affairs : true condition ⟨that's about the ~ of it⟩ b : true character or significance — used with *down* and *to* and usu. with *cut* or *chop* ⟨cut his opponent down to ~ by skillful questioning⟩

syn SIZE, DIMENSIONS, AREA, EXTENT, MAGNITUDE, VOLUME can signify, in common, the amount of space or, sometimes, time or energy occupied or used. SIZE usu. applies to things having length, width, and depth or height whether involving accurate measurements or merely a general impression of smallness or largeness; it often applies to things computed in terms of the individuals comprising them or the space occupied by the individuals or to things having qualities conceived of in terms of largeness or smallness ⟨as a voice⟩ ⟨a box two feet by three in *size*⟩ ⟨a house of small *size*⟩ ⟨the increase in the *size* of the reading public —Helen Sullivan⟩ ⟨his company ... has expanded under his management thus far to twice its original *size* in the number of its employees —*Current Biog.*⟩ ⟨the *size* of its power and potentialities —Rupert Emerson⟩ ⟨her remarkably clear and sweet voice is not of great *size* —*New Yorker*⟩ DIMENSIONS (pl. of *dimension*, a measurement in a single direction, as in width) is a close synonym of SIZE usu., however, implying more frequently an accurate measurement ⟨compute the exact *dimensions* of a building lot⟩ ⟨this book suggests the *dimensions* of the modern tasks of the federal government and of its chief executive —J.M.Blum⟩ ⟨the *dimensions* of the artist's genius —Herbert Read⟩ AREA applies to things measurable in two dimensions or directions only, for example, length and breadth ⟨as of the surface of the ground or a floor⟩ ⟨a parking lot with an *area* of 1500 square yards⟩ ⟨other lakes ... have an *area* of more than 10,000 acres —*Amer. Guide Series: Minn.*⟩ ⟨a relatively small population compared with the vast *area* served —*Canada Yr. Bk.*⟩ EXTENT chiefly applies to the measurement in one direction, usu. length (as of a driveway), often applying to something conceived of as if it had length; sometimes, however, it is used interchangeably with AREA or SIZE ⟨estimate to the *extent* of the territory from east to west⟩ ⟨the full *extent* of its extreme northern boundary —*Amer. Guide Series: Ariz.*⟩ ⟨a wide *extent* of territory —C.D.Forde⟩ ⟨the *extent* of his vocabulary —C.D.Lewis⟩ ⟨underestimate the *extent* of an enemy's vindictiveness⟩ MAGNITUDE, largely a mathematical and scientific term, may refer to size or two-dimensional extent or to something whose quantity, extent, or degree are expressible chiefly in mathematical figures ⟨a star of small *magnitude*⟩ ⟨an earthquake of sizable *magnitude* —Mary W. Shelley⟩ ⟨a European catastrophe of such appalling, and a scope so unpredictable —G.B.Shaw⟩ VOLUME, though sometimes close in meaning to SIZE, usu. refers to anything that can be measured in cubic measurements (as cubic feet) or is thought of in terms of cubic size ⟨the expanding air increased considerably the *volume* of the balloon⟩ ⟨the *volume* of the box⟩ ⟨a voice of small *volume*⟩ ⟨the *volume* of bank reserves —G.L.Harrison⟩ ⟨a much greater *volume* of credit —Rafael De Haro⟩ ⟨the *volume* of commercial airline passenger traffic —H.G.Armstrong⟩

— for size 1 : for the purpose of determining adequacy or proper fit — usu. used with *try* ⟨try on a hat *for size*⟩ ⟨try a dramatic role *for size*⟩ 2 : according to the various sizes ⟨these things are going to have to be separated *for size* —James Jones⟩ **— of a size** : of similar size ⟨the robin and the bluejay are much of *a size*⟩

²size \"\ *vb* -ED/-ING/-S [ME *sisen*, fr. *sise*, n.] *vt* 1 *archaic* : to fix the standard (as of weight, measure, or capacity) of : conform (something) to standard 2 *archaic* : to record (a portion of food or drink) as a financial obligation of a university student usu. by an appropriate entry in an account book : CHARGE 3 a : to make a particular class : bring to proper or suitable size ⟨... *sized* to fit anybody's living room —*advt*⟩ ⟨these cars are *sized* to the human frame, not to the human ego —Lewis Mumford⟩ ⟨they're *sized* for bill enclosure use —*Jewelers' Circular-Keystone*⟩ ⟨they ~ clothes to fit, not for children to grow into —Mary B. Picken⟩ ⟨chutes for dropping supplies are *sized* according to the weight of the load they are meant to carry —O.J.Mink⟩ b : COIN 1c 4 a : to arrange, grade, or classify according to size or bulk ⟨copper and nickel powders ... were *sized* by screening into the four ranges —*Symposium on Powder Metallurgy*⟩ b : to make in a series of graduated sizes conventionally identified by numbers or letters each representing a particular dimension or set of dimensions : grade (as clothing patterns) according to a set of specified measurements ⟨women's rings may be *sized* to 10; men's to 14 —*Sears, Roebuck Cat.*⟩ ⟨sport shirts *sized* to fit —*G. Fox & Co. Cat.*⟩ c : to check (as clothing) against patterns during manufacture 5 : to arrange (men) in units or formations according to stature ⟨first to ~ the corps of cadets —W.H. Baumer⟩ 6 : to size up ⟨could feel her listening, *sizing* me —Joseph Hitrec⟩ ~ *vi* 1 *archaic* : to order an allowance of food or drink from the buttery esp. of a university college 2 : to be equal in size, quality, power, or other particular characteristic : COMPARE — usu. used with *up* and often with *to* or *with* ⟨a yield that *sized* up very well with last year's⟩ 3 : to increase in size

³size \"\ *n* -s [ME *sise*, prob. fr. MF, setting, fixing, fr. OF, settlement, assize — more at ASSIZE] 1 a : any of various glutinous materials (as preparations of glue, flour, varnish, or resins) used for filling the pores in surfaces (as of paper, textiles, leather, or plaster) and in bookbinding for applying color or leaf to book edges or covers — compare GLAIR, GOLD SIZE

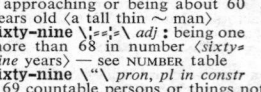

b : any material used in papermaking to prevent or retard the penetration of liquids **c :** the adhesive used in coating paper **2 :** a sticky substance used in place of ink when the printing is to be dusted with metallic powder

⁴size \ˈ"\ *vt* -ED/-ING/-S **1 :** to cover, stiffen, or glaze with or as if with size **:** treat with size **2 :** to compact (felt) by means of moisture, heat, and pressure esp. in hat making

⁵size *var of* SICE

⁶size \ˌsīz\ *adj* [¹*size*] **:** SIZED 1 — usu. used in combination ⟨has only a pond-*size* harbor —Christopher Rand⟩ ⟨conventional-*size* midtown blocks —Lewis Mumford⟩ ⟨the large economy-*size* box of a breakfast cereal⟩ ⟨bite-*size* candies⟩

sizeable *var of* SIZABLE

size block *n* **:** GAGE BLOCK

size bone *n* **:** a whalebone measuring six feet or more

sized \ˌsīzd\ *adj* [partly fr. ¹*size* + *-ed;* partly fr. past part. of ²*size*] **1 :** having a specified size or bulk — usu. used in combination ⟨a small-*sized* house⟩ ⟨a family-*sized* car⟩ ⟨a fair-*sized* crowd⟩ **2 :** arranged or adjusted according to size **3 a :** being up to standard in size **b :** of the same size

size down *vt* **:** to gradate or arrange from larger to smaller ⟨*size down* roofing slates from the eaves to the ridge⟩

size·man \ˈsīzmən\ *n, pl* **sizemen** [³*size* + *man*] **1 :** one who puts size on leather **2 :** a papermill worker who makes size

¹sizer *var of* SIZAR

²siz·er \ˈsīzə(r)\ *n* -S [²*size* + *-er*] **1 :** one that determines or sorts by sizes or checks for size ⟨an orange ~⟩ **2 :** one that shapes or surfaces articles to the required size ⟨timber ~⟩ **3 :** CLOCKER

³sizer \ˈ"\ *n* -S [⁴*size* + *-er*] **1 :** one that applies size **2 :** one that sizes felt hat bodies

sizer die *also* **sizing die** *n* **:** a die to finish threaded work to standard size

sizes *pl of* SIZE, *pres 3d sing of* SIZE

size stick *n* **:** a measuring stick or mechanical device used by shoe fitters to measure a wearer's foot from heel to toe or from heel to ball and the width of the foot at its widest point

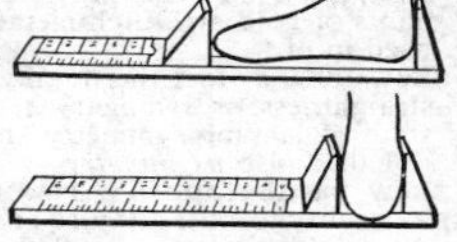

size stick

size up *vt* **:** to estimate or ascertain the character and ability of (a person) **:** form an opinion or judgment (as of a situation) ⟨*sizes up* the candidate quickly —W.L.Gresham⟩ ⟨at the stockyards the steers were *sized up* by two kinds of buyers —*advt*⟩ ⟨the power to *size up* a new problem —H.A. Overstreet⟩ ~ *vi* **:** to appear or be known as a result of being sized up ⟨here's the way the situation *sizes up* in key fields —*Newsweek*⟩ ⟨as the outlook *sizes up* . . . at this time —*U.S. News & World Report*⟩

size-up \ˈ≈,≈\ *n* -S [*size up*] **1 :** the action of sizing up (a person or thing) ⟨preventing a quick *size-up* of existing conditions —J.J.McCarthy⟩ **2 :** an evaluation arrived at by sizing up ⟨give a *size-up* of the applicants⟩

siz·i·ness \ˈsīzēnəs, -zin-\ *n* -ES *archaic* **:** the quality or state of being sizy **:** VISCOUSNESS

¹sizing *n* -S [fr. gerund of ²*size*] **1 :** the act or process of one that sizes **2 :** a fixed portion of food or drink ordered from the kitchen of an English university **3 sizings** *pl* **:** the coarsest particles of wheat endosperm broken out in the milling process **:** coarse middlings

²sizing *n* -S [fr. gerund of ⁴*size*] **:** ³SIZE

sizing tool *or* **sizing chisel** *n* **:** a wood-turning tool with a gauge clamped to it to determine the size of the wood turned

sizy \ˈsīzē, -zi\ *adj* -ER/-EST [³*size* + *-y*] *archaic* **:** VISCOUS, GLUTINOUS

¹sizz \ˈsiz\ *vi* -ED/-ING/-ES [prob. back-formation fr. ¹*sizzle*] **:** to hiss or to move with a hissing sound ⟨the bumblebee ~*ed* right under his straw hat —Feike Feikema⟩

²sizz \ˈ"\ *n* -ES **:** a hissing sound

¹siz·zle \ˈsizəl\ *vb* **sizzled; sizzled; sizzling** \-z(ə)liŋ\ **sizzles** [perh. freq. of *siss*] *vt* **1 :** to burn up or sear with scorching heat typically so as to produce a hissing sound ⟨the sun was beginning to ~ the whole wide valley —Richard Bissell⟩ **2 :** to affect painfully by heated language ⟨speakers *sizzled* the opposition⟩ ~ *vi* **1 a :** to make a hissing sound ⟨a dish of *sizzling* fat —Richard Llewellyn⟩ ⟨oil lamp which *sizzled* softly on his table —R.P.Warren⟩ ⟨powdery snow *sizzled* under their skis —Aldous Huxley⟩ ⟨only the desultory *sizzling* of some little bird —D.C.Peattie⟩ **b :** to produce the effect of making a hissing sound ⟨ink that ~*s* on the page —*Rotarian*⟩ ⟨everyone *sizzling* with enthusiasm —W.A.White⟩ ⟨the town *sizzled* with the news —Dorothy Parker⟩ **2 :** to move with or as if with a hissing sound ⟨lava *sizzling* down the snowy mountainside⟩ ⟨cars *sizzled* past us on the highway⟩ **3 :** to be in a state of partially repressed agitation caused esp. by deep anger or resentment ⟨*sizzling* because of the unsupported allegations⟩ **4 :** to perform or become performed at top form or in a noticeably improved manner ⟨the champion *sizzled* on the course today⟩ ⟨sales immediately began to ~⟩

²sizzle \ˈ"\ *n* -S **:** a hissing sound (as of something frying over a fire) ⟨there trailed in her wake a ~ of gossip —Marcia Davenport⟩

siz·zler \-z(ə)lə(r)\ *n* -S **:** one that sizzles; *esp* **:** SCORCHER

¹sizzling *adj* **:** that sizzles ⟨~ steaks⟩ ⟨a ~ commentary on investor psychology —Felix Belair⟩ ⟨~ political issues —J.A. Mayer⟩ **:** very hot ⟨a ~ spell of weather⟩ — **siz·zling·ly** *adv*

²sizzling *adv* **:** to a sizzling degree ⟨~ hot steaks⟩

sizzling heat *n* **:** a degree of heat (as about 400 to 450° F) that is approximately that of iron just hot enough to hiss when touched with a moistened finger

SJ *abbr, often not cap* [L *sub judice*] under consideration

sjam·bok \(ˈ)shamˌbäk, -ˈbək\ *n* -S [Afrik *sambok*, fr. Malay *cambok* large whip, fr. Hindi *cābuk* — more at CHAWBUCK] *southern Africa* **:** a heavy leather whip often of rhinoceros hide

SJC *abbr* Supreme Judicial Court

SJD \ˌesˌjāˈdē\ *abbr or n* -S [NL *scientiae juridicae doctor*] **:** a doctor of juridical science

sjo·gren·ite \ˈshōgrəˌnīt, ˈshə(r)g-\ *n* -S [Sw *sjögrenit*, fr. Hjalmar *Sjögren* †1922 Swed. mineralogist + Sw *-it* -ite] **:** a mineral $Mg_6Fe_2(OH)_{16}(CO_3).4H_2O$ consisting of a hydrous hydroxide and carbonate of magnesium and iron isomorphous with manasseite and barbertonite

sjt *abbr, often cap* serjeant

sk *abbr* **1** sack **2** sick **3** sink; sinking **4** sketch **5** skewbald **6** skewness **7** skip

SK *abbr* storekeeper

skaam·oog \ˈskäˌmōg\ *n* -S [Afrik, fr. *skaam* to be ashamed (fr. D *schamen*, fr. MD) + *oog* eye, fr. D, fr. MD *oge;* prob. fr. the habit of folding the tail over the head when caught; akin to OHG *ouga* eye — more at SHAME, EYE] *southern Africa* **:** a cat shark of the family Scyliorhinidae

skaapsteker *var of* SCHAAPSTEKER

skad *var of* SCAD

¹skaddle *var of* SCADDLE

²skad·dle \ˈskadᵊl\ *vi* -ED/-ING/-S [by alter.] *dial* **:** SKEDADDLE

skaff·ie \ˈskafi\ *n* -S [E dial. *skaff* light boat, skiff (fr. ME *skaf*, fr. MF *scaphe, escaffe*, fr. L *scapha*, fr. Gk *skaphē*) + E *-ie* — more at SCAPHOID] **:** a Scottish fishing boat having the stem raked and rounding and the stern raked and usu. main and mizzen dipping lugsails

¹skag *var of* SKEG

²skag \ˈskag, -a(ə)g, -aig\ *n* -S [origin unknown] *slang* **:** CIGARETTE

skag·it \ˈskajə̇t\ *n, pl* **skagit** *or* **skagits** *usu cap* **1 a :** a Salishan people of the Skagit and Stillaguamish river valleys, northwestern Washington **b :** a member of such people **2 :** a Salishan dialect often taken as representative of a group of dialects that includes also Nisqualli, Puyallup, Snoqualmie, Suquamish, and Swinomish

skaif *var of* SKEIF

skail *chiefly Scot var of* ⁴SCALE

skain *var of* SKEIN 1

skair \ˈskär\ *chiefly Scot var of* SCARE

skait \ˈskāt\ *archaic var of* ²SKATE, ³SKATE

skaith \ˈskāth\ *dial var of* SCATHE

skalawag *var of* SCALAWAG

skald *or* **scald** \ˈskȯld, ˈskäld\ *n* -S [ON *skāld* — more at SCOLD] **1 :** one of the ancient Scandinavian poets and historiographers **:** a Norse reciter and singer esp. of heroic poems and eulogies **2 :** a bard of an ancient Teutonic tribe

skald·ic *or* **scald·ic** \-dik, -dēk\ *adj* **:** of or relating to the Norse skalds or their poetry

skan·dhas \ˈskändəs\ *n pl* [Skt *skandha*] *Buddhism* **:** the five transitory personal elements of body, perception, conception, volition, and consciousness whose temporary concatenation forms the individual self

skarn \ˈskärn, kȧn\ *n* -S [Sw, lit., filth; akin to ON *skarn* dirt, dung — more at SCAT-] **:** contact metamorphic rock rich in iron

skart *var of* SCART

¹skat *or* **scat** \ˈskät, *usu* -äd.+V\ *n* -S [G, modif. of It *scarto* discard, fr. *scartare* to discard, fr. *s-* (fr. L *ex-*) + *-cartare* (fr. *carta* card) — more at CARD] **1 :** a three-handed card game played with 32 cards in which players bid for the privilege of attempting any of several contracts and value their hands according to the contract played, trump suit, points taken, and number of matadors **2 :** a widow of two cards in skat that may be used by the winner of the bid when various contracts are undertaken

²skat *var of* SCAT

¹skate \ˈskāt, *usu* -ād.+V\ *n, pl* **skates** *also* **skate** [ME *scate*, fr. ON *skata*] **1 :** any of numerous rays of *Raja* and related genera of the family Rajidae that have the pectoral fins greatly developed giving the animal a rhomboidal shape and that include the common gray skate (*Raja batis*) of Europe which sometimes weighs over 100 pounds and is extensively used as food, the barn-door skate, the little skate, and the thornback **2 a :** SKATE BOTTOM **b :** one of the units of gear making up a setline esp. in Pacific coast fisheries and consisting of several hundred fathoms of groundline with gangions and hooks attached — compare TUB

²skate \ˈ"\ *n* -S [modif. of D *schaats* skate, stilt, fr. MD *schaetse* stilt, fr. (assumed) ONF *escache* (akin to OF *eschace* stilt), perh. of Gmc origin; akin to OS *skakan* to depart — more at SHAKE] **1 a :** one of a pair of devices worn on the feet for skating on ice: as (1) **:** a shoe with a metal runner fastened to the sole — called also *ice skate;* see FIGURE SKATE, HOCKEY SKATE, RACING SKATE (2) **:** DOUBLE-RUNNER **b :** ROLLER SKATE **2** [³*skate*] **:** a period of skating ⟨went for a ~ on the pond⟩ **3 :** a sliding shoe fitting over a rail (as in a classification yard) to stop railroad cars not being retarded by brakes **4 :** a vertical fender (as a curved steel skid) fastened to the side of a ship's boat to fend it clear of the ship's side while lowering from davits on the high side of a listing ship

³skate \ˈ"\ *vb* -ED/-ING/-S *vi* **1 a :** to glide along on skates propelled by the alternate action of the legs **b :** to compete in a skating match ⟨picked to ~ against the visiting team⟩ **2 :** to slip or glide as if on skates ⟨bugs that ~ on top of the creek⟩ **3 :** to proceed in a superficial or venturesome manner (as over a dangerous subject) **:** pass lightly ⟨his ability deftly to ~ over subjects which Americans find unfit for mixed society — Ernest Beaglehole⟩ ~ *vt* **:** to go along or through by skating ⟨watched him ~ the length of the rink⟩ ⟨merely ~*s* the surface of the difficulties involved —*New Republic*⟩

⁴skate \ˈ"\ *n* -S [prob. alter. of ³*skite*] **1 :** a contemptible person ⟨these shyster ~*s* . . . just slip in like the boll weevil —*Tourist News*⟩ **2 :** a thin awkward-looking or decrepit horse **:** NAG **3 :** FELLOW ⟨the baseball throng beams upon the president and agrees that he is a pretty good ~ after all —*Los Angeles (Calif.) Examiner*⟩

skate·able \ˈskād.əbəl\ *adj* **:** suitable to skate on

skate barrow *n* **:** the egg case of a skate

skate bottom *n* **:** a square of canvas with a length of rope attached to each corner for storing a coiled skate of setline

skate machine *n* **:** a mechanism electrically controlled and electrically or pneumatically operated for placing a skate on or removing it from the rail

skate·mo·bile \ˈskātmōˌbēl\ *n* -S **:** a child's vehicle similar to a scooter moving on skates or skate wheels

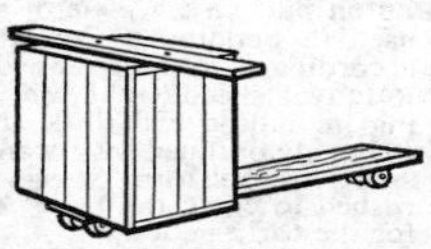

skatemobile

skat·er \ˈskād.ə(r), -ātə-\ *n* -S **1 :** one that skates **2 :** WATER STRIDER

skate sailing *n* **:** the sport of sailing on ice skates using a large sail attached to crossed sticks and held on the shoulders at an angle to the wind

skating *adj* **:** that is being skated upon or weighted ⟨the ~ foot⟩; *also* **:** that is on the same side of the body as the foot on which one is skating ⟨the ~ shoulder⟩ ⟨the ~ arm⟩

skating position *n* **:** a figure skating and folk dancing position in which partners are side by side with arms crossed in front and identical hands clasped

skat·ole *also* **skat·ol** *or* **scat·ole** \ˈskaˌtōl, -tȯl\ *n* -S [ISV *scat-* + *-ole*] **:** a crystalline compound C_9H_9N that has a disagreeable odor unless much diluted, that is found along with indole in the intestines and feces and also occurs in civet and several plants, but is usu. synthesized from propionaldehyde phenylhydrazone, and that is used in perfumes chiefly as a fixative; 3-methyl-indole

skatology *var of* SCATOLOGY

skaw *var of* SCAW

¹skean *or* **skeen** *or* **skene** *also* **skhian** \ˈs(h)kē(ə)n\ *n* -S [IrGael *scian* & ScGael *sgian;* ScGael *sgian* akin to IrGael *scian;* IrGael *scian* fr. MIr, knife; akin to OE *scēadan, scādan* to divide, separate — more at SHED] **:** DAGGER, DIRK **: a :** a bronze double-edged dagger anciently used in Ireland **b :** SKEAN DHU

²skean *or* **skeane** *var of* SKEIN

skean dhu \-ˈthü\ *n, pl* **skean dhus** [ScGael *sgian dubh*, lit., black skean] **:** a dagger worn by Scottish Highlanders in full dress

skean·ock·le *also* **skene·oc·cle** \ˈskēˌnäkəl\ *n* -S [ScGael *sgian-achlais*, fr. *sgian* skean + *achlais* armpit; akin to L *axilla* armpit — more at AXIS] *Scot* **:** a small dirk

skeat *var of* SCEAT

¹sked \ˈsked\ *n* -S [by shortening & alter.] **:** SCHEDULE

²sked \ˈ"\ *vt* **skedded; skedded; skedding; skeds** [by shortening & alter.] **:** SCHEDULE — **sked·der** \-də(r)\ *n* -S

¹ske·dad·dle \skəˈdadᵊl, skēˈ-\ *vi* **skedaddled; skedaddled; skedaddling** \-d(ᵊ)liŋ\ **skedaddles** [origin unknown] **:** to run away **:** leave hastily; *specif* **:** to take flight in a panic — **ske·dad·dler** \-d(ᵊ)lə(r)\ *n* -S

²skedaddle \ˈ"\ *n* -S **:** the act of skedaddling

skedge \ˈskej\ *also* **skedge·with** \-ˌwith\ *n* -S [Corn *skeswedhen, skeswŷth*, lit., shade tree, fr. *skēs* shade + *gwedhen, gwŷth* tree; akin to OIr *scāth* shadow and to OIr *fid* tree — more at SHADE, WOOD] **:** PRIVET 1a(1)

sked·lock \ˈskedˌläk, -dlək\ *n* [alter. of Sc *skeldock*] **:** JOINTED CHARLOCK

skee *var of* SKI

Skee–Ball \ˈ≈,≈\ *trademark* — used for an indoor target game in which a series of hard rubber balls are rolled along a slightly inclined wooden alley whose far end is curved upward so as to project the wall up and backward into one of several concentric circular scoring troughs whose score values increase as the circles decrease in size

skeel \ˈskēl, *esp before pause or consonant* -ēəl\ *n* -S [ME *skele*, of Scand origin; akin to ON *skjōla* pail, bucket; akin to OFris *skūl* hiding place — more at SHIEL] *dial chiefly Brit* **:** a wooden pail, bucket, or tub usu. having handles formed by staves extending above the rim

skeel·ing \ˈskēlən, -liŋ\ *or* **skil·ling** \ˈskil-\ *n* -S [ME *skelyng*, fr. *skel-* (of Scand origin; akin to ON *skjōl* shelter, cover) + *-inge, -ing, -yng -ing* — more at SHIEL] *dial Brit* **:** an outbuilding attached like a lean-to to another

skeely \ˈskēlē\ *archaic var of* SKILLY

skeen *var of* SKEAN

skeen arch *var of* SCHEME ARCH

¹skeet \ˈskēt, *usu* -ēd.+V\ *n* -S [ME *skete*] **:** a scoop on the end of a long pole formerly used for throwing water on the sails of a ship to tighten the canvas

²skeet \ˈ"\ *vb* -ED/-ING/-S [prob. alter. of ¹*scoot*] *vi* **1** *dial* **:** to move along quickly **:** SCOOT ⟨when you ~*ed* across the field —P.E.Green⟩ **2** *dial* **:** to cause a liquid to squirt ~ *vt, dial* **:** to cause to move along quickly or squirt ⟨you ~*ed* the water right in my ear —Carson McCullers⟩

³skeet \ˈ"\ *or* **skeet shooting** *n* -S [modif. of ON *skjōta* to shoot — more at SHOOT] **:** trapshooting in which clay targets are thrown in such a way as to simulate the angles of flight found in wing shooting

⁴skeet \ˈ"\ *n* -S [origin unknown] **:** a special hand recognized in some poker games that is composed of 9, 5, 2, and two other cards below the ten in rank (as 9, 6, 5, 3, 2) and no pair and that beats three of a kind but loses to a straight — called also *kilter, pelter*

¹skeet·er \ˈskēd.ə(r), -ētə-\ *n* -S [by shortening & alter.] **1 :** MOSQUITO **2 :** a small iceboat approximately 16 feet in length equipped with a single sail, a single steering runner in the front, and two runners in the rear

²skeeter \ˈ"\ *n* -S [³*skeet* + *-er*] **:** a skeet shooter

skee trap *n* [perh. so called fr. the resemblance of the trajectories of the targets to those of ski jumpers] **:** a trap used in trap and skeet shooting that is mounted in such a way as to make possible its inclination at any desired horizontal or vertical angle before the target is thrown — called also *joker trap*

skee·zicks *or* **skee·sicks** *or* **skee·zix** \ˈskēziks\ *n* -ES [origin unknown] **:** RASCAL ⟨you little ~⟩

skeg \ˈskeg\ *also* **skag** \ˈskag, -a(ə)g, -aig\ *n* -S [D *scheg, schegge;* akin to ON *skaga* to project — more at SHAG] **1 :** the afterpart of the keel of a vessel near the sternpost or a part in extension of the keel upon which the rudder rests; *esp* **:** the part connecting the keel with the bottom of the rudderpost in a single-screw vessel **2 :** the vertical triangular piece taking the place of the afterpart of a keel in a flat-bottomed boat **3 :** a protecting part that projects below the propeller of an outboard motor

skeg·ger \ˈskegə(r)\ *n* -S [origin unknown] **:** a young salmon

skeif *also* **skaif** \ˈskīf, -kāf\ *n* -S [D *schijf* skeif, disk; akin to OHG *scība* disk — more at SHEAVE] **:** a diamond cutter's polishing wheel

skeigh \ˈskēk\ *adj* [perh. of Scand origin; akin to Sw *skygg* shy — more at SHY] *chiefly Scot* **:** proudly spirited **:** SKITTISH — often used of a horse or a woman

skeily *var of* SKILLY

¹skein \ˈskān\ *n* -S [ME *skeyne, skayne*, fr. MF *escaigne*] **1** *or* **skean** *or* **skeane** \ˈ"\ **:** a loosely coiled length of yarn or thread wound on a reel in lengths suitable for a manufacturing process (as dyeing) or for sale as knitting wool or embroidery floss; *also* **:** such a bundle containing a given amount — compare HANK **2 :** something suggesting the twistings and contortions of a skein ⟨unravel the tangled ~ of evidence⟩ **3 :** a flock of wild fowl (as geese or ducks) in flight — compare GAGGLE **4 :** SPIREME

²skein \ˈ"\ *vt* -ED/-ING/-S **:** to wind into skeins

³skein \ˈskān\ *n* -S [D *scheen* narrow strip, shin, fr. MD *schene* — more at SHIN] **1** *also* **skain** \ˈ"\ **:** a trimmed strip of osier made from splits for basketwork **2 :** a metal thimble on an axletree arm

skein·er \ˈskānə(r)\ *n* -S **:** one that skeins: as **a :** an operator of a machine for winding thread, yarn, or twine into skeins **b :** a worker who winds unfinished cloth into skein form for boiling off

skel·der \ˈskeldə(r)\ *vb* -ED/-ING/-S [origin unknown] *vi, archaic* **:** to live by begging **:** BEG ~ *vt* **1** *archaic* **:** to obtain money from by fraud **:** CHEAT **2** *archaic* **:** to obtain (money) dishonestly

skel·et \ˈskelə̇t\ *n* -S [Gk *skeletos*, fr. *skeletos*, adj.] *archaic* **:** SKELETON

skelet- *or* **skeleto-** *comb form* [NL, fr. *skeleton*] **1 :** skeleton ⟨*skeleto*cyte⟩ **2 :** skeletal and ⟨*skeleto*muscular⟩

skel·e·tal \ˈskeləd.ᵊl, -lətᵊl\ *adj* [*skelet-* + *-al*] **1 :** of or relating to a skeleton ⟨~ material of the mound builders is abundant in many localities —Thomas Barbour⟩ **2 :** having the character of a skeleton, framework, or outline **:** SKELETON ⟨a large red and green buoy, with a ~ body like a derrick —Wirt Williams⟩ ⟨no more than a ~ survey of the life of the university —F.C.James⟩ **3 :** resembling a skeleton; *esp* **:** EMACIATED ⟨a nightmare population of gaunt men and ~ boys —Sydney Alexander⟩ **4** *of a soil* **:** belonging to the lithosol group and composed chiefly of rock fragments — **skel·e·tal·ly** \-ᵊlē, -ᵊli\ *adv*

skeletal muscle *n* **:** a muscle attached to the skeleton — distinguished from *smooth muscle* and *cardiac muscle*

skel·e·tog·e·nous \ˌskeləˈtäjənəs\ *adj* [*skelet-* + *-genous*] **:** forming skeletal tissue **:** OSTEOGENIC

skel·e·to·muscular \ˌskeləd.(ˌ)ō, -ə(ˌ)tō+\ *adj* [*skelet-* + *muscular*] **:** constituting, belonging to, or dependent upon the skeleton and the muscles that move it ⟨~ activity⟩ ⟨~ structures⟩

¹skel·e·ton \ˈskelətᵊn\ *n* -S [NL, fr. Gk, neut. of *skeletos* dried up, withered; akin to OE *sceald* shallow, *hellheort* terrified, MLG *schal* dull, clouded, insipid, MHG *hel* weak, Sw *skäll* watery, ON *hallæri* bad season, famine, Gk *skellein* to dry up, *sklēros* hard, harsh, stiff] **1 :** a supportive or protective structure or framework of an animal, a plant, or a part of an animal or plant: as **a :** the bones of a human being or other vertebrate; *broadly* **:** the bony or more or less cartilaginous framework supporting the soft tissues and protecting the internal organs **b :** any of various analogous structures in an invertebrate (as the mesh of spicules of a sponge, the shell of a brachiopod or mollusk, or the chitinous or partially calcareous covering of an arthropod) — see ENDOSKELETON, EXOSKELETON **c :** a rigid protective covering of a lower plant (as the frustule of a diatom) **d :** the vascular system of a vascular plant and esp. of an herbaceous plant or leaf in which it is a framework readily separable (as by weathering or retting) ⟨the lacy ~ of a leaf⟩ **2 :** something reduced to its minimum form or essential parts **3 :** an emaciated person or animal **4 :** something forming a structural framework: as **a :** the basic structure of a creative work (as a play) **b :** a written plan for a literary work having headings for main divisions **:** OUTLINE **c :** a rigidly connected frame of steel or reinforced concrete used in the construction of tall buildings that supports the external wall and distributes all loads and stresses to the foundation **d :** the framework of a molecular structure comprising a straight or branched chain or ring of atoms to which other atoms may be attached — compare NUCLEUS 2j, RING SYSTEM ⟨the carbon ~ of isoleucine⟩ **5 :** something shameful and kept secret (as in a family) — often used in the phrases *skeleton in the closet, skeleton in the cupboard* **6 :** a heavy steel-runnered sled capable of great speed and steered only by dragging the feet and shifting one's weight and used by Alpine tobogganers **7 :** the disposition of the pawns in a chess position — **skeleton at the feast :** someone or something that serves to bring unpleasant memories or prospects to the minds of pleasure-seekers

²skeleton \ˈ"\ *vt* -ED/-ING/-S **:** SKELETONIZE

³skeleton \ˈ"\ *adj* **1 :** of or having the character of a skeleton ⟨a ~ hand⟩; *specif* **:** having only the minimum form or essential parts ⟨a ~ plan⟩ ⟨a ~ wagon⟩ **2 :** consisting of the smallest number of persons who can care for an establishment and do essential work ⟨a ~ crew⟩ ⟨a ~ staff⟩ **3 :** of a structure having open interior parts ⟨a ~ spade⟩; *specif* **:** of or being a movement, dial, or timepiece with all but essential metal framework removed in order to allow the works to be observed **4** *of clothing* **:** PARTIAL ⟨a ~ lining⟩

skeleton chase *n* **:** a large narrow-framed printer's chase with no crossbars or slots for crossbars

skeleton construction *n* **:** a method of constructing high buildings in which the chief horizontal and vertical members are of rolled steel and the walls are for the most part supported at the floor levels by the steel frame itself

skeleton crystal *n* **:** an imperfect crystal arrested in development after the forming of the outline but before the filling in of the faces

skeleton dance *n* **:** a ceremonial dance in which dancers are costumed to represent skeletons or death; *also* **:** the dance of death in European folklore

skeleton form *n* **1 :** a form with limited printing areas (as used in printing blankbooks) **2 :** a form with scattered printing areas for printing a second color

skel·e·ton·ic \ˌskeləˈtänik\ *adj* **:** resembling or resembling that of a skeleton
skel·e·ton·iza·tion \ˌ==tᵊnəˈzāshən, -tᵊn,īˈz-\ *n* -s **:** the act or process of skeletonizing
skel·e·ton·ize \ˈ==tᵊn,īz\ *vb* -ED/-ING/-S *vt* **:** to produce in or reduce to skeleton form or strength ⟨~ a leaf⟩: as **a** (1) **:** to produce or reproduce in brief outline ⟨~ the plot of a novel in one paragraph⟩ (2) **:** to shorten (newspaper copy) for cable or headline purposes by eliminating nonessential words (as articles, personal pronouns) **b :** to reduce (as a regiment) to a number of men and officers far below the complement ⟨machinery was put in motion to bring men home early for discharge, to start *skeletonizing* units —T.R.Phillips⟩ **c :** to break up for colors **~** *vi* **1 :** to produce or reproduce something in skeleton form **2 :** to become a skeleton or like a skeleton
skel·e·ton·iz·er \-zə(r)\ *n* -s **:** one that skeletonizes; *specif* **:** any of various lepidopterous larvae that eat the parenchyma of leaves leaving the skeleton of veins and the upper or lower epidermis
skeleton key *n* **:** a key with a large part of the bit filed away so as to avoid the wards and thus enable it to open a low quality lock by manipulation

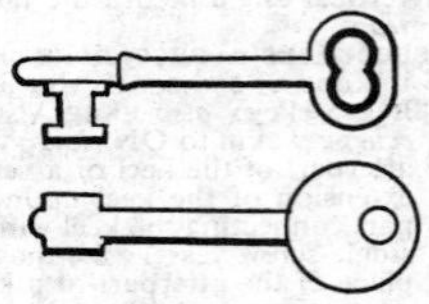
skeleton keys

skel·e·ton·less \ˈ===ləs\ *adj* **:** having no skeleton
skeleton pattern *n* **:** a pattern constructed in skeleton form in whose open spaces sand is inserted
skeleton proof *n* **:** a proof of a print or engraving with the inscription in hair strokes only
skeletons *pl of* SKELETON, *pres 3d sing of* SKELETON
skeleton shrimp *n* **:** an amphipod crustacean of *Caprella* or a related genus
skeleton suit *n* **:** a boy's tight-fitting suit with the trousers buttoned to the jacket worn in the 19th century
skeleton weed *n* **1 :** GUM SUCCORY **2 a :** a central No. American perennial composite weed (*Lygodesmia pincea*) with rosy purple flower heads on leafless rushlike stems that rise from a basal tufted rosette of elongated leaves — called also *purple skeleton weed* **b :** any of several other plants of the genus *Lygodesmia*
skel·e·tony \ˈskelətᵊnē\ *adj* **:** SKELETONIC
skelets *pl of* SKELET
¹skelf \ˈskelf\ *Scot var of* SHELF
²skelf \"\ *n* [perh. fr. ScGael *sgealb*] *Scot* **:** SLIVER, SPLINTER
skelic index \ˈskelik-\ *n* [*skelic* fr. Gk *skelos* leg + E *-ic* — more at CYLINDER] **:** an anthropometric index consisting of the ratio of the length of the leg to the length of the trunk multiplied by 100
skel·lat \ˈskelət\ *n* [ME (northern dial.) *skellet*, fr. ONF *escalete*, fr. *esquelle* small bell (of Gmc origin; akin to OHG *scella* small bell) + OF *-ete* -ette; akin to OHG *scellan* to resound, ring — more at SHILL] **1** *Scot* **:** a small bell; *esp* **:** HANDBELL **2** *Scot* **:** a shrewish woman
skel·ling·ton \ˈskeliŋtən\ *n* -s [by alter. (influence of names such as *Washington, Uffington*)] **:** SKELETON
¹skel·loch \ˈskelək\ *n* [prob. imit.] *Scot* **:** SCREECH, SCREAM
²skelloch \"\ *vi* -ED/-ING/-S *Scot* **:** SCREAM
skel·lum \ˈskeləm\ *n* -s [D *schelm*, fr. LG, fr. MLG, scoundrel, corpse, carrion; akin to OHG *skelmo* person deserving death, *scalmo* pestilence, corpse, and prob. to Lith *skelti* to split — more at SHELL] *chiefly Scot* **:** SCOUNDREL, SCAMP, RASCAL ⟨that ~ of a boy⟩
skel·ly \ˈskeli\ *n* -ES [prob. of Scand origin; akin to ON *skjalgr* wry, squinting — more at CYLINDER] *chiefly dial* **:** SQUINT
¹skelp \ˈskelp\ *vb* **skelped** \-pt\ *also* **skel·pit** \-pət\ **skelped** *also* **skelpit; skelping; skelps** [ME *skelpen*, prob. of imit. origin] *vt* **1** *dial Brit* **:** STRIKE, SLAP, BEAT **2** *dial Brit* **:** to drive with blows **3** *dial Brit* **:** to perform or accomplish in a brisk and lively fashion **~** *vi* **:** to walk in a brisk and lively manner **:** HUSTLE
²skelp \"\ *n* -S [ME, fr. *skelpen*, v.] *dial Brit* **:** a smart blow; *esp* **:** a slap with the palm of the hand
³skelp \"\ *n* -S [perh. fr. ScGael *sgealb* splinter, strip of wood] **:** a strip of metal (as wrought iron, steel) for making a hollow cylindrical piece or tube by bending it round longitudinally or helically and welding
⁴skelp \"\ *vt* -ED/-ING/-S **1 :** to form (as a plate or bar of iron) into a skelp by rolling **2 :** to bend round (a skelp) in tube making
⁵skelp \"\ *dial var of* SCALP
skelp·er \-pə(r)\ *n* -S **:** one that skelps
¹skelping *adj* [fr. pres. part. of ¹*skelp*] *chiefly Scot* **:** unusually large or outstanding of its kind
²skelping \"\ *n* -S [fr. gerund of ¹*skelp*] *dial* **:** WHIPPING, BEATING
¹skel·ter \ˈskeltə(r)\ *vi* -ED/-ING/-S [fr. *-skelter* (in *helter-skelter*)] **:** to run helter-skelter **:** SCURRY
²skelter \"\ *n* -S *chiefly dial* **:** a bustling rush
skel·to·nian \(ˈ)skelˈtōnēən, -nyən\ *adj, usu cap* [John *Skelton* †1529 Eng. poet + E *-an*] **:** SKELTONIC
skel·ton·ic \(ˈ)skelˈtänik\ *or* **skel·ton·i·cal** \-nəkəl\ *adj, usu cap* [John *Skelton* + E *-ic* or *-ical*] **:** of, relating to, or characteristic of the English poet John Skelton, his writings, or Skeltonics
skel·ton·ics \skelˈtäniks\ *n pl, usu cap* **:** short verses of an irregular meter much used by John Skelton having two or three stresses arranged sometimes in falling and sometimes in rising rhythm and usu. rhymed in couplets
sken \ˈsken\ *vi* **skenned; skenned; skenning; skens** [origin unknown] *dial Eng* **:** SQUINT
¹skene *var of* SKEAN
²ske·ne \ˈskē(,)nē\ *n, pl* **ske·nai** \-,nī\ [Gk *skēnē* — more at SCENE] **:** the structure in an ancient Greek theater behind the orchestra facing the cavea and being often of stone and of two stories of which the lower projects toward the orchestra, forms the proscenium, and serves as a background to the play — compare SCENE 4; see THEATER illustration
skene arch *var of* SCHEME ARCH
skeneoccle *var of* SKEANOCKLE
skeo \ˈskyō\ *n* -S [of Scand origin; akin to Norw *skjå* shed; akin to ON *skjōl* shelter, cover — more at SHIEL] **:** a shed of loose stones formerly used in the Shetland and Orkney islands for drying fish and meat
skep \ˈskep\ *n* -S [ME *skeppe* skep, skepful, fr. OE *sceppe* skepful, fr. ON *skeppa* bushel; akin to OHG *sceffil* bushel — more at SCHEPEL] **1 a :** a coarse round farm basket **b** *or* **skep·ful** \-fəl\ (1) **:** the quantity held by a skep (2) **:** any of various old units of capacity based on this quantity **2 :** BEEHIVE; *esp* **:** a domed hive made of twisted straw
skep·sis *also* **scep·sis** \ˈskepsəs\ *n* -ES [NL, fr. Gk *skepsis* examination, doubt, skeptical philosophy, fr. *skeptesthai* to look, consider] **:** philosophic doubt as to the objective reality of phenomena; *broadly* **:** a skeptical outlook or attitude
skep·tic *or* **scep·tic** \ˈskeptik, -tēk\ *n* -S [L or Gk; L *scepticus*, fr. Gk *skeptikos*, pl. *skeptikos* thoughtful, reflective, fr. (assumed) Gk *skeptos* (verbal of Gk *skeptesthai* to look, consider) + Gk *-ikos* -ic — more at SPY] **1 a :** one who believes the doctrine of skepticism or employs skepticism as a method **b** *usu cap* **:** a member of one of the ancient schools (as the Sophists) teaching skepticism **2 :** one who is disposed to or is in a state of skepticism **:** a doubting or incredulous person **3 :** a person marked by skepticism regarding religion or religious principles
skep·ti·cal \-tәkәl, -tēk-\ *adj* **1 :** of, relating to, or characteristic of a skeptic or skepticism ⟨~ arguments⟩ **2 :** characterized by skepticism ⟨a ~ listener⟩ ⟨a ~ look⟩ — **skep·ti·cal·ly** \-tәk(ә)lē, -tēk-, li\ *adv* — **skep·ti·cal·ness** \-kәlnәs\ *n* -ES
skep·ti·cism \-tә,sizәm\ *n* -S [NL *scepticismus*, fr. L *scepticus* skeptic + *-ismus* -ism] **1 a :** the doctrine that any true knowledge is impossible or that all knowledge is uncertain **:** a position that no fact or truth can be established on philosophical grounds ⟨total or radical ~⟩ **b :** a viewpoint that universally reliable knowledge is unattainable in particular areas of investigation ⟨theoretical or scientific ~⟩ ⟨moral ~⟩ ⟨metaphysical ~⟩ ⟨religious ~⟩ **c :** the method of suspended judgment, systematic doubt, or destructive criticism characteristic of skeptics — compare DOGMATISM, HUMISM, SOPHISM **2 :** an attitude of doubt or disposition towards incredulity in general or in regard to something particular (as a supposed fact) **3 :** doubt concerning but not necessarily denial of the basic religious principles (as immortality, providence, revelation) **:** FREETHINKING — compare AGNOSTICISM **syn** see UNCERTAINTY
skep·ti·cize \-,sīz\ *vi* -ED/-ING/-S **:** to indulge in skepticism
sker·rick \ˈskerik\ *n* -S [perh. irreg. fr. ¹*scar* (clinker)] *chiefly Austral* **:** the least bit **:** SEMBLANCE, TRACE ⟨not a ~ of food left over⟩
¹sker·ry \ˈskerē\ *n* -ES [origin unknown] *archaic* **:** a punt seating two
²skerry \"\ *n* -ES [of Scand origin; akin to ON *sker* skerry and to ON *ey* island — more at SCAR, ISLAND] **:** an insular rock or reef (as along the coast of Scotland or Scandinavia) **:** a rocky isle
¹sketch \ˈskech\ *n* -ES [D *schets*, fr. It *schizzo* sketch, splash, fr. *schizzare* to splash, squirt, prob. of imit. origin] **1 a :** a rough drawing representing the chief features of an object or scene and often made as a preliminary study **b :** a tentative draft or preliminary study (as for a literary work or musical composition) **2 :** a brief description (as of a person) or outline ⟨his ~ of the little born flirt devastating the hearts of the male cherubs at a children's ball —C.E.Montague⟩ ⟨a ~ of the rise of human culture —Benjamin Farrington⟩ **3 :** a short or slight creative work: **a :** a short literary composition somewhat resembling the short story and the essay but less formal and pointed than these and usu. intentionally slight in treatment, discursive in style, and familiar in tone **b :** a short instrumental composition usu. for piano **c :** a slight theatrical piece having a single scene; *esp* **:** a comic often burlesque variety or vaudeville act typically developed around a mishap or misunderstanding and involving a small cast or a single performer **4 :** a person peculiar or amusing in his actions or speech **syn** see COMPENDIUM
²sketch \"\ *vb* -ED/-ING/-ES *vt* **1 :** to draw, describe, or outline the chief features of **:** make a sketch of **:** ROUGH ⟨can ~ the look and attitude of a man in a few pithy sentences —Harry Hansen⟩ — often used with *in* or *out* ⟨the background is rapidly ~*ed* in, and only enough of it to serve as setting for the story itself —R.A.Hall b.1911⟩ ⟨it is the purpose of this paper to ~ out the broad outline of some of the areas within which research is under way —D.P.Cartwright⟩ **2 :** to execute in a superficial manner **:** do or make sketchily **:** SIMULATE ⟨his mother ~*ed* a hurried, amazed sign of the cross over her breast —Kay Cicellis⟩ **~** *vi* **1 :** to draw or paint a sketch ⟨docks where artists come to ~⟩ **2 :** to act in or as if in a theatrical sketch
sketchbook \ˈ=,=\ *n* **1 :** a published collection of literary sketches **2 :** a book containing drawing paper for sketches **3 :** a notebook of preliminary sketches
sketch·er \ˈskechə(r)\ *n* -S **1 :** one that sketches; *specif* **:** one that sketches designs for stage sets **2 :** LETTERER d
sketch·i·ly \-chəlē, -li\ *adv* **:** in a sketchy manner ⟨the spoon . . . having been only ~ washed —David Fairchild⟩
sketch·i·ness \-chēnəs, -chin-\ *n* -ES **:** the quality or state of being sketchy ⟨alarmed at the ~ of . . . security measures —Christopher Rand⟩
sketch map *n* **:** an outline map drawn from observation rather than from exact survey measurements and showing only the main features of the area
sketchmaster \ˈ=,==\ *n* **:** an instrument operating on the principle of the camera lucida and used for superimposing an image of an aerial photograph on a map
sketch plan *n* **:** a preliminary plan that is less detailed than a working drawing
sketch plate *n* **:** a plate of steel or iron of nonstandard shape used in building a ship and ordered from the rolling mill according to a dimensioned sketch
sketchy \ˈskechē, -chi\ *adj* -ER/-EST **1 :** depicting or describing in outline with little detail **:** of the nature of a sketch **:** roughly outlined **2 :** wanting in completeness, clearness, or substance **:** SLIGHT, SUPERFICIAL ⟨gulped a ~ breakfast and rushed to catch the train⟩ ⟨found only the *sketchiest* records for the early period⟩
ske·te \skäˈtē\ *n* -S [NGk *skētē*, fr. LGk *Skitis, Skētis*, desert in northern Egypt once famous for its many hermitages] **:** a settlement of Eastern Orthodox monks inhabiting a group of small cottages around a church and dependent upon a parent monastery
skeu·o·morph \ˈskyüə,mȯrf\ *n* -S [Gk *skeuos* vessel, implement + E *-morph*; akin to OE *hēgan* to perform, achieve, ON *heyja* to perform, and prob. to Russ *kutit'* to carouse] **:** an ornament or design representing a utensil or implement — **skeu·o·mor·phic** \ˌ==ˈmȯrfik\ *adj*
skev·ish \ˈskevish\ *n* -ES [origin unknown] **:** a No. American fleabane (*Erigeron philadelphicus*) with a hairy stem, spatulate toothed leaves, and corymbose or paniculate heads of showy pinkish purple flowers — called also *Philadelphia fleabane*
¹skew \ˈskyü\ *n* -S [ME, coping stone on a masonry gable, fr. AF *escu*, fr. OF, shield — more at ECU] *chiefly Scot* **:** a coping or coping stone on a masonry gable
²skew \"\ *vb* -ED/-ING/-S [ME *skewen* to skew, escape, fr. ONF *escuer* to shun, avoid, of Gmc origin; akin to OHG *sciuhen* to frighten off, make timid — more at SHY] *vi* **1 :** to take an oblique direction or course **:** move or turn aside **:** TWIST, SWERVE ⟨~*s* around in his chair⟩ **2 :** to look sideways or askance **~** *vt* **1 :** to make, set, or cut on the skew **:** turn or place at an angle **2 :** to give a bias or disproportionate weight to **:** DISTORT ⟨the list is badly ~*ed* in favor of the subjects with which I myself feel most at home —Bonaro W. Overstreet⟩ **3 :** to cause (a frequency distribution or its graphic curve) to lack symmetry
³skew \"\ *adj* **1 :** deviating from a straight line **:** set, placed, or running obliquely **:** DISTORTED, SLANTING **2 :** more developed on one side or in one direction than another; *specif* **:** lacking statistical symmetry ⟨for a symmetrical distribution the median is identical with the arithmetic mean, but for a ~ distribution it is not —*Statistical Methods in Research & Production*⟩
⁴skew \"\ *n* -S **1 :** a deviation from a straight line **:** an oblique course or direction **:** SLANT ⟨wearing her hat on the ~⟩ **2 :** deviation from rectangularity ⟨detects the ~ in cloth and controls the operation which straightens it —*Newsweek*⟩
⁵skew \"\ *vt* -ED/-ING/-S [origin unknown] **:** to remove loose particles of gold or silver leaf from with a soft brush
⁶skew \"\ *n* [origin unknown] *dial Eng* **:** a sudden gusty drizzle of rain
skew aileron *or* **skewed aileron** *n* **:** an aileron whose hinge line is set at an angle to the lateral axis of the airplane
skew arch *n* **:** an arch whose jambs are not at right angles with the face
skewback \ˈ=,=\ *n* -S **1 :** a course of masonry, a stone, or an iron plate having an inclined face against which the voussoirs of a segmental arch abut **2 :** a plate, cap, or shoe with an inclined face to receive the nut of a diagonal brace or rod in a truss or frame

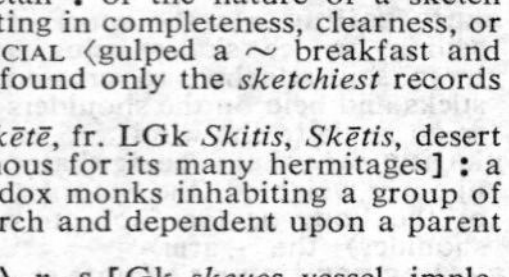

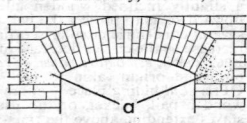

a skewbacks 1

¹skew·bald \ˈskyü,=\ *adj* [*skew-* (fr. *skewed*) + *bald*] *of an animal* **:** marked with spots and patches of white and some other color — used esp. of horses and sometimes distinguished from *piebald* when the latter is restricted to cases in which the colors are white and black **syn** see VARIEGATED
²skewbald \"\ *n* -S **:** a skewbald horse
skew bevel gear *or* **skew gear** *n* **:** a bevel gear in which the axes lie in different planes
skew bridge *n* **:** a bridge built obliquely from bank to bank
skew chisel *n* **:** a turning chisel with a straight cutting edge at an angle to the shank
skew curve *n* **:** SPACE CURVE
skew distribution *n* **:** an unsymmetrical frequency distribution having the mode at a different value from the mean
skewed \ˈskyüd\ *adj* [ME, prob. fr. *skew*, *skewe* cloud, sky (of Scand origin; akin to ON *ský* cloud) + *-ed* — more at SKY] **:** SKEWBALD
¹skew·er \ˈskyüə(r), -yü(ə)r, -üə\ *n* -S [prob. alter. of ¹*skiver*] **1 :** a pin of wood or metal for fastening meat to keep in form while roasting or to hold small pieces of meat and vegetables for broiling ⟨shish kebab served on ~*s*⟩ **2 :** any of various things shaped or used like a meat skewer: as **a :** an ornamental pin used to secure clothing or hair **b :** a pointed wooden rod at each end of a bobbin creel (as on a roving machine) on which the creel runs **c :** a pointed rod formed with a loop for a handle and used to secure a loose piece while ramming a mold **d :** a long slender bone artifact found in Hopewell archaeological sites and thought to have been used to pin matting or hides to the ground
²skewer \"\ *vt* -ED/-ING/-S **1 :** to fasten or pierce with a skewer ⟨~ a roast⟩ **2 :** to fasten or pierce as if with a skewer **:** TRANSFIX ⟨accidentally ~*ed* in the rear by the bayonet of another recruit —Earle Birney⟩ ⟨~*s* both the dunderheads of the fun-and-games department and the sacred cows in the newspaper hierarchy —W.W.Smith⟩ **3 :** to cause to penetrate like a skewer ⟨~*s* his criticism home⟩ — **skew·er·er** *n* -S
skew·er·ing \-riŋ, -rēŋ\ *n* -S **:** the act or process of cooking food on skewers
skewerwood \ˈ==,=\ *n* **1** *dial Eng* **:** a spindle tree (*Euonymus europaeus*) **2** *dial Eng* **:** RED DOGWOOD
skew facet *n* **:** one of the broad triangular facets which abut in pairs on the girdle of a brilliant between each pair of skill facets — called also *cross facet*
skew-gee \(ˈ)skyüˈjē\ *adv* (*or adj*) [perh. irreg. fr. ²*skew* + *gee* (to jibe)] **:** ASKEW
skew hinge *n* **:** a hinge with oblique knuckle joints (as a common rising hinge)
¹skewing *pres part of* SKEW
²skewing *n* -S **:** waste portions of gold leaf for remelting or remnants of gold or Dutch metal leaf available for reusing — usu. used in pl.
skew·ness *n* -ES **:** the quality or state of being skew **:** lack of straightness or symmetry **:** DISTORTION; *esp* **:** the quality or state of lacking symmetry shown by a frequency distribution — called also *asymmetry*
skew pantograph *n* **:** PLAGIOGRAPH
skew polygon *n* **:** a figure analogous to a polygon whose sides do not all lie in one and the same plane
skew putt *n* [¹*skew* + Sc *put* buttress, prob. fr. E *put* (throw, thrust)] **:** a stone at the foot of the slope of a masonry gable cut with a sloping surface and with a check to hold the coping stones
skew ray *n* **1 :** a ray in a symmetrical optical system that is neither parallel to nor intersecting the axis **2 :** a ray of a prism not perpendicular to the edge
skews *pl of* SKEW, *pres 3d sing of* SKEW
skew-symmetric \ˌ===ˈ==\ *adj, of a matrix* **:** such that the element in the *r*th row and *s*th column is the negative of the element in the *s*th row and *r*th column
skew-symmetric determinant *n* **:** a determinant whose matrix is skew-symmetric
skewwhiff \ˈ=,=\ *adj* (*or adv*) [perh. irreg. fr. ²*skew* + *whiff*, v.] *dial Eng* **:** ASKEW, AWRY ⟨put a patch on . . . pants without getting it ~ —Ruth Park⟩
skey \ˈskā\ *n* -S [Afrik *skei*, fr. D *schei*, fr. MD *scheide* dividing place, crossroads; akin to OHG *sceida* sheath, separation — more at SHEATH] **:** one of four slightly wedge-shaped bars that pass down through an ox yoke one on each side of the neck of an ox to hold the yoke in place and that are notched at the bottom for the riem
skhian *var of* SKEAN
skhul man \ˈsküil-\ *n, usu cap S* [Mugharet es-*Skhul*, cave on Mount Carmel, Palestine] **:** a strain of Palestine man showing distinct resemblances to Upper Paleolithic neanthropic man but retaining strongly developed brow ridges and associated with an early Mousterian type of culture
¹ski *also* **skee** \ˈskē *sometimes chiefly Brit* shē\ *n, pl* **skis** *or* **ski** *also* **skies** *or* **skiis** *or* **skees** *or* **skee** [Norw *ski*, fr. ON *skīth* ski, stick of wood; akin to OE *scīd* stick of wood, OHG *skīt* stick of wood, OE *scēadan, scādan* to divide, separate — more at SHED] **1 a :** one of a pair of narrow strips of wood, metal, or plastic of varying length and width and curving upward in front that are used esp. for gliding over snow **b :** a piece of material similar to a ski used as a runner on a vehicle **2 :** WATER SKI
²ski \"\ *also* **skee** *vb* **skied; skied; skiing; skis** *vi* **:** to glide on skis in travel or as a sport **~** *vt* **:** to travel or pass over on skis ⟨the trail . . . can only be ~*ed* when snow and weather conditions are favorable —*Amer. Guide Series: N.H.*⟩
skia- — see SCI-
ski·able \ˈskēəbəl *sometimes chiefly Brit* ˈshē-\ *adj* **:** passable on skis **:** suitable for skiing ⟨spectators donned their skis and broke the heavy crust to make the slope ~ —*Springfield (Mass.) Union*⟩
ski·a·gram \ˈskīə,gram\ *n* [ISV *sci-* + *-gram*] **1 :** a figure formed by shading in the outline of the shadow cast by an object **2 :** a shadowgraph made by X rays **:** an X-ray photograph **:** RADIOGRAPH
ski·a·graph \-,graf\ *n* [*sci-* + *-graph*] **:** SKIAGRAM 2
ski·ag·ra·pher \skīˈagrəfə(r)\ *n* -S [*skiagraph* + *-er*] **:** RADIOGRAPHER
ski·ag·ra·phy \-fē\ *n* -ES [ISV *sci-* + *-graphy*] **:** the art, science, or act of depicting or projecting shadows **:** the making of skiagrams esp. by means of X rays
ski·am·e·try \ˌ=ˈamətrē\ *n* -ES [*sci-* + *-metry*] *med* **:** the measurement of shadows: as **a :** the measurement of their movement in skiascopy **b :** the measurement of their intensity in X-ray photography
skiapod *var of* SCIAPOD
ski·a·scope \ˈskīə,skōp\ *n* [*sci-* + *-scope*] **:** a device for determining the refractive state of the eye by observing the movements of the retinal lights and shadows
ski·as·co·py \skīˈaskəpē\ *n* -ES [ISV *sci-* + *-scopy*] **1 :** RETINOSCOPY **2 :** FLUOROSCOPY
skib·by \ˈskibē, -bi\ *n* -ES [E dial. (western U. S.) *skibby* Japanese prostitute, prob. fr. Jap *sukebei* lewdness] **:** JAPANESE — usu. taken to be offensive
ski boot *n* **:** a rigid padded shoe that is usu. made of leather or plastic, extends just above the ankle, is securely fastened to the foot by various means (as laces, buckles, or hinges), and has a sole, heel, and toe that are locked into position in a ski binding

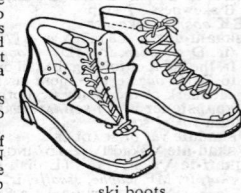

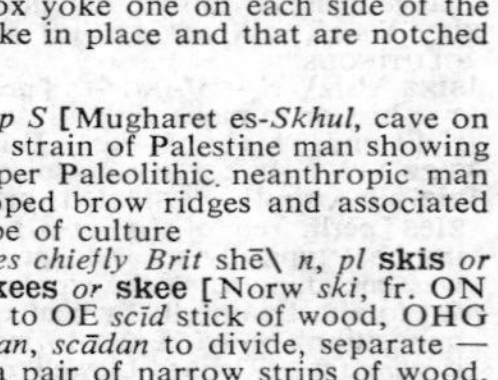
ski boots

skice \ˈskīs\ *vi* -ED/-ING/-S [Corn *scüsy*] *dial Eng* **:** to scurry about
¹skid \ˈskid\ *n* -S [perh. of Scand origin; akin to ON *skīth* stick of wood — more at SKI] **1 :** one of a group of objects (as planks or logs) used to support or elevate a structure or object ⟨commodities which are particularly susceptible to water damage should be on ~*s*, pallets or elevated platforms —*Nat'l Fire Codes*⟩: as **a :** one of a number of beams on which a small ship is constructed or repaired ⟨two landing craft which had come to grief on the coral were in the ~*s* —K.M.Dodson⟩ **b :** one of a number of beams on which a boat is elevated above a ship's deck **2 :** a wooden fender hung over a ship's side to protect it in handling cargo — usu. used in pl. **3 a :** a usu. iron shoe or clog attached to a chain and placed under a wheel to prevent its turning when descending a steep hill **:** DRAG **b :** a hook attached to a chain and used by catching round a spoke for the same purpose **c :** a brake for a power machine (as a crane) **4 :** a timber, bar, rail, pole, or log used in pairs or sets to form a slideway (as for an incline from a truck to the sidewalk) or such a set fastened temporarily or permanently to the bottom of a machine or structure to be slid ⟨gas-turbine power plants . . . may be

mounted on ~s and moved from place to place —*Modern Industry*); *specif* : one of the logs forming a skid road **5** [²*skid*] : the act of skidding : SLIP, SIDESLIP **6** : a runner used as a member of the landing gear of an airplane or helicopter — see TAIL SKID, WING SKID **7 skids** *pl* : a route to defeat, downfall, failure, destruction, or other disastrous situation ⟨a celebrated matador who has been on the ~s for some time —*New Yorker*⟩ ⟨will have to put the ~s under the pressure-groups who are trying to keep up the price of whatever they have to sell —*Sydney (Australia) Bull.*⟩ **8 a** *or* **skid platform** : a low platform of wood or metal mounted on wheels, legs, runners, or combinations thereof on which material is mounted for handling and moving (as by a fork truck) **b** : a varying quantity (as no more than 3000 pounds of paper) packed on a skid

²skid \"\ *vb* **skidded; skidded; skidding; skids** *vt* **1** : to apply a brake or skid to : slow or halt by a skid ⟨the guard got down to ~ the wheel for the descent —Charles Dickens⟩ **2 a** : to drag (logs) from the stump to a landing, skidway, or mill : YARD **b** : to haul along or slide on skids ⟨the new span will be *skidded* to the river by high powered winch equipment over heavily greased rails —*Windsor Star (Canada)*⟩ **c** : to raise, hoist, or store upon skids ⟨contents . . . should be *skidded* at least 4 inches above the floor level —*Nat'l Fire Codes*⟩ **d** : to package (as paper) on a skid **3** : to reinforce or repair (a road) with logs or poles **4** : to cause to skid ⟨*skidded* his car on an icy pavement —F.B.Gipson⟩ ~ *vi* **1** : to slide without rotating (as a wheel held from turning while a vehicle moves onward) **2 a** : to fail to grip the roadway; *specif* : to slip sideways on the road ⟨the truck *skidded* on the wet road⟩ **b** *of an airplane* : to slide sidewise away from the center of curvature when turning — compare SIDESLIP **c** : to cross an esp. slippery surface without effort or fall or nearly fall through loss of balance : SLIDE, SLIP ⟨*skidding* clumsily across the ice —Arthur Knight⟩ ⟨both horses *skidding* in the mud at every step —H.L.Davis⟩ **3** : to fall rapidly, steeply, or far ⟨sales of new models have *skidded* 60 percent —*Newsweek*⟩

skid box *or* **skid bin** *n* : a box mounted on skids

skid chain *n* : TIRE CHAIN

skidded *adj* : having skids or runners attached to facilitate handling ⟨~ freight⟩

skid·der \ˈskidə(r)\ *n* -s : one that skids or uses a skid: as **a** : a worker who skids logs **b** : an engine for hauling the cable used in skidding logs **c** : BUMMER 3

skid·ding \-diŋ, -dēŋ\ *n* -s [¹*skid* + *-ing*] : skids or material for skids

skidding hooks *or* **skidding tongs** *n pl* [*skidding* fr. gerund of ²*skid*] : tongs used in skidding logs; *specif* : a pair of hooks attached to a ring

skid·ding·ly *adv* [*skidding* (pres. part. of ²*skid*) + *-ly*] : in a skidding manner

skidding trail *n* [*skidding* fr. gerund of ²*skid*] : the path of a log being skidded

skid·dles \ˈskidᵊlz\ *n pl but sing in constr* [prob. blend of ²*skid* and *skittles* (pl. of ¹*skittle*)] : a game in which sticks are thrown at pins of different score value set up as the corners and center of a diamond — called also *stick bowling*

skid·doo *or* **ski·doo** \skiˈdü\ *vi* -ED/-ING/-S [prob. alter. of ¹*skedaddle*] : to go away : DEPART

skid·dy \ˈskidē, -di\ *adj* -ER/-EST : likely to skid or cause skidding ⟨cars and trucks littering the ~ roads —Noel Barber⟩

skidegate *usu cap, var of* SKITTAGET

skid engine *n* **1** : SKIDDER b **2** : an engine mounted on skids

skid fin *n* : a fore-and-aft vertical surface usu. placed above the upper wing of a biplane and designed to provide the vertical keel surface required for lateral stability

ski·di \ˈskēdē\ *n, pl* **skidi** *or* **skidis** *usu cap* **1** : a people of the Pawnee confederacy **2** : a member of the Skidi people

skidpan \ˈ=,=\ *n, Brit* : DRAG 3a(2)

skid road *n* **1** : a road along which logs are dragged to a skidway or landing often over heavy logs partly sunken at intervals of about five feet — called also *travois* **2 a** *West* : the part of a town frequented by loggers **b** : SKID ROW

skid row *n* [alter. (influenced by *row*) of *skid road*] : a district of cheap saloons, beaneries, flophouses, and employment agencies frequented largely by migrant workers, vagrants, and alcoholics

skidway \ˈ=,=\ *n* **1** : a usu. inclined platform on which logs are piled for loading or sawing **2** : a road or way formed of skids or along which objects are skidded

skie *obs var of* SKY

¹skied *past of* SKY

²skied *past of* SKI

ski·er *also* **skii·er** \ˈskēə(r)\ *sometimes chiefly Brit* ˈshē-\ *n* -s [*skier* fr. ²*ski* + *-er*; *skiier* fr. *skii-* (as in *skiing*) + *-er*] : one that skis

¹skies *pl of* SKY, *pres 3d sing of* SKY

²skies *pl of* SKI, *pres 3d sing of* SKI

skiey *var of* SKYEY

¹skiff \ˈskif\ *n* -s [MF or OIt; MF *esquif*, fr. OIt *schifo*, of Gmc origin; akin to OHG *skif* ship — more at SHIP] **1** : a small light sailing ship **2** : a light rowboat **3** : a boat with centerboard and spritsail light enough to be rowed and sometimes steered by an occupant's shifting his weight — called also *St. Lawrence skiff* **4** : a small fast powerboat

²skiff \"\ *vi* -ED/-ING/-S : to navigate in a skiff

³skiff \"\ *vb* -ED/-ING/-S [prob. alter. of ¹*skift*] *vi, Scot* : SKIM, FLIT ~ *vt, Scot* : to touch lightly

skiff·less \ˈ=ləs\ *adj* : having no skiff

skif·fling \ˈskifliŋ, -lēŋ\ *n* -s [prob. alter. of *scabbling*, gerund of *scabble*] : rough dressing of stone by knocking off projections

¹skift \ˈskift\ *vb* -ED/-ING/-S [ME *skiften* to shift, divide, fr. ON *skipta* to divide, change, be of importance — more at SHIFT] *dial Brit* : SHIFT

²skift \"\ *or* **skiff** \ˈskif\ *n* -s *dial* : something that is light: as **a** : a light fall of snow or rain **b** : WISP

³skift \ˈskift\ *dial var of* ¹SKIFF

ski·ing \ˈskēiŋ, -ēēŋ\ *sometimes esp Brit* ˈshē-\ *n* -s : the art or sport of sliding and jumping on skis

skiis *pl of* SKI

ski-jor·ing *or* **ski·ör·ing** \ˈskē,jōriŋ, =ˈ==\ *or* \"; ˈ=,(y)ər·iŋ, =ˈ(y)ər·iŋ\ *n* -s [modif. of Norw *skikjøring*, fr. *ski* + *kjøring* driving, fr. *kjøre* to drive; akin to ON *keyra* to drive and perh. to Skt *javate* he hurries on] : a winter sport in which a person wearing skis is drawn over snow or ice by a horse or vehicle

¹ski jump *n* **1** : a steeply inclined artificial course or track leveled off at its lower end and built at or near the top of a natural slope from which a skier makes a takeoff through the air **2** : the act or instance of a skier taking off from a ski jump esp. in competition

²ski jump *vi* : to jump on skis from a ski jump

skil \ˈskil\ *or* **skil·fish** \ˈ=,=\ *n, pl* **skils** *or* **skilfish** *or* **skilfishes** [Haida *sqil*] : SABLEFISH

skilful *var of* SKILLFUL

ski lift *n* : a power-driven conveyor for transporting skiers or sightseers up a long slope or mountainside and consisting usu. of a series of seats suspended from a motor-driven overhead endless cable

¹skill \ˈskil\ *n* -s *see sense 4* [ME *skile, skil*, fr. ON *skil* distinction, discernment, knowledge; akin to OE *scylian* to separate, part, MLG *schēlen* to distinguish, ON *skilja* to separate, divide, Goth *skilja* butcher, Lith *skėlti* to split — more at SHELL] **1** *obs* : CAUSE, REASON ⟨you have as little ~ to fear as I have purpose to put you to't —Shak.⟩ **2 a (1)** : knowledge of the means or methods of accomplishing a task ⟨~s disappear . . . when we fail to put them to work —T.W.Arnold⟩ **(2)** : the ability to use one's knowledge effectively and readily in execution or performance : technical expertness : PROFICIENCY ⟨revealed considerable ~ in the practice of law —Carol L. Thompson⟩ ⟨sufficient political ~ to govern wisely —J.G.Colton⟩ **b** : dexterity, fluency, or coordination in the execution of learned physical or mental tasks ⟨loss of motor ~ in the use of the hands —C.D.Martz & Frances Ekstam⟩; *specif* : technical competence without insight or understanding or the ability for further elaboration or development ⟨a volume of verses which show some ~ in versification, but little originality in thought or form —H.E.Starr⟩ ⟨frequently a person acquires certain reading ~s but never understands what he has read —John Haverstick⟩ **3 a** : a learned power of doing a thing competently : a developed or acquired aptitude or ability ⟨because of the influence which the language ~s exert on each other, the present trend is to teach them together —*Education Digest*⟩ ⟨the endless ~s the human hand is capable of developing —Abram Kardiner⟩ **b** : a craft requiring the use of related skills ⟨practiced the ~ of a carpenter⟩ **c** : a coordinated set of actions become smooth and integrated through practice ⟨thought canoeing was not a difficult sport or ~ —Ernest Beaglehole⟩ **4** *pl* **skill** : a skilled person ⟨immigration of ~ is . . . welcomed in all undeveloped areas —E.P.Hutchinson & W.E.Moore⟩ **5** *dial Brit* : discriminating taste : LIKING — usu. used with *of* ⟨he has a ~ of good wines⟩ **syn** see ART

²skill \"\ *vb* -ED/-ING/-S [ME *skilen*, fr. ON *skilja* to separate, divide] *vi* **1 a** : to make a difference : MATTER ⟨perhaps she was a soprano . . . it ~s not —Thomas Wolfe⟩ **b** : to be of help : AVAIL **2 a** *obs* : to have practical skill : be dexterous or competent **b** *archaic* : to have understanding : be knowing ~ *vi, dial Eng* : UNDERSTAND, COMPREHEND

skilled \ˈskild\ *adj* [¹*skill* + *-ed*] **1** : having skill : EXPERT, SKILLFUL ⟨one ~ in the science of mechanics —B.N.Cardozo⟩ **2** : of, relating to, consisting of, or requiring workers or labor with skill and training in a particular occupation, craft, or trade and full competence for a task ⟨a craft for those who wish to become ~ artisans —Maurice Graney⟩ ⟨a ~ electrician⟩ ⟨a far greater proportion of the population is engaged in ~ work in a truly mechanized society —David Goldknopf⟩ **syn** see PROFICIENT

¹skil·let \ˈskilət, *usu* -əd.+V\ *n* -s [ME *skelet*, prob. fr. *skele* pail + *-et* — more at SKEEL] **1 a** *chiefly Brit* : a small kettle or pot usu. having three or four often long feet and used for cooking on the hearth in front of an open fire **b** : FRYING PAN **2** : a flat mold in which a precious metal is cast for sale as bullion

²skillet \"\ *n* -s [origin unknown] : a thin veneer of wood used esp. in making matchboxes

skill facet *n* [so called fr. the skill required in placing such a facet correctly] : one of the narrow triangular facets that abut in pairs on the girdle of a brilliant at the corners of the stone

skill·ful *or* **skil·ful** \ˈskilfəl\ *adj* [ME *skilful*, fr. *skile, skil* skill + *-ful*] **1** : possessed of or displaying skill : having knowledge, readiness, and ability : well versed ⟨a ~ observer whose skill depended upon both native capacity and long practice —G.K.Chesterton⟩ ⟨one of the most ~ debaters and men of business in the kingdom —T.B.Macaulay⟩ **2** : accomplished with skill : done with trained proficiency ⟨~ use of precedent —G.W.Johnson⟩ ⟨less ~ efforts at perspective representation are not rare —Franz Boas⟩ **syn** see PROFICIENT

skill·ful·ly \-fəlē, -li\ *adv* : in a skillful manner

skill·ful·ness \-ləs\ *n* -ES : the quality or state of being skillful

skil·li·ga·lee \ˌskiləgəˈlē\ *n* -s [origin unknown] *chiefly Brit* : a thin broth or porridge usu. of oatmeal

skil·li·gil·lee *or* **skil·ly·goel·le** \"\ *n* -s [perh. alter. of *skilligalee*] : MARLIN

¹skilling *var of* SKEELING

²skil·ling \ˈskiliŋ, ˈshi-\ *n* -s [Sw, Norw, & Dan, fr. ON *skillingr*, a gold coin — more at SHILLING] : any of various old Scandinavian units of value equal to some small fraction of the Swedish, Norwegian, or Danish rix-dollars; *also* : any of the small coins representing one skilling unit

skil·lion \ˈskilyən\ *n* -s [alter. of *skeeling*] *Austral* : LEAN-TO

skill–less *or* **skil·less** \ˈskilləs\ *adj* **1** *archaic* : having no knowledge **2** : having no skill — **skill–less·ness** *n* -ES

skills *pl of* SKILL, *pres 3d sing of* SKILL

¹skilly \ˈskili\ *adj* -ER/-EST [¹*skill* + *-y*] *dial Brit* : SKILLFUL, SKILLED ⟨and the ~ use of words had not forsaken him —Maurice Walsh⟩

²skil·ly \ˈskilē, -li\ *n* -ES [by shortening & alter.] : SKILLIGALEE

skilo *or* **skil·lo** \ˈski(,)lō\ *n* -s [*skilo* alter. of *skillo*, fr. ¹*skill* + *-o*] : a game of rolling balls into depressions in a grid based on the cards used at bingo with the object of getting five balls in a row

skils *pl of* SKIL

¹skim \ˈskim\ *vb* **skimmed; skimmed; skimming; skims** [ME *skimmen*, prob. alter. of *scumen* — more at SCUM] *vt* **1 a (1)** : to clear (a liquid) of scum or floating substance ⟨~ boiling syrup⟩ **(2)** : to remove scum or floating matter from the contents of **b** : to remove (as film or scum) from the surface of a liquid ⟨foam rises as the liquid boils, and is *skimmed* off —*Amer. Guide Series: Tenn.*⟩ **c (1)** : to remove cream from (milk) by skimming **(2)** : to remove (cream) from milk by skimming **d** : to remove foreign particles from the surface of molten glass (in a pot or tank) ⟨*skimming* a glass pot before pouring —C.J.Phillips⟩ **e** : TOP 1f **f (1)** : to remove from the surface of a solid ⟨the dust could be *skimmed* from the cooking food —Russell Lord⟩ **(2)** : to remove a substance from the surface of (a solid body) ⟨then came a wind, *skimming* straw from the stacks —Adrian Bell⟩; *specif* : to remove roughnesses or irregularities from the surface of (a solid body) ⟨valve seats should be very lightly *skimmed* with a cutter —B.C.MacDonald⟩ **g (1)** : to remove the best or easiest obtainable contents from ⟨forests whose treasury of bird and beast and insect secrets had been only *skimmed* —William Beebe⟩ **(2)** : to take away (the most valuable or easiest obtainable contents) ⟨ore beds were *skimmed* and abandoned for richer deposits —D.A.Shepard⟩ ⟨nimble searchers after profits . . . ~ the cream off markets —Hartley Withers⟩ **2** : to read, study, deal with, or examine superficially and rapidly ⟨~s American poetry of the period —*College English*⟩; *specif* : to glance through (as a book) for the chief ideas or the plot ⟨the habit of *skimming* volumes in bookshops —*Time Lit. Supp.*⟩ **3** : to throw in a gliding path ⟨~ a hat across the room⟩; *specif* : to throw so as to ricochet along the surface of water ⟨taking a slate from the low wall and *skimming* it across the pond —Robert Graves⟩ **4 a** : to cover with or as if with a film or scum ⟨the standing water . . . was *skimmed* with ice —William Faulkner⟩ **b** : to put a finishing coat of plaster on **5** : to pass swiftly or lightly over : touch lightly, barely miss, or glide along in passing ⟨kingfishers . . . darted across the water, their wings just *skimming* the surface —David Walden⟩ ⟨~ the shores —Claudia Cassidy⟩ ~ *vi* **1 a** : to pass lightly or hastily : glide or skip along, above, or near a surface ⟨the plane ~s 200 feet above ground —A.C.Fisher⟩ ⟨*skimming* along the high road —D.S.Boyer⟩ **b** : to give a cursory glance or consideration ⟨*skimmed* through the overseer's report book —Eve Langley⟩ ⟨a flow of racy comment, *skimming* from one topic to another —Rose Macaulay⟩ — distinguished from *dip* **2** : to become coated with a thin layer of film or scum ⟨during the cold night the puddles *skimmed* over⟩ **3** : to put on a finishing coat of plaster

²skim \"\ *n* -s **1** : a thin layer, coating, or film ⟨bread with a ~ of jam on it —Anthony West⟩ ⟨a little ~ of ice in the ruts —William Faulkner⟩ **2** : the act of skimming ⟨the ~ of the swallows over the grass —Virginia Woolf⟩ **3** : something skimmed; *specif* : SKIM MILK **4** : a streak of dense seeds in glass

³skim \"\ *adj* **1** : that skims or is used for skimming ⟨~ net⟩ **2 a** : SKIMMED **b** : made of skim milk ⟨~ cheese⟩

skimback \ˈ=,=\ *n* [so called fr. its habit of skimming the water as it swims] : QUILLBACK 1

¹skim·ble–skam·ble \ˌskim(b)əlˈskam(b)əl\ *adj* [redupl. of *scamble*] : RAMBLING, UNCONNECTED, SENSELESS ⟨such a deal of *skimble-skamble* stuff as puts me from my faith —Shak.⟩

²skimble–skamble \"\ *n* -s : meaningless discourse : NONSENSE

skim coat *n* : FINISHING COAT 1

skim colter *n* : JOINTER c

skimeister \ˈ=,==\ *n* -s [part trans. of G *skimeister*, fr. *ski* + *meister* master, fr. OHG *meistar*, fr. L *magister* — more at MASTER] **1** : a skier with the best all-around performance in downhill, slalom, cross-country, and jumping competition **2** : a professional skier or skiing instructor

skim gate *or* **skimming gate** *n* : a gate or runner having a bridge to arrest the flow of slag

skimmed–milk white \ˈ=;=-\ *n* : a light bluish gray to light gray that is greener and lighter than glaucous gray or cinerous — compare MILK WHITE

skim·mel·ton \ˈskiməltən\ *or* **skim·mer·ton** \-mə(r)t-\ *n* -s [alter. of *skimmington*] *North* : SHIVAREE 1

¹skim·mer \ˈskimə(r)\ *n* -s [ME, alter. (influenced by *-er*) of *skymour*, fr. *skymen, skimmen* to skim + *-or, -our* -or] **1** : a utensil or implement used for skimming: as **a** : a flat perforated scoop or spoon used for skimming cooking liquids or lifting ripened cream from milk **b** : a broad-bladed jointer **c** : an implement to prevent dross or slag from running over with the molten metal from a ladle to a mold **d** : a device similar to a power shovel for skimming off the surface of the ground in grading **e** : a perforated shovel used in lifting salt out of an evaporating pan **2 a** : one that skims ⟨the structure of the modern news story is suited to the ~ —F.L.Mott⟩ **b** : one whose work is skimming (as dirt from the surface of a vat of oysters or slag from molten metal) **c** : a worker who sprinkles flux on molten magnesium to keep it from igniting when it is poured into molds **3** : any of several long-winged littoral marine birds of the genus *Rynchops* that are related to the terns, have the lower mandible compressed like a knife blade and much longer than the upper, fly rapidly along the surface of the water with the lower mandible immersed to skim out small marine animals **4 a** : WATER STRIDER **b** : a dragonfly of the genus *Libellula* **5** : a usu. straw flat-crowned hat with a wide straight brim

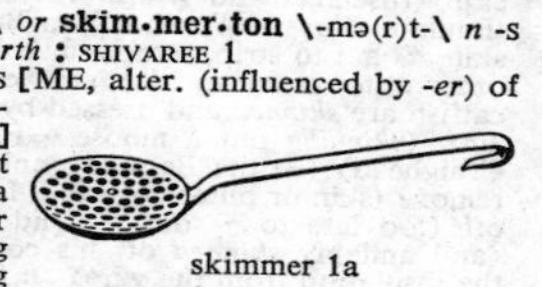

skimmer 1a

²skimmer \"\ *dial Brit var of* SHIMMER

skim·mia \ˈskimēə\ *n, cap* [NL] : a small genus of evergreen shrubs (family Rutaceae) of eastern Asia having small tetramerous flowers with a 2-celled to 5-celled ovary and red drupes

skim milk *also* **skimmed milk** *n* : milk from which the cream has been taken

skim·ming \ˈskimiŋ, -mēŋ\ *n* -s [ME *skemmyng*, fr. gerund of *skemmen, skimmen* to skim] **1** : that which is skimmed from a liquid ⟨do not add drosses, sweepings, or ~s —*Lubrication Engineering*⟩ **2** : the act or process of one that skims

skimming back *n* : a vat in which surplus yeast is skimmed from beer after the first fermentation

skimming dish *n* : a utensil for skimming : SKIMMER 1

skim·ming·ly *adv* [*skimming* (pres. part. of ¹*skim*) + *-ly*] : in a skimming manner

skim·ming·ton \ˈskimiŋtən\ *n* -s [*skimming* (fr. gerund of ¹*skim*) + *-ton* (as in surnames such as *Washington*); fr. the practice of representing the woman as beating her husband with a skimming ladle] **1** : one publicly impersonating and ridiculing a henpecked or cuckolded husband or his shrewish or unfaithful wife **2** *dial Eng* : a boisterous procession intended to ridicule an unfaithful spouse or a shrewish wife often with effigies and a mock serenade

skim·mi·ty \ˈskimədē, -mətē, -i\ *or* **skimmity ride** *n* -ES [*skimmity* alter. of *skimmington*] : SKIMMINGTON 2

¹skimp \ˈskimp\ *adj* [perh. alter. of ¹*scrimp*] : barely sufficient : SCANTY, MEAGER ⟨a thin woman whose ~ dress hung flat —Elizabeth M. Roberts⟩

²skimp \"\ *vb* -ED/-ING/-S *vt* : to give insufficient or barely sufficient attention or effort to or funds for : SCAMP ⟨their homes are all facade — ~*ed* under the superficial show —F.A. Swinnerton⟩ ~ *vi* : to save by or as if by skimping : SCRIMP ⟨we build schools without libraries, ~ on new-book budgets —Bice Clemow⟩ ⟨the two-dollar entry fee must have required a little ~*ing* —Dixon Wecter⟩

skimp·i·ly \-pəlē, -li\ *adv* : in a skimpy manner

skimp·i·ness \-pēnəs, -pin-\ *n* -ES : the quality or state of being skimpy

skimp·ing·ly *adv* : in a skimping manner

skimpy \ˈskimpē, -pi\ *adj* -ER/-EST : deficient in supply or execution esp. through skimping ⟨a ~ and inadequate training —Elspeth Mosscrop⟩ **syn** see MEAGER

skims *pres 3d sing of* SKIM, *pl of* SKIM

¹skin \ˈskin\ *n* -s *often attrib* [ME, fr. ON *skinn*; akin to OE *scinn* skin, MHG *schint* peel of a fruit, ON *skān* crust, W *ysgythru* to cut, scratch, and prob. to L *secare* to cut — more at SAW] **1 a** : the integument of an animal separated from the body with or without hair whether green, dry, tanned, or dressed; *specif* : that of a small animal (as a calf, sheep, or goat) as distinguished from the hide of a large animal **b** : the hide or pelt of a game animal and esp. of one to be hunted **c (1)** : the pelt of an animal prepared for use as a trimming or in a garment ⟨her neckpiece of four ~s⟩ ⟨it takes forty ~s to make a coat⟩ **(2)** : a sheet of parchment or vellum made from the whole or part of a hide **(3)** : BOTTLE 1b **(4)** : SEALSKIN 3; *also* : a plush covering for a ski used like a sealskin — usu. used in pl. **2 a** : the external limiting layer of an animal body esp. when forming a tough but flexible cover relatively impermeable from without while intact: as **(1)** : the 2-layered covering of the vertebrate body sometimes modified by the presence of bony plates (as in an armadillo) or scales (as in most fishes and reptiles) and consisting of an outer ectodermal epidermis that is more or less cornified and penetrated by the openings of various glands (as sweat and sebaceous glands in man) and an inner mesodermal dermis that is composed largely of connective tissue and is richly supplied with blood vessels and nerves **(2)** : the hypodermis and the overlying cuticle that it secretes in many invertebrates — compare EXOSKELETON, MUCOUS MEMBRANE **b** : an outer covering of a fruit or seed (as a rind, husk, or peel) ⟨a black eye caused by a swiftly hurled orange ~ —*Amer. Guide Series: N.C.*⟩ **c** : the epidermis of a plant **d (1)** : a membranous film or scum (as on boiling milk or on the surface of paints or varnishes) : PELLICLE ⟨how cold the gravy was getting — a ~ was forming on it —Agatha Christie⟩ **(2)** : a thin frozen coating ⟨a ~ of ice⟩ **e (1)** : an outermost layer or surface of an object ⟨the ~ of a casting⟩ ⟨the ~ of a diamond⟩ ⟨the ~ of an electric conductor⟩ **(2)** : a layer and esp. the outermost layer of nacreous matter composing a pearl **(3)** : the surface of a bituminous pavement **f** : the part of a furled sail that is on the outside and covers the whole **g** : a casing for sausage **h** : the rind of ham or bacon **3** : the life or physical well-being of a person ⟨when the troopship went down he took care that if anybody's ~ was saved it should be his —Peter Forster⟩ **4** : a sheathing or casing forming the outside surface of a structure ⟨steel for auto ~s —A.G.Tombs⟩: as **a** : a covering of planking or metal plates outside the framing that forms the sides and bottom of a ship : SHELL **b** : an exterior wall of a building: **(1)** : either of two panels that enclose a hollow space containing the framework ⟨external walls are of 11-inch cavity brickwork, with inner ~s of cellular flettons —*Architectural Rev.*⟩ **(2)** : thin weather-resistant stainless steel, aluminum, or other metal used alone or in combination with glass and other material to form a curtain wall **c** : an outer sheet covering of an airplane, missile, or satellite that is in an airplane usu. made of metal and designed to carry a portion of the stress **5** : PURSE, POCKETBOOK **6** : a contemptible person: as **a** : MISER, SKINFLINT **b** : one given to cheating : SWINDLER, SHARPER **7** : MADE=BEAVER **8** *slang* : DRUM **9** : SKINBALL **10** [short for *frogskin*] *slang* : DOLLAR **11** *slang* : HORSE **12** [²*skin*] *slang* : an unfavorable report or a reprimand — **in a whole skin** *or* **with a whole skin** : without bodily harm : safe and sound — **in one's skin** : wearing no clothes : NAKED ⟨in every section a man stood in *his skin* while a doctor examined his teeth or palpated his chest —Robert Lynd⟩ — **out of one's skin** : in or into unrestrained expression of joy, enthusiasm, vigor, surprise, or other emotion : EXCITEDLY ⟨people . . . always jump *out of their skins* when they hear our own artillery —R.M.Ingersoll⟩ — **the skin of one's teeth** : a very narrow margin ⟨escaped by *the skin of my teeth* —Job 19:20 (RSV)⟩ — **under one's skin** : beneath one's surface powers of resistance to emotional or intellectual excitation : so deeply penetrative as to irritate, stimulate, provoke thought, or otherwise excite ⟨that last had got *under his skin* a little . . . he lost his good humor —Mary Deasy⟩ — **under the skin** : beneath apparent or surface differences : at heart ⟨determined to confirm that women are all sisters *under the skin* —Elizabeth Taylor⟩

²skin \"\ *vb* **skinned** *or dial* **skun** \ˈskən\ **skinned** *or dial*

skun; skinning; skins *vt* **1 a :** to cover with or as if with skin ⟨fuselages and wings will be *skinned* with steel . . . or titanium alloys —Wernher Von Braun⟩ **b :** to heal over with skin **2 a :** to strip, scrape, or rub off the skin, peel, rind, or other outer covering of **:** remove a surface layer from ⟨huge catfish are *skinned* and dressed by hand —*Amer. Guide Series: La.*⟩ ⟨*skinning* out a moose —F.C.Craighead b.1916 & J.J. Craighead⟩ ⟨~ the Bermuda onion —Dione Lucas⟩ **b :** to remove (skin or outer covering) from an object **:** pull or strip off ⟨too late to ~ out the hide that night —Corey Ford⟩ ⟨and amiably *skinned* off his coat to help —R.V.Mills⟩ ⟨~ the insulation from the wire⟩ **c** (1) **:** to chip, cut, or damage the surface of ⟨*skinned* his hand on the rough rock⟩ ⟨saw the *skinned* fender⟩ (2) **:** to remove (a portion of a surface) by wearing, chipping, or cutting away from a body ⟨the movers *skinned* the paint off the front steps —Virginia D. Dawson & Betty D. Wilson⟩ **d** (1) **:** to slide (a single card) from the top of a pack in dealing (as in faro) (2) **:** to slide the cards off the top of (a pack) one by one **e** (1) **:** to peel a thin layer of paper from ⟨~ an album page⟩ (2) **:** to peel (a thin layer of paper) from a surface ⟨~ a stamp from an envelope⟩ **f :** to remove the patina from (a painting) in the process of restoration **3 a :** to strip of money or property **:** FLEECE ⟨determined to collect his army bounty from a town selectman who . . . had been trying to ~ him —Dixon Wecter⟩ **b :** to outdistance or defeat in a race or contest **c** (1) **:** to criticize, satirize, or otherwise unfavorably comment upon ⟨had once *skinned* me because . . . I seemed unable to take literature seriously —Bernard De Voto⟩ (2) *slang* **:** to administer a reprimand to or report a deficiency in ⟨he was *skinned* for dirty boots⟩ **4 :** to exhaust by excessive cultivation or exploitation **:** despoil of natural resources ⟨during the grain rush of the war years this raw new stretch . . . of farms was horribly *skinned* —Russell Lord⟩ **5 a :** to urge on and direct the course of (a draft animal) ⟨one talent he could turn to a profit — mules, *skinning* mules —H.G.Evarts⟩ **b :** to act as operator of (a caterpillar tractor) **6 :** to equalize the thickness of adhesive on (a pasted or glued surface) by placing a sheet of wastepaper over it and rapidly rubbing or pressing **~ *vi* 1 :** to become covered with or as if with skin ⟨these inks won't dry on the press . . . nor will they ~ in the can —*Graphic Arts Monthly*⟩ — usu. used with *over* **2 a :** to climb or descend — used with *up* or *down* ⟨when you leave you ~ up the rope —C.E.Rose⟩ ⟨*skinned* down inside ladders from the bridge deck —K.M.Dodson⟩ **b** (1) **:** to pass with scant room to spare **:** traverse a narrow opening — used with *through* or *by* ⟨the big ship barely *skinned* through the open draw⟩ (2) **:** to succeed or qualify by a narrow margin — used with *through* or *by* **c :** to pass or go hurriedly **:** SCURRY ⟨*skinned* . . . out the gate before she even had time to think —Helen Eustis⟩

syn SKIN, DECORTICATE, PEEL, PARE, and FLAY agree in meaning to divest of skin or an outer covering. SKIN can apply to any animal or to a vegetable or fruit ⟨*skin* a bear⟩ ⟨*skin* an orange⟩ DECORTICATE applies to the stripping of the bark of a tree, the husk of a seed, or the rind of a fruit ⟨cut down and *decorticate* a birch tree⟩ ⟨for the production of the best quality oil . . . the seeds are *decorticated* before being expressed in the cold —J.F.Thorpe & Martha Whiteley⟩ PEEL and PARE are usu. interchangeable but PEEL more generally applies when the skin or outer covering can be removed by stripping, PARE when cutting is necessary ⟨*peel* an orange⟩ ⟨*pare* an apple⟩ FLAY applies largely to persons or animals and implies a skinning under torture or by scourging ⟨a man nearly *flayed* alive for criminal attack upon a tribesman⟩

— skin a flint : to make a gain by the most disreputable means **— skin alive :** to torture or fleece callously or mercilessly **— skin the cat :** to grasp a horizontal bar, raise the feet and legs up under the bar, and turn over backward or forward

skin and bones *n* **:** a condition of extreme emaciation **:** excessive thinness

skinball \ˈ=,=\ *n* [²*skin* + *ball*; fr. the fact that the cards are skinned from the top of the pack] **:** a card game similar to faro in which players bet on which of certain cards will win or lose — called also *skin game, skinning*

skin beetle *n* **:** any of several beetles esp. of the genera *Trox* and *Dermestes* whose larvae feed on leather or hides

skin boat *n* **:** a boat made of skins stretched over a frame

skinch \ˈskinch\ *vb* -ED/-ING/-S [origin unknown] *vt, dial Brit* **:** to be stingy or niggardly in respect to (material or a person) **~ *vi* :** to be sparing — usu. used with *on* ⟨tried to ~ on the food⟩

skin-deep \ˈ=ˈ=\ *adj* **1 :** as deep as the skin ⟨the cut was ~⟩ **2 :** not thorough or lasting in impression **:** SUPERFICIAL ⟨discovered . . . that love is more than *skin-deep* —W.L.Gresham⟩

skin dive *vi* **1 :** to swim beneath the surface of water esp. at considerable depth without a diving helmet and suit but with a face mask, flippers, and a portable breathing device **2 :** GOGGLE 3

skin diver *n* **:** one that engages in skin diving esp. as a sport

skin effect *n* **:** an effect characteristic of current distribution in a conductor at high frequencies by virtue of which the current is greater near the surface of the conductor than in its interior resulting in an increase of resistance with increasing frequency

skinflint \ˈ=,=\ *n* [²*skin* + *flint*, n.] **1 :** a person who would save, gain, or extort money by any means **:** MISER, NIGGARD **2 :** an old or worn-out horse **:** PLUG, SKATE

skin-food \ˈ=,=\ *n* **:** any of various cosmetics (as creams) for improving the condition and appearance of facial skin

skin friction *n* **1 :** friction between a fluid and the surface of a solid moving through it or between a moving fluid and its enclosing surface **2 :** the part of the drag of an airplane or of the head resistance of a ship due to the friction of air or of air and water

skin·ful \ˈ=,fu̇l\ *n* -S **1 a :** the flesh and bones within a skin **:** BODY **b :** the contents of a skin bottle **2 a :** a large or satisfying quantity ⟨a proper ~ of food —Joseph Hergesheimer⟩ **b :** an intoxicating amount of alcohol ⟨roar in pubs with a ~ —R.P.Warren⟩

skin game *n* [²*skin*] **1 :** a swindling game or trick ⟨*skin games* running to fleece you as fast as you can get your money to the center —Andy Adams⟩ **2 :** SKINBALL

¹skin graft *vt* **:** to graft skin to

²skin graft *n* **:** a piece of skin of variable size and thickness cut from a donor area and transferred to the place to be repaired

skinhead \ˈ=,=\ *n, slang* **:** a person with a bald or close shaven head; *specif* **:** a marine boot

skin in *vt* **:** to apply a first coat of French polish to (furniture or woodwork)

¹skink \ˈskiŋk\ *vt* -ED/-ING/-S [ME *skinken*, fr. MD *schenken, schinken*; akin to OE *scencan* to pour out drink, give to drink — more at NUNCHEON] *chiefly dial* **:** to draw, pour out, or serve (drink)

²skink \ˈ"\ *n* -S [perh. fr. obs. D *schenk, schink* shank of an animal, ham; akin to OHG *scinka* shank, MLG *schenke, schinke* leg, shank — more at SHANK] **:** a soup made of the shin or hock of beef

³skink \ˈ"\ *n* -S [L *scincus*, fr. Gk *skinkos*] **:** any of numerous lizards that constitute the family Scincidae, usu. live in dry sandy places where they often burrow in the sand, and are typically small with small scales, a slightly notched tail covered with scaly papillae, and usu. well developed but sometimes reduced or wanting limbs

⁴skink \ˈ"\ *archaic var of* SKUNK

skink·er \-kə(r)\ *n* -S **1 :** one that serves liquor **:** TAPSTER **2** *obs* **:** a drinking vessel

¹skin·kle \ˈskiŋkəl\ *vi* -ED/-ING/-S [perh. blend of ²*skimmer* and *twinkle*] *chiefly Scot* **:** SPARKLE, GLITTER

²skinkle \ˈ"\ *vt* -ED/-ING/-S [perh. fr. ¹*skink* + *-le*] *chiefly Scot* **:** to scatter piecemeal **:** SPRINKLE

skin·less \ˈ=ləs\ *adj* [ME *skinles*, fr. ¹*skin* + *-les* -less] **1 :** having no skin or casing ⟨a ~ hot dog⟩ **2 :** easily moved **:** SENSITIVE ⟨that . . . defenseless ~ creature —Evelyn Whitehead⟩

skin maggot *n* **:** a maggot that is the larva of a tumbu fly

skin man *n* **:** one who covers the skeleton work of airplanes with sheet metal or plywood — called also *skinner*

¹skinned \ˈskind\ *adj* [ME *skynned*, fr. *skyn, skin* skin + *-ed*] **:** having a skin — often used in combination ⟨dark*skinned*⟩

²skinned *adj* [fr. past part. of ²*skin*] **:** having no turf ⟨~ infield⟩ ⟨~ racetrack⟩

skin·ner \ˈskinə(r)\ *n* -S [ME *skynner*, fr. *skyn, skin* skin + *-er*] **1 a :** one that deals in skins, pelts, or hides **b :** one that removes, cures, or dresses skins **2 :** one of a band of guerillas and irregular cavalry claiming attachment to either the British or American troops and operating in Westchester county in New York during the American Revolution — compare COWBOY 2a **3 a :** one that swindles, cheats, or engages in sharp bargaining **b :** a bet won at long odds **4 a :** a driver of draft animals **:** TEAMSTER ⟨~*s* driving six- and eight-horse teams —*Amer. Guide Series: Mont.*⟩ **b :** an operator of a large piece of construction equipment ⟨steam-shovel ~*s* —Clark Craig⟩ **5 :** SKIN MAN

skinner box *n, usu cap S* [after Burrhus F. *Skinner* b1904 Am. psychologist] **:** a laboratory apparatus in which an animal is caged for experiments in operational conditioning typically containing a lever that must be pressed by the animal to gain reward or avoid punishment

skin·nery \ˈskin(ə)rē\ *n* -ES [ME *skynnery*, fr. *skyn, skin* skin + *-ery, -erie* -ery] **:** a skinner's workshop or place of business

skin·ni·ness \ˈskinēnəs, -nin-\ *n* -ES **:** the quality or state of being skinny

skinning *n* -S [fr. gerund of ²*skin*] **:** SKINBALL

skinning loam *n* [*skinning* fr. gerund of ²*skin*] **:** a fine loam that is used for the last coating and forms the skin of a mold in founding

skin·ny \ˈskinē, -ni\ *adj* -ER/-EST **1 :** of the nature of or like skin **:** MEMBRANOUS **2 a :** thin and lacking flesh (as from emaciation) ⟨a ~ little guy, kind of funny, kind of sad —Barbara B. Jamison⟩ ⟨those ~ hands of his, withered beyond their years —Rex Ingamells⟩ **b :** lacking usual or desirable bulk, quantity, qualities, or significance ⟨a ~ old spirea bush —John Moore⟩ ⟨~ unimaginative settings —Whitney Balliett⟩ **3 :** of the nature of a skinflint **:** NIGGARDLY, STINGY **syn** see LEAN

skin on *vt* **:** to apply (as paint or varnish) in an excessively thin coat

skins *pl of* SKIN, *pres 3d sing of* SKIN

skin spot *n* **:** a disease of potato tubers caused by a fungus (*Oospora pustulans*) and characterized by circular spots that on coarse-skinned varieties resemble pimples and are similar in color to normal skin and on smooth-skinned varieties are dark and sunken with raised centers

skin test *n* **:** a test for susceptibility performed on the skin of the patient and used in detecting allergic hypersensitivity (as to pollens or foods) and in diagnosing infection (past or present) with diseases that produce local hypersensitivity — compare COCCIDIOIDIN, INTRACUTANEOUS TEST, PATCH TEST, SCRATCH TEST, TUBERCULIN TEST

¹skintight \ˈ=ˈ=\ *adj* **:** closely fitted to the figure ⟨playing tennis in ~ green shorts —*Sydney (Australia) Bull.*⟩

²skintight \ˈ"\ *n* -S **:** a skintight garment

skin·tle *also* **scin·tle** \ˈskintᵊl\ *vt* -ED/-ING/-S [origin unknown] **1 :** to stack (molded brick) with spaces between to allow ventilation for drying **2 :** to set (brick) in a wall irregularly so that the brick are out of line with the face of the wall ⅛ to ¼ inch or more

skin wool *n* **:** an inferior scoured wool obtained from sheep after death **:** PULLED WOOL

skinworm \ˈ=,=\ *n* **1 :** a caterpillar that is the larva of a moth (*Archips franciscana*) of the family Tortricidae that burrows beneath the skin of apples in the western U. S. **2 :** a grub that is the larva of a skin beetle

skiöring *var of* SKIJORING

¹skip \ˈskip\ *vb* **skipped; skipped; skipping; skips** [ME *skippen*, perh. of Scand origin; akin to ON *skopa* to take a run, Sw dial. *skopa* to hop, dance; prob. akin to OS *skop* poet — more at SCOP] *vi* **1 a** (1) **:** to move or proceed with a skip **:** move with leaps and bounds **:** move in a light dancing motion **:** CAPER, GAMBOL ⟨can ~ and frisk about with wonderful agility —William Cowper⟩ (2) **:** to move by bounding off one point after another **:** RICOCHET ⟨*skipping* across the surface of the water like a flung stone —C.L.Biemiller⟩ (3) **:** to proceed as if by exaggerated bounds ⟨the shock wave, which often ~*s* erratically, was felt . . . some 130 miles distant —*N.Y. Times*⟩ **:** HOP ⟨~ along the Florida coast towns in a . . . helicopter —Horace Sutton⟩ **b :** to move quickly, easily, and usu. blithely ⟨*skipped* happily to his hotel to interview him —Sinclair Lewis⟩ ⟨small yachts *skipped* here and there —Alan Villiers⟩ ⟨the opening chapters alternately plod and ~ along —Jay Leyda⟩ **c :** to leave hurriedly ⟨cut poles for a corral and put a couple of horses in it so we could ~ pretty fast —Bruce Siberts⟩ ⟨a warrant of arrest . . . was never served because the person *skipped* out —Erle Stanley Gardner⟩ esp. after getting funds by fraud or dishonest means ⟨the teller *skipped* with the till⟩ or to avoid paying a debt ⟨guests who ~ on their bills —Horace Sutton⟩ **d :** to move erratically or at random ⟨*skipping* through the country from one town to another⟩ **e :** to discuss or investigate quickly **:** SKIM ⟨bought the paper, calmly *skipped* through the interview —H.Ledig-Rowohlt⟩ **2 a :** to pass over or omit a topic, section, or line **:** move from one point to another by omitting or disregarding the intervals ⟨you may ~ through a book, reading only those passages here and there which concern you —L.R.McColvin⟩ ⟨a little bored by the passage . . . he ~*s* over it —Bernard De Voto⟩ ⟨the biography ~*s* from his infancy to his graduation from law school⟩ **b :** to pass from one grade in school to the next but one without going through the intermediate grade **c :** to leave out a step in a progression or series ⟨his heart *skipped* in terror⟩; *specif* **:** MISFIRE 1 — used of an internal combustion engine **d :** JUMP *vi* 3a(5) **~ *vt* 1 a :** to pass over without notice, mention, or attention **:** omit in reading, investigation, or discussion ⟨to ~ the old guard . . . two writers with definite talent must be noted —Richard Plant⟩ ⟨the scientists should ~ that part of the book —*London Calling*⟩ ⟨it ~*s* and dodges all the real questions —A.H.Vandenberg b. 1907⟩ **b :** to pass over (a step or stage in development or time) ⟨when an adjustment for the superior child is attempted, it sometimes takes the form of *skipping* a grade —J.D.Russell & C.H.Judd⟩ ⟨the festival concerts ~ a day —Claudia Cassidy⟩ **:** fail to participate in or do (a normal or regular function) ⟨the president *skipped* his regular Thursday press conference —*Newsweek*⟩ ⟨the three of us *skipped* chow and lit for town —Len Zinberg⟩ **c :** to pass over or by (a point, space, or area) ⟨separate related groups of paragraphs by *skipping* four blank lines —W.R. Parker⟩ ⟨they plan to ~ the larger cities on their trip⟩ **d :** to pass by or leave out (a step in a progression or series) ⟨~*s* every third line⟩ ⟨makes the strongest pulse beat faster and the weakest to ~ many beats —L.P.Stryker⟩ ⟨the tune ~*s* a note⟩ **e :** to fail or neglect to take, accept, order, or give ⟨if I've only stayed overnight and he has done nothing for me, I ~ the tip —Richard Joseph⟩ **2 a :** to cause to skip ⟨parents want their daughter or son . . . *skipped* to second grade the day he enters school —Caroline Tryon⟩ ⟨looking for flat stones to ~ in the sea —*Tomorrow*⟩ **b :** to drop (a bomb) in skip bombing ⟨*skipped* heavy bombs into their railroad-tunnel lairs —F.G.Vosburgh⟩ **3 :** to leap over lightly and with agility ⟨*skipped* the hedge and the wall⟩ **4 a :** to depart from quickly and secretly esp. under suspicion or after a misdemeanor ⟨built up a big load of debts, then *skipped* town with all his merchandise —J.P.Blank⟩ **b :** to stay away from without permission ⟨~ school⟩ ⟨*skipped* the staff meeting again⟩ **— skip bail :** to jump bail **— skip rope :** to jump rope

²skip \ˈ"\ *n* -S [ME *skippe*, fr. *skippen*, v.] **1 :** an act or instance of skipping: as **a :** a light blithe bounding step ⟨the ~ of the lamb and the caper of the kid —Douglas Kennedy⟩ **b :** a gait composed of alternating hops and steps **c :** a dance step consisting of a hop taking off and landing on the same foot with the free foot raised slightly in front or back **2 a :** a deliberate or accidental passing over or omission ⟨read the book without a ~⟩; *specif* **:** a melodic musical progression from one note to another at an interval greater than one scale step **b :** something skipped or to be skipped: as (1) **:** a small isolated spot or area left unintentionally when painting (2) **:** a depression in the surface of a board missed by the planer or finisher **c :** a small spot in planted ground where a crop fails to establish itself ⟨the seeder left many ~*s*⟩ **d :** SKIP STRAIGHT **3 a** [short for *skipkennel*] **:** FOOTMAN, LACKEY — compare SCOUT 4 **b :** a debtor who attempts to avoid paying by moving away without leaving a forwarding address

³skip \ˈ"\ *n* -S [alter. of *skep*] **1 a :** SKEP **b :** a basket, bucket, or open car mounted on wheels, rails, or vertical shafts for carrying men and materials (as in mining, quarrying, or manufacturing) **:** GUNBOAT 2 **c :** the container on a concrete mixer that receives the charge of aggregate and cement and is hoisted to discharge these materials into the drum **2 :** a slab of coal cut from a pillar or breast **3 skips** *pl* **:** thin brown papers of a grade suitable for lining containers (as for textiles)

⁴skip \ˈ"\ *n* -S [short for ²*skipper*] **1 :** the captain of a side in a game (as curling or lawn bowling) who advises his men as to the play and controls the action **2 :** SKIPPER

⁵skip \ˈ"\ *vt* **skipped; skipped; skipping; skips :** to act as skipper of (a curling or lawn bowling team)

ski pants *n pl* **:** pants worn for skiing that are ribbed or close-fitted at the ankle

ski pants

skip bomb *vt* **:** to attack by releasing delayed-action bombs from a low flying airplane near and parallel to the surface esp. so that they skip along the surface and strike the target

skipdent \ˈ=,=\ *n* [¹*skip* + *dent*] **:** an openwork fabric woven by skipping selected dents when drawing in the warp in the loom reed

skip distance *n* **:** the outer limit of the skip zone beyond which high-frequency radio signals are received satisfactorily

skip·e·tar \ˈskipə,tär, ,=ˈ=\ *n* -S *cap* [Alb *Shqiptarë*] **:** ALBANIAN 1

skip hoist *or* **skip elevator** *n* **:** ³SKIP 1b

skipjack \ˈ=,=\ *n* -S *see sense 2* **1 a :** a young conceited fop **b** *obs* **:** JOCKEY **2** *or pl* **skipjack :** any of various fishes that jump above or play at the surface of the water: as **a** (1) **:** any of various bonitos (as the Chile bonito or frigate mackerel) (2) *or* **skipjack tuna :** a rather small large-eyed fish (*Katsuwonus pelamis*) that is bluish above and silvery below with oblique dark stripes on sides and belly and with a series of small finlets following both dorsal and anal fins, that is widely distributed in warm seas, and that is an important food and sport fish — called also *oceanic bonito* **b :** TENPOUNDER **c :** RAINBOW RUNNER **d :** a common freshwater herring (*Pomolobus chrysochloris*) of eastern No. America; *also* **:** any of several related fishes (as an alewife or gizzard shad) **e :** BLUEFISH **f :** a small freshwater silversides (*Labidesthes sicculus*) of the southern U. S. **g :** a large pale green Australian percoid food fish (*Temnodon saltator*) **3 :** CLICK BEETLE **4 :** a small sailboat with bottom like a flat V and the sides vertical or nearly so

skipkennel \ˈ=,==\ *n* [¹*skip* + *kennel* (gutter)] **:** LACKEY, FOOTBOY

ski-plane \ˈ=,=\ *n* **:** a land-based airplane equipped with landing skis

skip mackerel *n* **:** BLUEFISH

skip·man \ˈ=mən\ *n, pl* **skipmen :** a worker who loads, unloads, or tends a skip

ski pole *n* **:** a metal-pointed pole or stick, made of steel or cane, fitted with a handstrap at the top and an encircling disk set a little above the point to keep it from sinking into deep snow, and used as an aid in skiing — called also *ski stick*

ski pole

skip·pable \ˈskipəbəl\ *adj* **1 :** capable of being skipped **2 :** liable to cause skipping ⟨the world's most ~ novel —*Times Lit. Supp.*⟩

skipped *past of* SKIP

¹skip·per \ˈskipə(r)\ *n* -S [ME *skippere* erratically active insect, one that skips, fr. *skippen* to skip + *-er, -ere* -er] **1 :** any of various erratically active insects: as **a :** CHEESE SKIPPER **b :** CLICK BEETLE **c** *South* **:** a maggot infesting meat **d :** WATER STRIDER **2 a :** one that skips ⟨the best readers are those that know how to skip, and I'm a good ~ —Meredith Nicholson⟩ **b :** a young thoughtless person **:** SKIPJACK **3 a :** the Atlantic saury (*Scombresox saurus*) or a related fish that jumps freely above the water **b :** LONG TOM 2b **4 :** any of numerous small stout-bodied lepidopterous insects of the superfamily Hesperioidea that differ from the typical butterflies in wing venation and the form of the antennae, are usu. somber in color, and have comparatively small wings, thickened antennae usu. hooked at the tip, a short swift flight, and larvae that usu. make a rudimentary cocoon **5 :** SKIP STRAIGHT

²skipper \ˈ"\ *n* -S [ME *skypper*, fr. MD *schipper* boatman, skipper, fr. *schip* ship + *-er*; akin to OE *scip* ship — more at SHIP] **1 a :** the master of a ship; *esp* **:** the master of a fishing, small trading, or pleasure boat **b :** the commander of a military or naval installation or unit **c :** the captain or first pilot of an airplane **2 a :** the captain of an athletic team **b :** the manager or coach of an athletic team (as a baseball team) **3 :** the conductor of a train **4 :** the adult leader of a sea explorer ship in the Boy Scouts of America **5 :** a dull blue

³skipper \ˈ"\ *vt* -ED/-ING/-S **1 :** to act as skipper or master of (a boat) **2 :** to act as coach or captain of (a team)

⁴skipper \ˈ"\ *n* -S [³*skip* + *-er*] **:** a skipman in a metal mine

skip·pered \-pə(r)d\ *adj* **:** infested with maggots

skip·per·ship \-pə(r),ship\ *n* **:** the position, duties, or skill of a skipper

skip·pery \-p(ə)rē, -ri\ *adj* [¹*skipper* + *-y*] **:** containing cheese skippers — used of cheese and meat

¹skip·pet \ˈskipət, *usu* -əd.+V\ *n* -S [ME *skipet* small receptacle, perh. fr. *skeppe, skippe* skep + *-et*] **:** a small box for covering and preserving a seal (as for a document)

²skippet *n* -S [perh. irreg. fr. ¹*skiff* + *-et*] *obs* **:** a small boat **:** SKIFF

skipping *pres part of* SKIP

skip·ping·ly *adv* [*skipping* (pres. part. of ¹*skip*) + *-ly*] **:** in a skipping manner

skipping rope *or* **skip rope** *n* [*skipping* fr. gerund of ¹*skip*] **:** JUMP ROPE

skipple *var of* SCHEPEL

skips *pres 3d sing of* SKIP, *pl of* SKIP

skip-stop \ˈ=,=\ *n* **:** the omission of intermediate vehicular stops (as of a bus or elevator) for operating advantage or emergency

skip straight *n* **:** a special hand recognized in some poker games that is composed of five cards in alternate sequence (as 3, 5, 7, 9, and jack) and beats two pairs but loses to three of a kind — called also *alternate straight, dutch straight, skip, skipper*

skiptail \ˈ=,=\ *n* **:** SPRINGTAIL

skip tender *n* [³*skip*] **:** CAGER 1a

skip tracer *n* **:** a person employed (as by an insurance company) to locate persons who disappear leaving unpaid bills

skip zone *n* **:** the area around a high-frequency radio transmitting station between the outer effective range of ground wave transmission and the inner limit of transmission by means of signals reflected from the ionosphere in which little or no signal reception is possible

skire thursday *n, usu cap S&T* [ME *skire thuresday* (trans. of ON *skīri-thōrsdagr*), fr. *skir* bright, pure (fr. ON *skīrr*) + *thuresday* Thursday; prob. fr. the practice of confessing one's sins on Maundy Thursday — more at SHEER] *obs* **:** MAUNDY THURSDAY

¹skirl \ˈskərl, *chiefly before pause or consonant* ˈskər·əl; *–R* ˈskəl *or* ˈskəil; *Scot usu* ˈskirl\ *vb* -ED/-ING/-S [ME (Sc) *skirlen, skrillen*, of Scand origin; akin to OSw *skrælla* to rattle, bang — more at SHRILL] *vi* **1 :** to utter or emit a shrill tone **:** SHRIEK **2 a** *of a bagpipe* **:** to emit the high shrill tone of the chanter; *also* **:** to give forth music **b :** to play the bagpipe **~ *vt* 1 :** to give forth (a shrill sound) **2 :** to play (music) on the bagpipe

²skirl \ˈ"\ *n* -S **1 :** a shrieking sound **:** SCREAM ⟨the ~ of a curlew —Vance Palmer⟩ **2 :** a high shrill sound produced by the chanter of a bagpipe

³skirl \ˈ"\ *vi* -ED/-ING/-S [origin unknown] **:** to fly or sweep in

a whirl : move or become moved in a twisting, curving, or flurrying path ⟨newspapers and old sacks ~*ed* a little in the gutters —P.D.Boles⟩

⁴**skirl** \"\ *n* -s : something that skirls, is skirled, or is formed by skirling ⟨~*s* of dust and wind and crumpled newspapers —Thomas Wolfe⟩

¹**skir·mish** \'skərmish, 'skəm-, 'skəim-, -mēsh\ *n* -ES [ME *skyrmissh*, alter. (influenced by ME *skirmysshen* to fence, brandish a sword, fr. MF *eskermiss-, escremiss-*, stem of *eskermir, escremir* to fence, of Gmc origin; akin to OHG *skirmen* to defend) of *skarmish, scarmuch*, fr. MF *escarmouche*, fr. OIt *scaramuccia*, of Gmc origin; akin to OHG *skirmen* to defend, *skerm, skirm* shield — more at SCHERM] **1** : a minor engagement in war usu. incidental to larger movements : combat between detached and small bodies of troops — distinguished from *pitched battle* **2** : a minor dispute or contest between opposing parties : a brisk preliminary conflict ⟨this verbal ~ is viewed here as the opening round in negotiations scheduled to start next Tuesday —*N.Y. Times*⟩

²**skirmish** \", *chiefly in pres part* -məsh\ *vi* -ED/-ING/-ES [ME *skyrmysshen*, alter. (influenced by ME *skirmysshen* to fence, brandish a sword) of *scarmysshen, scarmuchen*, fr. MF *escarmouchier*, fr. OIt *scaramucciare*, fr. *scaramuccia*, n.] **1 a** : to fight as skirmishers : engage in a skirmish **b** : to engage in a minor or preliminary argument ⟨would prevent the many would-be presidential candidates within the party from ~*ing* among themselves —*Newsweek*⟩ **2** : to search about (as for supplies) : scout around : SCRIMMAGE, RUMMAGE

skir·mish·er \-shə(r)\ *n* -s : one of a group of soldiers deployed in extended order as an advanced guard, a small independent attack force, or as cover for the front and flanks of a column

skirmish line *n* : a line of skirmishers; *esp* : the skirmishers in advance of a line of battle

¹**skirr** *also* **scur** \'skər(·)\ *vb* -ED/-ING/-S [perh. alter. of ¹*scour*] *vi* **1** : to leave hastily : FLEE ⟨birds ~*ed* off from the bushes —D.H.Lawrence⟩ **2** : to run, fly, sail, or otherwise move rapidly ~ *vt* **1** : to search about in ⟨~ the country round —Shak.⟩ **2 a** : to pass rapidly over : SKIM **b** *dial* : to cause to skim ⟨~ a stone⟩

²**skirr** \"\ *n* -s [prob. imit.] : a whirring, rasping, or roaring sound ⟨the ~ of a bird⟩ ⟨the occasional ~ of an automobile starting —*Harper's*⟩

skir·reh \'skirə\ *n* -s [origin unknown] : a cord used by masons in keeping brickwork or foundations straight and by surveyors and excavators in marking out sites

skir·ret \'skirət, *usu* -əd.+V\ *n* -s [ME *skirwhit*, by folk etymology (influence of ME *skir, skire* bright, pure and ME *whit* white) fr. MF *eschervi*, prob. modif. of Ar *karawyā* skirret, caraway — more at CARAWAY, SKIRE THURSDAY, WHITE] : an Asiatic herb (*Sium sisarum*) cultivated in Europe for its sweet edible tuberous roots

¹**skirt** \'skərt, 'skət, 'skəit, *usu* -d.+V\ *n* -s [ME, fr. ON *skyrta* shirt, kirtle — more at SHIRT] **1 a** (1) : the part of an outer garment or undergarment extending from the waist down that has a free hanging lower edge and is cut in one with the upper part of the garment or attached at the waistline ⟨the ~ of a jacket⟩ ⟨the sweeping ~ of a ball gown⟩ — often used in pl. ⟨gathered up her ~*s* and ran away⟩ (2) : a separate outer garment or undergarment for women and girls covering the body from the waist down **b** : either of two usu. leather flaps on a saddle covering the bars on which the stirrups are hung — see STOCK SADDLE illustration **c** : a cloth facing hanging loosely and usu. in folds or pleats from the bottom edge or across the front of a piece of furniture ⟨dressing table ~⟩ ⟨chair ~⟩ **d** : the outer part of a parachute canopy **e** : the lower branches of a tree when near the ground **2 a** : the rim, periphery, or environs of an area, territorial division, or natural feature ⟨the long white ~ of the salt desert lay awash —Dean Jennings⟩ — often used in pl. **b skirts** *pl* : the outlying parts of a town or city : OUTSKIRTS, SUBURBS ⟨unfenced pastures on the ~*s* of the village —Joseph Mitchell⟩ **3** : a part or attachment serving as a rim, border, edging, or endpiece of an object: as **a** : the lip of a bell **b** : an apron piece or border in a building (as a baseboard or the molded piece under a window stool) **c** : a decorative piece on furniture connecting the legs along the lower edge of the table top, chair seat, or base **d** : a protective guard or plating on machinery and appliances **e** : a sheet metal covering for the wheels and other working parts of a locomotive **f** : FENDER SKIRT **g** : the bottom portion of the vertical wall of a screw-on jar cap; *also* : the vertical portion of a can wall attached to the cap of a key-opened can **4** : the final portions of a period of time **5 a** : the diaphragm or midriff of an animal used as edible meat **b** *Brit* : a flank of beef **6** *slang* : GIRL, WOMAN ⟨the American soldiers' . . . reputation as perhaps the most tireless ~ chasers of all time and all peoples —D.L.Cohn⟩ **7** : the bearing surface of a piston consisting of the plain cylindrical portion below the ring ⟨neither the cylinder bore nor the piston ~ is perfectly stiff —H.F.Blanchard & Ralph Ritchen⟩ **8** : SKIRTING 3

²**skirt** \"\ *vb* -ED/-ING/-S *vt* **1** : to form the border or edge of : run along the edge of : BORDER ⟨the shell of mountains that ~*s* the southeast coast —W.B.Furlong⟩ ⟨~*ed* by a lofty iron railing —John Godley⟩ **2 a** : to provide a skirt for ⟨an old-fashioned full-*skirted* frock coat —O.S.J.Gogarty⟩ **b** : to furnish a border or guard for ⟨machines ~*ed* and fendered —*Newsweek*⟩ **3 a** : to go or proceed closely around or about : follow the outskirts of ⟨set out to ~ the marshes that lay between them and the fort —Kenneth Roberts⟩ ⟨the dusty path that ~*ed* the field —Ellen Glasgow⟩; *specif* : to go around or keep away from in order to avoid danger or discovery ⟨sent back word to ~ the frowning walls and make no contacts with the inhabitants —J.R.Perkins⟩ ⟨the friendly neighborhood cop whom everybody knows and the criminal ~*s* —George Barrett⟩ ⟨~*ed* right end on a 7-yard touchdown run —*N.Y. Times*⟩ **b** : to avoid (as a topic or question) because of difficulty, complexity, danger, or fear of controversy ⟨both candidates were seen as ~*ing* the referendums —*Current Biog.*⟩ **c** : to escape (as danger, death, or error) though coming very close : evade or miss by a very narrow margin ⟨an empiricist has to seek the justification . . . in the motivational make-up of man . . . yet to ~ the naturalistic fallacy —P.B.Rice⟩ ⟨unaware of having ~*ed* disaster —Edith Wharton⟩ **4** : to remove the skirtings from (a fleece of wool) ~ *vi* **1** : to be, lie, or move along an edge, border, or margin : follow a roundabout path ⟨the tanker . . . was expected to ~ around submerged obstacles —*N.Y. Times*⟩ **2** *of a hound* : to cut corners rather than follow the actual path of a fox

³**skirt** \'skirt, 'skərt\ *vi* -ED/-ING/-S [origin unknown] *Scot* : to hurry away

skirtboard \'⸗,⸗\ *n* **1** : BASEBOARD **2** : a side plate to protect conveyor chains and increase the capacity of a conveyor or catch spillage or redirect it to the conveyor belt

skirt cassock *n* : CASSOCK 2c

skirt-dance \'⸗,⸗\ *vi* [¹*skirt* + *dance*, v.] : to execute a skirt dance — **skirt-dancer** \'⸗,⸗⸗\ *n*

skirt dance *n* [¹*skirt* + *dance*, n.] **1** : a ballet dance popular in the 19th century distinguished by the dancer's manipulations of her long flowing and varicolored skirts or drapery **2** : a folk dance (as the chiapanecas) accompanied by the manipulation of full skirts or drapery

skirt·er \'skərd|·ə(r), 'skə̄|, 'skəi|, |t|\ *n* -s : one that skirts: as **a** : a hunter or hound that tends to go around rather than over obstacles; *also* : a dog that runs wide of the pack **b** : one that removes skirtings from fleeces

skirting *n* -s [fr. gerund of ²*skirt*] **1** : something that skirts: as **a** : BORDER, EDGING, ENCLOSURE; *specif* : SKIRT 3c **b** *or* **skirting board** *Brit* : BASEBOARD **2** : fabric (as wool) suitable for skirts **3 skirtings** *pl* : inferior or soiled wool trimmed from the edges of a fleece **4** : the act or process of one that skirts

skirting leather *n* : a leather used in the manufacture of saddles and bridles

skirt·ing·ly *adv* [*skirting* (pres. part. of ²*skirt*) + *-ly*] : in a skirting manner

skirt·less \'⸗ləs\ *adj* : having no skirt

skirtlike \'⸗,⸗\ *adj* : resembling a skirt esp. in forming an enveloping dependent covering for the lower part of something ⟨the ~ indusium of a fungus⟩

skirt-roof \'⸗,⸗\ *n* : a small usu. false portion of roofing between the stories of a building

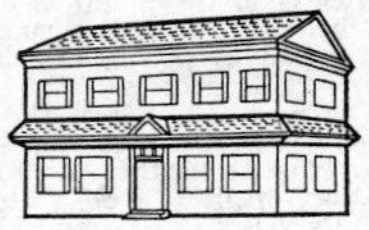

skirt-roof

skirts *pl of* SKIRT, *pres 3d sing of* SKIRT

skirty \'skər|d·|ē, 'skə̄|, 'skəi|, |t|, |i\ *adj* [*skirtings* + *-y*] *of wool* : containing excessive skirtings

ski run *n* : a slope or trail suitable for skiing

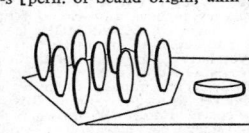

skis *pl of* SKI, *pres 3d sing of* SKI

skish \'skish\ *n* -ES [prob. blend of ³*skeet* and *fish*] : a target game for fishermen in which a small lead weight is cast at a set of targets placed flat on the surface of the water or sometimes on the ground

ski stick *n* : SKI POLE

ski suit *n* : a warm outfit for winter sports and play made in one-piece or two-piece style with a jacket top and pants usu. having ribbed cuffs

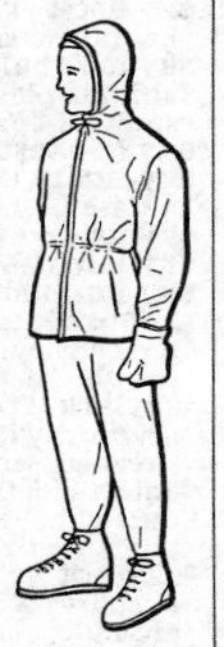

ski suit

¹**skit** \'skit, *usu* -id.+V\ *n* -s [ME *skytte*, of Scand origin; akin to Icel *skita* diarrhea; akin to ON *skīta* to defecate — more at SHIT] : SCOURS

²**skit** \"\ *vi* **skitted**; **skitted**; **skitting**; **skits** [prob. back-formation fr. *skittish*] **1** : to leap or start aside or away : be skittish : SHY **2** : to dance or jump about : CAPER, FLOUNCE

³**skit** \"\ *n* -s [perh. fr. ²*skit*] **1** : a jeering or satirical remark : JIBE, TAUNT **2 a** : a satirical or humorous story or sketch often outwardly serious; *esp* : PARODY ⟨a sophisticated and stylish ~ on typical review material —Barry Carman⟩ **b** (1) : a brief burlesque or comic sketch included in a dramatic performance (as a revue) (2) : a short serious dramatic piece included in a review or given separately; *esp* : one written, produced, and performed by amateurs ⟨the program . . . featured ~*s* by four church families on the ways religion can be brought into modern home life —*Springfield (Mass.) Union*⟩ **3** *dial Eng* : a sudden sharp shower or gust of rain

⁴**skit** \"\ *vb* **skitted**; **skitted**; **skitting**; **skits** *vi* : to make a jibe : make satirical remarks — used with *at* ~ *vt* : to satirize or caricature by means of a skit

¹**skite** \'skit, *usu* -īd.+V\ *vi* -ED/-ING/-S [prob. of Scand origin; akin to ON *skjōta* to shoot — more at SHOOT] **1** *chiefly dial* : to move quickly or hurriedly ⟨now ~ along to school⟩ **2** *chiefly Scot* : to strike an object with a glancing blow : RICOCHET, SKIP

²**skite** \"\ *n* -s **1** *chiefly dial* : a sudden glancing blow or impact **2** *dial* : TRICK, PRANK

³**skite** \"\ *n* -s [prob. fr. E dial. *skite* to defecate, fr. ME *skyten*, fr. ON *skīta*] *dial* : a disagreeable offensive person

⁴**skite** \"\ *vi* -ED/-ING/-S [prob. fr. E dial. *skite* to defecate] *chiefly Austral* : BOAST, BRAG

⁵**skite** \" *or* **skit·er** \-d·ə(r)\ *n* -s [*skite* fr. ⁴*skite*; *skiter* fr. ⁴*skite* + *-er*] *chiefly Austral* : BRAGGART, BOASTER

ski tow *n* **1** : a power-driven conveyor for pulling skiers to the top of a slope consisting usu. of an endless motor-driven moving rope which the skier grasps **2** : SKI LIFT

ski trooper *n* : a member of the ski troops

ski troops *n pl* : troops trained and equipped to maneuver and fight on skis

skit·swish \'skit,swish\ *n, pl* **skitswish** *usu cap* : COEUR D'ALENE

skit·ta·get \'skid·əgət, -d·ə,get\ *or* **skid·e·gate** \'skidəgət, -də,gāt\ *n, pl* **skittaget** *or* **skittagets** *or* **skidegate** *or* **skidegates** *usu cap* : HAIDA

skit·ta·get·an \,⸗⸗'gētᵊn, -'getᵊn\ *n, pl* **skittagetan** *or* **skittagetans** *usu cap* : HAIDA 3

¹**skit·ter** \'skid·ə(r), -itə-\ *vb* -ED/-ING/-S [prob. freq. of ¹*skite*] *vi* **1** : to pass or glide lightly or hurriedly: as **a** : to skip along a surface ⟨~*ing* across the ice on belly or back —S.H.Adams⟩ **b** : to skim along or scamper with bobbing motions : SCURRY, SKIP ⟨watch a rabbit ~ off into the woods —Grace Metalious⟩ **2** : to draw the hook of a fishing line through or along the surface of water with a twitching or quivering motion ~ *vt* : to cause to skitter ⟨~ stones across the pond⟩; *specif* : to impart a twitching motion to (a fishhook) when drawing through or along the surface of the water

²**skitter** \"\ *n* -s **1** : a light gliding or bobbing motion : SCURRYING, SCAMPER **2** : a sound of skittering : RUSTLE

skit·tery \-ərē, -ri\ *adj* -ER/-EST [¹*skitter* + *-y*] : SKITTISH

skit·tish \'skid·|ish, -it|, |ēsh\ *adj, sometimes* -ER/-EST [ME, fr. *skit-* (perh. of Scand origin; akin to ON *skjōta* to shoot) + *-ish* — more at SHOOT] **1 a** : excessively lively or frivolous in nature or action : CAPRICIOUS, IRRESPONSIBLE ⟨felt that for a minister the pastime was unduly ~ —Jean Stafford⟩ **b** : given to marked or rapid fluctuations : VARIABLE, UNSTABLE ⟨the ~ fads of musical fashion —Winthrop Sargeant⟩ **2** : easily frightened or agitated : given to shying : RESTIVE — used chiefly of horses **3 a** : COY, BASHFUL, SHY **b** : marked by extreme caution : FEARFUL, WARY ⟨old wooden bridges that were a nightmare for ~ drivers —Jack Westeyn⟩ — **skit·tish·ly** *adv* — **skit·tish·ness** *n* -ES

¹**skit·tle** \'skid·ᵊl, -itᵊl\ *n* -s [perh. of Scand origin; akin to Dan *skyttel* shuttle — more at SHUTTLE] **1 a skittles** *pl but sing in constr* : English ninepins played by pitching or sliding a wooden disk or rolling a wooden ball to knock down pins **b** : one of the pins used in skittles **2 skittles** *pl* : PLAY, ENJOYMENT — used chiefly in the phrase *beer and skittles* **3 skittles** *pl but sing in constr* : rapid informal play at chess with nothing at stake; *also* : a game so played

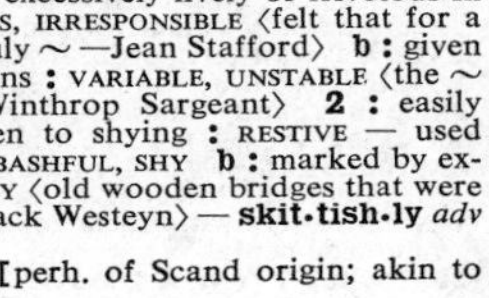

skittles 1b with disk

²**skittle** \"\ *vb* **skittled**; **skittled**; **skittling** \-itliŋ, -id·ᵊl-, -itᵊl-\ **skittles** *vi* : to play skittles ~ *vt* : to put out (several batsmen) easily in cricket — usu. used with *out*

skittle ball *n* : a heavy wooden disk used in skittles — called also *cheese*

skittle pool *n* : a game played on a billiard table with two white balls, a red ball, and a number of black and white pins in which counts are made by knocking down any of the white pins with the cue ball after contact with an object ball but if a black pin is knocked down the striker loses his entire score and must start anew

skit·tler \'skid·ᵊlə(r), -it(ᵊ)l-\ *n* -s : one that skittles

¹**skive** *or* **scive** \'skīv\ *vt* **skived** *or* **scived**; **skived** *or* **scived**; **skiving** *or* **sciving**; **skives** *or* **scives** [of Scand origin; akin to ON *skīfa* to slice, Icel *skīfa* disk — more at SHEAVE] : to cut off (as leather or rubber) in thin layers or pieces : SHAVE, PARE

²**skive** \"\ *n* -s : a skived or beveled part of a leather (as a shoe upper where it is seamed together)

³**skive** \"\ *n* -s [modif. of D *schijf* — more at SKEIF] : a diamond wheel : SKEIF

⁴**skive** \"\ *vi* -ED/-ING/-S [origin unknown] **1** *chiefly dial* : to dart or skim lightly and rapidly **2** *chiefly dial* : to depart in a hurry

¹**skiv·er** \'skivə(r)\ *n* -s [origin unknown] *dial* : SKEWER

²**skiv·er** \"\ *vt* -ED/-ING/-S : SKEWER, IMPALE

³**skiv·er** \'skīvə(r)\ *n* -s [¹*skive* + *-er*] **1** : a thin soft leather made of the grain side of a split sheepskin, usu. tanned in sumac and dyed, and used for hat linings, pocketbooks, and bookbindings **2** : one that skives: as **a** : a cutting tool a machine uses in splitting leather or skins **b** : a worker who bevels or pares leather, rubber, or fiber parts so that they will form a smooth joint

skiv·vy \'skivi\ *n* -ES [origin unknown] *Brit* : a female domestic servant

sklent \'sklent\ *vb* -ED/-ING/-S [ME *sclenten* to strike obliquely, alter. of *slenten* — more at SLANT] *vi* **1** *chiefly Scot* : to glance sideways : look askance **2** *chiefly Scot* : to cast aspersions ~ *vt, Scot* : to direct sideways : SLANT

sklim \'sklim\ *vb* [origin unknown] *Scot* : CLIMB

sklo·dow·skite \sklə'dȯf,skīt\ *n* -s [F, fr. Marja *Skłodowska* Curie †1934 Pol. born Fr. chemist + F *-ite*] : a mineral $Mg(UO_2)_2Si_2O_7.6H_2O$ consisting of a hydrous magnesium uranyl silicate that is isomorphous with uranophane

¹**skoal** \'skōl\ *n* -s [Dan *skål*, lit., bowl, cup; akin to ON *skāl* bowl — more at SCALE] : a toast to someone's health, well-being, or prosperity — often used interjectionally

²**skoal** \"\ *vi* -ED/-ING/-S : to drink an alcoholic beverage usu. as a toast

sko·be·loff green \'skōbə,lȯf-\ *n, often cap S* [prob. fr. the name *Skobeloff*] : a moderate bluish green that is greener, lighter, and stronger than porcelain green or sea blue

skoi·no·lon \'skȯinə,län\ *n* [NL, perh. irreg. fr. Gk *schoinos* rush, reed] *syn of* SCHOENOCAULON

sko·ko·mish \skō'kōmish, skə'-, -mēsh\ *n, pl* **skokomish** *or* **skokomishes** *usu cap* **1** : a Salishan people of western Washington **2** : a member of the Skokomish people

skolion *var of* SCOLION

skoliosis *var of* SCOLIOSIS

skol·ly \'skälē, -li\ *n* -ES [prob. modif. of Afrik *skorrimorrie* rascal, riffraff, fr. D *schorriemorrie, schorremorrie* riffraff, perh. modif. of Yiddish *soyrer-umoyre* rogue, good-for-nothing, hoodlum, fr. Heb *sorēr ūmōreh* stubborn and rebellious] *chiefly southern Africa* : a young hoodlum

¹**skoo·kum** \'skükəm\ *n* -s [Chinook jargon, powerful, evil spirit, fr. Chehalis *skukm*] : an evil spirit

²**skookum** \"\ *adj* [Chinook jargon] **1** : marked by strength or power ⟨was a ~ eater most times, but he pushed his bowl away —Arthur Mayse⟩ **2** : marked by excellent quality : FIRST-RATE ⟨as handsome and healthy as ~ apples —*Time*⟩

skookum-house \'⸗⸗,⸗\ *n* : JAIL ⟨had recently been arrested . . . put in the *skookum-house* . . . and fined —*Century Mag.*⟩

skop·lje \'skȯp,lā, -p,yä\ *adj, usu cap* [fr. *Skoplje*, city in southern Yugoslavia] : of or from the city of Skoplje, Yugoslavia : of the kind or style prevalent in Skoplje

skop·tsy \(,)skäpt'sē\ *n pl, usu cap* [Russ, pl. of *skopets*, lit., eunuch; akin to OSlav *skopiti* to castrate — more at CAPON] : members of an ascetic religious sect of dissenters from the Russian Orthodox Church dating prob. from the 18th century and stressing sexual abstinence

skraup synthesis \'skraůp-\ *n, usu cap 1st S* [after Zdenko H. *Skraup* †1910 Czechoslovak chemist] : the production of quinoline by heating aniline, glycerol, and sulfuric acid with an oxidizing agent (as nitrobenzene); *also* : any of various similar syntheses performed with aromatic amino compounds other than aniline

skreak *or* **skreek** \'skrēk\ *chiefly dial var of* SCREECH

skreich \'skrēk̠\ *chiefly Scot var of* SCREECH

skriegh \'skrēk̠\ *chiefly Scot var of* SCREECH

¹**skrim·shan·der** *or* **scrim·shan·der** \(ˈ)skim¦shandə(r)\ *or* **scrim·shan·dy** \-dē, -di\ *n, pl* **skrimshanders** *or* **scrimshanders** *or* **scrimshandies** [origin unknown] : SCRIMSHAW ⟨young seamen . . . examining . . . divers specimens of ~ —Herman Melville⟩

²**skrimshander** \"\ *vb* -ED/-ING/-S : SCRIMSHAW

skrimshank *var of* SCRIMSHANK

skryer *var of* SCRYER

skua \'skyüə\ *also* **skua gull** *n* -s [*skua* fr. NL, fr. Faeroese *skūgvur*; akin to ON *skūfr* skua, tassel, OE *scēaf* sheaf — more at SHEAF] : JAEGER 3; *esp* : a jaeger of the genus *Catharacta* — see GREAT SKUA

skul·dug·gery *or* **skull·dug·gery** *also* **scul·dug·gery** *or* **scull·dug·gery** \,skəl'dəg(ə)rē, -ri *also* '⸗,⸗(⸗)⸗\ *n* -ES [alter. of *sculduddery*] **1 a** : dishonest, underhanded, unfair, or unscrupulous behavior or activity ⟨suspects ~ in death of Londoner —*Saturday Rev.*⟩ ⟨counterfeiting is a prehistoric form of gainful ~ —St. Clair McKelway⟩ ⟨some alleged ~ in the state department —Elmer Davis⟩ ⟨won over to producing his major shows on the rival chain only by ~ —Herman Wouk⟩ **b** : proficiency in or a tendency toward such behavior or activity ⟨with such skill and ~ that nothing was suspected —*Time*⟩ ⟨the ~ in human nature —John Cournos⟩ **2** : an instance of skulduggery ⟨a stranger to those *skulduggeries* which have brought politics into disrepute —*New Republic*⟩

¹**skulk** *also* **sculk** \'skəlk\ *vb* -ED/-ING/-S [ME *skulken*, of Scand origin; akin to Dan *skulke* to shirk, play truant, Norw *skulka*, Sw *skolka*] *vi* **1** : to move in or as if in a stealthy, furtive, or cautious manner : SNEAK ⟨Indians ~*ing* through the tall sage —*Amer. Guide Series: Nev.*⟩ ⟨~ up and down with the air of a charity-boy, a bastard, or an interloper —R.W. Emerson⟩ **2 a** : to hide or conceal oneself often from cowardice or fear or sometimes with sinister intent ⟨children with ice-cream cones ~*ed* in the doorways, like abused cats —Jean Stafford⟩ ⟨scrambling over fence rails and ~*ing* in thickets —D.C.Peattie⟩ ⟨what bedevilled idiocy ~*s* behind that arrogant mask —Herbert Read⟩ **b** *chiefly Brit* : to avoid duty : MALINGER ~ *vt* : to avoid in a furtive or cowardly manner ⟨~ our obligation to our country⟩ **syn** see LURK

²**skulk** \"\ *n* -s [ME *skulke*, fr. *skulken*, v.] **1** *of foxes* : PACK, GROUP **2** : SKULKER

skulk·er \-kə(r)\ *n* -s [ME, fr. *skulken* to skulk + *-er*] : one that skulks

¹**skull** \'skəl\ *n* -s [ME *skulle*, of Scand origin; akin to Sw *skulle* skull; prob. akin to OHG *scollo* clod, lump, *scala* shell, husk — more at SHELL] **1 a** : the skeleton of the head of a vertebrate : the bony or cartilaginous case or framework that encloses and protects the brain and chief sense organs, supports the jaws, is cartilaginous in primitive forms (as cyclostomes and elasmobranchs) and in the embryos of all forms, but in higher vertebrates has the cartilage usu. replaced by bone and the structure made more complete by the union with it of other bones developed in membrane, and consists of the cranium, the bony capsules of the nose, ear, and eye, and the jaws **b** : the cranium together with those bones that are immovably fused with it (as the mammalian upper jaw) **2** : the seat of understanding or intelligence : MIND ⟨it penetrated his thick ~ what had happened —*Storyteller Weekly*⟩ ⟨a multitude of things that the ordinary sealed ~ rejects —J.M.Barzun⟩ **3 a** : the crown of the head ⟨an unattractive old man, with a bald yellow ~ —Ellen Glasgow⟩ **b** (1) : SKULLCAP 1b (2) : the top of a helmet ⟨the sides of the helmet were commonly hinged to the ~ —Christopher & Adrian Lynch-Robinson⟩ **4** : DEATH'S-HEAD **5** : a crust of solidified material (as metal, matte, or slag) that forms on the walls of a ladle or other vessel containing this material in the molten state — often used in pl.

²**skull** *var of* SCULL

skull and crossbones *n, pl* **skulls and crossbones** : a representation of a human skull over crossbones usu. used as a warning of danger ⟨stamped a *skull and crossbones* on the labels of poisonous drugs⟩

skullcap \'⸗,⸗\ *n* **1 a** : any of various close-fitting brimless cloth caps for indoor or outdoor wear — compare BEANIE, CALOT, YARMULKE, ZUCCHETTO **b** : a close-fitting steel or iron helmet **2** : a plant of the genus *Scutellaria* having a calyx that when inverted resembles a helmet with the visor raised **3** : a domed capping layer (as of rock) **4** : the top of the skull : CALVARIUM

skullcap speedwell *n* : MARSH SPEEDWELL

skull coral *n* : any of several bulky corals having closely set polyps and resembling the brain corals

skull cracker *n* : a heavy iron or steel ball swung or dropped by a derrick to demolish old buildings or compact bulky scrap for shipment — called also *ball breaker, wrecking ball*

skullduggery *var of* SKULDUGGERY

skulled \'skəld\ *adj* : having a skull — usu. used in combination ⟨long-*skulled*⟩ ⟨broad-*skulled*⟩

skullfish \'⸗,⸗\ *n* : a whale more than two years old

skullguard \'⸗,⸗\ *n* : a helmet worn by workers for protection against head injuries from falling objects

skull-pan \'⸗,⸗\ *n* : SKULLCAP 4

skull practice *or* **skull session** *n* **1** : a training class held by an athletic coach for planning strategy and diagraming plays ⟨hold *skull practice* an hour before school each morning —J.M.Blount⟩ **2 a** : a meeting for consultation, discussion, or the interchange of ideas or information ⟨just got through having a *skull session* with the county leaders —*New Yorker*⟩ **b** : intellectual exercise ⟨the product of intellectuals interested

in experiment, abstractions, erudite allusions and other *skull practice* —C.B.Taylor⟩
skun \ˈskən\ *dial past of* SKIN
¹skunk \ˈskəŋk\ *n, pl* **skunks** *also* **skunk** [of Algonquian origin; akin to Abnaki *segākw* skunk] **1 a** (1) **:** any of various common omnivorous New World mammals forming a subfamily of Mustelidae, showing typical warning coloration of brilliantly patterned black and white, and possessing a pair of muscular-walled perineal glands from which an intensely malodorous secretion is ejected when the animal is startled or in danger — see CONEPATUS, MEPHITIS, SPILOGALE; HOG-NOSED SKUNK, LITTLE SPOTTED SKUNK, STRIPED SKUNK (2) **:** any of various offensive-smelling Old World animals (as the teledu or the zoril) **b :** the fur of a skunk **2 a :** a contemptible ill-mannered person — used as a generalized term of abuse ⟨you're a low-down, foul-mouthed, impertinent ~ —Sinclair Lewis⟩ **3 :** an unidentified surface target detected visually or by radar — compare BOGEY
²skunk \"\ *vt* -ED/-ING/-S **1 a :** to subject to defeat **:** inflict defeat upon ⟨~*ed* the other candidate by a wide margin of votes⟩ **b :** to shut out (an opponent) in a game — compare ⁴LURCH **2 a :** to fail to pay (as a bill or a creditor) ⟨made a practice of ~*ing* hotels⟩ **b :** to deprive by or as if by cheating ⟨a man . . . who has been ~*ed* out of a summer vacation —Horace Sutton⟩
³skunk \"\ *n* -S [²*skunk*] **:** SHUTOUT
skunk bear *n* **:** WOLVERINE
skunkbill \ˈ=,=\ *n* **:** SURF SCOTER
skunk bird *or* **skunk blackbird** *n* [so called fr. the coloring of the male] **:** BOBOLINK
skunkbrush \ˈ=,=\ *also* **skunkbush** \ˈ=,=\ *n* **:** any of various shrubs having an offensive odor: as **a :** BEAR BRUSH **b :** SQUAWBUSH
skunk cabbage *n* **1 a :** a perennial herb (*Symplocarpus foetidus*) of the family Araceae of eastern No. America and Asia that sends up in early spring an offensive-smelling cowl-shaped brownish purple spathe that is followed in summer by a tuft of broad leaves **b :** a similar and related plant (*Lysichiton camstschatcense*) of the U.S. Pacific coast **2 :** PITCHER PLANT a
skunk currant *n* **:** a wild currant (*Ribes glandulosum*) native to the eastern U. S. that bears offensive-smelling red fruit
skunk·ery \ˈskəŋkərē, -ri\ *n* -ES **:** a place where skunks are bred and raised usu. for commercial purposes
skunk grass *n* [so called fr. its odor] **:** a grass of the genus *Eragrostis*
skunk porpoise *n* **:** SPECTACLED DOLPHIN
skunk spruce *n* **:** WHITE SPRUCE 1a
skunktail \ˈ=,=\ *also* **skunktail grass** *n* **:** SQUIRRELTAIL
skunk turtle *n* **:** MUSK TURTLE
skunkweed \ˈ=,=\ *n* **:** any of several offensive-smelling herbs: as **a :** SKUNK CABBAGE **b :** an annual Californian weed (*Gilia squarrosa*) **c :** a Rocky Mountain sticky-leaved herb (*Polemonium viscosum*) **d :** JOE-PYE WEED
skunky \ˈskəŋkē, -ki\ *adj* -ER/-EST **:** of, relating to, or having the characteristics of a skunk
skur·ry \ˈskər-|ē, ˈskə-r|, |i\ *chiefly Brit var of* SCURRY
skutch *var of* SCUTCH
skut·te·rud·ite \ˈskəd·ə,rə,dīt\ *n* -S [G *skutterudit*, fr. *Skutterud*, near Drammen, southern Norway + G *-it* -ite] **:** a mineral (Co,Ni)As_3 that consists of a native arsenide of cobalt and nickel and is isomorphous with smaltite, nickel-skutterudite, and chloanthite
¹sky \ˈskī\ *n* -ES *often attrib* [ME, cloud, sky, fr. ON *ský* cloud; akin to OE *scēo* cloud, *scua* shadow, OHG *scuwo*, ON *skuggi* shadow, Goth *skuggwa* mirror, Skt *skunāti* he covers — more at HIDE] **1 a :** the expanse of space surrounding the earth **:** the upper atmosphere — usu. used in pl. ⟨lifted his tiny hands to the *skies* —Sherwood Anderson⟩ **b :** the expanse appearing as a great vault or arch over the earth **:** FIRMAMENT ⟨the ~ was a cold stone-grey —Pearl Buck⟩ ⟨the daughter of earth and water, and the nursling of the ~ —P.B.Shelley⟩ ⟨behold a rainbow in the ~ —William Wordsworth⟩ ⟨a blue ~ of spring —William Allingham⟩ ⟨the infinitely perilous night ~ —V.V.Nabokov⟩ — often used in pl. ⟨promise in the *skies* neither of sun nor of snow —Jean Stafford⟩ ⟨the *skies* they were ashen and sober —E.A.Poe⟩ **2 :** HEAVEN 2 ⟨fate snatch'd her early to the pitying ~ —Alexander Pope⟩ — often used in pl. ⟨he rais'd a mortal to the *skies* —John Dryden⟩ **3 a :** meteorological conditions as manifested in the upper atmospheric regions — usu. used in pl. ⟨stormy *skies*⟩ ⟨the papers forecast clear *skies* tomorrow⟩ **b :** CLIMATE — usu. used in pl. ⟨our temperate English *skies* —G.G.Coulton⟩ ⟨creatures from neighboring fields and *skies* —R.W.Murray⟩ **4 :** SKY BLUE **5 :** an unrestricted or indefinite amount or degree of something — used in the phrase *the sky is the limit* — **to the sky** *or* **to the skies** *adv* **:** in an enthusiastic manner **:** EXTRAVAGANTLY ⟨praising their thinking *to the sky* —Bernard Kalb⟩
²sky \"\ *vb* **skied** *or* **skyed**; **skied** *or* **skyed**; **skying**; **skies** *vt* **1** *chiefly Brit* **:** to toss up (a coin) **:** FLIP ⟨*skied* a copper for heads or tails —S.H.Adams⟩ **2 a :** to hang (as a painting) above the line of vision ⟨have been *skied* or placed in obscure corners —*Carnegie Mag.*⟩ **b :** to place (as a person) in an inconveniently high place ⟨the world's press, *skied* up in the gallery —Mollie Panter-Downes⟩ **3 :** to hit (a ball) high into the air ⟨*skied* his simple pitch a full 40 yards short of the green —H.W.Wind⟩ **4 :** to pass (as cotton cloth) in dyeing through air on rollers (as for oxidizing the reduced form of a vat dye) ~ *vi* **1 :** to hit a ball high into the air ⟨the batter *skied* to the center fielder⟩ **2 :** to rise precipitously ⟨a way to keep insurance rates from *skying* —*Wall Street Jour.*⟩
sky·bal *or* **sky·bald** \ˈskībəl\ *n* -S [origin unknown] *dial Brit* **:** one that is worthless **:** GOOD-FOR-NOTHING
sky–blue \ˈ=;=\ *adj* [¹*sky* + *blue*, adj.] **:** of the color sky blue **:** AZURE, CERULEAN
sky blue *n* [*sky-blue*] **:** a variable color averaging a pale to light blue — called also *celestial, ethereal blue*
skyborne \ˈ=,=\ *adj* **:** AIRBORNE ⟨~ troops⟩
skycap \ˈ=,=\ *n* [¹*sky* + *-cap* (as in *redcap*)] **:** one who is employed to carry hand luggage at an airport — compare REDCAP
sky cavalry *n* **:** a lightplane reconnaissance unit often functionally integrated with surface cavalry units
skycoach \ˈ=,=\ *n* **:** a commercial airplane that provides low-cost transportation without sleeping accommodations or other special services
sky compass *n* **:** a device used by navigators for estimating the position of the sun when it is a few degrees below the horizon (as during long polar twilights)
sky control *n* **:** a gunnery control station aloft on a naval vessel
sky cover *n* **:** the extent to which the sky is obscured by clouds
sky–dome *n* **:** a dome that curves around and over the stage of a theater and represents the sky — compare CYCLORAMA
sky·er \ˈskī(ə)r, -īə\ *n* -S [²*sky* + *-er*] **:** a bowled ball that is skied by a batsman in cricket
skye terrier \ˈskī-\ *n* [*Skye*, island of the Inner Hebrides, northwest Scotland] **1** *usu cap S&T* **:** a Scottish breed of terrier having a long head with prick or pendent ears and close-set hazel eyes, a long low body with a short soft woolly inner coat and a long hard straight outer coat, a tail about 9 inches long, and short straight legs **2** *also* **skye** *usu cap S & often cap T* **:** a dog of the Skye terrier breed
sky·ey *or* **ski·ey** \ˈskīē\ *adj* [¹*sky* + *-y*] **:** of, relating to, or having the characteristics of the sky **:** EXALTED, LOFTY ⟨bright, ~ distances —Clara Laidlaw⟩ ⟨~ worlds of general principles —Ernest Barker⟩
sky father *n, often cap S&F* **:** the sky viewed (as in primitive theology) as the male member or masculine principle of the primordial parents — compare EARTH MOTHER
sky–flower \ˈ=,=\ *n* **:** GOLDEN DEWDROP
sky fog *n* **:** the fogging of a plate exposed for astronomical photography at night caused by the general light of the sky
sky·ful *also* **sky·full** \ˈskī,fu̇l\ *n* -S **:** as much or as many as the sky can accommodate ⟨chaotic ~ of crowding flakes —Thomas Hardy⟩ ⟨a ~ of bombers —Donald Armstrong⟩
sky–gazer \ˈ=,==\ *n* **:** a triangular skysail used esp. on clipper ships
sky glow *n* **:** a glow in the night sky deriving from an artificial source (as the lights of a city)
sky gray *n* **:** a light bluish gray that is redder and paler than chicory
sky green *n* **:** a light yellow green that is greener and deeper than glass green and greener and stronger than reed green
¹sky–high \ˈ=¦=\ *adv* [¹*sky* + *high*, adv.] **1 a :** high into the air ⟨men on the upper deck were flung *sky-high* —J.E.Macdonnell⟩ **b :** to an unusually or unprecedentedly high level ⟨raising taxes *sky-high* —Laura Krey⟩ ⟨lifted my spirit *sky-high* —Elmer Morriss⟩ **2 :** in an enthusiastic manner ⟨extolling the virtues of the crew *sky-high* —Frederick Way⟩ **3 :** to pieces **:** APART ⟨the thesis . . . was blown *sky-high* —*Times Lit. Supp.*⟩ ⟨blasted another popular myth *sky-high*⟩
²sky–high \"\ *adj* [¹*sky* + *high*, adj.] **:** excessively expensive **:** EXORBITANT ⟨spend *sky-high* sums —Norman Cousins⟩ ⟨top restaurants are often *sky-high* —T.H.Fielding⟩
skyhook \ˈ=,=\ *n* [¹*sky* + *hook*, n.] **1 :** a hook conceived as being suspended from the sky ⟨the nearest thing to hanging a roof from ~*s* and leaving out the walls entirely —*Popular Science Monthly*⟩ **2 :** a self-propelled carriage suspended from two or more cables and used for high-line hauling logs esp. in logging **3 :** SKYHOOK BALLOON
sky hook *vt* [*skyhook*] **:** to reinforce (a mine ceiling) by inserting bolts vertically into the secure rock above
skyhook balloon *n* **:** a large semitransparent helium-filled high-altitude plastic balloon used to carry instruments aloft for the study of cosmic rays
sky hooker *n* [¹*sky* + *hooker*] **:** TOP LOADER
sky·hoot \(ˈ)skī¦hüt\ *vi* [by alter.] **:** SCOOT — often used in the phrase *go skyhooting*
skying *pres part of* SKY
sky·ish \ˈskīish, -ēsh\ *adj* **:** SKYEY
sky·ko·mish \skīˈkōmish, -mēsh\ *n, pl* **skykomish** *or* **skykomishes** *usu cap* **1 :** an Indian people of the Skykomish river valley in Washington **2 :** a member of the Skykomish people
¹skylark \ˈ=,=\ *n* **1 :** a common Old World lark (*Alauda arvensis*) with dark brown upper parts, a buff throat and breast streaked with brown, and creamy white abdomen that inhabits chiefly open country and is noted for its song esp. as uttered in vertical flight **2 :** any of various birds (as Sprague's pipit) that resemble the skylark
²skylark \"\ *vi* **1 :** to run up and down the rigging of a ship in sport **2 :** to frolic in a playful or boisterous manner **:** fool around ⟨were ~*ing* on the hike —L.M.Uris⟩
³skylark \"\ *n* [²*skylark*] **:** ⁴LARK 1 ⟨full of gusto, and to him everything is a ~ —John Hersey⟩
sky·less \ˈ=ləs\ *adj* **:** having the sky obscured by clouds
¹skylight \ˈ=,=\ *n* **1 a :** the diffused and reflected light of the sky ⟨the flux density due to sunlight and ~ —H.G.Houghton⟩ **b :** the general background of illumination of the nighttime sky that includes light from both natural and artificial sources **:** AIRGLOW **2 :** an opening in a roof or a deck of a ship covered with translucent or transparent material (as glass or plastic) and designed for the admission of light

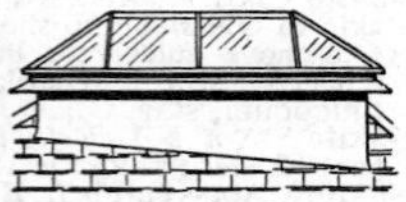

skylight 2

²skylight \"\ *vt* **:** to light (as a room) by a skylight
¹skyline \ˈ=,=\ *n* **1 :** an apparent line in the landscape at the juncture of earth and sky **:** HORIZON ⟨towers . . . rising above the ~ —A.B.Osborne⟩ **2 :** an outline (as of buildings or a mountain range) against the background of the sky ⟨the newer skyscrapers . . . along the ~ of New York —*Irish Statesman*⟩ ⟨the waving ~ of the foothills —C.W.Gordon⟩ **3 :** a cable stretched taut between two spar trees and used as a track along which logs are hauled — compare SLACKLINE **syn** see OUTLINE
²skyline \"\ *vt* **:** to outline against the sky ⟨let us be . . . *skylined* on earth's highest hill —Sean O'Casey⟩
skyline logging *n* **:** HIGH-LINE LOGGING
skyliner \ˈ=,==\ *n* [¹*sky* + *liner*] **:** AIRLINER
skylook \ˈ=,=\ *vt* **:** to survey (timber) from a position aloft
sky·man \ˈ=mən\ *n, pl* **skymen** *slang* **:** PARATROOPER
sky map *n* **1 :** a chart showing the positions of celestial bodies **:** STAR CHART **2 :** a pattern of varying degrees of glare on the underside of a cloud area caused by reflected light from the earth's surface
skymark \ˈ=,=\ *n* **:** an object appearing against the background of the sky ⟨the tower clock . . . is a familiar ~ —*Amer. Guide Series: N.Y.City*⟩
sky parlor *n* **:** a room at the top of a house ⟨sat hungry and cold in their *sky parlor*, looking down on a bystreet in the city — *N. Y. Herald Tribune*⟩
skyphos *var of* SCYPHUS
sky pilot *n* **:** CLERGYMAN; *specif* **:** CHAPLAIN
sky pipit *n* **:** SPRAGUE'S PIPIT
skyport \ˈ=,=\ *n* **:** HELIPORT
skyr \ˈskir\ *n* -S [Icel, fr. ON; akin to ON *skera* to cut — more at SHEAR] **1 :** sour curdled milk **2 :** a dessert prepared from sweet and sour cream with sugar
skyre \ˈskī(ə)r\ *vi* [prob. fr. obs. E *skyre, skire*, adj., bright, fr. ME *skir, skire* — more at SKIRE THURSDAY] *chiefly Scot* **:** to shine in a gaudy manner **:** GLITTER
sky–rider \ˈ=,==\ *n* **:** one who travels in or flies an airplane
¹skyrocket \ˈ=,==\ *n* **1 :** ³ROCKET 1 **2** *or* **skyrocket gilia :** a No. American biennial or perennial herb (*Gilia aggregata*) having flowers with linear reflexed lobes and often cultivated as an ornamental
²skyrocket \"\ *vi* **1 :** to rise abruptly and rapidly ⟨expenses, salaries, income, all ~*ed* —J.T.Farrell⟩ ⟨national advertising . . . has ~*ed* . . . within the last few years —F.W.Doepke⟩ **2 :** to act in an impulsive, thoughtless, or irrational manner ⟨you have . . . kept my feet on the ground when I was about to ~ —F.D.Roosevelt⟩ ~ *vt* **1 :** to cause to rise or increase abruptly and rapidly ⟨help ~ horsepower but add only a smidgen to torque —Frank Rowsome⟩ ⟨lavish touches which ~ costs —Frances W. Browin⟩ **2 :** to bring about the rapid and unexpected elevation of ⟨won instant success and ~*ed* its author to fame —Fanny K. Wister⟩
sky·rock·ety \-kəd·ē, -ətē, -i\ *adj* **:** resembling a skyrocket
sky·sail \ˈskī,sāl, -īsᵊl\ *n* **:** a sail set immediately above the royal — see SAIL illustration
skysail pole *n* **:** the part of the royal mast above the shoulder when skysails are carried — see SHIP illustration
skysail-yarder \ˈ=(,)=,==\ *n* [*skysail yard* + *-er*] **:** a ship having skysail yards
sky·scape \ˈskī,skāp\ *n* -S **1 :** a part of the sky with outlined terrestrial objects that can be comprehended in a single view ⟨gaps between the fluffy white mountains of the ~ —*McGill News*⟩ **2 :** a picture that includes an extensive view of the sky
sky·scrape \ˈ=,skrāp\ *vi* [back-formation fr. *skyscraper*] **:** to build a skyscraper ⟨city ruling . . . limits *skyscraping* to about twenty-two stories —*New Yorker*⟩
sky·scrap·er \-pə(r)\ *n* [¹*sky* + *scraper*] **1 :** a triangular skysail used on a clipper ship **2 :** one that is unusually tall ⟨that vegetable ~, the giant cactus —D.C.Peattie⟩; *esp* **:** a many-storied building ⟨a typical American ~, tall and narrow, with a spire and beacon —*Amer. Guide Series: Mich.*⟩
sky·scrap·ered \¦=¦=pə(r)d\ *adj* **:** having or marked by skyscrapers ⟨~ cities⟩
skyscraping \ˈ=,==\ *adj* [fr. *skyscraper*, after E *scraper: scraping*] **:** of, relating to, or having the characteristics of a skyscraper **:** very high ⟨a ~ building⟩
sky shade *n* **:** a screen that is usu. attached to the shutter or lens tube of a camera and is used for reducing the light from the sky
sky sign *n* **:** a usu. electric display sign on top of a building
skystone \ˈ=,=\ *n* **:** METEORITE
skysweeper \ˈ=,==\ *n* **:** a 75 millimeter antiaircraft gun that automatically locates and aims at a target and fires up to 45 rounds a minute by means of radar
sky train *n* **:** an airplane that has one or more unpowered aircraft (as gliders) in tow — called also *air train*
skytrooper \ˈ=,==\ *n* **:** PARATROOPER
skytroops \ˈ=,=\ *n pl* **:** PARATROOPS
sky truck *n* **:** a transport plane used for carrying heavy and bulky loads
sky·ward \ˈ=wə(r)d\ *also* **sky·wards** \-dz\ *adv* **1 :** to or toward the sky ⟨gaze ~⟩ **2 :** UPWARD ⟨spending by all consuming units shot ~ —E.W.Swanson⟩
sky wave *n* **:** a radio wave that is propagated by means of the ionosphere
skyway \ˈ=,=\ *n* **1 :** a route used by airplanes **:** AIRLANE, AIRWAY 2 **2 :** an elevated highway
skywrite \ˈ=,=\ *vi* **:** to engage in skywriting ⟨~ in long, slim letters —*Popular Science Monthly*⟩ ~ *vt* **1 :** to produce by means of skywriting ⟨~ a slogan⟩ **2 :** to give wide publicity to ⟨~ some of the ugly, underground truths of racial intolerance —John Mason Brown⟩
skywriter \ˈ=,==\ *n* **:** one that skywrites
skywriting \ˈ=,==\ *n* **:** writing formed in the sky by means of smoke or other visible substance emitted from an airplane
sl *abbr* **1** slate **2** slide **3** slip **4** slow
SL *abbr* **1** salvage loss **2** sea level **3** searchlight **4** [L *secundum legem*] according to law **5** seditious libeler **6** sergeant-at-law **7** *often not cap* [L *sine loco*] without place **8** single line **9** solicitor-at-law **10** sound locator **11** south latitude **12** squadron leader **13** stock length **14** streamline **15** sub-lieutenant **16** *often not cap* [L *suo loco*] in its place
sla \ˈslā\ *archaic var of* SLOE
¹slab \ˈslab, -lah(ə)b\ *n* -S [ME *slabbe, sclabbe*] **1 :** a comparatively thick plate or slice of something (as of metal, stone, wood, or food) ⟨a ~ of bread⟩ ⟨cut the marble into ~*s*⟩: as **a** (1) **:** the irregular outside piece cut from a log in squaring it or preparing it for being sawed into boards (2) *Austral & Africa* **:** a thick roughhewn plank (3) **:** a thin piece cut from a board in resawing (as for box making) **b :** a flat substantial piece of timber or stone forming the top of a table or counter **c :** a rectangular piece of iron or steel made by rolling an ingot so that the width of the section is at least twice the thickness — compare BLOOM **d :** PLATE 1h(2) **e :** a flat piece (as of stone, glass, or porcelain) on which drugs or colors are ground, printing ink distributed, or various substances (as ointments) are mixed **f :** concrete pavement (as of a road); *specif* **:** a strip of concrete pavement laid as a single unjointed piece **g :** a sheet of crystallized sugar before it is cut into cubes **h slabs** *pl* **:** fruit halves (as of apricots, peaches) flattened and matted together during drying **i** (1) **:** a flat rectangular architectural element that is usu. formed of a single piece or mass ⟨the use of a concrete foundation ~ in modern small houses⟩ ⟨the park included a dance ~⟩ — see SLAB BRIDGE (2) **:** a rectangular building having small depth in comparison with its length and usu. height and designed to provide optimum light and air distribution to the inside **2 :** firewood cut from lumber waste (as edgings) ⟨burned ~ except in the coldest weather⟩ **3 :** an offset of a bulb and esp. of a narcissus bulb
²slab \"\ *vb* **slabbed**; **slabbed**; **slabbing**; **slabs** *vt* **1 a :** to saw, divide, or form into slabs **b :** to remove an outer slab from (as a log) **2 a :** to cover (as a roadbed or roof) with slabs **b :** to support (as the sides of a shaft or well) with slabs **3 :** to put or stick on in slabs **:** apply thickly ⟨*slabbed* butter on the bread⟩ ⟨enjoyed *slabbing* paint onto the wall⟩ ~ *vi* **:** to prepare or form slabs **:** slab something esp. as an occupation ⟨spent the winter *slabbing* at the mill⟩
³slab \"\ *adj* [prob. of Scand origin; akin to obs. Dan *slab* slippery and prob. to Dan *slab* slime] **1** *dial chiefly Eng* **:** THICK, SLIMY, VISCID **2 :** sloppily sentimental; *also* **:** put on thickly **:** using profuse and exaggerated language ⟨prose too thick and ~⟩
⁴slab \"\ *n* -S [of Scand origin; akin to Sw dial. *slabb* slime, mud, *slabba* to roll in mud — more at SLAVER] *chiefly dial* **:** SLIME, MUD
⁵slab \"\ *n* -S [prob. short for *slab line*] **:** the slack part of a sail
slabbed tie *n* [*slabbed* fr. past part. of ²*slab*] **:** a railroad tie sawed to provide flat surfaces on the top and bottom only — called also *pole tie*
¹slab·ber \ˈslabə(r)\ *vb* -ED/-ING/-S [prob. fr. D *slabberen*, freq. of *slabben* to slaver, fr. MD — more at SLAVER] **1 :** SLOBBER, DROOL; *also* **:** DRIVEL **2 :** GORGE, BOLT
²slabber \"\ *n* -S **:** SLOBBER, SLAVER
³slab·ber \ˈslabə(r), -laab-\ *n* -S [²*slab* + *-er*] **:** one that slabs: as **a :** a saw for slabbing logs **b :** a machine for cutting soap into slabs **c :** MILLING MACHINE; *esp* **:** PLANOMILLER **d :** a person that forms slabs (as by cutting) or fixes slabs in place (as by cementing) **e :** an operator of any slabber
slab·ber·er \-labərə(r)\ *n* -S **:** one that slabbers
slab·bery \-bərē\ *adj* **:** like or covered with slabber **:** SLIPPERY, SLOPPY
slab·bi·ly \-bəlē\ *adv* [¹*slabby* + *-ly*] **:** in a slabby manner **:** as if made of something slabby
slab·bing \ˈslabiŋ, -laab-\ *n* -S [in sense 1, fr. ¹*slab* + *-ing*; in other senses, fr. gerund of ²*slab*] **1 :** SLABS **2 :** the cutting of a skip from the side of a pillar or face of coal **3 :** lamination of clay wares caused by rapid firing
slabbing cutter *n* **:** a plain milling cutter esp. when having a broad face
slabbing machine *n* **:** PLANOMILLER
slabbing mill *n* **:** a steel rolling mill that produces slabs
slab bridge *n* **:** a short-span bridge consisting of a reinforced-concrete slab resting on abutments
¹slab·by \ˈslabē\ *adj* -ER/-EST [prob. of Scand origin; akin to Sw dial. *slabb* slime, mud — more at SLAB] **1** *archaic* **:** WET, SLOPPY, MUDDY, MIRY **2 :** VISCOUS, JELLYLIKE
²slab·by \ˈslabē, -laabē\ *adj* [¹*slab* + *-y*] **1 :** covered or paved with slabs **2 :** made up of slabs **:** having the form of slabs ⟨~ fragments of rock⟩
slab door *n* **1 :** a rude door (as of a log cabin) made from rough slabbing **2 :** a door without panels and with a continuous smooth surface on both sides **:** FLUSH DOOR
slab house *n* **:** a pit house lined with stone slabs
slab line \ˈslab-, -laab-\ *n* [earlier *slabline*, part modif., part trans. of D *slaplijn*, fr. *slap* slack + *lijn* line] **:** a line or small rope by which seamen haul up the body of a course or topsail
slab·man \ˈslabmən, -ˌman\ *n, pl* **slabmen 1 :** a worker who cuts or piles up slabs (as of lumber) **2 :** ANGLESMITH **2 3 :** a worker who prepares hard candy mixture and pulls it to proper consistency for use
slab mill *n* **:** SLABBING CUTTER
slab–on–ground \ˈ=;=,=\ *adj* **:** marked by construction in which a foundation slab is laid directly on the ground without a basement ⟨*slab-on-ground* houses⟩
slab reef *n* **:** a small reef between tack and clew on the foot of a sail by which the sail may be made flatter
slabs *pl of* SLAB, *pres 3d sing of* SLAB
slab–sided \ˈ=¦==\ *adj* **:** having the rib cage narrow from side to side with flat sides and the ribs deficient in lateral curvature ⟨a *slab-sided* horse⟩; *also* **:** giving an effect of such a condition by reason of leanness or slenderness ⟨an airplane with a *slab-sided* fuselage⟩ ⟨*slab-sided* cheeks⟩
slabstone \ˈ=,=\ *n* **:** ³FLAG 3
slab tie *n* **:** a railroad tie made from the outside cut of a log
slab–top \ˈ=,=\ *adj* **:** having a cover in the form of a slab (as of reinforced concrete) ⟨a *slab-top* culvert⟩
slabwood \ˈ=,=\ *n* [¹*slab* + *wood*] **:** SLAB 2
¹slack \ˈslak\ *adj* -ER/-EST [ME *slak*, fr. OE *sleac*; akin to OS *slak* slack, OHG *slah*, ON *slakr* slack, L *laxus* slack, loose, spacious, *languēre* to be languid, Gk *lēgein* to leave off, stop, Skt *laṅga* lame] **1 :** not using due diligence, care, or dispatch **:** REMISS, INATTENTIVE, NEGLIGENT ⟨~ in service⟩ **2 a :** characterized by slowness, sluggishness, or lack of energy **:** wanting in life, vigor, or strength ⟨a ~ pace⟩ ⟨a very ~ performance⟩ **b :** moderate in some quality; *esp* **:** moderately warm ⟨a ~ oven⟩ **c :** blowing or flowing at low speed — used esp. of wind or tide **3 a :** not tight **:** not tense or taut **:** LOOSE, RELAXED ⟨a ~ rope⟩ **b :** lacking in firmness **:** WEAK, SOFT, UNSTEADY ⟨a ~ hand⟩ ⟨~ control⟩ **c** *of one edge of a roll of paper* **:** not wound as tightly as the other edge **4 a :** wanting in activity **:** not busy **:** DULL ⟨fall is our ~ season⟩ **b :** marked by a low level of activity **:** reduced below a desired, normal, or usual level ⟨employment is very ~⟩ **5 :** lacking in completeness, finish, or perfection ⟨the finish was much ~*er* than the design⟩ **6 a :** made with joints sufficiently tight for packing dried materials but not watertight ⟨~ cooperage⟩ **b :** concerned with or engaged in the making of slack cooperage **syn** see NEGLIGENT
²slack \"\ *vb* -ED/-ING/-S *vt* **1 a :** to be slack, inattentive, or negligent in performing, executing, or completing ⟨~ one's vigilance⟩ **b** *archaic* **:** to fail to take advantage of (as an opportunity) or use to advantage (as time) **c :** to moderate or slacken deliberately by or as if by relaxing one's energy, zeal,

grip, or other controlling factor : cause to lessen (as in speed, vigor, violence, fervor) ⟨~*ed* his pace as the sun grew hot⟩ — often used with *up* ⟨~ up one's effort⟩ **2** : to cause to be relaxed, loose, or otherwise free from tension : LOOSEN ⟨~ the girth while the horse is cooling⟩ ⟨~ a line⟩ — often used with an adverb (as *off, out*) ⟨~ off the sail⟩ **3 a** : to cause to abate : SLAKE 2 **b** : SLAKE 4 ~ *vi* **1 a** : to be or become slack : decline in some effort (as in speed, force, activity) : slow up : relax tension ⟨the wind ~*ed*⟩ **b** : to approach an end (as of activity) : cease to progress : ⟨our enthusiasm ~*ed* off⟩ ⟨retail business ~*s* down when employment drops⟩ **2** : to shirk or evade work or obligations : be or become a slacker, idler, or shirker **3** : SLAKE 3

³slack \"\ *adv* : SLACKLY

⁴slack \"\ *n* -s [ME *slak*, fr. ON *slakki*] **1** *dial Eng* : a pass between hills : GLEN **2** *dial Brit* **a** : a pool of water **b** : MARSH

⁵slack \"\ *n* -s [ME *sleck*, prob. fr. MD *slecke, slacke* slag, slack; perh. akin to MLG *slagge* slag — more at SLAG] : the finest screenings of coal produced at a mine and often containing slate and dirt that make it undesirable for fuel unless cleaned — called also *coom, culm*

⁶slack \"\ *n* -s [¹*slack*] **1** : cessation in movement or flow; *specif* : SLACK WATER **2** : a part of something that hangs loose without strain ⟨take up the ~ of a rope⟩ **3 a** : TROUSERS **b** : long pants for casual wear often of a looser cut than suit trousers and with pleats at the waist — usu. used in pl. but sometimes sing. in constr. **4** : a lull in activity : a dull season or period **5** : looseness of fit (as of a part in a mechanism) : BACKLASH **6** : the weak or stressless element in a rhythmic unit or foot : UNSTRESS

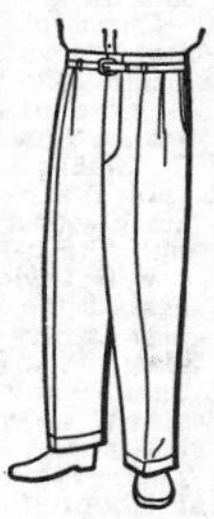

slacks 3b

⁷slack \"\ *n* [prob. short for *slack jaw*] *dial Eng* : impudent talk

⁸slack \"\ *n* -s [ME *slak* — more at SLAKE] : ³SLAKE

slack·age \ˈslakij\ *n* -s : amount of slack : SLACKENING

slack–baked \ˈ≈ˌ≈\ *adj* : inadequately or badly baked; *also* : imperfectly made or finished

slack coal *n* : ⁵SLACK

¹slack·en \ˈslakən\ *vb* **slackened; slackened; slackening** \-k(ə)niŋ\ **slackens** *vt* **1** : to render less active : hold back ⟨~ a flow of water⟩ ⟨~ one's interest⟩ : slow up : ABATE, MODERATE, RETARD ⟨~ one's speed⟩ **2** : to render slack (as by lessening tension, tautness, firmness) : LOOSEN ⟨~ sail⟩ ~ *vi* **1** : to become slack or slow or negligent : slow down ⟨determined not to ~ as a correspondent —Jane Austen⟩ **2** : to become less active : SLACK **syn** see DELAY

²slack·en *also* **slak·in** \ˈslakən\ *n* -s [modif. of obs. G *schlacken* (now *schlacke*), fr. or akin to MLG *slagge* slag — more at SLAG] : slag mixed with ores in smelting to promote their fusion

slack·en·er \-k(ə)nə(r)\ *n* -s : one that slackens

slackening *n* -s [fr. gerund of ¹*slacken*] : DECLINE, MODERATION

slack·er \ˈslakə(r)\ *n* -s : one that slacks: as **a** : a drawgate in a sluice **b** : a person who shirks work, responsibility, or an obligation; *esp* : one that evades military service in time of war

slack·er·ism \-kəˌrizəm\ *n* -s : the behavior of a slacker

slackest *superlative of* SLACK

slack–filled \ˈ≈ˌ≈\ *adj* [³*slack*] : incompletely or deceptively packed : abnormally or excessively loose-packed ⟨a *slack-filled* carton⟩

slack ice *n* : broken ice floating on quiet or slowly moving water

slacking *pres part of* SLACK

slack in stays *adj, of a ship* : slow in going about

slack jaw *n* : wearisome or impudent talk

slack–jawed \ˈ≈ˌ≈\ *adj* [³*slack*] : having the lower jaw dropped esp. as indicating amazement or stupidity ⟨stood *slack-jawed* yokels⟩ ⟨stood *slack-jawed* with surprise⟩

slackline \ˈ≈ˌ≈\ *n* **1** : a cable (as in a lumbering operation) suspended slackly between spar trees and adapted esp. to yarding downhill or across steep-sided canyons or gullies — compare SKYLINE **2** : a hoist that lowers an empty bucket by gravity with a slackline and applies cable tension to lift the loaded bucket on the return

slack·ly *adv* [ME *slackely*, fr. OE *sleaclīce*, fr. *sleac* slack + *-līce* -ly — more at SLACK] : in a slack manner : LOOSELY, CARELESSLY, INADEQUATELY

slack·ness *n* -ES [ME *slaknesse*, fr. OE *sleacness*, fr. *sleac* slack + *-ness*] **1** : the quality or state of being slack or behaving slackly **2** : something that is slack

slack rope *n* : a loosely stretched rope used by some ropewalkers and acrobats — compare TIGHTROPE

slacks *pres 3d sing of* SLACK, *pl of* SLACK

slack–sized \ˈ≈ˌ≈\ *adj, of paper* : so lightly sized as to be permeable to water with relative ease — compare HARD-SIZED

slack–spined \ˈ≈ˌ≈\ *adj* : WEAK, INEFFECTIVE ⟨*slack-spined* heedless leaders⟩

slack suit *n* : a comfortable man's or woman's suit for casual or sports wear or lounging consisting of a pair of slacks and jacket top or sport shirt often of the same material and color

slack–twisted \ˈ≈ˌ≈≈\ *adj* : lacking in firmness of fiber : weak in character or energy ⟨wanted no part of such a *slack-twisted* fellow⟩

slack water *n* **1** *or* **slack tide** : the period at the turn of the tide when there is little or no horizontal motion of tidal water **2** : a slowly moving or still body of water (as in a stream above a dam) **3** : ocean water marked by virtual absence of current **4** : a slackening of the current of a stream resulting from a logjam

¹slack–water \ˈ≈ˌ≈≈\ *adj* [*slack water*] **1** : marked by slack water ⟨a *slack-water* period⟩ **2** : carried on in slack water produced artificially (as by a lock or dam) ⟨*slack-water* navigation⟩

²slack–water \"\ *vt* : to produce slack water in (as a river) by a construction (as a dam, lock, or jetty)

slack wax *n* : yellow to dark-colored crude paraffin wax that is separated from part of the oil in paraffin distillate by chilling and pressing or by use of a solvent and that contains considerable residual oil — compare SCALE WAX

slack wire *n* : a wire slack rope

sladang *var of* SELADANG

¹slade \ˈslād\ *n* -s [ME, fr. OE *slæd*] **1** *dial chiefly Eng* : a little valley : RAVINE, GLEN — often used in place names **2** *dial chiefly Eng* : GLADE 1 **3** *dial chiefly Eng* : HILLSIDE

²slade \"\ *n* [origin unknown] : the sole of a plow **2** : PEAT SPADE

slae \ˈslā\ *chiefly Scot var of* SLOE

¹slag \ˈslag, -aa(ə)-, -ai-\ *n* -s [MLG *slagge*; prob. akin to MHG *slage* hammer, tool for striking, OE *slēan* to strike; prob. fr. the dross resulting from hammering or forging — more at SLAY] **1 a** : the dross of a metal; *specif* : a product of smelting containing mostly as silicates the substances not sought to be produced as matte or metal and having a lower specific gravity than the latter — called also *cinder* **b** : a similar substance that floats on molten impure steel during refining, protects the metal from oxidation, and removes unwanted substances chemically **2** : scoriaceous lava from a volcano **3** : a fused or partly fused and usu. glassy mass resulting from contact of bases with silica or silicates at high temperatures and often deliberately developed in enameling and glazing **4** : worthless matter : DEBRIS ⟨~ accumulations in the bottom of a wash tank⟩ ⟨nothing like a brisk walk to drag the ~ from your head⟩

²slag \"\ *vt* **slagged; slagged; slagging; slags** : to free from or convert into slag

slag block *n* : a masonry structural unit made from slag concrete

slag cement *n* : a pozzolana cement using slag as the pozzolana material

slag concrete *n* : concrete in which blast-furnace slag is used as the aggregate

slag furnace *or* **slag hearth** *n* : a metallurgical furnace in which lead ore is roasted and slagged for further treatment

slag·ger \-gə(r)\ *n* -s : a worker who removes slag from furnaces

slagging hole *n* : CINDER NOTCH

slag glass *n* : an opaque marbled glass

slag·gy \-gē,-gi\ *adj* -ER/-EST : of, relating to, containing, or resembling slag ⟨~ cobalt⟩ ⟨a ~ coal⟩

slag·less \-gləs\ *adj* : containing no slag — **slag·less·ness** *n* -ES

slag·man \-gmən\ *n, pl* **slagmen** : SLAGGER

slag sand *n* : slag crushed into fine particles and used esp. in mortar or concrete

slag–tap furnace *n* : a blast furnace or pulverized-fuel furnace with a tap opening in the bottom for removal of slag

slag wool *n* : a mineral wool made usu. from molten blast-furnace slag by the action of jets of steam under high pressure

slain *past part of* SLAY

slain·te \ˈslō(i)ntə\ *interj* [Ir *slāinte* health] *Irish* — used as a salutation or toast

¹slais·ter \ˈslāstə(r)\ *vi* -ED/-ING/-S [origin unknown] *dial Brit* : to be occupied with dirty, gooey, or messy materials : slop around

²slaister \"\ *n* -s *chiefly Scot* : a sloppy mess

slak·able *or* **slake·able** \ˈslākəbəl, -lak-\ *adj* : capable of being slaked

¹slake \ˈslāk, *in senses vi 3 & vt 4* " *or* ˈslak; *chiefly dial in other senses* ˈslak\ *vb* -ED/-ING/-S [ME *slaken*, fr. OE *slacian, sleacian*, fr. *sleac* slack — more at SLACK] *vi* **1** *obs* : to slacken one's efforts : FLAG, SLACK 1a **2** *archaic* : to become less violent, intense, or severe : grow less : ABATE, MODERATE ⟨no flood by raining *slaketh* —Shak.⟩ **3** : to become slaked : CRUMBLE, DISINTEGRATE ⟨lime may ~ spontaneously in moist air⟩ ~ *vt* **1** *obs* : SLACK 2 **2 a** *obs* : to make less : reduce in quantity or size : DIMINISH **b** *archaic* : to cause to be less acute : EASE, MITIGATE **c** : to cause to lessen (as in vigor, speed, force) : lessen the violence or fury of : MODERATE ⟨unwilling to ~ his anger⟩ **3 a** : to bring (as thirst) to an end with or as if with refreshing drink : SATISFY, ALLAY ⟨*slaked* our curiosity with an account of the night's happenings⟩; *also* : to make moist : WET ⟨land *slaked* with blood⟩ ⟨*slaking* our dry throats with melted snow⟩ **b** : to put out (as a fire) or cause to burn less strongly : DEADEN ⟨*slaking* all earthly desires⟩ **4 a** : to cause (as lime) to heat and crumble by treatment with water : HYDRATE **b** : to alter (as lime) by exposure to air with conversion at least in part to a carbonate : AIR-SLAKE

²slake \ˈslāk, ˈslak — *see* ¹SLAKE\ *n* -s [ME *slak*, fr. *slaken* to slake] : an act or an instance of slaking

³slake \ˈslāk\ *also* **slake kale** *n* -s [*slake* fr. ME *slak*, alter. of *slauk*, prob. fr. MIr *sleabhac* edible seaweed, slake] *Brit* : SLOKE 1; *also* : any of various confervoid freshwater algae

⁴slake \ˈslāk\ *vt* [alter. of earlier *slaik* to lick, daub, of Scand origin; akin to OSw *slekja* to lick, ON *sleikja* — more at LICK] *chiefly Scot* : DAUB, BESMEAR

⁵slake \ˈslāk\ *n* -s [by alter.] : ⁵SLACK

slaked lime \ˈslāk(t)-, ˈslak(t)-\ *n* : HYDRATED LIME

slake·less \-kləs\ *adj* : not capable of being slaked

slak·er \-kə(r)\ *n* -s : one that slakes: as **a** : a piece of equipment for slaking lime ⟨horizontal rotary ~*s*⟩ **b** : a worker who makes hydrated lime

slake trough *n* : a blacksmith's water tank for cooling forgings or tools

slakin *var of* SLACKEN

slaky \ˈslākē\ *adj* -ER/-EST [obs. E dial. *slake* mud, mire + E *-y*] : MIRY, MUDDY

sla·lom \ˈslälәm *also* ˈslal- *or* -ˌlōm *or* -ˌlōm; *also* ˈslalәm *sometimes* ˈslālәm\ *n* -s [Norw, lit., sloping track] : skiing in a zigzag or wavy course between upright obstacles (as flags); *also* : a race against time over such a course

¹slam \ˈslam, -laa(ə)m\ *n* -s [origin unknown] : a winning of all the tricks or points of a deal in a game of cards — see GRAND SLAM, LITTLE SLAM

²slam \"\ *n* -s [prob. of Scand origin; akin to Icel *slæma* to slam] **1** : a heavy blow or impact **2 a** : a noisy violent closing (as of a door) **b** : a banging noise; *esp* : one made by the slam of a door **3** : a cutting or violent criticism

³slam \"\ *vb* **slammed; slammed; slamming; slams** [of Scand origin; akin to Sw dial. *slämma* to slam, Norw *slemba, slemma*, Icel *slæma* and prob. to ON *slambra* to strike at something] *vt* **1** : to strike or beat vigorously or thoroughly : hit strongly : KNOCK ⟨*slammed* him about the head with a stick⟩ **2** : to shut forcibly and noisily : BANG ⟨wind often ~*s* the shutter⟩ **3 a** : to put in place with undue force or noise or in a great hurry : push, move, activate, or throw with impetuosity ⟨*slamming* the lid of the trunk⟩ ⟨~ home the bolt⟩ — often used with an adverb of direction ⟨*slammed* on the brake⟩ ⟨~ the window down⟩ **b** : to cause to occur through vigorous or impetuous action ⟨the batter *slammed* out a homer⟩ ⟨the committee determined to ~ through a new appropriation⟩ **4** : to criticize vigorously, brutally, or recklessly : abuse verbally ~ *vi* **1** : to make a banging noise **2** : to function (as in moving or working) with obvious and usu. noisy vigor ⟨ready to ~ into his chores⟩ ⟨a football player *slamming* into the line⟩ **3** : to utter verbal abuse — **slam the door** : to repel communication or contact usu. brusquely or arrogantly : refuse discussion or consideration ⟨*slammed the door* on the best chance of a peaceful settlement⟩ — **slam the door in one's face** : to refuse one entry or hearing

⁴slam \"\ *adv* **1** : with a slam ⟨~ went the doors⟩ **2** *dial* : CLEAR, COMPLETELY ⟨~ across the road⟩

¹slam-bang \(ˈ)≈ˈ≈\ *vi* : to behave boisterously ~ *vt* : BELABOR

²slam-bang \"\ *adv* **1** : with violence and noise **2** : without due thought or care : RECKLESSLY **3** : SLAM 2

¹slambang \"\ *adj* [*slam-bang*] **1** : unduly loud or violent ⟨a ~ clatter⟩ **2 a** : notably vigorous ⟨made a ~ effort to win⟩ **b** : exceptionally good : OUTSTANDING ⟨a ~ address that greatly impressed his auditors⟩

²slambang \"\ *n* : noisy clatter

slam·mock \ˈslamək\ *var of* SLOMMACK

SLAN *abbr, often not cap* [L *sine loco, anno, (vel) nomine*] without place, year, (or) name

slanch·wise \ˈslanch,wīz\ *or* **slanch·ways** \-wāz\ *adv* [*slanchwise* alter. of *slantwise; slanchways* alter. of *slantways*] : diagonally and usu. so as to face something ⟨turned ~ to watch the clouds⟩

SL and C *abbr* shipper's load and count

¹slan·der \ˈslandə(r), -laan-,-lān-\ *n* -s [ME *slaundre, sclaundre, sclandre*, fr. OF *esclandre, esclande, escandle* scandal, slander, fr. LL *scandalum* stumbling block, offense — more at SCANDAL] **1** : utterance of false charges or misrepresentations which defame and damage reputation **2** : a false tale or report maliciously uttered orally, tending to injure the reputation of another, and constituting a legal tort : a malicious oral utterance of false defamatory reports : malicious publication by speech of false tales or suggestions to the injury of another — compare LIBEL **3** *obs* : disgrace, shame, or reproach that falls on one usu. by reason of personal acts or character ⟨thou ~ of thy mother's heavy womb —Shak.⟩ **4** *obs* : a cause of sin : an obstacle to virtue **5** *obs* : a cause of disgrace or discredit to a body of which he is a part **syn** see DETRACTION

²slander \"\ *vb* **slandered; slandered; slandering** \-d(ə)riŋ\ **slanders** [ME *slaunderen, slaundren, sclaunderen, sclaundren*, fr. MF *esclandrer, esclander*, fr. OF, fr. *esclandre, esclande* slander] *vt* **1** : to hurt the reputation of by malicious utterance containing a false or injurious representation : utter slander against : DEFAME **2** *obs* : to bring shame or discredit to : DISGRACE **3** *obs* : to accuse unjustly : CHARGE, BLAME ~ *vi* : to utter or spread slander **syn** see MALIGN

slan·der·er \-dərə(r)\ *n* -s [ME *sclaunderer*, fr. *sclaunderen* to slander + *-er*] : one that utters or spreads slander

slanderful *adj* [ME *sclandirful*, fr. *sclandre* slander + *-ful*] *obs* : SLANDEROUS — **slanderfully** *adv*

slander of title : a false and malicious statement disparaging a person's title to property to his special damage; *broadly* : a disparagement of the property of a person by false and malicious statements to his special damage

slan·der·ous \-d(ə)rəs\ *adj* [ME *sclaundrous*, fr. *sclaundre* slander + *-ous*] **1** *obs* : being a source or occasion of scandal or disgrace **2** : containing or constituting slander : CALUMNIOUS ⟨a ~ utterance⟩ **3** : given to or uttering slander ⟨a ~ tongue⟩ — **slan·der·ous·ly** *adv* — **slan·der·ous·ness** *n* -ES

SL and T *abbr* shipper's load and tally

slane \ˈslān\ *n* -s [IrGael *sleaghān*] : PEAT SPADE

¹slang *chiefly dial past of* SLING

²slang \ˈslaŋ, -laiŋ\ *n* -s [origin unknown] *dial Eng* : a narrow strip of land

³slang \"\ *n* -s [origin unknown] **1** : language peculiar to a particular group: as **a** : the special and often secret vocabulary used by a class (as thieves, beggars) and usu. felt to be vulgar or inferior : ARGOT **b** : the jargon used by or associated with a particular trade, profession, or field of activity **2** : a nonstandard vocabulary composed of words and senses characterized primarily by connotations of extreme informality and usu. a currency not limited to a particular region and composed typically of coinages or arbitrarily changed words, clipped or shortened forms, extravagant, forced, or facetious figures of speech, or verbal novelties usu. experiencing quick popularity and relatively rapid decline into disuse **syn** see DIALECT

⁴slang \"\ *adj* **1** : of, constituting, or expressed in slang **2** : SLANGY, VULGAR, RAKISH

⁵slang \"\ *vb* -ED/-ING/-S *vt* **1** *slang, Brit* : CHEAT, SWINDLE, DUPE **2** *chiefly Brit* : to abuse with words : censure abusively or with harsh or coarse language ~ *vi* : to use slang or vulgar abuse : talk in a slangy manner

slang·i·ly \-ŋəlē, -li\ *adv* : in a slangy manner

slang·i·ness \-ŋēnəs, -gin-\ *n* -ES : the quality or state of being slangy

slang·ish \-ŋish, -ŋēsh\ *adj* : somewhat slangy — **slang·ish·ly** *adv*

slang·ism \-ŋˌizəm\ *n* -s : a slangy word or expression : slangy language

slang·kop \ˈslaŋ,käp\ *n* -s [Afrik, fr. D *slang* snake (fr. MD *slange*) + *kop* head, cup (fr. MD *coppe* drinking vessel); akin to OHG *slango* snake, *slingan* to wind, twist — more at SLING, CUP] : either of two southern African plants whose foliage is poisonous to cattle: **a** : a squill (*Urginea burkei*) **b** : a bulbous herb (*Ornithoglossum glaucum*) of the family Liliaceae

slang·ster \ˈslaŋztə(r), -aiŋ-, -ŋ(k)st-\ *n* -s [³*slang* + *-ster*] : a user of slang

slan·guage \ˈslaŋgwij, -laiŋ-, -wēj *sometimes* -ŋw-\ *n* -s [blend of ³*slang* and *language*] : slangy speech or writing

slangy \ˈslaŋē, -laiŋ-, -ŋi\ *adj* -ER/-EST **1** : given to vulgarity or flashiness **2 a** : of, relating to, or constituting slang **b** : containing or addicted to slang

slank *archaic past of* SLINK

¹slant \ˈslant, -aa(ə)-, -ai-, -á-\ *adv* [ME *slonte*, short for *aslonte* aslant — more at ASLANT] : ASLANT, OBLIQUELY

²slant \"\ *vb* -ED/-ING/-S [alter. of *slent*, fr. ME *slenten*, of Scand origin; akin to Sw *slinta* to slide, ON *sletta*; akin to MHG *sliten* to slide — more at SLIDE] *vi* **1** : to hit or strike obliquely : GLANCE — used with *against, on*, or *upon* **2** : to turn or incline from a right line or a level : lie or fall obliquely to a horizontal or perpendicular line : SLOPE ⟨the roof ~*s*⟩ ⟨where the field ~*s* to the river⟩ **3** : to take a diagonal course, direction, or path ⟨we ~*ed* across the river⟩ **4** : to have an inclination : TREND — used with *toward* ~ *vt* **1** : to cut or strike (something) obliquely : cut across at a sharp angle ⟨shafts of sunlight ~*ing* the earth —Carl Sandburg⟩ **2** : to turn from a direct line : give an oblique or sloping direction to ⟨~ a line⟩ **3** : to bend or incline (one) by training, urging, or similar effort **4** : to direct (written or spoken matter) to the interests of a particular audience or according to a particular interpretation : ANGLE ⟨a magazine ~*ed* for farm readers⟩; *specif* : to warp from objective presentation so as to favor a particular bias ⟨~ the news⟩

³slant \"\ *adj* **1 a** : inclined from a direct line whether horizontal or perpendicular : SLOPING ⟨a ~ line⟩ **b** : moving in an oblique path ⟨a ~ ray of light⟩ **2** : BIASED — used of a person or his faculties

⁴slant \"\ *n* -s [prob. alter. (influenced by ²*slant*) of *slent*, fr. ME, of Scand origin; akin to Sw *slänt* slope, slant, *slinta* to slide] **1** : a slanting direction, line, or plane : SLOPE, INCLINATION ⟨the east slope has a sharp ~⟩ ⟨sits at a ~⟩ ⟨lay a cloth on the ~⟩ **2** : something (as a slope or a shaft of light) that slants ⟨a ~ of sunlight fell between the branches⟩ ⟨puffing up the steep ~ and onto the highway⟩: as **a** : a short inclined passageway in a coal mine the course of which is diagonal to the main workings **b** : a slab with slanting depressions for artists' colors **c** : a sewer pipe that has one end beveled and is used for making a connection to a sewer **d** (1) : a culture medium solidified obliquely in a tube so as to increase the surface area ⟨a blood-agar ~⟩ — compare STAB 5a (2) : SLANT CULTURE **e** *or* **slant line** : DIAGONAL 4 **f** : a football running play in which the ball carrier moves obliquely toward the line of scrimmage **3** *chiefly dial* : an oblique or sarcastic remark : TAUNT **4 a** : a view from a particular angle : a peculiar or personal point of view, attitude, or opinion ⟨considered from a new ~⟩ ⟨you have a wrong ~ on the problem⟩ **b** : a slanting view : GLANCE ⟨take a ~ at him⟩

⁵slant \"\ *n* -s [alter. of earlier *slent* slant, spell (of weather), fr. ME, sprinkling, splash] : a light or brief breeze esp. over water : GUST

slant·able \-təbəl\ *adj* : capable of being slanted; *esp* : subject to biased interpretation

slant culture *n* : a culture (as of bacteria) made by inoculating the surface of a slant

slant dam *n* : RAFTER DAM

slant drilling *n* : drilling for oil or gas in other than a vertical direction

¹slant·er \-tə(r)\ *n* -s [²*slant* + *-er*] : one that slants something (as a person with a decidedly sloping handwriting)

²slan·ter \"\ *adj* [prob. modif. of D *slenter* trick, lie, shift, slow pace, loitering gait, fr. *slenteren* to saunter, loiter; akin to Sw *slinta* to slide — more at SLANT] *Austral* : TRICKY, UNFAIR, UNTRUTHFUL

slant–eye \ˈ≈ˌ≈\ *n* [back-formation fr. *slant-eyed*] : a person with slanting eyes; *esp* : one of Mongoloid ancestry — usu. taken to be offensive

slant–eyed \ˈ≈ˌ≈\ *adj* : having slanting eyes; *specif* : MONGOLOID

slant–front \ˈ≈ˌ≈\ *adj* : SLANT-TOP

slant height *n* **1** : the segment of a generating line of a right half cone lying between the vertex and the base **2** : the altitude of a side of a regular pyramid

slant·in·dic·u·lar \ˌslantˌinˈdikyələ(r)\ *adj* [blend of *slanting* and *perpendicular*] : somewhat oblique

slanting eye *n* : an eye with an epicanthic fold

slant·ing·ly *adv* : in a slanting manner : with a slant

slant·ing·ness *n* -ES : the quality or state of being or having a slant

slant·ing·ways \ˈ≈≈ˌwāz\ *or* **slant·ing·wise** \-ˌwīz\ *adv* : SLANTWISE

slant line *n* : SLANT 2e

slant·ly *adv* [³*slant* + *-ly*] : SLANTINGLY, SLOPINGLY

slant of wind : a local or passing variation of the wind from its general direction; *esp* : such a variation favoring a sailing vessel

slants *pres 3d sing of* SLANT, *pl of* SLANT

slant–top \ˈ≈ˌ≈\ *adj* : having a drop-front cover that lies at a slant when closed — used esp. of a desk

slant·ways \ˈ≈ˌwāz\ *adv* : SLANTWISE

slantwise \ˈ≈ˌ≈\ *adv (or adj)* : at a slant : moving or directed in a slanting position or direction

¹slap \ˈslap\ *n* -s [ME *slop*, fr. MD; akin to MHG *slupf* place to slip into, hiding place, sling, OHG *slupfen* to slip, slide, MD *slippen* to slip — more at SLIP] **1** *dial Brit* : a pass or notch between hills **2** *dial Brit* : OPENING, BREACH ⟨a ~ in the fence⟩

²slap \"\ *n* -s [LG *slapp*, of imit. origin] **1 a** : a quick sharp blow with the open hand ⟨a ~ on the cheek⟩ **b** : a quick sharp blow : SMACK ⟨used by hunters to protect their arm from the ~ of the bowstring —J.H.Howard⟩ **2** : a sharp noise like that produced by a slap ⟨listening . . . to the ~ and plunge of people in the water —Nadine Gordimer⟩ ⟨noise of construction — crashing slides of stone, whang of hammers, ~ of plaster —Ruth Adams⟩; *specif* : a noise resulting from play or slackness between parts of a machine (as in transmission gears) ⟨a bad piston ~⟩ **3 a** : REBUFF, INSULT ⟨words of praise like this are generally preliminary to a ~ —Erle Stanley Gardner⟩ — often used with *at* ⟨a ~ not only at this country but at all Asia —Robert Trumbull⟩ **b** : a sudden calamity : BLOW ⟨loyalty splintered under the ~ of a moderate economic setback —Samuel Lubell⟩ **4** : a quick try : GO — used with *at* ⟨have a ~ at the rabbits —F.E.Smedley⟩ **5** : an emphasized

brush of the foot usu. backward in tap dancing — **slap in the face :** a direct sharp insult or rebuff ⟨comfortable officers' clubs were, naturally, a *slap in the face* for enlisted men —*Tomorrow*⟩ — **slap on the wrist :** a gentle usu. ineffectual reprimand ⟨punishment will be more than just a *slap on the wrist* and will discourage recurring violations —Arthur Herrick⟩

³slap \"\ *vb* **slapped; slapped; slapping; slaps** [prob. fr. ²*slap*] *vt* **1 :** to strike usu. quickly and sharply with the open hand ⟨~ a child's face⟩ ⟨he ~*s* his knee⟩ ⟨~ the table⟩ **2 a :** to strike with a motion or sound like that of a blow with the open hand ⟨a pinch hitter *slapped* the ball —Vic Wall⟩ ⟨clothes *slapped* warm and dry with wind and sun —Janet Frame⟩ ⟨a *slapped* bull fiddle⟩ **b :** to cause to strike with a motion or sound like that of a blow with the open hand ⟨~ your feet on the floor⟩ ⟨women washing clothes in the canal ~ them . . . against stones —Christopher Rand⟩ **c :** to actuate (a trigger) with a sudden sharp pull rather than a slow squeeze **3 :** to place summarily and often carelessly ⟨carved a . . . bun into three horizontal slices, *slapped* two beef patties between them —*Time*⟩ ⟨little hats *slapped* against the back of the head —Lois Long⟩ — often used with *on* ⟨~ paint on a wall⟩ ⟨*slapping* new taxes on farm cooperatives —G.E.Cruikshank⟩ ⟨~ a quota restriction on foreign imports of fur —*New Republic*⟩ ⟨~ an additional fine on the violator —J.M. Flagler⟩ **4 :** CENSURE, REPRIMAND ⟨~ certain academic critics —Dudley Fitts⟩ ⟨*slapped* the workers who had gone on strike —Walter Sullivan⟩ **5 :** to take legal action against **:** SERVE ⟨~ him with a summons⟩ ~ *vi* **1 :** to strike usu. sharply with the open hand ⟨he ~*ed* with the palm of his hand on the table⟩ **2 :** to make a motion or sound similar to that of a blow with the open hand ⟨heelless slippers *slapping* on the stones —Claud Cockburn⟩ ⟨rain *slapped* at the stained-glass window —Berton Roueché⟩ ⟨the steady one, two, three, four beat of the *slapping* drums —*New Yorker*⟩ **syn** see STRIKE — **slap in the face :** INSULT, HUMILIATE ⟨*slapped in the face* by not being invited to the party⟩ ⟨*slapped* his own board *in the face* with a public statement —Irving Stone⟩ — **slap on the back :** BACKSLAP — **slap on the wrist** or **slap the wrist of** or **slap one's wrist :** to reprimand gently and usu. ineffectually ⟨*slapped on the wrist* for composing in too urbanized a manner —*Time*⟩ ⟨*slapped the wrists of* missionaries who demanded a show of forceful aid —D.L.Oliver⟩ ⟨*slapped his wrist* for reporting the story falsely⟩ — **slap together :** to construct or produce by constructing hastily and carelessly ⟨rude shanties *slapped together* —*Amer. Guide Series: Pa.*⟩ ⟨*slapped* the movie *together* in a month⟩

⁴slap \"\ *adv* [prob. fr. LG *slapp* with a sudden blow, suddenly, instantly, of imit. origin] **1 :** DIRECTLY, RIGHT, PLUMP, SMACK ⟨we hadn't sighted a thing . . . and then we ran ~ into her —Hugh MacLennan⟩ ⟨houses are ~ on the street; no sidewalk — not so much as a curb —Faubion Bowers⟩ **2** *dial* **:** COMPLETELY, ABSOLUTELY ⟨she was ~ out of black sewing cotton —Frances Gaither⟩

slap around *vt* **1 :** BUFFET, MANHANDLE ⟨drunks . . . have a way of becoming much less troublesome if they are *slapped around* a little —*Time*⟩ **2 :** to treat roughly, overbearingly, or harshly ⟨critics really *slapped* the play *around*⟩

¹slap–bang \ˈ=ˌ=\ *adj* [²*slap*] **:** marked by roughness and impetuousness of manner or method ⟨businessmen of the *slap-bang*, horn-blowing, bluff, good-natured . . . kind —Edna Ferber⟩ ⟨*slap-bang* . . . production methods —K.B.Butler⟩

²slap–bang \"\ *adv* **:** with excessive force, haste, and usu. noise **:** PRECIPITATELY ⟨yachts and . . . chasers ran *slap-bang* at 16 knots into a convoy —*Springfield (Mass.) Republican*⟩

slapdab \ˈ=ˌ=\ *adv* [⁴*slap* + *dab*] *chiefly South & Midland* **:** EXACTLY, RIGHT ⟨~ in the middle⟩

¹slapdash \ˈ=ˌ=\ *adv* [⁴*slap* + *dash*] **1 :** in a slapdash manner ⟨the house was put together ~⟩ **2 :** DIRECTLY, RIGHT, SMACK ⟨with a picture . . . ~ on the middle of it —Ward Moore⟩

²slapdash \"\ *adj* **:** HAPHAZARD, SLIPSHOD, SLOPPY ⟨the overture emerged as a ~ affair, marred not only by a rough and uncalculated style but by technical inaccuracies —Winthrop Sargeant⟩ ⟨a ~ excursion which fails to do justice to the abilities of any of its three authors —D.L.Olmsted⟩

³slapdash \"\ *n* **:** SLAPDASHNESS ⟨the case is being built carefully, not with ~ —*Kiplinger Washington Letter*⟩

slap·dash·ery \ˈ=ˌ=ərē\ *n* -ES [²*slapdash* + -*ery*] **:** SLAPDASHNESS ⟨~ of the London slums —*Newsweek*⟩

slap·dash·ness \ˈ=ˌ==\ *n* -ES **:** the quality or state of being slapdash **:** HAPHAZARDNESS, SLOPPINESS ⟨has amazing defects, flippancy, ~ —H.J.Laski⟩

slap down *vt* **1 :** to prohibit or restrain (a person or group) usu. abruptly and with censure from acting in a specified way **:** SQUELCH ⟨were *slapped down* with the . . . law regulating railroads —W.A.Lydgate⟩ **2 :** to put an abrupt stop to **:** SUPPRESS ⟨*slapped down* a Labor attempt to censure his government —*Time*⟩ ⟨open criticism of the regime is quickly *slapped down* by the police —Richard Mowrer⟩

¹slape \ˈslāp\ *adj* [ME, fr. ON *sleipr* — more at SLIP] *dial Eng* **:** SLIPPERY, SMOOTH

²slape \"\ *chiefly dial var of* SLEEP

slape end *n* **:** the end of a leaf in a leaf spring that is sharply bent back on itself to form a bearing surface to slide on a casting provided on the vehicle frame

slap·hap·pi·ness \ˈ=ˌ==\ *n*, *slang* **:** the quality or state of being slaphappy

slaphappy \ˈ=ˌ==\ *adj* [²*slap* + *happy*] *slang* **:** PUNCH-DRUNK, WITLESS ⟨~ with exhaustion —Ned Calmer⟩ ⟨it's driving me ~. In fact, I'm getting whacky —William Kozlenko⟩; *also* **:** buoyantly carefree **:** deliriously irrational **:** CRAZY ⟨~ abandon with which members . . . have been prying state secrets out of the administration —*New Yorker*⟩

slap in *vt* **:** to put in place hastily and usu. carelessly ⟨*slapped in* a new set of lyrics and put it to work as a singing commercial —*Time*⟩ ⟨new owners broke it and *slapped in* row crops —Russell Lord⟩

slap·jack \ˈslap,jak\ *n* [³*slap* + *jack* (as in *flapjack*)] **1 :** PANCAKE, FLAPJACK **2 :** a game in which playing cards are turned up one by one on a pile with the first player to slap his hand on any jack that appears acquiring the pile and the player who acquires the most cards winning

slap on *vt* **:** to put into effect usu. suddenly and decisively ⟨*slap on* the death penalty for narcotics smugglers —*Time*⟩ ⟨*slapped on* a hard money policy —T.R.Ybarra⟩

slapped *past of* SLAP

slap·per \ˈslapə(r)\ *n* -S **:** one that slaps; *specif* **:** a device that consists of two strips of canvas attached to a handle and is used for driving and directing cattle esp. in stockyards

slapping *adj* [fr. pres. part. of ³*slap*] **1 :** very rapid **:** RATTLING ⟨away we went at a ~ pace —T.C.Haliburton⟩ **2 :** very large **:** STRAPPING ⟨a ~ horse⟩

slap·py \ˈslapē\ *adj* -ER/-EST [³*slap* + -*y*] **:** marked by or productive of slapping ⟨~ tone-production marred what might otherwise have been one of the season's musical treats —Virgil Thomson⟩ ⟨thunderstorm suddenly gets ~ and twisty —*Flying*⟩

slaps *pl of* SLAP, *pres 3d sing of* SLAP

¹slapstick \ˈ=ˌ=\ *n* [²*slap* + *stick*] **1 a :** a device consisting of two flat pieces of wood fastened together at one end but loose at the other and sometimes used by an actor in farce to make a loud noise in simulation of a severe blow **b :** any of several similar devices: as (1) **:** two flat pieces of leather sewed together, weighted at the hitting end, and used as a club (2) **:** a stick hinged on one side to the top of a slate and clapped against the top to mark on a sound track the beginning of a movie take **2 a :** comedy that depends for its effect on fast, boisterous, and zany physical activity and horseplay (as the throwing of pies, the whacking of posteriors with a slapstick, chases, mugging) often accompanied by broad obvious rowdy verbal humor ⟨relies heavily on ~. Rosalind is trapped in the slats of a venetian blind, spanked by an exploding engine part in a hot-rod race, nearly strangled in an electric fan —*Time*⟩ ⟨the extravagant ~ comedy used by English pantomimists —M.E.McIntosh⟩ **b :** humor, language, or activity like that in slapstick comedy ⟨humor that ranges from arrant ~ to satire —*Newsweek*⟩ ⟨an exuberance and colloquial vigor that often only just stop short of ~ —F.W. Bateson⟩ **3 :** a flat strip of wood upon which an abrasive (as a piece of emery paper) is fixed for use in polishing or finishing work

²slapstick \"\ *adj* **:** of, relating to, or having the characteristics of slapstick ⟨~ comedy⟩ ⟨~ humor⟩ ⟨a ~ style⟩ ⟨his extravagant ~ English —B.D.Wolfe⟩

slap–up \ˈ=ˌ=\ *adj* [⁴*slap*] *chiefly Brit* **:** FIRST-RATE, FINE, EXCELLENT; *also* **:** ELEGANT, FANCY ⟨a *slap-up* feed — complete with sherry wine —C.G.Glover⟩ ⟨lured into the middle of a *slap-up* garden party —Christopher Isherwood⟩

slare \ˈsla(a)(ə)r\ *vi* [origin unknown] **1** *dial Eng* **:** to scuff the feet **2** *dial Eng* **:** SMEAR

slar·gan·do \slärˈgän(,)dō\ *adj* (*or adv*) [It, making slow, widening, verbal of *slargare* to make slow, widen, fr. *s*- (fr. L *ex*-) + *largare* to widen, loosen, fr. L *largus* abundant, generous — more at LARD] **:** ALLARGANDO — used as a direction in music

¹slash \ˈslash, -aa(ə)-, -ai-\ *vb* -ED/-ING/-ES [ME *slaschen*, prob. fr. MF *eslachier* to break] *vt* **1 :** to cut with sweeping strokes that are typically rapid and forceful or savage with or as if with a blade producing long cuts or slits and usu. without careful aim ⟨when our tools are blasted and our canvases ~*ed* —E.M.Forster⟩ ⟨the dog managed to ~ both his opponents severely —C.G.D.Roberts⟩ **2 :** to hit with a stroke like that used in slashing: as **a :** LASH, WHIP ⟨~ him with bridle reins and dog whips —Sir Walter Scott⟩ **b :** to strike swiftly and forcibly **:** DRIVE ⟨~*ed* the ball across the court⟩ **3 :** to wield with movements like those used in slashing ⟨~*ing* his bright sword somewhat aimlessly about —Evangeline Davis⟩; *esp* **:** CRACK ⟨~*ing* his whip so near the horse that the creature was frightened —Harriet B. Stowe⟩ **4 a :** to reduce to slash ⟨the growth has been ~*ed* by . . . scrub-cutting gangs —K.B. Cumberland⟩ **b :** to clear (land) by slashing down trees and bushes ⟨~*ed* fifty acres⟩ **5 a :** to advance (a thing) by or as if by slashing the obstacles in the way ⟨~*ed* his way through the Oregon wilderness —*Amer. Guide Series: Oregon*⟩ **b :** to move (a thing) swiftly and forcefully ⟨~*ed* the curtain across the light —Morley Callaghan⟩ **6 a :** to cut slits in (as a garment) so as to insert or expose an underlying contrasting color ⟨~*ed* cuff with inset bands of contrast —*Women's Wear Daily*⟩ **b :** to mark as if by slashing in such a manner **:** STREAK ⟨brown iris . . . ~*ed* with yellow —Willa Cather⟩ ⟨this gloom ~*ed* by a few bands of bright light —John Cheever⟩ ⟨great yellow flashes ~ the night —Guthrie Wilson⟩ **7 :** to criticize cuttingly and sweepingly **:** censure unsparingly ⟨~*ed* the administration for its policies⟩ **8 a :** to reduce sharply (as in amount or extent) **:** CUT ⟨~ the cost of fashion on every item in the store —*advt*⟩ ⟨would personally like to see the tax on corporations not just cut, but ~*ed* —*Wall Street Jour.*⟩ ⟨incidence of major crime in that area was ~*ed* by almost 50 percent —George Barrett⟩ **b :** to reduce the length of **:** SHORTEN ⟨editing would have ~*ed* this volume to half its size —Wayne Andrews⟩ **c :** to delete usu. by crossing out **:** EXPUNGE ⟨~*ed* many pages out of the typescript —F.A.Swinnerton⟩ **d :** remove by or as if by cutting **:** EXCISE ⟨~ twenty minutes out of the first act —Clemence Dane⟩ **9 :** to size (yarn) with a slasher ~ *vi* **1 :** to cut recklessly or savagely with or as if with a sword, knife, or razor ⟨these lads hacked and ~*ed* with the same tremendous spirit —Mark Twain⟩ **2 :** to fall, move, or advance with a sweeping cutting motion like that used in slashing **:** PELT, DASH, DRIVE ⟨a pouring night late in March, and the rain ~*ed* against the windows —Laura Krey⟩ ⟨the winds ~ before them —Marjory S. Douglas⟩ ⟨the rockets ~ groundward —*advt*⟩ **3 a :** to use unnecessary roughness in striking with one's stick at an opponent's stick in lacrosse **b :** to use unnecessary force when swinging the stick in playing the puck in ice hockey **syn** see CUT — **slash at 1 :** to attack swiftly and forcefully ⟨roar off runways . . . at minute intervals to *slash at* the communications of the . . . army —*Current History*⟩ **2 :** to censure unsparingly **:** EXCORIATE ⟨when you *slash at* my things —Dorothy C. Fisher⟩

²slash \"\ *n* -ES **1 a :** a long cut made by slashing **:** GASH **b :** a stroke or blow delivered with a slashing motion ⟨two revengeful ~*es* —H.G.Wells⟩ **2 :** an ornamental slit esp. for showing a lining, underlayer, or insertion in a contrasting color ⟨his paned hose were of velvet lined with purple silk, which garniture appeared at the ~*es* —Sir Walter Scott⟩ ⟨~*es* in the glaze to show the beige pottery beneath —*New Yorker*⟩ **3 :** a line or band of vivid or flashing color or light **:** STREAK ⟨peeping in yellow ~*es* through the trees —C.E.W. Bean⟩ ⟨~*es* of sunlight —Sylvia T. Warner⟩ **4 a :** an open tract in a forest strewn with debris (as logs, chunks of wood, bark, branches) from logging, wind, or fire **b :** the debris in such a tract **5** *also* **slash mark :** DIAGONAL 4 **6 :** a long straight cut or mark that is made in a garment or pattern and that usu. indicates or serves as the base for an opening or placket **7 :** REDUCTION, CUT ⟨5 to 10 percent price ~ in new cars —*Christian Science Monitor*⟩ ⟨substantial ~*es* in this year's defense outlays —Felix Belair⟩

³slash \"\ *n* -ES [prob. alter. (influenced by ¹*slush*) of ¹*plash*] **:** a low swampy area often overgrown with bushes **:** MARSH

slash–and–burn \ˈ=ˌ=ˌ=\ *adj* **:** characterized or developed by felling and girdling trees and then burning them to make land arable usu. for temporary purposes ⟨the *slash-and-burn* method of agriculture⟩

slashed *past of* SLASH

slash·er \-shə(r)\ *n* -S **:** one that slashes: as **a :** one that uses a slashing implement or weapon (1) **:** a bully esp. when boastfully wielding a weapon (as a sword or knife) **:** a slashing fellow **:** SWASHBUCKLER (2) **:** a prowler or other evildoer who uses a slashing instrument (as a knife or blade) as a weapon (3) **:** SWORDSMAN (4) **:** one that cuts down timber esp. in a wasteful or destructive manner (5) **:** one that tends an implement that slashes **b :** a weapon, implement, or machine that slashes: as (1) **:** SWORD (2) **:** KNIFE (3) **:** RAZOR (4) *dial Eng* **:** BILLHOOK (5) **:** an implement with an iron blade used in brickmaking to prod or slash the clay to detect stones (6) **:** a machine fitted with one or more coarse circular saws and used in lumbering for sawing logs, slabs, and scrap wood into pieces suitable for laths, pulpwood, or firewood or for transportation to the refuse burner (7) **:** a machine to apply size to warp yarns (8) **:** a cockfighting gaff with razor-edged sides and a sharpened tip

slashes *pres 3d sing of* SLASH, *pl of* SLASH

slash grain *n* **:** a grain produced by sawing wood so that the annual rings are parallel with the surface

¹slashing *n* -S [fr. gerund of ¹*slash*] **1 :** the act or process of slashing **:** the work of a slasher: as **a :** the illegal use of a slashing weapon (as a blade or knife) ⟨a three month sentence for ~ —*Springfield (Mass.) Union*⟩ **b :** the sizing of yarn by a slasher ⟨yarn sizing or ~ has become a fine art —H.R. Mauersberger⟩ **2 a :** an insert or underlayer of contrasting color revealed by a slash (as in a garment) ⟨the pink with the chocolate ~ in the skirt —R.P.Warren⟩ **b :** the slash that reveals such an insert or underlayer ⟨a different material being sewn under the ~*s* —Sophia Caulfeild & Blanche Saward⟩ **3 a :** an open tract of forest land covered with slash ⟨less forest and more open, hot, shadeless, weed-grown ~ —Ernest Hemingway⟩ **b :** the slash in such a tract ⟨dug out stumps, cut ~ —*Amer. Guide Series: Oregon*⟩ — usu. used in pl. ⟨using a power saw to salvage worthless pine ~*s* —Frank Cameron⟩ ⟨flinging aside the ~*s* —J.S.Qualey⟩

²slashing *adj* [fr. pres. part. of ¹*slash*] **1 :** incisively satiric **:** unsparingly critical or censorious ⟨his terrible ~ wit, his fine scorn of stupidity —John Reed⟩ ⟨a ~ attack on religious hypocrisy and scientific nonsense —R.A.Cordell⟩ **2 :** DASHING, SPIRITED, VIGOROUS ⟨a ~ fellow⟩ **3 :** HUGE, IMMENSE, SPLENDID ⟨a ~ fortune at her disposal —Charles Dickens⟩ **4 :** that strikes with a blow or a succession of blows like those used in slashing **:** PELTING, DRIVING, BITING ⟨~ southeaster⟩ **5 :** VIVID, BRILLIANT, FLASHING ⟨~ juxtapositions of blacks and whites —R.M.Coates⟩ ⟨bold ~ green canvas —*Sydney (Australia) Bull.*⟩ — **slash·ing·ly** *adv*

slash pine *n* [³*slash*; fr. the fact that caribbean pine esp. in Florida grows in slashes] **1 a :** CARIBBEAN PINE **b :** the strong hard heavy coarse-grained orange wood of the Caribbean pine **2 :** any of several pines (as the loblolly or longleaf pine) that grow in similar situations to or are used like the slash pine and esp. that are sources of turpentine and lumber in the southern U.S.

slash pocket *n* **:** a pocket suspended on the wrong side of a garment from a finished slit on the right side that serves as its opening

¹slat \ˈslat, *usu* -ad·+V\ *n* -S [ME *slat*, *sclat*, fr. MF *esclat* fragment, splinter, fr. OF — more at ÉCLAT] **1** *chiefly dial* **:** a piece of slate **:** SLATE **2 :** a thin narrow flat strip esp. of wood or metal: as **a :** LATH **b :** LOUVER **c :** STAVE **d :** a piece of wood about the length and half the diameter of a pencil that has been planed and grooved preparatory to receiving the lead in pencil manufacturing **e :** one of the thin flat members in the back of a slat-back chair **3 :** a sheepskin from which all or most of the wool has been removed and which has been air dried to preserve it for tanning **4 slats** *pl, slang* **a :** BUTTOCKS **b :** RIBS **5 :** an auxiliary airfoil at the leading edge of the wing of an airplane that is normally closed to form part of the regular contour of the wing but that may be opened to form a slot when flight conditions require it

²slat \"\ *adj* [ME *sclat*, fr. *sclat*, n., slat] **:** having or made of slats ⟨the ~ seat of the garden swing —Saul Bellow⟩ ⟨protected from the sun by ~ roofs —*Amer. Guide Series: Fla.*⟩

³slat \"\ *vt* **slatted; slatted; slatting; slats** [ME *slatten*, fr. *slat*, *sclat*, n., slat] **1 a :** to make or equip with slats ⟨small *slatted* houses over tombs —*Amer. Guide Series: La.*⟩ **b :** to stripe or bar as if with slats ⟨a single spread of green *slatted* with watercourses —Sheila Kaye-Smith⟩ **2 :** to close the slats of ⟨~ the Venetian blinds against the blaze of noon —Christopher Morley⟩

⁴slat \"\ *vb* **slatted; slatted; slatting; slats** [prob. of Scand origin; akin to ON *sletta* to slap, splash, throw, *sletta* to slide — more at SLANT] *vt* **1** *dial Eng* **:** to hurl or throw smartly against something else **:** toss or cast with force and vehemence **2** *dial Eng* **:** STRIKE, BEAT, PUMMEL ~ *vi* **1 :** to flap violently ⟨sails that ~ and belly in the wind —Hamilton Basso⟩ **2 :** to move with a motion or sound like that of a violently flapping sail ⟨the calms, with their exasperating rolling and *slatting* —W.H.Taylor⟩ ⟨rain . . . came in gusts, *slatting* and spattering against the rocky slopes —B.A.Williams⟩ ⟨boxcars *slatting* past at fifty miles an hour —Thomas Wolfe⟩

⁵slat \"\ *vi* [obs. F *esclater* (now *éclater*), fr. OF, to splinter, burst — more at ÉCLAT] *dial Eng* **:** SPLIT, CRACK

⁶slat \"\ *n* -S [IrGael] *Brit* **:** ¹KELT

slat–back \ˈ=ˌ=\ *adj* **:** having two or more horizontal or vertical slats; *esp* **:** LADDER-BACK — used of the back of a chair

slat bonnet *n* **:** a sunbonnet with a stitched brim stiffened by cardboard or wooden inserts

slatch \ˈslach\ *n* -ES [alter. of ¹*slack*] **1 :** a transitory breeze or its duration **2 :** an interval of fair weather ⟨a ~ in the storm —*Time*⟩ **3 :** a calm between breaking waves ⟨big waves generally come in groups of three, and then behind them there is a ~ —Hickman Powell⟩ **4 :** the loose or slack part of a rope

slat conveyor *n* **:** a conveyor consisting of one or more endless chains to which horizontal spaced slats are attached to form a moving support for the objects being conveyed

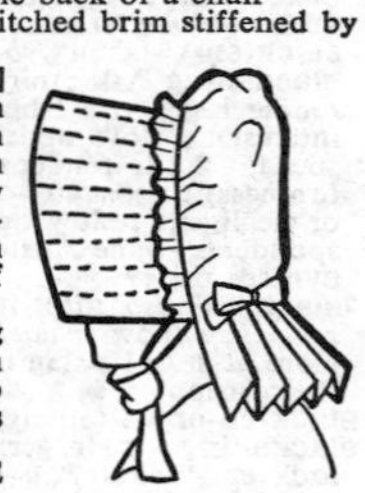

slat bonnet

¹slate \ˈslāt, *usu* -ād·+V\ *n* -S [ME *slate*, *sclate*, fr. MF *esclate*, fr. OF, fem. of *esclat* fragment, splinter — more at ÉCLAT] **1 a :** a thin flat slab, piece, or layer of laminated rock (as slate); *sometimes* **:** ¹BONE 8b **b :** a piece of slate or other construction material prepared in the shape of a shingle and used esp. for roofing and siding **:** TILE, SHINGLE ⟨roofing ~*s*⟩ ⟨roofs are covered with asbestos cement ~*s* —H.M.Dunnett⟩ ⟨roofing ~ is manufactured by a hand method and by a mill method —J.H.Bateman⟩ **2 :** a dense fine-grained rock produced by the compression of clays, shales, and various other rocks that develops a characteristic cleavage which may be at any angle with the original bedding plane and consisting essentially of sericite and quartz with biotite, chlorite, and hematite as principal accessories; *also* **:** a cleavable rock that resembles slate **3 a :** a tablet of slate or slatelike material used esp. by children for writing on usu. with chalk **b :** a tablet usu. of slate bearing take and scene numbers, date, director's name, or similar identifying data and photographed at the beginning or end of a movie take — compare SLAPSTICK 1b(2) **c** *Brit* **:** a slate on which a compositor in a piecework shop writes his name when he runs out of copy to set **d :** a hand instrument for writing braille consisting of a metal plate pitted with the six points of the braille cell and another metal plate above it with openings through which a stylus is pressed down into the pits one at a time to emboss points in desired position on paper placed between the two plates — called also *braille slate* **4 a :** a written or unwritten record of deeds or events ⟨leaving evaluation of the rest of the . . . to history —*New Republic*⟩ ⟨wiped the ~ clean of past mistakes —R.G.Woolbert⟩ **b** (1) **:** a list prepared in advance of candidates for appointment, nomination, or election (as to political or corporation office) ⟨the 10,000 names needed to put an independent ~ on the ballot —H.H.Martin⟩ ⟨the committee presents one ~ to be voted upon at the annual . . . meeting —*Saturday Rev.*⟩ (2) **:** the group of persons proposed for appointment, nomination, or election ⟨install a new ~ of officers for the coming year —*Springfield (Mass.) Daily News*⟩ **c :** a list of entrants in a horse race with the betting odds offered posted by a bookmaker **d :** a schedule of sports events ⟨the thirteen-game ~ includes home-and-home contests —*N.Y.Times*⟩ **5 a :** a dark purplish gray that is bluer and deeper than pigeon, redder, lighter, and stronger than charcoal, and bluer and darker than taupe gray **b :** any of various grays similar in color to common roofing slates — **clean slate :** a record unblemished by discreditable acts or measures ⟨left a *clean slate* for his successor in office⟩ — **have a slate loose** *chiefly Brit* **:** to be slightly defective mentally — **on the slate** *adv (or adj)* **1** *slang* **:** on credit **:** on a charge account ⟨give me another beer and put it *on the slate* —J.A.Lee⟩ **2** *Brit, of a compositor* **:** with one's name on the slate **:** without copy to set ⟨about one fourth of the time . . . is spent compulsorily *on the slate*, for which the compositor receives no remuneration —G. E.Rowles⟩

²slate \"\ *adj* [ME *sclate*, fr. *sclate*, n., slate] **1 :** made of slate ⟨a ~ roof⟩ **2 :** of the color slate **:** slate-colored ⟨a ~ dress⟩ **3 :** containing slate ⟨an Ordovician ~ belt⟩

³slate \"\ *vb* -ED/-ING/-S [¹*slate*] *vt* **1 :** to cover with slate or a slatelike substance ⟨~ a house⟩ ⟨the roof was *slated* instead of being thatched —C.K.Finlay⟩ **2 a :** to register or record the name of (a person or event) on a slate or in a schedule ⟨the party *slated* its candidates⟩ ⟨~ the game⟩ **b :** to schedule for or to schedule to occur or materialize at a specified time or in a specified place ⟨conclave is *slated* Sunday through next Thursday —*Sacramento (Calif.) Bee*⟩ ⟨elections *slated* in Japan next Sunday —*Newsweek*⟩ — usu. used with *for* ⟨market had been *slated* for Jan. 24–28 —*Retailing Daily*⟩ ⟨elections *slated* for July 1–2 —R.J.Kerner⟩ ⟨new ammonia plant is *slated* for the Midwest —*Wall Street Jour.*⟩ ⟨thunderstorms are *slated* for the northern Appalachians —*New Orleans (La.) Times-Picayune*⟩ **c :** to designate (a person or thing) for a specified function or purpose **:** act or be acted upon in a specified way at some time in the future **:** SCHEDULE, APPOINT ⟨*slated* for a prominent role in these plans —*Printers' Ink*⟩ ⟨who had been *slated* to start the game —Roscoe McGowen⟩ ⟨bill S246 *slated* for passage —W.A.Wittich⟩ ⟨work is *slated* to start shortly —P.S.Nathan⟩ ⟨*slated* to be converted into a . . . hospital —E.J.Kahn⟩ **d :** DESTINE, PREDESTINE, FOREORDAIN ⟨everything is . . . *slated* to fulfill a rational end —Harry Bear⟩ ⟨by aptitude, personality, and work he is obviously *slated* to go up —E.J. Fitzgerald⟩ **3 :** to flesh (hides) with a slater ~ *vi* **1 :** to make slates **2 :** to lay slates **3 :** to flesh hides with a slater

⁴slate \"\ *vt* -ED/-ING/-S [ME *slaiten*, irreg. fr. or akin to OE *slǣtan* to bait; akin to OHG *sleizen* to split, OE *slītan* to slit, tear — more at SLIT] *dial Brit* **:** to set a dog on **:** HOUND

⁵slate \"\ *vt* -ED/-ING/-S [prob. alter. of ⁴*slat*] **1 :** to thrash or pummel severely **2** *chiefly Brit* **:** to criticize or censure severely **:** BERATE ⟨*slated* him years later for having a part in the vilification —W.T.Scott⟩ ⟨severely *slated* for his pedantry, literary arrogance —R.G.Howarth⟩

slate black *n* **1 :** a nearly neutral slightly purplish black that is very slightly bluer and darker than sooty black and slightly redder and darker than neutral tint (sense 2) **2 :** a black pigment made by grinding black slate — compare MINERAL BLACK a

slate blue *n* : a variable color averaging a grayish blue that is redder and paler than electric, greener and less strong than copenhagen, redder, stronger, and slightly lighter than Gobelin, and greener and slightly paler than old china — called also *blue slate*
slate club *n, Brit* : a group of persons who save money in a common fund for a specified purpose (as distribution at Christmas)
slate–colored junco *also* **slate–colored snowbird** \'ˌ=ˌ==-\ *n* : a common junco (*Junco hiemalis*) of northeastern No. America that is dark slaty gray above with white underparts and outer tail feathers
slated *adj* [fr. past part. of ³*slate*] : SLATY 1 ⟨dark ~ clouds —Norman Mailer⟩
slate flour *or* **slate powder** *n* : a finely ground mineral that is obtained from slate and used esp. in the manufacture of gray paints
slate gray *n* : a light olive gray to medium gray — called also *oriental pearl, Russian gray*
slate green *n* : a grayish green that is yellower and duller than average bayberry or blue spruce (sense 2a)
slatelike \'=ˌ=\ *adj* : resembling slate (as in form, texture, composition, or color)
slate·man \'slātmən\ *n, pl* **slatemen** : a mine worker who handles rock or slate instead of coal — called also *rockman*
slate olive *n* : a dark greenish gray that is paler than sagebrush green and yellower and paler than muscovite
slate pencil *n* : a pencil of soft slate or of soapstone used for writing on a slate
slate–pencil sea urchin *n* : a large purple sea urchin (*Heterocentrotus mammillatus*) having stout heavy spines that resemble slate pencils
slate picker *n* : a person or a machine that picks slate and bone coal from coal
slate purple *n* : a dark grayish to dark reddish purple
¹**slat·er** \'slādə(r), -ātə-\ *n* -s [ME *sclater*, fr. *sclate* slate + -*er* — more at SLATE] **1** : one that slates; *esp* : a tool or machine with a blade of slate or similar stone used for fleshing hides **2** : SLATE PICKER **3 a** : WOOD LOUSE 1 **b** : any of various marine isopods — called also *sea slater*
²**slat·er** \"\ *n* -s [⁵*slate* + -*er*] *chiefly Brit* : one that censures sweepingly and violently : a severe critic
slaters' felt *n* : a tarred building paper used esp. under slate roofing
slates *pl of* SLATE, *pres 3d sing of* SLATE
slate tan *n* : a light olive gray that is deeper than piping rock and deeper and slightly redder than average covert gray
slate violet *n* : a grayish red that is bluer, less strong, and slightly darker than bois de rose, yellower and duller than appleblossom, and bluer and duller than Pompeian red
slate writer *n* : one that does slate writing
slate writing *n* : a spiritualistic or conjuring performance in which writing is mysteriously done upon a slate
slatey *var of* SLATY
slath \'slath, -ȧ-\ *n* -s [perh. of Scand origin; akin to Norw dial. *slōda*, a basket used in fishing] : the center of the bottom of a basket where the weaving is begun that is formed by crossing sticks at right angles and binding them

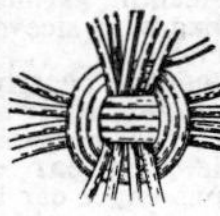
slath

¹**slath·er** \'slathə(r)\ *n* -s [origin unknown] : a great quantity : a lavish amount ⟨seems to be a ~ of public and private money available —Lee Rogow⟩ — often used in pl. ⟨~*s* of friends⟩ ⟨~*s* of luck⟩ — **open slather** *Austral* : FREE REIN ⟨asking to be allowed an *open slather* at an essential public service without being challenged —John Morrison⟩
²**slather** \"\ *vt* **slathered; slathered; slathering** \-th(ə)riŋ\ **slathers 1 a** : to spread thickly or lavishly — usu. used with *on* ⟨grabbed some bread and ~*ed* jam on it —P.E.Stevenson⟩ **b** : to spread thickly or lavishly on — usu. used with *with* ⟨~*ing* the cars with paint⟩ **2** : to use or spend in a wasteful or lavish manner : SQUANDER ⟨~*ed* money on ice cream —Dorothy C. Fisher⟩
slatier *comparative of* SLATY
slatiest *superlative of* SLATY
¹**slating** *n* -s [fr. gerund of ³*slate*] **1** : the work of a slater **2** : material used for slating : SLATE ⟨ordered ~ for the roof⟩ **3** : the movie-making process of preparing and photographing a slate ⟨original photography is often identified by ~ —W.H. Offenhauser⟩
²**slating** *n* -s [fr. gerund of ⁵*slate*] : a verbal or written lashing : a severely critical or censorious attack ⟨a hearty *slating* always does me good —H.L.Mencken⟩
slating nail *n* : a nail for use in nailing down slate roofing
slat·ish \'slād·ish\ *adj* [¹*slate* + -*ish*] : somewhat slate-colored ⟨the clouds . . . had taken a ~ tinge —Clark Russell⟩
slats *pl of* SLAT, *pres 3d sing of* SLAT
slatted *adj* [fr. past part. of ³*slat*] : having or made of slats ⟨a ~ blind⟩ ⟨~ crates⟩
slat·ter \'slad·ə(r)\ *n* -s [ME *sclatter*, fr. *sclat* slat + -*er* — more at SLAT] **1** *dial chiefly Eng* : SLATER **2** : a worker who removes slabs of soap from the frames in which they are formed
¹**slat·tern** \'slad·ə(r)n, -atə-\ *n* -s [prob. modif. of G *schlottern* to hang loosely, waddle, slouch (taken as a n.), fr. MHG *slottern, slattern, sluttern*; akin to D *slodderen* to hang loosely, *slodder* slovenly person, slut, Icel *sludda* clod of spittle, *slydda* sleet, slush, MHG *slote* mud, slime, *sloten* to stagger, shake, ON *slothra* to drag oneself forward, Goth *afslauthjan* to be anguished, shaken and prob. to ME *sloor* mud — more at SLUR] **1** : a person who is negligent of his appearance or surroundings; *esp* : an untidy slovenly woman ⟨two blowzy waitresses . . . ~*s* whose off-white aprons blended perfectly with their pasty cheeks —John Wain⟩ **2** : SLUT, PROSTITUTE ⟨there was a ~ or two . . . ladies of the profession —Bruce Marshall⟩
²**slattern** \"\ *adj* : SLATTERNLY ⟨~ hovels⟩ ⟨their gray ~ bodies —Liam O'Flaherty⟩
³**slattern** \"\ *vb* -ED/-ING/-S *vt* : to fritter away : WASTE — usu. used with *away* ⟨every fool who ~*s* away his whole time in nothings —Earl of Chesterfield⟩ ~ *vi* : to move or act in a slatternly manner
slat·tern·li·ness \-lēnəs, -lin-\ *n* -ES : the quality, state, or condition of being slatternly ⟨the room was . . . depressing from its ~ —Samuel Butler †1902⟩
¹**slat·tern·ly** \-lē, -li\ *adj* [¹*slattern* + -*ly* (adj. suffix)] **1** : untidy and usu. dirty through habitual neglect : SLOVENLY, UNKEMPT ⟨tatterdemalion, ~, slipshod women —E.C.Clayton⟩ ⟨streets terribly shabby and ~ and badly paved —Arnold Bennett⟩; *also* : CARELESS, DISORDERLY ⟨I am . . . ~; I seldom put, and never keep things in order; I am careless —Charlotte Brontë⟩ **2** : of, relating to, or characteristic of a slut or harlot
syn DOWDY, FROWZY, BLOWSY: SLATTERNLY stresses notions of slovenliness, unkemptness, and sordidness ⟨a small, *slatternly* looking craft, her hull and spars a dingy black, rigging all slack and bleached nearly white, and every thing denoting an ill state of affairs aboard —Herman Melville⟩ ⟨lived with them, in the *slatternly* apartment among the unwashed dishes in the sink and on the table, the odor of stale tobacco smoke, the dirty shirts and underwear piled in corners —R.P.Warren⟩ DOWDY may apply to a complete lack of taste typically marked by a blend of the untidy, unfit, or either drab or tawdry ⟨her shoes were bought a long time ago and have no relation to the dress, and the belt of her dress has become untied and is hanging down. She looks clean and *dowdy* —Lillian Hellman⟩ ⟨so dreadfully *dowdy* that she reminded one of a badly bound hymnbook —Oscar Wilde⟩ FROWZY suggests a lazy lack of neatness, order, and cleanliness ⟨a dumpy, *frowzy* woman, clad in old dress and apron —A.J.Coutts⟩ ⟨if a fully fed, presentably clothed, decently housed, fairly literate and cultivated and gently mannered family is not better than a half-starved, ragged, *frowzy*, overcrowded one, there is no meaning in words —G.B.Shaw⟩ BLOWSY suggests rude, loud, florid coarseness and lack of refinement ⟨a big *blowsy* Jezebel from the docks —Bruce Marshall⟩ ⟨the fat and *blowsy* wife bowed in an exaggerated fashion, never stopping the while to fan her red face vigorously —Louis Bromfield⟩

²**slatternly** \"\ *adv* [¹*slattern* + -*ly* (adv. suffix)] : in a slatternly manner
slat·tery \'slatəri\ *adj* [E dial. *slatter* to spill, splash, slop (perh. of Scand origin) + E -*y* (adj. suffix); akin to ON *sletta* to slap, splash — more at SLAT (throw)] *dial Eng* : RAINY, WET, SLOPPY
slatting *n* -s [fr. gerund of ³*slat*] **1** : SLATS **2** : the material from which slats are made
slaty *also* **slat·ey** \'slād·ē, -āt|, |i\ *adj* [¹*slate* + -*y*] **1** : of the nature or composition of, containing, or characteristic of slate ⟨a ~ texture⟩ ⟨a ~ cleavage⟩; *esp* : of a grayish cast suggestive of slate ⟨the ~ sky of dawn —Ethel Wilson⟩ ⟨house had a ~ impoverished look —Viola Meynell⟩ **2** : having mineral grains that are extremely small — used of rock foliation ⟨those with a ~ foliation have a very smooth cleaved surface —D.O.Woolf⟩
slaty gray aphid *n* : a plant louse (*Brevicoryne brassicae*) that infests various crop plants in New So. Wales
slaty gum *n* : any of several Australian eucalypts (as *Eucalyptus polyanthemos*) with slate-colored bark
¹**slaugh·ter** \'slȯd·ə(r), -ȯtə-\ *n* -s [ME *slauhter, slaughter*, of Scand origin; akin to ON *slātr* butcher's meat, *slātra* to slaughter; akin to OE *sleaht* slaughter, OHG *slahta*, Goth *slauhts*; derivative fr. the root of E ¹*slay*] **1 a** : the killing of animals ⟨the ~ of a hundred lions afforded him no recreation —Agnes Repplier⟩; *esp* : the butchery of cattle for market **b** : the killing of a person esp. in a bloody or barbarous manner ⟨was marked for ~ but escaped death and became the leader of the minority —E.E.Dale⟩ **2 a** : mass killing and bloodshed (as in war) : wholesale carnage : MASSACRE ⟨hoped that after the ~ it would be possible really to create . . . one world in peace —Alva Myrdal⟩ **b** : wanton destruction ⟨notwithstanding this wholesale ~, bird life is still plentiful —*Amer. Guide Series: Tenn.*⟩ ⟨half a century of . . . insensate ~ sufficed to destroy the magnificent forest —M.M.Quaife⟩ **c** *obs* : carnage personified ⟨besmeared and overstained with ~'s pencil —Shak.⟩ **3** : an act or instance of utter annihilation or defeat ⟨it was no longer a battle but a ~ —Robert Graves⟩ ⟨ended the ~ with a par 4 on the tenth hole to win by the awful margin of 9 and 8 —*New Yorker*⟩
²**slaughter** \"\ *vt* **slaughtered; slaughtered; slaughtering** \-ȯd·əriŋ, -ȯtər- *also* -ȯ·tr-\ **slaughters 1** : to kill (animals) for food; *esp* : BUTCHER **2 a** : to kill (a person) esp. in a bloody or barbarous manner : SLAY ⟨five men in a stolen car ~*ed* a paymaster and a factory guard —Phil Stong⟩ ⟨the number of people ~*ed* annually by cars —F.L.Allen⟩ **b** : to discredit or demolish completely ⟨tears through our literature ~*ing* Emerson, Thoreau, Melville, and Hawthorne —S.E.Hyman⟩ ⟨his team was . . . ~*ed* by Oklahoma —Eddie Beachler⟩ **c** *slang* : to make an irresistible impression on ⟨~*ing* them at the box office —*Metronome*⟩ **3 a** : to kill (people) in large numbers : MASSACRE ⟨overwhelming automatic firepower . . . proved too much for them, and 700 were ~*ed* in one day —Barrett McGurn⟩ **b** : to destroy in large quantities ⟨~*ed* fish in astronomical numbers —Henry LaCossitt⟩ ⟨timber was ~*ed* —Russell Lord⟩ **4** : to sell (securities) at a sacrifice
slaugh·ter·er \-ȯd·ərə(r), -ȯtər-, -ȯ·tr-\ *n* -s : one that slaughters: as **a** : KILLER **b** : BUTCHER, MEAT-PACKER — called also *slaughterman*
slaughterhouse \'=ˌ=ˌ=\ *n* [ME *slaughterhous*, fr. *slaughter* + *hous* house — more at HOUSE] **1** : an establishment where animals are butchered for market : ABATTOIR — called also *meatworks* **2** : something that resembles a slaughterhouse ⟨a political campaign is a ~ for issues and reputations —Norman Cousins⟩
slaughterhouse case *n* [so called fr. the fact that the matter at issue was the right of the city of New Orleans to regulate by law the carrying on of the butchering industry in that city] : one of a group of cases decided by the Supreme Court of the U.S. establishing that the police power of the states is not impaired by the fourteenth amendment to the Constitution
slaughtering *n* -s [fr. gerund of ²*slaughter*] : the butchering of animals for food ⟨custom ~ usu. includes the weighing of dressed carcasses —L.E.Zraick⟩
slaugh·ter·man \'slȯd·ə(r)mən, -ȯtə-\ *n, pl* **slaughtermen** [ME] **1** *archaic* : EXECUTIONER, SLAYER **2** : SLAUGHTERER b
slaugh·ter·ous \-ȯd·ərəs, -ȯtər- *also* -ȯ·tr-\ *adj* : of, relating to, or characterized by slaughter — **slaugh·ter·ous·ly** *adv*
slaugh·tery \-ȯd·ərē, -ȯtərē, -ȯ·trē\ *n* -ES [¹*slaughter* + -*y* (n. suffix)] **1** : KILLING, SLAUGHTER **2** : ABATTOIR
slaunch·ways \'slȯnch,wāz, -län-\ *adv* [alter. of *slantways*] *Midland* : DIAGONALLY, SLANTWAYS
slav \'släv, -a-, -ȧ-\ *n* -s *cap* [ME *Sclav*, fr. ML *Sclavus, sclavus* Slav, Slav held in servitude, slave] : a person speaking a Slavic language as his native tongue — see INDO-EUROPEAN LANGUAGES table
slav·dom \-vdəm\ *n* -s *usu cap* [*slav* + -*dom*] **1** : the whole body of Slavs **2** : the area inhabited by or under the influence of Slavs
¹**slave** \'slāv\ *n* -s [ME *sclave*, fr. OF or ML; OF *esclave* slave, fr. ML *Sclavus, sclavus* Slav, Slav held in servitude, slave, fr. LGk *Sklabos* Slav, fr. *Sklabēnoi* of or relating to the Slavs, fr. *Sklabēnoi*, pl., Slavs, of Slav origin; akin to OBulg *Slověne*, a Slavic group of people in the area of Thessalonike, ORuss *Slověne*, an East-Slavic group of people near Novgorod, *Slovutich* Dnieper river, Serb *Slavnica*, a river] **1 a** : a person held in servitude : one that is the chattel of another : BONDMAN, THRALL ⟨plantation life with ~*s*, indentured servants, or tenants —W.M.Kollmorgen⟩ ⟨begins her career as a ~, a pretty child bought from miserably poor parents under a contract —Lafcadio Hearn⟩ **b** *archaic* : a despicable person ⟨the . . . atheist, if earth bear so base a ~ —William Cowper⟩ **c** *obs* : an inconsequential person : FELLOW, JOKER ⟨oh ~*s*, I can tell you news, news you rascals —Shak.⟩ **2 a** : a servile or submissive follower : LACKEY ⟨his father's most abject ~ —Abram Kardiner⟩ **b** : a person completely subservient to a dominating influence : one who has surrendered control of himself ⟨all his life he had been a ~ to the land, harnessed to the elemental forces —Ellen Glasgow⟩ ⟨spineless ~*s* of tradition —Bennett Cerf⟩ **c** : one that labors for another : SERVANT ⟨a civilization in which machines are ~*s*, and all men may be free —W.H.Camp⟩ **d** (1) : a mechanical device that is directly responsive to another (as an electronic device for firing auxiliary flash bulbs); *esp* : a remote-control device for handling radioactive materials (2) : SLAVE STATION **3** : a toiler at hard monotonous work : DRUDGE ⟨~*s* in the Pentagon worked nights and through the holidays to revamp the budget —T.R.Phillips⟩ **4** : SLAVE ANT
²**slave** \"\ *vb* **slaved; slaved; slaving; slaves** *vt* **1 a** *archaic* : to reduce to bondage : ENSLAVE ⟨thou canst not ~ or banish me —John Marston⟩ **b** : to make directly responsive to another mechanism ⟨the gyro unit is continuously *slaved* to a compass —C.G.Yates⟩ **2 a** *archaic* : to employ at hard labor ⟨Egyptian kings built them monuments, wherein they *slaved* their whole nation —Martin Lister⟩ **b** : to wear out by hard work ⟨bullied . . . and *slaved* her half to death —H.G. Evarts⟩ ~ *vi* **1** : to work like a slave : TOIL, DRUDGE ⟨*slaved* sixteen hours a day for money to buy food —*Irish Digest*⟩ ⟨had to ~ hard to make . . . a showing at his school work —Archibald Marshall⟩ **2** : to traffic in slaves ⟨*slaving* was still active and profitable, in spite of the best efforts of the missionaries —A.W.Smith⟩
³**slave** \"\ *adj* **1** : held in servitude : ENSLAVED ⟨born of ~ parents⟩ ⟨activity to liberate ~ peoples in eastern Europe —Quincy Wright⟩ **2 a** : of, relating to, involving, or characteristic of slaves ⟨~ auction⟩ ⟨~ owner⟩ ⟨~ question⟩ ⟨with true ~ mentality . . . sacrifices himself to the group —Priscilla Robertson⟩ **b** : used for or restricted to the use of slaves ⟨~ ship⟩ ⟨~ quarters⟩ ⟨a ~ gallery extends across the . . . end of the nave —*Amer. Guide Series: N.C.*⟩ **c** : concerned with or dealing in slaves ⟨~ voyage⟩ ⟨~ trader⟩ **d** (1) : favoring or legally permitting slavery ⟨~ territory⟩ (2) : based on or characterized by slavery ⟨~ economy⟩ **3** : activated by remote control ⟨the device now tucked away behind the dials isn't properly a clockwork but a . . . ~ unit activated by an electric clock inside the bank —*New Yorker*⟩; *specif* : responding to manipulation of the master-end of the apparatus ⟨scientists manipulate radioactive material with in-three ~ hands —*Time*⟩
⁴**slave** \'släv, -a-, -ȧ-\ *archaic var of* SLAV

⁵**slave** \'slāv\ *n* -s *usu cap* **1 a** : an Athapaskan people living between the Rocky mountains and the Great Slave lake in the Northwest Territories of Canada — called also *Slavey* **b** : a member of such people **2** : the language of the Slave people
slave ant *n* : an ant enslaved by a slave-making ant
slave bracelet *n* : a chain-link bracelet often having a plain plaque or nameplate and often worn around the ankle — compare IDENTIFICATION BRACELET
slave clock *n* : the auxiliary apparatus of a precision astronomical clock that relieves the latter of nearly all the work and thus assures uniformity of performance
slave–drive \'=ˌ=\ *vt* [back-formation fr. *slave driver*] : to coerce relentlessly to action
slave driver *n* **1** : a supervisor of slaves at work **2** : a person in authority (as a foreman) who exacts extreme effort from his subordinates : RAWHIDER, SIMON LEGREE
slaveholder \'=ˌ==\ *n* : one that holds slaves
slaveholding \'=ˌ==\ *adj* : allowing slavery or inhabited by slaveholders ⟨the ~ South⟩ ⟨~ states⟩
slave labor *n* **1** : labor performed by slaves **2** : forced labor performed under duress ⟨deporting Belgian civilians into Germany for what amounted to *slave labor* —J.L.O'Brian⟩
slave·less \'slāvləs\ *adj* : being without slaves
slave·ling \-liŋ\ *n* -s [¹*slave* + -*ling*] : ¹SLAVE 2a
slave–making ant \'=ˌ==-\ *or* **slave maker** *n* : an ant (as the Amazon ant or the sanguinary ant) that attacks the colonies of ants of other species and carries off the larvae and pupae to be reared in its own nest as slaves
slave market *n* **1** : a market where slaves are exhibited and sold **2** : something that resembles a slave market ⟨imprisoned the free development of ideas almost to the point that we have . . . created an intellectual *slave market* —J.A.Brandt⟩; *specif* : EMPLOYMENT AGENCY
slaveocracy *var of* SLAVOCRACY
¹**slaver** \'slavə(r), -lāv-, -läv-, -lȧv-\ *vb* **slavered; slavered; slavering** \-v(ə)riŋ\ **slavers** [ME *slaveren*, of Scand origin; akin to ON *slafra* to slaver, Norw dial. *slevja*; akin to MD *slabben* to dirty, lap, slaver, Sw dial. *slabba* to roll in mud, G *schlabbern* to slaver, ON *slafast* to droop, slacken, Lith *slōbti* to grow weak, L *labi* to glide, slide — more at SLEEP] *vi* **1 a** : to let saliva dribble from the mouth : DROOL, SLOBBER ⟨a dog ~*s* over his food⟩ **b** : to have a craving : go in eager pursuit ⟨were ~*ing* after that small fortune —W.B.Mowery⟩ **2** : to voice elaborate praise or servile flattery : FAWN, ECSTASIZE ⟨spent years ~*ing* before the idol of American efficiency —*Times Lit. Supp.*⟩ ~ *vt* **1** *archaic* : to smear with or as if with saliva **2** *archaic* : to truckle to : FLATTER
²**slaver** \"\ *n* -s [ME, fr. *slaveren* to slaver] **1** : saliva dribbling from the mouth **2** *archaic* : effusive commendation or flattery : DRIVEL
³**slav·er** \'slāvə(r)\ *n* -s [¹*slave* + -*er*] **1** : one that is engaged in the slave trade ⟨warships, whalers, sealers and ~*s* . . . sailed from New England to the ends of the earth —Dana Burnet⟩ ⟨tough, cruel but desperately brave Arab ~*s* . . . rule the land —Rodney Gilbert⟩ **2** : WHITE SLAVER
¹**slavery** \'slav(ə)rē, -lāv-, -läv-, -lȧv-, -ri\ *adj* [ME, fr. ²*slaver* + -*y*] *archaic* : SLOBBERY, DRIVELING
²**slav·ery** \'slāv(ə)rē, -ri\ *n* -ES [¹*slave* + -*ery*] **1** : hard work : DRUDGERY, LABOR ⟨I never rowed — about the most awful form of ~ which mankind knows —A.P.Herbert⟩ **2 a** : submissiveness to a dominating influence : SUBSERVIENCE ⟨~ to habit⟩ ⟨deliverance of mankind from the long ~ of want, fear and cruelty —Leslie Rees⟩ **b** : control by imposed authority : SUBJECTION ⟨the . . . ~ of soldiers on the march —W.R.Inge⟩ ⟨all government without the consent of the governed is . . . ~ —Jonathan Swift⟩ **3** : the quality or state of being a slave : the practice or institution of keeping slaves : BONDAGE, SERVITUDE ⟨no one shall be held in ~ or servitude —*U.N. Declaration of Human Rights*⟩ ⟨neither ~ nor involuntary servitude, except as a punishment for crime . . . shall exist within the United States or any place subject to their jurisdiction —*U.S.Constitution*⟩ ⟨the inhuman exploitation of chattel ~ —Lewis Mumford⟩
slaves *pl of* SLAVE, *pres 3d sing of* SLAVE
slave state *n* **1** : a state of the U.S. in which Negro slavery was legal before the Civil War — compare FREE SOIL **2** : a nation subjected to totalitarian rule
slave station *n* : a transmitter in an electronic communication system (as in radio navigation) operated by remote control — compare MASTER STATION
slave trade *n* : traffic in slaves; *esp* : the buying and selling of Negroes for profit prior to the American Civil War
slav·ey \'slāvē, -vi\ *n* -s [¹*slave* + -*y* (dim. suffix)] **1** : DRUDGE; *esp* : a maid of all work **2** *usu cap* [⁵*slave* + -*y*] : ⁵SLAVE 1a
¹**slav·ic** \'slavik, -läv-, -lav-, -vēk\ *adj, usu cap* [*slav* + -*ic*] : of or relating to the Slavs or their languages
²**slavic** \"\ *n* -s *cap* : a branch of the Indo-European language family containing Belorussian, Bulgarian, Czech, Polish, Serbo-Croatian, Slovene, Russian, and Ukrainian — see INDO-EUROPEAN LANGUAGES table
slav·i·cist \-vəsəst\ *or* **slav·ist** \-lāvəst, -lav-, -läv-\ *n* -s *usu cap* [*slavicist* fr. ²*slavic* + -*ist*; *slavist* ISV *slav* + -*ist*] : a specialist in the Slavic languages or literatures
slav·i·cize \'slavə,sīz, -läv-, -lȧv-\ *or* **slav·ize** \-lä,vīz, -la,v-, -lȧ,v-\ *also* **slav·o·nize** \-lavə,nīz\ *or* **sla·von·i·cize** \slə'vänə,sīz, sla'v-\ *vt* -ED/-ING/-S *often cap* [*slavicize* fr. ¹*slavic* + -*ize*; *slavize* fr. *slav* + -*ize*; *slavonize* fr. obs. E *slavon* slavonian (fr. ML *Slavonia* land of the Slavs) + E -*ize*; *slavonicize* fr. ¹*slavonic* + -*ize*] **1** : to make Slavic in quality or characteristics : cause to become adapted to Slavism ⟨a *slavicized* German⟩ ⟨the region was *slavicized* within a few centuries⟩ **2** : to adapt to Slavic usage : alter to a characteristically Slavic form
slav·ik·ite \'slavə,kīt\ *n* -s [Czech *slavikite*, fr. František *Slavík* †1957 Czech mineralogist + Czech -*ite*] : a mineral $(Na, K)_2Fe_{10}(OH)_6(SO_4)_{13}.63H_2O(?)$ consisting of a hydrous basic sodium ferric sulfate and occurring as small greenish yellow rhombohedral crystals on weathered shales from Bohemia
slaving *pres part of* SLAVE
slav·ish \'slāvish, -vēsh *sometimes* ÷ -lav-\ *adj* [¹*slave* + -*ish*] **1 a** *archaic* : SLAVE 2a **b** : requiring hard work : LABORIOUS ⟨~ attention and practice were required —Richard Hayward⟩ **2 a** : resembling or characteristic of a slave : SPINELESS, SUBMISSIVE ⟨a ~ yes-man to the party bosses —S.H.Adams⟩ **b** *archaic* : of a despicable nature : CONTEMPTIBLE, LOW ⟨to lie is a ~ vice —James Astry⟩ **3** *archaic* : of a despotic nature : OPPRESSIVE ⟨shake off our ~ yoke —Shak.⟩ **4** : copying obsequiously or without originality : IMITATIVE ⟨out of the realm of mere ~ imitation of nature —Aldous Huxley⟩
syn see SUBSERVIENT
slav·ish·ly *adv* : in a slavish manner : SUBSERVIENTLY ⟨~ accepted the viewpoints of foreign scientists —Martin Gardner⟩ ⟨did not copy too ~ the designs of his predecessors —Edith Diehl⟩
slav·ish·ness *n* -ES : the quality or state of being slavish
slav·ism \'slä,vizəm, -la,v-, -lȧ,v-\ *also* **slav·i·cism** \-lavə,sizəm, -läv-, -lȧv-\ *n* -s *usu cap* [*slavism* ISV *slav* + -*ism*; *slavicism* fr. ¹*slavic* + -*ism*] **1 a** : Slavic traits or attitudes **b** : SLAVOPHILISM **2** : a characteristically Slavic word or expression occurring in another language
slav·oc·ra·cy *also* **slave·oc·ra·cy** \slā'väkrəsē\ *n* -ES [¹*slave* + -*o-* + -*cracy*] : a powerful faction of slave-owners and advocates of slavery in the South before the Civil War
slav·o·crat \'slāvə,krat\ *n* -s [fr. *slavocracy*, after such pairs as E *democracy*: *democrat*] : a member of the slavocracy — compare DOUGHFACE 2a
¹**sla·vo·nian** \slə'vōnēən, sla'v-, -ōnyən\ *n* -s *cap* [ML *Slavonia, Sclavonia* land of the Slavs, Slavonia (fr. *Slavus, Sclavus* Slav) + E -*an* (n. suffix) — more at SLAVE] : SLOVENE 1b
²**slavonian** \"\ *adj, usu cap* [ML *Slavonia* + E -*an* (adj. suffix)] **1** : SLOVENE **2** *archaic* : SLAVIC
slavonian grebe *n, usu cap S* : HORNED GREBE
¹**sla·von·ic** \slə'vänik, sla'v-, -nēk\ *adj, usu cap* [NL *slavonicus*, fr. ML *Slavonia* + L -*icus* -ic] : SLAVIC
²**slavonic** \"\ *n* -s *usu cap* **1** : SLAVIC **2** : OLD CHURCH SLAVONIC
slav·o·phile \'slavə,fīl, -läv-,-lȧv-\ *or* **slav·o·phil** \-,fil\ *n* -s *usu cap* [*slav* + -*o-* + -*phile, -phil*] : an advocate of Slavophilism

slav·oph·i·lism \slə'väfə,lizəm\ *n* -s *usu cap* [*slavophil* + *-ism*] **1** : advocacy of Slavic and specif. Russian culture over that of the West esp. as practiced by some members of the Russian intelligentsia in the middle 19th century **2** : PAN-SLAVISM

¹slaw \'slö\ *dial Brit var of* SLOW

²slaw \"\ *n* -s [by shortening] : COLESLAW

¹slay \'slā\ *vb* **slew** \-lü\ **slain** \-lān\ **slaying; slays** [ME *slan, slen,* fr. OE *slēan* to strike, beat, slay; akin to OHG *slahan* to strike, beat, ON *slā,* Goth *slahan* to strike, beat, MIr *slacaim* I beat] *vt* **1 a** : to deprive of life by force : put (a person) to death violently : MURDER ⟨began to throttle his enemy, meaning . . . to ~ him —Rudyard Kipling⟩ **b** : to strike down : KILL ⟨gradually they were eliminated, slaughtered by bullets or *slain* by disease —Philip Mason⟩ **2** : to put (an animal) to death esp. for food or as a sacrifice : SLAUGHTER ⟨growers *slew* laying hens when poultryless Thursday depressed prices —*advt*⟩ **3** : to stifle or destroy completely : ERADICATE, SUPPRESS ⟨these semiautomatic words and phrases should be *slain* —J.E.Gloag⟩ ⟨the great love she . . . had she was ~*ing* —Rose Macaulay⟩ **4** : to affect overpoweringly : OVERWHELM ⟨used to ~ myself with exhaustion —Eve Langley⟩ ⟨~*s* the girls with his rugged virility —C.J.Rolo⟩ ~ *vi* : to cause death : KILL ⟨no other infection so quickly ~*s* —*Jour. Amer. Med. Assoc.*⟩ **syn** see KILL

²slay *var of* SLEY

slay·er \'slā(ə)r, -le(ə)r, -leə\ *n* -s [ME *sleer,* fr. *slen* to slay + *-er*] : one that slays : KILLER

SLC *abbr, often not cap* straight-line capacitance

sld *abbr* **1** sailed **2** sealed **3** solder

slead \'slēd, -lād\ *n* -s [ME *slede,* fr. MD or MLG; — more at SLED] *chiefly dial* : SLED

¹sleave \'slēv\ *vb* -ED/-ING/-S [fr. (assumed) ME *sleven,* fr. (assumed) OE *slǣfan* to cut (whence *tōslǣfan* to cut up); akin to OE *tōslīfan* to split — more at SLIVE] *vt, obs* : to separate (silk thread) into filaments ~ *vi* : to separate into filaments ⟨the hair had *sleaved* out thin and fine —Aldous Huxley⟩

²sleave \"\ *n* -s **1** *obs* : ¹FLOSS 1 **2** : SKEIN ⟨sleep that knits up the raveled ~ of care —Shak.⟩

sleave silk *n, obs* : floss silk that is easily separated into filaments for embroidery

slea·zi·ly \'slēzəlē, -əli *also* 'slāz-\ *adv* : in a sleazy manner

slea·zi·ness \-zēnəs, -zin-\ *n* -ES : the state or quality of being sleazy

slea·zy \-zē,-zi\ *or* **slee·zy** \-lēz-\ *adj* -ER/-EST [origin unknown] **1 a** : lacking firmness of texture : having little substance : FLIMSY ⟨wore a ~ yellow coat and cheap high-heeled shoes —Wenzell Brown⟩ **b** (1) : carelessly made of inferior materials : SHODDY ⟨~ new apartment blocks, their broken rubble-salvaged brick unfaced —Flora Lewis⟩ (2) : marked by disrepair and cheapness : SHABBY ⟨a ~ rooming house sadly in need of paint⟩ **2 a** : marked by slightness : UNSUBSTANTIAL ⟨the series as a whole is ~ as history though frequently helpful as criticism —G.H.Genzmer⟩ **b** : marked by cheapness of character or atmosphere ⟨a ~ little gold digger —*New Republic*⟩ ⟨the ~ submerged seldom glimpsed underworld —J.B.Martin⟩ **c** : marked by low ethical standards ⟨outlaws about a dozen of the *sleazier* forms of competition —*Fortune*⟩ ⟨a ~ maneuver —H.C.Lodge⟩ **d** : marked by low artistic quality ⟨too many ~ spy stories —*Harper's*⟩

¹sled \'sled\ *n* -s [ME *sledde,* fr. MD; akin to MD & MLG *slede* sled, OHG *slito, slita,* ON *slethi,* OE *slīdan* to slide — more at SLIDE] **1** : a vehicle that moves by sliding usu. on a pair of runners esp. over snow or ice: as **a** : SLEDGE **b** *archaic* : SLEIGH **c** : a small sled designed to be used by children for coasting down snow-covered hills **d** : ROCKET SLED **2** : COTTON SLED **3** : the sliding contact of an underground trolley system that is drawn under the car

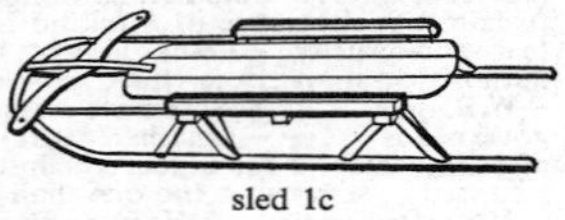

sled 1c

²sled \"\ *vb* **sledded; sledded; sledding; sleds** *vt* **1** : SLEDGE ⟨contraband goods were *sledded* over the ice —*Amer. Guide Series: Vt.*⟩ **2** : to harvest with a cotton sled ~ *vi* **1** : to ride on a sled ⟨a celebrated place for the boys in winter to ~ —J.F.Watson⟩ **2** *archaic* : to ride in a sleigh **3** : SLEDGE 2 ⟨*sledded* 70 miles up the Yukon —Jack London⟩

sled corrugator *n* : a device with sharp runners for opening small furrows for irrigation of cultivated fields

sled cultivator *n* : GO-DEVIL

sled·der \'sledə(r)\ *n* -s : one that sleds

sledding *n* -s [¹*sled* + *-ing*] **1 a** : the use of a sled ⟨enough snow for good ~⟩ **b** : the conditions under which one may use a sled ⟨the ~ last winter was exceptionally fine⟩ **2** : GOING 5 ⟨the appliance tax slash faces tough ~ in the final House-Senate conference —*Wall Street Jour.*⟩ ⟨envisioned easy ~ ahead —Ralph Cokain⟩ **3** : the action of harvesting with a cotton sled

sled dog *n* : a dog trained to draw a sledge esp. in the Arctic regions

¹sledge \'slej\ *n* -s [ME *slegge, slege,* fr. OE *slecg;* akin to MD *slegge* sledgehammer, ON *sleggja,* OE *slēan* to beat, slay — more at SLAY] : SLEDGEHAMMER

²sledge \"\ *vb* -ED/-ING/-S : SLEDGEHAMMER ⟨was *sledging* in the quarry⟩ ⟨were *sledging* out the wall —*Newsweek*⟩

³sledge \"\ *n* -s [D dial. *sleedse;* akin to MD *sledde, slede, sled* — more at SLED] **1** *Brit* : SLEIGH **2** : a vehicle with low runners that is used for transporting loads esp. over snow or ice **3 a** : a frame formerly used for stretching the yarns in the manufacture of rope **b** : a platform on runners that is weighted to maintain tension on rope while it is being laid

⁴sledge \"\ *vb* -ED/-ING/-S *vi* **1** *Brit* : to ride in a sleigh **2** : to travel with a loaded sledge esp. over snow or ice ⟨a small antarctic expedition . . . on which we would ~ and map the coastline —Finn Ronne⟩ ~ *vt* : to transport on a sledge ⟨millstones had been cut and laboriously *sledged* down the rough mountainsides —E.E.Evans⟩

sledge dog *n* [³*sledge*] : SLED DOG

¹sledgehammer \'=,==\ *n* [ME *slege hamer,* fr. *slege* sledge + *hamer* hammer] : a large heavy hammer that is usu. wielded with both hands and used esp. for driving stakes and breaking stone

²sledgehammer \"\ *vt* : to strike with or as if with a sledgehammer ⟨stills are officially ~*ed* at intervals —*Amer. Guide Series: Ind.*⟩ ⟨have been today ~*ing* your idea . . . into a sermon —Richard Whately⟩ ~ *vi* : to strike blows with or as if with a sledgehammer ⟨a racket of riveting and ~*ing* —Emily Hahn⟩ ⟨kept ~*ing* away on a procedural point —*Time*⟩

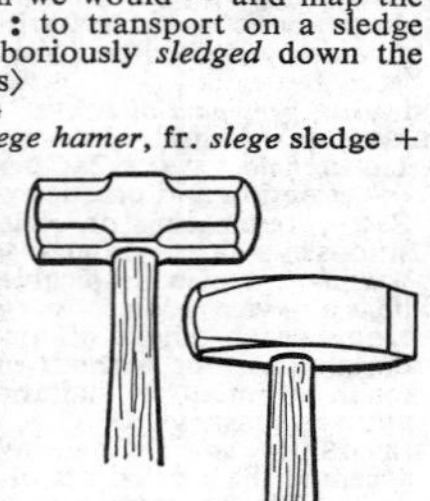

sledgehammers

³sledgehammer \"\ *adj* : marked by heavy-handed directness or the unsubtle use of force : BLUNT ⟨a plain direct ~ method —J.C.Powys⟩ ⟨trusting in ~ warfare —C.J.Rolo⟩

¹sledg·er \'slejə(r)\ *n* -s [³*sledge* + *-er*] : one that drives a sledge

²sledger \"\ *n* -s [¹*sledge* + *-er*] **1** : a strip mine worker who digs out coal, rock, or dirt with a sledge **2** : a worker who breaks up large stone into usable pieces with a sledge

sled harvester *n* [¹*sled*] : a wide flat horse-drawn implement equipped at its front end with a V-shaped knife that cuts cornstalks close to the ground

sled-length \'=,=\ *adv* : all out ⟨said he would join me *sled-length* in declining to yield —A.H.Vandenberg †1951⟩

sled lister cultivator *n* : a cultivator that has lister cultivating devices behind sled runners and a cultivator shield and that is used for cultivating row crops planted in furrows

sled marker *n* : a crop row marker consisting essentially of short sled runners and a platform from which a pipe rod with a small blade at the end extends to the side and makes a mark for the marker to follow on the return trip across a field

sleds *pl of* SLED, *pres 3d sing of* SLED

slee \'slē\ *dial Brit var of* SLY

sleech \'slēch\ *n* -ES [ME *sliche;* akin to MHG *slīch* shine — more at SLICK] *dial Brit* : ooze deposited by the sea or a river

sleechy \-chi\ *adj* [*sleech* + *-y*] *dial Brit* : OOZY, SLIMY

¹sleek \'slēk\ *vb* -ED/-ING/-S [ME *sleken,* alter. of *sliken* to slick] *vt* **1** : SLICK 1a, 1b, 2 **2** : to cover up : gloss over ⟨~*ed* over . . . his agitated expression —J.C.Powys⟩ ~ *vi* : SLICK

²sleek \"\ *adj* -ER/-EST [alter. of ²*slick*] **1 a** : smooth and shining usu. from good health or attentive care ⟨his ~ coat gleaming like mirror velvet —Alice Duncan-Kemp⟩; *also* : having sleek hair or fur ⟨steer and heifer calves — some of them so ~ and beefy that they had won blue ribbons —Lewis Nordyke⟩ **b** : being in a flourishing condition from or as if from attentive care ⟨animally alive, his naked brown body so ~ with health —Christopher Isherwood⟩ **2 a** : having a smooth or polished surface ⟨the metal felt ~ and warm to his touch —Stuart Cloete⟩ **b** : being wet and slippery ⟨cobbles were ~ with mud —Marguerite Steen⟩ **3** : disagreeably ingratiating or fawning : UNCTUOUS ⟨novels . . . in which every young man is ~ and feverish for an unattainable success —Marjory S. Douglas⟩ **4 a** : gracefully proportioned : SLENDER ⟨a ~ brunette in a green dress and fur jacket —J.J. Godwin⟩ ⟨the early engines, ~ and graceful —C.J.Allen⟩ **b** : fashionably or luxuriously trim or elegant ⟨~ figures in expensive clothes —Green Peyton⟩ ⟨~ establishments specializing in Peking duck —Jane Nickerson⟩ **c** : superficially stylish or elegant : FLASHY ⟨radiated merely the ~ and obvious aspects —J.S.Bowman⟩ **d** : having slender graceful lines : STREAMLINED ⟨a long ~ car gliding away —Andrew Buchanan⟩

³sleek \"\ *adv* : SLEEKLY

⁴sleek \"\ *n* -s : SLICK 1,2

sleek·en \'slēkən\ *vt* **sleekened; sleekened; sleekening** \-k(ə)niŋ\ **sleekens** [²*sleek* + *-en*] : to make sleek

sleek·er \-kə(r)\ *n* -s [¹*sleek* + *-er*] : SLICKER

sleek·it \'slēkət\ *adj* [Sc, fr. past part. of ¹*sleek*] **1** *chiefly Scot* : SLEEK, SMOOTH **2** *chiefly Scot* : CRAFTY, DECEITFUL

sleek-leaf \'=,=\ *n* [²*sleek* + *leaf*] : SAND MYRTLE

sleek·ly *adv* : in a sleek manner

sleek·ness *n* -ES : the quality or state of being sleek

sleekstone *n* [ME *slekstone,* fr. *sleken* to sleek + *stone*] *obs* : a stone for smoothing or polishing

sleek sumac *n* [²*sleek*] : SMOOTH SUMAC

sleeky \'slēkē, -ki\ *adj* -ER/-EST [²*sleek* + *-y*] **1** : SLEEK **2** *chiefly Scot* : having a fawning and deceitful character or quality

¹sleep \'slēp\ *n* -s [ME *slep, slepe,* fr. OE *slǣp;* akin to OHG *slāf* sleep, Goth *sleps,* OE *slǣpan* to sleep] **1 a** : the natural usu. regular suspension of consciousness during which the powers of the body are restored **b** : the suspension of consciousness caused by an abnormal physical condition or by artificial means ⟨the medium speaking for the first time . . . out of his mesmeric ~ —W.B.Yeats⟩ **2** : a state resembling sleep: as **a** : a state marked by inactivity or lack of awareness : TORPOR ⟨the depressed fellaheen who likewise are rousing from their centuries of ~ —D.M.Friedenberg⟩ **b** : DEATH **c** : a condition in plants that is marked by the closing of leaves or petals esp. at night **d** : complete quiet ⟨the ~ that is among the lonely hills —William Wordsworth⟩ **e** : a state marked by a diminution of feeling followed by tingling caused by pressure on a part of the body ⟨my foot has gone to ~⟩ **f** : the state of an animal during hibernation ⟨the ground hog's winter ~⟩ **3** : a period of sleep ⟨hoped for late morning ~*s* in his new home —Dorothy C. Fisher⟩ **4 a** : NIGHT ⟨not ten ~*s* have passed since the last of our fighting men returned —Mary Austin⟩ **b** : a unit of measurement indicating the distance that can be traversed in a period including a specified number of nights ⟨one of the Indian discoverers . . . said only that the mine was two ~*s* from the post —*Amer. Guide Series: Mont.*⟩ **5** : the signs of sleep : SLEEPINESS ⟨eyes heavy with ~⟩

²sleep \"\ *vb* **slept** \-lept, *esp before a consonant* -p\ **slept; sleeping; sleeps** [ME *slepen,* fr. OE *slǣpan;* akin to OHG *slāfan* to sleep, Goth *slepan,* L *labi* to slide, slip, sink, fall, and perh. to Gk *lobos* pod of a vegetable, lobe of the ear or other bodily organ; basic meaning: to hang loose] *vi* **1** : to rest in a state of sleep : be asleep ⟨is able to relax and always ~*s* well —C.B.Palmer b.1910⟩ ⟨*slept* at the club last night⟩ **2** : to be in a state resembling sleep: as **a** (1) : to lack awareness ⟨his judgment could neither ~ nor be softened —W.B.Yeats⟩; *specif* : to lack awareness and fail to take advantage (as of one's rights) ⟨the bill would favor claimants who have been ~*ing* on their rights —*U.S.Code*⟩ (2) : to lie dormant or inactive ⟨the ancestral idealism . . . that *slept* uneasily under the spell of middle-class ambitions —V.L.Parrington⟩ ⟨the seasons when nature ~*s* in seeds —Alan Devoe⟩ (3) : to remain quiet or motionless ⟨the day, immeasurably long, ~*s* over the broad hills —R.W.Emerson⟩ **b** : to lie dead ⟨two of them still ~ in an old graveyard —Dana Burnet⟩ **c** *archaic* : to have a diminution of feeling followed by tingling due to pressure on a part of the body **d** : to have the leaves or petals closed esp. at night **3** : to have sexual relations ⟨a lovely aristocratic woman who wants to ~ with him —H.C.Webster⟩ ⟨must have *slept* around —A.O.Myrer⟩ **4** : to wait until the next day before making a decision — usu. used with *on* ⟨said he would like to ~ on the proposition⟩ **5** *Scots law* : to lie over without being prosecuted for such a period as to become abeyant ~ *vt* **1** : to be slumbering in ⟨*slept* the sleep of the dead⟩ **2** *archaic* : to disregard because of indifference ⟨extraordinary that any body of men . . . should ~ obedience —Thomas Paine⟩ **3** : to get rid of by sleeping — used with *off* or *away* ⟨curls up along the base of the stone wall to ~ off his orgy of eating —Doris Cochran⟩ ⟨your oversize . . . berth is an airfoam invitation to ~ away business cares —*Wall Street Jour.*⟩ **4** : to spend in sleep — used with *away* or *out* ⟨if he is not doped to make him ~ away the hours of travel, he is shivering with fear —S.J.G.Ervine⟩ **5** : to bring (oneself) to a specified condition by sleeping ⟨retreated down to his own den . . . to ~ himself sober —Sir Walter Scott⟩ **6** : to provide with a place to sleep ⟨the place ~*s* 18 besides the servants —John Selby⟩

syn SLUMBER, DROWSE, DOZE, NAP, SNOOZE: SLEEP is the general term, applying to periodical repose with lack of consciousness; it lacks the connotations of the following. SLUMBER often applies to a light sleep; the word may sound somewhat literary ⟨the cradle of the *slumbering* babe —William Wordsworth⟩ DROWSE may suggest a dull or listless inactivity in which one may drift off to sleep ⟨quaint Spanish towns, with adobe houses and wide squares, sunk in their noonday sleep, — beautiful senoritas *drowsing* away the afternoon in hammocks —S.B.Leacock⟩ DOZE, close to DROWSE, may differ in applying to a deeper degree of sleep or sleepiness ⟨we laughed and *dozed,* then roused and read again —Vachel Lindsay⟩ As a verb NAP often applies to a sleeping or dozing when one should be alert and vigilant ⟨he *napped* again and when he opened his eyes he knew the sun was shining. He jumped out of bed, wondering about the time —Cortland Fitzsimmons⟩ ⟨caught *napping*⟩ SNOOZE may apply to a pleasant comfortable sleep between times ⟨having nothing to do, read a little Shakespeare and *snooze* —O.W.Holmes †1935⟩

sleepcoat \'=,=\ *n* : a man's knee-length coat with a tie belt similar in style to a pajama jacket

¹sleep·er \'slēpə(r)\ *n* -s *often attrib* [ME *sleper,* fr. *slepen* to sleep + *-er*] **1** : one that sleeps: as **a** : one that is inclined to sleep a great deal ⟨a great ~ and fond of his bed —W.M. Thackeray⟩ **b** : one that is asleep ⟨at such a distance from the ~ that their low words could hardly disturb her —Anthony Trollope⟩ **2** : a strong piece of wood or other material used as a support: as **a** (1) : a horizontal beam placed on or near the ground to support a floor or superstructure (2) : one of the heavy strips of wood that are set in or on a concrete floor base so that a wooden floor can be nailed down over the concrete base **b** : one of the knees that connect the transoms to the after timbers on a ship's quarter **c** *archaic* : the rafter of a roof valley **d** *chiefly Brit* : a railroad tie **e** : one of the longitudinal beams in a wooden bridge on which the transverse logs or planks are laid **3** : DORMOUSE **4 a** : a fish of the family Eleotridae **b** : GREENLAND SHARK **5 a** : a bet that is accidentally left standing on the layout of a gambling game **b** : a bet on a dead card in faro **6** : something (as a vehicle) that provides accommodation for sleeping: as **a** : SLEEPING CAR **b** : a truck with a sleeping compartment **7** : one that has no apparent importance and remains unnoticed for some time before becoming very important: as **a** : a racehorse that wins after a series of poor performances **b** : an article of merchandise having a value that is much greater than its recognized worth **c** : a book that sells well year after year without being advertised **d** : a movie whose box-office returns are out of proportion to the cost of its production and publicity and far exceed the expectations of the producers **e** : a piece of music that unexpectedly becomes a hit **f** : a provision, clause, or amendment inconspicuously introduced into legislation in the hope that it will be adopted without consideration before its actual intent or force is recognized by potential opponents **g** : a security apparently overlooked by investors and therefore selling too low in relation to the market as a whole **8** : a calf that has been earmarked but not branded **9 a** : RUDDY DUCK **b** : DOWITCHER **10** : a sleeping garment esp. for children: as **a** : pajamas often with feet **b** : a sleeping bag for babies **11** : an article of merchandise that sells slowly ⟨his unerring sense of what to buy, rarely gets stuck with ~*s* —E.O.Hauser⟩ **12** : a foal that is born comatose and usu. dies within a few days of birth due to intrauterine septicemic infection with one of the organisms (*Shigella equirulis* or *S. equuli*) commonly associated with navel ill **13** : a bowling pin that cannot be seen easily because it is directly behind another pin

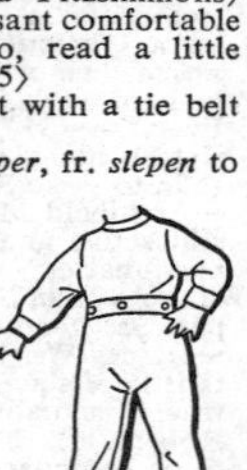

sleeper 10a

²sleeper \"\ *vt* -ED/-ING/-S : to earmark (a calf) so as to give the appearance of having been branded

sleep·ered \-pə(r)d\ *adj* [¹*sleeper* + *-ed*] : provided with sleepers

sleeper fire *n* : a forest fire that smolders for some time before bursting into a blaze

sleeper shark *n* : GREENLAND SHARK

sleep·ful \-pfəl\ *adj* [¹*sleep* + *-ful*] : marked by sleep ⟨a ~ night⟩ — **sleep·ful·ness** *n* -ES

sleepier *comparative of* SLEEPY

sleepiest *superlative of* SLEEPY

sleep·i·fy \'slēpə,fī\ *vt* -ED/-ING/-ES [*sleepy* + *-fy*] : to make sleepy

sleep·i·ly \-pəlē, -li\ *adv* : in a sleepy manner

sleep in *vi* **1** : to sleep where one is employed ⟨two maids who *sleep in*⟩ **2 a** : OVERSLEEP **b** : to sleep late intentionally ⟨was up too late and decided to *sleep in* the next morning⟩

sleep-in \'=,=\ *adj* [*sleep in*] : that sleeps at the place of employment ⟨five *sleep-in* servants —*New Yorker*⟩

sleep·i·ness \'slēpēnəs, -pin-\ *n* -ES **1** : the quality or state of being sleepy **2** : an abnormal condition in flowers (as carnations or snapdragons) marked by a partial closing of the petals

sleeping *pres part of* SLEEP

sleeping bag *n* **1** : a bag usu. of canvas or waterproof material and often warmly lined or padded in which one may sleep esp. outdoors **2** : a baby's sleeping garment resembling a bag with sleeves and a zipper closing

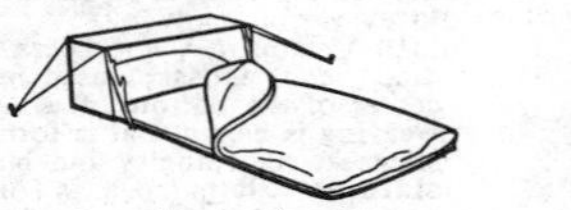

sleeping bag

sleeping beauty *also* **sleeping clover** *n* : a wood sorrel (*Oxalis acetosella*)

sleeping car *n* : a railroad passenger car having berths for sleeping

sleeping carriage *n, Brit* : SLEEPING CAR

sleeping lizard *n* : STUMP-TAIL

sleep·ing·ly *adv* [*sleeping* (pres. part. of ²*sleep*) + *-ly*] : SLEEPILY

sleeping partner *n* : a partner who takes no active part in the partnership to which he belongs and whose existence is often not known to the public

sleeping porch *n* : a porch or room having open sides or many windows arranged to permit sleeping in the open air

sleeping rent *n* : a fixed rent : a rent that is not determined by the amount of profits

sleeping sickness *n* **1** : a serious disease prevalent in much of tropical Africa that is characterized by fever, protracted lethargy, tremors, and loss of weight, is caused by either of two trypanosomes (*Trypanosoma gambiense* and *T. rhodesiense*), and is transmitted by tsetse flies — called also *African sleeping sickness, African trypanosomiasis* **2** : any of various viral encephalitides or encephalomyelitides of which lethargy or somnolence is a prominent feature; *esp* : EQUINE ENCEPHALOMYELITIS **3** *also* **sleeping disease** : SLEEPY DISEASE

sleeping suit *n* : ¹SLEEPER 10a

sleeping table *n* : a stationary buddle that is neither rotated nor shaken during the washing of the ore

sleep·less \'slēpləs\ *adj* [ME *slepeles,* fr. *slep* sleep + *-les* -less] **1** : not able to sleep : INSOMNIAC ⟨lay all that night ~ and yearning to go home —W.M.Thackeray⟩ **2 a** : affording no sleep ⟨troubles, cares, and ~ nights to him who wears the royal diadem —John Milton⟩ **b** : marked by absence of sleep ⟨the ~ sobriety of the drinker who has tried to go to sleep without drinks —Edmund Wilson⟩ **3** : unceasingly active ⟨the ~ ocean murmurs for all ears —William Wordsworth⟩ ⟨deserves the attention of every American citizen and the ~ concern of the responsible agencies of government —A.E. Stevenson b.1900⟩ — **sleep·less·ly** *adv* — **sleep·less·ness** *n* -ES

sleep movements *n pl* : movements (as nyctinasty or nyctitropism) in plants in which leaves or other organs assume positions suggestive of sleep

sleep out *vi* **1** : to sleep outdoors **2** : to go home at night from one's place of employment ⟨a cook who *sleeps out*⟩ **3** : to sleep away from home ⟨you can't *sleep out* . . . simply anything might happen to you —Edith Sitwell⟩

¹sleep-out \'=,=\ *n* -s [*sleep out*] **1** *Austral* : a place for sleeping outdoors; *esp* : SLEEPING PORCH **2** : an outing on which the participants sleep outdoors

²sleep-out \"\ *adj* [*sleep out*] : that sleeps at home rather than at the place of employment ⟨the *sleep-out* cooks and maids were coming to work —*New Yorker*⟩

sleep paralysis *n* : a complete temporary paralysis occurring in connection with sleep

sleeps *pl of* SLEEP, *pres 3d sing of* SLEEP

¹sleepwalk \'=,=\ *vi* [back-formation fr. *sleepwalking*] : to walk in one's sleep

²sleepwalk \"\ *n* : a walk taken in one's sleep

sleepwalker \'=,==\ *n* [¹*sleep* + *walker*] : SOMNAMBULIST

sleepwalking \'=,==\ *n* [¹*sleep* + *walking,* gerund of *walk*] : walking in one's sleep : SOMNAMBULISM

sleepwear \'=,=\ *n* : NIGHTCLOTHES 1

sleepy \'slēpē, -pi\ *adj* -ER/-EST [ME *slepy,* fr. *slep* sleep + *-y*] **1 a** (1) : having an inclination to sleep : ready to fall asleep : DROWSY ⟨is ~ and wants to go to bed⟩ (2) : inclined to sleep more than is usual for most people ⟨a ~ boy who is always late to school⟩ **b** : of, relating to, or characteristic of sleep ⟨has a ~ look on his face —Morris Fishbein⟩ **2** : marked by a state resembling sleep: as **a** : lacking alertness : SLUGGISH, LETHARGIC ⟨amateurs with a ~ sense of what is really at stake in the critic's business —R.E.Garis⟩ **b** : having little activity : quietly slow-moving ⟨this ~ little city lost among the gentle hills —Arnaldo Cortesi⟩ ⟨~ rivers lined with sycamores —*Amer. Guide Series: Ind.*⟩ **c** : having a dull glow rather than a sparkle ⟨even the best zircon is a bit ~ —F.B.Wade⟩ **3** : tending to induce sleep : SOPORIFIC ⟨will give you ~ drinks —Shak.⟩ ⟨the yellowhammer trills his ~ song in the noonday heat —L.P.Smith⟩ **4** : beginning to rot ⟨expect her to drop every minute like an overripe ~ pear —Frederick Marryat⟩

sleepy catchfly *n* : a No. American catchfly (*Silene antirrhina*) with small pink diurnal flowers

sleepy coot *n* : RUDDY DUCK

sleepy dick \'=,=dik\ *n* [*sleepy* + *Dick,* nickname for *Richard*] : STAR-OF-BETHLEHEM

sleepy disease *n* : any of several wilt diseases of plants; *esp* : a tomato wilt caused by either of two fungi (*Fusarium lycopersici* and *Verticillium alboatrum*)

sleepy grass *n* : a tall coarse grass (*Stipa robusta*) of the southwestern U.S. and northern Mexico that causes a deep sleep in horses or sheep that feed on it

sleepyhead \'=,=\ *n* **1** : a sleepy person **2** : RUDDY DUCK

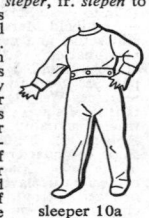

sleepy hollow chair \'≈≈,≈≈-\ *n, usu cap S&H* [fr. *Sleepy Hollow*, valley near Tarrytown, N.Y.] **:** a deep upholstered chair designed for comfort

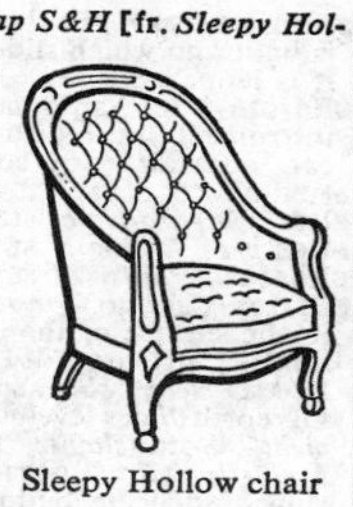
Sleepy Hollow chair

sleepy lizard *n* **:** STUMP-TAIL
sleepy sickness *n* **1** *Brit* **:** SLEEPING SICKNESS 1 **2** *Brit* **:** ENCEPHALITIS LETHARGICA **3** *NewZeal* **:** pregnancy disease of sheep
sleepy staggers *n pl* **:** FORAGE POISONING
sleer \'sli(ə)r\ *vi* -ED/-ING/-S [alter. (perh. influenced by ³*slur*) of *sneer*] *dial Eng* **:** MOCK, SNEER
¹sleet \'slēt, *usu* -ēd.+V\ *n* -S [ME *slete;* akin to MHG *slōz, slōze* hailstone, ON *slota* to hang down, ME *sloor* mud — more at SLUR] **1 :** precipitation in the form of frozen or partly frozen rain **:** fine driving icy particles **2 :** GLAZE 1a **3 :** a mixture or combination of rain and snow
²sleet \"\ *vi* -ED/-ING/-S [ME *sleten*, fr. *slete* sleet] **:** to shower sleet
sleety \'slēd.ē, -ēt\, |i\ *adj* -ER/-EST [¹*sleet* + -*y*] **:** consisting of, accompanied by, or of the nature of sleet
¹sleeve \'slēv\ *n* -S *often attrib* [ME *sleve, sleve*, fr. OE *slīefe;* akin to OE *slēfan* to slip (clothes) on, MD *slove* covering, apron, OE *slūpan* to slip, OHG *sliofan*, Goth *sliupan* to slip in, L *lubricus* slippery] **1 a :** a part of a garment covering an arm sometimes tied on at the shoulder or usu. set in by stitching at the armscye or cut with a body section of the garment (as a raglan or kimono sleeve) **b :** SLEEVELET ⟨postmistress in her brown paper ~*s* —James Stern⟩ **2 a :** a tubular part designed to fit over another part: as (1) *or* **sleeve axle :** a hollow axle or quill having relative movement to a shaft inside it (2) **:** a long bushing or thimble (3) *or* **sleeve coupling :** a piece of pipe or a thimble for covering a joint or for coupling two lengths of piping (4) **:** a longitudinally split quill or hollow mandrel for temporarily gripping a part (5) **:** a double tube of copper having a cross section like a figure 8 into which the ends of bare wires are pushed so that when the tube is twisted an electrical connection is made (6) **:** a pronged tubular spring used in a watch with a negative setting mechanism to set the stem in position (7) **:** a collar of coarse mesh wire screening placed around the base of a young tree or shrub to prevent injury by rodents (8) **:** a collar usu. of heavy paper placed around the base of a young plant (as a tomato) to prevent injury by grubs or cutworms **b :** an open-ended flat or tubular packaging or cover ⟨light bulbs in a ~⟩: as (1) **:** JACKET 3f (4) (2) **:** a protective cover usu. made of paper, cloth, or leather over board and slipped over a book to cover all but the fore edge and backbone **3 :** MANTLE 7a **4 :** SLEEVE TARGET — **up one's sleeve :** held secretly in reserve ⟨has an emergency plan *up his sleeve*⟩
²sleeve \"\ *vt* -ED/-ING/-S [ME *sleven*, fr. *sleve* sleeve] **1 a :** to furnish, cover, or surround with a sleeve **b :** to place (a part) as a sleeve upon another **2 :** to wipe off or away with the sleeve ⟨*sleeving* the sweat off his face —N.C.McDonald⟩
sleeve bearing *n* **:** a machine bearing in which the axle or shaft turns in a sleeve that is often grooved to facilitate distribution of lubricant to the bearing
sleeveboard \'≈,≈\ *n* **:** a small ironing board for pressing sleeves
sleeve brick *n* **:** a tubular firebrick used to line slag vents

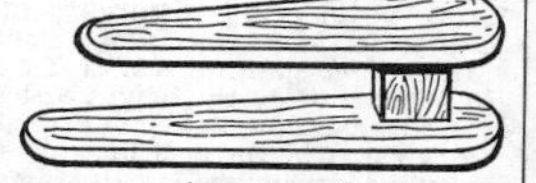
sleeveboard

sleeve button *n* **:** a button for fastening a cuff; *esp* **:** CUFF LINK
sleeved \'slēvd\ *adj* [¹*sleeve* + -*ed*] **1 :** made with sleeves ⟨~ garments⟩ **2 :** having sleeves of a particular type — usu. used in combination ⟨short-*sleeved*⟩ ⟨puff-*sleeved*⟩ ⟨long-*sleeved*⟩
sleeve dam *n* **:** a canvas dam for diverting part of the water from an irrigation ditch while the remainder flows through a sleeve whose opening can be regulated
sleeve dog *n* **:** a dog (as a Pekingese) small enough to carry inside the sleeve or in a muff
sleeve garter *n* **:** GARTER 1c
sleevehand *n, obs* **:** CUFF
sleeve·less \'slēvləs\ *adj* [ME *sleveles*, fr. OE *slīeflēas*, fr. *slīefe* sleeve + -*lēas* -less] **1 :** having no sleeve **2 a :** PROFITLESS, FUTILE ⟨the errand they were on was ~ —Virgilia Peterson⟩ **b** *Brit* **:** PETTY, FRIVOLOUS ⟨the ~ butterfly world —Llewelyn Powys⟩ — **sleeve·less·ness** *n* -ES
sleeve·let \-lət\ *n* -S [¹*sleeve* + -*let*] **:** a fitted covering for the forearm worn for protection or warmth
sleevelike \'≈,≈\ *adj* **:** resembling a sleeve
sleeve link *n* **:** CUFF LINK
sleeve nut *n* **:** a right-and-left nut
sleev·er \'slēvə(r)\ *n* -S [¹*sleeve* + -*er*] **1 a :** a garment worker who sews in sleeves **b :** a laundry worker who presses sleeves and neckbands of shirts on heated forms **2 :** a worker who reinforces the pouring openings of paper bags
sleeve target *n* **:** a tubular cloth target towed by an airplane for use in air and ground antiaircraft gunnery practice
sleeve valve *n* **:** an admission and exhaust valve on an internal-combustion engine that consists of one or two hollow sleeves fitting around the interior of the cylinder and moving as the piston moves so that openings in them come into line with inlet and exhaust ports in the cylinder at proper stages in the cycle
sleev·ing \'slēviŋ\ *n* -S [¹*sleeve* + -*ing*] **:** a braided, knitted, woven, or extruded tube used to slip over bare or weakly insulated conductors in an electronic assembly — called also *spaghetti*
sleezy *var of* SLEAZY
sleided *adj* [alter. (prob. influenced by *sleyed*, past part. of ²*sley*) of *sleaved*, past part of ¹*sleave*] *obs, of silk* **:** UNTWISTED
¹sleigh \'slā\ *n* -S [D *slee*, alter. of *slede*, fr. MD — more at SLED] **1 a :** a vehicle on runners used for transporting persons or goods on snow or ice — called also *sledge* **b** *dial* **:** a child's sled **2 :** the part of a gun carriage that supports the cannon, recoils with it, and guides it along the slides upon which the cannon moves in recoil
²sleigh \"\ *vi* -ED/-ING/-S **:** to drive or travel in a sleigh
³sleigh *var of* SLEY
sleigh bed *n* [¹*sleigh*] **:** a bed common esp. in the first half of the 19th century having a headboard and footboard that are solid and roll outward at the top
sleigh bell *n* **:** any of various bells commonly attached to a sleigh or to the harness of a horse drawing a sleigh: as **a :** CASCABEL 3 **b :** a hemispherical bell with an attached clapper often attached in series to a leather or metal strap fastened to a harness or sleigh
sleigh·er \'slāə(r), -le(ə)r, -leə\ *n* -S [²*sleigh* + -*er*] **:** one that sleighs
¹sleight \'slīt, *usu* -īd.+V\ *n* -S [ME *sleght, sleight*, fr. ON *slægth*, fr. *slægr* sly, crafty — more at SLY] **1 a :** deceitful craftiness **:** CUNNING, TRICKERY ⟨every interest did by right, or might, or ~, get represented —R.W.Emerson⟩ **b** (1) **:** mental or manual skill in making or performing **:** DEXTERITY, ADROITNESS ⟨a new ~ in the reading of poetry —R.P.Blackmur⟩ (2) **:** skill in a particular task **:** KNACK (3) *archaic* **:** SLEIGHT OF HAND 1 (4) **:** mental or physical quickness or agility **:** NIMBLENESS ⟨brilliant intuitions . . . and speculative hypotheses derived by ~ of mind from a fairly small number of works of the imagination —R.G.Davis⟩ **2 a :** a sly artifice **:** STRATAGEM, TRICK, SHIFT ⟨watching closely to discover by what mental artful ~ he would accomplish the miracle —Archibald Rutledge⟩ ⟨a wicked ~ that causes the assailant to put out his own shoulder —Lafcadio Hearn⟩; *specif* **:** SLEIGHT OF HAND 2 **b** *obs* **:** a skillfully executed pattern
²sleight *obs var of* SLIGHT
sleight of hand [¹*sleight*] **1 a :** expertness and adroitness in manual manipulation **:** manual dexterity **b :** skill and dexterity in the performance of juggling or conjuring tricks ⟨the simplest card trick defeats me if it demands *sleight of hand* —Geoffrey Household⟩ **c :** adroitness and cleverness in accomplishing a deception ⟨verbal *sleight of hand* —Marjorie Grene⟩ ⟨music that is free of self-conscious formulas and tricks of stylistic *sleight of hand* —Winthrop Sargeant⟩ **2 a :** a trick of conjuring or juggling requiring sleight of hand **b :** a cleverly executed trick or deception ⟨the *sleight of hand* by which a faction of the people as voters is invested with the authority of the people —Walter Lippmann⟩
sleighty \'slīd.ē\ *adj* [ME, fr. ¹*sleight* + -*y*] **1** *obs* **:** CUNNING, SLY, CRAFTY **2** *dial* **:** DEXTEROUS, SKILLFUL
slen·dang \'slen,daŋ, -dāŋ\ *n* -S [Malay *sĕlendang*] **:** a long narrow scarf worn esp. by Indonesian women
slen·der \'slendə(r)\ *adj, usu* -ER/-EST [ME *slendre, sclendre*] **1 a** (1) **:** spare in frame or flesh **:** not fleshy or large of bone ⟨a man of ~ build, being only five feet, five inches in height, and weighing less than one hundred pounds —D.Y.Thomas⟩; *esp* **:** gracefully slight ⟨she was like a feather in my arms, so ~, so ethereal —Jack London⟩ (2) **:** not robust **:** FRAIL ⟨as boy and girl neighbors, each of ~ health, they had enjoyed . . . playing the piano together —M.A.D.Howe⟩ **b** (1) **:** thin or insubstantial in proportion to breadth ⟨a ~ volume . . . of twenty-one pages —V.L.Parrington⟩ ⟨a ~ partition wall⟩ (2) **:** small or narrow in circumference or width in proportion to the length or height ⟨a ~ perpendicular steel framework tower —*Amer. Guide Series: Oregon*⟩; *esp* **:** delicately elongated in pleasing proportions ⟨a graceful portico of ~ columns —*Amer. Guide Series: N.C.*⟩ (3) **:** excessively thin and elongated **:** TENUOUS ⟨the new arrivals took over the defensive sector south of the airfield where the ~ line . . . had been punctured —H.L.Merillat⟩ **c :** limited in extent, size, quantity, capacity, or scope ⟨published a ~ list of generalized headings —John Lawler⟩ ⟨his critical powers were very ~ —G.C. Sellery⟩ **2 a** (1) **:** inadequate or barely adequate in quantity or supply **:** SCANTY, MEAGER ⟨compelled by ~ family finances to leave school early —E.M.Lustgarten⟩ (2) **:** barely adequate in dimensions or scope **:** NARROW, SCANT ⟨elected by a ~ margin⟩ ⟨a few attempts had been made to deepen and embank the natural streams, but with ~ success —T.B.Macaulay⟩ **b** (1) **:** inadequate to justify an inference, opinion, or action ⟨tended to start from some observation . . . and then elaborate on this ~ foundation a theory of the universe —Benjamin Farrington⟩ (2) **:** having slight or inadequate grounds or justification ⟨a ~ hope⟩ **c :** slight in significance, seriousness, or complexity ⟨the material is slighter, the texture more ~, and the formal exigencies shorter than the full-size sonata —Norman Demuth⟩ **3 a** (1) **:** FRONT — used of a vowel in some Celtic languages (2) **:** having the allophone that characterizes it when it is pronounced with a front vowel — used of a consonant in some Celtic languages **b :** characterized by or consisting of a tone that lacks fullness or volume ⟨fortunate in his recordings, for his rather ~ voice reproduces exceptionally well —P.L.Miller⟩ **syn** see THIN
slender aster *n* **:** an annual aster (*Aster exilis*) of the southwestern U. S. having usu. simple stems and thin linear upper leaves
slender bent grass *n* **:** ROUGH BENT
slender blue flag *n* **:** either of two irises: **a :** a dwarf iris (*Iris verna*) **b :** an eastern No. American iris (*Iris prismatica*) with stout ropy stolons and an acutely angled seed pod
slender deutzia *n* **:** JAPANESE SNOWFLOWER
slender foxtail *n* **:** a Eurasian annual weedy grass (*Alopecurus myosuroides*) that is locally established (as about seaports) in No. America
slender gooseberry *n* **:** MISSOURI GOOSEBERRY
slender grama *n* **:** a tufted perennial grama (*Bouteloua filiformis*) of Texas, Arizona, Mexico, and Panama having erect or spreading sparingly branched culms
slen·der·ish \-dərish\ *adj* **:** somewhat slender
slen·der·ize \-də,rīz\ *vt* -ED/-ING/-S **1 :** to make slender **2 :** to cause to appear slender
slender loris *n* **:** LORIS 1a
slen·der·ly *adv* [*slender* + -*ly*] **1 :** to a small degree **:** SLIGHTLY, SPARSELY ⟨~ endowed with natural resources —W.B.Fisher⟩ **2 :** in a slender manner ⟨a ~ built man⟩
slen·der·ness *n* -ES **:** the quality or state of being slender
slenderness ratio *n* **:** the ratio of the length of a structural member (as a column) to its least radius of gyration
slender rush *n* **:** a tufted wiry rush (*Juncus tenuis*) of wide distribution
slender vetch *n* **:** a Eurasian vetch (*Vicia tetrasperma*) with blue or purple flowers that is naturalized in eastern No. America — called also *lentil tare*
slender wheat grass *n* **:** a No. American grass (*Agropyron trachycaulum*) cultivated in the western U. S. for its excellent forage
¹slent \'slent\ *n* -S [ME — more at SLANT] *chiefly Scot* **:** SLOPE, PITCH, DECLIVITY
²slent \"\ *vi* -ED/-ING/-S [ME *slenten* — more at SLANT] **1** *dial Brit* **:** SLANT, SLOPE **2** *dial Brit* **:** to move or glance sideways
³slent \"\ *vt* -ED/-ING/-S [origin unknown] *archaic* **:** TEAR, SPLIT
slen·tan·do \slen'tän(,)dō\ *adv (or adj)* [It, fr. verbal of *slentare* to slow down, fr. *s-* away, off (fr. L *dis-* or *ex-*) + *lento* slow, fr. L *lentus* pliant, tough, slow — more at LITHE] **:** gradually decreasing in tempo — used as a direction in music
sle·pez \slə'pets\ *n* -ES [Russ *slepets*, lit., blind one, fr. *slepoĭ* blind] **:** a mole rat (*Spalax typhus*)
slept *past of* SLEEP
sleugh \'slü\ *Brit var of* ¹SLOUGH 1b
¹sleuth \'slüth\ *or* **sleuthhound** \'≈,≈\ *n* -S [*sleuth*, short for *sleuthhound*, fr. ME, fr. *sloth, sleuth* track of a person or animal (fr. ON *slōth*) + *hound*] **1 :** a hound that tracks by the scent; *specif* **:** BLOODHOUND **2 :** DETECTIVE; *broadly* **:** one that searches out and investigates obscure information, facts or phenomena ⟨been a good ~ and critic in assembling the text —T.D.Clark⟩
²sleuth \"\ *vb* -ED/-ING/-S *vi* **:** to act as a detective or investigator **:** follow a track, trace, or clue **:** search for information or facts ⟨assigned eleven reporters and five lawyers to ~ out the facts —*Time*⟩ ~ *vt* **:** to search into the affairs or follow the trail of (a person)
¹slew *past of* SLAY
²slew *var of* SLOUGH
³slew *var of* SLUE
⁴slew *also* **slue** \'slü\ *n* -S [IrGael *sluagh*] **:** a large number or quantity **:** LOT ⟨a whole ~ of uptown rowdies —Paul Gallico⟩ ⟨had ~*s* of work —Conrad Richter⟩
⁵slew \"\ *n* -S [origin unknown] **:** filling consisting of usu. three rods worked together — see BASKET illustration
¹slewed \-üd\ *adj* [fr. past part. of ³*slew* (to twist)] **:** somewhat intoxicated **:** TIPSY
²slewed \"\ *adj* [⁵*slew* + -*ed*] *of a basket* **:** filled in with slews woven around the stakes and by-stakes
slew·ing \'slüiŋ\ *n* -S [⁵*slew* + -*ing*] **1 :** the act of filling in in basketmaking with two or more rods worked together **2 :** SLEWS
¹sley *or* **slay** *or* **sleigh** \'slā\ *n* -S [ME *sleye, slay*, fr. OE *slege*, lit., act of beating, stroke; akin to OHG *slag* blow, ON *slagr*, OE *slēan* to strike, beat, slay — more at SLAY] **1 a :** a weaver's reed **b :** a movable frame in a loom that carries the reed **2 :** a guideway in a knitting machine **3 :** the number of warp ends per inch in a cloth **4 :** a device in a lace machine that contains small holes through which some warp ends pass and is used in selecting the pattern
²sley \"\ *vt* -ED/-ING/-S **:** to separate and arrange in a reed the threads of (the warp) — **sley·er** \-lāə(r), -le(ə)r, -leə\ *n* -S
sleyb *usu cap, pl of* SLUBBI
slg *abbr* sailing
slibbersauce *or* **slibber-slabber** *n* -S [*slibbersauce*, prob. fr. MLG *slibber, slipper* slippery (akin to OE *slipor* slippery) + E *sauce; slibber-slabber*, perh. redupl. of ¹*slabber* — more at SLIPPERY, SLABBER] *obs* **:** a sloppy or nauseating concoction used as food or medicine or as a cosmetic
¹slice \'slīs\ *n* -S [ME *sklise, slice*, fr. MF *esclice, esclisse* splinter, thin piece of wood, fr. OF, fr. *esclicier* to splinter — more at ²SLICE] **1 a :** a thin flat portion that is cut from something ⟨a ~ of bread⟩ ⟨a ~ of roast beef⟩ **b :** ¹CHIP 1i **c :** something that resembles a slice ⟨looked . . . through the narrow ~ of window in the tower room —Kay Boyle⟩ **2 a** *obs* **:** a spatula or paddle used esp. for mixing or spreading medical compounds **b :** a knife with a broad or wedge-shaped blade used esp. for serving food ⟨a fish ~⟩ **c** *archaic* **:** an iron bar flattened at one end for use as a fire shovel **d :** a tool with a flat blade for scraping or stripping (as for flensing a whale); *specif* **:** SLICE BAR **e** (1) **:** the removable sliding bottom of a printer's slice galley (2) **:** INK KNIFE **3 :** a part separated from the whole **:** SEGMENT, SHARE ⟨territorial claims to ~*s* of Antarctica —J.D.M.Blyth⟩ ⟨make a bid for a ~ of the . . . prize money —H.W.Young⟩ ⟨for plot must be substituted the reality of a ~ of life —F.B.Millett⟩
²slice \"\ *vb* -ED/-ING/-S [ME *sklicen*, fr. MF *esclicier, esclissier* to splinter, fr. OF, of Gmc origin; akin to OHG *slīzan* to tear apart — more at SLIT] *vt* **1 a :** to cut with or as if with a knife ⟨~ bread⟩ ⟨~ a melon in two⟩ ⟨~ hickory sapwood for chair-bottom splints —*Amer. Guide Series: Ark.*⟩ ⟨jets ~ the air like giant scythes —Claudia Cassidy⟩ ⟨production would be *sliced* by more than half —*Newsweek*⟩ **b :** to divide into segments as if by cutting ⟨the chimney's shade . . . ~*s* the glistening roof —Thomas Vance⟩ ⟨the data . . . have not been *sliced* in all the ways that they might —R.M.Goldman⟩ **2 a :** to cut off cleanly with or as if with a knife ⟨this machine ~*s* off a narrow edge from each envelope —J.R.Gregg⟩ ⟨the industry will be able to ~ $30,000,000 from its . . . annual fuel bill —D.C.Spaulding⟩ **b** (1) **:** to cut a passage through ⟨expressways . . . ~ our parks —Joseph Hudnut⟩ (2) **:** to make by or as if by slicing ⟨~ an opening in a wall⟩ ⟨troops . . . *sliced* their way through the crumpled resistance —*Police Gazette*⟩ **3 :** to stir, spread, or clear with a slice ⟨~ printer's ink⟩ ⟨~ a grate⟩ **4 :** to hit (as a golf ball or tennis ball) so that a slice results — distinguished from *drive;* compare ²HOOK 6b ~ *vi* **1 :** to cut or seem to cut cleanly ⟨the turbine blade . . . *sliced* into the fuel line —J.A.Michener⟩ ⟨wind . . . *slicing* through his overcoat as though it were the thinnest cotton —Irwin Shaw⟩ **2 a :** to move with a cutting action often on the diagonal ⟨the planes *sliced* on over —James Jones⟩ ⟨the luxury liner . . . *sliced* through the Atlantic today in quest of a speed record —*New Orleans States*⟩ ⟨the bull's horn *slicing* by his shoulder —Barnaby Conrad⟩ **b :** to hew a passage ⟨a four-lane superhighway . . . ~*s* through the craggy sierra —*Lamp*⟩ **3 a :** to put a slice on a stroke or ball **b** *of a ball* **:** to curve in flight in the direction of a slice
³slice \"\ *n* -S **:** a flight of a ball (as in golf, tennis, volley ball) that deflects to the right of a right-handed player or to the left of a left-handed player usu. as a result of being hit across its center line; *also* **:** a ball following such a course — compare HOOK, SPIN
slice·able \-səbəl\ *adj* **:** capable of being sliced
slice bar *n* [²*slice* + *bar*] **:** a steel bar with a broad flat blade for chipping or scraping operations (as breaking up clinkers or removing excess dirt from a trench wall)
sliced veneer *n* [fr. past part. of ²*slice*] **:** veneer that is sheared from the flat surface of a flitch or squared log
slice galley *n* [¹*slice*] **:** an old form of printer's galley having a sliding bottom for handling heavy forms
slice-of-life \'≈≈'≈\ *adj* [fr. the noun phrase *slice of life*, trans. of F *tranche de vie*] **:** of, relating to, or marked by the accurate transcription into drama or another art form of a segment of actual experience ⟨in these *slice-of-life* literary times, the novel that analyzes life at more than one level is somewhat of a rarity —Benjamin Appel⟩
slic·er \'slīsə(r)\ *n* -S [²*slice* + -*er*] **1 :** an implement designed for cutting: as **a :** a piece of cutlery for slicing food by hand ⟨roast ~⟩ ⟨fruit ~⟩ ⟨cheese ~⟩ **b :** a mechanically operated device usu. employing a revolving disk for slicing ⟨food ~⟩ ⟨veneer ~⟩ ⟨~ for sugar beets⟩ **c :** a lapidary's slitter **d :** CLIPPER 2b **2 :** a person using a cutting implement: as **a :** one that cuts materials (as butter, bread, fruit) by hand or by machine **b :** a worker who cuts slits in turpentine trees for the insertion of gutters

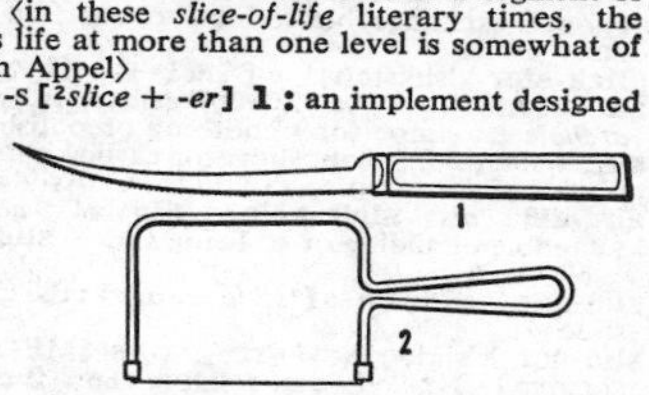
1
2
slicers 1a: *1* fruit, *2* cheese

slicht \'slikt\ *Scot var of* SLIGHT
¹slicing *n* -S [fr. gerund of ²*slice*] **:** the act or process or a result of cutting; *specif* **:** TOP SLICING
²slicing *adj* **:** of, relating to, or adapted for cutting ⟨~ blade⟩ ⟨~ method⟩
¹slick \'slik\ *vb* -ED/-ING/-S [ME *sliken;* akin to OE *nīgslīcod* newly smoothed, glossy, OHG *slīhhan* to glide — more at ²SLICK] *vt* **1 a :** to make (a surface) flat or slippery **:** LEVEL, POLISH ⟨a spatula is used to ~ . . . the flour on a board —*Correspondence Course in Flour Milling*⟩ ⟨men . . . were ~*ing* the skids with grease —James Dugan⟩ **b :** to give an elegant finish to **:** REFINE, SMARTEN ⟨~*ed* up and sentimentalized the . . . rough-hewn original story —*Time*⟩ ⟨called in a decorator to ~ it up, turning the . . . café into a restaurant de luxe —A.J.Liebling⟩ **c :** SLEEK 2 **2 a :** to give a smooth and glossy appearance to (the hair) esp. by combing with water or pomade **:** PLASTER ⟨hair ~*ed* down and then brushed up in a barber's curl above his left eye —B.A.Williams⟩ **b :** to make presentable **:** spruce up ⟨dress as if they were ~*ed* up for Saturday night in town —J.H.Jackson⟩ ⟨Mother was . . . a great one for keepin' things ~*ed* up —J.C.Lincoln⟩ ~ *vi* **1 :** to spruce up **:** make oneself presentable ⟨he ~*ed* up and courted her in the regular way —Helen Rich⟩ **2 :** to glide smoothly **:** SLIP ⟨the logs ~*ed* along without jamming or stranding —Hugh Fosburgh⟩
²slick \"\ *adj* -ER/-EST [ME *slike*, akin to MHG *slīch* slime, OHG *slīhhan* to glide, ON *slīkr* smooth, Gk *ligdēn* grazing the surface, *leios* smooth — more at LIME] **1 a :** having a glassy surface **:** SMOOTH, SLIPPERY ⟨waters ~ with oil —*Time*⟩ ⟨the grass was ~ from the night's dew, and the men slipped frequently as they moved downhill —Norman Mailer⟩ **b :** having surface glitter **:** polished but not profound **:** GLIB, GLOSSY ⟨an entertaining job of ~ writing, all surface and no depth —B.R.Redman⟩ ⟨turned out ~ and sound conventional likenesses in the best School of Fine Arts manner —*Time*⟩ **c :** lacking in complexity or originality **:** OBVIOUS, CONTRIVED ⟨the young gentlemen are altogether too pat, and the adventures which befall them altogether too ~ —Virginia Woolf⟩ ⟨neatly plotted story of the ~ variety, easily read, soon forgotten —Jerome Stone⟩ ⟨no ~ solutions, no easy cures are peddled —R.J.McCracken⟩ **2** *archaic* **:** SLEEK 1 ⟨fattens all their beasts of war, and makes them ~ and fine —John Fryer⟩ **3 a :** characterized by subtlety or nimble wit **:** CLEVER, INGRATIATING ⟨this ~ type of youngster anticipates exactly how adults will react to him and plays on their sensibilities —Agnes Meyer⟩ ⟨a good many ~ sales tricks —J.M. Guilfoyle⟩ ⟨approached this problem in . . . too unctuous and ~ a mood —A.M.Schlesinger b.1917⟩; *esp* **:** WILY ⟨a pair of ~ operators had given the district a bad name by salting a barren claim —Oscar Lewis⟩ **b :** characterized by expert proficiency **:** DEFT, SKILLFUL ⟨a notable level of ~ technical perfection in every department —Arthur Knight⟩ ⟨smooth ground attack and incredibly ~ passing attack —*New Yorker*⟩ **4 :** extremely good **:** FIRST-RATE **5 :** lacking identification marks **:** UNBRANDED — used of livestock on the range **6 a :** SLEEK 3 **b** *or* **slick-paper** \'≈,≈≈\ **:** of, relating to, being, or conforming to the standards of a slick ⟨~ fiction⟩ ⟨nationally circulated ~ and quality magazines —Paul Roberts⟩ ⟨appeals to the *slick-paper* or carriage trade —Rosemary Benét⟩
³slick \"\ *adv* **:** CLEVERLY, SMOOTHLY
⁴slick \"\ *n* -S **1 a :** something that is smooth or slippery ⟨snow left an icy ~ on the roads⟩; *esp* **:** a smooth patch of water often covered with a film of oil ⟨band ~*s* on the sea surface . . . are commonly seen along the shore when the wind is a light breeze —G.C. Ewing⟩ ⟨searchers spotted an oil ~ . . . and what might be the wreckage of a plane —*N.Y. Times*⟩ **b :** a film of oil ⟨an oily ~ drifted away from our boat —*Field & Stream*⟩ **2 :** an

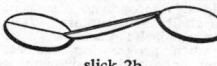

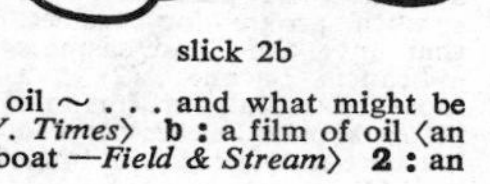
slick 2b

implement for producing a slick surface: as **a** : a flat paddle now usu. of steel for smoothing a sample of flour **b** : a foundry tool for smoothing the surface of a sand mold or unbaked core **3** : an unbranded range animal ⟨all of them added to their herds by branding ~*s* —Bruce Siberts⟩ — compare SLICK-EAR **4** : a shrewd or untrustworthy operator ⟨~*s* . . . exploited the plight of their brothers to ease their own paths —H.W.Baldwin⟩ **5** *chiefly Midland* : a treeless area in the southern Appalachians covered by a dense shrubby tangle usu. of rhododendron or mountain laurel **6** : a large-circulation consumer magazine printed on coated stock and usu. characterized by articles chosen for popular appeal and fiction limited to formulized stories with happy endings ⟨calculating editors of the ~*s*, who design moonshine to suit popular taste —Leo Marx⟩ — compare PULP 5a

⁵slick \"\ *or* **slick·er** \-kə(r)\ *vt* -ED/-ING/-S [*slick* fr. ²*slick; slicker* fr. *slicker*, n.] : to defraud cleverly : OUTSMART, TRICK ⟨explanations . . . only tended to confirm them in the notion that they were being ~*ed* —R.W.Riis & Webb Waldron⟩

slick–ear \ˈ=,=\ *n* [²*slick* + *ear*] : a range animal lacking an earmark : MAVERICK — compare SLEEPER 8, SLICK 3

slick·en \ˈslikən\ *vt* -ED/-ING/-S [²*slick* + *-en*] *chiefly dial* : to make slick

slick·ens \ˈslikənz\ *n pl* [prob. irreg. fr. *slick* finely pounded ore, fr. G *schlich* slime — more at SCHLICH] **1 a** : the thin layer of extremely fine silt sometimes deposited by flood waters of a stream **b** : finely pulverized material from a quartz mill or washings of lighter earth sluiced away in hydraulic mining **2** : SLICKENSIDE

¹slick·en·side \ˈslikən,sīd\ *n* [E dial. *slicken* smooth (alter. of ²*slick*) + *side*] : a smooth striated polished surface produced on rock by movement along a fault, a subsidiary fracture, a bedding plane, or at the bottom of a landslide — usu. used in pl. ⟨interpretation of the relative age of the faulting, on the basis of ~*s* alone, is difficult —J.D.Forrester⟩

²slickenside \"\ *vt* -ED/-ING/-S : to form slickensides upon

slick·er \ˈslikə(r)\ *n* -S [¹*slick* + *-er*] **1** : one that slicks: as **a** : a sharp-edged two-handled tool used for removing a thin layer of leather from hides to smooth them and reduce them to proper thickness **b** (1) : FLOAT 5d(1) (2) : GOOSENECK SLICKER **c** : a leather worker who uses a slicker **d** : a worker who lures hats **2** [²*slick* + *-er*] **a** : a bright yellow oilskin of loose full cut often worn with a matching sou'wester; *broadly* : RAINCOAT **b** : something that resembles an oilskin in style or smooth waterproof texture **3** [⁵*slick* + *-er*] **a** : a clever crook : SWINDLER, CHEAT; *sometimes* : a professional gambler **b** : a city dweller esp. of natty appearance or sophisticated mannerisms **4** [prob. fr. ¹*slick* + *-er*] : SILVERFISH 2

slickest *superlative of* SLICK

slicking *n* -S [fr. gerund of ¹*slick*] **1** : an act or process of making slick; *specif* : smoothing fine leathers by hand after setting by machine **2 slickings** *pl* : narrow veins of ore

slick·ly *adv* : in a slick manner : DEFTLY, SMOOTHLY

slick·ness *n* -ES : the quality or state of being slick

slickrock \ˈ=,=\ *n* [²*slick* + *rock*] : smooth slippery rock ⟨rough going over sand and ~ —S.W.Taylor⟩

slicks *pres 3d sing of* SLICK, *pl of* SLICK

slick spot *n* : an area usu. of a B horizon soil containing enough exchangeable sodium to interfere with the growth of most crops

slick·ster \ˈslikstə(r)\ *n* [⁵*slick* + *-ster*] : SLICK 4

slickstone \ˈ=,=\ *n* [ME *slikestone*, fr. *slike* slick + *stone*] *archaic* : a stone for smoothing or polishing

slid \ˈslid\ *adj* [prob. short for earlier *slidder* slippery, fr. ME, fr. OE *slidor;* akin to OE *slidrian* to slidder] *Scot* : SLIPPERY

slid·able *also* **slide·able** \ˈslīdəbəl\ *adj* [¹*slide* + *-able*] : capable of sliding or of being slid — **slid·ably** *or* **slide·ably** \-blē\ *adv*

slid·age \ˈslīdij\ *n* -S [¹*slide* + *-age*] : the charge for using a log slide

slid·der \ˈslidə(r)\ *vi* -ED/-ING/-S [ME *slideren* — more at SLITHER] **1** *chiefly dial* : SLIDE, SLIP **2** *chiefly dial* : SLITHER

slid·dery \ˈslidərē\ *adj* [ME *slidery*, fr. *slideren* to slidder + *-y*] **1** *chiefly dial* : offering insecure footing : SLIPPERY, SLICK **2** *dial Brit* : TRICKY, UNTRUSTWORTHY

¹slide \ˈslīd\ *vb* **slid** \ˈslid\ *or dial* **slod** \ˈsläd\ *or archaic* **slided**; **slid** *or archaic* **slid·den** \ˈslidᵊn\ **sliding; slides** [ME *sliden*, fr. OE *slīdan* to glide, slip, backslide; akin to MHG *slīten* to slide, Gk *olisthanein* to slip, glide, fall, Skt *sredhati* he errs, blunders, Gk *leios* smooth — more at LIME] *vi* **1 a** : to go with a smooth continuous motion : GLIDE ⟨fishes . . . *sliding* swiftly from your boat —*Amer. Guide Series: Fla.*⟩ ⟨a little red convertible *slid* up the . . . driveway —S.A.Offit⟩ ⟨shadows *slid* along the huge wooden tables —Sinclair Lewis⟩ **b** : to coast over a surface (as snow or ice) by means of gravity or momentum ⟨a startled dog ~*s* toward the skaters on all four feet⟩ ⟨~ downhill on a toboggan⟩ ⟨when the glacier *slid* down across New England —L.K.Porritt⟩ **c** : to drop down and approach a base in baseball along the ground usu. feet first with the weight of the body carried on one hip ⟨*slid* safely into third base ahead of the catcher's throw⟩ **2 a** (1) : to suffer a moral relapse : BACKSLIDE ⟨lead me in all thy righteous ways, nor suffer me to ~ —Charles Wesley⟩ (2) : to take a downward turn ⟨if the readjustment . . . ~*s* into a recession —*Fortune*⟩ **b** : to slip or fall by loss of footing ⟨stumbled over a log and *slid* down the slope⟩ **c** : to change position or become dislocated : SHIFT, SLIP ⟨the packages ~ from her arms⟩ ⟨rain *slid* off the smooth hide of the mountains —G.T.Nunn⟩ **3** : to become dissipated : VANISH ⟨it was inevitable that existentialism should ~ out of men's minds —Norman Cousins⟩ **4 a** : to slither along the ground : CRAWL, WRIGGLE ⟨began their advance, one *sliding* forward on his stomach —Georg Meyers⟩ **b** : to stream along : FLOW, POUR ⟨walked . . . along the dark *sliding* river —Irwin Shaw⟩ **5 a** : to pass effortlessly or unobserved : DRIFT — used of time ⟨how happily must my old age ~ away —Henry Fielding⟩ **b** : to become readily transferred or diverted ⟨his eye ~*s* from the printed page to the wonderful world outdoors⟩ **c** : to take a natural course ⟨finds it easier to let things ~ than to insist on strict observance of the rules⟩ **d** : to get along with a minimum of effort ⟨this means doing your best, not just *sliding* through —*Boy Scout Handbk.*⟩ **6 a** : to move softly or unobtrusively : disappear surreptitiously : SNEAK, STEAL ⟨*slid* behind the bole of a fir tree —F.V.W.Mason⟩ ⟨after playing to empty benches for two nights, they *slid* out of town —*Amer. Guide Series: Wash.*⟩ **b** : to pass easily or gradually ⟨~ into a reverie —John Masters⟩ **c** : to become gradually transformed ⟨may not godly authority imperceptibly ~ over into plain tyranny —V.L.Parrington⟩ **d** : to pass by gradations from one pitch to another without cessation of sound ⟨*sliding* . . . is another undesirable feature of singing —Sergius Kagen⟩ ~ *vt* **1 a** : to cause to glide or slip ⟨*slid* the car to the curb —Erle Stanley Gardner⟩ ⟨~ the left ski forward, then the right⟩ **b** : to traverse in a sliding manner ⟨firemen ~ the poles to the street floor⟩ **2** : to put or introduce surreptitiously ⟨*slid* the gun out of sight under his coat —Raymond Chandler⟩ ⟨the danger of . . . getting an emperor or a king or a dictator *slid* over on them —Dorothy C. Fisher⟩ **3** : to place (as an alphabetic sequence) beside another sequence in various juxtapositions at each of which the letters of one correspond one-to-one to those of the other

²slide \"\ *n* -S **1 a** : an act or instance of sliding: as (1) : a transit over a slippery surface ⟨a skier's hunger for more ~*s* . . . per weekend —William Gilman⟩ (2) : CHASSÉ (3) : the distance the fork moves after drop lock in a lever-escapement watch to reach the banking pin (4) : a sliding approach to a base in baseball — compare HOOK SLIDE **b** (1) *archaic* : a smooth progression ⟨verses, that have a ~, and easiness —Francis Bacon⟩ (2) : a lapse in morals or fortunes ⟨if he should . . . discover a bit of backward ~ in himself —H.A.Overstreet⟩ (3) : a downward turn ⟨action to halt the economic ~ —S.H. Slichter⟩ **c** (1) : a musical grace consisting of two or more small notes moving by adjacent degrees and leading to a principal note either above or below (2) : PORTAMENTO **2** : a sliding part or mechanism: as **a** : any of various clothing ornaments that slide on and hold by gripping ⟨tie ~⟩ ⟨belt ~⟩ **b** (1) : a U-shaped section of tube in the trombone that is pushed out and in to produce the tones between the fundamental and its harmonics (2) : a short tube that is used in most metal wind instruments to adjust the pitch **c** (1) : a moving piece (as the ram of a punch press) that is guided by a part along which it slides ⟨~ valve⟩ (2) : a guiding surface (as a feeding mechanism) along which something slides — compare CROSS SLIDE **d** : SLIDING SEAT **e** : a small runner to which something is attached to guide it along a track ⟨the luff of the sail . . . is sewn on to ~*s* which run in a metal track along the after side of the mast —F.E.Dodman⟩ **f** (1) : the knee of a composing stick (2) : a slugcasting-machine matrix for casting rules or borders **g** : a cryptographical device resembling a slide rule with a fixed member usu. carrying one alphabetic sequence and a double-length sliding member another one repeated **3 a** (1) : the descent of a mass (as of earth, rock, or snow) down a hill or mountainside ⟨a ~ of rock⟩ — used chiefly in combination ⟨land*slide*⟩ ⟨snow*slide*⟩ (2) : the track left by a slide (3) : a mass of debris deposited by a slide **b** : a dislocation in which one rock mass in a mining lode has slid on another : FAULT **4** : a drag or sledge for transporting heavy loads over a relatively smooth surface ⟨cut the last of the crop and . . . hauled it on a ~ to the tobacco barn —Elizabeth M. Roberts⟩ — called also *slider* **5 a** (1) : a slippery surface for coasting or sliding ⟨ski ~⟩ ⟨toboggan ~⟩ (2) : a chute with a flat polished bed sloping down from the top of a mounting ladder ⟨playground ~⟩ ⟨gave him a ~ for his swimming pool —*Brit. Books of the Month*⟩ **b** : a channel or track on which something is slid ⟨pushed the heavy door on the ~ and . . . followed him into the barn —Astrid Peters⟩ **c** : a sloping trough down which objects are carried by gravity ⟨log ~⟩ **d** : an inclined plane on moist soil adjoining water and smoothed by otters or occas. other aquatic mammals at play **e** *or* **slide stacker** : an inclined plane up which hay is drawn for stacking **6 a** : a usu. rectangular piece of glass on which an object is mounted for microscopic examination **b** (1) : a photographic transparency on a small plate or film suitably protected for projection — see FILMSLIDE, LANTERN SLIDE (2) : DARK SLIDE **7** : SCUFF 4

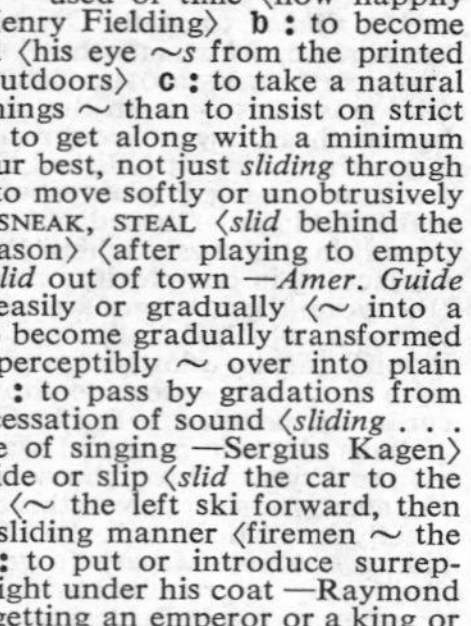

slide 5a (2)

slide–action \ˈ=,==\ *adj* : PUMP-ACTION

slide caliper *n* : CALIPER SQUARE

slide detector fence *n* : an electrically charged fence along a railroad track that when broken by a rock or earth slide automatically sets signals to halt trains from either direction until the obstruction is cleared

slide fastener *n* : ZIPPER

slidefilm \ˈ=,=\ *n* [²*slide* + *film*] : FILMSTRIP

slide–off \ˈ=,=\ *n* -S : SLIDE 1b (3)

slide pole *n* : POLE 2d

slid·er \ˈslīdə(r)\ *n* -S [¹*slide* + *-er*] **1** : one that uses or operates a slide: as **a** : a person that coasts over a slippery surface ⟨the hill was swarming with ~*s*⟩ **b** : a worker who slides covers onto commodities (as matches, tobacco) packed in slide-top boxes **2** : SLIDE 4 **3** : a sliding part or device; *esp* : a zipper pull ⟨the annoyance of a zipper that pops open behind the ~ —*N.Y. Times Mag.*⟩ **4** : any of various No. American freshwater edible turtles esp. of the genus *Pseudemys* **5** : a pitch in baseball that looks like a fast ball but curves slightly

slide rest *n* : an attachment for a machine tool (as a lathe or planing machine) designed to hold the tool or cutter firmly and to give it motion — compare FEED SCREW

slide–rock \ˈ=,=\ *n* **1** : SLIDE 3a (1) **2** : rock shards in talus

slide rule *n* : an instrument consisting in its simplest form of a

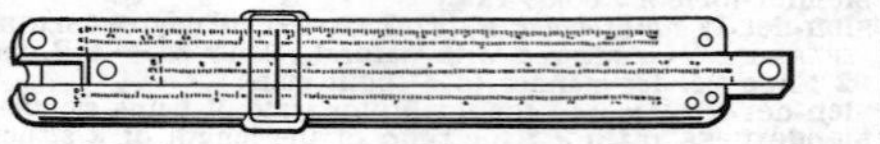

slide rule

ruler and a medial slide that are graduated with similar logarithmic scales labeled with the corresponding antilogarithms and used for rapid calculation

slides *pres 3d sing of* SLIDE, *pl of* SLIDE

slide stacker *n* : ²SLIDE 5e

slide valve *n* : a valve that opens and closes a passageway by sliding over a port; *specif* : such a valve often used in steam engines for admitting steam to the piston and releasing it and having a cuplike cavity in its face through which the exhaust passes

slideway \ˈ=,=\ *n* [¹*slide* + *way*] : a way along which something slides : GUIDEWAY, SLIDE

slide–wire \ˈ=,=\ *n* : a resistance-measuring device used as part of a Wheatstone bridge and consisting essentially of a straight or spiral wire divided by a sliding contact into two parts forming the whole or known portions of adjacent arms of the bridge

¹slid·ing \ˈslīdiŋ, -dēŋ\ *n* -S [ME, fr. gerund of *sliden* to slide] : the act of one that slides

²sliding \"\ *adj* [ME, fr. pres. part. of *sliden* to slide] **1 a** *obs* : PASSING, TRANSITORY **b** : of an unreliable nature : SHIFTY ⟨the gentleman with the ~ smile —John Galsworthy⟩ **2 a** : going with a smooth continuous motion : SLIPPING, GLIDING ⟨a ~ avalanche⟩ ⟨a ~ snake⟩ **b** *archaic* : moving smoothly : FLOWING ⟨naturalize the ~ rhymes . . . in English —J.R. Lowell⟩ **3 a** : designed to slip along the cord around which it is made : RUNNING ⟨~ knot⟩ **b** : adjusted by sliding ⟨the ~ fan windows are unusual —*Amer. Guide Series: La.*⟩ **c** : equipped with or characterized by a sliding part or mechanism ⟨a ~ piston⟩ ⟨~ calipers⟩ **4** : rising or falling in accordance with a standard of comparison ⟨rent is charged . . . in a ~ ratio to the wages of the tenant —Hewlett Johnson⟩ ⟨~ definition of an old man as anyone who is fifteen years older than you are —Alan Gregg⟩ — **slid·ing·ly** *adv*

sliding board *n* [¹*sliding*] : a playground slide

sliding bow *n* [²*sliding*] : a metal framework mounted on an electric locomotive or trolley car to connect with the overhead wire

sliding fit *n* [¹*sliding*] : a fit for mechanical parts that slide on one another

sliding friction *n* : the friction between two bodies that are in sliding contact — called also *kinetic friction*

sliding gear *n* [²*sliding*] : a change gear in which speed changes are made by sliding gear wheels along their axes so as to place them in or out of mesh

sliding–gear trans·mission *n* : a power-transmission system in which any given pair of gears is engaged by sliding one axially into mesh with the other

sliding growth *n* : GLIDING GROWTH

sliding gunter *n* : GUNTER RIG

sliding hinge *n* : a hinge that permits a sliding as well as a rotary movement (as of a door) — compare CLEANING HINGE

sliding keel *n* : CENTERBOARD

sliding microtome *n* : a microtome in which the object to be cut is fixed and the knife is carried obliquely across it — compare ROTARY MICROTOME

sliding rule *n*, *archaic* : SLIDE RULE

sliding scale *n* **1** : a wage scale geared to the selling price of the product or to the cost-of-living index but usu. assuring the worker a minimum rate **2 a** : a system for raising or lowering tariffs in proportion to the fall or rise of prices **b** : a flexible scale (as of fees or subsidies) adjusted to the needs or income of the individual ⟨the *sliding scale* of medical fees making it . . . possible to balance the losses with large fees from wealthy patients —Milton Terris⟩ ⟨advocate of a *sliding scale* for farm support prices —*Newsweek*⟩

sliding seat *n* : a rower's seat (as in a racing shell) that slides fore and aft — called also *slide*

sliding tumbler *n* : an internal member of a lock usu. of flat sheet metal that is adapted to slide in a guiding slot or groove in the lock as it is operated upon by the key — called also *plate tumbler;* compare LEVER TUMBLER

sliding ways *n pl* : the lower part of the cradle on which a ship is built and which slides down the ground ways with it when it is launched

slid·om·e·ter \slīˈdämədə(r)\ *n* [¹*slide* + *-o-* + *-meter*] : an instrument for indicating and recording shocks to railroad cars occasioned by sudden stopping

slied *past of* SLY

slier *comparative of* SLY

slies *pres 3d sing of* SLY

sliest *superlative of* SLY

slif·ter \ˈsliftə(r)\ *n* -S [origin unknown] *dial Eng* : a crack in the surface of the earth : CREVICE

¹slight \ˈslīt, *usu* -īd.+V\ *adj* -ER/-EST [ME *sleght, slight*, prob. fr. MD *slecht, slicht* smooth, simple, of slight measure; akin to OE *eorthslihtes* level with the ground, ON *slēttr* smooth, OHG *sleht*, Goth *slaihts*, ON *slīkr* smooth — more at SLICK] **1** *chiefly dial* : SMOOTH, CALM, SLEEK ⟨a ~ sea⟩ **2 a** : having a slim or delicate build : not stout or massive in body ⟨a ~ girl⟩ **b** : lacking in strength or substance : FLIMSY, FRAIL ⟨a ~ temporary construction⟩ **c** : deficient in weight, solidity, gravity, importance, or other esteemed quality : TRIVIAL, PALTRY, SUPERFICIAL ⟨a ~ argument⟩ ⟨a ~ attack of indigestion⟩ **3** *of persons* : of low rank : HUMBLE, MEAN **4** : small of its kind or in amount : SCANTY, MEAGER ⟨the rewards were ~⟩ ⟨a ~ odor of gas⟩ **syn** see THIN

²slight *n* -S *obs* : something (as an amount, quantity, or matter) that is slight or insignificant

³slight \ˈslīt, *usu* -īd.+V\ *adv* -ER/-EST **1** *obs* **a** : in small or slight degree : POORLY **b** : to a small degree : SOMEWHAT **2** : in a light or slender manner — usu. used in combination ⟨*slight*-built shapely persons⟩

⁴slight \"\ *vt* -ED/-ING/-S [ME *slighten*, fr. ¹*slight*] **1** *obs* : to make smooth or level; *also* : to level with the earth : OVERTHROW, RAZE **2** *obs* : to throw heedlessly or contemptuously **3 a** : to treat as slight or unimportant : disregard the significance of : make light of ⟨~ divine commands⟩ — sometimes used with *over* ⟨~*ed* his request over⟩ **b** : to treat with disdain or indifference : ignore discourteously ⟨~ a guest⟩ ⟨feel ~*ed*⟩ **c** : to perform or attend to carelessly and inadequately ⟨~ one's work⟩ **d** : SLUR 4 **syn** see NEGLECT

⁵slight \"\ *n* -S **1** : an act or an instance of slighting **2** : an instance of being slighted or treated indifferently or superciliously : a humiliating discourtesy : an affront to one's dignity

slight·er \-īd.ə(r)\ *n* -S : one that slights

slight falcon *n* [¹*slight*] : FALCON-GENTLE

slighting *adj* [fr. pres. part. of ⁴*slight*] : characterized by disregard or disrespect : DISPARAGING ⟨a ~ remark⟩ — **slight·ing·ly** *adv*

slight·ish \ˈslīd.ish\ *adj* [¹*slight* + *-ish*] : rather slight

slight·ly *adv* : in a slight manner or degree : SLENDERLY, LIGHTLY, CARELESSLY ⟨~ built⟩ ⟨touch ~⟩

slight negligence *n* [¹*slight*] : failure to exercise the great degree of care commonly exercised by an extraordinarily prudent person — compare GROSS NEGLIGENCE, ORDINARY NEGLIGENCE

slight·ness *n* -ES : the quality or state of being slight ⟨the ~ of the charge⟩ ⟨the ~ of her build⟩

slighty \ˈslīd.ē\ *adj* -ER/-EST [¹*slight* + *-y*] *chiefly dial* : SLIGHT

sli·go \ˈslī(,)gō\ *adj, usu cap* [fr. *Sligo*, county of Ireland] : of or from County Sligo, Ireland : of the kind or style prevalent in County Sligo

slily *var of* SLYLY

¹slim \ˈslim\ *adj* **slimmer; slimmest** [D, bad, inferior, crafty, fr. MD *slim, slimp* slanting, crooked, bad; akin to MHG *slimp* slanting, awry] **1** : of small diameter or thickness in proportion to the height or length : SLENDER ⟨a ~ person⟩ **2 a** : MEAN, WORTHLESS **b** : somewhat crafty : CLEVER, ADROIT ⟨a ~ rascal never at a loss for an answer⟩ **3 a** : inferior in substance, structure, quality, amount : SLIGHT ⟨a volume of ~ verse⟩ **b** : SCANTY, SMALL, SPARE ⟨a very ~ audience⟩ **syn** see THIN

²slim \"\ *vb* **slimmed; slimmed; slimming; slims** *vt* **1** *chiefly dial* : to do (as a task) carelessly or half-heartedly; *also* : to fail to make good use of (time) : LOAF **2** : to make slender or less : give an appearance of slimness to ⟨princess lines that ~ the waist⟩ ⟨~ your demands down⟩ ~ *vi* : to become slender

slim cake *n* : a plain Irish cake

¹slime \ˈslīm\ *n* -S [ME *slim, slime*, fr. OE *slīm;* akin to MHG & ON *slīm* slime, OHG *slīmen* to make smooth, L *lima* instrument for smoothing, file — more at LIME] **1** : soft moist earth or clay : viscous mud **2** : a viscous and usu. dirty or offensive substance : something felt to resemble viscous mud: as **a** : the original substance (as earth or clay) of the human body; *also* : a human being **b** *archaic* : BITUMEN **c** : a mucous or mucoid secretion of the skin of various animals (as slugs, land snails, hagfishes, catfishes) **d** : a product of wet crushing, consisting of ore ground so fine as to pass a 200-mesh screen — often used in pl. **e** : very wet inferior mortar **f** : a mass or coating of bacteria or algae growing in paper stock

²slime \"\ *vb* -ED/-ING/-S *vt* **1** : to smear or cover with slime : make slimy **2** : to remove slime from (as fish for canning) **3** : to crush or grind (ore) to a slime ~ *vi* : to become slimy

slime bacterium *n* : MYXOBACTERIUM

slimeball \ˈ=,=\ *n* [¹*slime* + *ball*] : a mass of cercariae enveloped in clear gelatinous material that constitutes the form in which some larval trematodes characteristically leave the snail host

slime body *n* : one of the discrete bodies of variable form, number, and distinctness that occur in a developing sieve-tube element, fuse prior to disintegration of the nucleus and form a viscous mass in the vacuole of the element, and are demonstrable after killing and fixing as a slime plug

slime disease *or* **slime sickness** *n* : any of several bacterial diseases of plants marked by slimy rot; *esp* : a destructive disease of tobacco caused by a bacterium (*Pseudomonas solanacearum*) and usu. contracted in the seedbed

slime flux *n* : a fluid or semifluid outflow from the bark or wood of a deciduous tree that is indicative of injury or disease

slime head *n* : a fish of the family Trachichthyidae

slime mold *also* **slime fungus** *n* : a plant of the class Myxomycetes

slime pit *n* : a pit yielding bitumen; *also* : a pit in which ore slimes are deposited

slime plug *n* : one of the funnel-shaped masses on each side of a sieve plate formed by aggregation of slime bodies (as in an injured sieve tube element)

slim·er \ˈslīmə(r)\ *n* -S [¹*slime* + *-er*] **1** : TOADFISH **2** : any of various devices (as a buddle or shaking table) for concentrating ore slime **3** [²*slime* + *-er*] : a worker who slimes something: as **a** : a cannery worker who cleans fish by hand **b** : a slaughterhouse worker who ties intestines into hanks and cleans them before they go individually to the casing-cleaning machine

slimesick \ˈ=,=\ *adj* : heavily populated with organisms capable of causing slime disease ⟨a ~ soil⟩

slime sponge *or* **slimy sponge** *n* : any of several marine encrusting sponges (class Demospongiae) lacking any form of skeleton

slime spot *n* : a colored or translucent spot in paper caused by a lump of slime in the stock that has been crushed in calendering

slime table *n* : SLIMER 2

slime thickening *n* : the thickening of an ore slime by the removal of clear water

slim file *n* : a file very narrow in proportion to its length

sli·mi·cide \ˈslīmə,sīd\ *n* -S [¹*slime* + *-i-* + *-cide*] : a chemical that prevents the growth of slime in paper stock

slim·i·ly \ˈslīmәlē, -li\ *adv* : in a slimy manner : so as to be slimy

slim·i·ness \-mēnəs, -min-\ *n* -ES : the quality or state of being slimy

slim–jim \ˈslim¦jim\ *n* -S [¹*slim* + *Jim*, nickname for *James*] : something (as a person) that is notably slender

slimline \ˈ=,=\ *adj* [¹*slim* + *line*] : of, relating to, or being a long small-diameter fluorescent lamp used esp. in a concealed location (as for showcase illumination)

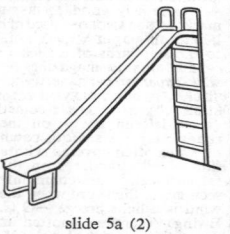

slim·ly *adv* **:** in a slim manner
slimmed *past of* SLIM
slimmer *comparative of* SLIM
slimmest *superlative of* SLIM
[1]**slimming** *adj* [fr. pres. part. of [2]*slim*] **:** giving an effect of slenderness ⟨a dress with ~ hipline⟩
[2]**slimming** *n* -s [fr. gerund of [2]*slim*] **:** the following of a regime (as of diet and exercise) designed to reduce the body weight
slim·mish \ˈslimish\ *adj* [[1]*slim* + *-ish*] **:** somewhat slight or slender ⟨~ evidence⟩
slim·ness *n* -ES **:** the quality or state of being slim
slim pickings *n pl* **:** little to be had or gained ⟨had *slim pickings* for supper⟩
slimp·sy \ˈslimpsē\ *adj* [alter. (influenced by [3]*limp*) of *slimsy*] **:** lacking in substance or sturdiness: as **a :** SLIMSY **b :** being in poor health **:** FEEBLE, PEAKED **c :** hanging limply **:** DROOPING
slims *pres 3d sing of* SLIM
slim·sy \ˈslimzē, -zi\ *adj* [blend of [1]*slim* and [1]*flimsy*] *of cloth* **:** lacking wearing qualities **:** FLIMSY, FRAIL
slimy \ˈslīmē, -mi\ *adj* -ER/-EST [ME, fr. [1]*slime* + *-y*] **1 :** of, relating to, resembling, or being slime **:** VISCOUS, GLUTINOUS; *also* **:** covered with or yielding slime **2 :** of such a character as to be highly distasteful **:** VILE, OFFENSIVE, VULGAR ⟨inexcusably ~ language⟩ ⟨a ~ traitor⟩ ⟨such ~ trickery⟩
slimy-backed \ˌ=ˌ=ˌ=\ *adj* **:** having a slimy back or surface
slimy salamander *n* **:** a No. American salamander (*Plethodon glutinosus*) secreting quantities of mucus from the body surface
[1]**sling** \ˈsliŋ\ *vb* **slung** \ˈsləŋ\ *or chiefly dial* **slang** \ˈslaŋ\ **slung; slinging; slings** [ME *slingen*, prob. fr. ON *slyngva* to hurl; akin to OE & OHG *slingan* to creep, wind, Lith *slinkti*] *vt* **1 :** to cast forcibly and usu. suddenly **:** HURL, FLING ⟨*sling* the net out to dry⟩ ⟨~ your coat over your shoulder⟩ **2 :** to throw (as a stone) with a sling ~ *vi* **1 :** to hurl missiles with a sling **2 :** to move with vigor as if slung ⟨~*ing* angrily out of the room⟩; *esp* **:** to stride along purposefully **:** SWING **syn** see THROW — **sling ink** *slang* **:** to write for publication — **sling one's hook** *Brit* **:** to go away **:** move on
[2]**sling** \"\ *n* -s **1 :** a slinging or hurling of or as if of a missile **:** a violent blow ⟨the ~*s* and arrows of outrageous fortune —Shak.⟩ **2 :** a fault in badminton committed when the racket makes a sliding contact with the shuttlecock
[3]**sling** \"\ *n* -s [ME, perh. fr. MLG *slinge*; akin to OHG *slinga* sling, *slingan* to creep, twist] **1 a :** an instrument for throwing stones or other missiles that usu. consists of a short strap with two strings fastened to its ends or with a string fastened to one end and a light stick to the other and that is used by whirling round until on loosing one end the missile is let fly with centrifugal force **b :** SLINGSHOT **2** *obs* **:** a small cannon **:** CULVERIN **3 a :** a usu. looped line (as of strap, chain, rope) used to hold securely something to be hoisted, lowered, carried, or suspended: as (1) **:** a strap forming a loop (as on a rifle, a pack, or a woman's purse) and used esp. to suspend the burden over the shoulder (2) **:** a hanging bandage suspended from the neck to support an arm or hand (3) **:** a strip of the upper of a shoe having a cutout back part that forms a strap fitting over the wearer's heel and holding the shoe in place **b :** a device based on or substituted for such a looped line and usu. fitted with hooks or tackles: as (1) **:** a chain or rope attached to a lower yard at the middle and passing around a mast near the masthead to support a yard — usu. used in pl.; see SHIP illustration (2) **:** a chain hooked at the bow and stern of a boat to hook the tackles to when it is lowered or hoisted aboard ship; *also* **:** a group of three or four wire legs spliced to a ring, fitted with shackles at their outer ends, and used for hoisting a man-of-war's boats with a crane (3) **:** SLING DOG 2 (4) **:** BUTT SLING (5) **:** a harness esp. constructed for supporting a sick animal in a standing position (6) **:** a device (as a rope net) for actually enclosing material to be hoisted or lowered by a tackle or crane (7) **:** the skeleton supporting frame of an elevator car and its attached guide shoes and cable beam **4 slings** *pl* **:** the middle part of a ship's yard **5 a :** a piece of wire with a handle at each end used for cutting potter's clay
[4]**sling** \"\ *vt* **slung; slung; slinging; slings 1 a :** to place in a sling for hoisting or lowering ⟨the load must be carefully *slung* if it is to be safely hoisted⟩ **b :** to move by slings ⟨~ a cask⟩ **2 :** to suspend by or as if by a sling ⟨~ a scaffold from a roof⟩ **3 :** to cut (clay for potting) with a sling **4 :** to suspend (a yard) from the masthead of an old-time war vessel by extra chains on going into action
[5]**sling** \"\ *adj* **1 :** attached to or suspended in or from a sling ⟨a ~ wagon⟩ ⟨wearing an alligator ~ bag over her shoulder⟩ **2 :** designed to be worn thrown loosely over the shoulders ⟨a ~ cape⟩
[6]**sling** \"\ *n* -s [origin unknown] **:** an alcoholic drink usu. made of whiskey, brandy, or esp. gin with plain or carbonated water, sugar, and sometimes bitters and often garnished with lemon or lime peel if cold or dusted with nutmeg if hot ⟨gin ~⟩ ⟨rum ~⟩
[7]**sling** \"\ *vi* **:** to drink slings
[8]**sling** \"\ *n* [fr. native name in Tibet, prob. modif. of *Sining, Hsining*, city of west central China, important trade station on route to Lhasa] **:** an Indian cloth of fine goat's wool
slingball \ˈ=ˌ=\ *n* [[3]*sling*] **:** a missile hurled from a sling
slingboard \ˈ=ˌ=\ *n* [[5]*sling*] **:** a strong wood floor to which ropes are attached at the corners so that it can be lifted by a ship's winch in handling cargo
sling cart *n* [[3]*sling*] **:** a cart to transport heavy loads in which the load is suspended by a chain attached to the axletree
sling chair *n* [[3]*sling*] **:** a chair formed of a metal or wooden frame to which a piece of canvas, leather, or other flexible material is loosely fitted

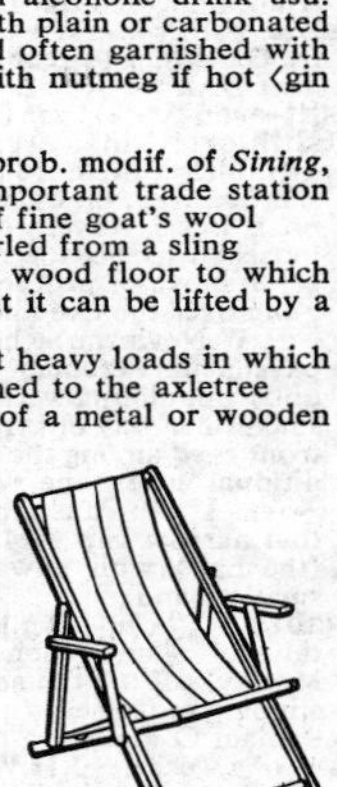

sling chair

sling dog *n* [[3]*sling*] **1 :** DOG 3b **2 sling dogs** *pl* **:** a pair of such dogs or crampons with the attached chain or rope — called also *sling*
slinge \ˈslinj\ *vi* -ED/-ING/-S [origin unknown] *dial Brit* **:** to hang around **:** LOAF
[1]**sling·er** \ˈsliŋə(r)\ *n* -s [ME, fr. *slingen* to sling, hurl + *-er*] **:** one that slings or uses a sling as a weapon; *esp* **:** a soldier of former times armed with a sling
[2]**slinger** \"\ *n* [[4]*sling* + *-er*] **1 :** one that uses a sling (as to support, hoist, or carry); *esp* **:** a workman that attaches slings to articles for hoisting **:** RIGGER **2 :** a device for centrifugally throwing oil into a bearing and usu. also for keeping dirt from getting into it
slinger ring *n* [[2]*slinger*] **:** a tubular ring fitted round the propeller hub of an airplane through which a spray of antifreeze solution is spread by centrifugal force over the propeller blades to prevent formation of ice
slinging *n* -s [fr. gerund of [4]*sling*] **:** a charge for attaching slings to a cargo
sling·man \ˈsliŋmən\ *n, pl* **slingmen** [[3]*sling* + *man*] **1** *archaic* **:** SLINGER **2 :** CRANE FOLLOWER
sling psychrometer *n* [[3]*sling*] **:** a psychrometer that can be whirled in the air until the reading of the wet-bulb thermometer reaches a constant value
sling pump *or* **sling-back pump** *also* **sling** *n* -s **:** a woman's shoe with a sling across the back and usu. an open toe
sling rope *n* **:** a rope used in fastening the pack on a pack animal
slings *pres 3d sing of* SLING, *pl of* SLING
slingshot \ˈ=ˌ=\ *n* [[1]*sling* + *shot*] **:** a forked stick with an elastic band attached that shoots small pellets (as pebbles or beans) and is used esp. by small boys in play and hunting **2 :** SLING 1a

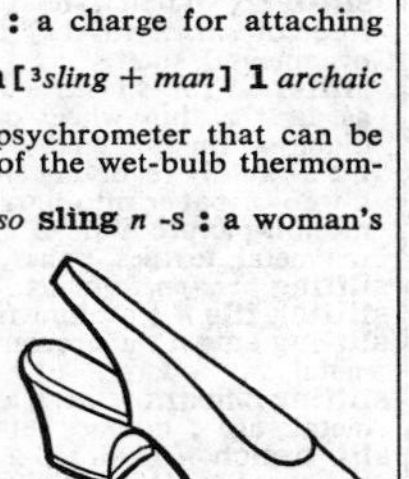

sling pump

slings·man \ˈsliŋzmən\ *n, pl* **slingsmen** [*sling's* (poss. of [3]*sling*) + *man*] **:** SLINGER
sling stay *n* [[3]*sling*] **:** any of the stay rods from which a crown bar of a steam boiler is suspended
slingstone \ˈ=ˌ=\ *n* [ME, fr. [3]*sling* + *stone*] **:** a stone to be thrown from a sling
sling strap *n* [[3]*sling*] **1 :** any of several long straps attached to a packsaddle for fastening the pack **2 :** SLING 3a (3)
sling unloader *n* **:** a hay unloader consisting of a rope sling which is laid on a wagon rack in advance, on which the hay is placed, and the ends of which in unloading are pulled together so that the entire load of hay may be lifted and transported (as by block and tackle) to the mow or stack
[1]**slink** \ˈsliŋk\ *vb* **slunk** \ˈsləŋk\ *or chiefly dial* **slinked** *or archaic* **slank** \ˈslaŋk\ **slunk; slinking; slinks** [ME *slinken*, fr. OE *slincan* to creep, crawl; akin to OSw *slinka* to creep, slink, MD *slinken* to sag, OE *slingan* to creep — more at SLING] *vi* **:** to go or move stealthily or furtively (as in fear, shame, sneaking) **:** creep or steal along or away **:** retire ignominiously ⟨~ behind an enemy⟩ ⟨*slunk* into a corner⟩ ~ *vt* **1 :** to give premature birth to — used esp. of a domestic animal ⟨a cow that ~*s* her calf⟩ **2 :** to move (as one's eyes) in a slinking manner **syn** see LURK
[2]**slink** \"\ *n* -s **1 a :** the young of an animal brought forth prematurely; *esp* **:** a calf brought forth before its time **b :** the flesh or skin of such a calf **2** *chiefly dial* **a :** an underdeveloped or undernourished creature **:** WEAKLING **b :** a slinking cowardly person **:** SNEAK **3 :** a stealthy slinking movement or pace ⟨a ~ of the eye⟩
[3]**slink** \"\ *adj* [[2]*slink*] **1 a :** born prematurely or abortively ⟨a ~ calf⟩ **b :** derived from a prematurely born animal ⟨~ meat⟩ **2** *chiefly dial* **:** starved looking **:** THIN, SCRAWNY
slink·er \-kə(r)\ *n* -s **:** one that slinks: as **a :** an animal (as a cow) that gives birth prematurely; *esp* **:** one that does so habitually **b :** LOAFER, SHIRKER, SLACKER
slink·i·ly \ˈsliŋkəlē\ *adv* **:** in a slinky manner
slink·i·ness \-kēnəs\ *n* -ES **:** the quality or state of being slinky
slink·ing·ly *adv* [*slinking* (pres. part. of [1]*slink*) + *-ly*] **:** in a slinking manner **:** so as to slink or seem to slink
slink lamb *n* [[3]*slink*] **:** a skin from a stillborn or a very young lamb
slinkskin \ˈ=ˌ=\ *n* [[2]*slink* + *skin*] **:** leather made from the skin of a slink
slinkweed \ˈ=ˌ=\ *n* [[1]*slink* + *weed*; fr. the belief that it causes cows to miscarry] **1 :** CARDINAL FLOWER **2 :** SWAMP LOOSESTRIFE
[1]**slinky** \ˈsliŋkē, -ki\ *adj* -ER/-EST [[2]*slink* + *-y*] *chiefly dial* **:** SLINK 2
[2]**slinky** \"\ *adj* -ER/-EST [[1]*slink* + *-y*] **1 :** characterized by slinking **:** stealthily quiet ⟨~ movements⟩ **2 :** sleek and sinuous in outline ⟨a ~ figure⟩; *esp* **:** following the lines of the figure in a gracefully flowing manner — used of woman's clothing ⟨a ~ evening gown⟩
[1]**slip** \ˈslip\ *vb* **slipped** *or archaic* **slipt** \ˈslipt\ **slipped** *or archaic* **slipt; slipping; slips** [ME *slippen*, fr. MD or MLG; akin to OHG *slipfen*, *slifan* to glide, slip, ON *sleipr* slippery, Gk *olibros* slippery, *leios* smooth — more at LIME] *vi* **1 a :** to move with a sliding motion ⟨he opened the door and she *slipped* under the wheel —Hamilton Basso⟩ ⟨the red rim of the sun ~*s* out of the sea —Richard Thruelsen⟩ **:** go or pass smoothly and easily ⟨let his mind ~ automatically into the trading routine —Walter O'Meara⟩ **b :** to move quietly and cautiously **:** go stealthily so as to escape notice **:** GLIDE, STEAL ⟨peeped out, saw no one, and thinking himself secure, *slipped* out into the road —David Garnett⟩ ⟨*slipped* from a doorway and followed him —T.M.Johnson⟩ **c :** to elapse quickly and smoothly **:** pass imperceptibly ⟨could see millions of years *slipping* by and the earth spinning still more dizzily —Waldemar Kaempffert⟩ **2 a** (1) **:** to escape from one's mind or consciousness ⟨lately, things seem to ~ away from me —Lenard Kaufman⟩ (2) **:** to become uttered through inadvertence or negligence ⟨her name *slipped* from his lips —Agnes S. Turnbull⟩ **b :** to pass quickly or easily away **:** become lost **:** ESCAPE ⟨the power of the upper classes to act as sole arbiters of taste and fashion was *slipping* from them —Jacquetta & Christopher Hawkes⟩ ⟨the money *slipped* through his fingers⟩ **3 :** to fall into error or fault **:** LAPSE ⟨he is most orthodox and rarely ~*s* —G.C.Sellery⟩ ⟨sometimes ~*s* into rather dreadful puns and hackneyed language —C.K.Kluckhohn⟩ **4 a** (1) **:** to slide out of place or away from a support or one's grasp **:** fall or change direction by sliding ⟨the books *slipped* to the floor⟩ ⟨the chisel *slipped* and cut his hand⟩ (2) **:** to undergo a slip ⟨the younger rock ~*s* from time to time, as some earth movement takes place —*Amer. Guide Series: Wash.*⟩ (3) *of a crystal* **:** to undergo internal sliding along a particular plane **b :** to slide on or down a slippery surface so as to fall or endanger one's balance ⟨had hurt his elbow through dropping his stick and *slipping* downstairs —Arnold Bennett⟩ **c :** to flow smoothly ⟨a gentle stream *slipping* down the face of the cliff —John Muir †1914⟩ **5 :** to get speedily or easily into or out of an article of clothing or wear ⟨began *slipping* into a pair of hip boots —*Buick Mag.*⟩ ⟨*slipped* into his coat⟩ **6 :** to let go of an anchor by letting the cable run overboard ⟨the captain gave the order to ~⟩ **7 a :** to suffer a gradual loss of one's health or capacities **:** DETERIORATE ⟨has *slipped* badly since his last illness⟩ **b :** to suffer a falling off in one's power, standing, or reputation ⟨more scared when he was successful than when he began to ~ —Delmore Schwartz⟩ **c :** to fall off from a standard or accustomed level by degrees **:** DECLINE ⟨as costs and prices rise, sales in some lines will ~ —*Time*⟩ **8 a :** to move the head or body quickly to either side to avoid being hit (as by an opponent's fist) **b :** SIDESLIP ~ *vt* **1 :** to cause to move easily and smoothly **:** SLIDE ⟨*slipped* a little mirror from her handbag —Willa Cather⟩ ⟨~*s* an airplane through openings in drifting clouds —William Beebe⟩ **2 a :** to get away from **:** ELUDE, EVADE ⟨*slipped* his pursuers⟩ **b :** to free oneself from **:** get out of ⟨his horse, having *slipped* the bridle —*Amer. Guide Series: Conn.*⟩ ⟨*slipped* the formal bonds that have held his comedy in restraint —Irving Kolodin⟩ **c :** to escape from (one's memory or notice) ⟨the appointment *slipped* his memory⟩ ⟨was so absorbed in his thoughts that the approaching storm *slipped* his attention⟩ **3 :** CAST, SHED ⟨the snake *slipped* its skin⟩ **4 a** *archaic* **:** NEGLECT, OVERLOOK — sometimes used with *over* **b :** to pass over or set aside **:** leave out of account or consideration **:** OMIT ⟨had *slipped* our claim until another age —Shak.⟩ **c** *obs* **:** to let (an appointed time) go by ⟨did command me to call timely on him; I have almost *slipped* the hour —Shak.⟩ **5 :** to put (a garment) hastily or carelessly — usu. used with *on* ⟨~ on a coat⟩ **6 :** to utter inadvertently ⟨never once did he ~ even the name of . . . that town —Will Irwin⟩ **7 a :** to let loose from a restraining leash or grasp ⟨the puppies were *slipped* and off they tore —*Manchester Guardian Weekly*⟩ **b :** to cause to slip open **:** RELEASE, UNDO ⟨*slipped* the knots that bound him⟩ ⟨in the darkness he *slipped* the night lock and went out —James Jones⟩ **c :** to loosen one's grip on or connection with **:** let go of ⟨*slipped* her lines and began the final leg of her homeward journey —*Crowsnest*⟩ ⟨with her tug *slipped*, she moved at gathering speed into the dark, open sea —J.E.Macdonnell⟩ **d :** to disengage from (an anchor) instead of hauling in ⟨ships began *slipping* their anchors, but her skipper . . . wouldn't ~ his —Max Hunn⟩ **:** get free of (an anchor cable) ⟨*slipped* its cable and made a run for the open sea⟩ **e** *Brit* **:** to detach (a slip carriage) en route ⟨knows all the stations where the train stops or where carriages are *slipped* —Bertrand Russell⟩ **8 a :** to insert, place, or pass quietly or secretly ⟨*slipped* the letter into his pocket when no one was looking⟩ ⟨the traditional paper *slipped* quietly into a learned journal —*Atlantic*⟩ ⟨*slipping* a wink to his brother —L.C.Douglas⟩ **b :** to give or pay on the sly ⟨*slipped* some money to the chief of police —Emmett Kelly⟩ **9** *of a domestic animal* **:** to give birth to prematurely **:** ABORT ⟨some cows ~ their calves in the early stages of pregnancy —*New Zealand Jour. of Agric.*⟩ **10 :** DISLOCATE ⟨*slipped* his shoulder⟩ **:** suffer the slipping of (one's foot) ⟨*slipped* his foot on the patch of oil and fell⟩ **11 :** PALM ⟨~ a card⟩ **12 a :** to transfer (a stitch) from one needle to another without working a stitch therein — compare DECREASE *vt* 2 **b** [*slip stitch*] **:** to sew (something) with slip stitches **13 a :** to avoid (a punch) by moving the body or head quickly to one side ⟨couldn't believe that he relied on speed of eye and head to ~ such punches —A.J.Liebling⟩ **b :** to cause (a descending parachute) to glide in a particular direction by pulling down on suspension lines on the side toward the desired direction so as to spill air out of the opposite side of the canopy — **slip a cog :** to make a mistake — **slip one's trolley** *slang* **:** to lose one's sanity **:** act irrationally — **slip something over :** to foist something on another **:** get the better of another by trickery or taking him unawares
[2]**slip** \"\ *n* -s [ME *slippe*, fr. *slippen* to slip] **1 a** (1) **:** a sloping ramp (as of stone) extending out into the water far enough to serve as a landing place for ships (2) **:** an inclined plane on which a ship is built or upon which it is hauled for repair (3) **:** a ship's berth between two piers or wharves **b :** a narrow passageway; *specif* **:** a mountain pass **:** DEFILE **2 :** the act or an instance of slipping out or away **:** secret or hurried departure, escape, or evasion ⟨under cover of night, gave his enemy the ~ and rejoined his convoy —Edward Breck⟩ **3 a :** a mistake in judgment, policy, or procedure **:** BLUNDER ⟨a ~ of presidential timing —*Time*⟩ ⟨one of the ~*s* a wise man sometimes makes —F.L.Mott⟩ **b :** a false step **:** a usu. slight offense or misdeed ⟨make a slight moral ~ — tell a lie, for instance, or smuggle a silk dress through the customhouse —O.W.Holmes †1894⟩ **c :** an unintentional and trivial mistake or fault **:** ERROR, LAPSE ⟨scan the purely mathematical reasoning to make sure that there are no mere ~*s* in it —A.N.Whitehead⟩ ⟨a ~ of the tongue⟩ **4 :** a leash or lead by which a dog is held and which is so made that it can be quickly slipped **5 a :** the act or an instance of slipping down or out of place or control ⟨a ~ on the ice⟩ **:** a sudden mishap ⟨many a ~ between the cup and the lip⟩ **b :** a movement dislocating the parts of a rock mass **:** the result of such a movement or a joint plane on which such a movement has taken place **:** a fault usu. of slight displacement; *specif* **:** one of the components of a fault movement that is confined to the plane of the fault **:** the displacement itself measured in a fault plane — see DIP SLIP, STRIKE SLIP, TOTAL SLIP **c :** displacement of one part of a crystal with respect to another along a particular plane — called also *slippage* **d :** a fall from some level or standard **:** DECLINE ⟨a ~ in stock prices⟩ **6 :** a garment or covering that slips on easily: as **a :** an undergarment made in dress lengths with shoulder straps or in skirt lengths as petticoats **b** *dial Brit* **:** a child's pinafore **c** *chiefly Brit* **:** BATHING SUIT **d :** a cloth covering for a pillow **:** PILLOWCASE **7 a slips** *pl, archaic* **:** the portions of the wings of a theater from which the scenes are slipped into place and where the actors stand just before their entrances **b** *Brit* **:** the sides of the upper gallery of a theater **8 a :** one of several cricket fielders positioned on the off side of the wicketkeeper and behind point **b slips** *n pl but sing in constr* **:** the part of the field in which the slips are placed — see CRICKET illustration **9 a :** the motion of the center of resistance of the float of a paddle wheel or the blade of an oar through the water horizontally; *also* **:** the difference between a ship's actual speed and the speed which it would have if the propeller worked in a solid **b** (1) **:** retrograde movement of a belt on a pulley or vice versa that is in excess of the movement due to expansion and contraction of the belt as its tension varies — compare CREEP 5b (2) **:** the sliding movement of a link relative to a link block that is due to swinging of the link (3) **:** relative motion of parts (as of a clutch or coupling) of a mechanism designed to have none **c :** the ratio of the difference between the operating and synchronous speed of an induction motor **d** (1) **:** a flow of fluid adjacent to a conduit wall that ceases to be laminar and slides along the surface as if it were a solid (2) **:** the amount of leakage past the piston and valves of a pump or the impellers of a blower usu. expressed as a percentage of the nominal flow **e :** the difference between the effective pitch of an airplane propeller and its mean geometrical pitch usu. expressed as a percentage of the latter **f :** a leakage of gas past the rotor of a gas meter **10 :** one of the projecting ends of the cords with which a book is sewed that are used to fasten the book to its covering boards **11 :** noncontagious abortion of a domestic animal ⟨this type of cow would breed itself out because of ~*s* and deaths in early spring —*New Zealand Jour. of Agric.*⟩ **12 a :** a disposition or tendency to slip easily ⟨good ~ is required of a plastic film to facilitate bag making —Walter Egan⟩ **b :** the quality of a paint or enamel that permits easy application with a brush **13 a :** SIDESLIP **b :** the act or an instance of slipping a parachute **14 :** CHASSÉ 1 **syn** see ERROR, WHARF
[3]**slip** \"\ *adj* [[1]*slip*] **1 a :** operating by slipping or sliding ⟨a ~ bar⟩ **b :** DETACHABLE ⟨a ~ compartment⟩ **2 :** having a slipknot **:** operated by means of a slipknot ⟨a ~ cord⟩ **3 :** capable of being released quickly ⟨a ~ bolt⟩
[4]**slip** \"\ *n* -s [ME *slippe*, prob. fr. MD and MLG, split, slit, flap of a garment] **1 a :** a small shoot or twig cut for planting or grafting **:** CUTTING, SCION **b :** DESCENDANT, OFFSPRING ⟨a lazy, conceited, wheyfaced ~ of gentility —Sir Walter Scott⟩ **c** (1) **:** a pineapple plant developing from a bud at the base of the fruit (2) **:** a rooted sweet potato sprout **2 a :** a long narrow strip of material ⟨~*s* of matchwood, bleached and split —Thomas Wood †1950⟩ ⟨a glass ~⟩ **b** (1) **:** a piece of paper used for a memorandum or record ⟨deposit ~⟩ ⟨sales ~⟩ (2) **:** a usu. small or narrow piece of paper used as an insert in a book or periodical ⟨a cancel ~⟩ ⟨an errata ~⟩ **c** (1) **:** a portion of the columns of a newspaper or other work struck off by itself (2) **:** GALLEY PROOF **3 a** (1) **:** a young and slender person ⟨a ~ of fourteen, just fresh from school —Richard Free⟩ (2) **:** a small and slender or undeveloped specimen — used with *of* ⟨a ~ of a girl⟩ ⟨a ~ of a boy⟩ ⟨an attractive little ~ of a coloratura soprano —Douglas Watt⟩ (3) *Austral* **:** a young pig **b :** a narrow stretch ⟨a thin ~ of gray beach and blue sea —May Sinclair⟩ **c :** a small or unusually narrow instance or example — used with *of* ⟨a ~ of a room which just held a trestle table and a couple of chairs —Edith C. Rivett⟩ ⟨in hard weather he stayed in his snug ~ of a house —Mary Webb⟩ **d :** a long seat or narrow pew in a church ⟨the interior has the old box pews, or ~*s*, each with an individual door —*Amer. Guide Series: Vt.*⟩ **4** *dial chiefly Eng* **:** a hank of yarn **5 :** an imperfectly castrated cockerel that is seldom able to reproduce but lacks the desirable meat-producing characteristics of the capon
[5]**slip** \"\ *vt* **slipped; slipped; slipping; slips 1 :** to write or note upon a slip ⟨this use of the word has been *slipped* and filed⟩ **2 :** to replace a book card in (a book) when returned to a library
[6]**slip** \"\ *vt* **slipped; slipped; slipping; slips** [ME *slippen* to cut off, prob. fr. MD or MLG, to split, slit] **:** to take cuttings from (a plant) **:** divide into slips ⟨~ a geranium⟩
[7]**slip** \"\ *n* -s [ME *slyp* slime, curds, fr. OE *slypa* slime, paste, pulp; akin to OE *slūpan* to slip — more at SLEEVE] **1 a :** a mixture of fine clay and water having the consistency of cream and used in the casting process, for the decoration of ceramic ware, or as a cement for handles and other applied parts **:** SLURRY **b :** enamel or glaze powdered and suspended in water and ready for application **2 :** SKINNING LOAM
[8]**slip** \"\ *vt* **slipped; slipped; slipping; slips 1 :** to convert into slip **2 :** to coat with slip
slipband \ˈ=ˌ=\ *n* [[2]*slip* + *band*] **:** one of the parallel lines on the crystal grains of a material stressed beyond its elastic limit that are visible only under a microscope and are produced by slippages inside the grains
slip bedding *n* **:** the contortion of the earth's stratification planes by slumping or related disturbance during sedimentation
slipboard \ˈ=ˌ=\ *n* [[3]*slip* + *board*] **:** a board sliding in grooves
slipbody \ˈ=ˌ=\ *n* [[2]*slip* + *body*] *Scot* **:** a loose bodice
slip carriage *or* **slip coach** *n* [[3]*slip*] *Brit* **:** a railroad coach or carriage designed to be detached at an intermediate station where the train does not stop
slipcase \ˈ=ˌ=\ *n* [[1]*slip* + *case*] **:** a protective container with one open end for books or other objects of similar shape and size — called also *slipcover*
slip casting *n* [[7]*slip*] **:** the process of forming clayware by pouring slip into plaster molds
slip coupling *n* [[3]*slip*] **1 :** a form of coupling adapted for use on slip carriages **2 :** a coupling designed to slip at heavy loads and thus relieve the duty on the driving unit
[1]**slipcover** \ˈ=ˌ=\ *n* [[1]*slip* + *cover*] **1 :** a cover that may be slipped off and on; *specif* **:** a protective or decorative usu. cloth or plastic covering for furniture (as sofas and chairs) that is usu. designed to fit closely **2 a :** a paper or fabric cover readily slipped on or off a book **:** JACKET **b :** SLIPCASE
[2]**slipcover** \"\ *vt* **:** to cover with a slipcover ⟨~ a chair in chintz⟩ ⟨an unusual decorative screen that you can ~ . . . to match the other fabric furnishings —*House Beautiful*⟩

slip decision *n* [⁴*slip*] **:** an advance or early and separate printing of a court's decision that is made available at or shortly after the time it is announced and before it is available in the regular court reports

¹slipe \'slīp\ *vt* -ED/-ING/-S [ME *slypen*] **1** *dial Brit* **:** to remove an outer covering from **:** PEEL, PARE, STRIP **2** *dial Brit* **:** to cut off **:** SLICE

²slipe \"\ *or* **slipe wool** *n* -S **:** pulled wool removed from skins by a lime process

³slipe \"\ *n* -S [ME, fr. MLG *slīpe, slēpe;* akin to MLG *slippen* to slip — more at SLIP] *dial Eng* **:** SLEIGH, SLED

⁴slipe \"\ *n* -S [origin unknown] *dial Brit & Midland* **:** a thin narrow strip esp. of land

slip face *n* [²*slip*] **:** the lee side of a dune where the slope approximates the angle of rest of loose sand that is generally about 33 degrees

slip form *n* [¹*slip*] **:** a form that can be moved slowly as concrete placing progresses and that is used extensively in building tall storage bins and occas. in widening existing pavements

slip friction *or* **slip friction clutch** *n* [²*slip*] **:** a friction clutch permitting slip when excessive power is transmitted

slip gage *n* [¹*slip*] **:** GAGE BLOCK

slip glaze *n* [⁷*slip*] **:** a glazing material applied in a liquid state before firing

slip grab *n* [³*slip*] **:** a pear-shaped link attachment for a whiffletree or evener that grips the skidding chain when the narrow end is down but otherwise permits the chain to slip — called also *grab link*

slip gun *n* **:** a single-action revolver having its trigger tied down or so altered that the piece may be fired by retracting the hammer and allowing it to fall

slip hook *n* **:** a hook so arranged as to be automatically or easily unhooked — called also *trip hook;* compare PELICAN HOOK

sliphorn \'ˌ=ˌ=\ *n* **:** TROMBONE

sliphouse \'ˌ=ˌ=\ *n* [⁷*slip*] **:** a building where slip is made

slip joint *n* [³*slip*] **1 a :** a telescopic joint between two parts (as a piece of tubing and packing material in a stuffing box) that permits the parts to move in a lengthwise direction **b :** a joint formed by slipping one part over another of nearly the same size and uniting the two (as by brazing) **2 :** a channel or groove cut in an existing wall to receive the ends of the brick of a new wall

slip–joint pliers *n pl but sing or pl in constr* **:** pliers having the joint adjustable to two positions so as to obtain either a wide or a narrow opening for the jaws

slip key *n* [⁴*slip*] **:** a cash register key that upon being depressed actuates a mechanism that certifies a sales slip usu. by printing on it pertinent information (as the number or amount of the sale)

slipknot \'ˌ=ˌ=\ *n* [³*slip*] **:** a knot that slips along the rope or line around which it is made; *esp* **:** one made by tying an overhand knot around the standing part of a rope

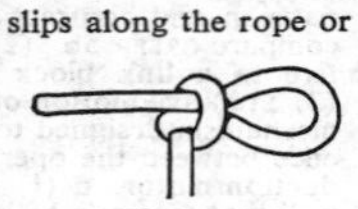
slipknot

slip–lasted \'ˌ=ˌ=ˌ=\ *adj* [¹*slip* + *lasted*, past part. of ⁷*last*] **:** manufactured by the California process — used of shoes

slip law *n* [⁴*slip*] **:** an early and separate print of a statute (as of the U. S. Congress) made available immediately after enactment and before the regular appearance of a permanent edition of collected statutes (as the statutes at large)

slip line *n* [²*slip*] **:** SLIPBAND

slip·man \'slipmən\ *n, pl* **slipmen 1 :** JACKER c(1) **2 :** one who operates a slip or wheeled scoop (as for moving earth or coal)

slip mortise *n* [¹*slip*] **:** a mortise cut through to the end of a piece

slipmouth \'ˌ=ˌ=\ *n* **:** any of numerous small compressed slimy bodied percoid fishes (genus *Leiognathus*) with highly protrusible mouths that are widely distributed in the Indian ocean and tropical parts of the Pacific and are often dried for food

slip noose *n* [³*slip*] **:** a noose with a slipknot

slip–off slope \'ˌ=ˌ=-\ *n* [¹*slip*] **:** a comparatively gentle slope often produced on the downstream face of a meander spur

slip–on \'ˌ=ˌ=\ *n* -S [¹*slip* + *on*] **:** an article of clothing that is easily slipped on or off: as **a :** a glove or shoe without fastenings **b :** a garment (as a girdle) that one steps into and pulls up **c :** PULLOVER

slipover \'ˌ=ˌ=ˌ=\ *n* -S **:** a garment or cover that slips over and off easily; *specif* **:** a sweater that is pulled on over the head

slip·page \'slipij, -pēj\ *n* -S [¹*slip* + *-age*] **1 :** the act or an instance of slipping out of place or failing to hold ⟨permits surgeon to tie with the finest of silk without ~ —*Armamentarium*⟩ ⟨the ~ of the tires on the ice⟩: as **a :** a shifting of threads in fabric when subjected to strain **b :** SLIP 5c **2 :** the act or an instance of falling off from a standard or level or the amount by which something falls off ⟨an indication of the ~ that can take place when training is let go —R.L.Moberly⟩: as **a** (1) **:** a loss in working (as in transmission of power) (2) **:** the difference between theoretical and actual output (as of power) **b** (1) **:** a lag in production of goods (2) **:** the difference between scheduled and actual production

slipped \'slipt\ *adj* [⁴*slip* + *-ed*] *of a heraldic plant* **:** having its stalk attached

slipped coat *n* [*slipped*, past part. of ⁸*slip* + *coat*] **:** FINISHING COAT

slipped disk *n* [*slipped* (past part. of ¹slip) + *disk*] **:** a protrusion of an intervertebral disk and its nucleus pulposus that produces pressure upon spinal nerves resulting in low back pain and often sciatic pain

slipped epiphysis *n* **:** EPIPHYSIOLYSIS

slipped tendon *also* **slipped tendon disease** *n* **:** perosis of poultry

slipped wing *n* **:** a fowl's wing that does not fold closely or that folds with some of the primaries extending below the secondaries

¹slip·per \'slipə(r)\ *adj* [ME *sliper, slipper* — more at SLIPPERY] **1** *chiefly dial* **:** SLIPPERY **2** *chiefly dial* **:** PLIANT, WILLOWY

²slipper \"\ *n* -S [ME, fr. *slippen* to slip + *-er*] **1 a :** a light shoe; *specif* **:** a low-cut shoe that is easily slipped on the foot, is held to the foot by means of the upper usu. without the aid of lacing or other fastening, and is made in various styles for either informal or formal indoor wear **b** *dial* **:** OXFORD 1 **2 a :** one that releases the leash of a hound in a coursing event **b :** ROSSER a **3 a :** SLIPPER BRAKE **b :** GIB 1 **4 :** something that is shaped like a slipper; *specif* **:** the lip of an orchid

³slipper \"\ *vb* -ED/-ING/-S *vt* **1 :** to strike with a slipper ⟨~*ed* him across the fingers⟩ **2 :** to put into slippers ⟨~*ed* her feet in bits of fluff —Truman Capote⟩ **~** *vi* **:** to walk in slippers **:** SHUFFLE ⟨~*ing* across the room from her bed —R.O.Bowen⟩

slipper animalcule *n* [²*slipper*] **:** a ciliated protozoan of the genus *Paramecium* (esp. *P. caudatum*) that is shaped somewhat like a slipper

slipper brake *n* **1 :** a metal plate or skid used under the wheel or pushed against the roadway or track to retard the motion of a vehicle **2 :** a metal plate slipped against a moving part of a machine to retard or stop its motion

slipper chair *n* **:** an often upholstered chair with short legs designed for bedroom use

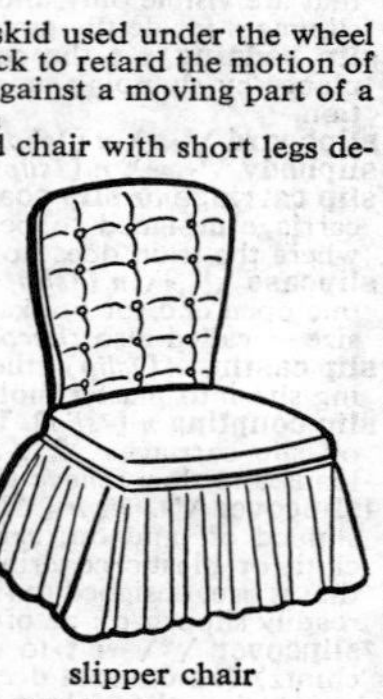
slipper chair

slip·pered \'slipə(r)d\ *adj* [²*slipper* + *-ed*] **1 :** provided with or wearing slippers ⟨the sixth age shifts into the lean and ~ pantaloon —Shak.⟩ **2 :** suggestive of or suitable to one wearing slippers **:** COMFORTABLE **:** RELAXED ⟨an easy, ~ prose —B.R.Redman⟩ ⟨the ~ ease of a small-town family man —*Time*⟩

slipperflower \'ˌ=ˌ=ˌ=\ *n* [²*slipper*] **1 :** SLIPPERWORT **2 :** SLIPPER PLANT

slipper foot *n* **:** SNAKE FOOT

slipper–foxed \'ˌ=ˌ=ˌ=\ *adj* [²*slipper* + *foxed*, past part. of *fox*] **:** having a vamp extending back over the heel and taking the place of the foxing or counter ⟨a *slipper-foxed* shoe⟩

slip·per·i·ly \'slip(ə)rəlē\ *adv* **:** in a slippery manner

slip·per·i·ness \-rēnəs, -rin-\ *n* -ES **:** the quality or state of being slippery

slipper limpet *or* **slipper shell** *n* [²*slipper*] **:** a mollusk of *Crepidula* or a related genus that is sometimes a serious pest of oyster beds

slipper plant *n* **1 :** a tropical American plant of the genus *Pedilanthus* having slipper-shaped involucres **2** *or* **slipper orchid :** LADY'S SLIPPER

slipper–root \'ˌ=ˌ=ˌ=\ *n* **:** a yellow lady's slipper (*Cypripedium parviflorum*)

slipper satin *n* **:** a strong heavy stiff satin with a high luster that is used chiefly for evening dresses and wraps and women's footwear

slipperweed \'ˌ=ˌ=ˌ=\ *n* **:** JEWELWEED

slipperwort \'ˌ=ˌ=ˌ=\ *n* **:** a plant of the genus *Calceolaria*

slip·pery \'slip(ə)rē, -ri\ *adj, sometimes* -ER/-EST [alter. (perh. influenced by LG *slipperig* slippery) of ME *sliper, slipper* slippery, fr. OE *slipor;* akin to MLG *slipper* slippery, OHG *sleffar*, MLG *slippen* to slip — more at SLIP (slide)] **1 a :** causing one to slide or fall down ⟨a new mountain road ~ with mud —Carleton Beals⟩ ⟨the ~ track made walking difficult —T.E. Lawrence⟩ **b :** tending to slide from the grasp **:** not easily held ⟨a running attack operated by half a dozen fast and ~ runners —Rogers Whitaker⟩ ⟨a ~ fabric⟩ ⟨a ~ fish⟩ **2 a :** not firmly fixed **:** UNCERTAIN, UNSTABLE ⟨to maintain his ~ position he needed more than cash, he needed prestige —G.W.Johnson⟩ **b :** not precise or fixed in meaning **:** AMBIGUOUS, ELUSIVE ⟨his style is so ~ that it is hard to tell what he really believes —J.N. Leonard⟩ ⟨the ~ term romanticism —M.W.Fishwick⟩ **3 a :** not to be trusted **:** SHIFTY, TRICKY ⟨those whom he knew to be ~ and double-faced —C.G.Bowers⟩ ⟨proved to be a ~ witness —Robert Coughlan⟩ **b :** marked by evasion, deceit, or trickery ⟨~ devices⟩ ⟨~ maneuvers⟩ **4 :** IMMORAL, WANTON ⟨~ looks of love —James Thomson †1748⟩

slippery dick *n* **:** a small brightly colored wrasse (*Halichoeres bivittatus*) of the warm western Atlantic

slippery elm *n* **1 a :** a No. American elm (*Ulmus rubra*) with rough leaves, short-pediceled flowers, and hard wood **b :** the wood of slippery elm **c :** the fragrant mucilaginous bark of slippery elm **2 :** FLANNELBUSH

slippery hitch *n* **:** a single hitch with the end doubled back under the standing part in such a way that a pull on the end releases the knot

slipperyroot \'ˌ=(ˌ=)ˌ=ˌ=\ *n* **:** a common comfrey (*Symphytum officinale*)

slippery slide *n* **:** SLIDE 5a(2)

slipping *pres part of* SLIP

slip plane *n* [²*slip*] **:** a plane surface through a crystal along which slip can take place under some conditions without apparently disrupting the crystal

slip proof *n* [⁴*slip*] **:** GALLEY PROOF

slip·py \'slipē, -pi\ *adj* -ER/-EST [¹*slip* + *-y*] **1 :** SLIPPERY ⟨the streets were still ~ and slimy from the rain —Bruce Marshall⟩ **2** *chiefly Brit* **:** ALERT, ALIVE, WIDE-AWAKE ⟨waiter, get this gentleman friend of mine a glass of port, and look ~ —E.F. Benson⟩

sliprail \'ˌ=ˌ=\ *n* [³*slip* + *rail*] *Austral* **:** one of a set of movable rails in a fence that can be taken out to form a gateway **:** DRAWBAR ⟨rode down toward the ~*s* of the scrubbers' paddock —F.D.Davison⟩

slip regulator *n* [²*slip*] **:** a usu. variable rheostat connected across the collector rings of a wound-rotor induction motor for regulating the speed or slip of the motor

slip ring *n* **:** COLLECTOR RING 1 — see MAGNETO illustration

slip rope *n* [³*slip*] **1 :** a rope by which a cable is secured preparatory to clearing hawse **2 :** a rope so fastened that it can easily and quickly be unfastened

slips \'slips\ *n pl but sing in constr* [fr. pl. of ²*slip*] **:** an accidental slipping of a taw from the hand of a marbles player as he is about to shoot

slip scraper *n* [³*slip*] **:** BUCK SCRAPER

slip seat *n* **:** a chair or settee seat either upholstered or made of rushes and built so as to rest in a rabbeted frame from which it can be lifted

slip seed *n* [⁴*slip*] **:** small sweet potatoes produced one year from cuttings for use as seed stock for the next year — compare CROP SEED

slip share *n* **:** a plowshare that is independent of the landside

slip sheet *n* [¹*slip*] **1 :** a sheet of paper placed between newly printed sheets to prevent offsetting **2 :** a protective sheet of paper placed between adjacent surfaces (as of bound books packed together)

slip–sheet \'ˌ=ˌ=\ *vt* [*slip sheet*] **1 :** to interleave (as printed sheets) with slip sheets **2 :** to protect (as books) with slip sheets

slip–shelled \'ˌ=ˌ=\ *adj* [³*slip*] **:** having a shell that slips off easily — used of nuts

slip·shod \'slip,shäd\ *adj* [¹*slip* + *shod*] **1 a :** wearing shoes or slippers that are loose or worn at the heel **b :** down at the heel **:** SHABBY ⟨~ shoes⟩ ⟨a small ~ girl in a dirty coarse apron —Charles Dickens⟩ **2 a :** careless and informal in style ⟨writes with the fluent ~ ease of a letter writer —*Edinburgh Rev.*⟩ **b :** not caring for or observant of exactness **:** lacking precision **:** INACCURATE ⟨is surprisingly ~ in his own use of words and his own thought —L.S.Woolf⟩ ⟨was at first a ~ observer . . . he had a positive distaste for exactitude —D.C. Peattie⟩ **c :** marked by indifference or carelessness **:** SLOVENLY ⟨these are days of fast, careless, ~ work —E.B.Barrett⟩ ⟨his own research is sketchy and frequently ~ —M.W.Straight⟩

syn SLOVENLY, UNKEMPT, DISHEVELED, SLOPPY: SLIPSHOD may imply an acceptance of the shabby, worn out, imperfect, unsound, or inexact that is careless, indifferent, or apathetic ⟨dressed hastily and roughly, in a *slipshod* way⟩ ⟨though facile, he had the conscientious craftsman's contempt for *slipshod* work —J.D.Spaeth⟩ SLOVENLY is a strong antonym for *neat* or *tidy* implying an extreme disorderly carelessness and lazy negligent indifference ⟨a long column — a *slovenly* column that marched irregularly and out of step —Kenneth Roberts⟩ ⟨she had become *slovenly* at home: she no longer reddened the hearth with pounded brick-dust, she no longer scrubbed the floor boards white and clean. Cobwebs hung in the corners —Lyle Saxon⟩ UNKEMPT implies negligent lack of ordinary care about grooming, smoothing, cleaning, refining, and maintaining ⟨a somewhat dilapidated house, badly in need of a new coat of paint. The garden round it was *unkempt* and weedy and the gate hung askew —Agatha Christie⟩ ⟨abandoned mills, general stores, and *unkempt* houses, an air of crumbling decadence prevailing in the sidehill settlement —*Amer. Guide Series: Vt.*⟩ DISHEVELED may suggest the ruffled disorder or disarray brought on by exertion, strenuous exercise, or coping with a series of exigent demands ⟨the white oxen of Clitumnus are loaded with gaudy flowers, and the dancing maidens are *disheveled* Maenads —J.A.Symonds⟩ SLOPPY may suggest a careless, loose, or messy abandon ⟨couldn't you even take the trouble to notice that you had a spot of soot on your nose tonight . . . why are you so *sloppy?* —Sinclair Lewis⟩

slip·shod·di·ness \-dēnəs\ *n* -ES [irreg. fr. *slipshod* + *-ness*] **:** SLIPSHODNESS

slip·shod·ness *n* -ES **:** the quality or state of being slipshod **:** SLOVENLINESS ⟨a combination of apparent ~ and actual precision —John Gunther⟩

slip sill *n* [³*slip*] **:** a sill that can be slipped into position between the jambs of an opening

slipskin \'ˌ=ˌ=\ *n* [¹*slip* + *skin*] **1 :** gray mold rot of grapes caused by a fungus of the genus *Botrytis* **2 :** a grape in which the skin slips readily from the pulp

slip·slop \'slip,släp\ *n* [redupl. of ²*slop*] **1** *archaic* **:** a watery food **:** a thin weak liquid **:** SLOPS **2** *archaic* **a :** a verbal blunder **:** MALAPROPISM **b :** a person given to making such blunders **3 :** shallow or meaningless talk or writing **:** TWADDLE ⟨the mass of ~ poured forth by the daily and weekly press —Frances Trollope⟩ ⟨the miserable, twaddling ~ that he is obliged to hear from and utter to her —W.M.Thackeray⟩ **4** [imit.] **:** a slip-slopping sound or movement ⟨the scurry of a hare, the ~ of my feet —J.A.Phillimore⟩

¹slip–slop \"\ *adj* [*slipslop*] **1** *archaic* **:** given to or marked by verbal blundering **2 :** lacking in solidity or content **:** INANE, WISHY-WASHY ⟨talked *slip-slop* commonplaces with them; they spoke of the country and the weather, and he of the city —Samuel Lover⟩

²slip–slop \"\ *vi* [imit.] **:** to move about in loose slippers or to make the flapping sound produced by or as if by such movement ⟨laid him in a crib and *slip-slopped* down to serve dinner —Anne Green⟩ ⟨his untidily shod feet *slip-slopping* on the wooden floor —Rafael Sabatini⟩

slipsole \'ˌ=ˌ=\ *n* [¹*slip* + *sole*] **1 :** a thin insole **2 :** a half sole inserted between the insole or welt and the outsole of a shoe to give additional height — called also *slip tap*

slipstick \'ˌ=ˌ=\ *n* [³*slip*] **:** SLIDE RULE

slip stitch *n* [¹*slip*] **1 :** a concealed stitch for sewing folded edges (as hems, facings, or appliqués) made by alternately running the needle inside the fold and picking up a thread or two from the body of the article **2 :** an unworked stitch; *esp* **:** a knitting stitch that is shifted from one needle to another without knitting in it

slip–stitch \'ˌ=ˌ=\ *vt* [*slip stitch*] **:** to sew with slip stitches ⟨*slip-stitch* facing to a garment⟩

slipstone \'ˌ=ˌ=\ *n* [¹*slip* + *stone*] **:** a small whetstone having a cross section like that of a wedge and usu. having one or both edges rounded

slip stopper *n* [²*slip*] **:** a cable stopper consisting of a short length of chain with a pelican hook at the end and intended to be used when the cable is let go suddenly

slipstream \'ˌ=ˌ=\ *n* [²*slip* + *stream*] **:** the stream of air driven aft by the propeller of an aircraft and having a velocity relative to the engine greater than that of the surrounding body of still air — called also *propeller race, race of the propeller*

slipstring \'ˌ=ˌ=\ *n* [¹*slip* + *string*] *archaic* **:** SCAPEGALLOWS

slip switch *n* [¹*slip*] **:** a crossing frog containing either one or two connecting tracks that serve as short turnouts

slipt *archaic past of* SLIP

slip tap *n* [¹*slip*] **:** SLIPSOLE 2

slip tongue *n* **:** a tongue that slips between two steel plates joining the fore hounds of a vehicle and into a stirrup supported under a crossbar with lengthwise movement of the tongue being prevented by a bolt that passes through holes in the tongue and steel plates

slip–tongue wheel *n* **:** a two-wheeled logging truck in which the load is suspended under an axle or arch and whose design is such that on a downgrade the end of the tongue slips out of a stirrup so as to let one end of the logs drop to the road and act as a brake

slip up *vi* [¹*slip* + *up*] **:** to make a mistake **:** BLUNDER ⟨*slipped up* in his calculations⟩

slipup \'ˌ=ˌ=\ *n* -S **:** the act or an instance of slipping up **:** MISTAKE ⟨through some ~ — a lost file, a technicality — I was to spend a few mistaken hours here —Andy Logan⟩

slipware \'ˌ=ˌ=\ *n* [⁷*slip*] **:** pottery coated with slip to improve the surface or change the color

slipway \'ˌ=ˌ=\ *n* [¹*slip*] **:** an inclined way: as **a :** one of the ways on which the cradle of a marine railway travels — usu. used in pl. **b :** BUILDING SLIP **c :** an inclined passageway in the stern of a whaling ship by which whales are hauled in

¹slit \'slit, *usu* -id·+V\ *vt* **slit; slit; slitting; slits** [ME *slitten;* akin to MHG *slitzen* to slit; akin to OE *slītan* to tear apart, OHG *slīzan*, ON *slīta*, Lith *skélti* to split — more at SHELL] **1 a :** to make a slit in **:** cut lengthwise **:** SLASH ⟨~ the huge envelope clumsily with the paper knife —Lawrence Durrell⟩ ⟨his two motorboats ~ the waters of the sound —Scott Fitzgerald⟩ **b :** to cut off or away **:** SEVER ⟨be his tongue ~ for his insolence —P.B.Shelley⟩ **2 :** to cut (as film or paper) into long narrow strips **syn** see CUT

²slit \"\ *n* -S [ME *slitte*, fr. *slitten* to slit] **:** a long narrow cut or opening ⟨a ~ in the jacket⟩ ⟨the window was no more than a ~ in the wall⟩: as **a :** a narrow opening in a dome or in the roof and sidewalls of an observing room through which a telescope is pointed at the celestial bodies **b :** a narrow usu. rectangular opening through which light or other emission is admitted (as to the collimator of a spectroscope) or through which it escapes (as from a black-body cavity) **c :** an aperture in the optical system of photographic sound recorders and reproducers that limits the height of the scanned area to less than a wavelength of the shortest wavelength signal to be recorded or reproduced

³slit \"\ *adj* **1 :** shaped like a slit **:** long and narrow ⟨fat-padded ~ eyes —Weston La Barre⟩ **2 :** having a slit ⟨a ~ skirt⟩ ⟨~ limpet⟩ **3 :** produced through a wide shallow opening formed at the free end of the tongue ⟨a ~ fricative such as \th\⟩ — compare GROOVE

⁴slit \"\ *vt* **slitted; slitted; slitting; slits :** to form into a slit **:** NARROW ⟨morning sunlight flooded in upon him, and he *slitted* his eyes against the glare —J.R.Ullman⟩

slit deal *n* [fr. past part. of ¹*slit*] **:** a deal board ⅝ of an inch thick — compare WHOLE DEAL

slit–drum \'ˌ=ˌ=\ *n* **:** a primitive drum orig. consisting of a tree trunk hollowed out like a boat and played by stamping

slite \'slīt\ *n* -S [fr. obs. *slite* to split, wear out, fr. ME *sliten*, fr. OE *slītan* to tear apart — more at SLIT] *dial Eng* **:** WEAR AND TEAR

slit–eyed \'ˌ=ˌ=\ *adj* [³*slit* + *eyed*] **:** having narrow eyes

¹slith·er \'slithə(r)\ *vb* **slithered; slithered; slithering** \-th(ə)riŋ\ **slithers** [ME *slideren, slitheren*, fr. OE *sliderian, slidrian*, freq. of *slīdan* to slide] *vi* **1 a :** to slide on or as if on a loose gravelly surface ⟨the sharp stones which were loosened as his toe caps ~*ed* over them —Fred Majdalany⟩ **b :** to move or proceed by slipping or sliding ⟨learnt to skate, ~*ing* over the five miles to and fro along the frozen . . . road —H.W.Nevinson⟩ ⟨horse-drawn sleds ~*ed* across the snowy pavement —Truman Capote⟩ **2 :** to walk or move in a sinuous undulating way **:** GLIDE ⟨a ~*ing* sinister creature who snakes her way out from her table —Leland Miles⟩ ⟨the brown trout ~*ed* among the shallow stones —W.C.Williams⟩ ⟨the traditional ticker tape ~*ed* down on the marching men —*Time*⟩ **~** *vt* **1 :** to cause to slide ⟨the wind had ~*ed* them through that narrow gap —Marguerite Lyon⟩ **2 :** to thin and taper (the hair) with upward strokes of a cutting edge along a small strand

²slither \"\ *n* -S **1 :** loose gravel **:** RUBBLE ⟨cascaded the great talus of ~ and reached the surf-belt of shingle —Christopher Morley⟩ **2 a :** the act or an instance of sliding **:** a gliding or slipping movement ⟨a ~ of his right foot on the wet pavement —Liam O'Flaherty⟩ ⟨was through the door with the smooth ~ of a weasel —J.H.Wheelwright⟩ **b :** a sound produced by or as if by a smooth gliding movement ⟨the soft ~ of the fountain in the sunk garden —Mary Austin⟩ ⟨heard the rush and ~ of breaking waves —William Beebe⟩

slith·ery \-th(ə)rē, -ri\ *adj* [¹*slither* + *-y*] **:** having a slippery surface, texture, or quality ⟨steep footpaths that are coated with ~ mud —Christopher Rand⟩ ⟨the ~ gloss of thick dust —Leslie Charteris⟩

slit lamp *n* [³*slit*] **:** a lamp for projecting a narrow beam of intense light into an eye to facilitate microscopic study (as of the conjunctiva or cornea)

slit·less \'slitləs\ *adj* **:** not having a slit ⟨a ~ spectroscope⟩

slitted *past of* SLIT

¹slit·ter \'slid·ə(r), -itə-\ *vt* -ED/-ING/-S [ME *sliteren, slitteren*, freq. of *slitten* to slit] **:** to cut the edge of (a garment) in ornamental slits

²slitter \"\ *n* -S [¹*slit* + *-er*] **1 :** a slitting machine or device: as **a :** a thin wheel of bronze or soft steel charged with diamond dust or emery for slitting or sawing precious stones **b :** a rapidly revolving sharpened disk for trimming or cutting a web of paper into narrower rolls **c :** a machine for slitting motion-picture film **2 :** an operator of a machine for slitting (as metal, textiles, paper, or plastics)

slitting *pres part of* SLIT

slitting file *n* **:** a blunt file of narrow lozenge section

slitting saw *n* **:** a circular saw or thin milling cutter for cutting metal

slitting shears *n pl* **:** a shearing machine for cutting sheet metal; *esp* **:** ROTARY SHEARS

slit trench *n* [³*slit*] **:** a usu. narrow and relatively shallow trench dug for individual protection during combat esp. against bomb and shell fragments — compare FOXHOLE

slitwork \'ˌ=ˌ=\ *n* [*slit* (past part. of ¹*slit*) + *work*] **:** thin boards used as sheathing

¹slive \'slīv\ *vt* -ED/-ING/-S [ME *sliven*, fr. (assumed) OE *slīfan* (whence *tōslīfan* to split); prob. akin to OE *slītan* to tear apart — more at SLIT] *dial chiefly Eng* **:** to slice off or cut through

2slive \"\ vi slove \'slōv\ slived; sliving; slives [obs. slive to cause to slip, slip (clothes) on, to slip away, fr. ME sliven, alter. of sleven, fr. OE slēfan to slip (clothes) on — more at SLEEVE] dial chiefly Eng : to move furtively : SIDLE

1sliv·er \'slivə(r), in sense 2 usu 'slīv-\ n -s [ME slivere, fr. sliven to slive + -ere -er] 1 a : a long slender piece cut or torn off : SPLINTER ⟨a piece of apple pie with a ~ of cheese on top —F.C.Othman⟩ ⟨was building up the fire with split logs and pine ~s —William Faulkner⟩ b : something that is small and narrow : FRAGMENT ⟨the initial quarrel over the ~s of land was intense —Foreign Policy Bull.⟩ ⟨a ~ of an apartment in an old-fashioned small hotel —Mollie Panter-Downes⟩ c : a piece of bait sliced from a small fish 2 a (1) : a loose soft untwisted strand or rope of textile fiber produced by a carding or combing machine and ready for drawing or roving (2) : a similar strand of wool fiber delivered by a carding machine and ready to be spun into yarn b : an untwisted strand of glass fibers produced from molten glass

2sliver \'slivə(r), 'slīv-\ vb -ED/-ING/-S vt 1 obs : to cut off in the form of a sliver ⟨slips of yew, ~ed in the moon's eclipse —Shak.⟩ 2 : to cut into slivers : reduce to slivers : SLICE, SPLINTER ⟨chopped the broccoli and ~ed the salad —Grace Reiten⟩ 3 : to cut slivers from (a fish) ⟨helped . . . to ~ porgies for the trawls —Sarah O. Jewett⟩ ~ vi : to become split into slivers ⟨the war decided that the United States should not ~ into two, three, or four fragments —Allan Nevins⟩

sliver lap n : cotton slivers combed into a wide strand and wound into a cylindrical roll

sliver lapper n [sliver lap + -er] : a textile machine for forming sliver laps; also : the operator of such a machine

sliv·o·vitz also **sliv·o·witz** or **sliv·o·vic** \'slivə,vits\ n -ES [Serbo-Croatian šljivovica, fr. šljiva, sliva plum; akin to Russ sliva plum — more at LIVID] : a dry usu. colorless plum brandy made esp. in Hungary and the Balkan countries

sliv·ver \'slivə(r)\ Scot var of SLOBBER

sloak var of SLOKE

sloa·nea \'slōnēə\ n, cap [NL, fr. Sir Hans Sloane †1753 Brit. naturalist] : a large genus of tropical timber trees (family Elaeocarpaceae) having alternate leaves, small apetalous flowers with numerous stamens, a spiny or hairy 4-valved capsule, and usu. very hard wood — see BREAKAX; compare IRONWOOD

sloat var of SLOTE

slob \'släb\ n -s [Ir slab, prob. of Scand origin; akin to Sw dial. slabb slime, mud — more at SLAB (mud)] 1 chiefly Irish a : MUD, MIRE, OOZE b : a tract of muddy ground; esp : 2FLAT 1a (2) 2 : a heavy sludge of sea ice 3 : a slack, ungainly, or common person : someone mean, rude, or undistinguished : BOOR, CLOD, VULGARIAN ⟨a bunch of ~s and stuffed shirts —H.A.Smith⟩ ⟨the translator who ignores or evades this responsibility is a ~ —Rolfe Humphries⟩

1slob·ber \'släbə(r)\ n -s [partly fr. ME slober mud, slush; partly fr. 2slobber; akin to MD slobbe slime, mud, mire, slobberen to walk through mud or mire, D slobber swill, slush and prob. to LG slubberen to sip, lap] 1 chiefly dial : a sloppy mess (as of rain and sleet or slush and mud) 2 : the slaver or drool of excessive salivation : spittle drooled from the mouth 3 : driveling, sloppy, or incoherent speech or expression : inarticulate utterance ⟨a mere helpless ~ of disconnected vowel noises —Henry James †1916⟩ ⟨some essays . . . I thought were ~, if that is worse than drool —O.W.Holmes †1935⟩ 4 slobbers \-z\ pl but usu sing in constr : excessive salivation; specif : more or less chronic drooling or salivation in rabbits usu. associated with excessive consumption of green feed but sometimes symptomatic of coccidiosis or of dental troubles

2slob·ber \"\ vb slobbered; slobbered; slobbering \-b(ə)riŋ\ slobbers [ME sloberen; akin to LG slubberen to sip, lap, sluf loose, slack, tired, OFris luf slack, tired, ON lūfa thick hair, MD lobbe thick underlip, Lith lūpa lip, slubnas slack, tired, drooping; basic meaning: slack, loose] vi 1 a : to let saliva fall or dribble from the mouth : DROOL, SLAVER ⟨bit . . . could cause a horse to ~ and bleed at the mouth —Bruce Siberts⟩ b : to let liquid spill or dribble from the mouth in eating or drinking 2 : to gush with effusive or unrestrained emotion or sentiment : indulge the feelings unchecked ⟨later writers ~ed over the mountains . . . with extensive extracts from the Lake poets —A.S.Pease⟩ ⟨when he reads the works of American historians . . . he can only ~ in abject frustration —C.M.Wilson⟩ ~ vt 1 a : to wet and smear with dribbling saliva or with food or drink spilled from the mouth ⟨the baby ~ed his bib⟩ b : to spill or let drip so as to smear or soil ⟨~ed the medicine on his nightclothes⟩ 2 a : to kiss very wetly or implant very juicy kisses on b : to utter or speak in a slurred, thick, or inarticulate way ⟨~ed one song out of his scraggy and ulcerous face —Robert Lynd⟩ 3 : to handle or perform in sloppy or slovenly fashion

slobberchops \'≈,≈\ n pl but sing or pl in constr [2slobber + chops (mouth)] : SLOBBERER

slob·ber·er \-bərə(r)\ n -s : one that slobbers

slob·ber·han·nes \,s(h)läbər'hänəs\ n -ES [G dial. schlabberhans, schlabberhannes sloppy eater, gossiper, fr. schlabbern to eat sloppily, slaver, gossip + Hans, Hannes, nickname for Johann, Johannes John — more at SLAVER] : a variation of the game of hearts in which the object is to avoid winning the first and last tricks and any trick containing the queen of clubs

slob·bery \'släb(ə)rē, -ri\ adj [ME slobery, fr. slober slobber + -y] 1 : MUDDY, SLUSHY, DIRTY ⟨a ~ and a dirty farm —Shak.⟩ 2 a : marked by drooling or slobbering b : marked by ungoverned or gushy sentimentality 3 : SLACK, SLOVENLY

slob·by \'släbē\ adj -ER/-EST [slob + -y] 1 : MUDDY 2 : SLOBBERY

slob land n 1 : muddy soil; esp : reclaimed alluvial land 2 : a tract of muddy soil

slob trout n : a trout from brackish water (as of an estuary)

1slock \'släk\ vt -ED/-ING/-S [ME sloken, of Scand origin; akin to ON slokinn extinguished, slokna to extinguish] dial Brit : QUENCH, DRENCH

2slock \"\ n -s [prob. fr. 1slock] chiefly Scot : DRINK, SWALLOW

3slock \"\ vt -ED/-ING/-S [ME slocken] dial Eng : ENTICE, LURE

slock·en \'släkən\ vt -ED/-ING/-S [ME slockenen, slokenen, of Scand origin; akin to ON slokna to extinguish, exhaust, loka to let hang loosely; akin to LG slokeren to hang loosely, MLG slūren to drag, trail — more at SLUR] chiefly Scot : QUENCH, EXTINGUISH

slod [alter. of earlier slode, fr. ME slood, fr. OE slād] dial past of SLIDE

sloe \'slō\ n -s [ME slo, fr. OE slāh, slā; akin to OHG slēha sloe, Sw slån sloe, L livēre to be blue — more at LIVID] 1 a : a small globose and pruinose dark-colored plum with astringent green flesh that is the fruit of the blackthorn and is used esp. for preserves and as a flavoring for liquors b : BLACKTHORN 1a 2 : any of various American wild plums 3 : BLACK HAW 1

sloe·ber·ry \'slō- — see BERRY\ n 1 : the fruit of the common juniper 2 : SLOE 1

sloebush or **sloetree** \'≈,≈\ n [sloebush fr. sloe + bush; sloetree fr. ME slotre, fr. slo sloe + tre tree — more at TREE] : BLACKTHORN 1a

sloe-eyed \'≈,≈\ adj 1 : having soft dark bluish or purplish black eyes 2 : having slanted eyes

sloe gin n : a sweet reddish liqueur consisting of grain spirits flavored chiefly with sloeberries from the blackthorn

1slog \'släg also -lȯg\ vb slogged; slogged; slogging; slogs [origin unknown] vt 1 a : to hit hard : BEAT b : DRIVE ⟨slogged his horse relentlessly on⟩ c (1) : to hit hard in cricket (2) : SCORE 2 a : to make (one's way) by dogged plodding (as in difficult terrain or in mud) b : to plod (one's way) perseveringly through a task or career esp. against difficulty, opposition, or adversity ⟨slogged his way steadily up through the business ranks⟩ ~ vi 1 : to plod heavily (as through mud) : tramp a long or arduous route ⟨slogged through the already softening drifts —Farley Mowat⟩ 2 : to work hard and steadily : PLUG ⟨been slogging away at this business for 15 years —Laurence Harvey⟩ syn see STRIKE

2slog \"\ n -s 1 a : a hard dogged march or tramp : a difficult or plodding advance b : a long drudgery of effort : hard plugging application ⟨that long central ~ of the war from Pearl Harbor to the invasion of Normandy —Geoffrey Crowther⟩ 2 : a hard hit at cricket

slo·gan \'slōgən\ n -s [alter. of earlier slogorn, fr. Gael sluagh-ghairm army cry, fr. sluagh army + gairm call] 1 a : a war cry or gathering word (as of a Highland clan in Scotland) : a rallying or battle cry b : a word or phrase used by a person or group to express a characteristic position or aim, a stand on a contested issue, or a goal of endeavor ⟨the whalemen's ~, "A dead whale or a stove boat" —Amer. Guide Series: Conn.⟩ ⟨a widespread decline of cognitive standards, exemplified, for example, in the popular ~ that "it all depends on the point of view" —T.M.Clarke⟩ ⟨years ago we repudiated the ~, "Peace at any price" —Laurence Sears⟩ 2 : a brief striking phrase used in advertising or promotion 3 a : a word or phrase imprinted on a piece of mail usu. with the cancellation as a commemorative or publicity device b : an advertising phrase imprinted on mail together with the postage by a postage meter

1slo·gan·eer \,slōgə'ni(ə)r\ n -s [slogan + -eer] : a coiner or user of slogans esp. for political or commercial purposes ⟨subtle ~s seeking to convert us to their views —H.G. Rickover⟩

2sloganeer \"\ vi -ED/-ING/-S : to phrase or disseminate a slogan in order to influence or stimulate thought or action

slo·gan·ize \'≈≈,nīz\ vt -ED/-ING/-S [slogan + -ize] : to cast in the form of a slogan : express tersely so as to induce action or instill opinion or belief ⟨scientists, to start a research program, must ~ it, must optimistically forecast great results from it, and report its progress in journalese —Science⟩

slog·ger \'slägə(r) also -lȯg-\ n -s [1slog + -er] : one that slogs: as a : PLODDER b : a hard-hitting pugilist or cricket batsman : SLUGGER c : a hard steady worker

1slogging n -s [fr. gerund of 1slog] 1 : PLODDING 2 : hard drudging work : PLUGGING ⟨it will require not merely general approval but desperately hard ~ at details in order to frame a practicable plan —Irish Statesman⟩

2slogging adj [fr. pres part. of 1slog] 1 : given to or marked by dogged hard work ⟨it is hard ~ work for the men in the field —K.W.Kuhne⟩ 2 : hard hitting : SLUGGING ⟨a ~ match⟩

slog·wood \'släg,≈, -lȯg-\ n [slog (perh. fr. 1slog) + wood] 1 : a West Indian timber tree (Beilschmiedia pendula) of the family Lauraceae 2 : the aromatic durable yellowish brown wood of the slogwood tree

slojd or **sloid** var of SLOYD

slo·ka \'shlōkə\ n -s [Skt śloka, lit., sound, fame, hymn, stanza; akin to śṛnoti he hears — more at LOUD] : a distich consisting of two lines of 16 syllables each or of four octosyllabic hemistichs that is the chief verse form of the Sanskrit epics

sloke or **sloak** \'s(h)lōk\ n -s [Ir sleabhac] 1 : any of various edible marine algae (as sea lettuce, red laver, and Irish moss) 2 : slime or scum in water

slok·en \'släkən\ var of SLOCKEN

1slom·mack \'sləmək, -läm-\ n -s [origin unknown] dial : an awkward, uncouth, or slovenly person : SLOB

2slommack \"\ vi -ED/-ING/-S dial : to be messy or ungainly

slom·macky \-kē\ adj, dial : repulsively untidy : MESSY

slone \'slōn\ n -s [prob. fr. ME slon, sloon, pl., sloes, fr. OE slān, pl. of slā sloe — more at SLOE] dial Eng : SLOE 1a

1sloom \'slüm\ n -s [ME slume, sloumbe — more at SLUMBER] dial Brit : a light sleep : DOZE, SLUMBER

2sloom \"\ vi -ED/-ING/-S [ME slumen, prob. fr. slume slumber] 1 dial Brit : DOZE, SLUMBER 2 dial Brit : to become weak and flaccid : DECAY, WASTE 3 dial Brit : to move or wander slowly or silently : DRIFT

sloomy \-mi\ adj, dial Brit : SLEEPY, SLUGGISH

1sloop \'slüp\ n -s [D sloep, prob. fr. F chaloupe — more at CHALOUPE] 1 : a fore-and-aft rigged boat with a single mast that is usu. stepped well forward and a single headsail jib — compare CUTTER 2 : SLOOP OF WAR 3 : LONGBOAT

2sloop \"\ n -s [origin unknown] 1 : a single sled or dray for supporting the front end of a log in hauling 2 : a pair of runners with bunks on which short logs may be loaded

3sloop \"\ vt -ED/-ING/-S : to haul (logs) down steep slopes on a dray or sloop

sloop·man \-mən\ n, pl sloopmen [1sloop + man] : a master or crewman of a sloop

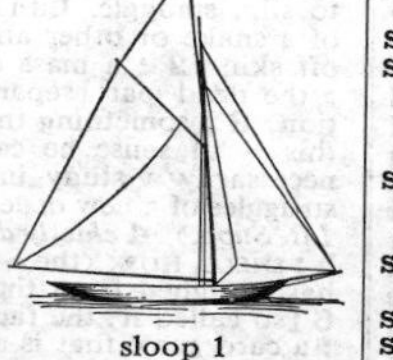

sloop 1

sloop of war 1 : a vessel rigged as a ship or as a brig or as a schooner and mounting from 10 to 32 guns 2 : a warship larger than a gunboat and carrying guns on one deck only 3 Brit : a small armed ship

sloosh \'slüsh\ n -ES [prob. alter. of 3slush] 1 : a lapping or sloshing sound 2 : an act of washing : WASH ⟨gave myself a good ~ with cold water —William Plomer⟩

sloot \'slüt\ n -s [D — more at SLUIT] chiefly Africa : SLUIT

1slop \'släp\ n -s [ME sloppe, prob. fr. MD slop; akin to OE oferslop surplice, stole, slop, ON sloppr slop and prob. to OE slūpan to slip — more at SLEEVE] 1 : a loose covering garment for workmen (as a smock, smock frock, apron, or overall) 2 a slops pl : the short full breeches worn by men of fashion in the late 16th century b dial : loose baggy trousers or a trouser leg — usu. used in pl. 3 a slops pl : clothing and other articles sold to sailors : a ship's small stores b : cheap ready-made clothing — usu. used in pl.

2slop \"\ n -s [ME sloppe, prob. fr. OE sloppe dung (as in cū-sloppe cowslip, lit., cow's dung); akin to OE slyppe, slypa slime, pulp, paste — more at SLIP] 1 : a mud puddle : soft mud : SLUSH 2 : thin tasteless drink or liquid food — usu. used in pl. ⟨the thin ~s provided on soup lines —Amer. Guide Series: Oregon⟩ ⟨had eaten the prison ~ without even suffering the gnawing pain of diarrhea —Douglass Cater⟩ 3 : the spilling or splashing of something liquid or moist or the material spilled or splashed ⟨washing up with ~s of water and bashing of plates —Richard Llewellyn⟩ ⟨shoves her glass in its own ~ over the bar —Brendan Gill⟩ 4 a (1) : food waste fed to animals : GARBAGE ⟨watching his pig eat ~s —P.E.Green⟩ (2) : a thin gruel for feeding animals ⟨a ~ of skim milk and bran⟩ b : excreted body waste — usu. used in pl. ⟨emptying other people's ~s —John Morrison⟩ 5 : STILLAGE 6 : sentimental or undiscerning effusiveness in speech or writing : GUSH

3slop \"\ vb slopped; slopped; slopping; slops vt 1 a : to spill (something) from a container b (1) : to splash (someone or something) with a liquid ⟨passing cars kept slopping him as they went through puddles⟩ (2) : to cause (a liquid) to splash ⟨slopped water from the pail he carried⟩ 2 : to slobber or spill liquid on ⟨beer drinkers kept slopping the bar⟩ 3 : to ladle, serve, or dish out clumsily or messily ⟨his red, swollen hands slopped oatmeal into our plates —Ruth Domino⟩ 4 : to eat or drink greedily or noisily : lap up : GOBBLE ⟨slopped up great tablespoonfuls of cereal —Hodding Carter⟩ ⟨so long as they could yap and ~ beer —Mickey Spillane⟩ 5 : to feed with slops ⟨slopped hogs . . . to get the money to go to college —Newsweek⟩ ~ vi 1 a : to plod or tramp in mud or slush ⟨slopped along muddy roads⟩ b : to slouch or lounge about in slack, slatternly, or slovenly style ⟨continental soldiers slopped about in a most unmilitary manner —Bruce Marshall⟩ ⟨for TV, they just ~ around in the living room —Newsweek⟩ 2 : to spill or splash over an edge (as of a container) ⟨carried the soup so unsteadily that it slopped over⟩ 3 : to go to excess in expression or conduct : be effusive or indiscriminate : GUSH — used with over ⟨when an ambitious feature writer ~s over —F.L.Mott⟩ 4 : to exceed, overrun, or overflow boundaries or limits — used with over ⟨my personal interests ~ over into related fields —Amer. Council of Learned Soc. Newsletter⟩ 5 a : to move or fit loosely ⟨the plug gage was worn and had begun to ~⟩ ⟨the spindle slopped in its bearing⟩ b : to make a rhythmic slapping sound (as of a loose-fitting machine part or of plashing waves) ⟨could hear his oars slopping in the rowlocks⟩

slop basin n, Brit : SLOP BOWL

slop book n : a record of clothing and supplies furnished to a British naval crew

slop bowl n : a basin or bowl for receiving the leavings of tea or coffee cups at the table

slop chest n : a store of clothing and personal requisites (as tobacco) carried on merchant ships for issue to the crew usu. as a charge against their wages

slop chute n 1 : a chute toward the rear of a ship for dumping garbage 2 slang : a tavern frequented by military men

slop culture n : a method of growing plants in which a nutrient solution is regularly poured over the surface of the sand or other medium in which the plants are growing, the surplus running through — compare DRIP CULTURE

1slope \'slōp\ adv [ME] archaic : in a sloping manner : ASLANT, OBLIQUELY

2slope \"\ adj : SLANTING, SLOPING ⟨stagger on the ~ decks —Alfred Tennyson⟩ — often used in combination ⟨slope-edged⟩ ⟨slope-sided⟩

3slope \"\ vb -ED/-ING/-S vi 1 : to move in or take an oblique direction : advance in or form a slanting line or course ⟨wide golden fans of light sloped down the canyons —Katharine N. Burt⟩ 2 : to incline from the horizontal or vertical : lie or fall in a slanting plane ⟨the bank sloped gently down to the water's edge —W.F.Davis⟩ 3 : GO, TRAVEL, WALK ⟨renounces her position and her inheritance, and ~s off into the night —Wolcott Gibbs⟩ ⟨pack and ~ out for cow country —C.T.Jackson⟩ ⟨eight dusty, hungry men sloped into the farm kitchen —Ronald Duncan⟩ ~ vt 1 a : to cause to incline or slant : give a slanting position or direction to : BEND ⟨the most obvious method of fitting a pattern to the body is to ~ or curve seam lines along body curves —Evelyn A. Mansfield⟩ b : to carry or place (a weapon) in a sloping position 2 : to form or make with a slanting shape or surface ⟨the same man will ~ his margin at one time to the right, at another time to the left —Stephen Paget⟩

4slope \"\ n -s 1 a : ground whose surface forms an angle with the plane of the horizon : a natural or artificial incline (as a hillside or terrace) : ACCLIVITY, DECLIVITY ⟨steep submarine ~s and steep-sided submarine canyons —F.P.Shepard⟩ b : a course on an open hillside prepared and graded for skiing — called also trail 2 : upward or downward slant or inclination : degree or extent of deviation from the horizontal or perpendicular ⟨the mountains reach 15,000 feet or higher, the average ~ of the flanking ranges being 60 degrees —Francis Kingdon-Ward⟩ 3 : the part of a continent descending toward and draining to a particular ocean ⟨the Pacific ~⟩ 4 : SLANT 2 5 a : the trigonometric tangent of the angle made by a straight line with the x-axis b : the derivative of a dependent variable y with respect to the independent variable x 6 : an inclined mine shaft; esp : the main incline in a colliery

slope angle n : the acute angle made by a meridional ray with the axis in a symmetrical optical system

slope arms n : a former command and position in the manual of arms with the piece carried as in left shoulder arms except that the muzzle was turned a little to the right or left

sloped adj [fr. past part. of 3slope] : having a slope : inclined from horizontal or perpendicular : formed or placed with a slant

slope-line approach n : a system of lights at an airport so arranged as to form a pair of sharply defined converging lines between which an airplane pilot may make a safe landing

slope·man \'slōpmən\ n, pl slopemen : a worker who grades slopes of excavations with hand tools

slop·er \-pə(r)\ n -s [3slope + -er] 1 : one that slopes: as a : a device for shaping the slopes of a railroad embankment b : a basic pattern for garment makers indicating the measurements for each size but having no fullness or design details 2 : SLOPEMAN

slope wash n 1 : SHEET EROSION 2 : earth material transported by sheet erosion

slope·ways \'≈,wāz\ adv : in a sloping position or direction : ASLANT

slopewise \'≈,≈\ adv, obs : SLOPEWAYS

sloping adj : having a slanting form, position, or direction : INCLINING, OBLIQUE

slop·ing·ly adv : in a sloping manner

slop jar n : a large pail often of china used variously in a house without running water to receive waste water from a washbowl, to collect the contents of chamber pots, or to serve as a chamber pot

slop-molding \'≈,≈≈\ n : the molding of brick in molds wet with water to prevent sticking in soft-mud process brickmaking — compare SAND-MOLDING

slop-over \'≈,≈≈\ n -s 1 : OVERFLOW 2 : EFFUSIVENESS, GUSH, SENTIMENTALITY

slop pail n : a pail for toilet or household slops

slopped adj [fr. past part. of 3slop] 1 : stained or wet with slops 2 : DRUNK, INTOXICATED ⟨~ to the eyes —Mitzi Martin⟩

slop·pi·ly \'släpəlē, -li\ adv : in a sloppy manner

slop·pi·ness \-pēnəs, -pin-\ n -ES : the quality or state of being sloppy

slopping pres part of SLOP

slop·py \'släpē, -pi\ adj -ER/-EST [2slop + -y] 1 a : muddy or slushy so as to spatter easily : SPLASHY ⟨those bogs can be great, ~ messes of treacle pudding in wet weather —Wynford Vaughan-Thomas⟩ ⟨the race was run over a ~ track —G.F.T. Ryall⟩ b : wet or smeared with slopped liquid or moist material : MESSY ⟨the oilcloth was sticky and ~ and smeared⟩ 2 of a garment : lacking formality or fastidiousness : ill fitted or worn carelessly 3 : feebly organized or directed : ill concerted or contrived : lacking firmness : CARELESS, LOOSE, SLOVENLY ⟨the misery of all those ~ words will fade as the correct, crisp sentence at last comes to her —L.B.Nicolson⟩ ⟨he was a ~ dresser —W.L.Gresham⟩ ⟨harden ~ thinking —Charlton Laird⟩ 4 : marked by excessive or indiscriminate sentimentality : EFFUSIVE, GUSHING, SOFT ⟨gives much of his time to ~ self-pity —E.F.Meagher⟩ 5 : disturbed with heavy waves : having a rough or choppy surface — used of lakes and seas ⟨hadn't the constitution to handle a heavy steering oar . . . in a ~ sea —R.S.Porteous⟩ 6 : DRUNK, INTOXICATED ⟨he had finished his fourth drink and was getting a little ~ —Edmund Wilson⟩ syn see SLIPSHOD

sloppy joe n 1 usu cap J : a man who is negligent of his clothes or personal appearance 2 : a loose baggy sweater for girls

slops pl of SLOP, pres 3d sing of SLOP

slopseller \'≈,≈≈\ n [1slop + seller] : a dealer in cheap ready-made clothing

slopshop \'≈,≈\ n : a slopseller's shop

slop sink n : a sink (as in a hospital) in which chamber pots and bedpans are emptied and washed and scrub water is thrown out

slopstone \'≈,≈\ n [2slop + stone] : a stone slab or table under a tap

slopwork \'≈,≈\ n [1slop + work] 1 a : the manufacture of cheap ready-made clothing b : slop clothing 2 [influenced in meaning by 2slop] : hasty slovenly work ⟨no ~ ever dropped from his pen —J.A.Froude⟩

slopworker \'≈,≈≈\ n : a worker making cheap ready-made clothing

slopy \'slōpē\ adj -ER/-EST [4slope + -y] : SLOPING

slorp \'slȯ(ə)rp\ dial Brit var of SLURP

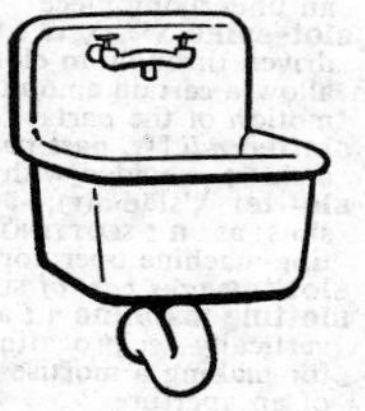

slop sink

1slosh \'släsh\ n -ES [prob. blend of 2slop and 1slush] 1 a : a wet sloppy condition underfoot : MUD, SLUSH b : a tramp through mud, slush, or puddles ⟨a half-mile ~ through a grove of sawed-off trees —Burgess Scott⟩ 2 : a thin poor drink 3 : the slap or splash of liquid (as waves or spilled water) ⟨listened to the ~ of the water against the barge —Willard Robertson⟩ 4 : a small quantity of liquid : DASH ⟨there seemed to be only a ~ of kerosine left⟩ 5 : BLOW, STROKE ⟨caught one chap a ~ on the ear he won't forget —Bruce Marshall⟩

2slosh \"\ vb -ED/-ING/-ES vi 1 : to slog or splash through water, mud, or slush : FLOUNDER ⟨rather than ~ over a soggy fairway —R.M.Hodesh⟩ 2 : to wander, walk, or loaf about 3 : to move with the lapping motion of a liquid : GURGLE, SPLASH ⟨his stomach ~ed with countless cups of coffee —K.M. Dodson⟩ ⟨the water ~ed around him, running down his legs —Bill Alcine⟩ ⟨saw about 20 gallons of water ~ing around the engine —Springfield (Mass.) Daily News⟩ ~ vt 1 a : to splash (something) about in liquid ⟨fills a pan with dry-cleaning fluid and ~es the hairpiece around in it —R.F.Wallace⟩ b : to splash (a liquid) about or on someone or something ⟨had finished systematically ~ing gasoline around —St. Clair

McKelway⟩ **c :** to splash (someone or something) with liquid ⟨workmen are ~*ing* down the open-air-café floors with water —Irwin Shaw⟩ **2 :** to pour hastily or clumsily ⟨was ~*ing* out the drinks behind the counter —Bruce Marshall⟩ **3 :** to gulp down **:** GUZZLE, SWILL ⟨the beer drinker would have to ~ down more than three quarts in less than three hours —*Newsweek*⟩ **4** *Brit* **:** BASH, PUNCH, SLAM, STRIKE ⟨you can't very well ~ a child —P.G.Wodehouse⟩

sloshy \-shē,-shi\ *adj* -ER/-EST **:** SLUSHY

¹slot \'slät, *usu* -äd·+V\ *n* -s [ME, fr. MD; akin to OFris & ON *slot* lock, bolt, OHG *sloz* lock, bolt, *sliozan* to lock, close — more at CLOSE] **1** *dial Eng* **:** a bolt or bar for fastening a door **2** *dial Eng* **:** SLAT

²slot \"\ *n* -s [ME, fr. MF *esclot*] **1** *chiefly Scot* **:** a hollow or depression; *specif* **:** the hollow running down the middle of the breast **2 a :** a long and narrow opening or groove **:** SLIT, NOTCH ⟨deliver mail through a ~ in a door⟩ ⟨the musket ~*s* in the fort's hand-hewn walls —J.H.Cutler⟩ ⟨information is coded by cutting ~*s* between adjacent vertical perforations —H.C.Zeisig & P.T.Martin⟩ ⟨spanner wrenches are made with one or two pins to fit into the holes or ~*s* of nuts, collars, sealing rings —T.G.Thompson & R.A.Peterson⟩ ⟨a coin ~ in a vending machine⟩ **b :** a narrow passage, enclosure, or space ⟨a ~ between islands⟩ ⟨they sat close together . . . in their ~ between the stacked, rattling ration boxes —Fred Majdalany⟩ **:** a small open compartment **:** PIGEONHOLE **c :** a passage of spanwise extent through an airplane wing located usu. near the leading edge and formed between a main and an auxiliary airfoil for improving the flow conditions over the wing at high angles of attack and thus increasing lift and delaying the stalling of the wing **3 :** a depression in the surface of an armature or stator of a dynamo-electric machine into which a portion of the winding is placed **4 a :** a place or a position in an organization, series, sequence, list, or program **:** NICHE ⟨athletes for athletic ~*s* on college teams —A.E.Lumley⟩ ⟨the chairman's ~⟩ ⟨her name was switched to the "contributing editors" ~ on the masthead —*Time*⟩ ⟨a TV show in the seven-o'clock ~⟩ **b :** the dealer's position in a gambling game **c** (1) **:** the position occupied by the copy editor on the inside of a horseshoe-shaped copydesk — compare RIM (2) **:** the position of copy editor **5** *slang* **:** SLOT MACHINE

³slot \"\ *vt* **slotted; slotted; slotting; slots 1 :** to cut a slot in **:** cut or shape by means of a slotting machine ⟨abrasive wheel . . . for cutting off or *slotting* any material —K.B. Lewis⟩ **2 :** to provide with slots ⟨the walls of the convent . . . were *slotted* for machine guns —Laurence Critchell⟩ ⟨a *slotted* collar⟩ **3 :** to pass through a slot ⟨velvet ribbon *slotted* through strands of wool —*Women's Wear Daily*⟩ **:** put into a slot

⁴slot \"\ *n, pl* **slot** [MF *esclot* horse's hoofprint, track, prob. of Scand origin; akin to ON *slōth* track] **1 :** the track of an animal (as a deer) **2 :** TRAIL

⁵slot \"\ *vt* **:** to follow the trail of **:** TRACK

slot bark graft *n* **:** a modified bark graft in which a wedge-shaped scion is inserted under a loosened tongue of bark on the stock

slot–drill \'⸗,⸗\ *vt* **:** to cut out (as a slot) with a traverse drill

slote *or* **sloat** \'slōt\ *n* -s [ME *sloot, slote* bolt, bar, crossbar, fr. MD *sloot, slot* slot — more at SLOT (bolt)] **:** any of several former devices for moving persons or scenery above or below a theater stage

sloth \'slȯth, -ō- *sometimes* -ä-; *sometimes* -ō- *for sense 1*, -ȯ- *or* -ä- *for sense 4*\ *n, pl* **sloths** \-ths,-thz\ [ME *slouthe, slowthe*, fr. *slou, slow* slow + *-the* -th — more at SLOW] **1 a :** disinclination to action or labor **:** SLUGGISHNESS, LAZINESS, IDLENESS, INDOLENCE ⟨the sun . . . is gentle, mellow, and ~ provoking —T.H.Fielding⟩ **b :** spiritual sluggishness and dejection that constitute one of the seven deadly sins **:** apathy and inactivity in the practice of virtue ⟨war may shake off . . . spiritual ~ —C.D.Lewis⟩ **2** *archaic* **:** SLOWNESS, TARDINESS **3 :** a pack of bears **4 a :** any of several slow-moving exclusively arboreal edentate mammals that inhabit tropical forests of So. and Central America, have esp. the front pair of limbs very long and provided with long curved claws, have rudimentary tail and external ears, have long coarse and crisp hair grayish or brownish in color but in the native habitat appearing more or less green and harmonizing with the moss and foliage due to a growth of commensal algae, have the habit of hanging from the branches back downward, and feed entirely on leaves, shoots, and fruits **b :** any of various related extinct edentates — see GROUND SLOTH **c :** any of various sluggish arboreal mammals (as the slow loris or the koala)

sloth bear *n* **:** a common bear (*Melursus labiatus*) of India and Ceylon that has long black hair and very large claws, a brownish muzzle, a white V-shaped mark on the breast, a long snout, and very mobile tongue and lips, that differs from ordinary bears in having very small molars and 4 instead of 6 upper incisors, and that feeds on fruit, insects, and honey

sloth·ful \-thfəl\ *adj* [ME *slotheful*, fr. *slouthe* sloth + *-ful*] **:** addicted to sloth **:** INACTIVE, SLUGGISH, INDOLENT ⟨not ~ anguish, is what you now require, but effort —Nathaniel Hawthorne⟩ ⟨municipal government was corrupt and ~ —H.A.Sinclair⟩ **syn** see LAZY

sloth·ful·ly \-fəlē, -li\ *adv* **:** in a slothful manner

sloth·ful·ness \-fəlnəs\ *n* -ES **:** the quality or state of being slothful ⟨that dim ~ of the spirit which a great sorrow . . . will bring —Mary Webb⟩

sloth monkey *n* **:** LORIS

slot·hound \'⸗,⸗\ *n* [⁴*slot* + *hound*] **:** SLEUTH 1

slot–lip aileron *n* **:** a combination of an aileron and a slot in which a small hinged flap controls the opening and closing of the slot

slot machine *n* **1 :** a machine (as a vending machine) whose operation is started by dropping a coin into a slot **2 :** a coin-operated gambling machine that pays off according to the matching of symbols on wheels spun by a handle — called also *one-armed bandit*

slot man *n* **:** a newspaper editor responsible for the layout of news items

slots *pl of* SLOT, *pres 3d sing of* SLOT

slot seam *n* **:** a seam with a decorative slit formed by bringing two folds together and stitching them onto an underlying piece

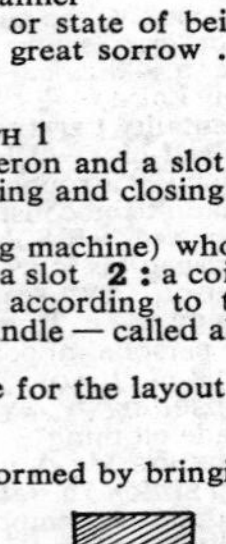

slot seam

slot–spike \'⸗,⸗\ *vt* **:** to secure by a spike driven through an elongated hole so as to allow a certain amount of relative endways motion of the parts

slotted *adj* [fr. past part. of ³*slot*] **:** having a slot **:** provided with slots

slot·ter \'släd·ə(r), -ätə-\ *n* -s **:** one that slots: as **a :** a SLOTTING MACHINE **b :** a slotting-machine operator

slotting *pres part of* SLOT

slotting machine *n* **:** a machine tool with a vertically reciprocating planing tool used for making a mortise or shaping the sides of an aperture

slot washer *n* **1 :** a lock washer having a slot cut in its edge to permit the driving of a nail or screw through it after the nut has been tightened to prevent the bolt or nut from turning **2 :** a washer slotted through from the outside to the central hole so that it may be inserted or removed with the bolt in place

slot winding *n* **:** a winding in which the wires are run in deep grooves (as in armatures of dynamos and motors)

sloubbie *usu cap, var of* SLUBBI

¹slouch \'slau̇ch\ *n* -ES [origin unknown] **1 a :** an awkward clownish fellow **:** LOUT **b :** one devoid of energy, ambition, or competence **:** an inefficient person **:** LOAFER, INCOMPETENT ⟨the ~ whom military drill has transformed into a man —Calvin Coolidge⟩ ⟨if you're only a clerk, you'll have to yield precedence to the ~ who holds the post of manager —M.F.A. Montagu⟩ — often used in negative constructions ⟨no ~ as a comedian⟩ ⟨no ~ at conversation⟩ ⟨a dancer who is no ~ on his feet⟩ **2 :** a gait or posture characterized by ungainly stooping of head and shoulders or undue relaxation of body muscles ⟨walked with shut lips and cold, cruel bearing, that had something of a ~ and a sneer in it —D.H.Lawrence⟩ ⟨all the regular prisoners had the same hollow-gutted ~ —R.O. Bowen⟩ **3 :** SLOUCH HAT **4 :** LAZINESS, SHIFTLESSNESS ⟨saw among them a good deal of ~ — mental, moral, and physical ~ —A.W.Long⟩

²slouch \"\ *adj* **1 :** DROOPING, PENDULOUS ⟨~ ears⟩ **2 :** SLOUCHING, SLOUCHY ⟨he slams ~ scribes —A.L.Hench⟩

³slouch \"\ *vb* -ED/-ING/-ES *vi* **1 :** to move, walk, stand, or sit with a slouch **:** assume or drop into a slouch **:** SLUMP ⟨the cur dog ~*ing* across the road —*Amer. Guide Series: Tenn.*⟩ ⟨~*ed* over to the telephone —S.H.Adams⟩ ⟨~*ed* behind the wheel —J.P.Marquand⟩ ⟨some of the others ~*ed* on the table around him —Vincent McHugh⟩ **2 :** to hang down flaccidly **:** DROOP ⟨a hat with a brim that ~*es*⟩ ~ *vt* **1 :** to cause to hang down or droop ⟨~ the hat over the eyes⟩ **2 :** to make in a slouching manner ⟨~*ed* his way along⟩ **3 :** to cause (the shoulders) to stoop ⟨his head drooped forward, his shoulders were ~*ed* down —O.E.Rölvaag⟩

⁴slouch \'slüch\ *n* -ES [prob. fr. ¹*slouch*] **:** a pipe by which an engine takes up water

slouch·er \'slau̇chə(r)\ *n* -s **:** one that slouches **:** SLOUCH ⟨modern man is an inveterate ~ . . . still rather a simian affair —*Time*⟩

slouch hat *n* **:** a soft usu. felt hat with a wide flexible brim

slouch·i·ly \'slau̇chəlē, -li\ *adv* **:** in a slouchy manner ⟨~ dressed⟩

slouch·i·ness \-chēnəs, -chin-\ *n* -ES **:** the quality or state of being slouchy

slouching *adj* [fr. pres. part. of ³*slouch*] **:** characterized by a slouch ⟨a tall but ~ figure standing at the bar —Richard Burke⟩ — **slouch·ing·ly** *adv*

slouchy \'slau̇chē, -chi\ *adj* -ER/-EST **1 :** slouching esp. in gait or posture **:** SLOVENLY ⟨the speaker presents a ~ and indifferent appearance —A.T.Weaver⟩ ⟨there is an indescribably constrained, ~, shabby look to all thus attired —Lafcadio Hearn⟩ **2 :** inefficient because lazy or unenergetic

¹slough \'slü, 'slau̇ *sometimes* 'sləf\ *n* -s [ME *slogh*, fr. OE *slōh*; akin to MHG *slouche* ditch] **1 a :** a place of deep mud or mire **:** MUDHOLE ⟨walk up steep rises in the road or help rescue horses stalled in a ~ —*Amer. Guide Series: N.J.*⟩ **b** *also* **slew** *or* **slue** \'slü\ (1) **:** a large wet or marshy place **:** SWAMP ⟨Indians are still living in primitive palm-thatched huts in the ~*s* of the Everglades —Merrill Folsom⟩ (2) **:** a small marshy place lying in a local depression of dry land (as on a prairie); *also* **:** a depression that becomes marshy or filled with water ⟨thousands of ~*s* and potholes went dry —I.N.Gabrielson⟩ **c** *also* **slew** *or* **slue** (1) **:** a side channel or inlet (as from a river) **:** a sluggish channel **:** a small backwater **:** BAYOU, POND ⟨lakes so close together and so intricately connected by rivers and ~*s* that they may almost be called continuous —Bernard DeVoto⟩ (2) **:** a creek in a marshland, tide flat, or bottomland ⟨a narrow tidal ~, over three miles long —*U. S. Board on Geog. Names Decisions*⟩ **2** *obs* **:** MUD, MIRE, OOZE **3 :** a state of moral degradation or spiritual dejection into which one sinks or from which one cannot free oneself **:** an engulfing depth of something (as sin or misery) **:** MORASS ⟨one of those tireless organizers who come to the rescue of doddering lodges and . . . bring them out of their ~*s* when all hope is gone —C.W. Ferguson⟩ ⟨high hopes ended in such a ~ of frustration, paralysis, and bitterness —W.W.Kaufmann⟩ ⟨music has just kept her nose above the ~ of realism, romance, and melodrama —Clive Bell⟩ ⟨the sooty ~ that submerges so many factory towns —*Amer. Guide Series: Vt.*⟩ ⟨a ~ of self-distrust⟩ ⟨a ~ of mediocrity⟩

²slough \"\ *vb* -ED/-ING/-S *vt* **1 :** to engulf in or as if in a slough **2** *slang* **:** ARREST, IMPRISON — usu. used with *in* or *up* ~ *vi* **:** to plod through mud ⟨lumberjacks ~*ing* through swampy lowlands —D.G.Hoffman⟩

³slough \'sləf\ *n* -s [ME *slughe, slouh*; akin to MHG *slūch* snake skin, hose, Norw *slo* fleshy part of a horn, D *sluiken* to slip, smuggle, Lith *šliaũžti* to glide, crawl] **1 :** the skin of a snake or other animal that sheds its skin; *esp* **:** the cast-off skin **2 :** a mass of dead tissue separating from an ulcer **:** the dead part separating from living tissues in mortification **3 :** something that may be shed or cast off ⟨when shall this ~ of sense be cast —A.E.Housman⟩ ⟨the book is . . . necessarily a study in sociology, concerning itself with the struggles of a new order in casting off the ~ of the old —*Times Lit. Supp.*⟩ **4** *chiefly dial* **a :** an outer skin, covering, or sheath **b :** SHELL, HUSK ⟨the ~ on a fruit⟩ **5 :** a mass of material that has sloughed from the side of a mine working or drill hole **6** [so called fr. the fact that it involves sloughing or discard] **:** a card game that is a variety of frog or solo

⁴slough \"\ *vb* -ED/-ING/-S *vi* **1 a :** to become shed or cast off ⟨a snake skin ~*s*⟩ ⟨the skin of my hand and forearm ~*ed* in patches —J.M.Savidge⟩ ⟨his clothes hung in rags, and some of them had ~*ed off* —Edison Marshall⟩ **b :** to shed or cast off one's skin ⟨the snake ~*s* annually⟩ **c :** to become encrusted with or as if with a slough: as (1) **:** to form a slough **:** separate in the form of dead tissue from living tissue ⟨a ~*ing* ulcer⟩ ⟨the dead tissue ~*s* slowly⟩ ⟨a ~*ing* of the colon⟩ — often used with *off* (2) **:** to cast off a thin film of scum or mass of bacterial growth or fungus ⟨a filter used in sewage disposal ~*s*⟩ **2 a :** to crumble and fall away **:** FALL, SLIDE ⟨fragments of rock ~ from the sides of a mine working or drill hole⟩ ⟨the track had disappeared with the ~*ing* of the surface rock —Francis Kingdon-Ward⟩ ⟨a worn stone building with stucco ~*ing* from its face⟩ ⟨stream banks that have a tendency to ~ at high-water level —*Carpentry*⟩ **b :** to drop or fall off **:** diminish in significance or intensity ⟨trade ~*s* off after Christmas⟩ **3 :** to slip from a bobbin or other package and tangle ⟨yarn ~*s*⟩ — usu. used with *off* ~ *vt* **1 a :** to cast off **:** throw off **:** ease off ⟨~ dead tissue⟩ ⟨many of the teeth are supported by soft tissue only; and several of them have been ~*ed* —E.C.Stafne⟩ ⟨a naked tired dark man, ~*ing* water off his thighs —Douglas Newton⟩ **b :** to get rid of, abandon, or discard as irksome, objectionable, deleterious, disadvantageous, outworn, or excrescent ⟨~*ed* their knapsacks —H.M. Robinson⟩ — usu. used with *off* ⟨~*ed off* the unimportant verbiage —P.D.Leedy⟩ ⟨the tendency in furniture . . . to ~ off many of its former crude and ungraceful characteristics —W.R. Storey⟩ ⟨author has ~*ed off* most of her more irritating sentimentalities —*Times Lit. Supp.*⟩ ⟨enlarged his understanding of religion by ~*ing* off most of the cosmological and theological lore associated with it —P.L.Holmer⟩ **2 :** to consume or waste away by forming a slough — usu. used with *away* ⟨the ulcer ~*ed* away the breast⟩ **3 :** to get rid of (a playing card) **syn** see DISCARD

⁵slough \'slü\ *var of* SLUE

⁶slough \'slau̇\ *vt* -ED/-ING/-S [prob. alter. (influenced by ⁴*slough*) of ⁶*slug*] *slang* **:** to strike heavily

slough bass *see* ¹SLOUGH\ *n* **:** LARGEMOUTH BLACK BASS

slough grass *see* ¹SLOUGH\ *n* **1 a :** either of two stout annual grasses (genus *Beckmannia*) with broad light green blades and 1-flowered or 2-flowered spikelets in two rows along one side of the rachis **b :** PRAIRIE CORDGRASS **c :** WESTERN WHEATGRASS 1 **2 :** TUSSOCK SEDGE

sloughi *often cap, var of* SALUKI

slough ice *see* ¹SLOUGH\ *n* **:** slushy ice or snow

slough of despond \ˌslüəvdə'spänd, ˌslau̇əv-, -dē's- *sometimes* -'de,s-\ [fr. The *Slough of Despond*, deep bog into which Christian falls on the way from the City of Destruction and from which Help saves him in the allegory *Pilgrim's Progress* (1678) by John Bunyan †1688 Eng. preacher and writer] **:** a state of extreme depression ⟨the country was in the *slough of despond* —Manfred Nathan⟩ ⟨men climbed out of the *slough of despond* on the ladder of Christian Platonism —Douglas Bush⟩

slough over \'sləf-\ *vt* [⁴*slough*] **:** SLIGHT, ²GLOSS 1 ⟨dwell on a few of the aspects of group work that are currently being *sloughed over* —W.H.Whyte⟩

¹sloughy *pronunc at* ¹SLOUGH + ē *or* i\ *adj* -ER/-EST [¹*slough* + -*y*] **:** full of sloughs **:** MIRY, MUDDY ⟨in a ~, weedy district —Willa Cather⟩ ⟨a ~ creek⟩

²sloughy \'sləfē, -fi\ *adj* [³*slough* + -*y*] **:** resembling or marked by the presence of the dead matter that separates from living flesh

slounge \'slünj\ *vb* -ED/-ING/-S [alter. (influenced by ¹*slouch*) of ¹*lounge*] *chiefly Scot* **:** LOUNGE, LOAF

¹slo·vak \'slō,väk, -vak, -väk\ *also* **slo·vak·ian** \(')⸗'⸗ēən\ *or* **slo·vac** *like* SLOVAK\ *n* -s *cap* [*slovak, slovac* fr. Slovak *Slovák*, lit., Slav; *slovakian* fr. Slovak *Slovák* + E *-ian*; akin to ORuss *Slověne*, an East-Slavic people — more at SLAVE] **1 a :** one of a Slavic people of eastern Czechoslovakia **b :** a member of such people **2 :** the Slavic language of the Slovak people

²slovak \"\ *or* **slovakian** \"\ *or* **slovac** \"\ *adj, usu cap* **1 :** of, relating to, or characteristic of the Slovaks **2 :** of, relating to, or characteristic of the Slovak language

slove *past of* SLIVE

¹slov·en \'sləvən *sometimes* -läv-\ *n* -s [ME *sloveyn*, of Flem or LG origin; akin to Flem *sloovin* gossip, woman of low character, LG *sluffen* to walk in a bedraggled manner, *sluf* loose, slack — more at SLOBBER] **1 :** one habitually negligent of neatness or cleanliness esp. in dress or person **:** one of extremely untidy habits ⟨local ~, who has since washed up, cleaned up —John Ciardi⟩ ⟨no slouchy ~ is he, but a scholar and a gentleman —W.A.White⟩ **2 :** one who is exceedingly lazy and slipshod in any way ⟨the difference between the unpunctual slacker and ~ and the model servant is very perceptible —G.B.Shaw⟩ ⟨a ~ in speech⟩

²sloven \"\ *adj* **1 :** SLOVENLY ⟨jargon . . . often ends as a ~ substitute for freshness and accuracy of statement —Dixon Wecter⟩ **2 :** UNCULTIVATED, UNDEVELOPED ⟨in this great ~ continent —Van Wyck Brooks⟩

¹slo·vene \'slō,vēn *sometimes* ⸗'⸗\ *or* **slo·ve·nian** \slō-'vēnēən, -nyən\ *n* -s *cap* [*slovene* fr. G *Slovene, Slowene*, fr. Slovene *Sloven; Slovenian* fr. G *Slovene* + E *-ian*; akin to OBulg *Slověne*, a Slavic people — more at SLAVE] **1 a :** a member of a southern Slavic group of people usu. classed with the Serbs and Croats and living in Yugoslavia **b :** a native or inhabitant of Slovenia — called also *Slavonian* **2 :** the language of the Slovenes

²slovene \"\ *or* **slovenian** \"\ *adj, usu cap* [*slovene* fr. ¹*slovene*; *slovenian* fr. G *Slovene*, n. + E *-ian* (adj. suffix)] **1 a :** of, relating to, or characteristic of Slovenia **b :** of, relating to, or characteristic of the Slovenes **2 :** of, relating to, or characteristic of the Slovene language

slov·en·li·ness \'sləvənlēnəs, -lin- *sometimes* -lä| *or* |ᵊml- *or* |bᵊml-\ *n* -ES **:** the quality or state of being slovenly

¹slov·en·ly \|vənlē, -li\ *adj* [¹*sloven* + *-ly* (adj. suffix)] **1 a :** having the habits of a sloven **:** negligent of neatness and order esp. in dress or person **:** SLIPSHOD **b :** lazily slipshod ⟨~ in thought⟩ **2 :** characteristic of a sloven **:** lacking neatness and order ⟨~ dress⟩ ⟨~ thinking⟩ ⟨~ habits⟩ ⟨~ grammar⟩ ⟨~ pronunciation⟩ ⟨~ workmanship⟩ **syn** see SLIPSHOD

²slovenly \"\ *adv* [¹*sloven* + *-ly* (adv. suffix)] **:** in a slovenly manner

slov·en·ness \|vən(n)əs\ *n* -ES *obs* **:** SLOVENLINESS

slov·en·ry \|vənrē\ *n* -ES [¹*sloven* + *-ry*] **:** SLOVENLINESS

slo·vin·cian \slō'vinch(ē)ən\ *n* -s *usu cap* [F *Slovince* (fr. G *Slowinze*, fr. Slovincian *Slovenec*) + E *-ian*; akin to Slovene *Sloven* Slovene] **:** an extinct Slavic language of Pomerania

¹slow \'slō\ *adj* -ER/-EST [ME *slow, slaw*, fr. OE *slāw, slǣw*; akin to OS *slēu* blunt, dull, weak, slow, OHG *slēo* blunt, dull, ON *sljōr, slær* blunt, dull, weak, Skt *srēvayati* he causes to fail] **1 a :** not quick in apprehending or comprehending **:** mentally dull **:** STUPID ⟨a ~ student⟩ ⟨a ~ mind⟩ ⟨offers ~ or retarded boys an adjusted program of education —*advt*⟩ ⟨the ~ learner, properly defined, is neither mentally nor emotionally retarded —Agnes Bass⟩ **b :** naturally inert or sluggish ⟨a ~ imagination⟩ **2 a :** lacking in readiness, promptness, or willingness **:** manifesting dilatoriness or extreme deliberation — often used with *in, of, to* ⟨they had been far too ~ in giving the colonies their independence —Hugh Gaitskell⟩ ⟨an unimaginative man, ~ of comprehension —*Times Lit. Supp.*⟩ ⟨many industries . . . have been ~ to develop the full value of research —*Defense Against Recession*⟩ **b :** not hasty or precipitate **:** not quickly aroused or excited ⟨~ to speak ill of a person —F.E.Ross⟩ ⟨a ~ theater audience⟩ **3 a :** moving, flowing, or proceeding without rapidity or at less than the usual speed ⟨a ~ stream⟩ ⟨a ~ train⟩ ⟨the robin has been mentioned as a ~ migrant —F.C.Lincoln⟩ **b :** exhibiting or characterized by retarded motion or speed ⟨a ~ advance⟩ ⟨~ marching⟩ ⟨~ music⟩ ⟨a ~ pace⟩ ⟨~ progress⟩ ⟨a ~ pulse⟩ ⟨a ~ tempo⟩ ⟨a ~ walk⟩ **c :** not acute ⟨a ~ disease⟩ **d** (1) **:** LOW, GENTLE ⟨a ~ fire⟩ (2) **:** heated to a relatively low baking temperature — compare SLOW OVEN **4 :** not happening in a short time **:** requiring a comparatively great length of time ⟨a ~ convalescence⟩ ⟨a ~ growth⟩ ⟨a ~ process⟩ **5 a :** having qualities that hinder or prohibit rapidity of movement, play, or action ⟨a ~ track is one in which the drying-out process has progressed to the stage where the footing is soft —Dan Parker⟩ ⟨her feet would sop in and out of the ~ mire —Elizabeth M. Roberts⟩ ⟨a ~ putting green⟩ **b** *of a wicket* **:** in such condition that a bowled cricket ball does not rebound with speed and liveliness — contrasted with *fast* **c :** not operating, taking effect, or responding to treatment immediately or quickly ⟨a ~ filter⟩ ⟨a ~ influence⟩ ⟨a ~ poison⟩ **d :** contributing to a lengthening of exposure time — used of a photographic lens or material **e :** draining slowly **:** WET — used of paper pulp; compare FREE 20a **6 a :** registering behind or below what is correct ⟨a ~ clock⟩ ⟨a ~ meter⟩ ⟨~ scales⟩ ⟨a ~ taximeter⟩ **b :** that is less than the time indicated by another method of reckoning ⟨standard time is an hour ~*er* than daylight-saving time⟩ **c :** that is behind the time with regard to a specified time or place ⟨local time (6 hrs. 36 min. 46.67 secs. ~ on Greenwich mean time) —G.B. & Charlotte L. Dyer⟩ ⟨Washington is several hours ~ on London⟩ **7 a :** lacking in life, animation, or gaiety **:** BORING ⟨somebody who's . . . so gay and daring that she'll think I'm ~ —Sinclair Lewis⟩ ⟨things were ~ around Times Square —Herbert Mitgang⟩ **b :** SLOWGOING, UNPROGRESSIVE ⟨a ~ town⟩ **c :** marked by reduced sales or patronage **:** not brisk **:** SLACK ⟨business here is a little ~ in summer —W.L.Gresham⟩ ⟨September is always a ~ month —Mary Jane Rolfs⟩ ⟨diamonds were particularly ~ —*Minerals Yrbk.*⟩ ⟨~ sales⟩ **8 :** not steep **:** GRADUAL ⟨a ~ taper⟩ ⟨a ~ spiral⟩ ⟨party climbed the comparatively ~ ascent —Frank Debenham⟩

syn SLOW, DILATORY, LAGGARD, DELIBERATE, and LEISURELY can apply to persons who take a longer time than is necessary, or sometimes desirable, to perform action or an action. SLOW, wide in its range of application, can apply to anything that is the opposite of quick ⟨a *slow* fuse⟩ ⟨a *slow* walker⟩ sometimes suggesting a more or less discreditable cause ⟨a *slow* careless worker⟩ ⟨*slow* wits⟩ ⟨*slow* in getting results⟩ or extreme care ⟨*slow* craftsmanship, careful and particular⟩ or a natural tempo ⟨*slow* growth⟩ ⟨a *slow* convalescence⟩ or a falling behind because of defect or difficulty ⟨a *slow* watch⟩ ⟨a *slow* train, held up by a storm⟩ DILATORY implies slowness resulting from inertia, procrastination, or indifference ⟨though *dilatory* in undertaking business, he was quick in its execution —Jane Austen⟩ ⟨the trial must not be protracted in duration by anything that is obstructive or *dilatory* —R.H.Jackson⟩ LAGGARD, more censorious than DILATORY, implies failure to do things on time or to observe a demand promptly, implying loitering or a wasting of time ⟨in its coverage of spot news events, radio has been especially *laggard* —R.H.Rovere⟩ ⟨a pupil *laggard* in getting assignments completed⟩ ⟨her body slender and motionless for a moment as though waiting for some *laggard* part to catch up —William Faulkner⟩ DELIBERATE suggests absence of hurry or agitation, or a slowness that is the result of care or calculation ⟨swung his axe steadily, with the *deliberate* measured strokes of a skilled woodsman —C.B.Nordhoff & J.N.Hall⟩ ⟨proceeding in the most *deliberate* and orderly manner —T.S.Eliot⟩ ⟨had been hurrying everyone since the first streak of light, suddenly became *deliberate* —Willa Cather⟩ LEISURELY also implies lack of hurry but suggests rather no pressure of time ⟨moving at a casual, almost *leisurely* pace —*Time*⟩ ⟨the mild wind and the blue skies with the *leisurely* clouds tenting among them —J.H.Wheelwright⟩

²slow \"\ *adv* -ER/-EST **:** SLOWLY ⟨how ~ time goes —Shak.⟩ ⟨I am going ~ until I am really on my feet again —H.J.Laski⟩ ⟨I would go pretty ~ on that —F.D.Roosevelt⟩ ⟨the engine is idling a trifle ~ —Walt Waron⟩

³slow \"\ *vb* -ED/-ING/-S *vt* **:** to make slow **:** slacken the speed of **:** RETARD ⟨investors were ~*ing* the market —*Time*⟩ ⟨the dirt track ~*ed* his pace —*Current Biog.*⟩ — often used with *up* or *down* ⟨a sudden storm will . . . only temporarily ~ down the movement of a freight train —J.N.Efferson⟩ ⟨reader is ~*ed* up by a stream of long words —Milton Hall⟩ ~ *vi* **:** to go slower **:** become slower ⟨the river . . . ~*s* on the flat bottom —Alexander Marshack⟩ ⟨the production of such vehicles ~*ed* a bit

—A.F.Harlow⟩ — often used with *up* or *down* ⟨go all day at high speed, begin to ~ up in the evening —R.S.Rubinow⟩ ⟨his doctor told him to ~ down —*N.Y. Times*⟩ **syn** see DELAY
⁴slow \"\ *n* -s **:** one that is slow
slowbelly \ˈ⸗⸗,⸗⸗\ *n, pl* **slowbellies** [¹*slow* + *belly*] **1 :** a slothful person **2 :** a heavy indolent glutton **:** HOG
slow board *n* **:** a track-side marker for indicating to railroad engineers the maximum permissible speed in restricted speed zones (as on curves and bridges)
slow-burning \ˈ⸗ˈ⸗⸗\ *adj* **:** burning slowly; *esp* **:** made of material treated to resist fire
slow coach *n* **:** one who is slow or is lethargic in temperament **:** one who thinks or moves slowly
slowdown \ˈ⸗,⸗\ *n* -s [fr. *slow down*, v.] **:** a slowing down ⟨a business ~⟩ ⟨an industrial ~⟩ ⟨a sales ~⟩; *specif* **:** a slowing down in the performance of duties by workers as a protest and means toward forcing compliance with demands — compare SIT-DOWN
slower *comparative of* SLOW
slowest *superlative of* SLOW
slow fever *n* **:** a fever that is not acute or a disease characterized by such fever; *esp* **:** INFECTIOUS ANEMIA
slow fire *n* **:** a class of rifle-marksmanship fire in which the time allowed for completing the number of shots is comparatively great (as one minute per round or longer)
slow-foot \ˈ⸗,⸗\ *adj* **:** SLOW-FOOTED
slow-footed \ˈ⸗ˈ⸗⸗\ *adj* **:** moving at a very slow pace **:** SLOW-GOING, PLODDING ⟨a *slow-footed* novel⟩ ⟨a *slow-footed* ship⟩ — **slow-foot·ed·ness** \ˈ⸗ˈ⸗⸗⸗\ *n* -ES
slowgoing \ˈ⸗ˈ⸗⸗\ *adj* **1 :** plodding along in easygoing fashion **2 :** not inclined to be enterprising **:** UNENERGETIC
slow·hound \ˈslō,⸗\ *n* [alter. (influenced by ¹*slow*) of obs. E *sloughhound*, prob. alter. (influenced by E ¹*slough*) of E *sleuthhound*] **:** SLEUTH 1
slow·ish \ˈslōish, -ō ēsh\ *adj* **:** somewhat slow ⟨a ~ reader⟩
slow loris *or* **slow lemur** *n* **:** LORIS 1b
slow·ly *adv* [ME *slowlich, slawly*, fr. OE *slāwlīce*, fr. *slāw* slow + *-līce* -ly — more at SLOW] **:** in a slow manner **:** not quickly, fast, rapidly, early, rashly, or readily **:** TARDILY
slow match *n* **:** a match or fuse made so as to burn slowly and evenly at a known rate and used for firing (as of blasting charges or fireworks)
slow motion *n* **:** the action in a projected motion picture apparently taking place at a speed much slower than that of the photographed action as a result of exposing the film at a rate much faster than that at which it is projected ⟨a scene in *slow motion*⟩
slow-moving \ˈ⸗ˈ⸗⸗\ *adj* **:** SLOW-FOOTED, SLOWGOING; *specif* **:** selling slowly
slow·ness *n* -ES [ME *slawnes*, fr. *slaw* slow + *-nes* -ness] **:** the quality or state of being slow
slow oven *n* **:** a baking oven heated to a temperature between 250° F and 325° F
slow-paced \ˈ⸗ˈ⸗\ *adj* **:** moving at a slow rate of speed **:** SLOW-FOOTED
slow pill *n, slang* **:** a depressant illegally administered to a race horse to slow his pace and prevent his winning
slow·poke \ˈslō,pōk\ *n* [¹*slow* + *poke*] **:** an annoyingly slow or slowgoing person **:** SLOW COACH ⟨journey even inquisitive ~*s* can make in a dawdling two days and a half —Claudia Cassidy⟩
slow-poke \"\ *vi* [*slow poke*] **:** to go like a slowpoke ⟨*slow-poked* up and down the river —Louis Armstrong⟩
slows \ˈslōz\ *n pl but sing in constr* [fr. pl. of ⁴*slow*] **:** MILK SICKNESS 1, TREMBLE 3
slow shrimp *n* **:** a small brightly colored Australian anomuran crustacean (*Axius plectorhynchus*)
slow-spoken \ˈ⸗ˈ⸗⸗\ *adj* **:** characterized by speaking slowly
slow-up \ˈ⸗,⸗\ *n* -s [fr. *slow up*, v.] **:** a slowing up; *specif* **:** a marked decline in activity
slow-witted \ˈ⸗ˈ⸗⸗\ *adj* **:** mentally slow **:** DULL
slow·worm \ˈslō,⸗\ *n* [alter. (influenced by ¹*slow*) of ME *slowurm, slaworm*, fr. OE *slāwyrm*, fr. *slā* (akin to Sw *slå* earthworm, Norw *slo* blindworm) + *wyrm* worm — more at WORM] **1 :** BLINDWORM 1 **2** *Austral* **:** a pygopodid lizard
sloyd *also* **slojd** *or* **sloid** \ˈslȯid\ *n* -s [Sw *slöjd* skill, skilled labor; akin to ON *slægth* cunning, sleight — more at SLEIGHT] **:** a system of manual training developed from a Swedish system and designed for training in the use of tools and materials but emphasizing training in wood carving as a means to this end
sloyd knife *n* **:** a single-blade woodworker's knife used in carving, trimming, or slicing

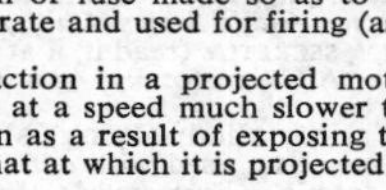

sloyd knife

SLP *abbr, often not cap* [L *sine legitima prole*] without lawful issue
slsmgr *abbr* sales manager
slsmn *abbr* salesman
slt *abbr* **1** searchlight **2** sleet
¹slub \ˈsləb, -lüb\ *n* -s [obs. D *slubbe*, fr. MD *slubbe, slobbe* slime, mud, mire — more at SLOBBER] *dial Eng* **:** a muddy or slushy mess
²slub \ˈsləb\ *n* -s [origin unknown] **:** a soft thick uneven section in a yarn caused accidentally by knotting during winding or by the inclusion of lint during spinning or intentionally by the twisting of two or more strands at different speeds or by the inclusion of short fibers during spinning
³slub \"\ *vt* **slubbed; slubbed; slubbing; slubs** [back-formation fr. *slubbing*] **:** to draw out and twist slightly (as slivers of wool)
⁴slub \"\ *n* -s **:** SLUBBING 2
slubbed *adj* [fr. past part. of ³*slub*] **:** made from yarns having decorative slubs
¹slub·ber \ˈsləbə(r)\ *vt* -ED/-ING/-s [prob. fr. obs. D *slubberen* to walk through mud or mire, to slubber, fr. MD *slubberen, slobberen* to walk through mud or mire — more at SLOBBER] **1** *dial chiefly Eng* **:** STAIN, SULLY ⟨~*ed* with . . . pedantry —John Milton⟩ **2 :** to perform in a slipshod fashion **:** run through hastily — usu. used with *over* ⟨~ over the business⟩
²slubber \"\ *n* -s [³*slub* + *-er*] **1 :** one that produces slubbing **2 :** partly twined or badly twined woolen thread
slub·ber·de·gul·lion \ˈsləbə(r)də,gəlyən, -dē,g-, ˌ⸗⸗⸗ˈ⸗⸗\ *n* [prob. irreg. fr. ¹*slubber*] *chiefly dial* **:** a dirty rascal **:** SCOUNDREL, WRETCH
slub·bi \ˈslübē\ *also* **so·lub·bi** *or* **sloub·bie** \slü-\ *n, pl* **sleyb** \ˈslāb\ *or* **su·lub·ba** \sə'lübə\ *usu cap* **:** a member of a nomadic Arab people living in an area extending from Damascus to Mosul in the north and in the Tigris-Euphrates region above Baghdad
slub·bing \ˈsləbiŋ\ *n* -s [*slub* of unknown origin + *-ing* (n. suffix)] **1 :** the act or process of drawing out and slightly twisting wool, cotton, or silk **2 :** slightly twisted roving
slubbing billy *n* **:** a machine for slubbing
¹slub·by \ˈsləbi, -lübi\ *adj* -ER/-EST [obs. D *slubbe* slub + E *-y* — more at SLUB] *chiefly dial* **:** MUDDY
²slub·by \ˈsləbē\ *adj* -ER/-EST [⁴*slub* + *-y*] *of a textile* **:** having slubs
slubcatcher \ˈ⸗,⸗⸗\ *n* [²*slub* + *catcher*] **:** a yarn inspection device on spoolers and winders consisting usu. of a narrow slit that stops slubs and thickenings
slub yarn *n* **:** a yarn with thick and thin sections alternating regularly or irregularly — compare SLUB
slud \ˈsləd, -lüd\ *also* **slud·der** \-də(r)\ *n* -s [of Scand origin; akin to Dan *slud* sleet, slush, Icel *slydda* — more at SLATTERN] *dial Eng* **:** a slippery mass (as of mud or slush)
¹sludge \ˈsləj\ *n* -s [prob. alter. of ¹*slush*] **1 :** MUD, MIRE; *esp* **:** a muddy deposit (as on tideland or river bed) **:** OOZE **2 :** a muddy or slushy mass, deposit, or sediment: as **a :** the precipitated solid matter produced by water and sewage treatment processes **b :** mud from a drill hole in boring **c :** muddy sediment in a steam boiler **d** (1) **:** SLIME 2d (2) **:** waste from a coal washery **e :** a precipitate or settling from oils; *esp* **:** one (as a mixture of impurities and acid) from mineral oils (as petroleum refined by sulfuric acid or oxidized in automotive engine lubrication or transformer cooling) **3 :** new sea ice forming in thin detached crystals **:** SLOB **4 :** a clump of agglutinated red blood cells; *specif* **:** SLUDGED BLOOD
²sludge \"\ *vb* -ED/-ING/-s *vt* **1 a :** to convert into sludge **b :** to fill in with sludge **c :** to clear of sludge **2 :** to form a sludge of (red blood cells) in small blood vessels **~** *vi* **:** to form sludge
sludge acid *n* **:** waste or spent sulfuric acid; *esp* **:** such acid derived from refining petroleum oils or crude benzenes
sludged blood *n* **:** blood in which the red blood cells become massed along the walls of the blood vessels and reduce the lumen of the vessels and the rate of blood flow
sludg·er \-jə(r)\ *n* -s **:** a device for sludging: as **a :** SAND PUMP **b :** SHELL PUMP **c :** a shovel for sludging out drains
sludgy \-jē,-ji\ *adj* -ER/-EST **:** full of sludge **:** MUDDY, SLUSHY
¹slue *var of* SLOUGH
²slue *also* **slew** *or* **slough** \ˈslü\ *vb* -ED/-ING/-s [origin unknown] *vt* **1 :** to turn (as a ship's spar) about a fixed point that is usu. the center or axis **2 :** to turn (something) about **:** TWIST, VEER — usu. used with *around* or *round* ⟨*slued* the boat around⟩ ⟨*slued* her head around⟩ ⟨they laughed and *slued* themselves round —Charles Dickens⟩ **~** *vi* **1 :** to turn, twist, or swing about **:** PIVOT — usu. used with *around* ⟨*slued* around in the saddle —A.B.Guthrie⟩ **2 :** to slide and turn or slip out of the course **:** SKID ⟨broke her towlines and *slued* across the channel —Marjory S. Douglas⟩
³slue *also* **slew** \"\ *n* -s **:** position or inclination after sluing ⟨get the mast on the right ~⟩
⁴slue *var of* SLEW
slue-foot \ˈ⸗,⸗\ *or* **slue-footed** \ˈ⸗ˈ⸗⸗\ *adj* **:** having big, clumsy, or turned-out feet
slue rope *also* **slew rope** *n* **:** a rope used in sluing (as a mast or spar)
¹sluff \ˈsləf\ *n* -s [alter. of ³*slough*] **1 :** SLOUGH **2 :** DISCARD 1
²sluff \"\ *vb* -ED/-ING/-s *vt* **:** DISCARD 1 **~** *vi* **:** to discard a playing card
¹slug \ˈsləg\ *n* -s [ME *slugge*, of Scand origin; akin to Sw & Norw dial. *slugga* to walk sluggishly, Norw dial. *sluggje* heavy slow person; akin to LG *slokeren* to hang loosely, MLG *slūren* to drag, trail — more at SLUR] **1 :** SLUGGARD **2** *archaic* **:** something (as a vessel, vehicle, or animal) that is slow-moving or sluggish **3 a :** any of numerous chiefly terrestrial pulmonate gastropods that are found in most parts of the world where there is a reasonable supply of moisture, are usu. placed in the family Limacidae though the group is prob. polyphyletic including descendants of shelled snails of several families, are closely related to the land snails but have the shell rudimentary and often buried in the mantle or wanting entirely, have the body when extended long and fusiform with the entire lower surface constituting the foot upon which the animal typically crawls over a film of mucous secreted by the skin, are mostly herbivorous, rasp at herbage with a well-developed radula, and often become serious pests of cultivated plants — see GARDEN SLUG **b :** SEA SLUG 2 **4 :** a smooth soft larva of a sawfly or moth that creeps like a mollusk: as **a :** PEAR SLUG **b :** ROSE SLUG
²slug \"\ *vb* **slugged; slugged; slugging; slugs** [ME *sluggen*, prob. of Scand origin; akin to Sw dial. *slugga* to walk sluggishly] *vi* **1 :** to rest idly **:** remain (as in bed) through laziness ⟨~ in sloth and sensual delight —Edmund Spenser⟩ **2 :** to move at a sluggish pace **:** LOITER ⟨*slugging* on their slow-gaited asses —William Tennant⟩ **~** *vt* **1 :** to spend (time) in dawdling or idling ⟨the wretch who ~s his life away —James Thomson †1748⟩ **2** *obs* **a :** to make sluggish **b :** DELAY, HINDER
³slug \"\ *n* -s [prob. fr. ¹*slug*] **1 :** a piece (as a lump, disk, or cylinder) of metal: as **a** (1) **:** a musket ball (2) **:** BULLET; *esp* **:** a revolver bullet **b** (1) **:** a piece of crude metal **:** NUGGET (2) **:** a piece of solid bulk metal roughly shaped for subsequent processing **c** (1) **:** one of the private gold coins issued in California in 1849 (2) **:** a $50 gold piece **d** (1) **:** a thin flat piece of metal formed from a sheet by punching **:** ¹BURR 3c (2) **:** a metal disk for insertion in a slot to operate an automatic machine; *esp* **:** one used illegally instead of a coin in such a machine (as a turnstile) **2 a :** a strip of metal similar to a printer's lead but usu. 6 point or larger **b** (1) **:** an identifying line placed by a compositor over matter set by him (2) **:** a line carrying a short title temporarily placed over one portion of matter set in separate takes — called also *galley slug* (3) **:** the short title itself (4) **:** GUIDELINE (5) **:** a line bearing a message or instruction (as a release date or the word *more*) **c :** a solid line either of characters or blank produced by a slugcasting machine **d** (1) **:** a scratch or tear in a negative or plate (2) **:** an anchor on a plate **3 :** a heavy nail or stud driven in a shoe or boot sole in shoe manufacturing **4 a :** a piece of magnetic material used to adjust the inductance of a coil **b :** a hollow metallic or dielectric cylinder used as a transforming element in a wave-guide system **5 :** a large flat-faced disk prepared for the purpose of mixing the ingredients in the manufacture of compressed pharmaceutical tablets **6 :** an irregular freshwater pearl — compare BAROQUE **7 :** a thickened place in a yarn or fabric caused usu. by lint or knots **8 :** a mass of half-roasted ore **9 a :** a small amount of liquor; *esp* **:** the quantity of drink taken in one swallow **:** SHOT, SNIFTER ⟨tossed down three stiff ~s of bourbon —Peter DeVries⟩ **b :** a detached mass of water or oil that causes impact or water hammer in a circulating system **10 :** the gravitational unit of mass in the fps system to which a pound force can impart an acceleration of one foot per second per second
⁴slug \"\ *vb* **slugged; slugged; slugging; slugs** *vt* **1 :** to load (as a gun) with slugs **:** insert a slug in ⟨~ a rifle⟩ ⟨~ a shoe⟩ ⟨~ a coin machine⟩ **2 :** to drive a soft lead bullet through (the bore of a rifle or pistol) in order to determine the exact bore diameter **3 a :** to add a printer's slug to (as a story) **:** insert a slug in (letterpress matter) **b :** to anchor (a printing plate) to a metal base by soldering metal projections into holes in the base **~** *vi* **:** to insert a slug (as in a shoe)
⁵slug \"\ *n* -s [perh. fr. ³*slug*] **:** a heavy blow; *esp* **:** one given with the fist ⟨an epidemic of slaps, ~s, and slights that has threatened to turn . . . bus conductors into public punching bags —*N.Y. Times*⟩
⁶slug \"\ *vb* **slugged; slugged; slugging; slugs** *vt* **1 :** to strike (as a person) heavily (as with the fist or a blunt instrument) ⟨~ a man with a length of pipe⟩ **2 a :** to drive or propel (a baseball) by batting hard ⟨~ the ball over the left field fence⟩ **b :** to achieve (as a two-base hit or a home run) by good batting ⟨~ four homers in one ball game⟩ **~** *vi* **1 :** to fight fiercely with a continuous exchange of heavy blows ⟨the two fighters were still *slugging* as the round ended⟩ ⟨the opposed armies *slugged* away in the same area for weeks⟩ **2 :** to move forward or push on vigorously against difficulties **:** PLOW ⟨a fighting leader who would ~ on through —Fletcher Pratt⟩ **syn** see STRIKE
¹slug·abed \ˈsləgə,bed\ *n* -s [¹*slug* + *abed*] **:** one who stays in bed after his usual or obligated time of getting up **:** SLUGGARD ⟨mothers getting their young ~s off to school⟩
²slugabed \"\ *adj* **:** of or relating to a slugabed ⟨~ habits . . . distressed him —Aldous Huxley⟩
slugcast \ˈ⸗,⸗\ *adj* [³*slug* + *cast*] **:** produced by slugcasting ⟨~ composition⟩
slugcasting \ˈ⸗,⸗⸗\ *n* [³*slug* + *casting*] **:** the mechanical casting of printer's slugs that are either keyboard assembled or hand assembled **:** LINECASTING
slug caterpillar *n* **:** ¹SLUG 4
slug·fest \ˈsləg,fest\ *n* -s [⁵*slug* + *-fest*] **:** a hard-hitting struggle or contest marked by a sustained and vigorous exchange of heavy blows: as **a :** a boxing match; *esp* **:** one marked by the frequent and sometimes lengthy exchange of hard punches and a minimum of defensive boxing **b :** a baseball game that is marked by heavy hitting and frequent scoring by both teams
¹slug·gard \ˈsləgə(r)d\ *n* -s [ME *sluggart, slogard*, prob. fr. *sluggy, sloggy* sluggish, lazy (prob. of Scand origin) + *-art, -ard* -ard; akin to Sw dial. *slugga* to walk sluggishly — more at SLUG] **:** an habitually lazy idle and inactive person ⟨go to the ant, thou ~; consider her ways, and be wise —Prov. 6:6 (AV)⟩ ⟨forecast a nation of ~s —Irwin Edman⟩
²sluggard \"\ *adj* **:** having the characteristics of a sluggard ⟨the people . . . depose the ~ king —J.G.Frazer⟩
slug·gard·ly \-lē,-li\ *adj* **:** lazily inactive **:** INDOLENT
slug·gard·ness *n* -ES [ME *slogardnes*, fr. *slogard* sluggard + *-nes* -ness] **:** the quality or state of being a sluggard **:** lazy inactivity **:** INDOLENCE
slugged *past of* SLUG
¹slug·ger \ˈsləgə(r)\ *n* -s [⁴*slug* + *-er*] **1 :** an operator of a slugging machine for nailing top lifts to shoe heels **2 :** a slugging machine used in shoe manufacturing
²slugger \"\ *n* -s [⁶*slug* + *-er*] **:** one that strikes hard or with heavy blows: as **a :** a prizefighter who punches hard but has usu. little defensive skill ⟨a boxer, not a ~ —Chandler Brossard⟩ **b :** a hard-hitting batter in baseball **c :** GOON 1 ⟨employers and labor organizations hiring . . . small armies of ~s —Walter Goodman⟩
¹slug·ging \ˈsləgiŋ, -gēŋ\ *n* -s [fr. gerund of ⁶*slug*] **:** illegal use of the fist or forearm on an opponent in football for which a penalty is usu. imposed
²slugging \"\ *n* -s [³*slug* + *-ing*] **:** the act or process of compressing pharmaceutical ingredients into disks — compare ³SLUG 5
slugging match *n* **:** SLUGFEST
slug·gish \ˈsləgish, -gēsh\ *adj* [ME *sluggus, sluggish*, fr. *slugge* sluggard + *-us, -ish* -ish — more at SLUG] **1 :** disinclined (as by nature, habit, or condition) to activity or exertion **:** INDOLENT, TORPID ⟨a ~ worker⟩ ⟨a ~ temperament⟩ ⟨some physicians are mentally ~ —*Fortune*⟩ ⟨many freshwater fishes . . . become ~ during cold weather —W.H.Dowdeswell⟩ **2 :** slow to respond (as to stimulation or treatment) **:** lacking in vigor, animation, or efficiency ⟨a ~ liver⟩ ⟨an old man whose reactions were so ~ he shouldn't have been driving a car —Erle Stanley Gardner⟩ ⟨tonic . . . for a clogged and ~ system —Emily Holt⟩ ⟨turn an otherwise good performance into a ~ one —Warwick Braithwaite⟩ **3 a :** markedly slow in movement, flow, or growth ⟨a ~ pace⟩ ⟨a ~ stream⟩ ⟨~, wallowing oil tankers —*Amer. Guide Series: Texas*⟩ ⟨his cataract of eloquence suddenly lagged to a ~ trickle —Herman Wouk⟩ ⟨several decades of ~ economic development —*Amer. Guide Series: Va.*⟩ **b :** economically inactive or slow-moving **:** DULL, STAGNANT ⟨a ~ market⟩ ⟨clothing sales were ~⟩ ⟨stock prices have remained notably ~ —*Fortune*⟩ **syn** see LETHARGIC
slug·gish·ly *adv* [ME *sluggusly*, fr. *sluggus* sluggish + *-ly*] **:** in a sluggish manner **:** SLOWLY, INDOLENTLY
slug·gish·ness *n* -ES [ME *sluggusnes*, fr. *sluggus* sluggish + *-nes* -ness] **:** the quality or state of being sluggish: as **a :** disinclination to activity **:** INDOLENCE ⟨mental ~⟩ **b :** slowness of movement ⟨silt adding to the ~ of the creek⟩ **c :** economic stagnancy ⟨the post-holiday ~ of department store sales⟩
slughi *often cap, var of* SALUKI
slug·horn \ˈsləg,hȯrn\ *n* -s [by folk etymology fr. earlier *slogorn* — more at SLOGAN] **1** *obs* **:** SLOGAN 1 **2 :** HORN, TRUMPET
sluglike \ˈ⸗,⸗\ *adj* **:** resembling a slug
slugline \ˈ⸗,⸗\ *n* **:** ³SLUG 2b, 2c
slugs *pl of* SLUG, *pres 3d sing of* SLUG
slug snail *n* **:** ¹SLUG 3
slug·wood \ˈslə,gwu̇d\ *n* [by alter.] **:** SLOGWOOD
slug worm *n* **:** ¹SLUG 4
¹sluice \ˈslüs\ *n* -s [ME *scluse*, fr. MF *escluse*, fr. LL *exclusa* dam, sluice, fr. fem. of L *exclusus*, past part. of *excludere* to shut out, exclude — more at EXCLUDE] **1 a :** an artificial passage for water (as in a millstream) fitted with a valve or gate for stopping or regulating the flow **b :** a body of water pent up behind a floodgate or water gate **2 :** a device for letting water in or out or holding it back: as **a :** a dock gate **:** WATER GATE, FLOODGATE **b :** VALVE, PIPE **3 a :** a stream flowing through a floodgate **b :** a conduit (as a channel or stream) that serves to drain or carry off surplus water **4 :** a long inclined trough or flume usu. on the ground (as for washing auriferous earth or floating down logs); *specif* **:** such a contrivance paved usu. with riffles to hold quicksilver for catching gold **5 :** something suggestive of a sluice: as **a :** a rushing or pouring stream **:** SPATE ⟨stopped the ~ of free advice —F.B.Gipson⟩ ⟨great ~s of rain —Carleton Beals⟩ **b :** a pent-up flood of emotion ⟨open the ~s of popular revolt —D.J.Dallin⟩
²sluice \"\ *vb* -ED/-ING/-s *vt* **1 :** to cause to flow or pour forth by or as if by floodgates **:** draw off by or through a sluice or sluiceway ⟨by this fresh blood that from thy manly breast I cowardly *sluiced* out —John Marston⟩ **2 a :** to wash with or in a stream of water running through or from a sluice **b :** to drench, wash, or scour with gushes or floods (as of water) **:** FLUSH, DOUSE ⟨~ earth in mining⟩ ⟨~ a pavement with a hose⟩ ⟨hydraulic jets ~ away soil layers bearing tin ore —W.R.Moore⟩ ⟨trying to ~ his face without wetting his cuffs —Richard Llewellyn⟩ **3 a :** to transport (as logs) in a sluice or float through a sluiceway **b :** to drive (logs) by releasing a sluice of water **~** *vi* **:** to pour from or as if from a sluice ⟨rain *sluicing* down to plaster his ragged shirt to his body —Marcia Davenport⟩ **syn** see POUR
sluice box *n* **:** a single section usu. about 12 feet long of a gold-mining sluice
sluice gate *n* **:** the sliding gate of a sluice
sluic·er \-sə(r)\ *n* -s **:** the keeper of a sluice
sluice valve *n* **1 :** SLUICE GATE **2 :** GATE VALVE **3 :** a watertight sliding valve in the watertight floors of a frame in shipbuilding
sluiceway \ˈ⸗,⸗\ *n* **1 :** an artificial channel into which water is let by a sluice; *specif* **:** SLUICE 4 **2 :** the opening in a splash dam for passage of logs **3 :** a channel through which a large volume of water has passed (as of meltwater from a glacier)
sluicy \ˈslüsē\ *adj* **:** falling copiously or in streams (as from a sluice) **:** STREAMING ⟨~ sheets of rain⟩
sluing arch *n* [*sluing* fr. pres. part. of ²*slue*] **:** SPLAYED ARCH
sluit \ˈslüt\ *n* -s [Afrik, fr. D *sloot* ditch, fr. MD; akin to MLG *slōt* ditch, puddle, bog, OFris *slāt* ditch, Sw dial. *slota* to be putrid, ME *sloor* mud — more at SLUR] *chiefly Africa* **:** a deep usu. dry ditch produced by the washing of heavy rains in a large natural fissure **:** GULLY, GULCH
¹slum \ˈsləm\ *n* -s *often attrib* [origin unknown] **1 :** a highly congested usu. urban residential area characterized by deteriorated unsanitary buildings, poverty, and social disorganization ⟨brought up in an unwholesome ~⟩ ⟨the ~s of the city⟩ ⟨~ clearance⟩ ⟨a ~ district⟩ ⟨creating a rural ~⟩ **2 :** cheap articles given as prizes in games of chance (as at carnivals)
²slum \"\ *vi* **slummed; slummed; slumming; slums :** to visit or frequent slums; *esp* **:** to make an excursion into slums out of curiosity or for pleasure — often used in the expression *go slumming* ⟨went *slumming* in their evening clothes⟩
³slum \"\ *n* -s [perh. fr. G *schlamm* slime, mud, fr. MHG *slam*; prob. akin to obs. E dial. *slemp* to slip away, ON *sleppa* to slide, slip, L *labi* to slide, slip, sink, fall — more at SLEEP] **1 :** SLIME **2 :** a passage at the bottom of a mining pit
⁴slum \"\ *n* -s [by shortening] **1 :** SLUMGULLION 1b **2 :** SLUMGULLION 3
¹slum·ber \ˈsləmbə(r)\ *vb* **slumbered; slumbered; slumbering** \-b(ə)riŋ\ **slumbers** [ME *slumberen, slumeren*, freq. of *slumen* to doze, prob. fr. *slume, sloumbe* slumber, fr. OE *slūma*; akin to MHG *slummern, slumen* to slumber, Norw *slum* sluggish, Norw dial. *sluma* to walk sluggishly, drag one's feet, ME *sloor* mud — more at SLUR] *vi* **1 a :** to sleep lightly **:** DOZE ⟨he who keeps Israel will neither ~ nor sleep —Ps 121:4 (RSV)⟩ **b :** to lie asleep ⟨the girl ~*ed* peacefully —Henry La Cossitt⟩ **2 a :** to lie or live as if sunk in sleep or stupor **:** be in a torpid state **:** HIBERNATE ⟨the . . . nation ~*ed* through more than two centuries of self-imposed isolation —Louis Wasserman⟩ **b :** to remain in a negligent or slothful state **:** IDLE ⟨the public conscience ~*s*⟩ ⟨~*ing* along until shocked into activity⟩ ⟨add to this a report I have been asked to do . . . and you will guess that I have not ~*ed* —H.J.Laski⟩ **c :** to lie dormant or latent ⟨below the surface ~*ed* deadly memories —*Times Lit. Supp.*⟩ **~** *vt* **:** to pass or spend (as time) in or as if in sleep — usu. used with *away* or *out* ⟨~*ing* away the best years for productive work⟩ **syn** see SLEEP
²slumber \"\ *n* -s [ME *slumbir, slummir*, fr. *slumberen, slumeren* to slumber] **1 a :** a state of sleep or repose **:** SLEEP ⟨it was no night for ~⟩ ⟨sank into a deep ~⟩ ⟨fills my ~ with tumultuous dreams —P.B.Shelley⟩ **b :** light sleep **:** DOZE ⟨at last fell into a ~, and thence into a fast sleep —John Bunyan⟩ **2 :** a moral, mental, or physical condition like sleep **:** LETHARGY, TORPOR ⟨a great writer arouses us from our dogmatic ~*s* —Zechariah Chafee⟩
³slumber \"\ *adj* **:** of, relating to, or intended for use during slumber ⟨a ~ cap⟩ ⟨a ~ robe⟩

slum·ber·er \-bərə(r)\ *n* -s [ME *slumbrer, slumerer,* fr. *slumberen, slumeren* to slumber + *-er*] : one that slumbers : SLEEPER
slumberland \ˈ⸗⸗,⸗\ *n* : an unreal country that is a realm of sleep
slum·ber·ous *or* **slum·brous** \ˈsləmb(ə)rəs\ *adj* [ME *slumbrous,* fr. *slumbir* slumber + *-ous*] **1 a :** inclined to sleep : heavy with sleep : SLEEPY, SOMNOLENT ⟨~ eyes⟩ ⟨lifting . . . her ~ little boy —Peggy Bennett⟩ ⟨her heavy ~ voice —Meridel Le Sueur⟩ **b :** CALM, PEACEFUL ⟨a ~ town⟩ ⟨a ~ Sunday in June —Maurice Walsh⟩ **2 :** inviting or inducing slumber : SOPORIFIC ⟨a ~ sound⟩ ⟨the ~ light is rich and warm —Alfred Tennyson⟩ **3 :** marked by, accompanied by, or suggestive of sleep or a condition like sleep : LETHARGIC ⟨a ~ peace pervaded every province —Pearl Buck⟩ ⟨a ~ administration⟩ — **slum·ber·ous·ly** *or* **slum·brous·ly** *adv* — **slum·ber·ous·ness** *n* -ES
slumber party *n* : an overnight gathering of teen-age girls usu. at one of their homes at which they dress in nightclothes but pass the night more in talking than sleeping
slum·bery \ˈsləmb(ə)rē\ *adj* [ME *slumbry,* fr. *slumbir* slumber + *-y*] : SLUMBEROUS
slum·dom \ˈsləmdəm\ *n* -s [¹*slum* + *-dom*] **1 :** a district of slums ⟨wandering through ~⟩ **2 :** the quality or state of being a slum ⟨a once fashionable district declining slowly into ~ —Osbert Lancaster⟩
slum·gul·lion \,sləmˈgəlyən, ˈ⸗,⸗⸗\ *n* [³*slum* + *gullion*] **1 a :** an insipid drink (as weak tea or coffee) **b :** a meat stew **2 :** the mixed blood, oil, and salt water that collect on the decks of a ship while the valuable parts of a whale are being handled **3 :** a usu. red muddy deposit in mining sluices
slumgum \ˈ⸗,⸗\ *n* [³*slum* + *gum*] : the residue consisting chiefly of propolis, cocoons, bits of wax, and honey that remains after removal of the readily extractable honey and wax from honeycombs
slumland \ˈ⸗,⸗\ *n* [¹*slum* + *land*] : an area of slums : SLUMDOM ⟨the town is one vast ~⟩
slum·mage \ˈsləmij\ *n* -s [³*slum* + *-age*] *Brit* : impurities that settle out in fermenting vessels and casks
slummed *past of* SLUM
slumming *pres part of* SLUM
slum·mock \ˈsləmək\ *var of* SLOMMACK
slum·my \ˈsləmē, -mi\ *adj* -ER/-EST [¹*slum* + *-y*] : of, relating to, or full of slums ⟨the ~ outskirts of the city⟩
¹**slump** \ˈsləmp\ *vb* -ED/-ING/-S [prob. of Scand origin; akin to Norw *slumpa* to fall, fall upon, Dan *slumpe* to stumble, fall upon, chance upon; akin to LG *slump* marsh, slime, L *labi* to slide, slip, fall — more at SLEEP] *vi* **1 a :** to fall or sink suddenly ⟨ice cracked and he ~*ed* through⟩ **b :** to drop suddenly : fall in a heap : slide down : COLLAPSE ⟨he ~*ed* to the floor with hardly a murmur —*Phoenix Flame*⟩ ⟨slipped on the parquet and ~*ed* headlong —Richard Llewellyn⟩ **2 :** to assume an awkwardly drooping posture or carriage ⟨~*ed* onto the leather davenport —J.A.Michener⟩ ⟨she walks slowly . . . ~*ing* at the waist —Constance Walsh⟩ **3 :** to fall off : DECLINE, SAG ⟨begins to make a place for himself and then . . . suddenly ~*s* —Edmund Fuller⟩ ⟨sales ~ badly in certain territories —E.H.Shanks⟩ **4 a :** to slip or settle down ⟨rock or earth ~*s* in a landslide or above a rock that is undergoing solution⟩ **b :** to settle slightly and spread out ⟨concrete or mortar will ~ when the form is removed⟩ ~ *vt* : to cause a slump in (a market) **syn** see FALL
²**slump** \ˈ", ˈslu̇mp\ *n* -s [LG, marsh, slime] *dial Brit* : a marshy or boggy place
³**slump** \ˈsləmp\ *n* -s [LG; akin to Fris *slompe* lump, slump, D *slomp*] *chiefly Scot* : a sizable group or quantity : LUMP, BULK
⁴**slump** \ˈ"\ *vt* -ED/-ING/-S *chiefly Scot* : to classify or consider together : LUMP ⟨~*ing* the . . . candidates together —*Scots Mag.*⟩
⁵**slump** \ˈ"\ *n* -s [¹*slump*] **1 a :** a marked decline or falling off (as in prices, activity, vigor) : DROP, SAG ⟨a ~ in theater attendance⟩ ⟨fear a ~ in the party vote⟩ ⟨a period of moral ~ —S.H.Adams⟩ ⟨the normal seasonal ~ in tuna deliveries —*Wall Street Jour.*⟩ **b :** a sustained decline in economic activity or in prices : DEPRESSION ⟨a worldwide ~⟩ ⟨a ~ in the wheat market⟩ ⟨the great waste of booms and ~*s* of the business cycle —Will Irwin⟩ ⟨lost all his money in the ~ —Dorothy Sayers⟩ **c :** a period of poor or losing play by a team or individual competitor in a sport : a losing streak ⟨one spring I was in a batting ~ —Ted Williams⟩ ⟨came out of its scoring ~ and won the consolation game —*Ice Hockey Guide*⟩ **2 :** the number of inches that a mass of concrete settles after the removal of a cone-shaped metal form into which the fresh concrete has been placed in three layers — see SLUMP TEST **3 :** a fall or downward slide (as of earth or rock) : LANDSLIDE **4** *chiefly NewEng* : a dessert made by dropping biscuit dough on cooking fruit ⟨apple ~⟩ ⟨blueberry ~⟩ — compare GRUNT 3
slump bedding *n* : SLIP BEDDING
slump test *n* : a test to determine the consistency of freshly mixed concrete by measuring the slump
slums *pl of* SLUM, *pres 3d sing of* SLUM
¹**slung** *past of* SLING
²**slung** \ˈsləŋ\ *chiefly Scot var of* SLING
slung·shot \ˈsləŋ,⸗\ *n* [¹*slung* + *shot*] : a weapon consisting of a small mass of metal or stone fixed on a flexible handle or strap
¹**slunk** *past of* SLINK
²**slunk** \ˈsləŋk\ *n* -s [¹*slunk*] : SLINK 1
slunkskin \ˈ⸗,⸗\ *n* [²*slunk* + *skin*] : SLINKSKIN
slup \ˈsləp\ *vt* **slupped; slupped; slupping; slups** [perh. alter. of ³*slop*] : to sip or swallow (as soup or beverage) greedily and noisily : SLURP ⟨there wasn't a sound at the table except for Uncle . . . slupping his soup —N.R.Nash⟩
¹**slur** *R* ˈslər, + *vowel* -lər·; -*R* -lə̄, + *suffixal vowel* -lər· *also* -lə̄r, + *vowel in a following word* -lər· *or* -lə̄ *also* -lə̄r\ *vb* **slurred; slurred; slurring; slurs** [prob. of LG origin; akin to LG *slurrn* to shuffle, drag the feet, MLG *slūren* to drag, trail — more at SLUR (to soil)] *vt* **1** *obs* : to slide (a die) so as to cheat : TRICK **2 a :** to slide or slip over without due mention, consideration, or emphasis : treat superficially or dissemblingly — often used with *over* ⟨the problem of the illegitimate child . . . is *slurred* over —C.W.Cunnington⟩ ⟨~ over certain facts in one's argument⟩ ⟨*slurring* over the significance of the letter —*Times Lit. Supp.*⟩ **b :** to perform (as a duty) hurriedly : SKIMP ⟨let him not ~ his lesson —R.W.Emerson⟩ ⟨wherefore ~ the . . . ceremony —Alfred Tennyson⟩ **3 a :** to perform (two or more successive musical tones of different pitch) in a smooth or connected manner **b :** to mark (notes) with a slur **4 :** to reduce, make a substitution for, or omit (a sound or succession of sounds that occurs or that would occur in speech regarded as exemplary) : make such reduction, substitution, or omission in one's utterance of (a word or phrase) ~ *vi* **1** *dial chiefly Eng* : SLIP, SLIDE ⟨~ on ice⟩ **2 :** DRAG, SHUFFLE ⟨*slurring* through ankle-deep water —W.E.M.Campbell⟩
²**slur** \ˈ"\ *n* -s **1** *obs* **a :** a glide in dancing **b :** a sliding of dice in an attempt to cheat **2 a :** a curved line ⁀ or ‿ connecting musical notes that are to be sung to the same syllable or performed without a break (as with one stroke of a bow) — called also *bind;* compare TIE **b :** the combination of two or more slurred tones **3 :** a slurring manner of speech **4** *or* **slur cam** *or* **slur cock :** a device for depressing the sinkers in knitting machines successively by passing over them

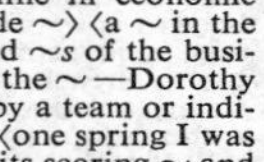

slur 2a

³**slur** \ˈ"\ *vb* **slurred; slurred; slurring; slurs** [obs. E dial. *slur* thin watery mud, fr. ME *sloor* mud; akin to MHG *slier* mud, MLG *slūren* to drag, trail, MD *sluren* to drag, trail, Norw dial. *slura* to hang loose, drag, Lith *slugti* to diminish, become small and prob. to Goth *slawan* to be silent; basic meaning: to hang loose, be slack] *vt* **1** *dial chiefly Eng* : to soil by smearing : BESMIRCH, SULLY **2 :** to cast aspersions upon : run down : DISPARAGE ⟨was always *slurring* her fellow workers⟩ ⟨*slurred* his integrity —Marguerite A. Brown⟩ **3 :** to make indistinct : OBSCURE, MASK ⟨with periods, points, and tropes he ~*s* his crimes —John Dryden⟩ **4 :** BLUR 1 ~ *vi* : to slip so as to blur or make slurs — used of a sheet being printed
⁴**slur** \ˈ"\ *n* -s **1 a :** an insulting or disparaging remark or innuendo : ASPERSION, CALUMNY ⟨his election was due to . . . last minute racial ~*s* on his opponent —William Cox⟩ ⟨the cowardly ~*s* of scandalmongers⟩ **b :** STAIN, BLOT, STIGMA ⟨his actions cast a ~ on his profession⟩ **2 :** a blurred or doubled spot or area in printed matter caused by the sliding of the paper on the printing surface at the moment of impression : MACKLE, SMUDGE
¹**slurp** \ˈslərp, -lə̄p, -ləip\ *vb* -ED/-ING/-S [D *slurpen* to lap, sip, slurp, fr. MD *slorpen;* akin to MLG *slorpen* to slurp, Norw *slurpe* to sip — more at ABSORB] *vi* : to make a sucking noise in the process of drinking or eating ~ *vt* : to eat or drink (soft food or liquid) noisily ⟨~*ing* porridge from a wooden spoon —Ogden Nash⟩
²**slurp** \ˈ"\ *n* -s : a noisy swallow or ingestion ⟨the puppy gobbled at the food in great ~*s* —Walter Karig⟩
¹**slur·ry** \ˈslər·ē, -lə·r|, |i\ *n* -ES [ME *slory;* prob. akin to ME *sloor* mud — more at SLUR] **1 a :** a watery mixture or suspension of insoluble matter (as mud, lime, plaster of paris, or wood pulp) ⟨a thin ~ of magnesia⟩ **b :** a mixture of raw materials with water in the manufacture of portland cement by the wet process **c :** a watery suspension of a fungicide or insecticide used esp. in seed treatment **d :** SLIP **2 :** REGULUS, MATTE
²**slurry** \ˈ"\ *vt* -ED/-ING/-S : to convert (as a powder or concentrate) into a slurry
³**slurry** \ˈ"\ *adj* : of, relating to, or involving the use of a slurry ⟨~ methods of seed treatment⟩
⁴**slurry** \ˈ"\ *vt* -ED/-ING/-S [ME *slorien,* prob. fr. *slory* slurry] *archaic* : SMEAR, SMIRCH
slurs *pres 3d sing of* SLUR, *pl of* SLUR
¹**slush** \ˈsləsh\ *n* -ES [perh. of Scand origin; akin to Norw *slusk* slop, slush, Sw *slask* wet, slushy weather] **1 a :** partly melted snow : watery snow **b :** a substance resembling melted snow (as a mixture of solid carbon dioxide and acetone) **c :** incoherent ice crystals formed during the early stages of freezing of salt water (as in the Arctic ocean) **2 a :** soft mud : MIRE ⟨the water was dirty with the ~ brought to the surface by the trampling —F.D.Davison⟩ **b :** liquid mud used in well drilling **c :** grout made of portland cement, sand, and water **3 :** refuse grease and fat from cooking esp. on shipboard **4 a :** a soft mixture of grease or oil and other materials for protecting the surface of metal parts against corrosion; *esp* : a mixture of white lead and lime for painting the bright parts of machines (as the connecting rods of steamboats) to preserve them from oxidation **b :** liquid enamel applied as a ground coat on metalware **5 :** SLUSH PULP **6 :** trashy and usu. cheaply sentimental material (as in a book, newspaper, or film) : RUBBISH, DRIVEL, MUSH ⟨syndicated ~⟩ ⟨the dramatic ~ known as soap operas —G.S.Perry⟩ **7** *dial Eng* : a sloppy person : SLOVEN
²**slush** \ˈ"\ *vb* -ED/-ING/-ES *vt* **1 :** to wet, splash, or soil with slush ⟨we were quite ~*ed* in the mire —R.T.Wilson⟩ **2 a :** to cover with a protective coating of paint or lubricating slush ⟨masts ~*ed* with linseed —W.P.Moore⟩ ⟨bearings . . . ~*ed* with two coatings of pure petrolatum —*Packing & Shipping*⟩ **b :** to apply a finishing material to roughly (as by dipping, spraying, or brushing) **3 :** to wash (as a deck) roughly or noisily : SLUICE ⟨waiting . . . for the bo'sun to come aloft to ~ the deck —Herman Smith⟩ **4 :** to fill in (as the joints of a wall or of a block pavement) with slush or grout — often used with *in* or *up* ⟨~ in well all the joints between the tile and brickwork —J.E.Ray⟩ **5 a :** to fill (old mine workings) hydraulically with fine waste material **b :** to transport (as ore or rock) in a scraper that is usu. drawn by a hoist and cable **6 a :** to pump (wet pulp) in paper manufacturing **b :** to extract surplus liquid from (pulp) ~ *vi* **1 :** to make one's way through slush : SLOSH, WADE ⟨~*ed* through the mire doggedly —*Century Mag.*⟩ ⟨~*ed* through waist-deep water —L.M.Uris⟩ **2 :** to make a splashing sound ⟨shoes ~*ing* in the mud —Shirley A. Grau⟩ ⟨the filthy gutter ~*es* —R.L.Stevenson⟩
³**slush** \ˈ"\ *n* -ES : a sound of or as if of slushing through soft mud or snow
slush-cast \ˈ⸗,⸗\ *vt* : to cast (as a hollow metal shape) by a process in which metal is poured into a metallic mold and immediately poured out leaving a thin solidified layer of the metal on the walls of the mold
slush casting *n* -s : a hollow casting made by the process of slush-casting
slush·er \-shə(r)\ *n* -s [²*slush* + *-er*] **1 :** one that slushes: as **a :** a worker who sprays filler over castings (as sinks or bathtubs) to make a smooth surface for the enamel coating **b :** a device for slushing **2 :** SCRAPER 1j
slush fund *n* **1 :** a fund raised from the sale of slush and other refuse (as formerly of warships) to obtain small luxuries or pleasures (as for the crew) **2 :** a fund for bribing public officials or carrying on corruptive propaganda on behalf of special interests ⟨a *slush fund* to corrupt legislatures, to purchase favors from public officers —W.O.Douglas⟩ ⟨had the support of the trucking interests with the richest *slush fund* in the state —*New Republic*⟩
slush ice *n* **1 :** ¹SLUSH 1c **2 :** FRAZIL
slush·i·ly \-shəlē, -li\ *adv* : in a slushy manner
slush·i·ness \-shēnə̇s, -shin-\ *n* -ES : the quality or state of being slushy : SENTIMENTALITY ⟨the ~ of young girls over a crooner⟩
slush·ing oil *n* : a semisolid oil or grease (as a mixture of petrolatum and rosin) used as a protective coating for bright metal surfaces
slush lamp *n* : a crude lamp burning slush, tallow, or grease
slushpit \ˈ⸗,⸗\ *n* : an excavation or diked area to receive sludge, mud, and discharged matter from an oil well
slush pulp *n* : paper pulp in water suspension
¹**slushy** \ˈsləshē, -shi\ *adj* -ER/-EST [¹*slush* + *-y* (adj. suffix)] : of, full of, or characterized by slush ⟨~ snow⟩ ⟨a ~ road⟩; *esp* : TRASHY ⟨pander to everything that's shoddy and ~ and third-rate in human nature —John Buchan⟩ ⟨~ songs —MacKinlay Kantor⟩ **syn** see SENTIMENTAL
²**slushy** \ˈ"\ *n* -ES [¹*slush* + *-y* (n. suffix)] **1** *slang* : a ship's cook **2** *Austral* : a cook's helper
slut \ˈslət, *usu* -əd·+V\ *n* -s [ME *slutte;* prob. akin to G dial. *schlote* slut, Sw dial. *slåta* slattern, D *slodder* slovenly person, slut — more at SLATTERN] **1 :** a lazy, careless, or slovenly woman : SLATTERN ⟨that ~ of a housekeeper —Margaret Kennedy⟩ **2 a :** a lewd or dissolute woman; *esp* : PROSTITUTE ⟨outrageously made up, her cheeks rouged to the eyes . . . she looked more of a ~ than any woman there —W.S.Maugham⟩ **b :** a saucy or brazen girl : HUSSY, MINX ⟨never knew any of these forward ~*s* come to good —Henry Fielding⟩ ⟨a whimsical ~ . . . who is off in peals of wanton laughter —D.B.Dodson⟩ **c :** a servant girl : MAID ⟨a most admirable ~ —Samuel Pepys⟩ **3 :** a female dog : BITCH **4** *dial* **:** a rude lamp or candle; *esp* : one made from a grease-soaked rag
¹**sluth·er** \ˈsləthə(r), -lu̇th-\ *vi* -ED/-ING/-S [alter. of ¹*slither*] *dial Eng* : to slip along : SHUFFLE, SLITHER
²**sluther** \ˈ"\ *n* -s *chiefly dial* : the act of shuffling or sliding
slut·tery \ˈsləd·ərē, -lətə-, -ri\ *n* -ES [*slut* + *-ery*] : SLUTTISHNESS
slut·tish \-d·|ish, -t|, |ēsh\ *adj* [ME, fr. *slutte* slut + *-ish*] : having the characteristics of a slut : SLOVENLY, DISORDERLY ⟨the servants awkward, ~, and slothful —Tobias Smollett⟩ ⟨his wife's careless tresses had ~ charm —Vera Caspary⟩ — **slut·tish·ly** *adv* — **slut·tish·ness** *n* -ES
slut·ty \|ē, |i\ *adj* -ER/-EST [ME, fr. *slutte* slut + *-y*] : SLUTTISH
slv *abbr* **1** sleeve **2** solvent
SLW *abbr, often not cap* straight-line wavelength
¹**sly** \ˈslī\ *adj* **slier** *also* **slyer** \-ī(ə)r, -īə\ **sliest** *also* **slyest** \-īəst\ [ME *sli, sleih, slegh,* fr. ON *slœgr* sly, crafty; akin to ON *slā* to strike, beat — more at SLAY] **1** *chiefly dial* **a :** wise in practical affairs : CANNY, SHREWD ⟨has a deal to say in his ~, dry, sententious, proverb way —Robert Burns⟩ **b :** displaying cleverness : INGENIOUS ⟨with ~ skill —Edmund Spenser⟩ **2 a :** artfully cunning : subtle in deceit : CRAFTY, GUILEFUL, WILY ⟨a ~ fox⟩ ⟨a ~ action⟩ ⟨a ~ scheme⟩ ⟨by ~ enticement gives his baneful cup —John Milton⟩ ⟨had played . . . many a ~ trick —Lyle Saxon⟩ ⟨a ~ way of prodding sales —*Business Week*⟩ **b :** trickily secret : SECRETIVE, FURTIVE ⟨he's a ~ one — had it up his sleeve all the time⟩ ⟨a ~ answer⟩ ⟨a ~ glance⟩ ⟨you have been very ~, very reserved with me —Jane Austen⟩ **3 :** lightly artful or mischievous : ARCH, ROGUISH ⟨~ jests⟩ ⟨a ~ wit⟩ ⟨churchmen, when off duty, were not averse to ~ irreverences —G.F.Whicher⟩ **4** *chiefly Austral* : carried on or sold clandestinely or illegally : ILLICIT, BOOTLEG ⟨a ~ trade⟩ ⟨selling ~ grog to the convicts —Colin Simpson⟩
syn CUNNING, CRAFTY, TRICKY, FOXY, INSIDIOUS, GUILEFUL, WILY, ARTFUL: SLY suggests devious, furtive, or secretive lack of candor or underhandedness ⟨the *sly* attack which undermines faith in our allies and among ourselves —Dean Acheson⟩ ⟨*sly* fellows to be watched —A.C.Whitehead⟩ CUNNING may apply to an overreaching, circumventing, or evading often by one of low intelligence and usu. by secret or devious means ⟨he's always slipping out at night. They're *cunning* as the devil, these naturals —Dorothy Sayers⟩ ⟨looked up with a *cunning* smile. "A servant can always know his master's secrets if he likes" —Charles Kingsley⟩ CRAFTY may describe adroitness at deceptive scheme and stratagem along with chary caution ⟨the Nazi insanity turned this mild man of conscience into a *crafty* plotter, collector of illegal funds, traffic manager of nocturnal convoys, distributor of forged passports —Hal Lehrman⟩ ⟨as truculent, as relentless in the fight, as *crafty* in legal subterfuge as the Erie men themselves —Matthew Josephson⟩ TRICKY may indicate shifty chicanery ⟨beneath all this glitter of chivalry lay the subtle, busy diplomatist . . . to all who dealt with him he was equally false and *tricky* —J.R. Green⟩ ⟨he avoided the mean and *tricky:* he was always an honorable foe —W.C.Ford⟩ FOXY may suggest practised, wary shrewdness ⟨concealment of his partnership in the Ballantyne firm and the publishing of many of his works either anonymously or under varied pseudonyms reveal a strain of *foxy* secretiveness —Edgar Johnson⟩ INSIDIOUS may apply to carefully masked underhandedness ⟨with the *insidious* undermining of respect for law and government, the vicious conception of republicanism made its appearance —V.L.Parrington⟩ GUILEFUL and WILY describe what is habitually marked by treacherous cunning or astute stratagem unctuously concealed ⟨nor trust in the *guileful* heart and the murder-loving hand —William Morris⟩ ⟨mistaking the light for a beacon, ships were lured to the treacherous reefs, there to be boarded and looted by the *wily* shoremen —*Amer. Guide Series: N.C.*⟩ ARTFUL may apply to calculating crafty deception employing the indirect or factitious ⟨if you can keep her from drink, but you can't keep her; she's that *artful* she'll get it under your very eyes, without you knowing it —Samuel Butler †1902⟩ ⟨as workingmen, under *artful* urging, began to blame the Chinese for all their wrongs —*Amer. Guide Series: Calif.*⟩ — **on the sly** *adv* : SURREPTITIOUSLY, SECRETLY ⟨read it, if at all, *on the sly,* to look for their names —A.C.Spectorsky⟩ ⟨got married *on the sly* —Helen Rich⟩
²**sly** \ˈ"\ *vi* **slied; slied; slying; slies :** to move slyly; *esp* : SLIP, SLINK — usu. used with *out* ⟨ready to ~ out the alley door, bent double —*Everybody's Mag.*⟩
sly *abbr* sloppy
slyboots \ˈ⸗,⸗\ *n pl but sing in constr* [¹*sly* + *boots*] : a sly, tricky person; *esp* : one who is cunning or mischievous in an engaging, diverting way : SCAMP, WAG ⟨the ~, how she wheedled him —W.S.Gilbert⟩ ⟨an adorable ~ of a child who was often naughty but always forgiven and indulged —Gore Vidal⟩
sly goose *n* : SHELDRAKE
sly·ly *also* **sli·ly** *adv* [ME *slily,* fr. *sli* sly + *-ly*] : in a sly manner: as **a :** SHREWDLY ⟨pointed his remarks by ~ wagging his forefinger —G.B.Shaw⟩ **b :** with covert cunning : SUBTLY ⟨offered her ~ insolent condolences on being married to a barbarian —Charles Kingsley⟩ **c :** in a surreptitious way : FURTIVELY ⟨glanced ~⟩ ⟨~ in love with their colleagues —H.T.Moore⟩ ⟨~ injected commercials —*New Yorker*⟩ **d :** ARTFULLY, ROGUISHLY
sly·ness *n* -ES [ME *sleghness, slinesse,* fr. *slegh, sli* sly + *-ness, -nesse* -ness] : the quality or state of being sly: as **a :** SHREWDNESS, CRAFTINESS ⟨a very weak position of which the bishop with praiseworthy ~ took full advantage —T.S.Eliot⟩ **b :** SECRETIVENESS ⟨led him to escape . . . the next morning with admirable ~ —Jane Austen⟩
¹**slype** *dial Eng var of* ³SLIPE
²**slype** \ˈslīp\ *n* -s [prob. fr. Flem *slijpe* place for slipping in and out, fr. MFlem *slijpen* to slip, slip out; akin to MD *slippen* to slip — more at SLIP] : a narrow passage; *specif* : one between the transept and chapter house or deanery in an English cathedral
sm *abbr* small
SM *abbr or n* -s [NL *scientiae magister*] Master of Science
SM *abbr* **1** senior magistrate **2** sergeant major **3** short meter **4** signalman **5** silver medalist **6** single deck **7** [L *sinistra mano*] left hand; mano sinistra **8** standard matched **9** state militia **10** stipendiary magistrate **11** surface measure **12** surgeon major
Sm *symbol* samarium
sma \ˈsmȯ, ˈsmä\ *Scot var of* SMALL
¹**smack** \ˈsmak\ *n* -s [ME, fr. OE *smæc;* akin to OFris *smek, smaka* taste, MD *smac, smake,* MLG *smak,* OHG *smoc,* ON *smekkr* taste, Lith *smaguriauti* to nibble, eat dainties] **1 :** characteristic taste or flavor : SAVOR; *also* : a slight or perceptible taste or tincture ⟨an orange with a bitter ~⟩ ⟨a ~ of the wood in cider⟩ **2** *obs* : LIKING, DELIGHT **3 :** a small quantity: as **a :** a trifling portion : little serving : TASTE ⟨a ~ of wine to each child⟩ **b :** a smattering of knowledge or information
syn see TASTE
²**smack** \ˈ"\ *vb* -ED/-ING/-S [ME *smacken,* alter. (influenced by *smack,* n.) of *smachen,* fr. OE *smæccan;* akin to OFris *smekka* to taste, MD *smaken,* OHG *smecken,* ON *smakka* to taste, *smekkr,* n., taste — more at ¹SMACK] *vt, archaic* : to perceive by taste or scent ~ *vi* **1 :** to have a taste or flavor ⟨wine that ~*s* of resin⟩ **2 :** to have a trace, vestige, or suggestion : reveal or retain a share, hint, or reminder — usu. used with *of* ⟨his talk ~*ed* of the sea⟩ ⟨the plan ~*s* of radicalism⟩
³**smack** \ˈ"\ *vb* -ED/-ING/-S [akin to MD & MLG *smacken* to strike, slap, throw] *vt* **1 a :** to close and open (lips) noisily and in rapid succession esp. in eating ⟨~*ing* his lips over the soup⟩ **b :** to consume (food or drink) with evident and sometimes noisy satisfaction **2 a :** to kiss vigorously with or as if with a smack ⟨~*ed* his cousin on the cheek⟩ **b :** to strike (as a person) in such a manner as to produce a smacking sound; *esp* : to strike with the palm of the open hand ⟨~ his ugly face⟩ **3 :** to move, place, or bring into contact with a smack ⟨~*ed* down the paper⟩ ⟨~*ing* her hands together⟩ ~ *vi* : to make or give a smack : do something with a smack
⁴**smack** \ˈ"\ *n* -s [akin to MD *smac* slap, throw, MLG *smak*] **1 :** a quick sharp noise made by rapidly compressing and opening the lips (as in gusto or kissing) **2 :** a loud kiss : BUSS ⟨a ~ on the cheek⟩ **3 :** a sharp slap with the palm of the open hand or sometimes with another flat surface; *broadly* : any quick sharp resounding blow ⟨hit the ball a powerful ~ with his bat⟩
⁵**smack** \ˈ"\ *adv* [⁴*smack*] **1 :** with the sudden violence of a smack : squarely and sharply : PLUMP ⟨ran ~ into the wall⟩ **2 :** as direct or as evident as a smack : COMPLETELY, UNDEVIATINGLY
⁶**smack** \ˈ"\ *n* -s [D *smak* or LG *smack;* prob. fr. MD & MLG *smacken* to strike, slap; fr. the slapping of the sail] **:** a sailing vessel (as a sloop or cutter) used chiefly in coasting and fishing: as **a** *Brit* : a large fishing vessel strictly fore-and-aft rigged — compare LUGGER **b** *also* **smack boat :** a fore-and-aft-rigged fishing boat having a well in which fish are kept alive — called also *well smack*
smack-dab \ˈ⸗ˈ⸗\ *adv* [⁵*smack* + *dab*] *dial* : SQUARELY, EXACTLY ⟨stood *smack-dab* in the middle of the parlor —Helen Eustis⟩
smacked *adj* [fr. past part. of ³*smack*] *chiefly Midland* : GROUND ⟨~ peanut hulls⟩
smack·er \ˈsmakə(r)\ *n* -s [³*smack* + *-er*] **1 :** one that smacks **2** *slang* : DOLLAR
smack·er·oo \,smakəˈrü\ *n* -s [alter. of *smacker*] *slang* : DOLLAR
¹**smacking** *adj* [fr. pres. part. of ³*smack*] **1 :** BRISK, LIVELY, SPANKING ⟨a ~ breeze⟩ **2 :** outstanding in some respect (as size or excellence) — **smack·ing·ly** *adv*
²**smacking** *n* -s [fr. gerund of ³*smack*] : the act of or sound made by one who smacks ⟨gave the child a good ~⟩ ⟨the ~ of the sail against the mast⟩
smacks·man \ˈsmaksmən\ *n, pl* **smacksmen** [*smacks* (gen. of ⁶*smack*) + *man*] : one of the crew of a fishing smack; *also* : the owner of a smack
smack-smooth \ˈ⸗ˈ⸗\ *adv (or adj)* [⁵*smack* + *smooth*] : so as to leave or involve no projection, irregularity, or imperfection
smaik \ˈsmāk\ *n* -s [ME] *Scot* : SCOUNDREL, RASCAL

smairt \'smärt\ *Scot var of* SMART

1small \'smȯl\ *adj* -ER/-EST [ME *smal*, fr. OE *smæl*; akin to OHG *smal* small, ON *smali* small cattle, Icel *smalr* small, Goth *smalista* smallest, L *malus* bad, Gk *mēlon* sheep, goat, Arm *mal* sheep, ram] **1 a :** slight in circumference esp. as compared with length or with another similar thing ⟨a ~ waist⟩ ⟨sausage casings made from the ~ bowel⟩ **b** *archaic* **:** narrow in width esp. as compared with length **2 a :** having little size esp. as compared with other similar things **:** not large or extended in dimensions, girth, or mass ⟨a ~ house⟩ ⟨~ lumps of coal⟩ ⟨the child is ~ for his age⟩ **b :** small in size by reason of incomplete growth **:** IMMATURE, YOUNG ⟨toys for ~ children⟩ ⟨~ plants for bedding⟩ **c** (1) **:** consisting of small pieces or units ⟨the branches yield ~ wood for burning⟩ (2) **:** LITTLE 1a(5) **d** *of a letter* **:** comparatively small in size, usu. less angular than the corresponding capital letter, and in print usu. having a body that does not extend above lower-case x height but in several letters having the overall height increased upward by an ascender or downward by a descender **3** *dial Eng* **:** fine in texture or in the size of constituent particles **:** not coarse or heavy ⟨a ~ misty rain⟩ **4 a :** of little influence, power, or authority **:** of low rank **:** lacking high position or status ⟨the ~ people who are the backbone of the nation⟩ **b :** lacking prominence in a particular sphere **:** minor in rank or ability **:** not noteworthy or great ⟨a ~ poets⟩: as (1) **:** being such to a limited degree **:** PETTY ⟨~ criminals⟩ (2) **:** having little capital or resources **:** operating on a limited scale in respect to assets, employees, and volume of business ⟨a ~ farmer⟩ ⟨~ manufactories⟩; *also* **:** having or serving a small clientele ⟨~ shops⟩ ⟨a ~ tradesman⟩ **5 :** lacking in strength: as **a** *of the voice* **:** GENTLE, SOFT **b :** very dilute; *esp* **:** deficient in or free from alcohol ⟨the wine was very thin and ~⟩ **6 a :** little in a way that is objectively measurable (as in quantity, amount, value, duration, extent) ⟨a ~ number⟩ ⟨a ~ salary⟩ ⟨a ~ distance away⟩ ⟨waited a ~ space of time⟩ **b :** made up of units that are few in number, little in size, low in value, or otherwise objectively small ⟨a ~ standing army⟩ ⟨~ change⟩ **7 a :** of little consequence, weight, or importance **:** INSIGNIFICANT ⟨a ~ fault⟩ ⟨played a ~ role in the show⟩ **b :** lacking in prominence **:** HUMBLE, MODEST ⟨living in a ~ way⟩ ⟨from such ~ beginnings⟩ **c** *of language* **:** PLAIN, SIMPLE **8 :** limited or slight in degree, intensity, scope, or similar quality **:** less and often markedly less than is usual, expected, or fitting **:** TRIFLING ⟨had ~ interest in public affairs⟩ ⟨paying ~ heed to his mother's warning⟩ ⟨suffered a ~ mishap⟩ **9 a :** lacking in largeness of spirit **:** not large-minded or generous **:** MEAN ⟨a ~ and cruel revenge⟩ ⟨a harsh ~ man⟩ **b :** HUMILIATED, HUMBLED ⟨never felt so ~ in his life⟩

syn SMALL, LITTLE, DIMINUTIVE, WEE, TINY, TEENY, WEENY, MINUTE, MICROSCOPIC, MINIATURE, and PETITE agree in meaning noticeably below the average in magnitude, esp. physical. SMALL and LITTLE are often interchangeable, but SMALL more frequently applies to things whose magnitude is formulated in terms of number, size, capacity, value, or significance ⟨a *small* audience⟩ ⟨a *small* child⟩ ⟨a *small* car⟩ ⟨*small* bills⟩ ⟨a *small* effect upon one's life⟩ ⟨a *small* reputation⟩ or modifies words like *quantity, amount, size,* or *capacity* ⟨a *small* quantity of flour⟩ ⟨rooms of a *small* size⟩ or limits intangible or generally immeasurable things ⟨a *small* mind⟩ ⟨a *small* personality⟩ ⟨a *small* prospect of succeeding⟩ LITTLE is usu. more absolute in implication, often carrying the idea of petiteness, pettiness, or insignificance in literal or figurative size, amount, quantity, or extent ⟨a *little* woman⟩ ⟨our *little* ambitions⟩ ⟨a *little* mind⟩ ⟨a *little* man in all qualities of character⟩ ⟨*little* hope of a cure⟩ LITTLE also often signifies a small amount, a small quantity, or a small extent of (something) ⟨a *little* meat⟩ ⟨a small house and a *little* land⟩ or carries a note of pathos, tenderness, or affection ⟨a *little* heart-rending smile⟩ ⟨a *little* adorable child⟩ DIMINUTIVE can stress not only smallness but often extreme, sometimes abnormal, smallness in comparison ⟨peasants who have wine for their ordinary drink, are of a *diminutive* size —Tobias Smollett⟩ ⟨a little black mustache and *diminutive* chin-beard —George Santayana⟩ ⟨*diminutive* houses and furniture fit only for dolls —W.H.Mallock⟩ ⟨these *diminutive* crabs are scavengers and live in holes in the mud at tide line —*Amer. Guide Series: Fla.*⟩ PETITE applies to a proportionally small but usu. pleasingly trim woman or girl ⟨*petite* in stature: her height is about five feet, her weight, 112 pounds —*Current Biog.*⟩ ⟨a *petite* actress with strong box-office appeal⟩ WEE is homely or dialect for DIMINUTIVE ⟨though my own interest quickened, my *wee* son, then aged one-and-a-half years, grew distinctly bored —O.S.Nock⟩ ⟨a *wee* drop of whiskey⟩ TINY goes farther than DIMINUTIVE in suggesting extreme littleness or smallness by comparison ⟨in my lapel was a *tiny* gold lizard —Victor Canning⟩ ⟨the poisonous ingredient which magnified will kill, but in *tiny* quantities will cure —B.N.Cardozo⟩ ⟨children who squat patiently over those *tiny* little holes in the ground where doodlebugs are thought to live —Carson McCullers⟩ ⟨a wee *tiny* voice⟩ TEENY and WEENY, occurring chiefly in children's or playful or humorous use, denote the same thing as DIMINUTIVE or WEE; the variant forms *teeny-weeny, teeny-tiny, teensy-weensy,* and similar reduplications, merely emphasize diminutiveness more or are more childish or playful ⟨a little *teeny* dog can make enough racket to attract neighbors' attention —*English Digest*⟩ ⟨two veteran progressive-school teachers who have grown a *weeny* bit tired of their energetic, articulate, expressive little charges —Dwight MacDonald⟩ ⟨a *teeny-weeny* little dwarf⟩ ⟨when I was a *teensy-weensy* little girl⟩ MICROSCOPIC applies to or suggests what is small or insignificant enough to be observed usu. only by the use of a microscope ⟨*microscopic* germs⟩ ⟨*microscopic* particles of dust⟩ ⟨the mill workers who labored twelve or thirteen or fourteen hours a day for a *microscopic* wage —F.L.Allen⟩ ⟨traverses rolling farm country, spans creeks, passes through *microscopic* settlements, and penetrates scrubby woodland —*Amer. Guide Series: Pa.*⟩ MINUTE means extremely small in an absolute sense, usu. on a microscopic or near-microscopic scale ⟨mollusks drill *minute* holes in the shells through which they suck the oyster —*Amer. Guide Series: Fla.*⟩ ⟨the *minute* and steady click of Mrs. Millington's needle —Walter de la Mare⟩ MINIATURE applies to what is complete but built, drawn, or made on a very small scale ⟨a *miniature* shower of pink petals —Harriet La Barre⟩ ⟨the park has a swimming pool for children, a *miniature* waterfall, and a small powerhouse and water-wheel —*Amer. Guide Series: Mich.*⟩ ⟨the child was a *miniature* version of the father⟩

2small \"\ *adv* -ER/-EST [ME *smale, smal*, fr. OE *smale*, fr. *smæl*, adj.] **1 :** in or into small-sized pieces **:** FINE ⟨grate ~⟩ ⟨the meat served ~ on toast⟩ **2** *obs* **:** to a slight extent or degree **:** very little **3 :** without force or loudness **:** FAINTLY, TIMIDLY ⟨you may speak as ~ as you will —Shak.⟩ **4 :** in a small way, manner, or size **:** in miniature **5 :** CONTEMPTUOUSLY, DISDAINFULLY ⟨think ~ of one's neighbors⟩

3small \"\ *n* -S [ME *smal*, fr. *smal*, adj.] **1 :** a part that is smaller and esp. narrower than the remainder or than adjacent parts ⟨the ~ of the back⟩; *esp* **:** the posterior part of a whale between the vent and the flukes of the tail **2 a smalls** *pl* **:** small-sized products (as notions, bread, rolls, screws) ⟨kept a good stock of ~s⟩ **b smalls** *pl, chiefly Scot* **:** small portions **:** DRIBLETS **c smalls** *pl, chiefly Brit* (1) **:** small articles of clothing (as underclothing) or household linen (2) **:** SMALLCLOTHES 1 **d :** coal, ore, or ore-bearing rock that passes through small meshes of a specified size — usu. used in pl. **e smalls** *pl, Brit* **:** articles of freight under a specified weight (as 200 pounds) for carriage of which an extra charge or surtax is made **3 smalls** *pl, slang* **:** RESPONSIONS — **by small and small :** by slow degrees **:** bit by bit

4small \"\ *vb* -ED/-ING/-S [ME *smalen*, fr. *smal*, adj.] *vt, obs* **:** to make small or less **:** LESSEN ~ *vi* **:** to become small or less **:** DIMINISH ⟨the road ~s in the distance⟩

small·age \-lij\ *n* -S [ME *smalege*, alter. of *smalache*, fr. *smal* small + *ache* wild celery, parsley — more at ACHE] **:** a strongly scented erect biennial herb (*Apium graveolens*) that is the wild form of the culinary celery and is widely distributed in moist situations in temperate regions

small ale *n* **:** a weak ale brewed with little malt and little or no hops as a mild and cheap drink

small and early *n* **:** an evening party (as an informal reception or dance) attended by comparatively few guests and breaking up early

small arm *n* **:** a firearm capable of being fired while held with one or both hands — usu. used in pl.

1small beer *n* **1 :** weak or inferior beer **2 :** something of small importance **:** insignificant matters **:** TRIVIA

2small beer *adv* **:** with contempt **:** SCORNFULLY — usu. used with a negative ⟨thought no *small beer* of themselves for having been out of their depths —Thomas Hughes⟩

small-beer \'=ˌ=\ *adj* [*1small beer*] **:** marked by little importance, significance, or worth **:** TRIVIAL ⟨finding a pleasure in these ~ chronicles —W.M.Thackeray⟩

small-billed water thrush \'=ˌ=-\ *n* **:** NORTHERN WATER THRUSH

small bluet *n* **:** a star violet (*Houstonia patens*)

small bond *n* **:** BABY BOND

small-bore \'=ˌ=\ *adj* **1 a** *of a firearm* **:** having a small or relatively small bore; *esp* **:** having a caliber of .22 inches — distinguished from *big-bore* **b :** of, relating to, or involving the use of small-bore firearms ⟨*small-bore* competition⟩ **2 :** narrow in outlook ⟨*small-bore* politicians⟩

small bower *n* **:** an anchor carried in the bow of a ship

small broomrape *n* **:** a broomrape (*Orobanche minor*) having a loose spike of flowers with two basal bracts and a corolla with rounded lobes — called also *hellroot*

small bugloss *n* **:** a Eurasian annual weed (*Lycopsis arvensis*) naturalized in No. America and having rough hairy leaves and small bluish flowers in one-sided racemes

small calorie *n* **:** CALORIE a

small cane *n* **:** a grass (*Arundinaria tecta*) having large sheaths enfolding the flowering shoots

small capital *n* **:** a letter having the form of and about two thirds the size of a capital letter (as in THESE WORDS) that is typically used for cross reference and in abbreviations (as A.D., B.C.) — abbr. *s. c., sm. cap.*

small chair *n* **:** a chair (as a side chair) that has no arms

small change *n* **1 :** money consisting of small coins — contrasted with *folding money* **2 :** something as trifling, petty, or as quickly circulated as small change

small circle *n* **:** a circle formed on the surface of a sphere by the intersection of a plane that does not pass through the center of the sphere; *specif* **:** such a circle on the surface of the earth — compare GREAT CIRCLE

small claim *n* **:** a debt or claim of small amount and esp. of an amount sufficiently small (as 50 dollars) to bring it within the jurisdiction of a special court of more or less expeditious or summary procedure

small-claims court *n* **:** a special court intended to simplify and expedite the handling of small debts or claims

smallclothes \'=ˌ=\ *n pl* **1 :** knee breeches esp. of the close-fitting type worn in the 18th and early 19th centuries **2 :** small articles of clothing (as underclothing, handkerchiefs, children's garments)

small coal *n* **1** *obs* **:** CHARCOAL **2 :** small-sized coal

small crabgrass *n* **:** a rather small somewhat glabrous and often purplish Eurasian grass (*Digitaria ischaemum*) that is widely naturalized and often a pest in lawns — called also *smooth crabgrass*

small cranberry *n* **:** EUROPEAN CRANBERRY

small debt *n, Brit* **:** SMALL CLAIM

small-debts court *n, Brit* **:** SMALL-CLAIMS COURT

small·en \'smȯlən\ *vt* [*1small* + *-en*] *dial* **:** to make smaller

smaller *adj* [fr. *smaller*, comparative of *1small*] **:** LESSER

smaller pine sawyer *n* **:** a pine sawyer (*Monochamus scutellatus*)

smallest *superlative of* SMALL

small fruit *n* **:** a low-growing plant (as a shrub, bramble, or herb) that produces table fruit; *also* **:** a fruit (as the strawberry, raspberry, or currant) produced on such a plant — compare BUSH FRUIT, CANE FRUIT, TREE FRUIT

small-fruited hickory \'=ˌ=-\ *n* **:** SMALL PIGNUT

small-fry \'=ˌ=\ *adj* [fr. the phrase *small fry*] **1 :** MINOR, UNIMPORTANT ⟨a *small-fry* politician⟩ **2 :** of, relating to, or made up of children **:** intended for children **:** CHILDISH ⟨*small-fry* sports⟩

small game *n* **:** game birds and mammals not classed as big game

small goods *n pl* **1 :** SMALL 2a **2** *Austral* **:** edible meat by-products

small grain *n* **:** a cereal (as wheat, oats, barley, rye, rice) having relatively small kernels or sometimes a relatively small plant as distinguished from a plant (as corn) with large kernels or sometimes from a cereal (as sorghum) with a large plant but small kernels or from a similarly cultured and used seed (as soybean) with a relatively small plant and large seeds

small-headed fly \'=ˌ=-\ *n* **:** a fly of the family Cyrtidae

small helm *n* **:** a helm at only a small angle to the keel of a ship

small henbit *n* **:** IVY-LEAVED SPEEDWELL

smallholder \'=ˌ=\ *n, chiefly Brit* **:** an owner or operator of a small holding

small holding *n, chiefly Brit* **:** a piece of land detached from a cottage, hired or owned by a laboring man, and cultivated to supplement his main income — compare ALLOTMENT

small honeysuckle *n* **:** a yellow honeysuckle (*Lonicera dioica*)

small horde *n, usu cap S&H* [trans. of Kirghiz *kitchi-juz*] **:** a division of the Great Horde

small hours *n pl* **:** hours of the early morning immediately following midnight — used with *the*

smalling *pres part of* SMALL

small intestine *n* **:** the anterior portion of the intestine that is lined with a complex glandular mucous membrane which secretes digestive enzymes and through which digested nutrients pass to enter the blood and lymph — see VILLUS; compare LARGE INTESTINE; see DIGESTION illustration

small·ish \'smȯlish, -lēsh\ *adj* [ME *smalish*, fr. *smal* small + *-ish*] **:** somewhat small **:** slightly below normal size

small laurel *n* **:** MOUNTAIN LAUREL 1

small-leaved linden *also* **small-leaved lime** \'=ˌ=-\ *n* **:** a large spreading European linden (*Tilia cordata*) that has small somewhat cordate dark green leaves and is often cultivated as a shade tree

small line *n* **:** a fishing line for use in shallow water ⟨a *small line* boat⟩

small magnolia *n* **1 :** EVERGREEN MAGNOLIA **2 :** SWEET BAY 2

small mean *n* **:** the second string of a viol — compare GREAT MEAN

small-minded \'=ˌ==\ *adj* **1 :** having few and petty interests, narrow sympathies, or rigid outlook **:** lacking breadth of mind ⟨a *small-minded* man⟩ **2 :** typical of a small-minded person **:** marked esp. by pettiness, narrowness, meanness ⟨*small-minded* conduct⟩ — **small-minded·ly** *adv* — **small-minded·ness** *n* -ES

small money *n* **:** SMALL CHANGE

smallmouth black bass *also* **smallmouthed black bass** *or* **smallmouth bass** *or* **smallmouthed bass** \'=ˌ=-\ *or* **smallmouth** \'=ˌ=\ *n* **:** a black bass (*Micropterus dolomieu*) that lives chiefly in cool clear rivers and lakes, is bronzy green above and lighter below, and has the angle of the jaw falling below the eye — compare LARGEMOUTH BLACK BASS

smallmouth buffalo *n* **:** a common buffalo fish (*Ictiobus bubalus*) that is usu. smaller and slenderer than the bigmouth and black buffalos and is a superior food fish

small·ness *n* -ES [ME *smalnesse*, fr. *smal* small + *-nesse* -ness] **1 :** the quality or state of being small **2 :** something that is small

small nettle *n* **:** an annual European weed (*Urtica urens*) naturalized throughout No. America and having stinging foliage and green flowers in lax elongating clusters that exceed the leaf petioles in length

small octave *n* **:** a musical octave that begins on the first C below middle C — see PITCH illustration

small part *n* **:** a minor role in a theatrical performance

small pastern bone *n* **:** the second phalanx of the functional digit of the foot of an equine

small people *n, chiefly dial* **:** FAIRIES

small pica *n* **:** an old size of type between long primer and pica and approximately 11 point

small pignut *n* **:** a smooth-barked hickory (*Carya ovalis*) with 5 to 7 leaflets; *also* **:** its nearly round small white nut

small potato *n* **:** someone or something of trivial importance or worth and usu. merely petty ⟨you are a *small potato* in the world —*Times Lit. Supp.*⟩ — usu. used in pl. but sing. or pl. in constr. ⟨he was *small potatoes* in my book⟩

1smallpox \'=ˌ=\ *n* [*1small* + *pox*] **1 :** an acute contagious febrile virus disease characterized by constitutional symptoms and successive stages of skin eruptions of which the last is marked by pustules, sloughing, and scar formation **2 :** BITTER PIT

2smallpox \"\ *vt* **:** to infect or scar with smallpox

smallpox plant *n* **:** a pitcher plant (*Sarracenia purpurea*)

small print *n* **:** FINE PRINT ⟨always read the *small print* —D.G. Gerahty⟩

small purple fringed orchis *n* **:** a rather small orchid (*Habenaria psychodes*) of moist parts of northeastern No. America with pink to rosy purple or occasionally white flowers distinguished by a broad lip deeply cleft into three lacerate segments

small reed *n* **:** REED BENT 1

smalls *pl of* SMALL, *pres 3d sing of* SMALL

small sagebrush *n* **:** a very low-growing sagebrush (*Artemisia nova*) of dry uplands of western No. America that is an important browse plant

small-scale \'=¦=\ *adj* **1 a :** small in scope; *esp* **:** having a small output or product ⟨a *small-scale* pilot plant⟩ ⟨*small-scale* farms⟩ **b :** occupied with or engaged in a small-scale operation ⟨a *small-scale* retailer⟩ **2** *of a map* **:** having a scale (as one inch to 25 miles) that permits plotting of comparatively little detail — compare LARGE-SCALE

small-seeded false flax \'=ˌ==-\ *n* **:** a weedy annual European false flax (*Camelina microcarpa*) that is a widely naturalized No. American weed, is similar to but generally smaller than gold of pleasure, and has been implicated in livestock poisoning when excessive amounts of the seed are present in feed

smallshot \'=ˌ=\ *n, slang* **:** a person of no importance or prominence

small slam *n* **:** LITTLE SLAM

small soapweed *n* **:** a short-stemmed or acaulescent yucca (*Yucca glauca*) of the central U. S. with usu. white-margined leaves and greenish white pendulous flowers

small solomon's seal *n, usu cap 2d S* **:** a low-growing Solomon's seal (*Polygonatum biflorum*) that is widely distributed in eastern No. America

small spelt *n* **:** EINKORN

small spikenard *n* **1 :** an American spikenard (*Aralia racemosa*) **2 :** WILD SARSAPARILLA 1

small stores *n pl* **:** articles of regulation issue clothing sold for cash by the supply officer of a naval ship or station to naval personnel

small strongyle *n* **:** CYLICOSTOME

small stuff *n* **:** spun yarn, marline, and other small rope that is used aboard ship and is usu. identified by the number of threads or yarns which it contains

smallsword \'=ˌ=\ *n* **:** a light tapering sword designed for thrusting and used esp. in the 18th century for dueling and fencing

small talk *n* **:** light or casual conversation **:** CHITCHAT

small-talk \'=ˌ=\ *vi* [*small talk*] **:** to engage in or be given to small talk

small tiger lily *n* **:** a tall-growing lily (*Lilium parvum*) of moist spots in the coastal mountains of the western U. S. that usu. produces large numbers of small funnelform purple-spotted yellowish orange flowers

small time *n* **:** theatrical and esp. vaudeville circuits where the pay is small and acts are shown three or more times a day

small-time \'smȯl¦tīm\ *adj* [*small time*] **:** belonging to a minor, small-scale, or local organization or to a petty gang obtaining only small returns **:** insignificant in performance and standing

small-tim·er \"+ə(r)\ *n* [*small time* + *-er*] **:** one that is small-time or belongs to a small-time group

small-toothed palm civet \'=ˌ=-\ *n* **:** any of several eastern Asian palm civets (genus *Arctogalidea*)

small-town \'=¦=\ *adj* [fr. *small town*, n] **:** of, belonging to, or characteristic of a small city or a large village, its life, or its inhabitants — usu. distinguished from *urban* and *metropolitan* ⟨*small-town* girls⟩ ⟨*small-town* customs⟩ ⟨a *small-town* outlook⟩

small-town·er \"+ə(r)\ *n* -S [*small town* + *-er*] **1 :** a resident of a small town **2 :** a person with small-town characteristics (as of thought or behavior)

small vehicle *n* **:** HINAYANA

smallware \'=ˌ=\ *n* **1** *Brit* **:** small articles of merchandise; *esp* **:** NOTIONS — usu. used in pl. **2** *Brit* **:** narrow fabrics

small white *n* **1 :** CABBAGE BUTTERFLY a **2 a** *usu cap S&W* **:** a British breed of small white hogs that tend to be somewhat chuffy and deficient in lean meat — compare LARGE WHITE **b :** an animal of the Small White breed

small woodbine *n* **:** YELLOW HONEYSUCKLE 1a

1smal·ly \'smȯlē\ *adv* [ME, fr. *smal* small + *-ly*] **1** *obs* **:** MINUTELY, SCANTILY **2** *obs* **:** in a small quantity, degree, or manner; *also* **:** not numerously or largely **3 :** on a small scale **:** DELICATELY, FINELY, SLENDERLY ⟨~ built⟩

2smally \'smȯlē, 'smälē, -li\ *adj* [*1small* + *-y*] *chiefly dial* **:** rather small

smalt \'smȯlt\ *n* -S [MF, fr. OIt *smalto*, of Gmc origin; akin to OHG *smelzan* to melt — more at SMELT] **1 :** a blue glass made by fusing potassium carbonate, silica, and cobalt oxide and used in powdered form chiefly as a colorant for glass and vitreous enamels — often used in pl. but sing. or pl. in constr. **2 :** a moderate blue that is redder and duller than average copen, redder and deeper than azurite blue, Dresden blue, or pompadour, and greener and deeper than luster blue — called also *cobalt glass, Dumont's blue, king's blue, powder blue, starch blue* **3 :** sand colored for use in producing a rough decorative long-wearing surface with paint

smalt green *n* **:** COBALT GREEN 2

smalt·ite \'smȯl,tīt\ *also* **smalt·ine** \-ltən, -l,tēn\ *n* -S [*smaltite* alter. of *smaltine*; *smaltine* F, fr. *smalt* + *-ine*] **:** a tin-white or gray isometric mineral $(Co,Ni)As_{3-x}$ of metallic luster that is an arsenide of cobalt and nickel and is isomorphous with skutterudite and chloanthite (hardness 5.5–6, sp. gr. 6.4–6.6)

smal·to \'smäl(,)tō\ *n, pl* **smaltos** \-ōz\ *also* **smal·ti** \-lē\ [It, smalt, smalto] **:** colored glass or enamel for use in mosaic work; *also* **:** a piece of such material

smaltz \'smȯlts\ *n* -ES [prob. alter. of *smalts*, pl. of *smalt*] **:** SMALT 1

smar·agd \'sma,ragd\ *n* -S [ME *smaragde*, fr. OF *smaragde, esmeragde, esmeraude, esmeralde* — more at EMERALD] **:** EMERALD

sma·rag·dine \smə'ragdən\ *adj* [L *smaragdinus*, fr. *smaragdus* emerald + *-inus* -ine — more at EMERALD] **:** of or relating to emerald **:** yellowish green in color like an emerald

sma·rag·dite \smə'rag,dīt\ *n* -S [F, fr. L *smaragdus* + F *-ite*] **:** a mineral consisting of a green foliated amphibole often derived from common diallage

smarm \'smärm\ *or* **smalm** \-äm\ *vb* [origin unknown] *vt, dial* **:** SMEAR ⟨more color in her cheeks, natural, than what they could ~ on out of a box —Richard Llewellyn⟩ ~ *vi* **:** GUSH, SLOBBER ⟨would ~ over me just the way they do over you —Robertson Davies⟩

smarmy \'smärmē\ *adj* -ER/-EST **1 :** SLEEK ⟨*smarmy*-headed —David Walker⟩ **2 :** unctuously or fulsomely flattering **:** SLOBBERY, GUSHING, OILY, INSINUATING ⟨young man with the ~ voice —Noel Coward⟩ ⟨coy and ~ —Bernard Hollowood⟩ ⟨~ insincerity —Eric Partridge⟩ ⟨a ~ little melody —*Time*⟩

1smart \'smär|t, -mȧ|, *usu* |d.+V\ *vb* -ED/-ING/-S [ME *smerten*, fr. OE *smeortan*; akin to MD *smerten, smarten* to pain, hurt, MLG *smerten*, OHG *smerzan* to pain, hurt, L *mordēre* to bite, Gk *smerdnos* terrible, fearful, *marainein* to waste away, Skt *mṛdnāti, mardati* he pulverizes, crushes, destroys, and perh. to L *mort-, mors* death — more at MURDER] *vi* **1 a :** to be the source or seat of a sharp stinging or cutting usu. local and superficial pain ⟨a cut that ~ed badly but was not serious⟩ ⟨face ~ed where his razor had scraped the skin⟩ ⟨rapid fatigue with burning and ~ing of the conjunctiva —H.G.Armstrong⟩ ⟨the ~ing of his wounded vanity —G.B.Shaw⟩ **b :** to cause or produce such a pain ⟨this liniment will ~⟩ ⟨a slap that was hard enough to ~⟩ **c :** to feel or have such a pain ⟨his skin was ~ing wherever the acrid fumes had come into contact with his skin⟩ ⟨and more than once under the lash of the cruel overseer⟩ ⟨this liniment will make you ~ but it will do you good⟩ **2 a :** to feel sharp mental pain or distress (as in re-

morse or in consequence of a real or fancied grievance) : suffer keenly in mind or feelings — usu. used with *under* ⟨~*ing* under the prickings of his own conscience⟩ ⟨~*ing*, evidently, under a sense of wrong —Susan Ertz⟩ ⟨had ~*ed* for years under his father's low opinion of him —Herman Wouk⟩ or with *from* ⟨~*ing* from his dismissal —R.A.Billington⟩ ⟨~*ing* from their defeats —*Wall Street Jour.*⟩ or sometimes with *over* ⟨~*ing* over the civil rights issue —R.E.Lee⟩ or *at* ⟨still ~*ing* at his too candid criticism —W.H.Hudson †1922⟩ ⟨then suddenly ~*ed* at her own pettishness —Sheila Kaye-Smith⟩ **b** : to suffer severely as a penalty — usu. used with *for* ⟨feared that someday he would ~ for this foolishness⟩ ⟨you will be made to ~ for this offense⟩ **~** *vt* : to cause to smart : act on as an irritant

²smart \"\ *adj* -ER/-EST [ME *smert, smart*, fr. OE *smeart*; akin to OE *smeortan* to smart — more at ¹SMART] **1 a** *archaic* : causing smarting : attended by smarting : arousing or marked by a sharp stinging or cutting pain ⟨their softest touch as ~ as lizard's stings —Shak.⟩ ⟨a ~ sensation⟩ **b** : so severe as to cause smarting ⟨a ~ thrashing⟩ ⟨winced under the ~ cut of the whip⟩ ⟨administered a ~ reproof⟩ **2 a** : marked by often sudden sharp intensity : showing sharp forceful activity ⟨brought the kettle to a ~ boil⟩ ⟨a ~ rally in oil stocks⟩ ⟨a ~ shock of surprise —Ambrose Bierce⟩ ⟨a ~ shower from the sinking sun —George Meredith⟩ **b** : marked by strength or pungency — used of liquors ⟨a ~ full-bodied wine⟩ ⟨I'm after bringing down a ~ drop —J.M.Synge⟩ **3 a** : marked by or suggesting brisk vigor, speedy effective activity, or spirited liveliness ⟨walking at a ~ pace⟩ ⟨a ~ trot⟩ ⟨a ~ gust of wind⟩ ⟨a brief but ~ skirmish⟩ **b** : seeming well suited to quick vigorous activity : not weak, flaccid, enervated, or obese ⟨a ~ physique⟩ **4 a** : having or showing mental alertness and quickness of perception, shrewd informed calculation, or contriving resourcefulness : BRIGHT, CLEVER, QUICK-WITTED ⟨wish I was ~ enough to invent something and maybe get rich —Sherwood Anderson⟩ ⟨~ children talk earlier and dull children talk later than the average —Morris Fishbein⟩ ⟨the race is no longer to the strong but to the ~ —F.V.Drake⟩ ⟨when are you going to get ~ and shut up for a while —Harvey Granite⟩ ⟨~ politics⟩ ⟨a ~ move⟩ ⟨a ~ investment⟩ ⟨~ management⟩ **b** : shrewd, sharp, and of questionable honesty esp. in the furthering of self-interest ⟨loaded with prizes for the ~ guys . . . full of booby traps for the unwary —W.H.Upson⟩ ⟨which a few ~ men at the top manipulated in their own interest —Elmer Davis⟩ ⟨making a fast buck . . . ~, a smooth operator —Marc Brandel⟩ **5 a** : marked by keen ready wit and repartee, amusing cleverness, or facetious pertness ⟨the essence of English ~ comedy is its combination of verbal distinction with intellectual impertinence —H.E.Clurman⟩ ⟨had been supposed to be clever and had said ~ things to him —Samuel Butler †1902⟩ **b** : impertinently witty or facetious : FLIP, FRESH, SAUCY ⟨gave his mother a ~ answer⟩ ⟨was punished for being ~⟩ ⟨an unpleasantly ~ attitude toward things that were not funny⟩ **6 a** : dashing in appearance : well turned out : NEAT, TRIM, SPRUCE, TIDY: (1) : showing the trimness of efficient design and careful maintenance : promising speed and reliable performance ⟨a ~ new yacht⟩ ⟨the ~*est* ship of the fleet⟩ ⟨drove his blooded horses to his ~ carriages —John Reed⟩ (2) : stylish in dress : showing careful attention to details of appearance : NATTY ⟨uniform of green faced with orange, *smart*-looking in spite of being patched —Kenneth Roberts⟩ ⟨trim and ~, from her bronze hair so well done to the end of her neat silver-slippered toe —Louis Bromfield⟩ **b** : showing fashion, elegance, richness, dash, modernity, or striking quality : appealing to sophisticated wealthier tastes ⟨the ~ suburban air —*Amer. Guide Series: N.Y. City*⟩ ⟨the hotel . . . is not at all ~ but very comfortable —Willa Cather⟩ **7** : characteristic of or patronized by exclusive ultrafashionable society ⟨the restaurant is small, exclusive, terribly ~ —T.H.Fielding⟩ ⟨locations which are considered ~ or chic because they are the property of privileged circles —Edward Sapir⟩ **8** *chiefly dial* : fairly large : CONSIDERABLE ⟨a ~ price for a broken-down car⟩ **syn** see INTELLIGENT

³smart \"\ *adv* -ER/-EST [ME *smerte, smarte*, fr. *smert, smart*, adj.] : in a smart manner : SMARTLY ⟨will make all his characters talk ~ or epigrammatically —Arnold Bennett⟩ ⟨frankly a good deal of a mug, indifferent to those who cannot play it ~ —Alfred Kazin⟩

⁴smart \"\ *n* -S [ME *smerte*; akin to MLG *smerte* pain, MD *smerte, smarte*, OHG *smerzo* pain, *smerzan* to pain, hurt — more at ¹SMART] **1** : a smarting pain; *esp* : a stinging local pain (as from an injury, blow, or irritant) ⟨a ~ in the eyes⟩ ⟨whimpering over the ~ from the liniment⟩ **2 a** : keen mental pain (as from grief, remorse, affliction, wounded feelings) : poignant distress ⟨only time would cure the ~ of their bereavement⟩ ⟨the ~ of being the underdog —Abram Kardiner⟩ ⟨was not the sort to get over ~*s* —Sir Winston Churchill⟩ **b** *archaic* : pain or distress inflicted or felt as punishment or retribution ⟨stand betwixt us and our deserved ~ —John Milton⟩; *also* : a cause of such pain ⟨a sword that thine enemy's ~ is —John Keats⟩ **3** : one that affects smartness (as in dress, speech, manners, attitudes) ⟨the wits and the ~*s* —Sir Walter Scott⟩ ⟨a young Broadway ~ —Joel Sayre⟩ **4** *dial* : a sizable amount

smar·ta \'smärd·ə\ *n* -S *usu cap* [Skt, fr. *smṛti* what is remembered] : a member of a large Hindu sect of Brahmans founded in the eighth century, guided chiefly by the traditions of the smriti, holding the doctrine of Advaita, worshiping all the principal deities equally, and thriving most in south India

smart al·eck *also* **smart-al·ec** *n, pl* **smart alecks** *also* **smart-alecs** \'smär\|d·ˌalə̇k, -mȧ\|, \|t\|-, -lēk, *dial* -ˌel-\ [*Aleck, Alec*, nickname fr. the name *Alexander*] : one that is offensively conceited and bumptious : a self-satisfied self-assertive cocky person with pretensions to cleverness : one combining in himself the characteristic traits of show-off and know-it-all

smart-al·eck·ism \-ˌkizəm\ *or* **smart-al·eck·ry** \-krē\ *n, pl* **smart-aleckisms** *or* **smart-aleckries** : the speech or behavior of a smart aleck : smart-alecky quality or characteristics

smart-al·ecky \-kē, -ki\ *or* **smart-aleck** *also* **smart-alec** *adj* : like, typical of, or being a smart aleck : marked by cockiness and conceit : concerned with or striving for smartness and cleverness for their own sake or at the expense of seriousness and responsibility ⟨had never talked that way to the *smart-aleck* kid before —J.H.Reese⟩ ⟨the *smart-aleck* way you were talking —Alexander Saxton⟩ ⟨dismayingly intelligent and a shade *smart-alecky* —Jean Stafford⟩ ⟨five *smart-alecky* collegians who conspired to rob the till —Bennett Cerf⟩

smarted *past of* SMART

smart up *adj* : made smart; *esp* : dressed up : spruced up ⟨a woman hates to go on a safari for a cab when she's all *smarted up* —Christopher Morley⟩

smart·en \'smärtᵊn, 'smȧt-\ *vb* **smartened; smartened; smartening** \-t(ᵊ)niŋ\ **smartens** [²*smart* + -*en*] *vt* : to make smart or smarter: **a** : to improve in appearance (as by making neat, trim, spruce, or stylish) ⟨a tightened and ~*ed* version of the modern sports coat —James Lauer⟩ — usu. used with *up* ⟨sent the kids along to ~ themselves up —John Christopher⟩ ⟨newly shaved and ~*ed* up —Thor Heyerdahl⟩ ⟨~ themselves up for the evening meal —Rebecca West⟩ ⟨~*ed* up with a new figurehead —Mollie Panter-Downes⟩ **b** : to make more brisk or vigorous ⟨~ the pace⟩ : brighten up : ENLIVEN — used with *up* ⟨old theme . . . has been ~*ed* up into a refreshing piece of whimsy —*New Yorker*⟩ **c** : to make more alert : sharpen the wits of — used with *up* ⟨could learn a lot . . . ~ you up no end —A.M.Shairp⟩ **~** *vi* **1** : to smarten oneself : become smart or smarter — used with *up* ⟨everybody tried to ~ up for the festival —Christopher Morley⟩ ⟨~ up boy . . . leave the dumbbells settle the war —Richard Bissell⟩ **2** : to become sharper or more vigorous or intense ⟨a ~*ing* wind⟩ ⟨~ into color as the sun rises —Amy Lowell⟩

smarter *comparative of* SMART

smartest *superlative of* SMART

smart grass *n* [⁴*smart*] : SMARTWEED

smarting *adj* [fr. pres. part. of ¹*smart*] : that smarts: **a** : causing or marked by an acute stinging or cutting sensation ⟨~ pain⟩ ⟨a ~ wound⟩ **b** : feeling or affected by sharp stinging pain ⟨~ eyes⟩ or acute mental distress ⟨~ vanity⟩ — **smart·ing·ly** *adv*

smart·ish \'smärd·ish\ *adj* [²*smart* + -*ish*] **1** : somewhat smart : fairly smart ⟨a ~ little bar —William Sansom⟩ **2** : of considerable importance or significance (as in amount, number, degree, quality) ⟨a ~ distance⟩ ⟨some ~ lambs . . . fat as snails —A.E.Coppard⟩

smart·less \'smärtlə̇s\ *adj* [⁴*smart* + -*less*] : free from smart

smart·ly *adv* [ME *smertly*, fr. *smert* smart + -*ly*] : in a smart manner : so as to be or seem smart: as **a** : VIGOROUSLY, SHARPLY ⟨paced ~ up and down —Thomas Hardy⟩ ⟨scratched his bare legs ~ —Willa Cather⟩ ⟨was spotted and ~ attacked by two English brigs —Parry Miller⟩ **b** : CURTLY ⟨was returned with the offending lines ~ pencilled out —Mollie Panter-Downes⟩ : SEVERELY ⟨reprimanded him ~⟩ **c** : to a notable degree : CONSIDERABLY ⟨~ improved buying —D.C. Morrill⟩ ⟨temperature rose ~⟩ **d** : NEATLY, TRIMLY, PRECISELY ⟨beds ~ turned down —C.W.Morton⟩ ⟨had executed all commands ~ and briskly⟩ ⟨with a plastic disk ~ balanced on his snout —R.N.Hill⟩ ⟨drilled and handled their weapons ~⟩ **e** : CLEVERLY, EFFICIENTLY, CAPABLY ⟨skillfully drawn and ~ administered city plans —Hal Burton⟩ ⟨Department of Agriculture was ~ on the job —*Sydney (Australia) Bull.*⟩ ⟨a ~ directed play⟩ **f** : PERTLY, WITTILY ⟨~ said⟩ ⟨~ turned phrases⟩ ⟨put it so ~ that it seemed to mean more than it did⟩ **g** : FASHIONABLY, STYLISHLY ⟨always dressed ~⟩ ⟨~ tailored black and white linen —Virginia Pope⟩ ⟨~ furnished⟩

¹smart money \'ˌ=ˌ==\ *n* [⁴*smart*] **1 a** : money allowed to British soldiers or sailors for wounds and injuries received **b** : a sum paid by an employer to an injured employee **2** : money paid to procure the release of a recruit for the British army **3** : PUNITIVE DAMAGES

²smart money \'=ˌ==\ *n* [²*smart*] **1** : money ventured by a bettor or speculator likely to have inside information; *sometimes* : investments made by alert experienced investors **2** : well-informed bettors or speculators

smart·ness *n* -ES [ME *smartnes*, fr. *smart* + -*nes* -ness] **1** *obs* : something causing smarting pain or distress **2** : the quality or state of being smart in expression, appearance, or movement : liveliness of wit or manner : BRISKNESS, SNAPPINESS ⟨~ of an epigram⟩ ⟨~ of a ship⟩ ⟨~ of a uniform⟩ ⟨~ of a salute⟩ ⟨~ of pace⟩ **3** : the quality or state of being ultrafashionable, elegant, or sophisticated ⟨~ of their address⟩ ⟨crowd . . . had a strong coloring of worldly ~ —Thomas Wolfe⟩ ⟨the ~ which is a characteristic achievement of most French girls —Frank Brookhouser⟩ **4** : ADROITNESS, CLEVERNESS, SHREWDNESS ⟨~ in business⟩ ⟨~ of a scheme⟩; *esp* : questionable shrewdness where self-interest is affected ⟨a certain degree of unscrupulous ~ —A.L.Guérard⟩

smarts *pres 3d sing of* SMART, *pl of* SMART

smart set *n* : ultrafashionable society

smartweed \'=ˌ=\ *n* [⁴*smart* + *weed*] **1** : any of various knotweeds (genus *Polygonum*) with strong acrid juice: as **a** : WATER PEPPER **b** : LADY'S THUMB **2** : a plant (as a nettle) that causes a burning sensation in contact with the skin

¹smarty *or* **smartie** \'smär\|d·ē, -mȧ\|, \|t\|, \|i\ *n* -ES [²*smart* + -*y*, -*ie*] : one that tries in a callow fashion to be witty or clever : SMART ALECK

²smarty \"\ *adj* -ER/-EST : having the characteristics of a smarty : SMART-ALECKY ⟨attempt to satirize . . . seems thin and even ~ —F.O.Matthiessen⟩ ⟨was full of ~ ideas and had no manners —Margery Allingham⟩

smarty-pants \'==ˌ=\ *n pl but sing in constr* : SMARTY

¹smash \'smash, -aa(ə)sh, -aish\ *vb* -ED/-ING/-ES [perh. blend of ³*smack* and *mash*] *vt* **1 a** : to break in pieces by violence : dash or crush to pieces : SHATTER ⟨~ a teacup⟩ ⟨~ a chair⟩ ⟨lifts his stick and ~*es* the chandelier —Edmund Wilson⟩ ⟨percussion wave that ~*ed* anything it hit at fifty yards —Wirt Williams⟩ ⟨bridge of his nose ~*ed* level with his face —G.B. Shaw⟩ ⟨typhoon ~*ed* all installations —*Americana Annual*⟩ ⟨X rays which ~ the genes and break up the chromosomes —Lee Hancock⟩ **b** : SPLIT 2a (3) ⟨a method of ~*ing* the atom —C.S.Kilby⟩ ⟨the cyclotron that ~*ed* the atom —J.W.Noble⟩ **2 a** (1) : to drive or throw violently esp. with a shattering or battering effect ⟨~ a stone through a window⟩ ⟨~*ed* a fist in his face⟩ ⟨~*ing* bombs into . . . enemy positions —*N.Y. Times*⟩ ⟨the shot ~*ing* an echo back from the gorge —Ernest Hemingway⟩ ⟨~ themselves against stone walls⟩; *also* : to bring about or effect in this way ⟨~*ed* a gap in the hedge —Adrian Bell⟩ ⟨had ~*ed* their way into Singapore two years before —Dave Richardson⟩ (2) : to handle (baggage) in a rough noisy manner **b** (1) : to hit violently : BATTER ⟨~ him in the face⟩ ⟨~ a door in⟩ ⟨~ down a fence⟩ (2) : to hit (as a tennis ball, a shuttlecock) with a very hard overhand stroke — compare DRIVE, KILL **3** : to destroy utterly as if by crushing to pieces or shattering : break up completely : cause to collapse : WRECK — often used with *up* ⟨~ a theory⟩ ⟨~ a tradition⟩ ⟨~ up an organization⟩ ⟨~ all resistance⟩ ⟨~ up a monopoly⟩ ⟨~ a revolt⟩ ⟨found his health ~*ed*⟩ ⟨~*ed* all production records⟩ **4 a** : to force (as into a new form, a more compact form) by pressure : MASH, PRESS ⟨caps to be worn ~*ed* sideways —Lois Long⟩ **b** : to compress (as folded book sections or assembled books) in order to give firmness and uniform bulk and eliminate a tendency to a wedge-shaped back from threads used in sewing — compare NIP 6a, SMASHING MACHINE **~** *vi* **1** : to move or become propelled with violence or crashing effect ⟨~*ed* into a tree⟩ ⟨~ through a thicket⟩ ⟨~*ed* over from the five-yard line for a touchdown⟩ ⟨raw wind ~*ing* against them —Irwin Shaw⟩ ⟨sea surges and ~*es* —Russell Lord⟩ **2** : to become utterly disrupted or wrecked; *esp* : to go bankrupt — often used with *up* ⟨~*ed* up during the slump⟩ **3** : to break up or go to pieces suddenly as a result of collision or pressure ⟨dish dropped from his grasp and ~*ed*⟩ ⟨had a horrible moment when things seemed to ~ inside me —Mary Deasy⟩ **4** : to execute a smash (as in tennis or badminton)

²smash \"\ *n* -ES **1 a** : a smashing blow ⟨a ~ on the jaw⟩ or attack ⟨two line ~*es* gained seven yards⟩ or the sound of a smashing blow ⟨~ of bat on ball⟩ ⟨the eternal ~ of a handball against the wall —Alfred Kazin⟩ **b** : an attacking shot in tennis or badminton in which the ball or shuttlecock is hit overhead with a powerful downward stroke and travels with great speed and usu. at a sharp angle to the floor or court **2 a** : the condition of being broken to pieces : a state of disaster ⟨the grand ~ that is inherent in every arms race —D.F.Fleming⟩ — often used in the phrases *go to smash, come to smash* ⟨had watched his plans go to ~⟩ ⟨felt his health going to ~⟩ **b** : a fabric defect caused by the breaking of warp or filling yarns **3 a** : a breaking or dashing to pieces or the sound of such breaking ⟨a ~ of crockery in the kitchen⟩; *esp* : a wreck due to collision : CRASH, SMASHUP ⟨a grade-crossing ~⟩ ⟨a bad ~ at the corner⟩ ⟨got in a ~ and a cyclist was killed —Margaret Kennedy⟩ **b** : utter collapse : FAILURE, RUIN, WRECK ⟨the ~ of all his hopes⟩; *esp* : business failure : BANKRUPTCY ⟨the bank ~*es* of 1893 —E.H.Collis⟩ **4 a** : a tall drink served with ice and garnished with fruit or mint and consisting of sprigs of mint, sugar, and soda water muddled in a glass to which is added an alcoholic liquor ⟨brandy ~⟩ ⟨whiskey ~⟩ **b** : a fruit beverage made with crushed or squeezed fruit ⟨cherry ~⟩ **5** : a striking success : HIT ⟨a box-office ~⟩ ⟨musical ~⟩ ⟨sang it for a ~ —R.G.Hubler⟩

³smash \"\ *adv* [²*smash*] : with a resounding crash : SMASHINGLY ⟨the stone went ~ through the window⟩

⁴smash \"\ *adj* [²*smash*] : being a smash : EXTRAORDINARY, OUTSTANDING, SMASHING ⟨~ hit⟩ ⟨the ~ best seller of the year —Orville Prescott⟩ ⟨~ musical show⟩ ⟨a ~ success⟩ ⟨two ~ record hits —Bill Simon⟩

⁵smash \"\ *n* -ES [origin unknown] **1** : counterfeit coin **2** : COIN ⟨twenty-nine dollars in bills and the rest in ~ —Croswell Bowen⟩ **3** *slang* : MONEY

⁶smash \"\ *vt* -ED/-ING/-ES : to pass (counterfeit coin)

smash·able \-shəbəl\ *adj* : capable of being smashed

smash-and-grab \ˌ=ˌ=ˈ=\ *adj, chiefly Brit* : committed by smashing a shop window and snatching articles displayed within ⟨a *smash-and-grab* robbery⟩

smashboard signal \'=ˌ=-\ *n* : a railroad signal the arm of which is designed to be broken when passed in the stop position

¹smash·er \'smashə(r), -aa(ə)sh-, -aish-\ *n* -S [¹*smash* + -*er*] **1** : something very large or fine or extraordinary of its kind ⟨hotel is a ~ with 1216 rooms —Hedda Hopper⟩ ⟨a ~ of a moustache —Bruce Marshall⟩ ⟨a ~ of a bride —Richard Llewellyn⟩ **2** : one that smashes or crushes ⟨a ~ of a blow⟩ ⟨heavy freight vehicles which are road ~*s* —John Kemp⟩: as **a** : a laborer who smashes slate or stone with a sledgehammer **b** : SMASHING MACHINE; *also* : an operator of such a machine **3** : a tennis or badminton player who is skilled in executing a smash ⟨can play the baseline but is also a volleyer, a ~ —Alice Marble⟩ **4** : a repairer of smashes in textiles — called also *smash fixer, smash hand, smash piecer* **5** *or* **smasher hat** *Africa* : a soft felt hat with a wide brim

²smasher \"\ *n* -S [⁶*smash* + -*er*] **1** : a receiver of stolen goods **2** : one that puts into circulation counterfeit coin or forged notes

smash·ery \-shərē\ *n* -ES [¹*smash* + -*ery*] : a state of smash : a smashed mass : DESTRUCTION

smashes *pres 3d sing of* SMASH, *pl of* SMASH

smash fixer *or* **smash hand** *or* **smash piecer** *n* : ¹SMASHER 4

smashing *adj* [fr. pres. part. of ¹*smash*] **1 a** : that smashes : CRUSHING ⟨a ~ blow⟩ ⟨~ defeat⟩ **b** : CRASHING ⟨~ chords⟩ **2** : that is a smash or a smasher : extraordinarily impressive or effective ⟨~ success⟩ ⟨a ~ victory⟩ ⟨~ display of power⟩ ⟨~ vote of confidence⟩ ⟨was ~ in that role⟩ ⟨an absolutely ~ costume⟩ ⟨a ~ blonde⟩ — **smash·ing·ly** *adv*

smashing machine *n* : a machine used by bookbinders to smash books or book sections

smashup \'=ˌ=\ *n* -S [fr. *smash up*, v.] **1** : a complete collapse ⟨the ~ of many an ancient civilization —Russell Lord⟩ ⟨warning signals of an economic ~ —*Time*⟩ ⟨an unexpected ~ in health⟩ ⟨trying to prevent a ~ of the family business⟩ **2** : a collision or crash esp. of one or more motor vehicles ⟨a head-on ~⟩ ⟨died in an early morning ~⟩

smatch \'smach\ *n* -ES [ME *smech, smach*, alter. (influenced by *smachen* to taste) of *smack* — more at SMACK] **1** : a slight touch or trace : HINT, SUGGESTION **2** : SMATTERING

smatch·et \'smachə̇t\ *n* -S [prob. fr. *smatch* + -*et*] *Scot* : a contemptible unmannerly person

¹smat·ter \'smad·ə(r), -atə-\ *vb* -ED/-ING/-S [ME *smateren*, prob. of imit. origin like MHG *smetern* to chatter, gossip, Sw *smattra* to clatter, crackle] *vt* **1** *obs* : SPOT, SPATTER, DEFILE **2** : to speak or utter so as to reveal a spotty or superficial knowledge ⟨to ~ French⟩ **3** : to dabble in : study bits of ⟨I have ~*ed* law . . . letters . . . geography —R.L.Stevenson⟩ **4** [influenced in meaning by *shatter*] *Scot* : to break in pieces : SHATTER **~** *vi* **1** : to talk superficially and disconnectedly : BABBLE, CHATTER **2** : to have a slight, superficial, and spotty knowledge : DABBLE

²smatter \"\ *n* -S **1** : slight piecemeal knowledge : SMATTERING ⟨a ~ of French⟩ **2** *Scot* : small bits : insignificant things : FRAGMENTS **3** : a heterogeneous collection : SMATTERING ⟨a weary ~ of applause —M.W.Straight⟩

smat·ter·er \-ərə(r)\ *n* -S : one that smatters or has a smattering knowledge

¹smattering *n* -S [fr. gerund of ¹*smatter*] **1** : an act of one that smatters ⟨learn a few languages then, and learn them well: a ~ is a frittering —A.L.Guérard⟩ ⟨a unified discipline instead of an elegant ~ —H.J.Muller⟩ **2** : superficial or piecemeal knowledge ⟨picked up a ~ of these languages when they were children —Demaree Bess⟩ ⟨a ~ of carpentry, house painting, bricklaying —Alva Johnston⟩ **3** : an inconsiderable number or amount esp. of similar but distinct individuals or parts : piecemeal collection : SMATTER ⟨weeks passed with only a ~ of lookers —Peter DeVries⟩ ⟨the ~ of Negroes in the balcony —Shelby Foote⟩ ⟨only a ~ of early writing had been printed —Charlton Laird⟩

²smattering \"\ *adj* [fr. pres. part. of ¹*smatter*] : that smatters or is a smattering ⟨~ knowledge of French⟩ ⟨~ dilettantes⟩ — **smat·ter·ing·ly** *adv*

smattery \-rē\ *adj* [²*smatter* + -*y*] : SMATTERING, SUPERFICIAL ⟨a ~ knowledge is equated to education —Eric Partridge⟩

smaze \'smāz\ *n* -S [*smoke* + *haze*] : a combination of haze and smoke similar to smog in appearance but less damp in consistency

sm cap *abbr* small capital

¹smear \'smi(ə)r, -iə\ *n* -S *often attrib* [ME *smere*, fr. OE *smeoru*; akin to OS & OHG *smero* fat, grease, lard, ON *smǫr, smjǫr* fat, butter, Goth *smairthr* fat, *smarna* dung, OIr *smir, smiur* marrow, Gk *smyrid-, smyris* powdered emery, *myron* unguent, perfume] **1 a** (1) *obs* : a fat oily substance : OINTMENT, GREASE (2) : a viscous or sticky substance **b** : a spot made by or as if by an unctuous or adhesive substance : BLOTCH, STAIN, SMUDGE **2** : material smeared on a surface (as of a microscopic slide or of a culture medium); *also* : a preparation made by smearing material on a surface ⟨a fecal ~⟩ ⟨vaginal ~⟩ **3** : a partial glaze on pottery produced by vapor or by brushing off the greater part of an applied glaze **4** : a play of a counting card on one's partner's trick **5** : a glissando esp. when produced on a trombone **6 a** : a deliberate and usu. unsubstantiated charge or accusation intended to foment distrust or hatred against the person or organization so charged ⟨pleaded calmly that those who expound unpopular doctrine be answered factually instead of by ~*s* —Saul Carson⟩ ⟨attack and personal ~ in the familiar manner of rumor and innuendo —Harry Conn⟩ **b** : SMEAR WORD

²smear \"\ *vt* -ED/-ING/-S [ME *smeren, smiren*, fr. OE *smierwan, smerwan, smirwan*; akin to MD & MLG *smeren* to grease, salve, anoint, OHG *smirwen*, ON *smyrva, smyrja* to anoint, *smǫr, smjǫr* fat, butter — more at ¹SMEAR] **1 a** (1) : to overspread with something unctuous, viscous, or adhesive : DAUB ⟨the wood looked new, so he ~*ed* it with oil and ashes —Lyle Saxon⟩ ⟨lived on bread ~*ed* with lard —C.J.Rolo⟩ (2) : to spread (a substance) over a surface ⟨~*ed* 10 minims of machine oil on a condenser lens —J.A.Knight⟩ **b** : to treat (as a wound) by overspreading with a thick or greasy medication **c** : to treat (as young sheep) with a salve to destroy vermin and mat the fleece **2 a** : to stain, smudge, or make dirty by or as if by smearing or rubbing : BESMIRCH, SULLY ⟨the hat . . . had been ~*ed* with grease and dirt in a minor airplane accident —Henry LaCossitt⟩ **b** : to give a quality or appearance to; *specif* : to vilify or blacken the reputation of by applying a debasing or odious epithet or by secretly and maliciously spreading gross charges and imputations ⟨people . . . whose opinions disagree with his; and whom he has ~*ed* by all sorts of distortions and misrepresentations —Elmer Davis⟩ **c** : to obliterate, obscure, blur, blend, or wipe out by or as if by smearing ⟨~*ed* the end of his cigarette on the tray —Hamilton Basso⟩ ⟨~ notes on a trombone⟩ **3 a** : to rush hard (the opposing ball carrier, passer, or kicker of a defensive football team) and throw for a loss **b** : to rout, repulse, or frustrate completely : SMOTHER **4** : FATTEN 1b(2) **5** : to prepare as a smear for microscopic examination : to make a smear of

smear·case *or* **smier·case** \'smirˌkās\ *n* [modif. of G *schmierkäse*, fr. *schmieren* to smear, spread (fr. OHG *smirwen*) + *käse* cheese, fr. OHG *kāsi* — more at SMEAR, CHEESE] *chiefly Midland* : COTTAGE CHEESE

smear dab *n* : a brown mottled flatfish (*Microstomus microcephalus*) of the coasts of northern Europe and Iceland that has a slimy skin and is highly esteemed as food; *also* : any of various other flatfishes

smear dock *n* : GOOD-KING-HENRY

smeared *adj* [fr. past part. of *smear*] : having color markings that are ill defined as if rubbed ⟨~ deerskin⟩

smear·er \'smirə(r)\ *n* -S : one that smears

smear·i·ness \-rēnə̇s\ *n* -ES : the quality or state of being smeary ⟨was conscious of the ~ of the tiled floor —Marjorie Brace⟩

smear·less \-rlə̇s\ *adj* : having no smears : UNSMEARED

smear-sheet \'=ˌ=\ *n* : a newspaper or periodical containing a high proportion of unfounded personal charges or vilification

smear word *n* : an epithet applied to a person or group in order to degrade, blacken, or make unjust or unfounded accusations ⟨time was . . . when independents in politics were rare and *mugwump* was a *smear word* —W.E.Binkley⟩ ⟨strained relations may be expressed in clique formation, subtle whispers and shrugs, *smear words*, discrimination in clubs and dances —F.J. Brown & J.S.Roucek⟩

smeary \'smirē, -ri\ *adj* -ER/-EST **1** : marked by or covered with smears ⟨the ~ marble-topped table —Nicholas Monsarrat⟩ ⟨every page . . . was a mess of ~ erasures —Robert Rice⟩ **2** : liable to cause smears : GREASY, ADHESIVE, VISCOUS ⟨~ white library paste —Pearl Kazin⟩

smec·tic \'smektik\ *adj* [L *smecticus* cleansing, fr. Gk *smēktikos*, fr. *smēktos* (verbal of *smēchein* to wash off, clean) + *-ikos* -ic — more at SMITE] **1 :** PURIFYING, DETERGENT **2 :** relating to, existing in, or being a mesomorphic state which is formed after the nematic state on cooling from a liquid melt and in which the orientation of the molecules or atoms is in parallel planes or layers

1smec·tym·nu·an \smek'timnəwən\ *n* -s *usu cap* [*Smectymnuus*, pseudonym formed fr. the initials of *S*tephan *M*arshall †1635, *E*dmund *C*alamy †1666, *T*homas *Y*oung †1655, *M*atthew *N*ewcomen †1669, and *W*illiam *S*purstowe †1666 Brit. Presbyterian clergymen + E *-an*] **1 :** one of a group of five 17th century English Presbyterian clergymen collaborating in a pamphlet attacking the episcopacy **2 :** an adherent of the Smectymnuans

2smectymnuan \"\ *adj, usu cap* **:** of or relating to the Smectymnuans

smed·dum \'smedəm\ *n* -s [fr. (assumed) ME, fr. OE *smedma, smeoduma*] **1** *chiefly Scot* **:** POWDER, DUST; *specif* **:** the flour or powder of ground malt **2** *Scot* **:** spirited vigor **:** SPUNK

1smeech \'smēch\ *n* -ES [ME *smech*, fr. OE *smēc, smȳc, smīc;* akin to OE *smoca* smoke — more at SMOKE] *dial Brit* **:** dense smoke

2smeech \"\ *vi* -ED/-ING/-ES *Brit* **:** to emit smoke or vapor

1smeek \'smēk\ *vt* -ED/-ING/-S [ME *smeken*, fr. OE *smēocan* to emit smoke, fumigate; akin to OE *smoca* smoke — more at SMOKE] *Scot* **:** to clean, cure, dry, drive out, or fumigate by means of smoke or fumes

2smeek \"\ *n* -S [ME *smek*, alter. (influenced by *smeken*) of *smech*] *chiefly Scot* **:** dense or black smoke — **smeeky** \-kī\ *adj* -ER/-EST

smeeth \'smēth\ *vt* -ED/-ING/-S [ME *smethen*, fr. OE *smēthan, smēthian*, fr. *smēthe*, adj., smooth — more at SMOOTH] *dial chiefly Brit* **:** SMOOTH

smeg·ma \'smegmə\ *n* -S [NL, fr. L, detergent, soap, fr. Gk *smēgma*, fr. *smēchein* to wash off, clean — more at SMITE] **:** the secretion of a sebaceous gland; *specif* **:** the cheesy sebaceous matter that collects between the glans penis and the foreskin or around the clitoris and labia minora

smegma bacillus *n* **:** an acid-fast bacterium (*Mycobacterium smegmatis*) found in smegma

1smell \'smel\ *vb* **smelled** \-ld\ *or* **smelt** \-lt\ **smelled** *or* **smelt; smelling; smells** [ME *smellen, smullen;* akin to MD *smölen* to smolder, scorch, LG *smelen, smölen* to smolder, scorch, MIr *smāl, smōl, smūal* fire, glow, Russ *smalit'* to scorch, singe; basic meaning: to smolder] *vt* **1 a :** to perceive by the excitation of the olfactory nerves **:** get the odor or scent of through stimuli affecting the sensory nerves of the nasal passages ⟨*smelt* growing things in the park —Ellen Glasgow⟩ **b :** to inhale the odor of (as for enjoyment or testing) **:** SNIFF ⟨~ stew cooking⟩ ⟨~ each perfume offered for sale⟩ **2 :** to detect or become aware of as if by the sense of smell or natural instinct ⟨the censors ~*ed* sex in every realistic literary creation —O.S.J.Gogarty⟩ ⟨very few fail to ~ the tension and the fear in the air of its cities —Patrick O'Donovan⟩ **3 :** to emit the odor of ⟨you ~ sherry, sir —W.M.Thackeray⟩ ~ *vi* **1 :** to exercise the sense of smell: as **a :** to be on the scent for something ⟨the dogs ran ~*ing* through the fields⟩ **b :** to inhale an odor ⟨~ at her salts⟩ **2 a** (1) **:** to have an odor or scent **:** give forth an aroma ⟨the air ~*s* of the sea —Gladys Taber⟩ ⟨lorries rolled by ~*ing* of rubber and oil —Paul Roche⟩ ⟨it ~*s* like violets⟩ (2) **:** to have or exhibit a characteristic aura or atmosphere **:** be suggestive ⟨the accounts . . . seemed to me to ~ of truth —R.S.Bourne⟩ ⟨elimination of anything ~*ing* of policy was necessary in order to secure unanimous agreement —R.C.Tolman⟩ **b** (1) **:** to have an offensive odor **:** STINK ⟨the canals are sewers and, in tactless truth, they ~ —Claudia Cassidy⟩ (2) **:** to appear evil, dishonest, ugly, or disreputable ⟨all this from the moral point of view ~*s* —A.F.Wills⟩ ⟨in the hands of certain people the word has begun to ~ —Lucien Price⟩ — **smell a rat :** to have a suspicion of something wrong — **smell of the lamp :** to bear marks of study and labor rather than of genius or inspiration **:** seem artificial ⟨to them a discussion of sovereignty in the abstract would have *smelt of the lamp* —C.A.Beard⟩ — usu. used of a literary composition — **smell one's oats :** to pluck up spirit and move with new energy when near one's goal — **smell the bottom** *or* **smell the ground** *of a ship* **:** to lose speed in shallow water and often to veer off course or become heavy on the helm

2smell \"\ *n* -S [ME *smel, smul;* akin to *smellen, smullen*, v. — more at 1SMELL] **1 a :** the act or power of perceiving odor **:** olfactory sensation or the capacity for it **:** OLFACTION ⟨canine behavior is largely oriented in terms of ~⟩ **b :** the one of the special senses that is concerned with the perception of the quality of a substance which is classified as odor, is mediated by the olfactory organ, is normally sensitive to volatile or dissolved material in extremely low concentration (as 0.00000001 mg. per liter), is conducted centrally by the olfactory nerve, and is coordinated esp. by centers in the hippocampal convolution **2 :** the property of a thing that affects the olfactory organs **:** a pleasant, unpleasant, or neutral odor ⟨the ~ of fat meat cooking in beans —Jean Stafford⟩ ⟨the sweet, intense ~ of overripe fruit —William Beebe⟩ **3 :** a quality pervading, suggestive of, or emanating from something **:** AURA, ATMOSPHERE ⟨there is a ~ of politics about all this which ill becomes responsible men in these times —*America*⟩ ⟨the authentic ~ and feel of a raw country —Mari Sandoz⟩ **4 :** an act or instance of smelling ⟨take a ~ of this wine⟩

syn SMELL, SCENT, ODOR, AROMA mean, in common, the quality of a thing that makes it perceptible to the olfactory sense, or something perceptible only to that sense. SMELL usu. indicates solely the sensation, usu. devoid of connotation, sometimes but rarely, however, as opposed to AROMA, carrying the suggestion of something unpleasant ⟨the *smell* of oranges and wooden boxes —Kay Fuller⟩ ⟨the spicy *smell* of tobacco —*Amer. Guide Series: Tenn.*⟩ ⟨like all houses . . . had its peculiar *smell* —Samuel Butler †1902⟩ ⟨about the town's political activity there was a *smell* to high heaven⟩ SCENT is associated, in one direction, with the natural odor of living things, esp. animals, and so carries rather vivid connotations; in being associated with the trail an animal leaves, it suggests a finer perception than SMELL; in being the word in Britain equivalent to the American *perfume*, it frequently suggests something pleasant ⟨the *scent* of rabbits roused the dog to alertness⟩ ⟨the *scents* of the countryside —Roy Lewis & Angus Maude⟩ ⟨the rich, vital *scents* of the ploughed ground —Ellen Glasgow⟩ ⟨vibrating among the pale petals of the lilies and setting free their *scent* in short waves of perfume —John Galsworthy⟩ ODOR is sometimes interchangeable with SMELL, often implying unpleasantness ⟨innumerable articles of manufacture carry with them characteristic *odors* —A.C.Morrison⟩ ⟨redolent with the *odor* of West Indian molasses, rum, spices, and China tea —*Amer. Guide Series: Maine*⟩ ⟨the fetid *odor* of a bog, the stench of a carcass in the woods, the delectable reek of ferment in the hay-crammed barn —D.C.Peattie⟩ AROMA suggests an odor that is penetrating or pungent and usu. pleasant as from something savory ⟨the *aroma* of cooking coffee⟩ ⟨African ginger lacks the fine *aroma* of Jamaica ginger but it has an intensely pungent odor —J.W.Parry⟩ ⟨the sweet, burned *aroma* of roasted meat and the penetrating, acid odor of hardwood smoke —Rufus Jarman⟩ ⟨the pervading *aroma* of decay and hopelessness —Harrison Smith⟩

— **smell of the lamp :** the appearance of having been produced by pedantry and plodding scholarship rather than vital inspiration ⟨when he speaks about economic or social issues the *smell of the lamp* hangs about every cliché-cluttered sentence —H.G.Nicholas⟩

smell·able \-ləbəl\ *adj* **:** capable of being smelled

smell·age \-lij\ *n* -S [2*smell* + *-age* (as in *lovage*)] **:** fragrant vegetation; *specif* **:** LOVAGE

smelled *past of* SMELL

smell·er \-lə(r)\ *n* -S **1 :** one that smells; *specif* **:** one that perceives, traces, or tests by the sense of smell **2 :** a tactile bristle **:** VIBRISSA **3 a :** NOSE **b :** a blow on the nose

smell-feast \'⸗,⸗\ *n* [1*smell* + *feast*] **:** one given to finding out and getting invited to good feasts **:** PARASITE, SPONGER

smell·ful \'smelfəl\ *adj, Austral* **:** SMELLY

smell·fun·gus \'smel,fəŋgəs\ *n* [after *Smelfungus*, a hypercritical traveler in *A Sentimental Journey through France and Italy* (1768) by Laurence Sterne †1768 Brit. novelist, who intended this character to satirize Tobias Smollett †1771 Brit. novelist for his descriptions in *Travels through France and Italy* (1766)] **:** a captious critic **:** FAULTFINDER

smell·ie \'smelē, -li\ *n* -S [2*smell* + *-ie*] **:** a motion picture having smells synchronized with the action

smell·i·ness \-lēnəs\ *n* -ES **:** the quality or state of being smelly

smelling *n* -S [ME, fr. gerund of *smellen* to smell — more at SMELL] **:** SMELL 1a

smelling bottle *n* **:** a bottle filled with smelling salts or a scent

smelling salts *n pl* **:** an aromatic preparation of ammonium carbonate (sense c) and ammonia water and often some scent used as a stimulant and restorative (as to avoid or relieve faintness or headache)

smelling-stick \'⸗⸗,⸗\ *n* **:** a common No. American sassafras (*Sassafras albidum molle*) with pubescent twigs and young leaves

smell-less \'smelləs\ *adj* **:** having no smell

smell out *vt* **1 :** to seek or find as if by smelling **:** ferret out ⟨its task remained unchanged: to *smell out* and sweep away ruthlessly all opposition to the dictator —W.C.Bullitt⟩ **2 :** to detect (a witch or one who causes disease or misfortune) by divination

smells *pres 3d sing of* SMELL, *pl of* SMELL

smell up *vt* **:** to fill with an esp. disagreeable odor ⟨the baggage man reported to the district supervisor that two trunks had *smelled up* his car —E.D.Radin⟩

smelly \'smelē, -li\ *adj* -ER/-EST **:** having a smell; *esp* **:** MALODOROUS

1smelt \'smelt\ *n, pl* **smelts** *or* **smelt** [ME, fr. OE; akin to Norw *smelte* whiting] **1 a :** any of various small fishes of the family Osmeridae and esp. of the genus *Osmerus* that closely resemble the trouts in general structure, are translucent greenish above, silvery on the sides, and silvery or white beneath, live along the coasts and ascend the rivers to spawn or are landlocked in lakes, and have delicate tender oily flesh with a distinctive odor and taste: as (1) **:** a common and commercially important food fish (*O. mordax*) of eastern No. America from Virginia northward (2) **:** SPARLING (3) **:** WHITEBAIT 2c **b :** any of various other salmonoid fishes: as (1) **:** any of several fishes of the family Argentinidae (as the capelin) (2) *Brit* **:** SMOLT (3) **:** a small freshwater fish (*Retropinna semoni*) of Australia and New Zealand that has a strong odor of cucumbers **2 :** any of various small fishes of groups other than Salmonoidea resembling the smelt: as **a :** any of several silversides (as a jack smelt, a top smelt, or a grunion) **b :** TOMCOD 1b **c :** SAND LAUNCE **d :** any of various freshwater cyprinid fishes **e :** SAND BORER **3** *obs* **:** an easy mark **:** SIMPLETON

2smelt *past of* SMELL

3smelt \'smelt\ *vt* -ED/-ING/-S [D or LG *smelten* (fr. MD & MLG, respectively); akin to OHG *smelzan* to melt, OSw *smælta*, OE *meltan* — more at MELT] **1 :** to melt or fuse (as ore) often with an accompanying chemical change usu. to separate the metal **2 :** FLUX, SCORIFY, REFINE, REDUCE

4smelt \"\ *n* -S **:** a product of smelting or fusing **:** MELT

5smelt \"\ *n* -S [origin unknown] **:** a half guinea

1smelt·er \-tə(r)\ *n* -S [3*smelt* + *-er*] **1 a :** one that smelts; *specif* **:** a furnaceman who smelts ore **b :** an owner or operator of a smeltery **2** *or* **smelt·ery** \-tərē\ **:** an establishment for smelting

2smelter \"\ *n* -S [1*smelt* + *-er*] **:** a smelt fisherman

smelt·er·man \'⸗⸗mən\ *n, pl* **smeltermen** [1*smelter* + *man*] **:** 1SMELTER 1a

smeuse \'smyüz, -üs\ *n* -S [prob. blend of 1*smoot* and *meuse*] *dial Eng* **:** a hole in a hedge or wall

smew \'smyü\ *n* -S [akin to Fris *smjunt* smew, D *smient*, MHG *smiehe*] **1 :** a merganser (*Mergus albellus*) of northern Europe and Asia that is the smallest of mergansers and one of the most expert divers of all ducks and is in the male white and black with a large white crest **2 :** HOODED MERGANSER

SMG *abbr* submachine gun

smick·er \'smikə(r)\ *vi* [prob. of Scand origin; akin to OSw *smikra, smikkra* to flatter, Dan *smigre;* akin to OE *smicer* handsome, elegant, *smācian* to flatter, OHG *smehhar* slender, bi*smītan* to defile, stain — more at SMITE] *archaic* **:** to ogle and smile amorously — used with *at* or *after*

smick·et \'smikət\ *n* [prob. dim. of *smock*] *dial Eng* **:** a woman's smock

smid·dy \'smidi\ *dial Brit var of* SMITHY

smid·gen *or* **smid·geon** *or* **smid·gin** \'smijən\ *also* **smidge** \'smij\ *n* -S [prob. alter. of *smitch*] **:** a small amount **:** BIT, MITE

smiercase *var of* SMEARCASE

smi·la·ce·ae \,smīlə'kāsē,ē\ *n pl, cap* [NL, fr. *Smilac-, Smilax*, type genus + *-aceae*] *in some classifications* **:** a family of herbs or somewhat woody vines (order Liliales) having leaves with one to five prominent parallel veins and dioecious flowers with six perianth segments succeeded by globose berries and being commonly included in the family Liliaceae — **smi·la·ca·ceous** \'⸗⸗'kāshəs\ *adj*

smi·la·ce·ae \smī'lāsē,ē\ [NL, fr. *Smilac-, Smilax* + *-eae*] *syn of* SMILACACEAE

smi·la·ci·na \,smīlə'sīnə\ *n, cap* [NL, fr. *Smilac-, Smilax* + *-ina*] **:** a genus of American and Asiatic plants (family Liliaceae) with alternate leaves and racemes or panicles of small white flowers succeeded by red, green, or black berries — see FALSE SOLOMON'S SEAL

smi·la·gen·in \,smīlə'jenən, smī'lajənən\ *n* -S [NL *Smilax* (genus name of *Smilax ornata*) + E *-genin*] **:** a steroid sapogenin $C_{27}H_{44}O_3$ that is obtained esp. from a sarsaparilla (*Smilax ornata*) and is stereoisomeric with sarsapogenin

smi·lax \'smī,laks\ *n* [NL, fr. L, a kind of oak, yew, bindweed, fr. Gk; perh. akin to Gk *smilē* woodcarving knife; fr. the use of oak in carving — more at SMITH] **1** *cap* **:** a large widely distributed genus of plants (family Liliaceae) having small greenish flowers in axillary umbels and erect often prickly stems that climb by means of petiolar tendrils — see CATBRIER, SARSAPARILLA **2** *pl* **smilaxes :** a delicate greenhouse twining plant (*Asparagus asparagoides*) of southern Africa having ovate, bright-green cladophylls and being used esp. by florists in bouquet work and as a pot plant

1smile \'smīl, *esp before pause or consonant* -īəl\ *vb* -ED/-ING/-S [ME *smilen;* akin to OE *smerian* to laugh at, LG *smilen* to smile, obs. D *smuilen*, OHG *smierōn*, MHG *smielen*, Sw & Norw *smila* to smile, L *mirus* wonderful, *mirari* to wonder, wonder at, Gk *meidian* to smile, Toch A *smi-*, Skt *smayate* he smiles] *vi* **1 :** to have, produce, or exhibit a smile ⟨by this time the infant . . . may even laugh or ~ at his mother —H.R. Litchfield & L.H.Dembo⟩ **2 a :** to look or regard with amusement, ridicule, contempt, or indulgence ⟨~ indulgently at his quiddities⟩ ⟨*smiled* at his own folly for engaging in such a business —Martin Gardner⟩ **b :** to look or seem to look with favor **:** bestow approval **:** be propitious ⟨could hardly be blamed for feeling that Heaven *smiled* on his labors —Sheila Rowlands⟩ ⟨circumstances happen to ~ around him —Glenway Westcott⟩ **c :** to look or appear pleasant or agreeable **:** present a gay, sparkling, thriving, or benignant aspect ⟨a lake, warm and *smiling* and margined with green trees and grass —*Amer. Guide Series: Oregon*⟩ ~ *vt* **1 a :** to affect in some way with a smile or by a smile ⟨*smiling* away his embarrassment —C.S.Forester⟩ **b :** to effect or accomplish by smiling ⟨you thanked them and *smiled* your way out of it before you started crying yourself —Fred Majdalany⟩ **2** *obs* **:** to regard with disdain **:** hold in contempt ⟨~ you my speeches, as I were a fool —Shak.⟩ **3 :** to express by a smile ⟨*smiling* his pleasure at the happy outcome —E.B.George⟩ ⟨*smiled* a doubt as to their capacity —Irving Howe⟩ **4 :** to form one's face into (a smile) ⟨*smiled* a filial smile —Charles Dickens⟩

2smile \"\ *n* -S **1 :** a change of facial expression involving a brightening of the eyes and an upward curving of the corners of the mouth with no sound and less muscular distortion of the features than in a laugh that may express amusement, pleasure, tender affection, approval, restrained mirth, irony, derision, or any of various other emotions ⟨an infectious public ~ —*Time*⟩ ⟨the slight superior ~ of the man who is sure that he has the future —O.W.Holmes †1935⟩ ⟨wears a fixed ~ on her made-up face —C.W.Mills⟩ **2 :** a bright, pleasant, gratifying, or encouraging appearance or aspect ⟨the ~ of sunlit sea half a mile or so away —Blanche E. Baughan⟩

smile·ful \-lfəl\ *adj* **:** SMILING

smile·less \'smī(ə)lləs\ *adj* **:** exhibiting no smile **:** SOLEMN — **smile·less·ly** *adv* — **smile·less·ness** *n* -ES

smil·er \'smīlə(r)\ *n* -S [ME, fr. *smilen* to smile + *-er*] **:** one that smiles

smil·et \'smīlət\ *n* -S [2*smile* + *-et*] **:** a little smile

smiley *also* **smily** \'smīlē\ *adj* [2*smile* + *-y*] **:** exhibiting a smile

smil·ing·ly *adv* **:** in a smiling manner

smil·ing·ness *n* -ES **:** the quality or state of exhibiting a smile

smi·lo \'smī(,)lō\ *or* **smilo grass** *n* -S [origin unknown] **:** a perennial mountain rice (*Oryzopsis mileacea*) native to the Mediterranean region and introduced into No. America

smi·lo·don \'smīlə,dän\ *n, cap* [NL, fr. Gk *smilē* woodcarving knife + NL *-odon* — more at SMITH] **:** a New World genus of Pleistocene saber-toothed tigers attaining the size of tigers and having upper canines that extend 7 inches or more below the lower jaw and a gape of fully 90 degrees

1smin·thu·rid \smin'thürəd\ *adj* [NL *Sminthuridae*] **:** of or relating to the Sminthuridae

2sminthurid \"\ *n* -S **:** a collembolan of the family Sminthuridae

smin·thu·ri·dae \-rə,dē\ *n pl, cap* [NL, fr. *Sminthurus*, type genus (fr. Gk *sminthos* mouse of non-IE origin; akin to Etruscan *isminthians* mouse — + *-urus*) + *-idae*] **:** a family of small jumping collembolans having a short rounded body — compare LUCERNE FLEA

1smirch \'sməch, 'smǝch, 'smǝich\ *vt* -ED/-ING/-ES [ME *smorchen*] **1 a :** to make dirty, stained, or discolored **:** SULLY, SOIL, TARNISH **b :** to smear with something that stains or dirties **:** apply a discoloring agent to ⟨with a kind of umber ~ my face —Shak.⟩ **2 :** to bring into disrepute **:** bring discredit or disgrace upon ⟨the kind of mentalities that delight in ~*ing* the names of public men —A.D.H.Smith⟩

2smirch \"\ *n* -ES **1 :** a dirty blurred mark or blot **:** SMEAR, STAIN **2 :** something that tarnishes a reputation **:** a moral flaw

smirchy \-chē\ *adj* -ER/-EST **:** marked with spots or stains **:** SMIRCHED, BEGRIMED

smi·ris \'smīrəs\ *n* -ES [Gk *smyris, smiris* — more at SMEAR] **:** EMERY

1smirk \'smərk, 'smǝk, 'smǝik\ *vi* -ED/-ING/-S [ME *smirken*, fr. OE *smearcian* to smile; akin to OE *smerian* to laugh at — more at SMILE] **:** to smile in an affected or conceited manner **:** smile with affected complaisance **:** SIMPER

2smirk \'smərk\ *adj, dial chiefly Brit* **:** pleasantly neat and trim **:** AGREEABLE

3smirk \'smərk, 'smǝk, 'smǝik\ *n* -S **:** an affected smile **:** SIMPER ⟨the solemnity of the ceremony was broken by ~*s*, whispered jokes, and repressed titters —Robert Graves⟩

smirk·er \-kə(r)\ *n* -S **:** one that smirks

smirk·ing·ly *adv* **:** in a smirking manner

smir·kle \'smərkəl\ *vi* -ED/-ING/-S [freq. of 1*smirk*] *chiefly Scot* **:** SMIRK, SMILE

smirky \'smərkē\ *adj* -ER/-EST **:** SMIRKING

smirr \'smər\ *var of* SMUR

smit \'smit\ *vt* [ME *smitten*, fr. OE *smittian;* akin to OFris *smitta* to dirty, defile, MLG *smitten*, OHG bi*smizzan*, bi*smīzan* — more at SMITE] *chiefly Scot* **1 :** STAIN, TARNISH **2 :** CONTAMINATE, SULLY — often used of persons **3 :** INFECT

1smitch \'smich\ *dial Brit var of* SMUTCH

2smitch \"\ *n* -ES [perh. fr. 1*smitch*] **:** SMIDGEN

1smite \'smī|t, *usu* |d.+V\ *vb* **smote** \'smō|\ *or archaic* **smit** \'smi|\ **smit·ten** \'smit°n\ *or* **smit** *or* **smote; smiting; smites** [ME *smiten*, fr. OE *smītan;* akin to MD *smiten* to strike, throw, OHG bi*smīzan* to defile, stain, OSw *smēta* to daub, smear, spread, Goth bi*smeitan* to anoint, Gk *smēn* to wipe off, cleanse, *smēchein* to wash off, clean, Arm *mic* dirt, and perh. to L *mittere* to let go, send, Av *hamista* cast down, suppressed; basic meaning: to rub, throw] *vt* **1 a :** to strike usu. hard esp. with the hand or something held in the hand ⟨blacksmiths *smiting* the anvil —Havelock Ellis⟩ ⟨*smote* the side of his head with the palm —Pearl Buck⟩ **b :** to knock down ⟨to ~ an enemy to the ground⟩ **c** *archaic* **:** to strike or pluck (as the strings of a harp) to produce musical sound ⟨the minstrel *smote* his harp and sang⟩ **d :** to shine upon suddenly ⟨morning sunlight *smote* for the first time mankind's very first space craft —W.F.Jenkins⟩ **2 a :** to kill or severely injure by or as if by smiting **:** afflict with sudden calamity, destruction, or injury **b :** to inflict punishment (as destruction, death, or severe injury) upon as if by a stroke ⟨the Lord had *smited* him for coveting —W.O.Mitchell⟩ **c :** to attack or afflict suddenly and injuriously ⟨the herd was *smitten* by foot-and-mouth disease —*Irish Digest*⟩ **3 :** to cause to strike ⟨*smote* his hand against his thigh⟩ ⟨~ cymbals together⟩ **4 :** to affect as if by striking forcefully or abruptly **:** impress suddenly ⟨little children *smitten* with the fear of hell —V.L. Parrington⟩ ⟨*smitten* by the view from a crossing ferry —*Newsweek*⟩ ⟨her conscience *smote* her that she should have so much and they should have so little —Rebecca West⟩ ~ *vi* **:** to deliver or deal a usu. heavy blow with or as if with the hand or something held in the hand ⟨the child over 16 who cursed or *smote* at parents might incur the death penalty —*Amer. Guide Series: N.J.*⟩ **syn** see STRIKE

2smite \"\ *n* -S **:** a heavy blow **:** a smiting with a hand, weapon, or implement

smit·er \'smīd·ə(r)\ *n* -S [ME, fr. *smiten* + *-er*] **:** one that smites

1smith \'smith\ *n* -S [ME, fr. OE; akin to OHG *smid* smith, ON *smithr* smith, craftsman, Goth aiza*smitha* coppersmith, Gk *smilē* woodcarving knife, and perh. to Lith *smailus* pointed, greedy; basic meaning to carve] **1 a :** a worker in metals — often used in combination ⟨gold*smith*⟩ ⟨iron*smith*⟩ ⟨platinum*smith*⟩ **b :** BLACKSMITH 1c **2 :** one who constructs, builds, or produces something **:** MAKER ⟨the ~ of his own fortune —Van Wyck Brooks⟩ — often used in combination ⟨ski*smith*⟩ ⟨tune*smith*⟩

2smith \"\ *vt* -ED/-ING/-S [ME *smithen*, fr. OE *smithian;* akin to OHG *smithōn* to forge, fashion, Goth ga*smithon* to produce; denominative fr. the root of E 1*smith*] **:** to make or fashion by beating metal into shape **:** forge on an anvil after heating ⟨~ a sword⟩ ⟨~ a blade⟩

smith·am \'smithəm\ *n* -S **:** ore in fine particles obtained usu. by sifting

smithcraft \'⸗,⸗\ *n* **:** the occupation or technique of a smith

smith·er·eens \,smithə'rēnz\ *also* **smith·ers** \'smithə(r)z\ *n pl* [*smithereens* fr. IrGael *smidirín*, dim. of *smiodar* fragment; *smithers* fr. IrGael *smiodar*] **:** BITS, FRAGMENTS ⟨blown to ~ in the dynamite pit —Mrs. Patrick Campbell⟩ ⟨broke their line and smashed their whole right all to ~ —*Yale Rev.*⟩

smith·ery \'smithərē, -ri\ *n* -ES [1*smith* + *-ery*] **1 :** the work, art, or trade of a smith **:** SMITHCRAFT **2 :** SMITHY 1

smith·field \'smith,fēld\ *adj, usu cap* [fr. *Smithfield*, town in the Union of So. Africa] **:** of or belonging to a southern African culture in the Würm glacial period characterized by hunting, rock painting, ground stone tools, and in the later stages by the introduction of pottery of the Bantu type

smithfield bargain *also* **smithfield match** *n, usu cap S* [fr. *Smithfield*, area in London, England where fairs were formerly held] **:** a marriage of convenience in which the size of the marriage settlement is the determining factor

smithfield ham *n, usu cap S* [fr. *Smithfield*, town in southeastern Va.] **:** uncooked ham cut with long shank attached, dry-cured, cold-smoked, and then aged by hanging in a dry room

smith·ian \'smithēən\ *adj, usu cap* [Adam *Smith* †1790 Scotch economist + E *-ian*] **:** of, relating to, or having the characteristics of Adam Smith or of his economic theories

smithing coal *n* **:** a grade of caking coal low in sulfur and ash used esp. by blacksmiths

smith·ite \'smi,thīt\ *n* -S [G. F. Herbert *Smith* †1953 Eng. mineralogist + E *-ite*] **:** a mineral $AgAsS_2$ consisting of a silver arsenic sulfide occurring in small red monoclinic crystals (hardness 1.5–2, sp. gr. 4.9)

smith-pe·ter·son nail \'smith'pēd·ə(r)sən-\ *n, usu cap S&P* [after Marius *Smith-Peterson* †1953 American orthopedic surgeon who designed it] **:** a flanged metal nail used to fix the femoral head in fractures of the femoral neck

smith's longspur \'smiths-\ *n, usu cap S* [after Gideon B. *Smith*, 19th cent. Am. physician] **:** a longspur (*Calcarius pictus*) of northwestern No. America

smith·son·ite \'smithsə,nīt\ *n* -s [James Smithson †1829 Brit. chemist and mineralogist + E *-ite*] **1 :** a usu. white or nearly white native zinc carbonate $ZnCO_3$ commonly reniform, botryoidal, stalactitic, or granular and distinguished from hemimorphite by its effervescence with acids (hardness 5, sp. gr. 4.30–4.45) **2 :** HEMIMORPHITE 1
smithwork \'=,=\ *n* **:** SMITHCRAFT
¹smithy \'smith|ē, |i, *esp Brit* -ith|\ *n* -ES [ME *smithi*, fr. ON *smithja;* akin to OE *smiththe* smithy, OHG *smitta* smithy, *smid* smith — more at SMITH] **1 :** the workshop of a smith; *esp* **:** BLACKSMITH SHOP — called also *smithery, stithy* **2 :** BLACKSMITH ⟨working with the village ~ —Judith Crist⟩
²smithy \"\ *vt* -ED/-ING/-ES **:** SMITH
smithy coal *n, Brit* **:** SMITHING COAL
smiting *pres part of* SMITE
smit·ing line \'smīd·iŋ-\ *n* **:** a line by which a sail stoppered with yarns is broken out from the deck
smitten *past part of* SMITE
smit·ting \'smitiŋ\ *adj* [fr. pres. part. of *smit*] *dial Brit* **:** INFECTIOUS
smit·tle \'smitᵊl\ *vt* [freq. of ²*smit*] **1** *dial Brit* **:** to infect esp. with a contagious disease **2** *dial Brit* **:** GRASP, SEIZE
smkd *abbr* smoked
smkls *abbr* smokeless
sml *abbr* small
smls *abbr* seamless
SMO *abbr* **1** senior medical officer **2** squadron medical officer
smoak \'smōk\ *archaic var of* SMOKE
¹smock \'smäk\ *n* -s *often attrib* [ME *smok*, fr. OE *smoc;* akin to OHG *smocco* adornment, ON *smokkr* woman's stomacher, OE *smūgan* to creep, MHG *smiegen* to press in tightly, ON *smjūga* to creep through, and prob. to ON *mjūkr* soft, gentle — more at MUCUS] **1 a** *archaic* **:** a woman's undergarment; *esp* **:** CHEMISE **b :** SMOCK FROCK **c :** a lightweight loose garment made usu. with smocking or gathering at the shoulders, short or long sleeves, and a front opening and worn esp. for protection of clothing while working **2** *obs* **:** WOMAN

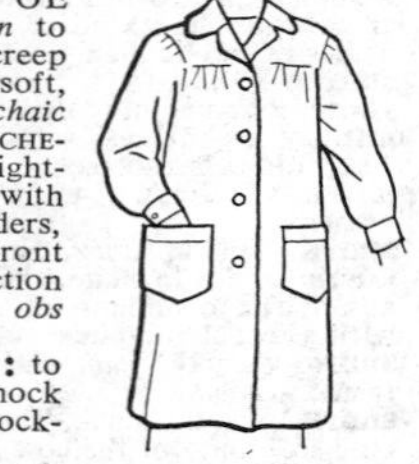
smock 1c

²smock \"\ *vb* -ED/-ING/-S *vt* **1 :** to provide with or clothe in a smock **2 :** to embroider or shirr with smocking ~ *vi* **:** to do smocking
smock–face \'=,=\ *n, archaic* **:** a pale effeminate face; *also* **:** a person having such a face
smock frock *n* **:** a loose shirtlike outer garment of coarse linen or cotton worn by workmen esp. in Europe
smocking *n* -s [fr. gerund of ²*smock*] **:** a decorative embroidery or shirring designed esp. to control fullness in garments and made by gathering cloth in regularly spaced round tucks held in place with fancy stitching
smock mill *or* **smock windmill** *n* [so called fr. the fancied resemblance of its shape to a person dressed in a smock] **:** a windmill whose cap alone turns round to meet the wind
smog \'smäg *also* 'smȯg\ *n* -s [blend of ¹*smoke* and *fog*] **1 :** a fog made heavier and darker by smoke and chemical fumes ⟨one of the worst ~*s* in London's history was . . . blamed for the deaths of 4000 people —Leonard Parkin⟩ **2 :** something resembling atmospheric smog **:** HAZE 2 ⟨behind the ~ of sophistry . . . lie two real issues —Robert Wuliger⟩
smog·gy \-gē\ *adj* -ER/-EST **:** characterized by or abounding in smog
smok·able *or* **smoke·able** \'smōkəbəl\ *adj* **:** fit for smoking
¹smoke \'smōk\ *n* -s *often attrib* [ME, fr. OE *smoca;* akin to OE *smēocan* to emit smoke, MD *smieken* to emit smoke, MHG *smouch* smoke, Gk *smychein* to smolder, Lith *smáugti* to suffocate, choke] **1 a** (1) **:** the gaseous products of burning carbonaceous materials made visible by the presence of small particles of carbon (2) **:** a similar incompletely burned volatilized product resulting from incomplete combustion and finally settling as soot — compare FLAME 1 **b :** a suspension of solid or liquid particles in a gas **:** FUME 1 **2 a** (1) **:** a mass or column of smoke ⟨the fifty ~*s* . . . curling from the valley —J.F.Cooper⟩ (2) **:** a smudge used esp. to drive away insects **b** *archaic* **:** FIRESIDE, HEARTH **3 a :** fume or vapor often resulting from the action of heat on moisture ⟨steeds . . . whose breaths dimmed the sun with ~ —John Lyly⟩ **b smokes** *pl* **:** dense white mists occurring in the dry season along the Guinea coast of Africa **4 :** visible or tangible evidence (as of secret activity) ⟨such a hell of a lot of ~ . . . that there must be enough flame to justify refusing a divorce —F.M.Ford⟩ **5 :** something of little substance, permanence, or value ⟨these aspirations and visions were only ~ —Van Wyck Brooks⟩ **6 :** something tending to cloud or obscure ⟨most of the ~ generated by the alleged conflict between poetry and science —C.I.Glicksberg⟩ **7 a** (1) **:** something to smoke **:** TOBACCO — often used in pl. ⟨what they spend each year on ~*s* is . . . less than what they spend on liquor — Dwight Macdonald⟩ (2) **:** CIGARETTE ⟨a reduction to seven cents a pack on ~*s* —G.E.Cruikshank⟩ **b** [²*smoke*] **:** an act or spell of smoking tobacco ⟨let's light our pipes and take a short ~ —A.B.Longstreet⟩ **8 a :** a pale blue that is redder and paler than average powder blue or Sistine and redder and duller than average cadet gray **b :** any of the colors of smoke viewed against various usual backgrounds (as smoke blue, smoke brown, smoke gray, smoke yellow) **c :** a nearly neutral slightly reddish dark gray that is darker than grebe or lead **9 a :** cheap liquor **b :** any of various drinks used as a substitute for liquor; *specif* **:** a drink consisting of wood alcohol and water **10 :** SPEED ⟨a pitcher with plenty of ~ on his fast ball⟩ **11 :** NEGRO — often taken to be offensive **12 :** SMOKE CAT
²smoke \"\ *vb* -ED/-ING/-S [ME *smoken*, fr. OE *smocian*, fr. *smoca*, n.] *vi* **1 a** (1) **:** to emit or exhale smoke ⟨hard by a cottage chimney ~*s* —John Milton⟩ (2) **:** to emit smoke as the result of faulty burning or inadequate draft ⟨the wick . . . flared and *smoked* —D.R.Murphy⟩ **b :** to give off something resembling smoke ⟨the marsh ~*s* in the sun⟩; *esp* **:** STEAM ⟨the horse's flanks *smoked*⟩ **2** *archaic* **:** to undergo severe pain or punishment **:** SUFFER ⟨some of you shall ~ for it in Rome —Shak.⟩ **3 a :** to spread like smoke ⟨a yellow mist far *smoking* o'er the interminable plain —James Thomson †1748⟩ **b :** to rise like or as if like smoke ⟨the anger of the Lord and his jealousy would ~ against that man —Deut 29: 20 (RSV)⟩ **4 a :** to inhale and exhale the fumes of tobacco or something resembling tobacco from a pipe, cigar, or cigarette ⟨has been *smoking* for six years⟩ **b :** to serve in a specified way for smoking ⟨the larger sizes *smoked* the best —Ben Riker⟩ **5** *archaic* **:** to have a notion or understanding of something **:** COMPREHEND **6 :** to go at a rapid rate **:** SPEED ⟨*smoked* along over the levels as fast as a pack in full cry —Rudyard Kipling⟩ **7** *Austral* **:** to run away **:** ABSCOND **8** *of a clay pigeon* **:** to break into small pieces **:** SHATTER ~ *vt* **1 :** to subject to the action of smoke: as **a :** FUMIGATE ⟨a good day for *smoking* ship —R.H.Dana⟩ **b :** to drive away (as mosquitoes) by smoke **c :** to blacken or discolor with smoke ⟨looked at the sun through *smoked* glasses —Ellen Glasgow⟩ **d :** to cure (as meat) by exposure to smoke ⟨*smoked* ham⟩ ⟨*smoked* salmon⟩ **e :** to stupefy (as bees) by smoke **2** *archaic* **:** to have an inkling or suspicion of **:** SUSPECT ⟨it's a capital notion . . . if he doesn't ~ the trick —Samuel Lover⟩ **3 a :** to inhale and exhale the smoke of **:** use in smoking ⟨*smoked* one cigarette after another⟩ ⟨*smoked* a pipe for many years⟩ **b :** to bring to a specified state by smoking ⟨if a man ~ himself to death —James I⟩ **4** *archaic* **:** to make fun of **:** RIDICULE ⟨*smoked* her and baited her and . . . drove her away —John Keats⟩ **5** *archaic* **:** to take notice of **:** OBSERVE ⟨~ his eyes, how they glare —John Wilson †1854⟩ **6 :** to cover with smoke so as to prevent enemy observation ⟨the wind and terrain were adaptable to *smoking* another mountainside on our right forward flank —G.E.Lynch⟩ **7 :** to cause (a clay pigeon) to break into small pieces
smokeable *var of* SMOKABLE
smoke ball *n* **1 :** a ball or case containing a composition that when ignited emits thick smoke **2 :** PUFFBALL **3 :** a pitch (as in baseball) having great speed
smoke beetle *n* **:** any of several buprestid beetles (genus *Melanophila*) that are attracted to smoke
smoke black *n* **:** a carbon black used as a pigment
smoke blue *n* **:** a dark bluish gray that is redder and darker than teal gray
smoke bomb *n* **:** a chemical bomb containing a smoke-producing substance; *esp* **:** any of various smoke flares that trail a streamer of smoke and are dropped from airplanes to mark targets for air attack, to screen targets from air attack, or to show wind direction over water
smokebox \'=,=\ *n* **:** a chamber in a steam boiler between the flues or flue tubes and the chimney or smokestack
smoke brown *n* **:** a nearly neutral very slightly olive dark gray — called also *asphalt, Vienna smoke*
smoke bush *n* **:** SMOKE TREE
smoke cat *n* **:** a domestic long-haired cat with a light silvery undercoat, ruff, and ear tufts and black topcoat and points; *also* **:** a similarly marked domestic short-haired cat
smoke chamber *n* **:** a part of a fireplace extending from the top of the throat to the bottom of the flue
smokechaser \'=,=\ *n* **:** a forest fire fighter; *esp* **:** one with light equipment that enables him to get to fires quickly — called also *fire chaser*
smoked *past of* SMOKE
smoke door *n* **:** a door in the roof above the gridiron of a theater opened in case of fire to draw the flames up and so prevent their spread to the auditorium
smoked pearl *n* **:** a purplish gray that is bluer than crane or granite and bluer and darker than cinder gray or zinc — called also *mitraille*
smoke–dry \'=,=\ *vt* **:** to dry or cure by means of smoke ~ *vi* **:** to become dried by means of smoke
smoked sheet *n* **:** sheet rubber dried by smoking
smoke eater *n* **1 :** FIRE FIGHTER **2 :** a device used with a smokejack in an enginehouse to draw smoke from a locomotive into a tank or pit for separating the solids in the smoke from the gas
smoke ejector *n* **:** a piece of fire apparatus used for ejecting smoke from a burning building by means of a blower
smoke explosion *n* **:** BACK DRAFT
smokefarthing \'=,==\ *n* [ME *smoke ffardyng*, fr. ¹*smoke* + *ffardyng, ferthing* farthing] **:** HEARTH MONEY — usu. used in pl.
smoke feeler *n* **:** EXHAUST-GAS ANALYZER
smoke–filled room \'=,=-\ *n* **:** a hotel room in which a small group of politicians carry on negotiations ⟨meet in a *smoke-filled room* to decide on . . . men and measures —D.D. McKean⟩
smoke fly *n* **:** any of several flies of a genus (*Microsania*) of the family Platypezidae that are attracted to smoke
smoke generator *n* **:** a mechanical device employing a special petroleum product that produces a smokelike screen to protect large areas from enemy observation
smoke gray *n* **:** a pale yellow green that is greener and slightly duller than oyster gray and yellower and less strong than average Nile
smoke helmet *n* **:** a gas mask used in fighting fire; *specif* **:** a gas mask connected by air hose to a pump or air line
smoke hole *n* [ME, fr. ¹*smoke* + *hole*] **:** a vent (as in a flue or roof) for smoke
smokehouse \'=,=\ *n* **1 :** a building where meat or fish is cured by means of dense smoke **2 :** a room where hides are softened in the manufacture of leather by means of smoke from a smoldering fire of spent tan
smokejack \'=,=\ *n* **1 :** a contrivance for turning a spit by a fly or wheel moved by the rising gases in a chimney **2 :** a flue built into the roof of an enginehouse to carry away the smoke and gases from the locomotive
smoke jumper *n* **:** a forest fire fighter who parachutes to locations otherwise difficult to reach
smoke·less \'smōkləs\ *adj* **1 :** producing little or no smoke ⟨~ fuel⟩ ⟨~ combustion⟩ **2 :** having little or no smoke ⟨the ~ air⟩ ⟨a ~ city⟩ — **smoke·less·ly** *adv* — **smoke·less·ness** *n* -ES
smokeless powder *n* **:** any of a class of propellants that produce less smoke on explosion than black powder, that typically consist of gelatinized cellulose nitrates either alone or mixed with nitroglycerin or other ingredients, and that are produced in various forms (as solid and perforated cylindrical grains for military use or as flakes and pellets for sporting use) but not in powder form — compare GUNPOWDER
smokelike \'=,=\ *adj* **:** resembling smoke
smoke mask *n* **:** SMOKE HELMET
smoke–oh \'=,=\ *n* -s [¹*smoke* + *oh*, interj.; fr. the practice of smoking during rest periods] *chiefly Austral* **:** a short rest period (as in the midmorning or midafternoon) for workers engaged esp. in manual labor **:** BREAK
smoke out *vt* **1 :** to drive out of a place of hiding or concealment by or as if by the use of smoke ⟨*smoked out* small game by ramming smoldering grass into a hole —*N.Y. Herald Tribune Bk. Rev.*⟩ ⟨came and *smoked* him *out* with tommy guns —Jean Stafford⟩ **2 :** to bring into the open **:** bring to public view or knowledge ⟨would *smoke out* the real intentions of the Syrian government —A.T.Steele⟩
smoke pipe *n* **:** a usu. thin metal pipe connecting a possible source of smoke to a chimney or smokestack
smoke plant *n* **:** SMOKE TREE
smoke pocket *n* **:** a steel angle enclosing the edge of the asbestos curtain in a theater for keeping smoke and flames from getting into the theater in case of fire
smoke pot *n* **:** a can containing a mixture that produces a smoke or smokelike screen
smoke proof *n* [¹*smoke* + *proof*, n.] **:** a test impression of a typefounder's punch obtained by blackening it in a flame and stamping it on paper
smokeproof \'=,=\ *adj* [¹*smoke* + *proof*, adj.] **:** impermeable to smoke; *specif* **:** designed to restrict the spread of smoke through a building — used esp. of a door or partition
smok·er \'smōkə(r)\ *n* -s **1 :** one that smokes: as **a :** a person who dries or preserves by smoke **b :** a person who smokes tobacco **c :** a ship or airplane discharging a smoke screen **d :** an apparatus for producing and directing a stream of smoke at bees so as to quiet them **e** *slang* (1) **:** STEAM LOCOMOTIVE (2) **:** HOTBOX **2 :** a railroad car or compartment in which smoking is allowed **3 :** an informal social gathering for men **4 :** SMOKING STAND
smoke room *n, chiefly Brit* **:** SMOKING ROOM
smoker's heart *n* **:** TOBACCO HEART
smok·ery \'smōkərē\ *n* -ES **:** a place where smoking is done
smokes *pl of* SMOKE, *pres 3d sing of* SMOKE
smoke sail *n* **:** a small sail hoisted close to the galley stovepipe in a head wind for carrying the smoke from the deck
smoke screen *n* **1 :** a screen or cloud of smoke: as **a :** a screen of smoke designed to hinder enemy observation of a military force, area, or activity **b :** a heavy smoke supplied by smudge pots and designed to protect orchards and other plantings from injury by frost **2 :** something designed to obscure, confuse, or mislead ⟨seek immunity from criticism behind a rhetorical *smoke screen* about academic freedom —Sidney Hook⟩
smoke shelf *n* **:** a shelf or baffle in a smoke flue designed to prevent downdraft
smoke shell *n* **:** a projectile that releases smoke on impact
smokestack \'=,=\ *n* **:** a chimney or funnel through which smoke and gases of combustion are discharged from a locomotive, ship, or building
smokestand \'=,=\ *n* **:** SMOKING STAND
smoke talk *n* **:** a talk given at a smoker
smoketight \'=¦=\ *adj* **:** impervious to smoke
smoke train *n* **:** a trail of dust and gas left by an exploding meteorite in its passage through the atmosphere
smoke tree *n* **1 :** either of two small shrubby plants of the genus *Cotinus* having large panicles of flowers on plumose pedicels that resemble a cloud of smoke: **a :** an Old World shrub (*C. coggygria*) — called also *Venetian sumac* **b :** an American shrub or shrubby tree (*C. obovatus*) — called also *chittamwood* **2 :** a spiny grayish green leguminous shrub (*Dalea spinosa*) of desert areas of the southwestern U.S. and Mexico that has very sparse foliage and terminal spikes of bluish violet flowers and that is a locally important honey plant yielding a light-colored honey of excellent flavor
smoke tunnel *n* **:** an experimental wind tunnel in which air movements are observed by means of smoke filaments released at suitable points
smoke up *vt* **:** to fill with smoke
smoke washer *n* **:** a device in which smoke is forced upward against a downward spray of water in order to remove the solid particles in the smoke
smoke yellow *n* **:** BEACH 3
smok·i·ly \'smōkəlē, -li\ *adv* **:** in a smoky manner
smok·i·ness \-kēnəs, -kin-\ *n* -ES **:** the quality or state of being smoky
smoking *adv* [fr. pres. part. of ²*smoke*] **:** to a smoking degree ⟨~ hot food⟩
smoking bean *n* [so called fr. the occasional use of the pods for smoking by boys] **1 :** CATALPA **2 :** the long pod of the catalpa
smoking car *n* **:** SMOKER 2
smoking concert *n, Brit* **:** FREE AND EASY 1a
smoking jacket *n* [so called fr. its orig. having been worn for after-dinner smoking] **:** a man's soft dressy jacket for wear at home — compare HOUSECOAT
smoking lamp *n* **:** a lamp on a ship kept lighted during the hours when smoking is allowed
smoking opium *n* **:** PREPARED OPIUM
smoking room *n* **:** a room (as in a hotel or club) set apart for smokers
smoking–room \'==,=\ *adj* [*smoking room*] **:** marked by indecency or obscenity **:** DIRTY, SMUTTY ⟨it is possible even in the *smoking-room* story to perceive some of the characteristics common to all storytelling —W.H.Auden⟩
smoking stand *n* **:** a wood or metal stand for holding an ashtray

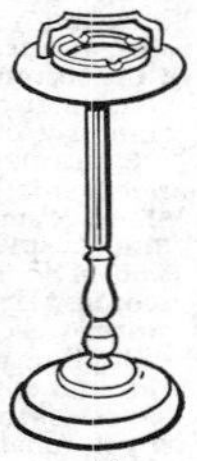
smoking stand

smoking tobacco *n* **:** tobacco suitable for the manufacture of cigarettes and pipe tobacco — compare BURLEY, MARYLAND
smok·ish \'smōkish\ *adj* [ME, fr. ¹*smoke* + *-ish*] **:** somewhat smoky
smo·ko \'smō(,)kō\ *var of* SMOKE-OH
smoky *also* **smokey** \'smōkē, -ki\ *adj* **smokier; smokiest** [ME *smoky*, fr. ¹*smoke* + *-y*] **1 a :** emitting smoke esp. in large quantities or in an offensive manner ⟨~ fireplaces⟩ ⟨a ~ torch⟩ **b :** emitting something that resembles smoke ⟨part the ~ flesh, enjoy the feast —Joel Barlow⟩ **2 a :** having the characteristics of or resembling smoke ⟨a ~ mist⟩: as (1) *obs* **:** having the obscuring or unsubstantial quality of smoke (2) **:** having a flavor or odor suggestive of smoke **:** tasting or smelling like smoke ⟨the ~ taste of Scotch whisky⟩ **b :** having a foggy or misty quality **:** HAZY ⟨the ~ outline of the farther shore —Valentine Williams⟩ ⟨the Great *Smoky* Mountains⟩ **3 a :** filled with or marked by the presence of smoke ⟨a ~ kitchen⟩ ⟨autumn is the *smokiest* season —Berton Roueché⟩ **b :** made dark or black by smoke ⟨~ rafters⟩ **4 :** of the color smoke **5 :** having the habit of smoking ⟨*smokey* young men . . . watching football matches —*London Daily News*⟩ **6** *archaic* **:** quick to detect or suspect **7** *of a voice* **:** marked by a low guttural quality suggestive of a torch singer
smoky fungus *n* **:** a parasitic fungus producing dark mycelium on the surface of fruit or twigs of its host
smoky quartz *n* **:** CAIRNGORM
smoky topaz *n* **:** a smoky quartz used for jewelry
¹smol·der *or* **smoul·der** \'smōldə(r)\ *n* -s [ME *smolder;* akin to MD *smölen* to smolder, scorch — more at SMELL] **1 :** SMOKE, SMOTHER, SMUDGE **2 :** a smoldering fire — compare BLAZE **3 :** a disease of narcissus bulbs caused by a fungus (*Botrytis narcissicola*)
²smolder *or* **smoulder** \"\ *vb* **smoldered** *or* **smouldered; smoldered** *or* **smouldered; smoldering** *or* **smouldering** \-d(ə)riŋ\ **smolders** *or* **smoulders** [ME *smolderen*, fr. *smolder*, n.] *vt* **1** *obs* **:** SMOTHER, SUPPRESS, SUFFOCATE **2 :** to blacken with fire or ashes ~ *vi* **1 :** to burn and smoke without flame ⟨the fuse ~*ed* and sputtered⟩ **:** waste away by slow combustion ⟨fire was ~*ing* in the grate⟩ — often used with *out* ⟨it took hours for the ruins to ~ out⟩ **2 :** to exist in a state of suppressed activity **:** be or continue liable to violent outbreak at any moment ⟨the feud ~*ed* for months with no actual shooting⟩ **3 :** to show scarcely suppressed or contained anger, hate, jealousy ⟨her tone was . . . conversational, although . . . her eyes were ~*ing* —James Hensel⟩
smol·der·ing·ly *adv* **:** in a smoldering manner
smo·lensk \smō'len(t)sk\ *adj, usu cap* [fr. *Smolensk*, city in western U.S.S.R.] **:** of or from the city of Smolensk, U.S.S.R. **:** of the kind or style prevalent in Smolensk
¹smolt \'smōlt\ *adj* [ME, affable, fr. OE, fair (of the weather); akin to MD *smout*, *smolt* fair (of the weather), calm, OSw *smultna* to become calm, OHG *smelzan* to melt — more at SMELT] *dial chiefly Eng* **:** SMOOTH, CALM
²smolt \"\ *n* -s [ME (Sc); prob. akin to OE ¹*smelt* — more at SMELT] **:** a salmon or sea trout between the parr and grilse stages when it is about two years old and silvery and first descends to the sea
¹smooch \'smüch\ *vt* -ED/-ING/-ES [prob. alter. of ²*smutch*] **:** SMUDGE, SMEAR, SOIL ⟨don't want you ~*ing* up these cards — W.L.Gresham⟩
²smooch \"\ *n* -ES **:** SMUDGE, SMEAR ⟨a ~ of lipstick on his collar⟩
³smooch \"\ *vi* -ED/-ING/-ES [alter. of ²*smouch*] **:** KISS, PET ⟨~*ing* in dark corners⟩
⁴smooch \"\ *n* -ES **:** KISS ⟨comes over and plants a big ~ on me —Richard Bissell⟩
smoochy \-chē\ *adj* **:** SMUDGY
smoodge *or* **smooge** \'smüj\ *vi* [perh. alter. of ²*smouch*] *chiefly Austral* **1 :** to curry favor in a fawning manner **2 :** ³SMOOCH
¹smoor \'smō(ə)r\ *var of* SMORE
²smoor \'smō(ə)r\ *chiefly Scot var of* SMUR
smoor·ich \'smōrək\ *n* [prob. imit.] *Scot* **:** a stolen kiss
smoot \'smüt\ *n* -s [of Scand origin; akin to ON *smātta* narrow lane; perh. akin to OE *smūgan* to creep — more at SMOCK] *dial Eng* **:** a narrow passageway; *esp* **:** one through which small animals may creep
¹smooth \'smüth\ *adj* -ER/-EST [ME *smothe*, fr. OE *smōth;* akin to OE *smēthe* smooth, OS *smōthi*] **1 a :** having a continuously even surface **:** being without roughness, points, bumps, or ridges esp. to the touch ⟨~ tabletop⟩ ⟨~ fabric⟩ ⟨~ skin⟩ ⟨~ lawn⟩ ⟨~ road⟩ **b :** being without bristles or hair ⟨my brother is a hairy man and I am a ~ man —Gen 27:11 (AV)⟩ **c :** not rough or scabrous **:** not pubescent **:** GLABROUS ⟨a ~ leaf⟩ **d** (1) **:** causing no resistance to a body sliding along its surface **:** FRICTIONLESS (2) *of a reflecting surface* **:** having surface irregularities small compared with the wave length of the reflected radiation **e :** less rough or harsh than is characteristic of the class ⟨~ file⟩; *sometimes* **:** having its points or ridges leveled by wear ⟨~ tire⟩ **2 :** free from all that would obstruct or impede progress **:** easily or comfortably traveled **:** presenting no obstacles or difficulties ⟨broad ~ highways⟩ ⟨trying to make his path ~*er* for him⟩ **3 a :** even and uninterrupted in flow or flight **:** continuously flowing or gliding **:** moving or proceeding without breaks, abrupt changes or transitions **:** not jerky, jolting, or jarring ⟨~ stream⟩ ⟨~ flow of words⟩ ⟨car came to a ~ stop⟩ **b :** capable of easy dexterity and effortlessly controlled movement ⟨~ dancer⟩ **c :** avoiding or minimizing what is harsh or unpleasant or objectionable **:** plausibly flattering **:** INGRATIATING ⟨deceived by the ~ talk of the salesman⟩ ⟨~ villain⟩ ⟨~ handling of an embarrassing situation⟩ ⟨~ explanations of suspicious conduct⟩ **4 a :** calm and unruffled in words, manner or behavior **:** SERENE, EQUABLE ⟨~ disposition⟩ **b :** AMIABLE, COURTEOUS, FRIENDLY **5 :** accompanied by calm weather **:** free from discomfort or difficulty ⟨~ channel crossing⟩ ⟨~ sailing from here on⟩ **6 a :** performed so that each tone within the musical phrase glides or flows into the next **:** LEGATO **b :** moving by small intervals — used of the progression of voice parts in harmonized music **7** *Greek grammar* **a** *of a vowel* **:** sounded without the aspirate **:** unaspirated ⟨~ vowel⟩ **b** *of a stop consonant* **:** being voiceless, unaspirated, and lenis **8 a :** agreeable or soothing to one's ear,

palate, feelings : BLAND, MILD ⟨~ tone of voice⟩ ⟨~ syrup⟩ ⟨~ wine⟩ **b** : free from lumps : having perfect blending of the elements ⟨~ batter⟩ ⟨~ salad dressing⟩ **c** : having the pungency (as of alcohol) moderated by blending of other ingredients ⟨a ~ cocktail⟩ **9** : relatively good — used esp. of a poker hand in lowball; compare ROUGH **10** : forming smooth colonies usu. made up of organisms that form no chains or filaments, show characteristic internal changes, and tend to marked increase in capsule formation and virulence — used of dissociated strains of bacteria; compare MUCOID **syn** see EASY, LEVEL, SUAVE

²smooth \"\ *vb* -ED/-ING/-S [ME *smothen*, fr. *smothe*, adj., smooth] *vt* **1** : to make smooth, level, or even on the surface : remove the surface inequalities and irregularities of ⟨~ soil in a flower bed⟩ ⟨~ the edge of a board⟩ ⟨~ cloth with an iron⟩ ⟨~ a rumpled bedsheet⟩ **2 a** : to free from what is harsh, crude, offending, or disagreeable : REFINE, POLISH ⟨~ verses⟩ ⟨sent to a school to ~ and polish his manners⟩ **b** : to make calm : SOOTHE **3** : to minimize (as a fault, a difference) in order to allay anger or ill-will : PALLIATE — often used with *over* ⟨~*ing* things over is practically a profession to mothers of families —Margaret Deland⟩ **4** : to free from obstruction or difficulty : make easy ⟨~*ed* his way with bribes⟩ **5 a** : to remove (as wrinkles, creases) from a surface ⟨~*ed* the lines of worry away with her cool fingertips⟩ **b** : to press or rub into a flat form ⟨nervously crumpling and ~*ing* out her handkerchief⟩ **c** : to remove expression from (one's face) : COMPOSE **6** : cause to lie evenly and in order : PREEN ⟨took off her hat and ~*ed* down her hair⟩ ⟨hen ~*ing* her ruffled feathers⟩ **7** : to change a broken line made up of sections of straight lines into (a curve); *specif* : to free (a graph) from irregularities by ignoring random deviations **8** : MONOPHTHONGIZE — used esp. of the change of a vowel before a back consonant in the Anglian dialects of Old English ⟨Anglian ~*ing* of *ēa* to *ē*⟩ ~ *vi* **1** *obs* : BLANDISH, FLATTER **2** : to become smooth ⟨the wind dropped and the waves ~*ed* down⟩

³smooth \"\ *adv* [ME *smothe*, fr. *smothe*, adj., smooth] : SMOOTHLY ⟨~ runs the water where the brook is deep —Shak.⟩

⁴smooth \"\ *n* -S [ME *smothe*, fr. *smothe*, adj., smooth] **1 a** : a smooth stretch (as of land); *specif* : MEADOW **b** : an intermittent space of smooth water **2** : the smooth part of anything : something that is smooth ⟨learn to take the rough with the ~⟩ **3** [²*smooth*] : act of smoothing or state of being smooth : a stroke which smooths ⟨give a ~ to his hair⟩ **4** [²*smooth*] : a smoothing implement **5** : the side of a tennis racket on which the binding strings form a continuous line ⟨calling rough or ~ to decide court and service⟩

smooth alder *n* : a common alder (*Alnus rugosa*) of the eastern U.S. with smooth bark and leaves green on both sides — called also *hazel alder*

smooth azalea *n* : TREE AZALEA

smoothbark \'=,=\ *n* : any of several eucalypts having the bark smooth except at or near the base of the trunk — compare STRINGYBARK

smooth beardtongue *n* : a commonly cultivated perennial herb (*Pentstemon laevigatus*) with showy slightly irregular tubular purple flowers

smooth–billed ani \'=,=-\ *n* : a common ani (*Crotophaga ani*)

¹smoothbore \'=,=\ *adj* [¹*smooth* + *bore*, n.] *of a firearm* : having a bore with a smooth surface — compare ⁴RIFLE

²smoothbore \"\ *n* : a smoothbore firearm

smooth breathing *n* [trans. of LL *spiritus lenis*] **1** : a mark ʼ placed over some initial vowels in Greek to show that they are not aspirated (as in ἄγειν pronounced \'ägān\) **2** : the absence of aspiration as indicated by the mark ʼ — called also *spiritus lenis;* compare BREATHING 2, ROUGH BREATHING

smooth brome *or* **smooth bromegrass** *n* : AWNLESS BROMEGRASS

smooth buckeye *n* : a common buckeye (*Aesculus glabra*)

smooth–chinned \'=¦=\ *adj* : BEARDLESS

smooth crabgrass *n* : a weedy European grass (*Digitaria ischaemum*) naturalized in No. America often becoming a troublesome pest

smooth curve *n* : a curve with a continuously turning tangent

smooth dogfish *also* **smooth dog** *n* : any of various dogfishes that lack spines in front of the dorsal fins — see SMOOTH HOUND; compare SPINY DOGFISH

smoothed *past of* SMOOTH

smoothen \'smüthən\ *vb* **smoothened; smoothened; smoothening** \-th(ə)niŋ\ **smoothens** *vt* : to make smooth ~ *vi* : to become smooth

¹smoother *comparative of* SMOOTH

²smooth·er \'smüthə(r)\ *n* -S **1** : one that smooths ⟨a ~ of the way for those who came after him⟩ **2** : one whose work is to make something smooth: as **a** : one who smooths sheet metal on a hammering machine **b** : one that bevels the edges of optical glass with an abrasive wheel **c** : one that removes blemishes from glassware by means of a gas flame **d** : one that smooths finished fountain pen points with emery paper **3** : a device or tool for smoothing : SLEEKER, SLICKER

smoothest *superlative of* SMOOTH

smooth–faced \'=¦=\ *adj* **1** : BEARDLESS **2** : having a smooth surface — usu. used of cloth **3** : bland in countenance or expression

smooth green snake *n* : a green snake (*Ophiodrys vernalis*) occupying a somewhat more northerly range than the rough green snake and having dark bluish green or almost blue perfectly smooth scales above and smooth ivory ventral plates

smooth hound *n* : a smooth dogfish (*Mustelus mustelus*) common in southern European waters; *broadly* : SMOOTH DOGFISH

smoothie *var of* SMOOTHY

smoothing *pres part of* SMOOTH

smoothing box *n* : BOX IRON

smoothing iron *n* **1** : FLATIRON **2** : an iron slicker used in leather manufacture

smoothing mill *n* : a revolvable sandstone wheel used with a stream of water for cutting and beveling glass or stone

smoothing plane *or* **smooth plane** *n* : a short finely set plane used for smoothing and finishing

smooth·ish \'smüthish\ *adj* : fairly smooth ⟨~ bark⟩

smooth joint *n* : TIGHT JOINT

smooth–leaved elm \'=,=-\ *n* : a European elm (*Ulmus carpinifolia*) used as an ornamental and having lustrous smooth leaves

smooth log *n* : a clean copy of a ship's log

smooth lungwort *n* : any plant of the genus *Mertensia; esp* : VIRGINIA COWSLIP

smooth·ly *adv* [ME *smothely*, fr. *smothe*, adj., smooth + *-ly*] : in a smooth manner : without roughness, abruptness, or interruption ⟨~ flowing speech⟩ : without difficulties ⟨not be assumed that rents and dues were all paid ~ —*Times Lit. Supp.*⟩

smooth meadow grass *n* : KENTUCKY BLUEGRASS

smooth muscle *n* : muscle tissue made up of elongated spindle-shaped cells having central nucleus and lacking cross striations that in vertebrates typically form thin sheets associated with visceral structures (as stomach and bladder) performing functions (as peristalsis) not under direct voluntary control and that constitute in most invertebrates the chief or only type of muscle present

smooth·ness *n* -ES [ME *smothenesse*, fr. *smothe*, adj., smooth + *-nesse* -ness] : the quality, state, or fact of being smooth : absence of irregularities of surface, movement, or functioning

smooth newt *n* : a common European newt (*Triturus vulgaris*) — called also *spotted newt*

smooth–running \'=¦==\ *adj* : that runs smoothly, frictionlessly, or efficiently ⟨*smooth-running* machinery⟩

smooths *pres 3d sing of* SMOOTH, *pl of* SMOOTH

smooth–shaven \'=¦==\ *adj* : having the face shaven clean of beard and moustache

smooth shelf fungus *n* : a fungus of the family Thelephoraceae

smooth skate *n* : BARN-DOOR SKATE

smooth snake *n* : a harmless European colubrid snake (*Coronella austriaca*) with smooth glossy scales

smooth–spoken \'=¦==\ *adj* : speaking smoothly : fluent and plausible in speech

smooth storax *n* : SPRING ORANGE

smooth sumac *n* **1** : a common No. American sumac (*Rhus glabra*) with glaucous stems and leaves **2** : DWARF SUMAC

smooth–taper drift *n* : DRIFT 4g

smooth tare *or* **smooth vetch** *n* : SLENDER VETCH

smooth tongue *n* : a genetic variation in cattle believed due to a recessive gene and marked by faulty differentiation of the lingual structures and anemia

smooth–tongued \'=¦=\ *adj* : ingratiating in speech : PLAUSIBLE, FLATTERING

smooth winterberry *n* : an often arborescent shrub (*Ilex laevigata*) that lacks prickles on the leaves

smoothy *or* **smooth·ie** \'smüthē, -thi\ *n, pl* **smoothies** [¹*smooth* + *-ie*] **1 a** : a person with polished manners **b** : one who behaves or performs with deftness, assurance, easy competence; *esp* : a man with an ingratiating manner toward women **c** : a smooth-tongued person **2** *slang* : SLICK 6

¹smore \'smō(ə)r\ *vb* -ED/-ING/-S [ME *smoren*, fr. OE *smorian* to suffocate, strangle] *dial Brit* : SMOTHER, SUPPRESS

²smore \"\ *n* -S *chiefly Scot* : dense smoke or stifling air

smor·gas·bord *R* 'smȯrgəs,bȯrd, -bōrd; –*R* 'smȯgəs,bō(ə)d, -bȯəd\ *n* -S [Sw *smörgåsbord*, fr. *smörgås* bread and butter, open sandwich (fr. *smör* butter + *gås* goose) + *bord* table; fr. a fancied resemblance of lumps of butter to geese; akin to ON *smör*, *smjör* fat, butter, to ON *gās* goose, and to ON *borth* table — more at SMEAR, GOOSE, BOARD] **1** : a luncheon or supper buffet offering a variety of foods and dishes (as hors d'oeuvres, hot and cold meats, smoked and pickled fish, sausages, cheeses, salads, relishes) **2** : MÉLANGE, HODGEPODGE

smør·re·brød \'smœrə,brœth\ *also* **smor·re·brod** \'smȯrə,-bräd\ *n* -S [Dan *smørrebrød*, fr. *smør* butter + *brød* bread; akin to ON *smör*, *smjör* fat, butter and to ON *brauth* bread — more at BREAD] : an hors d'oeuvre served in Danish style on a slice of buttered bread

smor·zan·do \smȯrt'sän(,)dō\ *also* **smor·za·to** \-ä(,)dō\ *adj* [*smorzando* fr. It, verbal of *smorzare* to tone down, reduce, alter. (influenced by *s-*, fr. L *ex-*) of *ammorzare* to moderate, weaken, extinguish, fr. (assumed) VL *admortiare* to extinguish, fr. L *ad-* + (assumed) VL *-mortiare* (fr. L *mortuus*, past part. of *mori* to die); *smorzato* fr. It, past part. of *smorzare* — more at MURDER] : growing slower and softer : dying away — abbr. *smorz.*; used as a direction in music

smote *past of* SMITE

¹smoth·er \'sməthə(r)\ *n* -S [ME, alter. of *smorther*, fr. *smoren* to smother, fr. OE *smorian* to suffocate, strangle; akin to MD *smoren* to suffocate, stew, MLG *smōren*, and perh. to MD *smölen* to smolder, scorch — more at SMELL] **1 a** : thick stifling smoke : a suffocating smudge or smoky condition **b** : a state of being stifled or suppressed : a smoldering or dampened fire **2** : a dense cloud of fog, foam, spray, snow, or dust ⟨logs . . . rolled and tossed in a creamy ~ —Kenneth Roberts⟩ ⟨come with her tail up in a ~ of flying sand —Mary H. Vorse⟩ **3** : a confused multitude or rush of things : WELTER ⟨~ of flowering creepers and climbers —Jean Devanny⟩ ⟨in a ~ of shoal-water waves that roll you down to leeward —S.E. Morison⟩

²smother \"\ *vb* **smothered; smothered; smothering** \-th(ə)riŋ\ **smothers** [ME *smotheren*, alter. of *smortheren*, fr. *smorther*, n.] *vt* **1** : to overcome or kill with smoke or fumes **2 a** : to destroy the life of by depriving of air ⟨~ a child with a pillow⟩ ⟨~ seedlings in a tight cold frame⟩ **b** : to overcome or discomfit through or as if through lack of adequate air ⟨such close quarters tend to ~ one⟩ **c** : to suppress (a fire) by excluding oxygen **3** : to cover or overlay oppressively: as **a** : to cause to smolder rather than blaze by or as if by covering ⟨~ a fire with too much coal⟩ **b** : to suppress or prevent expression, utterance, notice, or knowledge of as though by thick covering ⟨~ a secret⟩ ⟨he ~*ed* his rage⟩ ⟨the bill was ~*ed* in committee⟩ — often used with *up* **c** : to stop or prevent the growth, development, activity, or vitality of by or as if by thick cover or dense concentration around ⟨moralized, intellectualized, and nearly ~*ed* by Harvard —H.S.Canby⟩ ⟨little flowers ~*ed* by the weeds⟩ ⟨~ weeds in a field by planting sorghum⟩ **d** : to cover thickly, settle over, or blanket completely or restrictingly ⟨a record snow ~*ing* the valley⟩ **e** : to overcome quickly and completely : vanquish at once and render utterly helpless ⟨Belgian units ~*ed* by the invading Germans⟩ ⟨state ~*ed* Tech by a score of 52–0⟩ **f** : to hit (a golf ball) low along the ground through faulty execution of a lofting stroke **g** : to play (a bowled cricket ball) from above with a sharp downward defensive stroke **4 a** : to cook (meat, vegetables) in a covered pan or pot with very little liquid over low heat ⟨~*ed* round steak and onions⟩ ⟨~*ed* cabbage⟩ **b** : to serve (food) covered with other food cooked or uncooked ⟨gingerbread ~*ed* with whipped cream⟩ ⟨broiled steak ~*ed* with mushrooms⟩ ~ *vi* **1** : to suffer or die from lack of air ⟨were ~*ing* in the sultry heat⟩ ⟨the child ~*ed* in the locked chest⟩ **2** *dial Brit* : SMOLDER **3** : to undergo suppression, repression, extreme restraint, or concealment ⟨his anger ~*ed* and died⟩ **syn** see SUFFOCATE

³smother \"\ *n* -S : SMOTHERING

smoth·er·able \-ərəbəl\ *adj* : that may be smothered

smoth·er·a·tion \,sməthə'rāshən\ *n* -S : a smothering or state of being smothered : SUFFOCATION ⟨death by ~ in a mine cave-in⟩

smother crop *n* : a crop (as buckwheat, soybeans) sown for the purpose of suppressing persistent weeds

smothered mate *n* : a checkmate by a knight in chess when movement of the king is completely obstructed by his own men

smoth·er·er \'sməth(ə)rə(r)\ *n* -S : one that smothers ⟨after three days of a hundred-and-two-degree ~ —Alma Stone⟩

smother fire *n* : a smoldering fire

smother fly *n, Brit* : APHID

¹smothering *adj* [ME, fr. pres. part. of *smotheren* to smother] **1** : SUFFOCATING, STIFLING ⟨~ affection⟩ ⟨~ heat⟩ **2** : SMOLDERING — **smoth·er·ing·ly** *adv*

²smothering *n* -S [fr. gerund of ²*smother*] : a disease of tree seedlings occurring esp. in crowded nurseries and characterized by the growth of the leathery fruiting body of a fungus (*Thelephora terrestris*) about the seedling stem

smother–kiln \'=,=-,=\ *n* : a kiln in which pottery is blackened by admitting smoke in firing

smoth·ery \'sməth(ə)rē\ *adj* : tending to smother : STIFLING ⟨~ attic⟩ ⟨climbed up the bank and walked under the trees; it was soft and warm and ~ in there —Richard Bissell⟩

¹smouch \'smüch, 'smau̇ch\ *n* -ES [imit.] *dial* : a slobbery smacking kiss

²smouch \"\ *vb* -ED/-ING/-ES *chiefly dial* : to kiss esp. loudly or slobberingly

³smouch *n* -ES [alter. of *smous*] *obs* : JEW

⁴smouch \'smau̇ch\ *vt* -ED/-ING/-ES [prob. fr. ³*smouch*] : to get by stealing or trickery : FILCH, PILFER

⁵smouch *var of* SMUTCH

smoulder *var of* SMOLDER

smous *or* **smouse** *n, pl* **smouses** [D *smous*, prob. fr. Yiddish *shmues* talk, chat — more at SCHMOOZE] **1** *obs* : JEW **2** *So Afr* : an itinerant peddler

SMP *abbr, often not cap* [L *sine mascula prole*] without male issue

smri·ti *also* **smrti** \'smrid·ē\ *n* -S *often cap* [Skt *smṛti*, lit., what is remembered, fr. *smarati* he remembers — more at MEMORY] : the body of Hindu sacred writings containing traditional teachings (as on religious, domestic, and social practice) based on the Vedas and forming the class of shastras below the sruti

smry *abbr* summary

smstrs *abbr* seamstress

¹smudge \'sməj\ *vb* -ED/-ING/-S [ME *smogen*] *vt* **1 a** : to make a blurry splotch or streak (as of dirt) on : BEGRIME, SMUTCH, SOIL ⟨wiped his brow with his sooty hand, *smudging* it⟩ **b** : to soil as if by smudging ⟨the bright record for child welfare has been *smudged* occasionally by scandals —*Amer. Guide Series: Oregon*⟩ **2 a** : to rub, daub, or wipe in a smeary manner ⟨*smudging* out instead of erasing neatly his first hesitant strokes —*Time*⟩ **b** : to make indistinct : BLUR ⟨~ the clean line of the bridges with unnecessary parapets —*Times Lit. Supp.*⟩ ⟨careful distinctions are *smudged* and coarsened —*New Statesman & Nation*⟩ **3 a** : to smoke by means of a smudge (as in repelling mosquitoes); *specif* : to protect (an orchard, garden) against frost by means of a smudge — compare ORCHARD HEATING **b** : to cause (a fire) to smoke heavily ~ *vi* **1 a** : to make a smudge ⟨chalks that mark easily but do not ~⟩ ⟨they were *smudging* in the groves —Wright Morris⟩ **b** : to burn with little flame and much thick smoke **2** : to become smudged ⟨charcoal drawings ~ easily⟩

²smudge \"\ *n* -S **1 a** (1) : a blurry spot or streak : SPLOTCH, SMEAR ⟨left a ~ at the erasure⟩ ⟨~*s* made by cheap carbon paper⟩ (2) : an immaterial stain ⟨cleanse him of every last ~ of impropriety —Richard Hanser⟩ **b** : a smudged condition : SOILAGE **c** : an indistinct mass : BLUR ⟨ahead lay a chocolate brown ~ of land, huddled in mist —Gerald Durrell⟩ **2 a** : thick or suffocating smoke : SMOTHER **b** *or* **smudge fire** : a smoldering mass placed on the windward side (as of a tent) to repel insects or in an orchard or garden to prevent frost **c** : an apparatus for making a smudge fire **3** *Brit* : PLUMBER'S SOIL **4 a** : ONION SMUDGE **b** : a disease of wheat, rye, and barley caused by fungi of the genera *Helminthosporium* and *Alternaria* and characterized by brownish or black discoloration of the grains **5 a** : a bid of 4 by a player in auction pitch who is not in the hole that if made wins the game forthwith **b** : the winning of all four points in auction pitch; *also* : the reward for this which may be a doubled score or the winning of the game **c** : the game of auction pitch when either of the foregoing rules is incorporated **6** : a leukocyte that is degenerating

³smudge \"\ *vi* [origin unknown] *chiefly Scot* : to be quietly and slyly amused : laugh up one's sleeve

smudg·ed·ly \-jədlē\ *adv* [*smudged* (past part. of ¹*smudge*) + *-ly*] : in a smudged manner

smudge pot *n* : a container in which oil or other fuel is burned to produce a smudge (as in an orchard)

smudg·er \'sməjə(r)\ *n* -S : one that smudges; *specif* : a worker who smudges orchards or groves

smudg·i·ly \-jəlē\ *adv* : in a smudgy manner

smudg·i·ness \-jēnəs\ *n* -ES : the quality or state of being smudgy

smudgy \'sməjē, -ji\ *adj* -ER/-EST [²*smudge* + *-y*] **1** *dial Eng* : thick with smoke : SMOKY **2** *dial* : OPPRESSIVE, STIFLING — used esp. of weather **3** : soiled by smudging : BEGRIMED, STAINED **4** : lacking distinctness : BLURRED

¹smug \'sməg\ *adj* **smugger; smuggest** [prob. modif. of LG *smuck* neat, trim, fr. MLG, fr. *smucken* to dress, adorn; akin to MHG *smiegen* to press in tightly — more at SMOCK] **1** : presenting a smooth, well-groomed appearance : NEAT, SLEEK ⟨at one end of the promenade the clean, ~ town drifted into desultory fields —*Strand Mag.*⟩ **2** : giving an impression of scrupulous correctness and respectability ⟨you are looking ~, man; the honest innkeeper to the life —W.W.Jacobs⟩ **3** : marked by or suggestive of belief in one's own superiority, virtue, and respectability usu. accompanied by contented resistance to change, provincial lack of vision, or deprecation of others ⟨a ~ glow of self-congratulation radiated from the editorial pages of some of the most respectable newspapers —Max Ascoli⟩ ⟨people relax with a sense of ~ well-being because a law has been enacted which will take care of everything —D.W. Maurer & V.H.Vogel⟩ **syn** see COMPLACENT

²smug \"\ *vt* **smugged; smugged; smugging; smugs** : to make clean or neat : SPRUCE, SMARTEN

³smug \"\ *n* -S : a smug person : PRIG

⁴smug \"\ *vt* **smugged; smugged; smugging; smugs** [prob. back-formation fr. ¹*smuggle*] : to run away with in a sneaking manner : FILCH

smug·gle \'sməgəl\ *vb* **smuggled; smuggled; smuggling** \-g(ə)liŋ\ **smuggles** [LG *smuggeln, smuckeln* & D *smokkelen;* akin to OE *smūgan* to creep — more at SMOCK] *vt* **1** : to import or export secretly contrary to the law : bring into or take out of a country (merchandise, forbidden articles, or persons) contrary to law and with a fraudulent intent ⟨~ Chinese laborers⟩; *specif* : to import or export without paying the duties imposed by law ⟨by various ruses liquors were *smuggled* past the inspecting officers —W.M.Babcock⟩ **2** : to convey or introduce in a surreptitious manner ⟨escaped with his life by being *smuggled* out in a policeman's uniform —S.P.B.Mais⟩ ⟨~ a normative judgment into what purports to be a statement of fact —A.J.Ayer⟩ ~ *vi* : to import or export anything in violation of the customs laws

smug·gle·able \-gələbəl\ *adj* : that can be smuggled

smug·gler \'sməg(ə)lə(r)\ *n* -S [LG *smuggeler, smuckeler* & D *smokkelaar;* LG *smuggeler, smuckeler* fr. *smuggeln, smuckeln* to smuggle + *-er* (akin to G *-er*); D *smokkelaar* fr. *smokkelen* to smuggle] **1** : one that smuggles **2** : a ship employed in smuggling

smug·ly *adv* : in a smug manner

smug·ness *n* -ES : the quality or state of being smug ⟨the little smile of self-satisfaction that gave his face an aspect of ~ —*Strand Mag.*⟩

smur *or* **smurr** \'smər\ *n* [origin unknown] *dial* : a drizzly fog or mist

smur·ry \-rē\ *adj, chiefly dial* : MISTY, FOGGY, CLOUDY

¹smut \'smət, *usu* -əd·+V\ *vb* **smutted; smutted; smutting; smuts** [prob. alter. of earlier *smot* to stain, fr. ME *smotten*; akin to ME *-smoteren* to soil, stain, MHG *smutzen*, and prob. to Gk *mydan* to be damp — more at MOSS] *vt* **1** : to stain or mark with a black or dirty substance (as soot) **2** : to taint or affect with smut or mildew ⟨*smutted* corn⟩ **3** : SULLY, TAINT, DEFILE **4** : to clear of smut ⟨~ grain for the mill⟩ ~ *vi* **1** : to become affected by smut : become smutted ⟨treated grain will not ~⟩ **2** *Brit, of fish* : to rise at or feed on very small flies

²smut \"\ *n* -S **1 a** (1) : a dirty spot or condition : SOIL (2) : a patch of black or dark hair on an animal (as on the nose of a Himalayan rabbit) **b** : matter that soils or blackens ⟨her lace curtains . . . would already be darkened by the ~ of soft coal —Lewis Mumford⟩; *specif* : a particle of soot ⟨the chimney fire went by the garden was filled with smoke and ~*s* —David Garnett⟩ **2 a** (1) : any of various destructive diseases of cereal grasses and some other plants caused by parasitic basidiomycetous fungi of the order Ustilaginales and characterized by the transformation of various plant organs into dark brown or black often dusty masses of spores — see COVERED SMUT, FLAG SMUT, LOOSE SMUT (2) : any fungus producing such a disease **b** : a similar disease of figs caused by an ascomycetous fungus (*Aspergillus niger*) **3** : inferior soft coal containing much earthy matter and found esp. at the outcrop **4** : material (as jokes, pictures, stories) in which a subject is treated in a manner violating accepted standards of decency : verbal or graphic obscenity : matter felt to be morally fouling **5** *Brit* : any of various small flies (as the midge, gnat) **6** : a dark slate color appearing in a domesticated bird normally of another color

smut ball *n* **1** : the spore mass into which the ovary of the host is converted by the stinking smut organism — compare ²BUNT **2** : PUFFBALL

¹smutch \'sməch\ *or* **smouch** \'smüch, 'smau̇ch\ *n* -ES [prob. irreg. fr. ¹*smudge*] **1** : a soiling mark or trace : dirty spot : SMUDGE **2** : a corrupting or polluting influence or effect : BLOT **3** : SMUT, SOOT, GRIME

²smutch \"\ *or* **smouch** \"\ *vt* -ED/-ING/-ES **1** : to make black or dirty (as with soot) : SMUDGE **2** : DEFILE, SULLY, TAINT

smutchy \'sməchē\ *adj* -ER/-EST : DIRTY, STAINED, SMUDGED

smut fungus *n* : any fungus of the order Ustilaginales

smut gall *n* : an abnormal growth composed of the tissues of the host and a smut fungus (as in boil smut of corn)

smut grass *n* : a grass (*Sporobolus poiretii*) native to the West Indies but common in the southern U.S. that often has its tufted wiry stems and narrow panicles infested with a fungus (*Helminthosporium ravenelii*) — called also *blackseed, carpet grass*

smut mill *n* : a machine to rid grain of smut

smut sheet *n* : WASTE LEAF 1

smut·ter \'sməd·ə(r)\ *n* -S : one that smuts; *specif* : an operator of machinery for cleaning smut and other impurities from grain

smut·ti·ly \'sməd·ᵊlē, -ətl, |ᵊlī, |əl-\ *adv* : in a smutty manner

smut·ti·ness \|ēnəs, |in-\ *n* -ES : the quality or state of being smutty

smut·ty \|ē, |i\ *adj* -ER/-EST **1** : soiled or tainted with smut : affected with smut fungus : SMUTTED **2** : OBSCENE, INDECENT ⟨a ~ joke⟩ **3** : like smut in appearance (as in color) : SOOTY, DUSKY

smyn·thu·ri·dae \smin'thu̇rə,dē\ *syn of* SMINTHURIDAE

¹smyr·na \'smərnə, 'smėrnə, 'smėinə\ *adj, usu cap* [fr. *Smyrna* (now *İzmir*), Turkey, fr. L, fr. Gk] : IZMIR

²smyrna \"\ *n* -S *usu cap* **1** : a Turkish rug shipped from Smyr-

na **2 :** a modern industrial carpet produced in Smyrna **3 :** a domestic reversible chenille rug
¹smyr·nae·an \-nēən\ *n* -s *cap* [L *smyrnaeus*, adj. & n., Smyrnaean (fr. Gk *smyrnaios*, fr. *Smyrna*) + E *-an*, n. suffix] **:** a native or inhabitant of the ancient city of Smyrna in Asia Minor
²smyrnaean \"\ *adj, usu cap* [L *smyrnaeus* + E *-an*, adj. suffix] **:** of or belonging to Smyrna
smyrna fig *n, usu cap S* **:** a fig orig. grown near Smyrna that requires caprification in order to set fruit — compare COMMON FIG
smyr·ni·ote \-nē,ōt\ *n* -s *cap* [NGk *smyrniōtēs*, fr. *Smyrna* + Gk *-iōtēs* (as in *Sikeliōtēs* Siceliot)] **:** SMYRNAEAN
smyth sewing *or* **smythe sewing** \'smith-, 'smīth-\ *n, usu cap 1st S* [after David M. *Smyth* †1907 Am. inventor] **:** a mechanical method of attaching together the sections of books by means of thread passed through the folds
smy·trie \'smītri, 'smit-\ *n* -s [origin unknown] *Scot* **:** a miscellaneous collection of small creatures or things **:** BUNCH
sn *abbr* **1** sanitary; sanitation **2** [L *sine*] without
SN *abbr* **1** *often not cap* [L *secundum naturam*] naturally **2** serial number **3** shipping note **4** *often not cap* side note **5** *often not cap* [L *sine nomine*] without name
Sn *symbol* [LL *stannum*] tin
snab \'snab\ *n* -s [fr. or akin to Flem *snabbe* beak, beak of land; prob. akin to OHG *snabul* beak — more at NEB] *Scot* **:** the brow of a steep rise
¹snack \'snak\ *vb* [ME *snaken*, prob. fr. MD *snacken* to snap at, bite, chatter — more at SNATCH] *vi* **1** *dial* **:** to snatch something with the teeth **:** SNAP, BITE **2 :** to lunch esp. between meals ~ *vt* **1** *chiefly dial* **:** to go shares on **:** divide into portions and share **2** *chiefly Scot* **:** to seize by or as if by snatching
²snack \"\ *n* -s [ME *snake*, fr. *snaken*, v.] **1** *chiefly Scot* **a :** a snap or snatch with the teeth (as by a dog) **2 :** SHARE — often used in the phrase *go snacks* ⟨go ~s in the profits —*Temple Bar*⟩ **3 a :** a slight amount (as of liquor) **:** TASTE, BIT **b :** food served or taken informally usu. in small amounts and typically under other circumstances than as a regular meal ⟨had coffee and a ~⟩ ⟨took time for a ~ at noon⟩ ⟨dinner was a mere ~⟩
³snack \"\ *adj* [perh. fr. ²*snack*] **1** *chiefly Scot* **:** keenly alert **:** CLEVER, QUICK **2** *chiefly Scot* **:** SNAPPISH, PEEVISH
⁴snack \"\ *adv, chiefly Scot* **:** with dispatch **:** QUICKLY, SMARTLY
⁵snack \"\ *n* -s [origin unknown] **:** a fives ball
snack bar *n* **1 :** a public eating place where snacks are served usu. at a counter **2 :** a counter or shelf in a home at which a snack may be eaten
snack table *n* **:** a small portable table designed to hold food or drink for one person

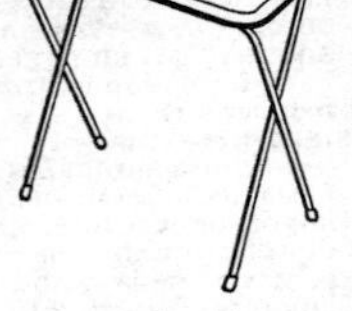
snack table

¹snaf·fle \'snafəl\ *n* -s [origin unknown] **1** *also* **snaffle bit :** a bridle bit the mouthpiece of which has one or more joints or links and which consists in its simplest form of two bars tapering to where they are joined by a single ring — see BIT illustration, BRIDLE illustration **2 :** a light or gentle restraint or check — compare CURB
²snaffle \"\ *vt* **snaffled; snaffled; snaffling** \-f(ə)liŋ\ **snaffles 1 a :** to fit or equip with a snaffle ⟨a *snaffled* bridle⟩ **b :** to restrain or check with or as if with a snaffle **2 a** *dial chiefly Brit* **:** STEAL, ROB **b :** to obtain by devious or irregular means **c :** to obtain without delay **:** snap up **syn** see RESTRAIN
³snaffle \"\ *vi* [prob. alter. of *snuffle*] *chiefly dial* **:** SNUFFLE, SNIFF
snaf·fles \-fəlz\ *n pl but sing or pl in constr* [fr. pl. of ¹*snaffle*; fr. the shape of the flowers] **:** a lousewort (*Pedicularis canadensis*)
¹sna·fu \(ˈ)sna¦fü\ *adj* [*s*ituation *n*ormal *a*ll *f*ouled *u*p] *slang* **:** snarled or stalled in confusion **:** AWRY
²snafu \"\ *n* -s *slang* **:** CONFUSION, MUDDLE
³snafu \"\ *vt* -ED/-ING/-S *slang* **:** to cause to be in a state of complete confusion and disorder **:** snarl up
¹snag \'snag, -aa(ə)g, -aig\ *vi* **snagged; snagged; snagging; snags** [perh. of Scand origin; akin to Icel *snagga* to quarrel, wrangle, and perh. to ON *snaga*, a kind of ax — more at ²SNAG] *dial chiefly Brit* **:** to scold aggravatingly **:** NAG, CARP
²snag \"\ *n* -s [of Scand origin; akin to Norw dial. *snag* projecting point on a headland, islet or skerry, ON *snagi* clothes peg, *snaga*, a kind of ax, and prob. to Norw *snake* to sniff around, snatch at something with the teeth — more at SNATCH] **1 a** (1) **:** a stub or stump remaining on a tree after a branch has been lopped off (2) **:** the rough stub remaining after a branch has been torn off (as by wind); *also* **:** such a roughly broken branch ⟨stumbling through underbrush and over the ~s that littered the ground⟩ **b :** a tree or a branch, log, or stump embedded in a lake or stream bed in such a manner that projecting parts constitute a hazard to navigation **c :** a standing dead tree from which parts or all of the top have fallen; *esp* **:** one that is more than 20 feet tall — compare STUB **d :** a short stub that is left temporarily to support the new growth from the scion when the stock is cut back after some side graft or more often budding operations **2 :** a rough sharp or jagged projecting part or unit **:** PROTUBERANCE: as **a :** a projecting tooth; *also* **:** a stump of a tooth **b :** one of the secondary branches of an antler **:** a small tine or a branch of a tine **3 :** a concealed or unexpected impediment, difficulty, or obstacle **4 a :** a jagged tear made by or as if by catching on a sharp projection **b :** an irregularity that suggests the result of tearing; *esp* **:** a pulled thread in fabric ⟨a *snag* in her stocking⟩ **5 a :** an irregular piece separated from a larger unit ⟨broke off a ~ of bread⟩ **b :** an indefinite amount ⟨came into quite a ~ of money⟩ **syn** see OBSTACLE
³snag \"\ *vt* **snagged; snagged; snagging; snags 1 :** to lop off (as branches) so as to leave snags **:** hew, trim, or cut roughly or jaggedly **2 a :** to catch on an underwater tree ⟨the boat was *snagged* near the right bank⟩ **b :** to catch (as wool) on sharp bushes or brush **c :** to catch (a line or hook) on underwater weeds or stones **d :** to catch (as clothes) on wire ⟨*snagged* his pants on the barbed wire fence⟩ **e :** to hook (a fish) in the body rather than in the mouth **f :** to hook (a fish) with a snagline **g :** to interrupt or interfere with as if by catching on a snag ⟨commerce . . . has been *snagged* by . . . lack of foreign exchange —*N.Y.Times*⟩ **3 a :** to clear (a river) of snags **b :** to remove rough protuberances from a foundry casting **4 :** to catch or obtain by quick, decisive, and often more or less irregular action ⟨~ a football pass from the opponent⟩ ⟨*snagged* a taxi —Frances Crane⟩ ⟨*snagged* the cake from the pantry while his mother was out⟩ ⟨worked out ways and means of *snagging* a rich husband —Polly Adler⟩
⁴snag \"\ *n* -s [origin unknown] *dial Brit* **:** SLOE, BLACKTHORN
snag boat *n* **:** a steamboat with an apparatus for removing impeding debris (as snags) from inland waters
snag·ged \-gəd\ *adj* **:** full of snags **:** SNAGGY, JAGGED; *also* **:** caught on or damaged by a snag
snag·ger \-gə(r)\ *n* -s [³*snag* + *-er*] **:** one that snags: as **a :** a billhook for trimming trees **b :** a foundry worker who chips or grinds excess metal from castings **c** *Austral* **:** an inexperienced shearer
snag·gle \-gəl\ *vt* -ED/-ING/-S [freq. of ³*snag*] **:** ³SNAG 4
snag·gled \-gəld\ *adj* [*snaggletooth* + *-ed*] *of teeth* **:** markedly uneven **:** irregularly projecting; *also* **:** broken or decayed to stumps
snaggletooth \'=ˌ=ˌ=\ *n* [E dial. *snaggle* irregularly shaped tooth (fr. ²*snag* + *-le*) + *tooth*] **:** an irregular, broken, or projecting tooth — **snaggletoothed** \'=¦=ˌ=\ *adj*
snag·gy \-gē, -gi\ *adj* -ER/-EST **:** full of snags ⟨a ~ pole⟩
snagline \'=ˌ=\ *n* **:** a line to which is attached a large number of unbaited fishhooks and which is anchored across the bottom of a river to entangle fish (as paddlefish) nosing about
snag·rel \'snagrəl\ *n* -s [origin unknown] **:** VIRGINIA SNAKEROOT
snags *pres 3d sing of* SNAG, *pl of* SNAG
snag scow *n* **:** a scow employed in pulling snags from inland waterways

snag tree *n* **:** BLACK GUM 1a
¹snail \'snāl, *esp before pause or consonant* -āəl\ *n* -s *often attrib* [ME, fr. OE *snægl*, *snægel*; akin to OS *snegil* snail, MHG *snegel*, OHG *snecko* snail, *snahhan* to creep, ON *snigill* snail, OIr *snaigim* I creep, Lith *snãke* snail; basic meaning: to creep] **1 :** a freshwater or marine or terrestrial gastropod mollusk esp. when having an external enclosing spiral shell — see BROWN SNAIL, EDIBLE SNAIL, GARDEN SNAIL, LAND SNAIL, VIOLET SNAIL; compare LIMPET, PTEROPOD, SLUG **2 :** a slow-moving or sluggish person or thing **:** one lacking in energy or activity **3 :** something suggesting a snail shell: as **a :** a snail clover or its pod — often used in pl. **b** *or* **snail wheel :** a spiral or volute-shaped cam (as in a watch)

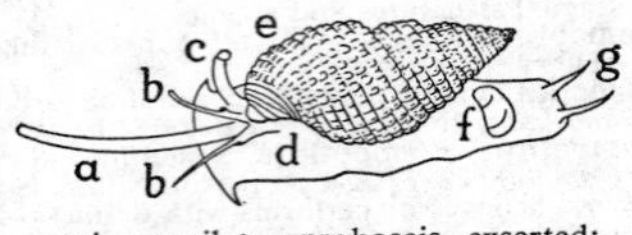

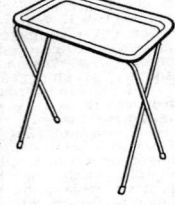

marine snail **:** *a* proboscis, exserted; *b,b*, tentacles; *c* siphon; *d* foot; *e* shell; *f* operculum; *g* caudal cirri

²snail \"\ *vb* -ED/-ING/-S *vi* **:** to move, act, or go slowly or lazily ⟨the train ~*ed* up the steep grade⟩ ~ *vt* **1 :** to form in or mark with a spiral — used chiefly in horology **2 :** to spend (time) like a snail or drone
³snail *n* [prob. by folk etymology] *obs* **:** CHENILLE 1
snail bore *or* **snail borer** *n* **:** a boring gastropod mollusk **:** DRILL
snail cloud *n* **:** CUMULOSTRATUS
snail clover *or* **snail medic** *n* **:** any of several medics having helicoid or spirally coiled pods (as *Medicago scutellata*)
snail countersink *or* **snail-head countersink** *n* **:** a countersink used esp. to bevel the ends of holes — see COUNTERSINK illustration
snaileater \'=ˌ==\ *n* **:** OPENBILL
snail·er \-lə(r)\ *n* -s [²*snail* + *-er*] **:** an operator of a machine used for snailing and polishing ratchet wheels for clocks and watches
snail·ery \-lərē, -ri\ *n* -ES **:** a place where edible snails are bred and fattened for market
snail fever *n* **:** SCHISTOSOMIASIS
snailfish \'=ˌ=\ *n* **:** SEA SNAIL 2
snailflower \'=ˌ==\ *n* **1 :** a perennial tropical American vine (*Phaseolus caracalla*) that is sometimes cultivated for its racemes of showy purple and yellow flowers and has the corolla keel coiled like a snail shell **2 :** SNAIL CLOVER
snail hawk *n* **:** EVERGLADE KITE
snail-horned \'=¦=\ *adj* **:** having short crooked horns suggesting a snail shell ⟨a *snail-horned* cow⟩
snail·ish \'snālish\ *adj* **:** suggesting a snail esp. in slowness or sluggishness — **snail·ish·ly** *adv*
snaillike \'=ˌ=\ *adj* **:** resembling a snail **:** SNAILISH
snail-paced \'=¦=\ *adj* **:** moving at or characterized by a snail's pace
snail-seed \'=ˌ=\ *n* **:** CAROLINA MOONSEED
snail-slow \'=¦=\ *adj* **:** SNAIL-PACED
snail's pace *n* [ME *snayles pas*] **:** an excessively slow pace or rate of speed ⟨business is progressing at a *snail's pace*⟩
snaily \'snālē\ *adj* [¹*snail* + *-y*] **1 a :** SNAILISH **b :** infested with snails **2** *Austral* **:** SNAIL-HORNED
snaith \'snāth, -th\ *dial Eng var of* SNATH
¹snake \'snāk, *dial* 'snek\ *n* -s *often attrib* [ME, fr. OE *snaca*; akin to MLG *snake*, ON *snākr*, *snōkr* snake, *snigill* snail — more at SNAIL] **1 a :** any of numerous oviparous or ovoviviparous scaly limbless reptiles (suborder Serpentes) with a very elongated body that are first known from the Cretaceous and are presumably derived from lacertilian ancestors, that have the branches of the mandible usu. connected in front by an elastic ligament so that the mouth is very distensible, the tongue forked, the tympanum of the ear lacking, the eye permanently covered by a transparent membrane, and one lung usu. reduced or absent, that in many forms produce venoms in modified salivary glands, that are usu. predaceous in habit killing their prey by constriction or by injection of venom through hollow or grooved fangs and swallowing it whole, and that are often valuable destroyers of rodents and other vermin **b :** an elongated limbless lizard or amphibian — not used technically; see GLASS SNAKE **c :** any of various vigorous voracious elongated fishes (as a pike, a pickerel, or a barracuda) — not used technically **2 a** *obs* **:** a poor, miserable, or cringing person **b :** a worthless contemptible fellow; *esp* **:** a perfidious ingrate **3 :** something felt to resemble a snake: as **a** *obs* **:** a tail, curl, or braid of a wig **b :** SERPENT 6 **c :** the flexible stem of a hookah **d :** an arrow buried flat in the grass **e :** PLUMBER'S SNAKE **f :** FISH TAPE **g :** a crooked surface flaw in rolled metal **h :** a baseball curve **i :** an explosive charge in a very long narrow metal case that can be pushed into a minefield by a tank and then exploded to clear a path sometimes of several hundred feet through the field **4** *usu cap* **a :** any of various Shoshonean peoples esp. of the northern Shoshoni, northern Paiute, and Comanche **b :** a member of such people
²snake \"\ *vb* -ED/-ING/-S *vt* **1 :** to wind (as one's way, one's body in crawling) so as to suggest a snake or snakelike movement **:** move sinuously ⟨a long wagon train *snaking* its way along the slope⟩ **2 a :** WORM 6 **b :** to bind (as backstays) together with small stuff **3 a :** to move (something) by dragging **:** drag forcibly ⟨*snaking* logs down the hill with a chain hitch⟩ ⟨*snaked* out the timber over an old tote road⟩; *also* **:** to move (logs) by skidding **b** *chiefly dial* **:** STEAL, SWIPE **4 :** to flaw (a log) in sawing into board by making a wavy cut ~ *vi* **1 a :** to crawl or move silently, secretly, or sinuously ⟨*snaking* softly through the brush⟩ **b :** to twist in the manner of a snake **:** progress in a spiral ⟨a narrow trail that ~s between the trees⟩ **c** *dial Eng* **:** to move stealthily **:** SNEAK **2** *of an arrow* **:** to bury itself in the grass in falling
snakebark \'=ˌ=\ *n* **:** a medium-sized timber tree (*Colubrina ferruginosa*) of Florida and the West Indies with yellowish brown durable wood
snakeberry \'=- — *see* BERRY\ *n* **1** *Brit* **:** BRYONY; *also* **:** the fruit of bryony **2 a :** RED BANEBERRY **b :** a bittersweet (*Solanum dulcamara*); *also* **:** its berry **c :** PARTRIDGEBERRY
snakebird \'=ˌ=\ *n* [so called fr. its snakelike neck] **1 :** any of various fish-eating birds constituting the genus *Anhinga*, having a very long slender neck, small head, and sharp-pointed bill, being mostly blackish brown varied on the upper parts with silvery gray or metallic greenish, chiefly frequenting inland streams, lakes, and swamps, and being very expert swimmers and divers **2** *dial Eng* **:** WRYNECK
snakebit \'=ˌ=\ *or* **snakebitten** \'=ˌ==\ *adj* **:** bitten by a venomous snake
snakebite \'=ˌ=\ *n* **1 :** the bite of a snake; *also* **:** the condition of having been bitten by a venomous snake characterized by stinging pain in the puncture wound, constitutional symptoms, and injury to blood or nerve tissue **2 a :** BLOODROOT 1 **b :** a common No. American wake-robin (*Trillium cernuum*) **3** *also* **snakebite remedy** *dial* **:** LIQUOR; *specif* **:** WHISKEY
snake buzzard *n* **:** SERPENT EAGLE
snake cactus *n* **:** a cactus (*Nyctocereus serpentinus*) having clustered cylindric stems and showy red flowers
snake cane *n* **:** a tropical So. American palm (*Kunthia montana*) having a ringed snakelike stem
snake charmer *n* **:** an entertainer who exhibits his professed power to charm or fascinate venomous snakes
snake crane *n* **:** CARIAMA 2
snake dance *n* **1 :** a ceremonial dance in which snakes or their images are handled, invoked, or symbolically imitated by individual sinuous actions **2 :** a group progression in a single-file serpentine path often in celebration of an athletic victory
snake doctor *n* **1 :** HELLGRAMMITE **2 :** DRAGONFLY
snake-eater \'=ˌ==\ *n* **1 :** MARKHOR **2 :** SECRETARY BIRD
snake eel *n* **:** any of numerous scaleless eels of the family Ophichthyidae having no caudal fin and the end of the tail projecting beyond the dorsal and anal fins, abounding in tropical seas, and being often spotted like some of the venomous sea snakes
snake eggplant *n* **:** an eggplant with long cylindric fruit that is curled at the end
snake eyes *n pl* **:** a throw of two aces in craps
snake feeder *n, Midland* **:** DRAGONFLY
snake fence *n* **:** WORM FENCE

snakefish \'=ˌ=\ *n* **1 :** RIBBONFISH 1b **2 :** LIZARD FISH
snakeflower \'=ˌ==\ *n* **1 :** BLUEWEED 1 **2 :** GREATER STITCHWORT **3 :** WHITE CAMPION a **4 :** STARFLOWER b
snake fly *n* **:** any of several insects of the suborder Raphidiodea having a large head and an elongated prothorax that suggests a neck
snake foot *n* **:** a pointed Dutch foot (as on Queen Anne furniture) — see FOOT illustration
snake gentian *n* **:** a lion's foot (*Prenanthes serpentaria*)
snake gourd *n* **1** *or* **snake cucumber :** SNAKE MELON **2 a :** a gourd (*Trichosanthes anguina*) with long contorted green and white edible fruits that become bright orange when fully ripe **b :** BOTTLE GOURD **c :** DISHCLOTH GOURD
snake-grass \'=ˌ=\ *n* **1 :** GREATER STITCHWORT **2 :** a common forget-me-not (*Myosotis scorpioides*) **3 :** SKUNK GRASS
snake hawk *n* **:** SWALLOW-TAILED KITE
snakehead \'=ˌ=\ *n* **1 :** a loose bent-up end of one of the strap rails or flat rails formerly used on railroads **2 a :** TURTLEHEAD **b :** GUINEA-HEN FLOWER **3** *also* **snakehead mullet** *or* **snake-headed fish** \'=¦==\ **:** a fish of the family Ophicephalidae
snake-hipped \'=ˌ=\ *adj* **:** having slender and usu. mobile hips
snakehips \'=ˌ=\ *n pl but sing in constr* **:** a swing dance with sideward foot twisting and resultant hip wriggling
snake hole *n* **1 :** a hole bored beneath a boulder and immediately against the bottom of it for blasting **2 :** any of various drill holes in quarrying or bench blasting
snakeholing \'=ˌ==\ *n* -s **:** blasting (as in mining or quarrying) by means of snake holes
snake in the grass 1 : a lurking or unsuspected danger **2 :** a secretly faithless friend
snake juice *n, dial* **:** strong drink; *esp* **:** bad whiskey
snake killer *n* **1 :** SECRETARY BIRD **2 :** ROADRUNNER
snake·less \-ləs\ *adj* **:** free from snakes ⟨the ~ isle⟩
snake·let \-lət\ *n* -s **:** a young or small snake
snakelike \'=ˌ=\ *adj* **:** resembling a snake esp. in elongate tapering form
snake lily *n* **1 :** BLUE FLAG **2 :** a climbing and twining herb (*Brodiaea volubilis*) that is native to the southwestern U.S. but cultivated elsewhere for its showy umbels of rose-red or pinkish flowers
snake line *n* **:** a small line passed around or between two ropes in a spiral or zigzag
snake·ling \'=liŋ\ *n* -s **:** SNAKELET
snake mackerel *n* **:** a long silvery deep-sea fish (*Gempylus serpens*) chiefly of tropical and southern seas that is highly esteemed for its rich oily flesh and is related to but slenderer than the typical escolar; *broadly* **:** ESCOLAR
snake melon *n* **:** a long sinuous white-fleshed melon that is technically a variety (*Cucumis melo flexuosus*) of the muskmelon but resembles a cucumber in texture and flavor and that is sometimes cultivated usu. as a curiosity — called also *snake gourd*
snake-milk \'=ˌ=\ *n* **:** FLOWERING SPURGE
snake moss *n* **:** a common club moss (*Lycopodium clavatum*)
snakemouth \'=ˌ=\ *also* **snakemouth pogonia** *n* **:** a showy bog orchid (*Pogonia ophioglossoides*) of eastern No. America and Japan having pink flowers suggestive of the open mouth of a snake
snake muishond *or* **snake weasel** *n* **:** a small slender burrowing African muishond (*Poecilogale albinucha*) with the top of the head white — compare STRIPED MUISHOND
snakeneck \'=ˌ=\ *n* **:** SNAKEBIRD 1
snake-necked \'=ˌ=\ *adj* **:** SIDE-NECKED
snake oil *n* **:** any of various substances or mixtures sold (as by a traveling medicine show) as medicine usu. without regard to their medical worth or properties
snake palm *n* **:** DEVIL'S-TONGUE 2
snakepiece \'=ˌ=\ *n* **:** a diagonal timber connecting the afterbody and the stern frame of a wooden ship
snake pit *n* **1 :** a hospital for mental diseases **2 :** a place of chaotic disorder and distress ⟨the *snake pit* of her alcoholism —John Barkham⟩
snake plant *n* **:** a plant of the genus *Sansevieria*
snak·er \'snākə(r)\ *n* -s **:** SKIDDER a, b
snakeroot \'=ˌ=\ *n* **1 :** any of numerous plants most of which have had repute as remedies for snake bites: as **a :** VIRGINIA SNAKEROOT **b :** BUGBANE 1 **c :** a plant of the genus *Sanicula* **d :** SENEGA ROOT **e :** BUTTON SNAKEROOT **f :** BLAZING STAR 3a **g :** WHITE SNAKEROOT **h :** a plant of the genus *Asarum*; *esp* **:** WILD GINGER 2a **i :** BITTERBUSH 2 **2 :** the root of a snakeroot
snakes *pl of* SNAKE, *pres 3d sing of* SNAKE
snakes and ladders *n pl but usu sing in constr* **:** a board game in which pictures of snakes and ladders retard or facilitate the players' progress
snake's-head \'=ˌ=\ *n, pl* **snake's-heads 1 a** *or* **snake's-head lily :** GUINEA-HEN FLOWER **b :** a woody composite herb (*Malacothrix coulteri*) with a spotted involucre that grows in dry areas of the southwestern U.S. **2 :** SNAKEHEAD 1
snake's-head iris *n* **:** a tuberous herb (*Iris tuberosus*) of the Mediterranean region having flowers that resemble a serpent's open mouth
snakeskin \'=ˌ=\ *n* **:** leather prepared from the skins of snakes
snake spit *n* **:** CUCKOO SPIT 1
snakestone \'=ˌ=\ *n* **1** *chiefly dial* **:** AMMONITE **2 :** a stone (as the adder stone) or a stony preparation popularly thought efficacious when applied to a snake bite **3 :** AYR STONE
snake's-tongue \'=ˌ=\ *n, pl* **snake's-tongues :** ADDER'S-TONGUE 1
snake turtle *or* **snake tortoise** *n* **:** LONG-NECKED TURTLE
snake violet *n* **:** BIRD'S-FOOT VIOLET
snakeweed \'=ˌ=\ *n* **:** any of several plants popularly associated with snakes (as in appearance, common habitat, or use in treatment of snake bite): as **a :** BISTORT **b :** SNAKEROOT **c :** any of various plantains **d :** a plant of the genus *Gutierrezia* **e :** POISON HEMLOCK 1
snake wire *n* **:** FISH TAPE
snakewise \'=ˌ=\ *adv* [¹*snake* + *-wise*] **:** so as to resemble a snake; *esp* **:** with a stealthy slithering snakelike movement
snake woman *n, usu cap S&W* **:** a male Aztec leader functioning as the principal executive officer in tribal affairs and ranking equal with the chief
snakewood \'=ˌ=\ *n* **1 :** NUX VOMICA 2 **2 :** an East Indian climbing shrub (*Rauwolfia serpentina*) whose twisted roots and stems resemble serpents **3 :** TRUMPETWOOD **4 :** FRANGIPANI **5 :** LETTERWOOD **6 :** SNAKEBARK **7 :** NAKEDWOOD 1
snakeworm \'=ˌ=\ *n* **:** a traveling mass of army worms of the genus *Sciara*
snak·i·ly \'snākəlē, -li\ *adv* **:** in a snaky manner
¹snaking *adj* [fr. pres. part. of ²*snake*] **1 :** WINDING, SINUOUS ⟨a ~ river⟩ **2 :** used in snaking ⟨a ~ chain⟩
²snaking *n* -s [fr. gerund of ²*snake*] **1 :** the act of one who snakes **2 a :** something that is snakelike in form or arrangement **:** COIL **b :** a persistent directional oscillation of an airplane
snak·ish \'snākish, -kēsh\ *adj* [¹*snake* + *-ish*] **:** rather snaky
snaky *also* **snakey** \-kē, -ki\ *adj* **snakier; snakiest** [¹*snake* + *-y*] **1 :** of, formed of, or covered or entwined with snakes ⟨a writhing ~ mass littered the den⟩ **2 :** resembling a snake **:** SNAKELIKE, SERPENTINE ⟨a ~ eel⟩; *usu* **:** having many convolutions **:** SINUOUS, WAVY, WRIGGLY ⟨~ ridges in the sand⟩ ⟨a ~ river⟩ **3 a :** of or typical of a snake ⟨a ~ cunning⟩ **b :** felt to share the characteristics of a snake (as in slyness, treachery, perfidiousness, venom, spitefulness) ⟨mean ~ ways⟩ ⟨~ treachery⟩ **4 :** abounding in snakes ⟨a ~ forest⟩ **5** *Austral* **:** ANGRY, EXASPERATED, TOUCHY
snal·ly·gas·ter \'snalē,gastə(r)\ *n* -s [perh. modif. of PaG *schnelle geeschter*, lit., quick spirits] **:** a mythical nocturnal creature that is reported chiefly from rural Maryland, is reputed to be part reptile and part bird, and is said to prey on poultry and children
¹snap \'snap\ *vb* **snapped; snapped; snapping; snaps** [D or LG *snappen*, fr. MD & MLG, respectively; akin to MHG *snappen* to snap, stumble, sway, chatter, ON *snapa* to snuffle, snap, and prob. to OHG *snabul* beak — more at NEB] *vi* **1 a :** to make a snap of the jaws **:** seize something with a snap of the mouth ⟨an ill-conditioned cur that ~s and snarls⟩ — usu. used with *at* ⟨fish *snapping* at the bait⟩ **b :** to grasp at something eagerly **:** make a pounce or snatch — usu. used with *at* ⟨*snapped* at the invitation⟩ ⟨ready to ~ at any chance for im-

provement⟩ **2 :** to utter sharp biting words **:** bark out irritable or peevish retorts — often used with *at* **3 a :** to break off or in two often with a short snapping sound **:** break suddenly (as under strain or tension) ⟨the twig *snapped*⟩ ⟨the taut cable finally *snapped*⟩ **b :** to give way under stress **:** suddenly yield usu. to the cumulative effect of some strain ⟨after three days of battle his nerve *snapped*⟩ **4 a :** to make a sound that is a snap **:** give out a sharp or crackling sound or a sudden report or click ⟨the fire *snapped* and crackled on the hearth⟩ ⟨damp clothes *snapping* on the line⟩ **b** *of a firearm* **:** to make a sharp sound by the falling of the hammer on an empty chamber or on a round that does not fire; *also* **:** MISFIRE **5 :** to move esp. abruptly in a particular direction or manner usu. in attaining a position of closure ⟨the lid *snapped* down⟩ ⟨her eyes *snapped* shut⟩ ⟨the bolt ~*s* home with a click⟩ **6 :** to emit sparks or flashes (as of wit or sarcasm) ⟨the conversation *snapped* back and forth⟩; *also* **:** to appear to scintillate **:** SPARKLE ⟨eyes *snapping* with fury⟩ ~ *vt* **1 a :** to seize with or as if with a snap of the jaws **:** grasp or snatch suddenly or unexpectedly ⟨the dog *snapped* the meat from the table⟩ ⟨the wind *snapped* the scarf from her hand⟩ **b :** to capture or take possession of suddenly **:** steal by adroitness ⟨ready to ~ up the very shoes from our feet⟩ **2 :** to secure (something) to one's own use or possession by prompt decisive action — usu. used with *up* ⟨quick to ~ up a bargain⟩ ⟨a prize to be *snapped* up cheaply⟩ ⟨~ up his offer⟩ **3 a :** to retort to or interrupt with a snappish, cutting, or crushing remark **:** speak to curtly and usu. irritably ⟨*snapped* him short with a curt acknowledgement⟩ ⟨*snapped* them a sharp reply⟩ **b :** to utter (words) curtly, harshly, or abruptly ⟨*snapping* out an answer without a moment's hesitation⟩ **4 a :** to break by snapping **:** break short or in two **:** break apart or into pieces ⟨the blow *snapped* the bone⟩ ⟨wind ~*s* many branches from the trees⟩ **b :** to harvest (as corn or cotton) by breaking from the stem **5 a :** to cause to make a snapping sound usu. in the course of some action or movement ⟨wind *snapping* the sheets on the line⟩ **:** cause to crack ⟨~ a whip⟩ **b :** to cause (as a handgun) to discharge by pulling the trigger **c :** to put into or remove from a particular position or state by a sudden movement or with a snapping sound ⟨~ the lock shut⟩ ⟨*snapped* the top from the bottle⟩ **d :** to make a snapping sound by moving (fingers) against one another **6 a :** to project with a snap **:** FILLIP ⟨snapped a spitball across the classroom⟩ **b :** to make, present, or do without prolonged preparation or delay ⟨~ into a performance or role⟩; *esp* **:** to fire (a projectile) without chance for careful aim ⟨*snapped* a shot at the fleeing bandit⟩ **c** (1) **:** to catch (a cricket batsman) out sharply (as from a snicked ball) — often used with *up* ⟨*snapped* up at the wicket⟩ (2) **:** to put (a football) in play from a position on the ground with a quick continuous motion of the hands **d** (1) **:** to take (a photograph) with a hand-held camera using an instantaneous exposure (2) **:** take a snapshot of ⟨*snapping* the scenery⟩ — **snap off one's head** *also* **snap off one's nose :** to speak to curtly, harshly, or discourteously by way of reply — **snap one's fingers at :** give no heed to **:** treat with contempt or indifference — **snap out of it :** to free oneself from something (as a mood or habit) by an effort of will **syn** see BREAK, JERK

²snap \"\ *n* -S **1 :** an abrupt closing (as of the mouth in biting or of scissors in cutting) **:** the action of one that bites or bites at something **:** a biting or snatching with the teeth or jaws ⟨the dog took a ~ at a flea⟩ ⟨a ~ of the scissors cut the string⟩ **2 a** *obs* **:** something snapped up as one's share of profits or booty **b :** a chance to make money easily or quickly; *specif* **:** an easy remunerative post or position **c :** something (as a task or course of study) that is easy and presents no problems ⟨it will be a ~ to win the game⟩ ⟨the literature course was a ~ for him⟩ **3 a :** a small amount **:** BIT, MORSEL ⟨cared not a ~ for his mother's advice⟩ **b** *dial chiefly Brit* **:** a small or hasty meal **:** SNACK; *esp* **:** a miner's lunch eaten while on shift **4 a :** an act or instance of seizing abruptly **:** a sudden gripping or snatching at something **:** a quick short brisk movement ⟨a ~ of the fingers⟩ **b :** a sudden sharp tearing or breaking ⟨felt the ~ of the bone parting⟩ **5 a :** a sudden sharp sound made by or as if by snapping something (as together, apart, into place, off) ⟨the ~ of a twig⟩ ⟨shut the book with a ~⟩ **b :** a brief sharp and usu. irritable speech or retort ⟨took me up with a ~⟩ **6 :** FELLOW, LAD **7 :** a sudden interval of harsh weather ⟨an unexpected cold ~⟩ — compare SPELL 3b **8 a :** a catch or fastening that closes or locks with a click (as one provided with a spring or with parts that fit tightly into each other) ⟨the ~ of a bracelet⟩ ⟨closed the ~*s* on the suitcase⟩ **b :** a device (as a snap hook or snap fastener) having such a catch **9 :** a thin brittle cooky ⟨a batch of lemon ~*s*⟩ ⟨a new chocolate ~⟩ — compare GINGERSNAP **10 a :** SNAP SHOT **b :** SNAPSHOT **c :** SNAPDRAGON **11 a** *or* **snap tool :** a tool having a usu. cup-shaped depression in one end and used in forming rivetheads in riveting **b :** SNAPHEAD **12 a :** the condition of being vigorous in body, mind, or spirit **:** ALERTNESS, ENERGY, GO ⟨a young man with plenty of ~⟩ **b :** a pungent pleasing quality (as of literary style) **:** SMARTNESS **13 :** a fruit that is snapped (as from the fruiting spur): as **a :** a whole mature cotton boll when harvested by snapping — usu. used in pl. **b :** SNAP BEAN **14 :** SCOTCH SNAP **15 a :** an act or instance of snapping a football **b :** CENTER 5a(1) — used chiefly in Canadian football

³snap \"\ *adv* [¹*snap*] **:** with a snapping movement or sound **:** with suddenness or violence **:** BRISKLY ⟨the sail went ~ in the freshening wind⟩

⁴snap \"\ *adj* [¹*snap*] **1 a** *chiefly Scot* **:** QUICK, SMART, ALERT **b :** snapped up or done in a snap **:** secured, given, done, carried through suddenly or without due process or deliberation ⟨a ~ judgment⟩ ⟨such ~ decisions⟩ **c :** called or taken without prior warning ⟨repeated calling of ~ votes has given the cabinet some severe scares —*Atlantic*⟩ **2 :** shutting, fastening, or otherwise coming together with a click or by means of a device that snaps ⟨a ~ lock⟩ ⟨~ closures⟩ ⟨a ~ action⟩ **3 :** unusually easy or simple ⟨a ~ course⟩

snap back *vi* **:** to make a quick or vigorous recovery

snapback \ˈ=ˌ=\ *n* -S [fr. *snap back*, v.] **1 :** a football snap **2 :** a sudden rebound or recovery ⟨predicted a ~ of the market from the present lows⟩

snap bean *n* **1 :** a bean grown primarily for its whole pods that are usu. broken in pieces and cooked as a vegetable while young and tender and before the seeds have become enlarged — see GREEN BEAN, WAX BEAN; compare SHELL BEAN **2 :** one of the edible pods of a snap bean

snap beetle *or* **snap bug** *n* **:** CLICK BEETLE

snapberry \ˈ=ˌ-\ — *see* BERRY\ *n* **:** CORALBERRY

snap-brim hat \ˈ=ˌ=-\ *also* **snap-brim** *n* **:** a hat usu. made of felt with the brim turned up in back and down in front and with a dented crown

snap catch *n* **:** SPRING CATCH

snap clutch *n* **:** any of several clutches used on major drive parts of harvesting and threshing machinery and so designed as to disengage when subjected to undue strains

snapdragon \ˈ=ˌ==\ *n* **1 a :** a garden plant of the genus *Antirrhinum* (esp. *A. majus*) having showy white, crimson, or yellow bilabiate flowers fancifully likened to the face of a dragon **b :** TOADFLAX **c :** JEWELWEED **2** *archaic* **:** a mummer's representation of a dragon with snapping jaws **3 :** a game in which the players snatch raisins or other tidbits from burning brandy and quickly eat them; *also* **:** any of the materials used in the game — called also *flapdragon* **4 :** a tongs used by glassmakers **5 :** a light to moderate yellow that is redder than amber yellow and stronger and slightly redder than buff (sense 4b)

¹snape \ˈsnāp\ *dial var of* SNEAP

²snape \"\ *vb* -ED/-ING/-S [origin unknown] *vt* **:** TAPER; *specif* **:** to bevel the end of (a timber) to fit against an inclined surface (as of a ship) ~ *vi* **:** to taper a timber

snap fastener *n* **:** a metal fastener consisting essentially of a ball and a socket attached to opposed parts of an article and used to hold meeting edges (as of a garment) together — see FASTENER illustration

snap flask *n* **:** a molding flask for small work having its sides separable and held together by latches so that the flask may be removed from around the sand mold

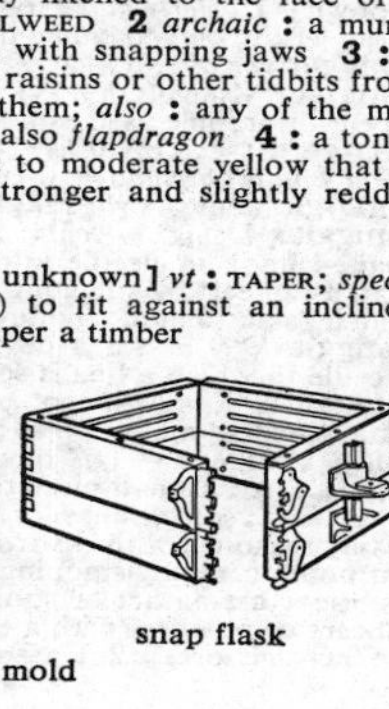

snap flask

snap gage *n* **:** a gage with inside measuring surfaces (as for calipering lengths or diameters)

snap·hance *or* **snap·haunce** \ˈsnap‚han(t)s, -hän\ *also* **snap·haan** \|n\ *n* -S [D *snaphaan* highway-man, snaphance (influenced in meaning by *snappen* to snap and *haan* hammer of a gun), fr. MD *snaphaen* highwayman, fr. *snappen* to snap, snatch + *haen* cock; akin to OHG *hani* cock — more at SNAP, CHANT] **1 a :** a primitive flintlock **b :** an old-time musket having such a lock **2** *obs* **:** a snap catch or spring catch

snaphead \ˈ=ˌ=\ *n* **1 :** a hemispherical or rounded head on a rivet or bolt **2 :** a riveting snap

snap header *n* **1 :** a half brick appearing like a header in a masonry face but not extending in beyond the facework **2 :** a bond stone not extending through the wall

snaphead rivet *n* **1 :** a rivet with head formed by a snap **2 :** a buttonhead rivet

snapholder \ˈ=ˌ==\ *n* **:** a holder (as a tool holder) actuated by a snap

snap hook *n* **:** SPRING HOOK

snapjack \ˈ=ˌ=\ *n, dial Eng* **:** GREATER STITCHWORT

snap·less \ˈ=ləs\ *adj* **:** having no snap **:** employing or requiring no snaps

snap link *n* **:** a link (as of a chain) with a gap in the side closed by a spring

snap lock *n* **:** a lock shutting with a catch or snap

snap mackerel *n* **:** BLUEFISH 1

snap molding *n* **:** molding with snap flasks

snap-on \ˈ=ˌ=\ *adj* [fr. *snap on*, v.] **1 :** designed to snap into position and fit tightly ⟨dishes with *snap-on* covers⟩ **2 :** attachable by means of snap fasteners ⟨a *snap-on* collar⟩

snap out *n, pl* **snap outs** [fr. *snap out*, v.] **:** a perforated leaf that can be pulled apart from the others in a set of printed tablet sheets

snap·pable \ˈsnapəbəl\ *adj* **:** capable of being snapped

snapped *past of* SNAP

snapped work *n* **:** masonry laid with considerable use of snap headers

¹snap·per \ˈsnapə(r)\ *vi* [ME *snaperen*; akin to MHG *snappen* to snap, stumble, sway, chatter — more at SNAP] **1** *chiefly Scot* **:** STUMBLE **2** *chiefly Scot* **:** to commit an error **:** make a slip

²snapper \"\ *n* -S *chiefly Scot* **:** a false step **:** SLIP, FAUX PAS

³snapper \"\ *n* -S [¹*snap* + *-er*] **1 :** something that snaps: as **a snappers** *pl* **:** CASTANETS **b :** a small usu. tasseled tip on a buggy whip **c :** CRACKER 2c **d** (1) **:** GREATER STITCHWORT (2) **:** BLADDER CAMPION a (3) **:** SNAP BEAN **e** (1) **:** SNAPPING TURTLE (2) **:** GREEN WOODPECKER (3) **:** CLICK BEETLE (4) **:** PHAINOPEPLA **f :** a bit of business, turn of phrase, or other matter that gives new orientation to a situation or utterance **g :** SNAP FASTENER **h :** a small clamshell bucket used esp. for collecting samples of deep-sea mud and ooze **2 :** a person that snaps or that snaps something esp. by way of occupation: as **a :** an irritable snappish individual **:** one who answers or speaks curtly and cuttingly **b :** a glassworker who uses a snapdragon **c :** a taker of snapshots **d :** ²CLIPPER a; *also* **:** a mine car brakeman or coupler **e :** SNAPPER-BACK **3** *pl sometimes* **snapper a :** any of numerous active carnivorous fishes (family Lutjanidae) of warm seas that are important as food and often as sport fishes, commonly resemble bass, attain a length of about two feet, and are usu. red or rose in deep-sea forms but often greenish above in shallow-water forms esp. when young **b :** any of several immature fishes (as the young of the bluefish, rosefish, or red grouper) that somewhat resemble a snapper **c :** an important sparid food fish (*Pagrosomus auratus* or *P. unicolor*) of Australia and New Zealand that is usu. pink or reddish with dark spots when young and becomes bright red when adult — see COCK SNAPPER **4** *slang* **:** WHOPPER

snapper-back \ˈ=(ˌ)=ˌ=\ *n* -S [*snap back* + *-er*] **:** a football player who snaps back the ball **:** CENTER

snapper shark *n* **:** MAKO

snapper-up \ˈ=ˌ=ˈ=\ *n, pl* **snappers-up** [*snap up*, v. + *-er*] **:** one that snaps something up ⟨a *snapper-up* of bargains⟩ ⟨a *snapper-up* of unconsidered trifles —Shak.⟩

snap·pi·ly \ˈsnapəlē, -li\ *adv* **:** in a snappy manner

snap·pi·ness \-pēnəs, -pin-\ *n* -ES **:** the quality or state of being snappy

snapping *adv* [fr. pres. part. of ¹*snap*] **:** NOTABLY, VERY, INTENSELY ⟨a ~ cold day⟩

snapping beetle *also* **snapping bug** *n* **:** CLICK BEETLE

snapping hazel *n* **:** WITCH HAZEL 2a(1)

snap·ping·ly *adv* **:** in a snapping manner **:** with snapping ⟨dogs threatening ~⟩

snapping mackerel *n* **:** BLUEFISH 1

snapping prawn *n, Austral* **:** SNAPPING SHRIMP

snapping shrimp *n* **:** any of numerous small shrimps (family Crangonidae) that make a sharp snapping sound with one of their chelae which is greatly enlarged

snapping tool *n* **:** a stamp for forcing a metal plate into a die to make an impression

snapping turtle *also* **snapping terrapin** *n* **1 :** any of several large and voracious American aquatic turtles of the family Chelydridae that seize their prey with a snap of their powerful jaws, have a strong musky odor, and are extensively used as food — see ALLIGATOR SNAPPER **2 :** SOFT-SHELLED TURTLE

snap·pish \ˈsnapish, -pēsh\ *adj* [¹*snap* + *-ish*] **1 a :** given to snapping irritable speech **:** TESTY, IRASCIBLE ⟨a ~ old man⟩ ⟨a ~ disposition⟩ **b :** arising from a harsh irascible nature **:** curt and ungracious **:** CUTTING ⟨a ~ answer⟩ **2 :** inclined or accustomed to bite or snap ⟨a ~ dog⟩ **syn** see IRRITABLE

snap·pish·ly *adv* **:** in a snappish manner **:** with a snap

snap·pish·ness *n* -ES **:** the quality or state of being snappish

snap point *n* **:** SNAPHEAD

snap·py \ˈsnapē, -pi\ *adj* -ER/-EST [¹*snap* + *-y*] **1 :** SNAPPISH **2 :** quickly made or done **:** QUICK, SUDDEN **3 :** full of or characterized by liveliness, briskness, pungency, smartness, or similar quality ⟨~ conversation⟩: as **a** *of weather* **:** CRISP, BRISK **b :** exhibiting a high degree of style or pleasing show ⟨~ clothes⟩ ⟨a ~ dresser⟩ **4 :** emitting or constituting sparks or a series of sharp quick reports **:** CRACKLING ⟨a ~ sound⟩ **5** *of a photographic negative or positive* **:** having a high degree of contrast **syn** see PUNGENT

snappy gum *n, Austral* **:** a eucalyptus (esp. *Eucalyptus haemastoma*) with notably soft or brittle wood

snap ring *n* **1 :** a spring ring that is sprung open and snapped into place in its groove and is used esp. for a piston or other retaining ring function **2 :** an oval or pear-shaped ring used by rock climbers to fasten a rope to a piton

snap-rivet \ˈ=ˌ==\ *vt* **:** to rivet by forming heads with a snap

snap roll *n* **:** a maneuver in which an airplane is made by quick movement of the controls to complete a full revolution about its longitudinal axis while maintaining an approximately level line of flight

¹snaps *pres 3d sing of* SNAP, *pl of* SNAP

²snaps \ˈsnaps, -näps\ *n, pl* **snaps** [Sw & Dan, lit., dram of liquor, fr. LG, dram, mouthful — more at SCHNAPPS] **:** an alcoholic beverage of Scandinavia consisting of ethyl alcohol flavored with various herbs

snapsack \ˈ=ˌ=\ *n* [LG *snappsack*, fr. *snappen* to snap + *sack*, bag, sack — more at SNAP, KNAPSACK] *archaic* **:** KNAPSACK

snapshoot \ˈ=ˌ=\ *vt* [back-formation fr. ¹*snapshot*] **:** to take a snapshot of

snap shooter *n* [⁴*snap* + *shooter*] **:** a gunner that is adept at snap shooting

snapshooter \ˈ=ˌ==\ *n* [*snapshoot* + *-er*] **:** a person that takes snapshots

snap shooting *n* [⁴*snap*] **:** shooting (as a rifle) quickly and without taking deliberate aim with the sights

snap shot *n* [⁴*snap*] **:** a quick shot (as with a rifle) made without deliberately taking aim with the sights

¹snapshot \ˈ=ˌ=\ *n* [⁴*snap* + *shot*] **1 :** a casual photograph made by rapid exposure and usu. with a small hand-held camera **2 :** a brief or transitory view; *also* **:** a mere segment ⟨the letters give us ~*s* of his progress⟩

²snapshot \"\ *adj* **1 :** of, relating to, or having the nature of a snapshot **2 :** produced or executed as hastily as a snapshot

³snapshot \"\ *vt* **snapshotted; snapshotted; snapshotting; snapshots :** SNAPSHOOT

snap·shot·ter \-ād·ə(r), -ātə-\ *n* -S *chiefly Brit* **:** SNAPSHOOTER

snap switch *n* **:** a manually operated electric switch with a blade which makes contact with a snap and in which the speed of making or breaking of the circuit is independent of the speed of operation of the switch

snap table *or* **snap-top table** *n* **:** a tip-top table whose top is held down by a snap catch

snap-the-whip \ˈ=ˌ=ˈ=\ *n* **:** CRACK-THE-WHIP

snap tool *n* **:** SNAP 11a

snap trap *n* **:** a trap that snaps shut when the bait or trigger is disturbed: as **a :** a trap designed to imprison an animal unharmed in a suitable container **b :** a guillotine mouse or rat trap

snap turtle *n* **:** SNAPPING TURTLE

snap up *n, pl* **snap ups** [fr. *snap up*, v.] **:** KIP-UP

snapweed \ˈ=ˌ=\ *n* **:** JEWELWEED

snap willow *n* **:** CRACK WILLOW

snapwood \ˈ=ˌ=\ *n* **:** SPICEBUSH 1

¹snare \ˈsna(a)(ə)r, ˈsne|, |ə\ *n* -S [ME, fr. OE *sneare*, fr. ON *snara*; akin to MD *snaer* cord, string, MLG *snāre* cord, string, OHG *snaraha*, *snarha* noose, snare, *snuor* cord, Gk *narkē* numbness — more at NARROW] **1 a :** a contrivance typically consisting of a running noose (as of wire or cord) by which a bird or other animal may be caught; *broadly* **:** TRAP, GIN **b :** something by which one is entangled, involved in difficulties, held fast, or impeded in one's progress; *often* **:** something deceptively attractive **:** a misleading lure **2** [prob. fr. D *snaar*, lit., cord, string, fr. MD *snaer*] **a :** one of the gut strings or metal spirals of a snare drum **b :** SNARE DRUM **3 :** a surgical instrument consisting usu. of a wire loop or noose that can be constricted by a mechanism in the handle and used for removing tissue masses (as tonsils, polyps, granulations)

²snare \"\ *vt* -ED/-ING/-S [ME *snaren*, fr. *snare*, n.] **1 a :** to capture or gain possession of by or as if by use of a snare ⟨pigeons *snared* in a trap⟩ ⟨*snaring* the ball out of the air⟩ **b :** to win or attain by artful or skillful maneuvers ⟨~ an important appointment⟩ **2 :** to cause to become enmeshed in unanticipated complexities, difficulties, or distress **:** entangle as if in a snare ⟨urban dissipations that ~ unwary countrymen⟩ **syn** see CATCH

snare drum *n* **:** the smaller common military double-headed drum having a snare or snares stretched across its lower head and sounded by means of two wooden drumsticks — called also *side drum*; see DRUM illustration

snare head *n* **:** the lower head of a snare drum across which the snares are stretched — compare BATTER HEAD

snare·less \ˈ=ləs\ *adj* **:** free from snares

snar·er \ˈsna(a)rə(r), ˈsner-\ *n* -S **1 :** one that snares **2 :** one that uses snares (as in hunting)

snark \ˈsnärk, ˈsnȧk\ *vi* [prob. alter. of *snork*] *dial Brit* **:** SNORE, SNORT

¹snarl *R* ˈsnärl, *chiefly before pause or consonant* -rəl, *–R* ˈsnȧl\ *n* -S [ME *snarle*, prob. fr. *snare* + *-le* (dim. suffix)] **1** *chiefly dial* **:** SNARE, NOOSE, GIN **2 a :** a tangle (as of hairs, thread, lines, plant growths) difficult or impossible to unravel ⟨a ~ of blackberry bushes and a matting underfoot of vine —Edmund Wilson⟩ ⟨a ~ of traffic⟩; *also* **:** a confused or disordered group or mass **:** SWARM ⟨a ~ of people arrived late⟩ **b :** a condition of complication or confusion making orderly procedure or progress difficult or impossible ⟨in the home of the direct primary . . . the system produced an inconclusive ~ —F.L.Paxson⟩ **syn** see CONFUSION

²snarl \"\ *vb* -ED/-ING/-S [ME *snarlen*, fr. *snarle*, n.] *vt* **1 a** *chiefly dial* **:** to catch in a snare or on a noose; *also* **:** hold fast in a knot or tangle **b** *obs* **:** STRANGLE **c** *obs* **:** to ensnare by arts or wiles as if by a noose; *also* **:** to bring (oneself) into a state of confused disorder **:** enmesh or entangle (oneself) in difficulties **2 :** to get into a tangle **:** cause to become knotted and intertwined ⟨~ one's hair⟩ **3 :** to make excessively or unduly complicated or confused ⟨~ a once simple problem⟩ ~ *vi* **:** to become tangled or snarled **:** be inclined to tangle ⟨this thread ~*s* easily⟩

³snarl \"\ *vb* -ED/-ING/-S [freq. of obs. E *snar* to growl, snarl; akin to MD *snarren* to hum, drone — more at SNORE] *vi* **1 :** to growl with a snapping or gnashing of the teeth (as of an angry dog) **:** utter angry or grumbling sounds with a display of teeth **2 :** to give vent to anger or irritation in rude surly language **:** quarrel, scold, complain, or otherwise show anger or disgust in a growling, snappish, or spiteful manner **3 :** to become expressed by a snarl ⟨their anger ~*s* forth in angry words⟩ ~ *vt* **1 :** to utter or express with a snarl or by snarling **2 :** to bring into a specified situation or condition by snarling ⟨~*ed* himself hoarse⟩

⁴snarl \"\ *n* -S **:** an act or the sound of snarling **:** a surly angry growl ⟨the ~ of the waves changed to a sullen roar⟩

⁵snarl \"\ *vt* -ED/-ING/-S [perh. fr. E dial. *snarl* knot in wood, fr. ¹*snarl*] **:** to form raised work upon the outer surface of (thin metal ware) by the repercussion of a snarling iron

⁶snarl \"\ *n* -S **:** an anvil whose horn has an upturned projecting point over which hollow sheet-metal work in process may be placed when it is to be ornamented with reliefs — compare SNARLING IRON

¹snarl·er \ˈsnärlər, ˈsnȧlə(r\ *n* -S [³*snarl* + *-er*] **:** one that snarls

²snarler \"\ *n* -S [⁵*snarl* + *-er*] **:** a user of a snarling iron

snarling iron *n* [*snarling* fr. gerund of ⁵*snarl*] **:** a tool with a long beak used in making raised work on metal surfaces by repercussion

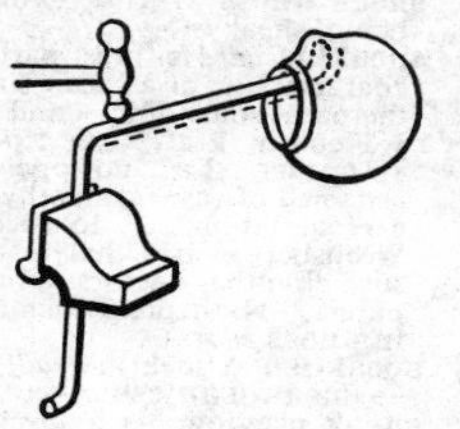

snarling iron

snarl·ing·ly *adv* **:** in a snarling manner **:** with a snarl ⟨answered ~⟩

snarl·ish \-lish\ *adj* [³*snarl* + *-ish*] **:** disposed to snarl **:** ugly-tempered

¹snarly \-lē, -li\ *adj* -ER/-EST [¹*snarl* + *-y*] **:** full of tangles and snarls **:** TANGLED ⟨~ yarn⟩

²snarly \"\ *adj* -ER/-EST [³*snarl* + *-y*] **:** marked by snarling ill nature **:** SURLY, PEEVISH

¹snash \ˈsnash\ *n* [origin unknown] *chiefly Scot* **:** INSOLENCE, ABUSE, IMPERTINENCE

²snash \"\ *vi, chiefly Scot* **:** to speak or act disrespectfully or insolently

snaste *n* [origin unknown] *obs* **:** the wick of a snuffed candle

¹snatch \ˈsnach\ *vb* -ED/-ING/-ES [ME *snacchen*, *snecchen*; akin to MD *snacken* to snap at, bite, chatter, MLG & MHG *snacken* to chatter, gossip, ON *snaka* to sniff around, Norw *snake* to sniff around, snap at with the teeth] *vi* **1** *obs* **:** to give a sudden snap (as in anger or attack) **:** make a snappish attack **2 :** to attempt to seize something suddenly by or as if by snapping **:** catch at something — often used with *at* ⟨~ at a rope⟩ ~ *vt* **1 :** to take or grasp abruptly or hastily **:** seize (something) hurriedly or in passing ⟨~ a pen⟩ ⟨~*ed* the first opportunity⟩ ⟨~*ing* a glance at his friend⟩; *often* **:** to seize or grab suddenly without permission, ceremony, due process, or legal or moral right **:** steal, win, or otherwise gain irregularly when catching another unawares ⟨~ a kiss⟩ ⟨~*ing* victory from defeat⟩ **2 a :** to remove with suddenness (as by pulling, tearing, concealing, rescuing) — often used with *away* or *off* ⟨~ off his burning clothes⟩ **b :** to remove by death ⟨~*ed* from the bosom of his family⟩ **3 :** to insert (a rope) in a snatch block **4 :** to catch (a fish) by intentionally hooking the body rather than the mouth **syn** see TAKE — **snatch one baldheaded :** to rebuke severely or caustically

²snatch \"\ *n* -ES [ME *snacche*, fr. *snecchen*, *snacchen*, v.] **1** *obs* **:** TRAP, SNARE **2 :** a snatching at or of something **:** a quick catching or grabbing: as **a :** a lift in which the weight is raised from the floor to the overhead position in one rapid motion — compare CLEAN AND JERK, PRESS **b** *slang* (1) **:** KIDNAPPING (2) **:** a demand for something (as money) — used chiefly in *put the snatch on* ⟨put the ~ on him for a cut of the take⟩ **3 :** a snatched opportunity or period of time **:** an occasional period (as a moment or hour) ⟨sleep only in ~*es*⟩ ⟨work by ~*es*⟩ **4 :** something (as a short period, spell, or stint, an excerpt from a song, a few bars of a melody, a fleeting glimpse, a disconnected portion of a story, a snack) as brief, fragmentary, or hurried as if snatched or done in snatched

time ⟨a ~ of spring in January⟩ ⟨sing ~es of old tunes⟩ ⟨you may have heard ~es of the story⟩ 5 *obs* : something (as a way of speaking or an argument) with a catch 6 a : SNATCH BLOCK b : SNATCH HOOK 7 a : VAGINA — usu. considered vulgar b : SEXUAL INTERCOURSE — usu. considered vulgar

snatch·able \-chəbəl\ *adj* : capable of being snatched

snatch block *n* : a block that can be opened on one side to receive the bight of a rope

snatched *adj* : that is snatched; *usu* : BRIEF, HURRIED ⟨a ~ moment of chat⟩

snatch·er \'snachə(r)\ *n* -s : one that snatches: as a : THIEF; *esp* : one that snatches purses or other articles from his victims b : BODY SNATCHER c : KIDNAPPER d : a slaughterhouse worker who removes viscera

snatch hitch *n* : an easily made and broken hook hitch that is used to hook an extra team to a load for pulling it over a difficult spot and then to unhitch quickly while the load is in motion

snatch hook *n* : a gang hook designed specif. for foul-hooking fish

snatch·i·ly \-chəlē\ *adv* : in snatches : so as to be snatchy

snatching *pres part of* SNATCH

snatch·ing·ly *adv* : in a snatching manner : HURRIEDLY

snatch line *n* : a line by which something (as a piece of theatrical scenery) is snatched into position

snatch pickup *n* : an action wherein a flying airplane hooks onto a glider or a person or object on the ground and carries or tows it away through the air

snatch team *n* : TOW TEAM

snatchy \'snachē, -chi\ *adj, often* -ER/-EST : done in or by snatches; *broadly* : marked by breaks in continuity : INTERRUPTED, SPASMODIC ⟨~ reading⟩ ⟨a ~ conversation⟩

snath \'snath, -neth\ *or* **snathe** \-nāth, -nath\ *or* **snead** \-nēd, -nad, -ned\ *or* **sneath** \-nēth, -nāth\ *n* -s [ME *snede*, fr. OE *snǣd*; akin to OE *snīthan* to cut, OHG *snīdan*, ON *snītha*; akin to Ukr *snit* block, chunk, Czech *snět* branch, and perh. to MIr *snēid* small, short] : the handle of a scythe

snav·vle \'snavəl\ *vt* [alter. of ²*snaffle*] *Austral* : to get hold of by fair means or foul : rustle up

snaw \'snȯ, 'snä\ *chiefly Scot var of* SNOW

snaz·zi·ness \'snazēnəs, -zin-\ *n* -ES : the quality or state of being snazzy

snaz·zy \-zē, -zi\ *adj* -ER/-EST [origin unknown] 1 : outstanding in style : conspicuously or flashily attractive ⟨his suit was pretty ~ —Wallace Stegner⟩ ⟨a pretty ~ place —Paul Gallico⟩ 2 : very pleasing ⟨smooth, ~ tunes —E.T.Canby⟩

snd *abbr* sound

SND *abbr* 1 *often not cap* sap no defect 2 static no delivery

1sneak \'snēk\ *vb* **sneaked** \-kt\ *or chiefly dial* **snuck** \'snək\ *or dial* **snook** \'snu̇k\ **sneaked** *or chiefly dial* **snuck**; **sneaking**; **sneaks** [akin to OE *snīcan* to creep, sneak along, ON *snikja* to hanker, Dan *snige* to sneak, OHG *snahhan* to creep — more at SNAIL] *vi* 1 a : to go stealthily or furtively : creep or steal so as to be unobserved ⟨would ~ out over the back fence to avoid boys who were laying for me —John Reed⟩ : SLINK ⟨~*ed* away after his ignominious defeat⟩ b : to get oneself out or past or through by furtive or artful means ⟨~ out of a difficulty⟩ ⟨his papers always ~ past the examiners⟩ 2 : to behave in a furtive or servile manner 3 : to cross a football goal line and score by a quarterback sneak — usu. used with *over* ~ *vt* 1 : to put, bring, or take in a furtive or artful manner : get surreptitiously ⟨~ in a stop at a bar⟩ ⟨~ Christmas gifts into the house⟩ ⟨~ a look at the book during the test⟩ ⟨~ a smoke while the nurse is out⟩; *specif* : steal in the manner of a sneak thief ⟨caught him ~*ing* tomatoes when he thought no one was home⟩ 2 a : to cause (radio or television sound) to come or go with a very gradual change of volume — used with *in* or *out* b : to bring in (radio or television sound) at a very low volume ⟨~ bar sounds⟩ **syn** see LURK

2sneak \"\ *n* -s 1 : a person who acts in a stealthy, furtive, or shifty manner : a sneaky person; *specif* : SNEAK THIEF 2 a : a stealthy or furtive move b : an unobserved departure or escape 3 : SNEAKER 3 — usu. used in pl. 4 : the opening lead of a singleton in a card game (as bridge) 5 : SNEAK PREVIEW 6 : QUARTERBACK SNEAK — **on the sneak** *adv* : in a clandestine manner ⟨speakeasies and clubs . . . operated *on the sneak* —Polly Adler⟩

3sneak \"\ *adj* 1 : carried on secretly : CLANDESTINE ⟨handbook operations . . . are now operating on a ~ basis —*New Orleans (La.) Times-Picayune*⟩ 2 : occurring without warning : SURPRISE ⟨a ~ attack⟩ ⟨a ~ flood⟩

sneak boat *n* : a boat used in approaching unobserved; *esp* : SNEAK BOX

sneak box *n* : a boat orig. built for duck shooting having a spoon-shaped bottom and deck with a small cockpit and a dagger board and usu. a boom and gaff mainsail and jib

sneak–cup *n* [¹*sneak* + *cup*] *obs* : one who fails to drink his share

sneak current *n* : an electric current that though too feeble to blow the usual fuse or to injure at once telegraph or telephone instruments will in time burn them out

sneak·er \'snēkə(r)\ *n* -s 1 : one that sneaks 2 : PUNCH BOWL 3 : a shoe usu. of canvas with a pliable rubber sole worn esp. for sports or hiking — usu. used in pl.; compare TENNIS SHOE

sneak·i·ly \-kəlē, -li\ *adv* : in a sneaky manner

sneak·i·ness \-kēnəs\ *n* -ES : the quality or state of being sneaky

sneaking *adj* [fr. pres. part. of ¹*sneak*] 1 : that sneaks or is characteristic of a sneak : FURTIVE, UNDERHAND ⟨felt . . . that there was something ~ and unclean about secret code messages —Fletcher Pratt⟩ 2 : MEAN, NIGGARDLY, PALTRY, CONTEMPTIBLE 3 a : not openly expressed as if something to be ashamed of ⟨a ~ sympathy for the rascal⟩ ⟨I have always had a ~ ambition . . . to become a conductor myself —Joseph Wechsberg⟩ b : that is a persistent conjecture ⟨had a ~ suspicion that doctors were only one step ahead of the general public —Nathaniel Benchley⟩ — **sneak·ing·ly** *adv* — **sneak·ing·ness** *n* -ES

sneak·ish \'snēkish\ *adj* : SNEAKY — **sneak·ish·ly** *adv* — **sneak·ish·ness** *n* -ES

sneak preview *n* : a special advanced showing of a motion picture usu. announced but not named

sneaks·by \'snēksbē\ *n* -ES [²*sneak* + -*sby* (as in such proper names as *Grimsby*, *Ormesby*)] : SNEAK

sneak shooting *n* : shooting from a sneak boat

sneak thief *n* : a thief who steals whatever he can reach without using violence or forcibly breaking into buildings

sneak–up \'=,=\ *n* -s [fr. *sneak up*, v.] : SNEAK

sneaky \'snēkē, -ki\ *adj* -ER/-EST : marked by stealth, furtiveness, or shiftiness : that sneaks or is done in a sneaking manner : characteristic of a sneak ⟨a ~ two-faced fellow who breaks all the rules when your back is turned⟩ ⟨called the policeman's hiding behind the billboard a ~ trick⟩

1sneap \'snēp\ *vt* -ED/-ING/-S [ME *snaipen*, prob. of Scand origin; akin to ON *sneypa* to dishonor, disgrace, Icel. to scold, rebuke, OSw *snöpa* to castrate, ON *snubba* to scold — more at SNUB] 1 *dial Eng* : CHIDE, REPROVE, CHASTEN ⟨she had a tongue for the ~*ing* of too casual boys —Arnold Bennett⟩ 2 *archaic* : to blast or blight with cold : NIP ⟨like an envious ~*ing* frost that bites the first born infants of the spring —Shak.⟩

2sneap \"\ *n* -s *archaic* : REBUKE, SNUB

sneath *var of* SNATH

sneb *var of* SNIB

1sneck \'snek\ *n* -s [ME *snekk*, *snekke*; prob. akin to ME *snecchen*, *snacchen* to snatch — more at SNATCH] 1 *dial Brit* : the latch or catch of a door 2 *chiefly dial* : a clicking sound

2sneck \"\ *vb* -ED/-ING/-S [ME *snekken*, fr. *snekk*, *snekke*, n.] *vt*, *dial Brit* : to fasten (a gate or door) with a latch ~ *vi*, *dial Brit* : LATCH

3sneck \"\ *vb* -ED/-ING/-S [origin unknown] *chiefly dial* : ¹SNICK

4sneck \"\ *vt* -ED/-ING/-S [origin unknown] : to lay (rubblework) with spalls and fragments to fill the interstices

5sneck \"\ *n* -s : a small roughly squared stone used in snecking

sneckdraw \'=,=\ *or* **sneck drawer** *n* [*sneckdraw* fr. ¹*sneck* + *draw* (v.); *sneck drawer* fr. ME *snek-drawer*, fr. *snek*, *snekk* sneck + *drawer*] *chiefly Scot* : a sly crafty person trying to worm his way in

sneck up *vi* [*sneck* of unknown origin] *chiefly dial* : to make oneself scarce — usu. used in the phrase *go sneck up*

sned \'sned\ *vt* [ME *sneden*, fr. OE *snǣdan* to cut off, slice — more at SNATH] *chiefly Scot* : to lop off (vegetation) : PRUNE

1sneer \'sni(ə)r, -iə\ *vb* -ED/-ING/-S [prob. akin to MHG *snerren* to chatter, gossip — more at SNORE] *vi* 1 *dial chiefly Brit* : to snort in the manner of an animal 2 a : to smile or laugh with facial contortions that express scorn or contempt b : to manifest derision, disdain, or contempt by speaking or writing in a scornfully jeering manner ⟨people are nowadays so cynical — they ~ at everything that makes life worth living —L.P.Smith⟩ 3 : to make a sound like a sneer ⟨a bullet ~*ing* overhead⟩ ~ *vt* 1 : to utter with a sneer or sneeringly ⟨~ a reply⟩ 2 *archaic* : to treat with sneers : sneer at **syn** see SCOFF

2sneer \"\ *n* -s : the act of sneering : a sneering expression, remark, or saying ⟨the lips are pursed in a scornful, supercilious ~ —Harry Luke⟩ ⟨the current ~ that both parties are without cardinal distinctive principles —*No. Amer. Rev.*⟩

sneer·er \-rə(r)\ *n* -s : one that sneers

sneer·ful \'=fəl\ *adj* : given to sneering

sneer·ing·ly *adv* : in a sneering manner

sneer·less \'=ləs\ *adj* : being without a sneer

sneery \-rē, -ri\ *adj, often* -ER/-EST : given to or marked by sneering

sneesh \'snēsh, -nish\ *n* [short for *sneeshing*] *dial Brit* : SNUFF

sneesh·ing \'snēshən, -nish-, -shiŋ\ *n* -s [alter. of *sneezing*, fr. gerund of *sneeze*] 1 *dial Brit* : SNUFF; *specif* : a pinch of snuff 2 *dial Brit* : a thing of little value or significance

1sneeze \'snēz\ *vb* -ED/-ING/-S [ME *snesen*, alter. of *fnesen*, fr. OE *fnēosan*; akin to MHG *pfnūsen* to snort, sneeze, ON *fnȳsa* to snort, Gk *pnein* to breathe] *vi* 1 : to make a sudden violent spasmodic audible expiration of breath through the nose and mouth usu. as a reflex act following irritation of the nasal mucous membrane 2 : to make a sound like a sneeze ⟨the last wind snarls and ~s —Thomas Hardy⟩ ~ *vt* 1 : to utter or give forth with a sneeze 2 : to cause to be or go by sneezing ⟨~ germs over everyone⟩ 3 *slang* : to place under arrest — **sneeze at** : to treat lightly : DESPISE, CONTEMN — usu. used in the phrase *not to be sneezed at* ⟨there must be many thousands more to whom two dollars is not to be *sneezed at* —*Saturday Rev.*⟩

2sneeze \"\ *n* -s 1 : the act or fact of sneezing : a sudden violent audible spasmodic expiration through the nose and mouth 2 *slang* : ARREST

sneeze gas *also* **sneezing gas** *n* : STERNUTATOR

sneeze·less \'=ləs\ *adj* : having no sneeze : being unlikely to cause sneezing

sneez·er \'snēzə(r)\ *n* -s 1 : one that sneezes 2 *slang* a : NOSE b : a drink of spirits c : one that is exceptional or superlative in some respect ⟨a terrible powerful man he was — a real ~ —T.C.Haliburton⟩ d : JAIL

sneezeweed \'=,=\ *n* 1 : any of several plants of the genus *Helenium*: as a : a No. American yellow-flowered perennial herb (*H. autumnale*) the odor of which is said to cause sneezing b : a stout perennial herb (*H. hoopesii*) of the western U.S. causing spewing sickness in sheep 2 : a weed (*Centipeda orbicularis*) of the family Compositae of Australia and Tasmania 3 : SNEEZEWORT 2

sneezewood \'=,=\ *n* 1 : a South African timber tree (*Ptaeroxylon utile*) of the family Meliaceae 2 : the hard valuable wood of the sneezewood tree that yields sawdust which causes sneezing

sneezewort \'=,=\ *n* 1 *obs* : WHITE HELLEBORE 2 : a strong-scented Eurasian perennial herb (*Achillea ptarmica*) resembling yarrow but having simple leaves and large flower heads 3 : SNEEZEWEED 1

sneezy \'snēzē, -zi\ *adj* -ER/-EST : given to or causing sneezing

1snell \'snel\ *adj* -ER/-EST [ME *snel*, *snell*, fr. OE *snell* quick, active, bold; akin to OHG *snel* strong, bold, agile, OS, fresh, active, bold, ON *snjallr* well-spoken, brave] 1 *chiefly dial* a : acting or moving swiftly : QUICK, EAGER b : SHARP-WITTED, ACUTE 2 : having a keen edge : PIERCING, BITING ⟨a ~ wind blew down the street — Christopher Morley⟩

2snell \"\ *adv* [ME, fr. *snel*, *snell*, adj.] *dial chiefly Brit* : QUICKLY, SWIFTLY, VIGOROUSLY

3snell \"\ *n* -s [origin unknown] : a short line (as of gut or nylon) by which a fishhook is attached to a longer line

4snell \"\ *vt* -ED/-ING/-S : to attach to or by a snell

snel·len test \'snelən-\ *n, usu cap S* [after Herman *Snellen* †1908 Dutch ophthalmologist] : a test for visual acuity presenting letters of graduated sizes to determine the smallest size that can be read at a standard distance

snell's law \'snelz-\ *n, usu cap S* [after Willebrord *Snell* van Royen (Willebrord *Snellius*) †1626 Dutch mathematician] : a law in physics: the ratio of the sines of the angles of incidence and refraction is constant for all incidences in any given pair of media for electromagnetic waves of a definite frequency

1snel·ly \'snel(l)ē\ *adv* [ME, fr. OE *snellīce*, fr. *snellic* smart, ready, quick, bold, fr. *snell* + -*līc* -ly] *dial chiefly Brit* : SNELL

2snelly \-ēli\ *adj* [¹*snell* + -*y*] *Scot* : CHILL, SHARP

snerp *var of* SNURP

1snew \'sn(y)ü\ *vi* [ME *sniwen*, *snewen*, fr. OE *snīwan*; akin to MD & MLG *snīen* to snow, OHG *snīwan* to snow, ON *snȳr* it is snowing, OE *snāw* snow — more at SNOW] *dial* : SNOW

2snew \"\ [ME] *dial past of* SNOW

SNF *abbr* solids not fat

1snib \'snib\ *also* **sneb** \'sneb\ *vt* **snibbed; snibbed; snibbing; snibs** [ME *snibben*, prob. of Scand origin; akin to obs. Dan *snibbe* to scold, rebuke, obs. Sw *snybba*, ON *snubba* — more at SNUB] 1 *dial Brit* : CHECK, RESTRAIN 2 *dial Brit* : REBUKE, SNUB 3 *dial Brit* : to put an end to : cut short

2snib \'snib\ *n* -s [ME *snybb*, fr. *snibben*, v.] *chiefly Scot* : REBUFF, SNUB

3snib \"\ *vt* **snibbed; snibbed; snibbing; snibs** [origin unknown] *Scot* : FASTEN, BOLT, BAR ⟨*snibbed* the door —J.M.Barrie⟩

4snib \"\ *n* -s [origin unknown] *dial Brit* : a door fastening : BOLT, CATCH

1snick \'snik\ *vb* -ED/-ING/-S [prob. back-formation fr. *snickersnee*] *vt* 1 : to cut slightly : SNIP, NICK ⟨the razor ~*ed* my Adam's-apple —*Sydney (Australia) Bull.*⟩ 2 : to strike sharply : pierce with a thrust 3 : to hit (a cricket ball) a glancing blow with the edge of the bat usu. inadvertently ~ *vi* : to cut, snip, or nick something ⟨~ at the skin until you can get a hold of the splinter with the tweezers —Peter Heaton⟩

2snick \"\ *n* -s 1 : a small cut : SNIP, NICK 2 a : the act or an instance of snicking (as in cricket) b : a snicked ball in cricket ⟨with the bat at an angle the most likely result is a ~ —*Calling All Cricketers*⟩

3snick \"\ *n* -s [alter. of ²*snack*] *chiefly dial* : SHARE — **go snicks** *chiefly dial* : SHARE

4snick \"\ *chiefly dial var of* ¹SNECK

5snick \"\ *vb* -ED/-ING/-S [imit.] *vt* : to put or move so as to make a clicking sound ⟨~*ed* his dagger in and out of the sheath —Donn Byrne⟩ ~ *vi* : to make a click ⟨bolts ~*ed* sharply as cartridges snapped into chambers —J.W.Bellah⟩

6snick \"\ *n* -s : a cutting or clicking noise ⟨the plane made a pleasant ~ as it shaved a long wooden curl —Luis Marden⟩ ⟨he clicked on the safety; it made a metallic ~ —Arthur Gordon⟩

7snick \"\ *n* -s [origin unknown] : a knot or irregularity in yarn or wire

1snick·er \'snikə(r)\ *or* **snig·ger** \'snigə(r)\ *vb* **snickered** *or* **sniggered; snickered** *or* **sniggered; snickering** \-k(ə)riŋ\ *or* **sniggering** \-g(ə)riŋ\ **snickers** *or* **sniggers** [imit.] *vi* 1 : to laugh in a slight, covert, or partly suppressed manner (as in derision or from embarrassment) ⟨they ~ at my graftin', and I laugh in my sleeve . . . at their penetration —T.C.Haliburton⟩ ⟨a fantastic caricature of the Edwardian dandy his grandfather probably ~*ed* at —P.D.Whitney⟩ ⟨like a small boy taking you into a corner to *snigger* at a bawdy story —H.J.Laski⟩ : TITTER ⟨chuckled at his readers, ~*ed* at his correspondents, smiled at his own folly —Martin Gardner⟩ 2 : to make a sound like a snicker ⟨the irreverent red squirrels . . . run and ~ at my approach —John Burroughs⟩ ~ *vt* : to utter with or express by a snicker

2snicker \"\ *or* **snigger** \"\ *n* -s : an act or sound of snickering : a slight, covert, or half-stifled laugh ⟨from innuendo, a dropped word here and there, a sly, meaningful ~ —H.A. Sinclair⟩ ⟨raises in you a ~ of derision, a smile of superiority —J.M.Barzun⟩

snick·er·er \'snik(ə)rə(r)\ *n* -s : one that snickers

snick·er·ing·ly *adv* : in a snickering manner

1snick·er·snee \'snikə(r)¦snē, ,==ˈ=\ *or* **snick and snee** \-kən¦\ *or* **snick–or–snee** \-kə(r)¦\ *vi* [alter. of earlier *steake or snye*, *stick or snee*, fr. D *steken of snijden* to thrust or cut or *steken en snijden* to thrust and cut] *archaic* : to engage in cut-and-thrust fighting with knives

2snickersnee \"\ *or* **snick–a–snee** \-kə\ *or* **snick–or–snee** \-kə(r)\ *n* -s 1 *archaic* : the act or practice of engaging in cut-and-thrust fighting with knives 2 : a large knife or sword

snick·et \'snikət\ *n* -s [³*snick* + -*et*] *dial Eng* : something very small or insignificant of its kind

1snick·le \'snikəl\ *vt* -ED/-ING/-S [origin unknown] *dial Brit* : SNARE, NOOSE

2snickle \"\ *n* -s *dial Brit* : SNARE, NOOSE

snick up *var of* SNECK UP

snid·dle \'snidᵊl\ *n* [ME *snyth hill*; prob. akin to OE *snīthan* to cut — more at SNATH] *dial Eng* : coarse grass or sedge

1snide \'snīd\ *adj* -ER/-EST [origin unknown] 1 a : COUNTERFEIT, SPURIOUS ⟨some contractors use ~ oils knowingly, and . . . some have doped linseed oil palmed off on them —Frederick Maire⟩ b : practicing deception : DISHONEST, CROOKED ⟨taken in by a ~ merchant⟩ c : designed to deceive : TRICKY ⟨this is a ~ bill, full of tricks and man-traps —H.L.Ickes⟩ 2 : MEAN, BASE, LOW, CHEAP ⟨has to take a ~ job in a ~ town —Fannie Hurst⟩ ⟨a ~ trick⟩ 3 : slyly disparaging : subtly derisive : INSINUATING ⟨she makes many a sharp comparison, but never a mean or ~ one —Bernardine Kielty⟩ ⟨draws a line between legitimate reporting and ~ muckraking —Don Weldon⟩ 4 : showing malice ⟨nothing very deep or ~, merely good, clean spoofing —*N.Y.World-Telegram*⟩

2snide \"\ *n* -s : a snide person or thing

sni·der \'snīdə(r)\ *n* -s *usu cap* [after Jacob *Snider* †1866 Amer. inventor] : a breech-loading rifle converted from a muzzle-loading rifle and used in the British military service in the late 1860s and early 1870s

snid·ery \-dərē\ *n* -ES [¹*snide* + -*ery*] : the practice of sly malicious disparagement

1sniff \'snif\ *vb* -ED/-ING/-S [ME *sniffen*; prob. akin to ME *snivelen* to snivel — more at SNIVEL] *vi* 1 a : to draw air audibly up the nose : smell or snuff with short audible inhalations ⟨lifted the lids of pots and pans, ~*ed* appreciatively —Winifred Bambrick⟩ ⟨~ at several perfumes before choosing one⟩; *also* : to clear the nose of mucus by sniffing ⟨got a runny nose and began to ~⟩ b : to make a sniffing noise (as to express disdain) ⟨asked what stipend he might expect, and on being enlightened . . . ~*ed* loudly and disdainfully —Elinor Wylie⟩ 2 : to show or express disdain or scorn : be contemptuous — usu. used with *at* ⟨like all who had read through the four volumes she could ~ at those who knew but the abridged versions —J.D.Hart⟩ 3 : take a curious or suspicious look ⟨turning . . . to politics, he might finance some lunatic group or ~ suspiciously around public libraries —T.D.Parrish⟩ ~ *vt* 1 : to smell or take by inhalation through the nose ⟨a pack of bloodhounds eagerly ~*ing* the ground⟩ : INHALE ⟨threw open the window and ~*ed* the fresh morning air⟩ ⟨addicts who ~ cocaine⟩ 2 : to utter or express with a sniff or with disdain or scorn ⟨men, she ~*ed*, were poor creatures —Laura Krey⟩ 3 : to recognize or detect by or as if by smelling ⟨excelled . . . in ~*ing* trouble before it began — *Times Lit. Supp.*⟩ — often used with *out* ⟨German shepherd dogs are parachuted in the Austrian Alps to ~ *out* survivors of avalanches —P.T.White⟩

2sniff \"\ *n* -s 1 : an act or sound of sniffing ⟨the aspirant must school and steel himself to ~s and sneers —H.L. Mencken⟩ ⟨the coughs, sneezes, and ~s of those who had colds⟩ 2 : a quantity that is sniffed ⟨got a good ~ of sea air⟩ 3 a : MUGGINS 1b b : the first doublet played in the game of muggins

sniff·er \'snifə(r)\ *n* -s : one that sniffs

sniff·i·ly \-fəlē, -li\ *adv* : in a sniffy manner : DISDAINFULLY, SNIFFINGLY ⟨listening to the volume of booing, he said rather ~, "I am not at all impressed" —*Time*⟩

sniff·i·ness \-fēnəs, -fin-\ *n* -ES : the quality or state of being sniffy

sniff·ing·ly *adv* : in a sniffing manner

sniff·ish \'snifish, -fēsh\ *adj* [¹*sniff* + -*ish*] : given to sniffing scornfully : HAUGHTY, DISDAINFUL, SUPERCILIOUS ⟨an essentially aristocratic movement — snobbish, and antidemocratic —H.L.Mencken⟩ — **sniff·ish·ly** *adv* — **sniff·ish·ness** *n* -ES

1snif·fle \'snifəl\ *vi* **sniffled; sniffled; snif·fling** \-f(ə)liŋ\ **sniffles** [freq. of ¹*sniff*] 1 : to sniff repeatedly to prevent mucus running from the nose (as in a cold) 2 : to speak with or as if with sniffling : SNIVEL

2sniffle \"\ *n* -s 1 : an act or sound of sniffling 2 **sniffles** *pl* a : the nasal symptoms (as discharge and congestion) associated with or characteristic of infection of the respiratory tract b : a head cold marked by nasal discharge 3 **sniffles** *pl but usu sing in constr* : bullnose of swine

snif·fler \-f(ə)lə(r)\ *n* -s : one that sniffles

sniffle valve *n* : SNIFTER VALVE

snif·fly \-f(ə)lē, -li\ *adj* : that sniffles

sniffy \'snifē, -fi\ *adj* : inclined to sniff haughtily or scornfully : DISDAINFUL, SUPERCILIOUS ⟨pay tradesmen . . . in the ~ manner of one whose main purpose in arriving at the shop was to take the dog for a walk —*Punch*⟩

snift \'snift\ *vb* -ED/-ING/-S [short for ¹*snifter*] *chiefly dial* : SNIFF

1snif·ter \'sniftə(r)\ *vi* [ME *snifteren*; prob. akin to ME *snivelen* to snivel — more at SNIVEL] *dial* : SNIFF, SNORT, SNUFFLE

2snifter \"\ *n* -s 1 *dial* a : SNIFF, SNORT b **snifters** *pl* : a cold in the head 2 *dial* : a severe wind or storm 3 *Austral* : one that is outstanding : RIPSNORTER 4 a : a small drink of distilled liquor b : a small amount of a narcotic ⟨takes an occasional ~ of opium —*Time*⟩ 5 : an addict who takes cocaine by inhaling it 6 : a large short-stemmed goblet with a bowl narrowing toward the top in which the aroma of brandy can be savored before drinking — called also *inhaler*

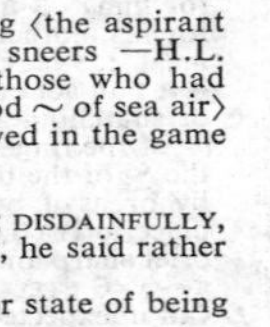
snifter 6

snifter valve *or* **snift·ing valve** *n* 1 : a small valve opening into the atmosphere from a cylinder, from a condenser, or from the air chamber of a steam pump to allow the escape or entrance of air and the release of accumulated water at each stroke of the piston — called also *sniffle valve* 2 : any of various valves (as in an internal combustion engine) resembling a snifter valve

snif·ty \'sniftē\ *adj* 1 : SNIFFY 2 : PETTY, MEAN

1snig \'snig\ *n* -s [ME *snygge*; perh. akin to OE *snægl* snail — more at SNAIL] *dial chiefly Eng* : a small eel

2snig \"\ *vt* **snigged; snigged; snigging; snigs** [origin unknown] 1 *chiefly dial* : to chop off : LOP 2 a *chiefly dial* : to drag jerkily b : to snake or drag (a log) with a rope or chain

1snigger *var of* SNICKER

2snig·ger \'snigə(r)\ *n* -s [prob. alter. of ²*sniggle*] *Brit* : a fish spear or grapple used esp. by salmon poachers

snig·gers \-gə(r)z\ *interj* [alter. of *God's nigs*, euphemism for *God's nails*] *archaic* — used as a mild oath

1snig·gle \'snigəl\ *vb* **sniggled; sniggled; sniggling** \-g(ə)liŋ\ **sniggles** [¹*snig* + -*le*] *vi* : to fish for eels by thrusting the baited hook or needle into their hiding places ~ *vt* 1 : to catch (an eel) by sniggling 2 : CREEP, CRAWL, SNEAK 3 : to catch (as a salmon) by direct snatching with a hook or snare

2sniggle \"\ *n* -s : a device used in sniggling eels; *esp* : a needle to which a line is secured at the middle

3sniggle \"\ *vi* [alter. of *snigger*] *chiefly dial* : SNICKER

snig·gler \-g(ə)lə(r)\ *n* -s : one that sniggles

1snip \'snip\ *n* -s [fr. or akin to D & LG *snip* small piece, snip] 1 a : a small piece that is snipped off ⟨cut a paper into ~s⟩; *also* : something very small : FRAGMENT, PARTICLE, BIT ⟨an essay seasoned with ~s from great poets⟩ b : a cut, incision, or notch made by snipping ⟨an armhole formed by a ~ in the fabric⟩ c : an act or sound of snipping : a single stroke of shears or scissors ⟨with a ~ of his shears⟩ ⟨heard the busy ~ of her scissors⟩ 2 : a small stripe or spot of white on an

animal's face; *esp* : a white spot between the nostrils of a horse **3** *archaic* : TAILOR **4** : a presumptuous or impertinent person (as a saucy girl) : UPSTART, MINX ⟨the little ~ — the nerve of her —Tom Walters⟩ **5** *archaic* : SHARE ⟨let me go ~ with you in this lie —John Dryden⟩ **6** *Brit* **a** : something certain of achievement : a sure thing ⟨it is a ~; we will get both of them, and also the guns —Nevil Shute⟩ **b** : a purchase certain not to disappoint : a good value for the price : BARGAIN, BUY ⟨a real ~⟩ ⟨one small donkey cart . . . a ~ at £15 —*Farmer's Weekly (So. Africa)*⟩

²snip \"\ *vb* **snipped; snipped; snipping; snips** [fr. or akin to D & LG *snippen* to snip; akin to MHG *snipfen* to snap the fingers] *vt* **1** *obs* : to snatch quickly : snap off; *also* : FILCH **2** : to cut with or as if with shears or scissors ⟨~ off the surplus thread⟩; *specif* : to clip suddenly or by bits ⟨~ his budget until it is within his income⟩ **3** *chiefly dial* **a** : to mar by snipping or chipping a piece from : CHIP **b** : CURB, CHECK **4** : to make a snip with (shears or scissors) ~ *vi* **1** : to make a cut with or as if with shears or scissors; *specif* : to make a short quick cut **2** : to make the characteristic short cutting sound of shears or scissors

¹snipe \'snīp\ *n, pl* **snipes** *also* **snipe** [ME, of Scand origin; akin to ON *snīpa* snipe; akin to MD *snippe* snipe, OHG *snepfa*, and prob. to OHG *snabul* beak — more at NEB] **1 a** : any of several game birds (genus *Capella*) that are widely distributed in the New and Old Worlds esp. in marshy areas, resemble but are slenderer than the related woodcocks and like these have very long slender bills with which they probe in mud after worms and other food, and are usu. variegated above with blackish brown, buff, and chestnut and barred on the tail and sides — see GREAT SNIPE, JACKSNIPE, WHOLE SNIPE, WILSON'S SNIPE **b** : any of various usu. slender-billed birds (as a dowitcher or some of the sandpipers and tattlers) of the suborder Charadrii and esp. of the families Charadriidae or Scolopacidae — usu. used with a qualifying term ⟨the red-breasted ~⟩ **2 a** : a contemptible person **b** *slang* : a railway section hand **c** *slang* : an enlisted man in the engineering division of a naval vessel **3** *slang* : a butt of a smoked cigar or cigarette **4** : an outdoor advertising poster **5** : an act of sniping **6** *usu cap* : a racing sailboat approximately 15½ feet long and Marconi sloop rigged

²snipe \"\ *vb* -ED/-ING/-S *vi* **1** : to shoot or hunt snipe **2 a** : to shoot at exposed individuals of an enemy's forces esp. when not in action from a usu. concealed and removed point of vantage ⟨a rifleman missed in mopping up the ridge *sniped* at anyone moving about the camp in an officer's uniform⟩ **b** : to aim a carping or snide attack (as at a competitor) : take damagingly critical or sly swipes ⟨other parties of all political shadings have been *sniping* at his regime —Robert Trumbull⟩ **3** : to post an advertising bill on an available surface (as a post, tree, wall) without permission ~ *vt* **1** : to shoot at from a usu. concealed and removed point of vantage ⟨~ the enemy column from the treetops⟩ **2** : to round the end of (a log) for easy skidding

snipe eel *n* : any of various long very slender deep-sea eels of the family Nemichthyidae having long sometimes recurved beaks — called also *thread eel*

snipefish \'ₛ,ₛ\ *n* : BELLOWS FISH

snipe fly *n* : a fly of the family Rhagionidae

snipe hinge *n* : an early American Colonial furniture hinge consisting of a pair of half-round iron wires doubled back like cotter pins, linked by the eyes, and clinched into the wood at the sharp outer ends

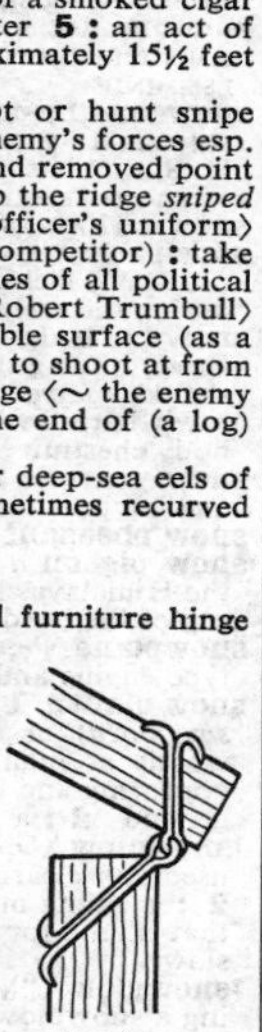

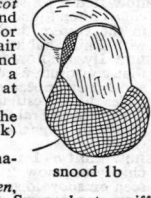

snipe hinge

snipe hunt *n* : a practical joke in which the victim is left in a remote spot holding a bag for fictitious snipe to run into

snipe-nosed \'ₛ,ₛ\ *adj* : SNIPY — used esp. of dogs

snip·er \'snīpə(r)\ *n* -S **1** : one that snipes: as **a** : one that fires at exposed men of an enemy's force **b** : a worker who snipes logs for skidding **2** : a prospector or placer miner who works abandoned claims

snip·er·scope \'ₛₛ,skōp\ *n* **1** : a device based on the principle of the periscope, attached to a rifle near the rear sight and projecting downward into a trench, and used by a soldier to aim and fire his rifle without exposing himself **2** : a snooperscope for use on a rifle or carbine

snip·i·ness \'snīpēnəs, -pin-\ *n* -ES : the quality or state of being snipy

snipped *past of* SNIP

snip·per \'snipə(r)\ *n* -S : one that snips: as **a** : a worker who trims off edges (as of hides or sheet metal) **b** : NICKER

snip·per·snap·per \'snipə(r),snapə(r)\ *n* [origin unknown] : WHIPPERSNAPPER

snip·pet \'snipət, *usu* -əd·+V\ *n* -S [¹*snip* + -*et*] : a small part, piece, or thing; *specif* : a brief literary quotation or quotable passage ⟨on notes ~*s* of information about a few African tribes —*Times Lit. Supp.*⟩

snip·pety \'snipəd·ē, -ətē, -i\ *adj* **1** : that is a snippet : ridiculously small : PETTY **2** : made up of snippets ⟨a rather ~ anthology⟩ **3** : unduly brief or curt : SNIPPY ⟨had been ~ to her former friends since she inherited money⟩

snip·pi·ness \-pēnəs, -pin-\ *n* -ES : the quality or state of being snippy

snipping *n* -S [fr. gerund of ²*snip*] : something snipped off or out : CLIPPING

snip·py \'snipē, -pi\ *adj* -ER/-EST [²*snip* + -*y*] **1** : SHORT-TEMPERED, TART, SNAPPISH **2** : unduly brief or curt : SNIPPETY, FRAGMENTARY **3** : putting on airs : SNIFFY, SUPERCILIOUS

snips \'snips\ *n pl but sing or pl in constr* [²*snip* + -*s*] : hand shears used esp. for cutting sheet metal

¹snip-snap \'ₛ;ₛ\ *adv* [¹*snip* + *snap*] : in a snip-snap fashion : with a snip-snap

²snip-snap \'ₛ,ₛ\ *vi* **1** : to indulge in snip-snap **2** : to make a snip-snap sound

³snip-snap \"\ *n* **1** : a series of snips with shears **2** : clever quick repartee

⁴snip-snap \'ₛ;ₛ\ *adj* : that is or makes a snip-snap : given to snip-snapping : SNIPPY, SNAPPISH

snip·snap·sno·rum \,snip,snap'snōrəm, -nȯr-\ *n* -S [LG *snipp-snapp-snarr, snipp-snapp-snorum*, fr. *snipp* + *snapp* + *snurr, snorum*, interjections used during play] : a game in which one player lays a card on the table, the others in turn must match its rank if able, the first to do so says *snip*, the second *snap*, and the third *snorum*, and the winner is the one who gets rid of all his cards first — called also *Earl of Coventry*

snip·tious \'snipshəs\ *adj* [¹*snip* + -*tious* (as in *pretentious, captious*)] *chiefly dial* : ATTRACTIVE, SMART, FINE

snipy *or* **snipey** \'snīpē, -pi\ *adj* [¹*snipe* + -*y*] **1 a** : resembling a snipe's bill **b** *of an animal* : having a long lean narrow head or muzzle **2** : abounding in snipe

snirl \'snərl\ *vb* [alter. of ²*snarl*] *chiefly Scot* : to curl up : TWIST, SNARL, WRINKLE

¹snirt \'snərt\ *n* [prob. of imit. origin] *chiefly Scot* : an unsuccessfully suppressed snort of laughter

²snirt \"\ *vb, chiefly Scot* : to snort esp. with laughter

snir·tle \'snərtᵊl\ *vi* [freq. of *snirt*] *Scot* : to laugh with snorts : SNIRT

snit \'snit\ *n* -S [origin unknown] : a state of agitation or excitement : STEW ⟨Wall Street brokers were in a ~ because nobody bought stocks —*Information Please Almanac*⟩

¹snitch \'snich\ *vb* -ED/-ING/-ES [origin unknown] *vi* : to give incriminating evidence against someone, esp. an associate : INFORM, TATTLE ⟨a Congressional witness doesn't have to ~ on far-past Red acquaintances if . . . his information serves no legislative purpose —T.R.Ybarra⟩ ~ *vt* [prob. fr. ¹*snatch*, influenced in meaning by ¹*snatch*] : to take by stealth ⟨~ a ride on the back of a streetcar⟩; *specif* : to steal (as something of small value) in a stealthy manner ⟨started out ~*ing* hubcaps and ended up stealing cars⟩ **syn** see STEAL

²snitch \"\ *n* -ES **1** *slang* : NOSE **2** : SNITCHER, INFORMER, STOOL PIGEON

snitch·er \-chə(r)\ *n* -S : one that snitches

snitch knot *n* : a weaving knot made by passing two free ends through a lark's head knot and tying the free ends in an overhand knot

¹snite \'snīt, *usu* -īd·+V\ *n* -S [ME, fr. OE *snīte*] *dial Eng* : SNIPE 1

²snite \"\ *vt* -ED/-ING/-S [ME *sniten*, fr. OE *snȳtan*; akin to MD *snuten* to blow the nose, OHG *snūzen*, ON *snȳta* to blow the nose, OHG *snuzza* nasal mucus — more at SNOT] *dial Brit* : to blow (the nose) without benefit of a handkerchief

snithe \'snīth\ *adj* [fr. obs. E *snithe* to cut, fr. ME *snithen*, fr. OE *snīthan* — more at SNATH] *chiefly dial, of wind or weather* : SHARP, PIERCING

snits *also* **snitz** *var of* SCHNITZ

¹sniv·el \'snivəl\ *vb* **sniveled** *or* **snivelled; sniveled** *or* **snivelled; sniveling** *or* **snivelling** \-v(ə)liŋ\ **snivels** [ME *snivelen, snevelen*, fr. (assumed) OE *snyflan* (whence *snyflung* sniveling); akin to OE *snofl* phlegm, mucus, D *snuffelen* to nose about, snuffle, MD *snof* head cold, MHG *snupfe* head cold, *snūfen, snūben* to snort, ON *snoppa* snout, Gk *nan* to flow — more at NOURISH] *vi* **1** : to run at the nose ⟨played with their noses ~*ing* because it was so early in the morning —John Paris⟩ **2** : to snuff mucus up the nose audibly : SNUFFLE **3** : to cry or whine with snuffling **4** : to speak or act in a whining, sniffling, tearful, or weakly emotional manner ⟨the actual people ~ every bit as piously as in the gravest legend —Bruce Lancaster⟩ ~ *vt* **1** : to bring into a specified or implied condition by sniveling **2** : to utter or express with or by sniveling ⟨don't come ~*ing* you'd like to go back with the pilot —Marguerite Steen⟩

²snivel \"\ *n* -S [ME *snevel*, fr. *snivelen, snevelen*, v.] **1** *archaic* : mucus in or from the nose **2** **snivels** *pl, dial* : HEAD COLD **3** : an act or instance of sniveling

sniv·el·er \-v(ə)lə(r)\ *n* -S : one that snivels; *esp* : a whiny or weakly emotional person

sniv·ely *or* **sniv·el·ly** \-v(ə)lē\ *adj* : marked by sniveling : weakly sentimental : TEARFUL, WHINY

SNLR *abbr* services no longer required

SNO *abbr* **1** senior naval officer **2** senior navigation officer

¹snob \'snäb\ *vi* [ME *snobben*, of imit. origin] *archaic* : to sob violently

²snob \"\ *n* -S [perh. alter. (influenced by ¹*snip* "tailor", with which it appeared in alliterative phrases) of *cobbler*] **1** *dial Brit* **a** : SHOEMAKER, COBBLER **b** : a shoemaker's apprentice **2 a** *archaic* : a person not belonging to the upper classes : one not an aristocrat : COMMONER, PLEBEIAN **b** : one who blatantly imitates, fawningly admires, or vulgarly seeks association with those he regards as his superiors ⟨a ~ . . . would put up with any affront . . . would ignore any rebuff . . . would swallow any rudeness to get asked to a party he wanted to go to —W.S.Maugham⟩ **c** (1) : one who tends to rebuff the advances of those he regards as inferior : one convinced of his superiority : one inclined to social exclusiveness ⟨a wealthy ~ . . . who was anxious to pursue his family tree —Wallace Clare⟩ ⟨incurable old-fashioned ~*s* who regard trade as beneath the dignity of their family —G.B.Shaw⟩ (2) : one rightly or esp. wrongly convinced of his superior knowledge or taste within a field or of the intrinsic superiority of his field of interest or hobby ⟨every seat taken by music lovers (not musical ~*s*) —Janet Flanner⟩ ⟨all of us, except a few academic ~*s*, know full well that a Ph.D. is no indication of good teaching —S.H.Horton⟩ **3** : a game based on cricket and played typically with a stick for a bat and a soft ball

³snob \"\ *vt* **snobbed; snobbed; snobbing; snobs** : to look down upon : SNUB

snob appeal *n* : qualities in a product (as high price, rarity, foreign origin, or association with an elite) that appeal to the snobbery in a purchaser ⟨whatever advantage the domestic has in price is offset by the imported's *snob appeal* —Barrett McGurn⟩ ⟨the *snob appeal* of articles made in the home of a former court attendant —Virginia A. Oakes⟩

snob·bery \'snäb(ə)rē, -ri\ *n* -ES [²*snob* + -*ery*] **1** : the quality of being snobbish : snobbish conduct or display : SNOBBISHNESS **2** : an instance of snobbish conduct or opinion; *also* : a snobbish trait of character ⟨the *snobberies* of empty, albeit high-sounding nomenclatures, from overseas —H.L.Mencken⟩

snob·bish \-bish, -bēsh\ *adj* : of, relating to, characteristic of, or befitting a snob — **snob·bish·ly** *adv* — **snob·bish·ness** *n* -ES

snob·bism \'snä,bizəm\ *n* -S : SNOBBERY

snob·by \-bē, -bi\ *adj* : SNOBBISH

snob·dom \'snäbdəm\ *n* -S : SNOBS

snob·ling \-liŋ\ *n* -S : a young or petty snob

Sno-Cat \'snō,kat, *usu* -ad·+V\ *trademark* — used for a tracklaying vehicle designed for travel on snow

¹snod \'snäd\ *adj* [ME (Sc dial.), perh. of Scand origin; akin to ON *snothinn* bald, *snöggr* shorn, bald — more at NOVACULITE] **1** *chiefly Scot* : SMOOTH, NEAT, TRIM, SLEEK **2** *chiefly Scot* : well-organized : ORDERLY

²snod \"\ *vt* **snodded; snodded; snodding; snods** *chiefly Scot* : to make smooth, neat, or trim : TIDY

snoek \'snük\ *n* -S [Afrik, fr. D, pike, fr. MD *snoec*] *Africa* : any of several vigorous active marine fishes: as **a** : BARRACOUTA **b** : BARRACUDA **c** : SNAKE MACKEREL; *also* : any of several closely related fishes

snoek·ing \-kiŋ, -kēŋ\ *n* -S : fishing for snoek

sno·ho·mish \snō'hōmish, snə'-, -mēsh\ *n, pl* **snohomish** *or* **snohomishes** *usu cap* **1 a** : a Salishan people of the lower Snohomish river valley and Whidbey island, Washington **b** : a member of such people **2** : a dialect related to Skagit

snoke \'snōk\ *var of* SNOOK

snol·ly·gos·ter \'snälē,gästə(r)\ *n* -S [prob. alter. of *snallygaster*] : an unprincipled but shrewd person

¹snood \'snüd\ *n* -S [fr. (assumed) ME, fr. OE *snōd*; akin to Old Gutnish *snōth* cord, OIr *snāth* thread, OE *nǣdl* needle — more at NEEDLE] **1 a** *Scot* : a fillet or band for the hair of a woman and esp. of an unmarried woman **b** : a net or fabric bag for confining a woman's hair pinned or tied on at the back of the head and sometimes attached to the back edge of a hat **2** : SNELL **3** : a fleshy protuberance at the base of the bill of a turkey

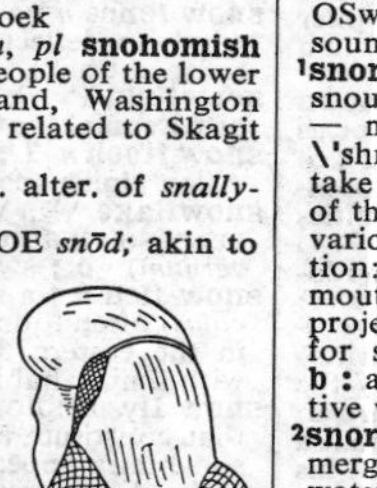

snood 1b

²snood \"\ *vt* -ED/-ING/-S **1** : to bind (the hair) with a snood **2** : to fasten (a hook) with a snell

snood·ing \-diŋ\ *n* -S [¹*snood* + -*ing*] : material for a snell

¹snook \'snük\ *vi* -ED/-ING/-S [ME *snoken*, prob. of Scand origin; akin to Norw & Sw *snoka* to sniff around, obs. Dan *snoge*, ON *snaka* — more at SNATCH] **1** *dial* : to pry about esp. while sniffing and smelling **2** *dial* : SNEAK

²snook \'snük, 'snůk\ *n, pl* **snook** *or* **snooks** [D *snoek* pike, snook, fr. MD *snoec* pike] **1 a** : a large vigorous marine percoid sport and food fish (*Centropomus undecimalis*) resembling a pike and widely distributed in warm seas — called also *robalo, sergeant fish* **b** : any of various other fishes of the family Centropomidae **2** [Afrik *snoek*, fr. D, pike] : SNOEK **3** : COBIA **4** : any of several needlefishes **5** *Austral* : a barracuda (*Sphyraena novae-hollandiae*)

³snook *dial past of* SNEAK

⁴snook \'snůk, 'snük\ *n* -S [origin unknown] : a gesture of derision consisting of a thumbing of the nose — usu. used in the phrase *cock a snook* ⟨small boy . . . consoles himself by cocking a ~ at the policeman's back —Joyce Cary⟩

¹snook·er \'snůkə(r)\ *n* -S [origin unknown] **1** *also* **snooker pool** : pool played with fifteen red balls having a value of one each and six variously colored balls having values of from 2 to 7 respectively on which the striker may play only after pocketing a red ball **2** : a ball that lies in the way of an opponent's direct shot in the game of snooker — often used in the phrase *lay a snooker*

²snooker \"\ *vt* -ED/-ING/-S **1** : to prevent (an opponent) from making a direct shot in the game of snooker by striking a ball so that it rests between the cue ball and the ball he is to play on **2** : THWART, DEFEAT

¹snool \'snül\ *n* -S [origin unknown] *Scot* : a cringing person

²snool \"\ *vb* -ED/-ING/-S *vt, Scot* : to reduce to submission : COW, BULLY ~ *vi, Scot* : CRINGE, COWER

¹snoop \'snüp\ *vb* -ED/-ING/-ES [D *snoepen* to buy or eat something on the sly, eat sweets, fornicate; akin to Fris *snobje* to buy sweets, Norw *snopa* to eat sweets, throw money away on sweets, ON *snoppa* snout, *snapa* to snuffle, snap — more at SNAP] *vi* : to look or pry in a sneaking or meddlesome manner : search intrusively or pryingly ⟨interception of telephone conversations . . . is an intrusion into the home . . . because its purpose and effect is to ~ into what goes on in the home —Wayne Morse⟩ ~ *vt* : to pry into, search for, or doggedly or exhaustively search out and examine the affairs, activities, or contents of ⟨knew he was around, they had ~*ed* him for days —Fletcher Pratt⟩

²snoop \"\ *or* **snoop·er** \-pə(r)\ *n* -S : one that snoops: as **a** : a prying meddler ⟨neighborhood ~*s* began gossiping —*Time*⟩ **b** : one employed as an inspector, investigator, detective, or spy ⟨a wartime censor — one of the 15,000 *snoopers* who . . . opened your mail —Mary Knight⟩ ⟨an increased number of *snoopers* dogging him —Joseph Wechsberg⟩ **c** : an airplane working alone to search out, observe, and sometimes attack targets

snoop·er·scope \'ₛₛₛ,skōp\ *n* : a device that enables a person to see an object obscured (as by darkness) by the use of infrared radiation sent out from the device and reflected back to it from the object to produce a visible image on a fluorescent screen

snoop·ery \'snüpərē\ *n* -ES : the act or practice of prying or meddling into the affairs of others ⟨reading the published letters of famous men . . . is legitimized and justifiable ~ —J.D. Adams⟩

snoopy \-pē, -pi\ *adj* -ER/-EST : given to snooping esp. for personal information about others that is not one's own concern ⟨the aloof but ~ master of thirty thousand employees —Brendan Gill⟩ **syn** see CURIOUS

snoose \'snüs, 'snüz\ *n* -S [Sw, Dan, & Norw *snus*, short for Sw & Dan *snustobak* & Norw *snustobakk* respectively, fr. Sw *snusa* to sniff, snuff & Dan & Norw *snuse* + Sw & Dan *tobak* tobacco & Norw *tobakk*] *dial* : SNUFF

¹snoot \'snüt, *usu* -üd·+V\ *n* -S [ME *snute* — more at SNOUT] **1 a** : SNOUT **b** *slang* : NOSE ⟨an overpowering compulsion to bust each other on the ~ —H.H.Martin⟩ **2 a** : a grimace expressive of contempt or disgust (made as ~ at us) **b** : SNOOK ⟨little boys making ~*s* across the fence —W.A.White⟩ **3** : a snooty person : SNOB

²snoot \"\ *vt* -ED/-ING/-S : to treat with disdain : look down one's nose at ⟨the aristocracy snubs the middle class as the middle class ~*s* the workers —*New Republic*⟩

snoot·ful \'ₛ,fůl\ *n* -S : enough alcoholic liquor to cause drunkenness ⟨afraid he'd get a real ~ if he had any more —Syd Bennington⟩

snoot·i·ly \'snü|dᵊlē, |t|, |ᵊli, |əl-\ *adv* : in a snooty manner

snoot·i·ness \|ēnəs, |in-\ *n* -ES : the quality or state of being snooty

snooty \'snüd·ē, -ütē, -i\ *adj* -ER/-EST [¹*snoot* + -*y*] : haughtily or arrogantly contemptuous : SUPERCILIOUS, SNOBBISH

snoove \'snüv\ *vi* [fr. earlier Sc *snoove* to twirl, turn, of Scand origin; akin to ON *snūa* to turn, twist; akin to OE *snūd* speed, haste, OHG *sniumi* hasty, rapid, Goth *sniumjan* to hurry, L *nēre* to spin — more at NEEDLE] : to walk smoothly and steadily : make a steady advance

¹snooze \'snüz\ *vi* -ED/-ING/-S [origin unknown] : to take a nap : DOZE, DROWSE **syn** see SLEEP

²snooze \"\ *n* -S : a short sleep : NAP ⟨settling himself deliberately for a ~ —Joseph Conrad⟩

snooz·er \-zə(r)\ *n* -S **1 a** : one that snoozes **b** : FELLOW, SCAMP **2** : ¹DOM PEDRO

snoo·zle \-zəl\ *vb* **snoozled; snoozled; snoozling** \-z(ə)liŋ\ **snoozles** [prob. fr. ¹*snooze* + -*le*] **1** *chiefly dial* **a** : CUDDLE, SNUGGLE **b** : NUZZLE **2** *chiefly dial* : DOZE

snoozy \'snüzē, -zi\ *adj* -ER/-EST : inclined to snooze : DROWSY

sno·qual·mie \snō'kwälmē, snə'-\ *n, pl* **snoqualmie** *or* **snoqualmies** *usu cap* [Snoqualmie *sdokwalbiuqᵘ*] **1 a** : a Salishan people of the Snoqualmie and Skykomish river valleys of west central Washington **b** : a member of the Snoqualmie people **2** : a dialect related to Skagit

¹snore \'snō(ə)r, -ō(ə)r, -ōə, -ȯ(ə)\ *vb* -ED/-ING/-S [ME *snoren*; akin to MLG & D *snorren* to drone, hum, MD *snarren* to drone, hum, MLG & MHG, to rattle, gossip, MHG *snerren* to chatter, gossip] *vi* **1** *chiefly Scot* : SNORT **2** : to breathe during sleep with a rough hoarse noise due to vibration of the uvula and the soft palate **3 a** : to make a sound as of snoring : ROAR, RUMBLE **b** *of a ship* : to cut the waves with a roar ⟨*snoring* along in a good twelve-knot breeze —Vincent McHugh⟩ **4** *dial* : DECLARE — used in the expression *I snore* ⟨I ~ I don't think there's much difference —T.C.Haliburton⟩ ~ *vt* **1** : to spend in snoring — used with *away* or *out* ⟨*snored* away the interval between their own arrival and that of the expected repast —Sir Walter Scott⟩ **2** : to utter with a snore

²snore \"\ *n* -S [ME, fr. *snoren*, v.] **1** : an act of snoring **2** : a noise of or as if of snoring ⟨the deep ~ of distant traffic —Margery Allingham⟩

snor·er \'snōrə(r), 'snȯr-\ *n* -S [ME, fr. *snoren* to snore + -*er*] : one that snores

snoring disease *n* : nasal granuloma of cattle and other ruminants usu. held identical to nasal schistosomiasis

snork \'snȯ(ə)rk, 'snȯ(ə)k\ *n* -S [fr. E dial. *snork* to snort, snore; akin to MD & MLG *snorken* to snore, MHG *snarchen*, OSw *snarka*, ME *snoren* — more at SNORE] *dial Eng* : a snoring sound : SNORT

¹snor·kel \'snȯrkəl, -ȯ(ə)k-\ *n* -S [G *schnorchel*, fr. G dial; snout, fr. *schnorchen* to snore, fr. MLG *snarchen* to snore — more at SNORK] **1** *or* **schnor·kel** *also* **schnor·chel** \'shnȯrkəl, -ȯ(ə)k-\ : a tube or pair of tubes housing air intake and exhaust pipes that can be extended above the surface of the water for operating submerged submarines **2** : any of various devices resembling a snorkel in appearance or function: as **a** : a plastic breathing tube fitted at one end with a mouthpiece and at the other with a valve that admits air when projecting above water and closes when submerged and used for swimming near the surface with the head underwater **b** : an air intake tube projecting above water on an automotive vehicle designed to travel submerged

²snorkel \"\ *vi* -ED/-ING/-S **1** *of a submarine* : to operate submerged on diesel engines with only a snorkel showing above water **2** : to swim near the surface of the water with submerged face breathing through a snorkel

¹snort \'snȯ(ə)rt, -ȯ(ə)t, *usu* -d·+V\ *vb* -ED/-ING/-S [ME *snorten*; prob. akin to ME *snoren* to snore — more at SNORE] *vi* **1 a** : to force air violently through the nose with a rough harsh sound ⟨a drover's pony . . . sipped the water, ~*ing* at its own shadow —Alice Duncan-Kemp⟩ **b** : to express scorn, anger, indignation, or surprise by a snort ⟨has been known to ~ impatiently at public acknowledgments of his skill —R.L. Taylor⟩ **2** *obs* : SNORE **3 a** : to emit explosive sounds like or in the manner of a snort ⟨the bleating and ~*ing* lyricism of the saxophone —F.J.Mather⟩ **b** : to travel with snorting or roaring sounds ⟨an old car was ~*ing* along the road without a muffler —Elizabeth Pollet⟩ ⟨the first iron horse that ever ~*ed* up these mountains —A.W.Long⟩ ~ *vt* **1** : to utter with or express by a snort ⟨the horse ~*ed* his relief at the removal of the heavy, burdened saddle and accouterments —Zane Grey⟩ **2** : to expel or emit with or as if with snorts ⟨a horse ~*ing* grass pollen out of his nostrils —H.L.Davis⟩ **3** : to inhale (a narcotic drug in powdered form) through the nostrils **syn** see EXCLAIM

²snort \"\ *n* -S **1** : an act or sound of snorting ⟨gave an astonished ~ of laughter —Kay Boyle⟩ ⟨was mingled with deep, hoarse ~*s*, and we knew that we had disturbed one of the big red deer —William Beebe⟩ **2** : a drink of usu. straight liquor taken in one draft **3** *Brit* : SNORKEL 1

snort·er \'snȯr|d·ər, -ȯ(ə)|d·ə(r), |tə-\ *n* -S [¹*snort* + -*er*] **1** : one that snorts **2** *dial Brit* : WHEATEAR **3** : something that is extraordinary, remarkable, or prominent : HUMDINGER ⟨made up his mind to preach the ~ of a sermon —Bruce Marshall⟩ ⟨a real ~ at chess⟩ : as **a** : a violent storm or wind ⟨blizzard wasn't long, but she was a ~ —C.T.Jackson⟩ **b** : a bowled ball in cricket that is exceptionally fast or accurate or difficult to play **4** : SNORT 2 **5** : an exhaust tube projecting above water on an automotive vehicle designed to travel submerged

snort·ing·ly *adv* : in a snorting manner

snorty \|d·ē, |t|, |i\ *adj* -ER/-EST : characterized by or given to snorting

¹snot \'snät, *usu* -äd·+V\ *n* -S [ME, fr. OE *gesnot*; akin to OFris *snotta* nasal mucus, MD & MLG *snotte*, OHG *snuzza*,

Norw *snott* nasal mucus, MIr *snūad* river, Gk *nan* to flow — more at NOURISH] **1 :** nasal mucus — usu. considered vulgar **2 :** a snotty person ⟨don't like young ~s like you —Irwin Shaw⟩

²snot \"\ *vt* -ED/-ING/-S **:** to blow or clear mucus from (the nose) — usu. considered vulgar

snot-rag \ˈ=,=\ *n* **:** HANDKERCHIEF — usu. considered vulgar

¹snot·ter \ˈsnäd·ə(r), -ätə-\ *n* -S [akin to ¹*snot*] *dial Brit* **:** nasal mucus

²snotter \"\ *vi* **1** *dial Brit* **:** to breathe noisily **:** SNORT, SNORE **2** *dial Brit* **:** SNIVEL, SNIFF ⟨stood blubbering and ~*ing* and twisting his hands —Bruce Marshall⟩

³snotter \" *or* **snort·er** \ˈsnȯr\|d·ər, -ȯ(ə)\|d·ə(r, \|tə-\ *n* -S [origin unknown] **:** a flat rope usu. of sennit secured to a yardarm to which a tripping line is bent and used to strip the lower lift and brace from the yardarm in sending down topgallant and royal yards in a ship of war **2 :** a loop or ring of rope or metal for receiving the lower end of a sprit

¹snot·ty \ˈsnäd·ē, -ätē, -i\ *adj* -ER/-EST [¹*snot* + -*y*] **1 :** foul with nasal mucus **:** VISCOUS, SLIMY **2 a :** meanly contemptible ⟨~ little scion of a degenerate family —Laurent Le Sage⟩ **b :** exhibiting unjustified or exaggerated pride **:** SNOOTY, SUPERCILIOUS ⟨you were so ~ when I called you up, I was afraid to talk to you —Dorothy Parker⟩

²snotty *or* **snot·tie** \"\ *n, pl* **snotties :** a midshipman, esp. in the British navy

snotty nose *n* **:** nasal myiasis of sheep

snotty-nosed \ˌ=ˈ=ˈ=\ *also* **snot-nosed** \ˈ=ˈ=\ *adj* **1 :** having a nose running or fouled with nasal mucus **2 :** small and contemptible **:** SNOTTY

snot·ziek·te \ˈsnȯt,zēktə\ *n* -S [Afrik *snotsiekte* (formerly spelled *snotziekte*), fr. *snot* nasal mucus (fr. MD *snotte*) + *siekte* disease, sickness — more at SNOT, LAMSIEKTE] *southern Africa* **:** malignant catarrh of cattle

snouch \ˈsnau̇ch\ *vt* -ED/-ING/-ES [origin unknown] **:** SNUB

¹snout \ˈsnau̇t, *usu* -au̇d·+V\ *n* -S [ME *snute, snoute;* akin to MD *snute* snout, G *schnauze*, Norw *snut* snout, and prob. to OHG *snuzza* nasal mucus — more at SNOT] **1 a** *obs* **:** the trunk of an elephant **b :** the long projecting nose of any of various mammals (as a swine); *also* **:** the anterior prolongation of the head of various animals ⟨a weevil with a long ~⟩ **:** ROSTRUM **c :** the human nose esp. when large or grotesque ⟨over the gruesomely fattened ~, her scarlet eyes stared —Jean Stafford⟩ **2 :** something resembling an animal's snout in position, function, or shape: as **a** (1) **:** PROW (2) **:** the projecting front of an automotive chassis **b** (1) **:** NOZZLE (2) **:** MUZZLE **c :** a projecting mass of rock **:** PROMONTORY **d :** the terminal face of a glacier

²snout \"\ *vb* -ED/-ING/-S *vt* **:** to furnish with a snout, nozzle, or point ~ *vi* **:** to dig with or as if with a snout **:** GRUB ⟨~*ed* into pails and old crocks in the back yard —Paul de Kruif⟩

snout beetle *n* **:** a beetle of the group Rhynchophora — see WEEVIL

snout butterfly *n* **:** a butterfly of the family Libytheidae having very long palpi carried extended in front of the head

snout·ish \ˈsnau̇d\|ish, -au̇t\|, \|ēsh\ *adj* **:** SNOUTLIKE ⟨a gross heavy face with a ~ look⟩

snout·less \ˈsnau̇tləs\ *adj* **:** having no snout

snoutlike \ˈ=,=\ *adj* **:** resembling a snout

snout machine *n* **:** a boring machine or mill in which the cutting tools are carried directly by the spindle without the interposition of a boring bar and the spindle is supported along its entire length by a projecting boss

snout mite *n* **:** any of numerous active slender usu. reddish mites (family Bdellidae) with well-developed and prolonged rostrum

snout moth *n* **:** a moth of the family Pyralididae; *broadly* **:** any of various moths mostly of this or related families having the labial palpi held out forward like a snout

snouty \ˈsnau̇d·ē, -au̇tē, -i\ *adj* -ER/-EST **1 :** SNOUTLIKE **2 :** having a snout and esp. a prominent or remarkable one ⟨the ~ little creatures became a symbol of pamperedness —*New Yorker*⟩

¹snow \ˈsnō\ *n* -S *often attrib* [ME *snaw, snow,* fr. OE *snāw;* akin to OHG *snēo* snow, ON *snær, snjōr,* Goth *snaiws,* L *niv-, nix,* Gk *nipha* (acc.), Lith *sniēgas*] **1 a :** small tabular and columnar white transparent often branched crystals of frozen water that are formed directly from the water vapor of the air at a temperature of less than 32°F and belong to the hexagonal system of crystallization **b** (1) **:** a descent or shower of snow crystals **:** SNOWFALL ⟨another big ~ fell the next day —Bruce Siberts⟩ (2) **:** a usu. consolidated mass of fallen snow crystals ⟨play in the ~⟩ (3) **:** a region or area covered with snow and often with permanent snow — usu. used in pl. ⟨the high ~s⟩ **2 :** something resembling snow (as in whiteness, coldness, or transitoriness): as **a :** a dessert made of stiffly beaten whites of eggs, sugar, and fruit pulp ⟨apple ~⟩ **b :** white hair — often used in pl. **c :** any of various congealed or crystallized substances resembling snow in appearance ⟨carbon dioxide ~⟩ ⟨very finely granulated copper sulfate ~⟩ **d** *slang* **:** COCAINE **e :** small transient light or dark spots on a television or radar screen resulting from the same causes as those that produce static in radio **3 :** a period of time consisting of one winter with or without the accompanying seasons — used chiefly in a representation of Amerindian speech ⟨forty ~s ago⟩

²snow \"\ *vb* **snowed** *or dial* **snew; snowed; snowing; snows** [ME *snawen, snowen,* fr. *snaw, snow,* n.] *vi* **1 :** to fall in or as snow — usu. used with *it* ⟨it had been ~*ing* all day⟩ **2 a :** to fall in the manner of snow ⟨soot ~*s* in my face —Isaac Rosenfeld⟩ **b :** to descend or become distributed in great quantities ⟨telegrams began to ~ on Congress —T.H.White b. 1915⟩ ~ *vt* **1 :** to cause to fall like or as snow ⟨watching the rhododendron ~ its petals on the dark pool —D.C.Peattie⟩ **2 a** (1) **:** to cover with or as if with snow **:** bury in or as if in snow — usu. used with *over* or *under* ⟨cars ~*ed* under by drifts⟩ (2) *slang* **:** to deceive, persuade, or charm glibly (as by the presentation of a large amount of information that is hard to check or the relation of fictitious exploits) ⟨remembered that a Marine should "~" his girl, and started telling her about his campaigns —Dan Levin⟩ **b :** to shut in or imprison with snow — used with *up* or *in* ⟨in the hidden valleys, whole families who, ~*ed* up, never set foot outside their houses from September to May —F.M.Ford⟩ **3 :** to whiten like snow ⟨hair ~*ed* by age⟩

³snow \"\ *n* -S [modif. of D *snauw,* prob. fr. LG *snau* beak, snout, snow (vessel); akin to MD *snauwen* to snap at, bite, MLG *snouwen* to snap at, MHG *snöuwen, snouwen* to snort, snap at, and perh. to MHG *snūben, snūfen* to snort — more at SNIVEL] **:** a square-rigged ship that differs from a brig in having a trysail mast close abaft the mainmast

snow apple *n* **:** MUSHROOM

snow azalea *n* **:** an evergreen shrub (*Rhododendron mucronatum*) with white flowers and bristly shoots

¹snowball \ˈ=,=\ *n* [ME, fr. *snow* + *ball*] **1 a** (1) **:** a small round mass of snow pressed into shape in the hand for throwing (2) **:** a large round mass of snow formed by rolling in snow until the desired size is attained **b :** shaved ice molded into a ball and flavored with fruit or other syrup **2** *also* **snowball bush :** any of several cultivated white-flowered shrubs of the genus *Viburnum* (as the guelder rose or the Japanese snowball) **3 :** something that snowballs ⟨watch the toll of the steel strike begin to mount in a ~ of statistics —*Christian Science Monitor*⟩

²snowball \"\ *vb* -ED/-ING/-S *vt* **1 :** to pelt with snowballs **:** throw snowballs at **2 :** to cause to increase or multiply at a rapidly accelerating rate ⟨helped the newly built organization to ~ its political influence —L.G.Reynolds⟩ ~ *vi* **1 :** to engage in throwing snowballs ⟨little boys, too, were ~*ing* —Virginia Woolf⟩ **2 a :** to increase, accumulate, expand, or multiply at a rapidly accelerating rate ⟨discontent would grow, sabotage increase, passive or overt resistance ~ —F.H.Hartmann⟩ ⟨the differences may ~ into a heated public controversy —*Current History*⟩ **b :** to progress rapidly and with great momentum

snowball cactus *n* **:** any of several cacti that have a covering of long cottony hairs

snowbank \ˈ=,=\ *n* **:** a mound or slope of snow

snow banner *n* **:** a stream of snow blown into the air from a mountain peak that is often pinkish and several miles in horizontal extent

snow bear *n* **:** RED BEAR

snowbell \ˈ=,=\ *n* **:** any of several plants of the genus *Styrax; esp* **:** a shrub or small tree (*S. grandifolia*) of the southeastern U. S. with showy clusters of fragrant white flowers

snowberry \ˈ=,- — *see* BERRY\ *n* **1 :** any of various shrubs of the genus *Symphoricarpos* that have white berries; *esp* **:** a low-growing No. American shrub (*S. albus*) with pink flowers in small axillary clusters **2 :** BLOLLY **2 3 :** CREEPING SNOWBERRY

snowbird \ˈ=,=\ *n* **1 a :** SNOW BUNTING **b :** a finch of the genus *Junco* **c :** FIELDFARE **d :** IVORY GULL **2 a** *slang* **:** a cocaine addict **b :** SKIER **3 :** one of a class of sailing dinghies of about 12 feet in length

snow blanket *n* **:** a surface accumulation of snow that serves to protect and water underlying vegetation

snow blight *n* **:** a disease of conifer seedlings caused by a fungus (*Phacidium infestans*) that attacks the needles under the snow, causes them to turn brown, and covers them with white mycelium

snow-blind \ˈ=ˈ=\ *or* **snow-blinded** \ˈ=ˈ=\|=\ *adj* **:** affected with snow blindness

snow blindness *n* **:** inflammation and photophobia caused by exposure of the unprotected eyes to ultraviolet rays reflected from fields of snow or ice ⟨suffering the excruciating agony of *snow blindness* after two weeks of futile searching in the empty plains —Farley Mowat⟩

snowblink \ˈ=,=\ *n* **:** a white glare in the sky over a snowfield that is brighter than iceblink

snowblower \ˈ=,==\ *n* **:** a machine using blasts of air to remove snow (as from a highway or railroad)

snow boot *n* **:** a boot reaching to the ankle or above for wear in snow

snowbound \ˈ=,=\ *adj* **:** shut in or blockaded by snow

snowbreak \ˈ=,=\ *n* **1 :** a melting of snow **:** THAW **2 a :** a breaking of trees by snow **b :** an area over which there has been such breakage **3 :** a protective barrier (as of planted trees along a highway or railroad) against drifting snow

snowbridge \ˈ=,=\ *n* **:** a bridge of snow across a crevasse in a glacier

snow-broth \ˈ=,=\ *n* **1 :** mixed snow and water **2 :** newly melted snow

snowbrush \ˈ=,=\ *n* **:** any of several white-flowered shrubs of the genus *Ceanothus; esp* **:** a spreading shrub (*C. velutina*) of the mountainous western U.S. with dark green cinnamon-scented leaves and abundant panicles of small white flowers

snow bunny *n* **:** a person and esp. a girl who is a beginner in skiing

snow bunting *n* **:** a finch (*Plectrophenax nivalis*) of northern regions that is related to the longspurs, breeds in the arctic regions, in winter often appears in large flocks both in Europe and the U. S. esp. during snowstorms, and has largely white plumage with upper parts usu. overcast with brown and red during winter and during the summer in the male with black — called also *snowflake*

snowbush \ˈ=,=\ *n* **:** a Polynesian shrub (*Breynia nivosa*) of the family Euphorbiaceae cultivated for the white and green mottled foliage of one of its horticultural varieties

snowcap \ˈ=,=\ *n* **1 :** a covering cap of snow (as on a mountain peak) **2 :** a very small Central American hummingbird (*Microchera albo-coronata*) having a shining white crown — **snow-capped** \ˈ=ˈ=\ *adj*

snow cock *or* **snow chukar** *n* **:** any of several large gallinaceous birds of the genus *Tetraogallus* living almost exclusively above timber line in the mountains of central and western Asia — see HIMALAYAN SNOW COCK

snow crab *n* **:** a specially equipped railroad car that draws snow from the sides of a track onto the track so that it may be thrown further to the side by a rotary plow

snowcraft \ˈ=,=\ *n* **:** skill and experience in judging snow conditions and behavior useful esp. for travel in mountainous regions

snow cup *n* **:** a cup-shaped indentation in snow at high altitudes caused by evaporation

snow devil *n* **:** a column of fine snow blown upward from a surface by the wind

snow·do·nian \(ˈ)snō\|dōnēən, -nyən\ *adj, usu cap* [*Snowdonia,* mountainous area in northwestern Wales + E *-an*] **:** of relating to, or situated in the area of Snowdonia

snowdrift \ˈ=,=\ *n* **1 a :** a bank of drifted snow **b :** drifting snow **2 :** SWEET ALYSSUM

snowdrop \ˈ=,=\ *n* **1 :** a plant of the genus *Galanthus; esp* **:** a bulbous European herb (*G. nivalis*) bearing nodding white flowers that often appear while the snow is on the ground **2 :** WOOD ANEMONE a

snowdrop anemone *n* **:** a Eurasian herb (*Anemone sylvestris*) having ternately cleft leaves and usu. solitary nodding fragrant white flowers

snowdrop tree *n* **1 :** a plant of the genus *Halesia; esp* **:** SILVER BELL **2 :** FRINGE TREE

snow dust *n* **:** snow borne by the wind in fine particles

snow eater *n* **:** CHINOOK 3b

snowed *past of* SNOW

snowfall \ˈ=,=\ *n* **:** a fall of snow; *specif* **:** the amount of snow that falls in a single storm or in a given period

snow fence *n* **:** a barrier stretched across the path of prevailing winds to deflect drifting snow (as from a building, road, or railroad track)

snowfield \ˈ=,=\ *n* **:** a broad level expanse of snow; *esp* **:** a mass of perennial snow as at the head of a glacier

snow finch *n* **1 :** BRAMBLING **2 :** any of several European and Asian alpine sparrows of the genus *Montifringilla*

snowflake \ˈ=,=\ *n* **1 :** a flake or crystal of snow **2 :** SNOW BUNTING **3 a :** a bulbous plant of the genus *Leucojum* (esp. *L. vernum*) **b :** SWEET WILLIAM

snow flea *n* **:** a small black leaping springtail (*Achorutes nivicolus*) often found in early spring on the snow in vast numbers in the eastern U.S.; *broadly* **:** any of several collembolans with similar habits

snow fly *or* **snow insect** *n* **1 :** any of several minute insects that constitute a genus (*Boreus*) of the order Mecoptera and sometimes appear on the snow in great numbers and in the males have vestigial wings but in the female are wingless **2 :** any of several small American stone flies (esp. *Taeniopteryx nivalis* or *Capnella pygmaea*) often seen on snow **3 :** SNOW GNAT

snow gnat *n* **1 :** a wingless crane fly (genus *Chionea*) found chiefly on snow **2 :** a gnat of the family Chironomidae often seen on snow in spring

snow goggles *n* **:** a piece of wood with two narrow slits used esp. by Eskimos for protection against snow blindness

snow goose *n* **:** any of several geese of the genus *Chen* that are usu. white with blackish primaries and a reddish or pinkish bill, breed chiefly in Arctic America, and migrate south — see ROSS'S GOOSE

snow grass *n* **:** any of several Australian grasses of the genera *Agrostis, Danthonia,* or *Poa*

snow grouse *n* **:** PTARMIGAN

snow guard *n* **:** any of several devices to prevent a slide of snow from a sloping roof

snow gum *n* **:** any of several eucalypts growing at higher elevations in Australia

snowhouse \ˈ=,=\ *n* **:** a house built of snow **:** a snow igloo

snow ice *n* **1 :** ice (as in a glacier) formed by the compacting of snow **2 :** whitish porous ice formed by the freezing of half-melted snow or ice

snowier *comparative of* SNOWY

snowiest *superlative of* SNOWY

snow·i·ly \ˈsnōəlē, -li\ *adv* **:** with or as snow

snow·i·ness \-ōēnəs, -ōin-\ *n* -ES **:** the quality or state of being snowy

snowing *pres part of* SNOW

snow-in-summer \ˌ=ˈ==\ *also* **snow-in-harvest** \ˌ=ˈ==\ *n* **:** any of several plants blossoming at harvesttime: as **a :** a mouse-ear chickweed (*Cerastium tomentosum*) with grayish tomentose foliage and rather large white flowers that is sometimes used as a low border about ornamental plantings **b :** a virgin's bower (*Clematis viorna*) of the eastern U. S. sometimes cultivated for its purplish flowers and showy plumose white achenes

snow job *n, slang* **:** a long involved effort at persuasion or deception with a vast amount of information or fictitious exploits ⟨he didn't talk much — no *snow job* about the money he'd had, the cars he'd owned, the women he'd known —*Prison World*⟩

snow knife *n* **:** a broad-bladed curved knife used by Eskimos for cutting and shaping blocks of snow in building snowhouses

snow lemming *n* **:** PIED LEMMING

snow leopard *or* **snow panther** *n* **:** a showily marked large cat (*Felis uncia*) of the high mountains of central Asia with a long heavy pelt that is grayish white irregularly blotched with brownish black in summer and almost pure white in winter

snow·less \ˈ=ləs\ *adj* **:** having no snow ⟨along the ~ ridges of the coast —Freya Stark⟩

snow lichen *n* **:** a cream-colored or pale gray lichen (*Cetraria nivalis*) with finely divided crinkled tips found on soil in high mountain areas of northern New England and the northern Rockies

snow light *n* **:** SNOWBLINK

snow lily *n* **:** GLACIER LILY

snow line *n* **1 :** the lower margin of a perennial snowfield **:** the elevation above which some snow remains throughout the year **2 :** the extreme limit from the equator within which no snow falls unmelted and which varies with physical conditions (as elevation and nearness to the sea)

snow·man \ˈsnō,man, -,maa(ə)n, -mən\ *n, pl* **snowmen 1 :** a representation of a man formed from snow and usu. from snowballs **2 a :** a person that works in or with snow **b :** a specialist in the study of snow **3 :** ABOMINABLE SNOWMAN

snowmelt \ˈ=,=\ *n* **:** water from melting of snow

snow·mo·bile \ˈ=-mō,bēl\ *n* -S [¹*snow* + *automobile*] **:** any of various automotive vehicles for travel on snow

snow mold *or* **snow rot** *n* **1 a :** a disease of cereals caused by a fungus (*Calonectria graminicola*) and characterized by abundant superficial white mycelium when the snow melts **b :** a similar disease esp. of turf grasses caused by a fungus of the genera *Typhula, Sclerotium* or *Fusarium* **2 :** a fungus causing a snow mold

snow mosquito *n* **:** any of several mosquitoes of the far north esp. of the genus *Aedes* with larvae that develop in the water from melting snow

snow mouse *n* **1 :** any of several pale-grayish voles of the Alps and other high mountains of central Europe **2 :** PIED LEMMING

snow-on-the-mountain \ˌ=ˈ==ˈ==\ *n* **1** *dial Eng* **:** SNOW-IN-SUMMER a **2 :** a spurge (*Euphorbia marginata*) of the western U. S. that has showy white-bracted flower clusters and is used as an ornamental

snow owl *n* **:** SNOWY OWL

snowpack \ˈ=,=\ *n* **:** a field of naturally packed snow that ordinarily melts slowly and yields water for irrigation or power during the early summer months

snow partridge *n* **1 :** a Himalayan gallinaceous bird (*Lerwa lerwa*) having the upper half of the legs feathered, the reddish shanks spurred, the upper parts of the body blackish and narrowly barred with white and rufous, and the under parts of the body chestnut **2 :** SNOW COCK **3 :** PTARMIGAN

snow pear *n* **:** a European pear (*Pyrus nivalis*) used esp. for making pear cider

snow pheasant *n* **1 :** SNOW COCK **2 :** EARED PHEASANT

snow pigeon *n* **:** a pigeon (*Columba leuconota*) of Tibet and the Himalayas having the back, neck, and rump white and the top of the head, ear coverts, and tail blackish

snowplane \ˈ=,=\ *n* **:** a snowmobile propelled by an airplane-type engine and pusher propeller

snow plant *n* **1 :** a fleshy bright red saprophytic herb (*Sarcodes sanguinea*) of the family Pyrolaceae growing in coniferous woods at high altitudes on the sierras of California often appearing and blossoming in early spring while snow is on the ground **2 :** a red-snow flagellate (*Chlamydomonas nivalis*)

¹snowplow \ˈ=,=\ *n* [¹*snow* + *plow*] **1 :** any of various devices used for clearing away snow (as from a road or railroad) **2 :** a skiing maneuver consisting of stemming with both skis that is used for coming to a stop, slowing down, or descending slowly

²snowplow \"\ *vi, of a skier* **:** to slow down or stop by executing a snowplow

snowplow turn *n* **:** an elementary skiing turn executed by shifting the weight to the ski opposite to the desired direction of the turn while keeping both skis in snowplow position

snow pudding *n* **:** a pudding made very fluffy and light by the addition of whipped egg whites and gelatin

snow pusher *n* **:** a concave scoop similar to a shovel used to remove snow by pushing on a long handle

snow quail *n* **:** WHITE-TAILED PTARMIGAN

snow roller *n* **:** a mass of snow rolled up by the wind that is usu. cylindrical with concave ends

snow rose *n* **:** a low shrub (*Rhododendron chrysanthum*) of cool regions in northeastern Asia sometimes cultivated for its pale yellow flowers

snows *pl of* SNOW, *pres 3d sing of* SNOW

snow scald *n* **:** a disease of cereals and turf grasses caused by fungi of the genus *Typhula* (esp. *T. gramum*) and characterized by white to gray or black mycelium and by reddish brown sclerotia in the roots, stem bases, and leaf sheaths

snowshed \ˈ=,=\ *n* **1 :** a shelter (as a long structure over an exposed part of a railroad) to protect from snow; *esp* **:** a shelter on a mountain or other slope to afford protection against snowslides **2 :** a watershed supplied largely by snowfalls

snow sheen *n* **:** SNOWBLINK

¹snowshoe \ˈ=,=\ *n* [¹*snow* + *shoe*] **1 :** any of various devices worn in pairs under the shoes to enable a person to walk on soft snow without sinking; *specif* **:** a light oval wooden frame strengthened by two crosspieces, strung with thongs, and attached to the foot **2 :** INDIAN YELLOW 2 **3 :** SNOWSHOE RABBIT

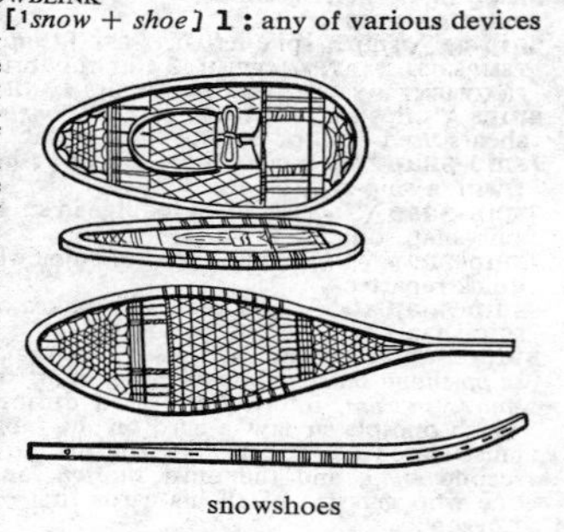

snowshoes

²snowshoe \"\ *vi* -ED/-ING/-S **:** to travel on snowshoes — **snow-shoeing** \ˈ=,==\ *n* -S — **snowshoer** \ˈ=,==\ *n* -S

snowshoe rabbit *n* [so called fr. the large, heavily furred feet in winter pelage] **:** a rather large chiefly northern No. American rabbit (*Lepus americanus*) with large heavily furred hind feet and a coat that is brown in summer but usu. white in winter

snowslide \ˈ=,=\ *n* **:** an avalanche of snow

snow snake *n* **:** an implement in the form of a staff several feet long hurled along ice or snowy ground in a No. American Indian game

snow static *n* **:** static resulting from the passage of a vehicle and esp. an airplane through snow or particles of ice

snowstorm \ˈ=,=\ *n* **1 :** a storm of falling snow ⟨alighted at the station in a raging ~ —Willa Cather⟩ **2 :** something resembling a snowstorm ⟨~*s* of white birds lighted on sandbars —J.M.Brinnin⟩

snowsuit \ˈ=,=\ *n* **:** an outfit for winter wear; *esp* **:** a one-piece or two-piece lined garment similar to a ski suit worn by children

snow sweeper *n* **:** a vehicle or car with revolving brushes for sweeping away snow (as from a road or railroad track)

snowthrown \ˈ=ˈ=\ *adj, of a tree* **:** bent or broken by the weight of snow

snow tire *n* **:** an automotive tire with a tread designed to give added traction on snow or ice

snow train *n* **:** a special train to a ski resort or other place suitable for winter sports

snow trillium *n* **:** EARLY WAKE-ROBIN

snow under *vt* **1 :** to overwhelm beyond the capacity for absorbing or dealing with something ⟨*snowed under* by corre-

spondence and paper work —Raymond Chandler⟩ **2 :** to defeat by a large margin ⟨*snowed* him *under* with some 4000 write-in votes for another candidate —H.H.Martin⟩

snow vine *n* **:** PEPPER VINE 2

snow vole *n* **:** SNOW MOUSE 1

snow water *n* **:** water from melted snow

snow–white \ˈ≈ˌ≈\ *adj* [ME *snawwhit, snowwhit,* fr. OE *snāwhwīt,* fr. *snāw* snow + *hwīt* white — more at SNOW, WHITE] **:** white as snow — **snow–white·ness** *n*

snowworm \ˈ≈ˌ≈\ *n* **:** any of several oligochaete worms of the family Enchytraeidae found living in or on snow

snow wreath *n* **1** *dial Brit* **:** SNOWDRIFT **2 :** a deciduous shrub (*Neviusia alabamensis*) of the family Rosaceae native to Alabama that is cultivated for its white feathery flowers

snowy \ˈsnōē, -ōi\ *adj* -ER/-EST [ME, fr. OE *snāwig,* fr. *snāw* snow + *-ig* -y] **1 a :** composed of snow or melted snow **b :** marked by, abounding in, or covered with snow ⟨the *snowiest* night of the year —Beverly Fields⟩ ⟨~ pastures —H.D.Thoreau⟩ **2 :** whitened by or as if by snow ⟨the ground was still ~ with fallen petals —Ellen Glasgow⟩ **:** SNOW-WHITE ⟨its beaches were of ~ coral sand —C.B. Nordhoff & J.N.Hall⟩

snowy campion *n* **:** a perennial smooth herb (*Silene nivea*) of the eastern U.S. with a much-inflated calyx and white notched petals

snowy egret *or* **snowy heron** *n* **:** a small white egret or heron (*Leucophoyx thula* or *Egretta thula*) that is about two feet long, ranges from the southern U.S. southward to Chile, and was formerly extensively hunted for its aigrettes

snowy lemming *n* **:** PIED LEMMING

snowy orchid *n* **:** a slender fringed orchid (*Habenaria nivea*) of eastern No. America with linear firm keeled leaves and white flowers

snowy owl *n* **:** a large diurnal arctic owl (*Nyctea nyctea*) that enters the northern parts of the U.S. and Europe in winter and has no ear tufts and plumage that is sometimes nearly pure white but usu. with dark brownish spots

snowy plover *n* **:** a small plover (*Charadrius alexandrinus nivosus*) of the Gulf coast and the western parts of the U.S. and Mexico that is light gray above with a dark patch on the crown, sides of the head, and each side of the breast and has the underparts and portions of the head white

snowy tree cricket *n* **:** a pale greenish or whitish yellow tree cricket (*Oecanthus fultoni*) widely distributed in No. America

snoz·zle \ˈsnäzəl\ *var of* SCHNOZZLE

SNP *abbr* soluble nucleoprotein

snr *abbr* senior

¹snub \ˈsnəb\ *vb* **snubbed; snubbed; snubbing; snubs** [ME *snubben,* of Scand origin; akin to ON *snubba* to scold, rebuke, Sw dial., to reproach, cut off; akin to MLG *snubbelen* to chide, and perh. to OHG *snabul* beak — more at NEB] *vt* **1 a :** to check or stop with a cutting retort or remark **:** restrain by reprimanding **:** REBUKE ⟨was quickly *snubbed* when he tried to intercede⟩ **b** *archaic* **:** UPBRAID, SCOLD **c :** to treat with contempt or neglect so as to humiliate or repress **:** ignore with or as if with disdain **:** slight designedly ⟨the ambassador was obviously *snubbed*⟩ ⟨his suggestions were *snubbed*⟩ ⟨whose only concerns were to make history and to ~ the history that had already been made —Jean Stafford⟩; *also* **:** to affect in a specified way by such treatment ⟨*snubbed* into silence⟩ **2 a** *obs* **:** to check or curb the growth or development of **b** *chiefly dial* **:** to break off the end of **:** NIP ⟨~ branches of a tree⟩ **c** *West* **:** DEHORN ⟨~ cattle⟩ **3 a :** to check suddenly (as a rope or chain that is running out) ⟨*snubbed* short, like a downstream trout when fairly hooked —*Century Mag.*⟩ **b :** to increase the tension of (as a rope or belt) by turning around a post, pin, or pulley **:** TAUTEN **c :** to check or restrain the motion of (an animal or thing) by turning an attached line around a post or other available anchoring point ⟨~ a horse to a tree⟩ ⟨as the lariat jerked tight, the rider instantly *snubbed* it tight around the saddle horn —D.A.Brown⟩ **d :** INHIBIT, SUPPRESS, RESTRAIN ⟨air springs *snubbed* out all the undulating motion —*Motor Life*⟩ **e :** to extinguish (a cigarette) by stubbing — usu. used with *out* ⟨*snubbed* the butt out in my saucer —Mickey Spillane⟩ **4 :** to turn the end of (a line) around a post or other available anchoring point **:** tie up short ⟨let the wagons down the steep slope by means of rope *snubbed* around trees —G.R.Stewart⟩ ⟨had *snubbed* the bronc's rein to his saddle horn —Colin Lofting⟩ **5 :** to enlarge (an undercut in a coal mine) by blasting or other means so that the coal rolls forward when it is broken down ~ *vi* **1 :** to snub someone or something **:** give snubs ⟨the ability to ~ and to tell useful fibs —R.H.Rovere⟩ **2 :** to tie up short against a bank or wharf ⟨one by one, the flatboats *snubbed* in at the bank —F.G.Slaughter⟩ ⟨a raft well piloted would outrun a flood and have to ~ up to the bank and wait for the floodwater to catch up —R.G.Lillard⟩ **3 :** to pull a restraining line up taut ⟨when a wind came up, the boat began to ~⟩ ⟨the horse *snubbed* back from the hitchrack⟩ **4 :** to enlarge an undercut in coal mining by blasting or other means so that the coal rolls forward when it is broken down

²snub \"\ *n* -S **1 :** an act or an instance of snubbing; *esp* **:** a rebuff or slight intended to check a person or his activity ⟨accepted every unjust rebuke and ~ as part of the day's routine —R.S.Porteous⟩ **2 a :** something that snubs **b :** SNUBBING POST ⟨no ~ in that corral —A.B.Guthrie⟩ **3** [*³snub*] **:** SNUB NOSE

³snub \"\ *adj* **1 :** used in snubbing ⟨~ rope⟩ ⟨~ line⟩ **2** *or* **snubbed :** BLUNT, STUBBY, STUMPY ⟨allowed a flicker of indulgent amusement to show itself upon his ~ features —Guy McCrone⟩ ⟨a small pyramid . . . a ~ figure, rather flat and inelegant —Isaac Rosenfeld⟩ — **snub·ness** *n* -ES

⁴snub \"\ *vi* **snubbed; snubbed; snubbing; snubs** [alter. of *¹snob*] *chiefly Midland* **:** SOB

⁵snub \"\ *n* -S *chiefly Midland* **:** SOB

snub·ber \ˈsnəbə(r)\ *n* -S **:** one that snubs: as **a :** a miner who breaks down the working face of a coal seam with a pick so that it will drop freely when blasted **b :** a device with a drum and a brake used with a cable for lowering logs or vehicles down a steep grade **c :** a device for snubbing a cable **d :** SHOCK ABSORBER

snub·bi·ness \-bēnəs, -bin-\ *n* -ES **:** the quality or state of being snubby

snubbing *n* -S **:** the act of one who snubs **:** SNUB, REBUKE, REBUFF

snub·bing·ly *adv* **:** in a snubbing manner

snubbing post *n* **:** a post around which a line is thrown to snub something

snub·bish \ˈsnəbish\ *adj, of the nose* **:** somewhat snub — **snub·bish·ness** *n* -ES

snub·by \-bē, -bi\ *adj* -ER/-EST **1 a :** SNUB ⟨a ~ nose⟩ **b :** SNUB-NOSED ⟨an impudent, vulgar, ~ little face —Aldous Huxley⟩ **2 :** giving snubs **:** inclined to snub ⟨a ~ manner⟩

snub nose *or* **snubbed nose** *n* **:** a short blunt nose; *esp* **:** one slightly turned up at the tip

snub–nosed \ˈ≈ˌ≈\ *adj* **:** having a snub nose **:** SNUB ⟨a *snub-nosed* revolver —Erle Stanley Gardner⟩

snub–nosed auklet *n* **:** CRESTED AUKLET

snub–nosed cachalot *n* **:** PYGMY SPERM WHALE

snub–nosed langur *or* **snub–nosed monkey** *n* **:** any of several rather large langurs (genus *Rhinopithecus*) of western China and Tibet that are distinguished by a large fleshy upturned nose

snub pulley *n* **:** a pulley placed to support an empty conveyor belt in its return

snubs *pres 3d sing of* SNUB, *pl of* SNUB

¹snuck \ˈsnək\ *chiefly dial past of* SNEAK

²snuck \"\ *n* -S [alter. of *²snack*] *chiefly dial* **:** SHARE — **go snucks** *chiefly dial* **:** SHARE

¹snudge \ˈsnəj\ *vi* -ED/-ING/-S [origin unknown] **1** *chiefly dial* **:** to be stingy and niggardly **2** *chiefly dial* **:** to cheat esp. in competition **:** FUDGE **3 :** to go about hunched over or as if in deep thought

²snudge \"\ *n* -S *archaic* **:** a niggardly miserly fellow

³snudge \"\ *vi* -ED/-ING/-S [prob. alter. of *²snug*] *chiefly dial* **:** SNUGGLE, NESTLE

¹snuff \ˈsnəf\ *n* -S [ME *snoffe*] **1 :** the charred part of a candlewick **2** *obs* **:** the leavings of a cup or glass of liquor **3 a** *obs* **:** UMBRAGE, PIQUE, OFFENSE — usu. used with *take* **b** *chiefly Scot* **:** a fit of resentment or indignation **:** HUFF

²snuff \"\ *vb* -ED/-ING/-S [ME *snoffen,* fr. *snoffe,* n.] *vt* **1 a :** to crop the snuff of (a candle) by pinching or by the use of snuffers so as to brighten the light **b :** to extinguish by or as if by the use of snuffers **:** make extinct **:** put an end to **:** KILL — usu. used with *out* ⟨just in case automation ~s out their jobs —A.H.Raskin⟩ **2** *obs* **:** CLEANSE, PURIFY ~ *vi* **1 :** to become extinguished — usu. used with *out* ⟨the lighted wick gutters, ~s out —Ernest Beaglehole⟩ **2** *slang* **:** DIE ⟨I'll love 'er till I ~ it —C.J.Dennis⟩ — often used with *out* ⟨what a place to ~ out in —Elizabeth Bowen⟩

³snuff \"\ *vb* -ED/-ING/-S [akin to D *snoffen, snuffen* to sniff, snuff, MD *snuven* to sniff, snuff, *snof* head cold — more at SNIVEL] *vt* **1 :** to draw in forcibly through the nostrils **:** sniff audibly ⟨~ up a solution of salt and water⟩ ⟨~ the fragrance of the clover⟩ ⟨among the irises and roses . . . ~*ing* in . . . the delicious scent —Virginia Woolf⟩ **2 :** to perceive or detect by smelling **:** SCENT, SMELL **3 :** to sniff at in order to examine — used of an animal ~ *vi* **1 :** to inhale through the nose noisily and forcibly **:** sniff or smell inquiringly **2** *archaic* **:** to sniff loudly in or as if in disgust ⟨the enemies of the church rage and ~ —Joseph Hall⟩ **3 :** to chew or inhale snuff **:** take snuff ⟨smoked and ~*ed* almost to the hour of her death —*Irish Digest*⟩

⁴snuff \"\ *n* -S **:** the act of snuffing **:** SNIFF, INHALATION

⁵snuff \"\ *n* -S [D *snuf* (short for *snuftabak,* fr. *snuffen* to sniff + *tabak* tobacco) & *snuif,* short for *snuiftabak,* fr. *snuiven* to sniff (fr. MD *snuven*) + *tabak*] **1 a :** a preparation of pulverized tobacco to be chewed, placed against the gums, or inhaled through the nostrils **b :** the amount of snuff taken at one time **:** PINCH **2 :** SCENT, SMELL, AROMA, ODOR **3** *or* **snuff brown :** MUMMY BROWN 2b — **up to snuff 1** *chiefly Brit* **a :** not easily deceived **b :** SOPHISTICATED, WORLDLY-WISE **2 :** in good shape or normal condition **:** up to an accepted standard ⟨looked more *up to snuff* than he had at any time since he won —G.F.T.Ryall⟩ ⟨one child mentally not *up to snuff* —Andy Logan⟩ ⟨if his judgment of red and green lights isn't *up to snuff* —Frederick Way⟩ ⟨if your work wasn't *up to snuff* . . . you'd hear about it quick enough —W.H.Whyte⟩

⁶snuff \"\ *vt* -ED/-ING/-S [origin unknown] **:** to lightly buff (the grain side of leather) so as to remove grain imperfections

snuff bottle *n* [*⁵snuff*] **:** an often elaborately decorated bottle for holding snuff

snuffbox \ˈ≈ˌ≈\ *n* **1 :** a small box for holding snuff usu. carried about the person **2** *dial Eng* **:** PUFFBALL

snuffbox bean *n* **1 :** a sea bean that is the large seed of a tropical liana **2 :** a plant (*Entada phaseoloides* or *E. scandens*) bearing the snuffbox bean and having tough ropy stems, pinnate leaves ending in a tendril, small spicate flowers, and gigantic sword-shaped woody pods divided into boxlike compartments

snuffbox fern *n* **:** MARSH FERN 1

snuff brush *n, chiefly Midland* **:** a stick or brush used in rubbing snuff on teeth or gums

snuff dipper *n* **:** one that dips snuff

¹snuff·er \ˈsnəfə(r)\ *n* -S [ME *snoffer,* fr. *snoffen* to snuff + *-er*]

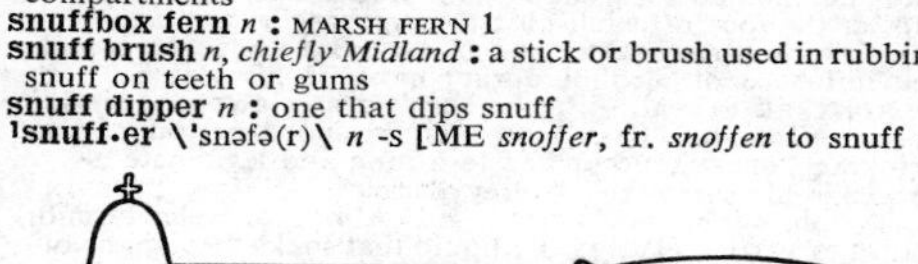

snuffer 1b

1 a : a device somewhat like a pair of scissors for cropping and holding the snuff of a candle when its light grows dim or is extinguished — usu. used in pl. but sing. or pl. in constr. **b :** a device for extinguishing candles consisting of a small hollow cone with a handle attached **2** *archaic* **:** one that snuffs out candles **3 :** a wire used to adjust the wick in a safety lamp — called also *pricker* **4 :** a means for extinguishing an electric arc or preventing ignition by it of combustible material **5 :** a cup-shaped device used for handling incendiary bombs

²snuffer \"\ *n* -S [*³snuff* + *-er*] **1 :** one that inhales esp. audibly through the nostrils **2 :** a user of snuff **3 :** PORPOISE

snuff·i·ness \-fēnəs, -fin-\ *n* -ES **:** the quality or state of being snuffy

¹snuffing *adj* [fr. pres. part. of *³snuff*] **:** that snuffs disagreeably or disdainfully **:** ARROGANT

²snuffing *n* -S [fr. gerund of *²snuff*] *archaic* **:** the snuff of a wick as removed by snuffers — usu. used in pl.

snuff·ing·ly *adv* **:** in a snuffing manner

snuff·ish \ˈsnəfish\ *adj* [*³snuff* + *-ish*] **:** SNIFFISH, TOUCHY

¹snuf·fle \ˈsnəfəl\ *vb* **snuffled; snuffled; snuffling** \-f(ə)liŋ\ **snuffles** [akin to D & LG *snuffelen* to nose about, snuffle — more at SNIVEL] *vi* **1 :** to snuff esp. audibly and repeatedly ⟨the tiny dog *snuffled* hungrily over the meat —T.B.Costain⟩ ⟨took her handkerchief . . . and *snuffled* into it —Jean Stafford⟩ **2 :** to breathe through an obstructed nose with a broken sound ⟨a herd of buffalo stomping and *snuffling* around —Jackson Burgess⟩ **3 a :** to speak in a nasal tone ⟨the old man *snuffled* indistinctly in reply⟩ **b** *archaic* **:** to speak in a canting sanctimonious manner **4 :** to make a sound like a snuffle ⟨the wind *snuffling* at the window⟩ ⟨a teletype ~s intermittently —*Lamp*⟩ **5 :** SNIVEL, WHIMPER ⟨the child merely *snuffled* a little⟩ ~ *vt* **1 :** to snuff up ⟨the wind is warm and the horse ~s it —Millen Brand⟩ **2 :** to snuff out ⟨dogs *snuffling* rabbits⟩ **3 :** to snuff at ⟨old hound that used to ~ your door and moan —R.P.Warren⟩ ⟨a snooping dog *snuffled* the thickets —George Heinold⟩

²snuffle \"\ *n* -S **1 a :** the act or fact of snuffling **b :** the sound made in snuffling ⟨the snort and ~ of the straining oxen —Victor Canning⟩ **2 :** a nasal twang ⟨talked with an adenoidal ~ —Earle Birney⟩ **3 snuffles** *pl* **:** SNIFFLES **4 snuffles** *pl but usu sing in constr* **:** a respiratory disorder in animals marked esp. by catarrhal inflammation and sniffling: as **a :** a contagious disease of rabbits characterized by nasal discharge, sneezing, rubbing of the nose, and gradual emaciation and caused by a bacterium (*Brucella bronchiseptica*) **b :** BULLNOSE 3

snuf·fler \-f(ə)lə(r)\ *n* -S **1 :** one that snuffles **2 :** one that uses cant

snuff·less \ˈsnəfləs\ *adj* [*²snuff* + *-less*] **:** not requiring snuffing ⟨~ candle⟩

snuf·fli·ness \-f(ə)lēnəs, -lin-\ *n* -ES **:** the quality or state of being snuffly

¹snuffling *n* -S [fr. gerund of *¹snuffle*] **1 :** the act of snuffling **2 :** SNUFFLE ⟨the ~s of obtuse furry animals grunting and nosing —Virginia Woolf⟩

²snuffling *adj* [fr. pres. part. of *¹snuffle*] **:** that snuffles; *specif* **:** SANCTIMONIOUS — **snuf·fling·ly** *adv*

snuf·fly \ˈsnəf(ə)lē, -li\ *adj* -ER/-EST [*¹snuffle* + *-y*] **:** SNUFFLING

snuff mill *or* **snuff mull** *n, Scot* **:** SNUFFBOX

snuffs *pl of* SNUFF, *pres 3d sing of* SNUFF

snuff stick *n, chiefly Midland* [*⁵snuff*] **:** SNUFF BRUSH

¹snuffy \ˈsnəfē, -fi\ *adj* -ER/-EST [*³snuff* + *-y*] **1 a :** SULKY, PEEVISH **b :** SHORT-TEMPERED **2 :** inclined to haughtiness **:** SUPERCILIOUS, DISDAINFUL ⟨among his mother's ~ colleagues —W.J.Locke⟩ ⟨a ~ seminary for young ladies —Sylvia T. Warner⟩

²snuffy \"\ *adj* -ER/-EST [*⁵snuff* + *-y*] **1 :** resembling snuff (as in color, consistency, or pungency) ⟨~ brown clothing⟩ ⟨~ soil⟩ **2 a :** addicted to the use of snuff ⟨a ~ old man —Henry Watterson⟩ **b :** having unpleasant habits **:** HORRID, DISAGREEABLE ⟨a singularly unattractive, ~ old man —Dorothy C. Fisher⟩ **3 :** soiled with snuff ⟨~ clothes⟩

snuffy ears *n pl but sing in constr* [*²snuffy*] *Austral* **:** LOOSE SMUT

¹snug \ˈsnəg\ *adj* **snugger; snuggest** [perh. of Scand origin; akin to Sw *snygg* tidy, neat, clean, ON *snöggr* shorn, bald — more at NOVACULITE] **1 a** *of a ship* **:** manifesting seaworthiness (as in design, compactness, or arrangements) **:** adequately prepared for a voyage or esp. for riding a storm **:** TAUT ⟨soon all was ~ aloft, and we were allowed to go below —R. H.Dana⟩ ⟨a comparatively ~ rigged vessel that could leave her three lower sails set in most weather —*Rudder*⟩ **b :** TRIM, NEAT, TIDY — used esp. of a person ⟨a ~ gentleman⟩ **c :** fitting closely but not tightly or uncomfortably **:** not loose or baggy ⟨a ~ coat⟩ ⟨a ~ fit⟩ ⟨install bearing retainer by pressing it on until it is ~ —H.F.Blanchard & Ralph Ritchen⟩ **2 a :** enjoying or affording warm secure shelter, safety from intrusion, and opportunity for placid ease and quiet contentment often in unpretentious quarters or quiet ways ⟨his home . . . the ~ haven to which his adventurous forebears retired at the end of their voyages —*Amer. Guide Series: Maine*⟩ ⟨a town that seems especially ~ in winter —Richard Joseph⟩ ⟨sit in the ~ little parlor —*Irish Digest*⟩ **b :** at rest, warmly covered, and safe from cold ⟨~ and warm under blankets and comforters —Willa Cather⟩ ⟨the fisherfolk were all ~ under thatch —G. W.Russell⟩ **c :** affording safe or protected anchorage ⟨the sailboat enthusiast's paradise of ~ harbors —R.W.Hatch⟩ **d :** compact, neat, orderly, and affording or suggesting comfortable sheltered ease or safe smoothness ⟨~ little shops that once offered Cornhill the best soups and jellies —Rebecca West⟩ ⟨a ~ little commune intent on its own affairs —John Buchan⟩ ⟨the street level was broken by three ~ doorways —Harriet LaBarre⟩ **e :** marked by pleasant ease, conviviality, friendly intimacy or cordiality, and secure privacy ⟨~ little dinners with old friends⟩ **3 a :** assuring or affording a degree of comfort and ease ranging from modest adequacy to gratifying ampleness ⟨a ~ little benefice, worth a hundred gold florins a year —Alan Moorehead⟩ ⟨family influence had installed him in a ~ ecclesiastical berth —H.O.Taylor⟩ ⟨his brother made a ~ fortune —Julian Dana⟩ **b** *chiefly Irish* **:** in comfortable financial circumstances **:** fairly well-to-do **4 a :** resorting to or offering safe concealment or a safe retreat ⟨lie ~ until the chase stops⟩ ⟨a ~ hideout⟩ **b** *dial* **:** marked by or given to secretiveness or taciturn reticence ⟨staying ~ about the arrangement⟩ **syn** see COMFORTABLE, NEAT

²snug \"\ *vb* **snugged; snugged; snugging; snugs** *vi* **1 a** *archaic* **:** to lie close **:** SNUGGLE — often used with *up* or *together* **b :** to move along close to a confining line or surface ⟨a horse *snugging* along the inner rail of the track⟩ **2 a :** to settle or lie down **:** NESTLE; *specif* **:** to go to bed ⟨dragged the old buffalo hide out to the covered wagon again, *snugged* in the hay and pulled all the horse blankets over us —C.T.Jackson⟩ **b :** to put something in a condition to resist a storm or other onslaught (as by lashing down movables) — often used with *down* ⟨with a good motor, one can *snug* down while approaching a harbor —H.A.Calahan⟩ ~ *vt* **1 :** to place in a snug or snuggled-up position **:** cause to fit closely ⟨a belt that ~s the waist⟩ ⟨~ the sole of a shoe to the upper⟩ ⟨overcoat collars turned up and *snugged* close to our necks —S.H. Adams⟩ ⟨she curled up . . . her head *snugged* between her shoulders —D.H.Lawrence⟩ — often used with *down* ⟨found his sons, *snugged* down in a lifeboat, pretending to be castaways —Archie Binns⟩ **2 :** to make snug ⟨push-up sleeves *snugged* by tiny buttons —*Californian*⟩ ⟨tidy up the fields and garden and ~ the place for winter —Hal Borland⟩ — often used with *down, in,* or *up* ⟨*snugged* the farm down for the winter —H.E.Giles⟩ ⟨farmers . . . *snugging* themselves in for the winter —L.C.Douglas⟩ ⟨children were *snugged* up in overcoats, mufflers, and mittens⟩ **3 :** to put away snugly **:** HIDE ⟨pick a pocket and ~ it in a featherbed —W.B.Yeats⟩ **4 a :** to prepare (a ship) for a gale esp. by reducing sail, lowering topmasts, or lashing down movables — usu. used with *down* **b :** to put in a condition to resist a storm or other onslaught — usu. used with *down* ⟨*snugging* down her hatches for the long voyage —W.J.Granbert⟩ ⟨move the aircraft to the parking place and *snug* it down for the night —Nevil Shute⟩ **5 :** to rub (as twine or rope) so as to make smooth and improve the finish

³snug \"\ *adv* **:** SNUGLY, NEATLY ⟨a coat that fits ~ across the shoulders⟩ ⟨in harbor, at night berthed ~ —Thomas Wood †1950⟩

⁴snug \"\ *n* -S *Brit* **:** a small private room or a back room in a public house

⁵snug \"\ *n* -S [prob. alter. of *²snag*] **1** *obs* **:** a jagged projection **2 :** a projecting piece **:** LUG; *esp* **:** one forged under the head of a bolt in order to prevent rotation in screwing up the nut

snug fit *n* **:** a fit (as of mechanical parts) with no allowance **:** the closest fit that can be assembled by hand for parts that are not to move against each other

snug·ger \ˈsnəgə(r)\ *n* -S [*²snug* + *-er*] **:** a device for snugging or making snug

snug·gery \-g(ə)rē, -ri\ *n* -ES [*¹snug* + *-ery*] **1** *chiefly Brit* **:** a snug cozy place ⟨underground *snuggeries* for foxes —W.W. Smith⟩; *esp* **:** a small warm comfortable room ⟨little smoking ~ at the end of the passage —W.F.De Morgan⟩ ⟨the inner room . . . was a perfect ~, with walls two feet thick and outside shutters to close at night and . . . rag rugs, red curtains, and feather cushions within —Flora Thompson⟩ **2** *Brit* **:** a parlor or alcove in a public house **:** SNUG

snug·gies \ˈsnəgēz, -giz\ *n pl* [*¹snug* + *-ies* (pl. of *-ie*)] **:** women's warm knitted undergarments; *esp* **:** pants of this type

snug·gish \-gish\ *adj* [*¹snug* + *-ish*] **:** somewhat snug

¹snug·gle \ˈsnəgəl\ *vb* **snuggled; snuggled; snuggling** \-g(ə)liŋ\ **snuggles** [freq. of *²snug*] *vi* **1 :** to move so as to come near to a person, animal, or thing for warmth or protection or in affection **:** get into or lie in a warm or comfortable position **:** CUDDLE, NESTLE ⟨a baby *snuggling* close to its mother⟩ ⟨~ up in a blanket⟩ ⟨allow aircrews to ~ cozily inside their leaden fuselage —Joseph Wechsberg⟩ ⟨a few houses *snuggling* against a hill⟩ ⟨before he *snuggled* down into the warm domesticity of winter —John Buchan⟩ ~ *vt* **1 a :** to draw (as oneself, one's head, or another) close esp. for comfort or protection or in affection ⟨the dog *snuggled* his muzzle under his master's arm⟩ ⟨kittens *snuggling* a mother cat⟩ **b :** to be or place in a position close to (someone or something) ⟨trapshots used to ~ their cheeks against the combs of their stocks —*Amer. Guide Series: Conn.*⟩ **2 :** to place in a snug position **:** make snug ⟨the ship experiment center is *snuggled* in an out-of-the-way spot —*All Hands*⟩ ⟨*snuggled* the bottle into a lower drawer —David Wagoner⟩

²snuggle \"\ *n* -S **:** the action of snuggling

snug harbor *n* **:** a cozy comfortable retreat; *esp* **:** a home for retired seamen

snug·ly *adv* **:** in a snug manner ⟨pipers, with their beribboned bagpipes ~ tucked —W.B.Ready⟩ ⟨while old tenants have sat ~ in their apartments paying a comparatively small rent —Gerda Luft⟩ ⟨extended series of small incidents that must fit ~ together —Arthur Knight⟩ ⟨music is no longer fitted so ~ to the word as before —Alfred Einstein⟩

snug·ness *n* -ES **:** the quality or state of being snug ⟨a fitted shirt . . . with . . . elastic sides and back for ~ —*Car Life*⟩

snum \ˈsnəm\ *vi* [origin unknown] *chiefly dial* **:** VOW, DECLARE — used in the phrase *I snum*

snurl *var of* SNIRL

snurp \ˈsnərp, -nəp\ *vi* [of Scand origin; akin to Sw *snäipa* to shrivel up, contract, Norw *snerpa,* Dan *snerpe;* akin to OHG *snerfan* to contract, shrivel up, ON *snarpr* rough, sharp, Goth *atsnarpjan* to touch, and perh. to OE *nearu* narrow — more at NARROW] *dial Eng* **:** to contract into a shriveled form **:** go to pieces

snuz·zle \ˈsnəzəl\ *vi* -ED/-ING/-S [blend of *²snug* and *nuzzle*] *dial Eng* **:** NESTLE, SNUGGLE

snw *abbr* snow

¹sny \ˈsnī\ *vi* -ED/-ING/-ES [origin unknown] *dial Eng* **:** ABOUND, TEEM

²sny \"\ *vi* -ED/-ING/-ES [origin unknown] **:** to bend upward — used esp. of the edge of a plank near the bow or stern of a ship

³sny \"\ *n* -ES **:** the upward curve of the edge of a plank esp. toward the bow or stern of a ship

¹so \(ˈ)sō, *when followed without pause by a stressed syllable sometimes* sə\ *adv* [ME *so, sa, swa,* fr. OE *swā;* akin to OHG *sō* so, ON *svā,* Goth *swa* so, *swe* as, OL *suad* thus, L *si* if, Gk *hōs* thus, so, Skt *sva* one's own — more at SUICIDE] **1 a :** in a manner or way that is indicated or suggested ⟨many farmers operated a tannery and ~ provided a convenient market for hides —W.M.Kollmorgen⟩ ⟨imposing a pattern which, ~ the author contends, the facts do not warrant —*Brit. Bk. News*⟩ ⟨~ it goes throughout the nation —F.L.Mott⟩ ⟨gave up the life of a missionary in the field to become an administrator . . . it was better ~ —Kemp Malone⟩ ⟨hold the shears right . . . incline the edge ~ —Thomas Hardy⟩ — often used to indicate an exact or close parallel (as between two actions or

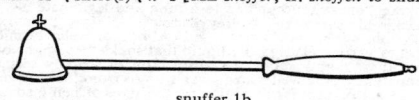

situations) ⟨just as in his absence during the war he required weekly reports from the manager . . . ~ now he kept up the same practice —H.E.Scudder⟩; often used with a following clause introduced by *that* or with an infinitive phrase introduced by *as* that shows the logical result or purpose of an action done in a specific manner with the following clause or phrase serving to indicate the desired manner as well as the outcome of the action ⟨the educated people of our country would have to be ~ trained that they could see the dialectical possibility of the opposites of the beliefs they possess —R.M. Weaver⟩ ⟨it ~ happened that . . . the first work bearing this title by a sociologist was published in the same year —L.A. White⟩ ⟨nothing in this constitution shall be ~ construed as to prejudice any claims of the United States —*U. S. Constitution*⟩ ⟨try to hit the snake on the head ~ as to stun it⟩; often used as a substitute in various expressions (1) to express the idea of an entire preceding clause or longer passage ⟨perhaps they take life seriously too, but if ~, that is only because there are things in life . . . worth taking seriously —Clive Bell⟩ ⟨this fly is the most common species of the horseflies, but even ~ it is not abundant —H.L. Van Volkenberg⟩ or (2) to express the idea of a preceding phrase ⟨there seems no logical necessity for local . . . organizations to fall into the hands of reactionaries even though the major national organizations have done ~ —Elmer Davis⟩ or (3) to express approval (as of an action performed in a particular way) sometimes interjectionally ⟨here, just let me turn that curl — there, ~ —T.E.Hook⟩ ⟨if it please you, ~; if not, why, ~ —Shak.⟩ **b :** in the same manner or way : ALSO, TOO ⟨always worked on a farm and ~ did his father⟩ ⟨if a metropolis had its hard decorum, ~ had a village —Carl Van Doren⟩ **c :** in the following manner : THUS ⟨for ~ the Lord said unto me, I will take my rest —Isa 18:4 (AV)⟩ **d :** forward or as if forward in a manner that is indicated or suggested : SUBSEQUENTLY, THEN ⟨~ home and to bed —Samuel Pepys⟩ **2 a (1) :** to an indicated or suggested extent or degree ⟨there is usu. some spirit of the age which historians can define, but the shape of things is seldom ~ clear to those who live them —J.W.Krutch⟩ — often used with a following clause that indicates the extent or degree ⟨the difficulties they encountered getting home ~ weakened him that he never recovered his strength —H.E.Starr⟩ ⟨was ~ eloquent he could sell refrigerators to the Eskimos —D.L. Graham⟩ ⟨the nest was . . . in ~ good a state of preservation that it might have been occupied the previous year —*Manchester Guardian Weekly*⟩ ⟨~ gradual was the growth . . . that 90 years after its founding it had but 107 students —*Amer. Guide Series: N.Y. City*⟩; often used with a following infinitive phrase usu. introduced by *as* that indicates the extent or degree by specifying a result or consequence ⟨gossip ~ persistent as to be impossible to ignore —T.H.White b.1915⟩ ⟨had been ~ kind to procure the child a new wardrobe —Mary Charlton⟩ (2) **:** to the same extent or degree : to such a degree : AS 1 — used chiefly in negative constructions with a following correlative element introduced by *as* ⟨see a bullfight . . . it won't be half ~ gory as you think —T.H.Fielding⟩ ⟨thought that his share wasn't ~ big as his brother's⟩ ⟨never . . . had the condition of the Puritans been ~ deplorable as at that time —T.B.Macaulay⟩ but also in positive constructions ⟨the river was . . . deep enough for a pleasure boat ~ small as theirs —G.K.Chesterton⟩ ⟨if my aunt thought I was defeated ~ easily as that, she . . . was mistaken —R.H.Sampson⟩ ⟨many of our best citizens intend starting to California ~ soon as they can —Pamela Clemens⟩; often used in adjurative phrases ⟨I did see him there, ~ help me⟩ **b :** to a great extent or degree : VERY, QUITE, EXTREMELY ⟨had . . . a life of their own, but it was all ~ patterned and convention-ridden —H.S.Bennett⟩ ⟨~ many of the subjects had been photographed ~ often —Norris Harkness⟩ ⟨said that he left her because he loved her ~⟩ — often used in mild negative understatements ⟨isn't ~ slow as a lawyer himself —G.A.Nichols⟩ **c :** to a definite but unspecified extent or degree ⟨I can only move ~ fast —Dave Beck⟩ **d :** most certainly : INDEED ⟨said, like a stolid little girl, "I am ~ pregnant" —Maude Hutchins⟩ ⟨"I didn't do it." "You did ~"⟩ **3** — used in place of an adjective to avoid repetition of the adjective ⟨susceptible, but not excessively ~, to the attractions of other women —Anthony Quinton⟩ ⟨is paralyzed but was not born ~⟩ **4 :** for a reason that has just been stated : THEREFORE ⟨the records deal mostly with business and ~ are not as valuable . . . as records of a more personal kind —*Notes & Queries*⟩ — **so far from** *prep* **:** rather than : instead of — used chiefly to give emphasis by pointing out a marked difference ⟨*so far from* abating, the pestilence grew in virulence —A.M.Young⟩ — **so fashion** *dial* **:** in an indicated way : so ⟨I'll knock *so fashion* and peep round the door —Robert Frost⟩

2so \"\ *conj* [ME *so, sa, swa,* fr. OE *swā*] **1 a :** with the result that ⟨the choral work was clean, ~ every word was distinguishable —Douglas Watt⟩ **b :** with the purpose that : in order that ⟨separate the marginal items by slashes ~ they won't run together —H.M.Silver⟩ **2 :** provided that — usu. used with *just* ⟨some people don't care who goes hungry just ~ they themselves get enough to eat⟩ **3 a (1) :** for that reason : THEREFORE ⟨when I speak of these matters I am always accused of being a snob, ~, to illustrate my point, I propose to quote —Nancy Mitford⟩ (2) **:** AND ⟨was getting rather tired by this time, ~ that is why he sang a complaining song —A.A.Milne⟩ **b (1)** — used as an introductory particle ⟨~ here we are at last⟩ occas. reduplicated ⟨~ ~, quoth he, these let this attend the time —Shak.⟩ and often to belittle a point under discussion esp. in the phrase *so what* ⟨he took a drink now and then . . . ~ what? He was a man —E.D.Radin⟩ ⟨I may be a numskull scholastically, but what I remember of my family — it was so wonderful. *So* I misspell a word —Helen Traubel⟩ (2) — used interjectionally to indicate awareness of a discovery (as of guilt) ⟨~, that's who did it⟩ or surprised dissent

3so \ˈsō\ *adj* [ME *so, sa, swa,* fr. OE *swā*] **1 :** conforming with actual facts : TRUE ⟨cocksure of many things that were not ~ —O.W.Holmes †1935⟩ **2 :** marked by a definite order ⟨insists on having his books just ~⟩

4so *pron* [ME, fr. *so, sa, swa,* adv.] **1 :** such as has been specified or suggested : the same ⟨became chairman . . . and remained ~ until his death —Marie A. Kasten⟩ ⟨"has she gone?" "I believe ~"⟩ — often used for emphasis at the beginning of a statement ⟨the last day? Why, ~ it is⟩ **2 :** something that approximates what has just been indicated ⟨I've known him 20 years or ~⟩ ⟨back in 1940 or ~ —C.D.Lane⟩ ⟨my joints are somewhat stiff or ~ —Alfred Tennyson⟩ **3 :** THIS ⟨then fold the paper like ~⟩

5so *var of* SOL

so *abbr* south; southern

SO *abbr* **1** seller's option **2** senior officer **3** sex offender **4** shipping order **5** ship's option **6** shop order **7** special order **8** staff officer **9** standing order **10** strikeout **11** suboffice **12** supply officer

1soak \ˈsōk\ *vb* **soaked; soaked** \-kt\ *also* **soak·en** \-kən\ **soaking; soaks** [ME *soken,* fr. OE *socian;* akin to OE *sūcan* to suck — more at SUCK] *vi* **1 :** to remain steeping in water or other liquid : to become saturated or softened by immersion ⟨let the beans ~ overnight⟩ ⟨put the clothes to ~⟩ ⟨likes to get in the tub and ~⟩ **2 a :** to enter or pass through something by or as if by pores or interstices : PERCOLATE, PERMEATE — often used with *into* ⟨rain ~s into the ground⟩ ⟨blood ~ing through the bandage⟩ ⟨the porous quality of the brick into which the light seemed to ~ as if absorbed —Herbert Read⟩ ⟨the warmth ~ed into his legs —Oliver La Farge⟩ ⟨dawn was ~ing into the sky over the tops of the trees —R.H.Newman⟩ **b :** to penetrate or affect the mind or feelings — usu. used with *in* or *into* ⟨waited for the remark to ~ in —O.S.J. Gogarty⟩ ⟨will let it ~ into my subconscious —W.H.Upson⟩ ⟨the idea of web defense ~ing into troops —Tom Wintringham⟩ **3 :** to drink alcoholic beverages intemperately or gluttonously ⟨~ing all night at the bar⟩ **4 :** to remain for a considerable time under heat treatment — used esp. of a metal in annealing ~ *vt* **1 :** to permeate so as to wet, soften, or fill thoroughly : SATURATE ⟨the meteorologist watched the solid drenching sheets ~ the ground —Hilbert Schenck⟩ ⟨unable to fire a shot because of ~ed cartridges and drowned powder horns —F.V.W.Mason⟩ ⟨two entire annual layers had been ~ed by the summer meltwater —Valter Schytt⟩ ⟨the house . . . made of sun-*soaked* red brick —Edith Sitwell⟩ ⟨an atmosphere ~ed with insatiable interest in international law —G.F.Renier⟩ **2 a :** to place (something) in a liquid or other surrounding element to wet or as if to wet thoroughly : SUBMERGE, STEEP ⟨~ the clothes before washing⟩ ⟨~ the negatives in an acid solution⟩ ⟨bread ~ed in milk —Agnes Repplier⟩ ⟨~ed overnight in vinegar and olive oil —*Amer. Guide Series: La.*⟩ ⟨~ed himself in the sunshine —Archibald Marshall⟩ ⟨his irony . . . was ~ed in vitriol —Max Lerner⟩ ⟨a drama ~ed . . . in blood and rape —Leslie Rees⟩ ⟨books ~ed in sentiment —Hubert Herring⟩ ⟨~ed himself in booze —V.P.Hass⟩ **b :** to engross the full attention of (a person) in deep and extensive study : imbue fully : IMMERSE ⟨~ yourself in art⟩ ⟨start right off not only to expose yourself to, but to ~ yourself in, those fields of knowledge —Bennett Cerf⟩ ⟨~ himself in American history —*Nieman Reports*⟩ ⟨until recently nearly all writers have been ~ed in classical and renaissance literature —A.N.Whitehead⟩ **3 a :** to drain or cleanse by washing or absorbing — usu. used with *out* ⟨~ the dirt out of the clothes⟩ ⟨apply a poultice to ~ out the poison⟩ **b (1)** *obs* **:** to exhaust or make poor by emptying or removing ⟨all plants that do draw much nourishment from the earth, and so ~ the earth, and exhaust it —Francis Bacon⟩ (2) **:** to levy an exorbitant or unreasonable charge against (a person or business concern) ⟨neither the newspaper nor its millionaire executives were ever ~ed very hard by the tax collectors —D.D.McKean⟩ ⟨~ the rich⟩ ⟨~ing the tourist is a popular . . . sport —A.T.Steele⟩ **4 a :** to draw in by or as if by suction or absorption ⟨down the coast bathers cavorted and ~ed sun —*Springfield (Mass.) Republican*⟩ — usu. used with *up* ⟨plaster walls ~ed up the rain —Virginia D. Dawson & Betty D. Wilson⟩ ⟨partitions ~ up sound —*advt*⟩ ⟨inserting the bar to a length that ~s up enough neutrons —Leon Svirsky⟩ ⟨~ed up the sunshine —Nelson Glueck⟩ ⟨electronics is ~ing up much of the surplus labor and plant space —R.B.Cole⟩ ⟨traveled . . . to ~ up the atmosphere there —Walter Sullivan⟩ ⟨philosophizing about the law does not amount to much until one has ~ed in the details —O.W.Holmes †1935⟩ **b :** to intoxicate (oneself) by drinking alcoholic beverages ⟨coming home half ~ed, he can hardly climb the stairs⟩ **5 :** to bake (bread) thoroughly **6 :** to beat or punish severely ⟨the jury comes in loaded to ~ an anarchist and a foreigner —Maxwell Anderson⟩ **7 :** to subject (as a metal) to prolonged heat treatment **8 :** to charge (a storage battery) at a low rate

2soak \"\ *n* -s **1 a :** the act or process of soaking : the state of being soaked ⟨might as well put them in ~ tonight —Ellen Glasgow⟩ **b :** the liquid in which something is soaked : STEEP 2: as (1) **:** a bath for softening dry hides (2) **:** an often hot medicated solution with or in which a body part is soaked usu. long or repeatedly esp. to promote healing, relieve pain, or stimulate local circulation **2** *Austral* **a :** wet land lying esp. at the foot of a hill **b :** a temporary swamp caused by overflowing surface water **c :** SPRING **3 a :** one who is under the influence of alcohol during most of his waking hours : DRUNKARD ⟨a real ~ . . . he hasn't drawn a sober breath in years —Hamilton Basso⟩ **b :** an extended period of hard drinking : SPREE ⟨succumbed to a long and legitimate ~ . . . to pickle his sorrows —Audrey Barker⟩ **4** *slang* **:** 1PAWN 2 ⟨got a job, but my bed's in ~ —E.C.Abbott & Helena Smith⟩

soak·age \-kij, -kēj\ *n* -s **1 :** liquid that soaks through or out; *also* **:** the amount gained by absorption or lost by seepage ⟨an analysis of the well water reveals no ~ from the cesspool⟩ **2 :** the act or process of soaking : the state of being soaked ⟨increase the ~ of rain into the geological layers which store water —*Sydney (Australia) Bull.*⟩ ⟨white oak . . . is impervious to ~ through the pores —F.P.Hankerson⟩

soakaway \ˈ=,=,=\ *n* -s [fr. *soak away*, v.] *Brit* **:** a depression in the earth's surface into which waters flow and naturally drain away : SINK

soak·er \ˈsōkə(r)\ *n* -s *obs* **1 :** one that drains or exhausts **2 a** [short for *old soaker*] *obs* **:** an experienced or elderly person **b :** SOAK 3a **3 :** a worker who carries out a soaking process: **a :** one who preshrinks woolen cloth with steam **b :** one who soaks hides to clean and soften them **4 :** a long soaking rain ⟨a real good ~ ought to do it . . . a real good all-day rain —C.O.Gorham⟩ **5 :** an absorbent cover of knitted wool for a baby's diaper — often used in pl.

soaking *adv* [fr. pres. part. of 1*soak*] **:** to a high degree : THOROUGHLY — usu. used in phrase *soaking wet*

soak·ing·ly *adv* [ME *sokingly*, fr. *soking* (pres. part. of *soken* to soak) + -*ly*] **1 :** in a slow and steady manner : GRADUALLY **2 :** in such manner as to wet thoroughly : DRENCHINGLY

soaking pit *n* **:** a deep furnace in which a steel ingot is allowed to stand until its temperature is equalized throughout in preparation for forging or rolling

soaks *pres 3d sing of* SOAK, *pl of* SOAK

so·an \sōˈän\ *also* **so·han** \sōˈhän\ *adj, usu cap* [fr. *Soan, Sohan*, tributary of the upper Indus river in the northwestern part of the Indian subcontinent] **:** of or relating to a Paleolithic culture of West Pakistan characterized by chopping tools

1so-and-so \ˈsōən,sō\ *n* -s **1 :** an unnamed or unspecified person or thing ⟨would argue as to whether *so-and-so's* badger could lick such-and-such a dog —*Amer. Guide Series: Nev.*⟩ ⟨the reason he didn't was *so-and-so* —Ring Lardner⟩ ⟨word meaning *so-and-so* —Alexander d'Agapeyeff⟩ **2 :** BASTARD 7 ⟨has often been called an unregenerate *so-and-so* by the opposition —Bill Hatch⟩ ⟨should have given the poor *so-and-so* another chance —Jean Stafford⟩ ⟨you old *so-and-so* . . . how are you, anyway —J.G.Cozzens⟩

2so-and-so \"\ *adv* **:** in an unspecified manner or fashion ⟨instructions were to feed them so-and-so and treat them *so-and-so* —H.G.Wells⟩

3so-and-so \"\ *adj* **:** BLANKETY-BLANK ⟨expurgate that profane gentleman's scathing narration of what he terms a *so-and-so* wild-goose chase —G.F.T.Ryall⟩ ⟨you can keep the *so-and-so* car —Harry Bennett⟩

1soap \ˈsōp\ *n* -s *often attrib* [ME *sope*, fr. OE *sāpe*; akin to MD *sepe* soap, OHG *seifa* soap, OE *sāp* amber, salve, L *sebum* tallow, grease, Toch A *sepal* salve] **1 a :** a cleansing and emulsifying agent that is made usu. either from fats and oils (as a mixture of tallow and coconut oil) by saponification with alkali in the boiling process or the cold process or from fatty acids by neutralization with alkali, that consists essentially of a mixture of water-soluble sodium or potassium salts of fatty acids, and that may contain other ingredients (as sodium carbonate or other builders, perfume, coloring agents, fluorescent dyes, disinfectants, or abrasive material) — sometimes distinguished from *detergent;* compare HARD SOAP, RESIN SOAP, SOFT SOAP, SURFACE-ACTIVE AGENT, TOILET SOAP **b :** a water-soluble salt of a single fatty acid or similar acid **c :** a usu. water-insoluble metal salt other than an alkali-metal salt of a fatty acid or similar acid (as a resin acid or a naphthenic acid) that may be a nuisance (as the calcium and magnesium soaps formed as a curd when ordinary soap is used in hard water) or that may be useful as a paint drier and for other purposes : METALLIC SOAP **2 :** soap as prepared esp. for the trade ⟨a full stock of ~s⟩ — **no soap :** to no purpose : with no results : no go ⟨tried to talk the buyer into redrawing the contract . . . but it was *no soap* —F.B.Gipson⟩ ⟨I was asked, I was cajoled . . . I was threatened — but *no soap* —F.H. La Guardia⟩

2soap \"\ *vt* -ED/-ING/-S **1 a :** to rub soap over or into esp. so as to make a lather or coating ⟨~ one's hands⟩ ⟨~ing the clothes⟩ ⟨~ed crosses on windows and automobiles —*Holiday*⟩ **b :** to treat or scour (as cloth) with a soap solution **2 :** to address in smooth or complimentary speech : FLATTER ⟨as I ~ed the dean I was sure of having one hearer in my favor —O.W.Holmes †1935⟩ — compare SOFT-SOAP

soap apple *n* **:** the bulb of a soap plant (*Chlorogalum pomeridianum*); *also* **:** the plant itself

soapbark \ˈ=,=\ *n* **1 a** *also* **soapbark tree :** a Chilean tree (*Quillaja saponaria*) with shining leaves and terminal white flowers **b :** the bark of the soapbark tree that because of its saponin content yields a soapy lather and is used in cleaning and in emulsifying oils — compare QUILLAIC ACID **2** *also* **soapbark tree :** any of several tropical American trees or shrubs of the genus *Pithecolobium* (as *P. bigeminum*) having saponaceous bark

soap·berry \ˈsōp- — *see* BERRY\ *n* **1 a** *also* **soapberry tree :** a tree of the genus *Sapindus* (esp. *S. saponaria*) **b :** the fruit of the soapberry tree that in the common form contains as much as 37 percent saponin **2 :** BUFFALO BERRY

soapberry family *n* **:** SAPINDACEAE

soap-boiler \ˈ=,==\ *n* **:** one that makes soap by boiling

1soapbox \ˈ=,=\ *n* **1 a :** a small box or receptacle designed to hold a bar of soap **b :** a packing box used for shipping soap **2 :** an improvised platform used by a self-appointed, spontaneous, or informal orator ⟨~es were carried openly into the classroom and mounted by the orators —Heywood Broun⟩ ⟨need no encouragement to leap on your ~ to tell it to the world —Norris Harkness⟩ ⟨novels are novels and rarely handy ~es —Robert Carson⟩

2soapbox \"\ *adj* **1 :** shaped like a soapbox ⟨architects of skyscrapers who found their ~ forms imposed by zoning laws —W.E.Cox⟩ **2 :** of, relating to, or delivered from a soapbox ⟨~ oratory⟩ ⟨distrustful of the whole pattern of ~ politics —Leslie Rees⟩ ⟨the park is the orating ground of the city's ~ evangels —*Amer. Guide Series: Oregon*⟩

3soapbox \"\ *vi* -ED/-ING/-ES **:** to indulge in soapbox oratory ⟨girls who ~ed for equal rights —Marybeth Weinstein⟩ ⟨joined picket lines and ~ed at breadlines —*Time*⟩ — **soap·box·er** *n*

Soap Box Derby *service mark* — used for a competition in which children usu. 11 to 15 years of age race homemade motorless single-seated vehicles down an inclined raceway

soap brick *n* **:** a small brick used in filling out a course

soap bubble *n* **:** a hollow iridescent globe formed by blowing a film of soapsuds from a pipe

soapbush \ˈ=,=\ *n* [*soap* + *bush*] **1 :** a deer brush (*Ceanothus integerrimus*) of the western U. S. that is an important browse and honey plant **2 :** SWEET PEPPERBUSH

soap dish *n* **:** a dish for holding soap; *esp* **:** a bathroom or kitchen fixture designed for holding soap

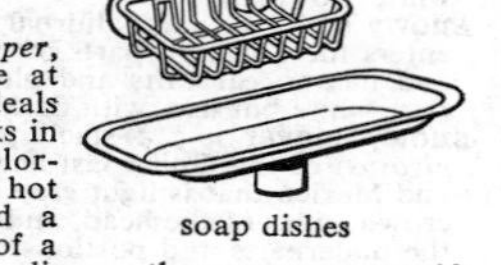

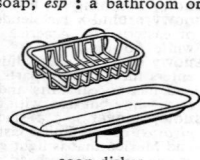

soap dishes

soap earth *n* **:** STEATITE

soaped *past of* SOAP

soap·er \ˈsōpə(r)\ *n* -s [ME *soper*, fr. *sope* soap + -*er* — more at SOAP] **1 :** one that makes or deals in soap **2 a :** a series of tanks in which printed cloth is made colorfast as it is run through a hot solution of water, soap, and a fixing agent **b :** an operator of a soaper **3 :** SOAP OPERA ⟨in radio . . . there were some 40 separate ~s a day —Gilbert Seldes⟩

soap·ery \ˈsōpərē\ *n* -ES [1*soap* + -*ery*] **:** a soap factory

soapfish \ˈ=,=\ *n* [*soap* + *fish*] **:** any of several fishes constituting the genus *Rypticus* (family Serranidae) of the warmer coasts of America and having scales that are smooth and soapy to the touch

soap flakes *n pl* **:** finely flaked soap prepared for marketing

soapier *comparative of* SOAPY

soapiest *superlative of* SOAPY

soap·i·ly \ˈsōpəlē\ *adv* **:** in a smooth or slippery manner

soap·i·ness \-pēnəs\ *n* -ES **:** the quality or state of being soapy

soaping *pres part of* SOAP

soaplees \ˈ=,=\ *n pl* [*soap* + *lees* (dregs)] **:** SPENT LYE

soap·less \ˈsōpləs\ *adj* **1 :** being without soap **2 :** UNWASHED, DIRTY

soapless soap *n* **:** DETERGENT c

soap lock *n* [*soap* + *lock*] **1 :** a lock of hair plastered down with soap — usu. used in pl. **2 :** a person wearing a soap lock

soapmaking \ˈ=,==\ *n* **:** the act, process, or occupation of manufacturing soap

soap nut *n* **1 :** the seed of a soapberry (*Sapindus saponaria*) used for making beads and buttons **2 :** the flat saponaceous pod of an East Indian woody vine (*Acacia concinna*); *also* **:** the plant itself

soap opera *n* [prob. so called fr. the fact that it was formerly often sponsored by soap manufacturers] **:** a radio or television serial drama performed usu. on a daytime commercial program and chiefly characterized by stock domestic situations and often melodramatic or sentimental treatment ⟨unadulterated *soap opera* — a banal story, dripping with sentiment — *Sat. Rev.*⟩

soap orange *n* **:** a wild orange (*Citrus aurantium saponacea*) of Guam and other Pacific islands that has an inedible fruit with saponaceous pulp

soap plant *n* **:** a plant having a part that may be used in place of soap: as **a :** a California plant (*Chlorogalum pomeridianum*) of the family Liliaceae **b :** SOAPWORT 1 **c :** any of several plants of the genera *Agave, Yucca,* and *Zigadenus* found in southwestern U.S. and adjacent Mexico **d :** a soapberry (*Shepherdia canadensis*) having leaves that are silvery on the lower surface

soap powder *n* **:** soap in powdered form made by grinding dried soap chips or by spray-drying crutched soap; *esp* **:** a mixture of soap with large amounts of one or more alkaline builders — compare WASHING POWDER

soaprock \ˈ=,=\ *n* [*soap* + *rock*; fr. its soapy feel] **:** STEATITE

soaproot \ˈ=,=\ *n* **1 :** any of several southern European herbs of the genus *Gypsophila* whose roots are used as a substitute for soap **2 :** SAND LILY **3 :** SOAPWORT 1 **4 :** SOAP PLANT a

soaps *pl of* SOAP, *pres 3d sing of* SOAP

soap stock *n* **:** the fatty material from which soap is made; *esp* **:** the foots obtained in refining or hardening oils that contain chiefly fatty acids or their salts and oil

soapstone \ˈ=,=\ *n* **:** a soft stone having a soapy feel and composed essentially of talc, chlorite, and often some magnetite — compare STEATITE

soapston·er \"+ə(r)\ *n* -s **:** a worker who uses powdered soapstone to clean molds and other equipment used in the rubber industry — called also *talcer*

soapsuds \ˈ=,=\ *n pl* **:** SUDS 2a, 2b

soap test *n* **:** a test for determining the hardness of water by adding just enough standard soap solution to produce a lasting lather

soap tree *n* **:** any tree that yields saponin; *specif* **:** SOAPBERRY

soapweed \ˈ=,=\ *n* **:** SOAP PLANT

soapwood \ˈ=,=\ *n* **1 :** WILD PEAR **2 :** any of several Australian trees with smooth pale yellowish wood **3 :** SOAPBARK 2

soapwort \ˈ=,=\ *n* **1 :** a European perennial herb (*Saponaria officinalis*) that is widely naturalized or escaped in the U.S. and has coarse pink or white flowers and leaves that yield a detergent when bruised — called also *bouncing Bet* **2 :** COWHERB **3 :** a plant of the family Sapindaceae

soapwort gentian *n* **:** an eastern No. American gentian (*Gentiana saponaria*) whose leaves and unexpanded flower buds resemble those of soapwort

soapy \ˈsōpē, -pi\ *adj* -ER/-EST **1 :** smeared with soap : covered with soap : LATHERED **2 :** containing or combined with soap or saponin ⟨~ water⟩ ⟨a ~ solution⟩ **3 :** resembling or having the qualities of soap : SLIPPERY, SMOOTH, SOFT ⟨talc and soapstone have a ~ feel⟩ **4 :** ingratiating or flattering in word or act : UNCTUOUS, SUAVE ⟨writes to me requesting in ~ terms what he calls an autographed photograph —O.W. Holmes †1935⟩ ⟨~ supplications for unity — *New Republic*⟩ **5 :** of, relating to, or having the characteristics of soap opera ⟨much of the nighttime drama was equally ~ —*Time*⟩ ⟨the midmorning stimulant that the radio now dishes out in ~ drama —Louise Baker⟩

1soar \ˈsō(ə)r, ˈsȯ(ə)r, -ōə, -ȯ(ə)\ *vb* -ED/-ING/-S [ME *soren*, fr. MF *essorer* to expose to the air for drying, throw up in the air, soar, fr. (assumed) VL *exaurare* to expose to the air, fr. L *ex-* 1ex- + *aura* air — more at AURA] *vi* **1 a :** to mount on wings : fly aloft or about ⟨larks ~ing into the sky⟩ ⟨birds ~ed lower and settled on rooftops —Joseph Hitrec⟩ — often used with *away* ⟨an early gull rose from the water . . . and ~ed away into the murk —Nevil Shute⟩ **b (1) :** to sail or hover in the air often at a great height : GLIDE ⟨vultures ~ing above the plain⟩ ⟨a few lilac-colored clouds ~ed overhead —G.A.Wagner⟩ (2) *of a glider* **:** to fly without engine power and by means of ascending air currents without loss of altitude **2 :** to go or move upward in position or status : RISE ⟨the final rocket . . . ~ed twice as high —Jan Struther⟩ ⟨~ed in his sophomore year to an eastern record —Eddie Beachler⟩ ⟨his reputation ~ing to its zenith —O.S.Nock⟩ ⟨the thermometer ~ed up past the century mark —*Sydney (Australia) Bull.*⟩ ⟨up from the eastern sea ~s the delightful day —A.E.Housman⟩ **3 :** to ascend to a higher or more exalted level : to go beyond earthly or mean things or con-

siderations : TRANSCEND ⟨young ~ing imaginations —John Reed⟩ ⟨his ~ing idealism —H.S.Commager⟩ ⟨his spirit ~ed —Stephen Crane⟩ ⟨a man whose desires ~ed beyond one room —Robertson Davies⟩ — often used with *above* ⟨~ed above the troubles of ordinary people —Marchette Chute⟩ ⟨~ above the facts —A.L.Guérard⟩ **4 a** : to rise to an imposing or majestic stature or height : TOWER ⟨mountainsides . . . ~ 3000 feet from the floor of the narrow valleys —M.J. Herskovits⟩ ⟨half-grown oaks and ~ing poplars —J.A.G. Hungerford⟩ ⟨soldiers filling the impressive square before the ~ing pillars and broad steps —Irwin Shaw⟩ **b** : to go or move to such a height : CLIMB ⟨~ing chairs and tramways of all sorts —William Gilman⟩ ⟨the motorist can be ~ing 284 feet above the ground at one point and boring through a tunnel . . . 30 seconds later —Richard Thruelsen⟩ **5** : to increase to an uncommon or unprecedented level or amount ⟨unemployment was ~ing —N.M.Clark⟩ ⟨food prices continued to ~ —*Current History*⟩ ⟨~ing hospital costs —Clarence Axman⟩ **6 a** : to sing or play usu. in the higher ranges in an impressive or moving fashion ⟨a soprano voice ~ing ecstatically above the orchestra —Dyneley Hussey⟩ ⟨the welling up of that climactic ~ing of symbolic song —Claudia Cassiday⟩ ⟨~ed effortlessly through two choruses —H.A.Sinclair⟩ **b** : to rise to a high and usu. moving pitch and cadence ⟨no matter what ~ing of verbal eloquence —Leslie Rees⟩ ⟨terse and rich in dialogue . . . the prose ~s in those amazing apostrophes —Douglas Stewart⟩ **7** : to move or go at a high rate of speed ⟨~ed down that road leaving a trail of dust behind —Frederick Way⟩ ⟨any skier who has ~ed down a slope —*Ford Times*⟩ ~ *vt* **1** *archaic* : to lift oneself high in (flight) ⟨whether thy soul ~s fancy's flights beyond the pole —Robert Burns⟩ **2** *archaic* : to ascend to or hover through (a height) ⟨~ing the air —John Milton⟩ **syn** see RISE

2soar \"\ *n* -s **1** : the range, distance, or height attained in soaring ⟨such ~s of fancy⟩ **2** : the act of soaring : upward flight ⟨the ~ of a lark⟩ ⟨the ~ of song and verse⟩

soar·able \'sōrəbəl, 'sȯr-\ *adj* : able to support soaring : permitting soaring ⟨~ winds⟩

soar falcon *or* **soar hawk** *n* [*soar* alter. (influenced by 1*soar*) of *sore* (as in *sorefalcon*)] : SOREFALCON

soaring *n* -s [fr. gerund of 1*soar*] : the act or process of soaring; *specif* : the art of operating a heavier-than-air craft without power and without loss of altitude by utilizing ascending air currents

so as *conj* **1 a** *obs* : so 1a ⟨I hope you shall receive honorable requital of his amicable ambassade *so as* you shall have no cause to regret his arrival —Elizabeth I⟩ **b** : so 1b ⟨repeated aloud *so as* there'd be no chance of a mistake —G.W.Brace⟩ **2** : provided that ⟨could play 'em a tune on any sort of pot you please, *so as* it was iron or block tin —Charles Dickens⟩

so·ave \sō'ävā\ *adj (or adv)* [It, fr. L *suavis* sweet — more at SWEET] : with sweetness or smoothness : in a gentle manner — used as a direction in music — **so·a·ve·men·te** \,sō,ävā'mentā\ *adv*

so·ay \'sō(,)ā\ *n* [fr. *Soay*, island of the Hebrides, where the breed originated] **1** *usu cap* : an old breed of small dark-brown or blackish sheep that are horned in both sexes **2** -s *often cap* : an animal of the Soay breed

1sob \'säb\ *vb* **sobbed**; **sobbed**; **sobbing**; **sobs** [ME *sobben*] *vi* **1 a** : to catch the breath audibly in a spasmodic contraction of the throat resulting from an intense emotional excitement **b** : to cry or weep with such convulsive catching of the breath ⟨began to ~ a little, like a hurt child —F. Tennyson Jesse⟩ **2** : to make a sound like that of a sob or sobbing ⟨the loud, rapid, painful, regular intake of *sobbing* breath —Arnold Bennett⟩ ⟨the doves ~ quietly in their cote —Edmund Blunden⟩ ⟨gives . . . the theme to the basses while the horns play a *sobbing* figure —Martin Cooper⟩ ~ *vt* **1** : to bring (as oneself) to a specified state or condition by sobbing ⟨*sobbed* himself to sleep⟩ **2** : to utter or pour forth with sobs ⟨had cried enough already, *sobbing* her loneliness into her pillow —Stuart Cloete⟩

2sob \"\ *n* -s [ME *sobbe*, fr. *sobben* to sob] **1 a** : an act of sobbing ⟨~s shook their bodies —George Meredith⟩ ⟨stood for a moment . . . a joyous ~ catching his throat —Wallace Markfield⟩ **b** *archaic* : an utterance or sound (as of effort or pain) similar to a sob **2 obs a** : the act of a horse in getting its wind **b** : an interval for a horse to rest **c** : REST, RELIEF **3** : a sound like that of a sob ⟨~s of the wind in the trees⟩

3sob \¦e,sō'bē\ *abbr or n* -s *often cap S&O&B* : SON OF A BITCH : BASTARD 7a ⟨what the administration needs most . . . is a ruthless ~ to run its politics —*Time*⟩

sobbed \'säbd\ *adj* [perh. alter. (influenced by 1*sob*) of *sopped*, past. part. of *sop*, v.] *chiefly dial* : thoroughly wet : SOAKED ⟨water-*sobbed* potatoes⟩

sob·ber \'säbə(r)\ *n* -s : one that sobs

1sob·bing \'säbiŋ\ *adj* [perh. alter. (influenced by 1*sob*) of *sopping*, pres. part. of *sop*, v.] *chiefly dial* : thoroughly wet : SOBBED, SOAKED ⟨his shoes are ~⟩

2sobbing \"\ *adv*, *chiefly dial* : to a high degree : THOROUGHLY — usu. used in the phrase *sobbing wet*

sob·bing·ly *adv* : in a sobbing manner : with sobs

sob·by \'säbē, -bi\ *adj* -ER/-EST [in sense 1, perh. alter. (influenced by 1*sob*) of *sop*, v., to soak, saturate + -*y*; in sense 2, fr. 2*sob* + -*y*] **1** *chiefly dial* : saturated with moisture : WET, SOGGY **2** : of or relating to sobs or weeping : SENTIMENTAL ⟨sad, ~ little stories in the magazines —*Metropolitan Mag.*⟩ ⟨endeavor to simulate the Italian style . . . results in too much that is strenuous, manifestly ~, and tortured —*Saturday Rev.*⟩

so being *conj* : provided that

so·be·it \sō'bēət\ *conj* [fr. the phrase *so be it*] *archaic* : provided that : as long as : IF ⟨the heart of his friend cared little whither he went ~ he were not too much alone —H.W. Longfellow⟩

1so·ber \'sōbə(r)\ *adj*, *usu* -ER/-EST [ME *sobre*, fr. MF, fr. L *sobrius* sober; akin to L *ebrius* drunk] **1 a** (1) : sparing in the use of food and drink : restrained in appetite : ABSTEMIOUS ⟨blank as to morals but comparatively ~ in his habits —Dorothy Sayers⟩ ⟨for him the ~ path of moderation appears to be infeasible —J.V.L.Casserley⟩ (2) *archaic* : moderate in amount or quantity — used esp. of food or drink⟩ **b** : not given or addicted to the use of intoxicating beverages : ABSTINENT ⟨meet all sorts of men, from ~ traveling missionaries . . . to drunken loafers —Rudyard Kipling⟩ **c** : free from the influence of intoxicating beverages : not drunk ⟨authorities state that a person whose blood contains less than 0.05 percent of alcohol is ~ —*Quarterly Jour. of Studies on Alcohol*⟩ ⟨smell of port wine, and did not appear to be quite ~ —Charles Dickens⟩ ⟨said he was cold ~⟩ **2 a** : indicating or expressing a thoughtful or grave character or intent ⟨if our pupils are to devote ~ attention to our instruction, we must set a high standard for ourselves —C.H.Grandgent⟩ ⟨had gone into battle . . . with the ~ insouciance, the lighthearted seriousness, so characteristic of the age —Walter Millis⟩ **b** (1) : marked by staid or sedate attitude or demeanor : GRAVE, SOLEMN ⟨a group of ~ merchants who detested the leveling tendencies —V.L.Parrington⟩ ⟨pensive nun, devout and pure, ~, steadfast, and demure —John Milton⟩ ⟨the ~ office of sexton —*Countryman*⟩ (2) : marked by an earnest or thoughtful demeanor or frame of mind : SERIOUS ⟨was unwontedly ~; his customary levity had . . . deserted him —W.H.Wright⟩ ⟨a ~ and experienced generation, grown old on the battlefields —Sigmund Neumann⟩ **3 a** *archaic* : patient or unruffled in bearing or movement : UNHURRIED ⟨pacing back his ~ way, slowly he gained his own array —Sir Walter Scott⟩ **b** : marked by quiet or calmness : PEACEFUL ⟨the sun sinking into a ~ sea⟩ **4** *archaic* : of indifferent value : SLIGHT, MEAGER **5** *chiefly Scot* **a** : in poor health : not well : FEEBLE, AILING **b** : UNPRETENTIOUS, HUMBLE **6 a** : indicating or expressing a temperate or moderate character or demeanor ⟨the Puritans . . . with their ~, thrifty, industrious life —Lewis Mumford⟩ ⟨soothes with ~ words their angry mood —John Dryden⟩ **b** : marked by temperance, moderation, or seriousness of character or demeanor ⟨the ~*est* and best man in that countryside, only a little hot and hasty now and then —George Eliot⟩ ⟨the people were quiet, ~, and friendly —Upton Sinclair⟩ **c** *archaic* : moderate in ambition or desire ⟨their ~ wishes never learned to stray —Thomas Gray⟩ **7** : quiet or neutral in color or decoration : SUBDUED ⟨wore no scarlet raiment, but clothed himself in ~ garments —H.O.Taylor⟩ ⟨skies that were ashen and ~ —George du Maurier⟩ ⟨a ~ Georgian colonial with simple details —*Amer. Guide Series: Mich.*⟩ **8 a** : showing no excessive or extreme qualities : RESTRAINED, REASONABLE, TEMPERED ⟨the writing is at once vivid and ~ —*Geog. Jour.*⟩ ⟨the cleanliness, order and ~ luxury of all the dwellings —Arnold Bennett⟩ ⟨the more ~ and less ecstatic types of church —W.L.Sperry⟩ **b** : carefully reasoned or considered : free from fancy or exaggeration : REALISTIC ⟨tried to subdue his riotous senses to the ~ dictates of reason —Ellen Glasgow⟩ ⟨was not a pose of youthful cynicism, but a ~ judgment confirmed by observation and experience —V.L.Parrington⟩ ⟨~ fact⟩ ⟨~ truth⟩ ⟨hope is followed by ~ and critical second thought —John Dewey⟩ **9** : dictated or guided by sane and sound reason : RATIONAL ⟨being sometimes mad, sometimes ~⟩

syn TEMPERATE, CONTINENT, UNIMPASSIONED: SOBER implies cool composure, dispassionate unprejudiced reason and analysis, or freedom from unreasonable excess ⟨a *sober* book, written without hysteria or excitement —A.T.Steele⟩ ⟨*sober* speech, thoughtfully reasoned and carefully prepared —Jack Gould⟩ ⟨no young giddy thoughtless maiden, full of graces, airs, and jeers — but a *sober* widow —W.S.Gilbert⟩ TEMPERATE implies moderation, self-control, and restraint operating against the excessive, extreme, extravagant, or violent ⟨his *temperate* advice at the early provincial congresses aroused some opposition among the more radical leaders —W.A. Robinson⟩ ⟨the delegates adopted a resolution threatening to rise in armed opposition if any attempt was made to coerce East Tennesseans into the Confederacy. Maynard urged the delegates to be more *temperate* —*Amer. Guide Series: Tenn.*⟩ CONTINENT indicates deliberate accustomed restraint on desires, esp. sexual desires ⟨had the circumstances of their lives given them opportunity they would have been sheer sensualists. Their strength was the strength of men geographically beyond temptation: the poverty of Arabia made them simple, *continent*, enduring —T.E.Lawrence⟩ UNIMPASSIONED indicates lack of ardor and fervor; it may imply accustomed rationality, stoicism, or coldness ⟨in weighed and measured *unimpassioned* words —Robert Browning⟩ ⟨Stephen spoke irritably. He was tired, excited, on fire, and Deborah seemed so *unimpassioned* —Mary Webb⟩ **syn** see in addition SERIOUS

2sober \"\ *vb* **sobered**; **sobered**; **sobering** \-b(ə)riŋ\ **sobers** [ME *sobren*, fr. *sobre* sober] *vt* **1** : to make (a person) serious, grave, or thoughtful ⟨an atmosphere of tense expectancy . . . that ~*ed* everyone —J.R.Perkins⟩ ⟨both had been ~*ed* and sharpened by wide experience —Willa Cather⟩ ⟨the buffet of Providence failed utterly to ~ her frivolous spirit —Robert Grant †1940⟩ ⟨a verdict for libel damages would have a tremendously ~*ing* effect on the guilty party —Norman Cousins⟩ **2** : to make (a drunken person) sober — usu. used with *up* ⟨trying to ~ him up before taking him home⟩ **3** : to make (something) neutral or dull in color ⟨the lacy green of trees . . . is ~*ed* by vast fields of brown earth —*Amer. Guide Series: Ark.*⟩ ~ *vi* **1** : to become sober: as **a** : to become serious or thoughtful ⟨had ~*ed* from youthful cavaliers into . . . astute businessmen —Francis Hackett⟩ **b** : to become neutral or dull in color or tone ⟨the sunset ~*ed* into twilight⟩ **c** : to become sober after being drunk ⟨came home drunk and then ate . . . when they ~*ed* —C.T. Jackson⟩ — usu. used with *up* ⟨the offender apologizes when he ~s up —Abram Kardiner⟩ **2** : to become settled or quiet — usu. used with *down* ⟨~*ed* down and married somebody else and was as sensible as anybody —Ellen Glasgow⟩ ⟨are so high from tension that they need half a dozen drinks to ~ —Alfred Bester⟩

soberer *comparative of* SOBER

soberest *superlative of* SOBER

so·ber·ing·ly *adv* : with a sobering effect ⟨embarrassed by the memory of experiences which even seemed ~ private —Neil Martin⟩

so·ber·ize \'sōbə,rīz\ *vb* -ED/-ING/-S [1*sober* + -*ize*] *vt* : to make sober ⟨the honor you have done me has its *soberizing* qualifications —*Times Lit. Supp.*⟩ ~ *vi*, *archaic* : to become sober

so·ber·ly *adv* [ME *sobrely*, fr. *sobre* sober + -*ly*] : in a sober manner

so·ber·ness *n* -ES [ME *sobrenes*, fr. *sobre* sober + -*nes* -ness] : the quality or state of being sober

sobersided \'==,==\ *adj* [1*sober* + *sided*] **1** : of a grave or serious nature : not given to levity : EARNEST, SEDATE ⟨the lean, ~, goateed, frock-coated types the cartoonists love —C.B.Palmer b. 1910⟩ ⟨~ historians of the 17th century —Lindesay Parrott⟩ **2** : wholly serious in viewpoint or treatment : unrelieved by humor or light touches : SOLEMN ⟨book is no piece of ~ pontificating —*Time*⟩ ⟨a ~ treatise on Congressional organization —R.H.Rovere⟩ ⟨the choreography . . . is ~ and sententious —*Musical America*⟩ — **sobersided·ness** *n* -ES

sobersides \'==,=\ *n pl but sing or pl in constr* [1*sober* + *sides*] : one who is sobersided ⟨is sure to give all but the ~ in the audience some pleasant moments —*Newsweek*⟩ ⟨drew a humorless ~ for his teacher⟩

sob·ful \'säbfəl\ *adj* : full of sobs : given to sobbing : drawing forth sobs ⟨in a ~ state⟩ ⟨a ~ story⟩

sobnd *abbr* southbound

sob·o·le \'säbə,lē\ *also* **so·bol** \'sō,bäl\ *or* **sob·o·les** \'säbə,lēz\ *n*, *pl* **sobo·les** \-ēz\ *also* **sobols** [L *soboles*, *suboles* sprout, shoot, offspring, fr. *sub-* + root of *-olescere* to grow — more at ADULT] : SUCKER, STOLON, SHOOT

sob·o·lif·er·ous \,säbə¦lif(ə)rəs\ *adj* [L *soboles* sprout + E -*iferous*] : producing shoots or suckers

so·bor \sə'bȯ(ə)r\ *n* -s *often cap* [Russ, fr. ORuss *sŭborŭ*] : an ecclesiastical synod, council, or assembly of the Eastern Orthodox Church

so·bor·nost \-r,nȯst\ *n* -s [Russ, lit., conciliarity, fr. *sobornyĭ* conciliar, fr. *sobor* council] : spiritual harmony based on freedom and unity in love : ECUMENICITY; *specif* : the principal of spiritual unity and religious community based on free commitment to a tradition of catholicity interpreted through ecumenical councils of the Eastern Orthodox Church — compare CONCILIARITY

so·bra·lia \sō'brālēə\ *n*, *cap* [NL, fr. Francisco M. *Sobral*, 18th cent. Span. physician and botanist + NL -*ia*] : a genus of tropical American terrestrial orchids having leafy stems and usu. brightly colored solitary or racemose flowers

so·brer·ol \sō'bre,rōl, -rōl\ *n* -s [ISV, fr. Ascanio *Sobrero* †1888 Ital. chemist + ISV -*ol*] : a crystalline alcohol $C_{10}H_{16}(OH)_2$ formed by oxidation of alpha-pinene

so·bri·e·ty \sə'brīəd·ē, sō'-, -īət, ¦i\ *n* -ES [ME *sobrietie*, fr. MF *sobrieté*, fr. L *sobrietat-*, *sobrietas*, fr. *sobrie-* (fr. *sobrius* sober) + -*tat-*, -*tas* -ty — more at SOBER] : the quality or state of being sober ⟨tried to establish rules of ~ in costume . . . to restrain the sartorial excesses —Rosaleen Mills⟩ ⟨able to force himself into ~ despite his alcoholic consumption —Wayne Hughes⟩ ⟨the ~, the earnestness, and the soul-searching . . . come out clearly —T.G.Bergin⟩ ⟨applied himself with scientific ~ to observation of his own life —R.L. Rusk⟩

so·bri·quet \'sōbrə,kā, -ket (*usu* -ked·+V), ,==¦=\ *or* **sou·bri·quet** \",'süb-\ *n* -s [F *sobriquet*, fr. MF *soubriquet*, tap under the chin, nickname] : an assumed name : a fanciful epithet or appellation : NICKNAME ⟨also had its purely local celebrities . . . with such picturesque ~s as "Rowdy Joe" and "Monte Joe" —*Amer. Guide Series: Texas*⟩ ⟨earned the lasting ~ of "Honest John" —G.A.Woods⟩ ⟨referred to it as "that hotbed of radicalism," a trite ~ —G.R.Stewart⟩

sobs *pres 3d sing of* SOB, *pl of* SOB

sob sister *n* **1** : a journalist who specializes in writing or editing sob stories or other material of a sentimental type ⟨the *sob sisters*, male and female, have filled the magazines and newspapers with sentimental homilies —A.Q.Maisel⟩ ⟨nothing of their marriage would be too intimate for the *sob sisters* to search out and serve to the public in syrupy prose —Vera Caspary⟩ ⟨for fear some . . . *sob sister* would track him down for one of those rags-to-riches human interest yarns —Budd Schulberg⟩ **2** : a sentimental and often impractical person esp. one engaged in good works ⟨the impression that psychiatrists are *sob sisters* who are actuated alone by sympathy for the offender —*Medico-Legal Jour.*⟩ ⟨describes the pacifists as paid agitators, sentimental *sob sisters* —*New Republic*⟩

sob story *n* **1** : a sentimental story or account designed chiefly to evoke sympathy or sadness ⟨the old *sob story* of youngsters sweltering in the blow rooms of the glass factories and spinning out their lives in cotton mills —*New Republic*⟩ **2** : a story or account designed to gain sympathy and used as an excuse or rationalization ⟨won't listen to your *sob stories* about absences —Evan Hunter⟩ ⟨your publisher's *sob stories* about how little he can afford —Julian Maclaren-Ross⟩

sob stuff *n* : a sob story or other material designed to make a sentimental or strongly emotional appeal ⟨the fineness and restraint of feeling that differentiate it from the coarsely and slushily sentimental child literature, the vulgar *sob stuff* —*Nation*⟩

soc *var of* SOKE

soc *abbr* **1** social; socialist **2** society **3** sociology **4** [L *socius*] companion **5** socket

soc·age *or* **soc·cage** \'säkij, -kēj\ *n* -s [ME *socage*, *sokage*, fr. *soc*, *sok*, *soke* soke + -*age* — more at SOKE] : a tenure of land by agricultural service fixed in amount and kind or by payment of money rent only and not burdened with any military service — see FREE SOCAGE, VILLEIN SOCAGE; compare BURGAGE

soc·ag·er \-jə(r)\ *n* -s : a tenant by socage : SOKEMAN

so–called \'=¦=\ *adj* **1** : commonly named : popularly so termed ⟨the privilege of the *so-called* pocket veto —*School & Society*⟩ ⟨his heavy working schedule did not keep the student out of *so-called* campus politics —*Current Biog.*⟩ ⟨closer cooperation with our traditional rivals in the *so-called* Ivy Group —J.B.Conant⟩ **2** : falsely or improperly so named or designated ⟨deceived by his *so-called* friend⟩ ⟨his *so-called* explanation further confuses the issue⟩

so–called dollar *n* : a dollar-size token or medal issued for commemorative purposes or for political propaganda (as an exposition medal or a token issued to propagandize bimetallism or free silver)

soc·cer \'säkə(r)\ *n* -s *often attrib* [by shortening & alter. (influence of -*er*) fr. *association* (in *association football*)] : a football game with 11 players on a side in which the ball is advanced by kicking or by propelling it with any part of the body except the hands and arms — called also *association football*

socdolager *var of* SOCKDOLAGER

soce \'sōs, 'sȯs\ *n pl* [prob. short for *associates*] *archaic* : COMRADES, FRIENDS — used as a term of address

so·cia·bil·i·ty \,sōshə'biləd·ē, -lət|, |i\ *n* -ES [ME *socibbilite*, fr. L *sociabilis* sociable + ME -*ite* -ity] **1 a** : the quality or state of being sociable : AFFABILITY ⟨smoke to relieve tension, to express ~ —Vance Packard⟩ **b** : the act or an instance of being sociable ⟨the midmorning coffee break and the other *sociabilities* —David Riesman⟩ **2** : relative tendency of individuals of one kind (as pine trees) to group themselves together or scatter among individuals of other kinds usu. expressed in terms of gregariousness or dispersion

1so·cia·ble \'sōshəbəl\ *adj* [MF or L; MF *sociable*, fr. L *sociabilis*, fr. *sociare* to join, share (fr. *socius* companion) + -*abilis* -able] **1** : inclined by nature to community life : inherently disposed to companionship or association with others of the same species : SOCIAL ⟨man is said to be a ~ animal —Joseph Addison⟩ ⟨all large ~ birds make noticeable preparations when about to take wing —E.A.Armstrong⟩ **2 a** : inclined to seek or enjoy companionship or social intercourse : AFFABLE, COMPANIONABLE, FRIENDLY ⟨I had been intensely ~, but now I had grown shy —Osbert Sitwell⟩ **b** : marked by or conducive to friendliness or pleasant social relations ⟨ask him to have a dinner and play some ~ pinochle —Mary Barrett⟩ ⟨no more ~ form of traveling to town has been devised than those old river steamers —E.H.Collis⟩ **syn** see GRACIOUS

2sociable \"\ *n* -s **1 a** [short for *sociable coach*] : an open four-wheeled carriage having two double seats facing each other and a box for the driver **b** : an S-shaped sofa designed to seat two persons partially facing each other **c** : a vehicle (as a tricycle or airplane) having a seat accommodating two persons side by side **2** : an informal party or group gathering for general entertainment and encouragement of sociability and frequently having a central activity or interest — called also *social* ⟨giving an ice cream ~ in the grove about the new courthouse —Willa Cather⟩ ⟨enjoying a strawberry ~ on a . . . church lawn —Irving Dilliard⟩

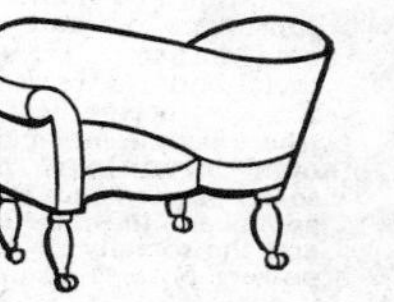

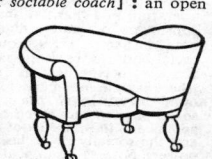

sociable 1b

so·cia·ble·ness *n* -ES : SOCIABILITY

sociable weaverbird *n* : a southern African weaverbird (*Philetairus socius*) that breeds in colonies having a compound nest in one great umbrella-shaped structure of grass placed in a tree

so·cia·bly \-blē, -li\ *adv* : in a sociable manner

1so·cial \'sōshəl\ *adj* [L *socialis*, fr. *socius* companion, ally, associate + -*alis* -al; akin to OE *secg* man, follower, companion, OS *segg*, ON *seggr* man, messenger, companion, Gk *aossein* to help, stand by, Skt *sakha* companion, friend, L *sequi* to follow — more at SUE] **1** : involving allies or confederates ⟨the *Social* War between the Athenians and their allies⟩ **2 a** : marked by or passed in pleasant companionship with one's friends or associates ⟨leads a very full ~ life⟩ ⟨spent a relaxed ~ evening⟩ : taken, enjoyed, or engaged in with friends or for the sake of companionship ⟨~ drinking⟩ ⟨a ~ game of bridge⟩ **b** : SOCIABLE ⟨difficult for him, although fundamentally a ~ character, to take any great pleasure in the company —Osbert Lancaster⟩ ⟨having to drive home, and not feeling very ~, I drank very little —Nigel Balchin⟩ **c** : composed of sociable persons or formed for the purpose of sociability ⟨a purely ~ club⟩ **d** : of, relating to, or designed for sociability or sociable gatherings ⟨the ~ director of the hotel⟩ ⟨the church has a large ~ hall⟩ **3 a** : forming or having a tendency to form cooperative and interdependent relationships with one's fellows : GREGARIOUS ⟨man is a ~ creature . . . one of the aims of education, therefore, is to teach man how to adjust himself to community living —M.B.Smith⟩ **b** : living together and breeding in more or less organized communities ⟨~ insects are less individuals than standardized, interchangeable units —Ralph Linton⟩ **c** *of a plant* : present in large numbers wherever present at all in nature : tending to grow in groups or masses so as to form a more or less pure stand — used esp. of forest trees **4 a** : of or relating to human society ⟨~ institutions⟩ ⟨the ~ implications of scientific progress⟩ : of or relating to the interaction of the individual and the group ⟨immature ~ behavior⟩ **b** : of, relating to, or concerned with the welfare of human beings as members of society ⟨~ legislation⟩ ⟨the ~ question⟩ **c** *Roman, civil, & Scots law* : of or relating to an association, partnership, or corporation **5 a** : of, relating to, or based on rank or status in a particular society or community ⟨move in different ~ circles⟩ ⟨did not accept him as their ~ equal⟩ ⟨a member of his ~ set⟩ **b** : of, belonging to, or characteristic of the upper classes ⟨a reactionary, solid, stuffy, and ~ —Rosemary Benét⟩ ⟨made fun of her being so ~ and high-tone —Lillian Hellman⟩ ⟨writes a column of ~ gossip⟩ **c** : FORMAL ⟨asked in a ~ voice, very deliberately, if she'd wakened me last night when she came in —Crary Moore⟩

syn GREGARIOUS, COOPERATIVE, CONVIVIAL, COMPANIONABLE, HOSPITABLE: SOCIAL now often indicates having to do with society in general as an interdependent group or as a phenomenon for study ⟨the desire for removing human error, clearing human confusion, and diminishing human misery . . . —motives eminently such as are called *social* —Matthew Arnold⟩ ⟨the *social* order⟩ ⟨plans for *social* reorganization⟩ In its older senses, still quite current, it describes easy pleasant conversational companionship with others conducted on the basis of friendship and equality and enjoyed for its own sake, without ulterior motive ⟨if at times everyone is telling at once it is evidently because of the *social* desire to contribute to the conversation, rather than because of the unsocial disposition to neglect one's neighbor's appreciation —W.C.

Brownell⟩ ⟨of a jovial, *social* disposition, with a host of friends —Allan Westcott⟩ GREGARIOUS indicates tending to flock together with others of one's kind and disliking a solitary existence: it may or may not connote enjoyable sociability ⟨renounced a life of solitude, and became a *gregarious* creature —William Cowper⟩ ⟨without intelligence, man is not social, he is only *gregarious* —Samuel Johnson⟩ ⟨as popular with the seeker after solitude as with the noisily *gregarious* —S.P.B. Mais⟩ ⟨the true Nevadan is *gregarious*, as his passion for clubs and other social circles indicates —*Amer. Guide Series: Nev.*⟩ COOPERATIVE indicates a willingness to work with others for a common end, subordinating immediate personal interests and wishes, and may suggest an attitude conducive to good morale throughout a group ⟨the *cooperative* efforts of all the allies⟩ ⟨while the development of armor called forth the skill of the smith, the multiplication of cannon demanded *cooperative* manufacture on a much larger scale —Lewis Mumford⟩ ⟨the cohesive, *cooperative* nature of American life as opposed to selfish individualism —Bradford Smith⟩ CONVIVIAL suggests jovial or merry enjoyment of others' company, particularly in situations in which eating or drinking is involved ⟨all the social and *convivial* joy and festivity that become youth —Earl of Chesterfield⟩ ⟨at the insistence of a *convivial* uncle and against her better inclination she permits herself to drink three glasses of champagne —Edmund Wilson⟩ COMPANIONABLE suggests a ready affability and warm sympathy that make association easy and pleasant ⟨blessed with a *companionable* roommate⟩ ⟨the trip was the more pleasant because our associates were *companionable*⟩ HOSPITABLE indicates a disposition to greet guests and visitors openly, generously, and warmly ⟨with a few rare exceptions which may arise from sheer lack of time to welcome all newcomers, Arizonans are warmhearted and *hospitable* —*Amer. Guide Series: Ariz.*⟩

²social \"\ *n* -s : SOCIABLE 2

social action *n* : an organized program of socioeconomic reform; *specif* : activity on the part of an interested group directed toward some particular institutional change ⟨a committee for the prevention of juvenile delinquency through *social action*⟩

social anthropology *n* **1** : the study of the social structure of nonliterate societies **2** : CULTURAL ANTHROPOLOGY

social ascidian *n* : any of various ascidians that reproduce by budding like the ordinary compound ascidians but that produce zooids each surrounded by a separate test though remaining connected by stolons

social bee *n* : any of numerous bees (as the bumblebees, honeybees, and stingless bees) of the superfamily Apoidea that live together in colonies

social brethren *n pl, cap S&B* : members of a small religious body organized in 1867 in Illinois on the basis of orthodox evangelical doctrines and a polity formed principally from Baptist and Methodist features

social casework *n* : CASEWORK

social climber *n* : one who attempts to gain a higher social position; *esp* : one ambitious to gain acceptance as a member of fashionable society ⟨the misery of the *social climber* to whose sumptuous party nobody will come —F.L.Allen⟩

social compact *n* : SOCIAL CONTRACT

social contract *n* [trans. of F *contrat social*] **1** : an agreement among individuals by which organized society is brought into being and which serves to regulate the relations of the members of a society with each other and with the government — compare CONTRACT THEORY, POPULAR SOVEREIGNTY, ROUSSEAUISM **2** : an agreement between the community and the ruler that defines and limits the rights and duties of each

social control *n* : the rules and standards of society that circumscribe individual action through the inculcation of conventional sanctions and the imposition of formalized mechanisms

social credit *n, usu cap S&C* : a doctrine that the capitalist system does not distribute sufficient income to keep itself in operation and that national dividends should be declared for consumers to assure a high level of consumption

social dance *n* **1** : a group dance or couple dance done for social and usu. recreational purposes — see BALLROOM DANCE **2** : a gathering held in a ballroom, in a home, or outdoors where people may participate in social dances

social darwinism *n, usu cap D* : an extension of Darwinism to social phenomena; *specif* : a theory in sociology: sociocultural advance is the product of intergroup conflict and competition and the socially elect classes (as those possessing wealth and power) possess biological superiority in the struggle for existence

social democracy *n* [trans. of G *sozialdemokratie*] : the principles and policies of social democrats or of a Social Democratic party

social democrat *n* [trans. of G *sozialdemokrat*] **1** *usu cap S&D* : a member of a Social Democratic party **2** : one who believes in and advocates a gradual and peaceful transition from capitalism to socialism by democratic means

social democratic *adj, usu cap S&D* [trans. of G *sozialdemokratisch*] : of or constituting a political party or group advocating social democracy

social disease *n* **1** : VENEREAL DISEASE **2** : a disease (as tuberculosis) whose incidence is directly related to social and economic factors

social disorganization *n* : a state of society characterized by the breakdown of effective social control resulting in a lack of functional integration between groups, conflicting social attitudes, and personal maladjustment

social distance *n* : the degree of acceptance or rejection of social intercourse between individuals belonging to diverse racial, ethnic, or class groups

social dividend theory of taxation : BENEFIT THEORY OF TAXATION

social dynamics *n pl but often sing in constr* : a branch of social physics that deals with the laws, forces, and phenomena of change in society

social engineering *n* : management of human beings with respect to their place and function in society : applied social science

social evil *n* : PROSTITUTION — used with *the*

social gospel *n* **1** : the application of biblical principles and esp. the teachings of Jesus to social problems **2** *usu cap S&G* : a movement in American Protestant Christianity initiated at the end of the 19th century and reaching its zenith in the first part of the 20th century and dedicated to the purpose of bringing the social order into conformity with the teachings of Jesus Christ

social group work *n* : GROUP WORK

social hedonism *n* : UNIVERSALISTIC HEDONISM

social history *n* **1** : history that concentrates upon the social, economic, and cultural institutions of a people — compare CULTURAL HISTORY **2** : the environmental history of an individual; *specif* : CASE HISTORY

social hygiene *n* : the practice of measures designed to protect and improve the family as a social institution; *specif* : the practice of measures aiming at the elimination of venereal disease and prostitution

social insect *n* : an insect that lives in a colony or community with other individuals of the same species

social insurance *n* : insurance against economic hazards (as loss of income due to unemployment, old age, disability, or death) affecting the individual and his family in which the government participates or secures the participation of the employer and the wage earner or self-employed individual — compare PRIVATE INSURANCE

so·cial·ism \ˈsōshəˌlizəm\ *n* -s **1** : any of various theories or social and political movements advocating or aiming at collective or governmental ownership and administration of the means of production and control of the distribution of goods: as **a** : FOURIERISM **b** : GUILD SOCIALISM **c** : MARXISM **d** : OWENISM **2 a** : a system or condition of society or group living in which there is no private property ⟨trace the remains of pure ~ that marked the first phase of the Christian community —W.E.H.Lecky⟩ — compare INDIVIDUALISM **b** : a system or condition of society in which the means of production are owned and controlled by the state — compare CAPITALISM, LIBERALISM **c** : a stage of society that in Marxist theory is transitional between capitalism and communism and distinguished by unequal distribution of goods and payments to individuals according to their work

¹so·cial·ist \-shələst, *in rapid speech* -shl-\ *n* -s [*social*ism + *-ist*] **1** : one who advocates or practices socialism **2** *usu cap* : a member of a socialist party or political group **syn** see COLLECTIVIST

²socialist \"\ *adj* **1 a** : of or relating to socialism ⟨~ theory⟩ ⟨~ ideas⟩ : adhering to or favoring socialism ⟨a ~ state⟩ ⟨a ~ thinker⟩ **b** : advocating, furthering, or constituting political, economic, or social measures or actions tending toward or regarded as tending toward socialism **2** *usu cap* : of, belonging to, or constituting a political party advocating or associated with the doctrines of socialism ⟨the major ~ parties prior to 1914 were all professedly Marxian —G.E.Hoover⟩; *specif* : of or constituting a minor political party in the U.S. formed by fusion after 1899 of the Social Democratic party and seceders from the Socialist Labor party and having its greatest influence and activity in the early 20th century — compare LABOR 2b

so·cial·is·tic \ˌsōshəˈlistik, -tēk\ *adj* [*social*ism + *-istic*] : of, relating to, or tending toward socialism ⟨government ~ development of peacetime atomic power —*New Republic*⟩

socialist labor *adj, usu cap* : of or constituting a minor U.S. political party formed in 1874 and advocating the attainment of socialism by economic rather than political action

so·cial·ite \ˈsōshəˌlīt, *usu* -īd·+V\ *n* -s *often attrib* [¹*social* + *-ite*] : a socially prominent person

so·ci·al·i·ty \ˌsōshēˈaləd·ē, -lət|, |i\ *n* -ES [L *socialitas*, fr. *socialis* social + *-itas* -ity — more at SOCIAL] **1 a** : the quality or state of being social : SOCIABILITY ⟨though capable of friendship, he is not always much disposed to general ~ —Adam Smith⟩ **b** : an instance of social intercourse : an act of sociability — usu. used in pl. ⟨reminded the other of their early *socialities* —J.G.Lockhart⟩ **2** : the tendency to associate with one's fellows or to form social groups ⟨mammals as a class are not naturally strong on ~ —*Harper's*⟩ : the fact or condition of being associated with others : FELLOWSHIP ⟨the moral sense demands that men should be bound together by ties of ~ —J.W.Beach⟩

so·cial·iza·tion \ˌsōshələˈzāshən, ˌsōshəˌlīˈ-\ *n* -s [in sense 1, fr. *socialism* + *-ization*; in other senses, fr. *socialize* (sense 1) + *-ation*] **1** : the action or process of making socialist or putting on a socialist basis : the state of being socialized ⟨made public ownership of land the first step in ~ —Irving Brant⟩ ⟨the country was quite prepared for ~ of the banking structure —*Accent*⟩ **2** : the process by which a human being beginning at infancy acquires the habits, beliefs, and accumulated knowledge of his society through his education and training for adult status — compare ENCULTURATION **3** : adoption (as by a juvenile court) of a sociological approach to legal procedure

so·cial·ize \ˈsōshəˌlīz\ *vb* -ED/-ING/-S *see -ize in Explan Notes* [in sense 1, fr. ¹*social* + *-ize*; in other senses, back-formation fr. *socialization*] *vt* **1** : to render social; *esp* : to fit or train for society or a social environment ⟨children are *socialized* according to a given cultural pattern —H.A.Murray & C.K. Kluckhohn⟩ **2 a** : to constitute on a socialistic basis ⟨~ the country⟩ : subject to collective or governmental ownership and control ⟨~ the land⟩ ⟨~ industry⟩ — compare NATIONALIZE **b** : to use for social purposes : adapt to social needs or uses ⟨*socializing* science in such a way as to make it more widely available for public use —Kimball Young⟩ **3** : to organize group participation in ⟨teaching that employs the *socialized* recitation instead of the question-and-answer method⟩ ~ *vi* : to participate actively in a social group : enter into or maintain personal relationships with others ⟨*socializing* at backyard barbecues —*Newsweek*⟩ ⟨let the students themselves decide with whom they want to ~ —Vannevar Bush⟩

socialized medicine *n* : administration by an organized group, a state, or a nation of medical and hospital services to suit the needs of all members of a class or all members of the population by means of funds derived from assessments, philanthropy, taxation, or other sources — compare STATE MEDICINE

so·cial·iz·er \-zə(r)\ *n* -s : one that socializes

social justice *n* : a state or doctrine of egalitarianism ⟨the causes of human freedom and of *social justice* —Sir Winston Churchill⟩ ⟨promote the common good and *social justice* —G.J.Schnepp⟩

so·cial·ly \ˈsōshəl|ē, |i, *in rapid speech* -shl|\ *adv* **1** : in a social manner ⟨~ popular⟩ ⟨~ active⟩ **2** : with respect to society ⟨intellectually his superior but ~ his inferior⟩ **3** : by society ⟨~ prescribed values⟩

social medicine *n* : organized investigation of social, genetic, and environmental factors influencing human disease and disability and promotion of methods of prevention of disease and health measures protective of individual and community

social–minded \ˈ≈≈ˈ≈≈\ *adj* : having an interest in society; *specif* : actively interested in social welfare or the well-being of society as a whole

so·cial·ness *n* -ES : SOCIALITY

social order *n* : the totality of structured human interrelationships in a society or a part of it

social organism *n* : society considered as an organic unit analogous to a physiological organism

social organization *n* **1** : the kinship structure of a culture or society esp. as constituted in a stabilized network of rules of descent and residence **2 a** : the system of relationships between persons and among groups with regard to the division of activity and the functional arrangement of mutual obligations within society **b** : the broad institutional interrelationships in a society

social parasitism *n* : a mixobiotic and dependent relation; *specif* : the relation of various ants that lack a worker caste to other kinds of ants within whose nests they dwell and upon whom they depend for all the services normally performed by a species' own workers

social pathology *n* : a study of social problems (as crime or alcoholism) that views them as diseased conditions of the social organism

social philosophy *n* : the study and interpretation of society and social institutions in terms of ethical values rather than empirical relations

social physics *n pl but usu sing in constr* **1** : the science of social phenomena subject to invariable natural laws — compare SOCIAL DYNAMICS, SOCIAL STATICS **2** : the quantitative study of human society : social statistics

social process *n* **1** : a consistent historical change within a society or social institution **2** : a characteristic mode of social interaction

social psychiatry *n* **1** : a branch of psychiatry that deals in collaboration with related specialties (as sociology and anthropology) with the influence of social and cultural factors on the causation, course, and outcome of mental illness **2** : the application of psychodynamic principles to the solution of social problems

social psychology *n* : the study of the manner in which the personality, attitudes, and motivations of the individual esp. as manifested in his behavior reciprocally influence and are influenced by the structure, dynamics, and behavior of the social groups with which he interacts

social realism *n* : a theory or practice (as in painting) of using appropriate representation and symbol to express a social or political attitude

social recovery *n* : an improvement in a psychiatric patient's clinical status without the implication of cure but sufficient to permit his return to his former social milieu

social reg·is·ter·ite \-ˈrejəstəˌrīt\ *n* -s [fr. *Social Register*, a trademark + E *-ite*] : one whose name is listed in a register of persons socially prominent

socials *pl of* SOCIAL

social science *n* **1** : the branches of science that deal with the institutions and functioning of human soiety and with the interpersonal relationships of individuals as members of society **2** : a science (as economics or political science) dealing with a particular phase or aspect of human society — compare BEHAVIORAL SCIENCE

social scientist *n* : a specialist in the social sciences

social secretary *n* : a personal secretary employed to handle social correspondence and appointments

social security *n* **1** : the principle or practice of public provision for the economic security and social welfare of the individual and his family (as through social insurance or assistance) **2 a** *sometimes cap* : a U.S. government program established in 1935, gradually extended since, and including provisions for old age and survivors insurance, contributions to state unemployment insurance, and old age assistance **b** : a deduction or payment made under the U.S. social security program ⟨deducted three dollars from his check for *social security*⟩ ⟨hasn't received his *social security* for this month⟩

social selection *n* : the differential action of social conditions or agencies on the longevity and reproductive rates of individuals and strains in the population ⟨war is a factor in *social selection*⟩

social service *n* : an activity designed to promote social welfare; *specif* : organized philanthropic assistance of the sick, destitute, or unfortunate (as by a hospital, church or charitable agency) : WELFARE WORK

social statics *n pl but usu sing in constr* : a branch of social physics that deals with the fundamental laws of the social order and the equilibrium of forces in a stable society

social structure *n* **1** : the internal institutionalized relationships built up by persons living within a group (as a family or community) esp. with regard to the hierarchical organization of status and to the rules and principles regulating behavior **2** : the social organization of a society constituting an integrated whole

social studies *n pl* : the part of a school or college curriculum concerned with the study of social relationships and the functioning of society and usu. including courses in history, government, economics, civics, sociology, geography, and anthropology

social system *n* **1** : the patterned series of interrelationships existing between individuals, groups, and institutions and forming a coherent whole : SOCIAL STRUCTURE **2** : the formal organization of status and role that may develop among the members of a relatively small stable group (as a family or club)

social telesis *n* : TELESIS

social unit *n* : a unit (as an individual, a family, or a group) of a society

social wasp *n* : a wasp that lives in a communal nest

social weaverbird *n* : SOCIABLE WEAVERBIRD

social welfare *n* : organized public or private social services for the assistance of disadvantaged classes or groups; *specif* : SOCIAL WORK

social whale *n* : BLACKFISH 2

social work *n* : any of various professional services, activities, or methods concretely concerned with the investigation, treatment, and material aid of the economically underprivileged and socially maladjusted — compare CASEWORK, COMMUNITY ORGANIZATION, GROUP WORK

social worker *n* : one engaged in social work; *specif* : a professionally trained specialist in social work

¹so·ci·ate \ˈsōs(h)ēət\ *n* -s [ME *sociat*, fr. L *sociatus*, past part. of *sociare* to join, share, fr. *socius* companion — more at SOCIAL] *archaic* : COMPANION

²so·ci·ate \-ēˌāt\ *vi* -ED/-ING/-S [L *sociatus*, past part. of *sociare* to join, share] *archaic* : ASSOCIATE ⟨desire to ~ with and to be in their company —Wallace Stevens⟩

so·ci·a·tion \ˌsōs(h)ēˈāshən\ *n* -s [LL *sociation-*, *sociatio* union, association, fr. L *sociatus* (past part.) + *-ion-*, *-io* -ion] **1** : a mode or process of social interaction whether associative or dissociative — compare FORMAL SOCIOLOGY **2 a** : an ecological association that is usu. rather stable and of essentially uniform composition **b** : a community that is subject to seasonal variation

so·ci·a·tive \ˈsōs(h)ēˌād·iv, -ōshəd·iv, -ōs(h)ēəd·iv\ *adj* [L *sociatus* (past part.) + E *-ive*] **1** : expressive of association ⟨the ~ case⟩ **2** : tending to produce social interaction : ASSOCIATIVE

so·ci·a·trist \sōˈsīəˌtrəst\ *n* -s [*sociatry* + *-ist*] : one who practices sociatry

so·ci·a·try \-rē\ *n* -ES [*socio-* + *-iatry*] : group psychotherapy through the use of sociometric techniques (as psychodrama or sociodrama)

so·cies \ˈsō(ˌ)shēz\ *n, pl* **socies** [NL, fr. E *sociation* + *-ies* (as in *species*)] : a transitory ecological society of a developmental community : a seral community comparable to a society

so·cié·taire \ˌsōˌsyāˈta(a)(ə)r\ *n* -s [F, lit., member of a group or society, fr. *société* society (fr. MF *societé*) + *-aire* -ary] : a full member of the acting company of the Comédie Française having a voice in the management and sharing in the profits — compare PENSIONNAIRE

so·ci·e·tal \səˈsīəd·ᵊl, sōˈ-, -īətᵊl\ *adj* [*society* + *-al*] : of or relating to society : SOCIAL ⟨~ evolution⟩ ⟨~ forces⟩ — **so·ci·e·tal·ly** \-ᵊlē\ *adv*

so·ci·e·tary \səˈsīəˌterē\ *adj* [*society* + *-ary*] : SOCIETAL

so·ci·e·tas \sōˈkēˌtäs, sōˈsīəˌtas\ *n, pl* **so·ci·e·ta·tes** \sōˌkēˈtäˌtās, sōˌsīəˈtād·(ˌ)ēz\ [L] *Roman & civil law* : SOCIETY 3c

societas le·o·ni·na \-ˌlāəˈnēnə, -ˌlēəˈnīnə\ *n* [LL] : LEONINE PARTNERSHIP

societas univ·er·so·rum bo·no·rum \-ˌünəvərˈsōrəmbəˈnōrəm, -ˌyünə(ˌ)vərˈs-\ *n* [LL] : a partnership including all the property of the partners however acquired : UNIVERSAL PARTNERSHIP

so·cié·té ano·nyme \sōsyātāänōnēm\ *n, pl* **sociétés anonymes** \"\ [F, lit., anonymous society; fr. the fact that it consists of silent partners] *in civil law systems* : a society or corporation in which liability is limited to the capital invested — compare COMMANDITE

société en com·man·dite \-äⁿkōⁿmäⁿdēt\ *n, pl* **sociétés en commandite** \"\ [F, lit., society in commandite] : COMMANDITE

so·ci·e·ties \səˈsīəd·ēz\ *n pl, usu cap* [fr. pl. of ¹*society*; fr. the fact that they were orig. organized into a number of separate societies] : CAMERONIANS

¹so·ci·e·ty \səˈsīəd·|ē, sōˈ-, -īət|, |i\ *n* -ES [MF *societé*, fr. L *societat-*, *societas*, fr. *socie-* (fr. *socius* companion) + *-tat-*, *-tas* -ty — more at SOCIAL] **1 a** : companionship or association with one's fellows : friendly or intimate intercourse : COMPANY ⟨what are lobster and claret compared with the ~ of those we love —W.S.Gilbert⟩ **b** : one's friends or companions : ACQUAINTANCES ⟨widen his range of feminine ~, hitherto restricted —Richard Sullivan⟩ **2** *archaic* : the quality or state of being connected : RELATIONSHIP **3 a** : a voluntary association of individuals for common ends; *esp* : an organized group living or working together or periodically meeting or worshiping together because of a community of interests or beliefs or a common profession : a corporate or cooperative body ⟨a ~ of lawyers⟩ ⟨an agricultural ~⟩ ⟨the Royal *Society*⟩ **b** (1) : an ecclesiastical division of a town in colonial New England — called also *precinct* (2) : a Congregationalist corporation connected with a local church in the U.S. and having control of the ownership of the church buildings as well as the determination and payment of the minister's salary — called also *parish* **c** *Roman, civil, & Scots law* : an association organized under law for some recognized civil or business purpose and having various forms (as of a corporation, a general partnership, a limited partnership, or a community property entity) — compare COMMANDITE, SOCIÉTÉ ANONYME **d** : an association or fraternity among nonliterate peoples; *esp* : one functioning as an esoteric or ritualistic organization ⟨the medicine *societies* of the No. American Indians⟩ ⟨the leopard ~ of West Africa⟩ **4 a** : an enduring and cooperating social group whose members have developed organized patterns of relationships through interaction with one another; *also* : the complex structure of social institutions of such a group **b** : a community, nation, or broad grouping of people having common traditions, institutions, and collective activities and interests **c** : an international social order or community of societies and institutions ⟨a ~ of nations⟩ ⟨the ideal of a Christian world ~⟩ **d** : an autonomous nonliterate or peasant group possessing a distinct cultural heritage ⟨a primitive ~ in New Guinea⟩ **5 a** : a community made up of an aggregate of persons : those who are responsible for the prevailing social order ⟨when I say ~ I mean more than people; I mean people bound together for an end —V.S.Pritchett⟩ **b** : a part of a community that is a unit distinguishable by particular aims or standards of living or conduct : a social circle or a group of social circles having a clearly marked identity ⟨move in polite ~⟩ ⟨in the judgment of good ~⟩ ⟨literary ~⟩ ⟨musical ~⟩ **c** : a part of the community that sets itself apart as a leisure class and that regards it-

self as the arbiter of fashion and manners ⟨in most towns and smaller cities there is an easily discernible social pattern with a local ~ on top —F.L.Allen⟩ ⟨introduced to ~ at a formal reception⟩ ⟨snubbed by ~⟩ **6 a** (1) **:** a unit assemblage of plants within an association or consociation characterized by a single species or a common habit ⟨the alder ~ within the sugar maple consociation⟩ ⟨an herbaceous ~ in open woodland⟩ (2) **:** ASSOCIATION 8 **b :** the progeny of a pair of insect parents when constituting a social unit (as a hive of bees) **7 :** an interdependent system of organisms or biological units ⟨the skin — the protector, conservator, and inquirer of the ~ of organs —Margaret Gilbert⟩ ⟨the biological organism, a ~ of cells —T.C.Schneirla & Gerard Piel⟩

²society \"\ *adj* **:** of, relating to, or characteristic of fashionable society ⟨with her outdated ~ face highly rouged —G.A. Wagner⟩ **:** dealing with the activities of fashionable society ⟨~ page⟩ ⟨~ reporter⟩

society finch *n* **:** a small white weaverbird that is prob. an artificial variety and possibly derived from an Asiatic bird (*Lonchura acuticauda*)

society islander *n, usu cap S&I* [*Society island* + E *-er*] **:** a native or inhabitant of the Society islands in French Oceania

society men *or* **society people** *n pl, usu cap S* [so called fr. their being orig. organized into separate societies] **:** CAMERONIANS

society screw *n* [fr. its adoption by the Royal Microscopical Society] **:** a standard screw thread for objectives and nosepieces on microscopes used throughout the world

socii *pl of* SOCIUS

¹so·cin·i·an \sō'sinēən\ *n* -s *usu cap* [NL *socinianus*, fr. Faustus *Socinus* (latinized form of Fausto Sozzini) †1604 Ital. theologian who developed Socinianism and his uncle Laelius *Socinus* (latinized form of Lelio Sozzini) †1562 Ital. theologian whose writings influenced the founding of the movement + L *-ianus* -ian] **:** an adherent of Socinus or Socinianism

²socinian \"\ *adj, usu cap* [NL *socinianus*] **:** of or relating to Socinus, the Socinians, or Socinianism

so·cin·i·an·ism \-ə,nizəm\ *n* -s *usu cap* [NL *socinianismus*, fr. *socinianus* socinian + L *-ismus* -ism] **:** the rationalistic doctrines and anti-Trinitarian theological movement originating in the middle of the 16th century in Italy and developed in Poland under the leadership of Socinus who denied the tenets of the Trinity, the divinity of Christ, the personality of the Devil, the native and total depravity of man, substitutionary atonement, the efficacy of the sacraments, and the eternity of future punishment and affirmed instead the tenets that Christ was a man miraculously conceived by the Virgin Mary, that the Holy Spirit is a power or influence exerted by God, that human sin is the imitation of Adam's sin, that salvation is something to be achieved by the imitation of Christ's virtue, and that the Bible is to be interpreted by and as being in accord with human reason

so·cin·i·an·is·tic \sō¦sinēə¦nistik\ *adj, usu cap* [*socinian* + *-istic*] **:** Socinian in character or tendency

so·cin·i·an·ize \sō'sinēə,nīz\ *vt* -ED/-ING/-S *usu cap* [*socinian* + *-ize*] **:** to cause to conform to Socinianism **:** imbue with Socinianism

socio- *comb form* [F, fr. L *socius* associate, companion — more at SOCIAL] **1 :** society ⟨*socio*graphy⟩ **:** social ⟨*socio*gram⟩ **2 :** social and ⟨*socio*educational⟩ ⟨*socio*political⟩ ⟨*socio*religious⟩ **3 :** sociological and ⟨*socio*legal⟩ ⟨*socio*psychiatric⟩

so·cio·biological \¦sōs(h)ē(,)ō+\ *adj* [*socio-* + *biological*] **1 :** relating to the interrelation of social science and biological science or joining their techniques **2 :** having both a social and biological factor

so·cio·biology \"+\ *n* [*socio-* + *biology*] **:** the study of society in terms of the methods and concepts of biological science

so·ci·o·cen·tric \¦sōs(h)ēō¦sen·trik\ *adj* [*socio-* + *-centric*] **:** concerned with or centered on one's own social group — compare EGOCENTRIC, ETHNOCENTRIC — **so·ci·o·cen·tric·i·ty** \,sōs(h)ēōsen·'trisəd·ē\ *n* -ES

so·ci·o·cen·trism \¦==='sen,trizəm\ *n* -s [ISV *sociocentric* + *-ism*] **:** a tendency to assume the superiority or rightness of one's own social group

so·ci·oc·ra·cy \,sōs(h)ē'äkrəsē\ *n* -ES [F *sociocratie*, fr. *socio-* + *-cratie* -cracy] **1 :** a theoretical form of government in which society as a whole has sovereign rights **2 :** the application of scientifically determined principles promoting the interests of society as a whole

so·ci·o·crat \'sōs(h)ēə,krat\ *n* -s [*socio-* + *-crat*] **:** one who advocates sociocracy

so·ci·o·crat·ic \¦===krad·ik\ *adj* [*socio-* + *-cratic*] **:** of or relating to sociocracy

so·cio·cultural \¦sōs(h)ē(,)ō+\ *adj* [*socio-* + *cultural*] **:** of, relating to, or involving a combination of social and cultural factors

so·cio·drama \"+\ *n* [*socio-* + *drama*] **1 :** a dramatic play in which several individuals act out assigned roles for the purpose of studying and remedying group or collective relationships — compare PSYCHODRAMA **2 :** the application of the principles of psychodrama to the study of intergroup tensions and conflict — **so·cio·dramatic** \"+\ *adj*

so·cio·dynamic \"+\ *adj* [*socio-* + *dynamic*] **:** causing or producing change in a society or social group ⟨morale is a ~ factor in a ship's company⟩

so·cio·economic \"+\ *adj* [*socio-* + *economic*] **1 :** of, relating to, or involving a combination of social and economic factors; *specif* **:** of or relating to income and social position considered as a single factor ⟨a scale to measure family ~ status⟩ **2 :** of or relating to social economics

so·cio·genesis \"+\ *n* [NL, fr. *socio-* + *genesis*] **:** the evolution of societies or of a particular society, community, or social unit

so·ci·o·ge·net·ic \¦sōs(h)ēōjə¦ned·ik\ *adj* [*socio-* + *-genetic*] **:** of, relating to, or contributing to sociogenesis ⟨~ factors⟩

so·ci·o·gen·ic \-ēō¦jenik\ *adj* [*socio-* + *-genic*] **:** produced or determined by society or social forces ⟨~ factors in mental health⟩

so·ci·o·gram \'sōs(h)ēə,gram\ *n* [*socio-* + *-gram*] **:** a sociometric chart plotting the structure of interpersonal relations in a group situation

so·ci·o·graph·ic \¦sōs(h)ēə¦grafik\ *adj* [*sociography* + *-ic*] **:** of or relating to sociography ⟨a ~ survey⟩

so·ci·og·ra·phy \,sōs(h)ē'ägrəfē\ *n* -ES [*socio-* + *-graphy*] **:** a branch of sociology that concentrates on the descriptive analysis of social groups

so·ci·o·log·ic \¦sōsēə¦läjik, -jēk *also* ¦sōsh(ē)ə¦-\ *or* **so·ci·o·log·i·cal** \-jəkəl, -jēk-\ *adj* [*sociologic* fr. F *sociologique*, fr. *sociologie* sociology + *-ique* -ic; *sociological* fr. *sociology* + *-ical*] **1 a :** of or relating to sociology or to the methodological approach of sociology **b :** involving one or more of the social sciences generally **2 a :** oriented or directed toward social needs and problems ⟨~ jurisprudence⟩ ⟨~ novels⟩ ⟨~ criticism⟩ **b :** social in nature ⟨only human society is truly ~⟩ **3 :** of or relating to interpersonal and collective relationships rather than to individual psychology — **so·ci·o·log·i·cal·ly** \-jək(ə)lē, -jēk-, -li\ *adv*

so·ci·ol·o·gism \,sōsē'äləjizəm *also* ,sōshē-\ *n* -s [*sociology* + *-ism*] **:** a sociologistic explanation or theory

so·ci·ol·o·gist \-jəst\ *n* -s [ISV *sociology* + *-ist*] **:** a specialist in sociology

so·ci·ol·o·gis·tic \¦sōsē¦älə¦jistik, -tēk *also* ¦sōshē-\ *adj* [*sociology* + *-istic*] **:** SOCIOLOGIC; *specif* **:** explaining social phenomena by sociologic principles alone ⟨a ~ interpretation admitting of no biologic or psychologic factors⟩

so·ci·ol·o·gize \,sōsē'älə,jīz *also* ,sōshē-\ *vt* -ED/-ING/-S [*sociology* + *-ize*] **:** to give a sociological character or interpretation to

so·ci·ol·o·gy \-ləjē, -ji\ *n* -ES [F *sociologie*, fr. *socio-* (fr. L *socius* associate, companion) + *-logie* -logy — more at SOCIAL] **1 :** the science of society, social institutions, and social relationships; *specif* **:** the systematic study of the development, structure, and function of human groups conceived as processes of interaction or as organized patterns of collective behavior **2 a :** the scientific analysis of a social institution as a functioning whole and as it relates to the rest of society ⟨the ~ of education⟩ ⟨the ~ of law⟩ ⟨the ~ of business⟩ **b :** an analysis or exposition of the socially significant traits of a specific group, class, or social milieu ⟨a ~ of the blind⟩ ⟨write a ~ of Victorian England⟩ **3** *Brit* **:** SOCIAL ANTHROPOLOGY **4 :** the study of social and behavioral interaction among lower animals (as in a flock of hens) **:** SYNECOLOGY

so·cio·medical \¦sōs(h)ē(,)ō+\ *adj* [*socio-* + *medical*] **:** of or relating to the interrelations of medicine and social welfare

so·ci·o·met·ric \¦sōsēə¦me·trik, -rēk *also* ¦sōsh(ē)ə¦-\ *adj* [*socio-* + *-metric*] **1 :** adapted for or used in the measurement of social phenomena ⟨a ~ scale⟩ **2 :** relating to or constituting a test in which the members of a group are invited to express their feelings with regard to one another

so·ci·om·e·trist \,sōsē'ämə·trəst *also* ,sōshē-\ *n* -s [*sociometry* + *-ist*] **1 :** a specialist in sociometry **2 :** one who administers sociometric tests

so·ci·om·e·try \-rē, -ri\ *n* -ES [ISV *socio-* + *-metry*] **:** the study (as by sociometric test, psychodrama, or sociodrama) of the patterns of interrelation existing in a group of people

so·ci·o·path \'sōs(h)ēə,path\ *n* -s [*socio-* + *-path*] **:** a sociopathic person

so·ci·o·path·ic \¦===¦pathik\ *adj* [*socio-* + *-pathic*] **:** of, relating to, or characterized by asocial or antisocial behavior ⟨a ~ personality⟩ — compare PSYCHOPATHIC PERSONALITY

so·ci·op·a·thy \,sōs(h)ē'äpəthē\ *n* -ES [*socio-* + *-pathy*] **:** the condition of being sociopathic

so·cio·political \¦sōs(h)ē(,)ō+\ *adj* [*socio-* + *political*] **:** of, relating to, or involving a combination of social and political factors

so·cio·psychological \"+\ *adj* [*socio-* + *psychological*] **1 :** of, relating to, or involving a combination of social and psychological factors **2 :** of or relating to social psychology

so·cio·sexual \"+\ *adj* [*socio-* + *sexual*] **:** of or relating to the interpersonal aspects of sexuality

so·ci·us \'sōshēəs\ *n, pl* **socii** \-ē,ī\ [L — more at SOCIAL] **1 :** ASSOCIATE, COLLEAGUE ⟨was procurator and ~ to the vice-provincial —R.J.Purcell⟩; *specif, cap* **:** the divine friend and companion of man **2 :** a unit in social relationships consisting of an individual

socius cri·mi·nis \-'krimənəs\ *n* [LL] **:** an associate or accomplice in crime **:** ACCESSORY

¹sock \'säk\ *n* -s *see sense 2a* [ME *socke, sokke*, fr. OE *socc*, fr. L *soccus*, a low-heeled light shoe, slipper, sock; akin to Gk *sykchos*, a shoe, sock, Av *haxa* sole of the foot] **1** *archaic* **:** a low shoe or slipper **2 a** *or pl* **sox** \-ks\ **:** a knitted or woven covering for the foot usu. extending above the ankle and sometimes to the knee and worn inside the shoe or other footwear **b :** a soft protective covering (as for the head of a golf club) resembling a sock **c :** SOCK LINING **d** [by shortening] **:** WIND SOCK **3 a :** a shoe worn by actors in Greek and Roman comedy **b :** comedy as a literary or theatrical form **:** the comic stage — compare BUSKIN 2b **4 :** a receptacle for savings ⟨in France, the money tends to disappear into the ~; here it goes into circulation —Frank Gorrell⟩ **5 :** a usu. white band of foot color extending to the fetlock ⟨a horse with three white ~s⟩ **6 :** STOCKING 2a

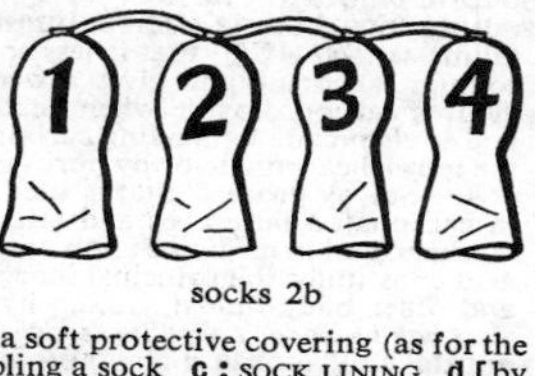

socks 2b

²sock \"\ *vt* -ED/-ING/-S **:** to furnish socks to **:** put socks on

³sock \"\ *n* -s [ME *sok, sokk*, fr. MF *soc*, fr. OF — more at SOCKET] *chiefly Scot* **:** PLOWSHARE

⁴sock \"\ *vb* -ED/-ING/-S [prob. of Scand origin; akin to ON *sökkva* to cause to sink, *sökkva* to sink — more at SINK] *vt* **:** to hit, strike, or apply forcefully ⟨hailstones as big as pullet eggs were ~*ing* me on the head —*Springfield (Mass.) Union*⟩ ⟨I pick a good one and ~ it —Babe Ruth⟩ ⟨~*ed* the hot iron to the calf's side —Lewis Nordyke⟩ ~ *vi* **:** to deliver a blow **:** HIT ⟨a miracle that a person as old . . . could ~ as hard or holler as loud as she could —J.T.Farrell⟩ ⟨the bull lunged forward and ~*ed* against the mattress shield that protected the horse —Barnaby Conrad⟩ — **sock it** *slang* **:** to act, speak, or express oneself forcefully or violently ⟨they may let you off the first time . . . but the second time they'll *sock it* to you —James Jones⟩ ⟨he really *socked it* to her . . . he had a great talent for obscenity and filth —Albert Morgan⟩

⁵sock \"\ *n* -s **1 :** a vigorous or violent blow ⟨got a ~ in the belly from somebody that made him plenty sick —H.A.Sinclair⟩ **2 :** FORCE, PUNCH ⟨surface-to-surface missiles will add new ~ to the Army's firepower —*Time*⟩

⁶sock \"\ *adj* [⁴sock] **1** *slang* **:** having a loud or forceful quality ⟨dazzling chorus work and ~ arrangements —Douglas Watt⟩ **2** *slang* **:** highly successful ⟨wrote a ~ first play and can't get on with a second —*Time*⟩

⁷sock \"\ *vi* [prob. imit.] *dial Eng* **:** SIGH

sock away *vt* [¹sock] *slang* **:** to put away (money) as savings or investment ⟨has *socked away* very little of his earnings with which to buy a ranch —*Life*⟩ ⟨had been *socking* money *away* at a faster rate —*Newsweek*⟩

sock·dol·a·ger *or* **sock·dol·o·ger** *also* **soc·dol·a·ger** \säk'däləjə(r)\ *n* -s [perh. alter. (influenced by ⁵sock) of *doxology*] **1 :** something that ends or settles a matter **:** a decisive blow or answer **:** FINISHER **2 :** something or someone outstanding or exceptional ⟨a blizzard — a real ~ —Lorna Slocombe⟩

¹sock·er \'säkə(r)\ *chiefly Brit var of* SOCCER

²socker \"\ *n* -s [⁴sock + *-er*] *slang* **:** one that socks; *specif* **:** a hard puncher

sock·er·oo \,säkə'rü\ *n* -s [alter. of ²socker] *slang* **:** a smash hit

¹sock·et \'säkət, *usu* -əd·+V\ *n* -s [ME *soket* spearhead shaped like a plowshare, support of a spear or pole, socket, fr. AF, dim. of OF *soc* plowshare, of Celt origin; akin to Corn *soch* plowshare, MIr *soc* plowshare, snout of a hog, OIr *socc* hog — more at sow (hog)] **1 a :** an opening or hollow that forms a holder for something **:** a hollow piece that serves as a standard or support for a pole, rod, shaft, or similarly shaped object ⟨the whip was in its ~ beside him —Kathleen Freeman⟩ ⟨put the flagpole in its ~⟩ ⟨a candle ~⟩ **b :** any of various hollows in body structures in which some other part normally lodges ⟨the bony ~ of the eye⟩ ⟨an inflamed tooth ~⟩; *esp* **:** the depression in a bone with which the rounded head of another bone fits in a ball-and-socket joint ⟨the acetabulum or ~ of the hip joint⟩ **c :** a cavity terminating an artificial limb into which the bodily stump fits ⟨suction ~⟩ **d :** BELL 5i **2 a :** a device to receive and grip the end of a thing (as a rope, tool, incandescent lamp, or shaft of a golf club) ⟨screwed the light bulb into the ~⟩ **b :** any of several fishing tools for catching the outside of pipe or tools lost in an oil well

²socket \"\ *vt* -ED/-ING/-S **1 :** to provide with or support in or by a socket **2 :** to insert, screw, or secure in a socket

socket-and-spigot joint \¦==='==-\ *n* **:** BELL-AND-SPIGOT JOINT

socket chisel *n* **:** a chisel that has a tapering hollow tang to receive a handle — see CHISEL illustration

socket head screw *n* **:** a screw having a recess or socket to fit a wrench for turning rather than a slot or external hexagonal or square shape

sock·et·less \'säkətləs\ *adj* **:** not provided or made with a socket

socket punch *n* **:** a hollow punch (as a belt punch) with a cutting edge forming a closed curve

socket washer *n* **:** a washer countersunk to receive a bolt head or nut

socket wood *n* **:** an Australian sassafras (*Daphnandra micrantha*) that has swellings resembling sockets at the branch bases

socket wrench *n* **:** a wrench in the form of a socket or a rod having a hollow end to fit a bolt or nut — compare BOX WRENCH

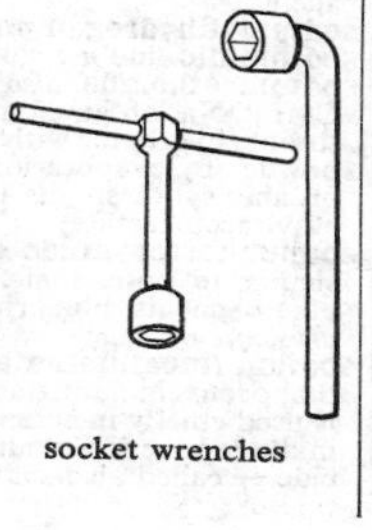
socket wrenches

sock·eye \'sä,kī\ *or* **sockeye salmon** *n* [by folk etymology fr. Salish dial. *suk-kegh* sockeye] **:** a small but very important Pacific salmon (*Oncorhynchus nerka*) attaining an average weight of about 5 pounds and ascending rivers chiefly from the Columbia northward to spawn in spring — called also *red salmon;* compare KOKANEE

sock in *vt* [¹sock; fr. the fact that indications by the wind sock may cause flights to be canceled] **1 :** to close in **:** CONCEAL ⟨bases . . . *socked in* with monsoon clouds squatting on the runways —Wesley Price⟩ **2 :** to restrict from flying ⟨planes *socked in* by fog⟩

socking *pres part of* SOCK

sock·less \'säkləs\ *adj* **:** being without socks

socklike \'=,=\ *adj* **:** resembling a sock

sock lining *n* **:** a thin piece of leather or other material inserted in a shoe over the insole

sock·man \'säkmən\ *archaic var of* SOCMAN

socko \'sä(,)kō\ *adj* [prob. fr. ⁵sock + ¹oh] **1** *slang* **:** SMASH ⟨some ~ successes in TV —Ethel Merman⟩ **2** *slang* **:** packing a wallop ⟨the ~ lines, the one-two punch lines —*Vogue*⟩

socks *pl of* SOCK, *pres 3d sing of* SOCK

sock suspenders *n pl, Brit* **:** men's garters

soc·le \'säkəl, 'sōkəl\ *n* -s [F, fr. It *zoccolo* sock, wooden shoe, socle, fr. L *socculus*, dim. of *soccus* sock — more at SOCK] **:** a projecting usu. molded member at the foot of a wall or pier or beneath the base of a column, pedestal, or superstructure — compare PLINTH

soc·man \'säkmən, 'sōk-\ *n, pl* **socmen** [ML *sochemannus, sokemannus* — more at SOKEMAN] **:** SOKEMAN

soc·man·ry \-nrē\ *n* -ES [by alter.] **:** SOKEMANRY

so·co \'sō(,)kō\ *n* -s [Pg *socó*, fr. Tupi *soco, çoco*] **:** any of several Brazilian herons; *esp* **:** any of certain night herons and bitterns

¹so·co·tran \sə'kō·trən\ *or* **so·co·trine** \-rən\ *or* **so·ko·tron** \-rən\ *adj, usu cap* [*Socotra, Sokotra*, island in the Indian ocean + E *-an* or *-ine*] **:** of, relating to, or characteristic of Socotra, an island in the Indian ocean off Cape Guardafui, Africa

²socotran *or* **sokotran** \"\ *n* -s *cap* [*Socotra, Sokotra* + E *-an* (n. suffix)] **:** a native or inhabitant of Socotra

soc·ra·te·an \¦säkrə¦tēən\ *adj, usu cap* [*Socrates* †399 B.C. Greek philosopher + E *-an*] **:** SOCRATIC

¹so·crat·ic \sə'krad·|ik, sō'-, -at|, |ēk\ *adj, usu cap* [L *socraticus*, fr. Gk *sōkratikos*, fr. *Sōkratēs* Socrates †399 B.C. Greek philosopher + *-ikos* -ic] **:** of or relating to the philosopher Socrates, Socratism, or the Socratics

²socratic \"\ *n* -s *usu cap* **1 :** a follower of Socrates **2 :** a member of one of the minor schools of Greek philosophy (as the Cynic, Cyrenaic, or Megarian) influenced by Socrates — called also *lesser Socratic, minor Socratic*

so·crat·i·cal \|əkəl\ *adj, usu cap* [L *socraticus* + E *-al*] *archaic* **:** SOCRATIC

so·crat·i·cal·ly \|ək(ə)lē\ *adv, usu cap* **:** in the Socratic method

socratic elenchus *n, usu cap S* **:** the method of questioning and cross examination used by Socrates

socratic induction *n, usu cap S* **:** the process of gradually arriving at generalizations through dialectical questions and answers — compare SOCRATIC METHOD

socratic irony *n, usu cap S* **:** pretended ignorance or willingness to learn from others assumed for the sake of making their errors conspicuous by means of adroit questioning

so·crat·i·cism \sə'krad·ə,sizəm\ *n* -s *usu cap* [¹socratic + *-ism*] **1 :** SOCRATISM **2 :** a Socratic trait or principle

socratic method *n, usu cap S* **:** the method of inquiry and instruction employed by Socrates esp. as represented in the dialogues of Plato and consisting of a series of questionings the object of which is to elicit a clear and consistent expression of something supposed to be implicitly known by all rational beings

soc·ra·tism \'säkrə,tizəm\ *n* -s *usu cap* [*Socrates* †399 B.C. Greek philosopher (fr. L, fr. Gk *Sōkratēs*) + E *-ism*] **:** the philosophy or the method of Socrates to whom are generally ascribed an intense ethical devotion that influenced all later Greek philosophy, the development of the inductive method, and the conception of knowledge or insight as the foundation of virtue — compare DIALECTIC, SOCRATIC METHOD

socy *abbr* society

¹sod \'säd\ *n* -s *often attrib* [ME *sod, sodde*, fr. MD or MLG *sode;* akin to OFris *sātha* sod] **1 a :** the upper stratum of the soil or humus that is filled with the roots of grass or other herbs **:** TURF, SWARD **b :** a piece or section of such sod (as for grassing a lawn) **2 a :** the grass-covered surface of the ground ⟨hired nesters to break ~ for 50 cents an acre —F.B.Gipson⟩ ⟨clambered on to the wet-soaked ~ of land —Michael McLaverty⟩ **b :** COUNTRY 2a — usu. used in the phrase *old sod* ⟨would take a trip to the old ~ —J.T.Farrell⟩

²sod \"\ *vt* **sodded; sodded; sodding; sods :** to cover with sod ⟨many gullies on the ridge have been *sodded* with grass —*Amer. Guide Series: Ark.*⟩ ⟨*sodded* earthen bunkers capped three walls —B.A.Roth⟩

³sod \"\ *adj, archaic, of food* **:** boiled or prepared by boiling; *sometimes* **:** SOGGY, UNPALATABLE

⁴sod \"\ [ME *soden* (past pl.), fr. OE *sudon*] *archaic past of* SEETHE

⁵sod \'säd\ *n* -s [short for *sodomite*] **:** BUGGER ⟨you bleary-eyed murderous ~ —Ernest Hemingway⟩ ⟨picture palace for the silly ~s to go and get rid of the rest of their minds in —Richard Llewellyn⟩ ⟨poor little ~'s out o' his mind —G.G.Carter⟩

sod *abbr* sodium

SOD *abbr* seller's option to double

so·da \'sōdə, *dial* -dē *or* -di\ *n* -s [It, barilla (from which soda is produced), soda, fr. (assumed) ML *soda* barilla (whence *sodanum* barilla), perh. fr. Ar *suwwād*] **1 a :** SODIUM CARBONATE; *esp* **:** the decahydrate of the normal salt **b :** SODIUM BICARBONATE **c :** SODIUM HYDROXIDE **2 a :** SODIUM OXIDE **b :** SODIUM — not used systematically ⟨nitrate of ~⟩ **3 a :** SODA WATER 2 **b :** ICE-CREAM SODA **4 :** the faro card that shows face up in the dealing box before play begins

soda alum *n* **:** sodium alum esp. in the isometric crystal form but not isostructural with potash alum — compare MENDOZITE

soda ash *n* **:** commercial anhydrous sodium carbonate Na_2CO_3 obtained as a grayish white powder or as lumps

soda biscuit *n* **1 :** a biscuit leavened with baking soda and sour milk or buttermilk **2 :** SODA CRACKER

soda bread *n* **:** a quick bread leavened with baking soda and sour milk

soda cracker *n* **:** a cracker leavened with bicarbonate of soda and cream of tartar

soda crystals *n pl* **:** SODIUM CARBONATE a(3)

soda fountain *n* **1 :** an apparatus with delivery tube and faucets for drawing soda water **2 :** the equipment necessary for the preparation and serving of sodas, sundaes, and ice cream; *also* **:** the counter at which such items are dispensed

soda-granite \'==¦==\ *n* **1 :** a granite containing more soda than potash **2 :** a granite rock differing from normal granite in containing a soda-plagioclase instead of orthoclase

soda jerk \'==,jərk, -,jōk, -,jəik\ *or* **soda jerker** \'==,==\ *n* [*soda jerk*, short for *soda jerker*, fr. *soda* + *jerker*] **:** a counterman at a soda fountain

soda lake *n* **:** ALKALI LAKE

soda lime *n* **:** a granular mixture of calcium hydroxide with sodium hydroxide or potassium hydroxide or both and sometimes with other substances (as kieselguhr) used to absorb moisture and acid gases esp. carbon dioxide (as in gas masks, in the rebreathing technique of inhalation anesthesia, and in oxygen therapy)

soda-lime glass *n* [*soda lime*] **:** a lime glass in which soda is used

so·da·list \'sōdᵊləst\ *n* -s *sometimes cap* [*sodality* + *-ist*] **:** a member of a sodality

so·da·lite \-də,līt, -dᵊl,īt\ *n* -s [*soda* + *-lite*] **:** a mineral $Na_4Al_3Si_3O_{12}Cl$ consisting of a sodium aluminum silicate with some chlorine that occurs commonly in dodecahedrons, that is transparent to translucent with a vitreous or greasy luster, that is white, greenish, gray, or blue in color, and that is found in various igneous rocks (hardness 5.5–6, sp. gr. 2.14–2.30)

so·dal·i·ty \sō'dalədē, -lətē, -i\ *n* -ES [L *sodalitat-, sodalitas* comradeship, association, club, fr. *sodalis* comrade — more at ETHICAL] **1 :** a grouping, association, or joining together based on common purpose or interest **:** BROTHERHOOD, COMMUNITY ⟨whether ape hordes are blood kin or mere territorial *sodalities* —Weston La Barre⟩ ⟨federal ~⟩ ⟨body of ardent and vocal supporters and a formidable ~ of hostile critics —R.J.B. Sellar⟩ **2 :** an organized society or fellowship **:** FRATERNITY, CLUB ⟨endless . . . *sodalities* into which people brigade them-

selves —John Buchan⟩; *specif* : a lay association of the Roman Catholic Church organized for devotional or charitable purposes **3** *obs* : a chapel used for sodality meetings and devotions

soda lye *n* : a solution (as used in soap-making) of sodium hydroxide

soda mesolite *n* : NATROLITE

soda mica *n* : PARAGONITE

so·da·mide \'sōdə‚mīd, sō'da‚ ‚məd\ *n* -s [*sodium* + *amide*] : SODIUM AMIDE

soda niter *n* : SODIUM NITRATE

soda process *n* : a method for making pulp by cooking wood chips at high temperature and pressure in an alkaline solution containing chiefly caustic soda

soda pulp *n* : pulp prepared by the soda process — compare SULFITE PULP, WOOD PULP

so·dar \'sō‚där, -dä(r\ *n* -s [*so*und *d*etecting *a*nd *r*anging] : an acoustical system operated like radar and initially developed to investigate the atmosphere directly overhead for the prediction of the weather

sodas *pl of* SODA

soda soap *n* : a usu. hard soap made with sodium hydroxide or sodium carbonate

soda-tremolite \‚==¦==‚=\ *n* : a mineral $Na_2CaMg_5Si_8O_{22}(OH)_2$ consisting of an amphibole that differs from tremolite in having sodium in place of half of the calcium

soda water *n* **1** : a weak solution of sodium bicarbonate with some acid added to cause effervescence **2 a** : a beverage consisting of water highly charged with carbonic acid gas that is effervescent when not under pressure and is used in the manufacture of soft drinks and with various liquors in highballs and other alcoholic drinks **b** *or* **soda pop** : a bottled soft drink consisting of such charged water with added flavoring and a sweet syrup

sod-bound \'=‚=\ *adj* [[1]*sod*] : impeded in growth or yield by a seemingly crowded condition of the sod usu. resulting from inadequate nitrates in the soil ⟨*sod-bound* grass⟩ ⟨*sod-bound* meadows⟩

sodbuster \'=‚==\ *n* : one that breaks the sod: **a** : a breaking or sod plow **b** : a farmer on a homestead **c** : FARMER; *esp* : a farm worker or tiller of the soil

sod cloth *n* : a heavy canvas or duck cloth that extends into the ground at the foot of a tent wall and serves to exclude vermin and rain

sod crop *n* : a crop (as flax or corn) grown on a field of freshly broken sod

sod culture *n* : the culture of fruit trees in sod with or without fertilizing or light tillage

sodded *past of* SOD

[1]**sodden** [ME *soden*, fr. OE] *archaic past part. of* SEETHE

[2]**sod·den** \'säd°n\ *adj* [ME *soden*, fr. *soden*, past part.] **1** *archaic* : BOILED **2 a** : dull or expressionless in cast or appearance from or as if from continued indulgence in alcoholic beverages ⟨a feeble smile crept over his ~ features —Joseph Furphy⟩ ⟨a burly, ~ red-faced man —S.E.White⟩ **b** : dull or mentally inert : TORPID, UNIMAGINATIVE ⟨is emotionally, intellectually, and spiritually . . . too ~ a character to carry the full weight of philosophical understanding —C.I. Glicksberg⟩ ⟨quickens their ~ . . . minds to some sort of glimmering conception of writing as an art —Dorothy C. Fisher⟩ **c** : wearisome or monotonous in delivery or effect : SPIRITLESS ⟨turns in a ~ performance, ranting endlessly about his daughter's conduct —John McCarten⟩ ⟨considering how many ~ and saccharine singers wandered through half a dozen variety shows —Bernard De Voto⟩ **3 a** : heavy with moisture or water : SOAKED, SATURATED ⟨the ~ drumming of the water on the caribou skins of the roof —Farley Mowat⟩ ⟨torrid atmospheric conditions which . . . had reduced the conductor's collar to a ~ wreck —*Sydney (Australia) Bull.*⟩ ⟨the sands were ~ with petroleum that killed fish, destroyed waterfowl —Walter Karig⟩ **b** : settled, unremitting, or oppressively heavy or inert ⟨living in clumsy and ~ ugliness —Galbraith Welch⟩ ⟨depicts ~ hopelessness in the dreary landscape —Curtis Dahl⟩ ⟨the ~ habits of a dead and inferior era —C.G. Burke⟩ ⟨the exhausted, ~ sleep of beasts —F. Tennyson Jesse⟩ ⟨too small a minority to leaven the ~ mass of a people long subject to absolutist rule —V.L.Parrington⟩ **c** : heavy or doughy because of imperfect cooking ⟨~ biscuits⟩ **4** : filled or weighed down with evil : SORDID ⟨exposing the ~ motives behind anti-Semitism —Carl Van Doren⟩ ⟨some very ~, very callous guys operate around these stock joints —Marcus Verner⟩ ⟨drunkenness is a ~ vice —Albert Mowbray⟩

[3]**sodden** \"\ *vb* **soddened; soddened; soddening** \-d(°)niŋ\ **soddens** *vt* : to make sodden: **a** : SOAK, SATURATE ⟨bread which has been ~*ed* in water —C.R.A.Martin⟩ **b** : to cause (one's mind) to become dull, stupid, or inert ⟨~*ed* by years of oppression and hardship⟩ **c** : to make (a person) flabby or bloated by alcoholic beverages ⟨a woman ~*ed* and mad with brandy —William Black⟩ ~ *vi* : to become soaked or saturated with moisture or water ⟨the sands ~ as the waves move in⟩

sod·den·ly *adv* : in a sodden condition or manner ⟨tramping ~ homeward through the dust —Booth Tarkington⟩

sod·den·ness \-d°n(n)əs\ *n* -ES : the quality or state of being sodden

sodding *n* -s [fr. gerund of [2]*sod*] **1** : the action of one that sods **2** : SOD, TURF

sod disease *n* [[1]*sod*] : a severe vesicular dermatitis esp. of the feet of young chickens and turkeys ranging on sod that is marked by swelling and frequent sloughing of toes and is thought to be due to a fungus infection

sod·dite \'sä‚dīt\ *n* -s [Frederick *Soddy* †1956 Eng. chemist + E *-ite*] : SODDYITE

[1]**sod·dy** \'sädē, -di\ *adj* -ER/-EST [[1]*sod* + *-y*] : consisting of, covered with, or abounding in sod : TURFY

[2]**soddy** \"\ *n* -ES [[1]*sod* + *-y*] : SOD HOUSE

sod·dy·ite \'sädē‚īt\ *n* -s [alter. of *soddite*] : a mineral $(UO_2)_{12}Si_5O_{22}.14H_2O$ consisting of a hydrous uranium silicate occurring in fine-grained pale-yellow aggregates or orthorhombic crystals

sod grass *n* [[1]*sod*] : a grass that forms good sod — compare SAINT AUGUSTINE GRASS

sod house *n* : a house with walls built of sod or turf laid in horizontal layers

so·dic \'sōdik\ *adj* [ISV *sod-* (fr. NL *sodium*) + *-ic*] : of, relating to, or containing sodium

so·dio \'sōdē‚ō\ *adj* [*sodio-*] : containing sodium in place of hydrogen

sodio- *comb form* [NL *sodium*] **1** : sodium and ⟨*sodio*aluminic⟩ ⟨*sodio*hydric⟩ **2** : containing sodium in place of hydrogen — used in names of organic compounds ⟨*sodio*malonic ester⟩ ⟨*sodio*nitromethane⟩

so·di·um \'sōdēəm\ *n* -s [NL, fr. E *soda* + NL *-ium*] : a silver white soft waxy ductile metallic element of the alkali metal group that has a low melting point and density and high electrical and thermal conductivity, that occurs abundantly in nature in combined form (as rock salt, Chile saltpeter, trona, borax, glauberite, albite), in soils, in the sea and other salt waters, in most plants, and in the animal body esp. in the fluids, that is usu. prepared by electrolysis of a mixture of fused sodium chloride and calcium chloride, that is very active chemically and oxidizes and tarnishes readily in air and burns with a yellow flame, that reacts violently with water to form sodium hydroxide and spontaneously ignitable hydrogen, that is stored under kerosine, other inert hydrocarbon liquid, or in tight containers protected from moisture and air, and that is used sometimes in the form of its amalgam or other alloys or in dispersions in hydrocarbon liquids in making tetraethyl lead and various sodium compounds (as sodium cyanide, sodium hydride, sodium peroxide), in organic synthesis (as in reducing esters to alcohols for making detergents), in metallurgy esp. for removing oxygen or various impurities, in sodium-vapor lamps, and as a heat-transfer agent esp. in cooling valves for internal-combustion engines — symbol *Na*; see ELEMENT table; compare RADIOSODIUM

sodium acetate *n* : either of two sodium salts of acetic acid: **a** : the hygroscopic crystalline normal salt CH_3COONa used chiefly in organic synthesis and photography and as a mordant or as an analytical reagent **b** : the acid salt $CH_3COONa.CH_3COOH$ used chiefly in inhibiting mold and rope in bakery products; sodium hydrogen acetate

sodium acid phosphate *n* : SODIUM PHOSPHATE 1a

sodium acid pyrophosphate *n* : SODIUM PYROPHOSPHATE a

sodium alginate *n* : ALGIN c

sodium alum *n* : a crystalline double salt $NaAl(SO_4)_2.12H_2O$ used similarly to potassium alum; sodium aluminum sulfate dodecahydrate — called also *soda alum*

sodium aluminate *n* : a crystalline compound $NaAlO_2$ used chiefly in water purification, in making synthetic zeolites, and in sizing paper

sodium aluminum fluoride *n* : SODIUM FLUOALUMINATE

sodium aluminum sulfate *n* : a salt $NaAl(SO_4)_2$ occurring either in the anhydrous form as a fine powder used as an acid ingredient of baking powder or in the hydrated forms mendozite and sodium alum

sodium amide *n* : a crystalline compound $NaNH_2$ that decomposes explosively in contact with water, that is usu. made by passing ammonia through molten sodium, and that is used chiefly in making sodium cyanide and in organic synthesis as a strongly basic condensing agent (as in the preparation of indoxyl for making indigo) — called also *sodamide*

sodium antimonate *n* : an antimonate of sodium; *esp* : the meta-antimonate $2NaSbO_3.7H_2O$ obtained as a granular powder and used chiefly as an opacifier for enamels

sodium arsenate *n* : an arsenate of sodium: as **a** : the poisonous secondary orthoarsenate Na_2HAsO_4 or its hydrates that are used chiefly in dyeing and in medicine **b** : the poisonous normal orthoarsenate $Na_3AsO_4.12H_2O$ used chiefly in making other arsenates and insecticides

sodium arsenite *n* : a poisonous substance that is obtained as a concentrated solution or dry powder by treating arsenic trioxide with sodium hydroxide, that consists in some cases of a mixture of sodium ortho-arsenite Na_3AsO_3 and sodium meta-arsenite $NaAsO_2$, and that is used chiefly as an insecticidal bait and weed killer

sodium aurothiosulfate *n* : GOLD SODIUM THIOSULFATE

sodium azide *n* : a poisonous crystalline salt NaN_3 used esp. to make lead azide

sodium benzoate *n* : a crystalline or granular salt C_6H_5COONa used chiefly as a food preservative

sodium biborate *n* : BORAX

sodium bicarbonate *also* **sodium acid carbonate** *n* : a crystalline salt $NaHCO_3$ that is less soluble in water than normal sodium carbonate and gives a weakly alkaline reaction, that evolves carbon dioxide when heated, that is found in nature and is also made by passing carbon dioxide into a solution of the normal carbonate or by purifying the intermediate product of the Solvay process, that is used chiefly in baking powders, in carbonated beverages and effervescent salts, in fire extinguishers, and in medicine as an antacid, and that with carbonic acid constitutes the principal inorganic buffer system of blood and other body fluids; sodium hydrogen carbonate — called also *baking soda, nahcolite, soda*

sodium bichromate *n* : SODIUM DICHROMATE

sodium bifluoride *n* : SODIUM FLUORIDE b

sodium bisulfate *also* **sodium acid sulfate** *n* : a crystalline salt $NaHSO_4$ that gives an acid reaction in solution, that is usu. made by the reaction of sulfuric acid with common salt or sodium sulfate, and that is used chiefly as a flux in pickling metals and as an acid ingredient in dyeing and cleaning compositions; sodium hydrogen sulfate — called also *niter cake*

sodium bisulfite *also* **sodium acid sulfite** *n* : either of two salts usu. obtained by passing sulfur dioxide through a solution of sodium carbonate: **a** : an unstable crystalline salt $NaHSO_3$ that is known esp. in solution and forms sodium metabisulfite on dehydration; sodium hydrogen sulfite **b** : SODIUM METABISULFITE

sodium borate *n* : a sodium salt of a boric acid; *esp* : BORAX — compare SODIUM PERBORATE

sodium borohydride *n* : a hygroscopic crystalline compound $NaBH_4$ that is flammable but remarkably stable in air and decomposes readily in water only above room temperature or in the presence of acid to yield hydrogen and sodium metaborate, that is made in various ways (as from methyl borate and sodium hydride or from diborane and sodium methoxide), and that is used chiefly as a reducing agent for organic compounds — called also *sodium tetrahydroborate*

sodium bromide *n* : a crystalline salt NaBr having a biting saline taste that is used similarly to potassium bromide esp. in medicine and photography

sodium cacodylate *n* : a poisonous deliquescent crystalline or granular salt $(CH_3)_2AsOONa.3H_2O$ used in medicine as an arsenical

sodium carbonate *n* : a sodium salt of carbonic acid: as **a** (1) : the hygroscopic crystalline anhydrous normal salt Na_2CO_3 that is moderately soluble in cold water and gives a strongly alkaline reaction, that was orig. obtained from the ash of sea plants but is now usu. produced by the Solvay process in light and dense forms, and that is used chiefly in making glass, soap powders and soap builders, in water treatment, in the manufacture of pulp and paper, and in the manufacture of sodium hydroxide and other chemicals — called also *soda ash*; compare LEBLANC PROCESS (2) : the crystalline monohydrate $Na_2CO_3.H_2O$ found in nature as thermonatrite and used similarly to the anhydrous salt in photography and medicine (3) : the efflorescent crystalline decahydrate $Na_2CO_3.10H_2O$ found in nature as natron but usu. made artificially by crystallization and used chiefly in washing and bleaching textiles — called also *sal soda, soda, washing soda* **b** : SODIUM BICARBONATE **c** : SODIUM SESQUICARBONATE

sodium carboxymethyl cellulose *n* : a gummy substance that is obtained as a hygroscopic powder or a granular solid by reaction of alkali cellulose and sodium chloroacetate, that is either soluble in water or swells in water, and that is used chiefly as a thickening, emulsifying, and stabilizing agent (as in sizes for textiles and paper and in pharmaceutical ointments) and as a bulk laxative and antacid in medicine : a sodium salt of carboxymethyl cellulose

sodium chlorate *n* : a hygroscopic crystalline salt $NaClO_3$ usu. made by electrolysis of common salt and used as an oxidizing agent (as in dye manufacture) and for the manufacture of perchlorates and esp. as a weed killer

sodium chloride *n* : SALT 1a

sodium chlorite *n* : a crystalline salt $NaClO_2$ usu. made by reaction of sodium hydroxide with chlorine dioxide from the reduction of a chlorate and used chiefly as a bleaching and oxidizing agent

sodium chromate *n* : a yellow crystalline salt Na_2CrO_4 made by roasting chrome ore with soda ash and used chiefly in making pigments and other chromium chemicals and in dyeing and processing textiles

sodium citrate *n* : a crystalline salt $Na_3C_6H_5O_7$ used chiefly in foods as a buffering agent, in pharmaceuticals as an alkalizer and cathartic, and in medicine as a blood anticoagulant

sodium cyanide *n* : a highly poisonous deliquescent crystalline salt NaCN usu. made by heating sodium amide with carbon and used chiefly in case-hardening and heat-treating steel, in the cyanide process, in electroplating, and in chemical synthesis

sodium diacetate *n* : SODIUM ACETATE b

sodium dichromate *n* : a poisonous red deliquescent crystalline salt $Na_2Cr_2O_7$ made by oxidizing sodium chromate and used in making pigments, tanning leather, dyeing, cleaning and protecting metals from corrosion, and as an oxidizing agent

sodium dihydrogen phosphate *n* : SODIUM PHOSPHATE 1a

sodium dioxide *n* : SODIUM PEROXIDE

sodium ethoxide *also* **sodium ethylate** *n* : a strong base C_2H_5ONa obtained in solution by reaction of sodium or sodium hydroxide with ethyl alcohol and as a hygroscopic white powder by evaporation of the excess of solvent and used in organic synthesis (as in the condensation of ethyl acetate to ethyl acetoacetate)

sodium ferrocyanide *n* : a yellow crystalline salt $Na_4Fe(CN)_6$ similar to potassium ferrocyanide and used in making iron blue pigments, blueprint paper, and dyes — called also *yellow prussiate of soda*

sodium fluoaluminate *n* : a crystalline complex salt Na_3AlF_6 that occurs in nature as cryolite, is also made synthetically, and is used chiefly in ceramics, in metallurgy esp. as an electrolyte in the production of aluminum from alumina, and as an insecticide — called also *sodium aluminum fluoride*

sodium fluoride *n* : either of two poisonous crystalline salts usu. made by reaction of hydrofluoric acid with soda ash: **a** : the normal salt NaF that is used in trace amounts in the fluoridation of water, in metallurgy, as a flux, as an antiseptic, and as an exterminator **b** *or* **sodium bifluoride** : the corrosive acid fluoride $NaHF_2$ used as a laundry sour, as a preservative esp. for biological specimens, and in tinning steel; sodium hydrogen fluoride

sodium fluoroacetate *n* : a poisonous powdery compound $CH_2FCOONa$ used as a rodenticide — called also *1080*

sodium fluosilicate *n* : a crystalline salt Na_2SiF_6 used chiefly as a laundry sour, as an insecticide, and in ceramics

sodium formate *n* : a deliquescent crystalline salt HCOONa made usu. by passing carbon monoxide (as in the form of producer gas) through heated sodium hydroxide and used chiefly in making formic acid, sodium oxalate, and oxalic acid and in the chrome tanning of leather

sodium hexametaphosphate *n* : a sodium metaphosphate glass formerly regarded as having the composition $(NaPO_3)_6$

sodium hydrate *n* : SODIUM HYDROXIDE — not used systematically

sodium hydride *n* : a flammable gray to white crystalline compound NaH that is made by reaction of hydrogen and sodium, that is decomposed by water to yield hydrogen and sodium hydroxide, and that is used chiefly in organic synthesis and in removing scale from metals

sodium hydrosulfide *n* : a hygroscopic crystalline compound NaSH used chiefly in dehairing hides; sodium hydrogen sulfide

sodium hydrosulfite *n* : a crystalline salt $Na_2S_2O_4$ made by reduction (as of sodium bisulfite or sulfur dioxide with zinc) and used as a reducing agent esp. in dyeing, printing, and stripping textiles and as a bleaching agent; sodium dithionite — not used systematically

sodium hydroxide *n* : a brittle white deliquescent solid NaOH that dissolves readily in water to form a strongly alkaline and caustic solution, that is made usu. by the electrolysis of common salt or by treating soda ash with hydrated lime, and that is used chiefly in making other chemicals, soap and detergents, rayon and cellulose film, and pulp and paper, in petroleum refining, and in bleaching and mercerizing — called also *caustic soda*; compare LYE

sodium hypochlorite *n* : an unstable salt NaOCl made usu. in aqueous solution by passing chlorine into sodium hydroxide solution and used chiefly as a bleaching agent and disinfectant — see JAVELLE WATER b

sodium hyposulfite *n* **1** : SODIUM THIOSULFATE **2** : SODIUM HYDROSULFITE

sodium iodide *n* : a crystalline salt NaI used like potassium iodide

sodium lactate *n* : a hygroscopic syrupy salt $CH_3CHOHCOONa$ used chiefly as an antacid in medicine and as a substitute for glycerol

sodium lamp *or* **sodium-vapor lamp** *n* : a gas discharge lamp using sodium vapor and designed esp. for lighting highways

sodium lauryl sulfate *n* : the crystalline sodium salt $C_{12}H_{25}SO_4Na$ of sulfated lauryl alcohol; *also* : a mixture of sodium alkyl sulfates consisting principally of this salt and used as an anionic detergent, wetting agent, and emulsifying agent

sodium light *n* : the yellow light of glowing sodium vapor consisting chiefly of two monochromatic portions of wavelength 5890 and 5896 angstroms corresponding respectively to the D_2 and D_1 Fraunhofer lines

sodium metabisulfite *n* : a compound $Na_2S_2O_5$ produced as an anhydrous solid or in aqueous solutions and used chiefly as a reducing agent, bleaching agent, and antichlor, in preserving foods and silage, as an antiseptic esp. in the fermentation industries, and in coagulating rubber latex

sodium metaphosphate *n* **1** : any of several crystalline sodium salts $NaPO_3$ or $(NaPO_3)_n$ of a metaphosphoric acid: as **a** : the water-soluble cyclic trimetaphosphate $(NaPO_3)_3$ or $NaPO_3$ I **b** : sodium Kurrol's salt $NaPO_3$ IV **2 a** : a water-soluble sodium phosphate glass having the composition of a sodium metaphosphate — called also *sodium (1:1) phosphate*; compare SODIUM HEXAMETAPHOSPHATE **b** : SODIUM PHOSPHATE GLASS

sodium metasilicate *n* : SODIUM SILICATE b

sodium molybdate *n* : a molybdate of sodium; *esp* : the normal salt Na_2MoO_4 that commonly crystallizes with two molecules of water and is used chiefly in making pigments and in chemical analysis

sodium morrhuate *n* : a pale-yellow granular salt administered in solution intravenously as a sclerosing agent esp. in the treatment of varicose veins

sodium nitrate *n* : a deliquescent crystalline salt $NaNO_3$ esp. occurring in crude form (as caliche) in Chile and also made by reaction of nitric acid and soda ash and used as a fertilizer, as an oxidizing agent (as in explosives), and in curing meat — called also *soda niter*; see CHILE SALTPETER

sodium nitrite *n* : a colorless or yellowish deliquescent salt $NaNO_2$ made usu. by absorption of nitrogen oxide in a solution of soda ash and used chiefly for diazotizing (as in dye manufacture) and in medicine

sodium nitroprusside *n* : a red crystalline salt $Na_2[Fe(CN)_5NO].2H_2O$ made usu. by reaction of a ferrocyanide and nitric acid or of a ferricyanide and nitrous acid and used chiefly in testing for sulfides with which it forms a violet color in alkaline solution; disodium penta-cyano-nitrosyl-ferrate

sodium orthosilicate *n* : SODIUM SILICATE a

sodium oxalate *n* : a poisonous crystalline salt $Na_2C_2O_4$ made by heating sodium formate and used chiefly as a source of oxalic acid and as a reagent in chemical analysis

sodium oxide *n* : an oxide of sodium; *esp* : the hygroscopic amorphous monoxide Na_2O that reacts violently with water to yield sodium hydroxide and that is obtained chiefly as an intermediate in the manufacture of sodium peroxide

sodium pentothal *n* : the sodium salt of thiopental

sodium perborate *n* : either of two crystalline or powdery substances that are compounds of sodium metaborate with hydrogen peroxide and are used chiefly as bleaching agents and oxidizing agents and in mouthwashes and dentifrices: **a** *or* **sodium perborate tetrahydrate** : the compound $NaBO_3.4H_2O$ or $NaBO_2.H_2O_2.3H_2O$ made by reaction of sodium peroxide with a solution of borax or by electrolysis of a solution of borax and sodium carbonate **b** *or* **sodium perborate monohydrate** : the compound $NaBO_3.H_2O$ or $NaBO_2.H_2O_2$ made by dehydration of the tetrahydrate

sodium perchlorate *n* : a crystalline salt $NaClO_4$ made usu. by electrolysis of sodium chlorate and used chiefly in making other perchlorates and perchloric acid

sodium peroxide *n* : a pale-yellow hygroscopic granular compound Na_2O_2 that reacts with water to form sodium hydroxide and hydrogen peroxide, that is made by passing hot dry air over metallic sodium and treating with oxygen the sodium oxide formed, and that is used chiefly as an oxidizing and bleaching agent and in making other peroxy compounds

sodium phosphate *n* **1** : an orthophosphate of sodium known in both anyhydrous and hydrated crystalline forms: **a** : the primary phosphate NaH_2PO_4 that with the secondary phosphate constitutes the principal buffer system of the urine and that is used chiefly in buffer compositions (as in acid cleaning compositions) — called also *monobasic sodium phosphate, monosodium phosphate, sodium acid phosphate, sodium dihydrogen phosphate* **b** : the secondary phosphate Na_2HPO_4 that is used chiefly in water treatment for precipitating polyvalent metals, in cleaning compositions, in process cheeses, in ceramic glazes and enamels, in the textile industry, and in medicine as a laxative and antacid — called also *dibasic sodium phosphate, disodium hydrogen phosphate, disodium phosphate* **c** : the tertiary phosphate Na_3PO_4 that is used chiefly in cleaning compositions and in water treatment — called also *tribasic sodium phosphate, trisodium phosphate* **2** : a phosphate of sodium that is not an orthophosphate — compare SODIUM METAPHOSPHATE, SODIUM PYROPHOSPHATE, SODIUM TRIPOLYPHOSPHATE

sodium phosphate glass *n* : any of various usu. water-soluble glassy substances that in many cases approximate a sodium metaphosphate in composition but are held to be mixtures of sodium polyphosphates and that are used chiefly as sequestering agents in water treatment, as deflocculating agents, and in

protecting metals from corrosion; *esp* : SODIUM METAPHOSPHATE 2a
sodium polysulfide *n* : any of several yellow compounds Na_2S_n containing two or more atoms of sulfur in the molecule (as sodium tetrasulfide Na_2S_4) made by dissolving sulfur in an aqueous solution of sodium sulfide or sodium hydroxide and used chiefly in making polysulfide rubbers
sodium potassium tartrate *n* : ROCHELLE SALT
sodium propionate *n* : a deliquescent crystalline salt CH_3CH_2COONa used as a fungicide (as in retarding the growth of mold in the baking and dairy industries)
sodium pyrophosphate *n* : any of four sodium salts of pyrophosphoric acid: as **a** : a crystalline acid salt $Na_2H_2P_2O_7$ used chiefly as a leavening agent, in acid cleaning compositions, and in electroplating; disodium dihydrogen pyrophosphate — called also *sodium acid pyrophosphate* **b** : the crystalline normal salt $Na_4P_2O_7$ used chiefly as a builder in soaps and detergents and as a deflocculant (as in treating drilling muds for oil wells) — called also *tetrasodium pyrophosphate*
sodium pyrosulfite *n* : SODIUM METABISULFITE
sodiums *pl of* SODIUM
sodium salicylate *n* : a crystalline salt HOC_6H_4COONa with a sweetish saline taste used chiefly in medicine as an analgesic, antipyretic, and antirheumatic
sodium sesquicarbonate *n* : a crystalline acid carbonate $Na_2CO_3.NaHCO_3.2H_2O$ or $Na_3H(CO_3)_2.2H_2O$ that occurs in nature as trona or is made synthetically from sodium carbonate and sodium bicarbonate and is used chiefly as a detergent — not used systematically
sodium silicate *n* : any of various water-soluble substances obtained in the form of crystals, glasses, powders, or aqueous solutions usu. by melting silica with a sodium compound (as sodium carbonate or sodium hydroxide): as **a** *or* **sodium orthosilicate** : a corrosive crystalline substance regarded as a salt Na_4SiO_4 or $2Na_2O.SiO_2$ of orthosilicic acid or as a mixture of sodium metasilicate with sodium hydroxide and used chiefly in heavy-duty cleaning compositions **b** *or* **sodium metasilicate** : a crystalline salt Na_2SiO_3 or $Na_2O.SiO_2$ either in the anhydrous or hydrated form used chiefly as a detergent **c** *or* **sodium sesquisilicate** : a corrosive crystalline salt regarded as intermediate in composition between sodium orthosilicate and sodium metasilicate and used in heavy-duty cleaning compositions — not used systematically **d** : WATER GLASS
sodium silicofluoride *n* : SODIUM FLUOSILICATE
sodium sulfate *n* : either of two crystalline sulfates of sodium: **a** : the bitter normal salt Na_2SO_4 occurring in nature as the mineral thenardite and in various salt lakes and brines and used chiefly in detergents, in the manufacture of wood pulp and rayon, and in dyeing and finishing textiles — see GLAUBER'S SALT, SALT CAKE **b** : SODIUM BISULFATE
sodium sulfide *n* : a sulfide of sodium; *esp* : a crystalline compound Na_2S usu. obtained by heating sodium sulfate with coal or hydrogen and used in dehairing hides, in the manufacture of sulfur dyes, as a solvent for these dyes, and as a reducing agent for the nitro group in making amines — compare [2]BLACK ASH 2, SODIUM HYDROSULFIDE, SODIUM POLYSULFIDE
sodium sulfite *n* : a sulfite of sodium: as **a** : the crystalline normal salt Na_2SO_3 used chiefly as a reducing agent, bleaching agent, and antichlor, in photographic developing and fixing baths, and in preserving foods **b** : SODIUM BISULFITE a **c** : SODIUM METABISULFITE
sodium sulfydrate *n* : SODIUM HYDROSULFIDE — not used systematically
sodium tetraborate *n* : BORAX
sodium tetrahydroborate *or* **sodium tetrahydridoborate** *n* : SODIUM BOROHYDRIDE
sodium thiocyanate *n* : a hygroscopic crystalline salt NaSCN made usu. by reaction of sodium cyanide with sulfur or sodium polysulfide and used chiefly in dyeing and printing textiles, in processing photographic color film, and as a weed killer
sodium thiosulfate *n* : a hygroscopic crystalline salt $Na_2S_2O_3$ that commonly crystallizes with five molecules of water, that is usu. made by the reaction of sodium sulfite solution with sulfur or of sodium sulfide with sulfur dioxide or in the recovery of sulfur from waste products (as spent oxide), and that is used as a fixing agent in photography, as a reducing agent, bleaching agent, and antichlor, in chemical analysis for the titration of iodine, and in medicine as an antidote in poisoning by cyanides or iodine — called also *hypo, sodium hyposulfite*
sodium tripolyphosphate *n* : a crystalline salt $Na_5P_3O_{10}$ used chiefly as a builder in soaps and detergents, as a sequestering agent, and as a deflocculating agent; penta-sodium triphosphate — not used systematically
sodium tungstate *or* **sodium wolframate** *n* : a tungstate of sodium; *esp* : the normal salt Na_2WO_4 that commonly crystallizes with two molecules of water, is usu. obtained during the extraction of tungsten from its ores, and is used chiefly in making other tungsten compounds and in fireproofing textiles
sodium-vapor lamp *n* : SODIUM LAMP
sod oil *n* [[3]*sod*] : degras recovered from treated skins by washing with alkali instead of by pressing
so·do·ku \'sōdə,kü\ *n* -s [Jap, fr. Chin (Cant) *shué* rat + *tûk* poison] : RAT-BITE FEVER b
sod·om \'sädəm\ *n* -s *usu cap* [fr. *Sodom*, city of ancient Palestine destroyed by God for its wickedness (Gen 18:20, 21; 19:24–28)] : a place notorious for vice or corruption
sodom apple *n, usu cap S* : APPLE OF SODOM
sod·om·ite \'sädə,mīt\ *n* -s [ME, fr. MF, fr. LL *Sodomita* inhabitant of Sodom, fr. LGk *Sodomitēs*, fr. *Sodoma* Sodom + Gk -*itēs* -ite] **1** *often cap* : one who practices sodomy — compare BUGGER **2** *usu cap* : a native or inhabitant of Sodom, a city located in ancient times in the region of the Dead Sea which with Gomorrah was destroyed for its wickedness
sod·om·it·ic \¦sädə¦mid·ik\ *adj, often cap* [LL *sodomiticus* of the inhabitants of Sodom, fr. *Sodomita* inhabitant of Sodom + L -*icus* -ic] : SODOMITICAL
sod·om·it·i·cal \id·əkəl\ *adj, often cap* [LL *sodomiticus* + E -*al*] **1** *obs* : given to or participating in the practice of sodomy **2** : of, relating to, or involving sodomy — **sod·om·it·i·cal·ly** \-id·ək(ə)lē\ *adv*
sodomitry *n* -ES *often cap* [MF *sodomiterie*, fr. *sodomite* + -*erie* -ry] *obs* : SODOMY
sod·om·ize \'sädə,mīz\ *vt* -ED/-ING/-S [*sodomy* + -*ize*] : to practice sodomy upon ⟨had begun the practice of *sodomizing* younger boys —David Abrahamsen⟩
sod·omy \'sädəmē, -mi\ *n* -ES [ME, fr. OF *sodomie*, fr. LL *Sodoma* Sodom (fr. Gk) + OF -*ie* -y; fr. the homosexual proclivities of the men of the city as narrated in Gen 19:1–11] : carnal copulation with a member of the same sex or with an animal : noncoital carnal copulation with a member of the opposite sex; *specif* : the penetration of the male organ into the mouth or anus of another — compare BESTIALITY, BUGGERY, CUNNILINGUS, FELLATIO, HOMOSEXUALITY, PEDERASTY
sod plow *n* [[1]*sod*] **1** : BREAKER 2b **2** : a plow for stirring cultivated meadows
sods *pl of* SOD, *pres 3d sing of* SOD
sod webworm *n* : GRASS WEBWORM
sodwork \'=,=\ *n* : a construction (as a revetment) made of sods piled up and packed closely together
soe *n* [ME *so, soe*, fr. OE *sā*; akin to ON *sār* large vessel — more at SAY] *obs* : a large wooden tub or pail
soerabaja *usu cap, var of* SURABAJA
soerakarta *usu cap, var of* SURAKARTA
so·ev·er \sə¦wevə(r), (,)sō'e-\ *adv* [-*soever* (as in *whosoever*)] **1** : to any possible or known extent : in any conceivable degree or manner — used after an adjective preceded by *how* or a superlative preceded by *the* ⟨how fair ~ she may be⟩ ⟨the most selfish ~ in this world⟩ **2** : of any or every kind that may be specified — used after a noun modified esp. by *any, no*, or *what* ⟨all who are perplexed in any way ~ —J.H.Newman⟩
SOF *abbr* sound on film
so·fa \'sōfə, *dial* -fē *or* -fi\ *n* -s [Ar *ṣuffah* a long bench] **1** : a carpeted and cushioned section of floor raised above the rest in some eastern Mediterranean lands for sitting on : DIVAN **2** : an upholstered couch or settee usu. with arms and a back and often convertible into a bed — compare LOUNGE
sofa bed *n* : an upholstered sofa that can be made to serve as a double bed by lowering its hinged upholstered back to horizontal position — compare SOFA 2, STUDIO COUCH
so·far \'sō,fär, -fȧ(r\ *n* -s [*sound fixing and ranging*] : a system for locating an underwater explosion at sea by triangulation based on the reception of the sound by three widely separated shore stations that is usable in a search for survivors who drop a special bomb into the sea (as from a lifeboat)
so far as *conj* : as far as
sofa table *n* : a moderate-sized oblong table with small leaves at the ends
sof·fi·o·ne \,säfē'ōnē, ,sōf-, -ō(,)nā\ *n, pl* **soffio·ni** \-ō(,)nē\ [It, fr. aug. of *soffio* puff, blast, fr. *soffiare* to blow, fr. L *sufflare* to inflate, blow upon — more at SUFFLATE] : a jet of steam usu. accompanied by other vapors that issues from the ground in a volcanic region
sof·fit \'säfət\ *also* **sof·fite** \", sä'fēt\ *n* -s [F *soffite*, fr. It *soffitto*, fr. (assumed) VL *suffictus*, past part. of L *suffigere* to fasten underneath — more at SUFFIX] : the underside of a part or member of a building (as of an overhang, ceiling, staircase, cornice, or entablature); *esp* : the intrados of an arch — compare PLANCIER
so·fia \÷sō'fēə, 'sōf- *sometimes* 'sōf-\ *adj, usu cap* [fr. *Sofia*, capital of Bulgaria] : of or from Sofia, the capital of Bulgaria : of the kind or style prevalent in Sofia
sof·kee \'säfkē\ *n* -s [Muskogee *safki*] *South* : a thin mush or gruel made of cornmeal
[1]**soft** \'sȯft *also* 'säft\ *adj* -ER/-EST [ME *softe, soft*, fr. OE *sōfte*, alter. (prob. influenced by *sōfte* softly) of *sēfte*; akin to OS *sāfti* soft, OHG *semfti*, and prob. to Goth *samjan* to please, ON *semja* to arrange, settle, make peace, Skt *samayati* he levels, regulates, *sama* level, same — more at SAME] **1 a** : pleasing or agreeable to the senses : bringing ease, comfort, or quiet ⟨the ~ influences of home⟩ — sometimes used interjectionally to enjoin silence or less haste ⟨~, who comes here —*Shak.*⟩ **b** : having the restfulness of sleep ⟨~ slumbers⟩ **c** (1) : having a bland or mellow rather than a sharp or acid taste or flavor (2) : containing no alcohol — used of beverages ⟨washing down hot dogs with ~ drinks⟩ **d** (1) : having only moderate contrast between light and shadow or between colors or color shades : not bright or glaring : SUBDUED ⟨the ~ shadows of a spring evening⟩ (2) : having or producing little contrast or a relatively short range of tones ⟨~ negative⟩ ⟨~ print⟩ ⟨~ paper⟩ ⟨~ lighting⟩ **e** (1) : free from loudness, harshness, or stridency : quiet in pitch or volume (2) *archaic* : making a low and gentle rather than a loud or harsh sound — used of a musical instrument (3) : MELODIOUS, PLEASING, SENSUOUS ⟨her voice was ~ and thrilling⟩ **f** *of the eyes* : having a liquid or gentle appearance ⟨~ brown eyes —Len Zinberg⟩ **g** : smooth or delicate in texture, grain, or fiber : not rough, coarse, or irritating to the touch ⟨a ~ cashmere⟩ **h** (1) : balmy, mild, or clement in weather or temperature ⟨~ summer nights —Sherwood Anderson⟩ (2) : moving or falling with slight force or impact : not violent ⟨outside there was a ~ rain —Martin Quigley⟩ ⟨~ breezes⟩ **2** : having a surface unbroken by heavy waves : CALM — used of a river or sea **3 a** *obs* : readily endured or supported : involving no severity, harshness, or strain **b** : demanding little work or effort : not toilsome or laborious : EASY, IDLE ⟨given to ~ living and dissolute practices⟩ ⟨young men who married ~ jobs —J.H.Reese⟩ **4 a** : sounding as in *ace* and *gem* respectively — used of *c* and *g* or their sound **b** *of a consonant* : VOICED **c** : constituting a vowel before which there is a \y\ sound or a \y\-like modification of a consonant or constituting a consonant in whose articulation there is a \y\-like modification or which is followed by a \y\ sound (as in Russian) — opposed to *hard*; compare PALATALIZATION **5 a** *archaic* : moving slowly and unhurriedly **b** : slow or moderate in burning — used of a fire **6** : rising gradually : ascending by moderate degrees ⟨a ~ slope⟩ ⟨a ~ crescendo⟩ **7** : having curved or rounded outline : blending easily into the general effect or view : not harsh or jagged ⟨~ hills against the horizon⟩ ⟨a pullover sweater with ~ shoulder lines⟩ **8 a** : evincing mildness of disposition or temper : showing gentleness, kindness, or mercy : COMPASSIONATE **b** (1) : exhibiting sympathetic understanding : tending to ingratiate or disarm : CONCILIATORY, ENGAGING, KIND, SUAVE ⟨a ~ answer turns away wrath —Prov 15:1 (RSV)⟩ ⟨could be great harm in accepting, at face value, whatever ~ words they may utter —*Springfield (Mass.) Republican*⟩ (2) : TENDER, SENTIMENTAL ⟨the ~ utterance of a loving heart⟩ **c** (1) : mild, lenient, or gentle in method or procedure ⟨adopted a policy of slow growth and ~ competition to allow other firms to establish themselves in the industry —A.D.H.Kaplan⟩ ⟨hopes . . . died in the awful gap between tough talk and ~ action —*New Republic*⟩ (2) : based on negotiation and conciliation rather than on a show of power or on threats ⟨had switched to a ~ line as the situation worsened⟩ **d** : emotionally susceptible or responsive : readily affected by sentiment : IMPRESSIONABLE, SUGGESTIBLE **e** : unduly susceptible to influence : readily affected, swayed, or imposed on : COMPLIANT ⟨said their teacher was ~⟩ **f** *obs* : of refined character or gentle breeding **g** : lacking firmness or strength of character : FEEBLE, UNMANLY **h** : amorously intent or emotionally involved or attracted — used with *on* ⟨had always been ~ on the neighbors' daughter⟩ **9 a** : weak or delicate in health or constitution : lacking robust strength, stamina, or endurance : enervated by ease or luxury : not hardened by exercise or effort **b** : weak or deficient mentally : FOOLISH, HALF-WITTED **10** *Scot & Irish* : DAMP, WET, DRIZZLY **11 a** : yielding or giving way to physical pressure : having a surface that does not firmly resist the touch : loose rather than dense in texture or consistency : comfortable or pleasant because not hard **b** : too moist or yielding to support weight : permitting (someone or something) to sink in — used of wet ground **c** : of a consistency that may be shaped or molded : COMPRESSIBLE, MALLEABLE **d** : easily magnetized and demagnetized ⟨magnetically ~ alloys are used for motors, transformers, and other electromagnetic devices⟩ **e** : lacking relatively or comparatively in hardness ⟨~ iron⟩ ⟨~ coal⟩ **12** : characterized by the practical absence of substances (as calcium and magnesium salts) that prevent formation of lather with soap — used of water and water solutions; compare HARD 1c (1) **13** : maturing as a ceramic glaze or object at a relatively low temperature **14** *of glass* **a** : capable of being annealed at a relatively low temperature **b** : readily scratched : having little mechanical hardness **15 a** : having relatively low penetrating power ⟨~ X rays⟩ **b** : *of an electron tube* : containing gas that adversely affects its characteristics **16** : not durable : PERISHABLE **17 a** : tending to decline in price under the influence of selling — used esp. of securities or commodities **b** *of money* : paper as distinct from metallic **c** *of currency* : not convertible into gold nor heavily backed by a gold reserve and typically unstable, low, or depreciating in value; *also* : available to borrowers in ample supply and at low interest rates **d** *of a currency* : not soundly backed nor readily convertible into foreign currencies except under restrictions or at considerable discounts ⟨has attempted, where possible, to shift purchases to ~ currency areas —T.C.Blaisdell⟩ **18** *of brick* : underburned because of its position in the kiln **19** : SOFTWOOD **20 a** *of paper* : being opaque and not brittle or crisp and having under the microscope a slightly fuzzy texture **b** : bound in paperback ⟨*soft*-bound book⟩ ⟨*soft*-back book⟩ ⟨~ bindings⟩ **21** *of news* : unimportant in its economic, political, or larger social bearing ⟨a ~ human-interest story⟩ — compare HARD **22** *of a foundry blast* : weak in force or pressure **23** : containing some of the solids of raw cane sugar that are removed in refining white sugar and being usu. brown and somewhat moist
syn SOFT, BLAND, MILD, GENTLE, LENIENT, and BALMY can mean, in common, pleasantly agreeable because devoid of harshness or roughness in the sensations evoked. SOFT suggests a tranquilizing sensation of mellowness esp. as devoid of pungency, vividness, intensity, stridency, and so on ⟨a *soft* color⟩ ⟨a *soft* voice⟩ ⟨a *soft* answer⟩ ⟨the *soft* glow of the lamp —Louis Bromfield⟩ ⟨a *soft* and smooth climate⟩ BLAND can be often interchanged with SOFT but more generally suggests smoothness and suavity, emphasizing more than SOFT the absence of what might disturb, irritate, stimulate, and so on ⟨it was hot and cold, sweet and sour, fiery and *bland* — all at the same time —Mary Lasswell⟩ ⟨a *bland* diet was prescribed with milk and cream with meals and between meals —*Jour. Amer. Med. Assoc.*⟩ ⟨a *bland* reply to a belligerent accusation⟩ ⟨from the south comes the *bland* air of the gulf —H.T.Kane⟩ ⟨the *bland* influence of encouraging words⟩ MILD and GENTLE both stress moderation and are usu. applied to things that are not, as they might be and often are, harsh, rough, strong, stimulating or violent, often, however, connoting positively pleasurable sensations, a pleasurableness induced by the very moderation of the thing, MILD possibly stressing more an induced mood of serenity, GENTLE possibly implying more an induced placidity and a sense of restrained power or force ⟨a *mild* drink⟩ ⟨a *mild* taste⟩ ⟨a *mild* winter⟩ ⟨a *mild* breeze⟩ ⟨his picture is *mild*, feeble, and contrived, whereas Picasso's is excited, bold, and hardy —J.T.Soby⟩ ⟨a good man, *mild*, charitable, and humane —Tobias Smollett⟩ ⟨a *gentle* hand⟩ ⟨his voice was soft; his manner *gentle* —Robert Tallant⟩ ⟨a tone of *gentle* authority —Martha Bacon⟩ ⟨contrasts of light, shade, and shadow should be *gentle* —A.S.Whiton⟩ LENIENT sometimes applies to something exerting an emollient, relaxing, or assuasive influence, often connoting (from another sense of the word) indulgence or kindliness ⟨a *lenient* hand on his brow⟩ ⟨the weather was *lenient* —H.L.Davis⟩ ⟨poured her a *lenient* rum and water —Christopher Morley⟩ BALMY, applied chiefly to atmospheric conditions, esp. to a breeze or a wind, often adds to the idea of soothing sensation on mind or senses the idea of refreshing influence or even fragrant quality ⟨the *balmy* summer air, the restful quiet —Mark Twain⟩ ⟨it was a lovely soft spring morning at the end of March, and unusually *balmy* for the time of year —Samuel Butler †1902⟩ ⟨the *balmy* trade winds and subtropical sunshine —P.J.C.Friedlander⟩
[2]**soft** \"\ *n* -s [ME, fr. [1]*soft*] **1 a** : the quality or state of being soft : SOFTNESS **b** : a soft object, material, or part ⟨the ~ of the thumb⟩ **2** : a soft or silly person **3 softs** *pl, Brit* : SHODDY
[3]**soft** \"\ *adv* [ME *softe, soft*, fr. OE *sōfte*; akin to OS *sāfto* softly, OHG *samfto*; all fr. a prehistoric WGmc adv. fr. the root of OE *sēfte* soft — more at [1]SOFT] : in a soft or gentle manner : SOFTLY
sof·ta \'sóftə, 'säf-\ *n* -s [Turk, fr. Per *sōkhtah* burnt, kindled (with love of knowledge)] : someone associated with the religious activities of a Turkish mosque; *esp* : a beginner in theological studies
softball \'=,=\ *n* [[1]*soft* + *ball*] **1** : a team game of seven innings closely resembling baseball but played on a smaller diamond with a larger ball under rules requiring an underhand pitch and forbidding a base runner to take a lead until the ball is pitched **2** : a smooth-seamed ball about 12 inches in circumference that is filled with kapok, covered with horsehide or cowhide, and used in the game of softball
soft-bill \'=,=\ *n* : any of numerous birds with rather fragile weak bills suitable for consuming insects and other small animals as food — compare HARD-BILL
soft black *n* : a vegetable black pigment (as vine black) used esp. in printing inks
soft-boiled \'=¦=\ *adj* **1** *of an egg* : boiled to a soft consistency **2 a** : SENTIMENTAL **b** : of or relating to literary expression regarded satirically as given to wholesome sentiment and moralism — opposed to *hard-boiled*
soft brome *or* **soft brome grass** *n* : SOFT CHEAT
soft chancre *n* : CHANCROID
soft cheat \'=¦chēt\ *or* **soft chess** \'=¦ches\ *n* [*soft cheat* fr. [1]*soft* + *cheatgrass*; *soft chess* fr. [1]*soft* + *chess*] : a weedy Old World grass (*Bromus mollis*) that is softly pubescent in all parts and is widely naturalized in No. America esp. on the Pacific coast; *also* : a very similar grass (*B. racemosus*)
soft clam *n* : SOFT-SHELL CLAM
soft coal *n* : BITUMINOUS COAL
soft commissure *n* : a commissure of gray matter connecting the optic thalami across the third ventricle of the brain
soft coral *n* : any member of the alcyonarian order Alcyonacea in which the polyp bases fuse into a fleshy mass partially supported by calcareous spicules and which are common in shallow tropical seas (as the Indian ocean)
[1]**soft corn** *n* **1** : an Indian corn (*Zea mays amylacea*) having kernels shaped like those of flint corn and composed almost entirely of soft starch — called also *flour corn, squaw corn* **2** : a soft and watery corn whether immature or prematurely frozen as distinguished from hard dry mature corn
[2]**soft corn** *n* : a usu. moist white corn between two toes
soft-cover \'=¦==\ *adj or n* : PAPERBACK
soft crab *n* : SOFT-SHELL CRAB
soft-cure \'=¦=\ *vt* : to cure (tobacco) slowly with limited heat
soft dough *n* : the early part of the dough stage of a cereal grain
soft·en \'sȯfən *also* 'säf- *sometimes* -ftən\ *vb* -ED/-ING/-S [ME *softnen*, fr. [1]*soft* + -*nen* -en] *vt* **1** : to lessen the severity of : make more endurable : ASSUAGE, MITIGATE ⟨have ~*ed* their puritanical code —Paul Blanshard⟩ ⟨pride in his heroism ~*ed* their grief⟩ **2 a** : to render gentle, mild, or compassionate : induce sympathy or mercy in : MELT ⟨the story should ~ the stoniest of hearts —J.D.Adams⟩ **b** : to reduce the harshness or rigor of : make milder or gentler : MOLLIFY ⟨~*ing* him to love by eloquent tenderness —T.L.Peacock⟩ **c** : to make effeminate or weak : leach away the strength or virility of : ENERVATE ⟨ease and luxury had ~*ed* their fiber⟩ **3** : to make less glaring, loud, or sharp : tone down the brightness, contrast, or sound of : round or blend the harsh lines or jagged angles of ⟨dusk and dark clouds were ~*ing* the daylight —Elyne Mitchell⟩ ⟨the contours of the bodies are ~*ed* —Leona Prasse⟩ **4 a** : to make less hard, solid, or compact (as by pounding or annealing) ⟨heat ~*s* iron⟩ **b** : to make less dry or brittle by use of an oil or grease : restore freshness, pliability, or luster to ⟨lotions that ~ dry skin⟩ ⟨used oil to ~ and preserve leather⟩ **c** : to make (hair) more receptive to dye by use of a bleaching solution **5** : to lessen the hardness of (water) esp. by removing or reducing the reactivity of calcium and magnesium ions (as by precipitation, ion exchange, or sequestration) **6** : to remove impurities from (lead) preparatory to desilverizing **7 a** : to weaken the military resistance and morale of esp. by preliminary bombardment or other harassment — often used with *up* **b** : to break the resistance or opposition of (a person) by physical or mental torture ⟨first we'll ~ you up with a little of the pistol-whipping I promised you —Hartley Howard⟩ **8** : to bring down (prices or market demand) ⟨adverse developments . . . have completely demoralized product prices, ~*ed* the price of crude, and are squeezing profits to a minimum —P.C.Spencer⟩ ~ *vi* : to become soft, gentle, pliable, or weak ⟨her expression ~*ed*⟩ ⟨foreign policy ~*ed* as the cold war reached a temporary lull⟩ ⟨thewind was ~*ing* —Vincent McHugh⟩
soft·en·er \-(ə)nə(r)\ *n* -s : one that softens: as **a** : a worker who softens hides, skins, or leather usu. by immersing or tumbling them in water **b** : a textile worker who waxes thread and yarn **c** : a machine or apparatus in which something is softened **d** : a substance added to something (as hard water, molten iron, or rubber in the process of manufacture) to make it soft, malleable, or plastic — compare PLASTICIZER
softening point *n* [*softening* (gerund of *soften*) + *point*] : the temperature or range of temperatures at which a substance softens
softer *comparative of* SOFT
softest *superlative of* SOFT
soft fiber *n* : any of various cordage or textile fibers (as flax, hemp, jute, or ramie) obtained from the stems of plants and typically of softer texture and greater length than hard fibers obtained from leaves : BAST 2
soft-finned \'=¦=\ *adj* [[1]*soft* + *fin* + -*ed*] : having fins in which the membrane is supported entirely or almost entirely by soft or articulated rays — used of the more advanced teleost fishes; opposed to *spiny-finned*
soft flame *n* : a thin shell of flame surrounding a core of unburned gas that is produced by using a small amount of primary air in the mixture and is used as a free flame (as in an oven)
soft focus *n* : unsharpness of a photograph due to intentional diffusion of the lens image
soft-focus \'=¦=\ *adj* [*soft focus*] **1** *of a photographic image* : having unsharp outlines **2** *of a lens* : producing an image having unsharp outlines
soft fold *n* : the fold that results when paper is lapped
soft fruit *n, chiefly Brit* : SMALL FRUIT

soft goods *n pl* **1** *Brit* : DRY GOODS **2** : goods that are not durable : perishable goods — used esp. of textile products
soft grass *n* : any of various grasses of the genus *Holcus; esp* : VELVET GRASS
soft grit *n* : finely ground corncobs, rice hulls, or other siliceous plant wastes used as a mild abrasive in air blasting
soft ground *n* **1** : a mixture of ordinary etching ground usu. with tallow or grease that is used chiefly to obtain textural lines and effects on the plate by pressing cloth or similar material into the ground or by drawing with a pencil on a piece of paper laid over it **2** : a process or effect in etching obtained by the use of soft ground
soft hail *n* : GRAUPEL
softhead \ˈ=ˌ=\ *n* [¹*soft* + *head*] **1** : a silly or feebleminded person : SIMPLETON **2** : a fatuous sentimentalist ⟨aren't they the ~*s*, the all too susceptible and sentimental imbeciles? —Aldous Huxley⟩
softheaded \ˈ=ˈ==\ *adj* [¹*soft* + *headed*] : having a weak, unrealistic, or uncritical mind : lacking judgment : IMPRACTICAL ⟨a ~ visionary —*Commonweal*⟩ — **soft·head·ed·ly** *adv* — **soft·head·ed·ness** *n* -ES
softhearted \ˈ=ˈ==\ *adj* [¹*soft* + *hearted*] : emotionally responsive : MERCIFUL, SYMPATHETIC, TENDER — **soft·heart·ed·ly** *adv* — **soft·heart·ed·ness** *n* -ES
soft hog *n* : a hog producing or expected to produce soft pork
softie *var of* SOFTY
softies *pl of* SOFTY
soft·ish \ˈsȯftish, -tēsh *also* ˈsäf-\ *adj* : somewhat soft
soft–laid \ˈ=ˌ=\ *adj* : having the strands twisted more loosely than those of medium-laid rope
soft lay *n* : a rope lay in which the yarns of the strands and the strands of the rope are loosely twisted to secure great strength on a straight pull
soft lead *n* : lead containing virtually no impurities other than the precious metals : lead that has been put through the process of softening
soft·ling \-ftliŋ\ *n* -S [¹*soft* + *-ling*] **1** : an effeminate person : WEAKLING **2** : something soft, small, or delicate
¹**soft·ly** *adv* [ME, fr. ¹*soft* + *-ly*] : in a soft manner — used interjectionally to enjoin silence or less haste
²**softly** *adj* [¹*soft* + *-ly*] *archaic* : SOFT, GENTLE, QUIET
soft maize *n* : SOFT CORN 1
soft maple *n* **1** : any of various maples with soft wood: as **a** : SILVER MAPLE **b** : RED MAPLE **c** : DWARF MAPLE **2** : the wood of a soft maple tree
soft–mud process *n* : a brickmaking process in which water and clay are mixed to a relatively soft consistency and inserted into molds — compare STIFF-MUD PROCESS, SAND-MOLDING, SLOP-MOLDING
soft mute *n* : MEDIA 1a
soft·ness \-f(t)nəs\ *n* -ES [ME *softnes*, fr. OE *sōftnes* ease, comfort, fr. *sōfte* soft + *-nes* -ness] : the quality or state of being soft
soft–nosed \ˈ=ˌ=\ *adj, of a bullet* : having a hard metal jacket that covers all but the nose and encloses a soft core and mushrooming upon striking an object
soft palate *n* : the membranous and muscular fold suspended from the posterior margin of the hard palate and partially separating the mouth cavity from the pharynx — called also *velum;* see UVULA
soft paste *n* **1** : a ceramic body containing refined clay and a glassy frit **2** *or* **soft–paste porcelain** : a soft low-fired translucent ware with a soft-paste body produced in Europe from the 15th through the 18th century — compare HARD PASTE
soft patch *n* **1** : a patch for a crack in a metallic vessel (as a steam boiler) consisting of a soft material (as putty) covered and held in place by a plate bolted or riveted fast **2** : a plate and gasket used as a temporary repair to cover a break or hole in a ship's hull
soft pedal *n* **1** : a foot pedal on a piano that reduces the volume of sound by shortening the stroke of the hammers or by shifting the hammers so that fewer strings are struck for each note **2** : something that muffles, deadens, or reduces effect : DAMPER
soft–pedal \ˈ=ˈ==\ *vb* [*soft pedal*] *vt* **1** : to use the soft pedal in playing (a musical passage) **2** : to play down (a fact, an aspect, or a consideration) : reduce the effect of : CONCEAL, DISGUISE, MUFFLE ⟨time for the club to *soft-pedal* the war heroics —Jack Gould⟩ ⟨this concern is evident, though *soft-pedaled* —*Atlantic*⟩ ~ *vi* **1** : to play a musical passage with the soft pedal **2** : to play something down : obscure or muffle a fact or consideration
soft phosphate *n* : a powdery impure form of tricalcium phosphate of low fertilizer value occurring in natural deposits of phosphate rock and separated from hard rock and pebble phosphates in fertilizer manufacture
soft pine *n* **1** : a soft-wooded pine; *specif* : an American white pine (*Pinus strobus*) **2** : the wood of a soft pine
soft poplar *n* : LARGE-TOOTHED ASPEN
soft porcelain *n* : a porcelain made of soft paste
soft pork *n* : pork made oily and flabby by feeding hogs on oily feeds (as peanuts or soybeans)
soft ray *n* : a fish's fin ray made up of numerous short slightly movable joints giving it some flexibility and usu. dividing into two or more slightly diverging branches — opposed to *spiny ray*
soft–rayed \ˈ=ˌ=\ *adj* **1** : having soft or articulated rays — used of the fins of some fishes **2** : having fins with soft or articulated rays — used of fishes; compare SPINY-RAYED
soft roe *n* : the testes of a fish : MILT
soft rot *n* : a mushy watery or slimy decay of plants or their parts caused by bacteria or fungi: as **a** : a disintegration of tissues (as of roots, tubers) caused by a bacterium (*Erwinia carotovora*) **b** : a highly destructive blue mold or storage rot of fruits caused by a mold (*Penicillium expansum*)
soft rush *n* : a nearly cosmopolitan rush (*Juncus effusus*) common in marshy areas and having furrowed or striate usu. soft culms — called also *round rush*
softs *pl of* SOFT
soft saw·der \-ˈsädə(r), -ˈsȯd-\ *n* [*soft* + obs. *sawder* solder, fr. ME — more at SOLDER] : FLATTERY, BLARNEY
soft–sawder \ˈ=ˈ==\ *vb* [*soft sawder*] *chiefly dial* : FLATTER
soft scale *n* : a scale insect (esp. family Coccidae) more or less active in all stages; *esp* : BROWN SOFT SCALE — compare ARMORED SCALE
soft sell *n* : the use of suggestion or persuasion in selling rather than aggressive pressure — compare HARD SELL
¹**soft–shell** \ˈ=ˌ=\ *adj* [¹*soft* + *shell*] **1** : having a soft or fragile shell esp. as a result of recent shedding **2** : moderate in policy or doctrine : avoiding extreme principles or measures ⟨the sort of *soft-shell* left-of-center man who is for free speech plus the good manners that ensure that nothing offensive will ever be said —Anthony West⟩
²**soft–shell** \ˈ=ˌ=\ *n* [¹*soft-shell*] **1** : SOFT-SHELLED CRAB **2** : SOFT-SHELL CLAM **3** : SOFT-SHELLED TURTLE **4** : MODERATE, LIBERAL
soft–shell clam *also* **soft–shelled clam** *n* : an elongated clam (*Mya arenaria*) of the east coast of No. America having a thin friable shell and long siphons and being considered esp. desirable for steaming
soft–shelled \ˈ=ˌ=\ *adj* : SOFT-SHELL
soft–shell crab *or* **soft–shelled crab** *n* : a crab that has recently shed its shell and has a very soft new one — distinguished from *hard-shell crab;* see BLUE CRAB
soft–shelled turtle *n* : any of numerous fiercely voracious aquatic turtles of the family Trionychidae having a flat, oval, or nearly round shell covered with soft leathery skin instead of with horny plates, a narrow head, nostrils at the end of a fleshy proboscis, and feet broadly webbed with but three claws and living in parts of Africa, Asia, and No. America, including the whole Mississippi valley, the Great lakes, and many southern rivers
soft–shoe \ˈ=ˌ=\ *adj* : of or relating to tap dancing done in soft-soled shoes without metal taps
soft silk *n* : silk with the natural gum removed
soft–sized \ˈ=ˌ=\ *adj* : SLACK-SIZED
soft snap *n* : a post, job, or course of study demanding little time or effort
soft soap *n* **1** : soap of a semifluid consistency made principally with potash or with soda by control of the fluidity by other factors (as the unsaturation of the fat used and the amount of water and glycerol present) and used chiefly in liquid soaps, in blending with hard soaps to increase solubility and lathering properties, and in medicine — see GREEN SOAP **2** : the art or device of persuasion and flattery : BLARNEY ⟨the master of the glad hand and the *soft soap* —H.A.Burton⟩
soft–soap \ˈ=ˈ=\ *vt* [*soft soap*] : to soothe or persuade with flattery or blarney ⟨*soft-soaped* him and got him to ride along by giving him an office —*Amer. Mercury*⟩
soft–soaper \ˈ=ˈ=ə(r)\ *n* : one that soft-soaps : FLATTERER
soft solder *n* **1** : an alloy of lead and tin that melts below 700° F and is used when melted to join metallic surfaces — compare HARD SOLDER, SILVER SOLDER **2** : SOFT SAWDER
soft–solder \ˈ=ˈ==\ *vt* [*soft solder*] : to repair or join with soft solder
soft sole *n* : a soft-soled shoe; *specif* : an infant's shoe made with a moccasin seam and soft leather sole

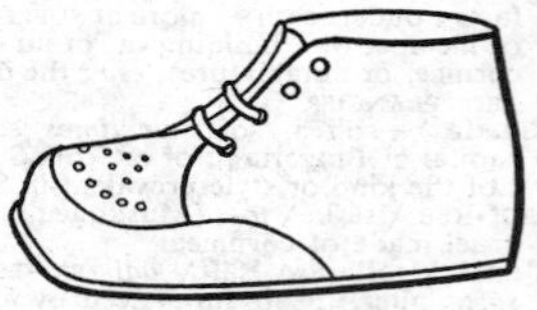

soft sole

soft–spoken \ˈ=ˈ==\ *adj* [³*soft* + *spoken*] : speaking softly : having a mild or gentle voice : SUAVE ⟨as *soft-spoken* as any curate —Heywood Broun⟩
soft spot *n* **1** : a sentimental weakness : an affectionate inclination : LEANING ⟨women have a *soft spot* for a man with a broken heart —Rearden Conner⟩ **2** : a vulnerable point ⟨the major *soft spot* in the West's armor —*World*⟩ **3** : any business or department of the economy that displays weakness ⟨some *soft spots* have appeared in a number of items, notably in stainless steel and in sheet and strip —*Wall Street Jour.*⟩
soft steel *n* : MILD STEEL
soft–stem bulrush *n* : GREAT BULRUSH b
soft thing *n* : SOFT SNAP
soft tick *n* : a tick of the family Argasidae — compare HARD TICK, IXODIDAE
soft toe *n* [¹*soft* + *toe*] **1** : the toe of a shoe without toe stiffening or toe box **2** : a shoe having a soft toe
soft touch *n* **1** : someone who can be easily talked into giving help (as a gift or loan of money) : EASY MARK ⟨recognized him early as a *soft touch* for a loan —John Lardner⟩ **2** : something easily performed or dispatched ⟨it's not a *soft touch;* it's a business⟩ **3** : an easily defeated opponent : someone readily victimized ⟨their traditional football rival promised to be a *soft touch* that year⟩
soft turtle *or* **soft tortoise** *n* : SOFT-SHELLED TURTLE
soft waste *n* : textile waste from processes prior to spinning that is usu. reworkable — compare HARD WASTE
soft wheat *n* : a wheat with soft starchy kernels that are high in starch but typically low in gluten and yield a weak flour esp. suitable for pastry and breakfast foods — compare HARD WHEAT
¹**softwood** \ˈ=ˌ=\ *n* **1** : the wood of a coniferous tree known orig. from soft European woods but including both soft and hard woods **2** [²*softwood*] : a tree that yields softwood : an arborescent conifer
²**softwood** \"\ *adj* **1** : having softwood or made of softwood **2** : consisting of immature and still soft and pliable tissue ⟨~ cuttings for propagating plants⟩
soft–wooded \ˈ=ˈ==\ *adj* **1** : having soft wood that is easy to work or finish **2** : SOFTWOOD 1
softy *or* **soft·ie** \ˈsȯftē, -ti *also* ˈsäf-\ *n, pl* **softies** [¹*soft* + *-y*] **1** : an excessively sentimental or susceptible person ⟨an old ~ with a weakness for the tingling effect on the spine of massive bands swinging into college songs —John McNulty⟩ **2** : a weak, effeminate, or foolish person ⟨easy polemic victories, won by browbeating *softies* on the other side —H.L.Varney⟩
¹**sog** \ˈsäg *also* ˈsȯg\ *vb* **sogged; sogged; sogging; sogs** [origin unknown] *chiefly dial* : SOAK
²**sog** \"\ *vb* [origin unknown] *dial Eng* : DROWSE
so·ga \ˈsōgə\ *n, pl* **soga** *or* **sogas** *usu cap* **1 a** : a Bantu-speaking people of the north shore of Lake Victoria in eastern Africa **b** : a member of the Soga people **2** : a dialect of Ganda spoken by the Soga people
¹**sog·di·an** *or* **sogh·di·an** \ˈsägdēən *also* ˈsȯg-\ *n* -S *cap* [L *Sogdiani* (pl.), fr. *sogdiani*, pl. of *sogdianus*, adj., Sogdian] **1** : a native or inhabitant of Sogdiana, a province of the ancient Persian Empire in the region of modern Bukhara **2** : an Iranian language of the Sogdian people
²**sogdian** *or* **soghdian** \"\ *adj, usu cap* [L *sogdianus*, fr. OPer *Sughuda* Sogdiana, province of the ancient Persian Empire + L *-anus* -an] **1** : of, relating to, or characteristic of ancient Sogdiana **2** : of, relating to, or characteristic of the people of ancient Sogdiana
sog·garth \ˈsägərth\ *n* -S [IrGael *sagart*, fr. L *sacerdot-*, *sacerdos* — more at SACERDOTAL] *Irish* : PRIEST
sog·gi·ly \ˈsägəlē, -li *also* ˈsȯg-\ *adv* : in a soggy manner
sog·gi·ness \-gēnəs, -gin-\ *n* -ES : the quality or state of being soggy: as **a** : WATERINESS, MARSHINESS ⟨the ~ of the land⟩ **b** : DULLNESS, PONDEROUSNESS ⟨the sometimes unbelievable ~ of their prose —T.E.Cooney⟩
¹**sog·ging** \-giŋ\ *adj* [fr. pres. part. of ¹*sog*] : SOAKING
²**sogging** \"\ *adv* : THOROUGHLY ⟨our clothes were ~ wet⟩
sog·gy \ˈsägē, -gi *also* ˈsȯg-\ *adj* -ER/-EST [¹*sog* + *-y*] **1** : saturated or heavy with water or moisture: as **a** : WATERLOGGED, SOAKED ⟨slosh over a ~ fairway —R.M.Hodesh⟩ ⟨a thick and ~ mat of fiber —*Monsanto Mag.*⟩ ⟨~ clothes⟩ ⟨~ shoes⟩ **b** : DAMP, HUMID ⟨the air of the lowlands seemed ~ and heavy —Ida Treat⟩ **c** : SODDEN ⟨~ bread⟩ **2** : heavily dull : HEAVY-FOOTED, PONDEROUS, SPIRITLESS ⟨a good deal of . . . ~ conversation about the state of the world —Wolcott Gibbs⟩ ⟨digest large portions of rather ~ educational literature —M.B.Smith⟩ ⟨a ~ prose that makes even sudden death seem tedious —Martin Levin⟩
¹**soh** \ˈsō\ *interj* [origin unknown] *archaic* — used as an expression of surprised annoyance or as a command to calm down
²**soh** *var of* SOL
sohan *usu cap, var of* SOAN
so–ho \sōˈhō\ *n* -ES [ME *so howe, so ho*] — used by hunters on sighting a hare as a call or exclamation; sometimes used interjectionally as an expression of angry surprise or discovery ⟨*so-ho*, caught in the act⟩
soia *var of* SOJA
soi–disant \ˌswädēˈzäⁿ\ *adj* [F, lit., saying oneself] : SELF-STYLED, SO-CALLED, PRETENDED — usu. used disparagingly ⟨a *soi-disant* artist⟩ ⟨this *soi-disant* novel —Anthony Boucher⟩ ⟨literary specialists (*soi-disant* or even authentic) —M.A.Pei⟩
soi·gné *or* **soi·gnée** \(ˈ)swänˈyā\ *adj* [F, fr. past part. of *soigner* to take care of, fr. ML *soniare*] **1** : taken care of painstakingly : elegantly maintained : MODISH ⟨a *soigné* restaurant⟩ ⟨simple but *soignée* dresses of black crêpe —*New Yorker*⟩ **2** : dressed with great care and elegance : WELL-GROOMED, SLEEK ⟨she was *soignée* in a platinum mink stole —*Time*⟩
¹**soil** \ˈsȯil, *esp before pause or consonant* -ȯiəl\ *vb* -ED/-ING/-S [ME *soilen*, fr. OF *soiller, souiller* to wallow, soil, fr. *soil* pigsty, boar's wallow, prob. fr. L *suile* pigsty, fr. *sus* pig — more at SOW] *vt* **1** : to stain or defile morally : CORRUPT, POLLUTE ⟨why ~ their ears with nasty knowledge —C.W. Cunnington⟩ ⟨~ one's mind with such paltry thoughts —Van Wyck Brooks⟩ **2** : to make unclean esp. superficially : DIRTY 1, SMUDGE, SPOT ⟨~ a rug⟩ ⟨a paste that ~*s* the hands⟩ ⟨his shoes . . . were ~*ed* now from the clay of the airfield —Kay Boyle⟩ ⟨the majestic river . . . ~*ed* with garbage —Herbert Agar⟩ **3** : to blacken or besmirch (as a person's reputation or honor) by word or deed : give a bad name to : SULLY, DISGRACE ⟨what hath she done, prince, that can ~ our mothers —Shak.⟩ **4** *chiefly Brit* : to paint (as a pipe) with plumber's soil ~ *vi* **1 a** : to wallow in mud — used esp. of a deer or wild boar **b** : to take refuge in water or in a marsh — used of hunted game **2 a** : to become soiled or dirty ⟨this fabric ~*s* easily⟩ **b** : to defecate involuntarily ⟨patients also showed infantile reactions . . . continually wetting and ~*ing* —*Digest of Neurology & Psychiatry*⟩
²**soil** \"\ *n* -S **1 a** : the action of soiling or the condition of being soiled : SOILAGE 1, STAIN, SPOT ⟨protect a dress from ~⟩ ⟨hands free from ~⟩ ⟨finger marks or any other kind of ~ —*New Yorker*⟩ **b** : moral defilement : CORRUPTION ⟨disburdening herself of the ~ of worldly frailties —Nathaniel Hawthorne⟩ **2** : something that soils or pollutes: as **a** : foreign matter : REFUSE ⟨metal surfaces . . . filled with all types of ~ —R.E.Marce⟩ **b** : SEWAGE ⟨conduits to carry away the ~⟩ **c** : DUNG, EXCREMENT **3** : PLUMBER'S SOIL
³**soil** \"\ *n* -S [ME, fr. AF, fr. L *solium* seat (influenced in meaning by L *solum* base, floor, ground, soil); prob. akin to L *sedēre* to sit — more at SIT] **1** : firm land : EARTH, GROUND ⟨underfoot the divine ~, overhead the sun —Walt Whitman⟩ ⟨she was as brown as the very ~ itself —Pearl Buck⟩ **2 a** : the upper layer of earth that may be dug or plowed; *specif* : the loose surface material of the earth in which plants grow usu. consisting of disintegrated rock with an admixture of organic matter and soluble salts — see HUMUS, NITRIFICATION **b** : the surface earth of a particular place with reference esp. to its composition or its adaptability (as for the farmer, builder, or engineer) ⟨sandy ~⟩ ⟨fertile ~⟩ ⟨a rich ~⟩ ⟨a ~ deficient in alkali⟩ **3** : COUNTRY, LAND ⟨seek your hero in a distant ~ —Thomas Gray⟩ ⟨left his native ~ never to return⟩ **4 a** : cultivated or tilled ground ⟨works on the ~⟩ **b** : the agricultural life or calling ⟨a son of the ~⟩ ⟨felt a closeness to the ~⟩ **5** : a medium in which something takes hold and develops ⟨countries where such misery exists are fertile ~ for Communist infiltration —*N.Y. Times Mag.*⟩ ⟨psychiatry flourished in the ~ of curiosity —R.S.Ellery⟩
⁴**soil** \"\ *n* -S [ME *soyle* boar's wallow, small pond, fr. MF *soil, souille* boar's wallow — more at ¹SOIL] : a tract of water (as a marsh or pool) in which hunted animals take refuge from their pursuers : REFUGE, SANCTUARY — used chiefly in the phrases *run to soil, go to soil, take soil*
⁵**soil** \"\ *vt* -ED/-ING/-S [origin unknown] **1** : to feed (livestock) in the barn or an enclosure with fresh grass or green food : FATTEN **2** : to purge (livestock) by feeding on green food
⁶**soil** \"\ *n* -S : SOILAGE
soil·age \ˈsȯilij, -lēj\ *n* -S [¹*soil* + *-age*] **1** : the act of soiling or condition of being soiled ⟨a fabric that resists ~⟩ **2** *archaic* : REFUSE, SEWAGE **3** [⁵*soil* + *-age*] : green crops cut for feeding confined animals
soil air *n* [³*soil*] : gases occupying the free pore space in soil
soil auger *n* : an auger for taking soil samples
soil binder *n* : a plant (as any of various grasses or stoloniferous plants) used to prevent or capable of preventing soil erosion usu. by forming dense mats of roots or of superficial growth
soil cap *n* : a layer of mantle rock
¹**soil–cement** \ˈ=ˌ=ˈ= *sometimes* ˈ=ˈ=ˌ=\ *n* : an intimate highly compacted mixture of pulverized soil and measured amounts of cement and water used chiefly as a base course for roads and street and airport paving
²**soil–cement** \"\ *adj, of a road* : having a hard base or surface composed of earth mixed with portland cement
soil colloid *n* : the colloidal complex of soils that consists chiefly of clay and humus and plays an important role in ion exchange and fertility
soil complex *n* : a mapping unit consisting of two or more recognized taxonomic units used in detailed soil surveys
soil conditioner *n* : a chemical substance (as gypsum) used to improve the structure of the soil and increase its porosity and crumbliness
soil conservation *n* **1** : the prevention or reduction of soil erosion and soil depletion by protective measures against water and wind damage **2** : management of soil so as to obtain the largest crop yields feasible and improve the soil at the same time
soil creep *n* : slow down-slope movement of earth materials under the influence of gravitation
soiled \ˈsȯi(ə)ld\ *adj* [³*soil* + *-ed*] : having soil of a specified character — used chiefly in combination ⟨rich-*soiled*⟩
soil family *n* : FAMILY 4g
soil fertility *n* : capacity of a soil to provide crops with essential plant nutrients
soil horizon *n* : HORIZON 2a
¹**soiling** *n* -S [fr. gerund of ⁵*soil*] **1** : the act or process of soiling or feeding green food to an animal **2** : SOILAGE 3
²**soiling** *n* -S [fr. gerund of obs. *soil* to spread with soil, to manure, fr. ³*soil*] : the act or process of spreading or filling with soil, dirt, or manure
soiling crop *n* [¹*soiling*] : a crop cut green and fed to livestock immediately without further curing or processing
soil·less \ˈsȯi(ə)lləs\ *adj* [³*soil* + *-less*] : carried on without soil ⟨the ~ growth of plants⟩ ⟨~ agriculture⟩
soil map *n* : a record on a map of an area showing soil types, drains, and other pertinent information
soil mechanics *n pl but sing or pl in constr* : the study of the physical properties and utilization of soils esp. in planning foundations for structures and subgrades for highways
soil miller *n* : any of several rotary cultivating devices for pulverizing soil
soil–moisture index *n* : ability of soil to supply moisture to plants
soil–moisture tension *n* : the force per unit area required to remove film water from soil
soil mulch *n* : DUST MULCH
soil phase *n* : a subdivision of a soil type that deviates from the typical character of the soil type
soil pipe *n* : a pipe for liquid wastes carrying human excrement
soil rot *n* : a rot caused by organisms in the soil; *specif* : pox of sweet potatoes
soils *pres 3d sing of* SOIL, *pl of* SOIL
soil science *n* : the study of soil as a natural product : PEDOLOGY
soil scientist *n* : a specialist in soil science
soil series *n* : any of various soils with similar profiles developed from similar parent materials under comparable climatic and vegetational conditions ⟨the Miami *soil series*⟩ — see SOIL TYPE
soil solution *n* : the film moisture in the soil together with its dissolved substances
soil stack *n* : a vertical soil pipe
soil stripe *n* : one of the alternating bands of finer and coarser material comprising a soil structure that are produced in sloping ground by solifluction — usu. used in pl.
soil structure *n* : the arrangement of soil particles in various aggregates differing in shape, size, stability, and degree of adhesion to one another
soil survey *n* : a systematic study of the soil of an area including classification and mapping of the properties, crop adaptations, and distribution of various soil types
soil type *n* : a member of a soil series distinguished primarily by texture ⟨the Miami silt is a distinctive *soil type* of the Miami series⟩
soil·ure \ˈsȯilyə(r)\ *n* -S [ME, fr. OF *soilleure*, fr. *soiller* to soil] **1** : the act of soiling : the condition of being soiled ⟨not making any scruple of her ~ —Shak.⟩ **2** : STAIN, SMUDGE ⟨a dry, light ~ of dead ashes —William Faulkner⟩
soily \ˈsȯilē\ *adj* -ER/-EST [³*soil* + *-y*] : having spots or stains : DIRTY ⟨on her ~ neck stealthily hangs her lady's jewels —Gordon Bottomley⟩
soi·ree *or* **soi·rée** \(ˈ)swäˈrā\ *n* -S [F *soirée* evening period, evening party, fr. MF, fr. *soir* evening, fr. L *sero* at a late hour, fr. abl. of *serum* late time, fr. neut. of *serus* late — more at SINCE] : an evening party or reception ⟨attending . . . ~*s* in her silk, penthouse parlor —Saul Bellow⟩ ⟨invited to ~*s* where the elite . . . displayed their shoddy splendor —Upton Sinclair⟩
soix·ante–neuf \ˌswäˌsäⁿtˈnə(r)f, -ˈnœf\ *n* -S [F, lit., sixty-nine] : simultaneous cunnilingus and fellatio : double fellatio : double cunnilingus
¹**soja** \ˈsȯi(y)ə, ˈsōjə, ˈsōyə, ˈsȯyə\ [NL, fr. D, soybean — more at SOYA] *syn of* APIOS
²**soja** \", *dial* ˈsōjē *or* -ōji *or* -ōdə *or* -ōdē *or* -ōdi *or* -ōə\ *also* **soja bean** \"-\ *or* **soia** *like* ²SOJA\ *n* -S [D *soja*] : SOYBEAN
¹**so·journ** \ˈsō,jərn, -jən, -jəin, =ˈ= *sometimes* səˈj-, *chiefly Brit* ˈsəj- *or* ˈsə,j- *or* -ˌjən\ *n* -S [ME *soiorn, soiourne*, fr. OF *sojorn*, fr. *sojorner* to sojourn] **1** : a temporary stay (as of a traveler in a foreign country) ⟨returned . . . after a long ~ in

Europe —Alan McCulloch⟩ ⟨a summer's ~ in the English countryside —Lucien Price⟩ ⟨the Israelite tradition of a prolonged ~ in Egypt —W.F.Albright⟩ **2** *archaic* **:** a temporary dwelling place ⟨long detained in that obscure ~ —John Milton⟩

²sojourn \"\ *vi* -ED/-ING/-S [ME *soiornen, soiournen,* fr. OF *sojorner,* fr. (assumed) VL *subdiurnare,* fr. L *sub-* under, during + LL *diurnum* day — more at JOURNEY] **:** to stay as a temporary resident **:** STOP ⟨~*ed* for a month at a mountain resort⟩ ⟨the right . . . to ~ there as long as they pleased —R.B.Taney⟩ **syn** see RESIDE

so·journ·er \-nə(r)\ *n* -S [ME *soiorner,* fr. *soiornen* to sojourn + *-er*] **:** one that sojourns ⟨missionaries and other ~*s* among primitive peoples —*Times Lit. Supp.*⟩: as **a** *obs* **:** GUEST, LODGER ⟨report what a ~ we have —Shak.⟩ **b** *archaic* **:** a student lodging in the house or school where he is taught

so·journ·ment \-nmənt\ *n* -S [²*sojourn* + *-ment*] *archaic* **:** SOJOURN

soke \ˈsōk\ *also* **soc** \ˈsäk, ˈsōk\ *n* -S [ME *soc, sok, soke,* fr. ML *soca,* fr. OE *sōcn* — more at SOKEN] **1 a** *Anglo-Saxon & early Eng law* **:** the right to hold court and do justice with the franchise to receive certain fees or fines arising from it **:** jurisdiction over a territory or over people **b :** any of various other jurisdictions or franchises: as (1) **:** FOLDAGE (2) **:** MILL SOKE **2 :** the district included in a soke jurisdiction or franchise

soke·man \ˈsōkmən\ *n, pl* **sokemen** [ME, fr. ML *sokemannus, sochemannus,* fr. OE *sōcn* soke + *man*] **:** a man who is under the soke of another **:** a tenant by socage

soke·man·ry \-rē\ *n* -ES [AF *sokemanerie,* fr. ML *sokemannus* sokeman + AF *-erie* -ry] **1 :** tenure of land subject to the soke of another — compare SOCAGE **2 a :** the quality or state of being a sokeman **b :** SOKEMEN

so·ken \ˈsōkən\ *n* -S [ME *socne, soken* soke, fr. OE *sōcn* act of seeking, inquiry, exercise of judicial power, jurisdiction, district of jurisdiction; akin to ON *sōkn* attack, action at law, parish, Goth *sokns* search, inquiry, OE *sēcan* to search — more at SEEK] **:** a district held by socage **:** SOKE 2

so·khor \(ˈ)sō¦kȯ(ə)r\ *n* -S [origin unknown] **:** any of several sturdily built burrowing cricetid rodents (genus *Myospalax*) of China, Manchuria, and southern Siberia that strongly resemble the American pocket gophers but may be distinguished from them by the greatly reduced eye and by absence of the external ear

so·kol \ˈsōˌkōl\ *n* -S *often cap* [Czech, lit., falcon; akin to Skt *śakuna* bird] **:** a member of any one of various Slavic gymnastic societies of Europe and the U.S.

sokotran *or* **sokotrine** *usu cap, var of* SOCOTRAN

so·ko·tri \səˈkō·trē\ *n, usu cap* [Ar *Suquṭrī*] **:** a South Arabic dialect very closely related to Mahri and spoken on the island of Socotra

¹sol \ˈsōl, *chiefly Brit* ˈsäl\ *also* **soh** *or* **so** \ˈsō\ *n* -S [*sol,* ME, fr. ML, fr. L *solve* purge, a word sung to this note in a medieval hymn to St. John the Baptist; *soh, so,* alterations of *sol* due to simplification of *-l l-* in singing the sequence *sol la* in the ascending scale] **1 :** the fifth tone of the diatonic scale in solmization **2 :** the tone *G* in the fixed-do system

²sol \"\ *vt, obs* **:** to sing sol to

³sol \ˈsäl, *in sense 3 "* or ˈsōl\ *n* -S [ME, fr. L — more at SOLAR] **1** *usu cap* **:** SUN **2 :** gold as used in alchemy **3** [Mex-Sp, fr. Sp, sun, fr. L] **:** the sunny side or section of a bullfight arena — compare SOMBRA

⁴sol \ˈsäl, ˈsōl\ *n* -S [ME, fr. MF — more at SOU] **:** an old French coin equal to 12 deniers or ¹⁄₂₀ livre; *also* **:** a corresponding unit of value

⁵sol \"\ *n, pl* **so·les** \ˈsō(ˌ)lās\ [AmerSp, fr. Sp, sun, fr. L; fr. the device on the coin] **1 a :** a Peruvian monetary unit equal to ¹⁄₁₀ libra or pound used before 1930 **b :** the basic monetary unit of Peru since 1930 — see MONEY table **2 :** a coin or note representing one Peruvian sol unit

⁶sol \ˈsäl, ˈsōl, ˈsōl\ *n* -S [*-sol* (as in *hydrosol, alcosol*), fr. *solution*] **1 :** a fluid colloidal system: as **a :** a dispersion of solid particles in a liquid colloidal solution — compare GEL **b :** AEROSOL 1 **2 :** a fraction of a high-molecular-weight compound (as rubber) that dissolves or disperses in a solvent (as ether)

sol *abbr* **1** soldier **2** solenoid **3** solicitor **4** soluble **5** solution

SOL *abbr* **1** shipowner's liability **2** strictly out of luck

¹so·la \(ˈ)sō¦lä\ *interj* [origin unknown] *obs* **:** HOLLO

²so·la *also* **so·lah** \ˈs(h)ō(ˌ)lä\ *n* -S [Hindi *solā*] **:** an East Indian shrubby herb (*Aeschynomene aspera*) the pith of which is used for making hats, swimming jackets, and toys — see TOPEE

³so·la \ˈsōlə\ *or* **sola bill** *n* [L *sola,* fem. of *solus* sole, only] **:** an unduplicated bill of exchange

⁴sola *pl of* SOLUM

¹sol·ace \ˈsäləs *sometimes* ˈsōl-\ *n* -S [ME *solas,* fr. OF, fr. L *solacium, solatium* fr. *solari* to console, comfort — more at SILLY] **1 :** comfort in grief **:** alleviation of grief or anxiety ⟨seek ~ in company⟩ ⟨give ~ to a friend⟩ **2 a** *obs* **:** RECREATION **b :** an offsetting diversion **3 :** something that gives solace **:** a source of relief or consolation ⟨books were his only ~⟩ **4** *archaic* **:** a penalty imposed on a member by a printers' chapel for a breach of the rules

²solace \"\ *vb* -ED/-ING/-S [ME *solacen,* fr. OF *solacier,* fr. LL *solaciare,* fr. L *solacium* comfort, solace] *vt* **1 :** to give comfort to in grief or misfortune **:** CONSOLE **2 a :** to make (as a place) cheerful **b :** to give (as oneself) diversion **:** ENTERTAIN, AMUSE **3 :** ALLAY, ASSUAGE, SOOTHE ⟨~ grief⟩ **4** *archaic* **:** to impose a solace on (a member of a printers' chapel) ~ *vi, obs* **:** to take or give solace or comfort or diversion **syn** see COMFORT

sol·ace·ful \-fəl\ *adj* **:** full of or tending to bring solace ⟨~ repose⟩

sol·ace·ment \-mənt\ *n* -S [²*solace* + *-ment*] **1 :** an act of solacing or the condition of being solaced **2 :** something that solaces

sol·ac·er \-ləsə(r)\ *n* -S **:** one that solaces

so·la·cious \səˈlāshəs, sōˈl-\ *adj* [ME, fr. MF *solacieus,* fr. OF, fr. *solas* solace + *-eus* -ous] *archaic* **:** affording solace

so·lan \ˈsōlən\ *n* -S [ME *soland,* fr. ON *sūla* pillar, gannet + *önd* duck — more at SILE, ANAS] **:** SOLAN GOOSE

so·la·na·ce·ae \ˌsōləˈnāsēˌē\ *n pl, cap* [NL, fr. *Solanum,* type genus + *-aceae*] **:** a large and economically important family of widely distributed, often strongly scented, and sometimes narcotic herbs, shrubs, or trees (order Polemoniales) having alternate leaves and flowers that are often showy and have five stamens and a 2-celled ovary of which each cell contains many ovules — see ATROPA, CAPSICUM, HYOSCYAMUS, LYCOPERSICON, NICOTIANA, PETUNIA, PHYSALIS, SOLANUM — **so·la·na·ceous** \ˌsōlə¦nāshəs\ *adj*

so·la·na·les \ˌsōləˈnā(ˌ)lēz\ *n pl, cap* [NL, fr. *Solanum* + *-ales*] *in former classifications* **:** an order of dicotyledonous plants comprising Solanaceae and related families that are now usu. included among the Polemoniales

so·land \ˈsōlən(d)\ *n* -S [ME — more at SOLAN] **:** SOLAN GOOSE

so·lan·der case \(ˈ)sō¦landə(r)-\ *also* **solander box** *or* **solander** *n* -S *often cap S* [after Daniel C. *Solander* †1782 Swed. botanist in England] **:** a protective often leather-covered and book-shaped case for books and documents usu. with a slide-on top that completely covers the contents

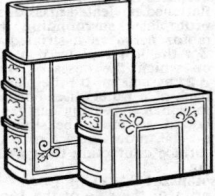

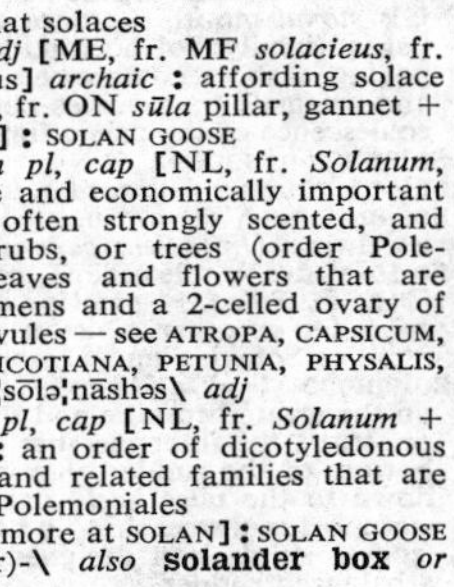
solander case

so·lan·dra \sōˈlandrə\ *n* [NL, after Daniel C. *Solander* †1782] **1** *cap* **:** a small genus of tall-climbing tropical American shrubs (family Solanaceae) having entire shining leathery leaves and large showy solitary white to yellow usu. fragrant flowers — see CHALICE VINE **2** -S **:** any plant of the genus *Solandra*

so·lan goose \ˈsōlən-\ *or* **so·lent goose** \-n(t)-\ *n* **:** a very large white gannet (*Sula bassana* or *Moris bassana*) with black wing tips

so·lan·i·dine \sōˈlanəˌdēn, -dən\ *also* **solanidine–t** *n, sometimes cap T* [*solanidine* ISV *solanine* + *-idine; solanidine-t* fr. *solanine* + *-idine* + *-t* (as in *solanine-t*)] **:** a crystalline steroidal alkaloid $C_{27}H_{43}NO$ obtained esp. by hydrolysis of solanine and also occurring with it naturally

so·la·nine \ˈsōləˌnēn, -ˌnən\ *also* **so·la·nin** \-nən\ *n* -S [F *solanine,* fr. L *solanum* nightshade + F *-ine*] **1** *also* **solanine–t** *usu cap T* [*solanine-t* fr. *solanine* + *t,* initial of NL *tuberosum* (specific epithet of *Solanum tuberosum,* a solanaceous plant from which it is produced), fr. L, neut. of *tuberosus* tuberous] **:** a bitter crystalline glycosidal alkaloid $C_{45}H_{73}NO_{15}$ that has the toxic properties of a saponin, that is obtained from several solanaceous plants (as potato sprouts and eyes, tomatoes, and the berries of black nightshade and bittersweet), and that on hydrolysis yields solanidine, glucose, galactose, and rhamnose **2 :** any of several glycosidal alkaloids (as solasonine) related chemically to solanine

so·la·no \səˈlä(ˌ)nō\ *n* -S [Sp, fr. L *solanus,* fr. *sol* sun + *-anus* -an — more at SOLAR] **:** a hot oppressive east wind of the Mediterranean region and esp. of the eastern coast of Spain; *also* **:** a cloudy rain-bringing wind of the same locality and direction

so·la·num \səˈlānəm, -län-\ *n* [NL, fr. L, nightshade, prob. fr. *sol* sun + *-anum,* neut. of *-anus* -an] **1** *cap* **:** the type genus of Solanaceae comprising herbs, trees, and shrubs that are widely distributed in tropical and temperate regions, have often prickly-veined leaves, cymose white, purple, or yellow flowers with a rotate corolla and five stamens with long connivent anthers, and a fruit that is a berry, and include several important food and ornamental plants — see EGGPLANT, POTATO; BITTERSWEET, JERUSALEM CHERRY; compare LYCOPERSICON **2** -S **:** any plant of the genus *Solanum*

¹solar \ˈsōlə(r), ˈsōl-\ *or* **sol·lar** \ˈsäl-\ *n* -S [ME *soler, solar,* fr. OE *soler, solar;* akin to MD *solre* loft, flat roof, MLG *solder,* OHG *solāri* loft; all fr. a prehistoric WGmc word borrowed fr. L *solarium* part of a house exposed to the sun — more at SOLARIUM] **1 :** an upper room or apartment (as a solarium, a chamber, a rood loft, or a garret); *esp* **:** an apartment for family use in a superior medieval residence ⟨the ladies gathered in the ~ while the lords drank in the great hall of the castle⟩ **2** *usu* **sollar** *or* **sol·ler** \ˈsälə(r)\ **:** a platform in a Cornish mine shaft and esp. between a series of ladders **:** a longitudinal partition forming an air passage between itself and the roof in a mine working

²so·lar \ˈsōlə(r) *sometimes* -ˌlär *or* -ˌlȧ(r\ *adj* [ME, fr. L *solaris,* fr. *sol* sun + *-aris* -ar; akin to OE & ON *sōl* sun, Goth *sauil,* Gk *hēlios,* Skt *sūra*] **1 :** of, derived from, or relating to the sun and its effects esp. on the earth and other celestial bodies **2 :** born under or subject to the influence of the sun **3 :** produced or operated by the action of the sun's light or heat; *also* **:** utilizing the sun's rays or heat ⟨a ~ engine⟩ — see SOLAR SALT, SOLAR TELEGRAPH **4 :** of, like, or connected with the sun as a deity or symbol of deity **:** descended from or sacred to a sun god **:** devoted to sun worship ⟨~ myths⟩ ⟨a ~ hero⟩

³solar \"\ *adj* [alter. (influenced by ²*solar*) of ²*sola*] **1 :** made of sola ⟨a ~ topee⟩ **2 :** intended for use in tropic regions ⟨~ clothing⟩

solar apex *n* **:** a point of the celestial sphere lying in the constellation Hercules toward which the sun and the solar system are moving with respect to the stars in the solar neighborhood at a rate of about 12 miles per second — compare ANTAPEX

solar attachment *n* **:** an attachment to a surveyor's transit or compass for determining the true meridian directly from the sun

solar battery *n* **:** a device consisting of one or more units for converting the energy of sunlight into electrical energy

solar compass *n* **:** SUN COMPASS

solar constant *n* **:** the quantity of radiant solar heat that is received normally at the outer layer of the earth's atmosphere and that has an average value of about 1.94 gram calories per square centimeter per minute

solar corona *n* **:** CORONA 2a(2)

solar cycle *n* **1 :** a cycle of disturbances in the sun and its atmosphere (as the fluctuation in the numbers and areas of sunspots or the form and shape of the corona) of an average length of about 11 years **2 :** CYCLE OF THE SUN

solar day *n* **1 :** the interval between transits of the apparent or mean sun across the meridian at any place **2 :** a period of one mean solar day containing 24 hours of solar minutes and seconds

solar diagonal *n* **:** an attachment for a telescope designed to permit direct observing of the sun by means of a prism that discards most of the unwanted heat and light

solar eclipse *n* **:** an eclipse of the sun by the moon — see ECLIPSE illustration

solar ecliptic limit *n* **:** the angular distance from the nodes of the moon's orbit within which an eclipse of the sun may or must occur when the sun and moon are in conjunction there

solar equation *n* **:** the correction of the epacts by —1 required in each century of the Gregorian calendar that begins with a common year instead of a leap year — compare LUNAR EQUATION

solar eyepiece *n* **:** an eyepiece for viewing the sun telescopically with means for diminishing the light and heat (as by partial reflection)

solar flare *n* **:** a sudden and temporary outburst of energy from a small area of the sun's surface that is usu. directly observable only in increased emission of a few spectral wavelengths (as in a hydrogen line and the lines of ionized calcium) but sometimes seen in white light

solar furnace *n* **:** a heating unit utilizing the rays of the sun concentrated by means of a concave mirror

solar heating *n* **:** space heating by capture and conversion of radiant energy from the sun — compare SOLAR FURNACE

solar hour *n* **:** the twenty-fourth part of a mean solar day

solar house *n* **:** a house equipped with glass areas and so planned as to utilize the sun's rays extensively in heating

so·lar·ism \ˈsōləˌrizəm\ *n* -S [²*solar* + *-ism*] **:** an interpretation of folk stories and ancient legends as primitive concepts of the nature and action of the sun — compare SOLAR MYTH 2

¹so·lar·i·um \sōˈla(a)rēəm, səˈl-, -ler-, -lār-\ *n, pl* **solar·ia** *see sense 2* \-ēə\ [L, sundial, part of a house exposed to the sun, flat house, terrace, fr. *sol* sun + *-arium* — more at SOLAR] **1 :** a Roman sundial or clock (as a water clock) **2** *pl also* **solariums :** an apartment exposed to the sun: as **a :** an apartment on the roof of an ancient dwelling **b :** the solar of a medieval residence **c :** a glass-enclosed porch or living room **:** SUN PARLOR **d :** a room (as in a hospital) for exposure of the body to sunlight (as in sunbathing) or for the treatment of illness by therapeutic light **3 :** a snail of *Architectonica* or a related genus **:** SUNDIAL SHELL

²solarium \"\ *n* [NL, fr. L, sundial] *syn of* ARCHITECTONICA

so·lar·i·za·tion \ˌsōlərəˈzāshən, -rīˈz-\ *n* -S [²*solar* + *-ization*] **1 :** an act or process of solarizing **2 :** a reversal of gradation sequence in the denser portions of the image obtained on the normal development of photographic films, plates, and papers after giving a very intense or long continued exposure **3 :** the inhibition of starch accumulation in leaves in the presence of intense illumination **4 :** alteration in the light-transmitting capacity of glass that follows prolonged exposure to sunlight or sometimes other radiations

so·lar·ize \ˈsōləˌrīz\ *vb* -ED/-ING/-S [²*solar* + *-ize*] *vt* **1 :** to expose to sunlight **:** affect or alter in some way by the action of the sun's rays **2 :** to interpret in terms of or color with solarism ⟨~ a myth⟩ **3 :** to subject (photographic materials) to solarization ~ *vi* **1 :** to solarize something **:** engage in solarizing **2** *of a photographic material* **:** to become affected by solarization

solar lamp *n* **:** ARGAND LAMP

solar letter *n* [trans. of Ar *alḥurūf ashshamsīya* — more at SUN LETTER] **:** SUN LETTER

solar mass *n* **:** the mass of the sun amounting to 2×10^{33} grams and being used as a unit for the expression of the masses of other stars, nebulas, and galaxies

solar microscope *n* **:** a projecting microscope using sunlight

solar motion *n* **:** the motion of the sun and solar system with reference to stars in the sun's neighborhood; *also* **:** any of the sun's other motions as a member of the galaxy — compare SOLAR APEX

solar myth *n* **1 :** a myth that concerns a sun god **2 :** a traditional story (as a folk tale or legend) that is interpreted as a primitive explanation of the course, motion, or influence of the sun — compare SOLARISM

solar noise *n* **:** radio noise emitted by the sun and its atmosphere

solar oil *n* **:** any of various mineral oils used esp. as fuel oils or insecticides: as **a :** gas oil from petroleum **b :** an intermediate fraction from crude shale oil

solar parallax *n* **:** the parallax of the sun being the angle subtended at the sun by the semidiameter of the earth, having an adopted value of 8″.80, and constituting the fundamental datum for the dimensions of the solar system

solar physics *n pl but sing or pl in constr* **:** a branch of astrophysics that deals with the constitution of the sun

solar plexus *n* [so called fr. the radiating nerve fibers] **1 :** a nervous plexus situated in the abdomen behind the stomach and in front of the aorta and the crura of the diaphragm, surrounding the coeliac axis and the root of the superior mesenteric artery, containing several ganglia of which the most important are the coeliac ganglia, and distributing nerve fibers to all the abdominal viscera — called also *coeliac plexus* **2 a :** the pit of the stomach **b :** a knockout or nerve-racking blow received in or as if in this spot

solar prominences *n pl* **:** great clouds of luminous hydrogen, calcium, sodium, and other gases floating above the sun's chromosphere, occas. erupting violently outward, and being esp. numerous in regions above sunspots

solar propagation *n* **:** a method of rooting cuttings involving use of a modified hotbed in which bottom heat is supplied by radiation of stored sun heat from bricks or stones in the bottom of the frame

solars *pl of* SOLAR

solar salt *n* **:** salt from seawater or other brine evaporated in the sun

solar star *n* **:** a star of spectral type G resembling the sun in spectrum

solar still *n* **:** a small device orig. designed for army and navy fliers forced down in the sea that converts salt water or contaminated water into drinking water by vaporization by the sun's rays and condensation

solar system *n* **:** the sun together with the group of celestial bodies that are held by its attraction and revolve around it

solar telegraph *n* **:** a telegraph for signaling by flashes of reflected sunlight — compare HELIOGRAPH 2

solar telescope *n* **:** a telescope designed for observations of the sun

solar tide *n* **:** the part of a tide due to the tide-producing force of the sun

solar time *n* **:** time either apparent or mean indicated by the sun **:** time expressed in units of mean solar time

solar tower *n* **:** a solar telescope in which light-gathering mirrors are placed at the top of a tall tower to permit the use of long-focus optics without the deterioration of image suffered in horizontal telescopes

solar trap *n* **:** a garden or terrace so oriented as to take advantage of the sun while protected from cold winds

solar type *n* **:** the spectral type of which the sun is the type object — used in designating stars

solary *adj* [L *sol* sun + E *-ary*] *obs* **:** SOLAR 1, 2

solar year *n* **:** the length of a year measured by the sun **:** TROPICAL YEAR

solas *pl of* SOLA

so·las·o·dine \səˈlasəˌdēn, -dən; ˌsäləˈsōˌdēn, -dᵊn\ *n* -S [*solasonine* + *solanidine*] **:** a crystalline steroidal alkaloid $C_{27}H_{43}NO_2$ closely related to solanidine and obtained by hydrolysis of solasonine

so·las·o·nine \səˈlasəˌnēn, ˌsäləˈsōˌnēn,-, -ˌnən\ *n* -S [*solaso-* (fr. NL *Solanum sodomaeum,* fr. *Solanum* + *sodomaeum,* neut. of *sodomaeus* of Sodom, fr. LL *Sodoma* Sodom, fr. Gk) + *solanine*] **:** a crystalline glycosidal alkaloid $C_{45}H_{73}NO_{16}$ obtained from several solanaceous plants (as *Solanum sodomaeum*) and closely related to solanine but yielding solasodine on hydrolysis — called also *solanine-S*

sol·as·ter \ˈsäˌlastə(r), ˌ=ˈ==\ *n, cap* [NL, fr. L *sol* sun + LL *aster* star — more at SOLAR, ASTER] **:** the type genus of Solasteridae comprising the sun stars — compare ROSE STAR

sol·a·ster·i·dae \ˌsäləˈsterəˌdē\ *n pl, cap* [NL, fr. *Solaster,* type genus + *-idae*] **:** a widely distributed family of long-spined starfishes (order Spinulosa) that are typically brightly colored and have numerous arms

sol·ate \ˈsäˌlāt, ˈsō-, ˈsō-,\ *vi* -ED/-ING/-S [⁶*sol* + *-ate*] **:** to change to a sol — compare GEL

so·la·ti·um \sōˈlāshēəm\ *n, pl* **so·la·tia** \-ēə\ [LL *solacium, solatium,* fr. L, solace — more at SOLACE] **:** something that alleviates or compensates for suffering or loss **:** COMPENSATION; *esp* **:** an additional allowance (as for injured feelings)

so·lay \səˈlā\ *vt* [alter. (due to printer's error) of ¹*splay*] **:** to cut (a bream) into serving portions

sold [ME *solde* (past), *sold* (past part.), fr. OE (northern & Midland dial.) *salde* (past), *gesald* (past part.)] *past of* SELL

sol·da·de·ra \ˌsōldəˈderə, ˌsäl-\ *n* -S [AmerSp, fr. Sp, female entertainer, woman of loose morals, lit., woman who works for pay, fr. *soldada* pay, fr. fem. of *soldado,* past part. of *soldar* to pay] **:** a woman that is a camp follower with a Latin-American and esp. a guerrilla military force

sol·da·do \sōlˈdä(ˌ)dō\ *n, pl* **soldados** *also* **soldadoes** [Sp, soldier, fr. past part. of *soldar* to pay, fr. *soldo, sueldo* a small coin, pay, salary, fr. LL *solidus, soldus* solidus] **:** a Latin-American soldier

sol·dan \ˈsäldən, ˈsōldən, ˈsōdᵊn\ *n* -S [ME, fr. MF, fr. Ar *sulṭān*] **1** *usu cap, archaic* **:** the sovereign of a Muslim country **:** SULTAN; *esp* **:** the sultan of Egypt **2 :** a Muslim ruler or prince

sol·da·nel·la \ˌsäldəˈnelə, ˌsōl-\ *n* [NL, fr. It, soldanella] **1** *cap* **:** a small genus of European low-growing perennial alpine herbs (family Primulaceae) having basal fleshy leaves and nodding scapose blue or pink flowers with the corolla lobes often fringed **2** -S **:** any plant of the genus *Soldanella*

¹sol·der \ˈsädə(r), ˈsȯd-, *chiefly Brit* ˈsōld-\ *n* -S [ME *souldour, sowder, sawder,* fr. MF *soldure, soudure, saudure,* fr. *solder, souder, sauder* to solder (fr. L *solidare* to make solid, join together, fr. *solidus* solid) + *-ure*] **1 :** a metal or metallic alloy used when melted to join metallic surfaces and usu. applied by means of a soldering iron or a blowpipe with a flux (as rosin, borax, or zinc chloride) to cleanse the surfaces; *esp* **:** an alloy of lead and tin so used **2 :** something (as a shared principle) that serves to unite or cement **:** a common bond

²solder \"\ *vb* **soldered; soldered; soldering** \-d(ə)riŋ\ **solders** *vt* **1 :** to unite or make whole by means of solder ⟨~ a joint in piping⟩ ⟨~ a leaky pot⟩ ⟨~ up a hole⟩ ⟨~ sheets of metal together⟩ **2 :** to bring into or restore to firm union as if by the use of solder **:** cause to adhere, knit, close up, or come together as if soldered ⟨a friendship ~*ed* by common interests⟩ — often used with *up* ⟨the union was ~*ed up* by concessions from both sides⟩ ~ *vi* **1 :** to use solder **:** make unions or repairs by means of solder ⟨was ~*ing* away at a free form when I got there⟩ ⟨workmen who like to ~⟩ **2** *obs* **:** to constitute a source of union **3 :** to become united or repaired by or as if by solder ⟨the joint ~*s* easily⟩

sol·der·able \-d(ə)rəbəl\ *adj* **:** capable of being soldered ⟨a ~ leak⟩ or of promoting union with solder ⟨a ~ coating⟩

sol·der·er \-dərə(r)\ *n* -S **:** one that solders; *esp* **:** a worker who joins or repairs metal parts with solder

¹soldering *n* -S [fr. gerund of ²*solder*] **1 :** an act or instance of using solder ⟨his ~ was very neat⟩ **2 :** SOLDER 1 **3 :** a joint, repair, or distinctive mark made by soldering **:** a soldered place ⟨the ~*s* should be polished clean⟩

²soldering *adj* **:** used in the process of uniting by solder ⟨~ tools⟩ ⟨a ~ flux⟩

soldering bolt *n* **1 :** SOLDERING IRON **2 :** ¹BIT 3a

soldering gun *n* **:** an electric soldering iron with a gun-type grip

soldering iron *also* **soldering copper** *n* **1 a :** a bit or bolt of copper made with a pointed or wedge-shaped end, furnished

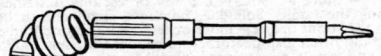

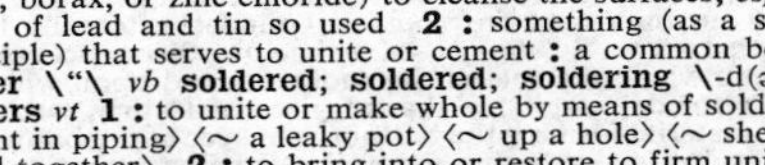
electric soldering iron

with a handle, and used for soldering **b :** a plumber's grozing iron **2 :** any of various usu. somewhat pointed or wedge-shaped electrically heated devices used for soldering
soldering nipple *or* **solder nipple** *n* **:** a plumbing nipple with a pipe thread on one end and the other end plain for soldering into the end of a pipe
soldering pot *n* **:** a small plumber's furnace (as one used by linemen)
sol·der·less \-də(r)ləs\ *adj* **:** lacking solder **:** containing no solder
soldi *pl of* SOLDO
¹sol·dier \'sōljə(r), *substand & dial* -ōj-, *chiefly Brit sometimes* -ōldyə(r)\ *n* -s *often attrib* [ME *souldiour, sodiour, soudier,* fr. OF *souldiour, soudier,* fr. *soulde, soude* pay, fr. LL *solidus, soldus* solidus] **1 a :** a person engaged in military service: as (1) **:** an officer or enlisted man serving in an army **:** a member of an organized body of combatants (2) **:** an enlisted man or woman in military service as distinguished from a commissioned or warrant officer (3) **:** PRIVATE 4a **b :** a skilled, experienced, or valorous warrior **c :** a member of the Salvation Army **2 :** one that fights for a cause, endures hardships, or otherwise conducts himself gallantly **:** a militant leader, follower, or worker ⟨~s in the cause of peace⟩ **3 :** any of various animals in some way (as habits, appearance) associated with soldiers: as **a** (1) **:** HERMIT CRAB (2) **:** FIDDLER CRAB **b** (1) **:** one of a caste of wingless sterile individuals that in most termites differ more or less from the workers in their larger size, very large head, and long jaws and that often perform a share in the work of the colonies (2) **:** one of a type of workers among some ants distinguished by exceptionally large head and jaws **c** (1) *dial Eng* **:** RED GURNARD (2) *southern Africa* **:** a silvery pink sparid food fish (*Cheimerius nufar*) widespread in the Indo-Pacific seas (3) **:** SQUIRRELFISH 1 **d :** SOLDIER BEETLE **e :** RED SPIDER **4 :** RED HERRING 1 **5 soldiers** *pl* **:** VIRGINIA STICKSEED **6 :** a person who shirks his work **:** LOAFER, DRONE **7 :** a brick that is placed on end in a wall with its narrow side exposed
²soldier \"\ *vi* **soldiered; soldiered; soldiering** \-(ə)riŋ\ **soldiers 1 a :** to serve or function as a soldier ⟨~*ed* in three wars⟩ **b :** to serve satisfactorily as a soldier **:** behave in a soldierly manner ⟨have to really ~ in such a crack outfit⟩ **2 :** to make a pretense of working while doing only enough to escape punishment or discharge **:** affect a pretense of busyness or working **:** loaf surreptitiously ⟨workers ~*ing* on the job⟩ **3** *chiefly dial* **:** BULLY
soldier ant *n* **1 :** SOLDIER 3b(2) **2 a :** BULLDOG ANT **b :** ARMY ANT
soldier beetle *n* **:** any of various usu. brightly colored and soft-bodied beetles of the family Cantharidae (as *Chauliognathus pennsylvanicus*) that frequent fruit and flowers and include several valuable predators on other insects
soldier bug *n* **:** any of numerous predatory bugs (family Pentatomidae) that suck the blood of other insects
soldier course *n* **:** a course of soldiers in masonry
soldier crab *n* **1 :** HERMIT CRAB **2 :** FIDDLER CRAB
soldierfish \'=,=\ *n* **1 :** SQUIRRELFISH 1 **2 :** RAINBOW DARTER **3 :** a small Australian cardinal fish (*Apogon fasciatus*) or a related fish (*A. conspersus*)
soldier fly *n* **:** any of numerous two-winged flies (family Stratiomyiidae) that are typically marked with colored stripes and have larvae which develop esp. in water, earth, or decaying wood
soldiering *n* -s [fr. gerund of ²*soldier*] **:** the life, service, or practice of one who soldiers
sol·dier·ize \'sōljə,rīz\ *vb* -ED/-ING/-S *vi* **:** SOLDIER 1a ~ *vt* **:** to convert into a soldier **:** force to soldier
soldierlike \'=,=\ *adj* [¹*soldier* + *like*] **:** SOLDIERLY
sol·dier·li·ness \-jə(r)lēnəs, -lin-\ *n* -ES **:** the quality or state of being soldierly
¹sol·dier·ly \-lē,-li\ *adj* [¹*soldier* + *-ly*] **:** being like or befitting a good soldier **:** BRAVE, MARTIAL, HEROIC
²soldierly \"\ *adv* **:** in a soldierly manner **:** so as to be soldierly
soldier of fortune : one who follows a military career wherever there is promise of profit, adventure, or pleasure; *also* **:** a mettlesome adventurer guided by similar aims
soldier prawn *n* **:** an edible Australian deep-water prawn (*Plesionika martia*)
soldier's buttons *n pl but sing or pl in constr* **:** a marsh marigold (*Caltha palustris*)
soldier's-cap \'==,=\ *n, pl* **soldier's-caps 1 :** DUTCHMAN'S-BREECHES **2 :** a monkshood (*Aconitum napellus*)
soldier's heart *n* **:** CARDIAC NEUROSIS
soldier's herb *n* **:** MATICO 1
sol·dier·ship \'sōljə(r),ship\ *n* **:** the status or condition of a soldier
soldiers' home *n* **:** an institution maintained (as by the federal or a state government) for the care and relief of military veterans
soldier's-plume \'==,=\ *n, pl* **soldier's-plumes :** PURPLE-FRINGED ORCHID a
soldier sprag *n* **:** a long sprag used esp. in New So. Wales to support a seam in a coal mine between the top of the holing and the roof
soldier's wind *n* **:** a beam wind favorable either coming or going
soldier turtle *n* **:** PAINTED TURTLE
soldier wood *n* **:** MABI 1
sol·diery \'sōlj(ə)rē, -ri\ *n* -ES [¹*soldier* + *-y*] **1 :** a body of soldiers **:** SOLDIERS, MILITARY **2 a :** the profession or training of a soldier **b :** the art or technique of soldiering
sol·do \'sōl(,)dō\ *n, pl* **sol·di** \-dē\ [It, fr. LL *solidus, soldus* solidus] **1 :** an Italian coin and corresponding unit of value of the 13th century **2 :** an Italian 5-centesimi piece or 1/20 lira
sold-out \(')=¦=\ *adj* **:** sold completely and esp. in advance ⟨had a *sold-out* house for both performances⟩
sold-up \(')=¦=\ *adj* **:** having the product for the production period in question sold in full or in advance ⟨many mills are reaching a *sold-up* position⟩
¹sole \'sōl\ *n* -s [ME, fr. MF, fr. L *solea* sandal (consisting of a sole with a strap across the instep); akin to L *solum* base, ground, soil] **1 a** (1) **:** the undersurface of a foot or that part of it which is placed on the ground in walking or standing (2) **:** the somewhat concave plate of moderately dense horn that covers the lower surface of the coffin bone in the horse, partly surrounds the frog, and is bounded externally by the wall **b :** FOOT **2 :** the part of a shoe or other article of footwear on which the sole of the foot rests and upon which the wearer treads; *specif* **:** a shaped piece of leather, rubber, or other material forming the bottom or a layer of the bottom of a shoe and often excluding the heel — compare HALF SOLE, INSOLE, MIDSOLE, OUTSOLE, SLIPSOLE; see SHOE illustration **3 :** the bottom or lower part of something or the base on which something rests: as **a** *obs* **:** the foundation or site of a building or city **b** (1) *chiefly dial* **:** the sill of a window or door (2) **:** the horizontal plate on which the studs of a partition bear (3) **:** SOLEPIECE (4) **:** either of two planks resting one on each side on a sliding ways and forming the foundation of the cradle that supports a ship during building **c :** the hearth or flooring of a furnace, oven, or other heating device **d :** the floor of drift, level, or working in a mine **e** (1) **:** the undersurface of a plane through which the blade projects (2) **:** the bottom of the body of a plow **f :** the floor of a cabin on a ship **g** *chiefly dial* **:** the underframe of a vehicle (as a wagon or cart) **h :** the bottom of the inside of a gas retort **i :** the flattened bottom surface of a golf club head **4 a :** the underlying layers of land and esp. of arable land **:** SUBSOIL **b :** the layer of intertwined roots that forms the base of sod or turf **c :** the bottom of a furrow **d :** the lowest part of a valley
²sole \"\ *vt* -ED/-ING/-S **1 :** to furnish with a sole ⟨~ a shoe⟩ **2 :** to serve as a base for or bottom of **3 :** to place the sole of (a golf club) on the ground (as in addressing a ball)
³sole \"\ *n* -s [ME, fr. MF, fr. L *solea* sandal, a flatfish (fr. its shape) — more at ¹SOLE] **1 :** any of various flatfishes constituting the family Soleidae, having a small mouth beyond which the snout projects more or less, reduced or rudimentary pelvic and often also pectoral and caudal fins, small gill openings, and small eyes placed close together, and including superior food fishes (as *Solea solea* of Europe) and others too small to be of commercial value — compare FLOUNDER **2 :** any of various flatfishes of families other than Soleidae esp. when for table use — usu. used with a qualifying term; see PETRALE SOLE, SAND SOLE
⁴sole \"\ *adj* [ME *soul, sool, sole* alone, celibate, fr. MF *seul, sol* alone, fr. L *solus;* prob. akin to L *sed, se* without — more at IDIOT] **1 :** having no spouse **:** UNMARRIED — used chiefly of women **2 :** having no companion **:** SOLITARY, LONELY ⟨sitting ~ by the hearth⟩ **3 a :** having no sharer (as in a right or status) **:** being the only one ⟨the ~ heir⟩ ⟨the ~ product of all this industry⟩ **b :** of unmatched quality or kind **:** UNIQUE **4 :** functioning (as in acting, working, moving) independently and without assistance or interference ⟨the ~ author of this scheme⟩ ⟨let conscience be the ~ judge⟩ **5** *obs* **a :** that is such and no other **:** MERE **b :** ALONE **6 :** belonging, granted, or attributed to the one person or group specified **:** independently accomplished, held, or developed **:** exclusively exercised **:** UNSHARED ⟨the ~ power of the Congress⟩ ⟨~ rights of publication⟩; *sometimes* **:** ENTIRE ⟨~ jurisdiction⟩ **syn** see SINGLE
⁵sole \"\ *adv* **:** SOLELY
⁶sole \"\ *vt* -ED/-ING/-S [origin unknown] **:** to pull roughly
¹so·lea \'sōlēə\ *n, cap* [NL, fr. L, a kind of flatfish — more at SOLE] **:** the type genus of Soleidae
²so·lea \sō'lēə\ *n* -s [MGk, fr. L, sandal, sill — more at ¹SOLE] **:** a platform or a raised part of the floor in front of the inner sanctuary in an Eastern Orthodox church on which the singers stand and the faithful receive communion
sole·cism \'sälə,sizəm *also* 'sōl- *sometimes* 'sōl-\ *n* -s [L *soloecismus,* fr. Gk *soloikismos,* fr. *soloikos* speaking incorrectly (lit., inhabitant of Soloi, fr. *Soloi,* city in ancient Cilicia where a corrupt form of Attic was spoken by colonists + Gk *-ikos* -ic) + *-ismos* -ism] **1 :** an ungrammatical combination of words in a sentence **:** a deviation from the idiom of a language or from the rules of syntax ⟨"he was independent *on* any patron" is a typical ~⟩; *also* **:** a minor blunder in speech **2 :** a deviation from the proper, normal, or accepted order **:** something (as a theory, situation, act) not consonant with logic, circumstances, known facts, or other standard **:** an absurd incongruity or incompatibility; *sometimes* **:** ANACHRONISM **3 :** a breach of etiquette or decorum **:** an unmannerly act or practice **:** IMPROPRIETY
sole·cist \-,səst\ *n* -s [LL *soloecista,* fr. Gk *soloikistēs,* fr. *soloikos* speaking incorrectly + *-istēs* -ist] **:** a user of solecisms; *also* **:** one who defies convention
sole·cis·tic \¦==¦sistik, -tēk\ *also* **sole·cis·ti·cal** \-təkəl, -tēk-\ *adj* [*solecist* + *-ic, -ical*] **:** relating to, constituting, or involving a solecism **:** INCORRECT, INCONGRUOUS, UNSEEMLY — **sole·cis·ti·cal·ly** \-tək(ə)lē, -tēk-, -li\ *adv*
sole·cize \'==,sīz\ *vi* -ED/-ING/-S [Gk *soloikizein,* fr. *soloikos* speaking incorrectly + *-izein* -ize] **:** to use solecisms **:** commit a solecism
sole·ciz·er \-zə(r)\ *n* -s [*solecize* + *-er*] **:** SOLECIST
sole corporation *n* [⁴*sole*] **:** CORPORATION SOLE
soled \'sōld\ *adj* [ME, fr. ¹*sole* + *-ed*] **:** having such or so many soles — usu. used in combination ⟨callous-*soled*⟩ ⟨triple-*soled*⟩ ⟨thin-*soled*⟩
sol·e·dad pine \'sälə,dad- *sometimes* 'sō\ *n, usu cap S* [fr. *Soledad* river, San Diego co., California] **:** TORREY PINE
so·le·idae \sə'lēə,dē\ *n pl, cap* [NL, fr. *Solea,* type genus + *-idae*] **:** a family of flatfishes (order Heterosomata) comprising the typical soles and distinguished from the typical flounders (family Pleuronectidae) by the extension of the dorsal fin high on the head and by the covered margin of the preopercle
so·le·i·form \sə'lēə,fórm, 'sōl-\ *adj* [L *solea* sandal + E *-iform* — more at SOLE] **:** shaped like a slipper **:** CALCEIFORM
¹so·leil \(')sō¦lā\ *adj* [F, sun, fr. (assumed) VL *soliculus,* dim. of L *sol* sun — more at SOLAR] **1 :** finished with a high luster ⟨*soleil* felt or velour⟩ **2 :** woven with a fancy warp rib
²soleil \"\ *n* -s **:** a fabric with a soleil finish or weave
sole leather *n* [¹*sole*] **1 :** a thick strong leather esp. for shoe soles **2** *also* **sole–leather kelp :** any of the larger kelps of the genus *Laminaria*
sole·less \'sōlləs\ *adj* **:** having no sole
sole·ly \'sōl(l)ē, -)i\ *adv* [⁴*sole* + *-ly*] **1 :** without an associate (as a companion or assistant) **:** SINGLY, ALONE ⟨go ~ on one's way⟩ **2 :** to the exclusion of alternate or competing things (as persons, purposes, duties) ⟨done ~ for money⟩ ⟨a privilege granted ~ to him⟩ ⟨rely ~ on oneself⟩
¹sol·emn \'säləm *sometimes* 'sōl-\ *adj* -ER/-EST [ME *solempne, solemne,* fr. MF, fr. L *sollennis, solennis, sollemnis, solemnis* regularly appointed, festive, solemn, prob. fr. *sollus* whole, entire (fr. Oscan; akin to Gk *holos* entire) + *-ennis* (fr. *annus* year) — more at SAFE, ANNUAL] **1 a :** marked by or performed, made, or uttered under circumstances that indicate a full and sober realization and acceptance of all that is involved and usu. accompanied by a specific religious sanction ⟨took a ~ oath on the Bible⟩ ⟨a ~ dedication to the cause of freedom⟩ **b :** made in due and proper form and so as to be legally binding **:** conforming to all legal requirements ⟨a ~ writ⟩ ⟨~ instruments⟩ ⟨made ~ affidavit⟩ ⟨a ~ declaration⟩ **2 a** *archaic, of a day or season* **:** given over to the performance of special rites or ceremonies usu. of a religious character **b :** carried out in accord with accepted religious forms or rites ⟨a ~ blessing⟩ ⟨a ~ curse⟩ **c :** observed or celebrated with unusual pomp and ceremony and usu. after a pattern established by liturgy or tradition ⟨a ~ festival⟩; *specif* **:** distinguished from other services by being celebrated with full liturgy ⟨a ~ high mass⟩ ⟨~ complines⟩ **3** *obs* **a :** SUMPTUOUS, SPLENDID **b :** NOTABLE, DISTINGUISHED **4 a :** notable for marked ceremony and formality **:** characterized by pomp, dignity, and elaborate attention to form ⟨a ~ state dinner⟩ **b** *obs* **:** being such in full form **:** conforming to what is usual in the thing specified **5 a :** of a kind fitted to excite serious reflections or exalted emotions **:** AWE-INSPIRING, SUBLIME ⟨these ~ scenes⟩ **b :** marked by grave sobriety and earnest serious sedateness **:** free from casualness or lighthearted levity ⟨the audience grew ~⟩ ⟨at this ~ moment⟩ ⟨spoke in a ~ and thoughtful manner⟩ **c :** of a serious nature **:** involving responsibility and strict adherence to duty imposed ⟨staked his life on the fulfilling of this ~ charge⟩ ⟨children are a ~ responsibility to their parents⟩ **6 :** SOMBER, GLOOMY ⟨a suit of ~ black⟩ **syn** see CEREMONIAL, SERIOUS
²solemn \"\ *adv* **:** SOLEMNLY
solemn form *n* **:** the form of probate of a will where the will is decreed in open court to be the last will and testament after notice to all interested persons and after hearing the testimony of the attesting witnesses
so·lem·ni·fy \sə'lemnə,fī\ *vt* -ED/-ING/-S **:** to make solemn
so·lem·ni·tude \-nə,tüd, -nə-,tyüd\ *n* -s [L *solemnis* + E *-tude*] **:** SOLEMNNESS
so·lem·ni·ty \sə'lemnəd·ē, -nətē, -i\ *n* -ES [ME *solempnite, solemnite,* fr. OF *solempnité, solemnité,* fr. LL *solemnitat-, solemnitas,* fr. L *solemnis* solemn + *-itat-, -itas* -ity] **1 :** formal or ceremonious observance of an occasion or event **:** such observance as a due of a particular occasion, person, or event ⟨welcomed the visiting statesman with fitting ~⟩; *esp* **:** solemn liturgical celebration of a sacrament, service, or feast day ⟨the *solemnities* of Easter⟩ **2 a :** a solemn event or occasion (as a season, rite, utterance, or feast day) **b :** an observance or proceeding according to due form **:** the formality necessary to make a thing done valid in law **3 :** a solemn condition or quality (as of mien) **:** the state of being serious, dignified, or awe-inspiring ⟨the ~ of his words⟩ ⟨an occasion of great ~⟩
sol·em·ni·za·tion \,sälemnə'zāshən, -,nī'z- *sometimes* ,sōl-\ *n* -s [ME *solemnyzacyoun,* fr. MF *solemnisation,* fr. ML *solemnization-, solemnizatio,* fr. LL *solemnizatus* (past part. of *solemnizare*) + L *-ion-, -io* -ion] **:** an act of solemnizing or the condition of being solemnized **:** CELEBRATION ⟨the ~ of a marriage⟩
¹sol·em·nize \'==,nīz\ *vb* -ED/-ING/-S *see -ize in Explan Notes* [ME *solempnisen,* fr. MF *solempniser,* fr. LL *solemnizare,* fr. L *solemnis* solemn + LL *-izare* -ize] *vt* **1 :** to hold, conduct, observe, or honor with due formal ceremony or solemn notice ⟨~ this sorrowing natal day to prove our loyal truth —Robert Burns⟩ **2 :** to perform with pomp or ceremony or according to legal forms; *esp* **:** to unite a couple in (marriage) with religious ceremony **:** celebrate (a marriage) with religious rites **3** *obs* **:** to exalt by praising **:** GLORIFY **4 :** to make solemn, serious, or exalted **:** DIGNIFY ~ *vi* **:** to grow solemn **:** speak or act with solemnity **syn** see KEEP
²solemnize \"\ *n* -s *obs* **:** SOLEMNIZATION
sol·em·niz·er \-zə(r)\ *n* -s **:** one that solemnizes
solemnlike \'==,=\ *adv* [*solemn* + *like*] *dial* **:** somewhat solemnly
sol·emn·ly *adv* [ME *solemnely, solemply,* fr. *solemne, solempne* solemn + *-ly*] **:** in a solemn manner **:** with solemnity ⟨~ sworn testimony⟩
solemn mass *n, often cap S&M* **:** a mass celebrated with full ceremony including the use of incense and music by an officiating priest assisted by a deacon and subdeacon
sol·emn·ness \-əmnəs\ *n* -ES **:** the quality or state of being solemn
solemn vow *n* **:** an absolute and irrevocable public vow taken by a religious in the Roman Catholic Church under which ownership of property by the individual is prohibited and marriage is invalid under canon law — compare SIMPLE VOW
so·len \'sōlən, -,len\ *n* [NL, fr. L, razor clam, fr. Gk *sōlēn* channel, pipe, a shellfish — more at SYRINGE] **1** *cap* **:** a genus (a type of the family Solenidae) of razor clams **2** -s **:** RAZOR CLAM
solen- *or* **soleno-** *comb form* [Gk *sōlēn-, sōlēno-,* fr. *sōlēn*] **:** channel **:** pipe **:** tube; *also* **:** tubular ⟨*Solenodon*⟩ ⟨*solenocyte*⟩ ⟨*solenostele*⟩
¹sole·na·cean \¦sälə¦nāsh(ē)ən, ¦sōl-\ *also* **sole·na·ceous** \-shəs\ *adj* [NL *Solēn* + E *-acean, -aceous*] **:** of, relating to, or resembling the Solenidae
²solenacean \"\ *n* -s **:** a solenacean mollusk
sole·ness *n* -ES [⁴*sole* + *-ness*] **:** the quality or state of being sole
sole·nette \(')sōl¦net, ¦sōlə¦n-\ *n* -s [irreg. fr. ³*sole* + *-ette*] **:** a small European sole (*Microchirus luteus*) about five inches long and of no commercial value
so·len·ho·fen stone \'s(ōlən,hōfən-, 'z(\ *n, usu cap 1st S* [fr. *Solenhofen,* village of west central Bavaria] **:** a limestone found at Solenhofen, Bavaria and valued for lithographic purposes
so·le·ni·al \sō'lēnēəl\ *adj* [NL *solenium* + E *-al*] **:** of, relating to, or involving a stolon
so·len·ich·thy·es \,sōlə'nikthē,ēz\ *n pl, cap* [NL, fr. *solen-* + Gk *ichthyes,* pl. of *ichthys* fish — more at ICHTHUS] **:** a small order of chiefly tropical marine fishes (as the bellows fishes, shrimpfishes, and cornetfishes) that are of varied and sometimes bizarre form but all have the small mouth at the end of a drawn-out tubular snout — compare THORACOSTEI
so·len·i·dae \sō'lenə,dē\ *n pl, cap* [NL, fr. *Solen,* type genus + *-idae*] **:** a family of marine clams (suborder Myacea) with elongated curved shells comprising the razor clams
so·le·ni·um \sō'lēnēəm\ *n, pl* **sole·nia** \-nēə\ [NL, fr. Gk *sōlēnion,* dim. of *sōlēn* channel, pipe] **:** STOLON
so·len·ne \sō'le(,)nā\ *adj* [It, fr. L *solemnis* — more at SOLEMN] **:** SOLEMN — used as a direction in music regarding mood — **so·len·ne·men·te** \sō,lenə'men·(,)tā\ *adv*
so·leno·concha \sō¦lēnə, -lenə-+\ *or* **so·leno·conchae** \"+\ *n pl, cap* [NL, fr. *solen-* + L *concha* shell — more at CONCH] *syn of* SCAPHOPODA
so·leno·cyte \sō'lēnə,sīt, -len-\ *n* -s [*solen-* + *-cyte*] **:** any of various modified tubular flagellated cells ocurring in the nephridia of the larvae of some annelids, mollusks, and rotifers and of a few lancelets — **so·leno·cyt·ic** \=¦==¦sid·ik\ *adj*
so·len·odon \sō'lēnə,dän, -len-\ *n* [NL, fr. *solen-* + *-odon*] **1** *cap* **:** a small genus (coextensive with the family Solenodontidae) of atypical and very rare insectivorous mammals of Cuba and Haiti that are nearly 2 feet long and have a long snout, short round ears, hard fur, a long scaly tail, 40 teeth, and a skull with no zygomatic arch **2** -s **:** any mammal of the genus *Solenodon* — **so·len·odont** \-nt\ *adj or n*
so·leno·gas·ter \=¦=¦gastə(r)\ *n* -s [NL *Solenogastres*] **:** APLACOPHORAN
so·leno·gas·tres \=,=ˈga(,)strēz\ [NL, fr. *solen-* + Gk *gastr-, gastēr* belly — more at GASTRIC] *syn of* APLACOPHORA
so·leno·glyph \=¦=,glif\ *n* -s [NL *Solenoglypha*] **:** a venomous snake with tubular erectile fangs
sole·nog·ly·pha \,sōlə'nägləfə, ,säl-\ *n pl, cap* [NL, fr. *solen-* + Gk *glyphein* to carve — more at CLEAVE] *in some classifications* **:** a group of venomous snakes with tubular erectile fangs comprising the families Viperidae and Crotalidae
sole·nog·ly·phous \¦=¦==fəs\ *or* **soleno·glyph·ic** \¦sōlənō-¦glifik, ¦säl-; sō¦lenə¦glifik, -¦len-\ *adj* [NL *Solenoglypha* + E *-ous* or *-ic*] **:** having tubular erectile fangs **:** belonging to the Solenoglypha
so·le·noid \'sōlə,nóid *sometimes* 'säl-\ *n* -s [F *solénoïde,* fr. Gk *sōlēnoeidēs* shaped like a pipe, fr. *sōlēn-* + *-oeidēs* -oid] **1 :** a coil of wire commonly in the form of a long cylinder that when carrying a current resembles a bar magnet so that a movable core is drawn into the coil when a current flows **2 :** a section of atmosphere bounded by two isobaric and two isosteric surfaces
so·le·noi·dal \¦==¦nóidᵊl\ *adj* **1 :** of, relating to, or constituting a solenoid **2 :** TUBULAR — used of a mathematical vector field whose divergence is 0 — **so·le·noi·dal·ly** \-ᵊlē\ *adv*
solenoid brake *n* **:** a brake in which the shoes are operated by the magnetic action of a solenoid
solenoid switch *n* **:** a switch operated by a solenoid
solenoid valve *n* **:** a valve operated by a solenoid
sole·nop·sis \,sōlə'näpsəs, ,säl-\ *n, cap* [NL, fr. *solen-* + *-opsis*] **:** a genus of small stinging ants including several abundant tropical and subtropical forms (as the fire ant and thief ant)
so·leno·stele \sō'lēnə,stēl, -len- *also* =¦=¦stēlē\ *n* [*solen-* + *stele*] **:** a siphonostele (as in some ferns) with phloem both internal and external to the xylem — **so·leno·ste·lic** \=¦==-¦stēlik\ *adj* — **so·leno·ste·ly** \=¦==,stēlē\ *n* -ES
so·le·no·stom·i·dae \sō,lenə'stämə,dē, -len-\ *n pl, cap* [NL, fr. *Solenostomus,* type genus + *-idae*] **:** a family of fishes (order Solenichthyes) that is coextensive with the genus *Solenostomus*
so·le·nos·to·mus \,sōlə'nästəməs\ *n, cap* [NL, fr. *solen-* + Gk *stoma* mouth — more at STOMACH] **:** a genus of small fishes (family Solenostomidae) of the tropical Indo-Pacific having a short compressed body and a long tubular snout and a female that carries her eggs in a pouch formed by the coalescence of the pelvic fins with the body
solens *pl of* SOLEN
solent goose *n* [alter. of *soland goose*] **:** SOLAN GOOSE
sol·en·tine \'sälən,tīn, -tēn\ *n* -s [alter. of *celandine*] **:** a jewelweed (*Impatiens capensis*)
so·le·oi·dei \,sōlē'óidē,ī\ *or* **so·le·oi·dea** \-dēə\ *n pl, cap* [NL, fr. *Solea* + *-oidei* or *-oidea*] *in some classifications* **:** a suborder or other division of Heterosomata comprising the families Soleidae and Cynoglossidae
solepiece \'=,=\ *n* [¹*sole* + *piece*] **1 :** a timber or girder laid on the ground to take and distribute the thrust of an upright or strut **:** the floor member of a frame **2 a :** a piece on the bottom of the rudder of a wooden ship designed to bring it down to the false keel **b :** a piece joining rudderpost and sternpost in a steel ship **c :** a projection from a ship's keel designed to support a balanced rudder
soleplate \'=,=\ *n* [¹*sole* + *plate*] **1 :** a flattened nucleated mass of soft granular protoplasm surrounding the end of a motor nerve in a striated muscle fiber **2 :** the lower plate of a stud partition on which the bases of the studs butt **3 a :** BEDPLATE **b :** the plate forming the back of a waterwheel bucket **c :** a plate to which a bearing can be wedged and bolted so as to be slightly adjustable **d :** the under surface of a flatiron **:** the surface contacting the material in pressing
soleprint \'=,=\ *n* [¹*sole* + *print*] **:** a print of the sole of the foot; *esp* **:** one made in the manner of a fingerprint and used particularly for the identification of an infant
sol·er \'sōlə(r)\ *n* -s [²*sole* + *-er*] **:** one that soles shoes or boots
so·le·ra \sō'lerə\ *n* -s [Sp, crossbeam, stone base, mother liquor, fr. *suelo* ground, floor, dregs, fr.

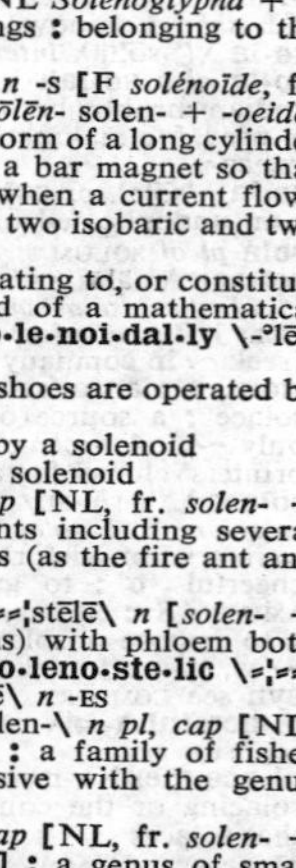

soleprint

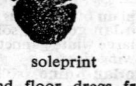

L *solum* ground, base] **1 :** a set of Spanish sherry vats arranged in tiers usu. three high in a storage shed **2** *also* **solera system :** a system evolved by the sherry producers of Jeres, Spain, whereby young wine in the vats of the top tier of a solera is successively blended into the more mature wine in the vats on the tier below to insure ultimate uniformity **3** *also* **solera sherry** *or* **solera wine :** a wine aged by the Spanish solera system

soles *pl of* SOL *or of* SOLE, *pres 3d sing of* SOLE

sole tile *n* [¹*sole*] **:** a tile with a concave top used esp. to pave sewers

sole tree *n* [¹*sole*] **:** a solepiece used in a mine (as for timbering headings)

so·le·us \'sōlēəs\ *n, pl* **so·lei** \-ē,ī\ *also* **soleuses** [NL, fr. L *solea* sole of the foot] **:** a broad flat muscle of the calf of the leg lying immediately below the gastrocnemius, arising from the back and upper part of the tibia and fibula and from a tendinous arch between them, and inserting by a tendon that unites with that of the gastrocnemius to form the Achilles' tendon

¹sol-fa \(')sōl¦fä, -fȧ, *chiefly Brit* (')säl-\ *n* -s [¹*sol* + *fa*] **1 :** SOL-FA SYLLABLES **2 :** GREAT SCALE **3 a :** SOLMIZATION **b :** an exercise sung in sol-fa syllables **4 :** TONIC SOL-FA

²sol-fa \"\ *vb* -ED/-ING/-S *vi* **1 :** to sing or practice the tones of the gamut or scale **2 :** to sing in sol-fa syllables **~** *vt* **:** to sing (as an air or song) to or in sol-fa syllables

sol-fa·er \-ə(r)\ *n* -s [²*sol-fa* + *-er*] **:** one that sol-fas

sol-fa·ist \-əst\ *n* -s [¹*sol-fa* + *-ist*] **:** a user or an advocate of the tonic sol-fa system

sol-fa syllables *n pl* **:** the eight modified Guidonian syllables *do, re, mi, fa, sol, la, ti, do* applied to reading music for the major scale and further modified for the chromatic scale ascending and descending to *do, di, re, ri, mi, fa, fi, sol, si, la, li, ti, do, ti, te, la, le, sol, se, fa, mi, me, re, ra, do* — compare MOVABLE-DO SYSTEM, SOLMIZATION

sol·fa·ta·ra \,sälfə'tärə, ,sōl-\ *n* -s [It, sulfur mine, sulphurous vent, fr. *solfo* sulphur, fr. L *sulfur*] **:** a volcanic area or vent that yields only hot vapors and gases in part sulfurous and represents a late stage of volcanic activity

sol·fa·taric \¦==¦tarik, -¦tär-\ *adj* **1 :** of or relating to a solfatara or its action **2 :** relating to, caused by, or denoting the transfer of mineral substances within the earth by sublimation or by the chemical and transporting action of steam

sol·fège \(')säl¦fezh\ *n* -s [F, fr. It *solfeggio*] **1 :** the application of the sol-fa syllables to the tones of the musical scale or to melodies or other voice parts **2 :** an exercise in scales; *specif* **:** a singing exercise using sol-fa syllables **3 :** practice in sight-singing using the sol-fa syllables

sol·feg·gio \säl'fe(,)jō, -ejē,ō\ *n, pl* **solfeg·gi** \-e(,)jē\ *also* **solfeggios** [It, fr. *solfeggiare* to sol-fa, fr. *solfa* sol-fa, fr. *sol* (fr. ML) + *fa* (fr. ML) — more at SOL, FA] **:** SOLFÈGE

sol·fe·ri·no \,sälfə'rē(,)nō\ *n* -s [fr. *Solferino*, village of northern Italy; fr. its being discovered soon after the battle fought there in 1859] **1 :** FUCHSINE 1 **2 :** a moderate purplish red that is redder, darker, and slightly stronger than average rose, redder and duller than violine pink, redder and paler than magenta rose, and redder and less strong than average fuchsia rose

solgel \'=¦=\ *adj* [⁶*sol* + *gel*] **:** involving alternation between sol and gel states — used esp. of protoplasmic phenomena ⟨~ transformations in the amoeba⟩

¹soli *pl of* SOLO

²so·li \'sō,lē\ *adj* [¹*soli*] **:** constituting a solo part usu. to be performed by a section or part of a section in an orchestra or a chorus ⟨~ parts⟩ ⟨~ strings⟩

soli- *comb form* [L, fr. *solus* — more at SOLE] **:** alone **:** solely ⟨*soli*loquy⟩ ⟨*soli*fidian⟩

so·lic·it \sə'lisət, *usu* -əd·+V\ *vb* -ED/-ING/-S [ME *soliciten*, fr. MF *solliciter*, *soliciter* to disturb, take care of (influenced in meaning by L *sollicitus* anxious), fr. L *sollicitare* to disturb, agitate, move, entreat, fr. *sollicitus* anxious, troubled, fr. *sollus* whole, entire (fr. Oscan; akin to Gk *holos* entire) + *citus*, past part. of *ciēre* to move — more at SAFE, HIGHT] *vt* **1** *archaic* **a :** to take charge or care of (as business) **:** MANAGE, FORWARD **b :** to act as solicitor or legal agent for or with reference to **2** *archaic* **:** to make anxious **:** DISQUIET, CONCERN **3 :** to make petition to **:** ENTREAT, IMPORTUNE ⟨~ the king for relief⟩; *esp* **:** to approach with a request or plea (as in selling or begging) ⟨~ one's neighbors for contributions⟩ **4 :** to move to action **:** serve as an urge or incentive to **:** INCITE **5 :** to strongly urge (as one's cause or point) **:** insist upon **6 a :** to entice or lead astray by or as if by specious arguments **:** lure on and esp. into evil **b** *obs* **:** to seek the favor of (a woman) usu. for the purpose of seduction **:** attempt to seduce **c :** to accost (a man) for immoral purposes and usu. in the character of a prostitute **7 :** to endeavor to obtain by asking or pleading **:** plead for ⟨~ an office⟩ ⟨~ alms⟩; *also* **:** to seek eagerly or actively **8 :** to demand as a requisite **:** call for **:** REQUIRE ⟨the situation ~*s* the closest attention⟩ **9 a** (1) **:** to have an effect on (a person or thing) through some natural influence or property (2) **:** to induce (as a phenomenon) by means of such influence or property ⟨~*ing* sparks by rubbing amber with flannel⟩ **b :** to seek to affect (as by moving, inducing, withdrawing) usu. by mild or gentle means ⟨~ a bowel movement with a laxative⟩ ⟨~ an arrow gently and draw it from a wound⟩ **10 :** to serve as a temptation or lure to **:** ATTRACT ⟨that fruit . . . ~*ed* her longing eye —John Milton⟩ **~** *vi* **1 :** to make solicitation **:** IMPORTUNE, PETITION: as **a :** to beg alms **b** *of a prostitute* **:** to offer illicit intercourse to a man **2 :** to serve as a solicitor **syn** see ASK

so·lic·i·tant \sə'lisəd·ənt, -isətənt\ *n* -s [L *sollicitant-*, *sollicitans*, pres. part. of *sollicitare* to solicit] **:** one who solicits

so·lic·i·ta·tion \sə,lisə'tāshən\ *n* -s [L *sollicitation-*, *sollicitatio*, fr. *sollicitatus* (past part. of *sollicitare*) + *-ion-*, *-io* -ion] **1 :** the pursuit, practice, act, or an instance of soliciting; *often* **:** ENTREATY, IMPORTUNITY ⟨yield to his ~*s*⟩ **2 :** the operation, influence, pressure, or other inducing effect of something that solicits or attracts or draws **:** a moving or drawing force **:** INCITEMENT, ALLUREMENT ⟨unable to resist the ~*s* of appetite⟩

soliciter *n* -s [ME, fr. *soliciten* to solicit + *-er*] *obs* **:** SOLICITOR

so·lic·i·tor \sə'lisəd·ə(r), -is(ə)tə-, *in rapid speech* 'sl-\ *n* -s [ME *solicitour*, fr. MF *soliciteur* prompter, agent, advocate, fr. *soliciter* to solicit, take care of] **1 :** one that solicits; *esp* **:** a person that acts as an agent in the soliciting of something (as contributions to charity, subscriptions to periodicals, or business for a firm) **2 a** (1) **:** a person formerly admitted to practice law in an English court of chancery or equity (2) **:** a person currently admitted to practice law and conduct litigation in any English court including the officers formerly called attorney-at-law and proctor but distinguished from the barrister in not having the right to plead in open court except in a few minor courts **b :** a law officer of a city, town, department, or government ⟨the city ~⟩ ⟨the ~ of the Interior Department⟩

solicitor general *n, pl* **solicitors general 1 :** the second law officer in the government of Great Britain appointed to assist the attorney general **2 :** an officer under the U.S. government appointed by the president to assist the attorney general **3 :** the chief law officer in some states of the U.S.

so·lic·i·tor·ship \-,ship\ *n* **:** the position or status of a solicitor

so·lic·i·tous \sə'lisəd·əs, -is(ə)təs\ *adj* [L *sollicitus* — more at SOLICIT] **1 :** full of concern or fears **:** APPREHENSIVE, TROUBLED, CONCERNED — often used with *about, for,* or *of* ⟨~ about the future⟩ ⟨~ for the welfare of one's country⟩ **2 :** full of desire **:** anxiously willing **:** EAGER ⟨~ to gain all the benefits⟩ ⟨not ~ to proceed in this affair⟩ **3 :** meticulously careful or attentive ⟨~ in matters of dress⟩ **4 :** manifesting or expressing solicitude or concern ⟨a ~ inquiry⟩ — **so·lic·i·tous·ly** *adv* — **so·lic·i·tous·ness** *n* -ES

so·lic·i·tress \-isə·trəs\ *n* -ES [*solicitor* + *-ess*] **:** a female solicitor

solicitrix *n* -ES [fr. *solicitor*, after such pairs as E *executor: executrix*] *obs* **:** a female solicitor

so·lic·i·tude \sə'lisə,tüd, -isə-,tyüd\ *n* -s [ME, fr. MF or L; MF *sollicitude*, fr. L *sollicitudin-*, *sollicitudo*, fr. *sollicitus* solicitous + *-tudin-*, *-tudo* -tude] **1 :** uneasiness of mind due to fear (as of evil, future developments, material want) **:** ANXIETY, DISQUIETUDE ⟨having few wants he had little cause for ~⟩ ⟨even the more peaceful hours . . . had beneath them a perpetual undercurrent of apprehensive ~ —Havelock Ellis⟩ **2 a :** urgently attentive and sometimes excessive care and protectiveness ⟨caring for the sick child with great ~⟩ **b :** an attitude of solicitous concern or attention ⟨inquired after her welfare with marked ~⟩ **3 :** a cause for or source of solicitude — usu. used in pl. ⟨worn by the ~*s* of daily life⟩ **syn** see CARE

so·lic·i·tu·di·nous \sə¦lisə¦tüd(ᵊ)nəs, -isə-¦tyü-\ *adj* [L *sollicitudin-*, *sollicitudo* + E *-ous*] **:** marked by solicitude **:** SOLICITOUS

¹sol·id \'säləd\ *adj* -ER/-EST [ME *solide*, fr. MF, fr. L *solidus*; akin to Gk *holos*, entire — more at SAFE] **1 a :** having an interior filled with matter **:** being without an internal cavity ⟨the knob is heavy because it is ~⟩ ⟨the stalks of some plants are not ~⟩ ⟨a ~ tire⟩ — opposed to *hollow* **b** (1) **:** set in type without leads or other spacing material between the lines **:** CLOSE ⟨a forbidding page full of ~ black paragraphs⟩ (2) **:** having no intervening space ⟨the ~ elements of a compound word⟩ **c :** not interrupted by any break or opening ⟨the outer walls ~ and windowless⟩ ⟨the law requires a driver to stay on his own side of the ~ line⟩ **2 a :** having or involving three dimensions **:** CUBIC ⟨a ~ paraboloid⟩ ⟨a ~ foot contains 1728 ~ inches⟩ **b :** of, relating to, or dealing with solid magnitudes ⟨a ~ equation⟩ — see SOLID GEOMETRY **3 a :** marked by density or compactness **:** of uniformly close and coherent texture or consistency **:** not disintegrated, loose, or spongy ⟨a ~ mass of rock⟩ ⟨rain fell in ~ sheets⟩ ⟨the surgeon scraped back to ~ healthy bone⟩ **b :** possessing or characterized by the properties of a solid **:** being neither gaseous nor liquid ⟨the pavement is not yet ~⟩ ⟨physics of the ~ state⟩ **4 :** of good and substantial quality or kind ⟨~ comfort⟩: as **a :** having merit or soundness ⟨based his decision on ~ reasons⟩ **b :** made firmly and well **:** STURDY ⟨a ~ chair⟩ ⟨firm ~ walls⟩ **c** (1) **:** full sounding and having a strong rhythmic drive ⟨~ jazz music⟩ (2) **:** excellent in every respect — used esp. of popular music **d** *of immunity* **:** capable of resisting severe challenge ⟨intradermal inoculation of the virulent agent in guinea pigs resulted in ~ immunity in all trials⟩ **5 :** united or consolidated so as to form an integral whole: as **a** *of time* **:** having no break or interruption ⟨stand for three ~ hours⟩ **b :** UNANIMOUS ⟨a ~ delegation⟩ ⟨the ~ vote of a delegation⟩ ⟨group opinion is ~⟩ **c :** united or joined in intimacy **:** being on good terms — used with *with* ⟨make oneself ~ with the chief⟩ **6 a :** having or marked by sound judgment or knowledge **:** thoroughly grounded ⟨~ thinkers⟩ ⟨~ learning⟩ **b :** SERIOUS-MINDED, RELIABLE, PRUDENT; *often* **:** well-established financially **:** having unimpaired credit ⟨~ New Englanders⟩ ⟨the ~ men of the community⟩ **c :** serious in purpose or character **:** not trivial **:** not vain or frivolous ⟨time for ~ reading⟩ **7 :** entirely of one substance, formation, kind, or character: as **a :** entirely of one metal **:** containing the minimum of alloy necessary to impart hardness ⟨~ gold⟩ **b :** being or consisting of a single uniform color or tone **c :** having decorative details worked on solid material ⟨a ~ frame⟩ **syn** see FIRM

²solid \"\ *adv* **:** SOLIDLY; *often* **:** UNANIMOUSLY

³solid \"\ *n* -s [ME, fr. L *solidum*, fr. neut. of *solidus*, adj.] **1 :** a magnitude that has the three dimensions length, breadth, and thickness **:** a part of space (as a cube, a sphere) bounded on all sides **2 a :** a substance that does not flow perceptibly under moderate stress, has a definite capacity for resisting forces (as compression, tension, strain) which tend to deform it, and under ordinary conditions retains a definite size and shape — compare GAS, LIQUID **b :** material in solution or suspension that when freed of solvent or suspending medium has the form and qualities of a solid — usu. used in pl. ⟨the ~*s* of the blood⟩ ⟨milk ~*s* include salts, protein, and sugar⟩ — see SOLIDS-NOT-FAT **3 :** something (as a substantial mass) that is solid: as **a :** a compact mass of masonry or comparable fabrication (as a wall or pier) as distinguished from one containing a void or an opening **b :** coal in place that has not been sheared, undercut, or similarly prepared for blasting **c** (1) **:** a solid color (2) **:** a printing plate having an entirely smooth surface without etching or design of any kind that is used for printing a solid color and esp. a tint (3) **:** one of the darkest or heaviest printing areas of a halftone as distinguished from middletone or highlight areas (4) **:** textile or other material of a solid color — usu. used in pl. **d :** a compound word whose members are joined together without a hyphen

sol·i·da·go \,sälə'dā(,)gō\ *n* [NL, fr. ML *soldago* an herb reputed to heal wounds, fr. *soldare* to make whole, make sound, fr. L *solidare*, fr. *solidus* solid] **1** *cap* **:** a very large genus of chiefly No. American herbs (family Compositae) that are distinguished from members of *Aster* by no definite characters but usu. have stems resembling wands, small heads with yellow or occas. white ray florets, and an inflorescence which varies from a thyrsoid panicle to axillary capitate clusters — see DYER'S-WEED, GOLDENROD **2** -ES **:** any plant of the genus *Solidago*

solid alcohol *n* **:** a product consisting of ordinary alcohol converted to a gel (as by means of a soap or calcium acetate) and used on a small scale as a fuel

solid angle *n* **:** the angular spread at the vertex of a cone or similar figure measured by the area intercepted on a unit sphere about the vertex as center by the cone surface

sol·i·dar·ic \¦sälə¦darik\ *adj* [*solidarity* + *-ic*] **:** having solidarity

sol·i·dar·i·ly \-¦derəlē\ *adv* **:** in a solidary manner **:** so as to be solidary

sol·i·da·rism \'säləda,rizəm\ *n* -s [*solidarity* + *-ism*] **1 :** SOLIDARITY **2 :** a theory in sociology: the mutual interdependence of members of society offers a basis for a social organization based upon solidarity of interests

sol·i·da·rist \-rəst\ *n* -s [*solidarity* + *-ist*] **:** an advocate of solidarism

sol·i·da·ris·tic \¦===¦ristik\ *adj* [*solidarist* + *-ic*] **:** of or relating to solidarity or solidarism **:** based on solidarism ⟨~ concepts⟩

sol·i·dar·i·ty \,sälə'darəd·ē, -rətē, -i *also* -der-\ *n* -ES [F *solidarité*, fr. *solidaire* solidary + *-ité* -ity] **1 :** an entire union of interests and responsibilities in a group **:** community of interests, objectives, or standards ⟨~ that knits together innumerable hearts —Joseph Conrad⟩ **2** *Roman, civil, & Scots law* **:** the quality or state of being solidary

sol·i·da·rize \'säləda,rīz\ *vi* -ED/-ING/-S [F *solidariser*, fr. *solidaire* + *-iser* -ize] **:** to come together **:** attain a state of solidarity ⟨the parties of the right failed to ~ in time⟩

sol·i·dary \-,derē\ *adj* [F *solidaire*, fr. MF, fr. L (*in*) *solidum* for the whole, involving all (fr. *in* + *solidum* whole sum, fr. neut. of *solidus* solid) + MF *-aire* -ary — more at IN, SAFE] **1 :** characterized by or manifesting community of interests and responsibilities **2 :** constituting or relating to an obligation in solido under Roman, civil, or Scots law wherein the parties thereto are bound jointly and severally for the entire debt or damages or for the full performance or object of the obligation, or wherein any one party entitled to such an obligation may receive the full debt, damages, performance, or object of the obligations and give a receipt or release binding all others entitled thereto — compare CORREAL

solid board *n* **:** a paperboard made of the same type of material throughout — distinguished from *combination board*

solid box *n* **:** a solid ring bearing for a shaft that is lined with babbitt metal, is not adjustable, and is used esp. on light machinery

solid bulb *n* **:** CORM

solid casting *n* **:** slip casting of ceramic material without pour-off of residue esp. for forming solid pieces or for hollow ware if the mold has a core

solid compound *n* **:** a compound whose components are solid in printing or writing — compare OPEN COMPOUND

solid die *n* **:** a hollow internally threaded screw-cutting tool made in one piece

solid-drawn \¦=¦=\ *adj* **:** drawn out from a heated solid bar esp. by a process of spiral rolling that first hollows the bar and then expands the cavity by forcing the bar over a pointed mandrel fixed in front of the rolls — used of a weldless tube

so·li·deo \,sōlə'dā(,)ō, -'thā-\ *n* -s [Sp, fr. the ML phrase *soli Deo sit gloria* to God alone be the glory; fr. the fact that it is removed only on approaching the sanctuary] **:** ZUCCHETTO

solider *comparative of* SOLID

solidest *superlative of* SOLID

solid geometry *n* **:** a branch of geometry that deals with the figures of three-dimensional space

solid hoof *n* **:** a hoof (as of a horse) that forms a continuous encasement of the distal part of a foot — compare CLOVEN FOOT

solid-hoofed \¦=¦=\ *adj* [*solid hoof* + *-ed*] **1 :** SOLIDUNGULATE **2 :** MULE-FOOT

solidi *pl of* SOLIDUS

so·lid·i·fi·able \sə'lidə,fīəbəl, =¦==¦===\ *adj* **:** capable of being solidified

so·lid·i·fi·ca·tion \sə,lidəfə'kāshən\ *n* -s [fr. *solidify*, after such pairs as E *ratify: ratification*] **1 :** an act or instance of solidifying **2 :** the condition of being solidified

so·lid·i·fi·er \='==,fī(ə)r, -īə\ *n* -s **:** one that solidifies

so·lid·i·fy \sə'lidə,fī\ *vb* -ED/-ING/-ES [¹*solid* + *-ify*] *vt* **:** to make solid or compact or hard: as **a :** to alter (a fluid) to a solid state ⟨~ concrete⟩ **b :** to give a feeling of reality to ⟨details that *solidified* the composition⟩ **c :** to cause to take on strength and assurance ⟨~*ing* one's knowledge⟩ **:** make secure, substantial, or firmly fixed ⟨stars that ~ public opinion⟩ **~** *vi* **:** to become solid **:** HARDEN ⟨hot paraffin *solidifies* as it cools⟩

solid injection *n* **:** the injection of atomized fuel oil into the combustion chamber of a diesel engine under the pressure of the liquid fuel itself — compare AIR INJECTION

sol·id·ish \'sälədish\ *adj* **:** comparatively solid

so·lid·i·ty \sə'lidəd·ē, -idətē, -i\ *n* -ES [MF *solidité*, fr. L *soliditat-*, *soliditas*, fr. *solidus* solid + *-itat-*, *-itas* -ity] **1 :** the quality or state of being solid **:** lack of an interior cavity **:** DENSITY, COMPACTNESS ⟨stone oppressed him with its indestructible ~ —Aldous Huxley⟩ ⟨felt the rubbery ~ as the club came down —Ernest Hemingway⟩ **2 :** the quality or character (as in a human being, act, institution) of being sound in a moral, mental, financial, or other comparable respect **3 :** something solid **:** a solid body **4** *archaic* **:** space within a closed surface **:** VOLUME **5 :** the ratio of the projected area of the blades of a rotor to the area swept by the blades

solid-looking \¦==¦==\ *adj* [¹*solid* + *looking*] **:** giving an impression of solid worth or substance ⟨*solid-looking* well-fed citizens⟩

sol·id·ly *adv* [¹*solid* + *-ly*] **:** so as to have or give an effect of solidity: as **a** (1) **:** STRONGLY, FIRMLY ⟨~ constructed furniture⟩ (2) **:** SECURELY ⟨set ~ on its base⟩ **b :** on soundly logical or reasonable grounds ⟨the result may be ~ inferred⟩ **c** *archaic* **:** SERIOUSLY, INTENSIVELY **d :** without reservation **:** WHOLLY, UNANIMOUSLY ⟨~ behind the move⟩ ⟨voted the precinct ~ for the party candidate⟩

solid-mouth \'==¦=\ *also* **solid-mouthed** \—¦=\ *adj, of a sheep* **:** having a complete set of teeth — compare BROKEN-MOUTHED

sol·id·ness *n* -ES **:** the quality or state of being solid

solid newel *n* **:** a newel into which the ends of winding stairs are built — distinguished from *hollow newel*

solid of revolution [³*solid*] **:** a mathematical solid conceived as formed by the revolution of a plane figure about an axis in its plane

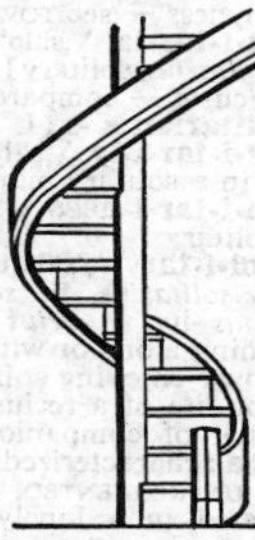

solid newel

solids *pl of* SOLID

solids-not-fat \¦==,=¦=\ *n pl but usu sing in constr* **:** the constituents of milk other than butterfat and water ⟨*solids-not-fat* is lowest in summer⟩

solid solution *n* [¹*solid*] **:** a homogeneous solid phase (as austenite) capable of existing throughout a range of chemical composition — used chiefly of crystalline materials; often distinguished from *intermetallic compound*; compare MIXTURE

solid system *n* **:** an underground electrical distribution system in which the conductors or cables are buried rather than pulled into ducts

sol·i·dum \'sälədəm\ *n* -s [L, neut. of *solidus* solid] **1 :** the dado of a pedestal **2 :** an entire sum **:** WHOLE — used in various phrases (as *in solidum, singuli in solidum*)

sol·id·un·gu·la \,sälə'dəŋgyələ\ *n pl, cap* [NL, fr. L *solidus* + *ungula* hoof — more at UNGULA] *in some classifications* **:** a group coextensive with Hippoidea

sol·id·un·gu·lar \¦==¦==lə(r)\ *also* **sol·id·un·gu·lous** \-ləs\ *adj* [L *solidus* solid + *ungula* hoof + E *-ar*, *-ous*] **:** SOLIDUNGULATE

¹sol·id·un·gu·late \-lət, -,lāt\ *adj* [L *solidus* solid + *ungula* hoof + E *-ate*] **:** having a single hoof on each foot ⟨horses and other ~ mammals⟩

²solidungulate \"\ *n* -s **:** a solidungulate animal

sol·i·dus \'säləd əs\ *n, pl* **sol·i·di** \-,dī\ [ME, fr. LL, fr. L *solidus* solid — more at SAFE] **1 :** an ancient Roman gold coin introduced by Constantine as successor to the aureus and used until the fall of the Byzantine Empire **2** [ML *solidus* shilling, fr. LL, a gold coin; fr. its use as a symbol for shillings] **:** DIAGONAL 4 **3 a** *also* **solidus curve** [L, solid, adj.] **:** a curve usu. on a temperature-composition diagram for a binary system that corresponds with a liquidus and that indicates temperatures below which only the solid phase can exist **b** *also* **solidus point :** the point of temperature at which a substance and esp. a metal or alloy is about to melt **:** incipient melting point

so·lier·i·a·ce·ae \sō,lirē'āsē,ē\ *n pl, cap* [NL, fr. *Solieria* genus of algae + *-aceae*] **:** a family of red algae (order Gigartinales) having multiaxial thalli and inhabiting the warmer seas

soli·fid·i·an \,sōlə'fidēən, ,säl-\ *n* -s [*soli-* + L *fides* faith + E *-ian* — more at FAITH] **:** one who holds that faith alone without achievement or personal merit is sufficient to insure salvation — compare NULLIFIDIAN

soli·fid·i·an·ism \-ēə,nizəm\ *n* -s **:** the doctrine of the solifidians

soli·fluction *also* **soli·fluxion** \¦sōlə, ¦sälə+\ *n* -s [L *solum* ground, soil + *-i-* + *fluction-*, *fluctio* act of flowing, fr. *fluctus* (past part. of *fluere* to flow) + *-ion-*, *-io* -ion — more at FLUID] **:** the slow creeping of wet soil and other saturated fragmental material down a slope resulting sometimes in the formation of small terraces **:** the selective movement of soil particles and rock waste in regions of perennially frozen ground by frost action and associated phenomena producing soil structures of various kinds and shapes — compare CONGELITURBATION — **soli·fluctional** \"+\ *adj*

so·lif·u·gae \sə'lifyə,jē\ *n* [NL, fr. pl. of LL *solifuga*, a venomous ant or spider, alter. of L *salpuga*] *syn of* SOLPUGIDA

soli·fuge \'sōlə,fyüj, 'säl-\ *n* -s [LL *solifuga*] **:** SOLPUGID

so·lif·u·ge·an \sə¦lifyə¦jēən\ *n* -s *or* **so·lif·u·gous** \-'lifyəgəs\ *adj* [LL *solifuga* + E *-ean* or *-ous*] **:** SOLPUGID

so·lif·u·gid \-'lifyəjəd\ *n* -s [NL *Solifugae* + E *-id*] **:** SOLPUGID

so·lig·e·nous \sō'lijənəs\ *adj* [L *solum* ground + E *-i-* + *-genous*] **:** produced by inflow of surface water or rise of ground water and not by locally precipitated water ⟨a ~ marsh⟩

so·lil·o·quist \sə'liləkwəst\ *n* -s [*soliloquy* + *-ist*] **:** one who soliloquizes

so·lil·o·quize \sə'lilə,kwīz\ *vb* -ED/-ING/-S *see* -IZE *in Explan Notes* [*soliloquy* + *-ize*] *vi* **:** to utter a soliloquy **:** talk to oneself **~** *vt* **:** to say, discuss, or address in a soliloquy

so·lil·o·quiz·er \-zə(r)\ *n* -s

so·lil·o·quiz·ing·ly \='==,===, =,==¦===\ *adv* [*soliloquizing* (pres. part. of *soliloquize*) + *-ly*] **:** in the manner of one that soliloquizes

so·lil·o·quy \sə'liləkwē, -wi\ *n* -ES [LL *soliloquium*, fr. L *soli-* + *loqui* to speak] **1 :** the act of talking to oneself **:** a discourse made by one in solitude to oneself **:** MONOLOGUE **2 :** a poem, a discourse, or an utterance of a dramatic character that has the form of a monologue or gives the illusion of being a series of unspoken reflections

so·li·lunar \¦sōlə+\ *adj* [L *sol* sun + E *-i-* + *lunar* — more at SOLAR] **:** LUNISOLAR

soling *pres part of* SOLE

so·ling·en \'zōliŋən, 'sō-\ *adj, usu cap* [fr. *Solingen*, city of northwest Germany] **:** of or from the city of Solingen, Germany **:** of the kind or style prevalent in Solingen

sol·ion \'säl+,-\ *n* -s [*solution* + *-ion*] **:** an electronic detecting and amplifying device whose operation depends on the movement of ions in a solution

soli·ped \'sälə,ped\ *n* -s [NL *soliped-*, *solipes*, fr. L *solidus* solid + *ped-*, *pes* foot — more at SAFE, FOOT] **:** SOLIDUNGULATE

solip·sism \'sōləp,sizəm, 'säləp-, sə'lip-\ *n* -s [L *sol*us alone + *ipse* self + E *-ism* — more at SOLE] **1 :** any of various extreme versions of subjective idealism: as **a** (1) **:** an epistemological theory that the self can know nothing but its own modifications and states (2) *or* **solipsism of the present moment :** an epistemological theory that the self knows or can know only its present modifications and states to the exclusion of future and past states **b** (1) **:** a metaphysical theory that the self is the only existent thing (2) **:** a metaphysical theory that all real entities are modifications and states of the self **:** EGOISM 1a **2 :** the adoption of epistemological solipsism as a premise for a general metaphysical or epistemological theory or as a scientific hypothesis **3 :** extreme indulgence of and concern with the self at the expense of social relationships esp. as expressed in a failure of artistic communication ⟨the poet today must navigate between . . . parochial ~ and commercial success —F.L.Utley⟩

solip·sist \-səst\ *n* -s [*solips*ism + *-ist*] **:** an adherent or advocate of solipsism ⟨the artist's egoism is outrageous . . . he is by nature a ~ and the world exists only for him to exercise upon it his powers of creation —W.S.Maugham⟩

solip·sis·tic \¦sōləp¦sistik, ¦säl-\ *or* **solip·sist** \'==,səst, sə'lip-\ *adj* **:** of or relating to solipsism or solipsists — **solip·sis·ti·cal·ly** \¦sōləp¦sistək(ə)lē, ¦säl-\ *adv*

so·liste \(')sō¦lēst\ *n* -s [F, fr. *solo* (fr. It) + *-iste* -ist — more at SOLO] **:** a minor solo dancer in ballet

sol·i·taire \'sälə,ta(a)|(ə)r, -te|, |ə *sometimes* ,==ˈ=\ *n* -s [F, fr. *solitaire* solitary, adj., fr. L *solitarius*] **1 :** SOLITARY 1 **2 a :** a single diamond or sometimes other gem set alone **b :** a piece of jewelry (as a ring) set with a single diamond ⟨her ear rings were magnificent ~*s*⟩ **3 :** a game designed for one person to play alone: as **a :** any of various card games that typically involve the arranging of cards dealt at random in a prescribed pattern — called also *patience;* see DOUBLE SOLITAIRE **b :** a game played on a board with pegs or balls in which the object is beginning with all the places filled except one to remove all but one of the pieces by jumping **4 :** a large usu. black silk neckcloth worn by men in the 18th century **5 a :** a flightless extinct bird (*Pezophaps solitaria*) related to the dodo but less clumsy and with a smaller bill and formerly inhabiting the island of Rodriguez in the Indian ocean **b :** any of several American fly-catching thrushes (genus *Myadestes*) noted for their sweet song and shyness — see TOWNSEND'S SOLITAIRE

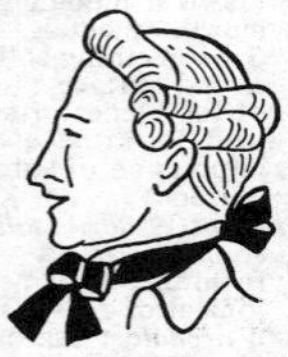
solitaire 4

sol·i·tar·ia \,sälə'terēə, -ta(ə)r-\ *n* -s [NL, fr. fem. of L *solitarius* solitary] **:** a nonmigratory phase occurring in some locusts — compare GREGARIA

solitarian *n* -s [L *solitarius* + E *-an*] *obs* **:** HERMIT, SOLITARY

sol·i·tar·i·ly \¦sälə¦terəlē, -li\ *adv* [ME, fr. ¹*solitary* + *-ly*] **:** in a solitary manner **:** in solitude

sol·i·tar·i·ness \-rēnəs\ *n* -ES **:** the quality or state of being solitary

¹sol·i·tary \'sälə,terē, -ri\ *adj, sometimes* -ER/-EST [ME, fr. L *solitarius*, fr. *solitas* aloneness (fr. *solus* alone + *-itat-*, *-itas* -ity) + *-arius* -ary — more at SOLE] **1 a :** being, living, or going alone or without companions ⟨a ~ traveler⟩ **b :** given to or enjoying solitude ⟨a person ~ by nature⟩; *also* **:** living the life of a recluse or hermit ⟨~ saint⟩ **c :** suffering from lack of companions **:** LONELY ⟨often alone but never ~⟩ **2 a :** characterized by seclusion, solitude, or lack of inhabitants **:** UNFREQUENTED, DESERTED, DESOLATE ⟨a ~ valley⟩ **b :** located in a lonely place ⟨a ~ mountain camp⟩ ⟨~ ruins⟩ **3 :** characterized by the lack or absence of companions **:** taken, passed, performed, endured, or otherwise dealt with alone ⟨a ~ ramble⟩ ⟨~ tasks⟩ ⟨lead a ~ life⟩ **4 :** SINGLE, INDIVIDUAL, SOLE ⟨a ~ example⟩ **5 a** *of a plant part or organ* **:** not forming part of a group or cluster of parts or organs **:** occurring singly and usu. one to a branch or stem ⟨flowers terminal and ~⟩ **b** *of an organism* **:** living or growing habitually alone **:** not gregarious, colonial, social, or compound ⟨~ tunicates⟩ ⟨some bees are ~ in habit⟩ ⟨some trees are ~ or sporadic in occurrence⟩ **syn** see ALONE, SINGLE

²solitary \"\ *n* -ES [ME, fr. ¹*solitary*] **1 :** one who lives or seeks to live a solitary life **:** RECLUSE, HERMIT **2 :** SOLITARY CONFINEMENT

solitary ant *n* **:** VELVET ANT

solitary bee *n* **:** any of various bees that do not live in colonies

solitary confinement *n* **:** confinement of a prisoner where he has no intercourse with others

solitary gland *n* **:** any of the small lymph follicles in the submucous tissue and mucous membrane of the intestine

solitary phase *n* **:** SOLITARIA

solitary sandpiper *n* **:** an American sandpiper (*Tringa solitaria*) that is similar in appearance and habit to the Old World green sandpiper and lays its eggs in abandoned nests in trees

solitary snipe *n, dial Eng* **:** GREAT SNIPE

solitary vireo *n* **:** a vireo (*Vireo solitarius*) of eastern No. America having the head bluish gray, the back green, and the wings with two white bars — compare BLUE-HEADED VIREO

solitary wasp *n* **:** any of numerous wasps (as the mud wasps and sand wasps) that do not live in colonies

solitary wave *n* **:** a single wave caused by some special disturbance (as a tidal wave)

soli·terraneous \¦sōlə, ¦sälə-+\ *adj* [L *sol* sun + E *-i-* + *terraneous*] **:** of or relating to the earth and sun; *specif* **:** constituting a period when solar and terrestrial conditions jointly affect weather

sol·i·tude \'sälə,tüd, -ə·,tyüd\ *n* -s [ME, fr. MF, fr. L *solitudin-*, *solitudo*, fr. *solus* alone + *-i-* + *-tudin-*, *-tudo* -tude — more at SOLE] **1 :** the quality or state of being alone or remote from society **:** SOLITARINESS, ISOLATION, SECLUSION **2 :** a solitary or lonely place (as a desert or wilderness) ⟨living in these ~*s*⟩ **3 a** *obs* **:** SOLENESS, UNIQUENESS **b** *archaic* **:** complete lack **:** DEARTH

sol·i·tu·di·nar·i·an \,==,tüdᵊn'erēən, ,==,tyü-\ *n* -s [L *solitudin-*, *solitudo* + E *-arian*] **:** RECLUSE

¹so·liv·a·gant \sō'livəgənt\ *n* -s [L *solivagus* wandering alone (fr. *soli-* + *vagus* wandering) + E *-ant* — more at VAGARY] **:** a solitary wanderer

²solivagant \"\ *adj* [L *solivagus* + E *-ant*] **:** rambling alone **:** marked by solitary wandering

sollar *or* **soller** *var of* SOLAR

sol·ler·et \¦sälə¦ret\ *n* -s [F *soleret*, *solleret*, fr. MF, dim. of OF *soller* shoe, fr. ML *subtelare*, fr. LL *subtel* hollow of the foot, fr. *sub-* + *talus* ankle] **:** a flexible steel shoe forming part of a medieval suit of armor — see ARMOR illustration

sol·lya \'sälēə, -lyə\ *n, cap* [NL, after Richard H. *Solly* †1858 Eng. botanist] **:** a genus of Australian woody vines (family Pittosporaceae) with evergreen entire leaves, nodding blue flowers in loose cymes, and oblong many-seeded capsules

sol·mi·zate \'sälmə,zāt\ *vb* -ED/-ING/-S [back-formation fr. *solmization*] *vt* **1 :** to sing or represent (music) by the syllables of solmization **2 :** SOL-FA ~ *vi* **:** to sing using solmization

sol·mi·za·tion \,sälmə'zāshən\ *n* -s [F *solmisation*, fr. *solmiser* to sol-fa (fr. *sol* — fr. ML — + *mi* — fr. ML — + *-iser* -ize) + *-ation* — more at SOL, MI] **:** the act, practice, or system of using a set of syllables to denote the tones of a musical scale — compare GREAT SCALE, GUIDONIAN SYLLABLES, SOL-FA SYLLABLES, SOLFÈGE

soln *abbr* solution

¹so·lo \'sō(,)lō\ *n, pl* **solos** \-lōz\ *also* **so·li** \-ō,lē\ [It, lit., alone, fr. L *solus* — more at SOLE] **1 a :** an air, strain, or a whole piece played by a single person or sung by a single voice with or without accompaniment **b :** a musical composition written for performance by one person **2 :** a performance (as a dance or a flight in an airplane) in which the performer has no partner or associate **3 a :** a bid or contract in various card games by which a player chooses to defeat two or more opponents without the benefit of having a partner **b :** a game in skat in which the player undertakes to play without use of the skat **c :** any of several card games in which a bid of solo is permissible **d :** a game derived from ombre

²solo \"\ *adv* (*or adj*) **1 :** without a companion **:** in solitude **:** ALONE ⟨experienced enough to fly ~⟩ ⟨left ~ to await the returning hunters⟩ **2 :** of, relating to, or being a solo **:** performed or for performance as a solo **:** UNACCOMPANIED ⟨a ~ air⟩ ⟨excellent ~ voices⟩ ⟨a ~ dance⟩

³solo \"\ *vb* **soloed**; **soloed**; **soloing** \-(,)lōiŋ, -ləwiŋ\ **solos** *vi* **:** to perform by oneself; *esp* **:** to fly solo in an airplane ~ *vt* **:** to fly (an airplane) solo

so·lod *or* **so·loth** \'sōlət\ *n, pl* **solo·di** *or* **solo·ti** \-lədē,-lətē\ *sometimes cap* [Russ *solod* malt; akin to Russ *sol'* salt, L *sal* — more at SALT] **:** any of an intrazonal group of dealkalized compacted clay soils of low productivity formed gradually through drainage and leaching of silty upper layers of solonetz soils

so·lod·iza·tion \,sōlədə'zāshən, -,dī'z-\ *n* -s **:** the process of solodizing or the process of becoming solodized

so·lod·ize \'sōlə,dīz\ *vt* -ED/-ING/-S [Russ *solod* malt + E *-ize*] **:** to develop (a soil and esp. solonetz) through dealkalizing processes including drainage and leaching into solod

so·lod·ous \'sōlədəs\ *adj* [*solod* + *-ous*] **:** made up of or constituting solod

so·lo·ist \'sōləwəst, -(,)lōəst\ *n* -s [¹*solo* + *-ist*] **:** one (as a singer or aviator) who performs a solo; *esp* **:** a performer of solos at an orchestral or choral concert

so·lo·is·tic \¦sōlə¦wistik, -lō¦is-\ *adj* [*soloist* + *-ic*] **:** of, relating to, or suitable for, performance by a soloist ⟨~ writing for wind instruments⟩

so·lo man \'sō(,)lō-\ *n, usu cap S* [fr. *Solo* river, Java] **:** a late Pleistocene Neanderthaloid man known from incomplete skulls and other skeletal remains found near Trinil in Java, usu. considered a distinct species (*Homo soloensis*), and being intermediate in many respects between Java and Peking man on the one hand and typical Neanderthal man on the other

sol·o·mon \'säləmən\ *n* -s *sometimes cap* [after King *Solomon* †*ab*933B.C. ruler of Israel who was famed for his wisdom as a judge] **:** a very wise man

sol·o·mo·nian \¦sälə¦mōnēən, -ōnyən\ *adj, usu cap* [King *Solomon* + E *-ian*] **:** SOLOMONIC

sol·o·mon·ic \-¦mänik\ *adj, usu cap* [King *Solomon* + E *-ic*] **1 :** of, relating to, produced by, or characteristic of the Hebrew ruler Solomon ⟨~ literature⟩ **2 :** marked by notable wisdom, reasonableness, or discretion esp. under trying circumstances ⟨a ~ compromise⟩

solomon seal *n, usu cap 1st S* [by alter.] **:** SOLOMON'S SEAL

solomon's lily *n, usu cap S* [after King *Solomon*] **:** BLACK CALLA

solomon's–plume \¦===¦=\ *n, pl* **solomon's–plumes** *usu cap S* **:** FALSE SOLOMON'S SEAL — often used in pl. with sing. or pl. constr.

solomon's seal *n, usu cap 1st S* **1 :** a mystic symbol that consists of two interlaced triangles arranged in a star with six points and often with one triangle dark and one light, is symbolic of the union of soul and body, and has been used as an amulet to guard against fever and other diseases — compare MAGEN DAVID **2** [so called fr. the resemblance of the scars on the rootstock to the symbol] **a :** a plant of the genus *Polygonatum* **b :** any of several plants felt to resemble the Solomon's seal: as (1) **:** TURQUOISEBERRY 1 (2) **:** FALSE SOLOMON'S SEAL

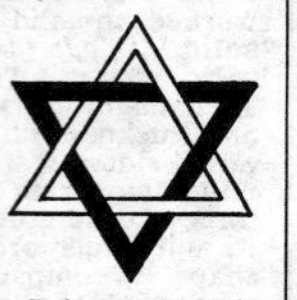
Solomon's seal

so·lon \'sōlən *also* -,län\ *n* -s [after *Solon* †*ab*559B.C. Athenian lawgiver and one of the Seven Wise Men of Greece] **:** a wise and skillful lawgiver or statesman; *broadly* **:** a member of a legislative body

sol·on·chak \¦sälən¦chak\ *n* -s *sometimes cap* [Russ, salt marsh, fr. *solonyĭ* salty, fr. *sol'* salt; akin to L *sal* salt — more at SALT] **:** any of an intrazonal group of strongly saline soils usu. light colored and without characteristic structural form and typically developed in poorly drained arid or semiarid areas vegetated mostly by halophytes

sol·o·netz *also* **sol·o·nets** \¦sälə¦nets\ *n, pl* **solonetzes** *also* **solonetz** *also* **solonetses** [Russ *solonets* salt not extracted by decoction, fr. *solonyĭ* salty] **:** any of an intrazonal group of dark hard alkaline soils showing columnar structure and containing sulfates, bicarbonates, and other soluble salts which evolve by leaching and alkalizing from solonchak in imperfectly drained semiarid regions — **sol·o·netz·ic** \-tsik\ *adj*

so long \=ˈ=\ *interj* **:** GOOD-BYE

so long as *conj* **1 :** during and up to the end of the time that **:** as long as **:** WHILE ⟨the different key words that we must use are all interconnected, and *so long as* some remain vague, others must . . . share this defect —Bertrand Russell⟩ **2 :** provided that ⟨could . . . do as they pleased *so long as* they attended lectures —John Reed⟩

so·lo·ni·an \sō'lōnēən, sə'l-\ *also* **so·lon·ic** \(')sō¦länik\ *adj* [*Solon* †*ab*559B.C. Athenian lawgiver + E *-ian*, *-ic*] **:** of, relating to, or characteristic of Solon, the ancient Athenian lawgiver or his legislation

solo organ *n* **:** a division of a pipe organ consisting of stops with an individual character suitable for solo effects

solos *pl of* SOLO, *pres 3d sing of* SOLO

solo stop *n* **:** an organ stop of individual tone quality suitable for solo effects

soloth *var of* SOLOD

soloti *pl of* SOLOD

solo whist *n* **:** a card game which is played with the full pack ranking as at whist and in which each player chooses one of seven different declarations he proposes to play

¹sol·pu·gid \säl'pyüjəd\ *adj* [NL *Solpugida*] **:** of or relating to the Solpugida

²solpugid \"\ *n* -s **:** an arachnid of the order Solpugida

sol·pu·gi·da \-jədə\ *n pl, cap* [NL, fr. *Solpuga*, genus of arachnids (fr. L *salpuga*, *solpuga*, *solipuga* a kind of venomous ant or spider) + *-ida*] **:** an order of hairy arachnids having a segmented thorax and abdomen, slender pedipalpi that resemble legs, and strong chelate chelicerae, showing in structure close relationship to the scorpions but breathing by means of tracheae and having no book lungs, and occurring widely in warm regions with the exception of Madagascar and Australia

sol·pu·gid·ea \,sälpyü'jidēə\ *or* **sol·pu·gi·des** \säl'pyüjə,dēz\ [NL, fr. *Solpuga* + *-idea*] *syn of* SOLPUGIDA

solr *abbr* solicitor

sols *pl of* SOL

sol·stice \'sälztəs, 'sōl-,'sòl-, -lst-\ *n* -s [ME, fr. OF, fr. L *solstitium*, fr. *sol* sun + *-stitium* (fr. *status*, past part. of *sistere* to come to a stand, cause to stand or stop); akin to L *stare* to stand, be stationary — more at SOLAR, STAND] **1 a :** one of the two points on the ecliptic at which its distance from the celestial equator is greatest and which is reached by the sun each year about June 22d and December 22d **b :** the time of the sun's passing a solstice which occurs on June 22d to begin summer in the northern hemisphere and winter in the southern and on December 22d to begin winter in the northern and summer in the southern hemisphere **c :** the summer solstice or its heat **2 :** a furthest or highest point **:** LIMIT

sol·sti·tial \(')säl¦stishəl, (')sōl-, (')sòl-, -¦st-\ *adj* [L *solstitialis*, fr. *solstitium* solstice + *-alis* -al] **:** of, relating to, or characteristic of a solstice and esp. the summer solstice **:** happening or appearing at a solstice or being associated with a solstice

sol·sti·tial·ly \-əlē\ *adv* [*solstitial* + *-ly*] **:** at or toward a solstice

solstitial point *n* **:** SOLSTICE 1a

solubbi *usu cap, var of* SLUBBI

sol·u·bil·i·ty \,sälyə'bilәd·ē, -lətē, -i\ *n* -ES [¹*soluble* + *-ity*] **1 :** the quality or state of being soluble **2 :** the amount of a substance that will dissolve in a given amount of another substance and is typically expressed as the number of parts by weight dissolved by 100 parts of solvent at a specified temperature and pressure or as percent by weight or by volume

solubility curve *n* **:** a graphic representation of the variation with changing temperature of the solubility of a given substance in a given solvent

solubility product *n* **:** the maximum product of the ionic concentrations or activities of an electrolyte that at one temperature can continue in equilibrium with the undissolved phase

sol·u·bi·li·za·tion \,sälyəbələ'zāshən, -(,)bil-, -,lī'z-\ *n* -s **:** the quality or state of being solubilized

sol·u·bi·lize \'==bə,līz\ *vt* -ED/-ING/-S *see -ize in Explan Notes* **:** to make soluble or increase the solubility of — compare EMULSIFY

solubilized vat dye *n* [fr. past part. of *solubilize*] **:** a vat dye in the form of a soluble sodium salt of a sulfuric acid monoester of its leuco compound — see DYE table I

sol·u·bi·liz·er \-zə(r)\ *n* -s [*solubilize* + *-er*] **:** an agent that increases the solubility of a substance

¹sol·u·ble \'sälyəbəl\ *adj* [ME, fr. MF, susceptible of being loosened or relaxed or dissolved, fr. LL *solubilis*, fr. L *solvere* to loosen, relax, dissolve + *-bilis* -able — more at SOLVE] **1 a** *archaic* **:** not constipated **:** evacuating normally **b** *obs* **:** having a laxative effect **:** inducing evacuation of the bowels **2 a :** susceptible of being dissolved in or as if in a fluid **:** capable of solution ⟨salt and sugar are ~ in water⟩ ⟨copper and zinc are completely ~ in the liquid state, but are only partially ~ in the solid state —G.E.Claussen⟩ — see FAT-SOLUBLE **b :** EMULSIFIABLE, DISPERSIBLE — used esp. of oils **3 :** subject to being solved **:** susceptible of being disentangled or explained **:** SOLVABLE ⟨a ~ puzzle⟩ ⟨such problems are perfectly ~⟩ — **sol·u·ble·ness** \-bəlnəs\ *n* -ES — **sol·u·bly** \-blē, -bli\ *adv*

²soluble \"\ *n* -s **:** something (as a substance or problem) that is soluble ⟨leaching of soil ~*s*⟩ — see DISTILLERS' SOLUBLES

soluble blue *n* **1** *often cap S&B* **:** any of several water-soluble acid dyes made by sulfonating the Spirit Blues and used in the form of salts chiefly in writing inks, in laundry blues, and as biological stains — see DYE table I (under *Acid Blue 22*) **2 :** a pigment dispersible in water that is made by treating an iron blue with sodium ferrocyanide or oxalic acid and is used chiefly in permanent writing inks and laundry blues

soluble coffee *n* **:** a fine powder or a mass of tiny crystal balls produced by dehydration from strong concentrates of brewed coffee and used for the quick preparation of beverage coffee without brewing

soluble dried blood *n* **:** a reddish brown powder made from defibrinated uncoagulated blood and used esp. in making water-resistant glues for plywood, as a clarifying agent, and as a stabilizer and spreader in emulsions (as insecticidal and fungicidal sprays)

soluble glass *n* **:** WATER GLASS 4a

soluble guncotton *or* **soluble cotton** *n* **:** PYROXYLIN 1

soluble nitrocellulose *or* **soluble nitrocotton** *n* **:** PYROXYLIN

soluble oil *n* **1 :** SULFONATED OIL **2 :** an emulsifiable oil (as a mineral oil containing a sulfonated oil or a soap as emulsifier) for use in the form of an aqueous emulsion as a cutting fluid, textile lubricant, or carrier for insecticides; *also* **:** the emulsion formed from such an oil

soluble starch *n* **:** a modified starch that is capable of dissolving in hot water to give a limpid solution and is formed from raw starch esp. by relatively mild treatment with acids, by oxidation, or by heating with glycerol — compare AMYLODEXTRIN

so·lum \'sōləm\ *n, pl* **so·la** *see sense 2* \-lə\ [NL, fr. L, base, ground, earth, soil] **1 :** SOIL, LAND; *esp* **:** a parcel of ground — used esp. in law **2** *or pl* **solums :** the layer of soil which lies above the parent material, in which the natural processes of soil formation take place, and which in well-developed soils is greatly altered from the parent material and includes the A- and B-horizons — called also *true soil;* distinguished from *topsoil*

so–lun *n, pl* **so–lun** \'sō¦lən\ *or* **so–luns** *usu cap* **:** a member of a Mongol people of Chinese Turkestan

so·lunar \sə, (')sä+\ *adj* [alter. of *sol-lunar*] **:** resulting from the combined action of sun and moon ⟨tides are a ~ phenomenon⟩; *esp* **:** of or relating to the effect of such action on biological systems ⟨computing ~ tables for hunters and fishermen⟩

so·lus \'sōləs\ *adv* (*or adj*) [L — more at SOLE] **:** without companions **:** in solitude **:** ALONE ⟨meditating ~ on the problems of life⟩ — often used in stage directions

solut *abbr* [L *solutus*] dissolved

solute \'säl,yüt *also* 'sō,lüt *sometimes* 'sōl,yüt\ *n* -s [L *solutus*, past part. of *solvere* to dissolve — more at SOLVE] **:** a dissolved substance; *esp* **:** a component of a solution present in smaller amount than the solvent

so·lu·tio \sō'lüd·ē,ō\ *n* [L, lit., loosening] *Roman & civil law* **:** performance of an obligation **:** PAYMENT, DISCHARGE, RELEASE

¹so·lu·tion \sə'lüshən *also* səl'yü-\ *n* -s [ME, fr. MF, fr. L *solution-*, *solutio* act of loosening, solving, fr. *solutus* (past part. of *solvere* to loosen, solve, dissolve) + *-ion-*, *-io* -ion — more at SOLVE] **1 a :** an action or process of solving a problem ⟨do your ~*s* quickly and without checking⟩ ⟨you may use tables in the ~ of the examples⟩; *also* **:** the fact or state of a problem's being solved ⟨a difficulty that admits of no ~⟩ **b :** an answer to or means of answering a problem **:** a clearing up **:** EXPLANATION, DENOUEMENT ⟨your ~ of the problem⟩ **c** (1) **:** a set of values of the variables of an equation that satisfies the equation (2) **:** any relation between the variables of a differential equation free from derivatives that upon differentiation yields the given differential equation **2 a** (1) **:** an act or the process by which a solid, liquid, or gaseous substance is homogeneously mixed with a liquid or less commonly a gas or solid which may consist of simple physical mixing of components or may involve chemical change ⟨when silver is dissolved in nitric acid the solute of the resulting ~ is not silver but silver nitrate formed by chemical interaction⟩ (2) *obs* **:** the process of altering material (as by dissolving, fusing, or distilling) through the agency of heat **b :** a mixture formed by a process of solution and having the same chemical composition and physical properties throughout although the concentration can undergo continuous variation within definite limits depending upon the conditions: as (1) **:** a single-phase liquid system in which the particles of dissolved solid, liquid, or gas are held to be molecules or ions — called also *true solution;* often distinguished from *emulsion, sol, suspension* (2) **:** a mixture of gases (3) **:** SOLID SOLUTION (4) **:** SOL **c :** the condition of being dissolved or of constituting the solute of a solution ⟨put the salt in ~ in as little water as possible⟩; *broadly* **:** a state of fluidity (as of material held in an emulsion or suspension) **d** (1) **:** a liquid containing a dissolved substance ⟨a watery ~ of unknown composition⟩ (2) **:** a liquid and usu. aqueous medicinal preparation with the solid ingredients soluble ⟨~*s* are easier to administer than powders⟩ **3 :** a bringing or coming to an end or into a state of discontinuity: as **a :** discharge of a contract by performance (as payment or release) **:** performance of an obligation **b** *obs* **:** a setting free **:** DELIVERANCE, DISCHARGE **c :** a separating from continuity of normally continuous parts **:** SEVERANCE ⟨a violent ~ of the continuity of a joint⟩ **d :** an interruption of continuity **:** DISRUPTION, BREACH, BREAK, DISPERSION ⟨watched the gradual ~ of the clouds as the storm moved on⟩

²solution \"\ *vt* -ED/-ING/-S **:** to apply a solution to; *esp* **:** to cement with a solution (as of rubber)

so·lu·tion·al \-shənᵊl,-shnəl\ *adj* **:** of, relating to, or constituting a solution

solution heat treatment *n* **:** heating of an alloy to a temperature at which a particular constituent will enter into solid solution followed by cooling at a rate fast enough to prevent the dissolved constituent from precipitating

so·lu·tion·ist \-sh(ə)nəst\ *n* -s [¹*solution* + *-ist*] **:** a solver of problems; *esp* **:** one who makes a practice or occupation of solving puzzles

solution plane *n* **:** a direction in a crystal of relatively easy solubility (as when the substance is under great pressure) ⟨chemical action along *solution planes* in minerals in rocks has often resulted in schillerization⟩

solution pressure *n* **:** the pressure by which the particles of a dissolved substance are driven into solution and which when equal to the osmotic pressure establishes equilibrium so that the concentration of the solution becomes constant

solutive *adj* [ML, fr. L *solutus* (past part. of *solvere* to loosen) + *-ivus* -ive] *obs* **:** tending to produce relaxation (as of the bowels) **:** LAXATIVE

sol·u·tiz·er \-zə(r)\ *n* -s [*solutize* + *-er*] **:** an agent (as an

organic salt or an organic solvent) for promoting solubility; *esp* : such an agent (as potassium isobutyrate) for use with a caustic solution in removing mercaptans from gasoline
so·lu·tre·an *or* **so·lu·tri·an** \sə'lü·trēən\ *adj, usu cap* [*Solutré*, village of east central France where remains of the period were found + E *-an* or *-ian*] : of or relating to an epoch of the Upper Paleolithic period following the Aurignacian, preceding the Magdalenian, and characterized by stone implements that are typically leaf-shaped and finely flaked on both sides and by the hunting of wild horses for food
solv *abbr* [L *solve*] dissolve
solv·abil·i·ty \,==ə'bilәd·ē, -lәtē, -i — *see* SOLVE\ *n* : the quality or state of being solvable
solv·able \'==əbəl — *see* SOLVE\ *adj* [*solve* + *-able*] **1** *obs* : able to pay one's debts : SOLVENT **2** *archaic* : SOLUBLE **3** : susceptible of solution or of being solved, resolved, or explained
¹solv·ate \'=,āt — *see* SOLVE\ *n* -S [*solvent* + *-ate*] : a chemical or physical combination of a solute with a solvent or of a dispersed phase with a dispersion medium — compare HYDRATE
²solvate \"\ *vb* -ED/-ING/-S *vt* : to convert into a solvate ⟨ions are *solvated* to a greater or lesser extent in polar solvents⟩ ⟨the polymer molecules are *solvated* by the plasticizer —Donald Druesedow & C.F.Gibbs⟩ ~ *vi* : to become or behave as a solvate
solvated *adj* [fr. past part. of ²*solvate*] : containing combined solvent ⟨a ~ hydrate⟩
solv·a·tion \=ə'āshən — *see* SOLVE\ *n* -S [²*solvate* + *-ion*] : the formation of a solvate; *also* : the state or degree of being solvated — compare HYDRATION, SOLVOLYSIS
sol·vay process \'säl,vā- *also* 'sól\ *n, usu cap S* [after Ernest *Solvay* †1922 Belg. chemist, its inventor] : a process for making sodium carbonate from common salt and limestone that is based on the sparing solubility of sodium bicarbonate and involves burning the limestone to lime and carbon dioxide, passing the carbon dioxide into a strong brine saturated with ammonia to precipitate sodium bicarbonate and leave ammonium chloride in solution, and converting the bicarbonate to soda ash by calcining — called also *ammonia soda process*
solve \'sälv, 'sólv *also* 'sä(ù)v *or* 'sóv\ *vb* -ED/-ING/-S [ME *solven*, fr. L *solvere*, *soluere* to loosen, free, pay, solve, dissolve, fr. *sed-*, *se-* apart (fr. *sed*, *se* without) + *luere* to release, atone for — more at LOSE] *vt* **1** *obs* : to set loose or free **2 a** : to find an answer, solution, explanation, or remedy for : arrive at a clear, definite, and satisfying answer to (the difficult, obscure, or urgent) ⟨the members of these commissions . . . ~ administrative difficulties, and save the state money —*Amer. Guide Series: Del.*⟩ **b** : to perform the operations required to solve (a mathematical problem) : work out **3 a** : to make payment of (as a debt or money) **b** : to free oneself of (an obligation) **4** : to cause to go into solution : DISSOLVE ~ *vi* : to solve something
syn RESOLVE, UNFOLD, UNRAVEL, DECIPHER: SOLVE is the most general in meaning and suggestion in this group; it applies to finding a satisfactory answer or solution, usu. to something of at least moderate difficulty ⟨the mystery and disquieting meaninglessness of existence . . . were *solved* for me now —L.P. Smith⟩ ⟨create a difficulty rather than *solve* one —A.M.Young⟩ RESOLVE, as contrasted with SOLVE, is likely to indicate analytic arrangement and consideration of the various phases or items of a problem or situation rather than finding a final solution or answer and is likely to suggest dispelling of confusion or perplexity by a clear formulation of questions or issues ⟨you may find it of some interest to be told that the law has had to struggle with these problems and to know how it has *resolved* them —B.N.Cardozo⟩ In some situations this process may achieve an answer, esp. a ready or summary one ⟨he was at the same time *resolving* successive tangles of intrigue against himself and his policy —Hilaire Belloc⟩ ⟨it was realized that the method of *resolving* apparent contradictions by liquidating one of the contradictories is not the way to arrive at true solutions —*Times Lit. Supp.*⟩ UNFOLD indicates continuous opening up, clarifying, making more and more clear and patent until a full solution or resolution is apparent ⟨went around and through and behind a situation, *unfolding* it . . . to include possibilities he hadn't known were upon its horizon —Mary Austin⟩ ⟨saw the great truth of evolution *unfolded* —Waldemar Kaempffert⟩ ⟨the method of *unfolding* the course of a plot must in some ways be different in a play meant for acting and in a book meant for reading —C.E.Montague⟩ UNRAVEL stresses the notion of making a clear and orderly rearrangement of something entangled or a simple ordering of something complicated, esp. by patient endeavor ⟨the details are difficult to *unravel* at this distance of time —H.O.Taylor⟩ ⟨a whole elaborate plot may be *unravelled* by discovering the one relevant detail —W. O.Aydelotte⟩ DECIPHER stresses the notion of finding the meaning or significance of something very obscure, clouded, cryptic, or enigmatic ⟨placing of a writer or other artist in his proper rank or in *deciphering* the less obvious intentions of his work —C.E.Montague⟩ ⟨the results, so far as they could be *deciphered* from the puzzling procedure and twisted combinations, confirmed what had gone before —*Atlantic*⟩
sol·ven·cy \'sälvənsē, 'sól-\ *n* -ES [¹*solvent* + *-cy*] : the quality or state of being solvent
sol·vend \'=,vend, =='=\ *n* -S [L *solvendus*, gerundive of *solvere* to dissolve] : a dissolved substance in a solution : SOLUTE
¹sol·vent \'sälvənt, 'sól-\ *adj* [L *solvent-*, *solvens*, pres. part. of *solvere* to pay, dissolve] **1** : able or sufficient to pay all legal debts ⟨a ~ merchant⟩ ⟨the estate is ~⟩ **2** : that dissolves or can dissolve : producing a solution or homogeneous mixture ⟨~ fluids⟩ ⟨the ~ action of water⟩ ⟨~ social influences⟩ — **sol·vent·ly** *adv*
²solvent \"\ *n* -S **1** : a substance capable of or used in dissolving or dispersing one or more other substances; *esp* : a liquid component of a solution present in greater amount than the solute : MENSTRUUM 1 ⟨water is a good ~ for many salts, alcohol for many resins, and ether for fats⟩ ⟨the best ~ for a material is usu. related to it in chemical structure —P.O.Powers⟩ — compare PLASTICIZER, THINNER **2** : something that provides a solution (as for a problem) ⟨no ~ has been found for the industrial stagnation⟩ **3** : something that dissipates, disintegrates, or otherwise eliminates or attenuates something and esp. something unwanted ⟨ridicule is a ~ of prejudice⟩
solvent dye *n* : any of a class of dyes that are soluble in varying degree in organic solvents and are usu. insoluble in water — see DYE table I
solvent naphtha *n* : a flammable liquid distillate containing principally xylenes and higher aromatic hydrocarbons, and usu. boiling higher than ligroin, obtained esp. from coal-tar light oils or coke-oven-gas light oils or from petroleum cracking, and used chiefly as a solvent and as a raw material for coumarone-indene resins
solv·er \'sälvə(r), 'sólv- *also* 'sä(ù)v- *or* 'sóv-\ *n* -S : one that solves
solves *pres 3d sing of* SOLVE
solving *pres part of* SOLVE
sol·vol·y·sis \säl'väləsəs, sól-\ *n* [*solvent* + *-o-* + *-lysis*] : a chemical reaction of a solvent and a dissolved substance with the formation typically of one or two or more new compounds : either hydrolysis or an analogous reaction (as alcoholysis or ammonolysis) in which a solvent other than water plays a role similar to that of water in hydrolysis — compare SOLVATION
sol·vo·lyt·ic \'==ə'lid·ik\ *adj* [*solvent* + *-o-* + *-lytic*] : of, relating to, or involving solvolysis
sol·vo·lyze \'==ə,līz\ *vt* -ED/-ING/-S [*solvent* + *-o-* + *-lyze*] : to subject to solvolysis
sol·vus \'sälvəs, 'sól-\ *n, pl* **sol·vi** \-,vī, -,vē\ *also* **solvuses** [NL, fr. L *solvere* to dissolve] : a curve on a temperature-composition diagram indicating the limits of solubility of one solid phase in another — compare LIQUIDUS, SOLID SOLUTION, SOLIDUS
soly *obs var of* SOLELY
soly *abbr* solubility
¹so·ma \'sōmə\ *n* -S [Skt; akin to Av *haoma* haoma, Gk *hyei* it is raining — more at SUCK] **1** : an East Indian leafless vine (*Sarcostemma acidum*) of the family Asclepiadaceae that yields a somewhat acidulous milky juice **2** : an intoxicating plant juice of ancient India used as an offering to the gods and as a drink of immortality by worshipers in Vedic ritual and worshiped in personified form as a Vedic god — compare HAOMA
²soma \"\ *n, pl* **so·ma·ta** \-məd·ə, -ətə\ *also* **somas** *often attrib* [NL *somat-*, *soma*, fr. Gk *sōmat-*, *sōma* body] **1** : the whole of any organism except its germ cells **2** [Gk *sōmat-*, *sōma*] : BODY 1a — opposed to *psyche*
-so·ma \'sōmə\ *n comb form* \-məd·ə, -ətə\ [NL *-somat-*, *-soma*, fr. Gk *sōmat-*, *sōma* body; akin to L *tumēre* to swell — more at THUMB] **1** : one having (such) a body — in generic names in zoology ⟨Dolicho*soma*⟩ ⟨Loxo*soma*⟩ and botany ⟨Crosso*soma*⟩ **2** *pl* **-somas** \-məz\ *or* **-soma·ta** : body ⟨actino*soma*⟩ ⟨hydro*soma*⟩ : region or portion of a body ⟨meso*soma*⟩
somaesthesia *or* **somaesthesis** *var of* SOMESTHESIA
so·mal \'sōməl\ *adj* [²*soma* + *-al*] : SOMATIC
so·ma·li \sō'mälē, sə'-\ *also* **so·mal** \-'mäl\ *n, pl* **somali** *or* **somalis** *also* **somal** *or* **somals** *usu cap* **1 a** : a very tall and dark Cushitic-speaking people of Somaliland apparently of mixed Mediterranean and negroid stock and almost universally Muslim **b** : a member of the Somali people **2** : the Cushitic language of the Somali people
so·ma·lia \sō'mälēə, sə'-, -lyə\ *adj, usu cap* [fr. *Somalia*, former Italian colony in East Africa] : of or from Somalia : of the kind or style prevalent in Somalia : SOMALIAN
¹so·ma·lian \-lēən, -lyən\ *adj, usu cap* [*Somalia* + E *-an*] **1** : of, relating to, or characteristic of Somalia **2** : of, relating to, or characteristic of the people of Somalia
²somalian \"\ *n* -S *cap* : a native or inhabitant of Somalia
somali shilling *also* **so·ma·lo** \-'mä(,)lō\ *n, pl* **somali shillings** *also* **soma·li** \-(,)lē\ *usu cap 1st S* **1** : the basic monetary unit of Somalia — see MONEY table **2** : a coin or note representing one Somali shilling
so many *adj* **1** : constituting an unspecified number ⟨reading . . . *so many* verses before bedtime because it was the Bible —Amy Lowell⟩ **2** : constituting a group or pack ⟨the noblesse stretched in pairs upon logs of wood like *so many* seals upon the rocks —Tobias Smollett⟩
so·ma·plasm \'sōmə,plazəm\ *n* [²*soma* + *-plasm*] : SOMATOPLASM
somat- *or* **somato-** *comb form* [NL, fr. Gk *sōmat-*, *sōmato-*, fr. *sōmat-*, *sōma* body] **1 a** : body ⟨*somatology*⟩ **b** : somatic ⟨*somatize*⟩ : somatic and ⟨*somatopsychic*⟩ **2** : soma ⟨*somatoplasm*⟩
-so·ma·ta \'sōməd·ə, -mətə\ *n pl comb form* [NL, fr. Gk *sōmata*, pl. of *sōmat-*, *sōma* body] : ones having (such) a body — in names of zoological taxa larger than a genus ⟨Hetero*somata*⟩
so·ma·te·ria \,sōmə'tirēə\ *n, cap* [NL, prob. irreg. fr. *somat-* + Gk *erion* wool] : the principal genus of eider ducks
so·mat·ic \sō'mad·ik, sə'-, -atik, -ēk\ *adj* [Gk *sōmatikos*, fr. *sōmat-*, *sōma* body + *-ikos* -ic] **1 a** : of, relating to, or affecting the body or esp. the soma : PHYSICAL, CORPOREAL ⟨~ posture⟩ ⟨~ attitudes⟩ **b** : of, relating to, or affecting the soma as contrasted with reproductive or germ cells ⟨~ cells⟩ **2 a** : of or relating to the wall of the body : SOMATOPLEURIC, PARIETAL — distinguished from *visceral* **b** : of or relating to the trunk — distinguished from *appendicular* **3** : MESOMORPHIC 2 **syn** see BODILY
so·mat·i·cal·ly \-ək(ə)lē, -ēk-, -li\ *adv* : in a somatic manner : in the soma : in terms of the body
somatic antigen *n* : an antigen of the body of the bacterial cell — distinguished from *flagellar antigen*
somatic cavity *n* : BODY CAVITY; *esp* : COELOM
somatic cell *n* : one of the cells of the body of an individual that become differentiated and compose the tissues, organs, and parts of that individual — distinguished from *germ cell*
somatic crossing-over *n* : crossing-over occurring during mitosis whether in germinal or somatic tissue
somatic mutation *n* : change originating in a somatic cell due to chance loss of genes or to genic change and constituting the cause of chimera formation
so·ma·tist \'sōməd·əst\ *n* -S [ISV *somat-* + *-ist*] **1** : an advocate of medical organicism **2** : one who seeks the causes of mental disorders in brain lesions and other physical conditions
so·ma·ti·za·tion \,sōməd·ə'zāshən, -ə,dī'z-, -ətə'z-, -ə,tī'z-\ *n* -S [ISV *somat-* + *-ization*] **1** : the production of physiological dysfunction often resulting in irreversible structural changes by the exaggeration and persistence of an emotional state **2** : the expression of psychological conflict through somatic symptoms including conversion hysteria
so·ma·tize \'sōmə,tīz\ *vb* -ED/-ING/-S [*somat-* + *-ize*] *vt* : to express (as psychological conflicts) through somatic symptoms ~ *vi* : to express psychological conflicts through somatic symptoms
somato- — see SOMAT-
so·ma·to·blast \'sōməd·ə,blast\ *n* [*somat-* + *-blast*] **1 a** : a cleavage cell of an annelid worm that is the precursor of most of the trunk ectoderm, the nervous system, and the nephridia **b** : cleavage cells descended from the primary somatoblast cell of an annelid **2** : the outer layer of cells of the nematogen of a dicyemid mesozoan
so·ma·to·chrome \-,krōm\ *n* [*somat-* + *-chrome*] : a nerve cell having a distinct cytoplasm around its nucleus and taking a deep stain with basic aniline dyes
so·ma·to·cyst \-,sist\ *n* -S [*somat-* + *-cyst*] : an air cavity in the float of a siphonophoran — **so·ma·to·cys·tic** \'===-'sistik\ *adj*
so·ma·to·derm \-,dərm\ *n* -S [*somat-* + *-derm*] : the mesodermal part of the somatopleure
so·ma·to·gen·ic \'===jenik\ *or* **so·ma·to·ge·net·ic** \-jə'ned·ik\ *adj* [*somat-* + *-genic* or *-genetic*] : originating in, affecting, or acting through the somatic cells — distinguished from *psychogenic*; compare BLASTOGENIC
somatogenic variation *n* : a nonheritable character imposed on the soma by environmental conditions
so·ma·to·logical \'===+\ *adj* : of or relating to somatology ⟨~ observations⟩
so·ma·tol·o·gy \,=='täləjē\ *n* -ES [NL *somatologia* study of the body, fr. *somat-* + L *-logia* -logy] : PHYSICAL ANTHROPOLOGY
so·ma·tome \'sōmə,tōm\ *n* -S [Gk *sōma* body + E *-tome* — more at -SOMA] : SOMITE — **so·ma·tom·ic** \'=='tämik\ *adj*
so·ma·to·metric \'sōməd·ə+\ *adj* [ISV *somat-* + *-metric*] : of or relating to somatometry
so·ma·tom·e·try \,=='tämə·trē\ *n* -ES : a branch of anthropometry that is concerned with measurement of the body
so·ma·to·phyte \'==d·ə,fīt\ *n* -S [ISV *somat-* + *-phyte*] : a plant composed of somatic cells that develop chiefly into adult tissue ⟨all higher plants are ~*s*⟩ — compare ASOMATOPHYTE
so·ma·to·phyt·ic \'===ˌfid|ik, -it|, |ēk\ *adj* : of, relating to, or being a somatophyte
so·ma·to·plasm \'==d·ə,plazəm\ *n* [*somat-* + *-plasm*] **1** : protoplasm of somatic cells **2** : somatic cells as opposed to germ cells — compare GERM PLASM
so·ma·to·plas·tic \'===ˌplastik\ *adj* [fr. *somatoplasm*, after E *plasm*: *plastic*] : of, relating to, or constituting somatoplasm
so·ma·to·pleure \'===,plù(ə)r, -ùə\ *n* -S [NL *somatopleura*, fr. *somat-* + Gk *pleura* side — more at PLEURISY] **1** : a complex layer of tissue in the embryo of a craniate vertebrate consisting of the outer of the two layers into which the lateral plate of the mesoderm splits together with the ectoderm that sheathes it externally and giving rise to the body wall and in amniote vertebrates to the amnion and chorion — compare SPLANCHNOPLEURE **2** : a part of an invertebrate embryo that corresponds to but is not necessarily homologous with the vertebrate somatopleure — **so·ma·to·pleu·ric** \'===ˌplùrik\ *adj*
so·ma·to·psychic \'===+\ *adj* [*somat-* + *psychic*] **1** : relating to an individual's notions regarding his own body ⟨a ~ delusion⟩ — compare PSYCHOSOMATIC **2** : of or relating to primary somatic diseases (as syphilis or chorea) which produce secondary mental symptoms
so·ma·to·psychological \'===+\ *adj* [*somat-* + *psychological*] : SOMATOPSYCHIC 2
so·ma·to·splanchnic \"+\ *adj* [*somat-* + *splanchnic*] **1** : of, relating to, or made up of the somatic and splanchnic layers of the mesoderm **2** : of or relating to the body and the viscera
so·ma·to·to·nia \,==='tōnēə\ *n* -S [NL, fr. *somat-* + *-tonia*] : a pattern of temperament typical of the mesomorphic individual and marked by predominance of physical over social or intellectual factors and exhibiting aggressiveness, love of physical activity, vigor, and alertness
¹so·ma·to·ton·ic \'==='tänik\ *adj* [NL *somatotonia* + E *-ic*] : exhibiting somatotonia
²somatotonic \"\ *n* -S : a somatotonic individual : MESOMORPH
so·ma·to·top·ic \'==='täpik\ *also* **so·ma·to·top·i·cal** \-pəkəl\ *adj* [*somat-* + *top-* + *-ic* or *-ical*] : of, relating to, or mediating the orderly and specific relation between particular body regions (as a hand or the tongue) and corresponding motor areas of the brain ⟨the ~ arrangement within the thalamus⟩
so·ma·to·trop·ic \'==='träpik\ *adj* [ISV *somat-* + *-tropic*] : promoting growth ⟨a ~ hormone⟩
so·ma·tot·ro·pin \,sōmə'tä·trəpən\ *also* **so·ma·tot·ro·phin** \-rəfən\ *n* -S [*somatotropin* ISV *somatotropic* + *-in*; *somatotrophin* alter. (influenced by *troph-*) of *somatotropin*] : a growth hormone of the anterior lobe of the pituitary body
¹so·ma·to·type \'sōməd·ə,tīp, sə'mad·ə,-\ *n* [*somat-* + *type*] **1** : body type : PHYSIQUE **2** : one of the types of body-build differentiated by a classificatory system : a classification of human body-build in terms of the relative development of ectomorphic, endomorphic, and mesomorphic components
²somatotype \"\ *vt* : to determine the somatotype of (as a human body) : classify according to physique
so·ma·to·ty·pol·o·gy \'===tī'päləjē\ *n* -ES [*somatotype* + *-o-* + *-logy*] : the study of somatotypes
-soma·tous \'sōməd·əs, ˌsōm-, -mətəs\ *adj comb form* [LL *-somatus*, fr. Gk *-sōmatos*, fr. *sōmat-*, *sōma* body — more at -SOMA] : having (such) a body ⟨macro*somatous*⟩
¹som·ber *or* **som·bre** \'sämbə(r) *sometimes* 'sōm-\ *adj* [F *sombre*] **1** : so shaded or full of shadows as to be dark and gloomy : lacking light or brightness : characterized by gloom or shadow : depressingly dark, dusky, or obscure ⟨narrow, ~ streets —*Amer. Guide Series: Va.*⟩ ⟨the bell-chamber was ~ and almost menacing —Dorothy Sayers⟩ **2 a** (1) : gloomy, sullen, melancholy, or dejected in appearance or mood ⟨the city made him ~ and restless —John Cheever⟩ (2) : of a serious mien : GRAVE ⟨~ . . . merchant dignitaries —J.H. Randall⟩ **b** : of a melancholy, dismal, or depressing character ⟨~ thoughts⟩ ⟨a ~ mood⟩ **3** : conveying gloomy suggestions or ideas : DEPRESSING, GRAVE, MELANCHOLY ⟨took on a more ~ and threatening aspect —*Emporia (Kans.) Gazette*⟩ ⟨know the truth, ~ though it may be —Sir Winston Churchill⟩ **4 a** *of color or a color* : of a dull or heavy cast or shade ⟨~ tone⟩ ⟨a more ~ hue⟩ **b** : having or characterized by a color : dark colored ⟨the ~ leaves of the copper beech —*Amer. Guide Series: N.J.*⟩ ⟨house . . . painted a ~ Puritan color —A.W.Long⟩ **syn** see SERIOUS
²somber *or* **sombre** \"\ *vb* **sombered** *or* **sombred**; **sombered** *or* **sombred**; **sombering** *or* **sombring** \-b(ə)riŋ\ **sombers** *or* **sombres** *vt* : to make somber ~ *vi* : to become or grow somber
³somber *or* **sombre** \"\ *n* -S : GLOOM
som·ber·ly *or* **som·bre·ly** *adv* : in a somber manner ⟨answered him flatly and ~ —Pearl Buck⟩ ⟨stared ~ at the . . . person —Booth Tarkington⟩
som·ber·ness *or* **som·bre·ness** *n* -ES : the quality or state of being somber
som·bra \'sämbrə\ *n* -S [MexSp, fr. Sp, shade, prob. modif. (influenced by Sp *sol* sun, fr. L) of L *umbra* — more at UMBRAGE, SOLAR] : the shady side or section of a bullfight arena — compare SOL
som·bre·ro \səm'bre(,)rō, säm-\ *n* -S [Sp, hat, canopy, fr. *sombra* shade] **1** *obs* : an Oriental sunshade **2** : a high-crowned hat made of felt or straw with a very wide brim usu. rolled at the edges and worn esp. in the Southwest and Mexico

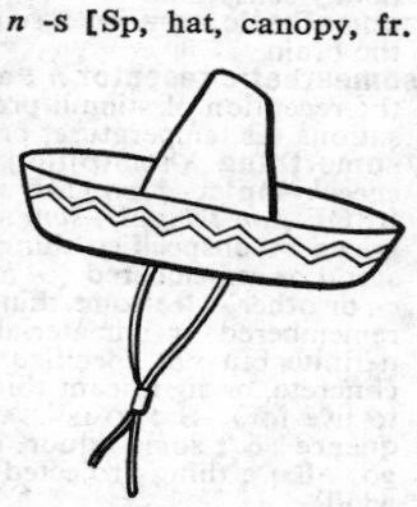
sombrero 2

som·brous \'sämbrəs\ *adj* [F *sombre* somber + E *-ous*] : characterized by or manifesting somberness : SOMBER ⟨an avenue of tall and ~ pines —H.W.Longfellow⟩ ⟨the ~ and heavy sound of the billows —Sir Walter Scott⟩
¹some \(')səm\ *adj* [ME *som*, adj. & pron., fr. OE *sum*, adj. & pron.; akin to OHG *sum*, adj. & pron., some, ON *sumr*, adj. & pron., some, Goth *sums*, adj. & pron., some, Gk *hamē* somehow, Skt *sama* any, *sama* level, equal, same — more at SAME] **1** : being one unknown, undetermined, or unspecified unit or being or thing ⟨~ person knocked at my door⟩ ⟨I'll do it ~ day⟩ — sometimes used as a correlative to *another* or *other* ⟨he is spending the summer at ~ beach or another⟩ ⟨~ day or other make us a visit⟩ **2** : being one, a part, or an unspecified number of something (as a class, group, species, collection, or range of possibilities) named or contextually implied : being an unspecified or ill-defined individual, kind, or example of something ⟨this criticism applies to ~ students only⟩ ⟨~ gems are hard but the majority are soft⟩ ⟨protective coloring occurs in ~ birds⟩ ⟨the hartebeest is ~ African animal⟩ ⟨requested help from ~ man in the audience⟩ **3** : worthy of notice or consideration : far from negligible : more or less important or striking ⟨that was ~ race⟩ ⟨that was ~ party⟩ **4** : being one of, one kind of, or an undetermined proportion of : being always at least one but often a few and sometimes all of — used as a sign of particularity to indicate that the logical proposition in which it occurs is asserted only of a subclass or certain existent members of the class denoted by the term which it modifies
²some \'səm\ *pron, sing or pl in constr* [ME *som*, adj. & pron., fr. OE *sum*, adj. & pron.] **1** : some one : one person or thing among a number ⟨~ of these days⟩ **2** : one indeterminate quantity, portion, or number as distinguished from the rest : a part of something (as a number or group of persons) ⟨~ had webbed feet, ~ had talons⟩ **3** : some more : an indefinite additional amount or degree ⟨he ran a mile and then ~⟩
³some \(')səm\ *indefinite article* [¹*some*] : being of an unspecified but appreciable or not inconsiderable quantity, amount, extent, or degree : more than a little : being in number at least or often more than a few ⟨we have ~ good honey⟩ ⟨there is ~ heat in this radiator⟩ ⟨they have ~ land by the river⟩
⁴some \'səm\ *adv* [¹*some*] **1** : ABOUT — usu. used before a numeral ⟨a village of ~ eighty houses⟩ ⟨~ two or three persons⟩ **2** : in some degree or extent : SOMEWHAT ⟨felt ~ better after just one mouthful⟩
¹-some \,səm; *when* n *immediately precedes, as in* "*winsome*", (t)səm\ *adj suffix* [ME *-som*, fr. OE *-sum*; akin to OFris *-sum* -some, OHG *-sam*, ON *-samr*, Goth *-sama* -some, *sama* same — more at SAME] : characterized by a (specified) thing, quality, state, or action ⟨awe*some*⟩ ⟨burden*some*⟩ ⟨cuddle*some*⟩ ⟨lone*some*⟩
²-some \"\ *n suffix* -S [ME (northern dial.) *-sum*, fr. ME *sum*, *som*, pron., one, a certain one, some, fr. OE *sum*, pron., one, a certain one, some, one of a group of (so many) members (in such expressions as *syxa sum* one of a group of six members) — more at SOME] : group of (so many) members and esp. persons ⟨four*some*⟩ ⟨two*some*⟩
³-some \,sōm\ *n comb form* -S [NL *-somat-*, *-soma* -soma — more at -SOMA] **1** : -SOMA 2 ⟨chromo*some*⟩ ⟨tropho*some*⟩ ⟨ecto*some*⟩ **2** : chromosome ⟨mono*some*⟩
⁴-some \"\ *adj comb form* [ISV, fr. NL *soma* body, fr. Gk *sōma* — more at -SOMA] : having (such) a body ⟨eury*some*⟩
¹some·body \'səm,bädē, -(,)bədē, -di\ *pron* [ME *sum body*, fr. *sum*, *som* some + *body*] : one or some person of no certain or known identity : a person indeterminate ⟨if you leave the door open ~ will be sure to come in⟩ ⟨there should be ~ at the office at this hour⟩
²somebody \"\ *n* : a person of position or importance ⟨think oneself a ~⟩ — often used without article ⟨the desire to be ~ is one of the strongest of human motives —*Amer. Quarterly*⟩
some·day \'səm,dā\ *adv* [ME *sum day*, fr. *sum*, *som* some + *day*] : at some time in the future ⟨~ a beginning must be made —Lewis Mumford⟩ ⟨may ~ choose to reassert themselves —John Gunther⟩
somedeal \'=,=\ *adv* [ME *somdel*, fr. OE *sume dǣle*, dat. of *sum dǣl* some part, fairly large amount, fr. *sum* some + *dǣl* part — more at DEAL] *archaic* : in some degree or measure : SOMEWHAT
somegate \'=,=\ *adv* [¹*some* + *gate* (way)] *Scot* : SOMEHOW, SOMEWHERE
somehow \'=,=\ *adv* : in one way or another : in some way not yet known or designated : by some means ⟨the thing must be done ~⟩ ⟨he lives ~⟩ ⟨the evidence needed was ~ obtained

—G.G.Coulton⟩ ⟨he has ~ or other got the entire management —Sir Walter Scott⟩

some·one \'səm(,)wən\ *pron* [ME *sum oon,* fr. *sum, som* some + *oon* one] **:** some person **:** SOMEBODY ⟨hoping that ~ will suddenly find out —*Contemporary Rev.*⟩ ⟨then you meet ~ . . . you like —John Van Druten⟩

someplace \'ᵻ,ᵻ\ *adv* **:** SOMEWHERE ⟨topples overboard ~ in the middle of the sea —Robert Evett⟩ ⟨really had ~ to go that day —*New Yorker*⟩ ⟨~ in this mess of masonry . . . was a girl —Richard Bissell⟩

somer *obs var of* SUMMER

som·ers \'səmə(r)z\ *adv* [alter. of *somewheres*] *chiefly dial* **:** SOMEWHERE

¹som·er·sault *also* **sum·mer·sault** \'səmə(r),sȯlt\ *n* -s [MF *sombresaut* leap, alter. of *soubresault,* prob. fr. (assumed) OProv *sobresaut,* fr. OProv *sobre* over (fr. L *super*) + *saut* leap, jump, fr. L *saltus* — more at OVER, SALT] **1 :** an act of turning end over end: as **a :** a stunt or maneuver in which a person stoops down and while remaining in a tuck position rolls end over end on the floor either forward or backward **b :** a leap or jump in which a person turns his heels over his head forward or backward before landing on the floor **c :** a front or back dive executed in tuck, pike, or layout position in which the diver rotates end over end one or more times before entering the water **2 :** an action held to resemble a somersault **:** a reversal of policy, tactics, or position **:** a complete overturn ⟨saying that our present Far Eastern policy represents a complete ~ —*New Republic*⟩ ⟨led Bulgaria in its complete ~ from the camp of the Axis into the fold of the Allies —E.P.Snow⟩

²somersault *also* **summersault** \"\ *vi* -ED/-ING/-S **:** to turn or execute a somersault

¹som·er·set *also* **sum·mer·set** -,set, *usu* -ed·+V\ *n* -s [by alter. (influence of *Somerset,* county in southwest England)] **:** SOMERSAULT

²somerset *also* **summerset** \"\ *vb* -ED/-ING/-S *vt* **:** to fling in a somersault **:** cause to turn a somersault **~** *vi* **:** SOMERSAULT

som·er·set·shire \'səmərsət,shi(ə)r; -məsət,shiə, -i(ə)r; -,set-, -,shə(r)\ *or* **som·er·set** \-,sə̇lt, -,se\, *usu* \d·+V\ *adj, usu cap* [fr. *Somersetshire, Somerset,* county in southwest England] **:** of or from the county of Somerset, England **:** of the kind or style prevalent in Somerset

som·er·ville \'səmə(r),vil, -,vəl\ *adj, usu cap* [fr. *Somerville,* city in northeast Massachusetts] **:** of or from the city of Somerville, Mass. ⟨a *Somerville* street⟩ **:** of the kind or style prevalent in Somerville

-somes *pl of* -SOME

som·esthesia \¦sōm+\ *also* **som·esthesis** \(')sōm+\ *or* **som·aesthesia** \¦sōm+\ *or* **som·aesthesis** \(')sōm+\ *n, pl* **somesthesias** *also* **somesthesises** [NL, fr. ²*soma* + *esthesia* or *esthesis*] **:** body sensibility including the cutaneous and kinesthetic senses

som·esthetic \¦sōm+\ *adj* [fr. *somesthesia,* after such pairs as E *anesthesia: anesthetic*] **:** of, relating to, or concerned with bodily sensations

somesthetic area *n* **:** a sensory area of either parietal lobe of the brain

somesthetic receptor *n* **:** a sensory end organ concerned with the reception of stimuli producing one of the generalized sensations (as temperature, pressure, position, or movement)

¹some·thing \'səm(p)thiŋ, -thēn, *in rapid, informal, or dial speech* -mpᵊm\ *pron* [ME *sum thing, sum thing* (noun phrase), fr. OE *sum thing,* fr. *sum* some + *thing*] **1 a :** some undetermined or unspecified thing **:** some thing not definitely understood or remembered ⟨~ must be done about it⟩ ⟨he muttered ~ or other⟩ **b :** some thing (as a name or part of a name) not remembered or immaterial ⟨the twelve ~ train⟩ **2 :** some definite but not specified thing **:** an unnamed but positive, concrete, or significant thing — opposed to *nothing* ⟨he has ~ to live for⟩ **3 :** SOMEWHAT **4 :** a person or thing of consequence **5 :** some liquor, drink, or food ⟨have ~ before you go⟩ **6 :** a thing projected or in prospect ⟨there was ~ in the wind⟩

²something \"\ *adv* [ME *sumthing,* fr. *sum thing, som thing* (noun phrase)] **1 :** in some degree **:** to some extent **:** SOMEWHAT ⟨the scarcely ambiguous answer was ~ softened —J.A. Froude⟩ ⟨~ under a quarter of an hour —G.N.Boothby⟩ ⟨a man of ~ less than mediocre abilities —Edmund Wilson⟩ **2 :** to a high degree **:** EXTREMELY, VERY ⟨raved ~ fierce⟩ ⟨swears ~ awful⟩

³something \"\ *n* [¹*something*] **:** a thing of an unspecified or indeterminate nature ⟨felt the presence of an unknown ~⟩

⁴something \"\ *vt* -ED/-ING/-S [¹*something*] **:** DAMN, CURSE

some·thing·ness *n* -ES **:** the quality or state of being something **:** real or material existence

¹some·time \'səm,tīm\ *adv* [ME *sum tim, sum time,* fr. *sum* some + *tim, time* time] **1 a** *obs* **:** at some past time **:** at a certain time or on a particular occasion in the past **:** ONCE ⟨there was ~ . . . founded a certain house —Friar Rush⟩ **b** *archaic* **:** in the past **:** at one time **:** in former times **:** FORMERLY ⟨a large marble stone ~ inlaid with brass —Edward Ledwich⟩ **2** *archaic* **:** once in a while **:** OCCASIONALLY, SOMETIMES ⟨but ~ fear is the beginning of wisdom —Timothy Puller⟩ **3 :** at one time or other hereafter **:** at some time in the future **:** on a future occasion ⟨I'll do it ~⟩ **4 :** at some indefinite or indeterminate time **:** at some not specified or definitely known point of time **:** at some time or other ⟨~ in 1710 or 1711 he was taken to a neighboring town —J.W.Krutch⟩ ⟨~ years ago a . . . sea had filled the valley —R.O.Easton⟩

²sometime \"\ *adj* **1 :** having been formerly **:** FORMER, LATE ⟨former military officer, ~ newspaper editor —Dixon Wecter⟩ ⟨~ professor of history at a nearby university⟩ **2** *South & Midland* **:** erratic in loyalties and dependability ⟨a ~ friend⟩

¹some·times \'səm,tīmz *also* (,)səm't-\ *adv* [¹*some* + *times,* pl. of *time,* n.] **1 :** on some occasions **:** at times **:** now and then **:** OCCASIONALLY ⟨writes . . . ~ in captious criticism of some policy or other —Ernestine Evans⟩ ⟨illustrated by excellent and ~ beautiful photographs —*Geog. Jour.*⟩ **2** *obs* **a :** ONCE **b :** FORMERLY

²sometimes \"\ *adj, archaic* **:** FORMER, SOMETIME ⟨excelled only by her ~ tutoress —Charlotte Smith⟩

some·way \'səm,wā\ *also* **some·ways** \-āz\ *adv* [*someway* fr. ME *sum way,* fr. *sum, som* some + *way; someways* fr. ME *som wayes,* fr. *sumes weis,* gen. of *sum wei* (noun phrase) some way, fr. *sum, som* some + *wei, way* way] **:** in some way or manner **:** by some means **:** SOMEHOW ⟨tried to make him ~ decent —James Joyce⟩ ⟨~ . . . finding money to buy things —W.A. White⟩

¹some·what \'səm,(h)wät, -,(h)wət, *usu* \d·+V; *sometimes* ᵻ'ᵻ\ *pron* [ME *somewhat,* fr. *som* some + *what*] **1 :** something (as an amount or degree) that is indefinite or unspecified **:** a part, more or less ⟨he told them ~ of his adventures⟩ ⟨neglect ~ of his duty⟩ **2 :** some unspecified, undetermined, or indeterminate thing **:** SOMETHING **3 :** one (as a previously specified person, thing, or action) having to a greater or lesser extent the character, qualities, or nature of something else ⟨he is ~ of a connoisseur⟩ **4 :** one (as a person or thing) that is important or noteworthy

²somewhat \"\ *adv* [ME *somwhat,* fr. *somwhat,* pron.] **:** in some degree or measure **:** to a certain slight or small extent **:** a little **:** SLIGHTLY ⟨the terrain roughens ~ as the watershed . . . is approached —*Amer. Guide Series: Texas*⟩ ⟨the total was ~ above earlier estimates⟩ ⟨speech in ~ different words —Edward Sapir⟩ ⟨the ~ ornately spired . . . church —*Amer. Guide Series: N.H.*⟩ ⟨~ at a loss for words⟩

³somewhat \"\ *n* -s [¹*somewhat*] **1 :** an undetermined or unspecified quality, character, or amount ⟨matter is an unknown ~ —George Berkeley⟩ **2** [trans. of G *etwas*] *Hegelianism* **:** a reality to which belongs negation as a limit **:** a limited reality

somewhen \'ᵻ,ᵻ\ *adv* **:** at some time or other **:** at some indefinite or unknown time **:** SOMETIME ⟨born somewhere and ~ —Marvin Farber⟩ ⟨imposed upon somebody, somehow, somewhere, and ~ —William James⟩

¹somewhere \'ᵻ(,)ᵻ\ *adv* [ME *somwher,* fr. *som* some + *wher* where] **1 a :** in or at some place unknown, unspecified, or undetermined **:** in one place or another ⟨a bleak farmhouse ~ in rural America —Harrison Smith⟩ **b :** in a book or other writing **:** in some part of a literary work ⟨makes a reference to it ~⟩ **2 a :** to some unknown or unspecified place ⟨he's ~ gone to dinner —Shak.⟩ ⟨go ~ out of town⟩ **b :** to a place unspecified or unknown but symbolizing positive accomplishment or progress ⟨getting ~ with his program —Michael James⟩ ⟨seemed to feel that the nine days of talks . . . had led ~ —*N. Y. Times*⟩ **3 :** APPROXIMATELY ⟨~ between five million and twenty million more Democrats —R.H.Rovere⟩ ⟨~ about nine o'clock⟩

²somewhere \"\ *n* -s **:** an undetermined or unnamed place ⟨~ in France⟩

somewheres \'ᵻ(,)ᵻ\ *adv* [¹*somewhere* + -*s*] *chiefly dial* **:** SOMEWHERE

somewhile \'ᵻ,ᵻ\ *adv* [ME *som while,* fr. *som* some + *while*] *archaic* **:** at some unspecified time **:** at one time or another **:** at times **:** SOMETIMES ⟨with which all lives worth living have been ~ brightened —John Nichol⟩

somewhiles \'ᵻ,ᵻ\ *adv* [¹*some* + *whiles,* pl. of *while,* n.] *archaic* **:** SOMEWHILE

somewhither \'ᵻ,ᵻᵻ\ *adv* **:** to some place **:** SOMEWHERE 2a ⟨the poor young king . . . must go ~ —Thomas Carlyle⟩

somewise \'ᵻ,ᵻ\ *adv* [ME *somwise,* fr. *som* some + *wise,* n.] **:** SOMEWAY — used chiefly in the phrase *in somewise* ⟨the father's, brother's love — was changed . . . in ~ —D.G. Rossetti⟩

-somi *pl of* -SOMUS

-so·mia \'sōmēə\ *n comb form* -s [NL, fr. ²*soma* + -*ia*] **:** condition of having (such) a body ⟨nano*somia*⟩

-so·mic \'sōmik, -mēk\ *adj comb form* [ISV ³-*some* + -*ic*] **:** having or being a body of chromosomes of which one or more but not all members exhibit (such) a degree of ploidy ⟨hexa*somic*⟩ ⟨mono*somic*⟩

som·ite \'sō,mīt\ *n* -s [ISV *som-* (fr. Gk *sōma* body) + -*ite* — more at -SOMA] **:** one of the longitudinal series of segments into which the body of many animals (as articulates and vertebrates) is more or less distinctly divided **:** METAMERE — **so·mit·ic** \sō'mid·ik\ *adj*

som·ma \'sämə\ *n* -s [It, summit, sum, fr. L *summa* — more at SUM] **:** the rim of a volcanic crater or caldera

som·me·lier \,sȯməl'yā\ *n* -s [F, wine steward, butler, fr. MF, court official charged with transportation of supplies, pack animal driver, fr. OProv *saumalier* pack animal driver, fr. *sauma* pack animal, load of a pack animal, fr. (assumed) VL *sauma* packsaddle (whence ML *sauma*), fr. LL *sagma* — more at SUMPTER] **:** a waiter in a restaurant who has charge of wines and their service **:** a wine steward

somnambul- *comb form* [NL, fr. *somnambulus* somnambulist, fr. L *somnus* sleep + -*ambulus* (as in *funambulus* funambulist) — more at SOMNOLENT, FUNAMBULIST] **:** somnambulism **:** somnambulist ⟨*somnambular*⟩

som·nam·bu·lant \säm'nambyələnt\ *adj* [*somnambul-* + -*ant*] **:** walking or addicted to walking while asleep

som·nam·bu·lar \-lə(r)\ *adj* [*somnambul-* + -*ar*] **:** of, relating to, or characterized by somnambulism

som·nam·bu·late \-,lāt, *usu* -ād·+V\ *vi* [*somnambul-* + -*ate*] **:** to walk when asleep

som·nam·bu·la·tion \ᵻ,ᵻᵻ'lāshən\ *n* [NL *somnambulation-, somnambulatio,* fr. *somnambul-* + L -*ation-,* -*atio* -ation] **:** the action of walking in sleep

som·nam·bule \ᵻ'ᵻ,byül\ *n* -s [F, fr. NL *somnambulus*] **:** SOMNAMBULIST

som·nam·bu·lic \(')säm¦nambyəlik\ *adj* [ISV *somnambul-* + -*ic*] **:** SOMNAMBULISTIC

som·nam·bu·lism \ᵻ'ᵻᵻ,lizəm\ *n* -s [NL *somnambulismus,* fr. *somnambul-* + L -*ismus* -ism] **1 :** the action of walking or the performance of other motor acts while asleep and specif. when the actions are not recalled after waking **2 :** an action performed while asleep

som·nam·bu·list \-ləst\ *n* -s [*somnambul-* + -*ist*] **:** one who is subject to somnambulism **:** one who walks in his sleep **:** SLEEPWALKER

som·nam·bu·lis·tic \(')ᵻ¦ᵻᵻ¦listik, -tēk\ *adj* **1 :** of, relating to, or affected by somnambulism ⟨a ~ state⟩ **2 :** of, relating to, or having the characteristics of a somnambulist

som·nam·bu·lis·ti·cal·ly \-tək(ə)lē\ *adv* **:** in the manner of a somnambulist ⟨moves about the stage ~ —Francis Fergusson⟩

somni- *comb form* [L, fr. *somnus*] **:** sleep ⟨*somni*facient⟩

som·ni·al \'sämnēəl\ *adj* [L, fr. LL *somnialis,* fr. L *somnium* dream + -*alis* -al; akin to L *somnus* sleep] **:** of or relating to sleep or dreams ⟨vivid recollections of . . . bizarre ~ experiences —H.W.Cushing⟩

¹som·ni·fa·cient \¦sämnə¦fāshənt\ *adj* [*somni-* + -*facient*] **:** HYPNOTIC 1

²somnifacient \"\ *n* **:** HYPNOTIC 1

som·nif·er·ous \(')säm¦nif(ə)rəs\ *adj* [L *somnifer* somniferous (fr. *somni-* + -*fer*) + E -*ous* — more at -FER] **:** tending to induce sleep **:** SOPORIFIC ⟨a ~ potion⟩ ⟨~ prose⟩ — **som·nif·er·ous·ly** *adv*

som·nif·ic \(')säm¦nifik\ *adj* [L *somnificus,* fr. *somni-* + -*ficus* -fic] **:** SOMNIFEROUS

som·nil·o·quist \säm'niləkwə̇st\ *n* -s [*somni-* + -*loquist* (as in *ventriloquist*)] **:** one who talks in his sleep

som·nil·o·quy \-kwē\ *n* -ES [ISV *somni-* + -*loquy* (as in E *ventriloquy*)] **:** the action or practice of talking in sleep

som·ni·o·sus \,sämnē'ōsəs\ *n, cap* [NL, fr. LL, sleepy, fr. L *somnium* dream + -*osus* -ose] **:** a genus of sharks (suborder Squaloidea) to which the Greenland shark belongs

som·nip·a·thy \säm'nipəthē\ *n* -ES [ISV *somni-* + -*pathy*] **:** abnormal or disordered sleep (as in a hypnotic state)

som·niv·o·len·cy \ᵻ'nivələnsē\ *n* -ES [*somni-* + -*volency* (fr. L *volentia* will, inclination, fr. *volent-, volens* — pres. part. of *velle* to will, wish — + -*ia* -y) — more at WILL] **:** SOPORIFIC

som·no·lence \'sämnələn(t)s\ *also* **som·no·len·cy** \-lənsē, -si\ *n, pl* **somnolences** *also* **somnolencies** [*somnolence* fr. ME *sompnolence,* fr. MF, fr. LL *somnolentia,* fr. L *somnolentus* somnolent + -*ia* -y; *somnolency* fr. LL *somnolentia*] **:** inclination to sleep **:** DROWSINESS, SLEEPINESS — compare HYPERSOMNIA

som·no·lent \-lənt\ *adj* [ME *sompnolent,* fr. MF fr. L *somnolentus,* fr. *somnus* sleep; akin to OE *swefn* dream, sleep, OHG *intswebben* to put to sleep, ON *svefn* dream, sleep, Gk *hypnos* sleep, Skt *svapna*] **1 :** tending to induce drowsiness or sleepiness ⟨the sound had a ~ effect⟩ **2 a :** inclined to sleep **:** heavy with sleep **:** DROWSY, SLEEPY ⟨fasting and watching had made him more than usually ~ —R.H.Barham⟩ **b :** marked by sleepiness, drowsiness, or slowness ⟨the ~ river scene⟩ ⟨a ~ country village⟩

som·no·lent·ly *adv* **:** in a somnolent manner **:** DROWSILY

som·no·rif·ic \¦sämnə¦rifik, -fēk\ *adj* [blend of *somnific* and *soporific*] **:** SOMNIFEROUS

¹so much *adv* [ME *so muche* (adverb phrase), fr. ¹*so* + *muche,* adv., much] **:** by the amount indicated or suggested ⟨if they lose their way, *so much* the better for us⟩

²so much *adj* [ME *so muche* (adjective phrase) such a quantity of, fr. ¹*so* + *muche,* adj., much] **1 :** of an equal amount — often used as an intensive ⟨the house burned like *so much* paper⟩ **2 :** of an unspecified amount — often used as an intensive ⟨the common notion of a classic or romantic literature is *so much* nonsense —Irving Kolodin⟩

³so much *pron* [ME *so muche,* fr. *so muche* (adjective phrase)] **1 :** something (as an amount or price) unspecified or undetermined ⟨charge *so much* a mile⟩ **2 :** that is all that can be or is to be said or done now ⟨*so much* for the history of the case⟩

so much as *adv* [ME *so muche as,* fr. *so muche* (adverb phrase) + *as*] **:** EVEN ⟨cannot recall that . . . their descendants were *so much as* mentioned in all that time —R.H.Shryock⟩

-so·mus \'sōməs\ *n comb form, pl* **-so·mi** \-,mī\ *or* **-somuses** [NL, fr. Gk *sōma* body — more at -SOMA] **:** one having (such) a body or (so many) bodies ⟨di*somus*⟩ ⟨nano*somus*⟩

¹son \'sən\ *n* -s [ME *sone,* fr. OE *sunu;* akin to OHG *sun* son, ON *sonr,* Goth *sunus,* Gk *hyios,* Skt *sūnu* son, *sūte* he begets] **1 a :** a male offspring of human beings ⟨a family consisting of two ~s⟩ **b :** a male child ⟨a playground for the ~s and daughters of the community⟩ **c :** a male who assumes the role or status of the offspring of human parents (as an adopted child or son-in-law) **d :** a male descendant — usu. used in pl. ⟨the modern-day ~s of early pioneers⟩ **2** *cap* **:** the second person of the Trinity **3 :** the male offspring of an animal (as a horse or dog) **4 :** a person closely associated with or deriving from a nation, school, race, belief, or any other formative agent ⟨a nation robbed by war of most of her ~s⟩ — often used with *of* ⟨the ~s of modern technology⟩

²son \'sōn\ *n, pl* **so·nes** \'sō(,)nās\ [AmerSp, fr. Sp, sound, prob. fr. OProv, fr. L *sonus*] **1 :** a folk song of Cuba, Mexico, and Central America **2 a :** a Latin American ballroom dance popular in Cuba and coastal Mexico **b :** the musical accompaniment of such a dance

son- *or* **soni-** *or* **sono-** *comb form* [L *son-, soni-,* fr. *sonus* — more at SOUND] **:** sound ⟨*sonal*⟩ ⟨*sonification*⟩ ⟨*sonobuoy*⟩

son *abbr* **1** sonata **2** southern

so·na·ble \'sōnəbəl\ *adj* [L *sonabilis* noisy, fr. *sonare* to sound + -*bilis* -able] **:** that may be sounded

so·nal \'sōnᵊl\ *adj* [*son-* + -*al*] **:** SONIC — **so·nal·ly** \-nᵊlē\ *adv*

so·nance \'sōnən(t)s\ *n* -s [L *sonare* + E -*ance*] **:** SOUND, SONANCY ⟨the far-off mellow ~ of a cowbell —Edna Ferber⟩

so·nan·cy \-nənsē, -si\ *n* -ES [¹*sonant* + -*cy*] **:** the quality or state of being sonant

¹so·nant \-nənt\ *adj* [L *sonant-, sonans,* pres. part. of *sonare* to sound — more at SOUND] **1** *of a speech sound* **:** VOICED — opposed to *surd* **2** *of a consonant* **:** SYLLABIC

²sonant \"\ *n* -s **1 :** a voiced sound **2 :** a syllabic consonant

so·nan·tic \sō'nantik\ *adj, of a consonant* **:** SYLLABIC

so·nant·ize \'sōnən,tīz\ *vt* -ED/-ING/-S **:** VOICE

¹sonant-surd \¦ᵻᵻ¦ᵻ\ *adj, of a sound* **:** beginning voiced and ending voiceless

²sonant-surd \"\ *n* **:** a sonant-surd sound

¹so·nar \sō'när\ *n* -s [Hindi *sonār,* fr. Skt *suvarṇakāra,* fr. *suvarṇa* gold (fr. *su-* good + *varṇa* color) + -*kāra* worker (fr. *kr̥noti* he makes); prob. akin to Skt *vr̥noti* he covers, holds back — more at WEIR, KARMA] **:** a member of a Hindu artisan caste of goldsmiths and silversmiths

²so·nar \'sō,när, -nä(r\ *n* -s [*sound navigation ranging*] **:** an apparatus that detects the presence and location of a submerged object (as a submarine or underwater mine) by means of sonic and ultrasonic waves which are reflected back to it from the object — compare ECHO RANGING, SOUND RANGING

sonar·man \'ᵻ,ᵻmən\ *n, pl* **sonarmen :** an enlisted man in the navy who operates sonar equipment

so·na·ta \sə'nädˑə, -ätə\ *n* -s [It, fr. *sonare* to sound, fr. L] **:** an instrumental musical composition: as **a :** an early instrumental composition in movements without characteristic structure — see SONATA DA CHIESA, SONATA DA CAMERA **b :** an extended composition for one or two instruments usu. in three or four movements which are contrasted in rhythm and mood but related in tonality and which usu. have an organic unity of sentiment and style — compare SONATA FORM

sonata da cam·era \-də'kam(ə)rə\ *n* [It, lit., chamber sonata] **:** a 17th and 18th century instrumental composition for two or more instruments with continuo consisting chiefly of dance movements

sonata da chie·sa \-dəkē'äzə\ *n* [It, lit., church sonata] **:** a 17th and 18th century instrumental composition for two or more instruments with continuo usu. in four movements of which one or more are in fugato style

sonata form *n* **1 :** the musical form of a sonata used not only in the sonata proper but also in the concerto, symphony, and string quartet and other chamber music **2 :** a type of musical structure distinctive of the first movement of the sonata usu. based on two themes or subjects presented in different keys often with transitional episodes and consisting of an exposition giving the principal subject in the tonic key and the secondary subject usu. in the dominant key if the tonic key is major but otherwise in the relative key, a development giving a full thematic working out of one or both subjects, and a recapitulation repeating both subjects in the original key and ending with a coda

son·a·ti·na \,sänə'tēnə\ *also* **son·a·tine** \¦sänə¦tēn\ *n, pl* **sonatinas** \,ᵻᵻ'tēnəz\ *or* **sonati·ne** \,ᵻᵻ'tē(,)nā\ *also* **sonatines** \¦ᵻᵻ¦tēnz\ [*sonatina* fr. It, dim. of *sonata; sonatine* fr. F, fr. It *sonatina*] **:** a short condensed sonata usu. with little or no development section

so·na·tion \sō'nāshən\ *n* -s [ML *sonation-, sonatio,* fr. L *sonatus* (past part. of *sonare* to sound) + -*ion-,* -*io* -ion] **:** a giving forth of sound **:** SOUNDING

son·chus \'säŋkəs\ *n, cap* [NL, fr. L, sow thistle, fr. Gk *sonchos*] **:** a genus of Old World herbs (family Compositae) comprising the sow thistles and having coarse often spiny-tipped foliage, heads of yellow flowers, and ribbed achenes crowned with soft white pappus

son·dage \(')sän¦däzh\ *n, pl* **son·dages** \-zh(əz)\ [F, lit., sounding, fr. *sonder* to sound + -*age* — more at SOUND] **:** a sounding of the earth (as by boring or digging) preliminary to archaeological excavation **:** a trial excavation

sonde \'sänd\ *n* -s [F, lit., sounding line — more at SOUND] **:** any of various devices for testing physical and meteorological conditions at high altitudes above the earth's surface

son·de·li \sän'dälē\ *n* -s [Kannada *sonḍili,* fr. *sunḍa* muskshrew + *ili* rat] **:** MUSKSHREW 1

sone \'sōn\ *n* -s [ISV, fr. L *sonus* sound — more at SOUND] **:** a subjective unit of loudness for a given listener equal to the loudness of a 1000-cycle sound that has an intensity 40 decibels above the listener's own threshold

sones *pl of* SON

song \'sȯŋ *also* 'säŋ\ *n* -s [ME *song, sang,* fr. OE; akin to OHG *sang* song, ON *söngr,* Goth *saggws* song, OE *singan* to sing — more at SING] **1 a :** the act of singing ⟨rejoice in ~⟩ **b :** the art of creating or singing vocal compositions ⟨a people famous for their ~⟩ **2 :** poetical composition ⟨a hero honored in ~ and story⟩ **3 a :** a short musical composition made up of mutually dependent words and music which together produce a unique aesthetic response — compare LIED **b :** a group or collection of such compositions ⟨gather and preserve popular ~ —Louise Pound⟩ **4 :** a distinctive sound **:** characteristic noise ⟨the ~ of the wind⟩ ⟨the ~ of birds⟩ **5 a :** a melody or musical setting for a lyric poem or ballad ⟨whistle a ~⟩ **b :** an instrumental composition displaying or suggesting the technique or quality of vocal music **6 a :** the words that are sung with or belong to a particular musical composition **:** LYRICS **b :** a poem of limited length often stanzaic and easily set to music ⟨Shakespeare's ~s⟩ **7 a :** a habitual, temperamental, or characteristic manner (as of speaking, reacting, or arguing) ⟨the same old ~ of the party politician⟩ **b :** a violent, abusive, or noisy reaction ⟨put up quite a ~⟩ **8 :** a small amount — used with *for* ⟨a house that sold for a ~⟩

song and dance *n* **1 :** a theatrical performance (as a vaudeville act) combining singing and dancing **2 :** a statement or explanation interesting in itself but not necessarily true or pertinent ⟨gave me a *song and dance* about how busy he was⟩

songbird \'ᵻ,ᵻ\ *n* **1 :** a bird that utters a succession of musical tones; *esp* **:** a bird of the suborder Passeres **2 :** a female singer

songbook \'ᵻ,ᵻ\ *n* **:** a collection of songs; *specif* **:** a book of hymns or other vocal music

song box *n* **:** SYRINX 3

songcraft \'ᵻ,ᵻ\ *n* **:** the art of making songs or verses

song cycle *n* **:** a group of songs based on the same general subject or having some other unifying feature

songfest \'ᵻ,ᵻ\ *n* **:** an informal session of group singing of popular or folk songs

song form *n* **:** the form of a song, dance, or similar short musical composition in binary or ternary measure

song·ful \'ᵻfəl\ *adj* **:** of or relating to singing **:** MELODIOUS — **song·ful·ly** \-fəlē, -li\ *adv* — **song·ful·ness** \-nə̇s\ *n* -ES

son·ghai \säŋ'gī\ *also* **son·ghoi** *or* **so'ngoi** *or* **son·ghay** \-'gī\ *n, pl* **songhai** *or* **songhais** *usu cap* **1 a :** a Sudanese people living below Timbuktu in the bend of the Niger that are mostly Muslim **b :** a member of such people **2 :** the language of the Songhai people used widely as a language of commerce throughout the middle Niger valley **3 :** a language family consisting only of Songhai and a few closely related languages or dialects (as perhaps Dyerma)

son·gish *also* **son·geesh** \sän'gēsh\ *n, pl* **songish** *or* **songishes** *also* **songeesh** *or* **songeeshes** *usu cap* **1 a :** a Salishan people of Vancouver Island and San Juan Island, Wash. **b :** a member of such people **2 :** the language of the Songish people

son·gle \'säŋgəl\ *n* -s [perh. alter. of E dial. (northern) *single* handful of gleaned grain, fr. E ²*single*] **1** *dial Eng* **:** a handful of gleaned grain **2** *dial Eng* **:** a small quantity

song·less \'ᵻləs\ *adj* **:** lacking in, incapable of, or not given to song — **song·less·ly** *adv*

song·let \'ᵻlə̇t\ *n* -s **:** a little song

songlike \'ᵻ,ᵻ\ *adj* **:** resembling or suggestive of song

song·man \ˈ⸗ˌmən\ *n, pl* **songmen** : a male choir singer

song of ascents *also* **song of degrees** *usu cap S&A&D* : any one of 15 psalms in the series Ps 120 to 134 sung by Hebrew pilgrims on their way to Jerusalem or possibly while ascending Mount Zion or the steps of the Temple — called also *Gradual Psalm, Pilgrim Psalm, Psalm of Ascents*

son·go fever \ˈsȯŋ(ˌ)gō-, ˈsäŋ-\ *n* [*Songo* river, Manchuria, where it was observed among Japanese soldiers in 1939] : epidemic hemorrhagic fever

songs *pl of* SONG

songsmith \ˈ⸗ˌ⸗\ *n* : a composer of songs

song sparrow *n* **1** : a common sparrow (*Melospiza melodia*) of eastern No. America about six inches long that is brownish above and white below with brownish streaks on the breast forming a blotch in the center and that is noted for its melodious song **2** : any of several western No. American birds that are varieties of the song sparrow and range from Alaska to Mexico

song·ster \ˈsȯŋ(k)stə(r), -ŋ(k)st- *also* ˈsäŋ-\ *n* -s [ME, singer, fr. OE *sangestre* woman singer, fr. *sang* song + *-estre* female agent — more at -STER] **1** : one that is skilled in song; *specif* : POET **2** : SONGBOOK; *esp* : a songbook containing popular songs

song·stress \-trə̇s\ *n* -ES [*songster* + *-ess*] : a female singer esp. of jazz

song thrush *n* **1** : an Old World thrush (*Turdus ericetorum*) that is olivaceous brown above and white below, tinged with buff on the breast, and spotted with blackish brown on the breast and sides — called also *mavis, throstle* **2** : WOOD THRUSH 1

songwriter \ˈ⸗ˌ⸗⸗\ *n* : a person who composes words or music or both esp. for popular songs

soni- — see SON-

son·ic \ˈsänik, -nēk\ *adj* [*son-* + *-ic*] **1** : having a frequency within the audibility range of the human ear — used of waves and vibrations; compare INFRASONIC, SUPERSONIC **2** : utilizing, produced by, or relating to sound waves ⟨~ altimeter⟩ **3** : of, indicating, or relating to the speed of sound in air : having a speed in air of about 1087 feet per second or about 741 miles per hour at sea level — compare HYPERSONIC, SUBSONIC, SUPERSONIC, TRANSONIC **4** : capable of uttering sounds — **son·i·cal·ly** \-nə̇k(ə)lē, -nēk-, -li\ *adv*

sonic barrier *n* : a sudden large increase in aerodynamic drag that occurs as the speed of an aircraft approaches the speed of sound and that is no longer an insurmountable obstacle to traveling faster than sound

sonic boom *n* : a sound resembling an explosion produced when a shock wave formed at the nose of an aircraft traveling at supersonic speed reaches the ground

sonic depth finder *n* : an instrument for determining the depth of a body of water or of an object below the surface by measuring the interval of time between the emission of a sound signal and the return of its echo from the bottom or the object

sonic mine *n* : a naval mine actuated by the sound of a ship's propeller or by the noise of water streaming along the hull

son·ics \ˈsäniks, -nēks\ *n pl but usu sing in constr* : acoustics esp. in its technological and supersonic aspects

so·nif·er·ous \səˈnif(ə)rəs, sōˈ-\ *adj* [*son-* + *-ferous*] : producing or conducting sound ⟨~ marine animals⟩

son·i·fi·ca·tion \ˌsänəfə̇ˈkāshən\ *n* -s [*son-* + *-fication*] : the act or process of producing sound (as the stridulation of insects)

son-in-law \ˈ⸗⸗ˌ⸗\ *n, pl* **sons-in-law** [ME *sone in lawe*] : the husband of one's daughter

son·less \ˈ⸗lə̇s\ *adj* : not possessing, bereft of, or never having had a son

son·ly *adj* : FILIAL

son·ne camera \ˈsänə-\ *n* [after Fred J. *Sonne* †1965 Am. engineer] : STRIP CAMERA

son·ne·ra·tia \ˌsänəˈrāsh(ē)ə\ *n, cap* [NL, fr. Pierre *Sonnerat* †1814 Fr. naturalist + NL *-ia*] : a genus (the type of the family Sonneratiaceae) of trees and shrubs having large flowers shaped like bells and succeeded by pulpy berries which in some members (as *S. acida*) are used as a condiment in India — see KAMBALA, PAGATPAT

son·ne·ra·ti·a·ce·ae \ˌ⸗⸗ˌ⸗shēˈāsēˌē\ *n pl, cap* [NL, fr. *Sonneratia*, type genus + *-aceae*] : a small family of tropical trees and shrubs (order Myrtales) having opposite leaves, large flowers with indefinite stamens, and pulpy often edible fruit

¹son·net \ˈsänə̇t, *usu* -ə̇d·+V\ *n* -s [It *sonetto*, fr. OProv *sonet* little song, fr. *son* song, sound (fr. L *sonus* sound) + *-et* — more at SOUND] **1** : a fixed verse form of Italian origin consisting of fourteen lines that are typically five-foot iambics rhyming according to a prescribed scheme; *also* : a poem in this pattern or more or less conforming to it — compare CURTAL SONNET, ENGLISH SONNET, PETRARCHAN SONNET, SPENSERIAN SONNET, TAILED SONNET **2** *obs* : a short usu. amatory poem

²sonnet \"\ *vb* **sonneted** *or* **sonnetted**; **sonneted** *or* **sonnetted**; **sonneting** *or* **sonnetting**; **sonnets** : SONNETIZE

¹son·ne·teer \ˌsänə̇ˈti(ə)r, -iə\ *n* -s [alter. (influenced by *-eer*) of earlier *sonnettier*, modif. (influenced by E ¹*sonnet*) of It *sonettiere*, fr. *sonetto* sonnet] **1** : a composer of sonnets **2** : a minor or insignificant poet

²sonneteer \"\ *vb* -ED/-ING/-S : SONNETIZE

son·net·ist \ˈsänəd·ə̇st\ *n* -s : SONNETEER

son·net·ize \-əˌtīz\ *vb* -ED/-ING/-S *vi* : to compose a sonnet ~ *vt* : to compose a sonnet on or to

son·net·ry \ˈsänə̇trē\ *n* -ES *archaic* **1** : poetry in sonnet form **2** : the writing of sonnets

sonnet sequence *n* : a series of sonnets often having a unifying theme

son·ny \ˈsənē, -ni\ *n* -ES [¹*son* + *-y*] : a young boy — used chiefly as a term of address

sono- — see SON-

so·no·buoy \ˈsänə+ˌ-\ *n* [*son-* + *buoy*] : a buoy equipped with a hydrophone for detecting underwater sounds and an automatic radio transmitter for transmitting the sounds and developed as a submarine detector to be dropped by parachute from aircraft for transmitting the coded sounds of submerged submarines to air and surface craft

son of a bitch *n, pl* **sons of bitches** : BASTARD 7 — sometimes considered vulgar; sometimes used interjectionally to express surprise or keen disappointment

son of a gun *n, pl* **sons of guns** **1** : SON OF A BITCH — sometimes used interjectionally **2** : a small firework in the form of a tablet that emits a loud crackling sound when scraped on a rough surface

son of god [ME *sone of God*] **1** *often cap S & cap G* : a superhuman or divine being; *specif* : an angel **2** *cap S&G* : God's Messiah — often used as a messianic title ⟨Jesus Christ, the *Son of God*⟩ **3** *cap G* : a person established in the love of God through acceptance of the divine will and guidance ⟨for all who are led by the Spirit of God are *sons of God* —Rom 8:14 (RSV)⟩ **4** *cap G* : an individual viewed in relation to God the Father

son of heaven *usu cap S&H* [trans. of Chin (Pek) *tien¹ tzu³*] : one of the former emperors of China

son of man [ME *sone of man*] **1** : a human being : MORTAL **2** *often cap S & sometimes cap M* : God's Messiah; *esp* : God's divine representative destined to preside over the final judgment of the world ⟨the coming of the Messiah, the *son of man*⟩

sono·graph \ˈsänəˌgraf\ *n* [ISV *son-* + *-graph*] : an apparatus by which sounds or seismic vibrations are recorded or translated into arbitrary phonetic symbols

son·o·luminescence \ˌ⸗⸗+\ *n* [*son-* + *luminescence*] : the emission of light by various liquids when traversed by high-frequency sound or ultrasonic waves of suitable intensity

so·no·ma oak \səˈnōmə-\ *n, usu cap S* [*Sonoma* County, Calif.] : CALIFORNIA BLACK OAK

so·nom·e·ter \səˈnäməd·ə(r), -ətə-\ *n* [ISV *son-* + *-meter*] **1** : MONOCHORD **2** : AUDIOMETER

son·o-radio buoy \ˈsä(ˌ)nō-\ *n* [*son-* + *radio* + *buoy*] : SONOBUOY

so·no·ra gum \səˈnōrə, -nȯrə-\ *n, usu cap S* [*Sonora*, state in northwest Mexico] : the acidulous gum resin of the creosote bush

sonora ironwood *n, usu cap S* : DESERT IRONWOOD

sonora lac *n, usu cap S* : a substance that resembles lac, is secreted by a scale (*Tachardiella mexicana*) living on the twigs of several Mexican leguminous shrubs, and is used locally for medicine

¹so·no·ran \səˈnōrən, -nȯr-\ *adj, usu cap* [*Sonora* + E *-an*] **1** : relating to, situated in, inhabiting, or coming from Sonora **2** : PIMAN 1 **3** : of, relating to, or being the arid division of the Austral biogeographic zone that includes the warmer parts of the western U. S. and central Mexico — see LOWER SONORAN, UPPER SONORAN

²sonoran \"\ *n* -s *cap* : a native or inhabitant of Sonora

sonoran coral snake *n, usu cap 1st S* : a coral snake (*Micrurus euryxanthus* or *Micruroides euryxanthus*) of western Mexico and the U. S. north to Colorado and Utah

so·no·rant \səˈnōrənt, -nȯr-\ *n* -s [*sonorous* + *-ant* (as in ²*sonant*)] **1** : RESONANT **2** : a nonvocalic resonant sometimes with the exclusion of \r\, \y\, and \w\

son·o·rif·er·ous \ˌsänəˌrif(ə)rəs\ *adj* [L *sonor* sound + E *-iferous*; akin to L *sonus* sound] : SONIFEROUS; *also* : RESOUNDING — **son·o·rif·er·ous·ly** *adv*

so·nor·i·ty \səˈnȯrəd·ē, -när-, -rətē, -i *sometimes* -nōr-\ *n* -ES [ML *sonoritat-, sonoritas*, fr. LL, melody, fr. L *sonorus* + *-itat-, -itas* -ity] **1 a** : the quality or state of being sonorous : SONOROUSNESS, RESONANCE **b** : a sonorous tone or speech **2** : the perceptibility or distinctness of speech sounds when spoken in a context in which stress, pitch, and sound duration are constant ⟨vowels possessing greater ~ than consonants⟩

son·o·riza·tion \ˌsänərəˈzāshən, -ˌrīˈz-\ *n* -s [It *sonorizzazione*, fr. *sonorizzare* to sonorize + *-azione* -ation] : VOICING ⟨~ of intervocalic consonants⟩

son·o·rize \ˈ⸗⸗ˌrīz\ *vb* -ED/-ING/-S [It *sonorizzare*, fr. *sonoro* sonorous, voiced (fr. L *sonorus* sonorous) + *-izzare* -ize] : VOICE — used esp. of intervocalic consonants in Italian

sono·rous \səˈnōrəs, -ˈnȯr-, ˈsänər-\ *adj* [L *sonorus*; akin to L *sonus* sound — more at SOUND] **1 a** : producing sound (as when struck) ⟨~ metals⟩ **b** : marked by or productive of loud sounds : NOISY ⟨a ~ water fall⟩ **2** : characterized by full or loud sound often with clear or rich tone, marked volume, or easy audibility ⟨a herald chosen for his ~ voice —J.G.Frazer⟩ **3 a** : marked by imposing or impressive effect or style ⟨the ~ sureness of pure philosophy —J.P.Marquand⟩ **b** : marked by excessively heavy high-flown grandiloquent or self-assured effect or style ⟨the cosmic poet, who indulges in vague generalities, magnificent and ~, about his universe —J.L.Lowes⟩ **4** : having a high or an indicated degree of sonority or number of sounds evaluated for sonority ⟨~ sounds like \ä\ and \ō\⟩ ⟨one of the least ~ of languages⟩ **syn** see RESONANT

sonorous figures *n pl* : figures (as the geometrical figures of sand on a plate of glass or metal when the bow of a violin is drawn along the edge) formed by the vibrations of a substance emitting a musical tone — called also *Chladni figures*

sono·rous·ly *adv* : in a sonorous manner ⟨a politician who spoke ~⟩

sono·rous·ness *n* -ES : the quality or state of being sonorous ⟨scores of phrases of splendid and empty ~ —S.H.Adams⟩

so·no·vox \ˈsōnəˌväks\ *n* -ES [*son-* + L *vox* voice — more at VOICE] : a device that transmits to the larynx recorded human or nonhuman sound whose vibrations substitute prosthetically or for unusual effect for those of the vocal cords

¹sons *pl of* SON

²sons *also* **sonse** \ˈsän(t)s\ *n* [partly fr. ME (Sc) *sons*, of Celt origin; akin to ScGael & IrGael *sonas* good fortune; partly fr. IrGael *sonas*] **1** *chiefly Scot* : health and happiness, good fortune, luck **2** *chiefly Scot* : ABUNDANCE, PLENTY

³sons \ˈsōnz\ *Scot var of* SOWENS

son·ship \ˈ⸗ˌship\ *n* : the relationship of son to father ⟨it at least brought a deepened realization of the significance of his ~ to God —K.S.Latourette⟩

son·stadt solution \ˈsänˌstat-\ *n, usu cap S* [after E. *Sonstadt*, 19th cent. Eng. chemist] : a heavy solution of mercuric iodide in potassium iodide having a maximum specific gravity of 3.2 — called also *Thoulet solution*

sonsy *or* **sons·ie** \ˈsän(t)sē\ *adj* [²*sons* + *-y*] **1** *chiefly dial* : bringing or having good fortune : LUCKY **2** *chiefly dial* : attractively buxom : COMELY **3** *chiefly dial* : cheerfully genial **4** *chiefly dial* : comfortably relaxed

son·tag \ˈsänˌtag\ *n* -s [after Henriette *Sontag* †1854 Ger. vocalist] : a crocheted or knitted cape with long ends crossed in front and fastened at the back

soo·chow *or* **su·chow** \ˈsüˌchau̇, -üˌjō\ *adj, usu cap* [fr. *Soochow* (*Suchow*), China] : of or from the city of Soochow in Kiangsu province, China : of the kind or style prevalent in Soochow

soodra *var of* SUDRA

soo·ey \ˈsüē, -üi\ *v imper* [prob. alter. of ¹*sow*] — used as a call to pigs

soogan *var of* SUGAN

¹soo·gee \ˈsüjē\ *vb* -ED/-ING/-S [perh. fr. Jap *sōji* cleaning] : to wash down (as the deck and paintwork of a ship) ⟨have his boys ~ the galley —Richard Bissell⟩

²soogee \"\ *n* -s : clean rope yarns used to wash with

soojee *var of* SUJI

sook \ˈsu̇k\ *or* **sook·ie** \-kē,-ki\ *v imper* [alter. of ¹*suck*] *dial* — used as a call to cows

sool \ˈsül\ *vt* -ED/-ING/-S [fr. dial. Brit *sowl, sole, sool* to pull by the ears, of unknown origin] **1** *Austral* : to incite (as a dog) to attack : SIC **2** *Austral* : to urge on

soo·la clover \ˈsülə\ *n* [*soola* modif. of Sp *sulla* — more at SULLA] : SULLA

soo markee *var of* SOU MARKEE

¹soon \ˈsün, ˈsu̇n\ *adv* -ER/-EST [ME *sone, soone*, fr. OE *sōna*; akin to OFris *sōn* immediately, OS & OHG *sān, sāno*] **1 a** : at once : without delay : IMMEDIATELY ⟨no ~*er* said than done⟩ **b** : before long : without undue time lapse ⟨smoke ~ disappears⟩ ⟨~ after sunrise⟩ ⟨results were ~ evident⟩ **2** : PROMPTLY, SPEEDILY, QUICKLY ⟨as ~ as possible⟩ ⟨the more help, the ~*er* done⟩ **3** : before the usual, expected, appointed, or actual time ⟨spring came ~ this year⟩ **4** : READILY, WILLINGLY ⟨as ~ walk as ride⟩ ⟨~*er* stay than go⟩ **5** : REASONABLY, ASSUREDLY, CERTAINLY ⟨as ~ expect a call from him as from anyone else⟩

²soon \"\ *adj* -ER/-EST [ME *sone, soone*, fr. *sone, soone*, adj.] **1** *chiefly dial* : EARLY **2** *archaic* : FAST, QUICK

soon·er \-nə(r)\ *n* -s [fr. *sooner*, compar. of ¹*soon*] **1** : a person settling on land in the early West before the official date of its being opened to settlement with a view to gaining the prior claim allowed by law to the first settler after the official opening **2** *usu cap* : OKLAHOMAN — used as a nickname

sooner or later *adv* : at some uncertain future time : SOMETIME

soop \ˈsüp\ *vb* [of Scand origin; akin to ON *sōpa* to sweep; akin to OE *swāpan* to sweep — more at SWOOP] *chiefly Scot* : SWEEP

¹soor \ˈsü(ə)r\ *chiefly Scot var of* SOUR

²soor \ˈsu̇(ə)r\ *n* -s [origin unknown] : ²THRUSH

soor·kee *or* **soor·ki** *or* **soor·ky** \ˈsu̇rkē\ *n, pl* **soorkees** *or* **soorkis** *or* **soorkies** [Hindi *surkhī*, fr. Per *surkhī*, lit., redness, fr. *surkh* red, fr. MPer *sukhr*; akin to Av *suXra-* bright, Skt *śukra*] *India* : brick pulverized and mixed with lime to form a mortar

soorma *var of* SURMA

¹soot \ˈsu̇t *also* ÷ˈsət *or* ˈsüt; *usu* |d·+V\ *n* -s [ME *sot, soot*, fr. OE *sōt*; akin to MLG & ON *sōt* soot, MD *soet*, OIr *sūide*, Lith *suodžioi* (pl.) soot, OE *sittan* to sit — more at SIT] **1** : a black substance formed by combustion or separated from fuel during combustion, rising in fine particles, and adhering to the sides of the chimney or pipe conveying the smoke; *esp* : the fine powder consisting chiefly of carbon that colors smoke and is the result of incomplete combustion — compare FLY ASH **2** : SOOTY BLACK

²soot \"\ *vt* -ED/-ING/-S : to coat, cover, or spread with soot : smudge or soil with soot

soot blowing *n* : removal of soot deposits on the tubes of a steam generator by a blast of air or steam

soot brown *n* : a grayish brown to yellowish brown that is stronger and slightly darker than mummy brown (sense 2b) and very slightly paler than gold bronze — called also *bister, pinecone, teakwood*

soot·er \|d·ə(r), ˈtə-\ *n* -s [¹*soot* + *-er*] : one that removes soot (as from the outside of a boiler)

soot·er·kin \ˈsüd·ə(r)kə̇n, ˈsüd-·\ *n* -s [prob. fr. (assumed) D dial. *zoetkijn*, dim. of D dial. *zoet* soot, fr. MD *soet* — more at SOOT] **1** : an afterbirth formerly held to be produced by Dutch women ⟨delivered of a ~ not unlike to a rat —John Cleveland⟩ **2** : something that is imperfect or unsuccessful; *esp* : an imperfect literary composition ⟨fruits of dull heat and ~s of wit —Alexander Pope⟩ **3** *archaic* : DUTCHMAN

sootfall \ˈ⸗ˌ⸗\ *n* : the descent of soot from an atmosphere contaminated with smokestack gases and dusts

¹sooth \ˈsüth\ *adj* -ER/-EST [ME *soth, sooth*, fr. OE *sōth*; akin to OHG *sand* true, ON *sannr* true, Goth *sunja* truth, Gk *eteos* true, Skt *sant, sat* being, existing, true, good, *satya* true, right, L *esse* to be — more at IS] **1** *archaic* : agreeing with or telling the truth **2** *archaic* : SOFT, SWEET

²sooth \"\ *n* -s [ME *soth, sooth*, fr. OE *sōth*, fr. neut. of *sōth*, adj.] **1** *archaic* **a** : TRUTH, REALITY **b** : FACT; *also* : TRUISM — used interjectionally **2** *obs* : CAJOLERY, BLANDISHMENT

soothe \ˈsüth\ *vb* -ED/-ING/-S [ME *sothen*, fr. OE *sōthian*, fr. *sōth*, adj.] *vt* **1** *obs* : to show, assert, or confirm the truth of : demonstrate or maintain as true **2** *obs* **a** : to uphold or back up; *also* : to humor by complying **b** : to gloss over : PALLIATE, EXTENUATE **3 a** : to please (a person) by or as if by attention or concern : PLACATE, MOLLIFY ⟨~ an angry crowd with promises⟩ **b** : to assuage or relieve as if by softening : ALLEVIATE ⟨~ an inflamed throat⟩ **4 a** : to bring comfort, solace, or reassurance to ⟨~ a troubled mind⟩ **b** : to lead to tranquility or equanimity : dispel the inner agitation of ⟨nature's *soothing* of the mind⟩ ⟨~ a frightened child⟩ ~ *vi* : to bring peace, composure, or quietude **syn** see CALM

¹sooth·er \-thə(r)\ *n* -s [*soothe* + *-er* (n. suffix)] : one (as a flatterer) that soothes

²sooth·er \ˈsüthə(r), ˈsu̇th-\ *vt* [*soothe* + *-er* (freq. suffix)] **1** *dial* : SOOTHE **2** *dial* : COAX, FLATTER

soothfast \ˈ⸗ˌ⸗\ *adj* [ME *sothfast, soothfast*, fr. OE *sōthfæst*, fr. *sōth* true + *fæst* fast — more at SOOTH, FAST] **1** *archaic* : firmly fixed in or founded on the truth : REAL, TRUE **2** *archaic* : TRUTHFUL

sooth·ful \ˈsüthfəl\ *adj* [ME *sothfol*, fr. *soth, sooth* truth + *-fol, -ful* -ful — more at SOOTH] *archaic* : TRUE, RELIABLE

soothing *adj* [fr. pres. part. of *soothe*] : having a quieting or sedative effect : CALMING, TRANQUILIZING ⟨~ syrup⟩ — **sooth·ing·ly** *adv* — **sooth·ing·ness** *n* -ES

sooth·less \ˈsüthlə̇s\ *adj* [²*sooth* + *-less*] *archaic* : lacking in faith or fidelity : TREACHEROUS, FALSE

sooth·ly \-thlē\ *adv* [ME *sothly, soothly*, fr. OE *sothlīce*, fr. *sothlic*, adj., true, truthful, fr. *sōth* true + *-līc* -ly — more at SOOTH] *archaic* : in truth : TRULY

¹sooth·say \ˈsüthˌsā *sometimes* -th-\ *n* -s [back-formation fr. *soothsayer*] **1** : PROVERB **2** : PROPHECY, SOOTHSAYING **3** : OMEN, PORTENT

²soothsay \"\ *vi* **sooth·said** \-ˌsed\ **soothsaid**; **sooth·say·ing** \-ˌsāiŋ\ **sooth·says** \-ˌsez\ [back-formation fr. *soothsayer*] : to practice soothsaying : PREDICT, FORETELL

sooth·say·er \-ˌsā(ə)r, -ˌse(ə)r, -ˌseə\ *n* [ME *sothseyer*, fr. *soth, sooth* truth + *seyer, sayer* sayer — more at SOOTH, SAYER] **1** : a speaker of truth or wisdom; *esp* : PROGNOSTICATOR **2** : MANTIS

sooth·say·ing \-ˌsāiŋ\ *n* [²*sooth* + *saying*] **1** : the act of foretelling events **2** : PREDICTION, PROPHECY

soot·i·ly *pronunc at* ¹SOOT +ᵊlē, əlī, |i\ *adv* : in a sooty manner

soot·i·ness *pronunc at* ¹SOOT +ēnə̇s, in-\ *n* -ES : the quality or state of being sooty

sooting *pres part of* SOOT

soot·less *pronunc at* ¹SOOT +lə̇s\ *adj* : lacking or not producing soot

sootlike \ˈ⸗ˌ⸗\ *adj* : resembling soot ⟨a black ~ material⟩

soots *pl of* SOOT, *pres 3d sing of* SOOT

¹sooty *pronunc at* ¹SOOT +ē,i\ *adj* -ER/-EST [ME *soty, sooty*, fr. *sot, soot* soot + *-y*] **1 a** : of or relating to soot : producing soot ⟨~ fires⟩ **b** : soiled or smutted with soot ⟨~ buildings⟩ **2** : of a dark color varying from soot brown to sooty black

²sooty \"\ *vt* -ED/-ING/-ES : to cover or soil with soot ⟨*sootied* clothing⟩

sooty albatross *n* : either of two dark-colored albatrosses (genus *Phoebetria*) common in far southern seas

sooty black *also* **soot** *n* : a nearly neutral slightly purplish black that is very slightly redder and lighter than slate black

sooty blotch *n* : a disease of apples and pears caused by an imperfect fungus (*Gloeodes pomigena*) and characterized by sooty blotches on the fruit

sooty kangaroo *n* : a large dark kangaroo (*Macropus fuliginosus*) found only on the Australian Kangaroo Island preserve

sooty mangabey *n* : a dark gray monkey (*Cercocebus fuliginosus*) of West Africa

sooty mold *n* **1** : a dark or black velvety coating of mycelium of various fungi growing in insect honeydew on the leaves, fruit, or other exposed parts of plants, when heavy often interfering with the normal metabolism of the plant, and being esp. common on plants of the genus *Citrus* **2** : a fungus (as members of the family Capnodiaceae and Meliolaceae) that causes or develops as a sooty mold on plants

sooty ore *n* : a black copper ore that is an impure form of chalcocite

sooty shearwater *or* **sooty petrel** *n* : a brownish black shearwater (*Puffinus griseus*) of the south Pacific that migrates in the nonbreeding season to the north Atlantic and north Pacific

sooty stripe *n* : a disease of sorghums caused by a fungus (*Ramulispora sorghi*) and characterized by elongate elliptic lesions which become sooty black as the sclerotia of the fungus develop

sooty tern *n* : a tern (*Sterna fuscata*) that is widely distributed on tropical coasts and is blackish above and white below

sooty wing *n* : a skipper of the genus *Pholisora*

¹sop \ˈsäp\ *n* -s [ME *soppe*, fr. OE *sopp*; akin to MLG *soppe* soup, broth, MD *sop* pot liquor, broth, sauce, OHG *sopfa* piece of bread soaked in milk, ON *soppa* soup, OE *sūpan* to swallow, sip, taste — more at SUP] **1** *chiefly dial* : a piece of food (as bread) dipped or steeped in a liquid before being eaten **2** *chiefly dial* : the liquid into which food is dipped before being eaten; *esp* : GRAVY **3** : a wet soppy mess **4** : a foolish spineless individual : MILKSOP **5** *dial Eng* : a tuft of damp green grass mixed in with hay **6** : a conciliatory or propitiatory bribe, gift, or advance ⟨as a ~ to the low-paid teachers . . . the board approved $400-a-year raises —*Time*⟩

²sop \"\ *vb* **sopped**; **sopped**; **sopping**; **sops** *vt* **1** : to steep or dip in or as if in a liquid ⟨~ bread in gravy⟩ **2** : to mop (as water) so as to leave a dry or semidry surface **3** : to give a bribe or conciliatory gift to ~ *vi* **1** : to become completely soaked **2** : to soak in : ooze through

sop *abbr* soprano

SOP *abbr* **1** senior officer present **2** standard operating procedure; standing operating procedure

sope \ˈsōp\ *n* -s [ME, fr. OE *sopa*; akin to OE *sūpan* to swallow, sip, taste — more at SUP] *dial chiefly Brit* : DRINK 3

soph \ˈsäf, ˈsȯf\ *abbr or n* -s sophomore

so·pha *archaic var of* SOFA

so·pher \ˈsōfər\ *n, pl* **so·pher·im** \-rə̇m, -ˌrēm\ *often cap* [Heb *sōphēr*] : SCRIBE 1

so·pher·ic \(ˈ)sōˈferik\ *adj, often cap* : of or relating to the sopherim or the literature associated with them

so·phia \sōˈfēə, ˈsäf-, ˈsōf-\ *n* -s *usu cap* [L, fr. Gk, fr. *sophos* skilled, clever, wise + *-ia* -y] : WISDOM; *specif* : divine wisdom — **so·phi·an** \-ən\ *adj, usu cap*

so·phi·an·ism \-əˌnizəm\ *n* -s *usu cap* : a theology or system of thought based on divine wisdom ⟨the *Sophianism* . . . represented by some of the outstanding Orthodox Thinkers of our time —Endre Ivanka⟩ — **so·phi·an·ist** \-ənə̇st\ *n* -s *usu cap*

soph·ic \ˈsäfik\ *or* **soph·i·cal** \-fə̇kəl\ *adj* [LL *sophicus*, fr. Gk *sophos* skilled, clever, wise + L *-icus* -ic, *-ical*] : of, relating to, or full of wisdom : INTELLECTUAL — **sophically** *adv*

sophies *pl of* SOPHY

sophi·ol·o·gy \ˌsäfēˈäləjē, ˌsōf-\ *n* -ES [*sophio-* (fr. *sophia*) + *-logy*] : SOPHIANISM

soph·ism \ˈsäˌfizəm\ *n* -s [alter. (influenced by MF *sophisme* & L *sophisma*) of earlier *sophim*, fr. ME, fr. MF *sophime*,

sophisme, fr. L *sophisma*, fr. Gk, clever device, artifice, sophism, fr. *sophizesthai* to become wise, act craftily, deceive, deal in sophisms, fr. *sophos* skilled, clever, wise] **1** : an argument that is correct in form or appearance but is actually invalid; *esp* : an argument used for deception, disputation, or the display of intellectual brilliance ⟨employ a ~⟩ — compare SKEPTICISM **2** : specious reasoning : SOPHISTRY 1 **3** : SOPHISTRY 4

soph·ist \-fəst\ *n* -S [L *sophista*, fr. Gk *sophistēs*, lit., master craftsman, expert, wise man, fr. *sophizesthai*] **1** *usu cap* : one of a class of teachers of philosophy and rhetoric in ancient Greece who became prominent about the middle of the 5th century B.C. and impressed by the conflicting opinions of the early nature philosophers developed subjectivistic, relativistic, and skeptical arguments, were the first to offer anything approaching systematic education beyond the elementary branches, and argued for the natural equality of men, but taught also the art of successful living and partly by virtue of their unorthodox opinions and their acceptance of pay for instruction gradually fell into disrepute **2** *sometimes cap* : a learned man, thinker, or sage **3** : a person employing sophistry : a fallacious reasoner

soph·is·ter \-tə(r)\ *n* -S [ME, fr. MF *sophistre*, fr. L *sophista*] **1** *obs* : SOPHIST 1 **2** : SOPHIST 3 **3** *obs* : a student in his third or fourth year esp. at an English university

¹so·phis·tic \(ˈ)sä¦fistik, sə'f-,sō'f-, -tēk\ *adj* [L *sophisticus*, fr. Gk *sophistikos*, fr. *sophistēs* + *-ikos* -ic] **1 a** : tending to or employing sophistry ⟨~ tyrants⟩ **b** : using sophisms ⟨~ rhetoricians⟩ **2** : of, relating to, or typical of sophists, sophistry, or the ancient Sophists ⟨a ~ age⟩ ⟨~ subtleties⟩ ⟨the ~ movement⟩

²sophistic \"\ *n* -S : the doctrines or procedures of the Sophists or a sophist; *also* : SOPHISTRY

so·phis·ti·cal \-təkəl, -tēk-\ *adj* [L *sophisticus* + E *-al*] **1** : SOPHISTIC **2** : resembling a sophism; *specif* : that appears to be plausible but is actually fallacious ⟨a ~ argument⟩ ⟨a ~ method⟩ — **so·phis·ti·cal·ly** \-k(ə)lē, -li\ *adv* — **so·phis·ti·cal·ness** \-kəlnəs\ *n* -ES

¹so·phis·ti·cate \sə'fistəkə̇t, -tēk-, -stə,kāt, *usu* \|d.+V\ *adj* [ME *sophisticat*, fr. ML *sophisticatus*, past part.] : SOPHISTICATED

²so·phis·ti·cate \-stə,kāt, *usu* -ād.+V\ *vb* -ED/-ING/-S [ME *sophisticaten*, fr. ML *sophisticatus*, past part. of *sophisticare*, fr. L *sophisticus* sophistic] *vt* **1** : to alter deceptively: as **a** : ADULTERATE ⟨rose oil is *sophisticated* with geraniol —R.N. Shreve⟩ **b** : to falsify (as a text, passage, or author) by interpolations, unwarranted changes, or misinterpretation **2** : to make artificial : deprive of genuineness, naturalness, or simplicity: as **a** *archaic* : DEBASE, SPOIL, CORRUPT **b** : to deprive of naïveté : DISILLUSION **3 a** : to make complicated or complex ⟨~ the mechanism of a watch⟩ **b** : to make aware of complexities and subtleties : REFINE ~ *vi* : ADULTERATE, CORRUPT, COMPLICATE

³sophisticate *like* ¹SOPHISTICATE\ *n* -S [¹*sophisticate*] : a sophisticated person

sophisticated \==,==\ *adj* [ML *sophisticatus* + E *-ed*] **1** : not in a natural, pure, or original state : ADULTERATED ⟨a ~ oil⟩ : amended unwarrantedly ⟨a ~ text⟩ **2** : deprived of native or original simplicity: as **a** : highly complicated : many sided : COMPLEX ⟨~ specifications⟩ ⟨a ~ search techniques would be needed to locate faint objects —*Space Handbk.*⟩ **b** : WORLDLY-WISE, KNOWING ⟨a ~ adolescent⟩ **3** : devoid of grossness : SUBTLE: as **a** : supremely cultured : finely experienced and aware ⟨a ~ columnist⟩ **b** : intellectually appealing : devoid of the obvious traditional or popular appeal ⟨a ~ novel⟩ — **so·phis·ti·cat·ed·ly** \==,===, =,==ǝ==\ *adv*

so·phis·ti·ca·tion \sə,fistə'kāshən\ *n* -S [ME *sophisticacioun*, fr. ML *sophistication-*, *sophisticatio*, fr. *sophisticatus* + *-ion-*, *-io* -ion] **1 a** : the use or employment of sophistry : sophistical reasoning : misrepresentation or falsification in argument **b** : SOPHISM, QUIBBLE **2** : an act of sophisticating : the quality or state of being sophisticated: as **a** : ADULTERATION, ADULTERANT; *also* : something adulterated **b** : the quality or the character of being intellectually sophisticated (as through cultivation, experience, or disillusionment) ⟨the text is simple and requires no scientific ~ to be understood —D.L.Wolfle⟩

so·phis·ti·ca·tive \=ǝ==,kād·iv\ *adj* : promoting sophistication : tending to sophisticate

so·phis·ti·ca·tor \-ād·ə(r)\ *n* -S : one that sophisticates; *esp* : one that adulterates

soph·is·try \'säfəstrē, -ri\ *n* -ES [ME *sophistrie*, fr. MF, fr. *sophistre* sophist + *-ie* -y — more at SOPHISTER] **1** : reasoning that is superficially plausible but actually fallacious ⟨his masterful but irresponsible ~⟩ **2** : the employment of sophisms : disputation in the actual or supposed manner of the Sophists ⟨rhetorical ~⟩ **3** : a sophistical argument; *specif* : SOPHISM ⟨a maze of *sophistries*⟩ **4** : the doctrines, principles, or practices of the ancient Sophists ⟨the history of ~⟩

sophists *pl of* SOPHIST

soph·o·cle·an \¦säfə¦klēən\ *adj, usu cap* [*Sophocles* †406 B.C. Greek tragic dramatist + E *-an*] : of, relating to, or characteristic of the Athenian tragic poet Sophocles or his dramas

soph·o·more \'säf(ə),m[ō(ə)r, -ˌō(ə)r, ǀȯ(ə)r, ǀōə, ǀȯ(ə), *esp in 2-syllable pronunc* 'sȯf-\ *n* -S [prob. fr. Gk *sophos* wise + *mōros* dull, foolish, stupid — more at MORON] **1** : a student in his second year or with second-year standing at a college; *also* : a student in his second year at a secondary school **2** : a person with two years of experience ⟨a ~ in organized baseball⟩

soph·o·mor·ic \¦=ǝ¦==, (ˌ)=¦==, *with last part* -ōrik, -or-, -rēk\ *adj* **1** : of, relating to, resembling, or characteristic of a sophomore **2 a** : exhibiting a firm and often aggressive conviction of knowledge and wisdom and unaware of limitations and lack of maturity : inclined to oversimplify : SUPERFICIAL **b** : falsely skeptical : given to shallow quibbling

so·pho·ra \sə'fōrə\ *n* [NL, fr. Ar *ṣufayrā'*, a tree of the genus *Sophora*] **1** *cap* : a genus of trees and shrubs (family Leguminosae) that are natives of the warmer parts of both hemispheres and have odd-pinnate leaves and rather showy flowers with a broad or rounded standard and oblong keel — see JAPANESE PAGODA TREE, KOWHAI, MESCAL BEAN **2** **2** -S : any plant of the genus *Sophora*

soph·o·rine \'säfə,rēn, -,rən; sə'fōrən\ *n* -S [ISV *sophor-* (fr. NL *Sophora*) + *-ine*] : CYTISINE

so·phros·y·ne \sə'fräs'n(ˌ)ē\ *n* -S [Gk *sōphrosynē*, fr. *sōphrōn* being of sound mind, prudent, reasonable (fr. *saos*, *sōs* whole, safe, sound + *-phrōn*; akin to Gk *phrēn* mind) + *-synē*, suffix used to form abstract nouns — more at THUMB, FRENETIC] **1** : TEMPERANCE **2** **2** : SELF-CONTROL **3** : PRUDENCE — contrasted with *hubris*

sophy *n* -ES [L *sophi*, pl. of *sophus*, fr. Gk *sophos*, fr. *sophos* skilled, clever, wise] *obs* : a wise man : SAGE

-so·phy \səfē\ *n comb form* -ES [ME *-sophie*, fr. OF, fr. L *-sophia*, fr. Gk *sophia* wisdom, fr. *sophos* skilled, clever, wise + *-ia* -y] : knowledge or wisdom concerning (something specified) : science or study of (something specified) ⟨anthropo*sophy*⟩ ⟨chiro*sophy*⟩ ⟨physio*sophy*⟩

sopite \'sō,pīt, 'sä,p-\ *vt* -ED/-ING/-S [L *sopitus*, past part. of *sopire* to put to sleep, fr. *sopor*] **1** : to put to sleep : LULL **2** : to put an end to (as a claim) : SETTLE

so·por \'sōpər, -,pȯ(ə)r\ *n* -S [L; akin to L *somnus* sleep — more at SOMNOLENT] : profound or lethargic sleep : STUPOR

sopo·rif·er·ous \¦säpə¦rif(ə)rəs, ¦sōp-\ *adj* [L *soporifer* (fr. *sopor* + *-ifer* -iferous) + E *-ous*] : characterized by or inducing sleep or stupor : SOPORIFIC — **sopo·rif·er·ous·ly** *adv* — **sopo·rif·er·ous·ness** *n* -ES

¹sopo·rif·ic \-fik,-fēk\ *adj* [prob. fr. F *soporifique*, fr. L *sopor* + F *-ifique* -ific] **1** : causing or tending to cause sleep ⟨a ~ drug⟩ ⟨a ~ speech⟩ **2** : of, relating to, or characterized by sleepiness or lethargy ⟨~ old men⟩ ⟨~ symptoms⟩ **3** : tending to dull or deaden awareness or alertness

²soporific \"\ *n* -S : something that is soporific ⟨the ~ of peace and prosperity —Peter Eckstein⟩; *specif* : a sleep-inducing drug or medicament

sopo·rif·i·cal \-fəkəl, -fēk-\ *adj* : SOPORIFIC — **sopo·rif·i·cal·ly** \-k(ə)lē, -li\ *adv*

sopo·rose \'==,rōs\ *adj* [*sopor* + *-ose*] : full of sleep : characterized by or manifesting morbid sleep or sleepiness

sopped *past of* SOP

sop·per \'säpə(r)\ *n* -S : one that sops

sop·pi·ness \'säpēnəs, -pin-\ *n* -ES : the quality or state of being soppy : WETNESS

sop·ping \'säpiŋ, -pēŋ\ *adv* [fr. pres. part. of ²*sop*] : EXTREMELY, VERY ⟨~ wet⟩

sop·py \-pē,-pi\ *adj* -ER/-EST **1** : soaked through : SATURATED : very wet or sloppy **2** *Brit* : MUSHY **2** **syn** see SENTIMENTAL

so·pra·ni·no \,sōprə'nē(,)nō\ *n* -S [It, dim. of *soprano*] : a musical instrument (as a recorder or saxophone) higher in pitch than the soprano

so·pranist \sə'pranəst *also* -rän- *or* -rȧn-\ *n* -S [¹*soprano* + *-ist*] : a treble singer

¹so·pra·no \-(,)nō, -,nə, *often* -nəw+V\ *n* -S [It, adj. & n., fr. *sopra* above + *-ano* -an] **1** : the highest voice part in 4-part mixed harmony **2** : the highest singing voice of women, boys, or castrati — compare ALTO **3** : a singer (as a woman) with a soprano voice

²soprano \"\ *adj* [It] **1** : relating to the soprano voice or part ⟨a ~ clef⟩ **2** : having a high or treble range ⟨a ~ saxophone⟩ ⟨~ solo⟩

soprano clef *n* : the C clef when it is on the first or lower line of the staff — see CLEF illustration

soprano recorder *n* : the highest of the four standard members of the recorder family — called also *descant recorder*

sops *pl of* SOP, *pres 3d sing of* SOP

sops in wine **1** : the clove pink once used to flavor wine **2** *also* **sops of wine** *usu cap S&W* : a red late summer apple of highly aromatic flavor

sop to cer·be·rus \-'sərb(ə)rəs\ *usu cap C* [after *Cerberus*, 3-headed dog guarding the entrance to Hades; fr. the sop given him by Aeneas in Vergil's *Aeneid* (6,417) to engage his attention while Aeneas slipped by — more at CERBERUS] : a concession or bribe to conciliate a person otherwise liable to be troublesome

so·ra \'sōrə\ *or* **sora rail** *n* -S [origin unknown] : a small short-billed No. American rail (*Porzana carolina*) numerous in marshes in the Atlantic states during its migrations

so·ral \'sōrəl\ *adj* [NL *sorus* + E *-al*] : of or relating to a sorus

sorance *n* -S [¹*sore* + *-ance*] *obs* : SORE, INJURY, DISEASE

¹sorb \'sȯ(ə)rb\ *n* -S *cap* [G *Sorbe*, fr. Sorbian *serb*] **1** : WEND **2** : WENDISH

²sorb \"\ *n* -S [F *sorbe* fruit of the service tree, fr. L *sorbum*] **1** : any of several Old World trees related to the apples and pears (as a wild service tree or rowan tree) **2** *or* **sorb apple** : the fruit of a sorb

³sorb \"\ *vt* -ED/-ING/-S [back-formation fr. *absorb* & *adsorb*] : to take up and hold either by adsorption or absorption : OCCLUDE

sor·bar·ia \sȯ(r)'ba(a)rēə\ *n, cap* [NL, fr. *Sorbus* + *-aria*] : a small genus of Asiatic shrubs (family Rosaceae) with some compound leaves (as at the base) and panicles of white flowers with 5 to 8 pistils

sor·bate \'sȯr,bāt, -bə̇t\ *n* -S [*sorbic* (*acid*) + *-ate*] **1** : a salt or ester of sorbic acid **2** : a sorbed substance

¹sor·be·fa·cient \¦sȯ(r)bə¦fāshənt\ *adj* [L *sorbēre* to suck up, swallow + *-facient*, *-faciens*, pres. part. of *facere* to make, do — more at ABSORB, DO] : producing or promoting absorption

²sorbefacient \"\ *n* : a sorbefacient substance

sorbent \'sȯrbənt\ *n* -S [³*sorb* + *-ent*] : a substance that sorbs

sor·bet \'sȯrbə̇t\ *n* -S [MF, fr. OIt *sorbetto*, fr. Turk *şerbet* — more at SHERBET] **1** *archaic* : SHERBET **3** **2** : a sherbet made with a mixture of fruits

¹sorb·ian \'sȯrbēən\ *adj, usu cap* [¹*Sorb* + *-ian*] : WENDISH

²sorbian \"\ *n* -S *cap* **1** : WEND **2** : WENDISH

sorb·ic acid \'sȯrbik-\ *n* [²*sorb* + *-ic*] : a crystalline diolefinic acid $CH_3(CH{=}CH)_2COOH$ obtained from the unripe fruits of the mountain ash or made synthetically and used chiefly as a fungicide and food preservative and in the form of esters in improving drying oils

sor·bi·tan \'sȯ(r)bə,tan\ *n* -S [*sorbitol* + *-an*] : an inner anhydride $C_6H_{12}O_5$ of sorbitol: as **a** : a synthetic compound made by chemical dehydration of sorbitol and used in making fatty acid esters (as the mono-oleate) and then ethers (as with a polyethyleneglycol) for use as emulsifiers and wetting agents; 1,4-anhydro-D-glucitol — called also *1,4-sorbitan* **b** : POLYGALITOL

sor·bite \'sȯr,bīt\ *n* -S [Henry C. *Sorby* †1908 Eng. geologist + E *-ite*] : tempered martensite having a distinctly granular appearance under the microscope — **sor·bit·ic** \(ˈ)=¦bid·ik\ *adj*

sor·bi·tol \'= bə,tōl, -tōl\ *n* -S [²*sorb* + *-itol*] : a crystalline faintly sweet hexahydroxy alcohol $CH_2OH(CHOH)_4CH_2OH$ that occurs esp. in mountain ash fruits, may be obtained by reduction of L-sorbose but is made industrially by reduction of D-glucose, and is used chiefly as a humectant and softener and in making sorbitan derivatives and ascorbic acid — called also D-glucitol; compare DULCITOL, MANNITOL

sor·bon·ist *also* **sor·bonn·ist** \(ˈ)sȯ(r)¦bänəst, -¦bən-\ *n* -S *usu cap* [MF *sorboniste*, fr. *Sorbonne*, a house for impoverished theological students at the University of Paris, now the site of the faculties of arts and letters of the University of Paris (after Robert de *Sorbon* †1274 Fr. theologian, its founder) + *-iste* -ist] **1** : a doctor of or theological student at the University of Paris **2** : a graduate of or student at the Sorbonne

sor·bose \'sȯr,bōs *also* -ōz\ *n* -S [ISV *sorbitol* + *-ose*] : a sweet crystalline unfermentable sugar $C_6H_{12}O_6$ of the ketohexose class existing in three optically isomeric forms; *esp* : the levorotatory L-form obtained from sorbitol by fermentation with an acetobacter (*Acetobacter xylinum*) and used chiefly in making ascorbic acid

sor·bo·side \-ˌbə,sīd, -səd *also* -,zīd *or* -zəd\ *n* -S [*sorbose* + *-ide*] : a glycoside that yields sorbose on hydrolysis

sorbs *pl of* SORB, *pres 3d sing of* SORB

sor·bus \'sȯrbəs\ *n* [NL, fr. L, service tree] **1** *cap* : a genus of trees and shrubs (family Rosaceae) distinguished from *Pyrus* and *Malus* by the pinnate leaves, three styles, and carpels that are not cartilaginous — see MOUNTAIN ASH **2** -ES : any tree of the genus *Sorbus*

sor·cer·er \'sȯ(r)s(ə)rə(r)\ *n* -S [modif. of MF *sorcier*, fr. (assumed) VL *sortiarius*, fr. L *sort-*, *sors* lot, chance, decision by lot + *-i-* + *-arius* -ary — more at SORT] : a person who practices sorcery : MAGICIAN, WIZARD

sor·cer·ess \ǀs(ə)rəs\ *n* -ES [ME *sorceresse*, fr. AF, fr. OF *sorcier* + *-esse* -ess] : a female sorcerer

sor·cer·ize \ǀsə,rīz\ *vt* -ED/-ING/-S [*sorcery* + *-ize*] : to transform by sorcery

sor·cer·ous \ǀs(ə)rəs\ *adj* [*sorcery* + *-ous*] : of or relating to sorcery : using sorcery : MAGICAL

sor·cery \ǀs(ə)rē\ *n* -ES [ME *sorcerie*, fr. OF, fr. *sorcier* sorcerer + *-ie* -y — more at SORCERER] : the use of power gained from the assistance or control of evil spirits esp. for divining : divination by black magic : NECROMANCY, WITCHCRAFT **syn** see MAGIC

sor·dar·ia \sȯ(r)'da(a)rēə\ *n, cap* [NL, fr. L *sordes* dirt, filth + NL *-aria* — more at SWART] : a genus of chiefly dung-inhabiting ascomycetous fungi (order Sphaeriales) having scattered hairy-necked perithecia with dark continuous ascospores

sor·des \'sȯr(,)dēz\ *n, pl* **sordes** [L] : foul matter : useless matter : REFUSE; *specif* : the crusts that collect on the teeth and lips in debilitating diseases with protracted low fever

sor·did \-dəd\ *adj* [L *sordidus*, fr. *sordes* dirt, filth — more at SWART] **1 a** : characterized by filth : FILTHY ⟨~ surroundings⟩ **b** : slatternly or foul in appearance : SLUTTISH ⟨a ~ mob⟩ **c** : covered with filth : DIRTY ⟨~ animals⟩ **2** : marked by baseness or grossness : VILE ⟨~ motives⟩ **3** : meanly avaricious : COVETOUS, NIGGARDLY **4** : of a dull or muddy color — used in the names of fishes or birds — **sor·did·ly** *adv*

sor·did·ness *n* -ES : the quality or state of being sordid

sor·dine \'sȯ(ə)r,dēn, =ˈ=\ *n* -S [MF *sourdine* — more at SOURDINE] **1** : a cone-shaped pipe inserted in the mouth of a trumpet to muffle its tone : MUTE **2** : SOURDINE 1a

sor·di·no \sȯr'dē(,)nō\ *n, pl* **sordi·ni** \-nē\ [It — more at SOURDINE] : ²MUTE

sor·dor \'sȯrdər, -,dȯ(ə)r\ *n* -S [NL, fr. L *sordes* dirt, filth + *-or* — more at SWART] : REFUSE, DREGS; *also* : SORDIDNESS

¹sore \'sō(ə)r, -ȯ(ə)r, -ōə, -ȯ(ə)\ *adj* -ER/-EST [ME *sar, sor, soor*, fr. OE *sār*; akin to OS & OHG *sēr* painful, sore, ON *sārr* sore, wounded, L *saevus* fierce, savage, cruel, OIr *sāeth* pain, Lith *šaižus* rough, sharp] **1** PAINFUL, DISTRESSING: as **a** : causing or involving physical suffering or risk ⟨a ~ wound⟩ **b** : painful from overuse, injury, or inflammation : SENSITIVE ⟨~ muscles⟩ ⟨a ~ eye⟩; *also* : affected by such pain ⟨~ from riding⟩ **c** : causing or likely to cause mental distress ⟨~ news⟩ ⟨a ~ subject⟩ **2** : attended by strenuous difficulties, hardship, or exertion ⟨in ~ straits⟩ ⟨~ struggles⟩ **3** : not readily placated or mollified : ANGERED, NETTLED, VEXED ⟨~ over a remark⟩ **syn** see BITTER

²sore \"\ *n* -S [ME *sar, sor, soor*, fr. OE *sār*; akin to OHG *sēr* pain, wound, ON *sār* sore, wound, Goth *sair* pain, OE *sār*, adj.] **1 a** : a place (as an ulcer or boil) in an animal body where the skin and flesh are ruptured or bruised and tender or painful **b** : a wound, bruise, or abrasion that has become infected : a suppurating ulcer or boil **c** : LESION **2** : DISEASE, SICKNESS, HARM **3** : a source or cause of pain or vexation : AFFLICTION, TROUBLE ⟨the ~s of official duties⟩

³sore \"\ *adv* [ME *sare, sore*, fr. OE *sāre* (akin to OS & OHG *sēro* sorely), fr. *sār*, adj.] : SORELY — often used in combination ⟨*sore*-afraid⟩

soredi- *comb form* [NL *soredium*] : soredium ⟨*soredi*ferous⟩ ⟨*sorediform*⟩ ⟨*soredioid*⟩

so·re·di·al \sə'rēdēəl\ *adj* [*soredi-* + *-al*] : relating to or like a soredium

so·re·di·oid \sə'rēdē,ȯid\ *or* **so·re·di·ose** \-,ōs\ *adj* [*soredi-* + *-oid* or *-ose*] : having the form or nature of a soredium : resembling or functioning as a soredium

so·re·di·um \sə'rēdēəm\ *n, pl* **sore·dia** \-dēə\ [NL, irreg. fr. Gk *sōros* heap + NL *-idium*; akin to L *tumēre* to swell — more at THUMB] : one of the vegetative gemmae on the surface of the thallus of a lichen consisting of a tuft of hyphae investing a few algal cells or gonidia — called also *brood bud, hologonidium*

sore-eyed pigeon \'=,=-\ *n* : SHEATHBILL

sorefalcon \'=,==\ *n* [*sore* (as in *sorehawk*) + *falcon*] : a peregrine falcon in the reddish plumage of the first year

sorehawk \'=,=\ *n* [ME *sor hawke*, fr. *sor* sorrel (fr. MF) + *hawke, hauk* hawk — more at SORREL, HAWK] : SOREFALCON

¹sorehead \'=,=\ *n* [prob. fr. the phrase *as mad as a bear with a sore head*] **1** : a person easily angered or disgruntled : one obdurately contentious and eager to find grievances or faults **2** [¹*sore* + *head*] : FOWL POX

²sorehead \"\ *adj* : irritated and disappointed esp. by having one's hopes frustrated ⟨~ politicians⟩

soreheaded \'=¦==\ *adj* : SOREHEAD — **sore·head·ed·ly** *adv* — **sore·head·ed·ness** *n* -ES

sore heels *n pl* : HORSEPOX

sore hocks *n pl* : an ulcerated condition of the undersurface of the forefeet or hind feet of a domestic rabbit

sor·el \'sȯrəl, 'sär-\ *n* -S [ME *sorelle, sorrel* (also, sorrel horse) — more at SORREL] *Brit* : a male fallow deer in the third year

sorel cement \"-\ *n* [fr. the name *Sorel*] : magnesium oxychloride cement consisting of magnesium chloride and calcined magnesia

sore·ly *adv* [ME *sarly, sorly, soorly*, fr. OE *sārlīce*, fr. *sārlīc*, adj., grievous, sad, painful, fr. *sār* sore + *-līc* -ly — more at SORE] : in a sore manner: as **a** : PAINFULLY, GRIEVOUSLY ⟨~ vexed⟩ **b** : SEVERELY, VIOLENTLY ⟨~ exerted⟩ **c** : EXTREMELY ⟨~ tired⟩

sore mouth *n* **1** : a highly contagious virus disease of sheep and goats that occurs esp. in young animals, is characterized by extensive vesiculation and subsequent ulceration about the lips, gums, and tongue, and rarely ends fatally but interferes with nutrition and may be complicated by secondary bacterial infection — called also *contagious ecthyma, scabby mouth* **2** : necrobacillosis affecting the mouth; *esp* : CALF DIPHTHERIA

soremuzzle \'=¦==\ *n* : SORE MOUTH 1

sore·ness *n* -ES [ME *sarnes, sornes*, fr. OE *sārnes*, fr. *sār* sore + *-nes* -ness] **1** : the quality or state of being sore: as **a** : PAINFULNESS ⟨the ~ of a sprain⟩ **b** : mental grief : DISTRESS ⟨the ~ of defeat⟩ **c** : SEVERITY, VIOLENCE ⟨the ~ of battle⟩ **2** : something sore or painful

sorer *comparative of* SORE

sores *pl of* SORE

sore shank *n* : rhizoctonia disease (as of tobacco)

sore shin *n* : a disease of tobacco, cotton, and other plants beyond the seedling stage caused by any of several soil fungi (as members of the genera *Corticium* and *Pythium*) that girdle the plant near the groundline

sorest *superlative of* SORE

sore throat *n* : painful throat due to inflammation of the fauces and pharynx

so·rex \'sȯr,eks\ *n* [NL, fr. L, shrew; akin to L *susurrus* murmur, hum — more at SWARM] **1** *cap* : a large and widely distributed genus (the type of the family Soricidae) of shrews with 32 reddish-brown-tipped teeth **2** -ES : any shrew of the genus *Sorex*

sor·ge \'zȯrgə\ *n* -S [G, fr. OHG *sorga* — more at SORROW] : CONCERN, CARE; *esp* : a feeling bordering on anxiety

sor·ghum \'sȯrgəm, -ȯ(ə)g-\ *n* [NL, fr. It *sorgo*, perh. fr. (assumed) VL *Syricum* (*granum*), fr. L *Syricum* (neut. of *Syricus* Syrian) + *granum* grain] **1 a** *cap* : an economically important genus of Old World tropical grasses that are sometimes naturalized in the New World, are widely grown for grain and herbage even in temperate regions, and are characterized by growth habit and stem form similar to that of Indian corn but have the leaves saw-toothed on their edges and the spikelets in pairs on a hairy rachis — see BROOMCORN, GRAIN SORGHUM, SORGO **b** -S : any plant of the genus *Sorghum*; *esp* : any cultivated plant (as a grain sorghum or a sorgo) derived from a common species (*S. vulgare*) **c** -S : the seeds of grain sorghum used as cereals and stock feed **d** -S : the stalks and leaves of sorghum used for fodder, hay, or silage **2** -S : syrup produced by evaporating from stems of any sorgo the juice which resembles cane sugar but contains a high proportion of invert sugars as well as starch and dextrin **3** -S : something cloyingly sweet or overly sentimental

sorghum brown *n* : WOOD ROSE 2

sorghum midge *n* : a minute gall midge (*Contarinia sorghicola*) whose larvae develop in the seed heads of sorghum, broomcorn, and wild grasses

sorghum smut *n* **1** : a smut attacking sorghum; *esp* : HEAD SMUT **2** : an organism causing a sorghum smut

sor·go *also* **sor·gho** \-(,)gō\ *n* -S [It *sorgo*] : any of various sorghums that are cultivated primarily for the sweet juice in their stems from which sugar and syrup are made and are also widely used for fodder and silage — called also *sweet sorghum*; compare GRAIN SORGHUM

sorgo syrup *n* : syrup made of sorghum

sori *pl of* SORUS

so·ric·i·dae \sə'risə,dē\ *n pl, cap* [NL, fr. *Soric-*, *Sorex*, type genus + *-idae*] : a family of small chiefly terrestrial long-snouted mammals (order Insectivora) that comprise the true shrews — compare ELEPHANT SHREW, TALPIDAE

so·ric·i·dent \sə'risə,dent, -dənt\ *adj* [L *soric-*, *sorex* shrew + *-i-* + *dent-*, *dens* tooth — more at SOREX, TOOTH] : having or characterized by teeth like those of shrews in which the middle pair of incisors are very large and the canines small and unspecialized

¹sor·i·cine \'sȯrə,sīn\ *adj* [L *soricinus*, fr. *soric-*, *sorex* shrew + *-inus* -ine] : of, like, or relating to a shrew or the Soricidae

²soricine \"\ *n* -S : SHREW

soricine bat *n* : a leaf-nosed bat (*Glossophaga soricina*) of Central and So. America

sor·i·coi·dea \,sȯrə'kȯidēə\ *n pl, cap* [NL, fr. *Soric-*, *Sorex* + *-oidea*] : a superfamily of insectivores consisting of the shrews, moles, and extinct related forms

sories *pl of* SORY

so·rite \'sō,rīt\ *n* -S [Gk *sōros* heap + E *-ite*] : ARCHAEOCYTE

so·ri·tes \sə'rīd·(,)ēz\ *n, pl* **sorites** \"\ [L, fr. Gk *sōritēs*, *sōreitēs*, fr. *sōros* heap — more at SORUS] **1** : an abridged form of stating a series of syllogisms in a series of propositions so arranged that the predicate of each one that precedes forms the subject of each one that follows and the conclusion unites the subject of the first proposition with the predicate of the last proposition — compare GOCLENIAN SORITES **2** : an aggregation of more or less related things, facts, or items

so·rit·i·cal \sə'rid·əkəl\ *also* **so·rit·ic** \-d·ik\ *adj* [*soritical*, fr. Gk *sōritikos* (fr. *sōritēs* + *-ikos* -ic) + *-al*; *soritic*, fr. Gk *sōritikos*] : of or relating to a sorites

sorn \'sȯ(ə)rn\ *vi* -ED/-ING/-S [origin unknown] *chiefly Scot* : to impose in order to obtain hospitality : SPONGE — **sorn·er** \-nər\ *n* -S *chiefly Scot*

sor·o·ban \'sȯrə,bän\ *n* -S [Jap, fr. Chin (Pek) *suan⁴ p'an²*, lit., reckoning board] : an abacus used by the Japanese that is a modification of the Chinese suan pan

so·ro·che \sə'rōchē\ *n* -S [AmerSp, fr. Quechua *surúchi*, lit., antimony; fr. the belief that the sickness is due to the presence of the metal in the Andes mountains] : mountain sickness esp. in the Andes

so·rop·ti·mist \sə'räptəməst\ *n* -S [blend of *sorority* and *optimist*] : a member of a club composed of professional women and women business executives associated primarily for service

so·ro·ral \sə'rōrəl\ *adj* [L *soror* sister + E *-al* — more at SISTER] : of, relating to, or in the relationship of a sister : SISTERLY

sororal polygyny *n* : a polygyny in which the wives are sisters — contrasted with *fraternal polyandry*; compare LEVIRATE, SORORATE

soro·rate \sə'rōrət, -ōr,āt; 'sȯrə,rāt\ *n* -S [L *soror* sister + E *-ate*] : the marriage of one man with two or more sisters usu. successively and after the first wife has been found to be barren or after her death — compare LEVIRATE, SORORAL POLYGYNY

so·ro·ri·al \sə'rōrēəl\ *adj* [L *sororius* sororal (fr. *soror* sister) + E *-al*] : SORORAL — **so·ro·ri·al·ly** \-ēəlē\ *adv*

so·ror·i·cide \sə'rȯrə,sīd\ *n* -S [in sense 1, fr. ML *sororicidium*, fr. L *soror* sister + *-i-* + *-cidium* -cide (killing); in sense 2, fr. L *sororicida*, fr. *soror* + *-i-* + *-cida* -cide (killer)] **1** : the act of killing one's sister **2** : a person who kills his sister

so·ror·i·ty \sə'rȯrəd·ē, -rär-, -ətē, -i\ *n* -ES [ML *sororitas*, fr. L *soror* sister + *-itas* -ity — more at SISTER] **1** : SISTERHOOD **2** : a society or club of girls or women (as in a college) — compare FRATERNITY

so·ro·rize \'sȯrə,rīz\ *vi* -ED/-ING/-S [L *soror* + E *-ize*] : to associate or hold fellowship as sisters — compare FRATERNIZE

so·rose \'sōr,ōs\ *adj* [NL sorus + E *-ose*] : bearing sori

so·ro·silicate \¦sōr(,)ō+\ *n* [Gk *sōros* heap + E *silicate*] : a class of polymeric silicates or a member thereof in which the silicon-oxygen groups are linked into limited clusters by sharing oxygen atoms (as in hemimorphite or in melilite or zunyite) and in some cases a portion of the silicon is replaced by aluminum — compare CYCLOSILICATE, INOSILICATE, NESOSILICATE, PHYLLOSILICATE, TECTOSILICATE

so·ro·sis \sə'rōsəs\ *n*, *pl* **soroses** \-ō,sēz\ *or* **sorosises** [fr. *Sorosis*, a woman's club incorporated in 1869] : an association of women (as for social purposes) : a women's club

so·ro·spo·rel·la \,sōrəspə'relə\ *n*, *cap* [NL, fr. Gk *sōros* heap + *spora* seed + NL *-ella* — more at SPORE] : a genus of imperfect fungi (family Moniliaceae) parasitic on various insect larvae and characterized by abundant chlamydospore production and verticillate conidiophores forming nonseptate hyaline spores

so·ro·spo·ri·um \,sōrə'spōrēəm\ *n*, *cap* [NL, fr. Gk *sōros* heap + NL *-sporium*] : a genus of smut fungi having teliospores united in more or less firm ball-like masses with the sori dusty at maturity and including several that cause head smuts in grasses

sorp·tion \'sȯrpshən\ *n* -S [back-formation fr. *absorption* & *adsorption*] : the process of sorbing by physical or chemical forces or both : ADSORPTION, ABSORPTION ⟨~ of gases and vapors by solids⟩ ⟨~ occurs wherever there is a surface or an interface —J.W.McBain⟩ — compare CHEMISORPTION, IMBIBITION 2a, OCCLUSION 3

sorp·tive \-ptiv\ *adj* : relating to sorption

sor·ra \'särə\ *also* **sor·roa** \-rwə\ *Irish & Scot var of* SORROW

¹sor·rel \'sȯrəl, 'sär-\ *n* -S [ME *sorelle*, fr. MF *sorel*, fr. *sorel*, adj., having the color sorrel, fr. *sor* reddish brown, prob. of Gmc origin; akin to MD *soor* dry, dried out, MLG *sōr* — more at SERE] **1** : an animal of a sorrel color: as **a** : a light bright chestnut horse often with white mane and tail **b** : a dark red roan horse **2** [fr. *sorrel*, adj., of the color sorrel, fr. ME *sorelle*, fr. MF *sorel*] : a brownish orange to light brown that is darker than caramel, slightly yellower than tawny, and redder than raw sienna

²sorrel \"\ *n* -S [ME *sorel*, fr. MF *surele*, fr. OF, fr. *sur* sour, of Gmc origin; akin to OHG *sūr* sour — more at SOUR] : any of various plants with sour juice: as **a** : ¹DOCK 1 **b** : a plant of the genus *Oxalis* — called also *wood sorrel* **c** : ROSELLE

sorrel dock *n* : GARDEN SORREL

sorrel family *n* : OXALIDACEAE

sorrel tree *n* **1** : SOURWOOD **2** : an Australian hibiscus (*Hibiscus heterophyllus*) with acid foliage **3** : STAGGERBUSH

sorrel vine *n* : a fleshy tropical American vine (*Cissus trifoliata*) with acid compound leaves

sor·ren·tine \'sȯrən·,tēn, sə'ren-\ *adj*, *usu cap* [It *sorrentino*, fr. *Sorrento*, seaport in southern Italy + It *-ino* -ine (fr. L *-inus*)] : relating to, situated in, inhabiting, or coming from Sorrento ⟨the *Sorrentine* peninsula⟩

sor·ren·to green \sə'rent·(,)ō-\ *n*, *often cap S* [fr. *Sorrento*, seaport in southern Italy] : a moderate bluish green that is bluer and deeper than porcelain green or sea blue

sorrento work *n*, *usu cap S* : inlaid fretwork (as in wood) esp. when made at or near Sorrento, Italy

sorrier *comparative of* SORRY

sorriest *superlative of* SORRY

sor·ri·ly \'särəlē, -li *also* 'sȯr-\ *adv* [ME *sarily*, *sorily*, fr. *sary*, *sory* sorry + *-ly* — more at SORRY] : in a sorry manner

sor·ri·ness \-rēnəs, -rin-\ *n* -ES [ME *sarines*, *sorines*, fr. OE *sārignes*, fr. *sārig* sorry + *-nes* -ness — more at SORRY] : the quality or state of being sorry

¹sor·row \'sä(,)rō, -rə *also* 'sȯ-; -,rəw, -,rō+V\ *n* -S [ME *sorge*, *sorwe*, *sorow*, fr. OE *sorg*; akin to OHG *sorga* care, sorrow, ON *sorg*, Goth *saurga* care, sorrow, OIr *serg* sickness, OSlav *sraga* sickness, Skt *sūrkṣati* he is concerned about something] **1 a** : uneasiness or anguish due to loss (as of something loved or familiar) : UNHAPPINESS, SADNESS ⟨~ at the loss of a friend⟩ **b** : a cause of grief or sadness : HARM, DAMAGE ⟨the great ~ of a conflagration⟩ ⟨transgressions that were ultimately a permanent ~⟩ **2** : contrition at having done or caused evil : PENITENCE **3** : a display of grief or sadness ⟨LAMENTATION ⟨uneasy in the presence of family ~⟩ **4 a** *chiefly Irish & Scot* (1) : MISCHIEF, MISFORTUNE (2) — used as an emphatic negative; often preceded by *the* ⟨the ~ a word or sign out of them —Seumas O'Kelly⟩ **b** *chiefly Scot* : PEST, RASCAL

syn GRIEF, HEARTACHE, ANGUISH, WOE, DOLE, REGRET: SORROW is the most general of these terms, implying a sense of loss or of guilt ⟨the widespread *sorrow* that his death aroused —Douglas Cleverdon⟩ ⟨anguish that wept aloud; misery that could find no voice; *sorrow* that was dumb —Oscar Wilde⟩ GRIEF is poignant or extended sorrow ⟨immune to *grief*, even at the death of a loved one⟩ HEARTACHE is usu. an all-embracing hidden sorrow springing from disappointment or loss, as of hope or love ⟨the *heartache* of war, signalized in defeat and death⟩ ⟨reach fame and success after many years of poverty and *heartache*⟩ ⟨the *heartache* of unrequited love⟩ ANGUISH is usu. excruciating or torturing grief or dread ⟨nothing but despair and *anguish* written in every line of Susanna's slim figure —Gerald Beaumont⟩ ⟨the *anguish* of intense fear⟩ WOE is deep or inconsolable misery induced by grief or anguish ⟨the suffering people whose *woes* he has not alleviated —W.P. Webb⟩ ⟨one builds a tight fence around the misfortune, and within that minute enclosure, one sits intent upon one's *woe* —H.A.Overstreet⟩ ⟨bowed now in his *woe* —Agnes S. Turnbull⟩ DOLE is woe given vent to in weeping, moaning, or wailing ⟨giving way to inconsolable, tearful *dole*⟩ REGRET implies a sorrow usu. not outwardly manifest and may designate pain of mind or spiritual anguish induced by disappointment, lost opportunity, or heartache, and ranging in intensity from the mildest of momentary unhappiness at an invitation declined to intense pangs of remorse for a wrong done, though usu. signifying only the lighter, less intense feelings ⟨intense *regret* for lost opportunities⟩ ⟨his bitter *regrets* for past happiness —T.S. Eliot⟩ ⟨in moments of *regret* we recognize that some of our judgments have been mistaken —M.R.Cohen⟩

²sorrow \"\ *vb* -ED/-ING/-S [ME *sorgen*, *sorwen*, *sorowen*, fr. OE *sorgian*; akin to OS *sorgon* to care, grieve, sorrow, OHG *sorgēn*, Goth *saurgan* to care, grieve, *saurga*, n.] *vi* **1** : to feel sorrow : GRIEVE ⟨~ over the death of a relative⟩ **2** : to express grief : LAMENT ⟨~ing at the graves of loved ones⟩ ~ *vt* : MOURN, LAMENT **syn** see GRIEVE

sor·row·er \-rəwə(r), -,rōə-\ *n* -S : one that sorrows

sor·row·ful \-rōfəl, -rəf-\ *adj* [ME *sorowful*, fr. OE *sorgful*, fr. *sorg* sorrow + *-ful*] **1** : full of or characterized by sorrow ⟨~ widows⟩ **2** : expressive of or inducing sorrow : SAD ⟨~ tale⟩ **3** : given to melancholy : PLAINTIVE ⟨a ~ disposition⟩

sor·row·ful·ly \-f(ə)lē, -li\ *adv* [ME *sorowfully*, fr. *sorowful* + *-ly*] : in a sorrowful manner

sor·row·ful·ness \-fəlnəs\ *n* -ES [ME *sorowfulnesse*, fr. *sorowful* + *-nesse* -ness] : the quality or state of being sorrowful : MISERABLENESS, SADNESS

sorrowing *adj* : given to grief, anguish, or lamentation — **sorrow·ing·ly** *adv*

sor·row·less \-,rōləs, -rəl-\ *adj* : being without sorrow : free of grief or trouble

sor·ry \'särē, 'sȯr-, -ri\ *adj* -ER/-EST [ME *sary*, *sory*, fr. OE *sārig*, fr. *sār* sore + *-ig* -y — more at SORE] **1** : grieved or grieving over the loss of some good ⟨was ~ to see it moved but I would be sorrier to see it destroyed —W.T.Scott⟩ : feeling sorrow, regret, or penitence ⟨she began to cry, poor thing, and I felt very ~ for her —W.S.Maugham⟩ ⟨was momentarily ~ that she had not read it —Arnold Bennett⟩ ⟨~ for past transgressions⟩ — often used interjectionally to express polite regret ⟨~, but I disagree⟩ ⟨~; I decline to yield —F.H.Case⟩ **2** : of melancholy, dismal, or gloomy mien : MOURNFUL, SAD ⟨through the ~ routine that follows on the heels of death —B.A.Williams⟩ ⟨the ~ truth is, this book ought not to have been accepted for publication —Kemp Malone⟩ **3** : inspiring blended sorrow, pity, scorn, and ridicule : worthlessly or wretchedly worn-out, unfit, or futile ⟨a ~ underpaid official⟩ ⟨fed us on such ~ chuck —Carl Sandburg⟩ ⟨for every good fur-catching dog, there are a hundred ~ ones —F.B.Gipson⟩ ⟨making a ~ spectacle of himself —Joseph Wechsberg⟩ **syn** see CONTEMPTIBLE

¹sort \'sȯ(ə)r\|t, -ó(ə)\|, *usu* \|d· +V\ *n* -S [ME, fr. MF *sorte*, prob. fr. ML & LL; ML *sort-*, *sors* sort, kind, fr. LL, way, manner, fr. L, lot, decision by lot, chance, fortune; perh. akin to L *serere* to bind together, join — more at SERIES] **1** : a group or kind established or set up permanently or temporarily on the basis of any characteristic in common ⟨a strange ~ of people⟩ — sometimes used as a zero plural with a preceding *these* or *those* and a following *of* ⟨those ~ of men⟩ **2 a** : a number of things used or adapted to be used together : SET, SUIT **b** *archaic* : GROUP, CROWD, FLOCK **3 a** : a method or manner of acting : WAY, FASHION, MANNER **b** : CHARACTER, QUALITY, DISPOSITION : NATURE ⟨people of an evil ~⟩; *also* : INDIVIDUAL, THING ⟨he is really not a bad ~ at all⟩ **4 a** : letter or character that is one element of a font **b** : a character or piece of type (as a symbol, piece fraction, or space) that is not part of a regular font **c** : a matrix that is not stored in a keyboard-controlled channel of a slugcasting machine and must be hand-inserted when used; *also* : a character cast or made from such a matrix **5 sorts** *pl* **a** : a grade of a natural resin (as a copal) characterized by largish pieces sorted usu. by color **b** : ungraded gum (as gum arabic) of various sizes **syn** see TYPE — **after a sort** : in a rough, unfinished, or haphazard way : after a fashion — **of sorts** *or* **of a sort** : of an inconsequential or mediocre quality ⟨a poet *of sorts*⟩ — **out of sorts** : out of temper : VEXED, ILL, DISTURBED

²sort \"\ *vb* -ED/-ING/-S [ME *sorten*, fr. *sort*, n.] *vt* **1** *obs* : to select as of a certain sort : CHOOSE; *also* : to distinguish between **2** *obs* : to assign by or as if by lot : ALLOT **3 a** : to put in a given place or rank according to kind, class, or nature ⟨~ mail⟩ : arrange according to chaarcteristics : CLASSIFY — often used with *out* ⟨~ out colors⟩ **b** : to separate (a particular thing) from a mass ⟨~ out a defective tool⟩ ⟨quickly ~ out some of the riddles resulting from repressed guilt —R.L. Jenkins⟩ **4** *chiefly Scot* : to furnish provision for; *esp* : to feed and bed down (an animal) **5** *chiefly Scot* **a** : to put to rights : put in order **b** : to put to rights morally by punishing or scolding ~ *vi* **1** : to join or associate with others esp. of the same kind — used with *with* ⟨~ with thieves⟩ **2** *obs* : to divine by or as if by lot : SOOTHSAY; *also* : turn out **3** *archaic* : SUIT, HARMONIZE, AGREE — used with *with*

sort·able \'sȯ(r)d·əbəl\ *adj* **1** : capable of being sorted **2** : SUITABLE, BEFITTING, PROPER — **sort·ably** \-blē\ *adv*

sor·ta·tion \sȯ(r)'tāshən\ *n* -S : the act or process of sorting ⟨the ~ of mail⟩

sort·er \'sȯrd·ər, -ó(ə)d·ə(r, \|tə-\ *n* -S : one that sorts: as **a** : one that sorts hides, skins, and leather according to grade, weight, thickness, and color **b** : one that sorts burned brick or tile according to color and hardness **c** : one that sorts fruit or other food products according to size or condition **d** : a clerical worker who sorts such items as bills, checks, correspondence, or statements (as for mailing or filing) **e** : a machine or device for selecting punched cards or arranging them in groups or in a predetermined order

¹sor·tie \'sȯrd·ē, -d(ə)l, \|t\|, \|i *also* ˌ≈'tē *sometimes* ≈'tē\ *n* -S [F, fr. MF, fr. fem. of *sorti*, past part. of *sortir* to escape, sally, go out] : a sudden or rapid emerging or issuing out: as **a** : the sudden issuing of troops from a defensive position to attack or harass the enemy : SALLY **b** : one mission or attack by a single plane **c** : the departure of a ship or group of ships from a harbor or anchorage

²sortie \"\ *vi* -ED/-ING/-S : to issue forth in a sortie : sally forth or go out; *specif* : to depart from a harbor or anchorage

sor·ti·lege \'sȯ(r)d·əlij, -)t³l-, -³l,ej\ *n* -S [ME, fr. ML *sortilegium*, fr. L *sortilegus* foretelling, fr. *sort-*, *sors* lot + *-i-* + *-legus* (fr. *legere* to gather, select, read) — more at SORT, LEGEND] **1 a** : the act of divination by lots — compare AUGURY **b** : the art or practice of divination by lots **2** : SORCERY, WITCHCRAFT, ENCHANTMENT ⟨the ~ of suddenly acquired wealth⟩ — **sor·ti·leg·ic** \¦≈≈¦ejik\ *or* **sor·ti·le·gious** \¦≈≈¦ējəs\ *adj*

sor·ti·leg·er \-ijə(r), -,ej-\ *n* -S : FORTUNE-TELLER

sorting boom *n* : a stout boom used to guide floating logs into the sorting jack

sorting jack *n* : a moored raft having a gap through which logs are floated to be sorted by their marks; *also* : the space where the sorting is done

sorting tracks *n pl* : yard tracks for sorting and classifying railroad cars in detail after they have passed through the classification tracks

sor·ti·ta \sȯ(r)'tēd·ə\ *n* -S [It, fr. fem. of *sortito*, past part. of *sortire* to come out, emerge, fr. F *sortir*] : an entrance aria in an opera

sor·ti·tion \sȯ(r)'tishən\ *n* -S [L *sortition-*, *sortitio*, fr. *sortitus* (past part. of *sortiri* to cast or draw lots, fr. *sort-*, *sors* lot) + *-ion-*, *-io* -ion — more at SORT] : the act of casting lots : determination or appointment by or as if by lot

sortment *n* -S [²*sort* + *-ment*] *obs* : ASSORTMENT

sort of \-ə(v), -ər\ *adv* : kind of ⟨acting *sort of* crazy —Scott Fitzgerald⟩ ⟨I *sort of* thought —Kenneth Roberts⟩ ⟨*sort of* squatly romanesque —James Dugan⟩

sorts *pl of* SORT, *pres 3d sing of* SORT

so·rus \'sōrəs, 'sȯr-\ *n*, *pl* **so·ri** \-ō,rī, -ȯ,rī\ [NL, fr. Gk *sōros* heap; akin to L *tumēre* to swell — more at THUMB] : a cluster of reproductive bodies or spores on a lower plant: as **a** : a clump of sporangia on a fertile frond of a fern **b** : a mass of spores bursting through the epidermis of the host plant of a parasitic fungus **c** : a cluster of gemmae on the thallus of a lichen

-so·rus \"\ *n comb form* [NL, fr. *sorus*] : one having sori of a (specified) kind — in generic names of plants ⟨Campto*sorus*⟩

sor·va \'sȯrvə\ *n* -S [Pg *sôrva* (also, serviceberry), fr. L *sorba*, pl. of *sorbum* serviceberry] **1** : COUMA **2** : the edible fruit of the couma **3** : the latex of the couma which yields a rubber — see BORRACHA

so·ry \'sōrē\ *n* -ES [L, fr. Gk *sōry*] : a black earth impregnated with vitriol; *also* : VITRIOLS

sos *abbr* sostenuto

SOS \¦e,sō'es\ *n* -S **1** : an internationally recognized signal of distress in radio code made of three dots, three dashes, three dots and used esp. by ships calling for help **2** : a call or request for help or rescue ⟨sent an ~ home for more cash⟩

SOS *abbr* **1** services of supply **2** [L *si opus sit*] if occasion require

soshed \'säsht\ *adj* [prob. alter. of E dial. *sossed* soaked, saturated, fr. past part. of E ²*soss*] : DRUNK, INTOXICATED

so·sie \sō'zē\ *n* -S [F, fr. *Sosie*, slave whose form Mercury assumes in the play *Amphitryon* (1667) by Molière †1673 Fr. playwright, fr. L *Sosia*, servant of the Greco-Roman mythological hero Amphitryon in the play *Amphitruo* by Titus Maccius Plautus †184 B.C. Roman playwright] **1** : a person having an exact likeness with another : DOUBLE **2** : TWIN; *esp* : an identical twin

¹so–so \'≈¦≈\ *adv* [redupl. of ¹*so*] : TOLERABLY, PASSABLY ⟨played golf only *so-so*⟩

²so–so \"\ *adj* : neither very good nor very bad : MIDDLING, PASSABLE, TOLERABLE, INDIFFERENT ⟨business has been only *so-so* lately⟩ ⟨tired of seeing *so-so* movies⟩

¹soss \'säs\ *n* -ES [ME *sos*, of imit. origin] *dial Brit* : MESS, SLOP

²soss \"\ *vb* -ED/-ING/-ES *vi* **1** *dial Brit* : MESS, SLOP **2** *dial Brit* : LAP ~ *vt*, *dial Brit* : LAP

³soss \"\ *n* -ES [prob. alter. of obs. E *sosh* thud, thump, of imit. origin] : THUMP

⁴soss \"\ *adv*, *dial Brit* : HEAVILY, PLUMP

⁵soss \"\ *vi* -ED/-ING/-ES *dial Brit* : to fall heavily

so·ste·nen·te *also* **so·sti·nen·te** \¦sōstə¦nentē, -en·(,)tā\ *adj* [It *sostenente*, fr. pres. part. of *sostenere* to sustain, fr. L *sustinēre* — more at SUSTAIN] : SUSTAINING; *sometimes* : SOSTENUTO

²sostenente *or* **sostinente** \"\ *n* -S [*sostenente* alter. of *sostinente*; *sostinente* short for *sostinente pianoforte*] : a device on a piano for attaining a sostenuto effect — compare SOSTINENTE PIANOFORTE

¹so·ste·nu·to \¦sōstə¦nüd·(,)ō\ *adj* [It, fr. past part. of *sostenere* to sustain] : SUSTAINED, PROLONGED — used as a direction in music to sustain the notes of a movement or passage to or beyond their full nominal value; *abbr. sost*

²sostenuto \"\ *n* -S : a movement or passage whose notes are markedly sustained or prolonged

sostenuto pedal *n* : a selective damper pedal on a piano that enables the performer to sustain selected tones or chords

sostinente pianoforte *n* [*sostinente* alter. of ¹*sostenente*] : one of several musical instruments (as melopiano, piano-violin) combining the ordinary piano with a mechanism for prolonging the tone produced by the strings — compare HARMONICHORD

¹sot \'sät, -äd·+V\ *n* -S [ME *sot*, *sott*, fr. OE] **1** *archaic* : FOOL, IDIOT **2** : a person dulled by excessive and continual drinking : a habitual drunkard

²sot \"\ *vb* **sotted**; **sotted**; **sotting**; **sots** [ME *sotten*, fr. *sott*, *sot* fool] *vt* **1** *archaic* : to make a fool or simpleton of : BEFOOL, STULTIFY, BEMUSE **2** : to waste in drunkenness : squander sottishly — usu. used with *away* ⟨~ away his time in taverns⟩ ~ *vi* : TIPPLE, GUZZLE

³sot \"\ *chiefly dial past of* SIT

⁴sot \"\ *adj* [fr. E dial. past part. of E *set*] **1** *dial* : SET, FIXED **2** *dial* : STUBBORN, OBSTINATE

so·ta·de·an \¦sōd·ə¦dēən\ *adj*, *usu cap* [L *sotade*us sotadean (fr. Gk *sōtadeios*, fr. *Sōtadēs* Sotades, 3d cent. B.C. Greek satirist) + E *-an*] : of, relating to, or characteristic of the ancient Greek poet Sotades or his notoriously scurrilous and licentious verse

sotadean verse *n* : a catalectic tetrameter of major ionics having the normal form ––⏑⏑ | ––⏑⏑ | ––⏑⏑ | ––

¹so·tad·ic \sō'tadik\ *adj*, *usu cap* [L *sotadicus*, fr. *Sotades* + L *-icus* -ic] : SOTADEAN

²sotadic \"\ *n* -S *usu cap* [L *sotadicus*, fr. *sotadicus*, adj., sotadic] : a Sotadean verse or poem : a scurrilous satire

sotadic verse *n*, *usu cap S* : palindromic verse

so·te·ri·al \sō'tirēəl\ *adj* [Gk *sōtēria* deliverance (fr. *sōtēr* savior + *-ia* -y) + E *-al*] : of or relating to salvation ⟨~ significance of biblical incidents⟩

so·te·ri·o·log·i·cal \sō¦tirēə¦läjəkəl\ *adj* : of or pertaining to soteriology

so·te·ri·ol·o·gy \sō,tirē'äləjē\ *n* -ES [Gk *sōtērion* deliverance, salvation (fr. *sōtēr* savior, fr. *sōzein* to save) + E *-logy*; akin to Gk *sōma* body — more at -SOMA] : a branch of theology that deals with salvation as the effect of divine agency

so that *conj* [ME, fr. OE *swā thæt*] **1** : SO 1 ⟨the turf roof of it had fallen entirely in *so that* the hut was of no use to me —R.L.Stevenson⟩ ⟨bombed out all the bridges *so that* the enemy could not retreat⟩ **2** *archaic* : provided that ⟨*so that* ye do not serve me sparrow hawks for supper, I will enter —Alfred Tennyson⟩

so·thi·ac \'sōthē,ak\ *also* **so·thi·a·cal** \sō'thīəkəl\ *adj*, *usu cap* [Gk *Sōthis* the star Sirius + E *-iac*, *-iacal* (as in *zodiac*, *zodiacal*)] : SOTHIC

so·thic \'sōthik, 'säth-\ *adj*, *usu cap* [Gk *Sōthis* the star Sirius + E *-ic*; fr. the fact that the year began when Sirius first appeared on the eastern horizon at sunrise] : relating to the ancient Egyptian year of 365¼ days or to the Sothic cycle

sothic cycle *n*, *usu cap S* : a period of 1460 Sothic years in the ancient Egyptian calendar being the time required for the beginning of the vague year of 365 days to return to its original place in relation to the sun after retrogressing through all the seasons

so·tho \'sō(,)thō\ *n*, *pl* **sotho** *or* **sothos** *usu cap* **1** : BASUTO 1 **2** : a group of closely related Bantu languages comprising Tswana, Northern Sotho, and Southern Sotho **3** : any of the Sotho languages; *esp* : Southern Sotho

so·tie \sō'tē\ *n* -S [F, fr. MF, lit., foolishness, farce, fr. *sot* fool + *-ie* -y] : a short topical and farcical play of medieval France performed in costumes combining contemporary dress and fantastic elements (as donkey's ears and cockscombs)

so·tol \'sō,tōl, ≈'≈\ *n* -S [AmerSp, fr. Nahuatl *tzotolli*] **1** : a plant of the genus *Dasylirion* (esp. *D. texanum* and *D. wheeleri*) of the southwestern U. S. and adjacent Mexico **2** [MexSp *sotol*, *sotole*, fr. *sotole* maguey leaf] : a distilled liquor made in northern Mexico esp. from the maguey — compare MESCAL, TEQUILA

sots \'säts\ *n pl* [PaG *satz* yeast, leaven, coffee grounds, fr. MHG *saz* settlement, sediment, seat (gen. *satzes*), fr. *sitzen* to sit, fr. OHG *sizzen* — more at SIT] *dial chiefly Midland* : YEAST

sot·ted \'säd·əd\ *adj* [ME, short for *assotted*, past part. of *assotten* to be a fool, make a fool of, become infatuated, fr. OF *assoter*, *asoter* to treat as a fool, fr. *a-* (fr. L *ad-*) + *sot* fool] : BESOTTED

sot·ter \'säd·ə(r)\ *vi* -ED/-ING/-S [prob. fr. G dial. *sottern*; prob. akin to OHG *siodan* to seethe — more at SEETHE] *chiefly Scot* : SIMMER, BUBBLE, SPUTTER

sot·tish \'säd·\|ish, -ät\|, \|ēsh\ *adj* [¹*sot* + *-ish*] : resembling a sot : DOLTISH, STUPID : very foolish; *also* : DRUNKEN — **sot·tish·ly** *adv* — **sot·tish·ness** *n* -ES

sot·to vo·ce \¦säd·(,)ō'vōchē, ¦sä(,)tō'-, -'vō(,)chā\ *also* **sotto** *adv (or adj)* [It *sotto voce* fr. It *sottovoce*, adv., lit., under the voice; *sotto* short for *sotto voce*] **1** : under the breath : in an undertone; *also* : ASIDE, PRIVATELY **2** : very softly ⟨play the finale *sotto voce*⟩

sou \'sü\ *n*, *pl* **sous** \'sü(z)\ [F, fr. MF, fr. OF *sol*, *solt*, fr. LL *solidus*, *soldus* solidus — more at SOLIDUS] **1** : ⁴SOL **2** : a 5-centime piece **3** : a smallest piece of money : PENNY, TRIFLE ⟨not a ~ lost⟩

sou *abbr* south; southern

sou·a·ri \sü'ärē\ *n* -S [F *saouari*, fr. Galibi *sawarra*] : a tree of the genus *Caryocar*

souari nut *n* : the large edible nutlike seed of any of various So. American trees of the genus *Caryocar* (as *C. nuciferum*) that yield a bland oil used in cookery

souari-nut family *n* : CARYOCARACEAE

sou·bise \(')sü¦bēz\ *or* **soubise sauce** *n* -S [F *soubise*, after Charles de Rohan, Prince de *Soubise* †1787 Fr. nobleman and military leader, fr. *Soubise*, village in western France that was an ancient seigneury of the Rohan family] : a white or brown sauce containing onions or onion purée

sou·bre·saut \,sübrə'sō\ *n* -S [F, leap, fr. MF *soubresault* — more at SOMERSAULT] : a ballet jump from and a landing on both feet in closed position

sou·brette \sü'bret\ *n* -S [F, fr. Prov *soubreto*, fem. of *soubret* affected, coy, fr. *soubra* to set aside, exceed, surmount, fr. L *superare* to go over, surmount — more at SUPERABLE] **1 a** : a lady's maid in comedies who acts the part of an intrigante : a coquettish maidservant or frivolous young woman — compare INGENUE **b** : an actress who plays such a part **2** : a soprano who sings supporting roles in comic opera

soubriquet *var of* SOBRIQUET

sou·chong \(')sü¦chȯŋ, -¦shȯ, -¦jȯ, ¦äŋ\ *n* -S [Chin (Pek) *hsiao³ -chung³* small sort] **1** : any of several Chinese black teas made from large leaves **2** : the coarser leaves obtained by screening fired tea

soudanese *usu cap, var of* SUDANESE

¹souf·flé \(')sü̇'flā\ *n* -s [F, fr. *soufflé*, adj., puffed, fr. past part. of *souffler* to blow, blow up, puff up, fr. L *sufflare* — more at SUFFLATE] **1** : an entrée or a dessert made with a white sauce, egg yolks and stiffly whipped egg whites, seasonings, and added ingredients (as tuna, cheese, chocolate) baked until puffed ⟨cheese ~⟩ — compare MOUSSE **2** : something (as an artistic creation) having a light delicate mixture ⟨happy endings and her ~ of fairies and folklore —*Time*⟩ **3** : a thin or sheer fabric made with large puffed designs and used for women's dresses

²soufflé \"\ *vt* souffléed; souffléing; soufflés : to cause (food) to puff up in cooking

³soufflé \"\ *adj* [F, fr. past part. of *souffler* to blow] **1** : of pottery : decorated with very small drops or sprinkles of color as if blown from a bellows **2** *or* souf·fléed \-ād\ [souffléed fr. ¹*soufflé* + -*ed*] : puffed by or in cooking ⟨~ omelette⟩ ⟨~ crackers⟩ ⟨~ mashed potato⟩

⁴souf·fle \'süfəl\ *n* -s [F, fr. *souffler* to blow, blow up] : a blowing sound heard on auscultation ⟨the uterine ~ heard in pregnancy⟩

soufflé potatoes *n pl but sing or pl in constr* [trans. of F *pommes de terre soufflées*] **1** : mashed potatoes with egg yolks, stiffly whipped egg whites, butter, and seasonings baked until puffed **2** : thinly sliced potatoes fried in deep fat of moderate temperature and then in fat of high temperature until puffed

sou·fri·ere \süfrē̇'a(ə)r\ *n* -s [F, fr. *soufre* sulfur (fr. L *sulphur*) + -*ière* -ier] : SOLFATARA

soufrière bird *n* : a solitaire (*Myadestes genibarbis sibilano*) of St. Vincent Island, West Indies, known only from the forested summit of the volcano La Soufrière

sougan *var of* SUGAN

¹sough \'saů̇, 'sǔ̇f\ *vb* -ED/-ING/-s [ME *swoghen, swoughen*, fr. OE *swōgan* to sound, rustle, moan; akin to OS *swōgan* to rustle, ON *sœgr* tumult, noise, Goth *gaswogjan* to groan, Lith *svagėti* to sound and perh. to Gk *ēchē̄, ēchos* sound — more at ECHO] *vi* **1 a** : to make a moaning or sighing sound ⟨wind ~*ing* in the branches⟩ **b** : to breathe or sigh noisily ⟨~*ing* in her sleep⟩ *c Scot* : to breathe one's last : DIE — used with *away* **2** *Scot* : to preach or pray in a whining tone ~ *vt* **1** *Scot* : to hum or whistle (a tune) softly **2** *Scot* : to utter or deliver (as a sermon) in a monotonous chanting tone

²sough \"\ *n* -s [ME *swogh, swough*, fr. *swoghen, swoughen* to sough] **1 a** : a moaning, murmuring, or sighing sound (as of the wind) **b** : a deep or noisy sigh **2** *Scot* : a flying report : RUMOR **3** *Scot* : the whiz of a missile or the hiss of a swung sword or club **4** *Scot* : a singsong manner of speaking esp. in preaching or praying — **a calm sough** *chiefly Scot* : SILENCE

³sough \'sǎf, 'saů̇\ *n* -s [ME *sough, swoughe, sogh*] **1** *Brit* : a wet place **2** *Brit* : DRAIN; *specif* : an adit for draining a mine

⁴sough \"\ *vt* -ED/-ING/-S *Brit* : to ditch for drainage : DRAIN

sought [ME *soughte* (past), *sought* (past part.), fr. OE *sōhte* (past), *gesōhte* (past part.)] *past of* SEEK

¹souk \'sük, 'sǔ̇k\ *chiefly Scot var of* SUCK

²souk *var of* SUQ

¹soul \'sōl\ *n* -s [ME *soule*, fr. OE *sāwol, sāwl*; akin to OHG *sēla, sēula* soul, ON *sāla*, Goth *saiwala*] **1** : the immaterial essence or substance, animating principle, or actuating cause of life or of the individual life **2 a** : the psychical or spiritual principle in general shared by or embodied in individual human beings or all beings having a rational and spiritual nature **b** : the psychical or spiritual nature of the universe related to the physical world as the human soul to the human body — compare LOGOS **c** *cap, Christian Science* : GOD b(6) **3 a** : the immortal part of man having permanent individual existence ⟨~s in paradise⟩ ⟨~s consigned to damnation⟩ — contrasted with *body* **b** : a person's total self in its living unity and wholeness — sometimes distinguished from *spirit* ⟨I pray God your whole spirit and ~ and body be preserved blameless —1 Thess 5:23 (AV)⟩ **4 a** : a seat of real life, vitality, or action : PERSONALITY, PSYCHE **b** : an animating or essential part : a vital principle actuating something ⟨the hidden ~ of harmony —John Milton⟩ ⟨the true French horn, the ~ of orchestral poetry —Ralph Vaughan Williams⟩ ⟨courageous minorities are the very ~ of a democracy —*New Republic*⟩ **c** : moving spirit : INSPIRER, LEADER ⟨~ of the rebellion⟩ ⟨~ of an enterprise⟩ **5 a** : man's moral and emotional nature as distinguished from his mind or intellect ⟨an indomitable ~ confronting a whole world, a whole culture —Lionel Trilling⟩ **b** : the quality of expression that effectively presents or arouses emotion and sentiment ⟨what is lacking most in these young dancers . . . is a feeling of ~ —Paul Tassovin⟩ **c** : a manifestation (as affection, generosity, charity, sympathy) of the moral nature ⟨a clever man lacking in ~⟩ ⟨with so much intelligence he needs less ~ than other people —Anne D. Sedgwick⟩ **d** : spiritual or moral force : FERVOR ⟨that America has no ~ and will not deserve to have one until she consents to plunge into the abyss of human suffering and sin —Wallace Fowlie⟩ **6** : human being : PERSON — used with a qualifying epithet ⟨a kindly ~⟩ ⟨dear ~⟩ ⟨poor ~⟩ *or* a number ⟨a village of barely a hundred ~s⟩ **7** : one having a good or noble quality in the highest degree : EXEMPLIFICATION, PERSONIFICATION ⟨he is the ~ of honor⟩ ⟨she is the ~ of generosity⟩ **8** *obs* : the base of a cannon *syn* see MIND

²soul \'sōl, 'sōl\ *vb* -ED/-ING/-S [fr. All *Souls'* Day] *dial Eng* : to go about on All Souls' Day singing and begging for soul cakes — **soul·er** \-lə(r)\ *n* -s

sou·lard crab *or* **soulard crab apple** \(')sü̇'lärd-\ *n, usu cap S* [after James G. Soulard, 19th cent. Am. horticulturist] : a hybrid tree (*Malus soulardii*) resembling the parent Iowa crab but having yellowish red fruit

soul bell *n* : PASSING BELL

soul cake *n* : a round or oval sweet bun traditionally eaten on All Souls' Day in England

souled \'sōld\ *adj* : having a soul : possessing soul and feeling — usu. used in combination ⟨whole-*souled* repentance⟩ ⟨brave-*souled* pioneers⟩

soule·tin \'sü̇l'tan\ *n* -s *cap* [F, fr. Soule, region in southwestern France] : a Basque dialect spoken in a district in the department Basses-Pyrénées in France

soul-force \'․,․\ *n* : SATYAGRAHA

soul·ful \'sōlfəl\ *adj* : full of or expressing feeling, emotion, or sentiment ⟨~ eyes⟩ ⟨~ pose⟩ — **soul·ful·ly** \-fəlē, -li\ *adv* — **soul·ful·ness** -ES

soul house *n* : a pottery model of a house set over a grave by the ancient Egyptians as a dwelling for the soul

soul·ish \'sōlish\ *adj* : relating to, involving, or suggesting the soul ⟨the ~ situations he discovers are real enough to be compulsory —Walter Lowrie⟩

soul kiss *n* : DEEP KISS

soul·less \'sōləs\ *adj* : having no soul ⟨~ corporation⟩ : lacking greatness or nobleness of mind or feeling ⟨~ grubbing for profits⟩ — **soul·less·ly** *adv* — **soul·less·ness** -ES

soul-mass \'sōmas\ *n* [ME *soulemasse*, fr. *soule* soul + *masse* mass — more at MASS] **1** *archaic* : a mass for the dead **2** *dial Eng* : ALL SOULS' DAY

soul mate *n* : one of two persons esp. of opposite sex temperamentally suited to each other : AFFINITY; *often* : a partner in an illicit relationship : LOVER, MISTRESS

soul priest *n* : a priest who offers prayers for the souls of the dead

soul scot *also* **soul shot** *or* **soul scat** *n* [*soul shot* fr. *soul* + *shot* (alter. of ME *scot* amount of money); *soul scat* alter. of *soul scot* — more at SCOT (amount of money)] : a mortuary fee or present paid to the clergy from a deceased's estate

soul-searching \'․,․,․\ *n* : anxious or conscientious deliberation : examination of one's conscience esp. with regard to deeper motives and values : SELF-ANALYSIS ⟨could never dismiss any suggestion however fantastic without hours of *soul-searching* —Christopher Isherwood⟩

soul-sick \'․,․\ *adj* : spiritually ill : very dejected or depressed — **soul-sick·ness** *n*

soul spirit *n* : PSYCHOPANNYCHY

soul-stuff \'․,․\ *n* : an impersonal essence vitalizing the body and believed by some peoples of Indonesia and Melanesia to permeate an individual's body and things in contact with his body and to be separable from the body either temporarily (as in dreams) or permanently (as in death)

soulth \'saů̇lth\ *var of* SOWLTH

¹soum \'süm\ *n* -s [prob. alter. of ¹*sum*] **1** *Irish & Scot* : the area of pastureland that will maintain one cow or a fixed number of other stock **2** *Scot* : the number of cattle or other stock that can be pastured on a determined amount of land

²soum \"\ *vt* -ED/-ING/-S *Scot* : to examine (land held in common) in order to determine the number of cattle or other stock that can be pastured

sou mar·kee *also* **soo markee** \'sümär'kē\ *n* [F *sou marqué*, lit., marked sou] **1** : a small 18th century French coin issued for the colonies and formerly circulating in the West Indies and on the No. American mainland **2** : something of little or no value : CONTINENTAL ⟨not worth a *sou markee*⟩

soun *obs var of* SOUND

¹sound \'saů̇nd\ *adj* -ER/-EST [ME *sound, sund*, fr. OE *gesund*; akin to OS *gisund* sound, OFris *sund* fresh, unharmed, healthy, OHG *gisunt* healthy, Goth *swinths* strong, healthy and prob. to Lith *sumdyti, siumdyti* to rouse, incite] **1 a** : free from injury or disease : ROBUST, WHOLESOME ⟨a young man . . . of good parentage, ~ in wind and limb —Henry Miller⟩ ⟨every tooth in her head was —W.M.Thackeray⟩ ⟨a ~ mind in a ~ body⟩ **b** : free from disease, abnormality, or defect impairing or likely to impair usefulness — used of a domestic animal and esp. of a horse; compare UNSOUND **c** : free from flaw, defect, or decay : UNIMPAIRED, UNBLEMISHED ⟨~ timber⟩ ⟨a ~ wine⟩ ⟨a ~ fruit⟩ ⟨the masonry . . . is still ~ —*Amer. Guide Series: N.C.*⟩ **2 a** : marked by solidity, firmness, or stability ⟨a building of ~ construction⟩ ⟨established a ~ foundation for future progress⟩ **b** : stable and resistant to volume change when used in construction work — used of hydraulic cements including portland, hydrated lime, quicklime, and aggregates for concrete **c** : solidly or securely based : RELIABLE ⟨a ~ economy⟩ ⟨a ~ society⟩ ⟨~ relationships⟩ **d** : financially secure : SAFE ⟨a ~ investment⟩ **3 a** : based on truth or right : free from error or fallacy ⟨~ advice⟩ ⟨a ~ argument⟩ ⟨~ reasoning⟩ ⟨~ criticism⟩ **b** : based on adequate knowledge or experience : CORRECT ⟨~ estimate of the military situation —Carl Bridenbaugh⟩ **c** : showing a high level of accuracy or polish : PRECISE ⟨~ scholarship⟩ ⟨paved the way for . . . a ~ and fruitful knowledge of antiquity —G.C. Sellery⟩ ⟨a ~ paragraph —L.B.Nicolson⟩ **d** *chess* : admitting of no variation advantageous to the opponent — used of a problem or combination **e** : founded in law : not defective : LEGAL, VALID ⟨a ~ title to land⟩ **f** : agreeing with accepted views : ORTHODOX ⟨~ in the faith⟩ ⟨preached ~ doctrine⟩ **4 a** : COMPLETE, THOROUGH ⟨a ~ revenge⟩ ⟨a ~ recovery⟩ **b** : deep and undisturbed — used of sleep ⟨a ~ sleep⟩ **c** : HARD, SEVERE ⟨a ~ whipping⟩ **5 a** : marked by loyalty and dependability : TRUSTWORTHY ⟨a ~ friend⟩ ⟨his shipmates pronounced him ~ to the kelson —Herman Melville⟩ **b** : showing high morale : not disaffected ⟨a robust and ~ people —Matthew Arnold⟩ **c** : showing good judgment : LEVEL-HEADED ⟨a man to have on a governing board⟩ *syn* see HEALTHY, VALID

²sound \"\ *adv* [ME, fr. ¹*sound*] : SOUNDLY — used with *asleep* and *sleep* and in combination ⟨~ asleep⟩ ⟨slept ~⟩ ⟨*sound*-thinking citizens⟩

³sound \"\ *n* -s *often attrib* [ME, fr. *son*, fr. L *sonus*; akin to OE *swinn* melody, OIr *senim* sounds, playing, OL *sonere* to sound, Skt *svanati* it sounds, resounds] **1 a** : the sensation perceived by the sense of hearing ⟨the pattern of nerve impulses arriving in the brain is associated with and subjectively experienced as ~ —Otto Stuhlman⟩ **b** : an auditory impression : NOISE, TONE ⟨the ~ of thunder⟩ ⟨~s of laughter⟩ ⟨the ~ of girls' voices —Pearl Buck⟩ ⟨from the passageway . . . the ~ of footsteps —Kenneth Roberts⟩ **c** : mechanical radiant energy that is transmitted by longitudinal pressure waves in air or other material medium and is the objective cause of the sensation of hearing ⟨the velocity of ~ in air at 32° F is about 1087 feet per second⟩ **2 a** : a speech sound ⟨a peculiar *r*-sound⟩ ⟨an \ó\-*sound*⟩ **b** : value in terms of a single speech sound or a succession of speech sounds ⟨Polish *prz* has pretty much the ~ of *bsch* in German hübsch —\psh\⟩ **3** *archaic* : RUMOR, TIDINGS ⟨the preachers . . . spread the glorious ~ —William Cowper⟩ **4 a** : noise without meaning : mere noise ⟨full of ~ and fury, signifying nothing —Shak.⟩ ⟨systems which . . . deal in ~s instead of sense —Jeremy Bentham⟩ **b** *obs* : underlying meaning : SIGNIFICANCE ⟨the word has no ~, as I may say, to me —Daniel Defoe⟩ ⟨the mental impression conveyed by a particular sound or expression : an accompanying implication : IMPORT, PORTENT ⟨that confession has a suspicious ~ to me⟩ **5** : distance within which a particular noise may be heard : EARSHOT, HEARING ⟨within ~ of his voice⟩ ⟨the lad was out of sight and out of ~ —S.H.Holbrook⟩ **6** : recorded auditory material (as on phonograph discs or motion-picture film) ⟨stereophonic ~⟩ ⟨with ~ there came . . . the need of good writing —Irving Pichel⟩

⁴sound \"\ *vb* -ED/-ING/-S [ME *sounen*, fr. MF *soner, suner*, fr. L *sonare*; akin to L *sonus* sound] *vi* **1 a** : to make a noise or sound (as with the voice or with an instrument) : produce an audible effect ⟨first taught speaking trumpets how to ~ —John Dryden⟩ ⟨a buzzing noise kept ~*ing* in his ears⟩ **b** : RESOUND ⟨~*ing* to strains of soft music⟩ ⟨the echoes of his clever talk were still ~*ing* —V.L.Parrington⟩ **c** : to give a signal by sound : SUMMON — used with *to* ⟨the bugle ~s to battle⟩ **d** *archaic* : to become known by word of mouth ⟨from you ~*ed* out the word of the LORD —1 Thess 1:8 (AV)⟩ **2 a** : to make or convey a certain impression : have a certain import when heard : SEEM, APPEAR ⟨~*s* good to me⟩ ⟨the whole thing ~*ed* incredible —Burtt Evans⟩ **b** *obs* : TEND, LEAN, INCLINE ⟨~ neither to matters of state nor of war —George Puttenham⟩ **c** : to become based or founded — used with *in* ⟨those remedies for rent which ~*ed* in contract —O.W. Holmes †1935⟩ ⟨~ in tort⟩ ⟨~ in damages⟩ ⟨motives ~*ing* in the need of divine salvation —H.O.Taylor⟩ **d** : to have or tend to have the character of a specified thing — usu. used with *in* ⟨~ in folly⟩ ~ *vt* **1** : to cause to sound (as a musical instrument) : PLAY, STRIKE ⟨~*ing* the gong for breakfast⟩ ⟨hear each instrumentalist ~ his A —Warwick Braithwaite⟩ ⟨the theme is ~*ed* by horns —Lucien Price⟩ ⟨the keynote⟩ ⟨~ a note of warning⟩ **2** : to put into words : VOICE ⟨how dares thy . . . tongue ~ this unpleasing news —Shak.⟩ ⟨encomiums are being ~*ed* —J.H.MacCormick⟩ **3 a** : to make known : PROCLAIM ⟨~ his praises far and wide⟩ ⟨~*ed* its purpose of enforcing its new regulations —Fred Russell⟩ **b** : to order, signal, or indicate by a sound ⟨~ a retreat⟩ ⟨a parley⟩ ⟨the clock ~s noon⟩ **4** : to examine the condition of (something) by causing it to emit sounds and noting their character ⟨~ a piece of timber⟩ ⟨~ the lungs⟩

⁵sound \"\ *n* -s [ME, fr. OE *sund* swimming, capacity for swimming, strait, sea & ON *sund* swimming, strait, sound; akin to MLG *sunt* narrow sea, strait, OHG *swimman* to swim — more at SWIM] **1 a** : a long and rather broad inlet of the ocean generally with its larger part extending roughly parallel to the coast **b** : a long passage of water connecting two larger bodies but too wide and extensive to be termed a strait (as a passage connecting a sea or lake with the ocean or with another sea or a channel passing between a mainland and an island) **2** : the air bladder of a fish

⁶sound \"\ *vb* -ED/-ING/-S [ME *sounden*, fr. MF *sonder*, fr. *sonde* sounding line, act of sounding, prob. of Gmc origin; akin to OE *sundgyrd* sounding rod, *sundlīne* sounding line, *sundrāp* sounding lead, ON *sund* strait, sound] *vt* **1** : to measure the depth of (as by a line and plummet) : FATHOM ⟨the crew must often ~ the bottom to be sure of enough water —Lyn Harrington⟩ ⟨~*ing* the distance to the bottom and to the ice overhead —W.R.Anderson & Clay Blair⟩ — see ECHO SOUNDING **2** : to try to find out (as by discreet questioning) the views or intentions of : feel out : PROBE ⟨~*ing* various senators as to their willingness to support him —Robert Graves⟩ — often used with *out* ⟨~ him out on the idea⟩ ⟨~*ed* out the old folks about marrying her —Seumas O'Kelly⟩ **3** : to explore or examine (a body cavity, as the bladder or urethra) with a sound **4** : to remove the sound and other organs from (fish) **5** : to carry down (the towline of a boat) when sounding — used of a whale ~ *vi* **1 a** : to ascertain the depth of water esp. with a sounding line ⟨there was fog . . . so they crept in, ~*ing* —*Christian Science Monitor*⟩ **b** : to look into or investigate the possibility : put out feelers ⟨sent commissioners . . . to ~ for peace —Thomas Jefferson⟩ **c** *of a lead*

: to go down ⟨deeper than did ever plummet ~ I'll drown my book —Shak.⟩ **2** : to dive suddenly straight toward the bottom — used of a fish and of a whale, esp. when hooked or harpooned ⟨get to the spot before the whale gathered its wits sufficiently to ~ —R.B.Robertson⟩ — **sound the well** : to measure the depth of water accumulated in the hold of a ship ⟨*sounded the well* . . . in Nos. 1 and 2 holds —F.W.Crofts⟩

⁷sound \"\ *n* -s [obs. *sound* sounding line, act of sounding, fr. MF *sonde*] : an elongated instrument or probe by which cavities of the body are sounded or explored for foreign bodies, constriction, or other abnormal conditions (as in the esophagus, urethra, uterus)

⁸sound \'saů̇n(d)\ *dial Brit var of* SWOON

sound·able \'saů̇ndəbəl\ *adj* [⁴*sound* + -*able*] : capable of being sounded ⟨one piano left ~ —Thomas Carlyle⟩

sound analyzer *n* : a harmonic analyzer for sound waves

sound barrier *n* : SONIC BARRIER

soundboard \'․,․ + *board*\ *n* [³*sound* + *board*] **1 a** : a thin resonant board (as the belly of a violin) so placed in an instrument as to reinforce its tones by sympathetic vibration — see VIOLIN illustration **b** : the top board of a wind-chest in an organ **2** : SOUNDING BOARD 1a

sound boarding *n* : boards that hold deafening in partitions or under floors to deaden sounds

sound boat *n* [fr. the Sound (Öresund), strait between Denmark and Sweden where these boats are common] : a double-ended deep-keel cutter-rigged Danish fishing boat

sound bone *n* [⁵*sound*] : a part of the backbone of a fish lying next to the sound

sound bow *n* [³*sound*] : the thick part of a bell against which the clapper strikes — see BELL illustration

sound box *n* **1** : a device in an acoustic phonograph using vibrating needle and thin diaphragm to convert phonograph record groove undulations into sound which is then amplified in a horn **2** : a hollow chamber in a musical instrument for increasing its sonority

sound cage *n* : SOUND PERIMETER

sound camera *n* : a motion-picture camera equipped to record a sound track simultaneously with the picture on a single film and in the form of either a photographic or a magnetic record

sound change *n* : phonetic or phonemic change

sound-condition \'․,․,․\ *vt* : to improve the acoustic properties of (as by absorption, damping, selective control, or reflection) ⟨*sound-condition* an auditorium⟩ — **sound-conditioned** \'․,․\ *adj* — **sound-conditioning** \'․,․(․)․\ *n*

sound-dead \'․,․\ *adj* : DEAD 10

sound effects *n pl* : effects that are imitative of sounds called for in the script of a play, radio or television program, or motion picture and are produced by various means (as phonograph records, musical instruments, or mechanical devices) ⟨before radio began to grow up in the 1920s, the technique of *sound effects* was extremely limited —Richard Hubbell⟩ ⟨a *sound-effects* girl . . . making radio noises like fire trucks, kisses, waterfalls, telephones —*Harper's*⟩

sound-effects man *n* : a technician (as in a radio or television studio) who produces sound effects

¹soun·der \'saů̇ndə(r)\ *n* -s [ME, fr. MF *sondre, sonre*, of Gmc origin; akin to OE *sunor* herd of swine, ON *sonar-* herd of swine, MHG *swaner* herd] : a herd of wild swine

²sound·er \"\ *n* -s [⁶*sound* + -*er*] : one that sounds: as **a** : a man who measures depths of water with a lead : LEADSMAN **b** : a device for making soundings — see DEPTH-SOUNDER

³sounder \"\ *n* -s [⁴*sound* + -*er*] : an electromagnetic instrument used in telegraphy that emits clicking sounds from which a message is interpreted

soundest *superlative of* SOUND

sound field *n* : a region in a material medium in which sound waves are being propagated

sound figures *n pl* : SONOROUS FIGURES

sound film *n* **1** : a motion-picture film carrying one or more sound records **2 a** : film intended for use in sound recording **b** : a strip of film carrying sound records in addition to the pictures

sound filmstrip *n* : SOUND SLIDEFILM

sound·ful \'saů̇ndfəl\ *adj* : full of sound : MELODIOUS ⟨a ~ crowd⟩ ⟨a ~ harp⟩

sound gear *n* : acoustic and sonic underwater submarine detection equipment

soundhead \'․,․\ *n* [³*sound* + *head*] **1** : an attachment for a motion picture projector containing apparatus for smoothing the motion of the film and for converting the sound record information into electrical signals **2** : the part of a motion-picture printer in which the sound track negative is printed onto the positive film

sound hole *n* : an opening in the belly or soundboard in stringed musical instruments serving to increase its elasticity for sympathetic vibration — see VIOLIN illustration

¹sound·ing \'saů̇ndiŋ, -dēŋ\ *n* -s [ME, fr. gerund of *sounden* to sound (measure depths) — more at SOUND] **1 a** : measurement by sounding **b** : the depth so ascertained — see ECHO SOUNDING **c** soundings *pl* : a place or part of a body of water where a hand sounding line will reach the bottom **2** : measurement of the condition of the atmosphere at various heights **3** : a probe, test, or sampling of opinion or intention : INQUIRY, INVESTIGATION ⟨has started ~s of farmer sentiment on future farm policy —*N.Y. Times*⟩ — **in soundings** *or* **on soundings** : in water not too deep to be fathomed by a hand sounding line : near the coast — **out of soundings** *or* **off soundings** : in water too deep to be fathomed by a hand sounding line

²sounding \"\ *adj* [ME *souning*, fr. pres. part. of *sounen* to sound — more at SOUND] **1** : EMITTING, REVERBERATING, RESONANT, RESOUNDING, SONOROUS ⟨~ brass and a tinkling cymbal —1 Cor 13:1 (AV)⟩ ⟨a ~ kiss —Osbert Sitwell⟩ ⟨the ~ cataract haunted me like a passion —William Wordsworth⟩ — often used in combination with a preceding adjective or adverb ⟨clear ~⟩ ⟨loud ~⟩ ⟨fine-*sounding* phrases⟩ **2** : HIGH-SOUNDING ⟨~ commonplaces⟩ ⟨apt to be taken in by ~ phrases —W.F.DeMorgan⟩ ⟨the ability to drop a ~ name with elaborate casualness —Clifton Fadiman⟩

sounding arrow *n* : WHISTLING ARROW

sounding balloon *n* [¹*sounding*] : a balloon sent aloft with self-registering instruments to record and often radio reports of meteorological data

sounding board *n* [*sounding* fr. gerund of ⁴*sound*] **1 a** : a board or structure placed behind or over a pulpit, rostrum, or platform to give distinctness and sonority to the sound (as voice or music) uttered from it — see BAND SHELL **b** : a device or agency that gives greater effect (as force, volume, or scope) to or helps propagate opinions or utterances ⟨Congressional hearings provide a *sounding board* comparable to question time in the House of Commons —*Economist*⟩ ⟨uses the newspapermen merely as a *sounding board* —*Atlantic*⟩ **2** : SOUNDBOARD 1 **3** : SOUND BOARDING

sounding lead *n* [ME] : a mass of lead at the end of a sounding line

sounding line *n* [ME] : a line, wire, or cord for sounding that is weighted at one end and is divided for sounding by hand into marks and deeps — called also *lead line*

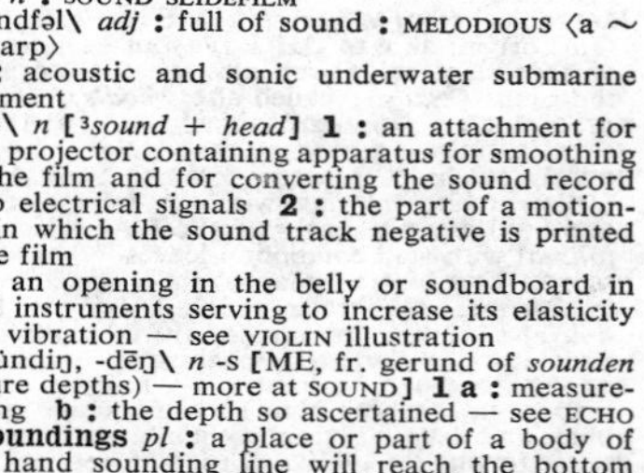

sound·ing·ly *adv* : in a sounding manner: as **a** : RESOUNDINGLY ⟨struck his chest —George Meredith⟩ **b** : IMPOSINGLY, IMPRESSIVELY ⟨pronounced the name⟩

sounding line: 1, 4, 6, 8, 9, 11, 12, 14, 16, 18, 19, 21, 22, 23, 24, deeps; 2, 3, 5, 7, 10, 13, 15, 17, 20, 25, marks

sound·ing·ness -ES : the quality or state of being sounding : SONOROUSNESS

sounding pipe *n* : a pipe in a water or oil tank on a ship for measuring depth of liquid

sounding rocket *n* **:** a rocket used to obtain information concerning the condition of the earth's atmosphere at various altitudes

sounding stop *n* **:** SPEAKING STOP

sounding tube *n* **:** a glass tube open at the bottom that is lowered to record water pressure and therefore depth as shown by the point reached within it by the water

sound intensity *n* **:** the intensity of a sound in a specified direction measured by the average rate at which sound energy passes through a unit area normal to that direction and commonly expressed in ergs per second per square centimeter

sound-intensity level *n* **:** the relative sound intensity at any point in a sound field as compared with a specified standard intensity that is usu. expressed in decibels above or below the standard

sound knot *n* [¹*sound*] **:** a knot in lumber that is as hard as the surrounding wood and is so solid and free from decay that it will retain its place in the piece

sound law *n* **:** PHONETIC LAW

sound lens *n* **:** a lens that brings sound waves to a focus (as by having walls of collodion film and being filled with a heavy gas which retards and consequently refracts sound waves)

¹**sound·less** \ˈsau̇ndləs, *in rapid speech* -nl-\ *adj* [obs. E *sound* act of sounding + E *-less* — more at SOUND (probing instrument)] **:** incapable of being sounded or plumbed **:** UNFATHOMABLE ⟨~ seas⟩ ⟨the ~ deep⟩

²**soundless** \"\ *adj* [³*sound* + *-less*] **:** making no sound **:** QUIET, SILENT ⟨tread sure and ~ —Lew Wallace⟩ ⟨his mouth moving in a brief, ~ prayer —Josephine Johnson⟩

sound·less·ly *adv* **:** in a soundless manner **:** without a sound **:** NOISELESSLY, SILENTLY ⟨a lion pacing ~ in his cage⟩ ⟨shot twice, he crumpled ~ to the ground⟩

sound·less·ness *n* -ES **:** the quality or state of being soundless **:** NOISELESSNESS, QUIETNESS ⟨the unnatural ~ was vaguely disturbing⟩

sound-level meter *n* **:** an apparatus for comparing sound-intensity levels usu. in decibels

sound line *n* [*sound* fr. obs. *sound* act of sounding] **:** the line fastened to a harpoon and carried down by a whale when sounding

sound·ly \-lē, -li\ *adv* [ME, fr. ¹*sound* + *-ly*] **:** in a sound manner: as **a :** on a solid basis **:** SECURELY ⟨has established himself ~ in his work —*Bull. of Bates Coll.*⟩ **b :** DEEPLY, PROFOUNDLY ⟨slept ~ through the storm⟩ **c** *obs* **:** in an orthodox manner **:** CORRECTLY **d :** THOROUGHLY ⟨the wound healed ~⟩ **e :** with good sense or judgment **:** in accordance with sound principles ⟨an organization administered ~⟩ ⟨teachers . . . ~ trained —Eric Ashby⟩ **f :** VIOLENTLY, SEVERELY ⟨shook her ~ —Pearl Buck⟩

sound man *n* **1 :** SOUND MIXER **2 :** SOUND-EFFECTS MAN

sound mixer *n* **:** one that controls the volume and tone of sound picked up by microphones (as on a motion-picture set) in order to obtain the desired effects for recording

sound money *n* [¹*sound*] **:** money not liable to sudden appreciation or depreciation in value **:** stable money; *specif* **:** a currency based on or redeemable in gold — compare PAPER MONEY, SOFT 17

sound motion picture *n* **:** a motion picture accompanied by synchronized recorded sound

sound·ness \ˈsau̇nnəs *also* -ndnəs\ *n* -ES [ME, fr. ¹*sound* + *-ness*] **:** the quality or state of being sound: as **a :** healthiness of body or mind ⟨the ~ of his constitution⟩ **b :** financial security **:** SOLVENCY ⟨appraising the ~ of the enterprise⟩ **c :** resistance to damage or disintegration **:** FIRMNESS, SOLIDITY ⟨assure . . . uniformity and structural ~ —*Steel*⟩ **d :** rightness of judgment or conception **:** LEVELHEADEDNESS ⟨the ~ of his educational theories —H.E.Starr⟩ **e :** ORTHODOXY ⟨convinced he had always doubted the ~ of my principles —Joseph Conrad⟩

¹**sound off** *vi* **1 a :** to play three chords before and after marching from right to left of the line of troops and back during a ceremonial parade or formal guard mount — used of the band or field music **b :** to play the sound off, march as indicated, and play the sound off again **2 :** to count cadence while marching **3 a :** to speak up in a loud voice **b :** to voice one's opinions freely, vigorously, and often somewhat belligerently ⟨*sounded off* on how publishers should run their papers —*Newsweek*⟩

²**sound off** *n* **:** the three chords sounded by the band or field music in a military ceremony — often used as a command

sound-on-film \ˌ==ˈ=\ *n* **:** SOUND FILM 1

sound perimeter *n* **:** an apparatus for testing the ability (as of a subject in a psychological experiment) to detect the location of sounds — called also *sound cage*

sound post *n* **:** a small post in an instrument of the viol or violin family set nearly under the bridge as a support and as a transmitter of vibrations to the back

sound-powered telephone \ˈ=ˌ==-\ *n* **:** a light telephone operated by current generated by the speaker's voice

sound pressure *n* **1 :** the difference between the actual pressure at any point in a sound field at any instant and the average pressure at that point — compare ACOUSTIC RADIATION PRESSURE **2 :** the amplitude of the sound pressure

sound printer *n* **:** an operator of a machine for transferring the sound image from the negative to the positive motion-picture film

sound projector *n* **:** a motion-picture projector equipped to reproduce photographically and magnetically recorded sound from one or more sound tracks in synchronism with picture projection from the same film

¹**soundproof** \ˈ=ˌ=\ *adj* [³*sound* + *proof*] **:** impervious to sound ⟨a ~ room⟩ ⟨a ~ studio⟩

²**soundproof** \"\ *vt* [back-formation fr. *soundproofing*] **:** to make soundproof **:** insulate so as to obstruct the passage of sound ⟨called for ~*ing* all floors, ceilings, and partitions⟩

soundproof·er \"+ə(r)\ *n* **:** a worker who installs material for soundproofing (as in automobile bodies)

soundproof·ing \"+iŋ\ *n* [¹*soundproof* + *-ing*] **:** the act or process of soundproofing ⟨the ~ of library cubicles⟩

sound ranging *n* **:** the location of enemy weapons and the adjusting of friendly fire by timing (as with microphones) sounds from accurately surveyed points — compare FLASH RANGING, SONAR

sound recorder *n* **1 :** a mechanism that records sound tracks for sound motion pictures on a separate film from the picture film **2 :** a device for recording sound on disc, tape, or film usu. by electronic means

sound recording *n* **1 :** the act or process of making a record of sound ⟨*sound recording* for 16-millimeter films⟩ **2 :** a film, disc, or tape recording of sound ⟨*sound recordings* for news broadcasts⟩

sounds *pl of* SOUND, *pres 3d sing of* SOUND

sound screen *n* **:** a motion-picture screen made of a porous material to facilitate the transmission of sound from a loud speaker placed behind it

sound shadow *n* **:** a region of relative silence behind a screen opaque to sound waves

sound shift *or* **sound shifting** *n* [trans. of G *lautverschiebung*] **:** PHONETIC CHANGE; *specif* **:** GRIMM'S LAW

sound slidefilm *n* **:** a filmstrip having accompanying sound on a separate disc or magnetic tape that is synchronized manually or automatically with each picture on the filmstrip — called also *sound filmstrip*

sound spectrogram *n* **:** a record produced by a sound spectrograph with time shown along the horizontal axis, frequency shown along the vertical axis, and intensity indicated by varying shades of darkness of the pattern

sound spectrograph *n* **1 :** an instrument that obtains a sound spectrum by analyzing a complex sound into its component elements **2 :** an electronic instrument that produces a time-frequency-intensity analysis of sound recorded on a magnetic tape loop by repeatedly playing the sound into a variable filter and recording the output by means of a stylus on electrically sensitive paper and by synchronizing the movement of the tape loop and the paper so that successive lines drawn by the stylus along the horizontal axis of the paper correspond to the shifting frequency range of the filter

sound stage *n* **:** a room or studio made acoustically suitable (as by soundproofing) for producing sound motion pictures

soundstripe \ˈ=ˌ=\ *n* **:** a longitudinal stripe of magnetic material on a photographic film on which a magnetic sound record is made

sound track *n* **:** the area on a motion-picture film that carries the photographic or magnetic sound record — compare SOUND STRIPE

sound truck *n* **:** a truck equipped with a loudspeaker for broadcasting speeches or music (as for an advertising purpose or in a political campaign) ⟨*sound trucks* drive slowly through the streets blaring forth the candidate's appeal⟩

sound-type \ˈ=ˌ=\ *n* **:** a speech sound whose articulation and acoustic effects are unlike those of any other speech sound **:** a member of the entire stock of allophones in one or more languages

sound wave *n* **1 :** ³SOUND 1b **2 sound waves** *pl* **:** longitudinal pressure waves in any material medium regardless of whether they constitute audible sound ⟨earthquake waves and ultrasonic waves are sometimes called *sound waves*⟩

sound wormy *n* [short for *sound wormy grade*] **:** a grade of lumber and esp. of chestnut and oak that contains many small wormholes

¹**soup** \ˈsüp\ *n* -S [F *soupe*, fr. OF, of Gmc origin; akin to ON *soppa* soup — more at SOP] **1** *often attrib* **:** a liquid food having as a base a meat, fish, or vegetable stock, being clear or thickened to the consistency of a thin puree or having milk or cream added, and often containing pieces of solid food (as meat, shellfish, pasta, or vegetables) **2 :** something having the consistency of soup: as **a :** a plastic mixture of solid material with liquid ⟨could not culture it in . . . any of the ~*s* used to grow bacteria —G.W.Gray b.1886⟩ ⟨manufacture . . . bookpaper from a ~ of shredded woodpulp —*Saturday Rev.*⟩; *specif* **:** a very wet concrete or mortar mix **b :** thick wet clouds or fog ⟨talk airplanes down through the ~ by . . . radar —*Boeing Mag.*⟩ **c :** nitroglycerin esp. as used by safecrackers ⟨drove to the powder house . . . to get some ~ for a safecracking job —*N.Y. Times*⟩ **d :** photographic developer ⟨while the prints were in the ~ —Florence Haas⟩ **e :** a thin solution of pyroxylin containing pigments used in coating fabrics (as for artificial leather) **3 :** an unfortunate predicament **:** HOT WATER — used in the phrase *in the soup* ⟨caught him red-handed and now he's in the ~⟩ — **from soup to nuts :** from beginning to end **:** in comprehensive detail ⟨complete equipment for the fisherman — rod, creel, waders, fancy flies, everything *from soup to nuts*⟩

²**soup** \"\ *vt* -ED/-ING/-S [fr. earlier *soup* substance injected into a racehorse to speed it up, fr. ¹*soup*] **:** to increase the power or efficiency of ⟨~*ing* the stock engine —*Hot Rod Mag.*⟩ — usu. used with *up* ⟨engineers had ~*ed* up the planes and some could climb as high as 20,000 feet —*All Hands*⟩ ⟨boys . . . buy old cars and ~ them up —Gregor Felsen⟩ ⟨suspended mikes — ~*ed* up to pick up a wider range of sounds —*Newsweek*⟩

³**soup** \"\ *n* -S **1** *slang* **:** HORSEPOWER **2** *slang* **:** added power of any kind ⟨using a rifle powder in a pistol cartridge can give a load with too much ~⟩

soup and fish *n* [so called fr. the kind of dishes served at formal dinners] **:** formal evening dress for men

soupbone \ˈ=ˌ=\ *n* **:** a shin, knuckle, or other bone suitable for making soup stock

soup·çon \(ˈ)süp¦sōⁿ\ *n* -S [F, suspicion, conjecture, hint, trace, fr. MF *sospeçon* suspicion — more at SUSPICION] **:** a little bit **:** TRACE, TOUCH ⟨a ~ of army rank had slipped . . . insidiously into his voice —J.D.Salinger⟩ ⟨great learning flavored with . . . a ~ of raillery —J.S.Schapiro⟩

souped-up \ˈ=ˌ=\ *adj* [fr. past part. of *soup up*, v.] **1 :** augmented in power or efficiency ⟨*souped-up* outboards have given new zoom to the water-ski business —*Newsweek*⟩ ⟨racing . . . at 100 miles per hour in *souped-up* jalopies —*Information Please Almanac*⟩ ⟨a *souped-up* fission bomb . . . may release more than ten times the explosive force —*Economist*⟩ **2 a :** heightened in impact **:** made more stimulating or sensational **:** DRAMATIZED ⟨extra billions . . . for a *souped-up* worldwide arms aid program —*Wall Street Jour.*⟩ ⟨sang a *souped-up* version of the national anthem —M.W.Straight⟩ **b :** made physically more attractive **:** GLAMORIZED ⟨a *souped-up* truck boasting luxury items that would make any trucker's mouth water —*Motor Transportation in the West*⟩ **c :** keyed up **:** OVERSTIMULATED ⟨to some *souped-up* American tastes this may seem . . . slightly old-fashioned —Anthony Boucher⟩

soupfin shark \ˈ=ˌ=-\ *also* **soupfin** *n* **:** any of various sharks whose fins when boiled form gelatin used by the Chinese in making soup: as **a :** a common shark (*Galeorhinus zyopterus*) of the California coast **b :** ²TOPE

soup kitchen *n* **:** an establishment dispensing soup, bread, and other minimum dietary essentials to the needy

¹**sou·ple** \ˈsüpəl\ *dial var of* SUPPLE

²**souple** \"\ *dial Brit var of* SWIPLE

³**souple** \"\ *or* **souple silk** *n* -S [*souple* short for F *soie souple* supple silk; *souple silk* part trans. of F *soie souple*] **:** partially degummed silk

soup-meagre \ˈ=ˌ==\ *n* [F *soupe-maigre*, lit., maigre soup] *archaic* **:** a broth made chiefly from vegetables or fish

soup plate *n* **:** a deep plate usu. having a wide rim and used for serving soup

soup spoon *n* **:** a spoon with a large or rounded bowl for eating soup

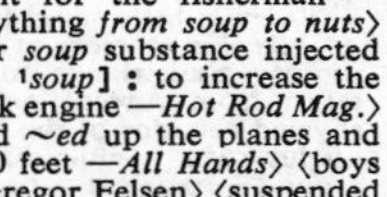

soup plate

soup up *vt* [²*soup*] **1 :** to increase the power of (a cartridge) by greatly increasing the powder charge in relation to the bullet weight **2 :** to heighten the impact of **:** make more exciting or colorful ⟨*souping up* textbook economics for popular consumption —Siegfried Mandel⟩ ⟨*souped up* his modest title with a jacket slogan —John Woodburn⟩

soupy \ˈsüpē, -pi\ *adj* -ER/-EST [¹*soup* + *-y*] **1 a :** having the consistency of soup ⟨a concrete mix should be *mushy* but not ~ —*Building, Estimating & Contracting*⟩ **b :** characterized by emotionalism **:** SENTIMENTAL, MAWKISH ⟨~ operetta melodies . . . made her cry —Mavis Gallant⟩ **2 :** densely foggy or cloudy ⟨~ weather⟩

¹**sour** \ˈsau̇(ə)r, ˈsau̇ə, *esp in the South* ˈsau̇wə(r\ *adj* -ER/-EST [ME, fr. OE *sūr*; akin to OHG *sūr* sour, ON *sūrr* sour, Lith *suras* salty, OSlav *syrŭ* moist, raw] **1 :** causing or characterized by the one of the four basic taste sensations produced chiefly by acids ⟨~ pickles⟩ ⟨~ green apples for pies⟩ — compare BITTER, SALT, SWEET **2 a** (1) **:** having the acid taste or smell of or as if of fermentation **:** RANCID, TURNED ⟨~ beer⟩ ⟨~ milk⟩ ⟨the smell of wet clothing is ~ —Norman Mailer⟩ (2) **:** of or relating to fermentation ⟨the ~ process for manufacturing starch⟩ **b :** smelling or tasting of decay **:** PUTRID, ROTTEN ⟨~ breath⟩ ⟨a dense drift of dead nettles — their ~ odor haunting the air —Walter de la Mare⟩ **c** (1) **:** proving unsound or unpopular **:** BAD, WRONG ⟨private lending institutions unloaded their ~ investments on the Treasury —Harrison Smith⟩ — usu. used with *go* or *turn* ⟨not enough people rented them and the project went ~ —*Reporter*⟩ ⟨a proposal which quickly turned ~ even in the Republican camp —*Economist*⟩ (2) **:** robbed of illusion **:** DISENCHANTED ⟨halfway through the book . . . went ~ on Marxism —Alfred Kazin⟩ **3 a :** of a disagreeable kind **:** UNPLEASANT, DISTASTEFUL ⟨find it easier if they . . . do not have to hear too often too much of the ~ truth —Walter Lippmann⟩ ⟨a ~ job, like washing up the dishes after a party —George Weller⟩ ⟨that's a ~ harbor in a sou'east gale —Mary H. Vorse⟩ **b :** of a cross or sullen nature **:** DOUR, MOROSE ⟨a ~ disgruntled man of small position —Margaret Mead⟩ ⟨take a ~ view of recent contributions of nuclear physics to human progress —J.B.Priestley⟩ **c :** expressive of ill humor or dissatisfaction **:** PEEVISH ⟨made a ~ grimace —L.C.Douglas⟩ **d :** taking a hostile attitude **:** DOWN — used with *on* ⟨unions are ~ on the new merger, and may . . . form a new group —*Kiplinger Washington Letter*⟩ **4 a :** acid in reaction and usu. needing drainage as well as liming — used of soil **b** *dial Brit* **:** disagreeable in texture or taste **:** HARSH, RANK — used of grass **5** *archaic* **:** INCLEMENT, MISERABLE — used of weather ⟨~ gusts of wind and rain —Archibald Lovell⟩ **6 a :** containing malodorous sulfur compounds (as hydrogen sulfide and mercaptans) — used esp. of natural gas, petroleum, and petroleum distillates; compare DOCTOR TEST **b :** inaccurate or inferior in quality **:** JARRING, POOR ⟨must hear the ~ note and correct it —C.W.Pearce⟩ ⟨his . . . drives were often wild, his putting ~ —*Time*⟩

syn ACID, ACIDULOUS, TART, DRY: SOUR is often interchangeable with ACID but in addition is applied to that which through fermentation has lost its sweet or neutral taste; it may or may not suggest rancidness ⟨*sour* wine⟩ ⟨*sour* bread⟩ ACID applies to that which has a biting taste in its natural or normal state ⟨*acid* fruits⟩ ACIDULOUS implies a degree of acidity ⟨mineral waters pleasantly *acidulous*⟩ while TART indicates a sharp but often an agreeable acidity ⟨cooks prefer *tart* apples for pies⟩ DRY applies to wines that are bland without being sweet. In more figurative senses, SOUR applies to the peevish or morose; ACIDULOUS and TART to asperity, pungency, or sharpness; ACID to the biting or caustic ⟨a *sour* man was Andrew Bogue that day, and *sourer* was he now. Nor word nor syllable would he utter —William Black⟩ ⟨she's none too well pleased about it. A discarded woman never is; she always turns *sour* on you —Max Peacock⟩ ⟨the *acidulous* tongue . . . had impaired working relationships with his British, Chinese, and American colleagues —John Fischer⟩ ⟨*tart* temper never mellows with age —Washington Irving⟩ ⟨his wit became *acid;* his letters are filled with caustic comment to sharpen the temper of those on the fighting line —V.L.Parrington⟩ DRY may suggest matter-of-fact impersonal presentation of the humorous, sarcastic, or ironic ⟨into these tiny paragraphs he packed his *dry* wit and his easy, good-natured satire on the follies of the day —Eleanor M. Sickles⟩ ⟨a story by Maupassant, *dry* and ironical in its beginning —V.S.Pritchett⟩

²**sour** \"\ *n* -S [ME, fr. ¹*sour*] **1 a** (1) **:** something acidulous ⟨film yeasts may develop on . . . pickles, including ~*s* and dills —*Crops in Peace & War*⟩ (2) **:** the primary taste sensation produced by acid stimuli **b :** something unpleasant or distasteful ⟨take the good with the bad, the sweet with the ~⟩ **2 :** an acid or acidic compound (as sodium fluosilicate) used in dilute water solution esp. in bleaching or laundering to neutralize alkali and decompose any remaining bleach or soap — compare GRAY SOUR 2, WHITE SOUR **3 :** a cocktail made with spirituous liquor, lemon or lime juice, sugar, and sometimes also soda water, shaken in ice and strained, and often served garnished with a maraschino cherry and slice of orange ⟨whiskey ~⟩ ⟨gin ~⟩

³**sour** \"\ *adv* -ER/-EST [ME, fr. ¹*sour*] **:** SOURLY

⁴**sour** \"\ *vb* -ED/-ING/-S [ME *souren*, fr. ¹*sour*] *vi* **1 a :** to become sour **:** FERMENT, ROT ⟨made a start of yeast in that keg . . . by letting some dough ~ in it —W.F.Harris⟩ ⟨there is no need for carpets to ~ from cleaning —*Boxoffice*⟩ **b :** to become acid or unproductive — used of soil **2 a :** to become peevish or morose ⟨a laughing girl, but she ~*ed* early and took to other ways —A.E.Coppard⟩ **b :** to lose interest **:** become disillusioned or fed up ⟨prospective investors ~*ed* when they found the company would pocket most of the proceeds⟩ — usu. used with *on* ⟨voters can ~ on a man who runs too many times for the same office —J.A. Morris b.1904⟩ **c :** to become impaired **:** go bad **:** DETERIORATE ⟨could . . . feel his grief ~*ing* into jealousy and resentment —Elizabeth Enright⟩ ⟨relations with his neighbors suddenly ~*ed* over the situation⟩ ~ *vt* **1 a :** to cause to ferment ⟨yeast is used to ~ the wort for beer⟩ **b :** to cause to spoil or become acidulous ⟨tainted vessels ~ what they contain —Philip Francis⟩ **c :** to make sour ⟨some grasses ~ land⟩ **2 a :** to cause to deteriorate **:** make distasteful **:** IMPAIR ⟨career was ~*ed* by inability to get along with . . . his colleagues —Lynn Montross⟩ ⟨a taste of Africa during two hunting trips . . . ~*ed* him for city life —*Newsweek*⟩ **b** (1) **:** to make cross or gloomy **:** DISGRUNTLE, IRRITATE ⟨everything in the galley had gone adrift and ~*ed* the cook —Llewellyn Howland⟩ (2) **:** to destroy the faith or enthusiasm of **:** DISAPPOINT, DISILLUSION ⟨refused to intervene . . . this ~*ed* many European idealists —Janet Flanner⟩ — usu. used with *on* ⟨~*ed* me on wealth, made me suspicious of the whole system —W.A.White⟩ **c** *obs* **:** to give a sour expression to ⟨~*ing* his cheeks —Shak.⟩ **3 :** to treat with a dilute acid solution esp. in bleaching, dyeing, and laundering **4 :** to macerate (lime) for plaster or mortar **syn** see EXACERBATE

sour ball *n* **:** a spherical piece of hard candy having a tart flavor — compare ACID DROP

sourball \ˈ=ˌ=\ *n* [*sour ball*] **:** a peevish person **:** GROUCH

sour·berry \ˈ=-*see* BERRY\ *n* **1 :** EUROPEAN CRANBERRY **2 :** LEMONADE BERRY

sourbush \ˈ=ˌ=\ *n* **1 :** FRENCH MULBERRY 1 **2 :** INDIAN TOBACCO 3

sour-cake \ˈ=ˌ=\ *n* **:** a sour leavened cake of oatmeal or rye

¹**source** \ˈsō(ə)rs, ˈsȯ(ə)rs, ˈsōəs, ˈsȯəs\ *n* -S [ME *sours*, fr. MF *sors*, fr. OF, past part. of *sordre*, *sourdre* to spring forth, rise, fr. L *surgere* to raise, rise — more at SURGE] **1 a :** the point of origin of a stream of water **:** FOUNTAINHEAD ⟨followed it from its ~ high in the mountains to its calmer reaches —*London Calling*⟩ **b** *archaic* **:** a natural spring or reservoir **:** FOUNT ⟨seven aqueducts brought water from distant ~*s* to Rome —Charles Merivale⟩ **2 a** (1) **:** a generative force or stimulus **:** CAUSE, INSTIGATOR ⟨reliance on local initiative . . . has always been a ~ of strength to American educational institutions —R.H.Wittcoff⟩ ⟨in almost all cases, the psychological ~ of cruel doctrines is fear —Bertrand Russell⟩ ⟨hills . . . are a ~ of scenic and recreational attraction —*Amer. Guide Series: Texas*⟩ (2) *usu cap* **:** ultimate reality **:** GOD ⟨felt close to the *Source* of all that is beautiful and true —Anna Kunz⟩ **b** (1) **:** a point of origin or procurement **:** FOUNTAIN, SUPPLIER ⟨brings us back to . . . the ~ of all significant artistic and intellectual effort — the struggles, aspirations, joys and sorrows of human beings —*Irish Digest*⟩ ⟨the principal ~ of the state's road funds was motor-vehicle fees —*Amer. Guide Series: Mich.*⟩ ⟨dried skim milk is a good ~ of protein for hogs —*Deerfield (Wis.) Independent*⟩ (2) **:** one that initiates or serves as a prototype **:** AUTHOR, MODEL ⟨the ~ of this fresh modern outlook is the prime minister —William Clark⟩ ⟨documenting . . . heavily the writer's ~*s* and his rational intentions —A.J.Guérard⟩ (3) **:** one that supplies information ⟨~*s* close to the chief executive report he is planning to request the Legislature to approve state purchase —E.M.Mills⟩ **c** *archaic* **:** genealogical lineage **:** ANCESTRY ⟨traced his ~ through the most Gothic gentlemen of Spain —Lord Byron⟩ **d :** a point of emanation ⟨it is desirable to have the light ~ accurately located —Terrell Croft⟩ **3 :** a firsthand document or primary reference work ⟨extensive work in the ~*s* — official records, manuscripts, letters, diaries, old books, newspapers —W.G.Carleton⟩ **syn** see ORIGIN

²**source** \"\ *vb* -ED/-ING/-S **:** ORIGINATE

source book *n* **:** a fundamental document or record (as of history, literature, art, or religion) upon which subsequent writings, compositions, opinions, beliefs, or practices are based; *also* **:** a collection of such documents ⟨these memoirs are . . . a *source book* for historians —Crane Brinton⟩

source material *n* **1 :** basic raw material ⟨requires . . . actual *source materials* in original languages on cultures, customs, economy —D.H.Clift⟩ ⟨ship nuclear *source materials* to allied nations —*Time*⟩ **2 :** PARENT MATERIAL

source region *n* **:** an extensive region of the earth's surface where large masses of air having uniform temperature and humidity conditions characteristic of the region originate

source rock *n* **:** a rock in which petroleum has originated ⟨oil passes from the *source rock* . . . into the more open spaces of a reservoir rock, where it can accumulate —W.G.Fearnsides & O.M.B.Bulman⟩

sour cherry *n* **1 a :** a rather small round-headed Eurasian tree (*Prunus cerasus*) with grayish bark, white to pinkish flowers, and bright red to almost black soft-fleshed acid edible fruits for which it is widely cultivated — compare SWEET CHERRY; see AMARELLE, MORELLO **b :** the fruit of this tree **2 :** an Australian tree (*Eugenia corynantha*) with sour-tasting red fruits

sour clover *n* **:** any of several plants of the genera *Melilotus* and *Trifolium; esp* **:** BITTER CLOVER

sour cream *n* **:** cream soured by the addition of a culture of lactic acid bacteria that produce lactic fermentation

sour crop *n* **:** moniliasis of poultry **:** THRUSH

sourcrout *or* **sourkrout** *var of* SAUERKRAUT

sour·dine \'sü(ə)r,dēn, ⸗'⸗\ *n* -s [F, fr. It *sordina, sordino,* fr. *sordo* silent, dull-sounding, deaf (fr. L *surdus*) + *-ina, -ino* (dim. suffixes) — more at SURD] **1 :** any of several obsolete musical instruments distinguished by their low or soft tone: as **a :** a trumpet used in giving soldiers the signal to march **b :** SPINET **2 :** 2MUTE 3

sour dip *n* **:** an acidic solution containing fermenting corn sugar and Epsom salts in which sole leather is dipped in tanning to improve color and feel

sour dock *n* [ME *sour docke,* fr. 1*sour* + *docke* dock — more at DOCK] **:** any of several docks with sour juice: as **a :** SHEEP SORREL 1 **b :** GARDEN SORREL **c :** CURLED DOCK **d :** CANAIGRE

sour dook \'sü(ə)r,dük\ *n* [1*sour* + *dook,* of unknown origin] *Scot* **:** BUTTERMILK

sourdough \'⸗,⸗\ *n* [ME *sour dogh,* fr. 1*sour* + *dogh* dough — more at DOUGH] **1 :** a leaven consisting of dough in which both alcoholic and lactic fermentation is active **2** [so called fr. the use of sourdough in making bread while camping] **:** a veteran inhabitant (as an old-time prospector) of Alaska or northwestern Canada — contrasted with *cheechako*

soured *past of* SOUR

1**sourer** *comparative of* SOUR

2**sour·er** \'saùrə(r)\ *n* -s **:** one that sours; *specif* **:** a worker who sours yarn in a solution

sourest *superlative of* SOUR

sour gnat *n, chiefly Midland* **:** any of various minute irritating insects (as an eye gnat or drosophila)

sour gourd *n* **1 a :** CREAM-OF-TARTAR TREE **b :** the acid fruit of the cream-of-tartar tree **2 :** BAOBAB

sour grapes *n pl* [so called fr. the fable ascribed to Aesop, legendary 6th cent. B.C. Greek author of fables, about the fox that tried to get at some grapes but finding that they were beyond his reach disparaged them by saying that they appeared to be sour] **:** disparagement of something that has proven unattainable ⟨his snide remarks about people who make the honor roll are nothing but *sour grapes*⟩

sour grass *n* **1 :** 1DOCK 1 **2 :** an American plant (*Xerophyllum tenax*) having stiff grasslike foliage **3 :** either of two tropical grasses (*Paspalum conjugatum* or *Tricholaena insularis*) the leaves of which are too sour for cattle to eat

sour greens *n pl* **:** a dock (*Rumex venosus*) of No. America having rose-colored veiny capsules

sour gum *n* **1 :** BLACK GUM — see TREE illustration **2 :** SOURWOOD

sour humus *n* **:** humus harmful to plant growth because of the presence of humic or similar acids

souring *n* -s [fr. gerund of 4*sour*] **1 :** an act or instance of turning sour **2** *archaic* **:** a substance (as lemon juice or vinegar) that causes souring

sour·i·quois \'sùrə,kwòi\ *n, pl* **souriquois** *usu cap* [F, of AmerInd origin] **:** MICMAC

sour·ish \'saùrish\ *adj* [ME, fr. 1*sour* + *-ish*] **:** somewhat sour **:** ACIDULOUS

sourjack \'⸗,⸗\ *n* [1*sour* + *jack*] **:** JACKFRUIT 2

sour lime *n* **:** 6LIME

sour·ly *adv* **:** in a sour manner ⟨complained ~ that it benefited only the bosses, as usual —Mollie Panter-Downes⟩

sour mash *n* **:** grain mash for brewing or distilling whose initial acidity has been adjusted to optimum condition for yeast fermentation by mash from a previous run

sour milk *n* **1 :** soured milk **2** *dial* **:** BUTTERMILK

sour milk cheese *n, North* **:** COTTAGE CHEESE

sour·ness *n* -ES [ME *sournes,* fr. OE *sūrness,* fr. *sūr* + *-ness* — more at SOUR] **1 :** the quality, state, or degree of being sour **:** ACIDITY **2 :** DISCONTENT, PEEVISHNESS

sour orange *n* **1 :** a tree (*Citrus aurantium*) much used as an understock in grafting **2 :** the fruit of the sour orange tree having somewhat bitter pulp and used esp. in making marmalade — called also *bitter orange, Seville orange*

sour plum *n* **1 :** EMU APPLE **2 :** any of several trees or shrubs of the genus *Ximenia*; *esp* **:** a tall much-branched often spiny shrub (*X. caffra*) of the northern Transvaal with greenish flowers in axillary clusters followed by orange-red to scarlet fruits

sourpuss \'⸗,⸗\ *n* [1*sour* + *puss* (face)] **:** GROUCH, KILLJOY

sour rot *n* **:** a soft slimy watery decay of citrus fruits caused by a fungus (*Oospora citri-aurantii*)

sours *pl of* SOUR, *pres 3d sing of* SOUR

sour salt *n* **:** CITRIC ACID

sour sap *n* **:** a winter injury of fruit trees in which there is a stagnation and fermentation of sap at the time uninjured trees are starting growth and which usu. results in death

sour scab *n* **:** CITRUS SCAB

sour·sob \'⸗,säb\ *n* [prob. alter. (influenced by 2*sob*) of *soursop*] **:** any of several plants of the genus *Oxalis*

soursop \'⸗,⸗\ *n* [1*sour* + *sop* (food)] **1 :** a small tropical American tree (*Annona muricata*) **2 :** the large succulent irregularly ovoid fruit of the soursop tree having short fleshy spines and a slightly acid fibrous pulp — called also *guanabana*; compare SWEETSOP

1**sour-sweet** \'⸗;⸗\ *adj* [trans. of MF *aigre-doux*] **:** sweet and sour at the same time ⟨*sour-sweet* molasses⟩; *esp* **:** pleasant but with an acid overtone ⟨a *sour-sweet* smile⟩

2**sour-sweet** \"\ *n* **:** something that is sour-sweet

sourtop \'⸗,⸗\ *also* **sourtop blueberry** *n* **:** CANADA BLUEBERRY

sour trefoil *also* **sour trifoly** *n* **:** a wood sorrel (*Oxalis acetosella*)

sour tupelo *n* **:** OGEECHEE LIME

sourveld \'⸗,⸗\ *n* [1*sour* + *veld*] **:** African veld that is largely covered with coarse seasonal perennial grasses and affords inferior grazing

sourweed \'⸗,⸗\ *n* **:** SHEEP SORREL

sourwood \'⸗,⸗\ *n* **:** a small tree (*Oxydendrum arboreum*) of the family Ericaceae common along the Alleghenies and having one-sided racemes of white flowers clustered in terminal panicles and sour-tasting leaves that turn brilliant red in the fall — called also *sorrel tree*

1**sous** \'sü\ *adj* [F, prep., under, fr. L *subtus,* adv., below, under; akin to L *sub* under — more at SUB-] **:** of subordinate rank **:** ASSISTANT — used chiefly in titles ⟨~ chef⟩

2**sous** *or* **souse** \'saùs\ *n, pl* **sous** *or* **souse** [MF *sous,* pl. of *sou* — more at SOU] **1** *archaic* **:** SOU ⟨grapes are a ~ a pound —J.A.Heraud⟩ **2** [so called fr. the fact that a hit in the ring entitled the archer to a sou] **a** *archaic* **:** the outermost ring of an archery target **b :** 1PETTICOAT 4a

3**sous** *pl of* SOU

sou·sa·phone \'süzə,fōn 'süsə,-\ *n* -s [John P. *Sousa* †1932 Am. bandmaster and composer + E *-phone*] **:** a large circular tuba similar to the helicon but having a flaring adjustable bell

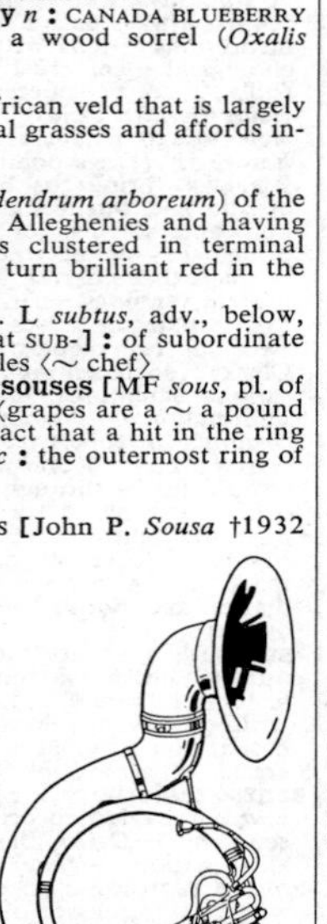
sousaphone

1**souse** \'saùs\ *vb* -ED/-ING/-S [ME *sousen,* prob. fr. MF *sous, souce,* n., souse, preservative] *vt* **1 :** to steep in a preservative **:** PICKLE ⟨counter loaded with *soused* herrings —A.J. Cronin⟩ **2 a :** to dip in or as if in water **:** IMMERSE, PLUNGE ⟨*soused* the squealing youngster up and down until . . . it was clean —A.W. O'Neil⟩ ⟨*soused* himself in the literature of the period before writing his term paper⟩ **b :** to wet thoroughly **:** DRENCH, SATURATE ⟨the engines arrived and *soused* the burning houses —George Meredith⟩ **3 a :** to shower or engulf completely **:** SOAK, SUBMERGE ⟨guns . . . *soused* the kopjes with shells —*London Daily News*⟩ **b :** to douse a person with **:** SLOSH, POUR ⟨*soused* one of the buckets in the drunk's face —W.A.White⟩ **4 :** to make drunk **:** INEBRIATE ⟨he was *soused,* but the look in his eyes, the rapt expression . . . weren't due only to drink —W.S.Maugham⟩ ~ *vi* **1 :** to become immersed or drenched; *esp* **:** BATHE **2 :** to get drunk **syn** see DIP

2**souse** \"\ *n* -s [ME *souse, souz, souce,* of Gmc origin; akin to OHG *sulza* salt water, pickled sausage, OS *sultia* salt water, MD *sulte* pickled pork, OE *sealt* salt — more at SALT] **1 a :** something that is pickled; *esp* **:** pork trimmings, fish, or shellfish chopped, seasoned, cooked, and molded for slicing **b :** a pickling solution **2** *chiefly dial* **:** EAR **3 :** an act or instance of drenching or immersion **:** DIP, WETTING ⟨the storm gets down his neck in an icy ~ —Robert Frost⟩ **4 a :** a habitual drunkard **:** TIPPLER ⟨a ~ on a bar stool —Raymond Chandler⟩ **b :** a drinking spree **:** BINGE ⟨a Sunday morning headache from a Saturday night ~⟩

3**souse** \"\ *n* -s [ME *sowce,* prob. of imit. origin] *chiefly dial* **:** a heavy blow

4**souse** *n* -s [ME *souce,* alter. of *sours* start of flight, source — more at SOURCE] *obs* **:** the start of a bird's flight or the stoop of a hawk intercepting it at this point

5**souse** \'saùs\ *vb* -ED/-ING/-S *vi, archaic* **:** to swoop down **:** PLUNGE ~ *vt, archaic* **:** to knock down by swooping upon

6**souse** \"\ *adv* **:** with a sudden swoop or splash ⟨~ went the sheep into a murky, muddy pool —Zane Grey⟩

7**souse** \"\ *vb* -ED/-ING/-S [prob. fr. 3*souse*] *vt, archaic* **:** to hit hard **:** beat severely ~ *vi, archaic* **:** to come down heavily

8**souse** \"\ *adv, chiefly dial* **:** with a strong impact **:** HEAVILY, DIRECTLY

souslik *var of* SUSLIK

sous-sous \'sü(,)sü\ *n* [modif. of F *sous-sus,* short for *dessous-dessus,* lit., "underover"] **:** SOUBRESAUT

sou·tache \(')sü¦tash\ *n* -s [F, fr. Hung *sujtás*] **:** a narrow rounded or flat braid with a characteristic herringbone pattern used as a decorative trimming (as on suits, dresses, uniforms)

sou·tane \(')sü¦tän\ *n* -s [F, alter. (influenced by 1*sous*) of MF *sottane,* fr. OIt *sottana,* fem. of *sottano,* fr. ML *subtanus,* adj., lower, under, fr. L *subtus* below, under + *-anus* -an; fr. its being worn under the vestments at religious services — more at SOUS] **:** a cassock worn by secular clergy of the Roman Catholic Church

sou·te·neur \,süt°n¦ər, +V -¦nər·; *-R* -¦nə, + *vowel in a word following without pause* -¦nər· *or* -¦nə *also* -¦nər\ *n* -s [F, lit., supporter, provider, fr. OF *susteneur,* fr. *sustenir* to support, provide, sustain + *-eur* -or — more at SUSTAIN] **:** PIMP 1b

sou·te·nu \,sütə¦nü\ *adj* [F, fr. past part. of *soutenir* to sustain, fr. OF *sustenir*] *of a ballet movement* **:** executed in a drawn-out manner **:** SUSTAINED

sou·ter *also* **sou·tar** \'sütə(r)\ *n* -s [ME *souter, sutor,* fr. OE *sūtere,* fr. L *sutor;* akin to L *suere* to sew — more at SEW] *chiefly Scot* **:** SHOEMAKER

sou·ter·lie·de·ken \'saùdə(r),lēdəkən\ *n* -s [D, fr. MD *souterliedekijn,* fr. *souter* psalter (prob. fr. OF *psautier, sautier*) + *liedekijn* little song, fr. *liet* song (akin to OHG *liod* song) + *-kijn* -kin — more at PSALTER, LAUD, -KIN] **:** one of a 16th century Netherlands collection of monophonic psalm tunes taken from current popular folk melodies and containing rhymed versions of the Psalms

sou·ter·rain \,süd·ə¦rān\ *n* [F, fr. *sous* under + *terrain* ground — more at SOUS, TERRAIN] **:** an underground passage or chamber

souter's clod *n, Scot* **:** a roll of coarse bread

1**south** \'saùth\ *adv* [ME *south, suth,* fr. OE *sūth;* akin to OFris *sūth* southward, ON *suthr,* OHG *sund-;* akin to OHG *sunna* sun — more at SUN] **:** to, toward, or in the south **:** SOUTHWARD

2**south** \"\ *adj* [ME, fr. OE *sūthan-,* fr. *sūthan,* adv.; akin to OHG *sundan* from the south; derivative fr. the root of E 1*south*] **1 a :** coming from the south ⟨a ~ wind⟩ **b** [ME, fr. OE *sūth-,* fr. *sūth,* adv.] **:** situated toward or at the south ⟨the ~ entrance⟩ ⟨the ~ country⟩ **2 :** situated in the direction of the right side of a church looking from the nave toward the altar or chancel

3**south** \"\ *n* -s [ME, fr. 1*south*] **1 a :** the direction of the south terrestrial pole **:** the direction to the right of one facing east **:** the direction to the right of one facing the sunrise when the sun is near one of the equinoxes **b :** the part of the sky lying to the right of an observer facing east **c :** the cardinal point directly opposite to north — abbr. *S;* see COMPASS CARD **d :** the direction along any meridian toward that pole of the earth viewed from which the earth's rotation is clockwise **e :** the direction on the celestial sphere to the right when one faces the direction of its apparent rotation **:** the direction to the right when one faces the direction of revolution around the sun of the earth and the principal planets **2** *usu cap* **a :** regions or countries lying to the south of a specified or implied point of orientation (as in the U. S. the states lying in general south of Mason and Dixon's Line and the Ohio river) **b :** something (as people, culture, or institutions) characteristic of the South ⟨for years the *South* could be depended upon to vote the straight Democratic ticket⟩ **3 :** the south wind **4** *often cap* **a :** the one of four positions at 90-degree intervals that lies toward the south **b :** a person (as a bridge player) occupying such a position in the course of a specific activity

4**south** \'saùth, 'saùth\ *vi* -ED/-ING/-S **1 :** to move or veer toward the south **2 :** to come to the meridian **:** cross the north-and-south line — used chiefly of the sun and moon

southabout \'⸗⸗,⸗\ *adv* (*or adj*) **:** about in tacking so as to head south; *broadly* **:** toward the south **:** SOUTHWARD

south africa *adj, usu cap S&A* [fr. *South Africa,* republic in southern Africa] **:** of or from South Africa **:** of the kind or style prevalent in South Africa **:** SOUTH AFRICAN

1**south african** *adj, usu cap S&A* [*South Africa* + E *-an,* adj. suffix] **1 :** of, relating to, or characteristic of southern Africa; *esp* **:** of, relating to, or characteristic of the Republic of South Africa **2 :** of, relating to, or characteristic of South Africans

2**south african** *n, cap S&A* [*South Africa* + E *-an,* n. suffix] **:** a native or inhabitant of the Republic of South Africa; *esp* **:** AFRIKANER

south african hunting dog *n, usu cap S&A* **:** AFRICAN HUNTING DOG

south african ruby *n, usu cap S&A* **:** CAPE RUBY

south african yellowwood *n, usu cap S&A* **1 :** a southern African timber tree (*Podocarpus elongatus*) **2 :** the hard yellow wood of the South African yellowwood tree

south america *adj, usu cap S&A* [fr. *South America,* continent of the western hemisphere] **:** of or from the continent of South America **:** of the kind or style prevalent in South America **:** SOUTH AMERICAN

1**south american** *adj, usu cap S&A* [*South America* + E *-an,* adj. suffix] **:** of, relating to, or characteristic of South America or its people

2**south american** *n, cap S&A* [*South America* + E *-an,* n. suffix] **:** a native or inhabitant of South America

south american blastomycosis *n, usu cap S&A* [so called fr. its being limited chiefly to South America and distinct from North American blastomycosis] **:** blastomycosis characterized by formation of ulcers on the mucosal surfaces of the mouth that spread to lips, nose, and cheeks, by great enlargement of lymph nodes esp. of the throat and chest, and by involvement of the gastrointestinal tract and caused by a fungus (*Blastomyces brasiliensis*)

south american bullfrog *n, usu cap S&A* **:** a large So. American toothed frog of the genus *Leptodactylus*

south american kino *n, usu cap S&A* **:** kino taken from a So. American tree (*Coccolobis uvifera*)

south american tulipwood *n, usu cap S&A* **:** TULIPWOOD 2a(1)

south american walnut *n, usu cap S&A* **:** CONACASTE

south·amp·ton \(')saù¦tham(p)tən, -aùth¦ha-\ *adj, usu cap* [fr. *Southampton,* England] **:** of or from the county borough of Southampton, England **:** of the kind or style prevalent in Southampton

south arabic *n, usu cap S&A* **:** a group of Semitic dialects spoken in southern Arabia from at least the third century B.C.

south australia *adj, usu cap S&A* [fr. *South Australia,* Australia] **:** of or from the state of South Australia **:** of the kind or style prevalent in South Australia **:** SOUTH AUSTRALIAN

1**south australian** *adj, usu cap S&A* [*South Australia* + E *-an,* adj. suffix] **1 :** of, relating to, or characteristic of South Australia **2 :** of, relating to, or characteristic of the South Australians

2**south australian** *n, cap S&A* [*South Australia* + E *-an,* n. suffix] **:** a native or inhabitant of South Australia

south bend \(')saùth¦bend\ *adj, usu cap S&B* [fr. *South Bend,* Ind.] **:** of or from the city of South Bend, Ind. ⟨*South Bend* factories⟩ **:** of the kind or style prevalent in South Bend

southbound \'⸗,⸗\ *adj* **:** traveling or headed in a southerly direction ⟨~ traffic⟩

1**south by east :** a compass point that is one point east of due south **:** S 11° 15′ E — abbr. *S b E, S by E;* see COMPASS CARD

2**south by east** *adv* (*or adj*) **1 :** toward south by east **2 :** from south by east

1**south by west :** a compass point that is one point west of due south **:** S 11° 15′ W — abbr. *S b W, S by W;* see COMPASS CARD

2**south by west** *adv* (*or adj*) **1 :** toward south by west **2 :** from south by west

south carolina *adj, usu cap S&C* [fr. *South Carolina,* south Atlantic state of the U. S., fr. 2*south* + *Carolina,* Eng. colony from which No. & So. Carolina were formed — more at CAROLINIAN] **:** of or from the state of South Carolina ⟨a *South Carolina* crop⟩ **:** of the kind or style prevalent in South Carolina **:** SOUTH CAROLINIAN

1**south carolinian** *adj, usu cap S&C* [*South Carolina* + E *-ian,* adj. suffix] **1 :** of, relating to, or characteristic of South Carolina **2 :** of, relating to, or characteristic of South Carolinians

2**south carolinian** *n, cap S&C* [*South Carolina* + E *-ian,* n. suffix] **:** a native or resident of the state of South Carolina

south celestial pole *n* **:** SOUTH POLE 1a

south central *adj, usu cap S&C* **:** of, relating to, or characteristic of the states of the lower Mississippi valley and east of the Rio Grande

south·cot·ti·an \saùth'käd·ēən\ *n* -s *usu cap* [Joanna *Southcott* †1814 Eng. woman + E *-ian*] **:** a follower of Joanna Southcott who claimed to be the bride of Christ and in the last year of her life prophesied that she would give birth to another Messiah

south dakota *adj, usu cap S&D* [fr. *South Dakota,* northwestern state of the U. S., fr. 2*south* + *Dakota* (*territory*), former region of the U. S. including No. & So. Dakota — more at DAKOTA] **:** of or from the state of South Dakota ⟨the *South Dakota* badlands⟩ **:** of the kind or style prevalent in South Dakota **:** SOUTH DAKOTAN

1**south dakotan** *adj, usu cap S&D* [*South Dakota* + E *-an,* adj. suffix] **1 :** of, relating to, or characteristic of South Dakota **2 :** of, relating to, or characteristic of South Dakotans

2**south dakotan** *n, cap S&D* [*South Dakota* + E *-an,* n. suffix] **:** a native or resident of the state of South Dakota

1**south·down** \'saùth,daùn\ *n* -s *usu cap* [fr. *South Downs,* England, where it was orig. bred] **:** an important English breed of small medium-wooled hornless mutton-type sheep — compare DOWN

2**southdown** \"\ *adj, usu cap* [fr. *South Downs,* England] **:** of, relating to, or characteristic of a range of pasture hills south of the Thames, England

1**south·east** \(')saù¦thēst, *in nautical pronunciation also* (')saù¦ēst\ *adv* [ME *southest,* fr. OE *sūthēast,* fr. *sūth* south + *ēast* east — more at SOUTH, EAST] **:** to, toward, or in the southeast **:** SOUTHEASTWARD

2**southeast** \"\ *n* -s [ME, fr. 1*southeast*] **1 a :** the general direction between south and east **b :** the part of the southern sky lying east of the observer's meridian **c :** the point of the compass midway between the cardinal points south and east **:** the point directly opposite to northwest — abbr. *SE;* see COMPASS CARD **2** *usu cap* **a :** regions or countries lying to the southeast of a specified or implied point of orientation **b :** something (as people or institutions) characteristic of the southeast ⟨the *Southeast* has benefited greatly from TVA⟩ **3 :** the southeast wind

3**southeast** \"\ *adj* [ME, fr. 1*southeast*] **1 :** coming from the southeast ⟨a ~ wind⟩ **2 :** situated toward or at the southeast ⟨the ~ corner of his ranch⟩

1**southeast by east :** a compass point that is one point east of due southeast **:** S 56° 15′ E — abbr. *SE b E, SE by E;* see COMPASS CARD

2**southeast by east** *adv* (*or adj*) **1 :** toward southeast by east **2 :** from southeast by east

1**southeast by south :** a compass point that is one point south of due southeast **:** S 33° 45′ E — abbr. *SE b S, SE by S;* see COMPASS CARD

2**southeast by south** *adv* (*or adj*) **1 :** toward southeast by south **2 :** from southeast by south

south·east·er \-tə(r)\ *n* **1 :** a strong southeast wind **2 :** a storm with southeast winds ⟨a good, solid ~ . . . smacks the windows with pelting rain —Wyman Richardson⟩

1**south·east·er·ly** \-tərlē, -li, *-R* -təl- *sometimes* -t°l-\ *adv* (*or adj*) [2*south* + *easterly,* adv. or adj.] **1 :** from the southeast ⟨~ gale⟩ **2 :** toward the southeast ⟨held a ~ course⟩

2**southeasterly** \"\ *n* [2*south* + *easterly,* n.] **:** a wind from the southeast ⟨it doesn't take one of those *southeasterlies* long to come up —Norman Lewis⟩

south·east·ern \-tə(r)n, *-R also* -t°n\ *adj* [2*southeast* + *-ern* (as in *eastern*)] **1** *often cap* **:** of, relating to, originating or dwelling in, or characteristic of a region (as of the U. S.) conventionally designated Southeast ⟨~ schools⟩ **2 :** situated toward or coming from the southeast ⟨the train comes in at the ~ station⟩

south·east·ern·er *R* -tə(r)nər, *-R* -tənə(r *also* -t°nə(r\ *n, usu cap* **:** a native or inhabitant of a southeastern region (as of the U. S.) ⟨the *Southeasterner* has his magnolias⟩

south·east·ern·most \-tə(r)n,mōst, *esp Brit also* -nməst\ *adj* **:** farthest to the southeast **:** most southeastern

1**south·east·ward** \-ēstwə(r)d\ *adv* (*or adj*) **:** toward the southeast **:** in a southeast direction ⟨rises in the mountains and flows ~⟩

2**southeastward** \"\ *n* **:** SOUTHEAST ⟨to the ~⟩

south·east·ward·ly *adv* (*or adj*) **:** toward or from the southeastward **:** SOUTHEASTERLY

south·east·wards \-dz\ *adv* **:** SOUTHEASTWARD

southed *past of* SOUTH

south·end \(')saù¦thend\ *or* **southend-on-sea** \(')⸗¦⸗⸗¦⸗\ *adj, usu cap both Ss* [fr. *Southend on Sea,* England] **:** of or from the city of Southend on Sea, England **:** of the kind or style prevalent in Southend on Sea

1**south·er** \'saùthə(r)\ *vi* -ED/-ING/-S [1*south* + *-er* (as in 1*batter*)] **:** to turn, veer, or shift to the south — used chiefly of the wind

2**souther** \"\ *n* -s [1*south* + *-er,* n. suffix] **:** a southerly wind ⟨the anchorage offers pretty fair protection from anything except a ~⟩

south·er·li·ness \'səthə(r)lēnəs\ *n* -ES **:** the situation of being southerly

1**south·er·ly** \-lē, -li\ *adj* [fr. 2*south,* after E 2*east:* 1*easterly*] **1 :** situated or directed toward the south ⟨ordered a ~ course —C.S.Forester⟩ **:** SOUTHERN ⟨there was a crack in its ~ wall —Earl Hamner⟩ **2 :** blowing from the south ⟨a ~ wind⟩

2**southerly** \"\ *adv* **1 :** from the south ⟨the wind blew ~⟩ **2 :** toward the south ⟨turned ~⟩

3**southerly** \"\ *n* -ES **:** a wind from the south ⟨the ~ came in with flood tide —G.W.Brace⟩

southerly buster *n* **:** BUSTER 3

south·er·most \-(r),mōst, *esp Brit also* -,məst\ *adj* [fr. 2*south,* after such pairs as E 2*east: eastermost*] **:** SOUTHERNMOST

1**south·ern** \'səthə(r)n\ *adj* [ME *southren,* fr. OE *sūtherne;* akin to OHG *sundrōni,* ON *suthrænn;* derivative fr. the root of E 1*south*] **1** *often cap* **a :** of, relating to, originating or dwelling in, or characteristic of a region conventionally designated South ⟨~ mansion⟩ ⟨~ belle⟩ **b :** being or characterizing the native speech of the r-dropping population of the southeastern U. S. — compare EASTERN 4, SOUTHERN MOUNTAIN **2 a :** lying toward the south ⟨patients on the ~ side of a hospital recover faster —Herbert Spencer⟩ **b :** coming from the south ⟨~ breezes⟩ **3** *of a sign of the zodiac* **:** situated south of the equator **:** AUSTRAL

2**southern** \"\ *n* -s [ME, fr. 1*southern*] **1** *usu cap* **:** an inhabitant of the South **:** SOUTHERNER 1 **2** *or* **southern dialect** *usu cap S* **:** the dialect of English spoken in the part of the U. S. that lies south of the southern boundary of Midland and includes most of the Chesapeake Bay area, the coastal plain and the greater part of the upland plateau in Virginia, North Carolina, South Carolina, and Georgia, and the Gulf states at least as far west as the valley of the Brazos in Texas

southern armyworm *n* **:** a climbing cutworm (*Prodenia eridania*) that is destructive to many vegetable crops in southern U. S.

southern bacterial wilt *n* **:** GRANVILLE WILT

southern balsam fir *n* **:** FRASER FIR

southern baptist *n, usu cap S&B* **:** a member of a body of Baptist churches organized in 1845 in the southern U. S. as the Southern Baptist Convention

southern black haw *n* : a coarse shrub or small tree (*Viburnum rufidulum*) chiefly of the southeastern U. S. having densely scurfy covering over all or parts of the leaves, petioles and branchlets
southern blight *n* : a disease of many vegetable and ornamental plants caused by a fungus (*Sclerotium rolfsii*) and characterized by girdling of the stem near the soil line and the production of round whitish to brown sclerotia on the stems — called also *southern stem rot*
southern blue gum *n* : a blue gum (*Eucalyptus globulus*)
southern bright *n* -s *usu cap S* : heat-cured tobacco grown in southeastern U. S., harvested by priming, and usu. used in cigarettes
southern buckthorn *n* : a shrub or small tree (*Bumelia lycioides*) of the southeastern U. S. with milky sap, smooth or silky oblong to narrowly obovate leaves, dense clusters of small white flowers followed by dark ovoid fruits, and very tough hard wood
southern buddhism *n, usu cap S&B* : HINAYANA
southern cabbage butterfly *n* : CABBAGE BUTTERFLY c
southern canary grass *n* : an annual grass (*Phalaris caroliniana*) with dense oblong panicles found in the southern U. S.
southern cattle fever *or* **southern fever** *n* : TEXAS FEVER
southern colonial *n, usu cap S&C* : the architectural style culminating in the fine Georgian mansions of the antebellum period
southern corn rootworm *n* : a corn rootworm that is the larva of the spotted cucumber beetle
southern cornstalk borer *n* : a brown-spotted grayish white caterpillar that is the larva of a straw-colored moth (*Diatraea crambidoides*) and is a destructive pest esp. of corn in the southern U. S.
southern crabapple *n* : a partially evergreen small tree (*Malus angustifolia*) native to southeastern U. S. but used as an ornamental having lance-oblong leaves and rose-colored flowers
southern cult *n, usu cap S&C* : a religious movement among the Indians of the southern U. S. in the 16th and 17th centuries assumed from certain naturalistic art styles in embossed copper plates, cut and engraved shell gorgets, pottery, and batons or maces found in archaeological sites
southern cypress *n* : a bald cypress (*Taxodium distichum*)
southern dewberry *n* : any of several brambles of the southern U. S.; *esp* : a dewberry (*Rubus trivialis*) with somewhat persistent foliage and oblong glossy black fruit
southern english *n, usu cap S&E* **1** : the English spoken in the South of England esp. by cultivated people native to or educated there and by many educated people in other parts of the British Empire **2** : SOUTHERN 2
south·ern·er \R ˈsəthə(r)nər, -R -thənə(r\ *n* -s **1** *usu cap* : a native or inhabitant of the South; *esp* : a native or inhabitant of the southern states of the U. S. **2** : a small light workhorse used chiefly in the southern U. S. for field labor, driving, and riding
southern flounder *n* : a dusky olive flounder (*Paralichthys lethostigmus*) of the south Atlantic and Gulf coasts of the U. S.
southern fox grape *n* : MUSCADINE 2
southern green stink bug *n* : a pentatomid bug (*Nezara viridula*) that is an important pest on citrus in Florida
southern hemisphere *n* : the half of the earth that lies south of the equator
south·ern·ism \ˈsəthə(r),nizəm\ *n* -s *usu cap* **1** : a locution or pronunciation characteristic of the southern U.S. ⟨can detect a phony ~ quicker than most theater men —Joshua Logan⟩ **2** : an attitude or trait characteristic of the South or Southerners esp. in the U.S. ⟨his *Southernisms* had been thoroughly rubbed away —Robert Lowell⟩
south·ern·ize \-,nīz\ *vt* -ED/-ING/-S *sometimes cap* [¹*southern* + *-ize*] : to imbue with qualities native to or associated with a southern region and esp. the southern states of the U. S.
southern leopard frog *n* : LEOPARD FROG 2
southern lights *n pl* : AURORA AUSTRALIS
south·ern·ly *adj* : SOUTHERLY
southern magnolia *n* : EVERGREEN MAGNOLIA
southern mongol *n, usu cap S&M* : PAREOEAN
southern moss *n* : SPANISH MOSS
south·ern·most \ˈsəthə(r)n,mōst, *esp Brit also* -nməst\ *adj* : farthest to the south : most southern
southern mountain *adj, often cap S&M* : being or characterizing the native speech of many mountain-dwellers of the southeastern U. S. who do not drop their r's — compare SOUTHERN 1b
southern paiute *n, usu cap S&P* **1** : PAIUTE 1 **2** : the language of the Southern Paiute people
southern pine *n* **1** *or* **southern pitch pine** : LONGLEAF PINE **2** : a pitch pine (*Pinus rigida*)
southern pine beetle *n* : a bark beetle (*Dendroctonus frontalis*) which attacks pines in southern and eastern parts of the U. S.
southern porgy *n* : SCUP b
southern prickly ash *n* : HERCULES'-CLUB 1a
southern red cedar *n* : a red cedar (*Juniperus silicicola*) of the southeastern U. S. differing from the eastern red cedar in having shorter thicker leaves with blunt apexes
southern red lily *n* : a bulbous herb (*Lilium catesbaei*) of the southeastern U. S. with showy scarlet purple-spotted flowers
southern red oak *n* : RED OAK 1b
southern right whale *n* : a right whale (*Eubalaena glacialis*) that is somewhat smaller than the Greenland whale and is widely distributed in temperate seas though nearly extinct in the North Atlantic through overfishing
southerns *pl of* SOUTHERN
southern senega *n* : SENEGA 2b
southern spatterdock *n* : a spatterdock (*Nuphar sagittifolium*) of flowing waters of the southeastern U. S. that has filmy submersed leaves and narrow oblong to lanceolate floating leaves, sometimes forms obstructive mats in larger streams, and is often planted in aquariums
southern stem rot *or* **southern root rot** *or* **southern wilt** *n* : SOUTHERN BLIGHT
southern sugar maple *n* : a tree (*Acer barbatum*) chiefly of the southeastern U. S. having whitish gray bark and flowers with a conspicuous long white beard projecting from the throat
southern white cedar *n* : a strong-scented evergreen tree (*Chamaecyparis thyoides*) somewhat resembling the American arborvitae but having smaller leaves and globose cones with peltate scales
southernwood \ˈ=,=\ *n* [ME *southernwode*, fr. OE *sūtherne wudu*, fr. *sūtherne* southern + *wudu* wood — more at SOUTHERN, WOOD] : a shrubby European wormwood (*Artemisia abrotanum*) naturalized in America and sometimes used in brewing beer — called also *old man*
southern yellow pine *n* : any of several pines; *esp* : LONGLEAF PINE
south ethiopic *n, usu cap S&E* : a subgroup of Afro-Asiatic languages including Amharic, Argobba, Harari, Gafat, Gurage
south geographical pole *n* : SOUTH POLE 1b
south·ing \ˈsau̇thiŋ\ *n* -s [¹*south* + *-ing*] **1 a** : difference in latitude to the south from the last preceding point of reckoning **b** : southerly progress : a going southward **2 a** : crossing of the meridian to the south of the zenith **b** : the distance of any celestial body south of the equator : south declination
south·land \ˈsau̇th,land, -,laa(ə)nd, -lənd\ *n, often cap* [ME, fr. OE *sūthland*, fr. *sūth* south + *land* — more at SOUTH, LAND] : land in the south : the south of a country ⟨most of Chile's hundred thousand Germans live in . . . her ~ —Hubert Herring⟩; *specif* : DEEP SOUTH ⟨bands from the ~ begin to jazz up their dance numbers —A.C.E.Schonemann⟩
south·land·er \-də(r)\ *n* : SOUTHERNER 1
southmost \ˈ=,=\ *adj* [alter. (influenced by ¹*most*) of ME *southmaist*, fr. OE *sūthmest*, superl. of *sūth* south] : SOUTHERNMOST
south·ness *n* -ES : the quality or state of being south
¹southpaw \ˈ=,=\ *n* [²*south* + *paw*] **1** : LEFT-HANDER; *specif* : a left-handed baseball pitcher **2** : a boxer who leads with the right hand and foot forward while guarding with the left hand
²southpaw \"\ *adj* **1** : habitually using the left hand : LEFT-HANDED ⟨a ~ pitcher⟩ **2** : done with the left hand ⟨a laboriously printed ~ note —John Mason Brown⟩
south polar distance *n* : the angular distance of a celestial body measured along its hour circle from the south celestial pole
south pole *n* **1 a** : the zenith of the heavens as viewed from the south terrestrial pole **b** *often cap S&P* : the southernmost point of the earth : the southern extremity of the earth's axis — see ZONE illustration **2** *of a magnet* : the pole that points toward the south when the magnet is freely suspended
¹south·ron \ˈsəthrən\ *adj, usu cap* [ME (Sc), alter. (influenced by *-on* as in *Briton*) of *southren* southern — more at SOUTHERN] *chiefly Scot* : SOUTHERN; *specif* : ENGLISH
²southron \"\ *n* -s *usu cap* : SOUTHERNER: as **a** *chiefly Scot* : ENGLISHMAN **b** *chiefly South* : a native or inhabitant of the southern states of the U. S.
souths *pl of* SOUTH, *pres 3d sing of* SOUTH
south sea *adj, usu cap both Ss* [fr. *South Seas*, the waters of the southern hemisphere] : of or relating to the seas of the southern hemisphere and esp. the south Pacific ⟨thatched huts and coconut palms of the *South Sea* islands⟩ ⟨*South Sea* pirate schooners with tall, raking masts, loaded to the gunwale with rum and gold bars —Peter Heaton⟩
south sea islander *n, usu cap both Ss&I* [*South Sea islands* + *-er*] : a native or inhabitant of the tropical islands of the South Pacific : POLYNESIAN
south-sea·man \(ˈ)=ˈ=mən\ *n, usu cap 1st S* [*South Sea* + *man*] : a sailing ship formerly running to or trading in the region of the South Seas
south sea rose *n, usu cap both Ss* : OLEANDER
south-seeking pole *n* : SOUTH POLE 2
south semitic *n, cap both Ss* : SOUTHWEST SEMITIC
south shields \-ˈshēldz\ *adj, usu cap both Ss* [fr. *South Shields*, England] : of or from the county borough of South Shields, England : of the kind or style prevalent in South Shields
south slav *n, cap both Ss* : a member of the Slovene, Croat, Serb, or Bulgarian peoples of the Balkans including the Serbo-Croatian speaking natives of Macedonia, Dalmatia, Bosnia and Herzegovina; *specif* : YUGOSLAV
¹south-southeast \(ˌ)=ˌ=ˈ=\ *adv (or adj)* [ME *south south est*] **1** : toward south-southeast **2** : from south-southeast
²south-southeast \"\ *n* : a compass point that is two points east of due south : S22°30′E — abbr. *SSE*; see COMPASS CARD
south-southerly \(ˈ)=ˈ===\ *n* [so called fr. an imitation of its cry] : OLD-SQUAW
¹south-southwest \(ˌ)=ˌ=ˈ=\ *adv (or adj)* **1** : toward south-southwest **2** : from south-southwest
²south-southwest \"\ *n* : a compass point that is two points west of due south : S22°30′W — abbr. *SSW*; see COMPASS CARD
south temperate *adj, often cap S&T* : of or relating to the south temperate zone of the earth lying between the tropic of Capricorn and the antarctic circle ⟨*south temperate* seas⟩ — see ZONE illustration
south terrestrial pole *n* : SOUTH POLE 1b
¹south·um·bri·an \(ˈ)sau̇ˈthəmbrēən\ *n* -s *cap* [²*south* + *-umbrian* (as in *northumbrian*)] : a native or inhabitant of Northern Mercia
²southumbrian \"\ *adj, usu cap* : of or relating to the northern part of the Anglo-Saxon kingdom of Mercia, south of Northumbria
¹south·ward \ˈsau̇thwə(r)d\ *adv (or adj)* [ME, fr. OE *sūthweard*, fr. *sūth* south + *-weard* -ward] : toward the south
²southward \"\ *n* : southward direction or part
south·ward·ly *adv (or adj)* : in a southern direction ⟨proceed ~ . . . through the great region of slaves —Hastings Lyon⟩
south·wards \-dz\ *adv* [ME *southwardis*, fr. OE *sūthweardes*, fr. *sūth* south + *-weardes* -wards] : SOUTHWARD
¹south·west \(ˈ)sau̇ˈthwest, *usual nautical pronunciation* -au̇ˈw-\ *adv* [ME, fr. OE *sūthwest*, fr. *sūth* south + *west*] : to, toward, or in the southwest : SOUTHWESTWARD
²southwest \"\ *n* [ME, fr. OE *sūthwest*, fr. *sūthwest*, adv.] **1 a** : the general direction between the south and west **b** : the part of the southern sky lying west of the observer's meridian **c** : the point of the compass midway between the cardinal points south and west : the point directly opposite to northeast — abbr. *SW*; see COMPASS CARD **2** *usu cap* **a** : regions or countries lying to the southwest of a specified or implied point of orientation **b** : something (as people or institutions) characteristic of the Southwest ⟨the *Southwest* is concerned over the problem of wetbacks⟩ **3** : the southwest wind
³southwest \"\ *adj* [ME, fr. ¹*southwest*] **1** : coming from the southwest ⟨a ~ wind⟩ **2** : situated toward or at the southwest
¹southwest by south : a compass point that is one point south of due southwest : S 33° 45′ W — abbr. *SW b S*, *SW by S*; see COMPASS CARD
²southwest by south *adv (or adj)* **1** : toward southwest by south **2** : from southwest by south
¹southwest by west : a compass point that is one point west of due southwest : S 56° 15′ W — abbr. *SW b W*, *SW by W*; see COMPASS CARD
²southwest by west *adv (or adj)* **1** : toward southwest by west **2** : from southwest by west
south·west·er \-tə(r)\ *n* **1** : a strong southwest wind ⟨for the ~ freshened, and blew three parts of a gale dead into the bay —Charles Kingsley⟩ **2** : a storm with southwest winds **3** : SOU'WESTER 2b
¹south·west·er·ly \-tərlē, -li, -R -təl- *sometimes* -tᵊl-\ *adv (or adj)* [fr. ²*southwest*, after E *west*: *westerly*] **1** : from the southwest ⟨a ~ weather pattern⟩ **2** : toward the southwest ⟨this part of US 277 extends ~, then south —*Amer. Guide Series: Texas*⟩
²southwesterly \"\ *n* : a wind from the southwest
south·west·ern \-tə(r)n, -R *also* -tᵊn\ *adj* [ME, fr. OE *sūthwesterne*, fr. *sūth* south + *westerne* western — more at SOUTH, WESTERN] **1** *often cap* : of, relating to, originating or dwelling in, or characteristic of a region conventionally designated Southwest ⟨~ ranchers⟩ ⟨~ pueblo towns⟩ **2** : situated toward or coming from the southwest
south·west·ern·er \R -tə(r)nər, -R -tənə(r *also* -tᵊnə(r\ *n, usu cap* : a native or inhabitant of a southwestern region (as of the U.S.)
southwest semitic *n, cap both Ss* : a division of the Semitic languages consisting of Arabic, South Arabic, and the Semitic languages of Ethiopia
¹south·west·ward \-twə(r)d\ *adv (or adj)* [²*southwest* + *-ward*] : toward the southwest : in a southwest direction
²southwestward \"\ *n* : SOUTHWEST ⟨to the ~⟩
south·west·ward·ly *adv (or adj)* : toward or from the southwest : SOUTHWESTERLY
south·west·wards \-dz\ *adv* [²*southwest* + *-wards*] : SOUTHWESTWARD
southwide \ˈ=,=\ *adj* : including or affecting all the southern states of the U.S. ⟨a ~ conference⟩ ⟨a ~ strike⟩
south ye·men \-ˈyemən, -ˈyām-\ *adj, usu cap S&Y* [fr. *South Yemen*, country in southern Arabian peninsula] : of or from the country of South Yemen : of the kind or style prevalent in South Yemen
¹sou·ve·nir \ˌsüvəˌni(ə)r, -niə\ *n* -s [F, fr. MF, fr. (*se*) *souvenir* to remember, fr. L *subvenire* to come to mind, to come up — more at SUBVENTION] **1** : an act of remembering : RECOLLECTION ⟨eking out her life of ~ in her palace —Eleanor Clark⟩ ⟨flitting ~ . . . of a regal gesture of her mother —Arnold Bennett⟩ **2** : something that serves as a reminder : MEMENTO, REMEMBRANCE ⟨the pressed flower is a ~ from her wedding bouquet⟩ ⟨brought him a pictorial ashtray as a ~ of the trip⟩ ⟨pockmarks in the masonry . . . are ~s of the bomb that exploded there —John Brooks⟩ **syn** see MEMORY
²souvenir \"\ *vt* -ED/-ING/-S : to take as a souvenir ⟨guests ~*ed* the green tulle and the pink tiger lilies which had adorned the Royal table —*Sydney (Australia) Bull.*⟩
souvenir sheet *n* **1** : a block or set of postage stamps or a single stamp printed on a single sheet of paper without gum or perforations and with margins containing lettering or design that identifies some notable event being commemorated **2** : MINIATURE SHEET 1
sou·ve·rain \ˈsüvəˌrāⁿ\ *n* -s [F, modif. (influenced by *souverain* sovereign, fr. OF *soverain*) of E ¹*sovereign*] : a gold coin of Brabant and the Low Countries issued from the early 17th century until supplanted by the Belgian coinage of 1832
¹sou·ward \ˈsau̇wə(r)d\ *adv (or adj)* [by contr.] : SOUTHWARD
²souward \"\ *n* -s : SOUTHWARD
sou'west·er \(ˈ)sau̇ˈwestə(r)\ *n* -s [by contr.] **1** : SOUTHWESTER ⟨exposure to . . . strong rain-bearing ~*s* —Katharine S. Woods⟩ **2 a** : a long oilskin coat with buckle fastenings worn esp. by sailors during stormy weather : SLICKER **b** : a hat with a wide slanting brim longer in back than in front and often having ear flaps that tie under the chin — called also *southwester*

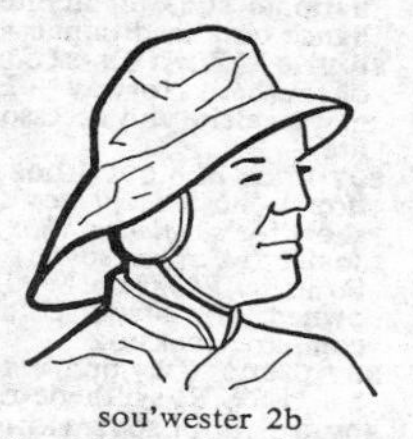
sou'wester 2b

sou·za·lite \ˈsözə,līt\ *n* -s [Antonio J. A. de *Souza*, 20th cent. Brazilian mineralogist + E *-lite*] : a mineral $(Mg,Fe)_3(Al,Fe)_4(PO_4)_4(OH)_6.2H_2O$ consisting of a hydrous basic phosphate of magnesium, iron, and aluminum found with scorzalite in Minas Gerais, Brazil
sov \ˈsäv\ *n* -s [short for ¹*sovereign*] *Brit* : SOVEREIGN, POUND
sov *abbr* **1** sovereign **2** soviet
SOV *abbr* shut-off valve
sovenance *n* -s [ME *sovenaunce*, fr. MF *sovenance*, *souvenance*, fr. (*se*) *sovenir*, (*se*) *souvenir* to remember + *-ance*] *obs* : REMEMBRANCE
¹sov·er·eign \ˈsäv(ə)rən, -vərn *sometimes* ˈsəv-\ *also* **sov·ran** \ˈsävrən\ *n* -s [*sovereign* alter. (influenced by ¹*reign*) of ME *soverein*, *soverain*, fr. OF *soverain*, fr. (assumed) VL *superanus*, fr. L *super* over, above + *-anus* -an; *sovran* alter. (influenced by It *sovrano* sovereign, fr. OIt, fr. OF *soverain*) of *sovereign* — more at SUPER-] **1 a** (1) : the supreme repository of power in a political state ⟨the ~ . . . is not himself bound by the law since the law is what he declares it to be —J.H.Hallowell⟩ (2) : the person wielding or exercising supreme political power in a political state — compare DICTATOR, MONARCH, RULER (3) : a political unit possessing or held to possess sovereignty ⟨a controversy between two ~*s* . . . the United States on the one hand and the state of California on the other —*U.S.Code*⟩ **b** : one that exercises supreme authority within a limited sphere : CHIEF, MASTER **c** : an acknowledged leader : ARBITER, SUPERIOR ⟨cupid . . . the anointed ~ of sighs and groans —Shak.⟩ ⟨the true ~*s* of a country are those who determine . . . its modes of thinking —Van Wyck Brooks⟩ ⟨the rose, ~ among flowers⟩ **2 a** : a gold coin of Great Britain worth 1 pound sterling or 20 shillings, issued from Henry VII to James I and as a coin having 123.274 grains of gold .9166 fine from George III **b** : a gold coin of Saudi Arabia equivalent to 40 riyals
²sovereign \"\ *also* **sovran** \"\ *adj* [*sovereign* alter. (influenced by ¹*reign*) of ME *soverein*, *soverain*, fr. MF *sovrain*, fr. OF, *soverain*, n., sovereign; *sovran* alter. (influenced by It *sovrano*) of *sovereign*] **1 a** : possessed of controlling power : RULING, PREDOMINANT ⟨the king could not be ~ if there were any immunities . . . outside his jurisdiction —Christopher Morris⟩ ⟨in the case of Palestine, the United Nations, for a brief period of history, was able to act as a ~ agent —A.S.Eban⟩ **b** : unlimited in extent : ABSOLUTE ⟨the ~ power of the pope over all forms of secular authority —G.H.Sabine⟩ **c** : enjoying autonomy : INDEPENDENT, SELF-GOVERNING ⟨a ~ state⟩ ⟨a move to unify command of the separate and ~ armed services⟩ ⟨the right of each individual to be a ~ personality —Geoffrey Bruun⟩ **2 a** : of the most exalted kind : SUPREME ⟨in . . . literary style the ~ virtue for the judge is clearness —B.N. Cardozo⟩ ⟨promote . . . the ~ good of the community —George Grote⟩ **b** : superlative in quality : EXCELLENT, UNSURPASSED ⟨their ~ sense of humor, never minding the joke that is turned against themselves —Sir Winston Churchill⟩ ⟨the veneration and respect due a ~ creative genius —Roland Gelatt⟩ **c** (1) : having generalized curative powers : POTENT ⟨diphtheria antitoxin is a specific and ~ remedy when given in sufficient amounts during the first 24 hours —K.F.Maxcy⟩ (2) : having universally beneficial application : EFFECTIVE ⟨special facets of past human culture remain potentially ~ for our current ills —H.H.Watts⟩ **d** : of an unqualified nature : UNMITIGATED, UTTER ⟨kissed the feet of their conquerors, but in ~ contempt —Vincent Sheean⟩ **e** : having undisputed ascendancy : LEADING, PARAMOUNT ⟨in recasting the . . . old theology, Calvin accepted as a ~ conception the idea of God as arbitrary and absolute will —V.L.Parrington⟩ **3** : of, relating to, characteristic of, or befitting a sovereign : ROYAL, UNRESTRICTED ⟨a ~ right⟩ ⟨~ equality⟩ **syn** see DOMINANT, FREE
sov·er·eign·ly *adv* [ME *soverainly*, fr. *soverain*, adj., sovereign + *-ly*] : in a sovereign manner : AUTONOMOUSLY, SUPREMELY
sov·er·eign·ty *also* **sov·ran·ty** \-ntē, -ti\ *n* -ES [*sovereignty* fr. ME *soveraintee*, *sovereintee*, fr. MF *soveraineté*, fr. *sovraine* (fem. of *sovrain* sovereign) + *-té* -ty; *sovranty* alter. (influenced by *sovran*) of *sovereignty*] **1** *obs* : supreme excellence or an example of it ⟨of all complexions the cull'd ~ do meet . . . in her fair cheek —Shak.⟩ **2 a** (1) : supreme power esp. over a body politic : DOMINION, SWAY ⟨the treaty provided for the cession . . . by Spain of its ~ over the territory of Puerto Rico —Antonio Fernós-Isern⟩ ⟨the gates of Hell shall not prevail against His Church — to believe otherwise is to deny the ~ of God —*Time*⟩ ⟨deprived the railroads of ultimate ~ in . . . rate-making —A.S.Link⟩ (2) : freedom from external control : AUTONOMY, INDEPENDENCE ⟨the chief cause of modern war has been the fallacy of absolute ~ of the national state —J.T. Shotwell⟩ ⟨~ is not an indivisible whole, since it can be partially ceded to a joint authority —*European Federation Now*⟩ ⟨his mind asserted itself with . . . a strong sense of its own ~ —Leon Edel⟩ **b** : royal position or authority ⟨let the emperor turn his nominal ~ into a real central and autocratic power —Hilaire Belloc⟩ **c** : controlling influence ⟨the ~ of a superior class which gains dominion through social, economic or religious prestige —J.S.Roucek⟩ **3** : one that is sovereign; *esp* : an autonomous state ⟨affirming . . . that Formosa and China are part of the same ~ —*New Republic*⟩
¹so·vi·et \ˈsōvē,et, -ēət *also* ˈsäv- *sometimes* ˈsə- *or* sōvˈyet *or* ˈsōv,yet *or* ˈsōvyət, *usu* -d·+V\ *n* -s [Russ *sovet* council, soviet, fr. ORuss *sŭvětŭ* council] **1** : an elected organizational unit in Communist countries : COMMITTEE, COUNCIL ⟨local ~*s* concern themselves with matters of public health, education, trade, urban improvement, and new construction —J.N.Hazard⟩ ⟨the system of ~*s* . . . provides an upward stream of political intelligence, suggestion and accounting from the lower organs and a downward stream of laws, decrees, and instructions from the apex —J.A.Corry⟩ — compare POLITBURO, PRESIDIUM **2** : a state organized on Communist lines ⟨peasants were willing to seize the land and proclaim a ~ —Clare & Harris Wofford⟩; *esp* : one of the associated republics of the U.S.S.R. ⟨incorporate — not in the Union as a ~ but as a member of her hierarchy —*Pleasures of Publishing*⟩ **3 soviets** *pl, usu cap* : the people, leaders, or armed forces of the U.S.S.R. ⟨the *Soviets* say they want an increase in East-West trade —*Wall Street Jour.*⟩
²soviet \"\ *adj, usu cap* : of, relating to, or associated with the U.S.S.R. or its inhabitants
so·vi·et·ism \-,izəm\ *n* -s *often cap* **1** : the principles or practices of a Soviet regime; *esp* : COMMUNISM ⟨fascism, socialism, and ~ have appeared as new and anticapitalistic forms in the contemporary world —A.M.Sievers⟩ ⟨compelled to listen to Russian radio music, and lectures about ~ —Alfred Bilmanis⟩ **2** : a characteristic expression or embodiment of Soviet ideology ⟨this operetta has a number of standard *Sovietisms* in it —Manny Farber⟩
so·vi·et·iza·tion \ˌsōvēəd·əˈzāshən, -ət|, |ˌīˈz-\ *n* -s *often cap* : conversion to the Soviet system ⟨Russian leadership still seeks security for the Soviet fatherland . . . through undermining of the capitalistic and socialistic democracies and their ultimate ~ —*Foreign Policy Bull.*⟩
so·vi·et·ize *pronunciation at* SOVIET + ,īz\ *vt* -ED/-ING/-S *often cap* [¹*soviet* + *-ize*] **1** : to bring within the Soviet orbit ⟨quotes their own words to prove that they won't be content until the world has been not only *Sovietized* but Russified —*New Yorker*⟩ **2** : to imbue with Soviet ideals or bring into line with Soviet policy ⟨tries to *Sovietize* the youth through Marxist-trained teachers and professors —*Education Digest*⟩ ⟨on the heels of the Communist armies march the Communist commissars, who . . . ~ the conquered territory —*N.Y.Times*⟩
so·vi·et·ol·o·gist \ˌsōvēəˈtäləjəst, -vēˈtä- *also* ˈsäv- *n* -s *often cap* [¹*soviet* + *-ologist* (as in *geologist*)] : a specialist in sovietism

soviet style *n, usu cap 1st S* **:** the U.S.S.R. version of the international style of architecture characterized by a heavier reliance on a traditional vocabulary of forms

sö·vite \'sœ̄,vīt\ *n* -s [*Söve,* area in Telemark, mountain region of southern Norway + E *-ite*] **:** a dike rock composed of magmatic calcite and accessory apatite, biotite, and manganophyllite

sov·khoz *also* **sov·khos** \(,)səf'kȯz, sȯv'-, säv'-, -ȯs\ *or* **sov·hoz** \-'hȯ-\ *n, pl* **sovkho·zy** \-ȯzē\ *or* **sovkhozes** [Russ, short for *sovetskoe khozyaĭstvo* soviet farm, fr. *sovetskoe,* adj., soviet (fr. *sovet* soviet) + *khozyaĭstvo* household, economy, farm, fr. *khozyain* head of the house, proprietor] **:** a state-owned farm of the U.S.S.R. paying wages to the workers — compare KOLKHOZ

sov·prene \'säv,prēn\ *n* -s [*soviet* + *-prene* (as in *neoprene*)] **:** a U.S.S.R. synthetic rubber of the neoprene type

sovran *var of* SOVEREIGN

sovs *pl of* SOV

[1]**sow** \'sau̇\ *n* -s [ME *sowe, suwe,* fr. OE *sugu;* akin to OE *sū* sow, OS *sū, suga,* OHG *sū,* ON *sȳr* sow, L *sus* hog, swine, Gk *hys,* Corn *hoch,* OIr *socc* hog, swine, Skt *sūkara* boar, hog, swine, Toch B *suwo* swine] **1 a :** the adult female of swine; *specif* **:** a female hog of any age that has farrowed — compare GILT **b :** the adult female of various mammals (as the cavy) **c** *archaic* **:** a fat slovenly woman **2 :** a movable protective shed; *specif* **:** CAT 3 **3 :** WOOD LOUSE 1 **4 a** (1) **:** a channel or runner that conducts molten metal to rows of molds in a pig bed (2) **:** mold of larger size than a pig **b :** a mass of metal solidified in such a mold **:** INGOT — compare [1]PIG 5a **c :** SALAMANDER **5** *chiefly Scot* **:** STACK, HEAP

[2]**sow** \'sō\ *vb* **sowed; sown** \'sōn\ *or* **sowed; sowing; sows** [ME *sowen, sawen,* fr. OE *sāwan;* akin to OHG *sāwen, sājen* to sow, ON *sā,* Goth *saian,* L *serere,* Lith *sėti* to sow, Skt *sīra* plow used for seeding, *sāyaka* one suitable for throwing; basic meaning: to drop, throw, scatter] *vi* **1 :** to plant or scatter seed ⟨farmers wait to plough and ~ until after the frost is out of the ground⟩ **2 :** to set something in motion **:** begin an enterprise ⟨may those who ~ in tears reap with shouts of joy —Ps 126:5(RSV)⟩ ~ *vt* **1 a :** to impregnate with or as if with seed ⟨surrounding fields have been *sown* . . . with squash, pumpkin and maize —*Science*⟩ ⟨insects are . . . *~ing* the lake surface with their eggs —D.C.Peattie⟩ **b :** to put into a growing medium **:** PLANT ⟨~ seeds in vermiculite⟩; *specif* **:** to broadcast (seed) over a wide area ⟨~ clover⟩ **c :** to spread thickly **:** introduce into a selected environment **:** DISTRIBUTE, IMPLANT ⟨half a million anchovy fingerlings were *sown* in the waters of the Gulf —Jack Raymond⟩ ⟨burying a drum of metallic sodium at sea . . . would be tantamount to *~ing* a mine —John Kobler⟩ **2 :** to set in motion **:** AROUSE, FOMENT ⟨moving . . . from town to village, *~ing* a suspicion here and a doubt there —Christine Weston⟩ ⟨~ timidity where there should be boldness —G.F. Kennan⟩ ⟨whatever a man *~s,* that he will also reap —Gal 6:7(RSV)⟩ **syn** see STREW

sow·able \'sōəbəl\ *adj* **:** fit for sowing

so·war \sō'(w)är\ *n* -s [Per *suwār* rider, fr. MPer *asbār, aspwār,* fr. OPer *asabāra-* horseman, fr. *asa-* horse + *-bāra-* carried by, rider] **1 :** a member of an Indian cavalry regiment **:** LANCER **2 :** a mounted orderly

sowback \'=,=\ *n* [[1]*sow* + *back*] **:** a long low hill **:** RIDGE — **sowbacked** \'=,=\ *adj*

sowbane \'=,=\ *n* [[1]*sow* + *bane*] **:** RED GOOSEFOOT; *also* **:** a related herb (*Chenopodium hybridum*) considered fatal to swine

sowbelly \'=,==\ *n* **:** fat salt pork or bacon **:** SIDE MEAT

sowbread \'=,=\ *n* [[1]*sow* + *bread;* fr. the fact that its rootstocks are eaten by swine] **:** a common wild cyclamen (*Cyclamen europaeum*) of central Europe having leaves that are dark green spotted with white above and carmine or white flowers **:** a related European herb (*Cyclamen neapolitanum*) often cultivated for its showy rose or white flowers

sow bug *n* [so called fr. its round shape] **:** WOOD LOUSE 1

sow·der \'sōdər\ *Scot var of* SOLDER

sow·ens \'sōənz, 'süə-\ *n pl but sing or pl in constr* [ScGael *sūghan* liquid of which sowens are made (fr. *sūgh* juice) + E *-s* (pl. suffix); akin to OHG *sūgan* to suck — more at SUCK] **:** a slightly fermented porridge made from the husks and siftings of oatmeal — compare FLUMMERY

sow·er \'sō(ə)r, -ōə\ *n* -s [ME *sower, sawere,* fr. OE *sāwere,* fr. *sāwan* to sow + *-ere* -er — more at SOW] **:** one that sows: as **a :** a planter of seed ⟨the simplest of mechanical *~s* —Walter Bally⟩ **b :** a distributor of various other objects ⟨a ~ of mines⟩ **c :** a fomenter of discord ⟨a ~ of sedition —*Times Lit. Supp.*⟩

sowf *or* **sowff** \'sau̇f\ *or* **sowth** \-au̇th\ *vt* [prob. alter. of [1]*sough*] *Scot* **:** to sing softly **:** HUM

sow-gelder \'=,==\ *n, archaic* **:** one that spays sows

sow·ing \'sōiŋ\ *n* -s *often attrib* [ME *sowing, sawing,* fr. gerund of *sowen, sawen* to sow] **:** an act or instance of scattering

sowl \'sōl\ *dial var of* SOUL

sowlth \'sau̇lth\ *n* [Ir *samhailt,* lit., likeness] *Irish* **:** GHOST

sowp \'sau̇p\ *chiefly dial var of* SUP

sowre \'sau̇(ə)r\ *archaic var of* SOUR

sows *pl of* SOW, *pres 3d sing of* SOW

sow thistle *n* [ME *sowethistel,* fr. earlier *sugethistel,* fr. OE *sugu* sow + *thistel* thistle — more at SOW, THISTLE] **:** any of several coarse often somewhat spiny annual or perennial weedy herbs constituting the genus *Sonchus,* being native to Europe but naturalized throughout most of the world, and growing esp. in cultivated soils where they are noxious weeds

sow-tit \'=,=\ *n* **:** a wood strawberry (*Fragaria vesca*)

sox *pl of* SOCK

soxh·let apparatus \'säkslət-\ *n, usu cap S* [after Franz von *Soxhlet* †1926 Ger. agricultural chemist, its inventor] **:** an apparatus for use in extracting fatty or other material with a volatile solvent (as ether, alcohol, or benzene) consisting of a vertical glass cylindrical extraction tube that has both a siphon tube and a vapor tube, that is fitted at its upper end to a reflux condenser and at its lower end to a flask so that the solvent may be distilled from the flask into the condenser whence it flows back into the cylindrical tube and siphons over into the flask to be distilled again

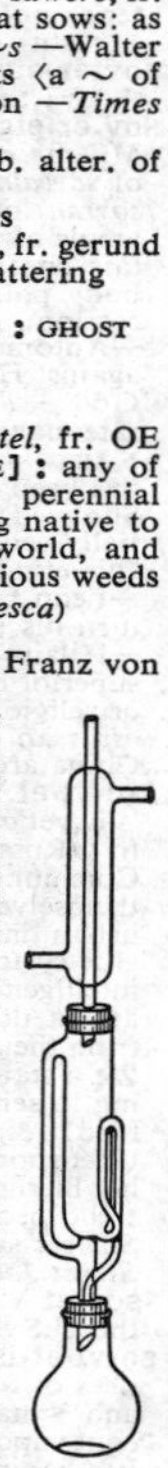

Soxhlet apparatus or extractor

soxhlet extraction *n, usu cap S* **:** extraction in a Soxhlet apparatus

soxhlet extractor *also* **soxhlet** *n, usu cap S* [after Franz von *Soxhlet* †1926] **:** SOXHLET APPARATUS; *esp* **:** the cylindrical extraction tube

soy \'sȯi, *dial* 'sōē *or* -ōi *or* -ōə\ *n* -s [Jap *shōyū,* fr. Chin (Pek) *chiang*^{4} *-yu*^{2}, lit., soybean oil] **1** *or* **soy sauce :** an oriental condiment consisting of a brown liquid sauce made by subjecting boiled beans (as soybeans) or beans and roasted wheat flour to long fermentation and then to long digestion in brine **2** *or* **soy pea :** SOYBEAN

soya *like* [2]SOJA\ *also* **soya bean** *n* -s [D *soja,* fr. Jap *shōyū* soy] **:** SOYBEAN

soyate \'sȯi,(y)āt, 'sō,yāt\ *n* -s [*soy* + *-ate*] **:** a mixture of salts of fatty acids from soybean oil ⟨cobalt ~⟩

soybean \'=¦=, *dial* ¦==¦=\ *n* [*soy* + *bean*] **:** an erect bushy hairy annual legume (*Glycine max*) native to Asia and extensively cultivated in China, Japan, and elsewhere whose seeds yield valuable products (as oil, flour, and meal) and whose plant is used for forage and soil improvement — called also *soja, soya*

soybean lecithin *n* **:** LECITHIN 2b

soybean milk *or* **soya milk** *n* **:** soybean flour or finely ground meal suspended in water and used as a substitute for milk

soybean oil *or* **soya-bean oil** *also* **soy oil** *n* **:** a pale-yellow drying or semidrying oil obtained from soybeans by expression or solvent extraction, containing principally glycerides of linoleic, oleic, linolenic, and palmitic acids and used chiefly as a food, in paints, varnishes, linoleum, printing ink, and soap, and as a source of phosphatides, fatty acids, and sterols — called also *Chinese bean oil*

soybean oil meal *or* **soybean meal** *n* **:** the ground protein-rich residue from the production of soybean oil used chiefly in animal feeds, in adhesives and plastics, in making synthetic protein fibers, and in fermentation media (as for the production of antibiotics)

soy flour *or* **soybean flour** *n* **:** a fine sifted hull-free soybean meal used esp. as human food

so·yot \sō'yōt\ *n, pl* **soyot** *or* **soyots** *usu cap* **1 a :** a Tatar people near the headwaters of the Yenisei in Siberia and Mongolia **b :** a member of such people **2 :** the Turkic language of the Soyot people

so·zol·ic acid \sō'zälik-, -'zōlik-\ *n* [*sozolic* ISV *soz-* (fr. Gk *sōzein* to save) + *-ol* + *-ic;* fr. its antiseptic character — more at SOTERIOLOGY] **:** a mixture of the ortho and para isomers of phenolsulfonic acid $C_6H_4(OH)SO_3H$ obtained as a syrupy liquid or crystalline solid by the action of sulfuric acid on phenol and used as an antiseptic

soz·zle \'säzəl\ *vb* -ED/-ING/-S [alter. of earlier *sossle,* prob. freq. of [2]*soss*] *vt* **1 :** to wash by splashing **:** SPLASH, SOUSE **2 :** to make drunk **:** INTOXICATE ⟨we will sit here and ~ ourselves into a nice coma —Noel Coward⟩ ~ *vi* **:** LOLL, LOUNGE

sozzled *adj* **:** DRUNK ⟨a ~ nightclub customer —Douglas Watt⟩ ⟨gets ~ on the smell of the cork —*Sydney* (*Australia*) *Bull.*⟩

sp *abbr* **1** space **2** spare **3** special; specialist **4** species **5** specific **6** specimen **7** speck **8** speech **9** speed **10** spell; spelled; spelling **11** spine **12** spirit **13** sponge **14** spoon **15** sport

SP *abbr or n* -s a shore patrolman

SP *abbr* **1** self-propelled **2** semipostal **3** shore patrol **4** short page **5** *often not cap* [L *sine prole*] without issue **6** *often not cap* single phase **7** *often not cap* single pole **8** small packet **9** small paper **10** small pica **11** smokeless powder **12** soil pipe **13** standpipe **14** starting point **15** starting price **16** static pressure **17** stern post **18** stirrup pump **19** stop payment **20** stretcher party **21** submarine patrol **22** subprofessional **23** supraprotest

spa \'spä, 'spȯ, 'spȧ\ *n* -s [fr. *Spa,* watering place in eastern Belgium] **1 a :** a mineral spring resorted to for cures **b :** a locality containing a mineral spring resorted to for cures ⟨the town used to be quite the fashionable ~ —Richard Joseph⟩ **c :** a resort hotel situated at a mineral spring **d :** any esp. fashionable resort locality or hotel ⟨ski instructor at a snow-*spa* —John Woodburn⟩ **2** *NewEng* **:** SODA FOUNTAIN

SPA *abbr* **1** special public assistance **2** subject to particular average

[1]**space** \'spās\ *n* -s *often attrib* [ME, fr. OF *espace,* fr. L *spatium* — more at SPEED] **1 a :** lapse of time between two points in time ⟨the brief intermission allowed little ~ to relax⟩ **b :** a period of time **:** SPELL ⟨now there was peace for a ~⟩; *esp* **:** a relatively short interval of time ⟨during the contemplative ~ after breakfast and before work —Rebecca West⟩ ⟨a brief resting ~⟩ — often used in the phrase *space of time* ⟨this ~ of time wrought many changes —I.M.Price⟩ **c :** a specified quantity of time **:** DURATION ⟨this continued by the ~ of two years —Acts 19:10 (AV)⟩ ⟨nine times the ~ that measures day and night —John Milton⟩ ⟨we stood for the ~ of a second or two —Francis Shean⟩ **2 a :** a limited extension in one, two, or three dimensions **:** a part marked off or bounded in some way **:** DISTANCE, AREA, VOLUME ⟨written communication across the intervening ~ was more quickly accomplished —R.H.Brown⟩ ⟨from the *~s* under the trees about the house one looked toward the south —Elizabeth M. Roberts⟩ ⟨~ left in a petroleum product container to allow for expansion during temperature changes —*Proving Ground*⟩ ⟨inner cells of land plants in contact with the outside air through the interconnecting intercellular *~s* —*Botanical Rev.*⟩ **b :** an extent or area set apart or available for a particular purpose ⟨the open-air lot would contain 945 parking *~s* —*Springfield* (*Mass.*) *Union*⟩ ⟨1800 square feet of floor ~⟩ ⟨the seating ~ of an auditorium⟩ ⟨down in the gasoline ~ deep in number five hold —K.M. Dodson⟩ **c :** an unobstructed area (as of land) ⟨an inner zone of parks, public gardens, and open *~s* —H.W.H.King⟩ ⟨between the clumps of nutmeg and azalea, wide open *~s* baked in the hot sunshine —R.L.Stevenson⟩ ⟨a land of wide open *~s* with a sparsely scattered population —*London Calling*⟩ ⟨men whom the free *~s* of thought frightened —V.L.Parrington⟩ ⟨the social area between built-up conventions and the wide open *~s* where riotous instincts roam at will —C.W.Cunnington⟩ **d** (1) **:** the shaped volume defined by architectural forms (as walls, roofs, courts, and wings) ⟨translations of architectural ~ into two dimensions —J.P.Coolidge⟩ ⟨the appropriate use of ~ in small rooms has not been fully solved —Gladys Miller⟩ (2) **:** the representation or effect of three-dimensional forms and volumes in painting; *also* **:** an instance of this ⟨the actual lines and colors and *~s* in a work of art —Clive Bell⟩ **3 :** one of the degrees between or above or below the lines of a musical staff **4 a** (1) **:** a three-dimensional entity that extends without bounds in all directions and is the field of physical objects and events and their order and relationships (2) **:** a part of space unaltered by removal of a material object **b** (1) **:** a mathematical model that pictures physical space as three-dimensional, as partly filled with material bodies, as capable of existence if all physical bodies were destroyed, and as determining but not determined by the relative positions of bodies **:** ABSOLUTE SPACE (2) **:** a mathematical model that pictures physical space as dependent on and solely determined by the relative position and direction of material bodies (3) **:** any of various mathematical models devised to explain observed or postulated phenomena inexplicable upon the assumption of a three-dimensional space unaltered by changes in the relations and state of material bodies — see SPACE-TIME **c :** the a priori form of one's experience of external phenomena **5 a :** the region beyond the earth's atmosphere — see OUTER SPACE **b :** all of the universe beyond the solar system **:** the sidereal universe ⟨interstellar ~⟩ **6 a :** a blank interval between words or lines in written or printed matter **b** (1) **:** a piece of type that is cast less than type high so as not to print and is used to separate words or characters in a line; *specif* **:** such type when narrower than an en quad — compare QUAD (2) **:** a blank area in printing caused by the use of such type; *also* **:** a comparable unexposed area in photocomposition **c :** the measure of room that a typewritten character occupies on the paper or that is left blank by one movement of the space bar ⟨indent the first line several *~s* —*Modern Language Assoc. Style Sheet*⟩ **d :** the measure of room that a line of typewriting occupies on the paper ⟨drop three *~s* and indent⟩ **7 a :** a mathematical aggregate of *n* elements and *n* dimensions **b :** a three-dimensional region **8 :** an expanse of empty air extending outward and downward from a particular point ⟨cornices which hung out over ~ on both sides —N. B. Clinch⟩ **9 :** a vague conception of distance and expansiveness induced by a listless or dreamy mental state ⟨was reminded of those dreamy spells of hers, the way she used to go drifting off into ~ —Hamilton Basso⟩ **10 :** a place left open in the pattern of a game of solitaire by the play of a card and made available for occupancy by another card **11 :** an interval in operation during which a telegraph key is not in contact **12 a :** LINAGE 1, 3 ⟨sell ~ for a newspaper⟩ ⟨~ in the newspaper is always restricted —F.L.Mott⟩ ⟨reproduced his delicate drawings badly, paid him by ~ —F.J.Mather⟩ **b :** time available on radio or television esp. to advertisers ⟨air ~ is even more valuable than paper ~ —Joanna Jonsson⟩ **13 :** accommodations obtained or available on a public transportation vehicle ⟨the passenger agent was pretty sure there wouldn't be ~ on the incoming flight —J.S.Redding⟩; *esp* **:** such accommodations when reserved in advance ⟨reserved his ~ two weeks ago⟩ — **in the mean space** *obs* **:** MEANWHILE

[2]**space** \"\ *vb* -ED/-ING/-S *vt* **1 :** to bound in space **:** determine the spatial limits of **2 :** to place at intervals **:** separate by periods of time **:** arrange with spaces between **:** INTERSPACE ⟨houses *spaced* as irregularly as pins on a map —*Amer. Guide Series: N.Y. City*⟩ ⟨~ the children born in a family⟩ — often used with *out* ⟨the farms were small, and *spaced* out from four to five miles apart —H.L.Davis⟩; see SPACE OUT ~ *vi* **:** to leave one or more blank spaces (as in a line of typing)

space absorption *n* **:** the attenuation of the light of stars and galaxies when it encounters interstellar matter within a galaxy or material in the relatively empty regions between galaxies **:** the reddening of starlight by interstellar matter

spaceband \'=,=\ *n* **:** a device consisting typically of a joined pair of thin reciprocally tapered steel wedges that is used as a variable-width space in keyboard slugcasting machines to expand and force the line of assembled matrices out to full measure so that a justified line is cast

space bar *n* **1 :** a bar (as on a typewriter) that on each depression causes the carriage to move one space to the left **2 :** a bar on a monotype keyboard each depression of which causes the setting of one justification space

space cadet *n* **1 :** a youthful astronaut in a space opera **2 :** a usu. juvenile enthusiast for space travel **3** *slang* **:** a pilot who shows off

space charge *n* **:** an electric charge (as the electrons in the region near the filament of a vacuum tube) distributed throughout a three-dimensional region as distinguished from the electrostatic surface charge on a conductor

space-charge effect *n* **:** the limitation of flow of plate current in an electron tube produced by repulsion exerted on electrons leaving the filament by the other electrons in the region between filament and plate

spacecraft \'=,=\ *n* **:** SPACESHIP

space curve *n* **:** a curve in three-dimensional space

space divider *n* **:** DIVIDER 9

spaced payment *n* **:** the payment of parts of a purchase price at stated intervals **:** payment by installments

space error *n* **:** a constant error in the comparison of magnitudes resulting from the differing locations of the magnitudes compared

space flight *n* **:** flight beyond the earth's atmosphere

space formula *n* **:** PERSPECTIVE FORMULA

space group *n* **:** a group or array of symmetry elements on the points of a space lattice

space heater *n* **:** a self-contained unit that warms a room or space by converting to heat in that space the fuel or electric energy supplied to it

space heating *n* **:** heating of spaces esp. for human comfort by any means (as by fuel, electricity, or solar radiation) with the heater either within the space or external to it

space isomerism *n* **:** STEREOISOMERISM

space key *n* **1 :** SPACE BAR 1 **2 :** a key on a monotype keyboard each depression of which causes the setting of a space of fixed width (as one em) **3 :** the key on a key punch that controls the spacing of holes in punched cards

space lattice *n* **:** a three-dimensional pattern of points so arranged as to determine by indefinite repetition sets of equally spaced parallel planes in various directions forming polyhedral cells (as in a honeycomb); *specif* **:** a set of such points occupied by the atoms of a crystal — compare BRAVAIS LATTICE, LATTICE CONSTANT

space·less \'spāsləs\ *adj* **1 :** having no limits **:** BOUNDLESS ⟨a timeless and almost ~ world of the imagination —R.A. Hall b.1911⟩ **2 :** occupying no space ⟨pure meanings, values, and norms are geometrically ~ —P.A.Sorokin⟩

space man \'=,man, -,maa(ə)n\ *n* **:** SPACE WRITER

space·man \-,man, -_mən, -,maa(ə)n\ *n, pl* **spacemen 1 :** one who travels or is in training for travel outside the earth's atmosphere **2 :** a visitor to the earth from outer space

space mark *n* **:** the symbol #

space medicine *n* **:** a branch of medicine that deals with the physiologic and biologic effects on the human body of rocket or jet flight beyond the earth's atmosphere — see AVIATION MEDICINE

space motion *n* **1 :** the motion of the earth and other solar system members as they travel through space with the sun **2 :** SPACE VELOCITY

space of fon·tana \-,fän·'tänə, -_fən--, -tanə\ *usu cap F* [after Felice *Fontana* †1805 It. physiologist] **:** any of the spaces between trabeculae of the posterior elastic lamina of the cornea through which the anterior chamber of the eye communicates with Schlemm's canal

space of ret·zi·us \-'retsēəs\ *usu cap R* [after Anders A. *Retzius* †1860 Swed. anatomist] **:** a space between the bladder and the symphysis pubis occupied by fatty tissue

space opera *n* **1 :** a novel, motion picture, radio or television play, or comic strip usu. of a stock type featuring interplanetary travel, beings of outer space often in conflict with the people of earth, and other similar science-fiction themes **2 :** the category of fiction or drama comprising space operas

space out *vt* **1 :** to fill out (a line) by increasing the interword spacing **2 :** to extend the vertical dimension of (a page or form) as by interlinear insertion of leads or furniture **:** BLANK 6

space perception *n* **:** the perception of direction, distance, size, and other spatial facts

spaceport \'=,=\ *n* **:** an installation for testing and launching rockets, missiles, and satellites

space quantization *n* **:** quantization in respect to direction in space ⟨the *space quantization* of an atom in a magnetic field whose quantum states correspond to a limited number of possible angles between the directions of the angular momentum and the magnetic intensity⟩

spac·er \'spāsə(r)\ *n* -s **:** one that spaces: as **a :** a device or piece for holding two members at a given distance from each other ⟨trucks which have *~s* between dual tires —*Motor Transportation in the West*⟩ ⟨wood *~s* holding the sides of a concrete form the proper distance apart⟩ ⟨when more than one layer of bars lies at the bottom of a beam or girder the layers are separated by *~s* —Theodore Crane⟩ **b :** a person or machine that spaces ties at proper intervals in railroad track **c :** a current-reversing device used esp. in cable telegraphy to increase speed of transmission **d :** SPACE BAR

spacer bar *n* **:** a bar used as a spacer (as in sling handling of crates)

space reddening *n, pl* **space reddenings :** an effect of selective space absorption in which the shorter wavelengths of the radiation of a star's or galaxy's light are reduced in intensity more than the longer wavelengths and cause the object to appear redder than it really is

space rule *n* **:** single rule in short regular lengths that is used chiefly in the printing of tables

spaces *pl of* SPACE, *pres 3d sing of* SPACE

space·ship \'spās(h),ship\ *n* **:** a man-carrying vehicle designed to operate in free space outside the earth's atmosphere

space stage *n* **:** an abstract stage setting consisting of a broad arrangement of platforms, flights of steps, and occas. other simple architectural elements backed by a usu. black cyclorama, the actors and properties being spotlighted to appear as if in a black void

space station *or* **space platform** *n* **:** a manned artificial satellite that is designed to revolve in a fixed orbit and serve as a base for scientific observation and experiment, the refueling of spaceships, or the launching of satellites or missiles

space suit *n* **1 :** a suit equipped with air supply and other elaborate provisions intended to make life in free space possible for its wearer **2 :** G SUIT

space-time \'=¦=\ *n* **1 :** the four-dimensional order within which every physical existent may be determined by specifying its three spatial coordinates and one temporal coordinate; *also* **:** the characteristic quality or set of properties of such an order **2 :** the whole or any circumscribed portion of physical reality that is a four-dimensional array of perduring extended things or of events or event particles **3 :** the primordial reality which has no qualities beyond the spatial and temporal and from which further qualities and higher levels of existence evolutionally emerge — compare EMERGENT EVOLUTION

space-time continuum *n* **:** a space of four dimensions which if described would have three space axes and one axis indicating variations in time

space velocity *n* **1 :** the velocity of a star's motion relative to the sun as determined from its proper motion, distance, and radial velocity — called also *space motion* **2 :** the number of volumes of gas or liquid usu. calculated to standard conditions that pass over or through one unit volume (as of a catalyst in a reaction tube) in unit time

space·ward \'spāswə(r)d\ *adv* **:** toward space

space washer *n* **:** a washer used for a distance piece (as on a mandrel)

space writer *n* **:** a writer (as a newspaper reporter or a copywriter) paid according to the space his matter fills in print

spacht·ling compound \'späk(t)liŋ-\ *n* [*spachtling* fr. G *spachteln* to spread with a spatula + E *-ing* — more at SPACKLE] **:** SPACKLE

spacial *var of* SPATIAL

spac·i·ness \'spāsēnəs, -āsin-\ *n* -ES **:** the quality or state of being spacy **:** ROOMINESS

spacing *n* -s **1 :** the act of providing with spaces or of placing at intervals ⟨the ~ of words in a line of type⟩ ⟨the ~ of

children born in a family⟩ **2 :** a spatial arrangement **:** an arrangement with intervening spaces ⟨the ~ of the planets at their present distances from the sun —F.L.Whipple⟩ **3 a :** SPACE ⟨the long end of roping at the tack provides a ~ when several flags are hoisted together —*Manual of Seamanship*⟩ ⟨neat ~*s* of white enamelled wood —Donn Byrne⟩ **b :** the distance between any two objects in a usu. regularly arranged series often measured from the center point of one object to that of the next **c** *of a lock* **:** the distance from the center of the keyhole to the center of the knob hub

spacing strip *n* **:** POLE STRIP

spa·cious \ˈspāshəs\ *adj* [ME, fr. MF *spacieux*, fr. L *spatiosus*, fr. *spatium* space, room + *-osus* -ous — more at SPEED] **1 :** marked by large or ample space: **a :** vast in area; *esp* **:** having broad open expanses ⟨contains within its ~ borders . . . many geographical, climatic, and economic divisions —H. S.Commager⟩ ⟨white villas . . . were scattered upon this ~ map —Nathaniel Hawthorne⟩ **b :** affording much room or space **:** not narrow or constricted **:** ROOMY ⟨a land of villages and ~ countrysides —C.J.Brosnan⟩ ⟨moved to a more ~, rambling residence on a hilltop —E.A.Weeks⟩ ⟨seemed so ~ and beautiful to stand high above the prairie and look around —O.E. Rölvaag⟩ **2 :** marked by largeness, magnitude, or scope: **a :** COMPREHENSIVE, WIDE, EXPANSIVE ⟨the ~ mountain air —R.M.Coates⟩ ⟨one great ~ golden morning followed another —J.C.Powys⟩ ⟨the topic is a ~ one, opening into many other fields —P.A.Wadsworth⟩ **b :** rich, varied, luxuriant or halcyon rather than circumscribed, inhibited, petty, or mean ⟨~ ease and generous enjoyment of life —*Times Lit. Supp.*⟩ ⟨a more ~ and stimulating existence than the farm could offer —H.L.Mencken⟩ ⟨the ~ life of the wealthy in that time before the great wars —H.W.Baehr⟩ **syn** see AMPLE

spa·cious·ly *adv* **:** in a spacious manner **:** on spacious lines **:** EXPANSIVELY ⟨in Cambridge the colleges are prominent and ~ spread out —S.P.B.Mais⟩ ⟨planned my life from the outset largely and ~ —Havelock Ellis⟩

spa·cious·ness *n* -ES **:** the quality or state of being spacious **:** BREADTH, AMPLITUDE, EXPANSIVENESS ⟨strong enough to walk out over the fields, at whose ~ she was amazed —Marcia Davenport⟩ ⟨out of this leisure they created a dignity, ease, and ~ in their lives —William Barrett⟩

spa·cis·tor \ˈspā,sistə(r)\ *n* -S [¹*space* + *-istor* (as in *transistor*)] **:** a high-frequency semiconductor amplifying device

spack *dial Brit past of* SPEAK

spack·le \ˈspakəl\ *vt* **spackled; spackled; spackling** \-k(ə)liŋ\ **spackles** [*Spackle*] **:** to apply a Spackle paste to **:** fill with Spackle paste

Spackle \"\ *trademark* — used for a dry powder usu. of gypsum plaster, glue, and silica flour that when mixed with water to form a paste is used as a filler or putty to fill in cracks or holes in a surface before painting

spackling compound *n* **:** a Spackle powder

spacy \ˈspāsē, -āsi\ *adj* -ER/-EST **:** characterized by space **:** ROOMY, LARGE ⟨contributed at rather ~ intervals to slightly known magazines —*Amer. Mercury*⟩

spad \ˈspad\ *n* -S [alter. of earlier *spud*, fr. ¹*spud*] **:** a nail one or two inches long made of iron, brass, tin, or tinned iron with a hook or eye at the head and used to mark stations in underground surveying (as of mines)

spad·able \ˈspādəbəl\ *adj* **:** capable of being spaded or shoveled ⟨~ sludge⟩

spa·da·ite \ˈspädə,īt\ *n* -S [G *spadait*, fr. L. di Medici-*Spada* + G *-it* -ite] **:** a mineral $MgSiO_2(OH)_2.H_2O(?)$ consisting of hydrous magnesium silicate

¹**spade** \ˈspād\ *n* -S [ME, fr. OE *spadu, spædu;* akin to OFris *spada* spade, OS *spado*, MHG *spat, spate*, Icel *spathi* spade, Gk *spathē* blade, Hitt *išpatar* spit, OHG *spān* chip of wood — more at SPOON] **1 a :** an implement for turning soil resembling a shovel, adapted for being pushed into the ground with the foot and having a heavy, usu. flat and oblong blade **b** (1) **:** the depth a spade reaches in digging ⟨ditches two ~*s* deep⟩ (2) **:** the total length of a spade **2 :** any of several spade-shaped instruments: as **a :** a cutting instrument used in flensing a whale **b :** a spade-shaped prong on the underside of the trail of a gun carriage that is embedded in the ground to check recoil of the carriage **c :** a long-handled tool similar in appearance to a garden spade used for compacting and smoothing vertical surfaces of freshly-placed concrete in forms **3 :** the horny formation on the heel of the spadefoot toad

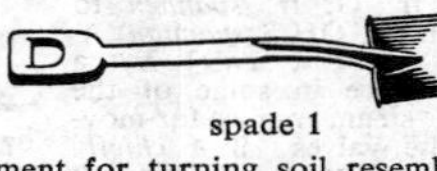

spade 1

²**spade** \"\ *vb* -ED/-ING/-S *vt* **1 a :** to dig up or out with a spade **:** pare off with a spade ⟨~ a garden⟩ ⟨~ a trench⟩ **b :** to place or cover with a spade ⟨~ plants in⟩ ⟨~ fertilizer under⟩ **2 :** to compact and smooth (a vertical surface of freshly placed concrete) by operating a spade up and down between the form and the concrete **~** *vi* **:** to use a spade **syn** see DIG

³**spade** \"\ *n* -S [origin unknown] **:** a three-year-old stag

⁴**spade** \"\ *n* -S [It *spada* or Sp *espada* sword (used as a mark on playing cards), both fr. L *spatha* spatula, broad sword, fr. Gk *spathē* blade — more at ¹SPADE] **1 a :** a usu. black figure ♠ impressed on each card of one of the four suits of a pack of playing cards **b :** a card marked with this figure **c spades** *pl* **:** the suit of cards marked with this figure ⟨he was strong in ~*s*⟩ **d :** an odd trick in bridge won or contracted for with spades as trumps ⟨I bid one ~⟩ ⟨four ~*s* bid and made⟩ **e spades** *pl* **:** the winning of the majority of the spades in casino; *also* **:** the score of one point for this **2** *slang* **:** NEGRO; *esp* **:** a dark-skinned Negro — usu. taken to be offensive — **in spades** *adv* [so called fr. the fact that spades are the highest suit in some card games (as bridge)] **1** *slang* **:** EMPHATICALLY, DECIDEDLY, DISTINCTLY, INTENSELY ⟨whether you realize it or not, you've got trouble — *in spades* —Jerry Bradley⟩ ⟨have thought him a stinker, *in spades*, for many years —Inez Robb⟩ ⟨it was a whirlwind romance, *in spades* —Larry Phelps⟩ **2** *slang* **:** without hesitation or glossing over **:** PLAINLY, FRANKLY, RELENTLESSLY ⟨he gave it to me *in spades* and there was nothing I could deny⟩ ⟨I was going to tell him off — *in spades* —Frank Bridges⟩

⁵**spade** \"\ *vt* -ED/-ING/-S [by folk etymology fr. *spay*] *chiefly dial* **:** SPAY

spade beard *n* [¹*spade* & ⁴*spade*] **1 :** an oblong beard with square ends **2 :** a beard rounded off at the top and pointed at the bottom

spade bit *n* **:** a bit having a piece of metal attached to the center of the bar in such a way that when the reins are pulled, the metal piece presses against the roof of the horse's mouth

spadebone \ˈ=,=\ *n, dial chiefly Eng* **:** SCAPULA 1a

spade casino *n* [⁴*spade*] **:** a variation of casino in which spades are worth one point each and the spade jack counts 2 making 24 points in all

spade edge *n* [¹*spade*] *of a shoe* **:** SCOTCH EDGE

spade face *n* **:** the exposed face or surface of a concrete structure that has been finished with the back of the spade

spadefish \ˈ=,=\ *n* **1 :** any of numerous short compressed deep-bodied fishes constituting the family Ephippidae and being widely distributed in warm seas; *esp* **:** a common bluish or dark gray food and sport fish (*Chaetodipterus faber*) of the tropical western Atlantic — called also *angelfish* **2 :** PADDLEFISH

spade foot \ˈ=ˈ=\ *n* **:** a terminal enlargement of the straight square furniture leg esp. of the late 18th century that sweeps outward in an abrupt curve on each side and then gradually tapers downward — see FOOT illustration

spadefoot \ˈ=,=\ *or* **spadefoot toad** *n, pl* **spadefoots** *or* **spadefoot toads :** any of several burrowing toads of the family Pelobatidae in which the inner bone of the tarsus has a strong sharp-edged horny sheath with which they dig

spade·ful \ˈspād,fu̇l\ *n* -S **:** as much as can be dug up or carried on a spade ⟨~ of earth⟩

spade graft *n, chiefly dial* **:** ¹SPADE 1b (1)

spade guinea *n* **:** a guinea of George III with a spade-shaped shield on the reverse

spade hand *n* **:** a timepiece hand in form of a spade

spade handle *n* **:** a forked end of a shaft or rod (as a connecting rod) in which a pin is held at both ends

spa·del·la \spəˈdelə\ *n, cap* [NL, prob. fr. LL *spada* sword (alter. of L *spatha* broad sword) + NL *-ella*] **:** a genus of marine worms (group Chaetognatha) resembling those of *Sagitta* but having a broader body and only one pair of lateral fins

spade lug *n* **1 :** a steel spade-shaped attachment to the rim of a tractor drive wheel to prevent slip during traction **2 :** a forked prong to be slipped under a screw or nut for making an electrical connection

spade·man \ˈspādmən\ *also* **spades·man** \-dzm-\ *n, pl* **spademen** *also* **spadesmen :** one who works with a spade **:** SPADER

spade money *n* **:** ancient Chinese money in the form of spade-shaped pieces of bronze

spad·er \ˈspādə(r)\ *n* -S **:** one that spades; *specif* **:** SPADING HARROW

spades *pl of* SPADE, *pres 3d sing of* SPADE

spadework \ˈ=,=\ *n* **1 :** work done with the spade **2 :** the hard plain preliminary drudgery in any undertaking ⟨between the periods of actual negotiations much ~ may be done by both sides in the form of collecting data and preparing for negotiations —D.C.Miller & W.H.Form⟩ — **spadeworker** \ˈ=,==\ *n*

spad·ger \ˈspajə(r)\ *n* -S [prob. alter. of *sparrow*] **1** *Brit* **:** HOUSE SPARROW ⟨always very quick on his feet, like a ~ —Margery Allingham⟩ **2** *slang* **:** a small boy

spa·di·ceous \spāˈdishəs, spəˈd-\ *adj* [L *spadic-, spadix* frond torn off a palm tree, brownish color of palm fronds + E *-eous* — more at SPADIX] **1 :** of a bright clear brown or chestnut color **2** [NL *spadic-, spadix* + E *-eous*] **:** bearing flowers on or constituting a spadix

spa·dici·flo·rae \=,disəˈflōr,ē\ *n pl, cap* [NL, fr. *spadic-, spadix* + *-i-* + *-florae* (fr. LL, fem. pl. of *-florus* -florous)] *in some classifications* **:** an order of monocotyledonous plants comprising the Palmales and Cyclanthales of other classifications

spa·dic·i·form \=ˈdisə,fȯrm\ *adj* [NL *spadic-, spadix* + E *-iform*] **:** resembling a spadix

spa·di·cose \ˈspādə,kōs\ *adj* [NL *spadic-, spadix* + E *-ose*] **:** SPADICEOUS 2

spa·dille \spəˈdil\ *n* -S [F, fr. Sp *espadilla*, dim. of *espada* sword (used as a mark on playing cards) — more at SPADE] **:** the highest trump (as the ace of spades in ombre or the queen of clubs in solo)

spading *pres part of* SPADE

spading fork *n* **:** a hand tool with flat tines for turning soil

spading harrow *n* **:** a disc harrow having rotating blades curved at the ends and assembled in the form of a sprocket wheel with the cutting edges out

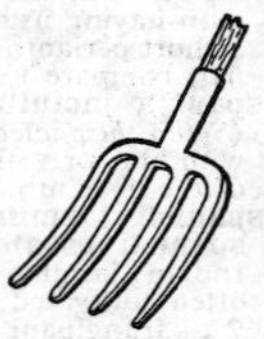

spading fork

spad·ish \ˈspādish\ *adj* [¹*spade* + *-ish* (after the phrase *call a spade a spade*)] **:** direct and blunt in manner of expression ⟨~ language⟩ — **spad·ish·ness** *n* -ES

spa·dix \ˈspādiks\ *n, pl* **spadi·ces** \spāˈdī(,)sēz, spəˈd-; ˈspādə,s-\ [NL, fr. L, frond torn off a palm tree, fr. Gk, fr. *span* to draw, pull, tear — more at SPAN] **1 :** a fleshy or succulent spike that is usu. subtended by or enclosed in a leaflike spathe and is the inflorescence characteristic of the arums and palms **2 :** a compressed cone-shaped organ of the male nautilus formed of four modified tentacles and their sheaths and supposed to represent a hectocotylus

spa·do \ˈspā(,)dō\ *n, pl* **spado·nes** \spāˈdō(,)nēz, spəˈd-\ [ME, fr. L *spadon-, spado*, fr. Gk *spadōn*, fr. *span* to draw, pull, tear — more at SPAN] **1 :** a castrated man or lower animal **2 :** an impotent person

spa·droon \spəˈdrün\ *n* -S [F dial. (Switzerland) *espadron*, alter. of *espadon* — more at ESPADON] *archaic* **:** a sword lighter than the broadsword and suitable for both cutting and thrusting

spads *pl of* SPAD

spae \ˈspā\ *vt* [ME *span*, fr. ON *spā* — more at SPY] *chiefly Scot* **:** FORETELL, PROPHESY

spaeman *n, pl* **spaemen** *Scot* **:** FORTUNE-TELLER, PROPHET, WIZARD

spaetz·le *or* **spätz·le** \ˈshpetslə, -lē\ *n, pl* **spaetzle** *or* **spaetzles** *or* **spätzle** *or* **spätzles** [G dial. (Alemannic) *spätzle*, dim. of *spatz* sparrow, dumpling, fr. MHG, sparrow, fr. *spar, spare* sparrow (fr. OHG *sparo*) + *-tz*, hypocoristic suffix (fr. OHG *-izo*) — more at SPARROW] **:** the strings and lumps that result when a batter made of eggs, milk, flour, and salt is run through a coarse colander into boiling liquid and that when cooked are used as additions to gravy, goulash, or other stews

spaewife *n, chiefly Scot* **:** a female fortune-teller **:** PROPHETESS, WITCH

spa·ghet·ti \spəˈged·ē, -et|, |i\ *n* -S [It, fr. pl. of *spaghetto* string, dim. of *spago* cord, string; akin to Sardinian *ispau* cord, string] **1 :** an alimentary paste made in solid strings of small diameter but larger than vermicelli — distinguished from *macaroni* **2** *or* **spaghetti tubing :** SLEEVING **3 :** a trimming with many cords resembling spaghetti for women's dresses

spa·gnuo·lo \,spänyəˈwȯ(,)lō\ *n* -S *cap* [It, lit., Spaniard, fr. *spagnuolo*, adj., Spanish, fr. (assumed) VL *Hispaniolus* — more at HISPANIOLIZE] **:** one of a group of Spanish and Portuguese Jews expelled from Spain in 1492 whose descendants scattered among the Balkan states speak Judeo-Spanish — compare LADINO 4, SEPHARDIM

spagyric \spəˈjirik\ *adj* [NL *spagiricus*] **:** ALCHEMIC, IATROCHEMICAL

spa·hi *also* **spa·hee** \ˈspä,hē\ *n* -S [MF *spahi*, fr. Turk *sipahi*, fr. Per *sipāhī* horseman, mounted soldier — more at SEPOY] **1 :** one of a corps of largely irregular Turkish cavalry disbanded after the suppression of the Janissaries in 1826 **2 :** one of a corps of Algerian native cavalry in the French army normally serving in Africa

spaik *or* **spake** \ˈspāk\ *Scot var of* ²SPOKE

¹**spain** \ˈspān\ *vt* -ED/-ING/-S [ME *spanen*, fr. OF *espanir*, of Gmc origin; akin to MD *spenen, spennen* to wean — more at SPEAN] *chiefly Scot* **:** WEAN

²**spain** \"\ *adj, usu cap* [fr. *Spain*, country in southwestern Europe] **:** of or from Spain **:** of the kind or style prevalent in Spain **:** SPANISH

spairge \ˈspärj, -perj\ *chiefly Scot var of* SPARGE

spait \ˈspāt\ *chiefly Scot var of* SPATE

spak \ˈspak\ [ME, fr. OE *spæc*] *dial Brit past of* SPEAK

spake [ME *spak*, fr. OE *spæc*] *archaic past of* SPEAK

¹**spa·lac·id** \spəˈlasəd\ *adj* [NL *Spalacidae*] **:** of or relating to the Spalacidae

²**spalacid** \"\ *n* -S **:** a rodent of the family Spalacidae

spa·lac·i·dae \-asə,dē\ *n pl, cap* [NL, fr. *Spalac-, Spalax*, type genus + *-idae*] **:** a family of Old World muroid rodents comprising the mole rats and extinct related forms — **spal·a·cine** \ˈspalə,sīn\ *adj*

spa·lax \ˈspā,laks\ *n, cap* [NL, fr. Gk, mole; akin to OHG *spaltan* to split — more at SPILL] **:** a genus (the type of the family Spalacidae) of mole rats

spald *var of* SPAULD

spale *also* **spail** \ˈspā(ə)l\ *n* -S [ME *spale, spalle*, perh. of Scand origin; akin to ON *spjald-, spölr* rail, bar, *spjald* square tablet — more at SPILL] **1** *dial Brit* **:** LATH, SPLINTER, CHIP **2 :** CROSS-SPALE

¹**spall** *also* **spawl** \ˈspȯl\ *n* -S [ME *spalle* — more at SPALE] **1 :** CHIP, FLAKE; *esp* **:** a small fragment broken from the face or edge of a material (as stone, metal, concrete, glass, or a ceramic product) and having at least one featheredge ⟨~*s* from marble-dressing operations —H.P.Chandler & Nan Jensen⟩ **2 :** a fragment removed from a rock surface by weathering ⟨few exfoliation ~*s* detach themselves from the parent mass in the form of lenses —*Jour. of Geol.*⟩ **3 :** CROSS-SPALE

²**spall** *also* **spawl** \"\ *vb* -ED/-ING/-S *vt* **1 :** to break up (ore) with a hammer usu. preparatory to crushing **2 :** to reduce (as irregular stone blocks) approximately to size by chipping with a hammer **3 :** to cause to break off in spalls ⟨avoid ~*ing* the concrete in drilling⟩ **~** *vi* **1 :** to break off chips, scales, or slabs from the surface or edge often as the result of a rapid change of temperature **:** EXFOLIATE ⟨the dead-burned magnesia produced does not ~ —R.N.Shreve⟩ — often used with *off* or *away* ⟨the ~*ing* off of the outer layers of a rock⟩ ⟨frost action . . . and other unavoidable influences tend to cause the mortar to ~ away from the joints —*Railway Engineering & Maintenance Cycl.*⟩ **2 :** to split off particles as the result of bombardment in such a manner that a large part remains — used of a surface, target, or nucleus

³**spall** \"\ *n* -S [alter. of *spauld*] *archaic* **:** SHOULDER

spall·ation \spȯˈlāshən\ *n* -S [²*spall* + *-ation*] **:** a nuclear reaction in which light particles are ejected as the result of bombardment (as by high-energy protons); *esp* **:** a reaction resulting in numerous products — distinguished from *fission*

spall·er \ˈspȯlə(r)\ *n* -S **:** one that spalls: as **a :** a machine for spalling ore **b :** a laborer who spalls ore

spalling *n* -S **:** loss of spalls from a face or edge (as of brick, stone, or concrete) due to any cause

spalling hammer *n* **:** a large hammer usu. with a flat face and straight peen for breaking and rough-dressing stone

spal·peen \(ˈ)spalˈpēn\ *n* -S [IrGael *spailpīn* common laborer, migratory workman, worthless person] **1** *chiefly Irish* **:** a common laborer **2** *chiefly Irish* **:** RASCAL 3 **3** *chiefly Irish* **:** a young boy

¹**spalt** \ˈspȯlt, -palt\ *vb* [prob. fr. G *spalten* to split, fr. OHG *spaltan* — more at SPILL] *dial* **:** SPLIT, SPLINTER

²**spalt** \"\ *n* -S **:** the residue left after cutting shingles from a bolt of wood

Spam \ˈspam, -paa(ə)m\ *trademark* — used for a canned meat consisting primarily of pork products

¹**span** [ME, fr. OE *spann*] *archaic past of* SPIN

²**span** \ˈspan, -paa(ə)n\ *n* -S [ME *spanne*, fr. OE *spann;* akin to OHG *spanna* span, ON *spönn* span, *spenna* to span — more at ³SPAN] **1 a :** the distance from the end of the thumb to the end of the little finger of a spread hand; *also* **:** an English unit of length based on this distance equal to 9 inches **b :** the distance between the tips of the middle fingers when the arms are stretched to the side as far as possible from the body **2 :** something conceived of as an extent, stretch, reach, or spread between two definite limits: as **a :** a limited often small space **b :** a portion of time; *esp* **:** the period of one's life on earth **3 a :** the distance between the supports of a transverse structural member or between the abutments of an arch **b :** a transverse member or the part of one which is between structural supports **:** ARCH, BRIDGE, TRUSS — see BRIDGE illustration **4 :** the amount of material that is grasped and dealt with in a single mental performance ⟨the ~ of attention⟩ ⟨memory ~⟩ **5 :** the maximum distance laterally from tip to tip of an airplane inclusive of ailerons or the lateral dimension of an airfoil — called also *spread*

³**span** \"\ *vb* **spanned; spanned; spanning; spans** [ME *spannen*, fr. OE *spannan;* akin to MD & MLG *spannen* to stretch, span, hitch up, fasten, OHG *spannan* to stretch, span, ON *spenna* to span, L *pendere* to weigh, Gk *span* to draw, pull, tear] *vt* **1 :** to grasp firmly **:** SEIZE **2 a :** to measure by or as if by the hand with fingers and thumb extended; *broadly* **:** to measure in any way ⟨watch the stars and your eye consciously ~*s* that distance —James Jones⟩ **b :** to encompass with or as if with the fingers **3** *obs* **:** to set a limit to **4 a :** to cross or reach over in space **:** TRAVERSE ⟨took us just three minutes to ~ the bay —Horace Sutton⟩ **b :** to extend across in time ⟨his active career . . . *spanned* the two decades —Vincent Starrett⟩ **5 a :** to form an arch over **:** spread, stretch, or extend across from one limit to another ⟨a rainbow *spanned* the lake —P.B.Shelley⟩ **b :** to cover (as a given space between supports) with a transverse member **6 :** to spread out **:** STRETCH ⟨little paths . . . with tree roots *spanned* across them —Katherine Mansfield⟩ **7 :** to bridge over ⟨a small stream, *spanned* by several rustic bridges —*Amer. Guide Series: Mich.*⟩ **~** *vi* **1 :** to swim along rising to the surface to breathe at more or less regular intervals — used of a whale **2 :** to move in the manner of a looper

⁴**span** \"\ *n* -S [of Scand origin; akin to ON *spann* pail, a measure of butter; akin to ON *spenna* to span — more at ³SPAN] **:** a unit of measure for butter formerly used in northern Scotland

⁵**span** \"\ *vt* **spanned; spanned; spanning; spans** [D *spannen* to stretch, span, hitch up, fr. MD — more at ³SPAN] **1 :** to stretch or pull tight **:** draw firmly ⟨he was on his knees . . . the seat of his trousers perilously *spanned* —Gladys Schmitt⟩ **2** *obs* **:** to cock with a spanner (as a firearm) **3 :** to confine by ropes or other lashings **:** to attach or fasten — often used with *in* **4** [Afrik, fr. MD *spannen*] *chiefly Africa* **:** to attach (a draft animal) to a vehicle

⁶**span** \"\ *n* -S [D, fr. MD, something stretched, team of animals, fr. *spannen* to stretch, span, hitch up — more at ³SPAN] **1 a :** a rope having its ends made fast so that a purchase can be hooked to the bight **b :** a rope made fast in the center so that both ends can be used (as with thimbles) as fairleads **c :** a rope made fast or secured between two uprights (as a jumper stay or the rope between davit heads) **2 a :** a pair of horses, mules, or other animals usu. matched in looks and action and driven together **b** [Afrik, fr. D] **:** a team of two or more pairs of oxen or other animals worked or driven together

⁷**span** \"\ *adv* [fr. *span-* (as in *span-new*)] **:** COMPLETELY ⟨~ white gloves⟩

span blocks *n* [⁶*span*] **:** two blocks each at one end of a span of rope at a masthead for studding-sail halyards

¹**span·cel** \ˈspan(t)səl\ *vt* **spanceled** *or* **spancelled; spanceling** *or* **spancelling; spancels** [LG *spanseln*, fr. *spansel*, n.] **:** to tie or hobble with or as if with a spancel **:** FETTER

²**spancel** \"\ *n* -S [LG *spansel*, fr. *spannen* to stretch, fasten, fr. MLG — more at SPAN] **:** a rope hobble or clog esp. for a horse or cow

span-clean \ˈspanˈ=, -paan-\ *adj* [⁷*span*] **:** extremely clean

span-counter \ˈ=,==\ *n* [³*span*] **:** an old English game in which a player tries to toss his counter within a span's distance of his opponent's — see SPAN-FARTHING

span·dex \ˈspan,deks\ *n* -ES [anagram of *expand*] **:** any of various synthetic textile elastic fibers that are long-chain polymers composed of at least 85 percent of a segmented polyurethane

span dog *n* [⁶*span*] **1 span dogs** *pl* **:** a pair of grappling dogs for hoisting logs and timber **2 :** an iron dog for holding a wooden stave to shape after bending while it cools

span·drel *or* **span·dril** \ˈspandrəl, -paan-\ *n* -S [ME *spaundrell*, dim. of AF *spaundre* spandrel, fr. OF *espandre*, *spandre* to spread, disperse — more at SPAWN] **1 a :** the wall or panel between the extrados of an arch and the next adjacent molding; *specif* **:** an ornamentally treated space between the right or left extrados curve and an enclosing right angle **b :** an area of the shape and nature of a spandrel **2 :** the triangular space beneath the string of a stair **3 :** an exterior wall panel which fills the space beneath a windowsill usu. extending to the top of the window in the story below **4 :** a corner space with scrollwork or other decorative filling between a rounded corner of a design and a squared corner of a rectangular frame line on a stamp

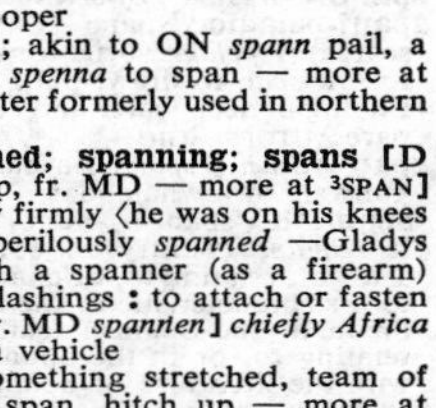

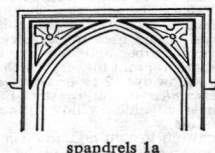

spandrels 1a

spandrel beam *n* **:** the exterior beam in steel or concrete construction that marks the floor level between stories

spandrel frame *n* **:** a triangular framing (as under a stair)

spandrel wall *n* **:** a wall on an extrados to fill the spandrels

¹**span·dy** \ˈspandē, -paan-, -di\ *adv* [alter. of ⁷*span*] **:** COMPLETELY ⟨a ~ new apartment house —*Time*⟩

²**spandy** \"\ *adj* **:** NEAT ⟨two pairs of ~ gloves —Louisa Alcott⟩

spane \ˈspān\ *var of* SPAIN

span-farthing \ˈ=,==\ *n* [³*span*] **:** a game played like span-counter but with farthings

¹**spang** \ˈspaŋ, -aiŋ\ *vb* -ED/-ING/-S [origin unknown] *vt, chiefly Scot* **:** THROW, BANG **~** *vi, chiefly Scot* **:** JUMP, LEAP

²**spang** \"\ *n* -S *chiefly Scot* **:** a sudden violent movement **:** JERK, LEAP, KICK

³**spang** \"\ *adv* **1 :** COMPLETELY ⟨the brooks were . . . all running ~ full to the very edge with snow-water —Dorothy C. Fisher⟩ **2 :** EXACTLY, SQUARELY, DIRECTLY ⟨this roomy place

is ~ in the middle of the theater district —Roger Angell⟩ ⟨jumped ~ onto my seat —G.W.Bagby⟩

4spang \"\ n -s [prob. of imit. origin] : a sharp loud often whining sound ⟨the canyon wall echoes to the ~ of the miner's hammer —Nature Mag.⟩ ⟨the ~ of a ricocheting bullet⟩

5spang \"\ vi -ED/-ING/-S : to make a spang : CRACK ⟨bullets buzzed in the air and ~ed into tree trunks —Stephen Crane⟩

spang·hew \'=,(h)yü\ vt -ED/-ING/-S [alter. of 1spang] dial Brit : to throw violently into the air; esp : to throw (a frog) into the air from the end of a stick

1span·gle \'spaŋgəl, -paiŋ-\ n -s [ME spangel, dim. of spang shiny ornament, spangle, prob. of Scand origin; akin to ON spang-, spöng spangle; akin to OE spang clasp, buckle, OHG spanga clasp, buckle, spannan to stretch, span — more at SPAN] 1 : a small disk or other geometric shape of shining metal or plastic used for sparkling ornamentation esp. on dresses and costumes 2 : something resembling or suggesting a spangle in sparkle and brilliance: as a : a small object that brightly reflects light ⟨a fox . . . wet with gold ~s of the dew —Edith Sitwell⟩ b : a glittering point of light 3 : a sparkle or glitter from or as if from spangles 4 : a glossy or shining mark on the end of a feather

2spangle \"\ vb spangled; spangled; spangling \-g(ə)liŋ\ spangles vt : to set or sprinkle with or as if with spangles : adorn with small brilliant objects : give a sparkling appearance or impression to ⟨the sky is . . . spangled with stars —Marjorie K. Rawlings⟩ ⟨yellow jasmine spangled the forest with gold —B.A.Williams⟩ ⟨an evening sheath . . . spangled with black sequins —Lois Long⟩ ~ vi : to glitter as if covered with spangles : GLISTEN, SPARKLE ⟨it spangled like a cold star —Eudora Welty⟩ ⟨its countless mirror lakes . . . glow and ~ —John Muir †1914⟩

3spangle \"\ n, pl spangle or spangles [origin unknown] : a measure of yarn formerly in use in Ireland and Scotland

spangled glass n : a late nineteenth century American clear glassware having crystalline fleckings usu. of mica suspended in the glass fabric

spanglegrass \'==,=\ n : SPIKE-GRASS a

span·gler \'spaŋg(ə)lə(r), -paiŋ-\ n -s : one that spangles

span·glet \-glət\ n -s : a tiny spangle

span·gly \-g(ə)lē, -li\ adj -ER/-EST [1spangle + -y] : covered with or resembling spangles : GLITTERING

spang–new \'spaŋ'=, -paiŋ-\ adj [alter. of span-new] : BRAND-NEW

spango·lite \'spaŋ(g)ə,līt\ n -s [Norman Spang, 19th cent. Am. mineralogist + E -o- + -lite] : a mineral $Cu_6Al(SO_4)(OH)_{12}Cl.3H_2O$ consisting of a hydrous basic sulfate and chloride of aluminum and copper in dark-green hexagonal crystals

span·iard \'spanyə(r)d\ n -s cap [ME Spaignard, Spaynard, Spanyeart, fr. MF Espaignart, Espaniard, fr. Espaigne Spain (fr. L Hispania) + -art, -ard -ard] 1 : a native or inhabitant of Spain 2 : a spear grass (Aciphylla colensoi) of New Zealand that grows in tufted clumps and has stiff but slender grassy leaf divisions

1span·iel \'spanyəl, chiefly archaic or dial -nᵊl\ n [ME spaynel, spaniell, fr. MF espaignol, lit., Spaniard, fr. OProv espanhol, fr. OIt spagnuolo — more at SPAGNUOLO] 1 a usu cap : any of numerous breeds of small or medium-sized mostly short-legged dogs usu. having long wavy hair, feathered legs and tail, and large drooping ears — see ENGLISH TOY SPANIEL, FIELD SPANIEL, WATER SPANIEL b -s sometimes cap : a dog of one of these breeds 2 -s : a cringing servile fawning person ⟨office seekers, . . . ~s well-trained to carry and fetch —Walt Whitman⟩

2spaniel \"\ vb -ED/-ING/-S vi : to play about like a spaniel : FROLIC, SPORT ~ vt : to follow esp. fawningly after ⟨the hearts that ~ed me at heels —Shak.⟩

spaning pres part of SPANE

spani·pelagic \¦spanə+\ adj [ISV spani- (fr. Gk spanios rare, scarce) + pelagic; orig. formed as G spanipelagisch; perh. akin to Gk span to draw, pull, tear — more at SPAN] of plankton : living in deep water and coming to the surface rarely — compare AUTOPELAGIC

span iron n [6span] : a harpoon usu. secured just below the gunwale of a whaleboat

1span·ish \'spanish, -nēsh\ adj, usu cap [ME Spainish, Spanish, fr. Spain, country in southwestern Europe + ME -ish] 1 a : of, relating to, or characteristic of Spain b : of, relating to, or characteristic of the Spanish people 2 : dominated by Spain or the Spanish ⟨sailed the Spanish Main⟩ 3 a : of, relating to, or in the Spanish language b : of or associated with the literature of Spain 4 : SPANISH-AMERICAN

2spanish \"\ n -ES see sense 2 1 cap : the Romance language of the largest part of Spain and of the countries colonized by Spaniards 2 pl in constr, cap : the people of Spain 3 also **spanish colonial** usu cap S & sometimes cap C : a style of architecture deriving from the missions and ranch houses of the Spanish settlers in the Southwest and Florida

spanish–american \¦==¦===\ adj, usu cap S&A 1 : of, relating to, or characteristic of the countries of America in which Spanish is the national language 2 : of, relating to, or characteristic of communities or sections of communities in the U. S. where Spanish Americans live

spanish american n, cap S&A 1 : a native or inhabitant of a Spanish-American country esp. of Spanish descent — compare LATIN AMERICAN 2 : a resident of the U. S. whose native language is Spanish and whose culture is of Spanish origin — compare ANGLO-AMERICAN

spanish bayonet n, usu cap S : any of several plants of the genus Yucca; esp : a stiff short-trunked plant (Yucca aloifolia) of the southern U. S. and tropical America with rigid spine-tipped leaves

spanish beard n, usu cap S : SPANISH MOSS 1

spanish billiards n, usu cap S : a game closely resembling pin pool except that winning and losing hazards and caroms are scored and that two points are counted for each pin knocked down by the cue ball after contact with an object ball

spanish bluebell n, usu cap S : SPANISH JACINTH

spanish bowline n, usu cap S : a knot that is similar to a bowline but has two separate loops and is used esp. as a sling for hoisting or lowering a man

spanish broom n, usu cap S 1 : a nearly leafless shrub (Spartium junceum) of the family Leguminosae of southern Europe and the Canary Islands that has green flexible twigs which are similar to rushes, are used in basketry, and yield a fiber and that has handsome fragrant flowers which yield a yellow dye 2 : a broom (Genista hispanica) of southwestern Europe having golden yellow flowers in heads

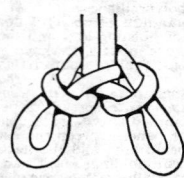

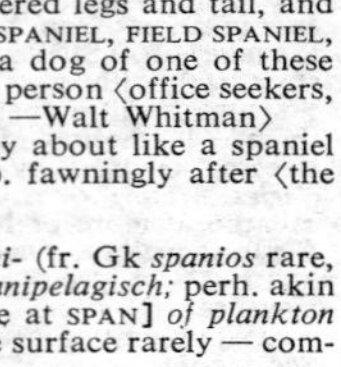
Spanish bowline

spanish brown n 1 usu cap S : earth having a dark reddish brown color because of the presence of iron oxide and used as a pigment — compare SPANISH OXIDE 2 often cap S : INDIAN RED 2b

spanish buckeye n, usu cap S : BUCKEYE 1c

spanish bugloss n, usu cap S : ALKANET 1a

spanish burton n, usu cap S : a tackle with two single blocks — see DOUBLE SPANISH BURTON, SINGLE SPANISH BURTON; BURTON illustration

spanish buttons n pl but sing or pl in constr, usu cap S : a perennial branching knapweed (Centaurea nigra) with hairy leaves and reddish purple to dark purple flowers

spanish carnation n, usu cap S : PRIDE OF BARBADOS

spanish cedar n, usu cap S 1 : any of several trees of the genus Cedrela; esp : a tropical American tree (C. odorata) 2 : the fragrant wood of Spanish cedar much used for cigar boxes — called also cigar-box cedar

spanish chalk n, usu cap S : a steatite from the Aragon region of Spain

spanish chestnut n, usu cap S 1 : a large tree (Castanea sativa) chiefly of the Mediterranean region with large nutritious nuts — called also sweet chestnut, Italian chestnut 2 : the nut borne by the Spanish chestnut

spanish clover n, usu cap S 1 : ALFALFA 2 : MEXICAN CLOVER 3 : PRAIRIE BIRD'S-FOOT TREFOIL

spanish cream n, usu cap S : a molded dessert made of eggs, sugar, milk, and gelatin

spanish curlew n, usu cap S 1 : HEN CURLEW 2 : WHITE IBIS 1

spanish dagger n, usu cap S 1 : a plant (Yucca gloriosa) of the southeastern U. S. resembling the Spanish bayonet but with shorter trunk and smoother leaves 2 : SPANISH BAYONET

spanish elm n, usu cap S 1 : a large tropical American tree (Cordia alliodora) 2 : the hard grayish wood of the Spanish elm used for building and for many other purposes

span·ish·er \'spanishə(r), -nēsh-\ n -s [Spanish (leather) + -er] 1 : one who treats embossed leather with a special solution and bakes it to obtain a two-tone effect 2 : a worker engaged in the production of Spanish leather

spanish fir n, usu cap S : an evergreen tree (Abies pinsapo) of the Pyrenees with stiff bright green foliage

spanish flag n, usu cap S 1 : a California rockfish (Sebastodes rubrivinctus) having conspicuous bands of red and creamy pink 2 : a West Indian fish (Gonioplectrus hispanus) of the family Serranidae with a bright-red body and yellow stripes along the head and back

spanish flesh n, often cap S : SEED PEARL 2

spanish fly n, usu cap S 1 : a brilliant green blister beetle (Lytta vesicatoria) common in the south of Europe 2 : CANTHARIS 2

spanish foot n, usu cap S : a foot on a piece of furniture curved outward with ridges resembling claws

spanish fox n, usu cap S : FOX 7b

spanish grain n, usu cap S : grain texture produced on fancy or upholstery leather by embossing

spanish grape n, usu cap S 1 : a wild grape (Vitis berlandieri) of Texas and Mexico 2 : the small purple tangy fruit of the Spanish grape

spanish green n, often cap S : VERDIGRIS 4

spanish grunt n, usu cap S : GRAY GRUNT

spanish guitar n, usu cap S : GUITAR

spanish heath n, usu cap S : an erect dense shrub (Erica lusitanica) native to western Europe but widely grown as an ornamental and having white or pink flowers produced profusely along the entire length of the branches

spanish heel n, usu cap S : a high leather-covered wooden heel having a straight breast — compare CUBAN HEEL, FRENCH HEEL, SPIKE HEEL

spanish hogfish n, usu cap S : LADYFISH b

spanish influenza n, usu cap S : pandemic influenza

spanish iris n, usu cap S : a bulbous iris (Iris xiphium) of the western Mediterranean region having usu. violet-purple flowers with a short perianth tube — called also xiphium iris; compare ENGLISH IRIS, PERSIAN IRIS

spanish jacinth n, usu cap S : a squill (Scilla hispanica) of Spain and Portugal with blue or white flowers resembling those of the hyacinth

spanish jasmine n, usu cap S 1 also **spanish jessamine** : a large-flowered East Indian jasmine (Jasminum grandiflorum) often cultivated for ornament and perfume 2 : a frangipani (Plumeria rubra)

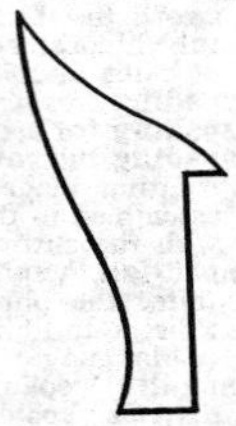
Spanish heel

spanish lady or **spanish ladyfish** n, usu cap S : LADYFISH b

spanish leather n, usu cap S : CORDOVAN 2

spanish lettuce n, usu cap S : INDIAN LETTUCE 3

spanish licorice n, usu cap S : LICORICE 1b

spanish lime n, usu cap S : GENIP 2

spanish lobster n, usu cap S : any of several large sluggish scyllarian crustaceans (genus Scyllarides) used as bait and sometimes for food in the West Indies

spanish mackerel n, usu cap S 1 : any of several mackerels of the genus Scomberomorus: as a : a mackerel (S. maculatus) that is bluish above with oval brown spots on the sides, is found during the warmer months off the American Atlantic coast from Cape Ann to Brazil, and often weighs six to ten pounds b : a related but unspotted mackerel (S. concolor) occurring on the Mexican and Southern California coast c : a large mackerel (S. commersoni) that is widespread in the tropical Indo-Pacific, attains a length of six feet, and weighs over 100 pounds 2 West : JACK MACKEREL a 3 : CHUB MACKEREL

spanish mahogany n, usu cap S : a mahogany obtained only from the West Indies and esp. from Santo Domingo and sometimes considered a distinct species (Swietenia macrophylla)

spanish measles n pl but sing or pl in constr, usu cap S : BLACK MEASLES 2

spanish moss n, usu cap S 1 : an epiphytic plant (Tillandsia usneoides) that forms pendant tufts of hairlike grayish green strands upon the trunks and branches of many trees in the southern U. S. and the West Indies — called also black moss, long moss, old-man's-beard 2 : a lichen (Ramalina reticulata) that forms lacelike masses on many trees in the Pacific coastal U. S.

spanish n n, usu cap S : the character ñ — compare TILDE

spanish needles n pl but sing or pl in constr, usu cap S 1 : the barbed achenes of any of several plants of the genus Bidens 2 : a common beggar-ticks (Bidens bipinnata) of the eastern U. S.

spanish oak n, usu cap S : any of several oaks of the southern U. S.; esp : RED OAK 1b

spanish ocher n, often cap S : OCHER ORANGE

spanish omelet n, usu cap S : an omelet served with a sauce containing chopped green pepper, onion, and tomato

spanish onion n, usu cap S : any of several large-bulbed mild-flavored onions

spanish oxide n, usu cap S : a dull red natural iron oxide pigment — compare INDIAN RED 1a, SPANISH BROWN

spanish oyster n, usu cap S, Bermuda : PEN SHELL

spanish oyster plant n, usu cap S : a tall biennial golden thistle (Scolymus hispanicus) of southwestern Europe that is sometimes cultivated for its edible roots which resemble but are larger and milder than those of salsify, for its foliage which is eaten like that of the cardoon, and for its flowers which are used as a substitute for saffron

spanish pack n, usu cap S : a pack of 40 playing cards resembling a 52-card pack but without eights, nines, and tens

spanish paprika n, usu cap S 1 : PIMIENTO 1 2 : a paprika produced from pimientos usu. in Spain

spanish peanut n, usu cap S : a peanut that has small pods and short rounded seeds and is sometimes grown as a forage plant

spanish pear n, usu cap S : AVOCADO

spanish pepper n, usu cap S 1 : PEPPER TREE 1 2 : PEPPER 3

spanish plum n, usu cap S 1 a : the red edible fruit of a tropical American hog plum (Spondias purpurea) — called also red mombin b : the tree that bears the Spanish plum 2 : FALSE SANDALWOOD 1

spanish potato n, usu cap S : SWEET POTATO

spanish red n, often cap S 1 : CARTHAMUS RED 2 : IRON-OXIDE RED

spanish rice n, usu cap S : rice cooked with onions, green pepper, and tomatoes

spanish rococo n, usu cap S : the more highly decorated and elaborate period of Spanish Renaissance architecture

spanish sage n, usu cap 1st S : a sage (Salvia lavandulaefolia) of western Europe that has small dark green leaves and is sometimes used as an adulterant of official sage

spanish salsify n, usu cap 1st S : SPANISH OYSTER PLANT

spanish sauce n, usu cap 1st S : BROWN SAUCE

spanish scroll n, usu cap 1st S : an ornamental scroll usu. for the foot of a chair or table consisting of a series of parallel flutes terminating in a sweeping spiral — see FOOT illustration

spanish sheep n, usu cap 1st S : MERINO 1b

spanish soldier n, usu cap 1st S : a spear grass (Aciphylla squarrosa) of New Zealand

spanish spoon n, usu cap 1st S : a long-handled shallow dipper or shovel used for digging postholes

spanish stopper n, usu cap 1st S : GURGEON STOPPER

spanish tea n, usu cap S 1 : MEXICAN TEA 2 : a West Indian shrub (Gesneria longiflora)

spanish thistle n, usu cap S : BUFFALO BUR

spanish toothpick n, usu cap S : a bishop's-weed (Ammi visnaga)

spanish topaz n, usu cap S : a yellow variety of rock crystal

spanish trefoil n, usu cap S : ALFALFA

spanish white n, usu cap S 1 : whiting used as a pigment 2 : bismuth subnitrate used as a pigment

spanish windlass n, usu cap S : a device for bringing together two taut lines (as for seizing) in which a small line is passed around the two, its ends are passed around a wooden roller, and a turn of each end is taken around a marlinespike by which the roller may be revolved and the lines hove together

spanish wine n, often cap S : PIGEON BLOOD

spanish yellow n, often cap S : a strong orange yellow that is slightly duller than bright maize or nasturtium yellow (sense 2)

1spank \'spaŋk, -paiŋk\ vb -ED/-ING/-S [imit.] vt 1 : to strike with or as if with the open hand; esp : to slap smartly on the buttocks ⟨in the olden days children were ~ed plenty —Benjamin Spock⟩ 2 : to thrust or propel with a spank ⟨"I like balloons," she said, ~ing it into the air with . . . her hand —Joseph Mitchell⟩ 3 : to reprimand severely ⟨we watch new American novelists being ~ed in the public prints —J.H. Burns⟩ ~ vi : to strike or fall with a spank ⟨the ball . . . would ~ into the round mitt —Richard Wilbur⟩

2spank \"\ n -s 1 a : a blow usu. with the palm of the hand : SLAP b : a blow resembling a spank ⟨raised his oar and brought it down flat on the water with a tremendous ~ —Saturday Rev.⟩ 2 : the sound produced by a spank

3spank \"\ vb -ED/-ING/-S [back-formation fr. 1spanking] vi 1 : to move quickly, dashingly, or spiritedly; esp : to drive or ride in a smart or stylish manner ⟨used to ~ around . . . in a smart rig that had yellow wheels trimmed in red —James Thurber⟩ 2 : to sail briskly ⟨sailing craft would come down ~ing before the breeze —Richard Jefferies⟩ ~ vt : to drive (as a horse, vehicle) smartly

1spank·er \-kə(r)\ n -s [origin unknown] 1 dial : one remarkable of its kind (as for size, speed, quality, appearance) 2 a : the fore-and-aft sail carried on the aftermast of a square-rigged ship — see SAIL illustration b : the aftermast and sail in a schooner of four or more masts c : the fifth mast of a six-masted or seven-masted schooner 3 : a horse capable of good speed : a fast trotter or pacer

2spanker \"\ n -s [1spank + -er] 1 a : one that spanks b : something used as an instrument for spanking ⟨some . . . shovel dirt in the path of the fire; others beat the flames with ~s —Philip Pollack⟩ 2 : a drop-hammer operator who straightens metal parts that become warped during forging

spanker boom n : the boom for a spanker — see SHIP illustration

1spank·ing \'spaŋkiŋ, -paiŋ-, -kēŋ\ adj [origin unknown] 1 : remarkable of its kind : unusual or distinctive in some manner ⟨rode the noble animal over the ~ leap —Samuel Lover⟩ ⟨her smocked . . . cotton brought up behind with a ~ bow —Mademoiselle⟩ 2 a : moving or capable of moving with a quick lively pace ⟨drove . . . by buckboard behind a ~ pair of the little mules —J.H.Allen⟩ b : DASHING, MERRY ⟨passed our house . . . at a ~ three miles an hour —Ben Riker⟩ ⟨like to be towed astern, riding surfboard . . . at a ~ clip —Jerome Ellison⟩ c : being fresh and strong : BRISK — usu. used of a breeze ⟨small boats dance on the clear blue waters in the ~ breeze —Bentz Plagemann⟩

2spanking \"\ adv : EXCEPTIONALLY, VERY ⟨put that away ~ clean last fall —Charles Boswell⟩ ⟨~ new modernistic structures, all concrete and colored glass —Ridgely Cummings⟩

spank·ing·ly adv : in a spanking manner : SPANKING

span–long \'=¦=\ adj [2span + long] : having the length of a span

spanned past of SPAN

span·ner \'spanə(r), -paan-\ n -s [fr. obs. E, instrument for winding the spring of a wheel lock, fr. G, fr. spannen to stretch (fr. OHG spannan) + -er — more at SPAN] 1 : a contrivance in some of the earlier steam engines for moving the valves 2 a chiefly Brit : WRENCH b : a wrench that has a jaw or socket to fit a nut or head of a bolt, a pipe, or hose coupling; esp : one having a tooth or one or more pins in its jaw to fit a hole or slot in an object 3 : a horizontal cross brace or collar beam 4 : a pendulum attachment for an ordinary sextant providing an artificial horizon for use when the sea horizon is obscured 5 : an embroidery-machine worker who adjusts fabric and frames

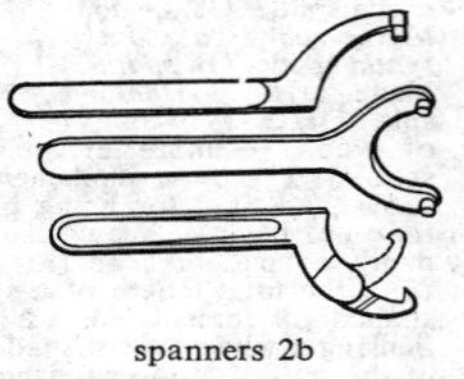
spanners 2b

span·ner·man \-mən\ n, pl spannermen 1 : a workman who tightens nuts or bolts with a spanner 2 : a worker who adjusts the rolls of a roughing mill to assure that iron and steel will be of the desired thickness

span–new \'span'=, -paan-\ adj [ME, part trans. of ON spānnȳr, fr. spānn chip of wood + nȳr new — more at SPOON] : BRAND-NEW

spanning pres part of SPAN

span of apprehension [2span] : the number of discrete stimulus objects to which a subject can simultaneously attend

span of attention [2span] 1 : SPAN OF APPREHENSION 2 : the duration of a subject's attention to a given task or set of stimuli

span roof n [3span] : a common roof having two slopes and one ridge with eaves on both sides

spans pl of SPAN, pres 3d sing of SPAN

spans and snops \-¦snäps\ n pl but sing in constr [spans fr. pl. of 2span; snops prob. alter. of snaps, pl. of snap] : an old game in which one player tries to shoot a marble against or to within a span of that of an opponent

span shackle n [6span] : a triangular or square shackle in the head of a large bolt driven through the forecastle deck to receive the heel of the fish davit

span·spek \'spänz,pek, -n,sp-\ n -s [Afrik, alter. of spaanspek, fr. spaans Spanisch (fr. D spaansch) + spek bacon, pork fat, fr. MD spec — more at SPECK] : a usu. somewhat pale-fleshed and moderately sweet muskmelon that is widely cultivated in southern Africa

spanwise \'=,=\ adj [2span + -wise] : directed, moving, or placed along the span of an airfoil — compare CHORDWISE

spanworm \'=,=\ n [3span + worm] : LOOPER 1

1spar \'spär, -pȧ(r\ vt sparred; sparred; sparring; spars [partly fr. ME sperren, fr. MD; partly fr. ME sparren, fr. OE gesparrian; akin to MD & OHG sperren to bolt, lock, hamper, ON sperra to bolt, bar, sparri beam, rafter — more at 2SPAR] 1 archaic : BOLT, BAR, FASTEN 2 a obs : SHUT, CLOSE b obs : to shut up : ENCLOSE

2spar \"\ n -s [ME sparre; akin to MD sparre beam, rafter, OHG sparro, ON sparri beam, rafter, OE spere spear — more at SPEAR] 1 archaic : RAFTER 2 a : a pole or moderately thick piece of timber b : a stout rounded typically solid piece of wood or metal (as a mast, boom, gaff, yard) used to support rigging — see SHIP illustration c (1) : one of the main longitudinal members of the wing of an airplane that carry the ribs (2) : LONGERON 3 : a thin doubled stick used in fastening thatch on roofs

3spar \"\ vt sparred; sparred; sparring; spars : to move or assist (a stranded ship) with a spar or with spar and tackle

4spar \"\ vb sparred; sparred; sparring; spars [prob. alter. of 2spur] vi 1 : to strike or fight with the feet or spurs like a gamecock 2 : to contest in words : WRANGLE ⟨the gabble of the vegetable men as they sparred with women at the open stalls outside their stores —Hortense Calisher⟩ 3 a : BOX; esp : to make offensive and defensive gestures without landing a blow in order to draw one's opponent and find or create an opening b : to engage in a practice or exhibition bout esp. of scientific boxing with a sparring partner 4 : to engage in a skirmish ⟨along the ground front . . . troops sparred in scattered fights —N.Y.Times⟩ 5 : to move or act slowly or inconclusively : STALL ⟨seems to ~ for time by asking that questions be repeated —Jerome Frank⟩ ~ vt : to teach (a gamecock) to fight : train for fighting

5spar \"\ n -s 1 a : a movement of offense or defense in boxing b : a sparring match or session 2 : a wrangle or dispute esp. between well-matched opponents : a contest of thrust and counter

6spar \"\ n -s [LG, fr. MLG; akin to OE spærstān gypsum,

chalk, *spæren* of plaster] **:** any of various nonmetallic usu. cleavable and somewhat lustrous minerals; *esp* **:** such a mineral occurring as gangue in a metalliferous vein — compare CALCSPAR, FELDSPAR, FLUORITE

[7]**spar** \"\ *n* -S *usu cap* [fr. *S*emper *Par*atus, motto of the U.S. Coast Guard fr. NL, always ready] **:** a member of the Women's Reserve of the U. S. Coast Guard formed during World War II

spar·a·ble \'sparəbəl\ *n* -S [alter. of *sparrowbill*] **:** a small headless nail used by cobblers to reduce wear on shoe soles

sparable tin *n* **:** tin ore in grains like sparables

spara·grass \'sparə,gras, -,grəs\ *n* [by folk etymology fr. *sparagus*] *chiefly dial* **:** ASPARAGUS

spar·a·gus \-,gəs\ *n* [modif. of L *asparagus*] *archaic* **:** ASPARAGUS

spa·ras·sis \spə'rasəs\ *n, cap* [NL, fr. Gk *sparassein* to tear, rend; akin to ON *spjörr* rag, Arm *p'ert'* piece ripped off of something, and perh. to OSlav *prǫžiti, prǫžati* to tear apart] **:** a genus of fungi (family Clavariaceae) having fleshy, much-branched, leafy sporophores — see YELLOW ROOT ROT

spa·rax·is \spə'raksəs\ *n* [NL, fr. Gk, act of retching; akin to Gk *sparassein* to tear, rend] **1** *cap* **:** a small genus of bulbous plants (family Iridaceae) that are native to the Cape of Good Hope and include several which are cultivated for their brilliantly colored flowers borne in fringed spathes — see WANDFLOWER **2** *pl* **sparaxis :** any plant, flower, or bulb of the genus *Sparaxis*

spar bridge *n* **:** a temporary bridge consisting of round timbers (as tree trunks) lashed together and usu. used for military purposes

spar buoy *n* **:** a buoy consisting of a spar anchored at one end usu. marking the port side of a channel — see BUOY illustration

sparce *var of* SPARSE

spar ceiling *n* **:** SPARRING

sparcity *var of* SPARSITY

spar deck *n* **:** an upper deck of light construction above the main deck

spar-decked \'=¦=\ *adj* **:** having a spar deck

spar-deck·er \'=¦dekə(r)\ *n* **:** a ship having a spar deck

spar-deck vessel *n* **:** a ship for both cargo and passengers that has two or more decks of lighter construction above the strength deck

[1]**spare** \'spa(a)|(ə)r, -pe|, |ə\ *vb* -ED/-ING/-S [ME *sparen*, fr. OE *sparian;* akin to OFris *sparia* to spare, OHG *sparōn, sparēn*, ON *spara;* derivatives fr. the root of E [2]*spare*] *vt* **1 :** to forbear to destroy, punish, or harm **:** preserve from punishment, injury, or evil **:** show mercy to ⟨~, O Lord, this miserable sinner⟩ ⟨many ships were sunk but a few were *spared*⟩ ⟨woodman, ~ that tree —G.P.Morris⟩ **2 :** to refrain from attacking, scolding, reprimanding, or speaking with necessary or salutary severity to ⟨his sermons *spared* neither high nor low, rich nor poor⟩ ⟨does not *spare* the U.N. and he recommends that it set its house in order —Chester Bowles⟩ **3 :** to relieve (someone) of the necessity of doing or undergoing something **:** EXEMPT ⟨~ him the trouble of answering⟩ ⟨wanted to ~ his parents the expense of sending him to college⟩ ⟨~ yourself quite a bit of . . . weeding —*New Yorker*⟩ **4 :** to refrain from **:** AVOID ⟨nothing is *spared* to . . . make you comfortable —T.H.Fielding⟩ **5 a :** to use stintingly or frugally **:** refrain from the free use or consumption of ⟨~ the rod and spoil the child⟩ — chiefly in negative use ⟨more pancakes, please, and don't ~ the syrup⟩ ⟨come at once and don't ~ the horses⟩ ⟨substantial homes with no *sparing* of paint —R.W. Hatch⟩ **b** *dial chiefly Brit* **:** SAVE 2a ⟨rob a poor man of all he had *spared* —Augusta Gregory⟩ **6 a :** to give up or part with as being not strictly needed **:** dispense with as surplus or extra ⟨could have better *spared* a better man —Shak.⟩ ⟨giving employment . . . to villagers who can be *spared* from the farms —*Geog. School Bull.*⟩ **b :** to have left over or as margin ⟨caught the train with a few minutes to ~⟩ ⟨that rug will cover the floor with a foot to ~⟩ **~** *vi* **1** *obs* **:** DESIST, STOP **2 :** to be frugal **:** live in a saving and stinting manner ⟨some will spend and some will ~ —Robert Burns⟩ **3 :** to refrain from executing judgment or punishment or taking vengeance **:** use mercy or kindness **:** be lenient — **and to spare :** in plenty **:** in superabundance **:** too much ⟨we have enough *and to spare* of bad novels⟩

[2]**spare** \"\ *adj* -ER/-EST [ME, fr. OE *spær;* akin to OHG *spar* spare, ON *sparr* spare, OSlav *sporŭ* abundant, OE *spēd* success, speed — more at SPEED] **1 :** not being used **:** held for future or emergency use ⟨~ bedroom⟩ ⟨~ tire⟩ ⟨~ anchor⟩ **2 :** being over and above what is necessary **:** not wanted **:** not presently needed **:** FREE, SUPERFLUOUS ⟨a hobby to occupy his ~ time⟩ ⟨have you any ~ cash you could lend me⟩ **3 :** not liberal or profuse **:** SPARING, CHARY ⟨habitually ~ of speech⟩ ⟨build up the truth of his characters through ~, pungent dialogue —Arthur Knight⟩ ⟨tale proceeds with a ~ and lucid simplicity —*Times Lit. Supp.*⟩ **4 :** lacking fat **:** somewhat thin **:** LEAN ⟨~, alert, and jaunty figure —Thomas Wolfe⟩ ⟨some like their beauty to be luxurious; others see beauty in the gaunt and the ~ —Richard Joseph⟩ **5 :** not abundant or plentiful **:** MEAGER, SCANTY ⟨~ diet⟩ ⟨~ vegetation⟩ **syn** see LEAN, MEAGER

[3]**spare** \"\ *n* -S [ME, fr. *sparen*, v.] **1** *obs* **:** an act of showing restraint or mercy — used esp. in the phrase *without spare* **2** *archaic* **:** PLACKET **3** *archaic* **:** frugal use **:** ECONOMY, FRUGALITY — used with *make* **4 a :** a spare tire **b :** a duplicate (as a battery, a pair of eyeglasses) kept in reserve **c** *chiefly Brit* **:** SPARE PART **d :** an extra member of a sports team **5 :** the knocking down of all 10 pins with the first 2 bowls of a frame in bowling — compare STRIKE **6 :** surplus clay trimmed off the mold in the slip-casting process

spare·able \'spa(a)rəbəl, -per-\ *adj* **:** that can be spared

spare hand *n* **:** an additional workman kept for incidental odd jobs or relieving a regular

spare·less \'=ləs\ *adj* [[3]*spare* + *-less*] *archaic* **:** UNSPARING

spare·ly *adv* [[2]*spare* + *-ly*] **1 :** SPARINGLY ⟨drinking gravely and ~ of the . . . punch —Irwin Shaw⟩ **2 :** SPARSELY, MEAGERLY ⟨rooms were ~ furnished —Elizabeth M. Roberts⟩ **3 :** LEANLY ⟨~ built, active little man⟩

spare·ness *n* -ES **:** LEANNESS, THINNESS, MEAGERNESS

spare part *n* **:** an extra part of a vehicle or machine kept for use in emergency or replacement

spar·er \'spa(a)rə(r), -per-\ *n* -S [ME *sparare*, fr. *sparen* to spare + *-are*, *-er* -er — more at SPARE] **:** one that spares; *esp* **:** one that reduces destruction of something (as a bodily substance) ⟨sugar in the diet may act as a ~ of protein⟩

spare·ribs \'spa(a)(r),ribz, -pe(r),ri-, -pa(a)ə,ri-, -peə,ri-\ *n pl* [by folk etymology fr. LG *ribbesper* smoked or pickled pork ribs roasted on a spit, fr. MLG, fr. *ribbe* rib + *sper* spit, spear; akin to OHG *rippi* rib and to OHG *sper* spear — more at RIB, SPEAR] **:** a cut of pork ribs and breastbone separated from the bacon strip

spares *pres 3d sing of* SPARE, *pl of* SPARE

spare-set \'=¦=\ *adj* [[2]*spare* + *set*, past part. of *set*] **:** spare in form **:** somewhat thin **:** GAUNT ⟨accosted by a graying, *spare-set* guest —S.H.Adams⟩

spar·ga·ni·a·ce·ae \(,)spär,gānē'āsē,ē\ *n pl, cap* [NL, fr. *Sparganium*, type genus + *-aceae*] **:** a monotypic family of monocotyledonous plants (order Pandanales) — see SPARGANIUM

spar·ga·ni·a·sis \,spärgə'nīəsəs\ *n, pl* **sparganiа·ses** \-īə,sēz\ [NL, fr. *sparganum* + *-iasis*] **:** SPARGANOSIS

spar·ga·nid \'spärgənəd\ *adj* [NL *sparganum* + E *-id*] **:** of or relating to a sparganum ⟨~ infestation⟩

spar·ga·ni·um \spär'gānēəm\ *n* [NL, fr. L *sparganion* bur reed, fr. Gk, dim. of *sparganon* swaddling band] **1** *cap* **:** a genus (coextensive with the family Sparganiaceae) of marsh or aquatic herbs of temperate regions with simple or branching stems, linear leaves, and monoecious flowers in globose heads — see BUR REED **2** -S **:** any plant of the genus *Sparganium*

spar·ga·no·sis \,spärgə'nōsəs\ *n, pl* **sparganoses** [NL, fr. *sparganum* + *-osis*] **:** the condition of being infected with Sparganum

spar·ga·num \'spärgənəm\ *n, pl* **sparga·na** \-nə\ *also* **sparganums** [NL, fr. Gk *sparganon* swaddling band; akin to Gk *speira* twist — more at SPIRE] **:** an intramuscular or subcutaneous vermiform parasite of various vertebrates including man that is the plerocercoid larva of a tapeworm — often used as though a generic name when referring to such a larva esp. when the adult is unknown ⟨*Sparganum proliferum* is a rare parasite of man⟩; compare LIGULA

[1]**sparge** \'spärj\ *vb* -ED/-ING/-S [prob. fr. MF *espargier* to sprinkle, fr. L *spargere* to scatter, strew, sprinkle — more at SPARK] *vt* **1 :** ROUGHCAST, PLASTER **2 a :** to moisten by sprinkling **:** SPRINKLE, BESPATTER; *esp* **:** to spray (mash) with hot water to extract the wort in brewing **b** (1) **:** to heat (a liquid) by means of live steam entering through a sparger (2) **:** to agitate (a liquid) by means of compressed air or gas entering through a sparger **~** *vi* **:** to scatter water about **:** SPRAY

[2]**sparge** \"\ *n* -S **:** a sprinkling or spraying; *also* **:** SPRAY

sparge pipe *n* **:** a horizontal perforated water pipe for flushing a urinal — called also *weeper*

sparg·er \-jə(r)\ *n* -S **:** one that sparges **:** SPRINKLER: as **a :** a vessel with a perforated cover for sprinkling clothes **b :** a device with perforated arms for sprinkling the grains in a mash tun **c :** a pipe having either perforations or nozzles through which steam, compressed air, or gas is forced into a liquid in a fermentation process

spar·hawk \'spär,=\ *n* [ME *sparhauk*, fr. OE *spearhafoc*, fr. *spearwa* sparrow + *hafoc* hawk — more at SPARROW, HAWK] *archaic* **:** SPARROW HAWK

[1]**spar·id** \'sparəd\ *adj* [NL *Sparidae*] **:** of or relating to the Sparidae

[2]**sparid** *n* -S **:** a fish of the family Sparidae

spar·i·dae \-rə,dē\ *n pl, cap* [NL, fr. *Sparus*, type genus + *-idae*] **:** a large and widely distributed family of deep-bodied marine percoid fishes including the porgies, scups, and sheepsheads that are related to the grunts and snappers but have some of the teeth along the sides of the jaw transformed into large blunt molars — see SEA BREAM

sparing *adj* [ME, fr. pres. part. of *sparen* to spare] **1 a :** economical in the use or expenditure of resources ⟨a ~ father and a spending son —John Clarke⟩ **b :** RETICENT ⟨~ in speech⟩ ⟨~ prose⟩ **2 :** MEAGER, SCANTY ⟨the map is ~ of information⟩ **3 :** capable of preventing or characterized by prevention of waste of a vital substance in metabolism ⟨carbohydrates are ~ agents of body proteins⟩ ⟨aureomycin may exert a ~ action on some vitamins⟩

syn SPARING, FRUGAL, THRIFTY, and ECONOMICAL can mean, in common, tending to save or make unwasteful use of one's money, goods, or resources. SPARING suggests abstention and restraint and can apply to the use of anything, although commonly applying to the use of money or goods ⟨the *sparing* use of words⟩ ⟨*sparing* in all matters of household expense⟩ FRUGAL suggests the absence of all luxury and implies simplicity and temperance ⟨Roman life was a *frugal* thing, sparing in food, temperate in drink, modest in clothing, cleanly in habit —John Buchan⟩ ⟨was *frugal* and he did not, like many of the villagers, spend his money freely at gambling or on foods too delicate for them —Pearl Buck⟩ THRIFTY implies a minimum wastefulness and often a maximum of saving, and usu. suggests industry and frugality ⟨a miserly man who hoards money out of avarice and a *thrifty* man who saves money out of prudence —William Empson⟩ ⟨a *thrifty* people — *thrifty* of property, of speech, of their emotions above all —H.S.Commager⟩ ECONOMICAL, often interchangeable with *thrifty* when the sparing use of money or resources is involved, more distinctly emphasizes prudent management or use of things to their best advantage ⟨an *economical* housewife⟩ ⟨*economical* methods of using building materials⟩ ⟨the *economical* use of words⟩

spar·ing·ly *adv* [ME, fr. *sparing* + *-ly*] **1 :** in a sparing manner **:** MEAGERLY, SCANTILY ⟨~ seasoned food⟩ ⟨~ soluble in water⟩ **2 :** with restraint **:** INFREQUENTLY

spar·ing·ness *n* -ES **:** the quality or state of being sparing

[1]**spark** \'spärk, -påk\ *n* -S [ME *sperke, sparke*, fr. OE *spearca, spærca;* akin to MD & MLG *sparke* spark, L *spargere* to scatter, strew, Gk *spargan* to swell, Skt *sphūrjati* it bursts forth, appears] **1 a :** a small particle of a burning substance thrown out by a body in combustion or remaining when combustion is nearly completed ⟨~*s* from a fire⟩ **b :** a hot glowing particle heated by friction and struck out at the impact of two hard objects (as flint and steel) **2 a :** a luminous disruptive electrical discharge of very short duration between two conductors separated by air or other gas **b :** a small arc of short duration (as often at dynamo brushes) **c :** the discharge in a spark plug **d :** the mechanism (as a button or lever) controlling the discharge in a spark plug **3 a :** a very small glittering body or surface or a transient flash of reflected light **:** SPARKLE **b :** a very small gem **:** SPARKLER; *specif* **:** DIAMOND **4 :** something that ignites or sets off an explosion, conflagration, or other manifestation of suddenly released force ⟨~ that set off the rebellion⟩ **5 :** a latent particle or vestige of some quality or capability having possibilities of growth or development **:** GERM ⟨discern the ~ of promise . . . the barb of fruitful controversy —August Fruge⟩ ⟨a ~ of decency still remained in him⟩ ⟨lacking the least ~ of wit or grace⟩ ⟨vital ~ in a man that makes him an artist —Philip Mason⟩ **6 sparks** *pl but sing in constr* **:** a radio operator on a ship **7 :** SPARK TRANSMITTER **8 :** a person interested in fires and fire fighting **:** BUFF 7a **9 :** GERANIUM LAKE 2

[2]**spark** \"\ *vb* -ED/-ING/-S [ME *sparken;* akin to MD & MLG *sparken* to spark, sparkle, OE *spearca* spark — more at [1]SPARK] *vi* **1 a :** to throw out sparks **:** SPARKLE ⟨the damp wood crackled and ~*ed*⟩ ⟨her eyes ~*ing* with fury⟩ **b :** to flash out or fall like sparks ⟨fireflies ~*ing* in the gathering darkness⟩ **2 :** to produce sparks **:** convert electrical energy into light and heat by ionization of the air or gas that separates the electrodes (as of a dynamo or a spark plug) **3 :** to respond with enthusiasm or ready acceptance ⟨~*ed* to the idea of an early wedding date⟩ **~** *vt* **1 :** to set off in a burst of activity **:** ACTIVATE ⟨these kindred spirits, articulate men with hair-trigger minds, ~ the president's thinking —Raymond Clapper⟩ **2 :** to stir into intense or sustained activity **:** inspire with zeal and energy **:** INCITE, STIMULATE ⟨a player ~*s* his team to victory⟩ ⟨his hit ~*ed* a rally that brought in four runs⟩ ⟨the discovery ~*ed* the police to fresh activity⟩ **3** *chiefly Scot* **:** SPATTER, SOIL

[3]**spark** \"\ *adj* [[1]*spark*] **:** of or relating to radio communication carried on with a spark transmitter ⟨~ set⟩ ⟨~ station⟩

[4]**spark** \"\ *n* -S [perh. of Scand origin; akin to ON *sparkr* lively, sprightly; perh. akin to OE *spearca* spark — more at SPARK] **1 :** a young, beautiful, witty woman **2 a :** a brisk showy gay man **:** BLADE, GALLANT **b :** a hot-tempered person **3 :** LOVER, BEAU

[5]**spark** \"\ *vb* -ED/-ING/-S *vt* **1** *obs* **:** show off — used with *it* **2 :** WOO, COURT ⟨the railroad didn't pay him to ~ a girl on its time —T.W.Duncan⟩ **~** *vi* **:** to engage in courting **:** go together as sweethearts

spark advance *n* **:** [2]LEAD 3d(2)

spark arrester *n* **1 :** a device for preventing the escape of sparks from a smokestack; *esp* **:** a framework of wire in the smokebox of a steam locomotive to arrest the escape of cinders **2 :** a device to minimize or prevent electric sparking at a place where a circuit is made and broken

sparkback *or* **sparked-back** \'=,=\ *n* **:** TURNSTONE

spark coil *n* **:** an induction coil for producing the spark for an internal-combustion engine

spark discharge *n* **:** an electric discharge accompanied by a spark **:** a disruptive discharge

sparked \'spärkəd, -påk-\ *adj* [obs. *spark* speck (fr. [1]*spark*) + *-ed*] *dial* **:** SPOTTED, STREAKED, VARIEGATED

spark·er \-kə(r)\ *n* -S **1 :** a small firework that gives out sparks **2 :** BEAU, LOVER **3** *Brit* **:** a ship's radio operator **4 :** IGNITER b

spark frequency *n* **:** the number of spark discharges per second in a radio transmitter

spark gap *n* **1 :** a space between two high-potential terminals (as of an induction coil) through which pass disruptive discharges of electricity in the form of sparks — see LIGHTNING ARRESTER illustration, SPARK PLUG illustration **2 :** a device consisting of two electrodes arranged to permit passage between them of disruptive discharges in the form of sparks

spark generator *n* **:** a generator of electric oscillations that utilizes the discharge of a condenser through a spark gap as the source of its alternating-current power

sparkier *comparative of* SPARKY

sparkiest *superlative of* SPARKY

spark·i·ness \-kēnəs, -kin-\ *n* -ES **1 :** the quality or condition of sparkling or of sending out sparks **:** LIVELINESS, VIVACIOUSNESS **2 :** the quality of being mottled or variegated

sparking lamp *n* **:** a small open oil lamp with floating wick

sparking plug *n, Brit* **:** SPARK PLUG

spark·ish \-kish\ *adj* [[4]*spark* + *-ish*] **1 :** like a gallant or beau **:** GAY **2 :** gaily dressed **:** SHOWY, DAPPER — **spark·ish·ly** *adv* — **spark·ish·ness** *n* -ES

spark knock *n* **:** the sound produced in an internal-combustion engine by operation with the spark too far advanced

[1]**spar·kle** \'spärkəl, -påk-\ *vb* **sparkled; sparkled; sparkling** \-k(ə)liŋ\ **sparkles** [ME *sparklen*, freq. of *sparken* to spark — more at SPARK] *vi* **1 a :** to throw out sparks **b :** to shine as if throwing out sparks **:** emit small flashes of light **:** SCINTILLATE, FLASH, GLISTEN ⟨dewdrops ~ in the morning sun⟩ **c :** to perform brilliantly ⟨the team hit well and *sparkled* in the field⟩ **2 :** to effervesce with bubbles of released carbon dioxide ⟨wine that ~*s*⟩ **3 :** to become lively or animated **:** show spirit and fire ⟨her eyes *sparkled* with anger⟩ ⟨the dialogue ~*s* with wit⟩ **~** *vt* **1 :** to cause to glitter or shine ⟨the sun *sparkled* wet grass⟩ **2 :** to show by or as if by flashes of light ⟨her eyes *sparkled* her pleasure at the compliment⟩

[2]**sparkle** \"\ *n* -S [ME, dim. of *sparke* spark — more at SPARK] **1 :** a little spark **:** SCINTILLATION **2 :** the quality of sending out or reflecting flashes of brilliant light ⟨~ of a diamond⟩ ⟨~ of the dancing waves⟩ **3 :** a slight trace **:** SHOWING ⟨now showed only an occasional ~ of his former high spirits⟩ **4 a :** ANIMATION, LIVELINESS, VIVACITY ⟨natural ~ animates her dialogue —*Current Biog.*⟩ **b :** EFFERVESCENCE **5 :** a small brilliant gem

[3]**sparkle** \"\ *vb* -ED/-ING/-S [ME *sparklen*, prob. alter. of *sparplen* — more at SPARPLE] *archaic* **:** DISPERSE, SCATTER

spark lead \'=,lēd\ *n* **:** the amount of advance by which the production of the spark in the cylinders of an internal-combustion engine precedes the arrival of the piston at the top dead center position

spar·kle·ber·ry \'spärkəl, -påk- —*see* BERRY\ *n* [prob. by alter.] **:** FARKLEBERRY

sparkle metal *n* **:** matte containing 74 percent copper

spar·kler \-k(ə)lə(r)\ *n* -S **:** one that sparkles: as **a :** DIAMOND **b :** a bright witty vivacious person **c :** a brilliant performer **d :** a firework that throws off brilliant sparks on burning **e :** a toy gun or pistol that produces sparks when the trigger is pulled

spark·less \'spärkləs, -påk-\ *adj* **:** producing no sparks ⟨~ electric switch⟩ — **spark·less·ly** *adv*

spark·let \-lət\ *n* -S **1 :** a small spark **:** a tiny point of light **2 :** a small sparkling or glittering object ⟨gown adorned with glass ~*s*⟩ **:** a small spot that is relatively bright against a dark background

spark lever *n* **:** a lever formerly mounted usu. on the steering post of a motor vehicle for controlling the timing of the ignition

sparkling *adj* [ME, fr. pres. part. of *sparklen* to sparkle — more at SPARKLE] **1 a :** having luster or sparkle **:** SHINING, GLISTENING **b :** reflecting brilliant flashes or points of light ⟨~ ice⟩ **2 a :** BRILLIANT, DAZZLING ⟨~ performance of a piano piece⟩ **b :** ANIMATED, LIVELY ⟨~ conversation⟩ **3 :** EFFERVESCENT; *specif* **:** bubbling due to escaping carbon dioxide gas — opposed to *still* ⟨~ Burgundy⟩ — **spar·kling·ly** *adv* — **spar·kling·ness** *n* -ES

sparkling water *n* **:** SODA WATER 2a

sparkling wine *n* **:** an effervescent table wine usu. white but occas. red containing on the average 12 percent alcohol by volume and carbonated by secondary fermentation — compare CHAMPAGNE, DESSERT WINE, TABLE WINE

spar·kly \-k(ə)lē, -li\ *adj* [[1]*sparkle* + *-y*] **:** tending to sparkle ⟨~ white teeth⟩

sparkover \'=,==\ *n* -S [fr. *spark over*, v.] **:** a disruptive electric discharge; *esp* **:** an undesired sparking (as in charging a Leyden jar) between two conductors ⟨high-voltage generator operating in a pressure chamber to prevent electrical ~ —*Science*⟩ ⟨~ potential⟩

spark photography *n* **:** photography in which an electric spark discharge provides the only illumination and which is used esp. for photographing rapidly moving objects

spark plug *n* **1 :** a part that fits into the cylinder head of an internal-combustion engine and carries two electrodes separated by an air gap across which the current from the ignition system discharges to form the spark for combustion **2 :** one that initiates, affords the impetus to, or is the most effective or dynamic force in an undertaking or work **:** PRIME MOVER, MAINSPRING ⟨supervisors are the *spark plugs* in any program of vocational education —E.A.Lee⟩ ⟨his responsibility to act as *spark plug* when his team is in the field —C.F.Stubblefield⟩ ⟨the profit motive as a *spark plug* of progress —S.T.Williamson⟩

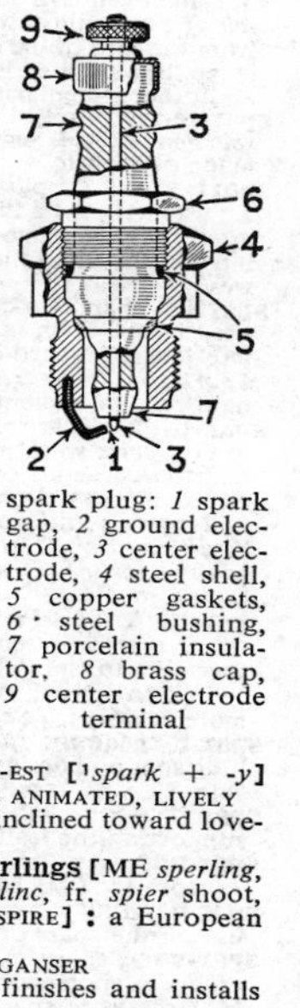

spark plug: *1* spark gap, *2* ground electrode, *3* center electrode, *4* steel shell, *5* copper gaskets, *6* steel bushing, *7* porcelain insulator, *8* brass cap, *9* center electrode terminal

sparkplug \'=,=\ *vt* [*spark plug*] **:** to initiate, give the impetus to, or play the chief role in (an undertaking) ⟨*sparkplugged* the new industrial and economic revolution —F.G.Slaughter⟩ ⟨*sparkplugging* their activities has been a group of dedicated physicians —Milton Silverman⟩

sparkproof \'=¦=\ *adj* **:** SPARKLESS

sparks *pl of* SPARK, *pres 3d sing of* SPARK

spark spectrum *n* **:** the spectrum of a substance (as a metal) produced by using light from sparks passing between electrodes composed of that substance — compare ARC SPECTRUM

spark transmitter *n* **:** a radio transmitting set using a spark generator

[1]**sparky** \'spärkē, -påk-, -ki\ *adj* -ER/-EST [[1]*spark* + *-y*] **1 :** showing or throwing out sparks **2 :** ANIMATED, LIVELY

[2]**sparky** \"\ *adj* -ER/-EST [[5]*spark* + *-y*] **:** inclined toward lovemaking or courting

spar·ling \'spärliŋ\ *n, pl* **sparling** *or* **sparlings** [ME *sperling*, fr. MF *esperling, esperlan*, fr. MD *spierlinc*, fr. *spier* shoot, blade of grass + *-linc* -ling — more at SPIRE] **:** a European smelt (*Osmerus eperlanus*)

sparling fowl *n* [*sparling*] *dial Eng* **:** MERGANSER

sparmaker \'=,==\ *n* **:** a carpenter who finishes and installs spars, masts, and cargo booms

spar·man·nia \spär'manēə\ *n, cap* [NL, fr. Andreas *Sparmann* †1820 Swed. naturalist + NL *-ia*] **:** a small genus of African shrubs or trees (family Tiliaceae) having cordate more or less lobed leaves and silky white flowers with imperfect outer stamens succeeded by echinate capsules — see AFRICAN HEMP

sparmate \'=,=\ *n* [[5]*spar* + *mate*] **:** SPARRING PARTNER

[1]**spar·oid** \'spa(a),ròid\ *adj* [NL *Sparus* + E *-oid*] **:** resembling or related to the Sparidae

[2]**sparoid** \"\ *n* -S **:** a sparoid fish

spar·ple \'spärpəl\ *vb* -ED/-ING/-S [ME *sparplen, sparpillen*, fr. MF *esparpeillier, esparpillier*, fr. (assumed) VL *sparpiliare*, perh. blend of L *spargere* to scatter, strew, sprinkle and *papilio* butterfly — more at SPARK, PAVILION] *archaic* **:** SCATTER, DISPERSE, ROUT, DISSEMINATE

sparred *adj* **:** made of or equipped with spars set at intervals

[1]**spar·ring** \'späriŋ, -pår-, -rēŋ\ *n* -S [ME, fr. *sparre* spar + *-ing*] **:** fore-and-aft battens secured to the reverse frames of a ship for cargo to rest against

[2]**sparring** \"\ *n* -S [fr. gerund of [4]*spar*] **1 :** scientific boxing **2 :** a skirmishing for advantage; *esp* **:** ARGUMENT, DISPUTE

sparring partner *n* **1 :** a boxer's companion for practice in sparring during training **2 :** one's mate in amicable wrangling or debating **:** a protagonist with whom to sharpen one's wits in argument

spar·row \'spa|(,)rō, |,rə; |,rəw, |,rō+V; *also* 'spe|\ *n* -S [ME *sparwe, sparowe, sparow*, fr. OE *spearwa;* akin to OHG *sparo* sparrow, ON *spörr*, Goth *sparwa* sparrow, Corn *frau* crow, Gk *sparasion*, a bird resembling a sparrow, *psar* starling, OPruss *spurglis* sparrow] **1 :** HOUSE SPARROW; *broadly* **:** any of various related birds of the genus *Passer* **2 :** any of numerous finches resembling the house sparrow in size and shape and in having

plumage streaked with brown or gray — see CHIPPING SPARROW, FIELD SPARROW, HEDGE SPARROW, SAGE SPARROW, SAVANNAH SPARROW, SONG SPARROW, TREE SPARROW **3** : MOUSE GRAY **4 a** : an undersized person **b** : one who is aggressively active and markedly self-reliant temperament

sparrowbill \'٭٭,٭\ *n* : SPARABLE

spar-row-grass \'٭٭٭,gras, -grəs\ *n* [by folk etymology fr. *sparagus*] *chiefly dial* : ASPARAGUS

sparrow hawk *n* [ME *sparowhauk*, fr. *sparowe*, *sparowe*, *sparow* + *hauk* hawk] **1 a** : a small Old World hawk (*Accipiter nisus*) similar in habits, size, and general coloration to the American sharp-shinned hawk **2 a** : a small No. American falcon (*Falco sparverius*) that is closely related to the European kestrel, is chiefly rufous and slaty blue above and buffy white with dark markings below, and feeds mostly on live insects (as grasshoppers) **3** : any of various hawks or falcons of small size: as **a** : PIGEON HAWK **b** : BUSH HAWK **4** : a small anvil used by silversmiths

spar-row-ish \'٭٭٭əwish\ *adj* : resembling or suggesting a sparrow — **spar-row-ish-ness** *n* -ES

sparrowlike \'٭٭٭,٭\ *adj* : resembling a sparrow

sparrow owl *n* **1** : PYGMY OWL **2** : LITTLE OWL

sparrow-tail *also* **sparrow-tailed** \'٭٭٭,٭\ *adj* : SWALLOW-TAILED

spar-rowy \'٭٭wē, -rōi, |i\ *adj* **1** : frequented by sparrows : infested with sparrows **2** : resembling a sparrow : SPARROWLIKE

spar-ry \'spär‿, -pär-, -ri\ *adj* [⁶spar + -y] : resembling, consisting of, or abounding with spar : SPATHIC (~ lode) (~ luster)

sparry iron *n* : SIDERITE

sparry limestone *n* : a coarsely crystalline marble

spars *pl of* SPAR, *pres 3d sing of* SPAR

¹sparse *vt* [L *sparsus*, past part. of *spargere* — more at SPARK] *obs* : SCATTER, DISPERSE, DISTRIBUTE

²sparse \'spärs, -pàs\ *adv* [L *sparsus*, past part.] : SPARSELY, THINLY

³sparse *also* **sparce** \"٭\ *adj* -ER/-EST [L *sparsus*, past part.] **1** : of few and scattered elements : having spaces between the component units : not thickly grown or settled : thinly scattered ⟨~ beard⟩ ⟨~ population⟩ ⟨~ shade of one willow tree —Eudora Welty⟩ *syn* see MEAGER

sparse-ly *adv* : in a sparse manner : SCANTILY, THINLY ⟨~ inhabited country⟩

sparse-ness *n* -ES : the quality or state of being sparse

spar-si-ty *also* **spar-ci-ty** \'spärsəd‿ē, -pàs-, -ətē, -i\ *n* -ES : the state of being sparse : SCANTINESS (~ of vegetation)

¹spar-tan \'spärt‿n, -pàt-\ *n* -S [ME, fr. L *Spartanus*, adj. & n., fr. *Sparta*, city in ancient Greece (fr. Gk *Sparta*, *Spartē*) + L *-anus* -an] **1** *cap* : a native or inhabitant of ancient Sparta **2** *usu cap* : a person of great courage and fortitude

²spartan \"٭\ *adj, usu cap* [L *Spartanus*] **1** : of or relating to Sparta in ancient Greece **2** : marked by simplicity, frugality, avoidance of comfort and luxury, strict self-discipline, severity of manner, brevity in speech, hardihood in the face of pain or danger ⟨love their homes and often derive a kind of *Spartan* satisfaction from running them —A.C.Spectorsky⟩ ⟨lived with *Spartan* simplicity ... eating frugal meals of farm produce and sleeping in a camp bed —N.Y.Times⟩ ⟨neat and *Spartan* look of military posts all over the world —Henriette Roosenburg⟩

spar-tan-ic \(')spär'tanik\ *adj, usu cap* [L *Spartanus* + E -ic] : SPARTAN — **spar-tan-i-cal-ly** \-nək(ə)lē\ *adv, usu cap*

spar-tan-ism \'spärt‿n,izəm, -pàt-\ *n* -s *usu cap* : the moral quality or traits ascribed to the ancient Spartans : austerity in mode of living or in self-discipline : indomitableness or endurance esp. under great stress; *also* : conduct characteristic of such moral quality or traits

spar-tan-ize \-‿n,īz\ *vb* -ED/-ING/-s *often cap* (¹*Spartan* + -ize] *vt* : to make Spartan in character : imbue with Spartan ideals ⟨tried to ~ his whole household⟩ ~ *vi* : to become Spartan in character : live in a Spartan manner

spar-tan-ly *adv, usu cap* : in a Spartan manner : with unflinching courage : with uncomplaining endurance of pain

spar-te-ine \'spärd‿ē,ēn, -,ē-ēn\ *n* -s [ISV *spart-* (fr. NL *Spartium* genus of shrubs, fr. L *spartum* broom + NL -*ium*) + -*eine*] : a liquid tetracyclic alkaloid $C_{15}H_{26}N_2$ obtained esp. from the tops of the common broom and used in the form of its crystalline sulfate esp. formerly in the treatment of tachycardia and other irregularities of the heart

spar-te-rie \'spärd‿ərē\ *n* -s [F, fr. *sparte* esparto (fr. L *spartum*) + -*erie* -ery — more at ESPARTO] : a fabric or articles made of esparto

spart grass \'spärt-\ *n* [L *spartum* — more at ESPARTO] **1** : ESPARTO **2** : a tall rather broad-leaved cordgrass (*Spartina alterniflora*) common in salt marshes of the eastern U.S. and introduced along the European coast and in the Pacific northwest

sparth \'spärth\ *n* -s [ME *sparthe*, fr. ON *spartha*] : a battle-ax used by the Irish in the middle ages

spar-ti-ate \'spärd‿ē,āt, -rshē-\ *n* -s *cap* [L *Spartiatēs*, fr. Gk *Spartiatēs*, fr. *Sparta*, *Spartē* Sparta] : a member of the dominant race of ancient Laconia : SPARTAN

spar-ti-na \'spärt‿nə\ *n* [NL, fr. Gk *spartinē* rope, cord; akin to Gk *speira* spiral — more at SPIRE] **1** *cap* : a small but widely distributed genus of grasses occurring chiefly in salt marshes along the coastal regions of Europe and No. and So. America and having stiff culms, panicled spikelets, and flowers with three glumes **2** *also* **spartina grass** -s : any grass of the genus *Spartina* — called also *cord grass*; see MARSH GRASS, SALT GRASS

spar-tle \'spärt‿l\ *vi* -ED/-ING/-s [D *spartelen*, fr. MD *spartelen*, *spertelen*, *sportelen*; akin to MLG *sparteln*, *sportelen*, *spertelen* to sprawl, thrash about, OHG *sprazzalōn*, Norw *spratla* to sprawl, thrash about, OHG *sprinzan* to jump up — more at SPRINT] *Scot* : to kick about : SPRAWL

spar torpedo *n* : an explosive charge mounted on the end of a long spar and designed to be carried to a target by an attacking ship

spar tree *n* : a tall tree trimmed and well-guyed and used for supporting the lead blocks for high-line logging

spar-us \'spa(a)rəs\ *n, cap* [NL, fr. L gilthead, fr. Gk *sparos* — more at SPEAR] : the type genus of the family Sparidae

spar varnish *n* : an exterior waterproof varnish suitable for use on the spars of ships

spar-ver \'spärvər\ *n* -s [ME *sperver*, *sparver*, fr. MF *espervier*, *esprevier* sparrow hawk, canopy bed, of Gmc origin; akin to MD *sperware* sparrow hawk, MLG *sparwer*, *sperwer*, OHG *sparwāri*] all fr. a prehistoric OHG-MD-MLG compound whose first element is represented by OHG *sparo* sparrow, and whose second element is represented by OHG *aro* eagle, altered under the influence of the suffix represented by OHG *-āri* -er — more at SPARROW, ERNE] *obs* : the canopy of a bed

spas *pl of* SPA

spasm \'spazəm\ *n* -s [ME *spasme*, fr. MF, fr. L *spasmus*, fr. Gk *spasmos*, fr. *span* to draw, pull, tear — more at SPAN] **1** : an involuntary and abnormal contraction of muscle or muscle fibers or of a hollow organ (as an artery, the colon, the esophagus) that consists largely of involuntary muscle fibers — compare CLONUS, TONUS **2** : a sudden violent and temporary activity, effort, or emotion : BURST, FIT ⟨a ~ of antagonism⟩ ⟨a ~ of economy⟩ ⟨a ~ of fear⟩ ⟨a ~ of grief⟩ ⟨a ~ of indignation⟩ ⟨a ~ of loneliness⟩ ⟨a ~ of nervousness⟩ ⟨a ~ of despair⟩

spas-mat-ic \(')spaz'mad‿ik\ *or* **spas-mat-i-cal** \-d‿əkəl\ *adj* [Gk *spasmat-*, *spasma* spasm (fr. *span* to draw, pull, tear) + E -ic, -ical] : SPASMODIC

spasm band *n* : a jazz band originating during the ragtime period, using chiefly improvised instruments (as cowbells, jug, kazoo), and later being composed primarily of youths performing esp. in the street

spasmed \'spazəmd\ *adj* : afflicted with spasms : marked by spasms

spas-mic \'spazmik\ *adj* : marked by spasms : SPASMODIC

spas-mod-ic \(')spaz'mädik, -dēk\ *or* **spas-mod-i-cal** \-dikəl, -dēk-\ *adj* [NL *spasmodicus*, fr. Gk *spasmōdēs* spasmodic (fr. *spasmos* spasm) + L -*icus* -ical] **1 a** : of, relating to, affected or characterized by a spasm **b** : resembling a spasm in being sudden and violent ⟨his body gave a ~ jerk forward —Anthony Trollope⟩ ⟨clutched at the doctor's hand with a ~ movement of despair —W.H.Wright⟩ **2** : act-

ing or proceeding fitfully or intermittently : lacking continuity of effort, production, or activity : INTERMITTENT ⟨a continuous discussion of international affairs, not a ~ action at times of crisis —Clement Attlee⟩ ⟨growth of the towns was —*Amer. Guide Series: Mass.*⟩ ⟨streamlining ... may prove chronic or ~ —C.C.Furnas⟩ **3** : subject to outbursts of emotional excitement — **spas-mod-i-cal-ly** \-dək(ə)lē, -dēk-, -li\ *adv*

spas-mo-dism \'spazmə,dizəm\ *n* -s [*spasmodic* + -ism] : spasmodic emotion

spas-mo-dist \-‿dəst\ *n* -s [*spasmodic* + -ist] : one that is spasmodic in word or manner

spas-mo-gen-ic \,spazmə'jenik\ *adj* [ISV *spasm* + -o- + -*genic*] : inducing spasm ⟨a ~ drug⟩

spas-mol-y-sis \spaz'mäləsəs\ *n, pl* **spasmoly-ses** \-lə,sēz\ [NL, fr. L *spasmus* spasm + NL -o- + -*lysis*] : the relaxation of muscle spasm

spas-mo-lyt-ic \,spazmə'lid‿ik\ *adj* [ISV, fr. NL *spasmolysis*, after such pairs as NL *hypnosis*: E *hypnotic*] : tending or having the power to relieve spasms or convulsions

¹spasmolytic \"٭\ *n* -s : a spasmolytic agent

spas-mo-neme \'spazmə,nēm\ *n* -s [*spasm* + -o- + -*neme*] : a contractile filament (as in various stalked protozoans)

spas-mo-phil-ia \,spazmə'filēə\ *n* -s [NL, fr. L *spasmus* spasm + NL -o- + -*philia*] : an abnormal tendency to convulsions, tetany, or spasms from even slight mechanical or electrical stimulation

spas-mo-phil-ic \,٭٭٭'filik\ *or* **spas-mo-phile** \'٭٭٭fīl\ *adj* [*spasm* + -o- + -*philic* or -*phile*] : of, relating to, or affected by spasmophilia

¹spas-tic \'spastik, -paas-, -pais-, -tēk\ *adj* [L *spasticus*, fr. Gk *spastikos* drawing, fr. (assumed) *spastos*, verbal of *span* to draw + -*ikos* -ic — more at SPAN] **1 a** : of, relating to, or characterized by spasm ⟨~ colon⟩ **b** : suffering from spastic paralysis ⟨~ child⟩ **2** : characterized by spasms esp. of movement or activity : SPASMODIC ⟨a ~ motion of alternate digging and ducking —Van Van Praag⟩

²spastic \"٭\ *n* -s : one suffering from spastic paralysis

spas-ti-cal-ly \-tək(ə)lē, -tēk-, -li\ *adv* : in a spastic manner ⟨the ~ gyrating performers —*Time*⟩

spas-tic-i-ty \٭'stisəd‿ē, -ətē, -i\ *n* -ES : the state of being spastic

spastic paralysis *n* : paralysis marked by tonic spasm of the muscles affected and by increased tendon reflexes — compare CEREBRAL PALSY

¹spat [ME *spatte* (past of *speten* to spit), fr. OE *spǣte*, past of *spǣtan* to spit; akin to OE (northern dial.) *spittan* to spit] *pas of* SPIT

²spat \'spat, *usu* -ad-+V\ *n, pl* **spat** *or* **spats** [origin unknown] **1** : a young oyster or other bivalve mollusk either before or after it first becomes adherent **2** : young oysters collectively ⟨he was in Paris ... still ~, still wearing his cutaway —Djuna Barnes⟩

³spat \"٭\ *vi* **spatted**; **spatted**; **spatting**; **spats** **1** : to emit spawn ⟨oysters ~⟩ **2** : to become permanently attached to some solid object — used of a mollusk and esp. of an oyster

⁴spat \"٭\ *n* -s [short for *spatterdash*] **1** : a covering for the instep and ankle usu. made of cloth or leather with a side closing and a strap under the instep and worn for protection or appearance — usu. used in pl. ⟨dressed in ~s, cutaway, and silk hat⟩ **2** : a fairing around the wheel of a fixed airplane landing gear

⁵spat \"٭\ *n* -s [prob. of imit. origin] **1 a** : a usu. petty quarrel that flares up quickly and is of short duration **2** *chiefly dial* : a quick sharp blow : SLAP **3 a** : something that spatters : a light splash ⟨a ~ of rain⟩ ⟨~s of mud⟩ **b** : a sound like that of rain falling in large drops ⟨the ~ of bullets against a stone wall⟩ *syn* see QUARREL

spats 1

⁶spat \"٭\ *vb* **spatted**; **spatted**; **spatting**; **spats** [prob. of imit. origin] *vi* **1** *chiefly dial* : SLAP **b** : to clap together (as the hands) **2** : to strike with a sound like that of rain falling in large drops ⟨bullets ... *spatting* the leaves —J.H.Stuart⟩ **b** : to quarrel usu. pettily or briefly and repeatedly ⟨a teen-ager *spatting* with her mother⟩ **2** : to strike or fall and strike with a sound like that of rain falling in large drops ⟨bullets were *spatting* down —R.H.Newman⟩

¹spa-tan-gid \spə'tanjəd\ *or* **spat-an-goid** \'spat‿n,gòid, spə'tan,gòid\ *or* **spat-an-goi-de-an** \,spat‿n'gòidēən\ *adj* [*spatangid* fr. NL *Spatangida*; *spatangoid* fr. NL *Spatangoida*; *spatangoidean* fr. NL *Spatangoida* + E -*ean*] : of or relating to the Spatangina

²spatangid \"٭\ *or* **spatangoid** \"٭\ *or* **spatangoidean** \"٭\ *n* -s : a sea urchin of the suborder Spatangina : HEART URCHIN

spa-tan-gi-da \spə'tanjədə\ *or* **spat-an-goi-da** \,spat‿n,gòidə\ *or* **spat-an-goi-dea** \-dēə\ *n pl, cap* [NL, fr. *Spatangus* + -*ida* or -*oida* or -*oidea*] *syn of* SPATANGINA

spat-an-gi-na \,spat‿n'jinə, -jēnə\ *n, pl, cap* [NL, fr. *Spatangus* + -*ina*] : a suborder of sea urchins (order Exocycloida) comprising numerous more or less flattened approximately heart-shaped sea urchins that exhibit considerable secondary bilateral symmetry — compare CLYPEASTRINA

spa-tan-gus \spə'tangəs\ *n, cap* [NL, fr. Gk *spatangēs*, a kind of sea urchin] : an ill-defined genus (the type of the family Spatangidae) of sea urchins including many of the commonest and best-known heart urchins

¹spatch-cock \'spach,käk\ *n* -s [prob. alter. of *spitchcock*] : a fowl split and grilled usu. immediately after being killed and dressed

²spatchcock \"٭\ *vt* -ED/-ING/-s **1** : to prepare (as a fowl) for eating or as if a spatchcock **2** : to introduce by or as if by interpolation or insertion ⟨task of attempting to ~ the new evidence into an existing framework —*Times Lit. Supp.*⟩ ⟨all the random majesty of the place appeared ~ed, rectified, and jumbled —John Cheever⟩

¹spate \'spāt, *usu* -ād-+V\ *n* -s [ME] **1** : FRESHET, FLOOD ⟨every waterfall roars in ~ —E.J.Moran⟩ ⟨an Arkansas River ~ —S.H.Adams⟩ ⟨a migration into the valley that continued in full ~ beyond the middle of the century —*Amer. Guide Series: Va.*⟩ **2** *chiefly Scot* : a sudden heavy rainstorm **3 a** : a large number or amount ⟨a ~ of books on gardening⟩ ⟨a ~ of cowboy movies⟩ ⟨a ~ of publicity⟩ **b** : a sudden or strong outburst : RUSH ⟨a ~ of anger⟩ ⟨a ~ of words⟩

²spate \"٭\ *vt* -ED/-ING/-s *chiefly Scot* : FLOOD

spat-fall \'٭‿,٭\ *n* [²*spat* + *fall*] : the settling and attachment of young bivalves (as oysters or mussels) to the substrate

spath \'spath, 'sh)pàt\ *n* -s [G *spat* (formerly spelled *spath*), fr. MHG *spat*, *spāt*; akin to OHG *spān* chip, thin slab of wood — more at SPOON] *archaic* : ⁶SPAR

spa-tha \'spathə, -pàthə\ *n, pl* **spathae** \-,thē, -,thī\ [L, fr. Gk *spathē* blade — more at SPADE] **1** : a broadsword with blunt point used by the ancient Greeks and Romans **2** : a long heavy sword used by Britons, Saxons, and Normans

spa-tha-ceous \spə'thāshəs, (')spà'th-, spà'th-, (')spà'th-\ *adj* [NL *spathaceus*] : having a spathe : resembling a spathe

spath-al \'spathəl, -th-\ *adj* [*spathe* + -al] : SPATHACEOUS

spathe \'spāth, -th\ *n* -s [NL *spatha*, fr. L, broadsword, fr. Gk *spathē* blade — more at SPADE] : a sheathing bract or pair of bracts subtending or enclosing an inflorescence on the same axis exhibiting much variation in form and coloring, and occurring typically in plants whose inflorescence is a spadix or in modified form in many monocotyledonous plants (as the irises)

spathed \-āthd, -atht\ *adj* : having a spathe

spath-ic \'spathik\ *adj* [*spath* + -ic] : resembling spar : FOLIATED, LAMELLAR, SPATHOSE

spathic iron *or* **spathic iron ore** *n* : SIDERITE

spathi-flo-rae \,spatho'flòr,ē, -pàth-,path-ī\ *n pl, cap* [NL, fr. *spatha* + -*i*- + -*florae* (fr. LL, fem. pl. of -*florus* -florous)] *syn of* ARALES

spa-tho-dea \spā'thōdēə, spà'th-,spa'th-\ *n* [NL, fr. *spatha* + -*odea*] **1** *cap* : a genus of tropical African evergreen trees (family Bignoniaceae) used as ornamentals in tropical and

subtropical regions and having large odd-pinnate or ternate leaves and showy orange or scarlet flowers in terminal panicles or racemes **2** *also* **spa-tho-dia** \"٭\ -s : any plant of the genus *Spathodea*

¹spath-ose \'spa,thōs\ *adj* [*spath* + -*ose*] : SPATHIC

²spath-ose \'spà,thōs, -thōs\ *also* **spath-ous** \-ّ‿thəs, -thəs\ *adj* [*spathe* + -*ose* or -*ous*] : SPATHACEOUS

spath-u-late \'spathyə,lāt, -ّ,lāt\ *adj* [LL *spathula*, *spatula* + E -*ate* — more at EPAULET] : SPATULATE (~ petals of a flower)

spa-tial *or* **spa-cial** \'spāshəl\ *adj* [*spatial* fr. L *spatium* space + E -*al*; *spacial* alter. of *spatial* — more at SPEED] **1 a** : of or relating to space ⟨~ pioneers will face such problems as ... cosmic radiation —*Time*⟩ ⟨elimination of ~ barriers by speedy transportation and communication —John Dewey⟩ ⟨the changing ~ distribution of our population —Sidney Goldstein⟩ **b** : subject to the conditions of space : limited by space ⟨it is one of the facts of our being that we are temporal and ~ —Norman Kelman⟩ **2** : occupying space : involving relations in space ⟨this ~ theme fulfills an ancient requirement of the art of architecture — namely, to balance artfully the building masses and open spaces —Walter Gropius⟩ — **spa-tial-ly** \-ّələ-,-əli\ *adv*

spatial isomerism *n* : STEREOISOMERISM

spa-ti-al-i-ty \,spāshē'aləd‿ē\ *n* -ES : the quality or state of being spatial — distinguished from *temporality*

spa-tial-iza-tion \,spāshələ'zāshən, -,lī'z-\ *n* -s : the act of spatializing

spa-tial-ize \'٭٭,līz\ *vt* -ED/-ING/-s [*spatial* + -*ize*] : to give spatial form to : think of as spatial or in space relations : localize in space ⟨man ... invented writing to ~, i.e. preserve, language —Susanne K. Langer⟩ ⟨our inveterate cognitive disposition to ~ everything —H.A.Murray⟩

spa-ti-ate \'spāshē,āt\ *vi* -ED/-ING/-s [L *spatiatus*, past part. of *spatiari*, fr. *spatium* space] : ROVE, RAMBLE, STROLL

spatio- *comb form* [L *spatium* — more at SPEED] **1** : space ⟨*spatiography*⟩ **2** : spatial and ⟨*spatiotemporal*⟩

spa-ti-og-ra-phy \,spāshē'ägrəfē\ *n* -ES [*spatio-* + -*graphy*] : a science that deals with space beyond the earth's atmosphere; *esp* : the description of the physical characteristics of the moon and the planets

spa-tio-tem-po-ral \,spāshē(,)ō+\ *adj* [*spatio-* + *temporal*] : having the quality of something that is at once extended and enduring : of or relating to the spatial and temporal together : of space-time ⟨the important elements of experience are ~ relations —M.M.Deems⟩ ⟨the ~ limits within which our reason functions —*Times Lit. Supp.*⟩ — **spa-tio-temporally** \"٭+\ *adv*

spats *pl of* SPAT, *pres 3d sing of* SPAT

spat-ted \'spad‿əd, -atəd\ *adj* [⁴*spat* + -ed] : furnished with or wearing spats ⟨he was in Paris ... still ~, still wearing his cutaway —Djuna Barnes⟩

¹spat-ter \'spad‿ə(r), -atə-\ *vb* -ED/-ING/-s [akin to Fris *spatte*, *spatterje* to spatter, splash, MD *spatten*, Flem *spetteren*] *vt* **1** : to splash with a liquid or with any wet substance : soil by splashing with drops or small portions ⟨~ the floor with grease⟩ **2** : to scatter by splashing : sprinkle around ⟨~ blood⟩ ⟨~ mud on one's clothes⟩ **3** : to cover with or as if with splashes or spots : SPOT ⟨the bare floor ~ed with moonlight —Amy Lowell⟩ ⟨green tweed ~ed with white silk flecks —*New Yorker*⟩ ⟨mistakes and misrepresentations ~ed throughout the whole article —*Times Lit. Supp.*⟩ **4** : to injure by aspersion : DEFAME ⟨as an advocate, he must praise the man whom, a year before, he had ~ed with ignominy —J.A. Froude⟩ ⟨satire ... has an awkward way of ~ing its author —*Listener*⟩ ~ *vi* **1** : to sputter as if ejecting something distasteful : SPLUTTER **2 a** : to jet or spurt forth in scattered drops ⟨by hitting the ferrule of the brush against the opposite wrist and causing dots of color to ~ upon the setting —H.F. Helvenston⟩ ⟨spray from one of the hoses ~ed over the longshoremen —Vernon Pizer⟩ **b** : to drop or fall with or as if with the sound of heavy drops of rain ⟨earth damp and fragrant from the dew which ~s from the overhanging trees —Tom Marvel⟩ ⟨water-stream blows ... and ~s into the basin with a light tinkling —Amy Lowell⟩

²spatter \"٭\ *n* -s **1 a** : the act or process of spattering or the state of being spattered : SPLASHING **b** : SPATTER DASH 2 **c** : the noise of spattering **2 a** : a drop or splash spattered on something : a spot or stain due to spattering ⟨clean mud ~s off clothing⟩ ⟨wipe grease ~s off the wall⟩ **b** : a small number or quantity : SPRINKLE ⟨a ~ of rain⟩ ⟨a ~ of applause⟩ ⟨heavy artillery fire and ~s of infantry raids —*Current History*⟩ ⟨a continual ~ of musketry fire —Kenneth Roberts⟩ **3** *West* : RUDDY DUCK

spatter cone *n* : a miniature volcanic cone on a crater floor or lava flow from which lava is ejected in drops or gobs

spat-ter-dash \"٭\ *n* [¹*spatter* + *dash*] : a usu. knee-high legging worn as a protection from water and mud — usu. used in pl.

spatterdash, 18th century

spatter dash \"٭\ *n* [¹*spatter* + *dash*] **1** : a finish produced on stucco by dashing a very thin mixture of cement and coarse sand against a surface of fresh mortar — called also *roughcast* **2** *usu* **spatter-dash** \"٭\ : a finish produced by spattering paint of a different color on a ground coat

spat-ter-dock \'spad‿ə(r),däk, -atə-\ *n* **1** : the common yellow water lily (*Nuphar advena*) of eastern and central No. America that grows freely in sluggish fresh or sometimes slightly brackish water (as in swamps or about the margin of ponds) **2** : a plant of the genus *Nuphar* — see SOUTHERN SPATTERDOCK

¹spattering *adj* [fr. pres. part. of ¹*spatter*] : that spatters — **spat-ter-ing-ly** *adv*

²spattering *n* -s [fr. gerund of ¹*spatter*] **1** : SPATTER, SPRINKLING ⟨a ~ of freckles across the bridge of her nose —Irwin Shaw⟩ ⟨only a ~ of irregular lights burned in the palace tenements —D.C.Peattie⟩ ⟨a ~ of applause —J.M. Flagler⟩ **2** : a method of painting stage scenery in which paint is spattered onto a surface

spatterware \'٭٭٭,٭\ *n* : earthenware that has spatterwork designs

spatterwork \'٭٭٭,٭\ *n* **1** : a process of reproducing designs by laying them on a surface and spattering the exposed parts with a tinting fluid **2** : a design made by spatterwork

spatting *pres part of* SPAT

spat-tle \'spad‿l\ *n* -s [ME *spatyl*, fr. MF *spatule* — more at SPATULE] **1** : SPATULA **2** : an implement for mottling a molded article with a pigment

spat-u-la \'spachələ\ *n* [LL — more at EPAULET] **1** -s : a flat thin flexible dull-edged usu. metal implement used esp. for scraping or mixing soft substances (as paint, plaster, ointment, frosting), scooping, or lifting (as in removing cookies from a pan) **2** *cap* [NL, fr. LL] : a genus of ducks consisting of the shovelers and often included in *Anas* **3** -s : a spatulate process on the body of an insect

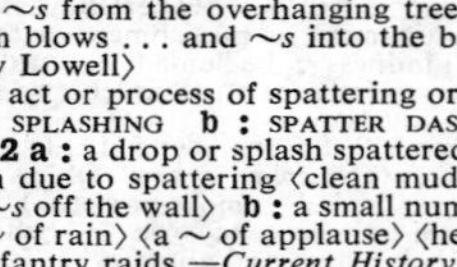

spatulas

spat-u-la-man-cy \-ّ,man(t)s)ē\ *n* -ES [LL *spatula* spatula, shoulder blade + E -*mancy*] : divination by means of an animal's shoulder blade

¹spat-u-late \'spachəlüt, -ّ,lāt\ *adj* [*spatula* + -*ate* (adj. suffix)] **1** : shaped like a spatula : spoon-shaped ⟨spreading her butter on her bread with her broad ~ hand —Jessie Roy⟩ ⟨a ~ leaf⟩ — see LEAF illustration **2** *of a hand* : having fingers shaped like spatulas and a palm either broad at the wrist and narrow at the base of the fingers or narrow at the wrist and broad at the base of the fingers usu. held by palmists to indicate energy, love of action, and independence of spirit

²spat-u-late \-ّ,lāt\ *vt* -ED/-ING/-s [*spatula* + -*ate* (v. suffix)] : to work or treat with a spatula ⟨after the powder has been incorporated in the water, the mass is *spatulated* thoroughly —M.G.Swenson⟩

spat-u-lat-ed \-ّ,lād‿əd\ *adj* [*spatula* + -*ate* + -*ed*] : SPATULATE

spat·u·la·tion \ˌ==ˈlāshən\ *n* -s : the act or process of spatulating or the condition of being spatulate

spat·ule \ˈspa(ˌ)chül\ *n* -s [ME, fr. MF, fr. LL *spatula* — more at SPATULA] **1** : SPATULA **2** : a spatulate organ or part

spat·u·li·form \ˈspachələˌfȯrm\ *adj* [*spatula* + *-iform*] : SPATULATE

spat·u·lose \-ˈspachəˌlōs\ *or* **spat·u·lous** \-_ləs\ *adj* [*spatula* + *-ose* or *-ous*] : SPATULATE

spätzle *var of* SPAETZLE

spaul *obs var of* ¹SPAWL

spauld *also* **spaul** \ˈspōl(d), -pal-\ *n* -s [ME *spalde, spaulde, spald,* fr. (assumed) OF *espalde,* var. of *espaule* — more at EPAULET] **1** *chiefly Scot* : SHOULDER **2** *chiefly Scot* : ¹LIMB 2

spa·vie \ˈspāvi\ *n* [by alter.] *chiefly Scot* : SPAVIN

spa·vied \-vid\ *also* **spa·viet** \-vit\ *adj, chiefly Scot* : SPAVINED

spav·in *also* **spav·ine** \ˈspavən\ *n* -s [ME *spavayne, spaveyne,* fr. MF *esparvain, espavain*] : SWELLING; *esp* : a bony enlargement of the hock of a horse immediately due to strain but associated with a hereditary predisposition

spav·in·dy \-vəndi\ *adj* [*spavined* + *-y*] *Irish* : SPAVINED

spav·ined \-nd\ *adj* [ME *spaveyned,* fr. *spavayne, spaveyne* + *-ed*] **1** : affected with spavin **2** : LAME, MAIMED ⟨broken-winded novels, or ~ verses —O.W.Holmes †1894⟩ ⟨an ancient coach and a string of ~ baggage cars —*Time*⟩ ⟨lawyers pictured him as a sad and ~ man, plagued with a bad heart —*Time*⟩

spaw *archaic var of* SPA

¹**spawl** \ˈspȯl\ *vb* -ED/-ING/-S [origin unknown] *archaic* : SPIT

²**spawl** *var of* SPALL

¹**spawn** \ˈspȯn *also* -pän\ *vb* -ED/-ING/-S [ME *spawnen,* fr. AF *espaundre,* fr. OF *espandre, spandre* to spread, disperse, fr. L *expandere* to spread out, expand — more at EXPAND] *vt* **1 a** : to produce or deposit (eggs or spawn) — used of an aquatic animal **b** : to induce (fish) to spawn — used esp. of an aquarium fish **c** : to strip spawn from (a ripe fish) esp. for hatchery rearing of fish **d** : to plant with mycelia of the common edible mushroom mostly in the form of spawn bricks ⟨~ beds for growing mushrooms⟩ **2** : to bring forth : GENERATE, PRODUCE ⟨a universe that ~s forth only ghouls and ogres —M.D.Geismar⟩ ⟨a blizzard ~*ed* in the Rocky mountains —*N. Y. Herald Tribune*⟩ ⟨impatience and irritation are often ~*ed* by ignorance or misunderstanding —A.E.Stevenson b. 1900⟩ ⟨slums which ~ the criminal elements —John Barkham⟩ ⟨this ideology is ~*ed* out of Communism —A.W. Barkley⟩; *esp* : to produce in great quantity ⟨no fewer than 500 private home-study schools . . . had been ~*ed* —J.M.Flagler⟩ ⟨hypotheses might be ~*ed* by the dozens —S.C.Pepper⟩ ⟨last year . . . ~*ed* books by the millions —Harrison Smith⟩ ⟨abundant rains, ~*ing* a profusion of desert wild flowers —*Los Angeles (Calif.) Examiner*⟩ ~ *vi* **1** : to deposit spawn ⟨silver fish that . . . madly push their way upstream to ~ —*Amer. Guide Series: Mich.*⟩ **2 a** : to give forth young esp. in large numbers or like spawn : REPRODUCE **b** : to develop in multitudes or masses

²**spawn** \"\ *n* -s [ME *spawne,* fr. *spawnen,* v.] **1 a** : the eggs of fishes, oysters, and other aquatic animals that lay many small eggs **b** : the fertilized eggs produced by one pair of fish at one time **2 a** : any product or offspring ⟨Spanish moss, that peculiar ~ of the South —Henry Miller⟩ ⟨our likes and dislikes are often blind, the ~ of instinct or habit —Harry Bear⟩ ⟨shooing away young ~s . . . who wanted the glory of having touched the wonderful red machine —Marcia Davenport⟩ **b** : offspring in great numbers or masses : numerous issue ⟨mules are ~ of Satan —Francis Yeats-Brown⟩ ⟨the ~ of careless dicta —B.N.Cardozo⟩ **3** : the seed, germ, or source of something ⟨democracy was . . . the very ~ of anarchy —V.L.Parrington⟩ ⟨the loom and shuttles made the old lady's garage apartment a ~ of noise —*Western Rev.*⟩ **4** : the mycelium of fungi esp. prepared usu. in the form of bricks for propagating mushrooms **5** : gelatinous matter : BREAK 6d ⟨the ~ of an oil⟩

spawneater \ˈ=,==\ *n* : SPOTTAIL SHINER

spawn·er \-_ə(r)\ *n* -s **1** : a mature female fish **2** : something that produces spawn

¹**spawning** *n* -s [ME *spawnynge,* fr. gerund of *spawnen* to spawn] **1** : the process of emitting spawn **2** : the collecting of spawn from ripe fishes

²**spawning** *adj* [fr. pres. part. of ¹*spawn*] **1** : emitting spawn **2** : FERTILE, PROLIFIC ⟨the ~ slums of our cities⟩

spawny \-ē\ *adj* : resembling spawn; *also* : SPAWNING

¹**spay** \ˈspā\ *vt* -ED/-ING/-S [ME *spayen,* fr. MF *espeer* to cut with a sword, pierce, fr. OF, fr. *espee* sword, fr. L *spatha* broadsword — more at SPATHE] : to remove or extirpate the ovaries of (as a sow or a bitch) : CASTRATE

²**spay** \"\ *n* -s **1** : a spayed animal **2** : SPAYING

³**spay** \"\ *or* **spay·ad** \-āəd\ *or* **spay·ard** \-āə(r)d\ *n* -s [ME *spayer, spayad*] : a male red deer in his third year

spaying *n* -s [fr. gerund of ¹*spay*] : the act of castrating a female animal

spd *abbr* **1** speed **2** sprayed

SPD *abbr, often not cap* steamer pays dues

spdl *abbr* spindle

¹**speak** \ˈspēk\ *vb* **spoke** \ˈspōk\ *or archaic* **spake** \ˈspāk\ *or dial Brit* **spak** \ˈspak\ **spo·ken** \ˈspōkən *sometimes* -kᵊŋ\ *or archaic* **spoke** *or dial Brit* **spak**; **speaking; speaks** [ME *speken,* fr. OE *sprecan, specan;* akin to OHG *sprehhan* to speak, Gk *spharageisthai* to crackle, Skt *sphūrjati* it roars, crackles] *vi* **1 a** : to utter articulate sounds with the ordinary modulation of the voice : TALK ⟨swallowed once or twice before she was able to ~ —Mary Austin⟩ ⟨does not find it necessary to ~ . . . at the top of his lungs —B.R. Redman⟩ **b** (1) : to give oral expression to thoughts, opinions, or feelings : engage in talk or conversation ⟨not for three years to ~ with any men —Alfred Tennyson⟩ ⟨why don't you ~ for yourself —H.W.Longfellow⟩ (2) : to extend a greeting ⟨are embarrassed . . . and they often blush when *spoken* to on the street —Carl Withers⟩ (3) : to be on speaking terms ⟨still are ~*ing* after a quarter century of collaboration —Lewis Nichols⟩ (4) : to give a rebuke or reprimand ⟨promised to ~ to the boy about his laziness⟩ **c** (1) : to express one's views before a group : make a talk or address ⟨*spoke* from one end of the state to the other during the campaign⟩ ⟨*spoke* to the club on gardening⟩ (2) : to address one's remarks — usu. used with *to* ⟨I should like to ~ to the nominations —*Report: Standard Oil Co. of N. J.*⟩ **2 a** : to give written expression to thoughts, opinions, or feelings : make a written statement ⟨as a writer of great talent he ~s with clarity and eloquence —R.K.Carr⟩ ⟨these lines . . . ~ of the saddest thing we know —H.A.Overstreet⟩ **b** : to express oneself ⟨science ~s in the conventionalized precision of mathematical language —T.H.Littlefield⟩ — often used in the phrase *so to speak* ⟨here he was at the enemy's gates, so to ~ —C.S.Forester⟩ **c** : to serve as spokesman ⟨associations presuming to ~ for higher education —J.K. Little⟩ ⟨the dominant interests of the electorate for whom they ~ —Cabell Phillips⟩ ⟨writers . . . ~ for their age —Caroline Gordon⟩ **3 a** : to give expression to thoughts, opinions, or feelings by other than verbal means ⟨eyes that ~ too plainly —W.S.Gilbert⟩ ⟨she said nothing at all but her strong fingers *spoke* for her —Louis Bromfield⟩ ⟨actions ~ louder than words⟩ **b** : to communicate by signals : SIGNAL ⟨our steamer *spoke* in a short, sharp blast —William Beebe⟩ **c** : to communicate by being interesting or attractive : APPEAL ⟨great music . . . is intelligible to children since it ~s directly to the emotions —A.N.Whitehead⟩ ⟨nature ~s to us . . . through our senses —Susanne K. Langer⟩ **4 a** : to make a request : ASK ⟨suppose you ~ for tea —Jane Austen⟩ **b** : to place an order ⟨among the companies which have *spoken* for these later models —Horace Sutton⟩ **5 a** : to make a characteristic or natural sound or noise ⟨and let the kettle to the trumpet ~ —Shak.⟩ ⟨all at once the thunder *spoke* —George Meredith⟩ **b** : to produce a musical sound readily and clearly ⟨discovered that the saxophone ~s easily —Deems Taylor⟩ **c** : to emit a sound on being fired ⟨the big guns that *spoke* so thunderously that wild night —H.L.Merillat⟩ **d** *of a hound* : to give tongue : BARK, BAY **6 a** : to bear witness : TESTIFY ⟨if his trial is held in absentia his dossier will ~ in his defense —Kay Boyle⟩ ⟨how the old tub took those tossing seas . . . *spoke* well for her builders —H.A.Chippendale⟩ **b** : to give proof or evidence : be indicative or suggestive ⟨his gold . . . *spoke* of riches in the land —Julian Dana⟩ ⟨schools and museums all ~ of the past —D.W.Brogan⟩ **c** : to serve as a symbol ⟨the acres of white marble . . . ~ for the purity of justice —John Mason Brown⟩ **d** : AUGUR ⟨his thrift and industry ~ well for his future⟩ ~ *vt* **1 a** (1) : to utter articulately and with ordinary modulation of the voice : PRONOUNCE ⟨once the words were *spoken* she was sorry —Carson McCullers⟩ ⟨~ the speech I pray you . . . trippingly on the tongue —Shak.⟩ (2) : to give a recitation of : DECLAIM ⟨little girls who were going to ~ pieces, fluttering about in white dresses —Della Lutes⟩ **b** : to make known by speech : express orally : DECLARE ⟨the English clergy *spoke* their mind very freely on the subject —L.F. Salzman⟩ **c** (1) *archaic* : to engage in talk or conversation with ⟨~*ing* him in that . . . tongue —P.J.Bailey⟩ (2) : ADDRESS, ACCOST — usu. used with *fair* ⟨a stranger came to the door at eve and . . . *spoke* the bridegroom fair —Robert Frost⟩ **d** : to make communication with : HAIL ⟨when you pass other yachts ~ them —H.A.Calahan⟩ **2 a** : to make known in writing : STATE ⟨letting the Bible ~ its message to them —J.C.Swaim⟩ ⟨in this passage the man himself is ~*ing* . . . his innermost convictions —H.O.Taylor⟩ **b** *obs* : to make reference to : MENTION ⟨~ me to her in the best language of affection —Robert Loveday⟩ **c** : to serve as spokesman for : REPRESENT ⟨the municipal council . . . had ceased to ~ the sense of the citizens —T.B.Macaulay⟩ **3** : to use or have the ability to use in talk or conversation ⟨has lived there and ~s both Spanish and Portuguese —H.G.Doyle⟩ **4 a** : to make known by other than verbal means : REVEAL ⟨his eager smile . . . *spoke* devotion —Hugh Walpole⟩ ⟨what color means, color alone can ~ —Louise Nicholl⟩ **b** : to give proof or evidence of : INDICATE, SUGGEST ⟨his various addictions . . . ~ the amateur —F.R. Leavis⟩ **c** *archaic* : to demonstrate clearly or undeniably : PROCLAIM ⟨his whole person . . . ~s him a man of quality —Richard Steele⟩ **d** : to announce by making a characteristic or natural sound ⟨these trumpets ~ his presence —Nicholas Rowe⟩ ⟨the tower-clock *spoke* night —Henry Treece⟩ **5** : to make a request of : ASK ⟨we'd like to ~ some friendly wraith to tell us news —*Bookman*⟩ **6** *archaic* **a** : DESIGNATE, CALL ⟨may'st thou live ever *spoken* our protector —John Fletcher⟩ **b** : to give a description of : DEPICT ⟨to ~ him true . . . no keener hunter after glory breathes —Alfred Tennyson⟩ **7** : to have the significance of : SIGNIFY ⟨another long passage that ~s volumes for the formalist viewpoint —Hunter Mead⟩ **8** : to bring into a specified state or position by or as if by speech ⟨*spoke* himself into the common council —*New Monthly Mag.*⟩

syn TALK, CONVERSE: SPEAK is a general term of wide application. It may on occasion differ from TALK in suggesting a weighty formality ⟨*speak* at a university commencement⟩ ⟨*speaking* as a guest of honor⟩ TALK in general may suggest less formality and is likely to implicate auditors or interlocutors ⟨we *talk* in the bosom of our family in a way different from that in which we discourse on state occasions —J.L.Lowes⟩ CONVERSE may imply interchange of opinions and ideas ⟨don't ever remember hearing my parents *converse,* and they never even chatted. My father would expound on law and ritual, my mother would listen —S.N.Behrman⟩

— **to speak of** : worthy of mention or notice ⟨the islanders had no trees *to speak of* —Harry Luke⟩

²**speak** \"\ *n* -s [ME *speke,* fr. *speken* to speak] *chiefly Scot* : SPEECH, TALK

³**speak** \"\ *n* -s [by shortening] : SPEAKEASY ⟨there would be token raids now and then but the ~ usually opened the next day —C.B.Davis⟩

speak·able \-kəbəl\ *adj* [ME *spekable,* fr. *speken* to speak + *-able*] **1** : capable of being spoken : fit to be spoken **2** *obs* : able to speak — **speak·able·ness** *n* -ES — **speak·ably** \-blē, -li\ *adv*

speak down *vi* : to speak in a condescending manner ⟨without once *speaking down* to the audience or without once sacrificing artistic quality —R.W.Sarnoff⟩

speakeasy \ˈ=,==\ *n* -ES : a place where alcoholic drinks are illegally sold ⟨asserts that his men are entitled to go into *speakeasies* without warrants and smash everything —*Nation*⟩

speak·er \ˈspēkə(r)\ *n* -s [ME *speker,* fr. *speken* to speak + *-er*] **1 a** : one that speaks ⟨an excellent ~ of French⟩ **b** : a person who addresses an audience : one who makes a public speech ⟨the ~ of the evening⟩ ⟨a forceful and logical ~⟩ **c** : one who acts as a spokesman for others; *specif* : a spokesman for an Indian nation or people in a council **2** : the presiding officer of a deliberative assembly; *esp* : the presiding officer of a popularly elected legislative body ⟨the *Speaker* of the House of Representatives is the leader of the majority party in that body —W.S.Sayre⟩ ⟨the ~ of the English House of Commons . . . long ago became a wholly disinterested and impartial moderator —F.A.Ogg & P.O.Ray⟩ **3** : a book of selections for declamation ⟨the readers and ~s used in the academies and colleges —E.C.Shoemaker⟩ **4** : LOUDSPEAKER ⟨from the ~ came a crackling static —Wirt Williams⟩

speak·er·ess \-kərəs\ *n* -ES [*speaker* + *-ess*] : a female speaker; *esp* : a woman serving as a presiding officer

speaker key *or* **speaker hole** *n* : a key or hole on a woodwind instrument to facilitate the production of the upper harmonics

speak·er·ship \ˈ=,=ˌship\ *n* [*speaker* + *-ship*] : the office of speaker in a legislative body

speakhouse \ˈ=,=\ *n* **1** *obs* : a room for conversation in a convent or monastery **2** : a large structure used for conferences or councils in some of the islands of the south Pacific

¹**speak·ing** \ˈspēkiŋ, -kēŋ\ *adj* [ME *speking,* fr. pres. part. of *speken* to speak] **1** : that speaks : capable of speech **2 a** : highly significant : ELOQUENT ⟨a ~ witness to their permanence —E.A.Freeman⟩ **b** : highly expressive ⟨a face profound and ~ in spite of its silence —Mary Lindsay⟩ **3** : resembling a living being or a real object : STRIKING, FAITHFUL ⟨the ~ portrait of the eldest daughter —Anita Marburg⟩ — **speak·ing·ly** *adv* — **speak·ing·ness** *n* -ES

²**speaking** \"\ *n* -s [ME *speking,* fr. gerund of *speken* to speak] **1 a** : the act or an instance of uttering words ⟨there has been fine ~ of noble language —*Scots Mag.*⟩ **b** : SPEECH, DISCOURSE ⟨so sweet his ~ sounded —William Morris⟩ **c** : STATEMENT, SAYING ⟨laying aside all malice . . . and all evil ~s —1 Pet 2:1 (AV)⟩ **2** : a political rally ⟨the farmers . . . had come in to attend the ~ —J.S.Buckingham⟩

speaking arc *n* : an arc lamp which is used as a telephone receiver and in which the telephonic current is superposed upon the normal current of the lamp

speaking choir *n* : a group organized for choral speaking

speaking part *n* : a dramatic role containing lines to be spoken

speaking pipe *n* : an organ pipe that sounds as contrasted with one that is only for display

speaking rod *n* : SELF-READING ROD

speaking stop *n* : a stop knob controlling a rank of pipes in a pipe organ

speaking terms *n pl* **1** : a mutual relationship limited to casual greeting or conversation — used in the phrase *on speaking terms* **2** : a mutual relationship of intimacy and trust — used with a negative and in the phrase *on speaking terms* ⟨the two brothers weren't on *speaking terms* for years⟩

speaking trumpet *n* : a trumpet-shaped instrument for intensifying and directing the sound of the human voice

speaking tube *n* : a pipe through which conversation may be carried on (as between persons in different parts of a building)

speak out *vb* [ME *speken out,* fr. *speken* to speak + *out*] *vi* **1** : to speak loud enough to be heard ⟨asked him to *speak up* or sit down⟩ **2** : to speak boldly or unreservedly ⟨stand up and *speak out* for the president's whole program —Sinclair Weeks⟩ ⟨*spoke out* . . . forthrightly against the carpetbag militia —*Amer. Guide Series: Ark.*⟩ **3** : to express an opinion freely and frankly ⟨everyone of us has the obligation to *speak out,* to exchange ideas —Wendell Willkie⟩ ~ *vt* : to make known verbally : DECLARE ⟨*spoke out* his mind and showed that he was not too well pleased —Augustus Jessopp⟩

speaks *pres 3d sing of* SPEAK, *pl of* SPEAK

speak up *vi* **1** : to speak strongly or vigorously — usu. used with *for* ⟨*speak up* for truth and justice —Clive Bell⟩ **2** : to speak loudly and distinctly ⟨was told to *speak up* as the people . . . could not hear him —B.L.K.Henderson⟩ **3** : to express an opinion freely and fearlessly ⟨we'll never find out how we feel about one another if we don't *speak up* —D.B.Chidsey⟩

speal *var of* SPEEL

speal·bone \ˈspēlˌbōn\ *n* [Sc *spealbane,* alter. of *spulebane,* fr. *spule* shoulder (of unknown origin) + *bane* bone, fr. OE *bān* — more at BONE] : the shoulder blade used by magicians or medicine men in divination

¹**spean** \ˈspēn\ *vt* [MD *spenen,* fr. *spene* teat; akin to OE *spane* teat, MHG *spenen* to entice, wean, ON *speni* teat, OIr *sine*] *chiefly Scot* : WEAN

²**spean** \"\ *n* -s [origin unknown] *dial Eng* : ¹PRONG 2

¹**spear** \ˈspi(ə)r, -iə\ *n* -s [ME *spere,* fr. OE; akin to OHG *sper* spear, ON *spjör* spears, L *sparus* hunting spear, Gk *sparos* gilthead]

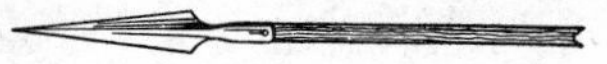

spear 1

1 : a thrusting or throwing weapon with a long shaft and sharp head or blade used in war or hunting **2** : something resembling a spear: as **a** : a transverse spike or pole in a cheval-de-frise **b** : a sharp-pointed instrument with barbs used in spearing fish **c** : the tip end of a fishhook with barb and point **d** : LANCE 2c **e** : a body part (as a stylet or barb) that resembles a spear **3** : SPEARMAN; *esp* : a soldier armed with a spear **4** : a light ray : BEAM ⟨the ~s of an aurora were stabbing upward to the zenith —S.H.Adams⟩ **5** : a tool used in recovering equipment lost in a drilled oil well — **under the spear** [fr. the ancient Roman practice of hanging up a spear as a sign that an auction was being held] *obs* : for sale at auction

²**spear** \"\ *adj* [ME *spere,* fr. *spere,* n.] **1** : of, relating to, or resembling a spear **2** : of or relating to the father : MALE ⟨the ~ side of the family⟩ — compare DISTAFF

³**spear** \"\ *vb* -ED/-ING/-S [¹*spear*] *vt* **1** : to pierce or strike with or as if with a spear ⟨learning how to ~ salmon⟩ ⟨~*ing* a cake . . . she put it on her plate —Clarissa F. Cushman⟩ **2** : to impale (cut stalks or plants) on a lath in harvesting tobacco **3** : to clean out (a hole) with a reamer **4** : to catch (as a baseball) with a sudden thrust of the arm ~ *vi* **1** : to thrust with or as if with a spear ⟨hundreds of sharks ~*ing* at the whale —H.A.Chippendale⟩ **2** : to make a way into or through something in the manner of a spear ⟨the headlight is a white shaft ~*ing* into a misty night —R.M.Neal⟩ ⟨the great cathedral ~s into the sky —Amy Lowell⟩

⁴**spear** \"\ *n* -s [alter. (influenced by ¹*spear*) of ¹*spire*] **1** *obs* : STEEPLE **2 a** : a usu. young blade, shoot, or sprout (as of grass) **b** (1) : a stalk of reed grass (2) *dial Eng* : REEDS; *esp* : reeds used for thatching

⁵**spear** \"\ *vi* -ED/-ING/-S : to thrust upward in a shoot, blade, or spear-shaped leaf ⟨how beautiful are oats when the first wavering ranks of green come ~*ing* bravely in the light —D.C. Peattie⟩

⁶**spear** \"\ *n* -s [alter. of ³*spire*] *Brit* : a rod to which the bucket of a mine pump is attached

spear·er \-rə(r)\ *n* -s : one that spears

speareye \ˈ=,=\ *or* **speareye shark** *n* [modif. (influenced by E *spear, eye*) of Afrik *spierhaai,* fr. *spier* muscle, blade (fr. MD; akin to OE *spīr* blade) + *haai* shark, fr. MD *haey* — more at SPIRE, HAYE] : a small coastal shark (*Mustelus punctulatus*) of the south Atlantic and Indian oceans that is grayish brown dotted with black

¹**spearfish** \ˈ=,=\ *n* [¹*spear* + *fish,* n.] **1** : any of several large powerful pelagic fishes of the genus *Tetrapturus* that are closely related to the marlins and sailfishes but have the first dorsal fin low in front and moderately elevated behind and are widely distributed but rare in all seas **2** : any of various fishes related to the spearfish

²**spearfish** \"\ *vi* [¹*spear* + *fish,* v.] : to fish with a spear: **a** : to catch fish by means of a barbed spear thrown by hand or propelled by a mechanical device and retrieved by an attached line **b** : to fish underwater with a spear

spearflower \ˈ=,==\ *n* [¹*spear* + *flower*] : a plant or flower of the genus *Ardisia*

spear grass *n* **1** : any of numerous grasses having spear-shaped inflorescences or stiff pointed leaves: as **a** : COUCH GRASS **b** : BENT 2d **c** : MEADOW GRASS **d** : DITCH REED **e** : SLENDER FOXTAIL **f** : PORCUPINE GRASS 1 **2 a** : a spearwort (*Ranunculus flammula*) **b** : a plant of the genus *Aciphylla* (family Umbelliferae) with prickly leaves; *esp* : a New Zealand perennial (*A. colensoi*)

spear gun *n* : a gun that propels a spear and is used in underwater spearfishing

spear hand *n, archaic* : the right hand

¹**spearhead** \ˈ=,=\ *n* [ME *spere-hed,* fr. *spere* spear + *hed* head] **1 a** : the sharp-pointed head of a spear **b** : something having a sharp-pointed end; *specif* : a sharp device on the end of a lath for piercing tobacco stalks that are to be hung on the lath during curing **2 a** : a military force that precedes others in a thrust or attack : the leading element in a military thrust or attack ⟨smashed the American ~ in savage fighting —F.V.W. Mason⟩ **b** : a leading element, force, or influence in an undertaking or development ⟨trained to act as the ~ of miners' demands against the management —Leo Wolman⟩ ⟨the ~ of propaganda is the slogan —S.H.Flowerman⟩ ⟨plastics might be said to be the ~ of the advance in synthetic materials —Howard Marshall⟩

²**spearhead** \"\ *vt* **1 a** : to take the lead in launching and pressing forward (a military thrust or attack) ⟨airborne troops ~*ed* a massed crossing of the river —Allan Taylor⟩ **b** : to precede in a military thrust or attack ⟨the dive bombers ~*ed* the panzer forces —C.C.Caldwell⟩ **2 a** : to take a leading role in (an undertaking or development) ⟨~*ed* the medical profession's efforts to improve physician-patient relationships —Milton Silverman⟩ ⟨~*ed* the romantic revolution —Florence Bullock⟩ **b** : to serve as leader of in an undertaking or development ⟨~*ed* a group of liberal Democrats who are supporting . . . the censure movement —Anthony Leviero⟩

spear hook *n* : SPRING HOOK 2

spear·ing \ˈspiriŋ, -rēŋ\ *n, pl* **spearing** [D *spiering* smelt, fr. MD *spierinc,* fr. *spier* spear; akin to OE *spere* spear — more at SPEAR] : a small lizard fish (*Trachinocephalus myops*) widespread in warm seas

spear javelin *n* [¹*spear*] : FRAMEA

spear lily *n* : a tall perennial herbaceous plant (*Doryanthes excelsa*) that is cultivated in warm regions for its showy globose heads of scarlet flowers with spreading perianths

spear·man \ˈ=mən\ *n, pl* **spearmen** [ME *spereman,* fr. *spere* spear + *man*] : one armed or equipped with a spear; *esp* : a soldier having a spear as a weapon

spearmint \ˈ=,=\ *n* [¹*spear* + *mint*] **1** : a common garden mint (*Mentha spicata*) that is widely cultivated for use in flavoring and esp. for its aromatic oil and that resembles peppermint but has slender interrupted spikes **2** : a moderate to strong green that is bluer and stronger than Hooker's green

spearmint oil *n* : an aromatic essential oil obtained from spearmint and used in flavoring

spearnose bat \ˈ=,=-\ *n* : any of several bats of the family Phyllostomatidae and esp. of the genera *Phyllostomus* and *Vampyrum* with a prominently pointed nose leaf

spear penny *n* [trans. of Welsh *ceiniog baladr*] : an exaction paid under ancient Welsh law to an injured person by a wrongdoer

spear plate *n* [¹*spear*] : STRAPPING PLATE

¹**spearpoint** \ˈ=,=\ *n* [ME *sperepoint,* fr. *spere* spear + *point*] **1** : the point of a spear **2** : SPEARHEAD ⟨the ~ of a general intellectual awakening —Mary Scrutton⟩

²**spearpoint** \"\ *vt* : SPEARHEAD

spear–point chisel *n* : a chisel with a triangular point for lathe-turning operations

spear pyrites *n* : a marcasite in twin crystals resembling the head of a spear

spear rod *n* [⁶*spear*] *Brit* : the main rod of a mine pump

spears *pl of* SPEAR, *pres 3d sing of* SPEAR

spear thistle *n* [¹*spear*] : BULL THISTLE 1

spear–thrower \ˈ=,==\ *n* : THROWING-STICK

spearwood \ˈ=,=\ *n* **1** : any of several Australian acacias with very hard heavy durable wood; *esp* : a widely distributed small or medium-sized tree (*Acacia doratoxylon*) with elongated slightly curved phyllodes and racemes of small flowers **2** : the wood of a spearwood used chiefly for cabinet work and small articles and by the aborigines for spears

spearwort \ˈ=,=\ *n* [ME *sperewort,* fr. OE *sperewyrt,* fr. *spere* spear + *wyrt* wort] : any of several crowfoots having spear-shaped leaves; *esp* : a Eurasian crowfoot (*Ranunculus flammula*) naturalized in Newfoundland

speary \'spirē, -ri\ *adj, usu* -ER/-EST **:** resembling a spear; *esp* **:** having a sharp point ⟨evergreens . . . point their ~ tops above the crest of bluffs —W.D.Howells⟩

speat \'spāt, spēt\ *chiefly Scot var of* SPATE

spec *abbr or n* **1** special; specialist; specialty **2** species **3** specific; specifically **4** specification **5** specimen **6** spectacle; spectacular **7** spectrum **8** speculation

speci- *or* **specie-** *or* **specio-** *comb form* [*species*] **:** species ⟨*speciogenesis*⟩ ⟨*speciation*⟩

¹**spe·cial** \'speshəl\ *adj, sometimes* -ER/-EST [ME, fr. OF or L; OF *especial*, fr. L *specialis* individual, particular, fr. *species* appearance, kind + *-alis* -al — more at SPY] **1 :** distinguished by some unusual quality **:** UNCOMMON, NOTEWORTHY, EXTRAORDINARY ⟨a ~ occasion⟩; *esp* **:** distinguished by superiority **2 :** regarded with particular favor and affection **:** DEAR, INTIMATE ⟨not a ~ friend of mine⟩ **3 a :** relating to a single thing or class of things **:** having an individual character or trait **:** PECULIAR, UNIQUE ⟨to this ~ evil an improvement of style would apply a ~ redress —Thomas De Quincey⟩ **b :** of or belonging to a particular species **:** constituting a species or kind ⟨a ~ concept⟩ **4 a :** supplemental to the regular **:** EXTRA ⟨a ~ edition of a newspaper⟩ **b :** assigned or provided to meet a particular need not covered under established procedures ⟨a ~ correspondent⟩ ⟨went west on a ~ train⟩ **5 :** confined to a definite field of action **:** designed or selected for a particular purpose, occasion, or other end **:** limited in range ⟨a ~ act of Congress⟩ ⟨a ~ branch of study⟩ ⟨a ~ student in college is not enrolled for the usual degree⟩ **6 :** containing particulars **:** DETAILED, SPECIFIC — opposed to *general* ⟨a ~ confession⟩

syn ESPECIAL, SPECIFIC, PARTICULAR, INDIVIDUAL: SPECIAL indicates the possessing of a quality, character, or identity of one's own, perhaps one out of the ordinary or conspicuously unusual ⟨a *special* diet for these cases⟩ ⟨*special* fatigue duty⟩ ⟨the women never drink in this manner, which is absolutely *special* to men —J.G.Frazer⟩ ⟨land that has *special* charm or outstanding beauty —S.P.B.Mais⟩ ⟨it's not like ordinary photographs. There's something *special* about it —Arnold Bennett⟩ ESPECIAL may add implications of preeminence or preference ⟨Gettysburg is of *especial* interest because of the famous battle —*Amer. Guide Series: Pa.*⟩ ⟨not one of his *especial* chums —Samuel Butler †1902⟩ SPECIFIC is applicable to special traits and characteristics in proportion as the group they characterize is limited; it often describes traits of an individual ⟨get down to *specific* cases⟩ ⟨the pressure on the universities, therefore, to educate men and women for *specific* vocations both increased and diversified —J.B.Conant⟩ ⟨some years ago we read with singular pleasure a new guidebook . . . its *specific* charm was simply that it left out all the gush —C.E.Montague⟩ PARTICULAR, often interchangeable with SPECIFIC, may differ from it in increasing suggestions of individual distinctness and decreasing those of membership in a group ⟨more than three years in the South were a happy experience and a liberalizing education for this *particular* northern boy —E.J.Benton⟩ ⟨any *particular* remark of a psychologist, if true, is unlikely to be startling —I.A.Richards⟩ ⟨a sense for *particular* beauties of nature, rather than a sense for Nature herself —Laurence Binyon⟩ INDIVIDUAL applies to what is clearly isolated or individualized from all else ⟨the *individual* idiosyncrasies of each member of the great family —Sherwood Anderson⟩ ⟨more faith in the collective opinion of all Americans than in the *individual* opinion of any one American —F.D.Roosevelt⟩ ⟨while the political influence of the baronage as a leading element in the whole nation thus steadily mounted, the personal and purely feudal power of each *individual* baron on his own estates as steadily fell —J.R. Green⟩

²**special** \"\ *adv* [ME, fr. ¹*special*] **:** SPECIALLY, ESPECIALLY

³**special** \"\ *n* -S [ME, fr. ¹*special*] **1 a** *obs* **:** a favorite or intimate friend or companion; *esp* **:** PARAMOUR **b :** a special thing **:** PARTICULAR — usu. used with *the* ⟨from the general to the ~⟩ **c** *obs* **:** SPECIES, KIND **d :** one outside of or in addition to the regular or normal number, quantity, series, range, or similar category ⟨not a regular, but a ~⟩ ⟨newsboys hawking the afternoon ~*s*⟩ ⟨a store featuring ~*s* on meats⟩ **2 :** one appointed or used for a special service or occasion ⟨the train was a ~ for the football game⟩ **3 a :** a special-delivery letter **b :** SPECIAL-DELIVERY STAMP

special ability *n* **:** an individual's ability in a particular subject (as music or mathematics) or in a particular function (as memorizing) as opposed to his general intelligence

special act *n* **:** an act of a legislature that is not of general application in all territory subject to the legislative power but affects private persons or only part of a class of persons in the same situation or only part of a more general subject matter or is intended to apply only in a particular subdivision of the entire territory subject to the legislative power

special administrator *n* **1 :** an administrator appointed to administer only a designated part of a decedent's assets **2 :** an administrator appointed ex parte without notice to all interested parties to conserve the assets of an estate usu. in some emergency (as in a will contest)

special agent *n* **1 :** an agent authorized by his principal to act in one undertaking or to act in a number of transactions not involving continuous service to the principal **:** an agent following particular instructions in a particular matter whose authority is limited to doing what is reasonable to fulfill those instructions — compare GENERAL AGENT **2 :** a representative of a property insurance company within a specified territory who supervises and assists local agents, recommends the appointment of new agents, and in some cases adjusts losses — called also *fieldman*

special appearance *n* **:** an appearance by a party in court for the sole purpose of attacking the jurisdiction of the court (as for lack of effective service or lack of power to adjudge the cause)

special area *n, Brit* **:** an area forming the subject of special legislation because of disproportionately severe depression and destitution

special assessment *n* **:** a specific tax levied on private property to meet the cost of public improvements that enhance the value of the property

special assumpsit *n* **:** EXPRESS ASSUMPSIT

special bail *n* **1 a :** BAIL ABOVE **b :** BAIL BELOW **2 :** bail given by responsible persons rather than that given solely as a matter of form

special bastard *n* **:** a bastard legitimated by marriage of its parents

special carrier *n* **:** PRIVATE CARRIER

special case *n* **:** a case the proceedings under which are different from those of the regular common law or equity actions: as **a :** an action or proceeding established by statute to provide new rights or remedies **b :** a case reserved for the decision of the court on a question of law, on a case stated, or on a finding of facts by the jury; *also* **:** a case prepared to be so submitted

special collection *n* **1 :** a memorial collection of printed works or manuscripts in a library **2 :** an aggregation of printed or other material of an author or on a special subject

special contract *n* **:** SPECIALTY CONTRACT

special court *n* **:** a court created for an exceptional and temporary purpose (as a commission to try alleged war criminals or a tribunal to hear claims for war damages against a state by nationals of the victorious state)

special court-martial *n* **:** a court-martial consisting of at least three officers, a trial judge advocate, and a defense counsel and having authority to impose no sentence in excess of six months' confinement or forfeiture of two thirds of six months' pay — compare GENERAL COURT-MARTIAL, SUMMARY COURT-MARTIAL

special creation *n* **:** the theoretical independent origin of each biological species through a special act of creation — opposed to *doctrine of descent*

special damage *n* **1 :** damage for which a defendant is responsible but which must be pleaded and proved by plaintiff to be recoverable **2 :** damage not ordinarily expected to be caused by defendant's wrong or breach of duty but in fact caused thereby under circumstances making defendant responsible **3 :** damage peculiar to a plaintiff because of his particular condition or the particular circumstances in which he finds himself, but not ordinarily implied from defendant's wrong or breach of duty **4 :** damage capable of being exactly measured in money or its equivalent as distinguished from damage which must be estimated and concerning which reasonable men might differ **5 :** CONSEQUENTIAL DAMAGE **6 special damages** *pl* **:** compensatory damages awarded for a particular harm or pecuniary loss for which special proof must be made

special delivery *n* **1 :** the delivery of a piece of mail of any class by postal messenger ahead of the regular carrier delivery on prepayment of a fee represented by a special-delivery stamp **2 a** *or* **special-delivery stamp :** a stamp affixed to a piece of mail to obtain special delivery service **b :** a piece of mail sent by special delivery

special demurrer *n* **:** a demurrer for some specified defect of form in a pleading

special deposit *n* **1 :** a deposit (as of valuables or securities) which is usu. primarily for security and in which the identical property deposited is to be returned to its owner — compare GENERAL DEPOSIT, IRREGULAR DEPOSIT **2 :** a deposit of money (as a savings or time deposit) in a bank that bears interest and is not subject to checking

special deputy *n* **:** a deputy authorized to exercise some special function on behalf of another official

special dividend *n* **:** a dividend that typically results from some windfall profit to a company and is not ordinarily expected to be repeated

special duty *n* **:** duty performed by an individual in military service with a unit or activity other than that to which he is assigned but at the same station — compare DETACHED SERVICE

special effect *n* **:** an often illusory effect introduced into a motion picture during processing of the film

special endorsement *n* **1 :** an endorsement on negotiable paper that limits the transfer to a particular person — compare RESTRICTIVE ENDORSEMENT **2 :** a statement on a writ of the nature of the claim or the scope of the relief sought

special finding *n* **:** a finding of a jury or judge sitting to try facts or some particular fact as established by the evidence in an action not including a rendering of a verdict or finding upon the entire matter in issue

special grace *n* **:** grace that relates to eternal salvation — distinguished from *common grace*

special handling *n* **:** the handling of a piece of parcel-post or fourth-class mail as first-class but not as special-delivery matter by the U.S. Post Office on prepayment of a fee represented by a special-handling stamp

special-handling stamp *n* **:** a stamp indicating payment of a fee for postal special handling

special hazard *n* **:** a potential cause of fire peculiar to a particular building or to a process of manufacturing — compare COMMON HAZARD

special injunction *n* **:** an injunction on motion granted to prevent threatened and irreparable injury **:** a temporary or preliminary injunction **:** a prohibitory injunction against specified acts or conduct

special interest *n* **1 :** a particular concern in something usu. by which one is directly affected **2 :** an individual, group, or corporation having a special interest in usu. a particular part of the economy and receiving or seeking through political pressure special advantages from the government often to the detriment of the general welfare — usu. used in pl.

spe·cial·ism \'speshə,lizəm\ *n* -S [¹*special* + *-ism*] **1 :** specialization in or confinement of interest to a particular field of study, activity, or interest **:** restriction of concern to one branch or aspect of a wider field (as of knowledge); *often* **:** excessive confinement to a specialty ⟨humanists decry the tendency to ~ in modern society⟩ **2 :** a field of specialization **:** a branch or aspect of something in which specialization exists ⟨the several medical ~*s*⟩ ⟨geomorphology and other ~*s* inside the fold of geography —J.K.Wright⟩

special issue *n* **1 :** an issue denying or traversing one or more material points of law or fact but not the whole declaration, complaint, or indictment — compare GENERAL ISSUE **2 :** an issue raised by pleadings that may be determinative of the entire case (as a plea of release or of infancy)

spe·cial·ist \'spesh(ə)ləst\ *n* -S *often attrib* [¹*special* + *-ist*] **1 :** a person who devotes or limits his interest to some special branch (as of an activity, business, art, or science): as **a :** a medical practitioner who limits his practice to a particular class of patients (as children) or of diseases (as skin diseases) or of technique (as surgery); *usu* **:** a physician who is qualified by advanced training and certification by a specialty examining board to so limit his practice **b :** a member of a stock exchange who concentrates his activity on a single stock or group of stocks traded at the same trading post and by executing orders for other brokers in such stocks as well as trading for his own account helps maintain a continuous market in the issues in question **c :** an enlisted man (as in the U. S. army) qualified for specialized duties and having a grade ranging from that of a corporal to that of a master sergeant but lacking the rank or command responsibilities of a noncommissioned officer **2 :** one that is extremely specialized in some physiologic respect (as in food habits)

spe·cial·is·tic \¦==shə¦listik\ *adj* [*specialist* + *-ic*] **1 :** concerned with or tending toward specialism **2 :** of, relating to, or typical of specialists

spe·ci·al·i·ty \,speshē'aləd·ē, -lətē, -i\ *n* -ES [ME *specialite, specialitie*, fr. MF or LL; MF *specialité*, fr. LL *specialitat-, specialitas* — more at SPECIALTY] **1 a :** a special or peculiar mark or characteristic **:** a distinctive or distinguishing and sometimes limiting or restrictive quality **:** PARTICULARITY **b specialities** *pl* **:** DETAILS, PARTICULARS **2 :** an object or class of objects marked by some special or peculiar characteristic **:** SPECIALTY 2a **3 a :** an aptitude or special skill in a particular endeavor (as a line of handicraft) **b :** SPECIALTY 3 **4 :** SPECIALTY 2a (1)

spe·cial·iza·tion \¦speshələ'zāshən, -,lī'z-\ *n* -S [*specialize* + *-ation*] **1 :** a making or becoming specialized **:** the quality or state of being specialized ⟨the ~ of industry⟩ **2 a :** adaptation in the structure of a body part to the performance of some particular function **:** differentiation that usu. tends toward greatly increased efficiency in one function at the expense of most other functions **b :** adaptation in the structure of an entire organism for life in particular surroundings or for particular habits **c :** a body part or organization adapted to a particular function, situation, or course of life

spe·cial·ize \'=shə,līz\ *vb* -ED/-ING/-S *see -ize in Explan Notes* [¹*special* + *-ize*] *vt* **1 :** to consider separately **:** ITEMIZE ⟨*specialized* each item —Vicki Baum⟩ **2 :** to limit in scope or interest **:** focus on a special area of knowledge or activity ⟨*specialized* his studies⟩ ~ *vi* **1 :** to go into detail **:** PARTICULARIZE ⟨first give a general outline, then ~⟩ **2 :** to concentrate one's efforts **:** develop or pursue a specialty ⟨~ in copyright law⟩ ⟨their restaurants ~ in Swedish cuisine —*Amer. Guide Series: N. Y.*⟩ ⟨the company ~*s* in jet engines⟩ **3 :** to undergo specialization; *esp* **:** to change adaptively ⟨many organisms ~ for a predacious existence⟩

specialized *adj* [fr. past part. of *specialize*] **1 :** designed or fitted for use or employment in one special line (as of occupation) so that change to another involves a loss in utility **2 :** characterized by or exhibiting biological specialization; *often* **:** highly developed **:** extremely differentiated esp. in a particular direction or for a particular end — compare GENERALIZED

spe·cial·iz·er \'==,līzə(r)\ *n* -S [*specialize* + *-er*] **:** SPECIALIST

special jury *n* **1 :** a jury formerly selected by the parties each striking a number of names (as 12 each) from the general list before the jury is impaneled — called also *struck jury* **2 :** a specially selected panel of jurors chosen by the court upon request of a party from a list of better educated or presumably more intelligent prospective jurors for a case involving complicated issues of fact or serious felonies — called also *blue-ribbon jury*

special law *n* **1 :** PRIVATE LAW **2 :** a local law applicable to a particular territory in a state or to a particular political subdivision thereof **3 :** a law unconstitutional because applying without justifiable reason to a particular member or members of but not to an entire class of persons or things in the same situation **:** a law that applies without reasonable basis to or in a particular territory rather than throughout the entire state

special library *n* **:** a privately owned library that forms a unit of a business firm or other organization, specializes in books and other material of special interest to the organization of which it is a part, and usu. serves only the staff or members of this organization

special license *n, Brit* **:** a license granting exceptional privileges; *specif* **:** a license from the Archbishop of Canterbury permitting a marriage to take place at any time or place and without usual preliminary formalities

special lien *n* **:** an attorney's charging lien against a judgment recovered by his efforts **:** PARTICULAR LIEN

spe·cial·ly \'spesh(ə)lē, -li\ *adv* [ME, fr. ¹*special* + *-ly*] **:** in a special manner **:** so as to be special **:** ESPECIALLY, PARTICULARLY

special master *n* **:** a master appointed by a court to hear the testimony and make findings of fact in a particular case, make a sale of property under court order, or carry out some other order of a court

spe·cial·ness *n* -ES **:** the quality or state of being special

special order *n* **:** a routine order issued by an authorized military headquarters that includes matter concerning individuals but is not of general interest — compare GENERAL ORDER

special partner *n* **:** a partner who may share in the profits of a general partnership registered under law, who contributes property to the capital thereof but must not exercise control over or be active in partnership affairs, and whose liability for partnership debts providing certain rules of law are observed is limited to his capital and interest in the firm assets — called also *limited partner;* distinguished from *general partner*

special partnership *n* **1 :** PARTICULAR PARTNERSHIP **2 :** LIMITED PARTNERSHIP

special plea *n* **:** a plea (as of infancy, statute of limitations or of frauds, discharge in bankruptcy or release) alleging new and affirmative matter as a defense without denying any allegations of the opponent **:** a plea in bar or in avoidance of what opponent alleges

special pleader *n* **1 :** a counsel who formerly devoted himself to drawing special counts and pleas **2 a :** a lawyer whose occupation is to draw pleadings, give opinions on matters submitted to him, and prepare the papers in various proceedings out of the usual course **b** *Brit* **:** a public officer, notary, barrister or solicitor occupied by such activities **3 :** one advocating a specific proposal (as a law) because of self-interest or on other bases than independent disinterested impartial judgment

special pleading *n* **1 :** the allegation of special or new matter to avoid the effect of matter pleaded by the opposite side and admitted, as distinguished from a direct denial of the matter pleaded **2 :** sophistical or misleading argumentation; *esp* **:** argument that presents one point or phase as if it covered the entire question at issue

special plea in bar : a plea in bar admitting the facts alleged but avoiding the action by setting forth particular and new matter — distinguished from *general issue;* compare ISSUE 6a

special power *n* **1 :** a power of appointment (as to testator's widow to appoint testator's estate to such of their issue as she should by her will appoint) created or reserved not for the benefit of the donee but for the benefit of persons or a class of persons that can be reasonably ascertained and not including the donee **2 :** a power described as such in a state statute where the persons or class of persons to whom the disposition of property under the power is to be made are expressly designated or where the power is to transfer, charge, or incumber any estate less than a fee simple

special privilege *n* **:** any privilege granted (as by a law or constitution) to an individual or group to the exclusion of others and in derogation of common right ⟨introduced a bill that would provide for *special privileges* such as tariff and other subsidies to domestic corporations⟩ ⟨the board . . . considered perhaps that scientists felt they were a group apart, entitled to *special privilege* or gentle treatment —Vannevar Bush⟩

special proceeding *n* **:** a judicial proceeding other than an action — used chiefly of such procedure under a code

special property *n* **:** a property right or qualified interest in property (as the interest of a bailee, pledgee, lawful possessor, a conditional vendee prior to full payment, or a lienholder) subordinate to the absolute, unconditional or general property or ownership

special retainer *n* **:** a retainer for a particular law service, case, or matter — distinguished from *general retainer*

special revelation *n* **:** religious revelation accessible only to a particular people or group of people ⟨the *special revelation* available to Christians through faith⟩ ⟨the *special revelation* of God's purposes in the history of Israel⟩ — compare GENERAL REVELATION

special rule *n* **:** a rule obtained from a court upon motion of counsel and not issuing as a matter of course **:** an interlocutory order made in a particular case — compare GENERAL RULE

specials *pl of* SPECIAL

special school *n* **:** a school for pupils who differ from the average so noticeably that they are not suited to ordinary schools; *esp* **:** a school for children of retarded development

special service school *n* **:** a unit in a system of military education (as in the U. S. Army) at which officers and enlisted men of the interested branch receive instruction in the subjects relating to their particular branch — compare GENERAL SERVICE SCHOOL

special service tariff *n* **:** a railroad or other shipping tariff containing regulations and charges for special services (as storage, demurrage, reconsignment, refrigeration)

special session *n* **1 :** an extraordinary session (as of a legislative body) **2 special sessions** *pl* **:** sittings held by two or more British magistrates or justices for the exercise of some special jurisdiction (as the licensing of alehouses) that can be exercised out of quarter sessions — compare GENERAL SESSIONS, PETTY SESSIONS

special settlement *n* **:** a settling of bargains usu. for new issues at a time other than the regular fortnightly settlement on the London stock exchange

special staff *n* **:** a part of the staff of a division or higher unit of an army including representatives of the artillery, engineers, ordnance, quartermaster, signal, and other branches — compare GENERAL STAFF, PERSONAL STAFF

special statute *n* **:** SPECIAL ACT

special term *n* **1 :** a term of court held by a single judge or for a special purpose — used of courts composed of several judges to describe the term at which one alone presides whose judgment may thereafter be reviewed by all or others sitting together **2 :** an extraordinary sitting of a court at a time other than that regularly fixed

special traverse *n* **:** a traverse not in absolute terms but with qualifications — compare COMMON TRAVERSE

special trust *n* **:** an active trust for the accomplishment of a specified purpose

spe·cial·ty \'speshəltē, -ti\ *n* -ES *often attrib* [ME *specialte*, fr. MF *especialté*, fr. LL *specialitat-, specialitas*, fr. L *specialis* special + *-itat-, -itas* -ity] **1 :** a particular, peculiar, or individual circumstance, detail, or characteristic **:** a distinctive or sometimes a restrictive mark or quality ⟨the *specialties* of one's lot in life⟩ **2 a :** an object or class of objects distinguished by some special characteristic, individual quality, or peculiarity: as (1) **:** a legal agreement (as a contract or deed) embodied in a sealed instrument — compare SPECIALTY CONTRACT (2) **:** a product of a special kind, made under a special patent, serving one special purpose or otherwise distinctive (as in excellence) ⟨apple pie was mother's ~⟩ ⟨the ~ of the house was seafood⟩ (3) **:** a security having some unusual character that makes it comparatively free from the influence of general market conditions (4) *or* **specialty good :** an item (as an automobile, novelty, piece of jewelry, or an art object) that has an attraction for the consumer other than price that tends to induce him to put forth special effort to obtain it, is usu. of relatively high unit value, is purchased infrequently in comparison with staple goods, and whose purchase is postponable ⟨a ~ dealer⟩ ⟨luxurious ~ shops⟩ **b :** the state of being special **:** possession of distinctive or peculiar or particular characteristics **3 :** something in which one specializes or of which

one has special knowledge: as **a :** a branch of knowledge, science, art, or business to which one devotes oneself whether as an avocation or a profession and usu. to the partial or total exclusion of related matters ⟨a chemist whose ~ is tropical alkaloids⟩ ⟨the major medical *specialties*⟩ **b :** a culture trait characteristic of or restricted to a limited group in a society

specialty contract *n* **:** a contract (as a deed or mortgage) depending for its validity upon the formality of its execution (as in being signed, sealed, and delivered) — called also *formal contract, special contract*

specialty mark *n* **:** insignia worn on an enlisted man's uniform that reveals his specialty or rating — compare RATING BADGE

special verdict *n* **:** a verdict setting forth the special findings of fact made by the jury on the material issues and leaving the court to make general finding for either party as the law requires on the facts so found

special vert *n* **:** trees in an English crown forest that provide food for deer

special warranty *n* **:** a limited warranty in a transfer or conveyance by which the grantor warrants the property transferred to be free of all liens and encumbrances made by, through, or under him

spe·ci·ate \ˈspēs(h)ēˌāt\ *vi* -ED/-ING/-S [back-formation fr. *speciation*] **:** to form species **:** differentiate into new species

spe·ci·a·tion \ˌ=ˌ=ˈāshən\ *n* -S [*speci-* + *-ation*] **:** formation of biological species or the processes leading to this end whether constituting gradual divergence from related groups (as by an extension of raciation) or occurring abruptly by combination or transformation of genomes (as in the formation of polyploid species) — compare MACROEVOLUTION, SALTATION — **spe·ci·a·tion·al** \ˌ=ˌ=ˈāshənᵊl, -shnəl\ *adj*

¹spe·cie \ˈspē(ˌ)shē, -shi *also* -(ˌ)sē *or* -si\ *n* -S [fr. the phrase *in specie*, fr. L, in kind] **:** money in coin ⟨required ~ payments⟩ — **in spe·cie** \ənˈzpē(ˌ)shē, ənˈsp-, -shi *also* -(ˌ)sē *or* -si; *in senses other than c* " *or* -pēs(h)ēˌē *or* -pekēˌā\ *adv* **:** in or with the same or like form or kind: as **a :** in kind **:** SPECIFICALLY ⟨his duties are *in specie* identical with your own⟩ **b :** in the identical form and without alteration or substitution — used chiefly in law ⟨an agreement to be carried out *in specie*⟩ **c :** in coin or coined money ⟨payment *in specie*⟩ **d :** in a like manner or with similar treatment ⟨ready to return insult *in specie*⟩

²specie \"\ *n* -S [back-formation fr. *species*] *nonstand* **:** SPECIES

specie- — see SPECI-

specie jar *n* [²*specie*] **:** a blown glass jar with sheet metal top formerly used for storage (as of herbs or stick candies)

specie payment *n* [¹*specie*] **:** payment in coin or bullion as distinguished from payment in paper money

¹spe·cies \ˈspē(ˌ)shēz, -shiz *also* -(ˌ)sēz *or* -siz\ *n, pl* **species** [L, appearance, form, kind, species, beauty — more at SPY] **1 a :** a class of individuals having common attributes and designated by a common name **:** a logical division of a genus or more comprehensive class **:** a subclass designated by adding to the name or connotation of a genus some specific difference that limits its application to a restricted group ⟨the triangle is a ~ of plane figure⟩ **b :** a limited kind or group having a distinguishing characteristic; *esp* **:** one capable of including variant individuals and of being subsumed in a more inclusive category ⟨mineral ~ are made up of varieties having common basic properties⟩ ⟨one ~ of tramp who wanders from workhouse to workhouse —Osbert Sitwell⟩ **c :** the race of man **:** human beings **:** HUMANITY ⟨progress of the ~ in science⟩ **d** (1) **:** a category of biological classification ranking immediately below a genus or subgenus and being denominated in taxonomic usage by a binomial that consists of the name of its genus followed by a Latin or latinized noun or adjective which is usu. not capitalized and agrees grammatically with the genus name **:** a group of intimately related and physically similar organisms that actually or potentially interbreed and are less commonly capable of fertile interbreeding with members of other groups, that ordinarily comprise differentiated populations limited geographically (as subspecies) or ecologically (as ecotypes) which tend to intergrade at points of contact, and that as a group represent the stage of evolution at which variations become fixed through loss of ability to exchange genes with members of other groups although formerly conceived to be the total progeny of a single distinctive specially created pair — compare NOMENCLATURE 4c; see SPECIFIC EPITHET (2) **:** an individual plant or animal or a kind of plant or animal belonging to a particular species — not used technically **e :** a particular kind of atomic nucleus, atom, molecule, or ion ⟨a great number of new nuclear ~ have been prepared within the last few years in the region of the natural radioactivities —*Science*⟩ ⟨all atoms of a particular radioactive ~ have the same probability of disintegrating —H.D.Smyth⟩ — compare ISOTOPE, NUCLIDE **2 a :** the consecrated eucharistic elements; *specif* **:** the accidents of the eucharistic bread and wine as distinguished in Roman Catholicism from their substance **b** (1) **:** a mental image, phantasm, or sensuous presentation (2) **:** an idea or object of thought that is the similitude of an object in nature whether in the guise of a modification of sense or of a purely intellectual correlative of the natural object; *broadly* **:** FORM, ASPECT, APPEARANCE **c** *obs* **:** a reflected image **:** REFLECTION **d** *obs* **:** an illusory image **:** PHANTOM **3** *obs* **:** the essential quality or distinguishing characteristic of something **4 a :** a component part of a compound medicine **:** SIMPLE **b :** a mixture of chopped or coarsely powdered vegetable drugs; *esp* **:** one used to prepare an aromatic tea or tisane ⟨a pectoral ~⟩ ⟨an emollient ~⟩ **5** *obs* **:** money of gold, silver, or other metal **:** COIN, SPECIE **syn** see CLASS

²species \"\ *adj* **:** constituting, being a member of, or selected from a biological species and not belonging to a horticultural variety of hybrid origin ⟨the China rose is a ~ rose⟩ ⟨native American ~ irises⟩

species-group \ˈ=(ˌ)=ˌ=\ *n* **:** ARTENKREIS

species-specific \ˈ=(ˌ)=ˌ=ˈ=\ *adj* **:** exhibiting or characterized by species specificity ⟨a *species-specific* reaction⟩

species specificity *n* **:** the phenomenon involved in the interaction of an agent (as a pathogen, drug, or antigen) and members of a given species that results in a reaction characteristic for that species — compare SUSCEPTIBILITY

spe·ci·es·ta·ler \ˈshpātsēˌstālər, -ēˌes,dāˌ-\ *n* -S [G *speziestaler*, fr. *spezies* specie (fr. L *species* species) + *taler* — more at TALER] **:** REICHSTALER

specif *abbr* **1** specific; specifically **2** specification

spec·i·fi·able \ˈspesəˌfīəbəl, ˌ=ˈ=ˌ=ˌ=\ *adj* **:** capable of being specified ⟨~ standards⟩ ⟨a ~ logical form⟩

¹spe·cif·ic \spəˈsifik, -fēk\ *adj* [LL *specificus*, fr. L *species* + *-ficus* -fic] **1 :** constituting or falling into the category specified ⟨~ fertilizing agents such as nitrogen or phosphate⟩ **2 :** having a real and fixed relationship to and usu. constituting a characteristic of **:** being peculiar to the thing or relation in question ⟨the ~ qualities of a drug⟩ ⟨a ~ distinction between vice and virtue⟩ ⟨~ symptoms of a disease⟩ **3 :** restricted by nature to a particular individual, situation, relation, or effect **:** PECULIAR ⟨faults ~ to past centuries⟩: as **a** *of a therapeutic agent* **:** exerting a definitive and distinctive influence on a particular part of the body or on the course of a particular disease ⟨quinine is highly ~ for malaria⟩ **b** *of a parasite* (1) **:** capable of living and reproducing in only one kind of host (2) **:** producing a particular disease **c** *of a disease* **:** caused by a particular pathogen (as a microorganism) **d** *of an antigen or antibody* **:** capable of reacting with but one antibody or antigen or with an antibody or antigen in but one way ⟨in complement fixation both antigen and antibody may be either ~ or nonspecific⟩ **4 a :** characterized by precise formulation or accurate restriction (as in stating, describing, defining, reserving) **:** free from such ambiguity as results from careless lack of precision or from omission of pertinent matter ⟨a ~ statement of faith⟩ ⟨~ analysis of the problem⟩ ⟨a ~ agreement⟩ **b :** intended for or restricted to a particular end or object ⟨a ~ deposit in a bank⟩ **5 :** of, relating to, or constituting a species and esp. a taxonomic species ⟨groups of ~ rank⟩ ⟨distinctive ~ characters⟩ **6 :** being any of various arbitrary physical constants and esp. one relating a quantitative attribute to unit mass, volume, or area ⟨~ luminous intensity is the luminous intensity per unit area of source⟩ — see SPECIFIC ENTROPY, SPECIFIC GRAVITY, SPECIFIC HEAT, SPECIFIC HUMIDITY **syn** see EXPLICIT, SPECIAL

²specific \"\ *n* -S **1 a :** something peculiarly adapted to its purpose, use, or situation **b :** a drug that has a specific mitigating influence on a disease ⟨quinine is a ~ for malaria⟩ **2 a :** a specific or characteristic quality, trait, mark, or other feature **b :** precise details or distinctions **:** PARTICULARS ⟨music frees us from the ~ and stirs the unconscious depths of our being⟩ **c specifics** *pl* **:** SPECIFICATION 4 ⟨work out the ~s required for putting his program into effect —*New Republic*⟩ **syn** see REMEDY

specific absorptive index *n* **:** absorbance of radiation per unit thickness of layer and concentration of solution

spe·cif·i·cal \-fəkəl\ *adj* [ME, fr. LL *specificus* + ME *-al*] *archaic* **:** SPECIFIC

spe·cif·i·cal·i·ty \ˌ=ˌ=fəˈkalədē, -lətē, -i\ *n* -ES [*specifical* + *-ity*] **:** the quality or state of being specific

spe·cif·i·cal·ly \spəˈsifək(ə)lē, -fēk-, -li\ *adv* [*specifical* + *-ly*] **1 :** in regard to the matter in question **:** with reference to a quality or condition that is specified or inherent ⟨water is ~ heavier than ice⟩ ⟨a product of ~ architectural imagination —R.W.Kennedy⟩ **2 :** with exactness and precision **:** in a definite manner ⟨~ denounced the new tax⟩

spe·cif·i·cate \-fəˌkāt\ *vt* -ED/-ING/-S [LL *specificatus*, past part. of *specificare* to specify — more at SPECIFY] **:** to give specificity to **:** SPECIFY

spec·i·fi·ca·tion \ˌspesəfəˈkāshən\ *n* -S [ML *specification-*, *specificatio*, fr. LL *specificatus* + L *-ion-, -io* -ion] **1 a** *obs* **:** the giving of a definitive or specific quality **b :** conversion of property and esp. of property belonging to another into a new kind of property by labor (as in manufacture); *also* **:** the acquisition of title in property so produced that results under Roman, Scots, or civil law when the article cannot be reduced to its original form **2** *obs* **:** natural or specific character **:** characteristic quality **3 :** the act or process of identifying or making specific through the supplying of particularizing detail **:** a decreasing of generality or vagueness (as of a concept) by determining or supplying characteristics that delimit a more precise applicability; *esp* **:** the replacement of a variable in a propositional function in symbolic logic by a specific value ⟨"the sky is blue" is obtained by ~ from "*x* is blue"⟩ **4 :** a detailed, precise, explicit presentation (as by enumeration, description, or working drawing) of something or a plan or proposal for something: as **a :** a written statement containing a minute description or enumeration of particulars (as of charges against a public officer or of the terms of a contract); *also* **:** a single article, item, or particular or an allegation of a specific act **b :** a written description of an invention or discovery for which a patent is sought that embodies the manner and process of making, constructing, compounding, and using and concludes with a specific and distinct claim of the part, improvement, or combination which the applicant regards as his discovery or invention — compare CLAIM **c :** a written or printed description of constructional work to be done (as in repairing a house or installing machinery in a factory) forming part of the contract, describing qualities of material and mode of construction, and giving dimension and other information not shown in the drawings — usu. used in pl.

spec·i·fi·ca·tive \ˈspesəfəˌkād·iv, spəˈsifə,-\ *adj* [LL *specificatus* + E *-ive*] **:** tending or serving to specify — **spec·i·fi·ca·tive·ly** \-d·əvlē\ *adv*

specific capacity *n* **:** the amount of water furnished under a standard unit head **:** the amount of water that is furnished under unit lowering of the surface of the water in a well by pumping

specific character *n* **:** a character distinguishing one species from another or from every other species of the same genus

specific charge *n* **1 :** a charge against specific identifiable property that is essentially the same in effect as a mortgage **2 :** the ratio of the electric charge on a particle to its mass

specific color *n* **:** a color having hue and saturation **:** a chromatic color

specific conductance *n* **:** CONDUCTIVITY

specific cost *n* **:** DIRECT COST

specific duty *n* **:** a duty assessed on an article of a given kind at a flat rate per unit of quantity (as a ton, bushel, or yard) without individual appraisal

specific dynamic action *n* **:** the effect of ingestion and assimilation of food and esp. of protein in increasing the production of heat in the body

specific energy *n* **:** the supposed specific quality of a sensory nerve that has been held to cause it to transmit a particular kind of sensation whatever the nature of the stimulus and that is usu. attributed to interpretive and correlative processes in the central nervous system

specific entropy *n* **:** entropy of a substance per unit mass (as per gram or per mole)

specific epithet *n* **:** the Latin or latinized noun or adjective that follows and agrees grammatically with the genus name in the name of a taxonomic species — called also *trivial name*

specific gravity *n* **:** the ratio of the density of a substance to the density of some substance (as pure water at its temperature of maximum density at 4° C) taken as a standard when both densities are obtained by weighing in air ⟨if one cubic inch of gold weighs in air 19.3 times as much as one cubic inch of water, the *specific gravity* of gold is 19.3⟩

specific-gravity balance *n* **:** a balance used for determining the specific gravity of a liquid or solid by means of the Archimedes' principle

specific-gravity bottle *or* **specific-gravity flask** *n* **:** a pycnometer having the form of a stoppered bottle

specific-gravity bulb *n* **:** a hollow glass bulb so weighted that it will float on a liquid of greater and sink in a liquid of less specific gravity than that marked on the bulb

specific heat *n* **1 :** the ratio of the quantity of heat required to raise the temperature of a body one degree to that required to raise the temperature of an equal mass of water one degree **2 :** the heat in calories required to raise the temperature of one gram of a substance one degree centigrade

specific humidity *n* **:** the mass of water vapor per unit mass of moist air

specific impulse *n* **:** the thrust produced per unit rate of consumption of the propellant usu. specified in pounds of thrust per pound of propellant used per second and forming a measure of the efficiency of performance of a rocket engine

specific ionization *n* **:** the number of ion pairs formed in a gas by an ionizing particle per unit length of its path

spec·i·fic·i·ty \ˌspesəˈfisəd·ē, -sətē, -i\ *n* -ES **:** the quality or state of being specific ⟨contribute a desirable note of ~ to the discussion —H.D.Gideonse⟩; *esp* **:** the condition of being peculiar to a particular individual or group of organisms ⟨host ~ of a parasite⟩

spe·cif·i·cize \spəˈsifəˌsīz\ *vt* -ED/-ING/-S **:** to make specific **:** give a specific quality to

specific key *n* **:** a key for a single cryptographic message or a small group of messages — compare PERIOD KEY

specific legacy *n* **:** a bequest of a particular identifiable and existing thing or part (as a specified animal) out of a testator's estate — compare GENERAL LEGACY

specific lien *n* **:** PARTICULAR LIEN

specific magnetization *n* **:** the ratio of the magnetization of a substance to the density obtained by dividing the magnetic moment of a specimen by its mass

specific modifier *n* **:** a gene that modifies the effect of one or more other genes

specific name *n* **:** the binomial name of a taxonomic species consisting of the name of its genus followed by a specific epithet

spe·cif·ic·ness *n* -ES **:** the quality or state of being specific

specific performance *n* **:** the performance of a legal contract exactly or substantially according to its terms — used chiefly with reference to such performance as decreed by a court of equity in a case where the common-law remedy of damages would be substantially inadequate and the specific performance not unjust to the defendant

specific rate *n* **:** an insurance rate specif. computed for a particular risk **:** SCHEDULE RATE

specific refractivity *n* **:** the refractivity of a medium divided by its density

specific resistance *n* **:** RESISTIVITY 2b

specific rotation *n* **:** the angle of rotation in degrees of the plane of polarization of a ray of monochromatic light that passes through a tube 1 decimeter long containing the substance in solution at a concentration of 1 gram per milliliter in a polarimeter

specifics *pl of* SPECIFIC

specific stain *n* **:** a dye used in histology and microchemistry that has a specific affinity for particular structural elements or chemical compounds

specific surface *n* **:** the ratio of the total surface of a substance (as an adsorbent) to its volume **:** surface area (as of a finely divided powder) per unit mass

specific volume *n* **:** the volume per unit mass of a substance **:** the reciprocal of the density

specific weight *n* **:** the weight of a substance per unit volume in absolute units equal to the density multiplied by the acceleration of gravity

spec·i·fi·er \ˈspesəˌfī(ə)r, -īə\ *n* -S **:** one that specifies (as by giving details or particulars); *esp* **:** a person who draws up specifications (as for obtaining a patent)

spec·i·fy \-ˌfī\ *vb* -ED/-ING/-ES [ME *specifien*, fr. OF *specifier*, fr. LL *specificare*, fr. *specificus* specific] *vt* **1 a :** to mention or name in a specific or explicit manner **:** tell or state precisely or in detail ⟨~ the uses of a plant⟩ ⟨clearly *specified* the one he meant⟩ ⟨the bequest *specifies* that the recipient must care for the cat⟩ **b :** to include as an item in a specification ⟨~*ing* oak flooring throughout⟩; *also* **:** to draw specifications of **2 :** to make specific **:** give a specific character or application to ⟨tensions that ~ personal conflicts⟩ **~** *vi* **:** to speak precisely or in detail **:** give full particulars **syn** see MENTION

spec·i·men \ˈspesəmən *sometimes* -esm-\ *n* -S [L, fr. *specere* to look, look at — more at SPY] **1 a :** a particular single item, part, aspect, or incident that is typical and indicative of the nature, character, or quality of others in the same class or group ⟨a ~ of the melodramatic fiction of the era —T.S. Eliot⟩ ⟨compared ~s of their handwriting⟩ ⟨repeated a ~ from which the tenor of the conversation could be readily inferred⟩ **b :** a sample or unit (as of merchandise, a mineral, or a plant) that is deliberately selected for examination, display, or study and is usu. chosen as typical of its kind ⟨a ~ cabinet⟩ ⟨~s of a new line of textiles⟩: as (1) **:** a printed sheet showing different styles and sizes of type (2) **:** a sample copy of a printed work; *specif* **:** a condensed sample containing enough of the typography, illustrations, maps, binding, and other features to give an adequate idea of the complete work (3) **:** a postage stamp printed as a sample and bearing the word *specimen* (4) **:** a portion of material for use in testing ⟨a fecal ~⟩ ⟨wool ~s for staple testing⟩ **2 a :** something that obviously belongs to a particular category but shows or is noticed by reason of some individual distinguishing character or peculiarity ⟨the scavenging pigs, the dirtiest, leanest, and hungriest ~s I have met with —V.G.Heiser⟩ **b :** INDIVIDUAL, PERSON ⟨turned out to be a queer ~⟩ ⟨~s like these fellows that hang around the docks⟩ **syn** see INSTANCE

specimen plant *n* **:** a plant grown for exhibition or in the open to display its full development as distinguished from one in a border or other planting

specio- — see SPECI-

spe·ci·os·i·ty \ˌspēshēˈäsəd·ē, -sətē, -i\ *n* -ES [ME *specioustee* beauty, fr. LL *speciositat-, speciositas*, fr. L *speciosus* beautiful + *-itat-, -itas* -ity] **1 :** the quality or state of being specious **2 :** a specious appearance or thing

spe·cious \ˈspēshəs\ *adj* [ME, fr. L *speciosus* beautiful, showy, plausible, fr. *species* appearance, beauty + *-osus* -ous — more at SPY] **1** *obs* **:** presenting a pleasing appearance **:** pleasing in form or look **:** SHOWY **2 :** superficially beautiful or attractive but not so in reality **:** deceptively beautiful **3 :** apparently right or proper **:** superficially fair, just, or correct but not so in reality **:** appearing well at first view **:** PLAUSIBLE ⟨~ reasoning⟩ ⟨a ~ claim⟩ **4 :** existing to our senses **:** actually known or experienced — see SPECIOUS PRESENT — **spe·cious·ly** *adv* — **spe·cious·ness** *n* -ES

specious present *n* **:** the time span of immediate consciousness **:** interval within which what is earlier may be distinguished from what is later though both are directly present to consciousness

¹speck \ˈspek\ *n* -S [ME *specke*, fr. OE *specca*] **1 a :** a small discoloration in or on something **:** SPOT, STAIN ⟨a ~ on paper or cloth⟩ ⟨covered with dark ~s⟩ **b :** a small discoloration revealing decay (as in fruit); *broadly* **:** FLAW, BLEMISH ⟨a reputation without a ~⟩ **2 :** a tiny bit of something **:** a small piece, particle, or amount **:** MITE ⟨put just a ~ of milk in the tea⟩ ⟨ore sparkling with ~s of gold⟩ ⟨the announcement failed to arouse a ~ of interest⟩ **3 a :** a bacterial or fungous disease of rice characterized by shriveled or specked grains **b :** a disease of plants characterized by small usu. circumscribed lesions — see BACTERIAL SPECK **4 :** something marked or marred with specks: as **a :** imperfect but usable fruit ⟨bought a basket of ~s for jelly⟩ **b :** a spotted or speckled fish ⟨when the big ~s begin biting⟩ **5 :** a small sand darter (*Ulocentra stigmaea*) common in the southeastern U. S.

²speck \"\ *vt* -ED/-ING/-S **1 :** to produce specks and esp. blemishes on or in **:** SPOT, SPECKLE **2 :** to remove specks from (as cloth)

³speck \"\ *n* -S [ME *spekke*] *dial Eng* **:** PATCH

⁴speck \"\ *n* [D *spek* (fr. MD *spec*) & G *speck*, fr. OHG *spek*; both akin to OE *spec, spic* bacon, blubber, ON *spik*, Skt *sphigī* buttock, *sphāyati* he increases, grows fat — more at speed] *chiefly dial* **:** fat meat: as **a :** BACON, SALT PORK **b :** the blubber of a whale or other marine mammal **c** *Africa* **:** the fat of the hippopotamus esp. when cured for use as bacon

⁵speck \"\ *vi* -ED/-ING/-S [by shortening and alter.] *Austral* **:** PROSPECT 1a

specked \ˈspekt\ *adj* [ME, fr. *specke* speck + *-ed*] **:** marked or marred with or as if with specks **:** SPOTTED, SPECKLED — **speck·ed·ness** \ˈspekədnəs\ *n* -ES

speckeldy *var of* SPECKLEDY

speck·er \ˈspekə(r)\ *n* -S **:** one that specks; *esp* **:** a worker that removes specks from something

speckfall \ˈ=ˌ=\ *n* [⁴*speck* + *fall*] **:** a fall rove through a block for hoisting blubber and bone aboard a whaler

speck finger *n* [²*speck* + *finger*] **:** ERYSIPELOID

speckier *comparative of* SPECKY

speckiest *superlative of* SPECKY

speck·i·ness \ˈspekēnəs, -kin-\ *n* -ES **:** the quality or state of being specky

¹speck·le \ˈspekəl\ *n* -S *often attrib* [ME *spakle, speckle*; akin to MD *speckel* speckle, OE *specca* speck] **:** a small mark, splotch, or speck; *esp* **:** an irregular natural speck (as of color) ⟨white eggs covered with purplish ~s⟩ ⟨a *speckle*-bellied goose⟩

²speckle \"\ *vt* **speckled; speckled; speckling** \-k(ə)liŋ\ **speckles 1 :** to mark with small spots or specks **:** SPECK, SPOT ⟨sunlight *speckling* the lawn⟩ ⟨decided to ~ the finish of the floor⟩ **2 :** to dot in the manner of speckles ⟨little lakes *speckled* the land⟩ ⟨a slope *speckled* with houses⟩

specklebelly \ˈ=ˌ=ˌ=\ *n* [¹*speckle* + *belly*] **1 :** WHITE-FRONTED GOOSE **2 :** GADWALL

specklebreast \ˈ=ˌ=\ *also* **speckle-breasted brant** \ˌ=ˈ=ˌ=-\ *or* **speckle-breasted goose** *n* **:** WHITE-FRONTED GOOSE

speckle-cheek \ˈ=ˌ=ˌ=\ *n* **:** CACTUS WOODPECKER

speck·led \ˈspekəld\ *adj* [ME *spacled*, fr. *spakle* speckle + *-ed*] **:** covered or marked with speckles **:** SPOTTED

speckled alder *n* **:** a common shrub (*Alnus rugosa*) of the north temperate zone with oval leaves and catkins that flower much before the leaves expand

speckled bass *n* **:** BLACK CRAPPIE

speckledbill \ˈ=ˌ=ˌ=\ *n* **:** SURF SCOTER

speckled blotch *or* **speckled leaf blotch** *n* **:** a disease of wheat caused by fungi of the genus *Septoria* and characterized by pinhead-sized light-colored leaf spots that later develop into blackish spore pustules

speckled brant *n* **:** WHITE-FRONTED GOOSE

speckled bullhead *n* **:** BROWN BULLHEAD

speckled crab *n* **:** an active shallow-water crab (*Araneus cribrarius*) that is found from Massachusetts to Brazil and is light brown thickly dotted with white or yellow

speckled hind *n* **:** a large grouper (*Epinephelus drummondhayi*) that is umber brown densely covered with small pearly-white or bluish dots and is a common food fish of the Florida coast

speckled moray *n* **:** HAMLET 2

speck·led·ness \ˈspekəldnəs\ *n* -ES **:** the quality or state of being speckled

speckled perch *n* **:** BLACK CRAPPIE
speckled trout *n* **1** *or* **speckle trout a :** BROOK TROUT **b :** RAINBOW TROUT; *broadly* **:** any of several trouts of the western U.S. **2 :** SPOTTED WEAKFISH
speckled turtle *or* **speckled tortoise** *n* **:** SPOTTED TURTLE
speckled wood *n* **1 :** LETTERWOOD **2 :** palmyra wood cut transversely so as to give a mottled effect
speck·ledy *also* **speck·eldy** \'spekəldē, -di\ *adj* [*speckled* + *-y*] **:** marked with spots or speckles
speckled yellows *n pl but usu sing in constr* **:** a manganese deficiency disease of table beets, sugar beets, and mangels marked by development of yellowish interveinal areas on the leaf that often turn brown and fall out
specklehead \'≈,≈\ *n* **:** BALDPATE 2
speckles *pl of* SPECKLE, *pres 3d sing of* SPECKLE
speck·less \'≈ləs\ *adj* **:** free from specks **:** UNMARKED, SPOTLESS; *esp* **:** perfectly clean — **speck·less·ly** *adv* — **speck·less·ness** *n* -ES
speckling *n* -S [fr. gerund of ²*speckle*] **:** speckled marking
speck·ly \'spek(ə)lē, -li\ *adj* -ER/-EST [¹*speckle* + *-y*] **:** marked with speckles **:** SPECKLED
¹specks *pl of* SPECK, *pres 3d sing of* SPECK
²specks \'speks\ *n pl* [alter. of *specs*] **:** GLASS 2b(2)
specky \-kē, -ki\ *adj* -ER/-EST [¹*speck* + *-y*] **:** marked or marred with specks or spots
specl *abbr* specialist
speclst *abbr* specialist
specs \'speks\ *n pl* **1** [contr. of *spectacles*] **:** GLASS 2b(2) **2** [pl. of *spec*] **:** SPECIFICATIONS
spectable *adj* [ME, fr. L *spectabilis*, fr. *spectare* to look, observe + *-abilis* -able] *obs* **:** VISIBLE; *also* **:** SIGHTLY
spec·ta·cle \'spektəkəl, -tēk- *also* -,tik-\ *n* -S [ME, fr. MF, fr. L *spectaculum*, fr. *spectare* to look at, watch, view, freq. of *specere* to look at, catch sight of — more at SPY] **1 a :** something exhibited to view; *usu* **:** something exhibited as unusual and notable **:** a remarkable or noteworthy sight **:** an impressive display esp. for entertainment **b :** an object of curiosity or contempt esp. by reason of silly or inappropriate behavior ⟨made a ~ of herself at the party⟩ **c** (1) **:** a public display appealing or intended to appeal to the eye by its mass, proportions, color, or other dramatic qualities ⟨a great dramatic ~⟩ ⟨a naval ~⟩ ⟨the opening ~ of a circus⟩ (2) **:** a motion picture employing massively impressive scenery and much crowd action, usu. set in past time, and commonly dealing with a historical or religious theme **2 :** a means of viewing or observing: as **a** *obs* **:** an object of glass (as a window or mirror) **b** (1) *obs* **:** an aid to vision (as a spyglass) (2) **:** GLASS 2b(2); *esp* **:** glasses that are supported by the ears as distinguished from goggles or pince-nez — usu. used in pl. and often with *pair* ⟨a new pair of ~s⟩ **3 :** any of various things felt to resemble a pair of glasses: as **a spectacles** *pl* **:** a colored marking on an animal either in the form of a double loop (as on the spectacled cobra) or of rings about the eyes (as on some birds) **b :** a frame containing the red and green lights of a railroad semaphore **c :** a device with two handles used to move well-boring tools **d spectacles** *pl, Brit* **:** a cricketer's score of nothing in each of his two innings in a single match **:** PAIR OF SPECTACLES

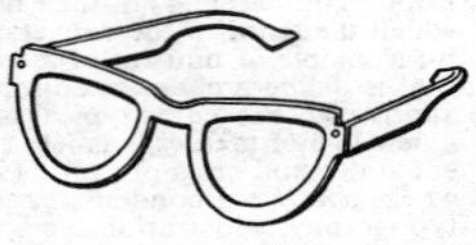
spectacles

spectacle clew *or* **spectacle iron** *n* **:** a steel device consisting of three rings at the clews of square sails into which three ropes or blocks can be hooked
spectacle coot *n* [short for *spectacled coot*] **:** SURF SCOTER
spec·ta·cled \-kəld\ *adj* [*spectacle, spectacles* + *-ed*] **1 :** having or wearing spectacles **2 :** having color markings or patches of naked skin suggesting a pair of spectacles ⟨~ alligator⟩
spectacled bear *n* **:** a bear (*Tremarctos ornatus*) of the Andes mountains
spectacled caiman *n* **:** a caiman with bony ridges about the eyes; *esp* **:** a common caiman (*Caiman sclerops*) that occurs from southern Mexico to the Argentine
spectacled cobra *n* **:** INDIAN COBRA
spectacled coot *or* **spectacled duck** *n* **:** SURF SCOTER
spectacled dolphin *n* **:** any of several dolphins (genus *Lagenorhynchus*) that are distinctively striped in black and white — called also *skunk porpoise*
spectacled eider *n* **:** a chiefly Siberian eider duck (*Somateria fischeri*) that has large white black-margined patches about the eyes
spectacled goose *n, Brit* **:** the common gannet (*Sula bassana*)
spectacled pelican *n* **:** a large predominantly white pelican (*Pelecanus conspicillatus*) of Australia and New Guinea that has the wings and hinder parts somewhat dusky to blackish
spectacled warbler *n* **:** a small Old World warbler (*Sylvia conspicillata*) with a dark slaty gray head and white eye rings
spectacle frame *n* **:** a frame at or near the sternposts through which both shafts pass in a twin-screw ship having the stern bossed out to surround both shafts
spectacle furnace *n* **:** a German shaft furnace with two tapholes
spec·ta·cle·less \-kəl(l)əs\ *adj* **:** having or wearing no spectacles
spectacle pod *n* **:** an annual cruciferous herb (*Dithyrea californica*) of the southwestern U.S. having thin fruits that resemble miniature spectacles
spectacle stone *n* **:** any of the ancient monumental stones of Scotland ornamented with connected or overlapping disks or rude spirals and probably of Celtic origin
¹spec·tac·u·lar \(')spek¦takyələ(r) *sometimes* spək't-\ *adj* [L *spectaculum* spectacle + E *-ar*] **1 :** of, relating to, or constituting a spectacle **:** adapted or intended to excite wonder and admiration by unusual display (as of pomp or scenic effects) ⟨a ~ play⟩ ⟨a ~ display of northern lights⟩ **2 :** of a kind to attract notice distinctly unusual or unexpected ⟨a ~ rise in prices⟩ ⟨a ~ scheme⟩ — **spec·tac·u·lar·i·ty** \(,)spek,takyə'larəd·ē *also* spək-\ *n* -ES
²spectacular \"\ *n* -S **:** something that is spectacular and esp. is designed to appeal to the eye as a spectacle **:** an unusual display (as of pomp or scenery): as **a :** an action or a sight of a sensational nature ⟨ever a lover of the ~⟩ **b :** a large custom-built advertising display usu. of electric or neon lights and designed to produce a special effect or unusual animation **c :** a long elaborately produced television show featuring noted entertainers
spec·tac·u·lar·ism \spek'takyələ,rizəm *also* spək'-\ *n* -S **:** the quality or state of being spectacular
spec·tac·u·lar·ly *adv* **:** in a spectacular manner
spec·tate \'spek,tāt\ *vi* -ED/-ING/-S [L *spectatus*, past part. of *spectare*] **:** OBSERVE, WATCH; *esp* **:** to be present as a spectator (as at a sports event)
¹spec·ta·tor \'spek,tād·ə(r), -atə-, ≈'≈≈\ *n* -S [L, fr. *spectatus* (past part. of *spectare* to look at, watch, view) + *-or* — more at SPECTACLE] **1 :** one that looks on or beholds; *esp* **:** one witnessing an exhibition (as a sports event) **2** *or* **spectator pump :** a woman's pump designed for casual wear with a medium to high heel and a leather upper often with contrasting color at the toe and heel

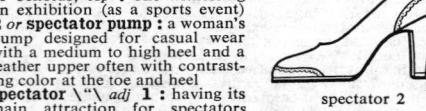

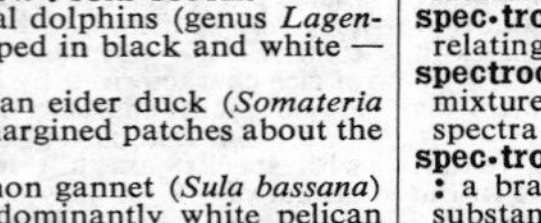
spectator 2

²spectator \"\ *adj* **1 :** having its main attraction for spectators **:** tending to attract spectators ⟨such ~ sports as racing⟩ **2 :** styled in an informal or casual manner and suitable for use by a spectator at a sports event ⟨a ~ frock⟩
spec·ta·to·ri·al \¦spektə¦tōrēəl, -tȯr-\ *adj* [¹*spectator* + *-ial*] **1 a :** of or relating to a spectator **b** *sometimes cap* [after *The Spectator* published in London 1711–12 by Joseph Addison †1719 and Richard Steele †1729] **:** suggesting the critical observations of a periodical essay
spec·ta·tor·itis \(,)spek,tād·ə'rīd·əs\ *n* -ES [¹*spectator* + *-itis*] **:** excessive indulgence in forms of amusement in which one is a passive spectator rather than an active participant
spec·ta·tor·ship \'≈,≈≈,ship, ≈'≈≈,≈\ *n* [¹*spectator* + *-ship*] **1** *obs* **:** the condition of being viewed or submitted for viewing **2 :** the condition of being a spectator esp. as distinguished from a participant
spec·ta·to·ry \(')spek¦tād·ərē\ *n* -ES [¹*spectator* + *-ory*] **:** a part of a building set apart for spectators; *also* **:** a body of spectators
spec·ta·tress \spek'tā·trəs, '≈,≈≈\ *also* **spec·ta·trix** \-·triks\ *n* -ES [*spectatress* fr. *spectator* + *-ess*; *spectatrix* fr. L, fem. of *spectator*] **:** a female spectator
spec·ter *or* **spec·tre** \'spektə(r)\ *n* -S [F *spectre*, fr. L *spectrum* appearance, specter, fr. *specere* to look — more at SPY] **1 :** a visible disembodied spirit **:** APPARITION, GHOST, PHANTOM **2 :** a ghostly and usu. fear-inspiring vision of the imagination **:** something that haunts or persistently perturbs the mind **:** PHANTASM ⟨the ~ of want⟩ **3 a :** STICK INSECT **b** *or* **specter crab :** GLASS CRAB **c :** SPECTER SHRIMP
specter bat *n* **:** a phyllostome bat; *esp* **:** a large tropical American leaf-nosed bat (*Vampyrum spectrum*)
specter candle *n* **:** BELEMNITE
spec·tered *or* **spec·tred** \-tə(r)d\ *adj* [*specter* + *-ed*] **:** peopled with specters
specter lemur *n* **:** TARSIER
specter of the brocken *usu cap B* **:** BROCKEN SPECTER
specter shrimp *n* **1 :** SKELETON SHRIMP **2 :** GHOST SHRIMP
spectra *pl of* SPECTRUM
spec·tral \'spektrəl\ *adj* [L & NL *spectrum* + E *-al*] **1 a :** of, like, or relating to a specter **:** GHOSTLY **b :** lacking in solid substance **:** FALSE, ILLUSORY **2 :** of or relating to a spectrum **:** made by the spectrum ⟨~ analysis⟩ — **spec·tral·i·ty** \spek'traləd·ē\ *or* **spec·tral·ness** \'spektrəlnəs\ *n* -ES — **spec·tral·ly** \-rəlē, -li\ *adv*
spectral bat *n* **:** SPECTER BAT
spectral distribution *n* **:** a function expressing analytically or graphically the relation between radiant or luminous flux per wavelength or frequency interval and wavelength or frequency
spectral lemur *n* **:** TARSIER
spectral line *n* **:** one of a series of linear images of the narrow slit of a spectrograph or similar instrument corresponding to a component of the spectrum of the radiation emitted by a particular source
spectral owl *n* **:** GREAT GRAY OWL
spectral type *n* **:** the type of a star according to a description of its spectrum by means of 10 principal spectral classes, decimal subdivisions of the classes, and symbols indicating special characteristics (as *e* for stars with bright lines, *d* for dwarfs, and *g* for giants)

PRINCIPAL SPECTRAL TYPES

TYPE	SURFACE TEMPERATURE (° KELVIN)	COLOR	MOST PROMINENT SPECTRAL LINES AND BANDS
O	50,000	blue	hydrogen, ionized helium, ionized oxygen, ionized nitrogen
B	20,000	bluish	hydrogen, helium
A	10,000	white	hydrogen
F	7,000	yellowish	hydrogen, ionized calcium
G	5,500	yellow	hydrogen, ionized calcium, metals
K	4,500	orange	ionized calcium, metals, cyanogen
M	3,000	red	titanium oxide, vanadium oxide
R	2,500	red	carbon, carbon compounds
S	2,400	red	zirconium oxide, lanthanum oxide
N	2,000	very red	carbon, carbon compounds

spectro- *comb form* [NL *spectrum*] **1 :** spectral and ⟨*spectro*chemical⟩ **2 :** of or relating to spectra ⟨*spectro*photography⟩ **3** [*spectroscope*] **:** combined with a spectroscope ⟨*spectro*polarimeter⟩
spec·tro·bolometer \¦spek(,)trō+\ *n* [*spectro-* + *bolometer*] **:** a combination of spectroscope and bolometer for determining the distribution of energy in a spectrum **:** SPECTRORADIOMETER
spec·tro·chemical \"+\ *adj* [*spectro-* + *chemical*] **:** of, relating to, or applying the methods of spectrochemistry
spectrochemical analysis *n* **:** the chemical analysis of a mixture of substances or of a complex substance by a study of spectra
spec·tro·chemistry \¦spek(,)trō+\ *n* [*spectro-* + *chemistry*] **:** a branch of chemistry based on a study of the spectra of substances
spec·tro·colorimetry \"+\ *n* [*spectro-* + *colorimetry*] **:** quantitative study of color by means of the spectrophotometer usu. for purposes of chemical analysis
spec·tro·gram \'spektr(ə),gram, -graa(ə)m\ *n* [ISV *spectro-* + *-gram*] **1 :** a photograph, map, or diagram of a spectrum **2 :** SOUND SPECTROGRAM
spec·tro·graph \-graf, -gaa(ə)f, -graif, -gräf\ *n* [ISV *spectro-* + *-graph*] **1 :** an apparatus for dispersing radiation into a spectrum and for photographing or mapping the spectrum — see CRYSTAL SPECTROGRAPH, MASS SPECTROGRAPH; compare SPECTROGRAM, SPECTROSCOPE **2 :** SOUND SPECTROGRAPH — **spec·tro·graph·ic** \¦≈≈¦grafik\ *adj* — **spec·tro·graph·i·cal·ly** \-fək(ə)lē\ *adv*
spec·trog·ra·pher \spek'trägrəfə(r)\ *n* -S [*spectrography* + *-er*] **:** SPECTROSCOPIST
spec·trog·ra·phy \-fē, -fi\ *n* -ES [ISV *spectro-* + *-graphy*] **:** the art or technique of using the spectrograph
spec·tro·heliogram \¦spek(,)trō+\ *n* [*spectro-* + *heli-* + *-gram*] **:** a photograph of the sun made by monochromatic light usu. of the hydrogen-alpha line in the red or the calcium K line in the violet and showing the sun's faculae and prominences
spec·tro·heliograph \"+\ *n* [ISV *spectro-* + *heli-* + *-graph*] **:** an apparatus for making spectroheliograms consisting of a spectroscopic camera used in combination with a telescope and provided with clockwork for moving the sun's image across the slit — **spec·tro·heliographic** \"+\ *adj*
spec·tro·he·lio·kinematograph \¦spek(,)trō¦hēlēō+\ *n* [*spectro-* + *heli-* + *kinematograph*] **:** a spectroheliograph equipped with a motion-picture camera
spec·tro·he·li·o·scope \,≈(,)≈'hēlēə,skōp\ *n* [ISV *spectro-* + *heli-* + *-scope*] **1 :** SPECTROHELIOGRAPH **2 :** an instrument similar to a spectroheliograph used for visual as distinguished from photographic observations — **spec·tro·he·li·o·scop·ic** \¦≈(,)≈¦≈≈≈¦skäpik\ *adj*
spec·trol·o·gy \spek'träləjē\ *n* -ES [L *spectrum* specter + E *-o-* + *-logy*] **:** the study of specters
spec·trom·e·ter \≈'trämәd·ə(r), -mətə-\ *n* [ISV *spectro-* + *-meter*] **1 :** an instrument used in determining the index of refraction by measuring the external angle of a prism of a substance and also its angle of minimum deviation for light of a given kind **2 :** a spectroscope fitted for measurements of the spectra observed with it — compare MASS SPECTROMETER

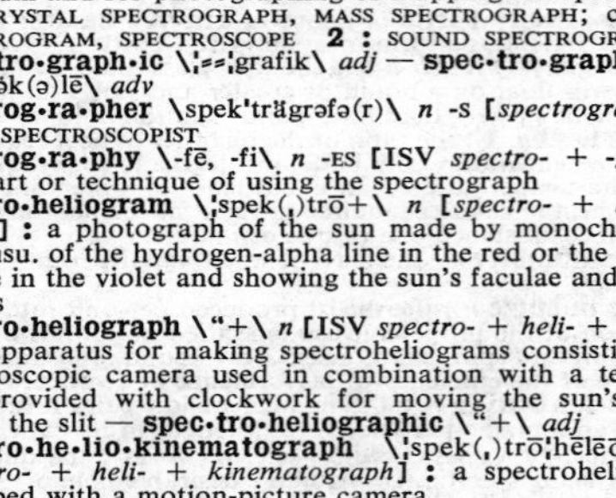

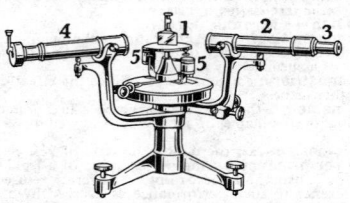

spectrometer: *1* prism, *2* telescope, *3* eyepiece, *4* collimator, *5*, *5* magnifying glasses

spec·tro·met·ric \¦spektrə¦me·trik\ *adj* [ISV *spectro-* + *-metric*] **:** of, relating to, or involving spectrometry or the spectrometer
spec·trom·e·try \spek'trämə·trē, -ri\ *n* -ES [ISV *spectro-* + *-metry*] **:** the art or process of using the spectrometer or of measuring wavelengths of rays of a spectrum
spec·tro·microscope \¦spek(,)trō+\ *n* [*spectro-* + *microscope*] **:** a microscope with a spectroscopic attachment — compare MICROSPECTROSCOPE — **spec·tro·microscopical** \"+\ *adj*
spec·tro·photoelectric \"+\ *adj* [*spectro-* + *photoelectric*] **:** varying in photoelectric sensitiveness according to the wavelength of the exciting light
spec·tro·photometer \"+\ *n* [ISV *spectro-* + *photometer*] **:** a photometer for measuring the relative intensities of the light in different parts of a spectrum
spec·tro·photometric \"+\ *adj* [ISV *spectrophotometer* + *-ic*] **:** of, relating to, or involving spectrophotometry or the spectrophotometer — **spec·tro·photometrically** \"+\ *adv*
spec·tro·photometry \"+\ *n* [ISV *spectrophotometer* + *-y*] **:** the art or process of comparing photometrically the relative intensities of the light in different parts of a spectrum **:** the use of the spectrophotometer
spec·tro·polarimeter \"+\ *n* [*spectro-* + *polarimeter*] **:** a combined spectroscope and polarimeter that is used for the determination of the rotatory power of solutions at different wavelengths
spec·tro·polariscope \"+\ *n* [*spectro-* + *polariscope*] **:** a combined spectroscope and polariscope **:** SPECTROPOLARIMETER
spec·tro·pyrheliometer \"+\ *n* [*spectro-* + *pyrheliometer*] **:** an instrument for measuring the energy distribution in the visible and ultraviolet spectrum of emitted radiation from the sun
spec·tro·pyrometer \"+\ *n* [*spectro-* + *pyrometer*] **:** an instrument for optical or spectrophotometric estimation of the temperature of an incandescent substance
spec·tro·radiometer \"+\ *n* [*spectro-* + *radiometer*] **:** an instrument for measuring the energy distribution of emitted radiation that is a combination of spectroscope and radiometer
spec·tro·radiometric \"+\ *adj* [*spectroradiometer* + *-ic*] **:** of, relating to, or involving spectroradiometry or the spectroradiometer
spec·tro·radiometry \"+\ *n* [*spectroradiometer* + *-y*] **:** the art or process of using the spectroradiometer in the study of radiant energy
spec·tro·scope \'spektrə,skōp\ *n* [ISV *spectro-* + *-scope*] **:** any of various instruments designed for forming and examining optical spectra and being so constructed that observations are made visually — compare SPECTROGRAPH, SPECTROMETER

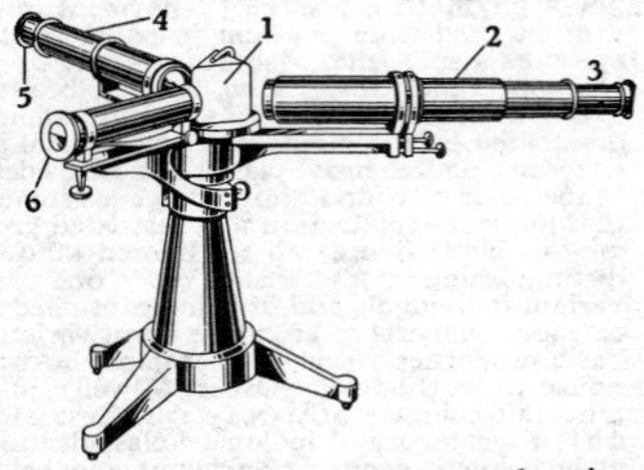

simple form of spectroscope: *1* prism, *2* telescope, *3* eyepiece, *4* collimator, *5* end with slit, *6* tube with micrometer

spec·tro·scop·ic \¦spektrə¦skäpik, -pēk\ *also* **spec·tro·scop·i·cal** \-pəkəl, -pēk-\ *adj* [*spectroscope* + *-ic*, *-ical*] **1 :** of, relating to, or involving spectroscopy or the spectroscope or sometimes spectrograph **2 :** dealing or concerned with spectroscopy — **spec·tro·scop·i·cal·ly** \-pək(ə)lē, -pēk-, -li\ *adv*
spectroscopic binary *n* **:** a binary star in which shifting of lines in the system's spectrum indicates orbital revolution
spectroscopic parallax *n* **:** the parallax of a star indicated by its absolute magnitude as deduced from the relative intensities of selected lines in its spectrum
spec·tros·co·pist \spek'träskəpəst\ *n* -S [ISV *spectroscope* + *-ist*] **:** one who uses the spectroscope **:** an expert in spectroscopy
spec·tros·co·py \-pē, -pi\ *n* -ES [ISV *spectro-* + *-scopy*] **1 a :** the production and investigation of spectra **b :** the art or process of using the spectroscope **2 :** the science of spectroscopic phenomena
spec·trous \'spektrəs\ *adj* [*specter* + *-ous*] **:** SPECTRAL
spec·trum \-trəm\ *n, pl* **spec·tra** \-rə\ *or* **spectrums** [NL, fr. L, appearance, image, specter — more at SPECTER] **1 a :** APPARITION, SPECTER **b :** AFTERIMAGE **2 :** an array of the components of an emission or wave separated and arranged in the order of some varying characteristic (as wavelength, mass, or energy): as **a :** a series of images formed when a beam of radiant energy is subjected to dispersion and brought to focus so that the component waves are arranged in the order of their wavelengths (as when a beam of sunlight that is refracted and dispersed by a prism forms a display of colors) — called also *color spectrum* **b :** ELECTROMAGNETIC SPECTRUM **c :** RADIO SPECTRUM **d** (1) **:** the range of frequencies of sound waves to which the human ear is sensitive — called also *acoustic spectrum, acoustical spectrum, sound spectrum* (2) **:** the range of frequencies of a particular sound (as a noise or a speech sound) **3 a :** an intergrading array in which the constituent elements are usu. not sharply isolable **:** a continuous sequence or range ⟨a wide ~ of opinions —Eugene Rabinowitch⟩ ⟨the total ~ of valid inference —J.T.Clark⟩ ⟨considerable deposits of a ~ of minerals ranging from platinum to mica —Smith Hempstone⟩ **b :** kinds of life forms associated with a particular situation (as an environmental region or sensitivity to an antibiotic); *also* **:** a conspectus of such forms
spectrum analysis *n* **:** the investigation of substances or bodies by means of their spectra; *specif* **:** SPECTROCHEMICAL ANALYSIS
spectrum-luminosity diagram *n* **:** a graph with the spectral type of each star plotted as the abscissa and the absolute magnitude as the ordinate
specula *pl of* SPECULUM
spec·u·lar \'spekyələ(r)\ *adj* [L *specularis* of a mirror, fr. *speculum* mirror + *-aris* -ar; in senses 3 & 4 influenced in meaning by L *speculari* to observe, examine — more at SPECULUM, SPECULATE] **1** *obs* **:** seen as if through a glass or in a mirror **:** REFLECTED **2 :** of, relating to, or having the qualities of a mirror **:** having a smooth reflecting surface or a metallic luster ⟨a ~ metal⟩ ⟨a ~ surface⟩ **3** *archaic* **:** concerned with, employed in, or assisting sight **4 :** offering an extensive prospect **:** providing a good view **5 :** of, relating to, or conducted with the aid of a medical speculum ⟨a ~ examination⟩ — **spec·u·lar·ly** *adv*
specular angle *n* **:** ANGLE OF REFLECTION
spec·u·lar·ia \,spekyə'la(a)rēə\ *n* [NL, fr. ML *speculum Veneris* campanula, lit., mirror of Venus + NL *-aria*] **1** *cap* **:** a small genus of annual herbs (family Campanulaceae) distinguished from *Campanula* by the rotate corolla and narrowly oblong ovary — see CORN VIOLET, VENUS'S LOOKING-GLASS **2** -S **:** any plant of the genus *Specularia*
specular iron *or* **specular iron ore** *n* **:** hematite with a metallic luster — called also *specularite*
specular reflection *n* **:** reflection (as of light by a mirror) at a surface having irregularities small as compared with the wavelength of the incident radiation
spec·u·late \'spekyə,lāt *sometimes* ÷ -kə-; *usu* -ād·+V\ *vb* -ED/-ING/-S [L *speculatus*, past part. of *speculari* to spy out, observe, examine, fr. *specula* watchtower, fr. *specere* to look, catch sight of — more at SPY] *vt, archaic* **:** to mull over in the mind **:** consider attentively or as an object of study **:** reflect upon ~ *vi* **1 a :** to ponder a subject in its different aspects, relations, and implications **:** indulge in contemplation **:** evolve ideas or theories by mental reexamination of a subject or matter and usu. without experimentation or introduction of new data **b :** to reason a priori **c :** to review something mentally or orally in an idle or casual manner and usu. with an element of doubt or without sufficient evidence to reach a sound or meaningful conclusion ⟨*speculating* about the chances of rain⟩ ⟨we may ~ about strangers⟩ **2 :** to enter into

a business transaction or other venture from which the profits, return of invested capital, or other good are conjectural because of the risks involved and knowingly assumed: as **a** : to purchase or sell with the expectation of profiting by anticipated but conjectural fluctuations in price **b** : to engage in hazardous business transactions for the chance of an unusually large profit; *esp* : to gamble on a stock or commodity market ⟨~ in coffee⟩ **syn** see THINK

spec·u·la·tion \ˌ==ˈlāshən\ *n* -s [ME, fr. LL *speculation-, speculatio* act of spying out, exploration, contemplation, fr. L *speculatus*, past part. of *speculari* to spy out, examine] **1 a** *archaic* : studious or profound consideration of some object or topic **b** : the faculty, act, or process of intellectual examination or investigation: as **(1)** : reasoning taking the form of prolonged and systematic analysis **(2)** : reasoning or theorizing about a matter that transcends experience and does not admit of demonstration : reasoning a priori **(3)** *Hegelianism* : reasoning that apprehends the unity of opposing categories, synthesizes them in a broader comprehension, and constitutes the thinking which explains objects of experience by their relation to the absolute personal reason **c** : contemplation or the theoretical as opposed to action or the practical **d** : light, casual, or superficial mental examination or study : mere guesswork or surmise ⟨his answer was obviously a product of ~ and not of serious thought⟩ **2** *archaic* : capacity for or exercise of the power of seeing: as **a** : comprehending or mental vision ⟨thou hast no ~ in those eyes —*Shak.*⟩ **b** : physical vision : the act of viewing : OBSERVATION **3 a** : a product of speculation: as **a** : a view, conclusion, opinion, or decision based on thought or attained by reasoning **b** : GUESS, CONJECTURE **4** *obs* : OBSERVER **5 a** : an act of speculating (as by engaging in business out of the ordinary, by dealing with a view to making a profit from conjectural fluctuations in the price rather than from earnings of the ordinary profit of trade, or by entering into a business venture involving unusual risks for a chance of an unusually large gain or profit) or the condition of being speculated in ⟨uncontrolled ~ is a danger to the national economy⟩ ⟨land ~ in the 19th century was as common as stock ~ today⟩ — contrasted with *investment* **b** : an individual transaction so entered into ⟨had a successful ~ in cotton futures⟩ **6** : a card game in which the players buy trumps from one another on a chance of getting the highest trump dealt and winning the pool

spec·u·la·tist \ˈ==ˌlād·əst\ *n* -s [*speculate* + *-ist*] : SPECULATOR

spec·u·la·tive \ˈspekyəˌlād·iv, -ˌlət, \|t\|, \|ēv *also* \|əv\ *adj* [ME *speculatif*, fr. MF, fr. LL *speculativus*, fr. L *speculatus* + *-ivus* -ive] **1 a** : involving, based on, or constituting speculation : not established by demonstration : THEORETICAL ⟨a ~ approach to a problem⟩ ⟨~ knowledge⟩ ⟨~ aspects of religion⟩ **b** : given to speculation : inclined to make or accept conclusions based on theory rather than demonstration : interested in abstractions ⟨the ~ intelligence⟩ ⟨a ~ writer⟩ **c** : forming an object of speculation : not subject to clear-cut demonstration or analysis ⟨~ matters⟩ ⟨a ~ concept⟩ **d** : marked by questioning curiosity : seeming to speculate ⟨gave him a ~ glance⟩ **2 a** *obs* : relating to or concerned with vision : VISUAL **b** : giving a wide prospect or view : constituting a vantage point for seeing ⟨a ~ height⟩ **3 a** : engaging in or making a practice of taking risks esp. in commercial matters ⟨a ~ trader⟩ **b** : involving relatively high risk and usu. an unusual potentiality for gain ⟨a ~ enterprise⟩ ⟨a ~ crop⟩; *also* : appealing primarily to speculators ⟨a ~ stock⟩ ⟨a ~ situation on an exchange⟩ **c** : concerned with economic speculation ⟨a ~ cycle⟩ — **spec·u·la·tive·ly** \\|əvlē, -li\ *adv* — **spec·u·la·tive·ness** \\|ivnəs, \|ēv- *also* \|əv-\ *n* -ES

speculative damages *n pl* : possible damages (as loss of anticipated profits depending on contingencies) not recoverable at law for lack of reasonable proof thereof : conjectural or contingent damages

speculative issue *n* : an issue of postage stamps unnecessary for postal requirements prepared chiefly for sale to collectors

speculative philosophy *n* **1** : a philosophy professing to be founded upon intuitive or a priori insight and esp. insight into the nature of the Absolute or Divine; *broadly* : a philosophy of the transcendent or one lacking empirical bases **2** : theoretical as opposed to demonstrative philosophy

speculative reason *n* : reason concerned with the supersensible — used esp. in Kantianism

speculative theology *n* : theology founded on or fundamentally influenced by speculation or metaphysical philosophy

spec·u·la·tor \-ˌlād·ə(r), -ātə-\ *n* -s [L, spy, lookout, examiner, fr. *speculatus* (past part. of *speculari* to spy out, examine) + *-or* — more at SPECULATE] : one that speculates: as **a** : a person who devotes himself to mental speculation or abstract reasoning : CONTEMPLATOR, THEORIST **b** *obs* : OBSERVER, LOOKOUT; *also* : SPY **c** : a person who speculates in business : one that engages in speculation (as in stocks, bonds, real estate) — contrasted with *investor*

spec·u·la·to·ry \ˈ==ləˌtōrē, -tȯrē, -ri\ *adj* [L *speculatus* + E *-ory*] **1** *obs* : concerned with or constituting occult speculation **2** *archaic* : SPECULATIVE 2b

spec·u·list \ˈspekyələst\ *n* -s [*speculate* + *-ist*] : one who observes or considers

spec·u·lum \-ləm\ *n, pl* **specu·la** \-lə\ *also* **speculums** [L, mirror, fr. *specere* to look, look at — more at SPY] **1** : a tubular instrument for insertion into the opening of a passage of the body esp. to facilitate visual inspection or medication ⟨vaginal ~⟩ ⟨nasal ~⟩ **2 a** : an ancient mirror usu. of bronze or silver **b** : a reflector of polished metal or of glass with a film of metal used in optical instruments **3** : a medieval treatise constituting a survey of life or of philosophy, history, and theology : a comprehensive, encyclopedic presentation of a subject aiming to be a compendium of all knowledge and usu. beginning with the Biblical account of creation, giving an outline of history, and thence passing chiefly to theology and scholastic philosophy **4** : a drawing or table showing the relative positions of all the planets (as in an astrological nativity) **5** : a patch of color covering the distal portion of the secondaries of most ducks and some other birds (as domestic fowls), exposed in the closed wing, variously colored and often with bluish or greenish iridescence or a frame of a different color, and usu. most brilliant in the adult male

speculum metal *n* : an alloy capable of taking a brilliant polish, used for making reflectors, and being commonly a hard brittle alloy of copper and tin in various ratios (as tin 33 to copper 67) with often a little arsenic, antimony, or zinc added to improve the whiteness

spe·cus \ˈspēkəs\ *n, pl* **specuses** *or* **specus** [L, cave, cavity, drain, channel; prob. akin to L *specere* to look — more at SPY] : the roofed channel in which the water of an ancient Roman aqueduct flows whether underground or raised on embankments or arches

sped *past of* SPEED

¹speech \ˈspēch\ *n* -ES [ME *speche*, fr. OE *spǣc, spēc, sprǣc, sprēc*; akin to OHG *sprāhha* speech, OE *sprecan, specan* to speak — more at SPEAK] **1 a** : the act of speaking : communication or expression of thoughts in spoken words ⟨~ is a means of producing in our hearers the images which are in us —Bertrand Russell⟩ **b** : interchange of spoken words : CONVERSATION, TALK ⟨wayfarers, after a first greeting, frequently plod on for miles without ~ —Thomas Hardy⟩ ⟨wanted to have ~ with him and could not —Arnold Bennett⟩ **c** : the sounding or speaking of a musical instrument **d** : a form or method of expression or communication ⟨so eloquent and poignant is his musical ~ that there is no other eloquence like it —A.T.Davison⟩ ⟨if another ship ever broke into ~ with flags or lamp, most ships' officers of that time panicked —Gavin Douglas⟩ **2 a** : something that is spoken : an uttered word : STATEMENT ⟨this was nearer a complaint than any ~ she had ever heard from him —Ellen Glasgow⟩ **b** : a usu. formal discourse delivered before or to an audience ⟨will make a ~ to the nation on television⟩ ⟨the queen read her ~ from the throne⟩ ⟨an impromptu ~⟩ **c** : a line or group of lines spoken at one time by a character in a play ⟨one of the most moving ~*es* in the play⟩ ⟨a dramatist with a fondness for writing long ~*es*⟩ **3 a** : a form of spoken communication or expression developed by a particular group of people (as of a nation, region, or class) : a language, dialect, or idiom ⟨had to begin by studying their ~ and creating a written language —*Amer. Guide Series: Minn.*⟩ ⟨wrote several treatises in his native ~ —William Grant⟩ ⟨Midland ~⟩ **b** : a manner, style, or pattern of speaking characteristic of a particular individual : a distinctive phonetic quality ⟨his ~ is slipshod and unclear⟩ ⟨his ~ is a peculiar blend of New England and the South⟩ **4 a** : the faculty of uttering articulate sounds or words : the faculty of expressing thoughts by words or articulate sounds : the power of speaking ⟨we stood for some moments, silent and trembling . . . at length I found my ~ —W.H.Hudson †1922⟩ **b** : the art or technique of clear and effective speaking : ELOCUTION, PUBLIC SPEAKING ⟨~ is one of the oldest subjects of study in organized instruction —F.H.Knower⟩ **5** *archaic* : common report : MENTION, TALK ⟨what was the ~ among the Londoners concerning the French journey —*Shak.*⟩ **syn** see LANGUAGE

²speech \"\ *vb* -ED/-ING/-ES *vi* : to make a speech ~ *vt* : to speak or make a speech to

speech center *n* : a brain center exerting control over the power of speech and being commonly situated in the cortex at the third left frontal convolution

speech community *n* : a group of people sharing characteristic vocabulary and grammatical and pronunciation patterns for use in their normal intercommunication ⟨the global English-speaking *speech community*⟩ ⟨the little *speech community* in the body-repair shop⟩

speechcraft \ˈ=,=\ *n* : skill in speech : RHETORIC

speech day *n* : the last day of the school year devoted to prize-giving and oral exercises at some British public schools

speech defect *n* : a defect in oral speech (as lisping or stuttering)

speech form *n* : LINGUISTIC FORM

speech·ful \ˈspēchfəl\ *adj* : full of speech : EXPRESSIVE, VOLUBLE — **speech·ful·ness** *n* -ES

speech house *or* **speech room** *n* : a room or hall used for audiences or conferences

speech·i·fi·ca·tion \ˌspēchəfəˈkāshən\ *n* -s [fr. *speechify*, after such pairs as E *specify: specification*] : the act or an instance of making speeches

speech·i·fi·er \ˈ==ˌfī(ə)r, -īə\ *n* -s [*speechify* + *-er*] : one that spouts speeches : DECLAIMER

speech·i·fy \-ˌfī\ *vi* -ED/-ING/-ES [¹*speech* + *-ify*] : to make a speech : DECLAIM, ORATE ⟨makes trips to ~ at industry conventions —F.C.Othman⟩ ⟨a good deal of pompous ~*ing* by the stay-at-homes —H.A.Overstreet⟩

speech island *n* [trans. of G *sprachinsel*] : a speech community within a different speech community ⟨Mexican Spanish *speech islands* in the southwestern U. S.⟩ — called also *linguistic island*

speech·less \ˈspēchləs\ *adj* [ME *specheles*, fr. OE *spǣclēas*, fr. *spǣc* speech + *-lēas* -less — more at SPEECH] **1 a** : unendowed with or deprived of the power of speech ⟨~ animals⟩ **b** : marked by lack of speech ⟨~ slumber⟩ ⟨~ death⟩ **2 a** : temporarily deprived of the ability to speak (as through injury, shock, or strong emotion) : struck dumb ⟨~ with exhaustion⟩ ⟨~ with grief⟩ **b** : refraining from speech : SILENT, RETICENT ⟨a shy and ~ person⟩ **c** : so as to deprive of speech : causing speechlessness ⟨the ~ fright of the captain —Herman Melville⟩ **3 a** *obs* : expressed or communicated without speech ⟨sometimes from her eyes I did receive fair ~ messages —*Shak.*⟩ **b** : done or experienced without speech : unattended by speech ⟨swaying back and forth in ~ content —Hamlin Garland⟩ **c** : not capable of being expressed in speech : beyond the power of speech ⟨a shape of ~ beauty did appear —P.B. Shelley⟩ **syn** see DUMB

speech·less·ly *adv* : in a speechless manner

speech·less·ness *n* -ES : the quality or state of being speechless

speechlike \ˈ=,=\ *adj* : resembling speech

speechmaker \ˈ=,==\ *n* : one who makes speeches

speechmaking \ˈ=,==\ *n* : the act or practice of making speeches

speech melody *or* **speech tune** *n* : the intonation of connected speech : the continual rise and fall in pitch of the voice in speech

speech organ *n* : any of the organs (as the larynx, tongue, or lips) playing a part in the production of articulate speech

speech-prefix \ˈ=ˌ=,=\ *n* : the usu. abbreviated name of a character in a play written or printed before each of his speeches in the play

speechreading \ˈ=,==\ *n* : LIPREADING

speech situation *n* : an instance of communication having as prerequisites a speaker, an utterance, and a hearer who interprets the utterance

speech sound *n* **1** : any one of the smallest recurrent recognizably same constituents of spoken language produced by movement or movement and configuration of a varying number of the organs of speech in an act of ear-directed communication **2** : PHONE **3** : PHONEME

speech stretcher *n* : an electronic instrument for speech analysis that halves the speed of recorded speech and avoids the reduced or lost intelligibility of reduced pitch by doubling the halved pitch

speechway \ˈ=,=\ *n* : a mode of speech common to a particular people, group, or region ⟨in the home, the family, the school, and the neighborhood we learn the ~*s* of our community —D.J.Lloyd⟩

¹speed \ˈspēd\ *n* -s [ME *spede*, fr. OE *spēd*; akin to OHG *spuot* prosperity, success, speed, *spāti* late, Goth *spediza* latecomer, L *spes* hope, *spatium* space, Lith *spētas* leisure, Skt *sphāra* extensive, *sphāyati* it increases, grows fat; basic meaning: to increase, expand] **1 a** *archaic* : good fortune : favorable issue : SUCCESS **b** *archaic* : something that falls to one's lot : FORTUNE ⟨send me good ~ this day, and show kindness unto my master —Gen 24:12 (AV)⟩ **c** *obs* : one that furthers success or provides favorable conditions ⟨now Hercules be thy ~, young man —*Shak.*⟩ **2 a** : the act, action, or state of moving swiftly : CELERITY, DISPATCH, SWIFTNESS ⟨this is the day of ~, of the atom, of wanting to get to places before you start —W.J.MacQueen-Pope⟩ ⟨the animal escaped pursuit by ~ rather than cunning⟩ **b** : rate of motion ⟨a heavy person who moved at a glacial ~⟩ ⟨drove at a reckless ~⟩; *specif* : rate of motion irrespective of direction : the magnitude of velocity expressed as a particular relationship ⟨the car maintained a ~ of 150 miles per hour⟩ ⟨a record made to be played at a ~ of 33⅓ revolutions per minute⟩ **c** : capacity or power of motion ⟨put all his ~ into the attempt to reach the ball before it hit the ground⟩ **d** : MOMENTUM ⟨set in motion an economic revival that gathered ~ with the hastening sense of crisis —Oscar Handlin⟩ **3 a** : swiftness of performance or execution : QUICKNESS ⟨as the minuteness of the parts formed a great hindrance to my ~, I resolved . . . to make the being of a gigantic stature —Mary W. Shelley⟩ ⟨a pastel sketch of flowers, full of life and ~ —Adrian Bell⟩ **b** : rate of performance or action ⟨trying to increase his reading ~⟩ **4 a** : the sensitivity of a photographic film, plate, or paper that is often expressed numerically according to one of several systems **b** : the light gathering power of a lens or optical system expressed as relative aperture **c** : the time during which a camera shutter is open **5** : a transmission gear in automotive vehicles ⟨shift to low ~⟩ **6 a** : character or level of performance or activity ⟨they need a new night watchman at the dam; that's about your ~ —Elmer Davis⟩ **b** : a person or thing suited to one's tastes : CUP OF TEA ⟨bottled beer and a cigar are about their ~ —A.J. Liebling⟩ **7** *of a baseball pitcher* : ability to throw a fast ball ⟨has a good curve, but no ~⟩ **syn** see HASTE — **at speed** *adv* : RAPIDLY ⟨the motorboat swung in a half circle, bore down upon them *at speed* —Erle Stanley Gardner⟩ ⟨sailed *at speed* across the wind —Eileen Robertson⟩

²speed \"\ *vb* **sped** \ˈsped\ *or* **speeded**; **sped** *or* **speeded**; **speeding**; **speeds** [ME *speden*, fr. OE *spēdan*; akin to MD *spoeden* to speed, OS *spōdian* to prosper, OHG *spuoten* to prosper, succeed; derivative fr. the root of E ¹*speed*] *vi* **1 a** : to experience good fortune : fare well : PROSPER ⟨regarding the quality of the sheep the shepherds led, asking if the rams ~*ed* —George Moore⟩ **b** : to get along : FARE, SUCCEED ⟨a forlorn hope at the best . . . I should like to know how you ~ —Charles Dickens⟩ **2 a** : to go or pass quickly ⟨the work *sped* on at a commendable rate until completed —I.M.Price⟩ ⟨his college years *sped* by —Alexander MacDonald⟩ **b** : to move with speed : make haste ⟨ordered an automobile and *sped* directly to the village —H.F.Wilkins⟩ ⟨fighter planes which ~ to intercept and identify —*Lamp*⟩ **c** : to go or drive at an excessive speed ⟨was ~*ing* on the icy highway and the car skidded⟩; *specif* : to drive at an illegal speed : exceed the speed limit ⟨~*ed* for a while but slowed down when he saw a police car⟩ **3** : to move, work, or take place at a faster rate — usu. used with *up* ⟨the heart ~*s* up and the blood pressure rises —H.G. Armstrong⟩ ⟨her embezzlements were ~*ing* up —R.T.Moriarty⟩ ~ *vt* **1 a** *archaic* : to cause or help to prosper : AID ⟨the Saxon bade God ~ him —Sir Walter Scott⟩ **b** : to promote the development or success of : ADVANCE, FURTHER ⟨two other things happened that *sped* the process —J.S.Martin⟩ ⟨increasing supply of banknotes and ~*ing* the inflationary trend —R.A.Billington⟩ **c** *archaic* : to bring to a state of satisfaction or sufficiency : SATISFY **2 a** : to cause to move quickly : HASTEN ⟨*sped* our craft forward —Nora Waln⟩ ⟨he *sped* his pen to complete his treatises on government —U.B.Phillips⟩ ⟨a camaraderie which *sped* the evening hours away all too quickly —Gwen Allmon⟩ **b (1)** : to expedite the departure of : aid in going or traveling ⟨some villager's departing soul was being ritually *sped* on its difficult road from earth to paradise —Arthur Grimble⟩ ⟨cops obligingly scattering traffic to ~ us on our way —Bennett Cerf⟩ **(2)** : to say good-bye to ⟨~ the parting guest⟩ **c** : to increase the rate of motion or operation of : ACCELERATE — usu. used with *up* ⟨~*ed* up the engine⟩ ⟨~*ed* up production⟩ **3** : to send out (as to a target) : DIRECT, DISCHARGE ⟨*sped* arrows from their heavy war bows —F.V.W. Mason⟩ ⟨these short essays . . . *sped* with so intense a seriousness —Edmund Wilson⟩ **4 a** *archaic* : to bring to completion : FINISH **b** *archaic* : DESTROY, KILL **5** : to set, adjust, or design to or for a definite speed

syn ACCELERATE, QUICKEN, HASTEN, HURRY, PRECIPITATE: SPEED, although usu. throwing stress upon the rapidity of motion or progress ⟨bullets *sped* only a few feet over the Americans' heads —Dave Richardson⟩ ⟨poised to *speed* down the runway —Richard Thruelsen⟩ is also generally used to emphasize the becoming rapid or the achievement of such rapidity as by acceleration or increasing efficiency ⟨his heart *speeded* a little as he neared the cluster of tents —L.C.Douglas⟩ ⟨linked with fourteen miles of highway connections, it *speeds* traffic by shunting through-vehicles away from congested areas and carrying them swiftly across the boroughs —*Amer. Guide Series: N. Y. City*⟩ ACCELERATE emphasizes an increase in rate of motion or progress, not necessarily implying rapidity ⟨*accelerate* your pace⟩ ⟨efforts to *accelerate* our technological progress —H.H.Curtice⟩ ⟨the development of the steamboat *accelerated* the stream of farm products flowing toward the South —*Amer. Guide Series: Ind.*⟩ QUICKEN often adds to the idea of an increase in rapidity the notion of an increase in animation in the action, often also throwing stress upon the shortening of time consumed ⟨how our steps *quickened* when we heard the exhilarating notes of the trumpets and drums —G.E.Fox⟩ ⟨the pace of discovery in geology has been *quickened* by applying the principles and techniques of modern physics —*Scientific American Reader*⟩ HASTEN may add the notion of urgency or of an earlier or sometimes premature outcome ⟨assembled a force of volunteers and . . . *hastened* to the relief of the village —*Amer. Guide Series: Minn.*⟩ ⟨as rapidly as physics and electronics are *hastening* the future —*Time*⟩ HURRY sometimes suggests the notion of a disturbing acceleration of pace and a consequent disorder in the activity or progress ⟨*hurry* home after dark⟩ ⟨events which were *hurrying* the war to the close —H.E.Scudder⟩ ⟨the need for responsive action *hurries* us along and prevents us from ever realising fully what the emotion is that we feel —Roger Fry⟩ PRECIPITATE implies usu. an unexpectedly sudden or abrupt motion or progress ⟨at that instant two animals *precipitated* against his calves, thereby nearly unbalancing him —John Buchan⟩ ⟨one of the bitter disputes was *precipitated* by the question of women's suffrage —*Amer. Guide Series: Tenn.*⟩ ⟨the false charges that the radicals had maliciously *precipitated* the strike —Oscar Handlin⟩

³speed \"\ *adj* [¹*speed*] : of or relating to speed : regulating, indicating, or attaining speed

¹speedball \ˈ=,=\ *n* : a game resembling soccer but permitting a ball caught in the air to be passed with the hands

²speedball \"\ *n, slang* : cocaine mixed with heroin or morphine

speedboat \ˈ=,=\ *n* : a launch or powerboat designed for high speed

speed·boat·ing \ˈ=,=ˌiŋ\ *n* : the act, art, or sport of managing a speedboat

speed box *n* : a box containing a speed-changing device for the main drive of a lathe or similar machine

speed change lane *also* **speed change area** *n* : an acceleration or deceleration lane

speed cone *n* **1** : STEPPED PULLEY **2** : one of a pair of conical pulleys connected by a short belt that can be adjusted to permit fine variations of speed

speed control *n* : equipment designed to operate automatically under certain conditions to keep the speed of a railroad train within a predetermined rate

speed counter *n* : a device for automatically counting the

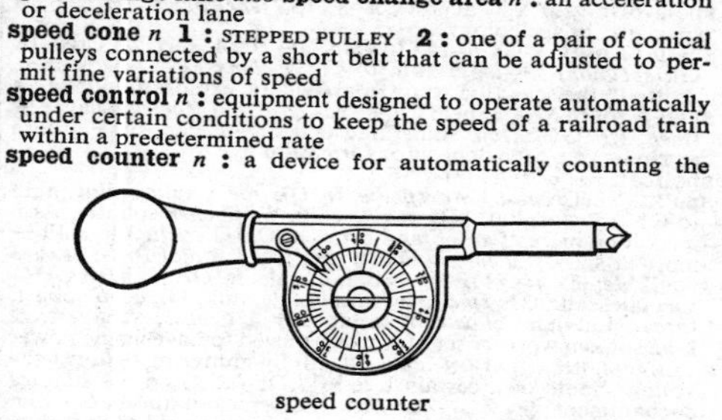

speed counter

revolutions of an engine or other machine — called also *counter*

speeded *past of* SPEED

speed·er \ˈspēdə(r)\ *n* -s [ME *speder*, fr. *spede* speed + *-er* — more at SPEED] : one that speeds: as **a** : any of various devices (as an attachment to a governor) for regulating the speed of a machine or part **b** *also* **speed frame** : a machine for drawing and twisting slivers to form rovings **c** : a small light usu. gasoline-operated vehicle with flanged wheels or solid rubber tires for operation on railroad tracks ⟨spent the next four days riding freight trains and gas ~*s* up and down the main line —H.L.Davis⟩ **d** : one who drives too fast or who exceeds the legal speed limit

speedflash \ˈ=,=\ *n* : SPEEDLIGHT

speed·ful \ˈspēdfəl\ *adj* [ME *spedeful*, fr. *spede* speed + *-ful*] *archaic* : full of speed : RAPID, SPEEDY

speed gear *n* : CHANGE GEAR

speedgun \ˈ=,=\ *n* : SYNCHRONIZER b

speed·i·ly \ˈspēdᵊlē, -dəl, \|i\ *adv* [ME *spedily*, fr. *spedy* speedy + *-ly*] **1** : in a speedy manner : QUICKLY, RAPIDLY ⟨an object traveling ~ through the air⟩ **2** : PROMPTLY, SOON ⟨you will ~ receive from me a letter of thanks for this —Jane Austen⟩

speed indicator *n* **1** *or* **speed gage a** : SPEED COUNTER **b** : TACHOMETER **2** : a device (as a display of canvas cones, a flashing or steady display of lights, or a display of flags) for showing the speed of a ship to other vessels in a formation

speed·i·ness \ˈspēdēnəs, -din-\ *n* -ES : the quality or state of being speedy

¹speeding *adj* [fr. pres. part. of ²*speed*] : moving with speed ⟨a ~ car⟩ ⟨the ~ earth⟩ — **speed·ing·ly** *adv*

²speeding *n* -s [fr. gerund of ²*speed*] : the act or action of going fast; *specif* : the act of operating a motor vehicle at an excessive or illegal speed ⟨was arrested for ~⟩

speedlamp \ˈ=,=\ *n* : SPEEDLIGHT

speed-length ratio *n* : the ratio of a ship's speed in knots divided by the square root of her length in feet

speed·less \ˈspēdləs\ *adj* [ME *spedeles*, fr. *spede* success, speed + *-les* -less] *archaic* : being without success

speedlight \ˈ=,=\ *n* : an electronic flash lamp : FLASHTUBE, STROBE

speed limit *n* : the maximum speed permitted by law in a given area under specified circumstances

speed·om·e·ter \spēˈdämәd·ә(r), -mәtә- *sometimes* spiˈd-\ *n* [¹*speed* + *-o-* + *-meter*] **1** : an instrument for indicating speed or velocity : TACHOMETER **2** : a device (as on an automobile) that measures distance as well as speed : ODOMETER

speed pulley *n* : SPEED CONE

speed reducer *n* : an apparatus for reducing speed

speeds *pl of* SPEED, *pres 3d sing of* SPEED

speed sprayer *n* : CONCENTRATE SPRAYER

speed·ster \ˈspēdztə(r), -dst-\ *n* -s [1*speed* + *-ster*] **1** : one that goes or moves at high speed : a person, animal, or vehicle that excels in speed **2** : SPEEDER d

speed test *n* : a psychological test for the maximum speed of performing a task that lies well within the subject's power — compare POWER TEST

speed trap *n* : a stretch of road watched by concealed officers or devices (as radar) to catch motorists who exceed a speed limit

speedup \ˈ=,=\ *n* -s [fr. *speed up*, v.] **1** : the act or action of speeding up : ACCELERATION ⟨a ~ in research and industrial technology is an integral part of the defense program —*U.S. Code*⟩ **2** : an acceleration of the rate of output required of a worker by an employer without increase in pay

speedway \ˈ=,=\ *n* **1** : a public road on which fast driving is allowed; *specif* : EXPRESSWAY **2** : a racecourse for automobiles or motorcycles

speed·well \ˈspē,dwel\ *n* -s [1*speed* + *well*] : an herb of the genus *Veronica; esp* : a common hairy perennial European herb (*V. officinalis*) with pale blue or lilac flowers in axillary racemes

speedy \ˈspēdē, -di\ *adj* -ER/-EST [ME *spedy*, fr. *spede* speed + *-y* — more at SPEED] **1** : rapid in motion : going or able to go quickly : SWIFT ⟨forced in time of war to use the heavier-type ~ vehicles —John Kemp⟩ ⟨a ~ runner⟩ **2** : marked by swiftness of motion or action : occurring, accomplished, or arrived at quickly ⟨a ~ journey⟩ ⟨a ~ recovery⟩ ⟨the ~ exhaustion of the soils that were being recklessly cropped —Lewis Mumford⟩ **3** : prompt in action or performance : QUICK ⟨the medication is ~ and effective⟩ **syn** see FAST

speedy cut *or* **speedy cutting** *n* : an injury to a horse's foreleg below the knee that is caused by the shoe of the opposite foot in running

1speel \ˈspē(ə)l\ *n* -s [ME, of Scand origin; akin to Norw *spel* flat stick, splinter, Sw *spjäla;* akin to ON *spjald* square tablet, OHG *spaltan* to split — more at SPILL] *dial chiefly Brit* : SPLINTER, STRIP

2speel \"\ *vb* -ED/-ING/-S [origin unknown] : CLIMB

speen·ham·land system \(ˈ)spēn¦hamlənd-\ *n, usu cap 1st S* [fr. *Speenhamland*, England, where it was first used] : a system of supplementing rural wage payments from local taxes first used in England in the latter part of the 18th century

1speer *or* **speir** \ˈspēr\ *vb* -ED/-ING/-S [ME (Sc) *speren, spiren*, fr. OE *spyrian* to seek after, follow a track; akin to ON *spyrja* to follow a track, *spor* spoor — more at SPOOR] *chiefly Scot* : ASK, INQUIRE

2speer \ˈspi(ə)r\ *n* -s [ME *spere*] *dial Eng* : SCREEN, PARTITION

speer·ings \ˈspērənz, -riŋz\ *n pl* [ME (Sc) *speringes, spiringes*, pl. of *spering, spiring* inquiry, information obtained by inquiry, fr. gerund of *speren, spiren* to inquire] : NEWS, TIDINGS

speis·ko·balt *also* **speiss·co·balt** \ˈs(h)pīˌskō,bȯlt *also* -bält\ *n* -s [G *speiskobalt*, fr. *speise* speiss + *kobalt* cobalt] : SMALTITE

speiss \ˈs(h)pīs\ *n* -ES [G *speise*, lit., food, fr. OHG *spīsa*, fr. (assumed) VL *spesa*, fr. LL *expensa* expense — more at EXPENSE] : a mixture of impure metallic arsenides produced as a regulus in smelting certain ores — compare MATTE

spek·boom \ˈspek,büm, -bōm\ *n* -s [Afrik, lit., fat tree, blubber tree, fr. D *spek* fat, blubber, bacon (fr. MD *spec*) + *boom* tree, fr. MD; akin to OHG *boum* tree — more at SPECK, BEAM] : PURSLANE TREE

speke's antelope \ˈspēks-\ *n, usu cap S* [after John H. *Speke* †1864 Eng. African explorer] : SITATUNGA

spe·lae·an *also* **spe·le·an** \spəˈlēən, (ˈ)spē¦l-\ *adj* [L *spelaeum, speleum* cave (fr. Gk *spēlaion*) + E *-an*] : dwelling or occurring in a cave

spel·der \ˈspeldər\ *vb* -ED/-ING/-S [obs. E *speld* to split open, spread open (fr. ME *spelden*, prob. alter. — influenced by *spelde* splinter — of *spalden* to split, spread open, fr. MLG, fr. OHG *spaltan* to split) + E *-er* (as in *batter*) — more at SPILL] *vt, chiefly Scot* : SPLIT ~ *vi, chiefly Scot* : STRETCH, SPRAWL

speld·ing \ˈspel(d)ən\ *n* -s [prob. fr. obs. E *speld* to split open + E *-ing*] *Scot* : STOCKFISH 1a

spel·dring *also* **spel·dron** \ˈspeldrən\ *n* -s [*speldring* prob. fr. *spelder* + *-ing; speldron* alter. of *speldring*] *Scot* : STOCKFISH 1a

spele·o·log·i·cal *also* **spelae·o·log·i·cal** \¦spēlēə¦läjəkəl, -pel-\ *adj* [*speleological* fr. *speleology* + *-ical; spelaeological* alter. (influenced by *spelaean*) of *speleological*] : of or relating to speleology

spele·ol·o·gist \,==ˈäləjəst\ *n* -s [ISV *speleology* + *-ist*] : a specialist in speleology

spele·ol·o·gy \-jē\ *n* -ES [ISV *speleo-* (fr. L *speleum* cave, fr. Gk *spēlaion*) + *-logy;* akin to Gk *spēlunx* cave, *speos* cave, grotto] : the scientific study or systematic exploration of caves

speleo·them \ˈ==ə,them\ *n* -s [*speleo-* (fr. L *speleum* cave) + *-them* (fr. Gk *thema* something laid down, deposit) — more at THEME] : a cave deposit or formation

spelican *var of* SPILLIKIN

spelk \ˈspelk\ *n* -s [ME *spelke*, fr. OE *spelc, spilc* splint; akin to ON *spjalk* splint, MD *spalke* chip, W *ffloch*en splinter, Arm *pʻelk* long piece of wood and prob. to OHG *spaltan* to split — more at SPILL] **1** *chiefly Scot* : SPLINTER **2** *dial Brit* : SPAR 3

1spell \ˈspel\ *n* -s [ME, speech, talk, tale, fr. OE; akin to OHG *spel* tale, talk, ON *spjall*, Goth *spill* tale, talk, Gk *apeilē* boast, threat, Latvian *pal'as* rebuke, abuse] **1 a** *obs* : STORY, TALE **b** : a spoken word or set of words believed to have magic power : CHARM, INCANTATION ⟨cause death by muttering ~s over the young shoots of a certain tree —W.D.Wallis⟩ **c** : a state of enchantment ⟨it was the voice that cracked the ~ — that pleasant, homely, wheedling voice which brought with it daylight and common sense —John Buchan⟩ **2** : a strong compelling influence or attraction ⟨even . . . enemies were unable to resist the ~ of his presence —Alvin Redman⟩ ⟨writing under the ~ of the slavery controversy —R.A.Billington⟩

2spell \"\ *vt* **spelled** \-ld\ **spelled; spelling; spells** : to put under or as if under a spell : BEWITCH, CHARM ⟨used witchcraft all these years to ~ the ladies —Ray Bradbury⟩

3spell \"\ *vb* **spelled** \-ld, -lt\ *or chiefly Brit* **spelt** \-lt\ **spelled** *or chiefly Brit* **spelt; spelling; spells** [ME *spellen*, fr. OF *espeller*, of Gmc origin; akin to OE *spellian* to relate, talk, MHG *spellen*, ON *spjalla* to talk, mention, Goth *spillon* to relate; denominative fr. the root of E 1*spell*] *vt* **1** : to read slowly and with difficulty ⟨yourselves may ~ it yet in chronicles —Robert Browning⟩ — often used with *out* ⟨laboriously ~ out a newspaper —*Time*⟩ **2 a** : to find out by study or investigation : DISCOVER — often used with *out* ⟨~ out a God in the works of creation —Robert Southey⟩ **b** : COMPREHEND, UNDERSTAND — often used with *out* ⟨found it hard to ~ out his meaning⟩ **c** : to give thought to : CONSIDER — often used with *over* ⟨she *spelt* over the names of the guests at the houses —George Meredith⟩ **3 a** : to name in order the letters of ⟨~*ed* the word correctly⟩ ⟨~*ed* the word incorrectly with two *e's*⟩ : write or print in order the letters of ⟨the two writers ~ the word in two different ways⟩ **b** : to make up (a word) : FORM, COMPOSE ⟨what word do these letters ~⟩ ⟨put the cards through a decoding machine to find out that the holes ~*ed* "order now" —F.W.Boardman⟩ **4** : to add up to : amount to : MEAN, SIGNIFY ⟨sensitiveness without impulse ~s decadence —A.N.Whitehead⟩ ⟨crop failure was likely to ~ stark famine —Stringfellow Barr⟩ ~ *vi* **1** : to form words with letters, symbols, or signs ⟨writes well, but ~s badly⟩ ⟨~*ed* with difficulty on his fingers —Helen Keller⟩ **2** : to make a suggestion : ASK, HINT ⟨never saw anybody in my life ~ harder for an invitation —Jane Austen⟩

4spell \"\ *n* -s [prob. alter. of ME *speld, spelde* spark, flake, splinter, fr. OE *speld* torch, ember; akin to Goth *spilda* tablet, Gk *sphallein* to cause to fall, OHG *spaltan* to split; basic meaning: split piece of wood — more at SPILL] **1** *dial chiefly Brit* : SPLINTER, FRAGMENT **2** *dial chiefly Eng* : BAR, RUNG **3** : the trap in the game of knur and spell **4** : a splinter raised from the back of an archery bow

5spell \"\ *vb* -ED/-ING/-S [ME *spelen* to spare, leave over, substitute, represent, fr. OE *spelian* to stand in the place of, represent; akin to OE *spala* substitute] *vt* **1** : to supply the place of for a time : take the turn of : RELIEVE ⟨four-carrier teams ~ each other every 15 minutes —*Nat'l Geographic*⟩ ⟨he and the other assistant stage managers ~*ed* each other —Mary McCarthy⟩ **2** : to allow an interval of rest to : REST ⟨it was midday, and we squatted there, ~*ing* the camels —I.L.Idriess⟩ **3** *Austral* : to interrupt grazing of (pasture) esp. in order to prevent transmission of disease among grazing animals ~ *vi* **1** : to work in turns ⟨she had learned to ~ at the oars and help in the camp work —Arthur Mayse⟩ **2** : to rest from work or activity for a time

6spell \"\ *n* -s [prob. alter. (influenced by ME *spelen* to substitute) of ME *spale* substitute, fr. OE *spala*] **1 a** *archaic* : a shift of workers **b** : a period of work taken by an individual or group in rotation with others : TURN ⟨as this work has to be done standing, it is generally shared between the assistants in ~s lasting perhaps three hours —*Choice of Careers: —Librarianship*⟩ **2 a** : an unbroken period spent in a specified job, occupation, or situation : HITCH ⟨a ~ of clerking . . . during his teens —Jerome Ellison⟩ ⟨a ~ of service in the tropics —D.W.Brogan⟩ ⟨became involved in a gambling scandal and did a ~ in prison —*Times Lit. Supp.*⟩ **b** *chiefly Austral* : a period of rest from work, activity, or use ⟨the tired musterers sitting down . . . and having a ten minutes' ~ and half a pipe —Mary S. Broome⟩ ⟨the motor bike was getting a ~ —F.S. Anthony⟩ **3 a** : an indeterminate period of time ⟨mark time for a ~ —*English Digest*⟩ ⟨a long ~ when he appeared to be petering out —A.M.Mizener⟩ **b** : a stretch of a specified type of weather ⟨a ~ of rain⟩ ⟨a long cold ~⟩ **4** : a period marked by illness, depression, or other abnormal physical or mental state ⟨take me some time to get her to her room if she has one of her weak ~s —Robertson Davies⟩ ⟨you mustn't excite yourself . . . you've had a bad ~ —Berton Roueché⟩ : a seizure of some specified sickness or symptom : ATTACK ⟨a ~ of dizziness, like a cough, is then a danger sign —Morris Fishbein⟩ ⟨prolonged coughing ~s —H.G.Armstrong⟩ — **by spells** *adv* : INTERMITTENTLY ⟨*by spells* she wept —Winston Churchill⟩

spell·able \ˈspeləbəl\ *adj* : capable of being spelled

spell·bind \ˈspel¦bīnd\ *vt* [fr. *spellbound*, after E 4*bound:* 1*bind*] : to bind or hold by or as if by a spell or charm : CHARM, FASCINATE ⟨~*ing* her little brother with tales of the wondrous anemones she had seen —P.A.Zahl⟩

spell·bind·er \-,bīndə(r)\ *n* : one that spellbinds ⟨because he is a poet he is a ~ —Gerald Bullett⟩; *specif* : a speaker (as a political orator, actor, or lecturer) able to seize and hold the attention of an audience by force of personality or eloquence ⟨a local ~ swayed the meeting into voting a resolution —John Bird⟩ ⟨the flashy ~ who popularizes himself instead of his subject —J.R.Adams⟩

spellbound \ˈ=¦=\ *adj* [1*spell* + *bound*] : held by or as if by a spell : FASCINATED ⟨can hold a reader almost ~ through every chapter —J.W.Lippincott⟩

spell down *vt* : to defeat in a spelling match

spelldown \ˈ=,=\ *n* -s : a spelling match that begins with all the contestants standing and ends when all but one have been forced by the rules to sit down after misspelling a word

spelled *past of* SPELL

1spell·er \ˈspelə(r)\ *n* -s [ME, fr. *spellen* to spell + *-er*] **1** : one that spells words ⟨the best ~ in the class⟩ **2** : SPELLING BOOK

2spell·er \"\ *n* -s [perh. fr. 4*spell* + *-er*] : a small branch from the crown of a deer's antler

spell·ful \ˈspelfəl\ *adj* : full of spells : ENCHANTING

spellican *var of* SPILLIKIN

spelling *n* -s [ME, fr. gerund of *spellen* to spell — more at SPELL] **1 a** : the act of one who spells : the formation of words by letters ⟨his ~ has improved⟩ **b** : the art or technique of forming words by letters according to accepted usage : ORTHOGRAPHY ⟨~ as a subject of instruction is in need of reexamination —*Education Digest*⟩ **2** : a sequence of letters composing a word ⟨where the dictionaries differed, either ~ would do —*Time*⟩

spelling bee *n* : a spelling match : SPELLDOWN

spelling book *n* : a book with exercises for teaching how to spell

spelling–bound \ˈ==,=\ *adj* : deaf to or intolerant of a pronunciation because of its discrepancy with its orthographic representation ⟨too *spelling-bound* to realize that the best-educated speakers often say \ˈsebᵊm\ for *seven*⟩

spelling pronunciation *n* : pronunciation of a word in which letters or syllables are given their usual sounds in analogous situations rather than the sounds heard among speakers who make greatest use of the word ⟨\ˈwȯ(r),sestə(r)\ instead of \ˈwu̇stə(r)\ for *Worcester*, or \ˈbōt,swān\ instead of \ˈbōsᵊn\ for *boatswain* are *spelling pronunciations*⟩

spelling reform *n* : a movement to modify conventional spellings so as to lessen or remove the differences between the orthography and the pronunciation of words — compare REFORMED SPELLING

spelling school *n* : a spelling match in rural schools esp. of the 19th century often serving as the occasion for a social event

spell out *vt* : to explain or state explicitly in unmistakable terms ⟨these views will be further *spelled out* in future speeches —*Newsweek*⟩ ⟨in a brief, seemingly unambitious book, without *spelling* anything *out* . . . gets a great deal said —*Time*⟩

spells *pl of* SPELL, *pres 3d sing of* SPELL

1spelt \ˈspelt\ *n* -s [ME, fr. OE, fr. LL *spelta*, of Gmc origin; akin to MHG & MD *spelte* split piece of wood, OHG *spaltan* to split; prob. fr. the splitting of the husk during threshing — more at SPILL] : a wheat (*Triticum spelta*) that is of no commercial importance in America but is grown to some extent in Germany and Switzerland and that has lax spikes with spikelets containing two light red kernels — called also *speltz;* compare EMMER

2spelt *chiefly Brit past of* SPELL

1spel·ter \ˈspeltə(r)\ *n* -s [prob. modif. (influenced by It *peltro* pewter) of MD *speauter* spelter — more at PEWTER] **1** : ZINC; *esp* : zinc cast in slabs for commercial use **2** : SPELTER SOLDER

2spelter \"\ *vt* -ED/-ING/-S : to solder with an alloy high in zinc

spelter solder *n* : a zinc solder (as one of three parts of zinc to four of copper) used in soldering copper, iron, and brass

spelt·oid \ˈspel,tȯid\ *n* -s [1*spelt* + *-oid*] : a variant in wheat having certain characteristics of spelt

speltz \ˈs(h)pelts\ *n* -ES [G *spelz* spelt, fr. OHG *spelza, spelta*, fr. LL *spelta* — more at SPELT] **1** : SPELT **2** : any of several varieties of emmer

spe·lun·car \spəˈləŋkə(r), (ˈ)spē¦l-\ *adj* [L *spelunca* cave + E *-ar*] : of or relating to a cave

spe·lunk·er \"\ *n* -s [obs. E *spelunk* cave (fr. ME, fr. MF or L) + E *-er;* MF *spelunque*, fr. L *spelunca*, fr. Gk *spēlunx* — more at SPELEOLOGY] : one who makes a hobby of exploring and studying caves : CAVER — compare SPELEOLOGIST

spe·lunk·ing \-kiŋ\ *n* -s [obs. E *spelunk* cave + E *-ing*] : the hobby or practice of exploring caves

spence \ˈspen(t)s\ *n* -s [ME *spence, spense*, fr. MF *despense* place for storing supplies, expense — more at DISPENSE] **1** *dial Brit* **a** : PANTRY **b** : CUPBOARD **2** *Scot* : an inner room usu. near the kitchen

1spen·cer \ˈspen(t)sə(r)\ *n* -s [after George John, 2d earl *Spencer* †1834 Eng. politician] **1** : a short double-breasted overcoat or jacket worn by men esp. in the 19th century **2** : a woman's fitted jacket of waist length or shorter

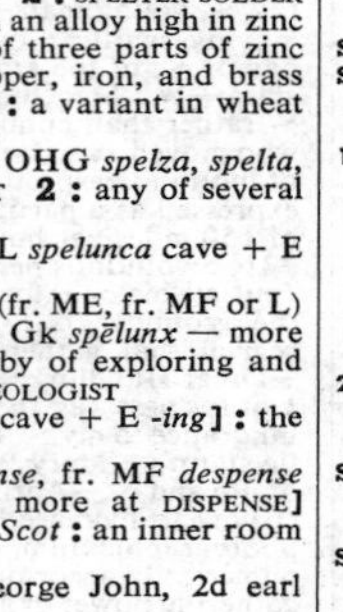
spencer 2

2spencer \"\ *n* -s [prob. fr. the name *Spencer*] **1** : a fore-and-aft sail formerly used abaft the foremast or the mainmast, hoisted upon a small supplementary mast, and set with a gaff and no boom **2** : a trysail abaft the foremast or mainmast

1spen·ce·ri·an \(ˈ)spen¦sirēən, -¦sēr-\ *adj, usu cap* [Herbert *Spencer* †1903 Eng. philosopher + E *-ian* (adj. suffix)] : of or relating to the philosopher Spencer or Spencerianism

2spencerian \"\ *n* -s *usu cap* [Herbert *Spencer* †1903 + E *-ian* (n. suffix)] : a follower of Spencer

3spencerian \"\ *adj, usu cap* [Platt Rogers *Spencer* †1864 Am. calligrapher the originator of the handwriting + E *-ian*] : of, relating to, or characteristic of a form of slanting handwriting

spen·ce·ri·an·ism \=ˈ===,nizəm\ *n* -s *usu cap* : the synthetic philosophy of Spencer that has as its central idea the evolution of the cosmos from relative simplicity to relative complexity through the operation of mechanical forces with the acme of evolution being the equilibration of these forces after which dissolution begins and the cosmos goes back to the ultimate state from which evolution started

spen·cer·ism \ˈspen(t)sə,rizəm\ *n* -s *usu cap* [Herbert *Spencer* †1903 Eng. philosopher + E *-ism*] : SPENCERIANISM

spen·cer·ite \-rīt\ *n* -s [Leonard J. *Spencer* †1959 Eng. mineralogist + E *-ite*] : a mineral $Zn_4(PO_4)_2(OH)_2.3H_2O$ consisting of a hydrous basic zinc phosphate occurring in pearly white scaly masses and small monoclinic crystals (hardness 2.7, sp. gr. 3.1)

spencer mast *n* : a small mast just abaft the foremast or mainmast and used to hoist the spencer

spen·cer roll \ˈspen(t)sə(r)-\ *n, usu cap S* [prob. after the name *Spencer*] : beef trimmed from the ribs, rolled, and used for short steaks or for a roast

1spend \ˈspend\ *vb* **spent** \-nt\ **spent; spending; spends** [ME *spenden*, fr. OE & OF; OE *spendan*, fr. L *expendere* to weigh out, expend; OF *despendre*, fr. L *dispendere* to weigh out — more at EXPEND, DISPENSE] *vt* **1** : to distribute or consume in payment or expenditure : pay out : EXPEND, DISBURSE ⟨~s money freely⟩ ⟨*spent* his inheritance within a few years⟩ **2 a** : to exhaust or wear out by use or activity ⟨the silver agitation had by this time *spent* its force —Marian Silveus⟩ ⟨gradually the hurricane *spent* itself —Francis Robinson⟩ ⟨*spent* himself in the service of humanity —D.S. & Jessie Jordan⟩ **b** : to make use of : EMPLOY ⟨prehistorians have *spent* their learning and ingenuity on reconstructing continental invasions —Jacquetta & Christopher Hawkes⟩ ⟨determined to ~ these new bullets . . . more profitably —H.H. Arnold & I.C.Eaker⟩ **c** : to consume wastefully : SQUANDER ⟨~ your rich opinion for the name of a night-brawler —Shak.⟩ **d** *archaic* : DESTROY **3** : to cause or permit to elapse : use the interval of : PASS ⟨have *spent* the greater part of the last year going up and down the countryside —S.P.B.Mais⟩ ⟨~s three hours a day on his studies⟩ ⟨*spent* his life in a quiet village⟩ ⟨~ the evening with his friends⟩ **4** : to give up : endure the loss of ⟨to royalize his blood, I *spent* my own —Shak.⟩ ⟨the ship *spent* its mast⟩ ~ *vi* **1** : to expend money or other possession ⟨~s without any thought for the next day⟩ **2** *chiefly dial* : to turn out or produce in a specified manner **3** : to become expended ⟨I have no skill to make money ~ well —R.W.Emerson⟩

syn EXPEND, DISBURSE: SPEND is the general term indicating a paying out of money or, sometimes, incurring obligations calling for its being paid ⟨*spend* a hundred dollars for a coat⟩ ⟨*spending* billions on wars⟩ It may apply to using, consuming, or exhausting without tangible or specific return ⟨*spend* time on the project⟩ ⟨*spend* one's life in government service⟩ EXPEND is often but not always applied to larger sums or more important materials and attributes ⟨more than twenty million dollars has been *expended* in the construction —*Amer. Guide Series: N.Y.City*⟩ ⟨during the war years we have *expended* our resources — both human and natural — without stint —H.S. Truman⟩ ⟨this eloquence was always *expended* in expounding the duties of the citizen —H.L.Mencken⟩ DISBURSE is sometimes interchangeable with EXPEND; it indicates a paying out or distributing, often from a public or corporation fund, sometimes by a person or agency other than the one doing the spending or expending ⟨state and federal funds *disbursed* for roads aggregated $34,514,584 —James Brewster⟩ ⟨waiting for the teller to *disburse* those complex payroll accounts —Christopher Morley⟩

— **spend one's mouth** *obs* : give tongue : BARK ⟨coward dogs most *spend their mouths* when what they seem to threaten runs far before them —Shak.⟩

2spend \"\ *n* -s : the act or process of spending money — used in the phrase *on the spend*

spend·able \ˈspendəbəl\ *adj* : capable of being spent : available for spending ⟨~ income⟩

spend–all \ˈ=,=\ *n* : SPENDTHRIFT

spend·er \ˈspendə(r)\ *n* -s [ME, fr. *spenden* to spend + *-er*] **1** : one that spends money; *esp* : one that spends lavishly : SPENDTHRIFT ⟨had become a ~ in his middle age —John Lardner⟩ **2** : one that uses up ⟨the most colossal ~s of resources in our history —Julian Dana⟩

spending *n* -s [ME, partly fr. gerund of *spenden* to spend & partly fr. OE *spendung*, fr. *spendan* to spend + *-ung* -ing — more at SPEND] **1** : the act of spending : EXPENDITURE ⟨the level of government ~⟩ **2** : the act of consuming : CONSUMPTION

spending money *n* : POCKET MONEY

spending unit *n* : an individual living alone or a family living together and pooling incomes to meet expenses

1spend·thrift \ˈspen(d),thrift\ *n* [1*spend* + *thrift* (savings)] **1** : one that spends or uses improvidently or wastefully ⟨mobilizing the populace against ~s at the public trough —J.R.Aswell & E.J.Michelson⟩ **2** : one who spends his estate (as by drinking or gambling) so as to expose himself or his family to want or suffering or to becoming a charge upon the public

2spendthrift \"\ *adj* : given to or marked by improvident expenditure or use : WASTEFUL ⟨~ property owners who have lived beyond their incomes —G.B.Shaw⟩ ⟨~ duplication of work —H.N.Southern⟩

spendthrift clause *n* : a provision sometimes included in a life insurance policy prohibiting the beneficiary from assigning or anticipating payments coming due and exempting such payments from the claims of creditors of the beneficiary

spend·thrift·i·ness \-ftēnəs, -ftin-\ *n* : the quality or state of being spendthrift : IMPROVIDENCE, WASTEFULNESS ⟨an almost incredible ~ of energy and talent —Carlos Baker⟩

spendthrift trust *n* : a trust created to provide a fund for the maintenance of another and to secure it (as by withholding from him the power to alienate his interest or put a charge upon it or to anticipate or assign the income) against his improvidence or incapacity

spend·thrifty \-ftē, -fti\ *adj* : SPENDTHRIFT

spe·ner·ism \ˈs(h)pānə,rizəm\ *n* -s *usu cap* [Philipp Jacob *Spener* †1705 Ger. Protestant theologian + E *-ism*] : the pietistic teaching of Spener

1spen·gle·ri·an \(ˈ)s(h)peŋ¦(g)lirēən\ *adj, usu cap* [Oswald *Spengler* †1936 Ger. writer on philosophy of history who developed the theory + E *-ian* (adj. suffix)] : of or relating to a theory of world history that holds that major cultures (as the Egyptian, Chinese, or Mayan) undergo similar cyclical developments from birth to maturity to decay, that modern western civilization also is undergoing such a development, and that its decline is consequently predictable

2spenglerian \"\ *n* -s *usu cap* [Oswald *Spengler* †1936 + E *-ian* (n. suffix)] : a follower of the historian Spengler or an advocate of a Spenglerian philosophy of history

spen·se·ri·an \(ˈ)spen¦sirēən, -¦sēr-\ *adj, usu cap* [Edmund *Spenser* †1599 Eng. poet + E *-ian*] : of or relating to the poet Spenser or his works

spenserian sonnet *n, usu cap 1st S* : a sonnet in which the lines are grouped into three interlocked quatrains and a couplet and the rhyme scheme is *abab, bcbc, cdcd, ee*

spenserian stanza *n, usu cap 1st S* : a stanza consisting of eight iambic pentameter lines and an alexandrine and having the rhyme scheme *ababbcbcc*

spent \ˈspent\ *adj* [ME, fr. past part. of *spenden* to spend — more at SPEND] **1 a** : used up : CONSUMED, EXPENDED ⟨the smell of ~ powder —R.H.Newman⟩ ⟨the air, breathed many times and ~ —Edna S. V. Millay⟩ **b** : exhausted of active or effective quality or components ⟨~ fuller's earth⟩ ⟨~ tanbark⟩ ⟨~ grain⟩ **2** : drained of energy or vitality : worn out : EXHAUSTED ⟨saw him come creeping home at dawn, panting and ~ —Pearl Buck⟩ ⟨two ~ old women —Edith Wharton⟩ **3** : exhausted of spawn or sperm — used esp. of fishes or of insects that have laid all their eggs; compare RIPE **4** *of an artificial fly* : tied to imitate the drooping wings of a natural insect that has dropped its eggs or is exhausted

spent acid *n* : acid weakened by use: as **a** : mixed acid that has been used in nitration **b** : acid that has been used in pickling metal articles

spent lye *n* : the alkaline glycerol-containing liquor that results on saponification of fat with boiling lye solution in soap-making and that is drawn off after cooling from the floating curd

spent oxide *n* : iron oxide that has been used in gas manufacture to purify coal gas by removing chiefly hydrogen sulfide and sometimes cyanogen, that generally has formed a coating on shavings and sawdust, and that may be used as a source of sulfur and of cyanogen compounds

spe·os \'spē,äs\ *n* -ES [Gk, cave — more at SPELEOLOGY] **:** an ancient Egyptian cave temple or tomb

speo·ty·to \,spēō'tīd·(,)ō\ *n, cap* [NL, fr. Gk *speos* cave + *tytō* night owl] **:** a genus of owls (family Strigidae) consisting of the burrowing owls

spe·rate \'spi,rāt\ *adj* [L *speratus*, past part. of *sperare* to hope; akin to L *spes* hope — more at SPEED] *archaic* **:** hoped for **:** to be hoped for **:** *esp* **:** giving some hope of being paid

spere *obs var of* [1]SPEER

sper·gu·la \'spərgyələ\ *n, cap* [NL, fr. ML, spurry, prob. fr. *spergere* to scatter, strew (alter. of L *spargere*) + L *-ula*, dim. suffix — more at SPARK] **:** a small genus of Old World annual herbs (family Caryophyllaceae) having subulate fascicled leaves, terminal cymes of pentamerous small white flowers, and 5-valved capsules — see CORN SPURRY

sper·gu·lar·ia \,==ˈla(a)rēə\ *n, cap* [NL, fr. *Spergula* + *-aria*] **:** a genus of chiefly maritime herbs (family Caryophyllaceae) with linear or setaceous and often fleshy leaves and pink or white flowers — see SAND SPURRY

sper·ling \'spərliŋ, -lən\ *n, pl* **sperling** *or* **sperlings** [ME — more at SPARLING] **1** *dial Brit* **:** SMELT; *esp* **:** SPARLING **2 :** a young herring

sperm \'spərm, -pəm,-pəim\ *n, pl* **sperm** *or* **sperms** [ME *sperme*, fr. MF *esperme*, fr. LL *spermat-, sperma*, fr. Gk; akin to Gk *speirein* to sow — more at SPROUT] **1 a :** the male fecundating fluid **:** SEMEN **b :** a male gamete: (1) **:** SPERMATOZOON (2) **:** SPERMATOZOID (3) **:** a sperm nucleus of an angiosperm **2** *archaic* **:** the seed, germ, or originative matter from which something develops **3 a :** SPERM WHALE **b :** a product of the sperm whale (as spermaceti or sperm oil)

sperm- *or* **spermo-** *or* **sperma-** *or* **spermi-** *comb form* [Gk *sperm-, spermo-*, fr. *spermat-, sperma* seed, sperm] **:** seed **:** germ **:** sperm **:** semen ⟨*spermophile*⟩ ⟨*spermangium*⟩ ⟨*spermatheca*⟩ ⟨*spermidine*⟩ ⟨*spermiduct*⟩

-sper·ma \"\ *n comb form* [NL, fr. fem. sing. of *-spermus* -spermous] **:** one having (such) a seed or germ — in generic names of plants ⟨Lepido*sperma*⟩

sper·ma·ceti \,==ˈsē|d·ē, -ˈsel, |t|, |ī\ *n* -S [ME *sperma cete*, fr. ML *sperma ceti* whale sperm, fr. LL *sperma* sperm + L *ceti*, gen. of *cetus* whale; fr. the belief that it was the coagulated semen of the whale — more at CETE] **1** *also* **spermaceti wax :** a white crystalline waxy solid that separates from sperm oil esp. from the head cavities and from the oils of related cetaceans, consists principally of cetyl palmitate and other esters of fatty acids, and is used chiefly in ointments, cosmetic creams, and candles **2 :** sperm oil containing spermaceti

sper·ma·duct *or* **sper·mi·duct** *or* **sper·mo·duct** \'=mə,dəkt\ *n* [*sperm-* + *duct*] **:** SPERMATIC DUCT

-sper·mae \'spər(,)mē, -pə(-, -pəi(-, -,mī\ *or* **-sper·me·ae** \-,mē,ē, -mē,ī\ *n pl comb form* [NL, fr. *-spermae*, fem. pl. of *-spermus* -spermous] **:** ones having (such) a seed or germ — in higher taxa in botany ⟨Angio*spermae*⟩ ⟨Gymno*spermae*⟩ ⟨Rhodo*spermeae*⟩

sper·ma·gone \'spərmə,gōn\ *n* -S [NL *spermagonium*] **:** SPERMOGONIUM

sper·ma·go·ni·al \;==ˈgōnēəl\ *adj* [NL *spermagonium* + E *-al*] **:** of, relating to, or being a spermagonium

sper·ma·go·ni·um *or* **sper·mo·go·ni·um** \,==ˈgōnēəm\ *n, pl* **spermago·nia** *or* **spermogo·nia** \-ēə\ [NL, fr. *sperm-* + *gonium*] **:** a flask-shaped or depressed receptacle in which spermatia are produced in various ascocarpous fungi and lichens — compare CONCEPTACLE, PYCNIUM

-sper·mal \ˈspərməl, -pəm-,-pəim-\ *or* **-sper·mous** \-məs\ *adj comb form* [*-spermal* fr. NL *-spermum* + E *-al*; *-spermous* fr. NL *-spermus*, fr. Gk *-spermos*, fr. *spermat-, sperma* seed, sperm — more at SPERM] **:** having (such or so many) seeds **:** seeded ⟨peri*spermal*⟩ ⟨poly*spermous*⟩ ⟨angio*spermal*⟩

sper·mal·ist \'spərməlǝst\ *n* -S [obs. E *spermal* relating to sperm (fr. E *sperm* + *-al*) + E *-ist*] **:** SPERMIST

sper·maph·y·ta \(,)spər'mafəd·ə\ [NL, fr. *sperm-* + *-phyta*] *syn of* SPERMATOPHYTA

sper·ma·phyte \'spərmə,fīt\ *n* -S [NL *Spermaphyta*] **:** SPERMATOPHYTE

sper·ma·phyt·ic \;==ˈfid·ik\ *adj* [*spermaphyte* + *-ic*] **:** SPERMATOPHYTIC

sper·mar·i·um \(,)spər'ma(a)rēəm\ *n, pl* **spermar·ia** \-ēə\ [NL, fr. *sperm-* + *-arium*] **:** SPERMARY

sper·ma·ry \'spərmərē\ *n* -ES [NL *spermarium*] **1 :** an organ in which spermatozoa are developed: **a :** TESTIS **b :** a sac dependent from a segmental septum of an oligochaete worm in which the later stages of sperm maturation take place **2 a :** ANTHERIDIUM **b :** POLLEN TUBE

sperm–aster \'=,==\ *n* **:** the centrosome and aster associated with the male pronucleus in the stage of fertilization preceding fusion of pronuclei and usu. giving rise to the first cleavage spindle of the zygote

spermat- *or* **spermato-** *comb form* [MF, fr. LL, fr. Gk, fr. *spermat-, sperma* seed, sperm — more at SPERM] **:** seed **:** spermatozoan ⟨*spermat*angium⟩ ⟨*spermato*phore⟩ ⟨*spermato*cyte⟩ ⟨*Spermato*phyta⟩

sper·ma·ta \'spərməd·ə\ *n pl* [NL, fr. *sperm-* + L *-ata*, neut pl. of *-atus* -ate] **:** HOMOEOMERIES

sper·ma·tan·gi·um \,spərmə'tanjēəm\ *n, pl* **spermatan·gia** \-ēə\ [NL, fr. *spermat-* + *-angium*] **:** a multicellular antheridium characteristic of some algae — compare SPERMATOCYST

sper·ma·teli·o·sis \,==,tēlē'ōsǝs, -,tel-\ *n* -ES [NL, fr. *sperm-* + Gk *teleiōsis* development] **1 :** SPERMIOGENESIS a **2 :** SPERMATOGENESIS

sper·ma·theca \;spərmə+\ *n* [NL, fr. *sperm-* + *theca*] **:** a sac connected with the female reproductive organs of most insects, many other invertebrates, and a few vertebrates (as some amphibians) that receives and retains the spermatozoa often for a long period and until the time for fertilizing the eggs — **sper·ma·thecal** \"+\ *adj*

spermathecal gland *n* **:** a gland in some insects connected with the spermatheca

spermatia *pl of* SPERMATIUM

sper·ma·tial \(')spər'māshəl, spər'm-\ *adj* [NL *spermatium* + E *-al*] **:** of, relating to, bearing, or being a spermatium

[1]**sper·mat·ic** \spər'mad·ik, (')spə'm-, (')spəi'm-, spə(r)'m-, -at|, |ēk\ *adj* [MF *spermatique*, fr. LL *spermaticus*, fr. Gk *spermatikos*, fr. *spermat-, sperma* seed, sperm + *-ikos* -ic] **1 :** relating to sperm or a spermary **:** carrying or full of sperm **:** resembling sperm **:** SEMINAL, TESTICULAR **2 :** REPRODUCTIVE, ORIGINATIVE, GENERATIVE

[2]**spermatic** \"\ *n* -S **:** a spermatic part (as an artery, canal, or vein)

spermatical *adj* [ME, fr. LL *spermaticus* + E *-al*] *obs* **:** SPERMATIC

sper·mat·i·cal·ly \|ək(ə)lē, |ēk-, -li\ *adv* **:** in a spermatic manner or relation

spermatic animalcule *n, archaic* **:** SPERMATOZOON

spermatic artery *n* **:** an artery that supplies blood to a testis and that in man is one of a pair which arises from the front of the aorta a little below the renal arteries and passes downward to the spermatic cord of the same side and along it to the testis

spermatic canal *n* **:** INGUINAL CANAL

spermatic capsule *n* **:** a transparent globular sac produced by the male of some mites, containing the spermatozoa, and serving to convey them to the female genital tract

spermatic cord *also* **spermatic funiculus** *n* **:** a cord that suspends the testis within the scrotum, contains the vas deferens and vessels and nerves of the testis, and extends from the internal abdominal ring through the inguinal canal and external abdominal ring downward into the scrotum

spermatic duct *n* **:** an efferent duct of a testis **:** a duct conveying sperm

spermatic fluid *n* **:** SEMEN

spermatic plexus *n* **:** the pampiniform plexus of the spermatic cord

spermatic vein *n* **:** any of the veins leading from the testes, being numerous in man, forming with tributaries from the epididymis the pampiniform plexus in the spermatic cord, and thence accompanying the spermatic artery and eventually uniting to form a single trunk which on the right side opens into the vena cava and on the left into the renal vein

sper·ma·tid \'spərməd·əd\ *n* -S [ISV *spermat-* + *-id*] **:** one of the cells formed by division of the secondary spermatocytes and differentiating into spermatozoa — compare OOTID

sper·ma·tif·er·ous \;spərmə'tif(ə)rəs\ *adj* [NL *spermatium* + E *-ferous*] **:** bearing spermatia

sper·ma·tin \'spərməd·ən\ *n* -S [ISV *spermat-* + *-in*; prob. orig. formed as F *spermatine*] **:** an albuminoid substance from semen

sper·ma·tio·phore \(,)spər'māshēə,fō(ə)r\ *n* -S [NL *spermatium* + E *-o-* + *-phore*] **:** a hypha that gives rise to spermatia

sper·ma·tism \'spərmə,tizəm\ *n* -S [*spermat-* + *-ism*] **1 :** emission of semen **2** [ISV *spermat-* + *-ism*] **:** SPERMISM

sper·ma·tist \-məd·əst\ *n* -S [ISV *spermat-* + *-ist*] **:** SPERMIST

sper·ma·ti·um \(,)spər'māshēəm\ *n, pl* **sperma·tia** \-ēə\ [NL, fr. Gk *spermation*, dim. of *spermat-, sperma* sperm — more at SPERM] **1 :** a nonmotile male gamete of a red alga that conjugates with the egg in the carpogonium **2 :** a nonmotile cell developed in various fungi and lichens by abstriction from a sterigma within a spermagonium and apparently functioning as a male gamete though sometimes considered a conidium (as a pycnospore)

sper·ma·ti·za·tion \,spərməd·ə'zāshən, -mə,tī'z-\ *n* -S [*spermatize* + *-ation*] **:** the quality or state of being spermatized

sper·ma·tize \'==,tīz\ *vb* -ED/-ING/-S [Gk *spermatizein* to sow, fr. *spermat-* + *-izein* -ize] *vi, obs* **:** to produce or shed sperm ~ *vt* **:** to mingle spermatia or rarely sperm with **:** fertilize or diploidize (as rust fungi) by means of spermatia

spermato- — see SPERMAT-

sper·mato·blast \(,)spər'mad·ə,blast, 'spərməd·-\ *n* [ISV *spermat-* + *-blast*] **:** a cell or structure producing sperm **:** SPERMATID — **sper·mato·blas·tic** \(,)=;==;blastik, ;===-\ *adj*

sper·mato·cele \(,)spər'mad·ə,sēl, 'spərməd·-\ *n* -S [NL, fr. *spermat-* + *-cele*] **:** a cystic swelling of the ducts in the epididymis or in the rete testis usu. containing spermatozoa

sper·mato·ci·dal \(,)spər;mad·ə;sīd·əl, ;spərməd·-\ *or* **sper·mi·ci·dal** \;spərmə;sīd·əl\ *adj* [*spermat-, sperm-* + *-cidal*] **:** capable of killing or used to kill spermatozoa

sper·mato·cide \-,sīd\ *or* **sper·mi·cide** \'spərmə,-\ *n* -S [*spermat-, sperm-* + *-cide*] **:** an agent that kills spermatozoa

sper·mato·cyst \(,)spər'mad·ə,sist, 'spərməd·-\ *n* [*spermat-* + *-cyst*] **1 :** SEMINAL VESICLE **2 :** a unicellular antheridium in an alga and fungus — compare SPERMATANGIUM — **sper·mato·cys·tic** \(,)spər;mad·ə;sistik, ;spərməd·-\ *adj*

sper·mato·cy·tal \(,)spər;mad·ə;sīd·əl, ;spərməd·-\ *adj* [*spermatocyte* + *-al*] **:** of, relating to, or being spermatocytes

sper·mato·cyte \(,)spər'mad·ə,sīt, 'spərməd·-\ *n* -S [*spermat-* + *-cyte*] **:** a cell giving rise to spermatozoa or spermatozooids — see PRIMARY SPERMATOCYTE, SECONDARY SPERMATOCYTE; compare ANDROCYTE, SPERMATID, SPERMATOGONIUM

sper·mato·genesis \,spərməd·ə, (,)spər,mad·ə+\ *n* [NL, fr. *spermat-* + *genesis*] **:** the whole process of male gamete formation including meiosis of a primary spermatocyte and transformation of the four resulting spermatids into spermatozoa — compare SPERMIOGENESIS

sper·mato·ge·net·ic \(,)spər;mad·əjə;ned·ik, ;spərməd·-\ *or* **sper·mato·gen·ic** \;spərməd·ə;jenik, (,)spər;mad·-\ *adj* [*spermat-* + *-genetic* or *-genic*] **:** of, relating to, or constituting spermatogenesis

sper·ma·tog·e·nous \;spərmə;täjənəs\ *adj* [*spermat-* + *-genous*] **:** producing sperm

sper·ma·tog·e·ny \-nē\ *n* -ES [*spermat-* + *-geny*] **:** SPERMATOGENESIS

sper·mato·go·ni·al \;spərməd·ə;gōnēəl, (,)spər;mad·-\ *also* **sper·mato·gon·ic** \-;gänik\ *adj* [NL *spermatogonium* + E *-al* or *-ic*] **:** of, relating to, or producing spermatogonia

sper·mato·go·ni·um \,===ˈgōnēəm, (,)=,==-\ *n, pl* **spermato·go·nia** \-ēə\ [NL, fr. *spermat-* + *gonium*] **:** a primitive male germ cell **:** a testicular cell from which gametes are ultimately produced by meiosis and metamorphosis

sper·ma·toid \'spərmə,tȯid\ *adj* [*spermat-* + *-oid*] **:** resembling sperm or a sperm cell **:** SEMINAL 1

sper·ma·tol·y·sis \,spərmə'täləsəs\ *n* [NL, fr. *spermat-* + *-lysis*] **:** dissolution of spermatozoa

sper·mato·lyt·ic \;spərməd·ə;lid·ik, (,)spər;mad·-\ *adj* [ISV *spermat-* + *-lytic*] **:** of, relating to, or promoting spermatolysis

sper·mato·pho·ral \(,)spər;mad·ə;fōrəl, ;spərməd·-; ;spermə;täfərəl\ *or* **sper·ma·toph·o·rous** \;spərmə;täfərəs\ *adj* [*spermatophore* + *-al* or *-ous*] **:** of, relating to, or being a spermatophore

sper·mato·phore \(,)spər'mad·ə,fō(ə)r, 'spərməd·-\ *n* -S [ISV *spermat-* + *-phore*] **1 :** a capsule, packet, or mass enclosing spermatozoa extruded by the male of various animals and functioning in the insemination of the female (as annelids, mollusks, arthropods, and some vertebrates) **2 :** SPERMATIOPHORE

spermatophore sac *n* **:** a terminal sac in a cephalopod that retains the spermatophores until ready for fertilization

sper·ma·toph·y·ta \,spərmə'täfəd·ə\ *n pl, cap* [NL, fr. *spermat-* + *-phyta*] *in some classifications* **:** a division of higher plants that is coordinate with Bryophyta and Pteridophyta and coextensive with the classes Gymnospermae and Angiospermae

sper·mato·phyte \(,)spər'mad·ə,fīt, 'spərməd·-\ *n* -S [NL *Spermatophyta*] **:** a plant of the division Spermatophyta **:** SEED PLANT — **sper·mato·phyt·ic** \(,)=;==;fid·ik, ;===-\ *adj*

sper·mato·plasm \(,)spər'mad·ə,plazəm, 'spərməd·-\ *n* -S [*spermat-* + *-plasm*] **:** protoplasm of a sperm cell — **sper·mato·plas·mic** \(,)=;==;plazmik, ;===-\ *adj*

sper·mator·rhea *or* **sper·mator·rhoea** \,spərməd·ə'rēə, (,)spər,mad·-\ *n* -S [NL, fr. *spermat-* + *-rrhea, -rrhoea*] **:** abnormally frequent or excessive involuntary emission of semen without orgasm

sper·mato·theca \,spərməd·ə, (,)spər,mad·ə+\ *n* [NL, fr. *spermat-* + *theca*] **:** SPERMATHECA

-sper·ma·tous \;spərməd·əs, -pəm-,-pəim-, -mətəs\ *adj comb form* [Gk *-spermatos*, fr. *spermat-, sperma* seed, sperm — more at SPERM] **:** having (such or so many) seeds **:** seeded ⟨macro*spermatous*⟩ ⟨angio*spermatous*⟩

sper·ma·toxic \;spərmə+\ *adj* [*sperm-* + *toxic*] **:** poisonous to spermatozoa

sper·ma·toxin \"+\ *n* [alter. of *spermotoxin*] **:** a substance (as an antibody) poisonous to spermatozoa or derived from spermatozoa and tending to prevent conception

sper·mato·zo·al \;spərməd·ə;zōəl, (,)spər;mad·-\ *also* **sper·mato·zo·an** \-ōən\ *or* **sper·mato·zo·ic** \-ōik\ *adj* [NL *spermatozoa* + E *-al* or *-an* or *-ic*] **:** of or relating to spermatozoa

spermatozoan \"\ *n* -S [NL *spermatozoa* + E *-an* (n. suffix)] **:** SPERMATOZOON

sper·mato·zo·id \,===ˈzōəd, (,)=,==-\ *n* -S [NL *spermatozoon* + ISV *-id*] **1 :** a motile male gamete of a plant (as an alga or a moss, a liverwort, a fern, or a gymnosperm) that is usu. produced in an antheridium and that swims freely by means of two or more anterior cilia prior to fusion with the egg or oosphere — compare SPERMATOZOON, SPERM NUCLEUS **2 :** SPERMATOZOON 1

sper·mato·zo·on \,===ˈzō,än, (,)=,==-, -ōən\ *n, pl* **spermato·zoa** \-ōə\ [NL, fr. *spermat-* + *-zoon*] **1 :** a motile male gamete of an animal produced in the male reproductive gland usu. in great numbers, varying greatly in form in different animals but usu. consisting of a rounded or elongate head made up chiefly of the greatly condensed nucleus, a thickened middle piece, and a long posterior flagellum that provides motility, discharged in a fluid semen or a gelatinous spermatophore, and under suitable conditions (as of moisture and temperature) capable of actively seeking the typically much larger passive ovum — compare FERTILIZATION, SPERMATOGENESIS **2 :** SPERMATOZOID 1

sper·ma·tu·ria \,spərmə'tu̇rēə, -mə·'tyu̇-\ *n* -S [NL, fr. *spermat-* + *-uria*] **:** discharge of semen in the urine

sperm candle *n* **:** a candle made of spermaceti

sperm cell *n* **:** a male gamete **:** a male germ cell — contrasted with *egg cell*

sperm center *or* **sperm centrosome** *n* **:** a sperm-aster presumably derived from the middlepiece of the fertilizing sperm **:** the aster of the first zygotic division

-spermeae — see -SPERMAE

spermi- — see SPERM-

-sper·mia \'spərmēə, -pəm-,-pəim-\ *n comb form* -S [NL, fr. *-spermus* -spermous + *-ia*] **:** condition of having or producing (such) sperm ⟨azoo*spermia*⟩

sper·mi·a·tion \,spərmē'āshən\ *n* -S [*sperm-* + *-ation*] **:** the discharge of spermatozoa from the testis

-sper·mic \'spərmik, -pəm-,-pəim-, -mēk\ *adj comb form* [NL *-spermicus*, fr. LL *sperma* sperm + L *-icus* -ic — more at SPERM] **1 :** -SPERMAL **2 :** being the product of (such) a number of spermatozoa **:** resulting from (such) a multiple fertilization ⟨a tri*spermic* egg⟩ ⟨poly*spermic* fertilization⟩

sper·mi·cide \'spərmə,sīd\ *var of* SPERMATOCIDE

sper·mi·dine \'spərmə,dēn, -dən\ *n* -S [*sperm-* + *-idine*] **:** a crystalline aliphatic triamine $H_2N(CH_2)_3NH(CH_2)_4NH_2$, found esp. in semen in association with spermine and structurally related to it and to putrescine

sper·mi·du·cal \;spərmə;d(y)ükəl\ *adj* [*spermiduct* + *-al*] **:** of, relating to, or being the sperm ducts — used esp. of glandular structures in oligochaetes

sper·mi·duct *or* **sper·mo·duct** \'spərmə,dəkt\ *var of* SPERMADUCT

-spermies *pl of* -SPERMY

sper·mig·er·ous \(;)spər;mijərəs\ *adj* [*sperm-* + *-gerous*] **:** carrying sperm

sperm·ine \'spər,mēn, -,mən\ *n* -S [*sperm-* + *-ine*] **:** a deliquescent crystalline aliphatic tetramine $[-CH_2CH_2NH(CH_2)_3NH_2]_2$ found in semen in combination with phosphoric acid, in blood serum and body tissues, and in yeast and also prepared synthetically

sper·mio·genesis \,spərmēō+\ *n* [NL, fr. *spermio-* (fr. *spermium*) + *genesis*] **1 :** transformation of a spermatid into a spermatozoon **2 :** SPERMATOGENESIS

sper·mio·teliosis \,spərmē(,)ō,telē'ōsəs, -tel-\ *n* -ES [NL, fr. *spermio-* (fr. *spermium*) + Gk *teleiōsis* development] **:** SPERMIOGENESIS 1

sperm·ism \'spər,mizəm\ *n* -S [ISV *sperm-* + *-ism*] **:** a theory formerly widely held in biology: the sperm contains the preformed germ of the embryo — compare OVISM

sperm·ist \-məst\ *n* -S [ISV *sperm-* + *-ist*] **:** an adherent of the theory of spermism

sper·mi·um \'spərmēəm\ *n, pl* **sper·mia** \-ēə\ [NL, prob. fr. Gk *spermeion* sperm, seed, fr. *sperma* — more at SPERM] **:** SPERMATOZOON — used usu. in pl.

sperm nucleus *n* **:** the nucleus of a male gamete; *esp* **:** either of the two nuclei that arise from the generative nucleus of a pollen grain and function in the double fertilization characteristic of seed plants

spermo- — see SPERM-

sper·mo·blast \'spərmə,blast\ *n* [*sperm-* + *-blast*] **:** SPERMATOBLAST — **sper·mo·blas·tic** \;==;blastik\ *adj*

sper·mo·carp \'==,kärp\ *n* -S [*sperm-* + *-carp*] **:** the oogonium together with the ensheathing cells that develop from underlying cells of the parent thallus after fertilization in various algae (as those of the genera *Chara* and *Coleochaete*)

sper·mo·center \'==+\ *n* [*sperm-* + *center*] **:** SPERM CENTER

sper·mo·derm \-,dərm\ *n* [*sperm-* + *-derm*] **:** TESTA

sper·mog·e·nous \(;)spər;mäjənəs\ *adj* [*sperm-* + *-genous*] **:** giving rise to sperms

sper·mo·gone \'spərmə,gōn\ *n* -S [NL *spermogonium*] **:** SPERMOGONIUM

spermogonium *var of* SPERMAGONIUM

sperm oil *n* [so called fr. its being found in the sperm whale] **:** a pale yellow oil that is found with spermaceti in the head cavities and blubber of the sperm whale, is classed chemically as a liquid wax, and is used chiefly as a lubricant (as for light machinery)

sper·mol·y·sis \(,)spər'mäləsəs\ *n* [NL, fr. *sperm-* + *-lysis*] **:** SPERMATOLYSIS

sper·mo·phile \'spərmə,fīl\ *n* -S [NL *Spermophilus*] **:** GROUND SQUIRREL 1c

sper·moph·i·lus \(,)spər'mäfələs\ [NL, fr. *sperm-* + *-philus*] *syn of* CITELLUS

sper·moph·y·ta \-mäfəd·ə\ [NL, fr. *sperm-* + *-phyta*] *syn of* SPERMATOPHYTA

sper·mo·phyte \'spərmə,fīt\ *n* -S [NL *Spermophyta*] **:** SPERMATOPHYTE — **sper·mo·phyt·ic** \;==;fid·ik\ *adj*

sper·mo·toxin \;spərmə+\ *n* [*sperm-* + *toxin*] **:** SPERMATOXIN

sper·mo·type \'spərmə,tīp\ *n* [*sperm-* + *type*] **:** a botanical type (as a neotype) obtained from a plant grown from the seed of a primary type (as a holotype)

sper·mous \'spərməs, -pəm-,-pəim-\ *adj* [*sperm-* + *-ous*] **:** resembling or made up of sperm

-spermous — see -SPERMAL

sperm·oviduct \'spərm+\ *n* [*sperm-* + *oviduct*] **:** HERMAPHRODITE DUCT

sperm receptor *n* **:** a hypothetical substance in the male gamete that is held to interact with fertilizin and egg receptor in the process of fertilization

sperm sac *n* **:** SPERMATHECA

-sper·mum \'spərməm, -pəm-,-pəim-\ *n comb form* [NL, fr. neut. of *-spermus* -spermous] **:** plant having (such) seeds or (such) a seed characteristic — in generic names ⟨Antho*spermum*⟩

sperm whale *n* [short for *spermaceti whale*] **:** a large toothed whale (*Physeter catodon* syn. *P. macrocephalus*) that has large conical teeth in the lower jaw only and no whalebone, attains a length of about 60 feet, has a large closed cavity in the head containing a fluid mixture of spermaceti and oil and a blubber yielding oil of superior quality, and produces ambergris as a pathological secretion of its intestines — called also *black whale;* see PYGMY SPERM WHALE

sperm–whale porpoise *n* **:** a beaked whale (*Hyperoodon ampullatum* syn. *H. rostratum*)

sperm whaling *n* **:** the search for and capture of sperm whales

-sper·my \,spərmē, -pəm-,-pəim-, -mi\ *n comb form* -ES [Gk *-spermia*, fr. *-spermos* -spermous + *-ia* -y] **1 :** state of having (such or so many) seeds ⟨gymno*spermy*⟩ **2 :** state of exhibiting or resulting from (such) a multiple fertilization ⟨poly*spermy*⟩

sper·o·na·ro \,sperə'nä(,)rō\ *also* **sper·o·na·ra** \-ärə\ *n, pl* **speronaros** *or* **speronaroes** [It *speronara*] **:** a large open boat rowed with oars but also having a lateen sail and used in southern Italian waters

sper·ry·lite \'sperē,līt, -rə,l-\ *n* -S [Francis L. *Sperry*, 19th cent. Canadian chemist + E *-lite*] **:** a platinum arsenide $PtAs_2$ occurring as a mineral near Sudbury, Ontario in grains and minute isometric crystals of a tin-white color and being the only compound of platinum known to occur in nature (hardness 6–7, sp. gr. 10.60)

sperse \'spərs\ *vb* -ED/-ING/-S [by shortening] *archaic* **:** DISPERSE

spes phthis·i·ca \'spā'stizəkə\ *n* [NL, phthisic hope] **:** a state of euphoria believed to occur in patients with pulmonary tuberculosis

spes re·cu·pe·ran·di \;spāsrə,kiipə'rän(,)dē\ *n* [LL] **:** hope of recovery of captured goods

spes·sart·ite \'spesə(r),tīt\ *also* **spes·sart·ine** \-,tēn, -,tən\ *n* -S [F, fr. *Spessart*, mountain range in southern Germany + F *-ite, -ine*] **:** a manganese aluminum garnet ideally $Mn_3Al_2(SiO_4)_3$ usu. containing iron, magnesium, or other elements in minor amounts — see GARNET 1

spet \'spā\ *n* -S [F, of Gmc origin; akin to OE *spitu* spit; fr. its long slender shape — more at SPIT (rod)] **:** a small barracuda (*Sphyraena sphyraena*) of southern Europe

[1]**spetch** \'spech\ *n* -ES [alter. of *speck* (patch)] **1 spetches** *pl* **:** parings and refuse of leather, hides, or skins used as a by-product (as for making glue) **2** *dial Brit* **:** a scrap (as of leather) for patching **:** PATCH

[2]**spetch** \"\ *vt* [prob. fr. [1]*spetch*] *dial Eng* **:** MEND, PATCH

[1]**spew** *also* **spue** \'spyü\ *vb* -ED/-ING/-S [ME *spewen*, fr. OE *spīwan*; akin to OHG *spīwan* to spit, ON *spȳja* to spew, Goth *speiwan* to spit, L *spuere*, Gk *ptyein* to spit, Skt *ṣṭhīvati* he spits] *vi* **1 :** VOMIT **2 :** to come in a flood or gush ⟨sewage ~*ed* over the yard⟩ ⟨a violently ~*ing* flood⟩ **3 a :** to ooze forth **:** EXUDE ⟨oil ~*ing* out of the wood⟩ ⟨water ~*ed* slowly from the saturated soil⟩ **b** *of soil* **:** to break away and slip (as when swollen with frost) ~ *vt* **1 :** to eject from the stomach **:** VOMIT ⟨~*ed* out a mass of undigested food⟩ **2 :** to cast forth with or as if with disgust **:** emit or eject with vigor or violence ⟨a volcano ~*ing* out lava⟩ ⟨~*ed* forth his contempt⟩ **3 :** to force out by or as if by pressure **:** EXTRUDE

[2]**spew** *also* **spue** \"\ *n* -S **1 a :** matter that is vomited **:** VOMITUS **b :** material that exudes or is extruded: as (1) **:** an oily or gummy exudate (as on the surface of leather or a recording disc) (2) **:** an overflow (as of rubber or metal) from a mold

2 *dial Brit* **:** an afterswarm of bees that is usu. the third or fourth of a season 3 *dial Brit* **:** a soggy piece of ground **:** an oozy patch esp. in a field

spew·er \-üə(r), -ü(ə)r, -üə\ *n* -s **:** one that spews

spewing sickness *n* **:** a disease of sheep and cattle caused by eating the sneezeweed (*Helenium hoopesii*) and characterized by weakness, rapid irregular pulse, nausea, and vomiting

spewy \-üï\ *adj* -ER/-EST [¹*spew* + -*y*] *of land* **:** excessively moist or marshy **:** tending to ooze out water ⟨fields too ~ to cultivate⟩

spey \ˈspā\ *Austral var of* SPAY

spey·e·ria \spīˈ(y)irēə\ *n, cap* [NL, fr. A. *Speyer*, 19th cent. Ger. lepidopterist + NL -*ia*] **:** a large genus of butterflies (family Nymphalidae) that contains the silverspots

spezia *adj, usu cap* [fr. La *Spezia*, seaport in northwest Italy] **:** LA SPEZIA

spg *abbr* 1 sponge 2 spring

sp gr *abbr* specific gravity

sph *abbr* sphere; spherical

sphac·e·lar·ia \ˌsfasəˈla(a)rēə\ *n, cap* [NL, fr. *sphacelus* gangrene + -*aria*] **:** a genus of small feathery brown algae (order Sphacelariales) similar to *Ectocarpus* but having the area of growth restricted to large dark brown apical cells

sphac·e·lar·i·a·les \ˌ=ˌ==ˈā(ˌ)lēz\ *n pl, cap* [NL, fr. *Sphacelaria* + -*ales*] **:** an order of small or medium-sized much branched parenchymatous brown algae (class Isogeneratae) that are found chiefly in the lower part of the intertidal zone and grow from apical cells on the branches

sphac·e·late \ˈsfasəˌlāt\ *vb* -ED/-ING/-S [prob. fr. (assumed) NL *sphacelatus*, past part. of *sphacelare* to become gangrenous, fr. NL *sphacelus* gangrene] *vi* **:** to become gangrenous **:** MORTIFY ~ *vt* **:** to cause to become gangrenous — **sphac·e·la·tion** \ˌ==ˈlāshən\ *n* -s

sphac·e·lat·ed \ˈ==ˌlād·əd\ *adj* [prob. fr. (assumed) NL *sphacelatus* + E -*ed*] **1 :** GANGRENOUS, SLOUGHED ⟨a ~ ulcer⟩ **2 :** WITHERED, DECAYED ⟨a ~ root⟩

spha·ce·lia \sfaˈsēlēə, sfəˈs-\ *n* -s [NL, fr. *sphacelus* gangrene + -*ia*] **:** the conidial stage of ergot (*Claviceps purpurea*) — called also *sphacelial stage* — **spha·ce·li·al** \-lēəl\ *adj*

sphac·e·lo·ma \ˌsfasəˈlōmə\ *n, cap* [NL, fr. *sphacelus* + -*oma*] **:** a form genus of imperfect fungi that is sometimes included in *Gloeosporium* but is usu. considered as distinct because of the firm acervulus suggestive of a cushion

sphac·e·lo·the·ca \ˌsfasəlōˈthēkə\ *n, cap* [NL, fr. *sphacelus* + *theca*] **:** a genus of smut fungi bearing teliospores in globose masses that are surrounded by a pseudoparenchymatous layer of tissue

sphac·e·lus \ˈsfasələs\ *n* -ES [NL, fr. Gk *sphakelos* gangrene] **:** GANGRENE, NECROSIS; *also* **:** a gangrenous or necrosed part or mass **:** SLOUGH

sphaer- *or* **sphaero-** *also* **spher-** *or* **sphero-** *comb form* [LL *sphaer-*, *sphaero-*, fr. L, fr. Gk *sphair-*, *sphairo-*, fr. *sphaira* — more at SPHERE] **1 :** ball **:** sphere ⟨*Sphaero*phorus⟩ ⟨calco*sphere*ite⟩ **2 :** spherical **:** consisting of spherical elements ⟨*sphaer*aphides⟩ ⟨*sphero*meter⟩

-sphae·ra \ˈsfirə, -fērə\ *n comb form* -s [NL, fr. L *sphaera* sphere — more at SPHERE] **:** ball **:** sphere — chiefly in taxonomic names ⟨Micro*sphaera*⟩

sphaer·al·cea \ˌsfiˌralˈsēə, -feˌr-\ *n, cap* [NL, fr. *sphaer-* + L *alcea*, a mallow, fr. Gk *alkaia* vervain mallow] **:** a large genus of chiefly tropical herbs (family Malvaceae) with showy pink or scarlet flowers and mostly globose fruit — see GLOBE MALLOW

sphaer·a·phis \ˈsfirəfəs, ˈsfer-\ *n, pl* **sphae·raph·i·des** \sfəˈrafəˌdēz\ [NL, fr. *sphaer-* + Gk *rhaphis* needle — more at RAPHIDE] **:** a spherical aggregation of raphides in a plant ce

sphae·rel·la \sfəˈrelə\ [NL, fr. *sphaer-* + -*ella*] *syn of* MYCOSPHAERELLA

sphaer·i·a·ce·ae \ˌsfirēˈāsēˌē\ *n pl, cap* [NL, fr. *Sphaeria*, type genus (fr. *sphaer-* + -*ia*) + -*aceae*] **:** a family of parasitic fungi (order Sphaeriales) having globose and sometimes necked or beaked perithecia usu. with ostioles — **sphaer·i·a·ceous** \ˌ¦==¦āshəs\ *adj*

sphaer·i·a·les \ˌ==ˈā(ˌ)lēz\ *n pl, cap* [NL, fr. *Sphaeria* + -*ales*] **:** a large order of ascomycetous fungi (subclass Euascomycetes) that usu. have hard dark perithecia with definite ostioles, that include many economically important plant parasites as well as large numbers of saprophytes, and that in recent classifications are often divided among several orders

sphae·rid·i·al \sfəˈridēəl\ *adj* [NL *sphaeridium* + E -*al*] **:** of, relating to, or being a sphaeridium

sphae·rid·i·um \-ēəm\ *n, pl* **sphaerid·ia** \-ēə\ [NL, fr. *sphaer-* + -*idium*] **:** one of the small organs found on or buried in the test of all recent sea urchins except the Cidaroida suggesting statoliths in structure and possibly subserving a similar function

¹**sphae·ri·id** \ˈsfirēəd\ *adj* [NL *Sphaeriidae*] **:** of or relating to the Sphaeriidae

²**sphaeriid** \"\ *n* -s **:** a mollusk of the family Sphaeriidae

sphae·ri·idae \sfəˈrīəˌdē\ *n pl, cap* [NL, fr. *Sphaerium*, type genus + -*idae*] **:** a cosmopolitan family of minute freshwater bivalve mollusks (suborder Submytilacea) including some that are intermediate hosts of trematode worms — see SPHAERIUM

sphae·ri·oi·da·ce·ae \ˌsfirēˌȯiˈdāsēˌē\ [NL, prob. fr. *Sphaeria*, genus of fungi + -*oides* -oid + -*aceae*] *syn of* SPHAEROPSIDACEAE

sphae·ri·ta \sfəˈrīd·ə, -rēd·ə\ *n, cap* [NL, fr. *sphaer-* + L -*ita* -ite] **:** a genus of amoeboid parasites of the cytoplasm of various algae and protozoans that are usu. considered lower fungi and placed in the order Chytridiales

sphae·rite \ˈsfiˌrīt\ *n* -s [G *sphärit*, fr. *sphär-* sphaer- + -*it* -ite] **:** a mineral consisting of a light gray or bluish hydrous aluminum phosphate in globular concretions

sphae·ri·um \ˈsfirēəm\ *n, cap* [NL, fr. Gk *sphairion*, dim. of *sphaira* ball, sphere — more at SPHERE] **:** a widely distributed genus (the type of the family Sphaeriidae) of small viviparous freshwater bivalve mollusks that have a thin light-colored shell and the siphons separate — see FINGERNAIL CLAM

sphaero- — see SPHAER-

sphaero·bo·la·ce·ae \ˌsfirōbəˈlāsēˌē, -fer-\ *n pl, cap* [NL, fr. *Sphaerobolus*, type genus (fr. *sphaer-* + Gk *bolos* throw) + NL -*aceae*; akin to Gk *ballein* to throw — more at DEVIL] **:** a monotypic family of fungi (order Nidulariales) in which the more or less spherical gleba is forcibly ejected at maturity

sphaero·car·pa·ce·ae \-ōˌkärˈpāsēˌē\ *n pl, cap* [NL, fr. *Sphaerocarpus*, type genus + -*aceae*] **:** a family of liverworts with bilaterally symmetrical gametophytes that is placed in the order Sphaerocarpales or sometimes included in Jungermanniales among the Anacrogynae — see SPHAEROCARPUS

sphaero·car·pa·les \-ā(ˌ)lēz\ *n pl, cap* [NL, fr. *Sphaerocarpus* + -*ales*] **:** a small order of Hepaticae comprising liverworts with an involucre around each archegonium — see SPHAEROCARPACEAE

sphaero·car·pos \-ōˈkärpəs, -ˌpäs\ [NL] *syn of* SPHAEROCARPUS

sphaero·car·pus \-pəs\ *n, cap* [NL, fr. *sphaer-* + -*carpus*] **:** the type genus of Sphaerocarpaceae comprising liverworts with a small many-lobed usu. orbicular thallus and with the spores nearly always remaining in tetrads at maturity

sphaero·cobaltite \ˌsfi(ˌ)rō, -fe(-+\ *n* [G *sphärokobaltit*, fr. *sphär-* sphaer- + *kobaltit* cobaltite] **:** COBALTOCALCITE

sphaero·coc·ca·ce·ae \ˌ=(ˌ)=ˌkäˈkāsēˌē\ *n pl, cap* [NL, fr. *Sphaerococcus*, type genus (fr. *sphaer-* + -*coccus*) + -*aceae*] **:** a family of red algae (order Rhodymeniales) having a much branched thallus with the cystocarps enclosed in semiglobular swellings of the peripheral tissues — see GRACILARIA — **sphaero·coc·ca·ceous** \ˌ¦=(ˌ)=¦kāshəs\ *adj*

sphaero·crystal \ˌ¦=(ˌ)=+ˌ-\ *n* [*sphaer-* + *crystal*] **:** SPHAERAPHIS

sphaeroid *var of* SPHEROID

sphaer·o·lite \ˈsfirəˌlīt, -fer-\ *n* -s [by alter.] **:** SPHERULITE

sphaer·o·lit·ic \ˌ¦==¦lid·ik\ *adj* [by alter.] **:** SPHERULITIC

sphae·ro·ma \sfəˈrōmə\ *n* [NL, fr. Gk *sphairōma* something made round, fr. *sphairoun* to make round, fr. *sphaira* ball, sphere — more at SPHERE] **1** *cap* **:** a genus (the type of the family Sphaeromidae) of marine isopod crustaceans having broad oval bodies that can sometimes be rolled into a ball, an abdomen of two segments, and well developed antennae and including destructive borers of pilings and other timbers — see ROCK-BORING ISOPOD **2** -s **:** any isopod of the genus *Sphaeroma*

sphaero·ne·ma \ˌsfirəˈnēmə, -fer-\ *n, cap* [NL, fr. *sphaer-* + -*nema*] **:** a genus of imperfect fungi (family Sphaeropsidaceae) having pycnidia with elongated necks and occurring chiefly on dead plant tissue

sphae·roph·o·rus \sfəˈräfərəs\ *n, cap* [NL, fr. *sphaer-* + -*phorus*] **:** a genus (the type of the family Sphaerophoraceae) of gymnocarpous lichens characterized by a foliaceous or fruticose thallus with terminal globose apothecia bearing continuous dark-colored ascospores

sphae·rop·lea \sfəˈräplēə\ *n, cap* [NL, fr. *sphaer-* + -*plea* (fr. Gk *pleos* full); akin to L *plenus* full — more at FULL] **:** a genus of unbranched filamentous green algae (order Cladophorales) having many chloroplasts in each cell arranged in transverse bands and producing more than one egg in each oogonium

sphae·rop·si·da·ce·ae \sfəˌräpsəˈdāsēˌē\ *n pl, cap* [NL, fr. *Sphaeropsid-*, *Sphaeropsis*, type genus + -*aceae*] **:** a very large family of imperfect fungi (order Sphaeropsidales) that include various important plant pathogens and are characterized by globose to spheroidal pycnidia with dark leathery or carbonaceous walls — **sphae·rop·si·da·ceous** \=¦==¦dāshəs\ *adj*

sphae·rop·si·da·les \=ˌ==ˈdā(ˌ)lēz\ *n pl, cap* [NL, fr. *Sphaeropsid-*, *Sphaeropsis* + -*ales*] **:** an order of imperfect fungi in which the conidia are produced in pycnidia or similar chambered cavities and which include both saprophytes and parasites

sphae·rop·sis \sfəˈräpsəs\ *n, cap* [NL, fr. *sphaer-* + -*opsis*] **:** a form genus of imperfect fungi (family Sphaeropsidaceae) having large unicellular dark pycnospores and including many forms that have been found to be imperfect stages of various other fungi (as members of the genus *Physalospora*)

sphaero·stil·be \ˌsfirōˈstil(ˌ)bē, -fer-\ *n, cap* [NL, fr. *sphaer-* + -*stilbe* (fr. Gk *stilbos* glistening) — more at STILBUM] **:** a genus of ascomycetous fungi (family Nectriaceae) characterized by red perithecia borne on slender stromatic stalks and 2-celled ascospores and including destructive root parasites esp. of tropical plants

sphaero·the·ca \-ˈthēkə\ *n, cap* [NL, fr. *sphaer-* + *theca*] **:** a genus of powdery mildews (family Erysiphaceae) having perithecia with one ascus and unbranched appendages that resemble hyphae — see HOP MILDEW

sphae·rot·i·lus \sfəˈräd·ᵊləs\ *n, cap* [NL, fr. *sphaer-* + Gk *tilos* fiber, fr. *tillein* to pluck] **:** a genus of bacteria (family Chlamydobacteriaceae) having filaments that exhibit false branching and reproducing by both conidia and swarmers

sphag·na·ceous \(ˈ)sfagˈnāshəs\ *adj* [NL *Sphagnum* + E -*aceous*] **:** of or relating to the genus *Sphagnum* or order Sphagnales

sphag·na·les \sfagˈnā(ˌ)lēz\ *n pl, cap* [NL, fr. *Sphagnum* + -*ales*] **:** an order of Musci that is coextensive with the genus *Sphagnum* and is often isolated in a separate subclass

sphag·ni·cole \ˈsfagnəˌkōl\ *n* -s [back-formation fr. *sphagnicolous*] **:** a sphagnicolous organism

sphag·nic·o·lous \(ˈ)sfagˈnikələs\ *adj* [*sphagnum* + -*i-* + -*colous*] **:** inhabiting or growing in sphagnum ⟨~ rotifers⟩

sphag·nob·rya \sfagˈnäbrēə\ *n pl, cap* [NL, fr. *Sphagnum* + -*brya* (fr. Gk *bryon* moss) — more at BRY-] *in some classifications* **:** a subclass of Musci coextensive with the order Sphagnales

sphag·no·phil·ic \ˌ¦sfagnə¦filik\ *adj* [*sphagnum* + -*o-* + -*philic*] **:** living or thriving in sphagnum

sphag·nous \ˈsfagnəs\ *adj* [NL *Sphagnum* + E -*ous*] **1 :** being or made up of mosses of the genus *Sphagnum* ⟨a heavy ~ growth⟩ ⟨~ plants⟩ **2 :** abounding in peat sphagnum ⟨a ~ bog⟩

sphag·num \ˈsfagnəm, -faig-\ *n* [NL, fr. L *sphagnos*, a moss, fr. Gk] **1** *cap* **:** a large genus (coextensive with the order Sphagnales) of atypical mosses that have a protonema which is not filamentous but resembles the prothallium of a fern, a pseudopodium which is derived from the gametophyte rather than the sporophyte as in other mosses, and leaves which contain abundant colorless aqueous tissue interspersed with chlorophyll-bearing cells and that grow only in very wet acid areas where their accumulated remains become compacted with other plant debris to form peat **2** *or* **sphagnum moss** -s **a :** any plant of the genus *Sphagnum* **b :** a mass of sphagnum plants ⟨damping off can often be prevented by covering the seeds with a thin layer of pulverized ~⟩ ⟨dehydrated ~ was used for surgical dressings during World War I⟩

sphagnum bog *n* **:** a bog containing sphagnum and usu. other characteristic and acid-tolerant plants (as pitcher plants of the genus *Sarracenia*, sundews, or heaths) and tending to form deposits of peat

sphagnum frog *n* [so called fr. the fact that it was orig. found in a sphagnum bog] **:** CARPENTER FROG

sphal·er·ite \ˈsfaləˌrīt\ *n* -s [G *sphalerit*, fr. Gk *sphaleros* deceitful, tripping, slippery (fr. *sphallein* to cause to fall) + G -*it* -ite; fr. its being often mistaken for galena — more at SPILL] **:** a widely distributed ore of zinc composed essentially of zinc sulfide ZnS but often containing iron, manganese, or other elements, occurring in isometric crystals or cleavable masses of resinous to adamantine luster and commonly yellow, brown, or black color, and having highly perfect dodecahedral cleavage (hardness 3.5–4, sp. gr. 3.9–4.1) — called also *blackjack, blende, false galena*

sphar·gis \ˈsfärjəs\ [NL] *syn of* DERMOCHELYS

¹**sphe·cid** \ˈsfesəd\ *adj* [NL *Sphecidae*] **:** of or relating to the Sphecidae

²**sphecid** \"\ *n* -s **:** a wasp of the family Sphecidae

spheci·dae \ˈsfesəˌdē, -fes-\ *n pl, cap* [NL, fr. *Sphec-*, *Sphex*, type genus + -*idae*] **:** a family of solitary wasps (superfamily Sphecoidea) having the first segment of the abdomen generally prolonged into a long smooth cylindrical petiole and including the mud daubers and some digger wasps

sphe·cius \ˈsfesh(ē)əs\ *n, cap* [NL, fr. *Sphec-*, *Sphex* — more at SPHEX] **:** a cosmopolitan genus of large solitary wasps (family Stizidae) including the cicada killer

¹**sphe·coid** \ˈsfēˌkȯid\ *adj* [NL *Sphecoidea*] **:** of or relating to the Sphecoidea

²**sphecoid** \"\ *n* -s **:** an insect of the superfamily Sphecoidea

sphe·coi·dea \sfəˈkȯidēə\ *n pl, cap* [NL, fr. *Sphec-*, *Sphex* + -*oidea*] **:** a superfamily of Hymenoptera comprising Sphecidae and related families and in some classifications the true bees — compare APOIDEA

spheges *pl of* SPHEX

sphegi·dae \ˈsfejəˌdē, -fēj-\ [NL, irreg. fr. *Sphec-*, *Sphex* + -*idae*] *syn of* SPHECIDAE

sphen- *or* **spheno-** *comb form* [NL, fr. Gk *sphēn-*, *sphēno-*, fr. *sphēn* — more at SPOON] **1 :** wedge **:** wedge-shaped ⟨*spheno*gram⟩ ⟨*Spheno*don⟩ **2 a :** of or relating to the sphenoid ⟨*spheno*tribe⟩ **b :** sphenoidal and ⟨*spheno*mastoid⟩ ⟨*sphen*ethmoidal⟩

sphen·acanthocephala \ˌsfēn+\ *n pl, cap* [NL, fr. *sphen-* + *Acanthocephala*] **:** a small order of Acanthocephala comprising a few parasites of birds that lack a true cephalic extrovert or proboscis

¹**sphe·nac·odont** \sfəˈnakəˌdänt\ *adj* [NL *Sphenacodontia*] **:** of or relating to the Sphenacodontia

²**sphenacodont** \"\ *n* -s **:** a sphenacodont reptile or fossil

sphe·nac·odon·tia \=ˌ=ˈdänchēə, -ntēə\ *n pl, cap* [NL, fr. *Sphenacodont-*, *Sphenacodon*, genus of reptiles (irreg. fr. *sphen-* + -*odont-*, -*odon*) + -*ia*] **:** a suborder of Pelycosauria comprising primitive Permian reptiles that resemble mammals

sphen·do·ne \ˈsfendəˌnē\ *n* -s [Gk *sphendonē* sling, sphendone — more at SPONDYL] **1 :** a headband worn by ancient Greek women **2 :** a semicircular part or place (as at the end of an ancient Greek stadium)

sphene \ˈsfēn\ *n* -s [F *sphène*, fr. Gk *sphēn* wedge; fr. a form of its crystals] **:** a mineral $CaTiSiO_5$ that is a silicate of calcium and titanium, and often contains columbium, chromium, fluorine, and other elements — called also *titanite*

sphen·ethmoid \(ˈ)sfēn+\ *adj* [*sphen-* + *ethmoid*] **:** of, relating to, or being a bone of the skull that surrounds the anterior end of the brain in many amphibians

sphe·ni·on \ˈsfēnēˌän\ *n* -s [NL, fr. *sphen-* + Gk -*ion*, dim. suffix] **:** the lower frontal apex of the parietal bone used as a reference point in craniometry

sphe·nis·ci·dae \sfəˈnisəˌdē\ *n pl, cap* [NL, fr. *Spheniscus*, type genus + -*idae*] **:** a family of birds (order Sphenisciformes) containing all the existing penguins

sphe·nis·ci·for·mes \=ˌ==ˈfȯr(ˌ)mēz\ *n pl, cap* [NL, fr. *Spheniscus* + -*iformes*] **:** an order of flightless aquatic birds comprising the penguins

sphe·nis·co·mor·phae \sfəˌniskəˈmȯrˌfē\ [NL, fr. *Spheniscus* + -*o-* + -*morphae*] *syn of* SPHENISCIFORMES

sphe·nis·cus \-ˈniskəs\ *n, cap* [NL, fr. Gk *sphēniskos* small wedge, dim. of *sphēn* wedge; fr. the shortness of the wings — more at SPOON] **:** a genus of penguins that is type of the family Spheniscidae and includes the jackass penguin

sphe·no·basilar *also* **sphe·no·basilic** \¦sfē(ˌ)nō+\ *adj* [*sphenobasilar*, fr. NL *sphenobasilaris*, fr. *sphen-* + *basilaris* basilar, irreg. fr. L *basis* base + -*aris* -ar; *sphenobasilic*, prob. fr. NL *sphenobasilaris* + E -*ic* — more at BASE] **:** of, relating to, lying between, or distributed to the sphenoid and the basilar part of the occipital bone

sphe·no·ce·pha·lia \ˌsfēnəsəˈfālyə\ *n* -s [NL, fr. Gk *sphēnokephalos* having a wedge-shaped head (fr. *sphēn-* sphen- + -*kephalos* -headed, -cephalous) + NL -*ia*] **:** SPHENOCEPHALY

sphe·no·ce·phal·ic \¦=ˌ=sə¦falik\ *or* **sphe·no·ceph·a·lous** \¦==¦sefələs\ *adj* [NL *sphenocephalia* + E -*ic* or -*ous*] **:** having a wedge-shaped head

sphe·no·ceph·a·ly \ˌ==ˈsefəlē\ *n* -ES [NL *sphenocephalia*] **:** the condition of being sphenocephalic

sphen·odon \ˈsfēnəˌdän, -fen-\ *n* [NL, fr. *sphen-* + -*odon*] **1** *cap* **:** a genus of reptiles comprising the tuatara, being distinguished from all other recent reptiles by the presence of a pineal eye, and usu. placed with the Rhynchocephalia but sometimes segregated in a distinct suborder **2** *or* **sphen·odont** \-änt\ -s [*sphenodont*, fr. NL *Sphenodont-*, *Sphenodon*] **:** an animal of the genus *Sphenodon* **:** TUATARA

sphen·odont \-änt\ *adj* [NL *Sphenodont-*, *Sphenodon*] **:** of or relating to the genus *Sphenodon*

sphe·no·frontal \¦sfē(ˌ)nō+\ *adj* [*sphen-* + *frontal*] **:** of, relating to, lying between, or distributed to the sphenoid and frontal bones of the skull

spheno·gram \ˈsfēnəˌgram, -fen-\ *n* [*sphen-* + -*gram*] **:** a cuneiform character (as in an inscription)

sphe·nog·ra·phy \sfəˈnägrəfē\ *n* -ES [*sphen-* + -*graphy*] **:** the art of writing in or deciphering cuneiform characters

¹**sphe·noid** \ˈsfēˌnȯid\ *also* **sphe·noi·dal** \(ˈ)sfē¦nȯidᵊl\ *adj* [*sphenoid*, fr. NL *sphenoides*, fr. Gk *sphēnoeidēs* wedge-shaped, fr. *sphēn* wedge + -*oeidēs* -oid; *sphenoidal*, fr. NL *sphenoidalis*, fr. Gk *sphēnoeidēs* + L -*alis* -al — more at SPOON] **1 :** of, relating to, or situated in the region of a compound bone of the base of the cranium of various vertebrates formed by the fusion of several bony elements with the basisphenoid and in man consisting of a median body from whose sides extend a pair of broad curved winglike expansions in front of which is another pair of much smaller triangular lateral processes while ventrally two large deeply cleft processes extend downward ⟨a ~ sinus⟩ **2** *usu* **sphenoidal a :** relating to or resembling a sphenoid **:** wedge-shaped **b :** having such symmetry that the general form is a sphenoid — used of a monoclinic crystal with a diad axis of symmetry

²**sphenoid** \"\ *n* -s **1 :** a sphenoid bone **2 a :** a wedge-shaped open form in the monoclinic system of crystallization consisting of two faces related by a diad axis of symmetry — compare DOME **b :** DISPHENOID

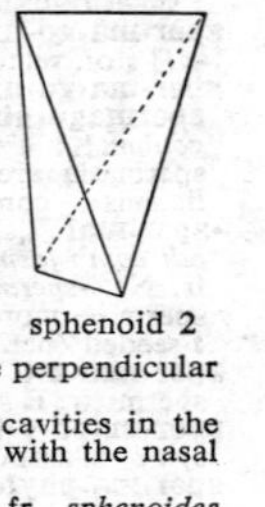

sphenoid 2

sphenoidal fissure *n* **:** a fissure between the greater and lesser wing of the sphenoid bone

sphenoidal group *n* **:** a group of the tetragonal system of crystalline symmetries of which the sphenoid is the typical form

sphenoidal process *n* **1 :** a process on the superior border of the vertical plate of the palatine bone articulating with the sphenoid **2 :** a backward prolongation of the cartilage of the nasal septum between the vomer and the perpendicular plate of the ethmoid

sphenoidal sinus *n* **:** either of two irregular cavities in the body of the sphenoid bone that communicate with the nasal cavities

sphe·noid·itis \ˌsfēˌnȯiˈdīd·əs\ *n* -ES [NL, fr. *sphenoides* sphenoid + -*itis*] **:** inflammation of the sphenoidal sinuses

spheno·lith \ˈsfēnᵊlˌith, -fen-\ *n* -s [*sphen-* + -*lith*] **:** a wedge-shaped intrusive mass of igneous rock

sphe·no·mandibular \¦sfē(ˌ)nō+\ *adj* [*sphen-* + *mandibular*] **:** of, relating to, or joining the sphenoid bone and the lower jaw

sphe·no·maxillary \"+\ *adj* [*sphen-* + *maxillary*] **:** of, relating to, or joining the sphenoid bone and the upper jaw

sphenomaxillary fissure *n* **:** the inferior orbital fissure

sphenomaxillary fossa *n* **:** PTERYGOPALATINE FOSSA

spheno-occipital suture \"+ . . . -\ *also* **spheno-occipital** *n* **:** the junction between the basisphenoid and basioccipital bones of the mammalian skull that in man is usu. closed by the age of 25

¹**sphe·no·palatine** \"+\ *adj* [ISV *sphen-* + *palatine*] **:** of, relating to, lying in, or distributed to the vicinity of the sphenoid and palatine bones

²**sphenopalatine** \"\ *n* **:** a sphenopalatine part; *specif* **:** SPHENOPALATINE GANGLION

sphenopalatine foramen *n* **:** a foramen between the sphenoidal and orbital parts of the vertical plate of the palatine bone; *often* **:** a deep notch between these parts that by articulation with the sphenoid bone is converted into a foramen

sphenopalatine ganglion *n* **:** an autonomic ganglion on the maxillary nerve in the pterygopalatine fossa receiving preganglionic fibers from the facial nerve by way of the greater superficial petrosal nerve, sending postganglionic fibers to the nasal mucosa, palate, pharynx, and orbit, and giving passage to sympathetic fibers from the carotid plexus — called also *Meckel's ganglion*

sphe·no·parietal \¦sfē(ˌ)nō+\ *adj* [*sphen-* + *parietal*] **:** of, relating to, lying between, or distributed to the region of the sphenoid and parietal bones ⟨~ fissure⟩

sphenoparietal index *n* **:** the ratio of the breadth of the skull from stenion to stenion to its greatest breadth multiplied by 100

sphe·noph·o·rus \sfēˈnäfərəs\ *n, cap* [NL, fr. *sphen-* + -*phorus*] **:** a genus of weevils whose larvae bore in the roots and stems of cereal and other grasses

sphe·no·phyl·la·les \ˌsfē(ˌ)nōfəˈlā(ˌ)lēz\ *n pl, cap* [NL, fr. *Sphenophyllum* + -*ales*] **:** an order of fossil plants (subdivision Sphenopsida) coextensive with the genus *Sphenophyllum*

sphe·no·phyl·lum \ˌsfēnəˈfiləm\ *n, cap* [NL, fr. *sphen-* + -*phyllum*] **:** a genus of Paleozoic fossil plants that are related to the club mosses and horsetails but are usu. placed in the separate order Sphenophyllales, that have jointed stems, cuneate leaves in whorls of three or multiples of three, and terminal cones or sporophylls, and that occur from the Devonian to the Permian

sphe·nop·sid \sfēˈnäpsəd\ *n* -s [NL *Sphenopsida*] **:** a plant or fossil of the subdivision Sphenopsida

sphe·nop·si·da \-psədə\ *n pl, cap* [NL, fr. *sphen-* + -*opsis* + -*ida*] **:** a subdivision of Tracheophyta comprising vascular plants (as the horsetails and extinct related forms) with jointed stems, small leaves usu. in whorls at distinct stem nodes, and sporangia in sporangiophores and including the orders Hyeniales, Sphenophyllales, and Equisetales — compare LYCOPSIDA, PSILOPSIDA, PTEROPSIDA

sphe·nop·ter·is \-ptərəs\ *n, cap* [NL, fr. *sphen-* + -*pteris*] **:** a form genus of Paleozoic fossil plants (fr. Cycadofilicales) based primarily on leaf blades with cuneate pinnules

sphe·no·squamosal \¦sfē(ˌ)nō+\ *adj* [*sphen-* + *squamosal*] **:** of, relating to, lying between, or distributed to the sphenoid and temporal bones of the skull ⟨~ suture⟩

¹**sphen·otic** \(ˈ)sfē¦näd·ik, -nōd-·\ *adj* [*sphen-* + -*otic*] **:** of, relating to, or being an element of the skull of many fishes situated above the prootic and often forming part of the posterior boundary of the orbit

²**sphenotic** \"\ *n* -s **:** a sphenotic bone or cartilage

¹**sphe·no·turbinal** \¦sfē(ˌ)nō+\ *adj* [*sphen-* + *turbinal*] **:** of, relating to, constituting, or situated near a pair of small curved plates of bone at the anterior and inferior part of the body of the sphenoid bone that in man remain attached to the sphenoid until the age of puberty

²**sphenoturbinal** \"\ *n* -s **:** a sphenoturbinal bone

spher- — see SPHAER-

spher·al \ˈsfirəl\ *adj* [LL *sphaeralis*, fr. *sphaer-* + L -*alis* -al] **1 a :** of, relating to, or having the form of a sphere **b :** resem-

bling a sphere esp. in perfection of symmetry or well-rounded excellence **2 a** : of or relating to the spheres of ancient astronomy **b** : suggesting the music of the spheres : HARMONIOUS
sphe·ral·i·ty \sfi'ralәd·ē\ *n* -ES : the quality or state of being spheral or spherical
spher·aster \(')sfi¦rastә(r)\ *n* -S [NL, fr. *sphaer-* + *-aster*] : a many-rayed sponge spicule with a spherical central body
sphe·ra·tion \sfi'rāshәn\ *n* -S [¹*sphere* + *-ation*] : the act or process of taking the form of a sphere
¹sphere \'sfi(ә)r, -iә, *chiefly South sometimes* 'spi-\ *n* -S *often attrib* [ME *spere*, fr. MF *espere*, fr. L *sphaera*, fr. Gk *sphaira* ball, sphere; perh. akin to Gk *spairein* to quiver — more at SPURN] **1 a** (1) : the apparent surface of the heavens of which half forms the dome of the visible sky, which is assumed to be spherical and everywhere infinitely distant from the earth, on which the celestial bodies seem to have their places, and on which the various astronomical circles (as of right ascension and declination, the equator, ecliptic) are conceived to be drawn : an ideal globe with the astronomical circles in their proper positions on it (2) : one of the concentric and eccentric revolving spherical transparent shells in which according to ancient astronomy stars, sun, planets, and moon are set and by which they are carried in such manner as to produce their apparent motions — compare MUSIC OF THE SPHERES **b** : a globe depicting such a sphere; *broadly* : GLOBE 1a **2 a** : a globular body : one whose major circumferences approximate to circles : BALL ⟨ruddy ~s burdening the apple boughs⟩: as (1) : a celestial body : PLANET, STAR (2) : a rounded differentiated structure (as a centrosome or idiosome) in protoplasm **b** (1) : a body or space bounded by one surface all points of which are equally distant from a point within that constitutes its center — see VOLUME table (2) : the bounding surface of such a body or space **3 a** : one of the concentric layers anciently believed to be formed by each of the elements earth, water, air, and fire **b** : natural, normal, or proper place ⟨fish in their underwater ~⟩ **c** : an order of society : social position or class **d** : a happier or heavenly region ⟨a future ~, where the injustices of life shall be rectified —W.E.H.Lecky⟩ **4 a** *obs* : a course or path encompassing a center : the orbit of a heavenly body : CIRCUIT **b** (1) : the area over which something acts, exerts influence, has its being or significance, or radiates : a domain or range of something (as action, knowledge, or influence) : field of action or existence : COMPASS, PROVINCE ⟨within her narrow ~ of action⟩ ⟨in the ~ of mundane affairs⟩ ⟨the case falls into the ~ of this act⟩ — compare CIRCLE 5b (2) : DENOTATION 4 **syn** see FIELD
²sphere \"\ *vt* -ED/-ING/-S **1** : to place in or as if in a sphere or among the spheres : raise aloft : ENSPHERE **2 a** : to form into a sphere : make round or spherical **b** : to make complete : PERFECT **3** : to enclose in or as if in a sphere : SURROUND **4** *archaic* : to send in a circuit : cause to turn in all directions : CIRCULATE
sphere crystal *n* : SPHAERAPHIS
sphere fungus *n* : a fungus of the order Sphaeriales
sphere gap *n* : a spark gap (sense 2) in which the electrode terminals are metal spheres
sphere·less \-lәs\ *adj* : lacking a sphere and esp. an orbit : WANDERING
sphere of influence **1** : a territorial area within which the political influence or the interests of one nation are held to be more or less paramount **2** : a region more or less under the control of a nation but not constituting a formally recognized protectorate
spheric \'sfirik, -fer-, -rēk\ *adj* [MF *spherique*, fr. LL *sphaericus*] : of or relating to a sphere or the spheres : resembling a sphere : SPHERICAL, ORBITAL ⟨~ shape⟩ ⟨~ geometry⟩
spheri·cal \-rәkәl, -rēk-\ *adj* [LL *sphaericus* (fr. Gk *sphairikos*, fr. *sphaira* sphere + *-ikos* -ic) + E *-al*] **1** : having the form of a sphere or of one of its segments : like a sphere : GLOBULAR, ORBICULAR ⟨a ~ body⟩ **2** : of or relating to a sphere : having to do with a sphere or with the properties of a sphere ⟨a ~ coordinate⟩ ⟨~ deviation⟩ **3** : of or relating to the celestial bodies or their spheres ⟨thieves . . . by ~ predominance —Shak.⟩ — **spheri·cal·ly** \-rәk(ә)lē, -rēk-, -li\ *adv*
spherical aberration *n* : aberration caused by the spherical form of a lens or mirror that gives different foci for central and marginal rays
spherical angle *n* : the angle between two intersecting arcs of great circles of a sphere measured by the plane angle formed by the tangents to the arcs at the point of intersection
spherical astronomy *n* : a branch of astronomy that deals chiefly with problems relating to the celestial sphere
spherical coordinate *n* : any of three coordinates in space two being obtained by constructing in a plane a polar coordinate system and the third being the angle between this plane and a fixed plane containing the polar axis
spherical excess *n* : the amount by which the sum of the three angles of a spherical triangle exceeds two right angles
spherical geometry *n* : the geometry of figures on a sphere
spheri·cal·i·ty \,sfirә'kalәd·ē, -fer-\ *n* -ES : ROUNDNESS, SPHERICITY
spherical lens *n* : a lens whose surfaces form portions of perfect spheres
spherical mirror *n* : a mirror with a surface that is either concave or convex and forms a portion of a true sphere
spheri·cal·ness *n* -ES : the quality or state of being spherical : spherical form
spherical perspective *n* : curvilinear perspective in which a picture is made upon a spherical surface
spherical polygon *n* : a figure analogous to a plane polygon that is formed on a sphere by arcs of great circles
spherical sailing *n* : sailing in which the earth is regarded as a spherical or spheroidal figure and allowance is made for the curvature of its surface in directing the course of a ship
spherical sector *n* : SECTOR OF A SPHERE
spherical triangle *n* : a spherical polygon of three sides
spherical trigonometry *n* : trigonometry applied to spherical triangles and polygons
spherical vault *n* : a vault having approximately the form of part of a sphere : a cupola of circular plan
spherical wedge *n* : the portion of a sphere included between two half planes that intersect in a diameter
sphe·ric·i·ty \sfә'risәd·ē\ *n* -ES [NL *sphaericitas*, fr. LL *sphaericus* spherical + L *-itas* -ity] : the quality or state of being spherical : ROUNDNESS; *esp* : the degree of perfection of the surface of a sphere
¹spherics \'sfiriks, -fer-, -rēks\ *n pl but sing in constr* [modif. (influenced by E *-s*, pl. suffix) of NL *sphaerica*, fr. fem. of LL *sphaericus* spherical] **1** : SPHERICAL GEOMETRY **2** : SPHERICAL TRIGONOMETRY
²spherics \"\ *var of* SFERICS
spherier *comparative of* SPHERY
spheriest *superlative of* SPHERY
spheri·form \'sfirә,fórm, -fer-\ *adj* [*sphaer-* + *-iform*] : SPHERICAL
sphering *pres part of* SPHERE
sphero- — see SPHAER-
sphero·crystal \'sfi(,)rō, -fe(-+,-\ *n* [ISV *sphaer-* + *crystal*] : a spherical crystal aggregate
sphero·cyte \'sfirә,sīt, -fer-\ *n* -S [ISV *sphaer-* + *-cyte*] : a more or less globular red blood cell that is characteristic of some hemolytic anemias — compare SPHEROCYTOSIS — **sphero·cyt·ic** \;==;sid·ik\ *adj*
sphero·cy·to·sis \,==,sī'tōsәs\ *n* -ES [NL, fr. ISV *spherocyte* + NL *-osis*] : a familial anemia in which the red blood cells are smaller than normal and spherical in form and which commonly accompanies congenital hemolytic jaundice
sphero·graph \'sfirә,graf, -fer-, -gräf\ *n* [*sphaer-* + *-graph*] **1** : two cardboards used esp. in navigation and astronomy, containing various circles, and turning upon each other in such a manner that any possible spherical triangle may be readily found and the measure of the parts read off by inspection **2** : a disk ruled with meridians and parallels in stereographic projection for the solution of problems in spherics
spheroid *or* **sphaeroid** \'sfi,róid, -fe,r-\ *n* -S [LL *sphaeroides* spherical, fr. Gk *sphairoeidēs*, fr. *sphaira* ball + *-oeidēs* -oid — more at SPHERE] : a figure resembling but not identical to a sphere; *esp* : an ellipsoid of revolution
sphe·roi·dal \(')sfi¦róidᵊl, sfә'r-\ *also* **spheroid** \'sfi,róid, -fe,r-\ *adj* : having the form of a spheroid : consisting of or characterized by spheroids — **sphe·roi·dal·ly** \(')sfi¦róidᵊlē, sfә¦r-, -ᵊli\ *adv*
spheroidal galaxy *n* : ELLIPTICAL GALAXY
spheroidal recovery *n* : a hypothetical more or less complete resumption by the earth of spheroidal form after distortion (as is sometimes held to follow periods of collapse to tetrahedral shape)
spheroidal state *n* : the state of a liquid (as water) when on being thrown on a surface of highly heated metal it gathers in flattened drops or round-edged masses that are at a temperature several degrees below ebullition and are without actual contact with the heated surface owing to a cushion of nonconducting vapor
sphe·roi·di·cal \sfә'róidәkәl, sfe'r-\ *adj* [*spheroid* + *-ical*] *archaic* : SPHEROIDAL — **sphe·roi·di·cal·ly** \-k(ә)lē\ *adv*, *archaic*
spheroid·ic·i·ty \,sfi,rói'disәd·ē, -fe,r-\ *n* -ES [*spheroidical* + *-ity*] : the quality or state of being spheroidal
spheroid·ism \'==,dizәm\ *n* -S **1** : the quality or state of being a spheroid **2** : spheroidal condition
spheroid·iza·tion \,==,dә'zāshәn, -,dī'z-\ *n* -S **1** : the act of spheroidizing steel **2** : the condition of steel that has been spheroidized
spheroid·ize \'==,dīz\ *vt* -ED/-ING/-S [*spheroid* + *-ize*] : to subject (an iron-base alloy) to prolonged heating near the critical temperature and then to slow cooling so that the iron carbide assumes a globular form — compare ANNEAL, HEAT-TREAT
spherome \'sfi,rōm, -fe,r-\ *n* -S [ISV *sphaer-* + *-ome*; orig. formed as F *sphérome*] : CYTOME
sphe·rom·e·ter \sfә'rämәd·ә(r)\ *n* [ISV *sphaer-* + *-meter*; orig. formed as F *sphéromètre*] : an instrument for measuring the curvature of a spherical surface

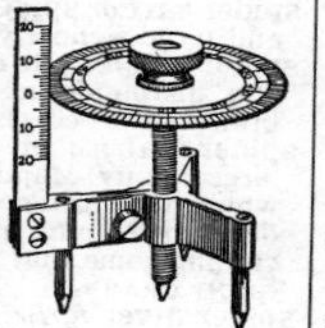
spherometer

sphe·roph·o·rus \sfә'räfәrәs\ *n*, *cap* [NL, fr. *spher-* + *-phorus*] : a genus comprising markedly pleomorphic gram-negative rod-shaped bacteria of uncertain systematic position and including various organisms associated with suppurative and necrotic processes in man and various lower animals — compare BULLNOSE
spheru·la \'sfir(y)әlә, -fer-\ *n*, *pl* **spheru·lae** \-,lē, -,lī\ *also* **spherulas** [NL, fr. LL *sphaerula* spherule] : a small spherical sponge spicule
spheru·lar \-lә(r)\ *adj* [*spherule* + *-ar*] : taking the form of or resembling a spherule
spheru·late \-lәt, -,lāt\ *adj* [*spherule* + *-ate*] : covered or set with spherules or tubercles
spherule \'sfi(,)rül, -fel, \r(,)yül\ *n* -S [LL *sphaerula*, dim. of L *sphaera* sphere — more at SPHERE] **1** : a little sphere or spherical body **2** [NL *spherula*] : SPHERULA
spheru·lite \'sfir(y)ә,līt, -fer-\ *n* -S [*spherule* + *-ite*] : a usu. spherical crystalline body made up of radiating crystal fibers, often found in vitreous volcanic rocks (as obsidian and perlite), and commonly constituting an intergrowth of quartz and feldspar
spheru·lit·ic \;==;lid·ik\ *adj* : of, relating to, made up of, or being spherulites
spheru·lit·ize \'==,lid·,īz\ *vt* -ED/-ING/-S : to convert into spherulites
sphery \'sfi(ә)rē\ *adj* -ER/-EST [*sphere* + *-y*] **1** : of, relating to, or suggestive of the heavenly spheres or the music of the spheres **2** : STARLIKE
sphet·er·ize \'sfed·ә,rīz\ *vt* -ED/-ING/-S [Gk *spheterizein*, fr. *spheteros* their own, their (fr. *spheis* they) + *-izein* -ize; akin to L *se* oneself — more at SUICIDE] : to take for one's own : APPROPRIATE
¹sphex \'sfeks\ *n* [NL, fr. Gk *sphēk-*, *sphēx* wasp] **1** *cap* : a genus of wasps that is the type of the family Sphecidae **2** *pl* **sphe·ges** \'sfē(,)jēz\ *also* **sphexes** : any wasp of the genus *Sphex*
²sphex \"\ [NL] *syn of* CHLORION
sphinc·ter \'sfiŋ(k)tә(r)\ *n* -S [LL, fr. Gk *sphinktēr* band, sphincter; akin to Gk *sphingein* to bind fast, L *spatium* space — more at SPEED] : an annular muscle surrounding and able to contract or close a bodily opening or channel ⟨the anal ~⟩ ⟨a ~ muscle⟩ ⟨suffering from *sphincter*algia⟩
sphinc·ter·al \-tәrәl\ *adj* : of, relating to, or functioning as a sphincter
sphincter ani \-'ā,nī, -'ä(,)nē\ *n* [NL] : ANAL SPHINCTER
sphinc·ter·ate \-tәrәt, -tә,rāt\ *or* **sphinc·trate** \-ŋ(k)trәt, -,trāt\ *adj* [*sphincter* + *-ate*] **1** : provided with or contracted by a sphincter **2** : constricted in the middle as if by a sphincter
sphinc·ter·ic \(')sfiŋ(k)¦terik\ *adj* : of, relating to, or being a sphincter
sphincter of od·di \-'ädē\ *usu cap 2d O* [after Ruggero *Oddi*, 19th cent. Ital. physician] : a complex sphincter closing the duodenal orifice of the common bile duct
sphinc·ter·ot·o·my \,sfiŋ(k)tә'räd·әmē\ *n* -ES [ISV *sphincter* + *-o-* + *-tomy*] : surgical incision of a sphincter
sphincter pu·pil·lae \-pyü'pi(,)lē, -pyü'pi,lī\ *n* [NL, pupilar sphincter] : a broad flat band of smooth muscle in the iris and surrounding the pupil of the eye
sphincter va·gi·nae \-vә'jī(,)nē\ *n* [NL, vaginal sphincter] : the female bulbocavernosus
¹sphin·did \'sfindәd\ *adj* [NL *Sphindidae*] : of or relating to the Sphindidae
²sphindid \"\ *n* -S : a beetle of the family Sphindidae
sphin·di·dae \-ndә,dē\ *n pl*, *cap* [NL, fr. *Sphindus*, type genus + *-idae*] : a family of small clavicorn tenebrionid beetles living in dry fungi on trees
sphinges *pl of* SPHINX
¹sphin·gid \'sfinjәd\ *adj* [NL *Sphingidae*] : of or relating to the Sphingidae
²sphingid \"\ *n* -S : a moth of the family Sphingidae : HAWKMOTH
sphin·gi·dae \-jә,dē\ *n pl*, *cap* [NL, fr. *Sphing-*, *Sphinx*, type genus + *-idae*] : a family of typically large heavy-bodied strong-flying moths with narrow elongated wings that comprise the hawkmoths
sphin·gine \'sfin,jīn, -jәn\ *adj* [L *sphing-*, *sphinx* + E *-ine*] : resembling a sphinx ⟨my most ~ smile —Aldous Huxley⟩
sphingo- *comb form* [ISV, fr. Gk *sphingein* to bind fast — more at SPHINCTER] **1** : deflection : bending ⟨*sphingo*meter⟩ **2** : sphingomyelin ⟨*sphingo*sine⟩
sphin·go·lipide *or* **sphin·go·lipid** \¦sfiŋ(,)gō+\ *n* [*sphingo-* + *lipide*, *lipid*] : any of a group of lipides (as sphingomyelins and cerebrosides) that yield sphingosine or one of its derivatives as one product of hydrolysis — compare GLYCOLIPIDE
sphin·gom·e·ter \sfiŋ'gämәd·ә(r), -iŋ'g-\ *n* [*sphingo-* + *-meter*] : an instrument for measuring the bending of a strut (as by deflection of beams of light)
sphin·go·myelin \¦sfiŋ(,)gō+\ *n* [ISV *sphingo-* (fr. Gk *sphingein* to bind fast) + *myelin*] : any of a group of crystalline phosphatides that are obtained esp. from nerve tissue and that on hydrolysis yield a fatty acid (as lignoceric acid), sphingosine or its saturated dihydro derivative, choline, and phosphoric acid
sphin·go·sine \'sfiŋgә,sēn, -,sәn\ *n* -S [ISV, irreg. fr. *sphingo-* + *-ine*] : an unsaturated amino glycol $C_{18}H_{33}(OH)_2NH_2$ obtained by hydrolysis of various sphingomyelins, cerebrosides, and gangliosides
sphinx \'sfiŋ(k)s\ *n* [ME *Spynx* the sphinx of Thebes who according to Greek legend destroyed all passers who could not solve the riddle she proposed until Oedipus guessed it and caused the sphinx to kill herself, fr. L *Sphinx*, fr. Gk, the sphinx of Thebes, person resembling the sphinx; akin to Gk *sphingein* to bind fast; prob. fr. the spell she cast — more at SPHINCTER] **1** *pl* **sphinx·es** \-iŋ(k)sәz\ *or* **sphin·ges** \-injēz\ **a** : an enigmatic monster in ancient Greek mythology having typically a lion's body, wings, and the head and bust of a woman; *also* : a monster resembling a Grecian sphinx in appearance or character **b** : a person who resembles the sphinx of ancient Greece esp. in enigmatic or inscrutable character or in speaking enigmatically **2** *pl* **sphinxes** *or* **sphinges** : an ancient Egyptian image in the form of a recumbent lion having a man's head, a ram's head, or a hawk's head **3** [NL, fr. L *Sphinx*] **a** *cap* : the type genus of Sphingidae formerly coextensive with the family but now including only a few hawkmoths with larvae that often assume a position suggestive of the Egyptian sphinx **b** *pl* **sphinges** *also* **sphinxes** : any moth of the genus *Sphinx* or family Sphingidae : HAWKMOTH **4** *pl* **sphinxes** *or* **sphinges** : a grayish yellowish brown that is darker than deer and slightly darker than acorn — called also *mustang* **5** *pl* **sphinxes** *or* **sphinges** [L, an ape, perh. chimpanzee, fr. Gk, an ape, fr. *Sphinx*] : SPHINX BABOON
sphinx baboon *n* : a large West African baboon (*Papio sphinx*) often kept in menageries
sphinx caterpillar *n* : the larva of a hawk moth
sphinx·ian \'sfiŋ(k)sēәn\ *adj* : of, relating to, or resembling a sphinx
sphinxlike \'=,=\ *adj* : resembling a sphinx esp. in enigmatic inscrutable quality
sphinx moth *n* : HAWKMOTH
sphoe·roi·des \sfә'rói(,)dēz\ *n*, *cap* [NL, fr. *sphoer-* (alter. of *sphaer-*) + L *-oides* -oid] : a common genus of globefishes
sphrag·ide \'sfra,jīd, -jәd\ *n* -S [L *sphragid-*, *sphragis*, fr. Gk, seal, signet; fr. the fact that it was sold in sealed packets] : LEMNIAN BOLE
sphra·gis·tic \sfrә'jistik\ *adj* [LGk *sphragistikos*, fr. Gk *sphragistos* sealed (fr. *sphragizein* to close with a seal, fr. *sphragis* seal + *-izein* -ize) + *-ikos* -ic] : of or relating to a seal or signet : dealing with seals ⟨~ studies⟩
sphra·gis·tics \-ks\ *n pl but usu sing in constr* [LGk *sphragistikē* (fem. of *sphragistikos* sphragistic) + E *-s* (pl. suffix)] : the science of seals and signets dealing esp. with their history, age, distinctions of types, manner of use, and legal function : SIGILLOGRAPHY
sp ht *abbr* specific heat
sphyg·mic \'sfigmik\ *adj* [Gk *sphygmikos*, fr. *sphygmos* pulse + *-ikos* -ic] : of or relating to the circulatory pulse
sphygmo- *comb form* [Gk, fr. *sphygmos*; akin to Gk *asphyxia* stopping of the pulse — more at ASPHYXIA] : pulse ⟨*sphygmo*gram⟩
sphyg·mo·chronograph \¦sfig(,)mō+\ *n* [*sphygmo-* + *chronograph*] : an instrument for recording the movements of the pulse
sphyg·mo·gram \'sfigmә,gram\ *n* [ISV *sphygmo-* + *-gram*] : a tracing made by a sphygmograph and consisting of a series of curves that correspond to the beats of the heart
sphyg·mo·graph \-raf, -räf\ *n* [ISV *sphygmo-* + *-graph*] : an instrument that when applied over an artery records graphically the movements or character of the pulse — **sphyg·mo·graph·ic** \¦==¦=\ *adj* — **sphyg·mog·ra·phy** \sfig'mägrәfē\ *n* -ES
sphyg·mo·manometer \¦sfig(,)mō+\ *n* [ISV *sphygmo-* + *manometer*; orig. formed as F *sphygmomanomètre*] : an instrument for measuring blood pressure and esp. arterial blood pressure
sphyg·mo·manometric \"+\ *adj* [ISV *sphygmomanometry* + *-ic*] **1** : obtained with a sphygmomanometer ⟨~ readings⟩ **2** : of or relating to sphygmomanometry — **sphyg·mo·man·ometrically** \"+\ *adv*
sphyg·mo·manometry \"+\ *n* -ES [*sphygmomanometer* + *-y*] : determination of blood pressure by use of the sphygmomanometer
sphyg·mom·e·ter \sfig'mämәd·ә(r)\ *n* [ISV *sphygmo-* + *-meter*] : an instrument for measuring the strength of the pulse beat
sphy·rae·ni·dae \-nә,dē\ *n pl*, *cap* [NL, fr. *Sphyraena*, type genus + *-idae*] : a monotypic family of large active elongated cylindrical small-scaled fishes (suborder Mugiloidea) having a large mouth with a projecting lower jaw and long strong teeth in jaws and palate — see BARRACUDA
sphy·ra·pi·cus \,sfīrә'pīkәs\ *n*, *cap* [NL, fr. Gk *sphyra* hammer + L *picus* woodpecker — more at PIE] : a genus of American woodpeckers consisting of the sapsuckers
sphyr·i·on \'sfirē,än, -ēәn\ *n*, *pl* **sphyrions** \-nz\ *or* **sphyr·ia** \-ēә\ [Gk, small mallet, small hammer, dim. of *sphyra* mallet, hammer] : MALLEOLAR POINT
sphyr·na \'sfәrnә\ *n*, *cap* [NL, modif. of Gk *sphyra* hammer] : a genus (the type of the family Sphyrnidae) of large voracious chiefly tropical sharks including the hammerhead shark
sphyr·ni·dae \'sfәrnә,dē\ *n pl*, *cap* [NL, fr. *Sphyrna*, type genus + *-idae*] : a family of sharks that have the head highly modified and that include the hammerheads and bonnetheads
spi·al \'spīәl\ *n* -S [ME (Sc) *spyale*, fr. ME *spyen*, *spien* to spy + *-ale*, *-aille* -al] **1** *obs* : ESPIAL, WATCH **2** *archaic* : SPY, SCOUT
spic *sometimes cap*, *var of* SPIK
spi·ca \'spīkә\ *n*, *pl* **spi·cae** \-ī,sē, -,sī\ *or* **spicas** [L, head (of grain); fr. the resemblance of the successive V-shaped crossings of the bandage to the rows on a head of grain — more at SPIKE] : a spiral reverse plain or plaster bandage used to immobilize a limb esp. at a joint ⟨hip ~⟩
spic-and-span *var of* SPICK-AND-SPAN
spi·car·ia \spī'ka(a)rēә\ *n*, *cap* [NL, fr. L *spica* + NL *-aria*] : a form genus of imperfect fungi (family Moniliaceae) characterized by nonseptate hyaline conidia borne in chains on verticillate conidiophores
spi·cate \'spī,kāt, *usu* -ād+V\ *adj* [L *spicatus*, past part. of *spicare* to furnish with heads of grain, arrange in the shape of heads of grain, fr. *spica*] : POINTED, SPIKED; *specif* : arranged in the form of a spike : resembling a spike ⟨a ~ inflorescence⟩
spi·cat·ed \-,kād·әd\ *adj* [L *spicatus* + E *-ed*] : SPICATE
¹spic·ca·to \spә'käd·(,)ō\ *adj* [It, past part. of *spiccare* to detach, make distinct] : performed with springing bow : ARCO SALTANDO — used as a direction in music for stringed instruments
²spiccato \"\ *n* -S : something (as technique, a performance, or a passage) that is spiccato
¹spice \'spīs\ *n* -S *often attrib* [ME, fr. OF *espice*, fr. LL *species* spices, fr. L, sight, outward appearance, sort, fr. *specere* to look — more at SPY] **1 a** : any of various aromatic vegetable products (as pepper, cinnamon, nutmeg, mace, allspice, ginger, cloves) used in cookery to season food and to flavor foods (as sauces, pickles, cakes) **b** : a substance or collection of substances used as a spice ⟨add ~ to a cake⟩ **2 a** *archaic* : a small portion, quantity, or admixture : DASH, TOUCH, TASTE **b** : something that enriches or alters the quality of a thing esp. in a small degree : something that gives zest or pungency : a piquant or pleasing flavor : RELISH ⟨our friends have all . . . a ~ of mischief in their constitutions —F.A. Swinnerton⟩ ⟨scandals a hundred years old usually lack ~ for anyone save the antiquary —Katharine F. Gerould⟩ **3** : a pungent or fragrant odor : PERFUME **4** : a brownish orange that is redder and duller than leather, stronger, slightly redder, and darker than gold pheasant, and slightly redder and darker than prairie brown, Windsor tan, Titian, or amber brown
²spice \"\ *vt* -ED/-ING/-S [ME *spicen*, fr. *spice*, n.] **1** : to season with spices : mix aromatic or pungent substances with : FLAVOR, SEASON ⟨~ a sauce⟩ **2** : to season as if with spices : make spicy, piquant, or pleasing ⟨his chapters are *spiced* with a wealth of curious and amusing detail —*Brit. Bk. News*⟩ ⟨these anecdotes, if *spiced* with derision, remained unflavored by malice —J.B.Cabell⟩ ⟨days of adventure, all the pleasanter for being *spiced* with danger —W.H. Hudson †1922⟩ — often used with *up* ⟨never misses a trick to ~ things up for the ordinary customer —Hal Lehrman⟩
spice·able \-sәbәl\ *adj* : capable of being spiced
spice·berry \'spīs- — *see* BERRY\ *n* **1** : WINTERGREEN 2a **2** : RED STOPPER **3** : SPICEBUSH
spice birch *n* : SWEET BIRCH
spice box *n* : a box holding or designed to hold spices; *esp* : a box fitted with smaller boxes for holding spices
spice brown *n* : a variable color averaging a moderate brown that is darker and very slightly yellower and stronger than auburn, redder, darker, and slightly stronger than chestnut brown, yellower and slightly duller than bay, and yellower and duller than toast brown

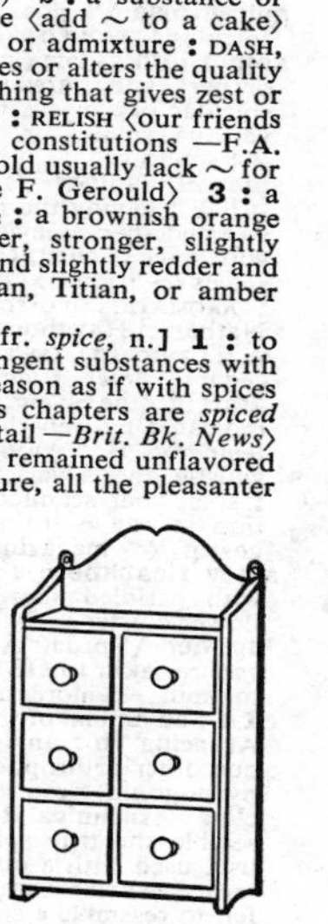
spice box

spicebush \'=,=\ *n* **1 :** an aromatic shrub (*Lindera benzoin*) bearing dense clusters of small yellow flowers followed by scarlet or yellow berries — called also *American spicebush* **2 :** any of several shrubs of the genus *Calycanthus*; *esp* **:** a tall upright shrub (*C. occidentalis*) with slightly fragrant brown flowers — compare CAROLINA ALLSPICE
spicebush swallowtail *n* **:** a rather dark swallowtail butterfly (*Papilio troilus*) of eastern No. America
spice currant *n* **:** GOLDEN CURRANT
spiced \'spīst\ *adj* [ME, fr. past part. of *spicen* to spice] **1 :** flavored with or as if with spice **:** SPICY **2** *obs* **:** NICE, DAINTY, SCRUPULOUS, SQUEAMISH **3 :** filled or impregnated with the odor of spices **:** FRAGRANT
spice·less \'=ləs\ *adj* **:** lacking spice **:** not spiced
spice nut *n* **:** a small crisp highly spiced cookie
spic·ery \'spīs(ə)rē\ *n* -ES [ME *spicerie*, fr. OF *espicerie*, fr. *espice* spice + *-erie* -ery] **1 :** SPICES **2 a** *archaic* **:** a storage place (as a pantry or warehouse) for spices **b** *obs* **:** a spice shop **c** *obs* **:** the department of the royal household connected with the keeping of spices **3 :** a spicy or aromatic quality **:** SPICINESS
spice tree *n* **:** CALIFORNIA LAUREL
spicewood \'=,=\ *n* **:** any of several trees or shrubs having spicy aromatic wood; *esp* **:** SPICEBUSH 1
spicey *var of* SPICY
spicier *comparative of* SPICY
spiciest *superlative of* SPICY
spi·ci·form \'spīsə,fȯrm\ *adj* [prob. fr. (assumed) NL *spiciformis*, fr. L *spici-* (fr. *spica* head of grain) + *-formis* -form — more at SPIKE] **:** shaped like a spike ⟨~ panicle⟩
spi·cig·er·ous \(')spī¦sij(ə)rəs\ *adj* [prob. fr. (assumed) NL *spiciger* spicate (fr. L *spici-* — fr. *spica* head of grain — + *-ger* -gerous) + E *-ous*] **:** SPICATE
spic·i·ly \'spīsəlē, -li\ *adv* **:** in a spicy manner **:** with seasoning (as of spices) **:** PUNGENTLY
spic·i·ness \-sēnəs, -sin-\ *n* -ES **:** the quality of being spicy **:** PUNGENCY
spicing *n* -S **:** SEASONING ⟨its liberal ~ of humor —Hywel Evans⟩
¹spick \'spik\ *n* -S [ME *spyk*, fr. OE *spic* — more at SPECK] *obs* **:** FAT, GREASE, BLUBBER
²spick \"\ *n* -S [MF *espic*, *spic*, fr. OProv *espic* head (of grain), fr. L *spica* — more at SPIKE] *dial Eng* **:** LAVENDER
³spick \"\ *adj* -ER/-EST [by shortening] **:** SPICK-AND-SPAN
⁴spick *sometimes cap, var of* SPIK
¹spick-and-span *or* **spic-and-span** \¦spikən¦span, -kəŋ¦-, -paa(ə)n\ *also* **spick-and-span-new** \¦==¦=¦=\ *adj* [*spic-and-span* alter. of *spick-and-span*, short for *spick-and-span-new*, fr. obs. E *spick* spike, nail (alter. of E ¹*spike*) + E *and* + *span-new*] **1 :** quite new **:** FRESH, BRAND-NEW ⟨a *spick-and-span* novelty⟩ **2 :** like new **:** spotlessly clean **:** SPRUCE ⟨his cottage was *spick-and-span* —J.B.Clayton⟩ ⟨a *spick-and-span* figure in his Panama hat and neat clothes —G.K.Chesterton⟩ ⟨automobile owner who likes to keep his car *spick-and-span* —*New Yorker*⟩ **syn** see NEAT
²spick-and-span *or* **spic-and-span** \"\ *adv* **:** in a spick-and-span manner ⟨clean the kitchen *spick-and-span*⟩
spick-and-spandy \-¦spandē, -aan-, -di\ *adj (or adv)* [by alter.] **:** SPICK-AND-SPAN
spick-and-span·ness \-nəs\ *n* -ES **:** the quality or state of being spick-and-span
spick·et \'spikət, *usu* -əd·+V\ *n* -S [ME *spyket*, alter. of ¹*spigot*] *chiefly South & Midland* **:** SPIGOT
spick·le \'spikəl\ *n* -S [by alter.] **:** SPICULE
spick·nel \'spiknəl\ *also* **spig·nel** \-ign-\ *n* -S [origin unknown] **:** a European perennial herb (*Meum athamanticum*) having finely divided strongly aromatic leaves and minute white flowers
spi·cose \'spī,kōs\ *adj* [L *spica* head (of grain) + E *-ose*] **:** having spikes ⟨~ flowers⟩ — **spi·cos·i·ty** \spī'käsəd·ē\ *n* -ES
spi·cous \'spīkəs\ *adj* [L *spica* head (of grain) + E *-ous*] **:** SPICOSE — **spi·cous·ness** *n* -ES
spic·u·la \'spikyələ\ *n, pl* **spicu·lae** \-,lē, -,lī\ [NL, fr. ML, arrowhead, alter. of L *spiculum* arrowhead, arrow] **:** SPICULE, PRICKLE
spic·u·lar \-lə(r)\ *adj* [prob. fr. (assumed) NL *spicularis*, fr. NL *spicula* & L *spiculum* + L *-aris* -ar] **:** of, relating to, or like a spicule **:** SPICULATE ⟨~ ice⟩
spicular cell *n* **:** IDIOBLAST 1a
spic·u·late \-lət, -,lāt, *usu* -d·+V\ *adj* [prob. fr. (assumed) NL *spiculatus*, fr. NL *spicula* & L *spiculum* + L *-atus* -ate] **1 :** covered with or having spicules **:** SPICULAR, PRICKLY **2 :** divided into small spikelets
spic·u·lat·ed \-,lād·əd\ *adj* [prob. fr. (assumed) NL *spiculatus* + E *-ed*] **:** SPICULATE
spic·u·la·tion \,=='lāshən\ *n* -S [*spicule* + *-ation*] **1 :** the formation of spicules **2 a :** the form and arrangement of spicules **b :** the spicular component of a sponge
spic·ule \'spi,kyül\ *n* -S [NL *spicula* & L *spiculum* small sharp organ or part, sting, arrowhead, arrow; L *spiculum* fr. *spica* head (of grain) + *-ulum* — more at SPIKE] **1 a :** a small fleshy point or appendage (as the sterigma in basidiomycetous fungi) **b :** SPIKELET **c :** the empty siliceous shell of a diatom **2 a :** one of the numerous small often very minute calcareous or siliceous bodies occurring in and serving to stiffen and support the tissues of various invertebrates (as the majority of sponges and alcyonarians and many radiolarians, holothurians, and compound ascidians) and having forms that are very varied and often characteristic of a species or other group **b :** a spikelike organ ⟨a copulatory ~⟩ **:** SPICULUM 1 **3 :** any minute slender pointed body **:** a needlelike body esp. of bony or other hard material ⟨~*s* of ice⟩ **4 :** a very small spikelike short-lived prominence appearing close to the chromosphere of the solar atmosphere and occurring in greatest numbers at the sun's poles
spic·u·lif·er·ous \¦spikyə¦lif(ə)rəs\ *adj* [prob. fr. (assumed) NL *spiculifer* spiculiferous (fr. *spiculi-* — fr. NL *spicula* & L *spiculum* — + *-fer* -ferous) + E *-ous*] **:** bearing spicules
spic·u·lose \'==,lōs\ *adj* [*spicule* + *-ose*] **:** having or full of spicules **:** SPICULIFEROUS
spic·u·lum \-ləm\ *n, pl* **spicu·la** \-lə\ [L, small sharp organ or part, sting, arrowhead, arrow] **1 :** any of various small spicular organs (as the spines of an echinoderm, the dart of various snails, or a copulatory bristle on a nematode) **2 :** SPICULE
spicy *also* **spicey** \'spīsē, -si\ *adj* **spicier; spiciest** [¹*spice* + *-y*] **1 :** having the quality of spice ⟨a ~ flavor⟩ ⟨clams had steamed in ~ seaweed —Marcia Davenport⟩ **2 :** flavored with spice **:** SPICED ⟨~ foods⟩ **3 :** producing or abounding in spices ⟨~ islands⟩ **4 :** having a fragrance suggestive of spices **:** AROMATIC ⟨blossoms of fervid hue and ~ fragrance —Nathaniel Hawthorne⟩ ⟨the sky is clear and clean, the air ~ —A.E.Coppard⟩ ⟨swampland, ~ with the odor of pine and cedar —*Amer. Guide Series: N.C.*⟩ **5 :** SPIRITED, PEPPERY, ZESTFUL ⟨the ~ and brisk quality of this adorable autocrat is indicated by well-chosen quotations —Agnes de Mille⟩ ⟨a ~ temper⟩ **6 :** PIQUANT, RACY ⟨uttering his famous shrill whistle and a variety of ~ language —*Current Biog.*⟩; *esp* **:** somewhat scandalous or salacious ⟨resisted every temptation to say ~ things in the footnotes —C.R.Sanders⟩ ⟨~ gossip⟩ ⟨~ magazines⟩ **syn** see PUNGENT
spicy fleabane *n* **:** a marsh fleabane (*Pluchea camphorata*) with petioled sharply serrate leaves and a round-topped flower cluster
¹spi·der \'spīdə(r)\ *n* -S *often attrib* [ME *spyder*, alter. of *spithre*; akin to OE *spinnan* to spin — more at SPIN] **1 a :** an animal of the order Araneida **b :** any of various other arthropods (as a pycnogonid) esp. of the class Arachnida that resemble the true spiders — usu. used with a qualifying term; see RED SPIDER **2 :** one felt to resemble a spider (as in appearance or in scheming) **3 :** a cast-iron frying pan orig. made with short feet to stand among coals on the hearth **4 :** a metal outrigger to keep a block clear (as of the mast) **5 :** a contrivance consisting of a frame or skeleton having radiating arms or members: as **a :** a frame for strengthening a core or mold in founding **b :** a casting forming the hub and spokes to which the rim of a wheel or pulley is secured **c :** the body or solid hub of a built-up piston **d :** a machine element consisting of a ring with projections outward **e :** a hub with radiating arms interposed between the shaft and the core of a dynamo or motor armature **6 a :** SPIDER CART **b :** SPIDER PHAETON **7 :** SPIDER NEVUS **8 :** SET GAGE **9 :** an obstruction in the teat of a cow; *esp* **:** a small irregular horny growth following bruises or other irritation **10** *often cap* **:** a solitaire or patience game played with two packs of cards dealt in a row of ten piles among which the cards are shifted to assemble them in complete suits **11 :** the part of a dynamic loudspeaker that properly positions the voice coil relative to the magnet and that usu. consists of a flexible fiber ring **12 :** a frame on an explosive mine that when pressed detonates the mine

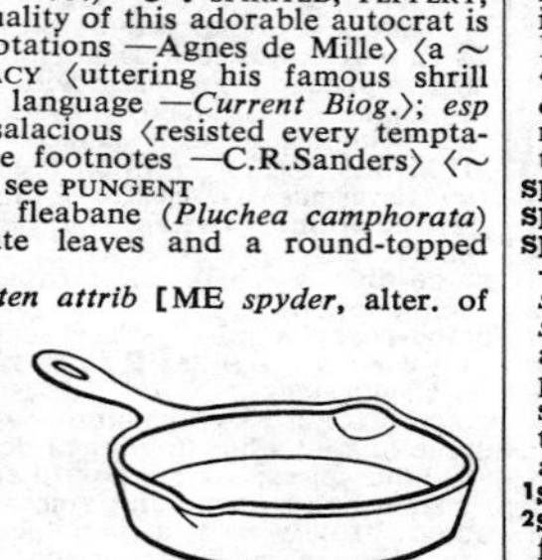
spider 3

²spider \"\ *vb* -ED/-ING/-S **:** to crack or shatter in a radiating pattern of thin lines ⟨the wall was . . . ~*ed* with cracks —A.R. Foff⟩
spider angioma *n* **:** SPIDER NEVUS
spider ant *n* **:** VELVET ANT
spider band *also* **spider hoop** *n* **1 :** a metal band around a ship's mast having sockets for belaying pins **2 :** a metal band around a ship's mast having eyebolts to which the lower ends of the futtock shrouds are secured
spider beetle *n* **:** any of various small destructive beetles of the genus *Ptinus* (as *P. fur* and *P. brunneus*) that resemble spiders and have larvae which feed on woolen goods, fur, feathers, flour, and seeds; *broadly* **:** a ptinid beetle
spider bug *n* **:** a bug of the genus *Ploiaria*
spider cart *or* **spider wagon** *n* **:** a light cart having a high body and large slenderly constructed wheels
spider cell *n* **:** one of the astrocytes typical of the white matter and distinguished from the mossy cells by very long unbranched processes
spider crab *n* **:** any of numerous oxyrhynchan crabs esp. of the large family Majidae having more or less triangular bodies which they often cover with kelp or other plants, a well-developed spiny rostrum, and extremely long legs and including some that are among the largest of crustaceans — see GIANT CRAB
spider diver *n, Brit* **:** LITTLE GREBE
spider fern *n* **:** RIBBON FERN 2
spiderflower \'==,=\ *n* [so called fr. the long stamens] **1 :** a plant of the genus *Cleome* **2 :** any of several shrubs of the genus *Tibouchina* whose flowers have long stamens — see BRAZILIAN SPIDERFLOWER **3 :** GREVILLEA 2
spider fly *n* **1 :** a sheep ked, bat fly, or similar usu. wingless parasitic dipterous insect **2 :** an artificial fly tied to imitate a spider or a spiderlike insect
spider hunter *n* **:** any of various relatively large long-billed East Indian sunbirds of the genus *Arachnothera*
spidering *pres part of* SPIDER
spider·less \'==ləs\ *adj* **:** lacking spiders **:** free of spiders
spiderlike \'==,=\ *adj* **:** resembling a spider (as in form or manner)
spider lily *n* **1 :** SPIDERWORT 1a **2 :** SAINT-BERNARD'S-LILY **3 :** any of several plants of the genus *Nerine* (as the Guernsey lily) **4 :** a plant of the genus *Hymenocallis*
spider line *n* **:** one of the bits of spider's web or fine platinum wires forming the reticle of an optical instrument **:** CROSS HAIR
spi·der·ling \'==,liŋ, -lēŋ\ *n* -S **1 :** a very young spider esp. where the brood remains on the back of the mother or in the egg sac for a time after hatching **2 :** a plant of the genus *Boerhavia*
spi·der·ly *adj* **:** resembling a spider **:** SPIDERY
spider milkweed *n* **:** a plant of the genus *Asclepiodora*
spider mite *n* **:** RED SPIDER
spider monkey *n* **:** any of numerous monkeys of *Ateles* or a related genus that range from southern Mexico to Paraguay, have long slender limbs, a thumb absent or rudimentary, and a very long and prehensile tail, and are preeminently fitted for arboreal life — see WOOLLY SPIDER MONKEY
spider nevus *n* **:** a nevus formed of dilated capillaries radiating like the legs of a spider
spider orchid *also* **spider orchis** *n* **:** any of various orchids (as members of the genus *Brassia*) having flowers with slender sepals or petals
spider phaeton *n* **:** a very high carriage of light construction with a covered seat in front and a footman's seat behind

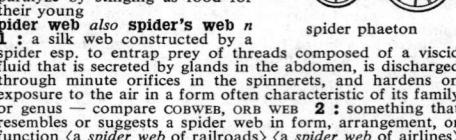

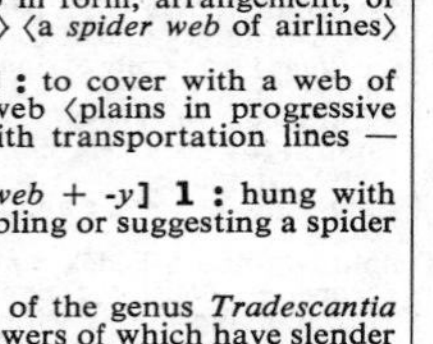
spider phaeton

spider plant *n* **1 :** SPIDERFLOWER 1 **2 :** SPIDERWORT 1a
spiders *pl of* SPIDER, *pres 3d sing of* SPIDER
spider shell *n* **:** SCORPION SHELL
spider wasp *n* **:** any of various solitary wasps that fill their brood cells with spiders which they kill or paralyze by stinging as food for their young
spider web *also* **spider's web** *n* **1 :** a silk web constructed by a spider esp. to entrap prey of threads composed of a viscid fluid that is secreted by glands in the abdomen, is discharged through minute orifices in the spinnerets, and hardens on exposure to the air in a form often characteristic of its family or genus — compare COBWEB, ORB WEB **2 :** something that resembles or suggests a spider web in form, arrangement, or function ⟨a *spider web* of railroads⟩ ⟨a *spider web* of airlines⟩ ⟨a *spider's web* of intrigue⟩
spider-web \'==,=\ *vt* [*spider web*] **:** to cover with a web of fine lines suggestive of a spider web ⟨plains in progressive countries are . . . *spider-webbed* with transportation lines —C.L.White & G.T.Renner⟩
spiderwebby \'==,==\ *adj* [*spider web* + *-y*] **1 :** hung with spider webs **:** COBWEBBY **2 :** resembling or suggesting a spider web ⟨~ cracks in ice⟩ ⟨~ trees⟩
spider wheel *n* **:** SPIDER 5b
spiderwort \'==,=\ *n* **1 a :** a plant of the genus *Tradescantia* the ephemeral usu. blue or violet flowers of which have slender hairy stamens **b :** any plant of the family Commelinaceae — called also *dayflower* **2 :** any of several plants (as the Saint-Bernard's-lily and Saint-Bruno's-lily) of genera other than *Tradescantia*
spiderwort family *n* **:** COMMELINACEAE
spi·dery \'spīdərē, -ri\ *adj, sometimes* -ER/-EST **1 a :** resembling or suggesting a spider (as in appearance, nature, or actions) **:** SPIDERLIKE ⟨eyes of horrid dark and ~ things —C.B. Fernald⟩ ⟨a ~ hand clad in a black kid glove —John Galsworthy⟩ ⟨a ~ disposition⟩; *specif* **:** long, thin, and sharply angular like the legs of a spider ⟨~ lines of scaffolding on the monument —Leslie Charteris⟩ or composed of elements having this appearance ⟨a ~ antenna reaching high in the sky —Horace Sutton⟩ ⟨~ bamboo bridges —Alan Moorehead⟩ ⟨write a ~ hand⟩ **b :** resembling or suggesting a spider web; *esp* **:** composed of fine threads or lines in a weblike arrangement ⟨~ lace⟩ **2 :** full of spiders **:** infested with spiders ⟨a ~ thicket⟩
spie *obs var of* SPY
spied *past of* SPY
spie·gel·ei·sen \'spēgə,līz°n\ *also* **spie·gel** *or* **spiegel iron** *n* -S [*spiegeleisen* fr. G, fr. *spiegel* mirror (fr. OHG *spiagal*, fr. L *speculum*) + *eisen* iron, fr. OHG *īsan*; *spiegel* short for *spiegeleisen*; *spiegel iron* part trans. of G *spiegeleisen* — more at SPECULUM, IRON] **:** a variety of pig iron containing 15 to 30 percent manganese and 4.5 to 6.5 percent carbon and used in steelmaking to recarburize and deoxidize the molten metal of the Bessemer converter or the open-hearth furnace — called also *mirror iron*; compare FERROMANGANESE
¹spiel *var of* SPEEL
²spiel \'spēl, *esp before pause or consonant* -ēəl\ *n* -S [short for *bonspiel*] *Scot* **:** a curling match
³spiel \"\ *vb* -ED/-ING/-S [G *spielen* to play, play music, gamble, fr. OHG *spilōn* to hop, dance, play; akin to OE *spilian* to revel, OFris *spilia* to play, *spil*, *spel* play, MD *spelen* to play, *spel* play, game, OHG *spil* play] *vi* **1 :** to play music ⟨with three or four you just ~ but with the whole band you got to work —Benny Goodman⟩ **2 :** to talk in a voluble often extravagant manner ⟨always ~*ing* about how scientists ought to rule the world, instead of . . . politicians —Sinclair Lewis⟩ ~ *vt* **:** to utter, express, or describe in a voluble often extravagant manner ⟨can quickly memorize answers to 250 questions and ~ them off long afterward —*Science News Letter*⟩
⁴spiel \"\ *n* -S **:** a voluble line of often extravagant talk usu. intended to persuade **:** PITCH
spiel·er \'spēlə(r)\ *n* -S [G, player, gambler, fr. OHG *spilāri* professional entertainer, fr. *spil* play + *-āri* -er] **1** *chiefly Austral* **a :** a person who earns a living by dishonest gambling **:** CARDSHARPER **b :** SHARPER, SWINDLER **2 a :** a person who attracts customers (as to a sideshow) by a voluble line of extravagant claims and skillful persuasion **:** BARKER **b :** one that spiels **:** the giver of a spiel; *specif* **:** a person with a voluble often exaggerated line of talk **c :** BARKER **b d :** a radio announcer (as for a commercial)
¹spi·er \'spīə(r), -īə\ *n* -S [ME *spiere*, fr. *spyen*, *spien* to spy + *-ere* -er] **:** one that spies
²spier \'spi(ə)r, -iə\ *n* -S [ME *spere*] **:** a fixed and often architecturally treated screen (as in the hall of an English manor house)
³spier \"\ *chiefly Scot var of* ¹SPEER
spies *pl of* SPY, *pres 3d sing of* SPY
¹spiff \'spif\ *n* -S [perh. fr. E dial. *spiff*, adj., smartly dressed, dandified] **:** PUSH MONEY
²spiff \"\ *vb* -ED/-ING/-S [E dial. *spiff*, adj.] **:** SPRUCE ⟨time to ~ up a bit before the company arrived⟩
spiffed *adj* [fr. past part. of ²*spiff*] **1 :** decked out **:** well attired **2** [prob. by shortening & alter. fr. *spiflicated*] **:** INTOXICATED
spiff·i·ly \'spifəlē, -li\ *adv* **:** in a spiffy manner
spiff·i·ness \-fēnəs, -fin-\ *n* -ES **:** the quality or state of being spiffy
spiff·ing \'spifiŋ, -fēŋ\ *adj* [E dial. *spiff*, adj. + E *-ing*] *slang* **:** SPIFFY ⟨a ~ cook and a top-notch dresser —Gertrude Atherton⟩
spiffy \-fē, -fi\ *adj* -ER/-EST [E dial. *spiff*, adj. + E *-y*] **1 :** fine looking **:** SMART ⟨you were sure ~ in your major's uniform —Lillian Ross⟩ **2 :** SPLENDID, EXCELLENT, CLEVER ⟨the ~ thing is to pull off the elections when they won't get balled up with national issues —*New Republic*⟩
spif·li·cate *or* **spif·fli·cate** \'spiflə,kāt, *usu* -ād·+V\ *vt* -ED/-ING/-S [origin unknown] **1 :** to overcome or dispose of by violence **2 :** BEAT
spiflicated *adj* **:** INTOXICATED
spif·li·ca·tion \,=='kāshən\ *n* -S **:** the act of spiflicating or state of being spiflicated
spig \'spig\ *n* -S *sometimes cap* [short for *spigotty*] **:** SPIK — usu. taken to be offensive
spi·ge·lia \spī'jēlyə, -lēə\ *n, cap* [NL, fr. *Spigelius* (latinized form of the name of Adriaan van den *Spieghel* †1625 Flem. botanist and anatomist) + NL *-ia*] **:** a large genus of American herbs (family Loganiaceae) with showy spicate flowers having valvate corolla lobes, and a 2-celled ovary — see PINKROOT
spi·ge·li·a·ce·ae \=,jēlē'āsē,ē\ [NL, fr. *Spigelia* + *-aceae*] *syn of* LOGANIACEAE
spi·ge·lian \=¦jēlyən, -lēən\ *adj, sometimes cap* [*Spigelius* + E *-an*] **:** relating to or discovered by the Flemish anatomist Adriaan van den Spieghel
spight \'spīt\ *n* -S [by alter.] *archaic* **:** SPITE
spignel *var of* SPICKNEL
spig·net *also* **spig·nut** \'spignət\ *n* -S [by alter.] **:** SPIKENARD 2a
¹spig·ot *also* **spig·got** \'spigət, -ikət, *usu* -əd·+V\ *n* -S [ME *spigot*, perh. fr. (assumed) OProv *espigot*, dim. of OProv *espiga* head (of grain), fr. L *spica* — more at SPIKE] **1 a :** a pin or peg used to stop the vent in a cask **b :** the plug of a faucet or cock **c :** FAUCET, COCK **2 :** the male end of a section of pipe that enters the hub end of the next section **3 :** a large usu. conical spinning tube associated with silk glands of a spider
²spigot \"\ *vt* **spigoted** *or* **spigotted; spigoted** *or* **spigotted; spigoting** *or* **spigotting; spigots :** to provide, plug, or pierce with or as if with a spigot
spigot-and-faucet joint \¦===¦==-\ *n* **:** BELL-AND-SPIGOT JOINT
spigot joint *n* **:** BELL-AND-SPIGOT JOINT
spig·ot·ty *or* **spig·go·ty** \-əd·ē, -otē, -i\ *n* -ES *sometimes cap* [prob. fr. the broken English utterance *no speaka de English* (meaning "I don't speak English") supposed to be much used by Spanish Americans] **:** SPIK — usu. taken to be offensive
spik *or* **spick** *or* **spic** \'spik\ *n* -S *sometimes cap* [alter. of *spig*] **:** SPANISH AMERICAN; *esp* **:** MEXICAN — usu. taken to be offensive
¹spike \'spīk\ *n* -S *often attrib* [ME *spike*, *spik*, prob. fr. MD *spike*; akin to MLG *spīker* spike, ON *spīk* splinter, Lith *speigliai* thorns, L *spina* thorn — more at SPINE] **1 a :** a very large nail; *specif* **:** one three or more inches long and often of square section (as a barge spike) **b :** a similar fastener used on railroads for securing rails to ties **2 :** a pointed piece of metal set with the point upward or outward **:** a pointed metal projection: as **a :** one of a row of pointed irons placed (as on the top of a wall) to prevent passage **b :** one of several metal projections set in the sole and heel of a shoe to improve traction (as in logging, baseball, track and field, golf) and made in varying size, shape, and number for different activities — compare CALK, CLEAT, CLIMBING IRON **c :** a needlelike steel spindle set upright in a base and used for temporary filing of papers (as restaurant bills, rejected newspaper copy) **3 :** something suggesting a spike (as in tapering to a point): as **a :** a young mackerel not over six inches long **b :** an unbranched antler of a young deer **c :** a backward projection on the rose comb of a fowl **4** *Brit* **:** a rigid adherent of high church dogma or ritual **5 :** SPIKE DISEASE **6 a :** SPIKE HEEL **b :** a spike-heeled shoe **7 spikes** *pl* **:** a pair of shoes having spikes attached **8** [²*spike*] **:** the act or an instance of spiking a volleyball — see SETUP **9 a :** the pointed element in a graph or tracing: as (1) **:** the sharp up-and-down deflections on a fever chart indicating high and low temperature levels ⟨had a fever with ~*s* to 102° F⟩ (2) **:** the pointed element in an electroencephalogram wave ⟨the ~ and dome pattern representing the discharges characteristic of petit mal epilepsy⟩ **b :** an unusually high and sharply defined maximum (as of amplitude in a wave train) **10** *slang* **:** HYPODERMIC NEEDLE

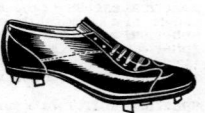

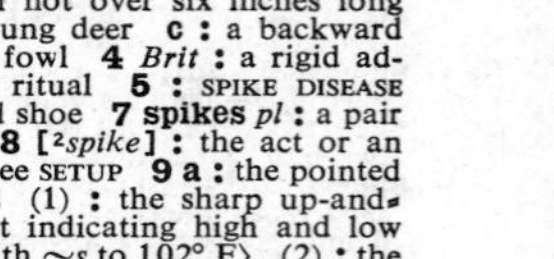
spikes 2b (baseball)

²spike \"\ *vb* -ED/-ING/-S *vt* **1 :** to fasten or fix with spikes ⟨all the track he owned had been laid and *spiked* —Bill Collins⟩ **2 a** (1) **:** to disable (a muzzle-loading cannon) temporarily by driving a spike into the vent (2) **:** to disable (a modern breech-loading cannon) by breaking or carrying away part of the breech mechanism **b :** to put an end to **:** suppress or cut off completely **:** QUASH ⟨~ the minority proposal and present one of their own⟩ ⟨~ the rumor by publishing a full account of the affair⟩ **3 a :** to pierce or impale with or on a spike ⟨~ an enemy with a bayonet⟩; *specif* **:** injure with the spikes on one's shoes ⟨in sliding the runner *spiked* the second baseman⟩ **b :** to reject (newspaper copy) by or as if by impalement on a spike ⟨the correspondent may wonder why his piece was *spiked* in favor of an item about the weather —Anthony Wigan⟩ **4 :** to set or furnish with spikes ⟨~ the bottoms of his climbing shoes⟩ **5 a :** to add alcohol or strong spirituous liquor to (beer or a nonalcoholic beverage) ⟨Frenchmen, accustomed to *spiking* coffee with cognac —*Newsweek*⟩ **b :** to increase the effect, interest, or attractiveness of **:** add strength or pungency to ⟨lighten the discussion by *spiking* it with dry humor⟩ ⟨geranium-pink ~*s* this kitchen and matches the flowers —Kay Hardy⟩ **6 :** to drive (a volleyball) into the opponents' court at a sharp angle with a hard downward blow delivered from a front line position — compare KILL *vt* 8 ~ *vi* **1 :** to form a spike **:** project like a spike ⟨docks which ~ outward from the eastern fringe of the city —E.K.Gann⟩ **2 :** to alternate sharply high points and low points in temperature as shown on a fever chart — **spike one's guns** *or* **spike the guns :** to nullify one's power of hostile action **:** frustrate one's hostile intentions

⟨*spiked the guns* of the opposition by exposing their equal involvement in the scandal⟩
3spike \"\ *n* -s [ME *spik* head (of grain), fr. L *spica* head (of grain), tuft (of a plant); akin to D *spie* peg, pin, L *spina* thorn — more at SPINE] **1 :** an ear of grain **2 :** an elongated indeterminate inflorescence similar to a raceme but having the flowers sessile on the main axis (as in common plantain) — see INFLORESCENCE illustration
4spike \"\ *dial Eng var of* 2SPICK
spikebill \ˈ=,=\ *n* **1 :** HOODED MERGANSER **2 :** MARBLED GODWIT
spike buck *n* **:** a male deer typically in its second year with unbranched antlers on both sides
spike bull *n* **1 :** a young male elk with unbranched antlers **2 :** a young bison with short sharp horns
spike camp *n* **:** a temporary or secondary camp site for a forestry crew accessible from the main camp
1spiked \ˈspīkt\ *adj* [3*spike* + *-ed*] **1 :** bearing ears **2 :** having a spiky inflorescence ⟨~ flowers⟩
2spiked \"\ *adj* [1*spike* + *-ed*] **:** having sharp points
spiked alder *n* **:** SWEET PEPPERBUSH
spike disease *n* [1*spike*] **:** a virus disease of the sandalwood tree in the Orient characterized by dwarfed growth of the shoots and narrow stiff crowded leaves
spiked loosestrife *n* **:** PURPLE LOOSESTRIFE
spiked willow herb *n* **1 :** PURPLE LOOSESTRIFE **2 :** SWAMP WILLOW HERB
spikefish \ˈ=,=\ *n* **:** SPEARFISH; *esp* **:** MARLIN
spike–grass \ˈ=,=\ *n* **:** any of several American maritime grasses having large or conspicuous spikelets: as **a :** SEA OAT; *also* **:** any of several related grasses of the genus *Uniola* **b :** SALT GRASS **c :** an annual grass (*Leptochloa fascicularis*) found in ditches and brackish meadows from New England to Florida
spike gun *n* **:** a machine for driving spikes in railroad ties
spike heath *n* **:** an erect but spreading shrubby evergreen heath (*Bruckenthalia spiculifolia*) of southern Europe and Asia Minor that has small bell-shaped pink flowers and is sometimes cultivated as an ornamental
spike heel *n* **:** a very high tapering heel used on women's shoes — compare FRENCH HEEL, SPANISH HEEL

spike heel

spikehorn \ˈ=,=\ *n* **1 :** SPIKE 3b **2 :** a deer having spikes
spike–kill \ˈ=,=\ *vt* **:** to make (a railroad tie) useless by repeated spiking
spike knot *n* **:** a knot in lumber sawed through lengthwise
spike lavender *n* [4*spike*] **:** a European mint (*Lavandula latifolia*) that is closely related to the true lavender and yields spike lavender oil — called also *French lavender*
spike lavender oil *or* **spike oil** *n* **:** a pale yellow fragrant essential oil obtained from spike lavender and used chiefly in scenting soap and in cosmetics
spike·let \ˈ=lət\ *n* -s [3*spike* + *-let*] **:** a small or secondary spike; *specif* **:** one of the small few-flowered bracteate spikes that make up the compound inflorescence of a grass or sedge — see WILD OAT illustration
spikelike \ˈ=,=\ *adj* [1*spike* & 3*spike* + *like*] **:** resembling a spike
spike·man \ˈ=mən\ *n, pl* **spikemen :** a spiker of railroad tracks
spike nail *n* [ME *spiknail,* fr. *spike, spik* spike + *nail*] *chiefly dial* **:** SPIKE 1a
spike·nard \ˈspīk,närd, -,nȧd, -,nə(r)d\ *n* -s [ME, fr. MF or ML; MF *spicanarde,* fr. ML *spica nardi* (trans. of Gk *nardou stachys*), fr. L *spica* head (of grain), tuft (of a plant) + *nardi,* gen. of *nardus* nard — more at SPIKE, NARD] **1 a :** a costly ointment with a musky odor valued as a perfume in ancient times — called also *nard* **b :** an East Indian aromatic plant (*Nardostachys jatamansi*) of the family Valerianaceae from the dried roots and young stems of which the ointment spikenard is believed to have been derived **2 a :** an American herb (*Aralia racemosa*) distinguished from wild sarsaparilla by its more aromatic root and its panicled umbels — called also *American spikenard* **b :** any of various other fragrant plants — usu. used in combination ⟨plowman's-*spikenard*⟩
spikenard tree *n* **:** HERCULES'-CLUB 3
spike–pitch \ˈ=,=\ *vi* [prob. back-formation fr. *spike-pitcher*] **:** to work as a spike-pitcher
spike–pitcher \ˈ=,==\ *n* [1*spike* + *pitcher;* fr. the use of a pitchfork] **:** a member of a threshing or baling crew who pitches bundles, headings, hay, or straw from a stack or derrick to the machine or who helps the hauler unload his wagon at the machine
spike potential *n* **:** the sharp wave of electric negativity that accompanies the passage of an impulse along a nerve and coincides in time of occurrence with the refractory period of the nerve
spik·er \ˈspīkə(r)\ *n* -s **1 :** one that spikes **2 :** a railroad trackman who drives spikes **3 :** a volleyball player who spikes the ball **:** an attack player
spike rush *n* [3*spike*] **:** a sedge of the genus *Eleocharis* — see HAIR GRASS
spikes *pl of* SPIKE, *pres 3d sing of* SPIKE
spiketail \ˈ=,=\ *n* **1** *or* **spiketail coat** \ˈ=,=-\ *or* **spiketailed coat** \ˈ=,=-\ **:** TAILCOAT **2 a :** PINTAIL 1a **b :** SHARP-TAILED GROUSE
spike team *n* **:** a team of three draft animals harnessed two abreast and one leading
spike–tooth harrow \ˈ=,=-\ *n* **:** a pulverizing and smoothing harrow equipped with straight steel teeth set in horizontal bars

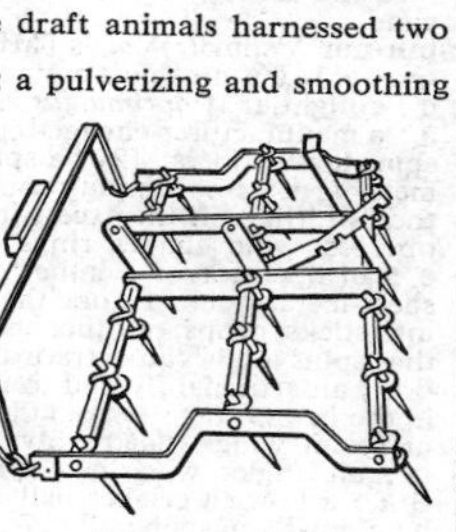
spike-tooth harrow

spiketop \ˈ=,=\ *n* **:** STAGHEAD
spike tub *n* [*spike* (alter. of 4*speck*) + *tub*] **:** a tub for blubber on a whaling ship
spikeweed \ˈ=,=\ *n* [1*spike*] **:** any of several annual Californian herbs of the genus *Centromadia* (family Compositae) with spiny involucral bracts; *esp* **:** a common summer annual (*C. pungens*) valued by beekeepers
spik·i·ly \ˈspīkəlē, -li\ *adv* **:** in a spiky manner
spik·i·ness \-kēnəs, -kin-\ *n* -ES **:** the quality or state of being spiky
spiking *pres part of* SPIKE
1spiky \ˈspīkē, -ki\ *adj* -ER/-EST [3*spike* + *-y*] **1 :** resembling the spike of a flower **2 :** bearing ears
2spiky \"\ *adj* -ER/-EST [1*spike* + *-y*] **1 :** having a sharp projecting point ⟨~ thorns⟩ **2 :** characterized by acerbity; *specif* **:** rigidly adhering to high church dogma or ritual
spiky jack *n, usu cap J, southern Africa* **:** SPINY DOGFISH
spi·lan·thes \spīˈlan(,)thēz\ *n, cap* [NL, fr. Gk *spilos* spot + NL *-anthes*] **:** a genus of widely distributed herbs (family Compositae) with opposite serrate leaves and yellow or whitish flowers in dense heads
1spile \ˈspīl, *esp before pause or consonant* -īəl\ *n* -s [prob. fr. D *spijl* stake, peg, fr. MD *spile;* akin to MHG *spīl* point, Icel *spila* skewer, Gk *spilas* reef, Latvian *spīle* wooden peg, L *spina* thorn — more at SPINE] **1** *chiefly dial* **a :** a small splinter of wood **:** SPILL **b :** a stake or post esp. when used for making a fence **2 a :** a large stake driven into the ground as a support for some superstructure **:** PILE **b :** FOREPOLE **3 a :** a small plug used to stop the vent of a cask **:** BUNG **b :** a tapering wooden pin used to stop the hole left in a ship's sheathing by a withdrawn spike or bolt **4 :** a small tube or spout inserted in a sugar maple tree for conducting sap
2spile \"\ *vt* -ED/-ING/-S **1 a :** to plug (as the hole in a cask) with a spile **b :** to draw off (liquor) through a spile **2 :** to supply (as a cask) with a spile **3 :** to make a small vent in (as a cask)
spilehole \ˈ=,=\ *n* **:** a small air hole in a cask or a maple tree **:** VENT
spileworm \ˈ=,=\ *n* [1*spile*] **:** SHIPWORM
spilikin *var of* SPILLIKIN
1spil·ing \ˈspīliŋ, -lēŋ\ *n* -s [origin unknown] **1 :** figures showing the distances from the edge of a template or straightedge to points along a curved part of a ship (as a bow plank or plate) — often used in pl. **2 :** the process of laying off the curvature of a structural part (as a beam or plate) on the material before cutting by taking the spiling **3 :** the curvature of a strake
2spiling \"\ *n* -s [1*spile* + *-ing*] **1 :** a set of piles **:** PILING **2 :** FOREPOLE
spi·lite \ˈspī,līt\ *n* -s [F, fr. Gk *spilos* spot, stain + F *-ite*] **:** a very fine-grained to dense and greenish to gray-green extrusive rock of the gabbro family often vesicular or amygdaloid and generally free from phenocrysts that is composed essentially of the same minerals as diabase and shows an ophitic texture with augite grains between laths of basic plagioclase — **spi·lit·ic** \=ˈlid·ik\ *adj*
1spill \ˈspil\ *vb* **spilled** \-ld,-lt\ *also* **spilt** \-lt\; **spilled** *also* **spilt; spilling; spills** [ME *spillen,* fr. OE *spillan;* akin to MD *spillen* to waste, squander, *spouden, spalden* to split, MLG *spalden,* OHG *spaltan* to split, ON *spjald, speld* square tablet, Goth *spilda* tablet, L *spolium* arms or armor stripped from an enemy, Gk *sphallein* to cause to fall, Skt *sphaṭati* it bursts; basic meaning: to split] *vt* **1** *archaic* **a :** KILL, DESTROY ⟨bade her command my life to save or ~ —Edmund Spenser⟩ **b :** to use or spend wastefully **:** WASTE, SQUANDER **c :** to make useless **:** RUIN, SPOIL **2 :** to cause (blood) to be lost by wounding ⟨rushed into battle eager to ~ their enemies' blood⟩ **3 :** to cause or allow to pour, splash, or fall out (as over the edge of a container) and be wasted, lost, or scattered ⟨fill your wine cup exactly full with a single toss of the bottle and without ~*ing* a drop —Lafcadio Hearn⟩ ⟨dropped the bag and ~*ed* sugar all over the floor⟩ ⟨felt of it and ~*ed* the cool tea on the brick floor and filled the bowl again —Pearl Buck⟩ ⟨2,000 plastic balloons ~*ed* out 2,000,000 leaflets —*Time*⟩ **4 a :** to relieve (a sail) from the pressure of the wind so that it can be more easily reefed or furled or to avoid capsizing or carrying away something **b :** to relieve the pressure of (wind) on a sail by coming about or by adjusting it with lines **5 :** to cause to fall from one's place (as on a horse or in a vehicle) **:** throw off, out, or down ⟨a bucking horse that ~*ed* everyone who tried to ride it⟩ **6 :** to give forth in an overflowing manner **:** pour freely ⟨a mockingbird . . . was ~*ing* his wild song over the moonlit woods —Rebecca Caudill⟩ **7 :** to let out (secret information) **:** DIVULGE ⟨would double-cross me and ~ some of the things I had told him —Polly Adler⟩ ~ *vi* **1** *obs* **a** (1) **:** to cause death or destruction (2) **:** PERISH, DIE **b :** DETERIORATE, SPOIL **2 a :** to flow, run, or fall out, over, or off with waste, loss, or scattering as the result ⟨don't shake the table or the coffee will ~⟩ ⟨light ~*ed* out through the windows —Frances & Richard Lockridge⟩ **b :** to cause or allow something to spill **:** waste a substance by letting it pour or fall out ⟨ate his ice cream, careful not to ~ on his new clothes⟩ **3 a :** to spread beyond bounds ⟨more than 1000 persons had filled the main ballroom and ~*ed* over into adjacent parlors —*Newsweek*⟩ ⟨they allow their private thoughts to ~ over into public statements —Norman Cousins⟩ **b :** to come, go, or pass with a turbulent rush **:** pour in an unrestrained, profuse, or disorderly manner **:** TUMBLE ⟨wave after wave of shouting crowds ~*ed* into . . . streets —*Time*⟩ ⟨the shelves of plays, pamphlets, prefaces, novels, and critical works which . . . ~*ed* from his pen —John Mason Brown⟩ **c :** to extend downward in precipitous or profuse disorder **:** descend as if overflowing ⟨the town ~*s* down a hillside and spreads into a valley —W.R.Moore⟩ ⟨great swags of lilac and laburnum ~ over ancient, weathered walls —*advt*⟩ **d :** to be full to overflowing ⟨the sidewalks . . . were soon ~*ing* over with workers —*Facts about Trailer Coaches*⟩ **4 :** to tell secrets **:** betray confidences ⟨would ~ in spite of the gang's threats⟩ **5 :** to fall from one's place (as on a horse or in a vehicle) **:** fall off, out, or down ⟨saw the motorcycle skid and the driver ~ in the dust⟩ — **spill the beans 1 :** to cause embarrassment by indiscreetly divulging information **2 :** to upset a plan or arrangement
2spill \"\ *n* -s **1 a :** an act or instance of spilling ⟨an undirected ~ of population into the suburban areas —Lewis Mumford⟩; *specif* **:** a fall from a place (as on a horse or in a vehicle) or an erect position (as in skiing) ⟨failing to clear the jump, horse and rider took a nasty ~⟩ ⟨broke his leg skiing when he took a ~ at a turn⟩ **b :** an abrupt decline in price ⟨stocks spurted most of the day then took a sharp ~ in the late trading —*New Orleans (La.) Times-Picayune*⟩ **2 a :** a quantity spilled ⟨fetch a cloth to mop up the ~ —Agnes M. Miall⟩ **b** *or* **spill light :** light that escapes from a concentration of theatrical or photographic light (as a spotlight cone) and produces illumination where it is not wanted **3 :** SPILLWAY
3spill \"\ *n* -s [ME *spille, spyll;* prob. akin to MD *spile* stake, peg — more at SPILE] **1 :** a bit of wood split off **:** SPLINTER **2 :** a slender piece of anything: as **a :** a metallic rod or pin on which something turns **b** (1) **:** a small roll or twist of paper or slip of wood used for lighting lamps, pipes, fires (2) **:** a paper sheath into which the tobacco is pushed in making a cigarette (3) **:** a roll or cone of paper serving as a container (as for a bunch of flowers) **c :** a peg or pin for plugging a hole (as in a cask) **:** SPILE **3 :** a scale-filled crack or seam in an ingot; *esp* **:** a lap due to careless rolling **4 :** a metal disk on a wooden rod used to remove matzoth from the oven
4spill \"\ *n* -s [perh. fr. 1*spill*] *archaic* **:** a small sum of money **:** GRATUITY
spill·able \-ləbəl\ *adj* **:** that can be spilled
spill·age \ˈspilij, -lēj\ *n* -s **1 :** the act or process of spilling ⟨replace antifreeze lost by ~⟩ **2 :** the quantity that spills or is spilled over ⟨a trough to divert any ~⟩
spill box *n* **:** a device for maintaining a constant head or pressure on a measuring weir or orifice; *specif* **:** a short flume with long wells at each end and a spillway over which the excess water flows
1spill·er \ˈspilə(r)\ *n* -s [1*spill* + *-er*] **1 :** one that spills **2 :** a bowl that results in a strike despite an inaccurate hit
2spiller \"\ *n* -s [alter. of 2*speller*] *archaic* **:** a branchlet on a deer's palm
3spil·ler \ˈspilə(r)\ *n* -s [IrGael *spilēar*] **1 :** a fishing line with many hooks **2 :** the final enclosure of a fish trap from which fishes are brailed into the fishing boat
spil·let \-lət, *usu* -əd·+V\ *n* -s [IrGael *spilēad*] *dial* **:** 3SPILLER
spill·flö·te \ˈspil,flād·ə, -lēd·ə, *G* ˈshpil,flœtə\ *n* -s [G, fr. *spille* spindle (fr. OHG *spilla*) + *flöte* flute, fr. MHG *vloite,* fr. OF *flaute, fleute;* akin to OHG *spinnan* to spin — more at SPIN, FLUTE] **:** a half-covered pipe-organ flue stop of 8-, 4-, or 2-foot pitch that is shaped like a spindle
spil·li·kin \ˈspiləkən, -lēk-\ *also* **spel·i·can** *or* **spel·li·can** \ˈspel-\ *or* **spil·i·kin** *or* **spil·li·ken** *n* -s [prob. alter. of obs. D *spelleken, spelleke* small peg, small pin, fr. MD *spellekijn* small pin, fr. *spelle, spelde* pin + *-kijn* -kin; akin to OE *speld* torch — more at SPELL] **:** JACKSTRAW 2
spill·ing \ˈspiliŋ, -lēŋ\ *n* -s **:** the loss of air from beneath the canopy of a parachute at the outer edges caused by deliberate manipulation of the parachute or by instability
spilling line *n* **:** a rope used for spilling a sail (as by hauling up the foot, brailing in an edge)
spillover \ˈ=,==\ *n* -s [fr. *spill over,* v.] **1 :** the act or process of spilling over; *also* **:** an instance of spilling over **2 :** a quantity that spills over **3 :** an extension of demand from one product to a related one because of insufficient supply
spillpipe \ˈ=,=\ *n* **:** CHAIN PIPE
spills *pres 3d sing of* SPILL, *pl of* SPILL
spill stream *n* **:** an overflow stream (as from a river)
spillway \ˈ=,=\ *n* **1 :** a passage (as a paved apron or channel) for surplus water over or around a dam or similar obstruction **2 :** a channel through which lake water or meltwater from a glacier flows or has flowed over a barrier (as of glacial drift)
spilly \ˈspilē, -li\ *adj* -ER/-EST [3*spill* + *-y*] *of wrought iron or steel* **:** defective from spills
spi·log·a·le \spīˈlägə(,)lē\ *n, cap* [NL, fr. Gk *spilos* spot + *galē, galeē* weasel, ferret — more at GALEA] **:** a genus of mammals (family Mustelidae) comprising the little spotted skunks
spi·lor·nis \spīˈlȯrnəs\ *n, cap* [NL, fr. Gk *spilos* spot + NL *-ornis*] **:** a genus of Asiatic and East Indian high-soaring diurnal birds of prey (family Accipitridae) that have long slender legs and short toes tipped by powerful claws and feed chiefly on reptiles
spi·lo·site \ˈspīlə,sīt\ *n* -s [G *spilosit,* fr. Gk *spilos* spot + G *-it* -ite] **:** a spotted schistose rock produced by contact metamorphism of clay slate usu. by diabase
spilt \ˈspilt\ *past of* SPILL
spilth \ˈspilth *also* -ltth\ *n* -s [1*spill* + *-th*] **1 :** an act or instance of spilling **2 a :** something spilled or freely poured out **b :** REFUSE, RUBBISH
1spin \ˈspin\ *vb* **spun** \ˈspən\ *or archaic* **span** \ˈspan, -paa(ə)n\ **spun; spinning; spins** [ME *spinnen,* fr. OE *spinnan;* akin to OHG *spinnan* to spin, ON *spinna,* Goth *spinnan* to spin, L *sponte* of one's free will, voluntarily, Gk *span* to draw, pull, tear — more at SPAN] *vi* **1 :** to draw and twist thread **:** make yarn or thread from fiber ⟨watched the jennies ~⟩ ⟨sat by the fireside *spinning*⟩ **2 :** to form a thread, web, or cocoon by extruding a viscous rapidly hardening fluid — used of a spider or silkworm **3 a :** to revolve or whirl rapidly **:** GYRATE, ROTATE ⟨little boys' tops were *spinning* in the spring afternoon⟩ ⟨round about him *spun* the landscape —H.W.Longfellow⟩ **b :** to turn quickly on one's heel **:** face about in place ⟨as one man we *spun* round —Rex Keating⟩ **c :** to rotate or whirl rapidly in dancing **d :** to feel as if revolving **:** be in a whirl **:** REEL ⟨her head was *spinning* at the finality and emptiness of the prospect⟩ **4 :** to stream or spurt (as blood or juice) in a thread or jet **5 :** to last out **:** EXTEND **6 a :** to move swiftly on wheels or in a vehicle ⟨Sunday trippers were *spinning* over the highway in flashing cars⟩ ⟨bicycles *spun* about an indoor track⟩ ⟨~*s* up the river in a little powerboat⟩ **b :** to pass quickly ⟨time ~*s* away when we are occupied⟩ **7** *Brit* **:** to fail in an examination **:** FLUNK **8 a :** to fish with spinning bait (as a spoon) **:** TROLL **b :** to fish with a fixed spool reel and light line **9 a** *of an airplane* **:** to fall in a spin **b :** to spiral rapidly downward **:** fall dizzily and out of control **:** be caught in a vortex ⟨watch a normal-seeming man ~ downward to madness and abnormality —James Kelly⟩ ~ *vt* **1 a :** to draw out and twist (fibers) into yarns or threads by hand or by machine ⟨mills that ~ cotton, flax, or wool⟩ **b :** to produce (yarn or thread) by drawing out and twisting a fibrous material **c :** to convert (pulp or chemical solutions) into rayon or other man-made filaments by extruding, solidifying, and winding **d :** to pass (an appropriate solution or melt) through a spinneret in the production of synthetic fibers (as rayon or nylon) **e :** to form (filaments) by extruding pulp or chemical solutions through spinnerets, solidifying, and winding **f :** to form (wire strands) into cable or wire rope **2 :** to form (a thread, web, or cocoon) by the extrusion of a viscous rapidly hardening fluid — used of a spider or a silkworm **3 a :** to form or produce in a manner resembling a spinning process **:** draw out slowly, by degrees, or at length **:** EXTEND, PROLONG, PROTRACT — usu. used with *out* ⟨possessed the ability to ~ a saga out of their escapades —Benjamin De Casseres⟩ ⟨~*s* a short-story plot into over 90,000 words of torpid action —Anthony Boucher⟩ ⟨~*s* out the small talk of a chance meeting —*Current Biog.*⟩ **b :** to evolve, express, or fabricate by processes of mind or imagination ⟨the most persistent risk that has always attended all *spinning* of yarns —C.E.Montague⟩ ⟨no more can the imagination ~ its fantastic tales of adventure —W.P.Webb⟩ ⟨*spun* a ritual full of cryptic references —C.W.Ferguson⟩ ⟨the theorists *spun* their theories —*Time*⟩ **c :** to make last **:** stretch out the duration of **:** extend in time or space — used with *out* ⟨*spinning* out his glass of port as long as possible —Elizabeth Goudge⟩ **4** *archaic* **:** to spend (time) to no effect — used with *out* **5 :** to cause to turn round rapidly **:** TWIRL, WHIRL ⟨boys *spun* their tops on the sidewalks⟩ **6 a :** to shape (a material) into threadlike form in manufacture ⟨*spun* gold⟩ **b :** to shape (glass) by a whirling process ⟨began to ~ glass flat by the crown method —Freda Diamond⟩ ⟨the bearings are centrifugally cast by *spinning* the rod with the center of its lower end . . . as the axis of rotation —H.F.Blanchard & Ralph Ritchen⟩ **c :** to form (metal hollow ware) on a mold on a lathe face plate with a roller or other hand tool ⟨a *spun* aluminum canister⟩ ⟨bowls of *spun* copper⟩ **7** *Brit* **:** to fail (a student) in an examination **:** FLUNK **8 :** to put together or construct (something likened to a spider's web) ⟨as the arctic radar net is *spun* —*Time*⟩ **9 :** to throw off (a fragment) by or as if by centrifugal force from a whirling object ⟨*spun* off a couple of independent companies from its corporate structure to satisfy the justice department⟩ **10 a :** to fish (a body of water) with a spinner or spinning bait **b :** to fish (a body of water) with a fixed spool reel and light line **11 :** to set (a phonograph disc record) rotating on a turntable **:** PLAY ⟨was *spinning* records on an all-night radio show⟩ **syn** see TURN
2spin \"\ *n* -s **1 a :** the act of spinning or twirling something ⟨the decision rested on the ~ of a coin⟩ **b :** the revolving or whirling motion imparted by spinning ⟨the ~ of a top⟩ ⟨the ~ given to a cricket ball by a bowler⟩ — compare 2ENGLISH 5, HOOK 6b, 3SLICE **c :** an excursion in a vehicle esp. on wheels ⟨an evening ~ in the car⟩ ⟨out for a ~ in a powerboat⟩ **2 a :** an aerial maneuver or flight condition consisting of a combination of roll and yaw with the longitudinal axis of the airplane inclined steeply downward so that it descends in a helix of large pitch and very small radius with its upper side on the inside of the helix while the angle of attack on the inner wing is maintained at an extremely large value **b :** a plunging descent or downward spiral ⟨when . . . the world enters upon the downward ~, it is desirable that each country should . . . stimulate revival —R.F.Harrod⟩ **c :** a mental whirl **:** a state of confusion or depression ⟨been in a ~ ever since the bankruptcy⟩ **3 a :** a system of velocities of any number of points all due to one and the same definite angular velocity about one and the same axis **b** (1) **:** the rapid rotation of an elementary particle (as an electron) on its own axis or of a system of such particles in orbital motion that is responsible for measurable angular momentum and magnetic moment (2) **:** the angular momentum associated with such rotation **4 :** a quick dance turn on the narrowest possible base **5** *Austral* **:** LUCK ⟨had a good ~ —Ruth Park⟩ ⟨had a tough ~ —Frank Sargeson⟩
spin- *or* **spini-** *or* **spino-** *comb form* [L *spin-, spini-* thorn, spine, fr. *spina* thorn, spine, spinal column — more at SPINE] **1 a :** spinal column **:** spinal cord ⟨*spino*gram⟩ **b :** of, relating to, or involving the spinal cord and ⟨*spino*thalamic⟩ **2 :** spine ⟨*spin*ate⟩ ⟨*spini*form⟩
spi·na \ˈspīnə\ *n, pl* **spi·nae** \-ī,nē\ [L, thorn, spine] **:** an anatomical spine or spinelike process
spina bi·fi·da \-ˈbīfədə, -ˈbif-\ *n* [NL, bifid spinal column] **:** a congenital cleft of the vertebral column with hernial protrusion of the meninges
spi·na·cea \spīˈnāshēə\ *syn of* SPINACIA
spina·cene \ˈspīnə,sēn, -pīn-\ *n* -s [ISV *spinac-* (fr. NL *Spinac-, Spinax* genus of sharks, prob. fr. Gk *spina,* a fish) + *-ene*] **:** SQUALENE
spi·na·ceous \spəˈnāshəs, (ˈ)spī¦n-\ *adj* [irreg. fr. NL *Spinacia* + E *-aceous*] **:** resembling or related to spinach ⟨~ herbs⟩
spin·ach *or* **spin·age** \ˈspinich, -nēch *sometimes* -nij *or* -nēj\ *n, pl* **spinaches** *or* **spinages** [MF *espinache, espinage,* fr. OSp *espinaca,* fr. Ar *isbānakh, isfānākh,* fr. Per *isfānākh*] **1 :** an annual potherb (*Spinacia oleracea*) native to southwestern Asia and cultivated widely for its edible leaves which are used as greens — called also *prickly-seeded spinach* **2 a :** something repellent, obnoxious, or nonexistent **:** something spurious or unwanted ⟨the bankers' pet . . . was just so much ~ as far as the plain people were concerned —Jay Franklin⟩ ⟨the ~ of controlled, cooperative effort —H.A. Moe⟩ **b :** an untidy overgrowth (as an untrimmed lawn or beard) **c :** an inessential, irrelevant, or inharmonious excrescence, addition, or decoration **:** FRILL ⟨a child . . . has no interest in literary and artistic ~ —Rochelle Girson⟩ ⟨might look at the externals of an airplane and see only struts, wires, and other such ~ —*Air World*⟩
spinach aphid *n, chiefly Brit* **:** GREEN PEACH APHID
spinach beet *n* **:** a beet that constitutes a variety (*Beta vulgaris cicla*) of the common beet, is used as an ornamental and potherb, has much-developed leaves, and lacks a fleshy root — called also *leaf beet*

spinach blight *n* **:** a mosaic disease of spinach caused by the cucumber mosaic virus

spinach carrion beetle *n* **:** a black carrion beetle (*Silpha bituberosa*) with a nocturnal black-and-white larva that feeds on spinach and other crop plants in the western U.S.

spinach dock *or* **spinage dock** *n* **:** PATIENCE 3

spinach flea beetle *n* **:** a small glossy bluish black beetle (*Disonycha xanthomelas*) that has a reddish or yellowish abdomen and feeds on spinach and beet leaves

spinach green *n* **:** a moderate yellow green that is greener and deeper than average moss green, duller and very slightly yellower than average pea green, duller than apple green (sense 1), and greener and duller than mosstone — called also *autumn green, gaudy green*

spinach leaf miner *n* **:** a maggot that is the larva of an anthomyiid fly (*Pegomya hyoscyami*) and mines the leaves of beets, spinach, chard, and other crop plants

spinach mustard *n* **:** TENDERGREEN

spinach yellows *n pl but usu sing in constr* **:** SPINACH BLIGHT

spi·na·cia \spə'nāshēə\ *n, cap* [NL, fr. It *spinace* spinach (fr. Sp *espinaca*) + NL *-ia*] **:** a small genus of Asiatic annual herbs (family Chenopodiaceae) having dioecious flowers without bracts and a pistillate calyx that becomes indurated over the one-seeded perianth — see SPINACH

spina ex·ter·na \-,ek'stərnə\ *n, pl* **spinae exter·nae** \-r,nē\ [NL, external spine] **:** a median bony point projecting from the anterior and ventral margin of the sternum of a bird

spina in·ter·na \-in'tərnə\ *n, pl* **spinae inter·nae** \-r,nē\ [NL, internal spine] **:** a median bony point projecting from the anterior and dorsal edge of the sternum of a bird and sometimes uniting with the spina externa

¹spi·nal \'spīn³l\ *adj* [LL *spinalis*, fr. L *spina* thorn, spine, spinal column + *-alis* -al — more at SPINE] **1 a :** of, relating to, or situated near the vertebral column, spinal canal, or spinal cord **b :** located in or affecting the vertebral column or spinal cord ⟨~ twinges⟩ ⟨degenerative ~ disease⟩ **2 a :** dependent upon the spinal cord **:** involving in its central nervous path only the spinal cord ⟨a ~ reflex⟩ **b :** having the spinal cord isolated in its functioning from the brain (as by surgical section) ⟨experiments with ~ animals⟩ **3 :** of or relating to a spine **4 :** resembling a spine **:** suggesting a backbone ⟨the two great ~ mountain-systems of the U.S. —Lewis Mumford⟩ **5 :** made for or fitted to the spine ⟨a ~ brace⟩

²spinal \"\ *n* -s **:** SPINAL ANESTHESIA

spinal accessory nerve *n* **:** ACCESSORY NERVE

spinal anesthesia *n* **:** anesthesia produced by injection of an anesthetic into the spinal subarachnoid space

spinal artery *n* **:** any of the arteries that supply the spinal cord and its membranes and adjacent structures, all arising as branches of the vertebral artery but anastomosing and being reinforced or continued by branches of intercostal and lumbar arteries which enter the intervertebral foramina

spinal canal *n* **:** the canal that is formed by the series of neural arches of the vertebrae and that forms a protective bony case about the spinal cord

spinal column *n* **:** the articulated series of vertebrae connected by ligaments and separated by more or less elastic intervertebral fibrocartilages that in nearly all vertebrates forms the supporting axis of the body and a protection for the spinal cord extending from the hind end of the skull through the median dorsal part of the body and to the end of the tail **:** BACKBONE, SPINE; *broadly* **:** the axial skeleton of the trunk and tail of a vertebrate which in the lowest vertebrates and in the embryos of all higher forms is represented by an elastic rod of cellular tissue enclosed in a fibrous sheath in which in higher forms cartilaginous or bony pieces develop and usu. unite in various ways in the different groups to form a longitudinal series of vertebrae — compare NOTOCHORD

spinal cord *n* **:** the thick longitudinal cord of nervous tissue that in vertebrates extends along the back dorsal to the bodies of the vertebrae and is enclosed in the spinal canal formed by their neural arches, is continuous anteriorly with the medulla oblongata, gives off at intervals pairs of spinal nerves to the various parts of the trunk and limbs, serves not only as a pathway for nervous impulses to and from the brain but as a center for carrying out and coordinating many reflex actions independently of the brain, and is composed largely of white matter arranged in columns and tracts of longitudinal fibers about a large central core of gray matter somewhat H-shaped in cross section and pierced centrally by a small longitudinal canal continuous with the ventricles of the brain

spinal fluid *n* **:** CEREBROSPINAL FLUID

spinal foramen *n* **:** an opening under the neural arch of a vertebra that forms a part of the spinal canal when the vertebrae are articulated

spinal ganglion *n* **:** a ganglion on the dorsal root of each spinal nerve that is one of a series of ganglia lodging cell bodies of sensory neurons

spi·nalis \spī'nāləs, -nal-; spə'nal-\ *n, pl* **spina·les** \-ā(,)lēz, -ä(,)lēz, -ä(,)lās\ [NL, fr. LL, spinal] **:** any of three muscles of the spinal column

spi·nal·ly \'spīn³lē, -³li\ *adv* **:** with respect to the spine **:** along the spine

spinal marrow *n* **:** MARROW 1b

spinal nerve *n* **:** any of the paired nerves that leave the spinal cord of a craniate vertebrate by way of the intervertebral foramina, supply muscles of the trunk and limbs, and connect with the nerves of the sympathetic system, that arise by a short motor ventral root and a short sensory dorsal root which bears a spinal ganglion close to the cord and unites with the ventral root just beyond the ganglion forming a nerve of mixed function which passes through the foramen and divides into two mixed nerves of which one supplies dorsal and the other ventral bodily structures, and that normally aggregate 31 pairs in man and are divided according to the part of the cord from which they arise into 8 cervical pairs, 12 thoracic pairs, 5 lumbar pairs, 5 sacral pairs, and one coccygeal pair

spinal puncture *n* **:** puncture of the subarachnoid space in the lumbar region of the spinal cord to withdraw cerebrospinal fluid or inject anesthetic drugs

spinals *pl of* SPINAL

spinal segment *n* **:** a segment of the spinal cord including a single pair of spinal nerves and representing the spinal nervation of a single primitive metamere

spi·na·sterol \spīnə+\ *n* -s [NL *Spinacia* (genus name of the spinach plant *Spinacia oleracea*) + E *sterol* — more at SPINACIA] **:** any of several unsaturated isomeric phytosterols $C_{29}H_{47}OH$ obtained esp. from spinach leaves or the oil from alfalfa seeds and distinguished by Greek letters ⟨*α-spinasterol*⟩

spi·nate \'spī,nāt\ *adj* [*spin-* + *-ate*] **:** bearing a spine **:** SPINIFORM

spi·na·tion \spī'nāshən\ *n* -s [*spin-* + *-ation*] **:** the distribution and arrangement of spines (as on an insect)

spin casting *n* **:** casting with a light lure or light natural bait and a very light line

spin chute *n* **:** a small parachute attached usu. at the tail to an airplane undergoing flight tests to retard descent and help the pilot regain control if a spin develops

¹spin·dle \'spind³l, *chiefly dial* -n³l — *compare* SPINDLY\ *n* -s [ME *spindel*, fr. OE *spinel*; akin to OFris *spindel* spindle, OHG *spinila* spindle, OE *spinnan* to spin — more at SPIN] **1 :** a long tapered pin or rod serving as an axis in spinning: **a :** a round stick with tapered ends that is twirled around to form and twist the yarn in hand spinning **b :** the long slender pin by which the thread is twisted in a spinning wheel and on which it is then wound **c :** any of the various rods or pins holding a bobbin in a spinning frame or other textile machine **d :** the pin in a loom shuttle **2 :** something shaped like a spindle **:** a fusiform piece or figure: as **a** *obs* **:** a long stalk or stem of a plant **b :** a spindle-shaped sensory nerve ending — see MUSCLE SPINDLE **c :** the spindle-shaped portion of the achromatic figure along which the mitotic chromosomes are distributed to the daughter nuclei and which is apparently a dynamic product of gelation of the nuclear sap actively concerned in the separation of the chromosomes in mitosis and is no longer regarded as a structural unit of elongated spindle fibers **d :** RACHIS **e :** SPINDLE SHELL **f :** SPINDLE TREE **3 :** any of various more or less slender pins or rods that are suggestive of a spinning-machine spindle which turns or on which something turns: as **a :** the bar or shaft usu. of square section that carries the knobs and actuates the latch or bolt of a lock **b** (1) **:** a turned often decorative piece (as in a baluster) (2) **:** NEWEL **c :** an upright rod or pipe on which the sweep arm revolves in sweeping up a foundry mold or which is used in making a core **d** (1) **:** a revolving piece esp. if less in size than a shaft (2) **:** a horizontal or vertical axle revolving on pin or pivot ends ⟨the live ~ of a lathe⟩ ⟨the ~ of a vane⟩ ⟨the ~ of a capstan⟩ (3) **:** a rod attached to a valve to move or guide it **e :** the part of an axle on which a vehicle wheel turns **4 :** a unit of length used in counting yarns (as flax or jute) ⟨a ~ of flax or jute equals 14,400 yards⟩ **5 a :** the upper main piece of a made mast **b :** a round usu. iron pile or pipe placed on a rock or shoal as an aid to navigation **6 :** the pin of a turntable over which a phonograph record fits

²spin·dle \'spind³l, *chiefly dial* -n³l — *compare pres part*\ *vb* **spindled; spindled; spindling** \-nd(³)liŋ, -nliŋ, -nlēŋ, -nlən\ **spindles** *vi* **1 a :** to shoot or grow into a long slender stalk **:** form a stem **b :** to become disproportionately or unwholesomely tall and slender **2 a :** to grow to stalk or stem rather than to flower or fruit **b :** to become thin and useless ~ *vt* **:** to impale, thrust, or perforate on the spike of a spindle file ⟨~ an order slip⟩

spin·dle·age *also* **spin·dlage** \'spind(³)lij\ *n* -s [¹*spindle* + *-age*] **1 :** textile spindle equipment **:** the total number of spindles in a mill or region **2 :** the active or potential textile production represented by a stated spindleage

spindle attachment *n* **:** CENTROMERE

spindleberry \'spind³l- — *see* BERRY\ *n* **:** any of several shrubby spindle trees with showy usu. reddish fruits

spindle body *or* **spindle organ** *n* **:** a spindle-shaped enlargement on the mycelium of a fungus of the family Cladochytreaceae

spindle cell *n* **:** a fusiform cell; *esp* **:** a slender nucleated element that is the thrombocyte of a lower vertebrate and is equivalent in function to the blood platelet of higher forms

spindle–cell sarcoma *n* **:** FIBROSARCOMA

spindled *adj* [fr. past part. of ²*spindle*] **1 :** long and slender like the stalk of a plant **2 :** equipped or made with spindles ⟨a chair with ~ back⟩ **3 :** spiked on a spindle file

spindle fiber *also* **spindle element** *n* **:** one of the apparent filaments constituting the mitotic spindle esp. when construed as an actual physical structure capable of exerting traction

spindle file *n* **:** a device with a projecting spike, nail, or hook on which to stick papers

spin·dle·ful \'spind³l,fu̇l\ *n* -s **:** as much as a spindle will hold

spindlehead \'==,=\ *n* **:** a headstock or tailstock for a spindle or boring bar

spindle–legged *US usu* '==¦legəd, *Brit usu* -gd\ *adj* **:** having long slender legs

spindle oil *n* **:** a light fluid lubricating oil from petroleum suitable for oiling the spindles of spinning machinery and also for other light high-speed machinery

spin·dler \'spind(³)lə(r)\ *n* -s [¹*spindle* + *-er*] **:** one that places reels of paper on the spindle of a rotary printing press

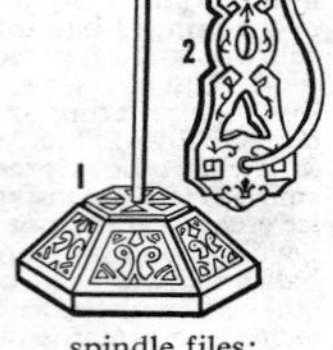

spindle files: *1* desk, *2* wall

spindles *pl of* SPINDLE, *pres 3d sing of* SPINDLE

spindle sander *n* **:** a sanding machine that carries the sand or sandpaper on its spindle — opposed to *belt sander*

spindle–shanked \'==¦=\ *adj* **:** having long slender legs **:** SPINDLE-LEGGED

spindleshanks \'==,=\ *n pl* **1 :** long slender legs **2** *sing or pl in constr* **:** a person having long slender legs

spindle shell *n* **1** *also* **spindle stromb :** any gastropod mollusk of the genus *Tibia* (family Strombidae) having a shell with a long conical many-whorled spire and a long slender anterior canal **2 :** a band shell of the genus *Fusinus* having a shell with a many-whorled spire and a very long straight canal

spindle sprout *or* **spinding sprout** *n* **:** the production of slender sickly shoots by potato tubers that accompanies some diseases (as leaf roll)

spindle stone *n* **:** TEMALACATL

spindletail \'==,=\ *n* **:** PINTAIL 1a

spindle temper *n* **:** a temper of steel characterized by the presence of about 1.125 percent carbon

spindle tree *n* **:** a shrub or tree of the genus *Euonymus; esp* **:** a small erect shrubby tree (*E. europaeus*) of Europe and western Asia with a pink capsule enclosing the orange fruit, tough white wood used esp. for spindles and skewers, and a powerfully cathartic principle in bark and fruit

spindle tuber *n* **1 :** a virus disease of the potato characterized by spindliness and uprightness of tops and by the formation of spindle-shaped tubers **2 :** POTATO MOSAIC

spindle–wood \'==,=\ *n* **:** the wood of a spindle tree

spin·dli·ness \'spin(d)lēnəs, -lin-\ *n* -ES **:** the quality or state of being spindly

¹spin·dling \-ind(³)liŋ, -inliŋ, -inlēŋ, -inlən\ *n* -s [fr. gerund of ²*spindle*] **1 :** the act or process of growing in a spindling manner **:** the growth of a plant to stalk rather than to flowers or fruit **2 :** a spindling person, plant, or object

²spindling \"\ *adj* [fr. pres. part. of ²*spindle*] **1 :** conspicuously or disproportionately long and slender or thin ⟨a tall, ~ ghost of a man —Van Wyck Brooks⟩ **2 :** lacking vitality, development, or strength **:** THIN, WEAK, INEFFECTUAL

spin·dly \-in(d)lē, -li\ *adj* -ER/-EST [¹*spindle* + *-y*] **:** exhibiting a tallness and thinness suggesting lack of strength or vitality **:** SPINDLING ⟨guards keep watch from a high, ~ lookout tower —Mollie Panter-Downes⟩ ⟨a sickly ~ child —*Times Lit. Supp.*⟩

spin·drift \'spin,drift\ *n* [alter. of Sc *speendrift*, fr. *speen* to drive before a strong wind (alter. of E ⁴*spoon*) + E *drift*] **1 :** sea spray **:** SPOONDRIFT **2 :** sand, dust, or snow driven before the wind like sea spray

spine \'spīn\ *n* -s [ME, thorn, spinal column, fr. L *spina* thorn, spine, spinal column; akin to Toch A *spin-* hook, Latvian *spina* twig, switch, Skt *sphya* flat sword-shaped piece of wood used in sacrifices] **1 a :** SPINAL COLUMN **b :** something resembling a spinal column in appearance, place, or function **:** something constituting a main strength, central axis, or chief support ⟨the land is flat and marshy before rising to a ~ of low hills —Robert Turley⟩ ⟨he has . . . ~ and starch, in a country sometimes lacking both —John Gunther⟩ ⟨give a ~ of significance to his butterfly existence —Tennessee Williams⟩ **c :** the backbone of a book **d :** the stiff springy quality desired in arrows **2 :** a stiff sharp-pointed plant process (as a modified leaf, leaf part, petiole, or stipule) — compare PRICKLE, THORN **3 :** a stiff sharp process of an animal body: **a :** a sharp-pointed protective outgrowth consisting of an enlarged and modified hair of a mammal (as a porcupine or a hedgehog) **b :** one of the processes that cover most parts of the body of a sea urchin, that serve for defense or for locomotion, and that are borne on rounded tubercles to which they are movably articulated **c :** a radiolarian spicule **d :** a spiny fin ray of a fish **e :** any of various processes esp. of bones **:** a spinous process (as of a vertebra or of the ilium); *specif* **:** a prominent ridge on the back of the scapula **4** *dial Eng* **:** SWARD, TURF **5** *dial Eng* **:** the surface layer or rind of meat **6 :** a pointed mass of viscous or solidified lava that occas. protrudes from the throat of a volcano

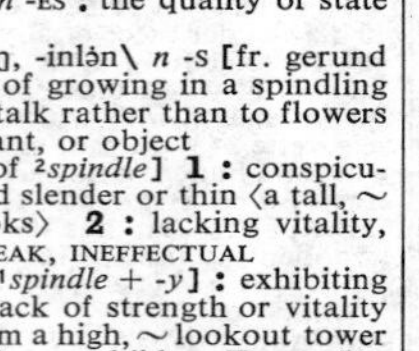

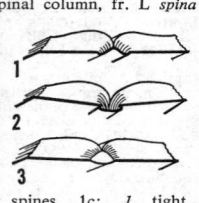

spines 1c: *1* tight, *2* flexible, *3* hollow back

spinebill \'=,=\ *n* **:** any of various honey eaters of the genus *Acanthorhynchus* having a slender curved and very sharp bill

spinebone \'=,=\ *n* [ME *spinboon*, fr. *spin, spine* spinal column + *boon* bone] **:** SPINAL COLUMN, BACKBONE

spine cell *n* **:** PRICKLE CELL

spined \'spīnd\ *adj* **:** furnished with a spine **:** SPINY

spine–finned \'=¦=\ *adj* **:** SPINY-FINNED

spinefoot \'=,=\ *n, pl* **spinefeet :** any of several rabbitfishes (genus *Siganus*) of the tropical Indo-Pacific capable of inflicting painful wounds with venomous fin spines

spine fusion *n* **:** surgical fusion of two or more vertebrae for remedial immobilizing of the spine

spi·nel \spə'nel *sometimes* 'spin³l\ *or* **spi·nelle** \spə'nel\ *n* -s [It *spinella, spinello*, dim. of *spina* thorn, fr. L; fr. the pointed crystals — more at SPINE] **1 a :** a mineral $MgAl_2O_4$ consisting of an oxide of magnesium and aluminum that is noted for its great hardness, that usu. forms octahedral crystals varying in color (as from colorless to ruby-red to black), and that is used as a gemstone — see ALMANDINE, BALAS, CEYLONITE, RUBICELLE, SPINEL RUBY **b :** a synthetic substance similar to the mineral spinel that is used as a gemstone, as bearings for watches and various instruments, and as a refractory **2 a :** a member of the spinel series **b :** a member of the spinel group **3 :** a substance (as a sulfide) that has a similar formula and the same crystal structure as a spinel

spine·less \'spīnləs\ *adj* **1 :** having no spines, thorns, or prickles **2 a :** having no spinal column **:** INVERTEBRATE **b :** lacking moral resolution, firmness, or strength of character ⟨a ~, craven fellow —John Lodge⟩

spine·less·ly *adv* **:** in a spineless manner **:** FEEBLY, IRRESOLUTELY

spine·less·ness *n* -ES **:** the quality or state of being spineless

spine·let \'spīnlət\ *n* -s **:** a small spine

spinel group *n* **:** a group of mineral oxides including the spinel series and having the general composition AB_2O_4 in which A represents magnesium, ferrous iron, zinc, or manganese or any combination of them and B represents aluminum, ferric iron, or chromium — see CHROMITE SERIES, MAGNETITE SERIES

spine·like \'=,=\ *adj* **:** resembling a spine

spi·nel·lid \spə'neləd\ *n* -s [ISV *spinel* + *-id*] **:** a member of the spinel group

spinel pink *n* **:** a moderate purplish red that is bluer and deeper than average rose, redder and deeper than violine pink, and redder and lighter than magenta rose

spinel red *n* **:** a strong red to purplish red that is duller than rose Neyron

spinel ruby *n* **:** a ruby spinel of a deep red color that is used as a gem — not used technically

spinel series *n* **:** a series of isomorphous mineral oxides $(Mg,Fe,Zn,Mn)Al_2O_4$ in the spinel group consisting of spinel, hercynite, gahnite, and galaxite

spine–rayed \'=¦=\ *adj* **:** SPINY-RAYED

spines *pl of* SPINE

spi·nes·cence \spī'nes³n(t)s\ *n* -s [NL *spinescentia*, fr. *spinescent-, spinescens* + L *-ia* -y] **1 :** SPININESS **2 :** SPINATION

spi·nes·cent \(')spī¦nes³nt\ *adj* [NL *spinescent-, spinescens*, fr. LL, pres. part. of *spinescere* to be thorny, incho. fr. L *spina* thorn] **:** becoming spiny **:** tapering to a sharp rigid point **:** tending toward spininess **:** SPINOSE, SPINULOSE

spin·et \'spinət, *usu* -əd.+V\ *n* -s [It *spinetta*, prob. fr. Giovanni *Spinetti* fl1503 Ital. spinet maker] **1 :** a small harpsichord similar to the virginal **2 a :** a compactly built upright piano of reduced height and usu. reduced keyboard suitable for limited space **b :** a small electronic organ

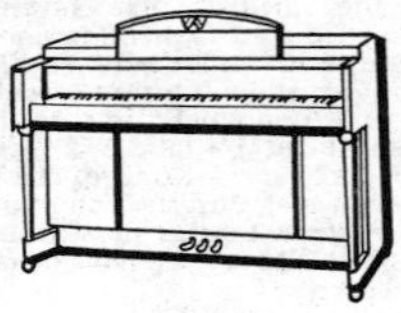

spinet 2

spinetail \'=,=\ *n* **1 :** SPINE-TAILED SWIFT **2 :** any of several So. and Central American birds of *Synallaxis, Siptornis*, or related genera of the families Dendrocolaptidae and Furnariidae **3 :** RUDDY DUCK

spine–tailed \'=¦=\ *adj* **:** having tail quills with sharp naked tips

spine–tailed swift *n* **:** a bird of the genus *Chaetura*

spinet desk *n* **:** a desk made from or in imitation of a spinet

spiney *var of* SPINY

spin fishing *n* **:** SPINNING 2

spin house *n* [trans. of D *spinhuis*] **:** SPINNING HOUSE

spini– — see SPIN-

spinier *comparative of* SPINY

spinies *pl of* SPINY

spiniest *superlative of* SPINY

spi·ni·fex \'spīnə,feks\ *n* [NL, fr. *spin-* + L *-fex* (fr. *facere* to do, make) — more at SPIN-, DO] **1 a** *cap* **:** a genus of chiefly Australian grasses the seeds of which bear an elastic spine — see SPINY ROLLING GRASS **b** -ES **:** any plant of the genus *Spinifex* **2** -ES **:** any of several Australian grasses of the genus *Triodia* that often form dense almost impassable growths and have stiff and sharp-pointed leaves

spi·ni·form \'spīnə,fȯrm\ *adj* [NL *spiniformis*, fr. *spin-* + L *-formis* -form] **:** like or being a spine

spin in *vi* **:** to crash in an aircraft **:** be out of control in any way

spin·i·ness \'spīnēnəs, -nin-\ *n* -ES **:** the quality or state of being spiny

spink \'spiŋk\ *n* -s [ME *spynke*, perh. of Scand origin; akin to Sw *spink* small bird, sparrow — more at FINCH] *dial Brit* **:** CHAFFINCH

spin·na·bil·i·ty \,spinə'bilәd·ē\ *n* **:** fitness for spinning **:** capability of being spun — used of textile fibers

spin·na·ble \'spinəbəl\ *adj* **:** suitable for spinning **:** capable of being spun

spin·na·ker \'spinəkə(r), -nēk-\ *n* -s [prob. irreg. fr. *Sphinx*, yacht that carried such a sail in 1866] **:** a large triangular sail set on a long light pole on the side opposite the mainsail on fore-and-aft rigged yachts and used when running before the wind

spin·ner \'spinə(r)\ *n* -s [ME *spinnere*, fr. *spinnen* to spin + *-ere* -er] **1 a** *archaic* **:** a spider that spins a web **b :** MAYFLY **c :** a nightjar (*Caprimulgus europaeus*) **2 :** one that spins: as **a :** a manufacturer engaged in spinning **b** (1) **:** a worker who spins textile fibers (2) **:** a spinning machine **c :** one that tins metal articles by dipping a basket of them in molten tin and then whirling off the excess in a spinning machine **d :** a lathe operator who shapes rings and other round jewelry forms **e :** an operator of a lathe for spinning shaped articles from sheet-metal stock **f :** one that rolls candy strips and cuts them into sticks, drops, or other shapes **3 :** the teller of a yarn **:** one that spins a tale ⟨an extraordinary ~ of yarns —I.L.Salomon⟩ **4 a :** an artificial fly tied to represent one of the Ephemeridae in the imago stage — see LURE illustration **b :** a spoon, blade, or set of wings that revolves when drawn through the water **c :** an angler who uses spinning tackle **5 :** SPINNERET 1 **6 a :** a bowled cricket ball to which spin has been imparted **b :** a bowler of such balls **7 :** SPINNER PLAY **8 :** a padded iron disk revolving for use in polishing stone **9 spinners** *pl* **:** fine wool of high spinning count **10 :** a streamline fairing usu. of sheet metal and roughly conical or paraboloid in form which is attached to a propeller boss and revolves with it **11 :** a movable arrow that is spun on its dial to indicate the number or kind of moves a player may make in a board game

spin·ner·et \,spinə¦ret\ *n* -s [*spinner* + *-et*] **1 :** an organ for producing threads of silk from the secretion of the silk glands **:** a spinning organ: **a :** one of the often distinctly jointed processes usu. numbering six and resembling nipples near the end of a spider's abdomen each bearing minute orifices by which the ducts of the silk glands open to emit streams of secretion that usu. join together to form a single thread **b :** an organ of some insect larvae having a function analogous to that of a spider's spinneret; *esp* **:** a tubule on the labium of many caterpillars by which a double thread made up of separate filaments from paired glands is extruded **2** *or*

spin·ner·ette \"\ [*spinnerette* fr. *spinner* + *-ette*] **:** a small metal plate, thimble, or cap with fine holes through which a cellulose or chemical solution is forced in the spinning of rayon, nylon, and other man-made filaments

spinner play *n* **:** a football play in which the ball carrier spins around in an attempt to deceive the opponents about the direction in which the play will go

spin·ner·ular \spə'ner(y)ələ(r); 'spinər,yül-, -nə,rül-\ *adj* **:** of or relating to spinnerets

spin·ner·ule \'spinə(r),yül, -nə,rül\ *n* -s [*spinner* + *-ule*] **:** one of many small tubes on the spinnerets of spiders for discharging the secretion of the silk glands

spin·nery \'spinərē\ *n* -ES [¹*spin* + *-ery*] **:** a spinning mill

spin·ney *also* **spin·ny** \ˈspinē\ *n, pl* **spinneys** *also* **spinnies** [MF *espinaye* thorny thicket, fr. *espine* thorn, fr. L *spina* — more at SPINE] *Brit* **:** a small wood with undergrowth **:** COPSE, THICKET

spinning *n* -s [ME *spinninge*, gerund of *spinnen* to spin] **1 a :** the operation or business of making fibers or filaments into yarn or thread **b :** the yarn or thread spun **2 :** a method of fishing with a light lure, a fixed spool reel, and light line **3 :** the drawing out of something (as a narration) to excessive length **4 :** rapid rotation ⟨the ~ of the planets⟩ **5 :** the shaping of hollow ware in a lathe by pressing a flat sheet of metal against a revolving form with a hand tool

spinning band *n* **:** ¹BAND 3c

spinning count *n* **:** the number of hanks of yarn that can be spun from one pound of washed combed wool of a given fineness ⟨wool with a *spinning count* of 80 is very fine while one of 40 is chiefly suitable for carpets⟩

spinning dial *n* **:** SPINNER 11

spinning frame *n* **:** a machine that draws, twists, and winds yarn — compare MULE, RING SPINNER

spinning gland *n* **:** SILK GLAND

spinning house *n* [ME *spynnyng hous* building used for spinning, fr. *spynnyng, spinninge* spinning + *hous* house] **:** a former house of correction for prostitutes esp. in England in which inmates were often made to work at spinning

spinning jen·ny \ˈ=‚=ˌjenē, -ni\ *n* [*spinning* + *Jenny*, nickname fr. the name *Jane*] **:** an early machine for spinning wool or cotton by means of many spindles

spinning lathe *n* **:** a lathe used for the shaping of metal hollow ware by pressing flat stock over a revolving form with a hand tool

spinning line *n* **:** a durable rope used to couple or uncouple lengths of pipe in oil well drilling

spinning machine *n* **1 :** a machine for spinning staple fiber or continuous filament into yarn **2 :** a machine for winding insulated covering on electric wires **3 :** a machine for shaping metal hollow ware

spinning mammilla *n* **:** SPINNERET 1

spinning mite *n* **:** RED SPIDER

spinning reel *n* **:** a fishing reel having a fixed spool on which the line is wound by means of an arm or bail actuated by turning the reel handle

spinning ring *n* **:** the circular track on which the traveler of a ring spinner slides

spinning rod *n* **:** a fishing rod designed for casting a spinning lure

spinning tube *n* **:** SPINNERULE

spinning wheel *n* [ME *spynnyngwhele*, fr. *spynnyng, spinninge* spinning + *whele, wheel* wheel] **:** a small domestic machine for spinning yarn or thread in which a wheel drives a single spindle and is itself driven by hand or by foot

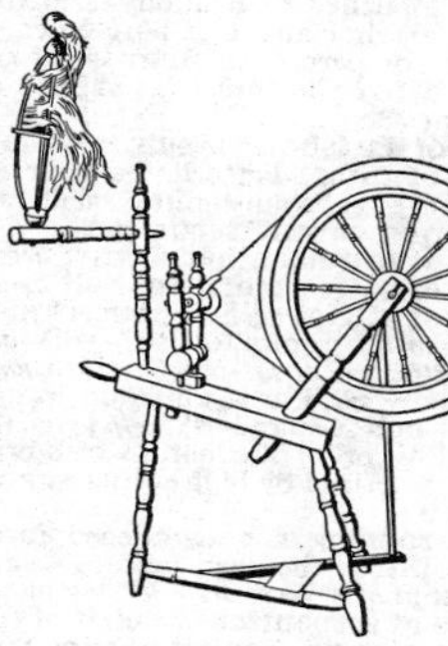

spinning wheel

spino- — see SPIN-

spi·no·blast \ˈspīnə‚blast\ *n* [*spin-* + *-blast*] **:** a free-floating statoblast provided with external barbs or hooks

spi·no·cerebellar \ˌspī(ˌ)nō+\ *adj* [*spin-* + *cerebellar*] **:** of or relating to the spinal cord and cerebellum

spinocerebellar tract *n* **:** any of four nerve tracts from the spinal cord to the cerebellum that arise two on each side from a group of large cells in the medial part of the base of the posterior columns of the spinal cord and pass to the cerebellum as both crossed and uncrossed fibers

spin–off \ˈ=‚=\ *n* -s [fr. *spin off*, v.] **:** a transfer of a distinctive business constituting one of two or more businesses owned by a corporation to a corporation controlled by it in return for a distribution to the stockholders of the distributing corporation of all the stock and securities in the transferee corporation without surrender of any stock or securities by the stockholders in the distributing corporation — compare SPLIT-OFF, SPLIT-UP

spi·no·gram \ˈspīnə‚gram\ *n* [*spin-* + *-gram*] **:** MYELOGRAM 2

spi·noid \ˈspī‚nȯid\ *adj* [*spin-* + *-oid*] **:** SPINELIKE

spino–olivary \ˌspī(ˌ)nō+\ *adj* [*spin-* + *olivary*] **:** connecting the spinal cord with the olivary body

spin·or \ˈspinər, -‚nȯ(ə)r\ *n* -s [¹*spin* + *-or*] **:** a quantity that resembles a vector with complex components in two- or four-dimensional space with complex coordinates and that is used esp. in the mathematics of the theory of relativity ⟨the geometrical picture of a two-component ~ requires two plane vectors . . . and these may be of arbitrary lengths and inclined to each other at any angle —*Scientific Monthly*⟩

spi·nose \ˈspī‚nōs\ *adj* [L *spinosus*, fr. *spina* thorn, spine + *-osus* -ose — more at SPINE] **:** full of spines **:** armed with spines **:** SPINELIKE — **spi·nose·ly** *adv* — **spi·nose·ness** *n* -ES

spinose ear tick *n* **:** an ear tick (*Otobius megnini*) of the southwestern U.S. and Mexico that is a serious pest of cattle, horses, sheep, and goats

spi·nos·i·ty \spīˈnäsəd·ē\ *n* -ES [LL *spinositat-, spinositas*, fr. L *spinosus* spinose + *-itat-, -itas* -ity] **1 a :** the state of having spines **b :** a thorny or prickly quality **:** something nettlesome or difficult (as in a problem or argument) **2 :** a rude or cutting remark or one likely to give pain

spinoso- *comb form* [*spinose* + *-o-*] **:** spinose and ⟨*spino*sodentate⟩

spi·no·tectal \ˌspī(ˌ)nō+\ *adj* [*spin-* + *tectum* + *-al*] **:** TECTOSPINAL

spi·no·thalamic \"+\ *adj* [*spin-* + *thalamic*] **:** connecting the spinal cord and thalamus; *also* **:** involving or affecting nerve fiber tracts connecting these parts

spi·nous \ˈspīnəs\ *adj* [*spine* + *-ous*] **1 :** difficult or unpleasant to handle or meet **:** BRISTLING, SHARP, THORNY ⟨a ~ humor⟩ **2 a :** having spines, thorns, or prickles ⟨a ~ plant⟩ **b :** having sharp processes (as of bone) ⟨the ~ appendage of a fish⟩ **c :** having the shape of a spine or thorn

spinous process *n* **:** SPINE 3e: as **a :** the median spinelike or platelike dorsal process of the neural arch of a vertebra **:** NEURAL SPINE **b :** a sharp posterior prolongation on each greater wing of the sphenoid bone **c :** a process on the head of the tibia between the articular surfaces for the condyles of the femur

spi·no·zism \spəˈnō‚zizəm\ *n* -s *usu cap* [ISV *spinoz-* (fr. Baruch *Spinoza* †1677 Du. philosopher) + *-ism*] **:** the philosophy of Spinoza whose fundamental ideas were that all reality is One Substance which has an infinite number of attributes of which only thought and extension are capable of being apprehended by the human mind, that all particular things and particular ideas or states of mind are modes or determinations of these two attributes and all such temporal existences are rigidly connected together in the One Substance in such a manner that all occurrences happen of necessity, and that human bondage to the passions and particular desires is due to an ignorance which fails to apprehend this inevitability so that freedom is to be won through understanding and acquiescing in this necessity and contemplative peace is to be found through the intellectual love of God — compare MONISTIC IDEALISM

spi·no·zist \-zəst\ *n* -s *usu cap* [ISV *spinoz-* (fr. Baruch *Spinoza*) + *-ist*] **:** an adherent of Spinozism or a specialist in Spinoza's philosophy

spino·zis·tic \spəˌnōˈzistik, ˌspī(ˌ)nōˈz-\ *adj, usu cap* **:** of, relating to, or typical of Spinoza or Spinozism

spinproof \ˈ=‚=\ *adj* **:** devised so as not to spin **:** incapable of spinning — used esp. of an airplane

spins *pres 3d sing of* SPIN, *pl of* SPIN

spin·ster \ˈspinztə(r), -n(t)stə-\ *n* -s [ME *spinnestere*, fr. *spinnen* to spin + *-estere* -ster] **1 a :** a woman whose occupation is to spin **b** *obs* **:** a man whose trade is spinning **2 a** *archaic* **:** an unmarried woman of gentle family **b :** an unmarried woman — often used as a legal term **3 :** a woman past the common age for marrying or one who seems unlikely to marry — called also *old maid*

spin·ster·hood \-‚hu̇d\ *n* **:** the state or condition of being a spinster **:** OLD MAIDHOOD

spin·ster·ish \-ərish\ *adj* **:** having the habits, appearance, or traits of a spinster **:** OLD-MAIDISH

spin·ster·ly \-ə(r)lē, -li\ *adj* **:** of, relating to, or characteristic of a spinster **:** OLD-MAIDISH

spin·stress \-nzt(ə)rəs, -n(t)st(-\ *n* -ES [*spinster* + *-ess*] **1 :** a woman who spins **2 :** SPINSTER

spin·stry \-rē\ *n* -ES [*spinster* + *-y*] **:** the occupation or product of spinning

spin·thar·i·scope \spinˈtharə‚skōp\ *n* [Gk *spintharis* spark + E *-scope*; akin to Gk *spinthēr* spark] **:** an instrument consisting of a fluorescent screen and a magnifying lens system for visual detection of alpha rays

spin the bottle *n* **1 :** the game spin the plate when played with a bottle **2 :** a method of choosing a performer (as a partner in a kissing game) according to whom the mouth of a bottle points to when it stops spinning

spin the plate *or* **spin the platter** *n* **:** a game in which something round (as a plate or platter) is spun on edge and the name of a player is called upon which the named player must catch the spinning object before it falls or pay a forfeit

spin·ther·ism \ˈspin(t)thə‚rizəm\ *n* -s [NL *spintherismus*, fr. Gk *spinthēr* spark + L *-ismus* -ism] **:** a subjective sensation as of sparks before the eyes

spin tunnel *n* **:** a vertical wind tunnel in which accurate scale models of aircraft are tested to determine their spinning characteristics

spi·nu·late \ˈspīnyə‚lāt\ *or* **spi·nu·lat·ed** \-ād·əd\ *adj* [*spinulate* fr. *spinule* + *-ate*; *spinulated* fr. *spinulate* + *-ed*] **:** SPINULOSE

spi·nu·la·tion \ˌspīnyəˈlāshən\ *n* -s [*spinule* + *-ation*] **:** an armature of spines or spinules

spi·nule \ˈspī(ˌ)nyül\ *n* -s [L *spinula*, fr. *spina* thorn, spine + *-ula* — more at SPINE] **:** a small or minute spine

spi·nu·les·cent \ˌspīnyəˈles³nt\ *adj* [*spinule* + *-escent*] **:** having small spines **:** somewhat spiny

spi·nu·lo·sa \ˌspīnyəˈlōsə\ *n pl, cap* [NL, fr. *spinulosa*, neut. pl. of *spinulosus* spinulose] **:** a cosmopolitan order of starfishes lacking conspicuous marginal plates and stalked pedicellariae and often occurring at great depths in the sea

spi·nu·lose \ˈspīnyə‚lōs\ *adj* [NL *spinulosus*, fr. L *spinula* spinule + *-osus* -ose] **:** covered with or having the form of small spines — **spi·nu·lose·ly** *adv*

spi·nu·lous \ˈspīnyələs\ *adj* [F *or* NL; F *spinuleux*, fr. NL *spinulosus*] **:** SPINULOSE

spin–up \ˈ=‚=\ *n* -s [fr. *spin up*, v.] **:** the acceleration of the wheels of an airplane by contact with the ground when touching down to land to a peripheral speed equal to the ground speed

spi·nus \ˈspīnəs, -pēn-\ *n, cap* [NL, fr. Gk *spinos* chaffinch — more at FINCH] **:** a genus of small active often brightly colored finches that commonly includes the siskins and the New World goldfinches and is sometimes considered to constitute a subgenus of *Carduelis*

¹**spiny** *also* **spin·ey** \ˈspīnē, -ni\ *adj* **spinier; spiniest** [*spine* + *-y*] **1 :** covered with spines **:** bearing several or many spines, prickles, or sharp processes **2 :** abounding with difficulties, obstacles, or annoyances **:** NETTLESOME, THORNY ⟨a ~ problem —A.C.Fisher⟩ **3 :** slender and pointed like a spine

²**spiny** \"\ *n* -ES *Africa* **:** any of several rabbitfishes of the genus *Siganus*

spiny amaranth *or* **spiny pigweed** *n* **:** THORNY AMARANTH

spiny anteater *n* **:** ECHIDNA

spiny catfish *n* **:** a small brown So. American freshwater naked catfish (*Doras cataphractus*) having the pectoral fins armed with hooked spines and a row of spinose bony plates along each side of the body and being sometimes kept in the tropical aquarium where it is an excellent scavenger

spiny clotbur *or* **spiny cocklebur** *n* **:** a European cocklebur (*Xanthium spinosum*) naturalized widely as a weed in waste grounds and having 3-branched spines at the axils of the leaves

spiny crawfish *n* **:** a large Australian crawfish (*Astacopsis serratus*) with a spiny carapace

spiny dogfish *n* **:** any of various dogfishes constituting the family Squalidae and distinguished by the presence of a spine in or immediately anterior to each dorsal fin: as **a :** a common very destructive dogfish (*Squalus acanthias*) of both coasts of the No. Atlantic that becomes about four feet long and has the fin spines stout and prominent **b :** a similar dogfish (*Squalus suckleyi*) of the Pacific coast of No. America

spiny dormouse *n* **:** a small Indian rodent (*Platacanthomys lasiurus*) with long bushy tail, pointed ears, and a pelage of mingled hairs and spines

spiny eel *n* **:** any of several strikingly colored eel-shaped freshwater fishes (order Opisthomi) of Africa and the East Indies having a long slender snout and an anterior dorsal fin consisting of free spines

spiny elm caterpillar *n* **:** the larva of the mourning cloak butterfly

spiny–finned \ˈ=ˌ=ˈ=\ *adj* **:** having fins with some spiny rays — opposed to *soft-finned*; used of members of the Acanthopterygii

spiny–haired rat \ˈ=ˌ=‚=-\ *n* **:** a small reddish southeastern Asiatic rat (*Rattus fulvescens* syn. *R. jerdoni*) having flat spines mingled with the hair

spiny–herb \ˈ=ˌ=‚=\ *n* **:** an annual desert plant of the genus *Chorizanthe* (family Polygonaceae) lacking sheathing stipules and having flowers borne in an involucre which is usu. one-flowered with bracts ending in bristles

spiny lobster *n* **:** an edible crustacean (family Palinuridae) that is distinguished from the true lobster by the simple unenlarged first pair of legs and by the spiny carapace — called also *lobster, rock lobster, sea crawfish*; compare CAPE CRAWFISH, LANGOUSTE

spiny mouse *n* **1 :** any of various mice of the genus *Acomys* that are closely related to the house mouse but distinguished by an almost entirely spiny coat, are native to the Mediterranean area, and are sometimes kept as pets in Europe **2 :** any of several New World fossorial pocket mice (as of the genus *Heteromys*) with spiny pelage

spiny oyster *n* **:** a bivalve mollusk of the family Spondylidae

spiny pocket mouse *n* **:** SPINY MOUSE 2

spiny rat *n* **1 :** any of various So. or Central American rats of *Echimys* and closely related genera having more or less bristly fur — called also *hedgehog rat, porcupine rat* **2 :** SPINY MOUSE 2

spiny ray *n* **:** a fin ray that is stiff, unbranched, pointed at the end, and lacking transverse segmentation, that occurs singly or grouped in the anterior part of the dorsal fin in many fishes or in the first dorsal when there are two as well as in the anal and ventral fins, and that was in former classifications the principal character of the group Acanthopterygii — opposed to *soft ray*

spiny–rayed \ˈ=ˌ=ˈ=\ *adj* **1 :** having spiny rays — used of a fin **2 :** having fins with one or more spiny rays **:** SPINY-FINNED — used of a fish, esp. of the Acanthopterygii; compare SOFT-RAYED

spiny rolling grass *n* **:** an Australian grass (*Spinifex hirsutus*) with long creeping stems that root freely at the joints and thus of value as a sand binder

spiny–skinned \ˈ=ˌ=ˈ=\ *adj* **:** having a skin covered with knobs, tubercles, or spines ⟨*spiny-skinned* fishes⟩

spio \ˈspī(ˌ)ō\ *n, cap* [NL *Spion-, Spio*, perh. fr. L *Spio*, one of the Nereids, fr. Gk *Speiō*] **:** a widely distributed genus (the type of the family Spionidae) of small burrowing marine polychaete worms without tentacles or palps but with enlarged dorsal cirri acting as gills

¹**spi·o·nid** \ˈspīənəd\ *adj* [NL *Spionidae*] **:** of or relating to the genus *Spio* or family Spionidae

²**spionid** \"\ *n* -s [NL *Spionidae*, family of marine polychaete worms, fr. *Spion-, Spio*, type genus + *-idae*] **:** a spionid worm

spir- *or* **spiri-** *or* **spiro-** *comb form* [LL *spir-*, fr. L *spira* — more at SPIRE] **1 :** coil **:** twist ⟨*Spir*anthes⟩ ⟨*spiri*valve⟩ ⟨*Spiro*chaeta⟩ **2 :** a chemical compound that contains one or more systems of two rings having a single atom in common with a resulting figure-eight arrangement of atoms ⟨*spiro*pentane⟩

spirable *adj* [L *spirabilis*, fr. *spirare* to breathe + *-bilis* -able] *obs* **:** capable of being breathed **:** RESPIRABLE

spi·ra·cle \ˈspirəkəl, -pīr-\ *n* -s [in sense 1, fr. ME, fr. LL *spiraculum*, fr. L, air hole, spiracle, fr. *spirare* to breathe; in other senses, fr. L *spiraculum* — more at SPIRIT] **1** *obs* **:** BREATH, SPIRIT **2 a :** a usu. small aperture giving a confined space communication with the outer air **:** a breathing hole **:** AIR HOLE, VENT **b :** a steam or gas vent on the surface of a lava flow **3 :** a breathing orifice: **a :** the blowhole of a cetacean **b :** an external tracheal aperture of a terrestrial arthropod that in an insect is usu. one of a series of small more or less elliptical apertures often having a valve and a protective sievelike structure or fringe of hairs and being located along each side of the thorax and abdomen usu. in 10 pairs but sometimes 11 or occas. fewer — see INSECT illustration **c :** one of the orifices or passages that open on the upper back part of the head of many elasmobranchs and some higher fishes (as a sturgeon or the bichir), communicate with the mouth cavity, represent the first postoral visceral clefts of the embryo, in rays serve instead of the mouth as the chief incurrent respiratory openings, and may contain a rudimentary gill **d :** the excurrent aperture of the gill chamber of a tadpole developing from two apertures that unite in a canal which opens on the left side of the body or rarely on the undersurface

spi·rac·u·lar \(ˈ)spīˈrakyələ(r), spəˈr-\ *adj* [*spiraculum* + *-ar*] **:** of, relating to, or serving as a spiracle

spi·rac·u·lum \-ˈ=ləm\ *n, pl* **spiracu·la** \-lə\ [L] **:** SPIRACLE

¹**spiraea** *var of* SPIREA

²**spi·raea** \spīˈrēə\ *n, cap* [NL, fr. L, a plant, perh. privet, fr. Gk *speiraia*, perh. fr. *speira* coil — more at SPIRE] **:** a large genus of shrubs (family Rosaceae) that are natives of temperate regions and have small perfect white or pink flowers in dense racemes, corymbs, cymes, or panicles each with five pistils which are alternate with the persistent calyx lobes and which ripen into follicles — see HARDHACK, MEADOWSWEET

¹**spi·ral** \ˈspīrəl\ *adj* [ML *spiralis*, fr. L *spira* coil + *-alis* -al — more at SPIRE] **1 a :** winding around a center or pole and gradually receding from or approaching it ⟨a ~ curve⟩ **b** (1) **:** HELICAL (2) **:** of, relating to, or resembling a spiral **2 :** having one or more strands twisted around a core yarn ⟨a ~ ply yarn⟩ **3 :** advancing to succeeding higher levels through a series of cyclical movements ⟨developed a ~ theory of social evolution⟩

²**spiral** \"\ *n* -s **1 a :** the path of a point in a plane moving around a centered point while continuously receding from or approaching it **b :** a three-dimensional curve (as a helix) with one or more turns about an axis **2 :** a single turn or coil in a spiral object **3 a :** something (as a piece of coiled wire or a winding staircase) having a spiral form ⟨a long blue ~ from his cigar ascended —John Galsworthy⟩ **b :** SPIRAL GALAXY **c :** a flight in a spiral path **:** a spiral flight **d :** a kick or pass in which a football rotates on its long axis while moving through the air **e :** a dance movement consisting of concentric circling with steadily diminishing or increasing diameter on a ground level or with rising and falling **f :** a free skating figure consisting of gliding on one foot with speed in a large circle with the body in arabesque position **g :** a synchronized swimming stunt consisting of at least four complete body revolutions executed with the body in a head downward vertical position with the ankles above water followed by complete submergence of the body **h** (1) **:** an easement curve (as in a railroad track) in which the change of degree of curve is uniform throughout its length (2) **:** a loop built where a railroad line ascends a steep slope for the purpose of gaining distance in order not to exceed the ruling grade **4 :** a continuously spreading and accelerating increase or decrease (as in costs, prices, or wages) ⟨a continuance of the upward ~ of prices —F.D.Roosevelt⟩ ⟨the vicious ~ of deflation —F.L.Allen⟩ ⟨the vicious ~ of arming and counterarming —B.N.Rau⟩ — see INFLATIONARY SPIRAL

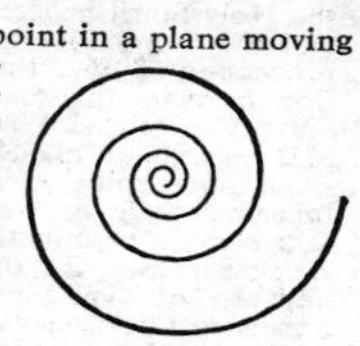

spiral 1a

³**spiral** \"\ *vb* **spiraled** *or* **spiralled; spiraled** *or* **spiralled; spiraling** *or* **spiralling; spirals** *vi* **1 a :** to go or move and esp. to rise or fall in a spiral course **:** wind in a spiral manner ⟨the path . . . ~*ed* up the hillside —Harlan Hatcher⟩ ⟨saw a column of cloud slowly ~ from nothingness —Victor Canning⟩ **b :** to follow a spiral path in ascending or descending ⟨our plane ~*s* down toward the . . . airdrome —W.L.White⟩ ⟨the birds ~*ed* high —Adria Langley⟩ ⟨we ~*ed* through the . . . cloud rift and landed —Lowell Thomas⟩ **2 :** to rise or fall in a continuously spreading and accelerating manner ⟨production ~*ed* upward⟩ ⟨the cost of living ~*ed* upward⟩ ⟨profits ~*ed* during the business boom⟩ **3 :** to revolve with a spiral pattern in dancing ~ *vt* **1 :** to form into a spiral **:** turn or twist spirally ⟨section foremen . . . ~*ed* the ends of their curves —*Engineering News*⟩ **2 :** to cause to rise or fall in a continuously spreading and accelerating manner ⟨inflation ~*ed* prices —Henry Coates⟩

⁴**spir·al** \"\ *adj* [¹*spire* + *-al*] **:** rising to a sharp point **:** tall and tapering or pointed like the spire of a building

spiral axis *n* **:** the axis of a twisted column drawn spirally in order to trace the circumvolutions without

spiral bandage *n* **:** a bandage wound in oblique turns around an extremity — see BANDAGE illustration

spiral bevel gear *n* **:** a bevel gear in which the tooth elements are curved lines (as helical lines)

spiral binding *n* **:** mechanical binding in which a continuous spiral wire or plastic strip is passed through holes at the gutter margin

spiral–bound \ˈ=ˌ=ˈ=\ *adj* **:** having or bound with a spiral binding ⟨a *spiral-bound* notebook⟩

spiral chute *n* **:** a continuous curved trough spiraled about a column for use in transporting materials to a lower level

spiral conveyor *n* **:** CONVEYER 2a (8)

spiral duct *n* **:** SPIRAL VESSEL

spi·rale \spīˈra(ˌ)lē, -rā(-, spəˈrä(ˌ)lā\ *n* -s [NL, fr. ML, neut. of *spiralis* spiral] **:** SPIRALIUM

spiral galaxy *n* **:** a galaxy exhibiting a central nucleus or barred structure from which extend concentrations of matter forming curved arms giving the overall appearance of a gigantic pinwheel — compare SPIRAL NEBULA

spiral ganglion *n* **:** a mass of bipolar nerve cells occupying the spiral canal of the organ of Corti and from their axons forming the cochlear branch of the eighth cranial nerve

spiral gear *or* **spiral gearing** *n* **:** a helical gear used to transmit power between nonparallel shafts

spiral grain *n* **:** a spiral or winding instead of the usual vertical arrangement in the vessels and other elements in the wood from a twisted tree

spiral head *n* **:** an index head whose spindle may be connected by gearing to the feed screw of a milling machine table for the purpose of cutting spirals

spi·ral·i·form \spīˈralə‚fȯrm\ *adj* **:** having or based upon the form of a spiral ⟨the ~ system in art⟩

spi·ral·ism \ˈspīrə‚lizəm\ *n* -s **:** the growth of a normally straight stem to form a spiral

spi·ral·i·ty \spīˈraləd·ē\ *n* -ES [ISV ¹*spiral* + *-ity*] **:** the quality or state of being spiral **:** the amount or degree of spiral curve

spi·ra·li·um \spīˈrālēəm\ *n, pl* **spira·lia** \-ēə\ [NL, fr. ML *spiralis* spiral + NL *-ium*] **:** one of the spirally twisted ribbonlike calcareous supports on the interior of the valve of various extinct brachiopods — see BRACHIOPOD illustration

spi·ral·iza·tion \ˌspīrələˈzāshən, -ˌlīˈz-\ *n* -s **:** the action or process of spiralizing ⟨~ of chromosomes⟩

spi·ral·ize \ˈ=‚=‚līz\ *vb* -ED/-ING/-S *vt* **:** to make spiral **:** wind, coil, twist, or cut in a spiral ~ *vi* **:** to gather into a spiral ⟨the chromosomes of the two nuclei begin to ~ —Esko Suomalainen⟩

spi·ral·ly \-rəlē, -li\ *adv* **:** in a spiral manner or course **:** in spiral lines or curves

spiral milling *n* **:** HELICAL MILLING

spiral nebula *n* **:** SPIRAL GALAXY — not used technically

spiral of archimedes *usu cap A* **:** ARCHIMEDEAN SPIRAL

spiral organ *n* **:** ORGAN OF CORTI

spiral reverse bandage *n* **:** a spiral bandage in which the oblique turns are reversed at each turn in order better to adapt to the part — see BANDAGE illustration
spirals *pl of* SPIRAL, *pres 3d sing of* SPIRAL
spiral spring *n* **:** a spring consisting of a wire coiled usu. in a flat spiral or in a helix
spiral stairs *n pl* **:** stairs that are circular in plan and consist entirely of winders
spiral valve *n* **:** a continuous spiral ridge of mucous membrane in the large intestine of fishes of the more primitive groups (as elasmobranchs, ganoids, dipnoans) that makes a number of complete turns increasing the surface for absorption and retarding the passage of food
spiral vessel *n* **:** a trachea or vessel having the walls spirally thickened — called also *spiral duct*
spiral wheel *n* **:** SCREW WHEEL
spi·ran \'spī,ran\ *or* **spi·rane** \-rān\ *n* -s [*spir-* + *-an* or *-ane*] **:** a spiro compound
spi·rant \'spīrənt\ *n* -s [ISV, fr. L *spirant-, spirans,* pres. part. of *spirare* to breathe — more at SPIRIT] **1 :** a consonant that is not a stop, affricate, nasal, voiced lateral, flap, trill, or semivowel (as in English \f\, \v\, \th\, \t͟h\, \s\, \z\, \sh\, \zh\, or \h\) **2 :** a consonant that is not a stop or affricate **3 :** a member of any classification intermediate between spirant (sense 1) and spirant (sense 2)
spi·ran·tal \(')spī¦rantᵊl\ *or* **spi·rant** \'spīrənt\ *adj* [*spirantal* fr. *spirant,* n. + *-al; spirant* ISV, fr. L *spirant-, spirans,* pres. part. of *spirare*] **:** of, relating to, or of the nature of a spirant
spi·ran·thes \spī'ran(t)(,)thēz\ *n, cap* [NL, fr. *spir-* + *-anthes*] **:** a large widely distributed genus of terrestrial orchids with slender often twisted spikes of white irregular flowers — see SCREW AUGER
spi·ran·tic \(')spī¦rantik\ *adj* **:** SPIRANTAL
spi·rant·ism \'spīrənt·,izəm\ *n* -s **:** spirantal nature ⟨in these sounds ~ is retained —R.F.Spencer⟩
spi·rant·iza·tion \,spīrəntə'zāshən, -rənt·,ī'z-\ *n* -s **:** the action or process of spirantizing
spi·rant·ize \'spīrənt·,īz\ *vt* ED/-ING/-S **:** to make spirantal
spi·ras·ter \(')spī¦rastə(r)\ *n* -s [NL, fr. *spir-* + *-aster*] **:** a spiral sponge spicule of one or more turns produced on the outside into several spines
spiration *n* -s [L *spiration-, spiratio* action of breathing, fr. *spiratus* (past part. of *spirare* to breathe) + *-ion-, -io* -ion] **1 a** *obs* **:** the action of breathing as a creative or life-giving function of the Deity **b** (1) **:** the act by or manner in which the Holy Spirit proceeds from the Father or from the Father and the Son (2) **:** the relation subsisting by virtue of this procession **2** *obs* **:** the action of breathing as a physical function of man and animals
¹spire \'spī(ə)r, -īə\ *n* -s [ME *spir, spire,* fr. OE *spīr;* akin to MD *spier* shoot, blade of grass, ON *spīra* stalk, L *spina* thorn, spine — more at SPINE] **1 :** a slender tapering blade or stalk (as of grass or grain) **2 a** *obs* **:** a germinating plant **:** SPROUT **b** *dial Brit* **:** SAPLING **3 :** the top or end of something and esp. of something held to taper to a point **:** the sharp tip **:** PINNACLE ⟨the ~ of a tree⟩ ⟨a ~ of flame⟩ **4 :** a conical heap or pile **:** a mass of pyramidal form ⟨~*s* of rock⟩ **5 a :** a steeply tapering roof or analogous pyramidal construction surmounting a tower or towerlike structure **b :** STEEPLE

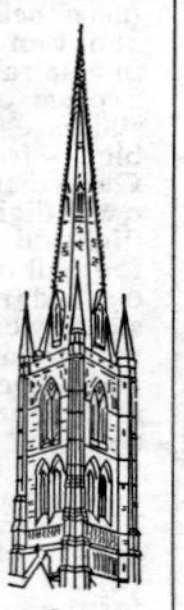
spire 5a

²spire \"\ *vi* -ED/-ING/-S [ME *spiren,* fr. *spir, spire,* n.] **1 :** to send forth or develop shoots **:** GERMINATE, SPROUT ⟨seeds ~ under suitable conditions⟩ **2** *of a plant* **:** to run to stalk or stem **:** become spindly **3 :** to shoot up into a spire **:** run up taperingly like a spire **:** mount or soar aloft ⟨a towering crag . . . *spired* up —Thomas Gray⟩
³spire \"\ *n* -s [L *spira* coil, twist, fr. Gk *speira;* akin to Gk *sparton* rope, esparto, Lith *springti* to choke on something] **1 :** SPIRAL **:** a sinuous winding (as of a serpent) **:** COIL, CURL, TWIST, WHORL **2 :** a series of curls or coils **3 :** the upper part of a spiral shell including the whole series of whorls except the last or body whorl **4 :** SPIRALIUM
⁴spire \"\ *vi* -ED/-ING/-S **:** to rise, fall, or otherwise move in or as if in a spiral **:** mount or soar spirally ⟨up, up ~*s* the song —Amy Lowell⟩
spi·rea *or* **spi·raea** \spī'rēə\ *n* -s [NL *Spiraea*] **1 :** a shrub of the genus *Spiraea* **2 :** any of several commonly cultivated plants that resemble members of the genus *Spiraea; esp* **:** a shrub (*Astilbe japonica*) often forced by florists for Easter blooming
spirea aphid *n* **:** GREEN CITRUS APHID
spire–bearer \'=,==\ *n* [³*spire* + *bearer;* trans. of NL *Spirifer*] **:** SPIRIFER 2
¹spired \'spī(ə)rd, -īəd\ *adj* [¹*spire* + *-ed*] **1 :** having a spire ⟨a ~ steeple⟩ ⟨a ~ church⟩ **:** characterized by spires ⟨a ~ English village —Mary Ross⟩ **2 :** tapering usu. to a sharp point **:** SLENDER, POINTED ⟨a ~ Englemann's spruce —R.L. Neuberger⟩
²spired \"\ *adj* [³*spire* + *-ed*] **:** having a spire **:** SPIRAL ⟨a ~ shell⟩
spire·let \'spī(ə)rlət\ *n* -s **:** a small spire **:** FLÈCHE
spire lily *n* **:** SUMMER HYACINTH
spi·reme \'spī,rēm\ *also* **spi·rem** \-rem\ *n* -s [G *spirem,* fr. Gk *speirēma, speirama* coil, fr. *speira* coil, twist — more at SPIRE] **:** a continuous thread observed in fixed preparations of cells in the prophase of mitosis that gives the appearance of being a strand of chromatin but is generally held to be an observational or technical artifact — compare CHROMOSOME
spire–steeple \'=,==\ *n, archaic* **:** a steeple surmounted by a spire **:** a church spire
spiri- — see SPIR-
spi·ri·cle \'spīrəkəl\ *n* -s [*spir-* + *-cle*] **:** one of the minute coiled threads in the coating of some seeds that uncoil when moistened
spi·ri·fer \'spīrəfə(r)\ *n* [NL, fr. *spir-* + *-fer*] **1** *cap* **:** a large genus (the type of the family Spiriferidae) of articulate brachiopods that have the arms supported within the shell by long spirally coiled spiralia which form a pair of cones with their apexes directed more or less laterally toward the ends of the long hinge line and that abound in Silurian, Devonian, and Carboniferous formations **2** *or* **spi·rif·er·id** \spī'rifərəd\ -s [*spiriferid* fr. NL *Spiriferidae* family of brachiopods, fr. *Spirifer,* type genus + *-idae*] **:** any brachiopod of *Spirifer* or a related genus — called also *spire-bearer*
spi·rif·era \spī'rif(ə)rə\ *syn of* SPIRIFER
spi·rif·er·a·cea \(,)spī,rifə'rāshēə\ *n* -s [NL, fr. *Spirifer* + *-acea*] **:** a suborder or superfamily of Brachiopoda comprising all the Telotremata with calcareous spiral supports for the arms
spi·rif·er·oid \(')spī¦rifə,rȯid\ *adj* [NL *Spirifer* + E *-oid*] **:** belonging to or characteristic of the genus *Spirifer* — see BRACHIOPOD illustration
spi·rif·er·ous \(')spī¦rif(ə)rəs\ *adj* [prob. fr. NL *spirifer* spiriferous (fr. *spir-* + *-fer* -ferous) + E *-ous*] **1 a :** having a spiral part or organ **b :** SPIRED **2** [*spirifer* + *-ous*] **:** containing or characterized by brachiopods of the suborder Spiriferacea — used esp. of rock
spi·ri·form \'spīrə,fȯrm\ *adj* [NL *spiriformis,* fr. *spir-* + L *-formis* -form] **:** resembling a spire or a spiral in form
spi·ril·la·ce·ae \,spīrə'lāsē,ē\ *n pl, cap* [NL, fr. *Spirillum* + *-aceae*] **:** a family comprising rigid more or less spirally curved elongate bacteria that lack endospores and always divide transversely and are sometimes included as a tribe in Pseudomonadaceae — **spi·ril·la·ceous** \¦==¦lāshəs\ *adj*
spi·ril·lar \(')spī¦rilə(r)\ *adj* [*spirillum* + *-ar*] **:** belonging to the genus *Spirillum* **:** resembling a spirillum
spi·ril·lary \'spīrə,lerē, (')spī¦rilərē\ *adj* [*spirillum* + *-ary*] **:** caused by spirilla
spi·ril·li·ci·dal \(,)spī,rilə'sīdᵊl, =¦==,==\ *adj* [*spirillum* + *-i-* + *-cidal*] **:** destroying spirilla ⟨~ action⟩
spi·ril·lum \spī'riləm\ *n* [NL, dim. of L *spira* coil, twist — more at SPIRE] **1** *cap* **:** a genus of bacteria formerly coextensive with the family Spirillaceae but now restricted to elongated forms having tufts of flagella at one or both poles and usu. living in stagnant water rich in organic matter — compare RAT-BITE FEVER, VIBRIO **2** *pl* **spiril·la** \-lə\ **a :** any bacterium of the genus Spirillum or of the group to which it belongs — compare SPIRILLACEAE **b :** SPIROCHETE
¹spiring *adj* [fr. gerund of ²*spire*] **:** rising taperingly to or as if to a point **:** soaring aloft **:** reaching to a great height ⟨~ summits of vast mountains —Thomas Pennant⟩ ⟨~ grass⟩
²spiring *adj* [fr. gerund of ⁴*spire*] **:** rising spirally ⟨a ~ stairway⟩
¹spir·it \'spirət, *chiefly dial* 'sper-; *usu* -əd·+V\ *n* -s *often attrib* [ME, fr. OF or L; OF *spirit, espirit, esperit,* fr. L *spiritus* spirit, breath; akin to ON *fīsa* to break wind, L *spirare* to breathe, and perh. to OSlav *piskati* to play a reed instrument] **1 :** the breath of life **:** the animating or vital principle giving life to physical organisms **2 a :** a supernatural being (as an apparition, specter, sprite, or elf) **b :** a supernatural, incorporeal, rational being or personality usu. invisible to human beings but having the power to become visible at will; *esp* **:** one held to be troublesome, terrifying, or hostile to mankind **c :** a supernatural being held to be able to enter into and possess a person ⟨possessed by a malign ~⟩ **d :** a being having an incorporeal or immaterial nature ⟨God is a ~ —Jn 4:24 (AV)⟩ **3** *usu cap* **a :** the active essence of the Deity serving as an invisible and life-giving or inspiring power in motion ⟨the *Spirit* of God was a silent partner in the production of many of these first Christian . . . sermons —H. H.Meyer⟩ **b :** one manifestation of the divine nature **:** one of the persons of the Trinity **:** HOLY SPIRIT ⟨at Pentecost the *Spirit* came down from heaven as cloven tongues of fire —D. C.Simpson⟩ **4 a :** SOUL ⟨into thy hands I commit my ~ —Lk 23:46 (RSV)⟩ **b :** a disembodied soul existing as an independent entity **:** the soul departed from the body of a deceased person **5 a :** temper or disposition of mind **:** DISPOSITION, MOOD — usu. used in pl. ⟨in good ~*s*⟩ ⟨in bad ~*s*⟩ **b :** mental vigor or animation **:** CHEERFULNESS, LIVELINESS, VIVACITY ⟨full of ~*s*⟩ **6 :** the immaterial intelligent or sentient part of a person **:** the vital principle in man coming as a gift from God and providing one's personality with its inward structure, dynamic drive, and creative response to the demands it encounters in the process of becoming **7 a :** the activating or essential principle of something (as an emotion or frame of mind) influencing a person **b :** an inclination, impulse, or tendency of a specified kind **8** *archaic* **:** the emotional source of hostile or angry feeling in a person **9** *often cap* **:** life or consciousness having an independent type of existence ⟨idealists maintain that the essential nature of the universe is ~⟩ ⟨pantheists assert that ~ pervades the universe⟩ **10** *archaic* **:** a movement of the air **:** a breath of wind **:** BREEZE, WIND ⟨the balmy ~ of the western gale —Alexander Pope⟩ **11 spirits** *pl* **:** bodily constitution that is the source of energy and strength **:** vital power **:** physical energy **:** the normal operation of the vital functions **12 :** a subtle substance (as a kind of breath or vapor) formerly held to permeate the blood and the principal body organs and to animate the body as a physical organism — usu. used in pl.; see ANIMAL SPIRITS, NATURAL SPIRITS, VITAL SPIRITS **13 spirits** *pl, obs* **:** mental constitution that is the source of perception and active thought **:** mental powers **:** INTELLECT ⟨his ~ should hunt after new fancies —Shak.⟩ **14 a :** a special attitude or frame of mind characterizing an individual or group **:** a character, disposition, or temper peculiar to and often animating a particular individual or group **b :** the frame of mind, feeling, or disposition characterizing something (as an action, consideration, or view) **15 a :** a lively or brisk quality in something **b :** stimulated or high characteristics (as liveliness, energy, vivacity, ardor, enthusiasm, or courage) in a person or his actions **16 :** an individual person considered with reference to characteristics of mind or temper **:** one having a character or disposition of a specified nature **17 :** a mental disposition characterized by firmness or assertiveness **:** ARDOR, COURAGE, METTLE **18 a** *archaic* **:** a liquid produced by distillation **b :** the flammable liquid containing ordinary alcohol and water as its main ingredients that is separated by distillation from any alcoholic liquor or mash and that is colorless and flavorless if highly rectified but that in the case of whiskey, brandy, or similar liquors derives its qualities from the nature of the source (as grain or fruit) from which it is made ⟨taxable distilled ~*s* —*U. S. Code*⟩ — often used in pl.; compare DISTILLED LIQUOR, METHYLATED SPIRIT, PROOF SPIRIT **c :** any of various volatile liquids obtained by distillation and sometimes by cracking (as of petroleum, shale, or wood) and used chiefly as fuels and solvents ⟨shale ~⟩ — often used in pl.; see MOTOR SPIRIT, PETROLEUM SPIRIT, WOOD SPIRIT **d :** ALCOHOL 3, RECTIFIED SPIRIT **e :** any of various usu. volatile organic solvents (as other alcohols, esters, ketones, or hydrocarbons) used similarly to alcohol — compare SPIRIT-SOLUBLE **19** *obs* **:** a volatile agent or essence that is a constituent and usu. life-giving element of a natural body ⟨the ~*s* . . . that are in all tangible bodies are scarce known —Francis Bacon⟩ **20 a :** the essential character of something **:** characteristic quality esp. as derived from individual genius or personal character **:** the pervading principle of something **b :** the prevailing tone or tendency ⟨the ~ of the age⟩ ⟨the ~ of the enterprise⟩ **c :** the general intent or real meaning of something (as a statement or law) — opposed to *letter* **21 :** an alcoholic solution of a volatile substance (as an essential oil) ⟨~ of peppermint⟩ **:** ALCOHOLATE 2 — called also *essence;* compare ELIXIR 2, TINCTURE **22 :** any of various solutions esp. of tin salts used as mordants in dyeing ⟨aniline ~⟩ ⟨scarlet ~⟩ **23 :** enthusiastic loyalty ⟨school ~⟩ ⟨class ~⟩ ⟨college ~⟩ **24** *Hegelianism* **:** the complex of human institutions (as family, society, state, and church) and productions in art, poetry, science, and culture **25** *cap, Christian Science* **:** ²GOD b(6) **syn** see COURAGE, VIGOR — **in spirits :** in a cheerful or joyful frame of mind **:** ANIMATED, ELATED, HAPPY — **out of spirits :** in a depressed frame of mind **:** LOW-SPIRITED
²spirit \"\ *vt* -ED/-ING/-S **1** *archaic* **:** to make (as the blood or a liquor) more lively or active ⟨our quick blood, ~*ed* with wine —Shak.⟩ **2 :** to infuse with energy, ardor, or life **:** ANIMATE, ENCOURAGE, INSPIRIT, STIMULATE ⟨some rum . . . to ~ me for what was before me —Daniel Defoe⟩ — sometimes used with *up* ⟨~ up our captives —Robert Browning⟩ ⟨inspire some . . . maid to ~ up her countrymen —Thomas Paine⟩ **3** *obs* **a :** to invest with a spirit or animating principle ⟨thy high commands must ~ all our wars —Alexander Pope⟩ **b :** to endow with a special spirit or character **4 a :** to carry off, make away with, or remove rapidly and secretly or mysteriously as if by the agency of a spirit ⟨seemed to ~ the things off the table without sound or effort —R.S.Surtees⟩ ⟨he ~*ed* from the files . . . canceled checks and other records —H.H.Martin⟩ — sometimes used with *away* ⟨residents . . . ~*ed* away the records —*Amer. Guide Series: La.*⟩ **b :** to convey to a destination in a secret or mysterious way ⟨managed to ~ the proprietor out of town —*Amer. Guide Series: Nev.*⟩ ⟨~*ed* his ensemble aboard a westbound liner —Ann M. Lingg⟩ — sometimes used with *away* ⟨was ~*ed* away to a secret hideaway —*Associated Press*⟩ **c :** to abduct or cause to disappear mysteriously **:** KIDNAP — usu. used with *away* ⟨women and children . . . ~*ed* away to America to be sold into bondage —*Amer. Guide Series: N.C.*⟩ ⟨the man was ~*ed* away, badly beaten, and sent back —J.A.Michener⟩ **5** *archaic* **:** to bring about **:** INSTIGATE — usu. used with *up* ⟨determined to ~ up a cruel war —John & William Langhorne⟩
spirit baptism *n, usu cap S* **:** baptismal purification by the Holy Spirit's entry into one's life as an indwelling force
spirit blue *n, often cap S&B* **:** any of several alcohol-soluble triphenylmethane dyes that are phenyl derivatives of pararosaniline or fuchsine — see SOLUBLE BLUE 1; DYE table I (under *Solvent Blue 3*)
spirit butterfly *n* **:** any of numerous delicate butterflies (genus *Ithomia*) of tropical America having gauzy wings nearly destitute of scales
spirit compass *n* **:** a liquid compass using a mixture of alcohol and water
spirit duck *n* **1 :** BUFFLEHEAD **2 :** GOLDENEYE
spirit duplicating *n* [*duplicating* fr. gerund of ³*duplicate*] **:** a duplicating-printing process utilizing master sheets that release color through type indentations when a colorless chemical fluid is applied
spir·it·ed \'spirəd·əd, -rətəd\ *adj* [¹*spirit* + *-ed*] **1** *obs* **:** impregnated with elements that activate or make more lively **2 :** full of life or vigor **:** characterized by or displaying animation **:** full of spirit or fire **:** showing energy or enterprise **:** having or suggesting vigor ⟨the ~ yet tractable bride —Henry Cavendish⟩ ⟨drawings of hunters and racehorses —Harrison Smith⟩ ⟨a ~ debate⟩ ⟨a ~ answer⟩ — often used in combination; see HIGH-SPIRITED, MEANSPIRITED, PUBLIC-SPIRITED
spir·it·ed·ly *adv* **:** in a spirited manner **:** with animation, liveliness, or vivacity ⟨writes directly and ~ —G.R.Crone⟩
spiritedness *n* -ES **:** the quality or state of being spirited **:** ANIMATION, LIVELINESS, VIVACITY ⟨her natural ~ detested the monotony —George Meredith⟩ — often used in combination ⟨mean-*spiritedness*⟩ ⟨public-*spiritedness*⟩
spir·it·ful \'spirətfəl\ *adj* **1** *archaic* **:** full of spirit or vigor **:** ANIMATED, SPIRITED, VIGOROUS ⟨a charming creature . . . but confoundedly smart and ~ —Samuel Richardson⟩ **2** *obs* **:** SPIRITUOUS 3
spirit ground *n* **:** an aquatint ground made by dissolving resin in spirits of wine, evaporating the spirits, and leaving a dry grain on the plate
spirit gum *n* **:** a solution of a gum (as of gum arabic in ether) used esp. for attaching a wig or other false hair to exposed parts of the skin
spir·it·ism \'spirəd·,izəm, -rə,ti-\ *n* -s **1 a :** a theory that mediumistic phenomena are caused by spirits of the dead **b :** the action or agency of such spirits **2 :** a belief that natural objects possess indwelling spirits — compare ANIMISM 2 **3 :** SPIRITUALISM 2
spir·it·ist \-əd·əst, -ətə-\ *n* -s **:** one who believes in or attempts to put in practice spiritism; *specif* **:** SPIRITUALIST
spir·it·is·tic \¦spirəd·¦istik, -rə¦tis-\ *adj* **:** of, relating to, or believing in spirits or phenomena connected with spirits
spir·it·ize \'spirəd·,īz, -rə,tīz\ *vt* -ED/-ING/-S **:** to implant a spirit in **:** imbue with spirits
spirit lamp *n* **:** a lamp in which a volatile liquid fuel (as alcohol) is burned ⟨made some coffee over a *spirit lamp* —Joseph Conrad⟩

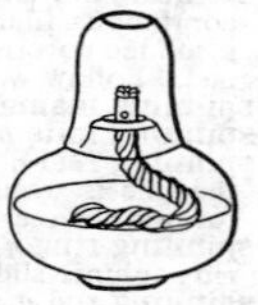
spirit lamp

spir·it·less \'spirətləs\ *adj* **1 :** destitute of spirit or vital principle **:** DEAD, LIFELESS ⟨the ~ body should be restored to the earth —Thomas Greenhill⟩ **2 :** wanting animation or cheerfulness **:** lacking lively or cheerful spirits **:** DEJECTED, DEPRESSED, DISPIRITED **3 :** destitute of vigor or energy **:** wanting life, courage, or fire **:** lacking ardor or boldness **syn** see LANGUID
spir·it·less·ly *adv* **:** in a spiritless manner
spir·it·less·ness *n* -ES **:** the quality or state of being spiritless
spirit level *n* **:** LEVEL 1a
spirit of ether : an anodyne mixture of approximately two parts alcohol and one part ether — called also *Hoffmann's drops;* compare COMPOUND SPIRIT OF ETHER
spirit off *vt* **:** to finish (as varnish or lacquer) with a coat of solvent
spirit of hartshorn *or* **spirits of hartshorn :** AMMONIA WATER
spirit of niter 1 : a liquid containing 68 or 70 percent by weight of absolute nitric acid with the remainder water **2 :** ETHYL NITRITE SPIRIT
spirit of nitrous ether : ETHYL NITRITE SPIRIT
spirit of salt *or* **spirits of salt** *archaic* **:** HYDROCHLORIC ACID
spirit of vitriol *archaic* **:** SULFURIC ACID
spir·i·to·so \,spirə'tō(,)sō, -)zō\ *adj* [It, fr. *spirito* spirit (fr. L *spiritus*) + *-oso* -ose (fr. L *-osus*) — more at SPIRIT] **:** ANIMATED — used as a direction in music
spir·it·ous \'spirəd·əs\ *adj* [¹*spirit* + *-ous*] **1** *archaic* **:** resembling or of the nature of spirit **:** PURE, REFINED **2** *obs* **:** characterized by high spirits **:** ARDENT, ANIMATED **3 :** SPIRITUOUS 3
spirit rapping *n* **:** an alleged form of communication with the spirits of the dead by raps — compare SPIRITUALISM 2
spirits *pl of* SPIRIT, *pres 3d sing of* SPIRIT
spirits of turpentine *or* **spirit of turpentine :** TURPENTINE 2a
spirits of wine *or* **spirit of wine :** RECTIFIED SPIRIT, ALCOHOL 3
spirit–soluble \¦==¦===\ *adj* **:** soluble in alcohol or other organic solvent used similarly — often distinguished from *oil-soluble* and *water-soluble* ⟨*spirit-soluble* dyes⟩ ⟨the *spirit-soluble* natural resins⟩
¹spir·i·tu·al \'spirəch(ə)wəl, -chəl *sometimes* -rēch-\ *adj* [ME *spirituel, spiritual,* fr. MF & ML; MF *spirituel,* fr. ML *spiritualis,* alter. (influenced by L *spiritus* spirit) of LL *spiritalis,* fr. L, of breathing, of wind, fr. *spiritus* spirit, breath + *-alis* -al — more at SPIRIT] **1 :** of, relating to, or consisting of spirit **:** of the nature of spirit rather than material **:** INCORPOREAL — contrasted with *earthy* **2 a :** of or relating to religious or sacred matters ⟨~ leaders⟩ **b :** SACRED ⟨~ songs⟩ **c :** ecclesiastical rather than lay or temporal ⟨lords ~ and temporal⟩ ⟨eight members, four ~ and four lay⟩ **3 :** of or relating to the moral feelings or states of the soul as distinguished from the external actions **:** reaching and affecting the spirit **4 a :** influenced or controlled by the divine Spirit **:** having a nature in which a concern for the Spirit of God predominates ⟨~ man⟩ **b :** proceeding from or under the influence of the Holy Spirit **:** concerned with religious values **:** seeking earnestly to live in a right relation to God ⟨a ~ Christian⟩ **c :** HOLY, DIVINE ⟨to become ~ and perfected⟩ **d :** RELIGIOUS ⟨Islam's ~ foundations⟩ **5 :** related or joined in spirit **:** spiritually akin **:** having a relationship one to another based on matters of the spirit ⟨her ~ home⟩ ⟨regarded her pastor as her ~ father⟩ ⟨came to believe himself the ~ heir of the French poet —Allen Tate⟩ **6** *archaic* **:** consisting of spirit **:** ALCOHOLIC, SPIRITUOUS 3 **7 :** of, relating to, or coming from the intellectual and higher endowments of the mind **:** INTELLECTUAL, MENTAL — contrasted with *animal* **8 :** highly refined in thought or feeling **9 :** SPIRITED, CLEVER, WITTY **10 :** having to do with spirits, ghosts, or similar supernatural beings or with the world which they are held to people **11 :** SPIRITUALISTIC
²spiritual \"\ *n* -s **1 spirituals** *pl* **:** things (as functions, offices, affairs, matters, or possessions) of a spiritual, ecclesiastical, or religious nature ⟨assigns supremacy to the pope in ~*s* and to the emperor in temporals —J.R.Lowell⟩ **2 :** a Negro religious song esp. of the southern U. S. distinguished by the graphic narrative method characteristic of the folk ballad and by strongly marked rhythm that is frequently emphasized in singing by swaying or other motions
spiritual bouquet *n* **:** an offering by a Roman Catholic of a number of promised or performed devotional acts undertaken on behalf of a person on special occasions (as name days or anniversaries) or of someone recently deceased esp. as an expression of sympathy
spiritual court *n* [ME *spirituall court,* fr. *spirituel, spiritual, spirituall* spiritual + *court*] **:** ECCLESIASTICAL COURT
spiritual director *n* **:** a confessor in the Roman Catholic Church whose advice and direction are regularly and frequently sought by one seeking spiritual advancement
spir·i·tu·al·ism \-ə,lizəm\ *n* -s [prob. fr. (assumed) NL *spiritualismus,* fr. ML *spiritualis* spiritual + L *-ismus* -ism] **1 :** a doctrine that all that exists is spirit **:** IDEALISM; *esp* **:** metaphysical idealism — compare MATERIALISM **2 a :** a belief that departed spirits hold intercourse with mortals usu. through a medium by means of rapping and other physical phenomena or during abnormal mental states (as trances) **b :** the doctrines and practices of spiritualists **3 :** the quality or state of being spiritual **:** spiritual nature or essence **:** SPIRITUALITY
spir·i·tu·al·ist \-ələst\ *n* -s [prob. fr. (assumed) NL *spiritualista,* fr. ML *spiritualis* spiritual + L *-ista* -ist] **1 :** one whose chief interest is in spiritual things and who tends to interpret things in a spiritual sense **:** a spiritually minded person **:** one whose ideas have a spiritual basis **2 :** one who maintains the doctrine of philosophical spiritualism **3 a :** one who believes in spiritualism **:** one who seeks intercourse with departed spirits **b** *usu cap* **:** a member of a religious organization practicing or believing in spiritualism
spir·i·tu·al·is·tic \¦spirəch(ə)wə¦listik, -chə¦l-, -tēk *sometimes* -rēch-\ *or* **spir·i·tu·al·ist** \'====ləst, '===¦ləst\ *adj* **:** of, relating to, or connected with spiritualism — **spir·i·tu·al·is·ti·cal·ly** \-¦listək(ə)lē, -tēk-, -)li\ *adv*
spir·i·tu·al·i·ty \,spirəch(ə)'waləd·ē, -lətē, -i *sometimes* -rēch-\ *n* -ES [ME *spiritualite,* fr. MF or ML; MF *spiritualité, espiritualité,* fr. ML *spiritualitat-, spiritualitas,* fr. *spiritualis* spiritual + L *-tat-, -tas* -ty] **1 :** something that in ecclesiastical law belongs to the church or to a person as an ecclesiastic or to

religion: as **a spiritualities** *pl* : spiritual or ecclesiastical things : ecclesiastical possessions or rights of a purely spiritual character : fees, dues, or tithes receivable by an ecclesiastic as such **b** : something having a spiritual character; *esp* : ecclesiastical property or revenue held or received in return for spiritual services — compare TEMPORALITY **2** : the whole body of clergy (as in a nation or country) : the body of spiritual or ecclesiastical persons : CHURCH, CLERGY ⟨subsidies . . . granted to the king by the ~ —Thomas Fuller⟩ — distinguished from *temporalty* **3** : sensitivity or attachment to religious values and things of the spirit rather than material or worldly interests ⟨a man of deep ~ —R.L.Patterson⟩ **4** *archaic* : something incorporeal; *specif* : SPIRIT **5** *obs* : the quality or state of being spirituous : VOLATILITY **6 a** : the quality or state of being spiritual **b** : something having a spiritual as distinguished from a worldly or material character **c** : existence purely in a spiritual state : the quality or state of being incorporeal

spir·i·tu·al·iza·tion \ˌspirəch(ə)wələˈzāshən, -chəlo-, -ˌliˈz- *sometimes* -rēch-\ *n* -s [prob. fr. (assumed) NL *spiritualization-*, *spiritualizatio*, fr. (assumed) NL *spiritualizatus* (past part. of *spiritualizare*) + L *-ion-*, *-io* -ion] : the action of spiritualizing or the state of being spiritualized

spir·i·tu·al·ize \ˈ···ˌlīz, ˈ···ˌlīz\ *vt* -ED/-ING/-S [prob. fr. (assumed) NL *spiritualizare*, fr. ML *spiritualis* spiritual + LL *-izare* -ize] **1** : to make spiritual : refine intellectually or morally : purify from the corrupting influences of the world : give a spiritual character or tendency to **2** *obs* : to convert into or impregnate with spirit : make volatile or spirituous **3** : to give a spiritual meaning to : take in a spiritual sense — opposed to *literalize* **4** : to endow with the nature and attributes of a spirit

spir·i·tu·al·iz·er \-ˌzə(r)\ *n* -s : one that spiritualizes

spiritual living *n*, *Brit* : BENEFICE

spir·i·tu·al·ly \ˈspirēch(ə)lē, -ch(ə)wəlē, -li *sometimes* -rēch-\ *adv* [ME *spiritualy*, *spiritualy*, fr. *spiritual*, *spiritual* spiritual + *-ly*] **1** : in a spiritual way : in connection with things of the spirit — distinguished from *materially* **2** : in an ethereal or supernatural manner : SUPERNATURALLY — distinguished from *naturally*

spiritually-mind·ed \ˈ···ˌ·ˈ·\ *adj* : having the mind set on spiritual things : filled with holy desires and purposes — SPIRITUAL

spiritual-minded·ness *n* -ES : the quality or state of being spiritually-minded

spir·i·tu·al·ness *n* -ES : the quality or state of being spiritual — SPIRITUALITY

spir·i·tu·al·ty *pronunc at* ¹SPIRITUAL + ˌtē\ *n* -ES [ME *spiritualte*, fr. MF *spiritualté*, fr. ML *spiritualitat-*, *spiritualitas* — more at SPIRITUALITY] **1 spiritualties** *pl* : SPIRITUALITY 1a ⟨a complete list of the ... temporalties and *spiritualties* belonging to a parish church —*English Historical Rev.*⟩ **2** : SPIRITUALITY 2 ⟨may regard the ~ of England . . . as a body completely organized —William Stubbs⟩

spir·i·tu·el *or* **spir·i·tu·elle** \ˌspirə̇ch(ə)ˈwel, -ˈel, |təˈwel, |·ˈtwel\ *adj* [*spirituel* fr. F, lit., spiritual; *spirituelle* fr. F, fem. of *spirituel* — more at SPIRITUAL] : having or characterized by a highly refined and esp. sprightly, bright, or witty nature ⟨writes with a tenderness which is ~ rather than spiritual —Malcolm Muggeridge⟩ ⟨a personality as *spirituelle* and knowing as any practicing *spirituelle* —Jean Stafford⟩

spir·i·tu·os·i·ty \ˌspirə̇ch(ə)ˈwäsəd·ē\ *n* -ES [fr. *spirituous*, after such pairs as E *generous*: *generosity*] : the quality or state of being spirituous ⟨~ of wines and liquors⟩

spir·i·tu·ous \ˈspirə̇ch(ə)wəs, -chəs, -·ˈrəd·əs, ·-rəd·əs *sometimes* -rēch-\ *adj* [prob. modif. (influenced by E ¹*spirit* and *-ous*) of Sp *espirituoso*, fr. *espíritu* spirit (fr. L *spiritus*) + *-oso* -ose (fr. L *-osus*) — more at SPIRIT] **1** *archaic* : spirited in character or behavior : ANIMATED ⟨her once gay and ~ behavior —Eliza Haywood⟩ **2** *archaic* : SPIRITUAL **3** : containing or of the nature of spirit : impregnated with alcohol obtained by distillation : ALCOHOLIC, ARDENT ⟨~ liquors⟩ ⟨~ beverages⟩

spir·i·tu·ous·ness *n* -ES *obs* : SPIRITUOSITY

spir·i·tus \ˈspirəd·əs, in *ecclesiastical use often* -pirē,t̪ūs *or* -pērē,t̪ūs\ *n* [NL, fr. L, spirit, breath] **1** : SPIRIT 21 **2** [LL, fr. L, spirit, breath] : BREATHING 2

spiritus as·per \-ˈaspə(r)\ *n* [LL] : ROUGH BREATHING

spiritus fru·men·ti \-früˈmentē, -n-,tī\ *n* [NL, lit., spirit of grain] : WHISKEY

spiritus le·nis \-ˈlānəs, -ˈlen-,-ˈlēn-\ *n* [LL] : SMOOTH BREATHING

spirit varnish *n* : an artificial varnish composed of a solution of natural or artificial resin, asphalt, or a cellulose ester (as pyroxylin) in a volatile solvent (as alcohol, spirits of turpentine, or amyl acetate) ⟨a common *spirit varnish* is a solution of shellac in alcohol⟩

spirit vinegar *n* : VINEGAR 1

spirit wrestler *n*, *usu cap* *S&W* [trans. of Russ *dukhoborets* Doukhobor] : DOUKHOBOR

spirit writing *n* : automatic writing held to be produced under the influence of spirits — compare PNEUMATOGRAPHY

spir·i·ty \ˈspirə̇d·ē\ *adj*, *dial* : SPIRITED, LIVELY

spirit yellow *n*, *usu cap* *S&T* : either of two solvent dyes — see DYE table I (under *Solvent Yellow 1* and *3*)

spi·ri·valve \ˈspirə,+,-\ *adj* [ISV *spir-* + *valve*, n.; prob. orig. formed in F] : having a spiral shell — used of a gastropod mollusk

spir·ket·ing \ˈspərˌkétiŋ\ *n* -s [obs. E *spirket*, *spurket* space between floor timbers of a ship forward or aft + E *-ing*] : planking consisting of timbers that are heavier than the ceiling and are worked above the waterways in a wooden ship — see SHIP illustration

spirketing plate *n* : the spirketing in a steel ship

spir·ling \ˈspərˌliŋ\ *n* [ME *spyrlyng*, fr. MD *spierlinc* — more at SPARLING] *chiefly Scot* : SPARLING

spi·ro- \ˈspī(,)rō\ *adj* [*spir-*] : of or relating to a compound or system that contains two rings having a single atom in common — compare SPIR- 2

¹spiro- *comb form* [ISV *spir-* (fr. L *spirare* to breathe) + *-o-* — more at SPIR-] : respiration ⟨*spirometer*⟩

²spiro- — see SPIR-

spiro·atom *n* : an atom (as a carbon atom) that is common to two rings in the molecule of a compound

spi·ro·cer·ca \ˌspirōˈsərkə\ *n*, *cap* [NL, fr. *spir-* + *-cerca* (fr. Gk *kerkos* tail)] : a genus of red filarial worms (family Thelaziidae) forming nodules in the walls of the digestive tract and sometimes the aorta of dogs and other canines esp. in warm regions

spi·ro·chae·ta \ˌspirōˈkēd·ə\ *n* [NL, fr. *spir-* + *-chaeta*] **1** *cap* : a genus (the type of the family Spirochaetaceae) of spirochetes distinguished by a flexible undulating body with the protoplasm wound spirally around an elastic axis filament and comprising as now restricted various chiefly aquatic forms or formerly these together with important pathogens now placed in the genera *Treponema*, *Borrelia*, and *Leptospira* **2** *or* **spi·ro·che·ta** \ˈ·\ *pl* **spirochae·tae** *or* **spiroche·tae** \-ēd·(,)ē\ : SPIROCHETE

spi·ro·chae·ta·ce·ae \ˌspirōkēˈtāsē,ē\ *n pl*, *cap* [NL, *Spirochaeta*, type genus + *-aceae*] : a comprising large coarsely spiral bacteria (order Spirochaetales) that are free-living in fresh or salt water or commensal in the body of oysters — compare TREPONEMATACEAE

spi·ro·chae·ta·les \ˌspirōˌkēˈtālēz\ *n pl*, *cap* [NL, fr. *Spirochaeta* + *-ales*] : an order of higher bacteria comprising slender elongated flexuous spiral forms in which the body makes up at least one complete turn of the spiral — compare SPIROCHAETACEAE, TREPONEMATACEAE

spi·ro·chet·al *or* **spi·ro·chaet·al** \ˌ···ˈkēd·ᵊl\ *adj* : caused by spirochetes ⟨~ jaundice⟩

spi·ro·chete *or* **spi·ro·chaete** \ˈspirə,kēt, *usu* -ēd·+V\ *n* -s [NL *Spirochaeta*] : a bacterium of the order Spirochaetales many of which cause severe diseases (as syphilis and relapsing fever)

spi·ro·chet·emia \ˌspirə,kēd·ˈēmēə\ *n* -s [NL, fr. *Spirochaeta* + *-emia*] : the abnormal presence of spirochetes in the circulating blood

spi·ro·che·tic *or* **spi·ro·chae·tic** \ˌ···ˈkēd·ik\ *adj* : of, relating to, or caused by spirochetes

spi·ro·che·ti·ci·dal \ˌ···ˌkēd·ə·ˈsīd·ᵊl\ *adj* [*spirochete* + *-i-* +

-cidal] : destructive to spirochetes esp. within the body of an animal host ⟨a ~ drug⟩

spi·ro·che·ti·cide *or* **spi·ro·chae·ti·cide** \ˌ···ˈkēd·ə,sīd\ *n* -s [*spirochete* + *-i-* + *-cide*] : an agent (as a drug) capable of killing spirochetes esp. within the human or animal body

spi·ro·chet·osis *or* **spi·ro·chaet·osis** \ˌ···ˌkēd·ˈōsəs\ *n* -ES [NL, fr. *Spirochaeta* + *-osis*] : infection with or a disease (as leptospirosis) caused by spirochetes

spi·ro·cyclic \ˈspirō +\ *adj* [*spiro-* + *cyclic*] : having flower parts in a spiral arrangement that changes phyletically to a cyclic arrangement

spi·ro·de·la \ˌspirəˈdēlə\ *n*, *cap* [NL, fr. *spir-* + *-dela* (fr. Gk *dēlos* visible, evident); fr. the fact that the spiral vessels are visible through the transparent tissues — more at ADEL-] : a genus of aquatic plants (family Lemnaceae) having a membranous spathe and a thallus with a cluster of several rootlets — see GREAT DUCKWEED

spi·ro·gram \ˈspirə,gram\ *n* [ˈspiro- + -gram] : a graphic record of respiratory movements traced on a moving drum

spi·ro·graph \-ˌraf,-ˌräf\ *n* [ISV ˈspiro- + -graph] : an instrument for recording respiratory movements commonly consisting of a spirometer together with a suitable recording device — see SPIROGRAPHIC

spi·ro·graph·ic \ˌspirəˈgrafik\ *adj*

spi·rog·ra·phis \spīˈrägrəfəs\ *n*, *cap* [NL, fr. *spir-* + LGk *graphis* embroidery, fr. Gk, stylus, fr. *graphein* to write — more at CARVE] : a genus of sabelloid annelids with bright-colored gill plumes arranged spirally

spi·ro·gy·ra \ˌspirəˈjīrə\ *n* [NL, fr. *spir-* + *-gyra* (fr. Gk *gyros* ring); akin to Gk *gyros* round — more at COWER] **1** *cap* : a genus of freshwater green algae (family Zygnemataceae) having spiral chlorophyll bands and forming slimy masses in still waters and slow streams **2** -s : any plant of the genus *Spirogyra*

spi·roid \ˈspī·ˌroid\ *also* **spi·roi·dal** \(ˈ)spīˈroidᵊl\ *adj* [*spiroid* fr. NL *spiroides*, fr. Gk *speiroeidēs*, fr. *speira* coil, twist + *-oeidēs* -oid; *spiroidal* ISV *spiroid* + *-al* — more at SPIRE] : resembling a screw : spiral in form

spi·ro·loc·u·line \ˈspī(ˌ)rō,läkyə,līn, -ˌlän\ *adj* [*spir-* + *loculus* + *-ine*] : having chambers arranged spirally — used of a foraminiferan shell

spi·rom·e·ter \spīˈrämə̇d·ə(r)\ *n* [ISV *spiro-* + *-meter*] **1** : an instrument for measuring the air entering and leaving the lungs (as in determining the vital capacity of the lungs) **2** : an instrument used in calibrating gas meters to measure and record the volume of gas

spi·ro·met·ric \ˌspirə̇ˈme·trik\ *adj* [ISV ˈspiro- + -metric] : of, relating to, or using a spirometer ⟨~ studies⟩ : of or relating to spirometry

spi·rom·e·try \spīˈrämə̇tr̄ē\ *n* -ES [ISV ˈspiro- + -metry] : measurement of air or gas by use of a spirometer

spi·ro·pentane \ˌspī(ˌ)rō +\ *n* [ISV *spir-* + *pentane*] : an unstable liquid hydrocarbon C_5H_8 made synthetically — compare STRUCTURAL FORMULA

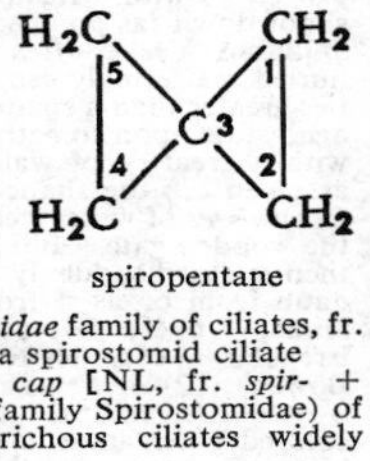

spir·or·bis \spīˈrȯrbəs\ *n*, *cap* [NL, fr. *spir-* + L *orbis* circle, disk — more at ORB] : a genus of small annelids (family Serpulidae) forming a spirally coiled calcareous tube

spiropentane

¹spi·ros·to·mid \(ˈ)spīˈrästəməd\ *adj* [NL *Spirostomidae*] : of or relating to the genus *Spirostomum* or family Spirostomidae

²spirostomid \ˈ·\ *n* -s [NL *Spirostomidae* family of ciliates, fr. *Spirostomum*, type genus + *-idae*] : a spirostomid ciliate

spi·ros·to·mum \spīˈrästəməm\ *n*, *cap* [NL, fr. *spir-* + *-stomum*] : a genus (the type of the family Spirostomidae) of large cylindrical elongated heterotrichous ciliates widely distributed in fresh and salt water

spi·ro·trich \ˈspirə,trik\ *n* -s [NL *Spirotricha*] : a spirotrichous protozoan

spi·rot·ri·cha \spīˈrä·trəkə\ *n pl*, *cap* [NL, fr. *spir-* + *-tricha*] : a large order consisting of euciliate protozoans with well-developed peristome and adoral zone of membranelles and general body cilia that are uniform or variously reduced and fused into body cirri and including the suborders Heterotricha, Oligotricha, and Hypotricha

spi·ro·trich·i·da \ˌspirəˈtrikədə\ [NL, fr. *spir-* + *trich-* + *-ida*] *pl*, *cap* [NL *Spirotricha*] : of or relating to the Spirotricha

spi·rot·ri·chous \(ˈ)spīˈrä·trəkəs\ *adj* [NL *Spirotricha* + E *-ous*] : of or relating to the Spirotricha

spirt *var of* SPURT

spir·tle *vt* [freq. of *spirt*] *obs* : SPATTER, SPLASH

spir·u·la \ˈspir(y)ələ\ *n* [NL, fr. LL, twisted cracknel, fr. L *spira* coil, twist + *-ula* — more at SPIRE] **1** *cap* : a genus (coextensive with a family Spirulidae of the order Decapoda) of small cephalopods related to the extinct belemnites, having a many-chambered shell coiled freely in a flat spiral that is comparable to the phragmocone of the belemnite shell and almost enveloped in the soft parts, and occurring in most tropic seas usu. at great depths from which the shells float to the surface and are cast on beaches, although complete specimens of the animal are rare **2** -s : a cephalopod of the genus *Spirula*

spiru·late \ˈspir(y)ə,lāt, ˈspir-\ *adj* [prob. fr. (assumed) NL *spirulatus*, fr. (assumed) NL *spirula* small coil fr. LL, twisted cracknel) + L *-atus* -ate] : spiral in form or arrangement

spi·ru·ra \spīˈrürə\ *n*, *cap* [NL, fr. *spir-* + *-ura*] : the type genus of Spiruroidea including various parasites of rodents

spi·ru·rid \(ˈ)spīˈrürəd\ *adj* [NL *Spiruridae*, *Spirurida*] : of or relating to the family Spiruridae or the order Spirurida

²spirurid \ˈ·\ *n* -s [NL *Spiruridae*, *Spirurida*] : a spirurid worm

spi·ru·ri·da \spīˈrürədə\ *n pl*, *cap* [NL, fr. *Spirura* + *-ida*] : an order of Aphasmidia comprising parasitic nematode worms with the esophagus cylindroid and not divided into three regions, six lips, no buccal stylet, and the musculature polymyarian and including the guinea worm, the filarial worms, and other parasites of vertebrates that all have complex life cycles requiring an invertebrate intermediate host

spi·ru·ri·dae \-,dē\ *n pl*, *cap* [NL, fr. *Spirura*, type genus + *-idae*] : a family of nematode worms having the adults parasitic in vertebrates and larval stages in insects and with related forms constituting a distinct superfamily of the order Spirurida — see ASCAROPS

¹spi·ru·roid \-ū,rȯid\ *adj* [NL *Spirura* + E *-oid*] : resembling or related to the Spiruroidea

²spiruroid \ˈ·\ *n* -s : a spiruroid worm

¹spiry \ˈspī(ə)rē, -ˌrī\ *adj* [ˈspire + -y] **1** : resembling a spire : tall, slender, and tapering to a point : rising in a slender, tapering form ⟨~ grass⟩ ⟨~ trees⟩ ⟨~ turrets⟩ **2** : abounding in spires ⟨~ towns⟩

²spiry \ˈ·\ *adj* [³spire + -y] *archaic* : of a spiral form : curving or coiling in spirals : CURLED, SERPENTINE, WREATHED ⟨hid in the ~ volumes of the snake —John Dryden⟩

spis·si·tude \ˈspisə,tüd, -ə-,tyüd\ *n* -s [ME *spite*, fr. L *spissitudo*, fr. *spissi-* (fr. *spissus*) + *-tudo* -tude] *archaic* : the quality or state of being thick, dense, or compact : DENSITY, VISCOSITY

spis·u·la \ˈspisələ, -izə-\ *n*, *cap* [NL, perh. irreg. fr. J. B. von Spix †1826 Ger. zoologist] : a genus of surf clams that includes a large yellowish white thick-shelled clam (*S. solidissima*) that is the common edible surf clam of the eastern coast of No. America

¹spit \ˈspit, *usu* |s + ⟨³spit⟩ -\ *n* [ME *spite*, fr. OE *spitu*; akin to MD *spit*, *spet* spit, OHG *spiz* spit, *spizzi* pointed, Icel *spīta* peg, L *spina* thorn — more at SPINE] **1 a** : usu. metal stationary or revolving slender pointed rod for holding meat and other foods while cooking before or over a fire **b** *archaic* : SWORD **c** *dial Brit* : a skewer on which fish (as herring) are hung to dry **d** : SPINDLE 1d **2 a** : a small point of land commonly consisting of sand or gravel deposited by waves and currents and extending into a body of water — compare BAR 2d **b** : a long narrow shoal extending from the shore

²spit \ˈ·\ *vt* **spitted**; **spitted**; **spitting** *spits* [ME *spiten*, fr. *spite*, n.] **1** : to thrust a spit through : fix upon a spit ⟨over the floor were spread the glowing embers of a fire; and across it . . . were *spitted* four whole sheep —Oscar Handlin⟩ **2** : to fix as if with a spit : IMPALE ⟨*spitted* him on a bayonet —Mack Morris⟩

³spit \ˈ·\, *dial* \ˈspel\ *vb* **spit** \ˈ·\ *or* **spat** \-pa\ **spit** *or* **spat**

also dial **spitted** \-pid·əd, -itəd\ *or* **spit·ten** \-pitᵊn\ **spitting**; **spits** [ME *spitten*, fr. OE (northern dial.) *spittan*, of imit. origin] *vt* **1 a** : to eject from the mouth (as saliva) : EXPECTORATE ⟨got a cigar, bit off the end and ~ it out —Wallace Stegner⟩ **b** (1) : to express (scorn, hatred, or malicious feelings) by or as if by spitting ⟨the old man simply *spat* his contempt and stumped away —Roderick Finkayson⟩ (2) : to utter with a spitting sound or scornful expression : utter in a scornful, malicious, venomous, rapid, or authoritative manner ⟨his father's face, *spitting* the one furious word —John Fountain⟩ ⟨*spat* out the words with unmistakable passion —Helen Howe⟩ **c** : to emit or eject as if by spitting : throw forth or out ⟨guns . . . capable of *spitting* heavy flak at guided missiles —*Science*⟩ ⟨a machine . . . cuts the hay as it goes along, places it, ties it with wire, then ~ it out the other side —Ralph Gustafson⟩; *specif* : to emit (precipitation) in driving particles or short scattered flurries ⟨the sky *spat* rain tentatively —*Springfield* (Mass.) *Republican*⟩ **2** : to set fire to : start burning ⟨~ a fuse⟩ ~ *vi* **1 a** (1) : to eject saliva as a gross insult or as a means of showing aversion or contempt — usu. used with such prepositions as *at*, *on*, or *upon* ⟨*spat* in their own black, ugly eyes —T.B.Costain⟩ ⟨*spat* contemptuously at the stove —R.H.Newman⟩ (2) : to possess or exhibit contempt — usu. used with the phrase *in the eye of* ⟨~s in the eye of commercialism with these words —*Ebony*⟩ **b** : to eject saliva : EXPECTORATE ⟨~ in the water and watched it bob away —R.O.Bowen⟩ ⟨*spits* onto the swept-up heap of rubbish —Herbert Gold⟩ **2** : to rain or snow slightly or with scattered drops or flakes : fall in flurries ⟨the rain ~s icily down —Kenneth Tynan⟩ **3 a** : to make a noise like that of expectoration : make a sudden short crackling or popping sound : SPUTTER ⟨the eggs ~ in the pan —A.R.Foff⟩ ⟨the motor coughed and ~ —R.S.Hillyer⟩ **b** : to emit something or become emitted with a spitting sound ⟨the bullets ~ into the sand below —H.H.Arnold & I.C.Eaker⟩ — **spit cotton 1** : to spit white cottony saliva esp. from thirst ⟨hadn't had a drink all morning and were *spitting cotton*, they were that thirsty —F.B.Gipson⟩ **2** : to be angry ⟨better look out; the sheriff's *spitting cotton* —R.B.House⟩ — **spit it out** : to say what is in the mind without further delay — **spit sixpences** *Brit* : to spit cotton

⁴spit \ˈ·\ *n* -s [ME, fr. *spitten*, v. — more at ³SPIT] **1 a** (1) : the secretion normally occurring in the mouth : SPITTLE, SALIVA, SPUTUM (2) : the act or an instance of spitting **b** (1) : a frothing expectoration resembling saliva exuded by spittlebugs (2) : SPITTLEBUG **2** : a short distance ⟨followed him into the woods about one good ~ from the door —William Faulkner⟩ **3** [so called fr. a former popular saying that a child with a great resemblance to its father looks as much like him as if it had been spit out of his mouth] : perfect likeness : COUNTERPART, IMAGE — usu. used in the phrase *spit and image* ⟨the spit and image of his father⟩ **4** : a falling of rain or snow in scattered particles : a sprinkle of rain or flurry of snow

⁵spit \ˈ·\ *n* -s [D, fr. MD; akin to MD *spitten* to dig, spade and prob. to OE *spitu* spit — more at ¹SPIT] **1** *chiefly Brit* : the depth of the blade of a spade **2** *chiefly Brit* **a** : a layer of earth as deep as the blade of a spade **b** : a spadeful of earth

spit·al *or* **spit·tle** \ˈspidᵊl, -itᵊl\ *n* -s [*spital* alter. (influenced by *hospital*) of *spittle*, fr. ME *spitel*, modif. of ML *hospitale*, fr. LL, hospice — more at HOSPITAL] : LAZARETTO, HOSPITAL; *esp* : a charitable institution of a lower class than a hospital for the needy, aged, or infirm

spit and polish *n* [so called fr. the practice of polishing objects such as shoes by spitting on them and then rubbing them with a cloth] **1** : the action of or materials for a thorough cleaning, polishing, and refurbishing ⟨presented himself for a *spit and polish* —Jessie Wall⟩ ⟨habituated to courtly rhetoric, which is emotion after *spit and polish* have been applied to it —Francis Hackett⟩ **2** : extreme attention to cleanliness, orderliness, smartness of appearance, and ceremonial esp. at the expense of operational efficiency ⟨reviews, parades, athletics, *spit and polish*, long-standing traditions, and automatic discipline are played up —R.A.Preston⟩

spit-and-polish \ˌ···ˈ·\ *adj* : marked by spit and polish ⟨embassies abroad can not do without their *spit-and-polish* doormen —*N.Y.Times*⟩ ⟨a full-time professional soldier, of the old *spit-and-polish* school —Evelyn Eaton⟩

spitball \ˈ·,·\ *n* **1** : paper chewed and rolled into a ball to be thrown as a missile **2** : a baseball pitch delivered after the ball has been moistened with saliva or sweat ⟨sounded the doom of the ~ . . . freak pitching deliveries —*Springfield* (Mass.) *Republican*⟩ — called also *spitter*

spit·ball·er \ˈ·,·ə(r)\ *n* : one that throws spitballs

spit·bug *n* : SPITTLEBUG

spitbox \ˈ·,·\ *n* : SPITTOON

¹spitch·cock \ˈspich,käk\ *n* [origin unknown] : an eel split and grilled

²spitchcock \ˈ·\ *vt* : to prepare as a spitchcock or in the manner of a spitchcock ⟨~ an eel⟩

spit curl *n* [prob. so called fr. its being sometimes plastered down with saliva] : a spiral curl that is usu. plastered on the forehead, temple, or cheek

¹spite \ˈspīt, *usu* -īd·+V\ *n* -s [ME, short for ¹*despite*] **1 a** *obs* : an injury, hurt, or disgrace incurred or inflicted ⟨it is a great ~ to be praised in the wrong place —Ben Jonson⟩ **b** *obs* : something that vexes : a petty annoyance **2 a** : often petty ill will or hatred toward another accompanied with the disposition to irritate, annoy, or thwart : envious or rancorous malice ⟨a little insignificant: not really hate at all, but ~ —C.D.Lewis⟩ **b** : an instance of spite : an individual malicious feeling : GRUDGE ⟨a normal child has no ~ against work until you have drilled one into him —C.E.Montague⟩ **syn** see MALICE — **in spite of** *prep* : in defiance or contempt of ⟨charged *in spite of* superior enemy forces⟩ : despite adverse effects of : in opposition to all efforts of ⟨*in spite of* careful preparation⟩

²spite \ˈ·\ *vt* -ED/-ING/-S [ME *spiten*, fr. *spite*, n.] **1** *obs* : to regard with spite : DISLIKE, HATE **2** : to treat maliciously (as by shaming or thwarting) ⟨children are still ready to ~ the older generation —E.H.Erikson⟩ **3 a** : to fill with spite **b** : ANNOY, OFFEND

spite fence *n* : an unsightly fence or wall that serves no useful purpose, is so constructed as to be an injury to adjoining property, and is erected and maintained maliciously for the purpose of injuring a neighbor (as by obstructing unreasonably his air, light, or view)

spite·ful \ˈspītfəl\ *adj*, *sometimes* **spitefuller**; *sometimes* **spitefullest** [ME, fr. ¹*spite* + *-ful*] : filled with or showing spite : having or exhibiting a desire to vex, annoy, or injure : MALIGNANT, MALICIOUS ⟨growing to hate the very sight of one another, becoming bitter, ~, jealous —W.H.Wright⟩ ⟨because the present law is ~ —A.E.Stevenson †1965⟩ — **spite·ful·ly** \-fəlē, -li\ *adv* — **spite·ful·ness** *n* -ES

spite·less \ˈspītləs\ *adj* : lacking spite : not motivated by spite

spite marriage *n* : a marriage entered into by one person to vex a third person with whom he is in love

spite of *prep* : in spite of ⟨exert your freedom, *spite of* the world —C.W.Hendel⟩

spite-work \ˈ·,·\ *n* : trouble or injury inflicted as revenge for a real or fancied grievance

spitfire \ˈ·,·\ *n* [²*spit* + *fire*, n.] **1** : one that emits fire (as a volcano or a cannon) **2** : a quick-tempered, fiery, or violently emotional person

spit in the ocean : poker in which each player is dealt a hand of cards facedown and combines them with cards faceup on the table to make a poker hand; *specif* : a game in which each player is dealt four cards, a fifth card is faced on the take, and the faced card and all others of the same rank are wild

spit·ish \ˈspīd·ish\ *adj* : SPITEFUL

spit-kit *also* **spit-kid** \ˈspit,kit, -kid\ *n* **1** : ASHTRAY **2** : a small ship (as a patrol boat)

spits *pl of* SPIT, *pres 3d sing of* SPIT

¹spit shine *n* : a very high gloss on a boot or shoe esp. when partially obtained by the application of saliva

²spit shine *vt* : to apply a spit shine to (a boot or shoe)

spit·stick \ˈspit,stik\ *or* **spit·stick·er** \-kə(r)\ *n* [*spitstick* alter. (influenced by *stick*) of *spitsticker*, fr. D *spitssteker*, fr. *spits* pointed (fr. MD, fr. MHG *spiz*, *spitze*, fr. OHG *spizzi*) + *steker* graver, one that pricks or thrusts, fr. MD, *steken* to stick, *steken* to sting, prick, thrust + *-er*; akin to OHG *stehhan* to sting, prick — more at SPIT, STICK] **1** : a graver that is used

esp. to outline designs **2 :** a small pointed chisel (as for making very small sloping cuts between the stones of a setting)
spitted *past of* ²SPIT *or dial past part of* ³SPIT
spitten *dial past part of* SPIT
¹**spit·ter** \ˈspid·ə(r), -itə-\ *n* -s [ME *spittere*, fr. *spitten* to spit + *-ere* -er] **1 :** one that ejects saliva from the mouth **2 :** a short length of fuse nicked to the powder core at about two-inch intervals so that when the fuse is ignited the nicks successively spit fire and are used to light the fuses of a round of loaded holes **3 :** SPITTING SNAKE
²**spitter** \"\ *n* -s [¹*spit* + *-er*] **:** a young deer whose antlers are beginning to shoot or become sharp **:** BROCKET, PRICKET
³**spitter** \"\ *n* -s [E dial. *spit* to spade (fr. ME *spitten* to dig, spade, fr. OE *spittan*) + E *-er*] *dial Brit* **:** SPADE
⁴**spitter** \"\ *n* -s [⁴*spit* + *-er*] **:** SPITBALL
spitting *n* -s [ME, fr. gerund of *spitten* to spit] **:** SPIT
spitting cobra *n* [*spitting* fr. pres. part. of ³*spit*] **:** a venomous elapid snake of the genus *Naja* that ejects its venom toward the victim without striking: as **a :** BLACK-NECKED COBRA **b :** RINGHALS
spit·ting image \ˈspitᵊn- *sometimes* -id·l\|iŋ- *or* -it\| *or* \|ēŋ-\ *n* [alter. (influenced by *spitting*, pres. part. of ³*spit*) of the phrase *spit and image*, fr. ⁴*spit*] **:** spit and image **:** SPIT 3
spitting snake *n* **:** a venomous snake (as a ringhals) that discharges its venom at an objective through the air without actually striking with the fangs
¹**spit·tle** \ˈspid·ᵊl, -itᵊl\ *n* -s [ME *spitel*, fr. OE *spitel;* akin to OE *spittan* to dig, spade, MD *spitten* to dig, spade, and prob. to OE *spitu* spit — more at SPIT] *dial Brit* **:** a spadelike implement **:** PEEL
²**spittle** \"\ *n* -s [alter. (influenced by ⁴*spit*) of ME *spetil*, fr. OE *spǣtl, spātl;* akin to OE *spittan* to spit — more at SPIT] **1 :** the fluid secreted by the salivary glands **:** SALIVA, SPIT **2 :** the frothy secretion of a spittle insect
³**spittle** *var of* SPITAL
spittlebug \ˈ==,=\ *n* **:** SPITTLE INSECT — usu. used in combination; see MEADOW SPITTLEBUG, PINE SPITTLEBUG, SARATOGA SPITTLEBUG
spittle insect *n* **:** any of numerous small leaping insects of the family Cercopidae with nymphs that live on plants and envelop themselves in a mass of white froth consisting of a fluid secreted from the anus in which bubbles of air are trapped
spit·toon \(ˈ)spiˈtün\ *n* -s [⁴*spit* + *-oon* (as in *balloon* or *doubloon*)] **:** a receptacle for spit; *esp* **:** a low cylindrical or round vessel (as of metal or earthenware) with a funnel-shaped top into which tobacco chewers spit periodically in the course of a chew — called also *cuspidor*

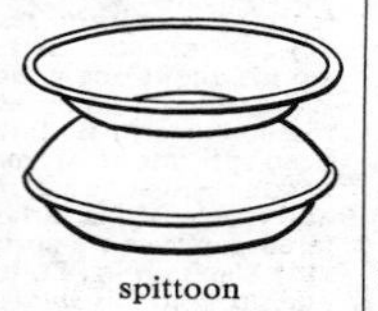
spittoon

spit up *vb* **:** REGURGITATE, VOMIT
spitz \ˈspits *sometimes* ˈshp-\ *n* -ES *sometimes cap* [G, fr. *spitz* pointed, fr. OHG *spizzi;* fr. the shape of the ears and muzzle — more at SPIT] **:** any of several dogs native to northern areas and distinguished by a broad strong stocky body with heavy double coat, a broad somewhat flat head with rather short muzzle and erect prick ears, and a heavily feathered tail tightly recurved over the back: as **a :** a dog regarded as ancestral to a modern breed exhibiting these qualities **b :** a dog of such a modern breed (as a chow chow, samoyed, or pomeranian) **c :** a medium-sized white dog descended from Pomeranian ancestors and often regarded as constituting a separate breed
spit·zer \-tsə(r)\ *n* -s [G, fr. *spitz* pointed (in *spitzgeschoss* pointed bullet) + *-er*] **:** a metal-jacketed pointed bullet
spitz·flö·te \ˈshpits,flǟd·ə, -lǣd·ə, *G* -lœtə\ *or* **spitz·flute** \ˈs(h)pits,flüt\ *n* -s [*spitzflöte* fr. G, fr. *spitz* pointed + *flöte* flute, fr. MHG *vloite*, fr. OF *flaute, fleute; spitzflute* part. trans. of G *spitzflöte* — more at FLUTE] **:** a labial pipe-organ stop with conical metal pipes of 8-foot, 4-foot, or 2-foot pitch and of flute quality
spiv \ˈspiv\ *n* -s [alter. of E dial. *spiff*, n., flashy dresser, fr. E dial. *spiff*, adj., smartly dressed, dandified] **1** *Brit* **:** one who gets his living by his wits without regular employment **:** PARASITE: as **a :** a hanger-on at a racetrack **b :** one engaged in petty black-marketeering and thievery **2** *Brit* **:** one who does not do his full share in an effort **:** SLACKER
spiv·ery *or* **spiv·very** \ˈspivərī\ *n* -ES *Brit* **:** the practice of a spiv **:** obtaining one's living without effort at the expense of others
spi·zel·la \spəˈzelə, spīˈz-\ *n, cap* [NL, fr. Gk *spiza* chaffinch + L *-ella* — more at FINCH] **:** a genus of small American finches including the chipping sparrow, the field sparrow, the tree sparrow, and related birds
spiz·zer·inc·tum \,spizəˈriŋ(k)təm\ *n* -s [E dial. (U.S.) *spizarinctum* cash, specie, prob. irreg. fr. E ¹*specie*] **:** the will to succeed **:** VIM, ENERGY, AMBITION
spk *abbr* speckled
spkl *abbr* sprinkle
spkr *abbr* **1** speaker **2** sprinkler
spl *abbr* special
SPL *abbr, often not cap* [L *sine prole legitima*] without legitimate issue
splach·na·ce·ae \splakˈnāsē,ē\ *n pl, cap* [NL, fr. *Splachnum*, type genus + *-aceae*] **:** a family of mosses (order Funariales) characterized by the swollen neck of the capsule and their growth upon dung or decaying animal tissues — **splach·na·ceous** \(ˈ)=ˈnāshəs\ *adj*
splach·noid \ˈsplak,nȯid\ *adj* [NL *Splachnum* + E *-oid*] **:** resembling or related to a moss of the genus *Splachnum*
splach·num \-ˌnəm\ *n, cap* [NL, fr. Gk *splanchnon* tree moss] **:** a genus (the type of the family Splachnaceae) of rather rare mosses distinguished by a capsule that bears spores only in the upper portion and by its colored lower half being much swollen and composed of loose tissue containing chlorophyll
splack·nuck \ˈsplak,nək\ *n* -s [coined by Jonathan Swift †1745 Eng. satirist as the name of an imaginary animal of approximately human size mentioned in his satire *Gulliver's Travels* (1726)] **:** an odd or peculiar person or animal
splake \ˈsplāk\ *n, pl* **splake** *or* **splakes** [blend of *speckled* (*trout*) and *lake* (*trout*)] **:** a hatchery-produced supposedly fertile hybrid between the American lake trout and the brook trout
splanch·nic \ˈsplaŋknik\ *adj* [NL *splanchnicus*, fr. Gk *splanchnikos*, fr. *splanchnon* entrail + *-ikos* -ic] **1 :** of or relating to the viscera **:** VISCERAL **2 :** of, relating to, affecting, involving, or being the splanchnic nerves
splanch·ni·cec·to·my \,=nəˈsektəmē\ *n* -ES [*splanchnic* + *-ectomy*] **:** excision of a segment of one or more splanchnic nerves to relieve hypertension
splanchnic nerve *n* **:** any of three important nerves situated on each side of the body, formed by the union of branches from the six or seven lower ganglia of the sympathetic system, and being a superior ending in the coeliac ganglion, a middle ending in the solar plexus, and an inferior ending in the renal plexus and part of the solar plexus
splanch·ni·cot·o·my \,splaŋknəˈkäd·əmē\ *n* -ES [*splanchnic* + *-o-* + *-tomy*] **:** surgical division of one or more splanchnic nerves
splanchno- *comb form* [NL, fr. Gk, fr. *splanchnon* entrail; akin to Gk *splēn* spleen — more at SPLEEN] **:** viscera ⟨*splanchno*megaly⟩ ⟨*splanchno*ptosis⟩
splanch·no·coele *or* **splanch·no·coel** \ˈsplaŋknə,sēl\ *n* -s [ISV *splanchno-* + *-coele, -coel*] **1 :** the embryonic body cavity when formed by splitting of the mesoderm into somatopleuric and splanchnopleuric layers **2 :** a visceral cavity esp. of a brachiopod
splanch·no·cranium \ˈsplaŋknə+\ *n* [NL, fr. *splanchno-* + *cranium*] **:** the portion of the skull that arises from the first three visceral arches and forms the supporting structure of the jaws — called also *viscerocranium;* compare NEUROCRANIUM
splanch·nol·o·gy \splaŋkˈnäləjē\ *n* -ES [NL *splanchnologia*, fr. *splanchno-* + *-logia* -logy] **:** a branch of anatomy concerned with the viscera
splanch·no·pleure \ˈsplaŋknə,plů(ə)r\ *n* -s [NL *splanchnopleura*, fr. *splanchno-* + *-pleura*] **:** a layer of tissue consisting of the inner of the two layers into which the lateral plate of the mesoderm splits in the embryo of a craniate vertebrate together with the endoderm internal to it and forming most of the walls and substance of the visceral organs — compare SOMATOPLEURE — **splanch·no·pleu·ric** \ˌ==ˈplůrik\ *adj*

¹**splash** \ˈsplash, -aa(ə)sh, -aish\ *vb* -ED/-ING/-ES [alter. of ⁴*plash*] *vi* **1 a :** to strike and dash about a liquid or semiliquid substance **:** cause the spattering of a liquid or thinly viscous substance ⟨the children ~⟩ ⟨~*ed* about in the bath —Elizabeth Goudge⟩ **b :** to move through or into a liquid or semiliquid substance and cause splashing ⟨~*ed* across the rich black loam of . . . fields sodden with irrigation water —Rex Keating⟩ ⟨~*ed* overboard and swam ashore —Harriot B. Barbour⟩ **2 a** (1) **:** to become splashed or spattered about or upon **:** spray around or on in drops, columns, sheets, or masses of liquid or semiliquid matter ⟨saw a drop of water ~ down upon the violet script and spread —Willa Cather⟩ ⟨the water ~*ing* out of the tubs upon the stones —Pearl Buck⟩ ⟨the road ~*ed* muddily —Christopher Bloom⟩ (2) **:** to become spread or scattered in the manner of a splashed liquid ⟨the sunlight ~*ed* over her deck and gear —Thomas Wood †1950⟩ **b :** to fall, strike, or move with a splashing sound ⟨kept awake by the ~*ing* of water from the faucet⟩ ⟨a brook ~*ing* over rocks⟩ ~ *vt* **1 a** (1) **:** to dash a liquid or thinly viscous substance upon or against **:** scatter liquid upon in large quantities ⟨poured water into the basin and began to ~ her face —Rumer Godden⟩ — compare SPATTER (2) **:** to soil or stain by a splashed liquid ⟨don't ~ your dress —Margaret Kennedy⟩ **b :** to cause to appear splashed or spattered **:** mark or overlay with patches of a different usu. contrasting color or of a different texture ⟨innumerable peaks, black and sharp, rose grandly into the dark blue sky . . . their sides streaked and ~*ed* with snow —John Muir †1914⟩ ⟨the white tulle is ~*ed* with segments of Alençon-type lace —*New Yorker*⟩ **c :** to cover (a plumbing joint) with melted solder **d :** to outline hastily or carelessly **:** draw, paint, write, or relate sketchily **:** SKETCH ⟨the verbal farce . . . ~*ed* out for us —*Listener*⟩ **e :** to place in a prominent position ⟨insurrectionary proclamations were ~*ed* on the walls of the capital —Bernard Frizell⟩ **f :** to give very conspicuous display to ⟨the papers ~*ed* stories about the dapper little general —*Newsweek*⟩ **2 a :** to strike and dash about (as water or mud) **:** cause (a liquid or thinly viscous substance) to spatter or toss about esp. with force ⟨she puffed and chugged, ~*ing* the brown waters behind her —Tom Marvel⟩ ⟨the pure bright colors which he confidently ~*ed* onto his canvases without even bothering to mix on his palette —*Time*⟩ **b :** to scatter in the manner of a splashed liquid ⟨the sunset colors were ~*ed* brilliantly across the skies —P.E.James⟩ **3 :** to move along (one's way) with splashing ⟨a man, wearing a rubber raincoat which glistened in the headlights . . . ~*ed* his way over toward the car —Erle Stanley Gardner⟩ **4 :** to cause to splash a liquid or other substance ⟨enjoy ~*ing* waterproof boots into deep puddles —Arnold Bennett⟩ **5 a :** to drive (logs) by releasing a head of water confined by a flood dam **b :** to flood (as a shallow river) with a flush of water (as for driving logs) **6 :** to shoot down (as an enemy airplane)
²**splash** \"\ *n* -ES *often attrib* **1 a** (1) **:** liquid hurled or being hurled scatteringly esp. with considerable force or in quantities greater than a spattering, as a result of a surface blow, and against or upon something ⟨the unskilled diver hit the surface with a great ~ of water⟩ ⟨a ~ of paint on his palette had assumed . . . the shape of a distorted skull —Herbert Read⟩ ⟨white ~*es* of water were plunging through the six-inch gap in the wooden gate —Bill Alcine⟩; *specif* **:** water impounded and then released suddenly (as for splashing logs) (2) **:** a spot or daub from or as if from splashed liquid ⟨a mud ~ on the fender⟩ **b** (1) *Brit* **:** a small shallow puddle or pond ⟨an irregular ~ of water to give away its foreignness —Elizabeth Bowen⟩ (2) *Brit* **:** a small amount of soda water ⟨Scotch and a ~ —J.A.Phillips⟩ **c :** a large or irregular conspicuous colored patch upon a background or surface **:** BLOTCH ⟨the blossoming trees dot the countryside with ~*es* of pastel color —*Amer. Guide Series: Texas*⟩ **2 a** (1) **:** the action of striking the surface of a liquid **:** the causing of a liquid to splash ⟨whose placid surface is broken by the swirl and ~ of pickerel and salmon —*Amer. Guide Series: Maine*⟩ (2) **:** the act or process of splashing logs (3) **:** a plunge of short duration and esp. accompanied by vigorous movements into water ⟨will find a warm shower relaxing and a short cold ~ immediately afterward stimulating —Morris Fishbein⟩ **b :** the action of a liquid striking or falling upon something ⟨the steady ~ of a light swell upon the shore⟩ **3 a :** a sound produced by or as if by a body striking upon or in a liquid ⟨tumbled with a sort of ~ upon the keys of a ghostly piano —Scott Fitzgerald⟩ **b :** a sound produced by or as if by a liquid falling, moving forward, being hurled against something, or oscillating back and forth ⟨heard the rain coming down in a ~ —Edmund Wilson⟩; *specif* **:** a splashing sound heard in succussion **4 a :** a vivid impression esp. resulting from conspicuous or ostentatious activity or appearance ⟨the son who has made the biggest ~ in the world —Green Peyton⟩ **b** (1) **:** the practice or an instance of ostentatious display ⟨his love of luxury and of ~ —M.D. Geismar⟩ ⟨hard to believe that the magnificence could increase after the first brilliant ~ —C.E.Abernethy⟩ (2) **:** a conspicuous featuring of an item in a newspaper or magazine ⟨the story got a robust front-page ~ —*Newsweek*⟩ ⟨~ headline⟩
splash back *n* **:** SPLASHBOARD
splash block *n* **:** a masonry block placed on the ground below a downspout to divert the water away from the building and to prevent ground washing
splashboard \ˈ=,=\ *n* **1 a :** DASHBOARD 1 **b :** a board or panel (as behind a kitchen sink) to protect against splashes **2 a :** a plank used to close a sluice or spillway of a dam **b :** FLASHBOARD
splash dam *n* **:** a flood dam used to retain a head of water for driving logs
splash·er \ˈsplashə(r), -aash-, -aish-\ *n* -s **1 :** one that splashes **2 :** a guard (as a splashboard) to keep off splashes
splash erosion *n* **:** erosion caused by the splash of falling raindrops
splashes *pres 3d sing of* SPLASH, *pl of* SPLASH
splash guard *n* **:** a flap suspended behind a rear wheel to prevent tire splash from muddying windshields of following vehicles
splash·i·ly \-shəlē, -li\ *adv* **:** in a splashy manner ⟨~ printed cotton kimonos —*New Yorker*⟩
splash·i·ness \-shēnəs, -shin-\ *n* -ES **:** the quality or state of being splashy
splash·ing·ly *adv* **:** in a splashing manner
splashings *n pl* [fr. gerund of ¹*splash*] **:** boiled liquor passed over the cooler and refrigerator in brewing and added in the fermentation vessel to reduce the wort to the required gravity

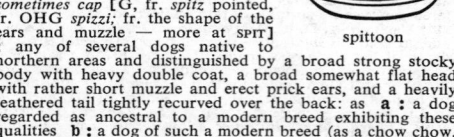

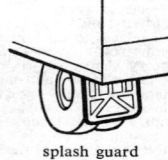

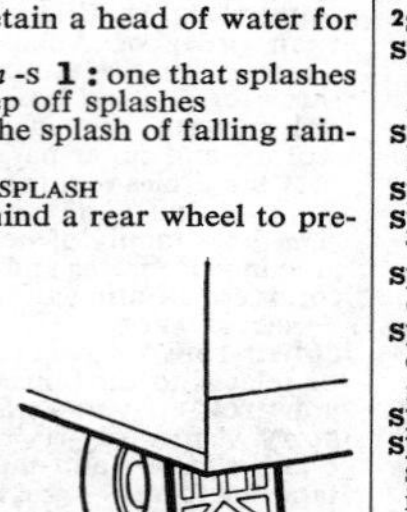
splash guard

splash-lubricate \ˈ=ˈ=,=\ *vt* [back-formation fr. *splash lubrication*] **:** to lubricate by splash lubrication
splash lubrication *or* **splash feed** *or* **splash system** *n* **:** lubrication of the parts in a crankcase and cylinder from the splashing about of oil by the crankpin and other moving parts
splash party *n* **:** a party at a swimming pool or beach featuring swimming and other water sports
splash plate *n* **:** a plate (as in the tender of a locomotive) to obstruct and weaken the surge of a surrounding mass of water in motion ⟨water is discharged through tubes located in the troughs, upon *splash plates* which break up the water and distribute it evenly —*Sweet's Catalog Service*⟩
splashy \ˈsplashē, -aash-, -aish-, -shi\ *adj* -ER/-EST [*splash* + *-y*] **1 :** full of dirty water **:** wet and muddy so as to be easily splashed about ⟨a youngster who could resist the temptation of a ~ rain puddle —Ellen L. Buell⟩ **2 :** moving or being moved with a splash or splashing sounds **3 :** tending to or exhibiting ostentatious display **:** SHOWY, SENSATIONAL ⟨a ~ half-page ad —E.J.Kahn⟩ **4 :** consisting of, being, or covered with colored splashes ⟨a short-sleeved dress of . . . black shantung has ~ yellow or white oblongs scattered over it —Lois Long⟩
¹**splat** \ˈsplat, *usu* -ad·+V\ *vb* **splatted; splatted; splatting; splats** [ME *splatten*] *vt* **:** to split open and spread out (a pike) for cooking ~ *vi* **1 :** to flatten on impact ⟨shooting snowballs that *splatted* on the black trunks —Saul Bellow⟩ **2 :** to make a sound characteristic of a bullet flattening on impact
²**splat** \"\ *n* -s **:** a single flat thin often ornamental member of a chairback rising from the seat-rail or one just above it to the top rail used on chairs of the Queen Anne and later styles; *also* **:** a similar horizontal member

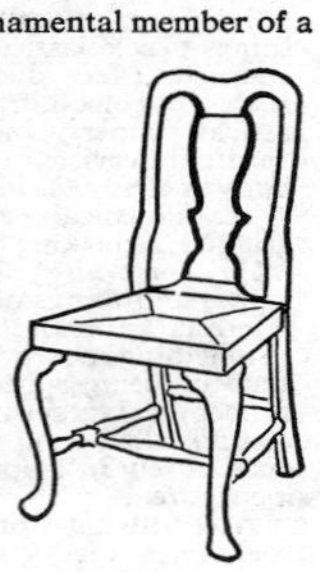
splat

³**splat** \"\ *n* -s [prob. alter. (influenced by ¹*splat*) of ⁸*plat*] *dial Eng* **:** a plot of ground; *also* **:** PATCH, SPOT, BLOTCH
⁴**splat** \"\ *n* -s [back-formation fr. ³*splatter*] **:** any of various splattering or slapping sounds ⟨~ of naked feet on concrete —Wallace Stegner⟩ ⟨the ~ of a bullet⟩
splatch *var of* SPLOTCH
splath·er \ˈsplathə(r)\ *vb* -ED/-ING/-S [prob. blend of ¹*splash* and ¹*blather*] **1** *dial Brit* **a :** SPLASH **b :** to spread about **2** *dial Brit* **:** to speak or tell confusedly
splathering *adj* **1 :** UNGAINLY, CLUMSY **2 :** CONFUSED, RAMBLING ⟨sends a long ~ telegram and never puts her address in it —J.B.Priestley⟩
¹**splatter** *n* -s [alter. of *spatule*] *obs* **:** SPATULA 1
²**splat·ter** \ˈsplad·ə(r), -atə-\ *vb* -ED/-ING/-S [prob. blend of ²*splash* and ¹*spatter*] **:** SPATTER, SPLASH
³**splatter** \"\ *n* -s **:** SPATTER, SPLASH
splat·ter·dock \ˈsplad·ə(r),däk, -atə-\ *n* **:** SPATTERDOCK
splat·ter·er \ˈsplad·ərə(r), -atə-\ *n* -s [²*splatter* + *-er*] *dial* **:** a coot (*Fulica americana*)
splatterfaced \ˈ==,=\ *adj* [alter. (influenced by ¹*splatter*) of *platter-faced*] **:** PLATTER-FACED
splatterwork \ˈ==,=\ *n* [¹*splatter* + *work*] **:** art work produced with or as if with a spatula
¹**splay** \ˈsplā\ *vb* -ED/-ING/-S [ME *splayen*, short for *displayen* to spread out, unfold — more at DISPLAY] *vt* **1 :** to cause to spread apart or open outward **:** EXPAND ⟨~*ing* large, meaty hands over the table —Nigel Dennis⟩ — usu. used with *out* ⟨~*ing* out their movable toes, they can move easily over marshy ground —C.D.Forde⟩ **2 :** to turn on one side **:** make oblique (as the side of a door or window) **3 :** to draw together (the ends of staves) in forming a barrel, tub, or bucket ~ *vi* **1 :** to become splayed **:** extend apart or outwards esp. in an awkward or clumsy manner ⟨the front wheels were ~*ing* like a llama's hoofs —A.W.Baum⟩ — usu. used with *out* ⟨four delicate legs that unite in a central shaft near the base and ~ out to support the top —Sheila Hibben⟩ **2 :** to lie at a slant **:** SLOPE, SLANT
²**splay** \"\ *n* -s **1 :** an outward or expanding slope or bevel esp. of the sides of a door or window by which an opening is made larger at one face of the wall than at the other or larger at each of the faces than it is between them **2 :** the degree of outward slope **:** SPREAD, EXPANSION ⟨the ~ of sheers is one-third of their effective length —*Manual of Seamanship*⟩
³**splay** \"\ *adj* **1 :** turned outward esp. in an awkward or ungainly manner ⟨~ knees⟩; *also* **:** broad and flat as from splaying **2 :** CLUMSY, UNGAINLY ⟨something ~, something blunt-edged, unhandy, and infelicitous —Matthew Arnold⟩
⁴**splay** \"\ *vt* [by alter.] *dial* **:** SPAY
splayed arch *n* **:** an arch with its opening at one side larger than at the other so that its intrados face is conical
¹**splayfoot** \ˈ=,=\ *n, pl* **splayfeet** [¹*splay* + *foot*] **:** a foot that is abnormally flattened and spread out; *specif* **:** FLATFOOT
²**splayfoot** \ˈ=,=\ *or* **splayfooted** \ˈ=ˈ=\ *adj* [*splayfoot* fr. ¹*splayfoot; splayfooted* fr. ¹*splay* + *footed*] **1 :** having a splayfoot **2 :** UNGAINLY, CLUMSY
splaymouthed \ˈ=ˈ=\ *adj* **:** having a mouth stretched into an awkward gape or grin
¹**spleen** \ˈsplēn\ *n* -s [ME *splen*, fr. MF or L; MF *esplen*, fr. L *splen*, fr. Gk *splēn;* akin to L *lien* spleen, OIr *selg*, OSlav *slězena*, Skt *plīhan*] **1 a :** a highly vascular ductless abdominal organ of vertebrates that resembles a gland in organization but is closely associated with the circulatory system playing a role in the maintenance of blood volume, production of some types of blood cells, recovery of material from worn-out red blood cells, and probably in the production of antibodies and that in man is a dark purplish flattened oblong object of a soft fragile consistency lying near the cardiac end of the stomach and consisting largely of reticuloendothelial and lymphoid tissue enclosed in a fibroelastic capsule from which trabeculae ramify through the tissue of the organ which is divisible into a loose friable red pulp in intimate connection with the blood supply and with red blood cells free in its interstices and a denser white pulp chiefly of lymphoid tissue condensed in masses about the small arteries **b** *archaic* **:** the seat of emotions and passions **:** the source of laughter **2 :** any of various passions or emotions or their manifestations: **a** *obs* **:** violent mirth or merriment; *also* **:** LAUGHTER ⟨haply my presence may well abate thy overmerry ~ —Shak.⟩ **b** *archaic* **:** a fit of anger, malice, or bad temper **c** (1) *obs* **:** a sudden impulse **:** WHIM, CAPRICE ⟨a thousand ~*s* bear her a thousand ways —Shak.⟩ (2) *obs* **:** a capricious temper **d** *obs* **:** a proud courageous impetuous temper **:** manly spirit ⟨leaden age, quick'ned with youthful ~ and warlike rage —Shak.⟩; *also* **:** IMPETUOSITY, HIGH-SPIRITEDNESS **e** (1) **:** latent malevolence or spite **:** violent feelings of anger or spite esp. when suddenly and explosively released ⟨his countrymen vented their ~ at his failure . . . by sending the unfortunate naval commander into exile —A.J. Toynbee⟩ (2) *obs* **:** a feeling of ill will **:** GRUDGE ⟨I have no ~ against you —Shak.⟩ **f :** extreme lowness of spirits **:** MELANCHOLY, DEPRESSION **syn** see MALICE
²**spleen** \"\ *vt* -ED/-ING/-S **:** to arouse the wrath of **:** ANGER
spleen amaranth *n* **:** a tropical American annual weed (*Amaranthus hybridus*) that has dark green or purple foliage and is widely naturalized in the U.S.
spleen·ful \ˈ=fəl\ *adj* **:** full of, displaying, or affected with spleen **:** SPLENETIC
spleen·ic \ˈsplēnik\ *adj* [¹*spleen* + *-ic*] **:** SPLENIC
spleen·less \-ləs\ *adj* **:** having no spleen; *specif* **:** SPLENECTOMIZED
spleen stone *n* **:** a green stone (as jade) formerly used for disorders of the spleen
spleenwort \ˈ=,=\ *n* [¹*spleen* + *wort;* fr. the belief that it has curative powers for disorders of the spleen] **1 :** a fern of the genus *Asplenium* **2 :** a fern of the genus *Athyrium*
spleenwort bush *n* **:** SWEET FERN 2
spleeny \ˈsplēnē, -ni\ *adj* -ER/-EST **1 :** full of or displaying spleen **2** *NewEng* **:** peevish and irritable with hypochondriac inclinations ⟨so ~ when they have the least little thing wrong with them⟩
splen- *or* **spleno-** *comb form* [LL, fr. L, fr. Gk *splēn-*, fr. *splēn* spleen — more at SPLEEN] **1 :** spleen ⟨*splen*ectomy⟩ ⟨*spleno*ma⟩ ⟨*spleno*lysis⟩ ⟨*spleno*rrhagia⟩ **2 :** spleen and ⟨*spleno*colic⟩ ⟨*spleno*lymphatic⟩
sple·nal·gia \spləˈnalj(ē)ə, splē-, splə-\ *n* [NL, fr. *splen-* + *-algia*] **:** pain (as neuralgic) in the region of the spleen — **sple·nal·gic** \(ˈ)splēˈnaljik, (ˈ)sple-, -lə-\ *adj*
sple·nat·ic \spləˈnad·ik\ *adj* [NL *splenaticus*, alter. of LL *spleneticus* splenetic — more at SPLENETIC] *obs* **:** arising from, due to, or affected by spleen **:** SPLEENFUL
splenative *adj* [*splen-* + *-ative*] *obs* **:** SPLENETIC
splen·cu·lus \ˈspleŋkyələs\ *n, pl* **splencu·li** \-ə,lī\ [NL, dim. of L *splen* spleen] **:** a small accessory spleen
splen·da·cious *or* **splen·da·ceous** *or* **splen·da·tious** \(ˈ)splenˈdāshəs\ *adj* [*splendid* + *-acious* (as in *loquacious*), *-aceous* (as in *pomaceous*), *-atious* (as in *ostentatious*)] **:** very splendid **:** GORGEOUS
splen·dent \ˈsplendənt\ *adj* [ME, fr. L *splendent-, splendens*, pres. part. of *splendēre* to shine] **1 :** shining glossily with light or reflected light ⟨~ planets⟩ ⟨~ luster⟩ **2 :** conspicuously eminent or illustrious
splen·did \-dəd\ *adj, often* -ER/-EST [L *splendidus*, fr. *splendēre* to shine; akin to Gk *splēdos* ashes, Skt *sphuliṅga* spark] **1 a :** marked by, manifestive of, adorned with, or maintained in showy magnificence **:** SUMPTUOUS ⟨a very long, narrow chamber — ~ with chandeliers, Oriental rugs, and gilt furniture —Christopher Rand⟩ ⟨the decoration of the public stage, so far from being merely passable, was strikingly ~ —Leslie Hotson⟩ **b :** brilliantly shining **:** RADIANT, LUSTROUS, BRILLIANT **c :** embellished as if with sumptuous

ornaments : FLORID, ORNATE ⟨his creed is set forth . . . in scores of phrases of ~ and empty sonorousness —S.H.Adams⟩ **2 a :** superior or preeminent in accomplishment or distinction : ILLUSTRIOUS, DISTINGUISHED ⟨a great man, a ~ figure in history —H.E.Scudder⟩ **b :** very good, fine, pleasant, or enjoyable : EXCELLENT, PRAISEWORTHY ⟨the ~ cement road —Adria Langley⟩ ⟨prompted by motives which are so ~ —Norman Angell⟩ ⟨the slavery issue offers a ~ illustration of this feature —C.A.M.Ewing⟩ **c :** remarkably pure, complete, or extreme as an embodiment of its type ⟨a miracle of ~ ugliness —Arnold Bennett⟩ ⟨its often ~ lack of intelligibility —C.W. Mills⟩ ⟨~ isolation⟩

syn SPLENDID, RESPLENDENT, GORGEOUS, GLORIOUS, SUBLIME, and SUPERB can all mean having or displaying extraordinarily impressive qualities. All of these terms, like most terms designating superlative qualities, are commonly used interchangeably in hyperbole or as mere indications of great satisfaction in or admiration of something ⟨a *splendid* dish of ice cream —Walt Whitman⟩ ⟨a *splendid* hiker⟩ ⟨a young ROTC student *resplendent* in Air Force blue —Land Kaderli⟩ ⟨a *gorgeous* fat bass voice —*Irish Digest*⟩ ⟨get yourself a *gorgeous* tan —*Read Mag.*⟩ ⟨the deserted boat deck to be a *gorgeous* place to kiss —I.V.Morris⟩ ⟨the *glorious* opportunity of intoxicating themselves at the public expense —J.G.Frazer⟩ ⟨*glorious* onion soup —Ernest Beaglehole⟩ ⟨*sublime* vacation areas —Laurence Lowry⟩ ⟨a *sublime* cocktail⟩ ⟨*superb* hunting and scenic attractions —Tom Marvel⟩ ⟨a *superb* toy⟩ but can be distinguished in more strict use. SPLENDID can apply to what outshines the usual in brilliancy, magnificence, or the like ⟨the courthouse with its portico and spire loomed *splendid* in the distance —Elinor Wylie⟩ ⟨draw the whole opera together in this one *splendid* moment —Robert Craft⟩ RESPLENDENT can apply to what seems to glow or blaze in beauty or splendor ⟨the stars of early evening were *resplendent* —Erle Stanley Gardner⟩ ⟨a *resplendent* butterfly —George Meredith⟩ ⟨she had shown how great and *resplendent* a thing love could be —J.W. Krutch⟩ GORGEOUS can stress a splendor of color or display, sometimes implying a showiness or undue but colorful elaborateness ⟨this *gorgeous* combination of all the hues of Paradise —Henry Adams⟩ ⟨a flair for the exotic and the *gorgeous* —F.O.Matthiessen⟩ ⟨a mass of *gorgeous* upholstery and a labyrinth of luxurious architecture —G.K.Chesterton⟩ GLORIOUS can suggest a radiant beauty or similar extraordinarily admirable quality ⟨all the *glorious* colors of this beautiful range, deep blue and purple in the shadows of the peaks, green and brown where grass and rock mingled —Bram Stoker⟩ ⟨a *glorious* display of fireworks⟩ SUBLIME can imply an elevation or exaltation in contemplation or an impossibility of fully grasping a thing's beauty, power, extent, nobility, or the like ⟨the *sublime* mountain scenery of the West Highlands —O.S.Nock⟩ ⟨the *sublime* but also terrible and sombre experiences and emotions of the battlefield —Sir Winston Churchill⟩ ⟨had been born into that world of stylized drama, of vanity, vulgar pomp and *sublime* grace —*Time*⟩ SUPERB can apply to what has reached or is at a peak of development, competence, grandeur, or magnificence ⟨*superb* political insight —A.M. Schlesinger b. 1917⟩ ⟨*superb* horsemanship⟩ ⟨a *superb* physique⟩ ⟨*superb* cunning⟩ ⟨a *superb* sunset⟩

splen·did·ly *adv* : in a splendid manner

splen·did·ness *n* -ES : the quality or state of being splendid : SPLENDOR, MAGNIFICENCE

splen·dif·er·ous \(ˈ)splenˈdif(ə)rəs\ *adj* [ME, fr. L *splendidus* + E *-ferous*] **1 :** SPLENDID, EXCELLENT, MAGNIFICENT ⟨the oil-rich who worked to live up to the ~ black fountains erupting on their lands —Le Roy Leatherman⟩ **2 :** deceptively splendid ⟨recalls to memory the splendid, or at least ~ days prior to 1929 —G.W.Johnson⟩ — **splen·dif·er·ous·ly** *adv* — **splen·dif·er·ous·ness** *n* -ES

¹splen·dor \ˈsplendə(r) *sometimes* -ˌdȯ(ə)r *or* -ȯ(ə)\ *n* -S *see -or in Explan Notes* [ME *splendure*, fr. MF *esplendour*, fr. L *splendor*, fr. *splendēre* to shine — more at SPLENDID] **1 a :** great brightness : brilliant luster : BRILLIANCY ⟨ahead shone the ~ of a showcase full of gold objects —Angélica Mendoza⟩ ⟨the color and delicacy and ~ of soap bubbles —Dorothy Barclay⟩ **b :** sumptuous display, ornament, or ceremonial : gorgeous show : MAGNIFICENCE, POMP, GLORY ⟨entertained at balls noted for their ~ and exclusiveness —*Amer. Guide Series: La.*⟩ **c :** BEAUTY ⟨the harsh ~ of barren mountains —Marion Wilhelm⟩ **d :** EXCELLENCE, VALUE, WORTH ⟨this eloquent and confident look should . . . open the eyes of many . . . to the ~ of their moral heritage —L.P.Curtis⟩ **2 a :** something that exhibits splendor ⟨the east was a ~ of forest fires —William Beebe⟩ **b :** something that contributes to splendor ⟨the vocabulary of poetry increased enormously its store . . . of vague ~*s* —J.L.Lowes⟩ — **in splendor** *of the sun* : represented heraldically with rays

²splendor \"\ *vb* -ED/-ING/-S *see -or in Explan Notes vi* : to proceed gloriously, radiantly, or resplendently ~ *vt* : to endow with splendor : ADORN ⟨the winter night is ~*ed* by the stars —Madeline Mason⟩

splen·dor·ous \-d(ə)rəs\ *also* **splen·drous** \-drəs\ *adj* : full of splendor : very bright : SPLENDID

sple·nec·to·mize \spləˈnektəˌmīz\ *vt* -ED/-ING/-S [*splenectomy* + *-ize*] : to excise the spleen of

sple·nec·to·my \-ˌmē, -mi\ *n* -ES [ISV *splen-* + *-ectomy*] : removal of the spleen by surgery

sple·ne·o·lus \spləˈnēələs\ *n, pl* **spleneo·li** \-əˌlī\ [NL, dim. of L *splen* spleen] : an accessory spleen

¹sple·net·ic \spləˈnedˌik, -netik, -ēk\ *adj* [LL *spleneticus*, fr. L *splen* spleen + *-eticus* -etic — more at SPLEEN] **1 :** of, relating to, or acting upon the spleen : SPLENIC **2 a** *obs* : having an improperly functioning spleen : afflicted with excessive spleen secretion **b** *archaic* : characterized by or liable to produce melancholy, depression, or moodiness ⟨I could be as *splenetic* as you . . . but my resolution is . . . never to be melancholy —William Cowper⟩ **3 :** marked by morose bad temper, sullen malevolence, or spiteful, peevish anger ⟨heavily biased . . . his book is also ~ in tone —*Times Lit. Supp.*⟩ ⟨~ and railing misanthropy —T.L.Peacock⟩ **syn** see IRASCIBLE

²splenetic \"\ *n* -S : a peevish irritable person

splenetical *obs var of* ¹SPLENETIC

sple·net·i·cal·ly \-ək(ə)lē, -ēk-, -li\ *adv* : in a splenetic manner

splenetic fever *n* : TEXAS FEVER

splen·e·tive \ˈsplenəd·iv\ *adj* [alter. of *splenative*] : SPLENETIC

¹sple·ni·al \ˈsplēnēəl\ *adj* [in senses 1 & 2, fr. NL *splenius* + E *-al*; in sense 3, fr. NL *splenium* + E *-al*] **1 :** of, relating to, or being a thin membrane bone on the inner side of the mandible of many vertebrates below mammals that resembles a splint and is usu. in close relation with the dentary **2 :** relating to a splenius muscle **3 :** of or relating to the splenium

²splenial \"\ *n* -S : a splenial bone

splen·ic \ˈsplenik, -lēn-, -nēk\ *also* **spleni·cal** \-nəkəl, -nēk-\ *adj* [*splenic* fr. L *splenicus*, fr. Gk *splēnikos*, fr. *splēn* spleen + *-ikos* -ic; *splenical* fr. L *splenicus* + E *-al* — more at SPLEEN] : of, relating to, or located in the spleen

splenic artery *n* : the branch of the coeliac artery that carries blood to the spleen and sends branches also to the pancreas and the cardiac end of the stomach

splenic fever *n* **1** *or* **splenic apoplexy** : ANTHRAX 2 **2 :** TEXAS FEVER

splenic flexure *n* : the sharp bend of the colon under the spleen where the transverse colon joins the descending colon

splenic pulp *n* : the characteristic tissue of the spleen

splenic vein *n* : the vein that carries blood away from the spleen, that in man is formed by five or six large branches which unite a short distance from the spleen, and that joins the superior mesenteric vein to form the portal vein

spleni·fi·ca·tion \ˌsplēnəfəˈkāshən, -len-\ *n* -S [F *splénification*, fr. *spléni-* splen- + *-fication*] : SPLENIZATION

sple·ni·tis \spləˈnīd·əs\ *n* -ES [NL, fr. Gk *splēnitis*, fr. *splēn* spleen + *-itis*] : inflammation of the spleen

sple·ni·um \ˈsplēnēəm\ *n, pl* **sple·nia** \-nēə\ [NL, fr. L, plaster, patch, fr. Gk *splēnion* bandage, spleenless person, spleenwort, dim. of *splēn* spleen — more at SPLEEN] : the thick rounded fold forming the posterior border of the corpus callosum and being continuous by its undersurface with the fornix

sple·ni·us \-nēəs\ *n, pl* **sple·nii** \-nēˌī\ [NL, fr. L *splenium* plaster, patch] : a flat muscle of each side of the back of the neck and upper thoracic region in man arising as a single muscle from the ligamentum nuchae, the spinous processes of the last cervical and six upper thoracic vertebrae, and the supraspinous ligament but dividing into a part that inserts into the mastoid process of the temporal bone and the occipital bone and a part that inserts into the transverse processes of the upper two or three cervical vertebrae — called also respectively *splenius capitis, splenius cervicis*

spleni·za·tion \ˌsplenəˈzāshən, -len-, -ˌnīˈz-\ *n* -S [F *splénisation*, fr. *spléni-* splen- + *-isation* -ization] : the condition of being or process of becoming like a spleen ⟨the ~ of the tissue of a congested lung⟩

spleno- — see SPLEN-

spleno·cyte \ˈsplēnəˌsīt, -len-\ *n* -S [ISV *splen-* + *-cyte*] : a macrophage of the spleen

spleno·gen·ic \ˌ⸗⸗ˈjenik\ *adj* [*spleno-* + *-genic*] : of splenic origin

sple·noid \ˈsplēˌnȯid\ *adj* [ISV *splen-* + *-oid*] : resembling a spleen

spleno·meg·a·ly \ˌsplēnəˈmegəlē, ˌsplen-\ *n* -ES [ISV *splen-* + *-megaly*] : enlargement of the spleen

splent *var of* SPLINT

splen·u·lus \ˈsplenyələs\ *or* **sple·nun·cu·lus** \spləˈnəŋkyələs\ *n, pl* **splenu·li** \-nyəˌlī\ *or* **splenuncu·li** \-kyəˌlī\ [NL, dim. of L *splen* spleen] : a rudimentary or accessory spleen

spleu·chan \ˈsplükən\ *n* -S [ScGael *spliùcan* & IrGael *spliúchán*] *Scot & Irish* : a pouch esp. for holding tobacco or money

¹splice \ˈsplīs\ *vt* -ED/-ING/-S [obs. D *splissen* to split ends into separate strands, splice, fr. MD; akin to MD *splitten* to split — more at SPLIT] **1 :** to fasten together esp. end to end and esp. in order to form a continuous length: as **a :** to unite (two ropes or two parts of a rope) esp. by sticking or tucking the strands of one rope or part between or around each other **b :** to unite (as spars, timbers, or rails) into a single length by lapping together two ends or by applying a piece that laps upon the two ends and binding or making fast; *specif* : to connect (railroad rails) end to end with joint bars **c :** to join (as two lengths of photographic film or paper or recording tape) by or as if by cementing or fusing the ends together; *also* : to transfer (as a sound or picture) to a recording or film by splicing in a piece of recorded tape or film ⟨an audience's laughs have been recorded and are *spliced* into the thirty-minute comedy film —Goodman Ace⟩ **2 :** to attach to, fix in, or join onto something ⟨~ a rope to a chain⟩ ⟨proposing to ~ upon the tariff bill an income tax —N.W.Stephenson⟩; *specif* : to graft (a slip or shoot) into stock by lapping or by applying a piece that laps and binding or making fast **3 :** to make, form, or repair by splicing ⟨bone and ivory knitting needles were often *spliced* in order to obtain the required length —Mary Thomas⟩ ⟨the broken girder can be *spliced* —*New Yorker*⟩ **4 :** to unite in marriage : MARRY ⟨asked the preacher to ~ them⟩ — **splice the main brace :** to give out or drink spirits on a special occasion or after great hardship or effort

²splice \"\ *n* -S **1 :** the act or result of joining or fusing esp. end to end: as **a :** a joining of two cords or ropes or two parts of the same cord or rope made by interweaving or intertwining the strands in such a way that the circumference of the joint is no greater or not much greater than the circumference of the rope — see CHAIN SPLICE, EYE SPLICE, LONG SPLICE, SHORT SPLICE **b :** a joining of the ends of long rigid objects (as spars, timbers, or rails) by lapping the ends or applying a piece lapping both ends and by making fast (as by binding or bolting) **c :** a fused or cemented joint in a length of photographic film or paper or recording tape **2 :** MARRIAGE, WEDDING **3 :** the part of the handle of a cricket bat that is inserted in the blade **4 :** SPLICING 2

splice bar *n* : JOINT BAR

spliced *adj* [fr. past part. of ¹*splice*] : reinforced with an extra thread at heel, foot, and toe — used of knitted hose

splice graft *n* : a plant graft made by cutting both stock and scion across obliquely, fitting the cut surfaces so that the cambiums are in contact, and tying — called also *whip graft*; see GRAFT illustration

splic·er \ˈsplīsə(r)\ *n* -S : one that splices; *specif* : a device for making splices in lengths of photographic film or paper

splicing *n* -S [fr. gerund of ¹*splice*] **1 :** a spliced section or part : SPLICE **2 :** a reinforcement of knitted hose with an extra thread at heel, foot, and toe

splicing chamber *n* : CABLE VAULT

¹spline \ˈsplīn\ *n* -S [origin unknown] **1 :** a thin wood, metal, or plastic strip : SLAT: as **a :** a loose tongue between two pieces of heavy subflooring used in place of a tongue-and-groove joint **b :** a flexible strip used as a guide in drawing curved lines **2 :** FEATHER KEY; *also* : a keyway for a feather key

²spline \"\ *vt* -ED/-ING/-S **1 :** to cut a keyway in for a feather key : SLOT ⟨a *splined* shaft⟩ **2 :** to attach or couple by means of a spline ⟨an exterior of cedar logs *splined* together —*Amer. Builder*⟩ ⟨shell and sleeve assembly *splined* to the armature shaft —Joseph Heitner⟩

spline shaft *n* : a splined shaft; *specif* : one having a number of equally spaced grooves cut in the shaft so as to form a series of projecting keys and fitting into an internally grooved cylindrical member

spline weight *n* : a usu. lead metal weight used for confining a spline to the desired curve — called also *dolphin*

¹splint \ˈsplint\ *or* **splent** \ˈsplent\ *n* -S *often attrib* [ME *splint, splent*, fr. MLG *splinte, splente*; akin to MD *splinte* splint, Norw *splint* wooden nail, wedge, OHG *spaltan* to split — more at SPILL] **1 :** a small plate or strip of metal — see SPLINT ARMOR **2 a** (1) *dial Brit* : LATH (2) : a thin strip of wood interwoven with others in caning (3) : a piece split off : SPLINTER (4) : a rigid or flexible material (as wood, metal, plaster, fabric, or adhesive tape) used to protect, immobilize, or restrict motion in a part ⟨an adhesive ~ on the chest⟩ ⟨a plaster ~ for a fractured leg⟩ ⟨a nasal ~ after rhinoplasty⟩ **b :** SAPWOOD **3 a :** an exostosis on the upper part of the cannon bone of a horse usu. on the inside of the leg — compare PEGGED SPLINT **b :** SPLINT BONE **4 :** SPLINT COAL

²splint \"\ *vt* -ED/-ING/-S **1 a :** to immobilize (as a broken bone) with a splint **b :** to support or brace with or as if with a splint **2 :** to protect against pain by reducing motion ⟨the patient ~*ed* his chest by a fixed position and shallow breathing⟩

splint·age \-tij, -tēj\ *n* -S : the application of splints

splint armor *n* : armor of usu. overlapping thin metal plates allowing the limbs to move freely

splint basket *n* : a usu. rectangular container having the sides and bottom formed from woven or braided splints crossed at right angles, and having some type of handle : MARKET BASKET 1a

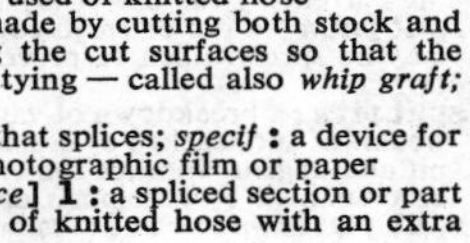

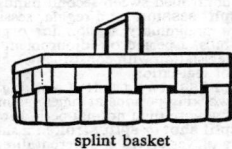

splint basket

splint bone *n* **1 :** one of the rudimentary metacarpal or metatarsal bones resembling a splint on either side of the cannon bone in the limbs of a horse and related animals **2 :** FIBULA

splint-bottom \ˈ⸗ˌ⸗⸗\ *or* **splint-bottomed** \ˈ⸗ˌ⸗⸗\ *adj, of a chair* : having a seat woven of splints

splint coal *n* [so called fr. its splintery fracture] : a very hard bituminous steam coal of dull appearance and laminated structure that gives out intense heat when burning — compare BRIGHT COAL

¹splin·ter \ˈsplintə(r)\ *n* -S [ME, fr. MD *splinter, splenter*; akin to MLG *splinte, splente* splint — more at SPLINT] **1 a** (1) : a thin often jagged or needlelike piece split or rent off lengthwise : SLIVER, CHIP, FRAGMENT ⟨gloves . . . protect a worker from sharp steel ~*s* —Michael Cawley⟩ ⟨the steering wheel . . . was knocked into ~*s* by an enemy shot —Edward Breck⟩ (2) : a small jagged or needlelike particle or flash ⟨flying ~*s* of ice —William Beebe⟩ ⟨irradiated for a moment now and then by ~*s* shooting through the darkness —E.K.Brown⟩ **b :** a usu. small group or faction broken away from an organization or body : a dissident faction ⟨this process does seem to split up the whole religious group into many ~*s* —J.O.Nelson⟩ **2 :** SPLINT **3 :** a minute, worthless, or insignificant piece or object ⟨carped at lesser breeds who failed in some ~ of the religious law —*Interpreter's Bible*⟩ ⟨contributed various ~*s* of hackwork —Clifton Fadiman⟩ ⟨no mere ~ of a peak, but a majestic mountain —Claudia Cassidy⟩

²splinter \"\ *vb* **splintered; splintered; splintering** \-ntəriŋ, -n·triŋ\ **splinters** *vt* **1 a :** to split, rend, or break into long thin pieces : SHIVER, SHATTER ⟨the walls were ~*ed* by the explosion⟩ **b :** to split into fragments, parts, or factions ⟨liberal opinion . . . was marshaled, integrated, and effective; it is ~*ed* now —G.W.Johnson⟩ ⟨ownership has been ~*ed* into so many tiny and inadequate parcels —J.D.McGoldrick⟩ **2** *obs* : SPLINT ~ *vi* **1 a :** to become split into long pieces : become shivered ⟨heard the thud of hooves lashing out and timbers ~*ing* —Robinson Jeffers⟩ **b** (1) : to become split into factions ⟨the politicians hope the veterans ~ and never wield their strength together —J.B.Martin⟩ (2) : to break away from an organization or entity : SECEDE ⟨will ~ off to form a third party —*Newsweek*⟩ **2 :** to fall or proceed in splinters ⟨the rain was ~*ing*, half frozen, against the kitchen window —Marjorie Housepian⟩

³splinter \"\ *adj* : of, relating to, belonging to, cast for, endorsed by, or being a faction or body broken away or independent from an original, larger, or primary organization or entity : FACTIONAL ⟨~ party⟩ ⟨~ group⟩ ⟨plagued by ~ politics —*Economist*⟩ ⟨the ~ votes . . . are considerably dispersed —Irving Kolodin⟩

splinter bar *n* **1** *Brit* : WHIFFLETREE **2 :** a crossbar in a coach or other vehicle to support the springs **3 :** a bar or other part in a wood-planing machine to decrease splintering of the fibers

splinter deck *n* : a less heavily armored deck usu. just below a ship's protective deck

splin·ter·ize \-təˌrīz\ *vb* -ED/-ING/-S [¹*splinter* + *-ize*] : SPLINTER

splin·ter·less \ˈsplintə(r)ləs\ *adj* : not liable to splinter

splinterproof \ˈ⸗⸗ˌ⸗\ *n* : a structure to protect against the splinters of bursting shells or bombs

splin·tery \ˈsplintərē, -n·trē, -ri\ *adj* **1 :** consisting of, resembling, or being embedded with splinters **2 a :** FRAGMENTARY **b :** NEEDLELIKE, ACICULAR, FIBROUS ⟨the ~ fracture of a mineral⟩

splints *pl of* SPLINT, *pres 3d sing of* SPLINT

splintwood \ˈ⸗ˌ⸗\ *n* : SAPWOOD

splinty \ˈsplintē, -ti\ *adj* [¹*splint* + *-y*] : SPLINTERY

¹splish-splash \ˈsplishˌsplash, -aa(ə)sh\ *vi* [redupl. of ¹*splash*] : to make a repeated splashing sound

²splish-splash \"\ *n* : a repeated splashing sound

¹split \ˈsplit, *usu* -id·+V\ *vb* **split** *or archaic* **splitted; split** *or archaic* **splitted; splitting; splits** [D *splitten*, fr. MD; akin to MLG *splīten* to split, MHG *slīzen*, OFris *splīta* to slit, OHG *spaltan* to split — more at SPILL] *vt* **1 a :** to divide or separate from end to end or in a lengthwise direction esp. sharply or suddenly or with force by cleaving or forcing apart usu. along a grain or a seam or by separating layers ⟨~ a board⟩ ⟨~ leather⟩ ⟨~ logs for firewood⟩ ⟨shock ~ the wall along a stud⟩ ⟨his trousers had been ~ down one leg⟩ ⟨girls come down to ~, clean, and pack the fish in barrels —Richard Joseph⟩ ⟨how to ~ clams on rocks —J.H.Wheelock⟩ ⟨~ open a roll and butter it⟩ ⟨~ a few sticks of kindling⟩: as (1) : to cause (a sail) to tear or rip ⟨a mainsail ~ by a gale⟩ : have (a sail) torn ⟨~ our mainsail in the storm⟩ (2) : to plough (a ridge) so as to cast the earth outward ⟨the ridges were ~ over the potatoes —Adrian Bell⟩ (3) : to divide (a pillar or post in a coal mine) by one or more roads (4) : to take (a rope) apart by separating the strands (5) : to cut (corrugated glass) to a desired width **b :** to affect as if by cleaving or forcing apart ⟨the whole plain . . . is gashed and torn and mauled and ~ —Thomas Wood †1950⟩ ⟨first bass of the season ~ the surface —Gertrude Schweitzer⟩ ⟨his face ~ by a huge yawn —John Wain⟩ ⟨the river ~*s* the town in two⟩ ⟨gorges which ~ the divide —R.L.Neuberger⟩ ⟨cloud was ~ with a flash of flame —R.H.Davis⟩ **2 a** (1) : to break up ⟨the wreck of a ship ~ upon a reef⟩ (2) : to tear or rend apart : BURST, RUPTURE ⟨warehouses *splitting* their sides with plunder —F.G.Slaughter⟩ (3) : to subject (an atom or atomic nucleus) to artificial disintegration esp. by fission **b :** to affect as if by breaking up or tearing apart : REND, SHATTER ⟨a roar that ~ the air⟩ ⟨series of explosives ~ our ears —J.B.Shaw⟩ : DISORDER, DISINTEGRATE ⟨mind is finally ~ asunder by her abnormal sexual jealousy —*Saturday Rev.*⟩ **3 :** to divide or separate into distinct parts or portions ⟨*splitting* the county into twenty-nine . . . rationing districts —Hal Burton⟩ ⟨scouts had been ~ into small detachments —Georg Meyers⟩ ⟨ornithologists have ~ these again into four more subspecies —Douglas Carruthers⟩ — often used with *up* ⟨*splitting* up the main colors into variants —C.W.H.Johnson⟩: as **a :** to divide between two or more persons : SHARE ⟨~ the loot⟩ ⟨~ up the cost⟩ ⟨~ the physics prize three ways⟩ ⟨~ a bottle of wine at dinner⟩ ⟨this pernicious practice of *splitting* fees —*Time*⟩ ⟨a man has a right to ~ his inheritance —Edward Sapir⟩ ⟨~ the pot at poker⟩ **b :** to divide into opposing factions, parties, or groups ⟨the solid South was ~ by internal revolt⟩ ⟨the issue ~ the village down the middle⟩ ⟨his candidacy ~ the labor vote⟩ **c :** to mark (a ballot) or otherwise cast or register (a vote) so as to vote for candidates of different parties ⟨usually ~ his ticket in national elections⟩ **d :** to divide (an air current) into separate currents (as in mine ventilation) **e :** to separate or break down (a chemical compound) into constituents : effect the cleavage of (as by hydrolysis : ¹CRACK 8 ⟨~ a fat into glycerol and fatty acids⟩ — sometimes used with *up* **f :** to remove by such separation — usu. used with *off* or *out* ⟨~ off carbon dioxide⟩ **g :** to divide (the stock of a corporation) by issuing a larger number of shares to existing shareholders usu. without increase in aggregate par value of capitalization for corporations with par value stock **h :** to win and lose an equal number of (as games or contests) ⟨~ a doubleheader⟩ ⟨~ the first four games⟩ **i :** to discard (one pair from a two-pair hand or one card of a pair) in draw poker to increase one's chance of improving the hand in the draw **j :** to bisect (a stamp) esp. into more than two pieces **4 :** to separate (the parts of a whole) by interposing something ⟨~ an infinitive⟩ ⟨~ the defense in hockey⟩ **5** *slang* : to reveal (as information, secrets) intentionally or unintentionally : BETRAY **6 :** to dilute (liquor) by adding water or a nonalcoholic liquid : CUT ~ *vi* **1 a :** to become divided or separated (as by cleaving, tearing) part from part or from end to end or in a lengthwise direction usu. along a grain or a seam or by the separating of layers ⟨the board ~ while he was driving the nail⟩ ⟨his coat had ~ at the seams⟩ ⟨fingernails showed a tendency to ~⟩ ⟨this wood ~*s* easily⟩ ⟨sails ~ in the storm⟩ **b :** to break apart or into pieces : break up ⟨ship ~*s* on the rock —Shak.⟩ : BURST, RUPTURE ⟨the jar ~ when the water froze⟩ ⟨fruit falls to the ground and ~*s* open⟩ **c** (1) : to part or open as if forced or torn apart by splitting ⟨the sky suddenly ~ open in a flash of lightning⟩ ⟨his face ~ into a wide grin⟩ (2) : to burst with laughter ⟨thought he would ~⟩ **2 a** (1) : to become divided up or separated off (as into parts, groups, parties, factions) ⟨stream ~*s* into numerous channels —G.R.Stewart⟩ — often used with *up* ⟨*splitting* up of a language into a number of dialects —Edward Sapir⟩ ⟨the group ~ up into two teams⟩ (2) : to break up into divergent or opposing groups ⟨began to ~ into left and right wings and then into smaller groupings —William Petersen⟩ ⟨court ~ four and four⟩ ⟨criticism, like religion, inevitably ~*s* into sects and schisms —C.I.Glicksberg⟩ ⟨~ into dissident groups —H.J. Laski⟩ (3) : *of a suit of cards* : to become divided evenly or as nearly so as possible **b :** to sever relations or connections esp. because of disagreement : SEPARATE ⟨~ after six years of marriage⟩ — often used with *with* ⟨had ~ with most of his former friends⟩ or with *from* ⟨caused such a furore by taking in a Negro and *splitting* from the national body —Cleveland Amory⟩ **3 :** to go very fast esp. at a run **4** *slang* : to betray confidence : let out a secret : act as an informer ⟨promised not to ~⟩ — often used with *on* ⟨on the point of *splitting* on the gang —Dorothy Sayers⟩ **5 :** to split one's vote **6 :** to apportion shares ⟨we all ~ equal and that was that —W.L. Gresham⟩ — often used with *with* ⟨said he would ~ with the others⟩ ⟨unwilling to ~ with anyone else⟩ **7 :** to turn up in a split — used of two cards of the same denomination dealt in faro **syn** see TEAR — **split hairs :** to make oversubtle or trivial distinctions : engage in hairsplitting — **split one's sides :** to laugh heartily or immoderately — **split openers :** to discard an essential part of the strength on which one has

opened in jackpot — **split straws :** to argue or quarrel over trifling differences — **split tacks :** to tack while an accompanying boat keeps on her course — used of one of two boats or skippers that have been on the same tack — **split the difference :** to reach agreement by compromise involving equal concessions esp. in a disagreement as to a price or to the conclusion of a contract

²split \"\ *n* -s **1 :** a narrow esp. lengthwise break or fissure made by or as if by splitting ⟨a small wedge driven into ~s in either end —Peter Heaton⟩ ⟨a spectacular flight through the deep ~ in the Andes —R.U. & Mary Light⟩ **:** CLEFT, CRACK, RENT: as **a** (1) **:** an acute-angled cut made in glassware with a grinding wheel (2) **:** a check in an article made of glass usu. extending from surface to surface **b :** a lengthwise separation of wood caused by the tearing apart of the wood cells **c :** an earmark on an animal made by slitting the ear — see EARMARK illustration **d :** a position of bowling pins left standing with space for one or more intermediate pins between them — compare RAILROAD **2 :** a piece of material that is split off or is made thin by splitting ⟨pegged or nailed the ~s together to get a big enough piece for the door —W.F.Harris⟩: as **a :** a splinter or fragment of wood **b :** a dent in the reed of a loom **c :** any of the underlying sections of a skin made by dividing it into two or more thicknesses **d :** any of the three or four strips into which osiers are cut for some kinds of basketwork — usu. used in pl. **e :** one of two or more narrow fabrics woven as one full-width cloth with selvage strips and then cut apart or split at these strips **3 a :** a breach or separation in an organized or normally cohesive group (as a political party or sect) or between partners or friends **:** DIVISION; *also* **:** a faction formed by such separation ⟨another ~ would just about end the party —S.H.Adams⟩ ⟨the ~ in the ranks of the Communist critics —C.I.Glicksberg⟩ ⟨exploiting ~s in the enemy camp —K.T.Chang⟩ ⟨a major ~ between the United States and most of the rest of the free world —McGeorge Bundy⟩ ⟨a rumored ~ between a famous acting couple⟩ **b :** any separation or division into or between esp. divergent or antagonistic elements or forces ⟨the ~ between the integrating and disintegrating tendencies —Lewis Mumford⟩ ⟨the fatal ~ between intellect and emotions —Hans Meyerhoff⟩ ⟨moral and religious ~s that are found in our very makeup as persons —John Dewey⟩ ⟨a very substantial ~ between the anxious egghead and the . . . lowbrow —Rosanna Shamray⟩ ⟨a ~ in his personality⟩ **4 :** the act or process of splitting: as **a :** a feat or the movement of lowering oneself to the floor (as by a dancer) or of leaping into the air (as by a gymnast or a figure skater) with the legs extended one to each side or one forward and one backward at right angles to the trunk **b :** the dealing of two cards of the same denomination in the same turn in faro with the result that the dealer takes half the bets on the card of that denomination **c :** SPLIT SHOT **d :** the act or process of splitting the stock of a corporation ⟨recent stock ~s —*Investor's Reader*⟩ ⟨approved a five-for-one ~ of the common stock —Richard Butter⟩ **5** *Brit* **a :** INFORMER **b :** PLAINCLOTHESMAN **6 :** a product of division by or as if by splitting: as **a :** any of the air currents in a mine formed by dividing a larger current; *also* **:** the workings ventilated by such a current **b :** a coal seam separated from another seam by a thick parting **c** *Brit* **:** a split roll or bun ⟨tea and cider passed around with cakes and ~s —A.T.Quiller-Couch⟩ **7 a :** a small bottle (of some drink) containing about half the quantity of the customary smaller commercial bottle used for that drink; *also* **:** a drink of half the usual quantity **:** half glass **b :** a brick of full length and width but half the usual thickness **c :** a share (as of booty, winnings, profits) claimed or promised **d :** an offset on a bulb (as in the narcissus) **e** (1) **:** the manner in which a suit is divided among the players in a card game (2) **:** an as nearly as possible even division of cards (as when four are divided 2-2 or five are divided 3-2) **f :** a piece of a bisected stamp **8 :** a mixed sweet composed of sliced fruit (as a banana divided lengthwise), ice cream, nuts, and syrups **syn** see BREACH

³split \"\ *adj* **1 :** CLEFT, DIVIDED, FRACTURED, ⟨~ collarbone⟩ ⟨~ lip⟩ ⟨came from a ~ home⟩ ⟨took a ~ vacation⟩ ⟨a badly ~ people⟩ ⟨was ~ between love and hatred —Carson McCullers⟩ ⟨were ~ on the question of women's rights⟩ ⟨executives betray a curiously ~ feeling —W.H.Whyte⟩ **2 :** that has been split or split off for use either singly or in combination ⟨fishing rod of ~ bamboo⟩ ⟨~ bandage⟩ ⟨~ hides⟩ **3** *of a stock* **:** that has been split ⟨~ shares⟩ ⟨a ~ issue⟩ **b** *of an order to buy or sell stock* **:** divided for execution part at one time and price and part at another **c** *of a stock quotation* **:** given in sixteenths rather than eighths **d :** divided on the London stock exchange into preferred ordinary stock and deferred ordinary stock **4** *of color printing* **:** using or done by means of a roller or ink fountain divided or adjusted to print two or more separate colors simultaneously ⟨~ fountain work⟩ ⟨~ roller method⟩ **5** *of a network or channel* **:** broken up to handle more than one program simultaneously **6 :** HETEROZYGOUS — used esp. by breeders of cage birds sometimes with *for* ⟨~ for both Cinnamon and Opaline —*All-Pets Mag.*⟩

splitbeak \ˈ=,=\ *n* **:** a touraco of the genus *Crinifer*

split bearing *or* **split box** *n* **:** a shaft bearing made in two pieces that are bolted together

split-board \ˈ=¦=\ *adj* **:** of or constituting a form of book construction in which the sewing tapes are anchored between laminated cover boards

split bond *n* **:** a bond in masonry that is formed by using face stretchers that are split lengthwise

split-bottom \ˈ=¦==\ *also* **split-bottomed** \ˈ=¦==\ *adj* **:** having a seat made of splits ⟨*split-bottom* chair⟩

split brilliant *n* **:** DOUBLE BRILLIANT

split buck *n* **:** an offensive play in football in which the quarterback fakes the ball to a back making a cross buck and then hands it to the fullback who goes thru the opposite side of the line

split call *n* **:** a telephone call on a party line that sounds on only half the telephones on the line

split chuck *n* **:** a hollow spring collet divided through the front into three equally spaced parts

split decision *n* **:** a decision in a boxing match reflecting a division of opinion among the referee and judges ⟨won a 10-round *split decision*⟩

split die *n* **1 :** a cutting or shaping die made in halves for convenience in making and economy in maintenance **2 :** a screw-thread die made in one piece with a slit from the outside to the central hole that makes it adjustable as to size

split-down \ˈ=,=\ *n* -s **:** the conversion of the outstanding shares of corporation stock into fewer shares

split fence *n* **:** a strong weighted V-shaped cribwork built on a hillside to deflect an avalanche

splitfinger \ˈ=,==\ *n* **:** a West Indian stomatopod crustacean (*Gonodactylus oerstedii*) that often cuts the fingers of its captor with its claws

split flag *n* **:** a swallow-tailed flag

split flap *n* **:** a hinged flap attached to the upper surface of a wing of an airplane usu. at the trailing edge to be raised for lateral control or to the lower surface of a wing to be deflected downward for giving increased lift and drag

split-foot \ˈ=¦=\ *adj, of hosiery* **:** having the sole and instep knitted of different yarns

split fraction *n, chiefly Brit* **:** PIECE FRACTION

split-hair \ˈ=¦=\ *adj* **:** minutely exact or precise ⟨this was *split-hair* stuff, this was walking tightrope on a split hair —Ira Wolfert⟩ ⟨a real model railroad runs to a *split-hair* schedule —J.C.Furnas⟩

split-half \ˈ=¦=\ *adj* **:** relating to, employing, or constituting a method of determining the reliability of a test by dividing the whole test into two halves presumably equivalent in difficulty and scoring the two halves separately ⟨*split-half* techniques⟩ ⟨*split-half* reliability⟩ ⟨*split-half* coefficients⟩

split hand *n* **:** a hand at bridge with no short suit **:** hand whose four suits are divided 4-3-3-3

split infinitive *n* **:** an infinitive with *to* having a modifier between the *to* and the verbal (as in "he hopes to really start")

split joint *n* **:** TONGUE JOINT

split jump *n* **:** a jump executed (as by a dancer) with legs extended horizontally and separated by 180 degrees

split key *n* **:** a key split at one end like a split pin and having similar uses

split kick *n* **:** a kick executed (as by a dancer) by raising a leg vertically upward

split-knob insulator \ˈ=¦=-\ *n* **:** a knob-shaped insulator split into two parts with either or both of the opposing surfaces notched for wires — see INSULATOR illustration

¹split-level \ˈ=¦==\ *adj* **:** divided vertically so that the floor level of rooms in one part is approximately midway between the levels of two successive stories in an adjoining part — used esp. of a dwelling with a one-story portion adjoining a two-story wing ⟨*split-level* design⟩ ⟨*split-level* architecture⟩ ⟨*split-level* house trailers⟩

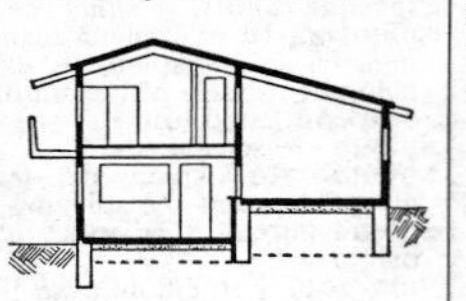
split-level in cross section

²split-level \"\ *n* **:** a split-level house

split-lift \ˈ=,=\ *n* **:** the piece of leather in a heel that attaches directly to the sole and is farthest from the top lift

split link *n* **:** a metal link consisting of two complete turns of a helix pressed flat together

split lug *n* **:** a lugsail divided below the yard along the line of the mast so that the forward part is practically a jib or foresail with its tack made fast in the bows and its clew shifted by sheets — see LUGSAIL illustration

split moss *n* **:** a moss of the order Andreaeales

split nut *n* **:** a screw nut split lengthwise so that it may be opened for quick adjustment

split off *vt* **:** to separate or remove by or as if by splitting ⟨*split* some kindling *off* from a log⟩ ⟨where only part of the assets of the corporation are *split off* into a new corporation —*U. S. Code*⟩ ⟨*split* the carbon dioxide *off*⟩ **~** *vi* **:** to separate oneself or become separated or removed by or as if by splitting ⟨pink-tinted granite existing in clean-cleaved layers that *split off* true and fine —Charles Rawlings⟩ ⟨ready to *split off* on the slavery question —S.H.Adams⟩ — often used with *from* ⟨blondness *splits off* from long-headedness —Ruth Benedict⟩ ⟨Miami are supposed to have *split off* from the Chippewa —*Amer. Guide Series: Mich.*⟩

split-off \ˈ=,=\ *n* -s [*split off*] **:** an act of splitting off or something that is split off from something else ⟨a succession of left-wing *split-offs*⟩; *specif* **:** a transfer of a distinctive business constituting one of two or more businesses owned by a corporation to another corporation controlled by the former accompanied by a surrender of part of the stock owned by the stockholders in the distributing corporation for stock in the controlled corporation — compare SPIN-OFF, SPLIT-UP

split page *n* **:** the first page of the second section of a newspaper

split pattern *n* **:** a pattern for a casting made in two or more pieces and doweled together to permit separate removal

split pea *n* **:** a dried hulled pea in which the cotyledons usu. split apart

split personality *n* **:** a personality structure ascribed to individuals and groups that is composed of two or more internally consistent groups of behavior tendencies and attitudes each acting independently of and apparently dissociated from the other ⟨the *split personality* of the manic-depressive —Allen Tate⟩ ⟨whole nation has had a *split personality* with respect to civil defense —F.P.Zeidler⟩ ⟨English department developed a *split personality* —Howard M. Jones⟩

split phase *n* **:** the phase difference of two or more currents into which a single-phase alternating current has been divided

split-phase \ˈ=¦=\ *adj* [*split phase*] **:** relating to or constituting an alternating single-phase current in a divided circuit when there is a difference of phase between the currents in the two branches

split-phase motor *n* **:** a motor run by a single-phase alternating current by the use of a phase splitter

split pin *n* **:** a pin or small cotter with one end split so that it may be spread open to prevent slacking back; *also* **:** SPRING COTTER

split pit *n* **:** a breakdown of various peaches caused by inherent weakness and marked by cracking and irregular breakup of the pit and degeneration of the embryo into a gummy mass often accompanied by gummosis of the fruit

split platen *n* **:** a business-machine platen divided so as to hold a form (as a ledger card) in one section and in the other a continuous listing tape on which is automatically typed or printed information (as credit posted) entered on the form

split pulley *or* **split rigger** *n* **:** a pulley made in semicircular halves for ease in applying to a shaft — called also *parting pulley*

split rail *n* **:** a fence rail split from a log

split ring *n* **1 :** a metal ring which consists of two complete turns of a helix pressed flat together and upon which objects (as keys) may be strung **2 :** a primitive form of commutator for a dynamo or motor consisting of a simple ring or cylindrical shell split axially with the parts insulated from each other **3 :** a metal ring used often along with bolts as a timber connector in heavy construction

split rivet *n* **:** a rivet with a bifurcated shank

split roof *n* **:** a roof made from strips split from straight-grained timber

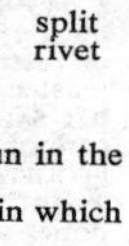
split rivet

split run *n* **:** a run (as of a newspaper or magazine) in which something (as an illustration or the wording of an advertisement) is changed part way through the run while remaining in the same position in the issue (as for testing the relative effectiveness of the two pieces of copy)

split S *n, often cap S* **:** a flight maneuver consisting of a half snap roll followed by a pullout to normal flight and accomplishing a 180 degree change in direction accompanied by a loss in altitude

splits *pres 3d sing of* SPLIT, *pl of* SPLIT

splitsaw \ˈ=,=\ *n* **:** RIPSAW

split scene *n* **:** a scene on the Elizabethan stage begun in the alcove but extending to the whole stage

split-scion graft \ˈ=¦=-\ *n* **:** a modified veneer graft in which the scion is split to form two scions

split screen *n* **:** a technique for projecting onto a television screen images from two cameras side by side or composed into a single picture

split second *n* **:** a fractional part of a second **:** any almost imperceptible period of time **:** FLASH, INSTANT ⟨happened in a *split second*⟩ ⟨one *split second* of surprise —Margery Sharp⟩

split-second watch *n* **:** a stopwatch with two independently controlled sweep-second hands

split session *n* **:** a regular session of a legislature divided into a preliminary session for organization and introduction of bills, a period of adjournment (as for discussion of proposed legislation with constituents), and a final session for enactment of legislation

split shift *n* **:** a shift of working hours divided into two or more working periods at times (as morning and evening) separated by more than normal periods of time off (as for lunch or rest)

split shot *or* **split stroke** *n* **:** a shot or stroke in croquet in which a player drives in different directions his own ball and another ball placed in contact

split shovel *n* **:** a device for sampling ground ore consisting of a series of parallel troughs separated by gaps of the same width as the troughs and provided with a handle for lifting

split skin *n* **1 :** a skin cut open along the belly and legs and spread out flat for drying **2 :** leather made from hides of large mammals whose skins are too thick in the natural state and are split into thinner layers for tanning

split stitch *n* **:** a fine chain stitch for outlining that is formed by bringing the needle through a soft thread

splitstone \ˈ=¦=\ *adj* **:** made of stones split along the bedding planes into units from one to six feet long and about four inches thick and having a height of one, two or three courses of brick ⟨~ hearth⟩ ⟨~ finish⟩

split switch *n* **:** a track structure used to divert rolling stock from one railroad track to another and consisting essentially of two movable point rails with necessary fixtures

split T *or* **split T formation** *n* **:** a variation of the football T formation in which the quarterback either moves along the line of scrimmage with the ball or keeps or pitches the ball depending on the play of the on side end

splittail \ˈ=,=\ *n* **1 :** a California market fish (*Pogonichthys macrolepidotus*) of the family Cyprinidae **2 :** PINTAIL **3 :** a tail in which some of the feathers are out of line

split-tail perch *n* **:** either of two surf fishes (*Phanerodon furcatus* or *Damalichthys vacca*) of the Pacific coast of No. America that have deeply forked tails and are common market fishes in California

splitted *archaic past of* SPLIT

¹split·ter \ˈsplid·ə(r), -itə-\ *n or vb* [LG *splittere*, fr. MLG; akin to MLG *spliten* to split — more at SPLIT] **:** SPLINTER

²splitter \"\ *n* -s [¹*split* + *-er*] **1 :** one that splits: **a :** a person (as a workman) who splits something: as (1) **:** a textile worker who splits warps according to the pattern for each beam (2) **:** an operator of a hide-splitting machine (3) **:** one that uses a resaw or a ripsaw (4) **:** one that splits plant shoots into strips for use in basketry (5) **:** a slaughterhouse worker who by sawing and cleaving lengthwise splits the backbone and neckbone of a cattle or hog carcass **b :** a device or an implement used in splitting something: as (1) **:** a tool used in splitting the edge of a plate in caulking before finally closing up the part so split (2) **:** a machine for splitting a hide or skin into two or more thicknesses (3) **:** a small narrow chisel used by stonemasons (as in carving, lettering) (4) **:** a butcher's implement for splitting a carcass (5) **:** any of various devices (as a riffle, a split shovel) for dividing a stream (as of water, ore, earth) into two or more parts **2 a :** one that makes overnice distinctions **:** HAIRSPLITTER; *also* **:** one that diffuses his efforts among many interests and accomplishes little **:** INCOMPETENT **b :** a taxonomist that regards every identifiable variant of living matter as a significant nameable natural unit — compare LUMPER

splitter·man \ˈ==mən\ *n, pl* **splittermen 1 :** an operator of a machine for cutting defects from wood and splitting it to size for pulp-making machines **2 :** BOLTER

split thumb *n* **:** SPLITFINGER

split ticket *n* **:** a ticket or ballot cast by a voter who splits his vote **:** ballot on which the voter has voted for candidates of more than one party — compare STRAIGHT TICKET

¹splitting *adj* [fr. pres. part. of ¹*split*] **:** that splits or causes to split: as **a :** causing a sensation of rending or piercing **:** very severe ⟨a ~ headache⟩ **b :** very fast or quick **c :** causing one's sides to split **:** very funny or comical ⟨~ farce⟩ ⟨~ laugh⟩

²splitting *n* -s [fr. gerund of ¹*split*] **:** something split off — usu. used in pl. ⟨~s of mica⟩

splitting chisel *n* **:** a steel chisel used by a stonecutter

splitting gun *n* **:** a pointed steel cylinder that is hollow for half its length and is used for splitting very large logs by means of an explosive charge of black powder that is loaded into the pointed end which is then driven into the center end of a log and the powder ignited

splitting plate *n* **:** a plate used for dividing a mold into halves (as in casting split pulleys)

split turning *n* **:** a turning (as of a baluster) split vertically and applied decoratively (as to the surface of a chest or cupboard) or used as a spindle in a chairback

¹split-up \ˈ=,=\ *n* -s [fr. *split up*, v.] **1 :** an act or result of splitting up **:** SEPARATION ⟨*split-up* of the Roman Empire —Sebastian De Grazia⟩ ⟨trying desperately to avoid a domestic *split-up*⟩ **2 a :** the act or process of splitting the stock of a corporation **:** SPLIT ⟨stock *split-ups* and stock dividends⟩ ⟨a tax-free *split-up*⟩ **b :** the breaking up of a corporation or interrelated group of corporations by legal compulsion or otherwise ⟨*split-up* of utility holding companies⟩ **c :** a transfer of a distinctive business constituting one of two or more businesses owned by a corporation to another corporation controlled by the former accompanied by the surrender of all stock owned by stockholders in the distributing corporation for new stock in both that and in the controlled corporations — compare SPIN-OFF, SPLIT-OFF

²split-up \ˈ=¦=\ *adj, of the hindquarters of a horse* **:** lacking substance **:** SHORT, NARROW; *esp* **:** lacking sound muscular development between the thighs

split vision *n* **:** an apparent ability to see out of the opposite corners of the two eyes at the same time **:** extraordinarily acute peripheral vision

split wheel *n* **:** SPLIT PULLEY

split wing *n* **:** a severely slipped wing

splitworm \ˈ=,=\ *n* **:** POTATO TUBERWORM

¹splodge \ˈspläj\ *n* -s [prob. alter. of ¹*splotch*] *chiefly Brit* **:** SPLOTCH ⟨rook dropped a ~ —Enid Bagnold⟩ ⟨thin green ~ of slime —Stephen Spender⟩

²splodge \"\ *vb* -ED/-ING/-S *vt, chiefly Brit* **:** SPLOTCH ⟨newsboys . . . trying to sell a few fresh-*splodged* violet words . . . that told us nothing at all —H.E.Bates⟩ **~** *vi, chiefly Brit* **:** SPLASH, SLOSH ⟨*splodged* about the streets —A.L.Rowse⟩

splodgy \-jē, -ji\ *adj* -ER/-EST *chiefly Brit* **:** SPLOTCHY ⟨big ~ brown hands —R.A.W.Hughes⟩

¹splore \ˈsplō(ə)r, -ȯ(ə)r\ *n* -s [origin unknown] **1** *Scot* **a :** FROLIC, MERRYMAKING, FESTIVITY **b :** a drinking bout **:** CAROUSAL **2** *Scot* **:** COMMOTION, BROIL

²splore \"\ *vi* **1** *Scot* **a :** FROLIC, REVEL **b :** RIOT **2** *Scot* **:** to make an ostentatious display **:** BRAG, BOAST

¹splosh \ˈsplàsh\ *vb* -ED/-ING/-ES [by alter.] **:** SPLASH ⟨~*ed* awkwardly through the black Pacific —E.K.Gann⟩ ⟨~*ed* along the rucked road —Adrian Bell⟩ ⟨~*ed* his feet about in the puddle⟩

²splosh \"\ *n* -ES **1 :** SPLASH ⟨plunge with a great ~ into the great social and political agonies of our time —V.S.Pritchett⟩ **2** *slang* **:** MONEY

³splosh \"\ *adv* **:** with a splash or a splashing sound — often used interjectionally

sploshy \-shē, -shi\ *adj* -ER/-EST **:** SLOPPY ⟨~ slush⟩

¹splotch \ˈsplàch\ *or* **splatch** \ˈsplach\ *n* -ES [*splotch* perh. blend of *spot* and *blotch*; *splatch* alter. (prob. influenced by *splash*) of *splotch*] **:** a contrasting patch **:** BLOT, BLOTCH **:** DAUB, SMEAR **:** SPOT, STAIN ⟨~*es* of rust⟩ ⟨a ~ of red paint⟩ ⟨his napkin a white ~ on the rug —Josephine Johnson⟩

²splotch \"\ *or* **splatch** \"\ *vt* -ED/-ING/-ES **:** to mark with a splotch **:** cover with splotches ⟨~*ed* face⟩ ⟨dark mass ~*ed* with white —Erskine Caldwell⟩ ⟨his record is ~*ed* and muddy —R.S.Allen⟩ ⟨paintings . . . ~*ed* with conventionally sharp colors —F.J.Mather⟩

splotch·i·ly \ˈsplächəlē, -li\ *adv* **:** in a splotchy manner **:** so as to be splotchy

splotch·i·ness \-chēnəs, -chin-\ *n* -ES **:** the quality or state of being splotchy

splotchy \-chē, -chi\ *adj* -ER/-EST **:** covered or marked with splotches

splty *abbr* specialty

splunge \ˈsplənj\ *vb* [blend of ¹*splash* and ¹*plunge*] *dial* **:** PLUNGE

¹splurge \ˈsplərj, -lə̄j, -ləij\ *n* -s [perh. blend of ¹*splash* and ¹*surge*] **1 :** an ostentatious or conspicuous demonstration or effort **:** burst of activity **:** great display ⟨without ~ or ostentation —*Fortune*⟩ ⟨last carefree ~s of pre-Depression film production —Arthur Knight⟩ ⟨frontier spirit was having its ~ —V.L.Parrington⟩ ⟨orgy of ~ characteristic of an easy-money period —S.H.Adams⟩ **2 a :** SPLASH ⟨dashing away in a ~ of foam —Rose Macaulay⟩ **b :** SPLOTCH ⟨imperfections . . . such as the ~ of the ink in a print —J.C.Tarr⟩

²splurge \"\ *vb* -ED/-ING/-S *vi* **1 :** to make a showy display ⟨of a grave and orderly demeanor . . . never *splurged* —G.D. Brown⟩ ⟨wild flowers ~ —*Time*⟩ **2 :** to indulge oneself in some unusual activity, expense, pleasure, luxury ⟨liked to ~ a bit on weekends⟩ — often used with *on* ⟨*splurged* on a steak and strawberries for dessert —Nancy Wilbur⟩ **3 :** to splash heavily **:** SLOSH **~** *vt* **:** to spend extravagantly, ostentatiously, or as a self-indulgence ⟨swarming into New Orleans to ~ millions during a five-day sports program —*Newsweek*⟩

splurgy \-jē, -ji\ *adj* -ER/-EST **:** given to or characterized by ostentatious display or extravagance

splurt \ˈsplər|t, ˈsplə̄|, ˈsplə̇i|, *usu* |d.+V\ *vb* -ED/-ING/-S [by alter.] **:** SPURT

¹splut·ter \ˈspləd·ə(r), -ətə-\ *n* -s [prob. alter. of ²*sputter*] **1 :** a confused noise (as of hasty speaking) ⟨a few ~s from the other end, then laughter —*N.Y. Herald Tribune*⟩ ⟨an occasional ~ of birds among the leaves —Gerald Durrell⟩ **2 :** a loud or violent splashing or sputtering ⟨dumped them overside with a sizzle and a ~ —C.S.Forester⟩ ⟨~ of rain came hissing down the chimney —J.C.Powys⟩ ⟨the flaming ~ of the volcano and the rending crash of the earthquake —W.E.Swinton⟩

²splutter \"\ *vb* -ED/-ING/-S *vi* **1 :** to speak hastily and indistinctly ⟨hardly a man in authority today who does not . . . ~ at some of the restrictions —F.L.Allen⟩ ⟨~*ed* about it being . . . too ill-considered —Louis Auchincloss⟩ **2 :** to make a series of sudden short crackling or popping sounds **:** SPUTTER ⟨bacon ~*ing* in the kitchen —Jan de Hartog⟩ ⟨steam hammer thudding . . . and the electric arcs ~*ing* —Gavin Casey⟩ **3 :** to hurry noisily **:** BUSTLE ⟨the last bus ~*ed* down the highway —D.C.Peattie⟩ ~ *vt* **1 :** to utter hastily and indistinctly **:** STAMMER ⟨he ~*s* a series of observations and analyses which are individually coherent —Robert Halsband⟩ — often used with *out* or *forth* **2 :** to scatter by or as if by splashing ⟨a plane . . . ~*ing* cannon fire —H.E.Bates⟩

splut·ter·er \-d·ərə(r), -tə-\ *n* -s **:** one that splutters

splut·tery \-rē, -ri\ *adj* **:** marked by spluttering **:** suggestive of spluttering ⟨voice was thin and ~ —Leslie Charteris⟩

SPM *abbr* **1** self-propelled mount **2** short particular meter **3** *often not cap* [L *sine prole mascula*] without male issue **4** smaller profit margin **5** *often not cap* strokes per minute

spn *abbr* specimen

SPO *abbr* sea post office

spode \'spōd\ *n* -s *usu cap* [after Josiah *Spode* †1827 Eng. potter] **:** ceramic ware (as bone china, stone china, or parian ware) made at the works established by Josiah Spode in 1770 at Stoke on Trent, England

spo·di·um \'spōdēəm\ *n* -s [ME, fr. L, fr. Gk *spodion*, dim. of *spodos* wood ash] **1** *obs* **:** a powder obtained as a product or residue of combustion (as soot from melting metals or vegetable ash) **2 :** bone or animal charcoal; *esp* **:** spent bone black from sugar factories used as fertilizer

spod·o·gram \'spädə,gram\ *n* [Gk *spodos* wood ash + E *-gram*] **:** a preparation of ash esp. of a woody portion of a plant that is used in investigating structure and the location of minerals in the plant

spo·dop·tera \spə'däptərə\ *n*, *cap* [NL, fr. Gk *spodos* wood ash + NL *-ptera*] **:** a genus of armyworms that includes numerous economically important pests

spod·u·mene \'späjə,mēn\ *n* -s [prob. fr. F *spodumène*, fr. G *spodumen*, fr. Gk *spodoumenos*, pres. part. of *spodousthai* to be burnt to ashes, fr. *spodos* wood ash; fr. its becoming ash-colored when exposed to the blowpipe] **:** a monoclinic mineral $LiAlSi_2O_6$ of the pyroxene group that is a lithium aluminum silicate of white to yellowish, purplish, or emerald-green color and that occurs in prismatic crystals often of great size (hardness 6.5–7, sp. gr. 3.13–3.20) — see HIDDENITE, KUNZITE

spof·fish \'späfish\ *adj* [prob. fr. E dial. *spoffle* (alter. of *spuffle*) + E *-ish*] **:** FUSSBUDGETY

¹spoil \'spȯil, *esp before pause or consonant* -ȯiəl; *dial* 'spī(ə)l\ *n* -s [ME *spoile*, fr. MF *espoille*, *espuille*, fr. L *spolium* hide stripped from an animal, armor stripped from an enemy, booty— more at SPILL] **1 a** (1) **:** the plunder taken in war **:** material, land, or property seized or confiscated by the victor of an armed aggression ⟨claim . . . colonies in Africa as its share of the ~*s* of war —Vera M. Dean⟩ (2) **:** arms or armor stripped from a defeated enemy **b :** something taken unlawfully usu. by stealth ⟨steal from the rich and give the ~*s* to the poor —E.V. Lucas⟩ **2 a :** the act or practice of plundering **:** SPOLIATION ⟨would have given their town up to ~ —Sir Walter Scott⟩ **b** *obs* **:** an act of plunder ⟨the man that hath no music in himself . . . is fit for treason, stratagems, and ~*s* —Shak.⟩ **c :** an object of plunder ⟨fire the palace, the fort . . ., leave to the foeman no ~ at all —Rudyard Kipling⟩ **3 a** *obs* **:** an injurious or destructive act **b :** the act of damaging **:** HARM, IMPAIRMENT, RUIN ⟨villainous company hath been the ~ of me —Shak.⟩ **4 a** *obs* **:** the cast skin of a snake **:** SLOUGH **b :** the cast skin of an animal; *also* **:** a treated animal hide ⟨moccasins of the ~ of deer⟩ **c spoils** *pl* **:** animal remains **5 a :** something that is gained by strength or special effort ⟨the ~*s* of a conservative industrial life —Van Wyck Brooks⟩ **b :** a collector's item (as an antique, rare book, or natural specimen) acquired by special and knowledgeable skill or search **6 :** public offices and their emoluments that are the peculiar property of a successful political party or faction to be bestowed for its own advantage — usu. used in pl. ⟨patronage and ~*s* . . . have helped to finance complete party machinery —D.D.McKean⟩ ⟨to the victors belong the ~*s* —W.L.Marcy⟩ **7 :** material (as refuse earth or rock) excavated usu. in mining, dredging, or excavating ⟨an artificial island built of ~ from dredging operations —*Amer. Guide Series: Texas*⟩ **8** [²*spoil*] **:** something imperfectly made **:** an object having flaws produced in the process of manufacture **9** [²*spoil*] **a :** a deal in spoil five in which no player wins the pool **b :** the act of winning a trick that causes this result

²spoil \"\ *vb* **spoiled** \-ld, -lt\ *or* **spoilt** \-lt\ **spoiled** *or* **spoilt; spoiling; spoils** [ME *spoilen*, fr. MF *espoillier*, fr. L *spoliare*, fr. *spolium* spoil] *vt* **1 a** *archaic* **:** to despoil (an enemy) esp. of armor and weapons on the field of battle **b** *archaic* **:** DIVEST, STRIP — often used with *of* ⟨made to ~ themselves of soiled arms —Edmund Spenser⟩ **2** *archaic* **:** to seize or take possession of by force or violence **:** PLUNDER ⟨enter into a man's house and ~ his goods —Mt 12:29 (AV)⟩ **3 :** to strip by violent means **:** ROB ⟨deliver him that is ~*ed* out of the hand of the oppressor —Jer 21:12 (AV)⟩ ⟨recovery of property of which it has been ~*ed* —W.E.Channing⟩ **4 :** to sack of valuable possessions **:** PILLAGE ⟨bind the strong man and then he will ~ his house —Mt 12:29 (AV)⟩ **5 :** DEPRIVE ⟨I may ~ the Egyptians of a proverb —J.L.Lowes⟩ **6 :** to cut up (a hen) **:** CARVE ⟨think of the pleasure of calling on the hostess for a ruling as to whether one was . . . ~*ing* a hen —Basil Davenport⟩ **7 :** to cause to decay or perish **:** cause to become of little or no use or value **:** seriously impair **:** MAR, RUIN ⟨the whole island . . . was inundated, and much valuable land ~*ed* —J.A.Steers⟩ ⟨more rain had fallen, the hay crop was *spoilt* —George Moore⟩ ⟨these thoughts . . . *spoilt* my sleep —Nevil Shute⟩ **8 a** *archaic* **:** DESTROY, KILL ⟨go down . . . and ~ them until the morning light, and let us not leave a man of them —1 Sam 14:36 (AV)⟩ **b** *obs* **:** to injure seriously **9 :** RAVISH ⟨am quite sure he would not ~ a virgin —Raymond Chandler⟩ **10 a :** to impair or injure the disposition or character of (a person) usu. by overindulgence, excessive adulation, or praise ⟨~*ed* by the high status accorded to them in their communities —Will Durant⟩ ⟨our only little girl, and . . . we ~ her —Margaret Deland⟩ **b :** to pamper excessively **:** CODDLE ~ *vi* **1 :** to practice plunder and robbery **2 :** to lose the best or valuable properties or qualities **:** become corrupted or tainted ⟨fruit will soon ~ in warm weather⟩ **3 :** to have an excessive desire esp. as a result of long deprivation **:** be extremely eager — usu. used with *for* ⟨was ~*ing* for a fight —Earle Birney⟩ **4 :** to play a defensive game often with marked emphasis on the thwarting of the opponents' efforts to start offensive movements ⟨~*ing* in soccer by constantly kicking the ball out of play⟩ **syn** see DECAY, INDULGE, INJURE

spoil·able \-ləbəl\ *adj* **:** capable of spoiling or of being spoiled

spoil·age \-lij, -lēj\ *n* -s **1 a :** the act of spoiling **b :** something that is spoiled or wasted (as sheets of paper in printing) **2 :** the process of decaying in foods esp. when caused by bacterial or fungal infection

spoil·a·tion \spȯi'lāshən\ *n* -s [alter. (influenced by ²*spoil*) of *spoliation*] **:** SPOLIATION

spoil bank *n* **:** a bank composed of waste earth which has been excavated

spoil·er \'spȯilə(r)\ *n* -s [²*spoil* + *-er*] **1 :** one that spoils: as **a :** one that plunders **:** PILLAGER, ROBBER ⟨estates soon became very great, tempting the ~ —G.G.Coulton⟩ **b :** one that corrupts, impairs, injures, or makes useless **2 :** a long narrow hinged or retractable plate that extends along the upper surface of an airplane wing and that may be raised above the surface for reducing the lift of the wing and increasing its drag

spoil five *n* [²*spoil* + *five*; fr. the rule that the game is spoiled if no one wins three of the five tricks] **:** a card game in which a pool is won by a player who wins three of the five tricks with a bonus for winning all five

spoil ground *n* **:** an area where excavated material is deposited

spoil heap *n* **:** a pile of refuse material from an excavation

spoil·ing \'spȯiliŋ\ *n* -s [ME, fr. gerund of *spoilen* to spoil] **:** an act of plundering or spoiling **:** a marauding raid

spoiling attack *n* [fr. *spoiling*, pres. part. of ²*spoil*] **:** a limited objective attack launched to disrupt enemy plans or operations

spoil–mold \'=,=\ *n* **:** WASTE MOLD

spoilsman \'=mən\ *n*, *pl* **spoilsmen** [*spoils* (pl. of ¹*spoil*) + *man*] **:** one who serves a cause or a party for a share of the spoils **:** one who makes or recognizes a demand for public office on the ground of partisan service

spoilsport \'=,=\ *n* [²*spoil* + *sport*] **:** one who spoils or mars sport or diversion ⟨was ~ enough to ask where the money was to come from —*Time*⟩

spoils system *n* **:** a practice of regarding public offices and their emoluments as so much plunder to be taken from the defeated party and distributed to members of the victorious party — opposed to *merit system*

spo·kan *or* **spo·kane** \spō'kan\ *n*, *pl* **spokan** *or* **spokans** *or* **spokane** *or* **spokanes** *usu cap* **1 a :** a Salishan people of northeastern Washington **b :** a member of such people **2 :** a dialect of Kalispel

spo·kane \(')spō'kan, -aa(ə)n, *by outsiders also* -kān\ *adj*, *usu cap* [fr. *Spokane*, city of eastern Wash.] **:** of or from the city of Spokane, Wash. ⟨*Spokane* churches⟩ **:** of the kind or style prevalent in Spokane

spo·kan·ite \-,nīt\ *n* -s *cap* [*Spokane*, city of Wash. + E *-ite*] **:** a native or resident of Spokane, Wash.

¹spoke [ME *spoken* (past pl. & past part.), alter. of *speken* (past pl. & past part.), fr. OE *spǣcon* (past pl.), *gespecen* (past part.)] *past & archaic past part of* SPEAK

²spoke \'spōk\ *n* -s [ME *spake*, *spoke*, fr. OE *spāca*; akin to OS *speca* spoke, MD *speke*, *speec*, OHG *speicha*, MD *spike* spike — more at SPIKE] **1 a :** the radius of a wheel **:** one of the small bars inserted in the hub of a wheel that serve to support the rim **:** a radiating bar or rod on a wheel — see WHEEL illustration **b :** something resembling a wheel spoke **2 :** a bar or rod designed to serve a specific purpose: as **a :** a rung of a ladder **b :** one of the poles used for bearing a coffin to the grave **c :** BALUSTER 1 ⟨the entrance hall was visible through the bannisters' ~*s* —Kay Boyle⟩ **3 :** one of the projecting handles of a steering wheel of a boat **4 a :** a bar of wood or metal to prevent the wheel of a vehicle from turning esp. in going downhill **:** CHOCK **b :** something that impedes **:** an obstacle to a course of action **:** OBSTRUCTION ⟨careless mistakes may be the ~ in the wheel of his advancement⟩ **5 :** STAKE 11 **6 :** a bar in drawnwork consisting of a solid row of buttonholing or overcasting across several threads **7 :** the length of rope that passes through the honda to the hand when spinning the rope

³spoke \"\ *vb* -ED/-ING/-S *vt* **1 :** to furnish with or as if with spokes **2 :** to block or impede with or as if with a spoke ⟨the scheme was my scheme and you might easily have *spoked* my wheel —F.W.Crofts⟩ ~ *vi* **:** to jut out like a spoke ⟨another road that *spoked* into their own —Thomas Wolfe⟩

⁴spoke *n* -s [prob. fr. ¹*spoke*, past part. of *speak*] **1** *dial Eng* **:** TALE, SPEECH **2** *dial Eng* **:** ENCHANTMENT

spoke auger *n* [²*spoke*] **:** a hollow cutter for forming a round tenon on the end of a spoke

spoke·less \-kləs\ *adj* [²*spoke* + *-less*] **:** having no spokes ⟨wagons with ~ wooden wheels —Alan Moore⟩

spo·ken \'spōkən\ *adj* [fr. past part. of ¹*speak*] **1 a :** expressed, told, or delivered by word of mouth **:** ORAL ⟨a ~ message⟩ **b :** used in speaking or conversation **:** UTTERED ⟨the ~ language⟩ **2 :** characterized by speaking in a specified manner — used in combination ⟨the Welsh-*spoken* schoolmaster —Gilbert Highet⟩ ⟨soft-*spoken*⟩ ⟨plain*spoken*⟩

spokeshave \'=,=\ *n* [²*spoke* + *shave*] **1 :** a drawing knife or small transverse plane with end handles for planing convex or concave surfaces **2 :** a notched concave scraper prob. used to shape curved or rounded artifacts

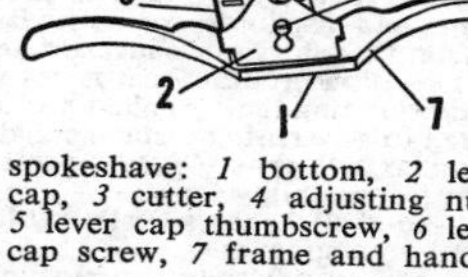

spokeshave: *1* bottom, *2* lever cap, *3* cutter, *4* adjusting nuts, *5* lever cap thumbscrew, *6* lever cap screw, *7* frame and handles

spokes·man \'spōksmən\ *n*, *pl* **spokesmen** [prob. fr. *spokes* (poss. sing. of ¹*spoke*, past part. of *speak* used as a noun) + *man*] **1 a :** one who speaks as the representative of another; *esp* **:** one delegated by others to express or present their views or opinions publicly ⟨acted as the industry ~ on current problems —*Current Biog.*⟩ ⟨a recognized ~ for the wage earners —William Green⟩ **b :** one that is or becomes an interpreter (as of an era) or an outstanding advocate (as of a cause) ⟨had the chance to become the ~ of the war generation —J.P.Bishop⟩ ⟨great statesmen . . . emerge as personalities and *spokesmen* for ideologies —F.L.Mott⟩ **2 :** one who makes a public address **:** ORATOR, SPEAKER

spokes·man·ship \-n,ship\ *n* **:** the position or status of a spokesman

spokes·woman \'spōks+,-\ *n*, *pl* **spokeswomen** [*spokes*man + *woman*] **:** a female spokesman

spokewise \'=,=\ *adv* [²*spoke* + *-wise*] **:** in a manner resembling the spokes of a wheel ⟨white dusty trails converge . . . ~ at the small Arab village —George Biddle⟩

spoky *adj* [²*spoke* + *-y*] *obs* **:** having or equipped with parts arranged like the spokes of a wheel

spo·li·ate \'spōlē,āt, *usu* -ād.+V\ *vb* -ED/-ING/-S [L *spoliatus*, past part. of *spoliare* to spoil] *vt* **:** to thoroughly despoil ~ *vi* **:** SPOIL 1 **syn** see RAVAGE

spo·li·a·tion \,==ˈāshən\ *n* -s [ME, fr. L *spoliation-*, *spoliatio*, fr. *spoliatus* (past part. of *spoliare* to plunder) + *-ion-*, *-io* -ion — more at SPOIL] **1 a :** the act of plundering **:** pillage or robbery in war **:** DESPOLIATION **b :** the state of having been despoiled or pillaged **2** *eccl & canon law* **a :** the appropriation of the fruits of a benefice whose incumbent has not yet resigned by one duly presented and instituted **b :** a process or writ for possession of a church or its fruits **3 :** injury done to or change made in a document by a stranger to the document — distinguished from *alteration* **4 :** the act of damaging or injuring esp. beyond reclaim or recovery ⟨the ~ of a magnificent piece of scenery —*Scots Mag.*⟩ **5 :** the destruction of a ship's papers or other documents showing its character and the nature of its business usu. when it is suspected of smuggling, carrying contraband of war, or being an enemy's ship that spoliates **:** SPOILER

spo·li·a·tor \'==,ād·ə(r)\ *n* -s [L, fr. *spoliatus* + *-or*] **:** one that spoliates **:** SPOILER

spo·li·a·to·ry \'spōlēə,tōrē\ *adj* [L *spoliatus* + E *-ory*] **:** of, relating to, or characterized by spoliation

¹spon·da·ic \(')spän'dāik, -āēk\ *also* **spon·da·i·cal** \-āəkəl, -āēkəl\ *adj* [*spondaic* fr. F or LL; F *spondaïque* fr. LL *spondaicus*, alter. of *spondiacus*, fr. Gk *spondeiakos*, fr. *spondeios* spondee; *spondaical* fr. LL *spondaicus* + E *-al*] **:** of, relating to, or constituting a spondee **:** consisting of spondees **:** characterized by spondees

²spondaic \"\ *n* -s **:** SPONDEE

spondaic hexameter *n* **:** a hexameter having a spondee instead of a dactyl in the fifth foot

spon·da·ize \'spändā,īz\ *vt* -ED/-ING/-S [*spondaic* + *-ize*] **:** to make spondaic

spon·de·an \spän'dēən, '===\ *adj* [L *spondeum* spondee + E *-an*] **:** having, consisting of, or characterized by spondees

spon·dee \'spän,dē\ *n* -s [ME *sponde*, fr. MF or L; MF *spondée*, fr. L *spondeum*, fr. Gk *spondeios*, fr. *spondeios* of a libation, fr. *spondē* libation; fr. its use in the solemn music accompanying a libation — more at SPOUSE] **:** a metrical foot consisting of two long or stressed syllables — symbol – – or óó

spon·di·a·ce·ae \,spändē'āsē,ē\ [NL, fr. *Spondias* + *-aceae*] *syn of* ANACARDIACEAE

spon·di·as \'spändē,as\ *n*, *cap* [NL, fr. Gk *spondias*, *spodias* bullace] **:** a small genus of tropical trees (family Anacardiaceae) having pinnate leaves and small flowers in terminal panicles, a free ovary that becomes in fruit a fleshy drupe, and astringent leaves and bark — see CIRUELA, HOG PLUM, MOMBIN, OTAHEITE APPLE

spon·du·licks *or* **spon·du·lix** \spän'düliks\ *n pl* [origin unknown] **1** *archaic* **:** FRACTIONAL CURRENCY **2 :** MONEY, FUNDS ⟨you certainly made the ~ fly —Joyce Cary⟩

spon·dyl \'spänd°l\ *or* **spon·dyle** \-n,dīl\ *n* -s [ME *spondyle*, fr. MF, fr. L *spondylus*, fr. Gk *sphondylos*, *spondylos* vertebra, whorl of a spindle, muscle of a bivalve, a kind of mussel; akin to Gk *sphendonē* sling, *sphadazein* to jerk, be restless, Skt *spandate* he quivers, MHG *spat* spavin] **1** *obs* **:** VERTEBRA **2 :** SPINY OYSTER

spondyl- *or* **spondylo-** *comb form* [Gk *spondylos* spondyl, whorl] **1 :** vertebra ⟨*spondyl*algia⟩ ⟨*spondylo*tomy⟩ **2 :** whorl ⟨*Spondylo*morum⟩

-spon·dy·li \'spändə,lī\ *n pl comb form* [NL, fr. L *spondylus* vertebra] **:** animals having (such) vertebrae — in names of higher taxa ⟨Diplo*spondyli*⟩ ⟨Lepo*spondyli*⟩

spon·dy·lic \(')spän'dilik\ *adj* [L *spondylus* vertebra + E *-ic*] **:** VERTEBRAL

¹spon·dy·lid \'spändələd\ *adj* [NL *Spondylidae*] **:** of or belonging to the Spondylidae

²spondylid \"\ *n* -s **:** a mollusk of the family Spondylidae

spon·dyl·i·dae \spän'dilə,dē\ *n pl*, *cap* [NL, fr. *Spondylus*, type genus + *-idae*] **:** a family of marine bivalve mollusks (order Filibranchia) comprising the spiny oysters

¹spon·dy·lit·ic \,spändə'lid·ik\ *adj* [NL *spondylitis* + E *-ic*] **1 :** of or relating to spondylitis **2 :** affected with spondylitis ⟨~ soldiers⟩

²spondylitic \"\ *n* -s **:** a person affected with spondylitis

spon·dy·li·tis \,spändə'līd·əs\ *n* -ES [NL, fr. *spondyl-* + *-itis*] **:** inflammation of the vertebrae ⟨tuberculous ~⟩ ⟨rheumatoid ~⟩

spon·dyl·i·um \spän'dilēəm\ *n*, *pl* **spondyl·ia** \-ēə\ [NL, fr. Gk *spondylion*, fr. *spondylos* muscle of a bivalve — more at SPONDYL] **:** a curved median plate for muscle attachment in the posterior part of one or both valves of a brachiopod

spon·dy·lo·cla·di·um \,spändələ'klādēəm\ *n*, *cap* [NL, fr. *spondyl-* + Gk *kladion* twig, dim. of *klados* branch — more at GLADIATOR] **:** a genus of imperfect fungi (family Dematiaceae) characterized by brown septate conidia borne in successive whorls on the conidiophores — see SILVER SCURF

spon·dy·loid \'spändə,lȯid\ *adj* [NL *Spondylus* + E *-oid*] **:** resembling or related to the Spondylidae

spon·dy·lo·lis·the·sis \,spändəlōlis'thēsəs\ *n* -ES [NL, fr. *spondyl-* + Gk *olisthēsis* dislocation, fr. *olisthanein* to slip, fall — more at SLIDE] **:** forward displacement of a lumbar vertebra and esp. of the fifth lumbar vertebra on the sacrum producing pain by compression of nerve roots

spon·dy·lo·mo·rum \,spändələ'mōrəm\ *n*, *cap* [NL, fr. *spondyl-* + L *morum* mulberry — more at MULBERRY] **:** a genus of colonial flagellates related to *Volvox*, having cells with four flagella, two contractile vacuoles, and a cup-shaped chromoplast, forming a 16-celled colony, and sometimes causing a contamination of water supplies

spon·dyl·ous \'spändələs\ *adj* [L *spondylus* spondyl + E *-ous*] *archaic* **:** VERTEBRAL

spon·dy·lus \"\ *n* [NL, fr. L, a kind of mussel, fr. Gk *spondylos* — more at SPONDYL] **1** *cap* **:** a genus of large, thick, inequivalve, usu. spinose and attached, bivalve mollusks (family Spondylidae) that are remarkable for perfection of the hinge **2** -ES **:** any mollusk of the family Spondylidae **:** SPINY OYSTER

-spon·dy·lus \"\ *n comb form* [NL, fr. L *spondylus* vertebra — more at SPONDYL] **:** animal having (such) vertebrae — in generic names ⟨Palaeo*spondylus*⟩

¹sponge *also* **spunge** \'spənj\ *n* -s *often attrib* [ME *sponge*, *spounge*, fr. OE *sponge*, fr. L *spongia*, *spongea*, fr. Gk *spongia*; akin to Gk *spongos* sponge—more at FUNGUS] **1 a :** the elastic porous mass of interlacing horny fibers that forms the internal skeleton of marine animals of low organization belonging to the phylum Porifera (as members of the genera *Hippiospongia* and *Spongia*) and that has great power of absorbing water and becomes soft when wet without losing strength — see GRASS SPONGE, TURKEY SPONGE, VELVET SPONGE, WOOL SPONGE **b :** any one of a large group of chiefly marine animals constituting the phylum Porifera that consist fundamentally of two layers of cells surrounding a central cavity, are permanently attached either solitary or in masses varying greatly in size, shape, color, and consistency, have skeletons composed variously of spongin (as in the commercial sponges) or a siliceous or a calcareous substance the interstices of which are filled with cells and pierced with a system of canals and small cavities opening on the surface through which a current of food-bearing water is maintained by collared flagellated cells lining the canal walls, and reproduce either asexually by budding or sexually by means of egg and sperm cells that form a free-swimming larva — see LEUCON, RHAGON, SYCON **2 a :** a piece of the skeleton of various marine sponges that is used for washing, cleaning, or erasing marks (as of chalk) from blackboards or slates; *also* **:** porous rubber or cellulose material used for washing or swabbing **b** *archaic* **:** something that effaces or blots out existing impressions, memories, or emotions **c** *obs* **:** a process or method of canceling or wiping off indebtedness without making payment **3 a :** a small pad made of multiple folds of gauze or of cotton and gauze used to mop blood from a surgical incision, to carry inhalable medicaments to the nose, or to cover a superficial wound as a dressing **b :** a porous dressing (as of fibrin or gelatin) applied to promote wound healing **c :** a plastic prosthesis used in chest cavities following lung surgery **4 :** a long-handled cylindrical swab for cleaning the bore of a cannon after discharge **5 :** SPONGE BATH **6 a :** a hard drinker **:** DRUNKARD **b :** one who lives upon others **:** a persistently idle or lazy dependent **:** SPONGER **c :** one from whom money may be extorted or information extracted **7 a :** porous elastic soil or a patch of such soil **b :** bread dough after it has been raised or converted into a light porous mass by yeast or leaven **c :** a dessert made light by the incorporation of air usu. through addition of whipped whites of eggs or of gelatin that is whipped after it has jelled ⟨pineapple ~⟩ **d :** LUFFA 3 **e** *obs* **:** pasty iron from a puddling furnace **f :** a metal (as lead, platinum) obtained in porous form usu. by reduction without fusion ⟨titanium ~⟩ — see PLATINUM SPONGE **g :** the egg mass of a crab borne by the female until the larvae hatch **8 :** a light olive brown that is slightly stronger than drab, less strong and slightly redder than average mustard tan, and deeper than the color dust **syn** see PARASITE

²sponge *also* **spunge** \"\ *vb* -ED/-ING/-S [ME *spongen*, fr. ¹*sponge*] *vt* **1 a :** to cleanse or wipe with or as if with a sponge ⟨~ a slate⟩ ⟨~ off his face⟩ ⟨~ the bore of a cannon⟩ **b :** to dampen with a sponge or cloth before ironing ⟨~ trousers⟩ **c :** to spruce up **:** make neat, fresh, and tidy **d :** to apply liquid to with a sponge ⟨~ a patient's back with alcohol⟩ **2 a :** to wipe out (as letters, numbers) with a sponge **:** ERASE, OBLITERATE — used often with *out* ⟨whole paragraphs had been *sponged* out⟩ **b :** to destroy all trace of **:** EFFACE ⟨every stain of his infected and corroding fingers will be *sponged* and . . . blasted from the surface of the earth —Sir Winston Churchill⟩ **3 a :** to stipple (a painted surface) by removing some of the wet paint with a sponge **b :** to decorate (a ceramic surface) by applying mucilaginous pigment with a sponge **c :** to smooth the edges of (ceramic ware) with a damp sponge before firing **4** *obs* **:** to squeeze money or information from **:** extort from **:** DRAIN **5 :** to get (as money, meals, comforts) without cost or return by imposing on generosity or hospitality ⟨nightclub entertainer . . . that ~*s* drinks from the guests —Anthony West⟩ **6 :** to take up or absorb with or as if with a sponge or as a sponge does **:** SOAK, SOP, SWAB — used usu. with *up* ⟨~ up spilled ink⟩ ⟨the state loan . . . managed to ~ up most of the available savings —D.C.McKay⟩ **7 :** to insert a piece of sponge in (a horse's nostril) to impair the breathing and so effect the loss of a race ~ *vi* **1 a :** to absorb, soak up, imbibe like a sponge **b :** to swell out like a sponge **2 a :** to get something at another's cost by imposing on hospitality or good nature ⟨beggar *sponging* for rum —R.L.Stevenson⟩ **b :** to live as a dependent or parasite — usu. used with *on* or *upon* ⟨do you expect to go on *sponging* on me the rest of your days —Marcia Davenport⟩ **3 :** to dive or dredge for sponges **4** *of a tobacco leaf* **:** to mottle in curing because of rapid beating or insufficient ventilation

sponge bag *n*, *Brit* **:** a waterproof case for holding a bath sponge and toilet articles

sponge–bag \'=,=\ *adj*, *Brit* [*sponge bag*; prob. fr. the frequent use of such fabrics for the outside of sponge bags] **:** CHECKED ⟨*sponge-bag* trousers⟩

sponge bath *n* **:** a bath in which water is applied to the body without actual immersion

sponge biopsy *n* **:** biopsy performed on matter collected with a sponge from a lesion

sponge boat *n* **:** a strongly built sailboat with a high bow used for obtaining sponges

sponge cake *n* **:** a cake made without shortening — distinguished from *butter cake*

sponge cloth *n* **1 :** RATINÉ 2 **2 :** any of various soft porous fabrics loosely woven esp. in honeycomb weave from coarse or nubby yarns and used for clothing, curtains, and cloths for cleaning machinery

sponge crab *n* **1 :** a female crab bearing an egg mass **2 :** any of several crabs commonly found in association with sponges: as **a** (1) **:** GRASS CRAB (2) **:** a crab of the group Dromiacea that decorates its back with sponges or ascidians **b :** any of several hermit crabs of the Pacific coast of No. America that excavate their homes in a living sponge (*Suberites latus*)

sponge finger *n, chiefly Brit* **:** LADYFINGER 2

sponge fly *or* **spongilla fly** *n* [so called fr. its being parasitic in its larva stage on sponges, including those of the genus *Spongilla*] **:** an insect of the family Sisyridae

¹sponge glass *n* **:** a glass-bottomed box or bucket for viewing the sea bottom from the surface in sponge fishing

²sponge glass *n* **:** CELLULAR GLASS

sponge gourd *n* **:** DISHCLOTH GOURD

sponge hook *n* **:** a 3-pronged curved hook attached to a long handle for detaching growing sponges from the bottom

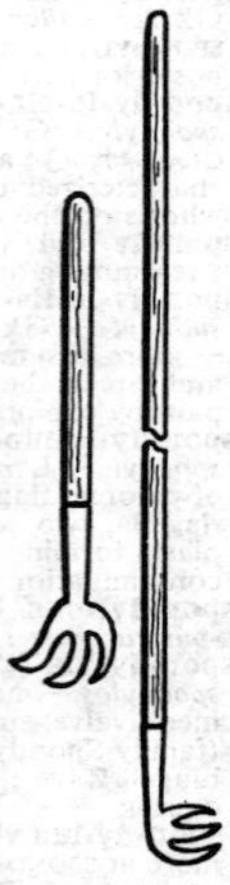

sponge hooks

sponge iron *n* **:** iron in porous form or containing many voids; *specif* **:** crude iron made by subjecting the oxide ore to a reducing gas without melting

spongelike \ˈ=,=\ *adj* **:** resembling a sponge **:** SPONGY, POROUS

sponge mushroom *n* **:** MOREL

spon·geous \ˈspənjəs\ *adj* [ME, fr. L *spongeosus*, fr. *spongea* sponge + *-osus* -ous] *archaic* **:** SPONGY

spong·er \ˈspənjə(r)\ *n* -s **1 :** a man or boat engaged in gathering sponges **2 :** one that sponges something: as **a :** one that smooths greenware with a sponge **b :** an operator of a machine for sponging and shrinking cloth **c :** an operator of a dough-mixing machine **3 :** a parasitical person **:** CADGER ⟨the feckless ~ is held in contempt —*Time*⟩ ⟨easy tolerance of ~*s* looking for a cinch rather than an education —Dixon Wecter⟩ **syn** see PARASITE

sponge rubber *n* **:** porous or cellular rubber resembling a natural sponge in structure that is made usu. by blowing with a gas (as carbon dioxide) liberated during vulcanization by a chemical (as sodium bicarbonate) incorporated in the rubber compound and that is used chiefly in making cushions, vibration dampeners, weather stripping, gaskets, insulation, and other molded products — compare FOAM RUBBER

sponges *pl of* SPONGE, *pres 3d sing of* SPONGE

sponge tree *n* **:** HUISACHE

spongework \ˈ=,=\ *n* **:** an irregular pattern of very small interconnecting cavities sometimes produced by solution in cave walls

spongi- *or* **spongio-** *comb form* [L *spongia*] **1 :** sponge ⟨*spongi*colous⟩ ⟨*spongio*logy⟩ **2 :** spongy ⟨*spongio*blast⟩

spon·gia \ˈspənjēə, ˈspän-\ *n, cap* [NL, fr. L, sponge] **:** a genus of tropical and subtropical sponges that includes various commercially important sponges and is the type of the family Spongiidae

¹-spongia \"\ *n comb form* [NL, fr. L *spongia*] **:** sponge — in generic names of sponges ⟨Astylo*spongia*⟩

²-spongia *pl of* -SPONGIUM

spon·gi·ae \-ē,ē\ [NL, fr. L, pl. of *spongia* sponge] *syn of* PORIFERA

-spongiae \"\ *n pl comb form* [NL, fr. L *spongiae*] **:** sponges — in names of orders and other higher groups of sponges ⟨Silici*spongiae*⟩

spon·gic·o·lous \spənˈjikələs, spän-\ *adj* [*spongi-* + *-colous*] **:** inhabiting sponges

spon·gi·da \ˈspənjədə, ˈspän-\ [NL, irreg. fr. *Spongia* + *-ida*] *syn of* PORIFERA

spon·gi·dae \-jə,dē\ [NL, irreg. fr. *Spongia*, type genus + *-idae*] *syn of* SPONGIIDAE

spongier *comparative of* SPONGY

spongiest *superlative of* SPONGY

spon·gi·idae \spənˈjīə,dē, spän-\ *n pl, cap* [NL, fr. *Spongia*, type genus + *-idae*] **:** a family of horny sponges (order Keratosa) that have solid spongin fibers enclosing an axial core — see SPONGIA

spon·gil·la \spənˈjilə, spän-\ *n, cap* [NL, fr. L *spongia* sponge + NL *-illa*] **:** a genus (the type of the family Spongillidae) of siliceous freshwater sponges that are usu. green in color and form incrustations on submerged objects — **spon·gil·lid** \-ləd\ *n* -s — **spon·gil·line** \-i,līn, -ilən\ *adj*

spongilla fly *var of* SPONGE FLY

spon·gi·ly \ˈspənjəlē\ *adv* **:** in a spongy manner **:** SPRINGILY, POROUSLY

spon·gin \ˈspənjən\ *n* -s [G, fr. L *spongia* sponge + G *-in*] **:** a scleroprotein constituting the chief constituent of the flexible fibers in the skeleton of commercial sponges and in part that of many other sponges

spon·gi·ness \ˈspənjēnəs, -jin-\ *n* -ES **:** the quality or state of being spongy

sponging *n* -s [fr. gerund of ²*sponge*] **1 :** DECATING **2 :** a cold-water or steam treatment for shrinking new woolen goods before cutting out garments

sponging house *n* [*sponging* (gerund of ²*sponge*) + *house*; fr. the extortionate charges made there for food and lodging] **:** a house usu. maintained by a bailiff for keeping debtors for a day to afford opportunity to come to terms with their creditors

spon·ging·ly *adv* [*sponging* (pres. part. of ²*sponge*) + *-ly*] **:** in a sponging manner

spon·gi·o·blast \ˈspənjēō,blast, ˈspän-\ *n* -s [ISV *spongi-* + *-blast*] **1 :** one of the ectodermal cells of the embryonic spinal cord or other nerve center that are at first columnar but become branched at one end and that give rise to the neuroglia cells **2 :** SPONGOBLAST

spon·gi·o·blas·to·ma \,=ˌ==blaˈstōmə\ *n, pl* **spongioblastomas** *or* **spongioblastoma·ta** \-məd·ə\ [NL, fr. ISV *spongioblast* + *-oma*] **:** a malignant tumor of the central nervous system or the brain composed of spongioblasts

spon·gi·o·cyte \ˈspənjēō,sīt, ˈspän-\ *n* -s [*spongi-* + *-cyte*] **:** a cell of the neuroglia

spon·gi·ol·o·gy \,spənjēˈäləjē, ,spän-\ *or* **spon·gol·o·gy** \späŋˈgä-\ *n* -ES [*spongiology* ISV *spongi-* + *-logy*; *spongology* fr. *spongo-* + *-logy*] **:** the study of sponges

spon·gi·o·plasm \ˈspənjēō,plazəm, ˈspän-\ *n* [ISV *spongi-* + *-plasm*; orig. formed in G] **:** CYTORETICULUM — **spon·gi·o·plas·mic** \,=ˌ==ˈplazmik\ *adj*

spon·gi·o·sa \,spənjēˈōsə, ,spän-\ *n* -s [NL, fr. *substantia spongiosa* spongy substance, fr. L *substantia* substance + *spongiosa*, fem. of *spongiosus* spongious] **:** the part of a bone (as much of the epiphyseal area of long bones) made up of spongy cancellous bone — compare COMPACTA

spon·gi·o·sis \-ˈōsəs\ *n* -ES [NL, fr. *spongi-* + *-osis*] **:** swelling localized in the epidermis and often occurring in eczema

spon·gi·ous \ˈspənjēəs\ *adj* [ME, fr. MF *spongieux*, fr. L *spongiosus*, fr. *spongia* sponge + *-osus* -ous] *archaic* **:** full of small cavities like sponge **:** SPONGY

spon·gi·o·zoa \,spənjēōˈzōə, ,spän-\ [NL, fr. *spongi-* + *-zoa*] *syn of* PORIFERA

-spon·gi·um \ˈspənjēəm, ˈspän-\ *n comb form, pl* **-spon·gia** \-ēə\ [NL, fr. L *spongia* sponge] **:** network of cells or fibrils ⟨neuro*spongium*⟩

spongo- *comb form* [Gk *spong-*, *spongo-*, fr. *spongos* — more at FUNGUS] **:** sponge ⟨*spongo*logy⟩

spon·go·blast \ˈspäŋgō,blast\ *n* [*spongo-* + *-blast*] **:** a cell that produces spongin — **spon·go·blas·tic** \,=ˌ=ˈblastik\ *adj*

spon·go·coel \ˈspäŋgō,sēl\ *n* -s [*spongo-* + *-coel*] **:** the internal cavity of a sponge discharging by way of the osculum

¹spon·goid \ˈspäŋ,gȯid, ˈspəŋ-\ *adj* [Gk *spongoeidēs*, fr. *spong-* spongo- + *-oeidēs* -oid] **:** resembling sponge **:** SPONGELIKE

²spongoid \"\ *n* -s **:** a spongelike animal or fossil

spon·gos·po·ra \spänˈgäspərə\ *n, cap* [NL, fr. *spongo-* + *-spora*] **:** a genus of organisms (family Plasmodiophoraceae) resembling the slime molds and characterized by spongelike spore balls each cell of which germinates — see POWDERY SCAB; compare PLASMODIOPHORA

spongy \ˈspənjē, -ji\ *adj* -ER/-EST [¹*sponge* + *-y*] **1 :** having the consistency of a sponge **:** being soft and full of cavities ⟨~ ice⟩ ⟨~ lava⟩ **:** being elastic, porous, and absorbent ⟨~ earth⟩ ⟨~ cheese⟩ ⟨~ roots⟩ **2 :** lacking in strength and solidity **:** not firm or solid ⟨~ area in an iron casting⟩ ⟨~ wood⟩ ⟨~ action of a steering gear⟩ ⟨cities suggest jittery nerves and ~ flesh —A.W.Long⟩ **3 :** moist and soft like a sponge full of water **:** SATURATED, SOGGY ⟨~ clouds⟩ ⟨~ moor⟩

spongy dry rot *n* **:** a dry rot (as of apples) caused by a fungus (*Colletrichum fructus*)

spongy parenchyma *n* **:** loosely and irregularly arranged parenchyma having numerous intercellular spaces found toward the lower surface within many leaves and consisting of irregular, lobed, or stellate cells — compare PALISADE PARENCHYMA

spon·sal \ˈspän(t)səl\ *adj* [L *sponsalis* of a betrothal, spousal — more at ESPOUSAL] **:** SPOUSAL

spon·sa·lia \spänˈsālēə\ *n pl* [L, betrothal — more at ESPOUSAL] **:** a formal promise or contract for a future marriage between persons competent to make such a contract

spon·si·ble \ˈspän(t)səbəl\ *adj* [short for *responsible*] *dial* **:** RESPONSIBLE, RESPECTABLE

spon·sion \ˈspänchən\ *n* -s [L *sponsion-*, *sponsio*, lit., solemn promise, pledge, fr. *sponsus* (past part. of *spondēre* to promise solemnly) + *-ion-*, *-io* -ion — more at SPOUSE] **1** *Roman law* **:** suretyship accessory to oral contracts and available only to Roman citizens **2 :** the act of becoming surety; *esp* **:** a formal pledge made on behalf of another **3 :** an act or engagement on behalf of a state undertaken by an agent not specially authorized or by one who exceeds the limits of his authority and requiring for validity ratification by the state

¹spon·son \ˈspän(t)sən\ *n* -s [prob. by shortening & alter. fr. *expansion*] **:** a projection from the side of a ship or a tank to act as a bearing or protection for some part: as **a :** a structure outside the normal hull of a vessel to give added deck room or stability or protection for paddle wheels or to afford a gun platform **b :** a gun platform projecting from the side of a warship or a tank to give a greater arc of fire **c :** an air chamber along the side of a canoe to increase its stability and buoyancy **d :** a light air-filled structure protruding from the hull of a seaplane to give it steadiness as it rests on water

²sponson \"\ *vt* -ED/-ING/-S **:** to equip with or install on sponsons

¹spon·sor \ˈspän(t)sə(r)\ *n* -s [L, fr. *sponsus* (past part. of *spondēre*) + *-or* — more at SPOUSE] **1** *Roman law* **:** one who binds himself to answer for another's default **:** SURETY **2 :** one who without request intervenes in behalf of another **3** [LL, fr. L, surety] **:** one who at the baptism of an infant or child professes the Christian faith in its name, and guarantees its religious education; *also* **:** one who presents a candidate for confirmation to the bishop **:** GODPARENT **4 :** one who assumes responsibility for some other person or thing: as **a :** one who presents and supports a legislative proposal **b :** an experienced salesclerk or salesperson who instructs and supervises new selling employees **c :** a teacher acting as adviser to a specified student activity ⟨~ to a student council⟩ ⟨homeroom ~⟩ ⟨~ for a class dance⟩ **d :** one who assumes responsibility for a paroled delinquent **5 a :** a corporation that organizes and usu. manages the distribution of the shares of an open-end investment trust **b :** an investment banker who underwrites and distributes a security issue **6 :** a business firm or a person who pays a broadcaster and the performer for a radio or television program that is not in itself commercial with the understanding that a limited portion of the time allotted is devoted to advertising a commercial product

²sponsor \"\ *vt* -ED/-ING/-S **:** to be or stand sponsor for **:** accept responsibility for

spon·so·ri·al \spänˈsōrēəl\ *adj* [¹*sponsor* + *-ial*] **:** of or relating to a sponsor

spon·sor·ship \ˈspän(t)sə(r),ship\ *n* **:** the state of being a sponsor **:** act of sponsoring **:** official or financial support

spon·ta·ne·i·ty \,späntəˈnēəd·ē, |āə-, -ətē, -i *sometimes* -tᵊnˈ|\ *n* -ES [LL *spontaneus* + E *-ity*] **1 :** the quality or state of being spontaneous ⟨the apparent ~ with which a new . . . type of art arose —Herbert Read⟩ ⟨~ of his laughter⟩ **2 :** the source of spontaneous action or expression **:** the quality, innate power, or influence that determines the character ⟨the free play of passion and thought, the graces and arts of life, all that springs from the ~ of nature —G.L.Dickinson⟩

¹spon·ta·ne·ous \spänˈtānēəs\ *adj* [LL *spontaneus*, fr. L *sponte* of one's free will, voluntarily — more at SPIN] **1 :** proceeding from natural feeling or native tendency without external constraint **:** VOLUNTARY ⟨~ expression of affection and gratitude⟩ ⟨a ~ modernist in theology and philosophy —George Santayana⟩ ⟨~ boycott⟩ ⟨~ obedience⟩ **2 :** arising from immediate natural impulse **:** UNPREMEDITATED, IMPULSIVE ⟨~ offer of assistance⟩ ⟨this diary has the ~ quality of a child's observations made for her own pleasure —Ellen L. Buell⟩ ⟨~ improvising on a melody⟩ **3 :** caused by internal energy controlled and directed internally **:** SELF-ACTING ⟨~ movement is characteristic of all living things⟩ ⟨proves that there must be ~ activity as well as derivative activity in the universe —C.H.Whiteley⟩ **4 :** produced without being planted or without human labor **:** NATIVE, INDIGENOUS ⟨~ growth of wood⟩ **5 a :** developing without apparent external influence or force or from some undiscoverable cause ⟨~ nosebleed⟩ ⟨~ fracture⟩ ⟨~ abortion⟩ **b :** not resulting from externally planned or intended modification or treatment ⟨~ remission of nervous symptoms⟩ ⟨~ recovery from a disease⟩ **6 :** occurring or seeming to occur in the natural course of things **:** not apparently contrived or manipulated ⟨the fact that the experiences are ~ and not laboratory products make these cases of the highest importance —W.H.Salter⟩

syn SPONTANEOUS, IMPULSIVE, INSTINCTIVE, AUTOMATIC, and MECHANICAL as applied to human acts (and, with appropriate adjustments, to the person performing the act, excepting possibly the word *automatic*) can mean activated (or acting) without apparent thought or deliberation. SPONTANEOUS applies to acts that come about so naturally, are so unselfconscious and so unaffected or unprompted by ulterior motive or purpose that they seem totally unpremeditated ⟨find ourselves making an immediate and *spontaneous* answer —W.T. Hastings⟩ ⟨his sentiment was *spontaneous* rather than introspective —H.S.Commager⟩ ⟨*spontaneous* laughter⟩ ⟨at ease with us . . . generally gay, always *spontaneous* and natural —Dorothy Bussy⟩ IMPULSIVE applies to apparently involuntary acts actuated suddenly and impetuously on the spur of the momentary feeling or spirit ⟨her childlikeness, her headlong sympathies, the *impulsive* traits that endeared —W.R. Benét⟩ ⟨*impulsive*, reckless and unreliable —A.E.Stevenson b. 1900⟩ INSTINCTIVE stresses the involuntary, often unconscious, character of an instantaneous, spontaneous act, suggesting the compulsion of native predisposition or long conditioning rather than of the will ⟨the *instinctive* movement of his agile frame —Nathaniel Hawthorne⟩ ⟨he did what he did *instinctively* and for no other reason than because it was most natural to him —Samuel Butler †1902⟩ ⟨long and laborious planning to carry out elaborately conceived intellectual effort was not her way. Everything was inborn, *instinctive*, spontaneous —Gamaliel Bradford⟩ AUTOMATIC and MECHANICAL both apply to acts which do not seem to engage the mind. AUTOMATIC usually stresses promptness and invariableness in a response to a given set of stimuli, as from long habit or repetition, often implying a training or discipline and sometimes a precision of response ⟨he said the right thing, performed the appropriate action, so unceasingly, day after day, night after night, that it had become simply *automatic* —Elizabeth Goudge⟩ ⟨his easy, *automatic* smile —Luke Short⟩ ⟨the artist's movements with the pencil were swift and *automatic*; in a few minutes the sketch was complete⟩ MECHANICAL, though it can apply to any act, usu. repeated, performed with little or no conscious ordering of movements, usu. connotes a lifelessness and perfunctoriness of response ⟨shorthand and typewriting, both of which are purely *mechanical* activities —George Sampson⟩ ⟨many of the situations which previously elicited emotional response come to be met in a *mechanical* or routine fashion —J.E.Anderson⟩ ⟨not with any interest or curiosity, but with a dull *mechanical* perception —Charles Dickens⟩

²spontaneous \"\ *adv, archaic* **:** SPONTANEOUSLY ⟨to her lips . . . the minstrel verse ~ came —Sir Walter Scott⟩

spontaneous amputation *n* **:** the spontaneous separation (as in some forms of gangrene) of a necrotic body part

spontaneous combustion *also* **spontaneous ignition** *n* **:** the outbreak of fire in combustible material (as oily rags or damp hay) that occurs without application of direct flame or spark and is usu. caused by slow oxidation processes (as atmospheric oxidation or bacterial fermentation) under conditions not permitting dissipation of heat

spontaneous generation *n* **:** ABIOGENESIS

spon·ta·ne·ous·ly *adv* **:** in a spontaneous manner **:** without external constraint ⟨children . . . will memorize favorite selections ~ —Dorothy Barclay⟩ ⟨woke up ~ at seven-fifteen⟩ **:** without premeditation ⟨acts so ~ that the consequences of his offense do not have time to sink in —R.S.Banay⟩

spontaneous magnetization *n* **:** the magnetization within each magnetic domain of a ferromagnetic substance in the absence of a magnetizing field

spon·ta·ne·ous·ness *n* -ES [¹*spontaneous* + *-ness*] **:** SPONTANEITY

spontaneous recovery *n* **:** reappearance of an extinguished conditioned response without further positive reinforcement

spon·toon \spänˈtün\ *also* **spon·ton** \ˈspäntᵊn\ *or* **es·pon·toon** \,espänˈtün\ *n* -s [F *sponton*, *esponton*, fr. It *spuntone*, *spontone*, fr. *punta* sharp point, fr. (assumed) VL *puncta* — more at POINT] **1 :** a half-pike formerly borne by subordinate officers of infantry **2 :** a policeman's club **:** TRUNCHEON

¹spoof \ˈspüf\ *vb* -ED/-ING/-S [fr. *Spoof*, a hoaxing game invented by Arthur Roberts †1933 Eng. comedian] *vt* **1 :** to deceive by a hoax **:** DELUDE ⟨managed to ~ and terrorize the local officials by impersonating a government inspector —Edmund Stevens⟩ ⟨who had often been ~*ed* but who was still anxious to get at the truth —*Saturday Rev.*⟩ **2 :** to make good-natured fun of often by means of a misrepresentation ⟨the witty screenplay . . . ~*s* this very quality —*Los Angeles (Calif.) Examiner*⟩ ⟨a deft satire . . . it . . . ~*s* traveling salesmen —Amy Loveman⟩ ⟨~ social customs —John McCarten⟩; *also* **:** KID, GUY ⟨they're kidding you . . . don't let them ~ you —Agnes N. Keith⟩ ~ *vi* **1 :** to use or practice deceit ⟨honesty pays . . . if I ~ I shall get found out —Thomas Wood †1950⟩ **2 :** to make fun of a person or thing often by means of a misrepresentation ⟨their type of gently ~*ing* satirical fantasy —*Time*⟩; *also* **:** KID, JOKE ⟨bring back a minstrel show man ~ about one oyster in the stew —*Springfield (Mass.) Union*⟩

²spoof \"\ *n* -s **1 a :** HOAX, FEINT ⟨one sees that the whole thing is a clumsy ~ —J.F.Runciman⟩ ⟨one day a supposed ~ might be the real thing —W.R.Frye⟩ **b :** HUMBUG, NONSENSE ⟨only don't try any more ~ about me —Joyce Cary⟩ **2 :** a light, amiable, humorous, but usu. telling takeoff (as on human nature, customs, or manners) **:** PARODY ⟨a pleasant ~ of all the moonstruck nonsense the movies have been dishing up —John McCarten⟩ ⟨those quiet, unpretentious, but deliciously funny ~*s* of national types and customs —Arthur Knight⟩

spoof·er \-fə(r)\ *n* -s **:** one that spoofs: as **a :** DECEIVER ⟨a ~ is inordinately insincere —*Dalhart (Texas) Texan*⟩ **b :** PARODIST ⟨the ~, the transient bubble-pricker lies in the theatrical deathbed —*Amer. Mercury*⟩

spoof·ery \-fərē\ *n* -ES [³*spoof* + *-ery*] **1 :** DECEIT **2 a :** good-natured ridicule **:** KIDDING, RIBBING ⟨British ~ that is sometimes so gentle that the humor is almost inaudible —*New Yorker*⟩ ⟨a compendium of ~ including cartoons, verse, and prose⟩ **b :** an instance of good-natured ridicule **:** SPOOF 2 ⟨the ballet . . . bringing this ~ of a house party to a realization less anachronistic than a literal reproduction —Irving Kolodin⟩

¹spook \ˈspük *sometimes* ˈspu̇k\ *n* -s [D, fr. MD *spooc*; akin to MLG *spōk* ghost] **1 :** GHOST, SPECTER, APPARITION, HOBGOBLIN ⟨the strange ~ . . . crept out of heaven on a windless night —S.V.Benét⟩; *specif* **:** an apparition in a spiritualistic séance ⟨became a spiritualist, believing in the power of ~*s* —*Amer. Mercury*⟩ **2** *slang* **:** a queer or strange person **:** ODDBALL ⟨a blind date? What is she, a real ~ —Oakley Hall⟩ **3** *slang* **:** GHOST-WRITER ⟨a writer signed to do the movie script as the ~ —Louis Messolonghites⟩ ⟨professional ~ . . . to ghostwrite a novel —David Dempsey⟩ **4** *slang* **:** NEGRO ⟨what's a ~? A Negro — like me —Robert Lowry⟩ ⟨stop talking like a ~ . . . I mean stop talking like most colored folks —Langston Hughes⟩

²spook \"\ *vb* -ED/-ING/-S *vt* **1 :** to inhabit or visit as a spook **:** HAUNT ⟨forces that ~ the old world —W.M.Meredith⟩ **2 a :** to stir up or excite (as a horse or steer) esp. by frightening ⟨if you come up too fast and ~ a deer it takes off —R.E.Maw⟩ ⟨the entire herd got ~*ed* and stampeded into the mountains —H.W.Anderson⟩ **b** *slang* **:** to frighten (a person) often so as to make run, freeze, or tremble **:** SCARE ⟨too shrewd a detective to ~ the pair with direct questions —Chris Edwards⟩ ⟨those kids had me ~*ed* all right . . . they wanted to kill somebody —Ernest Hemingway⟩ **3** *slang* **:** GHOSTWRITE ⟨~*ed* the reminiscences of the actor⟩ ~ *vi* **:** to flee, scramble, tremble, stampede, or balk as a result of fright ⟨wolves would ~ as the plane flew over —*Alaska Sportsman*⟩

spook·ery \-kərē\ *n* -ES [¹*spook* + *-ery*] **:** something that is concerned with or characteristic of spooks **:** something that is spooky ⟨exchange of *spookeries* between disembodied voices —Edmond Taylor⟩ ⟨with this ~ she mingles fragments of mysticism —*Nation*⟩

spookfish \ˈ=,=\ *n* **:** CHIMAERA

spook·i·ly \-kəlē\ *adv* **:** in a spooky manner ⟨trees rustled ~⟩

spook·i·ness \-kēnəs\ *n* -ES **:** the quality or state of being spooky ⟨skillful lighting gave . . . the right touch of ~ —*Carnegie Mag.*⟩

spook·ish \-kish, -kēsh\ *adj* [¹*spook* + *-ish*] **:** somewhat spooky ⟨big black-raftered kitchen looked ~ and weird —Lucy M. Montgomery⟩

spook·ism \-,kizəm\ *n* -s **:** belief in or the practice of communicating with spooks or spirits; *esp* **:** SPIRITUALISM ⟨dabbler in wireless and ~ has a specially equipped set which collects the voices of the dead —*Sydney (Australia) Bull.*⟩

spook·ist \-,kəst\ *n* -s **:** one who believes in or practices spookism

spooky \-kē, -ki\ *adj* -ER/-EST **1 :** resembling spooks or their appurtenances **:** SPECTRAL ⟨did your ~ friend walk last night —*Lippincott's Mag.*⟩ ⟨a ~ outfit of men who drove their stock by night —Will James⟩ ⟨saw a tall ~ staircase —Jean Stafford⟩ **2 :** of, belonging to, or concerning spooks **3 :** suggesting the presence or influence of ghosts **:** EERIE, UNCANNY, HAUNTING ⟨a very ~ place after dark —A.T.Walden⟩ ⟨the silence felt a bit ~ —W.H.Wright⟩ ⟨prescient to the point of being downright ~ —Milton Crane⟩ **4 :** NERVOUS, SKITTISH, JITTERY ⟨~ animals . . . who will buck from nothing more than high spirits —Alice Hager⟩ ⟨the gang was ~ after being questioned —J.K.Harris⟩

spook yeast *n* **:** EMPTINS

¹spool \ˈspül\ *n* -s *often attrib* [ME *spole*, *spule*, fr. MF or MD; MF *espole*, fr. OF, fr. MD *spoele*; akin to OHG *spuola* spool, bobbin, and prob. to OE *speld* thin piece of wood used as a torch — more at SPELL] **1 a :** any of several cylindrical devices which have a rim, ridge, or head at each end and commonly an axial hole for a pin or spindle and on which filamentary or ribbonlike material (as thread, yarn, ribbon, wire, cord, tape) is wound: as (1) **:** a small usu. wooden cylinder for holding sewing thread (2) **:** BOBBIN (3) **:** a holder for a field coil (4) **:** a holder on which sensitized photographic film or paper is wound esp. for use in a camera (5) **:** a holder for the ribbon of a typewriter or similar machine (6) **:** the part of a fishing reel upon which the line is wound **b :** something (as a capstan barrel) resembling or likened to such a spool **2 :** the material or the amount of material wound on a spool ⟨an hour-long ~ and . . . all the missing speeches . . . were recorded on it —Clemence Dane⟩ ⟨two ~*s* were needed to do the stitching⟩

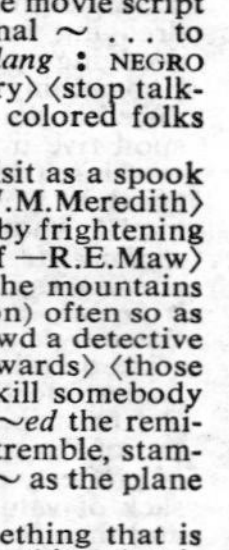

spool 1a(1)

²spool \"\ *vb* -ED/-ING/-S *vt* **1 :** to wind on a spool ⟨film is ~*ed* for use —R.N.Shreve⟩ ⟨skein yarns are ~*ed* —*Leavers*

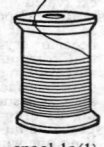

Lace⟩ **2 :** WIND ⟨~ the rope on the drum⟩ ⟨~ the thread off the bobbin⟩ ~ *vi* **1 :** to wind itself on a spool ⟨cause the cable to ~ properly —*advt*⟩ **2 :** WIND ⟨permitting the drilling line to ~ off the drum —*Primer of Oil Well Drilling*⟩

spool bed *n* **:** a wooden bed with spool-shaped turnings in the spindles and usu. in the rails and posts of the headboard and footboard

spool·er \-lə(r)\ *n* -s [²*spool* + *-er*] **1 :** a worker or machine that winds material (as thread, yarn, wire, cord, tape, film) on spools **:** WINDER **2 :** waste thrown off in spooling cotton yarn

spool heel *n* **:** a heel that has horizontal corrugations and is used on women's shoes

spool pin *n* **:** a spool-shaped pin tumbler used in some cylinder locks to foil picking attempts

spool turning *n* **:** a continuous turning in furniture that resembles rows of spools

spoolwood \ˈ=,=\ *n* [so called fr. its suitability for the making of spools] **1 :** PAPER BIRCH **2 :** the wood of paper birch

spoolwright \ˈ=,=\ *n* **:** a logger who chops out places in stumps or logs along a skid road for the insertion of spools to guide the skidding line

¹spoon \ˈspün *sometimes* ˈspu̇n\ *n* -s [ME *spone, spoon,* fr. OE *spōn;* akin to OHG *spān* splinter, chip of wood, ON *spānn, spōnn* chip, spoon, Gk *sphēn* wedge] **1** *obs* **:** a thin piece of wood **:** SPLINTER, CHIP **2 :** a usu. metal, plastic, or wooden eating or cooking implement consisting of a small oval or round shallow bowl with a handle — often used in combination ⟨~ maker⟩ ⟨baby ~⟩ ⟨jelly ~⟩ ⟨tea*spoon*⟩ **3 :** something that resembles a spoon in shape: as **a** *or* **spoon shovel :** a long bar with a small oval inclined blade at the end used in excavating deep narrow holes **b :** a lever that forms part of the stop motion on a drawing frame **4 :** SPOONFUL ⟨two ~*s* of sugar⟩ **5 :** WOODEN SPOON 1 **6** *slang* **:** SIMPLETON **7 :** a usu. metal or shell fishing lure shaped like the bowl of a spoon — see LURE illustration **8 :** a wooden golf club made with a slightly shorter and stiffer shaft and more loft than a driver or brassie and used through the green for long high shots — see WOOD illustration **9 a :** HORN SPOON 2 **b :** SCRAPER 1j **10 :** a smudged and crushed loop left in the ice by a figure skater who makes a faulty turn **11 :** a chrysanthemum with long tubular ray florets and a spoon-shaped tip

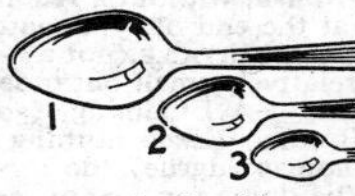

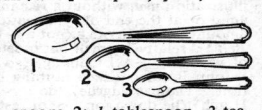

spoons 2: *1* tablespoon, *2* teaspoon, *3* coffee spoon

²spoon \"\ *adj* **1 :** used to hold spoons ⟨~ box⟩ ⟨~ rack⟩ **2 :** shaped like a spoon ⟨~ strainer⟩ or the bowl of a spoon ⟨~ shell⟩ **3 :** eaten with or suitable for eating with a spoon usu. because liquid or semisolid ⟨~ food⟩

³spoon \"\ *vb* -ED/-ING/-S *vt* **1 :** to take up and usu. transfer in a spoon ⟨they ~ their consommé —Mollie Panter-Downes⟩ ⟨~*ed* the tomatoes into the glass jars —H.D.Skidmore⟩ ⟨mother ~*ed* out bowls of porridge —Margaret Kennedy⟩ ⟨sat placidly ~*ing* up yogurt —*Time*⟩ ⟨the dredge ~*ed* up mud⟩ **2 :** to nestle close to and facing the back of (a person) while lying down **3** [prob. fr. the Welsh custom of an engaged man's presenting his fiancée with a love spoon] **:** to make love to by caressing, kissing, and talking amorously **:** PET, NECK ⟨have ~*ed* other women —Margaret W. Hungerford⟩; *sometimes* **:** WOO, COURT ⟨~*ing* his sister —Kenneth Grahame⟩ **4 :** to propel (a ball) by a stroke having a weak lifting motion ~ *vi* **1 :** to immerse a spoon (as into a liquid) ⟨~*ing* into a bowl of milk toast —William DuBois⟩ **2 :** to nestle close to and facing the back of a person while lying down ⟨sleepers ~*ing* together —Lee Meriwether⟩ — often used with *up* ⟨she tucked the bedclothes around him and then ~*ing* up she fell asleep —Willard Robertson⟩ **3 :** to make love by caressing, kissing, and talking amorously **:** NECK ⟨~*ed* out on the decks—Louis Armstrong⟩ **4 :** to spoon a ball (as a golfball)

⁴spoon \"\ *vi* -ED/-ING/-S [origin unknown] *of a boat* **:** to drive steadily before or as if before a strong wind

spoon–back \ˈ=,=\ *adj* [²*spoon*] **:** having a back curved slightly to fit the sitter's form — used esp. of chairs of the Queen Anne period

spoonbill \ˈ=,=\ *n* **1 :** any of several wading birds that constitute the family Plataleidae, are closely related to the ibises, and have the bill greatly expanded and flattened at the tip: as **a :** ROSEATE SPOONBILL — see BILL illustration **b :** a common wading bird (*Platalea leucorodia*) of southern Europe, Asia, and northeastern Africa that is pure white and crested **2 a :** SHOVELER **b** *dial Eng* **:** SCAUP DUCK **c :** RUDDY DUCK **d :** PADDLEFISH **3 :** SPOON-BILLED SANDPIPER

spoonbill cat *also* **spoon–billed catfish** *or* **spoonbill** *n* **:** PADDLEFISH

spoon–billed \ˈ=ˈ=\ *adj* **:** having the bill or snout expanded and spatulate at the end

spoon–billed duck *or* **spoon–billed teal** *or* **spoon–billed widgeon** *n* **:** SHOVELER

spoon–billed sandpiper *n* **:** a sandpiper (*Eurynorhynchus pygmeus*) that is characterized by a spatulate bill and inhabits northeastern Asia

spoon bit *n* **:** a wood-boring bit consisting of a grooved shank with a point shaped somewhat like the bowl of a spoon

spoon bow *n* **:** an overhanging bow of a ship whose underside is somewhat spoon-shaped

spoon bread *n, chiefly South & Midland* **:** bread made of cornmeal with or without added rice and hominy and mixed with milk, eggs, shortening, and leavening to a consistency that it must be served from the baking dish with a spoon — called also *batter bread*

spoon chisel *n* **:** a sculptor's bent chisel with the bezel on both sides

spoon·drift \ˈspün,drift\ *n* -s [alter. (influenced by ⁴*spoon*) of earlier *spenedrift,* fr. Sc *speendrift* — more at SPINDRIFT] **:** spray blown from waves during a gale at sea **:** SPINDRIFT

spoon end *n* [²*spoon*] **:** a concave end on a leaf spring to carry a swiveling member

spoon·er \ˈspünə(r)\ *n* -s [³*spoon* + *-er*] **1 :** one that uses a spoon implement ⟨~*s* being rapid professional handlers of the shovel —*Saturday Rev.*⟩ **2 :** one that makes love by spooning

spoon·er·ism \ˈspünə,rizəm\ *n* -s [William A. *Spooner* †1930 Eng. clergyman and educator noted for such lapses + E *-ism*] **:** a transposition of usu. initial sounds of two or more words that generally creates a comic effect (as in *votey heart* for *hearty vote, occupewing a pie* for *occupying a pew*); *esp* **:** such transposition done intentionally and so that the consequent formations are attested words (as in *tons of soil* for *sons of toil, ears and sparrows* for *spears and arrows*)

spoon·er·ize \-,rīz\ *vb* -ED/-ING/-S [Rev. William A. *Spooner* †1930 + E *-ize*] *vt* **:** to make a spoonerism of or in ⟨*spoonerized* recipes and words of advice to householders —*Current Biog.*⟩ ~ *vi* **:** to make spoonerisms

spooney *var of* SPOONY

spoon–fashion \ˈ=,==\ *adv* [¹*spoon*] **:** like spoons placed with the face of one fitting into the back of another ⟨sleep *spoon-fashion*⟩

spoon–feed \ˈ=,=\ *vt* **1 :** to feed (another) by means of a spoon **2 a :** to present (a thing) or to present a thing to (a person or group) so thoroughly or wholeheartedly as to preclude the need of independent thought, initiative, or self-reliance on the part of the recipient ⟨*spoon-feed* material to students⟩ ⟨poet should do all the work and *spoon-feed* his reader —*Fortnightly Rev.*⟩ ⟨claiming that you can prepare Indians for freedom by . . . *spoon-feeding* them —*Senior Scholastic*⟩ **b :** to present (information) or to present information to (a person or group) in a slanted version and with the intention of precluding questioning or revision on the part of the recipient ⟨*spoon-feeding* propaganda through the public schools —*Newsweek*⟩ ⟨fought . . . for free thought against *spoon-fed* thought —*Punch*⟩ ⟨the general public is being *spoon-fed* . . . more and more propaganda —Richard LaCoste⟩ ⟨a *spoon-fed* press⟩ ~ *vi* **1 :** to feed oneself or another by means of a spoon **2 a :** to present a thing so thoroughly or wholeheartedly as to preclude the need of independent thinking, initiative, or self-reliance on the part of the recipient ⟨our *spoon-feeding* pedagogy —H.G.Rickover⟩ **b :** to present information in a slanted version and with the intention of precluding questioning or revision on the part of the recipient ⟨altogether too much bureaucratic *spoon-feeding* about these proposals —*Contemporary Rev.*⟩ **c :** to accept passively that which has been spoon-fed ⟨has self-reliance superseded *spoon-feeding* —*Irish Statesman*⟩

spoonflower \ˈ=,==\ *n* [²*spoon* + *flower;* fr. the spoonlike end of the petiole] **:** YAUTIA a

spoon foot *n* **:** a foot (as on a table or chair) that projects out slightly from the leg and curves up to form a shape similar to that of the bowl of a spoon

spoon·ful \ˈ=,fu̇l\ *n, pl* **spoonfuls** \-lz\ *also* **spoons·ful** \-nz,-\ [ME *sponeful,* fr. *spone* spoon + *-ful*] **:** the amount of material a spoon contains or can contain; *specif* **:** TEASPOONFUL

spoonhunt \ˈ=,=\ *n* [*spoon*wood + *hunt* (of unknown origin)] *NewEng* **:** MOUNTAIN LAUREL 1

spoonhutch \ˈ=,=\ *n* [*spoon*wood + *hutch* (of unknown origin)] **:** BIG LAUREL

spoon·i·ly \ˈspünᵊlē\ *adv* **:** in a spoony manner ⟨how ~ I had managed my good fortune —G.J.Whyte-Melville⟩

spoon·i·ness *also* **spoon·ey·ness** \-nēnəs\ *n* -ES **:** the quality or state of being spoony ⟨restrained . . . from reciprocating my increasing ~ —T.A.Guthrie⟩

spooning *pres part of* SPOON

spoonlike \ˈ=,=\ *adj* **:** resembling a spoon (as in shape or function)

spoon meat *n* [²*spoon*] **:** food (as liquids or semisolids) eaten with or suitable for eating with a spoon ⟨live on *spoon meat* —Thomas Carlyle⟩

spoon nail *n* **:** KOILONYCHIA

spoon oar *n* **:** an oar having the blade so curved as to afford a better hold upon the water in rowing

spoons *pl of* SPOON, *pres 3d sing of* SPOON

spoon shovel *n* **:** SPOON 3a

spoon tool *n* **:** any of various more or less spoon-shaped molder's tools used for smoothing and finishing molds

spoonwood \ˈ=,=\ *n* [¹*spoon* + *wood;* fr. the use of its wood for making spoons] **:** MOUNTAIN LAUREL 1

spoonwood ivy *n* **:** SHEEP LAUREL

spoonwort \ˈ=,=\ *n* [trans. of D *lepelblad* or *lepelkruid*] **:** SCURVY GRASS 1

¹spoony *or* **spoon·ey** \ˈspünē\ *n, pl* **spoonies** *or* **spooneys** [¹*spoon* (simpleton) + *-y;* influenced in meaning by ³*spoon*] **:** one who is spoony ⟨a lackadaisical young ~ —Charles Dickens⟩ ⟨playing the lover . . . in the role of a ~ —H.E. Scudder⟩

²spoony *or* **spooney** \"\ *adj* **spoonier; spooniest** [¹*spoon* + *-y;* influenced in meaning by ³*spoon*] **1 :** SILLY, FOOLISH; *esp* **:** unduly emotional, sentimental, credulous, or indulgent **:** SOFT ⟨~ enough to let him get off —G.P.R.James⟩ ⟨even my jazz is like a ~ high-school kid's —H.L.Cliburn⟩; *esp* **:** enamored of or in love with to the point of being spoony — usu. used with *over* or *on* ⟨~ over Miss . . . to the point of idolatry —S.J.Perelman⟩ ⟨~ on a gypsy girl —Thomas Hughes⟩ **2 :** expressive or suggestive of spooniness ⟨not a ~ lovelorn effusion, but a good, rational, amusing letter —Bithia Croker⟩ ⟨~ ways and looks⟩

³spoony \"\ *n* -ES [*spoon*bill + *-y*] **:** SPOONBILL

spoony·ism *also* **spoon·ey·ism** \-nē,izəm\ *n* -s **:** SPOONINESS

¹spoor \ˈspu̇(ə)r, -ùə *sometimes* ˈspō(ə)r *or* ˈspōə *or* ˈspȯ(ə)r *or* ˈspȯ(ə)\ *n, pl* **spoor** *or* **spoors** [Afrik, fr. MD *spor, spoor;* akin to OE, OHG, & ON *spor* footprint, track, OE *spurnan* to kick — more at SPURN] **:** a mark (as a footprint), a trail, a scent, a sound, or droppings left by one (as a wild animal) that has passed **:** TRACK, SIGN ⟨~ of three large bulls . . . the tracks unusual in size —*Police Gazette*⟩ ⟨a ~ of blood from a slug in his right thigh —*Time*⟩ ⟨tell roughly how old a ~ is by the color and heat of the droppings —B.D.Nicholson⟩

²spoor \"\ *vb* -ED/-ING/-S [prob. fr. Afrik, fr. MD *sporen,* fr. *spor* spoor] *vt* **:** to track by a spoor ⟨~*ing* animals and interpreting every mark on the sand —Frank Debenham⟩ ~ *vi* **:** to track something by a spoor

spoor·er \-u̇rə(r), -ōrə-, -ȯrə-\ *n* -s **:** one that spoors

spor- *or* **spori-** *or* **sporo-** *comb form* [NL *spora* — more at SPORE] **:** seed **:** spore ⟨*sporo*cyst⟩ ⟨*sporangium*⟩ ⟨*spori*cide⟩

-spo·ra \spərə\ *n comb form* [NL, fr. *spora* seed, spore] **:** organism having (such) a sporal characteristic — in generic names ⟨Perono*spora*⟩ ⟨Iso*spora*⟩

spo·rad·ic \spəˈrad\|ik, spō'-, spȯ'-, -at\|, \|ēk\ *adj* [ML *sporadicus,* fr. Gk *sporadikos* scattered, fr. *sporad-, sporas* scattered; akin to Gk *speirein* to strew, sow — more at SPROUT] **:** occurring occasionally, singly, apart from other things of the same kind, or in scattered instances **:** SEPARATE, SINGLE, ISOLATED ⟨a ~ case of disease⟩ ⟨~ occurrence of a plant⟩ ⟨~ fighting⟩ — **spo·rad·i·cal·ly** \|ək(ə)lē, \|ēk-, -li\ *adv*

sporadic e layer *n, usu cap E* **:** a layer of ionization occurring irregularly within the E region of the ionosphere at heights of approximately 60 miles above the surface of the earth and occasionally being capable of reflecting radio waves of very high frequency back to earth at great distances

spo·ra·dic·i·ty \,spȯrəˈdisəd·ē\ *n* -ES **:** the quality or state of being sporadic

spo·ra·din \ˈspōrədən\ *n* -s [NL *Sporadina,* genus of gregarines, fr. Gk *sporad-, sporas* scattered + NL *-ina*] **:** a vermiform extracellular fully grown gregarine trophozoite that usu. lacks an epimerite — compare CEPHALIN

spor·al \ˈspōrəl, -pȯr-\ *adj* **:** of, relating to, or having the special characteristics of a spore **:** being a spore

spo·range \spəˈranj, ˈspōr,anj\ *n* -s [NL *sporangium*] **:** SPORANGIUM

sporangi- *or* **sporangio-** *comb form* [NL *sporangium*] **:** sporangium ⟨*sporangi*oid⟩ ⟨*sporangio*spore⟩

sporangia *pl of* SPORANGIUM

spo·ran·gi·al \spəˈranjēəl\ *adj* [NL *sporangium* + E *-al*] **:** of or relating to a sporangium **:** made up of sporangia

spo·ran·gif·er·ous \,spōranˈjif(ə)rəs\ *adj* [*sporangi-* + *-ferous*] **:** bearing sporangia

spo·ran·gi·form \spəˈranjə,fȯrm\ *adj* [*sporangi-* + *-form*] **:** having the form of a sporangium

spo·ran·gi·o·gen·ic \spəˈranjēō\|jenik\ *adj* [*sporangi-* + *-genic*] **:** producing sporangia

spo·ran·gi·oid \spəˈranjē,ȯid\ *adj* [*sporangi-* + *-oid*] **:** resembling a sporangium **:** SPORANGIFORM

spo·ran·gi·ole \-,ōl\ *n* -s [NL *sporangiolum*] **:** a small deciduous few-spored sporangium occurring along with larger sporangia that contain numerous spores in fungi of the family Mucoraceae

spo·ran·gi·o·lum \=,==ˈōləm\ *n, pl* **sporangio·la** \-lə\ [NL, dim. of *sporangium*] **:** SPORANGIOLE

spo·ran·gi·o·phore \spəˈranjēə,fō(ə)r\ *n* -s [*sporangi-* + *-phore*] **:** a stalk or receptacle bearing sporangia

spo·ran·gi·o·spore \-,spō(ə)r\ *n* [*sporangi-* + *spore*] **:** a spore that develops in a sporangium

spo·ran·gite \spəˈran,jīt\ *n* -s [NL *sporangium* + E *-ite*] **:** a fossilized spore case of a plant

spo·ran·gi·tes \,spōrənˈjīd·(,)ēz\ *n, cap* [NL, fr. *sporangium* + *-ites*] **:** a form genus of Paleozoic fossil organisms based on spores or spore cases apparently of plants of *Lepidodendron* and *Calamites* or related genera

spo·ran·gi·um \spəˈranjēəm, spō'-, spȯ'-\ *n, pl* **sporan·gia** \-ēə\ [NL, fr. *spor-* + Gk *angeion* vessel, receptacle — more at ANGI-] **:** a case within which spores that are usu. asexual are produced or borne: as **a :** a mother cell that in various bacteria, algae, and fungi produces one or a few cells endogenously **b :** the spore sac of a moss; *broadly* **:** CAPSULE 2b **c :** a complex structure in most ferns and related plants that contains numerous spores nourished by a tapetum and is usu. equipped with an annulus which aids in spore discharge **d :** MICROSPORANGIUM, MEGASPORANGIUM — compare GAMETANGIUM, GONIDANGIUM

¹spore \ˈspō(ə)r, ˈspȯ(ə)r, -ōə, -ȯ(ə)\ *n* -s [NL *spora,* fr. Gk *spora* act of sowing, seed; akin to Gk *sporos* act of sowing, seed, *speirein* to sow, strew — more at SPROUT] **1 :** a minute unicellular reproductive or resistant resting body that is often adapted to survive unfavorable environmental conditions and to produce a new vegetative individual when these conditions alter, is morphologically a mass of protoplasm usu. with a single definite nucleus and often with a cell wall and flagella, is capable of producing a new individual directly if asexual or only after union with another similar or dissimilar spore if sexual, and that occurs in many varieties differing in size, form, origin, and other characteristics — see ASCOSPORE, BASIDIOSPORE, CARPOSPORE, CHLAMYDOSPORE, CONIDIUM, ENDOSPORE, EXOSPORE, MEGASPORE, MICROSPORE, OOSPORE, TELIOSPORE, ZOOSPORE, ZYGOSPORE; compare SEED **2 :** any of various small multicellular resistant bodies (as a statoblast or gemmule) that are capable of reproducing a new individual

²spore \"\ *vb* -ED/-ING/-S *vi* **:** to produce or have spores **:** reproduce by or as if by spores ~ *vt* **:** to produce or multiply by or as if by sporing **:** SPAWN

-spore \,spō(ə)r, ,spȯ(ə)r, -ōə, -ȯ(ə)\ *n comb form* -s [NL *spora*] **1 :** spore having (such) a characteristic or origin ⟨pycnidio*spore*⟩ **2 :** spore membrane ⟨a dark epi*spore* enclosing a hyaline spore⟩

spore ball *n* **:** a multilocular body which becomes free like a spore and in which each cell is capable of germination (as in members of the genus *Spongospora*) or only some of the cells germinate (as in members of *Urocystis*)

sporebearer \ˈ=,==\ *n* **:** an organism that bears spores; *esp* **:** a bacterium that is difficult to destroy by sterilization because it produces heat-resistant spores

spore case *n* **:** a case containing spores **:** SPORANGIUM

spored \ˈspō(ə)rd\ *adj* [¹*spore* + *-ed*] **:** having spores — often used in combination

sporeformer \ˈ=,==\ *n* **:** an organism that forms spores **:** SPOREBEARER

spore fruit *n* **:** a specialized structure (as an ascocarp) that produces spores **:** FRUITING BODY

spore·ling \ˈspōrliŋ\ *n* -s [¹*spore* + *-ling*] **:** a young new individual developed from a spore; *usu* **:** a young sporophyte **:** PROTHALLIUM

spore mother cell *n* **:** one of the cells of the archespore of a spore-bearing plant whose final divisions result in the production of a spore and usu. of a tetrad of spores

spore print *n* **:** a deposit of spores of a fungus made by allowing the discharged spores to collect on paper or glass and form a print that gives a picture of the arrangement of the gills and of spore color

spore sac *n* **:** SPORE CASE: as **a :** a cavity of the theca of a moss **b :** ASCUS

spori- — see SPOR-

-spor·ic \ˈspōrik, -pȯr-, -pär-, -rēk\ *or* **-spor·ous** \ˈspōrəs, -pȯr-, ˌspərəs\ *adj comb form* [NL *spora* spore + E *-ic* or *-ous*] **:** having (such or so many) spores ⟨carpo*sporic*⟩ ⟨homo*sporous*⟩

spo·ri·ci·dal \ˌspōrəˈsīdᵊl\ *adj* [*spor-* + *-cidal*] **:** tending to kill spores

spo·rid \ˈspōrəd\ *n* -s [NL *sporidium*] **:** SPORIDIUM

spo·ri·desm \ˈspōrə,dezəm\ *n* -s [*spor-* + Gk *desmē* bundle, fr. *dein* to bind, tie — more at DIADEM] **:** a multicellular spore body or chain of independent spores

-spo·rid·ia \spəˈridēə, spō'-, spȯ'-\ *n pl comb form* [NL, fr. pl. of *sporidium*] **:** creatures bearing (such) small spores — in higher taxa in protozoology ⟨Micro*sporidia*⟩ ⟨Cnido*sporidia*⟩

spo·rid·i·al \-ēəl\ *adj* [NL *sporidium* + E *-al*] **:** of, relating to, or producing sporidia **:** developing from a sporidium

spo·ri·dif·er·ous \ˌspōrəˈdif(ə)rəs\ *adj* [NL *sporid*ium + E *-ferous*] **:** bearing sporidia

spo·rid·i·um \spəˈridēəm, spō'-, spȯ'-\ *n, pl* **sporid·ia** \-ēə\ [NL, fr. *spor-* + *-idium*] **:** a small spore; *esp* **:** one abjointed from a promycelium (as in various smuts and rusts) — compare BASIDIOSPORE

-spories *pl of* -SPORY

spo·rif·er·ous \-if(ə)rəs\ *adj* [*spor-* + *-iferous*] **:** bearing or producing spores

-spo·ri·um \ˈspōrēəm, -pȯr-\ *n comb form* [NL, fr. *spora* spore + *-ium*] **1** *pl* **-spo·ria** \-ēə\ *also* **-sporiums :** (such) a coat or layer of a spore wall ⟨endo*sporium*⟩ **2 :** plant having (such) a spore — in generic names ⟨Helmintho*sporium*⟩

sporo- — see SPOR-

spo·ro·blast \ˈspōrə,blast\ *n* [ISV *spor-* + *-blast*] **:** a cell of a sporozoan resulting from sexual reproduction and producing spores and sporozoites

spo·ro·bo·lo·my·ce·ta·ce·ae \spə,räbəlō,mīsəˈtāsē,ē\ *n pl, cap* [NL, fr. *Sporobolomycet-, Sporobolomyces,* type genus (fr. *spor-* + Gk *-bolos* + NL *-mycet-, -myces*) + *-aceae*] **:** a family of imperfect fungi (order Moniliales) characterized by scanty mycelium and propagation by both budding and repetition

spo·rob·o·lus \spəˈräbələs\ *n, cap* [NL, fr. Gk *spora, sporos* seed + *-bolos* (fr. *ballein* to throw) — more at SPORE, DEVIL] **:** a widely distributed genus of grasses having ample panicles with small one-flowered spikelets each with three glumes and grain that separates easily — see DROPSEED

spo·ro·carp \ˈspōrə,kärp, -pȯr-, -kȧp\ *n* -s [ISV *spor-* + Gk *karpos* fruit — more at HARVEST] **:** any structure in or on which spores are produced: as **a :** a multicellular body that develops from a fertilized archicarp or procarp of a red alga and produces asexual carpospores **:** CYSTOCARP **b :** a many-celled body (as an ascocarp) producing spores in a fungus **c :** the sporogonium of a moss **d :** an organized mass of sporangia in a fern ally of the families Salviniaceae and Marsileaceae

spo·roch·nus \spəˈräknəs\ *n, cap* [NL, fr. *spor-* + Gk *chnoos, chnous* dust, fine down — more at HYPOCHNUS] **:** a small genus (the type of the family Sporochnaceae) of brown algae characterized by tufts of fine elongated filaments terminating some of the branches of the thallus

spo·ro·cyst \ˈspōrə, ˈspȯrə+,-\ *n* [ISV *spor-* + *cyst*] **1 :** a unicellular resting cell that may give rise to asexual spores (as in various myxomycetes and algae) — compare SPORANGIUM **2 a :** a case or cyst secreted by some sporozoans preliminary to sporogony; *also* **:** a sporozoan encysted in such a case **b :** a saccular body that is the first reproductive form of a digenetic trematode in the molluscan host and buds off cells from its inner surface which develop into rediae within the cavity of the sporocyst — **spo·ro·cys·tic** \ˌ==+\ *adj* — **spo·ro·cys·tid** \"+\ *n* -s

spo·ro·cyte \ˈspōrə,sīt\ *n* -s [*spor-* + *-cyte*] **:** SPORE MOTHER CELL

spo·ro·do·chi·um \ˌspōrəˈdōkēəm\ *n, pl* **sporodo·chia** \-ēə\ [NL, fr. *spor-* + Gk *docheion* holder, receptacle, fr. *dechesthai, dekesthai* to receive, accept; akin to Gk *dokein* to seem good — more at DECENT] **:** an erumpent crowded cluster of conidiophores arising from a stroma in the form of a cushion (as in the Tuberculariaceae)

spo·ro·duct \ˈspōrə, ˈspȯrə+,-\ *n* [ISV *spor-* + *duct*] **:** minute tubes in the wall of the cyst formed by some gregarines for the exit of spores

spo·ro·genesis \ˌ==+\ *n* [NL, fr. *spor-* + L *genesis*] **1 :** reproduction by spores **2 :** spore formation

spo·ro·gen·ic \ˌspōrəˈjenik\ *adj* [*spor-* + *-genic*] **1 :** SPOROGENOUS **2 :** of, relating to, or involving sporogenesis ⟨a ~ cycle⟩

spo·rog·e·nous \spəˈräjənəs, spō'-, spȯ'-\ *adj* [*spor-* + *-genous*] **1 :** producing or adapted to the production of spores ⟨~ hyphae⟩ **2 :** reproducing by spores

spo·rog·e·ny \-nē\ *n* -ES [*spor-* + *-geny*] **:** SPOROGENESIS

spo·ro·gone \ˈspōrə,gōn, -pȯr-\ *n* -s [NL *sporogonium*] **:** SPOROGONIUM

spo·ro·go·ni·al \ˌ==ˈgōnēəl\ *adj* [NL *sporogonium* + E *-al*] **1 :** of, relating to, or producing sporogonia **2 :** SPOROGONIC

spo·ro·gon·ic \-ˈgänik\ *also* **spo·rog·o·nous** \spəˈrägənəs, spō'-, spȯ'-\ *adj* [*sporogony* + *-ic* or *-ous*] **:** of, relating to, involving, or produced by sporogony ⟨~ parasites⟩ ⟨a ~ cycle⟩

spo·ro·go·ni·um \ˌspōrəˈgōnēəm, -pȯr-\ *n, pl* **sporogo·nia** \-ēə\ [NL, fr. *spor-* + *-gonium* (as in *archegonium*)] **:** the sporophyte of a moss or liverwort consisting typically of a stalk bearing a capsule in which spores are produced, developing from a fertilized egg in the venter of the archegonium, and remaining permanently attached to the gametophyte by the base of the stalk which acts as an absorbing organ

spo·rog·o·ny \spəˈrägənē, spō'-, spȯ'-, -ni\ *n* -ES [ISV *spor-* + *-gony*] **:** reproduction by spores; *specif* **:** spore formation in a sporozoan by encystment and subsequent division of a zygote — distinguished from *schizogony*

spor·oid \ˈspō,rȯid\ *adj* [*spor-* + *-oid*] **:** resembling a spore

spo·ro·morph \ˈspōrə,mȯrf\ *n* -s [*spor-* + *-morph*] **:** a fossil pollen grain or spore

spo·ront \ˈspōr,änt\ *n* -s [ISV *spor-* + *-ont*] **:** a sporozoan (as a zygote or pansporoblast) that engages in sporogony

spo·ro·phore \'spōrə,fō(ə)r, -pȯr-, -fō(ə)r, -fōə, -fȯ(ə)\ *n* -s [ISV *spor-* + *-phore*] **:** a spore-bearing branch or organ **:** the part of the thallus of a sporophyte that develops spores, in fungi is often a conspicuous spore fruit (as in the mushrooms and other basidiomycetes) though sometimes a simple hyphal filament or a mass of hyphae, in ferns, mosses, and liverworts is practically equivalent to the sporophyte, and in seed plants constitutes the placenta — compare GAMETOPHORE — **spo·ro·phor·ic** \¦==¦fȯrik\ *adj*

spo·roph·o·rous \spə'räf(ə)rəs, spō'-, spȯ'-\ *adj* [NL *sporophorus*, fr. *spor-* + *-phorus* -phorous] **1 :** SPORIFEROUS **2** [*sporophore* + *-ous*] **:** of or relating to a sporophore

spo·ro·phyll *also* **spo·ro·phyl** \'spōrə,fil, -pȯr-\ *n* -s [ISV *spor-* + *-phyll*] **1 :** a spore-bearing leaf **:** a leaf more or less modified in form and structure that develops sporangia and may resemble and perform the functions of a foliage leaf (as in many ferns) or may be completely altered (as the spike of the adder's-tongue) — see MEGASPOROPHYLL, MICROSPOROPHYLL **2 :** a small foliaceous structure bearing the sporangia in a brown alga of the genus *Alaria* — **spo·roph·yl·lary** \spə'räfə,lerē\ *adj*

spo·ro·phyte \'spōrə,fīt, -pȯr-\ *n* -s [ISV *spor-* + *-phyte*] **:** an individual or generation of a plant exhibiting alternation of generations that bears asexual spores, is usu. not clearly differentiated in algae and fungi, is represented by the sporogonium in bryophytes, and in vascular plants is the conspicuous form ordinarily known — distinguished from *gametophyte* — **spo·ro·phyt·ic** \¦==¦fid·ik\ *adj*

spo·ro·plasm \'==,plazəm\ *n* -s [*spor-* + *-plasm*] **:** a mass of protoplasm that gives rise to or forms a spore; *esp* **:** the protoplasmic body that is released as an infective amoebula from a cnidosporidian cyst

spo·ro·sac \-,sak\ *n* [*spor-* + *sac*] **1 :** a simple degenerate gonophore of some hydroids that is often little more than a gonad and never medusoid **2 a :** SPOROCYST **b :** REDIA

spo·ro·thrix \-,thriks\ *n* -ES [NL *sporotrich-*, *sporothrix*, fr. *spor-* + Gk *trich-*, *thrix* hair — more at TRICHINA] **:** a fungus of the genus *Sporotrichum*

spo·ro·tri·cho·sis \,spōrə,trī'kōsəs\ *n, pl* **sporotricho·ses** \-kō,sēz\ [NL, fr. *sporotrichum* + *-osis*] **:** infection with or disease caused by fungi of the genus *Sporotrichum*, characterized by nodules and abscesses in the superficial lymph nodes, skin, and subcutaneous tissues, occurring esp. in man and horses, and usu. transmitted through entry of the fungus by way of a skin abrasion or wound (as from prick of a thorn)

spo·ro·tri·chot·ic \¦==¦kād·ik\ *adj* **:** of or relating to sporotrichosis ⟨~ lesions⟩

spo·rot·ri·chum \spə'rä·trəkəm\ *n* [NL, fr. *spor-* + Gk *trich-*, *thrix* hair — more at TRICHINA] **1** *cap* **:** a genus of saprophytic or parasitic imperfect fungi (family Moniliaceae) forming hyaline conidia either solitary or in groups and on short conidiophores — see SPOROTRICHOSIS **2** *pl* **sporotri·cha** \-kə\ **:** any fungus of the genus *Sporotrichum*

spor·ous \'spōrəs\ *adj* [*spore* + *-ous*] **:** SPORAL

-sporous — see -SPORIC

spo·ro·zoa \,spōrə'zōə, -pȯr-\ *n pl, cap* [NL, fr. *spor-* + *-zoa*] **:** a large class of strictly parasitic protozoans that pass through a complicated life cycle usu. involving alternation of a sexual with an asexual generation, often require two or more dissimilar hosts to complete their life cycle, are typically immobile and usu. intracellular parasites, and include many serious pathogens (as well as the malaria parasites, coccidia, and piroplasms) as well as apparently innocuous forms — see ACNIDOSPORIDIA, CNIDOSPORIDIA, TELOSPORIDIA — **spo·ro·zo·al** \¦==¦zōəl\ *adj* — **spo·ro·zo·an** \-zōən\ *adj or n*

spo·ro·zo·ite \,==¦zō,īt\ *n* -s [NL *sporozoon* + ISV *-ite*] **:** a small usu. motile and elongate infective stage of some sporozoans that is introduced into a definitive host by an intermediate host or by escape from a spore, is a product of sexual reproduction, and initiates an asexual cycle in the new host

spo·ro·zo·it·i·cide \,==zō¦id·ə,sīd\ *n* -s [*sporozoite* + *-i-* + *-cide*] **:** an agent selectively destructive of the sporozoite form of a sporozoan parasite

spo·ro·zo·on \,==¦zō,än\ *n, pl* **sporo·zoa** \-zōə\ [NL, sing. of *Sporozoa*] **:** SPOROZOAN

spor·ran \'spärən\ *n* -s [ScGael *sporan* purse] **:** a large pouch of skin with the hair or fur on that is worn in front of the kilt by Highlanders in full dress and used as a purse

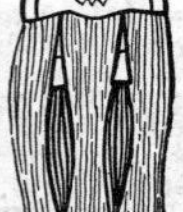

sporran

¹sport \'spō(ə)r\t, -pȯ(ə)\t, -ōə\, -ȯ(ə)\, *usu* \d·+V\ *vb* -ED/-ING/-S [ME *sporten*, short for *disporten* to disport] *vt* **1** *archaic* **:** to make (as oneself) merry **:** DIVERT, AMUSE, CHEER **2 a** *archaic* **:** to expend (money) in gambling **:** WAGER, BET **b :** to expend wastefully or carelessly (as in riotous living); *also* **:** to spend lavishly and ostentatiously **3 a :** to make public and usu. ostentatious display or use of **:** show off ⟨delighted to ~ his learning in company⟩ ⟨~*ing* the new sedan in the park⟩ **b :** to wear contentedly or with satisfaction ⟨~*ed* a trim little hat at church⟩ **c :** to keep or use as a possession ⟨every clerk hoping to ~ a horse some day⟩ **4** *Brit* **:** to close or keep (a door) closed usu. as an indication that one is too occupied for company **5** [²*sport*] **:** to put forth as a sport or bud variation ⟨the white rose ~*ed* a single red-flowered branch⟩ ~ *vi* **1 a :** to amuse oneself by light or playful activity (as by participation in a game or outdoor exercise) **:** FROLIC, ROMP ⟨lambs ~*ing* in the meadow⟩ **b :** to engage or participate in a sport and esp. an active field sport **2 a :** to treat sportively or lightly **:** deal in a sportive or light manner **:** MOCK **b :** to speak or act jestingly or slightly or without due or serious consideration — used with *with* ⟨~*ing* with things he scarcely hoped to understand⟩ **3** *archaic* **:** to bet habitually **4** [²*sport*] **:** to deviate or vary abruptly from type **:** give rise to a sport (as by bud variation) **:** MUTATE **syn** see PLAY — **sport one's oak** *Brit* **:** close one's door against interruption

²sport \"\ *n* -s [ME, short for *disport*] **1 a :** something that is a source of pleasant diversion **:** a pleasing or amusing pastime or activity **:** RECREATION ⟨spent the afternoon in ~ and play⟩ **b** *obs* **:** sexual dalliance **:** amorous play **c** *obs* **:** a theatrical performance **d :** a particular play, game, or mode of amusement: as (1) **:** a diversion of the field (as fowling, hunting, fishing, racing, or athletic games); *also* **:** any of various games (as bowling, rackets, basketball) or comparable diversions usu. played under cover (2) **:** a game or contest esp. when involving individual skill or physical prowess on which money is staked **2 a :** something light, playful, or frivolous and lacking in serious intent or spirit **:** PLEASANTRY, JEST **b :** superior or contemptuous mirth **:** MOCKING, MOCKERY, DERISION ⟨then make ~ at me, then let me be your jest —Shak.⟩ **3 :** an occupation that constitutes a diversion ⟨the same old domestic ~ of arguing at table and making up in bed⟩ **4 a :** something tossed or driven about in or as if in play **:** the helpless object of a force ⟨the prey and ~ of wintry winds⟩ ⟨seemed no more than the ~ of misfortune⟩ **b :** a subject of or butt for mirth, mockery, or derision **:** LAUGHING STOCK **5 :** a person interested in sports **:** SPORTSMAN: as **a :** a person with sporting instincts **:** one interested in sports chiefly for the gambling opportunities presented; *broadly* **:** GAMBLER **b :** a person enjoying a gay luxurious life **:** BON VIVANT **c :** a person living up to the high ideals of good sportsmanship esp. as a loser in any contest or situation **d :** a companionable or likable person; *often* **:** FELLOW, COMPANION, CHAP **6 :** an individual exhibiting in whole or in part a sudden spontaneous deviation from type beyond the normal limits of individual variation usu. as a result of mutation esp. of somatic tissue — compare BUD VARIATION **syn** see FUN, ²PLAY — **in sport** *adv* **:** in a light or jesting manner **:** without serious intent ⟨told him *in sport* that we would all go to Florida⟩

³sport \"\ *or* **sports** \lts\ *adj* **:** of, relating to, or suitable for sports and esp. outdoor sports **:** adapted to use in connection with sports ⟨a ~ roadster⟩ ⟨*sports* equipment⟩; *esp* **:** styled in a manner suitable for casual or informal wear ⟨*sports* coats⟩ ⟨a trim ~ shoe⟩

sport·abil·i·ty \,spōrd·ə'biləd·ē\ *n, archaic* **:** SPORTIVENESS

sport·er \'spōrd·ər\ *n* -s **1 :** one that sports (as a sportsman or a lavish spender) **2 :** one (as a dog or rifle) that is used in sport and esp. in the sport of hunting

sport finder *n* **:** ALBADA FINDER

sport fish *n* **:** a fish primarily of importance for the sport it affords anglers — compare COARSE FISH, GAME FISH, ROUGH FISH

sport·ful \'spōrtfəl, -pȯr-, -ōət-, -ȯ(ə)t-\ *adj* [ME, fr. ²*sport* + *-ful*] **1 a :** productive of sport or amusement **:** ENTERTAINING, DIVERTING **b :** having an inclination to lighthearted merriment **:** PLAYFUL, FROLICSOME; *usu* **:** inclined to jest or tease playfully **2 :** done in jest or for mere play **:** lacking serious intent **:** SPORTIVE — **sport·ful·ly** \-fəlē, -li\ *adv* — **sport·ful·ness** *n* -ES

sportier *comparative of* SPORTY

sportiest *superlative of* SPORTY

sport·i·ly \'spōrd·ᵊlē\ *adv* **:** in a sporty manner **:** so as to be or appear sporty

sport·i·ness \-d·ēnəs\ *n* -ES **:** the quality or state of being sporty

sporting *adj* [fr. gerund & pres. part. of ¹*sport*] **1 a :** SPORT **b :** suitable for or characteristic of a sportsman **:** marked by or calling for sportsmanship ⟨a ~ solution of the problem⟩ **c :** involving such risk as a sports contender may reasonably take or expect to encounter ⟨a ~ chance of success⟩ **2 a :** of, relating to, or preoccupied with dissipation and esp. gambling; *often* **:** FAST, FLASHY ⟨~ gents and their ladies⟩ **b :** engaged or used in prostitution **3 :** tending to produce sports usu. with exceptional frequency ⟨a ~ strain of evening primrose⟩

sporting blood *n* **1 :** instinctive love of sports **2 :** readiness to accept a challenge (as to a contest); *broadly* **:** DARING, COURAGE

sporting editor *n* **:** SPORTS EDITOR

sporting girl *or* **sporting woman** *n* **:** PROSTITUTE

sporting house *n* **1** *archaic* **:** a public place frequented by sportsmen or gamblers **2 :** BROTHEL

sport·ing·ly *adv* **:** in a sporting manner **:** so as to be sporting

sporting page *n* **:** SPORTS PAGE

sporting powder *n* **:** black powder or smokeless powder for use in sporting ammunition

spor·tive \'spōr|d·|iv, -pȯr|, -ōə|, -ȯ(ə)|, |t|, |ēv *also* |əv\ *adj* [²*sport* + *-ive*] **1 a :** tending to, engaged in, or productive or provocative of sport **:** GAY, FROLICSOME, PLAYFUL, MERRY **b :** not undertaken or done seriously **:** carried on or out in sport **c :** having an inclination for sexual encounter **:** ARDENT, LUSTY **2 :** relating to or connected with sports and esp. field sports **3 a :** produced as a sport **b :** tending to the production of sports **:** SPORTING 3 — **spor·tive·ly** \|əvlē, -li\ *adv* — **spor·tive·ness** \|ivnəs, |ēv- *also* |əv-\ *n* -ES

sportive lemur *n* **:** any of several small slender Madagascan lemurs constituting the genus *Lepilemur* — compare WEASEL LEMUR

sport·less \'=ləs\ *adj* **:** affording no sport **:** producing no sports

sport of kings 1 : horse racing **2 a :** FALCONRY **b :** HUNTING

¹sports *pres 3d sing of* SPORT, *pl of* SPORT

²sports *var of* SPORT

sports car *also* **sport car** *n* **:** a low-slung open or convertible automobile designed for high-speed transportation on regular roads and having rapid acceleration, more or less smooth horizontal lines, and usu. seats for two people

sports·cast \'spōrt,skast, -pȯr-, -ōət-, -ȯ(ə)t-, -aa(ə)st\ *also* **sport·cast** \-t,k-\ *n* -s [³*sport* + *broadcast*] **:** a radio or television broadcast of a sports event or of information about sports — **sports·cast·er** *also* **sport·cast·er** \-tə(r)\ *n* -s

sports·dom \-tsdəm, -tstəm\ *n* -s **:** the realm of sports; *esp* **:** the whole field of organized competitive sport

sports editor *also* **sport editor** *n* **:** a newspaper editor in charge of news about sports

sport shirt *n* **:** a soft shirt styled for casual wear with or without a tie or open at the neck and having long or short sleeves and usu. a square bottom for wear inside or outside the trousers

sports·man \'=mən\ *n, pl* **sportsmen :** a person who is active in sports: as **a :** one who engages in the sports of the field and esp. in hunting or fishing **b** *archaic* **:** one who gambles at cards or on sports and esp. on horse racing **:** a sporting man **c :** one who in sports is fair and generous **:** one who in any connection has recourse to nothing illegitimate **:** a person who is a good loser and a graceful winner

sports·man·like \'=₌,=\ *adj* **:** characteristic of a sportsman **:** consistent with the ideals of good sportsmanship

sports·man·ly *adj* **:** SPORTSMANLIKE

sports·man·ship \'==,ship\ *n* **1** *archaic* **:** skill or an instance of skillful performance in some sport **2 :** conduct becoming to a sportsman and involving fair honest rivalry, courteous relations, and graceful acceptance of results

sports page *n* **:** a page of a newspaper given over to sports news

sports section *n* **:** a section of a newspaper given over to sports news

sportswear \'=,=\ *n* -s **:** clothing suitable for wearing while engaged in an active sport (as tennis, golf, skiing) ⟨a store specializing in ~⟩; *also* **:** the wearing of such clothing or an occasion on which such clothing might suitably be worn ⟨sell clothing for ~⟩

sportswoman \'=,==\ *n, pl* **sportswomen :** a female sportsman

sportswriter \'=,==\ *n* **:** one who writes about sports esp. for a newspaper

sportsy \'spōrtsē\ *adj, sometimes* -ER/-EST [¹*sports* + *-y*] **1 :** suitable for sportswear **2 :** suggesting sportswear in design, motif, or cut **:** suitable for sport clothes

spor·tu·la \'spȯ(r)chələ\ *n, pl* **sportu·lae** \-chə,lē\ *also* **sportulas** [L, lit., little basket, dim. of *sporta* basket, fr. (assumed) Etruscan *spurta*, fr. Gk *spurid-*, *spuris*; akin to Gk *sparton* plaited rope, esparto — more at SPIRE (spiral)] **:** a gift (as of food or money) usu. from an ancient Roman to one of his clients and often at regular intervals or on prescribed occasions

sporty \'spōr|d·|ē, -pȯr|, -pōə|, -pȯ(ə)|, |t|, |i\ *adj* -ER/-EST **1 :** characteristic of a sport or a sportsman **:** SPORTSMANLIKE **2 a :** notably gay or dissipated **:** FAST, LOOSE ⟨ran around with a very ~ crowd⟩ **b :** FLASHY, SHOWY ⟨~ clothes⟩ **3 :** capable of giving or designed to give good sport **:** suitable for sport or for a particular sport ⟨a ~ little boat⟩ ⟨a ~ golf course⟩

spor·u·lar \'spȯryələ(r), -pär-\ *adj* [NL *sporula* sporule + E *-ar*] **1 :** of, relating to, or having the nature of a sporule **2 :** SPOROID

spor·u·late \-yə,lāt\ *vb* -ED/-ING/-S [back-formation fr. *sporulation*] *vi* **:** to undergo sporulation ~ *vt* **:** to transform into spores

spor·u·la·tion \,==¦lāshən\ *n* -s [NL *sporula* + ISV *-ation*] **:** the formation of spores; *esp* **:** division into many small spores (as after encystment) — **spor·u·la·tive** \'==,lād·iv\ *adj*

spor·ule \'spȯr,yül, -pär-\ *n* -s [F or NL; F *sporule*, fr. NL *sporula*, dim. of *spora* spore] **:** a small spore

-spory \,spōrē, ,spərē, -ri\ *n comb form* -ES [*-sporic* + *-y*] **:** the quality or state of having (such or such a number of) spores ⟨apo*spory*⟩ ⟨homo*spory*⟩

sposh \'späsh\ *n* [prob. blend of *slush* and ¹*posh*] *dial* **:** soft slushy mud or snow — **sposhy** \-shē\ *adj*

¹spot \'spät, *usu* -äd·+V\ *n* -s [ME *spotte, spot*; akin to MD *spotte* stain, speck, ON *spotti* small piece, bit] **1 :** a taint on character or reputation **:** blemish upon moral purity **:** DISGRACE, STIGMA, FAULT, REPROACH ⟨keep this commandment without ~ —1 Tim 6:14 (AV)⟩ ⟨the only ~ upon the family name⟩ **2 a :** a usu. disfiguring mark on a substance or body made by a deposit of foreign matter **:** discolored place **:** BLOT, SPECK, STAIN ⟨out, damned ~ —Shak.⟩ ⟨a dark ~ that might have been blood⟩ ⟨conscious of a grease ~ on his necktie⟩ ⟨tablecloth had many ~*s*⟩ ⟨one coat is guaranteed to cover all ~*s* and blemishes⟩ ⟨remove all common household ~*s* such as ink, oil, tar, paint, gum —*Sears, Roebuck Cat.*⟩ **b :** such a disfiguring mark or discolored place resulting from natural causes (as injury, disease) ⟨bruised ~ on an apple⟩ ⟨cut out several ~*s* of rot⟩: as (1) **:** a circumscribed area (as of different density, rarefaction) in an organ seen by means of X rays or an instrument (as an ophthalmoscope) ⟨a ~ on the retina⟩ ⟨left him with a ~ on his lungs —Green Peyton⟩ (2) **:** PIMPLE (3) **:** SUNSPOT (4) **:** NEVUS (5) **:** one of the circumscribed discolored areas produced on a plant (as upon leaves, fruits) by various fungi or by nonparasitic agencies — compare RUST **3 :** a small part or area differing to the eye (as in color, finish, composition) from the main ground or surface ⟨a leopard's ~*s*⟩ ⟨black silk with white ~*s*⟩ ⟨orchards made ~*s* of pink among the green meadows⟩ ⟨patterns of transparent ~*s* on photographic film —*Machine Literature Searching*⟩ ⟨added up the ~*s* on the dice⟩ ⟨set of dominoes with badly worn ~*s*⟩ ⟨combed his hair over a bald ~⟩ ⟨saw ~*s* before his eyes⟩: as **a** *obs* **:** BEAUTY SPOT, PATCH **b :** a blaze on a tree **c** (1) **:** a conventionalized design used on playing cards to distinguish suits and indicate values — called also *pip* (2) **:** any similar distinguishing device (as a numeral) used on objects (as billiard balls, paper money) in a set or series (3) **:** an object having a specified number of such designs or devices on its surface or bearing a specified distinguishing numeral ⟨played the six-*spot*⟩ ⟨sank the three-*spot* in the corner pocket⟩ ⟨handed the waiter a ten-*spot*⟩ **d** (1) **:** any of the small marks on the bed of a billiard or pool table indicating where balls are to be placed (2) **:** SPOT BALL (3) **:** SPOT STROKE **e** (1) **:** any of the circular marks painted on or embedded in the floor of a bowling alley to indicate the positions of the pins in tenpins and similar games (2) **:** the calculated spot part way down the alley at which a spot bowler aims when attempting to make a strike **f** (1) **:** a small character (as a star or diamond) used in printing as an ornament or eye-arresting device (2) **:** a small simple illustration usu. without a rectangular border or frame placed amid or at the end of type matter **4 a :** a small quantity or amount **:** BIT, PARTICLE ⟨not a ~ of room anywhere⟩ **b** *chiefly Brit* **:** a relatively small but indeterminate amount ⟨doing a ~ of wrestling —A.J.Liebling⟩ ⟨go over . . . for a ~ of lunch —John Brooks⟩ ⟨liked nothing better than a ~ of conversation —Thomas Sugrue⟩ ⟨do a ~ of big-game fishing —Alden Hatch⟩ ⟨lie down for a ~ of rest⟩ ⟨stopped for a ~ of beer⟩; *specif* **:** a smallish amount of liquor **:** DROP, DRINK ⟨could do with a few ~*s* —A.P.Gaskell⟩ ⟨how about having a ~⟩ **5 a :** a particular locality esp. of somewhat limited extent ⟨one of the most beautiful ~*s* in the world⟩ ⟨prepared to move the capital to a safer ~⟩ ⟨selected a ~ for the next annual meeting⟩ ⟨words from all the ~*s* on the earth —Charlton Laird⟩ ⟨any ~ . . . was more endurable than the place she was in —Ellen Glasgow⟩ ⟨hottest ~*s* . . . were Parliament itself, Spain, and Ireland —G.W.Johnson⟩ ⟨two foremost danger ~*s* in the East-West struggle —Carlyle Morgan⟩ **b :** a small extent of space ⟨the exact ~ where the crash occurred⟩ ⟨trying to find a dry ~ for a picnic⟩ ⟨found the right ~ behind the books, and the click of a sliding panel was heard —T.B.Costain⟩ ⟨X marks the ~⟩ ⟨looking for a quiet ~ to fish⟩ **c :** a locality or a building used or suitable for a particular purpose ⟨favorite vacation ~ for New Yorkers⟩ ⟨excellent picnic ~*s*⟩ ⟨his favorite fishing ~⟩ ⟨well-known gambling ~⟩ ⟨cleaning up the vice ~*s*⟩ ⟨famous dining ~*s* —*Ford Times*⟩; *esp* **:** NIGHTCLUB ⟨had a late dinner and then took in a few ~*s*⟩ ⟨tried another ~, where there was dancing —Molly L. Bar-David⟩ ⟨a Chicago jazz ~ —Martin Gardner⟩ **6 :** a small part or area differing from the whole to which it belongs ⟨represented on the tape by invisible magnetic ~*s* —*Univac*⟩ ⟨sensory ~*s* on the skin —R.S.Woodworth⟩ ⟨complained of a sore ~ in his throat⟩ ⟨finger detected a rough ~⟩ ⟨high ~*s* of each publishing season —William Peden⟩ ⟨another dark ~ appeared to be brightening as farm prices steadied —*Dun's Rev.*⟩ ⟨do not have excessively bright ~*s* in their pattern of mental abilities —R.J.Williams⟩ ⟨has ~ of very fine acting —Henry Huses⟩ **7 :** a small croaker (*Leiostomus xanthurus*) of the Atlantic coast of the U. S. that is highly esteemed as a panfish and that has a black spot behind the shoulders and 15 oblique dark bars **8 :** a particular position or situation esp. in order of priority (as in a place of employment, an organization, a program or schedule or on a slate or ticket) ⟨the top ~*s* in industry and finance —W.G. Hardy⟩ **:** BERTH, BILLET, POST ⟨finally found a ~ as a receptionist⟩ ⟨a Cabinet ~ here, an undersecretaryship there —E.J. Kahn⟩ ⟨been tried at every ~ except pitcher and catcher —W. B.Furlong⟩ ⟨if he ended up in my ~ one day —Louis Auchincloss⟩; *esp* **:** a place on a program of entertainment ⟨deserve a better ~ on the program —T.W.Duncan⟩ ⟨had a solo ~⟩ ⟨shifted him to a daytime ~⟩ ⟨engaged him for a 15 minute dramatic ~⟩ ⟨has several guest ~*s* lined up⟩ **9 spots** *pl* [³*spot*] **:** commodities (as merchandise and cotton) sold for immediate delivery **10 a** [by shortening] **:** SPOTLIGHT ⟨gallery ~*s*⟩ ⟨proscenium ~*s*⟩ ⟨an amber ~⟩ ⟨a battery of baby ~*s* —Christopher Morley⟩ ⟨individually lighted by a ~ in the ceiling —*Lamp*⟩ **b :** the spot of light that results from an electron beam hitting the phosphor in a picture tube and that traces out the television picture **11 a :** a situation with respect to conditions and circumstances **:** POSITION ⟨a tough ~⟩ ⟨in a fine ~ for rapid promotion⟩ **b :** a position of difficulty or embarrassment **:** FIX, PREDICAMENT ⟨was indeed in a dilemma — in a ~ —R.M.Lovett⟩ ⟨one of those ~*s* you get in —J.M.Cain⟩ **12 :** a brief interval between scheduled radio or television programs during which an announcement or advertisement is broadcast; *also* **:** the announcement or advertisement broadcast — **in spots :** at intervals **:** in some respects ⟨not unhappy — except *in spots* —Ellen Glasgow⟩ — **on the spot** *or* **upon the spot** *adv (or adj)* **1 :** before moving or without further consideration **:** at once **:** IMMEDIATELY ⟨decided *on the spot*⟩ **2 :** at the place where action is required ⟨sent to investigate *on the spot*⟩ ⟨found everything he needed right *on the spot*⟩ **3 a :** in a position of being held responsible or accountable or of being required to furnish a satisfactory explanation or reply **:** in trouble or difficulty **:** in a spot **b :** in a position of danger esp. of murder or assassination (as by way of reprisal) — often used in the phrase *put on the spot*

²spot \"\ *vb* **spotted; spotted; spotting; spots** [ME *spotten*, fr. *spotte, spot* spot] *vt* **1 a :** to taint or stain the character or reputation of **:** DISGRACE ⟨may I live *spotted* for my perjury —Francis Beaumont & John Fletcher⟩ **b** (1) *obs* **:** BLAME, ASPERSE (2) **:** give information against **2 :** to mark with a disfiguring or discoloring spot ⟨*spotted* his necktie⟩ **:** stain in spots **:** cover with spots ⟨trail of blood *spotted* the snow⟩ ⟨was *spotted* with mud from top to bottom⟩ ⟨fungus that ~*s* the leaves⟩ **3 :** to mark with a distinctive spot (as for ornament, identification) ⟨a book with edges *spotted* by hand⟩: as **a** *obs* **:** to affix a beauty spot to (the face) **b :** to put a blaze on (a tree) **:** mark (as a line or trail) with blazes **c** (1) **:** to mark (as watch or clock plates, flat surfaces of fine tools) with equally spaced whirls produced by a light abrasive (2) **:** to make a mark on (a surface) as a locating mark for laying out or other operations in machining **d :** to mark (as a railroad tie) by a spot of paint or other means as requiring particular attention **4 :** to single out **:** pick out **:** IDENTIFY: as **a :** to mark or note as a known criminal or as a suspicious person **b :** to pick out or choose in advance (one of a number of contestants) as the winner **c :** to pick out with the eye **:** catch sight of **:** DETECT, NOTICE, RECOGNIZE, SEE ⟨~ a mistake⟩ ⟨*spotted* the fire and turned in an alarm⟩ ⟨among the first to ~ the danger⟩ ⟨how to ~ a subversive⟩ ⟨*spotted* a friend in the distance⟩ ⟨*spotted* him at once for an American⟩ ⟨*spotting* airplanes⟩ **d** (1) **:** to locate (a position) accurately (as on the ground or on a map) ⟨~ the fall of a shell⟩ ⟨gunners were unable to ~ their shots⟩ ⟨*spotted* the position of the battery⟩ ⟨in *spotting* these crime locations . . . use one map with different colored tacks —V.A.Leonard⟩ (2) **:** to observe (a shot) on a target with s spotting scope **5 a :** to form or appear as spots on **:** DOT, STUD ⟨here and there figures *spotted* the twilight —Scott Fitzgerald⟩ ⟨aviation landing-fields with which California is *spotted* —Aubrey Drury⟩ ⟨small boats *spotting* a harbor⟩ **b :** to place in various spots **:** locate at intervals ⟨~ field telephones and observers strategically —*Motor Trend*⟩ ⟨men who represent the firm are *spotted* throughout the country —Victor Boesen⟩ **6 :** to place on an appointed or desired spot **:** put in position ⟨~ a billiard ball⟩ ⟨cameras were *spotted* about twenty feet from the judges' bench —S.J.Perelman⟩ ⟨*spotted* high in the top gallery, the voices floated easily through the hall —Irving Kolodin⟩ ⟨table is small enough to be *spotted* in tight quarters —*Flow Quarterly*⟩: as **a :** to place (as a freight car, truck, trailer, crane) in a desired position for loading or unloading **b :** to prick out or transplant (as young vegetable or flowering plants) **c** (1) **:** to fix in the beam of a spotlight ⟨mass spectacles in which individual acts were *spotted* —Winifred Bambrick⟩ ⟨door is sometimes *spotted* in this manner, with a special mat shaping the light beam —Herbert Philippi⟩ (2) **:** to direct or

focus on like a spotlight ⟨his genial smile was *spotted* on everyone in turn —Osbert Sitwell⟩ **d :** to schedule (as a performer, an act, a program) in a particular position or at a particular time **:** assign a spot to ⟨*spotted* the main bout at ten o'clock⟩ ⟨is *spotted* on a daily pop show —*Down Beat*⟩ ⟨if you have a good program, ~ it opposite another fine show —Gilbert Seldes⟩ **7 :** to rid of a spot or other small defect: as **a :** to touch out (as with India ink, opaque, pencil) defects consisting of clear spots in (a photographic negative) **:** remove similar spots on (a print) with transparent pigment — often used with *out* **b :** to remove a spot or mark from (a fabric) **8 :** to allow as a handicap ⟨*spotted* his opponent five points and still won easily⟩ ⟨~ him two strokes a hole⟩ **:** concede as an advantage ⟨will ~ his rival ten years but nevertheless expected to be the favorite —*N.Y. Times*⟩ ⟨an old timer . . . could have *spotted* the big elephant all his blubber and laid him low in a round —J.T.Farrell⟩ **~** *vi* **1 :** to become stained or discolored in spots ⟨fungus caused the leaves to ~⟩ ⟨cloth that tends to ~ in the rain⟩ **2 :** to make a spot **:** cause staining ⟨always said gin didn't ~ —Victoria Lincoln⟩ **3 :** to act as a spotter esp. in locating enemy targets ⟨was *spotting* for mortar fire —Mack Morriss⟩; *specif* **:** to locate targets for land batteries or warships from the air ⟨planes had spent the morning *spotting*⟩

3spot \"\ *adj* [1*spot*] **1 :** being, originating, or done on the spot or on or in or for a particular spot ⟨favored ~ control rather than general restrictions⟩ ⟨~ regulation of traffic —E. G.Mogren & W.S.Smith⟩ ⟨treatment of ~ unemployment —*New Republic*⟩: as **a** (1) **:** on hand for immediate delivery after sale — used of commodities ⟨~ wheat⟩ ⟨~ cocoa⟩ or of services ⟨~ cargo offering⟩ (2) **:** making a specialty of transactions in spot commodities ⟨~ broker⟩ **b** (1) **:** paid or ready for payment at once upon delivery of property purchased ⟨~ cash⟩ (2) **:** involving immediate cash payment ⟨a ~ transaction⟩ (3) **:** engaged in or making a specialty of cash transactions ⟨the ~ market⟩ ⟨a ~ firm⟩ **c :** designed to replace precisely a defective spot ⟨~ insert in a page of standing type⟩ ⟨~ patch for an electrotype⟩ **d :** originating at the scene of a newsworthy event ⟨~ coverage of a foreign election⟩ **e** (1) **:** broadcast between two scheduled radio or television programs or between parts of a scheduled program (as during a station break) ⟨20-second ~ announcements throughout the day —*New Republic*⟩ ⟨well placed ~ commercial campaign —S.H.Britt⟩ (2) **:** originating in or sent out from a local radio or television station for a national advertiser ⟨~ broadcasts⟩ ⟨use of electrical transcriptions in ~ broadcasting⟩ ⟨~ broadcasting . . . represents more than a third of all investment in television time —H.W.McMahan⟩ **2 :** made at random or restricted to a few key or sample places or instances ⟨an adequate job of ~ research, using only the principal references —W.N.Fenton⟩ ⟨a ~ test⟩ ⟨cross-country ~ check on current business —*Banking*⟩ ⟨a small ~ survey of where they go and what they like to eat —Jane Nickerson⟩; *also* **:** selected at random or as a sample ⟨~ questions⟩ ⟨a dozen ~ cities west of the Mississippi⟩

4spot \"\ *adv* [1*spot*] **:** for cash

spot anthracnose *n* **:** any of several plant diseases characterized by light-colored spots with tissue overgrowth forming a raised border; *specif* **:** such a disease caused by fungi of the genus *Sphaceloma* or its perfect stage *Elsinoë*

spot ball *n* **:** the cue ball in billiards marked with a black spot

spot–barred \ˈ=,=\ *adj* **:** constituting or relating to a game (as English billiards) in which the red ball is placed upon the center spot after two spot strokes

spot blight *n* **:** GREASE SPOT

spot blotch *n* **:** a disease of barley characterized by dark-colored elongated spots on the leaves caused by a fungus (*Helminthosporium sativum*) — compare NET BLOTCH

spot board *n* **:** a sighting board laid across the rails in advance of a railroad track-raising gang to indicate the required amount of lift

spot bowling *n* **:** bowling in which a bowler aims at a calculated spot part way down the alley rather than directly at the pins — compare HEADPIN BOWLING

spot card *n* **1 :** a playing card of rank two to nine inclusive **2 :** a playing card except an ace or face card but including the ten

spot–check \ˈ=¦=\ *vt* **:** to cause to undergo a spot check **:** sample quickly or roughly **:** test or investigate in a random manner ⟨*spot-checks* income tax returns —J.H.Lavely⟩ ⟨*spot-checked* for accuracy⟩ **~** *vi* **:** to make a spot check ⟨*spot-check* on . . . program reactions for advertisers —*Advertising Age*⟩

spot drawing *n* **:** a small decorative drawing usu. in black and white

spot–drill \ˈ=¦=\ *vt* **:** to drill a shallow hole or one just deep enough to locate a spot (as for use as a guide in further drilling)

spot–face \ˈ=¦=\ *vt* **:** to machine or face a spot of surface as the seat for a bolt head or nut

spot·fac·er \" + ə(r)\ *n* [*spot-face* + *-er*] **:** a counterbore for use in spot-facing

spot film *n* **:** a roentgenogram of a restricted area in the body taken by means of a radiolucent pressure cone that is pressed upon the spot to be radiographed

spotfin croaker \ˈ=,=-\ *n* [so called fr. the large black spot on the pectoral fin] **:** a large croaker (*Roncador stearnsii*) of the California coast that is metallic steel-blue above and silvery below and is a popular sport fish

spot fire *n* **:** a fire started by flying sparks or embers at a distance from the main fire

spot–grind \ˈ=¦=\ *vt* **:** to grind a spot of a surface or any small area

spot lamp *n* **:** SPOTLIGHT

spot lens *n* **:** a condensing lens in which the light is confined to an annular pencil by a small round diaphragm and which is used in dark-field illumination

spot·less \ˈspätləs\ *adj* **:** having no spot; *esp* **:** free from impurity or reproach **:** IMMACULATE, UNSPOTTED ⟨~ white linen⟩ ⟨~ kitchens⟩ ⟨shining ~ silver⟩ **:** BLAMELESS, IRREPROACHABLE, PURE, UNBLEMISHED ⟨his ~ youth⟩ ⟨had kept herself ~⟩ ⟨~ hero⟩ ⟨~ reputation⟩ — **spot·less·ly** *adv* — **spot·less·ness** *n* -ES

1spotlight \ˈ=,=\ *n* [1*spot* + *light*] **1 a :** a projected spot or circle of light used to illuminate brilliantly a single person or object or group on a stage while leaving the rest of the stage more or less unilluminated **b :** conspicuous public notice or attention or a place, occasion, or set of circumstances receiving such notice or attention ⟨held the political ~⟩ ⟨hated the ~⟩ ⟨their momentary place in the ~ —J.D.Hart⟩ ⟨wants to get out of the ~ —*Reporter*⟩ ⟨~ shifted westward last week —W.A. Howe⟩ **2 a** (1) **:** a device resembling a small searchlight with an adjustable reflector and consisting typically of an incandescent or arc light in a housing designed to direct a narrow intense beam of light upon a chosen small area (as of a stage or a photographic subject) (2) **:** such a device mounted on an adjustable bracket (as at the side of the windshield of an automobile) so that it can be adjusted to light up objects ahead or to the side **b :** something that illuminates as brilliantly and clearly as a spotlight ⟨series of talks . . . throwing a ~ round the world, illuminating continent after continent —*London Calling*⟩ ⟨throwing a ~ into certain hitherto dark corners of union policy —*Ethyl News*⟩ ⟨succinct penetrating ~s on the characters —Fanny Butcher⟩

2spotlight \"\ *vt* **1 :** to illuminate with or as if with a spotlight **:** direct a spotlight upon ⟨dreading the moment when . . . she would be *spotlighted*, pinpointed, impaled, focused upon —A.R.Marcus⟩ ⟨have the whole ghastly process of disintegration *spotlit* —Gwyn Thomas⟩ ⟨a program which ~s student musicians —D.R.Meltzer⟩ ⟨discoveries which have recently *spotlighted* this subject —R.W.Murray⟩ **2 :** JACK 1

spotlight·er \" + ə(r)\ *n* **:** one that uses a spotlight; *esp* **:** JACKLIGHTER

spot lighting *n* [1*spot* + *lighting*] **:** illumination of a part or the whole of an object to a brightness much greater than that of its surroundings by a beam or several beams of light from a distance

spotlike \ˈ=,=\ *adj* **:** resembling a spot

spot line *n* **:** a single line specially rigged to fly a piece of theatrical scenery that cannot be handled by the regular lines

spot–mill \ˈ=¦=\ *vt* **:** to mill a spot of a surface or any small area

spot news *n* **:** up-to-date immediately reported news ⟨*spot-news* pictures from the war fronts —John Larkin⟩

spot pass *n* **:** a pass (as in football, basketball, ice hockey) made to a predetermined spot usu. well down the field or court rather than directly to a player

spot plate *n* **:** a porcelain or glass plate usu. with several small depressions for use in spot tests

spot price *n* **:** the price of spot goods — contrasted with *future price*

spot rot *n* **1 :** JONATHAN SPOT **2 :** a general decay of apples in cold storage caused by a fungus (*Botrytis cinerea*) and characterized by brown spots each centering at a lenticel

spotrump \ˈ=,=\ *n* [1*spot* + *rump;* fr. the white spot on its tail] **:** HUDSONIAN GODWIT

spots *pl of* SPOT, *pres 3d sing of* SPOT

spot sheet *n* **:** a makeready sheet that has been spotted up

spots·man \ˈspätsmən\ *n, pl* **spotsmen :** one that spots, watches, or points out; *esp* **:** SMUGGLER

spot snapper *n* [so called fr. the red blotch below the soft dorsal fin] **:** any of several snappers; *esp* **:** LANE SNAPPER

spot stroke *n* **:** the pocketing of the red ball in English billiards in a top corner pocket from off its own spot so as to leave the cue ball in position for another winning hazard — see SPOT-BARRED

spot·ta·ble \ˈspäd·əbəl, -ätəb-\ *adj* **:** capable of being spotted; *esp* **:** that easily becomes spotted or stained ⟨~ fabrics⟩

spottail \ˈ=,=\ *n* **:** CHANNEL BASS

spottail shiner *n* **:** a common shiner (*Notropis hudsonius*) of lakes and larger streams of the central and northeastern U.S. that is distinguished by a black blotch at the base of the caudal fin

spot·ted \ˈspäd·əd, -ätəd\ *adj* [ME, fr. 1*spot* + *-ed*] **1 :** marked with spots ⟨the ~ coat of a leopard⟩ ⟨no ~ pony is ever pure Shetland —Ben Riker⟩ ⟨checked, ~, colored and printed petticoats —*Fashions & Fabrics*⟩ **2 a :** marked with disfiguring spots ⟨320 pages; front cover ~⟩ ⟨a ~ youth who lounged against the lorry —I.A.N.Henderson⟩ **b :** SULLIED, TARNISHED ⟨inherited a ~ name⟩ **3 :** characterized or attended by the appearance of spots **4** [fr. past part. of 2*spot*] **:** noticed by others **:** MARKED; *esp* **:** being under watch or suspicion **:** SUSPECTED **5** [fr. past part. of 2*spot*] **:** having an irregular distribution **:** scattered in spots **:** SPOTTY

spotted adder *n* **1 :** MILK SNAKE **2 :** HOGNOSE SNAKE

spotted alder *n* **:** WITCH HAZEL 2a(1)

spotted arum *n* **:** CUCKOOPINT

spotted asparagus beetle *n* **:** a chrysomelid beetle (*Crioceris duodecimpunctata*) that feeds on asparagus in Europe and the northeastern U.S.

spotted bass *n* **1 :** CHANNEL BASS **2 :** SPOTTED BLACK BASS

spotted bat *n* **:** JACKASS BAT

spotted black bass *n* **:** a black bass (*Micropterus pseudoplites*) intermediate in several respects between the largemouth and smallmouth black basses and wide-ranging in the central U.S.

spotted blenny *n* **:** OCELLATED BLENNY

spotted blister beetle *n* **:** a black-spotted gray beetle (*Epicauta maculata*) of the family Meloidae that is destructive in the adult stage to potatoes and other crops

spotted bowerbird *n* **:** a semigregarious bowerbird (*Chlamydera maculata*) of inland scrublands of Australia that builds a very large bower decorated with bright objects (as bleached bone or bits of glass)

spotted bur clover *n* **:** SPOTTED MEDIC

1spotted cat *or* **spotted catfish** *n* **:** a widely distributed black-spotted catfish (*Ictalurus lacustris*) of the Mississippi drainage and the southeastern U.S. that commonly attains a weight of five pounds and is regarded as superior to most catfishes as food

2spotted cat *n* **:** a wildcat with a blotched or spotted coat; *also* **:** the pelt of such a wildcat

spotted cavy *n* **:** PACA

spotted clover *n* **:** any of several plants of the genus *Medicago* that resemble clover; *esp* **:** SPOTTED MEDIC

spotted cowbane *or* **spotted hemlock** *n* **:** a tall biennial water hemlock (*Cicuta maculata*) of northeastern No. America with purple-mottled stems and clusters of tuberous roots that resemble small sweet potatoes and are extremely poisonous

spotted crake *n* **:** a small European rail (*Porzana porzana*) similar to the American sora — called also *spotted rail*

spotted cranesbill *n* **:** a common wild geranium (*Geranium maculatum*) of eastern No. America with deeply parted leaves and rose-purple flowers

spotted cucumber beetle *n* **:** a rather slender greenish yellow beetle (*Diabrotica undecimpunctata howardi*) that feeds as an adult on the foliage and flowers of various ornamental and crop plants and is a vector of wilt disease of cucurbit plants (as cucumbers and melons) — see SOUTHERN CORN ROOTWORM

spotted cuscus *n* **:** an Australian phalanger (*Phalanger maculatus*)

spotted cutworm *n* **:** a cutworm that is the larva of a noctuid moth (*Amathes c-nigrum*) and that feeds on various crop plants

spotted dead nettle *n* **:** a perennial dead nettle (*Lamium maculatum*) having usu. a pale blotch bordering the leaf midrib

spotted deer *n* **:** AXIS 1

spotted dick *n, often cap S&D* **1** *Brit* **:** SPOTTED DOG 1 **2 :** DALMATIAN 2

spotted dog *n* [prob. alter. of *spotted dick*] **1** *Brit* **:** a suet pudding containing raisins or currants **2 a :** a light-colored dog with dark spots **b** *often cap S&D* **:** DALMATIAN 2

spotted dogfish *n* **:** any of various dogfishes with a blotched or spotted skin; *esp* **:** a common European dogfish (*Scylliorhinus canicula*) sometimes used for food

spotted eagle *n* **:** a small eagle (*Aquila clanga*) ranging from southern Europe to China

spotted eagle ray *n* **:** an eagle ray (*Aetobatus narinari* or *Stoasodon narinari*) widely distributed in warm seas and having the upper surface more or less thickly covered with white or yellow spots — called also *spotted ray*

spotted fever *n* **:** any of various eruptive fevers: as **a :** TYPHUS **b :** ROCKY MOUNTAIN SPOTTED FEVER

spotted fever tick *n* **:** a tick that transmits the rickettsia of Rocky Mountain spotted fever; *esp* **:** a common tick (*Dermacentor venustus*) of western No. America

spotted–finned sunfish \ˈ==,=-\ *n* **:** a spotted sunfish (*Enneacanthus gloriosus*)

spotted flycatcher *n* **:** a flycatcher (*Muscicapa striata*) of Europe

spotted gar *n* **:** a widely distributed gar (*Lepisosteus productus*) of the eastern half of the U.S.

spotted goby *n* **:** a small European goby (*Gobius minutus*) that is gray with numerous dark spots and lives on sandy shores

spotted ground squirrel *n* **:** a brightly patterned ground squirrel (*Citellus spilosoma*) of the western U.S.

spotted grunter *n* **:** a large grunter (*Pomadasys operculare*) widely distributed in coastal waters and tidal estuaries of the Indian ocean and highly esteemed as a food and sport fish in southern Africa

spotted gum *n* **:** either of two Australian eucalypts (*Eucalyptus maculata* and *E. goniocalyx*) with dotted pale leaves

spotted hound *n* **:** a grayish brown black-spotted smooth dogfish (*Mustelus punctulatus*) that is common in warm seas of the Old World

spotted hyena *n* **:** a hyena (*Hyena crocuta* or *Crocuta crocuta*) of Africa south of the Sahara with the coat blotched with black

spotted jewelweed *n* **:** a common American jewelweed (*Impatiens biflora*) with mottled petals

spotted jewfish *n* **:** a grouper (*Promicrops itaiara*) of the West Indies and the west coast of Mexico that is one of the largest of all fishes

spotted knotweed *n* **:** LADY'S THUMB

spotted liver *n* **:** coccidiosis of the liver of the rabbit

spotted loco *or* **spotted locoweed** *n* **:** a perennial locoweed (*Astragalus lentiginosus*) of western No. America that has racemose flowers and often purplish mottled sparsely pubescent pods and is poisonous to livestock

spotted locust *n* **:** LOCUST 3a(2)

spot·ted·ly *adv* **:** SPOTTILY

spotted lynx *n* **:** a southern European lynx (*Lynx pardina*) now chiefly limited to the Spanish Pyrenees that is of a rufous color obscurely spotted with black

spotted medic *n* **:** a spreading annual medic (*Medicago arabica*) having yellow flowers, spotted leaflets, and coiled furrowed pods

spotted moray *n* **:** 2HAMLET 2

spotted–necked otter \ˈ==,=-\ *n* **:** a rather small brown nocturnal southern African otter (*Lutra maculicollis*) with pale markings on the throat and inguinal region

spotted nemophila *n* **:** FIVE-SPOT

spot·ted·ness *n* -ES **:** the quality or state of being spotted

spotted newt *n* **:** SMOOTH NEWT

spotted oak *n* **1 :** a water oak (*Quercus nigra*) **2 :** a black oak (*Quercus velutina*) **3 :** TEXAS RED OAK

spotted orchis *also* **spotted orchid** *n* **1 :** a Eurasian orchid (*Orchis maculata*) with purplish or whitish flowers spotted with purplish brown and palmate tubers **2 :** a leafless orchid (*Dipodium punctatum*) of Tasmania with rose-colored flowers

spotted parsley *n* **1 :** POISON HEMLOCK 1 **2 :** SPOTTED COWBANE

spotted pelidnota *n* **:** a large brownish orange beetle (*Pelidnota punctata*) with black dots on the thorax and elytra that feeds as an adult on grape foliage and as a larva in decaying wood

spotted rail *or* **spotted skitty** *or* **spotted water hen** *n* **:** SPOTTED CRAKE

spotted ray *or* **spotted sting ray** *or* **spotted whip ray** *n* **:** SPOTTED EAGLE RAY

spotted redshank *n* **:** a redshank (*Tringa erythropus*) that is larger than the common redshank and has orange-red legs

spotted rockfish *n* **:** STARRY ROCKFISH

spotted salamander *n* **:** any of various tailed amphibians having dark skin with usu. yellow spots or blotches: **a :** a European salamander (*Salamandra maculosa*) that is black with large yellow or orange blotches — called also *fire salamander* **b :** a common No. American amphibian (*Ambystoma maculatum* syn. *A. punctatum*) with glossy black skin spotted with yellow on the back

spotted sandpiper *n* **:** a common sandpiper (*Actitis macularia*) that breeds throughout No. America and frequents both fresh and salt water, that in summer has the underparts of the adult heavily spotted with black, and that has a plaintive whistling note and when walking or standing bobs its head and tail continually

spotted schaapsteker *n* **:** SCHAAPSTEKER a

spotted skate *n* **:** WINTER SKATE

spotted skunk *n* **:** LITTLE SPOTTED SKUNK

spotted spurge *n* **:** a common milky-juiced weed (*Euphorbia maculata*) of eastern No. America having spotted leaves

spotted sucker *n* **1 :** a sucker (*Minytrema melanops*) chiefly of small rivers of the central and southeastern U.S. that is marked by rows of small black dots occurring one on each scale **2 :** HOG SUCKER

spotted sunfish *n* **1 :** either of two small sunfishes (*Enneacanthus obesus* and *E. gloriosus*) of coastal streams of the eastern U.S. **2 :** STUMPKNOCKER

spotted tree *n* **:** LEOPARD TREE

spotted turtle *also* **spotted terrapin** *or* **spotted tortoise** *n* **:** a small American freshwater tortoise (*Clemmys guttata*) having a blackish carapace on which are scattered round yellow spots

spotted water hemlock *n* **:** SPOTTED COWBANE

spotted weakfish *or* **spotted sea trout** *or* **spotted squeateague** *n* **:** a weakfish (*Cynoscion nebulosus*) of the south Atlantic and Gulf coasts of the U.S.

spotted wilt *n* **:** TOMATO STREAK

spotted wintergreen *n* **:** a No. American evergreen herb (*Chimaphila maculata*) having white-mottled leaves and corymbose or umbellate white or pinkish flowers

spotted woodpecker *n* **:** any of several European and Asiatic woodpeckers having the plumage of variegated black and white: as **a :** GREAT SPOTTED WOODPECKER **b :** a bird (*Dendrocopos minor*) resembling but smaller than the great spotted woodpecker — called also *lesser spotted woodpecker*

spot·ter \ˈspäd·ə(r), -ätə-\ *n* -S **1 :** one that makes a spot; *esp* **:** one that makes or applies a distinctive spot (as for identification or guidance or to mark a defect): as **a :** a device for producing by abrasion frosted or mottled spots on a flat finished metal surface (as for decorative effect or on the ways of machine tools for better holding of lubricants) **b :** DOTTER 2 **c :** one that by means of a microscope locates the correct place for drilling a diamond to be used as a die and drills a tiny starting hole **d :** a device on a railroad car for marking irregularities in the track **e :** a logger who notches trees **f :** a small disk of black metal having a spindle through the center by which it is attached to the target in target practice to indicate the exact position of a hit — called also *spotting disk* **2 :** one that looks out for, keeps watch on, or singles out something ⟨a moralizer and a ~ of universal calamities —R.H. Rovere⟩ ⟨traveled all over the state . . . as a ~ on the trail of oil —Myron Brinig⟩: as **a** (1) **:** DETECTIVE, SPY; *esp* **:** a person privately employed (as by a railroad, a business establishment) to detect dishonesty and irregularities of a particular kind ⟨worked as a ~ for a bus company⟩ ⟨~s follow every move of player and dealer —Oscar Lewis⟩ (2) **:** one that checks attendance of workers by locating them on their jobs at various times of the day according to a daily record sheet (3) **:** INVESTIGATOR c **b** (1) **:** one that locates the position of an enemy target and that reports deviations of gunfire from the target; *specif* **:** a naval officer whose duty in battle is to observe the fall of shot and to estimate the corrections necessary to bring the shots on the target (2) **:** an airplane employed in spotting enemy positions or targets; *also* **:** an airman engaged in such spotting (3) **:** a civilian watcher whose duty is to report all approaching airplanes (as by type, direction, speed) **c** (1) **:** a member of a gang of thieves who locates buildings to be robbed (2) **:** one of a gang of hijackers who follows a stolen truck and signals the approach of police **d** (1) **:** an auctioneer's assistant who watches the buyers for bids (2) **:** one that sits with a sportscaster at an athletic event (as a football game) to help identify players **3 :** one that removes spots: as **a :** one that covers imperfections in a photograph by touching them up with a brush or pencil **b** (1) **:** a dry cleaner who removes stains from fabrics by local treatment (2) **:** a solvent used in removing such stains **4 :** one that places something on or in an appointed or desired spot ⟨automatic bowling-pin ~s —*Newsweek*⟩: as **a :** one that determines and designates where a load (as from a truck or crane) is to be deposited or a vehicle (as a railroad car, truck, trailer) is to be placed (as for loading, unloading, parking) **b :** CAR PINCHER **c :** CRANE FOLLOWER **d :** a device for moving a freight car into position for loading or unloading **5 :** one that places himself in position to give support or assistance to a tumbler or gymnast if needed to prevent injury

spot test *n* **1 a :** a test conducted on the spot to yield immediate results **b :** a test limited to a few key or sample points or a relatively small percentage of random spots **2 :** a chemical test carried out with one to several drops of solution of the sample and the reagent in which spots (as on filter paper or a spot plate) indicate results usu. by a change in color of the solution or formation of a precipitate

spot·ti·ly \ˈspäd·ᵊl¦ē, -ät¦, ¦əl¦, ¦i\ *adv* **:** in a spotty manner **:** so as to be spotty **:** without uniformity ⟨tackled on a major scale, and not just ~ —John Brooks⟩ ⟨account . . . is only ~ absorbing —Hollis Alpert⟩ ⟨rationality as well as unselfishness have existed ~ in the world —Priscilla Robertson⟩

spot·ti·ness \-äd·¦ēnəs, -ät¦, ¦in-\ *n* -ES **:** the quality or state of being spotty ⟨economical, clean heat without ~ or drafts —*Better Homes & Gardens*⟩ ⟨the ~ of American labor history is due largely to . . . the business cycles —Roger Burlingame⟩

spotting *pres 3d sing of* SPOT

spotting disk *n* [*spotting* (gerund of 2*spot*) + *disk*] **:** SPOTTER 1f

spotting scope *n* **:** a telescope for locating the strike of a bullet on a target

spot·tle \ˈspäd·ᵊl\ *vt* -ED/-ING/-S [2*spot* + *-le*] **:** SPOT, DOT

spot·ty \ˈspäd·¦ē, -ät¦, ¦i\ *adj* -ER/-EST [ME, fr. 1*spot* + *-y*] **1 a :** having many spots **:** marked with spots **:** SPOTTED **b** *obs* **:** DEFILED **2 :** occurring in spots **:** lacking uniformity (as in development, effect, quality) **:** IRREGULAR, PATCHY, UNEVEN ⟨~ attendance⟩ ⟨illumination was ~⟩ ⟨~ progress⟩ ⟨book is ~ . . . the whole work is not well integrated —A.L.Guérard⟩ ⟨a weak, ~ piece of music —Alfred Frankenstein⟩ ⟨program . . . was a rather ~ affair —Winthrop Sargeant⟩ ⟨a ~ public-school education, ending in his eleventh year —John Kobler⟩ ⟨medical care is ~ throughout the country —*Fortune*⟩ ⟨a poor musical director presiding over a ~ outfit —H.W.Wind⟩:

a *of a crop* **:** not evenly developed throughout the field **b :** active only in separated places or among a few isolated factors ⟨~ business⟩ ⟨a ~ market⟩ ⟨~ unemployment⟩

spot up *vt* **:** to paste patches of thin paper on (a makeready sheet) so as to give more impression to certain printing areas in a form

¹spot–weld \ˈ=,=\ *n* **:** a joint made by spot welding

²spot–weld *vt* **:** to weld two pieces at isolated spots rather than in a continuous seam

spot welding *n* **:** resistance welding in which the current and pressure are restricted to portions of the metal surfaces in contact

spot white *n* **:** SPOT BALL

spot zone *n* **:** SUNSPOT ZONE

spot zoning *n* **:** the illegal singling out of a small parcel of land within the limits of an area zoned for particular uses and permitting other uses for that parcel for the special benefit of its owners and to the detriment of the other owners in the area and not as a part of a scheme to benefit the entire area

¹spous·al \ˈspau̇zəl, -au̇zəl\ *n* -s [ME *sposail, spousaille,* fr. MF *espousailles* espousal — more at ESPOUSAL] **1** *obs* **:** the married state **:** WEDLOCK **2 a :** the action of espousing esp. in marriage **b :** NUPTIALS — usu. used in pl.

²spousal \"\ *adj* **:** of, relating to, or celebrating marriage **:** CONJUGAL, MATRIMONIAL, NUPTIAL ⟨~ rites⟩ ⟨a fitting symbol of ~ love —W.H.Gardner⟩ ⟨thy ~ bower —Louise Guiney⟩ — **spous·al·ly** \-əlē\ *adv*

¹spouse \ˈspau̇s *also* -au̇z\ *n* -s [ME *spuse, spouse,* fr. OF *spus, spous, espus* (masc.), *spuse, espouse* (fem.), fr. L *sponsus* (masc.) betrothed man, groom, *sponsa* (fem.) betrothed woman, bride, fr. *sponsus,* past part. of *spondēre* to promise solemnly, betroth; akin to Gk *spendein* to make a libation, promise, *spendesthai* to make a treaty, *spondē* libation, pl. treaty, Skt *spanti* he makes a libation] **1 :** a man or woman joined in wedlock **:** married person **:** HUSBAND, WIFE ⟨I that lady to my ~ had won —Edmund Spenser⟩ ⟨the accompanying ~ and children . . . travel at greatly reduced rates —P.J.C.Friedlander⟩ ⟨a responsible relative such as ~, father, mother, or child —*U.S.Code*⟩ ⟨free and full consent of the intending ~*s* —*U.N.Declaration of Human Rights*⟩ **2** *obs* **a :** BRIDE, BRIDEGROOM **b :** either one of a betrothed couple **:** FIANCÉ, FIANCÉE **3 a :** the church united in sacred bonds to God or to Christ **b :** a woman who by vow becomes an affianced of Christ **c :** God or Christ united in sacred bonds to the church

²spouse \ˈspau̇z, ˈspau̇s\ *vt* [ME *spousen,* fr. ¹*spouse*] **1** *obs* **:** to unite in marriage **:** give in marriage **2** *archaic* **:** ESPOUSE, WED **3** *obs* **:** AFFIANCE, BETROTH

spouse·hood \ˈspau̇s,hu̇d *also* -au̇z,-\ *n* [ME *spushod,* fr. *spuse* spouse + *-hod* -hood] *archaic* **:** the married state **:** MARRIAGE, WEDLOCK

spouse·less \ˈ=ləs\ *adj* [ME, fr. ¹*spouse* + *-less*] **:** having no spouse

¹spout \ˈspau̇t, *usu* -au̇d·+V\ *vb* -ED/-ING/-S [ME *spouten;* akin to MD *spoiten* to spout, MHG *spiuzen* to spit, ON *spȳta* to spit, *spȳja* to spew — more at SPEW] *vt* **1 :** to throw out (as liquid, vapor, granulated material, tiny objects) in a stream **:** eject in a jet ⟨gleaming metal faucet that ~*ed* clear water —Julian Dana⟩ ⟨farmhouse windows ~*ed* flame and smoke —F.V.W.Mason⟩ ⟨wells ~*ed* 200 barrels an hour —*Amer. Guide Series: Pa.*⟩ ⟨chewing snuff or ~*ing* the brown residue into a tin pail —Earle Birney⟩ — often used with *out* ⟨machines of steel which ~ out pins by the hundred million —G.B.Shaw⟩ ⟨causing the clams . . . to ~ out tiny streams of water —*Amer. Guide Series: Maine*⟩ **2 :** to speak or utter readily, volubly, and at length ⟨fairly ~*ed* technicalities —C.S.Forester⟩ ⟨~*ed* French like a Frenchman⟩ ⟨every cabdriver in town can ~ facts and gossip —John Durant⟩; *often* **:** to speak or utter in a pompous, oratorical, or grandiloquent manner **:** DECLAIM ⟨custom of these judges to ~ extravagant . . . harangues from the bench —C.G.Bowers⟩ ⟨~*ing* Latin invective —F.L. Windolph⟩ ⟨always goes around ~*ing* Shakespeare⟩ ⟨~*s* tag ends of wisdom —Leslie Rees⟩ **3** [²*spout*] *archaic* **:** PAWN **4** [²*spout*] **:** to fit or furnish with a spout ⟨had the roof repaired and the eaves ~*ed*⟩ ⟨teapot poured badly, had not been properly ~*ed*⟩ ~ *vi* **1 :** to issue with force in a strong stream or jet (as of liquid or other material discharged violently through a narrow opening) **:** SPURT ⟨oil was ~*ing* from Western lands —Van Wyck Brooks⟩ ⟨foamy bloody mucus ~*ed* from her mouth and nose —Grace Reiten⟩ ⟨illuminated by flaming jets which seemed to ~ from the trees —John Reed⟩ ⟨pure like a bubbling spring, a fountain ~*ing* out —F.N.Souza⟩ **2 :** to eject liquid or other material in a jet ⟨geyser was ~*ing* freely⟩ ⟨waves were ~*ing* high on the granite cliffs —C.L.Barrett⟩ ⟨he'd shy each time a clam ~*ed* —G.W.Brace⟩; *specif* **:** BLOW 5b **3 :** to talk or speak volubly or at length esp. in a pompous or grandiloquent manner **:** DECLAIM ⟨gave radio concerts, and politicians ~*ed* into the strange instruments —F.L.Allen⟩ ⟨~ about science and rationalism —Harold Strauss⟩

²spout \"\ *n* -s [ME *spoute;* akin to MD *spoite* spout, ME *spouten* to spout] **1 :** a tube, pipe, or conductor through which a liquid is discharged or by which it is conveyed in a stream from one place to another: as **a** (1) **:** a pipe (as in a gargoyle) for carrying off water from the roof of a building (2) **:** DOWNSPOUT (3) **:** GUTTER 2a — usu. used in pl. **b :** the part of a fountain or pump from which water issues **c** (1) **:** a projecting tube or lip for guiding the flow of a liquid poured from a receptacle ⟨broke the ~ off the teapot⟩ ⟨soldered a new ~ on the watering can⟩ (2) **:** a hollow metal device inserted in a hole bored in a maple tree to conduct the sap into a detachable pail **d :** BLOWHOLE 2 **e :** NOZZLE **2 a :** a discharge or jet of water or other fluid matter from or as if from a pipe esp. when ejected with some violence or when rising in a column ⟨surging uprush of invisible ~*s* of warm air —William Beebe⟩: as (1) **:** WATERSPOUT; *also* **:** a downpour of rain (2) **:** a spring of water (3) **:** the blowing of a whale **b :** something appearing as if spouted out ⟨a solitary dark ~ of smoke —Eric Linklater⟩ ⟨violent ~*s* and gusts of burning oil —Nevil Shute⟩ ⟨a rising ~ of debate on guns versus butter —*Fortune*⟩ ⟨a ~ of blasphemies —G.K.Chesterton⟩ **3** *also* **spout fish :** RAZOR CLAM **4 a :** a usu. enclosed trough or chute for conducting bulk materials (as flour, grain) to or from a receptacle **b :** a trough for conducting molten metal from a furnace to a ladle **c** (1) **:** a shoot or lift formerly used in a pawnbroker's shop for transferring pawned articles (2) *archaic* **:** PAWNSHOP **5 :** something resembling or suggestive of a spout on a roof or the spout of a vessel (as in discharging a liquid or in being in the shape of a pipe or a lip) ⟨eyes became two ~*s* —Shak.⟩ ⟨nest high up in the hollow ~ of the big fire-blackened gum —*Sydney (Australia) Bull.*⟩ **6 :** a rush of water to a lower level **:** CASCADE, WATERFALL — **up the spout** *adv* **1** *archaic* **:** in pawn **2 :** in a hopeless condition **:** in a bad way **:** beyond remedy

spout·ed \-au̇d·əd, -au̇təd\ *adj* [²*spout* + *-ed*] **1 :** having a spout ⟨~ ceremonial vessels⟩ **2 :** hollowed out in the form of a spout ⟨~ limb of a tree⟩

spout·er \-au̇d·ə(r), -au̇tə-\ *n* -s [¹*spout* + *-er*] **1 :** one that spouts: as **a :** an oil or gas well the flow of which has not been controlled by the engineers **b :** an oratorical or voluble speaker **:** SPEECHIFIER ⟨a ~ who thought he was an orator —W.A.White⟩ **c :** a whale that spouts **2 a :** a whaling vessel **b :** the master of a whaler **3** [²*spout* + *-er*] **:** a worker who controls the flow of grain through the machines and spouts of the milling process

spout hole *n* **1 :** a blowhole of a cetacean **2 :** a nostril of a walrus or seal

spout·ing \-au̇d·iŋ, -au̇t\, |ēŋ\ *n* -s [²*spout* + *-ing*] **1 :** the system of spouts used to convey rainwater from the roof of a building to the ground **2 :** material from which pieces for making spouts may be cut

spouting horn *n* [*spouting* (pres. part. of ¹*spout*) + *horn*] **:** a sea cave with an opening rearward or upward through which water spurts as waves enter the cave

spout·less \ˈspau̇tləs\ *adj* **:** having no spout

spoutlike \ˈ=,=\ *adj* **:** resembling a spout

spout·man \ˈ=mən\ *n, pl* **spoutmen 1 :** one who keeps a load (as of grain) level by moving the spout through which the load is being delivered **2 :** one who sets up the chutes and spouts through which concrete is transferred into molding forms

spouty \ˈspau̇d·ē\ *adj* -ER/-EST [¹*spout* + *-y*] **:** so wet as to spout water when walked on ⟨~ marshland⟩

spp *abbr* species

SPQR *abbr* **1** [L *senatus populusque Romanus*] the senate and the people of Rome **2** small profits, quick returns

spr *abbr* **1** sapper **2** sprinkled; sprinkler

sprach·ge·fühl \ˈshpräkgə,fu̅el\ *n* -s [G, fr. *sprache* language + *gefühl* feeling] **1 :** sensibility to conformance with or divergence from the established usage (as in form or idiom) of a language ⟨the dependable ~ of a skilled linguist⟩ **2 :** a feeling for what is linguistically effective or appropriate ⟨the ~ of the accomplished translator⟩

sprack \ˈsprak\ *adj* [prob. of Scand origin; akin to ON *sprækr* lively; akin to OE *spearca* spark — more at SPARK] *dial Brit* **:** ALERT, ACTIVE, LIVELY, NIMBLE

sprad·dle \ˈsprad°l\ *vb* **spraddled; spraddled; spraddling** \-d(°)liŋ\ **spraddles** [prob. of Scand origin; akin to Norw dial. *spradla* to thrash about, ON *sprathka* to kick, thrash about; akin to OHG *spratalōn* to thrash about, *sprinzan* to jump up — more at SPRINT] *vt* **1 :** to spread (the legs) in walking **:** STRADDLE **2 :** SPRAWL ~ *vi* **1 :** to go or walk with a straddling gait **:** STRADDLE **2 :** SPRAWL

spraddle leg *n* **:** perosis of young poultry

spraddle–legged \ *usu* ˈ=;=legəd, *Brit usu* -gd\ *adv (or adj)* **:** with the legs wide apart **:** STRADDLE-LEGGED

¹sprag \ˈsprag, -aa(ə)g, -aig\ *adj* [by alter.] *archaic* **:** SPRACK

²sprag \"\ *n* -s [perh. of Scand origin; akin to Sw dial. *spragg, spragge* branch — more at SPRIG] **1 :** a piece of timber or metal serving as a prop or brake: as **a :** a post for propping the ore or roof in a mine **b** (1) **:** a rod or shaft applied between the spokes of a wheel of a vehicle to prevent rotation (2) **:** a pointed stake or steel bar let down from a wagon or early automobile body at an angle to the ground to prevent the halted vehicle from rolling downhill

³sprag \"\ *vt* **spragged; spragged; spragging; sprags 1 :** to prop or sustain (as a mine roof) with a sprag **2 :** to check the motion of (a vehicle) by means of a sprag

⁴sprag \"\ *n* -s [origin unknown] **:** a young codfish

sprag·ger \-gə(r)\ *n* -s [²*sprag* + *-er*] **1 :** a worker who props coal beds with sprags for protection during mining or blasting **2 :** a worker who checks wheels (as of mine cars on inclines) with sprags

sprag road *n* [²*sprag*] **:** a gangway so steep that the wheels of ore cars have to be spragged when going down

sprague's grass \ˈsprāgz-\ *n, usu cap S* [after Isaac *Sprague* †1895 Am. illustrator of botanical works] **:** COUCH GRASS

sprague's pipit *n, usu cap S* [after Isaac *Sprague*] **:** a pipit (*Anthus spraguei*) found chiefly on the Great Plains — called also *Missouri skylark, sky pipit*

¹sprain \ˈsprān\ *n* -s [origin unknown] **1 :** a sudden or violent twist or wrench of a joint causing the stretching or tearing of ligaments and often rupture of blood vessels with hemorrhage into the tissues **2 :** the condition resulting from a sprain that is usu. marked by swelling, inflammation, hemorrhage, and discoloration — compare STRAIN **3** *also* **spraing** \-āŋ\ **:** internal brown spot of potatoes

²sprain \"\ *vt* -ED/-ING/-S **:** to weaken (a joint or ligament) by sudden and violent twisting or wrenching **:** stretch (ligaments) injuriously without dislocation of the joint — compare STRAIN

³sprain \"\ *vt* -ED/-ING/-S [back-formation fr. *spreined, sprent,* past part. of obs. *sprenge* to sprinkle — more at SPRENT] *archaic* **:** to sprinkle (seed) in sowing

sprain fracture *n* **:** the rupture of a tendon or ligament from its point of insertion at a joint with detachment of a splinter of bone

¹spraing \ˈspraŋ\ *n* -s [of Scand origin; akin to ON *sprang* lace, Norw *sprang,* a kind of embroidery; prob. akin to Norw *sprang* jump, OE *springan* to jump, spring — more at SPRING] *Scot* **:** a bright streak or stripe

²spraing \"\ *vt* -ED/-ING/-S *Scot* **:** to furnish or adorn with bright streaks or stripes

spraints \ˈsprānts\ *n pl* [ME *spraynetes,* fr. MF *espraintes,* pl. of *espreinte* piece of otter's dung, fr. fem. of *espraint,* past part. of *espraindre, espreindre* to express, squeeze out — more at EXPRESS] **:** otter's dung

sprang [ME, fr. OE] *past of* SPRING

spran·gle \ˈspraŋgəl, -aiŋ-\ *vb* **sprangled; sprangled; sprangling** \-g(ə)liŋ\ **sprangles** [ME *spranglen*] *vi* **:** to spread out in different directions **:** branch out **:** RAMIFY, STRAGGLE ⟨streams ~ over the countryside⟩ ~ *vt* **1 :** to cause to sprangle **:** DIFFUSE **2 :** to rough up the feathers of (an arrow) as by injury or carelessness

sprangletop \ˈ=,=,=\ *n* **1 :** a tall perennial rhizomatous grass (*Scolochloa festucacea*) that is widely distributed in wet lands and shallow water of northerly parts of the northern hemisphere and is a minor forage grass **2 :** a grass of the genus *Leptochloa; esp* **:** an erect wiry perennial grass (*L. dubia*) of the southern U.S. and southward to Argentina that is locally important for forage and hay

spran·gly \-g(ə)lē\ *adj, often* -ER/-EST [*sprangle* + *-y*] **:** SPREADING, SPRAWLING

¹sprat \ˈsprat, *usu* -ad·+V\ *or* **spret** \ˈspret, *usu* -ed·+V\ *n* -s [alter. of (assumed) ME *sprot,* fr. OE *sprott;* prob. akin to OE *sprūtan* to sprout — more at SPROUT] *dial Brit* **:** any of various rushes of the genus *Juncus*

²sprat \"\ *n* -s [alter. of earlier *sprot,* fr. ME, fr. OE *sprott;* prob. akin to OE *sprūtan* to sprout] **1 a :** a small European herring (*Clupea sprattus*) closely related to the common herring and the pilchard **b :** any of various other small or young herrings **2 :** any of numerous small fishes (as anchovy or bleak) not clearly distinguished in popular usage from members of the herring family (*Clupeidae*) **3 :** a small or insignificant person ⟨whip these young ~*s* —Jay Dugan⟩ ⟨a surly . . . ~ of a man —T.B.Costain⟩

³sprat \"\ *vi* **spratted; spratted; spratting; sprats :** to fish for sprats

sprat loon *n* [²*sprat*] **:** RED-THROATED LOON

sprat·ter \-ad·ə(r), -atə-\ *n* -s **:** one that fishes for sprats

sprau·chle \ˈspräk̲əl\ *vi* [prob. of Scand origin; akin to ON *sprökla* to thrash about, *sparka* to kick; akin to OE *spearca* spark — more at SPARK] *dial Brit* **:** CLAMBER, SCRAMBLE, SPRAWL

¹sprawl \ˈsprȯl\ *vb* -ED/-ING/-S [ME *sprewlen, sprawlen,* fr. OE *sprēawlian;* prob. akin to OE *sprūtan* to sprout — more at SPROUT] *vi* **1 a** *archaic* **:** to lie (as on the ground) thrashing or tossing about **:** struggle convulsively **b :** to creep or clamber with awkward movements of the arms and legs **:** SCRAMBLE ⟨the car slowly fell on its side and two figures ~*ed* out —Irwin Shaw⟩ **2 :** to lie or sit with arms and legs stretched out carelessly or awkwardly **:** spread out ⟨could ~ on her back in the little patch of grass —Elizabeth Janeway⟩ ⟨a child . . . ~*s* across her knees —Laurence Binyon⟩ ⟨the headmaster . . . was ~*ed* out in an easy chair —Grace Metalious⟩ **3 :** to spread or develop irregularly or ungracefully **:** STRAGGLE ⟨bushes are . . . allowed to ~ as they will —Fletcher Steele⟩ ⟨the city ~*s* without apparent logic or plan to the west, north, and south —*Amer. Guide Series: R. I.*⟩ ⟨this novel undeniably ~*s* —Sean O'Faolain⟩ ~ *vt* **1 :** to stretch out (the arms or legs) carelessly or awkwardly ⟨took a chair, ~*ed* out his legs —Erle Stanley Gardner⟩ **2 :** to cause to spread or develop irregularly or stragglingly **:** cause to move erratically **:** SCRAWL ⟨~*s* its . . . winding river across the state line —*Amer. Guide Series: Texas*⟩ ⟨languidly ~*ed* his signature over the document at her urging⟩

²sprawl \"\ *n* -s **1 :** the act, posture, or condition of sprawling ⟨sent him down in a long ~ —Vincent McHugh⟩ ⟨toppled backward to a ~ on the pavement —Scott Fitzgerald⟩ **2 :** an irregularly spread or scattered group or mass **:** a straggling array ⟨a bare and shadeless ~ of adobe barracks —Harvey Fergusson⟩ ⟨the increasing ~ of the curriculum —E.L.Vance⟩ ⟨the rich ~ of her hair —William Faulkner⟩ **3** *dial* **:** resolute spirit **:** SPUNK, GUMPTION ⟨chaps as hadn't the ~ to go a-soldiering —Flora Thompson⟩

sprawl·er \-lə(r)\ *n* -s **1 :** any of various European noctuid moths (esp. *Brachionycha sphinx*) or their larvae **2 :** HELLGRAMMITE

sprawling *adj* **1 :** characterized by clumsy spreading or stretching (as of the arms or legs) **:** UNGAINLY ⟨this ~ gait is characteristic of the crocodiles —W.E.Swinton⟩ **2 :** spreading or developing irregularly or erratically **:** STRAGGLING ⟨a treeless, ~ town with sandy streets —*Amer. Guide Series: Texas*⟩ ⟨a ~ book, discursive and prolix —Brendan Gill⟩ **3 :** carelessly irregular **:** SCRAWLY ⟨a letter written in a ~ hand⟩

sprawl·ing·ly *adv* **:** in a sprawling manner

sprawly \ˈsprȯlē, -li\ *adj* -ER/-EST **1 :** stretching or spreading out in an ungainly or irregular way **:** STRAGGLY, DIFFUSE ⟨an otter cub . . . a tiny, ~, furry handful —F.G.Turnbull⟩ ⟨a big, ~ city —G.S.Kaufman⟩ **2 :** laid on or drawn in an apparently careless fashion **:** SPLASHY ⟨an allover, ~ design of white rickrack —Lois Long⟩

¹spray \ˈsprā\ *n* -s [ME — more at SPRIG] **1 a :** a cluster or mass of small twiggy branches **:** small brushwood ⟨birch ~⟩ **b sprays** *pl, dial Eng* **:** twisted willow or hazel for thatching **2 a :** a usu. slim branch or shoot **:** SPRIG ⟨a ~ of apple blossoms⟩ **b :** a bunch or cluster of cut flowers arranged for decorative effect (as on a dress, dinner table, or coffin) ⟨shoulder ~⟩ **c :** something (as a decorative design, ornament, or brooch) resembling a spray ⟨a ~ of brilliants⟩ ⟨rhinestone-set shoulder ~ —*Fashion Digest*⟩ **3 :** a very light bluish green that is duller and slightly greener than average ice green **4 a :** an auxiliary gate, runner, or side channel in a founder's mold **b :** a group of castings made together and connected by sprues and not yet separated and trimmed

²spray \"\ *vi* -ED/-ING/-S **:** to spread out in the form of a spray **:** branch out ⟨orchids . . . ~*ed* from the bowl —Kathryn Grondahl⟩ ⟨branches of climbing vines ~*ed* up its sides —Frederick Faust⟩

³spray \"\ *n* -s [fr. obs. E *spray* to sprinkle, fr. MD *sprayen, spraeyen;* akin to MHG *spræjen, sprǣwen* to squirt, spray, Sw dial. *språ, språs* to sprout, Gk *speirein* to scatter, sow, sprinkle — more at SPROUT] **1 :** water flying in small drops or particles as blown from waves or thrown up by a waterfall ⟨~ cast up when the heavy rain pounded the flat porch rail —John Updike⟩ **2 a** (1) **:** a jet of fine medicated vapor used either as an application to a diseased part or to charge the air of a room with a disinfectant or deodorizer (2) **:** an instrument for applying such a spray **:** ATOMIZER — compare AEROSOL **b :** a jet of liquid (as water) dispersed by a sprayer **3 a** (1) **:** an application in suspension or solution of a pesticide (2) **:** the material so applied **b :** FOG 3a **c :** a device for applying a vaporized coating (as of paint)

⁴spray \"\ *vb* -ED/-ING/-S *vt* **1 :** to scatter or let fall (as a solution) in the form of spray ⟨~ a 1 percent solution from an atomizer onto the incision⟩ ⟨antibiotics and body powders that can be ~*ed* instead of dusted on —*Time*⟩ **2 a :** to throw spray upon ⟨the waves ~*ed* us with salt water⟩; *esp* **:** to cover entirely or partially with a liquid, a foam, or sometimes a dust by means of a sprayer or aerosol bomb (as for destroying bacteria or plant pests) **b :** to throw a liquid upon in the form of a spray ⟨stove exploded, ~*ing* them with flaming kerosine —*Pasadena (Calif.) Independent*⟩ **c :** to apply something to by atomizing and allowing to strike the surface in a uniform manner ⟨~*ed* the furniture with paint⟩ **d :** to fire upon scatteringly **:** strew with bullets ⟨opened fire ~*ing* them with buckshot —Meridel LeSueur⟩ ~ *vi* **1 :** to take the form of spray **:** scatter in fine particles ⟨the device causes the water to ~⟩ **2 :** to discharge a liquid as spray

⁵spray *var of* SPREE

spray boom *n* **:** a pipe with attached nozzles for distributing spray from a tank

spray calendar *or* **spray schedule** *n* **:** a table or chart indicating at what time or stage of development of a plant various pesticidal sprays should be applied

spray crab *n* **:** a small spiny grapsoid crab (*Percnow givvesi*) living on spray-washed rocks

spray drain *n* **:** a drain made by laying tree branches under earth **:** a covered brush drain

spray–dry \ˈ=;=\ *vt* **:** to dry (as milk, eggs, or soap) by bringing in the form of a spray into contact with hot air or other gases and often recovering in the form of a powder

spray·er \ˈsprāə(r)\ *n* -s **1 :** one that sprays: as **a :** one that sprays trees or crops with insecticides **b :** one that sprays surfaces with a coating substance (as paint, enamel, or waterproofing) **c :** one that sprays a finish on cloth **2 :** a device or machine for spraying: as **a :** a vehicle or an attachment to a vehicle for spraying liquids (as insecticides or fungicides) on plants and trees — compare TRACTION SPRAYER **b :** a device or instrument for spraying liquid drugs — compare ATOMIZER **c :** a device for spraying paint on a surface **:** ³SPRAY 3c, SPRAY GUN **d :** an apparatus for spraying liquids on a foundry mold or core

¹spray·ey \-āē\ *adj* [³*spray* + *-y*] **:** resembling water spray **:** carrying or throwing spray ⟨a ~ wind from the sea⟩

²sprayey \"\ *adj* [¹*spray* + *-y*] **:** consisting of, resembling, or branching out like the sprays of a tree or plant **:** TWIGGY

spray form *n* **:** the form of a tree or shrub as influenced by ocean spray

spray green *n* **:** a pale green that is bluer, lighter, and stronger than celadon gray, yellower, lighter, and stronger than bayberry gray, and bluer and lighter than aloes green

spray gun *n* **1 :** an apparatus resembling a gun for applying substances (as paints or insecticides) in the form of a spray **2 :** GUN 5b

spray nozzle *also* **spray head** *n* **:** an attachment to the end of a spray rod or hose that causes the liquid to be delivered finely and evenly as a spray

spray pond *also* **spray pool** *n* **:** a reservoir in which warmed water is cooled for reuse by evaporation of water discharged from nozzles in spray or mist form over the pond

sprays *pl of* SPRAY, *pres 3d sing of* SPRAY

spray strip *n* **:** a strip that projects from the forepart of a seaplane hull and deflects the spray thrown up when the hull is moving through the water

spray therapy *n* **:** roentgen irradiation of the entire body for therapeutic purposes

¹spread \ˈspred\ *vb* **spread; spread; spreading; spreads** [ME *spreden,* fr. OE *sprǣdan;* akin to OHG *spreiten* to spread, MLG & MD *spreiden, sprēden,* OSw *sprēda;* causative fr. the root of an intransitive v. represented by OHG *sprūtan* to spread, Sw *sprida;* akin to OE *sprūtan* to sprout — more at SPROUT] *vt* **1 a :** to cause to open out or extend over a larger area (as by unfurling, flattening out, or pulling taut) **:** EXPAND ⟨~ a carpet⟩ ⟨a ship with all sails ~⟩ ⟨hammered the metal to ~ it⟩ — often used with *out* ⟨~ out the newspaper⟩ ⟨~ out the roots carefully —Emily Holt⟩ ⟨city ~ out on a level terrain —*Amer. Guide Series: N. H.*⟩ **b :** to cause to reach or thrust out **:** stretch out **:** EXTEND ⟨~*ing* her arms wide to embrace him⟩ ⟨~*s* its wings for flight⟩ ⟨a tree ~*ing* its branches⟩ ⟨~ his hands, palms down on the table —Gilbert Millstein⟩ **c** (1) **:** to expose (one's hand or remaining cards) for the purpose of claiming all or some of the tricks yet to be played (2) **:** to lay down (a combination of cards having value under the rules of the game) **:** SHOW, MELD **2 a :** to distribute over an area **:** SCATTER, STREW ⟨~ fertilizer over the soil⟩ ⟨buildings . . . are around this central point —*Amer. Guide Series: Texas*⟩ ⟨has its armed forces ~ thinly all over the globe —*Wall Street Jour.*⟩ **b :** to distribute over a period of time **:** PROLONG, PROTRACT ⟨~ the cost of medical care⟩ ⟨the work had to be ~ over several weekends⟩; *specif* **:** to distribute (a limited amount of work) among as many workers and for as long as possible by shortening the work hours in a day or reducing the work days in a week **c :** to apply on a surface as an overlayer or cover ⟨~ butter on bread⟩ ⟨the varnish was ~ on every exposed part —Ben Riker⟩ **d** (1) **:** to cover or overlay with ⟨~ the floor with carpet⟩ (2) *archaic* **:** to cover or extend over completely **:** OVERRUN ⟨the velvet down that ~*s* his cheek —Thomas Moore⟩ **e** (1) **:** to prepare or furnish (as a table) for dining **:** SET ⟨~ the board⟩ ⟨~ the tables with the favorite dishes of their absent husbands —J.G.Frazer⟩ (2) **:** to lay out or set down (as a meal) **:** SERVE ⟨~ afternoon tea for us —Eve Langley⟩ ⟨supper was ~ —Thomas Hardy⟩ **f :** RECORD, ENTER ⟨moved . . . that the foregoing resolution be ~ upon the minutes —*Science*⟩ **3 a :** to make more widely known **:** PUBLISH, DISSEMINATE ⟨~ the news⟩ ⟨~ a man's fame⟩ ⟨~ the most glowing reports —T.B.Costain⟩ **b :** to cause to affect an increasing number **:** extend the range or incidence of ⟨~ a disease⟩ ⟨~ the habit of smoking —Olive Haseltine⟩ ⟨puerperal infection could be ~ in this way —Justina Hill⟩ **c :** DIFFUSE ⟨~ an effluvium⟩ **:** EMIT ⟨the hyacinth ~*ing* its fragrance⟩ **4 a :** to push apart by weight or force **:** make wider and flatter ⟨the locomotive ~*s* the rails⟩ ⟨~ a plate . . . and

had to be shod in the paddock —Richard Lane⟩ **b :** to separate (the lips) laterally and bring (them) close together vertically (as in the pronunciation of *ee* in *see*) — compare [6]ROUND 1c ~ *vi* **1 a :** to become dispersed, distributed, or scattered **:** flow out readily ⟨the rioters ~ throughout the city⟩ ⟨the odor ~*s* through the room⟩ ⟨a thin paint that ~*s* well⟩ **b :** to become known more widely **:** CIRCULATE ⟨the news ~⟩ ⟨the new ideas were ~*ing* —Tom Wintringham⟩ **c :** to increase in range, incidence, or influence ⟨the disease ~ through the island⟩ ⟨the panic ~ rapidly⟩ ⟨the academy idea had begun to ~ —J.P.Marquand⟩ **2 a :** to extend, grow, or stretch out in length or breadth **:** cover a greater area **:** EXPAND ⟨the city ~*s* over five square miles —*Amer. Guide Series: Mich.*⟩ ⟨the consequences of any big war ~ in circles to infinity —Dixon Wecter⟩ ⟨the shadow ~ across her face —Maude Hutchins⟩ **b :** to extend tendrils, shoots, or new growth **:** UNFOLD ⟨a vine remarkable for its tendency not to ~ and ramble —Willa Cather⟩ **c :** to become extended by heating, drawing, or compressing **d :** to project oneself into new activities ⟨he ~ out into other fields⟩ **3 :** to move apart (as from pressure or weight) **:** SEPARATE ⟨rails ~*ing* under the great weight⟩ ⟨the servant's mouth ~ in a placating grin —T.B.Costain⟩

syn DISSEMINATE, PROPAGATE, CIRCULATE, RADIATE, DIFFUSE: SPREAD, in the sense of broadcasting, publicizing, or making or becoming known widely, is without strong connotation, although it may suggest a scattered strewing ⟨scattered broadcast over the country at government expense, the report did much to *spread* knowledge of the northwest coast —R.A. Billington⟩ ⟨the taste for reading . . . slowly *spread* out toward the lonely clearings to the west —J.D.Hart⟩ DISSEMINATE means and suggests about the same things as SPREAD; it may connote the notion of a hoped-for useful fruition as of seed sown ⟨the need for a cooperative agency in the iron and steel industry for collecting and *disseminating* statistics and information —J.W.Hill⟩ PROPAGATE, applicable to complexes of notions rather than to specific facts or bits of information, may suggest fostering growth by making widespread and increasing the number of possible adherents ⟨mechanical societies sprang into existence, to *propagate* the creed with greater zeal —Lewis Mumford⟩ ⟨the outlandish philosophies that later sectaries were to *propagate* so diligently —V.L.Parrington⟩ CIRCULATE may suggest a passing from person to person as though in a circle and thus to become widely known ⟨this silly story that people are *circulating* —Thomas Hardy⟩ ⟨the satire, *circulating* in manuscript copies, had a great local vogue —E.V. Lucas⟩ RADIATE suggests sending out along radii from a nucleus; it is more likely to apply to matters affective than intellectual ⟨a unity of inspiration that *radiates* into plot and personages alike —T.S.Eliot⟩ ⟨the comments of Arthur Brisbane . . . *radiated* no warmth —A.W.Long⟩ DIFFUSE suggests to make known widely with permeation into small areas or crannies and an overall tingeing effect ⟨the drive behind the American ideal of a universally *diffused* education —Perry Miller⟩ ⟨once literacy has been generally *diffused* among the masses of a society, it tends to become indispensable —Helen Sullivan⟩

— **spread oneself :** to be lavish (as in effort, generosity, hospitality) ⟨*spread themselves* to entertain visiting delegates⟩

[2]**spread** \"\ *n* -S **1 a :** the act or process of spreading **:** EXPANSION, EXTENSION, DIFFUSION ⟨the ~ of wax under a seal⟩ ⟨the ~ of the great metropolis —*London Calling*⟩ ⟨the ~ of the plague through the city⟩ ⟨a gradual ~ of parliamentary democracy —Bertrand Russell⟩ **b :** the extent or capability of spreading ⟨the ~ of a sail⟩ ⟨elm . . . with a ~ of 146 feet —*Amer. Guide Series: Conn.*⟩ **c** (1) **:** DISPERSION 2a (2) **:** a continuous assemblage usu. of points in mathematics ⟨curves that are one-way ~*s*⟩ **2 :** something spread out: as **a :** a surface area **:** EXPANSE ⟨this giant ~ of land —A.B.Guthrie⟩ **b** *West* (1) **:** a ranch with all its appurtenances ⟨a cattle ~⟩ (2) **:** an expanse of range ⟨a ~ of 100,000 acres⟩ (3) **:** a herd of animals ⟨winter a ~ of 10,000 sheep⟩ **c :** the surface of a cut stone (as a diamond) in relation to its depth **d** (1) **:** a prominent display usu. occupying more than one column and esp. having pictorial illustration in a newspaper or periodical (2) **:** two facing pages (as of a magazine or newspaper) printed with matter that usu. runs across the fold (as a single advertisement or picture or part of an article to be read as a single page); *also* **:** the matter occupying these two facing pages **e :** SPREADHEAD **f** (1) **:** LAYDOWN (2) **:** an intentional exposure (as for the purpose of claiming tricks) of a player's entire hand (3) **:** a combination of cards in rummy that can be or is melded **:** SET (4) **:** the act of melding such a combination **3 :** something spread on or over a surface: as **a :** a food (as butter, jam, jelly, fruit or peanut butter, or deviled meat) used or made for use to spread on bread or crackers ⟨cheese ~⟩ **b :** a usu. sumptuous meal **:** FEAST, BANQUET ⟨a gigantic ~ in honor of the visiting prince —Robert Shaplen⟩ **c :** a plain or decorative cloth used as a cover for a table or a bed **4 :** the distance between two points **:** GAP, DIVERGENCE ⟨the wide ~ between theory and fact⟩: as **a :** the distance between the forelegs of certain quadrupeds (as dogs) **b :** distance from center to center (as of the cylinders of a duplex pump) in machinery **c :** the distance between gage lines at the heel or toe of a railroad frog **d :** SPAN **e** (1) **:** the difference between what the producer is paid for a product and what the consumer pays for it (2) **:** the difference between the highest and lowest price of a product for a given period (3) **:** STRADDLE **f** (1) **:** an option in a put and call in which the put price is different from the call price so that no profit is made unless the price falls or rises below or above the put or call price respectively by more than enough to cover the cost of the option (2) **:** an arbitrage transaction operated by buying and selling simultaneously in two separate markets (as Chicago and New York) when there is an abnormal difference in price between the two markets — see BACKSPREAD (3) **:** the difference between bid and asked prices (4) **:** the difference between any two prices for similar articles ⟨the ~ between the list price and the market price of an article⟩ **g :** DEVIATION f **5 :** something that spreads or fans out: as **a :** a salvo of torpedoes fired just ahead, at, and just abaft the target to ensure a hit **b :** SPREAD FORMATION **c :** a shot in billiards in which the cue ball is made to rebound from the object ball at a considerable angle to its original course

[3]**spread** \"\ *adj* [fr. past part. of [1]*spread*] **1 :** widely extended **:** EXPANDED **2 :** extending across two or more columns of a newspaper or periodical ⟨a two-page ~ advertisement⟩ **3 :** having insufficient depth so that its luster is below standard — used of a gem

spread·abil·i·ty \ˌ==ˈbiləd·ē, -lətē, -i\ *n* **:** ease or facility in spreading ⟨the ~ of butter⟩ ⟨the ~ of a paint⟩

spread·able \ˈ==bəl\ *adj* [[1]*spread* + *-able*] **:** capable of being spread ⟨a ~ plastic substance⟩

spreadboard \ˈ=,=\ *n* **:** a machine that spreads flax and hemp in ropemaking

spread eagle *n* [[3]*spread*; trans. of MF *aigle esployee*] **1 :** a representation of an eagle with wings raised and legs extended (as in an heraldic device or the silver insigne of the rank of colonel) **2 :** something resembling or suggestive of a spread eagle: as **a :** a man tied (as to a wheel) with arms and legs extended ⟨make a *spread eagle* of you —R.H.Dana⟩ **b :** a glide in figure skating executed with the skates heel to heel in a straight line **c :** a design used esp. in chair and bed backs (as designed by Duncan Phyfe) **3** [so called fr. the spread eagle on the Great Seal of the U. S.] **:** bombastic or high-flown expression esp. of U. S. chauvinistic sentiments ⟨a speech full of *spread eagle*⟩

[1]**spread-eagle** \ˈ=ˈ==\ *vb* -ED/-ING/-S [*spread eagle*] *vi* **1 :** to execute a spread eagle (as in skating) **2 :** to stand or move with the arms and legs stretched out **:** SPRAWL ⟨the boys *spread-eagled* across the cinders —J.A.Michener⟩ ~ *vt* **1 a :** to put into the position of a spread eagle **:** stretch out ⟨*spread-eagled* him on a log —R.P.Warren⟩ **b :** to spread over **:** stretch across **:** STRADDLE ⟨the company's plants *spread-eagled* the state⟩ **2 a :** to defeat completely **:** ROUT ⟨threatened to *spread-eagle* the field —Clifford Bloodgood⟩ **b :** to scatter (an opposing team) in football **c :** to break and spread (a wicket) with a bowled ball in cricket

[2]**spread-eagle** \"\ *adj* [*spread eagle*] **1 :** resembling or suggestive of a spread eagle ⟨sprawled in a *spread-eagle* position⟩ **2 :** marked by bombast and boastful exaggeration esp. of the greatness of the U. S. **:** VAINGLORIOUS ⟨to paint the biggest picture in the world was no inappropriate ambition for that *spread-eagle* era —Dixon Wecter⟩ ⟨a *spread-eagle* orator⟩ ⟨a *spread-eagle* speech⟩

spread-ea·gle·ism \-əˌlizəm\ *n* -S [*spread eagle* + *-ism*] **:** bombastic and vainglorious boasting of the greatness of the U. S. **:** SUPERPATRIOTISM, FLAG-WAVING ⟨resorted to some old-fashioned *spread-eaglelism* and even demagoguery —W.G. Carleton⟩

spread-eagle orchid *n* **:** a showy tropical American orchid (*Oncidium carthaginense*) having spreading petals

spreader \ˈspred·ə(r)\ *n* -S [ME *spreder*, fr. *spreden* to spread + *-er*] **1 :** one that spreads, scatters, or diffuses: as **a :** an implement for spreading material (as fertilizer, hay, sand, lime) over an area ⟨heavy trucks with sand ~*s*⟩ **b :** a small knife-shaped implement for use at the table esp. in spreading butter **c :** a worker in a bakery who spreads icing or filling (as on cookies) **d :** PLASTERER **e** (1) *also* **spreading machine :** a machine for coating fabrics esp. with rubber (2) **:** a tender of a spreading machine **f :** a wetting agent (as soap, oil emulsion, or casein) added to fungicides and insecticides to increase their spreading on foliage by lowering the surface tension **g** *or* **spreader dam :** a dike or trench forcing runoff water to disperse over a wide area instead of following a channel **2 :** one that spreads, stretches, or draws out something being processed: as **a :** one that layers cloth on a table for pattern cutting **b** (1) **:** a textile machine for combining and drawing flax fiber into a sliver (2) **:** a similar machine for straightening and evening fibers (as hemp) for rope making (3) **:** any of various textile machines for spreading out the warp threads during winding, fibers for drying, and loops on a knitting machine **c** (1) **:** TACKER a (2) **:** GAMBREL 2 **3 :** one that spreads, holds, or keeps apart: as **a :** a bar holding apart two stays or guys to stretch them and so stiffen a spar (as a topmast or jibboom) — compare CROSSTREE **b :** any of a series of crossbearers that supports a line of rails (as in an adit or heading) **c :** a bar that holds two whiffletrees apart **:** DOUBLETREE **d :** a stick or bar for holding apart the wires of a radio aerial **e :** a small bar or roll so placed as to ensure even tension across a web of paper entering a calender, winder, or printing press

spreader car *n* **:** a car with adjustable wings on each side for pushing earth away from a railroad track to widen the roadbed and for spreading ballast and ditching

spreader-sticker \ˈ=,=ˈ==\ *n* **:** a material or combination of materials added to sprays that causes the spray to spread and to stick to the sprayed foliage

spread footing *n* [[3]*spread*] **:** a footing in building construction that is shallow in proportion to its width and is usu. made of reinforced concrete

spread formation *n* [[3]*spread*] **:** a double or triple wing offensive formation in football in which the ends are spread three to five yards outside the tackles, the tailback plays seven to eight yards behind the line, and the other three backs are in flanking position close to the line so that they may move quickly downfield to receive a pass

spread glass *n* [[3]*spread*] **:** CYLINDER GLASS

spreadhead \ˈ=,=\ *n* [[3]*spread* + *head*] **:** a newspaper heading in large type usu. extending across two or more columns

spreading *pres part of* SPREAD

spreading adder *n* **:** HOGNOSE SNAKE

spreading board *n* **:** SETTING BLOCK

spreading cotoneaster *n* **:** a Chinese shrub (*Cotoneaster divaricata*) that has pink flowers, spreading branches, and red ellipsoid fruit and is used as an ornamental

spreading decline *n* **:** a disease of citrus trees caused by the citrus nematode and characterized by loss of feeder roots and subsequent progressive decline in vigor

spreading dogbane *n* **:** a milky-juiced No. American perennial herb (*Apocynum androsaemifolium*) having opposite entire leaves and loose spreading cymes of pinkish flowers in early summer — compare RHEUMATISM WEED

spreading factor *n* **:** HYALURONIDASE

spread·ing·ly *adv* **:** EXPANSIVELY, MANIFESTLY ⟨his deeper impression of something beautiful and ~ clear —Henry James †1916⟩

spreading yew *n* **:** any of several cultivated yews that are usu. derived from Japanese species and are characterized by low growth and much horizontal branching

spread misère *n* [[3]*spread*] **:** a misère game that the bidder plays with all his cards exposed

spread of risk : the extent to which an insurance company by selecting diversified and independent risks that are fairly uniform in size and sufficiently large in number can predict the losses thereon with reasonable accuracy by the law of averages

spreads *pres 3d sing of* SPREAD, *pl of* SPREAD

spread-set \ˈ=,=\ *vt* **:** to cause the metal of (saw teeth) to flow sidewise (as by swaging)

spready \ˈspredē\ *adj* -ER/-EST **:** having or constituting a hide 60 pounds or more in weight and 6½ feet or more in length — used of a steer or a hide ⟨~ native steers⟩ ⟨a ~ hide⟩

spreagh \ˈsprēk\ *n* -S [alter. of *spreath*] *Scot* **:** a cattle raid **:** FORAY

sprea·ghery *or* **spre·chery** \ˈsprēkəri\ *n* -ES [*spreagh* + *-ery*] **1** *Scot* **:** cattle lifting **:** PLUNDERING **2** *Scot* **:** BOOTY, PLUNDER

spreath \ˈsprēk\ *n* -S [ScGael *sprèidh* cattle, fr. L *praeda* booty — more at PREY] **1** *Scot* **:** PREY, BOOTY; *esp* **:** cattle carried off in a raid **2** *Scot* **:** a cattle raid **:** FORAY

spreck·led \ˈsprekəld\ *adj* [of Scand origin; akin to ON *sprek*lōtt speckled, *sprekla* spot; akin to MHG *spreckel* speckle, OE *spearca* spark — more at SPARK] *dial Brit* **:** SPECKLED

[1]**spree** \ˈsprē\ *or* **spray** \ˈsprā\ *n* -S [perh. alter. of *spreath*] **:** an unrestrained and usu. excessive indulgence in or outburst of any activity **:** SPLURGE, RAMPAGE ⟨a buying ~⟩ ⟨a speculative ~ —*Kiplinger Washington Letter*⟩ ⟨a fishing ~⟩; *esp* **:** an occasion, period, or bout of reckless merrymaking and usu. heavy drinking **:** BINGE, CAROUSAL ⟨inebriated after a ~ in town —*Amer. Guide Series: La.*⟩ — often used in the expressions *on a spree* and *go on a spree* ⟨a pair of undergraduates on a ~ —Lucien Price⟩ ⟨had gone on spending ~*s* —Truman Capote⟩

[2]**spree** \ˈsprē\ *vi* **spreed; spreed; spreeing; sprees :** to indulge in or go on a spree ⟨~*ing* around —Walt Whitman⟩

[3]**spree** \"\ *Scot & dial Eng var of* SPRY

spree drinker *n* **:** a chronic alcoholic who suffers from the compulsion to heavy periodic drinking **:** DIPSOMANIAC

spreeuw \ˈsprīü\ *n* -S [Afrik *spreeu* starling (formerly spelled *spreeuw*), fr. MD *spreeuwe, sprewe*] **:** any of several African starlings of glossy plumage

sprengel explosive \ˈspreŋgəl-, ˈshpreŋəl-\ *n, usu cap S* [after Herman J. P. *Sprengel* †1906 Brit. chemist born in Germany] **:** any of numerous high explosives formed by mixing just before use an oxidizing agent (as nitric acid or potassium chlorate) and a combustible ingredient (as nitrobenzene) neither of which by itself is explosive

sprengel pump *n, usu cap S* [after Herman J. P. *Sprengel*] **:** an air pump in which exhaustion is produced by drops of mercury running down a narrow tube and trapping bubbles of gas between them

sprengel tube *n, usu cap S* [after H. J. P. *Sprengel*] **:** a glass U tube with two capillary ends bent at right angles for use in determining specific gravity esp. of oils and fats by weighing it first filled with the substance to be tested and then filled with water — compare PYCNOMETER

[1]**sprent** \ˈsprent\ *vb* [ME *sprenten* to jump, spurt, of Scand origin; akin to Sw dial. *sprinta* to jump, hop — more at SPRINT] *vi, dial chiefly Brit* **:** RUN, LEAP, SPRINT ~ *vt, dial chiefly Brit* **:** SPRINKLE, SPLASH, SQUIRT

[2]**sprent** \"\ *n* -S **1** *dial chiefly Brit* **:** SPRINT, SPRING, LEAP **2** *dial chiefly Brit* **:** HASP, CATCH

[3]**sprent** \"\ *adj* [fr. past part. of obs. *sprenge* to sprinkle, scatter, fr. ME *sprengen*, fr. OE *sprengan*; akin to MD, MLG, & OHG *sprengen* to make jump, sprinkle, ON *sprengja* to cause to burst; causative fr. the root of E [1]*spring*] *archaic* **:** SPRINKLED ⟨the brown hair ~ with gray —Matthew Arnold⟩

spret *var of* SPRAT

sprier *comparative of* SPRY

spriest *superlative of* SPRY

[1]**sprig** \ˈsprig\ *n* -S [ME *sprigge*; prob. akin to OE *spræc* shoot of a plant, ME *spray*, MD *sproc* twig, sprig, MLG *sprik, sprok* dry twig, OHG *sprahhula* splinter, chaff, ON *sprek* stick, Sw dial. *spragg, sprägge* branch, and perh. to OE *spearca* spark — more at SPARK] **1 a :** a small shoot **:** TWIG ⟨a ~ of laurel⟩ ⟨a ~ of parsley⟩ ⟨the yard . . . completely bare, no weed no ~ of anything —William Faulkner⟩ **b :** a small division of grass used for propagation **2 a :** a small offshoot or side growth (as of a nerve or vein) **b** (1) **:** HEIR, SCION ⟨a young ~ of nobility —Peter Forster⟩ (2) **:** a young person ⟨a young ~ of a book reviewer —Clifton Fadiman⟩ **c :** a small specimen ⟨a ~ of vivid, unaffected idiom —John Woodburn⟩ **3 a :** an ornament (as a jeweled brooch or a decorative design) resembling a sprig, stemmed flower, or leaf **b :** a separate piece of lace (as a flower or foliage motif) usu. appliquéd to the ground **4 :** any of various pointed objects: as **a :** a small headless nail **:** BRAD **b :** GLAZIER'S POINT **c :** DOWEL **5 a :** PINTAIL 1a **b** RUDDY DUCK **c** *Scot* **:** HOUSE SPARROW

[2]**sprig** \"\ *vt* **sprigged; sprigged; sprigging; sprigs 1 a :** to drive sprigs or brads into **:** secure with sprigs ⟨boots, *sprigged* and screwed soles —*Queensland (Australia) Times*⟩ **b :** to attach (a part) to a piece of raw pottery ⟨~ a handle on the pitcher⟩ **2 :** to mark or adorn with the representation of small branches or plants **:** FIGURE 2a ⟨~ muslin⟩ ⟨white dimity *sprigged* with yellow rosebuds —*New Yorker*⟩ **3 a :** to propagate (a grass) by means of stolons or small divisions **b :** to strip (a shrub or plant) of sprigs ⟨~ a tobacco plant⟩

sprig budding *n* **:** BARK GRAFTING

sprig·ger \ˈsprigə(r)\ *n* -S **:** one that sprigs: as **a :** a machine for driving sprigs into shoes **b :** STRIPPER 1a

sprig·gy \-gē, -gi\ *adj* -ER/-EST **:** having sprigs or small branches ⟨~ branches⟩ ⟨a ~ pattern⟩

spright \ˈsprīt, *usu* -īd·+V\ *archaic var of* SPRITE

spright·ful \-tfəl\ *adj* [*spright* + *-ful*] **:** full of life or spirit **:** SPRIGHTLY — **spright·ful·ly** \-fəlē\ *adv* — **sprightful·ness** \-fəlnəs\ *n* -ES

spright·li·ly \-lələ̄, -li\ *adv* **:** in a sprightly manner **:** BRISKLY, ANIMATEDLY ⟨setting out on the ascent ~ —Louis Golding⟩

spright·li·ness \-lēnəs, -lin-\ *n* -ES **:** the quality or state of being sprightly: as **a :** gay liveliness **:** VIVACITY ⟨beneath her ~ . . . she was seriously inclined —Virginia Woolf⟩ **b :** PIQUANCY ⟨a ~ of flavor, a suggestion of the pineapple, the apricot, the orange —David Fairchild⟩

[1]**spright·ly** \ˈsprītlē, -li\ *adj* -ER/-EST [*spright* + *-ly*] **1 :** marked by a gay lightness and vivacity (as of movement or manner) **:** SPIRITED ⟨a short ~ dance⟩ ⟨a ~ young girl⟩ ⟨a ~ air⟩ ⟨a ~ style⟩ ⟨gradually through the afternoon her step had become less ~ —Douglass Wallop⟩ ⟨readers prefer ~ trash to dull excellence —H.S.Canby⟩ **2 :** having a distinctively piquant taste ⟨citrus fruits with a ~ blending of tartness and sweetness⟩ **syn** see LIVELY

[2]**sprightly** \"\ *adv* **:** in a sprightly manner **:** SPRIGHTLILY

sprigtail \ˈ=,=\ *n* **1 :** PINTAIL 1a **2 :** SHARP-TAILED GROUSE **3 :** RUDDY DUCK

sprigtailed \ˈ=,=\ *adj* **:** having a sharp-pointed tail ⟨a ~ mare⟩ ⟨a ~ duck⟩

[1]**spring** \ˈspriŋ\ *vb* **sprang** \ˈspraŋ, -aiŋ\ *or* **sprung** \ˈsprəŋ\ **sprung; springing; springs** [ME *springen*, fr. OE *springan*; akin to OHG *springan* to jump, spring, OFris & ON *springa* to jump, spring, Gk *sperchesthai* to hasten, Skt *sprhayati* he desires; basic meaning: to move fast, jump] *vi* **1 a** (1) **:** to undergo a sudden or violent change in place or position **:** DART, SHOOT ⟨the sparks *sprang* upward as he stirred the fire⟩ (2) **:** to have or display resiliency **:** move or be capable of moving by elastic force ⟨the two halves *sprang* back together again —C.L.Carmer⟩ **b :** to become shattered or cracked **:** BREAK, SPLIT ⟨the veneer ~*s* along the fracture —Andrew Wood & Thomas Linn⟩ **c :** to bend from a straight direction or plane surface **:** become warped **2 :** to issue with speed and force **:** break out ⟨the blood ~*s* from the wound⟩ ⟨the tears ~ from her eyes⟩ **:** issue as a stream ⟨out of these curiously shaped mounds ~*s* an unflagging supply of water —George Farwell⟩ ⟨turned on the first shining water tap, and watched the water ~, steaming, from it —Kay Boyle⟩ **3 a :** to grow as a plant ⟨white heather ~*s* on the mountainsides —Isabel Lawrence⟩ **b :** to issue by birth or descent ⟨both parents *sprang* from wealthy landowners —Cecil Sprigge⟩ ⟨*sprang* from a comfortable corner of the English middle class —J.M. Cameron⟩ **c :** to come into being **:** APPEAR, ARISE, EMERGE ⟨hope ~*s* eternal in the human breast —Alexander Pope⟩ ⟨the horror ~*ing* up in his eyes as it came to him —J.B. Benefield⟩ ⟨towns *sprang* into being where cattle trails and stage lines met —*Amer. Guide Series: Texas*⟩ **:** PROCEED, RESULT ⟨her anxiety had *sprung* from a definite cause —Ellen Glasgow⟩ **d** *archaic* **:** to become visible **:** DAWN ⟨at five the golden light began to ~ —John Keats⟩ **e :** to develop force **:** begin to blow — used with *up* ⟨a breeze suddenly *sprang* up⟩ **4 a :** to make a bound **:** move by means of a leap or leaps ⟨*sprang* toward the door, but was intercepted in her intended flight —T.L.Peacock⟩ ⟨*sprang* across the stream, inviting those who shared his views to follow him —*Amer. Guide Series: Maine*⟩ **b :** to start up suddenly (as from a covert) **c :** to leap or jump up **:** rise suddenly from a resting position ⟨I *sprang* to my feet, for anger had overtaken me —Edita Morris⟩ **5 a :** to stretch out in height or length **:** EXTEND ⟨from its corners ~ four slender minarets —Douglas Carruthers⟩ **b** *of a vault or arch* **:** to start rounding upward from the impost ⟨from rich entablatures ~ graceful arches supporting the vaulted ceilings —*Amer. Guide Series: Pa.*⟩ **6 a** *of a female domestic animal* **:** to show signs of approaching parturition (as by dropping of the enlarged abdomen and swelling of the udder) **b** *of an udder* **:** SWELL ~ *vt* **1 :** to cause to grow, arise, or develop ⟨hoped it would rain very soon, to ~ some new grass —Doris Lessing⟩ ⟨is *sprung* compellingly into life from a powerfully creative, romantic mind —*Times Lit. Supp.*⟩ **2 a :** to start (as game) from cover **:** cause to rise from the earth or from a covert **:** FLUSH ⟨~ a pheasant⟩ **b :** to put to a gallop ⟨*sprang* his horse in front of the ranks —C.L.Carmer⟩ **3 a** (1) **:** to undergo the splitting or cracking of ⟨the ship *sprang* a mast⟩ (2) **:** to bring about the splitting or cracking of ⟨the wind *sprang* the foremast of the ship⟩ **b :** to undergo the opening of (a leak) ⟨having grounded at the mouth of the river as a result of which it *sprung* a leak —*Hispanic Amer. Hist. Rev.*⟩ ⟨the radiator *sprung* a leak —John Steinbeck⟩ **4 a :** to cause to explode ⟨the disturbance of the steamer's approach ~*ing* a myriad of these floating mines —William Beebe⟩ **b :** CHAMBER 4 ⟨a borehole is *sprung* . . . by exploding in the bottom several charges of dynamite —*Blasters' Handbk.*⟩ **5 a :** to cause to shift place or position suddenly **:** make leap up or start forward or out ⟨the wind *sprang* some tiles from the roof⟩ **b** (1) **:** to operate or cause to operate by sudden pressure or movement ⟨*sprang* the watchcase open⟩ (2) **:** to cause to close or operate ⟨~ a trap⟩ (3) **:** to cause (a rattle) to sound by movement of a part **c :** to apply or insert by bending ⟨needed all his strength to ~ in the bar⟩ **d :** to bend by force ⟨~ the steel band⟩ **e :** to move, haul, or swing (a ship) by means of a spring line ⟨to get under way ~ the boat ahead —*Manual of Seamanship*⟩ **f :** to raise (the toe of a shoe last) above the ground line **6 a :** to start (a vault or arch) upward from the impost **b :** to put up (an arch) **c :** ARCH, CURVE ⟨the dog's ribs are well *sprung*⟩ **7 :** to pass over by leaping ⟨the horse *sprang* the narrow fence⟩ **8 :** to give, spend, offer, or pay out (money) ⟨there's nothing really immoral about ~*ing* ten cents for a ball of twine —R.P.Smith⟩ **9 :** to produce or disclose suddenly or unexpectedly ⟨the last page ~*s* a surprise bit of fireworks no reviewer should mention beforehand —*N.Y. Herald Tribune Bk. Rev.*⟩ ⟨my wife *sprung* a dinner party with nearly all my old secretaries on me —O.W.Holmes †1935⟩ **10 :** to make lame **:** STRAIN ⟨its near leg was *sprung* a little, maybe from being worked too hard too young —William Faulkner⟩ ⟨*sprang* every blessed muscle in my . . . leg —John Buchan⟩ **11** *slang* **:** to release or cause to be released from confinement, custody, or military service ⟨there'd be a lawyer down there to ~ him before I got the cell door shut —Leslie Ford⟩

syn SPRING, ARISE, RISE, ORIGINATE, DERIVE, FLOW, ISSUE, EMANATE, PROCEED, STEM can mean, in common, to come up or out of something into existence. SPRING stresses sudden or surprising emergence, esp. after a period of concealed existence

or preparation ⟨plants *spring* from seed⟩ ⟨the images that *spring* up in one's consciousness⟩ ⟨it is from the middle class that writers *spring* —Virginia Woolf⟩ ARISE emphasizes chiefly the mere fact of coming into existence or notice, conveying the idea of a vagueness of prior state; when used with *from* it implies a causal connection between subject and object ⟨an argument *arose* during the meal —Zechariah Chafee⟩ ⟨present uncertainties *arise* partly out of far-reaching changes in the American environment —J.D.Millett⟩ ⟨differences in English may *arise* from several causes —*English Language Arts*⟩ RISE and ARISE in this sense of to come into existence are often interchangeable, although RISE may possibly carry some connotation of literal or figurative ascent ⟨empires *rise* and fall within a single man's lifetime —Elspeth Huxley⟩ ⟨a church *rose* in the wilderness —*Amer. Guide Series: Conn.*⟩ ⟨from the South, at last, *rose* that bitter opposition which flowered in a bloody civil war —Carol L. Thompson⟩ ORIGINATE suggests a source or starting point, carrying the idea of inception at that source ⟨at one time it was believed that man *originated* in America —R.W.Murray⟩ ⟨within its area of 84,682 square miles *originate* three great river systems —*Amer. Guide Series: Minn.*⟩ ⟨adult fears *originating* in childhood insecurity⟩ DERIVE also suggests a source, though it usu. does not imply inception, usu. presupposing a prior existence in another form, person, or thing, and connoting descent as by endowment, transference, deduction, imitation, or reproduction ⟨the new playwrights *derive* from him —E.R.Bentley⟩ ⟨the principal income *derives* from coal mining —*Amer. Guide Series: Pa.*⟩ ⟨its criticism *derives* directly from English inspiration —Bernard Smith⟩ FLOW emphasizes often the abundance of the supply, often the ease of provision or production ⟨from the town's shaded public square *flows* justice —*Amer. Guide Series: Va.*⟩ ⟨masterpiece upon masterpiece *flowed* from his brush —*advt*⟩ ⟨a great generosity from which *flowed* gift after gift⟩ ISSUE suggests emergence into existence as from a womb, stressing somewhat a causal force ⟨three conclusions at least *issue* from the perusal —T.S.Eliot⟩ EMANATE applies chiefly to immaterial things, as law, principles, power, or thoughts, connoting the emergence or passage of something impalpable or invisible, suggesting less causal force than ISSUE ⟨the earlier reports which *emanated* from Dumbarton Oaks —Sir Winston Churchill⟩ ⟨the rain-drenched geranium bed, from which *emanated* an odor musky and sweet —J.C.Powys⟩ ⟨the impalpable aura of power that *emanated* from him —Osbert Sitwell⟩ ⟨the criminal organization . . . is extremely powerful, and part of its power *emanates* from the close-knit structure —D.W.Maurer & V.H. Vogel⟩ PROCEED stresses place of origin, or, sometimes, parentage, derivation, or cause ⟨*proceeding* from the premise that half the world does not know how the other half lives —*Dun's Rev.*⟩ ⟨the philosophic movement *proceeded* from little known thinkers and writers⟩ STEM suggests a growing out, as of a stem from a plant, and applies chiefly to things that come into existence through the influence of a predecessor, as a natural outgrowth or subordinate development ⟨one of twenty-five in the class, all but four *stemming* from Maine —M.L.Ernst⟩ ⟨these influences . . . *stem* from warfare, from medicine, from the arts, from religion —D.J.Struik⟩ **syn** see in addition JUMP

²spring \"\ *n* -s *often attrib* [ME, fr. OE; akin to OFris *spring*, OS & OHG *gispring* spring, OE *springan* to spring — more at ¹SPRING] **1 a :** a source of a body or reservoir of water (as of a river or well) ⟨a flowing body that begins in a hundred trickles and runnels and ~s high up in the mountains —Lewis Mumford⟩ **b** (1) **:** an issue of water from the earth **:** a natural fountain ⟨everybody lived in dugouts or small log houses on ~s or creeks —Bruce Siberts⟩ ⟨had to drill a well when their ~ ran dry⟩ (2) **:** a natural fountain having specified properties — usu. used in pl. ⟨mineral ~s⟩ ⟨sulfur ~s⟩ ⟨hot ~s⟩ (3) **:** something that resembles a fountain ⟨a ~ of pity, of affection . . . suddenly welled up within her —Winston Churchill⟩ **c :** a flow or seepage (as of a mineral) from the earth ⟨accumulations of oil which seeped to the surface in ~s —Bliss Isely⟩ ⟨tar ~s⟩ **2 a :** a source of something; *esp* **:** a hidden or ultimate source ⟨this habit of retirement to the inner ~s of being —H.S.Canby⟩ ⟨a custom, a belief, and art, however deep down its ~s, sooner or later rises into social consciousness —A.L.Kroeber⟩ **b** *archaic* **:** the beginning or first appearance of something ⟨never since the middle summer's ~, met we —Shak.⟩; *specif* **:** DAWN, DAYSPRING ⟨they arose early: and it came to pass about the ~ of the day —1 Sam 9:26 (AV)⟩ **c :** a first stage **:** a time or state of growth and development ⟨this thirteen-year-old girl, in whose flat childish body the ~ was beginning to stir —Edith Sitwell⟩ **d :** something that produces action or motion **:** CAUSE, MOTIVE ⟨laying open to his view the ~s of action in both parties —T.L.Peacock⟩ ⟨the ~s of human conduct —A. T.Weaver⟩ **3 :** an exceptionally high or low tide **:** SPRING TIDE **4 a** *chiefly dial* **:** a grove of young trees **:** PLANTATION **b** *chiefly dial* **:** a young undergrowth (as of trees or shrubs) **5 a** (1) **:** an elastic body or device that recovers its original shape when released after being distorted; *specif* **:** one designed for some specific use (as to check recoil, to diminish concussion and jar, to store up energy) — see BREGUET HAIRSPRING, MAINSPRING (2) **:** BEDSPRING **b :** a person likened to a spring (as in tension or contained energy) ⟨a steel ~ of a man —Claudia Cassidy⟩ **6 a :** the act or an instance of leaping up or forward **:** BOUND ⟨the cat made a ~ at the mouse⟩ ⟨took the steps at one ~⟩ ⟨that sudden and inexplicable ~ forward took place independently . . . in three different regions and cultures —T.I. Cook⟩ **b :** a low leap in which a dancer moves forward, backward, or sideward as weight is transferred from one foot to the other **c** *chiefly Scot* **:** a lively tune or dance ⟨took the pipes, and played a little ~ —R.L.Stevenson⟩ **7** *of teal* **:** a small flock **8 a :** the season between winter and summer reckoned astronomically as extending from the March equinox to the June solstice **b :** the season comprising the months of March, April, and May **c** *Brit* **:** the season comprising the months of February, March, and April **d :** the season reckoned astronomically in the southern hemisphere as extending from the September equinox to the December solstice **9 a :** capacity for springing **:** elastic power or force **:** ELASTICITY, RESILIENCE ⟨the ironing-out effect of passing trains on track which has a certain amount of ~ in it —O.S.Nock⟩ **:** BOUNCE, BUOYANCY, ENERGY ⟨there was a new ~ in their step —Bennett Cerf⟩ **b :** the action of flying back to a normal state or position from a sprung state or position ⟨the ~ of a bow⟩ **10 :** the point or plane at which an arch or vault curve springs from its impost **11 a :** a crack, fissure, or permanent deformation in a mast or yard **b** (1) **:** a line led from a ship's quarter to its cable so that by hauling in or slacking the line the ship can be made to lie in any desired position (2) **:** a line led diagonally from the bow or stern of a ship to some point upon a wharf and made fast to aid in springing the ship in to the wharf **12** *of a dog* **:** roundness of ribs **:** the state of having the ribs well arched **13 :** the furcula of a springtail **14 :** a more or less flexible pipe bend or elbow designed to accommodate slight changes in length **15 a :** the variation of a shoe at the toe and arch from a horizontal line **b :** a tension at the counter of a shoe caused by cutting the upper shorter at that place **16 a :** KING SALMON **b :** a pelt or fur taken in the spring and usu. no longer prime **syn** see JUMP, MOTIVE

³spring \"\ *vt* **springed** \-riŋd\ *or* **sprung** \-rəŋ\ **springed** *or* **sprung**; **springing**; **springs :** to fit with springs ⟨the ambulance . . . was the old kind, like a furniture van, but it was well *sprung* —Fred Majdalany⟩ ⟨there were ~*ed* bunks which folded into the wall —Bill Mauldin⟩

⁴spring \"\ *n* -s [alter. of *springe*] *chiefly dial* **:** NOOSE, SNARE

spring·ald \ˈspriŋəld\ *also* **spring·al** \-əl\ *n* -s [prob. fr. ME, a kind of catapult, fr. MF *espringale*, fr. OF, fr. *espringuier* to jump, dance, of Gmc origin; akin to OHG *springan* to jump, spring — more at SPRING] **:** a young man **:** STRIPLING ⟨have any penniless young ~ defy his parents to marry a green girl —J.H.Wheelwright⟩

spring azure *n* **:** a small blue American butterfly (*Lycaenopsis argiolus*) of the family Lycaenidae

spring back *n* [²*spring*] **:** HOLLOW BACK

springback \ˈ=,=\ *n* [fr. *spring back*, v.] **:** the capacity or tendency of a bent or shaped elastic material (as a metal) to revert to its original form ⟨the forming of magnesium . . . must be done at high temperatures to eliminate ~ —*Scientific American*⟩

spring base *n* **:** the distance between centers of suspension of an arched spring

spring beam *n* **:** a beam uniting the outboard ends of the paddle beams of a ship and assisting to support the side of a paddle box

spring beauty *n* **1 :** a plant of the genus *Claytonia* (esp. *C. virginica*) sending up in early spring a 2-leaved stem bearing several delicate pink flowers **2 :** a strong to vivid purplish red that is redder and slightly lighter than Tyrian pink

spring bed *n* **1 :** a spring mattress or a bed having a spring mattress **2 :** a long elastic steel plate that serves to press the fibers up to the cutters in a cloth-shearing machine

spring beetle *n* **:** CLICK BEETLE

spring binder *n* **:** a loose-leaf binder having a shaped spring-metal back that opens to receive or release the contents when the covers are opened wide and pressed back

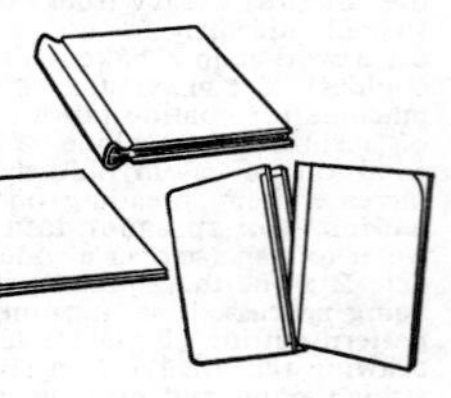
spring binder

springblade knife \ˈ=-,=-\ *n* **:** SWITCHBLADE KNIFE

spring block *n* **:** a block to which a spring is attached; *specif* **:** either of the distance pieces secured one above and the other below an elliptic car spring

springboard \ˈ=,=\ *n* **1 a :** a strong but flexible board of wood, metal, or glass resting on a fulcrum with one end secured and the other projecting over water and used for diving; *specif* **:** one usu. placed at a height of one or three meters above the water and used by fancy divers as a means of getting height for a dive **b :** a flexible board that is usu. secured at one end and is used as a takeoff device for certain gymnastic stunts **c :** a short iron-shod board that is inserted into a notched tree trunk and upon which the axman stands **2 :** a point of departure **:** JUMPING-OFF PLACE ⟨the idea is to use the convention as a ~ for the campaign —*New Republic*⟩ ⟨sees an opportunity ahead of making the chairmanship a ~ to higher things —*Atlantic*⟩

spring·bok \ˈ=,bäk, -,bək\ *n, pl* **springbok** *or* **springboks** [Afrik, fr. *spring* to jump (fr. MD *springen*) + *bok* male goat, male deer or antelope, fr. MD *boc*; akin to OHG *springan* to jump and to OHG *boc* male goat — more at SPRING, BUCK] **:** a swift and graceful southern African gazelle (*Antidorcas euchore*) noted for its habit of springing lightly and suddenly into the air and being dark buffy-brown with dark markings and white underparts and a white dorsal stripe that expands into a broad patch of white on the rump

spring bolt *n* **:** a bolt retracted by pressure and shot by a spring when the pressure is released — compare BULLET BOLT

spring brass *n* **:** common brass stiffened by cold working or heat treatment

springbuck \ˈ=,=\ *n, pl* **springbuck** *or* **springbucks** [part trans. of Afrik *springbok*] **:** SPRINGBOK

spring caliper *n* **:** a caliper having legs fastened together with a spring and pivot

spring cankerworm *n* **:** the variably colored looper larva of a widespread No. American geometrid moth (*Paleacrita vernata*) that largely resembles the fall cankerworm but has spines on the abdomen and emerges in spring

spring catch *n.* **:** a catch having a spring bolt

spring chair *n* **:** PERCH 3e

spring chicken *n* **1 :** a young table fowl of about three pounds in weight formerly available only from spring hatchings **2 :** a young person ⟨she looks youthful, but she's no *spring chicken*⟩

¹spring-clean \ˈ=ˈ=\ *vt* [back-formation fr. *spring-cleaning*] **:** to give a thorough cleaning to (a place) ⟨*spring-cleaned* the cabin even blacking the stovepipes and stoves —John Onslow⟩ ⟨starlings have started to *spring-clean* their nest box —*Manchester Guardian Weekly*⟩

²spring-clean \ˈ=,=\ *n, Brit* **:** SPRING-CLEANING

spring-cleaning \ˈ=ˈ==\ *n* [²*spring* + *cleaning*] **:** the act or process of doing a thorough cleaning of a place

spring cleavers *n pl but usu sing in constr* **:** a cleavers (*Galium aparine*)

spring clip *n* **1 :** a U-shaped piece of metal used to fasten a leaf spring to the axle of a vehicle **2 :** a small clip working with a spring (as for electrical terminal connections)

spring collet *n* **:** a tempered bushing slotted at the front end and tapered externally to fit another bushing so that when the collet is drawn backward axially (as by a screw action) it closes in and grips the work

spring corn *n* **:** CORN SNOW

spring cotter *n* **:** a cotter formed of elastic metal bent double and used as a split pin — called also *spring key*

spring cowslip *n* **:** a marsh marigold (*Caltha palustris*)

spring cress *n* **:** a small white-flowered cress (*Cardamine bulbosa*) common in wet places in eastern No. America

spring·dans \ˈspriŋ,dän(t)s\ *n* -ES [Norw, fr. *springe* to jump, spring (fr. ON *springa*) + *dans* dance, fr. ON, fr. OF *dance* — more at SPRING, DANCE] **:** a Norwegian leaping dance for men

spring die *n* **:** an adjustable screw-thread die that is made of a hollow cylinder cut away at one end and leaving prongs that are provided with cutting teeth on the inside and are taper-threaded on the outside

spring dwarf *n* **:** a disease of strawberry plants caused by an eelworm (*Aphelenchoides fragariae*) and characterized by twisting, stiffness, and glossiness of the leaves and shortening of the petioles esp. of the central leaves during the early part of the growing season

¹springe \ˈsprinj\ *n* -s [ME *springe, sprenge;* akin to OE *springan* to spring — more at SPRING] **1 :** a noose fastened to an elastic body and drawn close with a sudden spring to catch a bird or other animal **2 :** SNARE, TRAP ⟨the herd mind was always laying ~s to catch the unwary —V.L.Parrington⟩

²springe \"\ *vb* **springed; springed; springeing; springes** *vt* **:** to catch in a springe **:** ENSNARE ~ *vi* **:** to set a springe

³springe \", ˈsprinzh\ *adj, dial Eng* **:** SUPPLE, AGILE

springed *past of* SPRING

¹spring·er \ˈspriŋə(r)\ *n* -s [¹*spring* + -*er*] **1 a :** a stone or other solid laid at the impost of an arch **b :** the lowest voussoir in an arch — see ARCH illustration **c :** SKEWBACK **2 :** one that springs: as **a :** SPRINGBOK **b** (1) **:** SPRINGER SPANIEL (2) **:** a spaniel that flushes game by springing **c** *Africa* (1) **:** any active leaping mullet (2) **:** TENPOUNDER **d :** FLIPPER 2d **e :** WEDGER **3 :** a cow that is nearly ready to calve **4 :** NACHSCHLAG

²springer \"\ *n* -s [²*spring* + -*er*] **1 :** an Atlantic salmon that returns to fresh water in the spring **2 :** a young chicken that is larger than a broiler and smaller than a roaster **:** FRYER

³springer \"\ *n* -s [³*spring* + -*er*] **:** one that fits with springs; *specif* **:** a worker who fixes springs in place in seats that are to be upholstered

spring·er·le \ˈs(h)priŋərlə\ *n* -s [G dial. (Alemannic), lit.,

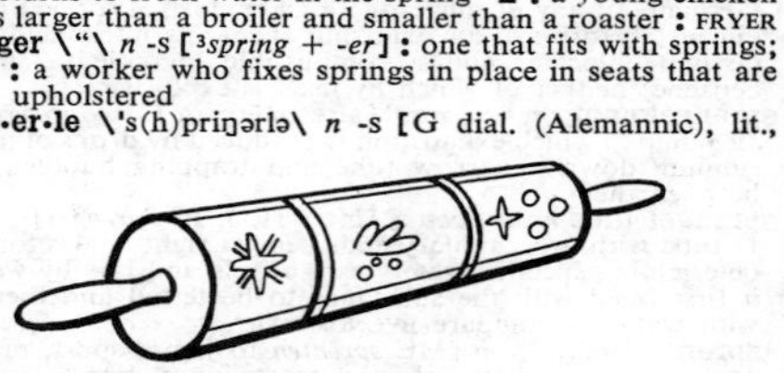
rolling pin used for springerle

hare, dim. of *springer* jumper, fr. MHG, fr. *springen* to jump (fr. OHG *springan*) + -*er* — more at SPRING] **:** a thick hard cookie that is usu. flavored with anise and has a design impressed in relief upon the dough by means of a carved board or rolling pin and that is traditionally eaten at Christmas in German-speaking countries

springer spaniel *n* [¹*springer*] **:** a medium-sized sporting dog of either of two breeds used chiefly for finding and flushing small game and having a flat or slightly waved coat usu. of white and another color, rather long legs, and a well-feathered tail carried low — see ENGLISH SPRINGER, WELSH SPRINGER SPANIEL

spring faucet *n* **:** a faucet that has to be kept open against the force of a spring that ordinarily keeps it closed

spring fever *n* **:** a lazy or restless feeling often associated with the onset of spring

¹spring·field \ˈspriŋ,fēld\ *adj, usu cap* [fr. *Springfield*, Mass., & *Springfield*, Ill.] **1 :** of or from the city of Springfield, Mass. ⟨a *Springfield* park⟩ **:** of the kind or style prevalent in Springfield **2 :** of or from Springfield, the capital of Illinois **:** of the kind or style prevalent in Springfield

²springfield \"\ *or* **springfield rifle** *n* -s *usu cap S* [fr. *Springfield*, Mass., where a United States Armory is located] **1 :** a breech-loading .45 caliber rifle used in the U. S. Army from about 1868 to 1893 and by U. S. volunteer troops in the Spanish-American War **2 :** a .30 caliber bolt-operated rifle adopted by the U. S. army in 1903 and used by U. S. troops in World War I — see RIFLE illustration

spring·field·er \-də(r)\ *n* -s *cap* [*Springfield*, Mass. & *Springfield*, Ill. + E -*er*] **:** SPRINGFIELDIAN

spring·field·ian \(ˈ)=ˈfēldēən, -dyən\ *n* -s *cap* [*Springfield*, Mass. & *Springfield*, Ill. + E -*ian*] **:** a native or resident of Springfield, esp. Springfield, Illinois or Springfield, Mass.

springfish \ˈ=,=\ *n* [²*spring* + *fish*] **1 :** MILLER'S-THUMB **2 :** SPRINGER 1

spring flood *n* [ME, fr. *spring* + *flood*] **1 :** SPRING TIDE **2 :** a flood (as from a river) occurring in the spring season

spring fly *n* **:** CADDIS FLY

springform \ˈ=,=\ *n* **:** a mold or pan having the upright rim fastened to the bottom by means of a clamp or spring that is released to detach the rim and facilitate removal of the molded or baked food

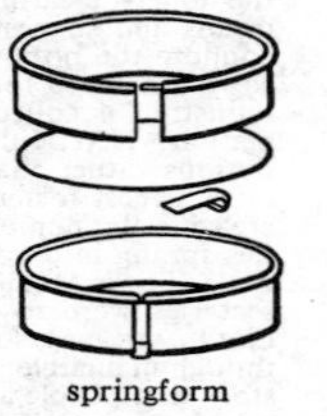
springform

spring frog *n* **1 :** GREEN FROG **2 :** LEOPARD FROG

spring grain aphis *n* **:** GREENBUG

spring green *n* **:** a variable color averaging a moderate yellow-green that is greener, lighter, and stronger than average moss green, mosstone, average pea green, or spinach green

spring gun *n* **:** SET GUN

spring·haas \ˈspriŋ,häs\ *n, pl* **springhase** \-äsə\ [Afrik, fr. *spring* to jump + *haas* hare, fr. MD *hase;* akin to OHG *haso* hare — more at SPRINGBOK, HARE] **:** JUMPING HARE

spring-hab·it·ed \ˈ=ˌhabəd·əd\ *adj, of wheat* **:** having growth of such a character as to mature and produce seed in one growing season from spring sowing — compare WINTER-HABITED

spring·halt \ˈspriŋ,=\ *n* [by alter.] **:** STRINGHALT

spring hammer *n* **:** a machine-driven hammer whose blow is caused or increased by the extension of a compressed spring or the expansion of a body of compressed air

springhare \ˈ=,=\ *n* [part trans. of Afrik *springhaas* — more at SPRINGHAAS] **:** JUMPING HARE

spring harrow *n* **:** SPRING-TOOTH HARROW

springhead \ˈ=,=\ *n* **:** FOUNTAINHEAD

spring heath *n* **:** a low European shrub (*Erica carnea*) with very early-blooming bell-shaped red flowers

spring heel *n* **1 :** a heel formed by bending the outsole over a thickness of leather between the sole and the upper at the heel **2 :** a low broad heel with wedge-shaped line at the breast that continues from the bottom of the heel to the surface of the sole at the shank

spring herring *n* **:** ALEWIFE 1a

spring hinge *n* **:** a hinge fitted with a spring to close an opened door automatically

spring hoe *n* **:** a hinged blade for a wheel hoe that is held by a spring so as to yield to obstructions

spring hook *n* **1 :** a hook with a spring snap in its end to prevent accidental unhooking — called also *snap hook* **2 :** a supplementary fishhook that springs down and secures a fish that takes the baited barbed hook — called also *snap hook, spear hook*

springhouse \ˈ=,=\ *n* **:** a small structure built over a spring and used as a cooling place (as for dairy products or meat)

springier *comparative of* SPRINGY

springiest *superlative of* SPRINGY

spring·i·ly \ˈspriŋəlē, -li\ *adv* **:** in a springy manner

spring·i·ness \-iŋēnəs, -iŋin-\ *n* -ES **:** the quality or state of being springy

springing *n* -s [ME, fr. gerund of *springen* to spring — more at SPRING] **1 :** the act, action, or process of one that springs **2 :** the architectural member that constitutes the first upward curvature of an arch or vault; *also* **:** the initial point of such curvature **3 :** the springs with which an automotive vehicle is equipped ⟨allow much softer ~ to be used at the front than the rear —*Country Life*⟩

springing bow *n* **:** a method of bowing stringed instruments so that the bow rebounds from the string — compare ARCO SALTANDO, SPICCATO

spring·ing·ly *adv* **:** in a springing manner

springing use *n* **:** a use that is limited to arise on the happening of a future event and is not dependent on any preceding use or estate and that is not in derogation of any prior estate or limited on a particular estate

spring iris *n* **:** a dwarf iris (*Iris verna*) with yellow spotted flowers resembling violets

spring key *n* **:** SPRING COTTER

spring lamb *n* **:** a market lamb born in late winter or early spring and sold fat off the dam usu. before July 1st; *also* **:** the meat of such a lamb

spring latch *n* **:** a latch that operates with a spring bolt

spring lay rope *n* **:** a composite rope having three wire and three fiber strands laid alternately around a fiber core

¹sprin·gle \ˈspriŋgəl\ *vt* -ED/-ING/-S [prob. by alter.] *archaic* **:** SPRINKLE

²springle \"\ *n* -s [prob. fr. ⁴*spring* + -*le*] **:** SPRINGE

spring leaf *n* **:** LEAF 2f (3)

spring·less \ˈ=ləs\ *adj* **1 :** being without a spring **:** lacking springs ⟨equipped with measuring rods and ~ scales —*Time*⟩ **2 :** lacking in elasticity or vitality ⟨looked at each other with wet eyes, and went off with ~ steps —Hall Caine⟩

spring·let \ˈ=lət\ *n* -s **:** a little spring **:** STREAMLET

spring ligament *n* **:** an elastic ligament of the sole of the foot that connects the calcaneus and navicular bone and supports the head of the astragalus

springlike \ˈ=,=\ *adj* **1 :** having the quality, characteristics, or effect of spring **:** VERNAL **2 :** resembling a spring or the action of a spring

spring lily *n* **:** a white-flowered dogtooth violet (*Erythronium albidum*)

spring line *n* **1 :** SPRING 11b **2 :** an imaginary line connecting the two opposite points at which the curve of an arch or vault begins

spring-load \ˈ=ˈ=\ *vt* **:** to apply force to or load by means of spring tension or compression

spring lock *n* **:** a lock that fastens with a spring bolt — distinguished from *deadlock*

spring needle *n* **:** a fine steel needle for machine knitting that has a butt at one end and a long flexible hook at the other that curves back to the shank of the needle

spring onion *n* **:** WELSH ONION

spring orange *n* **:** a white-flowered shrub (*Styrax americana*) of the southeastern U. S. having obovoid fruit

spring orchid *or* **spring orchis** *n* **:** SHOWY ORCHIS

spring peeper *n* **:** a small brown tree toad (*Hyla crucifer*) of the eastern U. S. and Canada that has an oblique dark-colored cross on the back, an angular mark between the eyes, and bars on the legs, that breeds in ponds and swamps in the spring, and that has a shrill piping call

spring pin *n* **:** an iron rod fitted between the springs and the axle boxes in locomotives to sustain and regulate the pressure on the axles

spring pole *n* **1 :** a flexible elastic pole used to act as a spring **2 :** an elastic wooden pole from which hand-operated percussion-drilling or other tools are suspended

spring-rail frog \ˈ=ˌ=-\ *n* **:** a frog having a movable wing rail held against the point rail by springs and normally presenting

an unbroken running surface to wheels using the main track but operating also to permit the passage of trailing wheels from a diverging track

spring ring *n* : PISTON RING

¹springs *pres 3d sing of* SPRING, *pl of* SPRING

²springs \'spriŋz\ *adj, usu cap* [fr. *Springs*, Union of South Africa] : of or from the city of Springs, Union of So. Africa : of the kind or style prevalent in Springs

spring salmon *n* : KING SALMON

spring saxifrage *n* : EARLY SAXIFRAGE

spring scale *n* : a scale in which the weight indications depend upon the change of shape or of dimensions of an elastic body or system of such bodies

spring scorpion grass *n* : EARLY SCORPION GRASS

spring set *n* : an arrangement of saw teeth in which alternate teeth are sprung to the right and left to make a saw kerf wider than the thickness of the blade

spring snow *n* : CORN SNOW

spring snowflake *n* : a snowflake (*Leucojum vernum*) with solitary very fragrant green-tipped white flowers borne in spring

spring starflower *n* : a spring-blooming onion-scented Argentine herb (*Spheion uniflora*) of the family Amaryllidaceae that is often cultivated for its bluish white flowers

spring stay *n* **1** : a heavy wire rope running horizontally between the mastheads of a schooner **2** : an auxiliary stay

spring steel *n* : a steel that is processed (as by cold drawing, cold rolling, or heat treating) to give it the elastic properties and yield strength useful in springs

spring switch *n* : a switch consisting of a pair of split switch points held in running position by a stiff coil spring and designed to return to that position after being thrown over by trailing wheels from the diverging route

springtail \'=,=\ *n* **1** : an arthropod of the order Collembola : COLLEMBOLAN **2** : the furcula of a collembolan

spring temper *n* : a temper induced in steel to increase its upper limit of elasticity by hardening and tempering in the ordinary way and then reheating until the steel assumes a bright blue color; *also* : a similar temper produced in brass by an extreme amount of cold rolling — **spring–tempered** \'=¦=='\ *adj*

springtide \'=,=\ *n* : SPRINGTIME ⟨in the ~ of his career⟩

spring tide *n* **1** : a tide of greater-than-average range between high and low tide that occurs twice each synodic month around the times of new and full moon when the tidal actions of the sun and moon are nearly in the same direction — compare FLOOD TIDE, NEAP TIDE **2** : a strong or heavy flow ⟨a *spring tide* of prosperity⟩

springtime \'=,=\ *n* [ME, fr. *spring* + *time*] **1 a** : the season of spring ⟨help him keep his business straighter when it grew more active in ~ —*New Yorker*⟩ **b** : YOUTH ⟨a man still in his prime but past his ~⟩ **c** : an early or flourishing stage of development ⟨the ~ of the national spirit, when the genius of the people formed customs and institutions —W.K.Ferguson⟩ **2** : a deep pink that is bluer, lighter, and stronger than average coral (sense 3b), bluer and deeper than fiesta, and yellower and deeper than begonia

spring tool *n* : a tool having a spring as an essential part of its construction: as **a** : a glassblower's tongs resembling sugar tongs without the spoon ends **b** : a lathe tool with a bend near the point to give a slight spring that makes possible a light finishing cut

spring tooth *n* : a flat coiled steel tooth (as on a cultivating or weeding machine) that digs deeply but springs backward on striking an obstruction

springtooth \'=¦=\ *vt* [*spring tooth*] : to cultivate with a spring-tooth implement

spring–tooth harrow \'=,=-\ *or* **spring–tooth drag** *also* **spring–tooth** *n* : a harrow with spring teeth

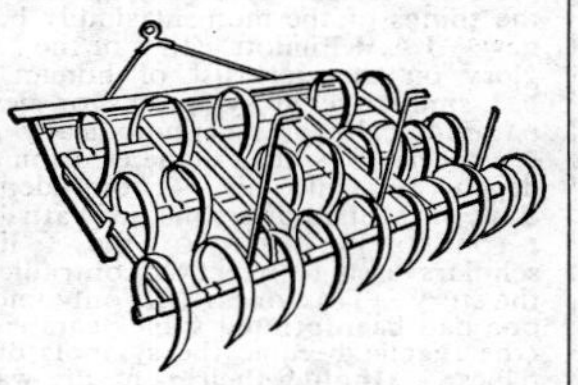

spring-tooth harrow

spring training *n* : a period usu. beginning on March 1st and extending until opening day that is used by professional esp. major league baseball teams for conditioning, practice, and exhibition games

spring–trip hoe \'=,=-\ *n* : a grain-drill furrow opener equipped with a spring hoe

spring vetch *n* : a vetch (*Vicia sativa*)

spring vetchling *n* : a European perennial herb (*Lathyrus vernus*) with nodding, racemose, violet-blue flowers

spring vise *n* **1** : a spring-actuated vise **2** : a vise for compressing springs

spring wagon *n* : a light wagon equipped with springs and formerly common on farms and ranches ⟨the *spring wagon* the boys used for hauling salt to the cattle —F.B.Gipson⟩

spring washer *n* : an elastic washer; *esp* : a strong flat spiral spring of one or two turns that is sharp-edged at the ends and used as a nut-locking device — compare LOCK WASHER

springwater \'=,==\ *n* [ME, fr. *spring* + *water*] : water from a natural spring — compare RAINWATER, SURFACE WATER

spring–well \'=,=\ *n* [²*spring* + *well*] : SPRING ⟨go down now to the *spring-well* and give him this —J.M.Synge⟩

spring wheat *n* : wheat that is sown in the spring and harvested in late summer or fall

springwood \'=,=\ *n* **1** : the portion of each annual ring of wood that develops largely early in the growing season and is softer, more porous, and lighter in weight than the adjoining summerwood because of its higher proportion of larger and thinner-walled cells — called also *earlywood;* compare SUMMERWOOD **2** : a thicket of young trees

springwort \'=,=\ *n* : a root held in European folklore to have magical properties

springy \'spriŋē, -iŋi\ *adj* -ER/-EST [²*spring* + -*y*] **1** : abounding with springs of water : SPONGY ⟨picking his way across the treacherous ~ country —Jeannie Gunn⟩ **2 a** : having an elastic quality : capable of springing back to its original shape after deformation ⟨made crossbows from the ~ horn of the musk ox —Farley Mowat⟩ **b** : having or marked by lightness and vigor of movement ⟨a ~ fellow, well set up —Amy Lowell⟩ ⟨a fine figure of a man tall, lithe, and agile, with a ~ step —A. Conan Doyle⟩ **c** : lively and resilient underfoot ⟨thickly covered with heath and ling and moor plants ~ to the tread —A.L.Rowse⟩ ⟨a ballroom with floor made ~ for dancing —*Amer. Guide Series: Md.*⟩ **syn** see FLEXIBLE

sprink *vt* [ME *sprinken*; akin to ME *sprenklen, sprinclen* to sprinkle — more at SPRINKLE] *obs* : SPRINKLE

¹sprin·kle \'spriŋkəl\ *vb* **sprinkled; sprinkled; sprinkling** \-k(ə)liŋ\ **sprinkles** [ME *sprenklen, sprinclen;* akin to MD, MLG, & MHG *sprenkel*, sprinkel spot, Icel *sprekla* spot, OE *spearca* spark — more at SPARK] *vt* **1 a** : to scatter in drops or particles ⟨it *sprinkled* rain late in the afternoon, just enough to remove some of the dust from the infield —*Nashville Tennessean*⟩ ⟨~ a little bird sand on the feeding board —William Powell-Owen⟩ **b** : to scatter widely : distribute sparsely ⟨a series of model houses *sprinkled* about the grounds —Betty Pepis⟩ **2 a** : to scatter over : BESPRINKLE, SPOT — usu. used with *with* ⟨*sprinkled* that roof with lightning rods —Eudora Welty⟩ ⟨his ill-fitting clothes were usually *sprinkled* with cigarette ashes —Samuel Lubell⟩ **b** : to scatter at intervals in or among : DIVERSIFY, DOT, INTERSPERSE — usu. used with *with* ⟨~*s* his programs generously with such light works —Green Peyton⟩ ⟨a propaganda tract *sprinkled* with glib half-truths —Theodore Brameld⟩ ⟨a heavily wooded section *sprinkled* with small lakes —*Amer. Guide Series: Pa.*⟩ **c** : to wet lightly ⟨*sprinkled* the flowers⟩ ⟨the rain *sprinkled* the grass⟩ **d** : to spatter small drops of color on the smoothly cut edges of (books) or acid on the surface of (smooth leather) ⟨*sprinkled* edges⟩ ⟨*sprinkled* calf binding⟩ **3 a** : to cleanse with or as if with a few drops of water : PURIFY ⟨our hearts *sprinkled* clean from an evil conscience —Heb 10:22 (RSV)⟩ **b** : to baptize by aspersion or by the application of a few drops of water ~ *vi* **1** : to scatter a liquid in fine drops ⟨shall ~ of the oil with his finger seven times —Lev 14:16 (AV)⟩ **2** : to rain lightly in scattered drops ⟨it began to ~⟩

²sprinkle \"\ *n* -S **1 a** : the act or an instance of sprinkling ⟨the ~ and trickle filter treatment of sewage —*Building, Estimating & Contracting*⟩; *specif* : a light rain ⟨a brief ~ that hardly wet the ground⟩ **b** : something scattered about or sparsely distributed ⟨they came out of the tunnel into a ~ of lights and houses —Katherine Mansfield⟩ ⟨gathering field peas or the last ~ of late cotton —Frances Gaither⟩ **c** : a small particle intended or suitable for sprinkling — usu. used in pl. ⟨covered it with chocolate ~*s* —Evan Hunter⟩ **2** : a mottled color effect

¹sprin·kler \'spriŋk(ə)lə(r)\ *n* -S [¹*sprinkle* + -*er*] **1** : a machine or device for sprinkling: as **a** : a vehicle or an attachment to a vehicle for sprinkling streets or roads **b** (1) : SPRINKLER HEAD (2) : SPRINKLER SYSTEM **c** : a device for spraying plants or lawns **d** : a device for distributing sewage on a filter bed **2** : one that sprinkles: as **a** : one that sprinkles timbers in mines with chemicals to make them proof against fire and rot **b** : one that sprinkles dry coal or dust in a mine with water to prevent explosions **c** : a laundry worker who uses a sprinkler to dampen clothes for ironing **3** : one that believes in baptism by aspersion rather than by immersion

²sprinkler \"\ *vt* -ED/-ING/-S : to provide with an automatic sprinkler system ⟨stressing the importance of having all schools ~*ed* —*Springfield (Mass.) Daily News*⟩

sprinkler head *n* : the outlet of a sprinkler system that is usu. a valve held closed by a strut having separable parts joined with solder of a predetermined melting point (as 160° F.) that fuses when exposed to fire temperatures and allows the head to open or by a quartz bulb containing a liquid that expands when heated and bursts the bulb

sprinkler leakage insurance *n* : insurance against loss resulting from damage to property caused by the accidental discharge of water from an automatic sprinkler system

sprinkler system *n* **1** : a system for protection against fire in which pipes are distributed for conveying water or other extinguishing fluid to outlets and that is usu. designed to function automatically with the action of heat on the automatic sprinkler head or on a controlling thermostatic system — see DRY-PIPE SYSTEM, WET-PIPE SYSTEM **2** : a system for sprinkling water to lay dust (as in coal mines)

sprinkling *n* -S [ME *sprenkling*, fr. gerund of *sprenklen, sprinklen* to sprinkle — more at SPRINKLE] **1** : the act or process of one that sprinkles **2 a** : a limited quantity or amount : a slight portion : MODICUM ⟨has a ~ of learning⟩ ⟨hasn't even a ~ of common sense⟩ **b** : a small quantity falling or made to fall in scattered drops or particles ⟨a ~ of snow⟩ ⟨a ~ of pepper⟩ **c** : a relatively small number distributed at random : SCATTERING ⟨the sandy soil of the plain had a light ~ of junipers —Willa Cather⟩ ⟨among them were thousands of artisans, a ~ of intellectuals, and political refugees —S.E. Morison & H.S.Commager⟩

sprinkling can *n* : a can used for sprinkling usu. in a flower bed — see CAN illustration

¹sprint \'sprint\ *vb* -ED/-ING/-S [of Scand origin; akin to Sw dial. *sprinta* to jump, hop, ON *spretta* to spurt, start up, jump up; akin to OE *gesprintan* to emit, utter, OHG *sprinzan* to jump up, Gk *spyrthizein* to jump up, OSlav *prędati* to jump, tremble, Skt *spardhate* he contends, fights] *vi* : to run or go at top speed esp. for a relatively short distance ⟨a rabbit ~*ing* back to cover from far out in the field —T.H.White b. 1906⟩ ~ *vt* : to traverse by sprinting

²sprint \"\ *n* -S **1** : the act or an instance of sprinting : a short run or burst of activity at top speed **2 a** : DASH 7b(1) **b** : a burst of speed in longer races ⟨a ~ at the finish⟩ **c** : a horse race of not more than a mile in distance

sprint·er \-tə(r)\ *n* -S : one that sprints; *esp* : one that competes in sprint races ⟨a champion ~⟩

sprint medley *n* : a medley relay run by a team of four men who run distances of 440 yards, 220 yards, 220 yards, and 880 yards respectively

sprint race *n* : a short footrace of usu. less than a quarter of a mile in distance that is run at top speed

¹sprit \'sprit, *usu* -id·+V\ *n* -S [ME *spret, sprit*, fr. OE *sprēot* pole, spear; akin to OE *sprūtan* to sprout — more at SPROUT] **1** *archaic* : a boat pole **2** : a spar that crosses a fore-and-aft sail diagonally from the mast near the tack of the sail to the upper aftmost corner that it extends and elevates

²sprit \"\ *vi* **spritted; spritted; spritting; sprits** [ME *sprutten*, fr. OE *spryttan;* akin to MHG *sprützen* to sprout, squirt, Norw *spruta* to spurt, squirt, OE *sprūtan* to sprout — more at SPROUT] : SPROUT, BUD, GERMINATE

³sprit \"\ *n* -S **1** : SHOOT, SPROUT **2** *chiefly Scot* : a reedy plant : RUSH **3** : a fine speck in unbleached linen — usu. used in pl.

sprite \'sprīt, *usu* -īd·+V\ *n* -S [ME *sprit*, fr. OF *esprit*, fr. L *spiritus* — more at SPIRIT] **1 a** *archaic* : inner being : SOUL ⟨his clear ~ yet reigns o'er earth —P.B.Shelley⟩ **b** : a disembodied spirit : GHOST, SHADE ⟨little ghost ~*s* of dust sprang up and danced across the shimmering plain —Francis Birtles⟩ **2 a** : ELF, FAIRY ⟨the witch, the ~, the goblin — where are they —E.A.Poe⟩ **b** : an elfish person ⟨he was a tricksy ~ for whom stone walls did not a prison make —Douglas Bush⟩ **3** *or* **sprite crab** : SAND CRAB 1b

sprite·li·ness \-lēnəs, -lin-\ *archaic var of* SPRIGHTLINESS

sprite·ly \-lē, -li\ *archaic var of* SPRIGHTLY

sprit·sail \'spritsəl (*usual nautical pronunc*), -,sāl\ *n* [ME *spretseil, spritseil*, fr. *spret, sprit* sprit + *seil* sail — more at SPRIT, SAIL] **1** : a sail extended by a sprit **2** : a sail formerly hung under the bowsprit from a yard

spritsail yard *n* : a yard across a bowsprit to support a spritsail

sprittail \'=,=\ *n* [¹*sprit* + *tail*] : PINTAIL 1a

sprit·ty *or* **sprit·tie** \'spridē, -itē, -i\ *adj* [³*sprit* + -*y*] *Scot* : full of rushes

spritz \'s(h)prits\ *vt* -ED/-ING/-ES [PaG *schpritze*, fr. MHG *sprützen* to sprout, squirt — more at SPRIT] *dial* : SPRAY, SQUIRT

spritz·er \-sə(r)\ *n* -S [G, fr. *spritzen* to squirt, spray (fr. MHG *sprützen* to sprout, squirt) + -*er*] : a drink of white wine and soda water

sproat \'sprōt, *usu* -ōd·+V\ *or* **sproat hook** *n* -S [after W. H. *Sproat*, 19th cent. Englishman who invented it] : a light fishhook with a gradual or flattened bend — see FISHHOOK illustration

sprock·et \'spräkət, *usu* -əd·+V\ *n* -S [origin unknown] **1** : a piece of wood fastened to the upper surface of a rafter to effect a change in the angle of the roof where it overhangs the wall of the building **2 a** : a tooth or projection (as on the periphery of a wheel) shaped so as to engage with a chain **b** : SPROCKET WHEEL **c** : a toothed cylinder or wheel that engages the perforations of a motion-picture film to carry it through a mechanism (as a projector)

sprocket wheel *n* : a wheel with cogs or sprockets to engage with the links of a chain or accurately pitched blocks on a cable — see CHAIN GEAR; BICYCLE illustration

sprod \'spräd\ *n* -S [origin unknown] : a sea trout smolt

sprot \'sprät, *usu* -äd·+V\ *archaic var of* SPRAT

¹sprout \'spraůt, *usu* -aůd·+V\ *vb* -ED/-ING/-S [ME *spruten, sprouten*, fr. OE *sprūtan;* akin to OFris *sprūta* to sprout, MD & MLG *sprūten*, OHG *spriozan* to sprout, Goth *sprauto* rapidly, W *ffrwst* haste, Gk *speirein* to scatter, sow, sprinkle, Arm *p'aratem* I disperse, take away; basic meaning: to scatter, sow] *vi* **1 a** : to grow, spring up, or come forth as a sprout ⟨vegetation that ~*ed* in a dried-up watercourse —Francis King⟩ ⟨feathers do not ~ uniformly, but grow in patches —J.M.Downs⟩ ⟨bowler hats banished by the war have been seen ~*ing* like mushrooms —*Britain Today*⟩ ⟨parodies ~*ed* like weeds —J.D.Hart⟩ — often used with *from, out*, or *up* ⟨a long, lean individual with whitish stubble ~*ing* from his lantern jaw —F.V.W.Mason⟩ ⟨limbs ~*ing* out two hundred feet from the ground —Norman Mailer⟩ ⟨giant shopping centers that have ~*ed* up across the country —*Newsweek*⟩ **b** : to send new shoots forth or up : to develop new growth : BUD, GERMINATE ⟨in that area the young grass ~*s* at least a month earlier —James Stevenson-Hamilton⟩ ⟨the bright green of the ~*ing* bracken —Algernon Blackwood⟩ ⟨potatoes kept too warm will ~ prematurely⟩ **2** : to expand enormously in bulk when heated — used esp. of some forms of graphite mica and esp. vermiculite ~ *vt* **1 a** : to send (as a sprout) forth or up : to cause (a new growth) to develop : GROW ⟨trees ~*ing* their new green leaves⟩ ⟨jurors who ~ beards during overnight deliberations —*N.Y.Times Mag.*⟩ **b** : to cause (a plant or seed) to burgeon or germinate ⟨the big rainy season . . . is as necessary for ~*ing* the seeds of the saguaro —D.C.Peattie⟩ **2** : to support or give rise to (something) in the manner of sprouting ⟨rooftops began to ~ antennae —*Amer. Guide Series: Wash.*⟩ ⟨the same soil can seemingly ~ suburban homes of rare beauty —E.H.Pickering⟩ ⟨may be ~*ing* neuroses like dandelions —G.W.Johnson⟩

²sprout \"\ *n* -S [ME, fr. *spruten, sprouten*, v.] **1** : the shoot of a plant: **a** : a shoot from the seed **b** : the young growth from a root or tuber **c** : a shoot or sucker from the root or trunk of a tree **2** : something similar or likened to a sprout in appearance or development: as **a** : a person in his early years : OFFSHOOT, SCION ⟨a ~ who wants to go to school but isn't old enough —*New Yorker*⟩ ⟨hanging around to listen were young ~*s*, 16, 18, seldom 20 —Mari Sandoz⟩ ⟨was now the turn of these young ~*s* to get their ears beaten back —*Key Reporter*⟩ **b** : a new growth or development ⟨small ~*s* of liberal thought and practice make their appearance —L.S.Fever⟩ ⟨new ~*s* included the only large aviation gas refinery —E.O.Hauser⟩ **3 sprouts** *pl* **a** : BRUSSELS SPROUTS **b** : BEAN SPROUTS **c** : KALE **4** : COPPICE 3

³sprout *vb* [prob. of Scand origin; akin to Norw *spruta* to spurt, squirt — more at SPRIT] *obs* : SPOUT, SPURT

sprout cell *n* : a cell developed by budding from a similar mother cell

sprout·er \'spraůd·ə(r), -aůtə-\ *n* -S : a device for germinating grains (as oats) for feeding livestock

sprout forest *n* : a forest consisting of trees grown from root or stump suckers

sprouting *n* -S **1** : the act or process of one that sprouts **2** : a new growth or shoot : SPROUT

sprouting broccoli *n* : BROCCOLI 2

sprouting crab grass *n* : an annual grass (*Panicum dichotomiflorum*) found chiefly in the southern U.S. that roots much at the lower nodes

sproutland \'=,=\ *n* : an area covered by a sprout forest

sprout·ling \'spraůtliŋ, -lēŋ\ *n* -S : a small sprout or offshoot ⟨a ~ of the giant tree —William Beebe⟩ ⟨his little ~ of a poem —Amy Lowell⟩

¹spruce \'sprüs\ *n* -S *often attrib* [fr. obs. *Spruce* Prussia, fr. ME, alter. of *Pruce*, fr. OF] **1 a** : an evergreen tree of the genus *Picea* marked by dense foliage forming a conical head and widely cultivated for ornament **b** : the light soft moderately strong wood of the spruce tree that is less resinous than pine and is used esp. for timbers, millwork, and musical instruments — compare FIR **c** : any of several other coniferous trees (as the Douglas fir) **2** : a variable color averaging a dark grayish green that is bluer and stronger than average ivy, bluer and darker than Persian green, and bluer, lighter, and slightly stronger than hemlock green **3** : SPRUCE BEER

²spruce \"\ *adj, often* -ER/-EST [perh. fr. obs. E *Spruce* (*leather*), a kind of smart leather imported from Prussia and used to make jerkins] **1** : SMART, ACTIVE, SPIRITED ⟨a ~, lively air, fashionable dress —Earl of Chesterfield⟩ ⟨the thick orchestral texture is well recorded and some of the chording is admirably ~ —Edward Sackville-West & Desmond Shawe-Taylor⟩ ⟨even pedestrian old stuff is pretty ~ under his editing, and the really good jokes take wing —D.T.W.McCord⟩ **2** : neat, clean-lined, or smart in appearance : TRIM ⟨how ~ he looks in his finery —W.E.M.Campbell⟩ ⟨had great neatness of person, and he continued to wear his ~ black coat and his bowler hat . . . in a dapper, jaunty manner —W.S.Maugham⟩ ⟨the store looked cheerful and ~ and spanking clean —Arthur Cavanaugh⟩

³spruce \"\ *vb* -ED/-ING/-S *vt* : to make (a person or thing) trim, smart, or spruce ⟨the interior . . . was so *spruced*, so glistening with white paint —Sylvia T. Warner⟩ ⟨*sprucing* himself for the party⟩ — often used with *up* ⟨bought a buggy and came to town *spruced* up in store clothes —W.A.White⟩ ⟨amusement arcades have *spruced* themselves up for the summer season —D.K.Keay⟩ ⟨a short collection of notions . . . some of them *spruced* up as epigrams, others running as long as a page —*New Yorker*⟩ ~ *vi* : to make oneself spruce — usu. used with *up* ⟨makes a mad dash for the comfortable waiting rooms . . . to ~ up a bit —Lynn Grok⟩ ⟨~ up, child, shoulders back, smile, look pleasant —*N.Y.Times*⟩

⁴spruce \"\ *adv, often* -ER/-EST : SPRUCELY

spruce aphid *n* : a small deep green aphid (*Elatobium abietinum*) that attacks the needles of spruces

spruce beer *n* : a beverage flavored with spruce: **a** : one made from spruce twigs and leaves boiled with molasses or sugar and fermented with yeast **b** : a fermented beverage made with an extract of spruce twigs and leaves

spruce beetle *n* : a beetle that attacks the spruce; *esp* : any of several bark beetles of the genus *Dendroctonus* whose larvae feed beneath the bark and often cause severe damage

spruce borer *n* : the larva of any of several beetles of the families Cerambycidae and Buprestidae or of various bark beetles that develops in the wood or beneath the bark of spruce trees

spruce bud midge *n* : a cecidomyiid fly (*Rhabdophaga swainei*) that causes bud gall on white spruce in eastern Canada

spruce bud moth *n* **1** : the adult of the spruce budworm **2** : an olethreutid moth (*Zeiraphera ratzeburgiana*) the larva of which feeds on spruce buds in northern U.S. and in Canada

spruce budworm *n* : a caterpillar that is the larva of a tortricid moth (*Choristoneura fumiferana*) and feeds on the needles of the terminal shoots of spruce, balsam fir, and other evergreen trees in the northern U.S. and in Canada

spruce coneworm *n* : the larva of a phycitid moth (*Dioryctria reniculella*) that feeds on young cones of spruce in the northeastern U.S. and eastern Canada

spruce extract *n* : waste sulfite liquor containing salts of ligninsulfonic acids and purified for use chiefly in tanning leather

spruce fir *n* [*spruce* fr. obs. E *Spruce* Prussia] : any of several spruces; *esp* : NORWAY SPRUCE

spruce foliage worm *n* : SPRUCE CONEWORM

spruce gall aphid *n* : any of several aphids of the genus *Adelges* that cause galls on the leaf shoots of spruce trees

spruce green *n* : SEA GREEN 1a

spruce grouse *or* **spruce partridge** *n* : a grouse (*Canachites canadensis*) of the forests of northern No. America chiefly north of the U.S. whose plumage is extensively barred with black with the adult male being nearly black below

spruce gum *n* : an oleoresinous exudation esp. from the red spruce or the black spruce used as a chewing gum or expectorant

spruce·ly *adv* [²*spruce* + -*ly*] : in a spruce manner : NEATLY, TRIMLY ⟨he dressed ~ —Robert Graves⟩ ⟨the buildings are ~ painted —*Amer. Guide Series: Wash.*⟩

spruce spider mite *or* **spruce mite** *n* : a dark green spiny mite (*Oligonychus ununguis*) that attacks spruce and other coniferous or deciduous trees in several parts of the U.S.

spruce·ness *n* -ES : the quality or state of being spruce ⟨the army leaves its marks of physical ~ —Dixon Wecter⟩ ⟨the curious confusion of ~ and squalor —W.C.Brownell⟩

spruce oil *n* : a colorless to light yellow pleasant-smelling essential oil obtained from the needles and twigs of various spruces and hemlocks and used chiefly in scenting soap and cosmetics and in medicinal preparations

spruce pine *n* **1** : any of various American pines with light soft wood: **a** : a pine (*Pinus glabra*) of the southern U.S. **b** : YELLOW PINE 1a **c** : WHITE PINE 1a **d** : LODGEPOLE PINE **2** : EASTERN HEMLOCK **3** : any of several spruces; *esp* : BLACK SPRUCE 1

sprucer *comparative of* SPRUCE

spruces *pl of* SPRUCE, *pres 3d sing of* SPRUCE

spruce sawfly *n* : any of several sawflies (family Diprionidae) whose larvae feed on spruce; *esp* : EUROPEAN SPRUCE SAWFLY

sprucest *superlative of* SPRUCE

spruce yellow *n* : a dark orange yellow to light yellowish brown that is very slightly yellower than cotrine

sprucing *pres part of* SPRUCE

sprucy \'sprüsē, -si\ *adj* -ER/-EST [²*spruce* + -*y*] : SPRUCE ⟨little tufts of white in her hair . . . looked real ~ —Alma Stone⟩ ⟨you don't look ~ like you did —J.C.Harris⟩

¹sprue \'sprü\ n -s [D *spruw*, fr. MD *sprouwe*; akin to MLG *sprüwe*, a kind of tumor] : a chronic deficiency disease characterized by a frothy fatty diarrhea and other digestive disturbances, a sore mouth and tongue, and macrocytic anemia that occurs in a tropical form which attacks chiefly adults and a nontropical form which begins usu. in childhood

²sprue \'\ n -s [origin unknown] **1 a** : the hole through which metal or plastics is poured into the gate and thence into a mold **b** : the waste piece cast in this hole : DROSS **2 a** : the part of each impression of a drop-forging die that receives the rough bar from which the forging is made and connects the edge of the die block with the gate or flash **b** : the waste portion of a drop forging that fills the sprue in the dies

³sprue \'\ n -s [origin unknown] : spindling asparagus

spru·er \'srü(r), -ü(ə)r, -üə\ n -s [²*sprue* + *-er*] : one that attends to the sprue occupying the gate in the process of casting iron

sprug \'sprəg\ n -s [origin unknown] *chiefly Scot* : HOUSE SPARROW

sprui·ker \'srükə(r)\ n -s [Austral. slang *spruik* to give a speech, make a barker's spiel (of unknown origin) + *-er*] *Austral* : BARKER

spruit \'srüt, -rät\ n -s [Afrik, shoot, small stream, fr. MD *sprute*, fr. *spruten* to sprout — more at SPROUT] : a small often dry tributary stream in southern Africa

sprung [ME *sprungen* (past pl. & past part.), fr. OE *sprungon* (past pl.), *sprungen* (past part.)] *past of* SPRING

sprung hock n : a horse's hock swollen from strain; *also* : the condition or the swelling : CURB

sprung rhythm n : a poetic rhythm designed to approximate the natural rhythm of speech and characterized by the frequent juxtaposition of single accented syllables and the occurrence of mixed types of feet (as the accentual trochee, dactyl, and first paeon) whose sequence is broken or interrupted by outrides

sprung weight n : weight supported by springs

¹sprunt \'sprənt, -rünt\ vi -ED/-ING/-S [prob. of Scand origin; akin to Sw dial. *sprunta* to jump, *sprinta* to jump, hop — more at SPRINT] *dial Eng* : to make a quick convulsive movement : JUMP, RUN

²sprunt \'\ n -s *dial Eng* : a spasmodic movement : SPRING

³sprunt \'\ adj [of Scand origin; akin to Sw dial. *sprant* lively, brisk, *sprinta* to jump, hop] *obs* : ACTIVE, BRISK, SPRUCE

spry \'sprī\ adj, usu -ER/-EST [perh. of Scand origin; akin to Sw dial *sprygg* very lively; perh. akin to Sw dial. *spragg*, *sprag* branch — more at SPRIG] : vigorously active : CHIPPER, NIMBLE, BRISK ⟨75 years old and ~ as a kitten —Winifred Bambrick⟩ ⟨his ~, youthful vigor and unimpaired energy —Hervey Allen⟩ ⟨their ~ cockney or colonial idiom —Leslie Rees⟩ syn see AGILE

spry·ly adv : in a spry manner : with spryness

spry·ness n -ES : the quality or state of being spry

SPS abbr, often not cap [L *sine prole superstite*] without surviving issue

spt abbr **1** seaport **2** split **3** support

¹spud \'spəd\ n -s [ME *spudde*; perh. akin to OE *spadu*, *spædu* spade — more at SPADE] **1** obs : a short knife : DAGGER **2** : any of various tools or mechanical devices like a spade or a chisel and with a short, thick or widened, and often curved blade: as **a** (1) : a sharp narrow spade sometimes with prongs instead of a smooth blade commonly having a long handle and used esp. for digging up large-rooted weeds (2) : a similarly shaped implement used for removing the bark from timber **b** : a small shovel with a crowbar point on one end used for digging holes under stumps — called also *stump spud* **c** (1) : a broad-bladed socketed stone or metal tool typical of midwestern and eastern No. America (2) : a socketed spearhead that is slipped on the end of a lath for spearing tobacco **d** : a long-handled chisel used for cutting holes through the ice **e** (1) : a small instrument shaped like a spade for removing foreign bodies esp. from the eye (2) : such an instrument for removing wax from the ear **f** : a reamer for enlarging a well around lost tools so that fishing tools can go over the lost article **g** : SPADE LUG **3** : POTATO **4 a** : one of usu. four sharp-pointed vertical posts or piles that can be forced by a tackle or by power through a socket in a floating or a land dredge or scow to anchor it **b** : one of the two foot pieces of the legs of the A-frame of a floating dipper dredge that are set in the banks of the ditch to steady the dredge and give it support **5 a** : a short connecting piece (as a piece of pipe between a cock and a supply pipe) **b** : a short thick insert or projection (as from a valve or ceramic piece) to which some other part is screwed **6** : percussion drilling used in starting a well in which a line is used to impart an up-and-down motion to the cable holding the tools to cause them to rise and fall

²spud \'\ vb spudded; spudded; spudding; spuds vt **1** : to dig, remove, or otherwise treat with a spud ⟨*spudding* up weeds⟩ **2** : to begin to drill (an oil well) by alternately raising and releasing a spudding bit with the drilling rig ⟨honor those who helped ~ America's first great gusher —*Christian Science Monitor*⟩ — often used with *in* ⟨expected that the well will be *spudded* in before the end of July —*Wall Street Jour.*⟩ ⟨an agreement to ~ in the first well within 30 days —Upton Sinclair⟩ **3** : to scrape off (as burrs caused by punching or reaming) around holes **4** : to anchor or hold steady (as a derrick or dredge) by means of spuds ⟨placed in position on the bay bottom and *spudded* in place by H-piles driven within the pipes —P.A.Hakman⟩ ~ vi **1** : to dig with a spud **2** : to begin to drill an oil well with a spudding bit ⟨company has *spudded* and yesterday was drilling at 582 feet —*Los Angeles (Calif.) Examiner*⟩ — often used with *in* ⟨the driller got busy . . . *spudding* in through the soft, wet earth —*Lamp*⟩

spud casing n : a well in the hull of a dredge through which a spud can be raised or lowered

spud·der \'spədə(r)\ n -s **1 a** : one that sets up and operates a well-drilling machine **b** : a light duty drilling rig used primarily to start a new well **2 a** : PEELER 1b **b** : a tool that removes bark from timber : BARKER, BARK SPUD

spudding bar n : a bar having a cutting end for spudding holes

spudding bit n : a broad dull drilling tool used for the preliminary boring of wells through earth down to rock or other solid substrata

spud·dle \'spəd³l\ vi [blend of ¹*spud* and *puddle*] *archaic* : PUDDLE

spud·dy \'spədē *also* 'spüdē\ adj -ER/-EST [¹*spud* + *-y*] : PUDGY

spue *var of* SPEW

spuf·fle \'spüfl\ vi [prob. of imit. origin] *dial Eng* : FUSS, BUSTLE

¹spule \'spül\ *Scot var of* SPOOL

²spule \'\ n -s [prob. alter. of *spauld*] *Scot* : SHOULDER

spule-bane \'\ n [²*spule* + *bane* (bone)] *Scot* : SHOULDER BLADE

¹spulzie \'spül(y)ē\ vb -ED/-ING/-S [alter. (z being taken as z) of earlier *spulzie*, fr. ME (Sc) *spulzien*, *spolyen*, fr. MF *espoillier* — more at SPOIL] *chiefly Scot* : PLUNDER

²spulzie \'\ n -s [alter. (z being taken as z) of earlier *spulzie*, fr. ME (Sc) *spolzei*, fr. MF *espoille*, *espuille* — more at SPOIL] **1** *chiefly Scot* : an act or instance of unlawfully and violently dispossessing a person of his movables **2** *chiefly Scot* : SPOIL, BOOTY

¹spume \'spyüm\ n -s [ME, fr. MF *espume*, *spume*, fr. L *spuma* — more at FOAM] : frothy matter raised on liquids by boiling, effervescence, or agitation : FROTH, FOAM, SCUM ⟨sea encumbered by rain-washed boulders and ruffed with sea ~ —Han Suyin⟩ ⟨swung down the gleaming incline while long feathers of ~ streamed out behind his horse —J.R.Ullman⟩ ⟨spat forth among men a ~ of things impure —H.O.Taylor⟩

²spume \'\ vb -ED/-ING/-S vi **1** : FROTH, FOAM ⟨a waterfall . . . steaming and *spuming* among the pebbles —Frederic Prokosch⟩ ⟨the yellow bench of reef *spuming* with surf — John Dos Passos⟩ ~ vt : to discharge or spout (something) like froth or foam — often used with *forth* ⟨volcanoes ~ forth fire and lava⟩

spu·mes·cence \spyü'mes³n(t)s\ n -s [¹*spume* + *-escence*] : the quality or state of being foamy or frothy

spu·mes·cent \(')'mes³nt\ adj [¹*spume* + *-escent*] : FROTHY, FOAMY

spu·moid \'spyü,mȯid\ adj [¹*spume* + *-oid*] : ALVEOLAR

spu·mo·ni \spü'mōnē, spə'm-\ \-,(,)nä\ n -s

[It *spumone*, aug. of *spuma* foam, froth, fr. L — more at FOAM] : ice cream molded in layers of different colors, flavors, and textures often with candied fruits and nuts and served in sections

spu·mose \'spyü,mōs, ₌'₌\ adj [L *spumosus*] : SPUMY

spu·mous \₌'₌, -məs\ adj [ME, fr. L *spumosus*, fr. *spuma* foam + *-osus* *-ous*, *-ose* — more at FOAM] : SPUMY

spumy \'spyü-, -mi\ adj, usu -ER/-EST [¹*spume* + *-y*] : marked by or covered with spume : of frothy or foamy consistency or appearance

spun [ME *spunnen* (past pl. & past part.), fr. OE *spunnon* (past pl.), *gespunnen* (past part.)] *past of* SPIN

spun-dyed \'₌'₌\ adj : dyed during the spinning process — used of a synthetic filament, staple, or yarn

¹spung \'spəŋ\ n -s [prob. alter. of ME *punge*, fr. OE *pung*; akin to MLG *punge* purse, OHG *scazfung*, ON *pungr*, Goth *pungs* purse, and perh. to OE *pocca*, *pohha* bag, pocket — more at POKE] *chiefly Scot* : PURSE

²spung \'\ vt, *Scot* : ROB

spunge *var of* SPONGE

spun glass n **1** : FIBER GLASS **2** : blown glass that has slender threads of glass incorporated in it often in the form of a spiral or network

spun hay n : hay twisted into ropes for convenient carriage

¹spunk \'spəŋk\ n -s [ScGael *spong* tinder, sponge, fr. L *spongia* sponge — more at SPONGE] **1** *dial Brit* **a** : a small portion or bit : SPARK, GLEAM **b** : a small fire **c** : ³MATCH 2a **2 a** : a wood or woody substance prepared for use as tinder : TOUCHWOOD, PUNK **b** : any of various fungi used to make tinder **3** : METTLE, PLUCK, COURAGE ⟨assigned themes on the ~ of great persons who had overcome physical handicaps —Robert Lowell⟩ ⟨enough ~ in the department to resent such an arrogant blow at its prestige —H.L.Ickes⟩ **4** : SPIRIT, LIVELINESS ⟨as for his musical efforts . . . who could play with such tremendous ~ —William Black⟩ ⟨a story told with rare ~, with the repetition and the surprise action small listeners love —N.Y. Herald Tribune Bk. Rev.⟩

²spunk \'\ vb -ED/-ING/-S vi **1** *Scot* : to come to light : become known — usu. used with *out* **2** *dial* : to assert oneself in a spirited or courageous manner : show spirit — usu. used with *up* ~ vt : to work up : muster — usu. used with *up* ⟨has ~ed up courage to tell the awful truth about the fallout —*New Republic*⟩

spunk·ie \'spəŋki\ n -s [¹*spunk* + *-ie*] **1** *Scot* : IGNIS FATUUS **2** *Scot* : LIQUOR **3** *Scot* : a spirited or quick-tempered person

spunk·i·ly \'spəŋkəlē, -li\ adv : in a spunky manner

spunk·i·ness \-kēnəs, -ki-\ n -ES : the quality or state of being spunky

spunky \-kē, -ki\ adj, usu ⟨ER/-EST **1** : full of spunk : COURAGEOUS, PLUCKY ⟨the children are ~ and determined —N.Y. Times Bk. Rev.⟩ **2** *dial Brit* : shining brightly : SPARKLING **3** : IRRITABLE, IRASCIBLE, TESTY ⟨that ~, crotchety, illiterate and wonderfully gifted maker of things —Brendan Gill⟩ ⟨cross and ~, and both too proud to speak —W.M.Carleton⟩ **4** : full of life : ANIMATED, SPIRITED ⟨was . . . an armful of ~ vitality —James Thurber⟩ ⟨were there for ~ debate —*Newsweek*⟩

spun rayon n : a yarn or fabric made wholly or chiefly of rayon staple ⟨butcher linen made of *spun rayon*⟩

spun silk n : a yarn or fabric made from short unreelable silk fibers that have been degummed — compare REELED SILK

spun sugar n : a garnish resembling floss made from sugar boiled to the long thread stage when the threads are gathered up and shaped into the desired forms or heaped upon a stick as a candy

spun yarn n **1** : a textile yarn spun from staple-length fiber **2** : a small rope or stuff formed of two or more yarns loosely twisted and used for seizings esp. on board ship

¹spur \R \'spor, + vowel 'spor-; -R \'spər, + suffixal vowel 'spor- *also* \spòr, + vowel in a following word 'spor- *or* 'spò *also* 'spòr'\ n -s often *attrib* [ME *spore*, *spure*, fr. OE *spora*, *spura*; akin to OHG *sporo* spur, ON *spori* spur, OE *spurnan* to kick — more at SPURN] **1 a** : a U-shaped implement with a pointed or rowel-tipped

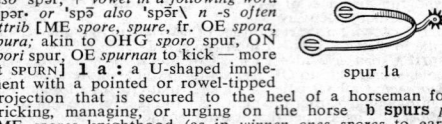

spur 1a

projection that is secured to the heel of a horseman for pricking, managing, or urging on the horse ⟨**b** spurs *pl* [ME *spores* knighthood (as in *winnen ones spores* to earn knighthood by a deed of valor)] : recognition and reward for achievement ⟨would have won his ~s had not a knee injury . . . put him out of the game —*Rugger*⟩ ⟨these guys have earned their battle ~s —L.M.Uris⟩ **2** : an inciting force or stimulus to action : GOAD, INCENTIVE ⟨he shot up fast, his ~ the determination to make money and a name —E.A.Weeks⟩ ⟨two professors were immediate ~s to trying her hand at writing —*Current Biog.*⟩ ⟨the book is a ~ to both the intellect and the imagination —Ellen L. Buell⟩ **3** : any of various diagonally set props, braces, or members usu. used in construction: as **a** : a brace (as a rafter or crossbeam) strengthening a post and some connected part : STRUT **b** (1) : a reinforcing buttress of masonry **c** (1) : a piece of timber fixed on the bilge ways before launching with the upper ends bolted to the vessel's side (2) : a curved piece of timber serving as a half-beam to support the deck where a whole beam cannot be placed (3) : SPUR SHORE **4** : a growth, formation, or projection suggestive of a spur in shape or relative size: as **a** : a stiff sharp spine (as on the wings or legs of a bird or insect); *esp* : a horny modification of the skin surrounding a bony core attached to the metatarsus of a cock's leg and used in fighting — see COCK illustration **b** : a bony outgrowth (as at a joint margin) : OSTEOPHYTE **c** : a projecting root or short branch of a tree: as (1) : a short branch bearing fruit buds (2) : a branch kept short by annual pruning (a vine cut to 4 ~s) **d** : a hollow projecting appendage of a corolla or calyx (as in larkspur or columbine) **5** : a sharp or pointed usu. metallic object similar to a spur: as **a** : a gaff for a gamecock **b** : a climbing iron : GAFF **c** : the bow ram of a warship **d** : a projection or prong on the arm of an anchor **e** : an article like a stilt resting on three points and having one pointing upward to support ceramic ware during firing **f** : the central point on an auger bit or lathe center **g** : ²GRIFFE 1 **h** : the metallic point on either end of a weaving shuttle **i** : the projection of the external hammer of a gun on which the thumb presses in cocking the weapon **j** : one of two or more adjustable buttons or spikes affixed to the back of a wall clock in order to allow the pendulum to swing clear of the walls **k** : one of several clamps with points attached to the hoop of a bass drum to prevent it from rolling and to hold it off the floor **l** : a bundle of several sheets of paper hung to dry in a loft **6** : an angular projection, offshoot, or branch extending out beyond or away from a main body or formation: **a** obs : an outer work or salient of a fortification **b** : a ridge or lesser elevation that projects from a mountain, a range of mountains, or a higher land surface to some distance at right angles or in a lateral direction ⟨the western edge is notched . . . by coves and valleys which break up into ~s . . . pointing towards the northwest —*Amer. Guide Series: Tenn.*⟩ **c** : a wing dam built out to deflect a river current **d** (1) : SPUR TRACK (2) : SIDING 3 (3) : a side or connecting road running from a main highway or turnpike ⟨problems . . . in the construction of thruway ~s —*N.Y. Times*⟩ **e** : a branch of a line of armine **7** : SPUR GEAR **8** : MOTIVE — **on the spur of the moment** : on impulse : prompted by the occasion : QUICKLY, SUDDENLY ⟨asked him how he could think up such language on the *spur of the moment* —Max Eastman⟩

²spur \'\ vb -ED/-ING/-S vt **1** : to prick (a horse) with spurs or to urge on : GOAD, INCITE ⟨*spurred*, fr. *spore*, *spure*, n.⟩ vt **1** : to prick (a horse) with spurs : to go at a faster pace ⟨*spurred* his horses along the crest of the ridge —Zane Grey⟩ **2** : to incite (a person or thing) to action or accelerated growth or development : URGE, STIMULATE ⟨general manager was ~ *spurred* by idealism —*Times Lit. Supp.*⟩ ⟨*spurred* his players to finish second —*Current Biog.*⟩ ⟨the war has *spurred* interest in the defense programs —*America*⟩ ⟨the rather pallid prose . . . inhibits rather than ~s the imagination —J.F.Muehl⟩ — often used with *on* ⟨his own needs ~ him on to invention —Ralph Linton⟩ ⟨*spurred* on by attractive commissions —G.M.Stephenson⟩ **3** : to furnish with spurs ⟨arriving all booted and *spurred*⟩ **4** *dial Eng* : to support or brace with a spur : PROP **5** : to cut back : PRUNE, TRIM ⟨number of main branches are *spurred* . . . to within

about two inches of their base —F.D.Smith & Barbara Wilcox⟩ ~ vi **1 a** : to hurry one's horse with spurs ⟨wheeling the white mustang, he *spurred* away —Zane Grey⟩ ⟨a wounded soldier *spurring* from the field with news of victory —A.B. Osborne⟩ **b** : to proceed in hurried fashion : RUSH ⟨*spurred* into the fray —S.H.Adams⟩ **2** : to strike out or fight with spurs — used of spur syn see URGE

³spur \'\ n -s [alter. of *spoor*] : the track of an animal (as an otter) : SPOOR

spur bit n : a boring bit having one or more spurs which scribe the periphery of the hole in advance of the cutting lips to guide the bit in the proper direction — compare TWIST BIT

spur blight n : a disease of raspberries caused by a fungus (*Didymella applanata*) that kills the fruit spurs and causes dark reddish or purple spots on the canes where the leaves arise and eventually browning and graying of the canes

spur-blind \'spər, ₌'₌-\ adj [alter. (influenced by ¹*spur*) of *purblind*] obs : quite or totally blind

spur budding n : a modified type of shield budding in which the scion consists of a twig or spur having more than one bud

spurdog \'₌,₌\ *also* spur dogfish n : DOGFISH 1

spur fowl n : any of several Indian gallinaceous birds of the genus *Galloperdix* related to the bamboo partridges and having two or more spurs on each leg

spurgall \'₌,₌, ₌'₌\ vt, *archaic* : to gall with or as if with a spur : INJURE, HARASS

spurge \'spərj, 'spōj, 'spaij\ n -s [ME, fr. MF *espurge*, *spurge*, purge, fr. *espurgier* to purge, fr. L *expurgare* — more at EXPURGE] **1** : any of several plants of the family Euphorbiaceae, esp. of the genus *Euphorbia* **2** : JAPANESE SPURGE **3** : ALLEGHENY SPURGE

spur gear *also* spur gear wheel n : the simplest form of toothed wheel used in machinery with radial teeth parallel to the axis of the wheel

spurge family n : EUPHORBIACEAE

spurge flax n **1** : an acrid evergreen European shrub (*Daphne gnidium*) with crowded narrow leaves and fibrous bark **2** : SPURGE LAUREL 1

spurge laurel n **1** : a low bushy Eurasian shrub (*Daphne laureola*) with oblong evergreen leaves and nearly scentless yellowish flowers **2** : MEZEREON 1

spurge moth n : a moth that feeds on euphorbias; *esp* : a European hawk moth (*Deilephila euphorbiae*) whose larva feeds on the leaves of devil's milk (*Euphorbia peplus*)

spur gear

spurge nettle n : a stinging American herb (*Jatropha stimulosus*)

spurge olive n **1** : MEZEREON **2** : a daphne (*Daphne oleoides*) of southern Europe related to the mezereon

spur-heeled \'₌,₌\ adj **1** : having a spur on the heel **2** : having the claw of the hind toe elongated and straight ⟨the larks are *spur-heeled*⟩

spu·ri·ae \'spyùrē,ē, -,pùrē,ī\ n pl [NL, fr. LL, fem. pl. of *spurius* false] : the feathers of the bastard wing of a bird

spu·ri·ous \'spyùrēəs, -pyùr- *sometimes* -ē- *or* -,pə-rē-\ adj [L & LL; LL *spurius* false, fr. L, of illegitimate birth, fr. *spurius*, n., bastard (often used as a praenomen)] **1** : of illegitimate birth : BASTARD ⟨her ~ firstborn —John Milton⟩ ⟨the dominions of both rulers passed away to their ~ or doubtful offspring —E.A.Freeman⟩ **2 a** : outwardly similar or corresponding to something without having its genuine qualities : FALSE, COUNTERFEIT ⟨the true ring by which . . . a fossilized survival may be known from a ~ reproduction —Thomas Hardy⟩ ⟨the ~ mechanical substitutes for knowledge and experience now provided through . . . the motion picture —Lewis Mumford⟩ ⟨prone to attach a ~ novelty to the things of the moment simply because they pretend to be new —J.A.R.Pimlott⟩ ⟨first of the . . . dictators to sweep to ~ glory on the upthrust of human arms —Milton Bracker⟩ **b** : simulative in symptoms or development without being pathologically or morphologically genuine ⟨~ labor pains⟩ ⟨~ species⟩ ⟨~ fruit⟩ ⟨the effusion of lymph which gradually degenerates into his ~ bony deposit —Robert Chawner⟩ **3 a** : of falsified or erroneously attributed origin or authorship : FORGED, INAUTHENTIC ⟨the ~ lines and passages which scholars used to reject as contradicting the genuine parts of the story —T.A.Jones⟩ ⟨the only known picture . . . albeit a ~ one had been printed some years earlier —James Monaghan⟩ ⟨the regalia became the symbols of sovereignty over all the tribes . . . though their ~ nature was obvious —A.M.Young⟩ **b** : of a deceitful or fictitious nature or quality : FRAUDULENT ⟨one of the worst features of the religious decadence . . . was the craftiness of such ~ types of men —Edwin Benson⟩ ⟨a completely ~ witness —M.S.Mayer⟩ ⟨the ~ explanations of the astrologers —G.A.L.Sarton⟩ **c** : faulty in reasoning or conclusion : ILLOGICAL, SPECIOUS ⟨~ inferences from obsolescent notions of causality and prediction —Ethel Albert⟩ ⟨no ~ argument, no appeal to sentiment . . . can deceive the American people —F.D.Roosevelt⟩ ⟨incomplete statistical evidence leads to ~ correlations⟩ **4** : marked by spuriousness or falseness ⟨additions which he inserted . . . to give them a ~ authenticity, into the original manuscript —R.D.Altick⟩ **5** : of an excrescent or superfluous character : undesirably intrusive : EXTRANEOUS ⟨the power output of a transmitter must be . . . free from ~ radiations —*Radio Amateur's Handbk.*⟩ ⟨designed . . . to operate so that ~ emissions and responses are completely eliminated —W.P.Corderman⟩ **6** : irrelevantly inapplicable : lacking correspondence to reality : vaguely ambiguous : PSEUDO ⟨if the terms of our discourse are incompatible or confused . . . then our alleged beliefs are not false, but ~ —Susanne K. Langer⟩ ⟨if, when he utters it, he is not talking about anything, then his use is not genuine one, but a ~ —Morris Weity⟩ syn see COUNTERFEIT

spurious claw n : a sturdy serrated bristle found on the feet of various spiders

spurious disk n : the small apparently circular disk of a star as seen in a telescope that limits the resolving power of the telescope and varies inversely with the diameter of the objective — called also *diffraction disk*

spurious fruit n : ACCESSORY FRUIT

spu·ri·ous·ly adv : in a spurious manner : PRETENTIOUSLY, FALSELY

spu·ri·ous·ness n -ES : the quality or state of being spurious

spurious primary or **spurious quill** n : the first or outer primary quill (as in certain singing birds) when rudimentary or much reduced in size

spurious vein n : a longitudinal thickening resembling a true vein or nervure and situated in the membrane of the wing of a fly between the radius and media — compare SYRPHUS FLY

spurious wing n : BASTARD WING

spurl \'spərl\ n -s [origin unknown] *Scot* : SCRAMBLE, SPRAWL

spur·less \'₌,ləs\ adj : having no spur

spur-ling \'spərliŋ, -ōl-, -ȯil-, -lēŋ-\ n [*spurling*, of unknown origin] **1 a** : a line by which the turning of a ship's wheel moves the indicator of a telltale **b** : a line stretched across the two forward shrouds of a ship with thimbles spliced in it to serve as a fairlead

spurling pipe n : a pipe or tube through which an anchor chain passes to the chain locker below the deck of a ship

¹spurn \'sparn, -pan, -pain\ vb -ED/-ING/-S [ME *spurnen*, fr. OE *spurnan*; akin to OFris *spurna* to kick, OS & OHG *spurnan*, ON *sporna* to kick, L *spernere* to despise, spurn, Skt *spairein* to quiver, Skt *sphurati* he kicks] vi **1** obs : to hit something with the foot : STUMBLE **2** obs : to strike something with the foot : KICK — often used with *at* ⟨~ not at stone walls⟩ **3** : to speak out or act against something in disdainful or contemptuous fashion — usu. used with *at* ⟨~ing fearlessly at danger and all enemies⟩ ~ vt **1** : to tread heavily upon (something) : KICK, TRAMPLE ⟨then the creature was off, silver hoofs ~ing the ground —Elizabeth Goudge⟩ ⟨would have ~ed him with his foot save that she did not want to rouse him —C.S.Forester⟩ — often used with *away* ⟨~ing away those who had helped him to power⟩ **2** : to reject (something) with disdain or contempt : SCORN ⟨used certain resources and ~ed others —Lewis Mumford⟩ ⟨~ed a suggestion that he carry a gun —*N.Y. Times*⟩ ⟨the ~ed lover assuaged his grief in violent activity —Saxe Commins⟩ syn see DECLINE

²spurn \"\ n -s [ME, fr. spurnen, v.] 1 : a blow delivered with the foot : KICK 2 : the act of spurning or kicking 3 : disdainful rejection : contemptuous treatment ⟨the insolence of office, and the ~s that patient merit of the unworthy takes —Shak.⟩

³spurn \"\ n -s [alter. of ¹spur] 1 archaic : the main root of a tree 2 archaic : a projecting part : SPUR 3 : a small short pillar of coal left within the seam to support the coal above during holing

spurn·er \-nə(r)\ n -s : one that spurns

spurnwater \'=,==\ n [ME spurnewater, fr. spurnen to spurn + water] : a low V-shaped barrier on the forward deck of a ship to throw off seas coming aboard

spur-of-the-moment \'=,==¦==\ adj [fr. the phrase (on the) spur of the moment] : occurring or developing without premeditation : hastily extemporized ⟨cumulative effect accomplished through . . . what had previously seemed merely spur-of-the-moment ideas —Irving Kolodin⟩ ⟨a human equation in live TV that gives it spur-of-the-moment touches —Dinah Shore⟩

spur pepper n : CHILI

spur pruning n 1 : a method of pruning grapevines in which the shoot of the previous season is cut back to a spur with one or two buds 2 : the removal (as from an apple tree) of fruiting spurs

¹spurred past of SPUR

²spurred \'spərd, 'spə̄d\ adj [ME spored, spurret, fr. spore, spure spur] 1 : wearing spurs 2 : having one or more spurs ⟨a ~ flower⟩ ⟨~ outgrowths from the gill covers⟩

spurred butterfly pea n : a butterfly pea of the genus Centrosema (esp. C. virginianum)

spurred gentian n : a plant of the genus Halenia (esp. H. deflexa)

spur·ri·er \'spər-ēə(r also 'spə·rē-\ n -s [ME sporier, fr. spore, spure spur + -ier — more at SPUR] : one that makes spurs

spurring pres part of SPUR

spurr·ite \'spər-,īt\ n -s [Josiah E. Spurr †1950 Am. geologist + E -ite] : a mineral $Ca_5(SiO_4)_2(CO_3)$ consisting of a calcium silicate and carbonate and occurring in light gray granular masses

spur rowel n, heraldry : a mullet pierced

spur·ry or spur·rey \'spərē\ n, pl spurries or spurreys [D spurrie, fr. MD sporie, fr. ML spergula — more at SPERGULA] 1 : a small white-flowered European weed (Spergula arvensis) with whorled filiform leaves 2 : any of several small herbs of the chickweed family

spur rowel

spur ryal or spur rial or spur royal n : the 15-shilling gold ryal of James I with a design on the reverse resembling the rowel of a spur

spurs pl of SPUR, pres 3d sing of SPUR

spur shore n : a timber or spar designed to hold a boat away from a pier wharf or quay

¹spurt also spirt \'spərt, 'spə̄l, 'spəi|, usu |d·+V\ n -s [origin unknown] 1 : a short period of time : MOMENT ⟨leaving for a ~ and returning shortly⟩ 2 a : a sudden and usu. brief burst or outbreak of effort, activity, or development ⟨in the pubertal phase . . . contains the most noticeable growth ~ —G.S.Blum⟩ ⟨the accidental and perhaps temporary ~ in population —S.H.Slichter⟩ ⟨has a little ~ of good fortune —Erle Stanley Gardner⟩ ⟨science and mathematics came in a four-century ~ and then stood still —A.L.Kroeber⟩ b : a quick burst or increase in speed of movement or progress ⟨put on an extra ~ and . . . slipped through a hole in the hedge —George Orwell⟩ ⟨his heads-up ball-playing saved many a game . . . in their late season ~ —Current Biog.⟩ c : a sharp or sudden increase or advance in business activity; also : the period of such a movement ⟨enjoying a ~ in sales —Vance Packard⟩ ⟨doing a nice business handling the annual ~ in the busy weeks before Christmas —Frederick Way⟩

²spurt also spirt \"\ vb -ED/-ING/-S vi : to make a spurt ⟨has ~ed into popularity —Jane Nickerson⟩ ⟨tucked the ball in, ~ed at him, driving hard —Irwin Shaw⟩ ⟨possibly its sales will ~ —Lloyd Mangrum⟩ ⟨stocks ~ed . . . then took a sharp spill —New Orleans (La.) Times-Picayune⟩ ~ vt : to cause (something) to make a spurt ⟨we ~ dress sales . . . every time we tie up with a smart society event —Women's Wear Daily⟩

³spurt also spirt \"\ vb -ED/-ING/-S [perh. akin to MHG spirzen, spürzen to spit, sprützen to sprout, squirt — more at SPRIT] vi : to gush suddenly or violently : SPOUT ⟨blood was seeping, not ~ing, from the head wound —Frances & Richard Lockridge⟩ ⟨hit the ground hard, the dust ~ing from beneath his boots —C.J.Clements⟩ ⟨saw smoke billow and flame ~ out —Philip Rooney⟩ ~ vt : to force out or expel (as a liquid) in a stream or jet : SQUIRT ⟨~s water from his mouth⟩

⁴spurt also spirt \"\ n -s 1 : a sudden forceful gushing or shooting forth : JET ⟨an intermittent wind with wild ~s of incredibly thin rain —J.C.Powys⟩ ⟨~s of rifle fire stabbed at them —Marjory S. Douglas⟩ ⟨little ~s of low-voiced conversation —H.L.Davis⟩ 2 : a quick surge of feeling or emotional outburst ⟨in a vicious ~ of temper, flung it into the fire —D.H.Lawrence⟩ ⟨sat there coughing, his sudden ~ of valor . . . knocked out of him —Max Peacock⟩ ⟨inspiration that came and went in ~s —Paul Hume⟩

⁵spurt also spirt \"\ vi -ED/-ING/-S [prob. alter. of ¹sprit] : to shoot up : SPROUT ⟨from the grass . . . flame-bright anemones ~ed —Elizabeth Bowen⟩ ⟨branches ~ from the trunk⟩

spur·tive \'spərd·iv\ adj [¹spurt + -ive] : of the nature of spurts : SPASMODIC, SUDDEN

¹spur·tle \'spərd·ᵊl\ n -s [origin unknown] 1 chiefly Scot : an implement similar to a spatula used to turn food (as griddle cakes) 2 chiefly Scot : a wooden stick for stirring porridge 3 chiefly Scot : SWORD

²spur·tle \'spər|d·ᵊl, 'spə̄|, 'spəi|, |tᵊl\ vb spurtled; spurtled; spurtling \|d·ᵊliŋ, |t(ᵊ)liŋ\ spurtles [freq. of ³spurt] vt : to cover with spatterings : SPRINKLE ~ vi : to break forth suddenly in a stream or spatter ⟨the white spurtling surf —Russell Thacher⟩

spur track n : a track that diverges from a main line : SIDING, BRANCH

spur tree n : a West Indian tree or shrub (Petitia domingensis) of the family Verbenaceae with fragrant white flowers

spur wheel n : SPUR GEAR

spurwing \'=,=\ n 1 : SPUR-WINGED GOOSE 2 : SPUR-WINGED PLOVER

spur-winged \'=¦=\ adj : having one or more horny spurs on the bend of the wings

spur-winged goose n : a long-legged African goose of the genus Plectropterus (esp. P. gambensis) having a strong spur on the bend of the wing

spur-winged plover n : any of various plovers; esp : a plover (Hoplopterus spinosus) of northern Africa and neighboring regions with a crested head and underparts chiefly black having a spur on the bend of the wing

spurwort \'=,=\ n : FIELD MADDER

sput·nik \'sputnik, -pət-,-püt-, -,nēk also -,nik; sometimes -püt(,)nyik or -püt(,)nyik\ n -s sometimes cap [Russ, traveling companion, satellite, fr. s, so with + put' path + -nik, suffix denoting a person engaged in or connected with something specified; akin to OSlav sŭ with, samŭ same, Skt sama equal, same, and to Skt patha way, path, course — more at SAME, FIND] : SATELLITE 2b ⟨first into space with a ~ —Newsweek⟩ ⟨successes in science, ~s, and rocketry —N.Y. Times⟩

¹sput·ter \'spəd·ə(r), -ətə-\ vb -ED/-ING/-S [akin to D sputteren to sputter, spuiten to spurt, spout — more at SPOUT] vt 1 : to spit or expel (particles of saliva or food) from the mouth with mildly explosive sounds : SPLUTTER ⟨cram your mouth so full that if you were to speak you must ~ the contents of it amongst the dishes and the company —Earl of Chesterfield⟩ 2 : to utter (words or ejaculations) hastily or explosively in confusion or excitement ⟨~ing protests he retired from the contest⟩ — often used with out ⟨began to laugh, ~ing out the story —Dawn Powell⟩ 3 : to deposit (a metallic film) by electric discharge in which positive gas ions bombarding the cathode cause it to eject atoms of the cathode metal with great speed ~ vi 1 : to spit or expel noisily from the mouth particles of food or saliva ⟨talks while he eats and ~s all over the place⟩ 2 : to speak, reply, or ejaculate explosively or confusedly from anger or excitement ⟨their response . . . ~ed in its indignation —F.L.Paxson⟩ 3 a : to make explosive or popping sounds in a spasmodic manner often with sparks or bursts of flame ⟨the car ~ed down the road —Elizabeth Pollet⟩ ⟨machine guns ~ed away hysterically —Erle Stanley Gardner⟩ ⟨candles . . . ~ before the shrines —Amer. Guide Series: Texas⟩ b : to cease acting or functioning with or as if with such a sputter ⟨the engine ~ed, spit, and died⟩ — usu. used with out ⟨the excitement . . . appeared to have ~ed out —Newsweek⟩

²sputter \"\ n -s 1 : confused and excited speech or discussion ⟨protesting with a good deal of ~⟩ 2 : the act or sound of sputtering ⟨can write their names now without a ~ of the pen —Thomas Hardy⟩ ⟨would come the distant cough, ~, choke, then catch, roar, and soon steady droning of the first planes —Benedict Thielen⟩

sput·ter·ing·ly adv : in a sputtering manner : with sputtering

sput·tery \'spəd·ərē, -ətə-, -ri\ adj : issuing in intermittent bursts : SPUTTERING, EJACULATORY

spu·tum \'spyüd·əm, -ütəm\ n, pl spu·ta \-d·ə, -tə\ also sputums [L, fr. neut. of sputus, past part. of spuere to spit — more at SPEW] 1 : something expectorated and usu. consisting of saliva with or without mucus or other materials from the respiratory passages 2 : the matter discharged from the air passages in diseases of the lungs, bronchi, or upper respiratory tract that contains mucus and often pus, blood, fibrin, or bacterial products

sputum cup n : a cup usu. made of paper or thin cardboard to receive and isolate the sputum of a patient with respiratory disease

¹spy \'spī\ vb spied; spied; spying; spies [ME spien, fr. OF espier, of Gmc origin; akin to OHG spehōn to watch, regard, spy, MLG spēen, MD spien; akin to ON spā to prophesy, L specere to look, species appearance, form, kind, species, Gk skeptesthai to view, look, consider, skopein to look at, examine, Skt paśyati he sees] vt 1 a : to watch (as a person) in a furtive or stealthy manner for the purpose of secretly obtaining information for usu. hostile purposes ⟨spies the enemy to determine his direction of march⟩ ⟨take command of the army and . . . sat with his glass, ~ing the movements across the water —H.E.Scudder⟩ b : to investigate or explore (a country or place) in a secretive or unobtrusive manner — usu. used with out ⟨made horseback trips about the vicinity, ~ing out the land —Julian Dana⟩ ⟨shareholders started ~ing out the landscape in quest of new prospects —Sydney (Australia) Bull.⟩ 2 : to scrutinize or examine (something) in detail ⟨~ing the exhibits at the fair⟩ 3 : to discover after some search : catch sight of : DESCRY, NOTICE ⟨the squire in the lead spied him . . . and reined in his horse —T.B.Costain⟩ ⟨spied the red camellias on the white marble mantel —Olive H. Prouty⟩ 4 : to search or look for intensively ⟨left at daylight in order to ~ their way . . . through the minefields —Herbert Hoover⟩ — usu. used with out ⟨sat at the feet of many European masters . . . ~ing out the secrets of their art —Brander Matthews⟩ ~ vi 1 : to observe or search for something : LOOK ⟨smoothing her gloves and ~ing downward at the folds of her mantle —Arnold Bennett⟩ ⟨you must ~ out for literature as you do for a qualified prescription clerk —Francis Hackett⟩ 2 a : to watch secretly : make furtive or stealthy observations — often used with into, on, or upon ⟨is usually ~ing into other people's business⟩ ⟨is above ~ing on his friends⟩ b : to seek strategic or related information about a country or people by secret methods of infiltration or investigation ⟨was sent into enemy territory to ~⟩ — usu. used with on or upon ⟨in order to ~ upon the British —Amer. Guide Series: Conn.⟩

²spy \"\ n -ES [ME spie, fr. OF espie, of Gmc origin; akin to OHG speho watcher, spy, spehōn to watch, spy — more at ¹SPY] 1 : one that spies: a : one who keeps secret watch upon a person or thing to obtain information ⟨spies who were able to mingle among politicians and gather hot gossip —W.A. Swanberg⟩ ⟨is a sneak, a ~, an informer —Jack London⟩ b : one engaged in seeking strategic or related information about a country or people by secret methods of infiltration or investigation : secret agent ⟨handicapped by a lack of decent military intelligence . . . had too few scouts and spies —F.V.W. Mason⟩; specif : one who acts in a clandestine manner or on false pretenses (as without regular uniform) to obtain information in the zone of operations of a belligerent with the intention of communicating it to the hostile party 2 [ME spie, fr. spien, v.] : the act or occasion of spying ⟨had the first ~ from a hillock in the glen —John Buchan⟩

spyglass \'=,=\ n : a small terrestrial telescope

sq abbr 1 sequence 2 [L sequens; sequentes; sequentia] the following 3 squadron 4 square

sqd abbr squad

sqdn abbr squadron

SQMS abbr staff quartermaster sergeant

sqn abbr squadron

sqq abbr [L sequentes; sequentia] the following

sqr abbr square

¹squab \'skwäb also -wȯb\ n -s see sense 1 [prob. of Scand origin; akin to Sw dial. skvabb, kvabb anything soft and thick, Norw dial. skvabb paplike mass; prob. akin to OS quappa eelpout, OBulg žaba toad] 1 or pl squab : a fledgling bird; specif : a fledgling pigeon that is about four weeks old and weighs about one pound ⟨the menu featured ~s en casserole⟩ 2 : one that resembles a squab; esp : a short fat person 3 a : COUCH b : a removable cushion used esp. in a chair or couch seat c chiefly Brit : the back part of an automobile seat

²squab \"\ adj 1 : of, relating to, or having the characteristics of a squab: a (1) : DUMPY, SQUAT ⟨his ~ white figure stopped growing at fat puppyhood —Haldane Macfall⟩ (2) : BROAD, THICK ⟨a ~ nose⟩ b : UNFLEDGED 2 obs : CURT, SHARP

³squab \"\ vb squabbed; squabbed; squabbing; squabs [prob. fr. ¹squab] vt 1 dial Brit : CRUSH, SQUASH 2 : to fill with stuffing (as a cushion) ~ vi, dial Brit : to squat down

⁴squab \"\ adv : PLUMP

⁵squab \"\ vb [perh. fr. ³squab] : SLOP, SPILL

squa·bash \'skwȯ,bash, -wä,b-\ vt -ED/-ING/-ES [blend of squash and bash] : to crush esp. with criticism : LAMBASTE ⟨his satire . . . ~ed at one blow a set of coxcombs —J.G.Lockhart⟩

squabbed \'skwäbd also -wȯbd\ adj [fr. past part. of ³squab] : ²SQUAB 1a(1) ⟨a ~ and thoroughly unattractive figure⟩

squab·ber \-bə(r)\ n -s [¹squab + -er] : a pigeon used for commercial breeding purposes

squab·bing \-biŋ\ adj [¹squab + -ing] : squab-producing ⟨~ pigeons⟩

squab·bish \-bish\ adj [²squab + -ish] : somewhat fat or squat

¹squab·ble \'skwäbəl also -wȯb-\ n -s [prob. of Scand origin; akin to Sw dial. skvabbel dispute, Norw skvabbe to chatter, babble, rant; prob. of imit. origin] 1 : a noisy altercation usu. over something insignificant : WRANGLE ⟨a mere ~ in the children's schoolroom —Alan Moorehead⟩ ⟨she could better endure a howling brawl . . . a shrill ~ of shrews —Jean Stafford⟩ 2 a : a futile, aimless, and usu. continuous quarrel : BICKERING ⟨because the committee has become the center of a political ~, it seems unlikely that anything will ever come of its activities —Henry LaCossitt⟩ b : a minor and often recurrent disagreement (as between groups) : DISPUTE ⟨recalled the jurisdictional ~s of the 15th century —Paul Johnson⟩ ⟨an unresolved ~ with the West —William Clark⟩ syn see QUARREL

²squabble \"\ vb squabbled; squabbled; squabbling \-b(ə)liŋ\ squabbles vi 1 : to quarrel noisily and to no purpose : WRANGLE ⟨fight and ~ among themselves in complete and vigorous disregard of any color line —Cabell Phillips⟩ ⟨doctors, nurses, the administrator, and the trustees squabbled constantly —Newsweek⟩ 2 of type : to become squabbled ~ vt : to disarrange (set type) so that the letters or lines stand awry or are mixed and need readjustment — compare ⁴PI

squab·bler \-b(ə)lə(r)\ n -s : one that squabbles

squab·bly \-b(ə)lē\ adj, usu -ER/-EST [¹squabble + -y] : tending toward or characterized by squabbling

squab·by \-bē\ adj -ER/-EST [¹squab + -y] : ²SQUAB 1a(1)

squab chicken n : a young chicken that weighs about 1 to 1¼ pounds and is usu. suitable for an individual serving

squac·co \'skwä(,)kō also -wȯ(-\ or squacco heron n -s [It dial. sguacco] : a small crested heron (Ardeola ralloides) that breeds in parts of Asia, Africa, and southern Europe

¹squad \'skwäd also -wȯd\ n -s [MF esquade, esquadre, fr. OSp & OIt; OSp escuadra, fr. escuadrar to square, fr. (assumed) VL exquadrare; OIt squadra, fr. squadrare to square, fr. (assumed) VL exquadrare; fr. the men being arranged in square formation — more at SQUARE] : a small group of individuals: as a : a group of military personnel organized as a team (as for drill or inspection) ⟨on command the ~ moves instantly, smartly, and smoothly —Drill & Ceremonies⟩; esp : a tactical unit that can be easily directed in the field by its leader ⟨using an 11-man rifle ~ for maneuverability and fire power⟩ b : a group engaged in a common effort or occupation ⟨a football ~⟩ ⟨a special police ~ of 30 men . . . was on duty —Springfield (Mass.) Daily News⟩ c : an auxiliary fire company equipped with special appliances

²squad \"\ vt squadded; squadded; squadding; squads : to arrange in squads

squad abbr squadron

squad car n : an automobile used by police that is equipped with short-wave radiophone connection with headquarters — called also cruise car, prowl car

squad·der \-də(r)\ n -s [¹squad + -er] : a member of a squad of police

squad leader n : an enlisted man usu. of noncommissioned officer rank in charge of a squad

squad·rol \(')skwä¦drōl, -wȯ¦d-\ n -s [blend of squad (car) and patrol (wagon)] : an automobile that is used by police both as a squad car and as an ambulance

squad·ron \'skwädrən also -wȯd-\ n -s [It squadrone body of soldiers arranged in square formation, squadron, aug. of squadra squad, fr. OIt] 1 : a unit of military organization: a : a cavalry unit that is higher than a troop and lower than a regiment — compare BATTALION b : a unit of naval administrative and tactical organization that consists of two or more divisions and sometimes additional vessels c (1) : an aviation unit (as of the U. S. Air Force) higher than a flight and lower than a group and composed of a headquarters and two or more flights (2) : a military flight formation 2 : a relatively large group of individuals ⟨since the war a ~ of younger symphonists has arisen —Score⟩ ⟨~s of birds wheel overhead —Amer. Guide Series: Fla.⟩ 3 obs : a division of a town or community or district in New England 4 : a unit of at least five air explorers of the Boy Scouts

squadron·ed \-nd\ adj : formed into or as if into a squadron

squadron leader n : a military officer (as in the British Royal Air Force) equivalent in rank to a major in the army

squad room n 1 : a room in a barracks used to billet soldiers 2 : a room in a police station where members of the force assemble (as for roll call or the assignment of duties)

squad tent n : a canvas shelter designed to accommodate a military squad

squad wagon n : a fire truck carrying a squad and its equipment

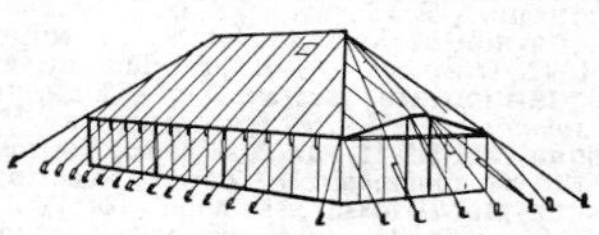

squad tent

squag·ga \'skwägə\ n -s [native name in Australia] : a scyllarian crustacean (Ibacus incisus) of Australia that is salmon red in color and reaches a length of eight inches

¹squail \'skwā(ə)l\ vb [origin unknown] vi, dial chiefly Brit : to throw a weighted stick (as at a bird or fruit on a tree) ⟨~ed at the pears with short sticks —Richard Jefferies⟩ ~ vt, dial chiefly Brit : to strike by throwing a stick

²squail \"\ n -s [back-formation fr. squails] : a disk or counter used in the game of squails

squails \-lz\ n pl but sing in constr [prob. alter. (influenced by ¹squail) of obs. E skayles a form of skittles or ninepins, alter. (prob. influenced by E skittles) of ME kayles kails — more at KAILS] : a game in which disks are driven or snapped from the edge of a table or board at a mark in the center

squa·lene \'skwā,lēn\ n -s [ISV squal- (fr. NL Squalus) + -ene] : a liquid acyclic triterpene hydrocarbon $[(CH_3)_2C{=}CHCH_2[CH_2C(CH_3){=}CHCH_2]_2]_2$ that is found esp. in the liver oil of various sharks but also in various plant oils, in yeast, and in human sebum, that is made synthetically from farnesol, that is formed enzymatically from mevalonic acid, and that is a biological precursor of various cyclic triterpenoids and of cholesterol and related steroids

squa·li \'skwā,lī\ [NL, fr. pl. of L squalus, a sea fish — more at WHALE] syn of PLEUROTREMATA

¹squal·id \'skwäləd also -wȯl- sometimes -wāl-\ adj, sometimes -ER/-EST [L squalidus — more at SQUALOR] 1 a : marked by filthiness and degradation usu. from neglect ⟨exchanged . . . ~ and savage dress for a suit of Dutch cloth —Francis Parkman⟩ ⟨ramshackle frame houses . . . notorious firetraps of ~ appearance —Amer. Guide Series: N. Y. City⟩ ⟨ministering every year to . . . the poorest, the sickest, the ~est human beings —Saturday Rev.⟩ ⟨rickety tables . . . surmounted by . . . overflowing ashtrays —John Wain⟩ ⟨rueful ~ poverty that crawled by every wayside —John Morley⟩ b : RUN-DOWN, SHABBY ⟨life at a fashionably ~ preparatory school —New Yorker⟩ 2 obs a : DRY b : SHAGGY 3 a : morally debased or repulsive : CONTEMPTIBLE, SORDID ⟨a sublime prophet . . . or a ~ quack —La Selle Gilman⟩ ⟨a series of rather ~ little affairs that everybody knew about and nobody mentioned —Ngaio Marsh⟩ b : lacking refinement or sophistication : CRUDE ⟨finds Voltaire's summary of ancient philosophy ~ —J.H.Seyppel⟩ ⟨such imagination as he can detect is usually commonplace or ~ —Bernard De Voto⟩ 4 : marked by an unwholesome appearance ⟨his complexion sallow and ~ —E.G.Bulwer-Lytton⟩ syn see DIRTY

²squa·lid \'skwāləd\ adj [NL Squalidae] : of or relating to the Squalidae

³squalid \"\ n -s : a shark of the family Squalidae

squa·li·da \'skwālədə\ [NL, fr. Squalus + -ida] syn of PLEUROTREMATA

squa·li·dae \-,dē\ n pl, cap [NL, fr. Squalus, type genus + -idae] : a family of sharks having a spine in each dorsal fin and comprising the spiny dogfishes and various chiefly small related forms

squa·lid·i·ty \skwä'lidəd·ē, -wȯ'-,-wā'-\ n -ES [LL squaliditas, fr. L squalidus squalid + -itas -ity] : the quality or state of being squalid

squal·id·ly adv : in a squalid manner

squal·id·ness n -ES : SQUALIDITY

squa·li·form \'skwālə,fȯrm\ adj [NL Squalus + E -iform] : resembling a shark or dogfish in form

¹squall also squawl \'skwȯl\ vb -ED/-ING/-S [of Scand origin; akin to ON skval useless chatter, skvala to talk noisily, cry out and perh. to ON skjalla to clash, clatter — more at SHILL] vi : to cry or cry out raucously : SCREAM ⟨a baby in the fire woke up and began to ~ —Victoria Sackville-West⟩ ⟨~ed in terror⟩ ~ vt : to utter in a strident voice ⟨one of the commonplace psalm tunes, ~ed by charity children —Court Mag.⟩

²squall also squawl \"\ n -s : a raucous cry : SQUAWK ⟨some clubs, while on the field, keep up a constant ~ of encouragement to their pitchers —R.O.Boyer⟩

³squall \"\ n -s [prob. of Scand origin; akin to Sw & Norw skval splash, ripple, rushing water and prob. to ON skval useless chatter] 1 : a sudden violent wind often accompanied by rain or snow 2 : a short-lived commotion resembling a squall ⟨his film career . . . has been . . . punctuated with the ~s of scandal —Arthur Knight⟩ : SQUABBLE ⟨she could hear another domestic ~ starting next door⟩ syn see WIND

⁴squall \"\ vi -ED/-ING/-S : to blow a squall ⟨the raw wind sagged with snow and the storms spat and ~ed —Helen Rich⟩

squall cloud n : a ragged light gray rolling cloud usu. located beneath the dark cloud mass of an advancing thunderstorm

squall·er \'skwȯlə(r)\ n -s : one that squalls; esp : a baby that cries excessively

squall line n 1 : an intersection or boundary between the cold and the warm winds of an extratropical cyclone or between the cold air of an advancing anticyclone and the warm air of a cyclone : COLD FRONT — called also wind-shift line 2 : a line of squalls often 50 to 200 miles ahead of a cold front

squally \'skwȯlē, -li\ adj -ER/-EST [³squall + -y] 1 a : marked

by squalls ⟨saw the vessel off, on a gray, ~ morning —James Dugan⟩ **b :** GUSTY ⟨the winds . . . are almost always high and ~ —C.D.Forde⟩ **2 :** marked by difficulty or disharmony **:** STORMY ⟨a couple whose home life has been extraordinarily ~ —John McCarten⟩

squa·loid \ˈskwā,lȯid\ *adj* [NL *Squalus* + *-oid*] **1 :** resembling a shark **2** [NL *Squaloidea*] **:** of or relating to the Squaloidea

squa·loi·dea \skwāˈlȯidēə\ *n pl, cap* [NL, fr. *Squalus* + *-oidea*] **1 :** a suborder of Pleurotremata comprising those sharks (as the spiny dogfishes) that have a compressed or rounded body but in some respects (as in adaptation to bottom-dwelling habits) approach the skates and rays — compare GALEOIDEA, NOTIDANOIDEA **2** *in some classifications* **:** a suborder or other division of elasmobranch fishes comprising the typical sharks — compare SQUATINA

squa·loi·dei \-ē,ī\ [NL, fr. *Squalus* + *-oidei*] *syn of* SQUALOIDEA

squal·or \ˈskwälə(r) *also* -wȯl- *or* -wāl-\ *n* -s [L, roughness, dirt, squalor; akin to L *squalēre* to be dirty, *squalidus* dirty, squalid, *squama* scale] **1 :** the quality or state of being physically squalid ⟨dwellings . . . sinking stage by stage from indigence to ~ —Lewis Mumford⟩ **2 a :** moral baseness **:** CORRUPTION ⟨presenting a picture of political ~ to the country —Russell Baker⟩ **b :** absence of intellectual sensitivity **:** CRASSNESS ⟨depressing ~ of the . . . mind —Dachine Rainer⟩

squa·lus \ˈskwāləs\ *n, cap* [NL, fr. L, a sea fish — more at WHALE] **:** a genus (the type of the family Squalidae) of sharks orig. comprising all the known sharks but now restricted to various typical dogfishes

squam \ˈskwäm *also* -wȯm\ *n* -s [fr. *Squam*, short for *Annisquam*, village in northeastern Mass., where it was orig. worn by fishermen] **:** SOU'WESTER 2b

squam- *or* **squamo-** *comb form* [L, fr. *squama*] **1 :** scale **:** squama ⟨*Squam*ata⟩ ⟨*squam*aceous⟩ **2 :** squamosal and ⟨*squamo*mastoid⟩ **:** squamously ⟨*squamo*cellular⟩

squa·ma \ˈskwāmə\ *n, pl* **squa·mae** \-,mē\ [L] **:** a scale or a structure resembling a scale: **a :** an alula, tegula, or calypter at the base of the wing above the halter of a dipterous insect **b :** the exopodite of the antenna (as of certain crustaceans) **c :** SQUAMOSA

squa·ma·ceous \skwəˈmāshəs\ *adj* [*squam-* + *-aceous*] **:** covered with or consisting of scales **:** SCALY, SQUAMOUS

squa·mal \ˈskwāməl\ *adj* [*squam-* + *-al*] **:** SQUAMOSAL

squa·ma·ta \skwəˈmäd·ə, -mād·ə\ *n pl, cap* [NL, fr. *squam-* + *-ata*] **:** an order of reptiles comprising the snakes and lizards and sometimes the extinct Pythonomorpha

squa·mate \ˈskwā,māt\ *also* **squa·mat·ed** \-mād·əd\ *adj* [LL *squamatus*, fr. *squama* + *-atus* -ate] **:** SCALY

squa·ma·tion \skwəˈmāshən, -wāˈm-\ *n* -s [*squam-* + *-ation*] **1 :** the state or condition of being scaly or scaled **2 :** the arrangement of scales on an animal **:** SCALATION

squame \ˈskwām\ *n* -s [F, fr. L *squama* scale] **:** SQUAMA

squa·mel·la \skwəˈmelə\ *n, pl* **squamel·lae** \-(,)lē, -,lī\ [NL, fr. *squam-* + *-ella*] **:** a diminutive scale or bractlet

squa·mel·late \skwəˈmelət, -wāˈm-; ˈskwāmə,lāt\ *adj* [NL *squamella* + E *-ate*] **:** SQUAMULOSE

squa·mel·lif·er·ous \;skwāmə;lif(ə)rəs\ *adj* [ISV *squamelli-* (fr. NL *squamella*) + *-iferous*] **:** bearing squamellae

squa·mel·li·form \skwəˈmelə,fȯrm\ *adj* [ISV *squamelli-* (fr. NL *squamella*) + *-iform*; orig. formed as F *squamelliforme*] **:** having the form of a squamella

squa·mi·form \ˈskwāmə,fȯrm\ *adj* [ISV *squam-* + *-iform*] **:** having the shape of a scale

squa·mi·pen·nate \;skwāmə;penət\ *adj* [NL *Squamipennes* + E *-ate*] **:** of or relating to the Squamipennes

squa·mi·pen·nes \,==ˈpe(,)nēz\ *n pl, cap* [NL, fr. *squam-* + *-i-* + *-pennes* (fr. L *penna* feather) — more at PEN] *in some classifications* **:** a suborder of Percomorphi comprising chiefly tropical marine fishes with a narrow deep body and usu. scaly bases on the dorsal and anal fins and including Chaetodontidae, Ephippidae, and various other families

squamish *var of* SQUAWMISH

squa·mo·columnar junction \;skwā(,)mō+...-\ *n* [*squam-* + *columnar*] **:** the region in the uterine cervix in which the squamous lining of the vagina is replaced by the columnar epithelium typical of the body of the uterus and which is a common seat of neoplastic change

squa·moid \ˈskwā,mȯid\ *adj* [*squam-* + *-oid*] **:** SCALY

squa·mo·sa \skwəˈmōsə, -wəˈm-, -ōzə\ *n, pl* **squamosas** \-z\ *or* **squamo·sae** \-ō,sē, -ō,zē, \ī\ [NL, fr. fem. of L *squamosus* squamous] **:** the squamous part of the temporal bone

¹squa·mo·sal \(ˈ)skwāˈmōsəl, skwəˈm-, -ōzəl\ *adj* [L *squamosus* squamous + E *-al*] **:** SCALELIKE **a :** SQUAMOUS **b** [NL *squamosa* + E *-al*] **:** of, relating to, or constituting a membrane bone of the skull of many vertebrates that is external and more or less dorsal to the auditory capsule and corresponds to the squamous portion of the temporal bone of man

²squamosal \"\ *n* -s **1 :** the squamosal bone **2 :** the pterotic of a teleost fish

squa·mose \ˈskwā,mōs\ *adj* [L *squamosus*] **:** SQUAMOUS — **squa·mose·ly** *adv* — **squa·mose·ness** *n* -ES

squa·mos·i·ty \skwāˈmäsəd·ē, -wəˈm-\ *n* -ES **1 :** the state or condition of being squamose **2 :** a scaly area (as on the body of an insect)

squa·mous \ˈskwāməs\ *adj* [L *squamosus*, fr. *squama* scale + *-osus* -ose — more at SQUALOR] **1 a :** covered with or consisting of scales **:** resembling a scale **:** SCALY ⟨a ~ stem or bulb⟩ ⟨~ epithelial cells⟩ **b :** of or relating to squamous epithelium **2 :** of, relating to, or constituting the anterior upper portion of the temporal bone of man and various mammals that is a thin sharp-edged form bearing the zygomatic process — **squa·mous·ly** *adv*

squamous cell *n* **:** a cell of or derived from squamous epithelium ⟨*squamous-cell* cancers⟩

squamous epithelium *n* **:** stratified epithelium that consists at least in its outer layers of small scalelike cells (as the epidermis of the human skin) — compare COLUMNAR EPITHELIUM

squams *pl of* SQUAM

squa·mu·la \ˈskwamyələ, -wām-,-wäm-\ *n, pl* **squamu·lae** \-,lē, -,lī\ [NL, fr. L, small scale, dim. of *squama* scale] **1 :** SQUAMULE **2 :** the tegula of a hymenopteron

squamu·late \-,lāt\ *adj* [*squamule* + *-ate*] **:** SQUAMULOSE

squamu·la·tion \,==ˈlāshən\ *n* -s [*squamule* + *-ation*] **:** a squamous arrangement

squamule \ˈ=(,)myül\ *n* -s [NL *squamula*] **:** a small scale: **a :** one of the scalelike lobes of the thallus of a lichen **b :** LODICULE

squamu·li·form \ˈ=myələ,fȯrm\ *adj* [ISV *squamul-* (fr. NL *squamula*) + *-iform*] **:** resembling a squamule

squamu·lose \-myə,lōs\ *adj* [*squamule* + *-ose*] **:** squamous with minute scales

¹squan·der \ˈskwändə(r) *also* -wȯn-\ *vb* **squandered; squandered; squandering** \-d(ə)riŋ\ **squanders** [origin unknown] *vt* **1 :** to cause to disperse or spread **:** SCATTER ⟨they drive and ~ the huge Belgian fleet —John Dryden⟩ **2 :** to expend extravagantly or foolishly esp. to the point of depletion **:** throw away **:** DISSIPATE ⟨tied up their fortunes in trust funds so that they could not be ~*ed* by their heirs —Lucien Price⟩ ⟨willing to ~ their lives on the gratuitous work that great art demands —Edmund Wilson⟩ ⟨the most brilliant journalist of my generation . . . often ~*s* his genius for invective —T.S.Eliot⟩ ⟨~*ing* away income by gambling —Bingham Dai⟩ ~ *vi* **1 :** ROAM, WANDER **2 :** to spend in a wasteful manner ⟨they often ~*ed*, but they never gave —Richard Savage⟩ **3 :** to scatter in various directions ⟨many of the enemy . . . ~*ed* like quail from a flushed covey —B.A. Williams⟩ **syn** see WASTE

²squander \"\ *n* -s **:** an act or instance of squandering **:** EXTRAVAGANCE

squan·der·er \-dərə(r)\ *n* -s **:** one that squanders; *esp* **:** WASTREL

squan·der·mania \,=də(r)+\ *n* [¹*squander* + *mania*] **:** the practice of spending money extravagantly esp. by a government ⟨within 6 months he had . . . begun history's most prodigious ~ —D.A.Reed⟩

squanter-squash \ˈskwäntə(r),=\ *n* [alter. of earlier *isquoutersquash* — more at SQUASH] **:** SUMMER SQUASH

squan·tum \ˈskwäntəm *also* -wȯn-\ *n* -s [prob. fr. *Squantum*, former Indian village in eastern Mass.] *NewEng* **:** CLAMBAKE 1a

squar·able \ˈskwa(a)rəbəl, -wer-\ *adj* **:** capable of being squared ⟨only theory ~ with the known facts⟩

¹square \ˈskwa(a)|(ə)r, -we|, |ə\ *n* -s [ME *squyre, square*, fr. MF *esquerre, esquarre*, fr. (assumed) VL *exquadra*, fr. (assumed) VL *exquadrare* to square, fr. L *ex-* ¹ex- + *quadrare* to square — more at QUADRATE] **1 :** an instrument with at least one right angle and two or more straight edges used to lay out or test right angles — see COMBINATION SQUARE, FRAMING SQUARE, TRY SQUARE, T SQUARE **2 a** *obs* **:** the corner or angle of a figure **b** *obs* **:** the side of a rectangle **c :** a rectangle with all four sides equal — see AREA table **3 a :** any of the quadrilateral spaces marked out on a board for playing games **b :** a square piece, surface, or area ⟨a quilt of ~*s* sewn together⟩ ⟨~ of pavement⟩ **c** *obs* **:** the bosom of a woman's dress **d :** a scarf of a square shape **4 :** the product of a number or quantity multiplied by itself ⟨81 is the ~ of 9⟩ **:** the second power of a number **5** *obs* **:** guiding principle **:** PATTERN, RULE, STANDARD **6 a** *obs* **:** justness of workmanship or of conduct **b** *obs* **:** exact proportion **:** REGULARITY **c** *obs* **:** quartile aspect **7 squares** *pl, obs* **:** MATTERS, AFFAIRS, THINGS — used in the phrase *how go the squares* **8 a** *Brit* **:** an open area enclosed by residential buildings and commonly laid out with trees, grass, walks, gardens **b :** an open place or area formed at the meeting of two or more streets ⟨village ~⟩ ⟨market ~⟩ **c :** BLOCK 5e (1), 5e(2) **9 a :** a body of troops formed in solid or hollow rectangle with the ranks that form the sides facing outwards ⟨the brave ~*s* of war —Shak.⟩ **b :** SQUARE DANCE 1 **c :** set 36b **d :** a figure in square dancing performed by moving successively forward, sideward, backward, sideward **10 a :** the upper part of the shank of an anchor to which the stock is attached **b :** the square-ended projection in a clock or watch turned by the key in winding ⟨winding ~⟩ **11 a :** a solid object or piece approximating a cube or having a square as its largest face ⟨~ of cheese⟩ ⟨butter ~*s*⟩ **b :** a molding of square section **c :** a rolled or machined piece (as of steel) with a square section ⟨rounds, bars, and ~*s* are available⟩ **12 :** an unopened cotton flower with its enclosing bracts **13 :** the portion of the board of a book cover that projects beyond the edge of the leaves at the top, fore edge, or bottom ⟨an adequate ~ at the fore edge⟩ **14 :** a builder's unit of floor or roof area equal to 100 square feet ⟨so many shingles per ~⟩; *also* **:** the number of roofing slates or shingles needed per square **15 :** a strong iron frame in a spinning mule to which the carriages are secured **16 :** a person who is an outsider or adversary because of the conventionality, conservatism, or respectability of his taste, behavior, or way of life **:** one who is not in the know **:** UNSOPHISTICATE; *also* **:** DUPE, SUCKER — compare BOURGEOIS, PHILISTINE — **at square** *obs* **:** in a state of opposition **:** at variance **:** at odds — **by the square** *obs* **:** PRECISELY, EXACTLY ⟨do you not know my lady's foot *by the square* —Shak.⟩ — **on the square** *adv (or adj)* **1 :** at right angles ⟨plants are set out *on the square* about 30 inches apart —F.D.Smith & Barbara Wilcox⟩ **2 :** in an open, fair manner **:** on the level **:** HONESTLY, HONORABLY ⟨operate a gambling game *on the square*⟩ **3 :** on terms of equality — **out of square 1 :** not at right angles **:** OBLIQUELY **2 :** not in order **:** not regular **:** out of true

²square \"\ *adj* -ER/-EST [ME, modif. (influenced by MF *esquarre* square) of MF *escarré*, past part. of *escarrer* to square, fr. (assumed) VL *exquadrare*] **1 a :** having four equal sides and four right angles **b :** forming a right angle ⟨~ corner⟩ **2 a :** having a width nearly equal to the height and rectangular rather than curving outline ⟨~ cabinet⟩ ⟨~ house⟩ **b :** of a shape suggesting strength and solidity ⟨~ jaw⟩ ⟨~ shoulders⟩ **c** *of a hand* **:** having the palm square at the wrist and at the base of square fingers and usu. held by palmists to indicate qualities of order, practicality, and common sense **d :** rectangular and equilateral in section ⟨~ tower⟩ ⟨~ rod⟩ ⟨pushing ~ pegs into round holes⟩ **3 a** *of a unit of length* **:** converted from a linear unit into a square unit of area having the same length of side **:** SQUARED ⟨~ foot⟩ **b :** being of a specified length in each of two equal dimensions — used after the term of measurement ⟨a room ten feet ~⟩ ⟨a 50 foot ~ courtyard⟩ **4 a :** exactly adjusted or correspondent **:** precisely constructed or aligned **b :** JUST, FAIR, HONEST, STRAIGHTFORWARD ⟨~ in all his dealings⟩ ⟨wanted to do the ~ thing⟩ ⟨a good, ~, explicit fallacy that can be squarely met and . . . refuted —C.S.Peirce⟩ **c :** leaving no balance **:** SETTLED ⟨make an account ~⟩ **d :** EVEN, TIED ⟨the golfers were all ~ on the 17th hole⟩ **e :** SUBSTANTIAL, SATISFYING ⟨~ meal⟩ **f** *of a horse's gait* **:** smooth and regular in movement **g :** having unsophisticated or conservative tastes esp. in entertainment **:** belonging to or characteristic of the respectable law-abiding tradition-bound classes of society ⟨~ audience⟩ ⟨some ~ music⟩; *also* **:** LEGITIMATE, LEGAL ⟨the car has ~ plates on it⟩ ⟨~ name⟩ **5 a :** set at right angles with the mast and keel — used of the yards of a square-rigged ship **b :** at right angles to a line drawn from wicket to wicket and usu. in line with the batting crease — used of cricket fielding positions, fieldsmen, and hits ⟨a ~ cut⟩; compare FINE **6 a :** markedly regular in rhythmic and harmonic structure ⟨~ melody⟩ **b** *of a military group* **:** based primarily on four units ⟨~ army division⟩ — compare TRIANGULAR **7 :** woven with an equal number of warp and weft threads per inch — **get square with :** to get even with **:** get satisfaction for an injury or insult from

³square \"\ *vb* -ED/-ING/-S [ME *squaren*, modif. (influenced by MF *esquarre* square) of MF *escarrer* to square, fr. (assumed) VL *exquadrare* — more at SQUARE (n.)] *vt* **1 a :** to form with right angles and straight edges or flat surfaces **:** make square or rectangular ⟨~ a building stone⟩ ⟨~ a timber⟩ ⟨~ the end of a board⟩ **b :** to measure in order to find or test the deviation from a right angle, straight line, or plane surface **:** apply a try square to **2 :** to bring approximately to a right angle ⟨thrust out his chin and *squared* his shoulders⟩ ⟨stood with feet apart and elbows *squared*⟩ ⟨~ the yards of a ship⟩ **3 a :** to multiply (a number or quantity) by itself **:** raise to the second power **b :** to find a square equal in area to ⟨~ a circle⟩ **c :** to be equal to a square of (a specified size) ⟨*squared* ten feet and ten inches —J.H.Bond⟩ **4 :** to compare with or reduce to a selected standard **:** ADJUST, REGULATE, SHAPE ⟨~ our actions by the opinions of others —John Milton⟩ **5 a :** to make even so as to leave no remainder or difference **:** BALANCE, SETTLE ⟨~ an account⟩ **b :** to even the score of (a contest) ⟨~ a ball game⟩ **6 :** to hold a quartile position respecting ⟨April, when Jupiter ~*s* his Pluto-Mars conjunction in the earthy sign of Taurus —*Time*⟩ **7 :** to mark the surface of (as a paper, a drawing) into squares — often used with *off* **8 a :** to set right **:** straighten out **:** bring into harmonious relation — used with *with* ⟨the corporation must, if it is to survive, ~ itself with the basic beliefs of the American people —E.C. Lindeman⟩ ⟨untamed feudal noble could ~ a good deal of anticlericalism with a conscience that had a . . . horror of . . . heresy —D.W.Brogan⟩ **b** (1) **:** to induce to favorable or satisfactory action or attitude by means of a bribe ⟨~ a watchman⟩ (2) **:** to settle by or as if by a bribe **:** FIX ⟨a friend in city hall can ~ the rap⟩ ~ *vi* **1 :** CONFORM, FIT — used with *with* ⟨making his story ~ with a larger independent body of ideas —Charles Frankel⟩ **2** *obs* **:** to take an opposite position **:** QUARREL — used with *with* **3 :** to settle matters; *esp* **:** to pay the bill — usu. used with *for* or *up* ⟨*squared* for his meal and left the diner⟩ ⟨~ up and go home⟩ **4 :** to take a fighting stance — often used with *up* or *off* ⟨surprised when he suddenly *squared* up to me⟩ ⟨a man *squared* off for his own pride in those days —Gene Tunney⟩ **syn** see AGREE — **square a valve :** to adjust the effective length of a slide-valve rod in a steam engine so that the valve will travel the proper distance past the steam edge of each port — **square by the lifts and braces :** to set the yards at right angles with the keel and with the mast

⁴square \"\ *adv* [²*square*] **1 :** STRAIGHTFORWARDLY, HONESTLY ⟨came ~ out with the truth⟩ ⟨always treated him ~⟩ **2 a :** so as to face or be face to face ⟨the house stood ~ to the road⟩ **b :** at right angles ⟨the path turned ~ to the left⟩ **3 :** with nothing intervening or deflecting **:** head on **:** DIRECTLY ⟨ran ~ into me⟩ ⟨coat buttoned ~ to the chin⟩ ⟨a hole lay ~ in the middle of the road⟩ **4 :** FIRMLY, SOLIDLY ⟨looked him ~ in the eye⟩ ⟨planted his great bulk ~ before his enemy⟩ **5 :** in a square shape **:** so as to form a square ⟨~ cut a diamond ~⟩ ⟨fold a sheet of paper ~⟩

square alphabet *n* **:** HEBREW ALPHABET 1

square and rabbet *n* **:** ANNULET

square away *vi* **1 :** to square the yards so as to sail before the wind **2 :** to put everything in order or in readiness **:** get ready ⟨is *squaring away* to write the first words of the new chapter —*Atlantic*⟩ **3 :** to take up a fighting stance ⟨a professional fighter he was being compelled to *square away* against —Hamilton Basso⟩ ~ *vt* **:** to put in order or readiness **:** make ready ⟨everything . . . is *squared away*, and satisfaction and contentment reign —W.W.Howells⟩ ⟨helped him *square away* his field scarf and button his blouse —L.M.Uris⟩

square back *n* **:** a flat backbone of a book — compare *round back*

square-backed fiddler \ˈ=,=-\ *n* **:** WOOD CRAB

square body *n* **:** the part of a ship in which the frames run perpendicular to the keel — compare CANT BODY

square bracket *n* **:** ¹BRACKET 4a

square cap *n* **:** MORTARBOARD 2

square capital *n* **:** a simply and elegantly formed erect Roman capital letter used in Roman inscriptions and in the early book hand modeled in the same style without a lowercase letter form — compare CURSIVE, RUSTIC CAPITAL, UNCIAL

square capitals

square center *n* **:** a lathe center with a 4-sided pyramidal point

square centimeter *n* **:** a unit of area equal to a square one centimeter long on each side — see METRIC SYSTEM table

square chain *n* **:** a unit of area equal to a square one chain long on each side or 0.10 acre or 4.047 ares

square check *n* **:** CROSS-CHECK 1b

squared *past of* SQUARE

¹square dance *n* **1 :** a set dance typically danced by four couples arranged to form a hollow square — compare COUNTRY-DANCE, QUADRILLE **2 :** a social gathering for square dancing **:** HOEDOWN 2a

²square dance *vi* **:** to take part in a square dance

square dancer *n* **:** a performer of or devotee to square dance

squared circle *n* **:** a boxing ring

square deal *n* **1 :** an honest and fair transaction or trade **2 :** a political program aiming at a fair consideration of the interests of all concerned

squared paper *n* **1 :** paper ruled or printed in squares **:** GRAPH PAPER **2 :** paper that has been trimmed by guillotine so as to be square on at least one corner

square-dress \ˈ=;=\ *vt* **:** SWAGE-SET

square drift *n* **:** DRIFT 4e

square-drill \ˈ=;=\ *vt* **:** to drill a square hole in

squared stone *n* **:** a stone roughly dressed and squared — compare ASHLAR

square edge and sound *n* **:** a specific grade of sawed timbers (as of yellow pine)

square engine *n* **:** an engine in which the stroke is equal to the diameter of the cylinder bore

squareface \ˈ=,=\ *n* [so called fr. a popular name for gin in So. Africa where it was formerly sold in square bottles] **:** cheap hard liquor

squareflipper \ˈ=;==\ *n* [²*square* + *flipper*] **:** BEARDED SEAL

square foot *n* **:** a unit of area equal to a square one foot long on each side — see MEASURE table

square frame *n* **:** a frame in the square body of a ship

square furlong *n* **:** a unit of area equal to a square one furlong on each side or 10 acres or 404.7 ares

square gait *n* **:** OPEN GAIT

squarehead \ˈ=,=\ *n* [²*square* + *head*] **1 :** BLOCKHEAD, DOLT **2 a :** GERMAN — usu. taken to be offensive **b :** SCANDINAVIAN; *esp* **:** SWEDE — usu. taken to be offensive

square-headed \ˈ=;==\ *adj* **:** having a square head ⟨a *square-headed* bolt⟩; *specif* **:** having a straight horizontal lintel or a flat arch ⟨a *square-headed* doorway⟩

square hebrew *n, cap H* **:** HEBREW ALPHABET 2

square inch *n* **:** a unit of area equal to a square one inch long on each side — see MEASURE table

square john \-ˈjän\ *n, sometimes cap J, slang* **:** a law-abiding citizen; *also* **:** one who is not addicted to dope

square joint *n* **:** STRAIGHT JOINT 2

square-jointed \ˈ=;==\ *adj, of a track* **:** having the rail joints opposite

square kilometer *n* **:** a metric unit of area equal to a square that is one kilometer long on each side — see METRIC SYSTEM table

square knot *n* **:** a knot made of two reverse half-knots and used to join the ends of two cords or to tie up and bind bundles and other objects

square knotting *n* **:** knot making for decorative design — compare MACRAME

square-law \ˈ=;=\ *adj* **:** designed so that one variable concerned in the operation is proportional to the square of another ⟨in a *square-law* detector tube the plate-current variations are proportional to the square of grid-voltage variations⟩

square league *n* **:** ¹LEAGUE 2

square leg *n* **:** a fielding position in cricket square with the receiving batsman and on the leg side; *also* **:** a player fielding in this position — see CRICKET illustration

square letter *n* **:** a letter having its horizontal lines at right angles to its up-and-down lines

square-lipped rhinoceros \ˈ=;=-\ *n* **:** WHITE RHINOCEROS

square·ly *adv* **1 :** in a square form or manner **2 a :** in a straightforward manner **:** JUSTLY, HONESTLY ⟨dealt ~ with his customers⟩ **b :** in a straight or direct manner ⟨looked him ~ in the eyes⟩

square·man \-mən\ *n, pl* **squaremen** *Scot* **:** one who uses a square for adjusting or testing his work: as **a :** CARPENTER **b :** STONECUTTER

square mark *n* **:** a mark placed upon running lines (as halyards or braces) to ensure their being secured always at the same point and giving a neat uniform appearance

square-marked toad \ˈ=;=-\ *n* **:** a widespread common toad (*Bufo regularis*) of Africa

square matrix *n, math* **:** a matrix with the number of rows and columns the same

square measure *n* **:** a unit or system of units for measuring area

square meter *n* **:** a unit of area equal to a square one meter on each side **:** CENTARE

square mile *n* **:** a unit of area equal to a square one mile long on each side — see MEASURE table

squaremouthed rhinoceros \ˈ=;=-\ *n* **:** WHITE RHINOCEROS

square-necked grain beetle \ˈ=;=-\ *n* **:** a small reddish beetle (*Cathartus quadricollis*) that feeds on dry cereal products — called also *red grain beetle*

square·ness *n* -ES [ME *squarenesse*, fr. ²*square* + *-nesse* -ness] **:** the quality or state of being square

square notation *n* **:** an early musical notation using square and oblong note heads

square of opposition : a square figure on which may be demonstrated the four logical oppositions by contrariety, subcontrariety, subalternation, and contradiction

square of the circle : QUADRATURE OF THE CIRCLE

square piano *n* **:** a piano having a horizontal frame, an oblong case, and strings parallel with the keyboard

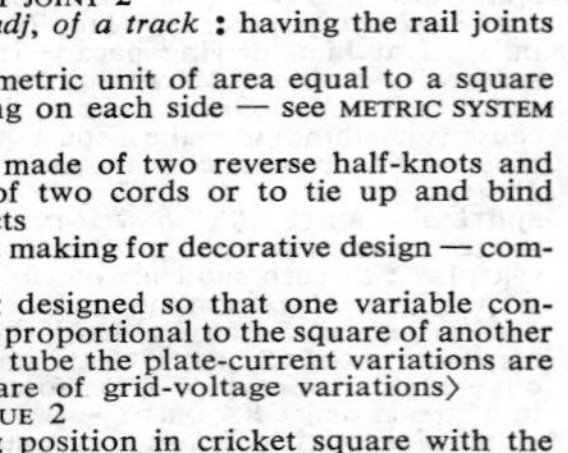

square piano

¹squar·er \ˈskwa(a)rə(r), -werə-\ *n* -s [ME, fr. *squaren* to square + *-er* — more at SQUARE] **1 :** one that squares; *esp* **:** a workman who squares timber or stone **2 :** a square broach **3 :** one who obtains permission (as by offering free passes) to post on private property material advertising a coming entertainment

²squarer *comparative of* SQUARE

square rig *n* **:** a sailing-ship rig in which the sails are bent to the yards carried athwart the mast and trimmed with braces — compare FORE-AND-AFT RIG

square-rigged \ˈ=;=\ *adj* **:** having or equipped with a square rig

square-rig·ger \ˈ=;rigə(r)\ *n* **:** a square-rigged craft

square rod *n* **:** a unit of area equal to a square one rod on a side — see MEASURE table
square root *n* **:** a factor of a number that when squared gives the number ⟨either +3 or −3 is the *square root* of 9⟩
squares *pl of* SQUARE, *pres 3d sing of* SQUARE
square sail \ˈ=səl, -ˌsāl\ *n* **:** a 4-sided sail extended on a yard suspended at the middle from a mast; *specif* **:** a sail set on a yard on the single mast or foremast of a fore-and-aft-rigged ship (as a sloop or schooner) — see SAIL illustration
square–serif \ˈ=ˌ=ˈ=\ *adj* **:** having strokes of equal weight and unbracketed serifs at right angles — used of printed letters
square set *n* **1 :** any of the rectangular sets used in the square-set system of mining **2 :** a group of four couples arranged in a square for a square dance
square set system *n* **:** a method of timbering a mine in which heavy timbers are framed together in rectangular sets 6 or 7 feet high and from 4 to 6 feet long so as to fill in as the ore body is removed by overhand stoping
square shake *n* **:** fair treatment **:** SQUARE DEAL
square shooter *n* **:** an honest person **:** one who plays fairly and justly
square–shouldered \ˈ=ˈ=ˌ=\ *adj* **:** having the shoulders high and well braced back **:** not round-shouldered
squarest *superlative of* SQUARE
square staff *n* **:** STAFF ANGLE
square stake *n* **:** a smith's stake with a square flat top — see STAKE illustration
square stance *n* **:** a golfer's stance in which both feet are parallel to the line of flight used primarily for distance shots — compare CLOSED STANCE, OPEN STANCE
square–stem \ˈ=ˌ=\ *n* **:** any of several plants with prominently angled stems: as **a :** a self-heal (*Prunella vulgaris*) **b :** OSWEGO TEA **c :** an American centaury (*Sabbatia angularis*)
square–stem spike rush \ˈ=ˌ=-\ *n* **:** a spike rush (*Eleocharis quadrangulata*) with square-angled stems
square stern *n* **1 :** a ship's stern having a transom and joining the counter timbers at an angle **2 :** a stern with no overhang
square table *n* **:** VIGENÈRE TABLEAU
squaretail \ˈ=ˌ=\ *n* **1 :** BROOK TROUT **2 :** a small dark long-bodied sluggish pelagic fish (*Tetragonurus cuvieri*) of the Atlantic, Pacific, and Mediterranean that has a compact armor of bony scales, a tail squarish in section, and flesh that is sometimes poisonous
square thread *n* **:** a screw thread so made that the sides, root, and crest of any section formed by a plane that passes through the thread axis are all equal theoretically to one half the pitch
square–thread \ˈ=ˈ=\ *vt* **:** to form a square thread on
square–tipped \ˈ=ˈ=\ *adj* **:** having the tip square
square–toed \ˈ=ˈ=\ *adj* **1 :** having the toe square ⟨*square-toed* boots⟩ **2 :** OLD-FASHIONED, CONSERVATIVE, PRIM — **square–toed·ness** *n* -ES
square up *vi* **:** to arrange one's self along with seven other dancers in a square set ready for square dance figures
square wave *n* **:** the rectangular wave form of a quantity which varies periodically and abruptly from one to the other of two uniform values
square weevil *n* **:** a So. American snout beetle (*Anthonomus vestitus*) closely related to the boll weevil
square wheel *n* **:** a wheel (of a car or locomotive) that has a flat spot on its rim
square yard *n* **:** a unit of area equal to a square one yard long on each side — see MEASURE table
squaring *pres part of* SQUARE
squaring lathe *n* **:** a lathe for shaping square pieces
squaring the circle **:** QUADRATURE OF THE CIRCLE
squar·ish \ˈskwa(a)rish, -wer-, -rēsh\ *adj* **:** somewhat square in form or appearance **:** resembling a square or block ⟨~ windows⟩ ⟨~ house⟩ — **squar·ish·ly** *adv*
1**squark** \ˈskwȯ(ə)rk, -ō(ə)k\ *n* -S [alter. of 2*squawk*] **:** SQUAWK, CROAK
2**squark** \"\ *vi* -ED/-ING/-S [alter. of 1*squawk*] **:** SQUAWK, CROAK
squar·rose \ˈskwaˌrōs, -waˌr-\ *also* **squar·rous** \-rəs\ *adj* [L *squarrosus* scurfy, scabby; akin to OSlav *skvrŭna* filth] **:** rough with divergent scales or processes; *esp* **:** having stiff spreading bracts ⟨a ~ involucre⟩ — **squar·rose·ly** *adv*
squar·ru·lose \-_r(y)əˌlōs\ *adj* [blend of *squarrose* and *-ule*] **:** somewhat squarrose
squar·son \ˈskwärsᵊn, -wäs-\ *n* -S [blend of *squire* and *parson*] **:** a landed proprietor who is also a clergyman of the Church of England
1**squash** \ˈskwäsh, -wȯ(i)sh, *substand* -wȯ(ə)rsh\ *vb* -ED/-ING/-ES [MF *esquasser*, fr. (assumed) VL *exquassare*, fr. L *ex-* 1ex- + *quassare* to shake, break into pieces — more at QUASH] *vt* **1 :** to press or beat into a pulp or a flat mass **:** CRUSH ⟨billycock hat ~*ed* low over his forehead —Robert Graves⟩ ⟨~ a fly on the windowpane⟩ **2 a :** to put down **:** SUPPRESS ⟨~ a revolt⟩ ⟨~ a strike⟩ **b :** DISCONCERT, SQUELCH ⟨first overshadowed by . . . his father, then ~*ed* by his contemptuous, ambitious wife —*Time*⟩ ~ *vi* **1 :** to lose shape and flatten out under pressure or impact ⟨guavas . . . fell ~*ing* to the ground —Edwin Granberry⟩ **2 :** to proceed with a splashing or squelching sound ⟨~*ing* through the mud⟩ **3 :** SQUEEZE, PRESS ⟨four of us managed to ~ into the back seat⟩ **4** *of an airplane* **:** to lose altitude in a horizontal position because of loss of airspeed **:** settle vertically
2**squash** \"\ *n* -ES **1** *obs* **:** something soft and easily crushed; *specif* **:** an unripe pod of peas **2 :** a sudden fall of a heavy soft body or the sound of such a fall **3 :** a squelching sound made by walking on oozy ground or in water-soaked boots **4 a :** a crushed mass ⟨the crash reduced the car to ~⟩ ⟨the tomatoes have all gone to ~⟩ **b :** a bit of tissue crushed between slide and cover glass and stained in situ, used esp. for cytological study of chromosomes **5** *Brit* **:** a drink of the sweetened juice of a citrus fruit usu. with added soda water **:** ADE ⟨orange ~⟩ ⟨lemon ~⟩ **6 a** *archaic* **:** a soft rubber ball used in the game of squash rackets **b :** SQUASH RACQUETS **7 a :** a crush of people massed together **b :** a crowded social function
3**squash** \"\ *adv* **:** with a squash or a squashing sound ⟨you must fall ~ into a bog —Thomas Gray⟩
4**squash** \"\ *n, pl* **squashes** *or* **squash** [by shortening & alter. fr. earlier *isquoutersquash*, fr. Natick & Narraganset *askútasquash*, lit., green thing eaten green] **1 :** any of various fruits of plants of the genus *Cucurbita* that are widely cultivated as a vegetable and for livestock feed: as **a :** SUMMER SQUASH **b :** WINTER SQUASH **c :** PUMPKIN 1a (2) **2** *or* **squash vine :** a plant that bears squashes
5**squash** \"\ *n* -ES [short for *musquash*] *archaic* **:** MUSKRAT
squash beetle *n* **1 :** a small American black-and-yellow striped beetle (*Acalymma vittata*) often very injurious to the leaves of squash and cucumber **2 :** SQUASH LADYBIRD
squash·ber·ry \ˈ=- — *see* BERRY\ *n* [4*squash* + *berry*] **:** the fruit of any of various plants (as the dockmackie) of the genus *Viburnum; also* **:** the plant itself
squash bite *n* **:** an impression of the teeth and mouth made by closing the teeth on modeling composition or wax
squash blossom *n* **:** hair dressed in large loops over each ear in a fashion formerly peculiar to Hopi girls
squash borer *also* **squash vine borer** *n* **:** a small clearwing moth (*Melittia satyriniformis*) or its larva that bores in the squash vine
squash bug *n* **:** a brownish black American insect (*Anasa tristis*) of the family Coreidae that is injurious to squash vines
squash flea beetle *n* **:** POTATO FLEA BEETLE

squash blossom

squash·i·ly \-shəlē\ *adv* **:** in a squashy manner ⟨slipped and sat down ~ in the muddy path⟩
squash·i·ness \-shēnəs\ *n* -ES **:** the quality of being squashy ⟨the most repulsive larva of all in its ~ —Compton Mackenzie⟩
squash ladybird *or* **squash ladybug** *n* **:** a ladybird (*Epilachna borealis*) that feeds both as larva and imago on the squash, pumpkin, melon, and cucumber
squash racquets *or* **squash rackets** *n pl but sing in constr* **:** a strenuous singles or doubles game played in a four-wall court with a long handled racket having a small round head and a small black rubber ball with slow bounce which can be played or caromed off any number of walls provided it reaches the front wall above the telltale before hitting the floor — called also *squash;* compare SQUASH TENNIS
squash tennis *n* **:** a racket game resembling squash racquets played by two people only in a four-wall court using a lively inflated ball the size of a tennis ball which bounces very fast and requires great speed in anticipation and turning though less speed of foot and in which points are scored only by the server
squashy \-shē\ *adj* -ER/-EST [1*squash* + *-y*] **1 :** easily squashed **:** very soft ⟨~ pillow⟩ **2 :** softly wet **:** BOGGY **3 :** soft because overripe ⟨~ melons⟩
squash yellow *n* **:** a variable color averaging a brilliant yellow that is redder and deeper than butter yellow or average daffodil and redder and stronger than lemon chrome
1**squat** \ˈskwä\|t *also* -wȯ\|; *usu* \|d· +V\ *vb* **squatted** *or* **squat; squatted** *or* **squat; squatting; squats** [ME *squatten*, fr. MF *esquater, esquatir*, fr. *es-* 1ex- (fr. L *ex-*) + *quatir, catir* to press, fr. (assumed) VL *coactire* to press together — more at DECATING] *vt* **1 a** *obs* **:** to bruise or lay flat with a blow **b** *obs* **:** CRUSH, REPRESS, SILENCE **2 :** to cause to crouch or sit on the ground ⟨*squatted* himself down before the fire⟩ **3 :** to occupy without title or payment of rent ⟨the rest of the mews had long been *squatted* by a low-class colony of private traders —Margery Sharp⟩ ~ *vi* **1 :** to crouch close to the ground to escape observation **:** COWER ⟨*squatting* hare⟩ **2 a :** to sit on one's haunches; *specif* **:** to crouch on the ground with legs fully drawn up before the body **b :** to sit cross-legged **c :** to take or keep a balanced position with knees fully bent and heels raised **d :** to stay persistently or obstinately seated **:** sit still and do nothing ⟨however solidly the officers of the court might ~ on their chairs —Earle Birney⟩ **3 a :** to settle on land without right or title or payment of rent **b :** to settle on public land under government regulation with the purpose of acquiring title **c :** to occupy without permission an abandoned or unguarded empty house **4** *of a ship* **:** to settle by the stern when under way at speed **5** *of clay ware* **:** to soften gradually and slump down
2**squat** \"\ *n* -S [ME, fr. *squatten* to crush, squat] **1** *chiefly dial* **:** a heavy fall or blow **2 a :** the act of squatting, crouching, or sitting **b :** the posture of one that squats ⟨horse threw himself into a ~ —F.B.Gipson⟩ **3 a :** a place where one squats; *esp* **:** the lair of a small animal ⟨~ of a hare⟩ **b :** a piece of land claimed by a squatter **4** *dial* **a :** a small mass of ore **b :** a mineral consisting of tin ore and spar **5 :** the amount of squatting of a ship under way ⟨allowance for the well-known ~ of Great Lakes vessels when close to the bottom in narrow channels —*Survey Graphic*⟩
3**squat** \"\ *adj* **squat·ter; squat·test** [fr. past part. of 1*squat*] **1 a :** bent into a sitting position typically resting the weight on the balls of the feet with the haunches close above the heels ⟨the catcher, ~ and ready for the pitch⟩ **b :** sitting on the ground with the body hunched and the legs bent ⟨sitting ~ around the fire⟩ **c :** crouching with the chest and belly close to the ground ⟨a hare ~ on the hillside⟩ **2 :** marked by closeness to the earth, lowness, or disproportionate thickness suggestive of a person squatting **:** gracelessly thick and wanting height or pleasing stature ⟨a ~ red smokestack between two stumpy masts —George Santayana⟩ **syn** see STOCKY
squat·a·ro·la \ˌskwädˌəˈrōlə, -rōlə\ *n, cap* [NL, fr. It dial., black-bellied plover] **:** a genus of birds (family Charadriidae) consisting of the black-bellied plover
squat·a·role *or* **squat·er·ole** \ˈ==ˌrōl\ *n* -S [NL *squatarola*] **:** BLACK-BELLIED PLOVER
squat board *n* **:** a horizontal plane (as a plate or extension of the hull) placed at the level of the water to prevent squatting
squat·i·na \ˈskwätᵊnə\ *n* [NL, fr. L, angelfish] **1** *cap* **:** a genus (coextensive with the family Squatinidae) of sharks having a broadly rounded head with winglike lateral extensions and a broad flattened body that resembles that of a ray and being sometimes placed in a separate suborder but usu. included in Squaloidea **2** -S **:** any shark of the genus *Squatina* **:** MONKFISH — **squat·i·nid** \-ᵊnəd\ *n or adj* — **squat·i·noid** \-ᵊnˌȯid\ *adj*
squat·ly *adv* **:** in a squat manner **:** so as to give a squat appearance ⟨building he envisioned was sort of ~ Romanesque —James Dugan⟩
squat·more \ˈskwätˌmō(ə)r\ *n* -S [2*squat* (fall) + *more;* prob. fr. its supposed healing effect on bruises] **:** HORNED POPPY
squat·ness *n* -ES **:** the quality of being squat
squat tag *n* **:** a game of tag in which one may escape being tagged by squatting before being touched — called also *stoop tag*
squat·tage \ˈskwädij\ *n* -S [1*squat* + *-age*] *Austral* **:** a property (as a sheep run or station) occupied by a squatter
squatted *past of* SQUAT
1**squat·ter** \ˈskwä\|d·ə(r) \|tə- *also* -wȯ\|\ *vi* -ED/-ING/-S [prob. of Scand origin; akin to Sw dial. *skvättra* to squander, Dan *skvatte* to sprinkle, Icel *skvetta* to squirt] **1 :** to go along through or as if through water ⟨a school of fish . . . ~*ing* across the bay in an arrowy rush —R.A.W.Hughes⟩ **2 :** to plunge about in or as if in water
2**squatter** \"\ *n* -S **:** a loud fluttering noise
3**squat·ter** \"\ *n* -S [1*squat* + *-er*] **1 :** one that squats: as **a :** one that settles on land without a right or title **b :** one that settles lawfully on government land with the intention of acquiring title **2 a :** PECTORAL SANDPIPER **b :** PARTRIDGE BRONZEWING **3 a :** a person occupying crown land in Australia for sheep raising under a lease or a license; *specif* **:** one holding a sheep run as freehold **b :** the owner or occupant of a sheep run or station in Australia; *specif* **:** one farming on a large scale, coming of a good family, or having a good education
squat·ter·ism \-əˌrizəm\ *n* -S [3*squatter* + *-ism*] **:** the practice of acquiring land by squatting
squatter sovereignty *n* **:** POPULAR SOVEREIGNTY 2 — usu. used disparagingly
squatter's right *n* **:** a right to occupancy of or title to land based on adverse possession for the statutory period of time
squatting *pres part of* SQUAT
squat·tish \ˈskwädish\ *adj* **:** somewhat squat
squat·tle \ˈskwädᵊl\ *vi* [freq. of 1*squat*] *archaic* **:** SQUAT, SETTLE
squat·toc·ra·cy \skwädˈäkrəsē\ *n* -ES [1*squat* + *-o-* + *-cracy*] **:** the wealthy and influential owners of sheep ranches in Australia ⟨were dependent upon the emerging ~ and the more highly paid government officials —Bernard Smith⟩
squat·ty \ˈskwä\|d·ē, \|t\, \|i *also* -wȯ\|\ *adj, sometimes* -ER/-EST [3*squat* + *-y*] **:** somewhat squat **:** DUMPY, THICKSET
squat vault *n* **:** a gymnastic vault in which the body is supported on both hands, the knees are flexed and drawn up toward the chest, and the legs pass between the arms as the body passes over the apparatus
squaw \ˈskwȯ\ *n* -S [of Algonquian origin; akin to Natick *squa* female creature, *squàas* woman, Narraganset *squàws*] **1 a :** an American Indian woman — compare SANNUP **b :** FEMALE, WOMAN, WIFE — usu. used disparagingly **2 :** an effeminate person **:** a man of womanish character — usu. used disparagingly **3 :** a form for holding a barrel during the process of crozing and chiming **4 :** a figure target representing a kneeling posture
squaw·ber·ry \ˈ=- — *see* BERRY\ *n* [prob. so called fr. the use of the twigs among the Indians in basketry work] **1 :** DEERBERRY 1 **2 :** PARTRIDGEBERRY 1 **3 :** any of several sumacs; *esp* **:** SQUAWBUSH 2
squawbush \ˈ=ˌ=\ *n* [so called fr. the use of the berries among Indians as a mordant in dyeing] **1 :** CRANBERRY TREE **2 :** a sumac (*Rhus trilobata*) of western No. America with unpleasantly scented trifoliolate or sometimes simple leaves and edible fruit **3 :** any of several shrubs of the genus *Cornus* **4 :** DWARF CORNEL
squaw cabbage *n* **1 :** INDIAN LETTUCE 3 **2 :** any of various plants of the family Cruciferae and esp. of the genera *Caulanthus* and *Streptanthus* believed to have been used as potherbs by the Indians
squaw carpet *n* **1 :** MAHALA MAT **2 :** MOUNTAIN MISERY
squaw corn *n* [so called fr. its extensive cultivation by the American Indians] **:** SOFT CORN 1
squaw currant *n* **:** a spineless shrub (*Ribes cereum*) native to the central and western U. S. having greenish white flowers and a crimson berry
squaw dance *n* **:** a round dance of the Plains Indians and Navaho in which the girls select partners
squaw–drops \ˈ=ˌ=\ *n pl but sing in constr* **1 :** CANCERROOT **2 :** SQUAWROOT 1
squaw duck *n* **:** EIDER
squawfish \ˈ=ˌ=\ *n* **1 :** any of several large cyprinid fishes (genus *Ptychocheilus*) of western No. America: as **a :** a dull-green silver-marked fish (*P. oregonensis*) of the Columbia river **b :** a closely related and nearly indistinguishable fish (*P. grandis*) of central and northern California and parts of the Colorado river system — called also *Sacramento pike* **2 :** a common surf fish (*Taeniotoca lateralis*) of the Pacific coast of No. America
squawflower \ˈ=ˌ=\ *n* **:** PURPLE TRILLIUM
squaw grass *n* **:** a turkey beard (*Xerophyllum tenax*) of the mountains of the Pacific northwest having small white or cream-colored flowers in many-flowered racemes — called also *pine lily*
squaw hitch *n* [prob. so called fr. its use among the Indians] **:** a knot used in tying a pack on an animal
squaw huckleberry *n* **:** DEERBERRY 1
1**squawk** \ˈskwȯk\ *vi* -ED/-ING/-S [prob. blend of 1*squall* and 1*squeak*] **1 :** to make a loud harsh abrupt raucous outcry ⟨the hens woke up ~*ing* with terror —George Orwell⟩ **2 :** to complain or protest loudly or vehemently or objectionably ⟨his fellow profs . . . ~*ed* about the bonfires the boys built —Christopher Morley⟩ **syn** see COMPLAIN
2**squawk** \"\ *n* -S **1 :** the act or noise of squawking **:** a harsh squall ⟨~ of auto horns⟩ ⟨~ of a parrot⟩ **2 a :** a noisy, raucous complaint **:** an undignified protest ⟨~*s* of taxpayers⟩ ⟨~*s* from motorists . . . that they have been gypped on speeding charges —*N.Y. Times*⟩ **3 :** BLACK-CROWNED NIGHT HERON
squawk box *n* **:** an intercommunication system speaker **:** LOUDSPEAKER ⟨the *squawk box* announced the kid was circling the ship —*Newsweek*⟩ ⟨interrupted me by buzzing the interoffice *squawk box* —Albert Morgan⟩
squawk duck *n* **:** a duck with brownish spots before and behind the eyes that is a hybrid of the mallard and teal or of the mallard and widgeon
squawk·er \-kə(r)\ *n* -S **:** one that squawks: as **a :** a toy that makes a squawking sound **b :** DUCK CALL **c :** one that complains or protests noisily **d :** INFORMER 3 **e :** SQUAWK BOX
squawking thrush *n* **:** MISTLE THRUSH
squawk sheet *n* **:** a report made out by a pilot listing defects observed in an airplane during the flight
squawky \-kē\ *adj* -ER/-EST [2*squawk* + *-y*] **:** HARSH, DISCORDANT, RAUCOUS
squawl *var of* SQUALL
squaw lettuce *n* **:** a waterleaf (*Hydrophyllum occidentale*) of the southwestern U. S. having flowers on stalks that are longer than the leaf stalks and that bear one or two heads of flowers
squaw man *n* **1 :** a white man married to an Indian woman and usu. living as one of her tribe **2 :** BARDASH
squaw mint *n* **:** PENNYROYAL 2
squaw·mish *or* **squa·mish** \ˈskwȯmish\ *n, pl* **squawmish** *or* **squawmishes** *or* **squamish** *or* **squamishes** *usu cap* **1 a :** a Salishan people of the British Columbia coast opposite Vancouver Island **b :** a member of such people **2 :** the language of the Squawmish people
squawroot \ˈ=ˌ=\ *n* [so called fr. its use among Indians as a remedy for female disorders] **1 :** a No. American scaly herb (*Conopholis americana*) that is parasitic on oak and hemlock and has a thick stem with yellow fleshy scales bearing small flowers in their axils **2 :** BLUE COHOSH **3 :** PURPLE TRILLIUM **4 :** YAMP
squaws *pl of* SQUAW
squaw sachem *n* **:** a woman who is a sachem or the wife of a sachem
squaw side *n* [so called fr. the custom among the squaws of some tribes of mounting from the right side of a horse] **:** the right side of a horse
squaw vine *n* **:** PARTRIDGEBERRY 1
squaw–weed \ˈ=ˌ=\ *n* **1 :** RAGWORT **2 :** WHITE SNAKEROOT **3** *also* **squaw waterweed :** PENNYROYAL 2 **4 :** SQUAWBUSH 2 **5 :** HORSEWEED 1
squaw winter *n* [so called fr. the fact that it often precedes Indian summer] **:** a brief early period of wintry weather occurring in the autumn
squaw wood *n* [so called fr. the fact that squaws could gather it since an axe was not needed] **:** the small dead limbs or branches under the live canopy of a tree
squax·on \ˈskwȯksən\ *n, pl* **squaxon** *or* **squaxons** *usu cap* **1 a :** a Salishan people of the southwest Puget sound area, Washington **b :** a member of such people **2 :** a dialect related to Skagit
squdge \ˈskwəj\ *vi* -ED/-ING/-S [prob. imit.] **1 :** OOZE ⟨black mud *squdging* up between their bare toes —M.O.Williams⟩ **2 :** to slosh around (as in ooze or mud)
squdgy \-jē\ *adj, sometimes* -ER/-EST [blend of 3*squat* and *pudgy*] **:** SQUAT, PUDGY ⟨a ~, ill-shaped body —Carleton Beals⟩
1**squeak** \ˈskwēk\ *vb* -ED/-ING/-S [ME *squeken*, prob. of imit. origin] *vi* **1 :** to utter or make a short shrill cry or noise ⟨heard the door . . . ~ upon its wooden hinges —Pearl Buck⟩ ⟨a long lean individual who ~*ed* with a nasal twang —H.A. Chippendale⟩ **2 :** to reveal a secret from or as if from fear of punishment **:** commit an act of betrayal ⟨if somebody ~*ed*, he was quickly smothered and gagged —F.N.Souza⟩ **3 :** to pass, succeed, or win by a narrow margin ⟨his party barely ~*ed* through in congress —G.W.Johnson⟩ ⟨by six months of hard cramming . . . he ~*ed* by the finals —H.H.Martin⟩ **:** barely manage to get by ⟨still ~*ing* by on the manpower available —*Newsweek*⟩ ~ *vt* **:** to utter in a shrill piping tone
2**squeak** \"\ *n* -S **1 a :** a sharp shrill usu. short and not very loud cry or sound of the human voice or of an animal ⟨gave a startled ~ as he entered —J.H.Wheelwright⟩ **b :** a sharp shrill piercing noise ⟨the ~ of oars in oarlocks —*New Yorker*⟩ ⟨the ~ and crunch of walking boots on powdery snow —Alan Devoe⟩ **2 a :** CHANCE, OPPORTUNITY ⟨gave him one more ~⟩ **b :** ESCAPE ⟨finally quashed by a 5 to 4 vote . . . a close ~ —H.R.Medina⟩ — usu. used in the phrase *have a narrow squeak* ⟨you've had a narrow ~, but we've pulled you through —O.Henry⟩
squeak·er \-kə(r)\ *n* -S **1 :** one that squeaks: as **a** (1) **:** a young pigeon **:** SQUAB — usu. used of racing pigeons (2) **:** a predominantly gray currawong (*Strepera versicolor*) **b** *Brit* **:** a young pig **c :** any of several African freshwater armored catfishes **d :** a rat kangaroo of the genus *Bettongia* **e :** a noisemaker or a toy instrument that squeaks **f** *Brit* **:** one that betrays **:** INFORMER **2 :** a contest won by a small margin ⟨pitched a 5 to 4 ten-inning ~⟩
squeaky \-kē, -ki\ *adj* -ER/-EST **:** of the nature of, emitting, or tending to emit squeaks ⟨his off-key ~ voice —Lynn Montross⟩ ⟨a ~ door⟩
1**squeal** \ˈskwēl, *esp before pause or consonant* -ēəl\ *vb* -ED/-ING/-S [ME *squelen*, prob. of imit. origin] *vi* **1 a :** to cry with a sharp shrill prolonged sound ⟨horses ~*ed* with terror —Kenneth Roberts⟩ ⟨the bird ~*ed* as if in sudden pain —E.A. Armstrong⟩ ⟨~ with delight⟩ **b :** to emit a usu. loud and prolonged shrill piercing noise ⟨chalk ~*ing* on a slate —John Lardner⟩ ⟨heard the brakes ~⟩ **2 a :** to turn informer **:** SQUEAK ⟨he trusted me and I ~*ed* —*Best True Fact Detective*⟩ — usu. used with *on* ⟨marked for death by other prisoners because . . . he ~*ed* on them —*Springfield (Mass.) Union*⟩ **b :** COMPLAIN, PROTEST ⟨individual interests . . . getting hurt . . . are apt to ~ —Bertrum Mycock⟩ ~ *vt* **:** to utter or express with or as if with a squeal ⟨pigs . . . ~ emphatic disapproval of their enforced journey —Leslie Stephen⟩
2**squeal** \"\ *n* -S **:** a shrill sharp somewhat prolonged cry or noise; *specif* **:** HOWL 5
squeal·er \-ēlə(r)\ *n* -S **:** one that squeals: as **a :** a European swift (*Apus apus* syn. *Micropus apus*) **b :** HARLEQUIN DUCK **c :** an American golden plover (*Pluvialis dominica*) **d :** a young squab pigeon **e** *dial* **:** WOOD DUCK 1 **f :** a young grouse, partridge, or quail **g :** INFORMER, BETRAYER
squeam \ˈskwēm\ *n* -S [back-formation fr. *squeamish*] **:** QUALM

squea·mish \'skwēmish, -mesh\ *adj* [ME *squaymisch*, alter. of *squaymous, esquaymous,* fr. AF *escoymous, escoymos*] **1 a :** having or being a stomach easily nauseated ⟨some babies seem to be born more ~ about lumps than others —Benjamin Spock⟩ **b :** inclined to become nauseated : QUEASY, QUALMISH **c :** affected with nausea : NAUSEATED ⟨the violent movement of the ship ... made me quite ~ —Jack London⟩ **2** *obs* : evincing distaste for familiarity : DISTANT, COLD **3 a :** inclined to be easily shocked or offended : PRUDISH **b :** characterized by great or excessive fastidiousness or scrupulousness in conduct or belief ⟨if he were to remain in politics he mustn't be ~ —M.R.Werner⟩ **c :** characterized by extreme fastidiousness about mental or esp. physical surroundings ⟨the mysterious horror of his paintings is heightened by the spellbinding richness of his pigments, and even the ~ do not easily turn away —J.T.Soby⟩ ⟨most psychologists have now abolished the mind and are a little ~ talking about the psyche —A.L.Kroeber⟩ **syn** see NICE
squea·mish·ly *adv* : in a squeamish manner
squea·mish·ness *n* -ES : the quality or state of being squeamish
squeamy \'skwēmē, -mi\ *adj* -ER/-EST [*squeam* + -*y*] : SQUEAMISH

¹squee·gee \'skwē͵jē *sometimes* �ₓ'ˈ\ *also* squil·gee \" *sometimes* 'skwil͵jē *or* ˈˈ\ *or* squil·la·gee \'skwilə͵jē, ˈˈ͵ˈ\ *n* -s [prob. imit.] **1 a :** a device that consists of a handle and a transverse piece at one end set with a blade of leather or rubber and is used for spreading, pushing, or wiping liquid material on, across, or off a surface (as a pavement, windowpane, or deck) **2 a :** a device constructed like a small squeegee and used (as by a photographer or lithographer) for wiping off excess moisture, transferring material evenly to a surface, or forcing ink, paint, or dye through a stencil or screen **b** *or* **squeegee roller** : a small rubber or plastic roller with a handle used esp. in printing and photography as a squeegee

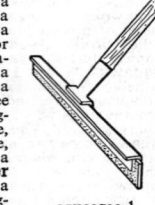
squeegee 1

²squeegee \"\ *vt* squeegeed; squeegees
squeegeeing; squeegees : to smooth, press, or wipe, spread, or remove with or as if with a squeegee (as when removing excess water or solution from the surface of a photographic film or paper)
squeez·abil·i·ty \͵skwēzə'biləd·ē\ *n* : the quality of being squeezable
squeez·able \'skwēzəbəl\ *adj* : capable of being squeezed; *specif* : easily subject to coercion or extortion — **squeez·able·ness** *n* -ES

¹squeeze \'skwēz\ *vb* squeezed \-zd\ *or dial* squoze \-wōz\ squeezed *or dial* squoze; squeezing; squeezes [earlier *squease,* alter. of obs. E *quease* to press, squeeze, fr. ME *queysen,* fr. OE *cwȳsan;* akin to Icel *kveisa* stomach cramps] *vt* **1 a (1) :** to exert pressure esp. on opposite sides or parts of : press together closely or tightly : COMPRESS ⟨nothing to do ... but ~ my friends' knees and drink my wine —Kenneth Roberts⟩ ⟨air that had been *squeezed* up so tight that he could not even move his hand through it very easily —J.B.S.Haldane⟩ **(2) :** HUG **(3) :** to pull back on (a trigger) with a steady slow pressure of the finger **b :** to cause to press upon an object ⟨*squeezed* the upper die smoothly down on the blank —John Craig⟩ **c (1) :** to extract or emit under pressure ⟨~ the juice from a lemon⟩ ⟨volcanoes formed by lava *squeezed* out of the earth in an exceedingly viscous condition —Howel Williams⟩ **(2) :** to bring into a specified state by or as if by pressure ⟨~ total budgetary outlays two to five billion dollars below the present level —Cabell Phillips⟩ **2 a (1) :** to gain to pass by pressure ⟨*squeezes* his hand into the hole and grasps the prize —James Stevenson-Hamilton⟩ **b (1) :** to gain (as valuables, services, or advantages) by extortionary means ⟨come to ~ his land from him in his extremity —Pearl Buck⟩ **(2) :** to force money, goods, or services from by extortionary means : OPPRESS ⟨the peasants, collectivization has been imposed at great cost —N.Y.Times⟩ **c :** to cause economic hardship to ⟨breaks in the supply line from the mainland periodically ~ the islanders —N.Y.Times⟩ ⟨not ... let the farmer be *squeezed* by lowered farm prices and high fixed costs —E.T.Benson⟩ **c :** to reduce the amount of (profits) ⟨climbing cost of cotton *squeezes* mill profits —Wall Street Jour.⟩ **3 :** to gain or procure as if by pressure : gain by hard work, adroit maneuvering, close attention to costs, or clever or dubious interpretation of facts ⟨the discount operator can ~ a profit out of a tiny markup —Advertising Age⟩ ⟨hard-working farmers ~ the last ounce from their holdings —T.H.Fielding⟩ ⟨thought that no new information can be *squeezed* from the premises of a syllogism —W.F.Dooney⟩ **4 a :** to crowd into or within a narrow area : cause to appear squeezed ⟨a single street *squeezed* between the railroad and the canal —Amer. Guide Series: Md.⟩ ⟨a small garage, into which, by much maneuvering, he could manage to ~ eight cars —General Motors Builds Its First 50 Million Cars⟩ **b :** to provide room, time, or opportunity for within a narrow compass ⟨brought before the courts every single case he could possibly ~ within its provisions —Richard Hayward⟩ — often used with *in* ⟨somewhere in this crowded early life ... managed to ~ in three years of piano lessons —Gilbert Millstein⟩ **5 :** to gain or win by a narrow margin ⟨just barely *squeezed* out controlling margins in the two houses of Congress —Cabell Phillips⟩ **6 :** to constrain (another player) to discard in bridge so as to unguard a suit **7 a :** to score (a run) by means of a squeeze play **b :** to bring home (a runner) from third base by means of a squeeze play — *vi* **1 :** to give way before pressure ⟨the corners of a gray cushion *squeezed* out around his fat back —Earle Birney⟩ **2 a :** to exert physical pressure **b :** to exert economic pressure ⟨would take at least two months for a strike to begin to ~ —Newsweek⟩; *specif* : to practice extortion or oppression **3 a :** to force a passage : make one's way by pressing ⟨we can all three ~ into my buggy —Ellen Glasgow⟩ ⟨a very stout lady, who could hardly ~ through the door —Fernando Sabino⟩ **b (1) :** to ease an automotive vehicle into another traffic lane esp. in preparation for a narrowed pavement ⟨~ to the right⟩ **(2) :** to ease into another traffic lane **4 :** to pass, succeed, gain a victory, or get by narrowly ⟨probably could ~ through the next five months of lean tax collections —N.Y.Times⟩ ⟨a measure *squeezed* through both houses —R.A.Billington⟩ **syn** see PRESS — **squeeze the shorts :** to put shorts under pressure to cover their commitments at higher prices (as by making stocks difficult to borrow or by spreading reports of a crop failure in commodities)

²squeeze \"\ *n* -s **1 a :** an act or instance of squeezing : a firm usu. steady and gradually increasing compression of an object esp. between two forces ⟨they give a ~ — not a slap — and exert maximum power only at the end of the stroke) ⟨trigger ~⟩ **b :** a pressing of one person's hand by another's ⟨friendly hands ... grasping our pencil-cramped fingers, and giving them a firm ~ and a hearty shake —Phoenix Flame⟩; *also* : HUG ⟨c (1) : the gradual closing of a mine working by the settling of the overlying strata **(2) :** a mine area undergoing a squeeze **d :** pressure or forcing caused by the shoving and crowding of a mass of people ⟨with one final ~, the crowd behind them pushed them along out of the gate —Dorothy C. Fisher⟩ **e :** the pressure with which paper is held against an inked printing surface esp. in a printing press **f :** the shrinkage in bulk of set type when subjected to the pressure of the quoins in locking up ⟨the compositor comes to know just how much allowance he should make for —R.W.Polk⟩ **g :** a sudden fatal crushing increase of pressure experienced by a diver as a result of any of various accidents **2 a :** a quantity squeezed or pressed out from something ⟨a ~ of lemon⟩ **b :** a group crowded together : CROWD ⟨a ~ of people —Emily Hahn⟩; *esp* : a crowded social gathering ⟨dinners, card parties, teas, ... and ~s —C.G.Bowers⟩ **c :** a facsimile impression of an object made in a plastic substance by forcing it into the depressions of the object **3** *Brit* : NECK **4** *Brit* : an article made of silk : SILK **5 a :** a commission charged by an oriental servant for service ⟨the servant won't let the salesman into the house unless he gets his ~ —Harper's⟩ **b :** an undercover but usu. recognized and tolerated profit made esp. by an oriental official or middleman on goods or valuables passing through his

hands, by an official on government financial transactions, or by anyone in a position that readily lends itself to exploitation **(2) :** GRAFT **c :** the practice of extorting squeeze ⟨resorted to ~ as a means of bringing their income more into proportion to what it cost them to stay alive —Virginia A. Oakes⟩; *also* : pressure applied to obtain squeeze ⟨the customary ~ applied to ... merchants —Darrell Berrigan⟩ **6 a :** an act or instance of squeezing the shorts **b :** financial pressure caused by a narrowing spread between two factors ⟨the ~ between low wages and high prices⟩ ⟨a ~ between high costs and stable selling prices⟩ **c (1) :** hardship, inconvenience, or difficulty caused by a shortage ⟨manpower ~⟩ ⟨housing ~⟩ or a tightening of fiscal controls or a withholding of assets ⟨credit ~⟩ or an economic blockade ⟨put a ~ on the city by strict inspection of entering transport⟩ **(2) :** the exploitation of hardship or inconvenience caused by a squeeze to gain an advantage **d (1) :** a play or situation in bridge in which one is squeezed — compare END PLAY **(2) :** a situation in canasta or rummy in which one must break up a valuable combination in order to retain a safe discard : SQUEEZE PLAY **7 :** a device for applying pressure or restraint: as **a** *slang* : a secret braking device for controlling a wheel of fortune **b :** a device for restraining cattle in a branding chute

squeeze bottle *n* : a bottle of flexible plastic that dispenses its contents by being pressed
squeeze-box \'ˈ͵ˈ\ *n* : ACCORDION
squeeze off *vt* : to fire (a round) by squeezing the trigger ~ *vi* : to fire a weapon by squeezing the trigger ⟨took a hard aim at the beast's shoulder and *squeezed off* —Edison Marshall⟩
squeeze play *n* **1 :** a prearranged baseball play used when there are less than two outs in which a runner on third base starts for home plate as the ball is being pitched and the batter attempts to bunt to give the runner time to score **2 :** the act or an instance of bringing pressure to bear in order to extort a concession or gain a goal : SQUEEZE ⟨was the victim of a *squeeze play* engineered by his foes ... and was forced to resign —L.A.Huston⟩
squeez·er \'skwēzə(r)\ *n* -s **1 a :** one that squeezes **b :** a mechanical contrivance that squeezes: as **(1) :** a device for pressing juice from fruit or vegetables ⟨lemon ~⟩ **(2) :** a wire-testing device somewhat like a lemon squeezer in which the wire is subjected to successive bendings until it breaks **(3) :** a pivoted lever device with an eccentric curved end used to curve metal bars or plates **(4) :** a machine for molding bricks **(5) :** a machine for shingling by squeezing — often used in pl.; see CROCODILE SQUEEZER **(6) :** a device for softening and compressing a cork to fit the mouth of a bottle **2 :** one that operates a squeezer **2 :** a playing card on which the value and suit are indicated in the upper left-hand corner

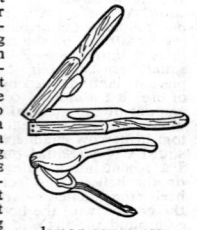
lemon squeezers

squeeze roll *n* : one of a pair of rollers designed to exert pressure on material passing between them
squeezes *pres 3d sing of* SQUEEZE, *pl of* SQUEEZE
squeeze track *n* : a photographic sound track of the variable density type whose width is manually varied to reduce noise
squeeze-up \'ˈ͵ˈ\ *n* -s [fr. *squeeze up,* v.] : a rock formation believed to have been squeezed up by volcanic pressure
squeezing *n* -s [fr. gerund of ¹*squeeze*] **1 :** the action of one that squeezes **2 a :** something that is squeezed out or only to be forced out by or as if by squeezing **b :** DREGS — usu. used in pl. **3 :** SQUEEZE 2c
squeezy \'skwēzē\ *adj* -ER/-EST [²*squeeze* + -*y*] : accompanied by or suggestive of squeezing; *specif* : CRAMPED, CONFINED
squeg \'skweg\ *vi* squegged; squegged; squegging; squegs [back-formation fr. *squegger* tube in which the valve oscillates, fr. *squegg-* (blend of *squeeze* and *wedge* + -*er*; fr. the oscillation's being a form of blocking of the grid)] : to oscillate in a highly irregular fashion esp. from too much unwanted feedback — used of an electronic system
¹squelch \'skwelch\ *n* -s [imit.] **1 a :** BLOW, BUFFET **b :** a dull heavy sound of or as if of a blow upon a soft body ⟨THUD ⟨he heard ... the ~ of turf as she ran toward him —Elizabeth Taylor⟩ **2 :** a sound of or as if of semiliquid matter under suction ⟨the ~ of mud⟩ **3 a :** the act or an instance of suppressing ⟨the producer ... boldly ignored the ~ and went right ahead ... in defiance of the industry's rules —Bosley Crowther⟩; *esp* : SQUELCHER **b** *or* **squelch circuit :** a circuit in an electronic receiver that cuts off the receiver entirely if the useful signal falls to too low a value and thereby avoids a situation where high noise signals are generated in the absence of wanted signals
²squelch \"\ *vb* -ED/-ING/-ES *vt* **1 a :** to flatten or stamp on so as to crush : crush by weight dropped or pressed from above **b (1) :** to completely suppress : QUELL ⟨a spirit here which a thousand years of misery had not ~ed —Henry Miller⟩ ⟨only three amendments were suggested ... and each was ~ed after a brief word —Dorothy Kahn⟩ **(2) :** SILENCE ⟨presiding at board meetings ... and ~ing shareholders in the middle of sentences —P.G.Wodehouse⟩ **2 :** to cause to emit or move with a sucking sound ⟨their broken shoes ~ing water —Marcia Davenport⟩ ~ *vi* **1 :** to emit a sound typical of an object being forcefully withdrawn from mire against the resistance of trapped air : emit a sucking or splashing sound ⟨have manure in my shoes and hear it ~ as I walked —Dylan Thomas⟩ **2 :** to move or proceed splashily in water, slush, or mire or with water or mud in one's shoes and produce a sucking or splashing sound ⟨~ through a miry farm gateway —Adrian Bell⟩ ⟨his feet inside the sodden seaboots ~ed icily whenever he moved —Nicholas Monsarrat⟩
squelch·er \-chə(r)\ *n* -s : one that squelches; *esp* : a retort that eliminates any possible reply
squelchy \-chē\ *adj* -ER/-EST [²*squelch* + -*y*] : likely to make a squelching sound : SOFT, PULPY
squench \'skwench\ *vb* [alter. of ¹*quench*] *dial* : QUENCH
squet \'skwet\ *n* -s [by shortening] : SQUETEAGUE
sque·teague *or* **squi·teague** \skwə'tēg\ *also* **sque·tee** \-'ˈ\, *pl* squeteague *or* squiteague *also* squetee [Narraganset *pesukwiteaug,* pl., lit., they make glue; fr. the practice of making glue from swimming bladders of weakfish] : GRAY TROUT 1; *also* : any of various other weakfishes — usu. used with a qualifying term; see SILVER SQUETEAGUE
¹squib \'skwib\ *n* -s [origin unknown] **1 a :** a small firecracker **b :** a broken firecracker the powder in which burns with a fizz **2 a (1) :** a small electric or pyrotechnic device used to ignite a charge **(2) :** a similar device to fire an igniter in a rocket **3 a :** a small explosive charge used to fire a larger one : DETONATOR **3 a :** a short humorous, satiric, or lampooning writing or speech ⟨the subject of ... some extremely ribald versified ~s —R.O.Altick⟩ **b :** a short carelessly written piece : SCRIBBLE ⟨continued to send ~s of one sort or another to the newspapers —J.W.Krutch⟩ **c :** FILLER 1d(1) ⟨his deeds and misdeeds hardly would have rated a ~ among the used-car ads —Newsweek⟩ **4** *chiefly Brit* : an insignificant or cowardly person
²squib \"\ *vb* squibbed; squibbed; squibbing; squibs *vi* **1 :** to speak, write, or publish squibs : dispute pettily **2 :** to fire or squirt a squib ~ *vt* **1 a :** to utter in an offhand manner **b :** to make squibs against : LAMPOON **2 :** to shoot off : FIRE
squib·bery \'skwibərē\ *n* -ES [¹*squib* + -*ery*] : the utterance or composition of squibs
squib·bish \-bish\ *adj* : somewhat like a squib
¹squid \'skwid\ *n, pl* squid *or* squids [origin unknown] **1 :** any of numerous 10-armed cephalopods typically having a long tapered body and a caudal fin on each side; *esp* : a cephalopod of *Loligo, Ommastrephes,* or a related genus that has the shell reduced to an internal chitinous structure shaped like a pen, often occurs in great schools, and is often used as fish bait and in many areas as food — see ARCHITEUTHIS, DIBRANCHIA; compare CUTTLEFISH **2 a :** bait prepared from a squid **b :** an artificial lure made in imitation of the natural squid used when trolling for tuna **3 :** a usu. metal weighted lure cast when surf fishing **4 :** a many-barreled antisubmarine weapon that fires charges ahead of a ship

²squid \"\ *vi* squidded; squidded; squidding; squids **1 :** to fish with or for squid **2 :** to cast with a squid lure; *specif* : to cast and retrieve a squid lure with rod and reel
squid·der \-də(r)\ *n* -s [²*squid* + -*er*] : a surf caster who uses artificial lures rather than natural bait
squidge \'skwij\ *n* -s [imit.] : SQUELCH 2
squidgy \-jē\ *adj* -ER/-EST [*squidge* + -*y*] : unpleasantly damp : CLAMMY ⟨fishermen in ~ rubber boots —Mary H. Vorse⟩ ⟨in the steamy atmosphere my skin had grown ~ as a toad's —Francis Kingdon-Ward⟩
squid hound *n* : STRIPED BASS
squid-jigger \'ˈ͵ˈˈ\ *n* -s : a group of fishhooks fastened together with radiating points for catching squid
squid-jigging \'ˈ͵ˈˈ\ *n* -s : the act or practice of hooking squid with a squid-jigger
squiffed \'skwift\ *or* **squiffy** \-fē, -fi\ *adj* [origin unknown] : INTOXICATED, DRUNK
¹squig·gle \'skwigəl\ *vb* squiggled; squiggled; squiggling \-g(ə)liŋ\ squiggles [blend of ¹*squirm* and ¹*wriggle*] *vi* **1 :** SQUIRM, WRIGGLE **2 :** to write or paint hastily : make scribbles ~ *vt* **1 :** SCRIBBLE ⟨didn't leave his mark on his correspondence —Bruce Bliven b. 1916⟩ **2 :** to cause to form or form in squiggles
²squiggle \"\ *n* -s : a short wavy twist or line : CURL, CURLICUE; *esp* : an esp. illegible hastily written bit of handwriting : SCRAWL, SCRIBBLE
squig·gly \-g(ə)lē, -li\ *adj* : WRIGGLING, WAVY, TWISTING
squilgee *or* **squillagee** *var of* SQUEEGEE
squill \'skwil\ *n* -s [ME, fr. L *squilla, scilla,* fr. Gk *skilla*] **1 a (1) :** a bulbous herb (*Urginea maritima*) of southern Europe and northern Africa that sometimes grows in gardens for its long racemes of small white flowers — called also *sea onion;* see RED SQUILL **(2) :** any of several other plants of the genus *Urginea* **(3) :** the bulbs of a squill (esp. *U. maritima*) **b :** a plant of the genus *Scilla* **2 a :** the cut and dried fleshy inner scales of the bulb of the white-rooted form of the squill (*Urginea maritima*) or of the younger bulb of a related plant (*U. indica*) of the Orient that contain one or more physiologically active glycosides and are used as an expectorant, cardiac stimulant, and diuretic **b :** the bulb of the red squill **3** [NL *Squilla*] : a crustacean of the genus *Squilla*
squil·la \'skwilə\ *n* [NL, fr. L, a small lobster, squill] **1** *cap* : a genus (the type of the family Squillidae) of stomatopod crustaceans that burrow in mud or beneath stones in shallow water along the seashore **2** *pl* squillas *or* squil·lae \-i͵lē, -i͵lī\ *also* squilla : any crustacean of *Squilla* or a related genus — called also *mantis prawn*
squill blue *n* : a light blue that is greener and duller than average forget-me-not (sense 2a) or della Robbia blue — called also *Diana*
squil·lid \'skwiləd\ *n* -s [NL *Squillidae*] : a stomatopod crustacean of the genus *Squilla* or family Squillidae
squil·li·dae \'skwilə͵dē\ *n pl, cap* [NL, fr. *Squilla,* type genus + -*idae*] : a family of stomatopod crustaceans — see SQUILLA
squil·loi·dea \skwə'lóidēə\ *n* [NL, fr. *Squilla* + -*oidea*] *syn of* STOMATOPODA
squin·a·cy \'skwinəsi, -wēn-\ *n* -ES [ME *swinacie, squinacy* quinsy, modif. of OF *esquinancie, squinancie* squinancy] *dial Brit* : PERITONSILLAR ABSCESS
squin·an·cy \-n(ə)si\ *n* -ES [ME, quinsy, fr. MF *esquinancie, squinancie,* fr. OF, alter. (influenced by Gk *synanchē* sore throat, fr. *syn-* + *anchein* to strangle) of *quinancie* quinsy, fr. LL *cynanche* sore throat, fr. Gk, fr. *anchein* to strangle : ANGER, QUINSY] **1** *obs* : PERITONSILLAR ABSCESS **2 :** a European perennial herb (*Asperula cynanchica*) with narrowly linear whorled leaves formerly thought to cure peritonsillar abscess
¹squinch \'skwinch\ *n* -s [alter. of obs. E *scunch* sconcheon, short for E *scuncheon*] **1 :** a support (as an arch, lintel, or corbeling) carried across the corner of a room under a superimposed mass (as an octagonal spire or drum resting upon a square tower) — compare PENDENTIVE **2 :** HAGIOSCOPE

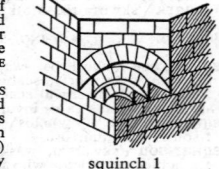
squinch 1

²squinch \"\ *vb* -ED/-ING/-ES [prob. blend of ²*squint* and ¹*pinch*] *vt* **1 :** to contort (as the face) as a signal or as an involuntary sign (as of pain) **b :** to forcefully but partially screw shut (the eyes) ⟨eyes, permanently ~ed against the sun —William Humphrey⟩ **2 :** to compress into a smaller bulk : make more compact ~ *vi* **1 :** FLINCH **2 :** to cause oneself or an object to take up less room ⟨he ~ed back into one corner —J.B.Clayton⟩ **3 :** SQUINT ⟨the fire so low she ~ed to see —R.P.Warren⟩
³squinch \"\ *adj* : characterized or affected by squinching: **a :** SQUINTED ⟨~ eye⟩ **b :** SCREWED, PINCHED ⟨~ face⟩
⁴squinch \'skwinch\ *var of* SQUENCH
squinch owl \'ˈ͵ˈ\ *n* [prob. fr. ³*squinch*] *South* : SCREECH OWL
¹squin·ny \'skwinē\ *vb* -ED/-ING/-ES [prob. fr. obs. E *squin* asquint (fr. ME *skuin*) + E -*y* (dim. suffix)] : SQUINT
²squinny \"\ *n* -ES : SQUINT
³squinny \"\ *adj* -ER/-EST : SQUINTY
⁴squinny \"\ *adj* -ER/-EST [prob. alter. (influenced by ¹*squinny*) of *skinny*] : long and narrow : SLENDER, THIN
⁵squinny \"\ *vi* -ED/-ING/-ES [origin unknown] : WEEP, FRET
¹squint \'skwint\ *adj* -ER/-EST [short for *asquint*] **1 a :** of an eye : looking or tending to look obliquely esp. with envy, disdain, or distrust **b :** characteristic of or likened to the appearance of a squint eye ⟨a ~ look⟩ **c** *of the eyes* : not having the visual axes parallel : CROSSED — compare STRABISMUS **2 a** *obs* : bearing indirectly **b :** OBLIQUE
²squint \"\ *vb* -ED/-ING/-ES *vi* **1 a :** to have an indirect bearing, reference, or aim **b :** to deviate from a true line : run obliquely **2 a (1) :** to look obliquely or askance or with a furtive glance **(2) :** to look suspiciously or with envy, malice, or disapproval **b :** to be cross-eyed or strabismic **c :** to look or peer with eyes partly closed (as when blinking from excess light or when sighting a gun) ~ *vt* **1 :** to cause (an eye) to look obliquely or to become crossed **2 :** to cause (an eye) to become partly closed or to peer while partly closed ⟨~ed his eyes as he stared up at the number —Erle Stanley Gardner⟩
³squint \"\ *n* -s **1 a :** STRABISMUS **b (1) :** the action, habit, or an instance of looking obliquely, furtively, or hastily ⟨detected him taking a hasty ~ at my certificate —Joseph Conrad⟩ **(2) :** an action, habit, or instance of screwing the eyes partly closed **c :** HAGIOSCOPE **2 :** a tendency from the ordinary : an inclination toward some object, course, or procedure : TREND, BENT
squint brick *n* **1 :** a brick cut or molded to an oblique angle **2 :** a brick shaped or molded to a special desired form
squint·er \'skwintə(r)\ *n* -s : one that squints
squint-eye \'ˈ͵ˈ\ *n* [back-formation fr. *squint-eyed*] : a cross-eyed person
squint-eyed \'ˈ͵ˈ\ *adj* **1 :** having the character of or having eyes that squint; *specif* : CROSS-EYED **2 :** having or exhibiting the character of envy, malice, or disdain : PREJUDICED, MALIGNANT ⟨*squint-eyed* with envy —Catherine D. Bowen⟩
squinting construction *n* : a grammatical construction that contains a word or phrase (as *sometimes* in "to die sometimes is noble") interpretable as modifying either what precedes or what follows and if interpreted in one way gives an unintended sense
squint·ing·ly *adv* : in a squinting manner
squint quoin *n* : a quoin at the corner of a building not forming a right angle
squinty \'skwintē, -ti\ *adj*, *sometimes* -ER/-EST [³*squint* + -*y*] : characterized by or affected with squinting ⟨~ eyes⟩
¹squire \'skwī(ə)r, -wī(ə)-\ *n* -s [ME *squier,* fr. OF *esquier, escuier,* fr. LL *scutarius* shield bearer — more at ESQUIRE] **1 :** a shield bearer or armor-bearer of a knight — compare PAGE **2 a :** a male attendant esp. on a great personage **b :** a man devotedly attendant on a lady : GALLANT, LOVER **3 a :** a member of the British gentry ranking below a knight and above a gentleman **b :** COUNTRY GENTLEMAN; *esp* : the principal landowner in a village or district **c (1) :** JUSTICE OF THE PEACE **(2) :** LAWYER **(3) :** JUDGE
²squire \"\ *vb* -ED/-ING/-s [ME *squieren,* fr. *squier* squire]

vt : to attend upon as a squire : serve as an escort to : ACCOMPANY, ESCORT ⟨girlhood, when she had gaily gone to parties, *squired* by boys her own age —Jean Stafford⟩ ~ *vi* : to function as or act the part of a country squire

squire·arch \ˈskwī(ə)ˌrärk\ *n* -s [back-formation fr. *squirearchy*] : a member of the squirearchy

squire·ar·chal \ˌskwīˈrärkəl, (ˈ)skwīˌrä-\ *or* **squire·ar·chi·cal** \-ärkəkəl\ *also* **squir·ar·chal** *like* SQUIREARCHAL\ *adj* [*squirearchal, squirearchical* fr. *squirearchy* + *-al* or *-ical*; *squirarchal* fr. *squirarchy* + *-al*] : of, relating to, characteristic of, or belonging to the squirearchy ⟨that image of the right life which has evolved from the aristocratic, ~, and higher official culture —Edward Shils⟩

squire·ar·chy *or* **squir·ar·chy** \ˈskwī(ə)ˌrärkē\ *n* -ES [¹*squire* + *-archy*] **1** : the gentry of a country : the landed proprietor class esp. with regard to its political influence ⟨two classes in the community struggling for supremacy: the land-owning ~ allied with the church, and the mercantile classes —C.J. Friedrich⟩ — used esp. of the English government prior to the Reform Bill of 1832 **2** : government by a landed gentry

squire·dom \ˈskwī(ə)rdəm\ *n* -s **1** : the rank, dignity, or estate of a squire **2** : SQUIREARCHY 1

squi·reen \(ˈ)skwīˈrēn\ *n* -s [¹*squire* + *-een*] *chiefly Irish* : a petty squire : a gentleman in a small way

squire·hood \ˈskwī(ə)rˌhu̇d\ *n* **1** : SQUIREDOM **2** : SQUIREARCHY 1

squire·less \-ī(ə)rləs\ *adj* : lacking a squire; *specif* : UNATTENDED, UNESCORTED

squire·ling \-liŋ\ *n* -s : a young or petty squire

squire·ly \-lē\ *adj* : of, relating to, resembling, or befitting a squire

squire·ship \-ī(ə)rˌship\ *n* : SQUIREDOM

squir·ess \-ī(ə)rəs\ *n* -ES [¹*squire* + *-ess*] : the wife of a squire

squir·ish \-rish\ *adj* : characteristic of, resembling, or befitting a squire

squirl \ˈskwər(-ə)l\ *n* -s [prob. blend of ²*squirm* and ²*twirl*] : FLOURISH, TWIST, CURLICUE ⟨signed with a ~ —Elizabeth Bowen⟩

¹**squirm** \ˈskwərm, -wə̄m, -wəim\ *vb* -ED/-ING/-S [perh. imit.] *vi* **1** : to twist about with contortions like an eel or a worm (as from nervousness, embarrassment, or excess of energy) ⟨sleek-haired subalterns who ~*ed* painfully in their chairs when they came to call —Rudyard Kipling⟩ **2 a** : to proceed or move with a writhing motion **b** : to extricate oneself by subtle maneuvering ⟨his reputation for honesty precluded any attempt to ~ out of an obligation —D.G.Hoffman⟩ **3** : to experience acute embarrassment, shame, anguish, remorse, or mental punishment ⟨preparing . . . a grueling cross-examination . . . in which he is going to make me ~ in front of the grand jury —Erle Stanley Gardner⟩ ~ *vt* **1** : to cause to squirm **2** : to execute or accomplish by means of a squirm ⟨~*ed* my way through the crowd —E.M.Benson⟩ **syn** see WRITHE

²**squirm** \"\ *n* -s : the action or an instance of squirming : WRIGGLE

squirmy \-mē,-mi\ *adj* -ER/-EST [¹*squirm* + *-y*] : given to or characterized by squirming ⟨the only other major horror of the barber business . . . is ~ kids —G.S.Perry⟩

squirr \ˈskwər(·)\ *vt* -ED/-ING/-S [prob. alter. of ¹*skirr*] *dial Brit* : to throw with a jerk or with the edge foremost

¹**squir·rel** \ˈskwər(·ə)l, -wəl,-wəil *also* -wə·rəl *sometimes* -wir(ə)l *or* -wer(ə)l\ *n, pl* **squirrels** *also* **squirrel** [ME *squirel, squerel*, fr. MF *esquireul, escuriuel*, fr. (assumed) VL *scuriolus*, dim. of (assumed) VL *scurius*, alter. of L *sciurus*, fr. Gk *skiouros*, fr. *skia* shadow + *oura* tail (akin to Gk *orrhos* buttocks) — more at SCENE, ASS] **1 a** (1) : a rodent of the family Sciuridae; *esp* : any of various widely distributed small to medium-sized usu. largely arboreal forms that have a bushy tail and long strong hind limbs which allow them to leap from branch to branch, feed largely on nuts and seeds which they commonly store for winter use, and include numerous small game animals and several economically important fur bearers — see BLACK SQUIRREL, FLYING SQUIRREL, GRAY SQUIRREL, GROUND SQUIRREL, RED SQUIRREL (2) : SCALETAIL (3) : the fur of a squirrel used in the fur trade; *esp* : the fur of a common Eurasiatic squirrel (*Sciurus vulgaris*) **b** *Austral* : any of various flying phalangers **2** : ⁴LEAD 5 **3** : one of the small rollers in a carding machine that work with the large cylinder

²**squirrel** \"\ *vt* -ED/-ING/-S : to store up for future use : HIDE, HOARD ⟨~*ed* away twice as much as he actually expects to use —John Fischer⟩

squirrel cage *n* **1** : a cage for a small animal (as a squirrel) that contains a cylinder revolving upon a horizontal axis when an animal moves within it **2 a** : something resembling a squirrel cage in construction; *specif* : a secondary winding for an induction motor consisting of cylindrically arranged copper bars with ends connected by short-circuiting rings — compare PHASE-WOUND **b** : something resembling a squirrel cage in senselessness or repetitiveness

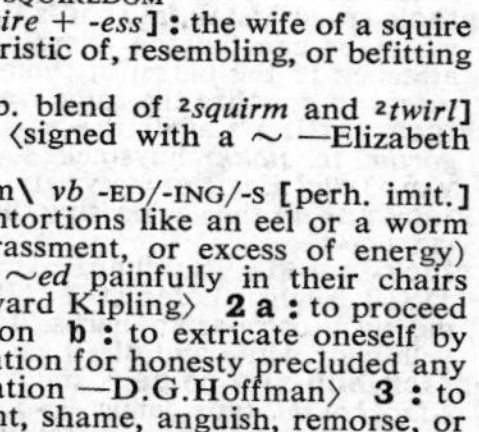

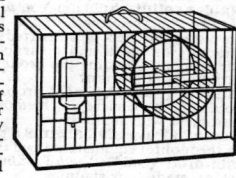

squirrel cage

squirrel–cage \ˈ≈(≈),≈\ *adj* [*squirrel cage*] **1** : consisting of or equipped with an induction motor squirrel cage ⟨*squirrel-cage* rotor⟩ ⟨*squirrel-cage* motor⟩ **2** : endlessly and ploddingly repetitive : constantly returning upon itself in the manner of a treadmill ⟨most of the talk and writing on human nature represents only *squirrel-cage* thinking —C.D.Dam⟩

squirrel corn *n* : a No. American herb (*Dicentra canadensis*) with delicate much-divided leaves and a scapose raceme of cream-colored flowers growing from a cluster of small tubers borne on the rootstock

squirrel cup *n* : a common No. American hepatica (*Hepatica americana*) with bluish to purple or sometimes white or pink flowers — usu. used in pl.

squirrel family *n* : SCIURIDAE

squirrelfish \ˈ≈(≈),≈\ *n* [prob. so called fr. the fact that the sound it makes out of water resembles the bark of a squirrel] **1** : any of numerous small fishes of the family Holocentridae; *esp* : a fish (*Holocentrus ascensionis*) of the West Indies, Bermudas, and adjacent areas that is usu. chiefly bright red with large eyes and large rough scales **2 a** : a pinfish (*Lagodon rhomboides*) **b** : a related grunt of the genus *Haemulon*

squirrel food *n* : any of several plants of the genus *Zigadenus*; *esp* : DEATH CAMAS

squirrel frog *n* : a small tree toad (*Hyla squirella*) of the southern U. S.

squirrel grass *n* : SQUIRRELTAIL 2

squirrel hake *n* : any of several hakes of the genus *Phycis*; *esp* : a common market fish (*P. chuss*) of the Atlantic coast south to Cape Hatteras

squirrel hawk *n* [so called fr. its fondness for ground squirrels] : FERRUGINOUS ROUGHLEG

squir·rel·ly *also* **squir·rely** \-lē,-li\ *adj* [¹*squirrel* + *-y*] : extremely odd : crazily peculiar or senseless ⟨just a ~ enough job to appeal to me —Mary McCall⟩

squirrel monkey *n* [so called fr. its being small and arboreal] **1** : any of several small soft-haired So. American monkeys of the genus *Saimiri* (syn. *Chrysothrix*); *esp* : a monkey (*S. sciurea*) having a long nonprehensile tail and being chiefly yellowish gray in color with a white face and black nose **2** : TITI **3** : TAMARIN; *esp* : a Panamanian tamarin (*Leontocebus geoffroyi*)

squirrel mouse *n* : DORMOUSE

squirrel phalanger *or* **squirrel opossum** *n* : FLYING PHALANGER; *esp* : a common Australian flying phalanger (*Petaurus sciureus*)

squirrel rifle *or* **squirrel gun** *n* [so called fr. its being suitable only for small game] : a small-bore rifle introduced into America about 1700 after the adoption of the patched bullet

squirrel's–foot fern *n* : BALL FERN

squirrel shrew *n* : TREE SHREW

squirreltail \ˈ≈(≈),≈\ *n* [¹*squirrel* + *tail*] **1** : a tufted perennial grass (*Sitanion hystrix*) that has very bristly spikes disarticulating above each node and resembles lyme grass **2** *also* **squirreltail grass** *or* **squirreltail barley** : any of several grasses of the genus *Hordeum* (as wall barley) with bushy spikes

squirrel tail *n* : a tail arched forward beyond a vertical from its anterior base — used chiefly of fowls

squirring *pres part of* SQUIRR

squirrs *pres 3d sing of* SQUIRR

¹**squirt** \ˈskwər|t, -wə̄|, -wəi|, *usu* |d.+V\ *vb* -ED/-ING/-S [ME *squirten, swirten*; akin to LG *swirtjen* to squirt] *vi* **1** : to eject liquid in a thin spurt **2** : to dart suddenly or quickly : move briskly **3** : to come forth in a sudden rapid stream from a narrow orifice : SPURT ~ *vt* **1** : to drive, eject, or inject in a fluid or gaseous stream ⟨~*ed* carbonated water into a glass —Erle Stanley Gardner⟩ **2** : to sprinkle, spatter, splash, or soak by squirting : force a stream of liquid upon ⟨load the hose attachment with soap powder and ~ your dirty car —*New Yorker*⟩ **3** : to cause to squirt a liquid, fluid, or gaseous substance ⟨merrily ~*ing* his seltzer bottle —*Springfield* (*Mass.*) *Union*⟩

²**squirt** \"\ *n* -s [ME, diarrhea, fr. *squirten* to squirt] **1** *dial* : DIARRHEA — usu. used in pl. and with *the* **2 a** : an instrument (as a syringe) for squirting a liquid **b** (1) : a small quick stream : JET, SPURT ⟨took the pipe from his mouth and sent a brown ~ of juice softly into the pebbles —John Hermann⟩ (2) : molten metal that is forced through an interstice in an improperly tightened line of matrices at the moment of casting in a slugcasting machine; *also* : an instance of such forcing through of metal **c** : the action or an instance of squirting **3 a** : an esp. young or small upstart or impudent person given to meddling beyond his competence or concern ⟨this young ~ is going too far —S.H.Holbrook⟩ **b** : a young child or youth : KID ⟨giving him nickels to buy lemon ice when he was a ~ —Bernard Malamud⟩

squirt can *n* : an oil can having a flexible bottom that when compressed forces oil out of a tapering spout

squirt·er \-d·ə(r), -tə-\ *n* -s **1** : one that squirts **2** *or* **squirter disease** [so called fr. the fact that the banana squirts when any pressure is applied] : a storage and market disease of bananas marked by dark watery rot of the pulp and caused by a fungus (*Nigrospora sphaerica*)

squirt gun *n* **1** : an often pistol-shaped device having a bulb that squirts out a liquid when pressed and being used for various purposes (as to spray plants or bushes) **2** : WATER PISTOL

squirting cucumber *n* : a Mediterranean plant (*Ecballium elaterium*) of the family Cucurbitaceae having oblong fruit that bursts from the peduncle when ripe and forcibly ejects the seeds

squirty \-d·|ē, -t|, |i\ *adj* -ER/-EST : of the nature of or characteristic of a squirt ⟨three times smarter than these ~ little naval officers —Kenneth Roberts⟩

¹**squish** \ˈskwish\ *vb* -ED/-ING/-ES [alter. (influenced by ¹*squirt*) of ¹*squash*] *vt* **1** : SQUASH ⟨~*ed* her nose against the window pane —R.W.Howard⟩ **2** : to cause to move in or eject a liquid or viscous substance with a splashing or sucking sound ⟨~*ed* his feet . . . deeper into the soft and comfortable mud —K.M.Dodson⟩ ~ *vi* : to move with or emit a sucking, gurgling, or splashing sound : SQUELCH ⟨their wet tennis shoes ~*ed* —Frank Noel⟩

²**squish** \"\ *n* -ES : a squishing sound

squishy \ˈskwishē\ *adj* -ER/-EST [¹*squish* + *-y*] : being soft, yielding, and damp : clammily viscous

¹**squit** \ˈskwit\ *n* -s [perh. alter. (influenced by ²*squirt*) of obs. E dial. *skit* skittish person, perh. fr. E ²*skit*] *Brit* : SQUIRT 3a

²**squit** \"\ *n* -s [by shortening & alter. fr. *squeteague* or *squetee*] : GRAY TROUT 1

squitch \ˈskwich\ *or* **squitch grass** *n* -ES [alter. of *quitch*] : COUCH GRASS 1a

squiteague *var of* SQUETEAGUE

¹**squit·ter** \ˈskwid·ə(r)\ *vb* -ED/-ING/-S [alter. (influenced by *-er* as in *blabber*) of obs. E *squit* to squirt, prob. of Scand origin; akin to Icel *skvetta* to squirt — more at SQUATTER] *dial* : SQUIRT

²**squitter** \"\ *n* -s *dial* : SQUIRT

squiz \ˈskwiz\ *n* [origin unknown] *Austral & NewZeal* : LOOK, GLANCE

squoze *dial past of* SQUEEZE

squush *or* **sqush** \ˈskwəsh, -wu̇sh\ *vb* -ED/-ING/-ES [alter. of ¹*squish*] *vt* : SQUASH ~ *vi* : SQUISH

squushy *or* **squshy** \-shē\ *adj* [alter. of *squishy*] : SQUASHY

sr *abbr* **1** seer **2** senior **3** *often cap* senor **4** *often cap* sir **5** *often cap* sister **6** [L *soror*] sister

SR *abbr* **1** saturable reactor **2** seaman recruit **3** sedimentation rate **4** self-rectifying **5** *often not cap* semantic reaction **6** senate resolution **7** sensibility reciprocal **8** service record **9** shipping receipt **10** short rate **11** *often not cap* small ring **12** social-revolutionary **13** sound ranging **14** special regulation **15** star route **16** stateroom **17** stimulus-response **18** storage room **19** subject ratio **20** supplementary regulation

Sr *symbol* strontium

sra *abbr, often cap* senora

SRA *abbr* sulfo-ricinoleic acid

sra·ban \ˈs(h)räbən\ *or* **sra·van** \-ävən\ *n, usu cap* [Skt *śrāvana*] : SAWAN

srad·dha *or* **shrad·dha** \ˈs(h)rädə\ *also* **sradh** \-d\ *n* -s [Skt *śrāddha*, fr. *śraddhā* belief — more at CREED] **1** : a Hindu rite or ceremony performed in behalf of departed ancestors **2** *Hinduism* : religious faith

sra dye \ˌesˌäˈrā-\ *n, usu cap S&R&A* [*sra* fr. sulfo-ricinoleic acid; fr. the use of this acid in treating the dye] : any of a group of disperse dyes — see DYE table I

sra·ma·na \ˈs(h)rəmənə\ *n* -s [Skt *śramana* — more at SHAMAN] *Buddhism* : a religious ascetic

sra·nan ton·go \ˌsränənˈtäŋ(ˌ)gō\ *n* : TAKI-TAKI

SR and CC *abbr* strikes, riots, and civil commotions

SR and O *abbr* statutory rules and orders

sra·va·ka \ˈs(h)rävəkə\ *n* -s [Skt *śrāvaka*, lit., hearer, listener; akin to Skt *śrnoti* he hears — more at LOUD] : a direct disciple of the Buddha

SRCC *abbr, often not cap* strikes, riots, and civil commotions

srch *abbr* search

sri *or* **shri** \ˈs(h)rē\ *n* -s [Skt *śrī* majesty, holiness — more at SETH] — used as a conventional title of respect when addressing or speaking of a distinguished Indian

sri·na·gar \srēˈnəgə(r), -ˈnäg-\ *adj, usu cap* [fr. *Srinagar*, city in northern India] : of or from the city of Srinagar, India : of the kind or style prevalent in Srinagar

srita *abbr, often cap* senorita

SRM *abbr* speed of relative movement

SRN *abbr* state registered nurse

SRO *abbr* **1** standing room only **2** statutory rules and orders

srta *abbr, often cap* senorita

sru·ti *or* **shru·ti** \ˈs(h)ru̇d·ē\ *n* -s [Skt *śruti* what is heard, fr. *śrnoti* he hears — more at LOUD] **1** *often cap* : the first class of shastras; *also* : a text of this class **2** : one of the microtones of the musical scale of India

ss *abbr* **1** *often cap both Ss* saints **2** *often cap both Ss* [L *sancti*] saints **3** *often cap both Ss* [L *sanctissimus*] most holy **4** scilicet **5** [L *scriptores*] authors **6** sections **7** [L *semis*] one half

SS *abbr* **1** Sabbath School **2** sacred Scripture **3** same size **4** screw steamer **5** secret service **6** selective service **7** semisteel **8** [It *senza sordini*] without mutes **9** set screw **10** shipside **11** shortstop **12** side seam **13** simplified spelling **14** single-screened **15** single sideband **16** slop sink **17** soap suds **18** social science; social security; social service **19** special session **20** staff surgeon **21** steamship **22** steel sash **23** Sunday school **24** [L *supra scriptum*] written above **25** sworn statement

s's *or* **ss** *pl of* S

SS and C *abbr* supersized and calendered

SSC *abbr* solicitor, supreme court

ss collar *n, cap both Ss* : COLLAR OF SS

SSE *abbr* south-southeast

s–shaped \ˈ≈,≈\ *adj, cap 1st S* : having the shape of a capital S

SSM *abbr* **1** squadron sergeant major **2** staff sergeant major **3** surface to surface missile

ssp *abbr* subspecies

SSR *abbr* Soviet Socialist Republic

SSS *abbr* **1** specific soluble substance **2** strong soap solution

s star *n, usu cap S* : a star of spectral type S — see SPECTRAL TYPE table

SSU *abbr* second, Saybolt universal

SSW *abbr* south-southwest

st *abbr* **1** *often cap* saint **2** stain **3** stamped **4** stand **5** stanza **6** start **7** state **8** statute **9** steam **10** steel **11** stem **12** stere **13** stet **14** stitch **15** stock **16** stone **17** stotinka **18** straight **19** strait **20** street **21** strophe **22** stumped

ST *abbr* **1** *often not cap* [It *senza tempo*] without regard to time **2** shipping ticket **3** *often not cap* short ton **4** single throw **5** sounding tube **6** standard time **7** static thrust **8** *often not cap* steam trawler **9** superintendent of transportation **10** surface tension

-st — see -EST

-st [fr. *-st* (superlative suffix)] *symbol* — used after the figure 1 to indicate the ordinal number first ⟨May 1*st*⟩ ⟨31*st* St.⟩

'st \st\ *vb* [by contr.] *archaic* : HAST ⟨thou'*st*⟩

sta *abbr* **1** *often cap* [It *santa*] saint **2** station; stationary; stationer **3** stator **4** statute

staa·ten·bund \ˈshtät'nˌbu̇nt\ *n* -s [G, fr. *staaten* (pl. of *staat* state) + *bund* federation, league — more at BUNDESSTAAT, BUND] : a league of states in which each participating state retains full sovereignty : CONFEDERACY 3 — contrasted with *Bundesstaat*

¹**stab** \ˈstab, -aa(ə)b\ *n* -s [ME *stabbe*] **1** : a wound produced by or as if by a pointed weapon; *specif* : STAB WOUND **2 a** : a thrust of a pointed weapon **b** : a jerky stroke (as with a bat, mallet, or club) **c** : a billiards shot in which the cue ball is stroked sharply to cause it to remain on the spot occupied by the object ball **d** : a hard jab in boxing **3** : a try made for a particular purpose ⟨a fish took a ~ at a fly —Richard Bissell⟩ ⟨a quick ~ into unknown country —L. J. Van Der Post⟩ **b** : ATTEMPT, GO, TRIAL ⟨the present reviewer's sections . . . devoted to phrase structure and clause structure represent only a ~ in this direction —R.A.Hall b. 1911⟩ ⟨speaks fluently in French, Italian, Spanish and German and makes a ~ at Hungarian —*Theatre Arts*⟩ ⟨making a ~ at aplomb —Marcia Davenport⟩ ⟨they didn't care to talk to him much even if he did make a ~ at conversation —Will James⟩ **4 a** : a sudden sharp sensation of pain : PANG ⟨a ~ of lumbago⟩ : a sudden strong feeling ⟨a ~ of anxiety⟩ ⟨a ~ of envy⟩ ⟨a ~ of joy⟩ ⟨a ~ of resentment⟩ **b** : a sharply delimited display of vivid color or light ⟨the ~ of the neon sign —*Saturday Rev.*⟩ ⟨a long ~ of lightning —Danforth Ross⟩ ⟨little ~*s* of flame shot from the chimney —O.S.Nock⟩ **5 a** : a culture medium solidified in an upright column in a tube so as to reduce the surface to a minimum — compare SLANT 2d(1) **b** : STAB CULTURE

²**stab** \"\ *vb* **stabbed; stabbed; stabbing; stabs** *vt* **1 a** : to wound by the thrust of a pointed instrument ⟨~ a man with a dagger⟩ **b** : to pierce with or as if with a pointed weapon ⟨cured me by *stabbing* me in the seat once a fortnight or so with a monstrous hypodermic syringe —G.B.Shaw⟩ ⟨~ an apple with a knife⟩ ⟨a derrick *stabbing* the sky —Ralph Gray⟩ : as (1) : to puncture (sheets, sections, or cover boards) to facilitate hand stitching or sewing in bookbinding (2) : to roughen the surface of (a brick wall) with a point to form a key for plaster **c** : PIERCE 5 ⟨poignant memories *stabbed* him —Marcia Davenport⟩ ⟨children coming home from the factory or the mine ~ the conscience —J.H.Plumb⟩ **2 a** : THRUST, DRIVE ⟨a fork that had been *stabbed* into the navel of a large orange —June W. Brown⟩ ⟨as you arrange the carding, ~ pins through it into the paper —Evelyn A. Mansfield⟩ ⟨man *stabbed* a thumb at a wisp of white ribbon —F.B.Gipson⟩ **b** : to strike (as a golf ball) with a jerky stroke **c** : to hit (a boxing opponent) with a hard jab **3** : to point (a bird) suddenly and without hesitation — used of a hunting dog ~ *vi* : to thrust or give a wound with or as if with a pointed weapon : make a stab : PIERCE ⟨his finger *stabbed* at a blank page —Jan Valtin⟩ ⟨small forces ~ northward looking for a fight —*Current History*⟩ ⟨the thought had *stabbed* through her like a knife —Ellen Glasgow⟩ ⟨misty blue peaks *stabbing* up out of rich forests —Allan Nevins⟩

³**stab** \ˈstab\ *n* -s [prob. alter. of *stob*] *chiefly Scot* : STAKE

⁴**stab** \"\ *n* -s [by shortening] *Brit* : ESTABLISHMENT — used of weekly or hourly wages paid by a printing house as distinguished from piecework payments ⟨~ work⟩ ⟨working on ~⟩

stab *abbr* **1** stabilize; stabilizer **2** stable

stab·ber \-bə(r)\ *n* -s **1** : one that stabs **2** : a sailmaker's marlinespike or awl : PRICKER

stabbing *adj* : that stabs : PIERCING ⟨master of the short, ~ phrase —*Times Lit. Supp.*⟩ ⟨~ glare of a fluorescent tube —Lewis Mumford⟩ ⟨knifelike, ~ or sharp pain —*Dental Abstracts*⟩ ⟨the ~ barb with which the stingaree was equipped —Francis Birtles⟩ — **stab·bing·ly** *adv*

stab cell *n* [part trans. of G *stabzelle*, fr. *stab* staff (fr. OHG) + *zelle* cell — more at STAFF] : a young blood granulocyte with densely staining unsegmented nucleus

stab culture *n* : a culture (as of bacteria) made by inoculating deep into a stab

¹**sta·bile** \ˈstāˌbəl, -ā,bīl *also* -ˌbēl *sometimes* ˈstabəl\ *adj* [L *stabilis* — more at STABLE] **1** : not moving : STATIONARY, STABLE **2** : not fluctuating : STEADY — compare LABILE 3 **3** : not decomposing readily : resistant to chemical change ⟨native proteins are never ~ —Otto Rahn⟩

²**sta·bile** \ˈstāˌbēl *sometimes* -ˌbīl *or* -ˌbil\ *n* -s : an abstract sculpture or construction typically made of sheet metal, wire, and wood — compare MOBILE

sta·bi·li·fy \stəˈbiləˌfī\ *vt* -ED/-ING/-ES : to make stable

stab·i·lim·e·ter \ˌstabəˈlimədə(r)\ *n* [*stability* + *-meter*] : a device for measuring or indicating stability; *specif* : an apparatus for recording the amplitude and frequency of the motions of an animal or child

sta·bil·i·tate \stəˈbiləˌtāt\ *vt* -ED/-ING/-S [ML *stabilitatus*, past part. of *stabilitare*, fr. L *stabilitas*] : to make stable

sta·bil·i·ty \stəˈbilədˌē, -lətē, -i *sometimes* stā'-\ *n* -ES [ME *stabilite*, fr. MF *estabilité*, fr. L *stabilitat-, stabilitas*, fr. *stabilis* stable + *-itat-, -itas* -ity — more at STABLE] **1** : the quality, state, or degree of being stable: as **a** : the strength to stand or endure without alteration of position or without material change : STEADINESS, FIRMNESS ⟨bridge . . . was frail, with little lateral ~ to withstand the gales —O.S.Nock⟩ ⟨these metals have a structural ~ that should ensure long life —Betty Pepis⟩ ⟨the ~ of a price is the degree to which it stays the same over time —A.P.Lerner⟩ ⟨a recession appeared that showed the lack of ~ in the economy —Oscar Handlin⟩ ⟨cultural ~ — a phenomenon which, in its psychological aspects, is called conservatism —M.J.Herskovits⟩ ⟨political ~, with its accompanying danger of political stagnation —W.C.Brownell⟩ **b** : the state of being in stable equilibrium **c** : the property of a body that causes it when disturbed from a condition of equilibrium or steady motion to develop forces or moments that restore the original condition ⟨the ~ of a projectile⟩ ⟨the ~ of a ship⟩ ⟨the ~ of an airplane⟩ **d** : resistance to decomposition or other chemical change or to physical disintegration ⟨a plastic with a heat ~ of up to 100° C⟩ ⟨salicylamide, an analgesic of wide compatibility and good ~ in pharmaceutical preparations —*Monsanto Mag.*⟩ **e** : PERMANENCE ⟨~ of a color⟩ **2 a** : steadiness or firmness of character, resolution, or purpose : CONSTANCY, STEADFASTNESS ⟨an idea so . . . dishonorable to the ~ of her lover —Jane Austen⟩ ⟨she lacks the ~ and discipline to keep her gift under control —*Time*⟩ ⟨each writer had to find or fashion for himself an artistic credo to serve as a center of ~ — Max Lerner & Edwin Mims⟩ **b** : a vow made by Benedictines and some other monks binding them to remain in the monastery in which they make their profession **c** : the state demanded by this vow

sta·bi·li·za·tion \ˌstābələˈzāshən, -bəˌlī'- *sometimes* ˌstab-\ *n* -s **1** : the act or process of stabilizing : the state of being stabilized **2 a** : the limitation (as by regulation) of fluctuations of business activity, prices, or employment **b** : the pegging of security prices usu. by an underwriting syndicate **c** : the keeping of the foreign exchange quotation of a currency within a narrow range either by making it convertible or by central bank or stabilization fund action **3** : the state of maximum adjustment between organisms and environment that is characteristic of an ecological climax community

stabilization fund *n* : a fund maintained by a government to control the foreign exchange quotation of its currency — called also *equalization fund*

sta·bi·lize \'stābə,līz *sometimes* 'stab-\ *vb* -ED/-ING/-S [*stabile* + *-ize*] *vt* **1 :** to make stable, steadfast, or firm ⟨sand fences were built and grasses planted to ~ the migratory ridges —*Amer. Guide Series: N.C.*⟩ ⟨advise me where the plant should be *stabilized* —P.A.Zahl⟩ ⟨religious faith . . . ~*s* one's life —Rufus Jones⟩ ⟨the recent arrivals . . . strengthened and *stabilized* the organization they discovered already in existence —Oscar Handlin⟩ **2 :** to make or hold steady **:** prevent fluctuations of **:** maintain at a constant level: as **a :** to maintain or to make it possible to maintain the stability of (as an airplane) by means of fixed surfaces or gyroscopic or other devices not manipulated by an operator ⟨a rocket *stabilized* by a gyroscope⟩ **b :** to limit fluctuations of (as business activity, prices, or employment) **c :** to establish a minimum price for (a security) by buying all offerings at that price **3 :** SET 40 ⟨a chemical treatment to ~ a fabric⟩ ~ *vi* **1 :** to become stable, firm, or steadfast ⟨prices received by farmers had *stabilized* —*Dun's Rev.*⟩ ⟨the birthrate has fallen and populations have tended to ~ —Gerard Piel⟩ ⟨when pulse and blood pressure respond and ~ —*Jour. Amer. Med. Assoc.*⟩ **2 :** to prevent regeneration by inserting resistors in the grid circuits of the electron tubes

syn STABILIZE, STEADY, POISE, BALANCE, BALLAST, and TRIM are seldom interchangeable but can mean, in common, to maintain or cause to maintain position or equilibrium. STABILIZE applies to what fluctuates or is unsteady and calls for regulation by an external force ⟨measures to *stabilize* and in the long run to enlarge farm income —*New Republic*⟩ ⟨if the stock rises, the fund can buy fewer shares; if the stock falls, it can buy more, thus tending to *stabilize* the market —*Time*⟩ STEADY applies to what loses, or is subject to loss of, its customary stability, and consequently rocks, shakes, flutters, or tips ⟨*steady* a table by putting a wedge under one leg⟩ ⟨while medics *steadied* trays of instruments against bomb concussions —Bill Alcine⟩ ⟨controlled elections *steadied* authoritarian regimes during the year —M.B.Travis⟩ ⟨a medicine to *steady* the nerves⟩ POISE applies chiefly to what maintains its equilibrium, either by an inherent proper distribution of balancing forces or by a discipline as of muscle or mind, under circumstances which would normally upset it, esp. external forces (as the law of gravity), or in a way that suggests imminent upset ⟨try to see a figure *poised* on a crag or jut of ice over a precipice —Marion Sheridan⟩ ⟨kingfishers *poise* on bare cypress limbs —*Amer. Guide Series: Fla.*⟩ ⟨the world is *poised*, uneasily, dangerously, on a point of decision —*London Calling*⟩ BALANCE also implies an equilibrium resulting from an even distribution of opposing forces but, unlike POISE, carries little suggestion of sustained equilibrium or of forces working to upset ⟨*balance* a pair of scales by putting like weights in both trays⟩ ⟨a military dictatorship of one man who *balances* and plays off the main forces of the country against each other —H.L.Matthews⟩ ⟨her humor . . . *balanced* between dignity and absurdity —*Current Biog.*⟩ BALLAST implies the addition of something heavy or solid to hold down, hold steady, or ensure the stability of something too light or too buoyant; in application to the mind or character it implies something counteracting volatility, frivolity, or uncertainty ⟨*ballast* a canoe in stormy weather with large stones⟩ ⟨the marriage seemed to *ballast* the normally flighty girl⟩ TRIM implies a proper balancing, as of a boat or ship, esp. by moving contents around so that it sits well or fulfills well any of the conditions that make for steadiness ⟨could be *trimmed* on an even keel . . . like scales, in which the weight on one side must be counterposed by a weight in the other —Richard Jefferies⟩ ⟨one man . . . can make quick work of loading and *trimming* a boxcar —*Industrial Equipment News*⟩

sta·bi·liz·er \-zə(r)\ *n* -S **:** one that makes stable: as **a** (1) **:** a substance added to an explosive esp. to make it less liable to spontaneous decomposition (2) **:** a substance added to a plastic or elastomer to maintain its desirable physical and chemical properties (3) **:** a substance added to an emulsion, foam, or other dispersion to prevent change **:** PROTECTIVE COLLOID ⟨~*s* used in the production of chocolate milk⟩ (4) **:** a substance (as gelatin) added to a food mix (as ice cream) to improve and maintain its quality (as of texture or body) **b :** a distilling column for decreasing the evaporative tendency of petroleum products (as gasoline) by removal of gaseous and low-boiling hydrocarbons **c :** a bar-shaped shock absorber for a vehicle (as an automobile) **d :** a gyroscope device to keep ships steady in a heavy sea — compare GYROSTABILIZER **e :** an airfoil providing stability for an airplane; *specif* **:** the fixed horizontal member of the tail assembly of an airplane **f :** a device to hold a tank gun on a target, while the tank moves over rough ground

¹sta·ble \'stābəl\ *n* -S [ME, fr. OF *estable*, fr. L *stabulum*, fr. *stare* to stand — more at STAND] **1 :** a building or part of a building in which domestic animals are lodged and fed; *esp* **:** such a building having stalls or compartments ⟨the horse ~ is in the main barn, the cow ~ is separate⟩ **2 a :** a group of racing horses under one ownership or management; *also* **:** the horses of such a group or the persons concerned with the ownership, operation, or management of such a group **b :** a group or staff of skilled people (as artists, comedians, speakers, writers) engaged to contribute their services or perform when called upon **:** POOL; *specif* **:** such a group of athletes (as boxers or tennis players) under the direction of a single manager **c :** a group of operable things under a single ownership or management ⟨a ~ of publications⟩ ⟨a ~ of racing cars⟩ **3 stables** *pl* **a :** military duty in the stables **b :** the bugle call to such duty

²stable \"\ *vb* **stabled; stabled; stabling** \-b(ə)liŋ\ **stables** [ME *stablen*, fr. MF *establer*, fr. L *stabulare*, fr. *stabulum*] *vt* **:** to put or keep (as animals) in a stable **:** HOUSE ⟨horses and cows were *stabled* on the lower floor —*Amer. Guide Series: N.C.*⟩ ⟨garage . . . redesigned to ~ neighborhood Cadillacs —*Newsweek*⟩ ~ *vi* **:** to dwell in or as if in a stable

³stable \"\ *adj, often* **stabler** \-b(ə)lə(r)\ *often* **stablest** \-b(ə)ləst\ [ME, fr. OF *estable*, fr. L *stabilis*, fr. *stare* to stand + *-abilis* -able — more at STAND] **1 a :** firmly established **:** not easily moved, shaken, or overthrown **:** SOLID, FIXED, STEADFAST ⟨so long upon the moving, rocking sea that the ~ land was a shock to us —Jack London⟩ ⟨the sawmill village with sawdust streets became a ~ community and was incorporated as a city —*Amer. Guide Series: Mich.*⟩ ⟨dictatorship always appears —*Christian Science Monitor*⟩ ⟨~ habits⟩ ⟨a ~ theory⟩ **b :** not subject to sudden change **:** subject to relatively limited fluctuation **:** DURABLE, UNVARYING ⟨~ currency⟩ ⟨a ~ economy⟩ ⟨a general trend toward a ~ population, rather than one that will continue to increase —K.F.Mather⟩ ⟨some industries are quite ~ inasmuch as no basic changes in technique occur for a long period of time —E.B.Alderfer & H.E.Michl⟩ ⟨a relatively ~ society, where class mobility is reasonably low, where the individual remains, both physically and socially, in the place in which he was born —Leslie Cheek⟩ ⟨the personnel of the Supreme Court remained relatively ~ —R.K.Carr⟩ **c :** ABIDING, ENDURING, PERSISTING, PERMANENT ⟨a ~ peace⟩ ⟨your name will travel widely over the world, but will have no ~ habitation —J.A.Froude⟩ **2 :** steady in purpose **:** firm in resolution **:** CONSTANT, UNWAVERING ⟨many boys are not emotionally ~ and, as a result, behave in a way that makes some adults believe them to be retarded —H.A.Delp⟩ ⟨~ personalities usually can handle any specific anxiety —R.V. Seliger⟩ **3 a :** placed so as to resist forces tending to cause motion or change of motion **:** designed so as to develop forces that restore the original condition when disturbed from a condition of equilibrium or steady motion ⟨an airplane is ~ if, when it is disturbed from a balanced condition of flight (whether level, climbing or gliding), its tendency is to return to that condition —*Skyways*⟩ **b :** of such structure as to resist distortion **c** (1) **:** not readily decomposing or changing otherwise in chemical composition or biological activity (as spontaneously or under the influence of heat, acid, or alkali) ⟨penicillin . . . is ~ at a point about neutrality —*Amer. Scholar*⟩ (2) **:** not readily changing in physical state or properties ⟨a ~ emulsion⟩ ⟨a ~ substance never changes spontaneously into a metastable one —Samuel Glasstone⟩ (3) **:** not spontaneously radioactive or observably so ⟨a ~ isotope⟩ ⟨a ~ nucleus⟩

stableboy \'ˌˌ\ *n* **:** a boy who works around a stable **:** HOSTLER

stable color *n* [³*stable*] **:** a color (as yellow, blue, bluish red, or bluish green) that keeps the same hue though it may lose saturation down to a dead gray as it is viewed in indirect vision

stable entry *n* [¹*stable*] **:** two or more horses owned by the same stable or having the same trainer that are grouped as a single entry in a race and bet on as a unit

stable equilibrium *n* [³*stable*] **:** a state of equilibrium of a body (as a pendulum hanging directly downward from its point of support) such that when the body is slightly displaced it tends to return to its original position — compare UNSTABLE EQUILIBRIUM

stable fly *n* [¹*stable*] **1 :** a two-winged fly (*Stomoxys calcitrans*) that is abundant about stables and often enters dwellings esp. in autumn and that resembles the common housefly but bites severely **2 :** a fly (*Muscina stabulans*) that is related to and similar to the stable fly — called also *false stable fly*

sta·ble·man \'ˌˌmən, -ˌman\ *n, pl* **stablemen :** a worker in a stable; *esp* **:** one who takes care of the horses

stablemate \'ˌˌ\ *n* **1 :** a horse stabled with another **:** one of two or more horses having the same owner **2 :** one of two or more boxers having the same manager

stable–meal \'ˌˌ\ *n, Scot* **:** the liquor bought to compensate an innkeeper for the accommodation of horses

sta·ble·ness *n* -ES [ME *stablenes*, fr. *stable* + *-nes* -ness] **:** STABILITY

stable oscillation *n* [³*stable*] **:** an oscillation (as of a pendulum, tuning fork, or airplane part) whose amplitude does not increase — compare UNSTABLE OSCILLATION

stable police *n pl* **:** enlisted men detailed to clean the stables or picket lines and to help in the care of the horses

sta·bler \'stāb(ə)lə(r)\ *n* -S [ME *stabyler*, fr. MF *establier*, fr. *estable* stable + *-ier* -er — more at STABLE] **:** one that keeps a stable

stablest *superlative of* STABLE

stabling *n* -S [ME, fr. gerund of *stablen* to stable — more at STABLE] **:** accommodation for animals in a building ⟨~ for 20 horses⟩; *also* **:** the building providing such accommodation ⟨a range of ~ across the court⟩

stab·lish \'stablish\ *vb* -ED/-ING/-ES [by shortening] *archaic* **:** ESTABLISH — **stab·lish·ment** \-shmənt\ *n* -S *archaic*

sta·bly \'stāblē\ *adv* [ME, fr. *stable* + *-ly*] **:** in a stable manner

stabs *pl of* STAB, *pres 3d sing of* STAB

stab stitch *n* **:** a stitch made with a needle held at a right angle to the cloth

stab wound *also* **stab incision** *n* **:** a small surgical opening made into the abdominal cavity for drainage or other purpose

stac *abbr* staccato

stacc *abbr* staccato

stac·ca·tis·si·mo \ˌstäkəˈtisəˌmō\ *adv* (*or adj*) [It, fr. *staccato* + *-issimo*, suffix denoting a high degree of (fr. L *-issimus*, superl. suffix)] **:** in a sharper and more detached staccato manner — used as a direction in music

¹stac·ca·to \stəˈkä|d·(ˌ)ō, -kȧ|, |(ˌ)tō\ *adj* [It, fr. past part. of *staccare* to detach, short for *distaccare*, fr. OIt, fr. MF *destacher*, fr. OF *destachier* — more at DETACH] **1 a :** cut short or apart in performing **:** DISCONNECTED ⟨~ notes⟩ ⟨~ chords⟩ **b :** marked by short clear-cut playing or singing of tones or chords ⟨a ~ style⟩ — compare LEGATO **2 :** having a sharp abrupt disjointed character or quality ⟨the ~ voice of the telegraph called from settlement to settlement —J.D.Hart⟩ ⟨the book is a series of ~ scenes —Joseph Frank⟩

²staccato \"\ *adv* **:** in a staccato manner — often used as a direction in music; *compare* TENUTO

³staccato \"\ *n, pl* **staccatos** \-ōz\ *or* **stacca·ti** \|d·(ˌ)ē, |(ˌ)tē\ **1 :** an abrupt and disconnected manner of performance (as of a musical instrument); *also* **:** a passage of music so performed **2 :** something (as a manner of expression) that is broken up into brief sharp bursts ⟨in his rapid conversational ~ —Dorothy C. Fisher⟩ ⟨heard the chugging of a tractor, the ~ of its motor coming louder —Kay Boyle⟩

⁴staccato \"\ *vt* -ED/-ING/-S **:** to play, utter, or sound in a staccato manner

staccato mark *n* **:** a pointed vertical stroke or a dot that is put over or under a musical note to be produced staccato

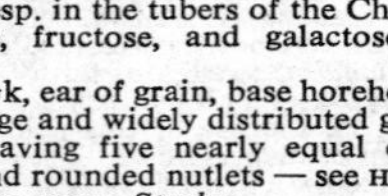

staccato marks

stach·er \'stakər\ *Scot var of* STAGGER

stach·y·bot·ryo·toxicosis \ˌstakə̇ˌbäˌtrēō+\ *n* [NL, fr. *Stachybotrys* + *-o-* + *toxicosis*] **:** a serious and sometimes fatal intoxication of horses fed on moldy hay that is due to a toxic substance elaborated by a mold (*Stachybotrys alternans*)

stach·y·bot·rys \ˌstakə̇ˈbä·trəs\ *n, cap* [NL, fr. Gk *stachys* ear of grain + *botrys* bunch of grapes, grape — more at STING] **:** a genus of imperfect fungi (order Moniliales) characterized by short usu. hyaline conidiophores with whorls of thick hyaline or brown sterigmata each bearing a spore or chain of spores

stach·y·drine \'stakəˌdrēn, -ˌdrən\ *n* -S [ISV *stach-* (fr. NL *Stachys*) + *hydr-* + *-ine*] **:** a crystalline alkaloid $C_7H_{13}NO_2$ found in various plants (as alfalfa or Chinese artichoke); the dimethyl betaine of proline

stach·y·ose \'stakēˌōs\ *n* -S [ISV *stach-* (fr. NL *Stachys*) + *-ose*] **:** a sweet crystalline sugar $C_{24}H_{42}O_{21}$ of the tetrasaccharide class that is found esp. in the tubers of the Chinese artichoke and yields glucose, fructose, and galactose on hydrolysis

sta·chys \'stākə̇s\ *n* [NL, fr. Gk, ear of grain, base horehound — more at STING] **1** *cap* **:** a large and widely distributed genus of herbs (family Labiatae) having five nearly equal calyx teeth, divergent anther cells, and rounded nutlets — see HEDGE NETTLE **2** -ES **:** any plant of the genus *Stachys*

stach·y·tar·phe·ta \ˌstakə̇tärˈfēd·ə\ *n, cap* [NL, fr. Gk *stachys* + NL *-tarpheta* (prob. irreg. fr. Gk *tarpheia*, fem. of *tarphys* thick; perh. akin to Gk *thrombos* lump — more at THROMB-] **:** a genus of chiefly tropical plants (family Verbenaceae) with solitary axillary flowers — see JAMAICA VERVAIN

stach·y·u·rus \ˌstakə̇ˈyu̇rəs\ *n, cap* [NL, fr. Gk *stachys* + NL *-urus*] **:** a small genus (coextensive with the family Stachyuraceae of the order Parietales) of Asiatic shrubs and trees having regular tetramerous flowers in long drooping racemes and small globose fruits

¹stack \'stak\ *n* -S [ME *stak*, fr. ON *stakkr*; akin to OE *staca* stake — more at STAKE] **1 :** a large pile (as of hay, grain in the sheaf, or straw) that is usu. nearly conical but sometimes rectangular, is commonly contracted at the top to a point or ridge, and is often thatched to shed rain **2 a :** a usu. orderly and systematically arranged pile or heap ⟨shuttled back and forth between the sink and the table, building her ~*s* of dried dishes —Lenard Kaufman⟩ ⟨keeps a great ~ of back copies of the magazine —Joseph Mitchell⟩ ⟨a ~ of wood⟩ ⟨a ~ of pancakes⟩ **b :** a large quantity or number ⟨there was a considerable ~ of evidence —G.A.Morran⟩ ⟨often spends his evenings working on ~*s* of papers he has brought home —*Current Biog.*⟩ ⟨has a ~ of money⟩ **3 :** an English unit of measure esp. for wood as fuel that is equal to 108 cubic feet **4 a :** CHIMNEY STACK **b :** a vertical pipe (as to carry off smoke) **:** CHIMNEY, FUNNEL, SMOKESTACK **c :** the part of a blast furnace or cupola above the hearth and melting zone **d :** the exhaust pipe of an internal-combustion engine — compare BAYONET STACK **e :** a fireplace and its chimney for cooking varnish **f :** a set of radiators in a cellar for heating apartments above by hot air conveyed through tin pipes; *also* **:** the tin pipe by which the heat is conveyed to an apartment **5 :** a rocky islet that is commonly steep-sided and near a cliffy shore and that has been isolated by wave erosion — compare CHIMNEY 2c **6 :** a pyramidal self-supporting pile of arms; *specif* **:** a pile composed of three rifles interlocked by their stacking swivels **7 a** (1) **:** a structure of bookshelves separated by narrow aisles that is one or more stories in height and is used for compact storage of books — usu. used in pl. (2) **:** the portion of a building housing such a structure — usu. used in pl. **b :** a collection of bookcases compactly arranged **8 :** a row of benches containing retorts for use in gas manufacturing **9 :** a number of usu. similar antennas mounted together and operated as part of a single radio system **10 :** an assembled set of calender rolls with the required accessories **11 :** AIR STACK **12 a :** an established quantity of chips sold at one time to a gambler (as in poker) — called also *takeout* **b :** the supply of chips belonging to a cardplayer at any given time

²stack \"\ *vb* -ED/-ING/-S [ME *stakken*, fr. *stak*, n.] *vt* **1 a :** to pile up **:** make into a usu. neat heap or pile ⟨so many millions so tightly packed and ~*ed* into such tall hives —G.S.Perry⟩ ⟨~*ed* the firewood in the cellar⟩ **b :** to place quantities of something on or in **:** LOAD ⟨the floor was ~*ed* high with bales of dry goods —Winston Churchill⟩ ⟨~ the bulkheads with cargoes from every port in the world —*Amer. Guide Series: N. Y. City*⟩ **2 :** to arrange in a stack ⟨~*ed* their arms and lowered their flag —*Amer. Guide Series: La.*⟩ **3 a :** to arrange (cards or a pack of cards) secretly for cheating ⟨the cards were ~*ed* against him⟩ **b :** to weight the composition of dishonestly or unfairly ⟨they ~*ed* juries and stole elections —*Springfield (Mass.) Daily News*⟩ ⟨charged . . . that the conference was ~*ed* against the supporters of federal aid —M.W.Straight⟩ **4 :** to assign (an airplane approaching an airport) by radio to a particular altitude and position within a group circling and waiting a turn to land **5 :** to make the belly of (an archery bow) high and narrow ~ *vi* **1 :** to form a stack **:** HEAP, PILE ⟨the containers are low in cost, set up easily and ~ well —*Appliance Manufacturer*⟩ **2 :** to form a line or group **:** ACCUMULATE — used with *up* ⟨long double lines of cars ~*ed up* on either side of the site —*Springfield (Mass.) Union*⟩

stacked *adj, slang, of a woman* **:** having a well developed figure **:** BUILT

¹stack·er \'stakə(r)\ *n* -S [²*stack* + *-er*] **:** one that stacks: as **a :** one whose work is stacking articles (as for transportation or storage) **b :** an elevator or blast tube attachment to a threshing machine for stacking the straw (as on a wagon) — compare WIND STACKER

²stack·er \'stakər\ *Scot var of* STAGGER

stack·freed \'stakˌfrēd\ *n* -S [origin unknown] **:** an eccentric wheel or cam having a spring pressing on it and formerly attached to the barrel of the earliest mainspring-driven timepieces to equalize the force transmitted

stack·garth \'stagə(r)th\ *n* -S [ME *stakgarth*, fr. ON *stakkgarthr*, fr. *stakkr* haystack + *garthr* yard — more at STACK, YARD] *dial Eng* **:** STACKYARD

stack gas *n* **:** the gas passing through a smokestack — compare FLUE GAS

stack·hou·sia \stakˈhau̇zēə\ *n, cap* [NL, fr. John *Stackhouse* †1819 English botanist + NL *-ia*] **:** a genus of xerophytic mostly Australasian herbs (family Stackhousiaceae) having yellow or white and often gamopetalous flowers

stack·hou·si·a·ce·ae \ˌstakˌhau̇zēˈāsēˌē\ *n pl, cap* [NL, fr. *Stackhousia*, type genus + *-aceae*] **:** a family of plants (order Sapindales) having a distinctly lobed ovary that produces a schizocarp

stacking swivel *n* **:** a swivel on a rifle for stacking it

stack process *n* **:** DUTCH PROCESS

stack room *n* **:** a room housing a library stack

stack silage *n* **:** silage made from chopped forage built into a pile above ground

stackstand \'ˌˌ\ *n* **:** a scaffolding for supporting a stack of hay or grain **:** RICKSTAND, STADDLE

stack up *vi* **1 :** to add up **:** TOTAL ⟨this is how things *stack up* today —*Time*⟩ **2 :** to measure up **:** COMPARE, MATCH — usu. used with *against* ⟨how does our product *stack up* against competitive products —Bud Wilson⟩ ⟨how does this ideal secretary *stack up* against the working secretary —Herbert Mitgang⟩

stackyard \'ˌˌ\ *n* **:** a yard or field containing straw or grain in stacks

stac·te \'staktē\ *n* -S [L, myrrh, fr. Gk *staktē*, fr. fem. of *staktos* oozing out in drops, fr. *stazein* to drip — more at STAGNATE] **:** a sweet spice used by the ancient Jews in preparing incense

stac·tom·e·ter \stakˈtäməd·ə(r)\ *n* [Gk *staktos* oozing out in drops + E *-meter*] **:** STALAGMOMETER

stad \'stät\ *n* -S [Afrik, town, city, fr. MD *stat, stad* place, town, city; akin to OE *stede* place — more at STEAD] *Africa* **:** a native village

stad·dle \'stadᵊl\ *n* -S [ME *stathel* base, foundation, support, fr. OE *stathol* (also, heavens, estate, farm); akin to OFris *stathul* base, foundation, OHG *stadal* barn, shed, ON *stöthull* milking shed, OE *stede* place — more at STEAD] **1 :** a small tree or sapling; *esp* **:** a small forest tree **2 a :** the lower part of a stack (as of hay) **b :** the supporting frame or base of a stack

stade \'stād\ *n* -S [MF *estade*, fr. L *stadium* — more at STADIUM] **:** STADIUM ⟨the circuit of the course was about six ~*s* —Richard Stillwell⟩

sta·der splint \'stādə(r)-\ *n, usu cap 1st S* [after Otto *Stader* *b*1894 Am. veterinarian] **:** a splinting device consisting of two stainless steel pins inserted in the bone above and below a fracture or break and a turnbuckle bar joining the pins for drawing and holding the broken ends together

¹stadia *pl of* STADIUM

²sta·dia \'stādēə\ *n* -S [It, prob. fr. L, pl. of *stadium*] **1 a :** STADIA ROD **b :** a surveying method using a stadia rod **2 :** an instrument with stadia hairs

stadia hairs *or* **stadia wires** *n pl* **:** horizontal cross hairs (as in a theodolite) equidistant from the central horizontal cross hair

¹sta·di·al \'stādēəl\ *adj* [*stadium* + *-al*] **:** of or relating to a stage, stadial, or stadium

²stadial \"\ *n* -S **:** a substage of a glacial stage; *esp* **:** one marked by a readvance of ice

stadia rod *n* **:** a graduated rod used with an instrument having stadia hairs to measure the distance from the observation point to the place where the rod is positioned by observation of the length of rod subtended by the distance between the stadia hairs when these are fixed or of the space between the stadia hairs when they are adjusted to cover a certain definite interval on the stadia rod

sta·dic \'stādik\ *adj* [*stadia* + *-ic*] **:** of or relating to a stadia

sta·dim·e·ter \stəˈdiməd·ə(r)\ *n* [*stadium* + *-meter*] **:** an instrument for measuring the distance of an object of known height

sta·di·um \'stādēəm\ *n, pl* **sta·dia** \-ēə\ *or* **stadiums** [ME, fr. L, fr. Gk *stadion*, alter. (influenced by *stadios* fixed, stable) of *spadion*, fr. *span* to pull, draw, tear — more at SPAN] **1 a** *also* **sta·di·on** \-ē,än\ [*stadion* fr. Gk] **:** any of various ancient Greek units of length equal to 600 Greek feet **b :** an ancient Roman unit of length equal to 625 Roman feet or 606.95 English feet **2 a :** a course for footraces in ancient Greece orig. one stadium in length **b :** a terraced structure with seats for spectators surrounding an ancient Greek running track and typically built in the shape of a long narrow horseshoe **c** *pl usu* **stadiums :** a large usu. unroofed structure with tiers of seats for spectators built in various shapes (as circular or elliptic) and enclosing a field usu. used for sports events (as baseball, football, track and field) — compare CIRCUS **3** [NL, fr. L] **:** a phase of development or growth **:** PERIOD; *specif* **:** the interval between any two successive molts in the development of an insect

Stadium Boot *trademark* — used for a usu. ankle-high fleece-lined boot worn by women and children for warmth

stadt·hold·er \'stat,hōldə(r)\ *also* **stad·hold·er** \-ad-,\ *n* -S [part trans. of D *stadhouder* (formerly spelled also *stadthouder*), fr. *stad* place, town, city (fr. MD *stat, stad*) + *houder* holder — more at STAD] **1 a :** a viceroy in a province of the Netherlands **b :** a chief executive officer of the United Provinces of the Netherlands **2 :** a viceroy or lieutenant governor of a region outside the Netherlands

stadt·hold·er·ate \-ə,rāt\ *n* -S **:** the office or position of a stadtholder

stadt·hold·er·ship \-ə(r),ship\ *n* **:** STADTHOLDERATE

stadt·house \'stat+,-\ *n* [part trans. of D *stadhuis* (formerly spelled also *stadthuis*), fr. *stad* town, city + *huis* house] **:** a town hall in a town or colony of the Netherlands

¹staff \'sta|f, |aa(ə)f, |aif, |äf\ *n, pl* **staffs** \|fs\ *or* **staves** \|vz, 'stāvz\ [ME *staf*, fr. OE *stæf*; akin to OHG *stab* staff, ON *stafr* staff, Goth *stabim* (dat. pl.) elemental substances, MIr *sab* shaft, staff, Gk *stemphylon* olive pulp, Skt *stabhnāti*, *stambhate* he supports — more at STAMP] **1 a :** a long stick carried in the hand for support in walking ⟨stumping with his ~ —Robert Browning⟩ ⟨my signs are a rainproof coat, good shoes, and a ~ cut from the woods —Walt Whitman⟩ **b :** a strong usu. rigid rod or bar used to hold or support something

⟨wears a corset with steel *staves* and braces —*Springfield (Mass.) Union*⟩ ⟨a number of hardwood *staves*, fixed crosswise —*Dyestuffs*⟩: as (1) *archaic* : SHAFT 1a(1) (2) : a round bar that is used as a crosspiece (as in a ladder or chair) : RUNG (3) : FLAGSTAFF ⟨twisting the flag around the ~ —*Boy Scout Handbk.*⟩ (4) : a pivoted arbor (as of a wheel or a pinion of a watch) (5) : a vertical bead molding at the angle between walls **c** : CLUB, CUDGEL ⟨a ~ is quickly found to beat a dog —Shak.⟩ **d** : something that upholds or sustains : PROP, SUPPORT ⟨his early successes will be the stout ~ which will support him —H.H.Arnold & I.C.Eaker⟩ **2 a** : a pole with a crook or cross that forms part of the insignia of an ecclesiastic (as a bishop) **b** : a rod carried as a symbol of office or position ⟨*staves* carried by the leading men of the society —L.M. Wulcko⟩ **c** : a rod used by a magician : WAND ⟨over them a gnarled ~ she shook —John Keats⟩ **d** : a small rod or other token handed to a railroad engineer as his authority to proceed over a particular section **3 a** *obs* : STANZA ⟨let me hear a ~ —Shak.⟩ **b** : the horizontal lines with their spaces on which music is written — called also *stave; compare* CLEF, LEDGER LINE **c** : a set of vertical lines for the placement of dance-movement symbols — compare LABAN SYSTEM **4** : any of various graduated sticks or rules used for measuring (as in shipbuilding, surveying) : ROD ⟨setting up gauging *staves*, against which the water level can be read —*Geog. Jour.*⟩ **5** *pl* **staffs** : the personnel responsible for the functioning of an institution or the establishment or the carrying out of an assigned task under an overall director or head ⟨put together an excellent ~ to assist him in his diplomatic mission⟩ ⟨a small ~ of servants takes care of the house⟩ ⟨is on the editorial ~ of the newspaper⟩: as **a** : the teaching and administrative personnel of an educational institution **b** : the doctors and surgeons regularly attached to a hospital and helping to determine its policies and guide its activities **c** : the personnel of an organization (as an industrial enterprise) that furnishes auxiliary and advisory services and does not participate directly in production — compare ³LINE 6j(2), LINE ORGANIZATION **d** (1) : the officers detailed to serve on the staff of the commander of a fleet or lesser unit (2) : the officers (as in the U.S. Navy) not eligible for command at sea **e** (1) : a group of officers in an army who assist (as by collection and analysis of information, organization of supplies and services, planning of operations) a commanding officer — see GENERAL STAFF, PERSONAL STAFF, SPECIAL STAFF, UNIT STAFF (2) : the noncombatant forces of an army — compare ³LINE 6e(1) **f** : the group of officers and aides appointed to attend upon and serve as escort to a civil executive (as a president or governor) — **at staff's end** *or* **at stave's end** *archaic* : at arm's length

²**staff** \"\ *vt* -ED/-ING/-S : to supply with a staff : provide the necessary personnel for ⟨a large modern plant, finely housed and ~ed —*Amer. Guide Series: N.H.*⟩ ⟨we are ~ing the faculties of other institutions —McGeorge Bundy⟩

³**staff** \"\ *adj* **1** : of, relating to, or constituting a staff ⟨~ work⟩ ⟨~ officers⟩ ⟨~ personnel⟩ **2** : having an auxiliary or advisory relationship to the stated objective of an organization ⟨the personnel department of a manufacturing concern performs a ~ function⟩

⁴**staff** \"\ *n* -s [prob. fr. G *staffieren* to trim, decorate — more at STAFFAGE] : a building material having a plaster of paris base and used in exterior wall coverings of temporary buildings

staf·fage \stə'fäzh\ *n* -s [G, fr. *staffieren* to trim, decorate (fr. LG *staffēren*, fr. MLG *stoffēren*, *staffēren*, fr. MD *stofferen*, fr. MF *estoffer* to stuff, trim, decorate) + F *-age* — more at STUFF] : the accessories of an artistic composition; *esp* : human or animal figures added as subordinate elements to the painting of a landscape

staff angle *n* : a corner of metal or wood set into the plaster so as to be flush with the wall surfaces forming an angle in order to secure the corner from injury

staff bead *n* **1** : a bead used to close the joint between a wooden frame and the adjacent masonry **2** : a molded or beaded staff angle

staff cell *n* [trans. of G *stabzelle*] : STAB CELL

staff corps *n* : the personnel of a staff branch of the military service

staff·er *pronunc at* STAFF + ə(r)\ *n* -s : a member of a staff; *specif* : a member of the editorial or reportorial staff of a newspaper, periodical, or press association — compare STRINGER

staf·fette \sta'fet\ *n* -s [MF *estaffette* — more at ESTAFETTE] *archaic* : ESTAFETTE

staff–herd \'≈,≈\ *vt* : to put (livestock) to graze esp. in charge of a herdsman

staff notation *n* : musical notation in which a staff is used — see PITCH illustration

staff of aesculapius *usu cap A* [after *Aesculapius*, Greco-Roman god of medicine, fr. L, fr. Gk *Asklēpios*] : a conventionalized representation of a staff branched at the top with a single snake twined around it that is used as a symbol of medicine and as the official insignia of the American Medical Association — called also *Aesculapian staff; compare* CADUCEUS

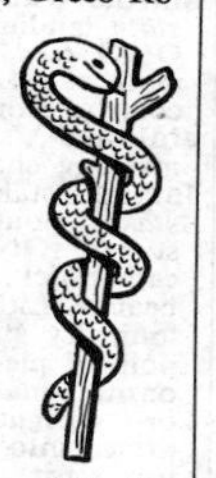
staff of Aesculapius

staff officer *n* **1** : an officer serving on a staff **2** : a member of the Salvation Army attached to a headquarters and responsible for administrative work or for work in a specialized field

staff of life : a staple of diet; *esp* : BREAD ⟨produced a *staff of life* about two feet in length, and cut off a good thick slice for each of them —C.B.Fairbanks⟩

staf·ford \'stafə(r)d\ *adj, usu cap* [fr. *Stafford*, England] **1** : of or from the municipal borough of Stafford, England : of the kind or style prevalent in Stafford **2** : STAFFORDSHIRE

¹**staf·ford·shire** \-d,shi(ə)r, -,shiə, -,shə(r)\ *adj, usu cap* [fr. *Staffordshire*, England] : of or from the county of Stafford, England : of the kind or style prevalent in Stafford

²**staffordshire** *or* **staffordshire ware** *n, usu cap S* : glazed ceramic ware produced in Staffordshire during the 18th and 19th centuries

staffordshire terrier *also* **staffordshire bullterrier** *n, usu cap S* : BULLTERRIER

staff ride *or* **staff walk** *n* : a tactical ride or walk for training in staff problems

staff rush *n* : a stiff tufted bog herb (*Juncus conglomeratus*) of the north temperate zone having isolated heads of chaffy flowers — called also *pith rush*

staffs *pl of* STAFF, *pres 3d sing of* STAFF

staff sergeant *n* : a noncommissioned officer rating in the army just below a platoon sergeant and above a sergeant, in the air force just below a technical sergeant and above an airman first class, and in the marine corps just below a gunnery sergeant and above a sergeant — see CHEVRON illustration

staff system *n* : a block system in which a suitably inscribed staff is delivered to the engineer of a train or caught up by the engine while moving as authority giving the right of way to a designated station

staff tree *n* : a tree or shrub of the genus *Celastrus*

staff–tree family *n* : CELASTRACEAE

staff vine *n* : BITTERSWEET 2b

¹**stag** \'stag, -aag, -aig\ *n* -s *see sense 1* [ME *stagge*, fr. OE *stagga;* akin to ON *andarsteggi* drake, Icel *steggi* drake, gander, tomcat, male fox, Sw *stagg*, a kind of stiff grass, OE *stingan* to sting — more at STING] **1** *or pl* **stag a** : the adult male of the red deer; *specif* : one five years of age or older — compare HIND **b** : the male of various other deer of the genus *Cervus* **c** : the male of various other large deer (as the caribou) **2** *chiefly Scot* : a young horse; *esp* : a young unbroken stallion **3** : a male animal castrated after the secondary sex characteristics have developed to such a point as to give it the appearance of a mature male **4 a** : a young male domestic fowl: (1) : a market fowl on which the spurs are developing and which is less tender than a fryer but still suitable for roasting (2) : a young gamecock that has not passed through its first full molt **b** *Brit* : TURKEY-COCK **5** *Brit* : INFORMER 3 **6** *Brit* : one who subscribes for shares of an announced issue of stock with the intention of selling at a profit as soon as possible **7 a** : a social gathering of men only ⟨automobile trips and luncheons for the ladies, and banquets and a ~ for the menfolks —*Daily Plumbers Trade Jour.*⟩ **b** : a person who attends a social gathering (as a dance) unaccompanied by someone of the opposite sex ⟨he joined the other ~s watching the dancers⟩ ⟨some of them come with their dates . . . but most of the girls are ~s —*Accent*⟩

²**stag** \"\ *vb* **stagged**; **stagged**; **stagging**; **stags** *vt* **1** *Brit specif* : to keep an eye on : spy on **2** : to cut down : SHORTEN; *specif* : to cut off (trousers) at the knees or just above the boot tops ⟨mackinaws and waist overalls, *stagged* at the boot tops —*Amer. Guide Series: Wash.*⟩ ~ *vi* **1** *Brit* : to turn informer **2** *Brit* : to speculate in stocks as a stag **3** : to attend a social function (as a dinner or dance) without a companion of the opposite sex : go stag ⟨had planned to ~ at the class dance —William Du Bois⟩

³**stag** \"\ *adj* **1 a** : restricted to men : for men only ⟨a ~ dinner⟩ ⟨a ~ party⟩ **b** : intended or suitable for a gathering of men only ⟨a ~ movie⟩ **2** : unaccompanied by someone of the opposite sex ⟨three ~ women in beautiful ermine coats —Speed Lamkin⟩

⁴**stag** \"\ *adv* : as a stag ⟨she had a cold, so he went along ~ —Victoria Lincoln⟩ ⟨many girls now prefer to dance ~ at a cotillion —*N.Y.Sun*⟩

stag beetle *n* : any of numerous mostly large lamellicorn beetles (as *Lucanus capreolus* of northeastern U.S. or *L. cervus* of Europe) that constitute the family Lucanidae and have males generally much larger than the females and with long and often branched mandibles suggesting the antlers of a stag and larvae which feed on the rotten wood of dead trees

stagbush *also* **stagbrush** \'≈,≈\ *n* : BLACK HAW 1

¹**stage** \'stāj\ *n* -s [ME, fr. OF *estage* (also, position, place,

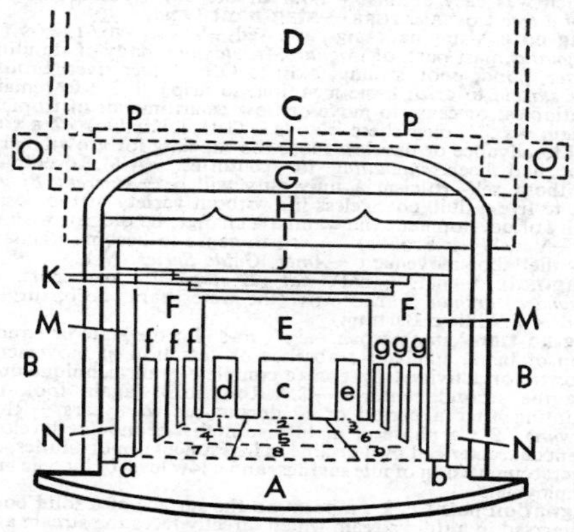

stage 2b(2): proscenium, *A;* wings, *B,B;* proscenium arch, *C;* flies, *D;* back flat, *E;* flats, *F,F;* asbestos curtain, *G;* grand drape, *H;* act drop, *I;* teaser, *J;* borders, *K,K;* returns, *M,M;* tormentors, *N,N;* fly gallery, *O,O;* bridge, *P,P;* *1* up right center; *2* up center; *3* up left center; *4* right center; *5* center; *6* left center; *7* down right center; *8* down center; *9* down left center; *a* right first entrance; *b* left first entrance; *c* center entrance; *d* right center entrance; *e* left center entrance; *f,f,f*, right side entrances; *g,g,g*, left side entrances

stay, habitation), fr. (assumed) VL *staticum*, fr. L *stare* to stand + *-aticum* -age — more at STAND] **1 a** : a story of a building : a horizontal division of a structure ⟨a low square tower in four ~s —*Amer. Guide Series: Md.*⟩ **b** : one of a series of positions or stations one above the other : GRADE, STEP ⟨the garden that sloped, ~ by ~ precipitously down to the water —F.M.Ford⟩ **c** : a set of shelves : SHELF; *specif* : a tier of shelves (as in a greenhouse) on which potted plants are placed ⟨the height of the glass above the greenhouse ~s —*So. African Garden Manual*⟩ **d** : the height of the surface of a river above an arbitrary zero point — see FLOOD STAGE **e** : the distance between two levels (as in hoisting) **2 a** : a raised platform for the better viewing of something by an audience ⟨spoke from a small ~ erected at the edge of the airport⟩ ⟨give order that these bodies high on a ~ be placed to the view —Shak.⟩ **b**(1) : the raised flooring in a theater or auditorium on which plays or other spectacles (as operas or ballets) are enacted (2) : the part of a theater between the proscenium and the rear wall including the acting area, wings, and storage space — called also *stagehouse* (3) : the dramatic art or profession : THEATER — usu. used with *the* ⟨attracted by the ~ ever since she was a child⟩ **c** : a place where something is exhibited or done : a center of attention or a scene of action ⟨all the world's a ~ —Shak.⟩ ⟨those diseases . . . now occupy the center of the medical ~ —R.J.Thomas⟩ ⟨the end of the eighteenth century set the ~ for a new middle-class struggle —Roy Lewis & Angus Maude⟩ **3 a** : a scaffold used to support workmen and their materials ⟨~s rigged overside swarmed with . . . shipfitters, busy removing crumpled shell plating —K.M.Dodson⟩ **b** : an elevated structure used for drying fish **c** : LANDING STAGE **d** : a platform used as a base or support; *specif* : the small platform of the stand of a microscope or polariscope on which an object is placed for examination **4 a** : a place of rest formerly provided for those traveling by stagecoach : STATION **b** : the distance between two stopping places on a road : a degree of advance in a journey ⟨proceeded by easy ~s, some of them spending the night near my camp —Douglas Carruthers⟩ **c** (1) : STAGECOACH ⟨sat on the slippery leather seat of the old ~ —Margaret Deland⟩ (2) : a motor vehicle that carries mail or passengers (3) : AIR STAGE **5 a** : a period or step in a process, activity, or development ⟨there were three ~s in the cutting process —G. S. & Helen McKearin⟩ ⟨came to bat with a teammate on base in the late ~s of a close ball game —W.B.Furlong⟩ ⟨aware of the ~s in child growth and development —*Current Biog.*⟩ **b** (1) : a period or phase in the course of a disease ⟨the preeruptive ~ of an eruptive fever⟩ ⟨sweating ~ of malaria⟩ (2) : one of two or more operations performed at different times but constituting a single procedure ⟨*2-stage* thoracoplasty⟩ ⟨the operation should be done in two or three ~s⟩ (3) : one of the four degrees indicating depth of general anesthesia ⟨~ of excitement⟩ ⟨~ of surgical anesthesia⟩ **c** : one of the steps into which the material development of man or a people is divided : a particular economy ⟨pastoral ~⟩ ⟨hunting ~⟩ ⟨nomadic ~⟩ **d** : a division of a culture or culture period with respect to time, content, or development **e** (1) : a minor subdivision of a stratigraphic series (2) : a part of a cycle of erosion in which the features of the landscape have characteristics that distinguish them from similar features in other parts of the cycle (3) : a subdivision of the Pleistocene epoch ⟨the Illinoian glacial ~⟩; *also* : STADIAL (4) : a particular phase in the historical development of a geologic feature ⟨the Calumet ~ of Lake Chicago⟩ **f** (1) : one of several periods whose beginning and end are usu. marked by some important change of structure in the development and growth of many animals and plants ⟨the larval ~⟩ — see INSTAR (2) : an organism in a specified stage ⟨the tadpole is the larval ~ of a frog⟩ **g** : one complete process or step (as of a fluid passing through one impeller of a multiple-impeller pump) — see PRESSURE STAGE, VELOCITY STAGE **h** : an element or part in a complex electronic contrivance; *specif* : a single tube with its associated components in an amplifier **i** : a propulsion unit of a rocket with its own fuel and container ⟨the first ~ raises all the ~s until its fuel is gone⟩ — **on the stage** *adv (or adj)* : in or into the acting profession ⟨has been *on the stage* for many years⟩ ⟨gave up his teaching career to go *on the stage*⟩

²**stage** \"\ *vb* -ED/-ING/-S *vt* **1** *archaic* : to furnish with a scaffold **2** : to put into a play or public show ⟨the quick comedians extemporally will ~ us —Shak.⟩ ⟨his play . . . *staged* only one woman character among airmen —Edmund Fuller⟩ **3 a** : to produce on the stage : put on ⟨*staged* the play in a spectacular fashion⟩ ⟨*staged* a number of new ballets this season⟩ ⟨*staged* the opera with new scenery⟩ **b** : to produce for public view ⟨~ a track meet⟩ ⟨~ a special art exhibition⟩ ⟨~ an elaborate parade⟩ **c** : to bring about or cause to take place esp. in a dramatic or spectacular manner ⟨*staged* a brief hunger strike yesterday —*N.Y.Times*⟩ ⟨*staged* huge protest demonstrations —Anne Bauer⟩ ⟨led his followers to ~ an attempt to release him from custody —L.S.B.Leakey⟩ ⟨the entirely unpredictable . . . weather had decided to ~ a clear sunny day in the middle of December —C.S.Forester⟩ **d** : to arrange or present for public effect : CONTRIVE ⟨*staged* a fake accident⟩ **4** : to place (potted plants) on a layer of sand, gravel, or other medium in a greenhouse **5** : to move (as military personnel, supplies, or equipment) to or establish in a new base in preparation for a further movement or a planned operation ⟨seize bases that would permit *staging* our aircraft forward —F.J.Sackton⟩ **6** : to protect (areas of a printing plate that require no further etching) with a resist of asphalt varnish or other solution ~ *vi* **1** : to travel by stage ⟨after four and a half days of continuous *staging* . . . he arrived —G.R.Stewart⟩ **2** : to establish a military base or position ⟨*staging* there for attacks —*Time*⟩ ⟨ordnance company *staging* for the night nearby —*Yale Rev.*⟩

³**stage** \"\ *adj* **1** : CONVENTIONALIZED, STEREOTYPED ⟨so French as to make him seem almost a ~ Frenchman —Osbert Sitwell⟩ ⟨the face of a ~ curate —Fred Majdalany⟩ **2** : of, relating to, or constituting a manner of pronouncing a language on formal occasions (as in stage acting or public speaking) that is not necessarily identical with any one dialect of the language and that seeks to avoid dialectal features that have the least currency among educated speakers

stage box *n* : a theater box over the proscenium

stage brace *n* : a brace used to support stage scenery (as flats) from behind

stage business *n* : BUSINESS 4

stage carriage *n* : STAGECOACH

stage cloth *n* : a cloth or hanging used about a stage; *specif* : a cloth to cover the floor of a stage

stagecoach \'≈,≈\ *n* : a heavy usu. four-in-hand closed coach formerly making regular trips between stations and carrying passengers and goods — see ROAD COACH

stagecraft \'≈,≈\ *n* : the art or practice of effective management of theatrical devices or techniques (as in dramatic composition, acting, directing)

staged *adj* **1 a** : written for or produced on the stage ⟨a ~ version of the novel⟩ **b** : deliberately planned and arranged for effect or deception : CONTRIVED ⟨not going to be taken in by one of those artfully ~ photographs —Philip Guedalla⟩ ⟨~ confessions and railings against sin —Nona B. Brown⟩ **2** : arranged or taking place in stages ⟨called for ~ reduction of both atomic and conventional weapons —*N.Y.Times*⟩

stage direction *n* : a description or direction written or printed in a play (as to describe a character or setting or to indicate a piece of stage business)

stage director *n* **1** : DIRECTOR 1c **2** : STAGE MANAGER

stage door *n* : an entrance to a theater reserved for actors and stage personnel and used also by authorized visitors

stage–door johnny *n, often cap J* : a man who frequents a theater for the purpose of courting an actress or chorus girl ⟨assumed the role of *stage-door Johnny* to serve papers on a burlesque queen —Ralph Ginzburg⟩

stage driver *n* : one that drives a stage

staged tower *n* : a tower in which the stories are strongly marked (as in a Chinese pagoda or a ziggurat)

stage effect *n* : a showy and artificial effect or contrivance ⟨sheer make-believe, *stage effect* and hocus-pocus —Isaac Deutscher⟩

stage fright *n* : nervousness or panic felt by a person appearing or due to appear before an audience — compare BUCK FEVER

stagehand \'≈,≈\ *n* : a stage worker who handles scenery and properties : SCENESHIFTER

stagehouse \'≈,≈\ *n* **1** : a house providing facilities for a stage and its passengers **2** : STAGE 2b(2)

stage–keeper \'≈,≈≈\ *n* : a stage attendant in the Elizabethan theater

stageland \'≈,≈\ *n* : the world of the theater ⟨a pure product of ~, and unrelated to any practical experiences of life —Agnes Repplier⟩

stage·man \'stājmən\ *n, pl* **stagemen** : one who works on a stage; *specif* : a worker who helps to prepare the stage for the shooting of motion pictures

stage–manage \'≈,≈≈\ *vt* [back-formation fr. *stage manager*] **1 a** : to arrange or exhibit with an eye to striking effect ⟨prewar pageantry, pictorially beautiful and brilliantly *stage-managed* —Mollie Panter-Downes⟩ **b** : to arrange or direct from behind the scenes ⟨arrest and trial had been *stage-managed* for a sinister purpose —*Atlantic*⟩ **2** : to act as stage manager for ⟨*stage-managed* a few more productions, but his heart was set on directing —E.J.Kahn⟩

stage management *n* **1** : the act or process of stage-managing **2** : the function of a stage manager

stage manager *n* : one that supervises the physical aspects of a stage production, assists the director during rehearsals, and is in complete charge of the stage during a performance

stage micrometer *n* : a finely divided scale ruled on a microscope slide and used to calibrate the filar micrometer

stage name *n* : a name by which an actor is known professionally

stageplank \'≈,≈\ *n* **1** : LANDING STAGE ⟨stood on the end of the ~ with the coil of rope in his hand —Mark Twain⟩ **2** : GANGPLANK ⟨the ~ was let down on schedule —Shelby Foote⟩

stag·er \'stājə(r)\ *n* -s [¹*stage* + *-er*] **1** : one that has experience : one that takes part (as in life, a profession, an activity) : HAND ⟨call the roll of the achievements of the new ~s —*Va. Quarterly Rev.*⟩ — usu. used in phrases with *old* ⟨a wise old literary ~ —Cyril Connolly⟩; compare OLD HAND 1 **2** *archaic* : ACTOR **3** : STAGE DRIVER **4** : one that applies an acid resistant to the parts of a rotogravure cylinder that are not to be etched

stage right *n* : a right generally protected by copyright to represent a work in a theater with living actors — usu. used in pl.

stag·ery \'stājərē\ *n* -ES [¹*stage* + *-ery*] : STAGECRAFT

stages *pl of* STAGE, *pres 3d sing of* STAGE

stage screw *n* : a tapered screw with a handle that resembles a corkscrew and is used to fasten stage braces to the floor

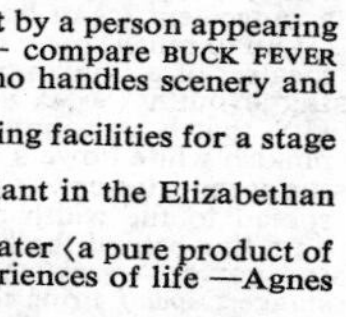
stage screw

stage set *n* **1** : an arrangement of scenery and properties for a particular scene in a play ⟨a house like a *stage set* —Dan Wickenden⟩ **2** : SETTING ⟨wonders if the best *stage set* for learning comes from casual and chance opportunities —Lucy S. Mitchell⟩

stage setting *n* **1** : the act or process of setting the stage **2** : STAGE SET

stage space *n* : the effect esp. in painting of a view limited by a complete block after a very short distance — compare DEEP SPACE

stagestruck \'≈,≈\ *adj* : fascinated by the stage; *esp* : seized by a passionate desire to become an actor ⟨the youthful who are ~ —John Mason Brown⟩

stage wagon *n* : a wagon used as a stagecoach esp. formerly in thinly settled areas

stage wait *n* : a marked and usu. awkward break in the continuity of the action during a theatrical performance

stage whisper *n* **1** : a loud whisper by an actor that is audible to the spectators but is supposed for dramatic effect not to be heard by one or more of the actors **2** : any distinctly audible whisper

stage–whisper \'≈,≈≈\ *vi* [*stage whisper*] : to speak in a stage whisper

¹**stagewise** \'≈,≈\ *adj* [¹*stage* + *wise*] : theatrically knowledgeable or effective ⟨a ~ director⟩ ⟨less commanding as musical compositions, but bright and ~ —C.M.Smith⟩

²stagewise \"\ *adv* [¹*stage* + *-wise*] **:** with respect to the stage : on the stage ⟨known ~ by another name⟩

stagey *var of* STAGY

stag·gard \'stag(ə)rd\ *or* **stag·gart** \-(r)t\ *n* -s [ME *staggard*, fr. *stagge* stag + *-ard*] **:** a male red deer in its fourth year

stagged *past of* STAG

¹stag·ger \'stag(ə)r, -aig-\ *vb* **staggered; staggered; staggering** \-g(ə)riŋ\ **staggers** [alter. of earlier *stacker*, fr. ME *stakeren*, fr. ON *stakra* to push, stagger, freq. of *staka* to punt, push, stagger; akin to MLG *staken* to push, OE *staca* stake — more at STAKE] *vi* **1 a :** to have difficulty in remaining erect **:** reel from side to side **:** stand or walk unsteadily **:** SWAY, TOTTER ⟨the man ~ed, with his stomach pushed out, under the weight of the demijohn —Jean Stafford⟩ ⟨an intoxicated motorist . . . ~s from his car —Wayne Hughes⟩ ⟨the last weary dancers ~ed off —Virginia D. Dawson & Betty D. Wilson⟩ **b :** to move on unsteadily : make headway or progress with difficulty ⟨the good little ship is ~ing along —E.J. Schoettle⟩ ⟨his coach ~ed through that wilderness of mud —James Stern⟩ ⟨an arrow : HOBBLE **d :** to get along or manage despite difficulties — used with *on* or *along* ⟨education, however, has managed to ~ on in spite of these pleasant diversions —F.J.Moffitt⟩ **2 :** to rock violently : SHAKE, TREMBLE, VIBRATE ⟨the whole fabric of the ship seemed to ~ —F.W.Crofts⟩ **3 :** to become doubtful and wavering in purpose, thought, or action : HESITATE ⟨at whose immensity even soaring fancy ~s —P.B.Shelley⟩ ⟨became ~ed and perplexed, a skeptic —Charles Lamb⟩ ~ *vt* **1 :** to cause to doubt or hesitate : make helpless : NONPLUS, PERPLEX ⟨a solution so bizarre as to ~ the imagination —*Newsweek*⟩ ⟨problems so intricate and laborious that they ~ the most patient mathematician —H.M.Davis⟩ **2 :** to cause to sway unsteadily : make reel or totter ⟨if a fighter is ~ed, watch closely to see how badly he is hurt —Jack Dempsey⟩ ⟨three young girls . . . doing work that would ~ most men —Louise D. Rich⟩ **3 :** to place alternately at equal distances on either side of a middle line: as **a :** to arrange ⟨as spokes or rivets⟩ on each side of a median line alternately **b** (1) **:** to plant alternately on each side of a median line (2) **:** to plant at irregular distances without reference to a definite line **c :** to arrange ⟨a file⟩ so that the tabs on the cards or folders are placed in different positions **4 :** to arrange in a series of overlapping or alternating periods ⟨the move to ~ city business hours to help ameliorate traffic congestion —*Sydney (Australia) Bull.*⟩ ⟨feeding is ~ed in three shifts between 11:45 and 1:30 —*Management Methods*⟩ **5 :** to adjust ⟨as the wings of a biplane⟩ so that the leading edge of one wing projects beyond the leading edge of another wing

²stagger \"\ *n* -s **1 staggers** *pl but usu sing in constr* **a :** an abnormal condition of domestic mammals and birds associated with damage to the central nervous system and marked by incoordination and a reeling unsteady gait **:** MEGRIMS — called also *blind staggers, mad staggers*; compare EQUINE ENCEPHALOMYELITIS, FORAGE POISONING, GID, ⁵KEEL **b :** CAISSON DISEASE **c :** a condition likened to the staggers ⟨as in disorientation⟩ ⟨a bad case of the verbal ~s —*Time*⟩ **2 :** a reeling or tottering movement of one trying to walk or stand **:** an unsteady gait or stance ⟨fling saddle and bridle on the horse and ride . . . into the last ~ of exhaustion —William Faulkner⟩ **3** *slang* **:** ATTEMPT, STAB **4 :** the amount of advance of the leading edge of an upper wing of a multiplane ⟨as a biplane⟩ over that of a lower that is expressed as percentage of gap and is measured from the leading edge of the upper wing along its chord to the point of intersection of this chord with a line drawn perpendicular to the chord of the upper wing at the leading edge of the lower wing with all lines being drawn in a plane parallel to the plane of symmetry

³stagger \"\ *adj* **:** marked by an alternating or overlapping arrangement ⟨as of hours of work or study⟩ ⟨a ~ system was set up to relieve overcrowding in the school⟩ ⟨adoption by the theatres of a ~ plan of curtain times —*N.Y.Times*⟩

staggerbush \'�⸱⸱⸱\ *n* **:** a shrub (*Lyonia mariana*) of eastern U.S. that is poisonous to stock and has clusters of nodding pinkish white flowers

staggered stance *n* **:** a football stance in which the feet are spread to the width of the hips and the toe of one foot is on a line behind the heel of the other foot

stag·ger·er \'-gərə(r)\ -\ *n* **:** one that staggers or causes to stagger; *specif* **:** one that shocks or astonishes ⟨the question, nevertheless, was a ~ —J.C.Lincoln⟩

stagger grass *n* **:** either of two plants with slender grassy leaves that are associated with poisoning of cattle or other livestock: **a :** a common atamasco lily (*Zephyranthes atamasco*) of the eastern U.S. which is reputed to cause staggers in horses **b :** FLY POISON 1

staggering *adj* **:** serving to stagger **:** ASTONISHING, OVERWHELMING ⟨in a few years proved an immediate and ~ problem —A.A.Berle⟩ ⟨represents a ~ investment in time, in skilled labor —Charlton Laird⟩ — **stag·ger·ing·ly** *adv*

staggering bob *n* [*bob* fr. E dial., very young calf, prob. fr. *Bob*, nickname for *Robert*] *dial Brit* **:** a very young calf

staggerweed \'⸱⸱⸱\ *n* **1 :** FIELD LARKSPUR **2 :** CORN WOUNDWORT **3 :** SQUIRREL CORN

stagger wire *n* **:** a wire connecting the upper and lower wings of an airplane and lying in a plane substantially parallel to the plane of symmetry

staggerwort \'⸱⸱⸱⸱\ *n* **:** a ragwort (*Senecio aureus*)

stag·gery \'stagərē\ *adj* **:** in a reeling condition **:** UNSTEADY ⟨slightly ~ about the legs, and did not disdain his father's hand beneath his elbow —Elizabeth Goudge⟩

stag·gie \'stagi\ *n* -s [¹*stag* + *-ie*] *Scot* **:** COLT

stagging *pres part of* STAG

stag·gy \'stagē\ *adj* -ER/-EST [¹*stag* + *-y*] **:** having the appearance of a mature male — used of female or castrated domestic animals

staghead \'⸱⸱⸱\ *n* **1 :** a dieback in which the shape of the projecting dead branches suggests a stag's horns **2 :** WITCHES' BROOM

stag-headed \'⸱⸱⸱⸱\ *adj* **:** having leafless dead limbs at the top ⟨*stag-headed* oak⟩

stag-head·ed·ness *n* -ES **:** the condition of being stag-headed

staghorn \'⸱⸱⸱\ *n* **1 :** a stag's horn used as a handle for a knife or for ornamental purposes **2 a** *or* **staghorn moss :** a club moss (*Lycopodium clavatum*) **b :** STAGHORN FERN **3 :** STAGHORN CORAL

staghorn calculus *n* **:** a calculus that branches in the shape of a stag's horns

staghorn coral *n* **:** any of several large branching corals of the genus *Acropora* that somewhat resemble antlers; *esp* **:** a coral (*A. cervicornis*) found in waters off Florida

stag-horned \'⸱⸱⸱\ *adj* **1 :** STAG-HEADED **2 :** having mandibles that are large and palmate or branched like an antler — used of a beetle

staghorn fern *n* **:** a fern of the genus *Platycerium*; *esp* **:** a commonly cultivated fern (*P. bifurcatum*) of Australia

staghorn sumac *n* **:** a small tree or shrub (*Rhus typhina*) of eastern No. America with velvety-pubescent branches and flower stalks, leaves that turn brilliant red in fall, and dense panicles of greenish yellow flowers followed by bright crimson fruits

staghound \'⸱⸱⸱\ *n* **:** a hound formerly used in hunting the stag and other large animals; *specif* **:** a large heavy hound that resembles and is held to be among the ancestors of the modern English foxhound

sta·gi·ary \'stajē⸱erē\ *n* -ES [ML *stagiarius*, fr. *stagium*, *estagium* term of residence (fr. OF *estage* stage) + L *-arius* -ary — more at STAGE] **:** a resident canon

stagier *comparative of* STAGY *or of* STAGEY

stagiest *superlative of* STAGY *or of* STAGEY

sta·gi·ly \'stājilē, -jə\ *adv* **:** in a stagy manner **:** THEATRICALLY

sta·gi·ness \-jēnəs, -jin-\ *n* -ES **:** the quality or state of being stagy **:** THEATRICALITY

staging *n* -s [partly fr. ME, fr. ¹*stage* + *-ing*; partly fr. gerund of ²*stage*] **1 :** SCAFFOLDING ⟨a ~ on which he was working —*Springfield (Mass.) Daily News*⟩ **2 a :** the business of running stagecoaches **b :** the act of journeying by stagecoaches **3 :** the act or art of putting a play on the stage ⟨the steadily evolving character development which is so vital to this kind of ~ —Henry Hewes⟩ **4 :** division of a process ⟨as the ex-

---

pansion of steam in a turbine⟩ into a series of steps or stages **5 :** the moving of troops or materiel forward in several stages or the assembling of troops or materiel in transit in a particular place

staging area *n* **:** an area in which troops are assembled and readied prior to a new operation or mission

stag·i·rite *also* **stag·y·rite** \'stajə⸱rīt\ *n* -s *cap* [L *Stagirites*, fr. Gk *Stagirités*, fr. *Stagiros*, *Stagira*, city in ancient Macedonia + Gk *itēs* -ite] **:** a native or inhabitant of Stagira ⟨Aristotle, the famous *Stagirite*⟩

stag jump *n* **:** a free jump in figure skating in which one leg is bent and drawn up toward the chest and the other extended behind

stag·mom·e·ter \stag'mäməd⸱ə(r)\ *n* [Gk *stagma* something that drips (fr. *stazein* to drip) + E -o- + *-meter* — more at STAGNATE] **:** an apparatus for the measurement of the number of drops per unit of volume of a liquid

stag·nance \'stagnən(t)s, -aig-\ *n* -s **:** STAGNANCY

stag·nan·cy \-gnənsē, -si\ *n* -ES **:** the quality or state of being stagnant

stag·nant \-gnənt\ *adj* [L *stagnans*, *stagnans*, pres. part. of *stagnare* to stagnate] **1 :** not running in a current or stream **:** not flowing **:** MOTIONLESS ⟨the ~ water looked uninviting —T.E.Lawrence⟩ **:** STALE ⟨the place was small and close, and the long disuse had made the air ~ and foul —Bram Stoker⟩ **2 a :** not advancing, developing, or growing **:** not active ⟨politically and economically a backward, ~ area —Stringfellow Barr⟩ ⟨something must be done to revive industry so long ~ —V.L.Parrington⟩ **b :** marked by a lack of vitality, activity, or interest **:** DULL ⟨seemed to wish to escape notice, which was easy at this ~ hour of the day —John Buchan⟩ **c** *of a tree* **:** OVERMATURE — **stag·nant·ly** *adv*

¹stag·nate \'stag⸱nāt, -aig-, *usu* -ād⸱+V\ *vb* -ED/-ING/-s [L *stagnatus*, past part. of *stagnare*, fr. *stagnum* body of standing water, pond, pool, swamp; akin to OBret *staer* river, brook, Gk *stazein* to drip; basic meaning: to drip] *vi* **1 :** to remain motionless or cease to move or flow ⟨maritime air of tropical origin ~ . . . over these islands —G.H.T.Kimble⟩ **2 a :** to fail to advance or develop **:** lose the capacity for growth ⟨arts that had been *stagnating* for centuries —A.M.Rosenthal⟩ ⟨without self-criticism a university will ~ —*Current Biog.*⟩ **b :** to live a dull, changeless life without variety or the possibility of development ⟨he wanted a change, he did not wish to ~ —Van Wyck Brooks⟩ ~ *vt* **:** to cause to become stagnant ⟨~ the labor movement —*Amer. Guide Series: N.Y.*⟩

²stag·nate \'⸱⸱⸱⸱\ *adj* [L *stagnatus*, past part. of *stagnare*] *archaic* **:** STAGNANT ⟨the water dark, deep, turgid, and ~ —William Bartram⟩

stag·na·tion \stag'nāshən, -aig-\ *n* -s **1 :** the state or condition of being stagnant **:** absence or cessation of movement, growth, or activity **:** TORPOR ⟨a complete ~ of technique during the second century —C.A.Robinson⟩ ⟨again took up painting after a period of ~ during the war years —Rhys Gwyn⟩ **2 :** a phase of mature capitalist economic development characterized by a decline in investment opportunities, an overaccumulation of idle savings, and a low level of income and employment

stagnation point *n* **1 :** a point on the surface of a solid body immersed in a fluid stream which directly faces the stream and at which the stream lines separate **2 :** a point near the leading edge or nose of a body placed in an airstream at which the airflow divides to go on either side of the body

stag·nic·o·la \stag'nikələ\ *n*, *cap* [NL, fr. L *stagnum* standing body of water, pond, pool + -i- + NL *-cola* — more at STAGNATE] **:** a genus of common freshwater snails (family Lymnaeidae) including intermediate hosts of the sheep liver fluke and of various trematodes of waterfowls that cause schistosome dermatitis in man

stag·nic·o·lous \-ləs\ *adj* [L *stagnum* + E -i- + *-colous*] **:** frequenting or living or thriving in stagnant water

stag·num \'stagnəm\ *n*, *pl* **stag·na** \-nə\ [L] **:** a pool of water without an outlet

stag·o·nos·po·ra \stag⸱ə'näspərə\ *n*, *cap* [NL, fr. Gk *stagon-, stagōn* drop (fr. *stazein* to drip) + NL -o- + *-spora* — more at STAGNATE] **:** a large cosmopolitan genus of imperfect fungi (family Sphaeropsidaceae) having oblong several-septate hyaline pycniospores and including some forms that cause leaf diseases of economic plants

stags *pl of* STAG, *pres 3d sing of* STAG

stag's horn *or* **stag's horn moss** *n* **:** STAGHORN 2a

stag's-horn sumac *n* **:** STAGHORN SUMAC

stag tick *n* **:** a fly (*Lipoptena cervi*) of the family Hippoboscidae that is parasitic upon the red deer and that has wings on attaining maturity but sheds them soon after settling on its host

stagworm \'⸱⸱\ *n* **:** the larva of a botfly that infests the stag and *esp* of a botfly of the genus *Cephenomyia*

stagy *also* **stagey** \'stājē, -ji\ *adj* **stagier; stagiest** [¹*stage* + *-y*] **:** having characteristics of the stage; *esp* **:** having an artificial and mannered quality **:** THEATRICAL ⟨his father's ~ gesturing for effect —Irwin Shaw⟩

stagyrite *cap, var of* STAGIRITE

¹stahl·ian \'stälēən, -lyən\ *adj, usu cap* [Georg Ernst Stahl †1734 Ger. physician and chemist + E *-ian*, adj. suffix] **:** of or relating to G. E. Stahl or his doctrine of animism

²stahlian \"\ *n* -s *usu cap* [Georg E. Stahl †1734 + E *-ian*, *n.* suffix] **:** an adherent of G. E. Stahl and his doctrines

¹staid \'stād\ *adj* [fr. past part. of ¹*stay*] **1 :** SETTLED, FIXED ⟨his ~ opinion⟩ **2 :** SOBER, GRAVE, SEDATE ⟨~ persons⟩ ⟨~ colors⟩ **syn** see SERIOUS

²staid *past of* STAY

staid·ly *adv*, *archaic* **:** in a staid manner

staid·ness *n* -ES **:** the quality or state of being staid **:** REGULARITY, SEDATENESS, SERIOUSNESS, STEADINESS

staig \'stāg\ *chiefly Scot var of* STAG

stail \'stāl, *esp before pause or consonant* -āəl\ *n* -s [alter. of ¹*stale*] *Brit* **:** a long straight wooden handle for a tool ⟨as a hoe⟩

¹stain \'stān\ *vb* -ED/-ING/-s [ME *steynen*, partly fr. MF *desteindre* to discolor & partly of Scand origin; akin to ON *steina* to paint — more at DISTAIN] *vt* **1 :** to discolor with foreign matter : make foul ⟨as with spots or blemishes⟩ **2 :** to impart to or suffuse with color ⟨like wine that ~s a pearly glass —Elinor Wylie⟩ **3 a :** to corrupt or defile morally : taint with guilt, vice, or corruption **b :** to inflict a stigma upon : bring reproach on **4** *obs* **:** to eclipse by superior beauty or excellence **5** *obs* **:** to obscure the luster of ⟨whether poverty . . . *staineth* nobility —Henry Peacham⟩ **6 :** to color ⟨as wood, glass, paper, or cloth⟩ by processes affecting chemically or otherwise the material itself **:** tinge with a color combining with or penetrating the substance ⟨~ wood with acids⟩ — compare DYE **7 :** to foil ⟨the scent of the quarry⟩ *esp* by the passage of hounds, horses, cattle, or other animals over the track ~ *vi* **1 :** to receive a stain **:** absorb coloring matter

²stain \"\ *n* -s **1 :** something that stains: as **a :** a discoloration by foreign matter **:** SPOT ⟨a ~ on his shirt⟩ ⟨water ~s⟩ ⟨weather ~s⟩ ⟨mineral ~s⟩ **b :** a discoloration of the skin **:** BLOTCH **c :** a natural spot of color different from the ground ⟨swift trouts, diversified with crimson ~s —Alexander Pope⟩ **2** *obs* **:** a cause of reproach or disgrace ⟨~ to thy countrymen, thou hear'st thy doom —Shak.⟩ **3 :** a taint of guilt ⟨as on one's character, conscience, or reputation⟩ **:** mark of disgrace or infamy **:** a usu. grave blemish **:** STIGMA, TARNISH ⟨on him had fallen . . . the ~ of the massacres —J.A.Froude⟩ ⟨degrades . . . the unhappy issue of the marriage by fixing upon it the ~ of bastardy —R.B.Taney⟩ **4 :** a dye, pigment, or preparation used in staining: **a :** a solution or dispersion of a dye or pigment in a vehicle ⟨as water, alcohols, or oils⟩ that is usu. thinner than a paint or other coating, transparent, and capable of penetrating the pores of wood or other material instead of forming a protective surface **b :** a dye or mixture of dyes used in microscopy to make visible minute and transparent structures, to differentiate tissue structures, or to produce specific microchemical reactions

stain·abil·i·ty \⸱⸱⸱⸱snə'bilə⸱dē, -lət⸱ē, -i\ *n* **:** the capacity of cells and cell parts to stain specifically and consistently with particular dyes and stains

stain·able \'⸱nəbəl\ *adj* **:** capable of being stained ⟨a ~ substance⟩

stained \'stānd\ *adj* [ME *steyned*, fr. past part. of *steynen* to

---

stain] **1 :** discolored with stains ⟨a ~ and tattered jacket⟩ — often used in combination ⟨her tear-*stained* cheeks⟩ **2 :** colored with stain ⟨a bookcase ~ and waxed⟩ — often used in combination ⟨a brown-*stained* house⟩

stained glass *n* **:** glass colored or stained; *esp* **:** window glass colored throughout by metallic oxides fused into it or remaining white and cased with colored glass or into whose surface the pigments have been burned

stained-glass \'⸱⸱⸱\ *adj* [*stained glass*] **1 a :** of, relating to, or concerned with stained glass **b :** made of or characterized by stained glass ⟨*stained-glass* windows⟩ **2 :** SANCTIMONIOUS ⟨the extirpation of *stained-glass* tones from the preaching of seminary students⟩ ⟨*stained-glass* attitudes⟩

stained paper *n* **:** paper colored on the surface in a calender stack

stain·er \'stānə(r)\ *n* -s [alter. (influenced by *-er*) of ME *steynour*, fr. *steynen* to stain + *-our* -or — more at STAIN] **:** one that stains: **a :** a worker who applies a coloring or finishing stain ⟨as to wood, furniture, or leather goods⟩ **b :** a worker who prepares the dyes for paper-coating mixtures **c :** a pigment used merely to give color to a paint, as distinguished from one that stains those with which they feed — see COTTON STAINER

stai·nier·ite \'stīnēə⸱rīt, stī'ni,r-\ *n* -s [D *stainieriet*, fr. Xavier *Stainier*, 20th cent. Belgian geologist + D *-iet* -ite] **:** a rare mineral CoO(OH) consisting of cobalt oxide-hydroxide and occurring in black mammillary masses

stain·less \'stānləs\ *adj* **1 :** free from stain, spot, blemish, or stigma **:** IMMACULATE ⟨the ~ purity of her private life —T.B. Macaulay⟩ ⟨a sea captain of ~ reputation —Llewellyn Howland⟩ **2 a :** highly resistant to stain, corrosion, or tarnish ⟨~ iron⟩ ⟨~ silver⟩ **b :** made principally of such a highly resistant material ⟨~ flatware⟩ ⟨~ sills⟩

stain·less·ness *n* -ES **:** the quality or state of being stainless

stainless steel *n* **:** an alloy steel practically immune to rusting and ordinary corrosion having as its essential alloying constituent chromium usu. 12 to 14 percent but sometimes more

stair \'sta(a)(ə)r, 'ste|, |ə\ *n* -s *often attrib* [ME *steir, steyer*, fr. OE *stæger*; akin to MD *steger, steiger* ladder, stair, OE *stīg* narrow path, *stīgan* to move, go up or down, OHG *stīgan* to go up, rise, ON *stīga*, Goth *steigan* to go up, rise, OIr *tiagu* I walk, Gk *steichein* to walk, go, Skt *stighnoti* he goes up, rises] **1 :** a series of steps or flights of steps connected by landings for passing from one level to another ⟨a steep ~ . . . provided access to the upper floor attics —G.E. Fussell⟩ ⟨climbing down the steep and tortuous ~ —H.S. Morrison⟩ — often used in pl. but sing. or pl. in constr. ⟨a narrow private ~s to connect the upper and lower rooms — Lewis Mumford⟩ ⟨lurked at the foot of one ~ —*New Yorker*⟩ ⟨ascended a ~s —Scott Fitzgerald⟩ **2 a :** any one step of a series for ascending or descending to a different level ⟨as within a building⟩ **b** *obs* **:** a step by which one progresses or may progress from one stage or elevation to another ⟨as in rank, dignity, preferment, wealth, or power⟩ **3 stairs** *pl* **:** LANDING STAGE

staircase \'⸱⸱⸱\ *n* [*stair* + *case*] **1 a :** the structure containing a stairway **:** an enclosure for stairs ⟨as of walls or railings⟩ **b :** a flight of stairs with the supporting framework, casing, and balusters **2 :** something resembling or held to resemble a staircase ⟨the dead stream was an interminable ~ of ledges —Alan Le May⟩ **3 :** RIVER 4

staircase curve *n* **:** HISTOGRAM

staircase shell *n* **1 :** WENTLETRAP **2 :** SUNDIAL SHELL

stair dance *n* **:** a tap dance performed up and down a small flight of stairs

stair horse *n* **:** one of the inclined members supporting a flight of stairs

stair rod *n* **:** a metal rod or its equivalent for holding a stair carpet in place in the angle between two steps

¹stairstep \'⸱⸱⸱\ *n* [*stair* + *step*] **1 :** a step in a flight of stairs **2 stairsteps** *pl* **:** a flight of stairs

²stairstep \"\ *vi* **:** to move up or down like the steps in a stairway ⟨narrow streets ~ up the slopes —*Geog. School Bull.*⟩

stair-step \'⸱⸱⸱\ *adj* **:** resembling the steps in a stairway ⟨*stair-step* levels of terrain⟩; *esp* **:** moving up or down like steps in a stairway ⟨*stair-step* inflation⟩

stair tower *n* **:** a clearly defined vertical shaft or tower containing stairs

stairway \'⸱⸱\ *n* -s **:** one or more flights of stairs and usu. connecting landings providing passage from one level ⟨as of a building⟩ to another

stairwell \'⸱⸱⸱\ *n* [*stair* + *well*] **:** a compartment extending vertically through a building in which stairs are located

stair wire *n* **:** a slender stair rod

staithe \'stāth\ *n* -s [ME *stathe*, of Scand origin; akin to ON *stöth* landing place, staithe; akin to OE *stæth* bank, shore, OHG *stad*, *stado* bank, shore, Goth *staths* place, stead — more at STEAD] *dial Eng* **:** a wharf for transshipment esp. of coal ⟨as from railroad cars into ships⟩

stak·age \'stākaj, -kēj\ *n* -s [²*stake* + *-age*] **:** the action of marking channels by stakes

¹stake \'stāk\ *n* -s *often attrib* [ME, fr. OE *staca*; akin to MLG *stake* pointed stick, stake, ON *lȳsistaki* candlestick, L *tignum* beam, Lith *stagaras* long dry stalk] **1 a :** a pointed piece of wood or other material driven or designed to be driven into the ground usu. for a specific purpose ⟨as a mark of a boundary, site, or claim, support for a plant, part of a framework, or a tethering rod⟩ **2 :** a post or other support to which a person is bound for execution usu. by burning **3 :** execution by burning at a stake **4 a :** something that is staked for gain or loss; *esp* **:** a sum of money or its equivalent risked **b :** the prize set in any contest — often used in pl. **5 :** a small anvil usu. having a tang to enter a hole in a bench top and used by smiths for light work **6 :** something that may be gained or lost ⟨as by the turn of events⟩ **:** something at stake **:** a permanent interest ⟨as in an enterprise or community⟩ ⟨have a ~ in the country⟩ **7 :** a sporting event in which a stake or prize is put up; *specif* **:** STAKE RACE **8 :** a territorial unit of Latter-day Saint Church jurisdiction comprising a group of wards and governed by a stake presidency **9 :** a wooden post formerly used in leather manufacturing to support a blunt semicircular steel blade over which skins are drawn to and fro to be stretched and softened **10 :** a stick inserted upright in a loop, eye, or mortise at the side or end of a vehicle ⟨as a cart, flatcar, or truck⟩ to retain the load **11 :** any of the longest foundation rods of a basket usu. usp. from the bottom — see BASKET illustration **12 :** a tool used by a slater **13 :** the part of a riveter frame that carries the stationary die **14 :** the part of stone or wood or both often elaborately ornamented and set up as a rover in archery **15 :** GRUBSTAKE — **at stake :** at issue **:** in jeopardy **:** INVOLVED, IMPLICATED ⟨his honor is *at stake*⟩

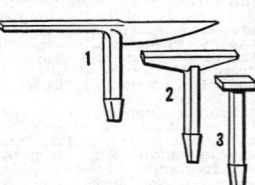

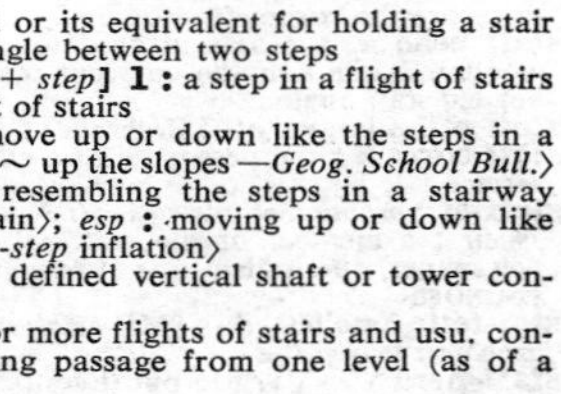

stakes 5: *1* beakhorn, *2* hatchet, *3* square

²stake \"\ *vb* -ED/-ING/-s [ME *staken*, fr. *stake*, n.] *vt* **1 :** to mark the limits of by stakes — usu. used with *out* or *off* **2 :** to tether ⟨an animal⟩ to a stake **3 :** to impale on or transfix with a stake ⟨as formerly in punishment⟩ **4 :** to risk ⟨as one's money or life⟩ upon the issue of competition or upon a future contingency **:** WAGER, VENTURE, BET **5 :** to fasten up or support ⟨as vines or plants⟩ with stakes **6 :** to work ⟨skins⟩ on a stake or in a staking machine in leather manufacturing **:** stretch and flex ⟨leather⟩ to soften it after tanning **7 a :** to back financially **:** support ⟨as a person or enterprise⟩ in order to further chances of success **b :** to advance ⟨as money or supplies⟩ to assist in or in expectation of future success **8 :** GRUBSTAKE ~ *vi* **1 :** to put up a bet **:** WAGER ⟨whether you ~ in pounds or in shillings —*advt*⟩ **2 :** to impale a wheel on the arbor of a clock or watch with the use of hollow punches and with the arbor resting in a die — **stake a claim :** to assert

title to something by or as if by placing stakes to satisfy legal requirements ⟨in order to *stake a claim* for a footing in Morocco —Wickham Steed⟩

stake and bound *n* **:** a dead hedge held in place between strong stakes that serves as an obstacle over which horses must jump esp. in fox hunting

stake-and-rider \ˈ=,=ˈ=\ *n* **:** a fence having a top bar supported by crossed stakes

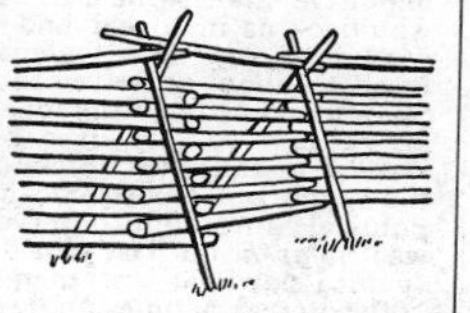

stake-and-rider

stake boat *n* **:** a boat moored to mark the course and esp. the starting point in a race

stake body *n* **:** an open motor-truck body consisting of a platform with stakes inserted along the outside edges to retain a load

stake down *vt* **:** to deposit (as a sum of money) as a wager or stake

stake driver *n* [so called fr. the belief that one of its notes resembles the sound of driving a stake into mud] **:** AMERICAN BITTERN

stakeholder \ˈ=,==\ *n* **1 :** a person entrusted with the stakes of two or more persons betting against one another and charged with the duty of delivering the stakes to the winner **2 :** a person entrusted with the custody of property or money that is the subject of litigation or of contention between rival claimants in which the holder claims no right or property interest

stake horse *n* **1 :** a horse that runs chiefly in stake races **2 :** a horse of superior quality

stakeman \ˈ=-mən\ *n, pl* **stakemen :** one who carries and sets stakes for a surveying party

stakemaster \ˈ=,==\ *n* **:** an official presiding over the stakes of shooting fields in archery

stake net *n* **:** a net held in position by stakes **:** TRAP NET

stake of zion *usu cap Z* [fr. *Zion*, height in the northeastern part of Jerusalem, Palestine that was once the site of Solomon's Temple and the seat of government of the kingdom of Judah] **:** STAKE 8

stake out *vt* **1 :** to assign (as a policeman) to a specified area usu. to conduct a surveillance **2 :** to maintain a police surveillance of (as a suspect or an area)

stakeout \ˈ=,=\ *n* -s [fr. *stake out*, v.] **:** a surveillance maintained by one or more policemen over an area or a person suspected of criminal activity ⟨a ~ was placed on the home —Courtney McClendon⟩

stake presidency *n* **:** the governing unit of a Latter-day Saint stake consisting of a president and two counselors and a high council of twelve

stak·er \ˈstākə(r)\ *n* -s [ME, fr. *staken* to stake + *-er* — more at STAKE] **1 :** one that stakes: as **a :** PERCHER c **b :** a worker who uses a handpress to press or rivet watch or clock parts together **2** [¹*stake* + *-er*] **:** a plant (as a tomato) of such size that it requires a stake for support when it is planted

stake race *also* **stakes race** *n* **:** a horse race in which the money stake or prize offered is the total contributed by the nominators — compare PURSE RACE

stakerope \ˈ=,=\ *n* **:** a rope for staking out an animal

stakes *pl of* STAKE, *pres 3d sing of* STAKE

stake truck *n* **:** a truck having a stake body

sta·khanov·ite \stəˈkänə,vīt, -kan-\ *n* -s *usu cap* [Alexei G. *Stakhanov* b1905 Russ. miner who devised a system of higher production + E *-ite*] **:** a worker esp. in the U.S.S.R. whose production is consistently above average and who is therefore awarded recognition and special privileges ⟨said here that *Stakhanovites* . . . make more money than members of the government —Joseph Wechsberg⟩

staking *pres part of* STAKE

stal·ace \ˈstaləs\ *n* -s [irreg. fr. Gk *stalaktos*] **:** a central mass of cells in the root cap of some plants that is evident because its cells are arranged in a distinctly regular radial fashion — called also *columella*

sta·lac·ti·form \stəˈlaktə,fȯrm\ *adj* [¹*stalactite* + *-iform*] **:** resembling a stalactite

¹**stalac·tite** \stəˈlak,tīt *sometimes* ˈstaləkˌ; *usu* -īd.+V\ *n* -s [NL *stalactites*, fr. Gk *stalaktos* dropping, dripping (fr. *stalassein* to let drop, drip) + L *-ites* -ite; fr. the dropping of the waters — more at STALE (urine)] **1 a :** a deposit of crystalline calcium carbonate (as calcite) resembling an icicle, depending from the roof or sides of a cavern, formed by waters that have become saturated with calcium bicarbonate by percolating through and partially dissolving the overlying limestone, and varying from white or colorless to yellow and brown or in some copper mines bright green or blue — compare STALAGMITE **b :** limestone so formed **2 :** a similar formation of some other material ⟨a ~ of lava⟩ **3 :** a small stalactiform projection used in overlapping tiers for ornamentation (as of a vault or capital) in Moorish architecture

²**stalactite** \"\ *or* **stalac·tit·ed** \-īd·əd\ *adj* **:** ornamented with successive rows of stalactites in Moorish architecture ⟨a ~ vault⟩ ⟨~ work⟩

stal·ac·tit·ic \ˌstalakˈtid·ik\ *also* **stal·ac·tit·i·cal** \-d·əkəl\ *or* **sta·lac·tic** \stəˈlaktik\ *or* **sta·lac·ti·cal** \-tə̇kəl\ *or* **stalac·tit·al** \ˌstalakˈtīd·əl, stəˈlak,tīd-\ *adj* [*stalactitic*, *stalactitical* fr. ¹*stalactite* + *-ic* or *-ical*; *stalactic*, *stalactical* fr. ¹*stalactite* + *-ic* or *-ical*; *stalactital* fr. ¹*stalactite* + *-al*] **1 :** of, relating to, or resembling a stalactite **2 :** covered with stalactites — **stal·ac·tit·i·cal·ly** \ˌstalakˈtid·ək(ə)lē\ *adv*

sta·lag \ˈs(h)tä,läg\ *n* -s [G, short for *stammlager* base camp, fr. *stamm* base, stem (fr. OHG *stam*) + *lager* camp, place to sleep, bed, fr. OHG *legar* bed — more at STEM, LAIR] **:** a German prison camp for noncommissioned or enlisted prisoners of war

sta·lag·ma \stəˈlagmə, -laig-\ *n* -s [NL, fr. Gk, drop] **:** STALAGMITE 1b

stalag·mite \stəˈlag,mīt, -ˈlaig- *sometimes* ˈstaləg-; *usu* -īd·+V\ *n* -s [NL *stalagmites*, fr. Gk *stalagma* drop, *stalagmos* dropping, dripping + L *-ites* -ite; akin to Gk *stalassein* to let drop, drip — more at STALE (urine)] **1 a :** a deposit of crystalline calcium carbonate more or less like an inverted stalactite formed on the floor of a cave by the drip of water saturated with calcium bicarbonate and often uniting with a stalactite in a complete column **b :** limestone so formed **2 :** a similar formation of some other material

stalagmite marble *n* **:** onyx marble often occurring in a stalagmitic deposit

stal·ag·mit·ic \ˌstaləgˈmid·ik\ *also* **stal·ag·mit·i·cal** \-d·əkəl\ *adj* [*stalagmite* + *-ic* or *-ical*] **:** having the shape or character of or found in stalagmites — **stal·ag·mit·i·cal·ly** \-d·ək(ə)lē\ *adv*

stal·ag·mom·e·ter \ˌstaləgˈmäməd·ə(r), -mətə-\ *n* [Gk *stalagmos* dropping, dripping + E *-meter*] **:** a device characterized by a capillary tube usu. with a flattened tip for determining either the number of drops in a given volume of liquid or the drop weight esp. for use in calculating the surface tension (as of blood or serum) — called also *stactometer* — **sta·lag·mo·met·ric** \stəˌlagməˈme·trik\ *adj* — **sta·lag·mo·met·ri·cal·ly** \-rə̇k(ə)lē\ *adv*

stal·ag·mom·e·try \ˌstaləgˈmämə·trē\ *n* -ES **:** the measurement of surface tension by means of a stalagmometer

¹**stale** \ˈstāl, *esp before pause or consonant* -āəl\ *n* -s [ME, fr. OE *stalu* wood to which harpstrings are fixed; akin to OE *stela* stalk, stem — more at STEAL] **1** *chiefly dial* **:** the stock of an implement (as a rake) **2** *dial Brit* **:** a rung of a ladder **3** *obs* **:** the shaft of an arrow or spear

²**stale** \"\ *adj* -ER/-EST [ME; akin to MD *stel* stale] **1** *obs, of malt liquor* **:** well aged **2 a :** altered in quality through the action of natural processes **:** having undergone physical changes while standing **:** not fresh; *esp* **:** impaired in flavor, odor, or texture by such changes ⟨kept the bread until it was too ~ to eat⟩ ⟨asked the nurse to empty the ~ water and get her a fresh pitcher⟩ **b :** having the unpleasant odor of something that has become stale ⟨a ~ courtyard⟩ **3 :** having lost a former novelty and power of pleasing **:** TRITE, COMMONPLACE ⟨~ and worn phrases —H.D.Gideonse⟩ ⟨news that was ~ by the time it reached him⟩ **4** *archaic* **:** past the age of vigor and attractiveness suitable for marriage **5 a :** impaired in legal force or effect by reason of laches or being allowed to rest without use, action, or demand **:** barred from enforcement by a statute of limitation ⟨a ~ affidavit⟩ ⟨a ~ debt⟩ **b** *of a check* **:** held an unreasonable time after issue before being presented for payment at a bank **6 :** showing a marked loss of vigor, enthusiasm, and effectiveness often due to monotony ⟨many of the old burlesque comics were going ~ for want of fresh material —Henry Hewes⟩ **7 a :** deficient in vitality usu. because of age ⟨a ~ culture of bacteria⟩ **b** *of land* **:** unsuitable as range for the same kind of poultry or livestock because of long use

³**stale** \"\ *vb* -ED/-ING/-S [ME *stalen*, fr. *stale*, n.] *vt* **1 :** to make stale ⟨a smell of previous food *staled* the air —Rose Thurburn⟩ **:** destroy the freshness of ⟨age cannot wither her, nor custom ~ her infinite variety —Shak.⟩ **2** *archaic* **:** to render common **:** CHEAPEN **3 :** to sweat (as sheepskins) at higher temperatures **4** *of an organism* **:** to make (as a culture medium) unsuitable by its metabolic activities for the growth of another kind of organism — used chiefly as a participle or gerund ⟨*staling* products of rhizoctonia⟩ ~ *vi* **:** to become stale: as **a :** to undergo progressive changes in quality of crust, crumb, texture, and flavor ⟨muffins that have *staled*⟩ **b :** to become wearisome, monotonous, or uninteresting ⟨the quickly passing invention of newspaper writers, vaudeville and stage personages . . . will soon ~ —J.P.Bishop⟩

⁴**stale** \"\ *n* -s [ME; akin to MLG *stal* urine of horses, *stallen* to urinate, Gk *stalassein* to let drop, drip and perh. to Lith *iželžti* to pour in] **:** urine of a domestic animal (as a horse)

⁵**stale** \"\ *vi* -ED/-ING/-S [ME *stalen*; akin to MLG *stallen* to urinate] **:** URINATE — used chiefly of camels and horses

⁶**stale** \"\ *n* -s [ME, bird used as a decoy, fr. AF *estale*, prob. modif. (influenced by OF *estaler* to set, place, fr. *estal* place, stand, stall, of Gmc origin) of OE *stæl-* decoy; akin to OE *stæl* place, stand, OHG *stellen* to set, place, stand — more at STALL] **1** *chiefly dial* **:** a person or thing that lures **:** LURE, DECOY **2** *archaic* **:** a person or thing used as a tool, pretext, or front for illicit or clandestine activity **3** *obs* **:** a butt for ridicule **4** *obs* **:** PROSTITUTE

stale·ly \ˈstā(l)lē, -)i\ *adv* **:** in a stale manner

¹**stalemate** \ˈ=,=\ *n* [obs. E *stale* stalemate (fr. ME, fr. AF *estale*, lit., fixed position, fr. OF *estal* place, position, stand, stall) + E ³*mate*] **1 :** a drawing position in chess in which only the king can move and although not in check can move only into check **2 :** a position from which neither contestant can derive a winning advantage **:** a drawn contest **:** DEADLOCK

²**stalemate** \"\ *vt* **:** to bring into a stalemate

stale·ness *n* -ES **:** the quality or state of being stale

staling *n* -s [fr. gerund of ³*stale*] **:** gradual decrease and eventual cessation of growth of a fungus in an artificial culture medium believed to be due wholly or in part to progressive increase of the metabolic products of the fungus itself

sta·lin·grad \ˈstälən,grad, -raa(ə)d — *see* DESTALINIZE *for other variants*\ *adj, usu cap* [fr. *Stalingrad*, former name of Volgograd, city in Southeastern U.S.S.R.] **:** of or from the city of Stalingrad, U.S.S.R. **:** of the kind or style prevalent in Stalingrad

sta·lin·ism \-lə,nizəm\ *n* -s *usu cap* [Joseph *Stalin* †1953 Russ. political leader + E *-ism*] **:** the political, economic, and social principles and policies associated with Stalin; *esp* **:** the theory and practice of communism developed by Stalin from Marxism-Leninism — compare BOLSHEVISM, LENINISM, MARXISM, TITOISM, TROTSKYISM

¹**sta·lin·ist** \-,nəst\ *n* -s *usu cap* [Joseph *Stalin* †1953 + E *-ist*] **:** a follower of Stalin **:** an adherent of Stalinism

²**stalinist** \"\ *adj, usu cap* [Joseph *Stalin* †1953 + E *-ist*, n. suffix] **:** of, relating to, or having the characteristics of Stalinism or Stalinists ⟨*Stalinist* communists⟩

sta·lin·ize \-,nīz\ *vt* -ED/-ING/-S *usu cap* [Joseph *Stalin* †1953 + E *-ize*] **:** to make Stalinist

sta·li·no \ˈstälə,nō, ˈstal-, -lyənə\ *adj, usu cap* [fr. *Stalino*, former name of Donetsk, city in southwestern U.S.S.R.] **:** of or from the city of Stalino, U.S.S.R. **:** of the kind or style prevalent in Stalino

¹**sta·lin·oid** \ˈstälə,nȯid, ˈstal- — *see* DESTALINIZE *for other variants*\ *adj, usu cap* [Joseph *Stalin* †1953 Russ. political leader + E *-oid*, adj. suffix] **:** favorable to or influenced by Stalinism ⟨*Stalinoid* Marxism⟩ ⟨*Stalinoid* propaganda⟩

²**stalinoid** \"\ *n* -s *usu cap* [Joseph *Stalin* †1953 + E *-oid*, n. suffix] **:** a Stalinoid person

sta·linsk \ˈstäl|,linzk, ˈstal|, |l,yi-, -n(t)sk\ *adj, usu cap* [fr. *Stalinsk*, former name of Novokuznetsk, city in southern U.S.S.R. in Asia] **:** of or from the city of Stalinsk, U.S.S.R. **:** of the kind or style prevalent in Stalinsk

¹**stalk** \ˈstȯk\ *vb* -ED/-ING/-S [ME *stalken*, fr. OE *bestealcian* to walk stealthily; akin to OE *stealc* steep, lofty, OSw *stjælke* stalk, stem, ON *stjölr* hinder part, tail — more at STEAL] *vi* **1** *obs* **:** to walk cautiously or furtively **:** STEAL, SLIP **2 :** to pursue quarry or prey stealthily or under cover (as behind a stalking horse) **:** STILL-HUNT ⟨deer are hunted chiefly by ~*ing* —*Encyc. Americana*⟩ — compare DRIVE **3 a :** to walk with a stiff ungainly stride ⟨long-legged water birds ~ along the shore⟩ **b :** to walk with long measured steps **:** stride loftily ⟨turned on his heel, and ~*ed* stiffly out —Kenneth Roberts⟩ **c :** to move in a silent deliberate manner — used of ghosts and half-personified evils ⟨a specter that ~*ed* along the castle walls at midnight⟩ ⟨the terror that ~*s* through the city⟩ ~ *vt* **1 a :** to pursue (as game) stealthily and often under cover for the purpose of killing ⟨~ deer⟩ ⟨~ an enemy patrol⟩ ⟨watch a tiger ~ its prey⟩ **b :** to pursue or follow in a stealthy, furtive, or persistent manner ⟨the man was ~*ing* him as remorselessly as if he were a criminal —*Time*⟩ **2 :** to move through, recur to, or follow as a specter or evil **:** DOG, HAUNT ⟨a nightmare that ~*s* his sleep⟩ ⟨the starvation that ~*ed* the winter-devastated land —*N. Y. Times Bk. Rev.*⟩ **3 :** to go through (an area) in search of prey or other quarry ⟨~ the woods for deer⟩

²**stalk** \"\ *n* -s [ME *stalke*, fr. *stalken* to stalk] **1 :** the act or process of stalking prey or other quarry **2 :** a stalking gait

³**stalk** \"\ *n* -s [ME *stalk*; akin to OSw *stjælke* stalk — more at STALK, v.] **1 a :** the main stem of an herbaceous plant often with its dependent parts (as leaves, twigs, fruit) ⟨a ~ of wheat⟩ — often used in combination ⟨*cornstalk*⟩ ⟨*beanstalk*⟩ **b :** a part of a plant by which an organ (as a leaf, fruit) is attached and supported: as (1) **:** the petiole of a leaf (2) **:** the peduncle or pedicel of a flower or fruit (3) **:** the stipe of an ovary (4) **:** the seta of a moss **c :** an organ-bearing stalk with the parts it bears ⟨bought a whole ~ of bananas⟩ **2 :** a slender upright object or supporting or connecting part: as **a :** a long narrow peduncle supporting some part of an animal body ⟨the ~ of the pituitary⟩ or the entire body ⟨the ~ or hydrocaulus that attaches a hydroid to the substrate⟩ ⟨the ~ of some crinoids is many times as long as the body it attaches⟩ **b :** the stack of a chimney **c :** an ornament in the Corinthian capital which resembles the stalk of a plant and from which the volutes and helices spring **3 :** an iron bar with projections that is inserted in a core to strengthen it **:** a core arbor

stalk·able \-kəbəl\ *adj* **:** that can be stalked

stalk borer *n* **:** an insect larva that bores in the stems of plants; *esp* **:** the larva of a noctuid moth (*Papaipema nebris*) that infests the raspberry, strawberry, tomato, aster, and other plants

stalk cell *n* **:** one of the two cells produced by division of the generative cell in the pollen grain of some gymnosperms that bears or supports the body cell

stalk-cutter \ˈ=,==\ *n* **:** an implement with rotating knives for chopping up cornstalks or cotton stalks in the field in preparation for plowing

stalk disease *n* **:** a stem rot and wilt of the potato caused by a fungus (*Sclerotinia sclerotiorum*)

stalked *adj* **:** having or borne on a stalk

stalked hydatid *n* **:** HYDATID OF MORGAGNI 1

stalked puffball *n* **:** a fungus of the family Tulostomaceae

stalk·er \ˈstȯkə(r)\ *n* -s [ME, fr. *stalken* to stalk + *-er* — more at STALK] **:** one that stalks; *esp* **:** one that stalks game

stalk-eyed \ˈ=ˈ=\ *adj* **:** having the eyes raised on a stalk — used chiefly of crustaceans

stalk-eyed fly *n* **:** a two-winged fly of *Diopsis* or related genera that has the eyes on the ends of stalks

stalk field *n* **:** a field of cornstalks from which the ears have been harvested

stalk·i·ly \-kəlē\ *adv* **:** in a stalky manner

stalk·i·ness \-kēnəs, -kin-\ *n* -ES **:** the quality or state of being stalky

stalking-horse \ˈ==,=\ *n* **1 :** a horse or a figure like a horse behind which a hunter stalks game **2 :** something used to cover up a secret project **:** MASK, PRETENSE **3 :** a candidate put forward to divide the opposition in the interest of some faction or to conceal the real candidacy of some other person

stalk·ing·ly *adv* **:** in a stalking manner

stalk·less \ˈ=ləs\ *adj* **:** having no stalk

stalk·let \-lət\ *n* -s [³*stalk* + *-let*] **:** a small or secondary stalk

stalklike \ˈ=,=\ *adj* **:** resembling a stalk

stalks *pres 3d sing of* STALK, *pl of* STALK

stalk shaver *n* **:** an implement on runners with knives cutting cornstalks or stubble at the ground surface for burning (as in the control of the European corn borer)

stalky \ˈstȯkē, -ki\ *adj* -ER/-EST [³*stalk* + *-y*] **1 :** having stalks **2 :** resembling a stalk **:** SLENDER

¹**stall** \ˈstȯl\ *n* -s *often attrib* [ME *stal, stall*, fr. OE *stall, steall*; akin to OHG *stal* stand, place, stall, *stellen* to set, place, ON *stallr* stand, stall, OL *stlocus* place, L *locus* place, *stolidus* dull, *stultus* foolish, Gk *stellein* to set up, make ready, send, Skt *sthalati* he stands] **1 a :** a place where horses or cattle are kept: (1) *obs* **:** STABLE (2) **:** a division of a stable or barn accommodating one animal and often enclosed except at the rear **b :** a compartment in a roundhouse for a locomotive **c :** a space marked off for the parking of a motor vehicle **2** *obs* **a :** a fixed position **:** STAND **b :** a place in or as if in a series **:** STATION, RANK **3 a :** a fixed seat in the chancel of a church usu. forming one of an attached row enclosed or partly enclosed at the back and sides and often having a canopy, separating arms or partitions, a seat that can tip up, a desk for books, and carved ornamentation; *esp* **:** such a seat on either side of the chancel of a cathedral or collegiate church serving as the official seat of a dignitary or residentiary canon ⟨the only minor canon . . . to obtain a prebendal ~ —Leslie Smith⟩ **b :** a long seat with back and arms for worshipers in a church **:** PEW **c :** one of the seats assigned to the knights in a British chapel associated with one of the higher orders of chivalry **d** *Brit* **:** a seat in the forward part of the main level of a theater — usu. used in pl. ⟨people who . . . can't afford the ~*s* and are ashamed to be seen in the gallery —G.B.Shaw⟩ **4 :** a booth, stand, or counter at which articles are displayed for sale or a business is conducted ⟨a candy ~ at a fair⟩ ⟨a shooting ~ at a carnival⟩ ⟨coffee ~⟩; *specif* **:** BOOKSTALL ⟨publishers try to get their most handsome volumes into the ~*s* just before Christmas —*Time*⟩ ⟨published as ~ ballads —Kenneth Lodewick⟩ **5 :** a protective sheath covering a single finger, thumb, or toe **:** COT **6** *chiefly Brit* **:** a tunnel in which coal is mined by the bord-and-pillar system **:** ROOM, BREAST **7 :** a small partially enclosed compartment ⟨a shower ~⟩: as **a :** CARREL **b :** a usu. roofless enclosure in which ore is roasted **8 stalls** *pl, Brit* **:** the occupants of the stalls in a theater

²**stall** \"\ *vb* -ED/-ING/-S [ME *stallen*, fr. ¹*stall*] *vt* **1 a :** to put into or keep in a stall ⟨the cattle were ~*ed* in the house —Gunnar Mickwith⟩ **b** *archaic* **:** to fatten by stall-feeding ⟨better is a dinner of herbs where love is than a ~*ed* ox and hatred —Prov 15:17 (AV)⟩ **c** *dial Brit* **:** to cause surfeit in **:** SATIATE **2** *obs* **:** to install in office orig. by formal induction into a stall of office or dignity in a church or chapel **3** *obs* **a :** to assign a place to **b :** to appoint beforehand **:** ARRANGE **c :** to arrange payment of (a debt) by portions due at different times **4 a :** to force to a standstill **:** hinder from going on ⟨help rescue horses ~*ed* in a slough —*Amer. Guide Series: N. J.*⟩ ⟨soldiers were ~*ed* here for four days by heavy enemy fire —Toni Howard⟩ **b** (1) **:** to cause (an engine) to stop from overload or poor fuel supply **:** KILL (2) **:** to cause (a motor vehicle) to stop by stalling the engine **c :** to cause (an airplane or airfoil) to go into a stall ~ *vi* **1** *obs* **:** to live in the same place **2 a :** to come to a standstill: as (1) **:** to stick fast in mire or snow (2) **:** to stop from engine overload or poor fuel supply **:** DIE **b :** to enter or experience a stall in flying

³**stall** \"\ *n* -s **:** the condition of an airfoil or airplane operating at an angle of attack greater than that corresponding to maximum lift that is characterized by flow breakdown and loss of effectiveness of the controls

⁴**stall** \"\ *n* -s [alter. (influenced by ¹*stall*) of ⁶*stale*] **1** *obs* **:** DECOY **2 :** a pickpocket's confederate who blocks the victim, distracts his attention (as by jostling), and screens the theft **3 :** something used to deceive others about one's intentions **:** DODGE, RUSE, BLIND **4 :** an artifice for delaying or impeding action

⁵**stall** \"\ *vb* -ED/-ING/-S *vi* **1 :** to serve as a pickpocket's stall **2 :** to keep a situation going by some device or trick until relief or change can be effected **:** play for time ⟨charged that he was ~*ing* when he did not answer promptly⟩ **3 :** to do less than one's best in a contest in order to deceive one's opponent for some purpose or to husband one's strength **4 :** to maintain possession of the ball (as in basketball) without endeavoring to score to prevent the possibility of a score by the opponents ~ *vt* **:** to divert or delay by evasion or deception ⟨many contractors ~ renegotiation, hoping new renegotiators will be named soon and give them a better break —*Kiplinger Washington Letter*⟩ — often used with *off* ⟨tried to ~ off his creditors till the expected check came⟩

stall·age \-lij, -lēj\ *n* -s [ME, fr. MF *estalage*, fr. OF, fr. *estal* place, stand, stall + *-age* — more at STALE (decoy)] **1** *Eng law* **:** the right of erecting a stall in a fair **2** *Eng law* **:** rent or toll paid for a stall

stall bar *n* **:** a piece of gymnastic apparatus used for corrective and strengthening exercises that consists of uprights about eight feet high and three feet apart secured to a wall and joined by horizontal wooden rungs at about 5-inch intervals

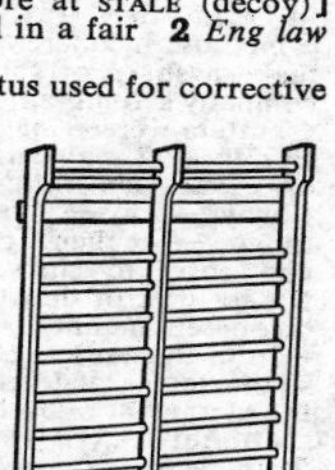

stall bar

stallboard \ˈ=,=\ *n* **1 a :** a display board formerly attached to the sill of a shop window and often hinging out into the street **b :** a stout sill or rail under the sash in a shop front **2 :** any of a series of successively higher floors on which excavated material is pitched (as in digging sewers)

stalled *adj* [fr. past part. of ²*stall*] *of an animal* **:** suffering from autointoxication usu. due to overfeeding

stall·er \ˈstȯlə(r)\ *n* -s **:** one that stalls

stall-feed \ˈ=ˈ=\ *vt* **:** to feed in a stall for fattening ⟨*stall-feed* an ox⟩

stalling speed *n* **:** the speed of an airplane in steady flight at its maximum lift coefficient

stal·lion \ˈstalyən\ *n* -s [ME *stalion, stalon*, fr. MF *estalon*, of Gmc origin; akin to OHG *stal* stall — more at STALL] **1 a :** a male horse not castrated **:** a male horse kept for breeding; *also* **:** a mature male of any equine mammal ⟨a zebra ~⟩ **b :** the male of any of various other animals (as dogs, sheep) when kept for or considered in respect to its worth as a stud **2** *obs* **a :** PARAMOUR **b :** COURTESAN **3 :** a man marked by vigorous maleness

stal·lion·er \-nə(r)\ *or* **stal·lion·eer** \ˌ==ˈni(ə)r\ *n* -s [*stallion* + *-er* or *-eer*] **:** one supervising or in charge of a stallion (as at public stud)

stallion plague *n* **:** DOURINE

stall·man \ˈ=mən\ *also* **stallkeeper** \ˈ=,==\ *n, pl* **stallmen** *also* **stallkeepers :** one who keeps a stall for selling goods (as books)

stall plate *n* **:** a plate with the arms of a knight affixed to his chapel stall

stall reader *n* **:** one that reads books at a bookstall

stallriser \ˈ=,==\ *n* [¹*stall* + *riser*] *Brit* **:** the part of a store front below a show window

stalls *pl of* STALL, *pres 3d sing of* STALL

stall-warning indicator \ˈ=,==-\ *n* **:** a flight instrument that warns the pilot that his airplane is approaching a stall

¹**stal·wart** \ˈstȯlwə(r)t *sometimes* -,wȯr|t *or* -,wȯ(ə)|; *usu* |d.+V\ *adj* [ME, alter. of *stalworth*, fr. OE *stælwierthe* serviceable, prob. contr. of *statholwierthe*, fr. *stathol* base, foundation, support + *wierthe* worth — more at STADDLE, WORTH] **1 :** STOUT, STURDY ⟨~ sons . . . well over six feet tall, lean,

long, and resilient —Green Peyton⟩ ⟨the ~ wall of the castle⟩ **2 :** BRAVE, VALIANT, RESOLUTE ⟨a number of ~ men and women who, not counting the cost to themselves, reported on . . . activities to the police —L.S.B.Leakey⟩ **syn** see STRONG

²stalwart \"\ *n* -s [ME, fr. ¹*stalwart*] **1 :** a sturdy or resolute person **2 a :** an unwavering partisan (as in politics) ⟨have ~*s* in both major political parties and have always chipped in heavily to both national campaign coffers —Harry Conn⟩ **b** *usu cap* **:** one of a faction of the Republican party between 1869 and 1877 having a very strong machine and subsequently opposing civil-service reform and conciliation toward the South — compare HALF-BREED 2a

stal·wart·ly *adv* [ME, fr. ¹*stalwart* + *-ly*] **:** in a stalwart manner

stal·wart·ness *n* -ES **:** the quality or state of being stalwart

stal·worth \'stȯl(,)wərth\ *archaic var of* STALWART

sta·men \'stāmən\ *n, pl* **stamens** \-nz\ *also* **stami·na** \'stāmənə, 'stam-\ [L, warp, thread, thread spun by the fates at one's birth to determine the length of his life, stamen; akin to Gk *stēmōn* warp, thread, OIr *sessam* act of standing, Skt *sthāman* station, Gk *histanai* to cause to stand; basic meaning: standing upright — more at STAND] **1** *obs* **:** a vital principle or force formerly regarded as the determining factor in longevity **2 :** a microsporophyll of a seed plant **:** the organ of the flower that gives rise to the male gamete, consists of an anther and a filament, is morphologically a spore-bearing leaf though sometimes exhibiting transition to a petal (as in a double flower), occurs usu. in fixed numbers in a given group, and thereby affords an important diagnostic character — see ANDROECIUM; compare PISTIL; see FLOWER illustration

sta·mened \-nd\ *adj* **:** having stamens

stam·in \'stamən\ *n* -s [ME, fr. OF *estamin*, fr. (assumed) VL *staminea*, fr. fem. of L *stamineus* made of threads, fr. *stamin-*, *stamen* thread + *-eus* -eous] **1 a :** a coarse woolen fabric of late medieval use esp. for undershirts of penitents **b :** a rough woolen fabric for clothing similar to linsey-woolsey **2 :** TAMMY

stamin- *or* **stamini-** *comb form* [L *stamin-*, *stamen*] **:** stamen ⟨*stamin*ody⟩ ⟨*stamini*ferous⟩

stam·i·na \'stamənə\ *n* -s [L, pl. of *stamen* warp, thread of life spun by the fates] **1** *pl in constr, archaic* **:** the essential or fundamental parts, elements, or nature of something esp. an organism **2** *pl in constr, archaic* **:** the innate capacities formerly regarded as conditioning or governing the duration of life **3 a :** the strength or vigor of bodily constitution **:** capacity for standing fatigue or resisting disease ⟨the chase, sometimes lasting for miles, calls for unlimited ~ from both dogs and men —*Amer. Guide Series: Tenn.*⟩ ⟨lack of ~ of the population is caused partly by the high rate of infection from parasitic and venereal diseases —Mary Tew⟩ **b :** strength or courage of conviction **:** staying power **:** PERSEVERANCE ⟨displayed little of the moral ~ which characterized the Puritan fathers —R.P.Stearns⟩ ⟨must acquire proficiency in defense and display ~ in purpose —D.D.Eisenhower⟩ ⟨exhibited enough ~ to disagree frequently with the great chief justice —*advt*⟩ ⟨evidence of the ~ of India's indigenous democracy —Vera M. Dean⟩ **c :** the capacity for standing hard or demanding use over an extended period **:** DURABILITY ⟨steelmakers use small amounts of vanadium alloys to give steel ~ —*Hot-Metal Magic*⟩ ⟨enduring ~ built into these trucks —*Newsweek*⟩ ⟨a locker with ~ and correctness of design —*Sweet's Catalog Service*⟩ **4** *archaic* **:** the chief source of support or strength ⟨the infantry is the ~ of a military force⟩ — sometimes pl. in constr.

stam·i·nal \-nᵊl\ *adj* [in sense 1, fr. *stamina* + *-al*; in sense 2, fr. *stamin-* + *-al*] **1 :** of, relating to, or constituting stamina **2 :** of, relating to, or consisting of a stamen

stam·i·nate \-ˌnāt, -ˌnət, -ˌnā\, *usu* |d·+V\ *adj* [*stamin-* + *-ate*] **1 :** having or producing stamens **2** *of a diclinous flower* **:** having stamens but no pistils — compare PISTILLATE; see AMENT illustration

stam·i·nif·er·ous \ˌstamə¦nif(ə)rəs\ *adj* [*stamin-* + *-ferous*] **:** bearing or having stamens

stam·i·node \'staməˌnōd\ *n* -s [NL *staminodium*] **:** STAMINODIUM

stam·i·no·di·um \ˌ==ˈnōdēəm\ *n, pl* **stamino·dia** \-dēə\ [NL, fr. *stamin-* + *-odes* -ode + *-ium*] **:** an abortive or sterile stamen (as in the flowers of the genus *Parnassia*)

stam·i·no·dy \'==ˌnōdē\ *n* -ES [*stamin-* + *-ody*] **:** the metamorphosis of other floral organs into stamens

stam·mel \'staməl\ *n* -s [prob. fr. *stamin* + *-el*] **1** *obs* **:** a coarse woolen clothing fabric usu. dyed red and used sometimes for undershirts of penitents **2** *or* **stammelcolor** \'==,==\ **:** the bright red color of this cloth

¹stam·mer \'stamə(r)\ *vb* **stammered; stammered; stammering** \-m(ə)riŋ\ **stammers** [ME *stameren*, fr. OE *stamerian*; akin to OS *stamarōn* to stammer, MD *stameren*, OHG *stamalōn*, *stamēn*, ON *stamma* to stammer, Goth *stamms* stammering, Lith *stumti* to push] *vi* **1 a :** to make involuntary stops and repetitions in uttering syllables and words **:** hesitate, falter, or block oneself in speaking ⟨is so nervous he ~*s* constantly⟩ ⟨shrank a little at his vehemence, but neither blushed nor ~*ed* —George Meredith⟩ — compare STUTTER **b :** to speak or write haltingly, confusedly, or unclearly ⟨where the pedant theologians mumble and ~, she is articulate —W.L. Sullivan⟩ ⟨living thoughts . . . in the 9th century began to ~ in Latin verses —H.O.Taylor⟩ ⟨appear a much more diffuse, ~*ing*, and incoherent writer than he is —Paul Welsh⟩ **c :** to make a sharp or rattling noise in a spasmodic fashion ⟨my company's light automatics ~*ed* furiously —John Masters⟩ ⟨shutters were ~*ing* and fidgeting at their hooks —Elizabeth Enright⟩ **2** *dial Brit* **:** STAGGER, STUMBLE ~ *vt* **1 :** to utter or speak (something) with involuntary stops or repetitions ⟨"why — why — " ~*ed* the youth struggling with his balking tongue —Stephen Crane⟩ ⟨~*ed* that he was afraid he had not any notes to show — worth seeing —George Meredith⟩ **2 :** to utter or deliver (something) in a confused, halting, or incoherent manner ⟨~*ed* a crude communism in the vernacular —John Buchan⟩ — often used with *out* ⟨contented with a very slight degree of learning, could scarcely ~ out the words of the sacrament —G.G.Coulton⟩

²stammer \"\ *n* -s **1 :** an act or instance of stammering **2 :** defective utterance **:** the involuntary interruption of utterance ⟨when he was at all agitated the ~ became a complete inhibition of speech —F.A.Swinnerton⟩

stam·mer·er \-mərə(r)\ *n* -s **:** one that stammers

stammering *n* -s [ME *stamering*, fr. gerund of *stameren* to stammer] **1 :** the act of one who stammers **2 :** a defective condition of speech characterized by involuntary stops and repetitions or blocking of utterance — compare STUTTERING

stam·mer·ing·ly *adv* **:** in a stammering manner **:** with stammering

stam·nos \'stamˌnäs\ *n* [Gk; akin to Gk *stēmōn* warp in an upright loom — more at STAMEN] **:** an ancient Greek wine jar with a wide mouth and with handles set horizontally on the shoulders

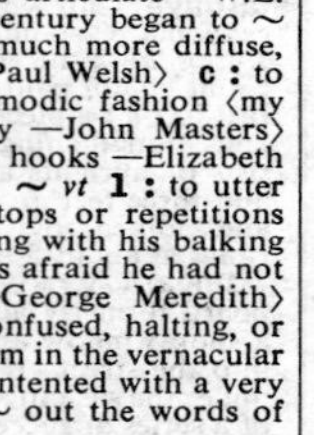

stamnos

¹stamp \'stamp, -aa(ə)mp, -aimp; *in senses 2a of vt & 2 of vi also* 'stämp *or* -tȯmp\ *vb* -ED/-ING/-s [ME *stampen*; akin to OE *stempan* to stamp, OHG *stampfōn*, ON *stappa* to stamp, L *temnere* to slight, despise, Gk *stembein* to shake up, handle roughly, Skt *stambhate*, *stabhnati* he supports] *vt* **1 :** to pound with a pestle or a heavy instrument; *specif* **:** to crush (ore) by pounding with a stamp **2 a** (1) **:** to strike or beat (something) forcibly with the bottom of the foot or by thrusting the foot downward ⟨the watch officer ~*ing* the deck —R.H. Davis⟩ ⟨~*ing* the mud off his boots⟩ ⟨~*ing* a trail in the deep snow —John Hunt & Edmund Hillary⟩ ⟨~*ed* an incongruous step . . . in a vain effort to dance to the music —Haldane MacFall⟩ (2) **:** to bring down (the foot) forcibly or noisily on the ground or floor ⟨~*s* his feet with rage⟩ ⟨~*ing* her heels with true regimental emphasis —T.B.Costain⟩ ⟨pass unscathed over this burning charcoal although they actually ~ their feet on it —J.G.Frazer⟩ **b :** to extinguish, eradicate, or do away with (something) by or as if by stamping with the foot ⟨are still trying to ~ the spread . . . following the war —T.H.Fielding⟩ — usu. used with *out* ⟨one small fire . . . was easily ~*ed* out —Frank Pemberton⟩ ⟨finally ~*ed* out the cattle thieves —*Amer. Guide Series: La.*⟩ ⟨medical authorities attempted to ~ it out by quarantine measures —*Amer. Guide Series: Fla.*⟩ ⟨strong monarchs are ~*ing* out privy conspiracy and rebellion —S.E.Morison & H.S.Commager⟩ **3 a :** to impress or mark (something) with a symbol or design in intaglio or relief with ink or coloring **b** *obs* **:** to print (a book) with such a process **c :** to impress or mark (something) with a device or design by means of a die and a blow or mechanical pressure **d :** to cut out, bend, or form by a blow or sudden pressure with a stamp or die **e** (1) **:** to impress (lettering or a design) with heated metal type or dies (2) **:** to impress (as a book) with lettering or a design ⟨~*ed* book covers⟩ ⟨~*ed* bindings⟩ ⟨~*ed* cloth⟩ **4 a :** to impress or mark (something) with a device or lettering to authenticate, certify, or register formal or official examination or sanction **b :** to impress (something) with an official mark, stamp, or adhesive label to certify that a government or state tax or duty has been paid **5 a** (1) **:** to adjudge or categorize (a person or thing) as being of good or bad repute or value ⟨little things . . . ~ a girl at her first informal beach party —Alex Atkinson⟩ ⟨long association with agrarian reform ~*ed* him as a radical in the eyes of . . . moderates —R.A. Billington⟩ ⟨~*ed* him as an artist of extraordinary skill and perception —Howard Barnes⟩ ⟨the account of the foundation . . . ~*s* it as fraudulent —G.C.Sellery⟩ (2) **:** to justify or lend approbation or sanction to (a person or thing) ⟨a consummate ability that ~*ed* him the peer of the greatest advocate of the age —W.J.Ghent⟩ ⟨the happy diction and the graceful phrase which literature has ~*ed* with its authority —E.G.Bulwer-Lytton⟩ **b** (1) **:** to mark (a person or thing) with a distinctive or lasting characteristic ⟨an art ~*ed* with great beauty —*Amer. Guide Series: Ind.*⟩ ⟨listlessness rather than vigor ~*s* most of the homeless men —*Amer. Guide Series: Minn.*⟩ ⟨~*ed* the works of Benedictine scholars with a character which they seldom lost —R.W.Southern⟩ (2) **:** to mark or mold one's physical features or appearance with (a distinctive characteristic or cast) **:** TRACE ⟨his paternity was ~*ed* so indelibly on his outer shell —T.B.Costain⟩ **c :** to be a conspicuous characteristic of (something) **:** DISTINGUISH ⟨the chief quality that ~*s* this study of jazz —R.L.Shayon⟩ ⟨corporate ties which had ~*ed* the old monasticism —R.W.Southern⟩ **d** (1) **:** to embed or deeply impress (a fact, idea, or effect) ⟨the Welsh characteristics are indelibly ~*ed* —Wilfrid Goatman⟩ — usu. used with *on* or *upon* ⟨the firm discipline of the Roman Military Academy was ~*ed* on him —L.C.Douglas⟩ ⟨one of the symbolic events that had ~*ed* itself on his mind as a child —Van Wyck Brooks⟩ (2) **:** to impose or firmly mark (an influence, quality, or development) — usu. used with *on* or *upon* ⟨concerned to ~ our civilization upon the world —Bertrand Russell⟩ ⟨developments which were to ~ a new form of papal authority on the church —R.W.Southern⟩ ⟨his genius was ~*ed* on the ecclesiastical architecture —G.M.Trevelyan⟩ ~ *vi* **1 :** to strike, beat, or crush in a manufacturing process **:** POUND ⟨fibers had been fermented, and then separated by . . . ~*ing* —R.K. Johnson⟩ **2 a :** to strike or thrust the foot forcibly or noisily downward ⟨men ~*ing* about with clanking swords —Richard Joseph⟩ ⟨men ~*ed* all over the decks —Anthony Carson⟩ ⟨steps would ~ into the kitchen —Nancy Hale⟩ ⟨~ round in a circle —Wilfred Thesiger⟩ ⟨officers' mounts ~*ed* and steamed before a . . . hitching post —F.V.W.Mason⟩ **b :** to push or beat something down by such stamping with the foot — usu. used with *on* ⟨~ on the accelerator —Green Peyton⟩ ⟨jumping and ~*ing* on the leaves⟩ **c :** to extinguish, extirpate, or do away with something by or as if by such stamping ⟨nearby householders were ~*ing* on the sparks to keep the brush fire from spreading⟩ ⟨decided to ~ on all utterances of a disloyal character —Zechariah Chafee⟩

²stamp \'stamp, -aa(ə)mp, -aimp; *in sense 4 also* 'stämp *or* -tȯmp\ *n* -s *often attrib* [ME *stampe*, fr. *stampen* to stamp] **1 :** a device or instrument for stamping: as **a :** a die or tool for impressing or marking a design or pattern (as of a coin, postage stamp, or plaque) on metal, paper, or other soft or absorbent material **b** (1) **:** a heavy pestle raised by water or steam power for crushing ore (2) **stamps** *pl* **:** STAMP MILL **c :** a bookbinder's embossing tool **d :** a machine for beating and softening hides **2 :** the impression, design, or mark made by stamping or imprinting with a die or tool: as **a :** such an impression or mark used to give authentication, distinctive value, or force to something (as a coin, a document, or goods) **b** (1) **:** an official mark or seal set on something (as a warrant or deed) chargeable with a government or state duty or tax or on papers legally requiring execution under certain conditions to signify that the duty or tax has been paid or the conditions fulfilled (2) **:** POSTMARK **3 a :** a cast, make, or kind marked by distinctive or peculiar qualities or characteristics **:** TYPE ⟨reformers of all ~*s* are prone to regard the existing order as sheer folly —H.J.Muller⟩ ⟨books of a serious ~ —Jane Austen⟩ ⟨does not indicate that the ideal field trial dog is of that ~ —W.F.Brown b. 1903⟩ **b :** a distinguishing or characteristic imprint, sign, or impression **:** MARK ⟨a poet who has left her ~ upon her generation —Sara H. Hay⟩ ⟨these works have the classic ~ upon them —Laurence Binyon⟩ ⟨the very ~ of genius —Alfred Kazin⟩ ⟨in its content and terminology the unmistakable ~ of the backwoods —*Amer. Guide Series: Ind.*⟩ **c :** the lasting imprint or residual impression of something **:** EFFECT ⟨sun and weather . . . and the deeper ~ of his new life have made him physically a stranger —Dixon Wecter⟩ ⟨the ~ of his character upon his style —Arnold Isenberg⟩ **d :** external appearance **:** physical cast or form ⟨the English look gave way to a Celtic ~ on the features of the inhabitants —Richard Joseph⟩ **e :** a sign or certification of worth based on judgment or opinion ⟨implied this to be the very highest ~ of juvenile merit —George Eliot⟩ ⟨carries the ~ of approval⟩ **4 :** an act of stamping; *esp* **:** a forceful downward stroke or step with the foot **5** *obs* **:** something stamped or impressed with a device **:** COIN, MEDAL **6 :** a picture made by an inked impression from an engraved surface **:** ENGRAVING, PLATE **7 a :** a stamped or printed device or slip of paper issued by a government or state at a fixed price and required by law to be affixed to or stamped on various papers or matter as evidence that the government charge or tax is paid — compare POSTAGE STAMP **b :** such a stamp privately printed or issued for any purpose of signification or certification **:** SEAL — compare TRADING STAMP **8 :** a card for gambling marked on the back by the manufacturer — compare READER **9 :** a section of a bloom nicked, partly cut through, or broken off to show the grain

stamp battery *n* **:** BATTERY 9

stamp book *n* **:** a book of or for stamps: as **a :** STAMP BOOKLET **b :** a collector's book for mounting stamps **:** a stamp album **c :** a book in which savings stamps are affixed until they are redeemed or deposited

stamp booklet *n* **:** a book of postage stamps consisting of a few panes of postage stamps separated by sheets of oiled paper stapled together in thin cardboard covers

stamp copper *n* **:** copper-bearing rock that has been or is to be stamped and washed before smelting

stamp duty *n* **:** STAMP TAX

stamped *past of* STAMP

¹stam·pede \(')stam¦pēd, -taam-\ *n* -s [AmerSp *estampida*, fr. Sp, loud noise, crash, fr. *estampar* to pound, stamp, of Gmc origin; akin to OHG *stampfōn* to stamp — more at STAMP] **1 a :** a wild headlong rush or flight of a number of animals usu. due to fright ⟨a ~ of wild animals is no place for a would-be observer —K.K.Darrow⟩ **b :** a sudden retreat or dispersion ⟨this was no disciplined march; it was a ~ —H.G.Wells⟩ **2 :** a sudden often impulsive action or mass movement of a number of persons having a common motive ⟨the migration took on the proportions of a ~ —*Amer. Guide Series: N. Y.*⟩ ⟨discovery of rich silver deposits sets off a ~ of miners —Howard Boston⟩ ⟨a steadily increasing ~ of farm boys escaping . . . farm work for the dullness of city life —M.B. Smith⟩ ⟨delays in delivery would have caused a ~ of postponements —F.A.Swinnerton⟩; *specif* **:** a sudden rush of voters or delegates to support a candidate esp. at a national political convention ⟨the favorite son, never sure that a . . . ~ may not take place at the next moment —H.R.Penniman⟩ ⟨worked desperately to stop the ~, but could not agree on a coalition candidate —I.G.Blake⟩ — compare BREAK 4j **3 :** an extended festival or gathering combining a rodeo, exhibitions, contests, and social events ⟨watched the Calgary ~ grow through the years . . . to a commercialized, supercolossal spectacle —*Time*⟩

²stampede \"\ *vb* -ED/-ING/-s *vt* **1 a :** to cause (as cattle) to run away in a headlong panic ⟨thunderstorms often ~ the cattle⟩ **b :** to cause (a group or army) to retreat or disperse frantically ⟨came the victor *stampeding* armies before him⟩ **2 :** to cause (a group or mass of people) to act or move in an impulsive, unreasoning, or hurried manner ⟨the taverners who would ~ us in to eat and drink —G.G.Coulton⟩ ⟨Indians were *stampeded* into violence —Oliver La Farge⟩ ⟨have refused to allow ourselves to be *stampeded* by fear —Hartley Shawcross⟩ ⟨attempting to ~ government representatives into giving him control over . . . workers —Douglass Cater⟩; *specif* **:** to cause (as voters or delegates) to rush suddenly to the support of a party, ticket, or candidate esp. at a national political convention ⟨observers consider that the . . . electorate was *stampeded* at last year's general election —John Hughes⟩ ⟨gained slowly at first, then shot forward with accretions of a 100 votes at a time, and *stampeded* the convention —H.R. Penniman⟩ ~ *vi* **1 a :** to take to sudden headlong flight in panic ⟨the alarmed herd *stampeding* across the veldt⟩ **b :** to retreat or disperse in a frenzied manner ⟨fired into the roof of the mosque, and the crowd of worshipers *stampeded* —*Time*⟩ **2 :** to move or act usu. in a group or mass in an impulsive, hurried, or unreasoning manner ⟨pulled up stakes and *stampeded* back to China, most of them perishing on the way —A.R.Williams⟩ ⟨prospectors . . . who *stampeded* into the Klondike —Ivor Jones⟩ ⟨companies will now ~ to release . . . their huge backlogs of modern movies —*Wall Street Jour.*⟩ ⟨has . . . *stampeded* out of every war into wholesale demobilization —T.R.Ybarra⟩

stam·pe·do \=ˈpē(,)dō\ *n* -s [AmerSp *estampido* crash, stampede, fr. Sp, loud noise, crash, fr. *estampar* to stamp] *archaic* **:** STAMPEDE

stamped paper *n* **:** postal stationery, postage and revenue stamps, and paper bearing imprinted revenue stamps

stamp·er \'stampə(r), -aam-, -aim-\ *n* -s [ME *stampere*, fr. *stampen* to stamp + *-ere* -er] **:** one that stamps: as **a** (1) **:** one that stamps designs (as on pottery, buttons, fabrics, leather goods) (2) **:** a worker who stamps identifying information on merchandise or its containers (3) **:** STAMPMAN (4) **:** an operator of a machine for stamping bronze or copper to powder **b** (1) **:** an implement for pounding or stamping; *esp* **:** a pestle or heavy metal piece attached to the lower end of a stamp in a stamp battery for crushing ore (2) **:** any of various stamping machines (as for powdering calcined flints or cleansing fabrics in a revolving vessel) **c :** a metal negative from which phonograph records are stamped

stamp hammer *n* **:** a power hammer that moves vertically

stamp·ic \'stampik\ *adj* [²*stamp* + *-ic*] **:** of or relating to stamps or philately ⟨paid ~ tribute to one of her pioneer airmen —L.A.Wolf⟩ ⟨a new issue of stamps is always an event in the ~ world —*Nat'l Stamp News*⟩

stamping *pres part of* STAMP

stamping ground *n* **:** a place much frequented **:** a favorite or habitual resort ⟨accounted for a pretty, tree-lined city on the old buffalo *stamping ground* —Margaret Cousins⟩ ⟨this part of the state was once the *stamping ground* of . . . the outlaw —*Amer. Guide Series: Texas*⟩ ⟨New Orleans is one of his family's *stamping grounds* —Robert Graves⟩

stamp iron *n* **:** a branding iron with the complete brand stamped on it

¹stamp·less \'=ləs\ *adj* [²*stamp* + *-less*] **:** being without stamps **:** not bearing any stamp

²stampless \"\ *or* **stampless cover** *n, pl* **stampless** *or* **stampless covers :** a philatelic cover that bears no adhesive stamp; *esp* **:** one transmitted before the beginning of official postal service or before the use of adhesive stamps

stamp·man \'=mən\ *n, pl* **stampmen :** an operator of a stamp mill — called also *stamper*

stamp mill *or* **stamping mill** *n* **:** a mill in which ore is crushed with stamps; *also* **:** a machine for stamping ore **:** BATTERY 9 — called also *quartz battery*

stamp rock *n* **:** ore or metal-bearing rock requiring stamping before further metallurgical treatment

stamps *pres 3d sing of* STAMP, *pl of* STAMP

stamp seal *n* **:** an ancient stone seal usu. engraved with figures of animals or sometimes (as in China) with characters for stamping identification on personal property — see BUTTON-SEAL

stamp tax *n* **:** a tax or duty collected by means of stamps required to be purchased and affixed to specified articles (as cigarettes, playing cards); *specif* **:** such a tax or duty on specified documents (as deeds, certificates of stock, promissory notes) necessary in legal proceedings — called also *stamp duty*

stan *abbr* **1** stanchion **2** standard

stance \'stan(t)s, -taa(ə)n-, -tain- *also* -tȧn-\ *n* -s [MF *estance* position, posture, fr. OF — more at STANCHION] **1** *chiefly Scot* **a :** STATION **b :** SITE **2 :** a place for standing; *esp* **:** a rock platform or ledge on a mountain where a climber can stand at ease or maintain balance without hand support **3 a :** a mode of standing or being placed **:** POSTURE ⟨the threatening ~ of a figure in a picture⟩ **b :** intellectual or emotional attitude **:** general standpoint ⟨moralizing and self-interested ~*s* were compatible —David Riesman⟩ **4 a :** the position of the feet of a golfer or batter preparatory to making a swing — see CLOSED STANCE, OPEN STANCE, SQUARE STANCE **b :** the position of both body and feet from which an athlete starts or operates ⟨crouching ~ of a boxer⟩ ⟨batting ~⟩

¹stanch *also* **staunch** \'stȯnch, -tän-, -tan-, -taa(ə)n-, -tain-, -tȧn-\ *vb* -ED/-ING/-ES [ME *staunchen*, *stanchen*, fr. MF *estancher*, fr. OF, fr. (assumed) VL *stanticare*, fr. L *stant-*, *stans*, pres. part. of *stare* to stand — more at STAND] *vt* **1 :** to check or stop the flowing of ⟨charity . . . ~*ing* the widow's tears —W.E.H.Lecky⟩ **:** stop the flow of blood from (a wound) **2** *archaic* **a :** ALLAY, SATISFY **b :** QUENCH, EXTINGUISH **3 a :** to stop or check in its course **:** put an end to ⟨have somewhat ~*ed* the drain on gold and dollar reserves —*Time*⟩ **b :** to make watertight **:** stop up ⟨~ a leak in a ship⟩ ~ *vi, archaic* **:** to cease flowing or bleeding

²stanch \"\ *also* **staunch** \"\ *n* -ES [ME *staunch*, fr. *staunchen* to stanch] **1** *obs* **:** something that stops or allays **2 :** a floodgate to accumulate water for flashing a boat over a shallow in a stream ⟨we have to have daylight to run the Thames ~*es* —C.S.Forester⟩

³stanch *var of* STAUNCH

stan·chel \'stanchəl\ *n* -s [perh. fr. MF *estanchielle*, dim. of OF *estanche* stay, prop — more at STANCHION] *dial* **:** STANCHION

stanch·er *pronunc at* STANCH + ə(r)\ *n* -s [ME, fr. *stanchen* to stanch + *-er*] **:** one that stanches; *esp* **:** STYPTIC

¹stan·chion \'stanchən, -taan-\ *n* -s [ME *stanchon*, fr. MF *estanchon* prop, supporting post, fr. OF, fr. *estance*, *estanche* position, act of staying, prop, fr. (assumed) VL *stantia* act of standing or staying, fr. L *stant-*, *stans* (pres. part. of *stare* to stand) + *-ia* -y — more at STAND] **1 :** an upright bar, post, prop, brace, or support (as for a roof, a ship's deck, an awning); *specif* **:** an iron mullion in a leaded window **2 :** a device that fits loosely around a cow's neck and limits forward and backward motion while commonly permitting a lateral swinging motion **3 :** a traffic sign mounted on a portable stand

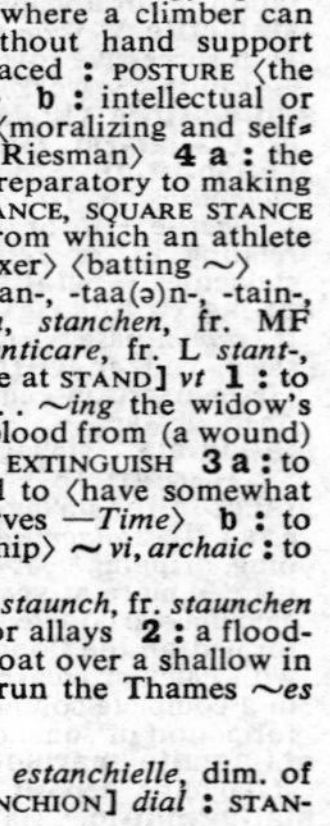

stanchion 2

²stanchion \"\ *vt* -ED/-ING/-s **1 :** to provide with stanchions **:** support, prop, or brace with or as if with a stanchion ⟨~*ing* themselves against the wind⟩ ⟨~ a sagging beam⟩ **2 :** to secure (as a cow) by a stanchion ⟨the herd was ~*ed* and fed⟩

stanchion gun *n* **:** a gun mounted on a pivot *esp* **:** a gun fixed to a boat for duck shooting

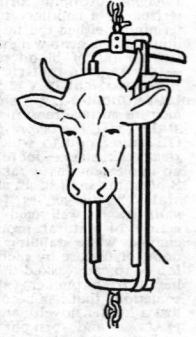

stanch·less \'=ləs\ *adj* [¹*stanch* + *-less*] **:** that cannot be stanched ⟨~ wound⟩ **:** CEASELESS ⟨the

innkeeper's ~ conversational flow —John Kobler⟩ — **stanch·less·ly** *adv*

¹stand \'stand, -aa(ə)nd\ *vb* **stood** \'stu̇d\ **stood; standing; stands** [ME *standen, stonden,* fr. OE *standan, stondan;* akin to OHG *stantan, stān* to stand, ON *standa,* Goth *standan,* L *stare,* Gk *histanai* to cause to stand, set, place, *histasthai* to be standing, *stēnai* to come to a stand, Skt *tiṣṭhati* he stands] *vi* **1 a :** to support oneself on the feet in an essentially erect position — compare LIE, SIT, KNEEL **b :** to be a specified height when fully erect ⟨~*s* six feet two in his socks⟩ ⟨a horse ~*ing* over fifteen hands at the shoulders⟩ **c :** to rise to an erect position **:** stand up **2 a :** to take up or maintain a specified position or posture ⟨~ aloof from an argument⟩ ⟨~ aside and let me pass⟩ ⟨asked the crowd to ~ back⟩ ⟨warned to ~ clear of the swinging boom⟩ ⟨~ at attention⟩ **b :** to hold one's ground **:** maintain one's position ⟨~ firm⟩ ⟨~ fast⟩ ⟨~ still⟩ **:** resist attack ⟨choose whether to run away or ~ and fight it out⟩ ⟨*stood* at bay facing his tormentors⟩ **3 a :** to assume and maintain a particular position or attitude with respect to some question or course of action ⟨how does he ~ on the disarmament question⟩ **:** be firm and steadfast in support or opposition ⟨has always *stood* firmly for states' rights⟩ **b :** to be in a particular state or situation ⟨~*s* revealed as a liar⟩ ⟨~*s* accused of betraying his friend⟩ ⟨his bank account *stood* at low level⟩ ⟨~*s* under heavy obligation to me⟩ **4 :** to hold a course at sea **:** sail in a specified direction ⟨~ out from the shore⟩ ⟨~ for the harbor⟩ **5** *obs* **:** HESITATE, SCRUPLE ⟨~ at murder⟩ **6 a :** to have or maintain a relative position in or as if in a graded scale of value or estimation ⟨~*s* first in his class⟩ ⟨~*s* high with his uncle just now⟩ **b :** to be in a position to gain or lose because of an action taken or commitment made ⟨~*s* to realize a handsome profit on his investment⟩ **7 a :** to choose to play a hand of cards as dealt (as in écarté or twenty-one) **b :** to accept the turnup as trump (as in seven-up) **8** *chiefly Brit* **:** to be a candidate for a position or office **:** RUN ⟨will ~ for reelection in his own district⟩ **9 a :** to rest or remain upright on a base or lower end ⟨a clock *stood* on the mantel⟩ ⟨a ladder ~*ing* against the wall⟩ — opposed to *lie* **b :** to occupy a place or location ⟨an elm ~*s* before the house⟩ ⟨the house ~*s* on a knoll facing the sea⟩ **c :** to be or stay upright in place ⟨trees still ~*ing* after the hurricane⟩ **d :** to stay or remain in the usual position of use ⟨left the dishes ~*ing* on the table⟩ **10 a :** to remain stationary or inactive ⟨the car *stood* in the garage for a week⟩ ⟨~ waiting for the green light⟩; *specif, of a vehicle* **:** to stay briefly (as for loading) in a public or private way **b** *of a liquid* **:** to lie or remain without flowing or circulating or being stirred or shaken up ⟨rainwater ~*ing* in stagnant pools⟩ ⟨let the wine ~ so that the lees will settle⟩ **c :** to gather slowly and remain ⟨sweat *stood* on his brow⟩ ⟨tears ~*ing* in her eyes⟩ **11 :** to be consistent **:** AGREE, ACCORD — used esp. in the expression *it stands to reason* **12 a :** to exist in a definite written or printed form ⟨copy a passage exactly as it ~*s* in the original⟩ ⟨the spelling of a name as it ~*s* in the early charters⟩ ⟨enforce a law just as it ~*s* in the record⟩ **b :** to remain valid or efficacious ⟨the order given last week still ~*s*⟩ **13** *of the wind, archaic* **:** to come from or be in a specified place or condition ⟨the wind ~*s* in the west⟩ **14 a** *of a hunting dog* (1) **:** POINT (2) **:** RANGE ⟨~*s* over more ground than is usual with hounds of other breeds —*Dog World*⟩ **b** *of a male animal* **:** to be available as a sire — used esp. of horses ⟨his sire now ~*s* in France⟩ ⟨the average stallion ~*s* for about seven years⟩ **c** *of a female animal* **:** to accept the male **:** be in heat ~ *vt* **1 a :** to endure or undergo successfully ⟨~ the cold⟩ ⟨~ the test of time⟩ ⟨how his motives would ~ a closer scrutiny⟩ **b :** TOLERATE, BEAR ⟨cannot ~ criticism⟩ ⟨can't ~ the thought of losing all that money⟩ **c :** to endure the presence of ⟨I never could ~ that fellow⟩ **2 :** to resist without yielding or retreating **:** remain firm in the face of ⟨~ gunfire⟩ ⟨~ a siege⟩ **3 :** to submit to **:** agree to abide by **:** accept the result of **:** RISK ⟨~ the judgment of a Roman senate —Joseph Addison⟩ ⟨brought back to ~ trial for forgery⟩ **4 a :** to perform the duty of ⟨as I did ~ my watch upon the hill —Shak.⟩ ⟨*stood* guard over the treasure⟩ **b :** to participate in (a formation) ⟨~ reveille⟩ **5 :** to pay the cost of (as a treat) **:** pay for ⟨I'll ~ you a dinner⟩ ⟨~*ing* drinks for the crowd⟩ **6 :** to set upright **:** cause to stand ⟨picked the child up and *stood* him on his feet⟩ ⟨~ a board on end⟩ **7** *of a hunting dog* **:** POINT, SET ⟨~ game⟩ **8 :** to make available (a stallion) for breeding esp. as a public stud **9 :** to provide standing room for ⟨this bus ~*s* 41 people⟩ **syn** see BEAR — **stand a chance** *or* **stand a show :** to have a likelihood or possibility ⟨he doesn't *stand a chance* with the champion⟩ — **stand and deliver** *archaic* **:** to halt and hand over valuables — **stand by 1 a :** to remain loyal or faithful to **:** SUPPORT, DEFEND ⟨*stand by* the Constitution⟩ ⟨*stood by* her husband through all his troubles⟩ ⟨a strong minority would always *stand by* the king —G.G.Coulton⟩ **b :** to stick to ⟨*stood by* all his promises⟩ **:** MAINTAIN **2 :** to get ready or in position to operate ⟨*stand by* the lifeboats⟩ — **stand by one's guns :** to stick to one's guns — **stand easy** *Brit* **:** to relax in formation **:** stand at ease — often used in commands to troops to give them a rest interval — **stand for 1 :** to be a symbol for **:** REPRESENT, SIGNIFY, DENOTE ⟨white *stands for* purity⟩ ⟨assumed that a consonantal letter *stood for* a consonant and a vowel —A.L.Kroeber⟩ **2 :** to acknowledge or declare as a guiding principle or ideal ⟨*stand for* decency⟩ **3 :** to put up with **:** PERMIT, ENDURE ⟨human sacrifice . . . was more than the Romans . . . could *stand for* —Stuart Piggott⟩ — **stand in hand** *chiefly dial* **:** to be serviceable or advantageous ⟨the architect was possessed of a . . . virtuosity which *stood* him *in hand* in his adopted land —Rexford Newcomb⟩ **:** BEHOOVE — **stand mute** *of a prisoner upon arraignment* **:** to make no answer or to refuse to plead directly or to put himself on trial — **stand on** *or* **stand upon 1 :** to depend upon **:** have a basis in ⟨*stand on* the fifth amendment⟩ **2 :** to insist on **:** regard as important ⟨he will *stand on* his rights⟩ ⟨never *stood on* ceremony with his friends⟩ ⟨*stand not upon* the order of your going —Shak.⟩ — **stand one's ground :** to maintain one's position **:** stand firm — **stand on one's own feet** *or* **stand on one's own legs 1 :** to support oneself **:** make a living **:** manage one's own affairs **2 :** to think or act independently — **stand over :** to watch closely and steadily and control the actions of — **stand pat 1 :** to choose to play one's hand as dealt in draw poker without resorting to the draw **2 :** to oppose or resist change; *specif* **:** to oppose any change in the tariff policy of the U.S. — **stand the gaff :** to bear up under trials and difficulties **:** endure stress and strain without weakening or yielding — **stand the racket 1 :** to sustain heavy expense incurred **2 :** to endure consequences — **stand to 1 :** to persevere in using with determination and courage **:** ply with zeal ⟨*stood to* their guns manfully⟩ ⟨now, boys, *stand to* the oars⟩ **2 :** to give support to **:** remain faithful to **:** stand by — **stand together :** to be consistent **:** AGREE — **stand treat :** to pay the cost of food, drinks, or entertainment for others in a group ⟨we all went to a baseball game, myself *standing treat* —Isaac Rosenfeld⟩

²stand \"\ *n* -s [ME *stand, stond,* fr. *standen, stonden* to stand] **1 a :** an act of stopping or staying in one place **b :** STANDSTILL ⟨the team was finally brought to a ~⟩ **2 a :** a halt (as in a retreat or flight) for defense or resistance **b :** a defensive effort of some duration or degree of success ⟨a gallant ~ at the bridge⟩ ⟨rallied his forces for a final ~⟩ ⟨a record 5th-wicket ~ by a cricket batsman⟩ ⟨desperate goal-line ~⟩ **c** (1) **:** a stop made by a touring theatrical company to give a performance ⟨a one-night ~⟩ (2) **:** a town where such a company stops for a performance **d :** a place for travelers to stop along a road ⟨the old ~ on the stage line —*Amer. Guide Series: Tenn.*⟩ **3 a :** a place or post where one stands **:** STATION, POSITION ⟨a beggar's customary ~ near the gate⟩ ⟨urged to take a definite ~ on the question of civil rights⟩ **b :** a place where the hunter stands awaiting the game that is being driven toward him **4 a :** the place taken by a witness for testifying in court **:** WITNESS-BOX ⟨took the ~ in his own defense⟩ **b :** a section of the tiered seats for spectators of an outdoor sport or spectacle; *also* **:** the occupants of such seats — usu. used in pl. ⟨a roar of applause from the ~*s*⟩ ⟨the ball went into the ~*s* behind third base⟩; compare GRANDSTAND **c :** a raised platform for viewing a race or other spectacle ⟨judges' ~⟩ ⟨the troops saluted as they passed the reviewing ~⟩ **d :** an outdoor platform for speakers or performers **e :** BANDSTAND **f :** a place where a stallion is made available for breeding **5 a :** a small often open-air structure for a small retail business ⟨cigar ~⟩ ⟨roadside fruit ~⟩ ⟨hot-dog ~⟩; *specif* **:** NEWSSTAND ⟨after the latest edition hit the ~*s*⟩ **b :** a site fit for business opportunity ⟨a good ~ for a drugstore⟩ **6 :** a place at which a vehicle regularly stops or is parked when waiting for passengers ⟨bus ~⟩ ⟨taxi ~⟩ **7** *archaic* **:** a large container: as **a :** CASK **b :** TUB ⟨~ of lard⟩ **c :** an open barrel **8** *dial* **:** ¹HIVE 2 **9 a :** a small table **b :** a frame on or in which something may be placed for support ⟨umbrella ~⟩ ⟨music ~⟩ ⟨reading ~⟩ ⟨salt and pepper ~⟩ ⟨~ for firing a rocket⟩ **c :** a base on which something may be placed for exhibit or use **:** STANDARD, PEDESTAL ⟨typewriter ~⟩ **10 a :** the state of the tide at high or low water when there is no sensible change of level **b :** STILLSTAND 2a **11 a** *chiefly Scot* **:** a complete set (as of clothes) **:** SUIT **b** *pl* **stand** *or* **stands** *chiefly Brit* **:** a complete set of arms for one soldier **c :** a set of two or more related rolls in a rolling mill **d :** a unit of drill pipe consisting of two or more lengths coupled together with threaded pipe couplings **e :** a unit of machinery (as for milking, cotton ginning) **12 :** a growth of plants (as trees); *esp* **:** the number or density on a given area ⟨a good ~ of corn⟩ ⟨a mixed ~ of hardwoods and conifers⟩ ⟨timber thinned to a proper ~⟩ — compare CATCH 8 **13** *Africa* **:** LOT 6b **14 :** the erect part of a turned-over collar from the neckline to the crease — compare FALL 1d(3) **15 :** a standing posture ⟨the tumblers ended the stunt in a ~⟩ — **at a stand :** at a standstill **:** in a perplexing situation

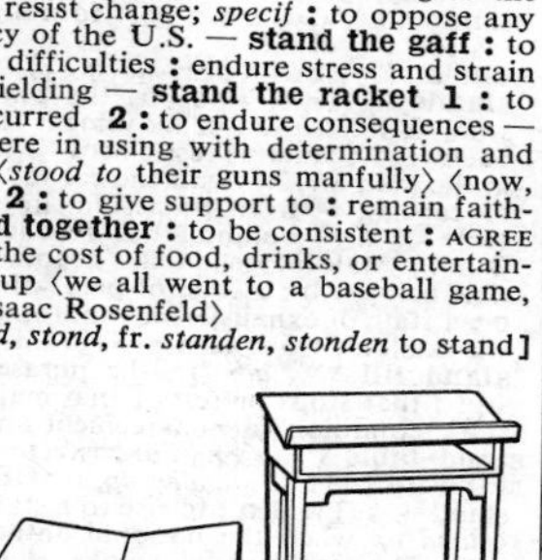
stands 9

stand·age \'standij\ *n* -s [¹*stand* + *-age*] **1** *Brit* **a :** space or permission for standing ⟨~ for cattle⟩ ⟨~ for bicycles⟩ **b :** a charge for permission to stand **2** *Brit* **:** a reservoir in which water accumulates at the bottom of a mine **:** SUMP

¹stan·dard \'standə(r)d, -aan-\ *n* -s [ME *standart, standard,* fr. MF *estandart, estandard* rallying place, flag to mark a rallying place, fr. OF, prob. of Gmc origin; fr. a compound whose first element is akin to OHG *stantan* to stand and whose second element is akin to OHG *ort* point, corner — more at STAND, ODD] **1 :** a pole or spear bearing some conspicuous object (as a banner) at the top formerly used in an army or fleet to mark a rallying point, to signal, or to serve as an emblem **2 a :** a long narrow tapering flag of considerable size and richness that is personal to an individual or corporation and bears heraldic badges, usu. a motto, and often other devices — distinguished from *banner* **b** (1) **:** the personal flag of the head of a state or of a member of a royal family — compare ROYAL STANDARD (2) **:** a distinctive flag adopted by a government that is not a monarchy for some distinguishing purpose served by the monarch's personal flag under a monarchy **c :** an organization flag carried by a mounted or motorized military unit ⟨regimental ~⟩ **d :** BANNER **e** *obs* **:** STANDARD-BEARER **3 a :** something that is established by authority, custom, or general consent as a model or example to be followed **:** CRITERION, TEST **b :** a definite level or degree of quality that is proper and adequate for a specific purpose **4 :** something that is set up and established by authority as a rule for the measure of quantity, weight, extent, value, or quality; *esp* **:** an original specimen measure or weight (as the international prototype meter and kilogram of the International Bureau of Weights and Measures) or an official copy of such a specimen used as the standard of comparison in testing other weights and measures **5 a :** the fineness of the metal used in coins and the legally fixed weight each coin should have when first minted **b :** STANDARD OF VALUE **6 a** *or* **standard hundred :** any of various units of quantity for timber; *esp* **:** a unit equal to 1980 board feet or 165 cubic feet — called also *Petersburg standard* **b :** STANDARD DEAL **7 a :** a carefully thought-out method of performing a task ⟨auditing ~*s*⟩ **b :** carefully drawn specifications covering manufacturing material or equipment **8** *Brit* **:** a grade in an elementary school ⟨had not gone beyond the fifth ~ of her country school⟩ **9 standards** *pl* **:** the punches (as H M O P h m o p) of a type font that are made first and that serve as a dimensional and design model for the other letters **10** [²*standard*] **:** STANDARD ENGLISH **11** *obs* **:** a complete assortment **:** SET, SUIT **12 :** a structure built for or serving as a base or support for something ⟨the ~ for a Sèvres vase⟩ ⟨~ for a set of flags⟩ ⟨power-line ~*s*⟩ ⟨~ for a sewing machine⟩ **13 a :** a tall candlestick in a church; *esp* **:** one of two or more set on a sanctuary or chancel floor **b :** STANDING CUP **c** *obs* **:** a large chest **:** COFFER **14 :** an inverted knee timber placed upon the deck of a ship instead of beneath it **15 :** a plant grown with an erect main stem so that it forms or resembles a tree: as **a :** a fruit tree and esp. an apple grafted on a stock that does not induce dwarfing and grown in an essentially natural form as distinguished from an espalier **b :** an herbaceous plant (as a fuchsia or geranium) pruned and trained to a single stem that is induced to branch when the desired height is attained by pinching out the apical growth **c :** a woody plant (as a rose or wisteria) that is budded on a tall stock and pruned and trained to produce a broad head of scion growth at the top of the stock **16 a :** the large upper posterior petal of some flowers (as the pea) — called also *banner, vexillum* **b :** one of the three inner usu. erect and incurved petals of an iris **17 a :** a tree permitted to remain after coppice felling **b :** a tree from one to two feet in diameter at breastheight **18** [²*standard*] **:** a musical composition that has become a part of the standard repertoire

syn STANDARD, CRITERION, GAUGE (*or* GAGE), YARDSTICK, TOUCHSTONE can designate, in common, any measure by which one judges a thing as authentic, good, or adequate or the degree to which it is authentic, good, or adequate. STANDARD applies to any authoritative rule, principle, or measure used to determine the quantity, weight, or extent, or esp. the value, quality, level, or degree of a thing ⟨each generation . . . has its own ideals and its own *standards* of judgment —S.M.Crothers⟩ ⟨the ideal of general cultivation has been one of the *standards* in education —C.W.Eliot⟩ ⟨each breed has a written *standard* of perfection which supposedly describes the ideal specimen —J.W.Cross⟩ CRITERION is the thing, whether formulated into a rule or principle or not, by appeal to which one arrives at or confirms a given judgment, as of value, quality, fitness, or correctness ⟨the sole *criterion* of the truth of illusion is its inner congruity —J.L.Lowes⟩ ⟨the size of sunspots is a meaningless *criterion* in predicting the havoc which may occur to radio transmission —C.L.Dawes⟩ ⟨no exact *criterion* for a just and fruitful apportionment of the surplus wealth —J.A.Hobson⟩ ⟨these laws . . . did establish useful *criteria* of conduct —Oscar Handlin⟩ GAUGE (*or* GAGE), concretely a standard measure or scale or an instrument for measuring something that fluctuates, as in size or height, can in extension apply to any standard measure whether tangible or not ⟨a piece of ⅛ inch thickness fiber or wood makes a convenient *gage* in setting brush holders —*Mill & Factory*⟩ ⟨the *gauges* Hollywood uses to measure a picture's importance —*Time*⟩ ⟨the degree of public acceptance of the opinions of leaders is the ultimate *gauge* of the importance and validity of those opinions —K.A.Rafferty⟩ ⟨the thickness *gage* has leaves of various thickness, and its function is to measure clearances in presswork —*Theory & Practice of Presswork*⟩ YARDSTICK, in this comparison, is a more or less figurative and informal term for any criterion, esp. for something intangible or immaterial ⟨no absolute or universal *yardstick* about what constitutes a frustration —Abram Kardiner⟩ ⟨the consumption of petroleum products, an accurate *yardstick* of economic growth —*Lamp*⟩ TOUCHSTONE, in this comparison, is any simple device by which authenticity or value may be determined, esp. an authentic or superior instance of a class of things by comparison with which another thing may be judged authentic or superior ⟨consistency is a *touchstone* by which the basic doctrine can often be distinguished from the propaganda line —L.C.Stevens⟩ ⟨a Marxist critic using economic determinants, social perspectives, and class consciousness as his *touchstones* —C.I.Glicksberg⟩ ⟨the chief *touchstone* to folklore is the manner in which it is transmitted: one man tells another, one man shows another —D.B.M.Emrich⟩ **syn** see in addition FLAG, MODEL

²standard \"\ *adj* **1 :** constituting or affording a standard for comparison, measurement, or judgment ⟨~ weight⟩ ⟨~ silver⟩ **2 a :** having qualities or attributes required by law or established by custom ⟨~ insurance policy⟩ ⟨window of ~ width⟩ ⟨~ milk⟩ ⟨~ ginger⟩ **b** *of a fruit or vegetable* **:** of medium-low to inferior quality **:** falling into the third and usu. lowest quality class generally marketed ⟨~ canned tomatoes are often a good buy for cooking⟩ **3 a :** regularly and widely available **:** readily supplied **:** not unusual or special ⟨~ brand of coffee⟩ ⟨~ model of automobile⟩ **b :** well-established and very familiar **:** not novel or experimental ⟨~ automobile transmission⟩ ⟨~ building practice⟩ **4 :** having recognized and permanent value ⟨~ history⟩ ⟨~ authors⟩ ⟨~ reference work⟩ ⟨~ biography⟩ **5 :** substantially uniform and well-established by usage in the speech and writing of the educated and widely recognized as acceptable and authoritative ⟨~ German⟩ ⟨~ pronunciation⟩ ⟨~ spelling⟩ ⟨~ grammar⟩ **6 :** grown in natural form **:** not trained to a wall or support ⟨~ fruit trees⟩ **7** *of a typewriter* **:** heavily constructed for constant service and designed for use on a desk or stand built for the purpose — compare PORTABLE, NOISELESS **8** *cryptography* **:** preserving alphabetic order ⟨DCBAZY . . . GFE is a reversed ~ sequence⟩

³standard \"\ *vt* -ED/-ING/-S **:** to determine the fineness of (as gold, silver)

standard atmosphere *n* **1 :** an arbitrary ideal set of atmospheric conditions (as used in calculations of aircraft performance); *specif* **:** the international standard specifying a temperature of 15°C and 760 millimeters pressure at sea level with a vertical temperature gradient of −6.5°C per kilometer up to 11 kilometers altitude and uniform temperature of −56.5°C above that level **2 :** ATMOSPHERE 5

standard-bearer \'==,==\ *n* [ME *standart berer,* fr. *standart* standard + *berer* bearer] **1 a :** one that bears a standard or banner **b :** the leader of an organization or movement ⟨the *standard-bearer* of a political party⟩ **2 :** STANDARD-WING

standard-bred \'==;=\ *adj* **:** bred to conform to predetermined standards; *specif* **:** of or relating to the Standardbred breed or an animal of this breed

standardbred \'==,=\ *n* **1** *usu cap* **:** an American breed of light trotting and pacing horses largely of Thoroughbred ancestry bred to attain a standard of speed (as a mile in 2:30 for trotters and in 2:25 for pacers) and noted for their endurance **2** -S *often cap* **:** a horse of the Standardbred breed

standard candle *n* **:** CANDLE 4

standard cell *n* **:** a cell of known electromotive force used in the potentiometer calibration of electrical instruments

standard coin *n* **:** a coin having an intrinsic value equal to its face value — compare TOKEN COIN

standard condition *n* **1 :** a condition specified in a series of scientific tests **2 standard conditions** *pl* **:** a temperature of 0°C and a pressure of 760 millimeters of mercury for use in a comparison of gas volumes

standard cost *n* **:** a predetermined cost based on cost factors assumed to be normal with which a correlated historical cost is compared — compare ACTUAL COST

standard deal *n* **:** a deal board usu. 3 in. x 9 in. x 12 ft. from which other sizes may be sawed

standard deviation *n* **:** the square root of the average of the squares of the deviations from the mean — symbol σ; called also *root-mean-square deviation*

standard distance *n* **:** a distance of 500 yards for capital ships or 250 yards for cruisers in a simple formation — compare DISTANCE 2b(2)

standard dropper *n* **:** DROPPER 4b

standard english *n, usu cap S & cap E* **1 :** the English taught in schools **2 :** English that is current, reputable, and national **3 :** the English that with respect to spelling, grammar, pronunciation, and vocabulary is substantially uniform though not devoid of regional differences, that is well-established by usage in the formal and informal speech and writing of the educated, and that is widely recognized as acceptable wherever English is spoken and understood **4 :** all words entered in a general English language dictionary that are not restricted by a label (as *slang, dial, obs, biol, Scot*)

standard error *n* **1 :** STANDARD DEVIATION **2 :** standard deviation divided by the square root of the number of items in a sample tested **:** the standard deviation of the sample mean

standard fit *n* **:** a fit having standardized allowance and tolerance

standard gage *n* **1 a :** a template, pattern, or other instrument for gauging the dimensions or shape of standardized parts **b :** MASTER GAGE **2 :** a railroad gage of 4 feet 8½ inches

standard gold *n* **:** gold of the legal fineness for coinage **:** COIN GOLD

standard gravity *n* **:** ACCELERATION OF GRAVITY

standard hole *n* **:** a hole machined to a standard of zero allowance plus a specified tolerance, any allowance in the fit being provided for in the size of the shaft intended to fit the hole — compare BILATERAL 5, STANDARD SHAFT

standard hundred *n* **:** STANDARD 6a

stan·dard·iz·able \'standə(r),dīzəbəl, ,==ˈ===\ *adv* **:** capable of being standardized

stan·dard·iza·tion \,standə(r)də'zāshən, -aan-, -(r),dī'-\ *n* -S **:** the act, process, or result of standardizing **:** the condition in which a standard has been achieved or effectively applied

stan·dard·ize \'standə(r),dīz, -aan-\ *vb* -ED/-ING/-S *see -ize in Explan Notes* [¹*standard* + *-ize*] *vt* **1 :** to reduce to or compare with a standard **:** determine the strength, value, or quality of by comparison with a standard ⟨~ a solution⟩ ⟨~ a voltmeter⟩ **2 :** to bring into conformity with a standard **:** make uniform ⟨*standardized* education⟩ ⟨*standardized* concert repertory⟩ **3 :** to arrange or order the component items of a test (as of intelligence, achievement, or personality) so that the probability of their eliciting a designated class of response varies with some quantifiable psychological or behavioral attribute, function, or characteristic ~ *vi* **:** to adopt a specified product or method as the only one to be produced or utilized ⟨believed the Russians had *standardized* on an A-bomb of considerably greater power —H.W.Baldwin⟩

standard knot *n* **:** a lumber knot that is sound and not over 1½ inches in diameter

standard length *n* **:** the distance on a fish from the tip of the snout or of the lower jaw if projecting forward to the base of the caudal fin

¹standard line *or* **standard route** *n* **:** a railroad line or route upon which the regular or highest rates apply **:** a fast-service route in distinction from slower and perhaps longer routes or from one that is partly by rail and partly by water — compare DIFFERENTIAL ROUTE

²standard line *n* **:** type casting in which all printed letters and figures regardless of size or style align at the bottom

standard meridian *n* **:** a meridian used for determining standard time

standard money *n* **:** a monetary unit which is designated by a government to serve as the basis of its currency system and into which other types of money in the country are convertible — compare STANDARD OF VALUE

standard of living *or* **standard of life 1 :** the necessities, comforts, and luxuries enjoyed or aspired to by an individual or group **2 :** a minimum of necessities, comforts, or luxuries that is essential to maintaining a person in customary or proper status or circumstances

standard of perfection *or* **standard of excellence :** a compilation of the desired qualities and characteristics of a breed of livestock usu. with indication of the faults to be esp. avoided

standard of value : the commodity that is made the measure of value in any comparison of values; *specif* **:** the basis of value in a monetary system — compare GOLD STANDARD

standard operating procedure *n* **:** STANDING OPERATING PROCEDURE

standard parallel *n* **:** CORRECTION LINE

standard pitch *n* **:** the geometrical pitch of an air propeller measured usu. at a point two-thirds of the radius

standard policy *n* **:** an insurance policy prescribed by statute or otherwise adopted generally by all insurers

standard port *n* **:** a port for which the tides are predicted in tide tables — compare SECONDARY PORT
standard rate *n* **:** a basic or minimum rate established for similar work or occupation within a plant, industry, or community by collective agreement or union rule or by law
standard rose *n* **:** TREE ROSE
standards *pl of* STANDARD, *pres 3d sing of* STANDARD
standard schnauzer *n* **:** a schnauzer of a variety that attains a height of 16¾ to 19¾ inches
standard score *n* **:** an individual test score expressed as the deviation from the mean score of the group in units of standard deviation
standard scottish *or* **standard scotch** *n, often cap 1st S & cap 2d S* **:** English as taught in Scotch schools
standard shaft *n* **:** a shaft machined to a standard of zero allowance minus a specified tolerance — compare STANDARD HOLE
standard silver *n* **:** COIN SILVER
standard solution *n* **:** a solution having a standard or accurately known strength that is used as a reagent in chemical analysis
standard spheroid *n* **:** the ellipsoid of revolution that most nearly coincides with the figure of the earth
standard star *n* **:** a star of known position and proper motion used as a standard in determining time, latitude, and the positions of other celestial bodies
standard test *n* **:** a test (as of intelligence, achievement, or personality) whose reliability has been established by obtaining an average score of a significantly large number of individuals for use as a standard of comparison
standard time *n* **1 :** the time of a region or country that is established by law or general usage as civil time **:** the mean solar time of a meridian that is a multiple of 15 arbitrarily applied to a local area or to one of the 24 time zones and designated as a number of hours earlier or later than Greenwich time **2 :** the amount of time required for a repeated operation by an experienced worker of average skill working at normal pace and with due allowance for relaxation and interruptions
standard unit *n* **:** standard deviation used as a unit of measurement of deviation
standard-wing \'=,=\ *n* **1 :** a bird of paradise (*Semioptera wallacii*) that has two long special feathers standing erect on each wing **2** *or* **standard-winged nightjar :** PENNANT-WINGED NIGHTJAR
standaway \'=,=,=\ *adj* [fr. the phrase *stand away*] **:** standing out from the body ⟨~ neckline⟩ ⟨~ skirt⟩
stand by *vi* [ME *standen by*, fr. *standen* to stand + *by*] **1 a :** to be near at hand **:** be present ⟨made the statement with several witnesses *standing by*⟩ **b :** to remain apart or aloof ⟨how can you *stand by* and let your son ruin himself⟩ **2 a :** to be or to get ready to act ⟨*standing by* to await instructions⟩ ⟨ordered to *stand by* to let go the anchor⟩ **b** *of a transmitting station* **:** to be ready to send signals **c** *of a receiving station* **:** to remain tuned in
¹standby \'=,=\ *n* -S [*stand by*] **1 a :** one to be relied upon esp. in emergencies **b :** a favorite or reliable choice or resource ⟨old ~s of the concert repertory⟩ ⟨good old Anglo-Saxon ~s of beef, lamb, mutton, ham, and domestic poultry —Thomas Barbour⟩ **2 :** one that is held in reserve ready for use **:** SUBSTITUTE
²standby \"\ *adj* [*stand by*] **1 :** held near at hand and ready for emergency use ⟨~ orchestra in a broadcasting station⟩ ⟨~ equipment⟩ ⟨~ crew for fire fighting⟩ ⟨~ power plant⟩ **2 :** relating to the act or condition of standing by ⟨~ period⟩ ⟨~ time⟩ ⟨~ agreement⟩ ⟨~ pay⟩
stand down *vi* **1 :** to sail with the tide or with the wind **2 :** to leave the witness stand **3** *chiefly Brit* **a :** to go off duty **b :** to retire from taking part (as in a game) or from a position of leadership
stand-down \'=,=\ *n* -S [*stand down*] **:** a period of time off **:** LAYOFF
stand-easy \'=,==\ *n* -ES [*stand easy*] **:** a command to troops to be at ease; *also* **:** the rest interval so authorized
stand·ee \(')stan¦dē, -aan-\ *n* -S [*stand* + *-ee*] **:** one that occupies standing room ⟨~s at a play⟩ ⟨~s in a ticket queue⟩ ⟨~s in a bus⟩
stand·er \'standə(r), -aan-\ *n* -S **1 :** one that stands ⟨~ of a watch⟩; *esp* **:** a member of a hunting party whose duty it is to wait in readiness for game to be driven within shooting range **2 :** BASE, SUPPORT
stander-by \'=='=\ *n, pl* **standers-by :** BYSTANDER
standfast \'=,=\ *n* -S [fr. the phrase *stand fast*] **:** a firm, fixed, or settled position
stand fire *n* [²*stand* + *fire*] **:** a forest fire that ignites the trunks of trees
standholder \'=,==\ *n* [²*stand* + *holder*] **:** an exhibitor in a fair or public exhibition
stand in *vt, chiefly Brit* **:** to be a (specified) expense to **:** COST **~** *vi* **:** to act as a stand-in — **stand in with :** to be in a specially favored position with; *esp* **:** to be in secret and usu. profitable alliance with
stand-in \'=,=\ *n* -S [*stand in*] **1 :** a preferred position **:** a place high in favor **2 a :** someone physically resembling an actor and employed to stand in the actor's place until lights and camera are ready **b :** SUBSTITUTE
¹standing *adj* [ME, fr. pres. part. of *standen* to stand] **1 :** upright on the feet or in place **:** ERECT ⟨~ audience⟩ ⟨~ timber⟩ **2 a :** not being used or operated ⟨~ factory⟩ **b :** not flowing **:** STAGNANT ⟨~ water⟩ **3 a :** remaining at the same level, degree, or amount for an indeterminate period ⟨made me a ~ offer of $10,000 for my house⟩ **b :** kept in use indefinitely **:** remaining valid ⟨one of the ~ problems in physics⟩ ⟨felt her childless state as a ~ reproach to her as a wife⟩ ⟨had a ~ joke with the elevator boy⟩ **c :** kept intact for printing or reprinting or for molding — used of set letterpress matter and sometimes of other printing surfaces (as lithographic stones) ⟨keep the type ~⟩ ⟨~ heads in a newspaper⟩ **4 :** established by law or custom **:** SETTLED, PERMANENT ⟨~ prohibition⟩ **5 a :** not movable **:** fixed in place ⟨~ washtub⟩ **b :** having a supporting base ⟨~ bowl⟩ **6 :** done from a standing position ⟨~ ovation⟩ ⟨~ jump⟩ ⟨race from a ~ start⟩
²standing \"\ *n* -S [ME, fr. gerund of *standen* to stand] **1 a :** a place to stand in **:** SITUATION **:** LOCATION **b :** a position from which one may assert or enforce legal rights and duties **c** *Brit* (1) **:** STABLE (2) **:** a stall (as in a stable) for a domestic animal **2 a :** length of service or experience esp. as determining relative place, rank, pay, or privilege ⟨candidates for the fellowship must be of postgraduate ~⟩ **b :** position or condition in society or in a profession **:** STATUS ⟨lawyer of high ~⟩; *esp* **:** good reputation ⟨among those at the meeting were several men of ~ in the community⟩ **c :** position relative to a standard of achievement ⟨left the college in good ~⟩ ⟨attained a ~ of B in his senior year⟩ or to achievements of competitors ⟨improved their ~ in the baseball league by two places⟩ **3 :** maintenance of position or condition **:** DURATION ⟨custom of long ~⟩ ⟨marriage of many years' ~⟩

STANDARD TIME IN 102 PLACES THROUGHOUT THE WORLD WHEN IT IS 12:00 NOON AT NEW YORK

CITY	TIME	CITY	TIME
Adelaide, Australia	2:30 A.M. next day	Los Angeles, California	9:00 A.M.
Alexandria, Egypt	7:00 P.M.	¹Madrid, Spain	6:00 P.M.
¹Amsterdam, Netherlands	6:00 P.M.	Manila, Philippines	1:00 A.M. next day
Anchorage, Alaska	7:00 A.M.	Melbourne, Australia	3:00 A.M. next day
Asunción, Paraguay	1:00 P.M.	Mexico City, Mexico	11:00 A.M.
Athens, Greece	7:00 P.M.	Miami, Florida	12:00 NOON
Auckland, New Zealand	5:00 A.M. next day	Montevideo, Uruguay	2:00 P.M.
Baghdad, Iraq	8:00 P.M.	Montreal, Quebec	12:00 NOON
Bangkok, Thailand	12:00 MIDNIGHT	¹Moscow, U.S.S.R.	8:00 P.M.
Belgrade, Yugoslavia	6:00 P.M.	Nairobi, Kenya	8:00 P.M.
Berlin, Germany	6:00 P.M.	Nome, Alaska	6:00 A.M.
Bogotá, Colombia	12:00 NOON	Oslo, Norway	6:00 P.M.
Bombay, India	10:30 P.M.	Ottawa, Ontario	12:00 NOON
Boston, Massachusetts	12:00 NOON	Panama City, Panama	12:00 NOON
¹Brussels, Belgium	6:00 P.M.	¹Paris, France	6:00 P.M.
Bucharest, Romania	7:00 P.M.	Peking, China	1:00 A.M. next day
Budapest, Hungary	6:00 P.M.	Perth, Australia	1:00 A.M. next day
¹Buenos Aires, Argentina	2:00 P.M.	Philadelphia, Pennsylvania	12:00 NOON
Cairo, Egypt	7:00 P.M.	Prague, Czechoslovakia	6:00 P.M.
Calcutta, India	10:30 P.M.	Quito, Ecuador	12:00 NOON
Cape Town, Republic of So. Africa	7:00 P.M.	Rangoon, Burma	11:30 P.M.
Caracas, Venezuela	1:00 P.M.	Regina, Saskatchewan	10:00 A.M.
¹Casablanca, Morocco	6:00 P.M.	Reykjavik, Iceland	4:00 P.M.
Chicago, Illinois	11:00 A.M.	Rio de Janeiro, Brazil	2:00 P.M.
Colombo, Sri Lanka (Ceylon)	10:30 P.M.	Rome, Italy	6:00 P.M.
Copenhagen, Denmark	6:00 P.M.	Saigon, Vietnam	1:00 A.M. next day
Delhi, India	10:30 P.M.	Saint John's, Newfoundland	1:30 P.M.
Denver, Colorado	10:00 A.M.	Saint Louis, Missouri	11:00 A.M.
Detroit, Michigan	12:00 NOON	Salt Lake City, Utah	10:00 A.M.
Djakarta, Indonesia	12:00 MIDNIGHT	San Francisco, California	9:00 A.M.
Dublin, Ireland	5:00 P.M.	San Juan, Puerto Rico	1:00 P.M.
Edmonton, Alberta	10:00 A.M.	Santiago, Chile	1:00 P.M.
Geneva, Switzerland	6:00 P.M.	São Paulo, Brazil	2:00 P.M.
Glasgow, Scotland	5:00 P.M.	Seattle, Washington	9:00 A.M.
Halifax, Nova Scotia	1:00 P.M.	Shanghai, China	1:00 A.M. next day
Havana, Cuba	12:00 NOON	Singapore	12:30 A.M. next day
Helsinki, Finland	7:00 P.M.	Sofia, Bulgaria	7:00 P.M.
Hong Kong	1:00 A.M. next day	Stockholm, Sweden	6:00 P.M.
Honolulu, Hawaii	7:00 A.M.	Sydney, Australia	3:00 A.M. next day
Houston, Texas	11:00 A.M.	Tehran, Iran	8:30 P.M.
Istanbul, Turkey	7:00 P.M.	Tel Aviv, Israel	7:00 P.M.
Jerusalem, Israel	7:00 P.M.	Tokyo, Japan	2:00 A.M. next day
Johannesburg, Republic of So. Africa	7:00 P.M.	Toronto, Ontario	12:00 NOON
Juneau, Alaska	9:00 A.M.	Vancouver, British Columbia	9:00 A.M.
Karachi, Pakistan	10:00 P.M.	Vienna, Austria	6:00 P.M.
Kuala Lumpur, Malaysia	12:30 A.M. next day	¹Vladivostok, U.S.S.R.	3:00 A.M. next day
La Paz, Bolivia	1:00 P.M.	Warsaw, Poland	6:00 P.M.
Leningrad, U.S.S.R.	8:00 P.M.	Washington, D.C.	12:00 NOON
Lima, Peru	12:00 NOON	Wellington, New Zealand	5:00 A.M. next day
¹Lisbon, Portugal	6:00 P.M.	Winnipeg, Manitoba	11:00 A.M.
London, England	5:00 P.M.	Zurich, Switzerland	6:00 P.M.

¹Time is one hour in advance of the standard meridian.

standing army *n* [¹*standing*] **:** a permanently organized army of paid soldiers — compare MILITIA
standing barrage *n* **:** a defensive barrage designed to be fired on a particular line
standing bevel *n* **:** a bevel whose angle is obtuse
standing block *or* **standing pulley** *n* **:** a fixed pulley block — distinguished from *running block*
standing committee *n* **:** a committee to consider subjects of a particular class arising during a stated period; *specif* **:** a permanent committee of a legislative body
standing crop *n* **:** a crop not cut or otherwise severed from the soil
standing cup *n* **:** a tall goblet with a foot and a cover
standing cypress *n* **:** a tall erect biennial or perennial leafy-stemmed herb (*Gilia rubra*) having the alternate leaves pinnately divided into slender needlelike leaflets and numerous largely scarlet flowers in a terminal panicle and being native to the southern U.S. but escaped from cultivation and naturalized in areas (as New England) outside its normal range
standing finish *n* **:** the part of the interior fittings esp. of a house that is permanent and fixed
standing height *n* **:** STATURE 1
standing initial *n* **:** a cockup initial
standing lug *n* **:** a lugsail whose yard is not dipped in tacking — compare DIPPING LUG; see LUGSAIL illustration
standing operating procedure *n* **:** established or prescribed tactical or administrative methods to be followed routinely for the performance of designated operations or in designated situations — called also *standard operating procedure;* abbr. *SOP*
standing order *n* **1 :** an instruction or prescribed procedure in force permanently or until specifically changed or canceled: as **a standing orders** *pl* **:** the rules for the guidance and government of parliamentary procedure which endure through successive sessions until vacated or repealed — distinguished from *sessional order* **b standing orders** *pl* **:** routine orders giving authority for the performance of certain prescribed acts for hospitalized patients by the personnel as distinct from specific orders written for a particular patient ⟨blood count and urinalysis on admission are *standing orders*⟩ **2 a :** an order for purchase that holds good until it is filled **b :** an order directing the automatic purchase of succeeding issues of a serial publication
standing part *n* **1 :** the part of a tackle made fast to the block or to any point or object — distinguished from *running part* **2 :** the part of a rope around which turns are taken with the running part in making a knot or bend **3 :** the part of a hook opposite the point
standing press *n* **:** a vertical press in which printed and folded sheets and books are piled and pressed
standing rigging *or* **standing gear** *n* **:** permanent rigging (as stays and shrouds) used primarily to secure the masts and fixed spars of a vessel or to support radio, radar, and other equipment carried aloft — compare RUNNING RIGGING
standing roast *n* **:** a rib roast from which only the heaviest parts of the vertebrae have been removed — compare ROLLED ROAST
standing room *n* [²*standing*] **:** space for standing; *esp* **:** accommodation available for spectators or passengers after all seats are filled
standing rope *n* [¹*standing*] **:** a rope permanently fastened and used as a guy
standing rules *n pl* **:** the rules of a society or organization for details of its government that are created by a majority vote and remain in force until repealed or annulled by a majority vote
standing salt *n* **:** SALTCELLAR
standing valve *n* **:** a foot valve at the bottom of an oil-well pump
standing vise *n* **:** a bench vise at which the operator stands while working
standing vote *n* **:** RISING VOTE
standing wave *n* **:** a single-frequency mode of vibration of a body or physical system in which the amplitude varies from place to place, is constantly zero at fixed points, and has maxima at other points (as at the nodes and antinodes respectively on a violin string or in an organ pipe) — called also *stationary wave;* compare TRAVELING WAVE
standing wave ratio *n* **:** the ratio of the maximum to the minimum signal voltage on a transmission line
standing ways *n pl* **:** GROUND WAYS
stand·ish \'stan(,)dish\ *n* -ES [origin unknown] **:** a stand for writing materials **:** INKSTAND
stand method *n* **:** a practice in forestry of securing reproduction from self-sown seed induced by successive cuttings of trees of different ages in the stand and leading to the development of a stand of trees of the same age
stand of colors : the flags carried by a military unit (as a regiment); *also* **:** a single such flag
stand off *vi* **1 :** to stay at a distance in social intercourse or acquaintance **:** be unapproachable or unobliging **2 :** to sail away from the shore **~** *vt* **1 a :** to hold at a distance **:** keep from advancing **:** REPEL ⟨taking cover they managed to *stand* the Indians *off* until they could make their escape —D.D. Martin⟩ **b :** to put off **:** STALL ⟨able to *stand off* his creditors⟩ **2** *Brit* **:** to remove temporarily from regular employment **:** lay off — **stand off and on** *of a sailing ship* **:** to remain near a coast by sailing toward and then away from the land ⟨*standing off and on* while the captain went ashore⟩
¹standoff \'=,=\ *adj* [*stand off*] **1 :** not cordial **:** not ready to agree or to make friends **:** RESERVED ⟨~ attitude⟩ **2 :** used for holding something (as an electric wire) at a distance from a surface ⟨~ insulator⟩ — see INSULATOR illustration
²standoff \"\ *n* -S [*stand off*] **1 :** the act of standing off **2** *Brit* **:** a rest from work **3 a :** a counterbalancing effect **:** NEUTRALIZATION **b :** TIE, DRAW, DEADLOCK
standoff coat *n* **:** a double coat (as of some dogs) in which thick underhair supports profuse long hair so that it stands out from the body
standoff half *n* **:** a rugby halfback whose position is between the scrum half and the three-quarter backs — called also *fly half*
stand·off·ish \(')stan¦dȯfish, -aan-, -fēsh\ *adj* [¹*standoff* + *-ish*] **:** somewhat cold and reserved **:** lacking cordiality ⟨~ manner⟩ — **stand·off·ish·ly** *adv* — **stand·off·ish·ness** *n* -ES
stand oil *n* **:** a thickened drying oil prepared orig. by exposing to sunlight and air and now usu. by heating **:** BODIED OIL; *esp* **:** linseed oil heated to about 600° F — compare LITHOGRAPHIC VARNISH
stand on *vi* [ME *standen on*, fr. *standen* to stand + *on*] **:** to continue on the same tack or course ⟨whether the approaching ship would *stand on* or give way⟩
stand out *vi* **1 a :** to appear as if in relief **:** PROJECT **b :** to be prominent or conspicuous **:** stick out ⟨success and affluence *stood out* all over him —Hamilton Basso⟩ **2 :** to steer away from shore **3 :** to be stubborn in resolution or resistance **:** not to yield ⟨if you're rich you can afford to *stand out* for a really good contract —Christopher Isherwood⟩ **~** *vt* **:** OUTLAST, ENDURE ⟨*stand out* a storm⟩
¹standout \'=,=\ *n* -S [*stand out*] **:** something outstanding **:** a thing or a person readily distinguishable from others because of excellence or uniqueness ⟨a ~ among the available candidates for the office⟩ ⟨the coat is a ~ in this year's fashions⟩
²standout \"\ *adj* **:** OUTSTANDING ⟨~ performance in an operatic role⟩
stand over *vi* **:** to await consideration or settlement at a later date ⟨resolution will *stand over* until the following session⟩ **~** *vt* **:** to put off **:** POSTPONE
standover \'=,==\ *adj* [fr. the phrase *stand over*] **:** making new growth the next year after harvest ⟨~ crop of sugar cane⟩ ⟨~ cotton⟩ — compare RATOON
¹standpat \'=,=\ *adj* [fr. the phrase *stand pat*] **:** of or relating to or characterized by the policy of standing pat **:** stubbornly conservative
²standpat \"\ *n* -S [fr. the phrase *stand pat*] **:** STANDPATTER
stand·pat·ter \(')stan(d)¦pad·ə(r), -taan-, -patə-\ *n* -S **:** one that stands pat esp. in political matters **:** one that resists or opposes change
stand·pat·tism *also* **stand·pat·ism** \-pad·,izəm\ *n* -S **:** the policy of standing pat **:** resistance to change **:** reluctance to take positive action ⟨~ is timidity —A.L.Guérard⟩
standpipe \'=,=\ *n* **:** a vertical pipe used for holding a liquid: as **a :** a high tank or reservoir that is used to secure a uniform pressure in a water-supply system **b :** a vertical pipe for water that is used to provide fire protection to the upper stories of a high building **c :** a manhole frame

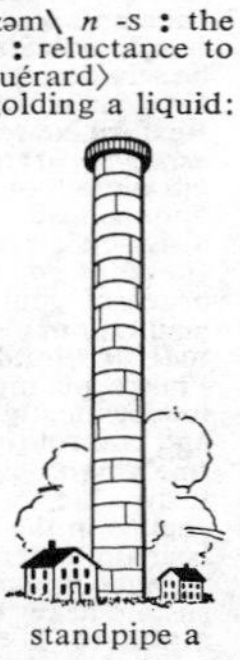

standpipe a

standpoint \'=,=\ *n* [trans. of G *standpunkt*] **:** a fixed point or station **:** a position from which objects or principles are viewed and according to which they are compared and judged ⟨arguing a question from the historical ~⟩ ⟨a good method from the ~ of economy⟩
standpost \'=,=\ *n* **:** a post forming a stand (as for a hydrant)
stands *pl of* STAND, *pres 3d sing of* STAND
¹standstill \=,=\ *n* -S [fr. the phrase *stand still*] **1 :** cessation of movement forward or backward **:** state of rest **:** STOP ⟨wheels sank in the mud and brought the car to a ~⟩ ⟨death was attributed to cardiac ~ from potassium intoxication —T.R.Harrison⟩ ⟨rate of new building has reached a ~⟩ **2 :** STILLSTAND 3 **3 a :** a state of deadlock ⟨negotiations were at a ~ for the time being⟩ **b :** a state of paralyzing indecision or bafflement **c :** a state of exhaustion or thorough defeat ⟨never met a man she couldn't work to a ~ —Frank Sargeson⟩
²standstill \"\ *adj* [fr. the phrase *stand still*] **:** that stands still **:** that stops or rests **:** that maintains things in a fixed or static condition ⟨a ~ agreement on nuclear testing⟩
stand-table \'=,==\ *n, dial* **:** TABLE
stand up *vb* [ME *standen up*, fr. OE *standan up*, fr. *standan* to stand + *up*] *vi* **1 a :** to rise to a standing position **:** stand erect ⟨*stand up* when the national anthem is played⟩ **b :** to rise vertically ⟨columns of smoke *standing up* to the sky —Ira Wolfert⟩ **2 :** to remain sound and intact under stress, pressure, attack, or close scrutiny ⟨a fieldpiece . . . reported to have *stood up* under the weak charges used —*Amer. Guide Series: Conn.*⟩ ⟨proof that would *stand up* in court —Ross Annett⟩ ⟨*stands up* well to rough treatment⟩ **~** *vt* **1 :** to set on end **:** cause to stand **2 :** to fail to keep an appointment with — **stand up for :** to defend against attack or criticism **:** JUSTIFY, SUPPORT ⟨he was my brother anyway and I'm going to *stand up for* him —Liam O'Flaherty⟩ ⟨has always *stood up for* the rights of the individual —Bradford Smith⟩ — **stand up to :** to meet (as a danger, or obligation) fairly and fully ⟨*stand up to* a promise⟩ ⟨urged by an immense pride to *stand up to* our job —A.W.Long⟩ **:** face boldly **:** defend oneself or one's interests against ⟨had enough nerve to *stand up to* the boss⟩ — **stand up with :** to be best man or bridesmaid for a wedding ceremony

1stand-up \'=,=\ *adj* [*stand up*] **1 a :** ERECT, UPRIGHT **b** *of a collar* **:** stiffened to stay upright without folding over **2 :** performed in or requiring a standing erect position ⟨*stand-up* lunch⟩ ⟨*stand-up* bar⟩ ⟨*stand-up* comedy act⟩ ⟨*stand-up* boxing stance⟩ **3** *of a fight* **:** characterized by the exchange of blows without maneuvering, dodging, or retreating ⟨a *stand-up*, knockdown brawl⟩ ⟨*stand-up* battle⟩

2stand-up \"\ *n* -s [*stand up*] **1 :** the quality of standing up to or enduring stress, strain, and wear; *specif* **:** the quality of wearing well when subjected to service **2 :** something that stands erect or is provided with a stand or support to hold it erect ⟨display samples mounted on *stand-ups*⟩ **3 :** the act of failing to keep an appointment

stane \'stān\ *Scot var of* STONE

stan·ford-binet test \'stanfə(r)d \ *or* **stanford revision** *n*, *usu cap S&B* [fr. *Stanford* University, California] **:** a revision of the Binet-Simon scale prepared at Stanford University **:** an individually administered intelligence test commonly employed with children

1stang [ME, fr. OE] *archaic past of* STING

2stang \'staŋ\ *n* -s [ME *stong, stang*, fr. ON *stöng;* akin to OE *steng* pole, *stingan* to thrust, sting, OHG *stanga* pole — more at STING] *dial Brit* **:** POLE, BAR

3stang \"\ *vb* -ED/-ING/-S [ME *stangen*, fr. ON *stanga* to prick, goad; akin to ON *stinga* to sting — more at STING] *vt, chiefly Scot* **:** STING ~ *vi, chiefly Scot* **:** STING, ACHE, THROB

4stang \"\ *n* -s [ME, sting, fr. *stangen* to stang] *chiefly Scot* **:** PANG

stan·ge·ria \stan'jirēə\ *n, cap* [NL, fr. William *Stanger* †1854 Eng. surveyor general in Natal + NL *-ia*] **:** a genus of So. African cycads with fernlike foliage and bracted strobiles

stan·hope \'stanəp, -n,hōp\ *n* -s [after Fitzroy *Stanhope* †1864 Brit. clergyman] **:** a gig, buggy, or light phaeton typically having a high seat and closed back

stan·ho·pea \stan'hōpēə\ *n* [NL, after Philip Henry, 4th Earl *Stanhope* †1855 Eng. botanist] **1** *cap* **:** a genus of tropical American epiphytic orchids having a single large leaf, a raceme from each pseudobulb, and large fragrant flowers of various colors and markings with nearly equal sepals and a greatly contorted lip **2** -s **:** any plant of the genus *Stanhopea*

stanhope press *n, usu cap S* [after Charles, 3d Earl *Stanhope* †1816 Eng. scientist, its inventor] **:** a hand-operated printing press that has a system of levers which cause the platen to descend with decreasing rapidity and with increasing force

stanhope process *n, usu cap S* [after Charles, 3d Earl *Stanhope*] **:** a method of stereotyping in which the matrix used is of heat-hardened gypsum and plaster

sta·nine \'stā,nīn\ *n* -s [*sta*ndard (*score*) + *nine*] **:** an aptitude score for aviation students ranging from 1 to 9 based on a battery of tests and weighted for ratings of pilot, bombardier, and navigator

sta·nit·sa *also* **sta·nit·za** \stə'nitsə\ *n* -s [Russ *stanitsa*, dim. of *stan* station, police district; akin to Skt *sthāna* station, locality, district, *tiṣṭhati* he stands — more at STAND] **:** a village or administrative district in the Cossack regions of Russia

1stank [ME, fr. OE *stanc*] *past of* STINK

2stank \'staŋk\ *n* -s [ME, fr. OF *estanc*, prob. fr. *estancher* to check or stop the flowing of — more at STANCH] **1** *dial Brit* **a :** POND, POOL **b :** a ditch containing water **2** *Brit* **:** a small dam **:** WEIR

3stank \"\ *vt* -ED/-ING/-S *Brit* **:** DAM

stank·ie \'staŋki\ *or* **stank hen** \'staŋk-\ *n* -s [*stankie* fr. *stank* (*hen*) (fr. *2stank*) + *-ie;* fr. its being found near stanks] *Scot* **:** GALLINULE

stann- *or* **stanni-** *or* **stanno-** *comb form* [LL *stannum* tin — more at STANNUM] **:** relating to or containing tin ⟨*stann*ide⟩ ⟨*stanni*ferous⟩ ⟨*stanno*type⟩ **:** stannic ⟨*stann*ane⟩ **:** stannous ⟨*stann*ite⟩

stan·nane \'sta,nān\ *n* -s [*stann-* + meth*ane;* fr. the analogy of its formula to that of methane, CH_4] **1 :** a compound of tin and hydrogen; *esp* **:** the unstable gaseous tetrahydride SnH_4 known chiefly in the form of organic derivatives **2 :** any of various organic derivatives of tin tetrahydride

stan·na·ry \'stanərē\ *n* -ES [ML *stannaria* tin mine, fr. LL *stannum* + L *-aria* -ary] **:** one of the regions in England containing tinworks and formerly placed under jurisdiction of special courts — usu. used in pl.

stan·nate \'sta,nāt\ *n* -s [*stann-* + *-ate*] **:** a salt [as sodium hexa-hydroxo-stannate $Na_2Sn(OH)_6$] of a stannic acid

stan·na·tor \sta'nād·ə(r)\ *n* -s [ML *stannator* tin-miner, irreg. fr. LL *stannum*] **:** a representative from a stannary sent to a stannary assembly

stan·ners \'stanə(r)z\ *n pl* [fr. (assumed) ME (Sc), perh. fr. OE *stǣner* stony ground; akin to OE *stān* stone — more at STONE] *chiefly Scot* **:** the small stones found near or in a body of water

stan·nic \'stanik, -nēk\ *adj* [prob. fr. F *stannique*, fr. LL *stannum, stagnum* tin + F *-ique* -ic —more at STANNUM] **:** of, relating to, or containing tin — used esp. of compounds in which this element is tetravalent; compare STANNOUS

stannic acid *n* [prob. fr. F *acide stannique*] **:** any of various amorphous acid substances that behave like hydrates of stannic oxide and yield stannic oxide when calcined: as **a :** a highly hydrated substance obtainable as a gelatinous precipitate by hydrolysis of stannic chloride by alkali or excess water and forming salts with more alkali — called also *alpha-stannic acid* **b :** a less highly hydrated substance obtainable as a powder by heating or drying alpha-stannic acid — called also *beta-stannic acid*

stannic chloride *n* **:** a mobile liquid compound $SnCl_4$ that fumes in moist air, that is made usu. by the action of chlorine on tin (as in recovering tin from scrap), that when mixed with a little water solidifies to a soft crystalline mass of the pentahydrate and with more water slowly hydrolyzes yielding hydrochloric acid, and that is used chiefly in making other tin compounds but was formerly used in weighting silk and as a mordant and in producing military smoke screens — called also *tin tetrachloride*

stannic oxide *n* **:** the dioxide SnO_2 of tin that occurs in nature as cassiterite, is produced artificially as a crystalline powder when anhydrous, and is used chiefly in ceramic colors, in vitreous enamels and glazes as an opacifier, in glass, and in polishes — see STANNIC ACID

stannic sulfide *n* **:** a yellow compound SnS_2 obtained in amorphous and crystalline forms — see MOSAIC GOLD 1

stan·nide \'sta,nīd\ *n* -s [ISV *stann-* + *-ide*] **:** a compound of tin with a more electropositive element or radical

stan·nif·er·ous \sta'nif(ə)rəs\ *adj* [*stann-* + *-iferous*] **:** containing tin ⟨~ glaze for pottery⟩

stan·nite \'sta,nīt\ *n* -s [G *stannit*, fr. *stann-* + *-it* -ite] **1 :** salt formed in solution when a stannous salt is treated with excess alkali **2** [*stann-* + *-ite*] **:** a mineral Cu_2FeSnS consisting of a steel-gray or iron-black sulfide of copper, iron, and tin, of a metallic luster occurring in granular masses — called also *tin pyrites* (hardness 4, sp. gr. 4.3–4.52)

stan·nous \'stanəs\ *adj* [ISV *stann-* + *-ous*] **:** of, relating to, or containing tin — used esp. of compounds in which this element is bivalent; compare STANNIC

stannous chloride *n* **:** a compound $SnCl_2$ obtained by the action of chlorine, hydrogen chloride or hydrochloric acid on tin either as an anhydrous solid or a crystalline dihydrate and used chiefly in tinning and as a reducing agent and catalyst —called also *tin dichloride;* see TIN CRYSTALS

stannous oxide *n* **:** the monoxide of tin SnO that is obtained as dark lustrous crystals usu. blue-black but sometimes varying in shade (as from brown and red to dark green) and that forms stannic oxide when heated in air

stan·num \'stanəm\ *n* -s [LL *stagnum, stannum*, fr. L, an alloy of silver and lead, prob. of Celt origin; akin to IrGael *stān* tin, Welsh *ystaen*, Corn & Bret *stēn*] **:** TIN — symbol *Sn*

stan·te ma·tri·mo·nio \'stän(,)tā,mä·trə'mōnē,ō\ [NL] **:** while the marriage is in force

stan·za \'stanzə, -aan-\ *n* -s [It, act or place of staying, abode, room, stanza, fr. (assumed) VL *stantia* act of standing or staying — more at STANCHION] **1 :** a division of a poem consisting of a series of lines arranged together as a unit **:** STROPHE; *esp* **:** a group of lines arranged together in a recurring pattern of metrical lengths and usu. a sequence of rhymes **2** *slang* **a :** a period of performing or showing in one place **:** STAND, ENGAGEMENT; *esp* **:** WEEK ⟨the play is to be held over for another ~⟩ ⟨signed the orchestra for the last ~ in June⟩ **b :** a period (as a half or an inning) into which the duration of a game is divided

stan·zaed \-əd\ *adj* [*stanza* + *-ed*] **:** arranged in, divided into, or composed of stanzas

stan·za·ic \(')stan¦zāik, -aan- -āək\ *also* **stan·za·i·cal** *adj* [*stanza* + *-ic, -ical*] **:** relating to or consisting of stanzas ⟨~ structure⟩ — **stan·za·i·cal·ly** *adv*

1stap \'stap\ *Scot var of* STEP

2stap \"\ *n* -s [origin unknown] *chiefly Scot* **:** a stave of a cask or tub

3stap \"\ *dial Brit var of* STOP

sta·pe·di·al \stə'pēdēəl\ *adj* [NL *staped-, stapes* + E *-ial*] **:** of, relating to, or located near the stapes

sta·pe·dio·vestibular \stə¦pēdē(,)ō+\ *adj* [*stapedi*al + *-o-* + *vestibular*] **:** of or relating to the stapes and the vestibule of the ear

sta·pe·di·us \stə'pēdēəs\ *n, pl* **stape·dii** \-dē,ī\ [NL, fr. *staped-, stapes*] **:** a small muscle of the middle ear of mammals that arises from the wall of the tympanum, is inserted into the neck of the stapes by a tendon that sometimes contains a slender spine of bone, and serves to check and dampen vibration of the stapes

sta·pe·lia \stə'pēlēə\ *n* [NL, fr. J. Bodaeus van *Stapel* †1636 Du. physician and botanist + NL *-ia*] **1** *cap* **:** a large genus of African evil-smelling asclepiads, with succulent leafless toothed stems like the joints of a cactus and oddly colored flowers that are often several inches across and in some a foot or more across **2** -s **:** any plant of the genus *Stapelia* — called also *carrion flower*

sta·pes \'stā(,)pēz\ *n, pl* **stapes** \"\ *or* **stape·des** \stə'pē,dēz\ [NL *staped-, stapes*, fr. ML, stirrup, alter. (prob. influenced by L *ped-, pes* foot) of LL *stapia*, prob. of Gmc origin; akin to OHG *stapfo* step — more at STEP, FOOT] **1 :** the innermost of the chain of ossicles of the ear of mammals which has the form of a stirrup, a base that occupies the fenestra vestibuli of the tympanum, and a head that is connected with the incus — see EAR illustration **2 :** the inner segment of the columella or sometimes the entire columella of the ear of many nonmammalian vertebrates

staph \'staf\ *n* -s [by shortening] **:** STAPHYLOCOCCUS 2

staph·i·sa·gria \,stafə'sāgrēə\ *n* -s [NL (specific epithet of *Delphinium staphisagria*), fr. L *staphis agria* stavesacre — more at STAVESACRE] **:** the ripe seed of the stavesacre (*Delphinium staphisagria*) used to kill head lice

staphyl- *or* **staphylo-** *comb form* [MF *staphyl-*, fr. L *staphyl-, staphylo-*, fr. Gk, bunch of grapes, uvula, fr. *staphylē* bunch of grapes, swollen uvula, uvula; akin to Gk *stemphylon* olive pulp — more at STAFF] **1 a :** bunch of grapes ⟨*Staphylo*coccus⟩ **b :** staphyloma ⟨*staphylo*tomy⟩ **2 a :** uvula ⟨*staphyl*ectomy⟩ **b :** palate ⟨*staphyl*ion⟩ **3 :** staphylococcic ⟨*staphylo*coagulase⟩ ⟨*staphylo*dermatitis⟩

staph·y·lea \,stafə'lēə\ *n, cap* [NL, fr. Gk *staphylē* bunch of grapes; fr. the clustered fruit] **:** a genus of shrubs or small trees (family Staphyleaceae) with opposite leaves and drooping panicles of white or pink flowers succeeded by inflated bladdery capsules — see BLADDERNUT

staph·y·le·a·ce·ae \,stafəlē'āsē,ē\ *n pl, cap* [NL, fr. *Staphylea*, type genus + *-aceae*] **:** a family of plants (order Sapindales) mostly of the north temperate zone that have compound leaves, perfect regular flowers with introrse anthers, and inflated capsular fruit — **staph·y·le·a·ceous** \¦===¦āshəs\ *adj*

1staph·y·lin·id \¦stafə¦linəd\ *adj* [NL *Staphylinidae*] **:** of or relating to the Staphylinidae

2staphylinid \"\ *n* -s [NL *Staphylinidae*] **:** a beetle of the family Staphylinidae

staph·y·lin·i·dae \,=='linə,dē\ *n pl, cap* [NL, fr. *Staphylinus*, type genus + *-idae*] **:** a family of beetles consisting of the rove beetles

staph·y·li·noi·dea \,stafələ'nȯidēə\ *n pl, cap* [NL, fr. *Staphylinus* + *-oidea*] **:** a superfamily of beetles including the Staphylinidae and several related families

staph·y·li·nus \,stafə'līnəs\ *n, cap* [NL, fr. Gk *staphylinos*, an insect, prob. fr. *staphylē* bunch of grapes] **:** the type genus of the family Staphylinidae

sta·phyl·i·on \stə'filē,än\ *n* -s [NL, irreg. fr. *staphyl-*] **:** the median point of the posterior edge of the hard palate

staph·y·lo·coagulase \¦stafə(,)lō+\ *n* [*staphyl-* + *coagulase*] **:** a coagulase from pathogenic staphylococci

staph·y·lo·coc·cal \¦stafəlō¦käkəl\ *adj* [NL *Staphylococcus* + E *-al*] **:** of, caused by, produced by, or being a staphylococcus ⟨~ group⟩ ⟨~ infection⟩ ⟨~ organism⟩

staph·y·lo·coc·ce·mia \,stafəlōkäk'sēmēə\ *n* -s [NL, fr. *Staphylococcus* + *-emia*] **:** the presence of staphylococci in the circulating blood — **staph·y·lo·coc·ce·mic** \¦====¦sēmik\ *adj*

staph·y·lo·coc·cic \¦stafəlō¦käksik, -sēk\ *adj* [ISV *staphylococc-* (fr. NL *Staphylococcus*) + *-ic*] **:** caused by a staphylococcus

staph·y·lo·coc·co·sis \,stafəlōkä'kōsəs\ *n* -ES [NL, fr. *Staphylococcus* + *-osis*] **:** infection with or disease caused by staphylococci; *esp* **:** a disease of poultry and usu. of young turkeys and chickens caused by a staphylococcus (*Staphylococcus aureus*) and characterized by acute septicemia or chronic arthritis

1staph·y·lo·coc·cus \,stafəlō'käkəs\ *n* [NL, fr. *staphyl-* + *-coccus*] **1** *cap* **:** a genus of nonmotile gram-positive spherical eubacteria (family Micrococcaceae) that occur singly, in pairs or tetrads, or in irregular clusters and as now usu. restricted comprise a few parasites of skin and mucous membranes — compare MICROCOCCUS **2** *pl* **staphylococ·ci** \-äk,sī\ **:** any bacterium of the genus *Staphylococcus; broadly* **:** MICROCOCCUS 2

2staphylococcus \"\ [NL, fr. *staphyl-* + *-coccus*] *syn of* MICROCOCCUS

staph·y·lo·ma \,stafə'lōmə\ *n* -s [alter. (influenced by LL *staphyloma*) of earlier *staphylome*, fr. MF, fr. LL *staphyloma*, fr. Gk *staphylōma*, fr. *staphylē* bunch of grapes + *-ōma* -oma] **:** a protrusion of the cornea or sclera of the mammalian eye

staph·y·lot·o·my \-'läd·əmē\ *n* -ES [NL *staphylotomia*, fr. Gk, fr. *staphyl-* + *-tomia* -tomy] **1 :** the cutting or removal of the uvula **2** [ISV *staphyl-* + *-tomy*] **:** the surgical removal of a staphyloma

1sta·ple \'stāpəl\ *n* -s [ME *stapel* staple, post, pillar, fr. OE *stapol* post, pillar; akin to MD *stapel* step, foundation, heap, emporium, OHG *staffal* step, ON *stöpull* pillar, tower, OE *steppan* to step — more at STEP] **1 a :** a U-shaped metal loop both ends of which are driven into a surface to hold the hook, hasp, or bolt of a lock, secure a rope, or fix a wire in place **b :** a small U-shaped wire both ends of which are driven through layers of thin and easily penetrable material (as paper or paperboard) and usu. clinched to hold the layers together **2 :** CHAPLET 4 **3 :** a mine shaft that is smaller and shorter than the principal one and joins different levels **4** *or* **stapling** [*stapling* fr. gerund of *2staple*] **:** an angle bar or plate that is fitted closely around the frames and structural members of a ship and passes through decks and bulkheads to secure oil-tightness or watertightness

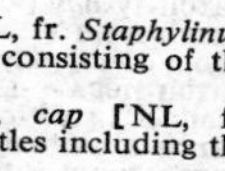
staples 1

2staple \"\ *vt* **stapled**; **stapled**; **stapling** \-p(ə)liŋ\ **staples** [ME *staplen*, fr. *stapel*, n.] **:** to provide with or secure by staples ⟨~ papers together⟩

3staple \"\ *n* -s [ME *staple, stapull*, fr. MD *stapel* emporium] **1 :** a town formerly and usu. by royal fiat used as a center for the sale or exportation of commodities (as wool, skin, and leather) in bulk **2 :** a place of supply **:** SOURCE, CENTER ⟨Whitehall naturally became the chief ~ of news —T.B. Macaulay⟩ **3 a :** a commodity that is produced regularly or in large quantities esp. for a wholesale market ⟨where . . . textiles and Welsh coal once led the list of exports, Britain's new ~*s* are . . . —*Time*⟩ **b :** the principal commodity of traffic in a market **:** a chief commodity or production of a place ⟨corn was the great ~ of the Old West —R.A.Billington⟩ **4 a :** a commodity for which the demand is constant and not dependent on variable factors (as season or fashion) ⟨sugar and flour are among a grocer's ~*s*⟩ **b :** something that enjoys widespread and constant use or appeal **:** something that is regular fare ⟨fish is one of the ~*s* of the grizzly's diet —Charles Mulvey⟩ ⟨news and weather reports are ~*s* of television variety shows —Philip Hamburger⟩ ⟨songs from his . . . shows are still . . . ~*s* all over the world —*Newsweek*⟩ **c :** the sustaining or principal element **:** CORE, SUBSTANCE ⟨the Bible . . . as the ~ of their intellectual and spiritual lives —D. R.Meyer⟩ ⟨the ~ of Roman education was always a study of the poets —E.E.Sikes⟩ ⟨the ~ of the satire is the wickedness of all paper-money issues —V.L.Parrington⟩ **5 :** the unworked or natural material from which textiles and other goods are manufactured **:** raw material **6 a** *or* **staple fiber** **:** natural fiber (as of raw wool, cotton, flax, or hemp) or synthetic fiber (as cut from continuous filaments of rayon or nylon) of relatively short length that when spun and twisted forms a yarn as distinguished from a filament **b :** the length of a piece of such textile fiber ranging from about one inch for some types of cotton to several feet for hemp ⟨tow is flax with short ~⟩

4staple \"\ *adj* **1** *obs* **:** of, relating to, or being a staple for commodities **2 :** used, needed, or enjoyed constantly usu. by many individuals **:** STANDARD ⟨such ~ items as sugar and flour⟩ ⟨the mesa was our ~ topic of conversation —Willa Cather⟩ ⟨a ~ romantic prop in the construction of historical fiction —E.J.Fitzgerald⟩ **3 :** produced regularly or in large quantities esp. for a wholesale market ⟨such ~ crops as wheat, rice, cotton, flax, sugarcane —V.A.Baker⟩ **4 :** PRINCIPAL, CHIEF ⟨the potato has long been the ~ crop here —*Amer. Guide Series: Va.*⟩ ⟨the ~ diet of all true Mexicans . . . is the tortilla —Green Peyton⟩ **5 :** being or made from textile staple ⟨~ fiber⟩ ⟨~ yarn⟩

5staple \"\ *vt* -ED/-ING/-S **1 :** to sort or grade (staple) according to its length ⟨~ cotton fiber⟩ **2 :** to convert (material that does not occur naturally as staple) into staple ⟨~ the filament rayon by cutting⟩

staple punch *n* **:** a punch for making two holes simultaneously to receive the points of a staple

1sta·pler \'stāp(ə)lə(r)\ *n* -s [*3staple* + *-er*] **1 :** one that deals in staple goods or in staple fiber **2 :** one that sorts staple according to its length

2stapler \"\ *n* -s [*2staple* + *-er*] **:** one that inserts staples (as in paper or wood): as **a :** a small usu. hand device for inserting the wire staples that bind papers together **b :** STAPLING HAMMER **c :** a workman who inserts staples with a hammer or machine

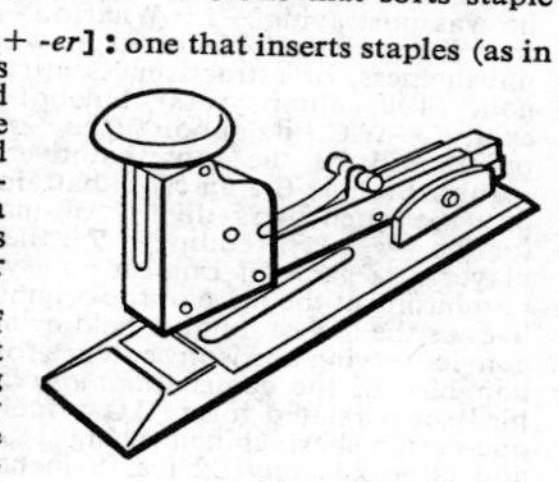
stapler a

staple right *n* [trans. of D *stapelrecht*] **:** a right of forcing any passing vessel either to pay duty or to sell its cargo in the market place orig. possessed by towns in the Netherlands and later introduced into the colony of New Netherland

stapling hammer *n* **:** a tool that resembles a hammer and is used to insert staples esp. in building material

stapp \'stap\ *n* -s [after John P. *Stapp* b1910 Am. biophysicist] **:** a unit of force caused by acceleration and equal to one G acting on a body for one second

stap·ple \'stapəl\ *Scot var of* 1STAPLE 3

staps *pl of* STAP

1star \'stär, 'stå(r\ *n* -s [ME *sterre*, fr. OE *steorra;* akin to OHG *sterro, sterno* star, ON *stjarna*, Goth *stairno*, L *stella*, Gk *astēr, astron* star, Skt *stṛbhis* (instrumental pl.) by means of stars] **1 a** (1) **:** an object (as a comet, meteor, or planet) in the sky resembling a luminous point and usu. only bright enough to be seen at night; *specif* **:** FIXED STAR (2) **:** a heavenly body (as the sun or moon); *also* **:** EARTH (3) *obs* **:** POLESTAR ⟨there's no more sailing by the ~ —Shak.⟩ **b** (1) **:** a self-luminous gaseous celestial body of great mass whose own gravitation produces high internal pressure and temperature resulting in atomic and nuclear processes that cause the star to emit electromagnetic radiation and to be observable in the visible region of the spectrum if its surface temperature is about 2500° absolute or higher, whose shape is usu. spheroidal, whose size may be as small as the earth or larger than the earth's orbit, and that often is composed of two or more stars in close gravitational association — see BINARY STAR, MULTIPLE STAR, SUPERGIANT, WHITE DWARF (2) **:** one of the self-luminous bodies belonging to a star cluster, globular cluster, star cloud, or galaxy **2 a** (1) **:** a planet or a configuration of the planets influencing one's destiny or fortune — usu. used in pl. (2) **:** fortune or fame esp. with regard to its waxing and waning ⟨during his lifetime he received no such acclaim . . . and . . . after his death his ~ had set apparently not to rise again —A.T.Davison⟩ **b** *obs* **:** DESTINY, FATE ⟨I was not born unto riches, neither is it I think my ~ to be wealthy —Sir Thomas Browne⟩ **3 a :** a conventional figure with five or more points that represents a star ⟨added another

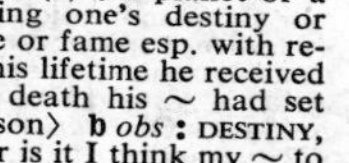
stars 3a

FIFTY IMPORTANT STARS

NAME AND PRONUNCIATION	CONSTELLATION
Achernar \'akər,när, 'ā-\	α Eridani
Albireo \al'birē,ō\	β Cygni
Alcor \'al,kȯr\	80 Ursae Majoris
Alcyone \al'sīə(,)nē\	η Tauri
Aldebaran \al'debərən\	α Tauri
Algenib \al'jenəb, -'ē-\	γ Pegasi
Algol \'al,gäl, -ȯl\	β Persei
Alioth \'alē,äth, -,ȯ-\	ε Ursae Majoris
Alkaid \al'kīd, -ād\	η Ursae Majoris
Almach \'al,mak\	γ Andromedae
Alphard \'al,färd\	α Hydrae
Alphecca \al'fekə\	α Coronae Borealis
Alpheratz \al'ferəts\	α Andromedae *or* δ Pegasi
Altair \al'tī(ə)r, -'ta(a)(ə)r\	α Aquilae
Antares \an'tarēz, aan'taar-\	α Scorpii
Arcturus \ärk't(y)u̇rəs\	α Boötis
Bellatrix \bə'lā·triks\	γ Orionis
Betelgeuse \'bed·ᵊl,jüz, -'ē-\	α Orionis
Canopus \kə'nōpəs\	α Carinae
Capella \kə'pelə\	α Aurigae
Castor \'kastər\	α Geminorum
Deneb \'de,neb, -,nəb\	α Cygni
Deneb Kaitos \-'kī¦d·əs, -kā¦, ¦,täs\	β Ceti
Denebola \də'nebələ\	β Leonis
Dubhe \'dübə, 'dəbə\	α Ursae Majoris
Elnath \'el,nath\	β Tauri
Fomalhaut \'fōməl,hȯt, -ə,lȯt, -,ō-\	α Piscis Austrini
Hamal \'haməl\	α Arietis
Markab \'mär,kab\	α Pegasi
Megrez \'mē,grez, -'e-\	δ Ursae Majoris
Menkar \'men,kär\	α Ceti
Merak \'mē,rak\	β Ursae Majoris
Mira \'mīrə\	o Ceti
Mirach \'mī,rak\	β Andromedae
Mirfak \'mi(ə)r,fak\	α Persei
Mizar \'mī,zär\	ζ Ursae Majoris
Phecda \'fekdə\	γ Ursae Majoris
Polaris \pō'la(a)rəs\	α Ursae Minoris
Pollux \'päləks\	β Geminorum
Procyon \'prōsē,än\	α Canis Minoris
Rasalgethi \,rasəl'jed·ē, -ethē\	α Herculis
Rasalhague \,rasəl'hägwē\	α Ophiuchi
Regulus \'regyələs\	α Leonis
Rigel \'rījəl, -īg-\	β Orionis
Scheat \shē'at, 'shē,at, 'shat\	β Pegasi
Schedar \'shedər\	α Cassiopeiae
Sirius \'sirēəs\	α Canis Majoris
Spica \'spīkə\	α Virginis
Thuban \'th(y)ü,ban\	α Draconis
Vega \'vēgə, -'ā-\	α Lyrae

~ to the flag⟩: as (1) : an unpierced mullet — used esp. in Scottish blazonry (2) : ESTOILE (3) : ASTERISK — compare REFERENCE MARK **b** : an often star-shaped ornament or medal worn as a badge of honor, authority, or rank or as the insignia of an order ⟨awarded the silver ~ for valor⟩ ⟨the single ~ of a brigadier general⟩ ⟨wearing a deputy sheriff's ~⟩ ⟨a campaign ribbon with three battle ~s⟩ **c** : one of a group of usu. four or five conventional stars used to place something in a scale of value ⟨his book could hardly rate three ~s for juvenile reading —*Sydney (Australia) Bull.*⟩ ⟨a five-*star* performance in modern research —J.T.Soby⟩ **4** : something resembling a star or a conventional star: as **a** : a white spot on the forehead of an animal and esp. on a horse **b** : one of the flashing or twinkling lights having no objective existence that are sometimes seen before the eyes esp. as the result of a blow ⟨a body blow that . . . filled his eyes with . . . ~s —F.V.W.Mason⟩ **c** [by shortening] : STARFISH **d** : a small mass of composition used in fireworks (as rockets or mines) that burns with a starlike effect in any of several colors **e** : a bright spot or flaw in the surface of steel that is the end of a pipe which has not been quite cut away **f** : STAR WHEEL **g** : the figure produced by joining the coils or circuits of a polyphase apparatus or system at a common center — see STAR CONNECTION, STAR WINDING **h** (1) : a light figure in a crystal that consists usu. of a bright center and one or more luminous lines radiating from it, is observed best under strong illumination, and is seen esp. in a cabochon-cut gemstone held in the proper orientation (2) : a gemstone showing asterism **i** : STAR FACET **j** : STAR CUT **k** : the multiple forking of a cloud track produced by multiple nuclear disintegration; *also* : a smaller pattern similarly produced in a photographic emulsion **l** : MILL 7c **5 a** (1) : the principal member of a theatrical or operatic company who usu. plays the chief roles (2) : a highly publicized performer whose appearance in a play or motion picture is a major guarantee of its success ⟨the films . . . create ~s out of young actors and actresses —*Britain Today*⟩ (3) : an outstandingly talented performer ⟨a ~ who unquestionably conveyed to the audiences the very essence of the character he was portraying —J.F.Wharton⟩ ⟨track ~⟩ **b** : something that is prominently featured or whose brilliance, distinction, unusualness, or attractiveness attracts attention ⟨a fish long gone (400 million years), but not forgotten, is the ~ of an exhibit —W.C.Fitzgibbon⟩ ⟨the ~s, from a spectator's standpoint, will be the representatives of the military services —John Brehl⟩ **6** : an esp. unattainable goal — often used in pl. ⟨the quenchless dignity of man, the ceaseless questing for the ~s —J.S.Redding⟩ **7** : the privilege open to the first player in a game of English pool who loses his three lives of purchasing at the price of the original stake as many additional lives as the lowest number held by any other player **8** *Brit* : a convict serving a prison sentence for the first time **9** : a hummingbird of the genus *Calothorax* (as the Lucifer hummingbird) or a related form **10** : one of a class of international one-design sharp-chined racing sloops that are Marconi rigged and approximately 22 feet 9 inches in overall length with a sail area of 281 square feet — **stars in one's eyes** : a feeling of elation or optimism ⟨an enamored young girl with *stars in her eyes*⟩

[2]**star** \"\ *vb* **starred; starred; starring; stars** *vt* **1** : to make (a person) into a star or constellation ⟨a mighty archer *starred* by the gods⟩ **2** : to sprinkle or adorn with or as if with stars : BESPANGLE, DOT ⟨meadows *starred* with buttercups and daisies —Kenneth Roberts⟩ **3 a** : to mark with a star as being superior or preeminent in some way ⟨a monument *starred* in the guidebook⟩ **b** (1) : to mark with or as if with an asterisk (2) : to run or fill out (as an improperly typeset line) with asterisks **4** : to present as a star : advertise or display prominently : FEATURE ⟨the movie ~s a famous stage personality⟩ **5** : to cause (molten antimony) to form starlike patterns on solidifying ~ *vi* **1 a** : to perform as or be a star : play the most prominent or important role ⟨under contract to produce and ~ in two pictures a year —*Current Biog.*⟩ **b** : to perform outstandingly ⟨the third baseman *starred* with a sensational catch⟩ ⟨the author *starred* as journalist, novelist, and playwright⟩ **2** : to become fractured in radiating cracks ⟨the glass *starred* but didn't shatter —*Dupont Mag.*⟩ **3** : to purchase additional lives in English pool **4** : to form starlike patterns on solidifying — used of antimony

[3]**star** \"\ *adj* **1 a** : of or relating to a star **b** : composed of stars ⟨~ belt⟩ **c** : shaped or arranged like a conventional star ⟨~ punch⟩ **2 a** : marked with a star as a distinguishing mark (as of importance or of excellence) **b** *Brit* : wearing a star that marks the prisoner who wears it as a first offender **3 a** : of, relating to, being, based upon, or concerned with a starred performer or a starring role ⟨~ system⟩ ⟨~ billing⟩ ⟨~ attraction⟩ ⟨~ actors are bad judges of plays —J.B. Priestley⟩ ⟨after his return to film work . . . he played ~ roles in six or more pictures —*Current Biog.*⟩ **b** : of outstanding excellence : PREEMINENT ⟨~ athlete⟩ ⟨~ pupil⟩ ⟨a ~ diplomat and intriguer —*Newsweek*⟩ ⟨~ mechanic⟩

[4]**star** \"\ *n* -s [ME, of Scand origin; akin to ON *störr* sedge; akin to OE *starian* to stare — more at STARE] *dial chiefly Brit* : BEACH GRASS, SEDGE

star anise *n* [so called fr. the shape of the fruit] : a tree of the genus *Illicium*; *esp* : CHINESE ANISE

star aniseed *n* [*star* (in *star anise*) + *aniseed*] : the dried fruit of the Chinese anise used as a spice

star anise oil *or* **star aniseed oil** *n* : a fragrant essential oil obtained from star aniseed and used chiefly as a flavoring agent, expectorant, and carminative — called also *anise oil*

star antimony *n* : refined metallic antimony characterized by crystalline patterns resembling stars or fern leaves on its surface — called also *star metal*

star apple *n* **1** : a tree of the genus *Chrysophyllum*; *esp* : an evergreen tropical American tree (*C. cainito*) that is often cultivated in warm regions for its showy foliage which is dark green above and golden and silky on the undersurface and for its edible purple fruits **2** [so called fr. the starlike figure formed by the carpels in cross section] : the fruit of a star apple

star begonia *n* : a rhizomatous begonia (*Begonia heracleifolia*) having leaves with pointed lobes suggestive of the shape of stars

star-blasting *n*, *obs* : a baleful influence supposed to be exerted by stars

starbloom \ˈ=,=\ *n* : a pinkroot (*Spigelia marilandica*)

[1]**star·board** \ˈstärbərd, ˈstȧbəd\ *n* [ME *sterbord* right side of a ship looking forward, fr. OE *stēorbord*, fr. *stēor*- rudder, steering oar + *bord* ship's side; fr. the early practice of steering a ship by means of an oar held in the water over the right side — more at STEER, BOARD] : the right side of a ship or airplane looking forward — opposed to *port*

[2]**starboard** \"\ *vt* : to turn or put (a helm or rudder) to the right

[3]**starboard** \"\ *adj* : of, relating to, or situated to starboard — see SHIP illustration

starboard bow *n* : the starboard surface of a ship's hull that curves inward to the stem — distinguished from *port bow*

star boarder *n* : a highly favored and privileged lodger

starboard tack *n* : the tack on which the wind comes from a sailing ship's starboard side

starboard watch *n* : the half of a ship's company that alternates with the port watch in working the ship in successive daily duty periods

star boat *n* : STAR 10

star·bo·lins *also* **star·bow·lines** \ˈstärbələnz\ *n pl* [perh. irreg. fr. [1]*starboard* + *-lings*, pl. of *-ling*, n. suffix] *archaic* : STARBOARD WATCH

starbright \ˈ=,=\ *adj*, *archaic* : bright as a star; *also* : studded with stars

star cactus *n* : a globular cactus of the genus *Astrophytum* with starlike clusters of spines — called also *bishop's cap*, *sand dollar*

star capsicum *n* : an ornamental Brazilian shrub (*Solanum capsicastrum*) that resembles the Jerusalem cherry

star carrier *n* : a mail carrier on a star route

star catalog *n* : a list of stars giving their positions for a given epoch, their magnitudes, and usu. other data

[1]**starch** \ˈstärch, ˈstȧch\ *vt* -ED/-ING/-ES [ME *sterchen*, prob. fr. (assumed) OE *stercan* to stiffen (whence OE *sterced*- firm, resolute); akin to OHG *sterken* to strengthen, OSw *stærkia* to starch, strengthen; causative fr. the root of OE *stearc* stiff, strong — more at STARK] **1 a** : to stiffen with or as if with starch ⟨the sheets were ~*ed* cool and smooth —Anton Vogt⟩ **b** : to make formal, precise or conventional : set into a rigid pattern ⟨dating from times when the English language had not yet been ~*ed* and formalized with definitions and rules of grammar —*Amer. Guide Series: Tenn.*⟩ **2** *obs* : to fasten or attach with starch paste

[2]**starch** \"\ *n* -ES [ME *sterche*, fr. *sterchen*, v.] **1 a** : a white odorless tasteless granular or powdery complex carbohydrate $(C_6H_{10}O_5)_x$ that is the chief storage form of carbohydrate in plants, is obtained commercially esp. from corn and potatoes, is hydrolyzed by acids to dextrins, hydrol, and finally glucose and by carbohydrases to dextrins or glucose, is insoluble in cold water but swells in hot water and cools to form a paste or gel, gives a characteristic blue color with iodine, is an important foodstuff, and is used otherwise chiefly in adhesives and sizes for paper and textiles, in laundering, and in pharmacy and medicine — compare CELLULOSE, CORNSTARCH, GLYCOGEN, SOLUBLE STARCH **b** : a substance used similarly to starch esp. for stiffening textile fabrics ⟨a permanent ~ for household use is usu. based on an emulsion of polyvinyl acetate or its copolymer with acrylic ester —K.G.Blaikie & M.S.W.Small⟩ **2** : a stiff formal manner : FORMALITY ⟨was there nothing in beautiful manners but foppery, prudery, ~, and affectation —Van Wyck Brooks⟩ **3** : a strengthening vitality : energy and resolution : resolute vigor ⟨he has . . . spine and ~, in a country sometimes lacking both —John Gunther⟩

[3]**starch** \"\ *adj* -ER/-EST : marked by a stiff formality or preciseness of manner

star-chamber \ˈ=ˈ==\ *adj* [*Star Chamber*, a court existing in England from the 15th century until 1641 that exercised wide civil and criminal jurisdiction under rules of procedure well suited to the purposes of absolutist sovereigns] **1** : of, relating to, constituting, or in the manner of a secret oppressive or irresponsible judicial body ⟨it took centuries of bloody struggle to outlaw *star-chamber* sessions, and the principle which requires judicial proceedings to be conducted in public still must be vigorously defended —*San Francisco (Calif.) News*⟩ **2** : of, relating to, constituting, or in the manner of a legislative or executive body that holds closed meetings ⟨*star-chamber* sessions of city councils and school boards —*Fortnight*⟩

star chart *n* : a chart showing the positions of the stars in a region of the sky

starch blue *n* : SMALT 2

starchboard \ˈ=,=\ *n* : a shallow wooden tray used as a container for the powdered starch in which molds or impressions for some candies are made

starch corn *n* : SPELT

star check *n* : STARSHAKE

starch equivalent *n* : the fat-producing capacity of an animal feed or ration expressed as the amount of starch required to produce the same amount of fat

starch·er \ˈstärchər\ *n* -s : one that starches; *specif* : a worker who starches cloth goods by hand or by machine

starch gum *n* : DEXTRIN

star chickweed *n* : GREAT CHICKWEED

starch·i·ly \ˈstärchəlē, ˈstȧch-, -li\ *adv* : in a starchy manner

starch·i·ness \-chēnəs, -chin-\ *n* -ES : the quality or state of being starchy ⟨the fresh ~ of her dress —Shirley A. Grau⟩; *esp* : a prim, prudish, or overly dignified formality ⟨deckhands . . . resent the growing ~ of the river cities —Murray Schumach⟩

starch layer *n* : ENDODERMIS

starch·less \-chləs\ *adj* : lacking starch

starch·ly *adv* [[3]*starch* + *-ly*] *archaic* : STARCHILY, FORMALLY

starch·man \-chmən\ *n*, *pl* **starchmen** : a worker in the starch room of a candy factory

starch·ness *n* -ES [[3]*starch* + *-ness*] : starchiness in conduct or manner : stiff formality

starch nitrate *n* : NITROSTARCH

starch room *n* : a room in which starch is applied to candies

starch sheath *n* : ENDODERMIS

starch star *n* : AMYLUM STAR

starch syrup *n* : a syrup made from starch; *esp* : CORN SYRUP

starchy \-chē, -chi\ *adj* -ER/-EST **1 a** : consisting of or containing starch ⟨~ roots⟩ **b** : resembling starch or something starched **2 a** : consisting of or having the characteristics of a stiff aloof and often prudish formality ⟨~ schoolmarms —William Manchester⟩ **b** : marked by a crotchety stiffness of manner or opinion : CRUSTY 2 ⟨a ~ retired colonel⟩

star cloud *n* **1** : a large luminous patch of the Milky Way that can be resolved with optical aid into great numbers of stars appearing to be more densely concentrated than in adjoining areas **2** : an enormous aggregation of stars forming one of the units comprising the nucleus or a spiral arm of a spiral galaxy

star cluster *n* : a relatively compact group of stars forming a gravitating unit and containing either not more than a few hundred stars or tens of thousands of stars

star color *n* : the apparent color of a star measured by its color index

star connection *n* : a method of connecting polyphase circuits in which one end of each phase line is connected to a common neutral point that may be connected to the earth as protection against lightning or to a wire to which all the other neutral points of the system are connected — compare DELTA CONNECTION

star coral *n* : any of numerous stony corals belonging to *Orbicella* and related genera in which the polyp cavities are round or polygonal and contain conspicuous radiating septa

star count *n* : a census of stars in a region of the sky usu. taken on the basis of magnitude, spectral type, or motion

star-crossed \ˈ=,=\ *adj* : not favored by the stars : ILL-FATED

star cucumber *n* : an herbaceous vine (*Sicyos angulatus*) that is native to No. America and that has branched tendrils, greenish white flowers, and prickly fruit

star cut *n* : a cut of a diamond or other gem marked by a hexagonal table bordered by six facets shaped like equilateral triangles — see CUT illustration

star day *n* : a day measured by the stars : SIDEREAL DAY

star density *n* **1** : the number of stars per unit area of a region of the sky **2** : the number of stars in a unit volume of space often expressed as per cubic parsec

star·dom \ˈstärdəm, ˈstȧd-\ *n* -s **1** : the status or position of a star ⟨a number . . . reached ~ in the various fields of entertainment —*Current Biog.*⟩ **2** : a body of stars ⟨a select body of guest soloists gathered from the ~ of European music centers —P.V.R.Key⟩

star drag *n* [so called fr. the five spokes on the fixture] : a friction brake on a saltwater fishing reel

star drill *n* : a drill for stone or masonry that has a star-shaped point and that operates by being struck with a hammer and rotated

star drum *n* : a drum (*Stellifer lanceolatus*) of the Atlantic and Gulf coasts of the U. S.

star-duckweed \ˈ=ˈ=,=\ *n* : a duckweed (*Lemna trisulca*) having fronds with very long stalks

stardust \ˈ=,=\ *n* **1** *usu* **star dust a** : a vast multitude of very small stars massed together in the night sky and suggestive of dust particles — not used scientifically **b** : COSMIC DUST — not used scientifically **2 a** : something twinkling in fine particles **b** : something light, fine, and ethereal : GOSSAMER **3** : a feeling or impression of romance, magic, or ethereality

[1]**stare** \ˈsta(a)(ə)r, ˈste(ə)r, ˈstæ(ə)\ *vb* -ED/-ING/-S [ME *staren*, fr. OE *starian*; akin to MD *staren* to stare, OHG *starēn*, ON *stara* to stare, L *strenuus* active, strenuous, Gk *stereos* solid, Lith *starinti* to stiffen; basic meaning: stiff] *vi* **1 a** : to look fixedly often with wide-open eyes (as in fear, wonder, surprise, or impudence) : fasten an earnest and prolonged gaze on an object or look blankly into space ⟨he *stared* into her eyes —Clarissa F. Cushman⟩ ⟨*staring* into the darkness beyond the circle of light —Sherwood Anderson⟩ **b** *archaic* : to glare in anger or madness **2 a** : to have a blank empty appearance ⟨*staring* rows of ghostly blue factory windows —*Amer. Guide Series: Mich.*⟩ **b** : to show oneself conspicuously ⟨loneliness . . . ~s between the lines of this volume —V.S.Pritchett⟩ ⟨*staring* white benches against the green —Fletcher Steele⟩ **3 a** *of hair* : to stand on end : BRISTLE **b** : to appear rough and lusterless — used of the coat of an animal out of condition ~ *vt* **1** : to have an effect upon by staring ⟨uncertain whether to ~ the eye out of its hole —Christopher Isherwood⟩ **2** : to look at with a searching or earnest overall gaze ⟨a fat old lady . . . with the most extraordinary insolence *stared* him up and down —H.J.Kaplan⟩ **syn** see GAZE — **stare one in the face** : to be undeniably and forcefully evident or apparent ⟨the significant difficulties that *stare us in the face* —George Sampson⟩

[2]**stare** \"\ *n* -s [ME, fr. *staren*, v.] **1** *archaic* : a state of fear or amazement **2** : the act or an instance of staring : a prolonged fixed gaze (as of fear, astonishment, or admiration)

[3]**stare** \"\ *n*, *pl* **stares** *also* **stare** [ME, fr. OE *stær* — more at STARLING] *archaic* : STARLING

sta·re de·ci·sis \ˌsta(a)rēdəˈsīsəs\ *n* [L, to stand by decided matters] : the doctrine or policy of following rules or principles laid down in previous judicial decisions unless they contravene the ordinary principles of justice — compare DICTUM

stare down *vt* : to cause to waver or submit by or as if by staring : overcome by calm resolute steadiness of purpose and action : OUTSTARE ⟨though the dog threatened to attack, he was *stared down*⟩ ⟨intending frankly to ~ her down —B.A. Williams⟩

star·er \ˈsta(a)rə(r), ˈster-\ *n* -s : one that stares

sta·rets \ˈstä,rets\ *n*, *pl* **star·tsy** \ˈstärtsē\ [Russ, lit., venerable old man, fr. *staryĭ* old — more at STOUR] : a spiritual director or religious teacher and counselor in the Eastern Orthodox Church : a spiritual advisor who is not necessarily a priest, who is recognized for his piety, and who is turned to by monks or members of the laity for spiritual guidance

starey *also* **stary** \ˈsta(a)rē\ *adj* **starier; stariest** : staring or given to staring; *specif* : wild, glaring, and fixed esp. as a result of ill health ⟨a dog with ~ eyes⟩

star facet *n* : one of the eight small triangular facets which abut on the table in the bezel of a brilliant — see BRILLIANT illustration

star feed *n* : a feeding device for a machine tool consisting of a star wheel attached to one end of the feed screw and a stop pin clamped so that it contacts with and turns the star wheel at each revolution of the toolhead

star field *n* : a region of the sky containing stars either as seen in a telescope or recorded on a photograph

starfish \ˈ=,=\ *n* : any of numerous echinoderms that constitute the class Asteroidea, that have a body of usu. five radially disposed arms coalescing at the center to form a disk on the lower surface of which is the mouth and containing prolongations of the body cavity and of the digestive tract and other organs, a skeleton composed of small more or less movable ossicles, and ambulacral areas occupying furrows along the under surface of each arm and bearing rows of tube feet by means of which the animal crawls and grasps its prey, and that feed largely on mollusks and esp. oysters

starfish flower *n* : a plant of the genus *Stapelia* (esp. *S. asterias*)

starflower \ˈ=,==\ *n* : any of several plants having star-shaped pentamerous flowers: as **a** : STAR-OF-BETHLEHEM **b** : a plant of the genus *Trientalis* (esp. *T. americana*) **c** : a chickweed of the genus *Alsine* **d** : a plant of the genus *Brodiaea*

starfruit \ˈ=,=\ *n* : a European water plant (*Damasonium stellatum*) of the family Alismataceae having spreading pointed carpels

star·ful \ˈstärfəl\ *adj*, *archaic* : full of stars : dotted thickly with stars

star gauge *n* **1** : an instrument for measuring bore diameters that consists of a long rod having a micrometer handle and a head fitted to receive adjustable radial steel points **2** : a count of the stars visible in standard areas in different portions of the heavens

star-gauge \ˈ=,=\ *vt* [*star gauge*] : to measure with a star gauge

star·gaze \ˈstär,gāz, -tȧ,-\ *vi* [back-formation fr. *stargazer*] **1** : to gaze at stars **2** : to gaze raptly or contemplatively

star·gaz·er \-zə(r)\ *n* [[1]*star* + *gazer*] **1 a** : one that gazes at the stars: as (1) : ASTROLOGER (2) : ASTRONOMER **b** : one that makes predictions and esp. unjustified predictions **2 a** : any of several marine percoid fishes belonging to the family Uranoscopidae that have the eyes on top of the head looking directly upward and that include several forms (as a common fish (*Astroscopus y-graecum*) of the eastern U. S.) that possess electric organs produced from the modified eye muscles **b** : any of various other fishes having the eyes on the top of the head **3** : a horse that carries its head too high

star·gaz·ing \-ziŋ, -zēŋ\ *n* -s [[1]*star* + *gazing*, gerund of *gaze*] **1** : the act or practice of a stargazer **2 a** : absorption in chimerical or impractical ideas **b** : ABSENTMINDEDNESS, DAYDREAMING

star gear *n* : a lobate somewhat star-shaped gear wheel used as a variable gear

star ghost *n* : a faint image often seen accompanying the main image of brighter stars and planets due usu. to reflection from lenses of an eyepiece or of a camera

starglory \ˈ=,==\ *n* : CYPRESS VINE 1

star grass *n* [[1]*star* + *grass*] **1** : an herb of the genus *Hypoxis* **2** : COLICROOT 1 **3** : BLUE-EYED GRASS **4** : WATER STARWORT **5** *Austral* : WINDMILL GRASS **6** : any of several grasses of the genus *Cynodon*; *esp* : GIANT STAR GRASS

star hummingbird *n* : STAR 9

star hyacinth *n* **1** : a spring-blooming European squill (*Scilla amoena*) with pale blue flowers **2** : a star-of-Bethlehem (*Ornithogalum umbellatum*)

starier *comparative of* STAREY *or of* STARY

stariest *superlative of* STAREY *or of* STARY

staring *pres part of* STARE

star·ing·ly *adv* **1** : in a staring manner : with a stare **2** : in an obtrusively obvious manner : GLARINGLY

star ipomoea *n* : a tropical American annual vine (*Quamoclit coccinea*) having red flowers, a long tube with yellow throat, and cupped spreading limb

star jasmine *n* : a Chinese woody vine (*Trachelospermum jasminoides*) with evergreen leaves and white fragrant flowers resembling jasmine flowers — called also *confederate jasmine*

star jelly *n* [so called fr. a popular belief that the gelatinous colonies fall from the stars] : any of several algae that form gelatinous colonies; *esp* : any of various algae of the genus *Nostoc* (esp. *N. commune*) that tend to form irregular or globular firm gelatinous pellets on marshy or frequently inundated ground

[1]**stark** \ˈstärk, ˈstȧk\ *adj* -ER/-EST [ME, stiff, strong, fr. OE *stearc*; akin to OHG *starc* strong, *gistorchanēn* to coagulate, ON *sterkr* strong, *storkna* to coagulate, Goth *gastaurknan* to become stiff, Lith *strėgti* to freeze, OE *starian* to stare — more at STARE] **1 a** : strongly constructed : STURDY, STOUT **b** : possessing physical strength : ROBUST, VIGOROUS **c** *chiefly Scot*, *of liquor* : STRONG, INTOXICATING **2 a** : lacking in flexibility or suppleness : rigid in or as if in death ⟨still unburied, lay along the wall, stiff and ~ —R.L.Stevenson⟩ ⟨~ with unbearable wet cold —Helen Rich⟩ **b** : conforming completely to pattern, precept, or doctrine : FIRM, UNBENDING, STRICT ⟨military strength, based of necessity on ~ discipline —H.J. Mackinder⟩ ⟨had a faith in law that was too ~ and literal —Irving Babbitt⟩ **3** : PURE, SHEER, UTTER ⟨~ brutality unredeemed by their tigerish grace —Miriam Allott⟩ ⟨~ denial was his plain course —Arthur Morrison⟩ ⟨~ nonsense⟩ **4** : violently stormy or windy : extremely inclement **5 a** [by shortening] : STARK-NAKED ⟨boys ~ except for breechclouts —Hervey Allen⟩ **b** : BLEAK, BARREN, DESOLATE ⟨the terrain has been rendered even more ~ by deforestation and consequent erosion —*Amer. Guide Series: Minn.*⟩ **c** (1) : having few or no ornaments, attachments, or appurtenances : appearing stripped : BARE, EMPTY ⟨rooms that were as ~ as the rooms of the white cottage had been crowded —D.B.Doner⟩ ⟨winter white offset by ~ branches —Constance Foster⟩ (2) : consisting of or presenting a simple, harsh, or blunt unadorned style or treatment ⟨critics and readers alike have commented on the ~ realism . . . of the torture scenes —Lionel Trilling⟩ ⟨a ~ description of a very graceful movement —Warwick Braithwaite⟩ **6 a** : furnishing or being furnished with an appearance of marked contrast from visual surroundings through outline, color, or texture ⟨crags in ~ outline against the sky⟩ **b** : sharply delineated : glaringly obvious ⟨there is one ~ antithesis which embraces . . . science, politics and philosophy

—Hugh Ross Williamson⟩ ⟨the ~ facts of power politics —John Mason Brown⟩ syn see STIFF

²stark \"\ adv 1 : STARKLY 2 : WHOLLY, ABSOLUTELY, QUITE ⟨~ mad⟩ ⟨rich men who were once ~ poor —Myron Brinig⟩ ⟨eyes shut and mouth ~ open —Douglas Newton⟩

³stark \'shtärk\ adv (or adj) [G, lit., strong, fr. OHG starc] : LOUDLY, FORTE — used as a direction in music

stark effect \'stärk-\ n, usu cap S [after Johannes Stark †1957 Ger. physicist] : the broadening or resolution into components of spectrum lines as the result of subjecting the source of light to an intense electric field — compare ZEEMAN EFFECT

stark·en \'stärkən\ vb -ED/-ING/-S [ME starknen, fr. ¹stark + -nen -en] : STIFFEN and shrank with decay —Waldo Frank⟩

stark·ly adv [ME, fr. OE stearclice strongly, fr. stearc stiff, strong + -lice -ly] : in a stark manner ⟨~ unable to achieve coherence —L.R.Ward⟩: as a : in sharp outline or contrast ⟨blackened stone walls rose ~ from the snow —F.V.W.Mason⟩ b : in a blunt or spare manner ⟨lit ~ by fluorescent lights —Christopher Rand⟩ ⟨state the problem in ~ realistic terms —Amer. Guide Series: N. Y.⟩

stark-naked \'≠≠,≠\ adj [alter. (influenced by ²stark) of start-naked, fr. ME start naked, stert naked, fr. start, stert tail + naked — more at START] : wholly naked : quite bare

stark·ness n -ES [ME starkenesse stiffness, fr. starke, stark stiff, strong + -nesse -ness] : the quality or state of being stark

star knot n : a usu. 5-stranded decorative knot tied in the end of a rope

star-leaved gum \'≠≠,≠\ n : SWEET GUM 1

star·less \'stärlǝs, -tǝl-\ adj [ME sterreles, fr. sterre star + -les -less] : without stars ⟨a ~ night⟩ — **star·less·ly** adv — **star·less·ness** n -ES

star·let \-lǝt, usu -ǝd-\ n -s 1 : a little star 2 : a young movie actress who is being coached and publicized for starring roles

starlight \'≠,≠\ n [ME sterrelight, fr. sterre star + light] : the light given by the stars

starlight blue n : a pale purplish blue that is paler and slightly bluer than hydrangea blue, bluer than haze blue, and bluer than moonstone blue

starlighted \'≠,≠\ adj : STARLIT

starlights \'≠,≠\ n pl 1 : DOVE'S-FOOT 2 : BLUET 1c

¹**starlike** \'≠,≠\ adj : resembling a star: as a : shining like a star ⟨a ~ light⟩ b : radiated like a star ⟨~ flowers⟩

²**starlike** \"\ adv : in the manner of a star

star lily n : SAND LILY

¹**star·ling** \'stärliŋ, -täl-, -lēŋ\ n -s [ME starling, sterling, fr. OE stærlinc, fr. stær starling + -linc, -ling -ling; akin to OE stearn, a bird, prob. fr. OHG stara starling, ON stari, L sturnus starling, OPruss starnite gull] 1 a : any of the family Sturnidae; esp : a dark brown or in summer plumage greenish black bird (Sturnus vulgaris) that has a metallic gloss, is spotted with yellowish white, lives sociably and builds nests around dwellings and structures, and is native to Europe but has been introduced in the U.S., Australia, and New Zealand where it is often a pest — see ROSE-COLORED STARLING b : an American bird of the family Icteridae 2 : BEAVER 6

²**starling** obs var of STERLING

³**star·ling** \'≠≠\ n -s [prob. alter. of stadling obs. E staddling, fr. ME stadeling, fr. (assumed) ME stadel foundation, support (alter. of ME stathel) + ME -inge, -ing -ing — more at STADDLE] : a projecting pointed or rounded structure of piles driven close together around a pier of a bridge and often filled with gravel or stone to protect the pier by breaking water, ice, or drift

starling's-egg green \'≠≠,≠\ n : COURT GRAY

star·ling's law \'stärliŋz-\ n, usu cap S [after Ernest H. Starling †1927 Eng. physiologist] : a statement in physiology: a muscle that is stretched within normal limits at the time of stimulation contracts more strongly than one that is completely relaxed

starling stone n : the petrified stem of a fossil fern (genus Psaronius) that shows in a polished cross section markings resembling those on the feathers of a starling

starlit \'≠,≠\ adj : lighted by the stars

star·lite \'stär,līt\ n -s [blend of starlight and -lite] : a blue zircon produced by heating a dark brown zircon from Thailand with potassium cyanide

star lot n : so called fr. the marking of such a lot with an asterisk in a catalog] : a small lot of baled wool (as three bales or less) to be sold at auction

star magnolia n : an early-blooming Japanese shrubby magnolia (Magnolia stellata) that is used as an ornamental and has fragrant often pink-tinged white star-shaped flowers blooming before the leaves unfold

star map n : a map often made by photography that gives the positions and magnitudes of the stars

star melanose n : a disease of citrus that results from late spring or summer sprays esp. of copper and is distinguished from melanose by the star-shaped longitudinally split lesions on the leaves

star metal n : STAR ANTIMONY

star-mop n : a tangle for catching starfish

starn \'stärn\ n -s [ME sterne, starne, of Scand origin; akin to ON stjarna star — more at STAR] Scot : STAR

starn·ie \-ni\ n -s [starn + -ie] Scot : STARLET 1

star-nosed mole \'≠,≠\ also **starnose** \"≠≠\ n : a common black long-tailed semiaquatic No. American mole (Condylura cristata) distinguished by a series of pink fleshy projections surrounding the nostrils

star nut palm n : a palm of the genus Astrocaryum

starny \'stärni\ adj [starn + -y] Scot : STARRY

star-of-bethlehem or **star-of-bethlehem** usu cap B [Bethlehem, ancient town in Judaea; prob. fr. a supposed resemblance of the flower to the star which according to Mt 2:9 guided the wise men from the East to the place where they were to find the child Jesus in Bethlehem] 1 : a plant of the genus Ornithogalum; esp : a common Old World herb (O. umbellatum) with greenish flowers that is naturalized in the eastern U. S. — called also sleepy dick 2 : AMAZON LILY 3 : an Australian plant (Chamaescilla corymbosa) of the family Liliaceae 4 : a Tasmanian plant (Burchardia umbellata) of the family Liliaceae 5 : any of several starflowers; esp : STARWORT 6 : BLUET 1c

star of david or **star of david** usu cap S&D : MAGEN DAVID

star of texas usu cap T [Texas, southwestern state of the U. S.] : an annual or biennial composite herb (Xanthium texanum) common in the prairie regions of the southern U. S. and also cultivated that has alternate leaves, yellow flower heads solitary or in pairs, and involucral bracts with a whitish margin

star-of-the-earth \'≠≠≠'≠\ n : BUCKHORN 3b(1)

star of the veldt n : DIMORPHOTHECA 2

star pepper n : BITTER PEPPER

star phlox n : any of several garden phloxes with narrow sharp-pointed often fringed or cut petals

star pine n : CLUSTER PINE

star place or **star position** n : the position of a fixed star usu. located by its right ascension and declination — compare MEAN PLACE

star plum n : STAR APPLE

star primrose n : a primrose that is a variety (Primula sinensis stellata) of the Chinese primrose in which the flowers occur superimposed in umbels

star quartz n : asteriated quartz

starred \'stärd, 'städ\ adj [ME sterred, fr. sterre star + -ed] 1 a : adorned with or as if with stars b : marked with or having the shape of a star 2 : affected in fortune by the stars

starred lizard n : an agamid lizard (Agama stellio) common about the eastern Mediterranean

star·rer \'stärə(r)\ n -s : a production starring a specified performer

star-ribbed vault var of STAR VAULT

star·ri·ly \'stärǝlē, -li\ adv : in starlike fashion, position, character, or manner ⟨the inhabitants of a world of thought ~ remote from theirs —Aldous Huxley⟩

star·ri·ness \-rēnǝs\ n -ES : the quality or state of being starry

starring pres part of STAR

star root n [so called fr. the fact that the leaves rise directly fr. the root and spread out in star shape] : DEVIL'S BIT b

star route n [so called fr. the fact that the star asterisk is used to designate such routes in postal publications] : a mail-delivery route in a rural or thinly populated area served by a private carrier under contract who takes mail from one post office to another or from a railroad station to a post office and usu. also delivers mail to private mailboxes along the route — compare RURAL ROUTE

star ruby n : an asteriated variety of ruby

star·ry \'stärē, -ri\ adj -ER/-EST [ME sterry, fr. sterre star + -y] 1 a : abounding with stars : adorned or studded with stars ⟨heavens⟩ b : of, relating to, consisting of, or proceeding from the stars : STELLAR ⟨~ light⟩ c : shining like stars : SPARKLING ⟨~ with gold and gem —A.E.Housman⟩ d : arranged in rays like those of a star : STELLATE 2 a : as high as or seemingly as high as the stars : AIRY ⟨~ speculations of what mankind may do —H.G.Wells⟩ b : aspiring to stardom ⟨the ~ scrambling of the twain —Osbert Sitwell⟩ 3 : composed of star performers : having an unusual number of stars in the cast ⟨you have to follow up one star program with another even more ~ —I.J.C.Brown⟩

starry campion n : a catchfly (Silene stellata) of the eastern U. S. having white somewhat star-shaped flowers

starry-eyed \'≠≠'≠\ adj : regarding an object or a prospect in an overly favorable light ⟨romantic enough to please the most starry-eyed girl —Times Lit. Supp.⟩; specif : VISIONARY ⟨may still think of this conception as radical, crackpot, starry-eyed and thoroughly unrealistic —A.L.Guérard⟩ ⟨starry-eyed advocates of world government in our time —Current History⟩

starry flounder n : a large dark brown mottled flatfish (Platichthys stellatus) of both coasts of the north Pacific that is distinguished by a small mouth with projecting lower jaw and star-shaped tubercles scattered over the head and body and is a commercially important food fish esp. along the California coast

starry grasswort n : GRASSWORT

starry magnolia n : STAR MAGNOLIA

starry puffball n : EARTHSTAR

starry ray n : a skate (Raja radiata) common on the European coasts and occasionally on the Atlantic coast of America having large dorsal spines with stellate bases

starry rockfish n : a rather small rockfish (Sebastodes constellatus) of the southern California and Lower California coast that is chiefly yellow to red above sprinkled with pale dots and fading to yellowish or pinkish white below

stars pl of STAR, pres 3d sing of STAR

star sapphire n : a sapphire that when cut with a convex surface and polished exhibits asterism resulting from there being microscopic crystals in various orientations within the gem

star saxifrage n : a small arctic or alpine saxifrage (Saxifraga stellaris) having small starlike white flowers

star scout n : a boy scout who has been awarded five merit badges — compare EAGLE SCOUT, LIFE SCOUT

starshake \'≠,≠\ n : a check in timber beginning near the heart and extending toward the surface in radial cracks or fissures — called also star check

star shell n [star + shell] 1 : a shell that on bursting releases a shower of brilliant stars and is used for signaling 2 : a shell with an illuminating projectile

starshell \'≠,≠\ n [star + shell] : a West Indian turban shell (Astraea longispina) having the margin of the whorls prolonged by hollow triangular spines; broadly : any of several other members of the genus Astraea

starshine \'≠,≠\ n : the glow of the stars : STARLIGHT

star·ship \'stär,ship\ n : a rocket or other ship designed for travel in interstellar space

starshoot or **starshot** \'≠,≠\ n -s : a star jelly (Nostoc commune)

star sight n : an observation of the altitude of a star made for navigational purposes

star skunk n : a common skunk of the genus Mephitis in which the normal white areas are reduced to one or two small white patches so that the coat is nearly all black

star-spangled \'≠≠,≠\ adj 1 : studded with stars 2 [fr. the fact that the flag of the U. S. has frequently been described as star-spangled since the composition of the patriotic song The Star-Spangled Banner in 1814 by Francis Scott Key †1843 Am. lawyer] a : of, relating to, or characteristic of the U. S. or its citizens ⟨ripsnorting star-spangled frontiersmen —R.A.Billington⟩ b : extremely patriotic with regard to the U. S.

star spot n : a bright or dark spot on the surface of a star inferred from photometric or spectroscopic observations and thought to be similar in nature to a sunspot

starstone \'≠,≠\ n : an asteriated stone; esp : STAR SAPPHIRE

star streaming n : real or apparent systematic drift of the stars

star system n 1 : a group of stars showing common characteristics of location and motion : GALAXY 2 : the dependence upon and extensive advertising of stars in motion pictures and the theater often to the extent of writing or altering a play or screenplay to fit a star's talents

¹**start** \'stärt, -tä\, usu \d-ə\V\ n -s [ME start, stert handle, tail, fr. OE steort tail; akin to MD stert, start, OHG sterz, ON stertr tail, OE starian to stare — more at STARE] : a curved or projecting part or section: as a : the curved or inclined front and bottom of a waterwheel bucket b : the lever of a gin driven around by a horse

²**start** \"\ vb -ED/-ING/-S [ME sterten; akin to MHG sterzen to move quickly, stand up stiffly, OE sterta to crease, OE starian to stare — more at STARE] vi 1 a : to move suddenly and violently from a state of stillness or rest : DART, JUMP, SPRING ⟨everywhere men and women ~ed from their beds at the shots —Marjory S. Douglas⟩ ⟨~ed to his feet angrily —Liam O'Flaherty⟩ — often used with up ⟨now falls on her bed, and then ~s up —Shak.⟩ b : to draw back : FLINCH, RECOIL ⟨she skipped forward to the pit . . . but she ~ed back in surprise —George Eliot⟩ c : to awaken suddenly ⟨~ed from my sleep with horror —Mary W. Shelley⟩ ⟨~ed from her reverie with a shiver —G.B.Shaw⟩ d : to react (as to something that frightens, surprises, or disgusts) with a sudden brief involuntary movement : become startled ⟨stepped stealthily, and ~ed when a twig snapped underfoot —Margaret Deland⟩ ⟨she never ~ or shows surprise —Rose Macaulay⟩ ⟨why do you ~ and seem to fear things that do sound so fair —Shak.⟩ 2 a : to issue, flow, or enter with sudden force : BURST ⟨blood ~ing from the wound⟩ ⟨tears ~ing from her eyes⟩ b : to arise, emerge, or break out suddenly ⟨in a few short paragraphs, the characters ~ into life⟩ — often used with up ⟨new settlements ~ed up all around them⟩ ⟨a man who ~ed up from obscurity⟩ c : to come into being, activity, or operation : BEGIN, COMMENCE ⟨the blood is all ready and waiting for a few days, only to ~ all over again —Justina Hill⟩ ⟨as soon as the battle ~ed, he left his command post —H.L. Merillat⟩ 3 : to protrude or seem to protrude : BULGE ⟨the men of the regiment, with their ~ing eyes and sweating faces —Stephen Crane⟩ : to work itself open or free : become loosened ⟨one of the planks has ~ed⟩ ⟨a nail has ~ed⟩ b : of an arrow : to be pulled suddenly out of the line of aim when loosed ⟨of book leaves : to extend beyond the regular free edge because loosened at the backbone 5 archaic : to deviate from one's course or duty : DESERT, REVOLT 6 a : to begin a forward movement : take off on a course or progress : set out ⟨the train is ready to ~⟩ ⟨the expedition ~ed north⟩ ⟨five cars ~ but only three finished⟩ b : to range from a specified initial point ⟨the rates ~ at ten dollars⟩ ⟨prices ~ with A⟩ ⟨a succession of expressions, ~ing with a gentle smile and finishing with a broad grin —Wilfred Campfield⟩ 7 a : to begin an activity or undertaking ⟨as soon as you're ready to play, we'll ~⟩ ⟨as a novelist, he ~s with a double handicap⟩ ⟨~ed in business on a shoestring⟩ b : to begin work ⟨when do I ~⟩ — sometimes used with in ⟨after a brief period of training⟩ c (1) : to be a contestant or entry in a race or field trial (2) : to be in the lineup at the beginning of a game (as baseball or football) ⟨despite his injury, he will ~ in center field⟩ ⟨a left-hander will probably ~ for the home team⟩ ⟨~ed at quarterback⟩ ~ vt 1 : to drive from a place of concealment into

the open : cause to move so as to be discovered : FLUSH ⟨~ed a deer on the banks of this stream —Amer. Guide Series: Vt.⟩ ⟨~ a hare⟩ 2 archaic : to disturb suddenly : STARTLE, ALARM ⟨every feather ~s you —Shak.⟩ 3 : to bring up for consideration or discussion : INTRODUCE, PROPOUND ⟨~ed a subject in which he expected him to shine —Jane Austen⟩ 4 a : to bring into being : INITIATE, ORIGINATE ⟨~ a story that his opponent was a crook⟩ ⟨~ed the modernist movement in art⟩ ⟨~ed the custom many years ago⟩ b : to set up : ESTABLISH, FOUND ⟨a college⟩ ⟨~ a newspaper⟩ 5 a : to cause to become loosened or displaced ⟨the pounding of the waves ~ed some of the rivets⟩ b : to break out ⟨~ the anchor⟩ c : to ease off : SLACKEN ⟨~ a rope⟩ 6 a : to discharge, empty ⟨~ the contents of the barrel into a new cask⟩ b : to begin the use of ⟨~ a new keg of beer⟩ ⟨a fresh loaf of bread⟩ 7 a : to set going : cause to move, act, or operate ⟨was unable to ~ the car⟩ ⟨wound the clock to ~ it running again⟩ ⟨~ed his son in business⟩ b : to cause (a motor) to begin running on its own ignition — often used with up c (1) : to enter in a race or contest ⟨plans to ~ the horse in only a few races this year⟩ (2) : to put into a game at the beginning ⟨~ed the rookie at third but took him out after three innings⟩ d : to begin the employment of : take on ⟨the company ~ed him at the same salary he had been getting on his previous job⟩ ⟨the station ~ed him as a news announcer⟩ e : to care for during the early stages of growth and development : initiate the raising or training of ⟨~ed chicks⟩ ⟨a well-started coonhound⟩ 8 : to perform the first stages or actions of : enter on ⟨~ed studying music at the age of three⟩ ⟨~ed to load the truck⟩ ⟨~ed what seemed like an impossible job⟩ syn see BEGIN

start something : to make trouble : create a disturbance ⟨a man with a chip on his shoulder who's always trying to start something⟩ — **to start with** : at the beginning ⟨standing cans in brine will not stop souring for several hours if the milk is warm —Farmer's Weekly (So. Africa)⟩

³**start** \"\ n -s [ME stert, fr. sterten, v.] 1 a : a sudden involuntary movement or reaction ⟨gave a little ~ of surprise —R.H.Davis⟩ ⟨jerked the reins so hard that her mother came out of her thoughts with a ~ —Margaret Deland⟩ : brief and sudden action or movement : BOUND ⟨nature does nothing by ~s and leaps —Roger L'Estrange⟩ ⟨does things by fits and ~s⟩ b obs : a sudden excursion or flight ⟨use your legs, take the ~, run away —Shak.⟩ d : a sudden capricious impulse or outburst : FIT, SALLY ⟨~s and aberrations of fancy welling up from springs of suppressed romance —Edith Wharton⟩ e : a sudden burst of sound or speech ⟨she did speak in ~s distractedly —Shak.⟩ 2 a : a beginning of movement, activity, or development : initial impulse, motion, or action ⟨made a good ~ in life⟩ ⟨the work is off to a promising ~⟩ ⟨the horse made a false ~ and had to be called back⟩ ⟨building ~s⟩ ⟨housing ~s⟩ b : a lead or handicap at the beginning of a race or competition : ADVANTAGE, HEAD START ⟨gave them a five minutes' ~ and then went after them⟩ ⟨the early sea trade of the inhabitants of the island world . . . gave them a ~ over their neighbors —Edward Clodd⟩ c (1) : the act or action of setting into motion : the imparting of motion ⟨gave the car a ~ by pushing it⟩ (2) : help in beginning or undertaking something ⟨gave him a ~ in his career or project⟩ ⟨gave him his ~ in business⟩ d : a place of beginning : point of departure ⟨five cars lined up at the ~⟩ ⟨selected the old mill as the ~ of the hike⟩ 3 : an unusual, interesting, or surprising incident or event : a peculiar circumstance ⟨of all the queer ~s . . . me, meeting you like this —Richard Dehan⟩ 4 a : something that has started : DISPLACEMENT b starts pl : book leaves that have started 5 : the act or an instance of being a competitor in a race or a member of a starting lineup in a game ⟨finished no worse than second in his last six ~s⟩ ⟨pitched an excellent game in his first ~⟩

start·er \'≠d-ə(r), 'tə(r)\ n -s 1 : one who initiates or sets going ⟨one of the ~s of the scientific revolution⟩: as a : an official who gives the signal to begin a race b (1) : DISPATCHER a (2) : DISPATCHER f c : one that does hat sizing 2 a (1) : one that enters a competition or sets out in a race ⟨a late ~ in the contest for the nomination⟩ ⟨an added ~ in the second race⟩ (2) : STARTING PITCHER b : one that begins to engage in an activity or process ⟨is not a tactful man, nor a slow, easy ~ —John Bird⟩ 3 : one that causes something (as a mechanism or process) to begin operating: as a : a controller that accelerates a motor to normal speed in one direction of rotation but that is not adapted for sustained use in positions intermediate between the off and full-on positions b : SELF-STARTER c : a strip of foundation placed in a frame or section in a hive to facilitate comb-building by honeybees d : material containing microorganisms used to induce a desired fermentation (as in making butter, cheese, or vinegar) and being either a sample of a natural population (as sour cream or vinegar) or a pure culture of a defined microorganism — compare FERMENT 1a e : a compound used to start a chemical reaction f : a specially prepared food or nutrient used to promote vigorous growth in very young animals or plants ⟨a calf ~⟩ ⟨a chick ~⟩ g : a device (as a drill or punch) used for starting a hole 4 a : something that is the beginning of a process, activity, or series : a first step ⟨will sink something over a million dollars into this plant just as a ~ —Green Peyton⟩ ⟨as a ~, the linguists began asking the names of everyday things —Time⟩ b (1) : a card that is cut and turned face up on the top of the stock after cribbage players have shuffled and dealt for the crib (2) : UPCARD c : EAVES TILE

starter set n : a small set of 16 or 20 dishes usu. comprising a service for four persons — compare PLACE SETTING

star thistle n : any of various plants of the genus Centaurea: as a : an annual or biennial herb (Centaurea calcitrapa) having a basal rosette of deeply toothed leaves, a much branched stem, and axillary or terminal heads of pinkish to purple tubular flowers surrounded by scales tipped with long stout yellow spines and being native to the Mediterranean region but widely distributed by commerce and in many places established as an aggressive weed b : BARNABY'S THISTLE c : BASKET FLOWER d : RUSSIAN KNAPWEED

starthroat \'≠,≠\ n : either of two Brazilian hummingbirds of the genus Heliomaster whose throat feathers have a metallic luster

star time n : SIDEREAL TIME

starting pres part of START

starting bar n : GEE-THROW

starting block n : a device that provides a runner with a rigid surface against which to brace his feet at the start of a race and that consists of two pedals or blocks mounted on either side of a frame usu. anchored in the ground

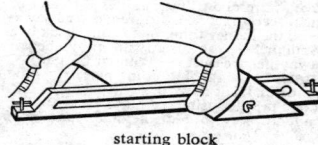

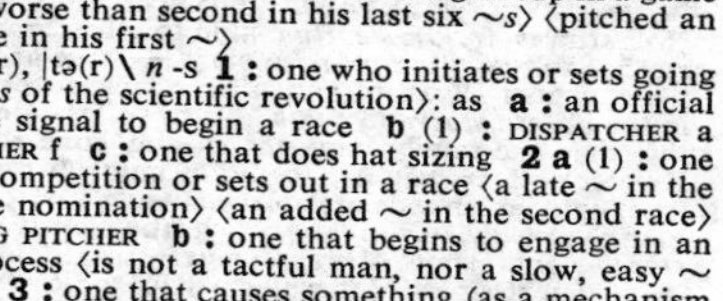

starting block

starting box n : RHEOSTAT

starting friction n : STATIC FRICTION

starting gate n : a mechanically operated barrier used as a starting device for a race

starting grid n : a paved area adjacent to the track on which automobiles line up for the start of a race 2 : a starting area on the track itself

starting hole n, archaic : a place of refuge : LOOPHOLE ⟨what trick, what device, what starting hole canst thou now find out to hide thee —Shak.⟩

start·ing·ly adv : in a starting manner ⟨why do you speak so ~ and rash —Shak.⟩

starting pitcher n : a baseball pitcher usu. used in regular rotation (as every fourth day) to start a game and usu. expected to pitch a complete game — compare RELIEF PITCHER

starting punch n : ³PUNCH 1a(4)

starting sheet n : a thin sheet of metal which is used as cathode in electrolytic refining and on which the refined metal is electrodeposited

starting torque n : the torque applied by an electric motor at standstill

¹**star·tle** \'stärt|d-əl, -tāl, |t²l\ vb startled; startled; startling \|d-əliŋ, |t(²)l-\ startles [ME stertlen, fr. sterten to start +

-*len* -le — more at START] *vi* **1** *chiefly Scot* **:** to run about wildly **2 a :** to move or jump suddenly as in surprise, fear, or alarm ⟨babies who ~ easily —Benjamin Spock⟩ ⟨the nervous creature who ~*s* at every sudden sound —J.H.Newman⟩ **b :** to awake suddenly from sleep or a dormant state ~ *vt* **1 :** to excite or rouse by sudden alarm, surprise, fear, or shock **:** frighten or affect suddenly and usu. not seriously **:** cause to start ⟨*startled* to see a ghostly silhouette of a submarine —Stewart Beach⟩ **2** *archaic* **:** to make irresolute **:** cause to waver ⟨can discover nothing that may ~ a discreet belief —Sir Thomas Browne⟩ **3 :** to bring into a specified state by or as if by startling ⟨ferns that the first rain ~*s* to green life —Marjory S. Douglas⟩ ⟨her blank face *startled* the end of his remark out of his mind —Ellen Glasgow⟩ **syn** see FRIGHTEN

²**startle** \"\ *n* -s **1 :** a sudden mild shock as of surprise or alarm **:** START **2 :** a marked tendency to display the startle pattern esp. under conditions of apparently inadequate stimulation

startle pattern *or* **startle reaction** *or* **startle response** *n* **:** the complex of psychophysiological changes that is elicited in an organism by an unexpected sudden stimulus (as a loud noise) and includes tremor, sweating, palpitation, dry mouth, and a feeling of fear or panic sometimes followed by escape or avoidance reactions

star·tler \ˈd·ᵊlə(r), ˌt(ᵊ)l-\ *n* -s **:** one that startles ⟨the investigation uncovered a ~⟩

startling *adj* **1 :** easily frightened **:** RESTLESS, SKITTISH **2 :** causing a momentary shock, fright, surprise, or astonishment by a mild or forcible demand upon the attention **:** consisting of or exhibiting shocking, bizarre, or extremely or mildly unusual features ⟨~ earthquake shocks —*Amer. Guide Series: Ind.*⟩ ⟨a ~ roadster, all streamlines and cream paint —Sinclair Lewis⟩ ⟨~ economies of expression —Margery Bailey⟩ — **star·tling·ly** *adv* — **star·tling·ness** *n* -ES

star·tlish \ˈd·ᵊlish, ˌt(ᵊ)l-\ *also* **star·tly** \ˈd·ᵊlē ˌt(ᵊ)lē\ *adj* **:** SKITTISH — **star·tlish·ness** *n* -ES

start–naked \ˈstärtˌnākəd\ *dial var of* STARK-NAKED

star tortoise *n* **:** an Indian tortoise (*Testudo elegans*) with a sculptured carapace, black with yellow markings, and two yellow stars on the black plastron

star trail *n* **:** a continuous line produced on a photographic plate by the image of a star during an exposure in which the camera or telescope does not follow the diurnal motion of the star or follows the motion of some other celestial body (as a comet) that is being photographed

starts *pl of* START, *pres 3d sing of* START

startsy *pl of* STARETS

star tulip *n* **:** MARIPOSA LILY

¹**start–up** \ˈ⸗,⸗\ *adj* [obs. E *start up*, past part. of E *start up*, v.] *archaic* **:** UPSTART

²**start–up** \"\ *n* -s [¹*start-up*] **1** *obs* **:** UPSTART ⟨that young *start-up* hath all the glory of my overthrow —Shak.⟩ **2** [fr. *start up*, v.] **:** the act or an instance of setting in operation or motion

start–ups \ˈstärtəps\ *n pl* [fr. *start up*, v.] **1** *obs* **:** low boots **2** *dial Eng* **:** LEGGINGS

star turn *n, chiefly Brit* **:** the featured skit or number in a theatrical production; *broadly* **:** the most widely publicized person or item in a group

star·va·tion \stärˈvāshən, stȧ'-\ *n* -s **:** the action or an instance of starving or the state of being starved

starvation wages *n* **:** wages insufficient to provide the ordinary necessities of life

star vault \ˈ⸗-\ *or* **star–ribbed vault** \ˈ⸗,⸗-\ *n* **:** a ribbed vault in which the ribs and liernes are arranged in a starlike pattern

starve \ˈstärv, ˈstȧv\ *vb* **starved; starved; starving; starves** [ME *sterven*, fr. OE *steorfan*; akin to OFris *sterva* to die, OHG *sterban* to die, OE *starian* to stare — more at STARE] *vi* **1** *obs* **:** DIE, PERISH **2 a :** to perish from lack of food — often used in the phrase *starve to death* **b :** to suffer extreme hunger ⟨all this time the family had *starved* and gone ragged —Conrad Richter⟩ **3** *archaic* **a :** to die of cold **b :** to suffer greatly from cold ⟨my hands are *starving* while I write in bed —Jonathan Swift⟩ **4 :** to suffer or perish from deprivation ⟨pupils are *starving* for means of expression —I.A.Richards⟩ ⟨his horse . . . almost *starved* for water —J.F.Dobie⟩ ⟨*starving* for lack of intellectual companionship —Robert Grant †1940⟩ ~ *vt* **1** *obs* **:** KILL, DESTROY **2 a :** to kill with hunger **b :** to deprive of nourishment ⟨seen men *starved*, beaten, herded like cattle —John Fountain⟩ **c :** to cause to capitulate by or as if by depriving of nourishment ⟨~ a person into submission⟩ ⟨*starved* him out by refusing to support his paper —W.E. Smith⟩ **d :** to attempt to cure (a disease) by restricting the diet of the affected person ⟨feed a cold and ~ a fever⟩ **3 a :** to destroy by or cause to suffer from deprivation ⟨*starved* the army of transport —F.M.Ford⟩ ⟨the company avoided bankruptcy by *starving* its depreciation reserves —M.W. Straight⟩ **b :** to suppress or extinguish (a fire) by cutting off fuel **4** *archaic* **:** to kill with cold

starved brood *n* **:** a diseased condition of the brood of the honeybee possibly due to an infectious disease

starved·ly \-vədlē, -vd-\ *adv* **:** in a starved manner **:** with little nourishment

starve·ling \ˈstärvliŋ, -tȧv-, -lēŋ\ *n* -s **:** one that starves **:** one that is thin from or as if from lack of nutriment

starv·er \ˈstärvər\ *n* -s **1 :** one that causes starvation **2 :** one that undergoes starvation

star violet *n* **1 :** either of two small herbs (*Houstonia patens* and *H. angustifolia*) of the central and southern U. S. **2 :** DEWDROP 2

star wheel *n* **:** a somewhat star-shaped disk used as a ratchet wheel (as in a repeating watch or the feed motion of any of various machines) — compare GENEVA STOP

star winding *n* **:** a winding used in a polyphase electric machine in which one terminal of each phase coil is connected to a common point and the other terminals are joined to the outside system — compare STAR CONNECTION

starwomen \ˈ⸗,⸗\ *n* **:** GEPHYREAN

starwort \ˈ⸗,⸗\ *n* [ME *sterrewort*, fr. *sterre* star + *wort*] **1 :** any of various chickweeds of the genus *Stellaria* **2 :** a plant of the genus *Aster* (as the stiff aster) **3 :** any of various plants of the genus *Callitriche* **4 :** GRUBROOT **5 :** COLICROOT

stary *var of* STAREY

¹**stash** \ˈstash, -aa(ə)-, -ai- *sometimes* -ā-\ *vt* -ED/-ING/-ES [origin unknown] **1** *chiefly Brit* **:** to put an end to **:** break up **:** STOP, QUIT ⟨~ the business⟩ ⟨~ it⟩ ⟨could ~ up any golden age . . . in about five minutes —H.G.Wells⟩ **2 :** to store in a usu. secret place for future use **:** put away **:** HIDE, CACHE ⟨had ~*ed* the money thinking to come back later and get it —Mickey Spillane⟩ — usu. used with *away* ⟨began systematically to ~ away her treasures —Truman Capote⟩

²**stash** \"\ *n* -ES **1 :** hiding place **:** CACHE; *esp* **:** one for moonshine or illicit narcotics ⟨fifty gallons left in the ~⟩ ⟨caught a dope peddler using the place as a ~⟩ **2 :** something stored or hidden away ⟨one of the chairs contains a considerable ~ of cash —*Time*⟩

stash·ie \ˈstashi\ *n* -s [perh. alter. of *ecstasy*] *Scot* **:** UPROAR

stasi- *comb form* [Gk *stasis* condition of standing, stoppage, stature, position — more at STASIS] **1 :** arrest of development **:** stoppage ⟨*stasi*morphy⟩ **2 :** erect posture ⟨*stasi*phobia⟩ **3 :** position ⟨*stasi*metric⟩

-sta·sia \ˈstāzh(ē)ə, -āsh-\ *n comb form* -s [NL, fr. Gk, fr. *statos* standing (fr. the stem of *histanai* to cause to stand) + *-ia* -y — more at STAND] **:** condition of standing **:** stoppage **:** -STASIS ⟨meno*stasia*⟩ ⟨enhypo*stasia*⟩

stas·i·mon \ˈstasəˌmän\ *n, pl* **stasi·ma** \-ˌmə\ *also* **stasimons** [Gk, fr. neut. of *stasimos* standing, stationary, fr. the stem of *histanai* to cause to stand] **:** one of the regular choral odes between two episodes in a Greek tragedy possibly sung with the chorus standing in its place in the orchestra — compare PARODOS

stasis \ˈstāsəs -tas-\ *n, pl* **stases** \-āˌsēz -aˌs-\ [NL, fr. Gk, condition of standing, standing still, stoppage, stature, condition, fr. stem of *histanai* to cause to stand + *-sis* — more at STAND] **1 :** a slowing or stoppage of the normal flow of fluid or semifluid material in an organ or vessel in the body: as **a :** slowing of the current of circulating blood in arteries or veins ⟨venous ~⟩ **b :** reduced motility of the intestines with retention of feces ⟨colon ~⟩ **2 :** an absence of circulatory convection currents in a mass of gas or liquid **3 :** a state of static balance or equilibrium among opposing tendencies or forces **:** QUIESCENCE, STAGNATION ⟨at a point of ~ artistically and spiritually . . . cannot develop any new creative activity —Harrison Smith⟩; *specif* **:** a state of stable and sometimes sterile equilibrium reached by a society **:** STAGNANCY ⟨the essential danger of mass media . . . lies in their ability to inflate existing consent to the point of a dull unanimity and so to achieve social and economic ~ —J.T.Klapper⟩

-stasis \ˈstāsəs, ˈsta|, stə|\ *n comb form, pl* **-stases** \|,sēz\ [NL, fr. Gk *stasis* condition of standing, standing still, stoppage] **1 :** slowing or stoppage of normal flow ⟨hemo*stasis*⟩ **2 :** inhibition of the growth without destruction of ⟨bacterio*stasis*⟩ ⟨fungi*stasis*⟩ **3 :** tendency toward maintenance of stability ⟨homeo*stasis*⟩ **4 :** retention **:** persistence ⟨tricho*stasis*⟩

stass·furt salt \ˈsta|sfə(r)t-, ˈs(h)tä|\ *n, usu cap 1st S* [fr. *Stassfurt*, Germany] **:** potash salt from large deposits in Germany

stat *abbr* **1** static **2** [L *statim*] immediately **3** stationary **4** statistical; statistician; statistics **5** statuary; statue **6** statute

stat- *comb form* [electro*static*] **:** electrostatic ⟨*stat*ampere⟩ — in names of electrical units

-stat \ˌstat, *usu* -ad·+V\ *n comb form* -s [NL *-stata*, fr. Gk *-statēs* one that causes to stand, fr. the stem of *histanai* to cause to stand — more at STAND] **1 :** apparatus or agent for keeping (something specified) stable or stationary ⟨gyro*stat*⟩ **2 :** device for regulating or for maintaining (something specified) in a constant state ⟨cryo*stat*⟩ ⟨rheo*stat*⟩ ⟨thermo*stat*⟩ **3 :** instrument for reflecting (something specified) constantly in one direction ⟨helio*stat*⟩ ⟨sidero*stat*⟩ **4 :** device for studying (something specified) in a state of rest ⟨hydro*stat*⟩ **5 :** agent causing inhibition of growth without destruction ⟨bacterio*stat*⟩ ⟨fungi*stat*⟩

stat·able *or* **state·able** \ˈstād·əbəl, -ātə-\ *adj* **:** capable of being stated ⟨philosophical problems . . . ~ as specific questions —J.E.Smith⟩

stat·al \ˈstād·ᵊl\ *adj* [¹*state* + *-al*] **1** *often cap* **:** of or relating to a state (as of the U.S. or India) ⟨~citizenship⟩ ⟨the ~economy⟩ **2 :** of or relating to a national government ⟨the sanctuaries of ~ authority —*Fortnightly Rev.*⟩ **3** *of a passive verb form* **:** expressing a state or condition (as *was closed* in "the door was closed all day") — contrasted with *actional*

stat·ampere \(ˈ)stad·+\ *n* [*stat-* + *ampere*] **:** the cgs electrostatic unit of current equal to about 3.3×10^{-10} ampere

sta·tant \ˈstātᵊnt\ *adj* [L *status* (past part. of *stare* to stand) + E *-ant*) — more at STAND] *of a heraldic beast* **:** standing with all feet on the ground and seen in profile ⟨a lion ~⟩

stat·coulomb \(ˌ)stat+\ *n* [*stat-* + *coulomb*] **:** the cgs electrostatic unit of charge equal to about 3.3×10^{-10} coulomb

¹**state** \ˈstāt, *usu* -ād·+V\ *n* -s *often attrib* [ME *stat*, fr. OF & L; OF *estat*, fr. L *status*, fr. *status*, past part. of *stare* to stand — more at STAND] **1 a :** a mode or condition of being **:** POSITION, NATURE ⟨this mortal ~⟩ ⟨our present ~ of knowledge⟩ ⟨the ~ of his health⟩ ⟨financial ~⟩ ⟨the unsanitary ~ of the building⟩ ⟨a ~ of readiness⟩ ⟨the married ~⟩ **b (1) :** a condition of mind or temperament ⟨a ~ of consciousness⟩ ⟨in a highly nervous ~⟩ **(2) :** a condition of abnormal tension or excitement (as from anger or fear) ⟨little things piled up on him and he got into a ~⟩ **c** *archaic* **:** the highest stage of development **:** ACME, CRISIS — usu. used of a disease **d :** a condition or form of a noun — compare ABSOLUTE STATE, CONSTRUCT STATE, EMPHATIC STATE **2 a :** a condition or stage in the physical constitution of something **:** STATE OF AGGREGATION ⟨the solid and liquid ~*s*⟩ ⟨water in the vaporous ~⟩ ⟨the best ~ of a metal for the purpose⟩ **b :** one of an indeterminate number of conditions in which an atomic system may exist that is characterized by definite quantities (as of energy, angular momentum, or magnetic moment) and separated from other conditions by finite differences in these quantities **c :** the physical condition of something at one stage in a process: as **(1) :** a stage of an engraved plate that is distinguished from another stage by a greater or less amount of work on the plate **(2) :** an impression from the plate in such a stage **(3) :** a condition of the unfired clay in ceramics ⟨green ~⟩ ⟨raw ~⟩ **(4) :** a variant (as in type setting or makeup) of an impression or issue of a book **(5) :** a stage in the growth or development of a plant or animal ⟨buttercups in the green ~⟩ ⟨the larval ~⟩ **3 a :** social position **:** RANK, STATION ⟨all luxuries befitting the ~ of a marquis —Charles Dickens⟩; *esp* **:** high rank **:** EMINENCE ⟨can this imperious lord . . . quit all his ~, descend, and serve again —Alexander Pope⟩ **b (1) :** elaborate or luxurious style or mode of living **:** MAGNIFICENCE ⟨has a wealthy lover and keeps a considerable ~ —Arnold Bennett⟩ **(2) :** formal dignity **:** POMP — usu. used with *in* ⟨rode in ~ to her coronation⟩ ⟨in solemn ~ . . . admitted to the fraternity —R.W. Southern⟩ ⟨lie in ~⟩ **c :** graceful dignity (as in bearing) ⟨keep some ~ in thy exit and vanish —Shak.⟩ ⟨perfect in shapeliness and ~ —A.C.Swinburne⟩ **d (1)** *obs* **:** a chair with a canopy and often on a dais **:** THRONE ⟨this chair shall be my ~ —Shak.⟩ **(2)** *archaic* **:** CANOPY **4 a :** a body of persons constituting a special class in a society **:** ESTATE, ORDER ⟨a division of governmental power between the several ~*s* . . . in the community —C.J.Friedrich⟩ **b states** *pl* **:** the members or representatives of the governing classes assembled in a parliament or diet (as in France before the Revolution, Scotland before the Union, and the United Netherlands) **:** ESTATE 3b **c** *obs* **(1) :** a person of high rank (as a noble) ⟨the bold design pleased highly those infernal ~*s* —John Milton⟩ **(2) :** the ruling persons (as in a country or town) **:** COUNCIL ⟨consult with the king and ~ —Francis Bacon⟩ **d :** the ruling body or government of a country **5 a :** a body of people permanently occupying a definite territory and politically organized under a sovereign government almost entirely free from external control and possessing coercive power to maintain order within the community **:** BODY POLITIC, COMMONWEALTH 2, NATION 1b ⟨for Aristotle the ~ was an association of men for the sake of the best moral life⟩ **b :** the political organization that has supreme civil authority and political power and serves as the basis of government ⟨the institutions of Church and ~⟩ **c :** a particular form of government or politically organized society ⟨the secular ~⟩ ⟨the fascist ~⟩ ⟨the welfare ~⟩ **d :** the embodiment of the ethical idea and the moral will of the community in Hegelian philosophy **e :** a colony of social animals (as ants or bees) with organization analogous to that of a human state **6 :** the operations, activities, or affairs of the government or ruling power of a country **:** the sphere of administration and supreme political power of a government ⟨matters of ~⟩ ⟨secrets of ~⟩ ⟨ministers of ~⟩ ⟨Department of ~⟩ **7** *often cap* **:** one of the bodies politic or component units in a federal system that is more or less independent and sovereign over internal affairs but forms with the other units a sovereign nation ⟨the United *States* of America⟩ ⟨the Indian ~*s*⟩ ⟨the ~*s* of Switzerland are called cantons⟩ **8 a :** a territory governed by a particular nation **b :** a territorial unit in which the general body of law is separate and distinct from the law of any other territorial unit **9** *obs* **:** PROPERTY, ESTATE 4c **10 a** *archaic* **:** STATEMENT, ACCOUNT **b** *Brit* **:** a periodic report of troop numbers and condition ⟨delivered a ~ of the troops⟩

syn CONDITION, MODE, SITUATION, POSTURE, STATUS: STATE, often interchangeable with CONDITION, may but does not always imply genuinely existent characteristics likely to be significant and enduring and discovered or announced after some analysis ⟨shall from time to time give to the Congress information of the *state* of the Union —*U.S.Constitution*⟩ ⟨wharves, piers and docks at the Atlantic ports were brought to what was a high *state* of efficiency for those days —A.F. Harlow⟩ ⟨in a *state* of some excitement, talking eagerly in a rather loud voice —J.D.Beresford⟩ CONDITION may more strongly imply the influence of circumstances on the way of existing, esp. of only temporary circumstances ⟨his mental *condition*⟩ ⟨in a delicate *condition*⟩ ⟨previous *condition* of servitude⟩ ⟨better working *conditions*⟩ ⟨the house is still in good *condition*⟩ ⟨certain weather *conditions*⟩ ⟨by no means relieved of his anxiety and fully aware of the excited *condition* of English opinion he could only await the issue —W.C.Ford⟩ MODE stresses external manifestation and suggests nothing of the concern with underlying reality that may be implicated by *state* ⟨the whole burden of her middle period is the attempt to reach a spiritual equilibrium through a formal *mode* of religious conversion —M.D.Geismar⟩ SITUATION, implying a being placed or located much more than a being formed or composed, may apply to any specific set of circumstances, perhaps individual or interesting ⟨the *situation* in fiction — the desperate girl appealing out of her misery to the Christian priest for help —Rose Macaulay⟩ ⟨he has already won for himself a personal *situation* unparalleled in postwar France, and with it a fighting chance to lead his country —Frank Gorrell⟩ ⟨a play upon a *situation* in which a surgeon is called upon to save the life of the lover of his wife —A.H.Quinn⟩ POSTURE, in this sense often a close synonym for SITUATION, may imply the shaping influence of personal inclination or decision ⟨the type of balance between military and civilian production which will permit us to maintain both a strong economy and a strong military *posture* —H.S.Truman⟩ ⟨showing me in a *posture* of comically servile deference to authority —F.R.Leavis⟩ STATUS may indicate one's state or condition as determined with some definiteness for legal administration or economic or social considerations ⟨new *status* of proprietor —Mary Austin⟩ ⟨the change in the *status* of the Negro, under the Thirteenth Amendment, from three fifths of a person to a whole person in computing state apportionment —Carol L. Thompson⟩ ⟨a married woman's *status* was determined entirely by that of her husband —F.A.Ogg & P.O.Ray⟩ ⟨big business has elevated the function of management to the *status* of the learned professions —*Nation's Business*⟩ ⟨my underprivileged *status* as an ex-convict —Frank O'Leary⟩

— **in a state of nature 1 :** naked as when born **:** NUDE **2 :** in a condition of sin **:** UNREGENERATE **3 :** UNCIVILIZED, UNTAMED

²**state** \"\ *vt* -ED/-ING/-S **1 a** *archaic* **:** to fix or settle in a position, rank, or condition **:** PLACE **b** *obs* **:** to confer possession on **:** vest a person in **c :** to set by or as if by regulation or authority ⟨meetings are held at *stated* times⟩ **2 a :** to express the particulars of **:** set forth **:** RECITE, REPORT ⟨~ the facts of a case⟩ ⟨~ the problem in full⟩ ⟨~ the account in dollars⟩ **b :** to put into words **:** FRAME, PHRASE ⟨~ the resolution as it is now to be voted upon⟩ **c (1) :** ASSERT, DECLARE ⟨authorities . . . ~ that a young man in good condition can cover up to a hundred miles a day —Richard Joseph⟩ **(2) :** ANNOUNCE ⟨the opening measures of the first movement where the horns ~ the first theme —Winthrop Sargeant⟩ **3** *obs* **:** to live in pomp or luxury — used with *it* ⟨began to ~ it . . . as high as ever before —Thomas Fuller⟩ **syn** see RELATE

-state \ˌ⸗\ *n comb form* -s [Gk *statos* standing, fixed, fr. the stem of *histanai* to cause to stand — more at STAND] **:** substance produced through a (specified) process ⟨ana*state*⟩ ⟨cata*state*⟩

stateable *var of* STATABLE

state account system *n* **:** PUBLIC ACCOUNT SYSTEM

state aid *n* **:** public monies appropriated by a state government for the partial support or improvement of some public local institution (as a library, hospital, or educational institution)

state attorney *or* **state's attorney** *n, usu cap S* **:** a legal officer appointed to represent a state in the courts **:** PROSECUTING ATTORNEY, DISTRICT ATTORNEY

state bank *n* **1 :** a bank owned, controlled, or operated by a government **2** *usu cap S* **:** a bank chartered by and operating under the laws of a state of the U.S. — compare NATIONAL BANK 1

state bird *n, usu cap S* **:** a bird selected (as by the legislature) as an emblem of one of the states of the U.S. ⟨the cardinal is the State bird of North Carolina⟩

state capitalism *n* **:** a system of capitalism in which capital is largely controlled or owned by the state

state church *n, often cap S&C* **:** ESTABLISHED CHURCH

state college *n* **:** a college that is financially supported by a state government, often specializes in a branch of technical or professional education, and often forms part of the state university

statecraft \ˈ⸗,⸗\ *n* **1 :** the art of conducting state affairs **:** state management **:** STATESMANSHIP ⟨one of the greatest problems of ~ now facing our nation —R.K.Carr⟩ — distinguished from *folkcraft* **2** *archaic* **:** wiliness or chicanery in political dealings ⟨a double treason . . . thought a masterpiece of ~ —T.B. Macaulay⟩

state crown *n, often cap S&C* **:** IMPERIAL STATE CROWN

stated *adj* [fr. past part. of ²*state*] **1 :** set or fixed (as by rule or custom) **:** ESTABLISHED, REGULAR ⟨the president shall, at ~ times, receive . . . a compensation —*U.S.Constitution*⟩ ⟨~ meetings are held on the first Thursday of every month⟩ **2 a** *obs* **:** unmistakably known **:** AVOWED **b :** set down explicitly **:** DECLARED ⟨allowing certain ~ exceptions⟩ ⟨the ~ value of stock⟩

stated account *n* **:** ACCOUNT STATED

stated case *n* **:** CASE STATED

stated clerk *n* **:** the chief executive officer of an American Presbyterian denomination ranking as the second highest elective officer of the denomination next below the moderator of the General Assembly

stat·ed·ly *adv* **:** as an established practice **:** REGULARLY ⟨took a very active part in the academy, visiting the school ~ —H.R. Warfel⟩

stated supply *n* **:** a clergyman who without formal installation supplies a pulpit for a limited time as a congregation's acting pastor

stated value *n* **:** the often arbitrary figure rather than the amount received at the time of issuance at which no-par-value stock is carried on the books of a corporation

state flower *n, usu cap S* **:** a flowering plant selected (as by the legislature or the school children of the state) as the floral emblem of a state of the U.S.

state guard *n* **:** a military force organized for use within a state in time of war or when the national guard has been called into federal service

state·hood \ˈstātˌhu̇d\ *n* **:** the quality, condition, or character of being a state: as **a :** the condition of national independence and sovereignty characterizing a state ⟨modern nationalism has . . . sought full expression in unified and independent ~ —J.S.Roucek⟩ **b :** the condition or status of one of the states of the U.S. ⟨the United States used to administer her territories before they achieved the dignity of ~ —H. W. Van Loon⟩

statehouse \ˈ⸗,⸗\ *n* **:** a building in which governmental affairs (as of a state legislature) are conducted; *specif* **:** a state capitol ⟨heated discussion of the governor's message in the corridors of the ~⟩

stateism *var of* STATISM

state·less \ˈstātləs\ *adj* **1 :** having no state ⟨looking forward to a ~ society⟩ **2 :** having no nationality **:** owing allegiance to no country ⟨considered himself a citizen of the world, voluntarily ~⟩ **3 :** having no citizenship whether from having lost citizenship in a state or from never having acquired effective citizenship in any state ⟨~ persons⟩

state·less·ness *n* -ES **:** the quality or state of being stateless **:** the condition of being without citizenship in any country ⟨methods by which ~ may be eliminated —*advt*⟩

state·let \ˈstātlət\ *n* -s **:** a small state ⟨the old . . . confederation of Teutonic states and ~*s* —H. W. Van Loon⟩

state·li·ly \ˈstātlәlē, -əli\ *adv* [¹*stately* + *-ly*] **:** in a stately manner **:** with impressive dignity **:** DIGNIFIEDLY, FORMALLY ⟨nobody danced more ~ —J.B.Cabell⟩

state·li·ness \-ātlēnəs, -lin-\ *n* -ES **:** the quality or state of being stately: as **a :** impressiveness in scale or proportion **:** MAJESTY, GRANDEUR ⟨who can deny to the architecture of nature a certain ~ —W.M.Dixon⟩ **b (1) :** imposing or courtly formality (as in appearance or manner) **:** ALOOFNESS ⟨his ~ often repelled people⟩ **(2) :** impressive dignity or loftiness **:** GRANDNESS ⟨a nobility and ~ of character —Sheldon Cheney⟩ **(3) :** elevation of style or expression **:** SUBLIMITY ⟨the ~ of biblical prose⟩

¹**state·ly** \ˈstātlē, -li\ *adj* -ER/-EST [ME *statly*, fr. *stat* state + *-ly*] **1 a** *obs* **:** showing consciousness of high birth or rank **:** HAUGHTY, UNAPPROACHABLE **b :** marked by lofty or imposing dignity **:** impressively formal **:** COURTLY, CEREMONIOUS ⟨contrasts of a ~ old order and a somewhat bumptious new —V.L.Parrington⟩ ⟨his wife looks on in ~ aloofness —H.J. Laski⟩ ⟨a ~ pace⟩ ⟨rising in the most ~ manner to open the door —W.M.Thackeray⟩ ⟨the ~ language of old worship —W.L.Sullivan⟩ **2 a :** impressive in size or proportions **:** MAJESTIC ⟨houses with ~ porticoes —*Amer. Guide Series: Va.*⟩

b : erect and imposing in outline or overall shape ⟨~ old elms⟩ **syn** see GRAND

²stately \"\ *adv* [ME *statly*, fr. *statly*, adj.] **:** in a stately manner: as **a** *obs* **:** in the grand style **:** IMPOSINGLY ⟨men come to build ~ sooner than to garden finely —Francis Bacon⟩ **b :** with a highly dignified or formal carriage or gait **:** CEREMONIOUSLY ⟨a figure . . . with solemn march goes slow and ~ —Shak.⟩

state medicine *n* **:** administration and control by the national government of medical and hospital services provided to the whole population and paid for out of funds raised by taxation — compare SOCIALIZED MEDICINE

state·ment \ˈstātmənt\ *n* -s [²*state* + *-ment*] **1 :** the act or process of stating, reciting, or presenting orally or on paper ⟨the ~ of a case⟩ ⟨strive . . . for economy of ~ —R.M.Coates⟩ ⟨permits an uninterrupted ~ of the argument —*Brit. Bk. News*⟩ **2 :** something stated: as **a :** a report or narrative (as of facts, events, or opinions) **:** ACCOUNT, RECITAL ⟨take a suspect's ~⟩ **b :** a single declaration or remark **:** ALLEGATION, ASSERTION ⟨his ~*s* were generally accepted at face value —Edith Diehl⟩ **3 :** PROPOSITION 3a **4 a :** the part of a declaration in a common law action that gives the facts on which the cause of action is based **b :** a formal declaration required by law or made in the course of some official proceeding (as a statement of a witness or of a position of a state in a diplomatic proceeding) **5 a :** a work of art (as in painting, music, or literature) or a part or an aspect of such a work that expresses most clearly and forcefully a theme, basic idea, or intention of the artist ⟨demands that the whole play shall be conceived and composed as ~ —F.R.Leavis⟩ ⟨this was cubism's last influential ~ —Janet Flanner⟩ **b :** the enunciation of a theme in a musical composition ⟨the initial musical ~ and . . . its melodic, rhythmic, and polyphonic deployment —P.H.Lang⟩ **6 :** a financial record or accounting ⟨a ~ of expenses⟩ ⟨a U. S. income tax withholding ~⟩; *specif* **:** a summary of an account showing the balance as of the beginning of, the credits and debts made during, and the balance due as of the end of the accounting period

statement form *or* **statement function** *n* **:** SENTENTIAL FUNCTION

statement of affairs : a statement for a financially embarrassed enterprise showing assets at book and realizable values and claims of creditors classified as preferred, secured, partly secured, and unsecured for the purpose of indicating probable amounts available to creditors in case of liquidation

statement of claim : a plaintiff's first pleading in the English High Court of Justice corresponding to the declaration in common law or the bill in chancery

statement of defense : a defendant's first pleading on an issue of fact in the English High Court of Justice corresponding to the plea in common law and to the answer in equity or under the codes of civil procedure

statemonger \ˈ=,==\ *n, archaic* **:** a dabbler in political affairs

state of aggregation : one of the three or more fundamental forms, conditions, or states of matter that are commonly considered to include the solid, liquid, and gaseous forms and often others (as the colloidal)

state of war 1 a : a state characterized by the actual existence of open armed hostilities (as between nations) regardless of a formal declaration of war by any party to the conflict **b :** a legal state that comes into being by formal declaration regardless of whether open armed hostilities have taken place, must be officially proclaimed at an end by a similar declaration, and is usu. characterized by such conditions that the rights and duties of belligerents and neutrals to act under the rules of international law applicable to war arise **2 :** the period of time during which a state of war is in effect

state police *n* **:** the police organized and maintained by a state as distinguished from those of a lower subdivision (as a city or county) of the state government

state prison *also* **state's prison** *n* **:** a prison maintained by the state; *esp* **:** the prison or penitentiary for the imprisonment of persons convicted of the more serious crimes (as felonies)

state prisoner *n* **:** POLITICAL PRISONER

sta·ter \ˈstād·ər, stäˈte(ə)r\ *n* -s [ME, fr. LL, fr. Gk *statēr*, a weight, standard coin, fr. the stem of *histanai* to cause to stand, set, place in a balance, weigh — more at STAND] **:** an ancient gold or silver coin of the Greek city-states of any of numerous standards

state religion *n* **:** a religion established by law as the only official religion of a state

stateroom \ˈ=,=\ *n* **1 :** an apartment of state in a palace or great house **2 a** *usu* **state-room** \"\ *archaic* **:** a commodious room on shipboard usu. for a captain or superior ship's officer **b :** CABIN 2a **3 :** a private room on a railroad car equipped with one or more berths and a toilet

states *pl of* STATE, *pres 3d sing of* STATE

state's attorney *n, usu cap S, var of* STATE ATTORNEY

state's evidence *n, often cap S* **1 :** one who gives evidence for the prosecution in U.S. state or federal criminal proceedings ⟨turned *state's evidence* against his pals —D.D.Martin⟩ — compare KING'S EVIDENCE **2 :** evidence for the government or prosecution in a criminal proceeding

states general *n pl, often cap S&G* [trans. of D *staten-generaal* & F *états généraux*] **:** a legislative assembly composed of members or representatives of the estates of a nation as distinguished from the states provincial (as the legislative assembly of France before the Revolution or the legislative assembly of the Netherlands from the 15th century to 1796) — compare ESTATE 3b

¹stateside \ˈ=,=\ *adj, often cap* [(*United*) *States* + *side*] **:** being in, going to, coming from, or characteristic of the U. S. as regarded from outside its continental limits ⟨transferred from Europe to ~ duty⟩ ⟨contrary to ~ custom⟩ ⟨reading a ~ magazine⟩

²stateside \"\ *adv, often cap* **:** in, to, or from the continental U.S. ⟨go ~⟩ ⟨before he could ship ~ —James Jones⟩

state·sid·er \"ə(r)\ *n, usu cap* **:** a native or inhabitant of the continental U.S. as regarded from outside its limits ⟨*Statesiders* employed in government offices on Guam⟩

states·man \ˈstātsmən\ *n, pl* **statesmen** [*state's* (genitive of ¹*state*) + *man*] **1 a :** one versed in the principles or art of government **:** POLITICIAN; *esp* **:** one actively engaged in conducting the business of a government or in shaping its policies ⟨an assembly of the *statesmen* of many nations⟩ **b :** one who exercises leadership wisely and without narrow partisanship in the general interest ⟨unhappily the republic was subject to men who were mere demagogues and in no sense *statesmen* —T.B.Macaulay⟩ ⟨the ~ differs from the ordinary politician in that he is able to envisage and inspire support for policies that are in the long run, best interests of the most people —J.H. Hallowell⟩ ⟨one of the academic *statesmen* of his era —N.M. Pusey⟩ **2** *dial Eng* **:** a countryman who owns and farms his own land

states·man·like \ˈ==,=\ *adj* **:** marked by the qualities (as wisdom, breadth of view, or diplomacy) of a statesman **:** befitting a statesman ⟨a man of ~ judgment —Marjory S. Douglas⟩ ⟨a ~ solution of the present perplexities —V.L.Parrington⟩

states·man·ly \-lē,-li\ *adj* **:** STATESMANLIKE

states·man·ship \-,ship\ *n* **1 :** the art or practice of conducting governmental affairs **:** political leadership ⟨those who are fit for the highest duties of ~ such as the final choice of means and ends —G.H.Sabine⟩ ⟨stupid, stubborn ~, without vision or imagination —C.G.Bowers⟩ **2 :** leadership characterized by wisdom, breadth of vision, or regard for the general welfare rather than partisan interest ⟨transforms opportunism into idealism, or politics into ~ —R.B.Perry⟩ ⟨forgot ~ and embraced politics —*N. Y. Herald Tribune Bk. Rev.*⟩ ⟨a task demanding a high level of educational ~ —J.D. Russell & C.H.Judd⟩ ⟨industrial ~⟩ ⟨labor ~⟩

state socialism *n* [trans. of G *staatssozialismus*] **:** socialism that advocates utilizing the power of the state to equalize income and opportunity (as by progressive income and inheritance taxes, by compulsory insurance against old age, unemployment, sickness, and accident, and by state administration of industries, public utilities, common carriers, banking, and housing)

state socialist *n* [trans. of G *staatssozialist*] **:** an advocate of state socialism

state-socialist \ˈ=ˈ=(=)=\ *adj* [*state socialist*] **:** of or relating to state socialism

states' right·er \ˈstāts'rīd·ə(r), -ītə-\ *n, often cap S&R* [*states' rights* + *-er*] **:** one that advocates strict interpretation of the U. S. constitutional guarantee of states' rights and is opposed to the exercise of federal authority in matters (as education, racial relations, or hours and working conditions) that he regards as the exclusive concern of the individual states

states' rights *n pl, often cap S&R* **:** all rights not vested by the Constitution of the U.S. in the Federal government nor forbidden by it to the separate states

states·wom·an \ˈstāt,swu̇mən\ *n, pl* **stateswomen** [*state's* (genitive of ¹*state*) + *woman*] **:** a woman who is active in politics or government; *esp* **:** one who holds high public office

state trading *n* **:** international agreements entered into by governments or government agencies for the sale or purchase of commodities

state tree *n, usu cap S* **:** a tree selected (as by the legislature) as an emblem of a state of the U.S.

state trial *n* **1 :** a trial for a political offense (as treason) **2 :** a trial that raises important questions of constitutional or international law

state university *n* **:** a university maintained and administered by one of the states of the U. S. as part of the state public educational system

state use system *n, often cap S* **:** the employment of prison labor in some states of the U. S. in the production of materials exclusively for use in institutions of the state or its subdivisions and not for sale — compare CONVICT LABOR SYSTEM

stateway \ˈ=,=\ *n* **:** a law or policy of government — contrasted with *folkway*

¹statewide \ˈ=ˈ=\ *adj* [¹*state* + *wide* (adj.)] **:** extending throughout a state **:** including all parts of a state ⟨a ~ celebration⟩ ⟨a ~ movement⟩ ⟨~ elective offices⟩

²statewide \"\ *adv* **:** throughout the state ⟨handbills . . . were distributed ~ —*New Republic*⟩

stat·farad \ˈstat+ˌ-\ *n* [*stat-* + *farad*] **:** the cgs electrostatic unit of capacitance equal to about 1.113×10^{-12} farads

stat·henry \"+ˌ-\ *n* [*stat-* + *henry*] **:** the cgs electrostatic unit of inductance equal to about 8.9×10^{11} henries

stath·mo·kinesis \ˌstath(ˌ)mō+\ *n* [NL, fr. Gk *stathmos* standing place, post (fr. the stem of *histanai* to stand) + NL *kinesis* — more at STAND] **:** interruption of mitosis (as by colchicine) — compare C-MITOSIS

¹stat·ic \ˈstad·ik, -at\, \|ēk\ *also* **stat·i·cal** \|əkəl, \|ēk-\ *adj* [*static* fr. NL *staticus*, fr. Gk *statikos* causing to stand, skilled at weighing, fr. *statos* (verbal of *histanai* to cause to stand, set, place on a balance, weigh) + *-ikos* -ic; *statical* fr. NL *staticus* + E *-al* — more at STAND] **1 a** *obs* **:** of, relating to, or used in weighing ⟨~ experiments⟩ ⟨~ chair⟩ ⟨~ barometer⟩ **b :** exerting force by reason of weight alone apart from effects of inertia ⟨~ load⟩ **2 :** of or relating to statics **:** of or relating to bodies at rest or forces in equilibrium — compare DYNAMIC **3 a :** showing little change **:** STABLE, STAGNANT ⟨the conception of a ~ universe⟩ ⟨a ~ population⟩ ⟨adjust to the realities of a fairly ~ environment —W.H.Whyte⟩ **b :** rigidly bound by traditional patterns and values **:** UNCHANGING ⟨dynamic modern society contrasted with ~ feudal society⟩ **4 a :** characterized by a lack of movement, animation, or progression ⟨creates ~ characters⟩ ⟨an enormous young woman who is ~ on stage —Roger Dettmer⟩ ⟨the novel is . . . a trifle ~, constructed in episodes —J.H.Jackson⟩ **b :** producing an effect of repose or quiescence ⟨a ~ design⟩ ⟨the Romanesque style is . . . ~ —Nikolaus Pevsner⟩ ⟨perfect fifths . . . sound relatively ~ —Virgil Thomson⟩ **c** *of a verb or verb form* **:** expressing mere existence or state as distinct from action — used esp. in the grammar of American Indian and African languages; compare ACTIVE 3b, NEUTER 1b, STATIVE **5 a :** standing or fixed in one place **:** STATIONARY ⟨a ~ installation⟩ ⟨a ~ dredge⟩ ⟨a ~ antiaircraft gun⟩ **b :** performed in place, on the ground, or in a stationary position ⟨~ firing of a rocket motor⟩ ⟨~ testing of a missile⟩ **c** *of water* **:** stored in a tank and not under pressure for use by pumping in case of fire **6 :** of, relating to, or constituting the labyrinthine sense **7 :** of, relating to, or producing stationary charges of electricity **:** ELECTROSTATIC ⟨~ charges due to friction⟩ ⟨a ~ machine⟩ **8 :** of, relating to, or caused by radio static

²static \"\ *n* -s **1 :** electrical discharges in the atmosphere (as lightning, corona, or electrical storms) **:** ATMOSPHERICS **2 :** atmospheric noise or disturbance resulting from accumulation of electric charges (as from snowflakes, household appliances, or power lines) on or near an antenna and interfering with radio reception

stat·i·cal·ly \|ək(ə)lē, \|ēk-, -li\ *adv* **1 :** with static electricity ⟨a wire charged ~⟩ **2 :** in a static manner **:** in stable or unchanging terms ⟨dealt with the problem ~ rather than dynamically⟩ ⟨conceives of life ~⟩

static balancer *n* **:** BALANCER SET 2

stat·i·ce \ˈstad·ə(ˌ)sē\ *n* [NL, fr. L, a plant of the genus *Armeria* (prob. thrift) that has astringent qualities, fr. Gk *statikē*, fr. fem. of *statikos* causing to stand, astringent — more at STATIC] **1** *cap, in former classifications* **:** a genus of low-growing usu. coastal herbs equivalent to the genera *Armeria* and *Limonium* of modern classification or sometimes synonymous with one or the other of these genera **2** -s **:** a plant of *Armeria* or the related genus *Limonium* **:** SEA LAVENDER, THRIFT

static electricity *n* **:** electricity in motionless charges (as on the terminals of an open-circuit battery or on hard rubber after it has been rubbed with cat's fur) or considered without reference to motion

static equilibrium *n* **:** equilibrium of a system whose parts are relatively at rest (as a steel truss resting on piers)

static field *n* **:** ELECTRIC FIELD

static friction *n* **:** the force between two bodies in contact that resists the initiation of sliding motion of one over the other **:** the force required to cause one of the bodies to begin to move when they are at rest — called also *starting friction*

static head *n* **:** the height of a column of water at rest that would produce a given pressure **:** HEAD 14b

static jet thrust *n* **:** the thrust developed by a jet-propulsion engine at rest with respect to the surrounding air

static line *n* **:** a cord or flexible cable attached at one end to a parachute pack and fitted at the other end with means for attachment to some part of an airplane to effect automatic opening of the parachute after the jumper clears the plane without the use of the manual rip cord

static marks *n pl* **:** markings produced by the light from an electrostatic discharge on a light-sensitive material and made visible by development

static metamorphism *n* **:** metamorphism in rock produced by pressure apart from any movement of the rock masses

static oceanography *n* **:** a branch of oceanography dealing with the physical and chemical properties of the ocean waters and the topography and composition of the ocean bottom

static pressure *n* **:** the force per unit area that is exerted by a fluid upon a surface at rest relative to the fluid

static propeller thrust *n* **:** the thrust developed by a propeller when rotating without translation in air that is still except for the effect of the propeller

static refraction *n* **:** the reciprocal of the far point distance of the eye — compare DYNAMIC REFRACTION

stat·ics \ˈstad·\|iks, -at\, \|ēks\ *n pl but usu sing in constr* [earlier *static* (fr. NL *statica*, fr. Gk *statikē* art of weighing, fr. fem. of *statikos* skilled in weighing) + *-s* — more at STATIC] **1 :** a branch of mechanics dealing with the relations of forces that produce equilibrium among material bodies — compare DYNAMICS **2 :** SOCIAL STATICS **3 :** the study of an economy that is active but unchanging in its fundamental relationships emphasizing rates of output rather than changes in these rates and dealing with single change and the timeless adjustment of the economy to this change rather than continuous changes and their time sequence

static sensation *n* **:** a sensation of the labyrinthine sense

static stability *n* **:** the degree of stable equilibrium of a body (as a suspended body, a floating ship, or an airplane in flight) capable of rotating out of its equilibrium position measured by the torque necessary to produce a given deflection

static theory *n* **:** STATICS 3

static thrust *n* **:** the thrust developed by an airplane engine that is at rest with respect to the earth and the surrounding air

static tube *n* **:** a usu. closed tube that is used for indicating static as distinct from impact pressure in a stream of fluid (as air), has perforations in its sides, is placed parallel to direction of flow, and has a conical forward end fitted with a branch tube so as to provide for a connection with a manometer

stating *pres part of* STATE

¹sta·tion \ˈstāshən\ *n* -s *often attrib* [ME *stacioun*, fr. MF *station*, *estation*, fr. L *station-*, *statio*, fr. *status* (past part. of *stare* to stand) + *-ion-*, *-io* -ion — more at STAND] **1 a** *archaic* **:** a state of standing still or being at rest **:** STILLNESS ⟨her motion and her ~ are as one —Shak.⟩ **b** *archaic* **:** STATIONARY POINT ⟨the planets in their ~*s* list'ning stood —John Milton⟩ **c** (1) **:** a stop or sojourn at one place **:** HALT ⟨having enjoyed my first ~ here . . . I again commenced my march —John Coulter⟩ (2) **:** tour of duty ⟨left after a short ~ there⟩ **2 :** the place or position in which something or someone stands or is assigned to stand or remain: as **a :** a post of duty ⟨a sentinel's ~⟩ ⟨waiters at their ~*s* in the dining room⟩ ⟨battle ~*s* on a ship⟩ **b :** the spot at which an instrument is planted or observations are made in surveying **c** (1) **:** one of the places on a machine tool where the work is subjected to a single operation (2) **:** a position on a conveyor system where materials are loaded or discharged **d :** an enlargement in a mining shaft or gallery used as a landing or passing place or for the accommodation of equipment (as a pump or tank) **e** (1) **:** a position of a ship in a formation or convoy (2) **:** the assigned position of each airplane relative to that of the flight leader in formation flying ⟨hold ~ on the leader⟩ **f** (1) **:** one of the 10 or more divisions on a ship's lines between forward and after perpendicular at which calculations (as of displacement) are made in shipbuilding (2) **:** one of the specified points along the keel or base line marking the places for the ship's frames **3 a :** the act or manner of standing **:** POSTURE ⟨maintain a firm ~⟩ ⟨~ was unsteady with the eyes open or closed —*Diseases of the Nervous System*⟩ **b :** the height and carriage of a gamecock **c :** any of the eight places from which a skeet shooter fires **4 :** a stopping place: as **a** (1) **:** a stopping place in a transportation route (as for taking on passengers or handling freight) (2) **:** the building or buildings connected with such a stopping place **:** DEPOT 3a, 3b (3) **:** an Air Force depot without flying facilities **b :** a place where a missionary stops as regularly as possible to conduct religious services and minister to the needs of the people **c :** one of the stations of the cross **d :** a Christian service held at one of a number of churches on a stated day (as every day in Lent, the ember days, and solemn feasts) **e** *Irish* **:** a priest's stay with a parishioner to confess the neighbors ⟨the night of a ~, when the priest was praising the place she had —Padraic Fallon⟩ **5 :** a sphere of life, duty, or occupation: as **a :** an army post ⟨spent five years at his first ~⟩ **b :** an area of residence (as formerly in India) for British military or civil officers in a district **c :** a place or region to which a government ship or fleet is assigned for duty **d :** a pioneer settlement **:** OUTPOST ⟨tribes were constantly interrupting stage service, attacking ~*s* —G.R.Stewart⟩ **e** *Austral* **:** RANCH **f :** MISSION STATION **g :** a single church of the Methodist denomination that is a pastor's sole charge as distinguished from a circuit of churches served by one clergyman **6 a :** social standing **:** RANK, POSITION ⟨married above his ~⟩ ⟨a woman of high ~⟩ ⟨the duties of the ~ in which we find ourselves —M.R.Cohen⟩ **b :** the ordinal position in which a number is drawn in lotteries and numbers games **7 a :** a region or situation where a particular kind of plant or animal lives **:** the most characteristic portion of its range **:** HABITAT, BIOTOPE **b :** the exact spot at which a given species or specimen is found or collected **8 a :** a place established and equipped for specialized observation and study of scientific phenomena ⟨a geologic ~⟩ ⟨a seismological ~⟩ ⟨an agricultural experiment ~⟩ **b :** an institution for studying living organisms in their natural surroundings ⟨a marine biological ~⟩ **c :** a place or location for ascertaining or tabulating tidal and current data **9 :** a place established to provide a public service: as **a :** FIRE STATION **b :** POLICE STATION **c :** a post office subsidiary to the headquarters post office of an area **:** a branch post office — see CLASSIFIED STATION, CONTRACT STATION **d** (1) **:** a complete assemblage of radio or television equipment including antenna, transmitting or receiving set, and signal making or reproducing device (2) **:** the place (as a room) in which a radio or television transmitting or receiving station is located **e :** a usu. outdoor place where merchandise is sold **:** STAND **10 :** STATION DAY

²station \"\ *vt* -ED/-ING/-S **:** to assign to or set in a station or position **:** POST ⟨~*s* his troops on a hill⟩ ⟨~*ed* himself at the only exit⟩ ⟨~*ed* a lady usher to watch a certain drama critic —Gilbert Millstein⟩

station agent *n* **:** a person on duty at a railroad station or depot whose responsibilities vary according to the size of the station — compare STATIONMASTER

sta·tion·al \-shənᵊl,-shnəl\ *adj* **:** of or relating to an ecclesiastical station ⟨a ~ indulgence⟩ ⟨a ~ cross⟩ ⟨a ~ mass⟩

sta·tion·ar·i·ly \ˌstāshəˈnerəlē, -li\ *adv* **:** in a stationary manner **:** MOTIONLESSLY ⟨hung ~⟩

sta·tion·ar·i·ness \-rēnəs, -rin-\ *n* -ES **:** the quality or state of being stationary: as **a :** FIXEDNESS, IMMOBILITY ⟨the ~ of the regiment⟩ **b :** STAGNATION ⟨the ~ of an industry⟩

sta·tion·ary \ˈstāshə,nerē, -ri\ *adj* [ME *stacionarye*, fr. MF & L; MF *stationnaire*, fr. L *stationarius*, fr. *station-*, *statio* station + *-arius* -ary — more at STATION] **1 a :** fixed in a station, course, or mode **:** standing still **:** IMMOBILE ⟨the shadow remained ~ —Jack London⟩ ⟨a ~ engine⟩ ⟨~ machinery⟩ **b :** not portable ⟨a ~ gun⟩ **c :** having no moving parts ⟨a ~ transformer⟩ **2 :** unchanging in condition **:** STABLE, STATIC ⟨the patient . . . remained relatively ~ —J.D.Teicher⟩ ⟨a ~ population⟩ ⟨a ~ period in philosophy⟩ ⟨no form of living speech can be ~ even though a standard be fixed —George Sampson⟩ **3** *archaic* **:** of or relating to a military post or garrison ⟨the ~ troops retired —Edward Gibbon⟩

stationary air *n* **:** the air that under ordinary circumstances does not leave the lungs in respiration

stationary engine *n* **:** a steam engine permanently placed; *specif* **:** a factory engine

stationary engineer *n* **:** one who operates stationary engines and related equipment

stationary engineering *n* **:** a branch of engineering concerned with the operation of stationary engines and related equipment

stationary flow *n* **:** STEADY FLOW

stationary front *n* **:** the boundary between two air masses neither of which is replacing the other — see FRONT illustration

stationary line *n* **:** INTERSTELLAR LINE

stationary point *n* **:** the point in a planet's apparent path among the stars where for a brief time it seems to be motionless because it is changing from direct to retrograde motion or vice versa

stationary state *n* **1 :** a stable or metastable quantum state **2 :** a condition taken as an operational concept in economic analysis in which economic processes merely reproduce themselves with no changes

stationary wave *n* **1** *or* **stationary vibration :** STANDING WAVE **2 :** a wave in which the water oscillates vertically without progressing

station bill *n* **:** a list of the crew and their duties in case of fire and other emergencies that is posted in the crew's quarters or another conspicuous place on a ship — compare QUARTER BILL

station break *n* **1 :** a pause in a radio or television program or between programs for announcement of the identity of the network or local station **2 :** an announcement or plug given during a station break

station day *n* **:** the fast of Wednesday and Friday in the early Christian church and in the Eastern Orthodox Church

stationed *past of* STATION

sta·tio·ner \ˈstāsh(ə)nə(r)\ *n* -s [ME *stacioner*, fr. ML *stationarius*, fr. *station-*, *statio* shop (fr. L, station) + L *-arius* -er — more at STATION] **1** *archaic* **:** a person engaged in the book trade: as **a :** BOOKSELLER **b :** PUBLISHER **2 :** one that sells stationery

station error *n* **:** the difference between the geodetic and the astronomical latitude or longitude of a place caused by a local deviation in the direction of gravity

sta·tio·nery \'stāshə,nerē, -ri *sometimes* -sh(ə)nər-\ *n* -ES *often attrib* [*stationer* + *-y*] **1 :** materials (as paper, pens, pencils, ink, blankbooks, ledgers, and cards) for writing or typing **2 :** letter paper usu. accompanied with matching envelopes **:** writing paper ⟨hotel ~⟩ ⟨write him on the company's ~⟩
station hospital *n* **:** a military hospital usu. located in a communications zone that gives treatment to troops stationed in its immediate area
station house *n* **:** a house at a post or station: as **a :** POLICE STATION **b :** FIRE STATION **c :** a usu. rural railroad station
stationing *pres part of* STATION
sta·tion·man \'stāshən,man, -,mən\ *n, pl* **stationmen :** one whose work is done from a particular place or station: as **a :** a bottomer in a mine **b :** one that loads and unloads fuel trucks or tank cars **c :** one that operates the controls at a steel rolling mill
stationmaster \'==,==\ *n* **:** an official in charge of the operation of a railroad station
station point *n* **:** the position of an observer that determines the perspective rendering of the objects or scene being represented in a drawing — compare LINEAR PERSPECTIVE
station pointer *n* **:** an instrument that has three arms of which the two outer are adjustable and the inner is fixed at the zero of a circle and that is used for locating on a chart the position of a place from which the angles subtended by three distant objects whose positions are known have been observed — see THREE-POINT PROBLEM
station pole *or* **station rod** *or* **station staff** *n* **1 :** a rod for marking stations in surveying **2 :** RANGE POLE **3 :** LEVELING ROD
stations *pl of* STATION, *pres 3d sing of* STATION
station selector *n* **:** the element of a radio receiving set that tunes in the signal from any station
stations of the cross *often cap S&C* **1 :** a series of 14 (as in the Roman Catholic and Anglican Churches) or more (as in the Eastern Orthodox Church) images or pictures that symbolize scenes of suffering in the successive stages of Christ's passion and are usu. located in a church or on the road to a church or shrine **2 :** a devotional exercise of a church in which a worshiper pauses before each of the stations of the cross, meditates, and recites appropriate prayers
station track *n* **:** a track at a railroad station on which trains are spotted to receive or discharge passengers and baggage as distinguished from a through track for the passage of trains — called also *house track*
station–type machine tool *n* **:** a machine tool having stations at which various operations are performed on the work
station wagon *n* **:** an automobile that resembles a sedan but has no separate luggage compartment and has a top less rounded in back, a tailgate, and one or more rear seats readily lifted out or folded to facilitate light trucking — called also *beach wagon*
statis *abbr* statistical
stat·i·scope *n* [by alter.] **:** STATOSCOPE
stat·ism *or* **state·ism** \'stād,izəm, -ā,ti-\ *n* -S [¹*state* + *-ism*; trans. of F *étatisme*] **:** concentration of all economic controls and planning in the hands of a highly centralized government ⟨abandoned her former reliance on ~ in favor of private enterprise —*World*⟩ — compare GOVERNMENTALISM 1
¹**stat·ist** \-ād·əst, -ātə-\ *n* -S [¹*state* + *-ist*] **1** *archaic* **:** one versed in state affairs **:** POLITICIAN ⟨hold it, as our ~s do, a baseness to write fair —Shak.⟩ **2** [trans. of F *étatiste*] **:** an advocate of statism ⟨our planners and ~s —Raymond Moley⟩
²**statist** \"\ *adj* **:** of, relating to, or advocating statism ⟨a ~ conception⟩ ⟨the partisans of the ~ formula —Gordon Wright⟩ ⟨matter-of-fact acceptance of a ~ and collectivist ideology —Henry Hazlitt⟩
³**stat·ist** \'stad·əst, -atə-\ *n* -S [G, back-formation fr. *statistik* statistics — more at STATISTICS] **:** one who collects statistics **:** STATISTICIAN
sta·tis·ti·cal \stə'tistəkəl, -istēk-\ *adj* [*statistics* + *-al*] **:** of, relating to, or dealing with statistics ⟨~ method⟩ ⟨a ~ tabulation⟩ ⟨a ~ study⟩ — **sta·tis·ti·cal·ly** \-istək(ə)lē, -tēk-\ *adv*
statistical engineering *n* **:** the application of statistical inference to engineering experiments
statistical graph *n* **:** a statistical frequency curve
statistical inference *n* **:** the making of estimates concerning a population from information gathered from samples
statistical mechanics *n pl but usu sing in constr* **:** a branch of physics dealing with the application of the principles of statistics to the mechanics of a system consisting of a large number of parts having motions that differ by small steps over a large range
statistical variable *n* **:** a variable having discrete values that differ through random causes and when arranged in order form a statistical distribution or array
stat·is·ti·cian \,stad·ə'stishən, -atə-\ *n* -S [*statistics* + *-ian*] **:** one versed in or engaged in compiling statistics
sta·tis·ti·cism \stə'tistə,sizəm\ *n* -S [*statistics* + *-ism*] **:** proneness to use statistics
sta·tis·tics \stə'tist|iks, |ēks\ *n pl but sing or pl in constr* [G *statistik* (fr. NL *statisticus*, adj., of state affairs, statistical, fr. L *status* state + *-isticus* -istic) + E *-s* — more at STATE] **1 :** a science dealing with the collection, analysis, interpretation, and presentation of masses of numerical data ⟨~ is a branch of mathematics⟩ **2 :** a collection of quantitative data ⟨~ are available on car ownership⟩ **3 statistic** *n sing* [back-formation fr. *statistics*] **a :** a single term or datum in a collection of statistics **b :** a quantity that describes a sample and is thus an estimate of a parameter of the population
stat·i·tron \'stad·ə,trän\ *n* -S [electro*static* + *-tron*] **:** ELECTROSTATIC GENERATOR
sta·tive \'stād·iv\ *adj* [NL *stativus*, fr. L *status* (past part. of *stare* to stand) + *-ivus* -ive — more at STAND] **:** expressing existence or state — compare ACTIVE 3b, STATIC 4c
stato- *comb form* [ISV, fr. Gk *statos*, verbal of *histanai* to cause to stand, set, place on a balance, weigh — more at STAND] **1 :** resting ⟨*stato*blast⟩ ⟨*stato*spore⟩ **2 :** balance **:** equilibrium ⟨*stato*receptor⟩ ⟨*stato*scope⟩
stat·o·blast \'stad·ə,blast\ *n* [ISV *stato-* + *-blast*] **1 :** a bud or germ in many freshwater bryozoans that is enclosed in a chitinous envelope in the parent body, generally serves to preserve the species in winter, and bursts and develops into a new individual in spring **2 :** an internal bud in some sponges that is somewhat analogous to the statoblast of a bryozoan **:** GEMMULE
stato·cyst \-,sist\ *n* [ISV *stato-* + *cyst*] **1 :** a cellular cyst containing one or more statoliths **2 :** an organ of equilibration and orientation that consists of a fluid-filled chamber containing a statolith and is widely distributed among invertebrate animals — compare LABYRINTHINE SENSE, OTOCYST
stat·ohm \'stad·+,-\ *n* [*stat-* + *ohm*] **:** the cgs electrostatic unit of resistance equal to about 8.9×10^{11} ohms
stato·kinetic \¦stad·ō+\ *adj* [*stato-* + *kinetic*] **:** of, relating to, or constituting a kinetic postural reflex that is initiated by stimulation of the semicircular canals through movements of the head and involves compensatory movements of the limbs and eyes — compare STATOTONIC
stat·ol·a·try \stād·'älə·trē\ *n* -ES [¹*state* + *-o-* + *-latry*] **:** worship of the state **:** advocacy of a highly centralized and all-powerful national government
stat·o·lith \'stad·ᵊl,ith\ *n* -S [ISV *stato-* + *-lith*] **1 a :** the calcareous body in a statocyst **b :** a similar body in the lagena of a fish or amphibian **2 :** any of various starch grains or other solid bodies in the cytoplasm that are thought responsible by their changes in position for changes in orientation of an organ or part — **stat·o·lith·ic** \¦==¦lithik\ *adj*
stator \'stād·ə(r), -tad-·\ *n* -S [NL, fr. L, one that stands, fr. *status* + *-or*] **:** a stationary part in a machine in or about which a rotor revolves: as **a** (1) **:** the stationary member of an electrical machine (as an induction motor) (2) **:** the stationary plates of a variable capacitor **b** (1) **:** the case enclosing a turbine wheel (2) **:** the body of stationary blades or nozzles of a turbine — compare ROTOR 1b
stato·receptor \¦stad·ō+\ *n* [*stato-* + *receptor*] **:** a sense organ for the reception of stimuli governing equilibration and orientation in space
stato·scope \'stad·ə,skōp\ *n* [ISV *stato-* + *-scope*] **1 :** a sensitive aneroid barometer for recording small changes in atmospheric pressure **2 :** an instrument for indicating small changes in the altitude of an airplane
stato·spore \-,spō(ə)r\ *n* [*stato-* + *spore*] **:** RESTING SPORE; *esp* **:** a thick-walled resistant spore formed within the frustules of various chiefly marine centric diatoms
stato·tonic \¦stad·ə+\ *adj* [*stato-* + *tonic*] **:** of, relating to, or constituting a tonic postural reflex that is initiated by stimulation of the utricle of the labyrinth through position of the head or movements of the neck muscles and involves alteration of skeletal muscle tone — compare STATOKINETIC
-stats *pl of* -STAT
statua *n* -S [ME, fr. L — more at STATUE] *obs* **:** STATUE ⟨here I will set up her ~ —Christopher Marlowe⟩
stat·u·a·rist \'stachəwərəst\ *n* -S [*statuary* + *-ist*] *archaic* **:** STATUARY 2
¹**stat·u·ary** \'stachə,werē\ *n* -ES [in sense 1, fr. L *statuaria*, fr. fem. of *statuarius* of a statue; in sense 2, fr. L *statuarius*, fr. *statuarius*, adj.] **1 a :** a branch of sculpture treating of figures in the round ⟨critics of painting and ~ —E.J.Banfield⟩ **b :** a collection of statues ⟨a group of ~, faintly seen —Matthew Arnold⟩ **2 :** one who practices the art of making statues **:** SCULPTOR ⟨a ~ might have modeled from it —Laurence Sterne⟩
²**statuary** \"\ *adj* [L *statuarius*, fr. *statua* statue + *-arius* -ary] **1 :** of or relating to statues ⟨the ~ art⟩ **2 :** consisting of or suitable for statues ⟨a ~ monument⟩ ⟨~ marble⟩
statuary bronze *n* **:** bronze whose surface has been treated with acid to produce the dark brown color frequently given to bronze statues
statuary marble *n* **:** marble of the purest white and of finely crystalline form used in architecture and sculpture
¹**stat·ue** \'sta(,)chü, -,chə, -,chü, +V *often* -,chəw\ *n* -S [ME, fr. MF, fr. L *statua*, fr. *statuere* to set up — more at STATUTE] **1 :** a likeness (as of a person or animal) sculptured, modeled, or cast in a solid substance (as marble, bronze, or wax) **:** IMAGE ⟨a bronze equestrian ~⟩ **2 statues** *pl but sing in constr* **:** a game in which the players dance or whirl around or are taken by the hand in turn and twirled about, freeze in whatever positions they find themselves in when a signal is given or the twirler lets go, and are judged on their poses

statue 1

²**statue** \"\ *vt* **statued; statued; statueing** *or* **statuing; statues 1 :** to adorn (as a walk or park) with statues ⟨a *statued* garden⟩ **2** *archaic* **:** to form a statue of **:** represent in statuary ⟨Herodotus sitteth *statued* —Robert Bridges †1930⟩
statue of liberty *usu cap S&L* [fr. the *Statue of Liberty* on Liberty Island in New York harbor; fr. the comparison of the upraised passing arm of the passer to the torch-bearing arm of the statue] **:** an offensive football play in which a back raises an arm as if to throw a pass and the ball is taken from his hand by a teammate who runs behind him
stat·u·esque \¦stachə¦wesk\ *adj* [¹*statue* + *-esque*] **:** resembling a statue: as **a** (1) **:** having a massive dignity or impressiveness **:** MAJESTIC ⟨a fine, ~ giant —Walter Lippmann⟩ (2) **:** strikingly well-proportioned **:** TALL, SHAPELY ⟨a ~ model⟩ ⟨she measures a ~ 5 feet 8 —Roger Dettmer⟩ **b** (1) **:** immobile or rigid in stance or posture ⟨~ great white heron —J.H.Baker⟩ ⟨~ soldiers⟩ (2) **:** coldly formal **:** INFLEXIBLE ⟨~ piety —W.M.Thackeray⟩ **c :** marked by classic harmony of form but little color, warmth, or feeling **:** MARMOREAL ⟨a composed, ~ little novel —*New Yorker*⟩ — **stat·u·esque·ly** *adv* — **stat·u·esque·ness** *n* -ES
stat·u·ette \¦stachə¦wet, *usu* -ed·+V\ *n* -S [F, dim. of *statue*] **:** a small statue usu. much smaller than life-size — compare FIGURINE
statu–quo–ite \,sta|(,)tü'kwō,īt, ,stal, |(,)chü-\ *n* -S [(*in*) *statu quo* + *-ite*] **:** an upholder of the existing state of affairs ⟨a perfectibilian and a *statu-quo-ite* were among the guests at this hall —*Times Lit. Supp.*⟩
stat·ure \'stachə(r)\ *n* -S [ME, fr. OF *stature, estature*, fr. L *statura*, fr. *status* (past part. of *stare* to stand) + *-ura* -ure — more at STAND] **1 :** natural height (as of a person or animal) in an upright position **:** standing posture ⟨a man of tall ~⟩ ⟨the fine ~ of the Indian males —*Amer. Guide Series: Oregon*⟩ **2 :** quality or status gained by impressive growth, development, or achievement **:** high caliber **:** PRESTIGE ⟨a playwright of ~ —Henry Hewes⟩ ⟨every piece of work you do adds something to your ~, increases the power and maturity of your experience —Thomas Wolfe⟩ ⟨continues to advance in ~ as a senior institution of learning —N.M.Pusey⟩ **syn** see QUALITY
stat·ured \¦stachə(r)d\ *adj* **:** having a specified stature — usu. used in combination ⟨short-*statured*⟩ ⟨fair-*statured* as the stately palm —Robert Southey⟩
sta·tus \'stā|d·əs, 'sta|, |təs *sometimes* 'stā| *or* 'stä|\ *n* -ES *often attrib* [L — more at STATE] **1 a :** the condition (as arising out of age, sex, mental incapacity, crime, alienage, or public station) of a person that determines the nature of his legal personality, his legal capacities, and the nature of the legal relations to the state or to other persons into which he may enter **b :** the condition of a political entity (as a state) determining its legal character in relationships with other political entities **2 a :** position or rank in relation to others (as in a social order, community, class, or profession) ⟨the ~ of a father⟩ ⟨the ~ of a doctor⟩ ⟨reduced to the ~ of a guerrilla leader —Woodrow Wyatt⟩ ⟨the city's ~ as a tourist attraction —Winthrop Sargeant⟩ — compare ROLE **b :** relative rank in a hierarchy of prestige ⟨the ~ of a corporation executive in the U.S.⟩ ⟨a rigid ~ system evolved during feudalism⟩ **c :** superior rank **:** high prestige **:** RECOGNITION ⟨academic ~ —Annabel Gray⟩ ⟨her connections gave her ~ in the group⟩ ⟨~ symbol⟩ ⟨~ anxiety⟩ ⟨the ~ seekers . . . continually straining to surround themselves with visible evidence of the superior rank they are claiming —Vance Packard⟩ **3 :** state of affairs **:** SITUATION ⟨the ~ of the negotiations between company and union officials⟩ ⟨the inventory ~⟩ **4 :** an abnormal condition of a person or animal **syn** see STATE
status asth·mat·i·cus \-az'mad·əkəs\ *n* [NL, lit., asthmatic state] **:** an attack of asthma of long duration characterized by dyspnea, cyanosis, exhaustion, and sometimes collapse
status ep·i·lep·ti·cus \-,epə'leptəkəs\ *n* [NL, lit., epileptic state] **:** a state in epilepsy in which the attacks occur in rapid succession without recovery of consciousness
status lym·phat·i·cus \-(,)lim'fad·əkəs\ *n* [NL, lit., lymphatic state] **:** a constitutional condition of the body marked by hyperplasia of the lymphatic tissue — called also *lymphatism*
status quo \,==·'kwō\ *n* [L, state in which] **:** the state in which something is **:** the existing state of affairs (as in political or social relationships) at the time in question ⟨seeks to preserve the economic *status quo*⟩ ⟨has a vested interest in the *status quo*⟩
status thy·mi·co·lym·phat·i·cus \-¦thīmə(,)kō(,)lim'fad·əkəs\ *n* [NL, lit., thymicolymphatic state] **:** a condition resembling status lymphaticus with conspicuous enlargement of the thymus
stat·ut·able \'stachəd·əbəl, -chətəb-\ *adj* [¹*statute* + *-able*] **:** made, introduced, regulated, or imposed by or in conformity to statute **:** STATUTORY, STANDARD ⟨~ provision⟩ ⟨~ age⟩ ⟨~ tonnage⟩
stat·ut·able·ness *n* -ES **:** the quality or state of being statutable
stat·ut·ably \-blē, -bli\ *adv* **:** in a statutable manner **:** conformably to the statutes
¹**stat·ute** \'sta(,)chül *also* -,chəl *sometimes* -,chü|; *usu* |d·+V\ *n* -S [ME *statut, statute*, fr. OF *statut, estatut, estatu*, fr. LL *statutum*, fr. L, neut. of *statutus*, past part. of *statuere* to stand up, set up, station, fr. *status* position, condition, state — more at STATUS] **1 :** something laid down or declared as fixed or established: as **a :** the edict of a ruler ⟨my acts, decrees, and ~s I deny —Shak.⟩ **b :** a law enacted by or by the authority of the supreme legislative branch of a government and esp. of a representative government **:** the written will of a legislature expressed with all the requisite forms of legislation as distinguished from the common or unwritten law — compare ACT, BILL, COMMON LAW, CONSTITUTION, DECREE, EDICT, ORDINANCE **c :** an act of a corporation or of its founder intended as a permanent rule or law ⟨the ~s of a university⟩ **d :** an international instrument setting up an agency and regulating its scope or authority ⟨the ~ of the Permanent Court of International Justice⟩ **2** *obs* **a :** STATUTE MERCHANT **b :** STATUTE STAPLE **3 :** STATUTE FAIR **4** [ME, influenced in meaning by *statue*] **:** STATUE
²**statute** \"\ *vt* -ED/-ING/-S [ME *statuten*, fr. *statut, statute*, n.] **:** to establish (a law) by statute **:** DECREE
³**statute** \"\ *adj* [¹*statute*] **:** fixed by statute **:** STATUTORY ⟨a ~ mile⟩ ⟨a ~ ton⟩
statute–barred \¦=(,)=¦=\ *adj* **:** barred by the statute of limitations
statute book *n* **1 :** an official, semiofficial, or recognized private collection of the statutes of a state or nation as a whole ⟨put a law on the *statute book*⟩ **2 :** the whole body of legislation of a given jurisdiction whether or not published as a whole
statute fair *or* **statutes fair** *n* **:** an annual fair formerly held in English towns and villages for the hiring of servants and farm laborers
statute merchant *n* [ME *statut marchand*, fr. AF *estatu marchaund*, lit., merchant statute] **:** a bond of record formerly in use in England giving the creditor power to seize the property of the debtor for failure to pay at a designated time
statute mile *n* **:** MILE 1a
statute of descent : a statute regulating the descent from ancestor to heir of real and sometimes other property — compare DESCENT 3c
statute of distribution : a statute regulating the distribution of the personal property or estate of a deceased person
statute of frauds : a statute designed to prevent fraudulent practices by requiring that various contracts and causes of action be evidenced by a writing signed by the party to be charged and varying in application to specific contracts according to British and U. S. state laws
statute of limitations *or* **statute of repose :** a statute assigning a certain time after which rights cannot be enforced by legal action — compare LACHES
statute roll *n* **:** a roll containing the engrossed text of a statute
statutes at large : statutes set forth in full in chronological order as enacted as distinguished from abridgments, revisions, codifications, or compilations; *specif* **:** a published compilation containing all the federal laws and resolutions public and private passed and all executive proclamations issued during a session of a congress
statutes of mortmain 1 : any of various English statutes restricting alienation of land in mortmain (as to an ecclesiastical corporation) for the purpose of preserving to the lords the feudal rights of relief, wardship, marriage, and escheat which conveyance in mortmain took away or of preventing undue accumulation of wealth in the hands of corporations **2 :** any of various statutes having purposes similar to those set forth in the English statutes of mortmain
statute staple *n* [ME, contr. of *statute (of the) staple*] **:** a bond of record formerly in use in England giving the creditor powers similar to those given by the statute merchant and acknowledged before the mayor of a staple
stat·u·to·ri·ly \¦stachə¦tōrəlē, -tȯr-, -li\ *adv* **:** in a statutory manner **:** by law ⟨~ created privileges —*New Republic*⟩
stat·u·to·ry \'stachə,tōrē, -tȯr-, -ri\ *adj* [¹*statute* + *-ory*] **1 :** of or relating to statutes ⟨~ matters⟩ **2 :** enacted, imposed, created, or regulated by statute ⟨a ~ age limit⟩ ⟨~ duty⟩ ⟨~ restrictions⟩ ⟨a ~ company⟩ ⟨~ attendance at chapel⟩
statutory bond *n* **:** COURT BOND
statutory civilian *n* **:** CIVILIAN 2
statutory crime *n* **:** STATUTORY OFFENSE
statutory declaration *n* **1** *Eng law* **:** a solemn declaration in lieu of an affidavit by a person conscientiously unable to take an oath **2** *Eng law* **:** a voluntary declaration by any person in an affirmation of documents (as written instruments or proofs of debts)
statutory foreclosure *n* **:** a foreclosure that is instituted by a suit in equity and involves the satisfaction of the debt to the extent made possible by a sale of the mortgaged property — distinguished from *strict foreclosure*
statutory guardian *n* **1 :** a guardian appointed by virtue of statutory authority **2** *Eng law* **:** a guardian appointed by deed or will by the father of minor children or by their surviving mother **:** TESTAMENTARY GUARDIAN
statutory instrument *n, Eng law* **:** a rule, order, or administrative regulation having the force of law promulgated by the crown in council, a minister, a local authority, a corporation or other body under power delegated by Parliament
statutory law *n* **:** the law declared by statute in the broadest sense as distinguished from the common or customary law or the law developed in ecclesiastical, equity, admiralty, or other courts without the aid of statute
statutory lien *n* **:** a lien given by statutory provisions and not otherwise existing
statutory next of kin : a blood relative of a person who in case of his death intestate will be entitled by virtue of a statute of distribution to take his personal estate — compare NEXT OF KIN
statutory offense *n* **:** a crime created by statute; *specif* **:** a criminal sexual offense (as rape or attempted rape)
statutory order *or* **statutory rule** *n, Eng law* **:** an administrative regulation promulgated pursuant to authority delegated by Parliament **:** STATUTORY INSTRUMENT
statutory period *n* **:** the period of time prescribed by a relevant statute of limitations
statutory rape *n* **:** sexual intercourse with a female whether willing or unwilling who is below an age fixed by the applicable statute as the age of consent
statutory referendum *n* **:** the submission of ordinary laws to the electorate after they have been passed by a legislative body
statutory rules *n pl, Scots law* **:** the acts of sederunt and acts of adjournal of the Court of Session and subordinate legislation set forth by orders in council and orders and regulations of government agencies and adopted under authority delegated by Parliament **:** STATUTORY INSTRUMENTS
statutory tenant *n* **:** a tenant whose tenancy has expired under the ordinary rules of law but who has rights by statute to pay rent and continue in occupation under rent control or other emergency legislation
statutory trust *n* **:** a trust created or authorized by statute (as for the care of animals or for the beneficiary of an action for wrongfully causing a person's death or for the social security trust funds)
stat·volt \'stat+,-\ *n* [*stat-* + *volt*] **:** the cgs electrostatic unit of potential difference equal to about 300 volts
staty *abbr* stationary
stau·cher \'stakər\ *Scot var of* STAGGER
stau·ding·er equation \'s(h)taùdiŋə(r)-\ *n, usu cap S* [after Hermann *Staudinger* †1965 Ger. chemist] **:** an equation for determining the molecular weight of polymeric materials that utilizes the viscosity of solutions of the polymer at definite concentrations
staum·rel \'stamrəl\ *adj* [Sc *staumer* to stagger, stumble (alter. of ¹*stammer*) + *-el*] *Scot* **:** HALF-WITTED
¹**staunch** *var of* STANCH
²**staunch** *or* **stanch** \'stȯnch, -ä-, -á- *sometimes* -a-, -aa(ə)-, -ai-\ *adj* -ER/-EST [ME, fr. MF *estanche*, fem. of *estanc*, fr. OF, fr. *estancher* to stanch] **1 a :** WATERTIGHT, SOUND ⟨a ~ ship⟩ **b :** strongly built **:** SUBSTANTIAL ⟨~ cabin⟩ **2 :** dependable to find, mark, or follow game ⟨~ hound⟩ ⟨drill his dog . . . to make him ~ on point —W.F.Brown b. 1903⟩ **3 :** constant and steadfast in loyalty **:** firm in principle **:** STEADY, TRUE ⟨the king's ~*est* followers⟩ ⟨~ defender of free speech⟩ ⟨~ friend⟩ ⟨~ ally⟩ **syn** see FAITHFUL
staunch·ly *or* **stanch·ly** *adv* [*staunch* + *-ly*] **:** in a staunch manner ⟨~ conservative⟩ ⟨a ~ defended principle⟩ ⟨he must hold the point ~ until his handler comes up —W.F.Brown b. 1903⟩
staunch·ness *or* **stanch·ness** *n* -ES **:** the quality of being staunch **:** LOYALTY, STEADFASTNESS
stau·ri·on \'stȯrē,än, -ēən\ *n* -S [NL, fr. LGk, small cross, dim. of *stauros* pale, stake, cross — more at STEER] **:** the point of intersection of the median and transverse palatine sutures

stauro- *comb form* [LL, fr. LGk, fr. Gk *stauros* pale, stake, cross] **:** cross ⟨*stauro*medusae⟩ ⟨*stauro*scope⟩
stau·rol·a·try \stȯ'räləträ\ *n* -ES [LL *staurolatria*, fr. LGk *stauro-* + LL *-latria* -latry] **:** worship of the cross or crucifix ⟨Satan's design in advancing ~ to the destruction of thousands of souls —Increase Mather⟩
stau·ro·lite \'stȯrə,līt\ *n* -S [F, fr. *stauro-* + *-lite*] **:** a mineral $(Fe,Mg)_2Al_9Si_4O_{23}(OH)$ consisting of a brown to black basic iron aluminum silicate in prismatic orthorhombic crystals often twinned so as to resemble a cross and generally found embedded in crystalline schists (hardness 7–7.5, sp. gr. 3.65–3.77) — **stau·ro·lit·ic** \;==;lid·ik\ *adj*

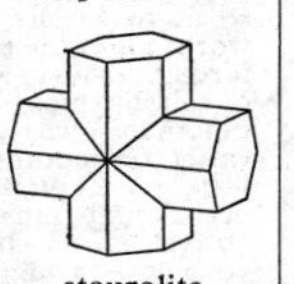
staurolite

stau·ro·medusae \;stȯ(,)rō+\ *n pl, cap* [NL, fr. *stauro-* + *medusae*, pl. of *medusa*] **:** an order of Scyphozoa comprising stalked or sessile jellyfish that have an aboral stalk ending in a sucker by which they attach themselves to marine plants and other objects, that both as larvae and adults are creeping or sessile, and that are limited to colder seas of both northern and southern hemispheres — **stauro·medusan** \"+\ *adj or n*
stau·ro·pe·gion \,stäurō'pē,yȯn\ *n, pl* **staurope·gia** \-ē(,)yä\ [MGk or NGk *staurop*ē*gion*, fr. MGk, act of fastening a cross on the spot where a church is to be built, fr. LGk *stauro-* + MGk *-pegion* (fr. *pēgnynai* to stick in, fix, fasten together) — more at PACT] *Eastern Church* **:** a church or monastery exempt from the jurisdiction of the local bishop and directly subject to the highest authority of the territorial church
stau·rop·ter·is \stȯ'räptərəs\ *n, cap* [NL, fr. *stauro-* + *-pteris*] **:** a genus of fossil plants frequent in the Carboniferous and known only from fronds which have the pinnae disposed in equal pairs
stau·ro·pus \'stȯrəpəs\ *n, cap* [NL, fr. *stauro-* + *-pus*] **:** a genus of chiefly Palaearctic medium-sized dull-colored moths (family Notodontidae) — see LOBSTER MOTH
stau·ro·scope \'stȯrə,skōp\ *n* [ISV *stauro-* + *-scope*] **:** a modified polariscope used to find the position of planes of light vibration in sections of crystals — **stau·ro·scop·ic** \;==;skäpik\ *adj* — **stau·ro·scop·i·cal·ly** \-pək(ə)lē\ *adv*
stau·ro·tide \'stȯrə,tīd\ *n* -S [F, fr. *staurot-* (irreg. fr. Gk *stauros* cross) + *-ide* — more at STEER] **:** STAUROLITE
¹stave \'stāv\ *n* -S [back-formation fr. *staves*, pl. of ¹*staff*] **1 :** a wooden stick **:** CUDGEL, STAFF **2 a :** any of the narrow strips of wood or narrow iron plates placed edge to edge to form the sides, covering, or lining of a vessel or structure — see BARREL illustration **b :** a piece shaped like a stave: as (1) **:** a bearing strip for an arch centering (2) **:** a slat of a hayrack **3 a :** any of the bars of a lantern pinion **b :** a bar or round of a rack or ladder **4 a :** a set of verses (as a stanza) ⟨forms that deviate from the common epic measure, such as the Northern lyrical ~*s* —W.P.Ker⟩ **b :** a letter of an alphabet **5 a :** a staff in music notation **b :** a bar or brief passage of music ⟨the quick, eager ~ of the chaffinch —*Scotsman*⟩ **6 :** BOWSTAVE **7 :** the stem of an acanthus leaf in classic architectural ornament
²stave \"\ *vb* **staved** \-vd\ *or* **stove** \-tōv\ **staved** *or* **stove; staving; staves** *vt* **1 a :** to break in the staves of (a cask) so that the wine or liquor is lost **b :** to lose or destroy (wine or liquor) by smashing the cask **2 a :** to cause a break in (a boat's hull) **:** smash (a hole) in a boat — often used with *in* ⟨whose deckhouse had been *stove* in by the tremendous seas —Homer Bigart⟩ **b :** to crush in **:** break inward ⟨*staved* in several ribs⟩ **3 :** to furnish with or form into staves **4 :** to thrust with great force ~ *vi* **1 a :** to come apart (as a cask or barrel) **:** break up **b :** to become stove in — used of a boat or ship **2 :** to walk or move rapidly **:** HURRY, RUSH — **stave and tail :** to interpose with the staff in bear baiting and hold back the dog by the tail
stave bolt *n* **:** a section of a log to be cut into staves
staved \'stāvd\ *adj* **:** equipped with or made of staves ⟨the ~ wooden tub —Merle Constiner⟩
stave oak *n* **:** WHITE OAK 1b
stave off *vt* **1 :** to beat off (an animal or person) with or as if with a staff or rod **:** drive or fight off **2 :** to ward or fend off (someone) **:** hold back **:** keep away ⟨let's *stave* the greaser *off* till dark —Zane Grey⟩ ⟨often had to *stave off* creditors —W.A. Swanberg⟩ **3 :** to forestall or prevent (something adverse) esp. at the last moment or in extremity **:** DEFLECT, AVERT ⟨the last form of credit that *staved off* foreclosure —*New Republic*⟩
stave pipe *n* **:** a pipe made of wooden staves
¹staver \'stāvər, -tav-\ *vi* [ME *staveren*] *chiefly Scot* **:** to walk restlessly or unsteadily
²stav·er \'stāvə(r)\ *n* -S [²*stave* + *-er*] **:** a bustling energetic person
staverwort \'==,=\ *n* [¹*staver* + *wort*] **:** TANSY RAGWORT
staves *pl of* STAFF *or of* STAVE, *pres 3d sing of* STAVE
staves·acre \'stāv,zākə(r)\ *n* [ME *staphisagre, staphisagrie*, fr. L *staphis agria*, fr. Gk, fr. *staphis, astaphis* raisin + *agria*, fem. of *agrios* wild, fr. *agros* field — more at ACRE] **1 :** a Eurasian larkspur (*Delphinium staphisagria*) having racemose purple flowers **2 :** the seeds of the stavesacre that contain delphinine, are violently emetic and cathartic, and are used in Eurasia as a fish poison
stavewood \'==,=\ *n* **1 :** PARADISE TREE 1 **2 a :** either of two Australian trees (*Tarrietia argyrodendron* and *T. actinophylla*) that are sometimes grown as ornamentals and yield hard heavy reddish brown lumber **b :** BUNGI-BUNGI
¹stav·ing \'stāviŋ\ *adj* [fr. pres. part. of ²*stave*] **:** POWERFUL, EXCELLENT
²staving \"\ *adv* **:** EXTREMELY
³staving \"\ *n* -S [¹*stave* + *-ing*] **:** material for forming staves **:** a quantity of staves **:** a casing of staves
¹staw \'stȯ\ [ME (Sc), alter. of ME *stal*, fr. OE *stæl*] *Scot past of* STEAL
²staw \"\ *chiefly Scot var of* STALL
³staw \"\ *n* [²*staw*] *chiefly Scot* **:** SURFEIT
¹stay \'stā\ *n* -S [ME *stey, stay*, fr. OE *stæg*; akin to MLG *stach* rope, stay, ON *stag* stay, G dial. (Alemannic) *stagen* to get stiff, OE *stēle, stȳle* steel — more at STEEL] **1 :** a large strong rope usu. of wire used to support a mast by being extended forward from the head of one mast down to some other or to some part of the ship **:** a fore-and-aft stay — compare BACKSTAY; see SHIP illustration **2 a :** a guy rope **b :** a tie piece to hold parts together or to contribute stiffness in engineering construction — compare STRUT — **at a long stay :** at such a small angle with the bottom as results when the anchor is not close in — used of an anchor cable — **at a short stay :** at such a large angle with the bottom as results when the anchor is close in — used of an anchor cable — **in stays** *adv* **1 :** in process of going about from one tack to another **2 :** in process of heading into the wind with sails shaking
²stay \"\ *vb* -ED/-ING/-S *vt* **1 :** to fasten or secure (as a smokestack) with or as if with stays **2 a :** to bring (a ship) about on the other tack **b :** to incline (a mast) forward, aft, or to one side by the stays and backstays ~ *vi* **:** to go about **:** TACK — used of a ship
³stay \"\ *vb* **stayed** \-ād\ *or* **staid** \"\ *or substand* **stood** \'stu̇d\ **stayed** *or* **staid** *or substand* **stood; staying; stays** [ME *steyen*, fr. MF *estei-, estai-*, stem of *ester* to stand, stop, stay, fr. L *stare* to stand — more at STAND] *vi* **1 :** to halt an advance **:** stop going forward **:** PAUSE ⟨if he paused here at all, he didn't ~ to found a city —Green Peyton⟩ **2 :** to stop doing something **:** CEASE — often used with *from* **3 :** to reach an end **:** become stopped — used of a process or action **4 a :** to remain somewhere or with someone rather than proceed or leave ⟨~ with us until the bridge is repaired —Victor Canning⟩ — often used with *on* ⟨proposed a brief visit but ~*ed* on for months⟩ **b :** to continue in a place or condition **:** remain unmoved or unaltered ⟨the instrument *staid* in tune for a greater period of time —A.E.Wier⟩ **c** (1) **:** to remain in the stomach — often used with *down* ⟨couldn't make spicy foods ~ down⟩ (2) **:** to satisfy appetite substantially — used of food **5 :** to stand firm **:** hold steadfast **6 :** to take up or maintain residence **:** LIVE, LODGE, VISIT ⟨~*ed* overnight at a waterfront hotel⟩ ⟨~*ed* with friends all along his route⟩ **7** *obs* **:** to wait quietly or passively **8** *obs* **:** to become deferred or kept waiting **:** become postponed **9** *obs* **:** HESITATE, DELAY, ABSTAIN **10 :** to keep even in a contest or rivalry — used with *with* ⟨was supremely confident that no rival could ~ with him —Allison Danzig & Joe King⟩ **11 :** to call a poker bet without raising — often used with *in* **12** *obs* **:** to be in waiting or attendance **13 a :** to remain in order to wait ⟨~*ed* neither for time nor tide⟩ ⟨~*ed* for me after the dinner⟩ **b :** to remain in order to share or participate — used with *for* ⟨urged them to ~ for tea⟩ ~ *vt* **1 :** to wait for **:** ABIDE, AWAIT ⟨I will not ~ thy questions —Shak.⟩ **2 :** to last out (a race, contest, or trial of endurance) **:** hold out for the extent or duration of **:** STICK ⟨should not be troubled to ~ the mile and a half —*Sydney (Australia) Bull.*⟩ ⟨we may not be able to ~ the course against moderately efficient tyranny —*Times Lit. Supp.*⟩ **3 :** to remain during **:** assist at **:** participate in ⟨she ~*ed* the sacrament —Jane Austen⟩ **4 :** to stop the progress or advance of **:** hold from proceeding **:** CHECK, DELAY, DETAIN, RESTRAIN ⟨the huge man in the red shirt ~*ed* his cudgel —Michael Arlen⟩ ⟨do something to ~ bloodshed —Charles Dickens⟩ ⟨might have ~*ed* the ruinous rise in prices —E.H.Youngman⟩ **5** *archaic* **:** to take or hold prisoner **6 :** to stop or keep something from moving **:** hold motionless **:** FIX **7 a :** to prevent, block, or stop from an action or proceeding **:** hold back ⟨there is nothing here . . . to ~ us in our flight —Virginia Woolf⟩ **b :** to stop or suspend the effect or progress of by judicial proceedings or executive mandate ⟨the court of appeals ~*ed* the order⟩ ⟨denied a motion by counsel to ~ the annual meeting⟩ **c** *archaic* **:** to cease from (an action, motion, or process) **8 :** to check the course of (a disease or an evil influence) **:** HALT ⟨that the plague may be ~*ed* from the people —1 Chron 21:22 (AV)⟩ **9 :** ALLAY, CALM, PACIFY ⟨~*ed* the civil war⟩ **10 :** to quiet the hunger of temporarily **:** appease the pangs of appetite of **:** SATISFY ⟨a glass of milk ~*ed* me until meal time⟩ ⟨offered him a snack to ~ his stomach⟩
syn REMAIN, WAIT, ABIDE, LINGER, TARRY: STAY, the most general of these verbs, suggests a continuance in one place for an appreciable time, often as, or in the manner of a visitor or guest ⟨*stay* at a hotel for a week⟩ ⟨*stayed* for the evening meal —Sherwood Anderson⟩ ⟨the itinerant weaver and the household loom *stayed* on in the smaller communities until late in the nineteenth century —*Amer. Guide Series: Mich.*⟩ REMAIN can add the idea of staying after the time of expected departure or a reasonable occasion for departure ⟨the others left but the officer *remained* for an hour more⟩ ⟨went to Europe in the spring of 1806, *remaining* over a year —M.H.Thomas⟩ ⟨no permanent ice *remains*, but snowbanks persist in places —Gladys Wrigley⟩ ⟨in earlier geological periods these were gigantic ranges; today only a few precipitous slopes *remain* —*Amer. Guide Series: Minn.*⟩ ⟨piles of stones *remain* to indicate the site of the mission's gristmill —*Amer. Guide Series: Tenn.*⟩ WAIT implies an event in the future, immediate or distant, for which one stays in anticipation ⟨*wait* for the guests to depart⟩ ⟨if we were to *wait* for the scientists to reach conclusions conducive to certitude, we would have a long wait —L.A.Foley⟩ ⟨when a man disregards current conventions he must *wait* for the future —O.W. Holmes †1935⟩ ABIDE signifies to stay for considerable time, suggesting long residence or a patient waiting or sometimes the staying of one who has found a place of respite or repose and has no immediate intention of leaving ⟨he must get out alone . . . into the wilderness and *abide* there hunting till he had built up his strength and regained his pride —Stuart Cloete⟩ ⟨here she was forced to *abide* —Thomas Hardy⟩ ⟨the foundation of a culture whose influence will *abide* while the world stands —Edward Clodd⟩ LINGER and TARRY both suggest a remaining or staying on in one place by a delaying of departure or of expected procedure in a given direction as from fondness for the place or situation or its concomitants or from uncertainty or recalcitrance ⟨the less casual visitor, with time to *linger*, senses the charm of the old church —*Amer. Guide Series: Texas*⟩ ⟨a young American who is *lingering* in Europe after the First World War —B.R.Redman⟩ ⟨she *lingered* for a few moments to talk with him —Sherwood Anderson⟩ ⟨numerous legends *linger* around this old dwelling —*Amer. Guide Series: Conn.*⟩ ⟨they did not *tarry* in the little settlement but sailed up the Ashley river, and chose a site 18 miles above the town —L.H.Beck⟩ ⟨that night after the guests had *tarried* long over their tea . . . the woman still lingered behind the stove —Pearl Buck⟩ **syn** see in addition DEFER, RESIDE
— **stay put :** to be firmly fixed, attached, or established **:** remain permanently
⁴stay \"\ *n* -S **1 a :** a bringing to a stop **:** the action of halting **:** the state of being stopped **:** CHECK **b :** a stopping or suspension of procedure or execution by judicial or executive order ⟨was asked to grant a ~ of execution —*N.Y.Times*⟩ **c :** the cessation of motion, progression, or action **:** a coming to a halt ⟨pressed forward without stop or ~⟩ **d** *obs* **:** something that causes a stop **:** HINDRANCE, OBSTACLE, OBSTRUCTION **2** *obs* **:** MODERATION, SELF-CONTROL **3** *obs* **:** a time of waiting or delay **:** DEFERMENT, POSTPONEMENT **4 :** a temporary residence or sojourn **:** a period of abode ⟨an extended holiday lengthened itself into a ~ of 16 years —J.T.Ellis⟩ **5 :** capacity for endurance **:** STAYING POWER **6 :** a fixed or stationary condition **:** a state without motion forward or back **:** STANDSTILL
⁵stay \"\ *n* -S [MF *estaie*, of Gmc origin; akin to MD *staen* to stand, OHG *stān, stēn* — more at STAND] **1 a :** something that serves as a prop **:** BRACE, SUPPORT ⟨special lid ~*s* and pneumatic dampers hold the lid open —*Nat'l Stamp News*⟩ **b :** someone or something that supports or helps **:** an object of reliance ⟨in this kingdom of illusions we grope eagerly for ~*s* and foundations —R.W.Emerson⟩ ⟨this great valiant class, the ~ of domestic England —Bernardine Kielty⟩ **2 a :** a corset stiffened with bones and esp. made in two pieces and laced together — usu. used in pl. **b :** the bones so used — usu. used in pl. **3 :** a series of plain or fancy stitches or a piece of cloth sewn into a garment for reinforcing points of strain, controlling fullness, or preventing stretching **4 :** a corner reinforcement in a rigid paper box
⁶stay \"\ *vb* -ED/-ING/-S [partly fr. MF *estaier*, fr. *estaie*, n.; partly fr. ⁵*stay*] *vt* **1 a :** to hold up or provide support for **:** PROP, SUSTAIN ⟨a hand on her uncle's chair to ~ herself from falling —George Meredith⟩ **b :** to provide moral support for **:** COMFORT, STRENGTHEN ⟨turned from the man whose friendship had ~*ed* him —Winston Churchill⟩ **2 :** to fix on as a foundation **:** GROUND, REST ⟨all my trust on thee is ~*ed* —Charles Wesley⟩ **3 :** to reinforce or strengthen with stays or supports of various kinds: as **a :** to sew stays into (as a corset) **b :** to reinforce (weak fur pelts) with fabric on the leather side ~ *vi* **1** *obs* **:** to be upheld **:** LEAN, REST — used with *on* or *upon* **2** *obs* **:** to place reliance or confidence **:** show trust **:** DEPEND — used with *on* or *upon* **syn** see BASE
¹stay-at-home \'stāət,hōm, *chiefly Brit* -ə,tōm\ *adj* [fr. the phrase *stay at home*] **:** remaining in one's residence, locality, or country **:** HOMEKEEPING ⟨a *stay-at-home* friend —Jerome Weidman⟩ ⟨while we were still overseas . . . *stay-at-home* doctors had taken over our practices —Milton Silverman⟩
²stay-at-home \"\ *n* **:** one that remains in his residence, locality, or country **:** one not given to wandering or travel **:** HOMEBODY ⟨travelogues that the *stay-at-homes* must additionally endure from the globe-trotters —Peter De Vries⟩
stay bar *n* [⁵*stay*] **:** a saddle bar passing through the mullions and secured to the jambs in an ornamental window to keep leaded glass in place
stay bolt *n* [⁵*stay*] **:** a bolt or short rod commonly threaded throughout its length and used as a stay to connect opposite plates (as in a steam boiler) that are subjected to a pressure tending to force them apart
stay-bolt tap *n* **:** a long combination cutting tool that successively reams, rough-taps, and finish-taps a stay-bolt hole
stayed *past of* STAY
¹stay·er \'stāə(r)\ *n* -S [⁶*stay* + *-er*] **:** one that stays: as **a :** one that upholds or supports **b :** BONER 1 **c :** an operator of a machine for joining and taping cardboard box parts
²stayer \"\ *n* -S [³*stay* + *-er*] **:** one that stays: as **a :** something that checks or restrains **b :** one having powers of endurance or perseverance ⟨fast horses — sprinters but not ~*s* —G.F.T.Ryall⟩
stay hole *n* [¹*stay*] **:** an opening in a staysail through which passes one of the hanks joining the sail to the stay
staying *pres part of* STAY
staying power *n* **:** capacity for endurance **:** STAMINA
stay-in strike *or* **stay-in** \'stā,in-\ *n* -S [fr. *stay in*, v.] **:** a slowdown or stoppage of work intended to bring pressure on an employer and concerted by workers who remain in their work place — compare LOCKOUT, SIT-DOWN
staylace \'=,=\ *n* [⁵*stay* + *lace*] **:** a corset lace
stay law *n* [⁴*stay*] **:** a moratory law **:** a law suspending or providing a means of suspending execution of judgments or sale on foreclosure or otherwise suspending legal remedies for a limited time
stay·less \'stāləs\ *adj* [⁵*stay* + *-less*] **1** *obs* **:** UNSUPPORTED **2 :** CORSETLESS
stay log *n* [⁵*stay*] **:** an eccentric arm mounted on a lathe as a support for a veneer flitch and permitting alteration of the sweep so as to secure enhanced grain effects in half-round veneer
stay·man convention \'stāmən-\ *n, usu cap S* [after Samuel M. *Stayman* b1909 Amer. bridge expert] **:** a convention in contract bridge of responding to an opening no-trump bid with an artificial bid in clubs to invite a rebid in a four-card major suit by the no-trump bidder if he has one
stay out *vt* [³*stay*] **1 :** to remain to or beyond the end of ⟨*stayed out* the whole long performance⟩ **2 :** linger after the departure of **:** OUTSTAY ⟨*stayed* her cousin *out*⟩
staypak \'stā,pak\ *n* -S [³*stay* + *pak*, alter. of *packed*] **:** wood densified by pressure and heat and stabilized by its lignin content with no added resin
stay pin *n* [⁵*stay*] **:** a crosspiece or stud in a link of a chain to prevent kinking
stays *pl of* STAY, *pres 3d sing of* STAY
stay·sail \'stāsəl (*usu nautical pronunc*), -ā,sāl\ *n* [¹*stay* + *sail*] **:** a fore-and-aft sail hoisted on a stay — see SAIL illustration
staysail schooner *n* **:** a schooner without the boom and gaff foresail and with the space between the fore and main masts filled by staysails of various shapes
stay tackle *n* [¹*stay*] **:** a tackle hooked to a stay and used to lift loads amidships in stowing or discharging holds
stay tap *n* [⁵*stay*] **:** STAY-BOLT TAP
stay tube *n* [⁵*stay*] **:** a fire tube with flared or threaded thickened ends that project through both tube sheets in a steam boiler so as to form stays
stbd *abbr* starboard
STC *abbr* **1** sensitivity-time control **2** short-title catalogue **3** single-trip container **4** state teachers college
std *abbr* **1** seated **2** standard **3** steward
STD \¦e,stē¦dē\ *abbr or n* -S [L *sacrae theologiae doctor*] **:** a doctor of sacred theology
ste *abbr, often cap* [F *sainte*] saint
¹stead \'sted, *dial* 'stid\ *n* -S [ME *stede*, fr. OE; akin to OHG *stat* place, ON *stathr*, Goth *staths*, L *statio* act of standing, station, *statim* on the spot, immediately, Gk *stasis* act of standing, position, Skr *sthiti* act of standing, position, *tiṣṭhati* he stands — more at STAND] **1** *obs* **:** LOCALITY, PLACE **2 :** FARMSTEAD 1 ⟨depicted a Tunisian cattle ~ and its animals —*Nat'l Geographic*⟩ **3 :** ADVANTAGE, AVAIL, SERVICE — used chiefly in the phrase *to stand one in good stead* ⟨took voluminous notes which later stood him in good ~ —W.O.Stevens⟩ ⟨this tradition stands primitive peoples in good ~ —Jane Nickerson⟩ **4 :** a frame on which a bed is laid **:** BEDSTEAD ⟨spool-turned cottage ~*s* —Muriel E. Sheppard⟩ **5 :** the office, place, or function ordinarily occupied or carried out by someone or something else ⟨was again placed in the deputy's ~ at the door —T.S.Stribling⟩ ⟨including rent controls, and the application in their ~ of indirect methods of inflation control —*Current Biog.*⟩ ⟨in the ~ of the traditional view —S.F.Mason⟩ **6** *Scot* **:** IMPRESS, TRACE, TRACK
²stead \'sted\ *vt* -ED/-ING/-S [ME *steden*, fr. *stede* stead] **1 :** to be of avail to **:** ASSIST, HELP, SUPPORT ⟨the great names cannot ~ him, if he have no life himself —R.W.Emerson⟩ **2 a** *archaic* **:** PLACE, SET **b** *obs* **:** to fill the place of **:** REPLACE ⟨advise this wronged maid to ~ up your appointment, go in your place —Shak.⟩ **3** *archaic* **:** to involve in difficulty or danger **:** BESET
¹stead·fast *also* **sted·fast** \'sted,fast, -aa(ə)st, -aist, -ȧst *also* -,fəst\ *adj* [ME *stedefast*, fr. OE *stedefæst*, fr. *stede* place, stead + *fæst* fast, fixed] **1 a :** firmly established **:** fixed in place or position **:** IMMOVABLE ⟨a castle, ~ among storms —Sinclair Lewis⟩ **b :** not subject to change **:** IMMUTABLE ⟨the most ~ of primitive environments, the ocean —Lewis Mumford⟩ ⟨the ~ doctrine of original sin —Ellen Glasgow⟩ **2 :** marked by unwavering steadiness **:** firm in belief, determination, or adherence **:** LOYAL, UNSWERVING ⟨our ~ friend, in peace or war, for many years —H.G.Doyle⟩ ⟨narrow of vision but ~ to principles —Agnes Repplier⟩ **syn** see FAITHFUL
²steadfast \"\ *adv* [ME *stedefast*, fr. *stedefast*, adj] **:** STEADFASTLY
stead·fast·ly \'=(;)==\ *adv* [ME *stedefastly*, fr. *stedefast* steadfast + *-ly*] **:** in a steadfast manner
stead·fast·ness \-s(t)nəs — *stressed* '=(;)==\ *n* -ES [ME *stedefastnesse*, fr. *stedefast* steadfast + *-nesse* -ness] **:** the quality or state of being steadfast
steadied *past of* STEADY
steadier *n* -S **:** one that steadies
steadies *pres 3d sing of* STEADY, *pl of* STEADY
stead·i·ly \'sted'lē, -dəl|, |i, *dial* 'stid- *also* 'stəd-\ *adv* **:** in a steady manner
stead·i·ment \'stedēmənt\ *n* -S [²*steady* + *-ment*] **:** an aid to steadiness **:** the state of being steadied
stead·i·ness \-dēnəs, -din\ *n* -ES **:** the quality or state of being steady
stead·ing \'stediŋ, -dēŋ\ *n* -S [ME *steding*, fr. *stede* stead + *-ing*] **1 a :** FARMHOUSE ⟨for their more permanent homes many of them owned small ~*s* —Jacquetta & Christopher Hawkes⟩ **b :** a small farm or homestead ⟨had left the affairs of the little ~ in a sad muddle —A.J.Cronin⟩ **2** *chiefly Scot* **:** the service buildings or area of a farm
stead·ite \'ste,dīt\ *n* -S [John Edward *Stead* †1923 Eng. metallurgist] **:** a eutectic of iron phosphide Fe_3P and iron that occurs as a microconstituent of high-phosphorus cast iron
stead of *prep, chiefly dial* [by shortening] **:** instead of
¹steady \'stedē, -di, *dial* 'stid- *also* 'stəd-\ *adj* -ER/-EST [¹*stead* + *-y*] **1 a :** firm in standing or position **:** not tottering or shaking **:** FIXED ⟨holding the box ~ on his shoulder with the other hand —Pearl Buck⟩ **b :** direct or sure in movement or action ⟨with hinged knees and ~ hand to dress wounds —Walt Whitman⟩ **:** UNFALTERING, UNSWERVING ⟨gave him a ~ look —Margaret Deland⟩ ⟨took ~ aim⟩ **c :** keeping nearly upright in a seaway **:** not easily tipped by an external force — used of a ship; compare ⁹CRANK, STIFF 7 **d :** serving to hold firm **:** STEADYING ⟨a ~ bearing⟩ **2 a :** marked by an even development, movement, or action **:** not varying in quality, intensity, or direction **:** REGULAR, UNIFORM ⟨a ~ pace⟩ ⟨a ~ breeze⟩ ⟨a ~ light⟩ **:** not changed, replaced, or interrupted **:** CONTINUOUS, UNINTERRUPTED ⟨from then on it was a ~ fight against misfortune —S.H.Adams⟩ ⟨continued to produce a ~ output of books —Evelyn G. Cruickshanks⟩ ⟨a ~ job⟩ ⟨a ~ girl friend⟩ **b :** showing little variation **:** recording little change in the weather ⟨the glass was ~ and the weather good with fair visibility —H.A.Chippendale⟩ **c :** not fluctuating or varying widely (as in price) **:** STABLE ⟨cattle were ~ to off 25 cents per hundredweight —*Wall Street Jour.*⟩ ⟨current quotations show no great improvement but they are *steadier* —*Chem. & Engineering News*⟩ **3 a :** not easily moved or upset **:** CALM, CONTROLLED ⟨~ nerves⟩ ⟨a ~ temper⟩ **:** DISCIPLINED, RESOLUTE ⟨the ~ valor of the warriors whom he had trained —T.B.Macaulay⟩ **b** (1) **:** constant in feeling, principle, purpose, or attachment **:** not fickle or wavering **:** STEADFAST ⟨a conservative and ~ people, are little attracted by tricky trends —*Exhibition of Swiss Bks.*⟩ (2) **:** consistent in performance or behavior **:** DEPENDABLE, RELIABLE ⟨there must be men to tend them, men as ~ as the wheels upon their axles —Aldous Huxley⟩ ⟨a good ~ ballplayer⟩ ⟨a ~ horse⟩ (3) **:** not easily frightened or thrown off ⟨a hound ~ on the scent⟩ **c :** not given to dissipation or excess **:** SOBER ⟨promised to marry another man, a good ~ farmer —Vance Randolph⟩ ⟨grown to be fine women, and good ~ mothers to their children —C.B.Nordhoff & J.N. Hall⟩
syn EVEN, CONSTANT, UNIFORM, EQUABLE: in relation to matters inanimate, STEADY indicates lack of variation, interruption, or change ⟨the light, small, but *steady* and persistent as before —Thomas Hardy⟩ ⟨he first imagined, and then demonstrated, that the geologic agencies are not explosive and cata-

clysmal, but *steady* and patient —C.W.Eliot⟩ and in relation to persons it may imply a balanced resolution and dependability, a strength of character under stress ⟨intoxicated as he was, he knew enough to charge the steward — a *steady* seaman be it remembered — with the present safety of the ship —Herman Melville⟩ ⟨statesmen, instead of being as they should be, at once mild and *steady*, are at once ferocious and inconsistent —T.B.Macaulay⟩ EVEN may indicate a level, plain quality without rough variation or elevation ⟨had been moving along in an *even* path . . . there was no apparent slope downward, and distinctly none upward —Theodore Dreiser⟩; when used of people it suggests a natural level calmness without the resolution implied by STEADY ⟨support with an *even* temper, and without any violent transports of mind, a sudden gust of prosperity —Henry Fielding⟩ CONSTANT implies a sameness, fixity, consistency, persistence, or regularity more or less measurable and lasting ⟨while there have been several clear and distinct changes in the pattern, the essence of the university tradition has through all these years remained *constant* —J.B.Conant⟩ In reference to persons, it may suggest either loyalty or unchanging fixity ⟨a loyal husband (*constant* if not faithful) —Agnes Repplier⟩ ⟨could never think of him as having been a young man . . . he always thought of him as an unchanging, a measured, deliberate, *constant* quantity, like a Greek letter in a mathematical formula —J.P.Marquand⟩ UNIFORM, less applicable to persons than the preceding words, stresses to a greater degree sameness and lack of variety in salient characteristics as indicated or implied ⟨the various tackle blocks and planks of the wooden ships were cut to *uniform* measure: building became the assemblage of accurately measured elements —Lewis Mumford⟩ ⟨the purpose of this is to afford a requirement of a reasonably *uniform* character for all states cooperating with the federal government —F.D. Roosevelt⟩ EQUABLE stresses lack of extremes and sudden marked changes ⟨a more *equable* winter climate in France —Osbert Sitwell⟩ ⟨in low *equable* tones, curiously in contrast to the strident babble with which natives are accustomed to make day hideous —Rudyard Kipling⟩ and applied to persons and their temperaments it may imply an unruffled complacence ⟨bridge, whist, baccarat, poker, roulette and Monte Carlo — at all these she won and lost, with the same *equable* sangfroid —Rose Macaulay⟩

2**steady** \"\ *vb* -ED/-ING/-ES *vt* **1 :** to keep from shaking, reeling, or falling : make or keep firm ⟨she swayed slightly and put a hand out to ~ herself —Nigel Balchin⟩ **2 a :** to bring under control : CALM, COMPOSE, QUIET ⟨drew a deep breath and *steadied* himself with an effort of will —Aldous Huxley⟩ **b :** to make serious or sober : keep from dissipation or irregular habits ⟨as he had no business or profession to ~ him, he traveled rapidly down the primrose path —G.C.Sellery⟩ **c :** to make constant, regular, or resolute ⟨was *steadied* in his determination for a career by his desire to win . . . approbation and love —Lawrason Brown⟩ **3 a :** to keep (a ship) on the course set : keep from veering off course **b :** to cause to proceed at an even pace ⟨~ the horse⟩ ~ *vi* **1 :** to settle down : become regular in habits or behavior ⟨led a wild life but *steadied* down after his marriage⟩ **2 :** to keep or return to a fixed position or course ⟨the statue tottered but then *steadied* on its base⟩ ⟨they swept round in a long gentle turn and *steadied* on the course —Nevil Shute⟩ **3 :** to become more stable ⟨another dark spot appeared to be brightening as farm prices *steadied* —*Dun's Rev.*⟩ **syn** see STABILIZE

3**steady** \"\ *adv* **1 :** in a steady manner : STEADILY ⟨the rain was coming down ~ —Richard Bissell⟩ ⟨these poets have seen the city ~ and seen it whole —Thomas Lask⟩ **2 :** on the course set : without veering from the direct line of course — used as a direction to the helmsman of a ship

4**steady** \"\ *n* -ES **1 :** one that is steady; *specif* : a boyfriend or girl friend with whom one goes steady **2 :** something that holds firm; *specif* : STEADY REST

steady flow *n* [1*steady*] **:** a flow in which the velocity of the fluid at a particular fixed point does not change with time — called also *stationary flow;* compare UNIFORM FLOW

steady-going \ˈ≈-ˌ≈-≈\ *adj* [3*steady*] **1 :** CONSTANT, REGULAR ⟨*steady-going* devotion⟩ **2 :** of steady habits : SERIOUS, SOBER ⟨a *steady-going* young man⟩

steady load *n* [1*steady*] **:** DEAD LOAD 1

steady motion *n* **:** motion in which the linear and angular velocity of either of them is constant

steady pin *n* [2*steady*] **1 :** DOWEL 1 **2 :** a device (as a pin or sunk key) used to prevent a pulley from turning on a shaft or spindle **3 a :** a long guide pin attached to a cope or pattern to enable it to be lifted vertically **b :** CORE PRINT

steady rest *n* **:** a rest in a lathe or grinding machine in which long round pieces of work may rotate but without eccentric movement — called also *center rest;* compare FOLLOW REST

steady state *n* **1 :** a state or condition of a system or process (as one of the energy states of an atom) that does not change in time **2 :** a condition of stability of a generator or electric system under normal fluctuations of load or voltage **3 :** a state of physiological equilibrium esp. in connection with a specified metabolic relation or activity

1**steak** \ˈstāk\ *n* -S [ME *steyke, steke,* fr. ON *steik;* akin to ON *steikja* to roast on a spit, *stik* stick, stake — more at STICK] **1 a :** a slice of meat cut from a fleshy part of a beef carcass usu. in cross section and usu. cooked or to be cooked by broiling : BEEFSTEAK — see BEEF illustration **b :** a similar slice of a specified meat other than beef ⟨ham ~⟩ ⟨veal ~⟩ **c :** a cross-section slice of a large fish ⟨halibut ~⟩ ⟨swordfish ~⟩ **2 :** ground beef prepared for cooking or for serving — see HAMBURGER STEAK, SALISBURY STEAK **3 :** FLANK STEAK

2**steak** \"\ *vt* -ED/-ING/-S **:** to cut (large fish) crosswise into steaks

steak hammer *n* **:** an implement for pounding meat to make it more tender by breaking down the tissue fibers

steak knife *n* **:** a table knife having a steel blade often with a serrated edge and a handle of any of various materials (as metal, wood, plastic)

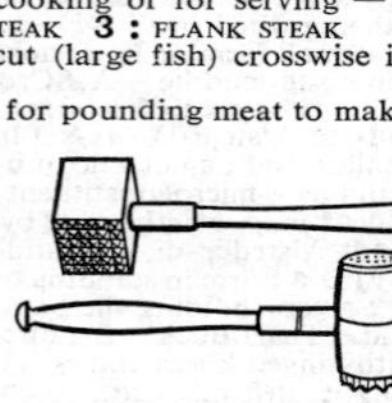
steak hammers

steak set *n* **:** a small carving set

1**steal** \ˈstē(ə)l, ˈstā(ə)l\ *n* -S [ME *stele* stalk, stem, handle, fr. OE, stalk, support; akin to ON *stjölr* hinder part, tail, Gk *stelea* handle of an axe, *stellein* to set up, make ready — more at STALL] **1** *dial Brit* **:** STALK, STEM **2** *dial Brit* **:** HANDLE, SHAFT

2**steal** \ˈstēl, *esp before pause or consonant* -ēəl\ *vb* **stole** \ˈstōl\ **sto·len** \ˈstōlən *sometimes* -ln\ *or chiefly dial* **stole** \-ōl\ *or dial chiefly Brit* **stoun** *or* **stown** \-ōn\ **stealing; steals** [ME *stelen,* fr. OE *stelan;* akin to OHG *stelan* to steal, ON *stela,* Goth *stilan,* and perh. to Gk *sterein* to deprive, bereave, rob, MIr *serbh* theft] *vi* **1 :** to practice theft : take the property of another ⟨you shall not ~ —Exod 20:15 (RSV)⟩ **2 a :** to leave secretly or unobtrusively ⟨he *stole* quietly out of the picture for ever —Richard Harrison⟩ **b :** to move furtively : attempt to come or go without attracting notice ⟨*stole* over at twilight for an inconspicuous inspection —Margaret Janes⟩ **c :** to move, glide, or elapse gently ⟨a tear *stole* down her cheek⟩ ⟨the months *stole* on⟩ **3 a :** to come upon one gradually or without warning ⟨the white, soft light that ~*s* upon half sleep near morning —Scott Fitzgerald⟩ ⟨shall we ~ upon them . . . at supper —Shak.⟩ **b :** to approach, enter, or take possession by imperceptible degrees ⟨anxiety was ~*ing* over her as if it emanated from her surroundings —Ellen Glasgow⟩ ⟨into her cheeks *stole* a lovely color —Edison Marshall⟩ **4** *of a base runner* **:** to advance from one base to the next without the aid of a hit or error ⟨are allowed to ~ without a signal —M.F.Mallette⟩ ~ *vt* **1 a :** to take and carry away feloniously and usu. unobserved : take or appropriate without right or leave and with intent to keep or make use of wrongfully ⟨*stole* a car from a parking lot⟩ ⟨*stole* money from the cash register⟩ ⟨who ~*s* my purse ~*s* trash —Shak.⟩ **b :** to appropriate (as another's conception or invention) and use as one's own ⟨*stole* the formula and began to manufacture the product himself⟩ : PLAGIARIZE ⟨his jokes were borrowed and *stolen* all over the country —Eleanor M. Sickels⟩ ⟨*stole* nearly all his plots —Agnes de Mille⟩ **c :** to take away by force or unjust or underhand means : deprive one of ⟨they've *stolen* our liberty from us, and we'll never get it back —Kenneth Roberts⟩ ⟨had *stolen* the nomination from him —A.S.Link⟩ **d** *archaic* **:** ABDUCT, KIDNAP ⟨such incidents as the child *stolen* by gypsies —E.A.Poe⟩ **e :** to take secretly or without permission ⟨*stole* a kiss from her before she could protest⟩ **f :** to take over : ADOPT, BORROW ⟨the various gyrations have been *stolen* from boxing, basketball, track —*This Week Mag.*⟩ **g :** to appropriate entirely to oneself or beyond one's proper share ⟨has to occupy the center of the stage and ~ the act —Constance Foster⟩ ⟨the young ladies ~ most of the limelight —O.S.Nock⟩ **2 a :** to move, convey, or introduce secretly : SMUGGLE ⟨*stole* a hand into hers —Rumer Godden⟩ ⟨watching for an opportunity to ~ their egg into some nest —John Burroughs⟩ **b :** to aim furtively : direct secretly ⟨*stole* several glances at him with a curiosity very natural under the circumstances —Joseph Conrad⟩ **c :** to accomplish in a concealed or unobserved manner ⟨might even ~ a visit —G.B.Shaw⟩ **3 :** to use (an interval of time) for an unscheduled, irregular, or secret purpose ⟨felt he was ~*ing* the time and using it for frivolous thoughts —Virginia D. Dawson & Betty D. Wilson⟩ ⟨~*ing* time off from her other clients to flit in and out of the workrooms —P.E.Deutschman⟩ **4 a :** to win away (as by persuasion or deception) : ENTICE ⟨this savage who *stole* your allegiance from me —T.B.Costain⟩ ⟨the obligation to refrain from deliberately ~*ing* each other's clients —H.S.Drinker⟩ **b :** to take possession of gradually and imperceptibly : withdraw or remove stealthily — often used with *away* ⟨shorter wind, paunches, and hardened arteries had begun to ~ away their lust for life —Dixon Wecter⟩ **5 :** to seize, gain, or win by trickery, skill, or daring ⟨a basketball player adept at ~*ing* the ball from his opponents⟩ ⟨show folks know how to ~ that extra bow —Goodman Ace⟩ ⟨a shrewd poker player who ~*s* many pots⟩: as **a** *of a base runner* **:** to gain (a base) by running without the aid of a hit or an error **b** *baseball* **:** to intercept and interpret correctly (an opponent's signal) ⟨false moves calculated to keep the enemy from ~*ing* the genuine sign —A.J.Daley⟩ **c :** to make (a run) in cricket by alert opportunism in circumstances where a run would not ordinarily be attempted **6** *of a hen* **a :** to make (a nest) in an out-of-the-way place **b :** to make use of (the nest) of another hen

syn PILFER, FILCH, PURLOIN, LIFT, PINCH, SNITCH, SWIPE, COP: these have in common the sense of to take another's possession without right, without his knowledge or observation. STEAL, the commonest and most general of the group, can refer to any act of taking without right although it suggests strongly a furtiveness or secrecy in the act ⟨*steal* a pocketbook⟩ ⟨*steal* jewels⟩ ⟨*steal* a kiss⟩ ⟨*steal* a glance at someone⟩ PILFER suggests stealing in small amounts ⟨the pantry mouse that *pilfers* our food —*Conservation in the U.S.*⟩ ⟨the ladies of unexceptionable position who are caught *pilfering* furs in shops —L.P. Smith⟩ ⟨*pilfer* the secret files of the foreign office —H.J. Morgenthau⟩ FILCH is close to PILFER but suggests more strongly the use of surreptitious means, esp. quick snatching ⟨the pursuit of a thief who had *filched* an overcoat —McKenzie Porter⟩ ⟨a lot of fellows were too hungry to wait, and so some of the rations were *filched* —Asa Autry⟩ ⟨a bulky, dark youth in spectacles . . . *filching* biscuits from a large tin —Dorothy Sayers⟩ PURLOIN usu. shifts the stress onto the idea of removal or making away with for one's own use, often becoming generalized to include such acts as plundering or plagiarism ⟨had *purloined* $386,920 from the New York realty management firm for which he worked, then absconded —*Time*⟩ ⟨added theft to her other sin, and having found your watch in your bedroom had *purloined* it —Samuel Butler †1902⟩ ⟨I hope to quote him is not to *purloin* —John Dryden⟩ LIFT, when it does not mean specif. to steal by surreptitiously taking from counters or displays in stores, is used frequently in spoken English in the sense of PURLOIN ⟨women shoplifters often work in gangs of three. Two act as shields while the third does the *lifting* —*Irish Digest*⟩ ⟨*lift* money from the cash register⟩ ⟨imitators who *lifted* everything except the shirt off his back —Scott Fitzgerald⟩ PINCH, SWIPE, SNITCH, and COP are virtually interchangeable with FILCH. PINCH and SWIPE are often used in place of STEAL to suggest an act morally less reprehensible ⟨loot having been *pinched* by him from the British ship *Mary Dyer* —*Sydney (Australia) Bull.*⟩ ⟨well-dressed crooks really did steal the Gold Cup at Ascot . . . drove up in a handsome car . . . and *pinched* the cup out of the Royal Enclosure —J.D. Carr⟩ ⟨the bloke who *pinched* my photographs —Richard Llewellyn⟩ ⟨hovering outside the dying butler's bedroom waiting to . . . pop in and *swipe* the old man's private notebooks —*Time*⟩ SNITCH possibly stresses more the removal by quick, furtive snatching ⟨while he was bathing, somebody *snitched* his uniform —P.G.Wodehouse⟩ ⟨*snitched* people's ideas without telling them —Dorothy Sayers⟩ COP usu. lays stress upon quick, often spur-of-the-moment filching or purloining ⟨some woman put on a dinner gown, mingled with guests, *copped* fifty thousand bucks in jewelry —Erle Stanley Gardner⟩ ⟨ran home and *copped* a piece of beefsteak from his old lady —J.T. Farrell⟩

— **steal a march :** to gain an advantage unobserved — **steal one's thunder :** to appropriate or adapt for one's own ends something effective (as an idea or plan) devised or thought out by another

3**steal** \"\ *n* -S **1 a :** the act or an instance of stealing : THEFT ⟨his hand went out and picked up the shears as if he had had that ~ in mind for many years —Wright Morris⟩ **b :** the act or an instance of stealing a base ⟨thrown out on an attempted ~⟩ **2 :** a fraudulent or questionable political action or deal ⟨this is the real ~ of the last 10 years —*New Republic*⟩ **3 :** BARGAIN ⟨was prepared to let it go, though it was a ~ at the price, for ten dollars —Reed Whittemore⟩

steal·able \-ləbəl\ *adj* [2*steal* + *-able*] **:** capable of being stolen ⟨though the invasion blueprints weren't stolen, they were ~ —Linnell Jones⟩

steal·age \-lij, -lēj\ *n* -S [2*steal* + *-age*] **:** STEALING, THEFT ⟨noted any increase in ~ from stores —*Christian Science Monitor*⟩

steal·er \-lə(r)\ *n* -S **1 :** one that steals ⟨base ~⟩ ⟨scene ~⟩ **2** *also* **steel·er** \"\ **:** the endmost plank or plate of a strake that ends short of the stem or stern

1**stealing** *n* -S [ME *steling,* fr. gerund of *stelen* to steal] **:** the act of one who steals ⟨accused of ~⟩ ⟨led the league in ~⟩

2**stealing** *adj* [fr. pres. part. of 2*steal*] **1** *archaic* **:** moving stealthily, softly, or imperceptibly **2 :** THIEVING ⟨helpful in the case of a ~ boy or girl —G.E.Gardner⟩ — **steal·ing·ly** *adv*

steals *pl of* STEAL, *pres 3d sing of* STEAL

stealth \ˈstelth *also* -ltth\ *n* -S [ME *stalthe, stelthe;* akin to OE *stelan* to steal] **1 a** *archaic* **:** the act or an instance of stealing : THEFT ⟨ingratitude makes it worse than ~ —Shak.⟩ **b** *obs* **:** something that is stolen : BOOTY ⟨pursue the ~ of pilfering wolf —John Milton⟩ **2 :** the act or action of going or passing furtively, secretly, or imperceptibly ⟨told him of your ~ unto this wood —Shak.⟩ ⟨the realization of it was creeping through her veins with the deadly ~ of a drug —J.C.Snaith⟩ ⟨with the ~ of years . . . she had lost a little bloom —Francis Hackett⟩ **3 :** FURTIVENESS, SLYNESS ⟨equaled this great wood-cat in ~, and far surpassed it in cunning and ferocity —Theodore Roosevelt⟩ — **by stealth** *adv* **:** in a clandestine manner : SECRETLY ⟨only seven were printed, anonymously, surreptitiously, and *by stealth,* during her lifetime —Louis Untermeyer⟩

stealth·ful \-fəl\ *adj* [*stealth* + *-ful*] *archaic* **:** STEALTHY

stealth·i·ly \-thəlē, -li\ *adv* **:** in a stealthy manner ⟨she looked out ~ through the blind of the little window —Charles Kingsley⟩ ⟨the public schools have ~ crept back into the hearts of the intellectuals —Edward Shils⟩

stealth·i·ness \-thēnəs, -thin-\ *n* -ES **:** the quality or state of being stealthy

stealthy \-thē, -thi\ *adj* -ER/-EST [*stealth* + *-y*] **1 :** slow, deliberate, and secret in action or character ⟨the ~ revolution that has produced machine-made society —F.B.Millett⟩ ⟨a ~ owl lived on the roof —E.W.H.Lumsden⟩ **2 :** intended to escape observation : FURTIVE ⟨a ~ sound⟩ ⟨a ~ glance⟩ ⟨a ~ movement⟩ **syn** see SECRET

1**steam** \ˈstēm\ *n* -S *often attrib* [ME *stem, steme,* fr. OE *stēam, stēm, stiem;* akin to D *stoom* steam] **1 a :** a vapor arising from some heated substance : EXHALATION ⟨a ~ of incense⟩ **b** *archaic* **:** stale air — often used in pl. ⟨every modest flower that needs the pure air and will not grow in ~*s* —James Martineau⟩ **2 a :** the invisible vapor into which water is converted when heated to the boiling point : water in the state of vapor — compare DRY STEAM, WATER VAPOR, WET STEAM **b :** the mist formed by the condensation on cooling of water vapor : visible vapor **3 a :** water vapor kept under pressure so as to supply energy for heating, cooking, or mechanical work; *also* **:** the power so generated ⟨full ~ ahead⟩ **b :** driving force : ENERGY, POWER ⟨had got here on his own ~, won a lot of scholarships —A.L.Rowse⟩ ⟨hit him a peach of a right . . . but the ~ was gone —A.J.Liebling⟩ **c :** emotional tension ⟨after six months of hard study, he felt the need to let off a little ~⟩ ⟨though not a demonstrative bird, the king penguin occasionally must let off ~ —A.N.T.Rankin⟩ **4 a :** STEAMSHIP ⟨travel by ~⟩ **b :** travel by or a trip in a steamship ⟨the sea voyage — a night and a day's ~ —J.P.O'Donnell⟩ **c :** the occupation of handling ships under steam ⟨a blue-water man who had come into ~ and the home trade to get an easier life —Thomas Wood †1950⟩

2**steam** \"\ *vb* -ED/-ING/-S *vi* **1 :** to rise in vapor : issue or pass off as vapor ⟨the heat ~*s* out of the forest —Robert Payne⟩ **2 a :** to give off steam or vapor ⟨the town ~*ed* in a listless heat —Vincent McHugh⟩ ⟨the cows . . . stood in the yards all day, ruminating and ~*ing* —Adrian Bell⟩ **b :** REEK ⟨at that time of year the boardwalk ~*s* with sophistication —*N.Y.Times*⟩ **3 a :** to move or travel by the agency of steam ⟨reaching the little riverside landing . . . after a day and a half of ~*ing* southward —Tom Marvel⟩ ⟨saw the train ~*ing* in —Edith Sitwell⟩ **b :** to move with energy or force as if by the agency of steam ⟨when he ~*s* into second base, say, on a long double —*Time*⟩ ⟨the racket smacked . . . and the white ball came ~*ing* across at me —R.P.Warren⟩ **4 :** to generate steam ⟨the boiler ~*s* well⟩ **5 :** to be angry : BOIL ⟨was still ~*ing* over the insult he had received⟩ ~ *vt* **1 :** to give out as fumes : EXHALE **2 :** to apply steam to ⟨women often like to ~ the skin by covering it with hot towels —Morris Fishbein⟩: as **a :** to cook by direct exposure to steam (as in a steamer) or in a vessel surrounded by steam (as in a double boiler) **b :** to expose (cloth) to the action of steam (as in dyeing or shrinking) **3 :** to convey by steamship **4 :** to move by the action of steam ⟨~*ing* a carrier through the Strait of Gibraltar —Walter Karig⟩ — **steam open :** to unglue by the action of steam ⟨*steam open* the envelope⟩

steam bath *n* **1 :** a bath of steam (as for use in a laboratory) — compare WATER BATH **2 :** a container for a steam bath

steam beer *n* **:** a highly effervescent beer brewed in the western U.S.

steam black *n, often cap S&B* **:** a natural dye — see DYE table I (under *Natural Black 4*)

steamblaster \ˈ≈ˌ≈≈\ *n* **:** one that cleans stone or brick structures with a spray of steam

steam blower *n* **:** a blower for producing a draft by a jet or jets of steam

1**steamboat** \ˈ≈ˌ≈\ *n* **:** a boat propelled by steam power; *esp* **:** one designed for river or coastal traffic

2**steamboat** \"\ *vi* **:** to go or travel by steamboat

steamboat gothic *n, usu cap G* [so called fr. its use in homes of retired steamboat captains in imitation of the style of river steamboats] **:** an elaborately ornamental architectural style used in homes built in the middle 19th century in the Ohio and Mississippi river valleys

steamboating \ˈ≈ˌ≈≈\ *n* [1*steamboat* + *-ing*] **:** the business or occupation of operating or working on a steamboat

steamboatman \ˈ≈ˌ≈≈\ *n, pl* **steamboatmen :** one engaged in running a steamboat

steamboat ratchet *n* **:** a sleeve internally threaded at the ends with opposing threads and equipped with a ratchet and handle so that when the sleeve is attached to the ends of two rods the rods may be pulled together by turning it

steam boiler *n* **:** a boiler for producing steam

steam box *n* **1 :** STEAM CHEST **2 :** a receptacle in which things are steamed

steam chest *n* **:** the chamber from which steam is distributed to a cylinder of a steam engine — called also *valve chest*

steam coal *n* **:** coal suitable for use under steam boilers

steam cock *n* **:** a cock for passage of steam; *specif* **:** the upper gauge cock in a steam boiler

steam coil *n* **:** a coil of pipe through which steam is passed

steam condenser *n* **:** CONDENSER 2e

steam cure *n* **:** vulcanization of rubber articles with direct exposure to steam

steam-distill \ˈ≈-≈ˈ≈\ *vb* [back-formation fr. *steam distillation*] *vt* **:** to subject to steam distillation ~ *vi* **:** to undergo steam distillation

steam distillation *n* **:** distillation (as of a substance essentially insoluble in water) assisted by steam that is usu. introduced as a current into the substance to be distilled and carries over with it quantities of the more volatile components to form an aqueous distillate on condensation ⟨by means of *steam distillations,* volatile organic liquids may be separated from relatively nonvolatile impurities —J.H.Perry⟩

steam dome *n* **:** DOME 4e

steamed *past of* STEAM

steam engine *n* **1 :** an engine driven or worked by steam; *specif* **:** a reciprocating engine consisting essentially of a piston driven in a closed cylinder by steam at a pressure initially much greater than that of the atmosphere and usu. connected rigidly by a piston rod to a crosshead whose reciprocating motion is usu. converted into rotary motion by a connecting rod, crankpin, crank, and crankshaft — compare STEAM TURBINE **2 :** LOCOMOTIVE

1**steam·er** \ˈstēmə(r)\ *n* -S [1*steam* & 2*steam* + *-er*] **1 a :** a vessel in which articles are subjected to steam **b :** a cooking utensil with a perforated insert to hold food to be steamed **2 a** (1) **:** STEAMSHIP (2) **:** a mechanically propelled ship **b :** an engine, machine, or vehicle operated or propelled by steam: as 1) **:** a fire engine having pumps operated by steam ⟨modern fire trucks ousting the rampaging old horse-drawn ~*s* —*Sat.Eve.Post*⟩ (2) **:** an automobile driven by steam **3 :** one that steams; *specif* **:** one that cleans or conditions with steam (as in the cleaning of electrolytic refining equipment, the preshrinking of cloth, the blending of tobacco) **4** [so called fr. its suitability for steaming] **:** SOFT-SHELL CLAM

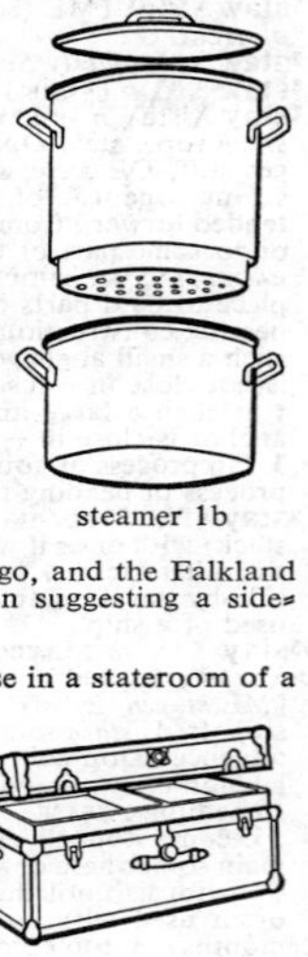
steamer 1b

2**steamer** \"\ *vi* -ED/-ING/-S **:** to go or voyage by steamer

steamer chair *n* **:** DECK CHAIR

steamer duck *n* **:** any of two flightless and one flying large sea ducks (genus *Tachyeres*) of Patagonia, Tierra del Fuego, and the Falkland islands that swim with a peculiar action suggesting a side-wheel steamboat

steamer rug *n* **:** RUG 2c

steamer trunk *n* **:** a trunk suitable for use in a stateroom of a steamer; *esp* **:** a shallow trunk that may be stowed beneath a berth

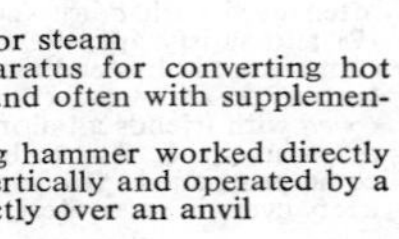
steamer trunk

steam fit *n* **:** a steamtight fit

steam fitter *n* **:** one that installs or repairs steam pipes or other equipment for heating, ventilating, or refrigerating systems

steam fitting *n* **:** the work or occupation of a steam fitter

steam fog *n* **:** fog formed by cold air flowing over a warm water surface

steam gauge *n* **:** a pressure gauge for steam

steam generator *n* **:** a large apparatus for converting hot water into steam at high pressure and often with supplementary coils to superheat the steam

steam hammer *n* **:** a power forging hammer worked directly by steam; *esp* **:** a hammer guided vertically and operated by a vertical steam cylinder located directly over an anvil

steam harrow *n* : a device resembling a spike-tooth harrow that is used for sterilizing soil (as in a greenhouse) with steam escaping from openings in short pipes forced into the soil

steam heat *n* : heat given off by steam in condensing

steam-heated \'꞉꞉꞉\ *adj* : provided with steam heat

steam heater *n* **1** : a radiator heated by steam **2** : a steam-heating apparatus consisting of a boiler, radiators, piping, and the necessary fixtures

steam heating *n* : a system of heating (as for a building) in which steam generated in a boiler is piped to radiators in the various parts of the system with the condensed steam being returned to the boiler for recirculation

steamier *comparative of* STEAMY

steamiest *superlative of* STEAMY

steam·i·ly \'stēməlē, -li\ *adv* : in a steamy manner

steam·i·ness \-mēnəs, -min-\ *n* -ES : the quality or state of being steamy

¹steaming *adj* [fr. pres. part. of ²steam] : giving out or constituting vapors or fumes ⟨drove in the big sleigh behind four ~ horses —Louis Bromfield⟩ ⟨there was a ~ mist in all the hollows —Charles Dickens⟩

²steaming *adv* : to a steaming degree ⟨the night was ~ hot⟩ ⟨the coffee was ~ hot⟩

³steaming *n* -s [fr. gerund of ²steam] : a distance traveled or to be traveled by a steamship in a specified time ⟨these rights did not extend farther than a distance of one hour's ~ from the coast —C.P.Stacey⟩

steam injector *n* : a steam-boiler injector

steam iron *n* : a pressing iron with a compartment holding water that is converted to steam by the iron's heat and emitted through the sole plate onto the fabric being pressed

steam jacket *n* : an outer casing enclosing a hollow space through which steam is circulated to heat the contents of an inner vessel

steam-jacket \'꞉꞉꞉\ *vt* [steam jacket] : to enclose in a steam jacket

steam joint *n* : a steamtight joint

steam knife *n* : a hollow-bladed knife heated by steam and used to uncap honeycombs

steam line *n* : a graph showing the temperature at which a liquid and its vapor are in equilibrium at any temperature

steam locomotive *n* : a locomotive using as motive power steam that is usu. self-generated in the locomotive's own boiler by the combustion of fuel (as coal or oil)

steam loop *n* : an arrangement of pipes by which water of condensation can be returned to the boiler without a pump or injector as a result of condensation of boiler steam in a loop of two vertical pipes connected by a horizontal one

steam metal *n* : a copper alloy specially designed to endure exposure to steam

steam navvy *n, Brit* : STEAM SHOVEL

steam nigger *n* : NIGGER 5

steam organ *or* **steam piano** *n* : CALLIOPE

steam packing *n* : packing made of material (as duck and rubber) resistant to the action of steam

steam point *n* : the normal boiling point of pure water that is used as one of the fixed points of the international temperature scale

steam port *n* : a port for steam; *esp* : one for live steam

steam power plant *n* : a plant using steam prime movers to drive electric generating apparatus

steam pump *n* : a pump driven by steam or directly by a steam engine; *specif* : a combined steam engine and pump with the piston rod and pump plunger directly coupled

steam railroad *n* **1** : a railroad for steam locomotives **2** : a railroad required to make reports in accordance with a uniform system of accounts for railroad companies prescribed by the U.S. Interstate Commerce Commission

steam ram *n* : a steam pump for deep wells that resembles a pulsometer in action

steam road *n* : STEAM RAILROAD

¹steamroller \'꞉꞉꞉꞉\ *n* **1** : a steam-driven road roller **2** : an irresistible or crushing power or force; *esp* : power ruthlessly exerted or applied to overcome opposition ⟨the ~ had passed over the insurgents, and the machine had won a new victory —Rev. of Reviews⟩

²steamroller \'꞉꞉꞉꞉\ *also* **steamroll** \'꞉꞉꞉\ *vb* -ED/-ING/-S [steamroller fr. ¹steamroller; steamroll, back-formation fr. ¹steamroller] *vt* **1** : to crush with a steamroller **2 a** : to overwhelm, crush, or coerce by greatly superior force ⟨~ the opposition⟩ ⟨the well-organized majority ~ed the conference into adopting its proposals without discussion⟩ **b** : to bring by overwhelming force or pressure ⟨~ed the bill through the legislature⟩ ⟨~ed the bill to defeat⟩ ~ *vi* : to move or proceed with irresistible force

steam room *n* : a room (as in a Turkish bath) that is heated to an extreme temperature by steam

steams *pl of* STEAM, *pres 3d sing of* STEAM

steamship *n* : a ship propelled by the power of steam : STEAMER

steam shovel *n* : a power shovel operated by steam

steam sizes *n pl* : the smallest sorted sizes of anthracite coal — compare PREPARED SIZES

steam still *n* : a still heated by steam; *esp* : one used in the production of gasoline and naphthas

steam-still \'꞉꞉꞉\ *vb* [¹steam + still (to distill)] : STEAM DISTILL

steam storage locomotive *n* : FIRELESS LOCOMOTIVE

steam table *n* **1 a** : a table having openings to hold containers of cooked food over steam or hot water circulating beneath them **b** : a steam-heated table for drying wet matrices in stereotyping **2** : a tabulation giving data relating to steam saturated at various temperatures and including usu. the pressure, specific volume, density, heat of vaporization, specific enthalpy, and specific entropy

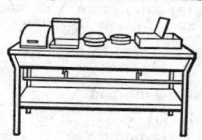

steam table 1a

steamtight \'꞉꞉꞉\ *adj* [¹steam + tight] : not permitting the leaking through of steam or of water under pressure of steam

steam trap *n* : a device that automatically obstructs the passage of steam (as from a pipe) but permits the escape of condensate or entrained air

steam trawler *n* : a small but strongly built steam-driven trawler equipped with an otter trawl

steam turbine *n* : a turbine that is driven by the pressure of steam which is discharged at high velocity against the turbine vanes

steam-turbine locomotive *n* : a locomotive propelled by a steam turbine

steam up *vb* [¹steam + up, adv.] *vt* **1** : to cover with steam or vapor ⟨his breath steamed up the window pane⟩ **2** : to supply with energy : give impetus to ⟨a drive for bigger government spendings to *steam up* the economy —Kiplinger Washington Letter⟩ **3** : to make angry or excited : AROUSE ⟨will find the injustice of the charges *steamed* him *up*⟩ ⟨will find the neighbors much more *steamed up* over economic issues —Time⟩ **4** *Brit* : to feed (a female domestic animal) heavily esp. before parturition in order to induce a heavy milk flow ~ *vi* : to become covered with steam ⟨his glasses *steamed up* as he came into the warm room⟩

steam valve *n* [¹steam] : a valve for regulating a supply of steam

steam vessel *n* **1** : a vessel propelled by steam : STEAMBOAT, STEAMSHIP, STEAMER **2** : a mechanically propelled vessel

steam whistle *n* : a whistle in which the sound is produced by the action of steam; *esp* : one attached to a steam boiler

steamy \'stēmē, -mi\ *adj* -ER/-EST **1** : consisting of or characterized by steam : full of steam ⟨from the *steamiest* tropics to the frozen polar regions —C.H.Curran⟩ **2** : marked by sensual heat : HEATED ⟨the object of some ~ yearnings on the part of the comely wife of an older colleague —John McCarten⟩ ⟨summarized the ~ little affairs to be related by the singer —Douglas Watt⟩

stean \'stēn\ *n* -s [ME *stene*, fr. OE *stæne*; akin to OHG *steinna* stone jug, OE *stān* stone] *dial chiefly Eng* : an earthenware container for liquids or foods

---

ste·ap·sin \stē'apsən\ *n* -s [Gk *stear* fat, suet + E -*psin* (as in *pepsin*) — more at STONE] : the lipase in pancreatic juice

stear- *or* **stearo-** *comb form* [ISV, fr. *stearic*] : related to or derived from stearic acid ⟨*stearamide*⟩ ⟨*stearo-di-oleins*⟩

stea·rate \'stē,rāt, 'sti,r-, *usu* -d-+\ *n* -s [stear- + -ate] : a salt or ester of stearic acid

stear·ic \('')stari̇k, 'stiˈr-\ *adj* [F *stéarique*, fr. Gk *stear* fat, tallow + F -*ique* -ic — more at STONE] **1** : relating to, obtained from, or resembling stearin or tallow **2** : of or relating to stearic acid or its derivatives ⟨~ esters⟩

stearic acid *n* **1** : a waxy crystalline saturated fatty acid $CH_3(CH_2)_{16}COOH$ that occurs esp. as a glyceride in tallow and other animal fats and in cocoa butter and other hard vegetable fats, that is obtained usu. by saponification of these fats or of hydrogenated oils (as soybean oil or cottoneed oil) or by hydrogenation of oleic acid, and that is used chiefly in mixtures with palmitic acid — called also *octadecanoic acid* **2** : a mixture principally of stearic acid and palmitic acid produced commercially usu. by pressing chilled fatty acid saponification products and used chiefly in rubber compounding, in candles, and in the form of metallic soaps and other derivatives in ointments and cosmetics, lubricants, and coatings

stea·rin \'stēərən, 'stir-\ *n* -s [F *stéarine*, fr. Gk *stear* fat, tallow + F -*ine*, -in, -ine] **1** : an ester of glycerol and stearic acid; *esp* : TRISTEARIN **2** *also* **stea·rine** \-, -rēn\ : the solid portion of any fat — distinguished from *olein*; compare OLEOSTEARIN **3** *usu* **stearine** : STEARIC ACID 2

stearin pitch *n* : ¹PITCH 1c

stea·rol·ic acid \,stēə'rōlik-, -räl-, (')sti̇ˈr-\ *adj* [stear- + -*olic*] : a crystalline acid $CH_3(CH_2)_7C≡C(CH_2)_7COOH$ of the acetylene series that is isologous with stearic acid and is obtained indirectly from oleic acid

stea·rone \'stēə,rōn, 'sti̇,r-\ *n* -s [stear- + -one] : a crystalline ketone $(C_{17}H_{35})_2CO$ obtainable by heating stearic acid with phosphorus pentoxide

stea·rop·tene \stēə'räp,tēn, sti̇'r-\ *also* **stea·rop·ten** \-ptən\ *n* -s [ISV stear- + Gk *ptenos* winged; akin to Gk *petesthai* to fly — more at FEATHER] : the portion of a natural essential oil that separates as a solid on cooling or long standing — distinguished from *eleoptene*

stear·o·yl \'stēərə,wil, 'stir-, -,wēl\ *n* -s [ISV stear- + -yl] : the radical $C_{17}H_{35}CO$- of stearic acid

stea·ryl \'stēə,ril, 'sti̇,r-, -ēl\ *n* -s [ISV stear- + -yl] **1** : STEAROYL **2** : the univalent radical $C_{17}H_{35}CH_2$- derived from stearyl alcohol

stearyl alcohol *n* : an unctuous solid alcohol $CH_3(CH_2)_{16}CH_2OH$ that occurs esp. in whale, porpoise, and dolphin oils but is usu. obtained in a mixture with other solid alcohols by hydrogenation of stearic acid and that has uses similar to those of cetyl alcohol — called also *1-octadecanol*

steat- *or* **steato-** *comb form* [Gk, fr. *steat-*, *stear* — more at STONE] : fat : tallow ⟨*steatolysis*⟩ ⟨*steatosis*⟩

stea·tin \'stēədən, -ətən\ *n* -s [NL *steatinum*, fr. *steat-* + L -*inum*, neut. of -*inus* -ine] : ⁷MULL 2

stea·tite \'stēə,tīt\ *n* -s [L *steatitis*, a kind of stone, fr. (assumed) Gk *steatitis*, *steatitēs*, fr. *steat-* + -*itis*, -*itēs* -ite] **1** : a massive talc having a grayish green or brown color and forming extensive beds : SOAPSTONE **2** : an insulating porcelain composed largely of steatite and used esp. in radio equipment —

ste·a·tit·ic \,stēə'tid·ik\ *adj*

ste·a·ti·tis \,stēə'tīd·əs\ *n* -ES [NL, fr. *steat-* + -*itis*] : YELLOW FAT

stea·tog·e·nous \,stēə'täjənəs\ *adj* [steat- + -*genous*] : producing fat : causing steatosis

ste·a·tol·y·sis \,stēə'täləsəs\ *n* [NL, fr. *steat-* + -*lysis*] : conversion of neutral fats into glycerol and free fatty acids

ste·a·to·ma \,stēə'tōmə\ *n, pl* **steatomas** \-məz\ *or* **stea·toma·ta** \-mədə, -ətə\ [NL *steatomat-*, *steatoma*, fr. L, fr. Gk *steatōmat-*, *steatōma*, fr. *steat-* + -*ōmat-*, -*ōma* -oma] **1** : a sebaceous cyst **2** : LIPOMA — **ste·a·toma·tous** \,꞉꞉꞉-\

ste·a·to·py·gia \,stēəd·ə'pij·ēə, -,pī-, |gēə\ *also* **ste·a·to·py·ga** \-'pīgə, ,stēə'täpəgə\ *n* -s [steatopyga fr. NL, fr. steat- + Gk *pygē* rump, buttocks; steatopygia fr. NL, fr. steat- + Gk *pygē* + NL -ia — more at FOG] : an excessive development of fat on the buttocks esp. of females that is common among the Hottentots and some Negro peoples — **ste·a·to·py·gous** \,stēəd·ə'pīgəs, ,stēə'täp-\ *adj* — **ste·a·to·py·gous** \,stēə'täpəgəs, ,stēəd·ə,pīgəs, ,stēd·ə|pijik\ *adj*

ste·a·to·py·gy \'stēəd·ə,pījē, -,īgē; ,stēə'täpəjē, -pəgē\ *n* -ES [NL *steatopygia*] : STEATOPYGIA

ste·a·tor·nis \,stēə'tórnəs\ *n, cap* [NL *Steatornith-*, *Steatornis*, fr. *steat-* + -*ornith-*, -*ornis*] : a genus (coextensive with the family Steatornithidae) consisting of the oilbird — see STEATORNITHES

ste·a·tor·ni·thes \,꞉꞉꞉'tórnə,thēz, -,tór'nī(,)thēz\ *n pl, cap* [NL, fr. pl. of *Steatornis*] : a suborder of Caprimulgiformes including the single genus *Steatornis*

ste·a·tor·rhea *or* **ste·a·tor·rhoea** \,stēə'rēə\ *n* -s [NL, fr. steat- + -*rrhea*] : an excess of fat in the stools resulting from any of several conditions

ste·a·to·sis \-'tōsəs\ *n, pl* **steato·ses** \-,ō,sēz\ [NL, fr. *steat-* + -*osis*] : FATTY DEGENERATION

stech \'stek\ *vb* [origin unknown] *vt, chiefly Scot* : CRAM, STUFF ~ *vi, chiefly Scot* : GORMANDIZE

steck·ling \'steklin, -lēn\ *n* -s [G, fr. *stecken* to stick, insert (fr. OHG *stecchen*) + -*ling* — more at STICK] : a small late-planted beet of a biennial root crop (as beet or carrot) that is usu. dug and stored over winter and replanted the next season for seed production

sted·dle \'stedᵊl\ *dial var of* STADDLE

stedfast *var of* STEADFAST

sted·man \'stedmən\ *n -s usu cap* [after Fabian *Stedman* 17th cent. Eng. printer, its inventor] : a system for ringing changes on a set of bells

stee \'stē\ *n* -s [alter. of ME *stie*, fr. ON *stigi*; akin to OE *stīge* ascent, descent, OHG *stega* flight of stairs, OE *stīgan* to go up — more at STAIR] *dial Eng* : LADDER

steed \'stēd\ *n* -s [ME *stede*, fr. OE *stēda* studhorse, stallion; akin to OE *stōd* stud — more at STUD] **1** : HORSE; *esp* : a spirited horse for state or war **2 a** : a horse of no mettle or distinction : NAG **b** : something (as a bicycle) ridden astride

steed·less \-l̇əs\ *adj* : lacking a steed

¹steek \'stēk\ *vb* [ME *steken* to pierce, fix, enclose; akin to MLG & MD *steken* to sting, prick, OHG *stehhan* — more at STICK] *chiefly Scot* : SHUT, CLOSE

²steek \"\ *n, chiefly Scot var of* STITCH

³steek \"\ *n* -s [prob. fr. ²steek] *Scot* : ⁴CLIP 5

steek·gras *or* **steek·grass** \'stēk,gras, ꞉꞉grás\ *n* -ES [Afrik *steekgras*, fr. *steek* prick, sting (fr. MD *steke*) + *gras* grass, fr. MD; akin to OE *stice* stitch and to OE *græs* grass — more at STITCH, GRASS] *southern Africa* : a grass of the genus *Aristida*

¹steel \'stēl, 'stēəl\ *n* -s [ME *stele*, *stel*, fr. OE *stēle*, *style*; akin to OHG *stahal* steel, ON *stāl*, Skt *stakati* he resists] **1** : commercial iron that contains carbon in any amount up to about 1.7 percent as an essential alloying constituent, is malleable when under suitable conditions, is distinguished from cast iron by its malleability and lower carbon content and when of low carbon content from wrought iron by its freedom from slag and by its method of manufacture, and is now usu. produced by refining molten pig iron in a bath that remains completely molten throughout the process — see ALLOY STEEL, BESSEMER STEEL, CARBON STEEL, ELECTRIC STEEL, MILD STEEL, STAINLESS STEEL; BESSEMER PROCESS, OPEN-HEARTH PROCESS **2 a** : steel as a material for manufactured articles **b** : the steel part of an article (as the blade of a knife) **3** : an instrument or implement of or characteristically of steel: as **a** (1) : WEAPON; *esp* : one used for thrusting or cutting — see COLD STEEL (2) : weapons or armaments of steel ⟨invaders are driven back by ~⟩ ⟨evils, for which the only remedy is blood and ~ —John Buchan⟩ **b** : an instrument for sharpening knives; *esp* : a fluted round rod of steel with a handle and used for this purpose ⟨butcher's ~⟩ **c** : a piece of steel for striking sparks from flint **d** : RAIL 3a,3b(3) ⟨lay ~⟩ ⟨end of ~⟩ **e** : a strip of steel used (as in corsets) for stiffening

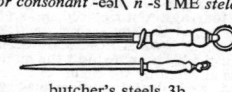

butcher's steels 3b

---

compare BONE 5b **4** : a steellike quality ⟨lacked the ~ a conquistador must have —Bernard De Voto⟩ ⟨the cold ~ of the intellect —Edward Sapir⟩ **5** : STEEL GRAY **6 a** : the steel manufacturing industry ⟨the growth of ~ since the end of the war —Howard Marshall⟩ ⟨Big Steel⟩ **b steels** *pl* : stocks or bonds of steel companies

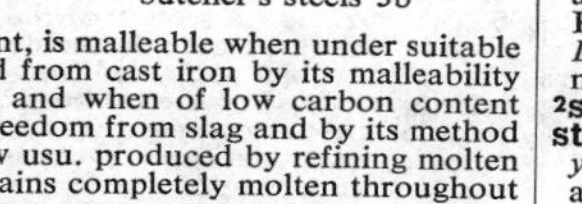

²steel \"\ *vt* -ED/-ING/-S [ME *stelen*, fr. *stele* steel] **1 a** : to overlay, point, or edge with steel ⟨~ a razor⟩; *esp* : to provide (an electrotype) with a nickel or iron-nickel compound face **b** : CASE HARDEN **2 a** : to cause to resemble steel (as in looks or hardness) **b** : to make hard or unbending : fill with strong resolution, unyielding determination, or stark insensibility ⟨was sick of the bareness and privation ... but was ~*ing* himself to hold out —Theodore Dreiser⟩ ⟨charge high rates and ~ their hearts against all compassion —G.G.Coulton⟩ ⟨strive rather to ~ them in a new and finer way —E.A.Mowrer⟩ **syn** see ENCOURAGE

³steel \"\ *adj* [¹steel] **1** : made of steel ⟨~ plate⟩ ⟨~ castings⟩ ⟨~ pen⟩ **2** : of or relating to the production of steel ⟨the ~ industry⟩ ⟨~ furnace⟩ **3** : resembling steel in one or more characteristics ⟨~ nerves⟩ ⟨~ courage⟩ -- often used in combination ⟨steel-jawed⟩ ⟨steel-willed⟩

steel band *n* [¹steel] : a band peculiar to the Caribbean islands and esp. Trinidad composed of percussion instruments typically cut out of oil barrels and usu. tuned to a definite pitch — called also *steel orchestra*

steel blue *n* [¹steel] **1** : a variable color averaging a grayish blue that is redder and paler than electric, greener and less strong than copenhagen, and redder than Gobelin **2** : STEEL GRAY **3** : PRUSSIAN BLUE 2 **4** : any of the blue colors assumed by steel at various temperatures in tempering — compare TEMPER COLOR **5** : an iron blue pigment

steel·bow \'stēl,bō, -bau\ *n* [ME *stelebow*, fr. *stele* steel + *bow* farm stock; fr. the understanding that the amount must be rigidly preserved and returned — more at BOWER (farm tenant)] **1** : the farming stock, implements, and other materials formerly supplied to a tenant farmer in Scotland by the landlord under a contract stipulating that these goods must be returned or compensated for at the expiration of the tenancy **2** : a type of contract formerly in use in Scotland under which a tenant farmer must at the expiration of his tenancy return to his landlord the farming goods supplied by the landlord or compensate him for them

steel bronze *n* [¹steel] : a bronze of about 92 percent copper and 8 percent tin hardened by compression and used as a substitute for steel in making guns — called also *Uchatius bronze*

steel-cage construction \,꞉꞉꞉-\ *n* : SKELETON CONSTRUCTION

steel-clad rope \,꞉꞉꞉-\ *n* : a hoisting rope whose strands have received an additional external serving of flat strip steel to secure additional wearing surface without a sacrifice of flexibility

steel concrete *n* : concrete reinforced with steel

steel-cut \,꞉꞉꞉\ *adj* **1** : ground or crushed between rolls fitted with cutting teeth into granules of uniform size and freed of powder and chaff ⟨*steel-cut* coffee⟩ ⟨*steel-cut* oats⟩ **2** : faceted with a steel tool — used esp. of buttons, buckles, and beads having an allover design of facets

steel driver *n* : a worker who before the adoption of the power drill drove a steel drill with a heavy hammer into rock or soil to make holes for blasting charges

steeled \'stē(ə)ld\ *adj* [ME *steled*, fr. OE *styled*, fr. *style* steel + -*ed*] : made of steel : edged, tipped, or armored with steel ⟨a ~ spear⟩ ⟨a ~ compartment of a battleship⟩

steel electrotype *n* : NICKELTYPE

steel emery *n* : an abrasive made in the same way as crushed steel but with an intensely hard temper

steel engraving *n* **1** : the art or process of engraving on steel **2** : an impression taken from an engraved steel plate

steeler *var of* STEALER

²steel·er \'stēlə(r)\ *n* -s [²steel + -er] **1** : one that steels; *esp* : a smith who steels edged tools **2** : one that inserts steels (as in corsets) : BONER

steel eraser *n* [³steel] : ERASER a

steel-face \,꞉꞉꞉\ *vt* : to make (a copper engraving or etching plate) more durable by electroplating with nickel steel

steelfaced electrotype \,꞉꞉꞉-\ *n* : NICKELTYPE

steel glass *n* : a mirror of steel

steel gray *n* : a nearly neutral slightly purplish dark gray that is lighter and slightly bluer than gunmetal — called also *Davy's gray*, *iron blue*

steel guitar *n* : HAWAIIAN GUITAR 1

steel hand *n* : a fishing tool used in well drilling to recover objects at the bottom of a well

steelhead \,꞉꞉꞉\ *n* **1** *or* **steelhead trout** : a large-sized silvery anadromous rainbow trout **2** *dial* : RUDDY DUCK

steel·ie *also* **steely** \'stēlē, -li\ *n, pl* **steelies** [³steel + -ie] : a steel playing marble

steel·i·fi·ca·tion \,stēlɔfə'kāshən\ *n* -s [fr. *steelify*; after such pairs as E *purify*: *purification*] : the act or process of converting iron into steel

steel·i·fy \'꞉꞉,fī\ *vt* -ED/-ING/-ES [¹steel + -*ify*] : to convert (iron) into steel

steel·i·ness \-lēnəs, -lin-\ *n* -ES : the quality or state of being steely

steel jack *n* : PUCELLAS

steel-jacketed \,꞉꞉꞉꞉꞉\ *adj, of a bullet* : having a steel jacket over a soft metal core

steel·less \'stēl(ə)əs\ *adj* : containing no steel : lacking steel

steellike \'stēl,līk\ *adj* : resembling steel : suggestive of steel (as in strength, severity, or relentlessness)

steelmaker \,꞉꞉꞉\ *n* **1** : one that makes steel : a steel manufacturer : an official of a steel manufacturing company

steelmaking \,꞉꞉꞉\ *n* : the process or business of manufacturing steel

steel-man \'꞉,man\ *n, pl* **steelmen** : STEELMAKER

steel marimba *n* : a musical instrument similar to a xylophone but having metal bars

steelmaster \,꞉꞉꞉\ *n* : STEELMAKER

steel mill *n* **1** : a mill (as for coffee or oats) that operates machines with steel grinding surfaces **2** : a mill where steel is manufactured

steel orchestra *n* : STEEL BAND

steels *pl of* STEEL, *pres 3d sing of* STEEL

steel square *n* : a carpenter's square made of steel

steel-trap \,꞉꞉꞉\ *adj* [fr. the phrase *as sharp as a steel trap*] : extremely quick and penetrating of intellect ⟨a *steel-trap* mind⟩

steel wool *n* : an abrasive material composed of long fine steel shavings and used esp. for scouring and burnishing

steelwork \,꞉꞉꞉\ *n* **1** : work in steel : articles or a part or the whole of any structure made of steel **2 steelworks** *pl but sing or pl in constr* : a shop or establishment where steel is made

steelworker \,꞉꞉꞉\ *n* : one that works in steel and esp. in the manufacturing of it

¹steely \'stēlē, -li\ *adj* -ER/-EST [steel + -y] **1** : made of steel : consisting of steel **2** : resembling steel (as in hardness, firmness, color, keenness, or chillness) ⟨night, with the ~ stars above —Aubrey Drury⟩ ⟨a ~ wind⟩ ⟨~ cymbals —Irving Kolodin⟩ ⟨nerves as ~ as those of a steeplejack —London Daily Telegraph⟩ ⟨~ fortitude⟩ **3** *of wool* : lacking the natural crimp and elasticity

²steely *var of* STEELIE

steel·yard \'stēl,yärd, -,yåd, -,yə(r)d\ *n* [prob. fr. ¹steel + *yard* (rod)] : a portable balance designed to be suspended (as from a hook or the free hand of the user) when in operation — called also *lever scales*

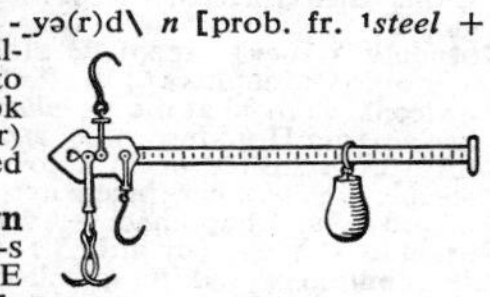

¹steen *or* **stein** *also* **steyn** \'stēn, 'stīn\ *vt* -ED/-ING/-S [ME *stenen* to stone, fr. OE *stænan*; akin to OHG *steinōn* to stone, Goth *stainjan*, ON *steina* to paint (with mineral colors), OE *stān* stone — more at STONE] : to line (an excavation) with stone, brick, cement, or similar material to prevent caving in or washing away of soil ⟨a well ⟨the bottom was but slightly ~*ed* and not watertight —G.E.Fussell⟩

steelyard

2steen *var of* STEAN

3steen \'stēn\ *adj* [prob. by shortening & alter. fr. *sixteen*] : UMPTEEN

steen-bok *or* **stein-bok** *also* **stein-bock** \'stēn,bäk\ *n, pl* **steenbok** *or* **steenboks** *or* **steinbok** *or* **steinboks** [Afrik *steenbok,* fr. MD *steenboc* ibex — more at STEINBOCK] : any small antelope of the genus *Raphicerus* (as *R. campestris*) of the plains of southern and eastern Africa

steen-bras *also* **steen-brass** \'stēn,bras\ *n, pl* **steenbras** *or* **steenbrases** *also* **steenbrass** *or* **steenbrasses** [Afrik *steenbras,* fr. *steen* stone (fr. MD) + *brasem* bream, fr. MD *brasem, bressem* — more at BREAM] : any of several southern African marine sparid food and sport fishes: as **a** : BISKOP **b** : RED STEENBRAS **c** : WHITE STEENBRAS

steening *or* **steining** *also* **steyning** *n* -s [fr. gerund of 1*steen*] : a lining (as for a well) of stone, brick, or other hard material to prevent caving in or washing away of soil

steenkirk *often cap, var of* STEINKIRK

steen-strup-ine \'stēnstrə,pēn, -n,strüpən\ *n* -s [Dan *steenstrupine,* fr. K. J. V. *Steenstrup* †1913 Dan. geologist + Dan *-ine*] : a mineral (La,Ca,Na)(Al,Fe,Mn)(Si,P)(O,OH,F)₄(?) consisting of a complex silicate, phosphate, and fluoride of the rare-earth metals, calcium, sodium, aluminum, iron, and manganese, and occurring in dark brown rhombohedral crystals

steenth \'stēn(t)th\ *adj* [3*steen* + *-th*] : UMPTEENTH

steen-tjie \'stēnchē\ *n* -s [Afrik, dim. of *steenbras*] : a small southern African sea bream (*Spondyliosoma emarginatum*)

1steep \'stēp\ *adj* -ER/-EST [ME *stepe,* fr. OE *stēap* high, steep, deep; akin to OE *stēap* cup, OFris *stāp* steep, OHG *stouf* high rock, cup, MHG *stief* steep, ON *staup* lump, knoll, hole in a road, cup] **1** : LOFTY, TALL, ELEVATED, HIGH — used chiefly of a sea ⟨ships steaming into ~ heavy seas —*Manual of Seamanship*⟩ ⟨the elusive periscope almost impossible to detect in such ~ seas —Stanley Rogers⟩ **2 a** : making a large angle with the plane of the horizon : having a side or slope approaching the perpendicular : PRECIPITOUS ⟨~ hills⟩ ⟨a ~ road⟩ ⟨area of cleared, ~ ground —Evan Williams⟩ **b** *of twill* : having an angle greater than 45 degrees in the twill line **3 a** : mounting or falling precipitously : HEADLONG ⟨a ~ flight of stairs⟩ **b** : characterized by a very rapid decline or increase ⟨the ~ but comparatively brief depression —Clark Warburton⟩ ⟨the persistently ~ fall in immigration —Peter Scott⟩ ⟨a period of ~ decline in our literary standards —Malcolm Cowley⟩ **4** : having precipitous or sharply pitched sides ⟨a ~ roof⟩ ⟨its ~ wooded valleys —R.M.Lockley⟩ **5** : difficult to accept, meet, or perform : ARDUOUS, EXTREME, EXCESSIVE, EXORBITANT, INCREDIBLE ⟨a ~ story⟩ ⟨a ~ tax⟩ ⟨prices are rather ~ ⟨a ~ task⟩

syn ABRUPT, PRECIPITOUS, SHEER: STEEP describes a slope or pitch likely to make ascent difficult or descent or fall sharp, rapid, rushing ⟨the trail ... then struck up the side of the mountain, growing *steeper* every foot of the way —H.D. Quillin⟩ ⟨a slope of water so *steep* that it made me giddy —R.L.Stevenson⟩ ABRUPT may apply to sudden protuberance or declivity, to sharply broken angles or levels ⟨occasionally the hills slope gently to the waterline, but more often the highlands rise into *abrupt* cliffs —*Amer. Guide Series: Minn.*⟩ ⟨high *abrupt* banks in places become hanging cliffs with a drop of 100 feet or more —*Amer. Guide Series: N.C.*⟩ PRECIPITOUS applies to inclines next to impossible to climb by ordinary procedures, to those approaching the perpendicular ⟨a mountainous region, fronting the Pacific, to which it presents, abruptly, a *precipitous* escarpment —*Amer. Guide Series: Oregon*⟩ ⟨a deep gorge, with *precipitous,* volcanic walls which no man could scale —Jack London⟩ SHEER may suggest an unbroken perpendicular expanse ⟨*sheer* cliffs that fell from the summit to the plain, more than a thousand feet —Willa Cather⟩ ⟨a *sheer* drop of 224 feet into a pool at the base of an overhanging cliff —*Amer. Guide Series: Oregon*⟩

2steep \"\ *adv* : STEEPLY ⟨the cliff rises ~ behind it —Edmund Wilson⟩ ⟨the roof ... was pitched very ~ to shed water —*Amer. Guide Series: Conn.*⟩ — often used in combination ⟨*steep*-ascending⟩

3steep \"\ *n* -s [1*steep*] : a precipitous place : a steep ascent or descent : an object having a steep side or slope ⟨too many thickets and swamps and ~s for practical traveling off the roads —G.W. Brace⟩ ⟨when the toiling cyclists climbed that ~ they had the flat road ... in front of them —O.S.J.Gogarty⟩

4steep \"\ *vi* -ED/-ING/-s : SLOPE; *esp* : to slope abruptly ⟨now the angle of ascent ~ed sharply —J.R.Ullman⟩

5steep \"\ *vb* -ED/-ING/-s [ME *stepen*; akin to Sw *stöpa* to steep, Dan *stöbe,* and prob. to OE *stēap* cup — more at 1*steep*] *vt* **1 a** : to soak or let stand in a liquid at a temperature under the boiling point (as for the purpose of cleansing, softening, bleaching, extracting a flavor, or germinating) : INFUSE, MACERATE ⟨rice grains are usually ~ed in a solution of sodium hydroxide⟩ ⟨~ coffee⟩ ⟨~ barley⟩ **b** : to soak (corn kernels) in warm water usu. containing a very small amount of sulfur dioxide in the manufacture of starch by the wet milling process **c** : to soak (cellulose pulp) in a dilute solution of sodium hydroxide for the production of alkali cellulose **2** : BATHE, WET, IMMERSE, MOISTEN ⟨~ed my wrists and laved my temples —R.L.Stevenson⟩ **3** : to saturate thoroughly : IMBUE ⟨the world was all ~ed in sunshine —D.H.Lawrence⟩ ⟨a man ~ed in the art of the past —Aline B. Saarinen⟩ ⟨they continued to ~ themselves in the classics —Gilbert Highet⟩ ⟨the annals of those ~ed in crime —Ellen Smith⟩ ~ *vi* : to undergo the process of soaking in a liquid (as water) under the boiling point ⟨the tea is ~ing⟩ ⟨rosemary ... ~ing in vinegar —J.H. Wheelwright⟩

6steep \"\ *n* -s [ME *stepe,* fr. *stepen* to steep] **1** : the state or process of being steeped ⟨put barley in ~ for forty-eight hours⟩ **2** : a bath or solution in which something is steeped (as in dyeing or cleansing) **3** : a tank in which a material (as corn or rice) is steeped ⟨the shelled corn is soaked in a ~ before milling ⟨the rice starch from the ~ is purified⟩

7steep \"\ *adj* [5*steep*] : used for steeping ⟨~ tank⟩ ⟨~ tub⟩

steepdown \"\ *adj* [1*steep* + *down,* adv.] : PRECIPITOUS

steep-en \'stēpən, -p*ə*m\ *vb* **steepened; steepened; steepening** \-p(ə)niŋ\ **steepens** [1*steep* + *-en*] *vt* : to make steeper : INCREASE ⟨ice sheets of successive glaciations have ~ed the valley sides —Samuel Van Valkenburg & Ellsworth Huntington⟩ ~ *vi* : to become steeper ⟨volcanoes have concave slopes that ~ to the summit —Howel Williams⟩ ⟨the slant of the line ~ed to the vertical —Arthur Mayse⟩

steep-er \'stēpə(r)\ *n* -s : one that steeps: as **a** : a container (as a tank or vat) in which something is steeped **b** : a worker who steeps barley for the manufacture of malt liquor

steepgrass \"\ *n* [6*steep* + *grass*] : a common butterwort (*Pinguicula vulgaris*) used like rennet

steep-i-ness \-pēnəs, -pin-\ *n* -ES [*steepy* + *-ness*] *archaic* : STEEPNESS

steep-ish \-pish, -pēsh\ *adj* : somewhat steep ⟨a very large field with a ~ slope —Roald Dahl⟩

1stee-ple \'stēpəl\ *n* -s [ME *stepel,* fr. OE *stīpel, stȳpel, stēpel* tower; akin to OE *stēap* steep — more at STEEP] **1 a** : a tall structure usu. composed of a series of diminishing stories finished at the top with a small spire or cupola surmounting the lower straight-sided story of a church tower **b** : the whole of a church tower **2** : something suggesting or having the shape of a steeple ⟨pressed together their fingertips to form ~s —Scott Fitzgerald⟩

2steeple \"\ *vb* **steepled; steepled; steepling** \-p(ə)liŋ\ **steeples** *vi* : to rise high in the air like a steeple ⟨looked at the *steepling* mast and loaded keel —Tom Hopkinson⟩ *vt* : to arrange in the form of a steeple or in a form suggestive of a steeple ⟨*steepled* her fingers in the childish gesture of prayer and happiness —Adria Langley⟩

3steeple \"\ *n* -s [by alter.] : STAPLE 1

steeplebush \"\ *n* [so called fr. its steeplelike inflorescences] : HARDHACK 1

1steeplechase \"\ *n* [so called fr. the use of church steeples as landmarks to guide the competitors] **1 a** : a race across country and over barriers (as fences, hedges, and ditches) ridden by a number of horsemen **b** : a similar obstacle race over a circular course typically situated on the inner

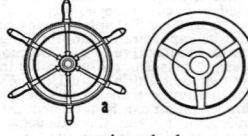

stee-ple 1a

periphery of a flat-racing track **2** : a usu. 2-mile footrace across country or over a prescribed course obstructed esp. by hurdles, hedges, and water jumps

2steeplechase \"\ *vi* : to run or ride in a steeplechase

steeplechaser \',⸗,⸗\ *n* **1** : one that rides or runs in a steeplechase **2** : an athlete or a horse trained to run in steeplechases

steeplechasing \',⸗,⸗\ *n* [fr. gerund of 2*steeplechase*] : the sport of riding in steeplechases

steeple clock *n* : an Early American pointed shelf clock with steeplelike finials bordering each side

steeple-crown \'⸗,⸗\ *n* **1** : a hat crown that is high and pointed like a steeple **2** : a hat with a steeple-crown — **steeple-crowned** \'⸗,⸗\ *adj*

steeple cup *n* : a usu. silver standing cup of early 17th century English origin with baluster stem supporting a conical bowl and with a domed cover carrying a steeplelike finial

stee-pled \'stēpəld\ *adj* [1*steeple* + *-ed*] : furnished with or having the form of a steeple : adorned with or having steeples ⟨a ~ hill⟩

steeple engine *n* : a vertical back-acting steam engine having the cylinder beneath the crosshead and chiefly used for donkey engines

steeple fork *n* : an earmark on an animal made by a cut removing a rectangular piece from the upper part of the ear — see EARMARK illustration

steeple hat *n* : a steeple-crowned hat

steeple headdress *n* : HENNIN

steeple-head rivet \'⸗,⸗,⸗\ *n* : a rivet having a head in the form of a cylindrical cone

steeplehouse \'⸗,⸗\ *n, archaic* : a church building — used esp. by the early Quakers

steeple hunt *n, archaic* : STEEPLECHASE

1steeplejack \'⸗,⸗\ *n* [*steeple* + *jack* (man)] : one whose work is building smokestacks, towers, or steeples or climbing up the outside of such structures to paint and make repairs

2steeplejack \"\ *vi* -ED/-ING/-s : to work as a steeplejack

steeple-less \'⸗ləs\ *adj* : having no steeple ⟨a ~ church⟩

steeplelike \'⸗,⸗\ *adj* : resembling or suggestive of a steeple

steeples *pl of* STEEPLE, *pres 3d sing of* STEEPLE

steeple skull *or* **steeple head** *n* : OXYCEPHALY

steepletop \'⸗,⸗\ *n* **1** : a top in the shape of a steeple; *specif* : an octagonal finial (as of an andiron or chair post) tapering to a point **2** [so called fr. its conical blowholes] : GREENLAND WHALE

steepling *pres part of* STEEPLE

steep-ly *adv* [1*steep* + *-ly*] **1** : at a sharp angle : ABRUPTLY, PRECIPITOUSLY, SHARPLY ⟨the train swept ~ down toward ... the Swiss border —Joseph Wechsberg⟩ ⟨the ground at once shelves ~ toward the north —James Whyle⟩ ⟨a ~ sloping roof⟩ **2** : at a rapid rate : SWIFTLY ⟨gasoline consumption rose ~ when rationing was ended —*Lamp*⟩ ⟨the ~ declining trend of the population —Alzada Comstock⟩ ⟨dropped ~ into unconsciousness —Irwin Shaw⟩

steep-ness *n* -ES [ME *stepnesse,* fr. *stepe* steep + *-nesse* -ness] : the quality or state of being steep : PRECIPITOUSNESS ⟨the ~ of a grade⟩

steeps *pres 3d sing of* STEEP, *pl of* STEEP

steep-to \'⸗,⸗\ *adj* [1*steep* + *to,* adv.] : PRECIPITOUS; *esp* : sloping almost perpendicularly downward — used esp. of a shore or shoal ⟨the north side of the cape is *steep-to* —U.S. *Coast Pilot: West Indies*⟩ ⟨found *steep-to* banks inside against which the ships would have to lie —S.E.Morison⟩

steep-up \'⸗,⸗\ *adj* [1*steep* + *up,* adv.] : STEEP, PRECIPITOUS, STRAIGHT-UP

steepwater \'⸗,⸗⸗\ *n* [6*steep* + *water*] : the solution resulting from steeping (as corn) in water in the manufacture of starch — see INOSITOL 1

steepweed \'⸗,⸗\ *or* **steepwort** \'⸗,⸗\ *n* [6*steep*] : STEEPGRASS

steepy \'stēpē, -pi\ *adj* [1*steep* + *-y*] *archaic* : STEEP, PRECIPITOUS ⟨climb the ~ cliffs —John Dryden⟩

1steer \'sti(ə)r, -iə\ *n, pl* **steers** *also* **steer** [ME *stere, steer,* fr. OE *stēor* young ox; akin to OHG *stior* young ox, ON *stjórr,* Goth *stiur,* Skt *sthavira, sthūra* stout, thick, broad, and perh. to L *taurus* bull, Gk *tauros,* MIr *tarb,* ON *thjórr* — more at 3STEER] **1 a** : a bull castrated before sexual maturity and usu. at an early age — see BEEF **b** : an ox less than four years old ⟨eight thousand head of ~ —Wright Morris⟩ **2** : an entire male bovine : BULL **3** : the hide of a steer

2steer \"\ *vt* -ED/-ING/-s : CASTRATE — used of a bullock

3steer \"\ *vb* -ED/-ING/-s [ME *steren,* fr. OE *stīeran;* akin to OHG *stiuren* to steer, ON *stȳra,* Goth *stiurjan* to establish; all fr. a prehistoric Gmc denominative verb fr. the root of OE *stēor-* rudder, steering oar; akin to ON *stȳri* rudder, *staurr* pale, stake, Gk *stauros* pale, cross, *stylos* pillar, Skt *sthavira, sthūra* stout, thick, *tiṣṭhati* he stands — more at STAND] *vt* **1 a** : to direct the course of : GUIDE, MANAGE, CONTROL ⟨~ a bill through the legislature⟩ ⟨~ed the conversation into his favorite channels —T.B.Costain⟩; *specif* : to direct the course of (as a ship) by means of a rudder or similar device or by other mechanical means ⟨~ an automobile⟩ ⟨~ a satellite⟩ **b** : to entice (a prospective customer or victim) to an illicit or disreputable establishment **2** : to set and hold to or pursue (a course) : WEND ⟨see that the boat was ~ing her right course for the Narrows —William Black⟩ ⟨an effort to ~ a course between inflation and deflation —*Biddle Survey*⟩ ~ *vi* **1** : to direct the course (as of a ship or automobile) ⟨~ by the stars⟩ ⟨take turns ~ing⟩ **2** : to direct one's course : pursue a course of action ⟨~ for home⟩ **3** : to be subject to guidance or direction : obey the helm ⟨an automobile that ~s well⟩ *syn* see GUIDE — **steer large** : to steer a ship off the wind — **steer small** : to steer a ship loosely with considerable shifting of the helm — **steer clear** : to keep entirely away (as from a danger) : direct one's course so as to avoid any chance of hindrance, contact, harm, or involvement ⟨tries to *steer clear* of controversial issues —Kathleen Teltsch⟩

4steer \"\ *n* -s [ME *stere,* fr. *steren* to steer] : something by which to steer: as **a** *obs* : RUDDER, HELM **b** : directions for steering a course ⟨gave us a ~ toward home⟩ **c** : a hint as to procedure : TIP ⟨give one a friendly ~⟩ ⟨never got a wrong ~ from me yet —H.A.Sinclair⟩ — see BUM STEER **d** : a steering mechanism or arrangement ⟨a truck with a four-wheel ~⟩

5steer \'stēr\ *adj* [ME *stere, steer;* akin to MLG *stūr* stiff, severe, OHG *stiuri, stūri* strong, proud, Skt *sthūra* stout, thick, broad — more at 3STEER] *chiefly Scot* : STRONG, ROUGH

6steer \'sti(ə)r\ *n, pl* **steers** *dial Brit var of* STIR

steer-abil-i-ty \,stirə'biləd-ē\ *n* : the quality or state of being steerable

steer-able \'stirəbəl\ *adj* [3*steer* + *-able*] : capable of being guided by steering ⟨a ~ balloon⟩; *also* : capable of being readily shifted ⟨~ antenna⟩

steer-age \'stirij\ *n* -s [ME *sterage,* fr. *steren* to steer + *-age*] **1** : the act or practice of steering ⟨the ~ of a ship⟩; *broadly* : DIRECTION, MANAGEMENT, GUIDANCE **2** : the effect of the helm on a ship : the manner in which an individual ship is affected by the helm **3** : a steering apparatus (as of a ship or agricultural implement) **4** *archaic* : a course steered **5 a** (1) *archaic* : a section of the underdeck of the afterpart of a ship situated near the rudder or immediately forward of the main cabin and used for passenger accommodations inferior to those of the cabin (2) : a section in a passenger ship for passengers paying the lowest fares and given inferior accommodations — compare TOURIST CLASS **b** : a compartment in a man-of-war located generally just forward of the wardroom and assigned to midshipmen and other junior officers for quarters

2steerage \"\ *adv* : with steerage accommodations ⟨traveled ~ to Panama —Carl Van Doren⟩

steerage passenger *n* : a passenger in the steerage

steerageway \'⸗,⸗\ *n* : a rate of motion sufficient to make a boat answer the helm : the slowest forward speed of a ship that will permit steering — compare STERNWAY ⟨the big ships in the van slowed down till they had almost lost ~ —Nicholas Monsarrat⟩

steer-er \'stirə(r)\ *n* -s **1** : one that steers: as **a** : STEERSMAN **b** (1) : an accomplice who directs persons to places where they may be swindled : CAPPER ⟨a ~ for a gambling game⟩ (2) : a person employed to entice patrons : TOUT ⟨a ~ for a

theater⟩ **2** : something (as a ship) that is steered or responds to steering in some specified way ⟨a quick ~⟩

steerhide \'⸗,⸗\ *n* [1*steer*] **1** : leather made from the hide of a steer **2** : CATTLEHIDE

steering *n* -s [ME *stering,* fr. gerund of *steren* to steer] **1** : the act of one who steers **2 a** : the response (as of a ship) to the action of steering **b** : STEERING GEAR **3** : MANAGEMENT, GOVERNMENT

steering arm *n* : an arm for transmitting the turning force from the steering gear to the drag link esp. of an automotive vehicle

steering bridge *n* : a bridge from which a ship can be steered

steering column *or* **steering post** *n* : the column carrying the steering wheel and enclosing connections to the steering gear of an automobile or other vehicle

steering committee *n* : a managing or directing committee; *specif* : a committee composed of leaders of the majority caucus that determines the order in which business shall be taken up in a U.S. legislative body

steering gear *n* : the mechanism by which something is steered: as **a** : the gear train and linkages between the steering control and road-wheel connections of an automobile **b** : any mechanism giving more powerful control over a boat rudder than that given by the simple tiller

steering head *n* : the assemblages of front-axle end and steering knuckle on which a front wheel of an automobile turns

steering knuckle *n* : a knuckle made to furnish a bearing for an automobile steering wheel, pivoted to the axle, and controlled in its swiveling motion by the steering gear

steering line *n* : the warm front of an extratropical cyclone where the tropical winds rise over the cooler easterly winds

steering lock *n* : the maximum angular range of the steered wheels of an automobile

steering oar *or* **steer oar** *n* : an oar used over the stern or on the quarter in place of a rudder

steering wheel *n* : a hand wheel by means of which one steers: as **a** : a wheel that controls the movements of a ship's rudder **b** : a wheel by which the direction of the road wheels of an automobile is controlled

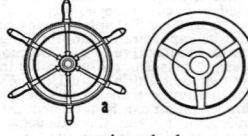

steering wheels

steer joint *n* [2*steer*] : an establishment (as a gambling house) that employs steerers

steer-less \'⸗ləs\ *adj* : lacking a steer

steers *pl of* STEER, *pres 3d sing of* STEER

steershead \'⸗,⸗\ *n* [1*steer*] : a low tuberous perennial herb (*Dicentra uniflora*) that is native to the mountains of western U.S. and has pink or white flowers few to a stalk and with the narrow outer petals strongly recurved

steers-man \'⸗mən\ *n, pl* **steersmen** [ME *steresman, stiersman,* fr. OE *stēoresman,* fr. *stēores-* (gen. of *stēor-* rudder, steering oar) + *man* — more at STEER] : one who steers: as **a** : one who steers a ship : HELMSMAN **b** : a worker who steers a raft of logs by means of an oar attached at the back of the raft

steersman-ship \'⸗⸗,ship\ *n* [*steersman* + *-ship*] : the ability a steersman has in steering a ship

steery \'stēri\ *n* [6*steer* + *-y*] *Scot* : COMMOTION, TUMULT

stees *pl of* STEE

1steeve \'stēv\ *adj* [ME *stef* (adv. *steve*)] *chiefly Scot* : STIFF, FIRM, STURDY — **steeve-ly** *adv, chiefly Scot*

2steeve \"\ *vt* -ED/-ING/-s [ME *steven,* prob. fr. Sp *estibar* or Pg *estivar* to pack tightly, fr. L *stipare* to press together, pack tightly — more at STIFF] : to stow esp. in a ship's hold : STUFF, PACK, STORE

3steeve \"\ *vb* -ED/-ING/-s [origin unknown] *vi, of a bowsprit* : to incline upward at an angle with the horizon or the line of the keel ~ *vt* : to set (a bowsprit) at an upward inclination

4steeve \"\ *also* **steev-ing** \-viŋ, -vēŋ\ *n* -s : the angle that a bowsprit makes with the horizon or with the keel ⟨was arranged with only slight ~ —E.W.White⟩

steever *var of* STIVER

ste-fan-boltz-mann law \'shte'bōlts,män\ *n, usu cap S&B* [after Josef *Stefan* †1893 Austrian physicist, its formulator, & Ludwig *Boltzmann* †1906 Austrian physicist who first demonstrated it] : a statement in thermal radiation: the total emissive power of an ideal black body is proportional to the fourth power of its absolute temperature

ste-fan's law \'shte,fänz\ *n, usu cap S* [after Josef *Stefan* †1893] : STEFAN-BOLTZMANN LAW

stef-fen process \'stefən-\ *n, usu cap S* [prob. fr. *Steffen,* name of its inventor] : a process for recovering sugar from beet molasses by adding powdered lime to precipitate the sugar as calcium sucrate

steffen's waste *n, usu cap S* : the filtrate obtained from the precipitation of calcium sucrate in the Steffen process and used chiefly as a source of amino acids (as glutamic acid or isoleucine)

1steg \'steg\ *n* -s [ME *stegge,* of Scand origin; akin to Icel *steggi* drake, gander — more at STAG] *dial Brit* : GANDER

2steg \"\ *n* [prob. fr. 1*steg*] *chiefly Scot* : STALK

steg- *or* **stego-** *comb form* [Gk *stegē, stegos* roof, fr. *stegein* to cover — more at THATCH] : covering plate or fold ⟨*stegodon*⟩ ⟨*stegocarpous*⟩

steg-a-no-gram \'⸗,⸗⸗,gram\ *n* [*steganography,* after such pairs as E *cryptography: cryptogram*] *archaic* : a cryptographic writing

steg-a-nog-ra-phy \,⸗⸗'nägrəfē\ *n* -ES [NL *steganographia,* fr. Gk *steganos* covered, reticent (fr. *stegein* to cover) + L *-graphia* -graphy] *archaic* : CRYPTOGRAPHY

steg-a-no-pod \'⸗⸗,⸗,päd\ *also* **steg-a-nop-o-dan** \,⸗⸗'näpədən\ *n* [*steganopod* fr. NL *Steganopodes; steganopodan* fr. NL *Steganopodes* + E *-an*] : a steganopodous bird

steg-a-nop-o-des \,⸗⸗'näpə,dēz\ *n* [NL, fr. Gk, pl. of *teganopod-, steganopous* web-footed, fr. *stegein* covered + *pod-, pous* foot] *syn of* PELECANIFORMES

steg-a-nop-o-dous \,⸗⸗'näpədəs\ *also* **steg-a-nop-o-dan** \-dən\ *adj* [NL *Steganopodes* + E *-ous, -an*] **1** : having all four toes webbed : TOTIPALMATE **2** : of or relating to the pelicans

-stege \,stēj\ *n comb form* -S [Gk *stegē* roof, fr. *stegein* to cover] : covering plate or fold ⟨gastrostege⟩ ⟨urostege⟩

stegh \'steg\ *var of* STECH

-ste-gite \stə,jīt\ *n comb form* -S [Gk *stegē* roof + E *-ite*] : segment of a carapace ⟨omostegite⟩

ste-go-bi-um \stə'gōbēəm\ *n, cap* [NL, fr. Gk *stegein* to cover + *-o-* + *-bium*] : a cosmopolitan genus of beetles (family Anobiidae) including the drugstore beetle

stego-car-pous \,stegō'kärpəs\ *adj* [*steg-* + *-carpous*] *of a moss* : having a capsule that opens by a deciduous lid

stego-ce-pha-lia \,⸗⸗səfālyə\ *n pl, cap* [NL, fr. *steg-* + Gk *kephalē* head + NL *-ia* — more at CEPHALIC] *in some esp former classifications* : an order or other division of Amphibia comprising all the pre-Jurassic and many later extinct typically tailed and salamandriform amphibians usu. with well-developed limbs and sometimes of large size — compare LABYRINTHODONTIA, LISSAMPHIBIA

1stego-ce-pha-lian \,⸗⸗'fālyən\ *adj* [NL *Stegocephalia* + E *-an*] : of or relating to the Stegocephalia

2stegocephalian \"\ *n* -s : a stegocephalian amphibian

stego-ceph-a-lous \,⸗⸗'sefələs\ *adj* [NL *Stegocephalia* + E *-ous*] : STEGOCEPHALIAN

stego-don \'stegə,dän\ *n, cap* [NL *Stegodont-, Stegodon,* fr. *steg-* + *-odont-, -odon* -odon] **1** *cap* : a genus of primitive Asiatic Pliocene and Pleistocene mammals that have molar teeth with relatively broad enamel ridges and but little cement and thus are intermediate between elephants and mastodons **2** : an animal or fossil of the genus Stegodon

stego-dont \-,nt\ *adj* -s [*stegodont* fr. NL *Stegodont-, Stegodon*] : STEGODON

stego-mus \-məs\ *n, cap* [NL, prob. fr. *steg-* + Gk *ōmos* shoulder — more at HUMERUS] : a genus of small short-necked 5-toed reptiles (order Thecodontia) with smooth dermal scutes found in the Triassic of the Connecticut valley

stego-my-ia \,⸗⸗'mī(y)ə\ *n* [NL, fr. *steg-* + *-myia*] **1** *cap, in some classifications* : a genus of mosquitoes including

the yellow-fever mosquito (*Aedes aegypti*) and several related mosquitoes **2** -s : any mosquito of the genus *Stegomyia*; *specif* : YELLOW-FEVER MOSQUITO
stego·saur \ˈ==ˌsȯ(ə)r\ *n* -s [NL *Stegosauria*] : a dinosaur of the suborder Stegosauria
stego·sau·ri \ˌ==ˈsȯˌrī\ [NL, pl. of *Stegosaurus*] *syn of* STEGOSAURIA
stego·sau·ria \ˌ==ˈsȯrēə\ *n pl, cap* [NL, fr. *Stegosaurus* + *-ia*] : a suborder of Ornithischia comprising numerous dinosaurs with strongly developed dorsal bony armor — compare STEGOSAURUS
¹stego·sau·ri·an \ˌ==ˈsȯrēən\ *adj* [NL *Stegosauria* + E *-an*] : of or relating to the Stegosauria
²stegosaurian \ˈ"\ *n* -s : STEGOSAUR
¹stego·sau·roid \ˌ==ˈsȯˌrȯid\ *adj* [NL *Stegosaurus* + E *-oid*] : resembling or related to the stegosaurs
²stegosauroid \ˈ"\ *n* -s : a stegosauroid dinosaur
stego·sau·rus \ˌ==ˈsȯrəs\ *n*, *cap* [NL, fr. *steg-* + *-saurus*] : a genus of large ornithischian dinosaurs of the Upper Jurassic rocks of Colorado and Wyoming being remarkable for their dermal armor and in the best-known species (*S. ungulatus*) having two rows of bony plates along the back
stegs *pl of* STEG
stei·ger·ite \ˈstīgəˌrīt\ *n* -s [George *Steiger* †1944 Am. chemist + E *-ite*] : a mineral $4AlVO_4.13H_2O$ consisting of hydrous aluminum vanadate and occurring in canary yellow masses in San Miguel valley, Calif.
steigh \ˈstā\ *var of* STEY
¹stein *var of* STEEN
²stein \ˈstīn\ *n* -s [prob. fr. G *steingut* stoneware, earthenware, fr. *stein* stone (fr. OHG) + *gut* goods, fr. *gut* good, adj., fr. OHG *guot* — more at STONE, GOOD] **1 a** : an earthenware mug esp. for beer commonly holding about a pint **b** : any large thick mug (as of glass) for beer holding sometimes as much as a quart **2** : the quantity of beer that a stein holds

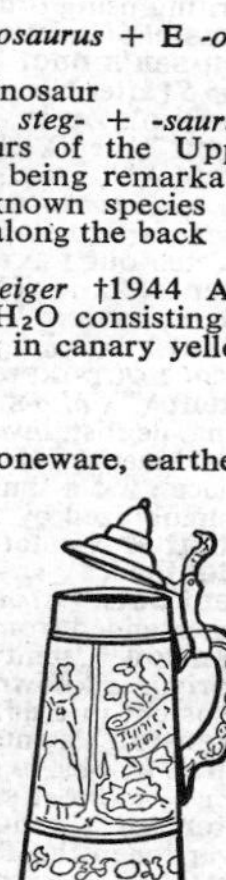

stein 1a

¹stein·bock \ˈstīnˌbäk\ *n* -s [G, fr. OHG *steinboc*; akin to OE *stānbucca* ibex, MD *steenboc*; all fr. a prehistoric WGmc compound whose first element is represented by OE *stān* stone and whose second element is represented by OE *bucca* buck — more at STONE, BUCK] : IBEX
²steinbock *var of* STEENBOK
steinbok *or* **steinbuck** *var of* STEENBOK
stein·heim man \ˈs(h)tīnˌhīm-\ *n, usu cap S* [fr. *Steinheim* am Murr, town of western Germany] : a Lower Paleolithic Neanderthaloid man having some neanthropic characteristics and known from a skull found associated with Acheulean artifacts in western Germany
stein·kern \ˈs(h)tīnˌkern\ *n* -s [G, fr. *stein* stone + *kern* kernel, grain, fr. OHG *kerno*; akin to OHG *korn* grain — more at CORN] : a fossil consisting of a stony mass that entered a hollow natural object (as a bivalve shell) in the form of mud or sediment, was consolidated, and remained as a cast after dissolution of the mold
stein·kirk *or* **steen·kirk** \ˈstēnˌkərk\ *n* -s *often cap* [F *steinkerke*, fr. the battle of *Steenkerke*, Belgium, 1692] : a cravat with long hanging ends loosely twisted or looped together and worn esp. in the 18th century by men and women
stein·mann pin \ˈstīnmən-\ *n, usu cap S* [after Fritz *Steinmann* †1932 Swiss surgeon] : a stainless steel spike used for the internal fixation of fractures of long bones
stein·metz coefficient \ˈstīnˌmets-\ *n, usu cap S* [after Charles P. *Steinmetz* †1923 Am. electrical engineer] : HYSTERESIS COEFFICIENT
stei·ron·e·ma \ˌstīrəˈnēmə\ *n, cap* [NL, fr. Gk *steiros* barren + NL *-nema*] : a small genus of No. American herbs (family Primulaceae) having yellow flowers with a rotate deeply lobed corolla — see LOOSESTRIFE 3
ste·la \ˈstēlə\ *or* **st·le** \ˈstēl *also* ˈstēlē\ *n, pl* **ste·lae** \-ēˌlē, -lī\ *or* **ste·lai** \-ˌlī\ *or* **steles** [*stela* fr. NL, fr. L, fr. Gk *stēlē*; *stele* fr. NL, fr. Gk *stēlē*; akin to Gk *stellein* to set up, make ready — more at STALL] **1** : a slab or pillar of stone usu. carved or inscribed and used for commemorative purposes (as to mark a grave) **2** : an inscribed area on a wall **3** : a monument in the form of a pillar
ste·lar \ˈstēlə(r)\ *adj* [*²stele* + *-ar*] : of, relating to, located in, or resembling a stele ⟨~ tissue⟩
stelar theory *n* : a theory in botany: stem and root are fundamentally alike anatomically since in both the cortex surrounds a central stele
¹stele \ˈstēl\ *n* -s [ME — more at STEAL] : HANDLE, SHAFT; *esp* : the wooden shaft body of an arrow
²stele \ˈ" *also* ˈstēlē\ *n* -s [NL, fr. Gk *stēlē* stela, boundary post or pillar — more at STELA] : the usu. cylindrical central portion of the axis of a vascular plant that consists of vascular tissue surrounded by a pericycle and often enclosing a central pith and that is in turn enclosed by cortex and in later life by a cork layer and other tissues of which all or part may be sloughed off with age — called also *vascular cylinder*; see ACTINOSTELE, DICTYOSTELE, EUSTELE, MERISTELE, POLYSTELE, PROTOSTELE, SIPHONOSTELE, SOLENOSTELE
-ste·lic \ˈstēlik\ *adj comb form* [*²stele* + *-ic*] : having (a specified number or kind of) steles ⟨*astelic*⟩
¹stell \ˈstel\ *vt* -ED/-ING/-S [ME *stellen*, fr. OE *stellan*; akin to MD & OHG *stellen* to set, place — more at STALL] **1** *Scot* : PUT, PLACE, FIX **2** : DELINEATE ⟨if truly a painter had *stell'd* thee there —Robert Bridges †1930⟩
²stell \ˈ"\ *n* -s [prob. fr. ¹*stell*] *chiefly Scot* : a protective enclosure for sheep or cattle
³stell \ˈ"\ *n* -s [origin unknown] **1** *dial Eng* : DITCH, DRAIN **2** *dial Eng* : BROOK
stel·lar \ˈstelə(r)\ *adj* [LL *stellaris*, fr. L *stella* star + *-aris* — more at STAR] **1 a** : of, relating to, or derived from the stars : ASTRAL ⟨an object of ~ size⟩ ⟨~ light⟩ ⟨~ spectrum⟩ **b** : composed of stars ⟨~ ornamentation⟩ **2** : of, relating to, or characteristic of a theatrical, operatic, or film star ⟨building or acquiring ~ names —W.J.Fadiman⟩ **3 a** : CHIEF, LEADING, PRINCIPAL ⟨given a ~ role⟩ **b** : OUTSTANDING, PREEMINENT, FIRST-RATE ⟨a ~ production⟩
stellar eclipse *n* : an eclipse of one star by another in a binary system
stellar energy *n* **1** : the internal energy of a star **2** : the energy radiated by a star **3** : the energy of the stars
stel·lar·ia \stəˈla(a)rēə\ *n, cap* [NL, fr. L *stella* star + NL *-aria*] : a genus of herbs (family Caryophyllaceae) having linear to ovate exstipulate leaves and flowers with deeply notched petals and three styles succeeded by ovoid capsular fruits
stellar interferometer *n* : an interferometer attachment to a telescope for measuring objects subtending very small angles (as close double stars)
stellar jay *n* [by alter.] : STELLER'S JAY
stellar nebula *n* [*stellar* + *nebula*] **1** : the nebulosity surrounding a star : a star's shell or envelope of nebulosity **2** : PLANETARY NEBULA
stellar parallax *n* : the heliocentric parallax of a star
stellar vault *n* : STAR VAULT
stel·lary \ˈstelərē\ *adj* [L *stella* + E *-ary*] *archaic* : STELLAR
stel·late \ˈsteˌlāt, *usu* -ād·+V\ *adj* [L *stellatus* set with stars, starry, shaped like a star, fr. *stella* star + *-atus* — more at STAR] : resembling a star (as in shape) : pointed, formed, or radiated like a star ⟨a ~ leaf⟩ ⟨a ~ ornament⟩ — **stel·late·ly** *adv*
stellate cell *n* : a cell with radiating cytoplasmic processes; *esp* : KUPFFER CELL
stellate–crystal fungus \ˈ=ˌ=ˈ==-\ *n* [so called fr. the stellate crystals of calcium oxalate formed in connection with the mycelium] *n* : a fungus (*Odontia sacchari*) frequently associated with diseased sugarcane
stel·lat·ed \ˈ=ˌlād·əd\ *adj* [L *stellatus* set with stars, stellate + E *-ed*] **1** : STELLATE **2** : ornamented or dotted with stars ⟨a ~ flag⟩
stellate ganglion *n* **1** : a composite ganglion formed by fusion of the inferior cervical and first thoracic ganglia of the sympathetic chain of a vertebrate animal **2** : a secondary ganglionic center on the course of the pallial nerve near the dorsal border of the internal wall of the mantle of a cephalopod
stellate ligament *n* : a branching ligament uniting the front of the head of a rib with the bodies of two vertebrae and the intervertebral disk between them
stellate reticulum *n* : a stellate arrangement of epithelial cells that in early stages makes up a large portion of the enamel organ
stel·lec·to·my \stəˈlektəmē\ *n* -ES [*stell*ate ganglion + *-ectomy*] : excision of the stellate ganglion
stelled *adj* [L *stella* star + E *-ed* — more at STAR] *obs* : studded with or as if with stars : STARRY
stel·ler·ine \ˈsteləˌrīn, -rən\ *n* -s [Georg W. *Steller* †1746 Ger. naturalist + E *-ine*] : STELLER'S SEA COW
¹stel·ler·oid \-ˌrȯid\ *adj* [NL *Stelleroidea*] : of or relating to the Stelliformia
²stelleroid \ˈ"\ *n* -s : an echinoderm of the division Stelliformia
stel·ler·oi·dea \ˌ==ˈrȯidēə\ [NL, fr. F *stelléride* starfish, (irreg. fr. L *stella* star) + NL *-oidea* — more at STAR] *syn of* STELLIFORMIA
stel·ler's eider \ˈs(h)telə(r)z-\ *also* **steller's duck** *n, usu cap S* [after Georg W. *Steller* †1746 Ger. naturalist] : an eider duck (*Polysticta stelleri*) of Alaska and eastern Asia having a white head and black collar
steller's jay *n, usu cap S* [after Georg W. *Steller*] : a blue jay (*Cyanocitta stelleri*) of western No. America with black to dark-blue fore and upper parts and a conspicuous high crest — see BLUE-FRONTED JAY, LONG-CRESTED JAY
steller's sea cow *n, usu cap 1st S* : an extinct large aquatic mammal (*Hydrodamalis gigas*) formerly common near the Asiatic coast of the Bering sea and having a relatively small head, no teeth, a laterally lobed tail, and a length of about 25 feet
steller's sea eagle *n, usu cap 1st S* : KAMCHATKAN SEA EAGLE
steller's sea lion *n, usu cap 1st S* : a north Pacific sea lion (*Eumetopia jubata*) that is the largest of sea lions
stel·let·ta \stəˈled·ə\ *n, cap* [NL, dim. of L *stella* star] : a genus of white encrusting sponges (class Demospongiae) with a feltlike covering of slender glassy spicules that is common near the low-tide mark along the Pacific coast of No. America
stel·lif·er·ous \stəˈlif(ə)rəs\ *adj* [L *stellifer* star-bearing, starry (fr. *stella* star + *-ifer* -iferous) + E *-ous*] : having star-shaped markings
stel·li·fi·ca·tion \ˌsteləfəˈkāshən\ *n* -s [fr. *stellify*, after such pairs as E *purify*: *purification*] : the action of stellifying
stel·li·form \ˈsteləˌfȯrm\ *adj* [NL *stelliformis*, fr. L *stella* star + *-iformis* -iform — more at STAR] : shaped like a star
stel·li·for·mia \ˌ==ˈfȯrmēə\ *n pl, cap* [NL, neut. pl. of *stelliformis*] *in some classifications* : a major division of Echinodermata consisting of the Asteroidea and Ophiuroidea
stel·li·fy \ˈsteləˌfī\ *vt* -ED/-ING/-ES [ME *stellifien*, fr. MF *stellifier*, fr. ML *stellificare*, fr. L *stella* star + *-ificare* -ify] : to turn into or as if into a star : place among the stars : GLORIFY ⟨therefore deserves to be *stellified* by British astronomers —John Ruskin⟩
stelling *pres part of* STELL
stel·lion·ate \ˈstelyənət, -ˌnāt, *usu* -d·+V\ *n* -s [LL *stellionatus*, fr. L *stellion-*, *stellio* crafty person (lit., a lizard marked with star-shaped spots, fr. *stella* star) + *-atus* -ate] *Roman, civil, & Scots law* : a fraud not distinguished by a more special name; *esp* : a sale of the same property to different persons or the sale of something as one's own which belongs to another
Stel·lite \ˈsteˌlīt\ *trademark* — used for any of various alloys composed essentially of 75 to 90 percent cobalt and 10 to 25 percent chromium with or without small amounts of other metals added and used esp. for cutting tools, hard wear-resistant surfaces, surgical instruments, and cutlery
stells *pres 3d sing of* STELL, *pl of* STELL
stel·lu·lar \ˈstelyələ(r)\ *adj* [LL *stellula* (dim. of L *stella* star) + E *-ar*] **1** : having the shape of a small star : STARRY ⟨a ~ light⟩ **2** : radiating like a star ⟨~ markings⟩
¹stem \ˈstem\ *n* -s *often attrib* [ME, fr. OE *stefn*, *stemn* stem of a plant or ship; *stefn* akin to MD *steven* stem of a ship, ON *stafn*, OE *stæf* staff; OE *stemn* akin to OHG *stam* stem of a plant, ON *stamn* stem of a ship, Gk *stamnos* wine jar, OE *standan* to stand — more at STAFF, STAND] **1 a** : the main and usu. wholly or predominantly aerial axis, trunk, or body of a tree or other plant; *specif* : the part of the body of a seed plant that originates from the plumule, constitutes the primary axis, produces and supports secondary branches, leaves, flowers, and other appendages, and differs from the root with which it is continuous in having or having a capacity for forming nodes, leaves, and buds, in developing a cuticle and stomata, and in lacking an endodermis and a protective cap over the meristem — see BULB, CORM, TUBER; compare RHIZOME, STOLON **b** : a plant part (as a petiole, peduncle, pedicel, or stalk) that supports one or more leaves, flowers, fruits, or fruiting bodies ⟨a flower with a long wiry ~⟩ ⟨the ~ of a mushroom⟩; *broadly* : any plant part (as the stipe of a kelp) that functions primarily in support **c** : a stalk of bananas including the fruit — compare HAND **2 a** (1) : a piece of timber or cast, forged, or rolled metal to which the sides of a ship are united at the fore end with the lower end scarfed to the keel and the bowsprit resting upon its upper end (2) *chiefly Scot* : a stem or sternpost esp. of a sharp-sterned boat **b** : the forepart of a ship : BOWS, PROW; *also* : a foremost position **3 a** : a line of ancestry : STOCK; *esp* : the main ancestral line from which the branches of a family may be considered to have arisen **b** : a fundamental or primitive line within a natural group of which other members of the group can logically be construed as descendants or offshoots **4 a** : the part of an inflected word that remains unchanged except by phonetic changes or variations throughout a given inflection, is sometimes identical with the root, but is often derived from it with some formative suffix ⟨the root *duc* serves as the ~ of Latin *dux* (duc), *ducis*, leader, and is developed with suffixes into *ducere*, to lead, *ductor*, leader, *ductus*, act of leading, *ductilis*, ductile⟩ **b** *obs* : an original word that serves as a basis for the formation of derivative words (as by the addition of suffixes) **5** : something felt to resemble a plant stem esp. in being an elongated process projecting from or supporting some structure: as **a** : a main or heavy stroke of a letter; *also* : BODY 10a — see TYPE illustration **b** : the short perpendicular line extending upward on the right or downward on the left from the head of a musical note **c** : the part of a tobacco pipe from the bowl outward; *usu* : the detachable mouthpiece of a tobacco pipe or a cigar or cigarette holder usu. provided with a rimmed mouth end — compare ¹BIT 2c **d** : the cylindrical and usu. solid support of a piece of stemware (as a goblet) **e** : a narrow elongated base or means of attachment by which a sessile animal is made fast ⟨the contractile ~ of a vorticellid⟩ ⟨the horny ~ of a colonial hydroid⟩ **f** : the recording tube of a measuring instrument (as a thermometer) **g** : a shaft of a watch having a threaded top to hold a winding crown and the lower end squared to fit into the winding wheels in the movement and used for winding — see STEM-WINDER **h** : the round portion in some locks about which the ordinary key turns **i** : one of the heavy vertical rods in a stamp battery to which the tappet and boss are attached **j** : a spindle or guide rod on a mechanical part ⟨the rod of a valve is a ~⟩ **k** : AUGER STEM **l** : a thread shank for a button **m** *slang* : a major way (as a street or railroad line) — usu. used in the phrase *main stem* — **from stem to stern** : THROUGHOUT, THOROUGHLY
²stem \ˈ"\ *vb* **stemmed; stemmed; stemming; stems** [ME *stemmen*, fr. ¹*stem* (stem of a ship)] *vi* **1** : to head in a particular direction or move forward against or irrespective of an obstacle ⟨a ship *stemming* on against a strong current⟩ **2** : to hold a straight course : STEER ⟨~ toward the sunset⟩ ~ *vt* **1** *archaic* : to oppose or cut with or as if with a ship's stem : RAM **2** *obs* : to hold (a ship) on course : STEER **3 a** : to make headway against (as an adverse tide, current, or wind) **b** : to check or progress against (something adverse) ⟨*stemming* the angry crowd⟩ ⟨*stemmed* the wild torrent of a barbarous age —Alexander Pope⟩
³stem \ˈ"\ *vb* **stemmed; stemmed; stemming; stems** [¹*stem* (stem of a plant)] *vi* **1** *archaic* **a** : to grow upward or rise erect like a stem **b** : to produce a stem **2 a** : to grow out or develop like a stem — usu. used with *from* ⟨an illness that ~s from a long-past accident⟩ ⟨our hopes ~ from the one previous success⟩ **b** : to have or trace one's origin or development from ⟨~ cherries⟩ ⟨~ tobacco leaves⟩ ~ *vt* **1** : to remove the stem or stem and midrib from ⟨~ cherries⟩ ⟨~ tobacco leaves⟩ **2** : to make stems for or fit with stems (as artificial flowers) **syn** see SPRING
⁴stem \ˈ"\ *vb* **stemmed; stemmed; stemming; stems** [ME *stemmen*, fr. ON *stemma*; akin to OE *stam* stammering, ON *stamr* stammering, blocked, *stamma* to stammer — more at STAMMER] *vt* **1 a** : to stop or dam up (as a river) **b** : to stop, check, or restrain by or as if by damming; *specif* : STANCH ⟨~ a flow of blood⟩ ⟨~ a wound⟩ **2** : to brace or set firmly (oneself or one's limbs) **3** : to ram or tamp (as a hole) in preparing to blast **4** : to turn (skis) in stemming ~ *vi* **1** : to restrain or check oneself; *also* : to become checked or stanched ⟨after a brief interval the bleeding *stemmed*⟩ **2** : to retard oneself by forcing the heel of one ski or of both skis outward from the line of progress
⁵stem \ˈ"\ *n* -s **1** : something that acts in opposition or resistance : CHECK, DAM **2** : an act or instance of stemming on skis
⁶stem \ˈ"\ *vt* [alter. of E dial. *steven* to bespeak, fr. ME *stefnen*, *stevenen* to appoint, specify, fr. OE *stefnan* to appoint, arrange, fr. *stefn* voice, time, occasion — more at STEVEN] *Brit* : to load or contract to load (a ship) with coal within an indicated time
stem anchor *n* [¹*stem*] : the bower anchor carried in the centerline hawsepipe on a clipper-bowed man-of-war
stem back *vb* [⁴*stem*] *vi* : to brace oneself to prevent being driven forward ~ *vt* : to hold in check : brace oneself against ⟨*stemming* the tide of opinion *back*⟩
stem blight *n* [¹*stem*] : a fungous blight (as of the peach caused by *Phoma persicae* or of cosmos caused by *Phomopsis stewartii*) primarily attacking the stems of plants
stem body *n* : the portion of a mitotic spindle that lies between the daughter chromosome groups during anaphase and telophase
stem·bok \ˈstemˌbäk\ *n, pl* **stembok** *or* **stemboks** [by alter.] : STEENBOK
stem borer *n* [¹*stem*] : an insect larva that bores in plant stems; *esp* : a cerambycid larva of the genus *Oberea*
stem break *n* : BROWNING 3a
stem–bud \ˈ=ˌ=\ *n* : PLUMULE
stem canker *n* : a canker disease affecting plant stems; *esp* : RHIZOCTONIA DISEASE
stem cell *n* : an unspecialized and usu. embryonic cell ancestral to one or more specialized cells ⟨one theory regards the hemocytoblast as a *stem cell* from which all the cellular elements of the blood arise⟩; *specif* : an embryonic cell destined to give rise to germ cells and often identifiable in early cleavage
stem christiania *n, often cap C* [⁵*stem*] : a turn in skiing begun by the stemming of one ski and completed by bringing the skis parallel into a christiania during the turn
stem–clasping \ˈ=ˌ==\ *adj* [¹*stem*] : AMPLEXICAUL ⟨a *stem-clasping* leaf⟩
stem climber *n* : a plant that climbs by twining
stem correction *n* : a correction applied to the readings of a precise thermometer to allow for the difference in temperature between the liquid in the stem and that in the bulb
stem cutting *n* : a piece of a plant stem or branch including at least one node used in propagation
stem eelworm *also* **stem nematode** *n* : BULB EELWORM
stem–end browning \ˈ=ˌ=-\ *n* : a storage disease of potatoes of undetermined cause characterized by brownish or black discoloration at the stem end of the tuber
stem–end rot *or* **stem–end decay** *n* : any of various rots (as of fruits) starting at the point of attachment to the plant (as decay of citrus fruits caused by fungi of the genera *Diplodia*, *Dothiorella*, and *Phomopsis*)
stemflow \ˈ=ˌ=\ *n* : rainfall reaching the ground in a forest by draining down the trunks of trees, as distinguished from that dripping from the canopy
stemform \ˈ=ˌ=\ *n* : original or ancestral form
stem ginger *n* : CANTON GINGER
stem girdler *n* : an insect that girdles (as with its jaws or ovipositor) the stems of plants
stemhead \ˈ=ˌ=\ *n* : the top of a ship's stem
stemhead plate *n* : a plate fastened at the bow of a sailboat and used as an attachment for the head stay
stem leaf *n* : a cauline leaf
stem length *n* : the height of the seated human body as measured from the seat of the chair occupied
¹stem·less \ˈ=ləs\ *adj* [¹*stem* + *-less*] : having no stem : ACAULESCENT
²stemless \ˈ"\ *adj* **1** [⁴*stem* + *-less*] : not capable of being stemmed **2** [²*stem* + *-less*] : impossible to steer or hold a course against
stemless gentian *n* [¹*stemless*] : a gentianella (*Gentiana acaulis*)
stemless lady's–slipper *n* : a moccasin flower (*Cypripedium acaule*)
stemless thistle *n* : a perennial Eurasian thistle (*Circium acaule*) with a rosette of spiny leaves and one or more usu. sessile crimson to reddish purple flower heads
stem·let \ˈstemlət\ *n* -s [¹*stem* + *-let*] : a small, slender, or young stem
stemlike \ˈ=ˌ=\ *adj* : resembling or sharing the function of a stem
stem–line \ˈ=ˌ=\ *n* : a long continuous line that is touched by short lines in ogham writing and that is typically the edge of an upright stone
stem·ma \ˈstemə\ *n, pl* **stem·ma·ta** \-məd·ə\ *also* **stemmas** [NL *stemmat-*, *stemma*, fr. L, garland, wreath, pedigree (fr. the garlands placed on ancestral images), fr. Gk, garland, wreath, fr. *stephein* to crown, enwreath] **1 a** (1) : one of the simple eyes of an insect : OCELLUS (2) : a facet of a compound eye of an arthropod **b** : a tubercle on which an antenna is borne **2 a** : a scroll (as among the ancient Romans) containing a list of family names with indication of genealogical or other relations : FAMILY TREE, PEDIGREE **b** : a tree showing the relationships of the manuscripts of a literary work
stem·mat·i·form \steˈmad·əˌfȯrm\ *adj* [NL *stemmat-*, *stemma* + E *-iform*] : formed like or resembling a stemma
stem·ma·tous \ˈstemad·əs\ *adj* [NL *stemmat-*, *stemma* + E *-ous*] : of, relating to, or being a stemma : OCELLAR
¹stemmed \ˈstemd\ *adj* [¹*stem* + *-ed*] : having or furnished with a stem — usu. used in combination ⟨long-*stemmed* roses⟩ ⟨a single-*stemmed* plant⟩ ⟨blue-*stemmed* grasses⟩
²stemmed *adj* [fr. past part. of ³*stem*] : having the stem or stems removed ⟨~ berries⟩ ⟨~ tobacco⟩
stem·mer \ˈstemə(r)\ *n* -s [³*stem* + *-er*] **1** : one that stems: as **a** : a miner's tamping bar for ramming in packing (as clay) over a blasting charge **b** : a machine or device for stemming fruits (as grapes or apples) **c** : STRIPPER 1a **d** : a worker who makes or applies stems of artificial flowers **2** [prob. fr. ¹*stem* (street) + *-er*] *slang* : a beggar seeking money from passersby along the street
stem·mery \-mərē, -ri\ *n* -ES [³*stem* + *-ery*] : a building or place in which tobacco is stemmed
stem·mi·ness \-mēnəs, -min-\ *n* -ES : the condition of being stemmy; *esp* : a tendency of some grasses to produce excessive stem that reduces their forage or hay value
stemming *pres part of* STEM
stem mother *n* [¹*stem*] : a sexually produced female that produces parthenogenetically a colony of offspring; *esp* : an aphid that develops from an overwintering egg and gives rise to the summer generation — compare FUNDATRIX
stem·my \ˈstemē, -mi\ *adj* -ER/-EST [¹*stem* + *-y*] : abounding in or mixed with stems; *esp* : consisting largely of stems ⟨a ~ hay from which most of the leaves have been lost in handling⟩ ⟨some grasses become very ~ when mature⟩
ste·mo·na \stəˈmōnə\ *n, cap* [NL, fr. Gk *stēmōn* warp, thread — more at STAMEN] : a small genus of Asiatic and Australian herbaceous twiners (family Stemonaceae) having alternate leaves and rather large perfect flowers with oddly appendaged somewhat monadelphous stamens
ste·mo·na·ce·ae \ˌstēməˈnāsēˌē\ *n pl, cap* [NL, fr. *Stemona*, type genus + *-aceae*] : a family of herbs (order Liliales) having regular perfect flowers with a 4-parted perianth in two series, four stamens, and a one-celled ovary — **ste·mo·na·ceous** \ˌ==ˈnāshəs\ *adj*

ste·mo·ni·tis \ˌ≈≈'nīdəs\ *n, cap* [NL, fr. Gk *stēmōn* warp, thread; fr. the threadlike strands of the capillitium] **:** a genus of slime molds (subclass Myxogastres) related to *Physarum* but having an evanescent sporangium and a capillitium formed from branches of the columella

-stemonous \ˈstēmənəs, -tem-\ *adj comb form* [fr. (assumed) NL *-stemonus*, fr. Gk *stēmōn* warp, thread — more at STAMEN] **:** having (such or so many) stamens ⟨diplo*stemonous*⟩ ⟨iso*stemonous*⟩

stem·phyl·i·um \stem'filēəm\ *n, cap* [NL, fr. Gk *stemphylon* olive pulp + NL *-ium* — more at STAFF] *in some classifications* **:** a genus that comprises imperfect fungi (order Moniliales) with dark greenish brown spores closely resembling those of *Alternaria* but borne singly rather than in chains and is often included in *Alternaria* or sometimes replaced by *Macrosporium*

stempiece \'≈,≈\ *n* [¹*stem* + *piece*] **:** a piece of timber attached to the stem of a wooden ship beneath the bowsprit for support or ornament

stem·ple *or* **stem·pel** \'stempəl\ *n* -s [prob. fr. LG *stempel;* akin to OE *stempan* to stamp — more at STAMP] **:** a crossbar of wood in a mine shaft serving some special purpose (as of a step, supporting timber, or strut)

stempost \'≈,≈\ *n* [¹*stem* + *post*] **:** the stem of a ship

stem–root \'≈,≈\ *n* **:** a root (as an adventitious or prop root) arising from a stem above the juncture of stem and basal root

stem–rooting \'≈ˌ≈≈\ *adj* **:** tending to form roots on the stem; *esp* **:** forming roots immediately above a basal bulb ⟨*stem-rooting* lilies⟩

stem rust *n* **1 :** a rust attacking the stem of a plant; *esp* **:** a destructive disease of wheat and various other grasses that is caused by a rust fungus (*Puccinia graminis*), is characterized by reddish brown lesions in the uredostage of the parasite and black lesions in the teliostage, and involves plants of the genera *Berberis* or *Mahonia* as alternate hosts of the parasite **2 :** the fungus causing stem rust

stems *pl of* STEM, *pres 3d sing of* STEM

stem sickness *n* **:** a disease of clover caused by the bulb eelworm (*Ditylenchus dipsaci*)

stem smut *n* **:** the common smut of rye caused by a fungus (*Urocystis occulta*) in which linear sori occur

stem·son \'stem(p)sən\ *n* -s [¹*stem* + *-son* (as in *keelson*)] **:** a piece of curved timber bolted to the stem, keelson, and apron in a ship's frame near the bow

stem stitch *n* **:** an embroidery outlining stitch (as for making stems); *esp* **:** an overlapping stitch that produces a corded appearance

stem turn *n* [⁵*stem*] **:** a skiing turn executed by stemming an outside ski

stem·wards \'stemwə(r)dz\ *adv* [¹*stem* + *-wards*] **:** toward a stem (as of a ship)

stemware \'≈,≈\ *n* **:** hollow ware (as for beverages or desserts)

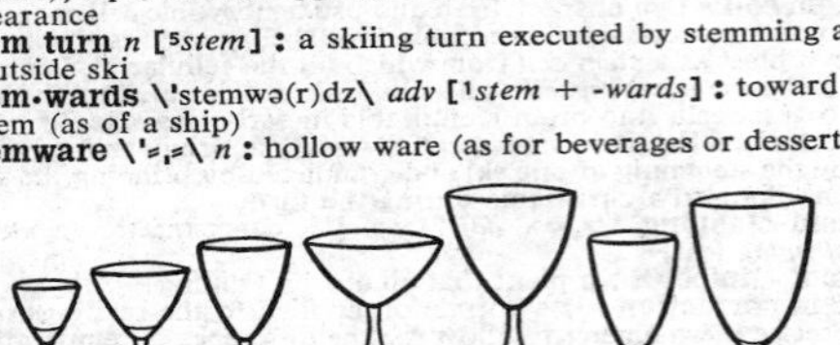

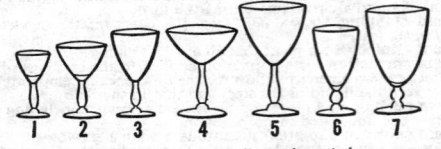

stemware: *1* cordial, *2* cocktail, *3* wine, *4* champagne, *5* goblet, *6* juice, *7* iced tea

of glass that consists of a rounded hollow body mounted on a usu. solid and basically cylindrical shaft which terminates in a flattened foot

stem–winder \'≈,≈≈\ *n* **1 :** a stem-winding watch **2 :** one that is first-rate of its kind

stem–winding \'≈ˌ≈≈\ *adj* **:** wound by an inside mechanism turned by the knurled knob at the outside end of the stem ⟨a *stem-winding* watch⟩

sten \'sten\ *or* **sten gun** *n* -s *usu cap S* [Major Sheppard, 20th cent. Eng. army officer + Mr. *Turpin*, 20th cent. Eng. civil servant, its designers + *England*] **:** a British machine carbine having only 45 parts and weighing from 6 pounds 6 ounces to 8 pounds that uses any rimless 9 millimeter ammunition

sten- *or* **steno-** *comb form* [Gk, fr. *stenos* narrow, close, scanty] **:** close **:** narrow **:** little ⟨*steno*bathic⟩ — opposed to *eury-*

sten *abbr* **1** stencil **2** stenographer; stenography

ste·nan·thi·um \stə'nan(t)thēəm\ *n, cap* [NL, fr. *sten-* + Gk *anthos* flower + NL *-ium* — more at ANTHOLOGY] **:** a genus of smooth bulbous perennials (family Liliaceae) of No. America and eastern Asia with long grasslike leaves and numerous small flowers in compound racemes — see BRONZE BELLS

¹stench \'stench\ *n* -ES [ME, fr. OE *stenc;* akin to OHG *stank* stench, OE *stincan* to emit a smell — more at STINK] **1 a :** an extremely disagreeable smell **:** offensive odor **:** STINK ⟨so many buffaloes were slaughtered . . . that the ~ was fearful —Mari Sandoz⟩ **b :** something resembling or producing the effect of a bad smell ⟨very idea . . . was ~ in his nostrils —C.A.Beard⟩ **c :** a strong heady odor ⟨sweet ~ of magnolia —*Newsweek*⟩ **2 :** something that has an offensive odor **:** ODORANT

²stench \"\ *vb* -ED/-ING/-ES *vi* **:** STINK ⟨~*ing* fumes issue from . . . crevices and holes —Robert Gibbings⟩ ~ *vt* **:** to cause to stink **:** annoy by stench ⟨the paint ~*es* the whole house⟩

stench bomb *n* **:** STINK BOMB

stench·ful \'≈fəl\ *adj* **:** full of disagreeable smells **:** REEKING

stench trap *n* **:** a trap for permitting outflow of sewage but preventing backflow of foul sewer gases

stenchy \'stenchē\ *adj* -ER/-EST [¹*stench* + *-y*] **:** having a stench

¹sten·cil \'sten(t)səl\ *n* -s [fr. (assumed) earlier *stansel*, fr. ME *stanselen* to ornament with sparkling colors or pieces of metal, fr. MF *estanceler*, *estenceler*, fr. *estencele* spark, fr. (assumed) VL *stincilla*, alter. of L *scintilla*] **1 a :** material (as a sheet of paper, metal, thin wax, or woven fabric) that is perforated with lettering or a design through which a substance (as ink, paint) is forced onto a surface to be printed **b :** color, ink, or metallic powder used in stenciling **c :** a pattern or design of figures or letters cut into a stencil **d :** an impression left on a surface after stenciling **2 :** a printing process using the stencil principle — compare INTAGLIO, LETTERPRESS, PLANOGRAPHY ⟨silk screen is a form of ~⟩ **3 :** something resembling a stencil **:** an uninspired or insipid repetition usu. of an original idea or plan ⟨the literary ~*s* that represent all cabdrivers as witty —Mark Murphy⟩

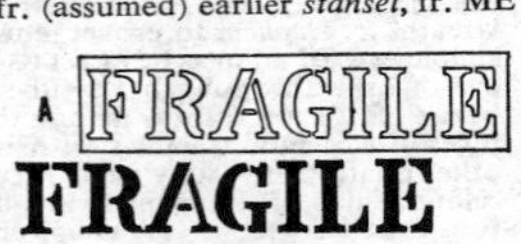

A stencil 1a; *B* stencil 1d

²stencil \"\ *vt* **stenciled** *or* **stencilled; stenciled** *or* **stencilled; stenciling** *or* **stencilling** \-s(ə)liŋ\ **stencils 1 :** to produce by or as if by means of a stencil ⟨~ an address on a packing case⟩ ⟨~ an interoffice memorandum⟩ **2 :** to mark or paint with an inscription or a design by means of a stencil ⟨curtains that you ~*ed* with such pride —Myrtle R. White⟩

stencil brush *n* **:** STIPPLE 3

sten·cil·er *or* **sten·cil·ler** \-s(ə)lə(r)\ *n* -s **:** one that stencils: as **a :** one whose work is decorating or identifying articles by means of stencils **b :** a worker who stencils patterns for the garment cutter

stenciling *or* **stencilling** *n* -s [fr. gerund of ²*stencil*] **:** the art or practice of one that stencils

sten·cil·iza·tion \ˌsten(t)sələ'zāshən, -ˌlī'z-\ *n* -s [*stencilize* + *-ation*] **:** the act or the product of stenciling esp. by mimeograph

sten·cil·ize \'sten(t)sə,līz\ *vt* -ED/-ING/-S [¹*stencil* + *-ize*] **1 :** STENCIL 2 **2 :** to cut into a stencil ⟨the . . . cushion shows through the *stencilized* openings —*Office Equipment Guide*⟩

stencil knife *n* **:** a knife with a wooden handle and a short sharp blade used esp. for cutting stencils and linoleum blocks

stencil paper *n* **:** strong tissue paper impregnated or coated with paraffin or other materials for stencils

¹stend \'stend\ *also* **sten** \'sten\ *n* -s [ME] *Scot* **:** JUMP, BOUND

²stend \"\ *also* **sten** \"\ *vi, Scot* **:** to jump up **:** LEAP, REAR

sten·der dish \'stendə(r)-\ *n, sometimes cap S* [after William P. *Stender* 19th cent. Ger. manufacturer] **:** a small circular glass dish with vertical walls and loosely fitting cover used in laboratories usu. to hold stains, culture media, or specimens

sten·dhal·ian \(')stanˈdälēən, -ta"(d)-, -ten'd-, -dal-, -lyən\ *adj, usu cap S* [*Stendhal* (pseudonym of Henri Beyle †1842 Fr. writer) + E *-an*] **:** of, relating to, or having the characteristics of Stendhal or his works ⟨a small but ardent public of *Stendhalian* experts —*Times Lit. Supp.*⟩

ste·ne·cious \stə'nēshəs\ *or* **ste·noe·cic** \-ēsik\ *adj* [*sten-* + Gk *oikos* house, dwelling + E *-ious* or *-ic* — more at VICINITY] **:** capable of adjusting to or surviving in only a narrow range of environments

steni·on \'stēnē,än, -ten-\ *n, pl* **stenia** \-nēə\ [NL, fr. *sten-* + *-ion* (as in *rhinion*)] **:** a point on the outer wall of either middle cranial fossa marking the least transverse diameter of the skull in that region

steno \'ste(,)nō\ *n* -s [by shortening] **:** STENOGRAPHER

steno- — see STEN-

steno·bath·ic \ˌstenəˈbathik\ *adj* [*sten-* + Gk *bathos* depth + E *-ic* — more at BATHOS] *of a pelagic organism* **:** living within narrow limits of depth — opposed to *eurybathic*

steno·ben·thic \ˌ≈≈ˈben(t)thik\ *adj* [*sten-* + Gk *benthos* depth + E *-ic* — more at BENTHOS] **:** STENOBATHIC

steno·car·dia \ˌ≈≈'kärdēə\ *n* -s [NL, fr. *sten-* + *-cardia*] **:** ANGINA PECTORIS — **steno·car·di·ac** \ˌ≈≈'≈dē,ak\ *adj*

steno·car·pus \ˌ≈≈'kärpəs\ *n, cap* [NL, fr. *sten-* + *-carpus*] **:** a small genus of Australian timber trees (family Proteaceae) with alternate or scattered leaves, umbellate or racemose red or yellow flowers, and leathery follicles with winged seeds — see WHEEL TREE 2

steno·cephalic \ˌ≈≈+\ *adj* [*sten-* + *-cephalic*] **:** having an abnormally narrow head

steno·ceph·a·ly \ˌ≈≈'sefəlē\ *also* **steno·ce·phal·ia** \-sə'fālyə\ *n, pl* **stenocephalies** *also* **stenocephalias** [NL *stenocephalia*, fr. *sten-* + *-cephalia* -cephaly] **:** abnormal narrowness of the head

steno·chrome \'≈≈,krōm\ *n* [*stenochromy*] **:** a print made by stenochromy

steno·chro·my \'≈≈,krōmē\ *n* -ES [ISV *sten-* + *-chromy*] **:** the printing at one impression of a varicolored design

ste·nog \stə'näg\ *n* -s [by shortening] **:** STENOGRAPHER

ste·nog·a·mous \stə'nägəməs\ *also* **steno·gam·ic** \ˌstenə'gamik\ *adj* [*sten-* + *-gamous*, *-gamic*] *of insects* **:** mating in a restricted space **:** requiring no nuptial flight — opposed to *eurygamous*

steno·gastric \ˌstenə+\ *adj* [*sten-* + *gastr-* + *-ic*] **:** having a slender abdomen — used esp. of various insects which later develop large swollen abdomens

steno·gas·try \'≈≈,gastrē\ *n* -ES [*sten-* + *gastr-* + *-y*] **:** a condition in various insects of having a slender abdomen — compare PHYSOGASTRY

steno·glos·sa \ˌ≈≈'gläsə, -lòsə\ *n pl, cap* [NL, fr. *sten-* + *-glossa*] **:** a suborder of Pectinibranchia containing many common marine snails (as the cone shells, olive shells, whelks) which have a concentrated nervous system, a radula, an unpaired esophageal gland, and usu. a well-developed proboscis and including the groups Rachiglossa and Toxoglossa

steno·glos·sate \ˌ≈≈'gläsət, -lòs-\ *adj* [NL *Stenoglossa* + E *-ate*] **:** of or relating to the Stenoglossa

steno·graph \'stenə,graf\ *vt* -ED/-ING/-S [back-formation fr. *stenographer*] **:** to write or report in stenographic characters

ste·nog·ra·pher \stə'nägrəfə(r)\ *n* -s [*stenography* + *-er*] **1 :** a writer of shorthand **2 :** one who is employed (as in an office) chiefly to take and transcribe dictation

steno·graph·ic \ˌstenə'grafik, -fēk\ *also* **steno·graph·i·cal** \-fəkəl, -fēk-\ *adj* [*stenography* + *-ic*, *-ical*] **:** of, relating to, or using stenography — **steno·graph·i·cal·ly** \-k(ə)lē, -li\ *adv*

ste·nog·ra·phy \stə'nägrəfē\ *n* -ES [Gk *stenos* narrow, close + E *-graphy*] **1 a :** a writing in shorthand esp. by using abbreviations or characters for whole words **b :** shorthand esp. written from dictation or oral discourse **c :** the making of shorthand notes and subsequent transcription of them esp. in typewriting **2 a :** a use of curtailed or reduced forms in representing **b :** a representation using such forms

steno·ha·line \ˌstenə'hā,līn, -ha,-, -ˌlən\ *adj* [ISV *sten-* + *-haline* (fr. Gk *halinos* of salt, fr. *hals* salt) — more at SALT] *of an aquatic organism* **:** unable to withstand wide variation in salinity of the surrounding water — opposed to *euryhaline*

steno·mer·ic \ˌ≈≈'merik\ *adj* [*sten-* + *mer-* + *-ic*] *of a femur* **:** strongly compressed laterally with a platymeric index of 100 or over

ste·nom·e·ter \stə'nämǝd·ə(r), -mətə-\ *n* [*sten-* + *-meter*] **:** an instrument for measuring distances consisting of a telescope mounted on a tripod and fitted with a micrometer screw so that the distance may be measured to a rod carrying two targets a known distance apart whose images are brought together in the telescope by the micrometer screw

steno·pa·ic \ˌstenə'pāik\ *also* **steno·pe·ic** *or* **steno·pae·ic** \-pēik\ *adj* [*sten-* + Gk *opaios* having a hole (fr. *opē* hole) + E *-ic;* akin to Gk *osse* (two) eyes — more at EYE] **:** having a small opening for the admission of light ⟨~ spectacles⟩

steno·pel·mat·i·dae \ˌ≈≈(,)pel'mad·ə,dē\ *n pl, cap* [NL, fr. *Stenopelmatus*, type genus + *-idae*] **:** a family of dull-colored orthopterous insects having compressed 3-jointed tarsi usu. wingless Orthoptera having compressed 3-jointed tarsi and a needle-shaped ovipositor and including the sand crickets and the cave crickets

steno·pel·ma·tus \-'mad·əs\ *n, cap* [NL, fr. *sten-* + Gk *pelmat-*, *pelma* sole of the foot — more at FELL] **:** the type genus of the family Stenopelmatidae

ste·noph·a·gous \stə'näfəgəs\ *adj* [ISV *sten-* + *-phagous*] **:** eating few kinds of foods — used esp. of an insect; compare EURYPHAGOUS, MONOPHAGOUS

steno·plastic \ˌstenə+\ *adj* [*sten-* + *plastic*] **:** exhibiting limited capacity for modification or adaptation to new environment **:** not capable of major evolutionary differentiation — opposed to *euryplastic;* compare PSEUDOPLASTIC — **steno·plas·ty** \'≈≈,plastē\ *n* -ES

stenos *pl of* STENO

ste·no's duct \'stā(,)nōz-\ *n, usu cap S* [after Nicolaus *Steno* (latinization of *Niels Stensen*) †1687 Dan. anatomist, its discoverer] **:** the duct of the parotid gland opening on the inner surface of the cheek opposite the second upper molar tooth

ste·nose \stə'nōs, -ōz\ *vt* -ED/-ING/-S [back-formation fr. *stenosis*] **:** to cause stenosis in

stenosed *adj* [fr. past part. of *stenose*] **:** affected with stenosis

ste·no·sis \stə'nōsəs\ *n, pl* **steno·ses** \-ō,sēz\ [NL, fr. Gk *stenōsis* act of narrowing, fr. *stenoun* to narrow, fr. *stenos* narrow, close] **1 :** a narrowing or constriction of the diameter of any passage, tube, or orifice ⟨mitral ~⟩ **2 :** a virus disease of the cotton plant marked by dwarfing, eroded or perforated leaf margins, and numerous sterile flower buds

steno·sper·mo·car·py \ˌstenə'spərmə,kärpē\ *n* -ES [*sten-* + *sperm-* + *-carpy*] **:** the production of abortive incompletely developed seeds (as in a seedless grape) with normal development of the berry — compare PARTHENOCARPY

steno·taph·rum \ˌstenə'tafrəm\ *n, cap* [NL, fr. *sten-* + Gk *taphros* ditch; akin to Gk *thaptein* to bury — more at EPITAPH] **:** a small genus of grasses found in Malaysia and along the seacoast of America and having creeping stems and one-flowered spikelets on one side of a flat corky rachis — see SAINT AUGUSTINE GRASS 1

steno·tele \'≈≈,tēl\ *n* -s [*sten-* + L *tela* warp threads, web — more at TELA] **:** PENETRANT a

steno·therm \'stenə,thərm\ *n* [back-formation fr. *stenothermal*] **:** a stenothermal organism

steno·thermal \ˌstenə+\ *also* **steno·thermic** \"+\ *adj* [prob. fr. G *stenotherm* stenothermal (fr. *sten-* + Gk *thermē* heat) + E *-al*, *-ic* — more at THERM] **:** resisting only slight changes of temperature — opposed to *eurythermal*

steno·thermophile \ˌ≈≈+\ *n* [*stenothermy* + *-o-* + *-phile*] **:** a stenothermophilic organism

steno·thermophilic \"+\ *adj* [*stenothermy* + *-o-* + *-philic*] **:** preferring a stenothermal environment

steno·ther·my \'stenə,thərmē\ *n* -ES [*stenothermal* + *-y*] **:** the quality or state of being stenothermal

ste·not·ic \stə'näd·ik, -ätik\ *adj* [fr. NL *stenosis*, after such pairs as NL *narcosis:* E *narcotic*] **:** relating to or having stenosis

steno·topic \ˌstenə'täpik\ *adj* [prob. fr. G *stenotop* stenotopic (fr. *sten-* + *-top*, fr. Gk *topos* place) + E *-ic* — more at TOPIC] **:** having a narrow range of adaptability to changes in environmental conditions — compare EURYTOPIC, STENOTROPIC

steno·trop·ic \ˌ≈≈'träpik\ *adj* [alter. (influenced by *-tropic*) of *stenotopic*] **:** having a narrow range of tolerance for variation in environmental conditions — compare STENOTOPIC

¹steno·type \'stenə+,-\ *n* [*steno-* (as in *stenography*) + *type*] **1 :** a letter or combination of letters representing a phonogram in stenotypy **2 :** a small machine somewhat resembling a typewriter that records by means of stenotypes

²stenotype \"\ *vt* **:** to record with a stenotype

steno·typ·ist \-pəst\ *n* [¹*stenotype* + *-ist*] **:** an operator of a stenotype

steno·typy \-pē, -pi\ *n* -ES [¹*stenotype* + *-y*] **:** a phonographic writing using ordinary script or printed letters

stens *pl of* STEN

sten·sen's duct *also* **sten·son's duct** \'sten(t)sənz-\ *n, usu cap S* [after Niels *Stensen* †1687 Dan. anatomist, its discoverer] **:** STENO'S DUCT

¹stent \'stent\ *chiefly dial var of* STINT

²stent \"\ *vt* -ED/-ING/-S [ME *stenten*, by shortening & alter. fr. *extenten* to stretch out, assess, fr. L *extentus*, past part. of *extendere* to stretch out — more at EXTEND] *chiefly Scot* **:** to stretch out **:** EXTEND

³stent \"\ *n* -s [ME, by shortening & alter. fr. *extente*] *chiefly Scot* **:** EXTENT 1

⁴stent \"\ *adj* [prob. contr. of Sc *stentit*, past part. of ²*stent*] *Scot* **:** OUTSTRETCHED, TIGHT

⁵stent \"\ *also* **stint** \'stint\ *n* -s [after Charles R. *Stent* †1901 Eng. dentist, inventor of the compound] **1 :** a compound or a mold made of the compound for holding some forms of graft in place **2 :** a similar object used as a stent (as a pad of gauze immobilized by sutures)

¹stent·er \-entə(r)\ *n* -s [²*stent* + *-er*] *Brit* **:** ¹TENTER

²stenter \"\ *vt* -ED/-ING/-S [¹*stenter*] *Brit* **:** ²TENTER

stent net *n* [⁴*stent*] **:** a net used in river fishing that is stretched or extended from the stake by which one end of it is anchored

sten·ton \'stent°n, -ntən\ *also* **stent·ing** \-tiŋ, -tēŋ\ *n* -s [origin unknown] **:** a short heading driven at right angles to a crosscut in a mining operation

¹sten·tor \'stentə(r)\ *n* -s [obs. *stent* to assess (by shortening & alter. fr. obs. *extent*, fr. ME *extenten* to stretch out, assess) + *-or* — more at STENT] *chiefly Scot* **:** a tax assessor

²sten·tor \'sten,tó(ə)r, -ó(ə), -ntə(r)\ *n* [after *Stentor*, Greek warrior in the Trojan War famed for his powerful voice, fr. L & Gk; L *Stentor*, fr. Gk *Stentōr*] **1** -s **:** a person having a powerful voice ⟨parliamentary ~*s* —*Time*⟩ **2** [NL, fr. L] **a** *cap* **:** a widely distributed genus of heterotrichous ciliate protozoans that have a trumpet-shaped body attached to the substrate by the smaller end with the mouth at the larger end, are often brightly colored, and are among the largest infusorians **b** -s **:** any protozoan of the genus *Stentor* **3** -s **:** HOWLER MONKEY

sten·to·ri·an \(')sten·'tōrēən, -tór-\ *adj* [²*stentor* + *-ian*] **:** extremely loud **:** capable of powerful utterance or sound ⟨proclaimed the fact in ~ tones —A.A.Berle⟩ ⟨the steamer's ~ foghorn —Nike Anderson⟩ **syn** see LOUD

sten·to·rine \'stentə,rīn, -ˌrən\ *adj* [NL *Stentor* + E *-ine*] **:** of or relating to the genus *Stentor*

sten·to·ri·ous \(')sten·'tōrēəs, -tór-\ *adj* [²*stentor* + *-ious*] **:** STENTORIAN — **sten·to·ri·ous·ly** *adv*

sten·to·ro·phon·ic \ˌstentərə'fänik\ *adj* [NL *stentorophonicus*, fr. Gk *Stentōr* Stentor + *-o-* + *phōnē* voice + L *-icus* -ic — more at BAN] **:** speaking or sounding very loud **:** STENTORIAN

sten·tor·phone \'stentə(r),fōn\ *n* [²*stentor* + *-phone*] **:** a large-scale loud open pipe-organ flue stop of 8-foot pitch

¹step \'step\ *n* -s *often attrib* [ME *step*, *steppe*, fr. OE *stæpe*, *stepe;* akin to OFris *stap*, *stepe* step, footstep, OHG *stapf*, *stapfo* step, footstep, OE *stæppan*, *steppan* to step — more at STEP (v.)] **1 :** something to put the foot on in ascending or descending: **a :** one of a flight of stairs consisting of a riser and a tread **b** (1) **:** a rung of a ladder (2) **:** a flat crosspiece of a stepladder **c :** a flat projecting or projectable footpiece for entering or alighting from a vehicle **d :** a foothold cut in a slope of earth, rock, or ice **2 a :** an advance or movement made by raising the foot and bringing it down in a different position ⟨took two ~*s* toward the door and stopped⟩ **b :** a combination of foot or of foot, leg, and body movements constituting a simple unit or a pattern that is repeated ⟨dancing . . . with such coincidence of ~ and gesture as only years of training could render possible —Lafcadio Hearn⟩ **c :** a pace in military drill — often used in combination ⟨goose ~⟩ **d :** manner of walking **:** STRIDE ⟨came in with his light lithe ~ —Adria Langley⟩ **e :** a mark or impression made by the foot **:** FOOTPRINT ⟨~*s* leading across the beach and disappearing at the water's edge⟩ **f :** the sound of a footstep ⟨heard his ~ on the stairs⟩ **3 a :** the space passed over by the movement of one foot beyond the other in walking ⟨twelve ~*s* or more from my mother's door —William Wordsworth⟩ **b** (1) **:** a short distance ⟨a store located just a ~ from the bank⟩ (2) **:** a distance for walking ⟨lives a good ~ down the road⟩ **c** *obs* **:** a short journey ⟨resolved to take a ~ to Paris for my health —Jonathan Swift⟩ **d :** the vertical distance of one of a set of stairs ⟨built the kitchen two ~*s* lower than the dining room⟩ **4 steps** *pl* **:** progress by or as if by walking **:** COURSE, WAY ⟨vengeance tend upon thy ~*s* —Shak.⟩ ⟨directed his ~*s* toward the river⟩ **5 a :** a degree, grade, or rank in a scale ⟨a ~ higher in the social scale⟩ ⟨rose several ~*s* in my opinion⟩ **b :** a stage in a gradual, regular, or orderly process ⟨achieve the initial ~ in this ambitious plan —Mason Wade⟩ ⟨guided her through every ~ of her career —Jerry Cotter⟩ **c :** promotion to the next higher grade or rank ⟨trusted you would get the ~ within . . . twelve months —Sir Walter Scott⟩ **d :** any one of a graded series of photographic exposures or tones **6 a :** a wood or metal frame on a ship designed to receive an upright shaft; *esp* **:** a block supporting the heel of a mast **b :** the lower bearing block on which a vertical shaft revolves **c :** one of the halves of a split-bearing bushing **7 :** an action, proceeding, or measure often occurring as one in a series ⟨took the unusual ~ of personally remonstrating with the president —W.C.Ford⟩ ⟨took ~*s* toward securing the mouth of the river against Spain —*Amer. Guide Series: La.*⟩ **8 :** pace with or as if with another ⟨two friends kept ~ beside me —A.E.Housman⟩ **9 :** a steplike offset or part usu. occurring in a series; *specif* **:** one of the series of parts of a cone pulley on which the belt runs **10 steps** *pl* **:** STEPLADDER ⟨from the early 18th century, library ~*s* were in use —J.E.Gloag⟩ **11 a :** a musical scale or staff degree **b :** the interval between two contiguous degrees of the staff or scale **c :** WHOLE STEP **12 a :** a steplike shoulder or bench on an otherwise smoothly rising hillside or slope **:** one of a series of terraces rising from a valley floor **b :** a steplike shelf or ledge in the vertical surface of a quarry or mine working **13 :** a change in direction in a line, a surface, or the construction of a solid body; *specif* **:** a break in the form of the bottom of a float or hull of a seaplane that is designed to reduce resistance when under way by rapidly reducing the wetted surfaces as speed increases and that serves to eliminate suction effect and improve longitudinal control in takeoff **14 a :** a change of place due to a motion of translation **b :** the translation that effects such a step — **in step** *adv (or adj)* **1 :** with each foot moving to the same time with the corresponding foot of others or in time to music ⟨walking *in step* with the other prisoners —C.K.Ogden⟩ **2 :** in harmony or agreement ⟨keep wages and salaries *in step* with economic conditions —*Report: Electric Auto-Lite Co.*⟩ **3 :** in phase — **on the step** *adv (or adj)* **:** in rapid movement over the water with the aft part of the float or hull off the water ⟨trailing a plume of spray . . . she went up *on the step* and was off into space —*Newsweek*⟩ — **out of step** *adv (or adj)* **:** not in step ⟨the second platoon was *out of step*⟩ ⟨the right of a man to be *out of step* with society —A.G.Hays⟩

²step \"\ *vb* **stepped** *or archaic* **stept** \-pt\ **stepped** *or archaic* **stept; stepping; steps** [ME *steppen*, *stepen*, *stapen*, fr. OE *stæppan*, *steppan;* akin to OFris *stapa*, *steppa* to step, MD *stappen*, OHG *stapfōn*, *stepfen* to step, ON *stappa* to pound, stamp — more at STAMP] *vi* **1 a :** to move in any direction by raising the foot and bringing it down in a different position or by moving each foot in succession **:** move the feet (as in walking) ⟨walked . . . to the barn and *stepped* into the saddle —Will Cook⟩ ⟨hunters ~ over the dead animal —J.G. Frazer⟩ ⟨*stepped* ashore at the ferry landing —Louis Brom-

field⟩ ⟨*stepped* off the curb and started walking down the hill —Dorothy Baker⟩ ⟨*stepped* out on deck to cool himself —E.K. Gann⟩ ⟨*stepped* down from the ladder⟩ ⟨~ aside to let the doctor pass⟩ ⟨the referee *stepped* between the two boxers⟩ **b** : DANCE ⟨that girl can really ~⟩ **2 a** : to go on foot : WALK ⟨what, you are *stepping* westward —Dorothy Wordsworth⟩ ⟨please ~ to the telephone⟩ ⟨*stepped* down to the corner for a newspaper⟩ **b** *obs* : to move forward : ADVANCE, PROCEED ⟨I am in blood *stepped* in so far —Shak.⟩ **c** : to go or be on one's way : DEPART — often used with *along* ⟨well, I must ~ *along* now⟩ **d** : to move at a brisk or lively pace ⟨they kept us *stepping* all right —W.L.Gresham⟩ **3 a** : to put the foot down : TREAD ⟨~ on a rusty nail⟩ **b** : to press down with the foot ⟨~ on the brake⟩ **4 a** : to come as if at a single step ⟨*stepped* into a fortune when his father died⟩ ⟨~ into a good job⟩ **b** *obs* : to enter suddenly and in a rash or thoughtless manner ⟨in hot blood hath *stepped* into the law —Shak.⟩ **5** : to stand erect with the lower end fixed in a step ⟨the foremast ~s abaft the forecastle⟩ ~ *vt* **1** : to take by moving the feet in succession ⟨rose and *stepped* three paces —Rudyard Kipling⟩ **2 a** : to move (the foot) in any direction : SET, PLACE ⟨the first man who *stepped* foot on the enemy's soil —S.G.W.Benjamin⟩ **b** : to move over or travel across on foot : TRAVERSE ⟨proud too ... of *stepping* this famous pavement —Virginia Woolf⟩ ⟨deer ~ the highways —Grace H. Flandrau⟩ **3** : to go through the steps of : PERFORM ⟨a minuet⟩ **4** : to make erect by fixing the lower end in a step ⟨a small pole *stepped* in a block of wood served as a mast —Bernard DeVoto⟩ **5** : to measure by steps ⟨have *stepped* more ground ... than any man in the country —Samuel Lover⟩ — often used with *off* or *out* ⟨~ off 50 yards⟩ **6** : to provide or furnish with steps : make steps in ⟨~ a key⟩ **7** : to construct or arrange in or as if in steps : build in steps ⟨was ... *stepped* to ensure that the winter rains did not wash the whole lot into the sea —Brendan Maguire⟩ ⟨the house is *stepped* down the slope —Siegfried Giedion⟩ ⟨craggy peaks with terraces *stepped* up the sides — *Time*⟩ — **step on it 1** : to increase the speed of a motor vehicle by pressing down on the accelerator **2** : to increase one's speed : hurry up

step- \~\ *comb form* [ME, fr. OE *stēop-*; akin to OFris *stiap-step-*, OHG *stiof-*, ON *stjūp-* step-, OE *āstēpan*, *āstȳpan* to deprive, bereave, OHG b*istiufen* to deprive of children or parents] : related by virtue of a remarriage (as of a parent) and not by blood ⟨*stepaunt*⟩ ⟨*stepcousin*⟩ ⟨*stepgrandchild*⟩

step-and-re·peat \~=≠≠\ *adj* : of, relating to, or employing a method in which successive exposures of a single image are made on a printing surface that is being prepared for gang printing

step back *vi* **1** : to yield ground by moving to the rear ⟨ordered the spectators to *step back*⟩ **2** : RECEDE ⟨end chimneys which *step back* unattached above the second story —*Amer. Guide Series: N.C.*⟩ ~ *vt* **1** : to construct (as a building) in an ascending series of steps or stages of diminishing width : build so that successive stories or groups of stories become farther and farther from the front, side, or back ⟨an octagonal tower ... rising sheer to 13 stories and then *stepped back* three times to a height of 327 feet —*Amer. Guide Series: N.Y.*⟩

step bearing *n* : a bearing that supports the lower end of a vertical shaft

step bolt *n* : CARRIAGE BOLT

step·broth·er \~=≠≠\ *n* [ME, fr. step- + *brother*] : a son of one's stepparent by a former marriage

step-by-step \~(,)~=≠\ *adj* : marked by successive degrees usu. of limited extent : GRADUAL ⟨approach on a *step-by-step* basis a closer association with other nations —Dean Acheson⟩

step-by-step telegraph *n* : an electric telegraph in which each letter of the message is indicated by a pointer on a dial

step chair *n* : a chair convertible into a stepladder

step·child \~=≠\ *n, pl* **stepchildren** [ME, fr. OE *stēopcild* orphan, fr. *stēop-* step- + *cild* child — more at CHILD] **1** : a child of one's wife or husband by a former marriage **2** : one that fails to receive proper care or attention ⟨music is ... a ~ in most of our academic institutions —P.H.Lang⟩

step chuck *n* : a lathe chuck with recessed shoulders of decreasing diameters for holding flat round work

step-cline \~=≠\ *n* [¹step] : an irregular or interrupted cline

step-cone pulley *n* : CONE PULLEY

step cut *n* : a cut for diamonds or esp. colored stones forming a series of straight facets that decrease in length as they recede from the girdle and so give the appearance of steps — compare TABLE CUT

step·dame \~=≠\ *n* [ME, fr. step- + *dame*] *archaic* : STEPMOTHER

step dance *n* : a dance in which steps are emphasized rather than gesture or posture; *esp* : a solo dance characterized by clogging, tapping, brushing, or kicking

step·daugh·ter \~=≠\ *n* [ME *stepdoughter*, fr. OE *stēopdohtor* (akin to MHG *stieftohter*, ON *stjūpdōttir*), fr. *stēop-* step- + *dohtor* daughter — more at STEP, DAUGHTER] : a daughter of one's wife or husband by a former marriage

step down *vt* **1** : to lower the voltage of (a current) by means of a transformer **2** : to decrease, retard, or mitigate by or as if by steps ⟨*stepping down* the intensity of the myth into mild contemporary equivalents —Malcolm Cowley⟩ ~ *vi* **1** : to retire or resign from a position of power or authority ⟨had *stepped down* from active management of the household —Irving Brant⟩

¹step-down \~=≠\ *adj* [*step down*] : that decreases, reduces, or retards; *specif* : that decreases voltage ⟨*step-down* transformer⟩

²step-down \~=≠\ *n* -s : a decrease or reduction in size or amount ⟨a *step-down* in dosage⟩

step·fa·ther \~=≠\ *n* [ME *stepfader*, fr. OE *stēopfæder* (akin to OFris *stiapfeder*, MHG *stiefvater*, ON *stjūpfathir*), fr. *stēop-* step- + *fæder* father — more at FATHER] : the husband of one's mother by a subsequent marriage

step fault *n* : DISTRIBUTIVE FAULT

step function *n* : a function of a single real variable in mathematics that remains constant throughout each of a series of adjacent intervals with the constant value varying from interval to interval

step gauge *n* **1** : a compound plug gauge consisting of several short cylindrical gauges of graduated diameters on the same axis **2** : a gauge that consists of a handled body in which a blade slides normally and that is used esp. for measuring shoulders or steps

step grate *n* : a fire grate in which the bars rise like steps

stephan- *or* **stephano-** *comb form* [Gk, fr. *stephanos* crown, fr. *stephein* to put round one's head, encircle, crown] : crown ⟨*stephanurus*⟩ ⟨*stephanone*⟩ ⟨*Stephanofilaria*⟩

steph·a·nan·dra \stefə'nandrə\ *n, cap* [NL, fr. stephan- + -*andra*] : a genus of deciduous Japanese and Chinese shrubs (family Rosaceae) with lobed or incised leaves and flowers with four or more petals and a single pistil that produces a follicle

steph·a·ne \'stefə(,)nē\ *n* -s [Gk *stephanē*, fr. *stephein* to put round one's head] : a headdress that consists of a metal band widest in the middle over the forehead and growing narrower toward the temples and that is often seen in ancient Greek statues of divinities

ste·pha·nian \stə'fānēən, -nyən\ *adj, usu cap* [F *stéphanien*, fr. (Sanctus) *Stephanus* (Latin form of Saint-Étienne, city in central France where a carboniferous basin representing this division is found) + F -*ien* -ian] : of or relating to a division of the Carboniferous — see GEOLOGIC TIME table

ste·phan·i·dae \-'fanə,dē\ *n pl, cap* [NL, fr. *Stephanus*, type genus (fr. Gk *stephanos* crown) + -*idae*; fr. the antennae] : a widely distributed family of slender ichneumon flies having many-segmented filamentous antennae and including some that as larvae are parasites on wood-boring insects

ste·pha·ni·on \-'fānēən\ *n* -s [NL, fr. Gk, dim. of *stephanos* crown] : the point where the coronal suture crosses the superior temporal line — see CRANIOMETRY illustration

steph·a·nite \'stefə,nīt\ *n* -s [G *stephanit*, fr. Archduke *Stephan* of Austria †1867 + G -*it* -ite] : a mineral Ag₃SbS₄ consisting of an orthorhombic iron black sulfide of silver and antimony and having metallic luster

steph·a·no·fi·lar·ia \stefənō-\ *n, cap* [NL, fr. stephan- + *filaria*] : a genus of filarial worms parasitic in the skin and subcutaneous tissues of ruminants and horses where they may cause dermatitis and extensive degenerative lesions — compare HUMP SORE

steph·a·no·fi·la·ri·a·sis \~=,≠filə'rīəsəs\ *n* [NL, *Stephanofilaria* + -*sis*] : infestation with or disease caused by worms of the genus *Stephanofilaria*

steph·a·no·kon·tae \-'kin-,(,)tē\ *n pl, cap* [NL, fr. stephan- + -*kontae* (as in *isokontae*)] *in some classifications* : a class or subclass that is approximately equivalent to Oedogoniales and includes green algae having zoospores with a crown or chaplet of cilia — compare HETEROKONTAE, ISOKONTAE

steph·a·nome \stefə,nōm\ *n* -s [*stephan-* + Gk *-nomos* distributor (fr. *nemein* to distribute) — more at NIMBLE] : an instrument for measuring the angular dimensions of fogbows and halos

steph·a·no·tis \~=≠'nōdəs\ *n* [NL, fr. Gk *stephanōtis* fit for a crown, fr. *stephanos* crown] **1** *cap* : a genus of Old World tropical woody vines (family Asclepiadaceae) with fragrant white flowers whose corolla has a cylindrical dilated tube and spreading limb — see MADAGASCAR JASMINE **2** -es : any plant of the genus *Stephanotis*

steph·a·nu·rus \-'nyurəs\ *n, cap* [NL, fr. stephan- + -*urus*] : a genus of nematode worms (family Strongylidae) including the kidney worm of swine

step-hop \~=≠\ *n* : a dance step consisting of a forward step followed by a hop on the same foot

step in *vi* [ME *stepen in*, fr. *stepen* to step + *in* — more at STEP] **1** : to make a brief informal visit : drop in ⟨*step in* and take your chocolate with her —Elizabeth Inchbald⟩ **2** : to enter into an affair or dispute often without invitation, permission, or welcome : INTERVENE ⟨if the local communities do not meet their responsibilities ... the federal and state governments will *step in* —C.F.Hood⟩

¹step-in \~=≠\ *adj* [*step in*] **1** *of clothing* : put on by being stepped into ⟨*step-in* dress⟩ ⟨*step-in* moccasins⟩ **2** : of or relating to step-in clothing ⟨*step-in* styles⟩

²step-in \~=≠\ *n* -s : an article of step-in clothing: as **a** : a shoe that resembles but usu. has a higher vamp than a pump **b step-ins** *pl* : a woman's short panties

step index *n* : an index cut into the fore edge of a book in the form of steps with the edge of each set of leaves preceding an indexed leaf being cut away — compare TAB INDEX, THUMB INDEX

step joint *n* : a joint used in fastening together the ends of two rails of different height and section

step·lad·der \~=≠\ *n* : a portable set of flat broad steps or treads with a frame hinged to the back for steadying

step·less \~=,ləs\ *adj* : having no steps

step·like \~=≠\ *adj* : resembling a series of steps

step·moth·er \~=≠\ *n* [ME *stepmoder*, fr. OE *stēopmōdor* (akin to MHG *stiefmuoter*, ON *stjūpmōthir*), fr. *stēop-* step- + *mōdor* mother — more at STEP, MOTHER] **1** : the wife of one's father by a subsequent marriage **2** : one that fails to give proper care or attention ⟨the monastery had got the credit of founding a school but had ... been a ~ to it —*Contemporary Rev.*⟩ **3** *dial* : HANGNAIL

step·moth·er·ly *adj* : of, relating to, or befitting a stepmother

step·ney \'stepnē\ *or* **stepney wheel** \~s *often cap* S [prob. fr. *Stepney* Street, Llanelly, Wales, where it was orig. manufactured] *Brit* : a spare spokeless automobile wheel with inflated tire

step-off \~=≠\ *n* [*step off*, v.] **1** : an act or instance of stepping off **2 a** : an abrupt dropping off of a shore line into deep water **b** : a place where such a dropping off occurs

step-on \~=≠\ *adj* [fr. *step on*, v.] : opened by means of a pedal ⟨14-quart *step-on* can in chrome-plated steel —*advt*⟩

step out *vi* **1** : to go away from a place usu. for a short distance and for a short time ⟨just *stepped out* for a while —Erskine Caldwell⟩ **2** : to go or march at a vigorous or increased pace **3** : DIE **4** : to engage in social activities : lead an active social life ⟨has really been *stepping out* this past year⟩ **5** : to be unfaithful — usu. used *on* ⟨hadn't been married two months before I knew he was *stepping out* on me —James Jones⟩

step-out \~=≠\ *n* : a well drilled outside but near a proved oil field

step·par·ent \~=≠\ *n* [step- + *parent*] : the husband or wife of one's mother or father by a subsequent marriage

steppe \'step\ *n* -s [Russ *step'*, fr. ORuss, lowland] **1** : one of the vast tracts in southeastern Europe or Asia that are usu. level and without forests **2** : arid land characterized by xerophilous vegetation and found usu. in large tracts and in regions of extreme temperature range and loess soil — compare GRASSLAND, PAMPA, PLAIN, PRAIRIE, SAVANNA

steppe cat *n* : MANUL

stepped \'stept\ *adj* [¹step + -*ed*] **1** : having a step or a series of steps : arranged or constructed in steps ⟨~ pyramids⟩ ⟨~ gables⟩ **2** *of an arch* : consisting of a series of concentric arches of diminishing radius set within one another

stepped footing *n* : a footing in which the desired width is secured by a series of steps in about the proportion of one unit of horizontal dimension to two units of vertical dimension

stepped gable *n* : a gable that diminishes in width by corbie-steps

stepped gauge *n* : STEP GAUGE

stepped gear wheel *n* : a gear wheel with two or more complete circular sets of teeth arranged adjacently on the same rim so that the corresponding teeth in the various sets form a series of steps

stepped key *n* : BIT KEY

stepped pulley *n* : a cone pulley with steps

stepped rack *n* : a rack made to mesh with a stepped gear

stepped screw *n* : an interrupted screw the divisions of whose surface are stepped

stepped-up \~=≠\ *adj* : AUGMENTED, ACCELERATED, INTENSIFIED ⟨a *stepped-up* sales campaign⟩

step·pe·land \~=≠\ *n* : STEPPE 2

step·per \'stepə(r)\ *n* -s : one that steps: as **a** : a horse with high action **b** : DANCER

step·ping *n* -s [ME, fr. gerund of *steppen* to step — more at STEP] **1** : an act or instance of moving the feet (as in walking) **2 a** (1) : lumber suitable for steps (2) : wood members esp. formed for use in constructing step treads **b** : an export grade of yellow pine and fir

stepping-off place \~=≠-≠\ *n* **1** : the outbound end of a transportation line **2** : a place from which one departs for unknown territory

stepping-stone \~=≠\ *n* [ME] **1 a** : a stone on which to step in walking (as in crossing a stream) **b** : a raised stone for facilitating an ascent or descent; *specif* : HORSE BLOCK **2 a** : means of progress or advancement ⟨the law was a *stepping-stone* to a career in politics —G.S.Bryan⟩ **3** : a place for a break in or as if in a journey ⟨this *stepping-stone* for airborne supplies on their way to far-flung fronts below the equator —Howell Walker⟩

step rate *n* : a rate that changes by regular gradations: as **a** : a life-insurance premium rate that increases or decreases each year **b** : a utilities rate whereby an increase in unit consumption results in a decrease in unit price

step rocket *n* : a multistage rocket whose sections are fired successively

steps *pl of* STEP, *pres 3d sing of* STEP

step·sis·ter \~=≠\ *n* [step- + *sister*] : a daughter of one's stepparent by a former marriage

step·son \~=≠\ *n* [ME *stepsone*, fr. OE *stēopsunu* (akin to MHG *stiefsun*, ON *stjūpsonr*), fr. *stēop-* step- + *sunu* son — more at STEP, SON] : a son of one's husband or wife by a former marriage

step·stone \~=≠\ *n* : a stone laid before an outside door as a step

step stool *n* : a stool with one or two steps that often fold away beneath the seat ⟨use a kitchen *step stool* to reach things on the higher shelves

stept *archaic past of* STEP

step table *n* : a small table surmounted by one short shelf or several progressively diminished shelves

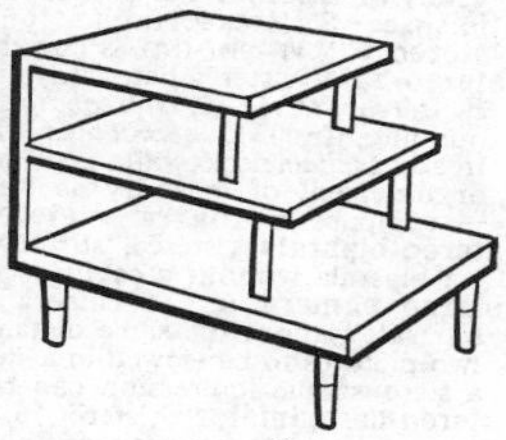

step terrace *n* : a stepped terrace on the levels of which farming is done

step trench *n* : a trench cut in a series of steps from the base to the top of a mound for determining the cultural levels of an archaeological site

step turn *n* : a turn executed in a downhill traverse by lifting the upper ski from the ground, placing it in the desired direction, weighting it, and bringing the other ski parallel

step table

step up *vt* **1** : to increase the voltage of (a current) by means of a transformer **2** : to increase, augment, or advance by or as if by steps ⟨the amount of salt mined can be materially *stepped up* —R.E.Crist⟩ ⟨radio and television have *stepped up* ... the tempo of the news —F.L.Mott⟩ **3** : to give a promotion to ⟨you're going to be *stepped up* to head clerk —Frederick Way⟩ ~ *vi* **1** : to come forward often in an interfering, inopportune, or unguarded manner ⟨time for teachers to *step up* and say that there is nothing wrong with teaching something —James Binney⟩ **2** : to undergo an increase ⟨world trade is *stepping up* —Kiplinger Washington Letter⟩ **3** : to receive a promotion ⟨*stepping up* to the chief executive's chair —*Current Biog.*⟩

¹step-up \~=≠\ *adj* [*step up*] : that increases, augments, or advances: as **a** *of a transformer* : that increases voltage **b** *of a lease* : that provides for increases in rent up to a maximum

²step-up \~=≠\ *n* -s : an increase or advance in size or amount ⟨a *step-up* in production⟩

step ward *n* : the ward of a lock or key nearest to the pin

step·way \~=≠\ *n* : a stepway

step wedge *or* **step tablet** *n* : an optical wedge in which the change in transmittance with distance along the wedge occurs in discrete adjacent steps

¹step·wise \~=≠\ *adv* : in a stepwise manner

²step·wise \"\ *adj* **1** : marked by or as if by steps : GRADUAL ⟨achieved in a ~ struggle for social reform —Fritz Tarnow⟩ ⟨a ~ chemical reaction⟩ **2** : moving step by step to adjacent musical tones ⟨a short melodic line ... containing mostly ~ progressions —Paul Hindemith⟩

-ster \stə(r), following a voiced consonant, as in "mobster", -ztə- *or* -stə-\ *n suffix* -s [ME -*ster*, -*stere*, -*estere*, fr. OE -*estre* female agent; akin to MD -*ster*] **1** : one that does or handles or operates ⟨spin*ster*⟩ ⟨taps*ter*⟩ ⟨teams*ter*⟩ **2** : one that makes or uses ⟨songs*ter*⟩ ⟨puns*ter*⟩ **3** : one that is associated with or participates in ⟨games*ter*⟩ ⟨gangs*ter*⟩

ster *abbr* **1** sterilization; sterilizer **2** sterling

ste·ra·di·an \stə'rādēən\ *also* **sterad** \'ste,rad, 'sti,r-\ *n* -s [*steradian* fr. *stere-* + *radian*; *sterad* short for *steradian*] : a unit of measure of solid angles that is expressed as the solid angle subtended at the center of the sphere by a portion of the surface whose area is equal to the square of the radius of the sphere

ste·ra·di·an·cy \stə'rādēənsē\ *n* -ES [*steradian* + -*cy*] : the radiant flux from a surface per steradian of solid angle in a specified direction per unit area of cross section of the emission perpendicular to that direction

ster·co·bi·lin \,stərkō'bīlən\ *n* -s [ISV sterco- (fr. L *stercus* excrement) + *bil-* (fr. L *bilis* bile) + -*in* — more at BILE] : UROBILIN; *esp* : a brown levorotatory pigment C₃₃H₄₆N₄O₆ found in feces and urine

ster·co·bi·lin·o·gen \,≠=,≠,-≠'bī'linəjən\ *n* -s [ISV *stercobilin* + -*o-* + -*gen*] : UROBILINOGEN

ster·co·ra·ceous \,stərkə'rāshəs\ *adj* [L *stercor-, stercus* + -*aceous*] : of or relating to dung : being or containing dung

ster·co·ral \'stərkərəl\ *adj* [ML *stercoralis*, fr. L *stercor-, stercus* excrement + -*alis* -al — more at DRECK] : of, relating to, containing, produced by, or being dung : FECAL ⟨~ living in or feeding on dung

stercoral pocket *n* : a pouched diverticulum of the hind intestine of a spider that serves as a reservoir for fecal material

ster·co·ra·nism \'stərkərə,nizəm\ *n, often cap* [ML *stercoranista* Stercoranist + E -*ism*] : the body of beliefs peculiar to Stercoranists

ster·co·ra·nist \-nəst\ *also* **ster·co·rar·i·an** \,stərkə-'ra(ə)rēən\ *n -s often cap* [*stercoranist* fr. ML *stercoranista*, fr. *stercoran-* (irreg. fr. L *stercor-, stercus* excrement) + L -*ista* -ist; *stercorarian* fr. L *stercorarius* stercoral + E -*an*] : one who holds that the consecrated elements in the Eucharist are subject to natural processes (as of digestion)

ster·co·ra·ri·i·dae \,stərkərə'rīə,dē\ *n pl, cap* [NL, fr. *Stercorarius*, type genus (fr. L *stercorarius* stercoral, fr. *stercor-, stercus* excrement + -*arius* -ary) + NL -*idae*] : a family of long-winged sea birds (suborder Lari) comprising the jaegers and skuas and being sometimes ranked as a subfamily of Laridae

ster·co·ra·ry \~=≠\ *n* -ES [ML *stercorarium* toilet, stercorary, fr. neut. of L *stercorarius* stercoral] *archaic* : a place (as a covered pit) for the storage of manure secure from the weather

ster·co·ra·tion \,≠=≠'rāshən\ *n* -S [L *stercoration-, stercoratio*, fr. *stercoratus* (past part. of *stercorare*) + -*ion-, -io* -ion] **1** *archaic* : the act of dressing with manure **2** : MANURE, DUNG

ster·co·ric·o·lous \,≠=≠'rikələs\ *adj* [L *stercor-, stercus* excrement + E -*i-* + -*colous*] : living in dung

ster·co·rite \'stərkə,rīt\ *n* -s [L *stercor-, stercus* + E -*ite*] : a native microcosmic salt HNaNH₄PO₄H₂O occurring in guano

ster·cov·o·rous \,≠=≠'kivərəs\ *adj* [L *stercus* excrement + E -*o-* + -*vorous*] : SCATOPHAGOUS — used esp. of an insect

ster·cu·lia \stə(r)'kyülēə\ *n* [NL, fr. L *Sterculius* god of cultivation and manuring, fr. *stercus* manure, excrement; fr. the fetid odor of some of the species — more at DRECK] **1** *cap* : a genus of tropical trees or shrubs (family Sterculiaceae) having palmate leaves, small paniculate unisexual flowers with 15 anthers, and an ovary with 5 cells that become distinct carpels in the fruit — see BOTTLE TREE, KALUMPANG **2** -s : any plant of the genus *Sterculia* — see STERCULIA GUM

ster·cu·li·a·ce·ae \~=≠=lē'āsē,ē, -lēˈāsēˌē\ *n pl, cap* [NL, fr. *Sterculia*, type genus + -*aceae*] : a large family of herbs, shrubs, or trees (order Malvales) distinguished mainly by the numerous monadelphous stamens and 2-celled anthers — see KURRAJONG

ster·cu·li·a·ceous \~=≠=lē'āshəs\ *adj* : of or belonging to the family Sterculiaceae

ster·cu·li·ad \-lē,ad\ *n -s* [NL *Sterculia* + E -*ad*] : a plant of the family Sterculiaceae

sterculia gum *n* : any of several vegetable gums that are similar in properties to tragacanth and often used as substitutes for it and that are obtained from tropical Asiatic trees of the genera *Sterculia* and *Cochlospermum* (esp. *S. urens* and *C. gossypium*)

ster·cu·lic acid \,(')stər'kyülik-\ *n* [NL *Sterculia* + E -*ic*] : a crystalline unsaturated fatty acid C₈H₁₇(CH₂)₇ COOH found as a glyceride in the seeds of a tropical tree (*Sterculia foetida*); 2-octyl-1-cyclo-propene-octanoic acid

stere \'sti(ə)r, -te-\ *n* -s [F *stère*, fr. Gk *stereos* solid] : a metric unit of volume equal to one cubic meter — see METRIC SYSTEM table

stere- *or* **stereo-** *comb form* [NL, fr. Gk, fr. *stereos* solid — more at STARE] **1** : solid : solid body ⟨*stereospondylous*⟩ ⟨*stereopticon*⟩ **2 a** : stereoscopic ⟨*stereocamera*⟩ **b** : having or dealing with three dimensions of space ⟨*stereochemistry*⟩ **c** : of, relating to, or considered with respect to stereochemistry ⟨*stereospecific*⟩

stere·id \'sterēd, 'stir-\ *n* -s [F *stéréide*, fr. Gk *stereoeidēs* of solid nature, fr. *stere-* + -*oeidēs* -oid] : a plant cell or cell derivative whose function is primarily mechanical support — compare SCLEREID

¹stereo \'sterē(,)ō, 'stir-\ *n* -s [by shortening] **1** : STEREOTYPE **2** [short for *stereoscopy*] **a** : a stereoscopic method, system, or effect; *esp* : stereoscopic photography **b** : stereoscopic photograph **3** [short for *stereophonic*] **a** : stereophonic reproduction **b** : a stereophonic sound system

²stereo \"\ *adj* [*stereo-*] **1 a** : STEREOSCOPIC **b** : STEREOTYPED

2 a : of, relating to, or involving three-dimensional space ⟨~ acuity of vision⟩ **b** : of or relating to the arrangement of atoms in space **3** : STEREOPHONIC

³stereo \"\ *vt* -ED/-ING/-S [by shortening] : STEREOTYPE

stereo·bate \ˈsterēə,bāt, ˈstir-, *usu* -ād.+V\ *n* -s [F or L; F *stéréobate*, fr. L *stereobata* foundation of a column or building, fr. Gk *stereobatēs*, fr. *stere-* + *-batēs* one that treads, fr. *bainein* to walk, go — more at COME] : a substructure or basement of masonry as visible above the ground level — compare STYLOBATE — **stereo·bat·ic** \¦===¦bad·ik\ *adj*

stereo·blastula \¦sterēə, ¦stir- +\ *n* [NL, fr. *stere-* + *blastula*] : a blastula without a cavity

stereo camera *n* : a camera having two matched lenses separated about the same distance as a person's eyes so that two pictures to be viewed in a stereoscope or projected to give a stereoscopic impression can be taken simultaneously

stereo·campimeter \¦sterē(,)ō, ¦stir- +\ *n* [*stere-* + *campimeter*] : a stereoscopic campimeter

stereo·chemical \¦sterēə, ¦stir- +\ *adj* [*stere-* + *chemical*] : of or relating to stereochemistry ⟨~ configurations of steroids⟩ — **stereo·chemically** \"+\ *adv*

stereo·chemistry \"+\ *n* [ISV *stere-* + *chemistry*] **1** : a branch of chemistry that deals with the spatial arrangement of atoms and groups in molecules **2** : the spatial relationship of atoms and groups in the molecule of a substance and its effect on the properties of the substance

stereo·chromatic \"+\ *adj* [*stereochromy* + *-atic*] : STEREOCHROMIC — **stereo·chromatically** \"+\ *adv*

stereo·chrome \ˈ===,krōm\ *n* -s [back-formation fr. *stereochromy*] : a stereochromic picture

stereo·chro·mic \¦===¦krōmik\ *adj* [ISV *stereochromy* + *-ic*] : of, relating to, or done by means of stereochromy — **stereo·chro·mi·cal·ly** \-mək(ə)lē, -li\ *adv*

stereo·chro·my \ˈ===,krōmē, -mi\ *n* -ES [ISV *stere-* + *-chromy*; orig. formed as G *stereochromie*] : a process of mural painting in which the pigment is fixed by a series of reactions between the lime, fluosilicic acid, and water glass

stereo·cilium \¦===+\ *n* [NL, fr. *stere-* + *cilium*] : one of the immobile processes that resemble cilia and occur on the free border of various epithelia

stereo·comparagraph \"+\ *n* [*stereocomparator* + *-graph*] : a plotting instrument using the stereoscopic principle of parallax for increased accuracy in making small-scale contour maps

stereo·comparator \"+\ *n* [ISV *stere-* + *comparator*; orig. formed as G *stereokomparator*] : a stereoscope used in making topographic measurements by the accurate comparison of stereoscopic photographs taken with an instrument having very great distance between the objectives or used in astronomy to detect small motions and brightness changes by stereoscopic examination of two photographs of the same celestial area taken at different times

stereo·fluoroscope \"+\ *n* [*stere-* + *fluoroscope*] : an instrument designed to give a three-dimensional image by fluoroscopy — **stereo·fluoroscopic** \"+\ *adj*

stereo·fluoroscopy \"+\ *n* [*stere-* + *fluoroscopy*] : stereoscopic fluoroscopy : use of the stereofluoroscope

stereo formula *n* : PERSPECTIVE FORMULA

stereo·gastrula \¦sterēə, ¦stir- +\ *n* [NL, fr. *stere-* + *gastrula*] : a gastrula with no cavity

stere·og·no·sis \,sterēäg'nōsəs, ,stir-\ *n* -ES [NL, fr. *stere-* + *-gnosis*] : ability to perceive or the perception of material qualities (as form, weight) of an object by handling or lifting it : tactile recognition

stere·og·nos·tic \¦===¦nästik\ *adj* [ISV *stere-* + *-gnostic*] : of, relating to, or involving stereognosis

stereo·gram \ˈsterēə,gram, ˈstir-, -raa(ə)m\ *n* [ISV *stere-* + *-gram*] **1** : a diagram or picture representing objects with an impression of solidity or relief **2** : STEREOGRAPH

¹stereo·graph \-,graf, -aa(ə)f, -aif, -âf\ *n* -s [ISV *stere-* + *-graph*] **1** : a pair of stereoscopic pictures or a picture composed of two superposed stereoscopic images prepared so as to give a three-dimensional effect when viewed with a stereoscope or with special spectacles — compare ANAGLYPH, VECTOGRAPH **2** : an instrument used in tracing the contours of skulls — compare STEREOGRAPHY **3** : STEREOTYPER

²stereograph \"\ *vt* **1** : to prepare (as a picture) for stereoscopic exhibition **2** : to take a stereoscopic photograph of **3** : STEREOTYPE 1c

stere·og·ra·pher \,sterē'ägrəfə(r), ,stir-\ *n* -s [*stereograph* + *-er*] : one that stereographs: as **a** : one that takes stereoscopic photographs **b** : STEREOTYPER

stereo·graph·ic \¦sterēə¦grafik, ¦stir-, -fēk\ *also* **stereo·graph·i·cal** \-fəkəl, -fēk-\ *adj* [*stereographic* prob. fr. (assumed) NL *stereographicus*, fr. *stereographia* stereography + L *-icus* -ic; *stereographical* fr. (assumed) NL *stereographicus* + E *-al*] : made or done according to stereography ⟨a ~ navigation chart⟩ — **stereo·graph·i·cal·ly** \-fək(ə)lē, -fēk-, -li\ *adv*

stereographic projection *n* : a map projection of a hemisphere showing the earth's lines of latitude and longitude projected onto a tangent plane by radials from a point on the surface of the sphere opposite to the point of tangency

stere·og·ra·phy \,sterē'ägrəfē, -fi\ *n* -ES [prob. fr. (assumed) NL *stereographia*, fr. NL *stere-* + *-graphia* -graphy] **1 a** : the art, process, or technique of delineating the forms of solid bodies on a plane : a branch of solid geometry showing the construction of all solids that are regularly defined **b** : demonstration of the five regular solids by models cut from flat material and folded **2** : stereoscopic photography

stereoing *pres part of* STEREO

stereo·isomer \¦sterēō, ¦stir- +\ *n* [ISV *stere-* + *isomer*] : any one of the isomers in an example of stereoisomerism ⟨~*s* have the same structure but differ in configuration —C.N. Webb⟩

stereo·isomeric \¦===+\ *adj* [*stereoisomerism* + *-ic*] : of, relating to, or exhibiting stereoisomerism ⟨the ability of living systems to discriminate between ~ forms of a chemical substance —J.S.Fruton & Sofia Simmonds⟩

stereo·isomeride \"+\ *n* [*stere-* + *isomeride*] : STEREOISOMER

stereo·isomerism \"+\ *n* [*stere-* + *isomerism*] : isomerism in which atoms are linked in the same order but differ in their arrangement in space — sometimes distinguished from *structural isomerism*; see GEOMETRIC ISOMERISM, OPTICAL ISOMERISM

stereo·kinesis \"+\ *n* [NL, fr. *stere-* + *-kinesis*] : a state of immobilization in an insect following strong mechanical stimulation

stere·ome \ˈsterē,ōm, ˈstir-\ *or* **stere·om** \-ē,äm\ *n* -s [G *stereom*, fr. Gk *stereōma* solid body, fr. *stereoun* to make solid, fr. *stereos* solid — more at STARE] : mechanical or strengthening tissue: **a** : rigid cellular tissue (as sclerenchyma and collenchyma) of a plant — compare MESTOME **b** : exoskeletal material of an invertebrate

stere·om·e·ter \,==ˈämәd·ə(r), -mәtə-\ *n* [ISV *stere-* + *-meter*; prob. orig. formed as F *stéréomètre*] **1** : VOLUMENOMETER **2** : an instrument used for measuring heights of earth features by means of stereoscopic pairs of aerial photographs

stereo·met·ric \¦==,ə¦me·trik, -rēk\ *adj* [NL *stereometricus*, fr. Gk *stereometrikos*, fr. *stereometria* stereometry + *-ikos* -ic] **1** : relating to stereometry; *usu* : having, characterized by, or representing a readily measurable solid form or volume ⟨a house . . . can have variety of interior but the outside is invariably a ~ body —Bruno Zevi⟩ **2** : made by or relating to a stereometer

stere·om·e·try \,==ˈämә·trē\ *n* -ES [NL *stereometria*, fr. Gk, fr. *stereos* solid + *-metria* -metry] : the measurement of volumes and other metrical elements of solid figures — distinguished from *planimetry*

stereo·micrograph \¦sterēə, ¦stir- +\ *n* [*stere-* + *micrograph*] : a stereoscopic micrograph

stereo·micrography \"+\ *n* [*stereomicrograph* + *-y*] : the art of producing stereoscopic micrographs

stereo·micrometer \"+\ *n* [*stere-* + *micrometer*] : an apparatus attached to an optical device (as a telescope) for measuring small angles in the field of view by noting the projection on squares seen with the other and naked eye

stereo·microscope \"+\ *n* [*stere-* + *microscope*] : a microscope having a set of optics for each eye so arranged that the sets view the object from slightly different directions and make it appear in three dimensions

stereo·pair \ˈ===+,-\ *n* [²*stereo* + *pair*] : a stereograph consisting of a pair of photographs

stereo·phonic \¦sterēə, ¦stir- +\ *adj* [ISV *stere-* + *phonic*] : giving, relating to, or constituting a three-dimensional effect of auditory perspective ⟨sound heard by both ears at once or reproduced through loudspeakers placed in different parts of an auditorium has a ~ quality⟩ ⟨the objective of ~ sound reproduction is to make clear to the listener the spatial aspects of the sound —Charles Fowler⟩ — compare MONOPHONIC — **stere·oph·o·ny** \,==ˈäfənē, ˈ== ə,fōnē\ *n* -ES

stereo·photogrammetric \¦sterēə, ¦stir- +\ *adj* [ISV *stereophotogrammetry* + *-ic*] : of or relating to stereophotogrammetry ⟨~ methods⟩

stereo·photogrammetry \"+\ *n* [ISV *stere-* + *photogrammetry*] : photogrammetry involving the use of stereoscopic photographs

stereo·photograph \"+\ *n* [*stere-* + *photograph*] : a stereoscopic photograph

stereo·photography \"+\ *n* [ISV *stere-* + *photography*] : stereoscopic photography

stereo·photomicrograph \"+\ *n* [*stere-* + *photomicrograph*] : a stereophotograph made through a microscope

stereo·photomicrography \"+\ *n* [*stereophotomicrograph* + *-y*] : the making of stereophotomicrographs

stereo·planigraph \"+\ *n* [ISV *stere-* + *planigraph*] : an instrument for making topographic maps from observations made with a stereocomparator

stereo·plasm \ˈsterēə,plazəm, ˈstir-\ *n* -s [ISV *stere-* + *-plasm*] : gelated protoplasm — **stereo·plas·mic** \¦==¦plazmik\ *adj*

stereo·plotting \¦===+\ *n* [*stere-* + *plotting*] : the plotting of a map (as a contour map) from aerial photographs by means of a stereoscopic device

stereo·projection \"+\ *n* [*stere-* + *projection*] : the projection of two photographs so as to give a stereoscopic effect

stere·op·sis \,sterēˈäpsəs, ,stir-\ *n* -ES [NL, fr. *stere-* + *-opsis*] : stereoscopic vision : capacity for depth perception

stere·op·ti·can \¦==¦äptəkən, -tēk-\ *adj* [NL *stereopticon* + E *-an*] : of, relating to, or like that produced by a stereopticon ⟨a figure with ~ definition⟩

stere·op·ti·cian \¦==,äpˈtishən\ *n* [NL *stereopticon* + E *-ian*] : one who tends a stereopticon (as for a lecturer)

stere·op·ti·con \,sterēˈäptəkən, -tə,kän\ *n* -s [NL, fr. *stere-* + Gk *optikon*, neut. of *optikos* optic — more at OPTIC] : a projector for transparent slides that is often made double so as to produce dissolving views

stereo·radiograph \¦sterēə, ¦stir- +\ *n* [*stere-* + *radiograph*] : a stereoscopic radiograph — **stereo·radiographic** \"+\ *adj* — **stereo·radiography** \"+\ *n*

stereo·regular \"+\ *adj* [*stere-* + *regular*] : possessing stereochemical regularity in the repeating units of a polymer structure ⟨linear and ~ addition polymers —N.G.Gaylord & H.F.Mark⟩ — **stereo·regularity** \"+\ *n*

stere·or·ni·thes \,sterēˈȯrnə,thēz, ,stir-, -,ȯrˈnī(,)thēz\ *n pl, cap* [NL, fr. *stere-* + *-ornithes*] *in former classifications* : an artificial or a composite order of very large Miocene Patagonian birds believed to be ratite and mostly included in the order Gruiformes — **stere·or·nith·ic** \¦==,ȯrˈnithik\ *adj*

stereos *pl of* STEREO, *pres 3d sing of* STEREO

stereo·scope \ˈsterēə,skōp, ˈstir-\ *n* [*stere-* + *-scope*] : an optical instrument for obtaining from two pictures (as photographs made for the purpose from points of view typically corresponding to the position of the two eyes) a single three-dimensional image by means of two lenses used one with each eye and set sometimes in conjunction with mirrors to deflect rays coming from corresponding points in the two pictures in such a manner as to produce the effect of originating at a single point

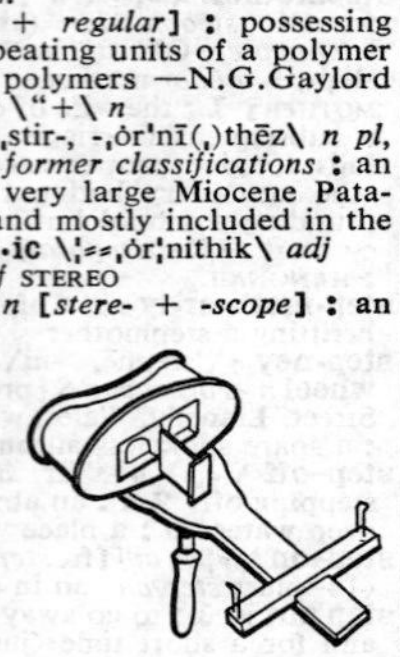

stereoscope

stereo·scop·ic \¦===¦skäpik, -pēk\ *also* **stereo·scop·i·cal** \-pəkəl, -pēk-\ *adj* [*stereoscopic* ISV *stereoscope* + *-ic*; *stereoscopical* fr. *stereoscope* + *-ical*] **1** : of or relating to stereoscopy or the stereoscope : characteristic of or adapted to the stereoscope **2** : characterized by stereoscopy ⟨~ vision⟩ — **stereo·scop·i·cal·ly** \-pək(ə)lē, -pēk-, -li\ *adv*

stereoscopic camera *n* : STEREO CAMERA

stereoscopic microscope *n* : STEREOMICROSCOPE

stereoscopic pair *n* : STEREOPAIR

stereoscopic radius *n* : the limiting distance at which objects are seen in stereoscopic relief amounting with unaided human vision to about 1500 feet

stereoscopic vision *n* : STEREOSCOPY 2

stere·os·co·py \,==ˈäskəpē, ˈ==ə,skōpē, -pi\ *n* -ES [ISV *stere-* + *-scopy*] **1** : a branch of science that deals with stereoscopic effects and methods by which they are produced **2** : the seeing of objects in three dimensions

stereo·selective \¦sterēə, ¦stir- +\ *adj* [*stere-* + *selective*] : stereochemically selective : relating to or being a reaction or process leading to a stereoisomer having one particular configuration regardless of the configuration of the reactant — compare STEREOSPECIFIC — **stereo·selectivity** \"+\ *n*

stereo·sonic \"+\ *adj* [*stere-* + *-sonic*] : STEREOPHONIC

stereo·specific \"+\ *adj* [*stere-* + *specific*] : stereochemically specific : relating to, being, or effecting a reaction or process in which a specific stereoisomer is formed esp. when the product is configurationally related to the reactant either by retention or reversal of the original configuration ⟨~ polymerization⟩ — compare STEREOSELECTIVE — **stereo·specif·ically** \"+\ *adv* — **stereo·specificity** \"+\ *n*

stereo·spon·dyl \,===ˈspänd°l\ *n* -s [NL *Stereospondyli*] : an amphibian or fossil of the order Stereospondyli

stereo·spon·dy·li \-də,lī\ *n pl, cap* [NL, fr. *stere-* + *-spondyli*] : an order of Labyrinthodontia or formerly a suborder of Stegocephalia including forms with stereospondylous vertebrae

stereo·spondylous \¦===+\ *adj* [*stere-* + *spondylous*] **1** : being or having vertebrae whose component elements are fused into a single piece ⟨most vertebrates are ~⟩ — opposed to *temnospondylous* **2** : of or relating to the order Stereospondyli

stereo·static \"+\ *adj* [ISV *stere-* + *static*; prob orig. formed as F *stéréostatique*] : GEOSTATIC

stereo·tac·tic \-¦taktik\ *adj* [fr. NL *stereotaxis*, after such pairs as NL *hypotaxis*: E *hypotactic*] : of, relating to, or involving stereotaxis — **stereo·tac·ti·cal·ly** \-tək(ə)lē\ *adv*

stereo·tax·is \,===ˈtaksəs\ *n* [NL, fr. *stere-* + *-taxis*] : a taxis in which contact esp. with a solid body is the directive factor

stereo·telescope \¦===+\ *n* [*stere-* + *telescope*] : TELESTEREOSCOPE

stereo·tom·ic \¦===¦tämik\ *or* **stereo·tom·i·cal** \-məkəl\ *adj* [*stereotomic* fr. F *stéréotomique*, fr. *stéréotomie* stereotomy + *-ique* -ic; *stereotomical* fr. *stereotomy* + *-ical*] : of or relating to stereotomy

stere·ot·o·mist \,==ˈäd·əməst\ *n* -s [*stereotomy* + *-ist*] : a practitioner of stereotomy

stere·ot·o·my \-mē, -mi\ *n* -ES [F *stéréotomie*, fr. *stéré-* stere- + *-tomie* -tomy] : the art or technique of cutting solids (as into arches); *esp* : the art of stonecutting

stereo·trop·ic \¦==ə¦träpik\ *adj* [ISV *stereotropism* + *-ic*] : of, relating to, or exhibiting stereotropism

stere·ot·ro·pism \,==ˈä·trə,pizəm\ *n* [ISV *stere-* + *tropism*] **1** : a tropism in which contact esp. with a solid body or a rigid surface is the orienting factor — compare HAPTOTROPISM **2** : STEREOTAXIS

¹stereo·type \ˈsterēə,tīp, ˈstir-\ *n* [F *stéréotype*, fr. *stéré-* stere- + *type*] **1 a** *archaic* : STEREOTYPY **b** : a solid metal duplicate of a relief printing surface that is made by pressing a molding material (as wet paper pulp, plaster of paris, clay, or flong) against it to make a matrix and then pouring molten metal into the matrix to make a casting which is sometimes faced with a harder metal (as nickel) to increase durability — compare ALUMINOTYPE, ELECTROTYPE **2** : something repeated or reproduced without variation : something conforming to a fixed or general pattern and lacking individual distinguishing marks or qualities; *esp* : a standardized mental picture held in common by members of a group and representing an oversimplified opinion, affective attitude, or uncritical judgment (as of a person, a race, an issue, or an event)

²stereotype \"\ *vt* **1 a** : to make a stereotype from (a relief printing surface) ⟨~ the pages of a newspaper⟩ **b** : to produce by stereotyping ⟨flat and curved *stereotyped* and electrotype plates —*Book Production*⟩ **c** : to emboss in braille characters by use of a stereotyper **2 a** : to fix in a lasting and usu. rigidly precise form **b** : to repeat without variation : make standardized or hackneyed **c** : to develop a mental stereotype about ⟨too easy to ~ and dismiss divergent groups⟩

stereotyped *adj* : produced by or as if by means of a stereotype : repeated by rote or without variation : lacking originality or individuality ⟨~ thinking⟩ ⟨~ manners⟩ ⟨~ concepts of other peoples —*Internat'l Social Sci. Bull.*⟩ **syn** see TRITE

stereo·typ·er \-,tīpə(r)\ *n* [ISV ²*stereotype* + *-er*] : one that stereotypes: as **a** : a worker who prepares stereotype plates **b** : a machine for embossing thin metal plates with braille characters for use in printing for the blind **c** *or* **stereotypist** : an operator of a stereotyper

stereo·typ·i·cal \¦===¦tipəkəl\ *also* **stereo·typ·ic** \-pik\ *adj* [¹*stereotype* + *-ical* or *-ic*] : of, relating to, or constituting a stereotype ⟨speaks . . . in terms ~ of the general attitude of the era —David Riesman⟩ — **stereo·typ·i·cal·ly** \-pək(ə)lē\ *adv*

stereotyping *n* [fr. gerund of ²*stereotype*] : the process, craft, or business of making stereotypes

stereo·typ·ist \ˈ===,tīpəst\ *n* [ISV ²*stereotype* + *-ist*] : STEREOTYPER c

stereo·typy \ˈ===,tīpē, -pi\ *n* -ES [ISV ¹*stereotype* + *-y*] **1** : the art or process of making or of printing from stereotype plates **2 a** : frequent and almost mechanical repetition of the same posture, movement, or form of speech (as in the mannerisms of dementia praecox) **b** : formation or a tendency to formation of mental stereotypes

stereo viewer *n* : STEREOSCOPE

stereo·vision \¦sterēə, ¦stir- +\ *n* [*stere-* + *vision*] : STEREOSCOPY 2

steres *pl of* STERE

ste·re·um \ˈstirēəm\ *n, cap* [NL, fr. Gk *stereos* solid — more at STARE] : a genus of fungi (family Thelephoraceae) having the sporophores resupinate or shelving and the basidial surface smooth — see SILVERLEAF

ster·hydraulic \¦ster+\ *adj* [prob. fr. F *stérhydraulique*, irreg. fr. *stéré-* stere- + *hydraulique* hydraulic] : relating to or being a hydraulic press producing pressure or motion by the introduction of a solid substance (as a screw, a rod, or a rope wound on a roller) into a cylinder previously filled with a liquid : resembling such a press in action or principle

steric \ˈsterik, ˈstir-, -rēk\ *adj* [ISV *stere-* + *-ic*] : relating to the arrangement of atoms in space : SPATIAL — **steri·cal·ly** \-rək(ə)lē, -rēk-, -li\ *adv*

steric hindrance *n* : hindrance of chemical action ascribed to the arrangement of atoms in a molecule

sterid \ˈsterəd, ˈstir-\ *also* **steride** \-,rīd, -,rəd\ *n* -s [*sterol* + *-id* or *-ide*] : STEROID — used to include sterols

ste·rig·ma \stəˈrigmə\ *n, pl* **sterigma·ta** \-məd·ə\ *also* **sterigmas** [NL, fr. Gk *stērigma* support, fr. *stērizein* to prop, support; akin to Gk *stereos* solid — more at STARE] **1** : one of the slender stalks at the top of the basidium of some fungi from the tips of which the basidiospores are abstricted; *broadly* : a stalk or filament from which conidia or spermatia are abjointed — compare PHIALIDE **2** : one of the persistent peg-shaped projections to which the leaves of some conifers (as spruces) are attached on the twigs — **ster·ig·mat·ic** \¦ste(,)rig¦mad·ik, -,rēg-\ *adj*

ster·i·lant \ˈsterələnt\ *n* -s [*sterile* + *-ant*] : a sterilizing agent; *esp* : an herbicide designed to completely eliminate a kind of plant and to have a rather persistent residual effect in the soil

ster·ile \ˈsterəl, -,rīl\ *adj* [L *sterilis*; akin to Gk *steira* sterile, Goth *stairo* sterile, Skt *starī* sterile cow] **1 a** : failing to produce or incapable of producing offspring ⟨a hybrid that is completely ~⟩ **b** : failing to bear or incapable of bearing fruit or spores ⟨a ~ tree⟩ ⟨~ fungous hyphae⟩ **c** : incapable of germinating ⟨~ spores⟩ **d** *of a flower* : lacking a gynecium : neither perfect nor pistillate **e** : having or producing no sori ⟨~ fern fronds⟩ **2** : characterized by deficient fruitfulness : BARREN: as **a** : deficient in plant life : unproductive of crops or other vegetation ⟨a ~ arid region⟩ ⟨an unusually ~ year⟩ **b** : deficient in ideas or originality of thought ⟨a ~ author⟩ ⟨~ prose⟩ **c** : free from living organisms and esp. microorganisms ⟨a ~ cyst⟩ ⟨dead ~ soil⟩ — compare STERILIZE **3** : serving no useful purpose : withheld from a normal use or function ⟨capital kept ~ through lack of initiative⟩ ⟨excessive and ~ reserves⟩

syn STERILE, BARREN, IMPOTENT, UNFRUITFUL, INFERTILE mean not having or not manifesting the power to produce offspring or bear fruit, literally or figuratively. STERILE implies literal inability, stressing some defect or lack in the reproductive functions; it has a strong figurative use, implying a lack or absence of creative vigor ⟨a *sterile* woman⟩ ⟨a *sterile* ram⟩ ⟨a *sterile* author⟩ ⟨the failure of the three characters to emerge as individuals makes their personal drama seem *sterile* —*Amer. Scholar*⟩ ⟨for him man is always the wanderer in the oppressive and *sterile* world of materialism —Alfred Kazin⟩ ⟨lies at an elevation of from 500 to 1,500 feet, and consists mainly of saline wastes and other *sterile* tracts —*Encyc. Americana*⟩ BARREN applies esp. to a female who has borne no offspring or is incapable of bearing offspring, stressing, literally and figuratively, the lack of issue ⟨a *barren* woman⟩ ⟨a *barren* soil⟩ ⟨nine *barren* years of marriage —Alice Lake⟩ ⟨I am very *barren* of American news —H.J. Laski⟩ IMPOTENT in this sense applies esp. to a male lacking the ability to engage in sexual intercourse and so to produce his kind, carrying more generally the implication of inability to act or suggesting some lack of manliness or natural vigor ⟨an *impotent* man⟩ ⟨nothing is quite so *impotent* in politics as a defeated candidate —W.A.White⟩ ⟨drove the choleric old man into a fit of *impotent* fury —Charles Reade⟩ UNFRUITFUL, interchangeable with BARREN though less forceful and absolute, has a more widespread figurative than literal use ⟨an *unfruitful* orchard⟩ ⟨an *unfruitful* enterprise⟩ ⟨*unfruitful* negotiations between belligerent states⟩ INFERTILE, a factual and neutral word, carries the sense of STERILE, esp. in literal application ⟨an *infertile* marriage⟩ ⟨an *infertile* valley⟩ ⟨an *infertile* line of research⟩

ster·ile·ly \-l(l)ē, -li\ *adv* : in a sterile manner : so as to be or remain sterile

ste·ril·i·ty \stəˈriləd·ē, steˈ-, -lətē, -i\ *n* -ES [ME *sterylite*, fr. MF *sterilité*, fr. L *sterilitat-*, *sterilitas*, fr. *sterilis* sterile + *-itat-*, *-itas* -ity] : the quality or state of being sterile

ster·i·liz·abil·i·ty \,sterə,līzəˈbiləd·ē, -lətē, -i\ *n* : the quality or state of being sterilizable

ster·i·liz·able \sterəˈlīzəbəl\ *adj* : capable of being sterilized

ster·i·liza·tion \¦==lәˈzāshən, -,līˈz-\ *n* -s **1** : the act or process of sterilizing: as **a** : the rendering of a body or material free from living cells and esp. microorganisms usu. by killing those present (as by heat) — see FRACTIONAL STERILIZATION; compare PASTEURIZATION **b** : a procedure by which a human or other animal is made incapable of reproduction — compare CASTRATION, SPAYING **c** : a preventing of a monetary factor from exerting its wonted influence ⟨~ of a gold reserve⟩ **2** : the condition of one that is sterile or sterilized

ster·i·lize \ˈsterə,līz\ *vt* -ED/-ING/-S *see -ize in Explan Notes* [*sterile* + *-ize*] : to cause to become sterile, barren, or unproductive: as **a** : to cause (land) to become unfruitful whether by exhaustion of fertility or deliberately by use of a sterilant **b** : to deprive of the power of reproducing (as by surgical removal or inhibition of function of the reproductive organs) : make incapable of germination or fecundation **c** (1) : to cause to become void of something desirable (as ideas, emotions, intelligence) ⟨parental pressure that ~*s* an inquiring young mind⟩ (2) : to make powerless, ineffective, or useless usu. by restraining from a normal function, relation, or participation ⟨capital *sterilized* by hoarding⟩; *specif* : to prevent (gold) from serving as a basis for a monetary expansion **d** : to free from living microorganisms usu. by the use of physical or chemical agents — compare PASTEURIZE

ster·i·liz·er \-zə(r)\ *n* -s **:** one that sterilizes something: as **a :** an apparatus for sterilizing by the agency of boiling water, steam, or dry heat — see AUTOCLAVE **b :** one whose work is sterilizing something (as food, materials, equipment)

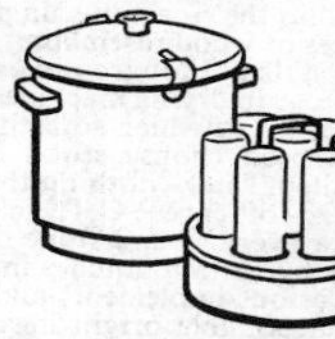
sterilizer for bottles

sterk·fon·tein ape–man \'sterkfən,tān-\ *n, usu cap S* [fr. *Sterkfontein,* farm near Johannesburg, So. Africa, where the specimens were found] **:** an extinct southern African anthropoid (*Australopithecus transvaalensis* or *Plesianthropus transvaalensis*) known from numerous parts of skulls, teeth, and other skeletal fragments recovered from cave bone breccia

ster·let \'stərlət\ *n* -s [Russ *sterlyad',* of Gmc origin; akin to OHG *sturio* sturgeon — more at STURGEON] **:** a small sturgeon (*Acipenser ruthenus*) found esp. in the Caspian sea and its rivers and highly esteemed for its flavor and its caviar

¹ster·ling \'stərliŋ, 'stəl-, 'stəil-, -lēŋ\ *n* -s [ME, prob. fr. (assumed) OE *steorling,* fr. OE *steorra* star + *-ling;* prob. fr. the star engraved on some of the early pennies — more at STAR] **1 a :** the silver penny of medieval England **b :** the legal currency of England and from 1707 of Great Britain **c :** British money **:** British foreign exchange **2 :** sterling silver or articles made of it ⟨a set of ~⟩ — compare PLATE 2, 3a **3 :** an Australian colonist born in England

²sterling \"\ *adj* [ME, fr. *¹sterling*] **1 a :** of, relating to, or calculated in terms of British sterling ⟨~ prices⟩ **b :** payable or involving payment in sterling ⟨a ~ bill⟩ ⟨~ exchange⟩ **2 a** *of silver* **:** having a fixed standard of purity from admixture or alloy that is usu. defined legally as represented by an alloy of 925 parts of silver with 75 parts of copper **b :** made of sterling silver **3 :** of full value or first quality **:** conforming to the highest standard **:** GENUINE ⟨~ merit⟩ ⟨a ~ character⟩ — **ster·ling·ly** *adv* — **ster·ling·ness** *n* -ES

sterling area *or* **sterling bloc** *n* **:** the United Kingdom and the countries that tie their currencies to the British pound sterling and pool their foreign exchange resources to a large extent

¹stern \'stərn, 'stən\ *n* -s [fr. (assumed) ME *sterne,* fr. OE *stearn,* a bird, prob. tern — more at STARLING] *dial Brit* **:** TERN

²stern \'stərn, 'stən, 'stəin\ *adj* -ER/-EST [ME *sterne, stirne, stierne,* fr. OE *styrne, stierne;* akin to OHG *stornēn* to startle, frighten, *storrēn* to project stiffly, Goth *andstaurran* to scold, OE *starian* to stare — more at STARE] **1 a :** having a definite hardness or severity of nature or manner **:** severely strict **:** EXACTING, UNCOMPROMISING, UNBENDING, INFLEXIBLE, RIGOROUS, AUSTERE ⟨equally ~ to himself and others⟩ ⟨a ~ discipline⟩ ⟨~ taskmasters⟩ **b** *obs* **:** lacking pity or mercy **:** CRUEL **c :** proceeding from or characteristic of a severe nature **:** expressive of severe displeasure **:** HARSH ⟨a ~ look⟩ ⟨returned a ~ answer⟩ **2 a :** forbidding or gloomy in appearance **:** lacking in pleasing or attractive aspects **:** INHOSPITABLE, UNINVITING ⟨a ~ coastline⟩ ⟨a ~ land demanding much and returning little⟩ **b :** rigorously severe in style **:** lacking enhancing ornamentation or softening detail ⟨a ~, sturdy, and purely utilitarian hall⟩ **3 :** of a compelling sort **:** INEXORABLE ⟨yielding to ~ necessity⟩ **4 :** of sturdy make or quality **:** having strong power to resist **:** STOUT ⟨made a ~ resolve to win⟩ ⟨only the ~*est* spirits can enjoy such a climate⟩ **syn** see SEVERE

³stern \"\ *adv* [ME *sterne, stirne,* fr. *sterne, stirne,* adj.] **:** in a stern manner **:** STERNLY — often used in combination ⟨facing us with *stern*-set face⟩

⁴stern \'stern\ *var of* STARN

⁵stern \'stərn, 'stən, 'stəin, *dial* 'stärn *or* 'stän\ *n* -s [ME *sterne,* prob. of Scand origin; akin to ON *stjōrn* act of steering, *stȳra* to steer — more at STEER] **1** *obs* **a :** the helm or tiller of a boat; *also* **:** RUDDER **b :** direction by or as if by a rudder **:** STEERAGE **c :** a post of management or direction ⟨sit at chiefest ~ of public weal —Shak.⟩ **2 :** the after or rear end of a ship; *specif* **:** the portion of the hull abaft the rudderpost or sternpost — see COUNTER illustration **3 :** a hinder or rear part of something **:** the last or a latter part: as **a :** BUTTOCKS, RUMP, BEHIND — not often in formal use **b :** TAIL 1a(1) — used of a hound — **by the stern** *adv* **:** with the stern lower in the water or sinking or settling first ⟨a boat anchored *by the stern*⟩ ⟨sank *by the stern*⟩

⁶stern \"\ *vb* -ED/-ING/-S [ME *sternen,* fr. *sterne* stern of a ship] *vt* **1** *obs* **:** STEER **2 :** to move (a boat) stern first ~ *vi* **:** to back water **:** row backward

⁷stern \"\ *adj* [*⁵stern*] **1 a :** of, relating to, or situated at or near the stern of a ship **b :** fastened or secured to or securing the stern **2 :** following, pursuing, or characterized by pursuit astern

stern- *or* **sterno-** *comb form* [F, fr. Gk, fr. *sternon* — more at STERNUM] **1 :** breast **:** sternum **:** breastbone ⟨*stern*algia⟩ ⟨*stern*ad⟩ **2 :** sternal and ⟨*sterno*cleidomastoid⟩

¹sterna *pl of* STERNUM

²ster·na \'stərnə\ *n, cap* [NL, fr. E *stern* tern — more at STERN] **:** a genus of typical terns (family Laridae) including forms that have a slender bill, narrow pointed wings, a forked tail, and mostly white coloration with a black cap and a bluish gray mantle

ster·nad \'stər,nad\ *adv* [*stern-* + *-ad*] **:** toward the sternum

ster·nal \'stərnᵊl, 'stən-, 'stəin-\ *adj* [NL *sternalis*] **1 :** of, relating to, or involving the sternum **2 a :** situated in the region of the sternum or a sternite **:** VENTRAL **b :** of or relating to a sternite

ster·na·lis \,stər'nāləs\ *n, pl* **sternales** \-(,)lēz\ [NL, sternal, sternalis, fr. *stern-* + L *-alis* -al] **:** a muscle nearly parallel to the sternum that is sometimes found on the surface of the pectoralis major

sternal rib *n* **1 :** a rib whose costal cartilage connects with the sternum **:** TRUE RIB **2 :** the ventral segment of a rib of some animals that represents an ossified costal cartilage

stern·berg cell \'stərn,bərg-\ *also* **sternberg–reed cell** \-'rēd-\ *n, usu cap S&R* [after Carl *Sternberg* †1935 Ger. pathologist] **:** a multinucleate acidophil giant cell found in the tissues in Hodgkin's disease

stern·ber·gia \,stərn'bər|gēə, |jēə\ *n* [NL, fr. Count Kaspar M. von *Sternberg* †1838 + NL *-ia*] **1** *cap* **:** a genus of low bulbous herbs (family Amaryllidaceae) native to the Mediterranean region but widely used as ornamentals and having ribbon-shaped leaves and autumn-blooming yellow flowers that resemble crocuses **2** -s **:** any plant of the genus *Sternbergia*

stern·berg·ite \'stərn,bər,gīt\ *n* -s [Count Kaspar M. von *Sternberg* †1838 Bohemian naturalist + E *-ite*] **:** a dark brown mineral ($AgFe_2S_3$) that is a silver iron sulfide and occurs in tabular crystals or soft flexible laminae

stern board *n* **1 :** a going or falling astern in sailing esp. as caused by missing stays **:** STERNWAY ⟨make a *stern board* into the wind⟩ **2 :** a board forming the flat part of the stern of a small ship

stern boat *n* **:** a ship's boat carried at or near the stern

sterncastle \'⸗,⸗⸗\ *n* [*⁵stern* + *castle*] **:** AFTERCASTLE

stern chase *n* [*⁵stern*] **1 :** a chase in which the pursuing vessel follows in the path of the vessel pursued ⟨a *stern chase* is a long chase⟩ **2 :** STERN CHASER

stern chaser *n* **:** a gun so placed (as on a warship) as to be able to fire astern at a vessel that may be in chase

ster·ne·bra \'stərnəbrə\ *n, pl* **sterne·brae** \-,brē, -brī\ [NL, fr. *stern-* + *-ebra* (as in *vertebra*)] **:** a segment of the sternum of a vertebrate — **ster·ne·bral** \-brəl\ *adj*

ster·nel·lum \,stər'neləm\ *n, pl* **sternel·la** \-lə\ [NL, fr. *stern-* + L *-ellum* -el] **:** the posterior plate of a thoracic sternite

sterner *comparative of* STERN

sternest *superlative of* STERN

stern fast *or* **stern line** *n* **:** a line used to secure a boat by the stern

sternforemost \'⸗'⸗(,)⸗\ *adv* [*⁵stern* + *foremost*] **:** with the stern in advance **:** BACKWARD; *also* **:** AWKWARDLY

stern frame *n* **1 :** the timbers in a wooden ship constituting the upper part of stern or counter **2 :** the forging or casting in a steel ship including in one piece the propeller post with boss, the sternpost with gudgeons, and the arch and solepiece

stern gallery *n* **:** a platform around the stern of an old wooden ship

stern hook *n* **:** a horizontal framework for strengthening the attachment of the sides to the sternpost of a ship

sterning *pres part of* STERN

ster·nite \'stər,nīt\ *n* -s [ISV *stern-* + *-ite*] **:** the ventral part or shield of a somite of an arthropod; *esp* **:** the chitinous plate that forms the ventral surface of an abdominal or occas. a thoracic segment of an insect — **ster·nit·ic** \(')stər¦nid·ik\ *adj*

stern knee *n* [so called fr. its shape] **:** STERNSON

stern·less \'⸗ləs\ *adj* [ME *sterneles,* fr. *sterne* stern + *-les* -less — more at STERN (rudder)] *obs* **:** RUDDERLESS

stern light *n* **:** a white running light displayed on the stern of a ship

stern·ly *adv* [ME *sternely,* fr. OE *styrnlic, stiernlic,* fr. *styrne, stierne* stern + *-lic* -ly — more at STERN (strict)] **:** in a stern manner **:** with sternness

stern·man \'⸗mən\ *n, pl* **sternmen** [*⁵stern* + *man*] **1** *obs* **:** STEERSMAN **2 :** one (as a rower or paddler) stationed at or occupying the stern of a craft

stern·most \'⸗,mōst *also chiefly Brit* -,məst\ *adj* [*⁵stern* + *-most* (as in *foremost*)] **:** farthest astern

stern·ness \-nnəs\ *n* -ES [ME *sternesse,* fr. *sterne* stern + *-nesse* -ness] **:** the quality or state of being stern

sterno- — see STERN-

¹ster·no·clei·do·mas·toid \,stər(,)nō¦klīdə¦ma,stȯid\ *adj* [NL *sternocleidomastoides,* fr. *stern-* + *cleid-* + *mastoides* mastoid] **:** of, relating to, or constituting a thick superficial muscle on each side arising by one head from the first segment of the sternum and a second from the inner part of the clavicle and inserted into the mastoid and occipital bone

²sternocleidomastoid \"\ *n* **:** a sternocleidomastoid muscle

ster·no·costal \¦stərnə+\ *adj* [*stern-* + *costal*] **:** of, relating to, or situated between the sternum and ribs

ster·no·fa·ci·a·lis \,stər(,)nō,fās(h)ē'aləs, -āl-, -äl-\ *n, pl* **sternofaciales** [NL, fr. *stern-* + *facialis,* alter. (influenced by *facialis* facial) of *fascialis* fascial] **:** an inconstant slip of muscle arising from the sternum and inserting into the fascia of the neck

¹ster·no·hyoid \"+\ *adj* [NL *sternohyoides,* fr. *stern-* + *hyoides* hyoid] **:** of or relating to the sternum and the hyoid bone or cartilage; *specif* **:** constituting a muscle on each side of the midline extending from the medial end of the clavicle and the first segment of the sternum to the body of the hyoid bone

²sternohyoid \"\ *n* **:** a sternohyoid muscle

ster·no·mastoid muscle \¦⸗⸗+-\ *n* [*stern-* + *mastoid*] **:** STERNOCLEIDOMASTOID

ster·no·scapular \"+\ *adj* [*stern-* + *scapular*] **:** connecting the sternum and scapula; *specif* **:** constituting a muscle that in many mammals helps to support the anterior part of the body upon the forelimbs

ster·no·the·rus \,⸗⸗'thirəs\ *n, cap* [NL, fr. *stern-* + Gk *thairos* pivot, axle] **:** a genus of No. American turtles of the family Kinosternidae — see MUSK TURTLE

¹ster·no·thyroid \¦⸗⸗+\ *adj* [NL *sternothyroides,* fr. *stern-* + *thyroides* thyroid] **:** of, relating to, or situated between the sternum and the thyroid cartilage; *specif* **:** constituting a muscle on each side of the body extending beneath the sternohyoid muscle

²sternothyroid \"\ *n* **:** a sternothyroid muscle

ster·no·tribe \'⸗⸗,trīb\ *adj* [*stern-* + *-tribe*] **:** touching the undersurface; *esp* **:** having stamens and pistils so arranged as to touch the sternum of a visiting insect ⟨~ flowers⟩

sternpost \'⸗,⸗\ *n* [*⁵stern* + *post*] **:** the principal and usu. vertical member at the after end of a ship extending from keel to deck and taking the after ends of the planking in a wooden ship and of the plates in a steel ship

sterns *pl of* STERN, *pres 3d sing of* STERN

stern sheets *n pl* **:** the space in the stern of an open boat not occupied by the thwarts

stern·son \'stərn(t)sᵊn\ *n* -s [*⁵stern* + *keelson*] **:** the end of a keelson to which the sternpost of a ship is bolted

stern tube *n* **1 :** a long bushing or bearing through the stern of a ship to support the after part of the propeller shaft **2 :** a torpedo tube located at the stern

ster·num \'stərnəm, 'stən-, 'stəin-\ *n, pl* **sternums** \-mz\ *or* **ster·na** \-nə\ [NL, fr. Gk *sternon* breast, chest, breastbone; akin to OHG *stirna* forehead, Skt *stīrṇa* spread, strewn, L *sternere* to spread out — more at STREW] **1 :** a bone or cartilage or a series of more or less distinct bony or cartilaginous segments lying in the median ventral part of the body of most vertebrates above fishes, connecting with the ribs or the shoulder girdle or with both, being in man about seven inches long, consisting in the adult of three parts, connecting with the clavicles and the cartilages of the upper seven pairs of ribs, and being in birds modified into a single broad bony plate that usu. bears a high median keel for the attachment of the wing muscles **:** BREASTBONE — see BAT illustration **2 a :** the ventral part of a somite of an arthropod **b :** the whole ventral wall of the arthropod thorax

ster·nu·ta·tion \,stərnyə'tāshən, -yü't-\ *n* -s [L *sternutation-, sternutatio,* fr. *sternutatus* (past part. of *sternutare,* freq. of *sternuere* to sneeze) + *-ion-, -io* -ion; akin to Gk *ptarnysthai* to sneeze, *ptarmos* act of sneezing, OIr *sreod*] **:** the act, fact, or noise of sneezing **:** SNEEZE

ster·nu·ta·tor \'⸗⸗,tād·ə(r)\ *n* -s [back-formation fr. *sternutatory*] **:** an agent (as a gas) that induces a flow of nasal secretion or causes sneezing

¹ster·nu·ta·to·ry \,stər'nyüd·ə,tōrē\ *or* **ster·nu·ta·tive** \-d·əd·iv, 'stərnyə,tād·iv, -yü,t-\ *adj* [*sternutatory* fr. LL *sternutatorius,* fr. L *sternutatus* (past part. of *sternutare*) + *-orius* -ory; *sternutative* fr. L *sternutatus* + E *-ive*] **:** inducing sneezing; *also* **:** of, relating to, or marked by sneezing

²sternutatory \"\ *n* -ES [LL *sternutatorium,* neut. of *sternutatorius* of sneezing] **:** STERNUTATOR

stern walk *n, chiefly Brit* **:** a gallery around the stern of an old-time man-of-war

stern·ward \'⸗wə(r)d\ *or* **stern·wards** \-dz\ *adv (or adj)* [*⁵stern* + *-ward, -wards*] **:** AFT, ASTERN

stern wave *n* **:** a wave formed at the stern of a boat under way — compare BOW WAVE

sternway \'⸗,⸗\ *n* **:** movement of a ship backward or with her stern foremost — compare STEERAGEWAY

stern·ways \'⸗,wāz\ *adv* [*⁵stern* + *-ways*] **:** toward the stern

stern wheel *n* **:** a paddle wheel at the stern of a boat

stern–wheeler \'⸗¦⸗⸗\ *n* **:** a paddle steamer having a stern wheel instead of side wheels

¹steroid \'sti(ə),rȯid, -te(-\ *n* -s [ISV *sterol* + *-oid*] **:** any of a class of compounds that are characterized by a polycyclic structure like that of the sterols and that usu. include the sterols and vitamin D as well as many other naturally occurring compounds (as the bile acids and various hormones and glycosides) — compare CHOLESTEROL illustration

²steroid \"\ *or* **ste·roi·dal** \stə'rȯidᵊl, ste'r-\ *adj* [*steroidal* fr. *¹steroid* + *-al*] **1 :** resembling a sterol esp. in chemical structure **2 :** of, relating to, or being a steroid

steroid hormone *n* **:** any of numerous hormones (as the sex hormones, cortisone, and adrenocortical hormones) characterized by steroid structure ⟨*steroid hormones* of animal origin —J.S.Fruton & Sofia Simmonds⟩

sterol \'ste,rōl, 'sti,r-, -rōl\ *n* -s [ISV, fr. *-sterol* (as in *cholesterol*)] **:** any of a class of solid complex cyclic alcohols (as cholesterol, ergosterol, and stigmasterol) that are widely distributed in the unsaponifiable portion of lipides in animals and plants and are characterized by a tetracyclic structure involving fusion of a cyclopentane ring to a partially or completely hydrogenated phenanthrene ring system

ster·ras·ter \stə'rastə(r)\ *n* -s [NL, fr. Gk *sterros* firm, solid (akin to Gk *stereos* solid) + NL *-aster* — more at STARE] **:** a spherical sponge spicule with many small rays

ster·rett·ite \'sterə,tīt\ *n* -s [Douglas B. *Sterrett* b1883 Am. geologist + E *-ite*] **:** a mineral $Al_6(PO_4)_4(OH)_6.5H_2O$ consisting of a hydrous basic aluminum phosphate

ster·rinck \'steriŋk\ *n* -s [prob. modif. of NL *Stenorhynchus,* genus of seals, fr. *sten-* + *-rhynchus*] **:** CRABEATER SEAL

ster·ro metal \'ste(,)rō-\ *n* [ISV *sterro* (fr. Gk *sterros* firm, solid) + *metal*] **:** a hard brass containing a little iron

-sters *pl of* -STER

ster·tor \'stərd·ər\ *n* -s [NL, fr. L *stertere* to snore + *-or;* akin to OIr *srennim* I snore, *sreod* act of sneezing — more at STERNUTATION] **:** the act or an instance of producing a snoring or rasping sound in respiration because of obstruction (as in sleep or coma) of air passages of the head

ster·to·rous \-d·ərəs\ *adj* [NL *stertor* + E *-ous*] **1 :** characterized by a harsh snoring or gasping sound **:** exhibiting or marked by stertor ⟨~ breathing⟩ **2 :** marked by snoring ⟨a ~ nap by the hearth⟩ **syn** see LOUD

ster·to·rous·ly *adv* **:** in a stertorous manner

ste·sich·o·re·an \stə¦sikə¦rēən\ *adj, usu cap* [*Stesichorus* †550? B.C. Greek poet + E *-an*] **:** of or relating to Stesichorus the chief early composer of Dorian lyrics and probable establisher of strophe, antistrophe, and epode as the normal structure for choral lyric

¹stet \'stet, *usu* -ed·+V\ *vt* **stetted; stetted; stetting; stets** [L, let it stand, 3d pers. sing. pres. subj. of *stare* to stand — more at STAND] **:** to annotate with the word *stet* or otherwise mark (as with a series of subscript dots) to nullify a previous order to delete or omit (a word or passage in a manuscript or printer's proof)

²stet \"\ *n* -s [by shortening] **:** STET PROCESSUS

³stet \"\ *vt* **stetted; stetted; stetting; stets :** to order a stet processus on

stetch \'stech\ *dial chiefly Brit var of* ¹STITCH 4

stet·e·feldt furnace \'sted·ə,felt-\ *n, usu cap S* [after Charles A. *Stetefeldt,* 20th cent. Am. mining engineer, its inventor] **:** a shaft furnace in which silver ores are desulfurized and chloridized by dropping them pulverized and mixed with salt through a heated atmosphere

steth- *or* **stetho-** *comb form* [F, fr. Gk *stēth-, stētho-,* fr. *stēthos*] **:** breast **:** chest ⟨*steth*arteritis⟩ ⟨*stetho*meter⟩

stetho·gram \'stethə,gram, -raa(ə)m\ *n* [*steth-* + *-gram*] **:** PHONOCARDIOGRAM

stetho·graph \-,graf, -raa(ə)f, -raif, -ráf\ *n* [ISV *steth-* + *-graph*] **:** an instrument that records graphically the heart sounds heard through a stethoscope — **stetho·graph·ic** \¦⸗⸗¦grafik\ *adj*

ste·thog·ra·phy \stə'thägrəfē, ste'-, -fi\ *n* -ES [ISV *steth-* + *-graphy;* prob. orig. formed as G *stethographie*] **:** PHONOCARDIOGRAPHY

ste·thom·e·ter \⸗'thäməd·ə(r), -mətə-\ *n* [ISV *steth-* + *-meter*] **:** an apparatus for measuring the expansion of the chest wall during respiration — **stetho·met·ric** \¦stethə¦me·trik\ *adj* — **ste·thom·e·try** \stə'thämətrē, ste'-\ *n* -ES

¹stetho·scope \'stethə,skōp *also* 'steth-\ *n* [F *stéthoscope,* fr. *stéth-* steth- + *-scope*] **1 :** an instrument used for the detection and study of sounds within the body (as chest, abdomen) that are conveyed to the ears of the observer through rubber tubing connected with an endpiece placed upon the area to be examined **2 :** an instrument resembling a stethoscope that is used to detect flaws in metal

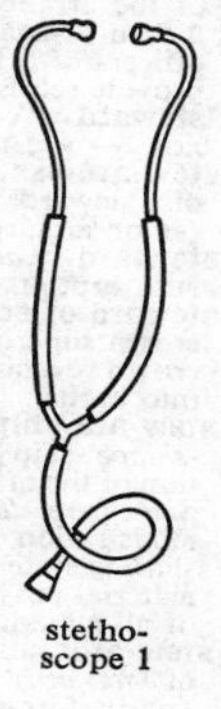
stethoscope 1

²stethoscope \"\ *vt* -ED/-ING/-S **:** to examine by means of a stethoscope ⟨*stethoscoped* the patient's chest⟩

stetho·scop·ic \¦⸗⸗¦skäpik, -pēk\ *or* **stetho·scop·i·cal** \-pəkəl, -pēk-\ *adj* [*stethoscope* + *-ic* or *-ical*] **:** of, relating to, or obtained or made by means of a stethoscope — **stetho·scop·i·cal·ly** \-pək(ə)lē, -pēk-, li\ *adv*

ste·thos·co·py \ste'thäskəpē, 'stethə,skōpē\ *n* -ES [ISV *stethoscope* + *-y*] **:** examination by means of the stethoscope

stet pro·ces·sus \'stet prō'sesəs\ *n* [L, let the process stop] **:** an entry in law staying all proceedings in an action; *also* **:** an order granting such a stay

stet·son \'stetsən\ *also* **stetson hat** *n* -s [fr. *Stetson,* a trademark] **:** a broad-brimmed felt hat with a high crown; *esp* **:** COWBOY HAT

stet·tin \(')s(h)te¦tēn\ *adj, usu cap* [fr. *Stettin* (now *Szczecin,* Poland), city in the former government district of Stettin in northern Prussia, Germany] **:** of or from the city of Stettin, Germany **:** of the kind or style prevalent in Stettin

Steu·ben \'st(y)übən *also* '⸗,bən\ *trademark* — used for glassware often of heavy design and decorated with engraved figures

stev *or* **steve** *abbr* stevedore

¹steve·dore \'stēvə,dō(ə)r, -dȯ(ə)r, -ōə, -ȯ(ə) *also* -v,d-\ *n* -s [Sp *estibador* packer, stower, fr. *estibar* to pack, stow, fr. L *stipare* to press together — more at STIFF] **:** one who works at or one who is responsible for the unloading of a ship in port

²stevedore \"\ *vb* -ED/-ING/-S *vt* **:** to work at or undertake responsibility for the loading and unloading of (a ship) ~ *vi* **:** to load or unload a ship **:** assume responsibility for loading and unloading cargoes ⟨talked you into coming to this town to ~ —R.F.Mirvish⟩

stevedore knot *or* **stevedore's knot** *n* **:** a stopper knot similar to a figure eight knot but with one or more extra turns

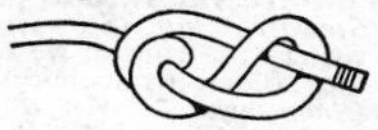
stevedore knot

stev·en \'stevən\ *n* -s [ME, fr. OE *stefn, stemn* voice, sound; akin to OFris *stifne, stemme* voice, OHG *stimna, stimma,* Goth *stibna*] **1** *dial chiefly Brit* **:** VOICE **2** *dial chiefly Brit* **:** NOISE, UPROAR

ste·ven·so·nian \,stēvən'sōnēən, -nyən\ *adj, usu cap* [Robert Louis *Stevenson* †1894 Scot. essayist, novelist and poet + E *-an*] **:** of, relating to, or characteristic of Robert Louis Stevenson or his writings **:** having the manner or style of Stevenson ⟨a real essay — *Stevensonian* . . . in its sustained and personal touch —August Heckscher⟩

ste·ven·so·niana \,⸗⸗,sōnē'anə, -'änə, -'ānə *also* -'ānə\ *n pl but sing in constr, usu cap* [NL, fr. Robert Louis *Stevenson* †1894 + NL *-ana*] **:** writings by or about Robert Louis Stevenson ⟨a collector and editor of minor *Stevensoniana* —*Yale Rev.*⟩

ste·via \'stēvēə, -vyə\ *n* [NL, irreg. fr. P. J. *Esteve* †1556 Sp. botanist + NL *-ia*] **1 a** *cap* **:** a genus of shrubs and herbs (family Compositae) chiefly of warm regions of the New World having glutinous foliage and white or purplish flowers **b** -s **:** any plant of *Stevia* or the related genus *Piqueria* **2** -s **:** WHITE SNAKEROOT

ste·vi·o·side \'stēvēə,sīd\ *n* -s [*stevios-* (irreg. fr. NL *Stevia,* genus name of *Stevia rebaudiana*) + *-ide*] **:** a hygroscopic crystalline intensely sweet glucoside $C_{38}H_{60}O_{18}$ obtained from the leaves of a Paraguayan shrub (*Stevia rebaudiana*)

¹stew \'st(y)ü\ *n* -s [ME *stu, stewe,* fr. MF *estuve,* fr. (assumed) VL *extufa,* fr. *extufare* to stew — more at STEW (v.)] **1 a** *obs* **:** a utensil used for boiling **b** *obs* **:** something resembling a stew ⟨I have seen corruption boil and bubble till it o'errun the ~ —Shak.⟩ **2 a :** a heated room where hot baths are furnished **b :** a hot bath **3 a :** BROTHEL ⟨squander every penny of their pay in waterfront ~*s* —*New Yorker*⟩ **b :** a district characterized by brothels; *typically* **:** a slum area — usu. used in pl. ⟨housed hundreds of free Negroes in the ~*s* of those days —*Reporter*⟩ **4 a :** food prepared by stewing in liquid (as water or milk); *esp* **:** a combination of fish or meat usu. with vegetables prepared in this way ⟨beef ~⟩ ⟨oyster ~⟩ **b :** something resembling a cooked stew: as (1) **:** a heterogeneous mixture ⟨a ~ of all the . . . measures ever suggested by anyone —R.H. Rovere⟩ (2) **:** a state of heat and congestion ⟨the tropical ~ of downtown Philadelphia —Alistair Cooke⟩ **5 :** a state of agitating excitement, worry, or confusion ⟨everyone went into a terribly silly ~ about it —Eve Langley⟩

²stew \"\ *n* -s [ME *stewe,* fr. MF *estui* case, tub, tank, fr. *estuier* to enclose, watch, prob. fr. (assumed) VL *studiare* to watch, guard, apply oneself to one thing, fr. L *studium* study — more at STUDY] **1** *Brit* **:** a tank or small pond for keeping fish often until they are wanted for cooking **2 :** an artificial bed of oysters

³stew \"\ *vb* -ED/-ING/-S [ME *stuen, stewen,* fr. MF *estuver,* fr. (assumed) VL *extufare,* prob. fr. L *ex-* ex- + (assumed) VL *tufus* hot vapor, fr. Gk *typhos* vapor, smoke; akin to L *fumus* smoke — more at FUME] *vt* **1 :** to boil slowly or with a simmering heat **:** to cook in a little liquid over a gentle fire without boiling ⟨~*ed* the beef for goulash⟩ **2** *archaic* **:** to keep con-

fined in or as if in a hot or stuffy atmosphere — usu. used with *up* **3** *archaic* : IMBUE, STEEP ⟨live . . . ~*ed* in corruption —Shak.⟩ **4** *obs* : to bathe in perspiration ⟨a reeking post, ~*ed* in his haste, half breathless, panting —Shak.⟩ **5** : to bring to an extreme state usu. by worry or excitement — usu. used with *up* ⟨so ~*ed up* with anxiety that he couldn't wait —John Morrison⟩ ~ *vi* **1** : to undergo cooking in or as if in a slow simmering manner : become cooked by stewing **2** : to swelter esp. from confinement in a hot or stuffy atmosphere ⟨a handful of . . . secretaries ~ in the cramped and cluttered Third Room —E.O.Hauser⟩ **3** : to study hard : SWEAT **4** : to become agitated or worried : FRET ⟨been ~*ing* over this thing all night —Erle Stanley Gardner⟩ — **stew in one's own juice** : to suffer the discomfort of conditions or circumstances brought about by oneself

¹stew·ard \ˈst(y)üə(r)d, -)ü(ə)rd, -)ůəd\ *n* -s [ME, fr. OE *stīweard, stigweard,* fr. *stī, stig* pen, hall, sty + *weard* ward — more at STY, WARD] **1** : one called to exercise responsible care over possessions entrusted to him ⟨a ~ of the time, talent, and treasure entrusted to his care⟩ **2 a** *obs* : an officer or employee of a household charged with the general administration of its affairs **b** : a head manager of a manor or estate presiding at the manorial courts, auditing accounts, conducting inquests and extents, and controlling the husbandry arrangements **c** : one employed on a large estate usu. to manage its affairs, supervise workmen, collect rents or income, and keep accounts **3** : SHOP STEWARD **4 a** : a magistrate appointed by the Scottish crown to exercise jurisdiction over lands forfeited to the crown **b** : an English judicial officer joining with the verderers in proceedings under the forest laws **5 a** : an officer in charge of finances (as of a guild or an English municipality) : a fiscal agent **b** : one of a body of officers in charge of the finances and some other temporal interests of a local Methodist church **6 a** (1) : one employed on board ship to do the catering and superintend culinary affairs (2) : an employee on a passenger ship who performs various services for the comfort and needs of the passengers ⟨room ~⟩ ⟨deck ~⟩ **b** : an employee on an airplane, bus, or train who manages the provisioning of food sometimes preparing and serving meals and who may attend to other duties (as seating or the checking of passenger lists, safety belts, and baggage) **7 a** : an officer of a college who has charge of the commons **b** : one appointed to supervise the provision and distribution of food and drink in an institution (as a hotel, club, hospital) **c** : one who operates a commissary **8 a** : one who actively directs affairs : MANAGER ⟨the ~*s* of a jockey club⟩ **b** *Brit* : a person who assists in the supervision of the arrangements of a large gathering of people : USHER **c** : an assistant to an animal show judge **9** : either of two officers of a Masonic lodge whose duties are to collect dues, provide refreshments, and perform other similar services

²steward \"\ *vb* -ED/-ING/-S *vt* : to act as a steward for : MANAGE ~ *vi* : to perform the duties of a steward

stew·ard·ess \-dəs\ *n* -ES : a woman who performs the duties of a steward; *esp* : one who attends to the needs of passengers (as on an airplane, ship, or train)

stew·ard·ly *adj* : characterized by careful management : CAREFUL, FRUGAL, PRUDENT

steward of scotland *cap 2d S* : a high officer of the Scottish crown superintending the royal household, administering the crown revenues, and having the privilege of leading the army into battle

stew·ard·ship \-ˌship\ *n* [ME *stewardshippe,* fr. *steward* + *-shippe* -ship] **1 a** : the office of steward **b** : the administration of the office of steward and of goods or duties entrusted to one's care **2** : the aspect of the religious life and church administration dealing with the individual's responsibility for sharing systematically and proportionately his time, talent, and material possessions in the service of God and for the benefit of all mankind

stew·ards·man \-dzmən\ *n, pl* **stewardsmen** [*stewards* (poss. of ¹*steward*) + *man*] : a naval enlisted man who serves food and performs other duties in officers' quarters

stew·ar·tia \st(y)üˈärsh(ē)ə, -rd·ēə\ *n, cap* [NL, irreg. fr. John *Stuart* †1792 3d Earl of Bute + NL *-ia*] : a genus of American and Japanese shrubs or trees (family Theaceae) having large solitary flowers with a 5-celled ovary which becomes a woody capsule — see SILKY CAMELLIA

stew·art·ite \ˈst(y)üə(r)ˌtīt\ *n* -s [*Stewart* mine, Pala, Calif., where it was orig. found + E *-ite*] : a mineral consisting of a hydrous phosphate of manganese that is brownish yellow in color, is usu. in minute crystals and tufts of fibers, and is found with hureaulite in several pegmatites

stew·art·ry \ˈst(y)üərtrī\ *also* **stew·ard·ry** \-rdrī\ *n* -ES [ME (Sc), fr. ¹*steward* + *-ry*] **1** : a former administrative district in Scotland under the jurisdiction of a steward **2** *chiefly Scot* : the office of a steward

stew·art's disease \ˈst(y)üə(r)ts-\ *n, usu cap S* [after Fred Carlton *Stewart* †1946 Am. plant pathologist] : a disease esp. of sweet corn caused by a bacterium (*Bacterium stewartii*) in which affected plants wilt, are stunted in growth, show leaf necrosis, and die prematurely

stew·art white trout \ˈst(y)üə(r)t-\ *n, often cap S&W* [after *Stewart White* (Stewart Edward White) †1946 Am. fiction writer] : a trout of western No. America prob. identical with the golden trout but often considered a separate species (*Salmo whitei*)

stewbum \ˈ=,=\ *n* [prob. fr. ¹*stew* + *bum*] : DRUNKARD

stewed \ˈst(y)üd\ *adj* [ME, fr. past part. of *stewen* to stew — more at STEW] **1** : cooked by stewing ⟨ate a dish of ~ prunes⟩ ⟨a meal of ~ chicken and rice⟩ **2** : DRUNK ⟨stagger out of the house ~ to the gills —Margaret Long⟩

stewing *pres part of* STEW

stewpan \ˈ=,=\ *n* [¹*stew* + *pan*] : a saucepan with a long handle used for stewing

stewpond \ˈ=,=\ *n* [²*stew* + *pond*] *Brit* : a pool or tank for keeping fish ⟨~*s* in which fishes were grown and fattened for the table —J.R.Norman⟩

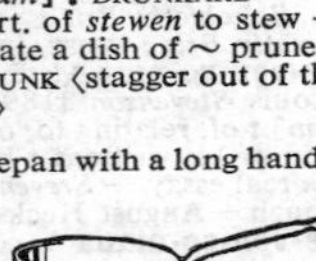
stewpan

stewpot \ˈ=,=\ *n* [¹*stew* + *pot*] : a saucepot with two hand grips used for stewing

stews *pl of* STEW, *pres 3d sing of* STEW

stey \ˈstā\ *adj* [ME (Sc) *stay*] *chiefly Scot* : STEEP

steyn *var of* STEEN

stf *abbr* **1** staff **2** stiff

stg *abbr* **1** staging **2** standing **3** sterling **4** storage

stge *abbr* storage

stgr *abbr* stringer

sth *abbr* south

STH *abbr* somatotropic hormone

sta·nak·va·si \ˌstänəkˈväsē\ *or* **sta·na·ka·va·si** \-kə'-\ *n* -s *usu cap* [Skt *sthānakavāsin,* fr. *sthānaka* secular place + *vāsin* living in, inhabiting; akin to Skt *tiṣṭhati* he stands and to Skt *vasati* he lives — more at STAND, WAS] : a member of a Jain sect originating in 1473 that rejects the use of all images and idols

sthene \ˈsthēn\ *n* -s [ISV, fr. Gk *sthenos* strength] : an mks absolute unit of force equal to 1000 newtons or 10^8 dynes

sthen·ic \ˈsthenik, -nēk\ *adj* [NL *sthenicus,* fr. Gk *sthenos* strength, force + L *-icus* -ic; perh. akin to Skt *saghnoti* he takes upon himself, is a match for] **1** : marked by excessive vitality or nervous energy : ACTIVE, STRONG ⟨~ fever⟩ **2** : indicative of strength and vigor ⟨the ~ personality type⟩ **3** : PYKNIC

sthn *abbr* southern

stib \ˈstib\ *n* -s [origin unknown] : RED-BACKED SANDPIPER

stib- *or* **stibi-** *or* **stibio-** *also* **stibo-** *comb form* [*stibium*] : antimony ⟨*stibiocolumbite*⟩ ⟨*stibophen*⟩

stib·amine \stibəˈmēn\ *n* [ISV *stib-* + *amine*] : a sodium salt of stibanilic acid injected chiefly in the form of a glucoside in the treatment of various tropical diseases

stib·anil·ic acid \ˌstibəˌnilik-\ *n* [*stib-* + *anilic*] : an unstable acid $NH_2C_6H_4SbO(OH)_2$ containing antimony that is analogous to arsanilic acid and is used in making organic antimonial drugs; *para*-amino-benzene-stibonic acid

stib·ble \ˈstibəl\ *chiefly Scot var of* STUBBLE

stib·bler \ˈstiblər\ *n* -s [origin unknown] *Scot* : a student of divinity licensed to preach but not called to a ministry

stibble–rig \ˈ==,=\ *n* **1** *Scot* : a field of stubble **2** *Scot* : the chief reaper

stib·i·al \ˈstibēəl\ *adj* [NL *stibialis,* fr. L *stibium* + *-alis* -al] : ANTIMONIC

stib·ic \ˈstibik\ *adj* [*stib-* + *-ic*] : ANTIMONIC

stib·i·co·nite \ˈstibəkəˌnīt\ *n* -s [modif. (influenced by *-ite*) of F *stibiconise,* fr. *stib-* + Gk *konis* dust — more at INCINERATE] : a mineral $Sb_3O_6(OH)$(?) consisting of a hydrous antimony oxide in yellowish masses or powder

stib·ine \ˈstiˌbēn\ *n* -s [ISV *stib-* + *-ine*] **1** : a colorless very poisonous gaseous compound SbH_3 of antimony and hydrogen that has a disagreeable odor and burns with a bluish green flame and that is usu. made by decomposing metallic antimonides with acid **2** : any of a class of organic compounds derived from stibine that are analogous to the arsines

sti·bin·ic acid \stəˈbinik-\ *n* [ISV *stibine* + *-ic*] : any of a series of organic acids of antimony having the general formula RR'SbOOH and analogous to the arsinic acids

stib·io·columbite \ˈstibē(ˌ)ō+\ *n* [*stib-* + *columbite*] : a mineral $SbCbO_4$ consisting of an oxide of antimony and columbium isomorphous with stibiotantalite

stib·i·o·pal·la·di·nite \ˌstibēōˈpalədəˌnīt\ *n* [*stib-* + *palladinite* PdO, fr. *palladium* + connective *-n-* + *-ite*] : a mineral Pd_3Sb that consists of a native alloy of palladium and antimony

stib·io·tantalite \ˈstibē(ˌ)ō+\ *n* [*stib-* + *tantalite*] : a mineral $SbTaO_4$ consisting of an oxide of antimony and tantalum isomorphous with stibiocolumbite

stib·i·ous \ˈstibēəs\ *adj* [*stib-* + *-ous*] : ANTIMONIOUS

stib·i·um \ˈstibēəm\ *n* -s [L *stibium, stibi, stimmi,* fr. Gk *stibi, stimmi,* fr. Egypt *stm*] **1** : ANTIMONY — symbol *Sb* **2** : STIBNITE; *esp* : stibnite used (as in ancient Egypt) as a cosmetic for painting the eyes

stib·nite \ˈstibˌnīt\ *n* -s [alter. (influenced by E *-ite*) of obs. E *stibine* stibnite, fr. F, fr. *stib-* + *-ine*] : a mineral Sb_2S_3 consisting of native antimony trisulfide occurring in prismatic orthorhombic crystals of lead gray color and brilliant metallic luster that show a highly perfect cleavage and are striated vertically and also in massive form and providing the chief source of antimony (hardness 2, sp. gr. 4.62)

sti·bon·ic acid \stəˈbänik-\ *n* [NL *stibonium* + E *-ic*] : any of a series of organic acids of antimony having the general formula $RSbO(OH)_2$ and analogous to the arsonic acids — compare STIBANILIC ACID

sti·bo·ni·um \stəˈbōnēəm\ *n* -s [NL, fr. *stib-* + ammon*ium*] : a univalent ion SbH_4^+ or radical SbH_4 derived from stibine and known only in the form of organic derivatives

stib·o·phen \ˈstibəˌfen\ *n* -s [*stib-* + *phene*] : a crystalline antimony derivative $C_{12}H_4Na_5O_{16}S_4Sb.7H_2O$ of pyrocatechol used in the treatment of various tropical diseases

¹stich \ˈstik\ *n* -s [Gk *stichos;* akin to Gk *steichein* to walk, go — more at STAIR] : a measured part of something written esp. in verse : LINE, VERSE

²stich \"\ *n* -s [G, sting, pricking, trick at cards, fr. OHG *stih* sting, pricking — more at STITCH] : a trick in various card games (as pinochle) that has scoring value because it is the last one

-stich \ˌstik\ *n comb form* -s [L *-stichon,* fr. Gk, fr. neut. of *-stichos* having (so many) rows or lines, fr. *stichos* row, line, verse] : poem or stanza consisting of (so many) lines ⟨*decastich*⟩ ⟨*heptastich*⟩

sti·cha·rion \stəˈkärˌyȯn\ *n, pl* **sticha·ria** \-(ˌ)yə\ [LGk, dim. of *stichē,* a kind of tunic, fr. Gk *stichos* row, line] : an ecclesiastical vestment made in the form of a tunic or long robe similar to an alb and worn by deacons and priests of the Eastern Orthodox Church

sti·che·ron \stəˈkiˌrän\ *n, pl* **stiche·ra** \-irə\ [MGk *sticheron,* fr. neut. of *sticheros* of verse, fr. Gk *stichos* row, line, verse] : a short hymn following usu. a verse from the Psalms in the Eastern Church

stich·ic \ˈstikik\ *adj* [Gk *stichikos,* fr. *stichos* + *-ikos* -ic] : of, relating to, or consisting of lines that are rhythmic units : arranged or divided by lines : serial in succession or recurrence — **stich·i·cal·ly** \-tikək(ə)lē\ *adv*

stich·id \ˈstikəd\ *n* -s [NL *stichidium*] : STICHIDIUM

sti·chid·i·um \stəˈkidēəm\ *n, pl* **stichid·ia** \-ēə\ [NL, fr. Gk *stichidion* small row, small line, dim. of *stichos* row, line] : a special branch of the thallus of a red alga bearing tetraspores and often fusiform

sticho·basidial \ˈstikō+\ *adj* [Gk *stichos* line + E *basidial*] : having the nuclear spindles of the basidia parallel to the longitudinal axis — compare CHIASTOBASIDIAL — **sticho·basidium** \"+\ *n*

stich·o·met·ric \ˌstikəˈme·trik\ *or* **stich·o·met·ri·cal** \-rəkəl\ *adj* : of or relating to stichometry : characterized by lines — **stich·o·met·ri·cal·ly** \-rək(ə)lē\ *adv*

sti·chom·e·try \stəˈkämə·trē\ *n* -ES [Gk *stichos* line + E *-metry*] **1 a** : a measurement of books by the number of lines they contain **b** : a list of documents stating how many lines each contains **2** : division of the text of a book into lines; *esp* : division of texts into lines fitted to the sense (as in manuscripts antedating the adoption of punctuation)

stich·o·myth·ia \ˌstikəˈmithēə\ *also* **sti·chom·y·thy** \stəˈkäməthē\ *n, pl* **stichomythias** *also* **stichomythies** [Gk *stichomythia,* fr. *stichomythein* to speak dialogue in alternate lines, fr. *stichos* row, line, verse + *mythos* tale, speech, myth — more at MYTH] : dialogue esp. of altercation or dispute delivered in alternating lines (as in classical Greek drama)

stich·o·myth·ic \ˌstikəˈmithik\ *adj* : of, relating to, or constituting stichomythia

sti·chos \ˈstiˌkäs\ *n, pl* **sti·choi** \-kȯi\ [Gk — more at STICH] : LINE, STICH, VERSE

stich·o·some \ˈstikəˌsōm\ *n* -s [Gk *stichos* row, line + E *-some*] : a column of glandular cells associated with the esophagus of various nematodes

-sti·chous \stəkəs\ *adj comb form* [LL *-stichus,* fr. Gk *-stichos,* fr. *stichos* row, line] : having (such or so many) rows or sides ⟨*diplostichous*⟩ ⟨*monostichous*⟩

sticht·ite \ˈstikˌtīt\ *n* -s [Robert *Sticht* †1922 Australian metallurgist born in U.S. + E *-ite*] : a mineral $Mg_6Cr_2(OH)_{16}(CO_3).4H_2O$ consisting of a hydrous carbonate and hydroxide of magnesium and chromium

¹stick \ˈstik\ *n* -s [ME *stikke, stik,* fr. OE *sticca;* akin to MLG *stikke* stick, OHG *stehho, stecko,* ON *stik, stika* stick, stake, OE *stician* to stick — more at ⁵STICK] **1** : a woody piece or part of a tree or shrub: as **a** (1) : a shoot, twig, or slender branch broken or cut off esp. when dry or dead (2) : BUD STICK **b** : a cut or broken branch or a piece of chopped wood used as or suitable for fuel — usu. used in pl. ⟨were able to find enough dry ~*s* to start a campfire⟩ ⟨cut a few ~*s* of kindling⟩ **c** : a stem or branch of any size cut or gathered for use esp. as construction material (as timbers, stakes, staves) or in manufacturing ⟨interwoven willow ~*s*⟩ ⟨cane ~*s* for oboes —*Time*⟩ ⟨in the postwar world ~*s* of timber will be shot full of strengthening plastic —*Science News Letter*⟩; *sometimes* : LOG ⟨the big ~*s* that housed early Americans and carried the canvas on tall Yankee clipper ships —*Monsanto Mag.*⟩ ⟨started with such a ~ I couldn't even move one end of it —G.W.Brace⟩ **2** : a long and relatively slender piece of wood in its natural form or shaped with tools and of a size that can be easily handled : ROD, STAFF, WAND ⟨cut himself a hiking ~⟩ ⟨the ~ of a skyrocket⟩ ⟨an apple on a ~⟩ ⟨manicure ~*s* of orangewood⟩ ⟨a burnt ~ of a match⟩: as **a** (1) : a wooden club or staff used as a weapon ⟨one hand resting on the white ~ in his belt —Kay Boyle⟩ ⟨cop in full kit, his ~ ready in his hand —R.O.Bowen⟩ — compare NIGHTSTICK (2) : something suitable for use as a means of compulsion ⟨programs carried on today are nowhere near large enough to be effective either as ~*s* or carrots —S.P. Hayes b.1910⟩ ⟨the ~ — the powerful instrumentalities of institutionalized violence —Julian Towster⟩ (3) : a beating with or as if with a stick ⟨got a fair share of the ~ —Brian James⟩ **b** (1) : DRUMSTICK (2) **sticks** *pl* : DRUMMER **c** : WALKING STICK ⟨tossed his hat and ~ on the table —Waldo Frank⟩ ⟨iron-pointed ferrule that distinguishes continental ~*s* —Hilton Brown⟩ **d** : any of various implements (as a baseball bat, billiard cue, golf club) used for striking or propelling an object in a game: as (1) : HOCKEY STICK ⟨all ~*s* shall be made of wood —*Official Ice Hockey Guide*⟩ (2) : CROSSE (3) **sticks** *pl* **a** : the staves thrown at the target figure in Aunt Sally **b** : the game of Aunt Sally (4) : an implement used by a croupier or stickman to retrieve thrown dice **e** (1) : a baton symbolizing an office or dignity; *also* : a person bearing or entitled to bear such a baton — compare GOLD STICK, SILVER STICK (2) : a musical conductor's baton ⟨though no professional conductor, handles the ~ astonishingly well —*N.Y.Times*⟩ **f** : one of the pieces of wood resembling laths that are used to suspend leaves and stalks of tobacco in curing barns and to suspend hands of tobacco in drying machines **3** : a piece, part, or bit of the total materials of which something (as a building) is constructed or composed ⟨house stood facing her, not a ~ of it changed —Allen Tate⟩ ⟨nothing there . . . not a windbreak tree, windmill, ~ of fence —C.T.Jackson⟩ ⟨had grown up in the town and knew every ~ and stone of it⟩ **4** : a piece of wood used as a tally by cutting notches in it or as a counter or token **5** : any of various implements and utensils shaped like a stick or having a possible origin in a stick: as **a** : CANDLESTICK **b** : a violin bow : FIDDLESTICK **c** (1) : COMPOSING STICK (2) : STICKFUL (3) : set type occupying two inches of one column esp. of a newspaper; *also* : copy for this amount of type (4) : the receiving galley of a slugcasting machine **d sticks** *pl* : a set of thin narrow rods or slats (as of wood, bone, ivory) on which the folding surface of a fan is mounted **e** *slang* : PISTOL **f** (1) : CHANTER 3 (2) : FIFE (3) : FLUTE **g** (1) : CONTROL STICK (2) : a gearshift lever of an automobile **h** : FOUNTAIN PEN **6** : something prepared (as by cutting, molding, rolling) in a relatively long and slender often cylindrical form (as for convenience in handling, ease of application or consumption) ⟨cinnamon ~*s*⟩ ⟨~ of candy⟩ ⟨~ of sealing wax⟩ ⟨~ of dynamite⟩ ⟨shaving ~⟩ ⟨chapsticks, lipsticks, and other cosmetic ~*s*⟩ ⟨cucumber ~*s*⟩ ⟨pound of butter in ~*s*⟩; *specif* : a marihuana cigarette : REEFER **7 a** : a quantity of eels consisting usu. of 25 eels **b** : a quantity of fish consisting of 25 pounds **8 a** : PERSON — used with a qualifying adjective ⟨queer ~⟩ ⟨a decent old ~ —Robert Graves⟩ ⟨they'd only been kidding you . . . they were good ~*s* —David Ballantyne⟩ **b** : a dull, inert, stiff, or spiritless person : one that lacks vigor, animation, or geniality ⟨this poor, dim ~ —Jean Stafford⟩ ⟨was also something of a ~ . . . rarely spoke to anyone who was not of her own social station —Aubrey Menen⟩ ⟨such a thing as carrying niceness too far — a girl could end by being a ~ —Hamilton Basso⟩ ⟨is a regular ~ on the stage —Emily Eden⟩ **c** : SHILL; *esp* : one working in a carnival **9 a** : a tree trunk or sometimes a tree suitable for timber ⟨next task is to get the big ~*s* out of the woods —D.C.Peattie⟩ ⟨a clear ~ of ninety feet was nothing unusual among these giants —G.W. Johnson⟩ **b** : a wood of timber trees **c sticks** *pl* (1) : wooded lands : rural districts : BACKCOUNTRY — used with *the* ⟨bringing in hordes of Indians from the ~*s* —*Guatemala News*⟩ ⟨back in the ~*s,* far from anything —Bill Wolf⟩ (2) : sections of a country remote from or held to be little touched by centers of civilization — used with *the;* compare BACKWOODS, PROVINCES ⟨in case you're from the ~*s,* I'll explain it to you —Willard Temple⟩ ⟨a musical comedy during its trial run in the ~*s* —J.M.Conly⟩ (3) : BUSH LEAGUES — used with *the* ⟨sent him back to the ~*s*⟩ **10 a** : an edible plant stem or stalk ⟨celery ~*s*⟩ ⟨stewed a few ~*s* of rhubarb⟩ **b** : the dry withered stem of a stiffish plant ⟨watering the dry ~*s* of hollyhock —Mari Sandoz⟩ **11 a** : MAST ⟨do my sailing with a rag and ~ —H.A.Calahan⟩ ⟨our eyes on the bobbing, varnished ~ of the dinghy —Vincent McHugh⟩ **b** : YARD **12** : a portion of alcoholic liquor (as brandy, rum) in a nonalcoholic drink ⟨a cup of tea with a ~ in it⟩ **13** : a single piece or article esp. of furniture ⟨upholstered almost every ~ of furniture herself —E.L.Howe⟩ ⟨some dusty ~*s* of Victorian furniture —Margery Allingham⟩ ⟨series of business failures that left him with hardly a ~ to his name⟩ **14** : LEG — usu. used in pl. ⟨fever left him weak on his ~*s*⟩ **15** : something constructed of sticks: as **a** : a cricket stump — usu. used in pl. **b** (1) : a racing or steeplechase hurdle (2) : any wooden obstacle (as a fence, gate, stile) to be hurdled (as in hunting) : TIMBER 4a **c** : a fireman's ladder **16 sticks** *pl* : a violation of the rules of field hockey by raising the stick above the shoulders at either the beginning or end of a stroke **17 a** : a number of bombs arranged for release or released one after another in quick succession from a bombing plane esp. in a spaced series across a target ⟨jettisoning its ~ of bombs —J.W.Bellah⟩ ⟨dropped a few ~*s* off target —Jack Alexander⟩ — compare SALVO **b** : a group of parachutists who jump or are assigned to jump one after another in quick succession ⟨our ~ was briefed again on various subjects —T.B.Bruff⟩ ⟨dropping two ~*s* of paratroopers simultaneously —J.G.Cozzens⟩ — **hold a stick to** *also* **hold sticks with** : compete with equally : survive comparison with — **to sticks** *adv* **1** : to pieces : COMPLETELY, THOROUGHLY ⟨beat being a farmhand all *to sticks*⟩ **2** *also* **to sticks and staves** : into fragments : to ruin : to the bad — **wrong end of the stick 1** *also* **short end of the stick** *or* **dirty end of the stick** : unfair or unfavorable treatment : a disadvantageous position **2** : a twisted or false version or account of something

²stick \"\ *vt* -ED/-ING/-S **1** : to arrange (lumber) in stacks esp. with stickers **2** : to provide a stick as a support for (as a plant, a vine) **3** : to set (type) in a composing stick : COMPOSE ⟨could . . . rustle news, solicit ads, ~ type, make up forms, put the paper to bed —S.H.Adams⟩

³stick \"\ *adj* **1** : resembling a stick in shape : prepared or made in the form of a stick ⟨~ licorice⟩ ⟨~ cinnamon⟩ ⟨a ~ deodorant⟩ **2** : made of or with sticks ⟨a ~ bridge⟩ ⟨~ chimney⟩ ⟨~ sling⟩

⁴stick \"\ *adv* : ALTOGETHER, COMPLETELY ⟨~ blind⟩ ⟨~ stark staring mad⟩

⁵stick \"\ *vb* **stuck** \ˈstək\ **stuck; sticking; sticks** [ME *stikken, stiken,* fr. OE *stician;* akin to OS *stekan* to stick fast, OHG *stehhan* to sting, prick, *stiken* to stick, prick, *stecchen* to stick, insert, ON *steikja* to roast, L *instigare* to urge on, incite, instigate, Gk *stizein* to tattoo, Skt *tejate* it is sharp; basic meaning: sharp] *vt* **1 a** : to pierce with something pointed: as (1) : to pierce with a pointed weapon : wound by a thrust of a pointed instrument : STAB (2) *chiefly dial* : to pierce with a horn or tusk : GORE (3) : to make a hole in with a pointed instrument : PUNCTURE ⟨man who could ~ a cow for clover bloat —*Time*⟩ **b** : to kill by piercing with a pointed instrument; *esp* : to kill (as a pig in butchering) by pressing a knife into the throat **c** : to strike (as fish) or hunt (as wild boar) with a spear ⟨~ salmon⟩ ⟨had *stuck* pigs in India⟩ **2** : to cause (as a pointed instrument) to penetrate : push or thrust so as to pierce or as if to pierce — used with *in* or *into* or with *through* ⟨died from a knife *stuck* in his back⟩ ⟨*stuck* a needle in her finger⟩ ⟨too thick to ~ a pin through it⟩ ⟨accidentally *stuck* his finger in his eye⟩ ⟨*stuck* his umbrella in my ribs⟩ ⟨test by ~*ing* a fork into the crust⟩ **3 a** : to fix, fasten, or secure in position by thrusting or pushing in esp. at a pointed or narrow end ⟨~ pins in a pincushion⟩ ⟨~ a marker in the ground⟩ ⟨~ candles in a birthday cake⟩ ⟨*stuck* a flower in his buttonhole⟩ ⟨*stuck* his pipe between his teeth⟩ ⟨a flower *stuck* behind his ear —Judson Philips⟩ ⟨had his pistol *stuck* in his belt⟩ ⟨*stuck* a feather in his hatband⟩ **b** (1) : to fix on a point or a pointed implement : IMPALE ⟨~ an apple on a fork⟩ ⟨kills a fowl, ~*s* it and the banana blossom on a spit —J.G.Frazer⟩ (2) : to mount (as an insect specimen) by transfixing with a pin **c** : to push, shove, thrust, or poke (as a part of the body) in a specified direction or into a specified place or position ⟨suddenly *stuck* his arm out⟩ ⟨*stuck* his hands behind him⟩ ⟨sitting with his feet *stuck* out into the aisle⟩ ⟨*stuck* his finger down his collar⟩ ⟨*stuck* his chin out pugnaciously⟩ ⟨an unpleasant way of ~*ing* his nose up in the air⟩ ⟨~*s* out his chest and struts away⟩ ⟨~ out your tongue and say "ah"⟩ ⟨prices jump . . . the minute you ~ your head inside the door —T.H.Fielding⟩ ⟨soldier foolish enough to ~ his head over the rock —Burtt Evans⟩ ⟨*stuck* his face into mine⟩ **4** : to put or set in a specified place or position ⟨the letter under the door⟩ ⟨~ a book back on its shelf⟩ ⟨~ a cake in the oven⟩ ⟨~ the washing in the machine⟩ ⟨~ their prepositions in front of the verbs —John Hilton⟩ ⟨*stuck* me in the shore patrol brig —R.O.Bowen⟩ ⟨*stuck* the prettiest girls in the front row⟩ ⟨*stuck* his hat on his head and left⟩ ⟨a cottage *stuck* down among a swarm of other cottages —Morley Callaghan⟩ ⟨*stuck* a few potted plants around the room⟩ **5 a** : to set or furnish with things fixed in or fastened on by or as if by piercing a surface ⟨~ a pincushion full of pins⟩ ⟨an orange *stuck* with cloves⟩ ⟨top of the wall had been *stuck* full of broken glass⟩ ⟨wore a coat *stuck* with badges⟩ **b** : to set or furnish with objects placed about ⟨a brisk trade in pretty things; buildings are *stuck* all over with

them —Clive Bell⟩ ⟨windows *stuck* full of plants and knickknacks on glass shelves⟩ **6 :** to attach by or as if by causing to adhere to a surface (as with pins or an adhesive) ⟨~ a stamp on a letter⟩ ⟨~ down the flap of an envelope⟩ ⟨~ a poster on the wall⟩ ⟨~ up a notice on the bulletin board⟩ ⟨~ a handle on a teapot with glue⟩ **7 a :** to compel to pay (as by beating in a game or gamble or by trickery or imposition) ⟨expert at ~*ing* his friends for drinks at liar's dice⟩ ⟨~ his host for the cost of several long-distance calls⟩ **b** (1) **:** CHARGE ⟨what do they ~ you for a meal⟩ (2) **:** OVERCHARGE **:** require to pay or spend exorbitantly ⟨everybody ~*s* the dogface —James Jones⟩ ⟨fixed the prices and . . . *stuck* the rich to favor the poor —Marcus Duffield⟩ **8 :** to run or plane (moldings) in a machine in contradistinction to working by hand **9 a :** to bring to a halt **:** prevent the movement or action of **:** keep from proceeding or going back ⟨could not move a yard among people without getting *stuck* —James Cameron⟩ ⟨prevent foreign matter from ~*ing* valve —*Air Tools*⟩ ⟨had been *stuck* there for a week by bad weather⟩ ⟨here he was, *stuck* in a shore job —Nevil Shute⟩ ⟨voice is *stuck* somewhere below his larynx —H.A.Overstreet⟩ ⟨got *stuck* halfway up the hill⟩ **b :** to cause to be at a loss **:** BAFFLE, NONPLUS, PUZZLE, STUMP ⟨*stuck* him with the first question they asked⟩ ⟨you can't ~ him about his native land —T.H.Fielding⟩ ⟨getting *stuck* for a word to rhyme with *moon* —R.K.Leavitt⟩ ⟨was *stuck* for a technique that would deal with them adequately —*New Yorker*⟩ **10 a :** to get the better of esp. fraudulently **:** CHEAT, DEFRAUD ⟨had been *stuck* several times in the past year by phony antique dealers⟩ **b :** to saddle with something disadvantageous or disagreeable — usu. used with *with* ⟨it is your car and you are *stuck* with it —Gregor Felsen⟩ ⟨had been *stuck* with the job of washing the dishes⟩ ⟨think you're going to ~ me with a bum rap like that —Courtney McClendon⟩ ⟨went back on the road again, *stuck* with a losing show —F.B.Gipson⟩ ⟨*stuck* with the most complex monetary system left on earth —Richard Joseph⟩ ⟨things like debt and family illness can ~ you —*Time*⟩ **11** *chiefly Brit* **:** BEAR, ENDURE, STAND, TOLERATE **:** put up with ⟨couldn't ~ that pace all day —Adrian Bell⟩ ⟨can't ~ this darned town any longer —Christopher Isherwood⟩ ⟨couldn't ~ life in some stuffy little house —T.H.Raddall⟩ ⟨none of the girls could ~ him —Edith C. Rivett⟩ — often used with *it* ⟨hoped she would try to ~ it a little longer —F.M.Ford⟩ ⟨don't know how I'm going to ~ it till Tuesday —Margaret Kennedy⟩ ⟨were going out to see if we could ~ it —A.R.Williams⟩ **~** *vi* **1 :** to hold to or be held in something tightly or firmly by or as if by being embedded or attached by adhesion: **a :** to become or remain fixed in place by means of a pointed end **:** have the point piercing or held fast in something ⟨was found with a knife ~*ing* in his heart⟩ ⟨thorn *stuck* in his finger and broke off⟩ ⟨javelin *stuck* in the ground where it fell⟩ ⟨arrow *stuck* in the target⟩ **b :** to become fixed or fast by or as if by entangling or miring typically after being impelled into a thickly viscous, gluey, or tacky mass ⟨boat *stuck* in the sand⟩ ⟨car *stuck* in the mud⟩ **c :** to become attached by or as if by gluing or plastering ⟨thin silk robe which *stuck* to his sweating barrellike torso —T.B. Costain⟩ ⟨glue had *stuck* to his fingers⟩ ⟨this stamp won't ~⟩ ⟨several pages had *stuck* together⟩ ⟨keep the biscuits from ~*ing* to the pan⟩ **2 a :** to remain in a place, situation, or environment **:** continue to stay often as though held firmly, made stationary, or attached ⟨*stuck* on the farm while his brothers traveled⟩ ⟨decided to ~ where he was⟩ **b :** to remain attached or fixed over a period of time as though imbedded in or holding to with tenacious strength or adhesive power ⟨two sentences ~ in my mind —Kenneth Roberts⟩ ⟨boyhood nickname had *stuck*⟩ ⟨anyone so beyond suspicion that no slander can ~ to him —Elmer Davis⟩ ⟨childhood fears that had *stuck* with him⟩ **c :** to remain effective **:** continue or endure esp. in the face of opposition or difficulty **:** have sufficient lasting power and effect to resist efforts to evade, nullify, or make inoperative ⟨many . . . reorganizations in the past have failed to ~ —*New Republic*⟩ — used chiefly in the phrase *make stick* ⟨making the requirements ~ —*New Republic*⟩ ⟨fifteen years before an arrest could be made to ~ —*N.Y.Times*⟩ **d** *chiefly Brit* **:** to put up with existing conditions or circumstances **e :** to refuse to declare in a card game **3 :** to hold to closely, persistently, or steadfastly **:** stay with or near: as **a :** to adhere tenaciously without deviation, digression, interruption, or wavering **:** PERSEVERE — usu. used with *to* ⟨his sermons . . . ~ too closely to the point to be entertaining —T.S.Eliot⟩ ⟨the faculty should ~ to education and abjure finance —R.M.Lovett⟩ ⟨~ to business⟩ ⟨would ~ to his gladiatorial work for the joy and thrill of it —C.E.Montague⟩ or with *at* ⟨~*s* at his job⟩ ⟨~*s* persistently at his studies⟩ **b :** to hold or cling (as to a position) with lasting fortitude and resolution despite attack, danger, or the weight of onerous burdens — usu. used with *to* ⟨call upon every American to ~ to his post until the last battle is won —H.S.Truman⟩ ⟨*stuck* to his ship till it sank⟩ ⟨~ to their boards no matter what happens around them —Margaret Biddle⟩ **c :** to remain (as through a series of developments often adverse, trying, or dire) resolute or unshaken in loyalty, friendship, or alliance — usu. used with *by* or *to* ⟨is full of good men . . . they'll help you and ~ by you —Sherwood Anderson⟩ ⟨a man who *stuck* to his friends⟩ **d :** to adhere with strict fidelity, sure reliability, and lack of modification or relaxation induced by temptation, convenience, or opposition — usu. used with *to* ⟨~ to a contract⟩ ⟨translation *stuck* closely to the original⟩ ⟨always *stuck* to his word⟩ sometimes with *by* ⟨*stuck* by his first account⟩ **e :** to keep close to in a quest, chase, vying, or competition matching or countering opposed efforts — usu. used with *with* or *to* ⟨was stronger than his opponent but the latter *stuck* with him and earned a draw⟩ ⟨managed to ~ to the leader's heels for two laps⟩ **4 :** to become fixed in position or hindered in progress or operation by reason of some obstacle or obstruction **:** become blocked or wedged **:** JAM, LODGE ⟨handle had *stuck*⟩ ⟨something had *stuck* in the pipe⟩ ⟨food *stuck* in his throat⟩ ⟨switch had a tendency to ~⟩ ⟨desk drawer always *stuck*⟩ **5 a :** to be reluctant or unwilling **:** be deterred (as by scruples) **:** BALK, HESITATE, SCRUPLE, STOP — usu. used with *at* ⟨was in a hole and would ~ at little to get out of it —John Buchan⟩ ⟨not one who would ~ at calling her at midnight —Aurelia Levi⟩ ⟨with someone else to do the thinking for him he would ~ at nothing —F.W.Crofts⟩ **b :** to be in difficulty **:** become baffled or nonplussed **:** BOGGLE — usu. used with *at* ⟨~ at grammar⟩ ⟨what we ~ at in most religious poetry is not the beliefs but the emotions —J.P. Bishop⟩ **c :** to be unable to proceed (as in a performance, a speech) ⟨memory failed him at the same place he had *stuck* the first time⟩ ⟨*stuck* in the middle of the verse⟩ **6 :** PROJECT, PROTRUDE ⟨had a book ~*ing* from his pocket⟩ ⟨spot the house by the air conditioner ~*ing* through the window⟩ ⟨aerial ~*s* up above the chimney⟩ ⟨nose of the car was ~*ing* out of the garage⟩ ⟨wreck of the tiny store ~*ing* up in the ruins —C.G.D. Roberts⟩ ⟨tail unit ~*ing* high up into the air —*London Calling*⟩ **syn** see ADHERE, DEMUR — **stick in one's craw** *also* **stick in one's crop** *or* **stick in one's gizzard :** to be difficult of digestion **:** be hard to accept **:** be offensive — **stick in one's throat** *of an utterance* **:** to be or become difficult or impossible to speak or repeat **:** remain unexpressed — **stick it on** *chiefly Brit* **:** to charge exorbitantly ⟨those country shops, it's something dreadful the way they *stick it on* —Victoria Sackville-West⟩ — **stick one's neck out :** to lay oneself open (as to attack, criticism, complaint, detection, punishment, reprisal) **:** run the risk of bringing down upon oneself a consequence detrimental to oneself (as by taking another's part, making a decision outside the scope of one's authority, passing judgment on a matter presumed to be beyond one's competence) ⟨when the testing time comes, he isn't afraid to *stick his neck out* —Jack Winocour⟩ ⟨her warmhearted, slaphappy way of *sticking her neck out* —C.J.Rolo⟩ ⟨economists *stuck their necks out* in the capacity of self-appointed forecasters —Fritz Machlup⟩ ⟨avoids *sticking his neck out* politically —*Scotsman*⟩ ⟨*stuck his neck out* many times for liberal causes —R.S.Allen⟩ — **stick together :** to remain united **:** act as a unit **:** stand by and support one another ⟨father seemed to want the family to *stick together* —Isa Glenn⟩ ⟨now or never for the states to find out how to *stick together* and make one nation —Dorothy C. Fisher⟩ ⟨*stick together* against the foreigner —H.L.Matthews⟩ ⟨we *stuck together* in negotiations —Hugh Gaitskell⟩ — **stick to one's fingers :** to be retained wrongfully ⟨as this currency passes from hand to hand, some of it inevitably *sticks to the fingers* that it touches —D.D.McKean⟩ — **stick to one's guns :** to maintain one's position esp. in the face of attack or opposition ⟨France has *stuck to its guns* as far as its principal demands . . . are concerned —Robert Strausz-Hupé⟩ — **stick to one's knitting :** to stick severely to business or to the matter at hand ⟨both airlines *stuck to their knitting* and improved the service on the respective routes —Horace Sutton⟩ — **stick to one's last :** to stick to what one knows best **:** remain within the field of one's special competence ⟨curators . . . shirk any responsibility for exhibits and . . . want to *stick to their lasts* in the research collections —Thomas Barbour⟩ — **stick to one's ribs** *or* **stick to the ribs :** to provide nourishment and protect against hunger ⟨liked a breakfast that would *stick to his ribs*⟩ — **stuck on :** captivated with **:** infatuated with **:** in love with ⟨a girl he had been *stuck on* for a while in high school⟩ ⟨many boys were *stuck on* her⟩ ⟨brought her out to the game with them and she got *stuck on* me —Ring Lardner⟩ ⟨pretty *stuck on* herself, too —S.H.Adams⟩

[6]**stick** \"\ *n* -s **1 :** a thrust with a pointed instrument **:** STAB **2 a :** a temporary stoppage **:** DELAY, STOP ⟨seemed to be at a ~⟩ **b :** something causing such a stoppage **:** IMPEDIMENT, OBSTACLE ⟨made no ~ at all⟩ **3 :** the quality or power of adhering or causing to adhere **:** adhesive tendency **4 :** a sticky substance; *specif* **:** the thick liquor obtained by evaporation of the liquid from tankage in rendering fats or tankage and mixed with garbage or solid residue from tankage for use as fertilizer or animal feed

stick·abil·i·ty \ˌstikəˈbiləd·ē\ *n* [[5]*stick* + *ability*] **:** ability to endure or persevere

stick·age \ˈstikij\ *n* -s [[5]*stick* + *-age*] **:** an act or the fact of sticking **:** tendency to stick **:** ADHESION ⟨belting conveys the raw dough pieces without ~ —*Bakers Digest*⟩

stick-and-dirt *or* **stick-and-mud** \ˌ=ˌ=ˈ=\ *adj* **:** made of sticks plastered with clay ⟨*stick-and-dirt* fireplace⟩ ⟨*stick-and-mud* chimneys, the type most often used —*Amer. Guide Series: Texas*⟩

stick and groove *n* **:** a primitive apparatus for kindling fire by friction consisting of a fire-plow and a hearth

stick around *vi* **:** to stay or wait about **:** remain nearby **:** LINGER ⟨was *sticking around* on the chance of being invited to come in⟩ ⟨somebody has to *stick around* and feed it —*New Yorker*⟩ ⟨*stick around* and you'll get your story —Mickey Spillane⟩

stick-at-it-ive \stiˈkad·əd·iv\ *adj* [fr. the phrase *stick at it* + *-ive*] **:** STICK-TO-ITIVE — **stick-at-itive·ness** *n* -ES

stick-at-nothing \ˈ=ˌ=ˌ==\ *adj* [fr. the phrase *stick at nothing*] **:** that hesitates or scruples at nothing to achieve its purpose **:** DETERMINED, UNSCRUPULOUS ⟨underhand, *stick-at-nothing* brute —Joseph Conrad⟩ ⟨*stick-at-nothing* methods⟩

stick-back \ˈ=ˌ=\ *adj* [[1]*stick* + *back*] **:** having a back with spindles driven into the seat and the top rail or bow ⟨Windsor chairs are *stick-back* chairs⟩ ⟨*stick-back* gig —*Amer. Guide Series: N.C.*⟩

stickball \ˈ=ˌ=\ *n* [[1]*stick* + *ball*] **:** baseball adapted to playing in streets or small areas and using a broomstick and lightweight ball

stick bean *n* **:** POLE BEAN

stick bowling *n* **:** SKIDDLES

stick bug *n* **1 :** STICK INSECT **2 :** SPIDER BUG **3 :** STILT BUG

stick-button \ˈ=ˌ==\ *n* **:** a common burdock (*Arctium lappa*)

stick candy *n* **:** hard candy molded in the shape of sticks or rods

stick caterpillar *n* **:** any of numerous caterpillars (family Geometridae) that assume the form of a stick or position of a twig when at rest

stick chair *n* **:** SEDAN CHAIR

stick control *n* **:** CONTROL STICK

stick dance *n* **:** any of various dances esp. of western Europe and India in which sticks are beaten against each other by two partners or by the two hands of a dancer

stick-dice \ˈ=ˌ=\ *n* -s **:** a game played by No. American Indians in which variously marked sticks are thrown in the air and scores are settled by the values of the marks that are uppermost when the sticks fall — called also *stick game*

sticked *past of* STICK

[1]**stick·er** \ˈstikə(r)\ *n* -s [[5]*stick* + *-er*] **1 :** one that pierces with a point: as **a** (1) **:** a slaughterhouse worker who sticks a knife into the neck of cattle, sheep, or hogs to sever the jugular vein — called also *bleeder* (2) **:** one that kills poultry by thrusting a knife through the roof of the mouth into the brain **b :** a weapon or implement for piercing as contrasted with slashing **c :** BRAMBLE, BUR, THORN **d :** a sharp projection on a shoe intended to give a racehorse better footing on a muddy track **e :** PINNER 2b **2 :** one that adheres or causes adhesion: as **a** (1) **:** one that sticks faithfully or unswervingly **:** one that remains constant ⟨was a stayer and a ~ —W.A.White⟩ (2) **:** one that persists (as in a task) or that shows powers of endurance ⟨both horse and rider were ~*s*⟩ (3) **:** STONEWALLER **b :** a commodity that does not sell rapidly **c :** an adhesive substance (as glue, casein, resin); *specif* **:** a substance added to a fungicide, insecticide, or other spray or dust to prevent removal of the active ingredients by weathering — compare SPREADER 1f **d** (1) **:** a slip of paper with gummed back (as a gummed label, seal, stamp, or philatelist's stamp hinge) that when moistened adheres to a surface against which it is pressed (2) **:** a label bearing the name of an independent candidate in an election sometimes used to stick over a regular name in voting by printed ballot (3) **:** a summons for a parking violation stuck to a motor vehicle **3 :** something or someone puzzling **:** POSER **4 a :** BILLPOSTER **b :** a worker who sticks or pastes one thing into or onto another: as (1) **:** one that inserts extra sheets or sections in newspapers or unbound pamphlets (2) **:** one that repairs marble slabs by sticking them together with shellac (3) **:** one that prepares small pieces of fur for shearing **5 :** a woodworking machine for working rods, moldings, and beadings

[2]**sticker** \"\ *n* -s [[1]*stick* + *-er*] **1 :** one that gathers sticks (as for fuel) **2 :** a wooden stick or strip placed between boards or plywood sheets stacked in piles to hasten drying and reduce warping — called also *crosser* **3 :** one that uses a stick (as in a game); *esp* **:** an athlete who handles his stick skillfully

sticker-up \ˈ==ˈ=\ *n* -s [*stick up* + *-er*] **1 :** one that finishes ware by sticking parts together **2** *chiefly Austral* **:** one that holds up another (as for robbery) **:** HIGHWAYMAN, BUSHRANGER **3** *Austral* **:** a primitive method of roasting meat on a wooden spit stuck in the ground and leaned over a fire

stick·ery \ˈstikərē\ *adj* [[1]*sticker* + *-y*] **:** PRICKLY ⟨hay that he didn't remember as being so ~ —*Southern Lit. Messenger*⟩

stickfast \ˈ=ˌ=\ *n* -s [fr. the phrase *stick fast*] **1 :** one that sticks or causes to stick firmly **2 :** an act of sticking fast

stickfast flea *n, Austral* **:** STICKTIGHT FLEA

stick figure *also* **stick drawing** *n* **:** a drawing representing a human or animal pose by single lines for all parts but the head which is shown usu. as a circle; *esp* **:** such a drawing showing the position of the body members in a dance or sport action

stick force *n* **:** the force exerted on the control column by the pilot of an airplane in flight

stick·ful \ˈstikˌfu̇l\ *n* -s **:** as much or as many as a stick will hold ⟨makes doughnuts and gives me a whole ~ —Helen Eustis⟩; *specif* **:** as much set type as fills a composing stick

stick game *n* **:** STICK-DICE

stick gig *n* **:** a lightweight two-wheeled carriage for one person

stick grenade *n* **:** a grenade with a handle **:** POTATO MASHER

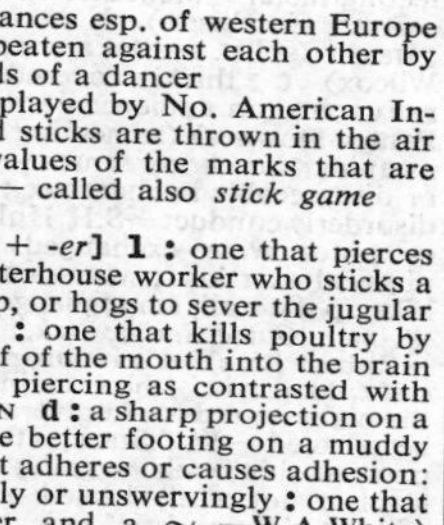

stick figures

stickhandle \ˈ=ˌ==\ *vi* [back-formation fr. *stickhandling*, fr. [1]*stick* + *handling*] **:** to maintain control of a puck (as in ice hockey) by clever and deceptive dribbling ⟨*stickhandled* across the ice and cut in from the other wing —H.W.Wind⟩

stick horse *n* **:** HOBBYHORSE 3a

stickied *past of* STICKY

stickier *comparative of* STICKY

stickies *pres 3d sing of* STICKY

stickiest *superlative of* STICKY

stick·i·ly \ˈstikəlē, -li\ *adv* **:** in a sticky manner ⟨~ hot⟩ ⟨squirming heap of maggots came ~ away —Kenneth Roberts⟩

stick-in \ˈ=ˌ=\ *n* -s [fr. *stick in*, v.] **:** STRANDER 2

stick·i·ness \ˈstikēnəs, -kin-\ *n* -ES **:** the quality or state of being sticky

[1]**stick·ing** \ˈstikiŋ, -kēŋ\ *n* -s [ME *stikking*, fr. gerund of *stikken* to stick — more at STICK] **1 :** the action of piercing or stabbing ⟨helpless as calves tied up for ~ —F.V.W.Mason⟩ **2 a :** the action of adhering, holding fast, or holding back; *specif* **:** the action of stonewalling in cricket **b :** material that sticks or has stuck; *specif* **:** GOUGE 4 **c :** an increase in the water resistance at high speed that delays or prevents the take-off of a seaplane **3 :** a molded edge worked on the rails or stiles of a door around the panels or lights

[2]**sticking** \"\ *n* -s [[1]*stick* + *-ing*] **1 :** sticks for use in supporting plants **2 :** the method or order employed in the use of drumsticks esp. in playing a snare drum

sticking knife *n* **:** a narrow-bladed knife used for killing animals (as poultry) by sticking

sticking-piece \ˈ==ˌ=\ *n, Brit* **:** a piece of beef cut from the lower part of the neck

sticking place *n* **1 :** the place where something stops and sticks fast ⟨screw your courage to the *sticking place* —Shak.⟩ **2 :** the place or point in the neck of an animal where the knife is stuck in slaughtering

sticking plaster *n* **:** an adhesive plaster for closing superficial wounds and similar uses

sticking point *n* **1 :** a place or position at which something sticks **:** STICKING PLACE ⟨go to war only when public opinion is aroused to the *sticking point* —T.K.Finletter⟩ **2 :** a particular (as an item in negotiations) resulting or likely to result in an impasse ⟨*sticking point* is the Soviet refusal to permit inspection of uranium deposits —*World Report*⟩

sticking salve *n* **:** a sticky salve (as for use on wounds)

sticking tommy *n* [*tommy* fr. the name *Tommy*] **:** a candlestick that is equipped with a sharp projecting point for sticking into a floor or wall

stick insect *n* **:** any of various insects of Phasmatidae and related families that are usu. wingless with a long round body sticklike in form and color and long legs often held rigidly in positions resembling twigs of the trees on which they live

stick-in-the-mud \ˈ=ˌ=ˌ=\ *n* -s **:** one that is slow, dilatory, old-fashioned, or unprogressive; *esp* **:** one that is ultraconservative **:** an old fogy ⟨*stick-in-the-muds* who would live out their days in one town —T.W.Duncan⟩

stick·it \ˈstikət\ *adj* [fr. Sc past part. of [5]*stick*, fr. ME *stikkyd*] **1** *Scot* **:** IMPERFECT, UNFINISHED ⟨a ~ job⟩ **2** *chiefly Scot* **:** having failed (as in one's intended profession) and given up ⟨a ~ minister⟩

stickjaw \ˈ=ˌ=\ *n* [[5]*stick* + *jaw*] **:** something (as candy or a pudding) that sticks the jaws together and is difficult to chew ⟨sticks of raspberry ~ —Ruth Park⟩

stick lac *n* **:** lac in its natural state that encrusts small twigs and the bodies of lac insects and is scraped off and dried in the shade to become the source of seed lac, lac dye, and shellac wax

[1]**stick·le** \ˈstikəl\ *adj* [ME *stikell*, fr. OE *sticol;* akin to OS *stekul* stony, rough, OHG *stehhal* steep, OE *stician* to stick — more at STICK] **1** *dial Eng* **:** STEEP **2** *dial Eng* **:** moving rapidly ⟨a mile of water . . . bright with ~ runs —R.D.Blackmore⟩

[2]**stickle** \"\ *n* -s **1** *dial chiefly Brit* **:** a rapid in a small stream ⟨the little runs and ~*s* —John Buchan⟩ **2** *chiefly Brit* **:** a line of persons placed across a shallow in a stream to prevent passage of an otter into water where it cannot be hunted

[3]**stickle** \"\ *vi* **stickled; stickled; stickling** \-k(ə)liŋ\ **stickles** [ME *stightlen, stiglen*, freq. of *stighten* to arrange, place, fr. OE *stihtan, stihtian* to rule, arrange, order; akin to ON *stétta* to support, establish, *stétt* pavement, stepping-stone, degree, rank, *stiga* to climb — more at STAIR] **1** *obs* **:** to separate combatants by intervening **:** act as umpire or mediator **2** *obs* **:** to participate actively **3 :** to contend or hold out esp. pertinaciously and usu. on finical or insufficient grounds **4 :** to feel hesitation or scruples **:** SCRUPLE **syn** see DEMUR

[4]**stickle** \"\ *n* -s **:** AGITATION, PERTURBATION **:** BEWILDERMENT, PERPLEXITY

stickleaf \ˈ=ˌ=\ *n* [[5]*stick* + *leaf*] **:** any of several rough-leaved herbs of the genus *Mentzelia*

stick·le·back \ˈstikəlˌbak\ *n* [ME *stykylbak*, fr. *stykyl-* (fr. OE *sticel* prick, goad, thorn) + *bak* back; akin to MLG *stekel* sticel goad, thorn, OHG *stihhil* goad, thorn, ON *stikill* point of a drinking horn, Goth *stikls* drinking vessel (prob. orig. pointed at the bottom), OE *stician* to stick — more at STICK, BACK] **1 :** any of numerous small fishes of the family Gasterosteidae that have two or more free spines in front of the dorsal fin and the ventral fins each reduced to one spine and a small ray, that are scaleless but often have the sides protected by bony plates, that occur in the northern hemisphere in brackish or fresh water or in the sea and are noted for their activity and vigor and for the curious nests which the males construct and guard during the breeding season, and that include the nine-spined stickleback and the two-spined or three-spined stickleback of both Europe and America and the fifteen-spined stickleback of Europe only as well-known forms **2 :** a cleavers (*Galium aparine*)

stick-leg \ˈ=ˌ=\ *adj* **:** having legs like sticks — used of a chair

stick·ler \ˈstik(ə)lə(r)\ *n* -s [[3]*stickle* + *-er*] **1 :** one that stickles: as **a** (1) *chiefly dial* **:** an umpire in a tournament or other test of strength or skill (2) *obs* **:** one that intervenes in a dispute **:** MEDIATOR **b** *obs* **:** one that participates actively or is an active partisan; *also* **:** MEDDLER **c** (1) *archaic* **:** one that opposes or raises objections — usu. used with *against* (2) **:** one that contends persistently and unyieldingly for something often of trifling importance (as a point of etiquette, a formality) — usu. used with *for* ⟨a ~ for formal clothes at formal functions —E.T.Hellman⟩ ⟨is no ~ for the more rigid military courtesies —Ed Cunningham⟩ ⟨a ~ for dignity —*Newsweek*⟩ **d** *archaic* **:** a backer in a contest **:** SECOND **2 :** something (as a problem, a question) that baffles or puzzles **:** POSER, STICKER ⟨not hard to diagnose. It's the cure that's the ~ —*Los Angeles (Calif.) Examiner*⟩

stick·less \ˈstikləs\ *adj* **:** having no stick

sticklike \ˈ=ˌ=\ *adj* **:** resembling a stick

stick·ling \ˈstikliŋ\ *n* -s [ME *stikeling;* akin to MLG *stekelink*, MD *stekeline*, OHG *sticheline;* all fr. a prehistoric WGmc compound whose 1st constituent is represented by OE *sticel* prick, goad, thorn, and whose 2d constituent is represented by E *-ing* — more at STICKLEBACK] **:** STICKLEBACK

stickly *adj* [[5]*stick* + *-ly*] *chiefly Scot* **:** PRICKLY, ROUGH

stick·man \ˈstikˌman, -ˌmaa(ə)n, -ˌmən\ *n, pl* **stickmen** [[1]*stick* + *man*] **1 :** one that handles a stick: as **a :** one that supervises the play at a dice table, calls the decisions, and retrieves the dice — called also *dealer* **b :** a player in any of various games played with a stick; *esp* **:** a lacrosse player **c** (1) **:** a worker who moves hogsheads of tobacco by means of a heavy curved stick or an iron bar — called also *hooker-out* (2) **:** a steelworker who moves bars or sheets with hand tongs **d :** CONDUCTOR 6 ⟨the superb ~ — the specialist in baton technique —*Newsweek*⟩ **2 :** STICK FIGURE

stick off *vb, obs* **:** to show to advantage

stick on *vi* **:** to hold fast **:** keep one's place (as on the back of a horse) **:** stay on ⟨was not a good rider but managed to *stick on*⟩

stick out *vi* **1 a :** to jut out **:** PROJECT, PROTRUDE **b :** to be prominent or conspicuous ⟨their writers' prejudices would often *stick out* —Curtis Brown⟩ ⟨antibourgeois notions of the analysts *stick out* all over —C.J.Friedrich⟩ **2 a :** to hold out **:** be persistent (as in a demand or an opinion) **:** refuse to come to agreement or make a settlement ⟨were *sticking out* for a higher price⟩ ⟨*stick out* for absolute domination —V.S. Pritchett⟩ ⟨a last ditcher, *sticking out* for the rigor of the law —D.B.W.Lewis⟩ **b** *of workmen* **:** STRIKE **~** *vt* **1 :** to endure (as something specified or conditions in general) or see through to the end ⟨*stuck* the first term *out* and then left⟩ ⟨*stuck out* the icy currents —*Newsweek*⟩ ⟨determined to *stick out* a California sojourn —R.G.Hubler⟩ — often used with *it* ⟨*stuck it out*, living on lemonade, glucose tablets and nerves —*Holiday*⟩ ⟨the people *sticking it out* where the dust is thickest and the gulches driest —Russell Lord⟩ ⟨too late now to do anything but *stick it out*⟩ **2 :** to maintain against a person ⟨*stuck* me *out* that . . . it was one of the six best comedies in English —Arnold Bennett⟩ **syn** see BULGE

1stick-out \ˈ=ˌ=\ *n* -s [*stick out*] **1 :** an act or fact of sticking out; *specif* **:** STRIKE 7a **2 :** one that sticks out
2stick-out \"\ *adj* [*stick out*] **:** sticking out; *esp* **:** PROTUBERANT, PROMINENT
stickpin \ˈ=ˌ=\ *n* [5*stick* + *pin*] **:** TIEPIN
stick rider *n* **:** a skier who makes excessive use of ski poles
sticks *pl of* STICK, *pres 3d sing of* STICK
stick salve *n* [5*stick*] **:** STICKING SALVE
stickseed \ˈ=ˌ=\ *n* [5*stick* + *seed*] **:** a plant of the genus *Lappula* characterized by its bristly fruit
sticktail \ˈ=ˌ=\ *n* [1*stick* + *tail*] **:** RUDDY DUCK
sticktight \ˈ=ˌ=\ *n* -s [fr. the phrase *stick tight*] **:** one that sticks or adheres closely: as **a :** BUR MARIGOLD **b :** STICKSEED
sticktight flea *n* **:** a tropical flea (*Echidnophaga gallinacea*) that is parasitic esp. on the heads of chickens and is a pest in the southern U.S.
stick-to-it·ive·ness \stikˈtüəd·|ivnəs, ə·t|\ *n* -ES [fr. the phrase *stick to it* + *-ive* + *-ness*] **:** dogged perseverance **:** RESOLUTENESS, TENACITY ⟨has drifted from job to job . . . and lacks *stick-to-itiveness* —Kendall Banning⟩ ⟨not so much a test of marriage as a test of *stick-to-itiveness* —Lewis Nichols⟩
stick·um \ˈstikəm\ *n* -s [5*stick* + *-um* (prob. alter. of *'em*)] **:** something that adheres or causes adhesion **:** a substance that sticks, sticks down, or sticks together ⟨a new ~ for his postage stamps —Bill Hatch⟩
stick up *vi* **:** to stand out from a surface **:** stand upright or on end **:** PROJECT ⟨grain of the wood tends to *stick up*⟩ ⟨a few pilings of an old wharf were still *sticking up* in the water⟩ ~ *vt* **1 a :** to hold up (as at the point of a gun) in order to rob ⟨*stick* a stagecoach *up*⟩; *also* **:** to enter and rob ⟨*stick up* a gas station⟩ ⟨had *stuck* several banks *up*⟩ **b :** to accost for money **:** solicit money from ⟨*stuck* him *up* for the community chest⟩ **2 :** to cook on a spit **3 a :** to finish (as raw clayware) by smoothing — compare FETTLE **b :** to attach (partly formed glass) to a hot iron rod or clamping tool for reheating — **stick up for :** to speak or act in defense of **:** stand up for **:** DEFEND, SUPPORT ⟨afraid to *stick up for* his own beliefs —Virginia Woolf⟩ ⟨haven't got a soul to *stick up for* me —Dorothy Sayers⟩ — **stick up to 1 :** to offer resistance to **:** stand up to ⟨*stick up to* a bully⟩ **2** *dial Brit* **:** 2COURT 2a
1stickup \ˈ=ˌ=\ *n* -s [*stick up*] **1 :** something that sticks up: as **a :** a stand-up collar **b :** COCKUP 2 **2 :** HOLDUP, ROBBERY ⟨a national wave of ~*s* —*Argosy*⟩ ⟨a grab-and-run ~ in a bank —Alan Hynd⟩ **3 :** graphic material (as lettering) that is pasted on a sheet usu. containing other printed matter; *also* **:** a process using such pasted matter ⟨a map with place-names added by ~⟩
2stickup \ˈ=ˌ=\ *adj* [*stick up*] **1 :** that projects upward or stands up stiffly ⟨~ collar⟩ ⟨hat with ~ trimming of feathers⟩; *specif* **:** COCKUP 1 **2 :** pasted on or prepared for pasting on ⟨~ lettering⟩
stickup man *also* **stickup** *n* -s **:** HOLDUP MAN
stick vat *n* **:** a tanning vat in which skins are suspended from wooden sticks
stickwater \ˈ=ˌ=ˌ=\ *n* [5*stick* + *water*] **:** a viscous quickly decomposing and evil-smelling liquor that is obtained as a by-product in the wet process of manufacturing fish meal and fish oil by cooking the fish with steam and pressing and that is often concentrated by evaporation for use in animal feeds as a source of vitamins and amino acids
stickweed \ˈ=ˌ=\ *n* [5*stick* + *weed*] **:** any of several plants having seeds that cling to wool or clothing: as **a :** RAGWEED 2a **b :** AGRIMONY **c :** a beggar's-lice (*Lappula virginica*) **d :** GUM SUCCORY
stickwork \ˈ=ˌ=\ *n* [1*stick* + *work*] **1 :** the use and management of one's stick in offensive and defensive techniques (as in lacrosse, polo, hockey) **2 :** batting ability in baseball
stickwort \ˈ=ˌ=\ *n* [5*stick* + *wort*] **:** AGRIMONY
1sticky \ˈstikē, -ki\ *adj* -ER/-EST [1*stick* + *-y*] **1 :** resembling a stick **:** WOODY **2 :** *of a person* **:** somewhat wooden **:** lacking animation
2sticky \"\ *adj* -ER/-EST [5*stick* + *-y*] **1 :** having the quality of adhering or of holding or retarding by or as if by adhesion **:** ADHESIVE ⟨stepped in something ~⟩ ⟨road was very ~ after the rain⟩ ⟨quaking and ~ area . . . has been a deathtrap for unwary animals —*Amer. Guide Series: Calif.*⟩: as **a** (1) *of a substance* **:** GLUEY, GLUTINOUS, VISCID, VISCOUS ⟨~ syrup⟩ ⟨paint was still ~⟩ ⟨wad of ~ chewing gum⟩ ⟨black ~ mud⟩ (2) **:** smeared or coated with a sticky substance ⟨table was ~⟩ ⟨wall had been painted and was still ~⟩ ⟨~ cinnamon buns⟩ ⟨how she ever got her face so ~⟩ **b** *of a turf wicket in cricket* **:** having a surface that is temporarily tacky or viscid from drying in the sun after being soaked with rain and that heavily favors spin bowlers **c** *of snow* **:** just beginning to melt **2 :** HUMID, MUGGY ⟨a ~ day⟩ ⟨a hot and ~ hour or two on shore —W.H.Ingrams⟩ **:** moist with perspiration with the clothing sticking to the body **:** CLAMMY, MESSY **3 :** offering or tending to offer resistance: as **a** *of a horse* **:** apt to hesitate at a fence or to jump from a standstill or a trot **b :** apt to impede or be impeded in movement or progress (as by wedging or blocking) ⟨~ windows⟩ ⟨~ valves⟩ ⟨found that control movement . . . was not ~, like many, but free and smooth —*Skyways*⟩ **c** (1) **:** resistant to change **:** not moving **:** RIGID ⟨~ prices⟩ ⟨consumer habits are probably more ~ than variations in the level of income are —H.W.Grayson⟩ ⟨labor supply is ~, perverse, and often unpredictable —L.R.Tripp⟩ (2) **:** hard to sell ⟨reported that television sets had become ~⟩ **:** difficult to secure payment on when due ⟨~ accounts receivable⟩ ⟨~ bank loans⟩ **d** (1) **:** inclined to make difficulties **:** hard to please **:** BALKY, FUSSY, METICULOUS, PARTICULAR ⟨tickets are available if you are not ~ about a special day —*Saturday Rev.*⟩ ⟨ought to be satisfactory to the *stickiest* State Department jurist —V.M.Fry⟩ (2) **:** DIFFICULT, TROUBLESOME ⟨a ~ question⟩ ⟨~ problems⟩ ⟨found the going ~⟩ ⟨the *stickiest* part of the whole operation —*New Yorker*⟩ **4 a :** DISAGREEABLE, PAINFUL, UNPLEASANT ⟨a rather ~ past she wanted to hide —J.B.Priestley⟩ ⟨seemed likely to come to a ~ end⟩ **b :** AWKWARD, STIFF, UNCOMFORTABLE ⟨after a rather ~ beginning became firm friends⟩ ⟨scarcely knew each other, and the talk was decidedly ~ —E.M.Forster⟩ ⟨when royalty is in the audience, things are generally very ~ —*New Yorker*⟩ **5 :** suggestive of a viscid substance or mass (as in lacking strength, solidity, or substance); *esp* **:** characterized by sentimentality **:** SACCHARINE, SLUSHY ⟨a ~ adagio —Wilder Hobson⟩ ⟨a long ~ death scene —*Time*⟩ ⟨a score as ~ as treacle —John McCarten⟩ ⟨invest childhood with a ~ but romantic gloss —Osbert Sitwell⟩
3sticky \"\ *vt* -ED/-ING/-ES **:** to make sticky ⟨children were *stickied* up with popcorn and lollipops and ice cream⟩
stickybeak \ˈ=ˌ=ˌ=\ *n* [2*sticky* + *beak*] *Austral* **:** an inquisitive person **:** BUSYBODY
sticky bomb *or* **sticky charge** *or* **sticky grenade** *n* **:** an explosive charge covered with an adhesive that when thrown against an object (as an armored vehicle) sticks until it explodes
sticky cockle *n* **:** NIGHT-FLOWERING CATCHFLY
sticky currant *n* **:** a leafy shrub (*Ribes viscosissimum*) of the western U.S. having black fruit and glandular hispid petioles and branchlets
sticky dog *n, cricket* **:** a wicket that has become sticky
sticky-fingered *also* **sticky-handed** \ˈ=ˌ=ˈ=ˌ=\ *adj* **:** given to stealing **:** apt to steal **:** LARCENOUS, THIEVING, THIEVISH
sticky-heads \ˈ=ˌ=ˌ=\ *n pl but sing or pl in constr* **:** GUMWEED
sticky laurel *n* **:** a buckbrush (*Ceanothus velutinus*) with gummy twigs and evergreen leaves
stic·ta \ˈstiktə\ *n, cap* [NL, fr. Gk *stiktē*, fem. of *stiktos* tattooed, spotted, fr. *stizein* to tattoo — more at STICK] **:** a large genus (the type of the family Stictaceae) of mainly tropical lichens having a foliaceous lobed thallus that is commonly coriaceous in texture
stic·ta·ce·ae \stikˈtāsēˌē\ *n pl, cap* [NL, fr. *Sticta*, type genus + *-aceae*] **:** a family of common foliaceous lichens comprising the two genera *Lobaria* and *Sticta*
stic·ti·form \ˈstiktəˌfȯrm\ *adj* [NL *Sticta* + E *-iform*] **:** resembling in form a lichen of the genus *Sticta*
stic·tis \ˈstiktəs\ *n, cap* [NL, irreg. fr. Gk *stiktos* tattooed, spotted] **:** a genus (the type of the family Stictidaceae) of fungi characterized by sunken pilose perithecia and filiform many-septate hyaline ascospores
stid·dy \ˈstidi\ *dial Brit var of* STITHY

stie *obs var of* STY
stied *past of* STY
stie·gel glass \ˈstēgəl-\ *n, usu cap S* [after Henry William *Stiegel* †1785 Am. glassmaker] **1 :** a late eighteenth century American flint or green glassware made in Pennsylvania; *esp* **:** fine flint glassware with engraved or enameled decoration **2 :** bubbly green glassware resembling some of the eighteenth century Stiegel glasswares
stieng \ˈstēŋ\ *n, pl* **stieng** *or* **stiengs** *usu cap* **1 :** a people related to the Cambodians and inhabiting Thudaumot province of So. Vietnam **2 :** a member of the Stieng people
sties *pres 3d sing of* STY, *pl of* STY
stieve *chiefly Scot var of* 1STEEVE
stife \ˈstīf\ *n* [perh. irreg. fr. 3*stifle*] *dial Brit* **:** a stifling fume or smell
1stiff \ˈstif\ *adj* -ER/-EST [ME *stif*, fr. OE *stīf*; akin to MD *stijf* stiff, MLG *stīf* stiff, ON *stīfla* to dam up, L *stipare* to press together, Gk *steibein* to tread on, Lith *stipti* to be stiff, Russ *stebel'* stalk] **1 a :** incapable of or resistant to being flexed or bent **:** RIGID ⟨wears a ~ collar⟩ ⟨sitting . . . on the edge of a ~ chair —Scott Fitzgerald⟩ ⟨a palace guardsman, ~ as a poker in his tall busby, stands sentinel⟩ ⟨knots in the gaskets were ~ with frost —C.B.Nordhoff & J.N.Hall⟩ **b :** exhibiting rigor mortis ⟨still unburied, lay . . . ~ and stark —R.L.Stevenson⟩ **c :** lacking in suppleness — used esp. of the muscles and joints ⟨my body was ~ from exertion as well as from cold —Jack London⟩ ⟨tried to smile . . . but her face felt ~ —Margaret Deland⟩ **d** *obs* **:** tightly stretched **:** TAUT ⟨another arrow forth from his ~ string he sent —George Chapman⟩ **e :** impeded in movement (as by friction) — used of a mechanism ⟨clocks whose mannikins went through . . . ~ and elegant movements —Lewis Mumford⟩ **f :** slowed or immobilized by intoxication **:** DRUNK ⟨after drinking . . . in that bar for two hours, I was pretty ~ —W.R.Hecox⟩ **2 a :** characterized by moral courage **:** FIRM, RESOLUTE ⟨has taken a ~ position that it has the power to forbid its contractors to bargain with unions —R.S.Brown⟩ ⟨kept a ~ upper lip for the term of his ordeal —Bruce Dearing⟩ **b :** characterized by obstinacy **:** STUBBORN, UNYIELDING ⟨took a rather ~ . . . stand in defense of his handiwork —Dexter Perkins⟩ **c :** characterized by independence or self-esteem **:** PROUD ⟨passeth by with ~ unbowed knee —Shak.⟩ ⟨too poor to go and too ~ to tell her the reason —*Time*⟩ **d** (1) **:** marked by reserve, decorum, or respect for ceremony **:** FORMAL, PUNCTILIOUS ⟨the easy warmth you knew has given place to a ~ courtesy —H.J.Laski⟩ ⟨brought his hand . . . to the visor of his cap in a ~ salute —Wirt Williams⟩ (2) **:** lacking in ease or grace **:** STILTED, UNBENDING ⟨a style which is lofty but not ~ —C.D.Lewis⟩ ⟨too arid and ~ a melody for song —M.F. Bukofger⟩ **3 :** hard fought **:** PUGNACIOUS, SHARP ⟨salmon give a ~ fight until landed —*Amer. Guide Series: Maine*⟩ ⟨she had driven a ~ bargain —Ann F. Wolfe⟩ ⟨heading into a year of ~ competition —Herbert Koshetz⟩ **4 a** *obs* **:** solidly constructed **:** STURDY, STALWART ⟨make you ready your ~ bats and clubs —Shak.⟩ **b** (1) **:** exerting great force **:** STRONG, VIOLENT ⟨a ~ west wind was whooping in off the prairies —F.B.Gipson⟩ (2) **:** of an energetic or powerful nature **:** FORCEFUL, VIGOROUS ⟨follow . . . on a ~ lope —Bruce Siberts⟩ ⟨landed . . . a ~ left to the head —*Ring*⟩ **c :** containing a relatively large amount of the main ingredient (as alcohol or a medicine) **:** POTENT ⟨a couple of ~ cocktails relaxed him completely⟩ ⟨a ~ dose of cod liver oil⟩ **5 a :** of a dense or glutinous consistency **:** THICK, VISCOUS ⟨the concrete is allowed to stand until it is quite ~ but still workable —*Building Estimating & Contracting*⟩ ⟨a grease that does a good job of protecting metal —*Monsanto Mag.*⟩ ⟨beat the egg whites until ~ —Ruth Hutchison⟩ **b :** consisting of or abounding in clay **:** HEAVY ⟨soils . . . that are wet and ~ —F.D.Smith & Barbara Wilcox⟩ **c :** thickly covered or completely filled **:** CROWDED, PERVADED ⟨an audience ~ with academic dignitaries —Mollie Panter-Downes⟩ ⟨something in the air, intangible, yet ~ with meaning, struck my senses —Edna S. V. Millay⟩ **6 a :** harsh or disagreeable in character **:** SEVERE, TOUGH ⟨get a ~ fine for disorderly conduct —S.H.Holbrook⟩ ⟨Nicaragua objected and ~ notes were exchanged —*Newsweek*⟩ **b :** demanding physical exertion **:** ARDUOUS, RUGGED ⟨~ terrain⟩ ⟨a ~ . . . hike up the trail, among jagged boulders and through crevasses —*Amer. Guide Series: Ark.*⟩ ⟨leading an orchestra is ~ work —Robert Rice⟩ **c :** requiring strenuous mental effort **:** DIFFICULT, EXACTING ⟨the examination was so ~ that none below the highest grades of university honors men . . . could hope to be selected —W.T.Stace⟩ ⟨the casual reader will find certain parts of this book ~ going —Ralph Linton⟩ **7 :** inherently not easily heeled over by an external force (as the wind) **:** righting itself quickly when tipped — used of a ship; compare 9CRANK, STEADY 1c **8 a :** excessive in amount **:** EXPENSIVE, STEEP ⟨the rent is a ~ $500 a week —Henry Hewes⟩ ⟨satellite goods paid a ~ duty to enter France —Stringfellow Barr⟩ **b :** maintaining a high level **:** tending to rise **:** BULLISH, UNYIELDING ⟨a ~ market⟩ ⟨buyers . . . find sellers ~ —*London Daily News*⟩ **9 :** UNGUARDED — used in a card game of a high honor that is a singleton
syn STIFF, RIGID, INFLEXIBLE, TENSE, STARK, and WOODEN can mean, in common, so firm or hard as to be difficult or impossible to bend literally or figuratively. STIFF, the most common, can apply to any degree of this condition or to something difficult to work or beat ⟨a *stiff* rod⟩ ⟨a book with *stiff* covers⟩ ⟨hinges that are a bit *stiff*⟩ ⟨a *stiff* pudding⟩ ⟨a *stiff* smile⟩ ⟨to stand straight and *stiff*⟩ RIGID applies to anything so stiff that bending will break it ⟨a *rigid* board⟩ ⟨the *rigid* wings of a plane⟩ INFLEXIBLE is like RIGID but stresses more the lack of suppleness or pliability ⟨an *inflexible* plastic material⟩ ⟨an *inflexible* shaft on a golf club⟩ TENSE, implying tautness, usu. applies to muscles or nerves strained in expectation of activity or by nervous excitement ⟨with muscles *tense* in position to spring⟩ ⟨nerves *tense* with anxiety⟩ STARK implies a stiffness associated with loss of life, warmth, and vitality, often connoting desolation, barrenness, or death ⟨told her once that cut flowers before they actually die . . . stretch themselves out with a palpable jerk, *stark* and rigid —J.C.Powys⟩ ⟨here all the surfaces remained *stark* and unyielding, thin and sharp, like impoverished old maids —George Santayana⟩ ⟨rats . . . danced comically before they died, and lay in the scuppers *stark* and ruffled —Sinclair Lewis⟩ WOODEN, in this application suggesting the hardness and lack of suppleness of wood, implies clumsiness, deadness or heaviness of spirit, or lack of grace or animation ⟨a face that was *wooden* with misery —Rebecca West⟩ ⟨*wooden* humorlessness —*Times Lit. Supp.*⟩ ⟨the *wooden* neatness of routine and failure —Howard Moss⟩
2stiff \"\ *adv, often* -ER/-EST [ME *stif*, fr. *stif*, adj.] **1 :** STIFFLY ⟨stood up straight and ~ —R.L.Stevenson⟩ ⟨wears a uniform that is starched ~⟩ **2 :** to an extreme degree **:** INTENSELY, SEVERELY ⟨bored ~⟩ ⟨scared ~⟩ ⟨advanced into the doctor's consulting room . . . was frightened ~ —Mary McCarthy⟩
3stiff \"\ *vt* -ED/-ING/-S [ME *stiffen*, fr. *stif*, adj.] **1 :** STIFFEN; *esp* **:** to remove the oil in (a French finish) with a rubber **2** *slang* **:** to withhold money from **:** CHEAT, CHISEL; *esp* **:** to refrain from tipping ⟨cabdrivers often get ~*ed*⟩
4stiff \"\ *n* -s [1*stiff*] **1 :** one that is stiff: as **a :** a stiffened article of clothing (as a collar or a petticoat) **b** *slang* (1) **:** negotiable paper **:** MONEY (2) **:** counterfeit bills or a forged check (3) **:** a letter, card, or legal document (as a certificate or license); *esp* **:** a note smuggled between prison inmates (4) **:** something (as a folded newspaper) used by a pickpocket to hide his maneuvers **c** (1) **:** CORPSE, CADAVER (2) **:** a haughty, prim, or boring person (3) **:** DRUNK (4) *slang* **:** CHEAP SKATE, TIGHTWAD; *esp* **:** one who tips poorly or not at all **2 a :** a crude or disreputable fellow **:** BUM, TRAMP ⟨looked like a mission ~ who had wandered uptown from the Bowery —Joel Sayre⟩ ⟨got the breaks, the lucky ~*s* —Jan Peerce⟩ **b :** a blue-collar worker **:** LABORER, HAND ⟨of first importance to every working ~, farmer and businessman in America —E.A.Lahey⟩ ⟨knew enough about the business to hire on as a construction ~ —*Time*⟩; *esp* **:** FLOATER 4 **3 :** a horse not intended to win or certain not to win a race ⟨no way even of knowing if his horse is trying to win or is a ~ just sent out for the exercise —Ernest Havemann⟩ **syn** see VAGABOND
stiff *abbr* stiffener
1stiff-arm \ˈ=ˌ=\ *vb* [fr. the noun phrase *stiff arm*, fr. 1*stiff* + *arm*, n.] **:** STRAIGHT-ARM

2stiff-arm \"\ *n* **:** STRAIGHT-ARM
stiff aster *n* **:** a wiry tufted perennial herb (*Aster linariifolia*) of the eastern U. S. with stiff erect rough stems, linear leaves, and large heads of violet flowers terminating the branchlets
stiff-backed \ˈ=ˈ=\ *adj* **1 :** rigidly erect ⟨a *stiff-backed* sergeant⟩ **2 :** punctiliously correct **:** HAUGHTY, UNBENDING ⟨a *stiff-backed* aristocrat⟩ ⟨*stiff-backed* Boston⟩
stiff·en \ˈstifən *also* -f°m\ *vb* **stiffened; stiffened; stiffening** \-f(ə)niŋ\ **stiffens** [ME *stiffnen*, fr. *stif*, adj., stiff + *-nen* -en] *vt* **1 a** (1) **:** to make stronger or more resolute **:** BOLSTER, SUPPORT ⟨busy . . . reordering his ship, and ~*ing* the morale of his crew —Llewellyn Howland⟩ ⟨felt the honor of the whole army rising within me and ~*ing* my backbone —R.H. Davis⟩ ⟨his papers are ~*ed* with solid facts and a scholar's indignation —E.A.Weeks⟩ (2) **:** to make tougher or more effective ⟨~ the armies . . . with an increasing leaven of mercenaries —J.E.M.White⟩ ⟨recommended ~*ing* the Refugee Relief Act —Dorothy Kahn⟩ (3) **:** to make more obstinate or intransigent ⟨a powerful will ~*ed* by many years of opposition —Helen Macafee⟩ **b** (1) **:** to make tight or hard **:** reduce in resilience **:** TAUTEN, IMMOBILIZE ⟨his sinews ~*ed* themselves in tense readiness —C.G.D.Roberts⟩ ⟨he was ~*ed* straight by a back trouble —A.C.Spectorsky⟩; *specif* **:** to knock out (a boxing opponent) ⟨~*ed* the . . . fighter in the first round —*Irish Digest*⟩ (2) **:** BENUMB ⟨spent his evenings ~*ing* himself with gin —V.S.Pritchett⟩ **c :** to make more stilted or inflexible **:** CONSTRICT, FORMALIZE ⟨poetic diction that has ~*ed* into corpses so many orthodox poetic dramas —Leslie Rees⟩ ⟨~*ed* one of the most picturesque of human beings . . . into a stock figure —Carl Van Doren⟩ **2 a :** to make denser or firmer **:** THICKEN, SOLIDIFY ⟨milk well ~*ed* with wheaten flour —G.E.Fussell⟩ ⟨phosphorus ~*s* and strengthens wire —*Monsanto Mag.*⟩; *specif* **:** to reinforce (as an article of clothing) by stitching, sizing, interfacing, interlining, wiring ⟨drapery ~*ed* with stiff starch —F.J.Mather⟩ ⟨hat brims are ~*ed* to hold their shape⟩ **b :** to alter the structure or ballast of (a ship) to prevent excessive heeling **:** STABILIZE **c :** to increase the ratio of inductance to capacity in (an electric circuit) **3 :** to cause to rise or be increased **:** fix at a high level ⟨~ prices⟩ ⟨~ the market⟩ ⟨a definite trend toward ~*ing* of money rates —*Wall Street Jour.*⟩ ~ *vi* **1 a :** THICKEN, HARDEN ⟨mud ~*s* as it dries⟩ **b :** to become physically taut or mentally inflexible ⟨~*ed* in her saddle and tossed her head —T.B.Costain⟩ ⟨my resolve to stick it out ~*ed* —V.G.Heiser⟩ ⟨young feelings ~ in senile works —Malcolm Cowley⟩ **2 :** to increase in strength or difficulty ⟨a ~*ing* breeze⟩ ⟨the climb ~*s* as we near the top⟩ **3 :** to become firmer ⟨stock prices ~*ed* in the final few hours of trading⟩
stiff·en·er \-f(ə)nə(r)\ *n* -s **:** one that stiffens: as **a :** a worker who sizes hats **b :** something (as buckram or a piece of paperboard) used for stiffening a manufactured article; *specif* **:** 5COUNTER 5 **c :** any of a number of vertical angles secured at intervals across the entire width of the web of a large plate girder to prevent buckling **d :** an angle iron, channel, or other structural shape used to increase the rigidity of plating on a ship's bulkhead — called also *stiffening bar* **e :** a structural member other than a flat sheet used to reinforce the frame of an aircraft — compare STRINGER **f :** an alcoholic bracer
1stiffening *n* -s [fr. gerund of *stiffen*] **1 :** the act or process of making or becoming stiff **2 :** STIFFENER
2stiffening *adj* [fr. pres. part. of *stiffen*] **:** making or becoming stiff ⟨a ~ truss for the floor of a suspension bridge⟩ ⟨the days of a ~ cold war —G.E.G.Catlin⟩
stiffening bar *n* **:** STIFFENER d
stiffer *comparative of* STIFF
stiffest *superlative of* STIFF
stiff gentian *n* **:** FIVE-FLOWERED GENTIAN
stiffing *pres part of* STIFF
stiff·ish \ˈstifish\ *adj* **:** moderately stiff: as **a :** fairly rigid or inflexible ⟨the zinnia is a ~ flower⟩ **b :** rather strong ⟨a ~ wind⟩ **c :** tending toward constraint or formality ⟨a ~ diplomatic dinner⟩ ⟨grand old lady, ~, but imposing —O.W. Holmes †1894⟩ **d :** pretty high **:** STEEP ⟨demanded a ~ advance —Burns Mantle⟩
stiff-lamb disease *or* **stiff lamb** *n* **1 :** a deficiency disease of lambs marked by muscular degeneration, difficulty in standing and walking, and general weakness and prostration and thought to be due to inadequate intake of vitamin E **2 :** a condition of young lambs marked by stiffness or lameness
stiffleg derrick \ˈ=ˌ=-\ *or* **stiffleg** *n* **:** a derrick whose framework rests on a fixed tripod of poles or timbers
stiff·ly *adv* [ME *stifly*, fr. *stif*, adj., stiff + *-ly*] **1 :** in a stiff manner **2 :** to an advanced degree of stiffness
stiff-mud process *n* **:** a brickmaking process in which a stiff mixture of water and clay is extruded in a continuous column through a die and individual bricks are cut by wires from the column as it emerges — compare SOFT-MUD PROCESS
stiff neck *n* **1 a :** fibrositis of the neck muscles **b :** TORTICOLLIS **2 a :** a proud or stubborn person **:** one with a haughty bearing **b :** OBSTINACY ⟨I know thy rebellion and thy *stiff neck* —Deut 31:27 (AV)⟩
stiff-necked \ˈ=ˈ=\ *adj* [trans. of Gk *sklērotrachēlos*] **1 :** characterized by arrogance or obstinacy **:** HAUGHTY, STUBBORN ⟨a *stiff-necked* aristocrat⟩ ⟨*stiff-necked* pride⟩ **2 :** STILTED ⟨it is *stiff-necked* . . . and at its best comes over with simple, not *stiff-necked* . . . unaffected power —*Times Lit. Supp.*⟩ **syn** see OBSTINATE
stiff-necked·ly \ˈ=ˈnekədlē, -ktlē\ *adv* **:** in a stiff-necked manner
stiff-necked·ness \-kədnəs, -ktn-\ *n* -ES **:** the quality or state of being stiff-necked **:** PRIDE, OBSTINACY
stiff·ness *n* -ES [ME *stifnesse*, fr. *stif*, adj., stiff + *-nesse* -ness] **1 a :** DENSITY, RIGIDITY ⟨14 kinds of varnish each differing in ~ —F.W.Hoch⟩ ⟨toothbrushes vary in the ~ of their bristles⟩ **b :** resistance (as of a structural beam) to bending under stress within the elastic limit — opposed to *compliance;* compare DEFLECTION 3a **c :** resistance of a ship to rolling **:** STABILITY **2 a :** lack of suppleness **:** INFLEXIBILITY ⟨pains in the limbs and growing ~, finally, paralysis —*Monsanto Mag.*⟩ **b :** firmness of attitude **:** RESOLUTION, OBDURACY ⟨unyielding ~ of will —O.J.Baab⟩ **c :** lack of ease or grace **:** punctilious conduct **:** FORMALITY, CONSTRAINT ⟨the ~ of conventional opera —Arthur Knight⟩ ⟨had given up his ~ and begun to laugh —Vicki Baum⟩
stiffs *pl of* STIFF, *pres 3d sing of* STIFF
stifftail \ˈ=ˌ=\ *n* **:** RUDDY DUCK
stiff upper lip *n* **:** a determined attitude or effort in the face of trouble — usu. used in the phrase *keep a stiff upper lip*
1sti·fle \ˈstīfəl\ *also* **stifle joint** *n* -s [ME *stifle*] **:** the joint next above the hock and near the flank in the hind leg of various quadrupeds (as horses and dogs) **:** the joint corresponding to the knee in man — see HORSE illustration
2stifle \"\ *vt* -ED/-ING/-S **:** to affect with dislocation of the stifle bone or disease in the stifle — usu. used in passive
3stifle \ˈstīfəl\ *vb* **stifled; stifled; stifling** \-f(ə)liŋ\ **stifles** [alter. of ME *stuflen, stufflen*, prob. modif. of MF *estouffer* to smother, suffocate] *vt* **1** *obs* **:** to kill by submersion **:** DROWN ⟨threw herself into a deep well, in which she was *stifled* —William Bosman⟩ **2 a :** to kill by depriving of oxygen **:** ASPHYXIATE, SUFFOCATE ⟨shall I not then be *stifled* in the vault —Shak.⟩ ⟨every living thing . . . must have perished slowly or suddenly, *stifled* by the mud —Francis Kingdon-Ward⟩ **b** (1) **:** to blanket or envelop to the point of suffocation **:** SMOTHER ⟨the oppressive air *stifled* her, and she felt that her breath . . . was suspended —Ellen Glasgow⟩ (2) *archaic* **:** to extinguish (fire) by covering **:** SNUFF ⟨travelers, armed with felt carpets, were endeavoring to ~ the flame —William Hazlitt †1893⟩ (3) **:** to mute by or as if by enveloping or screening **:** MUFFLE ⟨units can be insulated so they almost entirely ~ noise of operation —Jim Riggs⟩ **3 a :** to cut off (as the voice or breath) **:** SILENCE ⟨engulfing flames soon ~ their cries⟩ **b** *archaic* **:** to withhold from circulation **:** CONCEAL, SUPPRESS ⟨the papers he thought of too much value to be *stifled*, and advised the printing of them —Benjamin Franklin⟩ **c :** to withhold from expression **:** keep in check **:** REPRESS ⟨not the sort of man to ~ anger —J.E.Macdonnell⟩ **d :** to curb or quell by force **:** INHIBIT, RESTRAIN ⟨~ free speech by breaking up meetings . . . and confiscating pamphlets —Zechariah Chafee⟩ ⟨a belligerent right to ~ the trade of an

enemy —F.L.Paxson⟩ **e** *archaic* : to arrest the flow of : ABSORB, OBSTRUCT ⟨they stop and ∼ . . . the rays which they do not reflect or transmit —Isaac Newton⟩ **2** : to act as a deterrent to : deprive of initiative or vitality : DISCOURAGE, TRAMMEL ⟨the mountain barrier ∼s the commerce which might develop —P.E.James⟩ ⟨economic controls, which have . . . *stifled* our economy —A.E.Summerfield⟩ ⟨vital art is *stifled* by culture, which insists that artists . . . imitate old masters —Clive Bell⟩ ∼ *vi* **1** : to become suffocated by or as if by lack of oxygen : SMOTHER ⟨no need to ∼ in a hot kitchen this summer —*Better Homes & Gardens*⟩ ⟨my unsoiled name . . . will so your accusations overweigh, that you shall ∼ in your own report —*Shak.*⟩ **2** : to undergo repression or restraint ⟨why should I ∼ in a convent —P.B.Kyne⟩ **syn** see SUFFOCATE

⁴stifle \"\ *n -s* : a suffocating atmosphere ⟨the ∼ of the subway —*Everybody's Mag.*⟩

stifle bone *n* : the patella in the stifle of a quadruped

stifled *adj* : marked by suffocation or restraint : SMOTHERED, REPRESSED ⟨almost . . . with resentment —G.B.Shaw⟩ ⟨a politely ∼ yawn⟩ ⟨galvanize the ∼ energies of the nation —*Atlantic*⟩ — **sti·fled·ly** *adv*

sti·fler \"stif(ə)lə(r)\ *n -s* : one that stifles

stifling *adj* : producing suffocation or restraint : OPPRESSIVE, HAMPERING ⟨∼ heat⟩ ⟨stagnation under a ∼ orthodoxy —R.A.Lester⟩ — **sti·fling·ly** *adv*

stig·ma \'stigmə\ *n, pl* **stigma·ta** \stig'mäd·ə, 'stigmə|, stig'mä|, |tə\ *or* **stigmas** [L *stigma*, *stigma* mark, brand, fr. Gk, mark, tattoo mark, fr. *steizein* to tattoo — more at STICK] **1 a** *archaic* : a scar left by a hot iron : BRAND ⟨when a burning iron is put on the face of an evildoer, it leaveth behind it a . . . —Samuel Rutherford⟩ **b** : a mark of shame or discredit : DISGRACE, STAIN ⟨the ∼ of personal cowardice —William Peden⟩ ⟨the pathos and the ∼ of slavery —W.H. Sperry⟩ ⟨avoid the ∼ of being called unprogressive —W.H. Camp⟩ **c** : an identifying mark or characteristic ⟨the clothing and characteristic *stigmata* of the profession —R.P.Blackmur⟩ ⟨curmudgeonly inability to praise others which has ever been the ∼ by which we may recognize the ungenerous —Eric Partridge⟩; *specif* : a symptom of a physical or mental disorder ⟨∼s of the riboflavin deficiency state include ocular changes —*Therapeutic Notes*⟩ ⟨stigmata of degeneration, drug addictions, and nervous and mental diseases —H.G.Armstrong⟩ **d** : a mark or label indicating deviation from a norm ⟨a further ∼ is the tendency for most phrases to end on the tonic —Bruno Nettl⟩ **2 a** *stigmata pl* : marks resembling the wounds on the crucified body of Christ and believed to be supernaturally impressed upon the bodies of various persons (as St. Francis of Assisi) **b** : PETECHIA **3** [NL *stigmat-*, *stigma*, fr. L] **a** (1) : a spiracle of an insect or other arthropod or the opening into one of the lung sacs of an arachnid (2) : PTEROSTIGMA (3) : an androconium forming a conspicuously colored spot on the forewing of the male of various butterflies **b** : a portion of the pistil of a flower usu. apical on the style or ovary and often viscid or rough which receives the pollen grains and upon which they germinate — see FLOWER illustration **c** : the spot or projection on the surface of an ovary at which a Graafian follicle will rupture **d** (1) : the eyespot of a protozoan (2) : a nephridiopore of an annelid (3) : one of the small clefts or perforations in the branchial sac of an ascidian

stig·mal \'stigmal\ *adj* [*stigma* + -*al*] : of or relating to a stigma

stigmal plate *n* : a chitinized often sculptured or punctate plate covering a respiratory opening in various insect larvae and in ticks

stigmal vein *n* : a short vein extending obliquely from the stigma in various hymenopterous insects

stig·mar·ia \stig'ma(ə)rēə\ *n* [NL, fr. L *stigma* mark + NL -*aria*] **1** *cap* : a form genus of Carboniferous plants based on elongated, cylindrical, and sometimes branched structures that have rounded depressions scattered over the surface and are generally conceded to be underground portions of lepidodendrids (as of the genera *Sigillaria* and *Lepidodendron*) **2** *pl* **stigmariae** *also* **stigmarias** : any plant or fossil of the genus *Stigmaria* — **stig·mar·i·an** \-ēən\ *adj or n*

stig·mar·i·oid \-ē,ȯid\ *adj* [NL *Stigmaria* + E -*oid*] : resembling or related to a stigmaria

stig·mas·ter·ol \stig'mastə,rȯl, -rōl\ *n -s* [ISV *stigma-* (fr. NL *Physostigma*) + *sterol* — more at PHYSOSTIGMA] : a crystalline steroid alcohol $C_{29}H_{47}OH$ obtained esp. from the oil of Calabar beans and from soybean oil usu. in mixtures with sitosterols and used in the synthesis of progesterone

¹stig·mat·ic \(')stig'mad·ik, -at|, |ēk\ *adj* [ML *stigmaticus* branded, fr. L *stigmat-*, *stigma* mark, brand + -*icus* -ic — more at STIGMA] **1 a** *archaic* : having a physical blemish or deformity **b** : having or conveying a social stigma : CENSORIOUS, DETESTABLE ⟨the ∼ status usually accorded an occupying power —R.J.D.Braibanti⟩ **2** : STIGMAL, STIGMATIFEROUS **3** : of, relating to, or accompanying supernatural stigmata **4** : ANASTIGMATIC — used esp. of a bundle of light rays intersecting at a single point ⟨∼ spectroscope⟩ — **stig·mat·i·cal·ly** \-k(ə)lē, -ik, -li\ *adv*

²stigmatic \"\ *n -s* **1** *archaic* : one marked with a stigma **2** : one that is believed to bear supernatural stigmata ⟨one of the most remarkable ∼s in history —*Time*⟩

stigmatical [ML *stigmaticus* + E -*al*] : STIGMATIC ⟨he is deformed, crooked . . . in making, worse in mind —*Shak.*⟩

stigmatic cell *n* : LID CELL 1

stig·ma·tif·er·ous \ stigmə|tif(ə)rəs\ *adj* [prob. fr. (assumed) NL *stigmatifer* stigmatiferous (fr. L *stigmat-*, *stigma* + -*ifer* -iferous) + E -*ous*] : bearing a stigmata

stig·mat·i·form \stig'mad·ə,form, 'stigməd·-\ *adj* [prob. fr. (assumed) NL *stigmatiformis*, fr. L *stigmat-*, *stigma* + -*iformis* -iform] : having the form or appearance of a stigma

stig·ma·tism \'stigmə,tizəm\ *n -s* [L *stigmat-*, *stigma* + E -*ism*] : the condition of an optical system (as a lens or mirror) in which rays of light from a single point converge in a single focal point — compare ASTIGMATISM

stig·ma·tist \'stigməd·ə̇st\ *n -s* [L *stigmat-*, *stigma* + E -*ist*] : STIGMATIC 2

stig·ma·ti·za·tion \stigməd·ə̇'zāshən, -məd·ī'z-, -mə̇,tī'z-\ *n -s* [prob. fr. (assumed) NL *stigmatization-*, *stigmatizatio*, fr. ML *stigmatizatus* (past part. of *stigmatizare* to stigmatize) + L -*ion-*, -*io* -ion] **1** : an act or instance of stigmatizing ⟨a government ∼ which would deter the public from consideration of the opinions of the party —*Civil Liberty*⟩ **2** : the production of what are believed to be supernatural stigmata on the body

stig·ma·tize \'stigmə,tīz\ *vt* -ED/-ING/-s *see* -ize *in Explan Notes* [ML *stigmatizare*, fr. L *stigmat-*, *stigmata* + LL -*izare* -ize] **1 a** *archaic* : to brand with a hot iron **b** : to set a stigma upon : regard with opprobrium : CENSURE, DENOUNCE ⟨critics . . . America's technological good fortune as machine-worship —Adrienne Koch⟩ ⟨people who so much as whisper during a performance are . . . *stigmatized* as barbarians —Joseph Wechsberg⟩ **2** : to mark with stigmata ⟨a visit to the *stigmatized* seer —*U.S. Daily*⟩ **3** : DESIGNATE, IDENTIFY ⟨I wish . . . that the fates had not *stigmatized* me "writer" —Aldous Huxley⟩

stig·mo·de·ra \,stigmə'dirə, stig'mädərə\ *n, cap* [NL, prob. fr. *stigmo-* + L *dera* (fr. Gk *derē*, *deirē* neck) — more at DER-] : a large chiefly Australian genus of buprestid beetles many of which are brilliant green

stig·mo·nose \'stigmə,nōs *also* -,ōz\ *n -s* [*stigmo-* (fr. L *stigmat-*, *stigma*) + Gk *nosos* disease] : a disease characterized by translucent dots in leaves and spotting, dimpling, malformation, and sometimes dwarfing of fruits and caused by punctures made by small insects (as aphids, thrips, and leafhoppers)

sti·kine \stə'kēn\ *n, pl* **stikine** *or* **stikines** *usu cap* **1 a** : a Tlingit people along the Stikine River in Alaska **b** : a member of such people **2** : the language of the Stikine people

stilb \'stilb\ *n -s* [ISV, fr. Gk *stilbē* lamp] : a cgs unit of brightness equal to one candle per square centimeter of cross section perpendicular to the rays

stil·ba·ce·ae \stil'bāsē,ē\ *n pl, cap* [NL, fr. *Stilbum* + -*aceae*] *syn of* STILBELLACEAE

stil·ba·ceous \"\ \(')stil'bāshəs\ *adj* [NL *Stilbaceae* + E -*ous*] : of or relating to the Stilbaceae

stilb·am·i·dine \(')stil'bamə,dēn, -,dən\ *n* [*stilb-* (as in *stil-*

bene) + *amidine*] : a diamidine $[NH_2C(=NH)C_6H_4CH=]_2$ derived from stilbene and used chiefly in the form of its crystalline isethionate salt in treating various fungal infections (as systemic blastomycosis)

stil·bel·la \stil'belə\ *n, cap* [NL, fr. Gk *stilbos* glistening + -*ella*] : a genus (the type of the family Stilbellaceae) of imperfect fungi forming capitate synemata or coremia and bearing continuous hyaline conidia

stil·bel·la·ce·ae \,stilbə'lāsē,ē\ *n pl, cap* [NL, fr. *Stilbella*, type genus + -*aceae*] : a family of fungi of the order Moniliales — see STILBELLA

stil·bene \'stil,bēn\ *n -s* [ISV *stilb-* (fr. Gk *stilbos* glistening) + -*ene*] : an aromatic hydrocarbon $C_6H_5CH=CHC_6H_5$ occurring in cis and trans forms : *sym*-diphenyl-ethylene; *esp* : the more stable trans form obtained in large shining crystals (as by heating benzaldehyde with sulfur or by dehydrating benzyl-phenyl-carbinol) useful as phosphors (as in scintillation counters)

stilbene dye *n* : any of a class of usu. yellow to orange direct cotton azo dyes derived from stilbene; *also* : any of various fluorescent brighteners derived from stilbene

stil·bes·trol \stil'bes,trȯl, -rȯl\ *also* **stil·boes·trol** \" *sometimes* ,stilbō'es,-\ *n -s* [*stilbene* + *estrus* + -*ol*] **1** : DIETHYL-STILBESTROL

stil·bite \'stil,bīt\ *n -s* [F, fr. Gk *stilbē* lamp + F -*ite*; akin to Gk *stilbos* glistening] : a mineral $NaCa_2Al_5Si_{13}O_{36}.14H_2O$ of the zeolite family consisting of a hydrous silicate of aluminum, calcium, and sodium, being white when pure with pearly luster on the cleavage surface, often occurring in sheaflike aggregations of crystals and also in radiated masses, and considered by some to include heulandite (hardness 3.5-4, sp. gr. 2.09-2.21) — called also *desmine*

stil·bum \'stilbəm\ *n, cap* [NL, fr. Gk *stilbon*, neut. of *stilbos* glistening; akin to Gk *stilpnos* glistening and perh. to W *syllu* to gaze] *syn of* STILBELLA

stil-de-grain yellow \'stēldə,gran\ *n* [*stil-de-grain* fr. F *stil de grain* yellow lake] : DUTCH PINK 2

¹stile \'stī(ə)l\ *n -s* [ME, fr. OE *stigel*; akin to OHG *stigila* stile, OE *stigan* to go up — more at STAIR] **1 a** : steps or rungs to assist a person over a fence while remaining a barrier to livestock **b** : TURNSTILE **2** *archaic* : BARRIER, OBSTACLE ⟨a lift over the ∼ at a crisis of some importance to the party —*Manchester Examiner*⟩

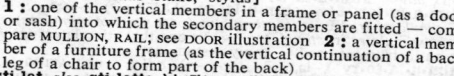

stile 1a

²stile *archaic var of* STYLE

³stile \'stī(ə)l\ *n -s* [prob. fr. D *stijl* post, doorjamb, fr. MD, post, prob. fr. L *stilus* stake, stylus] **1** : one of the vertical members in a frame or panel (as a door or sash) into which the secondary members are fitted — compare MULLION, RAIL; see DOOR illustration **2** : a vertical member of a furniture frame (as the vertical continuation of a back leg of a chair to form part of the back)

sti·let *also* **sti·lette** \'stīlə̇t, stī'let\ *n -s* [*stilet* fr. obs. F, stylet, stiletto, fr. MF, stiletto, fr. *-ette*) of stilet — more at STYLET] : STYLET 1 — **sti·let·ted** \-ə̇d·ə̇d, -ed·ə̇d\ *adj*

¹stil·let·to *also* **stil·let·to** \stə'led·ō, -e(,)tō\ *n, pl* **stilettos** *or* **stilettoes** [It *stiletto*, dim. of *stilo* dagger, stylus, fr. L *stilus* stake, stylus — more at STYLE] **1 a** : a slender dagger with a blade that is thick in proportion to its breadth — compare PONIARD **2** : something that resembles a dagger; *esp* : a pointed instrument for piercing holes for eyelets or embroidery — more at STYLE

²stiletto \"\ *vt* -ED/-ING/-s *archaic* : to stab or stab with or as if with a stiletto

stiletto fly *n* : any of numerous small or medium-sized predaceous dipterous flies of the family Therevidae that somewhat resemble the robber flies

¹still \'stil\ *adj* -ER/-EST [ME *stille*, fr. OE; akin to MD *stille* still, OHG *stilli* still, OE *steall* stall — more at STALL] **1 a** : devoid of or abstaining from motion : IMMOBILE, STATIONARY ⟨each movement has its center, its ∼ point —Isaac Rosenfeld⟩ ⟨sorrow loomed over her and time was ∼ —Ann Ryan⟩ **b** *archaic* : tending to remain in one place : SEDENTARY ⟨in his absence she was a ∼ personage —Charlotte Brontë⟩ **c** : having no effervescence : not carbonated ⟨∼ wine⟩ ⟨prefer sparkling fruit juices to the ∼ products —*Improvements in the Manuf. & Preservation of Grape Juice*⟩ — opposed to *sparkling* **d** : of, relating to, being, or designed for taking a static photograph as contrasted with a motion picture ⟨∼ camera⟩ ⟨∼ photography⟩ ⟨∼ projector⟩ **2 a** (1) : making no sound : disinclined to talk : QUIET, TACITURN ⟨∼ as a mouse⟩ ⟨her radio . . . was never ∼ —Mavis Gallant⟩ ⟨each with each patrols, in ∼ society, hand in hand —R.P.Warren⟩ (2) : calm in spirit : UNPERTURBED ⟨my soul was not ∼ enough for songs —George Macdonald †1905⟩ **b** : subdued in tone or volume ⟨music by the night wind sent through strings of some ∼ instrument —P.B.Shelley⟩ **3 a** : free from agitation : TRANQUIL, UNRUFFLED ⟨dived so smoothly that she scarcely rippled the ∼ water —C.B.Nordhoff & J.N.Hall⟩ **b** : free from noise or turbulence : PEACEFUL, SILENT ⟨the street was ∼, save for the twittering of birds —Winston Churchill⟩ ⟨the smack of fist against shoulder was sharp in the ∼ barracks —Mack Morriss⟩ ⟨∼ weather, and dry, powdery snow —O.E.Rölvaag⟩ **c** *archaic* : DULL, UNEVENTFUL ⟨save us . . . from a tedious day, or shine the dullness of ∼ away —William Cowper⟩ **4** *obs* : CONTINUED, PERSEVERING ⟨by ∼ practice, learn to know thy meaning —*Shak.*⟩

²still \"\ *vb* -ED/-ING/-s [ME *stillen*, fr. OE *stillan*; akin to MD & OHG *stillen* to still, ON *stilla*; derivative fr. the root of E ¹*still*] *vt* **1 a** : to cause to subside or die down : ALLAY, CHECK ⟨as suddenly as it had broken, the gale was ∼ed —Eric Linklater⟩ **b** : to put an end to : restore to order : PACIFY, SETTLE ⟨the threat of his coming had ∼ed the . . . revolt —John Buchan⟩ ⟨nominal unification . . . had not ∼ed interservice bitterness —*Time*⟩ **c** : to arrest the motion of ⟨before death ∼ed his hand —G.C.Sellery⟩ **2 a** : to gratify fully : APPEASE, ASSUAGE ⟨neither beef nor mutton could ∼ me —Francis Hackett⟩ **b** : to keep under control : OVERCOME, RESTRAIN, SUPPRESS ⟨drew a long breath and ∼ed her shuddering —Laura Krey⟩ ⟨unable to ∼ his persistent gambling instinct —T.H. White b. 1915⟩ **c** : to calm down : LULL, SOOTHE ⟨a magic voice that ∼ed and . . . comforted you —L.C.Douglas⟩ **3 a** : to repress the noise or clamor of : HUSH, SILENCE ⟨the once-thriving . . . metropolis is ∼ed by terror —Hal Lehrman⟩ ⟨sirens are ∼ed . . . when they pass hospital or convalescent homes —*Springfield (Mass.) Union*⟩ **b** : to cause to become quiet ⟨∼ed the people before Moses —Num 13:30 (AV)⟩ ∼ *vi* : to become motionless or silent ⟨∼ed the large hand and froze —Hugh MacLennan⟩ ⟨music from the dance band ∼ed —G.A.Wagner⟩ — often used with *down* ⟨the wind ∼s down —*Times Lit. Supp.*⟩ **syn** see CALM

³still \"\ *adv* [ME *stille*, fr. OE; akin to MD *stille* quietly, OHG *stillo*; adverb fr. the adjective represented by E ¹*still*] **1** : without noise or motion : QUIETLY ⟨the girl sat as ∼ as an image carved from marble —Louis Bromfield⟩ **2 a** : in a continuous or constant manner : ALWAYS, EVER ⟨remained for nearly a month . . . ∼ widening his acquaintance —W.C. Ford⟩ ⟨while we do his goodwill, He abides with us ∼ —J.H. Sammis⟩ **b** *archaic* : in an uninterrupted manner : PROGRESSIVELY ⟨∼ his courage with his toils increased —Alexander Pope⟩ **c** : in spite of a preceding event or consideration ⟨∼ have acne —Morris Fishbein⟩ ⟨this ∼ important truth —M.R.Cohen⟩ **3 a** : up to the present time ⟨ancient kitchen chimney place with its fireback and crane ∼ in position —John Durant⟩ ⟨∼ found in the homes of their ancestral homelands —*Amer. Guide Series: Minn.*⟩ **b** : at the time in question — used with implication of imminent change ⟨drink your coffee while it's ∼ hot⟩ ⟨∼ found them-

selves a good way from their unit by six o'clock —Earle Birney⟩ ⟨teacher noted what words the pupil ∼ did not know —Angell Mathewson⟩ **c** *obs* : without change in the future ⟨discern the coming on of years, and think not to do the same things ∼ —Francis Bacon⟩ **d** : to or at a greater distance : FARTHER ⟨west ∼, where the whitish sandy soil is thinly covered with grasses . . . cattle move and graze —Marjory S. Douglas⟩ **e** : in addition : beyond this ⟨six or seven hundred men . . . and occasionally more ∼ —Walt Whitman⟩ ⟨another example of cultural misunderstanding —A.A.Hill⟩ **4 a** *obs* : to a greater extent ⟨the guilt being great, the fear doth ∼ exceed —*Shak.*⟩ **b** : EVEN — used as an intensive to stress the comparative degree ⟨half a dozen little brigs . . . and eight clumsy gun vessels that were smaller ∼ —C.S.Forester⟩ ⟨placed him ∼ more in the wrong —W.C.Ford⟩

⁴still \"\ *n -s* [ME *stille*, fr. *stille*, adj., still — more at ¹STILL] **1** : a pervading calm or hush : QUIET, SILENCE ⟨the ∼ of the night⟩ **2 a** : a static photograph ⟨the instantaneous ∼ which a deer took of himself —*World's Work*⟩; *specif* : a specially posed photograph taken of the actors or scenes of a motion picture production for publicity or documentary purposes **b** : a photograph, map, or chart inserted into a television program **3** : STILL MAGAZINE

⁵still \"\ *conj* [³*still*] : BUT, NEVERTHELESS ⟨∼, all men, including dead men, can be wrong —Weston La Barre⟩ ⟨∼, aside from all other considerations, the relative importance seen in merit . . . may be a real issue —S.L.Payne⟩

⁶still \"\ *vb* -ED/-ING/-s [ME *stillen*, fr. OF *stiller*, fr. L *stillare* to drip, trickle — more at DISTILL] *vi, obs* : to trickle down in fine drops ∼ *vt, obs* : to exude or cause to fall in drops ⟨pricks the clouds, ∼s down the rain —Francis Quarles⟩

⁷still \"\ *vb* -ED/-ING/-s [ME *stillen*, short for *distillen* to distill — more at DISTILL] *vt* **1** : to subject to distillation ⟨∼ peaches for brandy⟩ **2** : to make or extract by distillation ⟨∼ brandy from peaches⟩ ∼ *vi* : to perform distillation : DISTILL ⟨∼ing was clearly against the law —H.E.Giles⟩

⁸still \"\ *n -s* [ME *stille*, fr. ⁷*still*] **1** : DISTILLERY 2 **2** : apparatus used in distillation comprising sometimes only the chamber in which the vaporization is carried out or at other times other distillation equipment: as **a** : a vessel or boiler together with a condenser for use in distilling alcoholic liquors or other liquids — compare POT STILL **b** : a fractionating column or tower with or without its condensing equipment and receiver for use in distilling various substances sometimes with decomposition ⟨ammonia ∼s⟩ ⟨turpentine ∼s⟩ ⟨petroleum topping ∼s⟩ ⟨cracking ∼s⟩ — compare RETORT, TAR STILL **c** (1) : equipment consisting essentially of an evaporator and a condenser for producing distilled water — called also *water still* (2) : a compact device for converting salt water to fresh water ⟨floating plastic solar ∼s⟩ **3** : a vessel in which manganese dioxide is treated with hydrochloric acid to form chlorine or a bleaching liquor — compare WELDON PROCESS

a simple retort form of still 2: *1* retort, *2* head, *3* tube, *4* condenser

⁹still \"\ *adj* -ER/-EST [⁸*still*] : of or relating to a still; *esp* : remaining as residual matter in a still after distillation ⟨∼ bottoms⟩ ⟨∼ coke⟩

¹stil·lage \'stilij\ *n -s* [modif. of D *stellage* scaffolding, fr. MD, fr. *stellen* to place + -*age* (fr. MF); akin to OHG *stellen* to place — more at STALL] **1** : a small table or stand (as for casks in a brewery) sometimes equipped with wheels **2** : a drying stone for ceramic ware shaped but not fired

²stillage \"\ *vt* -ED/-ING/-s : to place on a stillage

³still·age \"\ *n -s* [⁸*still* + -*age*] : the mash from an alcoholic fermentation after removal of the alcohol in a still ⟨simple screening of the ∼ gives distillers' dried grains —R.S.Aries⟩ — compare DISTILLERS' GRAINS

still alarm *n* : a fire alarm transmitted (as by telephone call or by voice communication with the unit directly concerned) without sounding the fire signal apparatus

still and all *adv* : after all : NEVERTHELESS

still and anon *or* **still an end** *adv* [*still and anon* fr. ³*still* + *anon*, fr. *and*, conj. + *anon*, adv.; *still an end* fr. ³*still* + *an end*, adv.] *obs* : from time to time : now and then

still and on *adv, chiefly Scot* : NEVERTHELESS, YET

stil·la·ti·tious \,stilə'tishəs\ *adj* [L *stillaticius*, fr. *stillatus*, past part. of *stillare* to drip, trickle] **1** : falling in drops **2** : DISTILLED

stil·la·to·ry \'stilə,tōrē\ *n -es* [ME *stillatorie*, fr. ML *stillatorium*, fr. L *stillatus* (past part. of *stillare* to drip, trickle) + -*orium* -ory] *archaic* : STILL, DISTILLERY

still-bay \'stil,bā\ *adj, usu cap* [*Still Bay*, southern coast of Cape Province, South Africa] : of or belonging to a Middle Pleistocene culture of East Africa and Cape Province characterized by flake tools and weapons resembling Mousterian and Solutrian types

still·birth \'s,⸗\ *n* **1** : the birth of a dead fetus — compare LIVE BIRTH **2** : a viable fetus that is born dead

¹still·born \'s,⸗\ *adj* **1** : dead at birth ⟨a ∼ child⟩ — compare LIVE-BORN **2** : failing from the start : disappointing all expectations : ABORTIVE, UNSUCCESSFUL ⟨a ∼ novel⟩ ⟨their first scheme died —J.W.Poling⟩ ⟨this ∼ treaty marked the failure of Germany to set up a new pattern of alliances —C.E. Black & E.C.Helmreich⟩

²stillborn \'s,⸗\ *n, pl* **stillborn** *or* **stillborns** : one that is stillborn ⟨antigens obtained from infants and ∼s —*Yr. Bk. of Urology*⟩ ⟨the greatest resuscitator of the ∼ known to dramatic art —*Everybody's Mag.*⟩

still box *n* : STILLING BASIN

still-burn \'s,⸗\ *vt* : to burn in the process of distillation

stilled *past of* STILL

¹stiller *comparative of* STILL

²stiller \'stilə(r)\ *n -s* [⁷*still* + -*er*] : DISTILLER

³stiller \"\ *n -s* [²*still* + -*er*] : one that calms or quiets

¹still·ery \'stilə(r)ē\ *n -es* [⁷*still* + -*ery*] : ⁸STILL

stillest *superlative of* STILL

still-fish \'s,⸗\ *vi* : to fish with the line and bait resting still or stationary in the water — **still-fish·er** \'s,⸗\ *n*

still head *n* : the top part of a still; *esp* : a fractionating column at the top of a still — compare COLUMN 3d

stillhouse \'s,⸗\ *n* : DISTILLERY 2

still hunt *n* **1** : a noiseless pursuit or ambushing of game (liked the test of holding a small bunch of buffaloes together in the *still hunt* as he picked them off —Mari Sandoz⟩ **2** : the covert pursuit of an object (the typical titled foreigner . . . on a *still hunt* for the American heiress —*N.Y. Sun*⟩; *esp* : a political campaign carried on secretly or underhandedly

still-hunt \'s,⸗\ *vb* [*still hunt*] **1** : to ambush or stalk a quarry : pursue game noiselessly esp. without a dog (in the *still-hunts*, he must be sufficiently versed in woodlore to outwit . . . animals —Don Stillman⟩ **2** : to lie in wait for or approach by stealth : AMBUSH, STALK ⟨impossible to *still-hunt* mountain lions; they were too alert —H.L.Davis⟩ — **still-hunt·er** \'s,⸗\ *n*

stil·li·cide \'stilə,sīd\ *n -s* [L *stillicidium*, fr. *stilla* (fr. *stilla* drop) + -*cidium* (fr. *cadere* to fall) — more at DISTILL, CHANCE] **1** *archaic* : a continual dripping **2** *Roman, civil, & Scots law* : the servitude of eavesdrop binding a servient tenement to receive from the dominant tenement rainwater from the eaves of a building located on the latter

stillier *comparative of* STILLY

stilliest *superlative of* STILLY

¹stilling *pres part of* STILL

²stil·ling \'stilin\ *n -s* [modif. of D *stelling* scaffolding, fr. MD *stellinge*, fr. *stellen* to place + -*inge* (akin to OE -*ing*, suffix forming nouns from verbs) — more at -ING] : STILLION

stilling basin *or* **stilling box** *or* **stilling pool** *or* **stilling well** *n* [*stilling* fr. gerund of ²*still*] : a depression in a channel or reservoir deep enough to reduce the velocity or turbulence of the flow — called also *still box*; compare ORIFICE BOX

stil·lin·gia \stə'linj(ē)ə, -inj(ē)ə\ *n* [NL, fr. Benjamin *Stillingfleet* †1771 Eng. botanist + NL -*ia*] **1** *cap* : a genus of widely

distributed herbs or shrubs (family Euphorbiaceae) with alternate leaves, monoecious spicate apetalous flowers, and capsular fruit — see QUEEN'S-DELIGHT **b** -s : any plant of the genus *Stillingia; often* : CHINESE TALLOW TREE **2** -s : the dried root of queen's-delight used as an alterative
stillingia oil *n* : a pale yellow drying oil obtained from the seeds of the Chinese tallow tree
stillingia tallow *n* : CHINESE TALLOW
stil·lion \'stilyən\ *n* -s [alter. of *stilling*] : a cradle for vats in a brewery : STILLAGE
still life *n, pl* **still lifes** *also* **still lives** [trans. of D *stilleven*] **1 a** : a picture consisting predominantly of inanimate objects ⟨so slow in painting *still lifes* that the flowers and fruit in his models would rot before he got them painted —Winthrop Sargeant⟩ **b** : something that resembles such a picture ⟨the novel will remain . . . just an interesting small-town *still life* in which figures are caught in careful needlepoint —James Kelly⟩ **2** : the category of the graphic arts concerned with inanimate objects as subject matter ⟨*still life* . . . is an excellent means of developing a sense of pictorial balance —*Amer. Photography*⟩
still liquor *n* **1** : spent liquid containing manganous chloride from chlorine stills — compare WELDON PROCESS **2** : bleaching liquor made in a still
still·man \'stilmən\ *n, pl* **stillmen 1** : one who owns or operates a still : DISTILLER **2** : a worker who controls the fermentation of beer **3** : one who tends distillation equipment (as in an oil refinery)
still·ness *n* -ES [ME *stilnesse*, fr. OE *stilnes*, fr. *stille*, adj., still + *-nes* -ness] **1 a** : freedom from agitation : CALMNESS, SERENITY ⟨brings with her beauty . . . a capacity for ~ and repose —E.R.Bentley⟩ **b** : absence of movement : IMMOBILITY, LIFELESSNESS ⟨the ~ is so absolute that it seems as if all the winds of the world had . . . dropped out of the air —J.C. Powys⟩ **2 a** : the quality or state of being soundless : QUIET, SILENCE ⟨knew by the ~ and the tenseness that we had reached the outer fringe of the front —Burgess Scott⟩ **b** : a soundless place or environment ⟨polar bears roam the great white ~*es*⟩ **3** *obs* : PATIENCE, FORTITUDE ⟨in peace . . . nothing so becomes a man, as modest ~ —Shak.⟩
still pack *n* : the pack of cards that is not in play when two packs are used (as in bridge) and is shuffled by the next dealer's partner
still return *n* : a fraction of distillate so impure that it must be redistilled
stillroom \'ˌ-,-\ *n* [[8]still] *Brit* : a room connected with the kitchen where liqueurs, preserves, and cakes are kept and tea, coffee, and other beverages are prepared
stills *pres 3d sing of* STILL, *pl of* STILL
still's disease \'stilz-\ *n, usu cap S* [after Sir George F. *Still* †1941 Eng. pediatrician] : rheumatoid arthritis in children
still·son wrench \'stilsən-\ *n* [fr. *Stillson*, a trademark] : a pipe wrench having an adjustable L-shaped jaw sliding in a sleeve that is pivoted to and loosely encircles the handle so that pressure on the handle increases the grip
[1]**stillstand** \'ˌ-,-\ *n* **1** : STANDSTILL **2 a** : an act or instance of stillstanding ⟨represent minor ~*s* locally preserved in the general emergence of the area —W.G.V.Bolchin⟩ **b** : STABILITY ⟨fairly long periods of ~ —C.A.Cotton⟩ **3** : an interval in the light cycle of a variable star when its brightness temporarily stops rising or falling and perhaps forms a secondary maximum or hump in the light curve
[2]**stillstand** \"\ *vi* : to remain stationary with respect to sea level or with reference to the center of the earth — used of a continent, island, or other land area
still water *n* : a part of a stream where the gradient is so gentle that no current is visible
[1]**stil·ly** \'still|ē, |i\ *adv* [ME, fr. OE *stillīce*, fr. *stille*, adj., still + *-līce* -ly] : CALMLY, QUIETLY ⟨~ she glided in —William Allingham⟩
[2]**still·y** \'stil|ē, |i\ *adj* -ER/-EST [perh. fr. [4]*still* + *-y*] : characterized by stillness : CALM, QUIET ⟨the sounds of this most ~ night are almost wholly of the faintly pulsing sea —E.J. Banfield⟩
stilp·no·mel·ane \,stilpnō'me,lān\ *n* -s [G *stilpnomelan*, fr. Gk *stilpnos* glistening + *melan-*, *melas* black — more at STILBUM, MULLET] : a black or greenish black mineral $K(Fe,Al)_{10}Si_{12}O_{30}(O,OH)_{12}$ (?) occurring in foliated plates, fibrous forms, and velvety bronze-colored incrustations and consisting of a hydrous iron aluminum silicate with a little potassium (sp. gr. 2.77–2.96)
stilp·no·siderite \,stilp(,)nō+\ *n* -s [G *stilpnosiderit*, fr. Gk *stilpnos* glistening + *sidēros* iron + G *-it* -ite] : LIMONITE
[1]**stilt** \'stilt\ *n* -s *see sense 4b* [ME *stilte* plow handle, crutch, stilt; akin to MD *stelte* wooden leg, crutch, OHG *stelza* stilt, OSw *stylta* crutch, OE *steall* place, position, stall — more at STALL] **1** *dial chiefly Brit* : CRUTCH **2** *dial chiefly Brit* : the handle of a plow **3 a** : one of two poles each with a rest or strap for the foot used to elevate the wearer above the ground in walking and usu. of sufficient length to be steadied at the top by the hand and arm **b** : something that resembles a stilt: as (1) : a pile or post serving to raise a building or other structure above ground or water level (2) : a vertical architectural member that raises the spring of an arch or vault above the apparent or elsewhere established impost (3) : a member placed above or below a column for additional height (4) : any of the piles forming the back of the sheet piling for a bridge starling (5) : a piece of hard-fired clay usu. three-armed with points on each side used to keep articles apart in a pottery kiln **c** : a precarious foundation ⟨rivals . . . can topple governments built on ~*s* as easily as they can hire assassins —Flora Lewis⟩ **4 a** : a long thin leg ⟨white stalky birds on ~*s* —Thomas Wood †1950⟩ **b** *also* **stilt plover**, *pl also* **stilt** : any of various notably long-legged three-toed limicoline birds of the genera *Himantopus* and *Cladorhynchus* related to the avocets, chiefly inhabiting inland ponds and marshes or brackish lagoons, nesting in small colonies, and being mostly white with a black mantle variously extended on the neck and head — called also *longlegs, stiltbird;* see BANDED STILT, BLACK-NECKED STILT, BLACK-WINGED STILT, WHITE-HEADED STILT

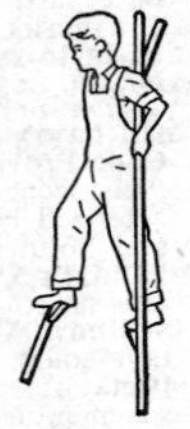
stilts 3a

[2]**stilt** \"\ *vb* -ED/-ING/-S *vt* : to raise on or as if on stilts; *specif* : to raise the spring of (an arch or vault) above the apparent or elsewhere established impost ~ *vi, chiefly Scot* : to walk awkwardly and stiffly : LIMP
stiltbird \'ˌ-,-\ *n* : STILT 4b
stilt bug *n* : any of various long-legged sluggish bugs (family Neididae) that are closely related to the coreid bugs
stilt·ed \'stiltəd\ *adj* **1 a** : supported on or as if on stilts ⟨a ~ railway trestle⟩ ⟨starting off . . . on her precarious heels with quick ~ steps —Warren Beck⟩ **b** : having the springing higher than the apparent level of the impost ⟨~ arch⟩ **c** : having long thin legs ⟨a ~ crane⟩ **2 a** : artificially elevated : POMPOUS, LOFTY ⟨their conversations are miracles of studied, ~ eloquence —B.R.Redman⟩ **b** : lacking in spontaneity : restricted by convention : FORMAL, STIFF ⟨a ~ letter of acknowledgment⟩ ⟨painting people and tigers . . . in a curiously flat and ~ way —Cyril Ray⟩ ⟨when people try to correct their speech . . . they develop a ~ pronunciation —Charlton Laird⟩ — **stilt·ed·ly** *adv*
stilt·ed·ness *n* -ES : the quality or state of being stilted
stilt·er \-ltə(r)\ *n* -s [[1]*stilt* + *-er*] : one that walks on or as if on stilts — called also *stiltwalker*
stil·ton \'stiltᵊn *also* -ltən\ *or* **stilton cheese** *n* -s *usu cap S* [*Stilton*, parish in Huntingdonshire, east central England, where it was originally sold] : a blue-veined cheese with wrinkled rind made of whole cows' milk enriched with cream and usu. aged two years
stilt palm *n* : a palm of the genus *Iriartea*
stilt petrel *n* : a long-legged black-and-white petrel of the genus *Fregetta*
stilt-root \'ˌ-,-\ *n* : a prop root of the mangrove
stilt sandpiper *n* : a rather rare American sandpiper (*Micropalama himantopus*) having very long legs and semipalmate feet and a bill somewhat expanded at the tip
stilt wheel *n* : the gauge-wheel attachment to a plow beam for limiting the plowing depth
stilty \'stiltē\ *adj* -ER/-EST **1** : suggestive of stilts **2** : STILTED
stilus *var of* STYLUS
stime \'stīm\ *also* **stim** \-tim\ *n* -s [ME (northern dial.) *stime, styme*] *chiefly Scot & Irish* : the smallest quantity : PARTICLE, GLIMMER
stim·part \'stimpə(r)t\ *n* -s [perh. contr. of *sixteenth part*] : LIPPY
stim·u·la·bil·i·ty \,stimyələ'biləd·ē, -bilətē, -i *sometimes* ÷-məl-\ *n* : the quality or state of being stimulable
stim·u·la·ble \'ˌ--ləbəl\ *adj* [*stimulate* + *-able*] : capable of being stimulated
stim·u·lan·cy \-lənsē\ *n* -ES [[2]*stimulant* + *-cy*] : stimulating quality
[1]**stim·u·lant** \'stimyələnt *sometimes* ÷-məl-\ *n* -s [L *stimulant-, stimulans*, pres. part. of *stimulare*] **1** : an agent that produces a temporary increase of the functional activity of a tissue (as the central nervous system) either by direct action (as by excitation) or indirect (as by removal of inhibiting influences) **2** : STIMULUS **3** : an alcoholic beverage — not used technically
[2]**stimulant** \"\ *adj* [L *stimulant-, stimulans*, pres. part. of *stimulare*] : that stimulates
stim·u·late \-,lāt, *usu* -ād.+V\ *vb* -ED/-ING/-S [L *stimulatus*, past part. of *stimulare*, fr. *stimulus* goad] *vt* **1** : to excite to activity or growth or to greater activity or exertion : stir up : GOAD, PRICK, ANIMATE ⟨crop loss might ~ a man to intenser fishing activity —V.W.Turner⟩ : LIVEN ⟨the very controversy his book aroused *stimulated* its sale —Eugene Exman⟩ : AROUSE ⟨establishing the fund . . . to ~ public interest in poetry —*College English*⟩ **2** : to function as a stimulus to; *esp* : to evoke the characteristic physiologic activity of (as a nerve or muscle) **3** : to arouse or affect by a stimulant drug ⟨the caffeine in coffee will ~ the patient⟩ **4** : to administer dope to (a racehorse) to speed running ~ *vi* : to act as a stimulant or stimulus ⟨an academic atmosphere that ~*s* rather than stultifies⟩ **syn** see PROVOKE
stim·u·lat·ing·ly *adv* : in a stimulating manner
stim·u·la·tion \,ˌ--'lāshən\ *n* -s [L *stimulation-, stimulatio*, fr. *stimulatus* (past part. of *stimulare*) + *-ion-, -io* -ion] **1 a** : the act or process of stimulating ⟨the ~ of trade by reducing tariffs⟩; *also* : STIMULATIVENESS ⟨enjoy the ~ of the metropolis with its cultural advantages⟩ **b** : the state of being stimulated : altered activity ⟨a test to detect ~ in racehorses⟩ **2** : the stimulating action of various agents on muscles, nerves, or a sensory end organ by which activity is evoked; *esp* : the reaction produced in a sensory end organ by a stimulus that initiates a nerve impulse and results in functional activity of an effector (as a muscle or gland) ⟨gastric secretion induced by ~ of the sense of smell⟩
stim·u·la·tive \'ˌ-,lād·iv, -,lə|, |t|, |ēv *also* |əv\ *adj* : having power or tending to stimulate — **stim·u·la·tive·ly** \|əvlē, -li\ *adv* — **stim·u·la·tive·ness** \|ivnəs, |ēv- *also* |əv-\ *n* -ES
stim·u·la·tor *also* **stim·u·lat·er** \-,lād·ə(r), -ātə\ *n* -s [*stimulator* fr. LL, fr. L *stimulatus* (past part. of *stimulare*) + *-or; stimulater* fr. *stimulate* + *-er*] : one that stimulates; *specif* : an instrument used to apply a stimulus
stim·u·la·to·ry \-,lə,tōrē, -tȯr-, -ri\ *adj* : STIMULATING
stim·u·lo·ge·nous \,ˌ--'läjənəs\ *adj* [*stimulus* + *-o-* + *-genous*] : developing as a consequence of stimulation
stim·u·lus \'stimyələs *sometimes* ÷-məl-\ *n, pl* **stimu·li** \-,lī *also* -,lē\ [L, goad, incentive; akin to L *stilus* stake, stylus — more at STYLE] **1** : something that rouses the mind or spirits or incites to activity : INCENTIVE ⟨the war proved a ~ to agriculture, industry, and commerce —*Amer. Guide Series: N.J.*⟩ **2** : something that produces a temporary increase of physiological activity in an organism or in any of its parts; *esp* : an agent (as an environmental change) capable of directly influencing the activity of living protoplasm (as by inducing a tropism, exciting a sensory end organ, or evoking muscular contraction or glandular secretion) — see HETEROLOGOUS STIMULUS, HOMOLOGOUS STIMULUS
stimulus diffusion *n* : diffusion in which one people receives a culture element from another but gives it a new and unique form
stimulus error *n* : an error in introspective observation of divining the object from which the stimulus comes instead of reporting the impression actually received
stimulus-object \'ˌ---,--\ *n* : the physical source of a stimulus : something that produces the energy for stimulation
stimulus-response \'ˌ----'-\ *adj* : representing the activity of an organism as composed of reactions to stimuli ⟨*stimulus-response* formula⟩ ⟨*stimulus-response* psychology⟩
stimulus threshold *n* : ABSOLUTE THRESHOLD
stimulus word *n* : a word to which the subject reacts (as in an association test)
[1]**sting** \'stiŋ\ *vb* **stung** \'stəŋ\ *or archaic* **stang** \'staŋ, -taiŋ\ **stung**; **stinging**; **stings** [ME *stingen*, fr. OE *stingan*; akin to ON *stinga* to sting, stab, Goth *usstangan* to pluck out, Gk *stachys* spike of grain, *stochos* target, aim, guess] *vt* **1 a** : to pierce or wound with a poisonous or irritating process (as a stinger or stinging hair) esp. so as to produce an inflammation or lesion ⟨a great aching welt where a mosquito had *stung* him⟩; *specif* : to wound with an ovipositor (as in laying eggs) ⟨destroy the fruit flies before they begin to ~ the fruit —*Farmer's Weekly* (*So. Africa*)⟩ **b** : to affect with quick sharp physical pain or smart ⟨driving hail that *stung* their faces⟩ ⟨ginger ~*s* the mouth⟩ ⟨smoke . . . began to ~ his eyes —Frank Cameron⟩ **2 a** : to cause to suffer sharp mental pain : pain keenly ⟨~ him with a sharp reproach⟩ ⟨had been *stung* by remorse⟩ **b** : to stir or incite by a sharp often painful stimulus : GOAD ⟨attacks . . . ~ him to a considerable rage —*English Digest*⟩ ⟨his suffering . . . *stung* their consciences to action —*Times Lit. Supp.*⟩ **3 a** : to get the better of in a financial dealing : OVERCHARGE, CHEAT ⟨never went again to the store that had *stung* him⟩ **b** *slang* : to compel to pay : submit a bill to : STICK, CHARGE ⟨how much did he ~ you for that —J.K. Ewers⟩ ~ *vi* **1** : to wound a person or thing with a sting ⟨scorpions ~ but snakes bite⟩ ⟨an insult that *stung* and rankled⟩ **2** : to feel a keen burning pain or smart ⟨a slap that made his hand ~⟩
[2]**sting** \"\ *n* -s [ME, fr. OE, fr. *stingan*, v.] **1 a** : the act of stinging; *specif* : the thrust of a stinger into the flesh **b** : a wound or pain caused by or as if by stinging ⟨apply wet baking soda to the ~⟩ ⟨crying from the ~ of a cut⟩ ⟨the ~ of sarcasm⟩ ⟨the quick ~ of tears came to her eyes —Edna Ferber⟩ **2** : STINGER 2 **3** : something that causes a keen pain or stimulation of mind : a stinging element (as the point of an epigram), force, quality, or capacity ⟨a smile that took the ~ out of his rebuke⟩ ⟨practice to put more ~ into his bowling at cricket⟩ **4** : a thin rod used for mounting a model for testing in a wind tunnel
sting and ling \,stiŋən'liŋ\ *adv* [Sc *sting* pole (fr. ME, alter. of *steng*, fr. OE) + *and ling*, fr. E *and*, conj. + Sc *ling* (prob. alter. of E *line*, n.); fr. the practice of carrying a load by a rope having both ends attached to a pole resting on the shoulders of the carriers; akin to D *steng* pole, OHG *stengil* stalk, OE *stingan* to sting] *Scot* : WHOLLY, BODILY
sting·a·ree \'stiŋərē, -ri *also* -ŋr-\ *n* -s [by alter.] : STINGRAY; *esp* : ROUND STINGRAY
sting bladder *n* : the larva of the sting moth
stinge \'stinj\ *vi* **stinged**; **stinged**; **stingeing**; **stinges** [back-formation fr. *stingy*] : to act stingily or parsimoniously ⟨not by ~ and paring —Sheila Kaye-Smith⟩
sting·er \'stiŋə(r)\ *n* -s [[1]*sting* + *-er*] **1** : one that stings; *specif* : a sharp blow or remark **2** : any of various sharp organs of offense and defense (as of a bee, scorpion, stingray, wasp) usu. connected with a poison gland or otherwise adapted to wound by piercing and inoculating a poisonous secretion **3** : a cocktail or after-dinner drink of approximately equal parts of white crème de menthe and brandy shaken in ice and strained before serving **4** *slang* : the machine gun or cannon mounted in the tail of an airplane
stingfish \'ˌ-,-\ *n* **1** : STONEFISH **2** : SCORPION FISH
stin·gi·ly \'stinjəlē, -li\ *adv* : in a stingy manner
stin·gi·ness \-jēnəs, -jin-\ *n* -ES : the quality or state of being stingy
stinging cell *also* **sting cell** *n* : NEMATOCYST
stinging hair *n* : a glandular hair whose base secretes a stinging fluid (as in nettles)
stinging lizard *n, South* : SCORPION
sting·ing·ly \'stiŋiŋlē, -ŋēŋ-, -li\ *adv* : in a stinging manner
sting·ing·ness *n* : the quality or state of being stinging
stinging nettle *n* : a plant of the family Urticaceae that bears stinging hairs: as **a** : a perennial Eurasian nettle (*Urtica dioica*) established in No. America and having broad coarsely toothed leaves **b** : WOOD NETTLE
stinging tree *n* : an Australian nettle tree (*Laportea gigas*)
sting·less \'stiŋləs\ *adj* : having no sting
stingless bee *n* : any of numerous social bees of *Melipona* and related genera (family Apidae) mainly of tropical America that lack a sting and store honey in waxen cells much like the hive bee to which they are related
sting moth *n* : an Australian moth (*Doratifera vulnerans*) whose larva is armed at each end of the body with four tubercles bearing powerful stinging hairs
stin·go \'stiŋ(,)gō\ *n* -s [irreg. fr. [2]*sting*] **1** *chiefly Brit* : strong ale or beer **2** *slang* : ZEST, ZIP
stingray \'ˌ-,-\ *n* : any of numerous rays of Dasyatidae and related families that have one or more large sharp barbed dorsal spines near the base of the whiplike tail capable of inflicting severe wounds, sometimes reach a large size, and in some forms (as on the American Pacific coast) are very destructive to oysters
stings *pres 3d sing of* STING, *pl of* STING
sting winkle *n* : a spinose marine gastropod mollusk (*Tritonalia erinacea*) of the family Muricidae
[1]**stin·gy** \'stinjē, -ji\ *adj* -ER/-EST [prob. fr. (assumed) E dial. *stinge*, n., sting + *-y*; akin to OE *stingan* to sting — more at STING] **1** *dial chiefly Eng* : BITING, SHARP **2 a** : reluctant to deal out, grant, or part with something : not generous : sparing or scant in giving or spending ⟨too ~ even to get a haircut before his wedding⟩ **b** : meanly scanty or small : MEAGER ⟨complained about his ~ allowance⟩ ⟨a ~ little attic room⟩
syn PARSIMONIOUS, PENURIOUS, CHEESEPARING, PENNY-PINCHING, MISERLY, CURMUDGEONLY, NIGGARDLY, TIGHT, TIGHTFISTED, CLOSEFISTED, CLOSE: STINGY, perhaps the most generally used term in this group, refers to notable want of generosity or liberality in giving, allotting, distributing, a want arising from a certain meanness of spirit ⟨couldn't help being *stingy*, since parsimony ran in their blood —Victoria Sackville-West⟩ ⟨had to request the thirteen states for tax levies, and since the states were jealous, *stingy*, and badly governed, they gave but grudging and inadequate help —Allan Nevins & H.S.Commager⟩ PARSIMONIOUS, PENURIOUS, CHEESEPARING, and PENNY-PINCHING refer to degrees and kinds of frugality. PARSIMONIOUS suggests extreme frugality with stingy wariness about expenditure ⟨a lonely bachelor life in caring for his property and in adding to it by *parsimonious* living —A.W. Long⟩ ⟨had now become strictly *parsimonious* . . . and . . . devoted every energy of his mind to save shillings and pence —Anthony Trollope⟩ PENURIOUS adds a suggestion of meanness to PARSIMONIOUS ⟨*penurious* restrictions upon the payment of legislators designed to discourage them —A.N.Holcombe⟩ CHEESEPARING suggests a parsimoniousness marked by petty mean little economies ⟨an example of *cheeseparing* economy at the dire risk of the national security —Walter Millis⟩ PENNY-PINCHING suggests greedy, wary parsimoniousness in avoiding expense ⟨a *penny-pinching* impresario who overlooked no opportunity to cut down the overhead —Bennett Cerf⟩ MISERLY, CURMUDGEONLY, and NIGGARDLY are derogatory or contemptuous terms for extreme illiberality and aversion to spending or dispensing. MISERLY suggests a morbid pleasure in hoarding, a sordid grasping meanness ⟨expenditure was parsimonious and even *miserly* —J.R.Green⟩ CURMUDGEONLY suggests mean stinginess and crusty irascibility ⟨the *curmudgeonly* old fool cutting off his wife with a bare pittance⟩ NIGGARDLY implies a stinginess in giving, granting, expending whereby one begrudges any contribution to the welfare or happiness of others ⟨we shall not be *niggardly* about this —Hugh Dalton⟩ ⟨*niggardly* monastic prescriptions with regard to gleaning —G.G.Coulton⟩ TIGHT, TIGHTFISTED, CLOSEFISTED, and CLOSE are somewhat informal expressions indicating reluctance and chariness about expending or contributing. TIGHT suggests a general chary stinginess of nature or temperament ⟨what in the name of God's the use of being so *tight* . . . you've got an expense account, haven't you —Dashiell Hammett⟩ TIGHTFISTED and CLOSEFISTED signify an accustomed reluctance to part with money and a careful vigilance against prodigality ⟨you English are a *tightfisted* race —T.B. Costain⟩ CLOSE, not so derogatory as the others, indicates either a certain stinginess or a marked caution about any expenditure ⟨he wasn't as tight as you . . . but he was a little bit *close* so the bargain hung fire —Dashiell Hammett⟩
[2]**stingy** \'stiŋē, -ŋi\ *adj* -ER/-EST [[2]*sting* + *-y*] : able to sting : having a sting or stinging hairs
[1]**stink** \'stiŋk\ *vi* **stank** \'staŋk, -taiŋk\ *or* **stunk** \'stəŋk\ **stunk**; **stinking**; **stinks** [ME *stinken*, fr. OE *stincan* to stink, emit a good or bad smell; akin to MD *stinken* to stink, OHG *stinkan* to emit a good or bad smell, and prob. to ON *stökkva* to leap, Goth *stigqan* to make war] **1** : to emit a strong offensive odor ⟨many of the men *stank* of cheap liquor —L.C. Douglas⟩ **2** : to be offensive to morality or good taste ⟨the business ~*s* to high heaven, and you . . . wouldn't dare have it aired before a court-martial —D.J.Greene⟩; *also* : to be in bad repute ⟨a scene of atrocities that will make its name ~ in history⟩ **3** : to possess something to an offensive degree ⟨tourists who are ~*ing* with money⟩ **4** : to be extremely or disgustingly bad in quality or execution ⟨his first performance *stank* and was mercilessly panned by the critics⟩
[2]**stink** \"\ *n* -s [ME, fr. *stinken*, v.] **1** : a strong offensive smell : a disgusting odor : STENCH **2** : an open or public outcry against something offensive : TO-DO ⟨made a big ~ over being accidentally shortchanged⟩ **3 stinks** *pl, Brit* : natural science as a subject of study ⟨science is called ~*s* . . . and neglected —*Spectator*⟩
stink·ard \'stiŋkə(r)d\ *n* -s **1 a** : a mean or contemptible person **b** *usu cap* : one of the common people in the social structure of the Natchez Indians — called also *stinker* **2** : an animal producing a foul odor; *specif* : TELEDU
stink·a·roo *or* **stink·er·oo** \,stiŋkə'rü\ *n* -s [irreg. fr. *stinker*] : STINKER ⟨this guy . . . is an insult to the integrity of the industry and a ~ —Otis Ferguson⟩
stink base *n* : PRISONER'S BASE
stink bell *n* : a fetid Californian herb (*Fritillaria agrestis*) common as a weed in grain fields
stinkbird \'ˌ-,-\ *n* **1** : HOATZIN **2** : any of various birds (as some wrens and sparrows) that leave a strong scent which may distract or confuse a bird dog
stink bomb *n* : a small bomb charged usu. with chemicals that gives off a foul odor on bursting
stinkbug \'ˌ-,-\ *n* : any of various hemipterous insects that emit a disagreeable odor: as **a** : a bug of the family Pentatomidae — called also *shield bug* **b** : SQUASH BUG
stinkbush \'ˌ-,-\ *n* **1** : a star anise (*Illicium floridanum*) of the southern U. S. **2** *Austral* : a tree (*Zieria smithii*) of the family Rutaceae
stink cat *n, Africa* : ZORIL
stinkdamp \'ˌ-,-\ *n* : sulfureted hydrogen occurring in mine workings
stink·er \'stiŋkə(r)\ *n* -s **1** : one that stinks: as **a** (1) : an offensive or disgustingly contemptible person ⟨a mean little ~ who kills puppy dogs —*Time*⟩ (2) *usu cap* : STINKARD 1b **b** : any of several large petrels (as the giant petrel) that feed on blubber and carrion and have an offensive odor **c** : something (as a play, motion picture) disgustingly poor in quality **d** *slang* : HOTBOX **2** *slang* : something extremely difficult ⟨said the three-hour examination was a real ~ and left him exhausted⟩
stink fly *n* : an insect of the family Chrysopidae
stink gland *n* : a gland that secretes a malodorous substance; *esp* : one of the thoracic or abdominal scent glands of hemipterous insects
stink grass *n* **1** : an ill-scented annual European grass (*Eragrostis megastachya*) that is nearly cosmopolitan as an introduced weed and may under certain circumstances be poisonous to livestock **2** : MOLASSES GRASS
stinkhorn \'ˌ-,-\ *n* : an ill-smelling fungus of the order Phallales; *esp* : a common fungus (*Phallus impudicus*) formerly used in preparing a salve for rheumatism — called also *carrion fungus;* compare DICTYOPHORA

¹stinking *adj* [ME *stinkinge*, alter. of *stinkende*, fr. OE *stincende*, pres. part. of *stincan* to stink] **1 :** RANK, OFFENSIVE **2** *slang* **:** offensively drunk — **stink·ing·ly** *adv* — **stink·ing·ness** *n* -ES

²stinking *adv* **:** to an extreme degree ⟨a ~ drunk bum⟩

stinking ash *n* **1 :** BOX ELDER **2 :** HOP TREE

stinking badger *n* **:** TELEDU

stinking benjamin *n, usu cap B* **:** PURPLE TRILLIUM

stinking cedar *n* **1** *or* **stinking yew :** an evergreen tree (*Torreya taxifolia*) of Florida with fetid leaves resembling those of the yew **2 :** CALIFORNIA NUTMEG

stinking chamomile *n* **:** MAYWEED 1

stinking clover *n* **:** ROCKY MOUNTAIN BEE PLANT

stinking goosefoot *n* **:** a European goosefoot (*Chenopodium vulvaria*) having strong-scented foliage and adventive in eastern No. America

stinking grass *n* **:** STINK GRASS 1

stinking gum *n* **:** an Australian gum tree (*Eucalyptus tereticornis*) whose leaves have a strong sour sickly smell

stinking horehound *n* **:** BLACK HOREHOUND

stinking iris *n* **:** an iris (*Iris foetidissima*) with purple flowers and evil-smelling leaves

stinking mayweed *n* **:** MAYWEED 1

stinking mustard *n* **:** PENNYCRESS

stinking nightshade *n* **:** HENBANE 1a

stinking pea *n* **:** a yellow-flowered shrub (*Cassia bahamensis*) of Florida and the West Indies with flat pods and fetid foliage

stinking pheasant *n* **:** HOATZIN

stinking poke *n* **:** SKUNK CABBAGE 1

stinking rog·er \-ˈräjə(r)\ *n, usu cap R* [*roger* fr. the name *Roger*] **1 :** any of various evil-smelling plants: as **a :** any of several figworts **b :** HENBANE **c :** BLACK HOREHOUND **2** *Austral* **:** a low-growing marigold (*Tagetes glandulifera*)

stinking smut *n* **:** ²BUNT

stinking wattle *n* **:** any of various evil-smelling Australian acacias; *esp* **:** GIDGEE 1a

stinking weed *n* **:** COFFEE SENNA

stinking wil·lie \-ˈwilē\ *n, usu cap W* [*willie* fr. *Willie*, nickname fr. the name *William*] **1** *NewZeal* **:** a ragwort (*Senecio jacobaea*) **2 :** PURPLE TRILLIUM **3 :** SAINT-JOHN'S-WORT

stinking willow *n* **:** MOCK LOCUST

stinko \ˈstiŋ(ˌ)kō\ *adj* [¹*stink* + *-o* (as in *blotto*)] *slang* **:** DRUNK

stink out *vt* **:** to drive out by or as if by subjecting to an offensive or suffocating odor

stinkpot \ˈ=,=\ *n* **1 a :** an earthen jar charged with materials of an offensive and suffocating smell formerly sometimes thrown upon an enemy's deck **b :** POWERBOAT **2 :** MUSK TURTLE **3 :** any of various petrels: as **a :** GIANT PETREL **b :** CAPE HEN **c :** SOOTY ALBATROSS

stinks *pres 3d sing of* STINK, *pl of* STINK

stinkstone \ˈ=,=\ *n* **:** a stone that emits a fetid smell on being struck or rubbed owing to decomposition of organic matter

stink turtle *n* **:** MUSK TURTLE

stink up *vt* **:** to cause to stink ⟨a dead whale washed ashore and *stank up* the countryside —*Time*⟩

stinkweed \ˈ=,=\ *n* **:** any of various strong-scented or ill-smelling plants: as **a :** PENNYCRESS **b :** JIMSONWEED **c :** a wall rocket (as *Diplotaxis tenuifolia* or *D. murinum*) having foliage that is fetid when bruised or crushed **d :** SAND ROCKET **e :** ROCKY MOUNTAIN BEE PLANT **f :** MARSH FLEABANE 1

stinkwood \ˈ=,=\ *n* **1 :** any of several trees with a wood of unpleasant odor: as **a :** either of two trees (*Ocotea bullata* and *Celtis kraussiana*) of southern Africa yielding tough useful timber **b** *Austral* **:** SAND-FLY BUSH **c :** a tree (*Foetidia mauritiana*) of the family Lecythidaceae of the Mascarene islands and Mauritius **d :** YELLOW BUCKTHORN **e :** BLACK GUM **f :** DOGWOOD 2d(1) **2 :** the wood of a stinkwood tree

stinkwort \ˈ=,=\ *n* **1 :** a fetid European herb (*Inula graveolens*) naturalized as a weed in Australia **2 :** JIMSONWEED

stinky \ˈstiŋkē, -ki\ *adj* -ER/-EST **:** that stinks **:** STINKING

stinky pin·ky \ˌstiŋkēˈpiŋkē\ *n* [prob. fr. *pinky* (var. of *pinkie*)] **:** a puzzle that consists in the defining of one phrase with another made up of words that rhyme ⟨*silly filly* is a *stinky pinky* for a foolish horse⟩

¹stint \ˈstint\ *vb* -ED/-ING/-S [ME *stinten, stenten* to cause to cease, cease, fr. OE *styntan* to blunt, dull; akin to ON *stytta* to shorten; causative fr. the root of the adjective represented by OE *stunt* dull, stupid, MHG *stunz* blunt, short, ON *stuttr* scant; akin to OHG *stōzan* to thrust, push, ON *stauta* to strike, Goth *stautan* to strike, L *tundere* to beat, Skt *tudati* he pushes, strikes, OE *stocc* stock — more at STOCK] *vt* **1** *archaic* **:** to put an end to **:** cause to stop or halt **:** STOP; *specif* **:** to check in growth **:** STUNT **2 a :** to restrain within certain limits **:** BOUND, CONFINE **b :** to limit or restrict with respect to a share or allowance **:** be sparing or frugal with ⟨they will ~ themselves for months to buy a phonograph or bicycle —*New Republic*⟩ **3** *Brit* **a :** to restrict (the use of a common pasture) to a determined number of cattle **b :** to divide (land) into rights of pasturage **c :** to limit (a person) in right of pasturage **4 :** to assign a fixed task to (a person) **:** allot a stint to **5 :** to cause (a mare) to get with foal — usu. used with *to* ⟨~*ed* to a Thoroughbred⟩ ⟨had over a hundred brood mares and began . . . ~*ing* the cream of them to him —J.L.Hervey⟩ ~ *vi* **1** *archaic* **:** STOP, CEASE, DESIST **2 :** to be sparing or frugal ⟨the stingy newspaper will ~ on its editorial costs —*Quill*⟩ ⟨one more mouth to feed, and we'll have to ~ more than we do now —Ellen Glasgow⟩

²stint \ˈstint\ *n* -S [ME, fr. *stinten, stenten*, v.] **1** *obs* **:** CESSATION, STOPPAGE, DELAY **2 :** RESTRAINT, RESTRICTION, LIMITATION; *esp* **:** severe or excessive limitations — often used in the phrase *without stint* ⟨during the war years we have expended our resources . . . without ~ —H.S.Truman⟩ **3** *Brit* **a :** the limited number of animals that may be grazed on a piece of common pasture **b :** the right to graze a limited number of animals on a piece of common pasture **4 :** a definite quantity or piece of work or activity assigned by another or set by oneself **:** period of work or activity ⟨did a ~ as a government livestock inspector —*New Yorker*⟩ ⟨started his one-minute ~ in the bell-ringing contest —*N.Y.Times*⟩ **:** TASK ⟨children had no hope of play before their ~*s* were satisfactorily performed —Blanche Sprague⟩ **syn** see TASK

³stint \ˈ"\ *n, pl* **stints** *also* **stint** [ME *stynte*, of unknown origin] **:** any of several small sandpipers: as **a :** RED-BACKED SANDPIPER **b :** LITTLE STINT **c :** TEMMINCK'S STINT **d :** LONG-TOED STINT **e :** LEAST SANDPIPER

⁴stint *var of* STENT

stint·ed·ly *adv* **:** in a stinted manner

stint·ed·ness *n* -ES **:** the quality or state of being stinted

stint·er \ˈstintə(r)\ *n* -S **:** one that stints

stint·ing·ly *adv* **:** in a stinting manner

stint·less \ˈstintləs\ *adj* **:** having no stint **:** CEASELESS, UNENDING

sti·on \ˈstīən\ *n* -S [¹*stock* + *scion*] **:** a plant consisting of a stock and a scion — **sti·on·ic** \(ˈ)stīˈänik\ *adj*

stip *abbr* **1** stipend; stipendiary **2** stipulation

sti·pa \ˈstīpə\ *n* [NL, fr. L *stupa, stuppa* coarse part of flax, tow — more at STUFF] **1** *cap* **:** a large widely distributed genus of grasses having a one-flowered spikelet and lemma terminating in a long twisted or bent awn — see BUNCHGRASS, FEATHER GRASS, ICHU, NEEDLEGRASS, PORCUPINE GRASS, SLEEPY GRASS **2** *also* **stipa grass** -S **:** any grass of the genus *Stipa*; *specif* **:** ESPARTO

¹stipe \ˈstīp\ *n* -S [NL *stipes*, fr. L, log, trunk of a tree; akin to L *stipare* to press together — more at STIFF] **1 :** a short stalk or support: as **a :** the stem supporting the cap or pileus of certain fungi **b :** the stemlike part of the thallus of many frondose algae **c :** the petiole of the frond of a fern; *also* **:** the woody caudex of a tree fern **d :** a stalklike prolongation of the receptacle beneath the ovary of a seed plant — compare ANTHOPHORE, CARPOPHORE, GYNOBASE, GYNOPHORE 1 **2 a :** STIPES 1 **b :** a branch of a graptolite colony — **stiped** \-pt\ *adj*

²stipe \ˈ"\ *n* -S [short for ²*stipendiary*] *chiefly Austral* **:** a stipendiary steward of a jockey club

sti·pel \ˈstīpəl\ *n* -S [NL *stipella*, dim. of *stipula* stipule] **:** the stipule of a leaflet

sti·pel·late \stīˈpelət, stəˈp-; ˈstīpəˌlāt, ˈstip-\ *adj* [NL *stipellatus*, fr. *stipella* stipel + L *-atus* -ate] **:** having stipels

sti·pend \ˈstīˌpend, -pənd\ *n* -S [ME *stipende, stipendy*, fr. L *stipendium*, fr. *stip-, stips* gift, alms + *-pendium* (fr. *pendere* to weigh, pay); perh. akin to L *stipare* to press together — more at STIFF, PENDANT] **1 :** a fixed sum of money typically modest in amount that is paid periodically in compensation for services (as of a clergyman or teacher) **:** SALARY **2 :** a regular allowance paid to defray living expenses; *esp* **:** a sum paid to a student under the terms of a fellowship or scholarship ⟨the scholarship may carry a ~ large enough to take care of the student's entire college expenses —*Harvard College Nat'l Scholarships*⟩ **syn** see WAGE

¹sti·pen·di·ary \stīˈpendēˌerē\ *adj* [L *stipendiarius*, fr. *stipendium* + *-arius* -ary] **1 :** receiving or compensated by wages or salary **:** performing services for a stated price or compensation ⟨a ~ curate⟩ **2 :** of or relating to a stipend

²stipendiary \ˈ"\ *n* -ES **:** one who receives a stipend: as **a** *Brit* (1) **:** a stipendiary clergyman (2) **:** STIPENDIARY MAGISTRATE **b** *archaic* **:** a mercenary soldier

stipendiary magistrate *n* **:** a salaried British magistrate who is a professional lawyer appointed under statutory provisions to act instead of or in cooperation with unpaid lay justices of the peace

sti·pen·di·um \stīˈpendēəm\ *n* -S [L] **:** STIPEND

sti·pend·less \ˈstīˌpendləs, -pən-\ *adj* **:** having no stipend

sti·pes \ˈstīˌpēz\ *n, pl* **stip·i·tes** \ˈstipəˌtēz\ [NL *stipit-, stipes*, fr. L, log, trunk of a tree; akin to L *stipare* to press together — more at STIFF] **1 :** PEDUNCLE: as **a :** the second basal segment of a maxilla of an insect or crustacean **b :** the second or rarely the first basal segment of the mandible of a millipede — compare MALA 2b **c :** either of the inner and outer platelike pieces that form the major portion of the deutomala of a myriapod **d :** EYESTALK **2 :** STIRPS 1

sti·pi·form \ˈstīpəˌfȯrm\ *also* **stip·i·ti·form** \ˈstipədəˌf-, stəˈpid-\ *adj* [*stipiform* fr. NL *stipiformis*, fr. *stipes* stipe, stipes + L *-iformis* -iform; *stipitiform* fr. NL *stipitiformis*, fr. *stipit-, stipes* stipe, stipes + L *-iformis* -iform] **:** resembling a stipe or stipes **:** STALKLIKE

stip·i·tal \ˈstipəd·ᵊl\ *adj* [NL *stipit-, stipes* + E *-al*] **:** of or relating to the stipes

stip·i·tate \ˈstipəˌtāt\ *adj* [NL *stipitatus*, fr. *stipit-, stipes* + L *-atus* -ate] **:** having or borne on a stipe ⟨a ~ pod⟩

stip·i·tat·ic acid \ˌstipəˈtad·ik-\ *n* [*stipitatic* fr. NL *stipitatum* (specific epithet of *Penicillium stipitatum*) (neut. of *stipitatus* stipitate) + E *-ic*] **:** a cream-colored solid acid $(HO)_2C_7H_3OCOOH$ related to tropolone and formed from sugar as a metabolic product of a mold (*Penicillium stipitatum*); 3,6-dihydroxy-4-oxo-cyclo-hepta-triene-carboxylic acid

stip·i·ture \ˈstipəˌchu̇(ə)r\ *n* -S [NL *Stipiturus*] **:** a bird of the genus *Stipiturus*

stip·i·tu·rus \ˌstipəˈtu̇rəs, -pə-ˈtyu̇-\ *n, cap* [NL, fr. L *stipit-, stipes* log + NL *-urus*] **:** a genus of small babblers comprising the Australian emu wrens

stip·pen \ˈstipən\ *n* -S [G, pl. of *stippe* speck, spot, fr. LG, fr. MLG, fr. *stippen* to prick] **:** BITTER PIT

¹stip·ple \ˈstipəl\ *vt* -ED/-ING/-S [D *stippelen* to spot, dot, fr. *stippel* speck, spot, fr. MD, dim. of *stip* point, dot, fr. *stippen* to prick; akin to MLG *stippen* to prick, MHG *steppen* to stitch, quilt, Russ *stebel'* stalk — more at STIFF] **1 :** to engrave essentially by means of dots and flicks — compare LINE ENGRAVING **2 a :** to make (as in paint, ink) by small short touches that together produce an even or softly graded shadow **b :** to apply (as paint) by repeated small touches **3 :** to produce an effect in as if by stippling **:** dot or spot with shade or color **:** SPECKLE, FLECK, STREAK ⟨sunlight that fell through the trees and *stippled* the sidewalks —Hamilton Basso⟩

²stipple \ˈ"\ *n* -S **1 a :** execution in graphic art by which gradation of light and shade is produced by separate touches of small points, larger dots, or longer strokes **b :** the effect so produced that may show every separate point or touch (as in prints from a stipple plate) or may resemble a mosaic in which the touches tend to run together (as in stippling in strokes from a brush filled with color) **c :** the spattered effect produced on book edges by sprinkling **d :** a finish of paper characterized by small raised dots **2 :** an effect (as in nature) resembling a stipple **3 :** a brush used in stippling

stipple board *n* **:** a drawing board prepared by coating and embossing in such a way that a mark made upon it with crayon or pencil produces the effect of a tone formed by minute dots

stippled *adj* **:** produced or applied by stippling **:** DOTTED, SPOTTED, SPECKLED

stipple engraving *n* **1 :** the act or process of engraving by stippling **2 :** the impression made from a stippled plate

stipple paper *n* **:** a paper similar to stipple board

stip·pler \-p(ə)lə(r)\ *n* -S **:** one that stipples; *specif* **:** an artist or a painter who stipples surfaces

stipple streak *n* **:** a virus disease of the potato characterized by leaf distortion, vein necrosis, and brittleness of stems and petioles

stippling *n* -S **1 :** a stippled effect **2 :** a spotted condition (as in basophilic red blood corpuscles, the retina in diseases of the eye, X rays of the lungs, bones)

stip·ply \-p(ə)lē, -li\ *adj* -ER/-EST **:** resembling stipple **:** somewhat stippled

stip·u·la \ˈstipyələ\ *n, pl* **stipu·lae** \-ˌlē, -ˌlī\ [NL] **:** STIPULE

stip·u·la·ble \ˈstipyələbəl\ *adj* [¹*stipulate* + *-able*] **:** that can be stipulated

stip·u·lar \ˈstipyələ(r)\ *adj* [NL *stipularis*, fr. *stipula* + L *-aris* -ar] **:** of, resembling, or provided with stipules **:** growing on or like stipules ⟨~ glands⟩ ⟨~ tendrils⟩

¹stip·u·late \ˈstipyəˌlāt, *usu* -ād.+V\ *vb* -ED/-ING/-S [L *stipulatus*, past part. of *stipulari* to make an express demand for some term in an agreement; akin to Umbrian *stiplatu* one that makes an express demand for some term in an agreement and perh. to L *stipare* to press together — more at STIFF] *vi* **1 :** to make an agreement or covenant with a person or company to do or forbear something **:** CONTRACT ⟨have *stipulated* for the future disposition and management of those funds —John Marshall⟩ **2 :** to make an express demand for some term in an agreement — used with *for* ⟨fulfilling . . . all the conditions of constraint for which we *stipulated* —Sacheverell Sitwell⟩ **3 :** to agree respecting the conduct of legal proceedings — used with *to* ⟨counsel on both sides will ~ to the receipt of such working papers . . . in evidence —*Jour. of Accountancy*⟩ ~ *vt* **1 :** to specify as a condition or requirement of an agreement or offer (as a contract, treaty, deed, will, law) **:** state as a stipulation ⟨in his will the latter *stipulated* that his sons should all be taught trades —H.E.Starr⟩ ⟨the terms of the Italian peace treaty had *stipulated* the return to Greece of the Dodecanese Islands —R.G.Woolbert⟩ **2 :** to give a guarantee of **:** PROMISE ⟨ceded to the French, who *stipulated* to erect no fortifications on these islands —Jedidiah Morse⟩ **3 :** to agree mutually concerning (conduct or evidence) during legal proceedings ⟨we'll ~ . . . that this man was employed to spy on his wife —Erle Stanley Gardner⟩

²stip·u·late \-lət\ *also* **stip·u·lat·ed** \-ˌlād·əd\ *adj* [*stipulate* fr. NL *stipulatus*, fr. *stipula* + L *-atus* -ate; *stipulated* fr. *stipulate* (fr. NL *stipulatus*) + *-ed*] **:** furnished with stipules

stipulated damages *n pl* **:** damages settled by liquidation **:** liquidated damages

stip·u·la·tion \ˌstipyəˈlāshən\ *n* -S [L *stipulation-, stipulatio*, fr. *stipulatus* (past part. of *stipulari*) + *-ion-, -io* -ion] **1 :** an act of stipulating or something stipulated **:** AGREEMENT, PROVISION: as **a :** an agreement between attorneys respecting the conduct of legal proceedings **b :** a bond or undertaking taken in admiralty courts **c** *Roman law* **:** a formal contract by oral question and answer imposing a duty on the promisor only **d :** a condition, requirement, or item specified in a contract, treaty, deed, will, or law **2 :** a stipulative definition or the process of specifying one **syn** see CONDITION

stip·u·la·tive definition \ˈstipyəˌlād·iv-, -ˌləd·iv-\ *n* [*stipulative* fr. ¹*stipulate* + *-ive*] **:** a declaration of a meaning that is intended to be attached by the speaker to a word, expression, or symbol and that usu. does not already have an established use in the sense intended — compare DICTIONARY DEFINITION

stip·u·la·tor \-ˌlād·ə(r)\ *n* -S [L, fr. *stipulatus* (past part. of *stipulari*) + *-or*] **1 :** one that stipulates **2 :** one that proposes a stipulative definition

stip·u·la·to·ry \-ləˌtōrē\ *adj* [¹*stipulate* + *-ory*] **1 :** of, relating to, or characterized by stipulation **2 :** constituted or contracted by stipulation ⟨~ obligations⟩

stip·ule \ˈsti(ˌ)pyül\ *n* -S [NL *stipula*, fr. L, stalk, straw; akin to L *stipes* log, trunk of a tree, *stipare* to press together — more at STIFF] **1 a :** one of the pair of leaflike or membranous appendages that arise at the base of the leaf in many plants, vary greatly in size and shape and in degree of adnation to the stem, to the petiole, or to each other, and become modified in some plants to form spines or tendrils and in others to perform all the functions of leaves — see OCREA **b** *also* **stip·u·lode** \ˈstipyəˌlōd\ [*stipulode* fr. *stipule* + *-ode*] **:** one of the leaflike structures arising together with the leaf from the cortex of the basal nodes in some algae of the genus *Chara* **2 :** a newly sprouted feather **:** PINFEATHER

stip·uled \ˈsti(ˌ)pyüld\ *adj* **:** STIPULATE

stip·u·lif·er·ous \ˌstipyəˈlif(ə)rəs\ *adj* [NL *stipulifer* stipuliferous (fr. *stipula* stipule + L *-ifer* -iferous) + E *-ous*] **:** bearing or producing stipules

stip·u·li·form \ˈstipyələˌfȯrm\ *adj* [*stipule* + *-iform*] **:** having the form of a stipule

¹stir \R ˈstər, + *vowel* -tər·; -R -tə̄, + *suffixal vowel* -tər· *also* -tə̄r, + *vowel in a following word* -tər· *or* -tə̄ *also* -tə̄r\ *vb* **stirred; stirred; stirring; stirs** [ME *stiren, steren*, fr. OE *styrian*; akin to MHG *stürn* to poke, incite, ON *styrr* disturbance, and prob. to Skt *tvarate* he hurries — more at TURBID] *vt* **1 a :** to impart movement to; *esp* **:** to cause the slightest movement or change of position of ⟨a faint smile *stirred* her lips —Kathleen Freeman⟩ ⟨tied so tightly he could scarcely ~ a finger⟩ ⟨the great warships easing slowly through the gates of the bay . . . and *stirring* the yachts at anchor —John Durant⟩ **b :** to disturb the quiet of **:** AGITATE ⟨little boats that barely ~ its mysterious black waters —Selby Paul⟩ ⟨coons, coyotes, and owls *stirred* the silence here and there —John Muir †1914⟩ **2 a** (1) **:** to pass a spoon or other implement through (a substance) with a continued circular movement for the purpose of mixing, blending, dissolving, cooling, or preventing sticking of the ingredients ⟨~ the batter until the dry ingredients are blended⟩ ⟨puts sugar in his tea and ~*s* it⟩ ⟨~*s* his pail of paint with a paddle⟩ (2) **:** to mix by or as if by stirring ⟨careful to ~ the ingredients well⟩ ⟨by *stirring* together a mass of . . . facts and superstitions, he arrived at a hierarchy of races —Martin Gardner⟩ — often used with *in* or *into* ⟨~ in the flour gradually to avoid lumping⟩ ⟨~ the beaten eggs into the milk⟩ **b :** to disturb the relative position of the particles or parts of ⟨~ the fire with the poker to make it burn again⟩ ⟨~ the topsoil⟩ — often used with *up* ⟨the cows would wade into the pool and ~ up . . . the mud on the bottom —Vicki Baum⟩ **3 :** BESTIR, EXERT ⟨the wife would . . . ~ herself to sweep the floor —Pearl Buck⟩ **4 :** to bring (a subject or question) into notice or debate **:** RAISE ⟨~ not questions of jurisdiction —Francis Bacon⟩ **5 a :** to excite to activity or strong feeling ⟨an instinct ~*s* her to feed the older girls —Weston La Barre⟩ **:** INCITE, INFLAME ⟨heroism that ~*s* orators to eloquence⟩ ⟨the increase of illiteracy in children . . . has *stirred* the conscience of the British public —*Britain Today*⟩ ⟨able, as a public speaker, to ~ people . . . to the point of tears —Stewart Cockburn⟩ **:** QUICKEN ⟨peace has no drums and trumpets to ~ the pulse —Amy Loveman⟩ — often used with *up* ⟨she *stirred* up her father to proclaim a campaign against the whites —Negley Farson⟩ **b :** to call forth (as a feeling, memory, or disposition) from a person or group **:** EVOKE ⟨men lacking an arm or leg *stirred* universal pity —Dixon Wecter⟩ ⟨this Vermont watering trough . . . will ~ nostalgic memories —J.H.East⟩ **:** PROVOKE ⟨the inquiry has *stirred* a hot controversy —*N.Y.Times*⟩ — often used with *up* ⟨abolitionists encouraged agitators to come South and ~ up discontent —Helen B. Woodward⟩ ~ *vi* **1 a :** to make a slight movement ⟨a light breeze was *stirring* in the lime trees —T.B.Costain⟩ **:** change one's position slightly ⟨a bed that squeaks if he so much as ~*s*⟩ **:** begin to move (as in rousing) ⟨girl on the floor *stirred*, moaned and sat up —Louis Bromfield⟩ **b :** to make the least movement or excursion **:** move or go at all **:** BUDGE ⟨so intent on this fantastic . . . narrative that she had hardly *stirred* —Walter de la Mare⟩ ⟨it was very wet all day and I didn't ~ out of the house —Lennox Robinson⟩ **2 :** to begin to be active **:** show signs of life ⟨already, although it was still dark, the life of the farm was *stirring* —Ellen Glasgow⟩ ⟨profound forces were *stirring* into a vigorous life that was soon to transform the culture of Europe —I.M.Price⟩ **3 a :** to move in or from a place (as amid prevailing quiet or after inactivity) ⟨in the barn back of the house she could hear the cattle *stirring* about —Sherwood Anderson⟩; *also* **:** to be up and about ⟨up and gone before the others were *stirring*⟩ **b :** to be active or busy **:** move in a brisk or vigorous manner ⟨seemed to be forever busy about something, *stirring* around in the midst of tumult and struggle —W.A.White⟩ **:** exert oneself ⟨the friends of the unfortunate exile . . . were *stirring* anxiously in his behalf —Charles Merivale⟩ **:** be in a state of excitement ⟨the discontents that had been *stirring* in him for at least fifteen years —Carl Van Doren⟩ **4 :** to become an object of notice **:** be current ⟨talk freely on everything that ~*s* —Isaac Watts⟩ **5 :** to pass an implement through a substance with a circular movement (as for the purpose of mixing) ⟨asked to lick the spoon she was *stirring* with⟩ **6 :** to be capable of being stirred ⟨add water till the mixture ~*s* easily⟩

syn STIR AND STIR (*up*), ROUSE, AROUSE, AWAKEN, WAKEN, RALLY can mean to inspire or drive someone from inactivity to action of some kind, or (with the exception of RALLY) to inspire or provoke. STIR and STIR (*up*) suggest provocation of a person or his imagination to activity often implying something latent awaiting provocation; or they can apply directly to an emotion or reaction of the person provoked ⟨obstacles only *stirred* the friars to greater efforts —R.A.Billington⟩ ⟨some of them *stir* the imagination and call forth emotions —Douglas Carruthers⟩ ⟨the present Diana had wakened his curiosity, had *stirred* his interest in her —George Meredith⟩ ⟨movements that begin by *stirring up* hostility against a group of people —John Dewey⟩ ⟨matters that *stir* heated controversy —F.A.Ogg & Harold Zink⟩ ROUSE, AROUSE, AWAKEN, and WAKEN all presuppose a state of repose, often sleep or a dormant condition. ROUSE suggests a suddenness in stirring to activity, esp. wakefulness, often applying to incitement by startling, frightening, or upsetting and sometimes suggesting ensuing turbulence ⟨*roused* out of sleep by a heavy pounding on the door —Joseph Wechsberg⟩ ⟨when he was *roused* he spoke with eloquence —R.M.Lovett⟩ ⟨the sight of the brisk flames *roused* the rioters —T.B.Costain⟩ ⟨poetry *roused* in her a clumsy and conventional enthusiasm —Virginia Woolf⟩ ⟨a *rousing* fight⟩ AROUSE is weaker in implication than ROUSE, often suggesting no more than to start into activity ⟨the fact *aroused* no curiosity —John Dewey⟩ ⟨busy *arousing* the public to the danger —W.G. Carleton⟩ ⟨*aroused* sleeping memories —R.L.Cook⟩ ⟨have sought to *arouse* prejudice and fear —F.D.Roosevelt⟩ AWAKEN and WAKEN, implying an ending of sleep, apply chiefly to the stirring to activity of mental or spiritual powers ⟨their assertion that you *awakened* them to think —Irwin Edman⟩ ⟨*awaken* the curiosity of the future scientist —J.B.Conant⟩ ⟨*awaken* the spirit of good will —V.L.Parrington⟩ ⟨employ their talents or *waken* the deepest interest in their lives —Thomas Wolfe⟩ ⟨*wakened* his latent powers of literary expression —C.A.Madison⟩ RALLY implies a gathering together of diffused or disorganized forces that stirs up or rouses, esp. to positive organized activity ⟨his smiling face *rallied* his friends —Claud Cockburn⟩ ⟨necessary to *rally* all the forces in the country in the name of freedom against a foreign foe —John Dewey⟩ ⟨the prisoner made an effort to *rally* his attention —Charles Dickens⟩

²stir \ˈ"\ *n* -S **1 a :** the state of being stirred **:** a state of disturbance, agitation, or activity **:** COMMOTION ⟨the entrance of the judge and a consequent great ~ . . . stopped the dialogue —Charles Dickens⟩ **:** RESTLESSNESS ⟨an age of ~ and change, a season of new wine and old bottles —John Galsworthy⟩ **:** FLURRY ⟨these visits brought a considerable ~ of . . . business in the provinces —R.W.Southern⟩ **b :** a reaction of widespread notice and discussion ⟨an exposé that created a considerable ~ in the press⟩ **:** IMPRESSION ⟨an obscure family that had till then made little ~ in the world⟩ **2 :** a slight or incipient movement, excitement, or emotion ⟨with every ~ of wind and wheel, the dust blows in choking brown clouds —Marjory S. Douglas⟩ ⟨everywhere there was a faint and genial ~ of spring in the air —Susan Ertz⟩ **3 :** an act of stirring **:** a stirring movement **:** POKE ⟨give the embers a ~⟩

syn STIR, BUSTLE, FLURRY, POTHER, FUSS, ADO: these six nouns all point to a manifest excitement or agitation accompanying

an action or event. STIR stresses a restless or brisk movement, usu. of a group or crowd ⟨a great *stir* about the manse that morning, and the boys were dressed in their Sunday clothes —William Black⟩ ⟨the announcement created quite a *stir* in the audience⟩ BUSTLE adds the idea of noisy, obtrusive, often self-important activity ⟨the streets are alive with the hurry and noise of a big city. Then the *bustle* subsides and relative calm is resumed —*Amer. Guide Series: N.C.*⟩ ⟨no such *bustle* of enthusiasm, no such in-and-out of busy workers —S.H.Adams⟩ FLURRY puts stress upon sudden, nervous, usu. short-lived activity, often suggesting undue haste ⟨a *flurry* of excitement⟩ ⟨set off a *flurry* of speculation in the world's oil industry —*Time*⟩ ⟨a *flurry* of ground fire exploded at almost the right altitude to catch the photographic plane —J.A.Michener⟩ POTHER and FUSS both imply unnecessary, often confused, activity or agitation, usu. over trifles. POTHER lays stress upon the agitation or confusion ⟨he was not unused to women, but he was unused to a *pother* of emotion over any one of them —Audrey Barker⟩ ⟨the great hydraulic firms were in a continual *pother* about the water rights —Julian Dana⟩ FUSS usu. stresses more the needlessness of the commotion ⟨those events . . . scarcely warranted the tremendous *fuss* subsequently made about them —Arnold Bennett⟩ ⟨much *fuss* is made of the right of the parent to order the life of his child —*Times Lit. Supp.*⟩ ADO usu. implies fussy activity and waste of energy ⟨everybody seems to know his job and to take over his duties without much *ado* —*Education Digest*⟩ ⟨among . . . speculators there always is considerable *ado* whenever the stock market drops below its preceding lows —*Newsweek*⟩

[3]**stir** \"\ *n* -S [by alter.] *Scot* : SIR

[4]**stir** \"\ *n* -S [origin unknown] *slang* : PRISON ⟨an international jewel thief just out of ~ and eager to get back to work —V.P. Hass⟩

stir *abbr* stirrup

stirabout \'==,=\ *n* -S [fr. *stir about*, v.] **1 :** a porridge of oatmeal or cornmeal boiled in water or milk and stirred during cooking **2 a :** STIR, TUMULT **b :** a bustling person **3 :** a combination of pinch shot and push shot used in pool when the cue ball and object ball are too close to a pocket to allow a cut stroke

stir bug *n, slang* : a person mentally unbalanced by prison life

stir crazy *adj, slang* : psychotic as a result of confinement in or as if in prison

stirk \'stәk\ *n* -S [ME, fr. OE *stirc;* akin to MLG *sterke* young cow, Icel *stirtla* sterile cow, L *sterilis* sterile — more at STERILE] **1** *Brit* **:** a young bull or cow esp. when more than one but less than two years old **2** *Brit* **:** FOOL

stir·less \'stərləs, -tәl-\ *adj* : devoid of stir : MOTIONLESS — **stir·less·ly** *adv* — **stir·less·ness** *n* -ES

stir·ling \'stərliŋ\ *Scot var of* STARLING

stir·ling cycle \'stər|liŋ-, -tәl|, -təi|, |lēŋ-\ *n, usu cap S* [after Robert *Stirling* †1878 Scot. engineer] : a cycle for an air engine using a regenerator and having for its indicator diagram two isothermals and two lines of constant volume

stirling engine *n, usu cap S* : an air engine using the Stirling cycle

stirling's formula *n, usu cap S* [after James *Stirling* †1770 Scot. mathematician] : a formula giving the approximate value of the factorial of any very large number

stir·ling·shire \-ŋ,shi(ə)r, ,shiə, -,shə(r)\ *or* **stirling** *adj, usu cap* [fr. *Stirlingshire, Stirling*, county in central Scotland] : of or from the county of Stirling, Scotland : of the kind or style prevalent in Stirling

stir off *vi* **1 :** to complete the process of boiling down syrup to a thickness at which the sugar crystallizes and is separated from the molasses **2 :** SUGAR OFF

stirp \'stərp\ *n* -S [L *stirp-, stirps*] **1 :** a line descending from a common ancestor : STOCK, LINEAGE **2 :** the sum of the determinants of whatever nature in a fertilized egg

stir·pi·cul·ture \'stərpə,kəlchər\ *n* [L *stirp-, stirps* + E *-i-* + *culture*] : the breeding of special stocks or races

stirps \'sti(ə)rps, 'stərps\ *n, pl* **stir·pes** \-ir,pās, -ər(,)pēz\ [L *stirp-, stirps* branch of a family, lineage, trunk, root — more at TORPID] **1 :** a branch of a family — usu. used in the phrase *per stirpes* **2 :** the person from whom a branch of a family is descended **3 a :** a large group of animals comparable to a superfamily **b :** a race or fixed variety of plants

stir·ra *or* **stir·rah** \'stirə\ *n* -S [prob. alter. of *sirrah*] *Scot* : BOY, FELLOW — compare SIRRAH

stir·ra·ble \'stər·əbəl *also* -tәrəb-\ *adj* : that can be stirred

stirred *past of* STIR

stir·rer \'stər·ə(r) *also* -tәrə(r\ *n* -S [ME *stirer, sterer*, fr. *stiren, steren* to stir + *-er*] : one that stirs: as **a :** a workman who stirs materials (as in baking, sugar refining) **b :** a stirring device in a seed planter **c :** a power-driven apparatus for stirring **d :** a utensil with a long stem and usu. a spoon end for mixing drinks

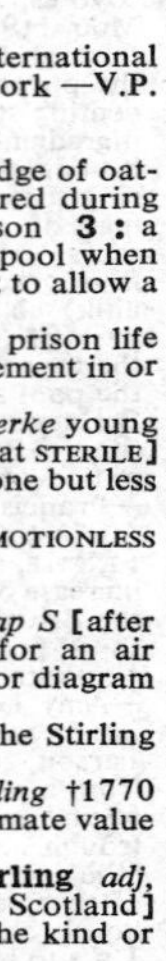
stirrer d

[1]**stirring** *n* -S [ME *stiringe, steringe*, fr. OE *styrung, styring*, fr. *styrian* to stir + *-ung, -ing* -ing] : the act of one that stirs : a moving or putting in motion : MOVEMENT, ACTIVITY, AGITATION, INCITEMENT ⟨his grandfather's barn at night with its . . . restless ~*s* of animals inside —J.P.Marquand⟩ ⟨had already felt little ~*s* of compunction —Mary Austin⟩

[2]**stirring** *adj* [ME *stiringe, steringe*, alter. of *stirende, sterende* that stirs, fr. OE *styrende, styriende*, pres. part. of *styrian* to stir] : that stirs; *esp* : EXCITING ⟨~ events such as wars and rescues⟩ ⟨inflamed their patriotism with a ~ oration on their threatened liberties⟩

stir·ring·ly *adv* [ME *steringli*, fr. *stiringe, steringe*, adj. + *-liche, -ly, -li* -ly] : in a stirring manner

stirring plow *n* : a plow with a high abruptly curved moldboard for turning the furrow slice of old land quickly but less completely than a breaker

stir·rup \'stər·əp, 'stə·rəp *also* 'stirəp *sometimes* 'sterəp, *chiefly in dial or substand speech* 'stərp\ *n* -S [ME *stirop*, fr. OE *stigrāp;* akin to OHG *stegareif* stirrup, ON *stigreip;* all fr. a prehistoric NGmc-WGmc compound whose first constituent is akin to OE *stīgan* to go up and whose second constituent is represented by OE *rāp* rope — more at STAIR, ROPE] **1 :** a ring or bent piece of metal, wood, or leather made horizontal in one part for receiving the foot of a rider, attached by a strap to a saddle, and used to aid in mounting and as a support while riding — see STOCK SADDLE illustration **2 :** a piece resembling a stirrup: as **a :** one used as a support or clamp in carpentry and machinery — compare HANGER 7 **b :** a flat usu. U-shaped steel bar or strap for receiving and supporting one end of a timber joist, beam, or girder **c :** a stirrup-shaped footrest (as used in working bellows) **3 :** a rope secured to a yard and having a thimble in its lower end for supporting a footrope — see SAIL illustration, SHIP illustration **4** [trans. of NL *stapes*] : STAPES **5 :** the part of a garment or device that passes under the instep

stirrup bar *n* **1 :** the horizontal piece of a stirrup **2 :** the bar from which a riding stirrup is suspended

stirrup cup *n* **1 :** a cup of wine or other drink taken by a rider about to depart **2 :** a farewell cup : a parting glass

stirrup iron *n* [ME (Sc) *stirrap irn*, fr. ME *stirrap, stirop* stirrup + *irn, iren* iron] : the metal loop of a riding stirrup

stirrup leather *or* **stirrup strap** *n* [*stirrup leather* fr. ME *stirop lethir*, fr. *stirop* stirrup + *lethir, lether* leather; *stirrup strap* fr. *stirrup* + *strap*] : the strap suspending a stirrup — see STOCK SADDLE illustration

stirruplike \'==,=\ *adj* : resembling a stirrup

stirrup pump *n* : a portable hand pump held in position by a foot bracket or stirrup and often used (as with a bucket) to supply a short hose for extinguishing small fires

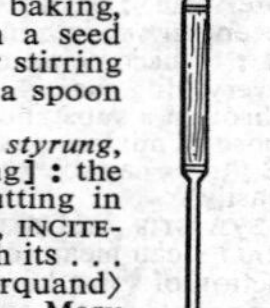
stirrup pump

stirrup-vase \'==,=\ *n* : PSEUDAMPHORA

stirs *pres 3d sing of* STIR, *pl of* STIR

stir-up \'=,=\ *n* -S [fr. *stir up*, v.] : an act of stirring up or state of being stirred up : AGITATION, TURMOIL

stir-up sunday \'=,=-\ *n, usu cap both Ss* [so called fr. the first words of the Anglican collect for the day, "Stir up, we beseech thee, O Lord, the wills of thy faithful people"] *Brit* : the Sunday next before Advent

[1]**stitch** \'stich\ *n* -ES [ME *stiche*, fr. OE *stice* stab, puncture, stitch in the side; akin to OHG *stih* sting, pricking, Goth *stiks* moment, OHG *stehhan* to prick — more at STICK] **1 :** a local sharp and sudden pain in the side (as in pleurodynia) **2 :** a single complete in-and-out movement of a threaded needle in sewing, embroidering, or suturing **3 a** (1) **:** a portion of thread left in the material after making one in-and-out movement with a threaded needle in hand sewing (2) **:** one of the separate lengths of thread, wire, or other material used to hold skin or flesh (as the edges of a wound or incision) during healing (3) **:** the interlocked section of the threads from needle and shuttle resulting from a single complete motion of the needle through the fabric in machine sewing **b :** the interlacing thread that joins the face and back of a double fabric in weaving **c :** a staple formed by a wire-stitching machine from a coil of wire (as for fastening pamphlets, cartons, novelties) ⟨a wire stitcher that applies ~*es* as fast as 300 a minute⟩ **4** *dial chiefly Brit* **:** a narrow ridge of arable land : a ridge between furrows **5 :** a least part : least bit ⟨a boat . . . with every ~ of canvas set —Benjamin Disraeli⟩ ⟨refused to do a ~ of work⟩; *specif* : the least bit of clothing ⟨left without a dry ~ on his back⟩ **6 :** a single loop of thread or yarn around a knitting needle, crochet hook, or other implement forming one of a series of links in knitted, crocheted, netted, or lace fabric ⟨drop a ~⟩ **7 a :** a stitch or series of stitches formed in a particular manner often for a particular purpose (as basting, buttonholing); *also* : a decorative pattern formed by a stitch (as a French knot) or series of stitches (as satin stitch) worked with a needle or hook through or on cloth or over canvas **b :** a method of fastening leaves (as of pamphlets) with thread or cord drawn by hand or machine through previously pierced holes or with wire staples — usu. used with a qualifier; see DOUBLE STITCH, SADDLE STITCH, SIDE STITCH **syn** see PAIN — **in stitches** *adv* : in a state of uncontrollable laughter ⟨keep cocktail parties *in stitches* with slapstick impersonations —*Time*⟩

[2]**stitch** \"\ *vb* -ED/-ING/-S [ME *stichen*, fr. *stiche*, n.] *vt* **1** *obs* **:** PIERCE, STAB **2 a** (1) **:** to fasten, join, or close with or as if with stitches ⟨~*ed* his team emblem onto his uniform⟩ ⟨~ the ends of the two strips together⟩ ⟨many literary travelers have . . . ~*ed* their impressions into skillful embroideries —Edward Sapir⟩ — often used with *up* ⟨~ up the rip⟩ (2) **:** to fasten together (signatures) by passing thread or wire through all the signatures at once — distinguished from *sew* (3) **:** to unite by means of staples ⟨~ the flaps of a fiber box⟩ **b :** to make, mend, or decorate with or as if with stitches : SEW ⟨~ a seam⟩ : EMBROIDER ⟨~ a sampler⟩ — often used with *up* ⟨~ up torn trousers⟩ **c :** to sew in a hasty manner — usu. used with *up* ⟨~ up a dress to wear this evening⟩ **d :** to sew by first puncturing (as shoe leather) with an awl or needle by hand or by machine **3** *dial* **:** to form (arable land) into ridges **4 :** to form the outline of (a design) on metal by prick-punching through a design on paper fixed to the metal **5 :** to strike or pierce at intervals in the manner of stitching ⟨machine guns ~*ed* the sides of buildings —*Springfield (Mass.) Union*⟩ ~ *vi* **1 :** to do needlework : SEW **2 :** to join something with wire stitches **3 :** to move in and out in a stitchlike manner

[3]**stitch** \"\ *n* -ES [perh. fr. ME *sticche* piece, fr. OE *stycce* — more at STOCK] *dial Eng* : a harvesting shock of about 12 sheaves

[4]**stitch** \"\ *n* [perh. fr. ME *sticche* piece] **1** *dial Eng* **:** DISTANCE 2c **2** *dial* **:** a period of time

stitch aloft *vt* : to stitch (as a shoe or the sole of a shoe) so that the stitches are exposed and not in a covered channel

stitch·bird \'stich,=\ *n* [so called fr. the resemblance of its call to the word *stitch*] : a nearly extinct honey eater (*Notiomystis cincta*) of North Island, New Zealand, of which the male has black, yellow, and white plumage

stitchdown \'=,=\ *n* -S [fr. *stitch down*, v.] **1 :** the stitching of the outward-turned lower edge of a shoe upper directly to the sole or sometimes with a welt added over the edge **2** *also* **stitchdown shoe :** a shoe made by the stitchdown process

stitch·er \'stichə(r)\ *n* -S : one that stitches: as **a :** a worker who joins or decorates articles or parts of articles with hand or machine stitching **b** (1) **:** a machine that joins (as box bottoms) using staples formed from a continuous coil of wire (2) **:** the operator of such a machine

stitch·ery \-chərē\ *n* -ES : NEEDLEWORK

stitching *n* -S **1 a :** the act of one that stitches **b :** work done by one that stitches **2 :** STITCHES; *esp* : a continuous line of stitches **3 :** SEWING

stitching horse *n* : a harness maker's clamp for holding work while it is being stitched

stitch in time : a timely action or remedy ⟨a *stitch in time* saves nine⟩

stitchlike \'=,=\ *adj* : resembling a stitch or stitching

stitch rivet *n* : one of several widely spaced rivets used to connect two or more parallel elements of a built-up structural member so that they will act as a unit and will not separate laterally

stitch-rivet \'=¦==\ *vt* [*stitch rivet*] : to connect with stitch rivets

stitch watermark *n* : a fortuitous watermark on a stamp caused usu. by the stitches in the wire of the paper machine

[1]**stitch weld** *n* : a joint made by stitch welding

[2]**stitch weld** *vt* : to unite by stitch welding

stitch welding *n* : resistance welding in which the weld is made linearly (as between rotating wheels) by a series of spot welds that are spaced rather than overlapping (as in seam welding)

stitch wheel *n* : PRICKER 2c

stitchwork \'=,=\ *n* : NEEDLEWORK; *esp* : TAPESTRY

stitchwort \'=,=\ *n* [ME *stichewort*, fr. OE *sticwyrt* agrimony, fr. *stice* stab, puncture, stitch in the side + *wyrt* herb — more at STITCH, WORT] : any of several plants of the genus *Stellaria*

stith \'stith\ *archaic var of* STITHY

stithy \'stithē, -thē\ *n* -ES [ME *stithy, stethy, stith, stethe*, fr. ON *stethi* (accus. *stethja*); akin to ON *stathr* place — more at STEAD] **1 :** ANVIL **2 :** SMITHY

[1]**stive** \'stīv\ *vb* -ED/-ING/-S [ME *stiven*, prob. fr. Sp *estibar* or Pg *estivar* to pack tightly — more at STEEVE] *vt* **1 :** to pack tightly : CROWD **2 :** to shut up in a warm close place : STIFLE, SUFFOCATE ~ *vi* : SUFFOCATE

[2]**stive** \"\ *n* -S [obs. D *stuive*, fr. MD *stuve, stuyve* pulverization; akin to MD *stuven, stieven* to raise dust, MLG *stūven* to raise dust, *stübbe* dust, OHG *stoub* dust, *stioban* to raise dust, *stuppi* dust, Goth *stubjus*] : DUST; *esp* : the floating dust in flour mills caused by grinding

[3]**stive** \"\ *chiefly Scot var of* [1]STEEVE

[1]**sti·ver** *or* **stui·ver** \'stīvə(r)\ *or* **stee·ver** \-tēv-\ *n* -S [D *stuiver*, fr. MD *stuyver, stuver*, a small coin; prob. akin to MLG *stūf* blunt, ON *stubbi* stub — more at STUB] **1 :** a unit of value of the Netherlands equal to $\frac{1}{20}$ gulden or 5 Dutch cents **2 :** a coin representing one stiver **3 :** the smallest amount of money ⟨not worth a ~⟩

[2]**stiv·er** \'stivə(r)\ *vb* -ED/-ING/-S [prob. irreg. fr. [1]*stiff*] *vi* **1** *dial Eng* **:** to stand up stiff : BRISTLE **2** *dial* **:** STAGGER, STRUGGLE ~ *vt, dial chiefly Eng* : to cause to stand up stiff : ROUGHEN

stivy \'stīvē\ *adj* [[1]*stive* + *-y*] : STUFFY

stiz·i·dae \'stizə,dē\ *n pl, cap* [NL, fr. *Stizus*, type genus (fr. Gk *stizein* to tattoo) + *-idae* — more at STICK] : a family of sphecoid wasps that includes the cicada killer

stizo·lo·bi·um \,stizə'lōbēəm, ,stīz-\ [NL, fr. *stiz-* (fr. Gk *stizein* to tattoo) + *-o-* + *-lobium* (fr. Gk *lobion* small lobe, dim. of *lobos* lobe) — more at SLEEP] *syn of* MUCUNA

stizo·ste·di·on \-'stēdēən\ *n, cap* [NL, fr. *stiz-* (fr. Gk *stizein* to tattoo) + *-o-* + *-stedion* (perh. irreg. fr. Gk *stēthion* small breast, dim. of *stēthos* breast)] : a genus of pike perches including the sauger and the walleye

stk *abbr* **1** sticky **2** stock **3** strake

stl *abbr* **1** stall **2** steel **3** stile

STL *abbr or n* -S [L *sacrae theologiae licentiatus*] : a licentiate in sacred theology

stlg *abbr* sterling

stm *abbr* storm

stmfr *abbr* steam fitter

stn *abbr* **1** stainless **2** station

stnd *abbr* stained

sto *abbr* **1** stoker **2** story

STO *abbr* sea transport officer

stoa \'stōə\ *n, pl* **sto·ae** \-ō,ē\ *or* **stoas** [Gk; akin to Gk *stylos* pillar — more at STEER] : an ancient Greek portico that is usu. long and walled at the back with a front colonnade opening on a public place and designed to afford a sheltered promenade or meeting place

stoach \'stōch\ *vb* -ED/-ING/-ES [origin unknown] *dial Eng* : TRAMPLE

stoat \'stōt, *usu* -ōd·+V\ *n, pl* **stoats** *also* **stoat** [ME *stote, stot*] : ERMINE 1a; *broadly* : any of various weasels that have a black-tipped tail — used esp. of the animal when in the brown summer coat

stoa·ting *also* **sto·ting** \'stōd·iŋ\ *n* -S [origin unknown] : invisible stitching used esp. by tailors for joining two edges of fabric

[1]**stob** \'stäb\ *n* -S [ME, stick, stump; akin to ME *stubb, stubbe* stub — more at STUB] **1** *chiefly dial* **:** STAKE, POST **2** *chiefly dial* **:** STUMP; *esp* : the stump of a small tree or a shrub

[2]**stob** \"\ *dial var of* STAB

stoc·ca·do \stə'käd·(,)ō\ *or* **stoc·ca·ta** \-d·ə\ *n* -S [OIt *stoccata*, fr. *stocco* estoc (fr. MF *estoc*) + *-ata* -ade — more at ESTOC] *archaic* : a thrust with a rapier (as in fencing) : STAB

sto·chas·tic \stə'kastik\ *adj* [Gk *stochastikos* skillful in aiming, proceeding by guesswork, fr. (assumed) *stochastos* (verbal of *stochazesthai* to aim at, guess at, fr. *stochos* target, aim, guess) + *-ikos* -ic — more at STING] : RANDOM ⟨~ processes⟩ ⟨~ variables⟩

sto·chas·ti·cal·ly \-stək(ə)lē\ *adv* : in a stochastic manner

[1]**stock** \'stäk\ *n* -S [ME *stok*, fr. OE *stocc;* akin to OE *stycce* piece, MD & OHG *stoc* stick, stump, trunk of a tree, OHG *stucki* piece, ON *stokkr* block of wood, trunk of a tree, *stykki* piece, MIr *tūag* ax, bow, *tōcht* part, piece, Skt *tujati, tuñjati* he pushes; basic meaning: to push, strike] **1 a :** a stump of a tree **b** *archaic* **:** a log or block of wood **c :** something held to resemble a log or stump of wood in having no life or consciousness; *specif* : IDOL — usu. used in the phrase *stocks and stones* ⟨all our fathers worshiped ~*s* and stones —John Milton⟩ **2 :** a supporting framework or structure: as **a :** the support of the block in which an anvil is fixed or of the anvil itself **b stocks** *pl* **:** the frame or timbers on which a ship rests while under construction ⟨the old-time shipyard in whose ~*s* were built so many . . . men-o'-war —S.P.B.Mais⟩ ⟨large ships would collapse in the ~*s* —S.F.Mason⟩ **c** *chiefly Scot* **:** the outer rail or edge of a bed **d :** the frame bearing the moving parts of a spinning wheel **e :** the casing surrounding and supporting a lock **f :** a frame in which an animal (as a horse or cow) may be slung or otherwise secured esp. for shoeing **3 :** a person who is dull, stupid, or lifeless like a block of wood ⟨they stood like ~*s*, stupidly listening —Dorothy C. Fisher⟩ **4 stocks** *pl* **:** a frame of timber with holes formerly used to confine the feet or the feet and hands of offenders commonly in a public place by way of punishment — compare PILLORY **5 a :** the main stem of a plant : TRUNK **b** (1) **:** a living plant or portion of a plant (as a root) designed or prepared for union with a scion in grafting and usu. supplying solely or predominantly underground parts to a graft; *also* : the portion of a grafted plant derived from the stock (2) *or* **stock plant :** a plant maintained primarily for the production of slips or cuttings **6 a :** the crosspiece of an anchor which cants it so that one of the flukes may enter the ground — see ANCHOR illustration **b :** the narrow part of a rudder above the blade **7 a** (1) **:** the source of a line of descent : the original progenitor : the original (as a man, a race, or a language) from which others have descended or have been derived ⟨one of . . . many sons might well become the ~ of a new dynasty —E.A.Freeman⟩ (2) *obs* **:** the original source from which something is derived ⟨the sun, the ~ of light —Thomas Fuller⟩ **b** (1) **:** the progenitor of a family and his direct descendants : the whole group of descendants of one individual : a line of descent : FAMILY, LINEAGE ⟨she comes of good ~⟩ (2) **:** a compound organism : a colony of individuals (as of interconnected zooids) — compare CLONE **c :** an infraspecific group usu. having unity of descent: (1) **:** a major anthropological division or primary race of mankind ⟨the main ~*s* of mankind are usu. held to be the Caucasoids, Mongoloids, and Negroids⟩ (2) **:** a race, subrace, or group of ethnically closely related people ⟨the Hamite ~ of northern Africa⟩ **d :** the living constituents of a biological group ⟨the ~ of a strain⟩ **e** (1) **:** a related group of languages (2) **:** a language family **8** *obs* **:** TRUNK 1b **9** *chiefly dial* **:** STOCKING — see NETHERSTOCK, UPPERSTOCK **10 a** *obs* **:** a sum of money set apart for a specific purpose (as to provide for expenses) **b** *obs* **:** capital for investment or direct use in a business : principal as distinguished from interest **c** *obs* **:** something constituting an endowment for a son or a dowry for a daughter **d** *archaic* **:** BASIS, GROUNDS — usu. used in the phrase *upon the stock of* **11 :** the block of wood from which a bell is hung **12 a :** the equipment, materials, or supplies (as of a farm or railroad) ⟨inspectors who report on the sufficiency of the works and ~*s* of railways —Homersham Cox⟩ — see DEAD STOCK, LIVESTOCK, ROLLING STOCK **b :** LIVESTOCK **13 a :** the wooden part into which the barrel, receiver, and action of a rifle or shotgun are fitted and by which the piece is held for firing **b stocks** *pl* **:** the often wooden parts fitted to the frame of a handgun to form the grip — compare BUTTSTOCK, TIPSTOCK **c :** the connecting arm between slide and shoulder piece in rapid-fire guns **d :** the long beam of general rectangular shape which forms the basis of the carriage body in field-gun carriages being securely fastened to the axletree, forming the connection with the limber in traveling, and affording the necessary third point of support when the gun is fired **14** *archaic* **a :** property that produces income : ASSETS **b :** the aggregate wealth of a nation **15 :** a hive of honeybees **16 :** the wooden or iron beam of a plow to which the handles, share, colter, moldboard, and landside are secured **17 a** (1) **:** the portion of a pack of cards not distributed to the players at the beginning of various games (2) **:** BONEYARD 3 **b** *obs* **:** HAND **18 :** the hub of a wheel **19** *chiefly Brit* **:** the capital that a firm employs in the conduct of business (as trading or investing) **20 a :** the part of a tally formerly given to the creditor in a transaction; *specif* : the part given in the English exchequer to the person having lent the monarch money on account **b** (1) **:** the debt or fund represented by such a stock or a series of such stocks; *specif* : the debt or fund due from a government or a private company or corporation to individuals for money loaned at interest and not divided into shares but instead being divisible and transferable in any amount desired not involving divisions smaller than a specified sum — compare CONSOL, MUNICIPAL SECURITY (2) *chiefly Brit* **:** a debt, fund, or capital bearing interest at a given rate percent in perpetuity and characterized by the principal not being payable unless at the option of the debtor **c :** a specific debt or fund of such character **d :** a security representing such a debt or fund — usu. used in pl. **21 :** a quantity of something accumulated for future use : a store or supply to be drawn upon ⟨lay in a ~ of provisions⟩ ⟨a girl should have . . . ~*s* of lovely clothes —Robertson Davies⟩ ⟨its members . . . put everything into a common ~ —Norman Goodall⟩ ⟨his own contribution to the general ~ of knowledge —Benjamin Farrington⟩ **22 :** a block of wood or metal frame which constitutes the body of a plane and in which the plane iron is fitted : a plane stock **23** *obs* **:** money invested by a person in a company or partnership **24 a :** any of various pubescent European and Asiatic herbs and subshrubs that constitute the genus *Matthiola*, bear racemes of usu. sweet-scented flowers with 4 long-clawed petals, and include numerous forms chiefly derived from the southern European species (*M. incana*) which are widely cultivated as ornamentals — see BRAMPTON STOCK, TEN-WEEK STOCK **b :** VIRGINIA STOCK **25 :** the butt or handle of an implement (as a whip, hunting crop, or fishing rod) **26 a :** the store of goods held by a merchant or manufacturer : the supply on hand : INVENTORY **b :** a quantity (as of completed parts or

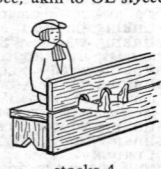

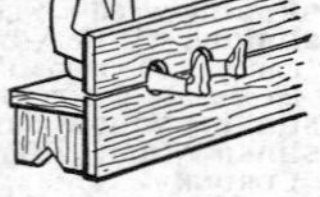
stocks 4

finished product) held esp. in a storeroom ready for delivery to customers ⟨no publishers' ~s remain of the German edition —*Brit. Bk. News*⟩ **c :** the supply of plants or of seeds of a kind of plant in a nursery, greenhouse, seed house, or other horticultural establishment **27 a :** a wide band or scarf worn about the neck commonly by men during the 18th century and often wrapped twice around and tied in front with a knot ⟨wearing a pearl stickpin in his ~ —Hamilton Basso⟩ **b :** a piece of material worn by some clergymen attached to a clerical collar and covering the chest **28 a :** the proprietorship element in a corporation divided into shares and represented by transferable certificates and giving to the owners a pro rata interest in the assets, the earnings, and except where withheld in the charter the voting power of the business — compare CAPITAL STOCK, COMMON STOCK, CONVERTIBLE, CUMULATIVE, FULLY PAID, GUARANTEED STOCK, NO-PAR, PAR, PARTICIPATING STOCK, PREFERRED STOCK, REDEEMABLE **b :** the proprietorship element of a particular corporation ⟨high quality growth ~s⟩ **c :** a share of such stock **d :** a security representing such a share **29** *Brit* **:** a hard solid brick that has been pressed in a mold — usu. used in pl. **30 :** liquid in which meat, fish, or vegetables are simmered and which is used as a basis for soup, stew, gravy, or sauce **31 a :** a beater in a fulling mill for cloth **b stocks** *pl* **:** a fulling mill for cloth **32 :** the handle or contrivance by which bits are held in boring **:** BITSTOCK, BRACE **33 :** the shorter of the two pieces comprising a square (as a carpenter's square) **34 :** an estimate, evaluation, or appraising survey of something (as of one's position, resources, or prospects) ⟨he took ~ and sought . . . to pick up the threads of his business —Milton Bracker⟩ ⟨the council . . . took ~ of the situation —F.L.Paxson⟩ **35 :** a holder for a threading die and esp. for any of a graduated set of dies for cutting screw threads on bolts and usu. having a pair of relatively long handles **36 :** a small metal container for holy oil used esp. in the Roman Catholic Church **37 a :** raw material from which something is manufactured **:** the basic material used in making or producing something ⟨paper ~⟩ ⟨film ~⟩ — see SOAP STOCK **b :** wood used in the construction of something **:** LUMBER ⟨the saw will cut round ~ to ¾ in. in diameter —*Industrial Equipment News*⟩ **c :** petroleum oil partly or completely refined that is to undergo further processing **38 :** confidence, faith, or value in something ⟨put little ~ in his testimony⟩ ⟨take no ~ in abstract rights —O.W.Holmes †1935⟩ ⟨did not at first take much ~ in it —M.R.Cohen⟩ **39 :** a body of igneous rock that is smaller than a batholith and intruded upward into older formations and that in ground plan is roughly circular or elliptical but in cross section may increase downward **40 stocks** *pl* **:** a machine for softening hides by beating or kneading **41 a :** the stump of a coppice which is expected to furnish new sprouts **b :** growth of a specified kind constituting a forest cover **42 :** material supplied to a break roll or reel in flour milling **43 :** STOCKPILE 2 **44 a :** STOCK COMPANY **b :** the production and presentation of plays by a stock company ⟨the beginning of resident ~ in Seattle —*Amer. Guide Series: Wash.*⟩ ⟨played bit parts in summer ~ —S.T. Williamson⟩ ⟨sold for films or released for ~ —*N.Y.Times*⟩ **45 :** the anterior individual of a chain of asexual annelid worms of *Nais* or related genera **46 a :** STUFF 2c **b :** wet pulp at any point in the manufacturing process **c :** paper on hand or in storage **47 :** a post bearing a holy-water vessel **48 :** the estimation in which someone or something is held ⟨his ~ with the electorate remains high —*Newsweek*⟩ **49 a :** STOCK CAR 2 ⟨racing modified ~s —W.L.Gresham⟩ **b :** a race involving stock cars ⟨winners . . . in the Class B ~s —*Springfield (Mass.) Union*⟩ **syn** see VARIETY — **in stock :** on hand **:** in the store and ready for delivery — **off the stocks 1 :** having been launched — used of a ship **2 :** completed and delivered **:** FINISHED ⟨a book *off the stocks*⟩ ⟨a piece of work *off the stocks*⟩ — **on the stocks** *adv (or adj)* **:** in preparation **:** under construction ⟨the dramatist has a play *on the stocks*⟩ ⟨a frigate is *on the stocks* in a British yard —Anthony Courtney⟩ ⟨through the years that this book has been *on the stocks* —*New Statesman & Nation*⟩ — **out of stock :** having no more on hand **:** sold out

²stock \"\ *vb* -ED/-ING/-S [ME *stokken*, fr. *stok*, n.] *vt* **1 :** to put (as a culprit) in the stocks **:** punish by confinement in the stocks **2** *archaic* **:** to dig or root up **:** EXTIRPATE — often used with *up* **3 :** to make pregnant (a female domestic animal) **:** IMPREGNATE **4 :** to provide (as a rifle, anchor, or bell) with a stock **:** fit to or with a stock **5** *archaic* **:** to make an investment of (funds) **:** put (capital) out at interest **:** INVEST **6 :** to provide with stock **:** equip with a stock of something **:** supply with material requisites **:** furnish with appropriate items ⟨retailers ~ed their shelves conservatively —*Dun's Rev.*⟩ ⟨he ~ed the farm with . . . Hereford cattle —*Amer. Guide Series: Maine*⟩ ⟨a bar . . . ~ed with gins and liquors —Scott Fitzgerald⟩ ⟨~ a stream with trout⟩ ⟨a good sound head . . . well ~ed with ideas —Rose Macaulay⟩ — sometimes used with *up* ⟨~ up the place with . . . new specimens —H.L.Davis⟩ **7 :** to let (a cow) retain milk for hours before sale to display the udder to advantage **8 :** to lay up a stock of **:** keep on hand esp. for sale **:** get or have (as merchandise) in stock ⟨stores that ~ everything from plowshares to lamp chimneys —*Amer. Guide Series: Ark.*⟩ ⟨most bookshops do not ~ encyclopedias —Evelyn Kirkland⟩ **9 :** to put (playing cards) into a pack esp. in such a way as to arrange for the purpose of cheating **:** STACK **10 a :** to graze livestock on (as pasture) **b :** to graze (livestock) on land and esp. grassland **11 :** to issue shares in or stocks of (a business enterprise) **12 :** to stamp or knead (as hides) with or as if with stocks in leather manufacturing **13 :** to deliver (logs) from the woods to a railroad or to a mill **14 :** to rough-machine with a stocking cutter ~ *vi* **1 :** to send out new shoots — used esp. of the crown of a plant or a severed trunk or branch **2 :** to put in stock or supplies — usu. used with *up* ⟨~ up for the holiday trade⟩ ⟨~ up on supplies⟩ **3 :** to swell or become swollen — used of a horse's legs and esp. of the part between the pasterns and the hock

³stock \"\ *adv* [ME *stok*, fr. *stok*, n.] **:** COMPLETELY — used in combination ⟨stood *stock*-still⟩ ⟨struck *stock*-dumb⟩

⁴stock \"\ *adj* [¹*stock*] **1 :** used or employed for constant service or application as if constituting a portion of a stock or supply **:** kept regularly in stock or ready for use or for immediate use ⟨a ~ size of paper⟩ ⟨a ~ model of an automobile⟩ ⟨cars must be clean and ~ —*Illustrated Speedway News*⟩ ⟨a ~ size⟩ **2 a :** suggesting something regularly kept in or as if in stock or ready for use **:** commonly used or brought forward **:** STANDARD ⟨the ~ answer to all these complaints —*Nation*⟩ ⟨humor depending upon ~ situations —*Amer. Guide Series: Tenn.*⟩ ⟨the ~ responses of the slick fictionist —L.O.Coxe⟩ ⟨a ~ jest among English gentlemen —V.L.Parrington⟩ **b :** COMMONPLACE, CONVENTIONAL, TRITE **3 a :** kept for breeding purposes **:** BROOD ⟨a ~ mare⟩ ⟨a ~ bull⟩ **b :** devoted to the breeding and rearing of livestock esp. beef cattle, horses, sheep, and hogs ⟨a ~ farm⟩ **c :** used by or intended for the use of livestock ⟨~ range⟩ ⟨~ train⟩ ⟨~ water⟩ **4 :** of, relating to, or having the characteristics of a stock company ⟨other plays which did not figure as ~ favorites —D.J.Rulfs⟩ ⟨~ actors⟩ **5 a :** employed in handling, checking, or taking care of the stock of merchandise on hand (as in a store or factory) ⟨a ~ girl⟩ ⟨a ~ clerk⟩ **b :** containing the stock **6 :** suitable for fattening ⟨~ cattle⟩

⁵stock \'shtäk, 'stäk\ *n* -S [G, fr. OHG *stoc* stick, stump, trunk of a tree — more at ¹STOCK] **:** STICK; *esp* **:** one used by skiers — sometimes used in combination ⟨alpenstock⟩

stock account *n, Brit* **:** a ledger account in bookkeeping with the credit side showing the original capital and additions and the debit side showing withdrawals and losses

¹stock·ade \(')stä¦kād\ *n* -S [Sp *estacada*, fr. *estaca* stake, pale (of Gmc origin; akin to OE *staca* stake) + *-ada* -ade (fr. LL *-ata*) — more at STAKE] **1 a :** a line of stout posts or timbers set firmly in the earth in contact with each other, usu. furnished with loopholes, and designed to form a barrier or defensive fortification **b :** a floating barrier of trees chained together to protect a pontoon bridge from floating objects **2 a :** an enclosure or pen made with posts and stakes **b :** an enclosure usu. surrounded by barbed wire in which prisoners are kept **3 :** piling that serves as a breakwater

²stockade \"\ *vt* -ED/-ING/-S **:** to surround, fortify, or protect with a stockade

stock·a·do \stä'kā(,)dō\ *archaic var of* STOCKADE

stock·age \'stäkij\ *n* -S [¹*stock* + *-age*] **:** the amount of military supplies and equipment on hand or scheduled to be on hand in controlled quantities in a given place ⟨build our ammunition reserve ~s to the point where we feel they should be —J.L.Collins⟩

stock-and-bill tackle \'ˌˌˌ-\ *n* **:** a small tackle to secure an anchor after it is hove up — called also *stock tackle*

stock·a·teer \ˌstäkə¦ti(ə)r\ *n* -S [¹*stock* + *-ateer* (alter. of *-eteer* —as in *racketeer*—)] **:** a broker dealing in fraudulent securities

stock beer *n* **:** a strong beer that keeps well

stock block *n* **:** a truncated obconical block of wood used as a pattern in making the hole for a stock fire in a forge

stock board *n* **1 :** a loose piece of wood plated with iron around the upper edge and forming the bottom of a brick mold **2 :** STOCK EXCHANGE **3 :** a board of an even width usu. 8, 10, or 12 inches

stock bonus *n* **:** a bonus paid to corporation executives and employees in shares of stock

stock book *n* **1 :** STOCK LEDGER **2 :** STUDBOOK, HERDBOOK **3 :** a book having pages with pockets for holding loose stamps (as stamps in a dealer's stock or the unmounted stamps of a collector)

stock bowler *n, chiefly Austral* **:** a regular bowler on a cricket team — compare CHANGE BOWLER

stockbreeder \'ˌˌˌ\ *n* **:** one that is engaged in the breeding and care of livestock for the market, for show purposes, or for racing

stock brick *n, Brit* **:** a hard solid brick that is burned in a clamp

stock·bridge \'stäk,brij\ *n* -S *usu cap* [fr. *Stockbridge*, Mass.] **:** a member of the Housatonic band of the Mahican which moved from Massachusetts in 1785 to join the Oneida in northern New York and later united with the Munsee in Wisconsin

stockbroker \'ˌˌˌ\ *n* **:** one that deals in or executes orders to buy and sell securities

stockbroking \'ˌˌˌ\ *or* **stockbrokerage** \'ˌˌ(ˌ)ˌ\ *n* **:** the business or work of a stockbroker

stock buckle *n* **:** a buckle for fastening a stock

stockcar \'ˌˌ\ *n* [¹*stock* + *car*] **:** a latticed railroad boxcar for carrying livestock

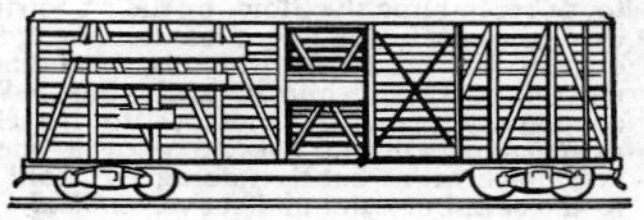

stockcar

stock car *n* [⁴*stock*] **1 :** an automotive vehicle of a model and type produced commercially and kept in stock for regular sales **2 :** a racing car having the basic chassis of a commercially produced assembly-line model

stock card *n* **:** a brush with bent wire teeth used for carding wool

stock cattle *n pl* **:** all cattle other than beef cattle and steers over three years of age; *esp* **:** cattle for breeding purposes

stock certificate *n* **1 :** a document issued by a joint-stock company to each of its shareholders certifying the amount and character of his holding **2 :** an instrument evidencing ownership of one or more shares of the capital stock of a corporation

stock chute *n* **:** a ramp for loading and unloading livestock

stock clerk *n* **:** one that receives and handles merchandise and supplies in a stock room

stock company *n* **1 a :** a corporation or joint-stock company of which the capital is represented by stock **b :** an insurance company owned and operated for the benefit of stockholders as contrasted with a mutual company **2 :** a theatrical company attached to a repertory theater; *esp* **:** one without outstanding stars

stock dividend *n* **1 :** the payment by a corporation of a dividend in the form of additional shares of its own stock — compare SPLIT-UP **2 :** the stock distributed in a stock dividend

stock dove *n* [ME *stokdouve, stokdove*, fr. *stok* stock + *douve, dove* dove; prob. fr. its living in hollow trees] **1 :** a common European wild pigeon (*Columba oenas*) resembling the rock pigeon but being darker colored and having the rump gray **2 :** an Asiatic dove (*Columba eversmanni*) related to the European stock dove

stock down *vt* **:** to sow (as plowed land) with seed of grass or other permanent forage crop

stock duck *n* **:** MALLARD

stock-dye \'ˌ¦ˌ\ *vt* **:** to dye (raw fibers) before processing and esp. spinning in the manufacture of textiles

stock eagle *n, dial Eng* **:** GREEN WOODPECKER

stocked *past of* STOCK

stock·er \'stäkə(r)\ *n* -S **1 :** one that makes or fits stocks esp. of guns **2 a :** a young animal (as a steer or heifer) suitable for being fed and fattened for market **:** a young or light feeder **b :** an animal (as a heifer) suitable for use in a breeding establishment **3 :** one that handles scrap in the stockyard of an iron or steel plant and loads materials for open-hearth melting **4 :** one that prepares stockers for market

stock exchange *n* **1 :** a building or room in which security trading is conducted on an organized system — compare EXCHANGE 5b **2 :** an association or group of people organized to provide an auction market among themselves for the purchase and sale of securities

stock fire *n* **:** a forge fire made in a stock — distinguished from *open fire*

stockfish \'ˌˌ\ *n* [ME *stokfish*, fr. MD *stocvisch*, fr. *stoc* stick, stump, trunk of a tree + *visch* fish; prob. fr. its having been dried on wooden racks; akin to OHG *fisc* fish — more at STOCK, FISH] **1 a :** fish (as cod, haddock, hake, or ling) dried hard in the open air without salt **b :** something held to resemble stockfish in being thoroughly beaten and flattened out ⟨as dead as a ~ —George Meredith⟩ ⟨sat mute as a ~ —Charles Dickens⟩ **2** *also* **stok·vis** \'stäk,fis\ [Afrik *stokvis*, fr. MD *stocvisch*] **:** a hake (*Merluccius capensis*) that is the basis of the leading commercial fishery of southern Africa

stock fly *n* **1 :** STABLE FLY **2 :** HORN FLY

stock guard *n* **:** a barrier for keeping livestock off railroad tracks

stockholder \'ˌˌˌ\ *n* **1 :** one that holds stock **:** an owner of stocks **:** SHAREHOLDER **2** *archaic* **:** the owner of large herds of cattle or sheep

stockholder of record : the person recorded on the books of the company as the owner of stock although often he is only an agent or trustee for the true owner

stockholding \'ˌˌˌ\ *n* **1 :** the state or fact of holding stock **:** ownership of stocks ⟨prohibition of unrestricted intercorporate ~ —W.Z.Ripley⟩ **2 :** a holding of stock **:** a specific number of stocks or shares owned — usu. used in pl. ⟨sell ~s he has in corporations —*Springfield (Mass.) Daily News*⟩

stock·holm \'stäk,hō(l)m\ *adj, usu cap* [fr. *Stockholm*, Sweden] **:** of or from Stockholm, the capital of Sweden **:** of the kind or style prevalent in Stockholm

stock·holm·er \-mə(r)\ *n* -S *cap* [Sw, fr. *Stockholm* + *-er*] **:** a native or resident of Stockholm, Sweden

stockholm tar *n, usu cap S* **:** pine tar used in shipbuilding and in the manufacture of cordage

stock·horn \'stäk,hȯrn\ *n* **:** an obsolete Scottish musical instrument similar to the Welsh pibgorn

stock horse *n* **:** a horse used in herding cattle on ranches

stockier *comparative of* STOCKY

stockiest *superlative of* STOCKY

stock·i·ly \'stäkəlē\ *adv* **:** in a stocky manner ⟨a ~ built man⟩

stock·i·nette \ˌstäkə¦net, *usu* -ed·+V\ *n* -S *often attrib* [alter. of earlier *stocking net*] **1** *or* **stockinette stitch :** a knitting pattern that produces a smooth surface on the face and is made on straight needles by alternating rows of knit stitch and purl stitch and on circular needles by knit stitch alone **2 a** *or* **stock·i·net** \"\ **:** a soft circular-knit usu. cotton fabric in stockinette stitch that has considerable natural elasticity, is often napped on the back, and is used esp. for bandages and infants' wear **b :** a garment, bag, or other article made from stockinette

¹stock·ing \'stäkiŋ, -kēŋ\ *n* -S [ME *stokking*, fr. gerund of *stokken* to stock — more at STOCK] **1 :** the action of making or fitting a stock (as to a rifle) **2 :** punishment by detention in the stocks **3** *Scot* **:** livestock and farm implements

²stocking \"\ *n* -S [¹*stock* (stocking) + *-ing*] **1 a :** a close-fitting covering for the foot and leg reaching above the knee and usu. knit of nylon, silk, wool, or cotton **b :** SOCK **2 :** something resembling or held to resemble a stocking: as **a :** a bandage or webbed support for the leg; *esp* **:** one woven or knitted with rubber and used in various disorders of the circulation — called also *elastic stocking* **b** (1) **:** a broad ring of color on the lower part of the leg of a biped or quadruped differing from the general color; *esp* **:** a white ring between the coronet and the hock or knee of a dark-colored horse (2) **:** the dark feathering of the neck of a Canada goose **c :** a knitted tube of fiber (as rayon) used in making incandescent mantles by impregnation (as with thorium nitrate) — called also *sock* — **in one's stocking feet :** having on stockings but no shoes ⟨went downstairs . . . *in his stocking feet* so as not to wake the others —Hugh MacLennan⟩

³stocking \"\ *vt* -ED/-ING/-S **:** to dress in stockings

stocking cap *n* **:** a knitted cone-shaped cap made usu. long with a tassel or pompon at the point and worn esp. for winter sports or play

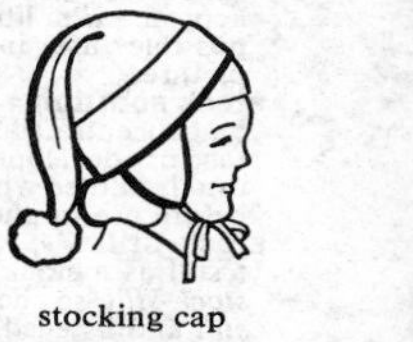

stocking cap

stocking cutter *n* **:** a milling gear cutter for removing stock with heavy cuts in preparation for finishing

stock·inged \-ŋd\ *adj* **:** wearing a stocking or stockings ⟨walks about in his ~ feet⟩

stock·ing·er \-ŋə(r)\ *n* -S **:** a stocking knitter or weaver

stocking frame *n* **:** a machine for knitting stockings or other knitted goods

stock insurance company *n* **:** an insurance company with capital contributed by stockholders who control its operations and reap any profits or sustain any losses which may result therefrom and with policies that are ordinarily nonparticipating and always nonassessable

stock-in-trade \'ˌˌˌ\ *n* **1 :** the equipment necessary to or used in the conduct of a trade or business: as **a :** the goods kept for sale by a shopkeeper **b :** the fittings and appliances of a workman **c :** the aggregate of things necessary to carry on a business **2 :** something held to resemble the standard equipment of a tradesman or business ⟨the light and frivolous charm which was her stage *stock-in-trade* —S.H.Adams⟩ ⟨its civic beauty, its *stock-in-trade*, is being ruined by parked cars —Janet Flanner⟩ ⟨this motive had been a *stock-in-trade* of medieval art —Verena Trudel⟩

stock·ish \'stäkish\ *adj* [¹*stock* + *-ish*] **1 :** resembling a stock **:** STUPID, BLOCKISH ⟨a dull, ~ character —R.L.Stevenson⟩ ⟨fell back into his ~, uncomprehending blankness —Dorothy C. Fisher⟩ **2 :** somewhat stocky ⟨~ of build⟩ — **stock·ish·ly** *adv*

stock·ist \'stäkəst\ *n* -S *Brit* **:** one (as a retailer or distributor) that stocks goods ⟨world's largest ~s of scientific periodicals —*advt*⟩

stock-job *vt* [back-formation fr. *stockjobber* & *stockjobbing*] *obs* **:** to deal with as or in the manner of a stockjobber

stockjobber \'ˌˌˌ\ *n* [¹*stock* + *jobber*] **:** one that deals in stocks: **a :** a member of the London stock exchange who deals speculatively with brokers or other jobbers and usu. specializes in one class of securities — called also *dealer, jobber* **b :** STOCKBROKER; *esp* **:** one held to be unscrupulous or to deal in stocks of doubtful worth

stockjobbing \'ˌˌˌ\ *n* -S [¹*stock* + *jobbing*] **:** the business of a stockjobber **:** the buying and selling of stocks **:** dealing in securities often on a speculative basis

stockjudging \'ˌˌˌ\ *n* -S **:** the appraisal of the quality of livestock in competitions or for educational purposes, either in respect to relative conformity of the animal to breed standards or to performance

stockkeeper \'ˌˌˌ\ *n* **1 :** one (as a herdsman or shepherd) having the charge or care of livestock **2 :** one that keeps and records stock (as in a warehouse) **:** one that keeps an inventory of goods on hand, shipped, or received

stock ledger *n* **1 :** STORES LEDGER **2 :** a book kept by a corporation in which are entered the names of the stockholders and the amount of the holding of each and sometimes other particulars

stock·less \'stäkləs\ *adj* **:** being without a stock ⟨a ~ anchor⟩

stock list *n* **1 :** a list of the stock issues admitted to dealings on an exchange **2 :** the list of stock issues with prices and volume of turnover published in a newspaper

stock lock *n* **:** a lock enclosed in a wooden case and attached to the face of a door

stockmaker \'ˌˌˌ\ *n* **:** one that makes stocks; *specif* **:** a workman employed in making the stocks of firearms

stock·man \'stäkmən, -k,man, -,maa(ə)n\ *n, pl* **stockmen 1 :** one occupied in the raising of livestock (as cattle or sheep): as **a** *Austral* (1) **:** COWHAND (2) **:** SHEPHERDER **b :** a ranch owner **:** one owning herds of cattle or sheep **2 :** one who keeps records or works on stock (as in a store or warehouse)

stock market *n* **1 a :** STOCK EXCHANGE 1 ⟨the New York *stock market*⟩ **b :** a market for particular stocks ⟨the bank *stock market*⟩ **c :** the market for stocks throughout a country ⟨the U.S. *stock market*⟩ **2 :** a market for the sale of livestock

stock melon *n* **:** CITRON

stock option *n* **:** an option giving to the holder the right to purchase a specified number of shares of stock from a corporation at a stated price and by a stated date and constituting a device widely used to provide supplementary compensation to corporation officers and employees

stock pass *n* **:** a culvert or bridge opening under a railroad track primarily for the passage of livestock (as cattle)

stock pea *n* **:** SOYBEAN

stock pigeon *n* **:** STOCK DOVE

¹stockpile \'ˌˌ\ *n* [¹*stock* + *pile*] **1 :** a pile of road metal stored on the roadside and used for road maintenance **2 :** a storage pile or heap of material (as ore or coal) at the surface of a mine **3 a :** a reserve supply of something essential (as processed food or a raw material) accumulated within a country for use during a shortage caused by emergency conditions (as war) ⟨strengthen its civil defense ~ of medical . . . supplies —D.D.Eisenhower⟩ ⟨built up ~s of strategic metals —Richard Rutter⟩ **b :** something held to resemble such a stockpile **:** a gradually accumulated reserve of something and esp. something vital or indispensable ⟨the ~ of basic research information has been seriously depleted —M.H.Trytten⟩ ⟨avert ~s of unsold cars —Bert Pierce⟩ ⟨assets include a ~ of . . . celluloid comedies and dramas —*Wall Street Jour.*⟩

²stockpile \"\ *vt* **1 :** to heap up (as coal or iron ore) **:** accumulate in piles **2 :** to place or store in or on a stockpile **3 :** to accumulate a stockpile of ⟨~ war materials in Europe —A.O.Wolfers⟩ ~ *vi* **:** to accumulate a stockpile

stockpiler \'ˌˌˌ\ *n* **:** one that stockpiles

stock plant *n* **:** ¹STOCK 5b(2)

stock·port \'stäk,pōrt, -pȯrt\ *adj, usu cap* [fr. *Stockport*, England] **:** of or from the county borough of Stockport, England **:** of the kind or style prevalent in Stockport

stockpot \'ˌˌ\ *n* **1 :** a pot in which stock (as for soup or gravy) is prepared **2 :** something held to resemble a stockpot ⟨the common ~ of melodramatic plots —G.B.Shaw⟩

stock power *n* **:** the irrevocable power of attorney used in making a transfer of a certificate of stock

stockproof \'ˌ¦ˌ\ *adj* **:** proof against livestock ⟨an electrified ~ fence⟩

stock purchase warrant *n* **:** a usu. transferable certificate entitling the holder to subscribe to corporate stock at a specified price and often attached to bonds or preferred stock to increase their salability

stock rail *n* **:** the fixed rail in a railroad track against which the switch rail operates

stock raiser *n* **:** one that raises livestock (as beef cattle, horses, sheep, or hogs)

stock raising *n* **:** the act or occupation of raising livestock

stock record *n* **:** STORES LEDGER

stockrider \'ˌˌˌ\ *n, Austral* **:** COWBOY 3a

stock room *n* **1 :** a storage place for supplies or goods used in a business **2 :** a room (as in a hotel) where commercial travelers may exhibit their goods **:** a sample room

stocks *pl of* STOCK, *pres 3d sing of* STOCK
stock saddle *n* **:** an often ornamented saddle used by cowboys and usu. made with a seat more bowl-shaped than the English saddle, a high pommel with a horn for holding the lariat, a high cantle, and broad skirts and fenders — called also *western saddle*

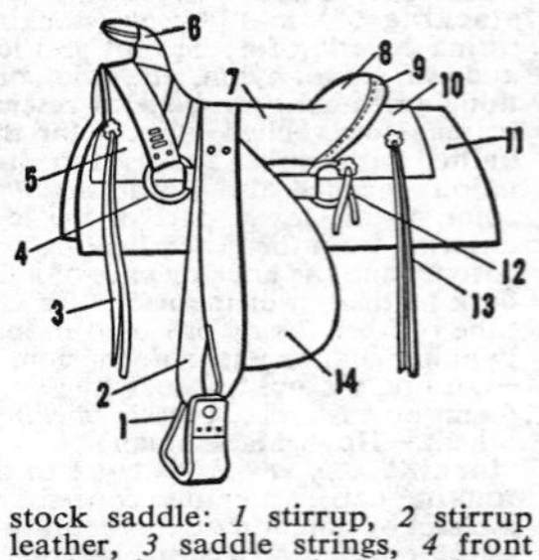

stock saddle: *1* stirrup, *2* stirrup leather, *3* saddle strings, *4* front rigging ring, *5* front jockey, *6* horn, *7* seat, *8* cantle, *9* cantle binding, *10* back jockey, *11* skirt, *12* flank rigging ring, *13* saddle strings, *14* fender

stock–share lease *n* **:** a lease based upon joint ownership of livestock and joint sharing of receipts and expenses by landlord and tenant on a rented farm
stock shot *n* [⁴*stock*] **:** a film clip (as of an historical event or a geographical area) usu. kept in a film library for possible use in future pictures
stock solution *n* [⁴*stock*] **:** a concentrated solution (as of developer) that usu. is diluted with water before use in photography
stock–still \ˈ=ˌ=\ *adj* [ME *stok still*, fr. *stok* stock (n.) + *still*] **:** still as a stock or fixed post **:** perfectly still ⟨her wits were *stock-still*, so she did not speak —Owen Wister⟩ ⟨stood *stock-still* and listened⟩
stockstone \ˈ=ˌ=\ *n* **:** a stone-bladed tool that is forced over the grain side of leather to stretch it and smooth the grain
stock system \ˈstäk-\ *or* **stock's system** *n*, *usu cap 1st S* [after Alfred *Stock*, 20th cent. German chemist] **:** a system in chemical nomenclature and notation of indicating the oxidation state of the significant element in a compound or ion by means of a Roman numeral that is used in parentheses after the name or part of the name designating this element and ending invariably in *-ate* in the case of an anion and that is placed above and to the right of the symbol for this element ⟨according to the *Stock system* nitrous oxide is named nitrogen(I) oxide, ferrosoferric oxide Fe_3O_4 is iron (II, III) oxide $Fe^{II}Fe^{III}{}_2O_4$, and potassium manganite is potassium manganate (IV) $K_2Mn^{IV}O_3$⟩
stock tackle *n* **:** STOCK-AND-BILL TACKLE
stocktaking \ˈ=ˌ=\ *n* -S **1 :** the action of checking or taking an inventory of goods or supplies on hand (as in a store or warehouse) ⟨business is interrupted by ∼ February first —*Hosiery & Underwear Rev.*⟩ **2 :** the action of estimating a situation at a given moment (as by considering resources and weaknesses or ground gained and lost) ⟨a sort of summing up and ∼ of his career thus far —Kenneth Rexroth⟩
stock tank *n* **:** a tank or artificial pond used for watering livestock
stock ticker *n* **:** TICKER b
stockturn \ˈ=ˌ=\ *n* **:** a measure of business volume constituted by the number of times the average inventory of merchandise is sold within a specified period of time usu. a year
stockwhip \ˈ=ˌ=\ *n*, *Brit* **:** a whip with a short handle and a long lash
stock width *n* **:** a piece of lumber cut in an even width from 4 to 12 inches — usu. used in pl.
stockwork \ˈ=ˌ=\ *n* [part trans. of G *stockwerk*, fr. *stock* stick, stump, trunk of a tree (fr. OHG *stoc*) + *werk* work — more at STOCK] **1 :** a system of working in ore when it lies not in strata or veins but in solid masses so as to be worked in chambers or stories **2 :** a body or tract of rock so charged with veinlets, nests, or impregnations of ore and esp. tin ore that it can be profitably mined
stocky \ˈstäkē, -ki\ *adj* -ER/-EST [¹*stock* + *-y*] **1 :** compact, sturdy, and relatively thick in build **:** short, firm, and solid in shape ⟨*stockier* and better plants are obtained from cuttings —F.W.Card⟩ **2** *dial Eng* **:** HEADSTRONG, BOISTEROUS **3 :** formal in character or manner **:** having a stiff, cold, or severe nature ⟨the ∼ virtues of integrity and piety —H.E.Scudder⟩
syn THICKSET, THICK, CHUNKY, STUBBY, SQUAT, DUMPY: STOCKY, like other words in this set in indicating a short and wide or thick build, is likely to be complimentary in suggesting compact sturdiness ⟨*stocky* though not chubby —W.A.White⟩ ⟨a *stocky* hard-hitting catcher⟩ THICKSET may describe a thick, solid, burly body ⟨too *thickset* for jockeying —John Masefield⟩ ⟨a *thickset* old policeman⟩ THICK as a synonym for THICKSET in reference to body build or form is dialectal, although it may be used for bodily parts ⟨*thick* lips⟩ ⟨*thick* legs⟩ CHUNKY may indicate a body type ample but robust and solid ⟨short and *chunky*, not quite fat —H.A.Sinclair⟩ ⟨a well-fed, *chunky*, healthy boy⟩ STUBBY, less apt than others in this set to describe human body types, indicates noteworthy lack of height or length and corresponding shortness ⟨outfielders' gloves have longer fingers . . . infielders' gloves have relatively *stubby* fingers —*New Yorker*⟩ SQUAT and DUMPY are usu. uncomplimentary. SQUAT may indicate unshapely lack of height as though suggesting a person squatting ⟨the *squat* misshapen figure that flattened itself into the shadow —Oscar Wilde⟩ ⟨anchored vessels of every sort from *squat* Baltic timber carriers —J.H.Wheelwright⟩ DUMPY may suggest short, lumpish gracelessness of body ⟨stumpy, *dumpy* girls with their rather coarse features, big buttocks and heavy breasts —Arthur Koestler⟩
stockyard \ˈ=ˌ=\ *n* **:** a yard for keeping stock; *specif* **:** an enclosure with stables, pens, and sheds which is usu. connected with a railroad and in which cattle, sheep, swine, and horses are kept temporarily for slaughter, market, or shipping
stockyard fever *or* **stockyard pneumonia** *or* **stockyards pneumonia** *n* **:** shipping fever of cattle
stød \ˈstœd\ *n* -S [Dan, lit., push, thrust; akin to MLG *stōt* push, thrust, OHG *stōz* push, thrust, *stōzan* to push, thrust — more at STINT] **:** a glottal modification occurring in Danish of the last part of a vowel or consonant sound or a glottal stop following a sound
stod·dard solvent \ˈstädə(r)d-\ *also* **stoddard's solvent** *n*, *usu cap 1st S* [fr. the name *Stoddard*] **:** a straight-run petroleum naphtha fraction of low flammability containing principally aliphatic hydrocarbons and conforming to specifications (as water-white color, distillation range 300° to 400°F, and flash point over 100°F) for use chiefly in dry cleaning — compare PETROLEUM SPIRIT
¹**stodge** \ˈstäj\ *vb* -ED/-ING/-S [origin unknown] *vt* **1 a :** to stuff full esp. with food ⟨the young will . . . be *stodged* with tea and buns —Mollie Panter-Downes⟩ **b :** to more than satisfy **:** SATIATE ⟨leaves me to ∼ myself with his *Times* —G.B.Shaw⟩ **2 :** to mix or stir up together ⟨all they ever do is ∼ some old jello and fruit⟩ ∼ *vi* **1 :** to trudge through or as if through muck and mire **:** tramp clumsily and heavily ⟨ought no longer to go *stodging* along in penury —F.M.Ford⟩ **2 :** GORGE ⟨he could eat . . . but he could not ∼ —J.M.Barrie⟩
²**stodge** \"\ *n* -S **1 :** a thick filling food (as oatmeal or stew) **2 :** something resembling stodge: as **a :** dull stupid ideas **b :** unimaginative tedious literary works ⟨the poor reading public soaked in life-long ∼ —*Sydney (Australia) Bull.*⟩ **3 :** a slow plodding person ⟨he's such a ∼ —Robertson Davies⟩
stodg·i·ly \ˈstäjəlē, -li\ *adv* **:** in a stodgy manner ⟨a ∼ respectable real estate man —Anthony Boucher⟩
stodg·i·ness \-jēnəs, -jin-\ *n* -ES **:** the quality or state of being stodgy ⟨were it not for a certain ∼ . . . this would have been a really fine performance —P.H.Lang⟩
stodgy \-jē, -ji\ *adj*, *sometimes* -ER/-EST [²*stodge* + *-y*] **1 a :** having a thick gluey consistency ⟨good ∼ mud —*Canadian Geog. Jour.*⟩ **b :** having a thick texture **:** HEAVY — used esp. of food ⟨gray, ∼ war bread stuns the stomach —F.V. & Katharine Drake⟩ **2 :** moving in a slow plodding way esp. as a result of physical bulkiness ⟨the cook's a ∼ German woman, a typical hausfrau —W.H.Wright⟩ ⟨an occasional group of ∼ sightseers —James Higgins & Gordon Donald⟩ **3 :** characterized by dullness **:** being without lightness or wit **:** BORING, PEDANTIC ⟨these volumes are not ∼ . . . they are extremely readable —G.E.Gardner⟩ ⟨many persons . . . become stilted and ∼ when they put pen to paper —Raymond Walters b.1912⟩ **4 :** devoid of excitement or interest **:** DULL, PROSAIC ⟨out on a peaceful rather ∼ Sunday boat trip —Edna Ferber⟩ ⟨not tied down by . . . the ∼ needs of mankind —Harriot B. Barbour⟩ **5 :** extremely old-fashioned in attitude or outlook **:** unwilling to yield to change ⟨received a pompously Victorian letter from his ∼ father —E.E.S.Montagu⟩ ⟨who had once been so eager and bright, be so ∼ now —Irwin Edman⟩ **6 :** lacking grace or distinction **:** DRAB ⟨∼ suburbs whose rows of frame dwellings contrast sharply with . . . opulent mansions —*Amer. Guide Series: N.Y.City*⟩ **7 :** having neither smartness nor style **:** DOWDY ⟨the clothes . . . look ∼ after the ones I've been seeing —Dodie Smith⟩ **8 :** adhering too much to tradition **:** stuck in the past **:** being without immediacy or innovation ⟨much better music than the ∼ efforts of most . . . composers —H.C.Schonberg⟩
stoep \ˈstüp\ *n* -S *chiefly Africa* [Afrik, fr. MD — more at STOOP] **:** PORCH 1
¹**stog** \ˈstäg\ *n* -S [prob. alter. of obs. *stock* estoc, thrust with an estoc, fr. MF *estoc* — more at ESTOC] *Scot* **:** STAB
²**stog** \"\ *vb* **stogged; stogged; stogging; stogs** [perh. alter. (influenced by *bog*) of ¹*stodge*] *vi*, *Scot* **:** TRUDGE, PLOD ∼ *vt* **:** to cause to be stuck **:** BOG
sto·gie *or* **sto·gy** \ˈstōgē, -gi\ *n*, *pl* **stogies** [fr. *Conestoga*, Pa.] **1** *also* **sto·ga** \-gə\ -S **:** a stout coarse shoe **:** BROGAN **2** *also* **sto·gee** \-gē, -gi\ -S **:** an inexpensive though not necessarily inferior cigar made in the form of a slender cylindrical roll ⟨still manufactures the . . . ∼*s*, which were favored by teamsters and were originally known as Conestogas —G.R. Stewart⟩ ⟨had happily smoked ∼*s* rolled by hand —*Time*⟩
¹**sto·ic** \ˈstōik, -ōēk\ *n* -S [ME, fr. L *stoicus*, adj. & n., fr. Gk *stōikos*, fr. *Stoa (Poikilē)* Painted Portico, a portico in Athens where Zeno taught (fr. *stoa* portico + *poikilē*, fem. of *poikilos* multicolored, painted) + *-ikos* -ic; akin to Gk *stylos* pillar — more at STEER] **1** *usu cap* **:** a member of a school of philosophy founded by Zeno of Citium about 300 B.C., extensively systematized by Chrysippus of Soli, and later developed and popularized by Seneca, Epictetus, and Marcus Aurelius **2 :** one apparently or professedly indifferent to pleasure or pain **:** one not easily excited or upset ⟨an absolute ∼ in the face of mishaps —Thomas Hardy⟩
²**stoic** \"\ *or* **sto·i·cal** \-ōəkəl, -ōēk-\ *adj* [*stoic* fr. L *stoicus*; *stoical* fr. ME, fr. L *stoicus* + ME *-al*] **1** *usu cap* **:** of, relating to, or resembling the Stoics or their doctrines **2 :** not affected by passion or feeling; *esp* **:** manifesting indifference to pleasure or pain ⟨the ∼ courage which enabled him to bear perhaps the most dreadful of human afflictions —W.S.Maugham⟩ ⟨she could only preach ∼ patience to herself —Douglas Bush⟩ ⟨a *stoical* person who does not allow a "mere pain" to interfere very much with what he is doing —Harold Shryock⟩ ⟨drenched to the skin but calm and suavely *stoical* —Elinor Wylie⟩ **syn** see IMPASSIVE
sto·i·cal·ly \-ōək(ə)lē, -ōēk-, -li\ *adv* **:** in a stoic manner ⟨imagined himself . . . ∼ accepting suffering without a word —Aldous Huxley⟩
stoi·chei·om·e·try \ˌstȯikīˈäm·ə·trē\ *chiefly Brit var of* STOICHIOMETRY
stoi·chi·o·met·ric \ˌstȯikēəˈme·trik\ *also* **stoi·chi·o·met·ri·cal** \-rəkəl\ *adj* [Gk *stoicheion* element + E *-metric*, *-metrical*] **:** of, relating to, employed in, or obtained by stoichiometry: as **a :** characterized by or being a chemical composition of definite proportions by weight ⟨the zinc oxide is no longer of ∼ composition but contains excess zinc atoms —E.E. Hahn⟩ ⟨the coating of lead dioxide obtained on the anode does not correspond to the ∼ formula PbO_2 —S.E.Q.Ashley⟩ — compare BERTHOLLIDE, DALTONIDE **b :** characterized by or being a proportion of substances or energy exactly right for a specific chemical reaction with no excess of any reactant or product ⟨combustion is initiated . . . where the fuel and air are close to the chemically correct or ∼ proportion —F.P.Durham⟩ ⟨by determining the amount of thrombin formed from known quantities of calcium, one is able to conclude whether the action of the latter is catalytic or ∼ —*Science*⟩ ⟨light quanta, like other chemical reactants, enter into the reaction in a ∼ manner —J.F.Bonner & A.W.Galston⟩ — **stoi·chi·o·met·ri·cal·ly** \-rək(ə)lē\ *adv*
stoi·chi·om·e·try \ˌstȯikēˈäm·ə·trē\ *n* -ES [Gk *stoicheion* + E *-metry*] **1 :** a branch of science that deals with the application of the laws of definite proportions and of the conservation of matter and also energy to chemical reactions and processes **2 a :** the quantitative relationship of constituents in a chemical entity ⟨aquo-cations of definite ∼ characterize crystalline salts —Therald Moeller⟩ **b :** the quantitative relationship between two or more substances esp. in processes involving physical or chemical change ⟨the ∼ and reversibility of ion exchange —Robert Kunin⟩
sto·i·cism \ˈstōəˌsizəm\ *n* -S **1** *usu cap* **:** the principles or the philosophical system of the Stoics who based an austere ethics on a pantheistic cosmology holding that the world is governed by and is the embodiment of logos, that it is man's duty to conform freely to natural law and his destiny, that virtue is the highest good, and that the wise man should be free from passion equally unperturbed by joy or grief **2 :** the principle or practice of showing indifference to pleasure or pain **:** repression of feeling **:** IMPASSIVENESS ⟨preparing himself with tranquil ∼ for the end —P.E.More⟩
stoi·rin \shōˈrēn\ *var of* STOREEN
stoit \ˈstȯt, ˈstȯit\ *vi* -ED/-ING/-S [perh. fr. D *stuiten* to stop, check, bounce; akin to OHG *stōzan* to push, thrust — more at STINT] **1** *chiefly Scot* **:** STAGGER, LURCH **2** *dial Eng* **:** to jump up
stoit·er \-tər\ *vi* -ED/-ING/-S *chiefly Scot* **:** STAGGER, LURCH
¹**stoke** \ˈstōk\ *vb* -ED/-ING/-S [D *stoken*, fr. MD, to thrust, poke, stoke; akin to MLG *stōken* to poke, MD *stuken* to push, shove, and prob. to OE *stocc* stock — more at STOCK] *vt* **1 :** to poke or stir up (as a fire) **:** tend the fire of **:** supply with fuel or something resembling fuel ⟨*stoked* the furnace expertly⟩ ⟨*stoked* the fire of his suspicions with lies⟩ **2 :** to feed abundantly or to excess **:** provide more than adequately with food ⟨the scouts *stoked* themselves for the long hike ahead⟩ ∼ *vi* **1 :** to poke or stir up a fire **:** tend the fires of furnaces **:** supply a furnace with fuel **2 :** to eat a big meal ⟨the gang fell to and *stoked* in silence —Ronald Duncan⟩
²**stoke** \"\ *n* -S [after Sir George G. *Stokes* †1903 Brit. mathematician and physicist] **:** the cgs unit of kinematic viscosity being that of a fluid which has a viscosity of one poise and a density of one gram per cubic centimeter
³**stoke** \"\ *or* **stoke–on–trent** \-ˈtrent\ *adj*, *usu cap S&T* [fr. *Stoke on Trent*, England] **:** of or from the city of Stoke on Trent, England **:** of the kind or style prevalent in Stoke on Trent
stokehold \ˈ=ˌ=\ *n* **1 :** a space in front of the boilers of a ship from which the furnaces are fed **2 :** a room containing a ship's boilers — called also *fireroom*
stokehole \ˈ=ˌ=\ *n* **1 :** the mouth to the grate of a furnace **2 :** the space in front of a furnace where the stokers stand
stok·er \ˈstōkə(r)\ *n* -S [D, fr. *stoken* to stoke + *-er*] **1 :** one employed to tend a furnace and supply it with fuel: as **a :** one that tends a marine steam boiler **b** *Brit* **:** a locomotive fireman **2 :** a machine for feeding a fire
stoker's cramp *n* **:** HEAT CRAMPS
stokes' aster \ˈstōks-\ *n*, *usu cap S* [after Jonathan *Stokes* †1831 Eng. botanist] **:** a perennial herb (*Stokesia laevis*) of the southern U.S. that is often cultivated and has large heads of usu. bluish flowers like asters — called also *cornflower aster*
sto·ke·sia \stōˈkēzh(ē)ə\ *n* [NL, fr. Jonathan *Stokes* + NL *-ia*] **1** *cap* **:** a monotypic genus of erect perennial herbs (family Compositae) with sometimes yellow or purple flower heads **2** -S **:** any plant of the genus *Stokesia* **:** STOKES' ASTER
stokes·ite \ˈstōkˌsīt\ *n* -S [Sir George G. *Stokes* †1903 Brit. mathematician and physicist + E *-ite*] **:** a mineral $CaSnSi_3O_9.2H_2O$ consisting of a hydrous silicate of calcium and tin and occurring in colorless orthorhombic crystals (hardness 6, sp. gr. 3.2)
stokes' law *n*, *usu cap S* [after Sir George G. *Stokes*] **1 :** a law in physics: the frequency of luminescence excited by radiation does not exceed that of the exciting radiation **2 :** a law in physics: the force required to move a sphere through a given viscous fluid at a low uniform velocity is directly proportional to the velocity and radius of the sphere
stokes litter *also* **stokes stretcher** *n*, *usu cap S* [after Charles F. *Stokes* †1931 Am. naval medical officer, its inventor] **:** a wire basket conforming in shape to the human body into which an injured, sick, or disabled person can be safely strapped

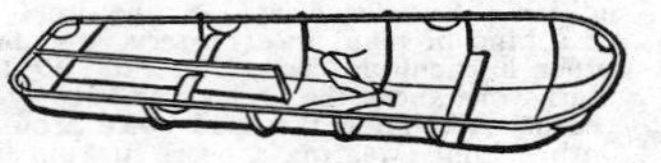

Stokes litter

stok·roos \ˈstäˌkrüs\ *n* -ES [Afrik (*wilde*) *stokroos*, fr. *wild* wild + *stokroos* hollyhock, fr. D, fr. *stok* stick (fr. MD *stoc* stick, stump, trunk of a tree) + *roos* rose, fr. MD *rose*, fr. L *rosa* — more at STOCK, ROSE] *Africa* **:** KENAF
stokvis *var of* STOCKFISH
sto·la \ˈstōlə\ *n*, *pl* **sto·lae** \-ōˌlē\ *or* **stolas** [L] **:** a long draped robe similar to the Greek chiton worn by women of ancient Rome
¹**stole** [ME *stole* (past), alter. (influenced by *stolen*) of *stal*, fr. OE *stæl*; ME *stole*, *stolen* (past part.), fr. OE *stolen*] *past & chiefly dial past part of* STEAL
²**stole** \ˈstōl\ *n* -S [ME, fr. OE, fr. L *stola*, fr. Gk *stolē* equipment, raiment, robe; akin to Gk *stellein* to set up, make ready, send — more at STALL] **1 a :** a long loose garment; *esp* **:** a garment similar to the stola or toga worn in ancient times **b :** STOLA **2 :** an ecclesiastical vestment consisting of a long narrow cloth band worn around the neck and falling from the shoulders of bishops and priests **3 :** a long wide scarf or similar covering worn by women usu. across the shoulders
³**stole** \"\ *vt* -ED/-ING/-S **:** to provide a stole for
⁴**stole** \"\ *n* -S [ME *stool*, lit., stool — more at STOOL] *archaic* **:** CLOSESTOOL
stoled \-ld\ *adj* [²*stole* + *-ed*] **:** having or wearing a stole
stole fee *n* [trans. of G *stolgebühre*] **:** a fee paid by a member of the laity to a priest for the administration of a sacrament or the performance of a rite in the Roman Catholic Church
stole mesh *n* **:** a double mesh in a fishnet
sto·len \ˈstōlən\ *adj* [ME, fr. past part. of *stelen* to steal — more at STEAL] **:** obtained or accomplished by theft, stealth, or craft **:** effected in secret ⟨∼ hours of pleasure⟩ ⟨managed a ∼ base to the delight of the crowd⟩
stol·id \ˈstäləd\ *adj*, *sometimes* -ER/-EST [L *stolidus* unmovable, dull, stolid — more at STALL] **:** having or expressing little or no sensibility **:** not easily aroused or excited ⟨a silent ∼ creature who took it all as a matter of course —Virginia Woolf⟩ ⟨spoke in ∼ tones —Ellen Glasgow⟩ **syn** see IMPASSIVE
sto·lid·i·ty \stəˈlidəd·ē, -ətē, -i\ *n* -ES [L *stoliditas*, fr. *stolidus* + *-itas* -ity] **:** the quality or state of being stolid ⟨all his ∼ seemed gone now; he was trembling —W.H.Hudson †1922⟩
stol·id·ly *adv* **:** in a stolid manner ⟨in the winter they had worked . . . enduring ∼ the snow and ice —Pearl Buck⟩
¹**stol·kjaer·re** \ˈstōlˌkyerə\ *n* -S [Norw *stolkjerre* (formerly spelled *stolkjærre*), fr. *stol* chair, seat (fr. ON *stōll*) + *kjerre* cart, fr. ON *kerra*, prob. fr. MD *carre*, *kerre*, fr. L *carra* — more at STOOL, CAR] **:** a 2-wheeled cart used in Norway with a front seat for two and a rear seat for the driver
²**stolkjaerre** \"\ *vi* **stolkjaerred; stolkjaerred; stolkjaerreing; stolkjaerres** **:** to ride in or drive a stolkjaerre
¹**stol·len** \ˈs(h)tōlən\ *n*, *pl* **stollen** [G, fr. MHG *stolle*, lit., post, support, fr. OHG *stollo*; akin to OHG *stellen* to set, place — more at STALL] **:** a repeated section in a meistergesang corresponding to the exposition in classical sonata form — compare ABGESANG
²**stollen** \"\ *n*, *pl* **stollen** *or* **stollens** [G *stolle*, *stollen*, fr. OHG *stollo* post, support] **:** a sweet yeast bread containing fruit and nuts usu. made in a long oval loaf
sto·lon \ˈstōlən\ *n* -S [NL, fr. L *stolon-*, *stolo* shoot, branch, sucker of a plant; akin to Arm *steln* branch, stalk, OL *stlocus* place — more at STALL] **1 a :** a horizontal branch from the base of a plant that is either above or below ground and produces new plants from buds at its tip or nodes (as in the strawberry) — called also *runner* **b :** a hypha produced on the surface and connecting a group of conidiophores (as in fungi of the genus *Rhizopus*) **2 :** a more or less prolonged extension of the body wall (as of an anthozoan, hydrozoan, bryozoan, or ascidian) from which buds are developed giving rise to new zooids and thus forming a compound animal in which the zooids usu. remain united by the stolon
sto·lon·ate \-lənət, -ləˌnāt\ *adj* [NL *stolon* + E *-ate*] **:** having stolons **:** arising from a stolon
sto·lo·nif·e·ra \ˌstōləˈnif(ə)rə\ *n*, *pl*, *cap* [NL, fr. *stolon* + *-i-* + L *-fera*, neut. pl. of *-fer* -ferous] **:** an order of alcyonarians comprising colonial polyps connected by stolons and supported by a skeleton of calcareous spicules which may be more or less fused into tubes — compare ORGAN-PIPE CORAL
sto·lo·nif·er·ous \ˌ=ˌ=ˈnif(ə)rəs\ *adj* [NL *stolon* + E *-iferous*] **:** bearing or developing stolons — **sto·lo·nif·er·ous·ly** *adv*
sto·lon·iza·tion \ˌstōlənəˈzāshən\ *n* -S [ISV *stolon-* (fr. NL *stolon*) + *-ization*] **:** the production of stolons
stolz·ite \ˈstōlˌzīt\ *n* -S [G *stolzit*, fr. Dr. *Stolz*, 19th cent. Bohemian scientist + G *-it* -ite] **:** a mineral $PbWO_4$ consisting of a native lead tungstate isomorphous with wulfenite and prob. with scheelite and powellite
stom- *or* **stomo-** *comb form* [NL, fr. Gk, fr. *stoma* — more at STOMACH] **:** mouth **:** stoma ⟨*stomodaeum*⟩ ⟨*stomoisia*⟩
sto·ma \ˈstōmə\ *n*, *pl* **stoma·ta** \-əd·ə *sometimes* ˈstäm-\ *also* **stomas** [NL, fr. Gk, mouth — more at STOMACH] **1 :** any of various small and simple openings or inlets (as an insect's spiracle) esp. in a lower animal; *esp* **:** one of the many minute openings among the cells of a serous membrane affording direct communication with the adjacent lymph channels **2 a :** one of the minute openings in the epidermis of leaves, stems, and other plant organs through which gaseous interchange between the atmosphere and the intercellular spaces within the leaf occurs; *usu* **:** the opening together with its associated guard cells and accessory cells **b :** STOMIUM 1 **c :** a fungal ostiole **3 :** an artificial permanent opening in the abdominal wall made in surgical procedures (as colostomy, cecostomy, ileostomy)
¹**-sto·ma** \stəmə\ *n comb form*, *pl* **-stoma·ta** \ˈstōməd·ə, -mətə *sometimes* ˈstäm-\ *also* **-stomas** [NL, fr. Gk *stoma*] **1 :** mouth **:** opening **:** stoma ⟨*hypostoma*⟩ **2** *or* **stomus** **:** creature with (such) a mouth or stoma — in generic names ⟨Bdello*stoma*⟩ ⟨Gnatho*stoma*⟩
²**-stoma** \"\ *or* **-stomata** \"\ *n pl comb form* [NL, fr. Gk *stomat-*, *stoma* mouth — more at STOMACH] **:** creatures with (such) a mouth or stoma — in higher taxa in zoology ⟨Gnatho*stoma*⟩ ⟨Plagio*stomata*⟩
³**-stoma** *pl of* -STOMUM
¹**stom·ach** \ˈstəmək, -mēk\ *n* -S *often attrib* [ME *stomak*, fr. MF *estomac*, fr. L *stomachus* gullet, esophagus, stomach, fr. Gk *stomachos*, fr. *stoma* mouth, opening; akin to MBret *staffu* mouth, W *safn* mouth, Av *staman-* mouth of a dog] **1 a :** a dilatation of the alimentary canal of a vertebrate communicating anteriorly with the esophagus and posteriorly with the duodenum, being typically a simple often curved sac with an outer serous coat, a strong complex muscular wall that contracts rhythmically, and a mucous lining membrane that contains gastric glands, being in some forms (as ruminants) constricted into several chambers that differ in function and structure, providing various digestive enzymes, and grinding and mixing food materials by its muscular action — compare CROP; see GASTRIC JUICE; GREATER CURVATURE, LESSER CURVATURE, PYLORUS; ABOMASUM, OMASUM, RUMEN **b :** a digestive cavity in an invertebrate animal; *esp* **:** a part of the alimentary canal more or less corresponding with the vertebrate stomach **c :** the part of the body that contains the stomach **:** the ventral part of the trunk **:** BELLY, ABDOMEN ⟨she lay on her ∼ reading⟩ ⟨a rash on the ∼⟩ **2 a :** desire for food caused by hunger **:** APPETITE ⟨had a good ∼ for dinner after their climb⟩ **b :** inclination or desire for something other than food — usu. used negatively ⟨had no ∼ for meeting such a rascal⟩ **3 a :** the seat or source of the feelings **:** emotional power or capacity to meet or withstand a demand on the feelings ⟨needed a strong ∼ to meet such challenges⟩ **b :** a particular disposition or mental attitude: as (1) *obs* **:** COMPASSION (2) *obs* **:** TEMPER, SPIRIT, VALOR (3) *obs* **:** PRIDE, ARROGANCE (4) *obs* **:** anger or a display of anger **:** SPLEEN
²**stomach** \"\ *vb* -ED/-ING/-S *vt* **1 :** to remember with anger

: take offense at **2** *obs* : ENRAGE, IRRITATE, OFFEND **3 a** : to bear without unfavorable reaction ⟨the prisoner could not ~ his food⟩ **b** : to bear without overt resentment : put up with : BROOK ⟨the legislators should not ~ the proposal⟩ **4** : NAUSEATE, DISGUST ~ *vi, obs* : to be angry : show anger : take offense : feel resentment

stomachache \ˈ==,=\ *n* : pain occurring in or in the region of the stomach

stom·ach·al \ˈstəməkəl\ *adj* : STOMACHIC

stom·ached \ˈstəmәkt\ *adj* [¹*stomach* + *-ed*] : having a stomach — used usu. in combination ⟨large-*stomached*⟩ ⟨weak=*stomached*⟩

stom·ach·er \ˈstəməkə(r), -mēk-\ *n* -s [ME *stomaker*, fr. *stomak* stomach + *-er*] **1** : the center front section of a waist or underwaist or a usu. heavily embroidered or jeweled separate piece for the center front of a bodice and worn by men or women in the 15th and 16th centuries and by women later **2** : a usu. large jeweled ornament worn by women on the front of a bodice

¹**stom·ach·ful** \ˈstəməkfəl, -mēk-\ *adj* [¹*stomach* + *-ful* (adj. suffix)] **1** *archaic* : OBSTINATE, STUBBORN **2** *archaic* : RESENTFUL, ANGRY **3** *archaic* : COURAGEOUS

²**stom·ach·ful** \-k,fu̇l\ *n* -s [¹*stomach* + *-ful* (n. suffix)] : a quantity sufficient to fill the stomach; *broadly* : all that one can stand or tolerate ⟨had a ~ of his abuse⟩

¹**sto·mach·ic** \stəˈmakik, -akēk\ *also* **sto·mach·i·cal** \-akəkəl, -akēk-\ *adj* [LL *stomachicus*, fr. Gk *stomachikos*, fr. *stomachos* stomach + *-ikos* -ic, -ical] **1** : of or relating to the stomach ⟨~ vessels⟩ **2** : strengthening to the stomach : exciting the action of the stomach ⟨a ~ cordial⟩ — **sto·mach·i·cal·ly** \-akək(ə)lē, -akēk-, -li\ *adv*

²**stomachic** \"\ *n* -s : a stimulant or tonic for the stomach

stomaching *n* -s [fr. gerund of ²*stomach*] *obs* : a feeling of bitterness, irritation, or anger : RESENTMENT

stom·ach·less \ˈstəməkləs\ *adj* : lacking a stomach

stomach piece *n* : APRON 2c (2)

stomach pump *n* : a suction pump with a flexible tube for removing liquids from the stomach

stomach tooth *n* [so called fr. the gastric disturbance that often attends its appearance] : a lower canine esp. of the first dentition

stomach tube *n* : a flexible rubber tube to be passed through the esophagus into the stomach for introduction of material or removal of gastric contents

stomach worm *n* : any of various nematode worms parasitic in the stomach of mammals or birds; *esp* : a worm (*Haemonchus contortus*) common in domestic ruminants — called also *barber's pole worm, twisted stomach worm*

stom·achy \ˈstəməkē\ *adj* **1** *dial Brit* : IRASCIBLE, IRRITABLE **2** : having a large stomach

sto·mal \ˈstōməl\ *adj* [*stom-* + *-al*] : of, relating to, or situated near a stoma ⟨a ~ ulcer⟩ ⟨the ~ closing mechanism⟩

stomas *pl of* STOMA

-stomas *pl of* -STOMA

stomat- *or* **stomato-** *comb form* [NL, fr. Gk, fr. *stomat-, stoma* — more at STOMACH] : mouth : opening : stoma ⟨*stomatitis*⟩ ⟨*stomatoscope*⟩

stomata *pl of* STOMA

¹-stomata *pl of* -STOMA

²-stomata — see ²-STOMA

stoma·tal \ˈstämədᵊl, ˈstōm-, -ətᵊl\ *adj* [*stomat-* + *-al*] : of, relating to, or constituting a stoma ⟨~ openings⟩

¹**sto·mate** \ˈstō,māt\ *n* -s [NL *stomat-, stoma*] : STOMA 2

²**stomate** \"\ *adj* [*stom-* + *-ate* (adj. suffix)] : STOMATOUS

-sto·mate \stə,māt\ *adj comb form* [*stom-* + *-ate*] : -STOMATOUS

sto·mat·ic \stəˈmad·ik\ *adj* [*stomat-* + *-ic*] : relating to or constituting a stoma

stoma·tit·ic \ˌstōməˈtid·ik, ˌstäm-\ *adj* [NL *stomatitis* + E *-ic*] : of, relating to, or constituting stomatitis ⟨a ~ disorder⟩

stoma·ti·tis \,==ˈtīd·əs\ *n, pl* **stomatit·i·des** \-ˈtid·ə,dēz\ *or* **stomatitises** [NL, fr. *stomat-* + *-itis*] : any of numerous inflammatory diseases of the mouth varying in symptoms with the cause and resulting from various local or systemic causes (as mechanical trauma, irritants, allergy, vitamin deficiency, disease of the blood, or infection) ⟨erosive ~⟩ ⟨vesicular ~⟩

stoma·to·dae·um *or* **stoma·to·de·um** \ˌstōməd·ōˈdēəm, ˌstäm-\ *n, pl* **stomato·daea** *or* **stomato·dea** \-ēə\ *also* **stomatodeums** [NL, fr. *stomat-* + *-odaeum, -odeum* (fr. Gk *hodaion*, neut. of *hodaios* being on the way, fr. *hodos* way) — more at CEDE] : STOMODAEUM

stoma·to·gas·tric \ˌstōmə(ˌ)d·ō, ˌstämə(ˌ)d·ō+\ *adj* [ISV *stomat-* + *gastric*] : of or relating to the mouth and the stomach; *specif* : constituting a system of nerves that ramify over the anterior portion of the alimentary canal in various invertebrates

stoma·to·graph \ˈstōməd·ə,graf, ˈstäm-, -rȧf\ *n* [*stomat-* + *-graph*] : an instrument for determining and recording variations in size of stomatal apertures (as of a leaf)

stoma·to·log·i·cal \ˌstōməd·ᵊlˈäjəkəl, ˌstäm-\ *also* **stoma·to·log·ic** \-jik\ *adj* : of or relating to stomatology

stoma·tol·o·gist \ˌstōməˈtäləjəst, ˌstäm-\ *n* -s : a specialist in stomatology

sto·ma·tol·o·gy \-jē, -ji\ *n* -ES [ISV *stomat-* + *-logy*] : a branch of medical science concerned with the mouth and its disorders

¹**stoma·to·pod** \ˈstōməd·ə,päd, ˈstäm-\ *adj* [NL *Stomatopoda*] : of or relating to the Stomatopoda

²**stomatopod** \"\ *n* -s : a crustacean of the order Stomatopoda : SQUILLA, MANTIS CRAB

stoma·top·o·da \ˌstōməˈtäpədə, ˌstäm-\ *n pl, cap* [NL, fr. *stomat-* + *-poda*] : an order of Crustacea coextensive with the division Hoplocarida — **stoma·top·o·dous** \ˌ==ˈtäpədəs\ *adj*

stoma·to·po·di·um \ˌstōməd·ōˈpōdēəm, ˌstäm-\ *n, pl* **stoma·topo·dia** \-ēə\ [NL, fr. *stomat-* + *-podium*] : a hypha of a parasitic fungus that passes through a stoma and commonly forms specialized haustoria within a parasitized leaf

stoma·tose \ˈstōmə,tōs, ˈstäm-\ *adj* [*stomat-* + *-ose*] : STOMATOUS

stoma·tous \-məd·əs, -mətəs\ *adj* [*stomat-* + *-ous*] : bearing stomata or having a stoma

-stoma·tous \ˈstäməd·əs, -tōm-, -mətəs\ *adj comb form* [prob. fr. NL *-stomatus*, fr. Gk *stomat-, stoma* mouth — more at STOMACH] : having (such) a mouth or opening : stomatous ⟨*cyclostomatous*⟩

-stome \ˌstōm\ *n comb form* -s [ISV, fr. NL *-stoma*] : mouth : opening resembling or functioning as a mouth ⟨*cytostome*⟩

¹**-stomi** *pl of* -STOMUS

²**-sto·mi** \stə,mī\ *n pl comb form* [NL, fr. Gk *stoma* mouth — more at STOMACH] : creatures having (such) a mouth or opening — in names of higher taxa in zoology ⟨*Plagiostomi*⟩ ⟨*Aulostomi*⟩ ⟨*Selachostomi*⟩

¹**-sto·mia** \ˈstōmēə\ *n comb form* -s [NL, fr. *stom-* + *-ia* -y] : mouth exhibiting (such) a condition ⟨*stenostomia*⟩

²**-stomia** \"\ *n pl comb form* [NL, fr. Gk *stomion* mouth — more at STOMION] : creatures sharing (such) a condition of the mouth — in names of higher taxa in zoology ⟨*Deuterostomia*⟩

¹**sto·mi·a·tid** \ˈstōmēəd·əd\ *adj* [NL *Stomiatidae*] : of or relating to the Stomiatidae

²**stomiatid** \"\ *n* -s : a fish of the family Stomiatidae

sto·mi·at·i·dae \ˌstōmēˈad·ə,dē\ *n pl, cap* [NL, irreg. fr. *Stomias*, type genus (irreg. fr. Gk *stoma* mouth) + *-idae* — more at STOMACH] : a family of small slender usu. scaleless deep-sea fishes having a short head that bears an enormous mouth full of long powerful teeth and a highly distensible stomach and with living and extinct related fishes forming a suborder of the order Isospondyli — compare DRAGONFISH

¹**sto·mi·a·toid** \ˈstōmēə,tȯid\ *adj* [NL *Stomiatidae* + E *-oid*] : resembling or related to the Stomiatidae

²**stomiatoid** \"\ *n* -s : a stomiatoid fish

-stomies *pl of* -STOMY

sto·mi·on \ˈstōmē,än\ *n, pl* **stomions** \-nz\ *or* **sto·mia** \-ēə\ [NL, fr. Gk, mouth, dim. of *stoma* mouth — more at STOMACH] : the midpoint of the oral fissure determined with the lips closed

sto·mi·um \ˈstōmēəm\ *n, pl* **sto·mia** \-ēə\ *also* **stomiums** [NL, fr. Gk *stomion* mouth] **1** : the thin-walled cells of the annulus marking the line or region of dehiscence of a fern sporangium **2** : the opening in an anther sac usu. between lip cells through which dehiscence occurs

stomo- — see STOM-

sto·mo·chord \ˈstōmə,kȯrd\ *n* [*stom-* + *-chord* (as in *notochord*)] : a structure in the proboscis of an enteropneust that has been construed as homologous with the chordate notochord — **sto·mo·chord·al** \ˌ==ˈkȯrdᵊl\ *adj*

sto·mo·dae·al *or* **sto·mo·de·al** \ˌstōməˈdēəl\ *adj* [NL *stomodaeum, stomodeum* + E *-al*] : of, relating to, or derived from a stomodaeum

stomodaeal food *n* : partly digested food regurgitated from the mouth by some social insects (as termites) and used to feed other members of the colony

sto·mo·dae·um *or* **sto·mo·de·um** \ˌ==ˈdēəm\ *n, pl* **stomodaea** \-ēə\ *also* **stomodaeums** \-ēəmz\ *or* **stomo·dea** \-ēə\ *also* **stomodeums** [NL, fr. *stom-* + *-odaeum, -odeum* (fr. Gk *hodaion*, neut. of *hodaios* being on the way, fr. *hodos* way) — more at CEDE] : the anterior ectodermal part of the alimentary canal or tract including all formed by invagination of the external body wall — compare PROCTODAEUM; see CTENOPHORE illustration

sto·moi·sia \stəˈmȯisēə\ *n, cap* [NL, perh. fr. *stom-* + Gk *oisos* agnus castus + NL *-ia* — more at WITHY] : a large genus of herbs (family Lentibulariaceae) widely distributed on wet shores and having rootlike bladder-bearing branches, minute or scalelike leaves, and racemose or solitary irregular often spurred mostly yellow flowers — compare BLADDERWORT

-sto·mous \stəməs\ *adj comb form* [NL *-stomus*, fr. Gk *stoma* mouth — more at STOMACH] : -STOMATOUS ⟨*gymnostomous*⟩

sto·mox·ys \stəˈmäksəs\ *n, cap* [NL, fr. *stom-* + Gk *oxys* sharp — more at OXY-] : a genus of blood-sucking flies that includes the stable fly (*S. calcitrans*) and is usu. placed in the family Muscidae but sometimes assigned to a separate family

¹**stomp** \ˈstämp, ˈstȯmp\ *vb* -ED/-ING/-S [alter. of ¹*stamp*] *vt* : STAMP 2 ~ *vi* **1** : STAMP 2 **2** : to dance a stomp — **stomp·er** \-pə(r)\ *n* -s

²**stomp** \"\ *n* -s **1** : STAMP 4 **2 a** : a jazz dance characterized by heavy stamping **b** : music for a stomp characterized by strong rhythmic drive and a rhythmic repetition pattern **3 a** : a shuffling counterclockwise line dance of Woodland Indians and derivatively of Oklahoma tribes with characteristic antiphonal singing **b** : the running step of this dance

³**stomp** *var of* STUMP

-sto·mum \ˈstōməm, *in sense 2* ˌstəməm\ *n comb form, pl* **-sto·ma** \-mə\ [NL, fr. Gk *stoma* mouth — more at STOMACH] **1** : mouth : opening : stoma ⟨*prestomum*⟩ **2** : creature with (such) a mouth — in generic names ⟨*Amphistomum*⟩ ⟨*Oesophagostomum*⟩

-sto·mus \stəməs\ *n comb form, pl* **sto·mi** \stə,mī\ [NL, fr. Gk *stoma* mouth] **1** : condition of having (such) a mouth ⟨*microstomus*⟩ **2** : creature with (such) a mouth — in generic names ⟨*Agonostomus*⟩ ⟨*Catostomus*⟩ ⟨*Phyllostomus*⟩

¹**-sto·my** \stəmē, -mi\ *n comb form* -ES [ISV, fr. NL ¹*-stomia*] : -STOMIA

²**-stomy** \"\ *n comb form* -ES [ISV *stom-* + *-y*] : surgical operation establishing a usu. permanent opening into (such) a part ⟨*enterostomy*⟩ or between (such) parts ⟨*esophagogastrostomy*⟩

stond \ˈständ\ *dial Eng var of* STAND

¹**stone** \ˈstōn\ *n* -s *see sense 3* [ME *stan, ston, stoon*, fr. OE *stān*; akin to OHG *stein* stone, ON *steinn*, Goth *stains* stone, L *stiria* icicle, Gk *stia, stion* pebble, *stear* fat, tallow, Skt *styāyate* it congeals, hardens; basic meaning: to harden] **1** : a concretion of earthy or mineral matter of igneous, sedimentary, or metamorphic origin: **a** (1) : such a concretion of indeterminate size or shape : BOULDER, PEBBLE ⟨~s rolling down the hill⟩ ⟨gathering ~s on the beach⟩ (2) : the substance of this concretion : ROCK ⟨the mountain is solid ~⟩ ⟨trees turned to ~ in the petrified forest⟩ **b** : such a concretion mined, quarried, or shaped in a definite form or size or for a specified function: as (1) : a building block ⟨demolish the structure a ~ at a time⟩ (2) : a paving block : COBBLESTONE ⟨building barricades of the very ~s of the streets⟩ (3) : a precious stone : GEM (4) : a mineral matter used for a particular ornamental or commercial purpose ⟨ornaments made of the rarer ~s — banded slate, rose quartz, steatite —*Amer. Guide Series: N.J.*⟩ (5) : a pillar or block of stone set as a monument or sign; *esp* : GRAVESTONE ⟨the burying ground, where you can find the ~s of veterans of the Revolution —J.P.Marquand⟩ (6) : a rounded missile fired from an arm or a sling ⟨six ~s for his sling⟩ (7) : a shaped piece of rock used in a feat of strength (as curling) (8) : MILLSTONE (9) : GRINDSTONE (10) : WHETSTONE (11) : a stand or table with a smooth flat top on which to impose or set type — called also *surface* (12) : a surface upon which a drawing, text, or design to be lithographed is drawn or transferred (13) : a watch jewel **2** : something resembling a small stone or pebble in shape, composition, or hardness: as **a** (1) : CALCULUS 1a (2) : a hard natural growth (as an otolith) found in an animal **b** : TESTIS **c** : HAILSTONE **d** (1) : the hard central portion of a drupaceous fruit (as a peach) (2) : a hard stonelike seed (as of a date) **3** *pl usu* **stone** : any of various units of weight ranging from 4 to 26 pounds: as **a** : an official British unit equal to 14 pounds **b** : a British unit for meat equal to 8 pounds — called also *Smithfield stone* **4** : any of the colors common in stone or weathered rock — see DEEP STONE, HONEY 6, LIGHT STONE, STONE GRAY **5** : CHINA STONE, CORNISH STONE **6** : a small crystalline contamination in glass comprising unmelted batch material or a particle of the melting vessel **7** : a playing piece used in backgammon

²**stone** \"\ *vb* -ED/-ING/-S [ME *stanen, stonen*, fr. *stan, ston, stoon*, n.] *vt* **1** : to hurl stones or sometimes other missiles at ⟨was *stoned* by abolitionists —Mari Sandoz⟩ ⟨began *stoning* us with empty beer cans —Leslie Waller⟩; *esp* : to kill by hitting with stones ⟨he shall be *stoned* or shot; whether beast or man, he shall not live —Exod 19:13 (RSV)⟩ **2 a** *obs* : to make (a person) hard or insensitive to feeling ⟨harsh deeds did ~ his heart⟩ **b** : to make numb or insensible (as from drink or narcotics) ⟨planned to ~ himself with vodka —Truman Capote⟩ **3** : to face, pave, or fortify with stones ⟨has dug a well and is *stoning* it⟩ **4 a** : to free from stones **b** : to remove the stones or seeds of (a fruit) ⟨500 grams of prunes *stoned* in advance —E.V.Knight⟩ **5 a** : to rub, scour, or polish (as leather, dies, machined metal) with a stone **b** : to sharpen with a whetstone ⟨the bit was . . . *stoned* and whetted to a razor edge —*Amer. Guide Series: Conn.*⟩ ~ *vi* : to form or develop a stone in the process of growing

³**stone** \"\ *adj* [¹*stone*] **1** : of, relating to, or made of stone **2** *often cap* : of or relating to the Stone Age ⟨~ culture⟩

stone age *n, usu cap S&A* : the first known period of prehistoric human culture characterized by the use of stone tools — see EOLITHIC, MESOLITHIC, NEOLITHIC, PALEOLITHIC; compare BRONZE AGE, IRON AGE

stone ax *n* [ME *stanax, stonax*, fr. OE *stānæx*, fr. *stān* stone + *æx* ax — more at AX] **1** : a stonecutter's ax : AXHAMMER **2** : a prehistoric stone implement similar to an ax head — compare GROOVED AX, HAND AX, PERFORATED AX

stonebass \ˈ=,=\ *n* : a large brown grouper (*Polyprion americanus*) of the eastern and southern Atlantic, the Mediterranean, and the seas about Tasmania and New Zealand

stonebird \ˈ=,=\ *n* **1** : GREATER YELLOWLEGS **2** : FINCH

stonebiter \ˈ=,==\ *n* : HAWFINCH

stone-blind \ˈ=ˈ=\ *adj* [ME *stane-blynde*, fr. *stan, ston, stoon* stone + *blynde, blind* blind] : totally blind — **stone-blindness** *n* -ES

stone blue *n* **1** : a variable color averaging a grayish blue that is redder and duller than electric or copenhagen, redder and darker than Gobelin, and duller and slightly redder than old china **2** : AZURITE BLUE

stoneboat \ˈ=,=\ *n* [ME (northern dial.) *stanboot* fr. *stan* stone + *boot* boat — more at STONE, BOAT] : a flat sledge or drag for transporting stones and other heavy articles or when weighted for smoothing tilled soil or breaking clods — called also *stone drag*

stone boiling *n* : boiling of a liquid by dropping hot stones into it

stone bolt *n* : a bolt grouted into masonry and used to support a member in place

stone borer *n* : an animal that bores stones; *esp* : any of various mollusks of the genus *Lithophaga*

stonebow \ˈ=,=\ *n* [ME *stonebowe*, fr. *stone, ston* stone + *bowe* bow — more at BOW] : a crossbow or catapult for shooting stones

stone brake *n* **1** : PARSLEY FERN b (2) **2** : a polypody (*Polypodium vulgare*)

stone bramble *n* : a European trailing bramble (*Rubus saxatilis*) with scarlet fruits made up of few drupelets

stonebrash \ˈ=,=\ *n* : land abounding in stones; *esp* : a subsoil of small stones or finely broken rock

stone brick *n* : a hard brick or firebrick made in Wales

stone-broke \ˈ=ˈ=\ *adj* : completely broke : lacking funds ⟨could smile at being *stone-broke* till the hundred a week came in —Leonard Merrick⟩

stone bruise *n* **1** : a sore spot on the bottom of the foot without laceration caused by a bruise by a stone or rounded object **2** : an injury to the casing of a pneumatic tire caused by forceful impact with a sharp or hard object

stone canal *n* : a tube in many echinoderms having a wall that contains calcareous deposits and leading from the circumoral ring of the water-vascular system to the madreporite

stone caribou *n* : a large dark caribou (*Rangifer arcticus stonei*) with heavy and well-developed antlers that is widely distributed from central Alaska northward to the arctic slopes

stonecat \ˈ=,=\ *n* : a catfish (*Noturus flavus*) of the Mississippi valley and Great Lakes area that is related to the smaller madtoms and like them has poisonous pectoral spines

stone cell *n* : BRACHYSCLEREID

stonechat \ˈ=,=\ *n* **1 a** : a common European singing bird (*Saxicola torquata*) of which the male has a black head, blackish wings and tail, rufous underparts, and white collar, wing spot, and upper tail coverts **b** : any of various other birds of the genus *Saxicola*; *specif* : WHINCHAT **2** : BLUE TIT

stone china *n* : an English chinaware resembling ironstone china; *broadly* : IRONSTONE CHINA

stone circle *n* : a circle of stones constructed by primitive or ancient peoples; *specif* : a circle of upright megaliths usu. enclosing a mound or dolmen — compare CROMLECH

stone clover *n* : RABBIT-FOOT CLOVER

stone coal *n* : ANTHRACITE

stone-cold \ˈ=ˈ=\ *adj* : completely cold : lacking warmth ⟨by the time he got back to his coffee it was *stone-cold*⟩

stone collar *n* : a large stone ring resembling a horse collar in size and shape and often bearing ancient symbolic decoration that is found in Mexico and the West Indies esp. in Puerto Rico

stone coral *n* : STONY CORAL

stone crab *n* **1** : a large edible crab (*Menippe mercenaria*) found on the southern coast of the U. S. and in the Caribbean area **2** : any of several spiny crabs of the genus *Lithodes*; *esp* : a crab (*L. maia*) of the European coasts

stone crayfish *n* : a freshwater crayfish (*Astacus torrentium*) of central Europe

stonecress \ˈ=,=\ *n* : a plant of the genus *Aethionema*

stone cricket *n* : a wingless cricket; *esp* : one of the genus *Ceuthophilus* (family Stenopelmatidae) that lives beneath stones and in cellars and caves : CAVE CRICKET

stonecrop \ˈ=,=\ *n* [ME *stancrop, stooncrop*, fr. OE *stāncrop*, fr. *stān* stone + *crop*] **1** : SEDUM 2; *esp* : a mossy European evergreen creeping sedum (*Sedum acre*) with pungent fleshy leaves and yellow flowers that has been widely introduced as a ground cover and is naturalized in many regions **2** : any of various crassulaceous plants of genera other than *Sedum* — usu. used with a qualifying term; see DITCH STONECROP

stone crusher *n* : a machine for crushing stone

stone curlew *n* **1** : a large-headed and large-eyed bird of the family Burhinidae that is somewhat nocturnal, frequents both open heaths and rocky shores, is widely distributed in the Old World and tropical America, and in some areas is highly regarded as a game bird — called also *thick-knee* **2** *dial Eng* : COMMON CURLEW **3** *South* : WILLET

stonecutter \ˈ=,==\ *n* **1** : one that cuts, carves, or dresses stone; *specif* : one that sharpens and repairs the buhrstones of a corn-grinding mill or cuts new ones **2** : a machine for dressing stone

stonecutting \ˈ=,==\ *n* : the art or process of cutting, carving, or dressing stone

stoned *adj* [past part. of *stone*] **1** : DRUNK **2** : being under the influence of a drug taken esp. for pleasure

stone-dead \ˈ=ˈ=\ *adj* [ME *standed*, fr. *stan* stone + *ded, deed* dead — more at DEAD] : as lifeless as a stone

stone-deaf \ˈ=ˈ=\ *adj* : totally deaf — **stone-deaf·ness** *n* -ES

stone devil *n* : HELLGRAMMITE

stoned horse *n* [fr. *stoned* having testes, fr. ¹*stone* (testis) + *-ed*] *dial Brit* : STALLION

stone drag *n* : STONEBOAT

stone dresser *n* : STONECUTTER

stone dressing *n* : the act or process of surfacing and shaping blocks of stone

stone dust *n* : ROCK DUST

stoneface \ˈ=,=\ *n* : LITHOPS 2

stone falcon *or* **stone hawk** *n* : MERLIN

stone fence *n* **1** *chiefly Midland* : STONE WALL **2** : a drink consisting of a mixture of cider and a spirituous liquor

stonefish \ˈ=,=\ *n* : any of several small dull-colored sluggish spiny scorpion fishes of *Synanceja* or a closely related genus that are widely distributed in shallow seas and about coral reefs of the tropical Indo-Pacific, often simulate seaweeds, and have dorsal spines associated with venom glands and capable of inflicting painful or occas. deadly injuries

stone fly *n* [ME *ston flye*, fr. *ston* stone + *flye* fly — more at STONE, FLY] : any of numerous insects constituting the order Plecoptera, having two pairs of membranous wings with the hinder pair folded in plaits and lying upon the abdomen when at rest, a large free prothorax, and long antennae and cerci, and characterized by an incomplete metamorphosis in which the nymphs are carnivorous, aquatic, and furnished with gills

stone fruit *n* : a fruit with a stony endocarp : DRUPE

stone gray *n* : an olive gray that is greener and lighter than nutria and greener and paler than rat — called also *crystal palace green*

stone-ground \ˈ=ˈ=\ *adj* : ground in a buhrstone mill ⟨white flour . . . was a great improvement over the gray, coarse *stone=ground* flour —R.M.Wilder⟩

stone hammer *n* [ME *stanehammer*, fr. *stane, stan, ston, stoon* stone + *hammer*] : SPALLING HAMMER

stonehand \ˈ=,=\ *n* : STONEMAN 1

stonehatch \ˈ=,=\ *n, Brit* : RING PLOVER

stonehearted \ˈ=ˈ==\ *adj* : STONYHEARTED

stone-horse \ˈ=,=\ *n* [¹*stone* (testis) + *horse*] *chiefly dial* : STALLION

stone indian *n, usu cap S&I* : ASSINIBOIN

stone·ite \ˈstō,nīt\ *n* -s *usu cap* [Barton W. *Stone* †1844 Am. evangelist + E *-ite*] : CHRISTIAN 1b(3)

stonelaying \ˈ=,==\ *n* -s : the laying of stones in the process of building; *specif* : the laying of a cornerstone of a building together with the accompanying ceremonies

stone·less \ˈstōnləs\ *adj* : having or containing no stone

stone lichen *n* : a lichen (as *Parmelia saxatilis*) growing on a rock substratum

stone life face *n* : LITHOPS 2

stone lifter *n* **1** : a device, apparatus, or machine for raising large stones **2** : a large-headed slender-bodied stargazer (*Kathetostoma laeve*) of shallow seas about Australia and New Zealand where it burrows through sand and mud and under stones by means of its powerful pectoral fins

stonelike \ˈ=,=\ *adj* : similar to stone

stone lily *n* : a fossil crinoid

stone·man \ˈstōnmən\ *n, pl* **stonemen** **1** : a compositor who imposes set type on a stone and locks it up in a chase **2 a** : a man working in stone **b** : one who drives stoneheads **3** : STONEMASON

stone marten *n* **1** : a marten (*Martes foina*) of central and southern Europe and Asia having a white patch on the breast and throat — called also *beech marten* **2** : the fur or pelt of the stone marten

stonemason \ˈ=,==\ *n* : a mason who builds with stone — **stonemasonry** \ˈ=,===\ *n*

stone mill *n* **1** : BREAKER 2c(4) **2** : a stone-dressing machine **3** : a flour mill with buhrstones instead of steel rollers — **stone-milled** \ˈ=ˈ=\ *adj*

stone mint *n* : DITTANY 3

ston·en \ˈstōnən\ *adj* [ME, fr. *ston, stoon* stone + *-en*] *dial chiefly Eng* : made of stone

stone net *or* **stone polygon** *or* **stone ring** *n* : an arrangement of rock fragments and soil particles in a polygonal pattern similar to a net with the finer materials concentrated in the central part of each net or polygon and the coarser materials in the borders as a result of congeliturbation or solifluction — usu. used in pl.

stone oak *n* **1** : a Javanese oak (*Quercus javensis*) having hard ridged acorns **2** : WHITE OAK 1b

stone ocher *n* : ocher found in hard globular masses

stone oil *n* : PETROLEUM

stone parsley *n* **1** : a slender herb (*Sison amomum*) of the family Umbelliferae that is native to Europe and Asia Minor and has aromatic seeds which are used as a condiment **2** : any plant of the genus *Seseli*

stone pine *n* **1** : SWISS PINE **2** : a pine (*Pinus pinea*) of southern Europe that has a wide-spreading flat-topped head and is much cultivated in warm countries for its sweet almondlike seeds — called also *umbrella pine* **3** : NUT PINE a

stone plover *n* : any of various shorebirds: as **a** : STONE CURLEW **b** : BLACK-BELLIED PLOVER **c** : RING PLOVER **d** : DOTTEREL

stone proof *n* : a printer's proof taken from a form on an imposing stone; *specif* : a rough proof made with mallet and planer

ston·er \ˈstōnə(r)\ *n* -S [ME *staner, stoner,* fr. *stanen, stonen* to stone + *-er* — more at STONE] : one that stones: as **a** : one that pelts with stones esp. with intent to kill **b** : one that walls with stones **c** (1) : a device for removing stones from stone fruit (as cherries) (2) : a device for cleaning stones from coffee or wheat **d** : a worker who removes bloom from tanned leather with pumice **e** : a worker who rubs rough edges and burrs from small watch parts or sharpens balance staffs with an oilstone

stone river *or* **stone run** *n* : ROCK STREAM

ston·ern \ˈstōnərn\ *Scot var of* STONEN

stone roller *n* **1** : HOG SUCKER **2** : a small common cyprinid fish (*Campostoma anomalum*) found chiefly in clear streams of the central U. S.

stoneroot \ˈ=,=\ *n* : HORSE BALM 1

stone runner *n* : any of numerous small shorebirds; *esp* : RING PLOVER

stones *pl of* STONE, *pres 3d sing of* STONE

stone sand *n* : finely crushed stone used in place of sand for concrete aggregate

stoneseed \ˈ=,=\ *n* : STONEWEED

stone sheep *or* **stone's sheep** *n, usu cap 1st S* : a dark brown northern mountain sheep (*Ovis canadensis stonei*) that is widely but sparsely distributed in the southern Yukon and northern British Columbia and Alberta

stoneshot \ˈ=,=\ *n, pl* **stoneshot** : a stone used as a missile

stone snipe *n* : any of several shorebirds; *esp* : GREATER YELLOWLEGS

stone–still \ˈ=ˈ=\ *adj* [ME *stanstill, stonstill,* fr. *stan, ston* stone + *still*] : still as a stone : MOTIONLESS ⟨sat *stone-still* for hours —Zane Grey⟩

stone stripe *n* : one of a set of roughly parallel bands of alternately finer and coarser rock debris that result from solifluction or congeliturbation on fairly steep slopes — usu. used in pl.

stone sucker *n* : LAMPREY

stone wall *n* **1** *chiefly North* : a fence made of stones; *esp* : one built of rough stones without mortar to enclose a field — called also *stone fence, rock fence* **2** : an immovable block or obstruction esp. in politics or public affairs ⟨the politicians battered against a *stone wall* of deep-seated popular distrust —*Political Science Quarterly*⟩ **3** : STONE FENCE 2

stone·wall \ˈstōn,wȯl\ *vb* [*stone wall*] *vi* **1** : to bat in cricket entirely or almost entirely defensively without trying to score runs **2** *chiefly Brit* : to engage in debate or use other parliamentary tactics for the purpose of consuming time and thus obstructing procedure or business : FILIBUSTER ⟨is ~*ing* for time in order to close the missile gap and . . . is actually opposed to negotiations —J.B.Reston⟩ **3** : to build or enclose an area with a stone wall ~ *vt, chiefly Brit* : FILIBUSTER ⟨~ debates . . . to postpone the voting stage —*Sydney* (*Australia*) *Sunday Telegraph*⟩ — **stone·wall·er** \-lə(r)\ *n* -S *Brit*

stoneware \ˈ=,=\ *n* : an opaque nonporous high-fired clayware that is well vitrified and intermediate in many respects between porcelain and earthenware, is often salt-glazed for utility pieces, and is used esp. for large storage vessels, tile, and ornamental wares — compare STONE CHINA

stoneware clay *n* : a clay suitable for making stoneware because of its plasticity, fusible minerals, and long firing range

stoneweed \ˈ=,=\ *n* : any plant of the genus *Lithospermum*

stonewood \ˈ=,=\ *n* : the hard close-grained wood of either of two Australian trees (*Callistemon salignus* and *Tarrietia actinophylla*); *also* : either of these trees

stonework \ˈ=,=\ *n* [ME *stonwerk, stoonwerk,* fr. OE *stānweorc,* fr. *stān* stone + *weorc* work — more at STONE, WORK] **1** : a structure or that part of a structure built of stone esp. with some artistic design or effect : MASONRY ⟨the pier . . . was accounted a most excellent piece of ~ —William Cowper⟩ ⟨a superb example of 14th century ~ with a magnificent timbered roof —S.P.B.Mais⟩ **2** : the process of working in stone : the shaping, preparation, or setting of stone **3** : mining that is done in shale or rock as distinguished from work done in coal

stoneworker \ˈ=,==\ *n* [ˡ*stone* + *worker*] : STONECUTTER 1

stonewort \ˈ=,=\ *n* **1** : a plant of the family Characeae that is often encrusted with calcareous deposits **2** : SCALE FERN

stone yellow *n* : YELLOW OCHER 1

sto·ney gate \ˈstōnē-\ *n* [after Bindon B. *Stoney* †1909 Ir. engineer] : a vertical gate moving on rollers and designed for controlling the flow of water from a reservoir or in a canal

ston·i·fy \ˈstōnə,fī\ *vt* -ED/-ING/-ES [ˡ*stone* + *-ify*] : PETRIFY

ston·i·ly \ˈstōnᵊlē, -nᵊli, -nəl-\ *adv* : in a stony manner : without apparent feeling or reaction : DUMBLY ⟨remains ~ indifferent to time and circumstance —Irving Kristol⟩ ⟨in prison sat down ~ to his fate —Marjory S. Douglas⟩ ⟨eyed him ~ —Kenneth Roberts⟩

ston·i·ness \-nēnəs, -nin-\ *n* -ES : the quality or state of being stony ⟨a bigness and a dilapidated dignity and a ~ which carry one back to the Middle Ages —D.H.Lawrence⟩

stoning *pres part of* STONE

stonish *obs var of* ASTONISH

stonishment *obs var of* ASTONISHMENT

stonk \ˈstäŋk\ *n* -S [perh. of imit. origin] : a heavy concentration of artillery fire ⟨call for a good ~ about five hours before our assault —*Infantry Jour.*⟩ ⟨loosed a ~ on them and wiped them off the face of the earth —Peter Rainier⟩

stonk·er \ˈstäŋkə(r)\ *vt* -ED/-ING/-S [origin unknown] **1** *Austral* : to hit hard : knock unconscious **2** *Austral* : to baffle completely : OUTWIT, FOIL

ˡ**stony** *also* **stoney** \ˈstōnē, -ni\ *adj* **stonier; stoniest** [ME *stany, stony, stoony,* fr. OE *stānig,* fr. *stān* stone + *-ig* -y — more at STONE] **1** : abounding in or having the nature of stone : full of or containing many stones : ROCKY ⟨an infertile ~ ridge —C.B.Hitchcock⟩ ⟨the ground was ~ under heel —David Goldknopf⟩ **2 a** : insensitive to pity or human feeling : HARDHEARTED, OBDURATE ⟨the city wasn't so ~ and inhospitable as she had believed —Ellen Glasgow⟩ ⟨the story should soften the *stoniest* of hearts —J.D.Adams⟩ ⟨presented a ~ front to . . . pleas for herself and the child —S.H.Adams⟩ **b** : manifesting no movement or reaction : DUMB, EXPRESSIONLESS ⟨their faces were ~, their eyes wide open and staring —Jan Valtin⟩ ⟨lighted her own cigarette . . . and smoked in ~, irritating silence —Clive Arden⟩ **c** : fearfully gripping : PETRIFYING ⟨man's . . . ~ knowledge of his own mortality —Maeve Brennan⟩ **3** *archaic* : consisting of or made of stones **4** : similar to stone in substance : HARD ⟨layers are spotted with the ~ remains of ocean forms —*Amer. Guide Series: Minn.*⟩ ⟨the shellfish crawls out of its . . . ~ case —R.W.Emerson⟩ **5** : STONEBROKE ⟨my father and I were ~ and had a lot of debts —Louis Bromfield⟩

²**stony** *vt* -ED/-ING/-ES [ME *stonien,* fr. MF *estoner* — more at ASTONY] *obs* : to numb the feelings or faculties of (a person) : STUPEFY, STUN

stony–broke \ˈ=ˈ=\ *adj* : STONE-BROKE

stony coral *n* : a coral with a hard calcareous skeleton

stonyhearted \ˈ=ˈ=,==\ *adj* : UNFEELING, CRUEL ⟨are used to being called heartless, or at least ~ —*New Yorker*⟩ — **stonyhearted·ness** *n* -ES

stony pit *n* : a virus disease of pears characterized by deep pitting and malformation of fruit

stony share *n* : a wingless moldboard plowshare designed for use in stony soils

ˡ**stood** [ME, fr. OE *stōd*] *past of* STAND

²**stood** *substand past of* STAY

stood·ed \ˈstüdəd\ *adj* [fr. dial. E past part. of ˡ*stand*] *dial Eng* : STALLED, STUCK

ˡ**stooge** \ˈstüj\ *n* -S [origin unknown] **1** : a subordinate participant in a comic act or dialogue whose function is to carry on repartee in such manner as to enable a principal comedian to make humorous remarks or appear in a humorous light : STRAIGHT MAN ⟨insults a ~ in the audience —A.J. Liebling⟩ ⟨some boy would play . . . ~ to him in order that this masterstroke of wit should be demonstrated —Robertson Davies⟩ **2 a** : one who plays a subordinate or compliant role to a principal or for some outside force or influence : CHARLIE MCCARTHY ⟨under such conditions directors are likely to be nothing more than paid ~s with far less independence of thought and action —*Corporate Concentration & Public Policy*⟩ ⟨the editor driven into exile . . . and the hoax of a newspaper perpetrated with the help of ~s —B.E.Nelson⟩; *specif* : a subversive agent acting for one government against another ⟨activities of their ~s in the countries of western and southern Europe —J.B.Reston⟩ **b** : PUPPET 4a ⟨a belief that dominion statesmen were . . . mere ~s for astute imperialist rulers —D.W.Brogan⟩ ⟨master strategists have infiltrated . . . ~s into the government —*Atlantic*⟩ **3** : a planted spy : STOOL PIGEON ⟨the company police . . . have ~s watching every move I make —Lawrence Lader⟩ ⟨detectives began contacting informers . . . in hopes that one of these ~s would help put the finger on the elusive bandit —Ray Strinnett⟩

²**stooge** \ˈ"\ *vi* -ED/-ING/-S **1** : to act as a stooge ⟨*stooged* for the comedian before starting his own show⟩ ⟨congressmen who ~ for the oil and mineral interests —*New Republic*⟩ **2** : to patrol or cruise in slow or routine flight ⟨two hours of *stooging* it . . . 16,000 feet would find you utterly numb and stiff when you landed —J.R.D.Braham⟩ — usu. used with *around* ⟨*stooging* around over the sea in all weathers —Ralph Michaelis⟩

ˡ**stook** \ˈstu̇k, ˈstük\ *n* -S [ME *stowke, stouk;* akin to MLG *stūke* tree stump, pile, sleeve, OHG *stūhha* sleeve, ON *stūka,* OE *stocu* sleeve, *stocc* stock — more at STOCK] **1** *chiefly Brit* : ˡSHOCK 1a **2** *Brit* : a pillar of coal left standing as a support for the roof of a mine

²**stook** \ˈ"\ *vb* -ED/-ING/-S *vt, chiefly Brit* : to arrange (as grain) in shocks ~ *vi, chiefly Brit* : to work at making shocks (as of grain) — **stook·er** \-kə(r)\ *n* -S *chiefly Brit*

stook·ie \-ki\ *n* -S [prob. fr. ˡ*stook* + *-ie*] *chiefly Scot* : FOOL

ˡ**stool** \ˈstül\ *n* -S [ME *stol, stool,* seat, chair, stool, fr. OE *stōl;* akin to OHG *stuol* chair, seat, ON *stōll* chair, seat, Goth *stols* chair, throne, OSlav *stolŭ* seat, throne, OE *standan* to stand — more at STAND] **1 a** : a device for sitting usu. consisting of a single wooden or upholstered seat without back or arms supported by three or four props or legs or by a central pedestal on which it may revolve **b** : a low bench or portable support used for stepping, kneeling, or resting the feet : FOOTSTOOL **c** : a base, standard, or small raised platform for supporting something : STAND **2** : a seat used as a symbol of office, authority, or precedence: as **a** : a bishop's seat; *also* : a bishop's see **b** : the seat of a western African chief or head of a lineage that is symbolic of his authority and of the line of continuity between his ancestors and their descendants; *also* : CHIEFTAINCY, KINGSHIP **3 a** : a seat used in evacuating the bowels or in urinating : COMMODE, WATER CLOSET **b** : the act of defecation ⟨violent straining at ~ —H.C.Hopps⟩ **c** : a discharge of fecal matter **4 a** : a tree stump or group of stumps with a common rootstock esp. when associated with suckers or watersprouts **b** : a plant crown from which parts (as shoots, stalks, or layers) grow out or are produced ⟨strong ~s can be layered year after year⟩ **c** : a shoot or growth from a stool : TILLER **d** : a stand of plants with developing stems or shoots ⟨a good ~ of timber⟩ **5 a** : the flat piece corresponding to the sill of a door against which a window shuts **b** : the narrow shelf fitted on the inside against the actual sill **6 a** : a small channel on the side of a ship for the deadeyes of the backstays **b** : a foundation of plates or angles for any auxiliary machinery, piping, or shafting of a ship **7 a** : a real or artificial bird used as a decoy **b** : a group of such decoys ⟨setting out the ~ upwind from the blind⟩ **8** : CULTCH 1a **9** : STOOL PIGEON ⟨among customs informers have been professional ~s —Horace Sutton⟩ — **fall between two stools** : to fail or come to naught because of inability to choose between or reconcile two alternative or conflicting courses of action ⟨a story of *falling between two stools* — the stool of election promises to balance the budget and reduce taxes, and the stool of the hideous cost of new weapons —Stewart Alsop⟩

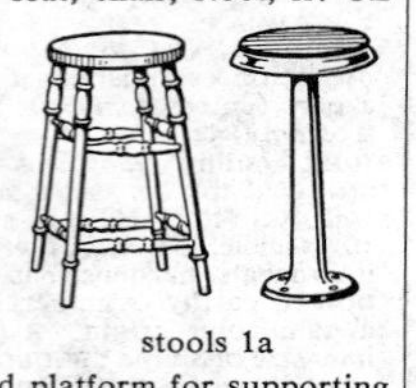

stools 1a

²**stool** \ˈ"\ *vb* -ED/-ING/-S *vi* **1** *archaic* : to evacuate the bowels : DEFECATE **2** : to form a stool : throw out shoots after the manner of a stool : TILLER **3** *of wildfowl* : to respond to the lure of a stool ⟨big flights ~*ing* into the decoys —Cameron Hawley⟩ **4** *slang* : to act as a stool pigeon ⟨once you're out of town you're fairly safe unless somebody ~s on you —C.R. Cooper⟩ ⟨~*ed* on a bank job . . . and got me four years —Raymond Chandler⟩ ~ *vt* : to lure (wildfowl) by means of decoys

stoolball \ˈ=,=\ *n* : an old English game resembling cricket played chiefly by women

stool bed *n* : a plot of ground in which plants are to be propagated by mound layering

stool end *n* : a supporting pillar of rock in a mine

stool·ie \ˈstülē, -li\ *n* -S [*stool* (*pigeon*) + *-ie*] : STOOL PIGEON ⟨~ . . . had turned in an imposing total of 281 counterrevolutionaries and other criminals —*Newsweek*⟩

stool·ing \ˈstüliŋ\ *n* -S [ˡ*stool* + *-ing*] : MOUND LAYERING

stool layering *n* : MOUND LAYERING

stool pigeon *n* **1** : a pigeon used as a decoy to draw others within a net **2** : a person acting as a decoy or informer; *esp* : a spy living among or sent into a group to report often to the police on the activities of its members ⟨served . . . as a *stool pigeon,* according to his fellow prisoners, and brought about the execution of a U.S. captain —*Time*⟩

stool shoot *n* : a lateral shoot produced on a woody plant in the absence of a terminal bud

stoon *or* **stoond** \ˈstün(d)\ *var of* STOUND

ˡ**stoop** \ˈstüp\ *vb* -ED/-ING/-S [ME *stupen, stoupen,* fr. OE *stūpian;* akin to MD *stupen* to bow, bend, ON *stūpa* to stand upright, to tower, Norw *stupa* to fall down, plunge, OE *stēap* high, steep, deep — more at STEEP] *vi* **1 a** : to bend the body forward and downward sometimes simultaneously bending the knees : LEAN ⟨the figures ~*ed* and rose with the lifting whips —Mary Austin⟩ ⟨he ~*ed* cowering to the ground —Pearl Buck⟩ ⟨he ~*ed* over his labor —Charles Dickens⟩ — often used with *down* ⟨~*ed* down to take a necklace . . . from the floor —Francis Yeats-Brown⟩ **b** : to stand or walk with a temporary or habitual forward inclination of the head, body, or shoulders ⟨~*ed* through the door of the camp —Lyndall Hadow⟩ ⟨~*ed* along the shore under the headwall of the beach —G.W.Brace⟩ ⟨stood before her, a tall, very thin man, ~*ing* a little —Michael Arlen⟩ **c** *Brit* : to lower the head in following a scent ⟨hounds . . . unlikely to ~ successfully for so weak a scent —E.G.W.W. Harrison⟩ **2** : to assume a position of subservience or subjection : humble oneself : BOW, SUBMIT ⟨~*ing* before the conqueror⟩ **3 a** : to descend from a superior rank, dignity, or status — usu. used with *to* ⟨couldn't believe that God ever ~*ed* to such trivial engagements —L.C.Douglas⟩ ⟨either the audience didn't measure up to his brand of humor, or he wouldn't ~ to theirs —H.J.Higdon⟩ ⟨that masculine dignity which forbids our ~*ing* to conquer . . . the common speech of a foreign people —G.G.Coulton⟩ **b** : to lower oneself morally or in a degrading fashion ⟨did not ~ habitually to falsehood and subterfuge to gain her end —Ellen Glasgow⟩ ⟨will ~ to robbing a bombed store —J.Coughlan⟩ ⟨he ~*ed* to fraud —Hilaire Belloc⟩ **4 a** *archaic* : to move down from a height : ALIGHT ⟨ready now to ~, with wearied wings and willing feet —John Milton⟩ **b** : to fly or dive down swiftly usu. to attack prey ⟨the big eagles were ~*ing* closer —David Walker⟩ ⟨when a falcon ~s for the kill he is traveling more than two miles a minute —H.M.Robinson⟩ ~ *vt* **1 a** : to cause (a person or thing) to move lower or bow down : PROSTRATE, OVERCOME **b** : DEBASE, DEGRADE ⟨~*ing* his talents to an unworthy cause⟩ **2** *obs* : to take or let down (as a sail or flag) **3 a** : to bend (a part of the body) forward and downward ⟨he ~*ed* his head to hers —Maurice Hewlett⟩ ⟨his shoulders were ~*ed* as if he were bearing a great bundle —Stephen Crane⟩ ⟨the bullocks . . . ~*ed* their heads to the grass —Adrian Bell⟩ **b** *dial Eng* : to cause (as a cask) to incline downward : TILT

²**stoop** \ˈ"\ *n* -S **1 a** : an act of bending the body forward : STOOPING **b** : a temporary or habitual forward bend of the back and shoulders ⟨walking bent for 50 yards before he can get the ~ out of his back —F.B.Gipson⟩ ⟨walked with a ~ as if laden with invisible burdens —Maurice Samuel⟩ **2** : the descent of a bird esp. on its prey : SWOOP ⟨the ~ of a hawk —V.C.Heilner⟩ ⟨hover . . . high above their quarry to descend in a terrific, vertical ~ on the unsuspecting larger bird —*Wyo. Wild Life*⟩ **3** : a lowering of oneself (as from a moral or dignified plane) : CONDESCENSION, CONCESSION

³**stoop** \ˈ"\ *n* -S [ME *stulpe, stowpe* post, pillar; akin to MLG *stolpe* beam, post, *stülpen* to turn upside down, OLG *stelpōn* to stagnate, ON *stolpi* post, pillar, Latvian *stulbs* post, and prob. to OHG *stellen* to place, set — more at STALL] **1** *dial Brit* : POST, PILLAR; *specif* : a large pillar (as of coal) left to support the roof of a mine **2** *Scot* : a chief supporter : PROP, MAINSTAY

⁴**stoop** *var of* STOUP

⁵**stoop** \ˈstüp\ *n* -S [D *stoep,* fr. MD; akin to OHG *stuofa, stuoffa* step of a building, MLG *stōpe* step of a building, OE *stæpe, stepe* step — more at STEP] : a porch, platform, entrance stairway, or small veranda at a house door ⟨mounted a folding stepladder chair on the front ~ and addressed them —Sinclair Lewis⟩ **syn** see BALCONY

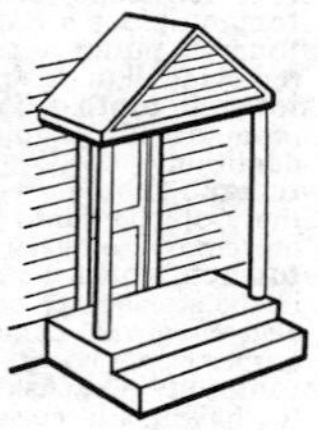

stoop

stoop and roop *adv* [origin unknown] *chiefly Scot* : COMPLETELY

stoopball \ˈ=,=\ *n* [⁵*stoop* + *ball*] : a game similar to baseball in which a player throws a ball against a stoop or building and runs to base while other players seek to capture the rebound and put him out — compare KICKBALL, PUNCHBALL

stoop crop *n* : a crop (as of a vegetable) that requires extensive hand labor and stooping in cultivating and harvesting

stooped *past of* STOOP

stooping *pres part of* STOOP

stoop·ing·ly *adv* : in a stooping manner : with a stoop

stoop labor *n* **1** : the work required or executed in cultivating or harvesting a stoop crop ⟨supports himself and his family by odd jobs and *stoop labor* in the fields —Dwight Macdonald⟩ **2** : workers employed to cultivate or harvest stoop crops ⟨migrant workers are imported by contract as *stoop labor* in the beet fields —Roscoe Fleming⟩

stoop laborer *n* : one that does stoop labor

stoops *pres 3d sing of* STOOP, *pl of* STOOP

stoop tag *n* : SQUAT TAG

stoor \ˈstu̇(ə)r\ *var of* STOUR

stoot \ˈstüt\ *dial Brit var of* STOUT

stoo·ter \ˈstōd-ə(r)\ *n* -S [D *stoter* (formerly spelled *stooter*), fr. MD, lit., one that pushes or rams, fr. *stoten* to push, stamp; akin to OHG *stōzan* to push — more at STINT] *archaic* : an old Dutch coin of base silver worth two and a half stivers

ˡ**stop** \ˈstäp\ *vb* **stopped** *or archaic* **stopt** \-pt\ **stopped** *or archaic* **stopt; stopping; stops** [ME *stoppen,* fr. OE *-stoppian;* akin to OFris *stoppia* to stop up, stuff, OLF *stuppon,* OHG *stopfōn;* all fr. a prehistoric WGmc word borrowed fr. (assumed) VL *stuppare* to stop with tow, fr. L *stuppa* tow — more at STUPE] *vt* **1 a** *obs* : to keep confined : prevent the escape of ⟨still the envious flood *stopped* in my soul, and would not let it forth —Shak.⟩ **b** : to hinder or prevent the passage of ⟨~ the inlets of fresh experience —Roger Fry⟩ ⟨applied a styptic pencil to ~ the blood⟩ **c** : to keep out : INTERCEPT ⟨weather-stripped the windows to ~ drafts⟩ ⟨most of the rain is *stopped* by the outer hills —Francis Kingdon-Ward⟩ **d** : to get in the way of : suffer the impact of : be wounded or killed by ⟨treats the male natives with bluster and hard knocks, even at the risk of *stopping* a shovel-headed spear —Leslie Rees⟩ ⟨easy to ~ a bullet along a lonely stretch of road —Harvey Fergusson⟩ ⟨*stopped* one in the last battle of the war⟩ **2** *chiefly Scot* : THRUST, PUSH, INSERT **3 a** (1) : to close up or block off access to (an opening) : PLUG ⟨sometimes they refuse to listen, and are seen to ~ their ears —B.N.Cardozo⟩ — often used with *up* ⟨the entrance to the cave was *stopped up* with rocks⟩ (2) : to close off (a burrow) from use esp. by foxes ⟨*stopped* the earths in the neighboring fields before the hunt⟩ **b** (1) : to make impassable : CHOKE, OBSTRUCT ⟨a narrow gangway, which one person could ~ —Anthony Trollope⟩ (2) : to fill or partially fill (a passage) with some obstruction — often used with *up* ⟨if your nose is badly *stopped up* for long, the infection may back up —*X-Rays & You*⟩ **c** (1) : to cover over or fill in (a hole or crevice) ⟨the hole in the window was *stopped* with a piece of cardboard —Christopher Isherwood⟩ ⟨built of hewn logs, the interstices *stopped* with clay —*Amer. Guide Series: N.C.*⟩ (2) : to pack (a horse's feet) with some substance ⟨at nightfall ~ the feet with wet tow —Richard Ford⟩ (3) : to dress over (as with plaster) : POINT 2a(1) (4) *chiefly Brit* : to put a filling in (a tooth) ⟨gnashed his formidable jaws, gleaming with teeth which had been newly *stopped* —S.H.Adams⟩ **4 a** : to cause to give up or change a mode of behavior or course of action ⟨tried to ~ him from continuing to make a fool of himself⟩ ⟨tried to ~ her from spending so much time before the mirror⟩ **b** : to keep from carrying out a proposed action : hold back : RESTRAIN ⟨pleaded with him to ~ him from resigning⟩ ⟨*stopped* him from making a speech that would have ruined him⟩ **5 a** : to interrupt or prevent the continuance or occurrence of : cause to cease ⟨teach people how to ~ burglaries in their homes or business places —Rufus Jarman⟩ ⟨unable to ~ the noise of the children⟩ ⟨*stopped* the epidemic⟩ **b** : DISCONTINUE ⟨*stopped* work at noon⟩ ⟨the phone *stopped* ringing⟩ **c** : to cause to discontinue operating or working ⟨*stopped* the presses to put in a new lead story⟩ **d** : to interrupt in a speech or statement ⟨*stopped* him short as he was trying to explain his mistake⟩ ⟨~ me if you've heard this one before⟩ **6 a** : to deduct or withhold (part or all of a sum due) in order to satisfy a claim or obligation ⟨each worker pays the equivalent of ten cents a week, which is *stopped* from his wages by the employer —D.W. & Jean Orr⟩ **b** : to instruct one's bank not to honor or pay ⟨~ a check⟩ ⟨~ payment on a check⟩ **7 a** : to arrest the progress or motion of : bring to a standstill : cause to halt ⟨*stopped* him with an upraised fat hand —Kenneth Roberts⟩ ⟨was *stopped* in his tracks by a shout from the barn —*Time*⟩ ⟨the violation consists in *stopping* goods in interstate commerce —T.W. Arnold⟩ ⟨*stopped* the car⟩ ⟨~ thief⟩ **b** : to check with a counter blow or movement : PARRY **c** : to check by means of a weapon : bring down ⟨missed his first shot, but *stopped* a bird with his second⟩ **d** (1) : to defeat in a prizefight by a knockout ⟨*stopped* his last opponent in three rounds⟩ (2) : to defeat in a game or contest ⟨*stopped* the opposing team by a wide margin⟩ **e** : to give pause to : BAFFLE, NONPLUS ⟨handles at a fast clip questions that have *stopped* the industrial experts —*N.Y. Times*⟩ **8 a** : to regulate the pitch of (as a violin string) by pressing with the finger **b** : to regulate the pitch of (a wind instrument) by closing one or more finger holes or by thrusting the hand or a mute into the bell **9 a** : to pay out (a cable) gradually in anchoring a ship **b** : to make fast (as a sail) with stops **10** *chiefly Brit* : ˡPINCH 1b (2) **11 a** : to hold an honor card and enough protecting cards to be able to block (a bridge suit) before an opponent can run off many tricks ⟨*stopped* his spades⟩ **b** (1) : to hold both of two honors

that can be melded in (a suit or rank) (2) **:** to prevent (a meld) by such holding ⟨the double ace of spades ~*s* 100 aces and a spade flush⟩ **12** *chiefly Brit* **:** PUNCTUATE **~ *vi* 1 a :** to cease activity or operation ⟨the motor *stopped*⟩ ⟨the rain *stopped*⟩ ⟨his heart *stopped*⟩ **b :** to come to an end **:** CLOSE, FINISH ⟨carried his bow over his shoulder, but the resemblance to the accepted picture *stopped* there —T.B.Costain⟩ ⟨then the din gradually dies down, the music ~*s* —Lafcadio Hearn⟩ **c :** to cease to extend ⟨the blue jacket *stopping* at his waist —Wirt Williams⟩ ⟨the highway ~*s* in the middle of nowhere⟩ **d :** to end abruptly **:** break off ⟨it doesn't end; it ~*s* —Arnold Bennett⟩ **2 a :** to cease to move on **:** stand still **:** HALT ⟨*stopping* for a moment in his walk —Edith Sitwell⟩ ⟨the horse *stopped* short at the fence⟩ ⟨*stopped* dead to listen for a suspicious sound⟩ **b :** to interrupt oneself in an activity or speech ⟨*stopped* for a while to have lunch⟩ ⟨*stopped* short when he discovered his error⟩ ⟨*stopped* to catch his breath⟩ **c :** to take time to consider **:** PAUSE ⟨had she *stopped* to think, she would have recalled . . . the plank there —Laura Krey⟩ **3 a :** to hold back **:** HESITATE ⟨doesn't ~ at the most outrageous lies⟩ ⟨~*s* at nothing to gain his ends⟩ **b :** to cease from a course of action **:** DESIST ⟨his tactics succeeded for a while, but he didn't know where to ~⟩ **4 a** (1) **:** to interrupt a trip (as for rest or a meal) ⟨decided to ~ at the next roadside restaurant for lunch⟩ — sometimes used with *off* ⟨*stopped* off on the way home to pick up some food⟩ (2) **:** to break one's journey ⟨decided to ~ for a few days at the state park⟩ — often used with *over* ⟨*stopped* over to visit his cousins⟩ (3) **:** to make a regularly scheduled halt (as for taking on or dropping passengers) ⟨the express train doesn't ~ at this station⟩ ⟨the bus ~*s* at the next corner⟩ **b :** to spend a short time **:** reside temporarily ⟨arranged to ~ at a hotel —Agnes S. Turnbull⟩ **c** *chiefly Brit* **:** REMAIN, STAY ⟨she'd ~ in bed all morning —Rosamond Lehmann⟩ ⟨his dad fell into that terrible rage with him because he had *stopped* out all night —Edith Sitwell⟩ **d :** to make a brief call **:** drop in — usu. used with *by* ⟨suggested that she ~ by that evening to talk things over —Polly Adler⟩ **5 :** to bring up a narrow wooden strip (as a molding) against a flat or curved surface **6 :** to become choked **:** CLOG ⟨the sink ~*s* up constantly because of the gooey messes the children pour into it⟩

syn QUIT, DESIST, CEASE, DISCONTINUE: STOP is a rather general term indicating suspending or interfering with moving or progressing ⟨the entrance of the judge, and a consequent great stir and settling-down in the court, *stopped* the dialogue —Charles Dickens⟩ ⟨you might as well try and *stop* a young tank —Rose Macaulay⟩ CEASE may differ in applying to conditions, states, or existences rather than to actions or activities ⟨*stopped* (but not *ceased*) the car⟩ ⟨the infielder *stopped* (but not *ceased*) the ball⟩ but often the two are interchangeable ⟨iron works . . . were erected here in 1795 but *ceased* activity in 1838 —*Amer. Guide Series: N.H.*⟩ ⟨these people suddenly *ceased* muttering, but redoubled their gesticulations —E.A. Poe⟩ CEASE may or may not carry with it the idea of gradual slow cessation of activity ⟨the soft woman gradually *ceased* her chirp —George Meredith⟩ ⟨outside in the street all noises suddenly *ceased* —Sherwood Anderson⟩ DESIST, a somewhat more formal word, is likely to indicate holding off, forebearing, refraining from going on, through self-restraint, consideration of others, expediency, or lack of success ⟨had *desisted* in his effort to press love upon her because they were to be married —Sherwood Anderson⟩ ⟨swindler and murderer *desisted* because they felt the latent strength of his personality —Osbert Sitwell⟩ DISCONTINUE is not a very expressive word; it stresses the fact of suspension of some activity, course, accustomed occupation, or habit and may be used more freely than others in this set with tangible objects ⟨*discontinue* the manufacture of motorcycles or motorbikes as part of the company's manufactures⟩ QUIT may suggest either finality or peremptoriness in a person's stopping an activity or employment or acceptance of defeat and futility in continuing an endeavor or struggle ⟨such of the owners as were not wedded to the industry *quit* —P.A.Rollins⟩ ⟨had no thought of *quitting* the struggle —Sir Winston Churchill⟩ **syn** see in addition RESIDE

— **stop one's mouth :** to make silent; *specif* **:** KILL ⟨threatened to *stop his mouth*⟩ — **stop the show :** to draw so much applause that the action on stage must temporarily halt ⟨a song that *stops the show* at every performance⟩ ⟨*stops the show* with her dance in the first act⟩

²stop \"\ *n* -s [ME, fr. *stoppen*, v.] **1 :** CESSATION, END, FINISH ⟨his death put a ~ to the project —J.W.Ellison b. 1891⟩ ⟨time, that takes survey of all the world, must have a ~ —Shak.⟩ **2 a** (1) **:** a graduated set of organ pipes of like kind and tone quality (2) **:** a corresponding set of vibrators or reeds of a reed organ (3) **:** STOP KNOB ⟨pulled out all the ~*s*⟩ **b :** a means of regulating the pitch of a musical instrument: as (1) **:** the closing of an aperture in the air passage of a wind instrument (2) **:** pressure of the finger upon a string of a string instrument **c :** a device in a harpsichord or similar instrument for modifying the power and quality of the tones produced **3 :** something that impedes, obstructs, or brings to a halt **:** IMPEDIMENT, OBSTACLE, OBSTRUCTION ⟨as soon as I had enough men I put out ~*s* on the motor road —*Yale Rev.*⟩ ⟨a groove is made on one side of a length of bone or horn and a raised knob or ~ is left at one end —Agnes Allen⟩: as **a :** DAM, WEIR **b** (1) **:** an opaque barrier for preventing the passage of light through certain portions of an optical system (as at the margin, in the axial zone, or in radial sectors); *specif* **:** the aperture of a camera lens (2) **:** a marking of a series (as of f-numbers) on a camera for indicating settings of the diaphragm **c :** a valve so placed to be used as a shutoff (as in disconnecting water or gas service) **d :** a drain plug **:** STOPPER **4 a** (1) **:** a device or piece (as a pin block, pawl, or strip of wood) for arresting or limiting motion or for determining the position to which a part will be brought (2) **:** a short feather key **b :** STOPWORK **c** (1) **:** a small piece of material (as canvas or line) used to bind or secure something ⟨secure a furled sail with ~*s*⟩ (2) **:** a projection on a mast or spar to support something or keep it from slipping down **d :** a bookbinder's hand tool used to stop a line at its intersection with another and thereby save mitering **e** (1) **:** MARGIN STOP (2) **:** a tabulator stop **5 a :** the act of impeding or bringing to a halt or the state of being impeded or brought to a halt **:** CHECK ⟨the shortstop made a great ~ on a hard grounder⟩ ⟨the train was brought to a sudden ~⟩ **b :** a guard or counter in boxing that prevents an opponent's blow from landing; *esp* **:** a blow delivered as the opponent is in the act of leading **c :** the act of preventing a goal (as in hockey, soccer) by catching or deflecting a shot **:** SAVE **6 a :** the act of coming to a halt **:** a cessation of motion or operation ⟨a brief ~ for mopping-up operations —*Current Biog.*⟩ ⟨within six months she was mastering spirals, sit-down spins and ~*s* —*Time*⟩ **b :** a halt in a journey or trip **:** STAY ⟨made a long ~ to visit the famous ruins⟩ ⟨the ship made a brief ~ to refuel⟩ **c :** a point or place for stopping ⟨an old town by the sea is a must ~ —Eleanor Early⟩; *specif* **:** a point at which a public means of conveyance (as a train, bus, or airplane) regularly stops to take on or let off passengers or goods **7 a** *chiefly Brit* **:** any of several punctuation marks ⟨if commas are used rightly the other ~*s* will sort themselves out —Ernest Gowers⟩ **b** — used in telegrams and cables to indicate a period **c :** a pause or break in a verse that marks the end of a grammatical unit **8 a** (1) **:** an order stopping payment (as of a check or note) by a bank (2) **:** the act of making such an order **b :** STOP ORDER **9 :** a consonant in the articulation of which there is a stage (as in the *t* of *apt*, the *p* of *apt*, and the *g* of *tiger*) when the breath passage is completely closed at the nose by raised velum and elsewhere by lips, tongue, or glottis — compare ²NASAL 2a **10 a :** a card in some games (as Michigan or fan-tan) that stops a sequence when played; *also* **:** the termination of a sequence by such a card **b stops** *pl but sing in constr* **:** any of several games having as an essential feature the stopping of play when the card specified to be played next is not available; *specif* **:** MICHIGAN **11 :** a depression in the face of an animal at the junction of forehead and foreface: as **a :** an indentation between muzzle and forehead in a dog (as a bulldog) — see DOG illustration **b :** an angular indentation between bill and forehead in some pigeons **c :** a line where the forehead meets the snout in a dolphin **12** *chiefly Brit* **:** one posted to prevent game animals from breaking away when located

³stop \"\ *adj* **1 :** serving to stop **:** designed to stop ⟨~ line⟩ ⟨~ signal⟩ ⟨~ valve⟩ **2 :** marked by stoppage of sound ⟨~ consonant⟩ ⟨~ articulation⟩

stop-and-go \¦==¦=\ *adj* **:** of, relating to, or involving frequent stops; *esp* **:** controlled or regulated by traffic lights ⟨*stop-and-go driving*⟩ ⟨*stop-and-go* highways⟩

stopback \'=,=\ *n* [fr. *stop back*, v.] **:** a condition in peach and pear nursery stock caused by the attack of the tarnished plant bug (*Lygus oblineatus*) and characterized by the death of the tender terminal bud of the principal shoot and the forcing of the development of lateral shoots

stopbank \'=,=\ *n*, *Austral* **:** LEVEE

stop bath *n* **:** an acid rinse bath between a photograph developer and the fixing bath used to check development of a negative or print by neutralizing the alkali in the developer — called also *short-stop*

stop bead *n* **:** a molding fastened to the inner side of a window frame on the face of the pulley stile and completing the groove in which the inner sash is to slide

stopblock \'=,=\ *n* **:** a bumping post or buffer at the end of a railroad track

stopboard \'=,=\ *n* **:** a board to restrain or check motion; *specif* **:** TOEBOARD

stop bud *n*, *Brit* **:** CROWN BUD

stop card *n* **:** a card (as in canasta) that when played on the discard pile prevents the taking of that pile

stop clock *n* **:** a timing device similar to a stop watch but larger in size usu. electrically operated and often designed for measuring very brief time intervals

stopcock \'=,=\ *n* **1 :** a cock for stopping or regulating flow (as through a pipe) **2 :** the turning plug, stopper, or spigot of a faucet

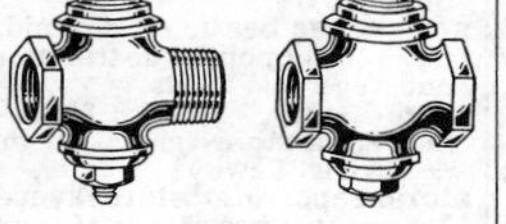

stopcocks

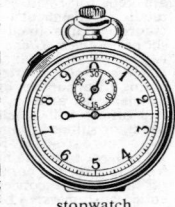

stop–cylinder press *n* **:** a cylinder press in which the cylinder revolves only when the bed makes its printing stroke and remains stationary on the return stroke — compare TWO-REVOLUTION PRESS

stop down *vt* **:** to reduce the effective aperture of (a lens) by means of a diaphragm **~ *vi* :** to make a lens opening smaller by means of a diaphragm

stop drill *n* **:** a drill with a collar on its shank to limit the depth of penetration

¹stope \'stōp\ *n* -s [prob. fr. LG *stope*, lit., step (of a building), fr. MLG *stōpe* — more at STOOP] **:** a usu. steplike excavation underground for the removal of ore that is formed as the ore is mined in successive layers — see BOTTOM STOPE, OVERHAND STOPE, RILL STOPE, SHRINKAGE STOPE

²stope \"\ *vb* -ED/-ING/-S *vi* **:** to mine by means of a stope **~ *vt* :** to extract (ore) from a stope

stope drill *n* **:** STOPER

stop·er \'stōpə(r)\ *n* -s **1 :** a drillman who works in a stope **2 :** a hammer drill mounted on a pneumatic feed cylinder and used for drilling vertical and inclined holes in stopes — called also *stope drill*

stop–fluted \'=¦==\ *adj* **:** having stopped fluting

stop fluting *n* **:** STOPPED FLUTING

stop gage *n* **:** a gage for determining the length of stock for a setup

¹stopgap \'=,=\ *adj* [*¹stop* + *gap*; after the phrase *stop a gap*] **:** serving to fill a gap **:** TEMPORARY ⟨only offered as a convenient ~ way of thinking of the phenomena —A.G.N.Flew⟩ ⟨a ~ measure⟩ ⟨a ~ program⟩

²stopgap \"\ *n* [*¹stop* + *gap*; after the phrase *stop a gap*] **1 :** something that serves as a temporary expedient **:** MAKESHIFT ⟨the export of goods and lending of money alone are only emergency ~*s* —R.P.Russell⟩ **2 :** one who occupies an office or position temporarily **:** SUBSTITUTE ⟨had simply been acting as a ~ for his brother-in-law —*Contemporary Rev.*⟩ **syn** see RESOURCE

stoping *n* -s [fr. gerund of *²stope*] **:** a process by which ore is stoped; *specif* **:** the process whereby intrusive igneous magmas are thought to make space for their advance by detaching and engulfing fragments of the invaded rocks

stop knob *n* **:** one of the handles by which the player of an organ draws or shuts off a particular stop or controls the mechanical accessories (as a coupler, tremolo)

stop·less \'stäpləs\ *adj* **:** having no stop — **stop·less·ness** *n* -ES

stoplight \'=,=\ *n* **1 :** a light on the rear of a motor vehicle that is illuminated when the driver presses the brake pedal to slow down or stop **2 :** TRAFFIC SIGNAL

stop log *n* **:** one of a set of usu. square pieces (as of wood or metal) that serve to form a dam or to check the flow of water

stop–loss \'=,=\ *adj* [*¹stop* + *loss*] **:** designed to prevent further loss

stop–loss order *n* **:** STOP ORDER

stop motion *n* **:** a device for stopping a machine or a part either automatically or at will

stop–motion *adj* **:** TIME-LAPSE

stop net *n* **1 :** a smaller seine auxiliary to a larger one to prevent the escape of fish **2 :** a net used to enclose a portion of shoreline at high tide so as to entrap fish as the tide goes out

stop netting *n* **:** the using of a stop net to catch fish

stop nut *n* **1 :** an adjustable nut used on an adjusting screw to limit motion in a particular direction **2 :** a nut with a fiber or plastic insert that binds it against vibration and eliminates the need for a lock washer or jam nut

stop off *vt* **1 :** to fill in solid (a part of a mold) where a part of the cavity left by a pattern is not wanted for the casting **2 :** to stop out

¹stop–off \'=,=\ *n* -s [fr. *stop off*, v.] **:** the act, privilege, or an instance of making a stopover

²stop–off \"\ *adj* [*stop off*] **:** serving to stop off ⟨various other *stop-off* coatings were tested and found to be unstable —*Chem. Abstracts*⟩

stop order *n* **:** an order to a broker to buy or sell at the market when the price of a security advances or declines to a designated level

stop out *vt* **1 :** to cover part of (a printing surface) with something that does not print or that prevents printing: as **a :** to cover (areas on a negative being prepared for photoengraving) with an opaque substance to prevent light action; *also* **:** to cover (areas on a plate) with a resist to prevent etching **b :** to cover a portion of (a case) with wax so as to prevent electrodeposition in an area that is to be blank in the finished electrotype **2 :** to cover (teeth) with black wax to make invisible

stopover \'=,==\ *n* -s [fr. *stop over*, v.] **1 a :** a stop at an intermediate point in one's journey **:** an interruption in a journey ⟨driving north with leisurely ~*s* to look at the animals —Alan Moorehead⟩ **b :** the act of breaking one's journey (as by train) with the privilege of continuing on a later conveyance of the same carrier **2 :** a stopping place on a journey ⟨the village is a delightful ~ for travelers —*Amer. Guide Series: Mich.*⟩

stop·pa·ble \'stäpəbəl\ *adj* [*¹stop* + *-able*] **:** capable of being stopped

stop·page \'stäpij, -pēj\ *n* -s [ME, fr. *stoppen* to stop + *-age* — more at STOP] **:** the act of stopping or the state of being stopped ⟨~ of hostile seaborne traffic —Walter Karig⟩ ⟨practically immune from ~*s* due to the weeds which infest so many of our waterways —Dick Gregson⟩: as **a :** deduction from pay as a fine or to reimburse an employer for a sum due from an employee **b :** obstruction of an organ of the body **c :** the stopping, seizure, or detention of a person, public carrier, or goods in transit (as for examination for contraband) **d :** the act or an instance of stopping payment **e :** STRIKE ⟨negotiations have broken down in other industries, and ~*s* are threatened —H.S.Truman⟩ ⟨government seizure of the railroads . . . to forestall a nationwide ~ —C.T.Lucey⟩ **f :** the complete obstruction of the breath passage or of the nonnasal part of it that is one stage in the production of some consonants — compare STOP 9 **g :** a failure of an automatic or semiautomatic firearm to extract or eject a spent case or to load or fire a new round

stoppage at source : the levying of taxes on the thing sought to be taxed (as income) at its source rather than on the person who receives the benefit or substance of it — called also *collection at source*; compare WITHHOLDING TAX

stoppage in transitu : the right of a seller of goods to stop them while on their way to the buyer and resume possession of them (as on discovery of the buyer's insolvency)

stop payment *n* **:** a depositor's order to a bank to refuse to honor a specified check drawn by him

stopped \'stäpt\ *adj* [ME, fr. past part. of *stoppen*] **1 a :** closed up or obstructed ⟨a ~ bottle⟩ ⟨a ~ nose⟩ **b** (1) *of an organ pipe* **:** closed at the top and producing thereby a pitch approximately an octave lower than that of an open pipe of the same length (2) *of a note* **:** obtained by stopping a string, pipe, or finger hole of a musical instrument **2 :** brought to a halt **:** CHECKED ⟨hang onto a ~ automobile or streetcar —Anthony Bailey⟩ **3 :** marked by stoppage ⟨~ consonant⟩ ⟨~ release⟩ **4** *of a bridge suit* **:** prevented from being run

stopped couplet *n* **:** CLOSED COUPLET

stopped diapason *n* **:** a foundation stop in a pipe organ consisting of wooden pipes closed at the top and sounding a powerful flute tone

stopped flute *n* **:** a flute filled for part of its length by a convex molding

stopped fluting *n* **:** a stopped flute or series of stopped flutes

¹stop·per \'stäpə(r)\ *n* -s [ME, fr. *stoppen* to stop + *-er* — more at STOP] **1 :** one that brings to a halt or causes to stop operating or functioning **:** CHECK ⟨do not appear to have been very effective bullet ~*s*, since the sheet of steel was so thin —J.C.Swaim⟩ ⟨conversation ~⟩ ⟨show ~⟩: as **a** (1) **:** a short piece of rope having a knot and lanyard at one end with a hook at the other (2) **:** a contrivance (as a length of rope or chain) to secure a rope or chain or to check it while running (3) **:** a device to secure a rowlock **b :** a device or appliance to stop machinery **c** (1) **:** a card that will stop the run of a suit (2) **:** both of two high cards whose possession by a pinochle player assures that no other player can make a certain meld **d :** a baseball pitcher depended on to win important games or to stop a losing streak of his team; *also* **:** an effective relief pitcher **e :** something that seizes the attention ⟨good pictures of babies, animals, and pretty girls are the conventional ~*s* because they are so high in human interest and attention value —Daniel Melcher & Nancy Larrick⟩ **2 :** one that closes, shuts, or fills up ⟨the rock was the ~ in the bottleneck —Burtt Evans⟩: as **a :** something (as a bung or cork) used to plug an opening ⟨oval bottles . . . with ground-glass ~*s* —Lois Long⟩ **b :** a composition to stop up holes **c :** one that applies a coating of stopping paste **d :** EARTH STOPPER **3 a :** any of several trees of the genus *Eugenia* (esp. *E. axillaris*) of Florida and the West Indies with hard close-grained wood **b :** WHITE STOPPER

²stopper \"\ *vt* -ED/-ING/-S **1 :** to close or secure with a stopper **:** fit a stopper on ⟨the big problem in wine manufacture was how to ~ the bottles —*Scots Mag.*⟩ **2 :** to close as if with a stopper **:** PLUG ⟨babies — their mouths ~*ed* up with pacifiers —Jean Stafford⟩

stopper knot *n* **:** a knot used to prevent a rope from passing through a hole or opening

stop·per·less \-(r)ləs\ *adj* **:** not having a stopper

stop·per·man \-(r)mən\ *n*, *pl* **stoppermen :** a foundry worker who makes or repairs fire-clay stoppers for ladles and sets them in place

stop·ping \'stäpiŋ, -pēŋ\ *n* -s [ME, fr. gerund of *stoppen*] **1 :** the act of one that stops ⟨a violinist whose ~ is phenomenal⟩ **2 :** material for stopping up or filling in a fissure or cavity **:** FILLING, PACKING ⟨the fleeting glimpse of gold ~ in his side teeth —Margery Allingham⟩ **3 :** a partition or door (as in a mine) to direct or prevent an air current **4 :** the placing of punctuation marks **:** PUNCTUATION **5 :** the solid end of an archery pile

stopping condenser *or* **stopping capacitor** *n* **:** a capacitor used in a circuit to prevent the flow of direct current but permit the flow of alternating current

stopping in transit : a special service by carriers that permits a shipper to unload part of a shipment at intermediate points and then send the remainder to a final destination at a through rate plus stopping charge

stop plank *n* **:** one of a set of planks set in grooves to form a dam — compare FLASHBOARD

stop plate *n* **:** a plate for stopping or limiting the travel of a part (as a rod or valve); *specif* **:** a plate serving as an end bearing for the axle of a railroad car to prevent or limit end play

¹stop·ple \'stäpəl\ *n* -s [ME *stoppell*, fr. *stoppen* to stop + *-ell* (suffix denoting an instrument)] **:** something that closes an aperture **:** STOPPER: as **a** (1) **:** a plug for closing a finger hole in a flute or flageolet to change the scale tone (2) **:** the plug in the end of a stopped organ pipe **b :** EARPLUG 2 ⟨a ~ must be fitted into the ear canal so that noise does not leak around the edges —*Nat'l Safety News*⟩

²stopple \"\ *vt* **stoppled; stoppled; stoppling** \-p(ə)liŋ\ **stopples :** to close the mouth of with or as if with a stopple **:** STOPPER

stop press *n* [*¹stop* + *press*] *chiefly Brit* **:** a space or column in a newspaper containing last-minute news items usu. printed from a fudge ⟨hadn't seen anything in the *stop press* or the early papers —Christopher Bush⟩

stop–press \'=,=\ *adj* [*¹stop* + *press*] **1 :** made or inserted while a printing press is stopped in the course of a run ⟨a *stop-press* alteration⟩ ⟨a *stop-press* correction⟩ **2 :** of up-to-the-minute significance or interest **:** TIMELY ⟨many a worthy book of scholarship might be all the better for . . . relating itself to the *stop-press* facts of life —James Cameron⟩

stop rod *n* **:** a stop-motion rod on a loom

stops *pres 3d sing of* STOP, *pl of* STOP

stop screw *n* **:** a screw for mounting or holding a stop

stop seine *n* **:** STOP NET 1

stop sign *n* **:** a usu. octagonal sign requiring vehicles to stop before entering or crossing a thoroughfare

stop street *n* **:** a street on which a vehicle must stop just before entering a through street

stopt *archaic past of* STOP

stop tester *n* **:** an instrument for determining the distance required to stop a vehicle by measuring its deceleration

stop thrust *n* **:** a counteroffensive movement made by a fencer to arrest an opponent's attack — compare TIME THRUST

stop valve *n* **:** a valve closed or opened at will (as by hand) for preventing or regulating flow (as of a liquid in a pipe); *specif* **:** the valve in an engine steam pipe for controlling or checking the passage of steam

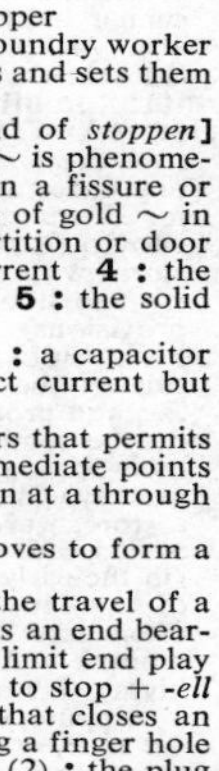

stop sign

stop volley *n* **:** a soft shot in tennis intended to carry just over the net short of the reach of one's opponent

stopwatch \'=,=\ *n* **:** a watch having a hand that can be started or stopped at will (as by pressing a small button on the edge of the watch) to register exact elapsed time (as of a race) — compare FLYBACK

stopwater \'=,==\ *n* [*¹stop* + *water*] **:** any of various devices or procedures for securing watertightness: as **a :** a plug of soft wood driven into a hole bored in the seam of a scarf **b :** canvas backed with red lead or other material and fitted between metal parts (as of a ship)

stopwork \'=,=\ *n* [*²stop* + *work*] **1 :** a device to prevent tight winding of the mainspring of a watch or clock — compare MALTESE CROSS **2** [*¹stop* + *work*] *Austral* **:** stoppage of work **:** STRIKE

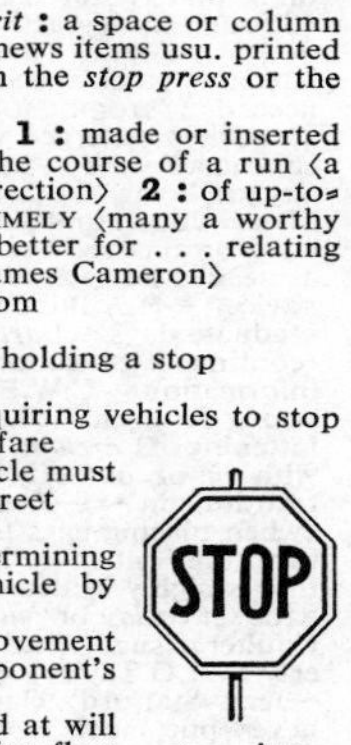

stopwatch

stor *abbr* storage

¹stor·able \'stōrəbəl, 'stȯr-\ *adj* [*¹store* + *-able*] **:** that may be stored ⟨reserves of ~ commodities —*New Republic*⟩ — contrasted with *perishable*

²storable \"\ *n* -s **:** something that may be stored for an extended period of time without serious loss from spoilage or

evaporation and without danger — usu. used in pl. ⟨~s such as wheat and cotton⟩

stor·age \'stō(ə)r-, 'stȯ-, -ōə, -ȯ(ə)\ *vb* -ED/-ING/-s [ME *storen*, fr. OF *estorer* to construct, restore, store, fr. L *instaurare* to renew, restore, perform, fr. *in-* [2]*in-* + *-staurare* (fr. a base akin to Gk *stauros* pole, stake) — more at STEER] *vt* **1** : FURNISH, PROVIDE, SUPPLY, FILL ⟨bins *stored* with grain⟩ ⟨his head was *stored* with chaotic but vivid impressions —Frances Gaither⟩; *esp* : to stock or furnish against a future time ⟨a ship with provisions⟩ **2** : to collect as a reserved supply : lay away : ACCUMULATE ⟨~ vegetables for winter use⟩ ⟨energy from the sun may be *stored* in the form of fat as well as carbohydrates . . . and proteins —R.E.Coker⟩ ⟨energy *stored* in a condenser can be computed —W.H.Timbie & Vannevar Bush⟩ — often used with *up* or *away* ⟨build dams to ~ up water —R.W. Murray⟩ ⟨memories *stored* away⟩ **3 a** : to leave or deposit in a store, warehouse, or other place for keeping, preservation, or disposal : CACHE, STOW ⟨potatoes *stored* in a basement⟩ ⟨in the early days of the passenger car it was almost unheard of to ~ it on the street —J.C.Ingraham⟩ ⟨the center mall is often used to ~ snow plowed from the pavement in winter months —A.G.Bruce & John Clarkeon⟩ ⟨honey *stored* in hives⟩ **b** : to record (information) in an electronic device (as a computer) from which the data can be obtained as needed **4** : to have space for : provide storage room for : HOLD ⟨elevators to ~ surplus wheat⟩ ~ *vi* **1** : to take on or store away supplies ⟨ships *storing* in the harbor⟩ **2** : to undergo storing esp. without spoilage ⟨foods should ~ well at room temperatures or in the refrigerator —Callie Cooney ⟨an egg that will ~ 60 percent longer —*Springfield (Mass.) Daily News*⟩

storage bellows *n pl but sing or pl in constr* : a chamber in a pipe organ in which the compressed air supplied by the blower is kept at a uniform pressure by means of weights or springs

storage car *n* : a railway car for hauling mail and parcels that do not require sorting and distribution en route — compare RAILWAY MAIL CAR

storage cell *or* **storage battery** *n* **1** : a cell that converts chemical energy into electrical energy by reversible chemical reactions and that may be recharged by passing a current through it in the direction opposite to that of its discharge — called also *accumulator*, *secondary battery* **2** : a connected group of two or more storage cells

storage in transit : the storing at an intermediate point of goods that are to be reshipped to their final destination within a prescribed period; *also* : the charge for such storage at through rates

storage life *n* : SHELF LIFE

storage spot *n* : a spotting of fruits and vegetables originating in storage; *specif* : a disease of citrus fruits characterized by light-colored or brown sunken spots of varying size and shape — called also *pox*

storage track *n* : a railroad yard track for cars awaiting use or other disposition

storage tube *n* : MEMORY TUBE

storage wall *n* : a built-in combination esp. of cabinets, closets, and open shelves set against or forming a broad wall space (as the side of a room)

storage yard *n* : a railroad yard for cars not in use

sto·rax \'stō-,raks, 'stȯ-\ *n* -ES [ME, fr. LL, storax, tree (of the genus *Styrax*) yielding storax, alter. of L *styrax* — more at STYRAX] **1** : a resin derived from various trees of the genus *Styrax* (*S. officinalis*) and formerly used for incense **2 a** : a balsam obtained from the bark of an Asiatic tree (*Liquidambar orientalis*) as a grayish brown fragrant liquid containing resin, styrene, and cinnamic acid and used as an expectorant and sometimes in perfumery — called also *Levant storax* **b** : a similar balsam from the sweet gum (*L. styraciflua*) — called also *American storax, sweet gum*; compare LIQUIDAMBAR **3** : a shrub or tree of the genus *Styrax*

storax family *n* : STYRACACEAE

[1]**store** \'stō(ə)r, 'stȯ(ə)r, -ōə, -ȯ(ə)\ *vb* -ED/-ING/-s [ME *storen*, fr. OF *estorer* to construct, restore, store, fr. L *instaurare* to renew, restore, perform, fr. *in-* [2]*in-* + *-staurare* (fr. a base akin to Gk *stauros* pole, stake) — more at STEER] *vt* **1** : FURNISH, PROVIDE, SUPPLY, FILL ⟨bins *stored* with grain⟩ ⟨his head was *stored* with chaotic but vivid impressions —Frances Gaither⟩; *esp* : to stock or furnish against a future time ⟨a ship with provisions⟩ **2** : to collect as a reserved supply : lay away : ACCUMULATE ⟨~ vegetables for winter use⟩ ⟨energy from the sun may be *stored* in the form of fat as well as carbohydrates . . . and proteins —R.E.Coker⟩ ⟨energy *stored* in a condenser can be computed —W.H.Timbie & Vannevar Bush⟩ — often used with *up* or *away* ⟨build dams to ~ up water —R.W. Murray⟩ ⟨memories *stored* away⟩ **3 a** : to leave or deposit in a store, warehouse, or other place for keeping, preservation, or disposal : CACHE, STOW

[2]**store** \"\ *n* -s [ME *stor*, fr. OF *estor*, fr. *estorer*] **1** : something that is stored or kept for future use ⟨~ for ten days⟩ ⟨through all his active years he drew heavily on his physical ~ —W.A.Slade⟩ **b stores** *pl* : articles (as of food) accumulated for some specific object and issued or drawn upon as needed : STOCK, SUPPLIES ⟨issue ~s upon proper written authority⟩ ⟨charged with payment for the coal, oil and other consumable ~s —*Railway Gazette*⟩ ⟨over 700 lb. of ~s — oxygen, tents, food, fuel, cookers, climbing gear — must be lifted —John Hunt & Edmund Hillary⟩ **c** : something accumulated or amassed : a source from which things may be drawn as needed : a reserve fund ⟨a ~ of provisions⟩ ⟨a ~ of sound advice —R.A.Billington⟩ ⟨their dwindling ~ of undergraduate days —*Dartmouth Alumni Mag.*⟩ — often used in pl. ⟨continued education . . . will provide increasing ~s of information —C.W.Eliot⟩ **2 a** *archaic* : LIVESTOCK **b** *Brit* : a young or unfinished meat animal suitable for growing on and fattening **3** *archaic* : POSSESSIONS **4** : STORAGE — usu. used with *in* or *out of* ⟨fresh fruits and vegetables, whether in transit or in ~ —*Fruit & Vegetable Storage & Pre-packaging*⟩ ⟨when placing eggs in ~ —*Dublin Sunday Independent*⟩ ⟨our furniture, out of ~ last week —Mary Shaw⟩ **5** : something that is highly valued or greatly relied upon : TREASURE — used with *set* or *lay* or *put* ⟨setting a great ~ on precedent —E.M. Coulter⟩ ⟨such schedules did not set light ~ on life and property —H.O.Taylor⟩ ⟨her mother set such ~ by the terrarium —Jean Stafford⟩ ⟨lay great ~ by tradition⟩ ⟨readers, who never put much ~ by the polite, personal essay —*Time*⟩ **6 stores** *pl* : the raw or unworked material supplies of a manufacturing concern **7** : a large quantity, supply, or number : ABUNDANCE ⟨intended to bake a ~ of brambles for you to take —G.W.Brace⟩ **8** : a place of deposit for goods esp. in large quantities : STOREHOUSE, WAREHOUSE, MAGAZINE ⟨meat ~⟩ ⟨rope ~⟩ ⟨explosives ~⟩ ⟨quartermaster's ~⟩ — see COLD STORE **9 a** : a business establishment where goods are kept for retail sale ⟨grocery ~⟩ ⟨furniture ~⟩; *esp* : a retail establishment having a large diversified stock of goods ⟨thoroughfares lined with modernized ~s and up-to-date shops —*Amer. Guide Series: Pa.*⟩ — see CHAIN STORE, DEPARTMENT STORE, RETAIL STORE; compare SHOP **b stores** *pl but sing or pl in constr, Brit* : a retail establishment often consisting of a number of departments **c** : a commercial establishment (as a bank, restaurant, or dry-cleaning shop) ⟨~s and offices will be closed for the holiday⟩ **d** : a building, room, or suite of rooms occupied by or suitable for occupancy by a store ⟨~ for rent⟩ ⟨several ~s under construction⟩ **10** *slang* : an establishment or setup used by swindlers as a front to gain the confidence of victims **b** : an establishment (as a carnival concession) employing shills or barkers to entice customers **11** : a space or compartment on a gameboard for the keeping of pieces when not in play **12** *chiefly Brit* : MEMORY 6 — **in store 1** : in a state of accumulation : in readiness : in preparation ⟨a faint promise of the excitement we had been told was *in store* for us —T.C.Roughley⟩ ⟨benefits which the activities of human intelligence may have *in store* for us —H.A.Kramers⟩ **2** *obs* : in abundance

[3]**store** \"\ *adj* **1 a** *or* **stores** : of, relating to, kept in, or used for a store ⟨~ barge⟩ ⟨the *stores* trucks are due on the dock

about the same time —Wirt Williams⟩ **b** : used for storing ⟨fill the big red ~ crock with water at night —Flora Thompson⟩ ⟨~ jar⟩ **c** : purchased from a store as opposed to natural or homemade : COMMERCIAL, MANUFACTURED, BOUGHT, READY-MADE ⟨~ clothes⟩ ⟨~ bread⟩ ⟨~ teeth⟩ **2** *archaic* : ABUNDANT, PLENTIFUL — used postpositively ⟨ships thou hast ~ —Alexander Pope⟩ **3** *Brit* : STOCK 3 **b** : suitable for fattening ⟨strolled past the pens of ~ cattle —Adrian Bell⟩

store-bought \',·,·\ *adj* : STORE 1c ⟨*store-bought* clothes⟩ ⟨a *store-bought* haircut⟩

store-boughten \',·,·\ *dial var of* STORE-BOUGHT

store card *n* : a token issued by a private business concern for relieving a public scarcity of small change or for advertising purposes

store cheese *n* : CHEDDAR; *esp* : sharp cheddar

stored *past of* STORE

sto·reen \stho'rēn\ *n* [IrGael *stóirín*, dim. of *stór* store, treasure, fr. E [3]*store*] *Irish* : DARLING

[1]**storefront** \',·,·\ *n* [[2]*store* + *front*] **1** : the front side of a store or store building facing a street ⟨old-time ~s with cast-iron columns —Richard Bissell⟩ **2** : a building, room, or suite of rooms having a storefront ⟨churches occupying ~s⟩

[2]**storefront** \"\ *adj* **1** : occupying a room or suite of rooms in a store building at street level and immediately behind a storefront ⟨operated from a ~ office —Val Adams⟩ **2** : of, relating to, or characteristic of a storefront church ⟨~ evangelists⟩

storefront church *n* : a city church that utilizes storefront quarters as a meeting place and that usu. holds services of a highly emotional nature

storehouse \',·,·\ *n* [ME *storhous*, fr. *stor* store + *hous* house] **1** : a building for storing goods (as provisions) : MAGAZINE, WAREHOUSE; DEPOT, STORE **2** : an abundant supply or source : REPOSITORY ⟨the sea is the world's greatest ~ of raw materials —J.P.Tully⟩ ⟨an author's memory is a ~ of sensations —R.W. Stallman⟩

storehouse beetle *n* : a ptinid beetle (*Gibbium psylloides*) that has a cosmopolitan distribution and is injurious to most animal and vegetable foods

store·keep \',·,·\ *vi* [back-formation fr. *storekeeper*] : to manage a store ⟨guess I'll buy him out and ~ for a while —Sinclair Lewis⟩

storekeeper *also* **storeskeeper** \'·,··\ *n* [[2]*store* + *keeper*] **1** : one that has charge of supplies (as military or naval stores) : a manager of a warehouse : STOCK CLERK; *specif* : an enlisted man (as in the U.S. Navy) who performs clerical and manual duty in the supply department of a ship or station **2** : one who operates a retail store : MERCHANT, SHOPKEEPER

storekeeping \'·,··\ *n* [[2]*store* + *keeping*] : the occupation of keeping a store : the management of a store

store·man *also* **stores·man** \'·mən\ *n, pl* **storemen** *also* **storesmen** \-·mən\ **1** : STOREKEEPER **2** : a man who stores goods (as in a storehouse)

store order *n* : an order for goods made out for an employee on the general supply store of a company

store pay *n* : payment for goods or work in articles from a shop or store

stor·er \'stōrə(r)\ *n* -s : one that stores: as **a** : one that maintains in store or places in storage **b** : one that lays aside for emergency : HOARDER

sto·re·ria \stə'rirēə\ *n, cap* [NL, fr. David H. *Storer* †1891 Am. obstetrician and naturalist + NL *-ia*] : a common genus of harmless No. American gray or brown colubrid snakes

storeroom \'·,·\ *n* **1** : a room for the storing of goods or supplies : LUMBER ROOM **2** : space for storing in a storehouse or repository **3** : STOREHOUSE 2 ⟨the prodigious ~ of his mind —F.H.Taylor⟩ ⟨his ~ of anecdotes and illustrations is rich and varied —Ben Bradford⟩ **4** : a room used or designed for the display of merchandise on sale

[1]**stores** *pres 3d sing of* STORE, *pl of* STORE

[2]**stores** *var of* STORE

storeship \',·,·\ *n* : a ship used to carry supplies

stores ledger *n* : a perpetual inventory record esp. of raw materials and manufacturing supplies

storewide \'·,·\ *adj* : including all or most merchandise throughout a store ⟨a ~ sale⟩ ⟨~ clearance⟩

storey *var of* STORY

storeyard \'·,·\ *n* : a yard that is used for storing goods or supplies

sto·ri·at·ed \'stōrē,ād·əd\ *adj* [ML *historiatus* historiated + E *-ed* — more at HISTORIATED] : HISTORIATED

sto·ri·a·tion \,··'āshən\ *n* -s [ML *historiatus* + E *-ion*] : ornamentation with designs representing historical subjects

[1]**sto·ried** \'stōrēd, 'stȯr-, -rid\ *adj* [[3]*story* + *-ed*] **1** : decorated with designs representing scenes from story or history ⟨a ~ frieze⟩ ⟨a ~ tapestry⟩ ⟨~ windows richly dight —John Milton⟩ **2** : having a history : celebrated in story or history : interesting from the stories that relate to it ⟨a country with a ~ past —Y.G.Heiser⟩ ⟨these are ~ mountains —Cornelius Weygandt⟩ ⟨a ~ family⟩

[2]**storied** *or* **sto·reyed** \'stōred, 'stȯr-, -rid\ *adj* [[3]*story*, *storey* + *-ed*] : having stories or a specified number of stories — often used in combination ⟨a two-*storied* house⟩ ⟨multi*storied* buildings⟩ **2** *of wood* : characterized by somewhat regular transverse rows when viewed in tangential section : having the appearance of ripple marks ⟨~ cambium⟩

sto·ri·er \'stōrēə(r)\ *n* -s [ME, fr. *storie* story + *-er* — more at STORY] **1** *obs* : HISTORIAN **2** : a teller of stories

stories *pres 3d sing of* STORY, *pl of* STORY

sto·ri·ette \,stōrē'et\ *n* -s [[1]*story* + *-ette*] : a brief story or tale

sto·ri·fy \'stōrə,fī\ *vt* -ED/-ING/-ES [[1]*story* + *-fy*] : to narrate or describe in story

storin *pres part of* STORE

sto·ris \'stōrəs\ *n, pl* **storis** [Dan, fr. *stor* large, big (fr. ON *stórr*) + *is* ice, fr. ON *īss* — more at STOUR, ICE] : a floating mass of closely crowded icebergs and floes

[1]**stork** \'stȯ(ə)rk, -ȯ(ə)k\ *n, pl* **storks** *also* **stork** [ME, fr. OE *storc*; akin to MLG & MD *storc* stork, OHG *storah* ON *storkr* stork, OE *stearc* stiff, strong; fr. its stiff legs — more at STARK] : any of various large mostly Old World wading birds having a long stout bill, constituting the family Ciconiidae, and related to the ibises and herons — see ADJUTANT BIRD, BLACK STORK, JABIRU, MARABOU, OPENBILL, SADDLE-BILL, WHITE STORK; compare WOOD IBIS

[2]**stork** \"\ *adj* [fr. the nursery story that children are brought into the world by storks] : relating to the birth of a child ⟨~ cards⟩ ⟨a ~ shower⟩

stork-billed kingfisher \'·,·-\ *n* : any of various long-tailed kingfishers (genus *Pelargopsis*) of southeastern Asia and the East Indies having a sharp-pointed bill with the culmen ridged at the base

storksbill \'·,·\ *n* **1** : a plant of the genus *Pelargonium* **2** : a plant of the genus *Erodium*; *esp* : ALFILARIA

[1]**storm** \'stȯ(ə)rm, -ȯ(ə)m\ *n* -s *often attrib* [ME, fr. OE; akin to OS & MD *storm*, OHG *sturm*, ON *stormr* storm, OE *styrian* to stir — more at STIR] **1 a** : a violent disturbance of the atmosphere attended by wind and usu. by rain, snow, hail, sleet, or thunder and lightning : TEMPEST — see TROPICAL STORM; compare CYCLONE, HURRICANE **b** : a heavy fall of rain, snow, or hail whether accompanied with wind or not **c** : stormy weather ⟨captured ... varying moods in sun, ~ and snow, —*Brit. Bk. News*⟩ **d** : wind having a speed of 64 to 72 miles per hour — see BEAUFORT SCALE TABLE **e** : a serious disturbance of any element of nature ⟨ionospheric ~⟩ — see MAGNETIC STORM **2** : a disturbed or agitated state : a sudden or violent commotion ⟨the economic ~s of the 1930s —*Woolworth's First 75 Years*⟩ ⟨the ~s of adolescence⟩ ⟨whose life has been a passage through ~s of emotion —P.E.More⟩ ⟨a ~ of birds in the ... trees —W.B.Yeats⟩ **3 a** : PAROXYSM, CRISIS **b** : a sudden increase in the symptoms of a disease ⟨thyroid ~⟩ **c** : a sudden heavy influx or onset ⟨the ~ of paperbacks now flooding the country —Harrison Smith⟩ ⟨the ~ of students now entering college⟩ **4** : a heavy discharge of objects (as missiles) or actions (as blows) ⟨a ~ of arrows⟩ ⟨a ~ of petals⟩ **5** : a tumultuous outburst ⟨a ~ of protest⟩ ⟨no words could be heard above the ~ of catcalls —E.S.Bates⟩ **6** : a violent assault on a defended position **7 storms** *pl* : STORM WINDOWS ⟨put up the ~s⟩ — **by storm** *adv* : by or as if by employ-

ing a bold swift frontal movement esp. with the intent of defeating or winning over quickly and completely ⟨attack a fort by storm⟩ ⟨take an audience by storm⟩

[2]**storm** \"\ *vb* -ED/-ING/-s [ME *stormen*, fr. *storm*, n.] *vi* **1 a** : to blow with violence ⟨the wind . . . ~ed at nearly 40 miles an hour —J.A.Michener⟩ **b** : to rain, hail, snow, or sleet esp. in a violent manner or with high wind — usu. used with *it* ⟨it was ~ing in the mountains⟩ **2** : to attack by storm ⟨armored divisions ~ing toward the city⟩ ⟨the attackers ~ed ashore at sunrise⟩ **3** : to be in or to exhibit a violent passion : RAGE ⟨~ing at the unusual delay⟩ **4** : to rush about or move impetuously, violently, or angrily ⟨the mob ~ed through the streets⟩ ⟨jumped into his clothes and ~ed over to the office —Nathaniel Benchley⟩ ⟨on such occasions the river ~s down in a rush —J.H.Moolman⟩ ~ *vt* : to attack, take, or win over by storm ⟨~ a fort⟩ ⟨trying to ~ the public by a mannerism —O.W.Holmes †1935⟩ ⟨they simply ~ed their audiences —Philip Carr⟩ **syn** *see* ATTACK

storm and stress *n, often cap both Ss* [trans. of G *sturm und drang*] : STURM UND DRANG

storm beach *n* : a low rounded ridge of coarse gravel or shingle constructed by storm waves at the inner margin of a beach beyond the reach of ordinary waves

stormbird \'·,·\ *n* **1** : PETREL; *esp* : STORM PETREL **2** : a bird (as the man-o'-war bird) thought to presage storms

storm blue *n* : a variable color averaging a grayish blue that is redder and less strong than electric, redder and duller than copenhagen, and redder and darker than Gobelin

storm boat *n* : a light fast craft used to transport attacking troops across streams

storm boot *n* : a woman's high-cut boot made of heavy waterproofed leather

stormbound \'·,·\ *adj* : cut off from outside communication by a storm or its effects : stopped or delayed by storms ⟨~ ports⟩ ⟨~ travelers⟩

storm breeder *n* : a cloud or weather condition regarded as portending storm; *also* : WEATHER BREEDER

storm cellar *or* **storm cave** *n* : CYCLONE CELLAR

storm center *n* **1** : the center of the area covered by a storm; *esp* : the place of lowest pressure in a cyclonic storm — compare EYE 2h **2** : a focus of controversy or disturbance : a central point around which trouble revolves

storm cloud *n* **1** : a cloud that portends a storm **2** : a threat of serious disturbance or trouble

storm coat *n* : a heavy lined fabric overcoat usu. waterproofed and with a fur collar

stormcock \'·,·\ *n* **1** : MISTLE THRUSH **2** : FIELDFARE **3** : GREEN WOODPECKER **4** : STORM PETREL

storm current *n* : a current caused by a storm wind

storm door *n* : an additional door placed outside an ordinary outside door to prevent entrance of wind, cold, and rain and to reduce heat losses — compare STORM WINDOW

storm drain *n* **1** : a drain carrying waste water other than sewage from a building to a stream sewer **2** : STORM SEWER

storm·er \'stȯrmər\ *n* -s : one that storms: as **a** : one that rages **b** : one that attacks by storm

storm flag *n* **1** : a small national flag flown (as at a U.S. Army post) only in stormy weather and measuring usu. 9 feet 6 inches by 5 feet **2** : a square red flag with a square black center displayed singly, in pairs, or in combination with various pennants to indicate the approach of a storm

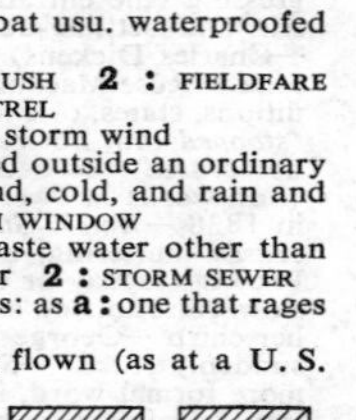

storm·ful \'stȯrmfəl\ *adj* : abounding with storms : STORMY — **storm·ful·ly** \-fəlē\ *adv* — **storm·ful·ness** *n* -ES

storm glass *n* : a vertical glass tube the contents of which are supposed to indicate changes in the weather by changes in their appearance

stormier *comparative of* STORMY

stormiest *superlative of* STORMY

storm·i·ly \'stȯ(r)məlē, -li\ *adv* : in a stormy manner

storm in a teacup : TEMPEST IN A TEAPOT

storm·i·ness \-mēnəs, -min-\ *n* -ES : the quality or state of being stormy ⟨~ increases toward the higher latitudes —P.E. James⟩

storming *adj* [fr. pres. part. of [2]*storm*] : that storms ⟨equity markets made a ~ start to the week —*Financial Times (London)*⟩

storming party *n* : a military party assigned to storm a position

storm jib *n* : a small jib used in stormy weather

storm lane *n* : a narrow belt over which storm centers pass with a certain degree of regularity and with frequency

storm lantern *or* **storm lamp** *n, chiefly Brit* : HURRICANE LAMP 1

storm·less \'stȯrmləs\ *adj* : having no storms — **storm·less·ness** *n* -ES

storm level *n* : the somewhat indefinite imaginary plane several feet above mean sea level to which storm waves occas. climb

storm mizzen *n* : a triangular sail set on a temporary stay abaft the mizzen

storm petrel *n* : any of various small petrels; *esp* : a small sooty black petrel (*Hydrobates pelagicus*) marked with white on wing and tail coverts and frequenting the north Atlantic and Mediterranean — called also *stormy petrel*

storm porch *n* : a small roofed structure designed to protect an outside door of a dwelling in cold weather

stormproof \'·,·\ *adj* : impervious to damage by storm : so tight as to exclude penetration by wind, rain, or snow in time of storm

storm rack *n* : FIDDLE 4

storm rubber *n* : a low-cut rubber overshoe having a high front that covers the instep

storms *pl of* STORM, *pres 3d sing of* STORM

storm sail *n* : any of numerous small strong heavy sails that are bent and set in stormy weather

storm sewer *n* : a sewer designed to carry water wastes except sewage **2** : STORM DRAIN

storm signal *n* **1** : a signal (as a flag, pennant, or cone) announcing the approach of a storm esp. of marked violence **2** : STORM WARNING 2

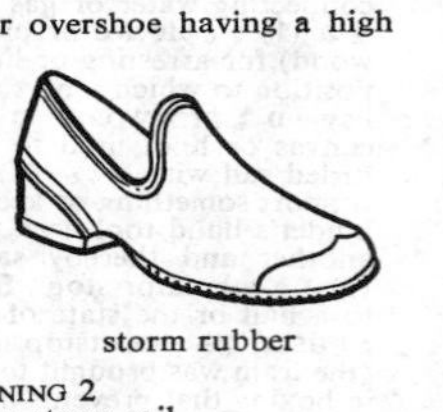

storm stay *n* : a temporary stay for a storm sail

storm thrush *n, Brit* : MISTLE THRUSH

storm tide *n* : a high tide that is significantly higher than normal due to onshore winds reinforcing tidal action

storm track *n* : the path of the center of a storm

storm trooper *n* **1** : a member of the shock troops **2** *sometimes cap S&T* : a member of the Sturmabteilung : BROWNSHIRT **3** : a member of a politico-military body similar in aims or function to the Sturmabteilung ⟨the *storm troopers* of some yet undefined totalitarianism —Dixon Wecter⟩

storm troops *n pl* **1** : SHOCK TROOPS **2** *sometimes cap S&T* : troops belonging to the Sturmabteilung of Nazi Germany

storm warning *n* **1 a** : a display of storm signals **b** : a notification (as a radio report) that gives warning of an approaching storm **2** : a happening that warns of a difficult or involved state of affairs lying ahead ⟨the *storm warnings* he sees for education —*Saturday Rev.*⟩ ⟨the surest *storm warning* that something exciting was about to happen —John Mason Brown⟩

storm welt *n* : a welt attached to a shoe between upper and sole around the outside edge of the sole so as to seal out moisture

storm wind *n* **1** : a heavy wind : a wind that brings a storm : the blast of a storm **2** : STORM 1d

storm window *n* **1** *or* **storm sash** : a sash placed outside an ordinary window as a protection against severe weather — compare STORM DOOR **2** : a dormer window or other protected window raised from a roof

stormy \'stȯrmē, 'stȯr)mē, -mi\ *adj* -ER/-EST [ME, fr. *storm* + *-y*] **1** : relating to, characterized by, or indicative of a storm : subject to storms : TEMPESTUOUS ⟨a ~ day⟩ ⟨a ~ autumn⟩ ⟨severed by a wide and ~ sea from the rest of the world —James Bryce⟩ **2** : marked by turmoil or fury : char-

storm flags 2: *1* hurricane, *2* SW storm

storm rubber

acterized by, subject to, or indicative of heated disagreements or strong emotional outbursts : PASSIONATE, TURBULENT ⟨a ~ conference⟩ ⟨a ~ life⟩ ⟨provoke ~ and uncontrollable emotional responses —Lewis Mumford⟩ ⟨a violent, ~ eloquence —J.L.Motley⟩ ⟨her deep ~ eyes —Thomas Hardy⟩ **3** : having alternating exacerbations and remissions of symptoms ⟨convalescence ran a ~ course⟩ ⟨the course of the disease is usually extremely ~ —Joseph Stokes⟩

stormy petrel *n* **1** : STORM PETREL **2** : one fond of strife : a harbinger of trouble ⟨became the *stormy petrel* of his time at home, at school —Floyd Stovall⟩

stor·nel·lo \stȯ(r)ˈne(,)lō\ *n, pl* **stornel·li** \-elē\ [It, prob. fr. *stornare* to turn aside, fr. OIt, fr. OF *destorner, destourner* — more at DETOUR] : a short Italian street song often consisting of only three lines rhyming *aba*

¹story \ˈstōrē, ˈstȯrē, -ri\ *n* -ES [ME *storie,* fr. OF *estorie, estoire,* fr. L *historia* — more at HISTORY] **1 a** *obs* : a connected narrative of important events esp. of the remote past **b** *archaic* : a historical record : a work of history **c** *archaic* : history as a branch of knowledge **2 a** : an account of some incident or event; *often* : a tale written or told esp. for the entertainment of children ⟨used to tell *stories* to his grandchildren at night —Vance Randolph⟩ **b** : a statement regarding the facts pertinent to a situation in question ⟨the man's ~ of the robbery was not convincing⟩ **c** : a detailed account of the career of a particular individual or of the sequential facts in a given case ⟨write the ~ of one's life⟩ ⟨the ~ of the ocean⟩ ⟨the ~ of atomic power⟩ ⟨the ~ of public housing⟩ **d** : ANECDOTE; *esp* : an amusing one ⟨his speech contained several good *stories*⟩ **e** : the events in the history of a person or thing that taken together are of sufficient interest and significance to serve as likely subject matter for an account ⟨there's a ~ in every one of your fellow passengers —Richard Joseph⟩ **f** : background information that clarifies a situation or affair ⟨what's the ~ on this deal⟩ ⟨get the whole ~ before commenting⟩ ⟨but figures give only part of the ~ —*New Republic*⟩ **3 a** : a prose or verse narrative of incidents arranged according to their time relationship : a fictional work that recounts objective events or a stream of thought or interactions of these **b** : a fiction that is shorter or has a more unified plot than the usual novel ⟨detective *stories*⟩ ⟨Western *stories*⟩; *specif* : SHORT STORY **c** : the intrigue or plot of a narrative or dramatic work; *broadly* : a narrative thread upon which a composition is based ⟨the ~ of a ballet⟩ **d** : a rewrite or condensation of a literary work in which dramatic values are emphasized and which serves as the basis of the script of a film play **4** : an historical, legendary, or literary subject depicted in sculptural or pictorial art ⟨~ pictures popular in the 19th century⟩ — compare HISTORY 4a(2) **5 a** *archaic* : a groundless rumor **b** : a widely circulated report or rumor ⟨a ~ going round⟩ **6** : FIB, LIE, FALSEHOOD **7 a** : the composition or telling of stories ⟨a feat long celebrated in song and ~⟩ **b** : TRADITION, LEGEND, ROMANCE ⟨castle walls and snowy summits old in ~ —Alfred Tennyson⟩ **8 a** : an account in a news organ or news broadcast ⟨human-interest ~⟩ ⟨feature ~⟩ **b** : the subject of a news account : material for news accounts ⟨the biggest *stories* of the year⟩ **9** : an arrangement (as of pictures or tableaux) that in sequence and often with the aid of accompanying text tells a connected narrative ⟨the first series of picture *stories* the photographer did —*Current Biog.*⟩

²story \"\ *vb* -ED/-ING/-ES [ME *storien,* fr. *storie,* n.] *vt* **1** *archaic* : to tell in historical relation : make the subject of a story : narrate or describe in story **2** : to adorn with a story or a scene from history ~ *vi* : to tell a story; *specif* : to tell a falsehood ⟨*storied* about his age⟩

³story *or* **sto·rey** \"\ *n, pl* **stories** *or* **storeys** [ME *storie,* fr. ML *historia, istoria* picture, story of a building, fr. L *historia* history, story (narrative); prob. fr. pictures adorning the windows of medieval buildings — more at HISTORY] **1 a** : a set of rooms on one floor level of a building excluding the attic level and usu. the cellar or basement level : the habitable space between two floors or between a floor and the roof of a building ⟨the first ~ of a house⟩ ⟨the attic ~⟩ ⟨a building ten *stories* high⟩ — often used in combination ⟨a single-*story* house⟩ ⟨a forty-*story* building⟩ — see HALF STORY; compare FIRST FLOOR, FLOOR, MEZZANINE, SECOND STORY **b** : a horizontal division of a building's exterior not necessarily corresponding exactly with the stories within **2** : one of a series of tiers arranged horizontally one over another ⟨beehives arranged in *stories*⟩ ⟨the three *stories* of the cave —J.H.Bretz⟩

story-and-a-half \ˈ≈≈≈≈ˈ≈\ *adj* : consisting basically of one story with additional minor rooms in the attic ⟨a *story-and-a-half* brick house⟩

storyboard \ˈ≈≈,≈\ *n* : a panel or series of panels on which is tacked a set of small rough drawings depicting consecutively the important changes of scene and action in a planned film or television show or act ⟨imperative to lay out the story of the film on a ~ —Raymond Spottiswoode⟩

storybook \ˈ≈≈,≈\ *n* : a book containing a story : a book of stories ⟨~s for children⟩

sto·ry·less \ˈ≈≈ləs\ *adj* : being without a story : UNSTORIED

story line *n* : the plot of a story or play ⟨novels with a strong *story line,* lots of action, and other surefire ingredients —Malcolm Cowley⟩

story pole *or* **story rod** *n* : a pole cut to the proposed clear height between finished floor and ceiling and often marked with minor dimensions (as for door trims and dadoes) that is used esp. by carpenters and bricklayers

storyteller \ˈ≈≈,≈≈\ *n* : a teller of stories: as **a** : one that relates anecdotes **b** : one that recites tales orally in public **c** : STORYWRITER **d** : FIBBER, LIAR **e** : one employed at a play center or library to tell stories to children

storytelling \ˈ≈≈,≈≈\ *n* : the telling of stories

storywriter \ˈ≈≈,≈≈\ *n* [ME *storiewriter,* fr. *storie* story + *writer*] : a writer of stories

stoss \ˈstäs\ *adj* [G *stoss-,* fr. *stossen* to push, thrust, fr. OHG *stōzan* — more at STINT] : facing toward the direction from which an overriding glacier impinges ⟨the ~ slope of a hill⟩ ⟨the ~ side of a knob of rock⟩ ⟨drumlins are ... steeper and broader on the ~ end —O. D. Von Engeln⟩ — opposed to *lee*

¹stot *also* **stott** \ˈstät\ *n* -S [ME *stot, stott,* fr. OE *stot;* akin to MLG *stūt* thigh, buttocks, OHG *stiuz* buttocks, ON *stūtr* horn, stump, ox, OHG *stōzan* to thrust, push — more at STINT] **1** *dial Brit* : a young bull **2** *dial Brit* : a usu. young steer

²stot \"\ *vb* **stotted; stotted; stotting; stots** [origin unknown] *vi* **1** *chiefly Scot* : BOUNCE, REBOUND, JUMP **2** *chiefly Scot* : to walk with an irregular step : STAGGER, LURCH ~ *vt, chiefly Scot* : BOUNCE ⟨a series of rebounds ... comparable to patting or *stotting* an india-rubber ball —Douglas Kennedy⟩

³stot \"\ *n* -S **1** *Scot* : REBOUND **b** : a hard blow **2** *Scot* **a** : JUMP; *esp* : a leap in dancing **b** : SWING, RHYTHM

stoter *var of* STOOTER

stoting *var of* STOATING

sto·tin·ka \stəˈtiŋkə\ *n, pl* **stotin·ki** \-kē\ [Bulg] **1** : a Bulgarian monetary unit equal to ¹⁄₁₀₀ lev — see MONEY table **2** : a coin representing one stotinka and issued only in 1901 and 1912

¹stot·ter \ˈstätə(r\ *vi* -ED/-ING/-S [freq. of ²stot] *dial Brit* : STAGGER, STUMBLE

²stot·ter \-tər\ *n* -S *Scot* : STUMBLE

stoun *dial chiefly Brit past part of* STEAL

¹stound *also* **stoun** \ˈstaund, ˈstün(d)\ *n* -S [ME *stund, stond, stound,* fr. OE *stund;* akin to OFris *stunde* time, hour, OHG *stunta* period of time, point in time, time, hour, ON *stund* period of time, hour, OE *standan, stondan* to stand — more at STAND] **1** *archaic* : TIME, WHILE, MOMENT **2 a** *chiefly Scot* : a throbbing pain : PANG, ACHE **b** *chiefly Scot* : THRILL **c** *archaic* : a loud noise : UPROAR

²stound *also* **stoun** \"\ *vi* -ED/-ING/-S *chiefly Scot* : to feel a pang : ACHE, SMART ⟨my heart it ~s with anguish —Robert Burns⟩

³stound *also* **stoun** \"\ *vt* -ED/-ING/-S [ME *stunden, stonden,* prob. fr. *stund, stound,* past part. of *stounen,* fr. OF *estoner* — more at ASTONY] *archaic* : to stupefy with or as if with a blow : STUN, ASTOUND

⁴stound \"\ *n* -S **1** *archaic* : STUPOR **2** *archaic* : a state of amazement

stoup *also* **stoop** \ˈstüp\ *n* -S [ME *stowp,* prob. of Scand origin; akin to ON *staup* cup — more at STEEP] **1** *chiefly Scot* : BUCKET, PAIL **2 a** : a container for beverages: as (1) : a large glass (2) : TANKARD (3) : FLAGON ⟨set me the ~s of wine upon that table —Shak.⟩ **b** : the contents of a stoup ⟨bade him come aboard and drink a ~ —Hope Muntz⟩ **3** : a basin at the entrance of a Roman Catholic church to contain holy water in which those entering may dip their fingers before blessing themselves

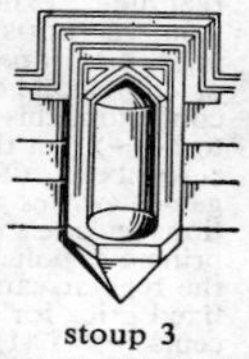
stoup 3

¹stour \ˈstü(ə)r\ *adj* [ME *stor, stur,* fr. OE *stōr;* akin to OFris *stōr* large, big, OS *stōri,* OHG *stuori,* ON *stōrr* large, big, Russ *staryĭ* old, Lith *storas* thick, OE *standan, stondan* to stand — more at STAND] **1** *chiefly Scot* : STRONG, HARDY **2** *chiefly Scot* : SEVERE, STERN, INFLEXIBLE **3** *obs* : having a coarse texture : ROUGH, STIFF **4** *chiefly Scot* : HARSH, RASPING, DEEP

²stour *also* **stoure** \"\ *n* -S [ME *stur, stour,* fr. OF *estor, estour, estur,* of Gmc origin; akin to OHG *sturm* storm, tumult, battle, combat — more at STORM] **1 a** *archaic* : BATTLE, FIGHT, CONFLICT **b** (1) *dial Brit* : TUMULT, UPROAR (2) *chiefly Scot* : STORM **2** *chiefly Scot* : DUST, POWDER **3 a** *archaic* : a time of tumult **b** *obs* (1) : TIME, OCCASION (2) : PLACE

³stour \"\ *vi* -ED/-ING/-S [alter. of ¹stir] *Scot* : to move quickly : FLY

stoury *also* **stour·ie** \ˈstüri\ *adj* [²stour + -y, -ie] **1** *dial Brit* : DUSTY **2** *dial Brit* : marked by driving snow

¹stoush \ˈstaush\ *vt* -ED/-ING/-ES [prob. of imit. origin] **1** *Austral* : to hit hard : STRIKE, THRASH **2** *Austral* : DEFEAT

²stoush \"\ *n* -ES *Austral* : FIGHT, BRAWL, VIOLENCE

¹stout \ˈsteüt\ *n* -S [ME, fr. OE *stūt;* prob. akin to ON *stūtr* horn, stump, ox — more at STOT] *dial Brit* : HORSEFLY

²stout \ˈstaut, *usu* -aud·+V\ *adj* -ER/-EST [ME, fr. OF *estout* bold, proud, arrogant, powerful, silly, of Gmc origin; akin to MLG *stolt* proud, arrogant, stately, MHG *stolz* proud, arrogant, stately, MD *stolt, stout* bold, brave, and prob. to OHG *stelza* stilt — more at STILT] **1 a** *obs* : FIERCE, MENACING **b** *archaic* : displaying insolent conceit : ARROGANT, HAUGHTY ⟨as ~ and proud as he were lord of all —Shak.⟩ **2** : characterized by physical or moral bravery : COURAGEOUS, VALIANT ⟨proves himself a ~ fellow in battle⟩ ⟨pioneers with strong backs and ~ hearts⟩ **3 a** *archaic* : expressive of opposition : DEFIANT, HOSTILE ⟨~ demeanor of the few bishops who refused to take the oaths —John Evelyn⟩ **b** *archaic* : unalterably set : OBSTINATE, STUBBORN ⟨this old ~ will and hardened heart —J.H.Newman⟩ **c** : perseveringly resolute : FIRM, STAUNCH ⟨a ~ pillar of the ... church —S.H.Holbrook⟩ **d** : relentlessly harsh : IMPLACABLE ⟨has now become a ~ foe of backsliders⟩ **4 a** : physically strong : LUSTY, POWERFUL ⟨the ~ vigorous frame ... fitted the peasant-preacher for the hard life he had chosen —J.R.Green⟩ **b** : sturdily constructed : DURABLE, SOLID ⟨their feet were protected by ~ boots —F.W.Mason⟩ ⟨~ wooden barricades ... have been built across the streets —Mollie Panter-Downes⟩ **c** : full of energy : VIGOROUS, FORCEFUL ⟨a ~ tail wind was giving a friendly boost —W.D. Patterson⟩ ⟨the nation is safer with ~ criticism going on in Washington —T.R.Ybarra⟩ **d** : physically healthy : HEARTY, ROBUST ⟨are you ~ enough to be the general nurse —Charles Lamb⟩ **e** : resistant to stress or pressure : TOUGH, RIGID ⟨a few yards of ~ rope for towing purposes —*Amer. Guide Series: Ariz.*⟩ ⟨room, within the ~ framework of routine, for more individual whim —Joyce Cary⟩ **5 a** : large in diameter — used of a plant or its parts ⟨a small tree with ~ spreading branches —W.C.L.Muenscher⟩ **b** : having body or substance — used esp. of liquor ⟨~ homemade beer —*Amer. Guide Series: Texas*⟩ **c** : excessively fat : CORPULENT, PORTLY ⟨a big ~ woman with ... an enormous bosom —Arnold Hill⟩ **d** : broad in proportion to length — used of an animal or its parts ⟨the vertebrae were ~ with slightly biconcave ends —W.E.Swinton⟩ **e** : of bulky proportions : HEAVY, THICK ⟨this ~ volume of over 400 pages —R.J.Cruikshank⟩ **syn** see FAT, STRONG

³stout \"\ *adv* [ME, fr. *stout,* adj.] *archaic* : STOUTLY

⁴stout \"\ *vi* -ED/-ING/-S [ME *stouten,* fr. *stout,* adj.] : to maintain a resolute or defiant attitude — usu. used in the phrase *to stout it out* ⟨a fool to resign ... he should have ~*ed* it out —Margaret Todd⟩

⁵stout \"\ *n* -S [²stout] **1** : a heavy-bodied brew that is darker and sweeter than porter and is made with roasted malt and a relatively high percentage of hops **2 a** : a fat person ⟨the genial ~ who sang —Bennett Cerf⟩ **b** : a clothing size designed for the large figure ⟨men's suits are available in longs, shorts, regulars, and ~s —*Women's Wear Daily*⟩

stout·en \ˈstautᵊn\ *vb* **stoutened; stoutened; stoutening** \-aút(ᵊ)niŋ\ **stoutens** [²stout + -en] *vt* : to make stout ⟨~ a resolve⟩ ~ *vi* : to become stout ⟨she's ~*ed* so she couldn't make the dress meet on her —Ellen Glasgow⟩

stouth \ˈstüth\ *n* [ME *stulth, stouth,* of Scand origin; akin to ON *stuldr* theft, *stela* to steal — more at STEAL] *Scot & dial Eng* : THEFT, ROBBERY

stouth and routh *n, Scot* : PLENTY

stouthearted \ˈ≈ˈ≈≈\ *adj* : having a stout heart or spirit: **a** : COURAGEOUS, VALIANT ⟨a ~ fellow who sustained the drag and turmoil of an active career in the deserts —Humphrey Bullock⟩ **b** : RECALCITRANT, STUBBORN ⟨hearken unto me, ye ~, that are far from righteousness —Isa 46:12(AV)⟩ — **stoutheart·ed·ly** *adv*

stoutheartedness *n* -ES : the quality or state of being stouthearted

stouth·rief \ˈstüth,rēf\ *also* **stouth·rife** \-rīf\ *n* [ME (Sc) *stouthreif,* fr. *stouth* + *reif*] *Scot* : robbery with violence

stout·ish \ˈstaud·ish\ *adj* : somewhat stout : inclined toward corpulence

stout·ly *adv* [ME, fr. *stout* + *-ly*] : in a stout manner: **a** : RESOLUTELY, STUBBORNLY ⟨stood ~ for the interests of the colony —J.T.Adams⟩ **b** : SOLIDLY, STRONGLY ⟨the square ordered to be ~ enclosed as protection in case of ... attack —*Amer. Guide Series: Del.*⟩ **c** : VIGOROUSLY ⟨applauded him ~ after each number —*New Yorker*⟩

stout·ness *n* -ES [ME *stoutnes,* fr. *stout* + *-nes* -ness] **1 a** *obs* : PRIDE, ARROGANCE **b** *archaic* : OBDURACY **c** : the quality or state of being strong physically or morally : FIRMNESS, FORTITUDE **2** : bulkiness of structure; *esp* : CORPULENCE

stouts *pl of* STOUT, *pres 3d sing of* STOUT

¹stove \ˈstōv\ *n* -S *often attrib* [ME, fr. MD or MLG, heated room, steam room; akin to OE *stofa* steam room, OHG *stuba* heated room, steam room, ON *stofa;* all fr. a prehistoric WGmc-NGmc word derived fr. (assumed) VL *extufa,* fr. *extufare* to heat with steam, fr. L *ex-* ¹ex- + (assumed) VL *tufus* steam, fr. Gk *typhos* smoke, steam — more at TYPHUS] **1** *obs* **a** : a steam room or hot air chamber for inducing sweating : STEW ⟨you shall sweat there ... as well as in all the ~s in Sweden —Ben Jonson⟩ **b** : a room heated by a furnace ⟨found him in his ~ with one hand dandling his child ... in the other holding a book —Thomas Fuller⟩ **2 a** : an apparatus (as a fixed or portable container of iron or porcelain) that burns fuel for cooking or heating — compare FRANKLIN STOVE, OIL-STOVE, OVEN, POTBELLY, RANGE **b** : a device that generates heat for special purposes (as for heating tools or heating air for a hot blast) — compare CHECKERWORK 3 **c** : KILN **d** : FOOT STOVE **e** *Brit* : GRATE **3** *chiefly Brit* : a hothouse usu. having a controlled humid atmosphere and used esp. for the cultivation of tropical exotics ⟨orchids requiring ~ conditions⟩; *broadly* : GREENHOUSE

²stove \"\ *vt* -ED/-ING/-S **1 a** *archaic* : to keep (a person) in a heated room ⟨mistaken medical opinions ... induced physicians to ~ their patients —Thomas Beddoes⟩ **b** : to subject to heat : dry in or as if in a stove ⟨the bars of soap ... are *stoved* by being placed on shallow trays in stacks in a long rectangular tunnel —T.P.Hilditch⟩ ⟨dirty clay pipes were *stoved* in a brick oven and restored —F.W.Burgess⟩ **2** *chiefly Brit* : to raise (plants) in a stove (sense 3) **3** *chiefly Scot* : STEW **4 a** : to expose (as damp yarn or cloth to be bleached or clothing to be disinfected) to sulfur dioxide **b** : to treat (a silk cocoon) with heat to kill the chrysalis

³stove *past of* STAVE

⁴stove \ˈstōv\ *vt* -ED/-ING/-S [fr. *stove,* past part. of ²stave] : STAVE 2

stove bolt *n* : a bolt with a round or flat slotted head and a square nut, resembling a machine screw but usu. having coarser threads and used for joining metal parts — see BOLT illustration

stove coal *n* : anthracite coal of a medium size but larger than chestnut — see ANTHRACITE table

stove distillate *n* : a distilled petroleum oil suitable for use in stoves

stove-in \ˈ≈ˈ≈\ *adj* [fr. past part. of *stave in,* v.] **1** : smashed inward ⟨a *stove-in* barrel —Cicely F. Smith⟩ **2** : STOVE-UP ⟨a *stove-in* horse —S.S.Field⟩

stove length *n* : a length of firewood suitable for use in a stove

stove lifter *n* : LIFTER 2d

¹sto·ven \ˈstōvən\ *n* -S [ME, fr. OE *stofn;* akin to ON *stofn* stump of a tree, *stūfr* stump — more at STUB] *dial Brit* : STUMP

²stoven \"\ *adj* [*stove* (past part. of ²stave) + *-en* (as in *gotten*)] : broken in : STAVED, SMASHED

stovepipe \ˈ≈,≈\ *n* **1** : pipe of large diameter usu. made of sheet steel in lengths and angular or curved pieces and used as a stove chimney or to connect a stove with a flue **2** *or* **stovepipe hat** : a very tall silk hat

stove plant *n* : a plant from a warm climate that has to be grown in a greenhouse to survive in temperate climates

stove polish *n* : a blacking (as graphite) used for polishing stoves

¹sto·ver \ˈstōvə(r)\ *n* -S [ME, modif. of AF *estovers* — more at ESTOVERS] **1** *dial chiefly Eng* : FODDER; *esp* : fodder for use in winter **2** : HAY, STUBBLE; *esp* : the refuse of a field crop (as the stalks and leaves of corn after the ears are harvested) used as feed for cattle ⟨corn ~⟩ ⟨sorghum ~⟩ — compare CORN FODDER

²stov·er \"\ *n* -S [²stove + *-er*] *chiefly Brit* : one that stoves; *esp* : a worker who tends a drying stove

stoves *pl of* STOVE, *pres 3d sing of* STOVE

stove-up \ˈ≈ˈ≈\ *adj* [fr. past part. of *stave up,* v.] : suffering physical discomfort caused by injury, illness, exercise, or overwork : BATTERED, WORN-OUT ⟨horses ... too old and *stove-up* for saddle work —F.B.Gipson⟩ ⟨several of the men were *stove-up* ... and even some of the women showed signs of having been kicked or stepped on —H.L.Davis⟩

stovewood \ˈ≈,≈\ *n* : wood sawed into stove lengths

¹stow \ˈstō\ *vb* -ED/-ING/-S [ME *stowen, stowe,* n., place, fr. OE *stōw;* akin to OFris *stō* place, OHG *stouwen* to complain, accuse, command, ON eld*stō* hearth, Goth *stojan* to judge, Gk *stylos* pillar — more at STEER] *vt* **1 a** *obs* : to put in a particular spot : PLACE ⟨his eye had ~*ed* her in his heart —William Warner⟩ **b** : to find at least temporary quarters for : HOUSE, LODGE ⟨~*ed* the patient in the hospital emergency room⟩ **2** *obs* : to put to use : BESTOW, SPEND ⟨there ~s his treasure —Edward Young⟩ **3 a** : to put away : keep in reserve : STORE ⟨small buildings where fishermen ~*ed* their gear —S.T. Williamson⟩ ⟨grabs the sheep and ~s it in the tucker-bag —William Power⟩ — often used with *away* ⟨taking his hat off, and wiping his head with the handkerchief ~*ed* away in its crown —Mary S. Broome⟩ **b** *obs* : to lock up for safekeeping : CONFINE ⟨the mariners all under hatches ~*ed* —Shak.⟩ **c** : to roll up (a sail) : FURL ⟨~ the jib⟩ **4 a** : to dispose in an orderly fashion : ARRANGE, PACK ⟨the cargo was ~*ed* in a thoroughly workmanlike ... manner —F.W.Crofts⟩ ⟨went on ~*ing* cigarettes on the shelf —David Ballantyne⟩ **b** : to fill with cargo : LOAD ⟨six warships ... ~*ed* to the hatches with scientific gear —Julian Dana⟩ **5** *slang* : to put aside : save for another time : STOP ⟨those ... not asking questions told those who were to ~ it, and give the lieutenant a chance —Frances & Richard Lockridge⟩ **6 a** *archaic* : to fill with contents : CROWD ⟨compared his mind to the magazine of a pawnbroker, ~*ed* with goods of every description —Sir Walter Scott⟩ **b** : to cram in (food) — usu. used with *away* ⟨the more of this heavenly food you can ~ away, the more you are admired —Hugh Cave⟩ **c** : to fill up (as a stope) with waste ~ *vi* : to fit into a storage space : PACK, STORE ⟨a stout rope ladder ... which ~s neatly in a box on the floor —P.W.Kearney⟩ ⟨the anchor ~s at the hawsepipe —A.M.Knight⟩ **syn** see SET

²stow \ˈstü, ˈstaü\ *vt* [origin unknown] *Scot & dial Eng* : CUT, CROP, TRIM

³stow *n* -S [by alter.] *obs* : STOVE

⁴stow \ˈstō\ *n* -S [by shortening] : STOWBORD

stow *abbr* stowage

stowable \ˈstōəbəl\ *adj* : capable of being stowed

stow·age \ˈstōij, -ōēj\ *n* -S [ME, fr. *stowen* to stow + *-age*] **1 a** : an act or process of stowing ⟨facilitate the ~ of wine casks —G.S.L.Clowes⟩ **b** : goods in storage or to be stowed ⟨crates and other ~ piled up on the dock⟩ **c** : the manner of stowing ⟨faulty ~ ... causes a cargo shift —E.B.Garside⟩ **2 a** : storage capacity ⟨she has excellent ~ for food and water —Peter Heaton⟩ **b** : a place or receptacle for storage ⟨a ~ in a London granary containing 500 tons of ... wheat —R.W. Owen⟩ ⟨booms situated amidships ... constituted the ~ for spare spars —*Manual of Seamanship*⟩ **3** : STORAGE ⟨jewels of rich and exquisite form ... and I am something curious, being strange, to have them in safe ~ —Shak.⟩

stow away *vi* : to secrete oneself aboard a vehicle as a means of obtaining transportation ⟨escaped internment by *stowing away* in an automobile trunk —*Newsweek*⟩

stowaway \ˈ≈≈,≈\ *n* -S [*stow away*] **1** : an unregistered passenger : one who stows away ⟨tickets were inspected and three ~s thrown off —John Masters⟩ **2** : a hiding place ⟨the window-seat top lifts up, and this makes another good ~ for toys —*London Daily Express*⟩

stow·bord *also* **stow·board** \ˈstō,bōrd\ *n* -S [*stowbord* alter. of *stowboard; stowboard* fr. ²stow + *board*] : a heading used by miners for stowing rubbish or waste

stowce *or* **stowse** \ˈstōs\ *n* -S [origin unknown] *archaic* : a windlass for hoisting ore

¹stow·er \ˈstauə(r)\ *n* -S [ME *stower, store,* of Scand origin; akin to ON *staurr* pole, stake — more at STEER] *dial Brit* : POLE, POST; *specif* : a punting pole

²stower \"\ *var of* ¹STOUR

³stow·er \ˈstō(ə)r\ *n* -S [¹stow + *-er*] : one that stows; *esp* : STEVEDORE

stown [ME (Sc) *stowin,* alter. of ME *stolen,* fr. OE] *dial chiefly Brit past part of* STEAL

stownet \ˈ≈,≈\ *n* [¹stow + *net*] : a funnel-shaped sprat trawl usu. made with several sections of different mesh which diminishes in size toward the small end and usu. anchored in a tideway

stowre \ˈstü(ə)r\ *var of* ¹STOUR

stows *pres 3d sing of* STOW, *pl of* STOW

stp *abbr* **1** stamp; stamped **2** stepping **3** stop; stopping

STP *abbr* standard temperature and pressure

stpd *abbr* stumped

str *abbr* **1** seater **2** steamer **3** straight **4** strainer **5** strait **6** stream **7** strength **8** stretch **9** striking **10** string; stringed **11** stroke **12** strophe **13** structural

STR *abbr* submarine thermal reactor

stra·bis·mal \strəˈbizməl\ *adj* [NL *strabismus* + E *-al*] : of, relating to, or typical of strabismus — **stra·bis·mal·ly** \-məlē\ *adv*

stra·bis·mic \-mik\ *adj* [NL *strabismus* + E *-ic*] **1** : STRABISMAL **2** : failing to perceive clearly or accurately : not based on straight clear observation or analysis ⟨a ~ judgment⟩

stra·bis·mom·e·ter \≈ˈ≈ˈmämәd-ə(r)\ *n* [NL *strabismus* + E *-o-* + *-meter*] : an instrument for measuring the degree of strabismus

strabis·mom·e·try \-ə·trē\ *n* -ES [NL *strabismus* + E *-o-* + *-metry*] : measurement of the degree of strabismus

stra·bis·mus \strəˈbizməs\ *n* -ES [NL, fr. Gk *strabismos,* act or condition of squinting, fr. *strabizein* to squint, fr. *strabos* squint-eyed + *-izein* -ize — more at STROPHE] : inability of one eye to attain binocular vision with the other because of imbalance of the extrinsic eye muscles — called also *manifest strabismus, squint;* see LATENT STRABISMUS

strad \ˈstrad, -aa(ə)d\ *n* -S *usu cap* [by shortening] : STRADIVARIUS

¹strad·dle \ˈstradᵊl\ *vb* **straddled; straddled; straddling** \-d(ᵊ)liŋ\ **straddles** [irreg. fr. *stride*] *vi* **1 a** : to part the legs wide : stand, sit, or walk, with the legs wide apart; *esp* : to sit astride **b** *of the legs* : to spread apart **2** : to spread out irregularly : SPRAWL ⟨branches *straddled* in every direction⟩ **3** : to be noncommittal : favor or seem to favor two apparently opposite sides **4** : to buy in one market and sell short in an-

other ~ *vt* **1 :** to stand, sit, or be astride of **2 :** to be noncommittal in regard to **:** favor or seem to favor both sides of ⟨~ an issue⟩ **3 :** to double (the blind) in playing poker **4 a :** to bracket with artillery fire **b :** to land a straddle on — used esp. of a firing ship with respect to a target

²straddle \"\ *n* -s **1 a :** the act or position of one who straddles **:** the act of standing, sitting, or walking, with the legs wide apart **b :** the distance between the feet or legs of one straddling **2 :** something that straddles or suggests straddling (as in sprawling irregular form or bracketing relation): as **a :** a vertical post (as one of those which support a horizontal set in a mine shaft) **b :** a gunnery salvo landing with part of its shots short of the target and part over the target **3 :** a noncommittal or equivocal position; *also* **:** assumption of such a position (as in politics) **4 a :** an option giving the holder the right to demand of the seller that he deliver at a particular price or compel him to accept at the same price within a specified time specified securities or commodities — compare SPREAD **b :** the state of being long in one market and short in another **5 :** a doubling of the blind in a draw poker game

³straddle \"\ *adv* [²*straddle*] **:** ASTRADDLE

straddleback \ˈ==,=\ *adv* **:** ASTRADDLE

straddlebug \ˈ==,=\ *n* **1 :** a long-legged insect (as a tumblebug) **2 :** a wooden tripod used to mark a boundary (as of a mining claim) **3 :** STRADDLE CARRIER

straddle carrier *n* **:** a vehicle that straddles a pile of lumber or other material, lifts it with adjustable arms, and moves it or loads it onto trucks or other vehicles

straddle–face \ˈ==,=\ *vt* **:** to face with a straddle mill

straddle–fashion \ˈ==ˈ==\ *adv* **:** ASTRADDLE

straddle–legged \ˈ==ˈlegəd, *esp Brit* -gd\ *adv (or adj)* **:** with the legs wide apart **:** astride of something **:** ASTRADDLE

straddle mill *n* **:** a side milling cutter esp. when used in pairs a fixed distance apart so as to straddle the work

strad·dler \ˈstrad(ᵊ)lə(r)\ *n* -s **:** one that straddles: as **a** *Brit* **:** a tool that straddles a railroad rail to bear upon the projecting ends of a tie plate and is used in driving tie plates into the track **b :** a weeding hoe that straddles a row

straddle trench *n* **:** a trench used as a latrine

straddle truck *n* **:** STRADDLE CARRIER

straddle vault *n* **:** a gymnastic vault in which the body passes over the apparatus in a sitting position with the legs spread wide to each side

straddleways \ˈ==,=\ *adv* **:** in a straddling manner

straddlewise \ˈ==,=\ *adv* **:** STRADDLEWAYS

strad·dling·ly *adv* **:** in a straddling manner **:** so as to straddle

strad·i·ot \ˈstradēət, *usu* -əd·+V\ *n* -s [MF, fr. It *stradiotto;* fr. Gk *stratiōtēs* soldier, fr. *stratia* army, military campaign, fr. *stratos* army, host — more at STRATUM] **:** a light cavalryman recruited esp. from Albania, Dalmatia, or Greece and employed in the Venetian and other armies in the 15th and 16th centuries

stradi·vari \,stradəˈvärē, ,sträd-, ,stradəˈva(a)rē\ *n* -s *usu cap* [after Antonio *Stradivari* †1737 Ital. violin maker] **:** STRADIVARIUS

stradi·vari·us \,stradəˈva(a)rēəs, ,strädəˈvärēəs\ *n* -ES *usu cap* [after Antonius *Stradivarius* (latinization of *Antonio Stradivari*)] **:** a stringed instrument (as a violin) made by Antonio Stradivari of Cremona whose instruments are famed for beauty of tone and design

¹strafe \ˈstrāf *sometimes* -raf *or* -räf\ *vt* -ED/-ING/-S [fr. the G phrase *Gott strafe England* God punish England, popular as a slogan of the Germans in World War I] **1 :** to rake (as ground troops or an airfield) with fire at close range and esp. with machine-gun fire from low-flying airplanes or formerly with artillery fire **2 :** to censure savagely — **straf·er** \-fə(r)\ *n* -s

²strafe \"\ *n* -s **:** a strafing attack

straf·for·di·an \strəˈfördēən\ *n* -s *usu cap* [Thomas Wentworth, 1st Earl of *Strafford* †1641 Eng. statesman + E *-ian*] **:** a follower of Thomas Wentworth, Earl of Strafford, esp. in the House of Commons in 1641

¹strag·gle \ˈstragəl, -raig-\ *vb* **straggled; straggled; straggling** \-g(ə)liŋ\ **straggles** [ME *straglen,* perh. irreg. fr. *straken* to move, proceed; akin to OE *streccan* to stretch — more at STRETCH] *vi* **1 :** to wander from the direct course or way **:** ROVE, STRAY; *specif* **:** to wander from a line of march or desert a line of battle **2 :** to wander off or become separated from others of its kind **:** be, become, or occur as if dispersed ⟨branches that ~ out too far⟩ ⟨hair *straggling* over her collar⟩ ~ *vt* **:** to spread scatteringly ⟨shabby houses were *straggled* along the slope⟩

²straggle \"\ *n* -s **:** a straggling body or arrangement (as of persons or objects) ⟨a man . . . with a ~ of a beard —J.C. Snaith⟩ ⟨a ~ of outbuildings⟩ ⟨a little ~ of mourners —Elizabeth Bowen⟩

strag·gler \-g(ə)lə(r)\ *n* -s [¹*straggle* + *-er*] **:** one that rambles without settled direction: as **a** *obs* **:** VAGABOND, TRAMP **b :** one that is separated by wandering off in some irregular manner from others ⟨crop the ~s in the hedge⟩ **c :** one that departs from the company to which he belongs or from the direct or proper course (as a bird that strays out of its usual range) ⟨sent a crew to round up the ~s from the herd⟩ **d** (1) **:** a soldier who wanders from his unit on the march or from the area assigned his unit (2) **:** a man who has been an unauthorized absentee from naval service for more than 72 hours but who has not been absent long enough to have been declared a deserter

straggling *n* -s [fr. gerund of ¹*straggle*] **:** the condition of one that straggles; *esp* **:** a statistical variation in some property (as in range or angle of travel of particles passing through matter)

strag·gling·ly *adv* [*straggling* (pres. part. of ¹*straggle*) + *-ly*] **:** in a straggling manner **:** so as to straggle

strag·gly \-g(ə)lē, -li\ *adj* -ER/-EST [¹*straggle* + *-y*] **:** spread out or scattered irregularly and without planned order **:** arranged as if by straggling into place ⟨a ~ hamlet⟩ ⟨a ~ beard⟩

strag·u·lum \ˈstragyələm\ *n, pl* **stragu·la** \-lə\ [NL, fr. L, covering, spread; akin to L *sternere* to spread out, strew — more at STREW] **:** the mantle of a bird

¹straight \ˈstrāt, *usu* -ād·+V\ *adv* -ER/-EST [ME *streght, streit,* fr. past part. of *strecchen* to stretch] **:** without deviation, delay, or other interruption: as **a :** in a manner involving no hesitation or delay **:** STRAIGHTWAY, IMMEDIATELY ⟨come ~ home⟩ **b :** in a direct and uninterrupted course **:** without curving or turning aside **:** DIRECTLY ⟨the arrow flew ~ to the mark⟩ ⟨the road ran ~ for several miles⟩; *also* **:** so as to penetrate usu. without deviation from course ⟨bored a hole ~ through the wall⟩ ⟨the tunnel goes ~ through the mountain⟩ **c :** with the body erect **:** UPRIGHT ⟨sentinel pines stood ~ along the crest⟩ **d :** in an honest or honorable manner ⟨a man willing to run ~ should make a success of this business⟩ ⟨swore to go ~ if he got out of the mess⟩ **e :** without hesitation or equivocation **:** STRAIGHTFORWARDLY, OPENLY ⟨~ denied the charge⟩ ⟨told him ~ we'd stand for no more loafing and neglect⟩

²straight \"\ *adj* -ER/-EST [ME *streght, streit, straight,* fr. past part. of *strecchen* to stretch] **1 a :** free from curves, bends, or angles **:** having no irregularities in course ⟨~ hair⟩ ⟨fine ~ timber⟩ ⟨an unusually ~ stream⟩ **b :** of, relating to, or constituting a one-dimensional continuum that is determined throughout its length by any two points included in it **:** taking the course like that of a taut uninterrupted cord made fast at opposite ends **:** progressing or projected in an unvarying direction **2 :** DIRECT, UNINTERRUPTED: as **a** (1) **:** leading or passing directly from one point to another ⟨sought a ~*er* way from his home to the office⟩ (2) **:** holding to a direct or proper course or method **:** proceeding directly and without disorder or confusion ⟨~ reasoning⟩ ⟨a ~ thinker⟩ **b :** CANDID, FRANK, STRAIGHTFORWARD ⟨a ~ speech⟩ ⟨a ~ answer to the charge⟩ **c :** coming directly from a trustworthy source ⟨a ~ tip on the horses⟩ **d :** composed of elements arranged in some logical order (as of descending values) ⟨following the ~ sequence of events⟩ **e :** having the cylinders of an internal-combustion engine arranged in a single straight line **f** *of type matter* **:** set in ordinary paragraphs of uniform width and without display lines, tabular matter, varied typefaces, or other features that tend to slow production **3** *chiefly Scot, of a mountain* **:** STEEP **4 a :** exhibiting no deviation from the vertical or horizontal **:** not leaning, bending, or inclining ⟨the picture is not quite ~⟩ **b** *of a cricket bat* **:** held with blade at right angles to the ground **5 :** exhibiting no deviation from what is established or accepted as usual, normal, or proper: as **a :** conforming to justice and rectitude **:** exhibiting truth, fairness, and honesty **:** UPRIGHT, FAIR, VIRTUOUS ⟨a ~ man of business⟩ ⟨known for his ~ dealing⟩ **b :** properly ordered or arranged **:** free from irregularity or confusion **:** correctly kept **:** CORRECT, NEAT ⟨in the general confusion, this room alone was ~⟩ ⟨his accounts were found to be ~⟩ ⟨set the kitchen ~⟩ **c :** free from extraneous matter **:** UNMIXED, UNDILUTED, UNMODIFIED ⟨played a ~ old rule game⟩ ⟨writes ~ humor⟩ **d :** making no exceptions or deviations in one's support of something accepted as right (as a principle, policy, party) ⟨a ~ Republican⟩; *also* **:** cast for all the regular candidates of a party ⟨a ~ ballot⟩ **e :** having a fixed price for each regardless of the number sold ⟨cigars 10 cents ~⟩ **f** (1) **:** not deviating from the general norm of human personality — used of dramatic representation or performers ⟨a ~ part⟩ ⟨an excellent ~ actor⟩ (2) *of music* **:** played or to be played as written usu. without improvisation or syncopation **g :** STRAIGHT-TIME **6 :** SEVERE, RIGID, STERN, RIGOROUS **7** *of a credit obligation* **a :** made without special security or endorsement **b :** repayable in full on a specified maturity date

³straight \"\ *vt* -ED/-ING/-S [ME *streghten* (Sc *strauchten*), fr. *streght* straight] **1** *obs* **:** STRETCH **2** *chiefly Scot* **:** STRAIGHTEN

⁴straight \"\ *n* -s [²*straight*] **1 :** something that is straight: as **a :** a straight line or arrangement ⟨the garden was laid out on the ~⟩ **b :** a level place, part, or area **:** PLAIN **c :** a straight extent (as of a road) **:** STRAIGHTAWAY; *esp* **:** the portion of a racetrack between the last turn and the winning post **d :** a true, honest, upright report or way of life **:** one involving no concealment, trickery, or dishonesty ⟨tell us the ~ of it⟩ ⟨had been on the ~ for several years⟩ **e :** a shoe adapted for wear on either foot and made with no deviation in the forepart of the foot in relation to the heel **f :** GRAIN 6d **2 a :** a sequence (as of shots, strokes, or moves) resulting in a perfect score in a game or contest **b :** first place at the finish of a horse race **:** WIN — compare PLACE, SHOW **3 :** a combination in a poker hand that consists of five cards in sequence but not all in the same suit and beats three of a kind but loses to a flush — see POKER illustration — **out of straight :** CROOKED, AWRY

straight a *adj, usu cap A* [²*straight* + *a*] **:** having or constituting a first-class record of achievement ⟨a *straight A* student through high school⟩

straight accent *n* **:** MACRON

straight and narrow *n* [prob. fr. ¹*strait;* fr. the admonition of Mt 7:14(AV), "strait is the gate and narrow is the way which leadeth unto life"] **:** the way of propriety and rectitude — used with *the* ⟨kept to the *straight and narrow* for the rest of his life⟩

straight angle *n* [²*straight*] **:** an angle whose sides lie in the same straight line but extend in opposite directions from the vertex **:** one that is equivalent to one half a complete turn, π radians, 180 degrees, or two right angles — compare ROUND ANGLE; see ANGLE illustration

straight arch *n* **:** a flat arch

¹straight–arm \ˈ=ˈ=\ *n* **:** an act or instance of warding off a football tackler with the arm fully extended from the shoulder, elbow locked, and the palm of the hand placed firmly against any part of his body — called also *stiff-arm*

²straight–arm \"\ *vt* **1 :** to ward off (an opponent) with or as if with a straight-arm **2 :** to clear (a passage) by using a straight-arm ~ *vi* **:** to use a straight-arm in warding off an opponent

¹straightaway \ˈ==,=\ *adj* [fr. the phrase *straight away,* fr. ¹*straight* + *away*] **1 a :** moving or projected away and on a straight or direct course ⟨a ~ shot at a low-flying bird⟩ ⟨a ~ bird⟩ ⟨a plane in ~ flight⟩ **b :** acting in one direction ⟨a ~ napper for textiles⟩ **2 :** constituting a straightaway ⟨the longest ~ bar in the hemisphere —Horace Sutton⟩ ⟨a ~ track⟩ **3 a :** constituting or presented in the form of an orderly progression ⟨a ~ story⟩ **b :** free from confusing disorder **:** CLEAR, STRAIGHTFORWARD ⟨written sometimes in ~ English, sometimes in lyrical double-talk —*Time*⟩ **4 :** IMMEDIATE ⟨a ~ gain in income⟩ ⟨made a ~ reply⟩

²straightaway \"\ *n* -s **:** a straight course: as **a :** the straight part of a closed racecourse; *also* **:** something that is straight **b :** a straight and unimpeded stretch on a highway or waterway

³straightaway \"\ *adv* **1 :** without hesitation or delay **:** IMMEDIATELY ⟨found an answer ~⟩ **2 :** from a straight position and without anticipatory shifts ⟨a baseball player who hits ~⟩

straight–backed \ˈ=ˈ=\ *also* **straight–back** \ˈ=ˈ=\ *adj* **:** having a straight back ⟨a *straight-backed* chair⟩

straight–billed curlew \ˈ=ˈ=-\ *n* **:** MARBLED GODWIT

straight bill of lading *n* **:** a nonnegotiable shipping document prescribed by law and consigning goods to a specific party — compare ORDER BILL OF LADING

straightbred \ˈ=ˈ=\ *adj* **1 :** carrying blood of a single breed, strain, or type ⟨a ~ Angus heifer⟩ — compare CROSSBRED **2 :** descended in all lines from one specified ancestor — compare LINEBRED

straight chain *n* **:** an open chain of atoms having no side chains (as the sequence of carbon atoms in normal butane $CH_3-CH_2-CH_2-CH_3$) — opposed to *branched chain*

straight–cut \ˈ=ˈ=\ *adj* **:** having the leaves cut lengthwise — used of smoking tobacco

straight dye *n* **:** a dye containing not more than a small amount (as less than 5 percent) of admixed substances excluding salt

straight dynamite *n* **:** DYNAMITE 1b

¹straightedge \ˈ=,=\ *n* [²*straight* + *edge*] **1 :** a bar or piece of wood, metal, or plastic (as a board or rule) having one or more long edges made straight within a desired degree of accuracy and used esp. for testing straight lines and surfaces or drawing straight lines **2 :** STRAIGHT RAZOR

²straightedge \"\ *vt* **:** to make the edge of (work) straight **:** test with a straightedge

straight·en \ˈstrātᵊn\ *vb* **straightened; straightened; straightening** \-t(ᵊ)niŋ\ **straightens** [²*straight* + *-en*] *vt* **:** to make straight: as **a :** to alter from a crooked to a straight form **:** cause to become straight or extended ⟨exercise helped to ~ the injured arm⟩ — sometimes used with *out* ⟨~*ed* himself out on the couch⟩ **b :** to make correct **:** put in order — usu. used with *out* or *up* ⟨~ out your accounts⟩ ⟨had to ~ up the house⟩ ⟨the doctor ~*ed* out her trouble⟩ **c :** to put on the correct road or course (as by reforming or explaining) — usu. used with *out* ⟨discipline without love never ~*ed* out anyone⟩ ⟨he misunderstood but a few words should ~ him out⟩ ~ *vi* **:** to become straight: as **a :** to bring the body to an erect position ⟨the wilting flowers ~*ed* in the rain⟩ — usu. used with *up* ⟨~ up, there's no excuse for slouching⟩ **b :** to alter for the better **:** reach a desirable adjustment — usu. used with *out* and sometimes with *up* ⟨determined to ~ up and make something of himself⟩ ⟨these problems tend to ~ out automatically⟩ — **straighten one's face :** to compose one's features **:** assume an aspect of sober concentration

straight·en·er \-t(ᵊ)nə(r)\ *n* -s **:** one that straightens ⟨a hair ~⟩; *esp* **:** one whose work is straightening or making level by hand or by machine

straighter *comparative of* STRAIGHT

straightest *superlative of* STRAIGHT

straight face *n* **:** a face giving no evidence of emotion and esp. of merriment — **straight–faced** \ˈ=ˈ=\ *adj*

straight flour *n* **:** flour recovered from bolted wheat meal and containing the whole product of milling except bran and shorts

straight flush *n* **:** a poker hand containing five cards of the same suit in sequence and except when there are wild cards being the highest-ranking hand — see ROYAL FLUSH; POKER illustration

straight–flute \ˈ=ˈ=\ *or* **straight–fluted** \ˈ=ˈ==\ *adj, of a drill* **:** having straight flutes

straightforth \ˈ=ˈ=\ *adv, archaic* **:** STRAIGHTFORWARD, STRAIGHTWAY

¹straightforward \ˈ=ˈ==\ *also* **straightforwards** \(ˈ)=ˈ==\ *adv* [¹*straight* + *forward, forwards*] **:** in a straightforward manner

²straightforward \"\ *adj* **1 :** proceeding in a straight course or manner **:** leading directly onward **:** DIRECT, UNDEVIATING **2 a :** free from circumlocution or obscurity **:** OUTSPOKEN, CANDID, FRANK, HONEST ⟨a ~ account of the accident⟩ ⟨their behavior was perfectly ~⟩ **b :** accurately defined or definable **:** CLEARCUT, PRECISE ⟨their responsibility is ~⟩ ⟨a case of ~ automatism⟩ — **straight·for·ward·ly** *adv* — **straight·for·ward·ness** *n* -ES

straight–from–the–shoulder \ˈ=ˈ===ˈ==\ *adj* [*straight from the shoulder,* phrase applied to a blow in boxing] **:** characterized by bold vigor of thought and presentation and by freedom from mincing or quibbling ⟨a *straight-from-the-shoulder* analysis of the problem⟩

straight–front \ˈ=ˈ=\ *adj* **:** having a straight front, edge, border, or other leading part

straight grain *n* **:** grain in wood characterized by wood fibers that run parallel to the long axis of the piece; *also* **:** a graining (as of leather) in which the distinctive elements run in straight lines — **straight–grained** \ˈ=ˈ=\ *adj*

straighthead \ˈ=,=\ *n* **:** a disease of the rice plant in which the heads remain sterile and therefore erect when normal heads are drooping and which is caused by disturbed water relations

straightheaded \ˈ=ˈ==\ *adj* [²*straight* + *headed*] **:** SQUARE-HEADED ⟨a ~ window⟩

straight hit *n, chiefly Austral* **:** a fielding position in cricket between long on and long off and usu. near the boundary; *also* **:** a player fielding in this position

straighting *pres part of* STRAIGHT

straight internship *n* **:** a medical internship in which the intern works under supervision in a single department or service ⟨had his *straight internship* in surgery⟩ — compare ROTATING INTERNSHIP

straight·ish \ˈstrād·ish, -āt|, |ēsh\ *adj* **:** somewhat straight

straightjacket *var of* STRAITJACKET

straight joint *n* **1 :** a continuous floor joint transverse to the length of the boards **2 :** a joint between pieces of wood without tongues, dowels, or other fittings — called also *square joint*

straight–laced *var of* STRAITLACED

straight life annuity *n* **:** an annuity for life **:** LIFE ANNUITY

straight life insurance *n* **:** ORDINARY LIFE INSURANCE

straight line *n* **:** a curve traced by a point traveling invariably in the same direction **:** a one-dimensional continuum of zero curvature **:** the collection of all points whose coordinates satisfy a linear equation in two-dimensional geometry or two simultaneous linear equations in three-dimensional geometry

straight–line \ˈ=ˈ=\ *adj* **1 :** being a mechanical linkage or equivalent device designed to produce or copy motion in a straight or approximately straight line **2 a :** having the principal parts arranged in a straight line ⟨a *straight-line* compressor having the steam and air cylinders in a straight line⟩ **b :** relating to or constituting a production system with parts or facilities arranged for performance of consecutive operations without backtracking or deviating from a straightforward course ⟨plant layout on a *straight-line* basis⟩ ⟨savings effected by *straight-line* organization⟩ **3 :** spread uniformly or spreading accumulation or payments uniformly and esp. in equal segments over a course covering a given term ⟨*straight-line* amortization of the discount on bonds⟩ ⟨comparison of results from a *straight-line* and a sinking-fund method⟩

straight–lined \ˈ=ˈ=\ *adj* **:** having straight lines **:** RECTILINEAR, UNDEVIATING; *also* **:** arranged in straight lines

straight–line depreciation *n* **:** periodic reduction in the book value of an asset by a fixed percentage of its original cost based on its estimated life — compare DEPRECIATION CHARGE

straight–line frequency condenser *n* **:** a variable condenser used in a tuned radio circuit in which a given change of setting of the movable plates corresponds to the same change of frequency for all settings

straight–line gale *n* **1 :** a gale of several days' duration blowing over the same region and from the same quarter **2 :** a long streak of violent wind not related to any deflection of isobars

straight–line method *n* **:** a method of calculating periodic depreciation that involves subtraction of the scrap value from the cost of a depreciable asset and division of the resultant figure by the anticipated number of periods of useful life of the asset — compare COMPOUND-INTEREST METHOD

straight–line rate *n* **:** a rate based on a straight price for each unit

straight·ly *adv* [ME, fr. ²*straight* + *-ly*] **:** in a straight manner **:** so as to be straight

straight man *n* **:** an actor or other entertainer whose main function is to feed lines to a comedian

straightneck \ˈ=,=\ *n* **:** a squash of summer crookneck type but having a straight neck

straight·ness *n* -ES **:** the quality or state of being straight

straight–of–breadth \,=ˈ=ˈ=\ *n* **:** DEAD FLAT

straight off *adv* [¹*straight* + *off*] **:** immediately and without hesitation **:** at once

straight organ *n* **:** a pipe organ containing no borrowed or unified stops

straight out *adv* **:** without concealment or hesitation **:** DIRECTLY ⟨told the whole story *straight out*⟩

¹straight–out \ˈ=ˈ=\ *n* -s [*straight out*] **:** a person who is uncompromising esp. in adhering to a political party or policy

²straight–out \ˈ=ˈ=\ *adj* [*straight out*] **1 :** acting without concealment, obliquity, or compromise **2 :** being such and no other **:** UNQUALIFIED, THOROUGHGOING ⟨*straight-out* resentment⟩

straight paper *n* [²*straight*] **:** negotiable paper signed or endorsed by one individual

straight peen *n* **:** a narrow round-edged peen of a hammer that is parallel to the handle — see PEEN illustration

straight poker *n* **:** closed poker in which players bet on the five cards dealt to them and then have a showdown without drawing

straight–pull \ˈ=ˈ=\ *adj, of a firearm* **:** having the motion of the bolt straight forward and back so that the locking and unlocking is effected without rotation ⟨a *straight-pull* rifle⟩

straight rail *n* **:** a carom billiards game in which points are scored by causing the cue ball with or without cushion contact to strike both object balls simultaneously or alternately

straight razor *n* **:** a razor with a rigid steel cutting blade that is hinged to a case which forms a handle when the razor is open for use — see RAZOR illustration

straight–run \ˈ=ˈ=\ *adj* **1 :** involving or produced in the course of petroleum refining by fractionation essentially without cracking or other pyrolytic change ⟨*straight-run* distillation⟩ ⟨*straight-run* gasoline⟩ **2** *of chicks* **:** sold as hatched; *specif* **:** not sexed

straights *pres 3d sing of* STRAIGHT, *pl of* STRAIGHT

straight shooter *n* [¹*straight*] **:** a thoroughly upright straightforward person

straight–side \ˈ=ˈ=\ *or* **straight–sided** \ˈ=ˈ==\ *adj* [²*straight*] **:** having straight sides

straight sinus *n* **:** a venous sinus of the brain formed by junction of the great cerebral vein and inferior sagittal sinus and terminating by confluence with the right and left transverse sinuses

straight ticket *n* **:** a ballot cast for all the candidates of one party — compare SPLIT TICKET

straight time *n* **1 :** the regularly established working time of employees during a standard period (as a week) excluding time lost through absence or gained through overtime ⟨in most industries *straight time* still exceeds 35 hours a week⟩ **2 :** the rate of pay applicable for straight-time work ⟨had 40 hours at *straight time* and 12 hours of overtime pay⟩

straight–time \ˈ=ˈ=\ *adj* [*straight time*] **1 :** constituting or taking place in straight time ⟨*straight-time* work⟩ ⟨40 *straight-time* hours⟩ **2 :** constituting or fixed at a regular base rate per hour, day, week, or month and excluding any overtime pay, merit bonus, shift differential, or commission ⟨a two dollar an hour *straight-time* rate⟩ ⟨*straight-time* pay⟩

straight–up \ˈ=ˈ=\ *adj* [fr. the phrase *straight up,* fr. ¹*straight* + *up*] **1 :** ERECT, UPRIGHT, PERPENDICULAR ⟨lilies nodding from tall *straight-up* stalks⟩ **2 :** timed exactly **:** being or ending at precisely the time stated or desired ⟨*straight-up* noon⟩

¹straightway \ˈ=ˈ=\ *adv* [ME *streght way,* fr. *streght* straight + *way*] **1 :** in a direct course **:** DIRECTLY ⟨his ashes invariably fell . . . either ~ or down one of the letter pages —J.D.Salinger⟩ **2 :** without delay or hesitation **:** FORTHWITH ⟨fell ~ to gambling⟩ ⟨~ the clouds began to drift apart⟩

²straightway \"\ *adj* [²*straight* + *way*] **:** having or affording a straight way; *esp* **:** allowing something (as a fluid) to pass directly ⟨~ valve⟩ ⟨~ flues⟩

straightway drill *n* **:** a straight-flute drill

straightway pump *n* **:** a pump with suction valves below and discharge valves above the plunger so arranged as to provide a straightaway flow of the fluid pumped

straightways \ˈ=,=\ *adv* [²*straight* + *-ways*] *archaic* **:** STRAIGHTWAY

straight whiskey *n* **:** pure unadulterated grain whiskey matured in new charred white oak barrels and being between 80 and 110 proof

straik \ˈstrāk\ *chiefly Scot var of* STROKE

¹**strain** \ˈstrān\ *n* -s [ME *streen, strene,* fr. OE *strēon, strīon* treasure, acquisition, procreation, progeny; akin to OE *strīenan* to gain, OHG *striunan* to gain, *gistriuni* gain, L *strues* heap — more at STRUCTURE] **1 a** *archaic* **:** OFFSPRING, CHILDREN **b :** a line descended or derived from a particular ancestral individual **:** PROGENY, DESCENDANTS ⟨the weakness of this royal ~ increased from generation to generation⟩; *also* **:** LINEAGE, ANCESTRY ⟨came of a sturdy peasant ~⟩ **c :** a selected group of organisms sharing or presumed to share a common ancestry and usu. lacking clear-cut morphological distinctions from related forms but having distinguishing physiological qualities (as high drought resistance in a plant, superior milk production in cattle, or increased virulence in a microorganism) ⟨a high-yielding ~ of winter wheat⟩; *broadly* **:** a specified infraspecific group (as a stock, line, or ecotype) **d :** a class of persons or things **:** KIND, SORT ⟨discussions of the highest ~⟩ **2 a :** inherited or inherent character, quality, or disposition ⟨may this valiant ~ remain a part of our national heritage⟩ **b :** a tendency or quality that is inherent though often incongruous as if inherited intact **:** TRACE, STREAK ⟨a ~ of madness in the family⟩ ⟨his character is marred by a ~ of fanaticism⟩ **3 a :** a period or other well defined short subdivision of a musical composition or movement; *often* **:** TUNE, AIR **b :** a distinct portion of an ode or other poem; *also* **:** a passage of verbal or musical expression **c :** a stream or outburst of forceful, vigorous, or impassioned speech **4 a :** the tenor, pervading note, burden, tone, manner, style, of an utterance (as a song, poem, speech, book) or of a course of action or conduct ⟨he spoke in a noble ~⟩ ⟨there was a ~ of woe in his story⟩ **b :** MOOD, TEMPER ⟨in a philosophizing ~⟩ **syn** see VARIETY

²**strain** \"\ *vb* -ED/-ING/-S [ME *streinen, strainen,* fr. MF *estreindre, estraindre,* fr. L *stringere* to bind tight, press together; akin to Gk *strang-, stranx* drop squeezed out, *strangos* twisted, flowing drop by drop, *strangalē* halter, MIr *srengim* I draw] *vt* **1 a :** to draw tight **:** cause to clasp firmly ⟨the bandage should be ~*ed* tightly over the scalded surface to minimize blistering⟩ **b :** to stretch to maximum extension and tautness ⟨the wire must be ~*ed* into position if the fence is to be firm and erect⟩ ⟨~ a canvas over a frame⟩ **2 a :** to exert (as oneself) to the utmost **:** put to great stress or effort **:** use or cause to function with extreme vigor ⟨~*ing* himself to a final burst of speed⟩ ⟨~*ed* her ear at the keyhole⟩ **b :** to injure (as oneself or a body part) by overuse or misuse ⟨~*ed* his heart by overwork⟩ ⟨~*ed* herself moving the piano⟩ — compare SPRAIN **c :** to injure by making too great a demand on or by exposure to excessive tension or other force ⟨the storm ~*ed* the timbers of the ship⟩ **d :** to cause a change of form or size in (a body) by application of external force **3 :** to squeeze or clasp tightly: as **a :** to press closely in one's arms **:** HUG — usu. used in the phrase *strain to one's breast* **b :** to compress painfully or harmfully **:** CONSTRICT **c** *obs* **:** to exert pressure upon so as to cause distress **:** AFFLICT **d** (1) **:** to take firmly in one's hand or grip ⟨~*ing* his hand in tearful farewell⟩ ⟨~*ed* her tense hands together⟩ (2) *obs* **:** to seize (prey) with the claws (3) *obs* **:** to grasp firmly and wield or brandish (a weapon) **4 a :** to cause to pass through a strainer or other separatory device (as a filter, cloth, or porous body) usu. by pressure, suction, or the force of gravity ⟨~ the gravy free from lumps⟩ **b :** to remove by straining — usu. used with *out* ⟨~ the lumps out of the gravy⟩ **5 a :** to stretch beyond its proper limit **:** do violence to in respect to intent or meaning ⟨a very ~*ed* interpretation of the passage⟩ ⟨the interests of justice are rarely served by ~*ing* the law⟩ **b :** to tax unduly ⟨it would ~ anyone's conscience to agree⟩ **6** *obs* **a :** to urge (as a request) with importunity **:** PRESS **b :** to squeeze out **:** EXTORT **7 :** to raise to a high degree, pitch, or emotional state ~ *vi* **1 a :** to make violent efforts **:** stretch or extend to a maximum in coping with an exerting or difficult task **:** STRIVE ⟨muscles ~*ing* to raise the stone⟩ ⟨his eyes ~ to catch a glimpse of the sea⟩ **b :** to sustain a strain, wrench, or distortion usu. in effecting an effort or resisting a force ⟨ships ~*ing* at their anchors⟩ **c :** to make a vigorous effort to eject something usu. from the body: as (1) **:** to retch in attempting to vomit (2) **:** to contract the muscles forcefully in attempting to defecate — often used in the phrase *strain at stool* **2 a :** to pass through a strainer or other separatory device **:** become filtered ⟨the liquid ~*s* readily⟩ **b :** to pass through something easily as if through a strainer **:** TRICKLE ⟨water ~*ing* through sandy soil⟩ **c :** to pass from something as if being separated with a strainer **:** OOZE, EXUDE ⟨muddy water ~*ed* from her hair⟩ ⟨juice ~*ing* from the overripe fruits⟩ **3 a :** to make great difficulty or resistance **:** BALK ⟨a horse ~*ing* at the lead⟩ ⟨ye blind guides, which ~ at a gnat, and swallow a camel —Mt 23:24 (AV)⟩ **b :** to take exception **:** SCRUPLE — usu. used with *at* ⟨anyone would ~ at such an interpretation⟩ **syn** see DEMUR — **strain a point :** to go beyond a usual, accepted, or proper limit or rule **:** stretch one's conscience or authority usu. because of exceptional circumstances ⟨willing to *strain a point* because of his excellent record⟩ — **strain courtesy** *archaic* **:** to be excessively or unnecessarily punctilious in the minutiae of courtesy **:** use an excess of civility

³**strain** \"\ *n* -s **1 :** an act of straining or the condition of being strained: as **a :** excessive physical or mental tension ⟨subject to severe ~ in action⟩; *also* **:** a force, influence, or factor causing such tension ⟨the wind pressure was a ~ on the ship's rigging⟩ ⟨her responsibilities were a constant ~⟩ **b :** excessive or difficult exertion or labor **:** a violent or overtaxing effort ⟨gave a great ~ and heaved the load aboard⟩ **c :** a hurt or injury of a body part or organ resulting or such as results from excessive tension, effort, or use ⟨suffered from heart ~⟩; *usu* **:** an injury resulting from a wrench or twist and involving overstretching of muscles or ligaments ⟨foot ~⟩ ⟨back ~⟩ — compare SPRAIN **d :** deformation of a material body and esp. of an elastic solid under the action of applied forces **2 :** something reachable only by straining **:** an unusual reach, degree, height, or intensity **:** PITCH ⟨a ~ of excitement quite beyond my reach⟩ **3** *archaic* **:** a misconstruction obtained by stretching a meaning (as of a word or passage) **:** a strained interpretation of something said or written **4** *obs* **:** the track or hoofmarks of a deer **syn** see STRESS

strain·able \ˈstrānəbəl\ *adj* **:** capable of being strained — **strain·able·ness** \-bəlnəs\ *n* -ES — **strain·ably** \-blē\ *adv*

strain band *n* [³*strain*] **:** a reinforcing band of canvas on a sail

strain diagram *or* **strain sheet** *n* **:** STRESS SHEET

strained \ˈstrānd\ *adj* [fr. past part. of ²*strain*] **1 :** subjected to great or excessive tension **:** WRENCHED, WEAKENED ⟨~ relations⟩ **2 :** done or produced with straining or excessive effort **:** FORCED ⟨~ wit⟩ **3 :** made uniform by or as if by passage through a strainer **4 :** distorted in sense **:** forced beyond what is reasonable or equitable — **strained·ly** \-n(ə)dlē, -lī\ *adv* — **strained·ness** \-nədnəs, -n(d)nəs\ *n* -ES

strain·er \ˈstrānə(r)\ *n* -s **1 :** one that strains something through or out: as **a :** a utensil or device (as a screen, sieve, or filter) to retain or hold back solid pieces or particles while a liquid passes through — compare COLANDER **b :** a worker that strains paper-coating mixtures to smooth and clean them **c :** an operator of a mill for breaking up devulcanized scrap rubber and removing the cord and fabric **2 :** any of various devices for stretching or tightening something ⟨a fence ~⟩: as **a :** a small rod with ends sharpened and bent at right angles used in basketry to keep a stake in position **b :** a reinforcement (as a strip of wood or a piece of glued canvas) for the back of a carriage panel

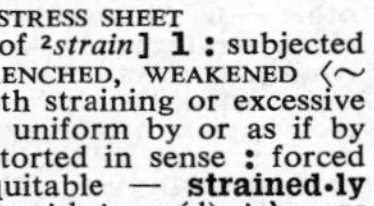

strainer 1a

strain gage *n* [³*strain*] **:** EXTENSOMETER

straining *pres part of* STRAIN

straining arch *or* **strainer arch** *n* [*straining arch* fr. *straining* (pres. part. of ²*strain*) + *arch*; *strainer arch* fr. *strainer* + *arch*] **:** a construction (as a flying buttress) that suggests an arch and is designed to resist end thrust

straining beam *or* **straining piece** *n* **:** a short piece of timber in a truss used to hold in place the ends of struts or rafters

strain·ing·ly *adv* [*straining* + *-ly*] **:** in a straining manner **:** so as to strain or produce a strain

straining sill *n* **:** a straining beam on the tie beam of a truss to resist at each end the foot of a diagonal strut

strain insulator *n* [³*strain*] **:** a strong electrical insulator used to insulate a wire in tension

strain·less \ˈ=ləs\ *adj* [³*strain* + *-less*] **1 :** free from strain or straining tension **2** *of a ring in a chemical compound* **:** characterized by bond angles in the structure that are approximately the same as those in comparable acyclic compounds ⟨~ 5- and 6-membered rings in natural organic products⟩ — compare BOAT FORM, CHAIR FORM; BAEYER STRAIN THEORY — **strain·less·ly** *adv*

strain·om·e·ter \strāˈnämədə(r)\ *n* [³*strain* + *-o-* + *meter*] **:** EXTENSOMETER

strains *pl of* STRAIN, *pres 3d sing of* STRAIN

strain shadows *n pl* **:** inhomogeneity of interference colors as seen with a polarizing microscope in a crystal that has been deformed

strainslip \ˈ=,=\ *n* **:** fracturing in rock accompanied by slight displacement **:** geologic faulting on a minute scale

strain theory *n* [³*strain*] **:** a theory in chemistry that accounts for strain in the structure of molecules; *esp* **:** BAEYER STRAIN THEORY

¹**strait** \ˈstrāt, *usu* -ād·+V\ *adj* -ER/-EST [ME *streit, strait, straight,* fr. OF *estreit,* fr. L *strictus,* fr. past part. of *stringere* to bind tight, press together — more at STRAIN] **1** *archaic* **a :** giving little room **:** not broad **:** NARROW ⟨~ is the gate, and narrow is the way, which leadeth unto life and few there be that find it —Mt 7:14 (AV)⟩ **b :** limited in space or time **:** RESTRICTED **c :** closely fitting **:** tightly drawn **:** CONSTRICTED, TIGHT, CLOSE **2** *archaic* **:** STRICT, RIGOROUS, EXACTING ⟨the ~*est* sect of our religion —Acts 26:5 (ASV)⟩ **3 a** *obs* **:** DEFINITE, EXACT **b** *chiefly dial* **:** strictly limited as to meaning or application **4 :** INTIMATE, FAMILIAR ⟨a ~ alliance⟩ **5 a :** DISTRESSFUL, DIFFICULT **b :** limited as to means or resources **:** STRAITENED **6** *obs* **a :** PARSIMONIOUS, MEAN, STINGY **b :** inadequate through scantiness of dimensions **syn** see NARROW

²**strait** \"\ *adv* [ME *streit,* fr. *streit,* adj.] **:** STRAITLY: as **a** *obs* **:** TIGHTLY; *also* **:** STINGILY **b** *obs* **:** SECURELY **c :** in a manner likely to cause hardship **:** OPPRESSIVELY **d** *obs* **:** STRICTLY, PRECISELY

³**strait** \"\ *n* -s [ME *streit, strait,* fr. *streit, strait,* adj.] **1 a** *archaic* **:** a narrow space or passage **b :** a comparatively narrow passageway connecting two large bodies of water ⟨the *Strait of Gibraltar*⟩ — often used in pl. **c :** a neck of land **d** *obs* **:** RAVINE, GORGE **2 straits** *pl, obs* **:** cloth of single width **3 :** a condition of distressing narrowness or restriction **:** a situation of perplexity or distress **:** DIFFICULTY, NEED — often used in pl. ⟨reduced to pitiful ~*s*⟩ ⟨in dire ~*s*⟩ **syn** see JUNCTURE

⁴**strait** \"\ *archaic var of* STRAIGHT

strait-bodied \ˈ=ˈ=\ *adj* [¹*strait* + *bodied*] *of a fitted garment* **:** made with stays

strait·en \ˈstrātᵊn\ *vb* **straitened; straitened; straitening** \-t(ᵊ)niŋ\ **straitens** [¹*strait* + *-en*] *vt* **1 a :** to make strait or narrow ⟨~*ed* the bed of the river with high embankments⟩ **b :** to hem in or confine usu. in a narrow space ⟨the arable land was ~*ed* between the mountains and the sea⟩ **2 a** *archaic* **:** to restrict (a person) usu. in respect to freedom or rights **b :** to make narrow in respect to scope, range, or similar property ⟨the decision of the court ~*ed* the range of his authority⟩ ⟨such experiences . . . ~ the mind —Osbert Sitwell⟩ **3 a :** to afflict physically or mentally **:** subject to distress, want, or anguish ⟨a man ~*ed* by misfortune⟩ **b :** to afflict or distress by reason of some deficiency — usu. used with *for* or *in* ⟨I am rather ~*ed* in time —William Cowper⟩ **c :** to cause to suffer or ebb by reason of insufficient funds **:** reduce (as oneself) to poverty ⟨~*ing* himself to keep up appearances⟩ ⟨old people living in ~*ed* circumstances⟩ **4** *obs* **a :** to make tense or tight **:** TIGHTEN **b :** to make more severe **:** increase the rigor of ~ *vi* **:** to become narrow **:** NARROW

¹**straitjacket** *or* **straightjacket** \ˈ=,==\ *n* [¹*strait* + *jacket*] **1 :** a cover or overgarment of strong material (as canvas) used to bind the body and esp. the arms closely in restraining violent motion of an irresponsible person (as one that is insane) **2 :** something that restricts or confines like a straitjacket ⟨escape the ~ of a one-crop economy —D.L.Cohn⟩

²**straitjacket** *or* **straightjacket** \"\ *vt* **:** to confine in or as if in a straitjacket ⟨society ~*ed* and enslaved the organic impulses —C.I.Glicksberg⟩

straitlace \ˈ=,=\ *vt* [back-formation fr. *straitlaced*] **:** to bind tightly with or as if with laces **:** CONFINE, RESTRAIN

straitlaced *or* **straightlaced** \ˈ=ˈ=\ *adj* [²*strait* + *laced*] **1 :** wearing or having a bodice or stays tightly laced **2 a** *obs* **:** stubbornly or rigidly self-contained and uncommunicative **:** STIFF, CONSTRAINED **b :** notably and usu. excessively strict in manners, morals, or opinion (as on matters of religion or propriety) **:** intensely or unreasonably scrupulous — **strait·laced·ly** \-stlē,-sədlē\ *adv* — **strait·laced·ness** \-stnəs, -sədn-\ *n* -ES

strait·ly *adv* [ME *streitly,* fr. *streit strait* + *-ly*] **:** in a strait manner **:** STRICTLY, NARROWLY

strait·ness *n* -ES [ME *streitnesse,* fr. *streit strait* + *-nesse* -ness] **:** the quality or state of being strait

straits dollar \ˈstrāts-\ *n, usu cap S* [fr. *Straits* Settlements, former British crown colony on the Strait of Malacca] **:** a dollar formerly issued by British Malaya and used in much of southern and eastern Asia and the East Indies

straits·man \ˈstrātsmən\ *n, pl* **straitsmen** \"\ [fr. the *Straits,* name used formerly to designate the Strait of Malacca, or Bass strait, Australia] **1 :** a ship equipped and suited for service in and about the Strait of Malacca **2** *usu cap* **:** a native or resident of Australia in the vicinity of Bass strait

straits tin *n, usu cap S* [fr. the *Straits*] **:** tin from the Malay peninsula constituting a market standard for high-quality tin

strait-waistcoat \ˈ=ˈ=(,)=\ *n, chiefly Brit* **:** STRAITJACKET

straitwork \ˈ=,=\ *n* [¹*strait*] *Brit* **:** mining by the bord-and-pillar system

¹**strake** \ˈstrāk\ *n* -s [ME; akin to OE *streccan* to stretch — more at STRETCH] **1 a :** an iron band made up of separate pieces by which the fellies of a wheel are secured to each other; *also* **:** one of the pieces making up such a band **b** (1) **:** a continuous band of hull planking or plates on a ship — see SHIP illustration (2) **:** the width of such a band **c :** one of the rings forming the shell of a steam boiler **d :** a run of clapboarding along the side of a house **2 a :** a striped marking usu. of a distinctive color from that with which it is associated **:** STREAK **b :** a narrow strip or stretch (as of land or mown grass)

²**strake** \"\ *vb* -ED/-ING/-S **:** STREAK

³**strake** \"\ *chiefly dial var of* STROKE

⁴**strake** [ME (northern dial.) *strake* (past), fr. OE *strāc* (past)] *obs var of* STRUCK

straked *adj* [¹*strake* + *-ed*] **:** having or equipped with strakes

stramash \ˈstraməsh, strəˈmash\ *n* -ES [prob. imit.] **1** *chiefly Scot* **a :** DISTURBANCE, COMMOTION, RACKET ⟨a terrible ~ to make about a wee lapse —J.D.Scott b. 1917⟩ **b :** BROIL, BRAWL ⟨provoked not a few ~*es* by asking . . . why they did not go back to their banks and braes —Wilson Neill⟩ **2** *chiefly Scot* **:** CRASH, SMASHUP ⟨a wild ~ into the other car —G.B. Shaw⟩

stramazon *n* -s [It *stramazzone,* fr. *stramazzare* to knock down, fr. *stramazzo* mat, mattress, fr. *strame* straw, litter, fr. L *stramin-, stramen*] *obs* **:** a descending cut or slash with the extreme edge of a sword delivered from the wrist

stra·min·eous \strəˈminēəs\ *adj* [L *stramineus* of straw, fr. *stramin-, stramen* straw, litter, fr. *sternere* to strew, spread out, lay flat — more at STREW] **1** *archaic* **a :** consisting of straw **b :** of the nature of or resembling straw; *specif* **:** VALUELESS **2 :** STRAW-COLORED

stram·mel \ˈstraməl\ *n* [prob. of F origin; akin to F dial. *étramiller* to scatter straw, fr. MF *estramer,* fr. OF *estraim* straw, fr. L *stramin-, stramen*] *chiefly Scot* **:** STRAW

stra·mo·ni·um \strəˈmōnēəm\ *n* -s [NL] **1 :** THORN APPLE **2 :** the dried leaf of the thorn apple that is used in medicine similarly to belladonna esp. in asthma and contains the alkaloids atropine, hyoscyamine, and scopolamine

stramp \ˈstramp\ *vb* -ED/-ING/-S [prob. blend of *stamp* and *tramp*] **1** *Scot & dial Eng* **:** STAMP **2** *Scot & dial Eng* **:** TRAMPLE

¹**strand** \ˈstrand, -aa(ə)nd\ *n* -s [ME *strand, strond,* fr. OE *strand*; akin to MLG & MD *strant* shore, beach, ON *strönd* border, edge, seashore, L *sternere* to spread out — more at STREW] **1 :** the land bordering a body of water **:** SHORE: as **a** (1) **:** the beach of the ocean, a sea, or an arm of the ocean (2) **:** the land alternately covered and uncovered by the tide **b :** the bank of a stream **2** *obs* **:** WHARF, QUAY **3** *archaic* **:** a faraway region

²**strand** *vb* -ED/-ING/-S *vt* **1 a :** to run, drive, or cause to drift onto a strand **:** run aground **:** BEACH ⟨pearly nautilus shells . . . have been found ~*ed* . . . far south —Joyce Allan⟩ ⟨left our boats ~*ed* —William Beebe⟩ **b :** to leave behind by or as if by the receding of water ⟨the cave suddenly drained off and ~*ed* the fish —*Amer. Guide Series: Tenn.*⟩ ⟨the skull . . . which the hurricane had left ~*ed* in the fork of a big water oak —W.F. Davis⟩ **2 :** to place in an unfavorable position **:** leave without means of coping with the surroundings ⟨when a wild and open land becomes . . . settled, certain men will be ~*ed* in the new, restricting, and alien environment —Francis Ratcliffe⟩; *specif* **:** to leave in an alien town or country without funds or means to depart ⟨he returned . . . almost penniless after paying his railroad fare from the . . . town where the company had been ~*ed* —*Current Biog.*⟩ ~ *vi* **:** to become stranded **:** become propelled onto a shore ⟨the ship ~*ed* at length on the island —Isobel Hutchison⟩

³**strand** \"\ *n* -s [ME *strand, strond, strund,* perh. fr. ¹*strand*] **1** *Scot & dial Eng* **a :** STREAM, CURRENT **b :** SEA **2** *Scot & dial Eng* **:** CHANNEL, GUTTER

⁴**strand** \"\ *n* -s [ME *strond,* of unknown origin] **1 a** (1) **:** fibers or filaments twisted, plaited, or laid parallel to form a unit for further twisting or plaiting into yarn, thread, rope, or cordage **:** one of the components of a plied yarn, thread, or rope ⟨6-*strand* embroidery floss⟩ (2) **:** one of the wires twisted together or laid parallel to form a wire rope or cable or an electrical conductor **b :** a thread, yarn, string, rope, wire, or cable esp. when of suitable length, strength, or construction for a particular purpose ⟨miles of open downland without a ~ of barbed wire —Anthony West⟩ ⟨the tug pulls, tightening the steel ~ —C.G.Bell⟩ **2 :** an element (as a yarn, thread, filament, or reed) of a woven or plaited material **3 :** an elongated or twisted and plaited body resembling a rope ⟨a ~ of pearls⟩ ⟨wet ~*s* of hair were plastered on her cheek —Sheila Kaye-Smith⟩ **4 :** a continuous patterned or structured whole forming a unity within a complex organization or activity ⟨several ~*s* of melody are heard at once —Robert Donington⟩ ⟨the wife comes back . . . to pick up the ~*s* of married life again —C.A.Lejeune⟩ **5** *South* **:** a pile of wood 8 feet by 4 feet by from 12 inches to 24 or 30 inches

⁵**strand** \"\ *vt* -ED/-ING/-S **1 :** to break a strand of (a rope) accidentally **2 a :** to form (as a rope) from strands **b :** to play out, twist, or arrange in a strand ⟨six pairs of copper wires insulated with polyethylene are ~*ed* around a steel core —*Annual Report of Amer. Tel. & Tel. Co.*⟩ ⟨fourteen hundred feet of . . . hose were ~*ed* from the catch basin over the hill to the reservoir —*Fyr-Fyter News*⟩ **3 a :** to lay a thread along an edge of (as a buttonhole) as a foundation for buttonholing **b :** to carry (an attached yarn) along the back in knitting having colored designs

strand·er \-də(r)\ *n* -s [⁵*strand* + *-er*] **1 :** a machine that makes strands into cable or rope **2 :** a steelworker who guides bars by the use of hand tongs from the roughing mill into other rolls for further processing — called also *edger, poke-in, pony rougher, stick-in*

strand fishery *n* [¹*strand*] **:** a fishery pursued from the shore rather than a boat

strandflat \ˈ=,=\ *n* **:** a wave-cut platform **:** an elevated wave-cut terrace

stranding *n* -s [fr. gerund of ²*strand*] **:** the running aground of a ship upon a strand, rock, or bottom so that it is fast for a time esp. when such a running aground is accidental or done to avoid a worse impending danger (as a sinking)

strand·less \ˈ=ləs\ *adj* [¹*strand* + *-less*] **:** having no shore ⟨a ~ expanse of water⟩

strandline \ˈ=,=\ *n* **:** SHORELINE, BEACH; *often* **:** a shoreline above the present water level

strand·loop·er \ˈstrand,lüpər\ *n* -s *usu cap* [Afrik, fr. *strand* shore (fr. MD *strant*) + *looper* runner, fr. MD *loper,* fr. *lopen* to run + *-er* — more at STRAND, LEAP] **1 :** one of a late prehistoric coastal race of southern Africa possibly related to both Bushman and Hottentot **2 :** a coast-dwelling Bushman

strand·man \ˈ= mən\ *n, pl* **strandmen** [⁵*strand*] **:** an operator of a machine for bending and cutting wire

strand mole *n* **:** MOLE RAT C

strand plover *n* [¹*strand*] *Brit* **:** BLACK-BELLIED PLOVER

strands *pl of* STRAND, *pres 3d sing of* STRAND

strand wolf *n* **:** BROWN HYENA

¹**strang** \ˈstraŋ\ *dial var of* STRONG

²**strang** *dial past of* STRING

¹**strange** \ˈstrānj\ *adj* -ER/-EST [ME, fr. OF *estrange,* fr. L *extraneus* external, foreign, strange, fr. *extra* outside — more at EXTRA-] **1 a :** of, relating to, coming from, characteristic of, or being a different country, region, or town **:** FOREIGN, ALIEN ⟨the immigrant press came . . . under surveillance . . . because of the ~ tongues in which most were published —Oscar Handlin⟩ **b :** not native to or naturally belonging in a place, body, or person **:** of external origin, kind, or character ⟨something ~ had been inhaled —*X-rays & You*⟩ **c :** belonging to or characteristic of an alien people or group ⟨lacked sympathy for ~ customs —Agnes Repplier⟩ ⟨there shall be no ~ gods among you —Ps 81:9 (RSV)⟩ **2 a :** not before known, heard, or seen **:** NEW, UNFAMILIAR ⟨the name . . . though it was ~ to me, was well known to some there —R.L.Stevenson⟩ ⟨sent to the front . . to join a ~ outfit under enemy fire —Gordon Harrison⟩ **b** (1) **:** exciting attention, curiosity, surprise, wonder, or awe because of novelty, eccentricity, or exceptional greatness, power, or attributes **:** out of the ordinary **:** strikingly uncommon or unnatural **:** UNUSUAL, EXTRAORDINARY, EXCEPTIONAL ⟨a ~ world indeed, replete with . . . even more weird inhabitants —F.G.Slaughter⟩ ⟨resorts to ~ shapes, odd forms without beauty —E.M.Bridge⟩ ⟨a ~ exaltation that was indefinable —Liam O'Flaherty⟩ (2) **:** difficult to comprehend or believe **:** UNACCOUNTABLE ⟨it's ~, the queer sort of people who win the lotteries —Ruth Park⟩ ⟨a ~ petulance that runs through the writings of the social engineers —W.H. Whyte⟩ **3 :** discouraging familiarities **:** RESERVED, DISTANT, COLD ⟨why did you break off our confidences and become quite ~ to me —G.B.Shaw⟩ **4 :** lacking skill, experience, knowledge, or acquaintance **:** UNACCUSTOMED, UNVERSED ⟨I know thee well; but in thy fortunes am unlearn'd and ~ —Shak.⟩

syn SINGULAR, UNIQUE, PECULIAR, ECCENTRIC, ERRATIC, ODD, QUEER, QUAINT, OUTLANDISH, CURIOUS: STRANGE, a rather general term, applies to the foreign, unnatural, inexplicable, or new or to anything unfamiliar that defies a ready explanation or commands attention by its novelty ⟨the headlands, snow-crowned, take on an icy glaze that sharpens their *strange* silhouettes —*Amer. Guide Series: Maine*⟩ ⟨a *strange* story of a mountain in Numidia which was inhabited by a commonwealth of cats —Agnes Repplier⟩ ⟨a *strange* sort of love, to be entirely free from that quality of selfishness which is frequently the chief constituent of the passion —Thomas Hardy⟩ SINGULAR may suggest individual strangeness of or as if of something unusual or notably different from others of its group; it may be a close synonym of STRANGE ⟨by the *singular* magic of his personality —Osbert Sitwell⟩ ⟨the taxi driver had lugged the parcel into the terminal for the woman, and then — proving himself a *singular* example of his species — had broken a ten-dollar bill for her when it developed that the clerk had insufficient change —E.J.Kahn⟩ ⟨*singular* that a woman of that age should flush so readily —W.S.Maugham⟩ UNIQUE may describe that which is singular (or individual) and unparalleled ⟨a privilege *unique* not only in the British Army but I believe in any army there has ever been —J.S.Bradford⟩ ⟨the *unique* task of setting up an observation post directly at the South Pole —Walter Sullivan⟩ ⟨a glass conservatory full of tropical

blossoms of quite *unique* and almost monstrous beauty —G.K. Chesterton〉 PECULIAR describes anything markedly different, unusual, or puzzling; it is sometimes a close synonym of the terms following 〈she had put herself in a *peculiar* light, namely, that of agreeing to marry when she was already supposedly married —Theodore Dreiser〉 〈the *peculiar* individuals are those whose behavior is odd and somewhat unpredictable —Carney Landis & Mary Bolles〉 ECCENTRIC implies a noticeably unusual deviation from the usual, normal, or established 〈what sort of burglars are they who steal silver, and then throw it into the nearest pond — it was certainly rather *eccentric* behavior —A. Conan Doyle〉 〈this architectural curiosity was erected in 1815 by an *eccentric* Irishman —*Amer. Guide Series: Va.*〉 ERRATIC may suggest a wandering or deviating, sometimes capricious, from the accustomed or expected so that predictability is impossible 〈geniuses are such *erratic* people —G.B.Shaw〉 〈his moods were *erratic*, and nobody could be certain how he would behave at any particular moment —Thomas Hardy〉 ODD may apply to a departure from normal tinged with the fantastic, whimsical, or paradoxical 〈the *oddest* sense of being herself invisible; unseen; unknown —Virginia Woolf〉 〈it was an *odd* argument that developed. Allnutt was perfectly prepared by now to throw away the life that had seemed so precious to him —C.S. Forester〉 〈it is *odd* that, when we whip her, Madam should love us the more —George Meredith〉 QUEER may describe the eccentric or odd slightly tinged with the questionable, dubious, reprehensible, or threatening 〈something *queer* floating by the bank. It was the body of an old woman, gutted, but not gutted enough to sink —Marjory S. Douglas〉 〈a *queer*, wild, half-starved, half-crazy loveliness —Katharine N. Burt〉 QUAINT may suggest a pleasing or attractive oddness usu. due to some old-fashioned suggestion 〈one of those *quaint* figures, in the stately ruff, the cloak, tunic, and trunk hose of three centuries ago —Nathaniel Hawthorne〉 〈*quaint* little tank engines, with tall chimneys, cowcatchers and highly polished steam domes —O.S.Nock〉 OUTLANDISH applies to what is odd as bizarre, foreign, barbaric, or exotic 〈wholly independent, and withal *outlandish*, they have left me a memory of pigtails and gongs and fluttering red paper —John Reed〉 CURIOUS, often interchangeable with others in this group, may apply to what merits or invites close scrutiny or examination through its strange or singular nature 〈*curious* and suspicious circumstances had of late been discovered —Rose Macaulay〉 〈the *curious* expression "pure serene" — Amy Lowell〉 〈the writ of habeas corpus has had a most *curious* history —Edward Jenks〉

²strange \"\ *adv* : STRANGELY

strange·ly *adv* [ME, fr. ¹*strange* + *-ly*] : in a strange manner

strange·ness *n* -ES [ME *strangenesse*, fr. ¹*strange* + *-nesse* -ness] : the quality or state of being strange

¹stran·ger \'strānjə(r)\ *n* -S [ME, fr. MF *estrangier* foreign, foreigner, fr. *estrange* strange, foreign] **1** : one who is strange: as **a** (1) : one who comes from a foreign land : FOREIGNER (2) : a resident alien; *specif* : GER **b** : one not in the place where his home is; *specif* : one in the family or house of another as a guest, visitor, or intruder 〈thy ~ that is within thy gates —Deut 5:14(AV)〉 **c** : a person or thing that is unknown or with whom one is unacquainted 〈a total ~〉 〈it's a ~ — and so was the young woman who owns it —Hartley Howard〉 **d** (1) : one who does not belong to or is not permitted to take part in the activities of a group, organization, or society (2) : someone not a priest : LAYMAN **e** : an acquaintance who has been long absent : an acquaintance who has not been seen for a longer period than usual **f** *or* **stranger in blood** : one who is not a relation; *specif* : one not closely enough related or not so circumstanced as to give rise to the consideration of love and affection 〈risk giving inheritance rights to offspring begotten by some ~ —H.M.Parshley〉 **g** : one not privy or party to an act, contract, or title : a mere intruder or intermeddler : one that interferes without right : a third party : VOLUNTEER 〈actual possession of land gives a good title against a ~ having no title〉 **h** (1) *obs* : something that is not indigenous : something (as a plant or animal) of exotic origin (2) : something not of the nature of or characteristic of a person, class, thing, or set of concepts **i** : a newborn child **2 a** : one ignorant of or unacquainted with a thing, person, fact, or set of ideas 〈a man of sociable disposition . . . though a ~ to books —C.H. Grandgent〉 〈no ~ to aesthetic studies —Joseph Frank〉 **b** : one spiritually alienated from an object or group 〈a ~ to his religion —Ruth Park〉 〈living as ~s to themselves —Marguerite Young〉 **3** : any of several things 〈as a tea leaf floating in a cup of tea〉 or occurrences 〈as a moth flying toward one〉 that according to folklore forebode the arrival of an unexpected visitor

²stranger \"\ *adj* [ME, fr. ¹*stranger*] : of, relating to, or being a stranger : FOREIGN, ALIEN

³stranger *vt* -ED/-ING/-S [¹*stranger*] *obs* : ESTRANGE, ALIENATE

stran·ger·hood \-,hu̇d\ *n* : the quality or state of being a stranger

stranger·ship \-,ship\ *n* [¹*stranger* + *-ship*] : STRANGERHOOD

strangest *superlative of* STRANGE

strange woman *n* [so called fr. the use of the expression in Prov 5:3(AV)] : PROSTITUTE

strang·ite \'straŋ,īt\ *n* -S *usu cap* [James J. *Strang* †1856 Am. religious leader + E *-ite*] : a member of a religious body that was organized by J. J. Strang in Wisconsin in 1844, that regards itself as the original and only true Church of Christ of Latter-day Saints, and that holds its founder to be the only legitimate successor to Joseph Smith

¹stran·gle \'straŋgəl, -aiŋ-\ *vb* **strangled; strangled; strangling** \-g(ə)liŋ\ **strangles** [ME *stranglen*, fr. MF *estrangler*, fr. L *strangulare*, fr. Gk *strangalan*, fr. *strangalē* halter — more at STRAIN] *vt* **1 a** : to compress the windpipe of until death results from stoppage of respiration : choke to death by compressing the throat with or as if with a hand or rope : THROTTLE **b** : to interfere with or obstruct seriously or fatally the normal breathing of 〈the bone wedged in his throat and *strangled* him〉 〈the tear gas *strangled* the convicts〉 **2 a** : to hinder the growth of (an organism) : deny a vital necessity (as air, water, or food) to : choke off or out **b** : to suppress, hinder, or halt the rise, expression, or development of by extreme restrictions or stringency 〈expression of biological needs is *strangled* by social pressures —Abram Kardiner〉 〈the states ~ local initiative —T.C.Desmond〉 〈*strangling* her trade would neither cause immediate hardship . . . nor stop an army —John Sparkman〉 **c** : to check free utterance of 〈a *strangled* gasp of anguish —O.E.Rölvaag〉 ~ *vi* **1** : to become strangled : undergo an esp. severe interference of breathing 〈she chokes very easily, and sometimes ~s —Grace Reiten〉 **2** : to die from or as if from interference with breathing 〈several prisoners in the hold *strangled*〉 **syn** see SUFFOCATE

²strangle \"\ *n* -S [by shortening] : STRANGLEHOLD

stranglehold \'≈,≈\ *n* [¹*strangle* + *hold*] **1** : an illegal wrestling hold by which one's opponent is choked **2** : a force, influence, or vantage point from which pressure might be brought to bear which chokes or suppresses freedom of movement, development, or expression

stran·gler \'straŋglə(r), -aiŋ-\ *n* -S **1** : one that strangles **2** *Brit* : CHOKE 2a

strangler fig *also* **strangler** *n* -S : any of several epiphytic vines or trees: as **a** : PITCH APPLE **b** : a fig (*Ficus aurea*) of the southeastern U.S. with sessile spheroidal or obovoid fruit — called also *golden fig*

strangler tree *n* : a plant of the genus *Clusia; esp* : PITCH APPLE

stran·gles \-gəlz\ *n pl but sing or pl in constr* [fr. pl. of obs. *strangle* act of strangling, fr. ME, fr. *stranglen* to strangle] : an infectious febrile disease of horses and other equines that is caused by a bacterium (*Streptococcus equi*), is characterized by inflammation and congestion of mucous membranes and a tendency to swelling and suppuration of the intermaxillary and cervical lymph nodes, usu. affects young animals, has a low mortality rate, and confers subsequent immunity after one attack — called also *colt distemper;* compare BASTARD STRANGLES

strangletare \'≈≈,≈\ *n* **1** : a European tare (*Vicia hirsuta*) with hirsute 2-seeded pods naturalized in No. America **2** : a broomrape of the genus *Orobanche*

strangleweed \'≈≈,≈\ *n* : DODDER

strangling fig *n* [*strangling* (pres. part. of ¹*strangle*) + *fig*] : STRANGLER FIG

¹stran·gu·late \'straŋgyə,lāt, -aiŋ-, *usu* -ād.+V\ *vb* -ED/-ING/-S [L *strangulatus*, past part. of *strangulare* to strangle] *vt* : STRANGLE, CONSTRICT ~ *vi* : to become constricted so as to stop circulation 〈the hernia will ~ and become painful〉

²strangulate \-,lət, -,lāt, *usu* -d.+V\ *adj* [L *strangulatus*] : strongly constricted as though compressed by bands 〈the ~ petiole of an ant or wasp〉

strangulated blade *n* [*strangulated* (past part. of ¹*strangulate*) + *blade*] : a prehistoric flint blade with opposing lateral notches on each margin

strangulated hernia *n* : a hernia in which the blood supply of the herniated viscus is so constricted by swelling and congestion as to arrest its circulation

stran·gu·la·tion \,≈≈'lāshən\ *n* -S [L *strangulation-, strangulatio*, fr. *strangulatus* (past part. of *strangulare* to strangle) + *-ion-, -io* -ion] **1** : the action or process of strangling or the state of being strangled 〈put to death by ~, the instrument of death being the cotton cloth —J.G.Frazer〉 **2** : inordinate compression or constriction of a tube or part (as the throat or bowel) esp. to a degree that causes a suspension of breathing, circulation, or the passage of contents **3** : the action or process of constricting, choking off, or killing natural, normal, or desirable growth, development, or activity 〈the gradual ~ of industry and individual initiative by bureaucracy —*Economist*〉

stran·gu·ry \'straŋgyərē, -aiŋ-, -ri\ *n* -ES [ME, fr. L *stranguria*, fr. Gk *strangouria*, fr. *strang-, stranx* drop squeezed out + *ourein* to urinate (fr. *ouron* urine) + *-ia* -y — more at STRAIN, URINE] : a slow and painful discharge of urine drop by drop produced by spasmodic muscular contraction of the urethra and bladder

stran·ner \'stranə(r)\ *n* -S [origin unknown] : a steelworker who guides bloom through rolling mills until sheets reach the right gauge

strany \'strani\ *n* -ES [origin unknown] *dial Brit* : a murre (*Uria troille*)

¹strap \'strap\ *n* -S *often attrib* [alter. of *strop* band or loop of leather or rope or metal, fr. ME, band or loop of leather or rope, fr. OE, thong for securing an oar; akin to MLG & MD *strop* strap, MHG *strupfe;* all fr. a prehistoric Gmc word borrowed fr. L *struppus, stroppus* band, thong, strap, fr. Gk *strophos* twisted band, cord — more at STROPHE] **1 a** : a band, plate, or loop of metal for binding objects together or for clamping an object in position; *also* : a flexible thin flat strip of metal fastened around a box, crate, bale, or bundle for security **b** : a projecting metal tang esp. when used for attaching or connecting **c** : metal strips, posts, or rods used for support or reinforcement **d** : a thin flat section of conducting material (as copper) forming part of an electrical connection **e** : a flat piece of lead in a storage battery to which the plates of a group are connected **2 a** : a piece of rope or metal passing around a block or deadeye holding it together and used for fastening it to something — called also *strop* **b** : a rope with its ends spliced together used esp. in slinging weights; *also* : a short cable with an eye at each end **3** : a narrow usu. flat strip or thong of a flexible material and esp. leather used variously (as for securing, holding together, or wrapping): as **a** : a strip of leather, cloth, or webbing fitted with a clasp or buckle for adjustment and used for fastening, securing, or holding together **b** : something made of a strap, a part of one, or of a combination of two or more forming a loop 〈a carriage ~〉 〈a ~ in a bus〉 **c** : a band (as of adhesive plaster) used to approximate edges (as of a wound) or to hold a dressing in position **d** : a strip of leather used for flogging; *also* : the use of a strap for inflicting punishment 〈a little boy who has been out later than he should and who is afraid . . . of getting his father's ~ —Vernon Jarratt〉 **e** : a piece of leather or strip of wood covered with a suitable material for sharpening a razor : STROP **f** : BELT 2 **g** : SHOULDER STRAP **h** : a flexible strap or belt (as of cloth to which an abrasive is glued and which runs over pulleys or over a pulley and a rod or plate) used for buffing **i** : any of several wide leather strips cut and fitted to blankbook backbones and extending upon the boards between bands **j** : a band or fillet used in strapwork **k** : a flattened strip of cable (as connected to an automobile storage battery) **l** : a strip of paper used to bind a bundle of paper currency **4** *or* **strap shoe** : a shoe fastened with a usu. buckled strap **5** *Brit* : CREDIT **6** *Irish* **a** : a forward impudent girl or woman : HUSSY **b** : HARLOT

²strap \"\ *vb* **strapped; strapped; strapping; straps** *vt* **1 a** (1) : to secure with or attach by means of a strap 〈*strapping* mail in bundles —*U.S.Post Office Manual*〉 〈*strapped* to the pulpit is a curious wooden megaphone —Charles Gordon〉 〈~ on an oxygen tank —Stuart Chase〉 (2) : to bind (as a sprained joint or painful muscles) with overlapping strips of adhesive plaster (3) : to constrict as if by a strap 〈his khaki bush shirt *strapped* him as though it were made with stays —Joseph Hitrec〉 〈a decent man *strapped* by dogma —*New Republic*〉 **b** : to fit, furnish, or equip with a strap 〈~ a book〉 〈~ the deadeye〉 **2** : to beat or punish with a strap 〈would not ~ his pupils —H.S.Canby〉 **3** : STROP **4** : to cause to suffer from an extreme scarcity 〈*strapped* its people to keep up the arms race —*Atlantic*〉 〈financially *strapped* due to the depression —Jerome Ellison〉 **5** : to rub down (a horse) : GROOM ~ *vi, Brit* : to busy oneself : apply oneself actively or energetically : buckle down

s trap *n, cap S* : an S-shaped trap used in plumbing

strap bolt *n* **1** : LUG BOLT **2** : a bolt with a flat portion in the center so that the whole may be bent into a U shape

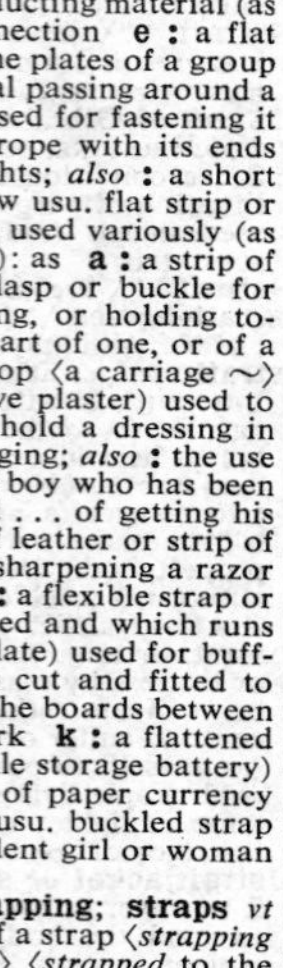

S trap

strap brake *n* : BAND BRAKE

strap drill *n* : a simple drill operated by means of a thong twisted about the shaft

strap fern *n* : a common tropical American fern (*Campyloneuron phyllitidis*) with long narrow strap-shaped leaves that is found in soil or as an epiphyte

strap game *n* : a swindling game in which a strap or belt is folded in the middle and then rolled up tightly with the victim betting that he can place a pencil in the loop so as to hold the strap when both ends are pulled

strap graft *n* : a graft similar to a bark graft except that the scion is so prepared that a flap of bark will cover the cut end of the stock and can be inserted under the bark of the stock on the side opposite the scion

strap hammer *n* : a heavy hammer (as a helve hammer or drop hammer) in which the head is suspended by a strap

straphang \'≈,≈\ *vi* -ED/-ING/-S [back-formation fr. *straphanger*] *chiefly Brit* : to ride in a conveyance as a straphanger

straphanger \'≈,≈≈\ *n* [¹*strap* + *hanger*] **1 a** : a passenger in a subway, streetcar, bus, or train who clings for support while standing to one of the short straps or similar devices running along the aisle **b** : a regular passenger on public transportation : COMMUTER **2** : a usu. curved piece of strap fastened at the ends and used to secure a pipe or rod suspended from above or against a vertical surface

strap hinge *n* : a hinge with long flaps by which it is fastened to the surface of a door and the adjacent wall — compare BUTT HINGE

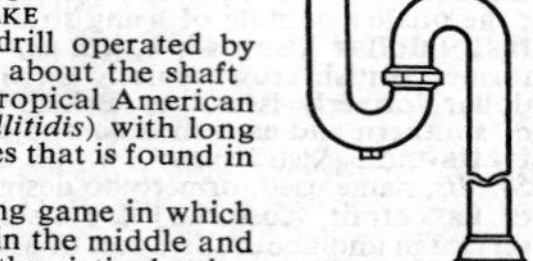

strap hinges

strap joint *n* : a joint formed by butting together the two pieces to be joined and riveting a metal strap to each piece

strap key *n* : TAPPING KEY

strap-laid \'≈;≈\ *adj* : consisting of or being flat rope made by stitching together side-by-side two cable-laid ropes

strap leather *n* : tanned cowhide leather used esp. for luggage straps

strap·less \'≈,lə̇s\ *adj* : having no strap; *specif* : made or worn without shoulder straps 〈~ bathing suit〉 〈~ evening gown〉

strap oyster *n, dial* : an uncommonly narrow oyster

¹strap·pa·do \strə'pä(,)dō, -pā(,)-\ *n* -S [modif. of It *strappata* sharp pull, strappado, fr. *strappare* to pull sharply, prob. of Gmc origin; akin to G dial. *strapfen* to stretch tight, MD *strof* tense, sharp] **1** : a former punishment or torture consisting of hoisting the subject by a rope sometimes fastened to his wrists behind his back and letting him fall to the length of the rope; *also* : a machine or device used in the infliction of this torture **2** *archaic* : a beating with or as if with a strap

²strappado \"\ *vt* -ED/-ING/-S *obs* : to punish or torture by or as if by the strappado

strap·pan \'strapən\ *Scot var of* STRAPPING

strapped *past of* STRAP

strap·per \'strapə(r)\ *n* -S [²*strap* + *-er*] **1** : a person unusually large, robust, or formidable **2** : one that uses a strap: as **a** : one that harnesses or grooms horses or takes care of horses in a stable **b** : one that attaches, removes, or attends to straps

¹strapping *adj* [fr. pres. part. of ²*strap*] : having or being a vigorously sturdy constitution : ROBUST — **strappingly** *adv*

²strapping *n* -S [fr. gerund of ²*strap*] **1 a** : the act or process of strapping; *esp* : a beating with or as if with a strap **b** : the application of adhesive plaster in overlapping strips upon or around (as a sprained ankle or the chest in pleurisy) to serve as a splint to reduce motion or to hold surgical dressings in place upon a surgical wound; *also* : material so used **2 a** : straps or material for straps **b** : a trimming for women's clothes made of one or more narrow bands of contrasting material or color and often applied over seams

strapping plate *n* : a long narrow strip of sheet iron or mild steel used as a strap in making a butt joint with two sections of a wooden main rod in a mine shaft

strap rail *n* : a railroad rail consisting of a metal strap placed upon a wooden rail

straps *pl of* STRAP, *pres 3d sing of* STRAP

strap-toothed whale \'≈;≈-\ *n* [so called fr. the shape of the base of its mandibular tooth] : a cowfish (*Mesoplodon layardi*) of southern seas having the front portion of the body gray and the hind portion black with yellow-tipped tail flukes

strapwork \'≈,≈\ *n* : decorative design of narrow fillets or bands folded, crossed, and sometimes interlaced

strapwort \'≈,≈\ *n* : a European maritime weed (*Corrigiola littoralis*) naturalized in eastern No. America

stras·bourg \'strä|s,bu̇rg, 'stra|, |z,b- *sometimes* 'strȯ|; -a|s,bərg, |z,b- *sometimes* -ȯ|\ *adj, usu cap* [fr. *Strasbourg*, city of northeast France] : of or from the city of Strasbourg, France : of the kind or style prevalent in Strasbourg

strasbourg goose *n, usu cap S* : a goose fattened so as to enlarge the liver for use in pâté de foie gras

strasbourg turpentine *n, usu cap S* : an oleoresin obtained chiefly from a silver fir (*Abies alba*)

strass \'stras\ *n* -ES [F *stras, strass*, prob. fr. the name of its inventor] : PASTE 4

strata *pl of* STRATUM

strat·a·gem \'strad·əjəm, -at|, |ējəm *also* |ə,jem\ *n* -S [It *stratagemma*, fr. L *strategema*, fr. Gk *stratēgēma*, fr. *stratēgein* to be a general, maneuver, fr. *stratēgos* general, fr. *stratos* army, host + *-ēgos* (fr. *agein* to lead) — more at STRATUM, AGENT] **1 a** : an artifice or trick in war for deceiving and outwitting the enemy **b** : a cleverly contrived trick or scheme for gaining an end 〈on our guard against the ~s of evil rhetoric —R.M.Weaver〉 **c** : skillfulness in the employment of stratagems : ability to devise cunning plans to gain an end 〈without ~, but in plain shock and even play of battle —Shak.〉 **2** *obs* : a violent or bloody act **syn** see TRICK

strat·a·gem·i·cal \¦≈≈'jemə̇kəl\ *adj* [*stratagem* + *-ical*] : characterized by stratagem — **strat·a·gem·i·cal·ly** \-mə̇k(ə)lē\ *adv*

stratal \'strā|d·ᵊl, |tᵊl, -ra| *also* -rä|\ *or* -rȧ|\ *adj* [NL *stratum* + E *-al*] : of or relating to a stratum or strata

strat·e·get·ic \¦strad·ə¦jed·ik\ *or* **strat·e·get·i·cal** \-d·ə̇kəl\ *adj* [*strategetic* fr. Gk *stratēgētikos*, MS var. (as if fr. *stratēgētos* — assumed verbal of *stratēgein* to be a general — + *-ikos* -ic) of *stratēgikos* strategic; *strategetical* fr. Gk *stratēgētikos* + E *-al* — more at STRATAGEM] : STRATEGIC

stra·te·gian \strə'tē|j(ē)ən\ *n* -S [*strategy* + *-an*] : STRATEGIST

stra·te·gic \-jik, -jēk\ *also* **stra·te·gi·cal** \-jə̇kəl, -jēk-\ *adj* [*strategic* fr. Gk *stratēgikos* of a general, fr. *stratēgos* general + *-ikos* -ic; *strategical* fr. Gk *stratēgikos* + E *-al* — more at STRATAGEM] **1** : of, relating to, or concerned with strategy 〈~ strength〉 〈~ considerations〉 〈on account of their ~ value to the enemy, I destroyed the bridges —R.H.Davis〉 **2** : marked by or done in accordance with strategy 〈this ~ retreat was the promise of victory —C.A. & Mary Beard〉 **3 a** : necessary to or of great value or importance in the initiation, conduct, or completion of a strategic plan 〈it is not probable that any enemy would attack . . . across thousands of miles of ocean, until it had acquired ~ bases from which to operate —F.D. Roosevelt〉 〈~ roads〉 〈the retention of a strong ~ reserve〉; *specif* : required for the conduct of war but obtainable at least in part only from outside the country — compare CRITICAL **b** : of great or vital importance within an integrated whole or to the taking place of a planned or unplanned occurrence 〈reinforced with belting leather at the corners and other ~ spots —*New Yorker*〉 〈at ~ points where agricultural products were processed . . . towns grew rapidly —*Amer. Guides Series: N.Y.*〉 〈there are four ~ areas of the economy: inventories, durables, business construction, and housing —H.H.Villard〉 〈constriction of arteries in ~ areas of the brain —*Jour. Amer. Med. Assoc.*〉 **4** : designed or trained to strike an enemy at the sources of his military, economic, or political power and esp. to destroy rear area bases and supply depots, industrial centers, and communications networks 〈~ bomber〉 〈~ air warfare〉

stra·te·gi·cal·ly \-jə̇k(ə)lē, -jēk-, -li\ *adv* [*strategical* + *-ly*] **1** : in a strategic manner : for purposes of strategy 〈deliberately and ~ condescending —L.A.Fiedler〉 **2** : with regard to strategy : from a strategical view 〈winning the war ~ and losing it politically —J.R.Newman〉

stra·te·gics \-jiks, -jēks\ *n pl but sing in constr* [L *strategica*, fr. Gk *stratēgika*, fr. neut. pl. of *stratēgikos* of a general] : STRATEGY

strat·e·gist \'strad·əjə̇st, -ratə-\ *n* -S [*strategy* + *-ist*] : one skilled in strategy

stra·te·gus \strə'tēgəs\ *or* **stra·te·gos** \", -,gäs\ *n, pl* **strate·gi** \-ē,jī\ *or* **strate·goi** \-ē,gȯi\ [L *strategus*, fr. Gk *stratēgos* — more at STRATAGEM] **1** : a leader of an ancient and esp. an ancient Greek army **2** : an officer associated with the hipparch as chief executive of the boule in the Achaean and Aetolian Leagues

strat·e·gy \'strad·əjē, -ratə-, -ji\ *n* -ES [Gk *stratēgia* office of a general, generalship, piece of strategy, fr. *stratēgos* general + *-ia* -y] **1 a** (1) : the science and art of employing the political, economic, psychological, and military forces of a nation or group of nations to afford the maximum support to adopted policies in peace or war (2) : the science and art of military command exercised to meet the enemy in combat under advantageous conditions — compare TACTICS **b** : a variety of or instance of the use of strategy 〈the ~ of the counterattack rather than of the offensive —H.W.Baldwin〉 〈collective security through a world organization is a ~ of defense like any other —J.T.Shotwell〉 **2 a** : a careful plan or method or a clever stratagem 〈vulnerable to one of three merchandising *strategies* —Vance Packard〉 〈drafted the ~ it followed in election campaigns —*Current Biog.*〉 **b** : the art of devising or employing plans or stratagems toward a goal 〈the clever manager's conception of political ~ —S.H.Adams〉

strat·for·dian \strat'fȯrdēən\ *n* -S *cap* [*Stratford* on Avon, municipal borough of central England and birthplace of William Shakespeare, or *Stratford*, city of southeast Ontario + E *-ian*] **1** : a native or resident of Stratford on Avon, England or of Stratford, Ontario **2** : one who believes that William Shakespeare was the author of the dramatic works usu. attributed to him

strath \'strath\ *n* -S [ScGael *srath;* akin to MIr *srath* wide valley, Welsh *ystrad* — more at STRATUM] **1** : a flat wide river valley or its bottomland **2** : a wide tract of level land embracing parts of several adjacent valleys **3** : a partially developed peneplain

strath·spey \(')strath¦spā\ *n* -S [fr. *Strath Spey*, district of northeast Scotland] **1** : a Scottish dance similar to but slower than the reel **2** : music for the strathspey : music having its duple or quadruple rhythm characterized by the Scotch snap

strath terrace *n* : a remnant of a dissected strath

strati *pl of* STRATUS

strati- *comb form* [NL *stratum*] : stratum 〈*strati*form〉 〈*strati*graphy〉

stra·tic·u·late \strəˈtikyələt, -ˌlāt\ *adj* [fr. (assumed) NL *straticulum* (dim. of *stratum*) + E *-ate*] **:** characterized by thin parallel strata

strat·i·fi·ca·tion \ˌstrad·əfəˈkāshən, -ratə-\ *n* -s [NL *stratification-, stratificatio*, fr. *stratificatus* (past part. of *stratificare* to stratify) + L *-ion-, -io* -ion] **:** the act or process of stratifying or state of being stratified **:** a stratified formation **:** disposal or growth in layers: as **a :** the arrangement of sedimentary rocks in layers **b :** the placing of seeds in damp sand, peat moss, or sawdust to facilitate germination that is a necessary procedure for seeds requiring moisture or low temperature or both during their resting period or afterripening period **c :** stratified variation in the richness of the mixture in a cylinder of an internal combustion engine **d** (1) **:** a formation of social classes, castes, strata, or levels into a hierarchy of prestige (2) **:** a graded system of individual statuses within a group, community, or organization **e :** arrangement (as of a forest) in vertical layers of vegetation so as to make maximum use of available light **f :** arrangement of the waters of a lake into hypolimnion and epilimnion separated by a thermocline as a result esp. of differences in specific gravity brought about by natural warming of the waters above the thermocline **g :** the division of a statistical population into groups on any basis esp. in order to select a sample from each group

stratification plane *n* **:** a division between two layers of sedimentary rock that often marks changes in the circumstances of deposition

stratified sample *n* [*stratified* (past part. of *stratify*) + *sample*] **:** a statistical sample obtained by breaking the universe down into smaller parts made up of relatively homogeneous units and taking a sample from each part

strat·i·form \ˈstrad·ə,fȯrm, -ratə-\ *adj* [*strati-* + *-form*] **1 :** having a stratified formation **:** consisting of roughly parallel bands or concentric zones **2** [NL *stratus* + E *-iform*] **:** having the form of a stratus

strat·i·fy \-ˌfī\ *vb* -ED/-ING/-ES [NL *stratificare*, fr. *stratum* + L *-ificare* -ify] *vt* **1 a :** to form, deposit, or arrange in strata ⟨*stratified* alluvium⟩ **b** (1) **:** to divide or arrange into classes, castes, or social strata ⟨important cultural differences often ~ husbands and wives . . . of the very same religious affiliation —M.L.Barron⟩ ⟨society was rather distinctly *stratified* into four classes —*Amer. Guide Series: N.C.*⟩ (2) **:** to divide into a series of graded statuses ⟨a *stratified* religious hierarchy⟩ **c :** to determine the arrangement and order of the strata of ⟨~ an archeological site⟩ **2 a :** to place (seed) in damp sand, peat moss, or sawdust **b :** to preserve (tree seeds) by spreading in layers alternating with sand, earth, or other moisture-holding medium ~ *vi* **:** to become arranged in strata ⟨convected heat . . . has a tendency to cause the air to ~ —P.D.Close⟩ ⟨all society . . . tends to ~ in lines of wealth distribution —V.L. Parrington⟩

stra·tig·ra·pher \strəˈtigrəfə(r)\ *n* -s [*stratigraphy* + *-er*] **:** a geologist who specializes in stratigraphy

strat·i·graph·ic \ˌstrad·əˈgrafik, -ratə-, -fēk\ *also* **strat·i·graph·i·cal** \-fəkəl, -fēk-\ *adj* [*stratigraphic* fr. *stratigraphy* + *-ic*; *stratigraphical* fr. *strati-* + *-graphical*] **:** of, relating to, or determined by stratigraphy — **strat·i·graph·i·cal·ly** \-fək(ə)lē, -fēk-, -li\ *adv*

stratigraphic geology *n* **:** STRATIGRAPHY 2

stratigraphic separation *or* **stratigraphic throw** *n* **:** PERPENDICULAR SEPARATION

stratigraphic sequence *n* **:** a chronologic succession of sedimentary rocks

stratigraphic trap *n* **:** a natural reservoir in which oil or gas may be confined because of changes in porosity and permeability of the strata rather than as a result of their structural attitudes

stra·tig·ra·phist \strəˈtigrəfəst\ *n* -s [*stratigraphy* + *-ist*] **:** STRATIGRAPHER

stra·tig·ra·phy \-fē, -fi\ *n* -ES [ISV *strati-* + *-graphy*] **1 :** the arrangement of strata esp. as to position and order of sequence **2 :** the branch of geology that deals with the origin, composition, distribution, and succession of strata **3 :** the determination of time sequence in the culture and physical types of peoples by study of the relative locations of the layers of material that are found in archaeological excavation — compare SHARD

¹strat·io·my·iid \ˌstrad·ēōˈmī(y)əd\ *or* **strat·io·my·id** \-ī̇əd\ *adj* [NL *Stratiomyiidae*] **:** of or relating to the Stratiomyiidae

²stratiomyiid \"\ *or* **stratiomyid** \"\ *n* -s **:** a fly of the family Stratiomyiidae **:** SOLDIER FLY

strat·io·my·ii·dae \ˌ===ˈmī(y)ə,dē\ *n pl, cap* [NL *Stratiomyia*, type genus (fr. Gk *stratios* of an army, warlike + NL *-myia*) + *-idae*] **:** a family of small often brightly colored two-winged flies comprising the soldier flies and having saprophagous or predacious terrestrial or aquatic larvae

¹strato- *comb form* [NL *stratus*] **:** stratus and ⟨*strato*cirrus⟩ ⟨*strato*cumulus⟩

²strato- *comb form* [*stratosphere*] **:** stratosphere ⟨*strato*=chamber⟩ ⟨*strato*-flying airplanes —*Science News Letter*⟩

strato·cirrus \ˌstrad·ō, -rā| *also* -ră| *or* -rȧ| + *n* [NL, fr. ¹*strato-* + *cirrus*] **:** a low dense cirrostratus cloud classed with the altostratus

stra·toc·ra·cy \strəˈtäkrəsē, -si\ *n* -ES [Gk *stratos* army + E *-cracy*] **:** a military government **:** government based on an army

strato·cumulus \ˌstrad·ō, -rā| *also* -ră| *or* -rȧ| +\ *n* [NL, fr. ¹*strato-* + *cumulus*] **:** stratified cumulus consisting of large balls or rolls of dark cloud which often cover the whole sky esp. in winter, give at times an undulated appearance, and do not bring rain — see CLOUD illustration

stra·ton·ic \strəˈtänik\ *or* **stra·ton·i·cal** \-nəkəl\ *adj, usu cap* [Gk *Stratōn* Strato, 3d cent. B.C. Greek philosopher + E *-ic* or *-ical*] **:** of, relating to, or typical of Strato of Lampsacus

stratose \ˈstrā,tōs, -ra,- *also* -rä,- *or* -rȧ,-\ *adj* [NL *stratum* + E *-ose*] **:** arranged in strata

strato·sphere \ˈstrad·ə,sfi(ə)r, -iə\ *n* [F *stratosphère*, fr. NL *stratum* + *-o-* + F *sphère* sphere, fr. L *sphaera* — more at SPHERE] **1 :** an upper portion of the atmosphere above seven miles more or less depending on latitude, season, and weather in which temperature changes but little with altitude, clouds of water are rare, and there is practically no deep convection — called also *isothermal region* **2 a :** a very high or the highest region on a graded scale ⟨meat prices are in the ~ —Joseph & Stewart Alsop⟩ ⟨the ~ of English society —*New Yorker*⟩ **b :** the top part of an object or region ⟨a sooty ~ of struts and girders —Berton Roueché⟩ ⟨the leafy ~ of the forest —Edmond Taylor⟩ **c :** a highly abstract or experimental field of endeavor ⟨a disembodied ~ of transcendental mathematics —A.L. Locke⟩ ⟨~ of modern art —D.C.Rich⟩

strato·spher·ic \ˌ===ˈsfirik, -fer-, -rēk\ *also* **strato·spher·i·cal** \-rəkəl, -rēk-\ *adj* [*stratosphere* + *-ic, -ical*] **1 :** of, relating to, or designed for use in the stratosphere **2 :** extremely high ⟨rearmament at ~ costs —Drew Middleton⟩ ⟨a severe critic whose standards are somewhat ~ —Rosalyn Krokover⟩ **3 :** remote from common sense or exact scientific thinking **:** MYSTICAL 3a, METAPHYSICAL 2a ⟨a solid point of reference by which to check . . . ~ philosophies of and about history —Garrett Mattingly⟩

stratous \ˈstrā|d·əs, |təs, -ra| *also* -rä| *or* -rȧ| **1** [NL *stratum* + E *-ous*] **:** composed of strata **2** [NL *stratus* + E *-ous*] **:** resembling stratus clouds

strato·volcano \ˌstra|d·ō, -rā| *also* -rä| *or* -rȧ|+\ *n* [NL *stratum* + E *-o-* + *volcano*; fr. its cone's being built up of successive layers of ash and lava] **:** a volcano composed of explosively erupted cinders and ash with occasional lava flows — contrasted with *shield volcano*

stratum \ˈstrā|d·əm, |təm, -ra| *also* -rä| *or* -rȧ|\ *n, pl* **strata** \-d·ə, -tə\ *also* **stratums** [NL, fr. L, spread, bed, fr. neut. of *stratus*, past part. of *sternere* to strew, spread out, lay flat; akin to Gk *stratos* (encamped) army, MIr *srath* wide valley — more at STREW] **1 :** a bed or layer artificially made **:** a coat of some material spread uniformly over a surface or upon another coat **:** LAYER ⟨the chaff, packed into a whole bay of the barn, was in strata —Adrian Bell⟩ **2 a :** a tabular mass or thin sheet of sedimentary rock or earth of one kind formed by natural causes and made up usu. of a series of layers lying between beds of other kinds **b :** BED **c :** a region of the sea or atmosphere that is analogous to a stratum of the earth ⟨winds tend to drive the surface water away . . . to be replaced by cold water upwelling from deeper *strata* —R.E.Coker⟩ **d :** a layer of tissue; *esp* **:** one of several superimposed membranes that go to make up an organ **e :** a layer in which archaeological material (as artifacts, skeletons, and dwelling remains) is found on excavation **f :** a vertical layer of vegetation (as of herbs, shrubs, or trees) in a plant community **3 a :** a part of a historical or sociological series representing a period or a stage of development ⟨the technique of skin dressing . . . belongs to an older ~ of Plains culture than the buffalo-skin tipi —Edward Sapir⟩ **b :** a socioeconomic level of society comprised of persons of the same or similar status esp. with regard to education or culture — compare CLASS ⟨wide *strata* of the intellectuals, professionals, and bureaucrats were penetrated ideologically —James Burnham⟩ ⟨the upper administrative *strata* of a typical large factory —E.H.Jacobson & S.E.Seashore⟩ **4 :** one of the sets considered as an integrated whole that make up an ordered, layered, or superimposed group of sets ⟨filtered down to him through different *strata* of thought —V.L.Parrington⟩ ⟨the whole subject of colds is overlaid by ~ upon ~ of folklore, superstition, and pseudoscience —C.H.Andrewes⟩ ⟨the more controversial mental *strata* lying between scientific, philosophical, and theological thought —*Times Lit. Supp.*⟩ ⟨the fairy-tale ~ of experience —F.R.Leavis⟩ **5 :** one of the divisions into which a population is divided in statistical stratification ⟨the counties of the United States may be grouped into 30 or more *strata* in terms of their population density —L.W.Doob⟩ **6 :** a group of linguistic phenomena characterized by the possession of common features (as of age or origin)

stratum corneum *n, pl* **strata cornea** [NL, lit., horny layer] **:** the outer more or less horny part of the epidermis including all the layers superficial to the Malpighian layer or only those that are superficial to the stratum granulosum and stratum lucidum

stratum ger·mi·na·ti·vum \-ˌjərmənəˈtīvəm\ *n, pl* **strata germinati·va** \-və\ [NL, lit., germinative layer] **:** the innermost layer of the epidermis consisting of a single row of columnar epithelial cells that continually divide and replace the rest of the epidermis as it wears away; *sometimes* **:** MALPIGHIAN LAYER

stratum gran·u·lo·sum \-ˌgranyəˈlōsəm\ *n, pl* **strata granulo·sa** \-sə\ [NL, lit., granulous layer] **1 :** a layer of granular cells lying immediately above the stratum germinativum in most parts of the epidermis **2 :** the layer of dentin in contact with the cementum of a tooth

stratum lu·ci·dum \-ˈlüsədəm\ *n, pl* **strata luci·da** \-də\ [NL, lit., lucid layer] **:** a thin somewhat translucent layer of cells lying superficial to the stratum granulosum in many parts of the epidermis

stratus \ˈstrā|d·əs, |təs, -ra| *also* -rä| *or* -rȧ|\ *n, pl* **strati** \-d·,ī, -,tī\ [NL, fr. L, past part. of *sternere* to spread out — more at STREW] **:** a cloud form characterized by relatively greater horizontal extension and comparatively lower altitude (2000 to 7000 feet) than the cumulostratus or cirrostratus — see CLOUD illustration

stratus cu·mu·li·for·mis \-ˌkyümyəliˈfȯrməs\ *n, pl* **strati cumulifor·mes** \-,mēz\ [NL] **:** a stratus cloud resembling the cumulus in form

stratus mac·u·lo·sus \-ˌmakyəˈlōsəs\ *n, pl* **strati maculo·si** \-ō,sī\ [NL, lit., spotted stratus] **:** MACKEREL SKY

straucht *or* **straught** \ˈsträkt\ *Scot var of* STRAIGHT

strauss·ian \ˈs(h)trau̇sēən\ *adj, usu cap* [Richard *Strauss* †1949 Ger. conductor and composer + E *-ian*] **:** of or relating to Richard Strauss or his musical compositions

stra·vage *or* **stra·vaig** \strəˈvāg\ *vi* [prob. by shortening and alter. fr. *extravagate*] *chiefly Scot* **:** SAUNTER, STROLL, WANDER

¹straw \ˈstrȯ\ *n* -s [ME *straw, stree*, fr. OE *strēaw, strē*; akin to OHG *strō* straw, ON *strā*, OE *strēowian, strewian* to strew — more at STREW] **1 a :** stalks of grain after threshing usu. mixed with leaves and chaff, used as bedding for cattle, for packing, for fodder, in papermaking, or woven, plaited, or braided for various uses (as for a hat) **b :** a natural (as buntal) or artificial (as nylon) fiber woven, plaited, or braided to serve various uses (as for a mat, hat, bag, shoe, or box) **c :** any of various dry or stalky residues of plant growth that are put to practical use (as for bedding or packing) — see PINE STRAW **2 :** a stalk or stem of grain (as of wheat, rye, oats, or barley); *also* **:** a stalk of buckwheat, beans, or peas **3 a** (1) **:** something of small worth or significance ⟨grateful for such ~*s* as the garden and the weather —Will Scott⟩ ⟨another ~ toward helping them carry out their project —Robert Grant †1940⟩ — usu. used in such phrases as *care a straw* ⟨didn't care a ~ about the case —O.W.Holmes †1935⟩ ⟨wasn't worth making a fuss about, because it didn't really matter a ~ —Ellen Glasgow⟩ (2) **:** something too insubstantial to provide support or help in a desperate situation ⟨clutches at the ~ of falsehood —H.M. Parshley⟩ ⟨even active unionists tend to grasp at strange ~*s* for support —Bob Senser⟩ (3) *or* **straw in the wind :** a slight fact that is an indication of a coming event ⟨some of the *straws in the wind* include an increase in the printing of paper yen —Lindesay Parrott⟩ **b :** CHAFF 3 ⟨the mass of irrelevant trivialities and repetitions in doubtful taste which form the ~ of a considerable part of this book —*Books Abroad*⟩ **c :** MAN OF STRAW **4 :** a thing made of straw: as **a** *obs* **:** PIPE 1a(1) **b :** STRAW HAT **c :** a prepared tube originally cut from a wheat straw for sucking up a beverage ⟨the nurse brought him some clear consommé and a bent glass ~ —Oakley Hall⟩ **5 :** a thing shaped like a straw; *esp* **:** a short narrow strip of pastry ⟨cheese ~*s*⟩ **6** *or* **straw yellow :** a pale yellow that is deeper than cream, deeper and slightly greener than ivory, and greener and stronger than leghorn — **in the straw** *adv (or adj)* **:** in childbed

²straw \"\ *vt* -ED/-ING/-S [ME *strawen*, fr. ¹*straw*] **1 :** to cover (a surface) with or as if with straw **2 :** to provide with straw ⟨steers ~*ed* to weather a blizzard —James Still⟩

³straw \"\ *adj* [¹*straw*] **1 :** made of straw ⟨~ basket⟩ ⟨~ seats⟩ ⟨~ broom⟩ **2 :** of, relating to, or used for straw ⟨~ barn⟩ **3 :** of the color of straw ⟨his ~ hair flopped wildly on his forehead —Wirt Williams⟩ **4 :** of little or no value **:** WORTHLESS **5 :** of, relating to, resembling, or being a man of straw ⟨a ~ structure which bore almost no resemblance to the Greek philosopher's manner of thinking —Martin Gardner⟩ ⟨purchase any property . . . either in his own name or by use of a ~ party —W.H.Husband & F.R.Anderson⟩ **6 :** of, relating to, or concerned with the discovery of preferences by means of a straw vote ⟨~ polls that seek to sample public opinion —W.E. Binkley & Malcolm Moos⟩ ⟨the poll . . . is conducted by seven crews of ~ takers —A.J.Liebling⟩

⁴straw \"\ *vt* -ED/-ING/-S [ME *strawwen, strawen*, fr. OE *strēawian, strēowian* to strew — more at STREW] **:** STREW **syn** see STREW

straw bail *n* **:** worthless or insufficient bail

straw ballot *n* **:** STRAW VOTE

straw bass *n* **:** LARGEMOUTH BLACK BASS

straw bed *n* **:** a mattress filled with straw

straw·berry \ˈstrȯ,berē, -b(ə)rē, -ri — *see* BERRY\ *n, often attrib* [ME, fr. OE *strēawberige*, fr. *strēaw* straw + *berige, berie* berry; perh. fr. the resemblance of the achenes on the surface to fragments of straw] **1 a :** a juicy edible usu. red fruit produced by a plant of the genus *Fragaria* and being an enlarged pulpy receptacle bearing numerous seedlike achenes rather than a true berry **b :** a plant of the genus *Fragaria* including many that are cultivated for their fruits **2 a :** a variable color averaging a moderate red that is very slightly yellower, lighter, and stronger than cerise, very slightly yellower, darker, and stronger than claret (sense 3a), lighter and very slightly yellower and stronger than Harvard crimson (sense 1), and bluer, slightly lighter, and very slightly stronger than Turkey red **b :** a grayish red that is bluer and deeper than appleblossom and bluer and darker than bois de rose **c** *of textiles* **:** a moderate purplish red that is bluer and deeper than average rose and redder and duller than violine pink **3 :** a small strawberry-colored mark or bruise

strawberry aphid *n* **:** any of several aphids that feed on strawberry plants; *esp* **:** a common and widely distributed aphid (*Chaetosiphon fragaefolii*) that is the chief insect vector of mosaic diseases of strawberries

strawberry bass *n* **:** BLACK CRAPPIE

strawberry blite *n* **:** an annual weedy herb (*Chenopodium capitatum*) of the north temperate zone with succulent stems, small greenish flowers, and red pulpy fruit — called also *strawberry pigweed*

strawberry blonde *n* **:** a woman of blonde complexion and yellowish red hair

strawberry bush *n* **1 a :** a No. American shrub (*Euonymus americanus*) having crimson pods and seeds with a scarlet aril **b :** ²WAHOO a **2 :** STRAWBERRY SHRUB

strawberry cactus *n* **:** a low caespitose cactus (*Echinocereus enneacanthus*) of southern Texas and Mexico

strawberry clover *n* **:** an Old World clover (*Trifolium fragiferum*) like the white clover but having an inflated pink or reddish calyx

strawberry comb *n* **:** a low rounded comb of a fowl that suggests a half strawberry and is characteristic of Malay and silky fowls — see COMB illustration

strawberry crab *n* **:** a small European spider crab (*Eurynome aspera*) having the back covered with pink tubercles

strawberry crinkle *n* **:** an insect-transmitted virus disease of the strawberry characterized by the development in young leaves of small chlorotic areas which fail to grow so that the leaf becomes crinkled and distorted

strawberry crown borer *or* **strawberry borer** *or* **strawberry root borer** *n* **:** a weevil (*Tyloderma fragariae*) whose larva bores in the crown of the strawberry

strawberry crown miner *n* **:** the caterpillar of a gelechiid moth (*Aristotelia fragariae*) which mines the leaves of strawberry plants

strawberry crown moth *n* **:** a clearwing moth (*Ramosia bibionipennis*) whose larva is destructive to strawberry, blackberry, and raspberry plants; *also* **:** an aegeriid moth with similar habits

strawberry fern *n* **:** a tropical American fern (*Hemionitis palmata*) sometimes cultivated for its roundish 3-parted coarsely lobed fronds

strawberry festival *n* **:** a community festival (as a card party, church supper, or bazaar) held usu. in strawberry season at which strawberry shortcake is served

strawberry finch *n* **:** AVADAVAT

strawberry flea beetle *n* **:** a small metallic blue or greenish American flea beetle (*Altica ignita*) that feeds on the foliage of strawberries

strawberry fly *n* **:** DEERFLY

strawberry gallbladder *n* **:** a gallbladder in which cholesterol is deposited in the lining of the organ in a pattern resembling the surface of a strawberry **:** CHOLESTEROSIS

strawberry geranium *or* **strawberry saxifrage** *n* **:** an eastern Asiatic saxifrage (*Saxifraga sarmentosa*) with numerous creeping stolons, round leaves, and racemes of small red-and-white flowers — called also *mother-of-thousands*

strawberry guava *n* **1 a :** a subtropical shrub or small tree (*Psidium cattleianum*) **b :** the dark-crimson fruit of this plant much used either fresh or preserved **2 :** FEIJOA

straw·ber·ry·ing \-iŋ, -ēŋ\ *n* -s [*strawberry* + *-ing*] **:** the act of gathering or looking for strawberries

strawberry leaf *n* **:** a representation of the leaf of a strawberry plant used as a symbol of the rank or estate of an earl, duke, or marquis

strawberry leaf roller *n* **:** any of several moth larvae that roll up and feed on strawberry leaves; *also* **:** a moth (esp. *Ancylis comptana*) whose larva is a strawberry leaf roller

strawberry leaf spot *or* **strawberry leaf blight** *also* **strawberry rust** *n* **:** a disease of the strawberry plant caused by a parasitic fungus (*Mycosphaerella fragariae*) and characterized esp. by the tan to white more or less circular spots with a usu. clear cut margin — compare LEAF SCORCH b

strawberry mark *n* **:** a birthmark consisting of a hemangioma that is somewhat like a strawberry in appearance

strawberry nettle *n* **:** a Polynesian plant (*Elatostema pedunculatum*) of the family Urticaceae with red fruits that resemble strawberries

strawberry pear *n* **1 :** the red ovoid slightly acid fruit of a West Indian cactus **2 :** a cactus (*Hylocereus undatus*) that bears strawberry pears and has triangular stems and large showy flowers

strawberry perch *n* **:** BLACK CRAPPIE

strawberry pigweed *or* **strawberry spinach** *n* **:** STRAWBERRY BLITE

strawberry pink *n* **:** a deep pink to yellowish pink

strawberry raspberry *n* **:** a low herbaceous or subshrubby Asiatic bramble (*Rubus illecebrosus*) cultivated for its large multi-parted leaves, large white flowers, and showy red edible fruits — called also *balloonberry*

strawberry roan *n* **1 :** roan with a decidedly red ground color **2 :** a horse of a strawberry roan color

strawberry root aphid *n* **:** an aphid (*Aphis forbesi*) that damages strawberries by sucking the sap from the roots

strawberry root weevil *n* **:** a small black beetle (*Brachyrhinus ovatus*) of the family Curculionidae whose larva lives in the soil and feeds on the roots or girdles the crown of strawberry plants

strawberry rootworm *n* **:** a grub that is the larva of a small brownish black-spotted leaf beetle (*Paria fragariae*) and that lives in the soil and feeds on the roots of strawberries

strawberry sawfly *n* **:** a small black sawfly (*Empria maculatus*) whose larva eats the leaves of the strawberry plant

strawberry shrub *n* **:** CAROLINA ALLSPICE

strawberry-shrub family *n* **:** CALYCANTHACEAE

strawberry slug *n* **:** the larva of a strawberry sawfly

strawberry tassel *n* **:** PURPLE MILKWORT

strawberry tomato *n* **:** GROUND-CHERRY 2; *esp* **:** a stout hairy annual herb (*Physalis pruinosa*) of eastern No. America with sweet globular yellow fruits

strawberry tongue *n* **:** a tongue that is red from the swollen congested papillae typical of scarlet fever

strawberry tree *n* **1 :** a European evergreen tree (*Arbutus unedo*) with fruit resembling strawberries and racemose white flowers — called also *Irish strawberry, madrona* **2 :** a strawberry bush (*Euonymus americanus*); *also* **:** ²WAHOO a

strawberry vine *n* **:** STRAWBERRY 1b

strawberry weevil *n* **1 :** a small weevil (*Anthonomus signatus*) that severs the stems of the strawberry and lays eggs in the buds **2 :** STRAWBERRY CROWN BORER

strawberry wine *n* **:** a dark red that is yellower and duller than cranberry and yellower, lighter, and stronger than average garnet or average wine

strawbill \ˈ=,=\ *n* **:** HOODED MERGANSER

strawboard \ˈ=,=\ *n* **:** board made of straw pulp and commonly used for packing and boxmaking

straw bond *n* **:** a bond whose sureties are worthless

straw boss *n* **1 :** an assistant to a foreman in charge of supervising and expediting the work of a small gang of workmen (as in a logging camp or factory or on a road gang) **2 :** a member of a group of workers who supervises the work of the others in addition to doing his own job

straw–boss \ˈ=,=\ *vt* [*straw boss*] **:** to function as a straw boss at or over ⟨was *straw-bossing* the dam work —*Reader's Digest*⟩

strawbreadth \ˈ=,=\ *n* **:** a very small distance

straw cat *n* **:** PAMPAS CAT

straw color *n* **:** a light yellow color like that of dry straw

strawed *past of* STRAW

straw·en \ˈstrȯən\ *adj* [ME, fr. ¹*straw* + *-en*] *archaic* **:** made of straw

straw fiddle *n* **:** a xylophone in which wooden bars are supported on rolls of straw

strawflower \ˈ=,=\ *n* **1 :** any of several everlasting flowers; *specif* **:** an Australian annual herb (*Helichrysum bracteatum*) much grown for its heads of chaffy brightly colored long-keeping flowers **2 :** any of several herbs of the genus *Uvularia*

straw hat *n* **:** a hat of woven or plaited straw

strawhat \ˈ=,=\ *or* **strawhat theater** *n* [*strawhat* fr. *strawhat theater*, fr. the former fashion of wearing straw hats in summer] **:** a summer theater ⟨prepares packages of his own which he distributes to his playhouses and to a few other ~*s* —Henry Hewes⟩

strawing *pres part of* STRAW

straw·ish \ˈstrȯish, -ēsh\ *adj* **:** somewhat resembling straw esp. in color

straw itch *n* **:** GRAIN ITCH

straw·less \ˈ=ˌləs\ *adj* **:** containing no straw
straw line *n* **:** a light cable used to haul the heavier cables of a rigging used in skidding logs
straw man *n* **:** MAN OF STRAW
strawmote \ˈ=ˌ=\ *n, dial Eng* **:** a single straw
straw-necked ibis \ˈ=ˌ=-\ *n* **:** an Australian ibis (*Threskiornis spinicollis* or *Carphibis spinicollis*) with modified feathers of the lower neck that are yellow and stiff and resemble straw
straw oil *n* **:** a high-boiling petroleum distillate similar to gas oil used chiefly in purifying coke-oven gas and other industrial gases
straw plait *n* **:** braided straw (as for making hats)
straw ride *n* **:** HAYRIDE
straws *pl of* STRAW, *pres 3d sing of* STRAW
straw sedge *n* **:** a common sedge (*Carex straminea*) of eastern No. America
strawsmear \ˈ=ˌ=\ *n* **1** *or* **strawsmall** \ˈ=ˌ=\ *Brit* **:** WHITETHROAT 1 **2** *Brit* **:** GARDEN WARBLER **3** *Brit* **:** WILLOW WREN
strawstack \ˈ=ˌ=\ *n* **:** a pile of grain straw from which the grain has been threshed
strawstacker \ˈ=ˌ==\ *n* [*strawstack* + *-er*] **:** one that piles straw in a stack
straw stem *n* **:** a wineglass stem pulled out of the substance of the bowl; *also* **:** a wineglass having such a stem
straw vote *n* **:** an unofficial vote (as taken at a chance gathering or by letters of inquiry) to indicate the relative strength of opposing candidates or issues — called also *straw ballot*
strawwalker \ˈ=ˌ==\ *n* **:** a device inside a thresher or combine that consists of reciprocating notched bars to push the straw to the rear of the machine
straw wine *n* **:** a sweet dessert wine that resembles liqueur and is produced from grapes partially dried often on straw and in the sun before fermentation
strawworm \ˈ=ˌ=\ *n* **1 :** CADDISWORM **2 :** any of several larval chalcid flies that injure the straw of wheat and other grains (as barley)
strawy \ˈstrȯi, -ȯē\ *adj* -ER/-EST [¹*straw* + *-y*] **1 :** of, relating to, resembling, consisting of, or containing straw **2** *obs* **:** WORTHLESS, TRIFLING
strawyard \ˈ=ˌ=\ *n, Brit* **:** a yard littered with straw for wintering or fattening livestock
straw yellow *n* **:** STRAW 6
¹**stray** \ˈstrā\ *vb* -ED/-ING/-S [ME *straien*, fr. MF *estraier* fr. (assumed) VL *extragare*, fr. L *extra-* outside + *vagari* to wander — more at EXTRA-, VAGARY] *vi* **1 a :** to wander from company, from confinement or restraint, or from the proper limits **:** rove at large ⟨leaving a gate open so that cattle ~ —Agnes M. Miall⟩ ⟨the two had ~*ed* apart where the woods were deepest —Mary Austin⟩ **b :** to leave a natural or accustomed habitat or environment ⟨fruit trees and ~*ed* garden flowers deep in the woods —Bernard DeVoto⟩ ⟨the most courteous . . . of eighteenth-century grands seigneurs ~*ed* out of his age into ours —Gerald Abraham⟩ ⟨of adults . . . at least one-tenth might never have ~*ed* outside in their lives —G.G. Coulton⟩ **2 a :** to roam about without fixed direction or purpose **:** wander at random ⟨fetid back alleys where we sometimes ~*ed* —Marvin Barret⟩ **b :** to move in a winding course **:** MEANDER **c :** to move without voluntary control or under external compulsion ⟨my hand automatically ~*s* towards my pocket —*Sydney (Australia) Bull.*⟩ ⟨eyes ~*ing* absently around the room⟩ **3 a** (1) **:** to engage temporarily or momentarily in sinful, immoral, or other than praiseworthy actions or thoughts **:** ERR (2) **:** to think or utter ideas contrary to or different from an accepted dogma ⟨those who ~*ed* from the party line —Kurt Glaser⟩ **b :** to become distracted from an argument or chain of thought **:** take up a tangential point ⟨I have ~*ed* from my . . . role of historian . . . to indulge in a bit of prophecy —J.B. Conant⟩ **4 :** to wander accidentally from a direct or chosen route **:** lose one's way **:** DEVIATE ⟨~*ed* off the road . . . in the dark of the moon —Mary Webb⟩ ⟨the unit ~*ed* across the border by mistake —*Springfield (Mass.) Union*⟩ **5 :** to present a haphazard or unkempt appearance ⟨black hair that ~*ed* carelessly about her face —Liam O'Flaherty⟩ ⟨a leading article (which regrettably ~*s* from page to page among the advertisements) —*Times Lit. Supp.*⟩ ~ *vt* **1** *archaic* **:** to cause to stray **2** *archaic* **:** to roam through or over
²**stray** \"\ *n* -S [ME, fr. AF *estray*, fr. OF *estraié*, past part. of *estraier* to stray] **1 a** (1) **:** a domestic animal that has left an enclosure or its proper place and company and wanders at large or is lost subject to impoundment and if unredeemed to forfeiture **:** ESTRAY (2) **:** an animal that has strayed ⟨the shepherd rounded up the flock's ~*s*⟩ (3) **:** an unidentified domestic animal (as a dog or an unbranded steer) wandering at large **b** (1) **:** a person or thing that strays or has strayed **:** a detached, isolated, or vagrant individual **:** STRAGGLER, WAIF ⟨harbored white renegades and ~*s* from hostile tribes —*Amer. Guide Series: Tenn.*⟩ ⟨do not own more than three books other than casual contemporary ~*s* —J.W.Krutch⟩ (2) **:** an animal or plant found outside its natural range or habitat or out of season **c** *obs* **:** a group of strayed animals, people, or things ⟨hast thou seen a ~ of bullocks and of heifers pass this way —Joseph Addison⟩ **2** [ME, fr. *straien* to stray] *archaic* **:** the act or process of going astray or of strolling aimlessly ⟨I would not from your love make such a ~ —Shak.⟩ **3** *Brit* **:** common land or pasturage; *also* **:** the right to allow one's stock to stray and feed thereon **4 a :** an electrical effect that is not produced by a transmitting station and that disturbs the reception of receiving apparatus **b :** an electric wave or current causing a stray — compare ATMOSPHERICS **5 :** an unexpected formation encountered in drilling an oil or gas well
³**stray** \"\ *adj* [²*stray*] **1 a :** escaped from confinement, supervision, or restraint or from a group of its kind ⟨~ cow⟩ ⟨~ dog⟩ ⟨~ child⟩ **b :** having been lost, misplaced, or forgotten ⟨the other fellows take handkerchiefs home and ~ coats sometimes —Janet Frame⟩ **2 :** wandering lost, aimless, or isolated from the normal or principal body, habitat, or course ⟨details picked up from ~ survivors —John Mason Brown⟩ ⟨account for every ~ traveller in the mountains —Owen Wister⟩ ⟨a ~ enemy group may at any time swoop down —Ed Cunningham⟩ **3 a :** occurring or appearing sporadically or at random ⟨~ acquaintances met with in hotel rooms and aeroplanes —*Geog. Jour.*⟩ ⟨the white dogwood were ~ handfuls of confetti in the young green —Horace Sutton⟩ **b :** touched upon or met with only in passing or in haste **:** OCCASIONAL, INCIDENTAL ⟨a series of scenes that (except for ~ ones) register honestly —John Kerry⟩ ⟨one or two ~ expressions that have evaded revision —*Times Lit. Supp.*⟩ ⟨a ~ weekly hour of hygiene —Hortense Calisher⟩ **c :** scattered about ⟨on our knees retrieving ~ cigarettes —A. Conan Doyle⟩ ⟨collecting ~ hairs from the farm horses' tails —W.P.Smith⟩ ⟨~ members of the congregation moved by the spirit may be prophesying in unknown tongues —W.L.Sperry⟩ **4 :** not serving any useful purpose **:** UNWANTED ⟨necessarily results in serious errors when ~ light . . . is not absorbed by the optical system —H.A.Stahl⟩ ⟨insulate them . . . so that no ~ current is introduced into the circuit —A.C.Morrison⟩ **5 :** written hastily or thoughtlessly and published in obscure or ephemeral journals ⟨wrote only one complete novel and a few ~ pieces and fragments —Henri Peyre⟩
strayaway \ˈ==ˌ=\ *n* -S [*stray* + *away*] **:** one that strays away
strayed *past of* STRAY
stray energy *or* **stray power** *n* **:** electrical losses (as in a dynamo) due to friction, hysteresis, or eddy currents as distinguished from the loss from electric resistance in the conducting apparatus
stray·er \ˈstrāə(r), -re(ə)r, -reə\ *n* -S **:** one that strays **:** STRAY
straying *pres part of* STRAY
stray line *n* **:** the portion of a log line which is run out to allow the chip to get clear of the stern eddies before the reckoning is begun
strays *pres 3d sing of* STRAY, *pl of* STRAY
strd *abbr* strand
¹**streak** \ˈstrēk\ *n* -S [ME *strek, streke, strik, strike*, fr. OE *strica* line, streak; akin to MD *streke* line, stroke, OHG *strich*, Goth *striks* line, stroke, L *striga* row, furrow — more at STRIKE] **1** *obs* **:** a linear mark or cut ⟨in the microscope . . . you may see the very ~*s* —Henry Power⟩ **2 a :** an irregular or indistinct stripe on the coat of an animal or the plumage of a bird ⟨a magnolia warbler . . . his bluish gray back and yellow breast crossed by a black band from which black ~*s* run downward —W.P.Smith⟩ **b** (1) **:** an irregular strip or line of contrasting color or texture causing variation in or on a surface ⟨faded ~*s* in a curtain where the sun hits it⟩ ⟨bacon with a thick ~ of lean⟩ (2) **:** an incision made by chipping a pine tree for obtaining turpentine **c :** the color of the fine powder of a mineral obtained by scratching, pulverizing, or rubbing against a hard white surface, often differing from the color of the mineral in mass, and being important as a distinguishing character esp. for minerals having metallic luster **d :** an imperfection in glass consisting of a wavy or colored line that distorts an image **e** (1) **:** a threadlike striation (2) **:** inoculum implanted (as with a needle drawn across the surface) in a line or stripe upon a solidified culture medium (3) **:** STREAK CULTURE **f** (1) **:** any of several virus diseases of plants (as the potato, tomato, raspberry, or sugarcane) resembling mosaic but usu. producing at least some linear markings — compare BLUESTEM 2, TOMATO STREAK (2) **:** a disease of sweet peas caused by a bacillus (*Erwinia lathyri*) and characterized by brownish spots or streaks on the stem, petioles, and leaves **3 a :** a narrow band of light ⟨the first grey ~*s* of dawn —R.S. Porteous⟩ ⟨a ~ of moonlight came in through the window —Sherwood Anderson⟩ ⟨burning oil flew outwards in a ~ —Nevil Shute⟩ **b :** a dart of lightning **:** BOLT ⟨in dazzling ~*s* the vivid lightnings play —William Cowper⟩ ⟨off like a ~, heading . . . down the homestretch —*N. Y. Times*⟩ **4 a :** a slight admixture (as of an inherent character) **:** STRAIN, TRACE ⟨the ~ of extreme stubbornness . . . was both his strength and his misfortune —J.K.Galbraith⟩ ⟨a ~ of Indian blood in him —A.W.Long⟩ **b :** a brief run (as of luck) ⟨when he hits a ~ . . . everything's dandy —Hamilton Basso⟩ **c :** a consecutive series (as of victories or defeats) ⟨had a long winning ~ and took the . . . lead —A.J.Liebling⟩ **d :** a short interval or transitory phase **:** FIT, SPELL ⟨got started on one of her talking ~*s* —Erskine Caldwell⟩ **5 a :** a long irregular strip (as of land or water) ⟨a ~ of deep green brush marks the course of a creek —*Amer. Guide Series: Ark.*⟩ **b :** a narrow layer (as of ore) **:** SEAM, VEIN ⟨struck a pay ~ at a thousand feet⟩
²**streak** \"\ *vb* -ED/-ING/-S *vt* **1 :** to make streaks on or in **:** STRIATE ⟨the water was ~*ed* with the sunset colors —R.H. Newman⟩ ⟨the sense of living nature seems to ~ some of his more recent pages —Cecil Sprigge⟩ **2 :** to prepare a streak culture of ~ *vi* **1 a :** to make streaks ⟨ribbons of rust ~ down . . . from patches of corrugated iron on the roof —James Reynolds⟩ **b :** to rush swiftly **:** BOLT, ROCKET ⟨lightning ~*s* from cloud to cloud⟩ ⟨reporters . . . ~*ed* through the crowd and out of the doors searching for telephones —Erle Stanley Gardner⟩ ⟨jet planes ~*ed* to three new transcontinental speed records —*Newsweek*⟩ ⟨when the nurse opened the door, the cat ~*ed* in —Henrietta Weigel⟩ **2 :** to become streaked ⟨hair beginning to ~ with gray⟩
³**streak** \"\ *vt* -ED/-ING/-S [ME *streken* to stroke, prob. fr. MD — more at STROKE] *obs* **:** RUB, SMEAR ⟨with the juice of this I'll ~ her eyes —Shak.⟩
⁴**streak** *archaic var of* STRAKE
⁵**streak** \ˈstrēk\ *var of* STREEK
streak culture *n* **:** a culture inoculated with a streak
streaked \ˈstrēkt, -kəd\ *adj* [fr. past part. of ²*streak*] **1 :** marked with or as if with stripes or linear discolorations **:** GRIZZLED, STRIATED ⟨~ hair⟩ ⟨~ lumber⟩ **2 :** physically or mentally disturbed **:** stricken with illness or anxiety **:** SICK, UPSET ⟨looked so ~ and so chopfallen, that I felt . . . sorry for him —T.C.Haliburton⟩
streaked-back plover \ˈ=ˌ=-\ *n* **:** TURNSTONE
streaked bass *n* **:** STRIPED BASS
streak·er \ˈstrēkə(r)\ *n* -S [¹*streak* + *-er*; fr. the usu. seven black stripes from gill cover to tail base of the yellow bass] **1 :** YELLOW BASS **2 :** WHITE BASS 1
streak·i·ly \-kəlē, -li\ *adv* **:** in a streaky manner
streak·i·ness \-kēnəs, -kin-\ *n* -ES **:** the quality or state of being streaky
streak lightning *n* **:** CHAIN LIGHTNING
streak plate *n* **:** a piece of white unglazed porcelain on which to test the streak of a mineral
streaky \ˈstrēkē, -ki\ *adj* -ER/-EST [¹*streak* + *-y*] **1 a :** resembling or characterized by streaks ⟨a smoky fleece . . . brushed to give a ~ effect —*Women's Wear Daily*⟩ **b :** marked with streaks ⟨fat legs and dirty, ~ face —Hugh Walpole⟩ **c :** having alternate streaks of fat and lean ⟨~ bacon⟩ **2 :** APPREHENSIVE ⟨as nervous and ~ about it as a cat on a hot rock —H.L.Davis⟩ **3 :** of mixed quality **:** VARIABLE, UNRELIABLE ⟨humans are the most ~ of conceivable things —H.G.Wells⟩
¹**stream** \ˈstrēm\ *n* -S *often attrib* [ME *strem, streme*, fr. OE *strēam*; akin to OHG *stroum, strōm* stream, ON *straumr* stream, OIr *sruaimm* river, OSlav *struja* flow, Gk *rhysis* flow, *rhein* to flow, Skt *sravati* it flows, *sarati* it runs, flows — more at SERUM] **1 a :** a body of running water flowing in a channel on the surface of the ground, in a cavern below the surface, or beneath or in a glacier ⟨cross the river . . . not far from where General Washington forded the ~ —Gladys Taber⟩ — compare CREEK, RIVER; see CURRENT table **b :** BROOK, RIVULET **2 a :** a steady succession (as of words or events) ⟨let loose a ~ of commentary and discussion —R.W.Southern⟩ ⟨life presents a perpetual ~ of problems —W.J.Reilly⟩ **b :** a constantly renewed supply ⟨the balanced budget . . . injects as much into the income ~ as it takes away —J.G.Gurley⟩ ⟨a steady ~ of material flowed into the Smithsonian from . . . all over the world —D.S. & Jessie Jordan⟩ **c :** a continuous procession moving in one direction ⟨sent a ~ of miners pouring . . . west —R.A.Billington⟩ ⟨a ~ of Sunday traffic⟩ ⟨goats followed him — a long ~ that pattered on small sharp hoofs behind him —Stuart Cloete⟩ **3 a :** an outpouring of a fluid from a source or container ⟨a ~ of water . . . from a fire nozzle —W.Y.Kimball⟩ ⟨pour a sticky ~ of syrup from a pitcher⟩ ⟨a reaction ~ can be switched from one line to the other —*Chem. & Engineering News*⟩ **b :** an effusion of a bodily fluid ⟨~*s* of sweat pour down his back⟩ **c :** an unbroken flow (as of gas or particles of matter) ⟨moisture was kept at a high level by a deep ~ of persistent northerly winds —*Farmer's Weekly (So. Africa)*⟩ ⟨an electric current is a ~ of . . . electrons —Leonard Engel⟩ **d** (1) **:** a valley glacier ⟨ice ~*s* coalesced to form a piedmont glacier —*Jour. of Geol.*⟩ (2) **:** a lava flow esp. long and narrow ⟨dated lava ~*s* —W.J.Miller⟩ (3) **:** sand grains moving or having moved downwind in a fairly continuous mass ⟨the dune advances . . . down the sand ~ —*Geog. Jour.*⟩ — compare ROCK STREAM **4 a :** a streak of light ⟨the ashen ~ of daybreak —Ellen Glasgow⟩ **b** *obs* **:** the tail of a comet ⟨saw another comet . . . but the ~ not so long as the former —John Evelyn⟩ **5 a :** a relatively narrow well-defined and usu. swift oceanic current ⟨the Gulf ~⟩ **b :** the center of a body of running water where the current is swiftest ⟨anchored out in the ~ and came ashore in a launch⟩ **c :** the propulsive current of running water ⟨floating straight, obedient to the ~ —Shak.⟩ ⟨row against the ~⟩ **d :** a prevailing attitude or group (in full accord with the main ~ of British policy —*New Statesman & Nation*⟩ **e :** a dominant influence or line of development ⟨the two ~*s* of heredity . . . that shaped his life —C.A.Dinsmore⟩ ⟨academicians, men out of the main creative ~ of their time —Donald Mintz⟩ ⟨eddies in the great ~ of baroque music —P.H.Lang⟩ **6 streams** *pl, archaic* **:** flowing waters ⟨a river . . . pours its ~*s* through a narrow vale —Sir Walter Scott⟩ **syn** see FLOW — **on stream :** in or into production ⟨the refinery could be *on stream* within four or five weeks —Clifton Daniel⟩ ⟨our Baton Rouge plant . . . will go *on stream*, it is expected, in June of this year —*Ethyl News*⟩
²**stream** \"\ *vb* -ED/-ING/-S [ME *stremen*, fr. *strem, streme* stream] *vi* **1 a :** to flow in or as if in a stream ⟨a river ~*s* to the sea⟩ ⟨firelight and dance music ~ out from its windows —Douglas Stewart⟩ ⟨a cooler wind was beginning to ~ through the . . . palms —Jean Boley⟩ ⟨capes and headlands . . . ~*ing* away into the west —H.H.Finlayson⟩ ⟨wealth ~*ing* through his fingers —Joseph Conrad⟩ **b :** to emit a beam of light **:** leave a bright trail ⟨a falling star ~*ed* down the blue vault —O.S.J. Gogarty⟩ **2 a :** to exude a bodily fluid in profuse amounts ⟨holding his pocket handkerchief before his ~*ing* eyes —Lewis Carroll⟩ **b :** to become saturated with a discharge of bodily fluid ⟨~*ing* with perspiration under the hot klieg lights⟩ **3 :** to become fully extended by or as if by a current **:** trail out at full length ⟨kelps, anchored to rocks while ~*ing* out in the water —R.E.Coker⟩ ⟨outthrust neck and ~*ing* legs are characteristic of its flight —*Nat'l Geographic*⟩ ⟨the boy, with hair ~*ing* back, was rushing helter-skelter down the hill —John Galsworthy⟩ **4 :** to pour in large numbers in one direction ⟨passengers . . . ~*ed* ashore on seven of the eight gangways —Vernon Pizer⟩ ⟨rooks went ~*ing* across the windy sky —Mary Webb⟩ ⟨innumerable requests and invitations . . . ~ in —Robert Bendiner⟩ ~ *vt* **1 :** to emit or cause to flow **:** EXUDE ⟨his eyes ~*ed* tears⟩ **2 :** to wave or display fully extended ⟨its radiator grille ~*ing* a flag —Kathryn Grondahl⟩ **3 :** to put into the water **:** allow (a tow) to run out to full length ⟨~ an anchor buoy⟩ ⟨~ a paravane⟩ ⟨~ a grass line so that the other ship can grapple it and pick it up —*Manual of Seamanship*⟩ **4 :** to subject to the action of water as a means of exposing ore **:** WASH ⟨slaves were ~*ing* the gravel for tin ore —Charles Kingsley⟩ **syn** see POUR
stream anchor *n* **:** a light anchor for use with a bower in narrow waterways
stream cable *n* **:** the cable of a stream anchor
stream capture *n* **:** CAPTURE 3
¹**stream·er** \ˈstrēmə(r)\ *n* -S [ME *stremer*, fr. *stremen* to stream + *-er* — more at STREAM] **1 a :** a flag that streams in the wind; *esp* **:** PENNANT **b :** a wavy band resembling a fluttering pennon ⟨clouds . . . like ~*s* of snow —O.E.Rölvaag⟩ **c :** a narrow free-floating strip (as of cloth or crepe paper) ⟨a hat with ~*s* down the back⟩ ⟨a hall festooned with ~*s*⟩ **d :** STREAMER FLY **e :** a ribbon poster esp. used in a window or store display and often having a single line of wording **f :** BANNER 4 **g :** a parachute that streams out from the pack but fails to blossom **2 a** *obs* **:** the tail of a comet **b :** a long gauzelike extension of the solar corona brighter at the base and fading to invisibility at the end, sometimes showing filamentous structure, and visible only during a total solar eclipse **c streamers** *pl* **:** AURORA BOREALIS **d :** a visible brush discharge streaming out from some part of an electric circuit or charged body — compare CORONA 2g **3 :** one that washes sand or gravel in search of ore **syn** see FLAG
²**streamer** \"\ *vt* -ED/-ING/-S **:** to provide or decorate with streamers
streamer fly *n* **:** any large wet fisherman's fly with long streamer feathers, hair, or other appendages extending out behind the hook and from the head
stream feeding *n* **:** a method of feeding in which sheets are overlapped as they approach the front guides on the feedboard of a printing press
streamflow \ˈ=ˌ=\ *n* **:** water flowing in a stream channel; *specif* **:** the velocity and volume of such water
¹**stream·ing** \ˈstrēmiŋ, -mēŋ\ *n* -S [ME *streming*, fr. gerund of *stremen* to stream — more at STREAM] **:** an act or instance of flowing; *specif* **:** CYCLOSIS
²**streaming** *adj* [fr. pres. part. of ²*stream*] **:** issuing in or suffused with streams **:** FLOWING, RUNNING ⟨a ~ cold⟩ ⟨a ~ umbrella⟩ ⟨a ~ sunset⟩ — **stream·ing·ly** *adv*
streaming potential *n* **:** a potential difference that arises across a capillary tube or membrane when a liquid is forced through it — compare ZETA POTENTIAL
stream jam *n* **:** a log jam that reaches neither shore — called also *center jam*
stream·less \ˈ=ləs\ *adj* **:** having no stream
stream·let \-lət\ *n* -S [¹*stream* + *-let*] **:** a small stream
¹**streamline** \ˈ=ˌ=\ *n, often attrib* [¹*stream* + *line*] **1 a :** LINE OF FLOW ⟨~*s* of liquid flowing in a constricted tube —H.B. Lemon & Michael Ference⟩ **b :** the path of a fluid particle relative to a solid body past which the fluid is moving in smooth flow without turbulence ⟨consider the ~*s* . . . around the plane parts —S.A.Moss⟩ **2 a :** a contour offering minimum resistance to a current ⟨probably no animal or plant in the water is without some touch of ~ —R.E.Coker⟩ ⟨the ~ of an airfoil⟩ ⟨the island . . . was formed generally in a ~ —Norman Mailer⟩ **b :** a fluid line ⟨~ may not improve the performance of a typewriter but it makes it look efficient⟩
²**streamline** \ˈ=ˌ=\ *vt* **1 a :** to adapt to a line of flow ⟨even without human assistance the controls of an airplane tend to ~ themselves⟩ **b :** to provide with a contour offering minimum resistance to a current ⟨the fish is the first organism to have its hind appendage . . . ~*ed* into it —A.L.Kroeber⟩ ⟨the nose is well ~*ed* with aluminum cowling giving a bullet-like appearance —*Aero Digest*⟩ **c :** to design with flowing contours ⟨~ apparatus for greater cleanliness and safety —D.E.Pierce⟩ **2 :** to bring up to date **:** renovate in appearance or attitude **:** MODERNIZE ⟨wants to ~ his people by treading on their fondest superstitions —Joseph Hitrec⟩ ⟨the archaic judiciary system has been ~*ed* —T.H.Fielding⟩ ⟨~ the text, to bring it closer to the contemporary stage —John Mason Brown⟩ **3 a :** to impose order or discipline upon **:** INTEGRATE, ORGANIZE ⟨everything is ~*ed* — doctrine, tactics, production, armaments, all integrated, all enshrined in a single dynamic —Lewis Hastings⟩ **b :** to make simpler or more efficient ⟨machines that extrude damp clay . . . ~ the work of clay modelers —*Ford Times*⟩ ⟨enacted legislation combining our armed forces into a single department of defense to ~ our defense machinery —*Think*⟩ **c :** to reduce to a minimum ⟨school terms were ~*ed* . . . to get the graduate sooner for industry —E.C.McVoy⟩
streamlined \ˈ=ˌ=\ *adj* **1 a :** affording minimum resistance to a current **:** contoured to reduce drag ⟨a ~ yacht⟩ ⟨~ engine nacelles⟩ ⟨~ hounds chase a fleeing mechanical rabbit —*Amer. Guide Series: Ark.*⟩ ⟨go easy on ice cream till we get the figure a bit more ~ —*Auckland (New Zealand) Weekly News*⟩ **b :** stripped of nonessentials **:** SIMPLIFIED, COMPACT ⟨a ~ ticket . . . replacing the long tickets previously used for transcontinental travel —*Wall Street Jour.*⟩ ⟨all-steel kitchens, ~ and efficient, with no empty spaces or useless nooks —Harriette Arnow⟩ **c :** effectively integrated **:** ORGANIZED ⟨the shrinking of the world . . . requires ~ and internationally uniform laws of aviation —*Air Transportation*⟩ **2 :** having fluid lines **:** CURVILINEAR ⟨~ watch bracelet⟩ ⟨~ pressure cooker⟩ **3 :** brought up to date **:** MODERNIZED ⟨jumped from the oxcart to the ultra ~ —*Holiday*⟩ ⟨has fashioned . . . a ~ version of the . . . novels —J.T.Winterich⟩ **4 :** of, relating to, or characteristic of streamline flow **:** LAMINAR ⟨the flow of the unagglutinated blood is laminar or ~ —*Science*⟩
streamline flow *n* **:** an uninterrupted flow (as of air) past a solid body in which the direction at every point remains unchanged with the passage of time **:** LAMINAR FLOW — compare TURBULENT FLOW
streamliner \ˈ=ˌ==\ *n* **:** one that is streamlined; *esp* **:** a streamlined train
streamlining *n* [fr. gerund of ²*streamline*] **1 a :** contouring for minimum resistance to a current ⟨the ~ of aircraft⟩ **b :** curvilinear design ⟨the ~ of household appliances is more decorative than functional⟩ **2 :** revision to increase efficiency or eliminate what is obsolete or nonessential **:** MODERNIZATION, SIMPLIFICATION ⟨the ~ of factory operations —*Nat'l Stationer*⟩ ⟨~ certainly reduced the number of opportunities for misunderstanding —*Jour. of Accountancy*⟩
stream of consciousness 1 : individual conscious experience considered as a series of processes, intrapsychic events, or experiences continuously moving forward in time — compare CONSCIOUSNESS 3 **2 :** INTERIOR MONOLOGUE
stream orchid *n* **:** a helleborine (*Epipactis gigantea*) native to western No. America and having greenish or purplish pendulous flowers — called also *giant helleborine*
stream piracy *n* **:** CAPTURE 3
streams *pl of* STREAM, *pres 3d sing of* STREAM
streamside \ˈ=ˌ=\ *n* **:** the land bordering on a stream
stream terrace *n* **:** one of a series of terraces cut usu. out of solid rock by successive changes in the regimen of a stream from alluviation to downcutting — called also *river terrace*; compare ALLUVIAL TERRACE
stream tin *n* **:** cassiterite occurring in the form of rolled fragments or pebbles in alluvial deposits
streamway \ˈ=ˌ=\ *n* **1 :** the current of a stream **2 :** the bed or course of a stream
streamwort \ˈ=ˌ=\ *n* [¹*stream* + *wort*] **:** a plant of the family Haloragaceae
streamy \ˈstrēmē, -mi\ *adj* -ER/-EST [ME *stremy*, fr. *strem, streme* stream + *-y* — more at STREAM] **1 :** abounding in streams **2 :** resembling or issuing in a stream
streb·li·dae \ˈstreblə͵dē\ *n pl, cap* [NL, fr. *Strebla*, type genus (fr. Gk *streblos* twisted, crooked) + NL *-idae* — more

at STROPHE] : a small widely distributed family of dipterous flies the adults of which are external parasites on bats

streek \'strēk\ *vb* -ED/-ING/-S [ME (northern dial.) *streken*, fr. OE *strec-*, stem of *streccan* to stretch] *vt* **1** *chiefly Sco* : STRETCH, EXTEND **2** *chiefly Scot* : to lay out (a dead body) ~ *vi* **1** : to fall or lie prostrate : stretch out **2** *obs* : to extend toward or to something : REACH

¹streel \'strē(ə)l\ *vi* [perh. fr. Ir *straoillim* I trail, *straoilleán* loiterer] **1** *chiefly Irish* : to saunter idly and aimlessly : trail along : STRAGGLE ⟨a group of tinkers ~*ed* into view —Mervyn Wall⟩ **2** *chiefly Irish* : to trail or float in the manner of a streamer ⟨the peat smoke ~*ing* off —Naomi Mitchison⟩

²streel \"\ *or* **streel·er** \-lər\ *n* -s *chiefly Irish* : an untidy slovenly person : SLATTERN

¹streen *obs var of* STRAIN

²streen \'strēn\ *n* [by shortening] *Scot* : YESTREEN

¹street \'strēt, *usu* -ēd-+V\ *n* -s [ME *strete*, fr. OE *strǣt*; akin to OFris *strēte* street, OHG *straza, strazza*; all fr. a prehistoric WGmc word borrowed fr. LL *strata* paved road, fr. L, fem. of *stratus*, past part. of *sternere* to spread out, throw down — more at STREW] **1 a** *obs* : a paved road : HIGHWAY ⟨until recently the Canterbury road was known as the *Street* —*Chicago Daily Tribune*⟩ **b** (1) : a public thoroughfare esp. in a city, town, or village including all area within the right of way (as sidewalks and tree belts) and sometimes further distinguished as being wider than an alley or lane but narrower than an avenue or boulevard and as separating blocks rather than penetrating them ⟨another alley that . . . gave on a through —Paul Bowles⟩ — contrasted with *road*; abbr. *st* (2) : the strip of a public thoroughfare reserved for vehicular traffic ⟨a pedestrian killed while crossing the ~⟩ (3) : a public thoroughfare including the property abutting it ⟨lives on a fashionable ~⟩ ⟨has an office on Main *Street*⟩ **c** : the roadway in front of or between the barracks or tents of a company or battery ⟨instruction in . . . shelter tent pitching, in the battery ~ —C.P.Smith⟩ **d** : a promising line of development or a channeling of effort ⟨in a crucial election year . . . was shrewdly working both sides of the ~ —*Time*⟩ ⟨this . . . method of furthering economic development can operate at full effectiveness only as a two-way ~ —*Atlantic*⟩ **2 a** : the people occupying property along a street ⟨the whole ~ is up in arms over the rezoning proposal⟩ **3** *usu cap a* : a district (as Wall Street, Fleet Street) identified with a particular profession ⟨the *Street's* top ten banking houses —*Time*⟩ ⟨came back as editor to the *Street* —*London Daily Chronicle*⟩ **b** : the people who work there ⟨railroads continued to act well in the opinion of the *Street* —*Wall Street Jour.*⟩ **4 a** : the life or profession of a prostitute ⟨found in opium dens . . . new contingents of women discovered on the ~ —Alfred Buchanan⟩ — usu. used in pl. ⟨a woman of the ~*s*⟩ **b** : the poor or derelict of a city ⟨children of the ~, clad in rags —Heinrich Harrer⟩ **c** *slang* : release from confinement : FREEDOM, LIBERTY ⟨you won't get to right back in when you make the ~ again —Nelson Algren⟩ **5** : the common man ⟨in Socrates the ~ conquered the intelligentsia and the aristocracy —C.P.Rodocanachi⟩ — **on the street** *adv (or adj)* **1** : out of doors in the city ⟨met him *on the street*⟩ **2 a** : idle, homeless, or out of a job ⟨his paper folded; and he's *on the street* —D.M.Mankiewicz⟩ **b** : in the company of the idle, homeless, or derelict in an urban area ⟨boys returning home . . . are amused at the bebops, forgetting their own days *on the street* —C.K.Myers⟩ — **up one's street** *also* **down one's street** : suited to one's abilities or tastes ⟨violence did not dismay them; it was right *down their street* —Raymond Chandler⟩

²street \"\ *adj* [ME *strete*, fr. *strete*, n.] **1** : of or relating to the thoroughfares of an urban area: as **a** : adjoining or giving access to a street ⟨~ door⟩ **b** : carried on or taking place in the streets ⟨~ fighting⟩ ⟨~ beggary⟩ **c** : living or working on the streets ⟨~ gamin⟩ ⟨~ vendor⟩ **d** : located in, used for, or serving as a guide to the streets ⟨fluorescent ~ lighting⟩ ⟨a ~ directory⟩ **e** : performing in or heard on the streets ⟨~ band⟩ ⟨~ music⟩ ⟨~ cries⟩ **f** (1) : suitable for wear on the street ⟨~ clothes⟩ ⟨~ makeup⟩ (2) : of a length that does not touch the ground — used of women's dresses in lengths reaching to the knee, calf, or ankle **2 a** : of or relating to the common man ⟨~ humor⟩ **b** : associated with the business of a particular street (as Wall Street) ⟨~ dollar market⟩ **c** : established by trading outside the exchange in a financial center ⟨~ price⟩ ⟨~ rate⟩ **3** : caused by a street virus ⟨~ distemper⟩

street arab *n, often cap A* : a homeless vagabond in the streets of a city and esp. an outcast boy or girl : GAMIN

street broker *n* : an independent stockbroker who trades elsewhere than on or near a financial exchange floor

streetcar \'‒‚‒\ *n* : a vehicle on rails used primarily for transporting passengers and usu. operating within the city limits — compare TROLLEY CAR

street certificate *n* : a stock certificate endorsed in blank by the registered owner and guaranteed by a broker that circulates freely from seller to buyer in the market without requiring a transfer on the books of the corporation

street cleaner *or* **street sweeper** *n* : one that cleans streets; *esp* : an employee of a municipal sanitation department

street edition *n* : an edition of a newspaper intended for sale on newsstands or street corners as distinguished from an edition intended primarily for home or office delivery

street elbow *n* : a pipe elbow with a female thread on one end and a male thread on the other

street·ful \'‒‚fu̇l\ *n* -s : as much or as many as a street will hold

street girl *n* : PROSTITUTE

streetlamp \'‒‚‒\ *n* : STREETLIGHT

street·let \'‒ lət\ *n* -s [*street* + *-let*] : a very narrow street

streetlight \'‒‚‒\ *n* : a light (as an arc lamp) usu. mounted on a pole and constituting one of a series spaced at intervals along a public street or highway

street loan *n* : CALL LOAN

street name *n* : a recognized broker, dealer, or bank in a financial district in whose name securities may be registered as a convenience for holding certificates and facilitating transfer; *specif* : NOMINEE 3

street offense *n, Eng law* : an offense (as loitering for purposes of prostitution, ringing doorbells without cause, posting bills without consent of the owner of the building, blowing horns or making noise to cause people to assemble) occurring in the street and classified as such by statute

street orderly *n, chiefly Brit* : STREET CLEANER

street organ *n* : a crude reed organ played on the streets and operated by turning a crank

street paper *n* : commercial paper sold through a dealer rather than to a bank and usu. of lower quality than bank paper

street piano *n* : a rudimentary mechanical piano played on the streets and operated by turning a crank or handle — called also *hurdy-gurdy*

street piano [illustration captions: **street elbow**, **street piano**]

street plate *n* : one of several steel plates that can be bolted to the track of a crawler tractor to provide a flat ground contact

street railway *n* : a line operating streetcars or buses

streets \'strēts\ *adv* [fr. pl. of *street*] : by a wide margin : far and away ⟨a nice woman, ~ above these other callers —Katherine Mansfield⟩ ⟨had run the house for thirty shillings a week less, and run it ~ better —F.M.Ford⟩

street virus *n* : virulent or natural virus (as of rabies) as distinguished from virus attenuated in the laboratory

streetwalker \'‒‚‒‒\ *n* : PROSTITUTE

streetwalking \'‒‚‒‒\ *n* : PROSTITUTION

street·ward \-wə(r)d\ *adv (or adj)* : toward the street

Stre·ga \'strāgə\ *trademark* — used for a sweet spicy orange-flavored yellow liqueur

streik \'strēk\ *Scot & dial Eng var of* STREEK

stre·litz·ia \strə'litsēə\ *n, cap* [NL, fr. Charlotte Sophia

†1818 Princess of Mecklenburg-*Strelitz* and wife of George III of England + NL -*ia*] : a small genus of usu. large African herbs (family Musaceae) resembling the banana, rarely having a woody base, and having rigid glaucous distichous leaves and richly colored flowers with three sepals and three very irregular petals — compare BIRD-OF-PARADISE

strem·ma·to·graph \'streməd·ə‚graf\ *n* [Gk *stremmat-, stremma* twist, thread (akin to Gk *strephein* to turn) + E -*graph* — more at STROPHE] : an instrument for determining the fiber stresses in rails under moving trains

streng·ite \'stren‚īt\ *n* -s [G *strengit*, fr. Johann A. *Streng* †1897 Ger. mineralogist + G -*it* -ite] : a mineral $FePO_4 \cdot 2H_2O$ consisting of a hydrous iron phosphate, occurring mostly in pale red botryoidal masses, and being isomorphous with variscite (sp. gr. 2.87)

strength \'stren(k)th, *chiefly in dial or substand speech* 'stren(t)th\ *n, pl* **strengths** \-ths, 'strenks\ [ME *strengthe, strenthe*, fr. OE *strengthu*; akin to OHG *strengida* strength, *strengi* strong — more at STRONG] **1 a** : moral courage : FORTITUDE, INTEGRITY ⟨surmount the horrors and humiliations of . . . defeat —Patrick O'Donovan⟩ ⟨the inner ~ of self-restraint —A.E.Stevenson b. 1900⟩ **b** : physical force or vigor : BRAWN, VITALITY ⟨the lion's natural weapons . . . ~ and cunning —James Stevenson-Hamilton⟩ ⟨as the day went on, her ~ lessened —Millen Brand⟩ **c** (1) : ability to produce an effect : INFLUENCE ⟨the ~ of his personal prestige —A.L. Funk⟩ ⟨a policy based on peace through ~ —R.M.Makins⟩ (2) : a quality of flour that determines the volume and texture of the loaf and depends on the amount and kind of protein present (3) : energy content ⟨testing the ~ of a new high explosive⟩ **d** *archaic* : healthy condition : PRODUCTIVENESS — used of soil ⟨westwardly . . . the soil again improves in ~ —Charles Vancouver⟩ **2 a** (1) : a source of power or influence ⟨the magnificent sense of history and tradition which is one of the ~*s* of the Roman Catholic Church —*Newsweek*⟩ (2) : a strong attribute or inherent asset ⟨make it clear what you consider are the ~*s* and weaknesses of the book —Raymond Walters b. 1912⟩ ⟨children . . . exhibit special gifts and ~*s* relatively early —Gertrude H. Hildreth⟩ ⟨it was Napoleon's ~ neither to admit defeat nor to be trapped by stubborn adherence to a ruinous course —Oscar Handlin⟩ **b** *archaic* : a secure retreat : FORTRESS, STRONGHOLD ⟨all the forts and ~*s* of the realm —Robert Barret⟩ **c** (1) : a strong position ⟨negotiate from ~⟩ (2) *obs* : a protective barrier : EMBANKMENT, FORTIFICATION **3 a** : military might ⟨made it easier for power-seeking nations to build ~ for the second world war —T.F. Hawkins⟩ **b** *obs* (1) : military forces (2) : a fighting force **c** *archaic* : ability to withstand assault ⟨castle's ~ will laugh a siege to scorn —Shak.⟩ **d** : ability to withstand stress or deformation : the quality of bodies by which they endure the application of force without breaking : TOUGHNESS, COHESION ⟨the ~ of igneous rocks⟩ ⟨the rubber does not attain full ~ until vulcanization is complete —*Dun's Rev.*⟩ — compare BREAKING STRENGTH, COMPRESSIVE STRENGTH, FATIGUE STRENGTH, TENSILE STRENGTH **e** (1) : the number of personnel or units on a military muster roll ⟨the struggle . . . was terrific, costing each side about one third of its ~ —*Amer. Guide Series: Tenn.*⟩ ⟨Commonwealth has a powerful ~ of naval bases around the world —Quentin Reynolds⟩ (2) : the authorized complement of a military unit ⟨suggested that we bring the regiment up to ~ with carefully certified officers —Oliver La Farge⟩ ⟨sufficiently valuable assistants to be put on the ~ —*Manchester Guardian Weekly*⟩ (3) : large numbers ⟨forces landed in ~ in three places —*Infantry Jour.*⟩ **f** : the number of personnel on a roster of any kind ⟨an employed ~ of 70,000 —*Country Life*⟩ **g** *archaic* : a sufficient number ⟨without . . . their crews he had no longer ~ enough to navigate the ship —George Anson⟩ **h** : available means of support : reserves that can be mobilized at will : RESOURCES ⟨economic and industrial . . . ~*s* of the Communist and anti-Communist blocs —N. Y. Times⟩ **4 a** (1) : velocity or amount of flow : relative quantity or degree : INTENSITY, VOLUME ⟨~ of the wind⟩ ⟨the ~ and direction of sea currents may vary considerably at different times of the year —W.H.Dowdeswell⟩ ⟨it is not sufficient to know merely the overall ~ of a wave . . . —S.S.Stevens⟩ (2) : the phase of a tidal current when its velocity is greatest; *also* : the velocity at that time **b** : fervor or predominant inclination : PROFOUNDNESS, VEHEMENCE — used of a mental or emotional attitude ⟨~ of conviction⟩ ⟨the overwhelming ~ of British opinion —A.P.Ryan⟩ **c** : degree of coloration or dilution : GRADATION, POTENCY ⟨each part of the engraving should print at its exact ~ —John Southward⟩ ⟨~*s* are given as percentages of alcohol by volume —O.A.Mendelsohn⟩ **d** : degree of ionization in solution — used of acids and bases; compare ACIDITY 1a, BASICITY 1 **e** : vigor of demand : rising tendency in prices ⟨~ in consumer buying⟩ ⟨stock markets were displaying remarkable drive and ~ —*London Financial Times*⟩ **5 a** *obs* : legal backing : AUTHORITY ⟨thou hast the ~ of laws —Shak.⟩ **b** : the true facts or general significance : GIST, TENOR ⟨intent to have an explanation . . . and I'll get the ~ of matters soon enough —Rex Ingamells⟩ **c** : degree of importance or credibility : SOUNDNESS, WEIGHT ⟨~ of an argument⟩ ⟨~ of legal evidence⟩ **6** : basis — used in the phrase *on the strength of* ⟨a fussy housewife scalding the entire pantry on the ~ of one ant in the cookie jar —H.L.Davis⟩ ⟨new sawmills were established on the ~ of anticipated canal trade —*Amer. Guide Series: Ind.*⟩ **6** : force of expression or treatment : clarity of definition ⟨it was this titan's spirit which gave such drive and ~ to the mightiest of his plays —John Mason Brown⟩ ⟨the film finds pictorial ~ in its fine blending of bare reality and shattering glitter —Cecile Starr⟩ ⟨the building masses are . . . well related, endowing the structure with a silhouette of great ~ —*Amer. Guide Series: N. Y. City*⟩ *syn* see POWER — **from strength to strength** : vigorously forward ⟨from one high point to the next ⟨the Horse of the Year Show goes *from strength to strength* . . . no waiting, no tedium —John Board⟩

strength deck *n* : the uppermost continuous deck that resists longitudinal bending

strength·en \-thən\ *vb* **strengthened; strengthened; strengthening** \-th(ə)niŋ\ [ME *strengthnen, strengthenen*, fr. *strengthe* strength + -*nen* -en] *vt* **1 a** : to give moral support to : ENCOURAGE, HEARTEN ⟨means of ~ the brethren and converting the pagans —*Episcopal Churchnews*⟩ **b** : to give added weight or incentive to : CORROBORATE, ENHANCE ⟨the probability of the ascription of this passage to Democritus is ~*ed* by the latest research —Benjamin Farrington⟩ **2 a** : to give added strength or vigor to ⟨a defensive position⟩ ⟨coarse foods ~ the jaws —Morris Fishbein⟩ ⟨although union membership has dropped off in some places, union organization has been . . . ~*ed* in other places —*Amer. Guide Series: N.C.*⟩ **b** : to increase in power or amount : improve in effectiveness ⟨his offices were regularly employed to ~ the personal machine of the governor —D.W. McConnell⟩ ⟨nothing . . . would so ~ the hand of democracy as the gift of literacy —Jerome Ellison⟩ ⟨our program of aid to scientific education . . . was enlarged and ~*ed* —*Report: Monsanto Chem. Co.*⟩ ⟨working together helps to ~ family life —Mary S. Switzer⟩ ⟨the course might be ~*ed*, further, by . . . more effective integration of movies, visual aids, and other motivational devices —S.B.Zuckerman⟩ **c** : to heighten the artistic effect of : make more expressive ⟨the design is ~*ed* by two slightly projecting corner piers —*Amer. Guide Series: Minn.*⟩ ~ *vi* **1** : to become stronger : increase in power or intensity ⟨the light ~*ed* minute by minute, and then the day came —John Connell⟩ ⟨intellectual faculties ~*ed*, and men . . . gained facility in moulding their Latin —H.O.Taylor⟩ **2** : to go higher : RISE ⟨the carrier's shares ~*ed* on the declaration of a 75-cent dividend —J.G.Forrest⟩

syn INVIGORATE, FORTIFY, ENERGIZE, REINFORCE: STRENGTHEN applies to any increasing of force, vigor, power, intensity, or effectiveness ⟨*strengthening* the shelf with an additional brace⟩ ⟨be silent if you can say nothing to *strengthen* me in my resolution —Israel Zangwill⟩ ⟨*strengthened* his entire staff with the specialists wherever they were needed —*Buick Mag.*⟩ ⟨a new science *strengthened* by proof and generalization —H.J.J. Winter⟩ INVIGORATE applies to whatever endows with vigor, vitality, animation, or energy ⟨fresh air and sunshine will help to *invigorate* the body and improve nutrition —Morris Fishbein⟩ ⟨gave their support to *invigorated* nationalist move-

ments —Oscar Handlin⟩ FORTIFY suggests strengthening often against attack of any sort, use calculated to impairment or enervation ⟨*fortified* by many recruits from the demobilized armies of Europe —C.E.Black & E.C.Helmreich⟩ ⟨*fortified*, her argument with quotations —H.O.Taylor⟩ ⟨*fortified* by 68 tables and 75 figures, as well as by the testimony of witnesses —D.D.McKean⟩ ENERGIZE may suggest a rousing into activity along with a strengthening and heartening to sustain that activity ⟨the imagining of beautiful settings can be more sensitizing, *energizing*, and exhilarating than the imagining or reporting of ugly settings —C.A. Smart⟩ ⟨when a man and woman are successfully in love, their whole activity is *energized* and victorious —Walter Lippmann⟩ REINFORCE applies to strengthening by augmenting with new forces or force, power, or effectiveness ⟨fresh troops *reinforcing* the defenders⟩ ⟨concrete *reinforced* with steel⟩ ⟨the simple country fare provided by the home farm was *reinforced* by a regular supply of more exotic dainties —Osbert Lancaster⟩ ⟨when we consider the codes of responsibility that exist in the various professions, we find generally that they do not usually come into being by means of legislation, although they may frequently be confirmed or *reinforced* by statutes —Lister Hill⟩

strength·en·er \-th(ə)nə(r)\ *n* -s : one that strengthens

¹strengthening *n* -s [fr. gerund of *strengthen*] **1** : an act or instance of reinforcing ⟨advised an immediate ~ of the faculty —J.E.Pomfret⟩ **2** *archaic* : REINFORCEMENT ⟨piers of brick or stone . . . to be a ~ to the building —B.G.Gerbier⟩

²strengthening *adj* [fr. pres. part. of *strengthen*] **1** : tending to strengthen ⟨a ~ element in the design —R.E.M.Wheeler⟩ **2** : increasing in strength or intensity ⟨objects became clearer in the ~ light⟩

strengthening card *n* : a queen, jack, ten, or nine led from a short suit in whist in the hope that it will establish a card in one's partner's hand

strength·ful \-thfəl\ *adj* [ME, fr. *strengthe* strength + -*ful* — more at STRENGTH] : full of strength : STRONG

strength·less \-thləs\ *adj* [ME *strentheles*, fr. *strenthe* strength + -*les* -less] : having no strength ⟨the ~ dead —A.E.Housman⟩ — **strength·less·ly** *adv* — **strength·less·ness** *n* -ES

strength of field *n* : FIELD INTENSITY

strengths *pl of* STRENGTH

strengthy \'stren(k)thi, -en(t)thi\ *adj* [ME *strengthy, strenthy*, fr. *strengthe, strenthe* strength + -*y*] *Scot & dial Eng* : STRONG

stren·u·os·i·ty \‚strenyə'wäsəd·ē, -sit·ē, -i\ *also* **stre·nu·i·ty** \stre'nyüə-\ *n* -ES [*strenuosity* fr. *strenuous* + -*ity*; *strenuity* fr. ME *strenuite*, fr. L *strenuitat-, strenuitas*, fr. *strenuus* strenuous + -*itat-, -itas* -ity] : the quality or state of being strenuous

stren·u·ous \'strenyəwəs\ *adj* [L *strenuus* — more at STARE] **1 a** : vigorously active : ENERGETIC ⟨to hustle and to be ~ . . . seem to be prominent American virtues —M.R.Cohen⟩ ⟨a tender sort of fancy rather than a ~ imagination —F.J. Mather⟩ ⟨implement the Full Employment Act by ~ measures —T.R.Ybarra⟩ **b** : intensely eager : FERVENT, ZEALOUS ⟨a family of intellectual energy and ~ Puritanism —F.A.Christie⟩ **2** : full of power : LUSTY, LOUD ⟨a mud puddle in ~ motion —Nathaniel Hawthorne⟩ ⟨the recorded tone is exemplary even in the most ~ fortissimo —Edward Sackville-West & Desmond Shawe-Taylor⟩ **3 a** : marked by or calling for physical energy or stamina : ARDUOUS, RIGOROUS ⟨relaxing . . . after a ~ day's work —Hervey Allen⟩ ⟨fog, high seas, and strong winds made the crossing a ~ one —M.M.Hunt⟩ **b** : marked by unusual difficulty or tension : HARD, EXACTING ⟨a ~ examination⟩ ⟨his occupation is sedentary from a physical standpoint, ~ from a nervous and mental standpoint —H.G.Armstrong⟩ *syn* see VIGOROUS

stren·u·ous·ly *adv* : in a strenuous manner : STRONGLY, VIGOROUSLY ⟨objected ~ to the stand his party was taking —J.D.Hicks⟩ ⟨campaigned ~ to increase the farm population —*Amer. Guide Series: Minn.*⟩

stren·u·ous·ness *n* -ES : STRENUOSITY

¹strep \'strep\ *n* -S [by shortening] : STREPTOCOCCUS 2

²strep \"\ *adj* : STREPTOCOCCAL

strep·era \'strepərə\ *n* [NL, fr. LL *streperus* noisy] **1** *cap* : a genus of bluish black Australian birds (family Cracticidae) often with snowy white undertail coverts **2** -s : any bird of the genus *Strepera* : CURRAWONG

strepho·sym·bo·lia \‚stref(ˌ)ō‚sim'bōlēə\ *n* -s [NL, fr. Gk *strepho-* (fr. *strephein* to turn) + *symbolon* sign, symbol + NL -*ia* — more at STROPHE, SYMBOL] : reversal or transposition of phrases, words, or letters or of any symbols esp. in reading — **strepho·sym·bol·ic** \-;sim'bälik\ *adj*

stre·pi·to·so \‚strepə'tō(ˌ)sō\ *adj (or adv)* [It, fr. *strepito* noise (fr. L *strepitus*) + -*oso* (fr. L -*osus* -ose)] : NOISY, IMPETUOUS — used as a direction in music

strep·i·tous \'strepəd·əs\ *also* **strep·i·tant** \-əd·ənt\ *adj* [*strepitous* fr. L *strepitus* noise, fr. *strepere* to make noise; *strepitant* fr. L *strepitant-, strepitans*, pres. part. of *strepitare*, freq. of *strepere* — more at OBSTREPEROUS] : characterized or accompanied by much noise : CLAMOROUS, NOISY, BOISTEROUS ⟨the *strepitant* racket of the streets — Christopher Morley⟩

strepo·gen·in \‚strepə'jenən; strā'pijənən, -‚nēn\ *n* -s [ISV *strepo-* (prob. fr. ¹*strep* + -*o*-) + -*genin*] : a peptide that is formed by partial hydrolysis of insulin and other proteins, that contains glutamic acid and other amino acid units, and that is essential for the growth of various microorganisms (as *Streptococcus pyogenes* and *Lactobacillus casei*) and of mice

strepsi- *comb form* [NL, fr. Gk, fr. *strepsis* act or instance of turning, fr. *strephein* to turn — more at STROPHE] : twisted ⟨*strepsitene*⟩

strep·sic·e·ros \strep'sisərəs, -‚räs\ *n* [NL, fr. L, addax, fr. Gk *strepsikerōs*, fr. *strepsi-* + -*kerōs* (fr. *keras* horn) — more at HORN] **1** *cap* : a large genus of African antelopes comprising the kudus, harnessed antelopes, nyalas, and related forms **2** *pl* **strepsiceros** : any antelope of the genus *Strepsiceros*

strep·si·ne·ma \‚strepsə'nēmə\ *n* -s [NL, fr. *strepsi-* + -*nema*] : chromatin threads in the strepsitene stage

strep·sip·te·ra \strep'sip(t)ərə\ *n pl, cap* [NL, fr. *strepsi-* + Gk, fr. *strepsis* act or instance of turning) + -*ptera* (fr. the twisted front wings)] : a group formerly included in the Coleoptera but now regarded as a separate order and comprising minute insects which are parasitic as larvae in other insects, in which the females remain permanently in the host and degenerate into a sac wherein the eggs hatch and the larvae develop, and finally undergo hypermetamorphosis in the course of larval development — compare STYLOPS, XENOS

strep·sip·ter·al \-('‚)‒;rəl\ *or* **strep·sip·ter·an** \-rən\ *or* **strep·sip·ter·ous** \-rəs\ *adj* [NL *Strepsiptera* + E -*al* or -*an* or -*ous*] : of or relating to the Strepsiptera

strep·sip·ter·on \-‚tə‚rän\ *or* **strep·sip·ter·an** \-‚rən\ *n* [*strepsipteron* fr. NL, fr. *Strepsiptera*; *strepsipteran* fr. NL *Strepsiptera* + E -*an*] : an insect of the order Strepsiptera

strep·si·tene \'strepsə‚tēn\ *n* -s [ISV *strepsi-* + -*tene*; prob. orig. formed as F *strepsitène*] : late diplotene in which the successive loops between chiasmata give the appearance of threads twisted together

strept- *or* **strepto-** *comb form* [NL, fr. Gk, fr. *streptos* twisted, pliant, fr. *strephein* to twist, turn — more at STROPHE] **1** : twisted ⟨twisted chain ⟨*Streptococcus*⟩ ⟨*streptaster*⟩ ⟨*Streptomyces*⟩ **2** : streptococcus ⟨*streptosepticemia*⟩ **3** : streptomycin ⟨*streptamine*⟩

strep·ta·mine \'streptə‚mēn, -mən\ *n* [*strept-* + *amine*] : a cyclic diamino alcohol $(HO)_4C_6H_6(NH_2)_2$ obtained from streptomycin or streptidine by alkaline hydrolysis

strep·tas·ter \'strep'tastə(r)\ *n* -s [NL, fr. *strept-* + -*aster*] : a sponge spicule having the form of a modified aster in which the rays do not meet at a common center but radiate from an axis

strep throat *also* **strep sore throat** *n* [²*strep*] : SEPTIC SORE THROAT

strep·ti·dine \'streptə‚dēn, -dən\ *n* [*strept-* + *-idine*] : a cyclic basic alcohol $(HO)_4C_6H_6[NHC(=NH)NH_2]_2$ that is obtained from streptomycin by acid hydrolysis and is a guanidine derivative related to scyllitol

strep·to·bacillary \‚streptō'‒\ *adj* [NL *streptobacillus* + E -*ary*] : caused by a streptobacillus

¹strep·to·bacillus \"+\ *n* [NL, fr. *strept-* + *Bacillus*] **1** *cap, in some classifications* : a genus of bacteria of obscure systematic position that is sometimes placed in Actinomyces and that includes a species (*S. moniliformis*) which causes one form of rat-bite fever **2** *pl* **strepto·bacilli** \-‚‒\ : any of

various bacilli in which the individual cells are joined in a chain

²streptobacillus \"\ [NL] *syn of* CLOSTRIDIUM

³streptobacillus \"\ [NL] *syn of* LACTOBACILLUS

strep·to·bi·o·sa·mine \ˌ==bīˈōsəˌmēn, -ˌmən\ *n* [*strept-* + *biose* + *amine*] **:** a glycosidic compound $C_{13}H_{23}NO_9$ structurally resembling a disaccharide, obtained along with streptidine from streptomycin by hydrolysis, and in turn yielding streptose and *N*-methyl-L-glucosamine on hydrolysis

strep·to·car·pus \ˌstreptəˈkärpəs\ *n* [NL, fr. *strepto-* (fr. Gk, fr. *streptos* twisted) + *-carpus*] **1** *cap* **:** a genus of usu. stemless African herbs (family Gesneriaceae) having showy blue or purple flowers that have two stamens and a funnel-shaped corolla with a 2-lipped limb and are followed by a linear spirally twisted capsule splitting into 2 or 4 valves — see CAPE PRIMROSE **2** -ES **:** any plant of the genus *Streptocarpus*

strep·to·coc·cal \ˌ==ˈkäkəl\ *or* **strep·to·coc·cic** \-äk(s)ik, -)ēk\ *adj* [NL *streptococci* + E *-al* or *-ic*] **:** of, relating to, or caused by streptococci ⟨a ~ sore throat⟩ ⟨~ organisms⟩

streptococcal mastitis *also* **streptococcic mastitis** *n* **:** bovine mastitis caused by infection of the udder with a streptococcus (*Streptococcus agalactiae* or occas. a related form), characterized by chronic progressive fibrotic changes in one or more quarters of the udder, passed readily from cow to cow in milking, and found most prevalent among stabled cattle esp. in winter

strep·to·coc·ci·ci·dal \ˌ==ˌkäk(s)əˈsīdᵊl\ *adj* [NL *streptococci* + E *-cidal*] **:** tending to kill streptococci

strep·to·coc·co·sis \ˌ==ˌkäˈkōsəs\ *n* -ES [NL, fr. *streptococci* + *-osis*] **:** infection with or disease caused by hemolytic streptococci

strep·to·coc·cus \ˌ==ˈkäkəs\ *n* [NL, fr. *strept-* + *-coccus*] **1** *cap* **:** a genus of nonmotile chiefly parasitic gram-positive bacteria (family Lactobacillaceae) that divide in only one plane, occur in pairs or chains but not in packets, do not form zoogleal masses nor ferment inulin, rarely have capsules, and include various important pathogens of man and domestic animals as well as forms important as starters in the manufacture of dairy products **2** *pl* **streptococ·ci** \-ä,kī, -ä(,)kē, -äk,sī, -äk(,)sē\ **a :** any bacterium of *Streptococcus* or a closely related genus **b :** a coccus occurring in chains

strep·to·dor·nase \ˌstreptōˈdȯrˌnās\ *n* -S [*strept-* + *deoxyribonuclease*] **:** a deoxyribonuclease from hemolytic streptococci that causes hydrolysis of deoxyribonucleic acid and deoxyribonucleoprotein outside of living cells or in the nuclei of degenerating cells and dissolves pus and that is usu. administered in a mixture with streptokinase

strep·to·ki·nase \ˈ==+\ *n* [*strept-* + *kinase*] **:** a proteolytic enzyme from hemolytic streptococci that is active in promoting dissolution of blood clots by catalyzing a fibrin-dissolving system present in the euglobulin fraction of blood and that is usu. administered in a mixture with streptodornase to remove clotted blood or fibrinous or purulent accumulations — see PLASMIN

strep·to·ly·sin \"+\ *n* [*strept-* + *lysin*] **:** an antigenic hemolysin that is produced by various streptococci (as *Streptococcus pyogenes*)

strep·to·my·ces \ˌ==ˈmīˌsēz\ *n* [NL, fr. *strept-* + *-myces*] **1** *cap* **:** the type genus of Streptomycetaceae comprising numerous bacteria that produce chains of conidia from aerial hyphae and including some that form antibiotics as by-products of their metabolism — see POTATO SCAB, STREPTOMYCIN **2** *pl* **streptomyces** \"\ *or* **streptomyce·tes** \-ˌmīˈsēd-ēz, -ētēz\ **:** any bacterium of the genus *Streptomyces*

strep·to·my·ce·ta·ce·ae \ˌ==ˌmīsəˈtāsēˌē\ *n pl, cap* [NL, fr. *Streptomycet-*, *Streptomyces*, type genus + *-aceae*] **:** a family of higher bacteria (order Actinomycetales) that form vegetative mycelia which rarely break up into bacillary forms, have conidia borne on sporophores, and are typically aerobic soil saprophytes but include a few parasites of plants or animals — see STREPTOMYCES

strep·to·my·cin \ˌ==ˈmīsᵊn\ *n* -S [NL *Streptomyces* + E *-in*] **:** an antibiotic organic base $C_{21}H_{39}N_7O_{12}$ that is produced by a soil actinomycete (*Streptomyces griseus*), that is active against many bacteria, and that is administered chiefly in the form of salts in the treatment of tuberculosis, tularemia, and other infections caused esp. by gram-negative bacteria — compare DIHYDROSTREPTOMYCIN

strep·to·neu·ra \ˌ==ˈn(y)u̇rə\ *n pl, cap* [NL, fr. *strept-* + *-neura*] **:** a large subclass of Gastropoda including the majority of marine, some freshwater, and the operculate land gastropods having the loop of visceral nerves twisted into a figure 8 with the right half crossing in dextral forms above the left, sexes usu. separate, and in most forms an operculum

¹strep·to·neu·ran \ˌ==ˈnyu̇rən\ *or* **strep·to·neu·ral** \-rəl\ *or* **strep·to·neu·rous** \-rəs\ *adj* [NL *Streptoneura* + E *-an* or *-al* or *-ous*] **:** of or relating to the Streptoneura

²streptoneuran \"\ *n* -S **:** a mollusk of the subclass Streptoneura

strep·tose \ˈstrepˌtōs *also* -ōz\ *n* -S [*strept-* + *-ose*] **:** an unstable hydroxy dialdehyde $(HO)_3C_4H_5(CHO)_2$ formed from streptomycin or streptobiosamine by hydrolysis; 3-*C*-formyl-5-deoxy-L-lyxose

strep·to·sty·lic \ˌstreptōˈstīlik\ *adj* [*strept-* + *-stylic*] **:** having the quadrate bone movably articulated with the squamosal — used of a reptile

strep·to·thri·cin \ˌ==ˈthrīsᵊn, -risᵊn\ *n* -S [NL *Streptothric-*, *Streptothrix* + E *-in*] **:** an antibiotic basic substance that is produced by a soil actinomycete (*Streptomyces lavendulae*) and is active not only against bacteria but to some degree against fungi

strep·to·thrix \ˈ==ˌthriks\ *n* [NL, fr. *strept-* + *-thrix*] **1** *cap, in some classifications* **:** a genus of higher bacteria that somewhat resemble molds, have branched filaments which abstrict conidia, and comprise forms now usu. placed in *Actinomyces* or in *Leptothrix* **2** *pl* **strep·to·thri·ces** \ˌ==ˈthrīˌsēz\ **:** any bacterium of the genus *Streptothrix*

strep·to·tri·cho·sis \ˌstreptōˌtrīˈkōsəs\ *also* **strep·to·thri·cho·sis** \-ˌthrī-\ *n* -ES [NL, fr. *Streptotrich-*, *Streptothrix*, *Streptothrix* + *-osis*] **:** actinomycosis caused by actinomycetes that do not form club-shaped bodies about the granules in lesions and usu. taking the form of a more or less chronic suppurative process that attacks chiefly mucous surfaces and lymph glands — compare FARCY 2

stre·py·an \strāˈpēən, ˈ===\ *adj, usu cap* [*Strepy*, village in eastern Belgium where implements of the culture were found + E *-an*] **:** of or relating to a pre-Chellean culture stage in Belgium characterized by primitive types of worked flints — compare MESVINIAN

¹stress \ˈstres\ *n* -ES *often attrib* [ME *stresse*, short for *distresse* distress — more at DISTRESS] **1** *obs* **:** DISTRESS 3b **2** *chiefly dial* **:** DISTRESS 1 **3 a :** a condition existing within an elastic material because of strain or deformation by external forces or by nonuniform thermal expansion and being expressed quantitatively always in units of force per unit area **b :** a physical, chemical, or emotional factor (as trauma, histamine, or fear) to which an individual fails to make a satisfactory adaptation, and which causes physiologic tensions that may be a contributory cause of disease ⟨continued ~ may result in gastric ulcer⟩ ⟨cramps before a school examination may be a response to the ~ of worry⟩ ⟨~ diseases are hazards of modern life⟩ — see ADAPTATION SYNDROME **4 a :** the state or condition of strain and esp. of intense strain **:** constraining force or influence **:** PRESSURE ⟨~ of circumstances⟩ ⟨~ of weather⟩ **b :** a condition held to be similar to such a state of strain **:** EMPHASIS, IMPORTANCE, SIGNIFICANCE, URGENCY, WEIGHT ⟨lay ~ on a particular argument⟩ **5** *archaic* **:** intense effort **:** strained activity or exertion toward the accomplishment of anything ⟨pursue, with ~ of mental faculties, a train of argument —Richard Polwhele⟩ **6 :** intensity of utterance given to a speech sound, syllable, or word producing relative loudness as its acoustic correlate — compare ACCENT; PRIMARY, SECONDARY, TERTIARY, WEAK **7 a :** relative force or prominence of sound in verse esp. when due to intensity or energy of utterance **:** volume or loudness of sound **b :** a syllable having relative force or prominence **:** a strong syllable **8 :** ACCENT 6a, 6c **9 :** the thickening of the stroke of a letter esp. when curved

syn STRESS, STRAIN, PRESSURE, TENSION, SHEAR, THRUST, and TORSION can apply in common to the action or effect of force exerted within or upon a thing. STRESS and STRAIN, the comprehensive terms, can be interchangeable in the basic sense above, but STRESS is technically applied to the force exerted when one body, or a part of one, presses upon, pulls upon, pushes against, or tends to stress, compress, or twist another body or part of one, STRAIN technically denoting the alteration in size or shape resulting from stress. PRESSURE commonly applies to a weighing down upon or a pushing against a surface ⟨the *pressure* of 3000 pounds upon the cement floor caused some cracking⟩ ⟨the *pressure* of air in the tire was about 30 pounds per square inch⟩ TENSION applies to the stress exerted and the strain effected by two forces pulling in opposite directions and causing or tending to cause extension ⟨the *tension* of a violin string⟩ ⟨the *tension* between an outward and a downward force⟩ SHEAR applies to a stress or strain occurring when a force in the plane of one area or section tends to cause it to slide upon a parallel plane or contiguous section ⟨the estimated *shear* in a layer of rock was not enough to cause a landslide⟩ THRUST applies to the pressure exerted by one part or structure against another, esp. when one member exerts a diagonal or horizontal outward thrust against the other ⟨the *thrust* of a rafter against a supporting wall⟩ TORSION applies to the strain or the deformation produced by twisting, esp. as displayed in a nonrigid body ⟨the *torsion* of a wire filament exposed to magnetic force tending to twist it⟩ ⟨the *torsion* strength of a metal column⟩

²stress \"\ *vt* -ED/-ING/-ES [ME *stressen*, partly by shortening fr. ME *distresse* distress & partly fr. MF *estrecier* to constrain, force, fr. (assumed) VL *strictiare*, fr. *strictia* constraint, force, stress, fr. L *strictus*, past part. of *stringere* to draw tight, press together — more at STRAIN] **1** *archaic* **a :** to subject to hardship, affliction, or oppression **b :** DISTRESS 3 **2 :** to subject to phonetic stress **:** ACCENT **3 :** to subject to physical stress **4 :** to lay stress on **:** place emphasis on **:** make emphatic **:** EMPHASIZE

stress accent *n* **1 a :** an accent or variation of prominence dependent on variation of stress **b :** a greater than minimal degree of stress given a vowel or syllable **2 :** a set of phonemes of stress

stress diagram *n* **:** a diagram that results from the graphical analysis of the stresses in a framed structure

stressed skin *n* **:** aircraft construction in which the torsion forces are resisted by shear in the usu. metal skin without aid of struts — compare MONOCOQUE

stresses *pl of* STRESS, *pres 3d sing of* STRESS

stress·ful \ˈstresfəl\ *adj* **:** full of or subject to stress ⟨emotional stability in ~ situation —P.M.Symonds⟩ ⟨living in these ~ times —*Commonweal*⟩ ⟨had been 12 ~ hours in the air —A.C. Fisher⟩

stress·ful·ly \-fəlē\ *adv* **:** in a stressful manner ⟨the plaintiff ~ contends —M.V.Barnhill⟩

stress-group \ˈ=,=\ *n* **:** a unit of speech sound constituted by a single primary stress and usu. marked by relatively open juncture or pause before and after **:** a single syllable with primary stress or a series of syllables united by the fact that among them there is only one with primary stress

stressless *adj* **:** having no stress **:** not accented — **stresslessness** *n* -ES

stress-meter \ˈ=,==\ *n* **:** STRESS-VERSE

stress-rhythm \ˈ=,==\ *n* **:** rhythm based on recurrence of stress

stress sheet *n* **:** a skeleton drawing of a structure (as a roof truss or a bridge) showing the stress to which each member will be subjected

stress-strain curve \ˈ=ˈ=-\ *n* **:** a chart or curve showing the relation between the load or stress on a structural member or specimen of material and the corresponding strain or deformation

stress-verse \ˈ=,=\ *n* **1 :** verse having rhythm produced by recurrence of stresses without regard to number of syllables or any fixed distribution of unstressed elements **2 :** verse having cadence produced by arrangement of stressed and unstressed syllables **:** accentual meter, as distinguished from meter based on temporal quantity

¹stretch \ˈstrech\ *vb* -ED/-ING/-ES [ME *strecchen*, *strechen*, fr. OE *streccan*; akin to OFris *strekka* to stretch, MD *strecken*, OHG *strecchan* to stretch, OE *stræc*, *strec* firm, rigid, MHG & MD *strac* straight, stiff, OHG *starēn* to stare — more at STARE] *vt* **1 :** to extend (as oneself, one's limbs, or one's body) in a reclining position — often used with *out* ⟨~*ed* himself out on the bed⟩ **2 :** to reach out **:** hold out **:** put forth **:** EXTEND ⟨~*ed* his arm to take the book —Cedomilj Mijatovic⟩ ⟨~*ed* forth a lean and quivering hand —Zane Grey⟩ ⟨the tree ~*ed* its branches over the road⟩ **3 a :** to extend in length ⟨~ one's arms⟩ ⟨~*ed* his legs cautiously⟩ **b :** to expand (wings) esp. for flight **4 :** to cause (as a person) to lie at full length: **a** *chiefly dial* **:** to lay out for burial **b :** to fell with or as if with a blow ⟨fired again . . . and ~*ed* him dying upon the sand —R.W. Thorp⟩ **5 a :** to cause the limbs of (a person) to be pulled or distended forcibly esp. in torture (as upon a cross or the rack) **b** *archaic* **:** to hang by the neck **:** execute by hanging **:** HANG **6 :** to straighten (oneself) esp. by rising to full height **:** draw up (one's body) from a cramped, stooping, or relaxed position **:** extend (as the arms or the legs) usu. in weariness ⟨awoke and ~*ed* himself⟩ **7 :** to bring to a rigid state of evenness or straightness by applying force at the ends or edges **:** pull taut ⟨tent . . . made of caribou skin ~*ed* on a framework —Ivor Jones⟩ **8 a** (1) **:** to expand, enlarge, or distend esp. by force **:** extend forcibly in length or width **:** enlarge in girth or capacity by pressure **:** draw or pull out ⟨~ . . . glass threads or fibers to the thinness necessary —Freda Diamond⟩ ⟨~ a hose into a building⟩ (2) **:** to expand as if by physical effort ⟨the understanding must be ~*ed* to take in the image of the universe —Francis Bacon⟩ **b :** to open wide ⟨tales . . . to ~ the wind eye of the oldest salts —Marjory S. Douglas⟩ **c :** STRAIN ⟨~*ed* his already thin patience⟩ **9 :** to cause to reach or continue (as from one point to another or across a space) ⟨~ a wire between two posts⟩ ⟨~ a curtain across the room⟩ **10 a** (1) **:** to amplify or enlarge beyond natural or proper limits **:** extend often unduly the scope, application, or meaning of ⟨~*es* the word . . . by giving it two entirely separate meanings —N.F.Busch⟩ ⟨the general-welfare clause . . . could easily be ~*ed* to give unlimited powers to the central government —Frank Meyer⟩ ⟨the law tacitly permits the rules to be ~*ed* —Norman Birkett⟩ ⟨~*ed* credibility far in reaching the solution —A.C.Ward⟩ (2) **:** to expand (as by improvisation) to fulfill a larger function ⟨~ the . . . appropriation to finance the relief of European children —Will Irwin⟩ ⟨~ one egg for two recipes —Molly L. Bar-David⟩ ⟨~ a budget⟩ **b :** to impair the accuracy of **:** exaggerate in narration ⟨~ the truth⟩ **11 :** to cause (a horse) to stand with the front legs stretched forward and the hind legs stretched backward **12 :** to extend or attempt to extend (a hit) into one involving one or more extra bases usu. by fast or daring running ⟨~ a single into a double⟩ ⟨cut down while trying to ~ the hit⟩ ~ *vi* **1 :** to press onward eagerly **:** proceed rapidly or energetically ⟨~ onward in thy fleet career —Sir Walter Scott⟩ **2** *obs* **:** to possess the capacity, force, or power to stand or endure strain ⟨so far as my coin would ~ —Shak.⟩ **3** *obs* **:** to possess a specified range of action **:** have a specified extent of application ⟨makes himself supreme lord . . . as far as his civil jurisdiction ~*es* —John Milton⟩ **4 a :** to become extended in length or in breadth or both **:** have a specified extent in space **:** be continuous to a certain point or over a certain distance or area **:** EXTEND, REACH, SPREAD ⟨pipeline . . . will ~ some 24.5 miles —*Wall Street Jour.*⟩ ⟨rolling fields ~ westward to the river's edge —*Amer. Guide Series: Conn.*⟩ ⟨attacks on a front that ~*es* from the mountains to the sea⟩ **b :** to extend over a continuous period of time ⟨their authorship ~*ed* . . . over a score of years —Leslie Rees⟩ ⟨this game . . . seems to ~ back to time immemorial —Geoffrey Boumphrey⟩ ⟨in the years which ~ ahead —Harold Wincott⟩ **5 :** to become extended or bear extension without breaking — used esp. of elastic or ductile substances ⟨rubber ~*s* easily⟩ **6 a :** to extend oneself, one's body, or one's limbs ⟨he awoke, yawned, and ~*ed*⟩ **b :** to lie down at full length ⟨~*ed* on the ground and took a nap⟩ ⟨between chores you ~*ed* by the fire —Mary Austin⟩ **7 :** to strain the truth **:** EXAGGERATE **8 :** to sail by the wind usu. under all sail **9 :** to exert oneself vigorously esp. in rowing **10 :** to stall for time (as by slowing the tempo of action) to enable a radio or television program to finish on schedule — **stretch a point :** to go beyond what is strictly warranted in making a claim or concession (as in an argument or bargain) — **stretch one's legs 1 :** to extend the legs; *specif* **:** to straighten the legs from a sitting position ⟨rose from the chair and *stretched his legs*⟩ **2 :** to take a walk in order to relieve the cramped feeling, stiffness, or fatigue caused by prolonged sitting **:** take a walk for exercise

²stretch \"\ *n* -ES **1 a** *archaic* **:** an act held to exceed the scope of authority, a commission, law, justice, propriety, or principle ⟨the unwarrantable ~ . . . which that house made in their last sitting —Thomas Paine⟩ **b :** an exercise (as of power, prerogative, or the law) held to be unwarranted **c** *archaic* **:** an instance of stretching the truth **:** an exaggerated statement **d :** an exercise of something (as the imagination or understanding) beyond ordinary or normal limits ⟨it was a ~ of his patience to hear himself addressed on a family matter —George Meredith⟩ ⟨not even by the longest ~ of the imagination can the sensitive listener be persuaded —Warwick Braithwaite⟩ **e :** an often undue extension of the scope or application of something ⟨a ~ of language⟩ **2 :** the extent to which something may be stretched **:** extreme reach ⟨defy the utmost ~ of your malice —Samuel Richardson⟩ ⟨one end is held at full ~ —Francis Yeats-Brown⟩ **3 :** the act of stretching or the state of being stretched: as **a :** the action of physically extending, expanding, or dilating something ⟨fixation of a muscle in ~ —C.R.Houck⟩ **b** (1) **:** the action of stretching the body or limbs (as in waking up or preparing to rest) ⟨that first comfortable ~ on the sand —*Read Mag.*⟩ (2) **:** the action of a baseball pitcher in fully extending himself (as by raising both arms with hands together over his head) before his windup and pitch **c :** a state of tension **:** the condition of being drawn taut ⟨the string . . . is kept at its ~ by means of a stiff piece of stick —Daniel Johnson⟩ ⟨keeping the thongs still upon the ~ —George Anson⟩ **4 a :** an extent in length **:** a continuous line, length, or distance **:** a continuous portion of something reckoned in length (as a journey, road, or river) ⟨a long ~ of the pipeline —Hardiman Scott⟩ ⟨killed all fish life in a ~ of creek —Bill Wolf⟩ ⟨suspended by . . . nothing except a ~ of stiff wire —P.E.Deutschman⟩ ⟨a particular ~ of speech —Bruce Pattison⟩ ⟨~*es* of narrative⟩ **b :** a continuous surface or expanse (as of land or water) ⟨~*es* of woodland dotted with lakes —*Amer. Guide Series: Maine*⟩ ⟨a tropical ~ of country in the south of India —Aubrey Menen⟩ **5 a :** a single prolonged period of time characterized by an activity or condition without intermission or interruption **:** an unbroken continuance of an activity or condition for a period of time ⟨he believed in regular ~*es* of work —Osbert Sitwell⟩ ⟨go on typing for eighteen hours at a ~ —Aldous Huxley⟩ ⟨pause . . . for unbearably long ~*es* —J.F.Wharton⟩ **b :** a continuous space, expanse, or period ⟨sustain unity of character over a ~ of time —Roger Manvell⟩ ⟨these notes were taken over a ~ of years —A.C.Ballard⟩ **c :** a run on one tack in sailing **d** *archaic* **:** a continuous journey or march **6 a :** an exertion of mental or physical powers **:** a state characterized by a straining of mind or body to the utmost ⟨keep the mind athletic and the upshot on the ~ —R.P.Blackmur⟩ ⟨keep his mental faculties at the ~ —J.N.Hall⟩ **b :** a strain or exhausting effort of mind **7 :** a walk to relieve the fatigue of prolonged sitting **8 a :** a sentence or term of imprisonment ⟨serving a ten-year ~ for counterfeiting —Bennett Cerf⟩ ⟨land a man in prison for quite a ~ —F.J.Warburg⟩ **b :** a period of service (as in the armed forces) ⟨did a short ~ in the infantry —Anthony Leviero⟩ ⟨during his ~ with a southern newspaper⟩ **9 :** the outward run of a mule carriage away from the rollers in spinning **10 a :** either of the straight sides of a racecourse ⟨a half-mile track with its shorter ~*es* —Jeremiah Tax⟩; *esp* **:** HOMESTRETCH 1 ⟨in the ~ the jockey looked back⟩ — see BACKSTRETCH **b :** the final or concluding stage (as in a baseball pennant drive or an election campaign) **11 a :** the capacity for being stretched **:** ELASTICITY ⟨no loss of ~ . . . or adhesive qualities —*Lancet*⟩ ⟨has a three-inch ~ to the yard —*New Yorker*⟩ **b :** liability to increase in size as a result of tension or moisture ⟨knit fabrics have considerable ~⟩

³stretch \"\ *adj* **:** characterized by a capacity to stretch **:** ELASTIC ⟨~ hosiery⟩ ⟨~ nylon⟩

stretch·abil·i·ty \ˌstrechəˈbiləd-ē, -lətē, -i\ *n* **:** the quality or state of being stretchable **:** ELASTICITY, RESILIENCE

stretch·able \ˈ=chəbəl\ *adj* **:** capable of being stretched ⟨~ bandages⟩

stretch·berry \ˈ=- — *see* BERRY\ *n* [³*stretch* + *berry*; fr. the elastic tissue in the pulp of the berries] **1 :** the fruit of a bristly or prickly greenbrier (*Smilax bonanox*) **2 :** the plant producing stretchberries

stretched *past of* STRETCH

stretch·er \ˈstrechə(r)\ *n* -S *often attrib* [ME *strecher*, fr. *strechen* to stretch + *-er* — more at STRETCH] **1 :** one that stretches: as **a :** a workman who stretches textiles or metal **:** a tender of a stretching machine **b :** a device or machine for stretching or expanding something (as a boot, carpet, fence, glove, saw, trousers, or wire) by applied force — often used in combination; see CURTAIN STRETCHER **c :** a stick or one of several sticks used to keep a fishnet expanded **d :** one of the rods pivoted at the ends to the ribs and to the tube that slides upon the handle in opening or closing an umbrella **e :** the frame upon which an artist's canvas is stretched for painting **f :** a piece of wood or metal used to spread the clews of a hammock **g :** one whose work is to straighten something specified ⟨iron ~⟩ ⟨silk ~⟩ ⟨spindle ~⟩ ⟨yarn ~⟩ **h :** a jointed rod or bar that when straightened raises a collapsible top or hood (as of a vehicle) **i :** a textile worker who operates a tenter **j :** an operator of a machine for shaping finger rings **k :** a machine operator who softens skins for hatter's fur **2 a :** a narrow crosspiece in a boat for a rower to brace his feet against — called also *boat stretcher* **b :** a temporary crosspiece to keep the sides of a boat from being crushed together **3 :** an overstretching of the truth **:** an exaggerated story or yarn **:** a tall tale ⟨a true book with some ~*s* —Mark Twain⟩ **4 :** a brick or stone laid with its length parallel to the face of the wall — compare BOND 6, HEADER **5 a :** a timber or rod used esp. when horizontal as a tie in framed work **b :** STRETCHER BAR **6 a :** TAIL FLY **b :** LEADER 1i(2) **7 :** the usu. horizontal bracing member or set of members reaching between and steadying the legs of a piece of furniture (as a chair or table) **:** a part of the underframing serving as a stay or brace between the legs **8 a :** a litter usu. made of canvas stretched on a frame for carrying disabled or dead persons **b** *chiefly Austral & NewZeal* **:** a folding canvas cot **9 :** a display folder simulating a book cover or series of covers (as for explanatory or advertising purposes)

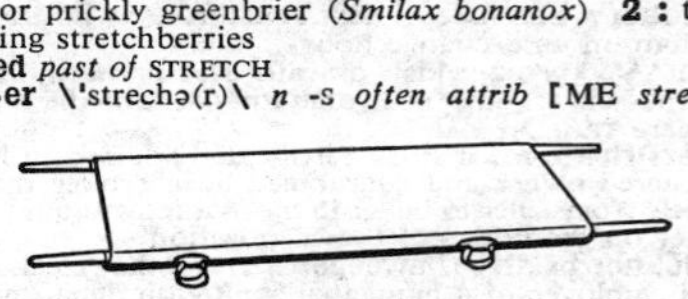

stretcher 8a

stretcher bar *n* **1 :** an extensible pillar attached to a rock drill to secure it in place **2 :** a bar or rod used as a distance piece

stretcher-bearer *n* **:** one who carries one end of a stretcher esp. for conveying sick or wounded from place to place (as from a battlefield to an ambulance)

stretcher bond *n* **:** a bond with all the bricks or ashlars laid as stretchers breaking joint

stretcher course *n* **:** a course in which all the bricks are laid as stretchers

stretcher key *n* **:** a thin wooden wedge pressed into the joints of a stretcher to tighten an artist's canvas

stretcher·man \ˈ==ˌmən\ *n, pl* **stretchermen :** an operator of a machine for stretching and flattening metal sheets

stretcher strip *n* **:** a side member of a stretcher used for oil or water-color painting

stretches *pres 3d sing of* STRETCH, *pl of* STRETCH

stretching *pres part of* STRETCH

stretching bond *n* **:** STRETCHER BOND

stretching course *n* **:** STRETCHER COURSE

stretch-out \ˈ=,=\ *n* -S [fr. *stretch out*, v.] **1 :** a system of industrial operation in which workers are required to do extra work and esp. to operate more machines than formerly

either with slight or with no additional pay **2 :** an economizing measure that spreads a limited quantity over a larger field than orig. intended; *specif* **:** a slackening of production schedules in defense planning so that a previously decided upon quantity of military goods will be produced over a longer period than initially stipulated

stretch runner *n* **:** a racehorse that makes a strong bid in the homestretch

stretch spinning *n* **:** the elongation of man-made textile filaments after they have left the spinneret but before they have finally solidified

stretchy \ˈstrechē, -chi\ *adj* -ER/-EST [¹*stretch* + *-y*] **1 :** having a capacity or tendency to stretch esp. unduly ⟨~ nylon⟩ **2 :** having length of body — used esp. of a pig

stretch yarn *n* **:** synthetic yarn that will stretch under tension and contract when released made from usu. thermoplastic filaments that have been given a permanently-set corkscrew twist and then plied or reverse-twisted and used esp. for hosiery

¹stret·to \ˈstred·(,)ō, -e(,)tō\ *adv* [It, lit., narrowly, closely, fr. *stretto* narrow, close, pressed together, fr. L *strictus*, past part. of *stringere* to draw tight, press together — more at STRAIN] **:** more quickly — used as a direction in music

²stretto \"\ *or* **stret·ta** \-edə, -etə\ *n, pl* **stret·ti** \-ed·(,)ē, -e(,)tē\ *or* **strettos** \-ed·(,)ōz, -e(,)tōz\ *or* **stret·te** \-ed·(,)ā, -e(,)tā\ *or* **strettas** [*stretto* fr. It, lit., narrow, close, pressed together; *stretta* fr. It, fr. fem. of *stretto*] **1 a :** the overlapping of answer with subject in a musical fugue **b :** the part of a fugue characterized by the cumulative effect of this overlapping **2 :** a concluding passage performed in a quicker tempo

streu·sel \ˈs(h)trȯi|zəl, |səl *sometimes* ˈstrü|\ *n* -S [G, lit., something strewn, sprinkling, fr. MHG *ströusel* something strewn, sprinkling, fr. *ströun, ströuwen* to scatter, strew, fr. OHG *strewen*] **:** a crumbly mixture of fat, sugar, and flour used on the top of coffee cake

streuselkuchen \ˈ==,==\ *n* [G, fr. *streusel* + *kuchen* cake — more at KUCHEN] **:** coffee cake that is baked with a topping of streusel

¹strew \ˈstrü\ *vb* **strewed; strewed** \-üd\ *or* **strewn** \-ün *sometimes* -üən\ **strewing; strews** [ME *strewen, strowen*, fr. OE *strēwian, strēowian*; akin to OHG *strewen* to strew, ON *strā*, Goth *straujan* to strew, L *sternere* to spread out, throw down, Gk *stornynai* to spread, strew, Skt *stṛṇāti* he scatters, strews] *vt* **1 :** to spread by scattering **:** SCATTER — used esp. of solids separated or separable into parts or particles ⟨the ground . . . upon which the poultry grower ~s his seed —S.R. Guard & Lloyd Graham⟩ ⟨the growth hormone . . . can be *strewn* freely on lawns —*Harvard Foundation Newsletter*⟩ ⟨obstacles being *strewn* along the water's edge —P.W.Thompson⟩ ⟨little balls of paper were ~*ed* over the bed —Arnold Bennett⟩ **2 :** to cover more or less thickly by or as if by scattering something over or on ⟨with flowers thy bridal bed I ~ —Shak.⟩ ⟨~*ed* the stones . . . with the straw —Padraic Colum⟩ ⟨the forest floor is *strewn* with large granite boulders —G.R.Stewart⟩ **3** *archaic* **:** to raze to the ground **:** cast down **:** lay low **4 :** CALM 1 **5 :** to become dispersed over as if scattered ⟨boulders that ~*ed* the mountainside —D.J.Rankin⟩ **6 :** to spread abroad **:** DISSEMINATE ⟨may ~ dangerous conjectures in ill-breeding minds —Shak.⟩ ~ *vi* **:** to strew seed

syn STREW, STROW, STRAW, SCATTER, SOW, and BROADCAST agree in meaning to throw, scatter, sprinkle, or spread around loosely or at intervals as by casting from the hand. STREW and the rarer STROW and STRAW imply spreading around more or less at random but suggesting a wide coverage ⟨*strew* a floor with rushes⟩ ⟨a sidewalk *strewn* with leaves⟩ ⟨clothes *strewn* around a room⟩ ⟨may *strow* the dust with holy water for her peace —John Bennett⟩ ⟨an ancient usage to *straw* the path that leads from her father's house to the family washing well with handfuls of these flowers —Llewelyn Powys⟩ SCATTER implies a separation of parts or pieces, distinctly suggesting a haphazard throwing about or dispersal of small units ⟨*scatter* toys all over the floor⟩ ⟨no railroad *scatters* its soot over the neat white frame houses —Corey Ford⟩ ⟨many bullets or shot which *scattered* out of the mouth of the gun —Tom Wintringham⟩ ⟨the majority of the dwellings being *scattered* over the town's edge —*Amer. Guide Series: Oregon*⟩ SOW, always implying the strewing of seed, applies to something like seed that can be disseminated throughout a group ⟨*sowed* the area with bombs —Nevil Shute⟩ ⟨*sow* seeds of reason and understanding throughout the world —A.E. Stevenson b. 1900⟩ ⟨*sowing* dissension in our ranks —Kenneth Roberts⟩ ⟨those problems with which literature is *sown* so thick —Virginia Woolf⟩ BROADCAST in this connection implies a scattering widely or in all directions ⟨*broadcast* very fine seed⟩ ⟨antitoxin should be used only in certain cases of exposed, susceptible individuals, not *broadcast* unnecessarily —Justina Hill⟩ ⟨university presses . . . all have one highly commendable objective — to help *broadcast* scholarship —B.L. Stratton⟩ ⟨used the Senate floor to *broadcast* the obscene objections that had been made against the confirmation —Sidney Hyman⟩

²strew \"\ *n* -S **:** a number of things scattered about **:** a disorderly mess ⟨a ~ of oak trunks lay everywhere —A.P. Terhune⟩

strew·er \ˈstrüə(r), -üə)r, -üə\ *n* -S **:** one that strews

strewing herb *n* **:** an herb formerly strewn over the floor in private rooms, banquet halls, churches, and similar places for the fragrance of flower or foliage

strew·ment \-mənt\ *or* **strew·ing** \-iŋ, -ēŋ\ *n* -S [*strewment* fr. ¹*strew* + *-ment*; *strewing* fr. ME *strewing, strowing*, fr. gerund of *strewen, strowen* to strew] *archaic* **:** something (as flowers) strewed or designed for strewing ⟨she is allow'd . . . her maiden ~*s* —Shak.⟩

stria \ˈstrīə\ *n, pl* **stri·ae** \-ī,ē, -ī,ī\ [L, furrow, channel, hollow — more at STRIKE] **1 :** a fillet esp. between flutes of columns or pilasters **2 a :** a minute groove or channel **:** a threadlike line or narrow band (as of color) esp. when one of a series of parallel grooves or lines ⟨the *striae* produced on a rock by rock fragments held in a glacier⟩ ⟨the *striae* on a shell⟩ ⟨the *striae* of the light in a vacuum tube⟩ **b :** a narrow structural band or line ⟨a ~ of nervous matter in the brain⟩ **3 :** an elongated imperfection in glass caused by variation in temperature of the furnace or by unequal density of materials used **4 :** a stripe or line (as on the skin) distinguished from the surrounding tissue by color, texture, or elevation ⟨the *striae* in the skin in pregnancy resulting from stretching and rupture of the elastic fibers⟩ **5 :** STRIÉ

stria lon·gi·tu·di·na·lis \-ˌlänjə,t(y)üdᵊnˈalə̇s, -äl-, -al-\ *n, pl* **striae longitudina·les** \-a(,)lēz, -ä(,)lēz, -ä,lās\ [NL, longitudinal stripe] **:** either of a pair of longitudinal elevations near the middle line of the upper surface of the corpus callosum

stri·ar·ia \strēˈa(a)rēə\ *n, cap* [NL, fr. L *stria* hollow + NL *-aria*] **:** a genus (the type of the family Striariaceae) of hollow filamentous brown algae of the north Atlantic having the filaments commonly tapering to either extremity

stri·a·tal \(ˈ)strī|ād·ᵊl, -ātᵊl\ *adj* [NL *striatus* striated + E *-al*] **1 :** of or relating to the corpus striatum **2 :** of or relating to the striae longitudinales

¹stri·ate \ˈstrī,āt, *usu* -ād.+V\ *adj* [NL *striatus*] **:** STRIATED

²striate \"\ *vt* -ED/-ING/-S [NL *striatus* striated] **:** to mark with or as if with striae

stri·at·ed \(ˈ)=|ād·əd, -ātəd\ *adj* [NL *striatus* striated (fr. L, past part. of *striare* to form furrows, fr. *stria* furrow, channel) + E *-ed*] **:** marked with parallel striae **:** showing narrow structural bands or lines ⟨a ~ crystal⟩ ⟨~ muscle fiber⟩

triated muscle *n* **:** muscle tissue made up of elongated multinuclear fibers enclosed in a delicate sarcolemma and marked by transverse dark and light bands that presumably indicate differing physical or chemical states of the cytoplasm, the fibers in vertebrates being bound together by a perimysium to form the muscles that clothe the skeleton of a vertebrate and are the organs productive of voluntary activity, and in arthropods forming all or most of the musculature

stri·a·tion \-ˈāshən\ *n* -S [²*striate* + *-ion*] **1 a :** the fact or state of being striated **b :** arrangement of striae **2 :** one of a series of parallel stripes or lines **:** STRIA **3 :** one of the alternate light and dark bands occurring in the discharge in the positive column of a vacuum tube between limits of low pressure due to alternate loss and recovery of electron energy through ionization and acceleration

stri·a·tum \-=ˈād·əm\ *n, pl* **stria·ta** \-ād·ə\ [by shortening] **:** CORPUS STRIATUM

stri·a·ture \ˈstrīəchə(r)\ *n* -S [L *striatura* fact of having furrows or channels, arrangement of furrows, fr. *striatus* (past part. of *striare* to form furrows, fr. *stria* furrow, channel) + *-ura* -ure — more at STRIKE] **:** STRIATION

strich *n* -ES [prob. modif. of L *strix* — more at STRIDENT] *obs* **:** SCREECH OWL

strick \ˈstrik\ *n* -S [ME *stric, strik*, prob. of LG or D origin; akin to MLG *strik* rope, MD *stric* knot, rope; akin to OFris *strik* rope, OHG *stric* rope, *stricchan* to rope, twine, OE *strician* to knit] **:** a bunch of hackled flax, jute, or hemp

strick·en \ˈstrikən\ *adj* [fr. past part. of ¹*strike*] **1** *archaic* **:** having reached an advanced stage — usu. used in the phrase *stricken in years* **2 :** having the contents leveled off even with the top ⟨a ~ measure of grain⟩ **3 :** hit or wounded by or as if by a missile ⟨a ~ deer that left the herd long since —William Cowper⟩ **4 a** (1) **:** afflicted with or overwhelmed by or as if by disease, misfortune, or sorrow ⟨was ~ at the height of his career⟩ ⟨wrapped the ~ man in his coat and sat down beside him —Irving Bacheller⟩ ⟨shows how a ~ region . . . can adjust valiantly to harsh conditions —Muna Lee⟩ — often used in combination ⟨grief-*stricken*⟩ ⟨palsy-*stricken*⟩ ⟨panic-*stricken*⟩ ⟨poverty-*stricken*⟩ (2) **:** showing the effect of or as if of disease, misfortune, or sorrow ⟨the whole company had a ~ look —Kenneth Roberts⟩ ⟨the most ~ landscape we had yet seen —George Farwell⟩ **b :** made incapable or unfit **:** INCAPACITATED ⟨destroyers . . . swarmed around the ~ vessel —*Springfield (Mass.) Union*⟩ — **strick·en·ly** *adv*

stricken field *n* **:** a field that has been the scene of a conflict **:** BATTLEGROUND

stricken hour *n* **:** a whole hour as marked by the striking of a clock

¹strick·le \ˈstrikəl\ *n* -S [ME *strikell*; akin to MD *strekel* strickle, ME *striche, strek* strickle, OE *strīcan* to pass over lightly, stroke — more at STRIKE] **1 :** an instrument for removing surplus grain from the top of a measure **2 a :** an instrument for whetting scythes **b :** a straightedge fed with an abrasive for sharpening knives arranged helically on a cylinder **3 :** a template consisting of a board or plate with a beveled edge of definite contour used to sweep or strike up a mold, core, or part of a mold in sand or loam

²strickle \"\ *vt* **strickled; strickled; strickling** \-k(ə)liŋ\ **strickles :** to smooth or form with a strickle

strict \ˈstrikt\ *adj* -ER/-EST [L *strictus*, past part. of *stringere* to draw tight, press together — more at STRAIN] **1 :** particularly severe in requirement **:** permitting no evasion ⟨had always been under the ~*est* orders not to enter —T.B.Costain⟩ ⟨the only court in equity capable of overruling ~ law —Henry Adams⟩ **2 :** maintained absolutely without deviation **:** COMPLETE, THOROUGH ⟨had been meeting his two friends only in ~ secrecy —Upton Sinclair⟩ ⟨occupy the position of ~ neutrality —E.M.Coulter⟩ **3** *archaic* **:** drawn close **:** TIGHT ⟨she wildly breaketh from their ~ embrace —Shak.⟩ **4 a** *bot* **:** of upright erect habit ⟨a ~ stem or plant⟩ **:** being straight and not lax or drooping ⟨a ~ inflorescence⟩ **b** *biol* **:** OBLIGATE **5 :** rigorous in exercising control **:** severely disciplinary ⟨though ~ in some ways she had shown herself unexpectedly lenient in others —Archibald Marshall⟩ **6 a** *archaic* **:** compressed in extent **:** CONSTRICTED, NARROW **b :** closely restricted ⟨remained in ~ custody⟩ **7** *archaic* **:** CLOSE, INTIMATE ⟨there never was a more ~ friendship —Richard Steele⟩ **8 :** inflexibly adhered to **:** firmly maintained ⟨demanded ~*er* discipline —E.W.Parks⟩ ⟨held his pupils under ~ control —L.M.Crosbie⟩ ⟨congestion . . . makes ~ supervision of speed imperative —*Amer. Guide Series: R.I.*⟩ **9 :** characterized by severity **:** rigorously austere ⟨aren't half so ~ now about mourning as they used to be —Arnold Bennett⟩ **10 :** completely accurate **:** EXACT, PRECISE ⟨in the ~ sense of the word every writer . . . deals with life —M.R.Cohen⟩ ⟨aim at ~ historical accuracy —G.G.Coulton⟩ **11 :** conforming closely to a set pattern **:** adhering rigidly to a conventionally fixed norm ⟨a development of several centuries into a ~ form —T.S. Eliot⟩ ⟨the opera is written in the ~ twelve-tone style —K.H. Wörner⟩ ⟨the verse . . . for all its freedom and variety, is nevertheless very ~ —F.R.Leavis⟩ **12 :** unswerving in conformance to principle ⟨an earnest and a ~ Moslem —W.N.Ewer⟩ ⟨regarded as uncanonical by all ~ churchmen —F.M.Stenton⟩ **syn** see RIGID

strict constructionist *n* **:** one who favors giving a narrow conservative construction of a given document or instrument; *specif* **:** one who favors a strict construction of the Constitution of the United States — compare LOOSE CONSTRUCTIONIST

strict counterpoint *n* **:** counterpoint limited harmonically to musical triads and first inversions in which appogiaturas and chromatic tones are forbidden and usu. divided into five species: (1) note against note of the cantus firmus; (2) two notes to one; (3) four notes to one; (4) syncopated; (5) figurate or florid

strict deposit *n, law* **:** SPECIAL DEPOSIT

strict foreclosure *n* **:** a proceeding in equity that determines by decree the amount due on a mortgage, fixes a time within which the mortgagor debtor must pay it, and vests in case of his default absolute title in the mortgagee forever free of any right of the mortgagor to redeem and that is often used where the value of the mortgaged property does not exceed the mortgage debt — distinguished from *statutory foreclosure*; compare LEGAL FORECLOSURE

stric·ti ju·ris \ˌstrik,tīˈjürə̇s, ˌstriktēˈyü-\ *adv* [L] **:** of or by strict law esp. as distinguished from equity

strict implication *n* **:** IMPLICATION 2b(2)

stric·tis·si·mi ju·ris \strikˈtisə,mīˈjürə̇s, -əmēˈyü-\ *adv* [L] **:** of or by the strictest law **:** having the law or the instrument or transaction creating the rights in question construed most strictly in favor of one and against the other party

strict law *n* **:** STRICTUM JUS 1

strict·ly *adv* [ME, fr. L *strictus* + ME *-ly* — more at STRICT] **:** in a strict manner **:** without latitude **:** CLOSELY, PRECISELY, RIGOROUSLY, STRINGENTLY, POSITIVELY ⟨the reporter was ~ on his own —Bruce Catton⟩ ⟨effectiveness as a novelist is so ~ a function of skill —Bernard DeVoto⟩ ⟨certain rules need to be ~ carried out —Agnes M. Miall⟩

strict·ness \-k(t)nə̇s\ *n* -ES **:** the quality or state of being strict **:** PRECISION, SEVERITY ⟨the orders of the . . . government had been executed with absolute ~ —W.H.G.Kingston⟩

strict settlement *n, Eng law* **:** a settlement in which in general there is a limitation of lands to a person for life and after his death to the eldest male child in succession with trustees to preserve contingent remainders and with certain rights being given to the younger children

stric·tum jus *or* **strictum ius** \ˌstriktəmˈjəs, -mˈyüs\ *n* [L, strict law] **1 :** the law by its letter without considering equities **2** *Roman law* **:** the jus civile of the city of Rome — compare PRAETORIAN LAW

stric·ture \ˈstrikchə(r)\ *n* -S [ME, fr. LL *strictura* contraction, stricture, fr. L *strictus* (past part. of *stringere* to draw tight, press together) + *-ura* -ure; in senses 4 & 5, influenced in meaning by L *strictus*, past part. of *stringere* to touch lightly, graze — more at STRAIN, STRIKE] **1 :** an abnormal narrowing of the lumen of a tubular organ from various causes (as inflammation, scar tissue, cancer) **:** CONSTRICTION **2** *obs* **:** a beam of light **:** SPARK **3 :** something that closely restrains or limits **:** RESTRICTION ⟨a ~ against disclosure of classified information —Douglass Cater⟩ ⟨a relaxation of tariffs and of ~*s* upon international currency —*Current Biog.*⟩ **4 :** an adverse criticism **:** critical remark **:** CENSURE ⟨wasn't keen about rousing her suspicions or ~*s* —David Walden⟩ **5** *obs* **:** a slight touch **:** SIGN, TRACE

strid \ˈstrid\ *n* -S [fr. the *Strid*, narrowest part of a channel of the Wharfe river in west central Yorkshire, England] **:** a narrow ravine **:** GORGE

strid·dle \ˈstridᵊl\ *vb* [back-formation fr. *stridling*] **1** *Scot & dial Eng* **:** STRADDLE **2** *Scot & dial Eng* **:** STRIDE

¹stride \ˈstrīd\ *vb* **strode** \-rōd\ **strid·den** \-ridᵊn\ **strid·ing** \-rīdiŋ\ **strides** [ME *striden*, fr. OE *strīdan*; akin to MLG *striden* to straddle, OHG *strītan* to quarrel, fight, ON *strītha* to fight, *strīthr* strong, hard, stiff, OE *starian* to stare — more at STARE] *vi* **1 a :** to stand with the legs wide apart **:** STRADDLE **b :** to give the appearance of standing astride ⟨hills rising from the water and the *striding* bridges —R.L. Shayon⟩ ⟨antennas would ~ north Atlantic icecaps —K.E. Mundt⟩ **2 :** to move or walk with or as if with long steps ⟨*strode* to the door —J.C.Lincoln⟩ ⟨was his custom to ~ up and down the street —*Amer. Guide Series: Oregon*⟩ **3 :** to take a very long step ⟨*strode* over the pail —Arnold Bennett⟩ ~ *vt* **1 :** BESTRIDE, STRADDLE **2 :** to pass over at a step **:** step over **3 :** to move or walk over, along, or about with or as if with long measured steps ⟨found the great man impatiently *striding* the floor —*Time*⟩

²stride \"\ *n* -S [ME *stride, stryde, strede*, fr. OE *stride*; akin to MLG *strede* stride, OE *strīdan* to stride] **1 a :** the distance measured by a long step **b :** the distance covered by a runner in one leg cycle **2 a** (1) **:** an act of striding **:** a lengthy walking step ⟨merely marched . . . briskly, stamping hard at every ~ —D.L.Busk⟩ ⟨walked . . . with a kind of finality in the ~, as though she had made up her mind —R.P.Warren⟩ (2) **:** something resembling a stride ⟨gathered many honors in his ~ through a long and useful life —A.W.Long⟩ ⟨a giant crane lifted steel girders with an effortless ~ —Louis Bromfield⟩ **b :** a long dance step **3 :** a standing position in which the legs are spread apart either laterally or forward and back **4 :** a stage of progress **:** a decisive movement toward a future goal **:** ADVANCE ⟨have made extraordinary ~*s* in invention —T.W.Arnold⟩ ⟨the ~*s* made in recent years in keeping the American public informed —Lou Smyth⟩ **5 a :** an act of locomotion consisting of a cycle of movements completed when an animal's feet regain the initial relative positions; *also* **:** the distance traversed in such a movement — used esp. of a horse **b :** the most effective natural pace **:** the full motion or height of activity ⟨he had just got into his ~ when the lady interrupted him with a remark —W.S.Maugham⟩ ⟨the laughter threw the Minister out of his ~, he . . . presently brought his remarks to a close —E.H.Collis⟩ **6 :** a manner of walking with distinctively long steps ⟨watched her lithe ~ . . . as she drew away —Zane Grey⟩ ⟨swinging his arms and stepping higher . . . so that his ~ was one of majesty —Roark Bradford⟩ **7 strides** *pl, Brit* **:** TROUSERS — **in stride** *adv* **:** without changing the normal pace **:** with no loss of equilibrium **:** without interference with regular activities ⟨if a man can't take his bad luck *in stride*, he isn't emotionally mature —P.B.Gilliam⟩

strideleg \ˈ=,=\ *or* **stridelegs** \ˈ=,=\ *adv, chiefly Scot* **:** ASTRIDE

stri·den·cy \ˈstrīdᵊnsē, -si\ *also* **stri·dence** \-dᵊn(t)s\ *n, pl* **stridencies** *also* **stridences :** the quality or state of being strident ⟨argued strongly but without ~ for idealism —Norman Cousins⟩ ⟨and the cities grew in size and in ~ —F.L. Allen⟩

stri·dent \-dᵊnt\ *adj* [L *strident-, stridens*, pres. part. of *stridere, stridēre* to make a harsh noise, to creak, hiss; akin to Gk *trizein* to screech, creak, hiss, *strix* owl, L *strix* screech owl; all of imit. origin] **1 a :** marked by insistent, discordant, harsh, shrill, or grating noise or sound **:** characterized by an annoying often abnormal sibilance ⟨his mouth opens . . . and from it comes a noise, a ~ sigh, a raucous moan —Douglas Newton⟩ ⟨the ~ babble with which natives are accustomed to make the day hideous —Rudyard Kipling⟩ ⟨talks at the top of a very high and ~ voice —Rose Macaulay⟩ **b :** having an unpleasant usu. irritating effect **:** loudly or obtrusively commanding notice or recognition **:** BLATANT ⟨the colors are pure, but they are not ~ —H.D.Walker⟩ ⟨his writing took on a faster tempo and a more ~ tone —Max Lerner⟩ **2 :** characterized by friction that is comparatively turbulent in that there are two friction-producing components in the articulation instead of only one ⟨\sh\, which has both tongue-teeth and tongue-palate friction, is ~, but \th\, which has tongue-teeth friction only, is not⟩ — compare MELLOW **syn** see LOUD, VOCIFEROUS

stri·dent·ly *adv* **:** in a strident manner ⟨the cheap alarm clock ticked ~ —T.O.Heggen⟩

strident stop *n* **:** AFFRICATE

strid·er \ˈstrīdə(r)\ *n* -S [¹*stride* + *-er*] **:** one that strides; *esp* **:** WATER STRIDER

strides *pres 3d sing of* STRIDE, *pl of* STRIDE

stri·dha·na \ˈstrē,dənə\ *also* **stri·dhan** \-dən\ *n* -S [Skt *strīdhana*, fr. *strī* woman + *dhana* property — more at DHAN] *Hindu law* **:** any property belonging to a woman; *esp* **:** property absolutely at her disposal and going to her heirs upon her death intestate

striding *pres part of* STRIDE

striding compass *n* **:** a compass on a theodolite for orientation

striding level *n* **:** a tube-shaped level fastened to a frame having two inverted Y's and mounted on a theodolite

strid·ling \ˈstridlən, -liŋ\ *or* **stridlings** \-lənz, -liŋz\ *adv* [ME *stridling, stridlinges*, fr. *striden* to stride + *-ling, -linges* -ling, -lings] *chiefly Scot* **:** ASTRIDE

stri·dor \ˈstrīdə(r)\ *n* -S [L, fr. *stridere, stridēre* to make a harsh noise] **1 :** a harsh, shrill, or creaking noise ⟨the pine grove, where . . . the boughs made a ~ —R.P.Warren⟩ **2 :** a harsh vibrating sound during expiration in cases of obstruction or spasm of the air passages ⟨laryngeal ~⟩

strids *pl of* STRID

strid·u·lant \ˈstrijələnt\ *adj* [*stridulation* + *-ant*] **:** STRIDULATING, STRIDULOUS

strid·u·late \-,lāt, *usu* -ād.+V\ *vi* -ED/-ING/-S [back-formation fr. *stridulation*] **:** to make a shrill often vibrating noise **:** produce a stridulation

strid·u·la·tion \ˌ==ˈlāshən\ *n* -S [F, fr. L *stridulus* shrill, squeaky + F *-ation*] **1 :** a usu. high pitched creaking or musical sound made by the males of many insects (as the katydids or crickets) and sometimes by the females by rubbing together specially modified parts of the body **2 :** the act of stridulating

strid·u·la·tor \ˈ==,lād·ə(r), -ātə-\ *n* -S [*stridulate* + *-or*] **:** one that stridulates

strid·u·la·to·ry \ˈ==lə,tōrē, -tȯr-, -ri\ *adj* [*stridulation* + *-ory*] **:** able to stridulate **:** used in stridulation **:** STRIDULOUS

strid·u·lent \ˈ==lənt\ *adj* [L *stridulus* shrill, squeaky + E *-ent*] **:** STRIDENT, STRIDULOUS

strid·u·lous \-ləs\ *adj* [L *stridulus*, fr. *stridere, stridēre* to creak — more at STRIDENT] **1 a :** making a shrill, creaking sound **:** SQUEAKY ⟨the ~ cries of the gulls —Jean Stafford⟩ **b :** having or producing the effect of a harshly unpleasant grating sound ⟨these harsh and ~ pieces . . . had an instantaneous success with the public —Oscar Cargill⟩ **2 :** characteristic of or affected with stridor — **strid·u·lous·ly** *adv*

strié \strēˈā\ *n* -S [F, fr. *strié*, adj., striated, fluted, grooved, fr. L *striatus*, past part. of *striare* to form furrows — more at STRIATED] **:** a striped design used esp. in textiles that consists of faint streaked vertical lines of color close in tone to the background

strife \ˈstrīf\ *n* -S [ME *strif*, fr. OF *estrif*, prob. fr. *estriver* to fight — more at STRIVE] **1 a :** the state or condition of distrust or enmity **:** often bitter sometimes violent conflict or dissension ⟨the grace of universal peace and the folly of human ~ —M.R. Cohen⟩ ⟨a law that . . . comes nearest to eliminating labor ~ —A.G.Larke⟩ **b :** an act of contention **:** FIGHT, QUARREL, STRUGGLE ⟨some twenty of them fought in this black ~ —Shak.⟩ ⟨was nominated for governor as a result of the factional ~ within the . . . party —H.C.Hockett⟩ **2 :** exertion or contention for superiority **:** a contest usu. for a desired goal or result ⟨a strange ~ of wishes, for and against —Thomas Hardy⟩ **3** *archaic* **:** the act of striving **:** earnest endeavor ⟨we will pay with ~ to please you —Shak.⟩ **syn** see DISCORD

strife·less \-ləs\ *adj* **:** free from strife

strif·fen *or* **strif·fin** \ˈstrifən\ *or* **strif·fon** \-fən\ *n* -S [prob. fr. ScGael *streafon* fringe, striffen] *dial Brit* **:** a thin skin **:** MEMBRANE

strift \ˈstrift\ *n* -S [fr. *strive*, after such pairs as E *thrive: thrift*] **1 :** the act of striving **2 :** STRIFE

strig \ˈstrig\ *n* -S [perh. alter. of ¹*string*] **1 a :** the footstalk of a leaf or flower **b** *dial Eng* **:** the rachis of a hop strobile **c :** the fruiting raceme of the common currant **2 :** a thin narrow part or attachment of various tools

¹stri·ga \ˈstrīgə\ *n, pl* **stri·gae** \-ī,jē, -ī,gī\ *or* **strigas** [NL, fr. L, furrow, windrow, swath — more at STRIKE] **1 :** a pointed appressed rigid hairlike scale or bristle **2 :** a flute in a column **3 :** STRIATION — **stri·gal** \-gəl\ *adj*

²striga \"\ *n, cap* [NL] **:** a genus of seed plants (family Scrophulariaceae) living as root parasites esp. on corn, sugarcane, and other grasses in the eastern tropics

stri·gate \ˈstrī,gāt\ *adj* [NL *striga* + E *-ate*] **:** having strigae

strig·e·ata \\,strijē'ăd·ə, -'ād·ə\\ *n pl, cap* [NL, fr. *Strigea,* genus of trematodes + *-ata*] *in some classifications* : a suborder of Prosostomata comprising digenetic trematode worms parasitic as adults in the blood or intestines of vertebrates and including such medically important forms as the schistosomes

¹strig·e·id \\'⸗⸗,əd\\ *adj* [NL *Strigeidae*] : of or relating to the Strigeidae

²strigeid \\"\\ *n* -s : a digenetic trematode of the family Strigeidae

stri·ge·i·dae \\strə'jēə,dē\\ *n pl, cap* [NL, fr. *Strigea,* type genus (prob. fr. *striga* bristle) + *-idae*] : a family of digenetic trematodes having the anterior end flattened or cuplike and the posterior end cylindrical and including various parasites of mammals and birds — see ALARIA

stri·ges \\'strī,jēz\\ *n pl, cap* [NL, fr. pl. of L *strix* screech owl — more at STRIDENT] *in some classifications* : a group of birds equivalent to Strigiformes formerly made a suborder of Coraciiformes or Raptores

strig·i·dae \\'strijə,dē\\ *n pl, cap* [NL, fr. *Strig-, Strix* type genus + *-idae*] : a family of birds (order Strigiformes): **a** *in former classifications* : a family coextensive with Strigiformes **b** *in some esp former classifications* : a family equivalent to Tytonidae **c** : a family comprising all the owls except the barn owls — compare TYTONIDAE; see BUBONIDAE

strig·i·for·mes \\,⸗⸗'fȯr,mēz\\ *n pl, cap* [NL, fr. *Strig-, Strix* + *-iformes*] : an order of birds of prey that comprises the owls and is usu. divided into the families Tytonidae and Strigidae

strig·il \\'strijəl\\ *n* -s [L *strigilis;* akin to L *stringere* to touch lightly, graze — more at STRIKE] **1** : an instrument usu. of metal or ivory used by the ancient Greeks and Romans for scraping the skin esp. after the athletic exercises of the palaestra and at the bath **2** : a pectinate structure in many insects at the apex of the front tibia formed from the tibial spur and used to clean the antennae and other parts of the body **3** : one of a group of undulating or slightly curved vertical channels, reedings, or flutings often carved on flat surfaces as ornament and used esp. in Roman architecture

strig·i·late \\'strijələt, -,lāt, *usu* -d·+V\\ *adj* [*strigil* + *-ate*] : having a strigil

strig·i·la·tor \\'⸗⸗,lād·ə(r)\\ *n* -s [*strigilate* + *-or*] : any of various myrmecophiles or termitophiles that feed by licking the surface of the bodies of the ants or termites with which they live

strig·i·lis \\'strijələs\\ *n, pl* **strigi·les** \\-ə,lēz\\ [L] : STRIGIL

strig·il·lose \\-ə,lōs\\ *adj* [NL *strigilla* (dim. of *striga* bristle) + E *-ose* — more at STRIGA] : finely strigose

stri·gine \\'strī,jīn, -,jən\\ *adj* [NL *Strig-, Strix* + E *-ine*] : relating to the Strigidae : OWLLIKE

stri·gol·nik \\strə'gälnik\\ *n, pl* **strigolniks** \\-ks\\ *also* **strigolni·ki** \\-nəkē\\ *usu cap* [Russ *Strigol'nik,* lit., cutter, shearer; akin to OSlav *strišti* to cut, shear, L *stringere* to touch lightly, graze; fr. the practice ascribed to the sect's leader of himself cutting the hair of new converts — more at STRIKE] : one of a Russian sect that broke away from the Eastern Orthodox Church in the 14th century in protest against the practice of charging fees for the administration of sacraments

stri·gose \\'strī,gōs, ⸗'⸗\\ *adj* [NL *strigosus,* fr. *striga* bristle + L *-osus* -ose — more at STRIGA] **1** : provided with strigae ⟨a ~ leaf⟩ — compare HISPID **2** : STRIATED : marked with fine closely set grooves

stri·gous \\'strīgəs\\ *adj* [NL *strigosus*] : STRIGOSE 1

strig·o·vite \\'strigə,vīt\\ *n* -s [G *strigovit,* fr. *Striegau,* Silesia (now Strzegom, Poland) + G *-it* -ite] : a mineral $Fe_3(Al,Fe)_3Si_3O_{11}(OH)_7$ consisting of a basic silicate of iron and aluminum of the chlorite group and occurring in dark green crystalline incrustations

strigs *pl of* STRIG

strig·u·la \\'strigyələ\\ *n, cap* [NL, dim. of *striga* bristle] : a genus (the type of the family Strigulaceae) of pyrenocarpous lichens characterized by minute rosettes growing on the surface of the leaves of tropical evergreens

strik·able \\'strīkəbəl\\ *adj* : capable of being struck

¹strike \\'strīk\\ *vb* **struck** \\'strək\\ **struck** \\"\\ *also* **strick·en** \\'strikən\\ **striking** \\'strīkiŋ\\ **strikes** [ME *striken,* fr. OE *strīcan;* akin to OFris *strīka* to pass over lightly, smooth, stroke, go, proceed, MLG *strīken,* OHG *strīhhan,* to pass over lightly, smooth, stroke, go, L *stria* furrow, channel, *striga* row, furrow, swath, *stringere* to touch lightly, graze, OPruss *strigli* thistle, OSlav *strišti* to shear, cut; basic meaning: to stroke] *vi* **1** : to take a course : PROCEED, GO ⟨*struck* into the woods and walked home along the . . . river —Jean Stafford⟩ ⟨you must ~ east from here —T.B.Costain⟩ ⟨*struck* off through the jungle on a trail along the foothills —H.L.Merillat⟩ ⟨the road . . . *struck* down into the sand hills —H.L.Davis⟩ **2 a** : to deliver or aim a stroke, blow, or thrust : HIT ⟨~ while the iron is hot⟩ ⟨~ at the dog with a stick⟩ ⟨~ at the nail with a hammer⟩ ⟨a rattlesnake ready to ~⟩ ⟨the hurricane *struck* . . . with the force of a battering ram —H.A. Chippendale⟩ ⟨the lightning *struck* again⟩ ⟨if trouble ~*s*⟩ ⟨a shortage of nurses when the epidemic *struck*⟩ **b** : to cast a stone in curling so as to hit and remove another from play **c** : to make a stroke with an oar **3 a** : to come into contact or collision ⟨*struck* against the stove as she fell⟩ **b** *of a ship* : to run aground : STRAND **c** *of light* : FALL ⟨the sunbeam *struck* full on his face⟩ **d** *of a sound* : to become audible ⟨hark! a deep sound ~*s* like a rising knell —Lord Byron⟩ **e** *of oyster spat* : to become fixed to something **f** *of a hound* : to find the scent of the quarry **4** : to delete, efface, or cancel something with or as if with a stroke of the pen ⟨a motion to ~ on the ground that there was no corroboration —R.B.Keech⟩ **5** : to lower a flag usu. as a sign of surrender ⟨pull alongside of the frigate to ascertain if she had *struck* —Frederick Marryat⟩ **6** : to attempt to bring about destruction, defeat, or overthrow as if by a blow or stroke ⟨had *struck* at the very heart of his faith —Mary Deasy⟩ ⟨ideas that ~ at the foundation of democracy⟩ **7 a** : to come to be indicated by the sounding of a clock, bell, or chime ⟨left the house just after six o'clock *struck*⟩ **b** : to make known the time of day by sounding ⟨the clock *struck* as he entered the room⟩ **8** *obs* : to cause suffering or pain ⟨this sorrow's heavenly; it ~*s* where it doth love —Shak.⟩ **9** : to go through a medium : PIERCE, PENETRATE ⟨a chill was *striking* through her flesh to the marrow of her bones —Ellen Glasgow⟩ ⟨an irresistible impulse to ~ nearer the heart of the truth —R.B.West⟩ **10** *obs* : STEAL, ROB **11 a** : to engage in battle : FIGHT ⟨exhorting the multitude to ~ for freedom —W.C.Taylor⟩ **b** : to make a military attack ⟨fast vessels which could ~ and get away —W.P.Webb⟩ ⟨bombers *struck* at the munitions factories⟩ **12** : PULSATE, THROB ⟨his heart *struck* heavily when the house was visible —George Meredith⟩ **13 a** : to produce fire with flint and steel ⟨~ on the tinder . . . give me a taper —Shak.⟩ **b** : to become ignited ⟨the match wouldn't ~⟩ **14** : to come suddenly or unexpectedly : LIGHT ⟨*struck* on a new plan to solve the problem⟩ **15 a** : to pull on a fishing rod in order to set the hook in the mouth of a fish **b** *of a fish* : to seize the bait **16** : to move quickly : DART, SHOOT ⟨has tossed a sheet of paper into the fire and seen it . . . ~ to flame —George Meredith⟩ **17 a** *of a plant cutting* : to take root **b** *of a seed* : GERMINATE **18** : to make an impression ⟨what ~*s* at a first reading —*Times Lit. Supp.*⟩ ⟨would ~ on pure minds with a force like mathematical demonstration —John Keble⟩ **19** : to engage in a temporary stoppage of work in order to bring about compliance with demands made on an employer ⟨voted to ~ for higher wages⟩ **20 a** : to take effect in the process of curing ⟨the salt has *struck*⟩ **b** : to cause a color to sink in (as in a glass coated with a composition and reheated) : become set **21** : to make a sudden beginning : LAUNCH ⟨the orchestra *struck* into another waltz⟩ **22** : to thrust oneself forward often in a sudden, unexpected, or vigorous manner ⟨sees no brawl but he must ~ into the midst of it —Sir Walter Scott⟩ **23** : to act or serve as the orderly of a military officer **24** : to form an arc (as between the two carbons of an electric arc) **25** : to have a geological strike **26** : to make a determined effort : work diligently : STRIVE ⟨as a boy . . . he had decided to ~ for a commission in the Royal Navy —J.A.Michener⟩ ⟨overborne by a sense of futility in *striking* for what seems unattainable —W.P.Webb⟩ ~ *vt* **1 a** : to deliver a stroke, blow, or thrust at : HIT ⟨~ the boy with the back of the hand⟩ ⟨~ the dog with a stick⟩ ⟨a deer *struck* by an arrow⟩ ⟨~ the whale with a harpoon⟩ ⟨a hurricane *struck* the town⟩ ⟨a house *struck* by lightning⟩ ⟨their herds are *struck* by an epidemic —Wilfred Thesiger⟩ ⟨this rise in living costs . . . ~*s* especially the poorer people of the country —P.E. James⟩ **b** (1) : to drive or remove with or as if with a blow ⟨*struck* the knife from his hand⟩ (2) : to remove or separate by or as if by cutting ⟨*struck* a branch from the tree⟩ **c** (1) *of a bird of prey* : to attack and sink the talons into (2) *of a snake* : to sink the fangs into **d** : to deliver or deal by or as if by some bodily action : INFLICT ⟨who would be free, themselves must ~ the blow —Lord Byron⟩ **e** : to produce by or as if by a blow or stroke ⟨waving wide her myrtle wand she ~*s* a universal peace —John Milton⟩ **2 a** (1) : to haul down (as a sail) (2) : to lower (as a flag) usu. as a sign of surrender ⟨made the ship — maybe with the aid of a ball across her bows — ~ her colors —Eva M. Tappan⟩ (3) : to lower (as a cargo) into a ship's hold — usu. used with *down* **b** : to dismantle and take away ⟨~ a stage set⟩ **c** (1) : to take down (a tent) ⟨shall be glad to help you ~ the tent —David Walker⟩ (2) : to take down the tents of (a camp) ⟨were to ~ camp at sunrise —Irving Stone⟩ **d** : to lower gradually (an arch or vault centering) so as to permit the arch or vault to reach safely its final state of equilibrium **3 a** : to bring suffering or death to as if with a blow ⟨heavily the hand of the Lord had *stricken* him —John Bruce⟩ **b** : to afflict suddenly : lay low ⟨was *stricken* with the bends —P.J.Costello⟩ ⟨was *struck* down at the height of his young glory —Richard Pollock⟩ **4 a** : to engage in (a battle) : FIGHT **b** : to make a military attack on ⟨the planes returned safely after *striking* their targets⟩ ⟨the first platoon *struck* the retreating enemy⟩ **5** : to delete, efface, or cancel with or as if with a stroke of the pen ⟨*struck* this appropriation from the defense budget —*Army-Navy-Air Force Jour.*⟩ ⟨have *struck* out a few pages which are merely a newspaper abridgment of an address —O.W.Holmes †1935⟩ ⟨*struck* down a . . . law requiring each state employe to take an oath —*N.Y.Times*⟩ ⟨demanded that the . . . professors be fired and the book *stricken* off the list —Green Peyton⟩ ⟨not only suppress the book but have it *struck* out of the catalog —G.B.Shaw⟩ **6 a** : to penetrate in a sharp or painful manner : PIERCE ⟨the news of the loss *struck* him to the heart⟩ **b** : to cause to penetrate ⟨his voice *struck* a chill into the girl's heart —A. Conan Doyle⟩ **c** : to send down or out ⟨trees that ~ deep roots⟩ **7** *obs* **a** : to rub gently ⟨~ his hand over the place and recover the leper —2 Kings 5:11(AV)⟩ **b** : to spread on a surface : SMEAR ⟨take of the blood and ~ it on the two side posts —Exod 12:7(AV)⟩ **8 a** : to level (as a measure of grain) by scraping off with a strickle what is above the rim **b** : to smooth or form (as a mold in founding) with a strickle — often used with *out* or *up* **c** : to dress and smooth (a mortar joint between bricks or stones) with a trowel **9 a** : to indicate by sounding ⟨the clock of the church . . . ~*s* the hours —Arnold Bennett⟩ ⟨her ship's bell is now being used . . . for *striking* the end of the day —H. A.Chippendale⟩ **b** : to cause to sound the time ⟨*struck* my repeater again and found that midnight was past —*Nat'l Observer*⟩ **10 a** (1) : to bring into forceful contact ⟨*struck* his head on a rafter⟩ ⟨~ the knee against the dashboard⟩ (2) : to shake (hands) in confirmation of an agreement ⟨let us ~ hands upon the bargain —Jane Austen⟩ (3) : to thrust suddenly ⟨*struck* the spurs in his horse and galloped away —Irving Bacheller⟩ **b** : to come into contact or collision with ⟨the car skidded and *struck* a tree⟩ ⟨a ship ~*s* the reef⟩ ⟨*struck* the table as he fell⟩ ⟨the hissing sound of the rain as it *struck* the river's surface —J.C.Powys⟩ **c** *of light* : to fall on ⟨the sun ~*s* him full in the face⟩ **d** *of a sound* : to become audible to ⟨nor shout nor whistle ~*s* his ear —William Wordsworth⟩ **e** *of a hound* : to find the scent of (the quarry) **11 a** : to cause to fall into a specified mental or emotional state ⟨at this they were all . . . *struck* into their dumps —John Bunyan⟩ **b** (1) : to cause to be affected with a strong emotion ⟨a sight that *struck* them with horror⟩ (2) : to cause (a strong emotion) to fall suddenly or enter ⟨eyes that ~ terror into junior clerks —Constance Foley⟩ **c** *archaic* : DEPRESS, SHOCK ⟨this *struck* . . . the enthusiasts of the King's side as much as it exalted the Scots —Gilbert Burnet⟩ **d** : to cause to become as a result of or as if of a sudden blow ⟨a stray bullet *struck* the man dead —Horace Sutton⟩ ⟨was reportedly *struck* dumb with stage fright —*Current Biog.*⟩ **12 a** : to cast (as candles) in a mold **b** : to convert (metal) into coins : MINT **c** (1) : to produce by stamping with a die or punch ⟨~ a medal⟩ (2) : to hit with a die or punch ⟨wanted coins that were sharply *struck* —*Numismatist*⟩ **d** : to cause (a hot tool or die) to make an impression in bookbinding **e** (1) : to produce (as a bank note) by imprinting : PRINT (2) : STAMP ⟨~ a handstamp⟩ **f** *obs* : to imprint on the mind ⟨those beauties which ~ a sort of melancholy —Earl of Shaftesbury †1713⟩ **13 a** : to produce (as fire) by or as if by the percussion of flint and steel ⟨could not be unaware that my remarks did not ~ fire —R.M.Lovett⟩ **b** : to cause to ignite by friction ⟨would have to ~ a match every now and then to read the compass —William Faulkner⟩ **14** : to make and ratify the terms of ⟨in this informal way the bargain is *struck* —W.T.C.King⟩ **15 a** : to play by strokes on the keys or strings ⟨~*s* the golden lyre —Alexander Pope⟩ **b** : to produce by or as if by playing a musical instrument ⟨~ a few chords on the piano⟩ ⟨he and his companions *struck* a discordant note in this firelit room —John Buchan⟩ **16** *obs* : STEAL, ROB **17 a** : to mark (as land) by plowing once up and down the field — often used with *off* **b** : to mark out (as a line) usu. with a compass or chalk line : DRAW **18 a** : to hook (a fish) by means of a sharp pull on the line ⟨rely on speed, not strength, when *striking* your trout —*Field & Stream*⟩ **b** *of a fish* : to snatch at (the bait) : SEIZE **19** *obs* : BROACH 3a **20 a** (1) : to come into the mind of : occur to ⟨it ~*s* me he has moved too far too fast —Irving Kolodin⟩ ⟨the oddity of the premature thanksgiving *struck* them both and they laughed —Israel Zangwill⟩ (2) : to appear to the judgment of : IMPRESS ⟨always *struck* strangers that way until the novelty wore off —J.P.Marquand⟩ ⟨no wonder they ~ us as silent —Thornton Wilder⟩ ⟨the young always ~ her as infinitely funny —G.W. Brace⟩ **b** : to make a strong impression on : appear remarkable to ⟨a spectacle . . . calculated to ~ a highly cultivated, a reflecting, an imaginative mind —T.B.Macaulay⟩ ⟨the name seemed to ~ them all —Jane Austen⟩ ⟨what *struck* me was that he told me very little that I cared to hear —O.W.Holmes †1935⟩ ⟨the first thing that *struck* me was the blue of the sky —Sam Pollock⟩ **c** : to catch and hold ⟨~*s* the attention and focuses the fugitive experience onto itself —Hunter Mead⟩ ⟨has painted the things that have *struck* her eye —*Newsweek*⟩ **21 a** : to transform by or as if by magic **b** : BEWITCH **22 a** : to precipitate (a dye) by a mordant **b** : to cause (a dye) to be adsorbed on an inert carrier in making an organic pigment **23** : to select the members of (a jury) : FORM **24** : to reach with a sounding line ⟨~ soundings⟩ **25** : to arrive at by the balancing, counterposing, or canceling out of opposing elements or considerations : achieve by or as if by computation or calculation ⟨~ the optimum balance between secrecy and openness —J.G.Palfrey⟩ ⟨for the time being a compromise has been *struck* —C.J.Friedrich⟩ ⟨~ an average⟩ ⟨~ a mean⟩ **26** : to make a request or demand of ⟨gaze at him and ~ him for his autograph —Mark Twain⟩ **27** : to smooth and stretch (as skins) while wet in leather manufacturing — often used with *out* **28** : to cause to become impregnated with salt in the process of curing **29** : to lade (as a liquor) into a cooler **30 a** (1) : to reach in the course of traveling : come to ⟨*struck* the main road after a short drive⟩ ⟨an easterly route that eventually ~*s* the river⟩ (2) : to succeed in reaching : ATTAIN ⟨after an unpromising beginning he finally *struck* his stride as a concert pianist⟩ **b** (1) : to come upon in or as if in the course of traveling : run across ⟨the most unpractical person I ever *struck* —Sheila Kaye-Smith⟩ ⟨the best sea story I have *struck* in years —H.J.Laski⟩ (2) : to come across in the course of prospecting or drilling : DISCOVER ⟨this peasant . . . had the luck to ~ water —Norman Douglas⟩ ⟨~ oil⟩ **31 a** : to engage in a temporary stoppage of (work) in order to bring about compliance with demands made on an employer **b** (1) : to engage in a strike against (an employer) (2) : to suspend or cripple the operation of (as a factory) by engaging in a strike **32** : to assume temporarily : take on ⟨*striking* what appeared to them to be most belligerent attitudes —Thomas Barbour⟩ ⟨~ a pose⟩ **33 a** : to place (a plant cutting) in a medium for growth and the development of roots ⟨less than 10 percent of the cuttings *struck* in sand finally rooted⟩ **b** : to propagate (a plant) esp. by means of cuttings **34** : to make one's way by taking : proceed along ⟨*struck* their path across the fields —Algernon Gissing⟩ **35** : to cause (an arc) to form (as between the carbon electrodes of an arc lamp) **36** : to form a thin preliminary deposit on (an article in an electroplating bath) at a rapid rate preliminary to a longer and slower deposition **37** *of an insect* : to oviposit on

syn STRIKE, HIT, SMITE, PUNCH, SLUG, SLOG, SWAT, CLOUT, SLAP, CUFF, BOX: of this group, all of which indicate the coming or bringing into contact with or as if with a sharp blow, STRIKE, HIT, and SMITE are the more general terms. STRIKE, the most general of the words, may indicate the motion of aiming or dealing the blow, the motion prior to contact with the hand, fist, instrument, weapon, or missile ⟨*strike* at the enemy and miss⟩ ⟨*strike* out at random⟩ It may indicate various types of contact from a light, often stroking contact ⟨the light breeze *struck* the ship on the north side⟩ to a forcible collision or blasting contact ⟨the car *struck* a post and overturned⟩ ⟨the lightning *struck* the house⟩ ⟨*strike* a man down with a heavy blow⟩ ⟨the enemy *struck* with full force⟩ It may suggest several types of physical or emotional effect or impression ⟨*strike* someone dead⟩ ⟨*strike* a line on paper⟩ ⟨*strike* out a name from a list⟩ ⟨to be *struck* by the beauty of the scenery⟩ ⟨grief-*stricken*⟩ ⟨conscience-*stricken*⟩ or it may be used to indicate any of the types of contact suggested by any of the other words in this group. HIT, although it is used in most of the situations in which STRIKE occurs, emphasizes more than STRIKE the physical or figurative contact with or impact upon an object, usu. something aimed at; it usu., though not necessarily, stresses forcefulness ⟨*hit* a child on the wrist⟩ ⟨the shell *hit* the tank and tore through the side⟩ ⟨the depression *hit* hard all elements of society⟩ ⟨*hit* the right road home⟩ ⟨*hit* the winning number in a lottery⟩ SMITE, largely a rhetorical or book word, usu. stresses the injuriousness or destructiveness of the contact and often suggests a motivation of anger or desire for vengeance ⟨with the hammer she *smote* Sisera, she *smote* off his head —Judg 5:26 (AV)⟩ ⟨conscience-*smitten*⟩ ⟨disease-*smitten*⟩ ⟨*smitten* with grief or love⟩ PUNCH, SLUG, SLOG, SWAT, and CLOUT are generally used to suggest the giving of various kinds of usu. sharp or heavy blows. PUNCH suggests a quick blow with or as if with the fist ⟨would handcuff everybody rather than face the risk of having their noses *punched* by somebody —G.B.Shaw⟩ SLUG emphasizes the heaviness of the impact and usu. suggests a certain viciousness in the delivery of the blow ⟨was attacked by an assault suspect, who *slugged* him with a 5-ft. iron pipe —*Time*⟩ SLOG emphasizes the heavy, usu. haphazard quality of the blows ⟨the two fighters were so tired they merely *slogged* rather than hit each other with clean, precise blows⟩ SWAT suggests a forceful, slapping blow, usu. with such an instrument as a bat, weapon, or flyswatter ⟨in off moments he would *swat* the regiment of cockroaches —Paul de Kruif⟩ ⟨*swat* flies⟩ ⟨*swat* a baseball out of the ball park⟩ CLOUT suggests a heavy careless blow usu. with the hand or fist ⟨a shoe *clouted* his skull and inflicted a fracture —Hugh McCrae⟩ ⟨they *clout* our heads the moment our conclusions differ from theirs —G.B.Shaw⟩ SLAP, CUFF, and BOX all suggest blows of varying force with the open hand. SLAP is the most general and indicates a sharp, usu. stinging blow with or as if with the palm of the hand ⟨*slap* a person in the face⟩ ⟨*slapped* the coverlet angrily —Kenneth Roberts⟩ CUFF suggests a blow often forcible enough to dizzy or throw off balance and often dealt with the back of the hand ⟨it was pointed out . . . that children could be hurried and delayed, *cuffed* and bribed, into becoming adults —Margaret Mead⟩ BOX suggests the delivery of an openhanded blow but is usu. limited to one against the ears ⟨the mother *boxed* her child's ears in a fit of temper⟩ **syn** see in addition AFFECT

— **strike a docket** *Brit* : to enter a creditor's affidavit and bond in bankruptcy

²strike \\"\\ *n* -s [ME *strik, strike,* fr. *striken,* v.] **1** *archaic* : a bunch of hackled flax, jute, or hemp prepared for drawing into slivers **2** *dial chiefly Eng* : a dry measure varying from two pecks to four bushels **3 a** : a strickle for leveling a surface by striking off superfluous material or for striking up a mold in founding **b** : a broad smooth stick for removing superfluous clay in molding bricks **4** : an act or instance of striking ⟨the ~ of a rattlesnake⟩ ⟨the ~ of the clock⟩ **5 a** : the unit quantity of malt used in making ale or beer **b** : excellence or strength of ale or beer ⟨three hogsheads of ale of the first ~ —Sir Walter Scott⟩ **6 a** : the impression on a coin, token, or medal made by a die or punch **b** (1) : the impression on a stamp made by a printing plate (2) : the impression on a stamp made by a handstamp **7 a** : a temporary stoppage of work by a body of workers designed to enforce compliance with demands (as changes in wages, hours, or working conditions) made on an employer — compare LOCKOUT, STAY-IN STRIKE **b** : a temporary stoppage of normal operations and activities designed as a protest against an action or condition ⟨a buyers' ~⟩ ⟨hunger ~⟩ **8 a** : the direction of the line of intersection of a horizontal plane with an uptilted bedding plane, vein, fault, slaty cleavage, schistosity, or similar geological structure **b** (1) : the trend of a linear geological feature or structure (2) : the orientation of a tabular particle in a sediment or rock **9 a** : a pull on a fishing rod designed to set the hook in the mouth of a fish **b** : a pull on a line made by a fish in taking the bait **10** : the mass of moist sugar crystals left in a pan after a boiling in the manufacture of sugar **11** : a sudden or unexpected stroke of good luck; *esp* : a sudden discovery of oil or of a rich vein of ore ⟨made a lucky ~ and in three months had realized a considerable fortune —H.W.H.Knott⟩ **12 a** : a pitched ball (as in baseball) recorded against a batter ⟨it's one-two-three ~*s,* you're out at the old ball game —Jack Norworth⟩: (1) : a pitch at which a batter swings and misses (2) : a pitch passing through the strike zone at which a batter does not swing (3) : a foul bunt not caught on the fly (4) : a foul ball hit with less than two strikes on the batter and not caught on the fly (5) : a foul tip caught by the catcher before it hits the ground **b** : a disadvantage that makes achievement difficult : HANDICAP ⟨his racial background was a second ~ against him —K.D.Miller⟩ **13** : an act or instance of knocking down all the bowling pins with the first ball of a frame — compare SPARE **14** : a piece of copper that carries an impression driven into it by a typefounder's punch and that after hand finishing becomes a matrix for forming the face of type **15 a** : an act of obtaining or attempting to obtain money by importunity, threat, or blackmail **b** *or* **strike bill** : a legislative bill designed to be harmful to a person or corporation if enacted into law and introduced in order to obtain a bribe for its withdrawal **16** : a striking mechanism (as for a clock) **17 a** : a part of a lock designed to be struck by another part **b** : a part of a lock that prevents a retracted bolt from shooting forward **c** : a metal fastening on a doorframe into which the bolt of a lock is projected in order to secure the door **18** : establishment of roots and plant growth (as by rooting of cuttings or germination of seeds) ⟨an excellent ~ of oats⟩ ⟨had a 70 percent ~ on his cuttings⟩ **19 a** : a thin initial electrodeposit **b** : an electrolyte used in making such a deposit **20 a** : cutaneous myiasis of sheep : FLY-STRIKE ⟨body ~⟩ ⟨tail ~⟩ ⟨blowfly ~⟩ — compare MULES OPERATION **b** : STRUCK 2 **21 a** : a military attack; *esp* : an air attack on a single objective ⟨air ~*s* on the more important road junctions —*Infantry Jour.*⟩ **b** : a group of airplanes taking part in such an attack ⟨in the afternoon a second ~ was flown off —Fletcher Pratt⟩ **22** : the amount of dye absorbed by the fiber but not diffused through it in the first brief period of dyeing **23** : the act or process of dismantling a stage set **24** : an individual unit of a design on china or other dinnerware in the decalcomania process

strike–a–light \\'⸗⸗,⸗\\ *n* : a device consisting of or including a piece of flint to be struck by steel or pyrites in order to obtain sparks

strike–anywhere match \\(')⸗'⸗⸗,⸗-\\ *n* : KITCHEN MATCH

strike back *vi* **1** : to return a blow ⟨*struck back* angrily at his opponent⟩ ⟨decided to *strike back* at the critics⟩ **2** : BACKFIRE 3

strike–back \\'⸗,⸗\\ *n* -s [*strike back*] : burning at the fuel injector of an air-fed burner : BACKFIRE 2b

strike below *vt* : to lower into or as if into a ship's hold : carry below ⟨perishables are stacked on deck under cover, awaiting rigid Navy inspection before they are *struck below* —*All Hands*⟩

strike benefit *or* **strike pay** *n* **:** a payment made by a union to provide subsistence to strikers ⟨well-financed unions always provide *strike benefits* covering the minimum cost of living —H.A.Millis & R.E.Montgomery⟩
strike board *n* **:** ⁵LUTE 2
strikebound \'⸗,⸗\ *adj* **:** subjected to a strike ⟨a ~ factory⟩
strikebreaker \'⸗,⸗⸗\ *n* **:** one engaged in strikebreaking: **a :** one hired to replace a striking worker **b :** one hired to supply replacements for striking workers
strikebreaking \'⸗,⸗⸗\ *n* **:** action designed to break up a strike
strike–dog \'⸗,⸗\ *n* **:** the dog of a pack that customarily first closes with game — called also *striker*
strike fault *n* **:** a geological fault whose trend coincides approximately with the strike of associated strata
strike in *vi* **1** *obs* **:** to enter into competition **:** TRY ⟨advises me to *strike in* for some preferment —Jonathan Swift⟩ **2** *obs* **:** to associate as a confederate or collaborator ⟨*strike in* with him and help him to dupe his father —John Dryden⟩ **3 a** *archaic* **:** to fall into or express agreement ⟨a shifting adversary . . . will *strike in* with any opinion —Richard Bentley †1742⟩ **b** *obs* **:** to prove compatible **:** fit in **4 :** to intervene or interrupt in a sudden or unexpected manner ⟨*strike in* with a foolish suggestion⟩ **5 :** to disappear from the surface with subsequent internal effects ⟨lived only a few days after the disease *struck in*⟩ **~** *vt* **1 :** IMPRINT ⟨presses adequate for *striking in* names and addresses⟩ **2 a :** to draw (a line) from one point on the surface of a sheet to another point with a ruling machine **b :** to make (perforations that do not extend from edge to edge) in a sheet
strike–in \'⸗,⸗\ *n* -s [*strike in*] **:** the relative penetration of ink into paper that is being printed
strike joint *n* **:** a joint whose horizontal direction is the same as that of the strike of the rock
strike·less \'strīkləs\ *adj* **:** marked by the absence of strikes
strike measure *n* **:** LEVEL MEASURE
strike note *or* **strike tone** *n* **:** the apparent pitch produced by a bell when it is first struck — compare HUM NOTE
strike off *vt* **1 :** to compose with facility **:** produce in an effortless manner ⟨*struck off* a sonnet for the occasion⟩ **2 :** to depict clearly and exactly **:** hit off ⟨had too much phlegm to *strike off* the grand passions or reach the sublime parts of painting —Tobias Smollett⟩ **3 :** to remove excess freshly placed concrete, mortar, or plaster from (a surface) by operating a straightedge over the forms or screeds
strike–off \'⸗,⸗\ *n* -s [*strike off*] **:** a straightedge used to remove excess freshly placed concrete, mortar, or plaster from a surface
strike out *vt* **1 :** to create or form with apparent ease **:** produce as if by a stroke ⟨*struck out* the fundamental method . . . now used by all aesthetic historians —Gilbert Highet⟩ **2 :** to enter vigorously and suddenly on ⟨breaking free from the family tradition and *striking out* a line of his own —Sheila Kaye-Smith⟩ **3 :** to retire (a baseball batter) by a strikeout ⟨allowed two walks and *struck out* eight⟩ **~** *vi* **1 :** to enter vigorously and suddenly upon a course of action ⟨had *struck out* for himself and refused to live the tame easy life that he could have lived —Frank Sargeson⟩ **2 :** to set out in a vigorous or sudden manner ⟨*struck out* in the direction . . . the miller had indicated —T.B.Costain⟩ **3 :** to make an out in baseball by a strikeout ⟨had a single, walked, and *struck out* twice⟩
strikeout \'⸗,⸗\ *n* -s [*strike out*] **:** an out in baseball resulting from a batter's being charged with three strikes
strikeover \'⸗,⸗⸗\ *n* -s [fr. the phrase *strike over*] **:** an act or instance of striking a typewriter character on a spot already occupied by another character
strike pan *n* **:** a vacuum pan with steam coils for increasing the rate of evaporation in sugar manufacturing
strike plate *n* **:** STRIKE 17c
strik·er \'strīkə(r)\ *n* -s [¹*strike* + *-er*] **1 :** one that strikes ⟨no blow can be struck but it recoils on the ~ —R.W.Emerson⟩ **2** *obs* **:** a dissolute person **3 :** STRICKLE **4 :** a player in any of several games who strikes: **a :** a batsman in cricket **b :** a billiards player whose turn it is at the table **c :** a player having last struck the ball in court tennis **d :** a player (as in squash) whose turn it is after the ball in play has hit the front wall **5 a :** a clock or watch that strikes **b :** any of various devices designed to strike: as (1) **:** the hammer of the striking mechanism of a clock or watch (2) **:** the part of the action that immediately delivers the blow to the primer of a firearm (3) **:** a small plunger intermediary between the firing pin and the primer that ignites the charge of a torpedo (4) **:** a device on a pen-ruling machine for raising and lowering a pen (5) **:** a device for putting a machine or part in gear with a driving mechanism (6) **:** a reciprocating projecting piece in a loom used to actuate a finger periodically to deliver the pick **6 a :** a worker engaged in any of various occupations that involve striking: as (1) **:** BLACKSMITH 1c (2) **:** one who dresses off the clay bricks with a strike in molding (3) **:** one who stretches and smooths wet hides and skins by hand or machine **b :** an oiler on a ship **c** (1) **:** a fisherman who rows a driveboat (2) **:** a shrimp fisherman who uses a trawl **7 a :** a worker who assists another: as (1) **:** one who assists a truck driver in loading and driving (2) **:** one who helps a furnaceman shape steel plates **b** (1) **:** an enlisted man detailed as an officer's orderly (2) **:** an enlisted man employed by an officer to do odd jobs for extra pay during off-duty hours **8 :** a worker who is on strike **9** *or* **striker plate :** STRIKE 17c **10 :** MORDANT 1 **11 :** STRIKE-DOG **12 :** a navy enlisted man who is working for a petty officer's rate
striker boat *n* **:** DRIVEBOAT
striker–out \'⸗⸗,⸗\ *n* -s [*strike out* + *-er*] **1 :** a player who receives the service in a racket game **2 :** SETTER 2h
strikes *pres 3d sing of* STRIKE, *pl of* STRIKE
strike shift *n* **:** the component of the shift parallel with the strike of a fault — compare DIP SHIFT
strike slip *n* **:** the part of a fault displacement that is recorded by the separation of orig. continuous beds or veins measured horizontally in the plane of the fault
strike–through \'⸗,⸗\ *n* -s [fr. *strike through*, v.] **:** the penetration of ink through paper that is being printed
strike up *vi* **1 :** to start singing or playing ⟨then an organ in a gallery *strikes up* —Arnold Bennett⟩ **2 :** to begin to be sung or played ⟨a march *struck up* and the parade began⟩ **~** *vt* **1 a :** to begin to sing or play ⟨the band *struck up* a set of waltzes —W.G.Smith⟩ **b :** to cause to begin singing or playing ⟨*strike up* the band⟩ **2 :** to cause to begin **:** set afoot ⟨easier to *strike up* acquaintanceships with local people —Richard Joseph⟩ ⟨*strike up* a conversation with the neighbors —W.H.Whyte⟩
strike valley *n* **:** a valley parallel to the strike of the underlying rocks of a region — called also *longitudinal valley*
strike zone *n* **:** the area (as between the knees and shoulders of a batter in his natural stance) over home plate through which a pitched baseball must pass to be called a strike
¹**striking** *n* -s [ME, fr. gerund of *striken* to strike — more at STRIKE] **1 :** an act or instance of one that strikes **2 a :** something (as a coin) produced by striking **b :** the things struck at one time ⟨a huge ~ of a token coinage —P.K.Anderson⟩ **3 :** STRIKE 6
²**striking** *adj* [fr. pres. part. of ¹*strike*] **1 :** that strikes; *esp* **:** attracting attention or notice through unusual or conspicuous qualities ⟨one of the most ~ and fearful figures in our early fiction —V.L.Parrington⟩ ⟨~ contradictions between what musical people admire and what they like —Virgil Thomson⟩ ⟨have been few more ~ examples of ingenuity —Edward Clodd⟩ ⟨beautiful tweeds . . . made into ~ suits —Catherine Paul⟩ **2 :** of, relating to, or constituting a device for striking on or putting in gear a machine or part of a machine **syn** see NOTICEABLE
striking angle *n* **:** ANGLE OF FALL
striking bag *n* **:** PUNCHING BAG
striking circle *n* **:** a semicircular area in front of each goal in field hockey which extends out from the goal line to a maximum distance of 15 yards and from which the ball must be hit in order to score a goal — see FIELD HOCKEY illustration
striking distance *n* **:** the distance through which it is possible to reach an object by striking **:** the distance at which a force is effective when directed at an object
striking energy *n* **:** the kinetic energy of a bullet at the instant of impact
striking hammer *n* **:** SLEDGEHAMMER
strik·ing·ly *adv* **:** in a striking manner **:** to a striking degree ⟨one of the most ~ picturesque bridges of any English town —S.P.B.Mais⟩
strik·ing·ness *n* -ES **:** the quality or state of being striking
striking–out machine \'⸗⸗,⸗-\ *n* **:** a machine used in the finishing of leather for smoothing and stretching — called also *setting-out machine*
striking pin *n* **:** PIN 8
striking plate *n* **:** KEEPER 2b
striking platform *n* **:** a prepared flat surface at right angles to the axis of a stone from which flakes are struck for the production of stone tools
striking reed *n* **:** BEATING REED
striking stile *n* **:** the stile of a door containing the lock — compare HANGING STILE
striking voltage *n* **:** the minimum voltage sufficient to arc across a given gap
¹**string** \'striŋ\ *n* -s [ME *streng, string*, fr. OE *streng*; akin to MD *strenge, stringe, strenc* rope, cord, strap, OHG *strang* rope, cord, ON *strengr* rope, cord, string, L *stringere* to bind tight, press together — more at STRAIN] **1 a :** a small cord (as of vegetable fiber) used to bind, fasten, or tie **:** a cord larger than a thread and smaller than a rope **b :** a gallows rope **c :** a cord for leading or controlling a person or an animal **:** LEASH **2 a** *archaic* **:** a cord (as a tendon or ligament) of an animal body **b :** a plant fiber (as a fine root, the vein of a leaf, or the tough fiber connecting the halves of a string-bean pod) **3 a :** the gut or wire cord of a musical instrument — see VIOLIN illustration **b strings** *pl* (1) **:** the bowed stringed instruments of an orchestra ⟨glanced at the golden forest of 52 ~*s* on my left . . . and gave the downbeat —Joseph Levine⟩ (2) **:** the players of such instruments esp. in an orchestra — compare WIND **4 :** BOWSTRING **5 :** a cord or drawstring used as a closure (as on an article of clothing or a bag) **6 a :** a group of objects threaded on a string esp. if enough to fill it ⟨a ~ of onions⟩ ⟨a ~ of fish⟩ **b :** the cord of a necklace **:** the thread on which beads or gems are strung ⟨a ~ of pearls⟩ **7 :** a cord or leather thong that ties together the leaves and covers of a book bound in the photograph-album style **8 :** a slender vein of ore in a mine **9 :** RIBBON 1c **10 a :** a series of things arranged in or as if in a line ⟨a ~ of cars waiting at a red light⟩ ⟨rapid formation of bars along the shore has produced a ~ of lagoons —P.E.James⟩ **b :** a group of business properties spread out or scattered geographically ⟨still visits the first drugstore of his ~ —*Monsanto Mag.*⟩ ⟨a ~ of filling stations⟩ ⟨a ~ of newspapers⟩ **11 a :** a column of animals, vehicles, or persons moving in single file **:** TRAIN **b :** the horses that belong to one stable or owner **:** STUD **c :** a group or set of horses or draft animals; *esp* **:** the group of saddle horses assigned to a cowhand for his exclusive use ⟨each rider had his ~ of two to six horses, usually belonging to the employer —W.S.Campbell⟩ — compare ³MOUNT 3b **12 a :** a recourse, means, or expedient by which to accomplish an end or purpose ⟨they have a second ~. The husband has farmed as a hobby all his life —Rebecca West⟩ ⟨he has two ~*s* to his bow⟩ **b :** a group of players or contestants ranked according to rated skill or proficiency ⟨the first ~ of the basketball team —Oakley Hall⟩ ⟨a second ~ quarterback⟩ **13 :** a series or succession in time **:** SEQUENCE ⟨his long ~ of single-handed successes made rich fare for . . . crime reporters —Al Spiers⟩ ⟨launched at once into a ~ of stories —Virginia D. Dawson & Betty D. Wilson⟩ **14 a :** one of the inclined sides of a stair supporting the treads and risers — see CLOSE STRING, OPEN STRING **b :** STRINGCOURSE **c :** an inside range of ceiling planks corresponding to the sheer strake of a ship and bolted to it **15 :** a cord used to manipulate a puppet **16 a :** a score or tally of an indoor game sometimes (as in billiards) marked by buttons threaded on a string or wire **b :** a fixed or standard number of turns at play in a game or competition **17** *billiards* **a :** BALKLINE 1 **b :** the action of lagging for break **c :** a wire strung with buttons usu. stretched above a table for the recording of points **18 :** the number of shots prescribed for each shooter in an event of a small arms target match ⟨a ~ of 10 or 20 shots —Townsend Whelen⟩ **19 :** LINE 12a **20 a :** proofs of matter set by one compositor usu. pasted in a strip to facilitate measurement of his work **b :** newspaper clippings of his printed stories pasted on a strip or sheet of paper as a record by a news correspondent paid by the line **21 strings** *pl* **a :** conditions or obligations attached to something ⟨it was his privilege to stay . . . there were no ~*s* attached —Morley Callaghan⟩ **b :** CONTROL, DOMINATION ⟨freed from the occupation's ~*s* —Lindesay Parrott⟩ **22 :** a yellowish gray that is paler and slightly greener than sand and greener and slightly duller than natural **23 :** a transparent line in glass resulting from the slow solution of a large grain of sand or foreign material **24 a :** a set of well-drilling tools and equipment esp. for percussion well drilling **b :** all of the casing or pipe of one size used in a well **25 :** a set of bombs dropped on a target in rapid succession **:** STICK **syn** see CONDITION — **on the string :** subject to one's influence **:** dangling at one's pleasure ⟨kept three suitors *on the string* for months⟩
²**string** \"\ *vb* **strung** \'strəŋ\ *or dial* **strang** \-raŋ,-raiŋ\ **strung** *also* **stringed; stringing; strings** [ME *strengen*, fr. *streng, string*, n.] *vt* **1 :** to fit (a bow) with a string **:** BRACE **2 a :** to equip (a musical instrument) with strings **b :** to bring the strings of (a musical instrument) to the required pitch **:** TUNE **3 :** to make tense **:** key up ⟨the whiskey had *strung* her up to recklessness —Dorothy Sayers⟩ **4 a :** to thread on or as if on a string ⟨*strung* beads by the hour⟩ **b :** to hang or thread (as a rope or wire) with objects ⟨*strung* the rope with the birds taken in our day's bag⟩ **c :** to tie, hang, or fasten with string **d :** to put together (as words or ideas) like objects threaded on a string ⟨words form the thread on which we ~ our experiences —Aldous Huxley⟩ **5 :** to hang (a person) by the neck **:** put to death by hanging ⟨*strung* him up from the nearest tall tree⟩ **6 :** to remove the strings of **:** clean of strings ⟨the beans have been *strung* —*Commonweal*⟩ **7 a :** to extend or stretch like a string ⟨*strung* electric light wires from tree to tree on the lawn⟩ **b :** to set out or stretch in a line, succession, or series ⟨merchants were ~*ing* their prosperous modern houses along this fairly new business thoroughfare —T.D.Clark⟩ **8 a :** to furnish (a book) with strings when binding **b :** to tie (the raised band of a book) with string or cord to preserve shape after covering **9 :** to thread (primed tobacco leaves) on twine or wire and attach to laths for hanging in the barn to dry **10 :** to pull (a wire) through the dies of a drawbench — used with *up* **11 :** to foist off a tall story on **:** pull the leg of **:** FOOL ⟨cowboys ~*ing* tenderfeet with tall tales —Carl Van Doren⟩ **~** *vi* **1 :** to be put to death by hanging **:** be hanged **2 :** to move, progress, or lie in a string or series ⟨the islands ~ along the coast⟩ ⟨the men were ~*ing* over the beach —Norman Mailer⟩ **3 :** to form into strings **:** become stringy (as a viscous material) **4 :** LAG 2b
³**string** \"\ *adj* [¹*string*] **1 :** of, containing, or like string **2 a :** STRINGED 1 **b :** relating to stringed musical instruments, the players of stringed instruments, or the music performed on stringed instruments ⟨~ orchestra⟩ **c :** imitating the tone quality of bowed stringed musical instruments ⟨~ stop of a pipe organ⟩
string *abbr* stringendo
string along *vi* **:** to go along ⟨prompts them to *string along* with the people's choice —*Time*⟩ **~** *vt* **1 :** to keep (someone) dangling or waiting ⟨told me to *string* him *along* —Dorothy Sayers⟩ **2 :** DECEIVE, FOOL ⟨let him *string* himself *along* with illusions and false expectations —H.L.Davis⟩
string and ray rot *n* **:** a disintegration of heartwood of the butts of oaks caused by a fungus (*Polyporus berkeleyi*)
string bag *n* **:** a bag made of string; *esp* **:** a mesh bag of heavy string with two handles at the top used for carrying packages

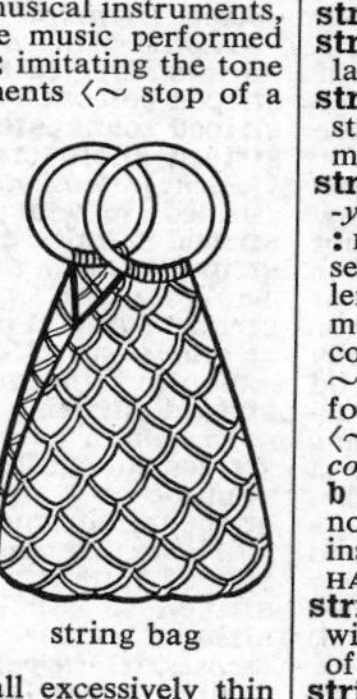
string bag

string bass *n* **:** CONTRABASS
string bean *n* **1 :** SNAP BEAN — used esp. of some older varieties that have stringy fiber on the sutures of the pods **2 :** a tall excessively thin person ⟨that *string bean* of a kid —R.F.Mirvish⟩
stringboard \'⸗,⸗\ *n* **:** a board or built-up facing used in stair building to cover the ends of the steps and hide the true string
string correspondent *n* **:** a news correspondent who is paid space rates
stringcourse \'⸗,⸗\ *n* **:** a horizontal band running around a building usu. on the outside ⟨a brick ~ between the first and second stories —*Amer. Guide Series: Va.*⟩ — compare BLOCKING COURSE
string development *n* **:** RIBBON DEVELOPMENT
stringed \'striŋd\ *adj* **1 :** having strings **2 :** produced by strings ⟨~ noise —John Milton⟩
stringed instrument *n* **:** a musical instrument whose tone is produced on taut strings by drawing a bow across them (as in the violin), by plucking them (as in the harp or guitar), by striking them (as in the piano), or by blowing upon them (as in the aeolian harp); *esp* **:** a member of the violin or viol family
strin·gen·cy \'strinjənsē, -si\ *n* -ES **:** the quality or state of being stringent: as **a :** RIGOR, SEVERITY, STRICTNESS ⟨the best parlor and the awful moral *stringencies* —G.W.Brace⟩ **b :** a pressing want or scarcity **:** tightness of money or credit ⟨financial ~ threatened to complete the ruin —*Amer. Guide Series: Mass.*⟩ **c :** cogency or convincing force of reasoning or argument ⟨theoretical ~⟩
strin·gen·do \strēn'jen(,)dō\ *adv* [It, verbal of *stringere* to press, squeeze, tie together, fr. L, to bind tight, press together — more at STRAIN] **:** with quickening of tempo (as to a climax) — used as a direction in music
strin·gent \'strinjənt\ *adj* [L *stringent-, stringens*, pres. part. of *stringere* to bind tight, press together — more at STRAIN] **1 :** sharp, astringent, or bitter to the senses esp. of taste ⟨the air was thin and clear, ~ with wood smoke —A.J.Cronin⟩ **2 a :** binding, drawing, or pressing tight ⟨the most ~ confinement that can be laid upon a human being —Lee Rogow⟩ **b :** marked by rigor, strictness, or severity **:** rigidly controlled by rule or standard **:** not loose or lax ⟨a tested touchstone of ~ thinking —Yakov Malkiel⟩ ⟨~ training in pioneer life —John Hersey⟩ ⟨extremely ~ libel laws —*Meet The British*⟩ ⟨colleges with the most ~ admissions requirements —N.O.Frederiksen⟩ **3 :** marked by money scarcity, credit strictness, or market decline ⟨money policies were more ~ —*Dun's Rev.*⟩ **syn** see RIGID
strin·gent·ly *adv* **:** in a stringent manner **:** STRICTLY ⟨game laws are ~ enforced —*Amer. Guide Series: Texas*⟩
string·er \'striŋə(r)\ *n* -s [ME *strynger*, fr. *streng, string* string + *-er*] **1 :** one that strings ⟨wire ~*s* sweated down the road, setting up lines —*Newsweek*⟩ **2 :** a string, rope, or wire often equipped with snaps on which fish are strung by a fisherman **3 a :** a narrow vein or irregular filament of mineral traversing a rock mass of different material **b :** a line or linear zone of specified objects or material ⟨narrow tongues of forest will . . . follow ~*s* of favorable soil —A.A.Nichol⟩ ⟨~*s* of gravel on a tidal flat⟩ ⟨~*s* of pumice⟩ **4 a :** a long horizontal timber used to connect uprights in a frame or to support a floor **b :** a string in stair building **c :** a tie in a truss **5 :** a longitudinal member in any of various kinds of construction: as **a :** such a member extending from bent to bent of a railroad bridge and carrying the track **b :** a longitudinal sleeper borne on the transverse ties of a railroad track **c :** a longitudinal girder, plank, or plate used in ship construction as a strengthening member — see SHIP illustration **d :** a longitudinal member used (as in a fuselage or wing) to reinforce the skin in a semimonocoque airplane **6 a :** STRING CORRESPONDENT **b :** a newspaper reporter who serves another publication or a news agency part time — distinguished from *staffer* **7 :** one that holds a specified competitive rating or is estimated as of specified excellence or efficiency — usu. used in combination ⟨pulled out his first-*stringers* after piling up a wide scoring margin⟩ ⟨sent their second-*stringer* to review the play⟩ **8 :** a sequence in rummy or panguingue
stringer lode *n* **:** a lode that consists of many small irregular reticulated stringers with the intervening country rock
stringer plate *n* **:** one of the plates forming the outer strake of a ship's deck and being usu. heavier than those used for the rest of the deck — see SHIP illustration
string figure *n* **1 :** a figure representing any of various objects that is made by passing a string around the fingers of both hands sometimes with the help of a second person ⟨anthropologists find the making of *string figures* common in many simple cultures⟩ — compare CAT'S CRADLE **2** *or* **string game :** a game of making string figures
string·ful \'striŋ,fu̇l\ *n, pl* **stringfuls** *also* **stringsful** \-ŋ,fu̇lz, -ŋz,fu̇l\ **:** the quantity or number of objects that can be threaded on a string
string galvanometer *n* **:** a galvanometer for measuring oscillating currents by the lateral motions of a silver-plated quartz fiber traversed by the current and stretched under adjustable tension perpendicular to the field of an electromagnet
string·halt \'striŋ,hȯlt\ *n* **:** a lameness in the hind legs of a horse caused by muscular spasms possibly of nervous origin and causing excessive flexure in locomotion — called also *springhalt*
string·halt·ed \-təd\ *also* **string·halty** \-tē\ *adj* **:** suffering from stringhalt — **string·halt·ed·ness** *n* -ES
string·i·ness \'striŋēnəs, -ŋin-\ *n* -ES **:** the quality or state of being stringy
stringing *n* -s [partly fr. ¹*string* + *-ing*; partly fr. gerund of ²*string*] **1 :** straight lines of inlay in furniture decoration **2 :** the threading of primed tobacco and attaching of it to laths **3 :** the gut, silk, or nylon with which a racket is strung
string insulator *n* **:** a series of two or more suspension insulators flexibly connected
string lead *n* **:** lead in thin strips
string·less \'striŋləs\ *adj* **:** having no strings
stringlike \'⸗,⸗\ *adj* **:** resembling a string (as in shape or tone)
string line *n* **:** BALKLINE 1
string·man \'striŋmən\ *n, pl* **stringmen :** STRING CORRESPONDENT
string organ *n* **:** a reed organ having a set of vibrators or free reeds joined by rods with wires or strings that are thus made to vibrate with them and give musical tones resembling those both of the harmonium and pianoforte
stringpiece \'⸗,⸗\ *n* **:** a long piece of heavy timber usu. used horizontally in a construction: as **a :** the heavy squared timber lying along the top of the piles forming a dock front or timber pier **b :** a temporary horizontal timber used in shoring — compare NEEDLE 4 **c :** STRING 14a
string proof *n* **:** the density at which a boiling syrup threads
string quartet *n* **1 :** a quartet of performers on stringed musical instruments usu. including a first and second violin, a viola, and a cello **2 :** a composition for string quartet
strings *pl of* STRING, *pres 3d sing of* STRING
strings·man \'striŋzmən\ *or* **string·man** \-ŋm-\ *n, pl* **stringsmen** *or* **stringmen :** a player on a stringed musical instrument
string tie *n* **:** a narrow necktie
string tone *n* **:** tone like that of a violin or related instrument

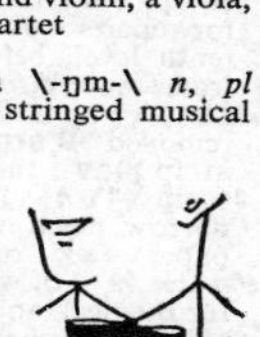
string tie

stringways \'⸗,⸗\ *n pl* **:** courses separated by strings for individual contestants (as in swimming, sprinting, and dog races)
stringy \'striŋē, -ŋi\ *adj* -ER/-EST [¹*string* + *-y*] **1 a :** consisting of strings or small threads **:** FIBROUS, FILAMENTOUS ⟨a ~ root⟩ **b** (1) **:** resembling or suggestive of a string **:** marked by length and thinness ⟨~ hair⟩ (2) **:** lean and muscular in build **:** SINEWY, WIRY ⟨~ old cowboys still rolling their cigarettes —J.B.Priestley⟩ ⟨his tough, ~ body —Georg Meyers⟩ **2 :** capable of being drawn out to form a string (as a glutinous substance) **:** GLUEY, ROPY, VISCID ⟨~ tenacious exudate —A.J.Steigman & C.H.Scott⟩ **3 a** *of cotton* **:** matted in rope form during poor ginning or picking **b** *of wool* (1) **:** slightly matted during scouring (2) **:** lacking normal crimp **4 :** having a tone like that of a violin or related instrument; *esp* **:** thin, edgy, and nasal in quality **5 :** STRINGHALTED
stringybark \'⸗⸗,⸗\ *n* **1 :** any of several Australian eucalypts with fibrous inner bark — compare SMOOTHBARK **2 :** the bark of a stringybark tree
stringybark pine *n* **:** an Australian cypress pine (*Callitris parlatorei*)

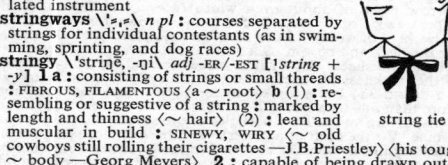

stringy kelp *n* **:** a kelp (*Alaria fistulosa*)
stringy sap *n* **:** an inferior sap of the sugar maple milky in color, ropy in texture, and deficient in sugar
¹strinkle *n* [ME *strenkil, strinkil,* prob. alter. (influenced by *strewen* to strew) of *sprenkil, sprinkil;* akin to ME *sprenklen* to sprinkle] *obs* **:** SPRINKLER; *esp* **:** ASPERGILLUM
²strin·kle \ˈstriŋkəl\ *vb* [ME *strenklen, strinklen,* prob. alter. of *sprenklen, sprinklen*] *chiefly dial* **:** SPRINKLE
stri·o·la \ˈstrīələ\ *n, pl* **strio·lae** \-ə,lē\ [NL, dim. of *stria*] **:** a faint or minute stria
stri·o·late \-ə,lāt\ *or* **stri·o·lat·ed** \-ād·əd\ *adj* [NL *striola* + E *-ate* or *-ated* (fr. *-ate* + *-ed*)] **:** having striolae
¹strip \ˈstrip\ *vb* **stripped** *also* **stript** \-pt\ **stripped** *also* **stript; stripping; strips** [ME *stripen, strepen, strupen, strippen,* fr. OE *-striepan, -strypan* to plunder, rob; akin to MD *stropen* to plunder, strip, OHG *stroufen*] *vt* **1 a :** to remove the clothing of **:** make naked **:** BARE ⟨~ the child completely for a doctor's examination —H.R.Litchfield & L.H.Dembo⟩ **b :** to divest (one) of outer garments ⟨*stripped* him of his robe⟩ ⟨*stripped* himself to the trunks⟩ **c :** to remove (as clothing) from a person **:** take off ⟨it was a privilege to help the king ~ off his shirt —*Irish Digest*⟩ **2 a :** to deprive (someone) of a uniform, the insignia of rank or office, or a decoration ⟨*stripped* two generals of their stars⟩ **b :** to divest (one) of honors, privileges, or functions ⟨*stripped* the sultan of both his legislative and executive powers —*New Statesman & Nation*⟩ **c :** to remove the externals or trappings of (something) **:** divest of adventitious or superficial matters ⟨*stripped* his proposition to the bare bones —A.H.Vandenberg †1951⟩ **3 :** to remove the accessory equipment of **:** DISMANTLE ⟨was sure the car would be either *stripped* or stolen —Kathryn Grondahl⟩ **4 :** to deprive (one) of possessions **:** PLUNDER, SPOIL **5 a :** to peel the rind, bark, or skin from **b :** to denude (a plant) of fruit or leaves **c :** to make bare or clear (as by cutting, grazing, or removing objects from) **:** empty off or out ⟨the church . . . was sold to a housebreaker who *stripped* it of its valuables —S.P.B.Mais⟩ **d :** to pull, tear, or scrape off (as skin or other covering) **:** wrest away ⟨*stripped* the feathers from fowl⟩ ⟨*stripped* the bark from trees⟩ ⟨*stripped* the film from a photographic plate⟩ ⟨~ the paint from a surface⟩ **6 :** to milk dry at the end of a milking by pressing the last available milk from the teats ⟨~ a cow⟩ **7 :** to remove (a ring or jewel) from finger or arm **8 a** (1) **:** to pick the cured leaves from the stalks of (tobacco) (2) **:** to remove strings of leaves of (primed tobacco) (3) **:** to remove tobacco strings from (laths) (4) **:** to pick, sort, and tie (tobacco leaves) into hands **b :** to remove the midrib from (tobacco leaves) **9 a :** to tear or damage the screw thread of (a bolt or nut) **b :** to cause impairment or distortion of (a screw thread) **10 :** to remove the overburden from (a mineral deposit) in mining **11 :** to bare (an ingot of steel) by removing the mold **12 a :** to remove fiber and embedded waste from (the teeth of a card) **b :** to transfer (carded fiber stock) from the carding cylinder to another **13 :** DEGUM **14 :** to separate (a plating or sheet of electrodeposited metal) from the base metal on which plated **15 a :** to remove the most volatile parts or lightest fractions of (as by distillation or by passage of steam or inert gas) **:** TOP ⟨~ coke-oven gas of benzene⟩ ⟨coke *stripped* by nitrogen purge gas —*Industrial & Engineering Chemistry*⟩ **b :** to separate (one or more components) from a mixture or solution ⟨in a natural-gasoline plant, gasoline fractions are *stripped* from rich oil —*Glossary of Terms Used in Petroleum Refining*⟩ **16 a :** to remove (a dye or part of the color) from yarn or fabric by boiling or treating with a chemical — compare DISCHARGE 6a **b :** to remove dye or part of the color from (yarn or fabric) — compare DISCHARGE 6b **17 :** to gather (as grass seed) with a mechanical beater or a hand comb that removes the seed heads for curing and subsequent threshing **18 a :** to lead from (a bridge hand) a series of winning cards that must be got rid of preparatory to executing an end play **b :** to remove (playing cards usu. of low rank) from a pack in a game requiring a smaller pack **19 :** to press eggs or milt out of (a fish) **20 :** to separate (a weapon) into the component parts **:** DISASSEMBLE ⟨could ~ and reassemble a machine gun in the dark⟩ **21 :** to remove the rigging of (a ship) **:** UNRIG **22 :** to draw all line from (a fishing reel) esp. during the run of a fish **23 :** to remove waste material from (a cut and creased board or sheet) before folding into a carton **24 :** to mount (a photographic negative or positive) in position on copy to be used for making a printing plate esp. by photoengraving — sometimes used with *in* **25 :** to remove (forms) from concrete after the concrete has hardened **26 :** to remove the old hair from (a dog) **:** PLUCK **27 :** to shear off surface metal from (a bullet) under excessive bore velocities ⟨found he was *stripping* bullets and fouling his gun barrel with overloads⟩ ~ *vi* **1 :** to take off clothes **:** undress wholly or partly ⟨ricksha men were enjoined not to ~ to the loincloth when at work —D.C. Buchanan⟩ ⟨we *stripped* in the dressing room —H.D.Schwartz⟩ **2 :** to separate or come off (as skin, bark, or rind) **:** PEEL **3 :** to strip tobacco **4 :** to undergo stripping — used of a bullet **5 :** to become damaged, distorted, or torn — used of a screw thread or a threaded part **6 :** to perform a striptease
syn DIVEST, DENUDE, BARE, DISMANTLE: STRIP may imply a pulling or tearing off or a rapid or thorough depriving of a covering, investment, or furnishing ⟨shot wayfarers from ambush, *stripped* the bodies to the skin —*Amer. Guide Series: Tenn.*⟩ ⟨a reading of the speech today, *stripped* of its emotional trappings —S.H.Adams⟩ ⟨had to sell even the few books that Sylvia had left him when she had *stripped* his house —F.M. Ford⟩ DIVEST may indicate a taking off or away of vesture or of whatever is vested in one as a distinction or mark of special privilege or treatment ⟨*divesting* capitalists of further increments of power —M.R.Cohen⟩ ⟨the king is thus *divested* of his kingship and now becomes merely a corpse —J.G.Frazer⟩ ⟨has begun to *divest* himself of his vast estates —William Clark⟩ DENUDE calls attention to the bareness or barrenness resulting from a stripping or divesting ⟨stripped of its vines and *denuded* of its shrubbery, the house would probably have been ugly enough —Willa Cather⟩ ⟨modern agriculture more and more *denudes* the land of the protective cover and food that wild creatures need —G.S.Perry⟩ BARE is a closer synonym to *uncover* or *reveal* than to STRIP; it seldom implies anything about the nature of the action but may implicate its purpose ⟨*bare* one's head in respect⟩ ⟨not afraid to strip themselves of a goodly portion of their clothes and *bare* their skin to the sun's rays —H.A.Overstreet⟩ ⟨the letter *bares* the motives of her own conduct —H.O.Taylor⟩ DISMANTLE now usu. indicates stripping a building, ship, or machine of furnishings and equipment ⟨his ship being laid up for a month and *dismantled* for repairs —Joseph Conrad⟩ ⟨this mine had been sunk to the tenth level, before the ore crusher, enginehouse, and headframe were *dismantled* —*Amer. Guide Series: Minn.*⟩
²strip \"\ *n* -s **1 :** tobacco leaf from which the midrib has been removed **2 strips** *pl* **:** milk strippings **3 :** STRIPTEASE **4** *also* **strip play :** the stripping of a bridge hand **:** ELIMINATION
³strip \"\ *n* -s [alter. of ME *stripe* — more at STRIPE] **1 a :** a narrow piece of about even width ⟨a ~ of cloth⟩ ⟨a ~ of paper⟩ ⟨a ~ of board⟩ **b :** a long narrow area of land or water ⟨a ~ of wood⟩ **2** *obs* **:** a decorative piece of cloth or lace for the neck and bosom **3 a :** a shallow cast ingot of brass for rolling into sheets **b :** a rolled piece of metal (as iron or steel) of the thickness of sheet metal but relatively long and narrow **4 :** COMIC 3a **5 a :** lumber under eight inches wide and not more than one inch thick **b :** ²STICKER 2 **6** *Brit* **:** a trough for transporting and settling particles of ore suspended in water at a mine **7 :** the draft of a pattern **8 :** three or more postage or other stamps or stickers attached in a row either horizontally or vertically — compare BLOCK 5g **9 :** a narrow piece of wood or metal on which usu. four to six electric-light bulbs are arranged in line and which is used in theatrical stage lighting **10 :** the path or course on which a race is run **11 :** the area usu. of rubber, cork, or linoleum on which a fencing bout takes place **12 :** AIRSTRIP
⁴strip \"\ *vt* **stripped; stripped; stripping; strips 1 :** to affix a strip of paper or cloth to (the edge of a pad) or over (the fold of a lining, section, cover, or insert of a book) either inside or outside usu. by machine **2 :** to split (rolled material) down the roll lengthwise by length
⁵strip \"\ *n* -s [AF *estrepe,* fr. OF *estreper* to estrepe] **:** ESTREPEMENT
⁶strip \"\ *vt* [ME *strypen* to move fast; prob. akin to MD *stripe* strip, stripe — more at STRIPE] *archaic* **:** OUTSTRIP
⁷strip \"\ *Scot var of* STRIPE
strip bridge *n* [¹*strip*] **:** DRAWBRIDGE
strip building *n* [³*strip*] *Brit* **:** the building of usu. low-cost dwellings in long parallel rows with minimum land use — compare HOUSING DEVELOPMENT, HOUSING PROJECT
strip camera *n* **:** a shutterless camera (as an aerial camera) in which the film moves past an exposing slit at a rate synchronized with that of the ground image
strip census *n* **:** an estimate of the numbers of a wild animal in an area by counting individuals along a typical strip and assuming a uniform population
strip count *n* **:** a piece tally of surfaced lumber based on the width, length, and thickness of the rough sizes used
strip–crop \ˈ=,=\ *vb* [³*strip* + *crop*] *vt* **:** to practice strip-cropping on ~ *vi* **:** to practice strip-cropping
strip–cropping \ˈ=,==\ *n* [fr. gerund of *strip-crop*] **:** the growing of separate crops in successive narrow strips that on sloping land follow an approximate contour and so check wind or water erosion — called also *strip farming*
strip cup *n* [¹*strip*] **:** a metal cup with the opening covered with a fine wire mesh or dark cloth into which foremilk is drawn for examination to detect gross abnormalities (as clots or ropiness) that may indicate the presence of disease in the udder
¹stripe \ˈstrīp\ *n* -s [ME; prob. akin to ⁴*stripe*] *Scot* **:** a small stream **:** RIVULET
²stripe \"\ *n* -s [ME, perh. fr. MLG *strippe* strap, lash; akin to MD *stripe* strip, stripe] **:** a stroke or blow with a rod or lash ⟨was laying on the prescribed number of ~*s* so lustily that the punished man's screams rent the air —F.V.W.Mason⟩
³stripe \"\ *vt* -ED/-ING/-S **:** to beat or lash with a rod or whip
⁴stripe \"\ *n* -s [ME, strip, fr. MD, stripe, strip; akin to OIr *sriab* stripe, OE *strica* line, streak — more at STREAK] **1 a :** a line or long narrow section of something differing in color or texture from the parts adjoining ⟨a white ~ down the center of the highway⟩ **b** (1) **:** a textile design consisting of vertical or horizontal lines or bands against a plain background and created by various weaving, printing, or finishing processes (2) **:** a fabric with a striped design **c :** a long narrow strip (as of land) **2 a :** a piece of gold, silver, silk, cotton, or other braid (as on the sleeve of a coat) used to indicate military rank or length of service — see HALF-STRIPE, SERVICE STRIPE **b :** CHEVRON **3 :** a distinct shade or variety (as of character, opinion, or partisan affiliation) **:** CLASS, KIND, SORT, TYPE ⟨men of a different moral ~ from the God-fearing, stolid farmers —Rex Lardner⟩ ⟨artists of every ~ —Celestine Sibley⟩ ⟨a man of paler ~ would be content to net for herring —J.W.Noble⟩ **4 a :** BARLEY STRIPE **b :** STREAK 2f **5 :** a narrow white mark extending down the face of a horse from between the eyes to the bridge of the nose **6 :** STRIPED BASS **7 stripes** *pl* **:** a prisoner's distinctive horizontally striped uniform **syn** see TYPE
⁵stripe \"\ *vt* -ED/-ING/-S **:** to make stripes on **:** form with lines of different colors or textures **:** variegate with stripes
stripe blight *n* **:** a disease of oats caused by a bacterium (*Pseudomonas striafaciens*) and characterized by water-soaked spots and streaks
stripe canker *n* **:** BLACK THREAD
striped \ˈstrīpt, -pəd\ *adj* [perh. fr. MD *stripet,* fr. *stripe* stripe, strip + *-et* -ed] **:** having stripes or streaks
striped alder *n* **1 :** a black alder (*Ilex verticillata*) **2 :** WITCH HAZEL 2a(1)
striped bass *n* **:** any of several fishes of the family Serranidae: as **a :** an anadromous sea bass (*Roccus saxatilis*) that is native to the Atlantic coast of the U. S. but introduced and common also on the Pacific coast, is olivaceous above and yellowish silvery on the sides and below, is marked with numerous longitudinal black stripes, is highly esteemed as a game fish and as food, and frequently reaches 20 and possibly sometimes 100 pounds in weight **b** (1) **:** WHITE BASS 1 (2) **:** YELLOW BASS
striped blister beetle *n* **:** a common No. American blister beetle (*Epicauta vittata*) that is sometimes a pest on alfalfa and other crops
striped bloodwort *n* **:** RATTLESNAKE WEED 1
striped cucumber beetle *n* **:** a yellowish black-striped beetle (*Acalymma vittata*) that feeds as a larva on the underground parts of cucumbers and other cucurbits and as an adult on foliage and flowers of cucurbits and other crop plants and that is a vector of bacterial wilt and of cucumber mosaic — compare CUCUMBER BEETLE
striped dace *n* **:** BLACKNOSE DACE
striped dogfish *n* **:** LUI-HAAI
striped dolphin *n* **:** SPECTACLED DOLPHIN
striped flea beetle *n* **:** a flea beetle (*Phyllotreta striolata*) having a yellow line on each elytron and being a pest of cabbage and other brassicas
striped gentian *n* **:** a marsh gentian (*Gentiana villosa*)
striped gopher *or* **striped ground squirrel** *n* **:** a ground squirrel that is striped; *esp* **:** THIRTEEN-LINED GROUND SQUIRREL
striped gourami *n* **:** a small labyrinth fish (*Colisa fasciata*) of India marked with alternate diagonal bands of red and blue that is sometimes kept in the tropical aquarium
striped grass *n* **:** RIBBON GRASS
striped grunt *n* **:** GRAY GRUNT
striped head *n* **:** HUDSONIAN CURLEW
striped hyena *n* **:** a strongly marked hyena (*Hyaena hyaena*) of parts of Africa and southern Asia east to India — see HYENA illustration
striped lizard *n* **:** RACE RUNNER
striped maple *or* **striped dogwood** *n* **:** a maple (*Acer pennsylvanicum*) of eastern No. America with striped bark and large thin 3-lobed leaves — called also *moosewood*
striped marlin *n* **:** a sport fish (*Makaira mitsukurii*) of the Pacific ocean that is purplish blue above with the back crossed by 15 light blue bands
striped mouse *n* **1 :** JUMPING MOUSE **2** *or* **striped rat :** any member of an African genus (*Arvicanthus*) of murid rodents having longitudinal dark stripes along the back
striped muishond *n* **:** a muishond (*Ictonyx striata*) that resembles a ferret in size and form and is often tamed — compare SNAKE MUISHOND
striped mullet *n* **:** a gray mullet (*Mugil cephalus*) of the European and American coasts and the Pacific ocean
striped muscle *n* **:** STRIATED MUSCLE
striped opossum *n* **:** any of several brightly marked nocturnal phalangers (genera *Dactylopsila* and *Dactylonax*) of Queensland and New Guinea having the fourth finger more or less strikingly elongated
striped–pants \ˈ=ˈ=\ *adj* [*striped pants;* fr. the wearing of striped trousers as semiformal attire] **:** overattentive to formality, protocol, or partying and social activity ⟨*striped-pants* diplomacy⟩
striped perch *n* **:** any of various more or less striped fishes resembling typical perch: as **a :** YELLOW PERCH **b :** a rainbow perch (*Hypsurus caryi*) **c** *Austral* **:** a small percoid fish (*Helotes sexlineatus*) blue and silver with narrow brown stripes along each side
striped polecat *n* **:** ZORIL
striped schaapsteker *n* **:** SCHAAPSTEKER b
striped shore crab *n* **:** a very common Pacific shore crab (*Pachygrapsus crassipes*) with a squarish carapace transversely striped usu. with purple and the chelae reticulated with purple
striped skunk *n* **:** any of several skunks of the genus *Mephitis*
striped snake *n* **:** a snake with longitudinal stripes on its back; *esp* **:** GARTER SNAKE
striped squirrel *n* **1 :** a squirrel with stripes on the back; *esp* **:** CHIPMUNK **2** *also* **striped spermophile :** THIRTEEN-LINED GROUND SQUIRREL
striped surf fish *or* **striped surf perch** *n* **:** a rainbow perch (*Taeniotoca lateralis*)
striped surmullet *n* **:** a mullet (*Mullus surmulletus*) of southern Europe
striped tree squirrel *n* **:** an Asiatic squirrel of the genus *Tamiops* that resembles the American chipmunk but is arboreal
striped tuna *n* **:** OCEANIC BONITO
stripe·less \ˈstrīpləs\ *adj* **:** having no stripes
strip·er \ˈstrīpə(r)\ *n* -s [in sense 1, fr. ⁵*stripe* + *-er;* in other senses, fr. ⁴*stripe* + *-er*] **1 :** one that stripes: as **a :** one that paints stripes (as on furniture, vehicle parts, or musical instruments) **b :** a worker who cuts and finishes expansion joints in concrete pavement **c :** a brush usu. with a tapering point for drawing stripes **d :** a knitting machine device that automatically changes yarns for patterns (as stripes) **2 :** a navy man who wears stripes on his sleeve to indicate rating or length of service — usu. used in combination; compare FOUR-STRIPER **3 a :** STRIPED BASS a **b :** WHITE BASS 1
stripe rust *n* **:** a rust of wheat, rye, barley, and other grasses caused by a fungus (*Puccinia glumarum*) that produces elongated yellow streaks of sori — called also *yellow rust, yellow stripe rust*
stripes *pl of* STRIPE, *pres 3d sing of* STRIPE
stripe smut *n* **1 :** a smut of grasses caused by a fungus (*Ustilago striaeformis*) and characterized by long narrow nearly black sori on leaves and sheaths **2 :** smut of rye caused by a fungus (*Urocystis occulta*)
strip farming *n* [³*strip*] **1 :** the distribution of farmlands into long strips for allotment to individual farmers formerly practiced in Europe to prevent unfairness caused by differing soils **2 :** STRIP-CROPPING
stripfilm \ˈ=,=\ *n* **:** FILMSTRIP
stripier *comparative of* STRIPY
stripiest *superlative of* STRIPY
strip–in \ˈ=,=\ *n* -s [¹*strip* + *in*] **1 :** a stripped photographic negative or positive **2 :** an instance of stripping in
strip·i·ness \ˈstrīpēnəs\ *n* -ES **:** the quality or state of being stripy
striping *n* -s [fr. gerund of ⁵*stripe*] **1 :** the act or process of marking with stripes ⟨worked for uniformity in the ~ of highways⟩ **2 a :** the stripes marked or painted on something **b :** a design of stripes
striplight \ˈ=,=\ *n* [³*strip*] **:** a row of small floodlights mounted on a trough reflector and used for theater borderlights, footlights, and general stage illumination
strip·ling \ˈstripliŋ, -lēŋ\ *n* -s [ME, prob. fr. *stripe* strip + *-ling*] **:** an adolescent boy or girl **:** one not yet fully matured into manhood or womanhood
strip map *n* [³*strip*] **:** a map (as for an aviator) showing only a narrow band of territory (as 500 miles long and 10 miles wide)
strip method *n* **:** a method of conservative lumbering by which timber is cleared in relatively narrow strips through a forest and reproduction on the cleared strips is obtained by the seed sown from the adjoining woodland
strip mill *n* **:** a rolling mill for producing long continuous strips of flat rolled metal
strip mine *or* **strip pit** *n* [¹*strip*] **:** a mine near the earth's surface that is worked by stripping; *esp* **:** a coal mine situated along the outcrop of a flat dipping bed
strip–mine \ˈ=ˈ=\ *vt* [*strip mine*] **:** to mine (an ore) from a strip mine
strip miner *n* [*strip mine* + *-er*] **:** a strip mine worker
strip·pa·ble \ˈstripəbəl\ *adj* [¹*strip* + *-able*] **:** capable of being stripped or pulled off ⟨~ vinyl coatings⟩ ⟨~ coal⟩
strip·page \-pij\ *n* -s [¹*strip* + *-age*] **:** material stripped from something (as branches from trees)
stripped *adj* [fr. past part. of ¹*strip*] **:** having clothes, a covering, or something accessory or superfluous removed ⟨a ~ automobile⟩ ⟨an athlete ~ to fighting weight⟩
stripped atoms *n pl* **:** atoms from which outer electrons have been removed permitting closer packing of the atoms and great densities — compare ATOMIC THEORY
stripped deck *n* **:** a pack of playing cards from which cards usu. of low rank have been removed (as in hearts and some poker games)
stripped·ness *n* -ES **:** the quality or state of being stripped
stripped plain *n* **:** a plain floored by a resistant flat-lying stratum from above which weaker rocks have been removed by erosion
strip·per \ˈstripə(r)\ *n* -s [¹*strip* + *-er*] **1 :** one that strips: as **a :** a worker who strips stems from moistened tobacco leaves and ties the leaves into books — called also *sprigger, stemmer* **b :** a worker who removes hides or skins from drying frames salvaging the tacks and piling the skins **c :** one of a group of workers who remove sheets of refined copper from the starting plates on which they were deposited by electrolysis **d :** a quarry worker who cleans up dirt left by a power shovel in exposing the rock **e :** one that strips fish of milt or roe **f :** one that strips photographic negatives or positives **2 :** a device that strips or peels (as bark from osier or insulation from wires) **3 a :** a machine that strips the seed heads from the stalks of grass and hay in harvesting **b :** an implement usu. with slots between revolving rolls for stripping cotton **c** *or* **stripper–harvester :** a harvester-thresher that beats the heads and grain from wheat or other crops without cutting the straw **4 a :** a metal plate or one of a pair of plates one on each side of a cutting die punch that strips the work from the punch and prevents it from being dragged up on the upstroke **b :** a machine for smoothing down files for subsequent recutting **c :** a metal point in a capstan for clearing away the cable as it unwinds **5 :** any of the various small card-clothed rollers in textile manufacturing that strip fiber from one cylinder and carry it to another and esp. from a worker to the main cylinder **6 a :** an apparatus in which volatile material is removed **b :** a solvent used to remove deposits (as paint or varnish) from surfaces **7 :** a card trimmed in a wedge shape so that it can be pulled easily from the pack (as by a cardsharper) **8 :** a cow that has nearly stopped giving milk **9 :** an oil well that has fallen off in production to a few barrels or less per day **10 :** STRIPTEASER ⟨a ~ in a honky-tonk —James Jones⟩ **11 :** STRIP MINER
stripper bolt *n* **:** SHOULDER SCREW
stripping *n* -s [ME, fr. gerund of *strippen* to strip] **1 :** the action of one that strips **2 :** something that is stripped: as **a strippings** *pl* **:** the last milk drawn at a milking usu. distinctly richer in fat and freer from bacteria than the foremilk **b :** OVERBURDEN 2a **3 :** DIGGING 2 **4 a :** the removal of cured tobacco leaves from the stalks or from the laths **b :** the removal of the foliage from the stem of a plant or flower **5 :** the shearing off of surface metal from a bullet that is driven at excessive velocity through a gun barrel by an overload of powder and fails to acquire spin from the rifling **6** [³*strip* + *-ing*] **:** material (as leather) that is cut into strips
stripping film *n* **:** photographic film supplied with an emulsion layer coated on the surface of a transparent film support such that all or selected portions of the processed or unprocessed emulsion may be easily removed as a continuous layer for transfer to another surface
stripping knife *or* **stripping comb** *n* **:** a metal blade with a serrated edge used for plucking or stripping the coat of a dog
strip·pit *or* **strip·ped** \ˈstripət\ *Scot & dial Eng var of* STRIPED
strip planking *n* [³*strip*] **:** the planking of a carvel-built boat or ship with narrow slightly tapered strips to make flush joints and a smooth outside hull as distinguished from the lap joints of a clinker-built boat
strip play *n* **:** STRIP 4
strip poker *n* [¹*strip*] **:** a poker game in which players pay their losses with articles of clothing that they take off
strips *pres 3d sing of* STRIP, *pl of* STRIP
strip survey *n* [³*strip*] **:** a valuation survey of a strip of forest land chosen as an average sample from which to estimate the value of a larger area
strip system *n* **:** STRIP FARMING 1
stript *past of* STRIP
¹strip·tease \ˈstrip,tēz\ *n* [¹*strip* + *tease*] **:** a burlesque act in which a female performer removes her clothing piece by piece in view of the audience
²striptease \"\ *vi* **:** to perform a striptease
strip·teas·er \-zə(r)\ *n* [*striptease* + *-er*] **:** an actress who performs a striptease — called also *ecdysiast, peeler, stripper, teaser*
strip template *n* [³*strip*] **:** POLE STRIP
strip·teuse \(ˈ)strip¦tərz, -¦tə̄z, -¦tüz, -¦təz\ *n* -s [¹*striptease* + *danseuse*] **:** STRIPTEASER
strip windows *n pl* [³*strip*] **:** RIBBON WINDOWS
stripy \ˈstrīpē\ *adj* -ER/-EST [³*stripe* + *y*] **:** having, occurring in, or marked by stripes or streaks
stri·sci·an·do \,strēshēˈän(,)dō\ *adv (or adj)* [It, fr. verbal of *strisciare* to drag, trail, fr. *striscia* track, trail, streak, prob. of imit. origin] **1 :** in a slurred or smooth manner — used as a direction in music **2 :** GLISSANDO

strive \ˈstrīv\ *vi* **strove** \ˈstrōv\ *also* **strived; striv·en** \ˈstrivən\ *or* **strived** *or chiefly dial* **strove; striving; strives** [ME *striven,* fr. OF *estriver* to fight, contend, of Gmc origin; akin to obs. D *strijven* to contend, endeavor, MHG *streben* to endeavor, Gk *striphnos* firm, hard, ON *strītha* to fight — more at STRIDE] **1 a :** to struggle in opposition or contention **:** carry on a conflict **:** CONTEND, CONTEST — used with *against* or *with* ⟨we ~ against butchers —Irwin Shaw⟩ ⟨~ not with your superiors in argument —George Washington⟩ **b :** to contend for dominance, mastery, or superiority **:** conduct war **:** FIGHT **c :** to compete as a rival **:** VIE ⟨grief and perplexity . . . ~ within her —Anne D. Sedgwick⟩ **d** *obs* **:** to struggle against physical obstacles **:** buck opposing forces, resistance, or difficulty **e :** to advance laboriously **:** make headway with effort **:** WORK ⟨*strove* not only for the advancement of learning but also for the conversion of the heathen —Kemp Malone⟩ **2 :** to devote effort or energy **:** try hard or earnestly **:** ATTEMPT, ENDEAVOR — often used with an infinitive ⟨*strove* to make the most of every minute —Osbert Sitwell⟩ ⟨a goal toward which he had always perseveringly *striven*⟩ **syn** see TRY

striv·er \-və(r)\ *n* -s [ME, fr. *striven* to strive + *-er*] **:** one that strives ⟨a man of talent and a true ~ after the highest human status —John Dollard⟩

¹striving *n* -s [ME, fr. gerund of *striven* to strive] **1 :** CONFLICT, CONTEST, RIVALRY ⟨there were strenuous ~*s* for place, profit, promotion, and power —D.C.Mearns⟩ **2 :** a straining effort ⟨these works cost him mighty ~*s* and struggles through long years —Abram Chasins⟩

²striving *adj* [ME, fr. pres. part. of *striven* to strive] **:** marked by strenuous effort, rivalry, or conflict — **striv·ing·ly** *adv*

¹strix \ˈstriks\ *n* -ES [L *strig-, strix* furrow, groove, flute; akin to L *striga* furrow — more at STRIKE] **:** a fluting of a column

²strix \"\ *n, cap* [NL *Strig-, Strix,* fr. L, screech owl — more at STRIDENT] **:** a variously restricted genus of owls: **a** *in former classifications* (1) **:** a large genus containing most owls except the barn owls (2) **:** a genus comprising the barn owls **b :** the type genus of the family Strigidae comprising owls that lack ear tufts and including the tawny owl and the barred owl

stroam *var of* STROME

strobe \ˈstrōb\ *n* -s [by shortening & alter. fr. *stroboscope*] **1 :** STROBOSCOPE **2 :** STROBOTRON ⟨~ photography⟩

strob·ic \ˈsträbik\ *adj* [Gk *strobos* action of whirling + E *-ic* — more at STROPHE] **:** having or appearing to have a spinning motion

strobic disk *n* **:** a disk marked with a set of concentric rings or toothed wheels that is moved in a circular path without causing it to revolve on its own axis causing the figures to appear to revolve on their axes

stro·bi·la \strəˈbīlə\ *n, pl* **strobi·lae** \-ī,lē\ [NL, fr. Gk *strobilē* plug of lint twisted so as to resemble a pine cone, fr. *strobilos* pine cone — more at STROBILUS] **:** a linear series of similar structures: as **a :** the chain of segments forming the body of a tapeworm **b :** the chain of individuals produced by repeated transverse fission of a scyphozoan scyphistoma larva — **stro·bi·lar** \-īlə(r)\ *adj*

strob·i·la·ceous \ˌsträbəˈlāshəs\ *adj* [NL *strobilaceus,* fr. *strobilus* strobile + L *-aceus* -aceous] **1 :** relating to or resembling a strobile **2 :** bearing strobiles

strob·i·late \ˈsträbə,lāt\ *vi* -ED/-ING/-S [back-formation fr. *strobilation*] **:** to become a strobila **:** undergo strobilation

strob·i·la·tion \ˌ≈≈ˈlāshən\ *also* **strob·i·li·za·tion** \ˌsträbələˈzāshən\ *n* -s [NL *strobila* + ISV *-ation, -ization*] **:** asexual reproduction by transverse division of the body into segments which develop into zooids, proglottids, or separate individuals in many coelenterates and worms

strob·ile *also* **strob·il** \ˈsträbəl\ *n* -s **1** [NL *strobilus*] **:** STROBILUS **2 :** a spike with persistent overlapping bracts that resembles a cone and is the pistillate inflorescence of the hop **3** [NL *strobila*] **:** STROBILA — **strob·i·lif·er·ous** \ˌsträbəˈlif(ə)rəs\ *adj*

strob·i·line \ˈsträbələn\ *adj* [NL *strobila* + E *-ine*] **:** STROBILACEOUS

strob·i·lo·cer·cus \ˌsträbəlōˈsərkəs\ *n, pl* **strobilocer·ci** \-ˈsər,sī\ [NL, fr. *strobila* + Gk *kerkos* tail] **:** a larval tapeworm that has undergone strobilization and everted from its bladder while still in the intermediate host

strob·i·loid \ˈsträbə,lȯid\ *adj* [NL *strobilus* + E *-oid*] **:** resembling or having to do with a strobilus ⟨a ~ theory of the descent of angiosperms⟩

strob·i·lo·my·ces \ˌsträbəlōˈmī,sēz\ *n, cap* [NL, fr. Gk *strobilos* whirling or twisted object + NL *-myces*] **:** a genus of fungi (family Boletaceae) similar to *Boletus* but with a shaggy scaly cap and the tubes not easily separating from the pileus

strob·i·loph·y·ta \ˌsträbəˈläfəd·ə\ [NL, fr. *strobilus* + *-o-* *-phyta*] *syn of* GYMNOSPERMAE

strob·i·lus \ˈsträbələs\ *n, pl* **strobi·li** \-bə,lī\ [NL, fr. LL, pine cone, fr. Gk *strobilos* whirling or twisted object, ball, top, pinecone, fr. *strobos* action of whirling — more at STROPHE] **1 a :** a conelike aggregation of sporophylls (as in the club mosses and horsetails) **b :** the cone of a gymnosperm **2 :** STROBILE 1b **3 :** STROBILA

strobilus theory *n* **:** a theory in evolutionary botany: the sporophyte of the vascular plant derives from a primitive form resembling or equivalent to a strobilus of sporophylls

stro·bo·scope \ˈstrōbə,skōp, -räb-\ *n* [Gk *strobos* action of whirling + ISV *-scope*] **:** an instrument that is used for observing motion in such a way that moving objects (as machine parts) appear to be slowed down or stationary, that is used esp. for determining speeds of rotation or frequencies of vibration, and that is made in the form of a revolving disk with holes around the edge through which an object is viewed or a rapidly flashing light that illuminates an object intermittently or a cardboard disk with marks to be viewed under intermittent light

stro·bo·scop·ic \ˌ≈≈ˈskäpik, -pēk\ *adj* [ISV *stroboscope* + *-ic*] **:** of, by means of, utilizing, or relating to a stroboscope ⟨~ effect⟩ ⟨~ photography⟩ ⟨~ light⟩—**stro·bo·scop·i·cal·ly** \-pək(ə)lē, -pēk-, -li\ *adv*

stro·bo·tron \ˈ≈≈,trän\ *n* -s [*stroboscopic* + *-tron*] **:** a gas-filled electron tube with a cold cathode used esp. as a source of stroboscopic light

strock·le \ˈsträkəl\ *n* -s [origin unknown] **:** a shovel with a turned-up edge used by glassworkers

strode *past of* STRIDE

stro·ga·noff \ˈstrógə,nȯf\ *adj* [after Count Paul *Stroganoff* 19th cent. Russ. diplomat] **:** sliced thin and cooked in a sauce of consommé, sour cream, mustard, onion, and condiments — used postpositively ⟨beef ~⟩ ⟨chicken ~⟩

¹stroke \ˈstrōk\ *vt* -ED/-ING/-S [ME *stroken,* fr. OE *strācian;* akin to MD *streken* to stroke, OHG *streihhōn* to stroke, *strihhan* to pass over lightly, smooth — more at STRIKE] **1 a :** to rub gently in one direction ⟨*stroking* his beard⟩ ⟨~ a cat's fur⟩ **b :** to pass the hand over gently in kindness or tenderness **:** CARESS, SOOTHE **2 a :** to smooth or arrange by repeatedly drawing the hand or a tool over or through **b :** to draw across a surface repeatedly in order to sharpen **:** WHET, HONE **3 :** to draw milk from (as a cow) esp. by stripping **4 :** to give a finely fluted surface to (a stone) — **stroke the wrong way :** to annoy by offending the tastes or prejudices of **:** RUFFLE

²stroke \"\ *n* -s [ME *stroke, strake;* akin to MLG *strek* stroke, MHG *streich,* OE *strican* to move, pass over lightly, stroke — more at STRIKE] **1 :** the act of striking with the hand; *esp* **:** a deliberately aimed swinging blow with a weapon or implement ⟨no man could withstand his sword ~⟩ ⟨dealt him several stinging ~*s* with the whip⟩ ⟨ringing ~*s* of the ax⟩ **2 :** a single unbroken movement without pause or reversal of direction ⟨sketched a likeness with a few ~*s* of a pencil⟩; *esp* **:** one of a series of repeated or to-and-fro movements ⟨~*s* of a pendulum⟩ ⟨painting with firm level ~*s*⟩ **3 a :** a blow on a drum; *esp* **:** a full accented beat as distinguished from a tap or a roll **b :** a striking of the ball in a game (as cricket, billiards, tennis) **c :** the act of striking or attempting to strike the ball that constitutes the scoring unit in golf ⟨win a match by two ~*s*⟩ ⟨accepted a penalty ~ for lifting the ball out of an unplayable lie⟩ ⟨a 10-*stroke* handicap⟩ **4 :** a sudden action or process producing an impact ⟨~ of lightning⟩ or a quick or unexpected result ⟨~ of fortune⟩ ⟨~ of luck⟩ **5 a** *obs* **:** the result or effect of a blow **:** INJURY **b** (1) **:** APOPLEXY (2) **:** LITTLE STROKE **6 a :** one of a series of propelling beats or movements against a resisting medium ⟨wing ~ of a bird⟩ ⟨swimming ~⟩ ⟨paddling with quick, stabbing ~*s*⟩ ⟨a rowing pace of 30 ~*s* to the minute⟩ **b :** the member of a rowing crew who sits nearest the stern and sets the tempo for the other rowers **7 a :** a vigorous or energetic effort by which something is done, produced, or accomplished ⟨brilliant diplomatic ~⟩ ⟨without doing a ~ of work⟩ ⟨~ of genius⟩ **b** *Brit* **:** a gratifying quantity of work or business **c :** a delicate or clever touch in a narrative or description or construction **:** a well-turned phrase or a deftly managed bit of plotting **d :** a series of moves and exchanges (in chess and checkers) resulting in a clear advantage for one side **8 a :** a movement of the arm or baton in beating time **b :** the movement of the bow in one direction on a stringed instrument **c :** HEARTBEAT **9 a :** the movement in either direction of a mechanical part (as a piston plunger, piston rod, crosshead) having a reciprocating motion **b :** the entire distance passed through in such a movement ⟨the piston is at half ~⟩ ⟨ratio of piston ~ to bore of a cylinder⟩ **10 :** the sound of a bell being struck ⟨at the ~ of twelve⟩ **11** *obs* **:** method or manner of touching or playing a musical instrument; *also* **:** MELODY **12** [¹*stroke*] **:** an act of stroking or caressing ⟨the ~ of wind and water on land —Russell Lord⟩ **13 a :** a mark or dash made by a single movement of an implement (as a pen, engraving tool, or brush) ⟨the ~ dividing numerator and denominator in the fraction ¾⟩ **b** *obs* **:** a distinguishing feature **:** CHARACTERISTIC **c :** one of the lines of a letter of the alphabet or other graphic character ⟨a typeface having great contrast between thick and thin ~*s*⟩ ⟨Bodoni has a lively quality caused by the contrast of the heavy ~*s* and the hairlines —W.S.Cowell⟩ **d :** a heavy line connecting the stems of two or more notes in a musical notation **14 :** the truth-functional operator that is the constant element in an alternative denial, that is commonly interpreted as "not both", that is symbolized |, and that can be used alone with only propositional symbols to construct a formally complete propositional calculus ⟨the alternative denial $p|q$ is read *p stroke q*⟩ — **at a stroke** *or* **at one stroke** *adv* **:** all at once **:** IMMEDIATELY ⟨his life savings wiped out *at a stroke*⟩

³stroke \"\ *vb* -ED/-ING/-S *vt* **1 a :** to mark with a short line ⟨dotted the *i*'s and *stroked* the *t*'s⟩ **b :** to cancel by drawing a line through — used usu. with *out* ⟨*stroked* out the last name on the list⟩ **c :** to join the stems of (musical notes) by a stroke **2 :** to set the stroke for (the crew of a rowing boat) **:** set the stroke for the crew of (a rowing boat) **:** row as stroke of **3 :** HIT ⟨~ a single over second base⟩; *esp* **:** to propel (a ball) with a controlled swinging blow ⟨~ a cue ball in billiards⟩ **4 :** to strike (a key) in typewriting **~** *vi* **1 :** to execute a stroke ⟨polo team showed bold riding and accurate *stroking*⟩ **2 a :** to pull an oar or serve as stroke ⟨*stroked* for the freshman crew —*Current Biog.*⟩ **b :** to row at a certain number of strokes a minute ⟨the crew was *stroking* at 32⟩ **3 :** to strike the keys in typewriting ⟨clean, even *stroking* is desirable for good impressions⟩

stroke function *or* **stroke operation** *n* [²*stroke*] **1 :** STROKE 14 **2 :** ALTERNATIVE DENIAL; *sometimes* **:** JOINT DENIAL

stroke hole *n* **:** a golf hole at which a stroke is received by a player in a handicap match

stroke in *vt* [¹*stroke*] *Brit* **:** to feed (a sheet) into a cylinder press

stroke·let \-klət\ *n* -s [²*stroke* + *-let*] **:** LITTLE STROKE

stroke oar *n* **1 :** the oar nearest the stern usu. on the port side **2 :** STROKE 6b

stroke play *n* **:** MEDAL PLAY

strok·er \-kə(r)\ *n* -s [¹*stroke* + *-er*] **1 :** one that strokes; *specif* **:** one who pretends to heal or cure by stroking **2** *Brit* **a :** a small tool with which sheets are stroked toward the grippers in hand-feeding a cylinder press **b :** a similarly functioning part in an automatic feeder

stroker-in \ˈ≈≈ˈ≈\ *n, pl* **strokers-in** *Brit* **:** one who hand-feeds sheets into a cylinder press

strokes *pres 3d sing of* STROKE, *pl of* STROKE

strokes·man \ˈstrōksmən\ *n* [*strokes* (gen. of ²*stroke*) + *man*] *archaic* **:** STROKE 6b

stroking *pres part of* STROKE

strok·ings \ˈstrōkiŋz\ *n pl* [fr. gerund of ¹*stroke*] **:** STRIPPING 2a

¹stroll \ˈstrōl\ *vb* -ED/-ING/-S [prob. fr. G dial. *strollen*] *vi* **1 :** to walk in a leisurely or idle manner **:** take a walk **:** SAUNTER, RAMBLE **2 :** to go habitually from place to place in search of occupation or profit **:** ROVE, WANDER ⟨~*ing* players⟩ ⟨~*ing* musician⟩ **~** *vt* **:** to walk at leisure along or about ⟨~ the streets of the village⟩

²stroll \"\ *n* -s **:** an idle and leisurely walk **:** RAMBLE ⟨go for a ~ in the country⟩

stroll·er \-lə(r)\ *n* -s [¹*stroll* + *-er*] **1 :** one that walks along in a leisurely manner **:** one that strolls or saunters ⟨Sunday afternoon ~*s*⟩ **2 a :** a wandering beggar **:** VAGRANT, TRAMP **b :** an itinerant peddler **3 :** a strolling player **:** an itinerant actor **4 :** a four-wheel usu. folding carriage designed as a chair in which a baby may be pushed ⟨the two-year-old prefers a ~ to a carriage⟩ — called also *go-cart*

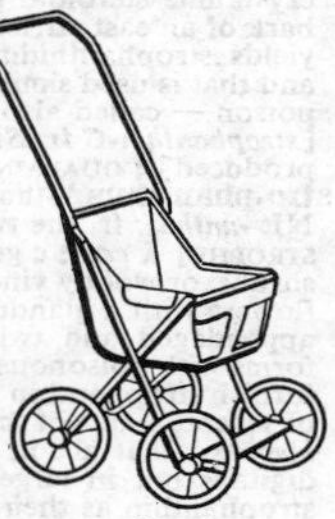

stroller 4

stroller tan *n* **:** MIKADO BROWN

stro·ma \ˈstrōmə\ *n, pl* **stroma·ta** \-məd·ə\ [NL *stromat-, stroma,* fr. L, bed covering, fr. Gk *strōmat-, strōma* bed covering, spread, bed, fr. *stornynai* to spread, strew — more at STREW] **1 a :** the supporting framework of an animal organ typically consisting of connective tissue **b :** the spongy protoplasmic framework of some cells (as red blood cells, muscle cells, nerve cells) **2 a :** a compact mass of fungous tissue on or in which perithecia or pycnidia are produced often intermingled with tissue of the host or substrate **b :** the proteinaceous matrix throughout which the granules of chlorophyll are dispersed in a chloroplast — **stro·mal** \-məl\ *adj* — **stro·ma·tal** \-məd·ᵊl\ *adj*

stro·ma·te·i·dae \ˌstrōməˈtēə,dē\ *n pl, cap* [NL, fr. *Stromateus,* type genus (fr. Gk *strōmateus* bed covering, a fish marked with patchwork colors, fr. *strōmat-, strōma* bed covering) + *-idae*] **:** a large family of chiefly small marine fishes (as the harvest fish and the dollarfish) having a short compressed body, smooth scales, feeble spines, and a series of toothlike processes in the esophagus behind the pharyngeal bones that with a few related forms constitutes a distinct suborder of Percomorphi — **stro·mat·e·oid** \strəˈmad·ē,ȯid\ *adj or n*

stro·mat·ic \strəˈmad·ik\ *adj* [NL *stromat-, stroma* + E *-ic*] **:** relating to, resembling, or constituting a stroma **:** STROMAL

stro·ma·tin \ˈstrōməd·ən\ *n* -s [ISV *stromat-* (fr. NL *stromat-, stroma*) + *-in*] **:** a protein in some respects comparable to keratin that is present in the stroma of some cells (as red blood cells)

stro·ma·top·o·ra \ˌstrōməˈtäpərə\ *n, cap* [NL, fr. *stromat-, stroma* + *-o-* + *-pora*] **:** a genus (the type of the family Stromatoporidae) of extinct hydrozoans that form thick concentric laminae of reticulated calcareous tissue with scattered tubules for the zooids and with related hydrozoans constitute extensive beds in various Paleozoic and esp. Devonian rocks — **stro·ma·top·o·roid** \ˌ≈≈ˈtäpə,rȯid\ *adj or n*

stro·ma·tous \ˈstrōməd·əs\ *adj* [NL *stromat-, stroma* + E *-ous*] **:** having or forming a stroma **:** affecting a stroma

stromb \ˈsträm(b)\ *n* -s [NL *Strombus*] **:** a mollusk or shell of the genus *Strombus* or family Strombidae

strom·bi·dae \-mbə,dē\ *n pl, cap* [NL, fr. *Strombus,* type genus + *-idae*] **:** a family of large marine gastropod mollusks (suborder Taenioglossa) comprising numerous chiefly tropical conchs — see STROMBUS

strom·bi·form \-mbə,fȯrm\ *adj* [NL *Strombus* + ISV *-iform*] **:** resembling a member of the genus *Strombus* in form

strom·bite \ˈsträm,bīt\ *n* -s [NL *Strombus* + ISV *-ite*] **:** a petrified shell of a gastropod of the genus *Strombus*

¹strom·boid \-,bȯid\ *adj* [NL *Strombus* + ISV *-oid*] **:** resembling or related to the genus *Strombus*

²stromboid \"\ *n* -s **:** a stromboid mollusk

strom·bo·li·an \strämˈbōlēən\ *adj, often cap* [*Stromboli,* volcano in the Lipari islands + E *-an*] **:** relating to volcanic eruptions that explode violently and eject incandescent dust, scoria, and bombs with little water vapor

strom·bus \ˈsträmbəs\ *n* [NL, fr. L, a kind of spiral snail, fr. Gk *strombos* a snail — more at STROPHE] **1** *cap* **:** a genus of marine gastropod mollusks (family Strombidae) having a heavy obconical shell with a short conical spire and usu. a much expanded outer lip, a horny operculum, a narrow foot, long snout, and long eye peduncles — see KING CONCH **2** -ES **:** any mollusk of the genus *Strombus*

strome \ˈstrōm\ *vi* [alter. of *stroam,* perh. blend of *stroll* & *roam*] *dial chiefly Eng* **:** STRIDE, STROLL

stro·mey·er·ite \ˈstrō,mīə,rīt\ *n* -s [G *stromeyerit,* fr. Friedrich *Strohmeyer* †1835 Ger. chemist + G *-it* -ite] **:** a steel gray mineral CuAgS consisting of silver copper sulfide of metallic luster and usu. occurring in compact masses (hardness 2.5–3, sp. gr. 6.15–6.3)

ström·ming \ˈstrœmiŋ\ *n* -s [Sw, fr. *ström* stream; akin to ON *straumr* stream — more at STREAM] **:** a small Baltic herring

stro·muhr \ˈstrō,mu̇(ə)r\ *n* -s [G, lit., stream clock, fr. *strom* stream (fr. OHG *strōm*) + *uhr* hour, clock, fr. MHG *ur* hour, fr. MLG or MD *ure,* fr. OF — more at STREAM, HOUR] **:** a rheometer designed to measure the amount and speed of blood flow through an artery

¹strong \ˈstrȯŋ *also* ˈstrāŋ\ *adj* **stron·ger** \-ŋgə(r)\ **stron·gest** \-ŋgəst\ [ME, fr. OE *strang;* akin to OHG *strango* strongly, *strengi* strong, brave, hard, ON *strangr* strong, severe, L *stringere* to bind tight, press together — more at STRAIN] **1 a :** having great muscular power **:** capable of exerting great bodily force ⟨~ as a bull⟩ **b :** accomplished or supported by marked physical power ⟨rows with a ~ stroke⟩ ⟨~ kick⟩ ⟨~ thrust with a spear⟩ **2 a :** able to bear or endure **:** ROBUST, RUGGED ⟨~ runner⟩ ⟨~ health⟩ **b :** able to withstand stress or violence **:** not easily broken or injured ⟨~ furniture⟩ **c :** tending to higher prices — sometimes distinguished from *firm* ⟨a ~ market⟩ **3 :** having or exhibiting moral or intellectual force, endurance, or vigor ⟨mistook an opinionated mind for a ~ one —C.H.Sykes⟩ ⟨~ ruler⟩ ⟨~ president⟩ **4 a :** having great resources of wealth ⟨~ bank⟩ ⟨~ national economy⟩ or of talent ⟨~ cast of actors⟩ ⟨among the ~*er* teams in the baseball league⟩ **b :** being of a specified effective number — used postpositively ⟨army 10 thousand ~⟩ ⟨each choir was over 150 ~ —Warwick Braithwaite⟩ **5 a :** striking or superior of its kind **:** capable of making a clear or deep impression esp. on the mind or imagination ⟨bears a ~ resemblance to his father⟩ ⟨~ picture⟩ **b :** effective or efficient esp. in a particular direction **:** able to accomplish a result ⟨if you are ~ on logic —W.J.Reilly⟩ **c :** MASSIVE, IMPORTANT ⟨~ vein of coal⟩ **d :** FULL 3e(1) **e** *of printing type or a slug* **:** cast slightly over point size **6 a :** having a particular quality in a great degree **:** intense in degree **:** CONCENTRATED ⟨~ salt solution⟩ ⟨~ coffee⟩ ⟨~ dislike⟩ ⟨~ light⟩ ⟨~ feelings of the farmers about foreign competition —Roy Lewis & Angus Maude⟩ **b :** EXTREME, UNCOMPROMISING ⟨~ views on raising children⟩ ⟨denounced in the ~*est* terms⟩ **c** *of a color* **:** high in chroma **d :** containing a large proportion of alcohol ⟨~ beer⟩ **e :** having a high degree of ionization in solution — used of an acid or a base ⟨hydrochloric acid and sulfuric acid are ~ acids⟩; compare WEAK 11 **f** *of tobacco* **:** having a high nicotine content or otherwise strongly flavored ⟨perique is a ~ tobacco⟩ **g :** having great refractive or magnifying power ⟨~ lens⟩ ⟨uses ~ eyeglasses⟩ **7** *obs* **:** GROSS, FLAGRANT, NOTORIOUS ⟨heinous, ~, and bold conspiracy —Shak.⟩ **8 :** URGENT, COMPELLING ⟨~ grounds for believing him guilty⟩ ⟨~ desire for recognition⟩ **9 :** ARDENT, ZEALOUS ⟨the whole family are ~ Republicans⟩ ⟨~ believer in astrology⟩ **10 :** moving with force or rapidity ⟨~ tide⟩ ⟨~ wind⟩ ⟨~ pulse⟩ **11 a** *obs* **:** DIFFICULT, HARD **b :** relatively hard to digest **:** SOLID ⟨~ foods⟩ **12 a :** not easily captured or subdued ⟨~ fortress⟩ ⟨~ military position⟩ **b :** well established **:** firmly fixed **:** not easily altered or eradicated ⟨~ prejudice⟩ ⟨~ belief⟩ ⟨~ custom⟩ **c :** not easily upset or nauseated ⟨~ stomach⟩ ⟨~ head for hard liquor⟩ **13 :** having an offensive or too intense odor or flavor ⟨~ cheese⟩ ⟨~ breath⟩ **14** *of soil* **:** PRODUCTIVE, FERTILE **15** *of flour or wheat* **:** containing a high percentage of gluten **:** cohesive and tenacious and producing bread of good texture and form **16 a** *of a verb* **:** forming its past tense by a change in the root vowel and its past participle usu. by the addition of *-en* with or without change of the root vowel (as *strive, strove, striven; break, broke, broken; drink, drank, drunk*) — opposed to *weak;* compare IRREGULAR **b** *of a noun or adjective declension* **:** retaining the old declensional endings characteristic of the vowel stems in Proto-Germanic — opposed to *weak* **17 a :** bearing a degree of stress greater than the minimal degree occurring in the language ⟨~ stress⟩ ⟨~ syllable⟩ ⟨~ ending of a line of verse⟩ **b :** EMPHATIC — used of forms of chiefly monosyllabic words (as pronouns, auxiliaries) that have minimal stress in some contexts ⟨*am* is a ~ form in "I'm not going today but I am going tomorrow"⟩ ⟨Modern English *off* descends historically from the old ~ form of *of*⟩ **18** *chiefly Austral* **a** *of wool* **:** broad-haired or coarse-fibered **b** *of sheep* **:** having such wool **:** STRONG-WOOLLED

syn STOUT, STURDY, STALWART, TOUGH, TENACIOUS: STRONG is a general term indicating marked physical power, great size or number, soundness for withstanding strain, or marked force, vigor, or intensity ⟨a *strong* constitution⟩ ⟨a *strong* army⟩ ⟨a *strong* brace⟩ ⟨*strong* liquor⟩ ⟨a *strong* color⟩ STOUT suggests power to resist or endure; of things it is applicable to a texture or construction resisting strain, and of persons to an ability to resist with undaunted resolution ⟨mooring the ship with *stout* ropes⟩ ⟨*stout* fences for keeping the cattle in⟩ ⟨the *stout* defenders of the fortress⟩ ⟨and let our hearts be *stout,* to wait out the long travail, to bear sorrows that may come, to impart our courage unto our sons —F.D. Roosevelt⟩ STURDY applies to what is marked by staying power or resistance arising from firm resolution, rugged or vigorous growth, or solid construction ⟨it was easy in this country to idealize the farmers as the *sturdy* yeomanry who embodied all the virtues associated with the original Anglo-Saxon love of liberty —John Dewey⟩ ⟨a kick delivered with all the strength of the blacksmith's *sturdy* leg sent him sprawling on all fours —C.B.Nordhoff & J.N.Hall⟩ STALWART may suggest a firm, strong dependability, often accompanied by notable mental or physical strength ⟨it is a hard life: those that survive are *stalwart,* rugged men, literally mighty men of valour who neither know nor desire comforts —L.D.Stamp⟩ ⟨a *stalwart* Federalist, he was a good hater of all Jacobins —V.L.Parrington⟩ TOUGH may suggest resistant, vigorous hardiness able to withstand hard strain and enervation ⟨a *tough* and durable material⟩ ⟨the *toughest* old salts imaginable — not pretty to look at, but fellows, by their faces, of the most indomitable spirit —R.L.Stevenson⟩ ⟨a *tough* ruthless power bent on dominating the world and suppressing our freedom —Vannevar Bush⟩ TENACIOUS implies a stubborn or resolute holding on, retaining, maintaining, or adhering despite forces that would discourage, weaken, dislodge, or thwart ⟨her power of recuperation was wonderful. There was something *tenacious* about that lily-frail body of hers, a clutch on existence which one could not reconcile with its patent weakness —Jack London⟩ ⟨stubborn, willful, *tenacious,* undiscouraged by adversity —T.H.Fielding⟩

— **strong for :** markedly prejudiced in favor of **:** attaching great importance to ⟨*strong for* hi-fi just now⟩

²strong \"\ *adv* [ME *stronge, strong,* fr. OE *strange,* fr. *strang* strong (adj.)] **:** STRONGLY ⟨had the love of adventure ~ in their Irish blood —*Irish Digest*⟩ ⟨still going ~ after 40 years of hard work⟩ ⟨reversible . . . topcoat . . . is coming back ~ —*New Yorker*⟩ ⟨wind blowing ~ from the West⟩

³strong \"\ *n* -s [¹*strong*] **:** FORTE 2

strong arm *n* **1 :** physical strength **:** POWER, FORCE ⟨*strong arm* of the law⟩ **2 :** undue force **:** VIOLENCE **3** *also* **strong-arm·er** \-ŋ,ärmər\ -s **:** a person using violence **:** THUG

¹strong-arm \ˈ≈,≈\ *adj* [*strong arm*] **:** having or using undue force **:** VIOLENT ⟨*strong-arm* methods of strike breaking⟩

²strong-arm \"\ *vt* **1 :** to use force upon **:** handle roughly

: beat up : ASSAULT ⟨*strong-armed* by a vice squad⟩ **2** : to intimidate by threat of violence ⟨*strong-arming* small business into paying protection money⟩ **3** : to rob by violence

strongback \ˈ=,=\ *n* **1** : a spar lashed from one boat davit to the other to which the boat is secured at sea **2** : a heavy timber or metal beam or bar for taking a strain; *specif* : a post to support a light deck used by passengers

strongbark *also* **strongback** \ˈ=,=\ *n* : a small tree (*Bourreria ovata*) of the family Ehretiaceae of southern Florida and the West Indies with strong hard brown wood streaked with orange and edible berries from which a beverage is made

strongbox \ˈ=,=\ *n* : a chest or case for money or valuables made very strongly : a small safe ⟨papers locked away in his ~⟩

strong breeze *n* : wind having a speed of 25 to 31 miles per hour — see BEAUFORT SCALE table

strong drink *n* [ME *strong drinke*, fr. ¹*strong* + *drinke* drink] : intoxicating liquor

stronger *comparative of* STRONG

strongest *superlative of* STRONG

strong gale *n* : wind having a speed of 47 to 54 miles per hour — see BEAUFORT SCALE table

strong grade *n* : a phase of an ablaut series of vowels that receives more than minimum stress

strongheaded \ˈ=¦==\ *adj* [¹*strong* + *headed*] : STUBBORN, HEADSTRONG — **strongheaded·ly** *adv* — **strongheaded·ness** *n* -ES

stronghearted \ˈ=¦==\ *adj* [ME *strong herted*, fr. ¹*strong* + *herted* hearted] : BRAVE, COURAGEOUS — **stronghearted·ness** *n* -ES

stronghold \ˈ=,=\ *n* [ME *strong holde*, fr. ¹*strong* + *holde* hold] **1** : a fortified place : a place of security or survival : FORTRESS, REFUGE ⟨one of the last ~s of the ancient Gaelic language —George Holmes⟩ **2** : a place occupied or dominated by a special group or faction ⟨a Puritan ~⟩

strong·ish \-ŋish, -ŋēsh\ *adj* : somewhat strong ⟨~ wind⟩

strong language *n* : markedly or unwarrantedly forcible or vehement manner of expression or choice of words

strong·ly *adv* [ME *strongliche*, fr. OE *stranglīce*, fr. *stranglic* strong, robust, fr. *strang* strong + *-līc* -ly (adj. suffix)] : in a strong manner : POWERFULLY, FORCIBLY, FIRMLY, BOLDLY, EMPHATICALLY

strong man *n* **1** : a man who exhibits feats of muscular strength ⟨*strong man* in a circus⟩ **2** : a man with the power of planning and executing work : a man capable of taking responsibility ⟨he is the *strong man* in their organization⟩ **3** : one who leads or controls by force of will and character or by military methods; *often* : DICTATOR

strong mayor *n* : a mayor in a mayor-council method of municipal government who is given by charter a large degree of control and responsibility — compare COUNCIL-MANAGER PLAN, WEAK MAYOR

strong-minded \ˈ=¦==\ *adj* : having a vigorous mind : marked by independence of thought and judgment — **strong-minded·ly** *adv* — **strong-minded·ness** *n* -ES

strong·ness *n* -ES [¹*strong* + *-ness*] : the quality or state of being strong : STRENGTH, VIGOR

strongpoint \ˈ=,=\ *n* : an organized tactical locality in a defensive position

strong room *n* **1** : a room for money or valuables specially constructed to be fireproof and burglarproof **2** : a special room for violently disturbed mental patients

strong sand *n* : molders' sand with an admixture of loam to increase its adhesiveness

strong side *n* : the side of a football formation having the greatest number of players

strong suit *n* **1** : a long suit that contains high cards **2** : a quality or characteristic in which one excels : one's forte

strong water *n* [trans. of NL *aqua fortis*] **1** *archaic* : ACID; *esp* : NITRIC ACID **2** *archaic* : distilled liquor

strong-weak \ˈ=ˈ=\ *adj* : having features of both strong and weak conjugations ⟨*tell, told* is a *strong-weak* verb⟩

strong-woolled \ˈ=ˈ=\ *or* **strong-wool** \ˈ=,=\ *adj*, *chiefly Austral* : having the relatively coarse-fibered wool characteristic of crossbred or mutton-type sheep; *also* : CROSSBRED

stron·gyle \ˈsträn,jīl\ *also* **stron·gyl** \-njəl\ *n* -S [NL *Strongylus*] **1** : any of various roundworms constituting the family Strongylidae and related to the hookworms; *esp* : a worm of *Strongylus* or closely related genera that is parasitic in the alimentary tract and tissues of the horse and may induce severe diarrhea and debility — compare CYLICOSTOME, PALISADE WORM **2** [NL *strongyla*, fr. Gk *strongylē*, fem. of *strongylos* round, compact — more at STRONGYLUS] : a rod-shaped biradiate sponge spicule with blunt ends

¹**stron·gy·lid** \-njələd\ *adj* [NL *Strongylidae*] : of or relating to the Strongylidae

²**strongylid** \"\ *n* -S : a nematode worm of the family Strongylidae

stron·gyl·i·dae \strän'jilə,dē\ *n pl*, *cap* [NL *Strongylus*, type genus + *-idae*] : a large family of nematode worms (suborder Strongylina) that are parasites of vertebrates and have a globular to cylindrical buccal capsule and a circlet of laminar processes about the mouth — see CHABERTIA, OESOPHAGOSTOMUM, STRONGYLUS

stron·gy·li·do·sis \,strănjələ'dōsəs\ *n* -ES [NL, fr. *Strongylidae* + *-osis*] : STRONGYLOSIS

stron·gyl·i·form \strän'jilə,fȯrm\ *adj* [*strongyle* + *-iform*] **1** : resembling strongyles **2** *of a larval nematode worm* : having the esophagus intermediate in character between the rhabditiform and filariform types

stron·gy·lin *or* **stron·gy·line** \ˈstränjələn, -jə,līn\ *n* -S [NL *Strongylina*] : a nematode worm of the suborder Strongylina

stron·gy·li·na \,stränjəˈlīnə\ *n pl*, *cap* [NL, fr. *Strongylus* + *-ina*] : a suborder of Rhabditida that comprises nematode worms parasitic as adults in vertebrates often with a complex life cycle involving an invertebrate larval host and includes important parasites (as the strongyles and the hookworms) of man and domestic animals

stron·gy·lo·cen·trot·i·dae \,stränjəlōsen'träd·ə,dē\ *n pl*, *cap* [NL, fr. *Strongylocentrotus*, type genus + *-idae*] : a large and nearly cosmopolitan family of typical sea urchins (order Centrechinoidea)

stron·gy·lo·cen·tro·tus \-ˈtrōd·əs\ *n*, *cap* [NL, fr. Gk *strongylos* round, compact + *kentrōtos* prickly, fr. *kentroun* to provide with a prick or sting, fr. *kentron* sharp point — more at STRONGYLUS, CENTER] : a widely distributed genus of sea urchins (family Strongylocentrotidae) that includes the common green urchin (*S. drobachiensis*) of the No. American coasts and the small purple urchin (*S. purpuratus*) of the Pacific coast as well as other common forms

¹**stron·gy·loid** \ˈstränjə,lȯid\ *adj* [NL *Strongyloidea*] : of or relating to the Strongyloidea

²**strongyloid** \"\ *n* -S [NL *Strongyloidea*] : a worm of the superfamily Strongyloidea

stron·gy·loi·dea \,==ˈlȯidēə\ *n pl*, *cap* [NL, fr. *Strongylus* + *-oidea*] : a superfamily of parasitic nematode worms (order Rhabditida) comprising the hookworms, strongyles, and related forms

stron·gy·loi·des \,stränjəˈlȯi,dēz\ *n*, *cap* [NL, fr. *Strongylus* + *-oides* -oid] : a genus (the type of the family Strongyloididae) of rhabditid nematode worms having both free-living males and females and parthenogenetic females parasitic in the intestine of various vertebrates and including some medically and economically important pests (as *S. stercoralis*) of man

stron·gy·loi·di·a·sis \,stränjə,lȯiˈdīəsəs\ *also* **stron·gy·loi·do·sis** \-ˈdōsəs\ *n* -ES [NL, fr. *Strongyloides* + *-iasis*, *-osis*] : infestation with or disease caused by nematodes of the genus *Strongyloides* occas. parasitic in the intestines of many vertebrates including man

stron·gy·lo·plas·ma·ta \,stränjəlōˈplazmədˑə\ *n pl*, *cap* [NL, fr. Gk *strongylos* round, compact + *plasmata*, pl. of *plasmat-*, *plasma* form, mold, body — more at STRONGYLUS, PLASMA] : inclusion bodies grouped taxonomically as organisms

stron·gy·lo·sis \,stränjəˈlōsəs\ *n* -ES [NL, fr. *Strongylus* + *-osis*] : infestation with or disease caused by strongyles

stron·gy·lote \ˈstränjə,lōt\ *adj* [Gk *strongylos* round + E *-ote* (as in *tylote*)] : having one end rounded — used chiefly of sponge spicules

stron·gy·lus \ˈstränjələs\ *n*, *cap* [NL, fr. Gk *strongylos* round, compact; akin to L *stringere* to bind tight, press together — more at STRAIN] : a genus (the type of the family Strongylidae) of parasitic nematode worms comprising worms with a pair of elongated buccal glands and including gastrointestinal parasites of the horse — see PALISADE WORM

stron·tia \ˈstränch(ē)ə, -ntēə\ *n* -S [NL, fr. E *strontian*] **1** : the strontium oxide SrO **2** : STRONTIUM HYDROXIDE — used chiefly commercially

stron·ti·an \-ən\ *n* -S [fr. *Strontian*, village in Argyllshire, Scotland, where it was discovered] : STRONTIUM

stron·ti·an·if·er·ous \¦stränch(ē)əˈnif(ə)rəs, -ˈäntēə¦-\ *adj* [*strontian* + *-iferous*] : containing or yielding strontian

stron·ti·an·ite \ˈstränch(ē)ə,nīt, -ˈäntēə,-\ *n* -S [*Strontian*, village in Argyllshire, Scotland + E *-ite*] : a mineral $SrCO_3$ consisting of native strontium carbonate and occurring as an orthorhombic, pale-green, white, gray, or yellowish mineral in masses of radiating needle-shaped or spear-shaped crystals or in fibrous massive forms (hardness 3.5–4, sp. gr. 3.68–3.71)

strontian white *n* : STRONTIUM WHITE

strontian yellow *n* **1** : strontium yellow or a pigment of the same color **2** : a brilliant greenish yellow that is greener and deeper than mimosa yellow

stron·tic \ˈsträntik\ *adj* [NL *strontium* + ISV *-ic*] : of or relating to strontium

stron·ti·um \ˈstränch(ē)əm, -ntēəm\ *n* -S [NL, fr. *strontia* + *-ium*] : a silver-white soft malleable and ductile bivalent metallic element of the alkaline-earth group that occurs only in combination esp. as strontianite and celestite, that is usu. obtained by electrolysis of its fused chloride or by thermal reduction of its oxide with aluminum, that turns yellowish in air, and that yields compounds capable of imparting a crimson color to flames and pyrotechnic compositions — symbol *Sr*; see ELEMENT table

strontium carbonate *n* : a crystalline salt $SrCO_3$ occurring naturally as strontianite and used chiefly in fireworks, in iridescent glass, and in making other strontium compounds

strontium hydroxide *n* : a deliquescent solid $Sr(OH)_2$ that forms a crystalline octahydrate, that dissolves in water to form a decidedly alkaline solution, and that is used chiefly in making soaps and greases and in refining beet sugar and recovering sugar from the molasses by the formation of insoluble sucrates

strontium 90 *n* : a heavy radioactive isotope of strontium having the mass number 90 and a half life of 25 years that is present in the fallout from nuclear explosions and is particularly hazardous because like calcium it can be assimilated in biological processes and deposited in the bones of human beings and animals — symbol Sr^{90} or ^{90}Sr; called also *radiostrontium*

strontium nitrate *n* : a salt $Sr(NO_3)_2$ that crystallizes from hot strong solutions in anhydrous form and from cold solutions as the tetrahydrate and that is used chiefly in fireworks, flares, and tracer bullets

strontium oxide *n* : an oxide of strontium; *esp* : the crystalline monoxide SrO resembling lime and barium monoxide

strontium salicylate *n* : a crystalline salt $Sr(C_7H_5O_3)_2.2H_2O$ used esp. formerly in medicine similarly to sodium salicylate

strontium sulfate *n* : a crystalline salt $SrSO_4$ occurring naturally as celestite and used chiefly in making other strontium compounds

strontium titanate *n* : a crystalline compound $SrTiO_3$ used chiefly as an additive to barium titanate ceramic bodies

strontium white *n* : strontium sulfate used as a pigment, extender, or filler

strontium yellow *n* : strontium chromate $SrCrO_4$ used as a yellow pigment although it has little tinting strength

strook *obs var of* STRUCK

stroop *var of* STROUP

stroot *obs var of* STRUT

¹**strop** \ˈsträp\ *n* -S [ME — more at STRAP] : STRAP: **a** : a short rope with its ends spliced to form a circle **b** : a band usu. of leather backed with liner canvas for sharpening a razor

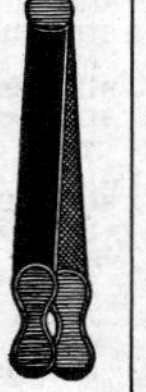

strop b

²**strop** \"\ *vt* **stropped; stropped; stropping; strops** **1** : to furnish (as a pulley block) with a strop **2** : to sharpen (a razor) on a strop

stroph- *or* **stropho-** *comb form* [Gk, fr. *strephein* to twist turn — more at STROPHE] : twisting : turning ⟨*strophosis*⟩ ⟨*strophocephaly*⟩

stro·phan·thi·din \strəˈfan(t)thədən\ *n* -S [ISV *strophanthin* + *-idin*] : a very toxic crystalline steroidal gamma-lactone $C_{23}H_{32}O_6$ obtained by hydrolysis of strophanthin, cymarin, and various other glycosides

stro·phan·thin \-thən\ *n* -S [NL *Strophanthus* + ISV *-in*] : any of several glycosides or mixtures of glycosides obtained from African apocynaceous plants of the genera *Strophanthus* and *Acocanthera*: as **a** *also* **strophanthin-K** [*strophanthin-K* fr. *Strophanthus kombé*, plant from which it is produced] : a bitter very toxic crystalline steroidal glycoside $C_{36}H_{54}O_{14}$ from the seeds and bark of an east African woody vine (*Strophanthus kombé*) that yields strophanthidin, cymarose, and glucose on hydrolysis and that is used similarly to digitalis and in Africa as an arrow poison — called also *k-strophanthin* **b** *also* **strophanthin-G** [*strophanthin-G* fr. *Strophanthus gratus*, plant from which it is produced] : OUABAIN **c** : CYMARIN

stro·phan·thus \-thəs\ *n* [NL, fr. Gk *strophos* twisted band + NL *-anthus*; fr. the twisted segments of the corolla — more at STROPHE] **1** *cap* : a genus of tropical Asiatic and African trees, shrubs, or woody vines (family Apocynaceae) that have showy flowers with a glandular calyx and a tubular corolla with five appendaged and twisted lobes and include several African forms with poisonous seeds as well as forms (as *S. kombé*) that furnish strophanthin **2** -ES : the dried cleaned ripe seeds of any of several plants of the genus *Strophanthus* (as *S. kombé* and *S. hispidus*) that are in moderate doses a cardiac stimulant like digitalis but in larger doses a violent poison and that have strophanthin as their most active constituent

stro·pha·ria \strəˈfa(a)rēə\ *n*, *cap* [NL, fr. Gk *strophos* + NL *-aria*] : a genus of brown spored gill fungi (family Agaricaceae) closely related to *Agaricus* but having gills and stipe united

stro·phe \ˈstrōfē, -fi\ *n* -S [Gk *strophē*, lit., act of turning, fr. *strephein* to twist, turn; akin to Gk *strophos* twisted band, cord, *streblos* twisted, crooked, *strabos* squint-eyed, *strobos* action of whirling, *strombos* whirling or spiral object, top, snail] **1** : the movement of the classical Greek chorus while turning from one side to the other of the orchestra — compare ANTISTROPHE **2 a** : a rhythmic system composed of two or more lines repeated as a unit; *esp* : such a unit recurring in a series of strophic units not all of which have the same internal structure — distinguished from *stanza*; compare ANTISTROPHE **b** : any arrangement of lines together as a unit : STANZA **c** : the part of a Greek choral ode sung during the strophe of the dance : the first of the three divisions of each section of a full Pindaric ode

stroph·ic \ˈsträfik, -rōf-, -fēk\ *also* **stroph·i·cal** \-fəkəl, -fēk-\ *adj* [*strophe* + *-ic*, *-ical*] **1** : relating to, containing, or consisting of strophes **2** : having the same music for successive stanzas of a song — compare THROUGH-COMPOSED — **stroph·i·cal·ly** \-fək(ə)lē\ *adv*

stroph·i·o·late \ˈsträfēə,lāt, -rōf-\ *adj* [NL *strophiolatus*, fr. *strophiolum* + *-atus* -ate] : furnished with a strophiole

stroph·i·ole \-ē,ōl\ *n* -S [NL *strophiolum*, fr. L, small wreath, dim. of *strophium* breastband, headband, fr. Gk *strophion*, fr. dim. of *strophos* twisted band, cord — more at STROPHE] **1** : an excrescence like a crest about the hilum of some seeds (as of spurge) **2** : CARUNCLE

stropho- — see STROPH-

stroph·o·me·na \,sträfəˈmēnə\ *n*, *cap* [NL, irreg. fr. Gk *strophōma* hinge (akin to Gk *strephein* to turn) + *mēnē* moon; fr. its hinge and concavo-convex shell — more at STROPHE, MOON] : a genus (the type of the family Strophomenidae) of extinct brachiopods having a long hinge, sharply limited muscle scars, and resupinate shell

stroph·o·men·i·dae \-ˈmenə,dē\ *n pl*, *cap* [NL, fr. *Strophomena*, type genus + *-idae*] : a family of Ordovician to Permian brachiopods that are usu. isolated in a distinct superfamily or suborder of Telotremata but are sometimes placed in a separate order — see STROPHOMENA

stroph·u·lus \ˈsträfyələs\ *n*, *pl* **strophu·li** \-yə,lī\ [NL, fr. Gk *strophos* twisted band — more at STROPHE] : a rash in infants marked by red or sometimes whitish papules surrounded by reddish halos and popularly associated with teething distress — called also *red gum, tooth rash*

stropped *past of* STROP

strop·per \ˈsträpə(r)\ *n* -S : one that strops; *esp* : a device for sharpening double-edged razor blades

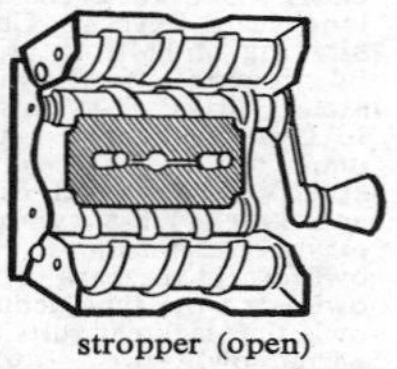

stropper (open)

stropping *pres part of* STROP

strops *pl of* STROP, *pres 3d sing of* STROP

strossers *n pl* [origin unknown] *obs* : TROUSERS

stroud \ˈstrau̇d\ *n* -S [prob. fr. *Stroud*, urban district of Gloucestershire, England, and woolen manufacturing center] **1** *also* **stroud·ing** \-diŋ\ : a coarse heavy woolen cloth usu. in plain weave formerly used in trade with No. American Indians **2** : a blanket or garment of stroud

stroup \ˈstrüp\ *n* -S [ME *stroupe*, fr. ON *strūpi*, *strjūpi*; akin to Norw dial. *strop* narrow opening, and prob. to Gk *stryphnos* astringent — more at STRUBBLY] **1** *dial chiefly Eng* : WINDPIPE **2** *chiefly Scot* : SPOUT

strove [ME *stroof* (past)] *past & chiefly dial past part of* STRIVE

strow \ˈstrō\ *vt* **strowed; strown** \-ōn\ *or* **strowed; strowing; strows** [ME *strowen* — more at STREW] *archaic* : SCATTER

syn see STREW

stroy *vb* -ED/-ING/-S [ME *struyen*, *stroyen*, short for *destruyen*, *destroyen* — more at DESTROY] *obs* : DESTROY

strsph *abbr* stratosphere

strub·bly \ˈstrəb(ə)lē, ˈstrůb-\ *adj* [PaG *schtruwwlich*; akin to OS *strūf* shaggy, OHG *strūben* to stand on end (of hair), MHG *strobel* shaggy, Gk *stryphnos* astringent, sour, harsh, Lith *strubas* lopped off short, OE *starian* to stare — more at STARE] *dial* : UNTIDY, UNKEMPT

struc *abbr* structure

¹**struck** [ME *strook* (past), fr. OE *strāc* (past)] *past of* STRIKE

²**struck** \ˈstrək\ *adj* **1** : affected strongly with love, affection, or fancy for — used with *with* or *on* ⟨~ with a girl⟩ ⟨~ on his dad —*Reader's Digest*⟩ **2 a** : closed or affected by a labor strike ⟨a ~ factory⟩ ⟨a ~ employer⟩ **b** : worked on or produced in a struck establishment ⟨~ work⟩ **3** : figured on the basis of contents being level with the top edge ⟨a sand-hauling truck with a ~ capacity of 15 cubic yards and a heaped capacity of 17 cubic yards⟩ **4** : affected by strike : FLYBLOWN ⟨~ sheep⟩

³**struck** \"\ *n* -S [²*struck*] **1** : STRIKE 20a **2** : enterotoxemia esp. of adult sheep

struck joint *n* **1** : a joint in which the mortar is recessed at the bottom with a trowel while the mortar is still green — see JOINT illustration **2** : a joint whose surface has been smoothed with a trowel

struck jury *n* : a special jury of 12 members selected from 48 taken by the sheriff indifferently from those qualified to act as special jurymen, reduced to 24 by the attorney for each side striking out the names of 12, and chosen from these 24 by the ordinary methods

struck measure *n* : LEVEL MEASURE

struct *abbr* structure

struc·tur·al \ˈstrəkchərəl, -ksh(ə)rəl\ *adj* **1 a** : of or relating to structure or a structure : affecting structure : used in building structures : CONSTRUCTIONAL ⟨a ~ error⟩ ⟨~ clay⟩ ⟨these metals have a ~ stability that should insure long life for the furniture in which they are used —Betty Pepis⟩ ⟨stands at the ~ center of the story —Charles Lee⟩ **b** : of or relating to the load-bearing members or scheme of a building as opposed to the screening or ornamental elements ⟨the ~ details of a house consist of floor joists, rafters, wall and partition studs, supporting columns . . . foundations —*Building, Estimating & Contracting*⟩ **c** : involved in or caused by structure esp. of the economy ⟨modern ~ unemployment⟩ **2** : of, relating to, or involving the physical makeup of a plant or animal body and esp. its plan of organization ⟨~ defects in the central nervous system —D.M.Hegsted & F.J.Stare⟩ ⟨the true wing is a ~ peculiarity of birds⟩ **3** : of, relating to, or resulting from the arrangement of rock bodies : resulting from the effects of folding or faulting of the earth's crust : TECTONIC ⟨a ~ plateau⟩ ⟨a ~ ridge⟩ ⟨a ~ valley⟩ **4 a** : of or relating to the social structure; *specif* : involving the arrangement of social status and stratification into a hierarchical class system **b** : stressing social structure and the interdependence of social institutions ⟨the ~ emphasis of social anthropologists⟩ **5** : concerned with or relating to structure rather than history or comparison ⟨~ linguistics⟩ : emphasizing the systematic relations of formal distinctions in a language ⟨~ grammar⟩

structural basin *n* : BASIN 4a

structural color *n* : a color or color component due to interference of light (as in thin films), diffraction (as by a grating), refractive dispersion (as in a rainbow), differential scattering, or differential polarization ⟨colors of most bodies are due largely to selective absorption with some superposed *structural color*⟩

structural engineering *n* : a branch of civil engineering dealing primarily with the design and construction of structures (as bridges, buildings, dams)

structural formula *n* : an expanded molecular formula show-

		structural formulas		
compound	molecular formula	with bonds	with covalent bonds and unshared electrons	with electrons
water	H_2O	H–O–H	H–Ö–H	H:Ö:H
acetic acid	$C_2H_4O_2$	CH_3-CO-O-H 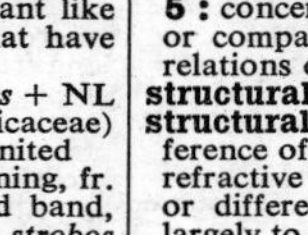	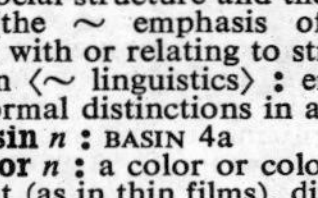	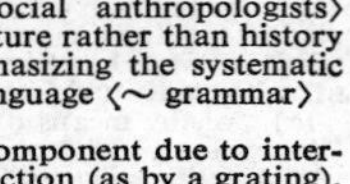
methyl formate	$C_2H_4O_2$	H-CO-O-CH_3 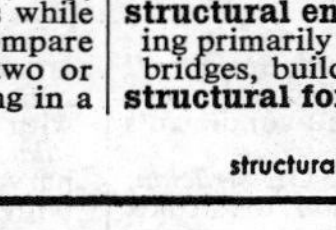		

ing the arrangement within the molecule of atoms and of bonds depicted usu. by lines or of valence electrons depicted usu. by dots — see KEKULÉ FORMULA, PERSPECTIVE FORMULA; compare BENZENE RING, OCTET 3; CHOLESTEROL illustration, CIS-TRANS ISOMERISM illustration, INDIGO illustration, MENTHANE illustration

structural–functional \¦=(=)=¦=(=)=\ *adj* **:** combining the approaches of the structuralist and functionalist schools of sociology and social anthropology; *specif* **:** analyzing established institutional relationships and their societal functioning

structural geology *n* **:** a branch of geology that deals with the form, arrangement, and internal structure of rocks — called also *geotectonic geology*

structural iron *n* **:** iron worked or cast in structural shapes

struc·tur·al·ism \'strəkchərə,lizəm, -ksh(ə)r-\ *n* -s **1 :** a theory that emphasizes the importance of structure as contrasted with function in mental life: as **a :** the introspective analysis of consciousness **b :** ORGANICISM b **2 :** the practice of structural methods in linguistics

structural isomerism *n* **:** isomerism in which atoms are linked in a different order — sometimes distinguished from *stereoisomerism;* compare POSITION ISOMERISM

¹struc·tur·al·ist \'strəkchərələst, -ksh(ə)r-\ *n* -s **1 :** an adherent or follower of structuralism **2 :** one stressing the more formal, organizational aspects of social life (as embodied in kinship regulations, marriage forms, clan and moiety systems)

²structuralist \"\ *also* **struc·tur·al·is·tic** \¦=(=)=¦listik\ *adj* **:** of or relating to structuralism

struc·tur·al·iza·tion \,strəkchərələ'zāshən, -ksh(ə)r-, -,lī'z-\ *n* -s **1 :** the process of structuralizing **2 a :** assimilation into a formal social structure ⟨the ~ of clerical duties⟩ **b :** embodiment of social and cultural patterns of thought in the individual personality ⟨the ~ of a person's outlook by his environment⟩

struc·tur·al·ize \'=(=)=,līz\ *vt* -ED/-ING/-s **:** to embody in structural or material form: as **a :** to embody (a function or group of functions) in an organic or other organizational structure **b :** to incorporate into a formal pattern or institution ⟨culture ~*s* individual behavior⟩

structural lumber *n* **:** lumber that is intended for use where working stresses are required and that is two or more inches thick and four or more inches wide

struc·tur·al·ly \-lē, -li\ *adv* **:** in a structural manner **:** in regard to structure

structural psychology *n* **:** STRUCTURALISM 1

structural steel *also* **structural** *n* -s **1 :** rolled steel in structural shapes **2 :** steel suitable for structural shapes

structural terrace *n* **:** a local flattening in an otherwise uniformly tilted series of strata

struc·tur·a·tion \,strəkchə'rāshən, -kshə'-\ *n* -s **1 :** the interrelation of parts in an organized whole **2 :** STRUCTURALIZATION 2b

¹struc·ture \'strəkchə(r), -ksh-\ *n* -s [ME, fr. L *structura,* fr. *structus* (past part. of *struere* to pile up, arrange, build) + *-ura* -ure; akin to L *strues* heap, *sternere* to spread out, throw down — more at STREW] **1 :** the action of building **:** CONSTRUCTION **2 a :** something constructed or built ⟨a laboratory housed in a temporary wooden ~⟩ ⟨the dam is a massive ~⟩ ⟨demolish any building, highway, road, railroad, excavation, or other ~ —T.W.Arnold⟩ ⟨a ~ of posts or stakes across a stream —F.W. Bradley⟩ ⟨~*s* experimented with . . . : oxygen-pressure suits, oxygen-pressure balloon gondolas and pressure cabin airplanes —H.G.Armstrong⟩ ⟨all vegetable fibrous ~*s* felted from a water suspension on a wire screen —*Paper & Paperboard*⟩; *esp* **:** a building of imposing size **:** EDIFICE ⟨the civic auditorium . . . is the city's most important public ~ —*Amer. Guide Series: Mich.*⟩ **b :** something made up of more or less interdependent elements or parts **:** something having a definite or fixed pattern of organization ⟨leaves and other complex plant ~*s*⟩ ⟨a glandular ~ at the base of the brain⟩ ⟨light provided by a fluorescent ~⟩ ⟨collapse the delicate, incomplete ~ of agreement —Kenneth Love⟩ ⟨the Nazi ~ of falsified facts and perverted history —Alfred Frankfurter⟩ ⟨any object which is in some sense an organized whole is said to have, or to be characterized by, ~ —W.C.Clement⟩ ⟨the political and institutional ~ of the Commonwealth has been built, and continues to develop, round this living core of tradition and culture —H.D.Hall⟩ ⟨events, or material objects, whose mutual spatial relationships are regarded as constant, constitute a ~ —L.A.White⟩ **3 :** the manner of construction **:** the way in which the parts of something are put together or organized **:** FORM, MAKEUP ⟨a rambling country house, basically Gothic in plan, ~, and mass —H.S.Morrison⟩ ⟨~ means the ways in which the stars are organized into clusters and other multiple systems —G.W.Gray b.1886⟩ ⟨primitive societies are . . . pretty rigid and uniform in ~ —J.D.Adams⟩ ⟨the ~ of a novel⟩ **4 :** the arrangement of particles or parts in a substance or body ⟨the ~ of soil⟩ ⟨the ~ of a plant⟩ ⟨the ~ of an animal⟩: as **a :** the arrangement and mode of union of the atoms in a molecule — compare CONSTITUTION 4 **b :** the attitude and relative positions of rock masses consequent upon deformative processes (as folding, faulting, and igneous intrusion) ⟨an anticlinal ~⟩ ⟨a basin-and-range ~⟩ ⟨an alpine ~⟩ **c :** the arrangement of a rock mass with respect to the larger features (as jointing, columnar and platy parting, bedding) — compare TEXTURE **5 :** the interrelation of parts as dominated by the general character of the whole ⟨economic ~⟩ ⟨financial ~⟩ ⟨personality ~⟩ ⟨political ~⟩ ⟨symphonic ~⟩ ⟨tax ~⟩ — see SOCIAL STRUCTURE **6 :** the elements or parts of an entity or the position of such elements or parts in their external relationships to each other: as **a** (1) **:** the components of a language (as phonemes, morphemes) and the way in which they are related — compare PHONEMICS, MORPHOPHONEMICS, MORPHOLOGY, SYNTAX (2) **:** the finite system of such components and their relations **b** (1) **:** the composition of conscious experience with its elements and their combinations (2) **:** GESTALT (3) **:** the anatomical basis of behavior consisting esp. of nerve and muscle tissue **7 :** the element that is common to all true interpretations of a logical or mathematical calculus

²structure \"\ *vb* **structured; structured; structuring** \-kchər, -ksh(ə)r + -iŋ\ **structures** *vt* **1 :** to form into an organized structure **:** BUILD, ORGANIZE ⟨the author has *structured* his book as a simple chronology —E.B.Pettet⟩ ⟨this book succeeds in *structuring* an admirable vantage point —J.G. Brin⟩ ⟨the male in the old-style mammal was largely *structured* for aggressive competition —Weston La Barre⟩ ⟨the way in which our collegiate education is *structured* —E.A.Walker⟩: as **a** (1) **:** STRUCTURALIZE (2) **:** to put into a meaningful frame of reference ⟨a theory to ~ empirical research⟩ ⟨the part of television in *structuring* public events⟩ **b :** to establish the relationship between components of: as (1) **:** to define the psychological relationships in ⟨~ a situation⟩ ⟨~ the perceptual field⟩ (2) **:** to formalize the role of (as a psychotherapist or a patient) (3) **:** to set up the rules or the agenda to be followed in (as an interview or a test) with respect to interpersonal conduct **2 :** to assign (a linguistic element) to a function or a relation within a system ~ *vi* **:** to function or become related — used of a linguistic element

structured *adj* **:** having definite structure **:** exhibiting organized structure or differentiation of parts

struc·ture·less \'==ləs\ *adj* **:** lacking definite structure or organization; *usu* **:** devoid of cells **:** HOMOGENEOUS ⟨a ~ membrane⟩ — **struc·ture·less·ness** *n* -ES

stru·del \'s(h)trüdᵊl\ *n* -s [G, lit., whirlpool, fr. MHG; akin to OHG *stredan* to bubble, Gk *rhothos* roar of the waves, noise, Skt *sarati* it flows — more at SERUM] **:** a sheet of paper-thin dough rolled up with any of various fillings and baked

¹strug·gle \'strəgəl\ *vb* **struggled; struggled; struggling** \-g(ə)liŋ\ **struggles** [ME *struglen*] *vi* **1 :** to make violent, strenuous, labored, or convulsive exertions or efforts against difficult or forceful opposition or impeding or constraining circumstances **:** STRIVE, CONTEND ⟨they *struggled* about the through as furiously as a litter of pigs —T.B.Costain⟩ ⟨with the driven rationality of church fathers *struggling* to formulate and express the accepted import of the Faith delivered to the saints —H.O.Taylor⟩ ⟨the story of the human spirit *struggling* with sin —R.A.Hall b.1911⟩ ⟨*struggled* bravely against poverty —C.M.Fuess⟩ ⟨the law has had to ~ with these problems —B.N.Cardozo⟩ ⟨the point of view I am *struggling* to attack —T.S.Eliot⟩ **2 :** to proceed with difficulty or with great effort ⟨*struggled* through ancient exits never big enough to handle the crowd —Claudia Cassidy⟩ ⟨the lamplight *struggled* out through the fog —Oscar Wilde⟩ ⟨fell over prostrate trees, sank into deep holes and *struggled* out —Willa Cather⟩ ⟨ancient Egypt was just *struggling* out of barbarism —Geoffrey Boumphrey⟩ ⟨the band *struggled* through the . . . national anthem —*Time*⟩ ⟨the college *struggled* along until 1855 —*Amer. Guide Series: La.*⟩ ~ *vt* **:** to bring to a desired state or condition by or as if by a struggle ⟨*struggled* down the last of his emotions —R.L. Stevenson⟩ **syn** see TRY

²struggle \"\ *n* -s **1 :** an act of earnest striving **:** a violent effort or exertion (as to obtain an object, overcome a difficulty, or avert an evil) ⟨if he makes no effort — shrinking without a ~ from his duty — he himself will not be the less certainly perish —Thomas De Quincey⟩ ⟨a ~ for freedom of thought⟩ ⟨a ~ with disease⟩ ⟨the boy had a ~ for a living⟩ ⟨the orchestra's ~ for survival⟩ **2 :** CONTEST, CONTENTION, STRIFE ⟨the ~ between the natural sciences and religion ended in an armistice —Zechariah Chafee⟩ ⟨attempts to express in musical form the ~ between sacred and profane love —Edward Sackville-West & Desmond Shawe-Taylor⟩ ⟨the ~ with communism⟩ ⟨a ~ over a political issue⟩ ⟨a legal ~⟩ ⟨in the course of the ~ he was made prisoner and harshly treated —E.M.Coulter⟩

struggle for existence : the automatic competition of the members of a natural population for a limited supply of vital necessities resulting in elimination of inadequately adapted individuals and hence in selection of the better-adapted as breeding stock — compare NATURAL SELECTION

strug·gler \-g(ə)lə(r)\ *n* -s **:** one that struggles

struggling *adj* **:** engaged in a struggle esp. to overcome poverty or obscurity ⟨a ~ artist⟩ ⟨a ~ school⟩ — **strug·gling·ly** *adv*

struld·brug \'strəl(d),brəg\ *n* -s *usu cap* [*Struldbrug,* one of a class among the inhabitants of the imaginary country Luggnagg, in the book *Gulliver's Travels* (1726) by Jonathan Swift †1745 Eng. satirist, composed of persons who can never die] **:** one of a class of imaginary persons who can never die but who are declared dead in law at the age of 80 and live on wretchedly at state expense

¹strum \'strəm\ *n* -s [ME *strom, strumme*] **:** STRAINER ⟨a wickerwork ~ for straining malt⟩ ⟨a metal ~ for a suction pipe of a pump⟩

²strum \"\ *vb* **strummed; strummed; strumming; strums** [imit.] *vt* **:** to play on or as if on (a stringed musical instrument) esp. in an offhand or careless way **:** THRUM ⟨~ a guitar⟩ ⟨the howling winds *strummed* the rigging —H.A.Chippendale⟩ ~ *vi* **:** to play on or as if on a stringed musical instrument ⟨a rain of missiles that *strummed* against the canvas —Lilian Brown⟩

³strum \"\ *n* -s **:** the act or sound of strumming ⟨the ~ of typewriters —John Summerson⟩

stru·ma \'strümə\ *n, pl* **stru·mae** \-ü,mē, -,mī\ [L, scrofulous enlargement of glands, goiter] **1 :** enlargement of an organ (as a breast or lymph gland); *specif* **:** GOITER **2** [NL, fr. L] **:** a cushion-shaped swelling on any organ; *esp* **:** a swelling at the base of the capsule in many mosses

stru·mel·la \strü'melə\ *n, cap* [NL, fr. L *struma* + NL *-ella*] **:** a form genus of imperfect fungi (family Tuberculariaceae) characterized by ovate nonseptate brown conidia

strum·mer \'strəmə(r)\ *n* -s **:** one that strums (as on a piano or mandolin)

stru·mose \'strü,mōs\ *adj* [L *strumosus* having a scrofulous swelling of glands, fr. *struma* + *-osus* -ose] **:** having a struma

stru·mous \-məs\ *adj* [L *strumosus*] **:** having, relating to, or connected with a struma; *specif* **:** GOITROUS

¹strum·pet \'strəmpət, *usu* -əd·+V\ *n* -s [ME *strumpet, strompet*] **:** PROSTITUTE, HARLOT

²strumpet \"\ *vt* -ED/-ING/-s **1** *obs* **:** DEBAUCH **2 :** to brand as a strumpet **3 :** BELIE, SLANDER

strung *past of* STRING

strung–up \'=¦=\ *adj* [fr. past part. of *string up,* v.] **:** HIGH-STRUNG

¹strunt \'strənt, -ru̇nt\ *n* -s [obs. E *strunt,* adj., stubby, perh. alter. of E ¹*stunt*] **1** *chiefly Scot & dial Eng* **:** the stump of a tail **2** *chiefly Scot & dial Eng* **:** a tail denuded of feathers or hair

²strunt \"\ *vt, dial chiefly Eng* **:** to dock (a tail)

³strunt \"\ *n* -s [origin unknown] *dial Brit* **:** DISPLEASURE, AFFRONT, OFFENSE

⁴strunt \'strənt\ *vi* [by alter.] *Scot* **:** STRUT

⁵strunt \"\ *n* -s [origin unknown] *Scot* **:** LIQUOR

¹strut \'strət, *usu* -əd·+V\ *vb* **strutted; strutted; strutting; struts** [ME *strouten,* fr. OE *strūtian* to exert oneself; akin to MHG *striuzen* to resist, ON *strūtr* conical upper part of a hood, L *struma* scrofulous enlargement of glands, goiter, OE *starian* to stare — more at STARE] *vi* **1 :** to become turgid **:** SWELL ⟨freshly cut unwilted tobacco plants ~ when exposed to rain⟩ **2 :** to walk with a lofty proud gait and an erect head; *esp* **:** to walk with pomposity or affected dignity **:** SWAGGER ⟨pompous little dictator swells with pride and importance as he ~*s* up and down his study —Martin Turnell⟩ ⟨when he has a little spurt of good fortune, he patronizes all his friends and starts to ~ —Erle Stanley Gardner⟩ ⟨the simple words have been made to ~ and posture and take on an emphasis which makes them ridiculous —Virginia Woolf⟩ ~ *vt* **1 :** to stretch or thrust out **:** PROTRUDE, BULGE, DISTEND ⟨should the udder still remain highly *strutted* —*Dairy Goat*⟩ **2 a :** to walk over with a swaggering gait **:** stride proudly over **b :** to deliver (as a speech or an actor's lines) in a swaggering manner **c :** to parade (as fine clothes or jewelry) with a show of pride ⟨the boys who labor in the music halls and show shops *strutted* their most elaborate accomplishments —*N.Y.Times*⟩ — **strut one's stuff** *slang* **:** to display one's best work **:** show off

²strut \"\ *n* -s **1 a :** a bar (as a member in a frame, structure, or machine) designed to resist pressure in the direction of its length ⟨a basement floor may be used as a ~ between opposite walls —C.W.Dunham⟩ ⟨a ~ supporting a rafter⟩ ⟨an airplane landing-gear ~⟩ ⟨a ~ of thin bone in the cavity of a long bone⟩ — compare BRACKET, STAY, TIE; see ROOF illustration **b :** an outboard support between the stern tube and the propeller on a ship having more than one propeller shaft **2 a :** the act of strutting **:** a pompous step or walk ⟨his walk was a self-important ~ —A.W.Turnbull⟩ **b :** OSTENTATION

³strut \"\ *vt* **strutted; strutted; strutting; struts** [²*strut*] **:** to provide, stiffen, support, or hold apart with or as if with a strut

strutbeam *n* **:** a beam used as a strut; *specif* **:** COLLAR BEAM

struth \'strüth\ *interj* [short for *God's truth*] — used as a mild oath

stru·thi·an \'strüthēən, -üth-\ *adj* [NL *Struthio* + E *-an*] **:** STRUTHIOUS

stru·thi·form \'strüthə,fȯrm, -üth-\ *or* **stru·thii·form** \-thēə-,fȯrm, -thē-\ *adj* [*struthi-* (fr. NL *Struthio*) + *-form* or *-iform*] **:** resembling an ostrich

stru·thio \'strüthē(,)ō, -üth-\ *n, cap* [NL *Struthion-, Struthio,* fr. LL, ostrich, irreg. fr. Gk *strouthos* ostrich, sparrow; perh. akin to OE *thrysce* thrush — more at THRUSH] **:** a genus (the type of the family Struthionidae) of birds comprising the African ostriches — **stru·thi·oid** \'==,ȯid\ *adj or n*

stru·thio·mi·mus \,==(,)=ˈmīməs\ *n, cap* [NL, fr. *Struthio* + *-mimus*] **:** a genus of small light-boned saurischian dinosaurs lacking teeth, resembling ostriches in size and proportions, and found in the Upper Cretaceous of Alberta, Canada

stru·thi·o·nes \,==ˈō,nēz\ *n pl, cap* [NL, fr. LL, pl. of *struthion-, struthio* ostrich] **1** *in former classifications* **:** a major division of Aves equivalent to Ratitae **2** *in some classifications* **:** a suborder or other group equivalent to Struthioniformes

stru·thi·on·i·dae \,==ˈänə,dē\ *n pl, cap* [NL, fr. *Struthion-, Struthio,* type genus + *-idae*] **:** a family of ratite birds (order Struthioniformes) comprising the African ostriches or made coextensive with the order or in former classifications including also the rheas and various other ratite birds

stru·thi·on·i·form \,==¦änə,fȯrm\ *adj* [NL *Struthioniformes*] **:** of or relating to the Struthioniformes **:** resembling an ostrich

¹stru·thi·on·i·for·mes \,==,==ˈfȯr,mēz\ *n pl, cap* [NL, fr. *Struthion-, Struthio* + *-iformes*] **:** an order of tall terrestrial birds (superorder Neognathae) comprising the ostriches and related extinct birds

²struthioniformes \"\ [NL, fr. *Struthion-, Struthio* + *-iformes*] *syn of* TINAMIFORMES

stru·thi·o·nine \'==,ə,nīn, -,nən\ *adj* [NL *Struthion-, Struthio* + E *-ine*] **:** STRUTHIOUS

stru·thi·ous \'==əs\ *adj* [L *struthio* ostrich + E *-ous*] **:** of or relating to the ostriches and related birds **:** RATITE

strut·ter \'strəd·ə(r), -ətə-\ *n* -s [ME *strouter* one that blusters, fr. *strouten* to swell, bulge, bluster + *-er* — more at STRUT] **:** one that struts

¹strutting *adj* [ME *stroutinge* that swells or bulges, fr. pres. part. of *strouten* to swell, bulge] **:** that struts — **strut·ting·ly** *adv*

²strut·ting \'strəd·iŋ, -ətiŋ, -ēŋ\ *n* -s [²*strut* + *-ing*] **:** STRUTS; *specif* **:** BRIDGING 2

strut·ty \'strəd·ē, -ətē, -i\ *adj* -ER/-EST **1 :** inclined or disposed to strut ⟨he was smallish and ~ —H.L.Davis⟩ **2 :** marked by a strut ⟨his ~, bull-like posture —Adria Langley⟩

stru·vite \'strü,vīt\ *n* -s [Sw *struveit,* fr. H. C. G. von *Struve* †1851 Russ. diplomat + Sw *-it* -ite] **:** a mineral $Mg(NH_4)(PO_4).6H_2O$ consisting of a hydrous ammonium magnesium phosphate and occurring in white orthorhombic-hemimorphic crystals (hardness 2, sp. gr. 1.7)

strych·nia \'striknēə\ *n* -s [NL, fr. *Strychnos*] **:** STRYCHNINE

strych·nic \-nik, -nēk\ *adj* [ISV *strychn-* (fr. NL *Strychnos*) + *-ic*] **:** of, relating to, or produced by strychnine ⟨~ poisoning⟩

¹strych·nine \'strik,nīn, -,nən, -,nēn\ *n* -s [F, fr. NL *Strychnos* + F *-ine*] **1 :** a very poisonous bitter crystalline alkaloid $C_{21}H_{22}N_2O_2$ obtained from various plants of the genus *Strychnos* (as nux vomica and St.-Ignatius's-bean) and used in medicine chiefly in the form of the sulfate or phosphate as a tonic and stimulant for the central nervous system and also as a rodenticide **2 :** NUX VOMICA 2

²strychnine \"\ *vt* -ED/-ING/-s **:** to poison by strychnine

strych·nin·ism \-,nizəm\ *n* -s [ISV ¹*strychnine* + *-ism*] **:** a toxic condition produced by the excessive use of strychnine **:** chronic strychnine poisoning

strych·nin·iza·tion \,=(,)nə'zāshən, -,nī'z-\ *n* -s [¹*strychnine* + *-ization*] **:** the act of strychninizing

strych·nin·ize \'=(,)nə,nīz\ *vt* -ED/-ING/-s [¹*strychnine* + *-ize*] **:** to subject to the action of strychnine

strych·nos \'striknəs, -,näs\ *n, cap* [NL, fr. L, nightshade, fr. Gk] **:** a large genus of tropical trees and woody tendril-climbing vines (family Loganiaceae) having 3- to 5-nerved leaves, cymose flowers with a salver-shaped corolla, and a 2-celled ovary that becomes in fruit a berry with a thick rind — see CURARE, NUX VOMICA, STRYCHNINE; compare BRUCINE

stry·mon \'strī,män\ *n, cap* [NL, prob. fr. Gk *Strymōn* Strymon, river in southwestern Bulgaria and northern Greece] **:** a large and widely distributed genus of hairstreak butterflies including a few (as *S. melinus*) with larvae that are destructive pests of various economic plants

strype *Scot var of* ¹STRIPE

STS *abbr* **1** serologic test for syphilis **2** special treatment steel

stsm *abbr* statesman

¹stu·art \'st(y)üə(r)t, -)ü(ə)rt, -)u̇ət, *usu* -d·+V\ *n* -s *usu cap* [*Stuart,* Scottish and English royal house] **:** a member or supporter of the British house of Stuart

²stuart \"\ *adj, usu cap* **:** of, relating to, or characteristic of the period or reigns of the Stuart kings of England — compare JACOBEAN, CAROLINE, RESTORATION

stu·ar·tia \st(y)ü'ärsh(ē)ə, -rd·ēə\ *syn of* STEWARTIA

¹stub \'stəb\ *n* -s *often attrib* [ME *stubb, stubbe,* fr. OE *stubb, stybb;* akin to ON *stubbi* stub, *stūfr* stump, Gk *stypos* stem, stump, *typtein* to beat, strike — more at TYPE] **1 a :** the part of a tree or plant that remains fixed in the earth when the stem is cut down or broken off **:** STUMP, SNAG ⟨solitary woodpeckers were drilling on the dead ~*s* —Hugh Fosburgh⟩ **b :** a short piece of a broken or trimmed branch remaining on the stem or trunk **2 :** something fashioned or worn to a short or blunt shape: as **a :** an old or worn nail or piece of iron **b :** FENCE 6 **c :** STUB TENON **d :** a short broad file with a handle projecting at an angle suitable for filing broad flat surfaces **e :** a pen with a short blunt nib **f :** a usu. cylindrical and often metallic protuberance used to tune or adjust the impedance of transmission lines at such high frequencies that conventional coils and condensers are impractical **3 :** a short blunt portion (as of a pencil, candle, or cigarette) remaining after the larger part has been broken off or used up **4 :** something that appears cut short or stunted **:** a rudimentary growth (as of a feather or horn) **5 a :** a small portion of each leaf (as of a checkbook or receipt book) permanently attached to the backbone for memoranda of the contents of the part filled out and torn away **b :** the portion of a ticket (as of admission or of a checking service) torn off and returned to the user for verification or identification **6 :** GUARD 9a, 9b **7 :** a vertical column at the extreme left side of a statistical or mathematical table usu. containing items of subject matter that are treated in vertical columns to its right **8 :** STUB TRACK

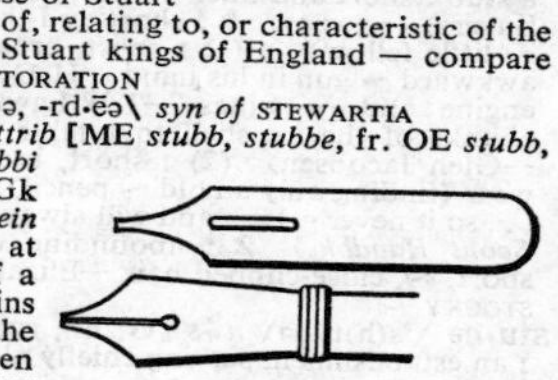

stubs 2e

²stub \"\ *vt* **stubbed; stubbed; stubbing; stubs** [ME *stubben,* fr. *stubb, stubbe,* n.] **1 a :** to grub or dig up by the roots **:** root out — usu. used with *up* ⟨*stubbing up* thornbushes⟩ ⟨the forest was gradually felled and *stubbed* up —A.C.Benson⟩ **b :** to remove trees, stumps, or scrub growth from (land) ⟨~*s* the heath to make his garden⟩ **c :** to hew or cut down (a tree) close to the ground **2 a** *archaic* **:** to reduce or wear down to a stub **b :** to make (as a knife or pencil) blunt at the point **3 :** to lame (a horse) by allowing to walk over stubs ⟨brought the horse home badly *stubbed*⟩ **4 a :** to crush or drive (as stone) into the ground **:** PULVERIZE **b :** to extinguish (as a cigarette) by crushing ⟨finished his cigarette, *stubbed* it on the floor —Victor Canning⟩ — often used with *out* ⟨smoked her cigarette . . . then she *stubbed* it out —Elizabeth Goudge⟩ **5 :** to strike (one's foot or toe) against a stub or stone ⟨*stubbed* his toe and fell heavily⟩ **6 :** GUARD 6 **7 :** to pluck the pinfeathers from (a fowl) ⟨birds are usually *stubbed* by female labor —W.P.Blount⟩

stub axle *n* **:** an axle supporting only one wheel and carried at the other end on the vehicle frame or some other support

stub·bi·ness \-bēnəs, -bin-\ *n* -ES **:** the quality or state of being stubby

¹stub·ble \'stəbəl\ *n* -s *often attrib* [ME *stuble, stubbel, stouple,* fr. OF *estuble, stuble,* fr. L *stupula* stalk, straw, alter. of *stipula* — more at STIPULE] **1 a stubbles** *pl* **:** a stump of a cultivated plant (as wheat, corn, clover, beans, or grasses) left in the ground after cutting or harvest ⟨the crisp fresh ~*s* dotted with shocked-up wheat and oats —Anthony West⟩ **b :** such stumps left in a field or area ⟨cattle are seen in the rice ~ during the fall and winter —*Amer. Guide Series: La.*⟩ **2 :** the straw of grain or other stalks remaining after the harvest **3 :** a rough surface or growth resembling stubble; *esp* **:** a short growth of beard ⟨the black unshaven ~ of his jaw —R.P. Warren⟩ **4 :** short wool left on the sheep after shearing ⟨leaves enough ~ to protect sheep from cold —*advt*⟩ **5 :** a blunt bristle (as in some mutant of drosophilas)

²stubble \"\ *vt* **stubbled; stubbled; stubbling** \-b(ə)liŋ\ **stubbles :** to leave in stubble **:** cover with stubble ⟨the *stubbled* prairies spread around her —Ethel Wilson⟩ ⟨black whiskers *stubbled* the small chin —K.M.Dodson⟩

stubbleberry \'== — *see* BERRY\ *n* **:** WONDERBERRY

stubble crop *n* **1 :** a crop (as soybeans, buckwheat, turnips) sown on stubble after the grain is harvested for turning under as green manure **2 :** a ratoon crop esp. of sugarcane

stubble field *also* **stubble** *n* -s **:** a field covered with stubble after harvesting

stubble goose *n* **:** GREYLAG

stubble mulch *n* **:** a lightly tilled mulch of stubble and plant residue left on the surface of the ground to prevent erosion, conserve moisture, and add organic matter to the soil

stubble–mulch farming *n* **:** TRASH FARMING

stubble plow *n* **:** a stirring plow with a steep moldboard for stubble land

stubble quail *n* **:** an Australian quail (*Coturnix pectoralis*)

stubble spurge *n* **:** SPOTTED SPURGE

stub·bly \'stəb(ə)lē, -li\ *adj* -ER/-EST **1 :** covered with stubble **:** STUBBLED ⟨our walk across ~ fields —May Sarton⟩ **2 :** resembling stubble ⟨having ~ hair —G.K.Chesterton⟩

¹stub·born \'stəbə(r)n\ *adj* [ME *stibourne, stuborn, stoburne,* perh. irreg. fr. *stubb, stubbe* stub — more at STUB] **1 a :** unreasonably or perversely unyielding in character or quality **:** PIGHEADED, MULISH ⟨break the ~ will which had been perverted at the source —Henry Miller⟩ ⟨jeopardized . . . by his ~ and tactless maneuvers —A.L.Funk⟩ ⟨~ carelessness⟩ ⟨~ rage⟩ **b :** fixed, resolute, or justifiably unyielding in character or purpose **:** DETERMINED, DOGGED ⟨the resources of the ~ mind, the stout heart —A.E.Stevenson b. 1900⟩ ⟨~ yeomen who parade their independence —V.L.Parrington⟩ ⟨~ conviction⟩ ⟨~ courage⟩ ⟨~ resistance⟩ **c :** unyielding, defiant, or resolute in cast or appearance ⟨had a ~ profile, like a willful horse —Katherine A. Porter⟩ ⟨under the ~ arch of their brows —Waiter O'Meara⟩ **2 a :** difficult to handle, work, or manage **:** RESISTANT, REFRACTORY ⟨was able to start a ~ fire engine —V.G.Heiser⟩ ⟨the lashes standing ~ and thick along the lowered lid —Kay Boyle⟩ ⟨sometimes the soil proved too ~ for even this hardy people —*Amer. Guide Series: N.H.*⟩ ⟨methods for dealing with ~ problems —Theodore Draper⟩ **b :** difficult to treat or cure **:** unresponsive to care **:** CHRONIC, PERSISTENT ⟨methods . . . dermatologists use today in treating ~ cases —Marjorie Vetter⟩ ⟨~ germ plasm's successive ways of surrounding itself with an ever more secure environment —Weston La Barre⟩ ⟨only a pathological condition could account for a depression so ~ and dangerous —L.C.Douglas⟩ **3 :** hard, stiff, or rigid in texture or substance ⟨in a lapidary inscription . . . shapes easy to cut in ~ material would be his chief concern —F.W Goudy⟩ ⟨gathering force . . . to break the ~, granite headlands —*Amer. Guide Series: Maine*⟩ **4 :** performed or carried on in a stubborn manner ⟨a result of long and ~ fighting —*Times Lit. Supp.*⟩ ⟨made a ~ living from repertory troupes for 8 years —*Current Biog.*⟩ **5 :** continually and unremittingly existent **:** ENDURING ⟨the ~ life of small religious bodies transplanted in America from Europe —W.L.Sperry⟩ ⟨the family . . . most ~ of all social units —Edward Sapir⟩ ⟨a ~ tradition of hope—A.M.Schlesinger b. 1917⟩ ⟨in the face of ~ facts —Norman Kelman⟩ **syn** see OBSTINATE

²stubborn \"\ *vt* -ED/-ING/-S **:** to make stubborn

stubborn child *n* **:** a minor (as in the state of Massachusetts) who refuses to submit to the lawful commands of parent or guardian and may be punished by six months imprisonment or by a fine — compare WAYWARD CHILD

stubborn disease *n* **:** a persistent virus disease of citrus characterized by shortened internodes resulting in stiff brushy growth, by the appearance of chlorotic leaves early in the season, and by a reduced crop of often acorn-shaped fruit — see ACORN DISEASE

stub·born·ly *adv* [ME *stoberlie,* fr. *stibourne, stuborn, stoburne* stubborn + *-lie, -ly* -ly] **:** in a stubborn manner **:** with stubbornness

stub·born·ness \-n(n)əs\ *n* -ES [ME *styburnesse, stobournesse,* fr. *stibourne, stuborn, stoburne* stubborn + *-nesse* -ness] **:** the quality or state of being stubborn

stub·by \'stəbē, -bi\ *adj* -ER/-EST [¹*stub* + *-y*] **1 a :** resembling a stub **:** short and thick or wide in growth or development ⟨~ fingers⟩ ⟨~ arms⟩ **b :** short and thickset in build **:** SQUAT ⟨a ~ little fellow⟩ **c** (1) **:** short, broad, or blunt in design ⟨an awkward ~ gun in his hand —H.D.Skidmore⟩ ⟨big air-cooled engine and ~ wings —T.W.Lawson⟩ ⟨might cause great chunks of the ice shelf to tumble down upon our ~ vessel —Glen Jacobsen⟩ (2) **:** short, broad, or blunt from use or wear ⟨finding only an old ~ pencil⟩ ⟨filing the flat of the blade . . . so it never gets ~ and will always bite into the wood —*Boy Scout Handbk.*⟩ **2 :** abounding with stubs **:** BRISTLY ⟨his short, ~, close-clipped hair —Elizabeth M. Roberts⟩ **syn** see STOCKY

stu·be \'s(h)tübə\ *n* -S [G, lit., room — more at BIERSTUBE] **:** an establishment serving chiefly alcoholic beverages and esp. beer

stub end *n* **:** either end of a connecting rod containing the bearing for the crankpin or the crosshead pin

stub–end feeder *n* **:** a feeder that connects a load with its only source of power

stub feather *n* **:** PINFEATHER

stub hoe *n* **:** a stout hoe for grubbing up stubs or stumps

stub mortise *n* **:** a mortise passing only part way through the timber

stubrunner \'=,==\ *n* **:** a corn planter or cotton planter furrow opener adapted for use in trashy soil

stubs *pl of* STUB, *pres 3d sing of* STUB

stub station *n* **:** a railroad station at which the tracks terminate — compare THROUGH STATION

stub switch *n* **:** a railroad switch in which the track rails are cut off squarely at the toe and the point rails are thrown to line up with the lead rails

stub tenon *n* **:** a tenon to fit a stub mortise

stub tooth *n* **:** a short gear tooth of great strength with a large angle of obliquity

stub track *n* **:** a track connected with another at one end only

¹stuc·co \'stə(,)kō\ *n, pl* **stuccos** *or* **stuccoes** [It, of Gmc origin; akin to OHG *stucki* piece, crust — more at STOCK] **1 a :** a material now usu. made of portland cement, sand, and a small percentage of lime and applied in a plastic state to form a hard covering for the exterior walls or surfaces of a building or structure **b :** a fine plaster of high quality used in the decoration and ornamentation of interior walls **2 :** STUCCOWORK **3 :** DEAUVILLE SAND

²stucco \"\ *vt* **stuccoed; stuccoed; stuccoing; stuccoes** *or* **stuccos 1 :** to overlay or decorate with stucco ⟨the doorcases are generally *~ed,* with Ionic or Roman Doric shafts supporting . . . pediments —*Country Life*⟩ **2 :** to coat (as a wall) with stucco ⟨streets lined with gray *~ed* houses —J.M.Brinnin⟩

stuccowork \'=(,)=,=\ *n* **:** decoration, design, or work done in stucco

stuck *past of* STICK

stuck·ling \'stəklən, 'stük-\ *n* [origin unknown] *dial Eng* **:** an apple turnover

stuck–up \'=,=\ *adj* [fr. past part. of *stick up*] **:** assuming or exhibiting an unwarranted attitude of superiority or self-importance **:** CONCEITED ⟨knew . . . that if she sat out the dance she would at once be damned as *stuck-up* —E.A.McCourt⟩

¹stud \'stəd\ *n* -S *often attrib* [ME *stod,* fr. OE *stōd;* akin to OHG *stuot* stud, ON *stōth* stud, OE *standan* to stand — more at STAND] **1 a :** a group of broodmares and stallions kept for breeding ⟨dictated the break-up of this mare's wonderful ~ —*London Calling*⟩ **b :** a group of animals kept or maintained for selective propagation ⟨a ~ of light canaries could very soon be transformed into one of dark selfs —*All-Pets Mag.*⟩ **2 :** an establishment or farm where horses are kept for breeding ⟨one of the most modern and well equipped trotting *~s* in this state —*Sporting Life*⟩ **3 a :** a group of horses bred or kept by one owner ⟨owner of a ~ of blooded horses —C.G.Bowers⟩ ⟨each omnibus claimed the services of a ~ of ten horses —Hugh McCausland⟩ **b :** a group of animals of a particular kind belonging to one owner ⟨my own ~ built from six generations of red siskin breeding —*All-Pets Mag.*⟩ **4 a** [by shortening] **:** STUDHORSE **b :** a male animal kept for breeding esp. for public use for a fee — compare BROOD 4 **c :** an outstanding plant selected for use in breeding because of inherent desirable qualities — used esp. of orchids **d** *slang* **:** a young male person ⟨an oily ~ in a second-hand sports jacket —Al Hine⟩ **5 :** STUD POKER — **at stud** *or* **in stud** *adv* **:** in the function of a stud **:** for breeding ⟨getting only 16 foals during the 11 years he stood *at stud* —Dennis Craig⟩ ⟨was placed *in stud* after being retired and had three foals —F.G.Menke⟩

²stud \"\ *n* -S *often attrib* [ME *stode,* fr. OE *studu;* akin to MHG *stud* prop, post, ON *stoth* post, OE *stōw* place — more at STOW] **1 a** *obs* **:** an upright prop or support used in a building **:** PILLAR, POST **b :** one of the smaller uprights in the framing of the walls of a building to which sheathing, paneling, or laths are nailed or fastened **:** SCANTLING **c :** the height of a room from floor to ceiling ⟨built a house at least 15 by 15 feet with a seven-foot ~ —*Springfield (Mass.) Republican*⟩ **2 :** something attached to, fixed in, or projecting from a surface: as **a :** a boss, rivet, or nail with a large head used (as on a shield, bridle, bag, or belt) for ornament or protection **b :** a solid button with a shank or eye on the back that is inserted through one or more eyelets usu. in a garment to serve as a fastener or ornament ⟨*~s* for a dress shirt⟩ ⟨~ earrings⟩ **3 :** a short branch of a plant or tree **:** STUB, SPUR **4 :** any of various infixed pieces (as a rod or pin) projecting from a machine and serving chiefly as a support or axis: as **a :** a short live spindle or mandrel (as in the change gear for a screw-cutting lathe) **b :** STUD BOLT **c :** a metal piece in a timepiece to which is attached the outer or upper coil of a hairspring **d :** a projecting pin or dowel on a loose piece used in pattern-making **e :** a chaplet with a baseplate and a disk top **f :** an iron brace across the link of a chain cable **g :** a part that conducts electric current from a terminal to a contact of a switch **h :** CLEAT

³stud \"\ *vt* **studded; studded; studding; studs 1 :** to furnish (a building or wall) with studs ⟨an old house with low-*studded* rooms⟩ **2 a :** to adorn, cover, or protect with studs ⟨likes to ~ her jewelry with semiprecious cabochons —*New Yorker*⟩ ⟨players . . . wearing a pair of *studded* shoes —Don Iddon⟩ ⟨gatehouse with original *studded* door —Nikolaus Pevsner⟩ **b :** to abound in or fill (a place or thing) in or as if in the manner of studs ⟨surrounding waters are *studded* with innumerable atoll-like reefs and small islands —*Amer. Guide Series: Mich.*⟩ ⟨its pansy-like red blossom *studded* thickly with tiny hairs tipped with . . . dew —Laura Krey⟩ ⟨figures of speech thickly ~ his work —J.G.Southworth⟩ **3 :** to mark or set (a place or thing) with a number of prominent objects ⟨several small islands ~ the broad sweep of water —*Amer. Guide Series: Maine*⟩ ⟨miles of green tundra . . . *studded* by scattered patches of trees —L.R.Huber⟩ **4 :** to secure with studs

stud *abbr* student

stud block *or* **stud box** *n* **:** a device for screwing home a stud bolt that consists of a rectangular block turned with a wrench — compare STUD DRIVER

stud bolt *n* **:** a bolt with threads on both ends designed to be screwed permanently into a fixed part at one end and to receive a nut on the other

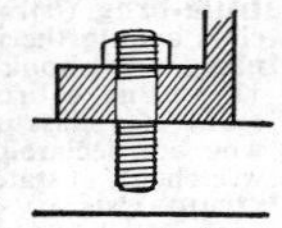

stud bolt

studbook \'=,=\ *n* **:** an official record of the pedigree of purebred animals (as horses and dogs); *also* **:** a book in which such records are published

stud chain *n* **:** a chain having links braced with studs

stud·der \'stədə(r)\ *n* -S **:** a worker who inserts watch hairsprings into studs

stud·die *or* **stud·dy** \'stədi, -tüdi\ *Scot & dial Eng var of* STITHY

studding *n* -S [fr. gerund of ³*stud*] **1 :** the uprights of the wall framing of a building **2 :** wood prepared for use as studding **3 :** the height of a room as determined by its studs

stud·ding sail \'stən(t)səl (*usual nautical pronunc*), 'stədiŋ ,sāl\ *n* [*studding* (of unknown origin) + *sail*] **:** a light sail set at the side of a principal square sail of a vessel in free winds to increase its speed — see SAIL illustration

studding–sail halyard bend *n* **:** a knot similar to a fisherman's bend used to secure a rope to a spar

¹stud·dle \'stədᵊl\ *n* -S [ME *stodul* sley of a loom, fr. OE *stōdla;* akin to MHG *stuodel* post, OE *standan* to stand — more at STAND] **:** a prop or stud used in timbering; *esp* **:** a piece or post separating the frames, rings, or sets used in timbering a mine shaft

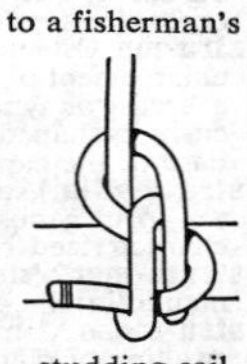

studding-sail halyard bend

²stud·dle \", 'stüd-\ *vt* [prob. alter. (influenced by ¹*stir*) of *muddle,* v.] *dial* **:** to muddy (as water) by stirring up **:** ROIL

stud driver *n* **:** a device for driving or firing home a stud usu. consisting of an impact wrench or a percussion torque tool — compare STUD BLOCK

stu·dent \'st(y)üdᵊnt\ *n* -S *often attrib* [ME, fr. L *student-, studens,* fr. *student-, studens,* pres. part. of *studēre* to be eager, be diligent, study — more at STUDY] **1 :** a person engaged in study **:** one devoted to learning: as **a :** one enrolled in a class or course in a school, college, or university **:** PUPIL **b :** one who independently carries on a systematic study or detailed observation of a subject ⟨a ~ of human nature⟩ ⟨to *~s* of ships and the sea, the Museum offers a valuable library —Dana Burnet⟩ **2** *often cap* **:** a member of a university foundation (as at Christ Church, Oxford)

student body *n* **:** the students of a school, college, or university

student council *n* **:** a group of students at a school or college elected by their fellow students to represent them in school government and usu. charged with drawing up and enforcing rules and penalties independently or with faculty assistance, coordinating extracurricular activities, and organizing the school's social life

student government *n* **:** the organization and management of student life, activities, or discipline by various student organizations (as the student council) in a school or college

student lamp *n* **:** an adjustable desk reading lamp with a tubular shaft, one or two arms to support a shaded light, and an oil reservoir; *also* **:** a similar electric lamp

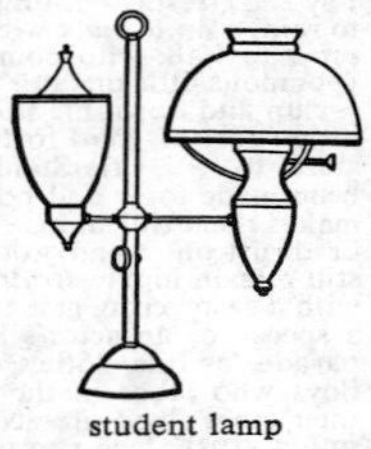

student lamp

stu·dent·ship \'==,ship\ *n* **1 :** the state or condition of being a student ⟨would not be a charge on her during the expensive years of ~ —O.S.J.Gogarty⟩ **2** *Brit* **:** a grant for university study — compare SCHOLARSHIP

student teacher *n* **:** one studying to be a teacher; *esp* **:** a student usu. in his last year at a college or teacher-training institution who is engaged in practice teaching at a demonstration school, in a public-school system, or at a cooperating private school

student teaching *n* **:** PRACTICE TEACHING

student volunteer *n* **:** a Protestant Christian student volunteering to devote his life to missionary work overseas

stud fee *n* **:** a fee paid the owner of an animal at public service by the owner of the female to be bred

studfish \'=,=\ *n* [prob. fr. ²*stud* + *fish*] **:** either of two brightly colored American killifishes: **a :** a killifish (*Xenisma catenatum*) of eastern Tennessee and the Ozark region **b :** a killifish (*X. stellifer*) of the Alabama river

studhorse \'=,=\ *n* [prob. fr. (assumed) ME *stodhors,* fr. OE *stōdhors,* fr. *stōd* stud + *hors* horse] **:** a stallion kept esp. for breeding

stud·ied \'stədēd, -did\ *adj* **1 :** well-read or versed in some branch of learning or activity **:** KNOWLEDGEABLE, LEARNED ⟨well ~ in geometry⟩ ⟨an able and ~ man⟩ **2 :** carefully considered or prepared **:** THOUGHTFUL ⟨the legal profession . . . gives its ~ acceptance to the program —*New Republic*⟩ ⟨his upright example . . . and carefully ~ lectures to the boys —Thomas Woody⟩ **3 :** produced or marked by conscious design or premeditation **:** intentionally conceived ⟨appareled for effect and so posed that its very casualness is ~ —John Mason Brown⟩ ⟨~ indifference⟩ ⟨~ insult⟩ ⟨~ dignity⟩ **syn** see DELIBERATE

stud·ied·ly *adv* **:** in or with a studied manner ⟨the ~ polite disrespect of our chamber-music halls —H.J.Foss⟩

stud·ied·ness *n* -ES **:** the quality or state of being studied

stu·dio \'st(y)üdē,ō, -(,)dyō\ *n* -S *often attrib* [It, lit., study, fr. L *studium* — more at STUDY] **1 a :** the working place of a painter, sculptor, or photographer **b :** a place for the study or practice of various performing or individual arts (as dancing, singing, acting) **2 :** a group of buildings including offices, laboratories, and stages where motion pictures are made **3 :** a room or place maintained and esp. equipped for the transmission of radio or television programs

studio apartment *n* **:** an apartment having a room with high ceiling and large windows similar to or serving as an artist's studio

studio couch *n* **:** an upholstered usu. backless couch that can be made to serve as a double bed by sliding from underneath it the frame of a single cot — compare SOFA BED

stu·dious \'st(y)üdēəs, -dyəs\ *adj* [ME, fr. MF or L; MF *studieux,* fr. L *studiosus,* fr. *studium* study + *-osus* -ose] **1 :** given to study **:** assiduous in the pursuit of learning ⟨a mind which had never found occasion to be ~ or analytical —S.H. Adams⟩ **2 a :** of, relating to, or concerned with study or learning ⟨a man of ~ and methodical habits —Harold Callender⟩ ⟨to read the great books . . . with intelligent appreciation is one of the last achievements of a ~ life—O.W.Holmes †1935⟩ **b :** favorable or suited for study or contemplation ⟨within these ~ walls⟩ **3 a :** diligent in purpose **:** of earnest intent ⟨if we were more ~ to write prose that could be read aloud with pleasure —A.T.Quiller-Couch⟩ **b :** marked by or evincing purposefulness or diligence ⟨a ~ effort was made to avoid representing the human figure realistically —R.W. Murray⟩ **c :** deliberately planned **:** STUDIED ⟨drove into the club with ~ calm . . . for the natives must not suspect that they were agitated —E.M.Forster⟩

stu·dious·ly *adv* [ME *studiousli,* fr. *studious* + *-li* -ly] **:** in a studious or studied manner ⟨followed his finger . . . and ~ copied letter by letter —Edward Bok⟩ ⟨real issues are kept ~ away from public notice —Christopher Hollis⟩

stu·dious·ness *n* -ES **:** the quality or state of being studious

¹stu·dite \'st(y)ü,dīt\ *n* -S *usu cap* [*Studius,* 5th cent. A.D. Rom. official + E *-ite*] **:** a Studite monk of the Eastern Orthodox Church

²studite \"\ *adj, usu cap* **:** of or relating to a monastery founded at Constantinople in the 5th century A.D. by a Roman official named Studius and reorganized by St. Theodore; *also* **:** of or relating to the rule codified in this monastery by St. Theodore

stu·di·um gen·er·a·le \'st(y)üdēəm,jenə'ra(,)lē, -rā(,)-; 'stüdēəm,genə'rä,lā\ *n, pl* **stu·dia genera·lia** \-dēə . . . ,lēə\ [ML, universal studying place] **:** a place or institute of studies where people from all parts of the world may come to study any subject; *esp* **:** a medieval university

stud link *n* **:** a link of a stud chain; *also* **:** the bracing member of such a link

studmaster \'=,==\ *n, Austral* **:** one owning or supervising a stud of sheep

stud–mate \'=,=\ *vt* **:** to breed (poultry) by mating selected pairs — compare FLOCK-MATE, PEN-MATE

stud poker *n* [¹*stud* + *poker*] **1 :** poker in which each player is dealt his first card facedown and his other four cards faceup with a round of betting taking place after each of the last four rounds **2 :** a variant (as seven-card stud) of stud poker

stud rivet *n* **:** SCREW RIVET

studs *pl of* STUD, *pres 3d sing of* STUD

stud welding *n* **:** the process of welding a stud to a plate or flat surface by the combined use of heat and pressure

stud wheel *n* **:** a wheel journaled on a stud

studwork \'=,=\ *n* **:** work supported, strengthened, held together, or ornamented by studs ⟨walls . . . of ~ with lath and plaster —Fiske Kimball⟩

¹study \'stədē, -di\ *n* -ES [ME *studie,* fr. OF *studie, estudie* state of perplexity or reverie, application of the mind to the acquirement of knowledge, study, fr. L *studium* eagerness, application of the mind to the acquirement of knowledge, study; akin to L *studēre* to be eager, be diligent, study and prob. to L *tundere* to beat — more at STINT] **1 :** a state of absorbed contemplation, perplexity, or reverie **:** ABSTRACTION ⟨paused and appeared to be in a deep ~ —Alexander MacDonald⟩ ⟨the long silences that meant I was lost in ~ —Eve Langley⟩ **2 a :** the application of the mental faculties to the acquisition of knowledge ⟨is in your own power greatly to improve . . . by ~, observation, and reflection —Earl of Chesterfield⟩ ⟨hours of ~ and careful thought —Bruce Payne⟩ ⟨years of ~ in school and college⟩ **b :** such application of the mind in a particular field or to a specific subject matter ⟨scholarship . . . which illuminates the ~ of the family —Lynn White⟩ ⟨taking up the ~ of history⟩ ⟨enter upon the ~ of law⟩ **c** (1) **:** a careful examination or analysis of a phenomenon, development, or question usu. within a limited area of investigation ⟨plunged into the ~ of latex —Clarence Woodbury⟩ ⟨*studies* have been made of individual cases and of groups of adolescents —H.R. Douglass⟩ — often used with *under* ⟨further reductions are under ~ —D.D.Eisenhower⟩ (2) **:** a paper or monograph in which such a study is published ⟨these two volumes constitute the ablest ~ on the iron and steel industry —*Current Biog.*⟩ ⟨publishes *studies* and reports⟩ **3 a :** a building or room furnished esp. with books and devoted to study or literary pursuits ⟨set out my typewriter in the ~ . . . to write —Worth T. Hedden⟩ **b** *obs* **:** the books contained in such a study or in a collection **c** *obs* **:** a place of learning **:** UNIVERSITY, STUDIUM GENERALE **d :** the lower level of the inner stage of an Elizabethan playhouse often used to represent an indoor scene **4 a** *obs* **:** an expressed inclination **:** DESIRE, INTEREST **b :** a consciously reasoned effort **:** PURPOSE, ENDEAVOR ⟨those favors which it will ever by my ~ to deserve —W.S.Gilbert & A.S.Sullivan⟩ ⟨it has been the ~ of my life to avoid those weaknesses —Jane Austen⟩ **5 a :** an organized branch or department of learning **:** SUBJECT ⟨what are your favorite *studies* —G.B.Shaw⟩ ⟨was . . . on the faculty of graduate *studies* —Edna Yost⟩ **b :** the activity or work of a student ⟨the curriculum for graduate ~ —E.B.Nyquist⟩ ⟨returning to his *studies* after vacation⟩ **c :** something that is the object of one's study ⟨was pompous and wonderfully conceited, his every word and every gesture a careful ~ —Marcia Davenport⟩ ⟨about the use of making this sugar . . . I said I made it my ~ —H.D.Thoreau⟩ **d :** something attracting close attention or examination usu. by reason of contrast or conflict ⟨it was quite a ~ to watch the faces round the table — in the struggle between good manners and amusement —Rachel Henning⟩ ⟨a ~ in conflicting emotions —T.B.Costain⟩ ⟨the whole show a ~ in tolerant condescension —David Driscoll⟩ **6 :** one who memorizes something (as a part in a play) — usu. used with a qualifying adjective ⟨is not considered a fast ~, but once he has learned a role he has it for good —H.C.Schonberg⟩ **7 a :** an artistic production in any of the fine arts intended as a preliminary outline or esp. as an experimental expression or interpretation of specific features or characteristics ⟨a number of his drawings were *studies* of beggars, clowns, cripples, and street musicians —*Current Biog.*⟩ ⟨a ~ in tunes, all of them beautiful and separate —Leonard Bernstein⟩ ⟨whether dancing in dramatic roles . . . or *studies* in pure dance —*Current Biog.*⟩ **b :** a literary work serving as an experimental or esp. as an exploratory analysis or portrayal of carefully observed features of character or motivation ⟨a particularly successful ~ of the type of grievance-ridden, unhappy . . . misfit —R.P.Fleming⟩ ⟨a topical ~ of life in a wartime services canteen —Leslie Rees⟩ ⟨a brilliantly intuitive ~ of war and the emotions of men in combat —*Time*⟩ **8 :** a musical composition usu. devoted entirely to a special problem of instrumental technique **:** ÉTUDE

²study \"\ *vb* -ED/-ING/-ES [ME *studien,* fr. OF *estudier,* fr. ML *studiare,* fr. L *studium,* n., study] *vi* **1 a :** to apply the mind to the acquirement of knowledge through reading and reflection, observation, or experiment ⟨he might have *studied* through the literature to the mind of that century —T.S.Eliot⟩ **b :** to undertake formal study of a subject or course ⟨*studied* at Manual Arts high school —Lillian de Tagle⟩ ⟨*studied* with the faculty of law at the university —*Current Biog.*⟩ ⟨*studied* under him at the university —*Current Biog.*⟩ **2** *dial* **a :** to consider deeply **:** MEDITATE, REFLECT — usu. used with *about* ⟨looking at the oil in the bottle and smelling it and tasting it, and *~ing* about what it meant —H.H. Martin⟩ **b :** to deliberate something with oneself **:** DEBATE ⟨stood digging a bare big toe into the dirt and *studied* awhile —F.B.Gipson⟩ — usu. used with *on* or *about* ⟨I'm *~ing* on whether I ought to sell —Jean Stafford⟩ **3 :** to consider something as one's aim **:** ENDEAVOR ⟨I *studied* to appear calm . . . so as to draw him on to say more —W.H.Hudson †1922⟩ ⟨appears to ~ to repress these things in his poetry —David Daiches⟩ **~** *vt* **1 a :** to read (a book or writing) in close detail often with the intent of learning for recall ⟨was set to *~ing* the Talmud for 15-hour stretches —*Current Biog.*⟩ ⟨stopped and *studied* a big sign in front of a large store —Irving Bacheller⟩ **b :** to learn (as a part) for playing ⟨you could . . . ~ a speech of some dozen or 16 lines — Shak.⟩ ⟨waiting in the wings *~ing* his part⟩ **2 a :** to apply the mind to the learning or understanding of (an area of knowledge) ⟨learns a good deal by simply *~ing* human nature⟩ ⟨*studies* the advances in his profession every free moment⟩ **b :** to occupy oneself with the formal study of (a subject, course, or activity) ⟨planning to ~ medicine⟩ ⟨*studies* the violin at the conservatory⟩ ⟨attends night school to ~ typing⟩ **c :** to do special reading about for a specific purpose — usu. used with *up* ⟨thought I knew something . . . because I'd *studied* it up in a book —Calder Willingham⟩ **3 :** to make a

plan for : PLOT, DESIGN ⟨he *studies* our overthrow and generally seeks our destruction —Robert Burton⟩ — usu. used with *out* ⟨works hard ~*ing* out a new system⟩ **4 a :** to observe or analyze in detail (a phenomenon, development, or question) usu. within a restricted area with a view to some action : INVESTIGATE ⟨experts ~ tides and ocean currents —H.M. Parshley⟩ ⟨~*ing* the mood of people in different quarters —Evelyn G. Cruickshanks⟩ ⟨~*ing* and attempting to solve the economic problem —*Current Biog.*⟩ **b :** to examine closely to understand or determine something ⟨each still ~*ing* the other with interest —Agnes S. Turnbull⟩ ⟨the brakeman . . . took advantage of each curve to ~ the train —*Monsanto Mag.*⟩ ⟨*studied* the flames as if seeking the answer . . . in their restive pattern —Walter O'Meara⟩ **5 :** to employ thought and careful attention in ⟨the epistle . . . was *studied* and recopied and elaborated —Anthony Trollope⟩ **6 :** to pay heed to or be solicitous for (a person's feelings or convenience) ⟨needed a home and a wife who would ~ his comfort —Edith Sitwell⟩ **syn** see CONSIDER

³study \ˈstədi, -tüdi\ *Scot & dial Eng var of* STITHY

study group *n* **:** a group of people joining in the study of a particular topic and usu. meeting at scheduled intervals to discuss individual observations, reading, and research

study hall *n* **1 :** a large room or hall in a school set aside for students to study and do homework in usu. under the supervision of a teacher or an older student **2 :** a period in a student's day scheduled for study and homework usu. in a study hall

study home *n* **:** a child-care institution; *esp* **:** one in which disturbed children undergo psychiatric observation and diagnosis

¹stuff \ˈstəf\ *n* -s [ME *stuff, stuffe,* fr. MF *estoffe* stuff, material, fr. OF, fr. *estoffer* to equip, stock — more at ²STUFF] **1 :** materials, supplies, or equipment used in various human activities: as **a** *obs* **:** military baggage : IMPEDIMENTA **b :** bullets or shells fired from a gun : PROJECTILES ⟨were throwing broadsides at him . . . and ~ was going past him from both sides and killing —Ira Wolfert⟩ ⟨our own ~ was pouring back on them, and the power of the weapons was impressive —Fred Majdalany⟩ **c** *obs* **:** the furnishings and chattels of a place or household **d :** PERSONAL PROPERTY, CLOTHING, POSSESSIONS ⟨my ~ is all unpacked —Joseph Dever⟩ **e :** MONEY ⟨he is out for the ~, and when he gets it he salts it away —P.G.Wodehouse⟩ ⟨is a moneyed writer burdened with even more of the ~ through inheritance —J.S.Sandoe⟩ **2 :** material to be manufactured, wrought, or used in construction : raw or partially prepared material: as **a :** building materials ⟨got all the ~ ready for building his house⟩ **b :** wood for use in carpentry ⟨well furred inside with clear half-inch pine ~ —Emily Holt⟩ **c :** fibrous pulp fully beaten and ready for the paper machine — called also *stock;* compare HALF STUFF **d :** a finished textile suitable for clothing; *esp* **:** wool or worsted material **e :** a composition of tallow, fats, and oil used to fill the pores of leather **f :** a mixture of tallow, tar, and turpentine used as a preservative on wooden ships **3** *chiefly Scot & Irish* **:** GRAIN, PULSE **4 a :** literary or artistic matter, productions, or compositions ⟨some contemporary . . . material, and some ~ on the early history of toleration —H.J.Laski⟩ ⟨most writers can't cut their own ~ —Claire Callahan⟩ — often used disparagingly ⟨seems to be all the same — the old picaresque ~ —Arnold Bennett⟩ **b :** material written for a newspaper or periodical : COPY ⟨turns in good ~ from his beat⟩ **c :** writing, discourse, or ideas of little value : RUBBISH ⟨novels are so full of nonsense and ~ —Jane Austen⟩ ⟨there is so much vulgar, trivial ~ on the air —D.W.Brogan⟩ ⟨mechanized organs of public opinion . . . are feeding us the same old ~ —Norman Woelfel⟩ **5 a :** an unspecified material substance or aggregate of matter ⟨investigating the age of the universe and the creation of the ~ of which it is made —George Gamow⟩ ⟨decided that hydrogen was the primordial ~ of the universe —Waldemar Kaempffert⟩ ⟨volcanic rock is curious ~⟩ **b :** a solid, liquid, or gaseous matter processed or synthesized for various uses: as (1) **:** a medical preparation : POTION (2) **:** an alcoholic beverage ⟨that ~'s too strong on an empty stomach —C.S.Barry⟩ (3) **:** NARCOTICS ⟨mentioned to me that if I needed any weed or ~ to let her know —J.B.Martin⟩ ⟨you've been pushing the ~ —Wenzell Brown⟩ (4) **:** COMMODITY, MERCHANDISE ⟨brings the ~ in by freight car⟩ ⟨when the ~ didn't move, advertised the lines widely —Susan Strom⟩ (5) **:** fissionable material ⟨plutonium . . . was the ~ of the early atom bombs —Bertram Mycock⟩ **6 a :** the fundamental material of which something is made or consists : ESSENCE ⟨tendencies that are part of the very ~ of warfare —Tom Wintringham⟩ ⟨the ~ of greatness⟩ ⟨the ~ of tradition⟩ ⟨the ~ of life⟩ **b :** the basic qualities of a person or character : capacity for accomplishment in an activity or mode of existence ⟨exhibits the ~ of manhood⟩ ⟨was not the ~ of which the revolutionary is made —Liam O'Flaherty⟩ ⟨must not expect to find in ordinary men the ~ of martyrs —Walter Lippmann⟩ ⟨she was of sterner ~ now —C.S.Forester⟩ ⟨proves that heroes are not made of pretty ~ —Frederic Morton⟩ **c :** the substance or material forming the basis of a literary work or artistic production ⟨their adventures are real and make the ~ of a stirring novel —H.U.Ribalow⟩ ⟨contained all the ~ of opera and was dramatically well-pointed —Norman Demuth⟩ ⟨slick work, but . . . he doesn't get down to the real ~ —Arnold Bennett⟩ **d :** a body of knowledge or subject matter ⟨philosophical physics . . . describes the ~ as a mathematical probability —W.L.Sullivan⟩ ⟨the procession of presidents and wars in . . . history is dull ~ indeed if presented in a vacuum —W.R.Steckel⟩ ⟨learning about the heavens from Ptolemy and his Arab commentators — real ~ at last —R.W. Southern⟩ ⟨this is primer ~ today to . . . meteorologists —Carey Longmire⟩ **7 a :** a mode or manner of acting or talking : the actions or talk of a person in specific circumstances ⟨rough ~ isn't tolerated —Bill Wolf⟩ ⟨no funny ~ now —Carl Jonas⟩ ⟨disturbing the peace, ~ like that —R.O.Bowen⟩ ⟨imagine a player getting away with that ~ today —Ted Williams⟩ **b :** an activity or branch of knowledge requiring specialized study, practice, or skill ⟨struck us as a lad who knew his ~ — who could handle affairs of state or breeze through a . . . luncheon with equal aplomb —*New Republic*⟩ ⟨with the plane's crew doing its ~ dodging the fireworks —T.B.Bruff⟩ **c :** an action, attitude, or development eliciting approval or commendation ⟨that's the ~, don't give up⟩ **8 :** LIVESTOCK ⟨beds down . . . on the outside edge of the herd away from the horned ~ —R.F.Adams⟩ ⟨box stalls are necessary for . . . young ~ —*Producing Farm Livestock*⟩ **9 a :** the spin or rotation imparted to a thrown, rolled, or hit ball to make it curve or change course ⟨no difference how hard you hit the ball or how much ~ you put on it in the way of spin . . . unless you have accuracy —J.D.Budge⟩ **b :** the speed or esp. the variety of pitches or curves of a baseball pitcher ⟨the greatest pitcher of my time . . . had tremendous ~ —Ted Williams⟩ ⟨has a wide assortment of curves, sliders, and slow ~ —Lou Boudreau⟩

²stuff \"\ *vb* -ED/-ING/-S [ME *stuffen,* fr. MF *estoffer* to equip, stock, fr. OF, prob. fr. MHG *stopfen* to stop up, stuff, fr. OHG *stopfōn* — more at STOP] *vt* **1** *obs* **:** as **a :** to supply (a fortification or commander) with stores, arms, or men : GARRISON **b :** to endow or equip (a person) with provisions, arms, or money **c :** to furnish (a house or place) with chattels, equipment, or accessories : STOCK **2 a** (1) **:** to fill (a receptacle) to fullness or distention by packing things in : CRAM ⟨had to . . . ~ the jar —Ida Pruitt⟩ — usu. used with *with* ⟨bags ~*ed* with papers —Van Wyck Brooks⟩ ⟨things you have to ~ your pockets with —Richard Joseph⟩ (2) **:** to insert a bill or communication in (an envelope) for mailing ⟨their fingers stiff from ~*ing* and addressing envelopes —George Sklar⟩ ⟨~*ed* and addressed the invitations —Carl Jonas⟩ **b :** to fill (as one's stomach) to fullness : SURFEIT ⟨got out the coffeepot . . . and before he could say a number she was ~*ing* him —Arthur Miller⟩ ⟨~*ing* ourselves with cake and sandwiches —Alice F. Webb⟩ ⟨beef calves . . . which he ~*s* for months with corn silage —John Bird⟩ ⟨~ a cold and starve a fever⟩ **c :** to prepare (meat or vegetables) for cooking or eating by filling or lining with a seasoned mixture ⟨~ed veal with bread crumbs and butter and sage . . . and onion —Margaret A. Barnes⟩ **d :** to fill (as a cushion or ticking) with a soft material or padding ⟨spent the morning ~*ing* the mattresses⟩ ⟨made of leather and ~*ed* with shoddy and cotton waste —*Amer. Guide Series: Conn.*⟩ **e :** to fill out the skin of (an animal or bird) for mounting **f :** to crowd (an interior or place) with people ⟨hopped aboard . . . the already ~*ed* rear of the bus —Eula Long⟩ ⟨the church was ~*ed* full —R.C.Wood⟩ **g :** to fill (as a hole or opening) by packing in material : stop up : PLUG ⟨~*ed* the keyhole to shut out prying eyes —*Amer. Guide Series: Conn.*⟩ ⟨~*s* woodchuck holes with rocks and dirt⟩ ⟨~*ing* the wound with cotton⟩ **h :** to furnish or fill (a house or room) to excess ⟨lived in attic rooms ~*ed* with fantastic objects and furniture —Virginia D. Dawson & Betty D. Wilson⟩ **3 a :** to clutter or fill (a person's mind) — usu. used with *with* ⟨those whose heads are ~*ed* with facts —A.J.P.Taylor⟩ ⟨has a mind ~*ed* with ideas, hungry for argument —Virginia Woolf⟩; often used disparagingly ⟨~*s* the people with lies that gag an honest man —Kenneth Roberts⟩ ⟨~*ed* right up to the ears with his own slogans —David Driscoll⟩ **b** (1) **:** to crowd or fill (as a work, book, or discourse) — usu. used with *with* ⟨the book is . . . ~*ed* with delectable stories —Mark Van Doren⟩; often used disparagingly ⟨tracts ~*ed* with a sodden morality —V.L.Parrington⟩ ⟨the appearance of a travelogue ~*ed* with melodrama —*Time*⟩ (2) **:** to expand or fill (a book or work) chiefly to enlarge the bulk or content : PAD — usu. used with *out* ⟨scanty material, ~*ed* out with appreciation and conjecture —T.S.Eliot⟩ ⟨~*ed* out their pages with platitudes —Virginia Woolf⟩ **4 :** to congest or block (as the nasal passages) ⟨sounded ~*ed up* . . . had been crying again —J.H.Reese⟩ ⟨his throat got ~*ed* —Liam O'Flaherty⟩ **5 a :** to insert or fit snugly or tightly : TUCK ⟨secret documents ~*ed* under his shirt —Bernard Kalb⟩ — usu. used with *into* ⟨got her ~*ed* into the closet —Robert Murphy⟩ ⟨~ the greenbacks into my wallet —H.A.Overstreet⟩ **b :** to cause to enter or fill : THRUST, PRESS — usu. used with *in* or *into* ⟨~*ed* it deep down in his mind —Richard Llewellyn⟩ ⟨knowledge . . . can never be knowledge that is ~*ed* in —H.A.Overstreet⟩ ⟨have ~*ed* too many of the facts . . . into my intellectuals —L.P.Smith⟩ ⟨any set mold into which the material has to be ~*ed* —Carlos Lynes⟩ ⟨~*ing* . . . any preoccupation with her concerns out of sight —Helen Howe⟩ **6 :** to impregnate (leather) for softening and preserving — usu. used with *with* ⟨the leather goods are ~*ed* with a mixture of hot oil and tallow, or fat liquored —*New Zealand Jour. of Agric.*⟩ **7 :** to fill (a ballot box) with fraudulent votes ⟨another type of corrupt practice is ~*ing* the ballot boxes —D.D.McKean⟩ ~ *vi* **:** to eat gluttonously : GORGE ⟨had finished ~*ing* in the dining room —H.A. Chippendale⟩ **syn** see PACK

³stuff *vt* [ME *stuffen,* fr. MF *estouffer*] *obs* **:** STIFLE, SUFFOCATE

stuff chest *n* **:** CHEST 1e

stuffed shirt *n* **:** a smug conceited usu. pompous person with an inflexibly conservative or reactionary attitude ⟨nothing of the *stuffed shirt* in him . . . never put on airs —W.S.Maugham⟩ ⟨at the heart of the legends . . . discovers a *stuffed shirt,* a faker, or a moral monster —DeLancey Ferguson⟩ ⟨a *stuffed shirt* with a starched mind⟩

stuff·er \ˈstəfə(r)\ *n* -s **1 :** one that stuffs: as **a** (1) **:** a worker who stuffs hides or skins with grease by hand or by machine (2) **:** a worker who stuffs articles (as sausage casings, dolls, cushions) **b** (1) **:** a worker who puts articles (as ads, bills, powder, folded garments) into envelopes or similar containers (2) **:** a clerk who sorts invoices or statements and inserts them in the proper ledgers for use by bookkeepers and posting clerks **2 a :** an enclosure (as a leaflet or blotter) inserted in an envelope in addition to a bill, statement, or notice usu. for advertising purposes **b :** a piece of cardboard or pieces of paper placed in an envelope that is mailed for a philatelic purpose **3 :** a series of extra threads or yarn running lengthwise in a fabric to add weight and bulk and to form a backing esp. for carpets

stuff gown *n* **1 :** a gown of stuff; *esp* **:** one that in England forms the distinctive garb of a junior barrister — compare SILK GOWN **2 :** a junior barrister

stuff·i·ly \ˈstəfəlē, -li\ *adv* **:** in a stuffy manner

stuff·i·ness \-fēnəs, -fin-\ *n* -ES **:** the quality or state of being stuffy

stuff·ing \ˈstəfiŋ, -fēŋ\ *n* -s **1 :** the act or process of one that stuffs **2 :** something that stuffs or fills: as **a :** a filling used to stuff upholstered furniture, cushions, bedding, or similar items **b :** a seasoned mixture used to stuff meat, vegetables, or eggs; *esp* **:** a composition (as for poultry) of bread, onion, celery, and condiments **c :** material of slight value added merely to fill space : PADDING ⟨saw that the author of it would need to . . . reject ~ and divagation —F.A.Swinnerton⟩ **d :** material used as stuffers ⟨printing classes can turn out excellent home-contact material, letter ~ —L.W.Kindred⟩ **3 :** INNARDS ⟨would knock the ~ out of an antagonist upon a point of dogma —O.W.Holmes †1935⟩

stuffing box *n* **:** a device that is designed to prevent leakage along a piston rod, propeller shaft, or other moving part passing through a hole in a cylinder or vessel containing steam, water, or oil and that consists of a box or chamber made by enlarging the hole and a gland to compress the contained packing

stuffing nut *n* **:** a nut used to tighten or adjust a stuffing box

stuff·less \ˈs-ləs\ *adj* **:** lacking stuff or substance ⟨a ~ sound —F. Tennyson Jesse⟩ ⟨a ~ ghost —Edna S. V. Millay⟩

stuff-over \ˈstə,fōvə(r)\ *also* **stuffed-over** \ˈstəf,tō-\ *adj* [*stuffover* alter. of *stuffed-over,* fr. *stuffed* (past part. of ²*stuff*) + *over,* adv.] *Brit* **:** OVERSTUFFED

stuffs *pl of* STUFF, *pres 3d sing of* STUFF

stuffy \ˈstəfē, -fi\ *adj* -ER/-EST **1** *obs* **:** containing stuff or substance : SUBSTANTIAL **2 :** SULLEN, ILL-HUMORED ⟨wrong feeding may have much to do with . . . ~, ill-natured, contractive individuals —H.A.Overstreet⟩ **3 a :** lacking oxygen : oppressive to the breathing : STALE, CLOSE ⟨it was hot and ~, and the air was gray with smoke —W.S.Maugham⟩ ⟨popping into the ~ little office —Vicki Baum⟩ **b :** stuffed or choked up ⟨the ~ feeling in the head —H.G.Armstrong⟩ **4 :** lacking in vitality or interest : DULL, STODGY ⟨a woodenly earnest, relentlessly ~ sort of fellow . . . not very strong on humor —Alan Devoe⟩ ⟨the press conference . . . was far from solemn and ~ —Stafford Derby⟩ **5 :** provincial in outlook : narrowly inflexible in standards of conduct : SELF-RIGHTEOUS ⟨am abiding by the rather involved, ~ code of ethics —R.L. Riggs⟩ ⟨resistance to ~ taboos and pieties —N.E.Nelson⟩ ⟨against the orders of a rather ~ police commissioner —S.H. Adams⟩

stug·gy \ˈstəgi, -tügi\ *adj* [origin unknown] *dial* **:** THICKSET, STOCKY, STURDY

stuiver *var of* STIVER

stull \ˈstəl\ *n* -s [perh. modif. of G *stollen* post, support, fr. OHG *stollo* — more at STOLLEN] **1 :** a round timber used to support the sides or back of a mine **2 a :** one of a series of props wedged between the walls of a stope to hold up a platform for supporting miners, ore, or waste or to protect miners from falling stones **b :** a platform held up by stulls

stull·er \-lə(r)\ *n* -s **:** one that places or works at stulls

stulm \ˈstəlm\ *n* -s [perh. modif. of G *stollen* adit, post, support] **:** an approximately horizontal passageway into a mine : ADIT

stul·ti·fi·ca·tion \,stəltəfəˈkāshən\ *n* -s [fr. *stultify,* after such pairs as E *fortify: fortification*] **:** the act or process of stultifying : the state of being stultified

stul·ti·fy \ˈ==,fī\ *vt* -ED/-ING/-ES [LL *stultificare* to make foolish, fr. L *stultus* foolish + *-ficare* -fy — more at STALL] **1 :** to allege or prove (oneself or another) to be of unsound mind so that the performance of some act may be avoided **2 a :** to cause to appear or be stupid, foolish, or absurdly illogical ⟨the dullards become more *stultified* than ever —C.H.Grandgent⟩ ⟨incidents will have occurred tending to ~ conclusions —James Stevenson-Hamilton⟩ ⟨how like the man to ~ himself, to prove all his own theories wrong —Clemence Dane⟩ ⟨the court did not ~ itself by claiming that its ruling fulfilled any logical, legal progression toward racial equality —C.S.Dowdey⟩ **b :** to impair, invalidate, or reduce to futility or uselessness esp. through debasing or repressive influences : FRUSTRATE, NULLIFY ⟨the psychiatrist *stultifies* his role if he allows such misunderstandings to develop —C.P.Printzlien⟩ ⟨demand for fresh leadership . . . is running smack into the ~*ing* seniority system —T.R.Ybarra⟩ ⟨the slavish traditionalism that *stultifies* most contemporary ecclesiastical art —*Time*⟩ ⟨centralization . . . *stultifies* their local initiative —Hugh McDiarmid⟩ ⟨*stultified* by the oppressive atmosphere of her earlier life —Martin Levin⟩

stul·til·o·quence \,stəlˈtiləkwən(t)s\ *n* -s [L *stultiloquentia,* fr. *stultus* foolish + *loquent-, loquens* (pres. part. of *loqui* to speak) + *-ia* -y] **:** senseless or silly talk : BABBLE — **stul·til·o·quent** \(ˈ)=;==kwənt\ *or* **stul·til·o·quen·tial** \,=;==;kwenchəl\ *adj*

stul·til·o·quy \-kwē\ *n* -ES [L *stultiloquium,* fr. *stultus* foolish + *-loquium* (fr. *loqui* to speak)] **:** STULTILOQUENCE

¹stum \ˈstəm\ *vt* **stummed; stummed; stumming; stums** [D *stommen,* fr. *stom,* n.] *archaic* **:** to renew (wine) by mixing with must and reviving fermentation

²stum \"\ *n* -s [D *stom* (approximate trans. of F *muet* in *vin muet* stum), fr. *stom,* adj., mute, fr. MD; akin to OFris *stumm* mute, OHG *stum* mute, OE *stamerian* to stammer] **:** unfermented or partly fermented grape juice; *esp* **:** must in which fermentation has been artificially arrested

¹stum·ble \ˈstəmbəl\ *vb* **stumbled; stumbled; stumbling** \-b(ə)liŋ\ **stumbles** [ME *stumblen, stomblen,* prob. of Scand origin; akin to Norw dial. *stumle* to stumble, Sw dial. *stumla;* akin to OE *stamerian* to stammer — more at STAMMER] *vi* **1 a :** to fall into sin, error, or waywardness : ERR ⟨though we *stumbled* and we strayed, we were led by evil counsellors —Rudyard Kipling⟩ ⟨man is *stumbling* blindly through a spiritual darkness —O.N.Bradley⟩ **b :** to falter through lack of knowledge or experience : BLUNDER ⟨people *stumbling* and learning and going forward to meet the realities of life and death —Marjorie Vetter⟩ ⟨his thought staggers, and reels and ~*s* —Martin Gardner⟩ ⟨how many people in the final survey will ~ over the same obstacle —S.L.Payne⟩ ⟨the problem that . . . other commanders had *stumbled* against —Tom Wintringham⟩ **c :** to come to a block or obstacle to belief ⟨~ at the doctrine of the elect⟩ : SCRUPLE, DEMUR **d :** to make a slip in speaking : MISPRONOUNCE, STAMMER ⟨voices that ~ and trip over proper names —F.L.Mott⟩ ⟨tongue *stumbled* at the start —T.B.Costain⟩ **2 :** to lose one's footing in walking or running so as to stagger or fall : TRIP ⟨*stumbled,* laughed, lay there a moment . . . then got up —O.E. Rölvaag⟩ ⟨*stumbled* and then, recovering herself, broke into a trot —Ellen Glasgow⟩ ⟨grumbled whenever we *stumbled* in a shell hole —J.P.O'Neill⟩ **3 a :** to walk or move in an unsteady or clumsy manner : STAGGER ⟨strained and *stumbled* in their exertions like fat sheep —Stephen Crane⟩ ⟨*stumbled* along the broken path —B.L.K.Henderson⟩ ⟨*stumbled* through the dark hall —Erskine Caldwell⟩ **b :** to proceed, speak, or act in a hesitant or faltering manner ⟨*stumbled* haphazardly through the 5th and 6th forms —Margaret A. Barnes⟩ ⟨*stumbled* through the first prayer —Maeve Brennan⟩ ⟨its plot creaks and ~*s* awkwardly —Orville Prescott⟩ ⟨the bassoon ~*s* along precariously —P.H.Lang⟩ **4 a :** to come or happen unexpectedly — usu. used with *on* or *upon* ⟨floundering around in the woods . . . *stumbled* on a blockhouse —P.W. Thompson⟩ ⟨cannot adventure very long with an electron microscope . . . without *stumbling* upon something new —L.A. White⟩ ⟨was so certain he had *stumbled* on the truth —T.B. Costain⟩ ⟨is looking for one thing and ~*s* on something much bigger —W.P.Webb⟩ **b :** to fall or move carelessly or inadvertently — usu. used with *into* ⟨was not long before he *stumbled* into a new folly —H.E.Scudder⟩ ⟨traveler who ~*s* into this world of passionate violence —Mark Schorer⟩ ⟨*stumbled* into a job —Frank O'Leary⟩ ⟨*stumbled* into immortality —David Dempsey⟩ ~ *vt* **1 :** to cause (a person or thing) to stumble : TRIP ⟨*stumbled* my shin against a bedpost to give pain to my rage —Herbert Gold⟩ **2 :** to cause to hesitate : CONFOUND, PERPLEX ⟨the problem ~*s* him⟩

²stumble \"\ *n* -s **1 :** a trip in walking or running : TUMBLE ⟨taking a bad ~⟩ **2 :** an inadvertent error : SLIP, BLUNDER ⟨conversation . . . is a mass of ~*s,* clumsy returns, and points missed —J.M.Barzun⟩ ⟨a republic . . . must needs make many ~*s* by the way —Katharine L. Bates⟩

stumblebum \ˈ==,=\ *n* **1 :** a punch-drunk, clumsy, or inept boxer ⟨was just a strawman built up craftily with knockouts over ~*s* —*Ring*⟩ **2 :** a clumsy, inept, or blundering person ⟨has filled most of his . . . staff with third-raters and ~*s* —E.K.Lindley⟩

stumbling block *n* **1 :** a bar or hindrance to righteous living **2 :** an impediment to belief or understanding : PERPLEXITY ⟨most difficult of statistical measurement and thus . . . the greatest *stumbling block* to the market analyst —S.B.Hunt⟩ **3 :** an obstacle in the way of a planned or progressive development or act ⟨*stumbling blocks* that the industry must be prepared to avoid —J.N.Robertson⟩

stum·bling·ly *adv* **:** in a stumbling manner ⟨as long as he could ~ follow their thoughts —Susan Ertz⟩

stum·bly \ˈstəmb(ə)lē, -li\ *adj* -ER/-EST **1 :** given to stumbling **2 :** apt to cause one to stumble ⟨weaved along ~ forest paths —*Newsweek*⟩

stu·mer *also* **stu·mour** \ˈst(y)ümə(r\ *n* -s [origin unknown] **1** *Brit* **:** FRAUD, SHAM; *esp* **:** a bad or forged check **2** *Brit* **:** FAILURE, DUD, WASHOUT; *esp* **:** a horse that loses a race usu. through fixing **3** *Brit* **:** MISTAKE, BONER

stum·mel \ˈs(h)tüməl\ *n* -s [G, lit., stump, butt, fr. OHG *stumbal* stump, piece cut off; akin to OE *stæf* staff — more at STAFF] **:** the bowl and shank of a tobacco pipe

¹stump \ˈstəmp\ *n* -s [ME *stumpe, stompe;* akin to MD *stompe, stomp* stub, stump, *stomp* blunt, OHG *stumpf* stub, stump, *stumpf* mutilated, OE *stempan* to stamp — more at STAMP] **1 a :** the basal portion of a limb or other part of the body remaining after the rest of it is removed ⟨the ~ of his severed hand —Hamilton Basso⟩ ⟨closure of the duodenal ~ —F.W.Bancroft⟩ **b :** a rudimentary or vestigial growth or part of an organism ⟨the cervical ~⟩ ⟨motor nerve ~⟩ **2 a :** the part of a tree or plant remaining in the earth after the stem or trunk is cut off : STUB — compare SNAG **b :** a walnut stub including the underground portion that is used in making veneers **c :** the base of a tree **d :** the stalk of a plant after the leaves have been removed ⟨cabbage ~*s*⟩ **3 a :** LEG — usu. used in pl. ⟨stir your ~*s,* step lively⟩ **b :** an artificial leg ⟨wore . . . a heavy wooden ~, which made a wooden sound as he walked —Osbert Sitwell⟩ **4 a :** the remaining part of something that has been worn down or used up : STUB ⟨pencil ~⟩ ⟨cigarette ~⟩ **b :** the portion of a worn or broken tooth remaining in the gum ⟨having the ~*s* extracted⟩ **c :** a mountain peak reduced from a former height or size by some natural force ⟨~*s* of much higher mountains of an earlier day —W.W.Atwood †1949⟩ **d :** the stub of a ship's mast ⟨the hulks or prison ships were old vessels reduced to their ~*s*⟩ **5 a stumps** *pl* **:** hair cut down or growing close to the skin : STUBBLE **b :** PINFEATHER **6 a :** a short pillar used as a barrier or marker : POST **b :** a small pillar at the entrance to a room in a mine **7 a :** one of the three pointed rods used in cricket that are stuck in the ground and topped with two bails to form a wicket **b** [short for *stumper*] **:** WICKETKEEPER **8 a** *archaic* **:** a tree stump used as a platform esp. by a political speaker **b :** a place or occasion for political public speaking ⟨supported it actively on the ~ and was elected —J.C.Yonge⟩ **9 a :** a small piece or projection in a lock for the attachment of another part or the reception of a screw or a rivet **b :** FENCE 6 **10 :** a miniature anvil in a watchmaker's staking set — **go on the stump** *or* **take the stump :** to go before the public or about the country as a political speaker or supporter of a cause ⟨*went on the stump* in his home state —S.H.Adams⟩ ⟨*took the stump* in a state campaign —*Springfield (Mass.) Republican*⟩ — **up a stump** *slang* **:** blocked in one's efforts : NONPLUSSED, PERPLEXED ⟨problems that sometimes got me *up a stump* —O.W.Holmes †1935⟩

²stump \"\ *adj* **:** shaped like or suggesting a stump ⟨a ~ arm⟩

³stump \"\ *vb* -ED/-ING/-S *vt* **1 :** to cut off a part of : reduce to a stump : TRIM ⟨~*ing* the plants⟩ **2 :** to dismiss (a cricket batsman who is out of his ground in attempting to play a bowled ball) by breaking the wicket with the ball — sometimes used with *out;* abbr. *st* **3 a :** to challenge to do something difficult or daring **b :** to block the progress or efforts of : PERPLEX, CONFOUND ⟨a mystery that still ~*s* everyone —*New Yorker*⟩ ⟨to become a universal genius and ~ the experts —*Nation's Business*⟩ ⟨a problem that had ~*ed* the mind of man for ages —M.R.Cohen⟩ **4 a :** to dig out by the roots ⟨~*ed* all the trees on the place⟩ **b :** to take or burn

stumps out of (land) ⟨land . . . which we hoped to ~ and plow ready for sowing —Alice F. Webb⟩ **5** *chiefly Brit* **a :** to pay out or come across with (money) — usu. used with *up* ⟨have been very decent and ~*ed* up half a quid each —Dorothy Sayers⟩ **b :** to cause (a person) to become penniless ⟨coming home from the races ~*ed*⟩ **6 :** to travel over (a region) making political speeches or supporting a cause ⟨~*ed* the country by air, train, and automobile caravans —T.L.Stokes⟩ ⟨was ~*ing* the country for the league —Dixon Wecter⟩ **7 a :** to walk over heavily or clumsily ⟨~*ing* the deck by the hour⟩ ⟨rising laboriously to the tips of my . . . shoes, I ~*ed* the width of the bed and back again —Agnes deMille⟩ **b :** to strike (as the toe) against something : STUB ⟨those stupid roads . . . where you ~*ed* your toe all the time —Samuel Selvon⟩ ~ *vi* **1 :** to walk heavily or noisily : STUMBLE ⟨spat his contempt and ~*ed* away —Roderick Finlayson⟩ ⟨~*ed* through the puddles —Mollie Panter-Downes⟩ ⟨~*ing* along eagerly on his iron support —T.B.Costain⟩ **2** *chiefly Brit* **:** to pay over money — usu. used with *up* ⟨if this was a bank, they'd have to ~ up —Richard Llewellyn⟩ **3 :** to go about making political speeches or supporting a cause ⟨~*ed* harder than ever, covering every county in the state —*Time*⟩ — often used with *for* ⟨~*ing* for these devices and their morale-building . . . virtues —David Riesman⟩

⁴stump \"\ *n* -S : DARE, CHALLENGE

⁵stump \"\ *or* **stomp** \'stämp\ *n* -S [F or Flem; F *estompe*, fr. Flem *stomp*, *stomp*, lit., stub, fr. MD *stompe*, *stomp* — more at ¹STUMP] **:** a short thick roll of leather or paper cut to a point or any similar implement used to rub down the lines of a crayon or pencil drawing in shading it or for shading drawings by producing tints and gradations from crayon in powder

⁶stump \'stəmp\ *vt* -ED/-ING/-S **:** to tone or treat (a crayon drawing) with a stump

stump·age \-pij, -pēj\ *n* -S **1 :** the value of or price paid for timber as it stands uncut in the woods **2 :** uncut marketable timber ⟨growing scarcity of accessible cedar ~ —*Jour. of Forestry*⟩

stump·er \'stəmpə(r)\ *n* -S **:** one that stumps: as **a :** one that removes tree stumps **b :** WICKETKEEPER **c :** a perplexing or difficult question : POSER ⟨a real question . . . a ~ —Benjamin DeMott⟩ **d :** STUMP SPEAKER ⟨the most indefatigable campaigner and best . . . ~ —Hodding Carter⟩ **e :** one that adjusts the mandrel on a tube-welding machine **f :** an operator of a felting machine

stumping *n* -S **:** a method of cultivating various plants (as blueberry bushes) by cutting mature bushes to the ground and covering the stubs with a mixture (as peat and sand) that is rich in humus

stump·ish \'stəmpish, -pēsh\ *adj* **:** of, relating to, or suggesting a stump ⟨called him a ~ man —H.S.Canby⟩

stump-jumper \'=,==\ *n* **1** *slang* **:** STUMP SPEAKER **2** *slang* **:** a person from a backwoods area

stump-jump plow \'=,=-\ *also* **stump-jumper** \'=,==\ *n* **:** a plow so constructed as to pass over the stumps or roots in newly cleared land

stumpknocker \'=,==\ *n* **:** a small brown-speckled sunfish (*Lepomis punctatus*) of the southeastern U.S. resembling the bluegill and esteemed as a panfish

stumpland \'=,=\ *n* **:** land full of the stumps of trees ⟨the best forests had been reduced to great stretches of ~ —*Amer. Guide Series: Minn.*⟩

stump·less \'= ,ləs\ *adj* **:** cleared of stumps

stump mast *n* **1 :** a lower mast with no topmast rigged **2 :** a broken mast

stumpnose \'=,=\ *n* [trans. of Afrik *stompneus*] *Africa* **:** any of several sea breams: as **a :** SILVER BREAM a; *esp* **:** WHITE STUMPNOSE **b :** RED STUMPNOSE

stump rot *n* **1 :** a disease of the tea bush in which the main central stem is rotted by a tooth fungus (*Irpex destruens*) **2 :** BUTT ROT

stumps *pl of* STUMP, *pres 3d sing of* STUMP

stump sock *n* **:** a special sock worn over an amputation stump with various types of prostheses

stump speaker *n* **:** one that does stump speaking

stump speaking *n* **:** speaking addressed to the general public during a political campaign or in support of a cause ⟨avoided public office and *stump speaking* but . . . engaged actively in party management —L.C.Hatch⟩

stump speech *n* **:** a speech made in the course of stump speaking

stump spud *n* **:** SPUD 2b

stumpsucker \'=,==\ *n* [¹*stump* + *sucker*] **:** CRIBBER b

stump sucker *n* [¹*stump* + *sucker* (shoot)] **:** a shoot growing from a stump

stump-tail \'=,=\ *or* **stump-tailed lizard** \'=¦=-\ *n* **:** an Australian scincoid lizard (*Trachysaurus rugosus*) having a short thick tail resembling its head in form

stump-tailed macaque *or* **stump-tailed monkey** *n* **:** a dark reddish brown pink-faced short-tailed macaque (*Macaca speciosa*) found in eastern Asia from Tibet to Indochina and Malaysia

stump topmast *n* **:** a topmast with no topgallant mast rigged

stump tracery *n* **:** tracery in late German Gothic architecture in which the molded bar seems to pass through itself in its convolutions and is then cut off short so that a section of the molding is seen at the end of each similar stump

stump tree *n* **:** KENTUCKY COFFEE TREE

stumpwood \'=,=\ *n* **1 :** wood from the base of a tree **2 :** STUMP 2b

stump work *n* **:** an elaborate colored embroidery with intricate padded designs and scenes in high relief esp. popular in 17th century England

¹stumpy \'stəmpē, -pi\ *adj* -ER/-EST [¹*stump* + -*y*] **1 :** full of short hard stalks or stubble ⟨walking through the ~ grass⟩ **2 a :** short and thick like a stump ⟨his ~ old umbrella —G.K.Chesterton⟩ ⟨bunches of ~ chimneys —Nigel Dennis⟩ ⟨a squat red smokestack between two ~ masts —George Santayana⟩ ⟨a ~ building⟩ **b :** having a short thick build : STUBBY ⟨is a block of a woman, thick and ~ and wide —Claudia Cassidy⟩ ⟨~ ungainly figure —R.H.Sampson⟩ **3 :** full of or abounding in stumps ⟨a hand-to-mouth existence on wheat and corn grown in ~ clearings —*Appalachia*⟩

²stumpy \"\ *n* -ES **1 :** one that is stumpy or has a stump **2 :** a pole-masted Thames barge **3** *Brit* **:** MONEY, CASH

stums *pres 3d sing of* STUM, *pl of* STUM

¹stun \'stən\ *vt* **stunned; stunned; stunning; stuns** [ME *stonen*, *stunen*, modif. of OF *estoner* — more at ASTONY] **1 a :** to cause to lose consciousness (as by a blow or concussion) ⟨gone about like a man half *stunned* —Rose Macaulay⟩ ⟨could ~ a rabbit or a squirrel with a stone —Helen Eustis⟩ **b :** to bewilder or daze with noise, clamor, or din : BENUMB ⟨a deafening crash *stunning* the ear drums —Fred Majdalany⟩ ⟨*stunned* into speechlessness by the abruptness and violence of the assault —W.A.Swanberg⟩ ⟨had been *stunned* by the terrific . . . bombardment —P.W.Thompson⟩ **2 a :** to shock or paralyze with strong emotional impression : STUPEFY ⟨still too *stunned* and dazed by the suddenness with which events had happened —Samuel Butler †1902⟩ ⟨*stunned* and reeling under her invective —D.G.Gerahty⟩ ⟨almost *stunned* by the surprise —A.W.Long⟩ **b** (1) **:** to overcome with astonishment or disbelief : CONFOUND, PERPLEX ⟨preparing a statement to ~ the company when we got the floor —Stuart Chase⟩ ⟨*stunned* me the other day by telling me she had attended a bullfight —G.S.Weight⟩ (2) **:** to overcome with pleasure or beauty ⟨the natural beauty of the desert ~*s* the visitor⟩ **3 a :** to bruise (as building stone) so as to cause spalls in the surface **b :** to scratch roughly (as by coarse sand under the saw in the kerf) **syn** see DAZE

²stun \"\ *n* -S **1 :** the effect of something that stuns : SHOCK ⟨the ~ of the blow . . . did not even dent his massive skull —James Jones⟩ ⟨bucklings and crashes and then the inside ~ of an explosion —Saul Bellow⟩ **2 :** one of the various strokes of the cue in snooker

stun·dism \'s(h)tün,dizəm\ *n* -S *usu cap* [Russ *shtundizm*, fr. *shtunda* + -*izm* -ism] **:** the religious movement of the Stundists or their principles and practices

stun·dist \-,dəst\ *n* -S *usu cap* [Russ *shtundist*, fr. *shtunda* Stundism, body of Stundists (fr. G *stunde* lesson, hour, fr. OHG *stunta* point in time, hour) + -*ist*; fr. their meetings for Bible study or prayer — more at STOUND] **:** one of a Russian denomination of Protestants originating about 1860 under German influence and emphasizing evangelical piety

stun·do-baptist \'s(h)tün(,)dō+\ *n*, *usu cap S&B* [*stundist* + -*o-* + *baptist*] **:** an adherent of a Russian religious movement originating in the 19th century with the union of various Stundists and Russian Baptists

stung [ME *stungen* (past pl. & past part.), fr. OE *stungon* (past pl.), gestungen (past part.)] *past of* STING

stunk [ME *stunken* (past pl. & past part.), fr. OE *stuncon* (past pl.), *stuncen* (past part.)] *past of* STINK

stun·kard \'stəŋkərd\ *adj* [origin unknown] *Scot* **:** STUBBORN, SULLEN

stunned *adj* **1 :** affected by stunning **2 :** caused by or as if by stunning ⟨the hurt look and the ~ silence —Robert Payne⟩ ⟨a ~ sensation held her emotions imprisoned —Ellen Glasgow⟩ ⟨for a ~ moment she lay, wondering —Dorothy Sayers⟩

stun·ner \'stənə(r)\ *n* -S **:** one that stuns: as **a :** something that amazes or astounds; *esp* **:** an unexpected event or development ⟨the ~ was what happened . . . on Saturday —G.F.T.Ryall⟩ **b :** a person or thing of unusual qualities or attractiveness ⟨the flashiest kind of girls — genuine ~*s* —R.L.Taylor⟩ ⟨would make a ~ of a table decoration —*New Yorker*⟩

stunner hitch *n* **:** a double Blackwall hitch

stun·ning \'stəniŋ, -nēŋ\ *adj* **1 a :** causing or capable of causing a state of bewilderment, shock, or insensibility ⟨its black powder blew forth a ~ detonation and volume of smoke —S.E.White⟩ ⟨with one ~ blow, laid the poor fellow senseless on the floor —R.L.Stevenson⟩ **b :** causing a high degree of surprise, astonishment, or consternation ⟨the sharecroppers' strike . . . came as a ~ protest against landlords —V.P.Hass⟩ ⟨no more ~ tax bills —J.H.Reese⟩ ⟨~ defeat⟩ ⟨~ collapse⟩ ⟨~ announcement⟩ **2 a :** of excellent quality or effect : SPLENDID, FIRST-RATE ⟨the book is a ~ piece of workmanship —*Current Biog.*⟩ ⟨the product of one of the most ~ talents today —Ann F. Wolfe⟩ **b :** emotionally impressive : ASTOUNDING, SENSATIONAL ⟨a breathtaking and . . . ~ midair extravaganza —*Monsanto Mag.*⟩ ⟨contributed ~ decorations for the adornment of sacred buildings —Edgar Levy⟩ ⟨a ~ performance⟩ ⟨a ~ recording⟩ **c :** extremely attractive : HANDSOME, GOOD-LOOKING ⟨was quite ~ . . . had a beautiful high-bosomed figure —Helen B. Woodward⟩ ⟨huge areas of glass, ~ colors, unusual new fabrics —*Newsweek*⟩ ⟨many ~ photographs of Canada's backwoods wilderness —William Murray⟩

stun·ning·ly *adv* **:** in a stunning manner **:** with a stunning effect ⟨sensitively directed and ~ photographed —Arthur Knight⟩ ⟨printed up two ~ handsome brochures —R.H. Rovere⟩

stun·poll \'stən,pōl\ *n* [irreg. fr. ¹*stone* + *poll*] *dial Eng* **:** a stupid person : DUNCE

stuns *pres 3d sing of* STUN, *pl of* STUN

stun·sail *or* **stun·s'l** \'stən(t)səl\ *n* [by contr.] **:** STUDDING SAIL

¹stunt \'stənt, *dial* " *or* -tûnt\ *adj* [prob. of Scand origin; akin to ON *stuttr* short, scant — more at STINT] **1** *chiefly dial* **:** STUBBORN, ANGRY **2** *chiefly dial* **:** STUNTED, UNDERSIZED, CURTAILED, BLUNT **3** *chiefly dial* **:** ABRUPT

²stunt \"\ *vb* -ED/-ING/-S *vt* **:** to hinder the normal growth, development, or progress of : DWARF, CHECK ⟨covered largely with ~*ed* pine woods —*Amer. Guide Series: N.J.*⟩ ⟨heifers will be ~*ed* and ruined, as they will calve at 18 months —*Farmer's Weekly (So. Africa)*⟩ ⟨physical and mental development became ~*ed* during . . . childhood —Dorothy Gardner⟩ ⟨superabundance of mechanical diversions ~*ed* men's souls —Bruce Marshall⟩ ~ *vi*, *archaic* **:** to become arrested in growth or development ⟨undernourished plants will ~⟩

³stunt \"\ *n* -S [²*stunt*] **1 :** a check in growth **2 :** a plant or animal that has been checked in growth; *esp* **:** a dwarfed plant **3 :** a disease of plants in which reduction in size is a marked symptom: as **a :** a virus disease of chrysanthemum characterized by smaller plants and leaves, smaller and often much earlier flowers, and bleaching of flower color esp. of the red and bronze varieties **b :** a similar virus disease of dahlia **c :** a disease of lettuce caused by a fungus of the genus *Pythium*

⁴stunt *vb* [prob. alter. of ³*stump*] *Scot* **:** STAMP

⁵stunt \"\ *n* -S [prob. alter. of ⁴*stump*] **1 a :** a feat or performance displaying notable strength or skill : TRICK ⟨a moored float with diving board and tower permits aquatic ~*s* —*Amer. Guide Series: Maine*⟩ ⟨standing with one foot on the seat, sitting on the handlebars, and similar ~*s* —W.L. Gresham⟩ ⟨one of his ~*s* . . . was to fly between two trees where the opening was narrower than his wingspread —*Amer. Guide Series: Calif.*⟩ **b :** a book or work marked chiefly by the display or exercise of skill or ingenuity : TOUR DE FORCE ⟨in a way this book is a ~, for the portraits are actually medallion heads —*New Yorker*⟩ ⟨the kind of literary ~ one remembers much more respectfully from a youthful reading than from a mature rereading —John Mason Brown⟩ ⟨too trickily written . . . too discontinuous in its drama to be more than a serious ~ —*Time*⟩ **2 :** an unusual feat or act performed or undertaken chiefly to gain attention or publicity ⟨in a money-raising ~ for the sports fund, he was fined a penny for every inch of waistline —Keith Ellis⟩ ⟨won the trip in a radio program advertising ~ —W.H.Davenport⟩ ⟨looked upon filibustering as a publicity ~ —Lindsay Rogers⟩

⁶stunt \"\ *vb* -ED/-ING/-S *vi* **1 a :** to perform stunts ⟨~*ed* without nets or any safety devices —Saul Bellow⟩ ⟨lugged a unicycle up the trail and ~*ed* on the summit —Andrew Hamilton & Chandler Harris⟩ **b :** to do stunts with an airplane ⟨its pilot was ~*ing* and . . . took a nose dive —Jean Stafford⟩ **2 :** to do unusual or startling things to attract attention or gain publicity ⟨sentimentalists, political agitators . . . and ~*ing* newspapers —A.A.Calwell⟩ ~ *vt* **:** to do stunts with (an airplane)

stunt·ed·ness *n* -ES **:** the quality or state of being stunted

stunt man *n* **:** one who professionally doubles for an actor in the performance of dangerous stunts

stunty \'stəntē, -ti\ *adj* -ER/-EST **:** characterized by stunts **:** given to performing stunts : FLASHY ⟨his advertising was flamboyant, ~, tricky —Don Wharton⟩ ⟨~ flying⟩

stu·pa \'st(y)üpə\ *n* -S [Skt *stūpa*] **:** a hemispherical or cylindrical mound or tower artificially constructed of earth, brick, or stone, surmounted by a spire or umbrella, and containing a relic chamber; *esp* **:** a Buddhist mound forming a memorial shrine of the Buddha — compare CHAITYA, DAGOBA

¹stupe \'st(y)üp\ *n* -S [ME *stupe*, *stuppe*, fr. L *stupa*, *stuppa* coarse part of flax, tow, fr. Gk *styppē*; perh. akin to Gk *styphein* to contract, be astringent, Skt *stukā* tuft of hair] **:** a cloth wrung out of hot water for external application sometimes with an added medicament as an irritant to stimulate local circulation ⟨a turpentine ~⟩

²stupe \"\ *vt* -ED/-ING/-S **:** to foment (a part of the body) with a stupe

³stupe \"\ *n* -S [short for ²*stupid*] *slang* **:** a stupid person : FOOL

stu·pe·fa·cient \¦st(y)üpə¦fāshənt\ *adj* [L *stupefacient-*, *stupefaciens*, pres. part. of *stupefacere* to stupefy] **:** bringing about a stupor : STUPEFYING

²stupefacient \"\ *n* -S **:** something promoting stupefaction : NARCOTIC

stu·pe·fac·tion \¦==¦fakshən\ *n* -S [NL *stupefaction-*, *stupefactio*, fr. L *stupefactus* (past part. of *stupefacere*) + -*ion-*, -*io* -ion] **:** the quality or state of being stupefied

stu·pe·fac·tive \¦==¦faktiv\ *adj* [ML *stupefactivus*, fr. L *stupefactus* (past part. of *stupefacere*) + -*ivus* -ive] *archaic* **:** STUPEFACIENT

stu·pe·fi·er \'==,fī(ə)r, -īə\ *n* -S **:** one that stupefies

stu·pe·fy \'st(y)üpə,fī\ *vb* -ED/-ING/-ES [MF *stupefier*, modif. (influenced by MF -*fier* -fy) of L *stupefacere*, fr. *stupēre* to be benumbed, be astonished, be stupefied + *facere* to make — more at DO] *vt* **1 a :** to make physically stupid, dull, or insensible : BENUMB ⟨concoctions of hemp and mandragora . . . to ~ the sensibilities of individuals who must undergo pain —*Science*⟩ ⟨people warped and *stupefied* by pellagra responded quickly to balanced diet —*Amer. Guide Series: Tenn.*⟩ **b :** to blunt or deaden the faculties of perception and understanding of ⟨such a power . . . enervates, extinguishes, and *stupefies* a people —Alexis de Tocqueville⟩ ⟨has not *stupefied* his countrymen into imitating his own mannerisms —*Times Lit. Supp.*⟩ ⟨the whole ~*ing* theological word game —H.J.Muller⟩ **2 :** to shock with surprise, astonishment, or consternation : STUN, ASTOUND ⟨the shape of the monolith . . . and the fanged feline deity left me wondering and *stupefied* —Angélica Mendoza⟩ ⟨was *stupefied* by the impact of this tragedy —B.A. Williams⟩ ⟨the amount of work their painstaking delicacy . . . represented was ~*ing* to think of —H.L.Davis⟩ ~ *vi* **:** to become stupid, dull, or torpid **syn** see DAZE

stu·pe·fy·ing·ly *adv* **:** in a stupefying manner **:** with a stupefying effect

stu·pen·dous \st(y)ü'pendəs, ÷ -njəs\ *adj* [L *stupendus*, gerundive of *stupēre* to be astonished] **1 :** causing astonishment or wonder : AWESOME, MARVELOUS ⟨that retribution follows guilt, in ways the most mysterious and ~ —Sheridan Le Fanu⟩ ⟨the still surviving walls and moats which form so ~ a feature of the place —*Country Life*⟩ ⟨a ~ occasion⟩ ⟨a ~ silence⟩ **2 :** of amazing size or greatness : PRODIGIOUS ⟨a ~ field of grass on which . . . some 10,000 wild animals were roaming —Alan Moorehead⟩ ⟨a facade ~ in its proportions —O.S.Nock⟩ ⟨~ labors⟩ ⟨~ demand⟩ ⟨~ war production⟩ ⟨~ uproar⟩ **syn** see MONSTROUS

stu·pen·dous·ly *adv* **:** in a stupendous manner **:** to a stupendous degree ⟨her nose ~ aquiline —Charles Dickens⟩ ⟨a group of ~ ignorant men⟩

stu·pen·dous·ness *n* -ES **:** the quality or state of being stupendous

stu·pent \'st(y)üpənt\ *adj* [L *stupent-*, *stupens*, pres. part. of *stupēre*] *archaic* **:** CONFUSED, BEWILDERED, DUMBFOUNDED

stu·pe·ous \-pēəs\ *adj* [L *stupeus*, *stuppeus* made of tow, fr. *stupa*, *stuppa* tow + -*eus* -eous] **:** resembling tow **:** having long loose scales or matted filaments : STUPOSE

¹stu·pid \'st(y)üpəd\ *adj* -ER/-EST [MF *stupide*, fr. L *stupidus*, fr. *stupēre* to be benumbed, be astonished, be stupefied; akin to Gk *typtein* to beat, strike — more at TYPE] **1 a :** slow of mind : UNIMAGINATIVE, OBTUSE, INSENSITIVE ⟨came to regard them as ~, sensual, veritable children of Adam —V.L.Parrington⟩ ⟨will defy the most phlegmatic and ~ spectator to behold it without admiration —Tobias Smollett⟩ ⟨bellowed into his ear as if he were deaf instead of ~ —Anthony Trollope⟩ **b :** given to unintelligent decisions or acts : UNTHINKING, IRRATIONAL ⟨while he may be wrong . . . he is never ~ —G.W.Johnson⟩ ⟨consider myself at least ~ for not having profited from many opportunities —Emery Neff⟩ ⟨reality is right under your ~ nose —Lionel Trilling⟩ **c :** lacking intelligence or reasoning power : BRUTISH ⟨getting the better of ~*er* beasts —G.A.Morgan⟩ **2 a :** dulled in feeling or sensation **:** being in a state of stupor : TORPID ⟨~ with drink —Sherwood Anderson⟩ ⟨~ with the lust of gain and the sloth of slavery —Van Wyck Brooks⟩ ⟨let fall the ~ inanimate limbs of the gone wretch —George Meredith⟩ **b :** incapable of feeling or sensation : INANIMATE ⟨nothing is quite so ~ as a fact —A.L.Guérard⟩ ⟨the ~ rain came down in buckets —J.W.Ellison b.1929⟩ **3 :** marked by or resulting from dullness or unintelligent thinking : SENSELESS ⟨a ~ refusal to be realistic —W.F.Hambly⟩ ⟨appalling capacity of collective man for ~, blind, self-destructive behavior —H.J. Muller⟩ ⟨takes everything seriously in a ~ and unimaginative fashion —K.T.Bluth⟩ ⟨it is ~ to wait until a probable enemy has gained a foothold from which to attack —F.D.Roosevelt⟩ **4 :** lacking interest or point : DREARY, BORING ⟨went to an awfully ~ evening . . . Monday night —Rachel Henning⟩ ⟨would not have minded his going to this ~ lunch —A.J. Cronin⟩ ⟨a really ~ performance⟩ **5** *dial Eng* **:** OBSTINATE, MULISH

syn DULL, DENSE, CRASS, DUMB: STUPID applies to a sluggish, slow-witted want of intelligence or comprehension, often congenital or accustomed; it may apply to a senseless, benumbed, or dazed condition ⟨so *stupid* and so obstinate that it was impossible to get him to do or understand anything —Anthony Trollope⟩ ⟨*stupid* with liquor and unable to understand that the ambulance had already gone —Scott Fitzgerald⟩ ⟨sleepy and *stupid* after a broken night and a hard day's work —Dorothy Sayers⟩ DULL strongly implies sluggish labored slowness of mind, with utter lack of quickness, brightness, or liveliness ⟨a *dull*, ambitionless, vegetating individual —J.A.Brussel⟩ ⟨with its impotent ruling classes and its *dull* and puritanical middle classes —Edward Shils⟩ DENSE applies to a blockheaded thick imperviousness or insensitive obtuseness ⟨she never offered to take me over the house, though I gave her the broadest hints — she's very *dense* —Clive Arden⟩ CRASS suggests a fatheaded grossness precluding delicacy, discrimination, or refinement ⟨in deep disgust at the farrier's *crass* incompetence to apprehend the conditions of ghostly phenomena —George Eliot⟩ ⟨a *crass* bonehead capable of sneering at the progress of the human race —Don Marquis⟩ DUMB may apply to an imperceptive vexatious obtuseness ⟨that the nutmegs were easily sold and eagerly bought is beside the story; the wonder is that we Southerners were so *dumb*, we did not know the difference —Erskine Caldwell⟩ ⟨I guess I was pretty *dumb* that morning, but a fellow in love never sees beyond his own nose —Vicki Baum⟩

²stupid \"\ *n* -S **:** a stupid person ⟨the generals were ~*s* —Stephen Crane⟩ ⟨such a ~ with my hands —John Selby⟩

stu·pid·i·ty \st(y)ü'pidəd·ē, -dətē, -i\ *n* -ES [MF *stupidité*, fr. L *stupiditat-*, *stupiditas*, fr. *stupidus* + -*itat-*, -*itas* -ity] **1 :** the quality or state of being stupid ⟨induced more by sudden alarm, coupled with blindness and ~ —James Stevenson-Hamilton⟩ **2 :** a stupid idea or act ⟨was keeping a diary of the captain's *stupidities* —Joanna Spencer⟩ ⟨tensions that lead to the *stupidities* of war —P.S.Henshaw⟩

stu·pid·ly *adv* **:** in a stupid manner

stu·pid·ness *n* -ES **:** the quality or state of being stupid : STUPIDITY

stuping *pres part of* STUPE

stu·por \'st(y)üpə(r)\ *n* -S [ME, fr. L, fr. *stupēre* to be benumbed, be astonished, be stupefied] **1 :** a physical or mental condition characterized by great diminution or suspension of sense or feeling : NUMBNESS, STUPEFACTION ⟨sleep produced by a bromide is . . . more of a ~ than natural sleep —D.W. Maurer & V.H.Vogel⟩ ⟨in a drunken ~ sold his wife to another —*Brit. Bk. News*⟩; *specif* **:** a chiefly mental condition marked by absence of spontaneous movement, greatly diminished responsiveness to stimulation, and usu. impaired consciousness — compare COMA **2 :** a state of apathy or torpor resulting often from stress or shock ⟨was in a ~ of mental weariness —Sherwood Anderson⟩ ⟨had collapsed for a moment in a ~ of pain —Marguerite Steen⟩ ⟨discomforts were minor, almost unnoticed in the leaden ~ of marching —Norman Mailer⟩ ⟨have recovered from the ~ of defeat —Sigmund Neumann⟩

stu·por·if·ic \¦==¦rifik\ *adj* **:** causing stupor ⟨was all ready to knock myself out with something really ~ —Christopher Morley⟩

stu·por·ose \'==,rōs\ *adj* [ML *stuporosus*, fr. LL, inducing stupor, fr. L *stupor* + -*osus* -ose] **:** STUPOROUS ⟨if so much drug is given that the patient becomes ~ —*Lancet*⟩ ⟨the patient . . . gradually became more anergic, ~, and silent in interviews —W.C.M.Scott⟩

stu·por·ous \-rəs\ *adj* [ML *stuporosus*] **:** attended or affected with stupor ⟨chronic intoxication may be manifested . . . by a dull, ~, almost comatose condition —D.W.Maurer & V.H.Vogel⟩ ⟨in demented children . . . ~ and hallucinatory conditions are rare —*Psychological Abstracts*⟩ ⟨stargazers as well as ~ bookworms —Charles Michelson⟩

stu·pose \'st(y)ü,pōs\ *adj* [ML *stuposus*, *stupposus*, fr. L *stupa*, *stuppa* tow + -*osus* -ose — more at STUPE] **:** composed of or having tufted or matted filaments like tow

stupp \'stəp, 'stüp\ *n* -S [G; prob. akin to OHG *stoub* dust — more at STIVE] **:** a black deposit obtained in distilling mercury ores and consisting of a mixture of soot, hydrocarbons, mercury and its compounds, and other dust

stuprate *vt* -ED/-ING/-S [L *stupratus*, past part. of *stuprare*, fr. *stuprum* defilement — more at TYPE] *obs* **:** to have sexual intercourse with (a woman); *esp* **:** RAPE

stupration *n* -S [prob. fr. (assumed) NL *stupration-*, *stupratio*, fr. L *stupratus* (past part. of *stuprare*) + -*ion-*, -*io* -ion] *obs* **:** the act of violating a woman : SEDUCTION, RAPE

stu·prum \'st(y)üprəm\ *n* -s [L, defilement, dishonor, stuprum] **1** *Roman & civil law* **:** sexual intercourse between a man and an unmarried woman other than one in slavery or concubinage **2** *Roman & civil law* **:** illicit intercourse contrary to morality **3** *Roman & civil law* **:** unchastity of a woman

stu·pu·lose \'st(y)üpyə,lōs\ *adj* [NL *stupulosus*, fr. L *stupa*, *stuppa* tow + *-ula* + *-osus* -ose] **:** covered with fine short hairs

stur·di·ly \'stərdəlē, 'stəd-, 'stəid-, -li\ *adv* [ME, fr. ¹*sturdy* + *-ly*] **:** in a sturdy manner

stur·di·ness \-dēnəs, -din-\ *n* -ES [ME *sturdinesse*, fr. ¹*sturdy* + *-nesse* -ness] **:** the quality or state of being sturdy

¹**stur·dy** \'stərdē, 'stəd-, 'stəid-, -di\ *adj* -ER/-EST [ME, fr. OF *estourdi*, *estordi* stunned, thoughtless, rash, past part. of *estourdir*, *estordir* to stun, fr. (assumed) VL *exturdire* to be dizzy as a thrush that is drunk from eating grapes, fr. L *ex-* + *turdus* thrush — more at THRUSH] **1** *obs* **:** brave, resolute, or fierce in combat **2** *archaic* **a :** difficult to manage **:** stubbornly rebellious **b :** OPINIONATED, OBSTINATE **3 a :** resistant to destruction **:** firmly built or constituted **:** STOUT ⟨a ~ peasant cottage of stucco and unpainted wood —Ida Treat⟩ ⟨the ~ oaks of the forest⟩ ⟨the *sturdiest* types of airplanes —F.J. Brown & J.S.Roucek⟩ **b :** resistant to disease or unfavorable weather **:** HARDY ⟨the *sturdiest* of creepers, facing the ferocious winds of the hills, the tremendous rains . . . and bitter frost —Richard Jefferies⟩ ⟨sumac and huckleberry hiding the less ~ flowers —*Amer. Guide Series: Minn.*⟩ **c :** sound or enduring in design or execution **:** SOLID, SUBSTANTIAL ⟨his ~, matter-of-fact exegesis with its resolute rejection of forced and fantastic interpretation —H.E.W.Fosbroke⟩ ⟨all delicate veining and spongy texture very unlike the ~ Maine landscapes he used to do —Carlyle Burrows⟩ ⟨conducts a ~ performance of the overture —Irving Kolodin⟩ **4 a :** characterized by or reflecting physical strength or vigor **:** ROBUST ⟨was a ~, handsome, high-colored woman —Carl Van Doren⟩ ⟨compact, broad, and ~ of limb —Joseph Conrad⟩ **b :** characterized by or expressive of mental vigor or vitality **:** UNSWERVING, RESOLUTE ⟨a ~ race, self-reliant and independent in temper —Allan Nevins & H.S.Commager⟩ ⟨developed into the *sturdiest* of fighters for reform —L.G.Vander Velde⟩ ⟨our democratic faith was ~ —F.D.Roosevelt⟩ ⟨~ common sense⟩ **syn** see STRONG

²**sturdy** \"\ *n* -ES **:** GID

sturdy beggar *n* **:** an able-bodied beggar or recipient of charity or relief who is capable of earning his own living

stur·geon \'stərjən, 'stəj-, 'stəij-\ *n* -s [ME, fr. OF *estourjon*, *esturgon*, of Gmc origin; akin to OE *styria* sturgeon, OHG *sturio*, ON *styrja*] **1 a :** any of various usu. large ganoid fishes of *Acipenser* and related genera that are widely distributed in the north temperate zone in both fresh and salt water, that have a heterocercal tail, a prolonged head with a toothless protrusile mouth on its undersurface, and an elongate body covered with tough skin protected by five rows of bony plates, and that are valued for their flesh and esp. for their roe which is made into caviar — compare BELUGA, STERLET **b :** fresh or cured sturgeon flesh **2 :** any of several fishes (as a paddlefish) related to and somewhat resembling the true sturgeons

stur·ine *also* **stur·in** \'stər-,ēn, -ər-ən, 'st(y)ü,rēn, -ürən\ *n* -s [ISV *stur-* (fr. NL *sturio* — specific epithet of the sturgeon *Acipenser sturio* —, fr. ML, sturgeon, of Gmc origin; akin to OHG *sturio* sturgeon) + *-ine* or *-in*] **:** a protamine in the spermatozoa of sturgeon

sturm's theorem \'stu̇rmz-\ *n*, *usu cap S* [after Jacques Charles François *Sturm* †1855 Fr. mathematician] **:** a theorem by which the number and position of the real roots between given limits of an algebraic equation are determined

sturm und drang \,shtu̇r,mu̇nt'dräŋ\ *n*, *usu cap S&D* [G, storm and stress, fr. *Sturm und Drang* (1776), drama by Friedrich Maximilian von Klinger †1831 Ger. dramatist and novelist] **1 :** a literary movement of the latter half of the 18th century in Germany characterized by a revolt against the strictures that the Enlightenment and a sterile imitation of French literature imposed, by the exaltation of nature, intuition, and inborn genius as the wellsprings of literature, and by works that typically are loosely constructed, written in realistic language, and marked by rousing action and high emotionalism and that frequently deal with the individual in revolt against the injustices of society **2 :** storm and stress **:** TURMOIL ⟨can no longer endure the buffetings of fate, the *Sturm und Drang* of life —*Times Lit. Supp.*⟩

stur·nel·la \,stər'nelə\ *n*, *cap* [NL, fr. L *sturnus* starling + *-ella*] **:** a genus of passerine birds (family Icteridae) including the meadowlarks

stur·ni·dae \'stərnə,dē\ *n pl*, *cap* [NL, fr. *Sturnus*, type genus + *-idae*] **:** a large family of passerine birds consisting of the Old World starlings and related birds and having ten primaries and characters somewhat intermediate between the crows and the American grackles — see STURNUS

stur·nine \'stər,nīn, -,nən\ *adj* [LL *sturninus* colored like a starling, fr. L *sturnus* starling + *-inus* -ine] **:** of, relating to, or resembling a starling

stur·noid \-,nȯid\ *adj* [NL *Sturnus* + E *-oid*] **:** resembling or related to the starlings

stur·nus \-,nəs\ *n*, *cap* [NL, fr. L, starling — more at STARLING] **:** the type genus of Sturnidae including the common starling

stur·shum \'stərshəm, 'stəsh-, 'stəish-\ *also* **stur·tion** \-shən\ *n* -s [by shortening & alter.] **:** NASTURTIUM

¹**sturt** \'stərt\ *n* [ME, contention, wrangling, alter. of *strut*, *strout* contention, combat; akin to MHG *strūz* combat, OE *strūtian* to exert oneself — more at STRUT] *chiefly Scot* **:** DISTURBANCE, TROUBLE ⟨amid the ~ of war —*Edinburgh Rev.*⟩ ⟨memories of early ~ and strife —John Buchan⟩

²**sturt** \"\ *vb* [ME *sturten* to fight, wrangle, fr. *sturt*, n.] *chiefly Scot* **:** STARTLE, STIR, VEX, ANNOY

sturt·ite \'stərd,īt\ *n* -s [Charles *Sturt* †1869 Eng. explorer + E *-ite*] **:** a mineral $Mn_3FeSi_4O_{11}(OH)_3.10H_2O(?)$ consisting of a rare hydrous silicate of iron, manganese, calcium, and magnesium and occurring in black compact masses

sturt's desert pea \'stərts-\ *also* **sturt pea** *n*, *usu cap S* [prob. fr. the name *Sturt*] **:** a glory pea (*Clianthus speciosus*) that is a sprawling shrubby perennial with long villous stems and pinnate leaves, that is noted for its scarlet black-marked flowers, and that is widely distributed in dry parts of Australia

stuss \'stəsh\ *n* -ES [Yiddish *shtos*, *stos*, fr. G *stoss* push, blow, fr. OHG *stōz* push, thrust — more at STØD] **:** faro in which cards are dealt by hand and the banker takes all bets on splits

stut \'stət, 'stu̇t\ *vb* [ME *stutten*] *dial* **:** STAMMER, STUTTER

¹**stut·ter** \'stəd-ə(r), -ətə-\ *vb* **stuttered; stuttered; stuttering** \-əd-əriŋ, -ətər-, -ə·tr-\ **stutters** [freq. of *stut*, fr. ME *stutten*; akin to D *stotteren* to stutter, MLG *stotern*, *stōtern* to stutter, OHG *stōzan* to thrust, push, L *tundere* to beat — more at STINT] *vi* **1 a :** to speak with involuntary disruption or blocking of speech (as by spasmodic repetition or prolongation of vocal sounds) — compare STAMMER **b :** to make sounds similar to or in the manner of a stutter ⟨thunder which ~*ed* far away in the distant ranges —Jean Stafford⟩ ⟨listens to the ~*ing*, muttering rumble of war —*Times Lit. Supp.*⟩ ⟨the one candle ~*ing* like an idiot's tongue —Edith Sitwell⟩ **2 :** to move or act in a halting or spasmodic manner ⟨schools are ~*ing* to an end —*Isis*⟩ ⟨a brilliant idea stands still and ~*ing* —V.S.Pritchett⟩ ~ *vt* **:** to say, speak, or sound with or as if with a stutter ⟨can only ~ his reply⟩ —often used with *out* ⟨the telegraph ticked the gladdest message . . . when it ~*ed* out its first letters —L.D.Lewis⟩ — **stut·ter·er** *n*

²**stutter** \"\ *n* -s **1 :** an act or instance of stuttering ⟨can hardly speak without a ~⟩ ⟨the ~ of the rain along the balconies —Elizabeth Bowen⟩ ⟨the heavy ~ of aerial fire —Walt Sheldon⟩ **2 :** STUTTERING 2 ⟨had a ~ but he was quite understandable —O.S.J.Gogarty⟩

stuttering *n* -s **1 :** the act of one who stutters **2 :** a disorder of vocal communication marked by involuntary disruption or blocking of speech (as by spasmodic repetition or prolongation of vocal sounds), by fear and anxiety, and by a struggle to avoid speech errors — compare STAMMERING

stut·ter·ing·ly *adv* **:** in a stuttering manner

stutt·gart \'s(h)tu̇t,gär|t, -tu̇t-, -gäl *sometimes* 'stət-; *usu* |d· +V\ *adj*, *usu cap* [fr. *Stuttgart*, city in southern Germany] **:** of or from the city of Stuttgart, Germany **:** of the kind or style prevalent in Stuttgart

stuttgart disease *also* **stuttgart's disease** *or* **stuttgart dog plague** *or* **stuttgart syndrome** *n*, *usu cap Stuttgart* **:** canine leptospirosis; *esp* **:** a severe highly contagious form of canicola fever marked by predominantly renal infection with nephritis and uremia, intense calf diphtheria, and bloody vomitus and diarrhea and commonly leading to collapse and death

stuttgart pitch *n*, *usu cap S* **:** INTERNATIONAL PITCH 2

stwd *abbr* steward

s-twist \'=,=\ *n*, *cap S* **:** a crossband twist

stwy *abbr* stairway

¹**sty** *or* **stye** *vi* **stied; stied; stying; sties** [ME *styen*, fr. OE *stīgan* to go up — more at STAIR] *obs* **:** ASCEND, MOUNT, CLIMB, RISE

²**sty** *also* **stye** \'stī\ *n*, *pl* **sties** *also* **styes** [ME *sty*, fr. OE *stī*, *stig* sty, pen, hall; akin to ON *-stī* sty and perh. to OE *stān* stone — more at STONE] **1 :** a pen or enclosure for swine **:** enclosed housing for swine **2 a :** an unkempt or filthy abode or lodging place ⟨her house was a perfect ~⟩ **b :** a low or vicious place **:** one catering to the viler instincts ⟨a ~ of immorality⟩

³**sty** \"\ *vb* **styed; styed; stying; sties** [ME *styen*, fr. OE *stigian*, fr. *stī*, *stig*, n.] *vt* **1 :** to pen up (swine) **2 :** to lodge or keep in or as if in a sty ~ *vi* **:** to live in a sty

⁴**sty** *or* **stye** \"\ *n*, *pl* **sties** *or* **styes** [short for obs. E *styan*, fr. (assumed) ME *styan*, alter. of OE *stīgend*, fr. *stīgan* to go up, rise] **:** an inflamed swelling of a sebaceous gland at the margin of an eyelid

sty·ca \'stīkə\ *n* -s [irreg. fr. OE (Northumbrian dial.) *stycas* lepta (in a translation of the Gospels at Mk 12:42); akin to OE *stycce* piece — more at STOCK] **:** a debased copper sceat issued by the kings of Northumbria during the 7th to 9th centuries

styf·siek·te \'stāf,sēktə, 'stīf-\ *or* **styf·ziek·te** \-,zē-\ *n* -s [Afrik *styfsiekte*, fr. *styf* stiff (fr. D *stijf*, fr. MD) + *siekte* disease, sickness, fr. MD, fr. *siek*, *siec* ill, sick — more at STIFF, SICK] *Africa* **:** aphosphorosis of cattle marked by faulty bone structure and lameness — compare LAMSIEKTE

styg·ian \'stij(ē)ən\ *adj*, *often cap* [L *stygius* stygian (fr. Gk *stygios*, fr. *Styg-*, *Styx* Styx, mythical stream considered to be the chief river of the subterranean world of the dead) + E *-an*] **:** of, relating to, or associated with the river Styx: as **a :** HELLISH, INFERNAL, GLOOMY **b :** characteristic of death **:** DEATHLY ⟨upon those roseate lips a ~ hue —William Wordsworth⟩ **c :** INVIOLABLE ⟨a ~ oath⟩

¹**styl-** *or* **stylo-** *comb form* [L *stylo-*, fr. Gk *styl-*, *stylo-*, fr. *stylos* — more at STEER] **:** pillar ⟨*Styl*aster⟩ ⟨*stylo*lite⟩

²**styl-** *or* **styli-** *or* **stylo-** *comb form* [*styl-* fr. earlier *stil-*, fr. L, stalk, fr. *stilus* stake, stalk, stylus; *styli-* fr. earlier *stili-*, fr. ML *styli-* stylus, fr. L *stilus*; *stylo-* fr. *styl-* + *-o-*] **1 :** style **:** styloid process ⟨*styl*ate⟩ ⟨*styli*ferous⟩ ⟨*stylo*graphic⟩ **2 :** of or relating to a styloid process and ⟨*stylo*mastoid⟩

sty·lar \'stīlə(r)\ *adj* [alter. of earlier *stilar*, fr. L *stil-* + E *-ar*] **1 :** of, relating to, or having the character of a style in writing **2 a :** of, relating to, or constituting an elongated process ⟨a ~ prominence on a shell⟩ **b :** leading to the ovary of a seed plant ⟨a ~ canal⟩

-sty·lar \,stīlə(r)\ *adj comb form* [Gk *stylos* pillar + E *-ar*] **:** having (such or so many) pillars **:** having (such) columniation ⟨amphi*stylar*⟩ ⟨hepta*stylar*⟩

stylar-end rot \,==-\ *n* **:** a disorder of limes and sometimes lemons that is of unknown cause and is characterized by a pale firm area of decay about the stylar end of the fruit

sty·las·ter \stī'lastə(r), -laas-\ *n* [NL, fr. ¹*styl-* + *-aster*] **1** *cap* **:** a genus of delicate usu. pink hydrocorals (order Stylasterina) **2** -s **:** any coral of the genus *Stylaster* or sometimes of the order Stylasterina

sty·las·te·ri·na \stī,lastə'rīnə, -rēnə\ *n pl*, *cap* [NL, fr. *Stylaster* + *-ina*] **:** an order of hydrocorals (class Hydrozoa) that are closely related to the millepores with which they were formerly included in the order Hydrocorallina

sty·late \'stī,lāt\ *adj* [prob. fr. (assumed) NL *stylatus*, fr. NL ²*styl-* + L *-atus* -ate] **1 :** having a persistent style ⟨~ ovaries⟩ **2 a :** bearing a style or stylet ⟨~ insects⟩ **b :** having the form of a stylet ⟨a ~ ovipositor⟩

¹**style** \'stīl, *esp before pause or consonant* -īəl\ *n* -s [ME, alter. (prob. influenced by Gk *stylos* pillar) of *stile*, fr. L *stilus* stake, stylus, manner of writing, style; akin to Av *staēra* mountain peak, OHG *stehhan* to prick — more at STICK] **1 :** an instrument used by the ancients in writing on waxed tablets and made with one of its ends sharp and the other blunt, smooth, and somewhat expanded for the purpose of making erasures by smoothing the wax **2 a :** mode of expressing thought in oral or written language: as **(1) :** a manner of expression characteristic of an individual, a period, a school, or other identifiable group (as a nation) ⟨a classic ~⟩ ⟨a flowery 18th century prose ~⟩ **(2) :** the aspects of literary composition that are concerned with mode and form of expression as distinguished from content or message ⟨his ~ is so graceful that one regrets he has nothing to say⟩ **(3) :** the manner, tone, or orientation assumed in discourse ⟨spoke in the ~ of a master to slaves⟩ ⟨took a very lofty ~ with us⟩ **b :** the custom followed (as in a business, editorial, or printing office) in spelling, capitalization, punctuation, and typographic arrangement and display **3 a :** a proper, generally recognized, or legally acceptable appellation **:** an official, distinctive, or honorific designation **:** mode of address **:** NAME, TITLE ⟨the king did not have the ~, Majesty, until the 16th century⟩ ⟨were in partnership under the ~, Acme Trading Company⟩ **b :** an attributive or qualifying designation ⟨gave himself the ~ of scholar⟩ **4 a :** manner or method of acting or performing esp. as recognized or sanctioned by some standard (as of law or custom) ⟨gave them a hearty welcome in the old-country ~⟩; *often* **:** one that is distinctive or characteristic of or attributed to some group or period ⟨singing in the Italian ~⟩ ⟨Renaissance ~ of painting⟩ ⟨oppressed by the formal ~ of the court⟩ **b :** a way or manner of living or behaving that is deemed elegant or in accord with fashion **:** a fashionable luxurious mode of life **:** fashionable elegance ⟨lived in ~⟩ ⟨a woman of ~⟩ **c (1) :** the peculiarly distinctive technique or methods characteristic of or identified with a particular individual usu. in the performance of a particular activity ⟨easy to recognize him by his ~ on the course⟩ **(2) :** an individual's typical way of life **:** his attitudes and their expression in a self-consistent manner as developing from childhood **d :** movement and manner in dancing as evolved in relation to a dance type, sex, tribe, region, or period **5 :** something felt to resemble the ancient style (as in appearance or use): as **a (1) :** the gnomon of a dial whose shadow marks the hour on the dial **(2) :** a pen or other writing instrument esp. as a symbol of authorship **(3) :** a blunt pointed surgical instrument **(4) :** a pointed tool used in engraving **:** GRAVER **(5) :** ETCHING NEEDLE **(6) :** a phonograph needle **:** STYLUS **b :** the usu. elongated portion of a pistil that connects the ovary with the stigma of a plant **:** a filiform prolongation of a plant ovary bearing a stigma at its apex — see FLOWER illustration **c (1) :** a slender bristle or other elongated process on an animal (as on the anal region or at the tip of the antenna of an insect or crustacean) **(2) :** a uniradiate sponge spicule that is blunt at one end **(3) :** a central calcareous process in the gastropores or sometimes also in the dactylopores of a coral of the order Stylasterina **(4) :** any of several small cusps or elevations of the cingulum of a molar tooth — see HYPOSTYLE, MESOSTYLE, METASTYLE, PARASTYLE **(5) :** EMBOLUS 3 **6 a (1) :** a quality that gives distinctive excellence to something (as artistic expression) and that consists esp. in the appropriateness and choiceness of the elements (as subject, medium, form) combined and the individualization imparted by the method of combining **(2) :** distinction of structural quality (as line, color, design, decoration) in dry goods (as for apparel, fabrics, interior decoration) **(3) :** the overall appearance and carriage of an animal esp. as an expression of personality and competence in action **b (1) :** a particular type of architecture based on distinctive qualities of design or decoration ⟨churches in the Gothic ~⟩ **(2) :** a combination of shape and ornamentation distinguishing an extensive group of artifacts (as ceramics) **c :** a general category based on somewhat similar characteristics (as of outward appearance) ⟨a modern ~ of furniture⟩ ⟨a Roman ~ of profile⟩ **syn** see FASHION

²**style** \"\ *vb* -ED/-ING/-S *vt* **1 :** to designate (as a person) by an identifying term **:** TERM, NAME, CALL ⟨an old lawyer *styled* judge by his friends⟩ ⟨does not hesitate to ~ himself scientist⟩ **2 :** to impart a particular style to ⟨carefully *styled* prose⟩: as **a :** to cause to conform to a customary style (as for publication) ⟨took hours to ~ the manuscript⟩ **b :** to design and make in accord with the prevailing mode; *esp* **:** to impart a new or distinctive design or quality to ⟨dresses *styled* for summer sports⟩ **c :** to impart a fashionable quality to (as by advertising) in order to stimulate sales **:** make stylish ⟨a campaign to ~ the new model⟩ ~ *vi* **:** to impart a style or stylish quality to something; *esp* **:** to make an article fashionable by advertising

³**style** \"\ *archaic var of* STILE

¹**-style** \,stīl\ *n comb form* [LL *-stylon*, fr. L, neut. of *-stylos* characterized by the presence of (so many) pillars, fr. Gk, fr. *stylos* pillar — more at STEER] **1 a :** structure characterized by the presence of (so many) pillars ⟨poly*style*⟩ **b :** structure with pillars ⟨cyrto*style*⟩ **2 :** animal part felt to resemble a pillar ⟨blasto*style*⟩ ⟨pygo*style*⟩

²**-style** \"\ *adj comb form* [L *-stylos*, fr. Gk, fr. *stylos* pillar] **:** characterized by the presence of (so many) pillars ⟨di*style*⟩

stylebook \'=,=\ *n* **:** a book explaining, describing, or illustrating the prevailing, accepted, or authorized style ⟨a dressmaker's ~⟩ ⟨a government ~ for printers⟩

styled \'stī(ə)ld\ *adj* [¹*style* + *-ed*] **:** having a specified style or number of styles — used in combination ⟨hetero*styled*⟩ ⟨short-*styled*⟩

style·dom \'= dəm\ *n* -s **:** the world of fashion

style·less \'stī(ə)lləs\ *adj* **:** lacking in style **:** UNSTYLISH ⟨a ~ costume⟩ — **style·less·ness** *n* -ES

stylelike \'=,=\ *adj* **:** resembling a style esp. in elongated pointed form ⟨a ~ process⟩

style of life **:** STYLE 4c(2)

style pen *n* **:** a stylographic pen

styl·er \'stīlə(r)\ *n* -s **:** STYLIST 2

style sheet *n* **:** a compilation of style rules often in the form of a card, pamphlet, or booklet

sty·let \'stīlət, *usu* -əd+V\ *n* -s [F, stylet, stiletto, fr. MF *stilet* stiletto, fr. OIt *stiletto* — more at STILETTO] **1 a :** a slender surgical probe **b :** a thin wire inserted in a catheter to maintain rigidity or in a hollow needle to maintain patency **2 a :** a style of a flowering plant **b :** a relatively rigid slender elongated organ or appendage on an animal **:** a small style **3 :** a small poniard **:** STILETTO **4 :** a pointed instrument or tool for making marks (as in graving)

sty·let·ed \-lәd·әd\ *adj* **:** having a stylet

sty·let·i·form \stī'led·ə,fȯrm\ *adj* **:** resembling or having the shape of a stylet

style up *vt* **:** to give a stylish or fashionable turn to (as something essentially utilitarian) **:** modify so as to impart style to ⟨*styled up* country denims trim enough for street wear⟩

stylewort \'=,=\ *n* [*style-* (fr. NL *Stylidium*) + *wort*] **:** a plant of the family Stylidiaceae

styli *pl of* STYLUS

styli- — see STYL-

-sty·lic \,stīlik, -lēk\ *adj comb form* [Gk *stylos* pillar + E *-ic*] **:** being or having (such) a connection of the jaw and skull ⟨hyo*stylic*⟩ ⟨strepto*stylic*⟩

sty·lid·i·a·ce·ae \(,)stī,lidē'āsē,ē\ *n pl*, *cap* [NL, fr. *Stylidium*, type genus + *-aceae*] **:** a family of herbs or shrubs (order Campanulales) of the southern hemisphere and esp. Australasia that have simple leaves and clustered perfect or unisexual flowers with a slightly irregular corolla followed by capsules bearing seeds with fleshy endosperm — **sty·lid·i·a·ceous** \(,)=,==,'āshəs\ *adj*

sty·lid·i·um \stī'lidēəm\ *n* [NL, fr. ¹*styl-* + *-idium*] **1** *cap* **:** the type genus of the family Stylidiaceae comprising mostly Australian herbaceous perennials that have racemes, panicles, or corymbs of showy flowers commonly with elastic stamens and are often cultivated as greenhouse ornamentals **2** -s **:** any plant or flower of the genus *Stylidium*

-stylies *pl of* -STYLY

sty·lif·er·ous \(')stī'lif(ə)rəs\ *adj* [²*styl-* + *-ferous*] **:** bearing one or more styles

sty·li·form \'stīlə,fȯrm\ *adj* [alter. of earlier *stiliforme*, fr. NL *stiliformis*, fr. ML *styli-* stylus + L *-formis* -form — more at STYL-] **:** resembling a style or stylus **:** bristle-shaped; *esp* **:** terminating in a long slender point ⟨a ~ antenna⟩

styling *n* -s [fr. gerund of ²*style*] **1** [fr. gerund of ²*style* "to shape or design by means of a stylus"] **:** ornamentation done with a style or stylus **2 :** the act or process of correcting a literary work with the purpose of improving the method or manner of expression **3 a :** the act or process of imparting a stylish quality or a particular style to; *esp* **:** the alteration of the style of something usu. to increase the sales appeal or utility or to improve the appearance **b :** the way in which something is styled

sty·li·on \'stīlēən\ *n*, *pl* **sty·lia** \-ēə\ *also* **stylions** [NL, irreg. fr. ²*styl-*] **:** an anthropometric reference point consisting of the end of the styloid process of the radius — called also *styloid point*

styl·ish \'stīlish, -lēsh\ *adj* **:** having style **:** conforming to an accepted standard and esp. to one of current fashion — **styl·ish·ly** \-ləshlē, -lēsh-, -li\ *adv* — **styl·ish·ness** *n* -ES

styl·ism \'stī,lizəm\ *n* -s [ISV ¹*style* + *-ism*; prob. orig. formed as F *stylisme*] **:** concern with style (as in art or literature) as an end in itself **:** undue preoccupation with style

styl·ist \-,ləst\ *n* -s [ISV ¹*style* + *-ist*] **1 :** one who is a master or model of style: as **a (1) :** a writer or speaker who is eminent in matters of style **(2) :** a critic of literary style **b :** a sports performer noted for precision and excellence in form **2 :** one who develops, designs, or advises on styles ⟨a fashion ~⟩ ⟨a hair ~⟩ ⟨an industrial ~⟩: as **a :** one who decides points of style or makes or enforces style rules (as in a publishing house or editorial office) **b :** a coordinator of fashions in a store

sty·lis·tic \(')stī'listik, -tēk\ *also* **sty·lis·ti·cal** \-tәkәl, -tēk-\ *adj* [*stylistic* ISV *stylist* + *-ic*; *stylistical* fr. *stylistic* + *-al*] **:** of or relating to style esp. in the use of language — **sty·lis·ti·cal·ly** \-tək(ə)lē, -tēk-, -li\ *adv*

sty·lis·tics \-tiks, -tēks\ *n pl but sing or pl in constr* [ISV *stylist* + *-ics*] **1 :** an aspect of literary study that emphasizes the analysis of various elements of style (as metaphor and diction) **2 :** the study of the devices in a language (as rhetorical figures and syntactical patterns) that produce expressive value

sty·lite \'stī,līt\ *n* -s [LGk *stylitēs*, fr. Gk *stylos* pillar + *-itēs* -ite — more at STEER] **:** one of a class of ascetics who lived as hermits on the tops of pillars chiefly in Syria and after the time of the famous pillar hermit Simeon Stylites († A.D.459) — called also *pillar saint*

styl·iza·tion \,stīlə'zāshən, -,lī'z-\ *n* -s [ISV *stylize* + *-ation*] **1 :** the quality or state of being stylized **2 :** an act or instance of stylizing

styl·ize \'stī(ə),līz\ *vt* -ED/-ING/-S *see -ize in Explan Notes* [trans. of G *stilisieren*] **:** to cause to conform to a style **:** give a formal quality to by causing to conform to a set plan or style **:** CONVENTIONALIZE: as **a :** to cause (an object represented in sculpture or in pictorial art) to conform to a style of expression often extreme in character rather than to the appearance of nature **b :** to design (theatrical matter) according to a stylistic pattern esp. so that the mise-en-scène, costumes, and other elements are illustrative of the idea of the play **c :** to emphasize inherent rhythmic or pictorial qualities of (a movement in dancing) so as to enhance artistic rather than natural effects; *also* **:** to employ such emphasis as the basis of (one's technique) in designing or staging dances

¹**sty·lo** \'stī(,)lō\ *n* -s [by shortening] **:** STYLOGRAPH

²**stylo** \"\ *n* -s [modif. of NL *Stylosanthes*] **:** a leguminous plant (*Stylosanthes gracilis*) grown in warm parts of Australia for pasture

stylo- — see STYL-

sty·lo·bate \'stīlə,bāt\ *n* -s [L *stylobates*, *stylobata*, fr. Gk *stylobatēs*, fr. *stylos* pillar + *-batēs* one that treads, fr. *bainein* to walk, go — more at COME] **:** a continuous flat coping or pavement on which a row of architectural columns is supported; *esp* **:** the uppermost step of a stereobate supporting a peristyle — see SUBBASE

sty·lo·ce·rite \,stīlō'si,rīt\ *n* -s [¹*styl-* + *cer-* (fr. Gk *keras* horn) + *-ite* — more at HORN] **:** an often spinous process on the outer aspect of the first antennae of a crustacean — see NATANTIA

sty·lo·chus \'stīləkəs\ *n*, *cap* [NL, fr. ²*styl-* + Gk *ochos* one that holds, fr. *echein* to have, hold — more at SCHEME] **:** a genus (the type of the family Stylochidae) of large polyclad flatworms with an oval flat body, short tentacles, and pharynx with several accessory lobes

sty·lo·glos·sus \,stī(,)lō'gläsəs, -glȯs-\ *n*, *pl* **styloglos·si** \-lä,sī, -lȯ,sī\ [NL, fr. ²*styl-* + *-glossus* (fr. Gk *glōssa* tongue) — more at GLOSS] **:** a muscle arising from the styloid process of

the temporal bone and inserted along the side and underpart of the tongue

sty·lo·go·nid·i·um \ˌstī(ˌ)lō+\ *n* [NL, fr. ²*styl-* + *gonidium*] : PYCNOSPORE

sty·lo·graph \ˈstīləˌgraf, -raa(ə)f, -aif, -.af\ *n* [²*styl-* + *-graph*] : a stylographic pen

sty·lo·graph·ic \ˌ�milgrafik, -ˈfēk\ *also* **sty·lo·graph·i·cal** \-fəkəl, -ˈfēk-\ *adj* [*stylographic* + *-al*] **1** : of, relating to, or used in stylography ⟨~ tablets⟩ **2** : of, relating to, or being a fountain pen that has a fine writing point fitted with a needle which by the pressure of the point on a surface is pushed back to release the flow of ink ⟨a ~ pen⟩ ~ *writing⟩* — **sty·lo·graph·i·cal·ly** \-fək(ə)lē, -ˈfēk-, -li\ *adv*

sty·log·ra·phy \stīˈlägrəfē, -fi\ *n* -ES [²*styl-* + *-graphy*] : a mode of writing or tracing lines by means of a style or similar instrument on cards or tablets

sty·lo·hy·al \ˌstī(ˌ)lōˌhīal\ *n* -s [²*styl-* + *hyoid* + *-al*, adj. suffix] : an element of each side of the hyoid arch between the epihyal and tympanohyal that appears as a distinct element of the anterior cornu of the hyoid bone in many mammals — see STYLOID PROCESS

sty·lo·hy·oid \ˌ⸱(ˌ)⸱hī,ȯid\ *also* **sty·lo·hy·oi·de·us** \ˌ⸱⸱(ˌ)⸱- hī'ȯidēəs\ *n, pl* **stylohyoids** \-dz\ *also* **stylohyoi·dei** \-dē,ī\ [NL *stylohyoideus*, fr. ²*styl-* + *hyoides* hyoid bone + L *-eus* *-eous*] : a slender muscle connecting the back part of the styloid process and the body of the hyoid bone

sty·loid \ˈstīˌlȯid\ *adj* [NL *styloides*, fr. Gk *styloeidēs*, fr. *stylos* pillar — fr. L *stilus* *styl-* (irreg. — influenced by Gk *stylos* pillar — fr. L *stilus* stylus) + *-oeidēs* *-oid* — more at STYLE] : resembling a style : STYLIFORM — used esp. of slender pointed skeletal processes

styloid point *n* : STYLION

styloid process *n* : any of several long slender pointed bony processes; *esp* : one from the lower side of the temporal bone of man corresponding to the tympanohyal and stylohyal of other mammals

sty·lo·lite \ˈstīlə,līt\ *n* -s [ISV ¹*styl-* + *-lite*] : a small longitudinally grooved column of the same material as the rock in which it occurs often resulting from the slipping under vertical pressure of a part capped by a shell through adjacent parts not so capped though one or more layers (as of limestone) may be affected by stylolitic structure throughout where there is no capping object — **sty·lo·lit·ic** \ˌ⸱⸱ˈlid-ik\ *adj*

sty·lo·man·dib·u·lar \ˌstī(ˌ)lō+\ *adj* [²*styl-* + *mandibular*] : of, relating to, or being a ligament connecting the styloid process of the temporal bone and the angle of the lower jaw

sty·lo·mas·toid \"+\ *adj* [²*styl-* + *mastoid*] **1** : of, relating to, or being a foramen that occurs on the lower surface of the temporal bone between the styloid and mastoid processes and forms the termination of the facial canal **2** : of or associated with the stylomastoid foramen ⟨~ vessels⟩

sty·lo·met·ric \ˌstīlə̷me·trik\ *adj* : of, relating to, or involving the methods of stylometry

sty·lom·e·try \stīˈlämə-trē, -tri\ *n* -ES [¹*style* + *-o-* + *-metry*] : the study of the chronology and development of an author's work based esp. on the recurrence of particular turns of expression or trends of thought

sty·lom·ma·toph·o·ra \ˌstī,lämə'täfərə\ *n pl, cap* [NL, fr. ¹*styl-* + Gk *ommat-, omma* eye + NL *-o-* + *-phora*; akin to Gk *ōps* eye — more at EYE] : a suborder of Pulmonata comprising gastropods with the eyes situated at the tips of the tractile tentacles and including the common land snails and slugs — **sty·lom·ma·toph·o·rous** \(')⸱⸱'täfərəs\ *adj*

sty·lo·nych·ia \ˌstīlə'nikēə\ *n, cap* [NL, fr. ¹*styl-* + *onych-* *-ia*] : a common genus of marine and freshwater, ovoid or reniform, hypotrichous ciliates related to *Oxytricha* and distinguished by long well-developed caudal cirri

sty·lo·pha·ryn·ge·us \ˌstī(ˌ)lōfə'rinjēəs, -ˌfarən'jēəs\ *or* **stylopharyn·gei** \-je,ī\ [NL, fr. ¹*styl-* + *pharyngeus*, adj.; pharyngeal — more at PHARYNGEAL] : a slender muscle connecting the base of the styloid process and side of the pharynx

¹sty·lo·pid \ˈstīlopəd, -,pid\ *adj* [NL *Stylopidae*] : of or relating to the Stylopidae

²stylopid \"\ *n -s cap* [NL *Stylopidae*] : an insect of the family Stylopidae; *broadly* : STYLOPS 2

sty·lop·i·dae \stīˈläpə,dē\ *n pl, cap* [NL, fr. *Stylop-, Stylops*, type genus + *-idae*] : a family of insects (order Strepsiptera) that have protuberant eyes and are parasites of other insects (as bees)

sty·lo·piza·tion \ˌstīlopə'zāshən, -,pī'z-\ *n -s* [NL *Stylop-, Stylops* + E *-ization*] : the condition of being or the process of becoming stylopized

sty·lo·pized \ˈstīlə,pēzd\ *adj* [NL *Stylop-, Stylops* + E *-ize* + *-ed*] : altered by the presence of a parasitic stylops usu. with inhibition of normal sexual development so that an intersexual state results ⟨a ~ female wasp⟩

sty·lo·po·di·um \ˌstīlə'pōdēəm\ *n, pl* **stylopo·dia** \-dēə\ [NL, fr. ²*styl-* + *-podium* (fr. Gk *podion* small foot, base) — more at PEW] : a disk-shaped or conical swelling or expansion at the base of the style in plants of the family Umbelliferae

sty·lops \ˈstīˌläps\ *n* [NL *Stylop-, Stylops*, fr. ¹*styl-* + *-op-, -ops -ops*] **1** *cap* : a large genus (the type of the family Stylopidae) comprising many of the better known strepsipterans **2** *pl* **stylops** *or* **stylopses** : any insect of the genus *Stylops*; *broadly* : an insect of the order Strepsiptera

stylos *pl of* STYLO

sty·lo·san·thes \ˌstīlə'san(ˌ)thēz\ *n, cap* [NL, fr. Gk *stylos* pillar + NL *-anthes* — more at STEER] : a genus of herbs (family Leguminosae) that are widely distributed in warm regions and have pinnately trifoliolate leaves and yellow flowers in small terminal or axillary clusters — see PENCIL FLOWER, STYLO

sty·lo·spore \ˈstīlə,spō(ə)r\ *n* [ISV ¹*styl-* + *-spore*; prob. orig. formed in F] : PYCNOSPORE

sty·lo·typ·ite \ˈstīlə,tī,pīt\ *n -s* [G *stylotyp* stylotypite (fr. styl- ¹*styl-* + *typ* type, fr. LL *typus*) + E *-ite* — more at TYPE] : a mineral (Cu,Fe,Ag)₃SbS₃ that is a sulfide of antimony, copper, silver, and iron and occurs in black orthorhombic crystals (hardness 3, sp. gr. 4.7-5.2)

-sty·lous \ˈstīləs\ *adj comb form* [¹*style* + *-ous*] : having (such) a style or (such or so many) styles — in descriptive terms in botany ⟨dolichostylous⟩ ⟨monostylous⟩

sty·lus *also* **sti·lus** \ˈstīləs\ *n, pl* **sty·li** \-ī,lī\ *also* **styluses** [in sense 1, fr. NL, alter. (prob. influenced by Gk *stylos* pillar) of L *stilus* stake, stylus; in other senses, modif. (prob. influenced by Gk *stylos* pillar) of L *stilus* — more at STYLE] **1 a** : STYLE 5b **b** : STYLE 5c, STYLET 2b; *esp* : any of various small pointed processes on the external genitalia of an insect **2** : INDICATOR, POINTER; *esp* : the gnomon of a sundial **3** : an instrument for writing or marking: as **a** (1) : STYLE 1 (2) : an ancient writing instrument for use on papyrus or parchment **b** (1) : a hard-pointed piece (as of glass or other material) used for tracing or writing on carbon paper so as to make impressions on the paper beneath the carbon (2) : a hard-pointed pen-shaped instrument for drawing, tracing, lettering, shading, ruling, or handwriting on stencils used in a reproducing or duplicating machine **c** (1) : NEEDLE 5b (2) : a cutting tool used to produce an original record groove during disc recording — called also *cutting stylus* **d** : a hard-pointed instrument for punching the dots in writing braille with a braille slate **e** : a device that traces a recording (as of a kymograph or an electrocardiograph) on paper

-sty·ly \ˌstīlē, -li\ *n comb form* -ES [ISV ¹*style* + *-y*] : condition of having (such or so many) styles — in botanical terms ⟨heterostyly⟩

styme *var of* STIME

¹sty·mie \ˈstīmē, -mi\ *n -s* [perh. fr. Sc *stymie* person with poor eyesight, fr. E *styme* + *-ie*] **1** : a condition that exists on a golf putting green when the ball nearer the hole lies in the line of play of another ball **2** : a thoroughly distressing and thwarting situation

²stymie \"\ *vt* **stymied; stymied; stymieing; stymies** : BLOCK, CHECK, THWART ⟨~ a plan⟩

stym·pha·lian \(')stim'fālēən, -lyən\ *adj, usu cap* [Gk *Stymphalios* Stymphalian (fr. *Stymphalos* Stymphalus, mountain in Arcadia near the lake formerly called Stymphalis and now called Zaraka) + E *-an*] : of or relating to Lake Zaraka in Arcadia that according to Greek mythology was haunted by man-eating birds slain by Hercules

sty·phe·lia \stīˈfēlē, -lyə\ *n, cap* [NL, fr. Gk *styphelos* rough + NL *-ia*; perh. akin to Gk *typtein* to beat, strike — more at

TYPE] : a large genus of mostly Australasian heathlike shrubs (family Epacridaceae) having the calyx and corolla usu. colored alike

styph·nate \ˈstif,nāt\ *n -s* [ISV *styphn-* (in *styphnic acid*) + *-ate*] : a salt of styphnic acid

styph·nic acid \ˈstifnik-\ *n* [ISV *styphn-* (fr. G — in G *styphninsäure* styphnic acid —, irreg. fr. Gk *stryphnos* astringent) + *-ic* — more at STRUBBLY] : an explosive yellow crystalline astringent acid $(NO_2)_3C_6H(OH)_2$ obtained usu. by nitration of resorcinol; 2,4,6-trinitro-resorcinol — compare PICRIC ACID

styp·sis \ˈstipsəs\ *n -s* [NL, fr. LL, astringency, contraction, fr. Gk, fr. *styphein* to contract + *-sis*] : the application or use of styptics

¹styp·tic \ˈstiptik, -tēk\ *adj* [ME *stiptik*, fr. L *stypticus*, fr. Gk *styptikos*, fr. (assumed) Gk *styptos* (verbal of *styphein* to contract, be astringent) + Gk *-ikos -ic* — more at STUPE] **1 a** : having an astringent effect : tending to contract or bind **b** : having a harsh, acrid, or acid effect or flavor ⟨the laughter they excite is more ~ than warm —R.A.Cordell⟩ **2** : tending to check bleeding ⟨the ~ effect of cold⟩; *esp* : having the property of arresting oozing of blood (as from a shallow surface injury) when applied to a bleeding part ⟨a ~ agent⟩ — compare HEMOSTATIC

²styptic \"\ *n -s* [ME *stiptik*, fr. LL *stypticum*, fr. Gk *styptikon*, fr. neut. of *styptikos*, adj.] : an agent (as a drug) having a styptic effect

styp·ti·cal \-təkəl\ *adj, archaic* : STYPTIC

styptic collodion *n* : a collodion preparation containing a styptic (as tannin) and used on minor cuts and wounds to stop bleeding

styptic cotton *n* : cotton prepared by impregnating with a styptic agent and drying and applied to minor wounds to stop bleeding

styp·tic·i·ty \stip'tisəd-ē\ *n -ES* [ME *stipticite*, fr. ML *stypticitat-, stypticitas*, fr. L *stypticus* styptic + *-itat-, -itas -ity*] : styptic quality : ASTRINGENCY

styptic pencil *n* : a cylindrical stick of a paste vehicle medicated with a styptic substance (as alum) and applied to small wounds to stop bleeding

styptic weed *n* : a senna (*Cassia occidentalis*)

sty·ra·ce·ae \stīrə'kāsē,ē, -stīr-\ *n pl, cap* [NL, fr. *Styrac-, Styrax*, type genus + *-aceae*] : a widely distributed family of shrubs and trees (order Ebenales) having flowers with a 5-lobed corolla and 10 stamens and a dry or drupaceous fruit — see STYRAX — **styra·ca·ceous** \ˌ⸱⸱'kāshəs\ *adj*

styra·cin \ˈstirəsən, 'stir-\ *n -s* [F *styracine*, fr. L *styrac-, styrax* + F *-ine* -in] : a crystalline compound $C_{18}H_{16}O_2$ extracted esp. from storax and balsam of Peru; cinnamyl cinnamate

sty·rac·i·tol \stīˈrasə,tȯl, -tōl\ *n -s* [NL *Styrac-, Styrax* + E *-itol*] : a crystalline heterocyclic polyhydric alcohol $C_6H_{12}O_5$ that is obtained from the fruit of a Japanese shrubby tree (*Styrax obassia*) or made synthetically and that is an inner ether of D-mannitol; 1,5-anhydro-D-mannitol

sty·rax \ˈstī,raks\ *n* [L *styrac-, styrax* storax, tree (of the genus *Styrax*) yielding storax, fr. Gk *styrak-, styrax*] **1** -ES : STORAX 1, 2 **2** [NL *Styrac-, Styrax*, fr. L] *a cap* : a large genus (the type of the family Styracaceae) of shrubs and trees that have usu. pubescent leaves and pendulous racemes of flowers with the petals distinct or slightly united and that include forms yielding commercially important resins — see BENZOIN 1, STORAX 1 **b** -ES : any plant of the genus *Styrax* : STORAX 3

styre·nate \ˈstīrə,nāt, 'stir-\ *vt* -ED/-ING/-S [*styrene* + *-ate*] : to combine with styrene, alpha-methyl-styrene, or a similar polymerizable monomer ⟨*styrenated* drying oils, and *styrenated* alkyds as a base for many protective coatings —*Encyc. of Chem. Technol.*⟩ — **styre·na·tion** \ˌ⸱⸱'nāshən\ *n -s*

styrene \ˈstī,rēn *also* 'sti,r-\ *n -s* [ISV *styr-* (fr. L *styrax*) + *-ene*] **1 a** : a fragrant mobile liquid unsaturated hydrocarbon $C_6H_5CH=CH_2$ that is obtained by the distillation of storax or the decomposition of cinnamic acid or more often from ethylbenzene either by catalytic dehydrogenation or by oxidation to acetophenone followed by partial reduction and dehydration, that polymerizes in the presence of air or peroxides to yield polystyrene, and that is used chiefly in making synthetic rubber, resins, and plastics and in improving drying oils — called also *phenylethylene, vinylbenzene*; see GR-S **b** : POLYSTYRENE **c** : STYRENE PLASTIC **2** : a bivalent radical –CH⟨CH₆- H₅⟩CH₂– derived from styrene by breaking of the double bond — called also *phenylethylene*

styrene plastic *n* : any of various synthetic plastics made from styrene by polymerization or copolymerization

¹styr·i·an \ˈstirēən\ *n -s cap* [*Styria*, province of southeastern Austria + E *-an*, n. suffix] : an inhabitant or native of Styria

²styrian \"\ *adj, usu cap* [*Styria* + E *-an*, adj. suffix] : of or relating to Styria

sty·rol \ˈstī,rȯl, 'sti,r-, -rōl\ *n -s* [ISV *styr-* (fr. L *styrax*) + *-ol*; prob. orig. formed as G] : STYRENE 1a

styryl \ˈstīrəl, 'stir-\ *n -s* [ISV *styr-* (fr. L *styrax*) + *-yl*] : a univalent radical $C_6H_5CH=CH-$ derived from styrene by removal of one of the hydrogen atoms attached to the omega carbon atom

styth *or* **stythe** \ˈstīth, -th\ *n -s* [prob. alter. of *stife*] *dial Brit* : BLACKDAMP

SU *abbr* **1** sensation unit **2** service unit **3** set up **4** Siemens's unit

sua·be flute \ˈswäbə-\ *n* [*suabe* prob. modif. of L *suavis* sweet — more at SWEET] : a wood flute organ stop of 4-foot pitch with a bright clear tone

suabian *usu cap, var of* SWABIAN

su·abil·i·ty \ˌsüə'biləd-ē, -ˌlət-ē, -i\ *n* : the quality or state of being suable

su·able \ˈsüəbəl\ *adj* [*sue* + *-able*] : capable of being sued : subject to be called to answer in court — **su·ably** \-blē, -bli\ *adv*

su·ae·da \sü'ēdə\ *n, cap* [NL, fr. Ar *suwayd*] : a genus of herbs and shrubs (family Chenopodiaceae) bearing fleshy terete leaves and small flowers with a persistent 5-lobed perianth — see BURROWEED, SEA BLITE, SEEPWEED

sua·kin gum \ˈswäkən-\ *n, usu cap S* [*Suakin*, seaport on Red sea, northeastern Sudan] : TALHA GUM

suan pan *or* **swan pan** \ˈswän'pän\ *n* [Chin (Pek) *suan⁴-p'an²*, lit., reckoning board] : an abacus employed by the Chinese and containing balls movable along rods held by a wooden frame

su·ant \ˈsüənt\ *var of* SUENT

sua·rez·ian \(')swä'rezēən\ *adj, usu cap* [*Francisco Suárez* †1617 Span. theologian + E *-ian*] : of, relating to, or typical of the Spanish Jesuit Francisco Suárez or his political, philosophical, and theological doctrines

sua·rez·ian·ism \-ə,nizəm\ *n -s usu cap* : the theories of Francisco Suárez characterized by criticism of the concept of the divine right of kings, by belief that a ruler derives his authority directly from the people and only indirectly from God, and by a moderate scholasticism differing from Thomism primarily in rejecting a real though accepting a rational distinction between essence and existence and in a tendency to Molinism

sua·si·ble \ˈswāsəbəl, -āzə-\ *adj* [LL *suasibilis*, fr. L *suasus* (past part. of *suadēre* to advise, urge) + *-ibilis -ible*] : capable of being persuaded : easily persuaded

sua·sion \ˈswāzhən\ *n -s* [ME, fr. L *suasion-, suasio*, fr. *suasus* (past part. of *suadēre* to advise, urge) + *-ion-, -io* -ion; akin to L *suavis* sweet — more at SWEET] : the act or an instance of urging, convincing, or persuading : PERSUASION ⟨moral ~⟩

¹sua·sive \ˈswäsiv, 'ēv *also* -āz\ *or* \əv\ *adj* [L *suasus* (past part.) + E *-ive*] : tending to persuade : having a capacity for persuading : PERSUASIVE ⟨a ~ speaker⟩ ⟨~ eloquence⟩ — **sua·sive·ly** \əv-\ *adv* — **sua·sive·ness** \ivnəs,|əv-\ *n*

²suasive \"\ *n -s* : something (as a force, speech, or influence) that exerts a suasive effect

sua·so·ria \swə'sōrēə, -ȯr-\ *n, pl* **suasori·ae** \-rē,ē, -ī\ [L, fr. fem. of *suasorius* persuasive, fr. *suasus* + *-orius -ory*] : an ancient Roman oration dealing with a problem of conscience

suave \ˈswäv, -ä-\ *adj, often* -ER/-EST [MF, fr. L *suavis* pleas-

ant, sweet — more at SWEET] **1** : blandly pleasant esp. to the senses ⟨the ~ light of afternoon —Elinor Wylie⟩ ⟨wind laden with the ~ odor . . . of madonna lilies —Norman Douglas⟩ **2 a** : smoothly affable and polite though often without deep interest or sincerity : superficially gracious in manner ⟨a ~ greeting⟩ ⟨affable, ~, moderate men, all of them perfectly and smugly convinced of their respectability —Ezra Pound⟩ **b** : smooth in performance or finish : highly finished ⟨a ~ mastery of technique⟩ ⟨a ~ surface⟩ ⟨one could wish that the book . . . was somewhat *suaver* in style —*Newsweek*⟩

syn URBANE, DIPLOMATIC, BLAND, SMOOTH, POLITIC: SUAVE suggests polished, smooth, well-mannered facilitation of easy and frictionless dealings with others, with affability, politeness, and persuasiveness all markedly checked from offensive excess or obvious fulness ⟨his voice was so smooth and *suave* as his countenance . . . murmuring his regret for having missed us at his first visit —A. Conan Doyle⟩ ⟨they could be as *suave* in advancing their bromides as we could be gauche in establishing our originalities —John Mason Brown⟩ URBANE suggests blended well-mannered and composed cultivation, poise, and wide social experience and an inbred or studied courtesy facilitating pleasant social relationships ⟨so *urbane*, sophisticated, and cultured that a stranger, meeting the Congressman for the first time, would be likely to think he had grown up in the lobby of the Waldorf-Astoria rather than in the backwoods of Missouri —Volta Torrey⟩ ⟨an active, *urbane*, gregarious gentleman . . . who likes to dine out, is fond of travel, is interested in people, and keeps his enthusiasm for life —Rosemary Benét⟩ DIPLOMATIC stresses the tactfulness necessary to ensure lastingly smooth relationships ⟨busy, active, *diplomatic* managing of the party —E.E.Hale⟩ BLAND stresses lack of irritation and implies a placid outlook, mild disposition, general affability, and complaisant benignness ⟨a distinguished-looking old cleric with a sweet smile and a white tie, he's just honorable and *bland* —George Santayana⟩ ⟨polished in his manners, exquisitely neat in his appearance and his *bland* conversation never rose above a calm level —Ruth Garland⟩ SMOOTH suggests an easy suavity making for pleasant, frictionless relationships ⟨they themselves were *smooth* in manner, and they saw to it that in their presence life had no rough edges —Mary Webb⟩ POLITIC suggests expedient, shrewd, and tactful handling of others by diplomacy, manipulation, or ingratiation ⟨the mayors and corporations as a rule guided their cities through difficult times with *politic* shrewdness —Edwin Benson⟩ ⟨the generosity shown by the *politic* conqueror to his prisoners —W.H.Prescott⟩

suave·ly *adv* : in a suave manner : with suavity

suave·ness *n* : the quality or state of being suave : SUAVITY

suav·i·ty \ˈswävəd-ē, 'swäv-, -və̄t-, -i *sometimes* 'swav-\ *n -ES* [ME *suavitee*, fr. MF *suavité*, fr. L *suavitat-, suavitas* pleasantness, sweetness, fr. *suavis* pleasant, sweet + *-itat-, -itas -ity*] **1** : the quality or state of being suave: as **a** (1) : mildness and pleasantness to the sense of smell or taste : FRAGRANCE ⟨eggs and butter and perhaps a bit of onion give both flavor and ~ —Scott Seegers⟩ (2) : pleasing sweetness (as of sound or expression) ⟨music performed with great ~⟩ **b** : the condition of being blandly pleasing to the mind : superficial and urbane agreeableness ⟨replied with ~⟩ ⟨the ~ of their manners⟩ **2** : something that is suave : AMENITY — usu. used in pl. ⟨the *suavities* of polite society⟩

¹sub \ˈsəb\ *adj* [short for *subordinate*] : AUXILIARY, SUBORDINATE, SECONDARY ⟨a ~ post office⟩ ⟨a ~ theme in a music⟩

²sub \"\ *n -s* [by shortening] : SUBSTITUTE

³sub \"\ *vb* **subbed; subbing; subs** [in sense 1, short for ²*substitute*; in sense 2, short for *subsistence*] *vi* **1** : to act and esp. work as a substitute ⟨*subbing* for the absent men⟩ **2** *chiefly Brit* : to provide or accept a portion of wages in advance as a subsistence allowance ~ *vt* **1** [by shortening] : SUBEDIT **2** [by shortening] : SUBIRRIGATE **3** [short for *substratum*] : to apply a substratum to (a photographic film or plate)

⁴sub \"\ *n -s* [by shortening] : SUBMARINE

⁵sub \"\ *n -s* [short for *substratum*] : a photographic substratum

sub- *prefix* [ME, fr. L, under, below, from below, up, near, further, after, fr. *sub*, prep. — more at UP] **1** : under : beneath : below ⟨*subsoil*⟩ ⟨*subcutaneous*⟩ ⟨*subpier*⟩ ⟨*subdominant*⟩ ⟨*subhymenial*⟩ **2 a** : subordinate : secondary : next lower than or inferior to ⟨*subcenter*⟩ ⟨*subfreshman*⟩ ⟨*subgenus*⟩ **b** : subordinate portion of : subdivision of : derived from ⟨*subcommittee*⟩ ⟨*subculture*⟩ ⟨*subdistrict*⟩ ⟨*subscience*⟩; *also* : with repetition (as of a process) so as to form, stress, or deal with subordinate parts or relations ⟨*subclassify*⟩ ⟨*sublet*⟩ ⟨*subbranch*⟩ ⟨*subcontract*⟩ **3 a** : somewhat : slightly : less than completely or perfectly : inadequately : less than normally ⟨*subacid*⟩ ⟨*subdominant*⟩ ⟨*subovate*⟩ ⟨*subarcuate*⟩ ⟨*subclinical*⟩ ⟨*subacute*⟩ ⟨*subconvulsive*⟩ **b** (1) : containing only a relatively small proportion or less than the normal amount of (such) an element or radical ⟨*suboxide*⟩ — not used systematically; compare PROT- **c** : basic — in names of salts ⟨*subacetate*⟩ ⟨*subnitrate*⟩; not used systematically **4 a** : almost : nearly ⟨*subalate*⟩ ⟨*subcaulescent*⟩ ⟨*subabdominal*⟩; SUBakhmimic⟩ **b** : falling nearly in the category of and often adjoining : bordering upon ⟨*subadult*⟩ ⟨*subarid*⟩ ⟨*subarctic*⟩ **c** : immediately following: after ⟨*subapostolic*⟩ ⟨*sub-Mycenaean*⟩

sub *abbr* **1** subaltern **2** subcontractor **3** sublieutenant **4** submerge : submerged **5** subordinate **6** subscriber; subscription **7** subsidiary **8** suburb; suburban **9** subway **10** supplementary unemployment benefit

sub·ab·dom·i·nal \ˌsəb+\ *adj* [*sub-* + *abdominal*] : of a ventral fin : situated nearly far enough back to be considered abdominal

sub·ac·count \"+\ *n* [*sub-* + *account*] : a subordinate or secondary account (as in a business record)

sub·ac·e·tate \ˌsäb+\ *n* [*sub-* + *acetate*] : a basic acetate ⟨verdigris is a ~ of copper⟩

sub·ac·id \"+\ *adj* [L *subacidus*, fr. *sub-* + *acidus* acid — more at ACID] **1 a** : moderately sour to the taste ⟨~ fruit juices⟩ **b** : somewhat biting (as in manner, style, or presentation) : rather tart ⟨~ prose⟩ ⟨a little ~ kind of . . . impatience —Laurence Sterne⟩ **2 a** : containing less than the normal or usual amount of acid ⟨a ~ salt⟩ **b** : having a hydrogen-ion concentration of 5.5 to 6.0 — used esp. of leaf-mold soils — **sub·acid·ly** \"+\ *adv* — **sub·acid·ness** \"+\ *n*

sub·acid·i·ty \ˌ⸱+\ *n* : the quality or state of being subacid; *esp* : HYPOCHLORHYDRIA

sub·acute \ˌsäb+\ *adj* [*sub-* + *acute*] : moderately acute ⟨a ~ angle⟩: as **a** : having a tapering but not sharply pointed form ⟨a ~ flower petal⟩ ⟨large ~ spines on some sea urchins⟩ **b** (1) : falling between acute and chronic in character ⟨~ endocarditis⟩ (2) : less marked in severity or duration than a corresponding acute state ⟨~ pain⟩ ⟨~ inflammation⟩ — **sub·acute·ly** \"+\ *adv*

sub·adult \ˌsäb+\ *n* [*sub-* + *adult*] : an individual approaching the adult age or the termination of the growing period : one that has passed through the juvenile period but has not yet attained typical adult characteristics

sub·aer·i·al \ˌsäb+\ *adj* [*sub-* + *aerial*] : taking place in the open air : situated or occurring on or immediately adjacent to the surface of the earth: as **a** : of, relating to, or taking place on a land surface as distinguished from a subaqueous or subterranean ⟨~ erosion⟩ ⟨a ~ valley⟩ **b** : situated or growing at or just above the surface of the ground ⟨~ roots⟩ — **sub·aerially** \"+\ *adv*

sub·aes·thet·ic \"+\ *adj* [*sub-* + *aesthetic*] : involving or occurring at a level below the developed aesthetic ⟨~ motor functioning out of which art accomplishments can develop —A.L.Kroeber⟩

sub·age \ˈsəb+ˌ-\ *n* [*sub-* + *age*] : a distinguishable subdivision of a geologic age usu. characterized by the occurrence of some specific phenomenon (as a deposition of loess or a glacial recession)

sub·agen·cy \ˌsäb+\ *n* [*sub-* + *agency*] : a subordinate agency commonly originated by the agency to which it belongs rather than by the primary authority from which its parent agency stems ⟨government agencies spawning *subagencies*⟩

sub·agent \"+\ *n* [*sub-* + *agent*] : a subordinate agent : a person to whom an agent delegates with the authorization of his principal the performance of some duty, act, or responsibility owed by him to the principal

su·bah \ˈsüba\ *n* -s [Per *sūba* province, fr. Ar] **1 :** a province or division of the Mogul Empire or its government **2 :** SUBAHDAR

su·bah·dar *or* **su·ba·dar** \ˌ==ˈdär\ *n* -s [Per *ṣūbadār*, fr. *ṣūba* province + *-dār* having, holding, fr. OPer *dar-* to hold] **1 :** a governor of a subah **2 :** the chief native officer of a native company in the former British Indian army having a position equivalent to that of captain

su·bah·dary \-ˈdärē, -ri\ *or* **su·bah·ship** \ˈsübə,ship\ *n, pl* **subahdaries** *or* **subahships** [*subahdary* fr. *subahdar* + *-y*; *subahship* fr. *subah* + *-ship*] **:** the office or jurisdiction of a subahdar **:** SUBAH 1

sub·akhmimic *also* **sub·achmimic** \¦səb+\ *n* -s *usu cap* [*sub-* + *Akhmimic*, *Achmimic*] **:** a late dialect of Coptic standing between Sahidic and Akhmimic

sub·alary \¦səb+\ *adj* [*sub-* + *alary*] **:** situated under the wings

sub·alate \"+\ *adj* [*sub-* + *alate*] **:** having a form suggesting a wing esp. in being thin and somewhat triangular

sub·alimentation \¦səb+\ *n* [*sub-* + *alimentation*] **:** insufficient or inadequate nutritional intake

sub·alkaline \¦səb+\ *adj* [*sub-* + *alkaline*] **:** having a hydrogen-ion concentration of 8.0 to 8.5 — used esp. of soils of various limestone or salt-marsh regions

sub·allocate \"+\ *vt* [*sub-* + *allocate*] **:** to provide a share of from a source or supply provided or available to one or more subordinate agencies ⟨the provincial treasury will ~ funds to the districts⟩ — **sub·allocation** \"+\ *n*

sub·almoner \¦səb+\ *n* [*sub-* + *almoner*] **:** an under almoner **:** an assistant to an almoner

sub·alpine \"+\ *adj* [*sub-* + *alpine*] **1 :** of or relating to the region about the foot and lower slopes of the Alps **2 :** of, relating to, or constituting high upland slopes immediately below the timberline ⟨spruce and fir are characteristic ~ floral elements⟩ — compare MONTANE

subalpine fir *n* **:** ALPINE FIR

¹sub·al·tern \səˈbȯltə(r)n *sometimes* ˈsəbˌbȯ-, *chiefly Brit* ˈsəbəltən\ *adj* [LL *subalternus*, fr. L *sub-* + *alternus* alternate, fr. *alter* other (of two) — more at ALTER] **1 :** ranked or ranged below **:** inferior in status or quality **:** SUBORDINATE ⟨the congenitally ~ type of man —H.L.Mencken⟩: as **a :** relating to or typical of subordinate status ⟨~ fears⟩ **b :** held or holding from one who is himself a vassal ⟨a ~ manor⟩ ⟨a ~ vassal⟩ **c** *chiefly Brit* **:** holding a rank below that of captain **2** [ML *subalternus*, fr. LL, subordinate] **:** particular with reference to a related universal or general ⟨"some S is P" is a ~ proposition to "all S is P"⟩

²subaltern \"\ *n* -s **1 a :** a person holding a subordinate position or being inferior in respect to some quality or characteristic ⟨natural ~s, ill-trained and uninterested⟩ **b** *chiefly Brit* **:** a commissioned officer below the rank of captain **2** [ML *subalternus*, fr. *subalternus*, adj.] **:** a subaltern proposition **:** a logical subalternate

sub·al·ter·nant \ˌsəˌbȯlˈtərnənt, -bal-\ *n* -s [ML *subalternus* + E *-ant*] **:** SUPERALTERN

¹sub·alternate \(ˌ)səb+\ *adj* [ML *subalternatus*, past part. of *subalternare* to subordinate, fr. LL *subalternus* subordinate] **1 :** inferior in quality or status **:** SUBORDINATE ⟨a ~ art⟩ ⟨a study ~ to his earlier work⟩ **2** [*sub-* + *alternate*] **:** nearly alternate but with a tendency to become opposite ⟨the secondary lateral veins of a pinnate leaf are often ~⟩ — **sub·alternately** \"+\ *adv*

²subalternate \"\ *n* **:** a particular logical proposition that follows by immediate inference from a universal one of like quality and identical terms

sub·alternation \"+\ *n* [ML *subalternation-*, *subalternatio*, fr. *subalternatus* (past part. of *subalternare* to subordinate) + L *-ion-*, *-io* -ion] **1 :** the quality or state of being subalternate **:** succession by turns **:** SUBORDINATION **2 :** the relation of a logical subalternate to a superaltern — see OPPOSITION 2a(2)

subaltern genus *n* **:** a logical genus that may be a species of a higher genus ⟨the genus *book* is a *subaltern genus* since it is also a species of the genus *printed matter*⟩ — compare TREE OF PORPHYRY

sub·al·ter·ni·ty \ˌsəˌbȯlˈtərnəd·ē, -bal-\ *n* -ES [¹*subaltern* + *-ity*] **:** the quality, state, or position of being subaltern

sub·angular \¦səb+\ *adj* [*sub-* + *angular*] **:** somewhat angular **:** free from sharp angles though not smoothly rounded ⟨~ quartz particles⟩ — **sub·angularly** \"+\ *adv*

sub·antarctic \"+\ *adj* [ISV *sub-* + *antarctic*] **:** of, relating to, or being a region just outside the antarctic circle

su·ba·nun \süˈbäˌnün\ *n, pl* **subanun** *or* **subanuns** *usu cap* [Cebuan, fr. Subanun *Subanen*, fr. *subà* upstream + *-nen* people, language] **1 a :** any of the pagan peoples on the Zamboanga peninsula of western Mindanao, Philippines **b :** a member of such people **2 :** the Austronesian language of the Subanun peoples

sub·apical \¦səb+\ *adj* [*sub-* + *apical*] **:** situated below or near an apex — **sub·apically** \"+\ *adv*

sub·aponeurotic \"+\ *adj* [*sub-* + *aponeurotic*] **:** lying beneath an aponeurosis

sub·apostolic \"+\ *adj* [*sub-* + *apostolic*] **:** of, relating to, or being the age immediately following that of the apostles ⟨the ~ church⟩

sub·apparent \"+\ *adj* [*sub-* + *apparent*] **:** imperfectly apparent **:** perceived with difficulty ⟨a ~ shadowing⟩

sub·appressed \"+\ *adj* [*sub-* + *appressed*] **:** imperfectly or partially appressed ⟨~ pubescence on a leaf⟩

sub·apterous \¦səb+\ *adj* [ISV *sub-* + *apterous*] **:** BRACHYPTEROUS

sub·aquatic \"+\ *adj* [ISV *sub-* + *aquatic*] **1 :** SUBAQUEOUS **2 :** somewhat aquatic ⟨a marginal ~ flora⟩

sub·aqueous \"+\ *adj* [*sub-* + *aqueous*] **1 a :** being or found under water or beneath the surface of water ⟨viewing the ~ fauna from a glass-bottomed boat⟩ **b :** adapted for use under water **:** SUBMARINE ⟨a ~ helmet⟩ **c :** suggesting or typical of the underwater world (as in remoteness or dimness) ⟨a soft ~ light⟩ ⟨the ~ world of the underconscious —Vernon Young⟩ **2 :** formed or taking place in or under water ⟨~ canyons⟩

sub·arachnoid \"+\ *adj* [ISV *sub-* + *arachnoid*] **:** of, relating to, or situated under the arachnoid membrane ⟨~ processes⟩: as **a :** constituting the space between the arachnoid membrane and the pia mater **b :** involving the subarachnoid space and the fluid that is contained therein ⟨a ~ meningitis⟩

su·ba·rae·an *or* **su·ba·re·an** \ˌsübəˈrēən\ *n* -s *usu cap* [*subaraean* prob. fr. NL *Subaraeus* Subaraean (fr. *Subartu*, ancient region of northern Mesopotamia inhabited by the Subaraeans) + E *-an*; *subarean* fr. *Subartu* + E *-ean*] **1 :** a member of an ancient people inhabiting the region stretching westward from the Zagros mountains of Iran **2 :** a language of uncertain relationship used by the Subaraeans and esp. by the Mitannians

sub·arch \ˈsəb+ˌ-\ *n* [*sub-* + *arch*] **:** a subordinate arch esp. when one of two or more grouped in a larger arch

sub·arctic \¦səb+\ *adj* [ISV *sub-* + *arctic*] **:** of, relating to, or being regions immediately outside of the arctic circle or regions that for various reasons (as altitude) are similar to these in climate or conditions of life — compare ALPINE

sub·arcuate \"+\ *also* **sub·arcuated** \"+\ *adj* [*sub-* + *arcuate* or *arcuated*] **:** somewhat arched or bowed

sub·arcuation \"+\ *n* [*sub-* + *arcuation*] **:** the construction of subordinate arches under a main arch; *also* **:** arches so constructed

sub·area \"+\ *n* [*sub-* + *area*] **:** a subdivision of an area

sub·arid \"+\ *adj* [*sub-* + *arid*] **:** moderately or slightly arid **:** characterized by or constituting a climate somewhat deficient in moisture — compare SUBHUMID

sub·artesian \¦səb+\ *adj* [*sub-* + *artesian*] **:** of, relating to, or being water that rises naturally in a well to a height appreciably above that of the surrounding water table but does not flow out of the well

sub·ascending \"+\ *adj* [*sub-* + *ascending*] **:** rising somewhat obliquely upward from a flattened basal attachment ⟨a ~ keel on a papilionaceous flower⟩

sub·assemble \"+\ *vt* [back-formation fr. *subassembly*] **:** to fabricate (as parts) into a subassembly **:** prepare (a structural unit) as a subassembly

sub·assembler \"+\ *n* [*subassemble* + *-er*] **:** a worker that puts together subassemblies in the process of manufacture

sub·assembly \"+\ *n* [*sub-* + *assembly*] **1 :** a structural unit manufactured or assembled separately but designed to be incorporated with other units in the final assembly of a finished product **2 :** the act or process of preparing subassemblies ⟨a ~ line⟩

sub·astral \¦səb+\ *adj* [*sub-* + *astral*] **:** located lower than the stars; *specif* **:** TERRESTRIAL ⟨lowly ~ beings⟩

¹sub·astringent \"+\ *adj* [*sub-* + *astringent*] **:** mildly astringent

²subastringent \"\ *n* **:** a subastringent substance

sub·atlantic \"+\ *adj, usu cap A* [ISV *sub-* + *Atlantic* ocean] **1 :** located beneath the Atlantic ocean ⟨a *sub-Atlantic* cable⟩ **2 :** of, relating to, or being a postglacial climatic period believed to have begun in northwestern Europe about 850–500 B.C. and to be continuing in existence at the present time

sub·atmospheric \"+\ *adj* [*sub-* + *atmospheric*] **:** less or lower than that of the atmosphere ⟨~ temperatures⟩

sub·atomic \"+\ *adj* [*sub-* + *atomic*] **:** of, relating to, or being the phenomena occurring inside of atoms or particles smaller than atoms ⟨the harnessing of ~ energy —Bernard Jaffe⟩

sub·audible \"+\ *adj* [*sub-* + *audible*] **1 :** having a frequency or intensity below the limit of hearing **2 :** scarcely perceptible to the ear ⟨a ~ conversation⟩ ⟨a ~ humming sound⟩

sub·au·di·tion \ˌsəˌbȯˈdishən\ *n* [LL *subaudition-*, *subauditio*, fr. *subauditus* (past part. of *subaudire* to understand, fr. L *sub-* + *audire* to hear) + L *-ion-*, *-io* -ion — more at AUDIBLE] **1 :** the act of understanding or supplying something not expressed **2 :** something that is understood or supplied in comprehending a text

sub·au·di·tur \ˌsəˌbȯˈdīd·ə(r), -ī,tər\ *n* -s [LL, it is understood, 3d pers. sing. pres. indic. of *subaudire* to understand] **:** something understood or implied in connection with what is expressed

sub·au·rale \ˌsəˌbȯˈra(ˌ)lē, -rā-, -rä-\ *n* -s [NL, fr. neut. of *subauralis* of below the ear, fr. L *sub-* + NL *auralis* of the ear, fr. L *auris* ear + *-alis* -al — more at EAR] **:** an anthropometric landmark consisting of the lowest point on the lobe of the ear when the head is held in the eye-ear plane

sub·auricular \¦səb+\ *adj* [*sub-* + *auricular*] **:** situated below the ear

sub·average \"+\ *adj* [*sub-* + *average*] **:** of a lower level or quality than some norm ⟨~ minds⟩ ⟨~ education⟩

sub·axillary \"+\ *also* **sub·axillar** \"+\ *adj* [*sub-* + *axillary* or *axillar*] **1 :** situated below the axilla **2 :** situated below or beneath an axil ⟨a ~ bud⟩

sub·basal \"+\ *adj* [*sub-* + *basal*] **1 :** situated near or below a base or basal part ⟨a ~ color band on an insect wing⟩ **2** [*subbase* + *-al*] **:** of, relating to, or constituting a subbase

sub·base \ˈsəb+ˌ-\ *n* [*sub-* + *base*] **1 a :** another base, foundation, or other underlying support placed below that which ordinarily forms the base **b :** the lowermost part of a base; *specif* **:** the lowest member of an architectural base (as when divided horizontally) or of a baseboard or pedestal **c :** material placed under or designed for use under a base **2 :** an alternate or satellite air base subordinate to a main air base commander either directly or administratively or logistically

sub–base \ˈ=ˌ=\ *n* [¹*sub* + *base*] **:** a submarine base

sub·basement \¦səb+\ *n* [*sub-* + *basement*] **:** a basement or an underground story or one of several such located below the true basement of a building

sub·bass \ˈsəb+ˌ-\ *n* [*sub-* + *bass*] **:** a 16- or 32-foot pipe organ stop used usu. in a pedal organ

subbed *past of* SUB

sub·bifid \¦səb+\ *adj* [*sub-* + *bifid*] **:** somewhat or incompletely forked ⟨a ~ tongue⟩

sub·bing \ˈsəbiŋ, -bēŋ\ *n* -s [fr. gerund of ²*sub*] **1 :** an act of serving as a substitute **2 :** SUBIRRIGATION **3** [¹*sub* + *-ing*] **:** SUBSTRATUM e

sub·bituminous \¦səb+\ *adj* [*sub-* + *bituminous*] **:** of, relating to, or being coal of lower rank than bituminous coal but higher than lignite

sub·boreal \"+\ *adj* [ISV *sub-* + *boreal*] **1 :** very cold **:** approaching the frigid ⟨a ~ climate⟩ **2 :** of, relating to, or constituting a postglacial period preceding the boreal and characterized by relatively warm dry climate **3 :** of, relating to, or constituting a biogeographic zone that approaches the boreal in climatic condition

sub·bot·nik \səˈbȯtnik\ *n, pl* **subbotni·ki** \-nəkē\ *also* **subbotniks** *usu cap* [Russ, fr. *subbota* Saturday (fr. L *sabbatum* Sabbath, Saturday) + *-nik* (as in *raskolnik*) — more at SABBATH] **:** SABBATARIAN 3

sub·bourdon \¦səb+\ *n* [*sub-* + *bourdon*] **:** a 32-foot covered wood pedal stop in a pipe organ of large scale

sub·brach·i·al \¦səbˈbrakēəl\ *also* **sub·brach·i·an** \-ēən\ *adj* [*subbrachial* fr. NL *subbrachialis*, fr. L *sub-* + *brachialis* brachial; *subbrachian* fr. NL *Subbrachiales* + E *-an* — more at BRACHIAL] **:** located beneath or nearly beneath a pectoral fin ⟨ventral fins ~⟩

sub·brach·i·a·les \ˌsəbˌbrakēˈā(ˌ)lēz\ *n pl, cap* [NL, fr. pl. of *subbrachialis* subbrachial] *in some esp former classifications* **:** a division of soft-finned fishes having the ventral fins beneath or nearly beneath the pectoral fins

sub·brachycephal \¦səb+\ *n* [NL *subbrachycephalus*, fr. *sub-* + *brachycephalus* brachycephal] **:** a subbrachycephalic individual

sub·brachycephalic \"+\ *adj* [NL *subbrachycephal*us + E *-ic*] **:** having a cephalic index of 80–83

sub·brachycephaly \"+\ *n* [NL *subbrachycephal*us + E *-y*] **:** the quality or state of being subbrachycephalic

¹sub·branch \ˈ=+ˌ-\ *vi* [*sub-* + *branch* (v.)] **:** to divide into subbranches

²subbranch \"\ *n* [*sub-* + *branch* (n.)] **1 :** a branch of a branch ⟨complex organizations that ramify into branches and ~es⟩ **2 :** a branch (as of a business firm) that is of secondary importance and usu. less complete in function or service than a main branch

sub·breed \"+ˌ-\ *n* [*sub-* + *breed*] **:** a distinguishable race or strain within a breed

sub·cabinet \¦səb+\ *n* [*sub-* + *cabinet*] **1 :** a cabinet designed to form a base (as for a piece of apparatus) **2 :** an unofficial advisory group selected by some U.S. presidents esp. from members of the several executive departments

sub·calcarine \"+\ *adj* [*sub-* + *calcarine*] **:** situated below the calcarine fissure

sub·caliber \"+\ *adj* [*sub-* + *caliber*] **1 :** smaller than the caliber of a gun ⟨a ~ projectile⟩ **2 :** of, relating to, used in, or effected by firing a subcaliber projectile

sub·callosal \"+\ *adj* [*sub-* + *callosal*] **:** situated below the corpus callosum ⟨the ~ gyrus⟩

sub·campanulate \"+\ *adj* [ISV *sub-* + *campanulate*] **:** somewhat ventricose at the base and usu slightly recurved at the margin **:** not quite bell-shaped ⟨a mushroom with a ~ pileus⟩

sub·capillary \¦səb+\ *adj* [ISV *sub-* + *capillary*] **:** of less than capillary dimensions ⟨~ pores in rock⟩

sub·capsular \"+\ *adj* [*sub-* + *capsular*] **:** situated or occurring beneath or within a capsule ⟨a ~ abscess⟩ ⟨~ cataracts⟩

sub·caption \"+\ *n* [*sub-* + *caption*] **:** a secondary headline (as in an advertisement)

sub·carbide \"+\ *n* [*sub-* + *carbide*] **:** a carbide having less than the ordinary proportion of carbon ⟨~ of iron $Fe_{24}C$ is reputed to be a constituent of commercial iron⟩

sub·carbonate \"+\ *n* [*sub-* + *carbonate*] **:** a basic carbonate (as bismuth subcarbonate)

sub·carboniferous \¦səb+\ *adj or n, usu cap* [*sub-* + *carboniferous*] **:** MISSISSIPPIAN

sub·carcinogenic \"+\ *adj* [*sub-* + *carcinogenic*] **:** inadequate to produce a carcinogenic effect

sub·cardinal \"+\ *adj* [*sub-* + *cardinal* (vein)] **:** of, relating to, situated near, or being either of two veins in the mammalian embryo or the adult of some lower vertebrates that develop one on each side in the abdominal region ventromedial to the mesonephros and in the mammal participate in the formation of the inferior vena cava and the renal veins

sub·carinate \"+\ *adj* [ISV *sub-* + *carinate*] **:** somewhat or incompletely keeled ⟨a ~ scale⟩

sub·carrier \"+\ *n* [*sub-* + *carrier*] **:** a low-frequency carrier in an electronic system (as a telemetering system or a multichannel radio system) used to modulate a main carrier and often being itself modulated to carry information

sub·cartilaginous \"+\ *adj* [MF *subcartilagineux*, fr. *sub-* + *cartilagineux* cartilaginous — more at CARTILAGINOUS] **1 :** partially cartilaginous **2 :** situated under a cartilage

sub·casing \"+\ *n* [*sub-* + *casing*] **:** a rough frame that forms a base over which the finish casing of a door or window opening is applied

sub·cast \"+ˌ-\ *n* [*sub-* + *cast*] **:** a secondary swarm (as of bees)

sub·caste \"+ˌ-\ *n* [*sub-* + *caste*] **:** a subdivision of a caste

¹sub·caudal \¦səb+\ *adj* [*sub-* + *caudal*] **:** situated under or on the ventral side of the tail ⟨a ~ pouch⟩

²subcaudal \"\ *n* **:** a subcaudal plate or shield

sub·caudate \"+\ *adj* [*sub-* + *caudate*] **:** having an imperfect or abridged prolongation ⟨a ~ wing of a butterfly⟩

sub·caulescent \"+\ *adj* [ISV *sub-* + *caulescent*] **:** nearly acaulescent

sub·celestial \"+\ *adj* [*sub-* + *celestial*] **:** situated beneath the heavens; *specif* **:** MUNDANE

sub·cellar \"+\ *n* [*sub-* + *cellar*] **:** a cellar beneath a story wholly or partly underground; *usu* **:** a cellar under a cellar **:** SUBBASEMENT

sub·center \"+\ *n* [*sub-* + *center*] **:** a secondary center; *esp* **:** a center (as for business, shopping, amusement) located outside the main business area of a city

sub·central \"+\ *adj* [*sub-* + *central*] **1 :** located under a center: as **a :** situated below the central sulcus **b :** situated below the centrum of a vertebra **2 :** nearly central **:** not quite central — **sub·centrally** \"+\ *adv*

sub·cerebral plane \¦=+-\ *n* [*sub-* + *cerebral*] **:** an anthropometric landmark consisting of the plane passing through a line crossing the lower angles of the parietal bones and the point where the superciliary ridge joins the cheek bone

sub·chairman \¦səb+\ *n* [*sub-* + *chairman*] **:** a substitute or subordinate chairman

sub·chanter \"+\ *n* [*sub-* + *chanter*] **1 :** SUCCENTOR **2 :** VICAR CHORAL

sub·chapter \"+\ *n* [*sub-* + *chapter*] **:** a subdivision of a chapter (as of a code of laws)

subchaser \ˈ=ˌ==\ *n* [¹*sub* + *chaser*] **:** SUBMARINE CHASER

sub·chela \¦səb+\ *n, pl* **subchelae** [NL, fr. *sub-* + *chela*] **:** a grasping organ of the limbs of some crustaceans (as of the genus *Squilla*) in which the terminal segment folds back against the next one

sub·chelate \"+\ *adj* [*sub-* + *chelate*] **1 :** imperfectly chelate **2** [NL *subchela* + E *-ate*] **:** ending in a subchela

sub·chief \ˈsəb+ˌ-\ *n* [*sub-* + *chief*] **:** a subordinate chief **:** a chief of secondary rank or authority

sub·chloride \¦səb+\ *n* [ISV *sub-* + *chloride*] **1 :** a binary chloride containing a relatively small proportion of chlorine ⟨calomel is the ~ of mercury⟩ **2 :** a basic chloride (as an oxychloride)

sub·chondral \"+\ *adj* [*sub-* + *chondral*] **:** situated below or beneath cartilage

sub·chordal \"+\ *adj* [*sub-* + *chordal*] **:** situated below the notochord

sub·chorionic \"+\ *adj* [*sub-* + *chorionic*] **:** underlying the chorion

sub·choroid \"+\ *adj* [*sub-* + *choroid*] **:** lying or occurring between the choroid coat of the eye and the retina

sub·cinc·to·ri·um \ˌsəbˌsiŋ(k)ˈtōrēəm\ *or* **suc·cinc·to·ri·um** \ˌsəkˌsiŋ(k)ˈtōrēəm, ÷ ˌsəˌsi-\ *n* -s [LL, fr. L *subcinctus*, *succinctus* (past part. of *subcingere*, *succingere* to tuck up, gird about) + *-orium* -ory — more at SUCCINCT] **:** a vestment consisting of an ornamental square of cloth suspended from the girdle and worn by the pope of the Roman Catholic Church when celebrating a solemn mass

sub·cin·gu·lum \ˌsəbˈsiŋgyələm\ *n* -s [LL *subcingulum*, *succingulum*, fr. L, girdle, fr. *subcingere*, *succingere* to tuck up, gird about + *-ulum* (neut. of *-ulus* -ule)] **:** a vestment consisting of a girdle or belt circling the waist from which hangs the subcinctorium of the papal vestments when the pope of the Roman Catholic Church is celebrating a solemn mass

sub·circular \¦səb+\ *adj* [*sub-* + *circular*] **:** nearly circular **:** not quite circular

sub·civilized \"+\ *adj* [*sub-* + *civilized*] **:** partially civilized

sub·claim \"+ˌ-\ *n* [*sub-* + *claim*] **:** a subordinate claim **:** a claim dependent on or arising out of another

sub·clamatores \¦səb+\ *n pl, cap* [NL, fr. *sub-* + *Clamatores*] *in former classifications* **:** a superfamily of passerine birds comprising the broadbills

sub·clan \ˈsəb+ˌ-\ *n* [*sub-* + *clan*] **:** a subdivision of a clan commonly tracing descent from a particular ancestor and forming a single community

sub·class \"+ˌ-\ *n* [*sub-* + *class*] **:** a primary division of a class: as **a :** a biological taxonomic category below a class and above an order **b :** SUBSET

sub·classify \¦səb+\ *vt* [*sub-* + *classify*] **:** to form or formulate a detailed classification of **:** divide into subclasses

sub·clause \ˈsəb+ˌ-\ *n* [*sub-* + *clause*] **:** a subordinate clause

sub·clavate \¦səb+\ *adj* [*sub-* + *clavate*] **:** somewhat club-shaped

sub·cla·via \ˌsəbˈklāvēə\ *n* -s [NL, fr. fem. of *subclavius* subclavian] **:** SUBCLAVIAN ARTERY

¹sub·cla·vi·an \¦səbˈklāvēən\ *adj* [NL *subclavius* (fr. L *sub-* + *clavis* key) + E *-an* — more at CLAVICLE] **:** located under the clavicle **:** of, relating to, or being a subclavian part

²subclavian \"\ *n* -s **:** a subclavian part

subclavian artery *n* [trans. of NL *subclavia arteria*] **:** the proximal part of the main artery of the arm or forelimb extending in man from its point of origin to the outer border of the first rib and arising on the right side from the innominate artery and on the left from the arch of the aorta — see AXILLARY ARTERY

subclavian groove *n* **:** either of two grooves for the passage of the subclavian artery and vein along the first rib

subclavian muscle *n* [trans. of NL *subclavius musculus*] **:** SUBCLAVIUS

subclavian vein *n* **:** the proximal part of the main vein of the arm from the end of the axillary vein at the level of the first rib to its junction with the internal jugular vein to form the innominate vein

sub·cla·vi·us \ˌsəbˈklāvēəs\ *n, pl* **subcla·vii** \-vēˌī\ [NL, fr. *subclavius*, adj., subclavian] **:** a small muscle on each side of the body extending from the first rib and its cartilage to the under surface of the clavicle

sub·climax \¦səb+\ *n* [*sub-* + *climax*] **:** a stage or community in an ecological succession immediately preceding a climatic or regional climax; *esp* **:** such a stage or community when held in relative stability for a long time or indefinitely through edaphic or biotic influences or by fire — compare DISCLIMAX

sub·clinical \"+\ *adj* [*sub-* + *clinical*] **:** marked by only slight abnormality and not being such as to give rise to overt symptoms **:** not detectable by the usual clinical tests ⟨a ~ infection⟩ ⟨a ~ vitamin deficiency⟩ — **sub·clinically** \"+\ *adv*

sub·clone \"+ˌ-\ *n* [*sub-* + *clone*] **:** a selected line within a clone

sub–cloud car \¦=¦=-\ *n* **:** a car which may be lowered from an airship by means of a cable to a position below obscuring clouds to permit observation of the ground

sub·clover \¦səb+\ *n* [by shortening] **:** SUBTERRANEAN CLOVER

sub·coastal \"+\ *adj* [*sub-* + *coastal*] **:** situated below a coast — used of a submerged plain of a continental shelf

subcoat \ˈ=ˌ=\ *n* [*sub-* + *coat*] **:** a coat or layer of material underlying another coat; *usu* **:** a coat (as of paint) applied before and intended to form a base for an outer coat

sub·collateral \¦səb+\ *adj* [*sub-* + *collateral*] **:** of, relating to, or being a convolution of the tentorial surface of the temporal lobe of the cerebrum lying external to the collateral fissure

sub·collegiate \"+\ *or* **sub·college** \"+\ *adj* [*sub-* + *collegiate* or *college*] **:** offered to or adapted to the needs of students not intending or inadequately prepared to attend college ⟨courses at the ~ level⟩ ⟨studies of ~ grade⟩

sub·columnar \¦səb+\ *adj* [*sub-* + *columnar*] **:** partially or imperfectly columnar

sub·coma \ˈsəb+\ *adj* [*sub-* + *coma*] **:** inadequate to produce coma ⟨~ doses of insulin⟩

sub·commission \"+\ *n* [*sub-* + *commission*] **:** a secondary or subordinate commission

sub·commissioner \"+\ *n* [*sub-* + *commissioner*] **1 a :** a commissioner subordinate in rank or authority to another **2 :** a member of a subcommission

sub·committee \"+\ *n* [*sub-* + *committee*] **:** a committee forming a subdivision of a primary or standing committee from which its responsibility and authority derive and usu. being charged with a specific or limited function

sub·company \"+\ *n* [*sub-* + *company*] **:** a subsidiary company (as of an industrial corporation)

sub·conchoidal \"+\ *adj* [*sub-* + *conchoidal*] **:** partially or indistinctly conchoidal ⟨a rock with ~ fracture⟩

sub·conical \"+\ *or* **sub·conic** \"+\ *adj* [*sub-* + *conical or conic*] **:** nearly or approximately conical **:** approaching a cone in form

sub·conjunctival \"+\ *adj* [ISV *sub-* + *conjunctival*] **:** situated or occurring beneath the conjunctiva ⟨~ hemorrhage⟩ — **sub·conjunctivally** \"+\ *adv*

1sub·conscious \ˈsəb+\ *adj* [*sub-* + *conscious*] **1 :** existing in the mind but not immediately available to consciousness **:** affecting thought, feeling, and behavior without entering awareness ⟨~ motive⟩ ⟨~ reflex⟩ — compare UNCONSCIOUS **2 :** imperfectly conscious **:** partially but not fully aware ⟨the persistence of ~ dream activity for several minutes after waking —*Psychological Abstracts*⟩ — **sub·consciously** \"+\ *adv* — **sub·consciousness** \"+\ *n*

2subconscious \"\ *n* **:** the mental activities just below the threshold of consciousness; *also* **:** the aspect of the mind concerned with such activities that is an entity or a part of the mental apparatus overlapping, equivalent to, or distinct from the unconscious

sub·contiguous \"+\ *adj* [*sub-* + *contiguous*] **:** almost touching

sub·continent \"+\ *n* [*sub-* + *continent*] **1 :** a landmass (as Greenland) of great size but smaller than any of the usu. recognized continents **2 :** a vast and more or less self-contained subdivision of a continent ⟨the Indian ~ stretches northward into the Himalayas and comprises all of the Indian peninsula including Pakistan⟩ — **sub·continental** \"+\ *adj*

1sub·contract \"+\ *vb* [*subcontract* n.v.] *vt* **1 :** obs **:** to cause to be betrothed a second time **2 a :** to take or bid on (as work) as a subcontractor **b :** to offer (as one phase of contracted work) to subcontractors ~ *vi* **1 :** to act as a subcontractor **:** take or depend on subcontractors **2 :** to offer work to subcontractors **:** depend on subcontractors for the performance of work contracted

2sub·contract \"+\ *n* [*sub-* + *contract* (n.)] **:** a contract under or subordinate to a previous or prime contract; *specif* **:** an agreement to perform a specified part or all of the work or to provide specified materials or all materials required for the completion of another contract

sub·contractor \"+\ *n* [*sub-* + *contractor*] **:** an individual or business firm that contracts to perform part or all of another's contract **:** a maker or performer of subcontracts

sub·contraoctave \"+\ *n* [*sub-* + *contraoctave*] **:** the musical octave that begins on the fourth C below middle C — see PITCH illustration

sub·contrariety \"+\ *n* [fr. ¹*subcontrary*, after E *contrary*] **:** the relation existing between subcontrary propositions in logic **:** the relation of two propositions with identical terms which is such that both may be true but both cannot be false — see OPPOSITION 2a(2)

1sub·contrary \"+\ *adj* [LL *subcontrarius*, fr. L *sub-* + *contrarius* contrary — more at CONTRARY] **1 :** contrary in an inferior degree; *specif* **:** having the relation of subcontrariety

2subcontrary \"+\ *n* **:** a subcontrary proposition in logic

sub·convulsive \"+\ *adj* [*sub-* + *convulsive*] **1 :** inadequate to produce convulsion ⟨~ doses of insulin⟩ **2 :** approaching the convulsive in character ⟨a ~ reaction to noise⟩

sub·cool \"+\ *vt* [*sub-* + *cool*] **:** SUPERCOOL

sub·coracoid \"+\ *adj* [*sub-* + *coracoid*] **:** situated or occurring under the coracoid process of the scapula ⟨a ~ dislocation of the humerus⟩

sub·cordate \"+\ *adj* [*sub-* + *cordate*] **:** incompletely cordate **:** nearly heart-shaped ⟨a ~ leaf⟩

sub·corneous \"+\ *adj* [*sub-* + *corneous*] **1 :** situated under a horny part or layer **2 :** partially horny

sub·cortex \"+\ *n* [NL, fr. *sub-* + *cortex*] **:** the parts of the brain (as the corpus striatum and internal capsule) immediately adjoining the cerebral cortex

sub·cortical \"+\ *adj* [*sub-* + *cortical*] **:** situated beneath or below a cortex; *usu* **:** of, relating to, involving, or being nerve centers below the cerebral cortex ⟨~ lesions⟩ ⟨~ sensation⟩ — **sub·cortically** \"+\ *adv*

sub·costa \"+\ *n* [NL, fr. L *sub-* + *costa* rib — more at COAST] **:** the subcostal vein of an insect's wing

1sub·costal \"+\ *adj* [NL *subcostalis*] **1 :** situated below a rib ⟨a ~ muscle⟩ **2 :** of, relating to, or being the primary vein of an insect's wing next behind the costal vein

2subcostal \"\ *n* -s [NL *subcostalis*] **:** a subcostal part (as a muscle or wing vein)

subcostal artery *n* **:** either of a pair of arteries that are the most posterior branches of the thoracic aorta and course beneath the last pair of ribs

subcostal cell *n* **:** one of the cells between the costal and subcostal veins of an insect's wing

sub·cos·talis \ˌsəbˌkäˈstäləs, -täl-, -tûl-\ *n, pl* **subcostales** \-ə(ˌ)lēz, -ā(ˌ)läs\ [NL, fr. *subcostalis* situated below or within the rib, fr. *subcosta* + L -*alis* -al] **:** any of a variable number of small muscles arising on the inner surface of a rib and inserted into the inner surface of the first, second, or third rib below

sub·coxa \ˈsəb+\ *n* [NL, fr. *sub-* + *coxa*] **:** the proximal part of the coxa of an arthropod appendage esp. when forming an element distinct from the coxa — **sub·coxal** \"+\ *adj*

sub·crepitant \"+\ *adj* [*sub-* + *crepitant*] **:** partially crepitant **:** indistinctly crepitant

sub·crescentic \"+\ *adj* [*sub-* + *crescentic*] **:** nearly or irregularly crescentic

sub·critical \"+\ *adj* [*sub-* + *critical*] **1 :** less or lower than critical in respect to a specified factor: as **a** *of temperature* **:** lower than that critical for the hardening of a metal **b** *of a mass of fissionable material* **:** of insufficient size to sustain a chain reaction **2 a :** occurring at or involving the use of subcritical temperatures ⟨~ annealing⟩ **b :** constituting or designed for use with fissionable material of subcritical mass ⟨a ~ reactor⟩ ⟨storing fissionable material in ~ chunks⟩ — **sub·critically** \"+\ *adv*

sub·crossing \"+\ *n* [*sub-* + *crossing*] **:** a minor or secondary crossing (as over a railway line)

sub·crust \ˈsəb+, -ˈ\ *n* [*sub-* + *crust*] **:** a layer underlying a crust; *esp* **:** the lower course of a bituminous macadam or concrete roadbed

sub·crustal \ˈsəb+\ *adj* [ISV *sub-* + *crustal*] **:** situated, acting, or occurring below a crust and esp. the crust of the earth

sub·crystalline \"+\ *adj* [*sub-* + *crystalline*] **:** obscurely crystalline **:** partially crystallized

sub·cultural \"+\ *adj* [*sub-* + *cultural*] **1 :** of, relating to, or constituting a subdivision of a social culture ⟨a special ~ framework within the Anglo-American area —John Gillin⟩ **2 :** existing prior to or on a lower level than that of cultural integration ⟨persistence of ~ traits⟩ ⟨~ experiences⟩

1sub·culture \ˈsəb+\ *n* [*sub-* + *culture*] **1 a :** a culture (as of bacteria) derived from another culture **b :** an act or instance of subculturing or of producing a subculture **2 :** an ethnic, regional, economic, or social group exhibiting characteristic patterns of behavior sufficient to distinguish it from others within an embracing culture or society ⟨a criminal ~⟩ ⟨southern regional ~ in the U.S.⟩

2subculture \"\ *vt* **:** to culture (as bacteria) anew on a fresh medium by inoculation from an older culture

sub·curative \"+\ *adj* [*sub-* + *curative*] **:** inadequate to produce a cure ⟨~ amounts of one drug may become curative when given with another⟩

sub·current \"+\ *n* [*sub-* + *current*] **:** an obscure or secondary current (as of thought)

sub·cutaneous \"+\ *adj* [LL *subcutaneus*, fr. L *sub-* + *cutis*

---

skin — more at HIDE] **1 :** situated or occurring beneath the skin ⟨~ fat⟩ **2 :** intended for use or made under the skin ⟨HYPODERMIC ⟨a ~ injection⟩ ⟨~ needles⟩ **3 :** living beneath the skin ⟨a ~ parasite⟩ — **sub·cutaneously** \"+\ *adv*

subcutaneous mite *n* **:** a widely distributed mite (*Laminosioptes cysticola*) that is an internal parasite of the fowl, turkey, goose, and some other birds

sub·cuticle \ˈsəb+\ *n* [NL *subcuticula*] **:** a layer (as of cells or fibers) lying beneath or forming the inner aspect of a cuticle **:** HYPODERMIS

sub·cuticula \"+\ *n* [NL, fr. *sub-* + *cuticula*] **:** SUBCUTICLE

sub·cuticular \"+\ *adj* [NL *subcuticula* + E -*ar*] **1 :** of, relating to, or being a subcuticle **2 :** [*sub-* + *cuticular*] **:** situated or occurring beneath a cuticle ⟨~ differentiation⟩

sub·cutis \ˈsəb+\ *n* [NL, fr. LL, beneath the skin, fr. L *sub-* + *cutis* skin] **:** the deeper part of the dermis

sub·cycle \"+, ¦+\ *n* **:** a float propelled like a bicycle and used by a lifeguard at a beach

sub·cylindrical \ˈsəb+\ *also* **sub·cylindric** \"+\ *adj* [*sub-* + *cylindrical, cylindric*] **:** nearly cylindrical

subd *abbr* subdivision

sub·deacon \ˈsəb+\ *n* [ME *subdecon, subdekene*, fr. LL *subdiaconus*, fr. L *sub-* under, below + LL *diaconus* deacon — more at SUB-, DEACON] **1 :** one in holy orders who ranks below a deacon and whose duties in the Eastern Orthodox and Roman Catholic Churches include the preparation of holy vessels for the Eucharist or mass **2 :** an ecclesiastic whose duty is to read the epistle in various religious services ⟨in the Protestant Episcopal Church, the epistoler is called a ~ regardless of his order of the ministry⟩

sub·deaconate \"+\ *n* [*subdeacon* + -*ate*] **:** SUBDIACONATE

sub·deaconry \"+\ *n* [*subdeacon* + -*ry*] **:** the order or office of subdeacon

sub·dean \"+\ *n* [ME *subdene, sudene*, fr. MF *souzdeien*, fr. ML *subdecanus*, fr. L *sub-* + LL *decanus* dean — more at DEAN] **:** an under dean **:** the deputy or substitute of a dean

sub·deanery \"+\ *n* [*subdean* + -*ery*] **:** the office or rank of subdean

sub·deb \ˈsəb+\ *n* [by shortening] **:** SUBDEBUTANTE

sub·debutante \"+\ *n* [*sub-* + *debutante*] **1 :** a young woman on the verge of becoming a social debutante **2 :** a girl in her middle teens ⟨styles for ~s⟩

sub·decanal \"+\ *adj* [ML *subdecanus* subdean + E -*al*] **:** of or relating to a subdean or subdeanery

sub·decimal \"+\ *adj* [*sub-* + *decimal*] **:** resulting from division by a multiple of ten

sub·deity \"+\ *n* [*sub-* + *deity*] **:** a minor member of a pantheon **:** a subordinate deity of a polytheistic religious system

1sub·delegate \"+\ *n* [ML *subdelegatus*, fr. L *sub-* + ML *delegatus* delegate — more at DELEGATE] **:** one who is deputy for a delegate; *often* **:** one to whom a delegated power or responsibility is transferred usu. for a particular case or situation

2sub·delegate \"+\ *vt* [ML *subdelegatus*, past part. of *subdelegare* to subdelegate, fr. L *sub-* + *delegare* to delegate] **:** to transfer (as a power or right delegated to oneself) to another ⟨~ legislative powers to an executive branch⟩ — **sub·delegation** \ˈsəb+\ *n*

sub·dentate \ˈsəb+\ *also* **sub·dentated** \"+\ *adj* [*sub-* + *dentate, dentated*] **:** partially or imperfectly dentate ⟨leaves with margins ~⟩

sub·depot \"+\ *n* [*sub-* + *depot*] **:** a military depot that operates under the jurisdiction of another depot and usu. performs only specified depot functions

sub·derivative \"+\ *n* [*sub-* + *derivative*] **:** a word derived from a derivative ⟨*friendliness* is a ~ from *friendly* which is derived from *friend*⟩

sub·dermal \"+\ *adj* [*sub-* + *dermal*] **:** SUBCUTANEOUS

sub·desert \"+\ *n* [*sub-* + *desert*] **:** a stretch of arid land that is less arid than typical desert

sub·diaconal \ˈsəb+\ *adj* [LL *subdiaconalis*, fr. *subdiaconus* subdeacon + L -*alis* -al — more at SUBDEACON] **:** of or relating to a subdeacon or a subdeaconry

sub·diaconate \"+\ *n* [LL *subdiaconatus*, fr. *subdiaconus*, fr. L *sub-* + -*atus* -ate] **:** the office or rank of a subdeacon

sub·diapente \"+\ *n* [*sub-* + *diapente*] **:** a fifth below — used as a direction in music

sub·dilution \"+\ *n* [*sub-* + *dilution*] **1 :** a fractional dilution of a solution of known concentration ⟨prepared 0.1, 0.01, and 0.001 molar ~s from a molar solution⟩ **2 :** the act of preparing a subdilution ⟨obtained an accurate solution by ~⟩

sub·dimension \"+\ *n* [*sub-* + *dimension*] **:** one of the partial dimensions or dimensions of constituent elements that make up the dimensions of an object

sub·disjunctive \"+\ *adj* [NL *subdisjunctivus*, fr. L *sub-* + *disjunctivus*, adj., disjunctive — more at DISJUNCTIVE] **:** a disjunctive conjunction connecting words or word groups that have the same reference ⟨in "report to the chairman or head of the department" *or* is a ~⟩

sub·dividable \ˈsəb+\ *adj* [*subdivide* + -*able*] **:** capable of being further divided **:** suitable for subdividing

sub·divide \"+\ *vb* [ME *subdividen*, fr. LL *subdividere*, fr. L *sub-* further + *dividere* to divide — more at SUB-, DIVIDE] *vt* **1 :** to further divide (what has already been divided) **:** divide the parts of into more parts ⟨the functional divisions were then subdivided⟩ **2 :** to divide into several parts ⟨bulkheads — the ship into watertight compartments; *esp* **:** to divide (a tract of land) into building lots **:** lay out a subdivision on (unimproved land) ~ *vi* **:** to separate or become separated into parts — **sub·divider** \"+\ *n*

sub·divisible \ˈsəb+\ *adj* [*sub-* + *divisible*] **:** susceptible of subdivision

sub·division \"+\ *n* [LL *subdivision-, subdivisio*, fr. *subdivisus* (past part. of *subdividere* to subdivide) + L -*ion-, -io* -ion] **1 a :** the act or process of subdividing **b :** an instance or example of subdividing **2 :** something produced by subdividing: as **a :** a part made by subdividing ⟨a ~ of a taxonomic division⟩ **b :** a tract of land surveyed and divided into lots for purposes of sale — compare DEVELOPMENT — **sub·divisional** \"+\ *adj*

sub·dolichocephalic \ˈsəb+\ *also* **sub·dolichocephalous** \"+\ *adj* [*subdolichocephalic* n. NL *subdolichocephalus*: subdolichocephalic person (fr. *sub-* + *dolichocephalus*) + *dolichocephal*] + E -*ic*; *subdolichocephalous* fr. NL *subdolichocephalus*] **:** having a cephalic index of 77.7–80 — **sub·dolichocephalism** \"+\ *n* *or* **sub·dolichocephaly** \"+\ *n*

sub·do·lous \ˈsäbdələs\ *adj* [L *subdolus*, fr. *sub-* + *dolus* fraud, deceit — more at TALE] **:** somewhat sly **:** CRAFTY, CUNNING, ARTFUL

sub·dominance \"+\ *n* **:** the quality or state of being subdominant

1sub·dominant \"+\ *adj* [*sub-* + *dominant*] **1 :** incompletely dominant **2 :** being or having the quality of a subdominant ⟨~ chords⟩ ⟨~ life-forms in an ecological community⟩

2subdominant \"\ *n* [*sub-* + *dominant* n.] **:** something dominant to an inferior or partial degree: as **a :** the fourth musical degree of the major or minor scale (as F in the scale of C) **b :** a species or life-form that is ecologically important but subordinate in influence to the dominants of a community or is characteristic of a structural subunit or partial area of a community ⟨shrubs may be prominent ~s in a forest community⟩ ⟨sometimes forbs behave as seasonal ~s in grasslands⟩

sub·dorsal \"+\ *adj* [*sub-* + *dorsal*] **:** situated nearly on the dorsal surface — **sub·dorsally** \"+\ *adv*

sub·drain \ˈsəb+, -ˈ\ *n* [*sub-* + *drain*] **:** a perforated or plain underground drain

sub·drainage \ˈsəb+\ *n* [*sub-* + *drainage*] **:** natural or artificial drainage from beneath

sub·drill \"+\ *vt* [*sub-* + *drill*] **:** to drill (a hole) to a size that leaves sufficient metal for finishing by reaming

sub·du·able \səbˈd(y)üəbəl\ *adj* **:** capable of being subdued

sub·du·al \səbˈd(y)üəl\ *n* -s [*subdue* + -*al* (n. suffix)] **:** the act of subduing

sub·duct \səbˈdəkt\ *vb* [L *subductus*, past part. of *subducere* to withdraw] *vt* **:** WITHDRAW, SUBTRACT, DEDUCT, REMOVE

sub·duc·tion \"+\ *n* -s [L *subduction-, subductio*, fr. *subductus* (past part. of *subducere*) + -*ion-, -io* -ion] **1 a :** the act of taking away **:** WITHDRAWAL **b :** arithmetical subtraction; *also* **:** DEDUCTION **2 :** the act or process of subduing **:** SUBJECTION

---

sub·due \səbˈd(y)ü\ *vt* -ED/-ING/-S [ME *subduen, sodewen* (prob. influenced in meaning by L *subdere* to put under, subdue), fr. MF *soduire* to seduce, deceive (prob. influenced in meaning by L *seducere* to seduce), fr. L *subducere* to withdraw, lit., to lead up, lead away, fr. *sub-* up, further + *ducere* to lead — more at SEDUCE, SUB-, TOW] **1 :** to conquer by force or by superior power and bring into subjection **:** VANQUISH, CRUSH ⟨where Norman forces *subdued* the English⟩ **2 a :** to bring (as a person) into subjection or order by or as if by persuasion, intimidation, or threat of punishment ⟨~ a wilful child⟩ **b :** to bring under control esp. by an exertion of the will **:** CURB ⟨*subduing* her foolish fears⟩ ⟨determined to ~ this unruly desire⟩ **3** *archaic* **:** to bring (a disease) under control by treatment **3 :** to prepare (land) for the growing of crops **:** bring under cultivation **4 :** to reduce the intensity or degree of **:** make less prominent **:** tone down ⟨with an effort *subdued* his angry speech⟩ ⟨voices became *subdued* as the twilight deepened⟩ ⟨a soft hairdo helped to ~ her heavy features⟩ **syn** see CONQUER

subdued *adj* [fr. past part. of *subdue*] **1 :** brought under control by or as if by military conquest **2 :** reduced or lacking in force, intensity, or vividness **:** toned down ⟨~ colors⟩ ⟨a ~ voice⟩ **3 :** characterized by broadly rounded elements as if weathered or eroded ⟨~ landforms⟩ ⟨a ~ topography is typical of old landmasses⟩ **syn** see TAME

sub·dued·ly \-ü(ə)dlē, -li\ *adv* **:** in a subdued manner

sub·dued·ness \-ü(ə)dnəs\ *n* -ES **:** the quality or state of being subdued

sub·du·er \səbˈd(y)üə(r), -dü(ə)r, -düə\ *n* -s **:** one that subdues

subduing *adj* **:** tending to produce subdual ⟨~ reflections⟩ — **sub·du·ing·ly** *adv*

sub·dural \ˈsəb+\ *adj* [ISV *sub-* + *dural*] **:** situated or occurring under the dura mater or between the dura mater and the arachnoid membrane ⟨the ~ space⟩ ⟨~ hemorrhage⟩ — **sub·durally** \"+\ *adv*

sub·dwarf \ˈsəb+, -ˌ\ *n* [*sub-* + *dwarf*] **:** a star having higher surface temperature for its mass and luminosity than is usual to stars of the main sequence and therefore having relatively high density and lying to the left of the main sequence on the spectrum-luminosity diagram

sub·economic \ˈsəb+\ *adj* [*sub-* + *economic*] **1 :** lacking in economic importance ⟨a pest present in ~ numbers⟩ **2 :** not justifiable on purely economic grounds ⟨~ public housing projects⟩

sub·edit \"+\ *vt* [back-formation fr. *subeditor*] **1 :** to act as subeditor of **2** *chiefly Brit* **:** COPYREAD

sub·edition \"+\ *n* [*sub-* + *edition*] **:** an issue of a printed work bibliographically categorized as of lesser status than an edition because done from plates leased from the original publisher or reproduced by photolithography from an original printing

sub·editor \"+\ *n* [*sub-* + *editor*] **1 :** an assistant editor **2** *chiefly Brit* **:** COPYREADER — **sub·editorial** \"+\ *adj*

sub·editorship \"+\ *n* [*sub-* + *editorship*] **:** the position or status of a subeditor

sub·effective \"+\ *adj* [*sub-* + *effective*] **:** inadequate to produce an effect ⟨~ treatment with a carcinogen⟩

sub·elliptic \"+\ *adj* *or* **sub·elliptical** \"+\ *adj* [*subelliptic* ISV *sub-* + *elliptic*; *subelliptical* fr. *sub-* + *elliptical*] **:** somewhat elliptic

sub·encephalon \ˈsəb+\ *n* [NL, fr. *sub-* + *encephalon*] **:** the midbrain and hindbrain together

sub·endemic \"+\ *adj* [*sub-* + *endemic*] **:** largely localized in one natural area **:** occurring mostly in one environment ⟨a ~ flora⟩

sub·endocardial \"+\ *adj* [*sub-* + *endocardial*] **:** situated or occurring beneath the endocardium or between the endocardium and myocardium ⟨~ blood loss⟩

sub·endorse \"+\ *vt* [*sub-* + *endorse*] **:** to provide with a secondary or additional endorsement — **sub·endorsement** \"+\ *n*

sub·endothelial \ˈsəb+\ *adj* [*sub-* + *endothelial*] **:** situated under an endothelium

sub·enfeoff \"+\ *vt* [*sub-* + *enfeoff*] **:** SUBINFEUDATE

sub·entire \"+\ *adj* [*sub-* + *entire*] **1 :** almost entire **2 :** having few denticulations

sub·entitle \"+\ *vt* [*sub-* + *entitle*] **:** to provide with a subtitle

sub·entry \ˈsəb+\ *n* [*sub-* + *entry*] **:** an entry (as in a catalog or an account) made under a more general entry

sub·epicardial \"+\ *adj* [*sub-* + *epicardial*] **:** situated or occurring beneath the epicardium or between the epicardium and myocardium

sub·epidermal \"+\ *adj* [*sub-* + *epidermal*] **:** lying beneath or constituting the innermost part of the epidermis

sub·epithelial \"+\ *adj* [*sub-* + *epithelial*] **:** situated or occurring beneath an epithelial layer; *sometimes* **:** SUBCUTANEOUS

sub·equal \"+\ *adj* [NL *subaequalis*, fr. L *sub-* + *aequalis* equal — more at EQUAL] **:** approximately but not exactly equal

sub·equatorial \"+\ *adj* [ISV *sub-* + *equatorial*] **:** approximately equatorial; *usu* **:** of, relating to, or constituting a region just outside the equatorial region

sub·equivalve \"+\ *adj* [ISV *sub-* + *equivalve*] **:** having shell valves that are slightly unequal in size ⟨a ~ mollusk⟩

su·ber \ˈsübə(r)\ *n* -S [L, prob. of non-IE origin; akin to the source of Gk *syphar* wrinkled skin] **:** corky plant tissue **:** PHELLEM; *esp* **:** the outer bark of the cork oak

su·ber·ate \-ə,rāt\ *n* -s [F *subérate*, fr. *subér-* (in *subérique* suberic) + -*ate*] **:** a salt or ester of suberic acid

sub·erect \ˈsəb+\ *adj* [*sub-* + *erect*] **:** standing or growing in a nearly erect position **:** ASCENDING ⟨a ~ shrub⟩

su·be·re·ous \(ˌ)sü¦birēəs\ *or* **su·ber·ic** \-ˈberik\ *adj* [L *bereous*, fr. *suber* + -*eous; suberic*, fr. *suber* + -*eus* -eous; *suberic* fr. L *suber* + E -*ic*] **:** of, relating to, or derived from cork **:** SUBEROSE

su·ber·ite \-ə,rīt\ *n* -s [NL *Suberites*] **:** a sponge of the genus *Suberites* or family Suberitidae

su·ber·i·tes \ˌsü¦əˈrīd-(ˌ)ēz\ *n, cap* [NL, fr. L *suber* cork oak, cork + NL -*ites*] **:** a genus (the type of the family Suberitidae of the class Demospongiae) of fleshy, erect or encrusting monaxial sponges that have no microscleres or spongin, that have megascleres shaped like needles with heads, and that include forms which often live on shells occupied by hermit crabs

su·ber·iza·tion \ˌsübərəˈzāshən, -ˌrī-\ *n* -s [ISV *suberize* + -*ation*] **:** conversion of plant cell walls into water-impervious corky tissue through infiltration with suberin — compare CUTINIZATION, LIGNIFICATION

su·ber·ize \ˈsübə,rīz\ *also* **su·ber·in·ize** \-ˈ\ *vt* -ED/-ING/-S *also* -ize in *Explan Notes* [*suberize* fr. L *suber* cork oak, cork + E -*ize; suberinize* fr. *suberin* + -*ize*] **:** to cause or effect the suberization of

su·ber·one \-ə,rōn\ *n* -s [F *subérone*, fr. *subér-* (in *subérique* suberic) + -*one*] **:** CYCLOHEPTANONE

su·ber·ose \-ə,rōs\ *also* **su·ber·ous** \-ərəs\ *adj* [NL *suberosus*, fr. L *suber* cork oak, cork + -*osus* -ose — more at SUBER] **:** having a corky texture resulting from or like that resulting from suberization

su·ber·yl·ar·gi·nine \ˌsübərəl+\ *n* [*suberyl* (fr. F *subéryle*, fr. *subér-* — in *subérique* suberic + -*yle* -yl) + *arginine*] **:** a monoamide derived from suberic acid and arginine and obtained by hydrolysis of bufotoxins

suberic acid *n* [F *subérique*, fr. L *suber*] **:** a crystalline dicarboxylic acid HOOC(CH$_2$)$_6$COOH obtained usu. by alkaline hydrolysis of suberin or by oxidation of cork, castor oil, or ricinoleic acid with nitric acid; octane-dioic acid

sub·esophageal \"+\ *adj* [*sub-* + *esophageal*] **:** situated or occurring under the esophagus

sub·essential \"+\ *adj* [*sub-* + *essential*] **:** important but not absolutely essential

sub·falcate \ˌsəb+\ *adj* [*sub-* + *falcate*] **:** nearly but not quite falcate **:** irregularly falcate

sub·family \"+\ *n* [ISV *sub-* + *family*] **:** a taxonomic category next below a family ⟨a ~ of languages⟩; *specif* **:** a biological taxonomic category below a family and above a genus — see -INAE

sub·fauna \"+\ *n* [NL, fr. *sub-* + *fauna*] **:** a localized fauna

sub·febrile \"+\ *adj* [ISV *sub-* + *febrile*] **:** of, relating to, or constituting a body temperature very slightly above normal but not febrile

sub·fertile \"+\ *adj* [*sub-* + *fertile*] **:** of less than normal fertility though still capable of producing fertilization ⟨~ semen⟩

¹sub·feu \"+,-\ *n* [*sub-* + *feu*] **:** a feu held of a vassal as such

²sub·feu \ˌsəbˈfyü\ *vb* **:** SUBINFEUDATE

sub·fibrous \ˌsəb+\ *adj* [*sub-* + *fibrous*] **:** somewhat fibrous ⟨a ~ consistency⟩

sub·fief \ˈsəb+,-\ *n* [*sub-* + *fief*] **:** a fief that is granted out of and is part of another fief

sub·fix \ˈsəb,fiks\ *n* [*sub-* + *-fix* (as in *prefix*)] **:** a subscript sign, letter, or character

sub·floor \ˈsəb+,-\ *n* [*sub-* + *floor*] **:** a rough floor laid as a base for a finished floor

sub·flooring \ˌsəb+\ *n* [*sub-* + *flooring*] **1 :** SUBFLOORS ⟨the ~ of a building⟩ **2 :** material for use in a subfloor ⟨the cheapest pine ~⟩

sub·flora \"+\ *n* [NL, fr. *sub-* + *flora*] **:** a localized flora

sub·fluoride \"+\ *n* [*sub-* + *fluoride*] **:** a fluoride containing a relatively small proportion of fluorine ⟨silver ~ Ag_2F⟩

sub·fluvial \"+\ *adj* [*sub-* + *fluvial*] **1 :** situated, taking place, or formed at the bottom of a body of water (as a river) ⟨~ cables⟩ ⟨a ~ deposit of silt⟩ **2 :** passing under a river ⟨a ~ tunnel⟩

sub·focal \"+\ *adj* [*sub-* + *focal*] **:** located or occurring below the focus of attention **:** not clearly conscious

sub·foreman \"+\ *n* [*sub-* + *foreman*] **1 :** a supervisory employee subordinate to a foreman **2 :** a member of a work crew functioning esp. temporarily as a foreman **:** a working foreman

sub·form \ˈsəb+,-\ *n* [*sub-* + *form*] **:** a subordinate or derivative form ⟨~*s* of the Gothic in 19th century writing⟩

sub·fornicate \ˌsəb+\ *adj* [*sub-* + *fornicate*] **:** somewhat arched

¹sub·fossil \"+\ *adj* [ISV *sub-* + *fossil*] **:** of less than typical fossil age though not strictly recent **:** having lost the organic constituents (as fats and proteins) produced in vital activities but not yet having had them replaced (as by mineralization)

²subfossil \"\ *n* **:** a subfossil specimen

sub·fossorial \"+\ *adj* [*sub-* + *fossorial*] **:** showing some modification adaptive to a fossorial way of life ⟨an insect with ~ forelimbs⟩

sub·foundation \"+\ *n* [*sub-* + *foundation*] **:** a secondary foundation **:** SUBGRADE

sub·fraction \"+\ *n* [*sub-* + *fraction*] **1 :** a fraction of a fraction **2 :** a small fraction — **sub·fractional** \"+\ *adj*

sub·frame \ˈsəb+,-\ *n* [*sub-* + *frame*] **:** a secondary frame: as **a :** a frame for the attachment and support of a finish frame (as of a window or door) **b :** a frame for the support of panels used as a wall finish

sub·freezing \ˌsəb+\ *adj* [*sub-* + *freezing*] **:** lower than is required to produce freezing **:** characterized by a temperature lower than 0° C ⟨~ temperatures⟩ ⟨~ conditions⟩

sub·fulgent \"+\ *adj* [*sub-* + *fulgent*] **:** somewhat shining **:** moderately lustrous

sub·functional \"+\ *adj* [*sub-* + *functional*] **:** having little or no apparent function ⟨a ~ appendage on an insect⟩

sub·fusc \ˌsəbˈfəsk\ *adj* [L *subfuscus* brownish, dusky, fr. *sub-* near, almost + *fuscus* dark brown, blackish — more at SUB-, DUSK] **1 :** SUBFUSCOUS **2 :** having little of brightness or appeal **:** DRAB, DINGY ⟨the moment when the word *Austerity* was to take to itself a new ~ and squalid twist of meaning —Osbert Sitwell⟩ ⟨that gray, impoverished, ~ community —Marguerite Steen⟩

sub·fus·cous \-skəs\ *adj* [L *subfuscus*] **:** somewhat fuscous **:** DUSKY

subg *abbr* subgenus

sub·galea \ˌsəb+\ *n* [NL, fr. *sub-* + *galea*] **:** a segment of the maxilla of an insect usu. attached to the stipes and bearing the galea

sub·gallate \"+\ *n* [*sub-* + *gallate*] **:** a basic gallate (as bismuth subgallate)

sub·generic \"+\ *also* **sub·generical** \"+\ *adj* [*subgeneric* ISV *sub-* + *generic*; *subgenerical* fr. *sub-* + *generical*] **:** of, relating to, or constituting a subgenus — **sub·generically** \"+\ *adv*

sub·genital \"+\ *adj* [*sub-* + *genital*] **:** situated below the genital organs

sub·genotype \"+\ *n* [*sub-* + *genotype*] **:** a species that is the type of a subgenus

sub·genus \"+\ *n* [NL, fr. L *sub-* + *genus*] **:** a category in biological taxonomy below a genus and above a species

sub·giant \"+\ *n* [*sub-* + *giant*] **:** a star of such color and luminosity that it falls above the main sequence of the spectrum-luminosity diagram yet is not in the region of ordinary giant stars

sub·gingival \ˌsəb+\ *adj* [*sub-* + *gingival*] **:** situated or occurring beneath the gums and esp. between the gums and the basal part of the crowns of the teeth ⟨~ deposits of tartar⟩

sub·glabrous \"+\ *adj* [ISV *sub-* + *glabrous*] **:** imperfectly glabrous **:** slightly rough or hairy

sub·glacial \"+\ *adj* [*sub-* + *glacial*] **1 :** of, relating to, or formed in or by the bottommost part of a glacier or the area immediately underlying a glacier ⟨~ channels⟩ ⟨the ~ floor⟩ **2 :** POSTGLACIAL ⟨postglacial (or ~) stream-cut canyons —*Jour. of Geol.*⟩ — **sub·glacially** \"+\ *adv*

sub·glenoid \"+\ *adj* [*sub-* + *glenoid*] **:** situated beneath the glenoid fossa of the shoulder

sub·globose \"+\ *adj* [*sub-* + *globose*] **:** imperfectly or nearly globose — **sub·globosely** \"+\ *adv*

sub·glottal \"+\ *adj* [*sub-* + *glottal*] **:** SUBGLOTTIC

sub·glottic \"+\ *adj* [ISV *sub-* + *glottic*] **:** situated or occurring below the glottis

sub·grade \ˈsəb+,-\ *n* [*sub-* + *grade*] **1 :** a subordinate level in a scale (as of rank or quality) ⟨~ is used in some classifications at a supraphylar level⟩ **2 :** a layer (as a stratum or surface) immediately beneath some principal layer; *specif* **:** a surface of earth or rock leveled off to receive the foundation of a structure (as a road, pavement, building, sewer) or the ballast of a railroad

sub·graywacke \ˌsəb+\ *n* [*sub-* + *graywacke*] **:** a graywacke characterized by introduced mineral cement and deposition from normal subaqueous currents

¹sub·group \ˈsəb+,-\ *n* [*sub-* + *group*] **:** a subordinate group usu. of individuals sharing some common quality that makes them distinguishable from other members of a major group to which they belong ⟨the Britannic ~ of the Celtic languages —Isidore Dyen⟩ ⟨the ~ of the professional criminal . . . has basic similarities . . . to the subgroup of the industrialist —R.K.Merton⟩

²sub·group \ˈ≈,≈\ *vt* **:** to divide into subgroups

sub·gular \ˌsəb+\ *adj* [*sub-* + *gular*] **:** situated on the lower part of the throat ⟨a ~ scale on a reptile⟩

sub·halide \"+\ *n* [*sub-* + *halide*] **:** a halide (as a subchloride) containing a relatively small proportion of halogen

sub·harmonic \"+\ *n* [ISV *sub-* + *harmonic*] **:** a component of a periodic wave having a frequency that is an integral submultiple of the fundamental frequency ⟨the ~ having half the fundamental frequency is the second ~⟩ — compare HARMONIC

¹sub·head \ˈsəb+,-\ *n* [*sub-* + *head*] **1 :** any of the heads under which each of the main divisions of a subject may be subdivided **2 :** a heading or caption subordinate to a main headline, heading, or title esp. when inserted as a divider between sections (as of a newspaper or periodical article or story or the text of a book)

²sub·head \ˈ≈,≈\ *vt* **:** to provide (as a manuscript or discourse) with subheads **:** introduce by a subhead

sub·heading \ˌsəb+\ *n* [*sub-* + *heading*] **:** SUBHEAD

sub·health \ˈsəb+,-\ *n* [*sub-* + *health*] **:** imperfect health **:** a condition of reduced vigor in the absence of overt ailment

sub·he·dral \ˌsəbˈhēdrəl\ *adj* [*sub-* + *-hedral*] **:** incompletely bounded by crystal planes **:** partly faced

sub·hepatic \ˌsəb+\ *adj* [ISV *sub-* + *hepatic*] **:** situated or occurring under the liver

sub–himalayan \"+\ *adj, usu cap H* **:** situated under or at the foot of the Himalaya mountains

sub·holding company \ˌsəb+-\ *n* [*sub-* + *holding company*] **:** a holding company in which a controlling interest is held by another holding company

¹sub·ho·los·te·an \ˌsəbhəˈlästēən\ *adj* [NL *Subholostei* + E *-an* (adj. suffix)] **:** of or relating to the Subholostei

²subholostean \"\ *n* -S [NL *Subholostei* + E *-an* (n. suffix)] **:** a ganoid fish of the order Subholostei

sub·holostei \"+\ *n pl, cap* [NL, fr. *sub-* + *Holostei*] *in some classifications* **:** an order comprising ganoid fishes that are generally more primitive than the Holostei and being more or less equivalent to the order Archistia

sub·horizontal \ˌsəb+\ *adj* [*sub-* + *horizontal*] **:** not quite horizontal in position or orientation

¹sub·human \"+\ *adj* [*sub-* + *human*] **:** less than human: as **a :** failing to attain the level (as of morality or intelligence) associated with normal human beings ⟨a ~ child⟩ ⟨treating the natives as ~⟩ **b :** unsuitable to or unfit for human beings ⟨~ conditions of life⟩ ⟨a ~ spectacle⟩ **c :** approaching that normal to man ⟨a dog with ~ intelligence⟩ **d :** of, relating to, or belonging to an infrahuman group ⟨the ~ primates⟩ ⟨the army ant . . . presents the most complex instance of organized mass behavior . . . in any ~ animal —T.C.Schneirla & Gerard Piel⟩

²subhuman \"\ *n* **:** a subhuman individual; *esp* **:** a person so deficient in ordinary human characteristics as to seem a member of a different species ⟨such moronic ~*s* —*Time*⟩

sub·humanity \ˌsəb+\ *n* **1 :** subhuman behavior **2 :** SUBHUMANS

sub·humid \"+\ *adj* [*sub-* + *humid*] **:** not quite humid **:** slightly to moderately humid and usu. more humid than subarid

sub·hyaline \"+\ *adj* [*sub-* + *hyaline*] **:** somewhat or imperfectly hyaline

sub·hymenium \"+\ *n* [NL, fr. *sub-* + *hymenium*] **:** the hypothecium of a fungus

sub·icteric \"+\ *adj* [ISV *sub-* + *icteric*] **:** very slightly jaundiced **:** indicative of a slight jaundice ⟨a ~ tint in the skin⟩

su·bic·u·lar \səˈbikyələ(r)\ *adj* [NL *subiculum* + E *-ar*] **:** of, relating to, or constituting a subiculum

su·bic·u·lum \-ləm\ *n, pl* **subicu·la** \-lə\ [NL, fr. L *subic-*, *subex* underlayer, support (fr. *subicere*, *subjicere* to throw under) + *-ulum* (neut. of *-ulus* -ule) — more at SUBJECT] **1 a :** a part of the hippocampal convolution that borders the fissure of the hippocampus **b :** the entire hippocampal gyrus **2 :** a felted mass of hyphae forming a basal stratum in which perithecia or pycnidia are situated

sub·imaginal \ˌsəb+\ *adj* [NL *subimagin-*, *subimago* + E *-al*] **:** of, relating to, or being a subimago

sub·imago \"+\ *n* [NL, fr. *sub-* + *imago*] **1 :** a stage in the development of some insects (as the mayflies) between the nymph and imago in which the insect is able to fly but becomes mature only after a further molt **2 :** an insect in the subimaginal stage — see DUN

sub·incandescent \"+\ *adj* [*sub-* + *incandescent*] **:** heated but below the point of incandescence

sub·incise \"+\ *vt* [back-formation fr. *subincision*] **:** to perform subincision upon

sub·incision \"+\ *n* [*sub-* + *incision*] **:** a ritual mutilation performed as a part of puberty rites among some native Australian and Fijian groups that involves slitting the underside of the penis with permanent opening of the urethra

¹sub·index \"+\ *n* [*sub-* + *index*] **1 :** a mathematical subscript **2 :** an index to a division of a main classification

²subindex \"\ *vt* **:** to make a subindex of or for ⟨provide with a subindex⟩

sub·indicative \"+\ *adj, archaic* [obs. E *subindicate* to indicate slightly (fr. LL *subindicatus*, past part. of *subindicare* to subindicate, fr. L *sub-* + *indicare* to indicate) + E *-ive* — more at INDICATE] **:** slightly or indirectly indicative

sub·in·feu·date \ˌsə,binˈfyü,dāt, *usu* -ād.+V\ *also* **sub·in·feud** \-ˈfyüd\ *vt* [back-formation fr. *subinfeudation*] **:** to make subinfeudation of

sub·infeudation \ˌsəb+\ *n* [*sub-* + *infeudation*] **:** the granting of feudal lands by a vassal lord to another to hold as vassal of himself rather than of his own superior; *also* **:** the relation or tenure of a vassal so holding land

sub·infeudatory \"+\ *n* -ES [*subinfeudation* + *-ory*] **:** a tenant holding by subinfeudation

sub·influent \ˌsəb+\ *n* [*sub-* + *influent*] **:** an organism functioning like but less effectively than an influent in an ecological community

sub·inguinal \ˌsəb+\ *adj* [*sub-* + *inguinal*] **:** situated below Poupart's ligament

sub·inoculate \"+\ *vt* [*sub-* + *inoculate*] **:** to introduce (infective material) from a laboratory strain into a potential host — used esp. of a virus — **sub·inoculation** \"+\ *n*

sub·integumental \"+\ *adj* [*sub-* + *integumental*] **:** situated or occurring under an integument; *specif* **:** SUBCUTANEOUS

sub·intelligential \"+\ *adj* [*subintelligential* fr. LL *subintelligent-*, *subintelligens* (pres. part. of *subintelligere* to understand implicitly, fr. L *sub-* secretly, under + *intelligere* to understand) + E *-al*] **:** implying something beyond what is obvious to the mind **:** INTIMATING

sub·in·tel·lig·i·tur \ˌsə,bintᵊlˈijəd·ər\ *n* -S [LL, it is implicitly understood, 3d pers. sing. pres. indic. of *subintelligere*] *archaic* **:** a meaning or understanding (as of a statement) implied but not expressed

sub·intent \ˌsəb+\ *n* [*sub-* + *intent*] **:** a subordinate meaning, purpose, or proposal

sub·interval \"+\ *n* [*sub-* + *interval*] **:** an interval that is a subdivision of a larger or major interval (as in music or mathematics)

sub·intestinal \"+\ *adj* [*sub-* + *intestinal*] **:** situated beneath or on the ventral aspect of an intestine

sub·intimal \"+\ *adj* [*sub-* + *intimal*] **:** situated beneath an intima and esp. between the intima and media of an artery

sub·introduce \"+\ *vt* [LL *subintroducere*, fr. L *sub-* secretly, under + *introducere* to introduce — more at SUB-, INTRODUCE] **:** to bring in secretly or surreptitiously

sub·involution \"+\ *n* [ISV *sub-* + *involution*] **:** partial or incomplete involution ⟨~ of the uterus⟩

sub·irrigate \"+\ *vt* [*sub-* + *irrigate*] **:** to water from beneath (as by the periodic rise of a water table); *esp* **:** to irrigate below the surface (as by a system of underground porous pipes) — **sub·irrigation** \ˌ≈+\ *n*

su·bi·ta·men·te \ˌsü,bēd·əˈmen·(,)tā\ *adv* [It, fr. *subito*, adj., sudden, fr. L *subitus*] **:** SUBITO — used as a direction in music

sub·i·ta·ne·ous \ˌsəbəˈtānēəs\ *adj* [L *subitaneus* — more at SUDDEN] **:** formed or taking place suddenly or unexpectedly **:** SUDDEN, HASTY; *esp* **:** undergoing or ready for immediate development ⟨~ summer eggs that develop without a period of dormancy⟩

sub·item \ˌsəb+\ *n* [*sub-* + *item*] **:** an item (as a brief note) that forms a subdivision of a larger topic

su·bi·to \ˈsübēd·(,)ō\ *adv* [It, fr. L, fr. *subitus* sudden, unexpected — more at SUDDEN] **:** IMMEDIATELY, SUDDENLY — used as a direction in music

su·bi·ya \süˈbē(y)ə\ *n, usu cap* **:** an archaic Bantu language of Northern Rhodesia

subj *abbr* **1** subject; subjective; subjectively **2** subjunctive

sub·ja·cen·cy \(,)səbˈjāsᵊnsē, -si\ *n* -ES **:** the quality or state of being subjacent

sub·ja·cent \-sᵊnt\ *adj* [L *subjacent-*, *subjacens*, pres. part. of *subjacēre* to lie under, fr. *sub-* + *jacēre* to lie — more at ADJACENT] **:** lying under or below: as **a :** lower than though not directly below ⟨hills and ~ valleys⟩ **b :** occurring below the surface ⟨a ~ fire⟩ **c :** antecedent and in some degree causative **:** UNDERLYING ⟨can infer a set of ~ causal events, when only the effects are available for direct scrutiny —A.C.Danto⟩ ⟨the factors in a crime⟩ — **sub·ja·cent·ly** *adv*

¹sub·ject \ˈsəbjəkt, -jekt *sometimes* -,jekt\ *n* -S [ME *suget*, *subget*, fr. MF, fr. L *subjectus* subject, inferior (fr. *subjectus*, past part.) & *subjectum* foundation, subject of a proposition (trans. of Gk *hypokeimenon*), fr. neut. of *subjectus*, past part. of *subjicere*, *subicere* to bring under, throw under, fr. *sub-* + *-jicere*, *-icere* (fr. *jacere* to throw) — more at JET] **1 :** one that is placed under the authority, dominion, control, or influence of someone or something: as **a :** one bound in allegiance or service to a feudal superior **:** VASSAL **b** (1) **:** one subject to a monarch or ruler and governed by his law (2) **:** one who lives in the territory of, enjoys the protection of, and owes allegiance to a sovereign power or state — compare CITIZEN 2 **c** *obs* **:** a person under the spiritual oversight, care, or direction of a religious superior **d** *obs* **:** those who owe allegiance to a particular sovereign or rule **:** CITIZENRY **2 a** *obs* **:** the material from which a thing is formed **:** material substance **b** (1) **:** that of which a quality, attribute, or relation may be affirmed or in which it may inhere **:** the theme of a discourse or predication **:** the identical reference of related thoughts **:** a material either physical or ideal in which differences may appear (2) **:** SUBSTRATUM; *esp* **:** substantive reality that is material or essential being (3) **:** something that sustains or is embodied in thought or consciousness **:** the thinking agent **:** the mind, ego, or reality of whatever sort that supports or assumes the form of mental operations — distinguished from *object* ⟨the individuality of the organism corresponds to, though it is not necessarily identical with, the psychological ~, while to the environment and its changes corresponds the objective continuum —James Ward⟩ **3 :** something that forms a basis (as for action, study, discussion, or use): as **a** (1) **:** the underlying theme or topic of a branch of knowledge or study ⟨the ~ of mathematics is quantities and their manipulations⟩ (2) **:** a branch of knowledge or study esp. when arranged and formulated for teaching as an integrated part in a system of studies ⟨each pupil took courses in five ~*s* including electives⟩ ⟨found the ~ of chemistry difficult⟩ **b :** REASON, MOTIVE, CAUSE ⟨a ~ of dispute⟩ ⟨gave them no ~ for complaint⟩ **c** (1) **:** one that is acted upon (as in an operation or process) ⟨a ~ of debate⟩ ⟨the helpless ~ of his cruelty⟩ (2) **:** an individual whose reactions or responses are studied (as in the testing of a physiological or psychological phenomenon) ⟨the ~*s* of a nutritional experiment⟩ ⟨the ~ was cued to run a maze⟩ (3) **:** a dead body for anatomical study and dissection **d** (1) **:** something concerning which something is said or done **:** a thing or person treated of ⟨let's say no more on that ~⟩ ⟨treated religion as the first and greatest of ~*s*⟩ ⟨the ~ of your essay⟩ ⟨a ~ worthy of a great dramatist⟩ (2) **:** something (as an incident, scene, figure, group) that is represented or indicated in a work of art **e** (1) **:** **subject term :** the term of a logical proposition that denotes what the proposition is about; *also* **:** matter denoted by such a term **:** the topic of an affirmation or denial — contrasted with *predicate* (2) **:** a word or word group denoting that of which something is affirmed or predicated **:** a term that is construed with or without modifiers as the nominative of a verb and is grammatically either a noun or a word, phrase, or clause used as a noun equivalent **f** (1) **:** the principal theme or melodic phrase on which a musical composition or movement is based (2) **:** the antecedent or dux of a contrapuntal work (as a fugue or canon) **g :** a plant having particular horticultural qualities or suitable for a definite site or effect ⟨make good hedge ~*s*⟩ ⟨a difficult ~ only suitable for the expert with fully equipped greenhouse⟩ **syn** see CITIZEN

²subject \"\ *adj* [ME *suget*, *subget*, fr. MF, fr. L *subjectus*, past part.] **1 :** falling under or submitting to the power or dominion of another ⟨children ~ to their parents⟩: as **a :** owing allegiance to or being a subject of a particular sovereign or state ⟨a colony is ~ to the mother country⟩ ⟨a ~ race⟩ **b :** SUBJECTED **c :** OBEDIENT, SUBMISSIVE ⟨be ~ to the laws⟩ **2 a :** suffering a particular liability or exposure ⟨~ to very severe draughts⟩ ⟨~ to temptation⟩ **b :** PRONE, DISPOSED ⟨very ~ to colds⟩ **3** *archaic* **:** situated under or below **:** SUBJACENT **4 :** likely to be conditioned, affected, or modified in some indicated way **:** having a contingent relation to something and usu. dependent on such relation for final form, validity, or significance ⟨democratic representatives whose acts are ~ to discussion and criticism —M.R.Cohen⟩ ⟨a treaty ~ to ratification⟩ **syn** see LIABLE

³sub·ject \səbˈjekt *sometimes* ˌsəbˈjekt\ *vb* -ED/-ING/-S [ME *subjecten*, fr. L *subjectare* to put under, freq. of *subjicere*, *subicere* to bring under — more at SUBJECT (n.)] *vt* **1 a :** to bring under control or dominion **:** SUBJUGATE ⟨~*ing* primitive peoples to colonial rule⟩ **b :** to reduce to subservience or submission **:** make (as oneself) amenable to the discipline and control of a superior ⟨a servant should ~ himself to his master⟩ **2 a :** to make liable **:** PREDISPOSE ⟨his conduct ~*ed* him to needless suffering⟩ **b :** to make accountable **:** SUBMIT ⟨refused to ~ himself to their judgment⟩ **c :** to make (a piece of commercial paper) subject to discount **3** *obs* **:** to cause to lie beneath or below **4 :** to cause to undergo or submit to **:** make submit to a particular action or effect **:** EXPOSE ⟨hated to ~ his wife to such company⟩ ⟨unwilling to ~ himself to any inconvenience⟩ ~ *vi, obs* **:** to be or become subject

sub·ject·able \-təbəl\ *adj* **:** capable of being made subject

subject card *n* **:** a catalog card serving as a subject entry in a library card catalog

subject catalog *n* **:** a catalog in which books or other materials are listed only under the subjects treated and arranged alphabetically or by classes

subject cataloging *n* **:** a form or portion of the library cataloging process that not only describes a title but classifies it and assigns subject headings — contrasted with *descriptive cataloging*

subjected *adj* [fr. past part. of ³*subject*] **1 a :** brought into a state of subjection **:** made subject **:** SUBJUGATED **b :** SUBMISSIVE, OBEDIENT **2** *archaic* **:** situated below **:** LOW-LYING — **sub·ject·ed·ly** *adv* — **sub·ject·ed·ness** *n* -ES

sub·ject·hood \-,hu̇d\ *n* **:** the status or position of a subject person

sub·jec·ti·fi·ca·tion \(,)səb,jektəfəˈkāshən\ *n* -S [fr. *subjectify*, after such pairs as E *fructify*: *fructification*] **:** the act or process of subjectifying

sub·jec·ti·fy \(,)səbˈjektə,fī\ *vt* -ED/-ING/-ES [¹*subject* + *-ify*] **:** to identify with a subject or interpret in terms of subjective experience

sub·jec·tion \(,)səbˈjekshən\ *n* -S [ME *subjeccioun*, fr. MF *subjection*, fr. LL *subjection-*, *subjectio*, fr. L, act of bringing under, fr. *subjectus* (past part. of *subjicere*, *subicere* to bring under) + *-ion-*, *-io* -ion — more at SUBJECT] **1 a** *obs* **:** the exercise of lordship or control **:** lordly sway or rule **b :** the act of subduing or subjecting **:** SUBJUGATION ⟨planned the ~ of the rebels⟩ ⟨determined on the ~ of his baser nature⟩ **2 :** the quality or state of being subject and esp. under the power, control, or government of another ⟨the general ~ of women prior to the 20th century⟩: as **a** *obs* **:** obedient submissiveness **:** SUBORDINATION **b** *archaic* **:** a legal obligation (as by contract or pledge) to submit to the will of another **:** HOMAGE **c** *archaic* **:** the condition of being under obligation or liability **3 :** attachment of a subject to a predicate in logic — compare PREDICATION

sub·jec·tion·al \-shənᵊl, -shnəl\ *adj* **:** of, relating to, or involving subjection

¹sub·jec·tive \(,)səbˈjektiv, -tēv *also* -təv\ *adj* [ME, relating to submissiveness, fr. ML *subjectivus*, fr. L *subjectus* (past part. of *subjicere*, *subicere* to bring under) + *-ivus* -ive] **1 :** of, relating to, or constituting a subject: as **a** *obs* **:** of, relating to, or characteristic of one that is subject esp. in lack of freedom of action or in submissiveness **b** [LL *subjectivus*, fr. L *subjectum* subject of a proposition + *-ivus* -ive — more at SUBJECT] **:** being or relating to a grammatical subject; *specif* **:** NOMINATIVE **2 a :** of or belonging to the real or essential being of that which supports qualities, attributes, or relations **:** SUBSTANTIAL, REAL — compare OBJECTIVE 1b(1) **b** (1) *Kantianism* **:** of, relating to, or determined by the mind, ego, or consciousness as the subject of experience and knowledge ⟨~ reality⟩ (2) **:** characteristic of or belonging to reality as perceived or known as opposed to reality as it is in itself or independent of mind **:** PHENOMENAL — compare OBJECTIVE 1b(2) **c :** of, relating to, or being whatever in experience or knowledge is conditioned by merely personal characteristics of mind or by particular states of mind as opposed to what is determined only by the universal conditions of human experience and knowledge — compare OBJECTIVE 1b(3) **3 :** arising from within or belonging strictly to the individual often as contrasted with something modified by the physical or social environment or by the presence of

an interpreter: as **a :** peculiar to a particular individual modified by individual bias and limitations **:** PERSONAL ⟨a ~ impression⟩ ⟨~ judgments⟩ **b :** arising from conditions within the brain or sense organs and not directly caused by external stimuli ⟨~ sensations⟩ **c :** placing undue stress on one's opinions, fancies, or moods **:** excessively or moodily introspective **d :** arising out of or identified by means of an individual's attention to or awareness of his own states and processes ⟨a ~ symptom of disease⟩ ⟨a ~ study of fatigue⟩ **e :** lacking in reality or substance **:** existing in the mind alone **:** ILLUSORY, FANCIFUL **f** (1) **:** making prominent the individuality of a writer or an artist (2) **:** modified or affected by the personal views, mental and emotional background, or other special characteristics of the artist ⟨a ~ painting⟩ ⟨~ writers⟩ — **sub·jec·tive·ly** \-tə̇vlē, -li\ *adv* — **sub·jec·tive·ness** \-tivnə̇s, -tēv- *also* -təv-\ *n* -ES

²**subjective** \"\ *n* -S **1 :** something that is subjective ⟨the overemphasis of the individual and the ~ in modern philosophy —John Dewey⟩ **2 :** NOMINATIVE

subjective complement *n* **:** a grammatical complement relating to the subject of an intransitive verb ⟨in "he had fallen sick" *sick* is a *subjective complement*⟩

subjective idealism *n* **1 :** the theory that nature does not have any real existence independent of perceiving minds **:** BERKELEIANISM **2 :** the doctrine that an absolute ego dialectically evolves the world **:** FICHTEANISM — contrasted with *objective idealism*

subjective theory *n* **:** MORAL THEORY

subjective time *n* **:** time that is subjectively experienced; *specif* **:** the subjective feeling of duration with its absolute given present — called also *experiential time, private time;* contrasted with *objective time*

subjective utility *n* **:** the utility or satisfaction an article gives to an individual based upon his personal judgment and desires rather than upon market judgment

subjective validity *n* **:** validity relative to the conditions of the thinking subject either to the universal limitations of human experience and knowledge or to personal limitations (as ignorance) or circumstances of individual judgment

subjective verb *n* **:** an intransitive verb

sub·jec·tiv·ism \(ˌ)səbˈjektə̇ˌvizəm\ *n* -S [ISV ¹*subjective* + *-ism*] **1 a :** any of various epistemological theories that limit knowledge to conscious states and elements; *specif* **:** SUBJECTIVE IDEALISM **b :** any of various theories, doctrines, or viewpoints that attach great or supreme importance to the subjective elements in experience: as (1) **:** KANTIANISM (2) **:** the doctrine that truth is relative to human nature **:** PROTAGOREANISM **2 :** either of two doctrines in ethics: **a :** the supreme good or the end of ethical conduct is the realization of some type of subjective experience or feeling (as pleasure) **b :** individual feeling or apprehension is the ultimate criterion of the good and the right

sub·jec·tiv·ist \-_vəst\ *n* -S **:** an adherent or advocate of subjectivism

sub·jec·tiv·is·tic \(ˌ)=ˌ==ˈvistik, -tēk\ *adj* [ISV *subjectivist* + *-ic*] **:** of or relating to subjectivism

sub·jec·tiv·i·ty \ˌsəbˌjekˈtivəd·ē, -jək-, -vətē, -i\ *n* -ES [NL *subjectivitat-, subjectivitas,* fr. *subjectivus* subjectivistic (fr. LL & ML, subjective) + L *-itat-, -itas* -ity — more at SUBJECTIVE] **1 :** subjective character, quality, state, or nature esp. in an artistic or literary work **:** the individuality of an artist as expressed through his work or performance **2 :** SUBJECTIVISM **3 :** the quality of an investigator that affects the results of observational investigation (as in scientific observation) by reason of the individual and peculiar characteristics and reaction of or response to the media by the aid of which the investigations are conducted — compare PERSONAL EQUATION **4 :** the testing of truth solely by standards which can be applied only by the individual subject making the judgment (as by some subjective impression or feeling or by an arbitrary individual purpose or will to believe) instead of by some objective criterion accessible to others (as logical reasoning, history, verification in generally accessible experience) or even by some traditional external authority frankly recognized as such

sub·jec·tiv·iza·tion \(ˌ)səbˌjektə̇vəˈzāshən, -ˌvīˈz-\ *n* -S **:** an act or instance of subjectivizing

sub·jec·tiv·ize \(ˌ)=ˈ=tə̇ˌvīz\ *vt* -ED/-ING/-S [¹*subjective* + *-ize*] **:** to make subjective **:** handle (as data) in a subjective manner

sub·ject·less \ˈsəbjə̇ktlə̇s, -jēk-\ *adj* **:** having no subject or subjects

subject matter *n* [ME *matere subject,* trans. of LL *materia subjecta,* trans. of Gk *hypokeimenē hylē,* lit., underlying matter] **1** *archaic* **:** matter acted upon (as in a process or by a skill) **:** material from which something is formed **2 :** matter presented for consideration: as **a :** the essential facts, data, or ideas that constitute the basis of spoken, written, or artistic expression or representation; *often* **:** the substance as distinguished from the form esp. of an artistic or literary production **b :** a subject of thought or study; *often* **:** conveyable material (as information, knowledge, skill) actually made available by a branch of knowledge or in a course of study **:** the available factual content of a branch or course as distinct from technique or method of instruction or factors inherent in the individual learner **c :** the topic of dispute in a legal matter

subject-object \ˈ==ˈ==\ *n* **1 :** something that is at once subject and object **2 a :** the ego as object of its own knowledge **b :** a self-conscious being (as man)

subject-objectivity \ˈ==ˌ=ˌ=ˈ===\ *n* **:** the essential character or status of a subject-object

subject-predicate \ˈ==ˈ===\ *adj* **1 :** of, relating to, characterized by, or taking the form of analysis into subjects and predicates analogous to the basic grammatical structure of the Indo-European languages ⟨*subject-predicate* logical structure⟩ **2 :** having the form of a predicate attached to a subject ⟨a *subject-predicate* proposition⟩

subjects *pl of* SUBJECT, *pres 3d sing of* SUBJECT

subject·ship \ˈ==ˌship\ *n* **:** the status or condition of a subject individual

subject substantive *n* **:** a simple grammatical subject

subject-superject \ˈ==ˈ=ˌ=\ *n* **:** a subject that is a superject

subject term *n* **:** SUBJECT 3e(1)

sub·join \ˌsəbˈjȯin, ˌsəbˈ-\ *vt* [MF *subjoin-,* stem of *subjoindre* to subjoin, fr. L *subjungere,* lit., to bring under, subjugate, fr. *sub-* + *jungere* to bring together, join — more at YOKE] **:** to add after something and esp. something said or written **:** place immediately after or next to ⟨let me ~ another example⟩; *esp* **:** to annex (subordinate or supplementary matter) as an appendix ⟨~*ed* a statement of expenses to his report⟩

sub·join·der \-ndə(r)\ *n* -S [*sub-* + *-joinder* (as in *rejoinder*)] **:** an additional remark

sub·joint \ˈsəb+ˌ-\ *n* [*sub-* + *joint*] **:** a secondary joint (as of a segment of an arthropod limb)

sub ju·di·ce \ˌsəbˈyüdəˌkā, -ˈjüdəˌsē\ *adv* [L] **:** before a judge or court **:** under judicial consideration **:** not yet decided

sub·ju·ga·ble \ˈsəbjəgəbəl\ *adj* [L *subjugare* to subjugate + E *-able*] **:** capable of being subjugated

sub·ju·gate \-ˌgāt, *usu* -ād.+V\ *vt* -ED/-ING/-S [ME *subjugaten,* fr. L *subjugatus,* past part. of *subjugare* to bring under the yoke, subjugate, fr. *sub-* + *jugare* to join, yoke, fr. *jugum* yoke — more at YOKE] **1 :** to bring under the yoke of power or dominion **:** conquer by force and compel to submit as a subject to the government of another ⟨colonial powers *subjugating* native peoples⟩ **2 a :** to force to submit to control and governance **:** make submissive or subject **:** MASTER ⟨~ a wild horse⟩ ⟨*subjugated* his unruly nephew⟩ **b :** to bring or hold under strict control or into a subordinate position ⟨had to ~ his own feeling⟩ **syn** see CONQUER

sub·ju·ga·tion \ˌ=ˈgāshən\ *n* -S [LL *subjugation-, subjugatio,* fr. L *subjugatus* (past part.) + *-ion-, -io* -ion] **:** an act of subjugating or the state of being subjugated ⟨the distinction between outright conquest and ~ on the one hand and mere military occupation on the other —E.H.Litchfield⟩ ⟨~ of personal inclination to the good of the group⟩

sub·ju·ga·tor \ˈ==ˌgād·ə(r), -ātə-\ *n* -S [L, fr. *subjugatus* (past part. of *subjugare*) + *-or*] **:** one that subjugates

sub·jugular \ˌsəb+\ *adj* [*sub-* + *jugular*] **:** situated nearly far enough forward to be jugular — used of the ventral fins of some fishes

sub·junc·tion \səbˈjəŋ(k)shən\ *n* [LL *subjunction-, subjunctio,* fr. L *subjunctus* (past part.) + *-ion-, -io* -ion] **1 :** an act of subjoining or the state of being subjoined **2 :** something subjoined ⟨a ~ to a sentence⟩

¹**sub·junc·tive** \-tiv, -tēv *also* -təv\ *adj* [LL *subjunctivus* (trans. of Gk *hypotaktikos*), fr. L *subjunctus* (past part. of *subjungere* to subjoin) + *-ivus* -ive — more at SUBJOIN] **:** of, relating to, or constituting a verb form or set of verb forms that represents an attitude toward or concern with a denoted act or state not as fact but as something entertained in thought as contingent or possible or viewed emotionally (as with doubt, desire, will) ⟨the ~ mood⟩ ⟨*bless* in "God bless you" and *write* in "I suggest that he write a letter" are ~ verb forms⟩ — compare IMPERATIVE, INDICATIVE

²**subjunctive** \"\ *n* -S **1 :** the subjunctive mood; *also* **:** a verb or verbal form denoting it **2 :** SUBJUNCTIVE EQUIVALENT

subjunctive equivalent *n* **:** a verb phrase formed in English with a modal auxiliary (as *shall, should, may, might*) and functioning in a manner comparable to the subjunctive mood

sub·junc·tive·ly \-tə̇vlē, -li\ *adv* **:** in a subjunctive manner **:** with a subjunctive ⟨expressed his doubt ~⟩

subjv *abbr* subjunctive

sub·kingdom \ˈsəb+\ *n* [*sub-* + *kingdom*] **1 :** a subordinate kingdom **2 :** a primary division of a taxonomic kingdom

¹**sub·labial** \"+\ *adj* [*sub-* + *labial*] **:** situated below a lip or labium

²**sublabial** \"\ *n* **:** a sublabial part **:** INFRALABIAL

sub·laciniate \ˌsəb+\ *adj* [*sub-* + *laciniate*] **:** partially or imperfectly laciniate

sub·lanceolate \"+\ *adj* [*sub-* + *lanceolate*] **:** nearly lanceolate

sub·lap·sar·i·an \ˌsəbˌlapˈsa(a)rēən, -ser-\ *adj or n* [NL *sublapsarius* (fr. L *sub-* + *lapsus* lapse, fall + *-arius* -ary) + E *-an* — more at LAPSE] **:** INFRALAPSARIAN

sub·lap·sar·i·an·ism \-əˌnizəm\ *n* -S [*sublapsarian* + *-ism*] **:** INFRALAPSARIANISM

sub·late \ˌsəˈblāt\ *vt* -ED/-ING/-S [L *sublatus* (suppletive past part. of *tollere* to take away, lift up), fr. *sub-* up + *latus* carried, suppletive past part. of *ferre* to carry — more at SUB-, TOLERATE, BEAR] **1** *obs* **:** to take away **:** REMOVE **2 a** (1) **:** NEGATE, DENY (2) **:** CANCEL, ELIMINATE **b :** to cancel but also preserve and elevate (an element in a dialectic process) as a partial element in a synthesis ⟨evil is not evaded, but *sublated* in the higher religious cheer of these persons —William James⟩

¹**sub·lateral** \ˌsəb+\ *adj* [*sub-* + *lateral*] **:** situated near a side (as of the body)

²**sublateral** \"\ *n* **:** a channel (as in an irrigation or sewage system) leading to or from a main lateral; *usu* **:** a channel of least importance

sub·la·tion \səˈblāshən\ *n* -S [LL *sublation-, sublatio,* fr. L, act of lifting up, fr. *sublatus* (suppletive past part. of *tollere* to lift up, take away) + *-ion-, -io* -ion] **1 :** the act of taking or carrying away **:** REMOVAL **2 :** the act or process of sublating

sub·la·tive \səˈblād·iv\ *adj* [L *sublatus* + E *-ive*] **:** able or tending to take away **:** concerned with taking something away ⟨the ~ case of the Magyar language⟩

sub·leader \ˈsəb+\ *n* [*sub-* + *leader*] **1 :** a person in a position of authority but subordinate to a leader of greater prominence **2** *chiefly Brit* **:** an article or paragraph (as in a periodical) in a prominent but not the first position

¹**sub·lease** \ˈ=+ˌ-\ *n* [*sub-* + *lease*] **:** a lease by a tenant or lessee to another person of part or all of the leased premises for a shorter term than his own term and under which he retains some rights or interest under his original lease **:** a derivative lease — compare ASSIGNMENT

²**sub·lease** \ˈ=+\ *vt* **:** to make or obtain a sublease of ⟨~*s* her apartment from a friend⟩

sub·lenticular \ˌsəb+\ *adj* [*sub-* + *lenticular*] **:** approaching the lenticular **:** almost doubly convex in outline

sub·lessee \"+\ *n* [*sub-* + *lessee*] **:** a tenant under a sublease

sub·lessor \"+\ *n* [*sub-* + *lessor*] **:** one that grants a sublease

¹**sub·let** \ˌsəb+\ *vb* [*sub-* + *let*] *vt* **1 :** to convey by or as if by renting one's rights in (rented or leased property) **:** SUBLEASE; *esp* **:** to turn over to another one's right of occupancy of (rented or leased housing) **2 :** to contract that another shall perform all or a specified part of (a contract held by oneself) ~ *vi* **:** to obtain something by subletting ⟨in large cities it is often possible to find excellent temporary quarters by *subletting*⟩

²**sublet** \"\ *n* **:** property and esp. housing obtained by or available for subletting ⟨a pleasant ~ near the park⟩

sub·lethal \ˌsəb+\ *adj* [ISV *sub-* + *lethal*] **:** less but usu. only slightly less than lethal ⟨~ doses of a poison⟩

sub·leukemic \"+\ *adj* [*sub-* + *leukemic*] **:** not marked by the presence of excessive numbers of white blood cells in the circulating blood ⟨~ leukemia⟩

sub·level \ˈsəb+\ *n* [*sub-* + *level*] **:** a level that is lower than another express or implied level ⟨a ~ of physiological activity⟩ ⟨the use of ~ caving in mining large bodies of ore⟩

sub·license \"+\ *n* [*sub-* + *license*] **:** a subordinate license granted to another by one already having a license

sub·licensee \"+\ *n* [*sub-* + *licensee*] **:** a subordinate licensee **:** a holder of a sublicense

sub·lieutenancy \"+\ *n* [*sub-* + *lieutenancy*] *chiefly Brit* **:** the status or position of a sublieutenant

sub·lieutenant \"+\ *n* [*sub-* + *lieutenant*] *chiefly Brit* **:** an officer ranking next below a lieutenant

sub·lim·able \səˈblīməbəl\ *adj* [¹*sublime* + *-able*] **:** capable of being sublimed ⟨a ~ chemical⟩

¹**sub·li·mate** \ˈsəbləˌmāt, *usu* -ād.+V\ *vb* -ED/-ING/-S [L *sublimatus,* past part. of *sublimare* to lift up, raise — more at SUBLIME] *vt* **1** *obs* **a :** to elevate to a place of dignity or honor **b :** to give a more elevated character to **2** [ML *sublimatus,* past part. of *sublimare* to refine, sublime, fr. L, to raise, lift up] **a :** to cause to sublime ⟨~ sulfur⟩ **b** *archaic* **:** to improve or refine as if by subliming **c** *obs* **:** to get or extract by or as if by subliming **3 :** to direct the energy of (an impulse) from a primitive aim to one that is higher in the cultural scale esp. in the course of psychoanalysis ⟨~ sexual curiosity into artistic or scientific production⟩ ~ *vi* **:** to undergo sublimation **:** be or become sublimed

²**sub·li·mate** \-ˌmāt, -_mə̇t, *usu* -d·+V\ *n* -S [ML *sublimatum,* fr. neut. of *sublimatus,* past part. of *sublimare* to sublime] **1 :** MERCURY CHLORIDE b **2 :** a chemical product obtained by sublimation

sub·li·ma·tion \ˌ==ˈmāshən\ *n* -S [ME *sublimacion* act or process of subliming, fr. MF & ML; MF *sublimation,* fr. ML *sublimation-, sublimatio,* fr. *sublimatus* (past part. of *sublimare* to sublime) + L *-ion-, -io* -ion] **1 :** the act or process of sublimating: as **a :** the act or process or an instance of subliming of a chemical entity — compare DISTILLATION 1, EVAPORATION 1a **b** [LL *sublimation-, sublimatio* act of raising, fr. L *sublimatus* (past part. of *sublimare* to raise, lift up) + *-ion-, -io* -ion; trans. of G *sublimierung*] **:** discharge of instinctual energy and esp. that associated with pre-genital impulses through socially approved activities **2 a :** a product of sublimating **b :** the condition of being sublimated — **sub·li·ma·tion·al** \ˌ==ˈmāshənᵊl, -shnəl\ *adj*

sublimation pressure *n* **:** the pressure of equilibrium at a definite temperature of a vapor in contact with its solid

sublimation vein *n* **:** a vein of mineral matter formed by condensation from the vaporous state

sub·li·ma·tive \ˈsəbləˌmād·iv\ *adj* [*sublimation* + *-ive*] **:** tending to produce or assist in the production of psychic sublimation

sub·li·ma·tor \-ˌmād·ə(r)\ *n* -S [¹*sublimate* + *-or*] **:** one that sublimates

¹**sub·lime** \səˈblīm\ *vb* -ED/-ING/-S [ME *sublimen,* fr. MF *sublimer,* fr. ML *sublimare* to refine, purify, sublime, fr. L, to lift up, raise, fr. *sublimis* uplifted, high] *vt* **1 a :** to cause to pass from the solid to the vapor state by the action of heat and again condense to solid form ⟨many chemicals (as naphthalene, benzoic acid, and iodine) are *sublimed* to rid them of impurities⟩ **b :** to produce, purify, or release by heating a containing mixture ⟨~ pure sulfur from an unpure mixture⟩ **2** [F *sublimer,* fr. L *sublimare*] **a :** to elevate or exalt esp. in dignity or honor **:** render finer (as in purity or excellence) **b :** to convert (something inferior) into something of higher esteem or worth ⟨selfishness *sublimed* into care for the public welfare⟩ **3 :** to cause to rise upward ⟨the sun's hot rays ~ the morning dew⟩ ~ *vi* **1** *of a chemical entity* **:** to undergo sublimation **:** pass directly from the solid to the vapor state ⟨ammonia vapor ~*s* from solid crystals⟩ **2 :** to become elevated or exalted (as in dignity or honor) **:** become finer (as in purity or excellence)

²**sublime** \"\ *adj* -ER/-EST [L *sublimis* uplifted, high, sublime, fr. *sub-* up + *-limis* (fr. *limin-, limen* threshold) — more at SUB-, LIMB] **1 a :** lofty in conception or expression **:** grand or exalted in thought or manner ⟨the *sublimest* lines in English prose⟩ ⟨a ~ style difficult to maintain⟩ **b :** elevated or exalted in character **:** of outstanding spiritual, intellectual, or moral worth ⟨in a ~ spirit of sacrifice⟩ ⟨~ devotion⟩ ⟨a ~ Christian leader⟩ **c :** tending to inspire awe or uplifting emotion usu. by reason of elevated beauty, nobility, grandeur, solemnity, or similar character ⟨the ~ beauty of that night⟩ ⟨a ~ peace settled about us⟩ **d :** outstanding as such **:** very great **:** NOTABLE ⟨turned out to be a ~ husband⟩ ⟨you ~ idiot⟩ ⟨the ~ stench in a city of evil smells —W.H.Hudson †1922⟩ **2 a** *archaic* **:** high in place **:** raised to a great height **:** lifted up **b** *obs* **:** lofty of mien **:** HAUGHTY, PROUD **c** (1) **:** of exalted rank or high estate (2) *usu cap* **:** SUPREME — used in a style of address (as to former Turkish sovereigns) **3** *obs* **:** elevated by joy **:** ELATED **syn** see SPLENDID

³**sublime** \"\ *n* -S **1 :** things that are sublime **:** the sublime aspect of anything **:** the quality of sublimity — usu. used with *the* ⟨we see little of the literary ~ in current writing⟩ ⟨from the ~ to the ridiculous⟩ **2 :** the supreme degree or utmost point **:** ACME

sublimed blue lead *n* **:** BLUE LEAD 2

sublimed sulfur *n* **:** sulfur that has sublimed; *esp* **:** FLOWERS OF SULFUR

sublimed white lead *n* **:** a white pigment composed essentially of basic lead sulfate and formed by fuming lead ore of a particular type

sub·lime·ly *adv* **1 :** in a sublime manner **:** with sublimity **2 :** UTTERLY, COMPLETELY ⟨~ content⟩ ⟨~ self-satisfied⟩

sub·lime·ness *n* -ES **:** the quality or state of being sublime

sub·lim·er \səˈblīmə(r)\ *n* -S **:** one that sublimes

sub·liminal \ˌsəb+\ *adj* [*sub-* + L *limin-, limen* threshold + E *-al* — more at LIMB] **1 :** falling below the threshold of stimulation (as for nerve or muscle) **:** inadequate to produce a sensation or a perception **:** too small for discrimination **2 a :** existing or functioning outside the area of conscious awareness **:** influencing thought, feeling, or behavior in a manner unperceived by personal or subjective consciousness ⟨~ perception⟩ ⟨the ~ mind⟩ — compare SUBCONSCIOUS, SUPRACONSCIOUS, UNCONSCIOUS **b :** designed to influence the mind on levels other than that of conscious awareness and esp. by presentation too brief to be consciously perceived ⟨~ techniques in TV advertising⟩ — **sub·limi·nal·ly** \-nᵊlē, -ᵊli\ *adv*

subliminal self *also* **subliminal** *n* -S **:** the portion of an individual's personality that lies below or beyond the reach of his personal awareness — compare SUBCONSCIOUS, SUPRACONSCIOUS, UNCONSCIOUS

sub·lim·i·na·tion \ˌ=ˌ==ˈnāshən\ *n* -S [*subliminal* + *-ation*] **:** the use of subliminal techniques (as in advertising)

subliming *pres part of* SUBLIME

sub·lim·i·ty \səˈblimədˌē, -mətē, -i\ *n* -ES [L *sublimitas,* fr. *sublimis* high, sublime + *-itas* -ity — more at SUBLIME] **1 :** something that is sublime: as **a :** exalted character, ideals, or conduct **:** noble quality or elevation (as of thought, feeling, style) **b :** high dignity, honor, or position **:** exalted office or status — sometimes used as a title or form of address **c :** the highest or supremest level, degree, phase, or development of something **:** ACME **2 :** the quality or state of being sublime and esp. of awakening awe, reverence, or a similar emotion or of producing a sense of vastness, power, or similar quality

sub·limize \ˈsəbləˌmīz, səˈblīˌ-\ *vt* -ED/-ING/-S [²*sublime* + *-ize*] **:** to give a sublime character to

sub·line \ˈsəb+ˌ-\ *n* [*sub-* + *line*] **:** a subdivision of a line (sense 6a)

sub·linear \ˌsəb+\ *adj* [*sub-* + *linear*] **1 :** almost linear ⟨a ~ arrangement of parts⟩ **2 :** placed below a line of written or printed characters

sub·lineation \"+\ *n* [*sub-* + *lineation*] **:** UNDERLINING

sub·lingua \ˌ=+\ *n, pl* **sublinguae** [NL, fr. L *sub-* + *lingua* tongue — more at TONGUE] **:** a process or fold covered with modified or hardened mucous membrane and occurring on the floor of the mouth in some animals (as lemurs)

sub·lingual \"+\ *adj* [NL *sublingualis,* fr. L *sub-* + ML *lingualis* lingual — more at LINGUAL] **1 :** situated or occurring under the tongue **2 :** of, relating to, or situated near the sublingual gland

sublingual gland *n* **:** a small salivary gland on each side of the mouth lying beneath the mucous membrane in a fossa in the mandible near the symphysis

sub·literary \ˌsəb+\ *adj* **:** of a quality below that acceptable as standard literature ⟨~ fiction . . . does not bother to blur the distinction between bad and good —G.P.Winship⟩

sub·literate \"+\ *adj* [*sub-* + *literate*] **:** imperfectly literate ⟨letters from ~ folk —J.G.Randall⟩

sub·literature \"+\ *n* [*sub-* + *literature*] **:** impermanent literature: as **a :** inferior literature that does not survive the test of time **b :** written material (as reports) duplicated in impermanent form (as by mimeographing or microfilming) usu. primarily for use by the staff of the issuing organization

sub·lithographic \"+\ *adj* [*sub-* + *lithographic*] *of limestone* **:** approaching in texture the fine grain of lithographic limestone

¹**sub·littoral** \"+\ *adj* [*sub-* + *littoral*] **:** situated, occurring, or formed on the watery side of a shoreline or littoral zone ⟨~ deposits⟩ **:** constituting the sublittoral ⟨a distinct ~ zone⟩

²**sublittoral** \"\ *n* **:** the deeper part of the littoral portion of a body of water: **a :** the region in an ocean between the lowest point exposed by a low low tide and the margin of the continental shelf **b :** the region in a lake between the deepest-growing rooted vegetation and the hypolimnion

sub·lobular \"+\ *adj* [*sub-* + *lobular*] **:** situated at the bases of the lobules of the liver

sub·luminous \"+\ *adj* [*sub-* + *luminous*] **:** partially luminous **:** approaching the state of luminosity

sub·lunar \"+\ *adj* [LL *sublunaris*] **:** SUBLUNARY

sublunar point *n* **:** the point on the earth's surface at which the moon is in the zenith

¹**sub·lu·nary** \ˈsəblüˌnerē, ˌsəbˈlünərē\ *adj* [modif. (influenced by ²*lunary*) of LL *sublunaris,* fr. L *sub-* + *lunaris* lunar — more at LUNAR] **1 :** situated beneath the moon or within the orbit of the moon — compare SUPERLUNARY **2 :** characteristic of or pertinent to this world **:** TERRESTRIAL, MUNDANE ⟨in a religious epoch those whose main interest is in secular affairs tend . . . to find transcendental motives for ~ action —Aldous Huxley⟩ — compare TRANSLUNARY **syn** see EARTHLY

²**sublunary** *n* -ES *obs* **:** something sublunary

sub·lunate \ˌseb+\ *adj* [*sub-* + *lunate*] **:** nearly crescentic in form

sub·lustrous \"+\ *adj* [*sub-* + *lustrous*] **:** somewhat or imperfectly lustrous

sub·luxated \"+\ *adj* [*subluxation* + *-ed*] **:** partially dislocated ⟨a ~ vertebra⟩

sub·luxation \"+\ *n* [NL *subluxation-, subluxatio,* fr. L *sub-* + LL *luxation-, luxatio* dislocation — more at LUXATION] **:** partial dislocation (as of one of the bones in a joint)

subm *abbr* **1** submarine **2** submerge; submerged

sub·machine gun \ˌsəb+-\ *n* [*sub-* + *machine gun*] **:** a lightweight automatic or semiautomatic portable firearm designed usu. for firing from the shoulder or hip

sub·main \ˈ=+ˌ-\ *n* [*sub-* + *main*] **:** a main (as in a sewer, gas, electrical, or drainage system) having a number of lesser mains feeding into or branching from it but being itself subsidiary to a larger main

sub·maintenance \ˌ=+\ *adj* [*sub-* + *maintenance*] **:** inadequate for the maintenance of bodily health ⟨a ~ ration⟩

sub·man \ˈ=+ˌ-\ *n, pl* **submen** [*sub-* + *man*] **:** a man or a being who has human characteristics in a very inferior degree **:** a brutal or stupid man

sub·marginal \ˌsəb+\ *adj* [*sub-* + *marginal*] **1 :** situated near a boundary **:** adjacent to a marginal part or structure ⟨a ~ cell in an insect wing⟩ **2 a :** less than marginal **:** falling below the minimum necessary for some end (as the obtaining of an economic return or the living of a normal life) ⟨attempting to crop ~ hill farms⟩ ⟨the children in the one fourth of our

nation that subsist on ~ levels —Leon Eisenberg⟩ ⟨a ~ diet⟩ **b :** dealing with or dependent upon something (as a way of life) that is submarginal ⟨~ farmers⟩ — **sub·marginally** \"+\ *adv*

sub·marginate \"+\ *also* **sub·margined** \"+\ *adj* [*sub-* + *marginate* or *margined*] **:** having a border near the edge or margin

¹sub·marine \"+\ *adj* [*sub-* + *marine*] **1 :** being, acting, growing, or used under water and esp. in the sea ⟨~ boats⟩ ⟨~ plants⟩ **2 :** suggestive of the undersea world ⟨an illusive ~ glimmer⟩

²submarine \"\ *n* -s **1 :** a submarine organism (as a plant or coral) **2 :** something (as an explosive mine) designed to function underwater; *specif* **:** a submersible ship armed with torpedoes, guns, and guided missiles and propelled by diesel engines, electric motors, or nuclear-powered steam turbines that operates below the surface of the sea — compare TORPEDO BOAT

³submarine \"\ *vb* -ED/-ING/-S [²*submarine*] *vt* **:** to make an attack upon or to sink by means of a submarine and esp. by torpedoing ~ *vi* **1 :** to be, move, or function beneath the sea: as **a :** to handle a submarine **b :** to swim or dive underwater **2** *of a defensive lineman in football* **:** to throw the head and shoulders beneath the knees of two opposing players and then draw the feet up so that the opponents slide over the back

submarine bell *n* **:** an underwater sound transmitting device using the strokes of a bell to send messages or to send at stated intervals a signal as an aid to navigation in a fog

submarine canyon *n* **:** CANYON 1b

submarine chaser *n* **:** a boat fitted to operate offensively against submarines

submarine geology *n* **:** geology of the ocean floor

submarine process *n* **:** a method of color correcting an offset printing plate by rubbing away details of dots under water

sub·ma·rin·er \ˌsəbməˈrēnə(r); ˌsəbˈmarənə(r) *also* -mer-\ *n* -s [²*submarine* + *-er*] **:** a member of a submarine crew

submarine sandwich *also* **submarine** *n* [so called fr. its shape] **:** POOR BOY

submarine sentry *n* **:** KITE 7a

submarine telegraph *n* **1 :** the sending of a message or messages by means of submarine telegraph cable **2 :** a system of communication by means of submarine telegraph cable

submarine telegraph cable *or* **submarine cable** *n* **:** a telegraph cable laid under water to connect stations separated by water

submarine telephone *n* **:** a system of signaling under water (as from a buoy to a ship) by the use of submerged bells and special receivers

sub·master \ˈsəb+ˌ\ *n* [ME, fr. *sub-* + *master*] **:** a subordinate or assistant master; *usu* **:** an assistant or deputy principal of a school

sub·mature \"+\ *adj* [*sub-* + *mature*] **:** incompletely matured or differentiated — used esp. of a topographic feature — **sub·maturely** \"+\ *adv*

sub·maxilla \"+\ *n, pl* **submaxillae** *also* **submaxillas** [NL, fr. *sub-* + *maxilla*] **:** the lower jaw or inferior maxillary bone; *specif* **:** the human mandible

¹sub·maxillary \"+\ *adj* [*sub-* + *maxillary*] **1 :** of, relating to, or situated below the lower jaw **2 :** of, relating to, or associated with the submaxillary gland

²submaxillary \"\ *n* **:** a submaxillary part (as an artery, bone, ganglion, or gland)

submaxillary ganglion *n* **:** an autonomic ganglion situated on the lingual branch of the mandibular nerve above the deep part of the submaxillary gland, receiving preganglionic fibers from the facial nerve by way of the chorda tympani, sending postganglionic fibers to the submaxillary and sublingual glands, and giving passage to sympathetic fibers from the external maxillary plexus

submaxillary gland *n* **:** a salivary gland inside of and near the lower edge of the mandible on each side and discharging by Wharton's duct into the mouth under the tongue

sub·maximal \ˈsəb+\ *adj* [*sub-* + *maximal*] **:** almost maximal

sub·medial \"+\ *adj* [*sub-* + *medial*] **1 :** SUBMEDIAN **2 :** lying under the middle — **sub·medially** \"+\ *adv*

sub·median \"+\ *adj* [*sub-* + *median*] **:** situated next to a median part or the midline ⟨a ~ tooth on the radula of a mollusk⟩

sub·mediant \"+\ *n* [*sub-* + *mediant*] **:** the sixth musical degree (as A in the scale of C) of the major or minor scale midway between the subdominant and the upper tonic — called also *superdominant*

submen *pl of* SUBMAN

sub·men·tal \ˈsəbˈmentᵊl\ *adj* [in sense 1, fr. *sub-* + *mental*; in sense 2, fr. NL *submentum* + E *-al*] **1 :** situated under the chin **2 :** of or relating to the submentum

submental artery *n* **:** a branch of the external maxillary artery that passes near the submaxillary gland and is distributed to the muscles of the jaw

sub·men·tum \ˌsəbˈmentəm\ *n, pl* **submen·ta** \-tə\ [NL, fr. *sub-* + *mentum*] **:** the basal part of the labium of an insect

sub·merge \səbˈmərj, -məj, -məij\ *vb* -ED/-ING/-S [L *submergere*, fr. *sub-* + *mergere* to plunge — more at MERGE] *vt* **1 :** to cause to pass under water **:** put under water ⟨~ your hand to test the heat of the water⟩ **2 :** to cover or overflow with water **:** INUNDATE ⟨the stream overflowed and *submerged* the town⟩ **3 :** to lose sight of, obscure, or cover up as if under a layer of water ⟨personal lives *submerged* by professional responsibilities⟩ ⟨the original argument was *submerged* in irrelevancies⟩ ⟨~ oneself in trivia⟩ ~ *vi* **1 :** to plunge into water or other fluid **2 :** to become submerged, buried, or covered as if by a fluid **syn** see DIP

submerged *adj* [fr. past part. of *submerge*] **1** *of a plant* **:** SUBMERSED **2 :** sunk in poverty and misery ⟨the ~ tenth of society that lacks all that makes life pleasant⟩ **3 :** HIDDEN, CRYPTIC ⟨a ~ gene effect⟩

submerged-tube boiler \ˈ=ˈ=,=-\ *n* **:** a steam boiler in which the tubes emerge below the waterline in the steam drum

sub·merge·ment \-mənt\ *n* -s [ISV *submerge* + *-ment*] **:** SUBMERSION

sub·mer·gence \-jən(t)s\ *n* -s **1 :** the quality or state of being submerged **2 a :** the act of submerging something **b :** the distance or degree to which something is submerged

sub·mer·gent \-nt\ *adj* **:** partly submerged **:** incompletely submerged

sub·mer·gible \-jəbəl\ *adj* **1 :** capable of being submerged ⟨a ~ body⟩ **2 :** capable of functioning under water ⟨a ~ pump⟩

sub·mer·sal \-səl\ *adj* [¹*submerse* + *-al*] **:** marked by or occurring during submersion ⟨a ~ period⟩ ⟨~ activities of amphibians⟩

¹sub·merse \səbˈmərs, -məs, -məis\ *vt* -ED/-ING/-S [L *submersus*, past part. of *submergere* to plunge under, submerge] **:** SUBMERGE

²submerse \"\ *adj* [L *submersus*, past part.] *of a plant* **:** SUBMERSED

sub·mersed \-st\ *adj* [L *submersus* (past part. of *submergere*) + E *-ed*] **:** SUBMERGED: as **a :** covered with water **b :** growing or adapted to grow under water

¹sub·mers·ible \-səbəl\ *adj* [ISV ¹*submerse* + *-ible*] **:** SUBMERGIBLE

²submersible \"\ *n* -s **:** a boat capable of submerging **:** SUBMARINE

sub·mer·sion \səbˈmər|zhən, -mə|, -məi|, |sh-\ *n* -s [LL *submersion-, submersio*, fr. L *submersus* (past part. of *submergere* to plunge under, submerge) + *-ion-, -io* -ion] **1 :** the act or process of submerging **2 :** the quality or state of being submerged

sub·metallic \ˈsəb+\ *adj* [*sub-* + *metallic*] **1 :** somewhat or imperfectly metallic ⟨a ~ luster⟩ **2 :** METALLOID ⟨such ~ elements as bismuth⟩

sub·meter \"+\ *n* [*sub-* + *meter*] **:** one of two or more meters for measuring different sections of a supply

sub·metering \"+\ *n* -s [*submeter* + *-ing*] **:** the retail sale through individual meters to tenants in large office or apartment buildings of electric current or gas purchased for the entire building by the owners at wholesale rates

sub·microgram \"+\ *adj* [*sub-* + *microgram*] **:** having a mass less than one microgram

sub·micron \"+\ *n* [NL, fr. *sub-* + *micron*] **:** a very small particle that can be seen only with the ultramicroscope; *specif* **:** one less than 1×10^{-4} centimeters in diameter

sub·microscopic \"+\ *adj* [ISV *sub-* + *microscopic*] **1 :** too small to be resolved and made visible by the ordinary light microscope — compare ULTRAMICROSCOPIC **2 :** of, relating to, or dealing with the very minute ⟨the ~ world⟩

sub·miliary \"+\ *adj* [ISV *sub-* + *miliary*] **:** less than miliary **:** smaller than a millet seed ⟨~ lesions⟩

sub·miniature \"+\ *adj* [ISV *sub-* + *miniature*] **:** smaller than miniature **:** very small — used esp. of a very compact assembly of electronic equipment

subminiature camera *n* **:** a miniature camera using film 16 millimeters wide for still photography

sub·miniaturization \ˌsəb+\ *n* -s [*subminiature* + *-ization*] **:** the action or process of making something subminiature ⟨the ~ of electronic components⟩

sub·minimal \"+\ *adj* [*sub-* + *minimal*] **:** smaller than the minimum that is required for a particular result ⟨a ~ stimulus⟩

sub·min·is·ter \səbˈminəstə(r)\ *vt* [L *subministrare*, fr. *sub-* + *ministrare* to serve — more at MINISTER] *archaic* **:** SUPPLY, FURNISH

sub·miss \səbˈmis\ *adj* [L *submissus*, past part. of *submittere* to let down, lower — more at SUBMIT] **1** *archaic* **:** SUBMISSIVE, HUMBLE **2** *archaic* **:** low in tone **:** SUBDUED

sub·mis·si·ble \-səbəl\ *adj* [L *submissus* + *-ible*] **:** capable of being submitted **:** SUBMITTABLE

sub·mis·sion \səbˈmishən\ *n* -s [ME, fr. MF, fr. L, act of letting down, lowering, fr. *submissus* (past part. of *submittere* to let down) + *-ion-, -io* -ion] **1 a :** a legal agreement by which parties engage usu. under the penalties of a bond to submit matters of controversy between them to the decision of arbitrators named or unnamed **b :** an act of submitting something (as for consideration, inspection, or comment) ⟨the ~ of his sketch for the mural⟩ **c (1) :** something that is submitted ⟨received more ~s than we could possibly publish⟩ **(2) :** a point of view, theory of a case, or proposal advocated ⟨included the ~ that 300,000 people should move out to new industrial towns —Eric Keown⟩ **2 a :** the condition of being submissive **:** humble or compliant behavior **:** humble or submissive deference in conduct or bearing **b submissions** *pl, archaic* **:** behavior expressive of submission **:** humbly deferent conduct **3 :** an act of submitting; *usu* **:** a yielding of power or authority or a surrendering of person and power to the control of another **4** *obs* **:** CONFESSION

sub·mis·sion·ist \-shənəst\ *n* -s **:** one who advocates submission

sub·mis·sive \səbˈmisiv, -sēv *also* -səv\ *adj* [L *submissus* (past part.) + E *-ive*] **:** inclined or ready to submit **:** expressing submission **:** YIELDING, OBEDIENT, HUMBLE ⟨~ demeanor⟩ ⟨a ~ race⟩ **syn** see TAME

sub·mis·sive·ly \-səvlē, -li\ *adv* **:** in a submissive manner **:** so as to be or appear submissive

sub·mis·sive·ness \-sivnəs, -sēv- *also* -səv-\ *n* -ES **:** the quality or state of being submissive

sub·miss·ly \səbˈmislē\ *adv* [*submiss* + *-ly*] *archaic* **:** HUMBLY, SUBMISSIVELY

sub·mit \səbˈmit, *usu* -id.+V\ *vb* **submitted; submitted; submitting; submits** [ME *submitten*, fr. L *submittere* to let down, lower, set under, fr. *sub-* + *mittere* to send, throw — more at SMITE] *vt* **1 a :** to yield to the will or authority of **:** SURRENDER ⟨~s his will to divine authority⟩ ⟨~ an undertaking . . . to the Senate —Vera M. Dean⟩ **b :** to cause to be subjected ⟨*submitting* himself to a series of literary influences —F.B.Millett⟩ ⟨~ metal to high heat and pressure⟩ **2 a** *obs* **:** to expose to peril or danger ⟨*submitting* me unto the perilous night —Shak.⟩ **b** *archaic* **:** LOWER, BEND ⟨will ye ~ your necks —John Milton⟩ **3 a :** to send or commit for consideration, study, or decision **:** REFER ⟨~ a question to the court⟩ ⟨texts of revised and new conventions, to be *submitted* to the International Red Cross Conference —J.S.Pictet⟩ **b :** to present or make available for use or study **:** OFFER, SUPPLY ⟨~ a report⟩ ⟨~ a manuscript to a publisher⟩ ⟨always ~ your judgment to others with modesty —George Washington⟩ **c :** AFFIRM, SUGGEST ⟨I ~ that it was the wrong decision —E. M.Zacharias⟩ ~ *vi* **1 a :** to bow to the will or authority of another **:** YIELD ⟨~ to an alien law —Frank Altschul⟩ **b :** to allow oneself to become subjected ⟨~ to an interview⟩ ⟨~ to an operation⟩ **2 a :** to grant precedence **:** DEFER ⟨~ to . . . superior intelligence, political wisdom and tough leadership —M.S.Handler⟩ **b :** to become resigned **:** acquiesce uncritically ⟨was obliged to give up the point and ~ —Jane Austen⟩ ⟨the inhabitants . . . will no longer ~ to the evils of the trade —E.V.Buckholder⟩ **syn** see YIELD

sub·mit·tal \-mid.ᵊl, -itᵊl\ *n* -s **:** an act of submitting

sub·mit·tance \-itᵊn(t)s\ *n* -s **:** SUBMISSION

sub·mit·ter \-id.ə(r), -itə-\ *n* -s **:** one that submits

sub·mit·ting·ly *adv* **:** in a submitting or submissive manner

sub mo·do \ˌsəbˈmō(ˌ)dō\ *adv* [LL] **:** under a qualification, condition, or restriction

sub·molecule \ˈsəb+\ *n* [ISV *sub-* + *molecule*] **:** a particle of less than molecular dimensions or state of organization

sub·montane \ˈsəb+\ *adj* [LL *submontanus*, fr. L *sub-* + *montanus* of a mountain — more at MOUNTAIN] **1 :** lying or passing under a mountain or range of mountains ⟨a ~ stream⟩ **2 :** situated at the foot or near the base of a mountain or range of mountains — **sub·mon·tane·ly** *adv*

sub·motive \"+\ *n* [*sub-* + *motive*] **:** a subordinate, secondary, or hidden motive

sub·mountain \"+\ *adj* [*sub-* + *mountain*] **:** lying under a mountain

sub·mucosa \"+\ *n* [NL, fr. *sub-* + *mucosa*] **:** the layer of areolar connective tissue directly under a mucous membrane — **sub·mucosal** \"+\ *adj*

sub·mucous \"+\ *adj* [ISV *sub-* + *mucous*] **:** lying under or involving the tissues under a mucous membrane

submucous coat *n* **:** SUBMUCOSA

sub·multiple \ˈsəb+\ *n* [*sub-* + *multiple*] **:** a number or quantity that divides another exactly ⟨8 is a ~ of 72⟩

sub·mundane \"+\ *adj* [*sub-* + LL *mundanus* of the earth, of the world — more at MUNDANE] **:** UNDERGROUND, SUBTERRANEAN

sub·muscular \"+\ *adj* [*sub-* + *muscular*] **:** situated beneath a muscle or muscular layer

sub-mycenaean \"+\ *adj, usu cap M* **:** belonging to a date and style later than the Mycenaean but before the distinctly Greek

sub·mytilacea \"+\ *n pl, cap* [NL, fr. *sub-* + *Mytilacea*] **:** a subborder of Eulamellibranchia comprising bivalve mollusks with an equivalve shell, an external ligament, a mantle that is only slightly closed, and siphons that if present are short

sub·narcotic \"+\ *adj* [*sub-* + *narcotic*] **:** somewhat narcotic; *esp* **:** insufficient to produce deep sleep ⟨barbiturates in ~ amounts⟩

sub·na·sale \ˌsəb,nāˈz|a(,)lē -ˈs|, |āl-, |äl-\ *n* -s [NL, fr. *sub-* + *nasale*, neut. sing. of *nasalis* nasal, fr. L *nasus* nose + *-alis* -al — more at NOSE] **:** SUBNASAL POINT 2

sub·nasal point \ˈsəb+-\ *n* [*sub-* + *nasal*] **1 :** ACANTHION **2 :** a point on the living where the nasal septum and the upper lip meet in the midsagittal plane — called also *subnasale*

sub·nascent \"+\ *adj* [L *subnascent-, subnascens*, pres. part. of *subnasci* to grow beneath, fr. *sub-* + *nasci* to be born — more at NATION] **1** *obs* **:** growing beneath **2 :** growing up or arising from beneath something

sub·nation \"+\ *n* [*sub-* + *nation*] **:** a subdivision of a nation often distinguished by community of culture and interests rather than by administrative dependency ⟨the South is . . . a ~ with its own history, its own patterns of behavior and its own national consciousness —Malcolm Cowley⟩ — **sub·national** \"+\ *adj*

sub·neural \"+\ *adj* [*sub-* + *neural*] **:** situated under the central nervous system

sub·nitrate \"+\ *n* [ISV *sub-* + *nitrate*] **:** a basic nitrate (as bismuth subnitrate) — compare OXYNITRATE

sub·niv·e·an \ˌsəbˈnivēən\ *adj* [fr. *sub-* + L *niveus* of snow + E *-an* — more at NIVEOUS] **:** situated or occurring under the snow ⟨~ burrows and runways —W.A.Fuller⟩

sub nom·i·ne \ˌsəbˈnämə,nā, -,nē, -ˈnōmə,nā\ *adv* [L] **:** under the name **:** under the caption or title

¹sub·normal \ˈsəb+\ *n* [in sense 1, fr. NL *subnormalis*, fr. L *sub-* + *normalis* normal; in sense 2, fr. ²*subnormal* — more at NORMAL] **1 :** the projection of the normal of a curve on the x-axis **2 :** one who is below the range of normality; *esp* **:** a person of subnormal intelligence

²subnormal \"+\ *adj* [ISV *sub-* + *normal*] **1 :** lower or smaller than normal ⟨a ~ temperature⟩ ⟨repeated ~ harvests⟩ **2 :** having less of something and esp. of intelligence than is normal ⟨~ children⟩ — **sub·normality** \"+\ *n* — **sub·normally** \"+\ *adv*

sub·no·ta·tion \ˌsəb,nōˈtāshən\ *n* [LL *subnotation-, subnotatio* act of signing underneath, fr. L *subnotatus* (past part. of *subnotare* to mark underneath, fr. *sub-* + *notare* to mark, sign, note) + *-ion-, -io* -ion — more at NOTE] **:** a written answer to an inquiry addressed by a private citizen upon some matter of law or policy to an emperor, sovereign, or pope

sub·nucleus \ˈsəb+\ *n* [NL, fr. *sub-* + *nucleus*] **:** a subdivision of a nucleus esp. of nervous tissue

sub·nutrition \"+\ *n* [*sub-* + *nutrition*] **:** inadequate feeding (as of livestock) whether quantitative or qualitative

sub·oblique \ˈsəb+\ *adj* [*sub-* + *oblique*] **:** not quite oblique

sub·obsolete \"+\ *adj* [*sub-* + *obsolete*] **:** not clearly defined **:** OBSCURE ⟨a ~ marking on an insect wing⟩

sub·occipital \"+\ *adj* [NL *suboccipitalis*, fr. L *sub-* + ML *occipitalis* occipital — more at OCCIPITAL] **1 :** situated below the occipital bone **2 :** situated below the occipital lobe of the brain

suboccipital nerve *n* **:** the first cervical nerve

sub·oceanic \"+\ *also* **sub·ocean** \"+\ *adj* [*sub-* + *oceanic* or *ocean*] **1 :** situated, taking place, or formed beneath the ocean or the bottom of the ocean ⟨~ light⟩ ⟨~ oil resources⟩ **2 :** concerned with the sea bottom ⟨~ physiography⟩

sub·octave \"+\ *n* [*sub-* + *octave*] **1 a :** a range of tones lower than two octaves below middle C **b :** SUBCONTRAOCTAVE **2 :** SUBOCTAVE COUPLER

suboctave coupler *n* **:** an organ coupler for making the tone an octave below sound together with the tone struck

¹sub·ocular \"+\ *adj* [LL *subocularis*, fr. L *sub-* + LL *ocularis* of the eyes — more at OCULAR] **:** situated below the eye

²subocular \"\ *n* **:** a subocular part; *esp* **:** one of the small scales between the eye and the upper labials of some reptiles

sub·oesophageal ganglion \ˈsəb+ . . . -\ *n* [*suboesophageal* fr. *sub-* + *oesophageal*] **:** a ganglionic mass formed in an insect by the fusion of the nerve ganglia of the 4th, 5th and 6th body segments

sub·office \"+\ *n* [*sub-* + *office*] **:** a secondary office (as of a post office or bank) that often provides only some of the services of the corresponding main office

sub·officer \ˈsəb+\ *n* [*sub-* + *officer*] **:** a subordinate officer

sub·opaque \"+\ *adj* [ISV *sub-* + *opaque*; prob. orig. formed in F] **:** partially or imperfectly opaque **:** nearly opaque

sub·operation \"+\ *n* [*sub-* + *operation*] **:** a subordinate operation; *usu* **:** an operation that forms a specific phase of a larger operation or process ⟨dividing the process into ~s⟩

sub·opercle \"+\ *n* [NL *suboperculum*, fr. *sub-* + *operculum*] **:** a bony plate immediately below the opercle in a gill cover of a fish

¹sub·opercular \"+\ *adj* [in sense 1, fr. *sub-* + *opercular*; in sense 2, fr. NL *suboperculum* + E *-ar*] **1 :** situated below an opercle **2 :** of, relating to, or being the subopercle

²subopercular \"\ *n* **:** a subopercular part; *esp* **:** SUBOPERCLE

sub·operculum \ˈsəb+\ *n* [NL] **:** SUBOPERCLE

sub·opposite \"+\ *adj* [*sub-* + *opposite*] **:** nearly opposite ⟨leaves ~⟩

sub·optimal \"+\ *adj* [ISV *sub-* + *optimal*] **:** less than optimal ⟨a ~ diet⟩

sub·optimum \"+\ *adj* [NL, fr. *sub-* + *optimum*] **:** SUBOPTIMAL

sub·oral \"+\ *adj* [*sub-* + *oral*] **:** situated or occurring beneath the mouth

sub·orbicular *also* **sub·orbiculate** *or* **sub·orbiculated** \"+\ *adj* [*suborbicular, suborbiculate* ISV *sub-* + *orbicular* or *orbiculate*; *suborbiculated* fr. *sub-* + obs. E *orbiculated*, fr. L *orbiculatus* orbiculate + E *-ed*] **:** nearly orbicular **:** approximately circular

¹sub·orbital \"+\ *adj* [*sub-* + *orbital*] **1 :** situated beneath the orbit of the eye; *also* **:** SUBOCULAR **2 :** being or involving less than one orbit ⟨the first manned ~ flight —Courtney Sheldon⟩

²suborbital \"\ *n* **:** a suborbital part (as a bone)

sub·order \ˈsəb+\ *n* [*sub-* + *order*] **1 :** a subdivision of an order ⟨a soil ~⟩; *esp* **:** a taxonomic category below an order and above a family **2 :** a smaller or subordinate architectural order as distinguished from the principal or main supporting order

sub·or·di·na·cy \səˈbȯ(r)dᵊnəsē, -ᵊnəsi *sometimes* -dən-\ *n* -ES **:** the quality or state of being subordinate **:** SUBORDINATION

sub·ordinal \ˈsəb+\ *adj* [NL *subordin-, subordo* suborder, fr. L *sub-* + *ordo* order] **:** of, relating to, or constituting a suborder

sub·ordinary \"+\ *n* [*sub-* + *ordinary*] **:** any of several common heraldic bearings less important than an ordinary

¹sub·or·di·nate \səˈbȯrd(ᵊ)nə̇t -ō(ə)d- *sometimes* -dᵊnə̇|, *or* -dᵊn,ā|, *or* -də,nā|; *usu* |d.+V\ *adj* [ME *subordinat*, fr. ML *subordinatus*, past part. of *subordinare* to place in a lower order, fr. L *sub-* + *ordinare* to put in order — more at ORDAIN] **1 :** placed in a lower order, class, or rank **:** holding a lower or inferior position ⟨making the executive ~ to the legislative branch of government⟩ ⟨a ~ branch of study⟩ ⟨~ peoples⟩ **2 :** of, relating to, or involving subordination or subordinates: as **a :** submissive to or falling under the control of a higher authority ⟨a ~ kingdom⟩ **b :** of, belonging to, or constituting a clause that functions as a noun, adjective, or adverb in a larger sentence ⟨~ construction⟩ ⟨~ clause⟩ **c :** grammatically subordinating ⟨~ conjunction⟩ — **sub·or·di·nate·ly** *adv* — **sub·or·di·nate·ness** *n* -ES

²subordinate \"\ *n* **:** one that is subordinate: as **a :** one who stands in order or rank below another — distinguished from *principal* **b :** a member of an ecological community other than a dominant

³sub·or·di·nate \-dᵊn,āt *sometimes* -də,nāt, *usu* -ād.+V\ *vt* [ML *subordinatus*, past part. of *subordinare* to subordinate] **1 :** to place in a lower order or class **:** make or consider as of less value or importance ⟨~ one creature to another⟩ **2 :** to make subject or subservient ⟨~ the passions to reason⟩

subordinating *adj* **:** having the capacity to subordinate or the function of subordinating; *usu* **:** introducing a subordinate clause **:** joining a subordinate to a main clause ⟨*if* in "I will come if I can" and *until* in "they fished until it was dark" are ~ conjunctions⟩ — **sub·or·di·nat·ing·ly** \ˈ=ˈ==,===, =,=ˈ===\ *adv*

sub·or·di·na·tion \sə,bȯ(r)dᵊnˈāshən *sometimes* -dəˈnā-\ *n* [ML *subordination-, subordinatio*, fr. *subordinatus* (past part. of *subordinare*) + *-ion-, -io* -ion] **1 :** the act of subordinating (as by making secondary or subject): as **a :** arrangement or classification into grades or ranks from highest to lowest **b :** the doctrine or practice under the law of bankruptcy and equity by which particular claims under the equities may not be paid before others or before sufficient assets are available to first meet such others or by which particular claims are allowed conditionally rather than wholly disallowed **c :** expression in the form of a subordinate clause **d :** arrangement of arches in architectural orders **2 a :** the quality or state of being subordinate to another **:** inferiority of rank or dignity **b :** the quality or state of being subordinate to authority **:** obedient submission — opposed to *insubordination* **3 a :** an arrangement produced by an act of subordination **b** *obs* **:** GRADE, RANK; *also* **:** a position of inferior status

sub·or·di·na·tion·ism \-shə,nizəm\ *n* -s **:** a doctrine in theology: the second and third persons of the Trinity are subordinate (as in order or essence) to the first person and the Holy Spirit is subordinate to the Son

sub·or·di·na·tion·ist \-sh(ə)nə̇st\ *n* -s **:** a person adhering to the doctrine of subordinationism

sub·or·di·na·tive \səˈbȯ(r)dᵊn,ād.iv, -d(ᵊ)nəd.-\ *adj* **:** tending to or expressing subordination: as **a :** grammatically subordinating **b** *linguistics* **:** having only one head — used of an endocentric construction (as *my books*); opposed to *coordinative*

sub·orn \səˈbȯ(ə)rn, -ō(ə)n\ *vt* -ED/-ING/-S [MF *suborner*, fr. L *subornare*, fr. *sub-* secretly, under + *ornare* to furnish, prepare, embellish — more at ORNATE] **1 a :** to induce (as

a person) by secret or underhanded means to do some improper or unlawful thing : incite secretly : INSTIGATE ⟨~ed government to the unlawful purposes of business —H.M. Kallen⟩ **b** : to induce or persuade (a person) to commit perjury; *also* : to obtain (testimony) by such action **2** *obs* **a** : to make secret or stealthy provision of **b** : EQUIP, SUPPLY **3** *obs* : to bring forward in support of an unworthy object

sub·or·na·tion \ˌsəbˌȯ(r)ˈnāshən, ˌsäb-\ *n* -S [MF, fr. ML *subornation-, subornatio*, fr. L *subornatus* (past part. of *subornare* to suborn) + *-ion-, -io* ion] : an act or instance of suborning: as **a** : the procuring of some end by secret, underhanded, or improper methods : the inducing (as by bribes or persuasion) of someone to do something improper or unlawful **b** (1) : the crime of procuring a person to commit perjury (2) : testimony procured by subornation : perjured testimony

sub·orn·er \səˈbȯrnər, -ˈȯ(ə)nə(r)\ *n* -S : one that suborns

sub·os·cines \ˌsäb+\ *n pl, cap* [NL, fr. sub- + *Oscines*] *in former classifications* : a superfamily of birds equivalent to the suborder Menurae

su·bo·ti·ca \ˈsübəˌtētsə, ˌ‥‥ˈ‥‥\ *adj, usu cap* [fr. *Subotica*, Yugoslavia] : of or from the city of Subotica, Yugoslavia : of the kind or style prevalent in Subotica

sub·ovate *or* **sub·ovated** \"+\ *adj* [sub- + *ovate* or obs. E *ovated*, fr. L *ovatus* ovate + E *-ed* — more at OVATE] : not quite ovate : approximately ovate

sub·ovoid \"+\ *adj* [ISV sub- + *ovoid*] : not quite ovoid : approximately ovoid

sub·oxide \"+\ *n* [ISV sub- + *oxide*] : an oxide (as carbon suboxide) containing a relatively small proportion of oxygen — compare PROTOXIDE

sub·pallial \"+\ *adj* [sub- + *pallial*] : occurring under a pallium; *usu* : situated beneath or derived from structures beneath the pallium of the brain

subpar \ˈsəb+\ *adv (or adj)* [sub- + *par*] : below a standard or normal level : less than par

subpar *abbr* subparagraph

sub·paragraph \ˈsəb+\ *n* [sub- + *paragraph*] : a subordinate paragraph esp. of a formally drafted document (as a contract or law)

sub·parallel \"+\ *adj* [sub- + *parallel*] : nearly parallel : not quite parallel

sub·passage \"+\ *n* [sub- + *passage*] : the passage of a strain of microorganisms obtained from one kind of animal through another (as for increasing its virulence)

sub·pectinate \"+\ *adj* [ISV sub- + *pectinate*] : somewhat pectinate : imperfectly pectinate

sub·pectoral \"+\ *adj* [ISV sub- + *pectoral*] **1** : situated under the pectoralis muscles **2** : situated or seeming to arise beneath the chest

sub pe·de si·gil·li \ˌsäbˈpēˌdāsēˈgi(ˌ)lē\ *adv* [L, lit., under the foot of the seal] : under seal

sub·peduncular \ˈsäb+\ *adj* [sub- + *peduncular*] : situated beneath a peduncle and esp. beneath one of the peduncles of the brain

sub·periosteal \"+\ *adj* [sub- + *periosteal*] : situated or occurring beneath the periosteum ⟨~ bone deposition⟩ — **sub·periosteally** \"+\ *adv*

sub·permanent \"+\ *adj* [sub- + *permanent*] : moderately permanent : PERSISTENT — **sub·permanently** \"+\ *adv*

subpermanent magnetism *n* : a metastable state of magnetization that is liable to loss through vibration or mechanical shock

sub·petiolar \ˈsäb+\ *adj* [sub- + *petiolar*] : concealed within the base of the petiole ⟨the leaf buds of the plane tree are ~⟩

sub·phonemic \"+\ *adj* [sub- + *phonemic*] : ALLOPHONIC, PHONETIC ⟨in Italian, \n\ is merely a ~ variant of \n\⟩

sub·phrenic \"+\ *adj* [ISV sub- + *phrenic*] : situated or occurring below the diaphragm

sub·phylar \"+\ *adj* [NL *subphylum* + E *-ar*] : of, relating to, or constituting a subphylum

sub·phylum \"+\ *n* [NL, fr. sub- + *phylum*] : a primary division of a phylum

sub·pial \"+\ *adj* [sub- + *pial*] : situated or occurring beneath the pia mater

sub·placenta \"+\ *n* [NL, fr. sub- + *placenta*] : DECIDUA

sub·plantigrade \"+\ *adj* [sub- + *plantigrade*] : having the heel raised when walking but standing flat-footed ⟨many carnivores are ~⟩

sub·plate \ˈsäb+ˌ-\ *n* [sub- + *plate*] : a plate (as of metal) placed beneath something usu. for protection or support

sub·platyhieric \ˈsäb+\ *adj* [sub- + *platyhieric*] : having a sacrum of moderate length and breadth with a length-breadth index of 100 to 106 — compare DOLICHOHIERIC, PLATYHIERIC

sub·pleural \"+\ *adj* [ISV sub- + *pleural*] : situated under the pleura and the body wall — **sub·pleurally** \"+\ *adv*

sub·plinth \ˈsäb+ˌ-\ *n* [sub- + *plinth*] : a plinth under and projecting slightly beyond a principal plinth

sub·plot \"+ˌ-\ *n* [sub- + *plot*] **1** : a subordinate plot in fiction or drama **2** : a subdivision of a plot (as of land)

subplow \"+ˌ-\ *vb* [sub- + *plow*] : SUBTILL

¹sub·poe·na *also* **sub·pe·na** \səˈpēnə, ÷-ēnē, ÷-ēnä\ *sometimes* (ˌ)səbˈp- *or* ÷-pēnyə\ *n* -S [ME *suppena, sub pena*, fr. L *sub poena* under penalty; fr. the opening words of the writ] **1** : a writ commanding a person designated in it to attend court under a penalty for failure — see SUBPOENA AD TESTIFICANDUM, SUBPOENA DUCES TECUM **2** : the process by which a defendant in an equity action is commanded to appear and answer the plaintiff's bill

²subpoena *also* **subpena** \"\ *vt* -ED/-ING/-S : to serve or summon with a writ of subpoena ⟨had been ~ed to appear at the inquest —Kamala Markandaya⟩

sub poe·na \ˌsäbˈpēnä\ *adv* [L] : under penalty

subpoena ad tes·ti·fi·can·dum \-ˌad,testə̇fəˈkandəm\ *n, pl* **subpoenas ad testificandum** [NL, under penalty to give testimony] : a writ commanding a person to appear in court for testifying as a witness

subpoena du·ces te·cum \-ˈdüˌkäsˈtākəm, -tāˌküm\ *n, pl* **subpoenas duces tecum** [NL, under penalty you shall bring with you] : a writ commanding a person to produce in court certain designated documents or other evidence ⟨the district attorney started serving *subpoenas duces tecum* on witnesses —Erle Stanley Gardner⟩

sub·poe·nal \səˈpēnᵊl *sometimes* (ˌ)səbˈp-\ *adj* [¹subpoena + *-al*] : required or done under penalty

sub·polar \ˈsäb+\ *adj* [ISV sub- + *polar*] : not quite polar : SUBARCTIC, SUBANTARCTIC

sub·population \"+\ *n* [sub- + *population*] **1** : an identifiable fraction or subdivision of a population **2** : a specific biotype within a natural population

sub·port \ˈsäb+ˌ-\ *n* [sub- + *port*] : a subordinate or secondary port (as of entry)

sub–post office \ˈsäb+\ *n, Brit* : a branch post office : a postal station

sub·potency \"+\ *n* [sub- + *potency*] : reduced capacity to transmit hereditary characters

sub·potent \"+\ *adj* [sub- + *potent*] : less than usu. or normally potent; *esp* : exhibiting genetic subpotency

sub·prefect \"+\ *n* [sub- + *prefect*] : an official subordinate to a prefect; *esp* : a French administrative official in immediate charge of an arrondissement — **sub·prefectorial** \"+ˌ-\ *adj* — **sub·prefecture** \"+\ *n*

sub·press \ˈsäb+ˌ-\ *n* [sub- + *press*] : a small press mounted usu. between the bed and ram of a larger main punch press, used for small and delicate work (as on jewelry), and having its plunger actuated by the slide of the main press

sub·principal \ˈsäb+\ *n* [sub- + *principal*] **1** : an assistant or subordinate principal (as of a school) **2** : a secondary or bracing rafter **3** : an open diapason subbass in a pipe organ

sub·prior \ˈsäb+\ *n* [ME, fr. ML, fr. sub- + *prior* — more at PRIOR] : the vicegerent or assistant of a prior

sub·problem \"+\ *n* [sub- + *problem*] : a problem that is contingent on or forms a part of another more inclusive problem

sub·professional \"+\ *adj* [sub- + *professional*] **1** : functioning or qualified to function at a level below the professional but distinctly above the clerical or labor level and usu. under the direct supervision of a professionally trained person ⟨~ and clerical workers⟩ **2** : designed to provide a founda-

tion and background for professional training ⟨the premedical course is basically ~ education⟩

sub·pubescent \"+\ *adj* [sub- + *pubescent*] : somewhat hairy

sub·punch \ˈsäb+ˌ-\ *vt* [sub- + *punch*] : to punch to a size smaller than the finished dimension so that sufficient material is left for finishing (as by drilling or reaming)

sub·purlin \ˈsäb+\ *n* [sub- + *purlin*] : a light architectural member resting on purlins and purlins usu. running at right angles to them

sub·pyrenean \"+\ *adj, usu cap P* : situated at the foot of or to the south of the Pyrenees mountains

sub·quadrangular \ˈsäb+\ *adj* [sub- + *quadrangular*] : nearly quadrangular : quadrangular but with the corners rounded

sub·quadrate \ˈsäb+\ *adj* [sub- + *quadrate*] : nearly square : square but with the corners rounded

¹sub·quality \ˈsäb+\ *n* [sub- + *quality*] : an underlying quality ⟨a ~ of beauty running through his serious writing⟩

²subquality \"\ *adj* [sub- + *quality* (adj.)] : of an inferior quality ⟨~ products⟩

sub·race \ˈsäb+\ *n* [sub- + *race*] : a subdivision of a race; *esp* : a division of a primary human race that is developed in a limited area by inbreeding, social selection, and environmental influences — **sub·racial** \ˈsäb+\ *adj*

sub·radius \ˈsäb+\ *n* [NL, fr. sub- + *radius*] : a radius of the fourth order in some coelenterates that intervenes halfway between an adradius and the adjacent perradius or interradius

sub·ramose *also* **sub·ramous** \"+\ *adj* [NL *subramosus*, fr. L *sub- + ramosus* branched — more at RAMOSE] : somewhat branched: as **a** : having blunt short processes or projections that are arranged like branches **b** : having few or sparse branches

sub·range \ˈsäb+ˌ-\ *n* [sub- + *range*] : a subordinate range (as of hills)

sub·rational \ˈsäb+\ *adj* [sub- + *rational*] : almost or nearly rational

sub·reader \"+\ *n* [sub- + *reader*] : an underreader in the Inns of Court formerly reading the texts discoursed on by the reader

sub·recent \"+\ *adj* [sub- + *recent*] : of, relating to, or being a period of indefinite and variable duration extending from the final part of the Pleistocene to the full establishment of the geologically Recent

sub·rectangular \"+\ *adj* [sub- + *rectangular*] : approximately rectangular

sub·refraction \"+\ *n* [sub- + *refraction*] : a state of refraction (as of the atmosphere) that is less than normal and is usu. associated with a sharp vertical gradient of some physical factor (as temperature)

sub·region \"+\ *n* [ISV sub- + *region*] **1** : a subdivision of a region ⟨economic ~s of the U.S.⟩ **2** : one of the primary divisions of a biogeographic region — **sub·regional** \"+\ *adj*

sub·regulus \ˈsäb+\ *n* [LL, fr. L sub- + *regulus* prince, petty king, fr. *reg-, rex* king + *-ulus -ule* — more at ROYAL] : a petty prince : a vassal ruler

sub·rent \ˈsäb+ˌ-\ *n* [sub- + *rent*] : rent from a subtenant

sub·rep·ta·ry \ˈsäˌbreptərē\ *adj* [L *subreptus* (past part. of *subrepere* to creep under, crawl, fr. sub- + *repere* to creep) + E *-ary* — more at REPTILE] : adapted primarily to crawling ⟨a mollusk with a broad ~ foot⟩

sub·rep·tion \(ˌ)səˈbrepshən\ *n* -S [LL *subreption-, subreptio*, fr. L, act of stealing, fr. *subreptus* (past part. of *subripere* to snatch away, take away secretly) + *-ion-, -io* ion — more at SURREPTITIOUS] **1 a** : secret, underhanded, unlawful or unfair representation through suppression or fraudulent concealment of facts **b** : a deduction drawn from such representation **2** *canon & Scots law* : the obtaining of or attempting to obtain a dispensation from ecclesiastical authority or a gift from the sovereign by concealing the truth — distinguished from *obreption*

sub·rep·ti·tious \ˌsäˌbrepˈtishəs\ *adj* [L *subreptitius, subrepticius* secret, clandestine, surreptitious, fr. *subreptus* (past part. of *subripere*) + *-itius, -icius -itious*] **1** : of, relating to, or involving subreption **2** *obs* : SURREPTITIOUS — **sub·reptitiously** *adv*

sub·reputable \ˈsäb+\ *adj* [sub- + *reputable*] : of slightly questionable reputation

sub·resin \"+\ *n* [ISV sub- + *resin*] : the part of a natural resin that dissolves in hot alcohol and is deposited on cooling — **sub·resinous** \"+\ *adj*

sub·ri·dent \ˌsäˌbrīdᵊnt\ *adj* [L *subrident-, subridens*, pres. part. of *subridere* to smile, fr. sub- + *ridere* to laugh — more at RIDICULOUS] : wearing or offered with a smile ⟨a ~ answer⟩ — **sub·ri·dent·ly** *adv*

sub·rigid \ˈsäb+\ *adj* [sub- + *rigid*] : not perfectly rigid; *usu* : designed to resist shock by reason of inherent flexibility ⟨a ~ framework⟩

sub·risive \-ˈrīsiv, -riz|, -rīz|\ *adj* [L *subrisus* (past part. of *subridere* to smile) + E *-ive*] : SMILING ⟨the sudden ~ humor that lighted his gray eyes —Leslie Ford⟩

sub·ro·gate \ˈsäbrōˌgāt\ *vt* -ED/-ING/-S [L *subrogatus*, past part. of *subrogare* to substitute — more at SURROGATE] : to put in the place of another : SUBSTITUTE; *esp* : to apply the legal doctrine of subrogation to

sub·ro·ga·tion \ˌ‥‥ˈgāshən\ *n* [ME *subrogacioun* substitution, fr. MF *subrogation*, fr. ML *subrogation-, subrogatio*, fr. L *subrogatus* (past part.) + *-ion-, -io* ion] **1** : an act of subrogating: as **a** : the substitution of one for another as a creditor so that the new creditor succeeds to the former's rights in law and equity : a legal operation by which a third person who pays a creditor succeeds to his rights against the debtor as if he were his assignee — compare SUBSTITUTION 1a **b** : succession by an insurance company after payment of a loss to the insured's rights against the party responsible for the loss (as against a person negligently or willfully causing fire damage to insured property) **2** : the legal relation created by an act of subrogation

sub·ro·gee \ˌ‥‥ˈjē\ *n* -S [*subrogate* + *-ee*] : one who acquires by subrogation rights belonging to another

sub·ro·gor \-ˈgȯ(ə)r\ *n* -S [*subrogate* + *-or*] : one who yields rights to another in subrogation

sub ro·sa \ˌsäˌbrōzə\ *adv* [NL, lit., under the rose; fr. the ancient custom of hanging a rose over the council table to indicate that all present were sworn to secrecy and prob. connected with the legend that Cupid gave a rose to the god of silence Harpocrates to keep him from revealing the indiscretions of Venus] : without publicity or notice : COVERTLY, PRIVATELY, CONFIDENTIALLY

sub–rosa \"\ *adj* [*sub rosa*] : designed to be secret or confidential : shunning publicity : SECRETIVE ⟨a *sub-rosa* report⟩ ⟨a *sub-rosa* group⟩

sub·rostral \ˈsäb+\ *adj* [sub- + *rostral*] : situated beneath or below a rostrum

sub·rotund \"+\ *adj* [L *subrotundus*, fr. sub- + *rotundus* round — more at ROUND] : nearly but not quite round : ROUNDISH

sub·rounded \"+\ *adj* [sub- + *rounded*] : partially rounded; *esp* : exhibiting such wear that some but not all edges are rounded ⟨~ sand⟩

sub·routine \"+\ *n* [ISV sub- + *routine*] : a subordinate routine; *esp* : a usu. coded specific instruction by which a digital computer is guided to perform a precisely defined mathematical or logical operation

subs *pl of* SUB, *pres 3d sing of* SUB

subs *abbr* **1** subscription **2** subsidiary **3** subsistence **4** substantive **5** substitute

sub·salicylate \ˈsäb+\ *n* [sub- + *salicylate*] : a basic salicylate (as bismuth salicylate)

sub·saline \"+\ *adj* [sub- + *saline*] : somewhat salty : salty but not excessively so

sub·sample \"+\ *n* [sub- + *sample*] : a sample or specimen obtained by subsampling : a subordinate sample ⟨~s are . . . representative to a lesser degree than the total samples —J.C.Davies⟩

²subsample \"\ *vt* [sub- + *sample* (v.)] : to draw samples from (a previously screened or selected group or population) : sample a sample of

²subsample \"\ *n* : a sample or specimen obtained by subsampling : a subordinate sample ⟨~s are . . . representative to a lesser degree than the total samples —J.C.Davies⟩

sub·saturated \ˈsäb+\ *adj* [sub- + *saturated*] : approximately but not completely saturated — **sub·saturation** \"+\ *n*

sub·scale \ˈsäb+ˌ-\ *n* [sub- + *scale* (plate)] : an oxidation product developed within the substance of rather than on the surface of a metal

¹sub·scapular \ˈsäb+\ *adj* [NL *subscapularis*, fr. sub- + *scapularis* scapular] : situated under the scapula : of or relating to the ventral or in man the anterior surface of the scapula; *esp* : being a body part (as an artery or a vein or muscle) that courses in whole or in part beneath the scapula

²subscapular \"\ *n* : a subscapular part

subscapular artery *n* : the largest branch of the axillary artery arising opposite the lower border of the subscapularis muscle and passing back to the inferior angle of the scapula to anastomose with arteries of that region

subscapular fascia *n* : a thin sheet of fascia fixed to the circumference of the subscapular fossa

subscapular fossa *n* : the concave depression of the anterior surface of the scapula

sub·scap·u·lar·is \ˈsäbˌskapyᵊ'la(ə)rᵊs\ *n* -ES [NL, fr. *subscapularis*, adj., subscapular] : a large triangular muscle that fills up the subscapular fossa, arises from the surface of the scapula, and is inserted into the lesser tubercle of the humerus

sub·science \ˈsäb+\ *n* [sub- + *science*] : a branch of a science that has developed some degree of specialization and autonomy in its own right ⟨geometry is a ~ of mathematics⟩

sub·scleral \"+\ *adj* [sub- + *scleral*] : SUBSCLEROTIC

sub·sclerotic \"+\ *adj* [sub- + *sclerotic*] : situated or occurring between the sclerotic and choroid coats of the eyeball

sub·scribe \səbˈskrīb, -bˈsk-\ *vb* [ME *subscriben*, fr. L *subscribere*, fr. sub- + *scribere* to write — more at SCRIBE] *vt* **1** : to write (as one's name) underneath : sign (one's name) to a document **2 a** : to sign with one's own hand : give consent to or bind oneself to the terms of (something written) by appending one's name **b** : to attest by appending one's name ⟨officers ~ their official acts⟩ **c** *obs* : to sign away : RESIGN, YIELD **d** (1) : to promise to give ⟨each man *subscribed* ten dollars⟩ (2) : CONTRIBUTE ⟨~ . . . that which it can do best —W.J.Haley⟩ **3** *chiefly Brit* : to give support to or concur in : FAVOR, SANCTION ⟨unable to . . . ~ their beliefs —T.E.Lawrence⟩ **4** *obs* : to declare with or as if with signature : PUBLISH ⟨I will ~ him a coward —Shak.⟩ ~ *vi* **1** : to sign one's name to a letter or other document **2 a** : to give approval to something written by signing — often used with *to* ⟨found him unwilling to ~ to the agreement⟩ **b** : to set one's name to a paper in token of promise to give something (as a sum of money); *also* : to give something in pursuance of a promise so made **c** (1) : to enter one's name for a publication (as a book or newspaper) or service — usu. used with *for* and sometimes with *to* (2) : to agree to take and pay for something (as stock) by signing one's name to a formal agreement; *esp* : to make a signed application for securities of a new offering — usu. used with *for* ⟨*subscribed* for 1000 shares⟩ **3** *obs* : to become surety **4** *obs* : YIELD, SUBMIT **5 a** : to be in accord : ACQUIESCE, AGREE — usu. used with *to* ⟨~ to a doctrine⟩ **b** : ADHERE, BELONG ⟨~ to the masculine gender⟩ **syn** see ASSENT

sub·scrib·er \-bə(r)\ *n* : one that subscribes: as **a** : one that signs something (as a letter, document, agreement) **b** : one that agrees or consents **c** : one that favors, aids, or supports (as by money contribution, moral influence, personal membership) **d** : an individual having commercial telephone equipment installed on his premises

¹sub·script \ˈsäbˌkript, -bˌsk-\ *n* [L *subscriptus*, past part. of *subscribere* to write underneath] : something written below (as a subscript sign or letter); *esp* : a subscript character affixed to a symbol to distinguish it in its class

²subscript \"\ *adj* [L *subscriptus*, past part. of *subscribere*] : written below or beneath: as **a** : being a usu. smaller character printed or written immediately below another character ⟨the ~ cedilla of ç⟩ **b** : being a usu. smaller character printed or written lower than but not immediately below another ⟨the ~ 2 of H₂O⟩ — compare ADSCRIPT, SUPERSCRIPT

sub·scrip·tion \səbˈkripshən, -bˈsk-\ *n, often attrib* [ME *subscripcioun*, fr. L *subscription-, subscriptio* thing written underneath, subscription, fr. *subscriptus* (past part. of *subscribere* to write underneath) + *-ion-, -io* ion] **1 a** : a formal approval or acceptance of some outline of principles (as of ecclesiastical articles of faith) attested by the signing of one's name **b** : the act of signing one's name (as in attesting or witnessing a document) **c** : consent, agreement, approval, or support conveyed or such as would be conveyed by signed confirmation **2** : something that is subscribed: **a** : matter appended at the end of a document or writing; *esp* : a signed response from a sovereign written below a written inquiry as to a matter of law or policy — compare RESCRIPT **b** : a written name : SIGNATURE; *also* : a paper to which a signature is attached *c obs* : SUBSCRIPT **d** (1) : a sum subscribed ⟨his ~ to a fund⟩ (2) : the whole amount realized from or pledged by subscribers to a particular offering ⟨the ~ amounted to over 3000 dollars⟩ **e** (1) : a method of issuing a published work in which the publisher agrees to a concession in price to those who buy in advance of publication — see SUBSCRIPTION BOOK (2) : a purchase by prepayment of the future issues of a periodical usu. for a fixed period (as a year) ⟨renewed her ~ to the journal⟩ (3) : application to purchase securities of a new issue **f** : a method of offering or supporting a series of public performances (as of plays or concerts) **g** : a part of a prescription that contains directions to the pharmacist **3** *obs* : SUBMISSION, OBEDIENCE

subscription book *n* **1** : a book containing a list of subscribers **2** : a book sold by subscription usu. through personal solicitation by an agent

subscription edition *n* **1** : an edition published after a required number of subscriptions has been guaranteed **2** : an edition usu. in a special format and binding sold only to subscribers

sub·scrip·tion·ist \-sh(ə)nə̇st\ *n* : one who seeks or canvasses for subscriptions

subscription library *n* : a lending library to which borrowers pay a membership fee either instead of or in addition to a specific charge for books borrowed

subscription list *n* : a list or record of subscriptions and subscribers

subscription warrant *n* : a certificate or other document constituting legal evidence of a subscription right

sub·sea \ˈsäbˌsē\ *adj* [sub- + *sea*] : SUBMARINE, UNDERSEA

sub·sect \ˈsäb+ˌ-\ *n* [sub- + *sect*] **1** : a sect directly derived from another **2** : a minor sect

sub·section \ˈsäb+\ *n* [sub- + *section*] **1** : a subdivision or a subordinate division of a section ⟨~ of a report⟩ **2** : a subordinate part or branch ⟨a ~ of a gene⟩

sub·segment \"+\ *n* [sub- + *segment*] : a subordinate segment; *specif* : a distinguishable portion of an arthropod appendage that appears to be but is not morphologically homologous to a true segment ⟨~s of the insect tarsus⟩

sub·sel·li·um \(ˌ)səbˈseleəm\ *n, pl* **sub·sellia** \-ēə\ [L, fr. sub- + *sella* seat, chair — more at SETTLE] : a low seat or bench; *esp* : MISERICORD

sub·semitone \ˈsäb+\ *n* [sub- + *semitone*] : the leading note of a key in medieval music : SUBTONIC

sub·sense \ˈsäb+ˌ-\ *n* [sub- + *sense*] : a subordinate division of a sense

sub·sensible \ˈsäb+\ *adj* [sub- + *sensible*] : deeper than the reach of the senses : situated beyond sensory perception

sub·septate \"+\ *adj* [sub- + *septate*] : imperfectly septate : having a partial septum

sub·se·quence \ˈsäbsə̇kwən(t)s, -bsēk-, -ˌkwen-, *also* -bzˌ)k- *or* -b(ˌ)sk- *sometimes* -bzə(ˌ)k- *or* -bzē(ˌ)k-\ *n* [LL *subsequentia* that which follows, succession, fr. L *subsequent-, subsequens* (pres. part.) + *-ia*] **1** : the quality or state of being subsequent **2** : something that comes subsequently : a later or following event

¹sub·se·quent \-nt\ *adj* [ME, fr. L *subsequent-, subsequens*, pres. part. of *subsequi* to follow closely, fr. sub- near, closely + *sequi* to follow — more at SUE] **1** : following in time : coming or being later than something else ⟨~ events⟩ ⟨a period ~ to the war⟩ **2** : following in order of place : SUCCEEDING ⟨a ~ clause in a treaty⟩ **3** [so called fr. its being subsequent in origin to the system of which it is a part] : developed along a belt of underlying weak rock and therefore adjusted to the regional structure ⟨~ stream⟩ — **sub·se·quent·ly** *adv* —

²subsequent \"\ *n* **1** : one that follows after in time or in position **2** : a subsequent stream

subsequent condition *n* : CONDITION SUBSEQUENT

subsequent drainage *n* **:** drainage by means of a subsequent stream

sub·se·quen·tial \¦=·=¦kwenchəl, ¦=¦kw-, ¦=¦skw-\ *adj* [*subsequent* + *-al*] **:** SUBSEQUENT — **sub·se·quen·tial·ly** \-ch(ə)lē, -li\ *adv*

subsequent to *prep* **:** at a time later or more recent than **:** SINCE ⟨*subsequent to* our discussion⟩

subsequent valley *n* **:** a valley eroded by a subsequent stream

sub·sere \'səb+,-\ *n* [*sub-* + *sere*] **:** a secondary succession arising after an ecological climax community has been interrupted (as by fire or human agency)

sub·serosa \¦səb+\ *n* [NL, fr. *sub-* + *serosa*] **:** subserous tissue

sub·serous \"+\ *adj* [ISV *sub-* + *serous*] **:** located under a serous membrane ⟨a ~ uterine fibroid⟩

sub·serve \(,)səb'sərv, -'səv, -'səiv\ *vb* [L *subservire*, fr. *sub-* + *servire* to serve — more at SERVE] *vi* **:** to hold or function in a subordinate position in respect to something ⟨the lesser need must ~ to the greater⟩ ~ *vt* **1 a :** to serve as an instrument or means in carrying on (as an activity) or out (as a plan) or in furthering the ends of (as a person) ⟨if we are going to ~ the purpose for which rent control was adopted —*Congressional Record*⟩ **b :** to function for or serve to promote the betterment, welfare, or effectiveness of ⟨an organism in which every part has its place and ~*s* the whole —Frank Thilly⟩ **c :** to be in accord with **:** accord honor or respect to ⟨Napoleon's star rose as long as he *subserved* the great ideas of the French revolution —Lucien Price⟩ **2** *archaic* **:** to avail (oneself) of something

sub·ser·vi·ate \-vē,āt\ *vt* -ED/-ING/-S [¹*subservient* + *-ate*] **:** to reduce to a subordinate or subservient place or condition

sub·ser·vi·ence \-vēən(t)s\ *also* **sub·ser·vi·en·cy** \-nsē, -nsi\ *n, pl* **subserviences** *also* **subserviencies** [L *subservire* to be subservient, to subserve + E *-ence* or *-ency*] **1 :** the quality or state of functioning in serving or promoting **:** the condition of one that subserves ⟨these proposals are made in ~ to the end in view⟩ **2 :** the quality or state of being subordinate or subordinated to something ⟨~ to sensation —Marjorie Grene⟩ ⟨the emancipation of American literature from its ~ to England —*Amer. Guide Series: Mass.*⟩ **3 a :** excessive willingness to submit to the control or demands of another ⟨repudiated the administration's ~ to foreign interests⟩ **b :** servile inferiority **:** obsequious servility ⟨felt no ~ in working for him —Emery Neff⟩

¹**sub·ser·vi·ent** \-nt\ *adj* [L *subservient-, subserviens*, pres. part. of *subservire* to be subservient, to subserve] **:** fitted or disposed to subserve: as **a :** useful in an inferior capacity **:** SUBORDINATE **b :** serving to promote some end **c :** obsequiously submissive **:** SERVILE, TRUCKLING

syn SERVILE, MENIAL, SLAVISH, OBSEQUIOUS: SUBSERVIENT implies compliance and obedience, perhaps abject and marked by cringing or truckling, of one very conscious of a subordinate, dependent position ⟨the *subservient* smirk which comes only of generations of tip-seeking ancestors —Jack London⟩ ⟨editors and journalists who express opinions in print that are opposed to the interests of the rich are dismissed and replaced by *subservient* ones —G.B.Shaw⟩ SERVILE is likely to suggest the mean submissive cringing or fawning of a slave ⟨*servile* and fawning as he had been before, he was now as domineering and bellicose —Jack London⟩ ⟨the manner of a prince doling out favors to a *servile* group of petitioners —Theodore Dreiser⟩ MENIAL may suggest lower domestic tasks and offices; it may suggest degradation or sordidness ⟨competing against a mass of unemployed, they accepted the most *menial* and worst paid jobs —Oscar Handlin⟩ ⟨the scullery boy peeled the potatoes and did other *menial* tasks out on the open platform —O.S.Nock⟩ SLAVISH, in this sense derived from and suggesting *slave*, may connote abjectness, debasement, or extremely hard drudging toil ⟨which attacks the poor companion bore with meekness, with cowardice, with a resignation that was half generous and half hypocritical — with the *slavish* submission —W.M.Thackeray⟩ OBSEQUIOUS may suggest fawning, unctuous, or sycophantic compliance with and attention to those being served ⟨brutal and arrogant when winning, they are bootlicking and servilely *obsequious* when losing —D.L.Cohn⟩

²**subservient** \"\ *n* -S **:** one that is subservient

sub·ser·vi·ent·ly *adv* **:** in a subservient manner **:** with subservience

sub·ser·vi·ent·ness *n* -ES **:** SUBSERVIENCE

sub·sessile \¦səb+\ *adj* [NL *subsessilis*, fr. L *sub-* + *sessilis* low, dwarf (of plants) — more at SESSILE] **:** nearly but not quite sessile

¹**sub·set** \'səb+¦-\ *vb* [*sub-* + *set* (v.)] *Scots law* **:** SUBLET

²**sub·set** \'səb+,-\ *n* [*sub-* + *set*] **:** a set (as of data) that is itself an element of a larger set; *esp* **:** a mathematical set each of whose elements is also an element of a given set

sub·sexual \¦səb+\ *adj* [*sub-* + *sexual*] **:** approaching but not clearly characterizable as sexual ⟨a ~ parthenogenetic reproduction involving nuclear changes analogous to meiosis but without reduction⟩

sub·shining \"+\ *adj* [*sub-* + *shining*] **:** somewhat lustrous

sub·shock \'səb+,-\ *adj* [*sub-* + *shock*] **1 :** inadequate to produce fully developed insulin shock ⟨~ doses of insulin⟩ **2 :** of, relating to, or constituting insulin shock therapy in which the dosage is kept below the level necessary to produce deep coma

sub·shrub \"+,-\ *n* [*sub-* + *shrub*] **1 :** a perennial plant having woody stems except for the terminal part of the new growth which is killed back annually **2 :** UNDERSHRUB 2

sub·shrubby \"+-,\ *adj* [*sub-* + *shrubby*] **:** somewhat shrubby **:** like or being a subshrub

sub·side \səb'sīd\ *vi* -ED/-ING/-S [L *subsidere*, fr. *sub-* + *sidere* to sit down, sink; akin to L *sedēre* to sit — more at SIT] **1 :** to sink or fall to the bottom **:** SETTLE, PRECIPITATE **2 :** to tend downward **:** become lower **:** DESCEND; *esp* **:** to flatten out so as to form a depression ⟨the soil *subsided* over the old dump⟩ **3 :** to let oneself settle down **:** EASE, SINK ⟨*subsided* into a chair⟩ **4 :** to fall into a state of quiet **:** cease to rage **:** settle down **:** become tranquil **:** ABATE ⟨the sea ~*s*⟩ ⟨the tumult will ~⟩ ⟨the fever has *subsided*⟩ **syn** see FALL

sub·sidence \səb'sīdᵊn(t)s, 'səbsədən-\ *n* -S [L *subsidentia*, fr. *subsident-, subsidens* (pres. part. of *subsidere* to subside) + *-ia*] **1 :** something (as a sediment in a liquid) that has subsided **2 :** the act or process of subsiding **:** a falling, lowering, or flattening out ⟨the ~ of waves after a storm⟩ ⟨his anger underwent a quick ~⟩

sub·siden·cy \-nsē\ *n* -ES [L *subsidentia*] *archaic* **:** SUBSIDENCE

sub·sident \-nt\ *adj* [L *subsident-, subsidens*, pres. part. of *subsidere* to subside] **:** falling to the bottom **:** SUBSIDING

sub·sid·er \səb'sīdə(r)\ *n* -S **:** one (as a settling tank or separator) that subsides or permits of or accelerates the process of subsidence

sub·sid·i·ar·i·ly \(,)səb¦sidē¦erəlē, -li *also* ÷ -'sidər-\ *adv* **:** in a subsidiary manner **:** so as to be subsidiary

sub·sid·i·ar·i·ty \-,sidē'arəd-ē\ *n* -ES **1 :** the quality or state of being subsidiary **2 :** a theory in sociology: functions which subordinate or local organizations perform effectively belong more properly to them than to a dominant central organization

¹**sub·sid·i·ary** \(,)səb'sidē,erē, -ri *also* ÷-dər-\ *adj* [L *subsidiarius* of or relating to a reserve, fr. *subsidium* army reserve, subsidy + *-arius* -ary] **1 a :** functioning in the provision of aid, support, or other benefit usu. in a subordinate or inferior status or capacity ⟨a ~ device⟩ ⟨a ~ subject in a course of study⟩ ⟨~ details that lend finish to the ensemble⟩ **b** (1) **:** of secondary importance or prominence **:** SUPPLEMENTARY, MINOR, TRIBUTARY ⟨a ~ stream⟩ ⟨~ crops⟩ (2) **:** belonging to or controlled by another ⟨a ~ company⟩ **2 a :** of, relating to, or constituting a subsidy ⟨a ~ payment to an ally⟩ **b :** aided or maintained by a subsidy ⟨raised a force of ~ troops⟩

²**subsidiary** \"\ *n* -ES **:** one that is subsidiary: as **a :** ASSISTANT **b :** a subordinate theme or motive in music; *esp* **:** one occurring as subject of an episode in an extended work **c** *also* **subsidiary company :** a company wholly controlled by another that owns more than half of its voting stock — compare AFFILIATE 2b(1) **d :** a subsidiary goal in polo

subsidiary cell *n* **1 :** ACCESSORY CELL **2 :** a cell of an elevated circular group of cells surrounding the base of a multicellular hair in the epidermis of some plants

subsidiary coin *n* **:** a coin esp. of silver of a denomination smaller than the basic monetary unit (as half-dollar, quarter, dime) — compare MINOR COIN

subsidiary ledger *n* **:** a ledger which is supplementary to a controlling account in a general ledger and in which detailed accounts of a like class are kept

subsiding reservoir *n* **:** SETTLING RESERVOIR

sub·si·diz·able \'səbsə,dīzəbəl, 'səbzə-, ,==¦===\ *adj* **:** capable of being subsidized

sub·si·di·za·tion \,==də'zāshən, -,dī'z-\ *n* -S **1 :** the act or practice of subsidizing **2 :** money or other benefits obtained as a subsidy

sub·si·dize \'səbsə,dīz *sometimes* 'səbzə-\ *vt* -ED/-ING/-S *see -ize in Explan Notes* [*subsidy* + *-ize*] **:** to furnish with a subsidy: as **a :** to purchase the assistance of by the payment of a subsidy **b :** to aid or promote (as a private enterprise) with public money ⟨~ a steamship line⟩ — **sub·si·diz·er** \-zə(r)\ *n* -S

sub·si·dy \'səbsədē, -di *also* 'səbzə-\ *n* -ES *often attrib* [ME *subsidie*, fr. L *subsidium* army reserve, support, help, fr. *subsidere* to settle down, subside — more at SUBSIDE] **1** *archaic* **:** something intended to aid, support, or comfort **2 :** a grant or gift of money or other property made by way of financial aid: as **a :** a sum of money formerly granted by the British Parliament to the crown and raised by extraordinary or special taxation in distinction from the proceeds of the customs or other taxes levied by royal prerogative **b :** money or other support exacted by a ruler usu. for a special purpose or occasion **c :** money granted by one state to another (as to a friendly power to aid in the prosecution of a war) **d :** a grant of funds or property from a government (as of the state or a municipal corporation) to a private person or company to assist in the establishment or support of an enterprise deemed advantageous to the public either as a simple gift or a payment of an amount in excess of the usual charges for a service (as in carrying the mails) or funds to aid in establishing or maintaining a service or equipment larger or more powerful than the state of trade would warrant (as for the building and keeping in service of ships designed for use as cruisers and auxiliaries in war); *broadly* **:** an entire payment from a government for services (as for carrying mail) which includes both compensation for actual services and a subsidy proper

sub·sieve \'səb+,-\ *adj* [*sub-* + *sieve*] **:** of, relating to, made up of, or being particles small enough to pass freely through a 44 micron separatory sieve ⟨the ~ fraction of a clay⟩ ⟨particles in the ~ range⟩

sub si·len·tio \,səbsə'lenchē,ō, -b,sī'l-; -bsə'lentē,ō\ *adv* [L] **:** under or in silence **:** without notice being taken or without making a particular point of the matter in question ⟨assumed *sub silentio* that the Supreme Court would have the power to review . . . legislation —J.P.Roche⟩

sub·silicate \¦səb+\ *n* [ISV *sub-* + *silicate*] **:** a basic silicate

sub·silicic \"+\ *adj* [*sub-* + *silicic*] **:** containing little silica ⟨a ~ rock⟩ — distinguished from *persilicic*

sub·sill \'səb+,-\ *n* [*sub-* + *sill*] **:** a secondary sill (as under a shop front or on a mudsill)

sub·sinuous \¦səb+\ *adj* [*sub-* + *sinuous*] **:** imperfectly sinuous **:** nearly but not quite sinuous

¹**sub·sist** \səb'sist\ *vb* -ED/-ING/-S [LL *subsistere* to stay alive, exist, be, fr. L, to remain standing, stand up, fr. *sub-* up + *sistere* to stand, cause to stand; akin to L *stare* to stand — more at SUB-, STAND] *vi* **1 a :** to have existence **:** be or remain alive **:** BE ⟨enabling a noble action to ~ as it did in nature —Matthew Arnold⟩ **b :** PERSIST, CONTINUE **2** *archaic* **:** to exist in a particular way or condition or have a particular form **3 :** to be maintained with food and clothing **:** have the necessities of life ⟨the town ~*s* on what mining activities remain —*Amer. Guide Series: Calif.*⟩ ⟨many adult persons can ~ . . . on less than half the amount of protein recommended —*Science*⟩ **4 a :** HOLD, OBTAIN; *specif* **:** to hold true or good ⟨relations ~ between terms⟩ **b :** to have existence as a concept rather than in fact; *specif* **:** to be conceivable as the subject of a true statement ⟨"the round square does not ~" is just as true as "the present King of France does not exist" —Bertrand Russell⟩ ~ *vt* **1** *obs* **:** to keep up or in existence **:** keep alive **2 :** to support with provisions **:** FEED, MAINTAIN ⟨~*ing* troops off the country⟩

²**subsist** \"\ *n* -S [short for *subsistence*] *Brit* **:** payment of wages on account

sub·sist·ence \-tən(t)s\ *n* -S *often attrib* [ME, fr. LL *subsistentia* (trans. of Gk *hypostasis*), fr. *subsistent-, subsistens* (pres. part. of *subsistere* to exist, be) + L *-ia*] **1 a** (1) **:** existence in reality **:** the condition of having substance or constituting an independent identifiable entity ⟨an abstraction without real ~⟩ (2) *obs* **:** condition or manner of existing (3) **:** HYPOSTASIS 2 (4) *archaic* **:** something that exists in reality **:** a material or substantial entity (5) **:** the condition of remaining in existence **:** PERSISTENCE (6) **:** INHERENCY ⟨~ of a quality in a body⟩ **b** *Scholasticism* (1) **:** the mode by which substance becomes individualized (2) **:** something in a reality by reason of which it is what it is (3) **:** a singular rational component of the human personality that is wholly self-contained and endowed with inalienable rights **c** (1) **:** the metaphysical status of something that subsists (sense 4b) (2) **:** the character possessed by whatever is logically conceivable **2 :** means of subsisting: as **a :** the irreducible minimum (as of food and shelter) necessary to support life ⟨a barren land providing no more than ~⟩ **b :** a mode of obtaining or a source of the necessities of life **:** LIVELIHOOD ⟨his small patrimony was enough for a ~⟩ ⟨won his ~ dealing in the castoffs of other people⟩ **c :** a source or supply of food ⟨their livestock was their sole ~⟩ **d** *or* **subsistence money** *or* **subsistence allowance** (1) **:** money given in advance (as to a soldier or workman) to meet the basic needs of life while awaiting a payday (2) **:** an allowance for expenses incurred in performance of a duty while temporarily away from one's residence (3) **:** a cash allowance to a member of a military organization given in lieu of food **3 :** the providing of the necessities to animal life **:** the furnishing of support ⟨farming is no easy means of ~⟩ **syn** see LIVING

subsistence economy *n* **:** an economy which is not based on money, in which buying and selling are absent or rudimentary though barter may occur, and which commonly provides a minimal standard of living — compare SUBSISTENCE FARMING

subsistence farming *or* **subsistence agriculture** *n* **1 :** farming or a system of farming designed to provide all or essentially all the goods required by the farm family usu. without any significant surplus for sale ⟨primitive farming is normally *subsistence farming*⟩ — compare GENERAL FARMER, MIXED FARMING, MONOCULTURE **2 :** farming or a system of farming that produces a minimum and often inadequate return to the farm operator **:** economically marginal farming — compare SHARECROPPER

subsistence homestead *n* **:** a piece of realty comprising a dwelling unit and sufficient land for the raising of supplementary food for a family not primarily dependent on the land for livelihood

subsistence stores *n pl* **:** military stores consisting principally of articles of the ration but including also other items (as candy, toilet articles) needed by the individual

subsistence theory *n* **:** a theory in economics: wages tend toward the lowest level that will provide subsistence — compare IRON LAW OF WAGES, WAGE-FUND THEORY

sub·sist·en·cy \-nsē\ *n* -ES [LL *subsistentia*] *archaic* **:** SUBSISTENCE

¹**sub·sist·ent** \səb'sistənt\ *adj* [LL *subsistent-, subsistens*, pres. part. of *subsistere* to stay alive, exist, be — more at SUBSIST] **1 :** having being **:** SUBSISTING ⟨a ~ spirit⟩ **2 :** INHERENT ⟨qualities ~ in matter⟩

²**subsistent** \"\ *n* -S **1 :** something (as an object or substance) having existence **2 :** an abstract entity

sub·sis·ten·tial \(¦)səb,si¦stenchəl\ *adj* [LL *subsistentia* existence, substance, reality + E *-al*] **:** of or relating to subsistence and esp. to the hypostases in the Trinity or to one of them

sub·sist·ing·ly *adv* **:** so as to subsist **:** in a subsisting manner

sub·sizar \¦səb+\ *n* [*sub-* + *sizar*] **:** a subsidized student (as at Cambridge University) ranking below a sizar in achievement and amount of stipend

sub·size \'səb+¦-\ *adj* [*sub-* + *size*] **:** of less than usual, standard, or normal size

sub·social \¦səb+\ *adj* [*sub-* + *social*] **:** incompletely social **:** tending to associate gregariously but lacking fixed or complex social organization ⟨~ insects⟩

sub–society \"+\ *n* **:** a social subgroup or subculture

¹**sub·soil** \'səb+,-\ *n* [*sub-* + *soil*] **:** the stratum of weathered material that underlies the surface soil

²**subsoil** \"\ *vt* **:** to turn, break, or stir the subsoil of

sub·soil·er \-ə(r)\ *n* -S **:** one that subsoils land: as **a** (1) **:** SUBSOIL PLOW (2) **:** an attachment to a lister that prepares a seedbed in the bottom of the furrow (3) **:** an attachment to a plow frame for breaking up the plow sole **b :** the operator of a subsoiler

subsoil plow *n* **:** a plow without a moldboard that is used for stirring without turning over the deeper soil usu. beneath previously plowed furrows

sub·solar \¦səb+\ *adj* [*sub-* + *solar*] **:** situated under the sun **:** having the sun in the zenith; *specif* **:** situated between the tropics

subsolar point *n* **:** the point on the earth's surface at which the sun is in the zenith — compare CIRCLE OF POSITION

sub·sonic \¦səb+\ *adj* [ISV *sub-* + *sonic*] **1 :** of, relating to, or being a speed less than that of sound in air — compare SONIC, TRANSONIC **2 :** moving, capable of moving, or utilizing air currents moving at a subsonic speed **3 :** INFRASONIC 1

subsonic flow *n* **:** directed motion of a fluid medium in which the velocity is less than that of sound in the medium throughout the region under consideration

sub·space \'səb+,-\ *n* [*sub-* + *space*] **:** a space each of whose points is contained in a given space but which does not itself contain all the points of the given space

sub·specialty \¦səb+\ *n* [*sub-* + *specialty*] **:** a subordinate field of specialization (as in medicine) ⟨proctology was formerly considered a ~ of surgery⟩

sub·speciation \"+\ *n* -S [NL *subspecies* + E *-ation*] **:** formation of or division into subspecies **:** RACIATION

sub spe·cie ae·ter·ni·ta·tis \,səb¦spekē,ā,ī,ternə'täd·əs\ *adv* [NL, lit., under the aspect of eternity] **:** in its essential or universal form or nature

sub·species \¦səb +\ *n* [NL, fr. L *sub-* + *species*] **:** a subdivision of a species: as **a :** a taxonomic category that is the lowest generally used taxon, ranks immediately below a species, and designates a morphologically distinguishable group whose members are at least partially isolated geographically but interbreed successfully with members of other subspecies of the same species where their ranges adjoin and overlap **b :** a named subdivision (as a race or variety) of a taxonomic species — not used technically **syn** see VARIETY

sub·specific \"+\ *adj* [*sub-* + *specific*] **1 :** of, relating to, or constituting a subspecies ⟨~ rank⟩ ⟨a ~ distinguishing character⟩ **2 :** of less than specific rank or significance ⟨a ~ race⟩ — **sub·specifically** \"+\ *adv*

sub·spherical \"+\ *adj* [*sub-* + *spherical*] **:** imperfectly spherical **:** nearly but not quite spherical **:** SPHEROIDAL — **sub·spherically** \"+\ *adv*

sub·spiniform \"+\ *n* [*sub-* + *spiniform*] **:** a part or process (as on an insect) that suggests a spine

sub·spinous \"+\ *adj* [*sub-* + *spinous*] **1 :** somewhat spinous **2 a :** situated beneath the spinal column **b :** INFRASPINOUS

sub·spontaneous \"+\ *adj* [*sub-* + *spontaneous*] **:** occurring only indirectly under the influence of man ⟨many plants make a ~ establishment in new areas when grazing alters the previous flora⟩

subst *abbr* **1** substantive **2** substitute

sub·stage \'səb+,-\ *n* [*sub-* + *stage*] **1 :** a subdivision of a stage and esp. of a geological stage **2 :** an attachment to a microscope by means of which accessories (as mirrors, diaphragms, condensers or Nicol prisms) are held in place beneath the stage of the instrument

sub·stalagmite \¦səb+\ *n* [*sub-* + *stalagmite*] **:** a compact noncrystalline deposit of calcium carbonate — **sub·stalagmitic** \"+\ *adj*

sub·stance \'səbztən(t)s, -bst-\ *n* -S [ME, fr. OF, fr. L *substantia*, fr. *substant-, substans* (pres. part. of *substare* to stand under, stand firm, fr. *sub-* + *stare* to stand) + *-ia* — more at STAND] **1 a :** essential nature **:** ESSENCE — used esp. of the divine nature and then distinguished from *hypostasis* ⟨being of one ~ with the Father —*Nicene Creed*⟩ **b :** a fundamental part, quality, or aspect **:** essential quality or import **:** the characteristic and essential part ⟨the ~ of his address⟩ ⟨distinguish a question of ~ from one which is merely procedural —*Va. Law Rev.*⟩ ⟨considering the plan in its ~ as well as its practical advantages⟩ **c** *Christian Science* **:** ²GOD b(6) **2** [trans. of Gk *ousia*] **:** something that underlies all outward manifestations whether unique (as in monism), one of two (as in dualism), or one of a large or infinite number (as in pluralism) **:** ultimate reality whether material or spiritual **:** the abiding part of existence or an existing thing as distinguished from what is accidental to it **:** the real essence or nature of a thing: as **a** *Aristotelianism & Scholasticism* (1) **:** the primary category presupposed by all the others **:** something that is the real subject of predication and cannot itself be predicated of anything **:** SUBJECT ⟨~ . . . is that which is neither predicable of a subject nor present in a subject; for instance, the individual man or horse —E.M.Edghill⟩ (2) **:** the essence of an existing thing **:** something that makes a thing what it is or gives it its essential nature (3) **:** something that supports attributes or modes or exists as the material of individuation **:** SUBSTRATUM (4) **:** an individual being considered as an existent entity **:** a subsistent entity compounded of matter and form (5) **:** GENUS 2 (6) **:** UNIVERSAL 2a (3) — compare NOMINALISM, REALISM 2 **b** *Cartesianism* (1) **:** something that depends on no other thing for its existence (2) **:** something that depends only on God for its existence **c** *Spinozism* **:** the universal underlying principle that exists and can be conceived independently of any other thing — compare MODE 6 **d** *Leibnizianism* **:** MONAD 1c **e :** an unknowable imperceivable entity that is the bearer of qualities ⟨if any-one will examine himself concerning his notion of pure ~ . . . he will find he has no other idea of it at all, but only a supposition of he knows not what support of such qualities which are capable of producing simple ideas —John Locke⟩; *also* **:** a complex of qualities together with its unknowable bearer **f** *Humean philos* **:** a collection of qualities regarded as constituting a unity ⟨the idea of a ~ . . . is nothing but a collection of simple ideas, that are united by the imagination, and have a particular name assigned them, by which we are able to recall . . . that collection —David Hume †1776⟩ **g** *Kantianism* **:** a permanent subsisting imperishable substratum necessary for the existence and perception of change in time **:** that which must be posited in order to assume the duration of a thing rather than a succession of phenomena ⟨we can only give to a phenomenon the name of ~ because we admit its existence at all times —Friedrich Max Müller⟩ **3** *archaic* **:** an underlying assurance **:** BASIS, GROUND **4 a :** material from which something is made and to which it owes its characteristic qualities ⟨the special ~*s* of nerve tissue⟩ ⟨a fabric of unknown ~⟩ **b** (1) **:** a distinguishable kind of physical matter (2) **:** a piece or mass of such substance ⟨struck by some hard ~⟩ ⟨an oily ~⟩ ⟨cork is a ~ with distinctive properties⟩ **c :** matter of definite or known chemical composition **:** an identifiable chemical element, compound, or mixture — sometimes restricted to compounds and elements ⟨water is a liquid derived from two gaseous ~*s*⟩ **5 :** material possessions **:** ESTATE, PROPERTY, RESOURCES ⟨a man of ~⟩ **6 a** *obs* **:** the whole amount or tally of something **:** QUANTITY **b :** the greater part **:** MAJORITY ⟨dissipated the ~ of his fortune in a few short years⟩ **c** *or* **substance number :** BASIS WEIGHT **7 :** a material object as distinguished from something shadowy or visionary; *also* **:** SOLIDITY, SUBSTANTIALITY ⟨an old building but of marked ~⟩ — **in substance** *adv* **:** in respect to essentials **:** SUBSTANTIALLY, FUNDAMENTALLY ⟨accurate *in substance*⟩

sub·stance·less \-ləs\ *adj* **:** lacking in substance **:** deficient in matter, content, or worth ⟨a ~ charge⟩

substance of schwann *usu cap 2d S* \-'shw|än, -'shf|, -'shv|\ [after Theodor *Schwann* †1882 Ger. anatomist] **:** MEDULLARY SHEATH

¹**sub·standard** \¦səb + \ *adj* [*sub-* + *standard*] **:** deviating from or failing to attain to or qualify under some standard or norm: as **a** (1) **:** of a quality lower than that specified as acceptable under a standard prescribed by law ⟨~ canned goods⟩ (2) *of housing* **:** deficient in amenities (as sanitary accommodations,

living space, safety facilities, or maintenance) in respect to a standard set by legal or other authoritative sources **b :** conforming to a pattern of linguistic usage existing within a speech community but not that of the prestige group in that community in choice of word (as *set*, for *sit*), form of word (as *brung*, for *brought*), pronunciation (as *twicet*, for *twice*), grammatical construction (as the boys *is* growing fast), or idiom (as *all to once*, for *all at once*) — compare NONSTANDARD **c :** constituting a greater than normal chance of loss to an insurer due to some inherent and determinable cause (as poor health or unusual fire hazard) ⟨a ~ life⟩ ⟨a ~ risk⟩; *also* **:** covering a substandard risk usu. in return for an extra premium ⟨~ insurance⟩ **d** *of motion-picture film* **:** narrower than 35 millimeters

²substandard \"\ *n* [in sense 1, fr. *sub-* + *standard*, n.; in sense 2, fr. ¹*substandard*] **1 :** a secondary standard used in measurement and esp. to check the accuracy of commercial measuring devices (as scales) **2 :** something (as a way of living) that is substandard

sub·stan·tia \səbz'tanch(ē)ə, -b'st-\ *n, pl* **substanti·ae** \-chē,ē\ [NL, fr. L, substance] **:** anatomical material, substance, or tissue

sub·stan·tia·ble \-ch(ē)əbəl\ *adj* [*substantiate* + *-able*] **:** capable of being substantiated

¹sub·stan·tial \səbz'tanchəl, -b'st-, -taan-\ *adj* [ME *substancial*, fr. LL *substantialis*, fr. L *substantia* substance + *-alis* -al — more at SUBSTANCE] **1 a :** consisting of, relating to, sharing the nature of, or constituting substance **:** existing as or in substance **:** MATERIAL ⟨~ life⟩ ⟨the ~ realities⟩ ⟨most ponderous and ~ things —Shak.⟩ **b :** not seeming or imaginary **:** not illusive **:** REAL, TRUE ⟨the ~ world⟩ ⟨a mere dream neither ~ nor practical⟩ **c :** being of moment **:** IMPORTANT, ESSENTIAL **2 a :** adequately or generously nourishing **:** ABUNDANT, PLENTIFUL ⟨set a ~ table⟩ ⟨after that too ~ dinner⟩ **b :** possessed of goods or an estate **:** moderately wealthy **:** WELL-TO-DO ⟨a ~ man⟩; *often* **:** having a good and well-maintained income-producing property ⟨a ~ farmer⟩ ⟨the more ~ tradesmen⟩ **c :** considerable in amount, value, or worth ⟨made a ~ gain on the transaction⟩ **3 a :** having good substance **:** firmly or stoutly constructed **:** STURDY, SOLID, FIRM ⟨a ~ house⟩ ⟨~ cloth⟩ **b :** having a solid or firm foundation **:** soundly based **:** carrying weight ⟨a ~ argument⟩ ⟨~ evidence⟩ **4 a :** being that specified to a large degree or in the main ⟨a ~ victory⟩ ⟨a ~ lie⟩ **b :** of or relating to the main part of something **syn** see MASSIVE

²substantial \"\ *n* -s [ME *substancial*, fr. *substancial*, adj.] **:** something that is substantial: as **a :** something having substance or actual existence **b :** something having good substance or actual value **c :** something of moment **:** an important or material matter, thing, or part

substantial damages *n pl* **:** damages which bring about actual economic loss or for which compensation in a substantial amount are awarded as distinguished from nominal damages awarded only to vindicate a legal right

substantial form *n* [ME *forme substancial*, trans. of ML *forma substantialis*, trans. of Gk *ousiōdes eidos*] **:** the form or nature that according to the scholastics gives to an individual substance its specific or generic character

sub·stan·ti·a·lia \=,=chē'alēə\ *n pl* [NL, fr. neut. pl. of LL *substantialis* substantial] *Scots law* **:** the formally essential parts of a deed

sub·stan·tial·ism \=ˈ=chə,lizəm\ *n* -s **:** either of two doctrines in philosophy: **a :** one holding that constant realities or substances underlie phenomena **b :** one holding that matter is a real substance rather than an aggregation of centers of force

sub·stan·tial·ist \-ˌləst\ *n* -s **:** a proponent of a doctrine of substantialism

sub·stan·ti·al·i·ty \=,=chē'alədē, -lətē, -i\ *n* -ES [LL *substantialitas*, fr. *substantialis* substantial + L *-itas* -ity] **:** the quality or state of being substantial **:** CORPOREITY, MATERIALITY

sub·stan·tial·ize \=ˈ=chə,līz\ *vt* -ED/-ING/-S **:** to make substantial **:** give substance to

sub·stan·tial·ly \səbz'tanch(ə)lē, -b'st-, -taan-, -li\ *adv* [ME *substancially*, fr. *substancial* + *-ly*] **:** in a substantial manner **:** so as to be substantial

sub·stan·tial·ness \-chəlnəs\ *n* -ES **:** SUBSTANTIALITY

substantial right *n* **:** a legal right affecting or involving a matter of substance as distinguished from matters of form **:** a right materially affecting those interests which a man is entitled to have preserved and protected by law **:** a material right

substantia ni·gra \-'nīgrə, -'nig-\ *n, pl* **substantiae ni·grae** \-(ˌ)grē\ [NL, lit., black substance] **:** a layer of deeply pigmented gray matter in the midbrain separating the cerebral peduncles from the tegmentum above

substantia pro·pria \-'prōprēə\ *n, pl* **substantiae propri·ae** \-ē,ē\ [NL, lit., the tissue proper] **:** the layer of lamellated transparent fibrous connective tissue that makes up the bulk of the cornea of the eye

sub·stan·ti·ate \səbz'tanchē,āt, -b'st-, -taan- *sometimes* -n(t)sē-, *chiefly substand* -nchə,wāt; *usu* -ād.+V\ *vt* -ED/-ING/-S [NL *substantiatus*, past part. of *substantiare* to substantiate, fr. L *substantia* substance — more at SUBSTANCE] **1 :** to impart substance or material form or being to **2 a :** to put into concrete form **:** EMBODY **b :** to make solid or firm **3 :** to establish the existence or truth of by proof or competent evidence **:** VERIFY ⟨~ a charge⟩ **syn** see CONFIRM

sub·stan·ti·a·tion \=,=='āshən, *chiefly substand* =,=='wāshən\ *n* -s **1 :** an act of substantiating (as by proving) **2 :** something adduced as proof **:** EVIDENCE — **sub·stan·ti·a·tive** \=ˈ===,ād·iv, *chiefly substand* =ˈ==,wā-\ *adj*

sub·stan·ti·a·tor \=ˈ==,ād·ə(r), -,ātə-, *chiefly substand* -,wā-\ *n* -s **:** one that substantiates something

sub·stan·ti·fi·ca·tion \səbz,tantəfə'kāshən, -b,st-\ *n* -s [fr. *substantify*, after such pairs as E *magnify: magnification*] **:** an act or product of substantifying

sub·stan·ti·fy \=ˈ==,fī\ *vt* -ED/-ING/-ES [ML *substantificare*, fr. L *substantia* substance + *-ficare* -fy] **1 :** to give substance or substantive character to **2 :** SUBSTANTIVATE

sub·stan·tious \səbz'tandiəs, -b'st-\ *adj* [MF *substancious*, *substancieus*, fr. OF *substance* + *-ious*, *-ieus* -ious] *chiefly Scot* **:** HEAVY, POWERFUL, SUBSTANTIAL, EFFECTUAL

sub·stan·ti·val \ˌsəbztənˈtīvəl, -bst-\ *adj* **:** of, relating to, or having the nature or function of a substantive — **sub·stan·ti·val·ly** \-vəlē\ *adv*

sub·stan·ti·vate \'səbztəntə,vāt, -bst-; səbz'tantə,v-, -b'st-\ *vt* -ED/-ING/-S **:** to convert into or use as a substantive ⟨the tendency to ~ adjectives⟩ — **sub·stan·ti·va·tion** \,==tə'vāshən, =,=-\ *n* -s

¹sub·stan·tive \'səbztəntiv, -bst-\ *n* -s [ME *substantif*, fr. MF, fr. *substantif*, adj., having or expressing substance, fr. LL *substantivus* self-existent, substantive] **1 a :** a word or part of speech that names or identifies something **:** a noun or noun equivalent (as a pronoun, phrase, or absolute adjective) ⟨in "the good die young" *good* is a ~⟩ **b :** a categorematic term **2 :** an independent thing or person **:** a self-existent entity

²substantive \", *in senses other than 2c & 3 also* səbz'tantiv *or* -b'st- *or* -taan- *or* -ⁿtēv *or* -ntəv\ *adj* [ME, fr. LL *substantivus*, fr. L *substantia* substance + *-ivus* -ive — more at SUBSTANCE] **1 :** having the character of an independent self-subsistent entity or thing **:** existing in its own right **:** not derivative or dependent **:** SELF-CONTAINED **2 a** (1) **:** having the character or status of or referring to something that is real rather than apparent **:** FIRM, SOLID (2) **:** enduring or permanent as distinguished from transitory **b :** belonging to the essence or intrinsic nature of the substance as distinguished from something that is accidental or qualifying **:** ESSENTIAL **c :** betokening or expressing existence ⟨the ~ verb is the verb *to be*⟩ **d** (1) **:** of, relating to, or being a dye that requires no mordant or a dyeing process involving such a dye **:** DIRECT — opposed to *adjective* (2) **:** having a specific affinity for a fiber (as wool or cellulose) **3 a :** having the nature or function of a grammatical substantive ⟨a ~ phrase⟩ **b :** relating to or having the character of a noun or pronominal term in logic **:** CATEGOREMATIC — contrasted with *adjective* **4 :** considerable in amount or numbers **:** SUBSTANTIAL **5 :** definite rather than contingent in status ⟨a ~ appointment to an office⟩

substantive expression *n* **:** a word or combination of words that functions as a substantive

substantive genitive *n* **:** a genitive that includes in its denotation the meaning of a qualified noun to be understood with it ⟨in "I spent the night at my brother's" *brother's* is a *substantive genitive* carrying the implication "residence"⟩

substantive law *n* **:** a branch of law that prescribes the rights, duties, and obligations of persons to one another as to their conduct or property and that determines when a cause of action for damages or other relief has arisen — compare ADJECTIVE

sub·stan·tive·ly \-ntəvlē, -li\ *adv* **1 :** in a substantive manner **:** in substance **:** ESSENTIALLY **2 :** as a substantive ⟨the phrase is here used ~⟩

sub·stan·tive·ness \-ntivnəs, -ntēv-, -ntəv-\ *n* -ES **:** the quality or state of being substantive

substantive right *n* **:** a right (as of life, liberty, property, or reputation) held to exist for its own sake and to constitute part of the normal legal order of society — compare REMEDIAL RIGHT

sub·stan·tiv·i·ty \,səbztən'tivəd·ē, -bst-\ *n* -ES **1 :** SUBSTANTIALITY **2 :** the attraction between a substance (as dye) in solution and a fiber — compare AFFINITY 2b

sub·stan·tiviza·tion \,==(,)tivə'zāshən, səbz,tantəv-, -b,sta-, -,vī'z-\ *n* -s **:** an act or instance of substantivizing

sub·stan·tivize \'== ti,vīz, ='=tə,v-\ *or* **sub·stan·tize** \'==-,tīz\ *vt* -ED/-ING/-S [*substantivize* fr. ¹*substantive* + *-ize*; *substantize* fr. ¹*substantive* + *-ize*] **:** to convert into or use as a substantive ⟨an adjective can easily be *substantivized*⟩

sub·station \'səb+,-\ *n* [*sub-* + *station*] **:** a station subordinate or subsidiary to another station: as **a :** a station which is subsidiary to a central station and at which high-tension electricity from the central station is transformed to electricity lower in potential and converted if desired to continuous current or to alternating current of a different frequency **b :** a small post-office station (as a contract station in a drug store or a station set up at a convention for handling philatelic mail) **c :** a subordinate station that rebroadcasts messages from a primary station of a communication system

substellar point \ˌ'səb+. . .-\ *n* [*substellar* fr. *sub-* + *stellar*] **:** the point on the earth's surface at which a particular star is in the zenith

sub·sternal \"+\ *adj* [ISV *sub-* + *sternal*] **:** situated or perceived beneath the sternum ⟨~ pain⟩

substile *var of* SUBSTYLE

sub·stit·u·end \səbz'tichə,wend, -b'st-\ *n* -s [NL *substituendum*] **:** something that can be or is substituted in a logical relation

sub·stit·u·en·dum \(,)=,=='wendəm\ *n, pl* **substituen·da** \-də\ [NL, fr. neut. of L *substituendus*, gerundive of *substituere* to substitute] **:** something that is to be substituted in a logical relation

¹sub·stit·u·ent \=ˈ==wənt\ *n* -s [L *substituent-*, *substituens*, pres. part. of *substituere* to substitute] **:** something that is or may be substituted; *usu* **:** an atom or group substituted for another or entering a molecule in place of some other part that is removed ⟨aniline derivatives containing an alkyl or halogen ~ —*Veterinary Bull.*⟩

²substituent \"\ *adj* **:** functioning as a substituent

sub·sti·tut·abil·i·ty \,səbztə,tüd·ə'biləd·ē, -bst-, -tə-,tyü-, -ütə-, -lətē, -i\ *n* **:** capacity for being substituted **:** the quality or state of being substitutable

sub·sti·tut·able \'==,==bəl\ *adj* **:** capable of being substituted or sometimes of substituting (as for one another)

¹sub·sti·tute \'səbztə,tüt, -bst-, -tə,tyüt, *rapid often* -bz,t(y)üt *or* -b,st(y)-; *usu* -üd +V\ *n* -s [ME, fr. L *substitutus*, past part. of *substituere* to put under, put in the place of, substitute, fr. *sub-* + *-stituere* (fr. *statuere* to set, place, stand up) — more at STATUTE] **1 :** a person who takes the place of or acts instead of another: as **a :** an heir instituted under Roman, civil, or Scots law to succeed to property in case another heir named cannot or will not accept the succession **:** a conditionally appointed heir named to take possession in case another heir loses his ownership through default of some condition (as under a will or settlement) **b :** a person who enlists for military service in the place of a conscript or drafted man **2 :** something that is put in place of something else or is available for use instead of something else ⟨honey is an excellent ~ for sugar in many recipes⟩: as **a :** something cheaper or inferior that is used instead of a standard article ⟨margarine is not a ~ but a distinctive article⟩ ⟨use of galvanized iron as a ~ for lead in flashing⟩ **b :** an artificial product used to replace a natural ⟨a valuable milk ~ prepared from soybeans⟩ **c :** a word or grammatical feature that replaces another word, a phrase, or a clause, in a context ⟨a pronoun serves as a ~⟩ **3 a :** any of several connections used for joining oil-well appliances that are of different sizes or that have different joint details — called also *sub* **b :** a special tool or part used in place of a regular tool **syn** see RESOURCE

²substitute \"\ *vb* -ED/-ING/-S [L *substitutus*, past part. of *substituere* to substitute] *vt* **1 a :** to put in the place of another **:** EXCHANGE ⟨~ a new technique for the old one⟩ **b :** to introduce (as an atom or group) by substitution ⟨~ sulfur for oxygen in a molecule⟩ **2** *obs* **:** to invest with delegated authority **:** designate as a delegate **3 :** to replace with another ⟨~ yesterday's steady opinions with the latest fancies⟩ ⟨names like *Jane* are always *substituted* by the pronoun *she* —R.A.Hall b. 1911⟩ **4 :** to nominate (a person) to take a remainder — compare SUBSTITUTION 1a(3) **~** *vi* **:** to function, serve, or act as a substitute

³substitute \"\ *adj* [L *substitutus*, past part. of *substituere*] **1 :** serving as or fitted for use as a substitute ⟨a ~ food⟩ **2 :** involving the use of substitutes ⟨~ feeding of infants⟩

substitute broker *n* **:** a person making a profession of securing military substitutes esp. during the American Civil War

substituted *adj* [fr. past part. of ²*substitute*] **:** put in the place of another: as **a :** appointed by a person to take the place of himself or another or of something else and esp. to act in his own stead or to act on the happening of a particular event in the stead of another **:** appointed by substitution ⟨a ~ executor⟩ ⟨a ~ legacy⟩ **b :** having been subjected to a substitution reaction or having some of its parts replaced ⟨alcohol is a ~ water⟩ ⟨methylamine is a ~ ammonia⟩

substituted service *n* **:** the service of a legal writ, process, or summons otherwise than by personal service (as by leaving it at a defendant's place of business or residence or with his agent, by mail, or by publication)

substitute fiber *n* **:** a living parenchyma cell with the form of a fiber, simple pits, and relatively thick walls that occurs esp. in sapwood

sub·sti·tut·er \-üd·ə(r), -ütə-\ *n* -s **:** one that substitutes

sub·sti·tut·ibil·i·ty *n* -ES [by alter.] **:** SUBSTITUTABILITY

sub·sti·tu·tion \,səbztə'tüshən, -bst-, -tə'tyü-\ *n* -s *often attrib* [ME *substitucion*, fr. MF *substitution*, fr. LL *substitution-*, *substitutio*, fr. L *substitutus* (past part. of *substituere* to substitute) + *-ion-*, *-io* -ion] **1 :** the substituting of one person or thing for another: as **a** *Roman law* (1) **:** the nomination of someone to be heir upon the failure of an heir previously named to take an inheritance — called also *common substitution*, *vulgar substitution* (2) **:** the similar nomination of a person to take as heir in place of or to succeed a descendant under puberty and in the potestas of the testator in case of the descendant's failure to take the inheritance or on his death before puberty or to succeed a descendant of any age who is a lunatic (3) **:** a designation by a testator that names one to whom property is to be handed over by the person named as heir or by his heir and that gives rise to a fideicommissum; *also* **:** a designation under civil law of a person to succeed to another as beneficiary of an estate used as a means of settling property and involving a fideicommissum **b :** the replacing of a quantity by its equal or of a variable by a value of it or of an algebraic expression or function by one that is equal in value **c** (1) **:** a chord that produces an unexpected or less likely resolution in place of a likelier resolution (2) **:** a change of fingers on a digital of a keyboard instrument **d :** a chemical reaction in which one or more atoms or groups in a molecule are replaced by equivalent atoms or groups to form at least two products; *esp* **:** the replacement of hydrogen in an organic compound by another element or group ⟨the ~ of one chlorine atom for one hydrogen atom of methane gives methyl chloride⟩ — often contrasted with *addition*; compare EXCHANGE 2e **e :** the replacing of a linguistic form by a substitute in a context **f** (1) **:** the replacing in Greek or Latin prosody of a foot required or expected at a given place in a given meter by another which is equivalent in temporal quantity (2) **:** the using in a metrical series in modern prosody of a foot other than the prevailing foot of the series or of a silence that replaces expected sound and occupies the time of a foot or syllable — compare INVERSION, IONIC DISPLACEMENT **g** (1) **:** the deceptive replacing of one material or product by another of less worth (2) **:** the natural economic tendency for the less costly of two or more operations or agencies to replace the more costly **h** (1) **:** the turning from an obstructed desire to another desire whose gratification is socially acceptable (2) **:** the turning from an obstructed form of behavior to a different and often more primitive expression of the same tendency ⟨a ~ neurosis⟩ (3) **:** the reacting to each of a set of stimuli by a response prescribed in a key ⟨a ~ test for speed of learning new responses⟩ **2 :** something that functions as a substitute or exists in a particular relation as a result of an act of substituting: as **a :** material substituted ⟨the ~ was found to be harmless⟩ **b :** a sound change consisting in the replacement or apparent replacement of one vowel or consonant by another **c :** an instance of linguistic substitution **d :** a cipher or method of ciphering that replaces message letters or polygraphs with substitutes

sub·sti·tu·tion·al \ˌ==(·)ˌt(y)üshənᵊl, -shnəl\ *adj* **:** of, relating to, or constituting substitution — **sub·sti·tu·tion·al·ly** \-ᵊlē, -əl|, |i\ *adv*

sub·sti·tu·tion·ary \-shə,nerē, -ri\ *adj* **:** of or relating to substitution; serving by way of a substitute **:** SUBSTITUTIONAL

substitution instance *n* **:** a statement in logic derived from a statement form by substitution of constants for variables

substitution rule *n* **:** a principle in logic specifying what expressions may be substituted for one another ⟨a *substitution rule* specifying that the definiendum may replace the definiens⟩

substitution tables *n pl* **:** tables of sentences in which equivalents may be substituted for their elements and which are used esp. in grammar drill

substitution vein *or* **substitution deposit** *n* **:** a metalliferous vein formed by the partial or complete substitution of the vein material for the original rock or mineral — called also *replacement vein*

sub·sti·tu·tive \'səbztə,tüd·|iv, -bst-, -tə-,tyü-, -üt|, |ēv *also* |əv\ *adj* [L *substitutus* (past part.) + E *-ive*] **:** tending to afford or furnish a substitute **:** suitable as a replacement **:** making or capable of substitution ⟨~ behavior⟩ — **sub·sti·tu·tive·ly** \|əvlē, -li\ *adv*

sub·story \ˌ'səb +\ *n* [*sub-* + *story*] **:** a lower story; *specif* **:** a layer of forest growth that does not reach to the canopy ⟨a ~ of shrubby growth and young replacement⟩

sub·stract \səbz'trakt, -b'st-\ *vb* -ED/-ING/-S [ML *substractus*, past part. of *substrahere* to draw from beneath, withdraw, alter. (influenced by L *subs-*, var. of *sub-*) of L *subtrahere* — more at SUBTRACT] **:** SUBTRACT ⟨so far from adding to, it will ~ from, the quantity of labor necessary —Jeremy Bentham⟩

sub·strac·tion \-kshən\ *n* -s [ML *substraction-*, *substractio*, fr. LL *substractus* (past part.) + L *-ion-*, *-io* -ion] **1 :** SUBTRACTION ⟨rendering back to us with additions or ~s, the beauty which existing things have of themselves presented to him —Thomas Carlyle⟩ **2 :** secret misappropriation of property and esp. from a decedent's estate **:** EMBEZZLEMENT

sub·stratal \ˌsəb +\ *adj* [*substratum* + *-al*] **:** of or relating to a substrate or substratum **:** BASIC, UNDERLYING

¹sub·strate \'səbz,trāt, -b,st-\ *n* -s [ML *substratum*] **1 :** SUBSTRATUM **2 a :** ¹BASE 2b(1), CARRIER 9b **b :** the base on which an organism lives ⟨the soil is the ~ of most seed plants while rocks, soil, water, tissues, or other media are ~s for various other organisms⟩ **3 a :** a substance acted upon (as by an enzyme) ⟨an enzyme-*substrate* complex⟩ **b :** a source of reactive material (as a nutritive medium) ⟨cultures developing on a nutrient agar ~⟩

²substrate \"\ *adj* **:** of, relating to, forming, or taking place in a substrate; *sometimes* **:** BASIC, FUNDAMENTAL

sub·stra·tist \ˌsəbzˌtrād·əst, -bˌst-\ *n* -s [*substratum* + *-ist*] **:** one that explains some feature of a language by reference to a substratum

sub·stra·tive \-ād·iv\ *adj* [*substratum* + *-ive*] **1 :** of, relating to, or constituting a substrate or substratum **2 :** UNDERLYING, FUNDAMENTAL

sub·stratose \ˌsəb+\ *adj* [*sub-* + *stratose*] **:** indistinctly or irregularly stratified

sub·stratosphere \"+\ *n* [ISV *sub-* + *stratosphere*] **:** the region of the atmosphere just below the stratosphere — **sub·stratospheric** \"+\ *adj*

sub·stratum \ˌsəb+\ *n, pl* **substrata** *also* **substratums** [ML, fr. neut. of L *substratus*, past part. of *substernere* to spread under, strew under, fr. *sub-* + *sternere* to strew — more at STREW] **:** something that is laid or spread under or that underlies and supports or forms a base for something else **:** an underlying structure, layer, or part **:** FOUNDATION: as **a** (1) **:** a permanent characterless support of properties of a thing or reality **:** substance as a support of attributes (2) **:** such a support regarded as a cause of a thing or its properties **b :** the material of which something is made and from which it derives its special qualities ⟨protoplasm is the material ~ of life⟩ **c :** a layer of rock or earth beneath the surface soil; *specif* **:** SUBSOIL **d :** SUBSTRATE 2, 3 **e :** a thin coating (as of hardened gelatin) on the support of a photographic film or plate to facilitate the adhesion of the sensitive emulsion **f :** a language that is extinct in a particular region but is believed by some linguists to have left traces of its structure in a current or more recently introduced language of that region as a result of imperfect learning of the introduced language by the native population

sub·striate \"+\ *adj* [*sub-* + *striate*] **:** marked indistinctly with striations

sub·struct \(ˌ)səbzˌtrəkt, -bˌst-\ *vt* -ED/-ING/-S [L *substructus*, past part. of *substruere* to build beneath, fr. *sub-* + *struere* to arrange, build — more at STRUCTURE] **:** to build or lay beneath

sub·struc·tion \-kshən\ *n* -s [L *substruction-*, *substructio*, fr. *substructus* (past part.) + *-ion-*, *-io* -ion] **:** the underlying or supporting part of a fabrication (as a building or dam) — **sub·struc·tion·al** \-kshənᵊl, -shnəl\ *adj*

sub·structural \ˌsəb +\ *adj* **:** of, relating to, or constituting a substructure

sub·structure \"+\ *n* [*sub-* + *structure*] **:** UNDERSTRUCTURE, GROUNDWORK: as **a :** the foundation of a building or other structure **b :** the earth roadway supporting the ballast and track of a railway line

sub·stylar \"+\ *adj* **:** of or relating to the substyle

sub·style *or* **sub·stile** \'səbz,tīl, -b,st-\ *n* [*sub-* + *style* or obs. E *stile* style, fr. ME — more at STYLE] **:** a straight line on which the gnomon of a dial is erected and which constitutes the common section of the face of the dial and a plane perpendicular to it passing through the gnomon

sub·sulfate \ˌsəb+\ *n* [*sub-* + *sulfate*] **:** a basic sulfate

sub·sul·tive \səb'səltiv\ *adj* [L *subsultus* (past part. of *subsilire* to leap up) + E *-ive*] **:** SUBSULTORY

sub·sul·to·ry \-tərē\ *adj* [L *subsultus* (past part. of *subsilire* to leap up, fr. *sub-* up + *-silire*, fr. *salire* to leap) + E *-ory* — more at SUB-, SALLY] **:** involving irregularity of movement or advance **:** BOUNDING, LEAPING

sub·sum·able \(ˌ)səb'süməbəl *sometimes* -b'zü-\ *adj* **:** capable of being subsumed

sub·sume \-m\ *vt* -ED/-ING/-S [*sub-* + L *sumere* to take up, take — more at RESUME] **1 :** to view, list, or rate as component in an overall or more comprehensive classification, summation, or synthesis **:** encompass as a part, example, or phase **:** classify as part of a larger schema or judge as a specific instance governed by a general principle ⟨Newtonian physics has not been overthrown so much as *subsumed* into a more embracing scheme —*Times Lit. Supp.*⟩ **2** *obs* **:** ASSUME, DEDUCE; *also* **:** to sum up **:** SUMMARIZE **syn** see INCLUDE

sub·summation *n* [irreg. (influence of *summation*) fr. *subsume* + *-ation*] **:** an act or product of subsuming

sub·summit \ˌsəb+\ *adj* [*sub-* + *summit*] **:** situated or occurring somewhat below an adjacent summit

sub·sump·tion \səb'səm(p)shən\ *n* -s [NL *subsumption-*, *subsumptio*, fr. *subsumptus* (past part. of *subsumere* to take under, subsume) + L *-ion-*, *-io* -ion] **1 :** the minor premise in the former syllogistic criminal procedure under Scots law containing an affirmation of the accused's guilt, a narrative of the material facts, or comparable matter **2 a :** something that is under the sumption of a presentation in formal logic **:** the minor premise of a syllogism **b :** something that is subsumed

⟨apprehension is a ~ under cognition⟩ **3 a :** the act or process of subsuming **:** a bringing under a major category **b :** the condition of something that is subsumed

sub·sump·tive \-(p)tiv\ *adj* **:** of, relating to, assuming the nature of, or containing a subsumption

sub·suretyship \ˌsəb+\ *n* [*sub-* + *suretyship*] **:** the relation between two or more sureties who are bound to answer for the same duty where one has the whole duty of performance with respect to the other

[1]**sub·surface** \"+\ *n* [*sub-* + *surface*] **1 :** soil situated just above the subsoil; *broadly* **:** rocks or other earth materials near but not exposed at the surface of the ground **2 :** the portion of a body of water that lies immediately below the surface

[2]**subsurface** \"\ *adj* **1 :** being, occurring, or used under a surface ⟨~ printing⟩ ⟨a ~ flow of water⟩ **2 :** of, relating to, or being something located or concealed beneath a surface (as of the ground) ⟨~ riches⟩

subsurface tillage *n* **:** a method of stirring the soil with underground blades that leave stubble or other vegetation on or near the surface — called also *subtillage*; compare TRASH FARMING

subsurface tiller *n* **:** an implement designed to loosen soil below the soil surface

sub·system \ˈsəb +\ *n* [*sub-* + *system*] **:** a secondary or subordinate system — **sub·systemic** \"+\ *adj*

sub·tack \ˈsəb+ˌ-\ *n* [*sub-* + *tack*] **:** a sublease under Scots law

sub·tangent \ˈsəb+\ *n* [*sub-* + *tangent*] **:** the projection on the x-axis of the portion of the tangent to a curve between the x-axis and the point of tangency

sub·tartarean \"+\ *adj* [*sub-* + *tartarean*] **:** being or living under Tartarus

sub·tectal \"+\ *adj* [*sub-* + L *tectum* roof (akin to L *tegere* to cover) + E *-al* — more at THATCH] **:** of, relating to, or being the alisphenoid bone in the skull of a fish

sub·teen \ˈ=ˌ=\ *n* [*sub-* + *teen*] **:** a child approaching adolescence; *esp* **:** a girl under 13 years of age for whom clothing in the size range 8–14 is designed

sub·temperate \ˈsəb+\ *adj* [*sub-* + *temperate*] **1 :** slightly temperate **:** somewhat less than typically temperate ⟨a ~ climate⟩ **2 :** of or relating to the colder parts of the temperate zones

sub·tenancy \"+\ *n* **:** the quality or state of being a subtenant

sub·tenant \"+\ *n* [*sub-* + *tenant*] **:** one who rents something (as a tenement or land) of one who is himself a tenant in respect to the property in question

sub·tend \səbˈtend, ˌsəbˈt-\ *vt* -ED/-ING/-S [L *subtendere* to stretch beneath, fr. *sub-* + *tendere* to stretch — more at THIN] **1 a :** to lie opposite to ⟨a hypotenuse ~*s* a right angle⟩ ⟨an arc ~*s* an angle at the center of a circle⟩ **b :** to mark off **:** DELIMIT ⟨a coral atoll, circular in form, ~*ed* a shallow lagoon —J.A.Michener⟩ **2 a :** to underlie so as to include ⟨lesser loyalties which this supreme loyalty ~*s* —C.C.Morrison⟩ **b :** to occupy an adjacent and usu. lower position to and often so as to embrace or enclose ⟨a bract ~*ing* a flower⟩

subtense \-n(t)s\ *adj* [L *subtensus*, past part. of *subtendere* to stretch beneath] **:** of, relating to, or constituting an object (as a pole or rod of known length) used to ascertain a distance without actual measurement by observing the subtended angle from a given point ⟨~ method⟩ ⟨~ transit⟩

sub·tentorial \ˈsəb+\ *adj* [*sub-* + *tentorial*] **:** situated or occurring under the tentorium ⟨a ~ tumor⟩

sub·tenure \"+\ *n* [*sub-* + *tenure*] **:** the tenure of a subtenant

sub·terete \"+\ *adj* [*sub-* + *terete*] **:** not precisely cylindrical **:** nearly terete

sub·ter·fuge \ˈsəbtə(r)ˌfyüj\ *n* -S [LL *subterfugium*, fr. L *subterfugere* to run away secretly, fr. *subter-* (fr. *subter*, adv. & prep., secretly, under) + *fugere* to run away; akin to L *sub*, prep., under, below, up — more at UP, FUGITIVE] **1 a :** deception by artifice or stratagem to conceal, escape, avoid, or evade ⟨employing ~ to get her own way⟩ **b :** a deceptive device or stratagem ⟨malingering or some other ~ is resorted to in order to save face —H.G.Armstrong⟩ **2** *obs* **:** a place of retreat or concealment **:** REFUGE **syn** see DECEPTION

sub·terminal \ˈsəb+\ *adj* [*sub-* + *terminal*] **:** situated or occurring near but not precisely at an end ⟨a ~ collapse⟩ ⟨a ~ band of color on the tail feathers⟩

[1]**sub·ter·rane** \ˌsəbtəˈrān\ *adj* [L *subterraneus*] **:** SUBTERRANEAN

[2]**subterrane** \"\ *or* **subterrain** \"\ *n* -S [L *subterraneum* subterranean place, fr. neut. of *subterraneus* subterranean] **1 :** the bedrock or the rocks beneath a particular geological formation **2 :** SUBTERRANEAN

[1]**sub·ter·ra·nean** \-nēən, -nyən\ *or* **sub·ter·ra·ne·ous** \-nēəs\ *adj* [*subterranean* fr. L *subterraneus* underground subterranean + E *-an*; *subterraneous* fr. L *subterraneus*, fr. *sub-* + *-terraneus* (fr. *terra* ground, earth + *-aneus*, fr. *-anus* -an) — more at TERRACE] **1 :** being or lying under the surface of the earth **:** situated in the earth or underground ⟨~ springs⟩ — opposed to *surficial* **2 a :** functioning, operating, or suitable for operating beneath the surface of the earth **b :** existing, functioning, or working in secret **:** HIDDEN — **sub·ter·ra·nean·ly** *adv*

[2]**subterranean** \"\ *n* -S [L *subterraneus* + E *-an* (n. suffix)] **1 :** one who lives, develops, or works underground **2 :** an underground cave or room **:** CAVERN

subterranean caterpillar *n* **:** any of various large grayish black caterpillars that are larvae of moths of the genus *Oxycanus*, live in burrows in the ground, and emerge at night to feed on the foliage of grass and other pasture plants — see PORINA

subterranean clover *n* **:** a low-growing spreading and branching annual clover (*Trifolium subterraneum*) prob. native to the Mediterranean region, valued for pasturage esp. in Australia and in parts of No. America, and burying the ripening seed heads in the soil like the peanut

sub·ter·rene \ˌsəbtəˈrēn\ *adj or n* [L *subterrenus*, fr. *sub-* + *terrenus* of earth, earthly, fr. *terra* earth] **:** SUBTERRANEAN

[1]**sub·terrestrial** \ˈsəb +\ *adj* [*sub-* + *terrestrial*] **:** SUBTERRANEAN

[2]**subterrestrial** \"\ *n* **:** one (as an animal) that lives underground

sub·tertian malaria \"+. . .-\ *n* [*subtertian* fr. *sub-* + *tertian*] **:** FALCIPARUM MALARIA

sub·tetanic \ˈsəb+\ *adj* [*sub-* + *tetanic*] **:** of less than tetanic force **:** approaching tetany or tetanus and esp. in form or degree of contraction ⟨a ~ convulsion⟩

sub·thalamic \"+\ *adj* [*sub-* + *thalamic*] **1 :** situated below the thalamus **2** [NL *subthalamus* + E *-ic*] **:** of or relating to the subthalamus ⟨a ~ nucleus⟩

sub·thalamus \"+\ *n* [NL, fr. *sub-* + *thalamus*] **:** the ventral part of the thalamus

sub·thoracic \"+\ *adj* [ISV *sub-* + *thoracic*] *of the ventral fins of some fishes* **:** situated not quite far enough forward to be thoracic

sub·threshold \"+\ *adj* [*sub-* + *threshold*] **:** inadequate to produce a response ⟨~ dosage with a drug⟩ ⟨a ~ stimulus⟩

sub·ti·a·ba \ˌsübtēˈäbə\ *n, pl* **subtiaba** *or* **subtiabas** *usu cap* **1 a :** an Indian people of western Nicaragua **b :** a member of such people **2 :** a Supanecan language of the Subtiaba people

sub·tile \ˈsəd·ᵊl, -ə(b)tᵊl,-əbtəl\ *adj, sometimes* **subtiler** \-əd·ᵊlə(r), -ət(ᵊ)lə-, -btᵊlə-, -btələ-\ *sometimes* **subtilest** \-əd·ᵊləst, -ət(ᵊ)lə-, -əbtᵊlə-, -əbtələ-\ [ME *subtile*, *subtil*, fr. MF *subtil*, alter. (influenced by L *subtilis* fine, thin, subtle) of OF *soutil*, *sotil* subtle — more at SUBTLE] **1 :** SUBTLE: as **a :** of a delicate or tenuous nature **:** ELUSIVE ⟨a ~ aroma⟩ ⟨the ~ threads of life —D.L.Sharp⟩ **b :** marked by craft or cunning **:** ARTFUL, WILY ⟨fishing . . . is made the ~ excuse for getting away again for a day among the plants —*Amer. Botanist*⟩ **2 a :** keenly perceptive ⟨a ~ sense⟩ **b :** keenly felt or perceived ⟨a ~ joy⟩ — **sub·tile·ly** \-əd·ᵊl(l)ē, -ət(ᵊ)l(l)ē, -əbtᵊl(l)ē, -əbtəl(l)ē, \|i\ *adv*

sub·ti·lin \ˈsəbtələn\ *n* -S [*subtil-* (fr. NL *subtilis*, — specific epithet of *Bacillus subtilis* — fr. L, thin, fine, minute) + *-in*] **:** a polypeptide antibiotic or mixture of antibiotics that is similar to bacitracin and is produced by a soil bacterium (*Bacillus subtilis*)

sub·til·ist \ˈsəd·ᵊləst, ˈsə(b)tᵊl-, ˈsəbtəl-\ *n* -S [*subtile* + *-ist*] **:** one given to subtlety

sub·til·i·ty \ˌsəbˈtiləd·ē, -lətē, -i\ *n* -ES [ME *subtilite*, fr. MF *subtilité*, alter. (influenced by L *subtilis*) of *sutilté*, *soutilleté* — more at SUBTLETY] **1 :** SUBTLETY **2 :** something that is subtile or subtle

sub·til·iza·tion \ˌsəd·ᵊləˈzāshən, ˌsə(b)tᵊl-, ˌsəbtəl-, -ᵊlˌīˈz-, -əˌlīˈz-\ *n* -S **:** an act or instance of the practice of subtilizing **:** SUBTLETY

sub·til·ize \ˈsəd·ᵊlˌīz, ˈsə(b)tᵊlˌīz, ˈsəbtəˌlīz\ *vb* -ED/-ING/-S *see -ize in Explan Notes* [ML *subtilizare*, fr. L *subtilis* fine, thin, subtle + LL *-izare* -ize] *vt* **:** to make subtile: as **a :** RAREFY, REFINE, SUBLIMATE, EXALT **b :** to clarify and sharpen (as the mind or senses) **:** make keen **c :** to treat with subtlety **:** introduce fine-drawn or nice distinctions into the use, discussion, or interpretation of ⟨~ words⟩ ⟨*subtilized* his activities⟩ **~** *vi* **:** to use subtlety **:** analyze, argue, or deal with materials in a subtle fashion ⟨*subtilized* more than other poets⟩

sub·til·iz·er \-zə(r)\ *n* -S **:** one that subtilizes

sub·till \ˈsəbˌtil\ *vb* [*sub-* + *till*] *vt* **:** to practice subsurface tillage on **~** *vi* **:** to practice subsurface tillage

sub·till·age \-lij\ *n* [*sub-* + *tillage*] **:** SUBSURFACE TILLAGE

sub·til·ty *like* SUBTLETY\ *n* -ES [ME *subtiltee*, alter. (influenced by L *subtilis*) of *sutilte* subtlety — more at SUBTLETY] **:** subtlety or an instance of it

[1]**sub·title** \ˈsəb+ˌ-\ *n* [*sub-* + *title*] **1 a :** a secondary title ⟨in *Uncle Tom's Cabin, or Life Among the Lowly* the ~ is *Life Among the Lowly*⟩ — called also *alternative title* **b :** an explanatory title ⟨in *The Behavior of Organisms: an Experimental Analysis* the ~ is *an Experimental Analysis*⟩ **2 a :** a printed translation of foreign language dialogue appearing near the bottom of the screen of a motion picture **b :** a printed statement or fragment of dialogue appearing between the scenes of a silent motion picture and usu. clarifying an immediately following scene

[2]**subtitle** \"\ *vt* **:** to give a subtitle to

sub·titular \ˈsəb+\ *adj* [fr. *subtitle*, after E *title: titular*] **:** of, relating to, or being a subtitle

sub·tle \ˈsəd·ᵊl, ˈsətᵊl\ *adj* **subtler** \-d·ᵊlə(r), -t(ᵊ)lə-\ **subtlest** \-d·ᵊləst, -t(ᵊ)lə-\ [ME *sutil*, *sotil*, fr. OF *soutil*, *sotil*, fr. L *subtilis* finely woven, fine, thin, refined, keen, subtle, fr. *sub-* + *-tilis* (fr. *tela* web); akin to L *texere* to weave — more at TECHNICAL] **1 a :** DELICATE, ELUSIVE ⟨~ aroma of sandalwood⟩ ⟨~ lights and shadows⟩ ⟨fawn fled with shy and ~ steps —Elinor Wylie⟩ **b :** difficult to understand **:** OBSCURE ⟨found the . . . situation ~, not to say opaque —Ruth McKenney⟩ **c :** hard to distinguish or describe **:** IMPERCEPTIBLE, INTANGIBLE ⟨~ distinctions among consonants⟩ ⟨intuitions . . . too ~ to be formulated —B.N.Cardozo⟩ ⟨~ hints of impending disaster —Leland Miles⟩ **2 a :** PERCEPTIVE, REFINED ⟨a great artist's ~ vision —Herbert Read⟩ ⟨China's complex and ~ language —*Time*⟩ **b :** marked by insight or sensitivity ⟨~ music⟩ ⟨a ~ characterization⟩ ⟨~ proportions of the Parthenon⟩ **3 a** (1) **:** SKILLFUL, INGENIOUS ⟨a clever and ~ diplomat —Charlton Laird⟩ (2) **:** demanding skill or ingenuity ⟨as ~ as the delicate incision of a great surgeon —Ezra Pound⟩ **b :** characterized by craft or indirection **:** DEVIOUS, WILY ⟨a ~ scheme⟩ ⟨~ diplomacy and wary tactics —Arnold Bennett⟩ **c :** having a covert and usu. injurious effect **:** INSIDIOUS ⟨a ~ insinuation⟩ ⟨a ~ technique of infiltration —C.E.Black & E.C. Helmreich⟩ — **subtleness** \-d·ᵊlnəs, -tᵊl-\ *n* -ES

sub·tle·ty \ˈsəd·ᵊltē, ˈsətᵊl-, -ᵊlti\ *n* -ES [ME *sutilte*, *sotilte*, fr. OF *sutilté*, *soutilleté*, *sutilitet*, fr. L *subtilitat-*, *subtilitas*, fr. *subtilis* fine, subtle + *-itat-*, *-itas* -ity] **1 :** the quality or state of being subtle: as **a :** the quality of being tenuous, intangible, indefinable, abstruse, or remote **b :** mental acuteness or penetrativeness **:** the power or practice of drawing delicate distinctions; *also* **:** the quality in a mental operation or its product that results from such power **2 :** something that emanates from a subtle person or mind: as **a :** a fine-drawn or delicate distinction **:** a refinement of analysis, perception, or comprehension ⟨avoid *subtleties* in a popular discussion⟩ **b :** an ingenious contrivance; *esp* **:** a decorative and sometimes edible confection made in an ornamental design **c :** an instance of craft or guile ⟨the *subtleties* of a twisted mind⟩ **3 :** something that is subtle and esp. tenuous, impalpable, or difficult to perceive or trace

sub·tly *also* **sub·tle·ly** \ˈsəd·ᵊl|ē, ˈsət(ᵊ)l|, |i\ *adv* [ME *sutelly*, *sotily*, *sotilich*, fr. *sutil*, *sotil* subtle + *-ly*, *-lich* -ly] **:** in a subtle manner **:** with subtlety **:** so as to be subtle

[1]**subtone** \ˈsəb+ˌ-\ *n* [*sub-* + *tone*] **:** UNDERTONE

[2]**subtone** \"\ *adj* **:** relating to or constituting clarinet playing esp. of popular music in which the tones are played very softly and usu. in the lower register with little wind pressure from the player

sub·tonic \ˈsəb+\ *n* [*sub-* + *tonic*] **:** the seventh degree of the musical scale

sub·torrid \"+\ *adj* [*sub-* + *torrid*] **:** SUBTROPICAL

[1]**sub·total** \"+\ *adj* [*sub-* + *total*] **:** somewhat less than complete **:** nearly total ⟨~ removal of the thyroid gland⟩

[2]**subtotal** \"\ *n* [*sub-* + *total* (n.)] **:** the sum of part of a series of figures

[3]**subtotal** \"\ *vt* **:** to determine a subtotal for ⟨~*ing* each column⟩ **~** *vi* **:** to determine subtotals

sub·tract \səbˈtrakt\ *vb* -ED/-ING/-S [L *subtractus*, past part. of *subtrahere* to draw from beneath, withdraw, fr. *sub-* + *trahere* to pull, draw — more at TRACE] *vt* **1** *archaic* **:** to withdraw or take away orig. by stealth **:** WITHHOLD; *also* **:** to take away (common land) by enclosing **2** *archaic* **:** to remove (as oneself) from some specified situation **:** take elsewhere **3 :** to take away (as a part, a quantity, or a number) by deducting — used with *from* or *out of* ⟨~ 5 from 9⟩; compare SUBTRACTION **c ~** *vi* **:** to perform a subtraction **:** calculate by subtraction

sub·tract·er \-ktə(r)\ *n* -S **:** one that subtracts

sub·trac·tion \-kshən\ *n* -S [ME *subtraccion*, fr. LL *subtraction-*, *subtractio*, fr. L *subtractus* (past part. of *subtrahere*) + *-ion-*, *-io* -ion] **:** an act, operation, or instance of subtracting: as **a :** the withdrawing or withholding from one a right (as customary services, fealty, rents, suit and service, conjugal rights, and tithes) to which he is entitled **b :** a process of logical abstraction whereby one class is excepted from another in which it is naturally included or a connotation is withdrawn from another connotation which includes it **c :** a mathematical process in which one number or quantity is deducted from another and which can be generalized by the formula $m-s=r$ in which the remainder r when added to the subtrahend s always reproduces the minuend m **:** the inverse of addition — **sub·trac·tion·al** \-kshənᵊl, -kshnəl\ *adj*

subtraction sign *or* **subtraction mark** *n* **:** a mathematical symbol used to indicate that a particular quantity is to be subtracted from another to which it is joined by the symbol **:** a symbolic representation of the relation of subtrahend and minuend — symbol —

sub·trac·tive \-ktiv, -ktēv *also* -ktəv\ *adj* **1 :** tending to subtract **:** constituting or involving subtraction ⟨a ~ error in spelling⟩ ⟨a ~ correction⟩ **2 :** formed by absorption of light passing through component colorants in turn — see SUBTRACTIVE PRIMARY **3 a :** being or relating to a process of reducing each of the densities of a photographic image by an approximately constant amount **b :** of or relating to the controlled mixing or superposition of several colored substances (as dyes or pigments) that selectively absorb and transmit or reflect light to form a colored positive photographic image ⟨a ~ process⟩ — compare ADDITIVE 5 — **sub·trac·tive·ly** \-ktəvlē, -li\ *adv*

subtractive primary *n* **:** one of a set of colorants comprising red, yellow, and blue or more exactly magenta, yellow, and cyan each of which is capable of absorbing from the spectrum of incident daylight some part that the others would reflect and which are therefore combinable to produce a maximum number of object colors — compare ADDITIVE PRIMARY

sub·tra·hend \ˈsəbtrəˌhend\ *n* -S [L *subtrahendum*, neut. of *subtrahendus*, gerundive of *subtrahere* to withdraw] **:** a quantity that is to be deducted from a minuend in the mathematical operation of subtraction

sub·translucent \ˈsəb+\ *adj* [*sub-* + *translucent*] **:** translucent only at the edges ⟨~ minerals⟩

sub·transparent \"+\ *adj* [*sub-* + *transparent*] **:** imperfectly or partially transparent **:** SEMITRANSPARENT

sub·treasurer \"+\ *n* [*sub-* + *treasurer*] **:** a subordinate treasurer; *specif* **:** an assistant treasurer of the U. S. formerly in charge of a subtreasury

sub·treasury \"+\ *n* [*sub-* + *treasury*] **:** a subordinate treasury or place of deposit; *specif* **:** any of nine former branch treasuries of the U. S.

sub·triangular \"+\ *adj* [NL *subtriangularis*, fr. L *sub-* + LL *triangularis* triangular — more at TRIANGULAR] **:** nearly but not quite triangular ⟨a ~ skull⟩

sub·tribe \ˈsəb+ˌ-\ *n* [*sub-* + *tribe*] **1 :** a subdivision of a tribe **2 :** a small or subordinate tribe

[1]**sub·tropical** *also* **sub·tropic** \"+\ *adj* [ISV *sub-* + *tropical* or *tropic*] **1 :** nearly tropical **:** of, relating to, or being the regions bordering on the tropical zone **2** *of a plant* **:** requiring climatic conditions typical of subtropical regions to survive ⟨even near the equator vegetation at 5000 feet is ~ rather than tropical⟩

[2]**subtropical** \"\ *n* **:** a plant requiring a subtropical environment to thrive

sub·tropics \ˈsəb+ˌ-\ *n pl* [*sub-* + *tropics*] **:** subtropical regions

sub·truncate \"+\ *adj* [*sub-* + *truncate*] **:** nearly but not quite truncate ⟨a ~ fin⟩

sub·tu·ber·ant \ˌsəbˈt(y)üb(ə)rənt\ *adj* [*sub-* + *-tuberant* (as in *protuberant*)] **:** of, relating to, or being a mountain supposedly formed by the lifting action of underlying intrusive igneous rock

sub·type \ˈsəb+ˌ-\ *n* [*sub-* + *type*] **:** a type that is subordinate to or included in another type ⟨the blood group ~*s*⟩

sub·typical \ˈsəb+\ *adj* [*sub-* + *typical*] **1 :** of or relating to a subtype **2 :** deviating somewhat from a type

subu·late \ˈsəbyəˌlāt, ˈsüb-, -lət\ *adj* [NL *subulatus*, fr. L *subula* awl + *-atus* -ate; akin to OHG *siula* awl, OSlav *šilo* awl, L *suere* to sew — more at SEW] **:** linear and tapering to a fine point ⟨a ~ leaf⟩

subu·li·corn \-ləˌkȯrn\ *adj* [ISV *subuli-* (fr. L *subula* awl) + *-corn*] **:** having or being subulate antennae

subu·lu·ra \ˌ==ˈlürə\ *n, cap* [NL, fr. L *subula* awl + NL *-ura*] **:** a genus of nematode worms (family Heterakidae) including a common parasite (*S. brumpti*) of the ceca of gallinaceous birds

sub·umbonal \ˈsəb+\ *adj* [*sub-* + *umbonal*] **:** situated beneath or forward of the umbones of a bivalve shell

sub·umbrella \"+\ *n* [*sub-* + *umbrella*] **:** the concave undersurface of the bell-shaped or disk-shaped body of a jellyfish — **sub·umbrellar** \"+\ *adj*

sub·ungual \"+\ *also* **sub·un·gui·al** \"+ˈəŋgwēəl\ *adj* [*subungual* ISV *sub-* + *ungual*; *subungual* alter. (influenced by L *unguis* nail, claw) of ISV *subungual* — more at NAIL] **:** situated under a nail, hoof, or claw ⟨a ~ abscess⟩

sub·ungulata \ˈsəb+\ *n pl, cap* [NL, fr. *sub-* + *Ungulata*] *in some classifications* **:** a major division of Eutheria comprising the mammalian orders Hyracoidea, Proboscidea, and sometimes Sirenia together with a variable group of extinct forms — **sub·ungulate** \"+\ *adj or n*

sub·unit \"+\ *n* [*sub-* + *unit*] **:** a secondary or subordinate unit **:** a unit that forms a discrete part of a more comprehensive unit

[1]**sub·urb** \ˈsəˌbərb, -ˌbəb, -ˌbəib *sometimes* -ˌbə(r)b\ *n* -S [ME, fr. L *suburbium*, fr. *sub-* under, near + *urb-*, *urbs* city — more at SUB-] **1 a :** an outlying part of a city or town **:** a smaller place adjacent to or sometimes within commuting distance of a city ⟨the Connecticut shore has become a ~ of New York City⟩ **b suburbs** *pl* **:** the residential area on the outskirts of any city or large town — used with *the* ⟨live in the ~*s*⟩ **2 suburbs** *pl* **:** the near vicinity **:** PERIPHERY, ENVIRONS ⟨carries them to the brink of rebirth and the ~*s* of destruction —R.P. Blackmur⟩

[2]**suburb** \"\ *adj* **1 :** SUBURBAN **2** *obs* **a :** of or characteristic of life in the suburbs of the City of London in the 16th and 17th centuries **b :** LOOSE, DISSOLUTE

[1]**sub·ur·ban** \səˈbər|bən, -ˈbə̄|, -ˈbəi|\ *adj* [L *suburbanus*, fr. *sub-* + *urb-*, *urbs* city + *-anus* -an] **1 :** of, relating to, inhabiting, or located in the suburbs ⟨a ~ home⟩ **2 :** characteristic of life in the suburbs: as **a** *obs* **:** SUBURB 2, DISSOLUTE **b :** lacking in finish or elegance **:** PROVINCIAL **c :** blending or characterized by the blending of the urban and rural ⟨~ recreation⟩ ⟨a ~ point of view⟩

[2]**suburban** \"\ *n* -S **1 :** a dweller in the suburbs **:** SUBURBANITE **2 :** STATION WAGON

sub·ur·ban·ite \|bəˌnīt, *usu* -īd·+V\ *n* -S **:** a dweller in the suburbs

sub·ur·ban·iza·tion \səˌbərbənəˈzāshən, -ˌbə̄b-,-ˌbəib-,-ˌnīˈz-\ *n* -S **:** the quality or state of being suburbanized

sub·ur·ban·ize \ə'==ˌnīz\ *vt* -ED/-ING/-S **:** to make suburban **:** give a suburban character to ⟨*suburbanizing* the untamed places —Wilfred Thesiger⟩

sub·ur·ban·ly *adv* **:** so as to be suburban

sub·urbed *pronunc at* [1]SUBURB +d\ *adj* **:** having a suburb

sub·ur·bia \səˈbərbēə, -ˈbə̄b-,-ˈbəib-\ *n* -S [[1]*suburb* + *-ia*] **1 :** the suburbs of a city **2 a :** suburbanites as a distinctive social element **b :** the manners, styles, and customs typical of suburban life

sub·ur·bi·car·i·an \ˌsəˌbərbəˈka(a)rēən\ *adj* [LL *suburbicarius* (fr. L *sub-* + LL *urbicarius* of the city, fr. L *urbicus* of the city — fr. *urb-*, *urbs* city + *-icus* -ic — + *-arius* -ary) + E *-an*] **:** being in the suburbs or near the city **:** of or relating to the suburbs ⟨one of the ~ dioceses surrounding the city of Rome⟩

sub·vaginal \ˈsəb+\ *adj* [*sub-* + *vaginal*] **:** situated under or inside a sheath

sub·valuation \"+\ *n* [*sub-* + *valuation*] **:** a secondary or subordinate valuation; *specif* **:** a valuation under Scots law of the teinds made by the subcommissioners and validated only through confirmation by the High Commission or since 1707 by the Teind Court

sub·varietal \"+\ *adj* [*subvariety* + *-al*] **1 :** of or relating to a subvariety ⟨a ~ character⟩ **2** [*sub-* + *varietal*] **:** of less than varietal significance ⟨~ variations⟩

sub·variety \"+\ *n* [*sub-* + *variety*] **:** a minor variety or strain in a more general one **:** a subdivision (as a strain or line) of a variety

[1]**sub·ven·tion** \səbˈvenchən\ *n* -S [ME *subvencioun* state subsidy, fr. MF *subvention*, fr. LL *subvention-*, *subventio* act of giving aid, assistance, fr. L *subventus* (past part. of *subvenire* to come to help), fr. *sub-* up + *venire* to come) + *-ion-*, *-io* -ion — more at SUB-, COME] **1 :** a providing of assistance or support; *esp* **:** the granting of financial aid (as to an undertaking) **2 :** aid and esp. pecuniary aid granted either to an individual or an organization: as **a :** ENDOWMENT **b :** a subsidy from a government or foundation

[2]**subvention** \"\ *vt* -ED/-ING/-S **:** to provide with a subvention **:** support by means of subventions **:** SUBSIDIZE

sub·ven·tion·ize \-chəˌnīz\ *vt* -ED/-ING/-S **:** SUBVENTION

sub·verbal \ˈsəb+\ *adj* [*sub-* + *verbal*] **:** NONVERBAL

sub·ver·sion \səbˈvər|zhən, -vəl, -vəi| *also* |sh- *sometimes* ˌsəbˈv- *or chiefly in rapid speech* səˈv-\ *n* -S [ME *subversioun*, fr. MF *subversion*, fr. LL *subversion-*, *subversio*, fr. L *subversus* (past part. of *subvertere* to overturn, overthrow) + *-ion-*, *-io* -ion] **1 :** the act of subverting or state of being subverted **:** overthrow from the foundation **:** utter ruin **:** DESTRUCTION ⟨~ of a government⟩ **2** *obs* **:** a cause of overthrow or destruction

sub·ver·sion·ary \|zhəˌnerē, |sh-, -ri\ *adj* **:** SUBVERSIVE

[1]**sub·ver·sive** \|siv, |ēv *also* |z| *or* |əv\ *adj* [L *subversus* (past part. of *subvertere*) + E *-ive*] **:** tending to subvert **:** having a tendency to overthrow, upset, or destroy ⟨hypocrisy is a vice ~ of manhood⟩; *esp* **:** intended to bring about the overthrow of a government by unlawful means — **sub·ver·sive·ly** \|əvlē, -li\ *adv* — **sub·ver·sive·ness** \|ivnəs, |ēv- *also* |əv-\ *n* -ES

[2]**subversive** \"\ *n* -S **:** a person engaged in subversive activities or planning or attempting to subvert legally constituted authority esp. by the employment of unconstitutional means

sub·ver·siv·ism \-ˌvizəm\ *n* -S **:** the quality or state of being subversive

sub·vert \səbˈvər|t, -vəl, -vəi| *sometimes* ˌsəbˈv- *or chiefly in rapid speech* səˈv-; *usu* |d·+V\ *vb* [ME *subverten*, fr. MF *subvertir*, fr. OF, fr. L *subvertere* to turn upside down, overturn, overthrow, fr. *sub-* down, under + *vertere* to turn — more at WORTH] *vt* **1 :** to overturn or overthrow from or as if from a foundation **:** ruin utterly **:** RAZE, DEMOLISH ⟨who . . . labor to ~ these great pillars of human happiness —George Washington⟩ **2 :** to pervert or corrupt (a person) by an undermining of morals, allegiance, or faith **:** ALIENATE ⟨propaganda that ~*s* foreign-born citizens⟩ **3 a :** to bring to nothing, destroy, or greatly impair the existence, sovereignty, influence, wholeness of esp. by insidious undermining ⟨tear

down our free institutions and ~ our form of government into a tyranny —*New Republic*) **b :** to make invalid or futile **:** CONFUTE, DEFEAT ⟨amorous sweet things, enough to make one fancy the adage ~*ed* that stolen fruits are sweetest —George Meredith⟩ **~** *vi* **:** to overthrow something completely **:** DESTROY, OVERTURN **syn** see OVERTURN

sub·vert·er \|d·ə(r), |tə-\ *n* -s **:** one that subverts

sub·vert·ible \|d·əbəl, |təb-\ *adj* **:** capable of being subverted

sub·vertical \¦səb+\ *adj* [*sub-* + *vertical*] **:** nearly but not quite vertical

sub·visible \"+\ *adj* [*sub-* + *visible*] **:** invisible unless magnified

sub·vitreous \"+\ *adj* [*sub-* + *vitreous*] **:** not quite vitreous

sub·vocal \"+\ *adj* [*sub-* + *vocal*] **:** characterized by the occurrence in the mind of words in speech order with or without inaudible articulation of the speech organs ⟨thinking is ~ talking⟩ — **sub·vocally** \"+\ *adv*

sub·vo·la \¦səb¦vōlə, 'səbvələ\ *n* [NL, fr. L *sub-* + *vola* hollow of the hand, palm, sole] **1 :** the interval between the second and fifth fingers **2 :** the hypothenar eminence

sub·water \¦səb+\ *vt* [*sub-* + *water*] **:** to furnish water to (plants) below the surface of the ground so that the water rises about the roots by capillary attraction **:** SUBIRRIGATE

¹sub·way \'səb,wā\ *n* [*sub-* + *way*] **1 :** an underground way or gallery: as **a :** a passage under a street (as for pedestrians, electric cables, water mains) **b :** a usu. electric railway built partly or entirely underground and usu. for local transit in metropolitan areas **c :** UNDERPASS **2 :** a subway train ⟨the ~ pounds along over a steel viaduct —Blake Ehrlich⟩

²subway \"\ *vi* -ED/-ING/-S **:** to travel by subway

sub·weight \'səb+,-\ *n* [*sub-* + *weight*] **:** a section of an assembled weight (as a unit of an elevator counterweight)

sub·xerophilous \¦səb+\ *adj* [*sub-* + *xerophilous*] *of a plant* **:** preferring but not confined to a dry habitat

sub-zero \"+\ *adj* **1 :** registering less than zero on some scale, esp. Fahrenheit ⟨*sub-zero* temperatures⟩ **2 :** characterized by or suitable for sub-zero temperature ⟨*sub-zero* weather⟩ ⟨*sub-zero* clothing⟩

sub·zone \'səb+,-\ *n* [*sub-* + *zone*] **:** a subdivision of a zone **:** a secondary or subordinate zone

suc *abbr* **1** succeeded **2** successor **3** suction

succ *abbr* **1** succeeded **2** successor

suc·cade \(,)sə'kād\ *n* -s [ME *socade*, fr. MF *succade*, *sucrade* sweet, candied fruit, succade, fr. OProv *sucrado*, adj., sweet, sugary, sugared, fr. past part. of *sucra* to sugar, fr. *sucre* sugar, fr. OIt *zucchero* — more at SUGAR] **:** a preserve or confection made from fruit **:** preserved or crystallized fruit

succah *var of* SUKKAH

suc·ce·da·ne·ous \¦səksə¦dānēəs\ *adj* [L *succedaneus*, fr. *succedere* to succeed] **:** of, relating to, or serving as a succedaneum **:** SUBSTITUTED

suc·ce·da·ne·um \-ēəm\ *n, pl* **succedaneums** \-ēəmz\ *or* **succeda·nea** \-ēə\ [NL, fr. neut. of L *succedaneus*] **1 :** one that succeeds to the place of another **:** SUBSTITUTE **2** *obs* **:** REMEDY, MEDICINE

suc·ce·dent \sək'sēdᵊnt\ *adj* [L *succedent-, succedens*, pres. part. of *succedere* to succeed] **1 :** SUCCEEDING, SUBSEQUENT **2 :** of or relating to the 2d, 5th, 8th, and 11th mundane houses

suc·ceed \sək'sēd *sometimes* sik-\ *vb* -ED/-ING/-S [ME *succeden*, fr. L *succedere* to go up, follow after, follow, succeed, fr. *sub-* up, after + *cedere* to go, proceed, yield — more at SUB-, CEDE] *vi* **1 a :** to come next after or replace another in an office, position, or role or in possession of an estate **:** fill a vacancy in an inherited, elective, or appointive position ⟨upon the death of his father he ~*ed* to a considerable fortune and to his father's position as rector —J.D.Wade⟩; *specif* **:** to inherit sovereignty, rank, or title ⟨upon the death of the president the vice-president would ~⟩ ⟨an instructor in biology . . . before ~*ing* to the chairmanship of the department of biology —*Current Biog.*⟩ **b :** to follow or take place after another esp. in a natural, prescribed, or necessary order, course of events, or development ⟨one idea would ~ to another with a rush —Osbert Sitwell⟩ ⟨slate has ~*ed* to thatch, and brick to timber —T.B.Macaulay⟩ ⟨the ~*ing* fifteen years . . . were uneventful —J.C.Fitzpatrick⟩ **2 a :** to turn out well **:** result favorably according to plans or desires ⟨the formula and ingredients that finally ~*ed* remain the top company secrets —*Monsanto Mag.*⟩ **b :** to attain a desired object or end **:** accomplish what is attempted or intended **:** be successful ⟨~*ed* in regaining the offensive after a smashing defeat —*Reporter*⟩ ⟨mental abilities high enough to enable them to ~ in college —*Clearing House*⟩ **c :** to attain to or be in a thriving, prosperous, or popular state ⟨will produce high quality grapes for wine on gravels where hardly any other crop will ~ —G.G.Weigend⟩ ⟨~*s* with our public —E.R. Bentley⟩ **3** *obs* **:** to turn out **:** RESULT, EVENTUATE ⟨whether the manner of their operation would ~ contrary —Richard Waller⟩ **4** *obs* **:** APPROACH ⟨will you to the cooler cave ~ —John Dryden⟩ **5** *obs* **:** to become the property of a person through inheritance **:** DESCEND ⟨a ring . . . that downward hath ~*ed* in his house from son to son —Shak.⟩ **~** *vt* **1 a :** to be the event or thing immediately following on or one of the items or events following upon in an ordered sequence or chain of events ⟨simplicity of concept ~*s* complexity of calculation —E.T.Bell⟩ ⟨the past is merely a series of messes, ~*ing* one another by discoverable laws —E.M.Forster⟩ ⟨the cathedral ~*ed* a frame building —*Amer. Guide Series: Ark.*⟩ **b :** to come after or follow in an office, position, role, or title **:** fill a vacancy as heir or elected or appointed successor to ⟨~*ed* her father as keeper of the lighthouse —*Amer. Guide Series: R.I.*⟩ **2** *obs* **:** to fall heir to **:** INHERIT **3** *obs* **:** to follow the example of ⟨~ thy father in manners as in shape —Shak.⟩ **4 :** to make successful **:** cause to prosper

syn SUCCEED, PROSPER, THRIVE, and FLOURISH can mean in common to attain the desired end, or increase or enlarge in that attainment. SUCCEED means to gain one's purpose ⟨*succeed* in passing a civil service examination⟩ ⟨*succeed* in business⟩ ⟨*succeed* in becoming president⟩ ⟨this government *succeeded* for seventy years —J.P.Boyd⟩ PROSPER implies continued success ⟨if a genuine democratic revolution should *prosper* —H.N.Brailsford⟩ ⟨education *prospers* by economy —R.W.Livingstone⟩ ⟨the oyster-fishing industry that *prospered* here in the middle-nineteenth century —*Amer. Guide Series: N.Y. City*⟩ THRIVE adds to PROSPER the idea of vigorous growth ⟨dictatorship *thrives* on poverty and war *thrives* on dictatorship —*New Republic*⟩ ⟨the era in which most American firms were born and *thrived* —C.F.Robinson⟩ ⟨the lumber industry *throve* during the boom days by meeting the needs of rush building —*Amer. Guide Series: Texas*⟩ FLOURISH suggests a thriving or prospering, esp. during a period when the thing is at the peak of its development or productivity ⟨if physics and chemistry and biology have *flourished*, morals, religion, and aesthetics have withered —J.W.Krutch⟩ ⟨three expensive but *flourishing* weeklies devoted to absolutely nothing but the life of the rich and the titled —Aldous Huxley⟩ ⟨the demagogue *flourishes* most luxuriantly where negligence is flagrant and the abuse of power is arrogant —A.W.Long⟩ **syn** see in addition FOLLOW

suc·ceed·er \-də(r)\ *n* -s [ME, fr. *succeden* to succeed + *-er*] *archaic* **:** SUCCESSOR

succeeding *n* -s [ME *succeding*, fr. gerund of *succeden* to succeed] *obs* **:** CONSEQUENCE, RESULT

suc·cent \sək'sent\ *vb* -ED/-ING/-S [back-formation fr. *succentor*] *vt* **:** to sing the close or second part of (a verse) esp. in responsive singing **~** *vi* **:** to act as succentor

suc·cen·tor \-tə(r)\ *n* -s [LL, leader, succentor, fr. L *succentus* (past part. of *succinere* to sing to, sing after, fr. *sub-* to, after + *canere* to sing) + *-or* — more at SUB-, CHANT] **1 :** one that succents **2 :** a precentor's deputy or assistant esp. in a monastery or cathedral

suc·cen·tu·ri·ate \¦sək,sen¦t(y)ürēət, -ē,āt\ *adj* [L *succenturiatus*, past part. of *succenturiare* to recruit into a Roman century, fr. *sub-* + *centuriare* to divide into hundreds — more at CENTURIATE] **:** SUPPLEMENTAL, ACCESSORY ⟨a ~ placental lobe⟩

suc·cès de scan·dale \sək,sādə,skäⁿ'däl\ *n* [F, lit., success of scandal] **:** the reception accorded a work of art that wins popularity or notoriety because of the scandalous nature of its contents or of its relation to a scandal ⟨so antireligious and sacrilegious that they . . . achieved a tumultuous *succès de scandale* —H.E.Clurman⟩ ⟨a *succès de scandale* won by its anecdotes about the members of the . . . aristocracy —Anthony West⟩

suc·cès d'es·time \-ā,de'stēm\ *n* [F, lit., success of esteem] **:** the reception accorded a work of art that wins critical respect but not popular success ⟨the satirical comedies which had brought him a small amount of money and a large *succès d'estime* —*Atlantic*⟩

suc·cès fou \-ā'fü\ *n* [F, lit., mad success] **:** an extraordinary success ⟨the performance . . . according to one of the more ecstatic members of the entertainment committee . . . was a *succès fou* —Cornelia O. Skinner⟩

suc·cess \sək'ses *also* sik-\ *n* -ES [L *successus*, fr. *successus*, past part. of *succedere* to follow, succeed — more at SUCCEED] **1** *obs* **:** something that ensues **:** OUTCOME, CONSEQUENCE, ISSUE ⟨what is the ~ —Shak.⟩ **2** *obs* **a :** COURSE, SEQUENCE, SUCCESSION **b :** a group that proceeds in temporal sequence; *specif* **:** LINEAGE **3 a :** the degree or measure of attaining a desired end **:** kind of fortune ⟨the poor ~ of the book disgusted him —Aldous Huxley⟩ ⟨the ~ of the performance is judged by its volume and enthusiasm —*Amer. Guide Series: Fla.*⟩ **b :** a succeeding fully or in accordance with one's desires **:** favorable termination of a venture ⟨I believe very little in the fortune . . . to which men attribute their ~*es* and reverses —George Meredith⟩ ⟨in pursuing this task she had, at first, cheering hopes of ~ —Matthew Arnold⟩; *specif* **:** the attainment of wealth, position, esteem, favor, or eminence ⟨the first book has been published and had a great ~ —L.L. Day⟩ **4 a :** a person achieving success ⟨as a dance student . . . was . . . an immediate ~ —*Current Biog.*⟩ ⟨a ~ as a rich man's wife —Pearl Buck⟩ **b :** an undertaking that succeeds or confers success ⟨the play was an immediate ~⟩ ⟨a remarkable series of ~*es* in experimentation⟩

suc·cess·ful \-esfəl\ *adj* **1 :** resulting or terminating in success **:** having the desired effect ⟨a ~ experiment⟩ **2 :** gaining or having gained success; *esp* **:** having attained wealth, position, or fame ⟨a ~ writer⟩ ⟨a ~ banker⟩ **3** *of a plant or animal group* **:** represented by diverse forms and occupying a wide variety of ecological niches — **suc·cess·ful·ly** \-fəlē, -li\ *adv* — **suc·cess·ful·ness** *n* -ES

suc·ces·sion \sək'seshən *also* sik-\ *n* -s [ME, fr. MF or L; MF, fr. L *succession-*, *successio*, fr. *successus* (past part. of *succedere* to follow, succeed) + *-ion-*, *-io* -ion] **1 a :** the order in which or the conditions under which one person after another succeeds to a property, dignity, title, or throne — compare APOSTOLIC SUCCESSION **b :** the right of a person or line to succeed **c :** the line having such a right **2 a :** the act or process of following in order of time or place **:** a repeated following up of one by another **:** SEQUENCE **b** (1) **:** the change in legal relations by which one person comes into the enjoyment of or becomes responsible for one or more of the rights or liabilities of another person ⟨a son's ~ to the estate of his father⟩ ⟨the ~ of one king to another⟩ **:** the act or process of one person's taking the place of another in the enjoyment of or liability for his rights or duties or both; *also* **:** the right or duty to take another's place by succession or the rights and duties succeeded to — see SINGULAR SUCCESSION, UNIVERSAL SUCCESSION (2) **:** the act or process of a person's becoming beneficially entitled to a property or property interest of a deceased person whether by operation of law upon his dying intestate or by testamentary disposition **c :** the whole estate of a deceased including all assets and all liabilities **d :** the action or process of one state taking over or following upon another and becoming entitled to the former's rights and position in international law **e :** the continuance of corporate personality ⟨a corporation which has unlimited ~⟩ **f** (1) **:** the process of change in the biological population of an area as the available competing organisms respond to the environment (2) **:** the sequence of identifiable ecological stages or communities in this process esp. from barrenness to climax **:** SERE ⟨the highlights of the ~ were the weed, grass, and forest communities, developed in that order⟩ **g :** the process of change in an inhabited area through invasion by a different human population group or through a different utilization of real estate ⟨the ~ from residence to business in an urban district⟩ **3 a :** a series of descendants, heirs, successors, or members of a dynasty following by right and in order from an initial member ⟨for him and for his ~ granted a tribute —Shak.⟩ ⟨had no antecedent and no fit ~ —Henry Adams⟩ **b** *obs* (1) **:** a group of people of somewhat homogeneous age succeeded to their ancestors **:** GENERATION (2) **:** succeeding generations **:** POSTERITY **c :** a number of persons or things that follow each other in sequence **:** a continuous and uninterrupted series ⟨preserved . . . by a ~ of private owners —C.P.Fitzgerald⟩ ⟨a ~ of rooms, one after the other, extending over a great length —*Amer. Guide Series: La.*⟩ **d :** a group, type, or series that succeeds or displaces another; *specif* **:** an inclusive stratigraphic sequence involving any number of stages, series, or systems, or parts thereof

suc·ces·sion·al \-shənᵊl, -shnəl\ *adj* **1 :** of, relating to, or forming part of a succession ⟨a ~ forest⟩ **2 :** in a regular order **:** CONSECUTIVE — **suc·ces·sion·al·ly** \-ᵊlē, -əl|, |i\ *adv*

successional speciation *n* **:** gradual evolution from and replacement of one species by another

succession duty *n, chiefly Brit* **:** INHERITANCE TAX 1

suc·ces·sion·ist \-sh(ə)nəst\ *n* -s **:** one who upholds the validity and necessity of the apostolic succession

succession of crops 1 : sustained seasonal production of a particular crop either by repeated sowings or by selecting varieties maturing at different times **2 :** the culture of two or more short-life crops planted in turn

succession state *n* **:** one of a number of states that succeed a former state in sovereignty over a certain territory

succession tax *n* **1 :** ESTATE TAX **2 :** INHERITANCE TAX 1

suc·ces·sive \sək'sesiv, -esēv *also* sik- *or* -esəv\ *adj* [ME, fr. ML *successivus*, fr. L *successus* (past part. of *succedere* to follow, succeed) + *-ivus* -ive] **1** *obs* **a :** inherited or capable of being inherited by succession **:** descending or transmissible to the next in a succession **:** HEREDITARY **b :** inheriting by succession **c :** being the next to inherit **2 a :** following in succession or serial order **:** following one upon another **:** coming in order **:** CONSECUTIVE ⟨their fourth ~ victory⟩ ⟨the product of the ~ labors of innumerable men —Lewis Mumford⟩ **b :** being a successor or one of a group of consecutive successors to a person, thing, or item ⟨the idea of a world order, ~ to both the pagan and the Christian —Paul Rosenfeld⟩ ⟨the book . . . was followed by many ~ editions —J.T.Howard⟩ **c :** characterized by or manifesting succession **:** produced or arranged in succession ⟨the angles between ~ points may be measured —R.E.Davis⟩ — **suc·ces·sive·ly** \-əsivlē, -li\ *adv* — **suc·ces·sive·ness** \-esivnəs, -esēv- *also* -esəv-\ *n* -ES

suc·ces·siv·i·ty \(,)sək,se'sivəd·ē\ *n* -ES **:** the quality or fact of being successive **:** successive development

suc·cess·less \sək'sesləs *also* sik-\ *adj* **:** being without success **:** UNSUCCESSFUL — **suc·cess·less·ly** *adv* — **suc·cess·less·ness** *n* -ES

success line *n* **:** LINE OF THE SUN

suc·ces·sor \sək'sesə(r) *also* sik-, *archaic* ¦səksə¦sȯ(ə)r\ *n* -s [ME *successour*, fr. OF, fr. L *successor*, fr. *successus* (past part. of *succedere* to follow, succeed) + *-or* — more at SUCCEED] **:** one that follows; *esp* **:** a person who succeeds to a throne, title, or estate or is elected or appointed to an office, dignity, or other position vacated by another

suc·ces·sor·ship \-,ship\ *n* **:** the quality or state of being a successor

successor state *n* **:** SUCCESSION STATE

success story *n* **:** a real or fictitious narrative of a poor or unknown person who rises to fortune, acclaim, or brilliant achievement

succi *pl of* SUCCUS

succin- *or* **succino-** *comb form* [L *succin-*, *sucin-*, fr. *succinum*, *sucinum* amber] **1 :** amber ⟨*succinic* (acid)⟩ ⟨*succinite*⟩ ⟨*succiniferous*⟩ **2 :** succinic acid ⟨*succinamide*⟩ ⟨*succinonitrile*⟩

suc·cin·a·mate \(,)sək'sinə,māt; ,səksə'namət, -ə,māt\ *n* -s [*succinamic* + *-ate*] **:** a salt or ester of succinamic acid

suc·ci·nam·ic acid \¦səksə¦namik-\ *n* [*succinamide* + *-ic*] **:** a crystalline compound $H_2NCOCH_2CH_2COOH$ that is the half amide of succinic acid

suc·cin·a·mide \(,)sək'sinə,mīd; ,səksə'naməd, -ə,mīd\ *n* [ISV *succin-* + *amide*] **:** a crystalline compound $H_2NCOCH_2CH_2CONH_2$ that is the amide of succinic acid

suc·ci·nate \'səksə,nāt\ *n* -s [ISV *succin-* + *-ate*] **:** a salt or ester of succinic acid

suc·cin·chlorimide \¦səksən+\ *n* [*succin-* + *chlorimide*] **:** a crystalline compound $C_2H_4(CO)_2NCl$ that has an odor like that of chlorine and is used as a disinfectant and chlorinating agent; *N*-chloro-succinimide — not used systematically

suc·cinct \sək'siŋ(k)t *also* ,sək'si- *or* ÷ sə'si- *or* ÷ ,sə'si-\ *adj, often* -ER/-EST [ME, fr. L *succinctus*, past part. of *succingere* to gird from below, tuck up, gird about, fr. *sub-* under, up + *cingere* to gird — more at SUB-, CINCTURE] **1 a** *archaic* **:** encircled with or as with a girdle **b** *archaic* **:** adorned, wrapped, or bound up by a girdle **c :** supported by a band of silk around the middle ⟨the ~ pupa of a butterfly⟩ **2 a :** marked by brief and compact expression or by extreme compression and lack of unnecessary words and details ⟨the displacement of the long-drawn-out epic similes by pithy and ~ comparisons —J.L. Lowes⟩ **b :** brief to the point of curtness ⟨a very ~ refusal⟩ **3 :** lacking fullness in cut **:** CLOSE-FITTING ⟨~ little nipped-in suits —Lois Long⟩ **syn** see CONCISE

suc·cinct·ly \-ŋ(k)tlē, -ŋklē, -li\ *adv* **:** in a succinct manner **:** with concise and precise brevity

suc·cinct·ness \-ŋtnəs, -ŋkn-\ *n* -ES **:** the quality or state of being succinct

succinctorium *var of* SUBCINCTORIUM

suc·cin·ea \(,)sək'sinēə\ *n, cap* [NL, fem. of L *succineus* of amber, fr. *succinum* amber; fr. the color of the shell] **:** a cosmopolitan genus (the type of a family Succineidae) of amphibious or terrestrial pulmonate snails

suc·ci·ne·idae \,səksə'nēə,dē\ *n pl, cap* [NL, fr. *Succinea*, type genus + *-idae*] **:** a family of small often amber-colored snails (suborder Stylommatophora) that comprises the amber shells — see SUCCINEA

suc·cin·ic acid \(¦)sək¦sinik-\ *n* [F *succinique*, fr. *succin-* + *-ique*] **:** a crystalline dicarboxylic acid $HOOCCH_2CH_2COOH$ that occurs widely both free and combined (as in amber, lignite, turpentine oils, and animal fluids), that is formed in the Krebs cycle and in various fermentation processes, that is usu. made by hydrogenation of maleic acid or fumaric acid, and that is used chiefly as an intermediate (as for pharmaceuticals and synthetic resins); butane-dioic acid — compare MALIC ACID

succinic anhydride *n* **:** a crystalline cyclic compound $C_2H_4(CO)_2O$ obtained by dehydration of succinic acid and used similarly as an intermediate

succinic dehydrogenase *n* **:** an iron-containing flavoprotein enzyme that catalyzes often reversibly the dehydrogenation of succinic acid to fumaric acid in the presence of a hydrogen acceptor (as a phenazine dye) and that is widely distributed esp. in animal tissues, bacteria, and yeast — see SUCCINOXIDASE

succinic oxidase *n* **:** SUCCINOXIDASE

suc·ci·nif·er·ous \¦səksə¦nif(ə)rəs\ *adj* [*succin-* + *-iferous*] **:** yielding amber

suc·ci·ni·mide \(,)sək'sinə,mīd; ,səksə'ni,mīd, -məd\ *n* [ISV *succin-* + *imide*] **:** a crystalline cyclic imide $C_2H_4(CO)_2NH$ obtainable (as by heating with ammonia) from succinic acid or succinic anhydride

suc·ci·nite \'səksə,nīt\ *n* -s [in sense 1, fr. F, fr. *succin-* + *-ite*; in sense 2, fr. G *succinit*, fr. *succin-* + *-it* -ite] **1 :** amber-colored grossularite **2 :** AMBER

succino- — see SUCCIN-

suc·cin·oxidase \¦səksən+\ *n* [*succin-* + *oxidase*] **:** the entire complex system containing succinic dehydrogenase and cytochromes that catalyzes the reaction between succinate ion and molecular oxygen with the formation of fumarate ion ⟨in rat liver cells, ~ activity is associated with the mitochondria, and in heart muscle it is localized in particles . . . that correspond cytologically to the mitochondria of other tissues —J.S.Fruton & Sofia Simmonds⟩

suc·ci·nyl \'səksənᵊl, -,nil\ *n* -s [ISV *succin-* + *-yl*] **1 :** the bivalent radical $-OC(CH_2)_2CO-$ of succinic acid **2 :** the univalent radical $HOOC(CH_2)_2CO-$ of succinic acid — not used systematically

suc·ci·nyl·choline \¦==(,)=+\ *n* [*succinyl* + *choline*] **:** a basic compound that has an action like that of curare and that is administered intravenously chiefly in the form of its crystalline dihydrochloride $C_{14}H_{30}Cl_2N_2O_4.2H_2O$ as a skeletal relaxant in surgery

suc·ci·nyl·sulfathiazole \"+\ *n* [*succinyl* + *sulfathiazole*] **:** a crystalline sulfa drug $C_{13}H_{13}N_3O_5S_2$ used esp. for treating gastrointestinal infections

suc·ci·sa \sək'sīsə, -īzə\ *n, cap* [NL, fr. fem. of L *succissus*, past part. of *succidere* to cut from below, fr. *sub-* + *-cidere* (fr. *caedere* to cut) — more at CONCISE] **:** a genus of European herbs (family Dipsacaceae) differing from the closely related *Scabiosa* chiefly in having the scales of the receptacle as long as the flowers — see BLUE SCABIOUS

suc·civ·o·rous \(,)sək'sivərəs\ *adj* [ISV *succi-* (fr. L *succus*, *sucus* juice, sap) + *-vorous* — more at SUCCULENT] **:** PHYTOSUCCIVOROUS

¹suc·cor \'səkə(r)\ *n* -s *see -or in Explan Notes* [ME *succur*, *sucur*, *socur*, fr. earlier *sucurs*, *socours*, taken as pl., fr. OF *secors*, *sucors*, fr. ML *succursus*, fr. L, past part. of *succurrere* to run up, run to help] **1 a :** relief from difficulty, want, or distress **:** AID, HELP, ASSISTANCE **b :** something that furnishes relief ⟨religion was their chief ~ —*Time*⟩ **c** *or* **succors** *pl* **:** military assistance in supplies and esp. men **:** REINFORCEMENTS ⟨can no longer draw ~ from this ally —Matthew Arnold⟩ ⟨the inconsiderable ~*s* . . . were easily intercepted —Edward Gibbon⟩ **2** *chiefly dial* **:** a sheltered place **:** a building used as a shelter **:** REFUGE

²succor \"\ *vt* -ED/-ING/-S *see -or in Explan Notes* [ME *sucuren*, *soucouren*, fr. OF *secorir*, *sucurir*, fr. L *succurrere* to run up, run to help, help, fr. *sub-* up + *currere* to run — more at SUB-, CURRENT] **1 :** to go to the aid of (one in difficulty, want, or distress) **:** HELP; *specif* **:** to provide with reinforcements or supplies **:** RELIEVE ⟨an escort vessel . . . sent to ~ four vessels . . . under attack by submarine —E.L.Beach⟩ **2 :** to cure, alleviate, or mitigate ⟨attempts to ~ the various distresses of these people —Jerome Stone⟩ **3** *chiefly dial* **:** to provide a shelter for

suc·cor·ance \-rən(t)s\ *n* -s [¹*succor* + *-ance*] **:** DEPENDENCE

suc·cor·er \-rə(r)\ *n* -s [ME *socourer*, fr. MF *secoreor*, *sucureor*, fr. OF, fr. *secorir*, *sucurir* to help + *-eor* -or] **:** one that succors

suc·cor·rhea *or* **suc·cor·rhoea** \,səkə'rēə\ *n* -s [NL, fr. *succo-* (fr. L *succus*, *sucus* juice, sap) + *-rrhea*, *-rrhoea* — more at SUCCULENT] **:** excessive flow of a juice or secretion

suc·co·ry \'səkərē\ *n* -ES [alter. (prob. influenced by MD *suckereie* succory, modif. — influenced by MD *suker* sugar — of *cichorei*, fr. MF *cichorée*) of ME *cicoree* — more at SUIKERBOS, CHICORY] **1 :** CHICORY 1; *broadly* **:** a plant of the genus *Cichorium* **2 :** any of various composite plants other than the chicory — used in combination; see BLUE SUCCORY, GUM SUCCORY, LAMB SUCCORY

succory blue *n* **:** CHICORY 3

suc·co·tash \'səkə,tash, -taa(ə)sh, -taish\ *n* -ES [of Algonquian origin; akin to Narraganset *msəkwataš* something broken into pieces (as corn from the cob), succotash, Natick *msəkutahas*] **1 :** a mixture of lima beans or shell beans and kernels of green corn cooked together **2 :** a mixture of two grain crops (as oats and barley) sown together

¹succoth *or* **succot** *or* **succos** *pl of* SUCCAH

²succoth *or* **succot** *or* **succos** *cap, var of* SUKKOTH

suc·cu·ba \'səkyəbə\ *n, pl* **succu·bae** \-,bē\ [LL, prostitute] **:** SUCCUBUS

suc·cu·bous \'səkyəbəs\ *adj* [L *succubare* to lie under + E *-ous*] **1** *of leaves* **:** being so arranged that the posterior margin of each overlaps the anterior margin of the next older **2 :** having succubous leaves ⟨~ liverworts⟩ — compare INCUBOUS

suc·cu·bus \'səkyəbəs\ *n, pl* **succu·bi** \-,bī\ [ME, fr. ML, alter. (influenced by LL *incubus*) of LL *succuba* prostitute, lit., one who lies under, fr. L *succubare* to lie under, fr. *sub-* + *cubare* to lie down — more at HIP] **1 :** a demon assuming female form to have sexual intercourse with men in their sleep — compare INCUBUS **2 :** DEMON, FIEND **3 :** STRUMPET, WHORE

suc·cu·lence \'səkyələn(t)s\ *n* -s [F, prob. fr. (assumed) NL *succulentia*, fr. L *succulentus* succulent + *-ia* -y] **1 :** the quality or condition of being succulent **:** JUICINESS **2 :** fresh or juicy food of wild or cultivated plant origin ⟨fodder should contain some ~⟩; *also* **:** SILAGE

suc·cu·len·cy \-nsē,-nsi\ *n* -ES [prob. fr. (assumed) NL *succulentia*] : SUCCULENCE

¹suc·cu·lent \-nt\ *adj* [L *succulentus, suculentus,* fr. *succus, sucus* juice, sap; akin to L *sugere* to suck — more at SUCK] **1 a** : full of juice : JUICY ⟨roasted ~ fresh meat —Charles Rawlings⟩ **b** *of a plant* : having fleshy and juicy tissues **2** : full of vitality, freshness, or richness — **suc·cu·lent·ly** *adv*

²succulent \"\ *n* -S **1** : a succulent plant (as a cactus) **2 succulents** *pl* : SUCCULENCE 2

succulent feed *n* : SUCCULENCE 2

suc·cu·lom·e·ter \ˌsəkyəˈlämədə(r)\ *n* [*succulence* + *-o-* + *-meter*] : an instrument for measuring the moisture content of a fresh or processed vegetable product (as an ear of corn)

suc·cumb \səˈkəm\ *vi* -ED/-ING/-S [F & L; F *succomber,* fr. L *succumbere* to fall down, yield, fr. *sub-* + *-cumbere* to lie down (akin to L *cubare* to lie down) — more at HIP] **1** : to yield and cease to resist or contend before a superior strength, overpowering appeal or desire, or inexorable force ⟨~*ed* to her drowsiness —Willa Cather⟩ ⟨the free economic system ~*ed* to the strains of war —C.E.Black & E.C.Helmreich⟩ **2** : to cease to exist : DIE ⟨disease ravaged the voyagers, more than half of whom ~*ed* —*Amer. Guide Series: N.C.*⟩ ⟨590 businesses ~*ed* —*Dun's Rev.*⟩ **syn** see YIELD

suc·cum·bence \səˈkəmbən(t)s\ *or* **succumbency** \-nsē\ *n, pl* **succumbences** *or* **succumbencies** [*succumbence* fr. *succumb* + *-ence; succumbency* prob. fr. ML *succumbentia* failure in a cause, fr. L *succumbent-, succumbens* (pres. part. of *succumbere*) + *-ia* -y] : the act or process of succumbing

¹suc·cur·sal \səˈkərsəl\ *adj* [F *succursale,* fr. ML *succursus* assistance, help + F *-ale* (fem. of *-al*) — more at SUCCOR] : of the nature of a branch or offshoot : SUBSIDIARY, AUXILIARY ⟨a ~ church of a cathedral⟩ ⟨a ~ bank⟩

²succursal \"\ *also* **suc·cur·sale** \"\ *n* -S [F *succursale,* fr. *succursale,* adj., succursal] : a succursal institution (as a dependent monastery or a branch of a business)

suc·cus \ˈsəkəs\ *n, pl* **suc·ci** \ˈsəˌkī, ˈsəkˌsī\ [L — more at SUCCULENT] : JUICE; *specif* : expressed juice (as of a fruit) for medicinal use

succus en·ter·i·cus \-ˌenˈterəkəs\ *n* [NL, intestinal juice] : a fluid that is secreted in small quantity by Lieberkühn's glands of the small intestine, is highly variable in constitution, and typically contains various enzymes (as erepsin, lipase, and lactose), enterokinase, mucus, salts, and water

suc·cus·sa·to·ry \səˈkəsəˌtōrē\ *adj* [obs. E *succussation* shaking, succussion (fr. ML *succussation-, succussatio,* fr. L *succussatus* — past part. of *succussare,* freq. of *succutire* to throw up from below — + *-ion-, -io* -ion) + E *-ory*] : characterized by up-and-down vibrations of short amplitude — used of an earthquake; compare SUSSULTATORY

suc·cus·sion \səˈkəshən\ *n* -S [L *succussion-, succussio,* fr. *succussus* (past part. of *succutere* to throw up from below, fling up, fr. *sub-* up + *quatere* to shake) + *-ion-, -io* -ion — more at SUB-, QUASH] : the action or process of shaking or the condition of being shaken esp. with violence: **a** : a shaking of the body to ascertain if fluid is present in a cavity and esp. in the thorax **b** : the splashing sound made by succussion

suc·cus·sive \-ˈkəsiv\ *adj* [L *succussus* (past part. of *succutere*) + E *-ive*] : SUCCUSSATORY

¹such \(ˌ)səch, (ˌ)sich (*i is less frequent when stress is primary*), *chiefly dial* (ˌ)sech\ *adj* [ME *such, swuch, swulch, swilch,* fr. OE *swilc, swelc, swylc;* akin to OHG *sulīh, solīh* such, ON *slīkr,* Goth *swaleiks;* all fr. a prehistoric Gmc compound whose first and second constituents respectively are represented by OE *swā* so and by OE *gelīc* like — more at SO, LIKE] **1 a** : of a kind or character about to be indicated, suggested, or exemplified ⟨will do ~ things as counsel an immigrant on buying a second-hand car —Robert Crichton⟩ ⟨a bag ~ as a doctor carries⟩ ⟨coarse fish, ~ as carp, catfish, and the like —Alexander MacDonald⟩ **b** : having a quality to a degree to be indicated ⟨his joy at seeing her was ~ that he wept —Henry La Cossitt⟩ ⟨had organized with ~ success that after four years of operation he was able to retire —Frank Monaghan⟩ **2 a** : having a quality already or just specified — used to avoid repetition of a descriptive term ⟨never to accept a thing as true unless it appears to me clearly and evidently to be ~ —R.B.Sewall⟩ **b** : of this or that character, quality, or extent : of the sort or degree previously indicated or implied ⟨had snorted with disdain at ~ vulgarity —C.S.Forester⟩ ⟨were rejoicing over ~ plenty of water —Henry Lapham⟩ ⟨by ~ a rigorous process of natural selection, those that reach maturity are tough —H.L.Hoskins⟩ **c** : previously characterized or specified : AFOREMENTIONED ⟨to take possession . . . of any horse for any of the purposes aforesaid and to detain ~ horse —*Australian Jockey Club*⟩ **3** : of so extreme a degree or quality ⟨this is ~ nonsense⟩ ⟨I never ate ~ food before⟩ ⟨I've never seen ~ a crowd⟩ ⟨~ a day⟩ **4** : not conspicuous of its kind : neither better nor worse : MEDIOCRE ⟨the meal, ~ as it was, was served quickly⟩ ⟨the house, ~ as it is, is at your disposal⟩ **5** : of the same class, type, or sort : in the same category : SIMILAR ⟨established twenty ~ libraries in the colonies —G.H.Doane⟩ ⟨in all ~ matters . . . developed an extraordinary efficiency —F.J. Mather⟩ **6** : such and such ⟨a simple matter to report that these films were shown in ~ a place to so many people —Cecile Starr⟩

²such \"\ *pron* [ME *such, swilch,* fr. OE *swelc, swilc,* fr. *swelc, swilc,* adj.] **1** : such a person or thing or such persons or things ⟨the father of ~ as dwell in tents —Gen 4:20 (AV)⟩ ⟨a general philosophy of life, if it may be called ~ —T.S.Eliot⟩ **2** : someone or something that has been or is being stated, implied, or exemplified ⟨~ was the result of his efforts⟩ ⟨if ~ is the decision, nothing further should be done⟩ ⟨~ is life⟩ **3** : someone or something similar : a person or thing of the same kind ⟨regarded a little water coloring and ~ as a polite accomplishment —Alfred Werner⟩ ⟨ship . . . planes and munitions and ~ in return for raw materials —*New Republic*⟩ — **as such** \ˈaz-ˌsəch, əzˈs-\ *adv* : in itself ⟨*as such* the gift was worth little⟩

³such \"\ *adv* [ME *such, swilch,* fr. OE *swelce, swilce,* fr. *swelc, swilc,* adj.] **1 a** : to such a degree : SO ⟨I have never seen ~ tall buildings⟩ ⟨~ a fine person⟩ **b** : ESPECIALLY, VERY ⟨physically, he was not in ~ good shape —Jay Leyda⟩ ⟨hasn't been in ~ good spirits the last few days⟩ **2** : in such a way ⟨the light is refracted ~ that the point of light appears as a streak —H.G. Armstrong⟩

¹such and such *pron* [ME] : something not specified or not requiring to be specified ⟨made him lay himself out to prove that *such and such* is the true view of the facts —*Notes & Queries*⟩ ⟨showed very clearly that *such and such* was often true —K.A.Menninger⟩

²such and such *adj* : not specifically mentioned or designated : not yet specified : not requiring specification now ⟨what we have objectively before us is *such and such* a race or group of people —A.L.Kroeber⟩

such a one *pron* [ME *such an on*] **1** : one of this or that kind : one of a specified or understood kind ⟨he knows who is a likely witch and takes *such a one* in hand by commonsense methods —W.W.Howells⟩ **2 a** : one of a kind to be indicated or specified ⟨*such a one* as may be found in any small town⟩ **b** : one of the same kind ⟨just *such a one* as his father⟩ **3** *archaic* : someone not named ⟨telling you then . . . that *such a one* and *such a one* were past cure —Shak.⟩

¹suchlike \ˈ=ˌ=\ *adj* [ME, fr. ¹*such* + *like*] : of like kind : SIMILAR ⟨a locker which normally held stationery, ink, and ~ equipment for writing —William McFee⟩

²suchlike \"\ *pron* [ME, fr. ¹*suchlike*] **1** : persons or things of the same kind or of similar character ⟨waiters, kitchen hands and ~ —*Times Lit. Supp.*⟩ ⟨gorgeously colored feminine finery — gowns and ~ —Haldane Macfall⟩ **2** : someone or something of the same sort : a similar person or thing ⟨less often a nobleman than a tramp or ~ —C.W.Cunnington⟩

such·ness *n* -ES **1** : the quality or state of being such : essential or characteristic quality ⟨without any apparent regard to the ~ of her environment, she sat down —J.D.Salinger⟩ **2** *Buddhism* : nameless and characterless reality in its ultimate nature — called also *tathata, thusness*

¹suchow *usu cap, var of* SOOCHOW

²su·chow \ˈsüˌchau̇, -ˈjō\ *adj, usu cap* [fr. *Suchow,* China] **1** : of or from the city of Suchow in Shantung province, China **2** : of the kind or style prevalent in Suchow **2** : IPIN

suchwise \ˈ=ˌ=\ *adv* [ME] *archaic* : in such a manner : SO

¹suck \ˈsək\ *vb* -ED/-ING/-S [ME *soken, souken,* fr. OE *sūcan;* akin to OHG *sūgan* to suck, ON *sūga,* L *sugere* to suck, MBret *sunaff* juice, Gk *hyei* it is raining, Lith *sunkti* to filter, ooze, Toch B *swese* rain] *vt* **1 a** (1) : to draw (a liquid) into the mouth by a partial vacuum caused by motion of the mouth; *specif* : to draw (milk) from a breast or udder by motion of the mouth or lips (2) : to draw or remove by application of the tongue or lips : LICK, LAP ⟨~ food particles from the tongue⟩ (3) : to draw by or as if by a vacuum created by application of the mouth to a tube ⟨~ the membrane from the throat, using a tube —Morris Fishbein⟩ ⟨the bee that ~*s* from mountain heath her honey —William Wordsworth⟩ (4) : to draw by or as if by suction, absorption, inhalation ⟨a vacuum pump ~*s* the steam out of the cloth —Werner Von Bergen & H.R.Mauersberger⟩ ⟨was nearly ~*ed* under by a bog —*Brit. Bk. News*⟩ ⟨the pull of gravity . . . would ~ the blood away from his head —J.A. Michener⟩ ⟨the sun ~*ed* up the rain . . . —H.L.Merillat⟩ **b** *archaic* : to absorb (a characteristic) in infancy ⟨thy valiantness was mine, thou *suck'st* it from me —Shak.⟩ **c** : to gather or exhaust a supply of ⟨~*ed* away their specie reserves —S.E. Morison & H.S.Commager⟩ ⟨the bemused spinster ~*ing* culture from galleries —H.S.Canby⟩ ⟨~*ing* strength all round for the savage struggle —Liam O'Flaherty⟩ **d** : to affect and esp. involve in an enterprise by compulsion or deceit ⟨all of us . . . have been ~*ed* out of our native soil and scattered in every unlikely corner of the world —Michael Howard⟩ — usu. used with *in* or *into* ⟨inadvertently ~*ed* into the . . . intrigue —Martin Levin⟩ ⟨~*ed* into . . . jury duty —H.J.Laski⟩ ⟨found themselves . . . ~*ed* in as the purveyors of gossip —Alan Barth⟩ **2 a** (1) : to draw liquid or semifluid substance from by a partial vacuum caused by motion of the mouth ⟨~ an orange⟩; *specif* : to suck milk from (a breast or udder) (2) : to draw from or consume by applying the lips or tongue to or across the surface of or by or as if by a vacuum created by applying the mouth to a tube ⟨~ out the trachea —A.R.Koontz⟩ ⟨~ a lollipop⟩ (3) : to apply the mouth or its parts to in the manner of a child sucking the breast ⟨~*s* his thumb⟩ ⟨~*ing* his empty pipe —Ellen Glasgow⟩ **b** : to gather or exhaust the resources, strength, or vitality of ⟨a body ~*ed* and wasted by disease⟩ **3** : SUCKLE, NURSE **4** : to fawn upon ~ *vi* **1 a** : to draw milk from a breast or udder **b** : to draw something in by or as if by producing a vacuum ⟨the thirsty hot winds above ~ constantly at the soil —W.P.Webb⟩ **c** : to draw air — used of a pump that fails to draw fluid because of low water or a defective valve **d** : to draw in the mouth over or around an object in the manner of a child at the breast ⟨pensively . . . and slowly ~*ed* at his pipe —Haldane Macfall⟩ **2** : to flow or splash against a shore somewhat forcefully and in waves esp. so as to undermine or wash away part of its substance ⟨the tide drained and ~*ed* at the mud flats —Nicholas Monsarrat⟩ **3** : to become sucked so as to make a sound or motion ⟨his pipe ~*ed* hollowly —Walter Machen⟩ ⟨flanks ~*ed* in and out, the long nose resting on his paws —Virginia Woolf⟩ **4** : to act in an obsequious manner ⟨when they want votes . . . the candidates come ~*ing* around —W.G.Hardy⟩ — **suck dry** : to draw all the vitality, resources, or strength of : EXHAUST ⟨several centuries of essentialist thought have *sucked dry* reality —*Modern Schoolman*⟩ — **suck the blood of 1** : to exhaust the financial resources of **2** : to exhaust the vitality of — **suck the monkey 1** *Brit* : to drink from the bottle; *also* : to drink liquor from a cask by means of a straw or tube inserted in a small hole **2** *Brit* : to drink rum from a coconut emptied of its milk — **suck up to** *slang* : to truckle to : APPLE-POLISH ⟨*sucked up to* the boss for advancement —*Fortune*⟩

²suck \"\ *n* -S [ME *souke,* fr. *souken* to suck] **1 a** : the act of sucking; *specif* : the act of sucking milk ⟨a child at ~⟩ **b** : a sucking movement or force ⟨the strong ~ of the undertow⟩ **2** *obs* : milk drawn or to be drawn from the breast **3** : a small draft : SIP **4** : WHIRLPOOL **5** *slang* : an obsequious person : TOADY; *also* : the influence an obsequious person has over another

³suck \", ˈsu̇k\ *var of* SOCK

suck-bottle \ˈ=ˌ==\ *n* : NURSING BOTTLE

suck-egg \ˈ=ˌ=\ *n* **1** : a young, foolish, or contemptible person **2** : an animal (as a weasel or cuckoo) that sucks eggs

¹suck·en \ˈsəkən\ *n* -S [alter. of *soken*] *Scots law* : the lands subject to the thirlage of a mill

²sucken \"\ *adj* [short for obs. E *bond-sucken,* fr. E *bond* (bound) + ¹*sucken*] *Scot* : being or belonging to a suckener

suck·en·er \-k(ə)nə(r)\ *n* -S *Scots law* : a tenant bound to grind his grain at the mill of a sucken

¹suck·er \ˈsəkə(r)\ *n* -S [ME *soker, souker,* fr. *soken, souken* to suck + *-er* — more at SUCK] **1 a** : one that sucks esp. a breast or udder : SUCKLING; *specif* : an unweaned domestic animal **b** : a device for creating or regulating suction (as a piston or valve in a pump) **c** (1) : a plaything consisting of a soft leather disk suspended from a string that when wet clings to a surface of an object and lifts it (2) : a pipe or tube through which something is drawn by suction (3) : one of several cup-shaped vacuum-operated rubber devices to pick up and carry material in bookbinding; *specif* : one that feeds material in a folding or gathering machine **d** (1) : an organ in various animals for adhering or holding consisting in its simplest form of a soft pad or disk often somewhat concave that when closely applied to an object adheres as a result of atmospheric pressure : a sucking disk — see ECHINOCOCCUS illustration (2) : a mouth (as of a leech) adapted for sucking or adhering or both (3) : a tube foot of an echinoderm ending in a sucking disk **2** : a person who lives by extortion or parasitism **3 a** : a shoot originating from the roots or lower part of the stem of a plant and usu. developing rapidly often at the expense of the plant; *also* : an accessory propagative shoot ⟨a ~ of pineapple⟩ **b** : HAUSTORIUM **4 a** : any of numerous freshwater fishes of the family Catostomidae that are closely related to the carps but are distinguished from them by the structure of the mouth which usu. has thick soft lips and of the lower pharyngeal bones, that live and feed near the bottom, that in the case of larger forms ascend small streams and brooks to spawn, that have inferior flesh frequently eaten in regions where they are abundant, and that except for two Asiatic species are confined to No. America — see BUFFALO FISH, HOG SUCKER, REDHORSE **b** : any of various marine or freshwater true fishes (as the lumpfish, remora, or clingfish) with a sucking organ or mouth like that of a sucker — often used with a qualifying adjective **c** : HAGFISH **d** : LAMPREY **5** : LOLLIPOP b **6 a** (1) : a person easily cheated or deceived; *specif* : a mark for a gambler or confidence man (2) : a person irresistibly attracted by a specific type of object ⟨I've always been a ~ for animal acts —Al Hine⟩ **b** : GREENHORN **c** : a customer or frequenter of a circus, carnival, gambling establishment, or racetrack or a nonprofessional investor in securities **d** : ILLINOISAN — used as a nickname

²sucker \"\ *vb* **suckered; suckered; suckering** \-k(ə)riŋ\ **suckers** *vt* **1** : to remove suckers from ⟨~ tobacco⟩ **2** : to make a sucker of : CHEAT, DECEIVE, SWINDLE ⟨got ~*ed* out of six grand —Gerald Hughes⟩ ~ *vi* : to form or send out suckers ⟨corn ~*s* abundantly⟩

sucker bait *n* : a lure (as the promise of easy money) to attract a person to be swindled

sucker bet *n* : a bet offered at incorrect odds

suck·ered \-kə(r)d\ *adj* : provided with suckers

suck·er·el \ˈsək(ə)rəl\ *n* -S [¹*sucker* + *-el*] : a slender somewhat compressed sucker (*Cycleptus elongatus*) of the Mississippi drainage that is dark or bluish gray above and lighter below, has a small head and eyes, and may attain a weight of over five pounds

suckerfish \ˈ==ˌ=\ *n* : SUCKER 4; *esp* : REMORA

sucker foot *n* **1** : one of the terminal prolegs of a caterpillar **2** : one of the tube feet of an echinoderm

sucker-footed bat \ˈ==ˌ==-\ *n* : a small golden-furred Madagascan insectivorous bat (*Myzopoda aurita*) having adhesive suckers on the soles of the feet

sucker list *n* : a list of the names, addresses, and sometimes telephone numbers of persons who are likely to be purchasers or donors, to whom advertising matter might profitably be sent, or to whom personal application might be made ⟨purchased a *sucker list* from another seller of watered stock⟩ ⟨on the *sucker lists* of all the local charities⟩

sucker mouth *n* : the small oval cavity left by the disarticulation of the seed in oats

sucker rod *n* : a jointed rod connecting a pump plunger in a well with a walking beam or pumping jack at the surface

sucker shift *n* : a deceptive shift in football used to lure opposing linemen offside

suckfish \ˈ=ˌ=\ *n* **1** : REMORA **2** : a Pacific coast clingfish (*Caularchus maeandricus*) found in tide pools

suck fly *n* [so called fr. the fact that it sucks the sap from the leaves] : TOBACCO BUG

suckhole \ˈ=ˌ=\ *n* **1** *dial* : WHIRLPOOL **2** *dial* : a spot of quicksand

suck in *vt* **1** : CHEAT, DECEIVE **2** : to contract, flatten, and tighten (the abdomen) by inhaling deeply

suck-in \ˈ=ˌ=\ *n* -S [*suck in*] *Brit* : the process of being cheated : DECEPTION, FRAUD ⟨you never got such a *suck-in* in all your life —Frank O'Connor⟩

sucking *adj* [ME *souking,* fr. pres. part. of *souken* to suck — more at SUCK] **1** : not yet weaned ⟨~ pig⟩ **2** : very young : not full-fledged ⟨~ dove⟩

sucking coil *n* : a coil that draws in an iron core when carrying current

sucking fish *n* **1** : REMORA **2** : LAMPREY

sucking louse *n* : a louse of the order Anoplura characterized by possession of mouthparts adapted to sucking the body fluids of the host — compare BIRD LOUSE

sucking stomach *n* **1** : a food reservoir in some sucking insects connected with the esophagus by a tube **2** : the crop of an insect **3** : a widening of the posterior esophagus in spiders that functions as a pump

sucking wound *n* : a perforating wound of the chest through which air enters and leaves during respiration

¹suck·le \ˈsəkəl\ *vt* **suckled; suckled; suckling** \-k(ə)liŋ, -lēŋ\ **suckles** [prob. back-formation fr. ¹*suckling*] **1 a** : to give suck to **b** : REAR, FOSTER, NOURISH ⟨*suckled* on miracles, religious and astrological —Josephine Pinckney⟩ **2** : to nurse at or from : SUCK **3** : to take in as nourishment ⟨from whose lusty, healthy breast my father had *suckled* the first of that fine strength —Rafael Sabatini⟩

²suckle \"\ *also* **sucklebush** \ˈ==ˌ=\ *n, pl* **suckles** *also* **sucklebushes** [*suckle* fr. ME *sokel* clover, honeysuckle, short for *honysokel, honysoukel* honeysuckle; *sucklebush* fr. ²*suckle* + *bush* — more at HONEYSUCKLE] : HONEYSUCKLE

¹suck·ler \-k(ə)lə(r)\ *n* -S [¹*suckle* + *-er*] **1** : SUCKLING **2** : an animal that suckles its young : MAMMAL

²suckler \"\ *n* -S [²*suckle* + *-er*] *dial Eng* : the flowering head of a clover

¹suck·ling \ˈsəkliŋ, -lēŋ\ *n* -S [ME *sokeling,* fr. *soken* to suck + *-ling* — more at SUCK] : a young child or animal before it is weaned

²suckling \"\ *n* -S [ME *sokeling,* fr. *sokel* suckle + *-ing*] **1** *also* **suckling clover** : HOP CLOVER **2** : a tall-growing European honeysuckle (*Lonicera periclymenum*) sometimes cultivated for its richly fragrant flowers

suck-rock \ˈ=ˌ=\ *n* : CHITON 2

sucks *pres 3d sing of* SUCK, *pl of* SUCK

suckstone \ˈ=ˌ=\ *n* : REMORA

SUCL *abbr* set up in carloads

su·clat \səˈklät\ *n* -S [Hindi *suqlāt,* fr. Per *saqalāt* a rich cloth] *India* : any of various woolens; *specif* : European broadcloth

sucr- *or* **sucro-** *comb form* [ISV, fr. F *sucre,* fr. OF — more at SUGAR] : sugar ⟨*sucro*acid⟩

sucr *abbr* successor

su·crase \ˈsüˌkrās, -āz\ *n* -S [ISV *sucr-* + *-ase*] : INVERTASE

su·crate \ˈsüˌkrāt, -krət\ *n* -S [ISV *sucr-* + *-ate*] : a metallic derivative of sucrose ⟨strontium ~⟩ — compare SACCHARATE 2

¹su·cre \ˈsü(ˌ)krā\ *n* -S [Sp, after Antonio José de *Sucre* †1830 So. American liberator] **1** : the basic monetary unit of Ecuador — see MONEY table **2** : a coin representing one sucre

²sucre \"\ *adj, usu cap* [fr. *Sucre,* Bolivia] : of or from Sucre, the constitutional capital of Bolivia : of the kind or style prevalent in Sucre

su·cri·er \ˌsükrēˈā\ *n* -S [F, fr. *sucre* sugar + *-ier* -er] : a sugar bowl usu. with cover

su·crose \ˈsüˌkrōs *also* -ōz\ *n* -S [ISV *sucr-* + *-ose*] : a sweet water-soluble crystalline dextrorotatory nonreducing disaccharide sugar $C_{12}H_{22}O_{11}$ that occurs naturally in most land plants esp. in the juices, fruits, and roots and that is hydrolyzed by mineral acids or by invertase into equal parts of D-glucose and D-fructose — compare SACCHAROSE; GLUCOSE illustration

¹suc·tion \ˈsəkshən\ *n* -S *often attrib* [LL *suction-, suctio,* fr. L *suctus* (past part. of *sugere* to suck) + *-ion-, -io* -ion — more at SUCK] **1 a** : the act or process of sucking ⟨suck the membrane from the throat . . . by direct mouth-to-mouth ~ —Morris Fishbein⟩ **b** *Brit* : the imbibing of liquor **2 a** (1) : the act or process of exerting a force upon a solid, liquid, or gaseous body by reason of a reduced air pressure over part of its surface (2) : the force so exerted ⟨~ on the upper surface of an airplane wing⟩ ⟨surfaces that adhere through ~⟩ ⟨pumped up by ~⟩ **b** : the drawing in an internal-combustion engine of a gaseous mixture during the suction stroke; *also* : the power or capacity to draw in such mixture **c** *or* **suction drainage** : the act or process of removing secretions or fluids from hollow or tubular organs or cavities by means of a tube and a device (as a suction pump) that operates on negative pressure **3** : the capacity for absorbing moisture or wet paint **4** : the amount the share point of a moldboard plow is turned down to cause the share to descend or be drawn into the soil a predetermined distance **5** : a pipe, fitting, or other device used in a machine that operates by suction

²suction \"\ *vt* -ED/-ING/-S : to remove from a body cavity or passage by suction ⟨a small amount of mucus could be ~*ed* through the trachea —Leon Unger⟩

suction anemometer *n* : an anemometer consisting of an inverted siphon half-filled with water that measures a difference in water level due to the wind's force

suction box *n* **1** : a box with a perforated cover over which the wire of a paper machine passes and to which suction is applied in order to remove water from the wet paper web **2** : a box connected with a suction pump and used (as for drying or cleaning) in a manufacturing process

suction cleaner *also* **suction sweeper** *n* : VACUUM CLEANER

suction couch *n* : a rotary suction box that functions also as a couch roll

suction cup *n* : a cup of glass or of a flexible material (as rubber) in which a partial vacuum is produced when applied to a surface and which is used variously (as to bring blood to the surface of the skin, for traction or holding, or as part of a plunger)

suction dredge *n* : a dredging machine using a centrifugal pump to draw up mud, sand, and silt through a suction tube

suction force *or* **suction pressure** *or* **suction tension** *n* : DIFFUSION PRESSURE DEFICIT

suction pump *n* : a common pump in which the liquid to be raised is pushed by atmospheric pressure into the partial vacuum under a retreating valved piston on the upstroke and reflux is prevented by a nonreturn valve in the pipe

suction socket *n* : a socket on an artificial leg that is held to the stump by the suction of negative pressure maintained within the socket

suction stop *also* **suctional stop** *n* : a voice stop in the formation of which the air behind the articulation is rarefied with consequent inrush of air when the articulation is broken — compare PRESSURE STOP

suction stroke *n* : the stroke of the piston in an internal-combustion engine that effects the drawing in of the gaseous mixture to the engine cylinder

¹suc·to·ria \ˌsəkˈtōrēə\ *n pl, cap* [NL, fr. neut. pl. of *suctorius* suctorial] : a class of complex protozoans (subphylum Ciliophora) which have cilia only early in development and in which the mature form is fixed to the substrate, lacks locomotor organelles or cytostome, and obtains food through specialized suctorial tentacles — compare ACINETA, PODOPHRYA

²suctoria \"\ [NL] *syn of* HIRUDINEA

³suctoria \"\ [NL] *syn of* SIPHONAPTERA

⁴suctoria \"\ [NL] *syn of* RHIZOCEPHALA

suc·to·ri·al \ˌsəkˈtōrēəl\ *adj* [NL *suctorius* (fr. L *suctus* — past part. of *sugere* to suck — + *-orius* -ory) + E *-al*] — more at SUCK] **1** : adapted for sucking : serving to draw up fluid

or to adhere by suction ⟨~ mouths⟩ **2 a :** provided with suctorial organs ⟨a ~ fish⟩ **b :** living by sucking the blood or juices of animals or plants **3** [NL *Suctoria* + E *-al*] **:** of or relating to the Suctoria

suc·to·ri·an \ˌsəkˈtōrēən\ *n* -s [NL *Suctoria* + E *-an*] **1 :** a suctorial animal **2 :** one of the Suctoria

su·cu·pi·ra \ˌsükəˈpirə\ *n* -s [Pg, fr. Tupi *sucupira, sapupira*] **:** any of several tropical So. American timber trees esp. of the genera *Bowdichia* or *Diplotropis* of the family Leguminosae; *also* **:** the hard heavy dark wood of a sucupira that resembles acapu and is used esp. for wagon hubs and in shipbuilding

su·cu·ri \ˌsükəˈrē\ *or* **su·cu·riu** \ˌsükəˈrē,ü\ *or* **su·cu·ru·ju** \ˌsukərəˈzhü\ *or* **su·cu·ry** \ˌsükəˈrē\ *n, pl* **sucuris** *or* **sucurius** *or* **sucurujus** *or* **sucuries** [Pg *sucuri, sucuriu, sucuriju,* fr. Tupi *sucuriuh*] **:** ANACONDA 2

¹sud \ˌsəd, (ˌ)sůd\ *Scot & dial Eng var of* SHOULD

²sud \ˈsəd\ *var of* SUDS

su·da·dero \ˌsüdəˈde(ˌ)rō\ *n* -s [Sp, sweat cloth, handkerchief, saddle cloth, fr. *sudar* to sweat, fr. L *sudare* — more at SWEAT] **:** a broad piece (as of leather) attached to a stirrup strap to protect a rider's leg from sweat

su·da·men \süˈdāmən\ *n, pl* **sudam·i·na** \-damənə\ [NL *sudamin-, sudamen,* fr. L *sudare* to sweat — more at SWEAT] **:** a transient eruption of minute translucent vesicles caused by retention of sweat in the sweat glands and in the corneous layer of the skin and occurring after profuse perspiration

su·dam·i·nal \(ˈ)süˈdamənᵊl\ *adj* [NL *sudamin-, sudamen* + E *-al*] **:** of or relating to sudamen ⟨~ eruptions following severe sweating —H.F.Swift⟩

¹su·dan \(ˈ)süˈdan, -daa(ə)n *sometimes* -dän *or* -dån\ *adj, usu cap* [fr. the *Sudan,* region of north central Africa] **1 :** of or from the Sudan in northern Africa between the Sahara and the rainy tropics extending from the Atlantic ocean to the mountains of Ethiopia or to the Red sea **:** of the kind or style prevalent in the Sudan **:** SUDANESE **2 :** of or from the Republic of the Sudan in northeastern Africa **:** of the kind or style prevalent in the Republic of the Sudan **:** SUDANESE

²sudan \"\ *n* -s **1** *often cap* **:** a dark grayish yellow to light olive brown **2** *usu cap* **:** any of several azo solvent dyes some of which have a specific affinity for fatty substances and are used as biological stains — see DYE table I

sudan brown *n, often cap S* **:** a moderate to strong brown that is redder than oak and yellower and slightly darker than Vassar tan — called also *brown bread*

¹su·da·nese *also* **sou·da·nese** \ˌsüdᵊnˈēz, -dəˈnēz, -ēs\ *n, pl* **sudanese** *also* **soudanese** *cap* [*sudanese* fr. the *Sudan,* region of north central Africa + E *-ese; soudanese* fr. F *soudanais,* fr. *Soudan* the Sudan + *-ais* -ese] **1 :** a native or inhabitant of the Sudan belonging to one of various racial and linguistic groups including Arab and Arabic-speaking peoples, peoples of Hamitic affiliation (as the Tuaregs), and numerous Negro and negroid peoples **2 :** a native or inhabitant of the former Anglo-Egyptian Sudan or the Republic of the Sudan in northeast Africa

²sudanese *also* **soudanese** \"\ *adj, usu cap* **:** of or relating to the Sudan, to the former Anglo-Egyptian Sudan, or to the Republic of the Sudan **:** SUDAN

sudan IV *also* **sudan** *n* -s *usu cap S* **:** a red disazo solvent dye used chiefly as a biological stain and in ointments for promoting (as in the treatment of burns, wounds, or ulcers) the growth of epithelium — called also *scarlet red;* see DYE table I (under *Solvent Red 24*)

sudan grass *also* **sudan** *n* -s *usu cap S* **:** a vigorous tall-growing annual grass (*Sorghum vulgare sudanensis*) with usu. prominently awned spikelets that is adapted for growth in semiarid regions and is widely cultivated for hay and fodder

sudan gum *n, usu cap S* **:** gum arabic collected in the Sudan chiefly from one species of acacia (*Acacia senegal*) — compare KORDOFAN GUM

¹su·dani \süˈdanē, -ni *sometimes* -dän- *or* -dån-\ *adj, usu cap* [Ar *Sūdānīy* of the Sudan, fr. *Sūdān* the Sudan] **:** SUDANESE

²sudani \"\ *n* -s *cap* **1 :** SUDANESE **2 :** an Arabic dialect spoken in the Sudan

¹su·dan·ic \(ˈ)=ˈ=ik, -ēk\ *adj, usu cap* [fr. the *Sudan* + E *-ic*] **:** SUDANESE

²sudanic \"\ *n, cap* **:** the languages neither Bantu nor Hamitic spoken in a belt extending from Senegal to southern Sudan one large part of which has been shown to be related and with Bantu to form the Niger-Congo family and another large part of which forms the Chari-Nile family

su·dan·iza·tion \(ˌ)süˌdanəˈzāshən, ˌsüdᵊn-\ *n* -s *usu cap* **:** the act or process of Sudanizing ⟨the rate at which *Sudanization* of the administration, judiciary and security forces is to take place —*Economist*⟩

su·dan·ize \süˈdaˌnīz, ˈsüdᵊnˌīz\ *vt* -ED/-ING/-S *often cap* [*sudanese* + *-ize*] **:** to make Sudanese; *esp* **:** to staff with Sudanese

sudano- *comb form, usu cap* [¹*sudan*] **1 :** Sudanese **:** Sudanese and ⟨*Sudano*-Guinean⟩ **2 :** Sudan dye ⟨*sudanophil*⟩ ⟨*sudanophobic*⟩

su·dan·o·phil \süˈdanəˌfil\ *or* **su·dan·o·phil·ic** \(ˌ)=ˌ==ˈfilik\ *adj* [*sudano-* + *-phil* or *-philic*] *of a tissue or tissue element* **:** staining selectively with Sudan dyes; *also* **:** containing lipoid — **su·dan·o·phil·ia** \(ˌ)=ˌ==ˈfilēə\ *n* -s

su·dar·i·um \süˈda(a)rēəm\ *n, pl* **sudar·ia** \-ēə\ [L, fr. *sudare* to sweat + *-arium* -ary — more at SWEAT] **1 :** a linen square carried by the upper classes in Roman times (as for wiping perspiration from the face) **:** HANDKERCHIEF **2 :** an image of the face of Christ painted on a cloth and used as an aid to devotion **:** VERONICA **3 :** SUDATORIUM

su·da·ry \ˈsüdərē\ *n* -ES [ME, fr. L *sudarium*] **1** *archaic* **:** SUDARIUM **2** *obs* **:** WINDING-SHEET, SHROUD **3 :** HUMERAL VEIL

su·da·tion \süˈdāshən\ *n* -s [L *sudation-, sudatio,* fr. *sudatus* (past part. of *sudare* to sweat) + *-ion-, -io* -ion] **:** SWEATING

su·da·to·ri·um \ˌsüdəˈtōrēəm\ *n, pl* **sudato·ria** \-ēə\ [L, fr. *sudatus* + *-orium*] **:** a sweat room in a bath

¹su·da·to·ry \ˈsüdəˌtōrē\ *adj* [L *sudatorius,* fr. *sudatus* + *-orius* -ory] **:** producing sweating

²sudatory \"\ *n* -ES [L *sudatorium*] **:** SUDATORIUM

sud·bur·ite \ˈsədbəˌrīt\ *n* -s [fr. *Sudbury* district, Ontario, Canada + E *-ite*] **:** a basic hypersthene-bearing basalt composed of bytownite, hypersthene, augite, and magnetite, often vesicular, and sometimes somewhat metamorphosed

sudd \ˈsəd\ *n* -s [Ar, lit., obstruction] **:** floating vegetable matter that is composed chiefly of papyrus stems and an aquatic grass (*Vossia procera*) often intermixed with ambatch and that forms obstructive masses in the upper White Nile

¹sud·den \ˈsədᵊn\ *adj* [ME *sodain, sodein,* fr. MF *sodain, sudain,* fr. L *subitaneus,* fr. *subitus* sudden, unexpected, fr. past part. of *subire* to come up, occur unexpectedly, fr. *sub-* up + *ire* to go — more at SUB-, ISSUE] **1 a :** happening without previous notice or with very brief notice **:** coming or occurring unexpectedly **:** not foreseen or prepared for ⟨caught out walking by a ~ thundershower⟩ ⟨took a ~ almost miraculous turn for the better⟩ **b :** changing angle or character all at once **:** PRECIPITOUS ⟨slopes gradually downwards toward the ~ drop of the icefall —John Hunt and Edmund Hillary⟩ **:** ABRUPT ⟨this ridge forms an important and ~ break between the land of abundant ground water . . . and the dry land —P.E.James⟩ **c :** come upon or met with unexpectedly ⟨watching for ~ turns in the road⟩ **2 a :** characterized by or manifesting hastiness **:** RASH, HEADLONG ⟨a red setter . . . too ~ to be a friend —May Sarton⟩ **b** *obs* **:** characterized by swift action **:** FAST-MOVING, QUICK, ALERT ⟨appearing goodly to the ~ eye —John Milton⟩ **3 a** *archaic* **:** made, provided, brought about, or acting in a short time **:** PROMPT, IMMEDIATE ⟨he acquaints the citizens with the king's peril . . . and requests their ~ assistance —John Cleveland⟩ ⟨hire assassins or put ~ poison in my evening drink —P.B.Shelley⟩ **b** *obs* **:** executed or executing on the spur of the moment **:** IMPROMPTU, EXTEMPORE ⟨do it without invention, suddenly, as I with ~ . . . speech purpose to answer —Shak.⟩ **c** *obs* **:** shortly to come or be **:** EARLY, SOON ⟨tomorrow, in my judgment, is too ~ —Shak.⟩ **syn** see PRECIPITATE

²sudden \"\ *adv* **:** SUDDENLY ⟨~ I heard a voice —Alfred Tennyson⟩

³sudden \"\ *n* -s *obs* **:** an unexpected occurrence **:** EMERGENCY — **of a sudden** *or* **on a sudden** *also* **on the sudden** *adv* **:** sooner than was expected **:** at once **:** SUDDENLY ⟨withdrew his opposition all *of a sudden* —W.M.Thackeray⟩ ⟨the driver had swerved *on a sudden* to avoid a file of geese —Ellen Glasgow⟩ ⟨an effect, *on the sudden,* of real sublimity —Walter Pater⟩

sudden death *n* **1 :** unexpected death that is instantaneous or occurs within minutes from any cause other than violence ⟨*sudden death* following coronary occlusion⟩ ⟨from battle and murder and from *sudden death,* good Lord, deliver us —*Bk. of Com. Prayer*⟩ **2 :** decision by a single throw of dice or toss or spin of a coin in gambling **3 a :** a single full game played to break a tie **b :** competition to break a tie that terminates the moment one side scores or gains the lead in an overtime period or play-off **4 :** a disease of cloves (as in Zanzibar and Madagascar) of unknown cause marked by the extreme rapidity with which death of the tree follows a slight chlorosis and wilting

sud·den·ly *adv* [ME *sodeinliche,* fr. *sodein* sudden + *-liche* -ly] **:** in a sudden manner

sud·den·ness \-dᵊn(n)əs\ *n* -ES **:** the quality or state of being sudden

sud·dent \-dᵊnt\ *dial var of* SUDDEN

suddenty *n* -ES [ME *sodeinte, sodentie,* fr. MF *sodeineté,* fr. *sodein* sudden + *-té* -ty] *obs* **:** SUDDENNESS — **of a suddenty** *or* **on a suddenty** *adv* **1 :** SUDDENLY **2** *Scots law* **:** without premeditation

sud·dle \ˈsədᵊl, ˈsůd-\ *n or vb* [prob. fr. MHG *sudelen;* akin to G dial. *sudel* swamp, bog, Gk *hyei* it is raining — more at SUCK] *Scot & dial Eng* **:** STAIN, SOIL

sud·dy \ˈsədē, -di\ *adj* -ER/-EST [*sud* + *-y*] **:** SUDSY

¹su·de·ten \süˈdātᵊn\ *also* **su·det·ic** \(ˈ)=ˈded·ik\ *adj, usu cap* [fr. *Sudeten,* mountain ranges in northern Czechoslovakia] **1 :** of, relating to, or being a semicircular chain of mountain ranges in the provinces of Bohemia and Silesia extending around the northern and western borders of Czechoslovakia **2 :** of, relating to, or being all the borderlands of Bohemia and Moravia

²sudeten *or* **sudeten german** \"\ *n* -s *cap S&G* **:** a German-speaking native or inhabitant of the Sudeten region

su·do·motor \ˌsüdō+\ *adj* [*sudo-* (fr. L *sudor* sweat) + *motor*] *of nerve fibers* **:** controlling the activity of sweat glands

su·do·rif·er·ous \ˌsüdəˈrif(ə)rəs\ *adj* [LL *sudorifer* sudoriferous (fr. L *sudor* sweat + *-ifer* -iferous) + E *-ous*] **:** producing or conveying sweat ⟨~ glands⟩ ⟨a ~ duct⟩

¹su·do·rif·ic \-fik\ *adj* [NL *sudorificus,* fr. L *sudor* sweat + *-i-* + *-ficus* -fic — more at SWEAT] **:** causing or inducing sweat **:** DIAPHORETIC ⟨~ herbs⟩

²sudorific \"\ *n* -s **:** a sudorific agent or medicine

su·do·rip·a·rous \ˌsüdəˈripərəs\ *adj* [NL *sudoriparus,* fr. L *sudor* + *-i-* + *-parus* -parous] **:** SUDORIFEROUS

su·dra *also* **shu·dra** \ˈs(h)üdrə\ *n* -s *usu cap* [Skt *śūdra*] **1 :** a member of the fourth ancient Hindu varna formed chiefly from conquered non-Aryans and assigned by classical law to menial occupations involving manual labor **2 :** a Hindu belonging to one of a large group of modern lower castes traditionally derived from the ancient Sudra varna — compare BRAHMAN, HARIJAN, KSHATRIYA, VAISYA

¹suds \ˈsədz\ *n pl but sing or pl in constr* [prob. fr. MD *sudde, sudse* (sing.) marsh, bog; akin to OE *sēothan* to seethe — more at SEETHE] **1 a** *obs* **:** FILTH, DREGS **b :** DUMPS — usu. used in the phrase *in the suds* **2 a :** water impregnated with soap and typically containing bubbles and froth **:** a foamy soap solution **b :** the froth or bubbles formed on soapy water ⟨arms white with ~⟩ **c :** a washing in water containing suds ⟨trousers usually require only one ~ —N.J. Berg⟩ **3 a :** FOAM, FROTH ⟨the ~ cast up by the waves⟩ **b** *slang* **:** BEER **4** *also* **sud :** soapy waste liquor formed by the scouring of wool before bleaching and containing grease

²suds \"\ *vb* -ED/-ING/-ES *vt* **:** to wash (as a garment) in suds ~ *vi* **:** to form suds ⟨a soap that ~*es* easily⟩

sudsy \ˈsədzē, -zi\ *adj* -ER/-EST [¹*suds* + *-y*] **:** full of suds **:** FROTHY, FOAMY

¹sue \ˈsü\ *vb* **sued; sued; suing; sues** [ME *suen, suwen, siwen, sewen,* fr. OF *sivre, suivre, suir,* fr. (assumed) VL *sequere,* fr. L *sequi* to follow, come or go after; akin to Gk *hepesthai* to follow, Skt *sacati* he accompanies, follows] *vt* **1** *obs* **a :** to go in pursuit of **:** try to overtake **:** CHASE **b :** to come after (as in time, order, or logical sequence) **:** ensue upon **:** result from **c :** to be a follower or servant or attendant or disciple of **d :** to guide or govern by (as an intention, one's will) **e :** to engage in as a pastime, occupation, or profession **:** PRACTICE **f :** to follow up **:** PROSECUTE, CONTINUE **2 :** to make petition to or for **:** SOLICIT, URGE **3 :** to pay court or suit to **:** WOO **4 a** *early Eng law* (1) **:** to follow or attend upon (a feudal superior) or to resort to (the superior's mill) for the grinding of grain (2) **:** to follow or seek (a court) in order to assist the court in administering justice usu. as a doomster or in order to obtain justice (3) **:** to follow (a person) to a court in order to act as a witness or compurgator in an action in the court **b :** to follow or go to (a court) in order to obtain legal redress ⟨*sued* the court for a writ of recovery⟩ **c :** to seek justice or right from (a person) by legal process **:** bring an action against **:** prosecute judicially **d :** to proceed with (a legal action) and follow up to proper termination **:** gain by legal process ~ *vi* **1 :** to follow someone or something **2 :** to make a request or application **:** PETITION, ENTREAT, PLEAD — usu. used with *for* or *to* **3 :** to pay court or suit **:** WOO ⟨he loved . . . but *sued* in vain —William Wordsworth⟩ **4 a** *early English feudal law* **:** to perform the duties or part of one who sues a superior court or person **b :** to take legal proceedings in court **:** seek in law ⟨~ for damages⟩

²sue *var of* SEW

sue and labor clause *n* [¹*sue*] **:** a clause ordinarily inserted in a marine insurance policy by which the insured contracts to sue, labor, and travel for, in, and about the defense, safeguard, and recovery of the insured property and the insurer agrees to bear his proportion of the expenses voluntarily incurred therefor

¹suede *or* **suède** \ˈswād\ *n* -s *often attrib* [fr. the phrase *suède gloves,* part translation of F *gants de Suède* Swedish gloves] **1 :** leather finished by buffing with an emery wheel usu. on the flesh side to produce a napped surface and used esp. for handbags, shoes, gloves, sports coats **2** *or* **suede cloth :** a woven or knitted fabric of wool, cotton, rayon finished with a very short smooth nap to give the texture and appearance of suede leather and used for sportswear, shirts, gloves **3 :** a light to moderate brown that is slightly yellower than tanbark or mocha bisque — called also *café crème*

²suede *also* **suède** \"\ *vb* -ED/-ING/-S *vt* **:** to give a suede finish or nap to (a fabric or leather) ~ *vi* **:** to give cloth or leather a suede finish

¹su·ent \ˈsüənt\ *adj* [alter. of ME *suaunt, suante* following, agreeable, smooth, fr. MF *suiant, suant,* pres. part. of *suir* to follow — more at SUE] **1** *dial* **:** SMOOTH, EVEN, REGULAR, STEADY **2** *dial* **:** EQUABLE, AGREEABLE **3** *dial* **:** PLACID, QUIET, GRAVE, DEMURE — **su·ent·ly** *adv, dial*

²suent \"\ *adv, dial* **:** in a suent manner

sue out *vt* [ME *suen out,* fr. *suen* to sue + *out*] **:** to obtain by suit **:** petition for and take out or apply for and obtain in judicial proceedings ⟨*sue out* a writ in chancery⟩ ⟨*sue out* a pardon⟩

su·er \ˈsüə(r), ˈsů(ə)r, -üə\ *n* -s [ME, fr. *suen* to sue + *-er*] **:** one that sues

suer·te \ˈswer(ˌ)tā\ *n* -s [Sp, lot, chance, luck, suerte, fr. L *sort-, sors* lot, chance — more at SORT] **:** a skilled movement or pass in a bullfight

su·et \ˈsüət, *usu* -əd·+V\ *n* -s [ME *swet, sewet,* fr. (assumed) AF *suet, sewet,* dim. of AF *sue, seu,* fr. L *sebum* tallow, suet — more at SOAP] **:** the hard fat about the kidneys and loins in beef and mutton that when melted and freed from the membranes forms tallow — compare LEAF FAT

suet pudding *n* **:** a boiled or steamed pudding made with chopped suet, flour, bread crumbs, raisins, and spices

su·ety \-d·ē, -t|, |i\ *adj* [*suet* + *-y*] **:** of, full of, or like suet

sueve \ˈswēv\ *n* -s *cap* [LL *Suevus,* fr. L *suevus* Suevian (adj.), fr. *Suevi*] **:** SUEVIAN

sue·vi \ˈswāˌ(ˌ)vē, -wēˌvī\ *or* **sue·bi** \-bē,-bī\ *n pl, cap* [L *Suevi, Suebi,* of Gmc origin; akin to G *Schwaben* Swabians] **:** SUEVIANS

¹sue·vi·an \-ˌvēən\ *n* -s *cap* [L *Suevi* + E *-ian,* n. suffix] **:** one of an ancient Germanic people prob. of many distinct tribes mentioned by Caesar as dwelling east of the Rhine and by Tacitus as extending to the Elbe and the Baltic; *also* **:** one of a Germanic horde from this region that overran France and Spain early in the 5th century A.D.

²suevian \"\ *or* **sue·vic** \-ˌvik\ *adj, usu cap* [L *Suevi* + E *-ian,* adj. suffix, or *-ic*] **:** of or relating to the Suevians

su·ez \süˈez, süˈez, *chiefly Brit* ˈsüiz\ *adj, usu cap* [fr. *Suez,* seaport city of Lower Egypt] **:** of or from the city of Suez, Egypt **:** of the kind or style prevalent in Suez

suf *abbr* suffix

suff *n* -s [origin unknown] *obs* **:** the shoreward surge of the sea

suff *abbr* **1** sufficient **2** suffix **3** suffragan

suf·fect \(ˌ)səˈfekt\ *n* -s [L (*consul*) *suffectus,* fr. *consul* + *suffectus,* past part. of *sufficere* to put in place of — more at SUFFICE] **:** a Roman consul elected to complete the term of one who vacated office before the end of the year

suf·fer \ˈsəfə(r)\ *vb* **suffered; suffered; suffering** \-f(ə)riŋ\ **suffers** [ME *soffren, suffren, sufferen,* fr. OF *soffrir, souffrir,* fr. (assumed) VL *sufferire,* fr. L *sufferre* to bear up, endure, suffer, fr. *sub-* up + *ferre* to bear — more at SUB-, BEAR] *vt* **1 :** to submit to or be forced to endure the infliction, imposition, or penalty of **:** bear as a victim ⟨~ martyrdom⟩ ⟨~ a year's imprisonment⟩ **:** to be subjected to physical or mental pain because of **:** endure with distress ⟨~ thirst⟩ ⟨~ insults⟩ **:** to feel keenly or acutely ⟨~ pain of body⟩ ⟨~ grief of mind⟩ **:** labor under ⟨the greatest handicap which our side ~*s* in entering the political conference —Willson Woodside⟩ **2 :** to go or pass through (as harm or loss) **:** UNDERGO ⟨most or all genes ~ mutational changes from time to time —Theodosius Dobzhansky⟩ **:** EXPERIENCE ⟨the company ~*ed* a 35% drop in sales the first quarter —*Wall Street Jour.*⟩ **:** SUSTAIN ⟨records that had ~*ed* damage during storage⟩ **3 :** to endure or undergo without sinking **:** have power to resist or sustain **:** to bear up under **:** SUPPORT ⟨~ through half an hour of standing in line for the sake of a five-minute ride⟩ — used chiefly in negative statements ⟨shrubs that cannot ~ a cold winter⟩ ⟨never able to ~ the slightest pain⟩ **4 a :** not to forbid or hinder **:** ALLOW, PERMIT ⟨in later years ~*ed* his beard to grow long —K.W.Colgrove⟩ **b :** to put up with **:** TOLERATE ⟨too proud of its revolutionary tradition to ~ dictatorship gladly —W.L.Burn⟩ **5** *chiefly dial* **:** to cause pain or suffering to ~ *vi* **1 :** to submit to or endure death, affliction, penalty, or pain or distress ⟨contracted rheumatoid arthritis and ~*ed* intensely⟩ ⟨make him ~ for his mistake⟩; *sometimes* **:** to endure such willingly or patiently ⟨martyrs who ~*ed* for Christ's sake⟩ **2 :** to be the one acted upon as distinguished from the one acting ⟨matter cannot act — it can only ~⟩ **3 :** to sustain loss or damage ⟨business ~*s* greatly from a long-continued depression⟩ **4 a :** to be in a state of disability (as from ill health, anxiety, error) **:** be subject to something disabling ⟨too many of them ~ from nervous or heart disabilities —H.W.Baldwin⟩ ⟨~*s* from the fallacy of supposing that everyone feels as he does⟩ **b :** to be at a disadvantage **:** labor under a handicap ⟨for years the school had ~*ed* from lack of funds —*Amer. Guide Series: Mich.*⟩ ⟨the story ~*s* by comparison with the shorter ones —Louise Anderson⟩ ⟨the men . . . ~*ed* from no lack of self-esteem —Van Wyck Brooks⟩ **syn** see BEAR, EXPERIENCE, LET

suf·fer·able \-f(ə)rəbəl\ *adj* [ME *suffrable,* fr. MF *soufrable,* fr. OF, fr. *souffrir* to suffer + *-able*] **1** *obs* **a :** able to suffer or endure **:** PATIENT **b :** ALLOWABLE, PERMISSIBLE **2 :** that can be suffered **:** ENDURABLE, TOLERABLE — **suf·fer·able·ness** \-nəs\ *n* -ES — **suf·fer·ably** \-blē,-bli\ *adv*

suf·fer·ance \ˈsəf(ə)rən(t)s\ *n* -s [ME *suffrance,* fr. OF *soufrance,* fr. *souffrir* to suffer + *-ance*] **1 :** patient endurance **:** forbearance under provocation **:** LONG-SUFFERING ⟨still have I borne it with a patient shrug, for ~ is the badge of all our tribe —Shak.⟩ **2** *archaic* **:** an act, state, or instance of suffering **:** PAIN, MISERY ⟨~*s* that you had borne —Shak.⟩ **3 :** consent or sanction that is not explicit but is implied by a lack of interference or the failure to enforce a prohibition **:** toleration of something that is usu. disapproved or illegal **:** passive or tacit permission — used usu. with *on, by,* or *through* ⟨he remains here on ~⟩ ⟨by ~ only were they allowed to enter the country⟩; *specif* **:** the legal condition of one continuing in the possession of an estate after his right to it has expired and without express leave from the owner — used with *at* or *by* ⟨a tenant at ~⟩ ⟨estates by ~⟩ **4 :** power or ability to endure or withstand **:** ENDURANCE ⟨it is beyond ~⟩ **5 :** BILL OF SUFFERANCE

sufferance wharf *n* **:** a licensed private wharf where dutiable goods may be kept until the duty is paid

suf·fer·er \-fərə(r)\ *n* -s [ME *suffrer,* fr. *suffren* to suffer + *-er*] **:** one that suffers; *esp* **:** one that endures or undergoes suffering or who sustains inconvenience or loss ⟨a new drug giving relief to hay fever ~*s*⟩ ⟨emergency aid given to flood ~*s*⟩

¹suffering *n* -s [ME *suffring,* fr. gerund of *suffren* to suffer] **1 :** the state or experience of one who suffers **:** the endurance of or submission to affliction, pain, loss **2 :** a pain endured or a distress, loss, or injury incurred ⟨rise from a bed of ~⟩ ⟨experience untold ~⟩ ⟨endured many ~*s*⟩ ⟨no one . . . better prepared by habitual ~ —Jane Austen⟩ **syn** see DISTRESS

²suffering *adj* [ME *suffring,* fr. pres. part. of *suffren* to suffer] **1 a :** that suffers **b :** characterized by or proceeding from suffering **2 :** ILL, SICK ⟨is he very ~ —Owen Wister⟩ — **suf·fer·ing·ly** *adv*

suf·fete \ˈsəˌfēt\ *n, pl* **suf·fetes** \-ˌfēts, ˈsəfəˌtēz\ [L *sufet-, sufes, suffet-, suffes,* of Punic origin; akin to Heb *shōphēṭ* judge] **:** one of the two annually elected chief magistrates of ancient Carthage

suf·fice \səˈfīs *sometimes* -īz\ *vb* -ED/-ING/-S [ME *suffisen, sufficen,* fr. MF *suffis-,* stem of *suffire,* fr. L *sufficere* to put under or in place of, provide, suffice, fr. *sub-* under, in place of + *-ficere* (fr. *facere* to do, make) — more at SUB-, DO] *vi* **1 :** to be enough **:** to meet or satisfy a need **:** to be adequate or sufficient ⟨a hint will ~⟩ ⟨ten bombs *sufficed* to destroy the fort⟩ — often used with an impersonal *it* ⟨~ it that without leisure there is no liberty —G.B.Shaw⟩ **2 :** to measure up to a standard **:** satisfy all requirements **:** be competent, capable, equal to a task ⟨what words or tongue of seraph can ~ —John Milton⟩ **3** *obs* **:** to permit within fixed limits **:** allow or admit of something ~ *vt* **1 :** to be enough for (a person) **:** give a sufficiency to **:** satisfy the needs or appetite of ⟨education that *sufficed* our forefathers⟩ ⟨enough food to ~ an army⟩ **2 :** to serve to satisfy (a want, appetite) **:** APPEASE ⟨this ~*s* present needs⟩ **3** *obs* **a :** to be capable of **b :** supply adequately **:** REPLENISH, FURNISH ⟨the power appeased, with winds *sufficed* the sail —John Dryden⟩

suf·fic·er \-īsə(r) *sometimes* -īzə-\ *n* -s **:** one that suffices

suf·fi·cience \səˈfishən(t)s\ *n* -s [ME, fr. LL *sufficientia*] *archaic* **:** SUFFICIENCY

suf·fi·cien·cy \-nsē,-nsi\ *n* -ES [LL *sufficientia,* fr. L *sufficient-, sufficiens* sufficient + *-ia* -y] **1 :** sufficient means to meet one's obligations or satisfy one's needs **:** COMPETENCY; *also* **:** a modest but not parsimonious scale or way of living **:** adequate comfort **2 :** the quality or state of being sufficient or adequate to the end proposed **:** ADEQUACY ⟨question the ~ of the equipment⟩ **:** ENOUGH ⟨eat a ~⟩ **3 :** the character or fact of being qualified **:** ABILITY, CAPACITY ⟨the ~ of present laws to meet a severe financial crisis⟩ **4 :** CONCEIT, SELF-CONFIDENCE, SELF-SUFFICIENCY ⟨the master had not flinched . . . nor . . . did he betray the least ~ —R.L.Stevenson⟩

¹suf·fi·cient \-nt\ *adj* [ME, fr. L *sufficient-, sufficiens,* fr. pres. part. of *sufficere* to suffice] **1 :** marked by quantity, scope, power, or quality to meet with the demands, wants, or needs of a situation or of a proposed use or end ⟨an ample sum, one ~ to supply those wants of hers —Thomas Hardy⟩ ⟨have not ~ information to state the exact damage —F.D. Roosevelt⟩ **2** *archaic* **:** adequately qualified or competent **3** *obs* **a :** excessively self-confident **b :** WEALTHY, WELL-TO-DO **4** *archaic* **:** well-made **:** SUBSTANTIAL **5** *of a bid in bridge* **:** higher in rank than the bid over which it is made

syn ENOUGH, ADEQUATE, COMPETENT: SUFFICIENT is likely to refer to a quantity or scope that meets the demands of a specific situation ⟨like ninety-nine percent of those who are taught the classics, I never acquired *sufficient* proficiency to read them with pleasure —Bertrand Russell⟩ ⟨a pinch from his snuffbox was an honor *sufficient* to turn the head of a young

enthusiast —T.B.Macaulay〉 ENOUGH, often placed after the noun it modifies, as in *men enough, money enough*, is less exact and more approximate than SUFFICIENT in its suggestion 〈my country! and 'tis joy *enough* and pride for one hour's perfect bliss to tread the grass of England once again —William Wordsworth〉 ADEQUATE may suggest barely meeting a requirement, with nothing excessive or ample remaining 〈vocabulary . . . was perfectly *adequate* to the clear and forceful statement of his ideas —Aldous Huxley〉 ADEQUATE is wider in its sphere of use than SUFFICIENT or ENOUGH 〈you can get along quite comfortably if you're just *adequate*, but it's different with an artist —W.S.Maugham〉 COMPETENT, usu. not used in reference to counting or physical measurement like others in this set, may be entirely complimentary or may imply some of the slighting suggestion of ADEQUATE 〈her *competent* steely mind never rested —Rebecca West〉 〈*competent* narrative or exposition, skilled but not beautiful or artistic writing such as deserves the name of literature —Samuel Alexander〉

²sufficient \"\ *n* -S : SUFFICIENCY, ENOUGH 〈ate till he had ~〉

sufficient condition *n* **1** : a cause, ground, or condition such that if it be given the thing in question is assured **2** : CONDITION 2a(3)

suf·fi·cient·ly *adv* [ME, fr. ¹*sufficient* + *-ly*] : in a sufficient manner or to a sufficient degree

suf·fi·cient·ness *n* -ES [¹*sufficient* + *-ness*] : SUFFICIENCY

sufficient reason *n* **1** : LAW OF SUFFICIENT REASON **2** : SUFFICIENT CONDITION

sufficing *pres part of* SUFFICE

¹suf·fix \'səˌfiks\ *n* -ES [NL *suffixum*, fr. L, neut. of *suffixus*, past part. of *suffigere* to fasten underneath, fasten to, fr. *sub-* + *figere* to fasten — more at DIKE] **1** : an affix occurring at the end of a word, base, or phrase — compare PREFIX **2** : SUBINDEX 1

²suf·fix \", (ˌ)sə'f-\ *vt* -ED/-ING/-ES [partly fr. L *suffixus*, past part. of *suffigere* to fasten to; partly fr. ¹*suffix*] : to add or annex to the end of a word, base, or phrase : attach as a suffix

suf·fix·al \'səˌfiksəl, (ˌ)ˌ='==\ *or* **suf·fix·i·al** \(ˌ)səˌfiksēəl\ *adj* [¹*suffix* + *-al* or *-ial*] : of, relating to, or being a suffix

suf·fix·a·tion \ˌsəˌfik'sāshən\ *n* -S [²*suffix* + *-ation*] : formation or inflection by means of suffixes

suf·flam·i·nate \sə'flaməˌnāt\ *vt* -ED/-ING/-S [L *sufflaminatus*, past part. of *sufflaminare* to check, brake, fr. *sufflamin-, sufflamen* brake, fr. *sub-* + (assumed) L *flagmen, flamen* chock, prop; akin to OE *balca* ridge — more at BALK] : OBSTRUCT, IMPEDE

suf·flate \(ˌ)sə'flāt\ *vt* -ED/-ING/-S [L *sufflatus*, past part. of *sufflare* to blow up, inflate, fr. *sub-* up + *flare* to blow — more at SUB-, BLOW] : to blow up; INFLATE, INSPIRE

suf·fla·tion \(ˌ)sə'flāshən\ *n* -S [L *sufflation-, sufflatio*, fr. *sufflatus* + *-ion-, -io* -ion] : an act or instance of sufflating; *specif* : INSPIRATION

suf·fo·cate \'səfəˌkāt, *usu* -ād.+V\ *vb* -ED/-ING/-S [L *suffocatus*, past part. of *suffocare* to choke, stifle, fr. *sub-* + *fauces, foces* (pl.) throat] *vt* **1** : to stop the respiration of (as by strangling or asphyxiation) : deprive of oxygen by any means : make unable to breathe **2** *obs* : to compress so as to impede or prevent breathing 〈let not hemp his windpipe ~ —Shak.〉 **3 a** : to overcome or make extremely uncomfortable by want of cool fresh air **b** : to impede or stop the development, growth, or activity of as though by depriving of air ~ *vi* : to become suffocated: **a** : to die from being unable to breathe 〈the children locked in the chest *suffocated*〉 **b** : to be very uncomfortable through lack of air 〈she was *suffocating* in the hot little kitchen〉 **c** : to become checked, stultified, or enervated in growth or development

syn ASPHYXIATE, STIFLE, SMOTHER, CHOKE, STRANGLE, THROTTLE: SUFFOCATE commonly refers to conditions in which breathing is impossible through lack of available oxygen or through presence of noxious or poisonous gas 〈prisoners *suffocated* in the underground dungeon〉 SUFFOCATE also refers to situations in which breathing is impossible because mouth and nose are covered 〈*suffocating* under the mud and earth which had fallen over his head〉 ASPHYXIATE is likely to refer to situations in which death comes through poisonous gases in the air or through lack of sufficient oxygen 〈*asphyxiated* by the chlorine gas in the cellar〉 STIFLE is likely to refer to situations in which breathing is difficult or impossible through lack of adequate fresh air and, often, presence of heat 〈closing a hatch to stop a fire and the destruction of a cargo was justified even if it was known that doing so would *stifle* a man below —O.W.Holmes †1935〉 SMOTHER is likely to be used in situations in which the supply of oxygen is inadequate for life; it often suggests a deadening pall of smoke, dust, or other impurity in the air 〈*smothered* by the dust after the explosion〉 〈a smell of soot which *smothered* the scent of wistaria and iris —Louis Bromfield〉 SMOTHER also refers to situations in which the mouth and nose are covered so that one cannot breathe 〈was *smothered* with a cushion〉 CHOKE suggests difficulty in breathing through constriction, obstruction, or extreme irritation within the throat 〈*choked* to death by a brutal marauder〉 〈*choking* on a chicken bone lodged in the throat〉 〈*choking* as he breathed the acrid smoke〉 STRANGLE also refers to constriction of the throat, obstruction of the windpipe, or irritation but it is more likely to indicate fatality or quite serious condition 〈fingers itched to *strangle* him —R.W. Buchanan〉 〈*strangling* on a chicken bone〉 THROTTLE may suggest external compression of the throat done forcefully for the purpose of subduing or overcoming resistance 〈heartbeats . . . so violent that they seemed . . . *throttling* hands to her throat —Edith Wharton〉

suf·fo·cat·ing·ly \'==ˌ===, ˌ=='===\ *adv* [*suffocating* (pres. part. of *suffocate*) + *-ly*] : in a suffocating manner

suf·fo·ca·tion \ˌsəfə'kāshən\ *n* -S [L *suffocation-, suffocatio*, fr. *suffocatus* + *-ion-, -io* -ion] : the act of suffocating or state of being suffocated : stoppage of breathing — compare ASPHYXIA

suf·fo·ca·tive \'səfəˌkāt·iv\ *adj* [L *suffocatus* + E *-ive*] : tending or able to choke or stifle 〈~ catarrh〉

¹suf·folk \'səfək *sometimes* -ˌfōk *or* -ˌfōk\ *adj, usu cap* [fr. *Suffolk*, county of eastern England] : of or from the county of Suffolk, England : of the kind or style prevalent in Suffolk

²suffolk \"\ *n* **1** *usu cap* : any of several English breeds of livestock: as **a** : a breed of black-faced hornless sheep derived in part from the Southdown, producing excellent mutton, but having a light fleece and being somewhat rangy **b** : a breed of chestnut-colored draft horses having a deep heavy body, a large head, and short legs — called also *Suffolk punch* **2** -S *often cap* : an animal of any of the Suffolk breeds

suffolk punch *n, usu cap S* : SUFFOLK 1b

suffr *abbr* suffragan

¹suf·fra·gan \'səfrəgən, -rēl, ÷ |jən\ *n* -S [ME *suffragan*, fr. MF, fr. ML *suffraganeus*, fr. *suffragium* support, assistance, intercessory prayer — more at SUFFRAGE] **1** *or* **suffragan bishop a** : a diocesan bishop (as in the Roman Catholic Church and the Church of England) subordinate to a metropolitan **b** : BISHOP SUFFRAGAN **c** : a Protestant Episcopal bishop elected by a diocese as assistant to the diocesan without right of succession, having no share in the jurisdiction of the diocese, and taking such duties as are assigned to him from time to time — compare BISHOP COADJUTOR **2** *obs* : ASSISTANT, DEPUTY, AGENT

²suffragan \"\ *adj* **1** : of or being a suffragan **2** : subordinate to a metropolitan or archiepiscopal see

suf·fra·gan·ship \-ˌship\ *n* [¹*suffragan* + *-ship*] : the office or rank of a suffragan

¹suf·frage \'səfrij, -rēj, ÷ 'səfər-\ *n* -S [in senses 1 & 2, fr. ME, fr. MF, fr. ML *suffragium* vote, support, assistance, prayer for intercession, fr. L, vote, political support, interest, prob. fr. *sub-* + *fragor* noise (of vote by acclamation); in other senses, fr. L *suffragium* — more at BRAY] **1** : an intercessory prayer or petition (as in a liturgy) — usu. used in pl. **2** *obs* : AID, HELP, ASSISTANCE **3 a** : a vote of assent given by a member of a body to a proposal or nomination — usu. used in pl. **b** : an opinion or decision in favor of a person or thing : APPROVAL, SANCTION **4** : an object (as a pebble or paper ballot) used for voting **5 a** : the vote or opinion of a group of persons : CONSENSUS **b** : a vote given in deciding a controverted question or election : the casting of a vote 〈no state shall be deprived of its equal ~ in the senate —*U.S.Constitution*〉 〈refrain from any word that may . . . influence your ~s in the election —Edward Gibbon〉 **6** : the right or privilege of voting in political matters or the exercise of such right; *esp* : the right or power to participate in electing public officials and adopting or rejecting legislation in a representative form of government : FRANCHISE — see MANHOOD SUFFRAGE, UNIVERSAL SUFFRAGE, WOMAN SUFFRAGE

²suffrage \"\ *vb* -ED/-ING/-S [L *suffragare, suffragari*; akin to L *suffragium* vote, support] *vi, obs* : to give one's vote, approval, or support ~ *vt, archaic* : to elect, sanction, or support by one's suffrage

suf·frag·ette \ˌsəfrə'jet, -rē'j-, *usu* -ed.+V\ *n* -S [¹*suffrage* + *-ette*] : a woman who militantly advocates suffrage for her sex

suf·frag·ett·ism \-ed.ˌizəm,-eˌti-\ *n* -S : militant advocacy of the extension of suffrage to women

suf·frag·i·nis \sə'frajənəs\ *n* -ES [NL *os suffraginis*, lit., bone of the suffrago] : the long bone of the pastern that is a common site of fracture in racehorses

suf·frag·ism \'səfrəˌjizəm, -rē,j-\ *n* -S [¹*suffrage* + *-ism*] : advocacy of the extension of suffrage (as to women)

suf·frag·ist \-jəst\ *n* -S [¹*suffrage* + *-ist*] : one who advocates an extension of suffrage (as to women)

suf·fra·go \sə'frā(ˌ)gō\ *n* -S [NL *suffragin-, suffrago*, fr. L, prob. fr. *sub-* + *frangere* to break — more at BREAK] **1** : the hock of a horse **2** : the tarsal joint of a bird : KNEE

suf·fru·tes·cent \ˌsəˌfrü'tes³nt\ *adj* [NL *suffrutescent-, suffrutescens*, fr. L *sub-* + NL *frutescent-, frutescens* frutescent, fr. L *frutex* shrub + *-escent-, -escens* -escent — more at FRUTICOSE] *of a plant or stem* : having a base that is somewhat woody and does not die down each year

suf·fru·ti·cose \(ˌ)sə'früd-əˌkōs\ *also* **suf·fru·ti·cous** \(ˌ)sə'früd·əkəs\ *adj* [NL *suffruticosus*, fr. L *sub-* + *fruticosus* fruticose] : woody and perennial at the base but remaining herbaceous above 〈a low ~ perennial〉

suf·fru·tic·u·lose \ˌsə(ˌ)frü'tikyəˌlōs\ *adj* [NL *suffruticulosus*, fr. L *sub-* + NL *fruticulosus* fruticulose, fr. *fruticulus* (dim. of L *frutic-, frutex* shrub) + L *-osus* -ose] *of a lichen* : somewhat or imperfectly fruticose

suffs *pl of* SUFF

suf·fumigate \(ˌ)sə+\ *vt* [L *suffumigatus*, past part. of *suffumigare* to fumigate from below, fr. *sub-* + *fumigare* to fumigate] : to fumigate from below : send fumes upward upon

suf·fumigation \(ˌ)sə+\ *n* [LL *suffumigation-, suffumigatio*, fr. L *suffumigatus* + *-ion-, -io* -ion] **1** : the act or process of suffumigating (as in magic rites or in treatment) **2** : a fume, smoke, or vapor used in suffumigating

suf·fus·able \sə'fyüzəbəl\ *adj* : that can be suffused

suf·fuse \sə'fyüz\ *vt* -ED/-ING/-S [L *suffusus*, past part. of *suffundere* to pour underneath, suffuse, fr. *sub-* + *fundere* to pour — more at FOUND (melt)] **1** : to spread over or through in the manner of fluid or light : FLUSH, FILL 〈when purple light shall next ~ the skies —Alexander Pope〉 **2** : to pour so as to overspread **syn** see INFUSE

suf·fused·ly \-z(ə)dlē\ *adv* [*suffused* (past part. of *suffuse*) + *-ly*] : in a suffused manner

suf·fu·sion \sə'fyüzhən\ *n* -S [L *suffusion-, suffusio*, fr. *suffusus* + *-ion-, -io* -ion] **1** : the act or process of suffusing or state of being suffused with something; *specif* : the spreading of a fluid of the body into the surrounding tissues 〈a ~ of blood〉 **2** : a coloring spread over a surface (as the face)

suf·fu·sive \-üsiv,-üziv\ *adj* [L *suffusus* + E *-ive*] : that suffuses : tending to overspread or to diffuse itself

¹su·fi \'süfē\ *n* -S *usu cap* [Ar *ṣūfīy*, lit., (man) of wool, fr. *ṣūf* wool; prob. fr. the woolen dress worn by the ascetic] : an ascetic Muslim mystic : an adherent of Sufism

²sufi \"\ *adj, usu cap* : of or relating to the Sufis or Sufism

su·fic \-fik\ *adj, usu cap* [¹*sufi* + *-ic*] : SUFISTIC

su·fism \-ˌfizəm\ *also* **su·fi·ism** \-ˌfēˌiz-\ *n* -S *usu cap* [¹*sufi* + *-ism*] : ascetic Islamic mysticism originating in the 8th century and developing esp. in Persia into a system of elaborate symbolism of which the goal is communion with the deity through contemplation and ecstasy

su·fis·tic \(')sü'fistik\ *adj, usu cap* [¹*sufism* + *-istic*] : of, relating to, or in accordance with Sufism

sug *abbr* suggested; suggestion

su·ga·mo \sü'gä(ˌ)mō\ *n* -S [Jap] : an aquatic plant (*Phyllospadix scouleri*) of the family Potamogetonaceae that occurs along the north Pacific coasts from the northwestern U.S. to Japan and is grown in Japan for fertilizer and fiber

su·gan *or* **soo·gan** *or* **sug·gan** \'sügən, 'süg-,'səg-\ *n* -S [IrGael *sūgān*; akin to ScGael *sūgan* sugan] **1** *chiefly Irish* : a hand-twisted rope of straw or heather **2** : a coarse blanket used by cowboys and ranchmen

¹sug·ar \'shu̇g(ə)r\ *n* -S [ME *sucre, sugre, suger*, fr. MF *çucre, sucre*, fr. ML *zuccarum, succarum*, fr. OIt *zucchero*, fr. Ar *sukkar*, fr. Per *shakar*, fr. Prakrit *sakkara*, fr. Skt *śarkarā* gravel, grit, sugar; akin to Skt *śarkara* pebble] **1 a** : a sweet crystallizable substance that consists entirely or essentially of sucrose, that is colorless or white when pure and usu. yellowish to brown otherwise, that occurs naturally in the most readily available amounts in sugarcane, sugar beet, sugar maple, sorghum, and sugar palms, that is obtained commercially principally by processing the juice expressed from sugarcane or the aqueous extract of sliced sugar beets and refining so that the final product is the same regardless of the source, and that forms an important article of human food and is used also chiefly as a condiment and preservative for other foods and for drugs and in the chemical industry as an intermediate — see BEET SUGAR, BROWN SUGAR 1, CANE SUGAR, INVERT SUGAR, MAPLE SUGAR 1, SACCHAROSE **b** : any of a class of water-soluble compounds (as glucose, fructose, xylose, sucrose, maltose, or raffinose) that vary widely in sweetness, comprise the simpler carbohydrates, include not only the monosaccharides but also the oligosaccharides, may be reducing or nonreducing, and typically are optically active **2** : a unit (as a spoonful, cube, or lump) of sugar 〈how many ~s in your tea〉 **3** : SUGAR BOWL 〈offering ~s, creamers in styles to match —*Edison Electric Appliances Cat.*〉 **4** *slang* : MONEY 〈undergoing an operation that cost heavy ~ —Mickey Spillane〉 〈spend my good ~ on a taxi —*Auckland (New Zealand) Weekly News*〉 **5** — used as an interjection to express annoyance or disappointment

²sugar \"\ *vb* **sugared; sugared; sugaring** \-g(ə)riŋ\ **sugars** [ME *sugren*, fr. *sugre* sugar] *vt* **1** : to make pleasing, palatable, or deceptively attractive : SWEETEN, SUGARCOAT 〈novels heavy with moral teaching and ~*ed* with romance —*Amer. Guide Series: N.Y.*〉 〈~*ing* the reproach with the expression of endearment —Vicki Baum〉 — often used with *over* or *up* 〈with devotion's visage . . . we do ~ o'er the devil himself —Shak.〉 〈his inclination to ~ up reality —David Tilden〉 **2** : to sprinkle sugar on : mix sugar with : put sugar into 〈~ a cake〉 〈~ the mixture to taste〉 〈~ tea〉 ~ *vi* **1** : to form sugar 〈continued stirring will cause a syrup to ~〉 **2** : to become granular in texture : GRANULATE 〈a varnish that ~s〉

³sugar \"\ *adj* [¹*sugar*] **1** : made or derived from sugar **2** : having the sweetness of sugar **3** : attracted to sugar **4** : used with sugar or in the making of sugar

⁴sugar \"\ *usu cap* — a communications code word for the letter *s*

sugar ant *n* : an ant that is attracted to sweet foods: as **a** : PHARAOH ANT **b** : any of several Australian ants of the genus *Camponotus*

sugar apple *n* **1** : SWEETSOP 2 **2** : BIRIBA

sugar ash *n* : BOX ELDER

sugar bag *n* **1** *Austral* : a wild bees' nest **2** *Austral* : honey from a wild bees' nest

sugar basin *n, Brit* : SUGAR BOWL

sugar beet *n* : a white-rooted beet grown for the sugar in its roots

sugar beet eelworm *or* **sugar beet nematode** *n* : a widely distributed destructive nematode worm (*Heterodera schachtii*) native to the Old World but found in several areas of No. America that attacks the roots of sugar beets

sugar beet root aphid *n* : a root aphid (*Pemphigus populivenae*) that causes severe injury to sugar beet, beet, and mangel crops in the western U.S.

sugar beet root maggot *n* : the larva of a fly (*Tetanops myopaeformis*) of the family Otitidae that infests the roots of sugar beets in the western U.S. and parts of Canada

sugarberry \'==-= — *see* BERRY\ *n* **1** : a hackberry with sweet edible fruits: as **a** : the common eastern hackberry (*Celtis occidentalis*) **b** : a large hackberry (*C. laevigata*) chiefly of the lower Mississippi valley that has orange or yellow fruit **2** : JUNEBERRY

sugarbird \'=ˌ=\ *n* [prob. trans. of Afrik *suikervogel*] **1** : any of various honeycreepers, honey eaters, and sunbirds that suck the nectar of flowers **2** : EVENING GROSBEAK

sugar bowl *n* : a bowl-shaped vessel that has usu. two handles and a cover and is used for holding sugar or sugar cubes

sugar bowl

sugar brake *n* : SENSITIVE FERN

sugar bush \'=ˌ=\ *n* **1** *or* **sugar grove a** : a grove or collection of sugar maples **b** : a woods in which sugar maples predominate — called also *sugar orchard* **2** *usu* **sugar-bush** [trans. of Afrik *suikerbos*] : any of several plants of the genus *Protea*; *esp* : a southern African shrub (*P. mellifera*) **3** *usu* **sugar-bush** : an evergreen shrub or small tree (*Rhus ovata*) of the southwestern U.S. with reddish yellow flowers in dense spikes and glandular hairy fruits

sugar camp *n, chiefly Midland* : SUGAR BUSH

sugar candy *n* [ME *sugre candy* — more at CANDY] **1** : hard candy made from pure sugar **2** : something sweet or pleasant

sugar-candy \'==ˌ==\ *adj* [*sugar candy*] : deliciously and usu. cloyingly sweet 〈*sugar-candy* novels —*Irish Statesman*〉

sugarcane \'==ˌ=\ *n* **1** : a stout tall perennial grass that is usu. considered to constitute a species (*Saccharum officinarum*) but is known only as a cultigen or escape in warm or tropical regions, occurs in distinct forms with characteristic qualities and different chromosome numbers and possibly constitutes a hybrid complex, and has flat 2-ranked leaves, many-jointed stalks, and a large terminal flower cluster — see NOBLE CANE, SUGAR 1 **2** : sugarcane plants 〈a plantation of ~〉

sugarcane beetle *n* : a destructive beetle (*Euetheola rugiceps*) that burrows in the base of the sugarcane

sugarcane borer *n* : the larva of a pyralidid moth (*Diatraea saccharalis*) that bores in sugarcane in the southern U.S. and the West Indies

sugarcane gummosis *n* : COBB'S DISEASE

sugarcane leafhopper *n* : a jassid bug (*Perkinsiella saccharicida*) injurious to sugarcane

sugarcane mosaic *n* : an important virus disease of sugarcane characterized by chlorotic streaking of the leaves, stunting of the plants, and a greatly reduced yield of sugar

sugarcane smut *n* **1** : a disease of sugarcane caused by a smut fungus (*Ustilago scitaminea*) **2** : the fungus causing sugarcane smut

sugarcane wax *n* : a wax that occurs as a thin layer on the outside of the stem of the sugarcane, that is usu. obtained as a by-product in the manufacture of cane sugar as a hard green to brown or tan solid, and that is used chiefly in polishing materials

sugarcoat \'==ˌ=\ *vb* [¹*sugar* + *coat* (v.)] *vt* **1** : to coat (as a food or drug) with sugar or candy 〈~ almonds〉 〈~ pills〉 **2 a** : to make (something difficult, harsh, or unpleasant) superficially easy, attractive, or palatable : SWEETEN 〈~*ing* the classics for children〉 〈~*ed* the punishment with promises of future rewards〉 **b** : to conceal (something ugly or evil) under a deceptively pleasing exterior : gloss over 〈adept at ~*ing* their vicious purpose〉 〈~ the real facts〉 ~ *vi* : to embellish something harsh or unpalatable : conceal a bitter truth by glossing over it 〈makes a practice of ~*ing*〉

sugarcoating *n* [fr. gerund of *sugarcoat*] **1** : the act or process of sugarcoating **2** : something that sugarcoats 〈using fiction as a ~ for their lectures —*Dial*〉

sugar corn *n* : SWEET CORN

sugar crop *n* : a crop (as sugarcane or sugar beets) grown for the extraction of sugar

sugar daddy *n* : a wealthy older man lavishing gifts and luxuries on a young woman whom he squires about or keeps as his mistress 〈the air of a chorus girl who has just been given a bracelet by her *sugar daddy* —Louis Bromfield〉

sugar diabetes *n* : DIABETES MELLITUS

sugar eat *or* **sugar lick** *or* **sugar party** *n* : SUGARING OFF 2

sugared *adj* [ME *sugred, sucred*, fr. *sugre, sucre* sugar + *-ed*] **1** : containing sugar : SWEETENED 〈~ water〉 **2** : deliciously appealing or alluring : HONEYED 〈~ temptation〉 **3** : SUGARCOATED 〈~ almonds〉 〈a ~ speech〉

sug·ar·er \'shu̇gərə(r)\ *n* -S [¹*sugar* + *-er*] *Brit* : SHIRKER

sugar grape *n* : SAND GRAPE

sugar grass *n* : any saccharine sorghum; *esp* : SORGO

sugar gum *n* : either of two Australian gum trees (*Eucalyptus corynocalyx* and *E. gunnii*) having sweetish leaves that livestock browse upon

sugarhouse \'==ˌ=\ *n* : a building where sugar is made or refined; *specif* : a shed where maple sap is boiled and maple syrup and maple sugar are made

sugarhouse molasses *n* : thin molasses remaining after refining of sugarcane

sug·ar·i·ness \'shu̇g(ə)rēnəs, -rin-\ *n* -ES : the quality or state of being sugary

sugaring *n* -S [fr. gerund of ²*sugar*] **1** : the act or process of making sugar **2** : granulation found in some marbles and thought to be caused by the differential expansion coefficients of the grains

sugaring off *n, pl* **sugaring offs 1** : the act or process of converting maple syrup into sugar **2** : a party held at the time of sugaring off at which the refreshments consist of doughnuts, pickles, and boiled-down maple syrup poured on snow — called also *sugar eat*

sugar lerp insect *n* : a psyllid bug (*Spondyliaspis eucalypti*) that secretes large amounts of lerp honey

sug·ar·less \'shu̇g(ə)rləs\ *adj* : containing no sugar 〈~ tea〉

sugarloaf \'==ˌ=\ *n* [ME *sugerlaf*, fr. *suger* sugar + *laf* loaf] **1** : refined sugar molded into a solid cone 〈in my boyhood in eastern Europe a ~ was still a familiar object —E.G.Gudde〉 **2** : a hill or mountain resembling a sugarloaf in its conical or conoidal shape

sugar-loaf \'==ˌ=\ *also* **sugar-loafed** \"t\ *adj* : shaped like a sugarloaf : CONOIDAL 〈a *sugar-loaf* mountain〉

sugar maple *n* : any of several maples having a sweet sap; *specif* : a maple (*Acer saccharum*) of eastern No. America having gray bark, 3- to 5-lobed leaves, flowers in nearly sessile corymbs, and hard close-grained wood that is much used for cabinetwork esp. in the curly-grained form and having sap that is the chief source of maple syrup and maple sugar — see BIRD'S-EYE MAPLE; TREE illustration

sugar-maple borer *n* : a maple borer that attacks sugar maple and is the larva of a black and yellow beetle (*Glycobius speciosus*)

sugar mite *n* : any of several mites of the genus *Glycyphagus* that often infest unrefined sugar and dried fruits

sugar mule *n* : a large mule suitable for work on a sugar plantation — distinguished from *cotton mule*

sugar off *vi* : to complete the process of boiling down the syrup in making maple sugar until it is thick enough to crystallize : approach or reach the state of granulation

sugar of lead : LEAD ACETATE a

sugar on snow : maple syrup boiled to the soft-ball stage and poured on snow or ice

sugar orchard *n, chiefly New Eng* : SUGAR BUSH

sugar palm *n* : any of several palms yielding sugar: as **a** : GOMUTI **b** : NIPA 3a **c** : a Philippine palm (*Corypha elata*)

sugar pea *n* : EDIBLE-PODDED PEA

sugar pear *n* **1** : JUNEBERRY **2** : a cultivated pear noted for its sweet flavor

sugar pine *n* : a lofty pine (*Pinus lambertiana*) of California and Oregon having leaves in fives, cones often 18 inches long, a soft reddish brown wood that is used for interior finishings and shingles, and heartwood that yields a sugary exudate

sugarplum \'==ˌ=\ *n* **1** : a small candy or confection usu. in the form of a ball or disk : COMFIT, SWEETMEAT 〈ready-made . . . as hand for glove or tongue for ~ —Robert Browning〉 〈visions of ~s danced in their heads —Clement Moore〉 **2** : something suggestive of a sugarplum (as in sweetness or desirability): as **a** : sweet words : FLATTERY 〈pelt with gilt ~s —Anthony Trollope〉 **b** : a gift or bribe offered to conciliate a person : SOP 〈stop his mouth with a ~〉 **c** : something esp. choice of its kind : PLUM 4b, PRIZE **3** : JUNEBERRY

sugar puncture *n* **:** puncture of a definite region in the medulla oblongata resulting in glycosuria
sugars *pl of* SUGAR, *pres 3d sing of* SUGAR
sugar sand *n* **:** granular mineral matter present in boiling maple syrup before filtration
sugar sheath *n* **:** the parenchyma surrounding the xylem in the root of the sugar beet
sugar shell *n* **:** a spoon for serving sugar that often has a bowl molded in the form of a seashell
sugarsop \ˈ=ˌ=\ *n, archaic* **:** a sweetened and spiced sop
sugar sorghum *n* **:** SORGO
sugar squirrel *or* **sugar opossum** *n* **:** a small widely distributed Australian opossum (*Petaurus breviceps*) that is largely silvery gray with a bushy and often white-tipped tail and that in habits and appearance much resembles a flying squirrel
sugar-stick \ˈ=ˌ=\ *n* **:** STICK CANDY ⟨jars of striped *sugar-stick* —*Spectator*⟩
sugar-tit *also* **sugar-teat** \ˈ=ˌ=\ *n* **:** sugar tied up in a nipple-shaped cloth for a child to suck ⟨fighting, while all these legislators were sucking *sugar-tits* —Kenneth Roberts⟩ ⟨*sugar-tit* children . . . coddled and comforted —Lillian Smith⟩ — called also *pacifier*
sugar tongs *n pl* **:** a pair of usu. silver tongs with claw-shaped or spoon-shaped ends for serving lump sugar

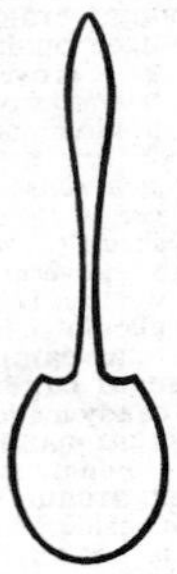
sugar shell

sugar tree *n* **1 :** SUGAR MAPLE **2 :** an Australian shrub or small tree (*Myoporum platycarpum*) with linear leaves and small white flowers
sugar vinegar *n* **:** vinegar made from refuse sugary or starchy materials by alcoholic and acetic fermentations
sugar wood *n* **1 :** SUGAR MAPLE **2 :** SUGAR TREE 2
sug·ary \ˈshu̇g(ə)rē, -ri\ *adj* [¹*sugar* + *-y*] **1 :** containing, resembling, or tasting of sugar **:** sweet with sugar ⟨~ food⟩ ⟨~ flavor⟩ ⟨~ delicacies⟩ **2 a :** exaggeratedly or ostentatiously sweet (as in manner or expression) **:** SACCHARINE, HONEYED ⟨a ~ smile⟩ ⟨her soft, ~ voice —Katherine Mansfield⟩ ⟨~ amiability coated . . . an inherent weakness in her own psyche —Margaret Hay⟩ **b :** cloyingly sweet **:** SENTIMENTAL ⟨~ verses⟩ ⟨~ melodies⟩ ⟨~ and unconvincing . . . fiction —Katharine F. Gerould⟩ **3 :** having a granular texture ⟨~ marble⟩
sug·bu·ha·non \ˌsəgˈbüəˌnän\ *n, usu cap* [Cebuan *Sugbu* Cebu Island + *-hanon* language of] **:** CEBUAN 2
sugg *abbr* suggested; suggestion
suggan *var of* SUGAN
sug·gest \sə(g)ˈjest\ *vb* -ED/-ING/-S [L *suggestus*, past part. of *suggerere* to put under, heap up, furnish, suggest, fr. *sub-* + *gerere* to bear, wage — more at CAST] *vt* **1 :** to put (as an idea, proposition, or impulse) into the mind: as **a** *obs* (1) **:** to seek to influence the mind of **:** URGE ⟨two spirits do ~ me still —Shak.⟩ (2) **:** to insinuate esp. an evil or false thought into the mind of **:** TEMPT, SEDUCE ⟨what serpent hath ~*ed* thee —Shak.⟩ **b :** to call forth (as a desire or mood) **:** AROUSE, EVOKE ⟨indirectly ~ the desired attitude —Dorothy Barclay⟩ ⟨the pleasant voice that enticed and ~*ed* the most improbable falsehoods from witnesses —Rose Macaulay⟩ **c :** to mention (something) as a possibility **:** put forward by implication **:** HINT, INTIMATE ⟨~ that a change of government is necessary⟩ ⟨~ strongly . . . that he bring his wife along for the interview —W.H.Whyte⟩ **d :** to propose (something) as desirable or fitting ⟨~ a stroll after lunch⟩ ⟨~*ed* several thesis subjects⟩ ⟨~*ed* . . . a special committee to work on plans for a possible settlement —*New Republic*⟩ **e :** to offer (as an idea or theory) for consideration **:** present as a hypothesis **:** THEORIZE ⟨this, I ~, is what happened⟩ ⟨~*ed* the conception of poetry as a living whole —T.S.Eliot⟩ ⟨~*s* other reasons why music is powerful in the building . . . of personality —H. A.Overstreet⟩ **2 a :** to call or bring to mind (as an idea, mood, or object) by a process of logical thought or natural association of ideas **:** give rise to the idea of **:** EVOKE ⟨the explosion . . . ~*ed* sabotage —F.L.Paxson⟩ ⟨the scientist ~*s* an ant, putting forth great efforts to lug one . . . apparently unimportant grain of sand —Oliver La Farge⟩ ⟨a setting which is brilliantly ~*ed* —*Times Lit. Supp.*⟩ ⟨the folk customs that ~ themselves for study —Phyllis Greenacre⟩ **b :** to serve as an incentive, motive, or reason for **:** INSPIRE, PROMPT ⟨a short story ~*ed* by an actual incident⟩ ⟨television may ~ new forms and expression —Leslie Rees⟩ ⟨this incident ~*s* significant reflections —M.R.Cohen⟩ ⟨physical comfort . . . ~*s* that students shall occupy alternate seats —*College of William & Mary Cat.*⟩ **3 :** to give an indication or impression of **:** imply the presence of **:** ADUMBRATE, SHADOW ⟨open gambling that ~*ed* collusion with public officials⟩ ⟨his impulsive gestures ~*ed* a passion he had never shown to her —Morley Callaghan⟩ ⟨admirable works, yet they ~*ed* . . . aloofness from the sordid realities —V.L.Parrington⟩ ~ *vi* **1** *obs* **:** to work insidiously upon a person's mind **:** TEMPT ⟨devils . . . do ~ at first with heavenly shows —Shak.⟩ **2 :** to arouse ideas or feelings by a process of association
syn IMPLY, HINT, INTIMATE, INSINUATE: SUGGEST may involve communicating or implanting an idea by calling attention to some notion likely to be associated with it by starting a mental association naturally leading to the notion in question ⟨the business of words in prose is primarily to state; in poetry, not only to state, but also (and sometimes primarily) to *suggest* —J.L.Lowes⟩ ⟨a steamer on the Thames or lines of telegraph inevitably *suggest* the benefits of civilization, man's triumph over Nature —L.P.Smith⟩ IMPLY is close to SUGGEST in denotation and connotation; it differs in seeming to require more analytical or systematic inference to grasp the implied meaning ⟨had always *implied* that there had been something irregular in Dr. Winter's accounts —Edith Wharton⟩ ⟨an era when the scientific point of view no longer *implies* this determinism —Edmund Wilson⟩ HINT refers to communication by slight, indirect, or covert suggestion, with a minimum of straightforward implicit expression ⟨as thou with wary speech . . . hast *hinted* —John Keats⟩ ⟨repeatedly *hinted* at in political thought —Alex Comfort⟩ INTIMATE may stress delicacy as contrasted with blunt forthrightness in expression ⟨*intimated* that there had been danger in his coming just then —Arnold Bennett⟩ ⟨"I never put it so strong as that," said the old lady, looking rather shocked. She had *intimated* as much many times —Archibald Marshall⟩ INSINUATE often indicates covert indirect reference artfully introduced and usu. calculated to depreciate or denigrate ⟨the *insinuated* scoff of coward tongues —William Wordsworth⟩ ⟨the voice that *insinuates* that Jews and Negroes and Catholics are inferior excrescences on our body politic —Max Lerner⟩
sug·gest·ibil·i·ty \=ˌ=əˈbiləd-ē, -lətē, -i\ *n* -ES **:** the quality or state of being suggestible **:** susceptibility to suggestion or influence ⟨the ~ of an actor⟩ ⟨surgically induced malleability and ~ . . . make reeducation possible —*Digest of Neurology & Psychiatry*⟩ ⟨the itching ~ of irresolute and halfhearted men —Ralph Bates⟩
sug·gest·ible \=ˈ=əbəl\ *adj* [*suggest* + *-ible*] **:** easily influenced by suggestion **:** susceptible mentally to external influences esp. to the opinions of others ⟨a bewildered, ~ boy —H.N.Fairchild⟩ ⟨the hypnotic subject is very ~ —G.H. Estabrooks⟩ ⟨whipped up their . . . pathologically ~ population into a frenzy —E.A.Hooton⟩ ⟨too ~ to possess a style of his own —F.O.Matthiessen⟩
sug·ges·tio fal·si \sə(g)ˌjes(h)chēˌōˈfòl(t)ˌsī\ *n* [NL] *law* **:** suggestion of an untruth **:** false statement as opposed to suppression of the truth — compare SUPPRESSIO VERI
sug·ges·tion \sə(g)ˈjes(h)chən\ *n* -S [ME, act of suggesting, fr. MF, fr. L *suggestion-, suggestio*, fr. *suggestus* (past part. of *suggerere* to suggest) + *-ion-, -io* -ion] **1** *obs* **:** incitement to evil **:** INSTIGATION, TEMPTATION ⟨thy ~, plot, and damned practice —Shak.⟩ **2 a :** the act or process of suggesting ⟨a letter written at a friend's ~⟩ **b :** something suggested: as (1) **:** PROPOSAL ⟨his ~*s* . . . had the force of commands —S.H. Adams⟩ (2) **:** INTIMATION, HINT ⟨his whispered ~ of something significant about to happen —Sherwood Anderson⟩ (3) **:** PROMPTING, INSPIRATION ⟨strange . . . that I should need a ~ from the *Iliad* —Thomas De Quincey⟩ **3 :** information given without oath in a legal action **:** an entry on the record for the action of the court of a material fact or circumstance (as the death or insolvency of a party) **4 a :** the process by which one thought leads to another esp. through association of ideas **:** the power of imaginative or artistic re-creation of experience **:** EVOCATION ⟨fear of the dark . . . seems to be entirely due to ~ —Bertrand Russell⟩ ⟨poetry achieves its finest effects by ~⟩ ⟨stimulates the observer with extraordinary ~ in his paintings —Howard Devree⟩ **b :** the act or process of impressing something (as an idea, attitude, or desired action) upon the mind of another ⟨visual ~ . . . far more powerful than the written word —Roy Lewis & Angus Maude⟩ ⟨situational factors influencing the process of ~ —T.E.Coffin⟩ **c :** a means or process of influencing attitudes and behavior hypnotically ⟨produced a hypnotic state very rapidly and by extremely simple ~ —C.P.Oberndorf⟩ **5 :** a slight indication or touch **:** SOUPÇON, TRACE ⟨a ~ of blue in the gray⟩ ⟨a sprightliness of flavor, a ~ of the pineapple, the apricot, the orange —David Fairchild⟩
sug·ges·tive \-estiv, -tēv *also* -təv\ *adj* [L *suggestus* (past part. of *suggerere* to suggest) + E *-ive*] **1 a :** giving a suggestion or hint **:** INDICATIVE, SIGNIFICANT ⟨the list is ~ rather than comprehensive⟩ ⟨his choice of writers is ~ of his bias —V.L.Parrington⟩ ⟨the peculiar distribution is very ~ —F.A. Geldard⟩ ⟨pediments on the wings, ~ of gable ends —*Amer. Guide Series: R.I.*⟩ **b :** full of suggestions **:** stimulating thought **:** PROVOCATIVE, SEMINAL ⟨provided a ~ running commentary on the era —Lloyd Morris⟩ ⟨a great variety of ~ ideas —M.R.Cohen⟩ **c :** stirring mental associations **:** PREGNANT, EVOCATIVE ⟨hauntingly ~ stories⟩ ⟨the poetry is . . . elusive and ~ —Richard Eberhart⟩ **2 :** suggesting or tending to suggest something considered improper or indecent **:** OFF-COLOR, RISQUÉ ⟨~ song lyrics⟩ ⟨a sly, ~ wink —A.M.Sampley⟩ ⟨a magazine of smutty jokes and ~ pictures —*Sydney (Australia) Bull.*⟩
sug·ges·tive·ly \-tə̇vlē, -li\ *adv* **:** in a suggestive manner **:** MEANINGFULLY, SIGNIFICANTLY ⟨picks up the empty bottle ~ —Erle Stanley Gardner⟩
sug·ges·tive·ness \-tivnə̇s, -tēv- *also* -təv-\ *n* -ES **:** the quality or state of being suggestive: as **a :** stimulation to thought **:** INSPIRATION ⟨your ~ . . . and affection have enriched life to me —O.W.Holmes †1935⟩ **b :** EVOCATIVENESS ⟨his writing was . . . possessed of an extraordinary power of ~ —J.T. Farrell⟩ **c :** intimation of or allusion to something held improper or obscene ⟨~ tended to take the place of honest bawdry —W.B.Adams⟩
sug·gil·la·tion \ˌsə(g)jəˈlāshən\ *n* -S [L *sugillation-, sugillatio*, fr. *sugillatus* (past part. of *sugillare, suggillare* to beat black and blue) + *-ion-, -io* -ion] **:** ECCHYMOSIS, BRUISE; *esp* **:** one that develops post-mortem ⟨~*s* of the head are not reliable signs of infanticide —*Ciba Clinical Symposia*⟩
sugh \ˈsü, ˈsüf, ˈsük\ *chiefly Scot var of* SOUGH
su·gi \ˈsü(ˌ)gē\ *n, pl* **sugi** *or* **sugis** [Jap] **:** JAPANESE CEDAR
su·i·ci·dal \ˌsüəˈsīdᵊl\ *adj* [¹*suicide* + *-al*] **1 :** of the nature of, relating to, or tending toward suicide **:** SELF-DESTRUCTIVE ⟨medical examiner said that death was ~ —*Springfield (Mass.) Daily News*⟩ ⟨the ~ implications of thermonuclear attack —Denis Healey⟩ ⟨mountain travel at that season was ~ —R. A.Billington⟩ **2 :** characterized by an impulse to commit suicide ⟨~ insanity⟩ ⟨I have had influenza and . . . feel ~ —G.B.Shaw⟩ **3 :** destructive of one's own interests ⟨knew it would be ~ to voice his true opinions in such a group⟩
su·i·ci·dal·ly \-ᵊlē, -ᵊli\ *adv* [*suicidal* + *-ly*] **:** in a manner suggestive of, tending toward, or risking self-destruction or the destruction of one's own interests **:** SELF-DESTRUCTIVELY ⟨the attack was . . . dangerous, almost ~ so —Frank Yerby⟩ ⟨the ouzel . . . flies ~ through a waterfall —Irving Petite⟩ ⟨a country ~ weakening its economy⟩
¹**su·i·cide** \ˈsüəˌsīd\ *n* -S [L *sui* (gen.), *sibi* (dat.), *se* (accus. & abl.) oneself + E *-cide*; akin to OE *sīn* his, OHG *sih* (accus.) oneself, *sīn* his, ON *sik* (accus.) oneself, *sinn* one's own, Goth *sik* oneself, *seins* his, L *suus* one's own, Gk *he* (accus.) oneself, *hos, heos* one's own, Skt *sva* oneself, one's own] **1 a :** the act or an instance of taking one's own life voluntarily and intentionally **:** SELF-DESTRUCTION ⟨the death was adjudged a ~⟩ **b :** the deliberate and intentional destruction of his own life by a person of years of discretion and of sound mind **:** FELO-DE-SE 2 ⟨civilizations . . . in which ~ was considered a completely honorable act —*New Republic*⟩ **c :** ruin of one's own interests ⟨drove into revolt or artistic ~ every student with an ounce of vitality in him —Clive Bell⟩ ⟨the proposal . . . is likely to be an invitation to political ~ —Frank Gorrell⟩ **2 :** one that commits or attempts self-murder **:** FELO-DE-SE 1 ⟨had a ~'*s* temperament, careless of life —J.H.Plumb⟩
²**suicide** \"\ *vb* -ED/-ING/-S *vi* **:** to commit suicide ⟨the unfortunate man had *suicided* —D.D.Martin⟩ ~ *vt* **:** to put (as oneself) to death **:** KILL ⟨after Brutus, aged twelve, had *suicided* himself —E.M.Forster⟩
³**suicide** \"\ *adj* **1** [¹*suicide*] **:** constituting a suicide ⟨his ~ brother —E.A.Mowrer⟩ ⟨the problem of the ~ blonde —J.P. O'Donnell⟩ **2** [¹*suicide*] **a :** resulting in or likely to result in the death of the individual or a high proportion of deaths in a participating group or unit — usu. used of a military or naval operation ⟨one-way ~ bombing missions⟩ ⟨supposed to make any attempt at invasion a ~ attack —*Coast Artillery Jour.*⟩ **b :** engaging in or intended to engage in such an operation ⟨~ pilot⟩ ⟨a ~ squad⟩ ⟨leaving a ~ force . . . to fight a rearguard action —F.B.Gipson⟩
suicide clause *n* **:** a provision limiting the liability of an insurer to a return of net premiums paid if a policyholder whether sane or insane commits suicide within a stipulated period
¹**su·id** \ˈsüə̇d\ *or* **su·id·i·an** \(ˈ)süˈidēən\ *adj* [*suid* fr. NL *Suidae*; *suidian* fr. NL *Suidae* + E *-ian*] **:** of or relating to the Suidae
²**suid** \"\ *or* **suidian** \"\ *n* -S **:** a swine of the family Suidae
su·idae \ˈsüəˌdē\ *n pl, cap* [NL, fr. *Sus*, type genus + *-idae*] **:** a family of nonruminant artiodactylous mammals consisting of the wild and domestic swine but in modern classifications excluding the peccaries
su·iform \ˈsüəˌfȯrm\ *adj* [NL *Suiformes*] **:** of or relating to the Suiformes
su·ifor·mes \ˌsüēˈfȯrˌmēz\ *n pl, cap* [NL, fr. L *sus* swine, hog + NL *-iformes* — more at SOW] *in some classifications* **:** a suborder of Artiodactyla that comprises numerous nonruminant mammals including swine, peccaries, hippopotamuses, and extinct related forms
sui·gen·der·ism \ˌsüˌīˈjendəˌrizəm, ˌsüēˈj-\ *n* -S [L *suus* one's own + E *-i-* + *gender* + *-ism* — more at SUICIDE] **:** the state or the period of development (as in childhood or early adolescence) in which one becomes chiefly interested in or attracted toward persons of the same sex — contrasted with *altrigenderism*
sui ge·ner·is \ˌsüˌīˈjenərə̇s; ˌsüēˈje-, -ēˈge-\ *adj* [L, of its own kind] **:** constituting a class alone **:** UNIQUE, PECULIAR ⟨possesses certain *sui generis* qualities —John Mason Brown⟩ — usu. used predicatively or postpositively ⟨the man is *sui generis* —John McCarten⟩ ⟨a history book *sui generis* —Max Wolff⟩
sui heredes *pl of* SUUS HERES
sui ju·ris \ˌsüˌīˈju̇rə̇s, ˌsüēˈyü-\ *adj* [L, lit., of one's own right or authority] **1 :** having full legal capacity to act on one's own behalf **:** not subject to the authority of another — opposed to *alieni juris* **2 :** qualified to enjoy full civil rights (as of holding public office or serving on a jury)
sui·ker·bos *also* **sui·ker·bosch** \ˈsākə(r)ˌbäs, ˈsük-, -bȯs\ *or* **sui·ker·bos·sie** \-sē\ *n, pl* **suikerboses** *also* **suikerbosches** *or* **suikerbossies** [*suikerbos, suikerbosch* fr. Afrik, fr. *suiker* sugar (fr. MD *suker*, fr. MF *sucre*) + *bos, bosch* bush, fr. MD *bosch*; *suikerbossie* fr. Afrik, fr. *suiker* + *bossie*, dim. of *bos* — more at SUGAR, BUSH] **:** SUGAR BUSH 2
sui·mate \ˈsüˌī, ˈsüē+ˌ-\ *n* -S [L *sui* (gen.) of oneself + E *mate* — more at SUICIDE] **1 :** checkmate forced by the side that is checkmated — called also *self-mate* **2 :** a chess problem in which suimate is required
su·ina \süˈīnə, -ˈēnə\ *n pl, cap* [NL, fr. L *sus* swine, hog + NL *-ina*] **:** a division of Artiodactyla (suborder Suiformes) that comprises the swine, peccaries, and closely related extinct forms and is occas. enlarged so that it becomes almost exactly coextensive with Suiformes
su·ine \ˈsüˌīn\ *adj* [NL *Suina*] **:** of or relating to the Suina
suing *n* -S [fr. gerund of ¹*sue*] **:** legal prosecution **:** SUIT
su·int \ˈsüənt, ˈswint\ *n* -S [F, fr. MF, fr. *suer* to sweat, fr. L *sudare* — more at SWEAT] **:** the dried perspiration of sheep that is deposited in the wool chiefly in combination with fatty acids and that is rich in potassium salts — compare YOLK
suio·goth \ˈswēō, ˈsüyō+ˌ-\ *n, cap* [NL *Suiogothi* (pl.) Goths of southern Sweden, fr. L *Suiones* + LL *Gothi* Goths] **:** a Scandinavian Goth; *esp* **:** a Goth from southern Sweden
sui·o·nes \ˈswēəˌnēz, süˈīə-\ *n pl, usu cap* [L, of Gmc origin; akin to ON *Svíar* Swedes — more at SWEDE] **:** an ancient Teutonic people of what is now Sweden
sui·pes·ti·fer infection \ˌsüˌīˈpestəfə(r)-, ˌsüēˈ-\ *n* [NL *suipestifer* (specific epithet of *Salmonella suipestifer*, a bacterium causing the disease), fr. L *sus* swine + *-i-* + *pestifer* pestilential — more at SOW, PESTIFEROUS] **:** NECROTIC ENTERITIS
¹**suit** \ˈsüt, *usu* -üd·+V\ *n* -S [ME *siute, sute, suite* act of following, pursuit, petition, retinue, attendance, sequence, set of things, esp. of clothes, fr. OF *sieute, siute* act of following, pursuit, retinue, attendance, fr. fem. of (assumed) OF *sieut* (past part. of OF *suir* to follow), fr. (assumed) VL *sequitus*, past part. of (assumed) VL *sequere* to follow — more at SUE]

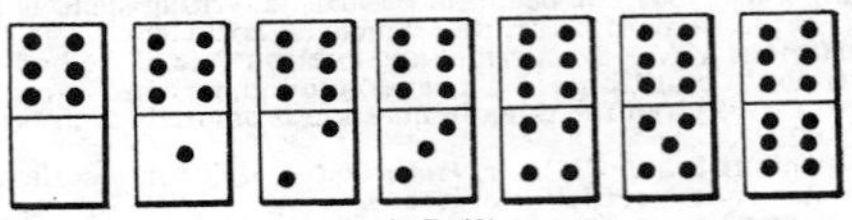
suit 7a(2)

1 *archaic* **a :** an act of following (as game or a quest) **:** PURSUIT **b :** SUITE 1 ⟨in his ~ was . . . a young gentleman —Meriwether Lewis⟩ **2 a :** attendance (as at a royal court or a manor) owed according to feudal law by a vassal to his king or lord ⟨~ to some form of court was incumbent upon all landholders —F.M.Stenton⟩ **b :** the required resort of a tenant to a particular mill for his grinding — compare SUCKEN **3 a :** recourse or appeal to a feudal superior for justice or redress of grievances ⟨made ~ to the king in council⟩ **b :** the attempt to gain an end by legal process **:** prosecution of right before any tribunal **:** LITIGATION ⟨an added reason for early institution of ~ —Joseph Schneider⟩ **c :** an action or process in a court for the recovery of a right or claim **:** a legal application to a court for justice ⟨a civil ~⟩ ⟨a criminal ~⟩ ⟨a ~ in chancery⟩ ⟨no ~ . . . having been instituted to recover the debt —*Detroit Law Jour.*⟩ **4 :** an act or instance of suing or seeking by plea or entreaty **:** PETITION, APPEAL ⟨his ~ to the Muse —*Nation*⟩; *specif* **:** solicitation in marriage **:** COURTSHIP, WOOING ⟨mocks all her wooers out of ~ —Shak.⟩ ⟨had her father's consent to his ~⟩ **5 a :** SUITE 2 — used chiefly of armor, sails, clothes, and cards and counters in games ⟨a ~ of medieval armor⟩ ⟨~*s* of sails for . . . racing yachts —*Amer. Guide Series: N.Y. City*⟩ **b** *of hair* **:** HEAD 3a, GROWTH ⟨a beauty with big quick eyes and a heavy ~ of hair —Elizabeth M. Roberts⟩ **6 :** a set of garments **:** OUTFIT, COSTUME: as **a** *obs* **:** LIVERY; *esp* **:** that of the members of a retinue **b** *archaic* **:** HABIT; *esp* **:** one worn by a religious **c :** UNIFORM **d :** an outer costume of two or more parts that harmonize or match in material and color (as a jacket, vest, and trousers for men or a jacket and skirt for women) **e :** BATHING SUIT **f :** a set of underwear **g :** a costume designed to be worn for a special purpose or under particular conditions ⟨gym ~⟩ ⟨space ~⟩ **7 a** (1) **:** all the cards in a pack of playing cards bearing the same spot or symbol (as spades or hearts) — called also *color* (2) **:** all the bones in dominoes bearing the same number ⟨the ~ of sixes⟩ (3) **:** all the counters in a game (as tiles in mah-jongg) having the same name or symbol **b :** all the cards or counters given a special function by the rules of a game though not necessarily similarly marked ⟨a trump ~⟩ **c :** the cards or counters held by a player in a particular suit ⟨a 5-card ~⟩ **d :** the suit led or last played ⟨follow ~⟩ **8 :** AGREEMENT, HARMONY ⟨manual strength . . . in ~ with the ferocity of his manners —Agnes Bennett⟩ **syn** see PRAYER
²**suit** \"\ *vb* -ED/-ING/-S *vi* **1** *obs* **:** to make a plea **:** PETITION, SUE **2 :** to be in accordance **:** AGREE, SQUARE — usu. used with *with* ⟨the position ~*s* with his abilities⟩ ⟨steady principles . . . which will ~ with common practice and experience —David Hume †1776⟩ **3 :** to be appropriate, acceptable, or satisfactory ⟨a restaurant . . . that would ~ —F.W.Crofts⟩ ⟨she'll ~, and we'll make her feel at home —Rex Ingamells⟩ ~ *vt* **1** *obs* **:** to arrange (as materials) in a set or order **:** ASSORT **2** *obs* **a :** to appeal for **:** BEG ⟨if we had merit to deserve it, we needed not ~ it of God —William Struther⟩ **b :** to ask the hand of in marriage **:** COURT, WOO **3 :** to outfit with clothes **:** DRESS ⟨did ~ me all points like a man —Shak.⟩ ⟨~*ed* in black⟩ **4 :** to make agree or harmonize with something **:** ACCOMMODATE, ADJUST, FIT, ADAPT — usu. used with *to* ⟨~ the action to the word⟩ ⟨you must ~ your frock to his flowers —Oscar Wilde⟩ ⟨~ their game to their opponents —Robert Collis⟩ **5 a :** to be proper or right for or appropriate to **:** accord with **:** BEFIT ⟨the right word . . . is the one that ~*s* the time and the occasion —E.S.McCartney⟩ ⟨a long handle that did not ~ my grip —O.S.J.Gogarty⟩ **b :** to be becoming to **:** MATCH ⟨a lipstick that ~*ed* her coloring⟩ ⟨the Bible name ~*s* you —Katharine N. Burt⟩ **6 a :** to answer the needs, desires, or requirements of **:** PLEASE ⟨~*s* me fine⟩ ⟨an arrangement that ~*ed* him perfectly⟩ ⟨something to ~ every palate —Peter Forster⟩ ⟨the weather exactly ~*s* us —Martha Kean⟩ **b :** to provide or furnish (as a customer) with something (as merchandise) that proves satisfactory **:** SATISFY ⟨aim to ~ all our patrons⟩
suit·abil·i·ty \ˌsüd·əˈbiləd·ē, -üt∂-, -lətē, -i\ *n* **:** the quality or state of being suitable: as **a :** COMPATIBILITY ⟨a marriage of pure inclination and ~ —Charles Dickens⟩ **b :** FITNESS, QUALIFICATION ⟨unfounded accusations reflecting on their loyalty and ~ —Sidney Hook⟩ ⟨the ~ of the land for cultivation⟩ **c :** APPROPRIATENESS ⟨due regard for . . . ~ of style —L.R.McColvin⟩
¹**suit·able** \ˈsüd·əbəl, -üt∂-\ *adj* [²*suit* + *-able*] **1** *obs* **:** matching or correspondent (as in character, condition, or kind) **:** LIKE, SIMILAR ⟨in his face youth smiled celestial and to every limb ~ grace diffused —John Milton⟩ **2 a :** adapted to a use or purpose **:** FIT ⟨food ~ for human consumption⟩ ⟨a ~ stream for canoeing⟩ ⟨a style ~ for news announcements —F.L.Mott⟩ **b :** appropriate from the viewpoint of propriety, convenience, or fitness **:** PROPER, RIGHT ⟨a movie ~ for children⟩ ⟨a ~ employment⟩ ⟨clothes ~ for the occasion —James Laver⟩ ⟨pronounced a ~ epitaph —W.R.Inge⟩ **c :** having the necessary qualifications **:** meeting requirements **:** APT, QUALIFIED ⟨find a ~ actor for the role⟩ ⟨looked about for a ~ art school⟩ **syn** see FIT
²**suitable** \"\ *adv, archaic* **:** in a suitable manner **:** CONFORMABLY ⟨clothed and attended ~ to their father's birth —Eliza Parsons⟩
suit·able·ness *n* -ES [¹*suitable* + *-ness*] **:** SUITABILITY
suit·ably \-blē, -bli\ *adv* **:** in a suitable manner: as **a** *obs* **:** CONFORMABLY ⟨brutes . . . act ~ to their whole nature —Joseph Butler⟩ **b :** APPROPRIATELY ⟨trying to look ~ scandalized —H.W.Carter⟩ ⟨a testimonial address, ~ engraved —*Amer. Guide Series: Md.*⟩ **c :** FITLY, RIGHTLY ⟨the only director to stage the play ~⟩ **d :** in accordance with requirements **:** PROPERLY ⟨~ treated metal⟩
suit and service *also* **suit service** *n* [¹*suit*] **1 :** the obligation of being in attendance at a feudal court and of serving one's suzerain **2 :** HOMAGE, FEALTY; *also* **:** one's full duty
suitcase \ˈ=ˌ=\ *n* [¹*suit* + *case*] **:** TRAVELING BAG; *esp* **:** one that is rigid, flat, and rectangular
suitcase farmer *n* **:** a grower of wheat or other crops who lives outside the community except during the plowing, seeding, and harvesting seasons, often has a farm without buildings, and does much of the farming by hired custom operators

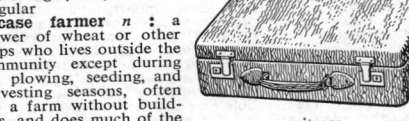

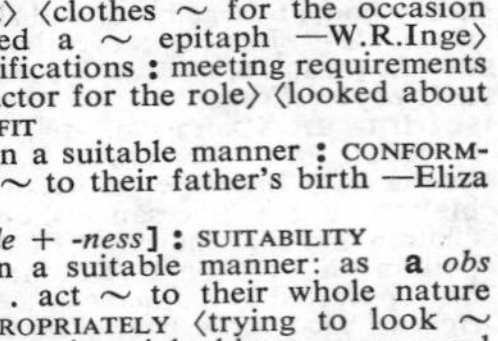
suitcase

suit court *n* **:** the feudal court in which tenants owe attendance

suit-dress \ˈ=,=\ *n* **:** a woman's two-piece costume that consists usu. of a lightweight jacket and skirt and is worn either as a dress or suit

suite \ˈswēt, *esp in sense 2e* ˈswē| *or* ÷ˈsü|; *usu* |d.+V\ *n* -s [F, alter. of OF *siute* — more at SUIT] **1 :** a company of followers or attendants **:** RETINUE; *esp* **:** the personal staff (as assistants and secretaries) accompanying a ruler, diplomat, or dignitary on official business ⟨he and his ~, including his wife, secretarial attachés, and servants —H.A.Chippendale⟩ **2 :** a series or group of things forming a unit or constituting a complement or collection **:** SET: as **a** (1) **:** a group of rooms designed for occupancy as a unit **:** APARTMENT ⟨a ~ of offices⟩ ⟨executive ~⟩ ⟨bridal ~⟩ ⟨the house . . . contains ninety ~s of three to six rooms —*N.Y. Times*⟩ (2) **:** two adjoining bedrooms in a railroad car having a removable partition for separate or joint occupancy **b** (1) **:** an instrumental musical form in vogue during the 17th and 18th centuries consisting of a series of usu. 3 to 5 dances (as allemande, gigue) in the same or related keys often with an elaborate prelude — compare SONATA (2) **:** a modern instrumental composition in several movements having sometimes almost the dimensions of a symphony but wholly free as to the character and number of its movements (3) **:** a long orchestral concert piece in suite form that is an arrangement by either the original composer or another of material drawn from a longer work (as an opera or ballet) **c :** a collection of rocks having some characteristic in common (as rock type or origin) **d :** SERIES 6a **e :** a set of matched furniture for a room ⟨a bedroom ~⟩ ⟨had a three-piece ~ in the living room⟩ **3 :** SEQUEL ⟨the same inevitable ~ of rationalizations —Norman Mailer⟩

¹suit·ed \ˈsüd·əd, -ütəd\ *adj* [¹*suit* + *-ed*] **:** dressed in a suit — often used in combination ⟨velvet-*suited*⟩

²suited \ˈ"\ *adj* [fr. past part. of ²*suit*] **1 :** CONFORMABLE, AGREEABLE ⟨the language of every speech community is ~ to the interests of that culture —Stuart Chase⟩ **2 :** ADAPTED, APT ⟨farmlands particularly ~ to the growing of sugar beets —*Amer. Guide Series: Mich.*⟩

sui·ter's grass \ˈsüd·ə(r)z-\ *n, usu cap S* [prob. fr. the proper name *Suiter*] **:** a reed fescue (*Festuca elatior arundinacea*) that resembles orchard grass and is sometimes cultivated esp. in the northeastern U.S. for grazing

suithold \ˈ=,=\ *n* **:** a feudal tenure of a superior in consideration of suit at his court

suit·ing \,süd·|iŋ, -üt|, |ēŋ\ *n* -s [¹*suit* + *-ing*] **:** a fabric for men's and women's suits

¹suit·or \ˈsüd·ə(r), -ütə-\ *n* -s [ME *suter, sutor, suitor,* fr. AF *suter, suitor,* fr. L *secutor* follower, pursuer, fr. *secutus* (past part. of *sequi* to follow) + *-or* — more at SUE] **1** *archaic* **:** one of a retinue **:** FOLLOWER **2 a :** one in attendance upon a feudal superior **b :** one that petitions or entreats **:** PLEADER, PETITIONER ⟨she hath been a ~ to me for her brother —Shak.⟩ ⟨a petition, signed by the parties . . . who are ~s for the bill —T.E.May⟩ **c :** one that sues at law or prosecutes an action in a court of justice **:** a party to a suit **:** LITIGANT **3 :** one that courts a woman or seeks to marry her **:** WOOER ⟨had difficulty choosing between her two ~s⟩ ⟨a ~ for the old king's daughter —A.C.Whitehead⟩

²suitor \ˈ"\ *vb* -ED/-ING/-S *vi, archaic* **:** to behave as a suitor **:** court a woman ~ *vt, archaic* **:** to seek (a woman) in marriage **:** WOO ⟨the miller's son . . . ~*ed* me —Sir Walter Scott⟩

suit-preference signal *n* **:** the play or discard in contract bridge of an unnecessarily high card to ask one's partner to lead the higher of two available suits and of a low card to ask him to lead the lower

suits *pl of* SUIT, *pres 3d sing of* SUIT

suit service *var of* SUIT AND SERVICE

sui·vez \(ˈ)sw(ʸ)ē¦vā\ *v imper* [F, 2nd pl. imper. of *suivre* to follow, fr. OF — more at SUE] **1 :** FOLLOW — used as a direction in music for the accompanist or orchestra to follow the soloist **2 :** SEGUE 2

su·ji *or* **su·jee** \ˈsü(,)jē\ *n* -s [Hindi *sūjī*] *India* **:** wheat granulated but not pulverized

¹suk \ˈsük\ *n, pl* **suk** *or* **suks** *usu cap* **1 :** a Nilotic people on the Ethiopian border and in the region of Lake Baringo in Kenya **2 :** a member of the Suk people

²suk *var of* SUQ

su·key *also* **su·kie** *or* **su·ky** \ˈsükē\ *or* **suke** \-k\ *n, pl* **sukeys** *also* **sukies** *or* **sukes** [fr. *Sukey,* nickname for *Susanna*] *dial* **:** TEAKETTLE

su·kha·va·ti \sə'kävəd·ē, -ˈkəv-\ *n* -s *usu cap* [Skt *sukhavatī, sukhāvatī,* fr. fem. of *sukhavat, sukhāvat* blissful, fr. *sukha* bliss, happiness, fr. neut. of *sukha* running smoothly, agreeable, happy, fr. *su* good, well + *kha* cavity, axle hole, fr. *khanati* he digs — more at HYGIENE] **:** PURE LAND

su·ki·ya·ki \skēˈ(y)äkē, ,sukē-, ,sükē-\ *n* -s [Jap, prob. fr. *suki* spade + *yaki* roast] **:** meat, soybean curd, onions, bamboo shoots, and other vegetables cooked in soy sauce, sake, and sugar usu. at the table

suk·kah *or* **suc·cah** \ˈsùkə, -(,)kä\ *n, pl* **suk·koth** *or* **suk·kot** \ˈsù,kōt(h), -,kōs, -kəs\ *or* **suk·kos** \-,kōs, -kəs\ *or* **sukkahs** *or* **suc·coth** *or* **suc·cot** *or* **suc·cos** *or* **succahs** [Heb *sukkāh*] **:** a booth or shelter with a roof of branches and leaves erected near a home or in or near a synagogue and used esp. for meals and for temporary residence during the celebration of the Sukkoth festival

suk·koth *or* **suk·coth** *or* **suk·kot** *or* **suk·kos** *or* **suc·cot** *or* **suc·cos** \ˈsù,kō(t)h, -,kōs, -kəs\ *n pl but sing in constr, usu cap* [Heb *sukkōth,* pl. of *sukkāh* thicket, hut, booth, arbor] **:** a Jewish religious festival of thanksgiving celebrated orig. as an autumn harvest festival that is commemorative of the temporary shelters of the Jews during their wandering in the wilderness and that begins on the 15th day of Tishri and lasts 7 days or 9 days with the annexed holidays of Shemini Atzereth and Simhath Torah — called also *Feast of Booths, Feast of Tabernacles*

suklat *var of* SUCLAT

su·ku·ma \sə'kümə\ *also* **su·ku** \-ü\ *n, pl* **sukuma** *or* **sukumas** *also* **suku** *or* **sukus** *usu cap* **1 :** a Bantu-speaking people living south of Lake Victoria in East Africa that is the largest community of Tanganyika **2 :** a member of the Sukuma people

sul- *comb form* [*sulfonic*] **:** sulfonic ⟨*sul*tam⟩ ⟨*sul*tone⟩

su·la \ˈsülə\ *n, cap* [NL, fr. ON *sūla* gannet, pillar — more at SILE] **:** a genus (the type of the family Sulidae) of sea birds comprising the boobies

sul·cal \ˈsəlkəl\ *also* **sul·car** \-kə(r)\ *adj* [NL *sulcus* + E *-al or -ar*] **1 :** of or relating to a sulcus **2 :** GROOVE

sul·cate \ˈsəl,kāt\ *also* **sul·cat·ed** \-,kād·əd\ *adj* [*sulcate* fr. L *sulcatus,* past part. of *sulcare* to furrow, plow, fr. *sulcus* furrow; *sulcated* fr. L *sulcatus* + E *-ed*] **:** scored with furrows **:** furrowed or grooved esp. lengthwise

SULCL *abbr* set up in less than carloads

sul·co-marginal \¦səl(,)kō+\ *adj* [L *sulcus* + E *-o-* + *marginal*] **:** situated at the margin of the spinal cord adjacent to the ventral median fissure

sul·cu·lus \ˈsəlkyələs\ *n, pl* **sulcu·li** \-yə,lī\ [NL, dim. of *sulcus*] **:** a small sulcus

sul·cus \ˈsəlkəs\ *n, pl* **sul·ci** \-l,sī\ [NL, fr. L, furrow; akin to Gk *holkos* track, trace, furrow, *helkein* to drag, pull, OE *sulh* plow, measure of land (cultivated by one plow), Arm *helg* slow, sluggish, Toch B *sälk* to pull, drag forward] **:** FURROW, GROOVE, FISSURE; *esp* **:** a shallow furrow on the surface of the brain separating adjacent convolutions

sulcus lu·na·tus \-lü'nād·əs\ *n, pl* **sulci luna·ti** \-ā,tī\ [NL, crescent-shaped groove] **:** a small inconstant semilunar furrow on the lateral surface of the cerebral hemisphere reputed to occur most often in the brains of primitive peoples

sulcus of ro·lan·do \-rō'lan(,)dō, -län-\ *usu cap R* [after Luigi *Rolando* †1831 Ital. anatomist] **:** CENTRAL SULCUS

sulcus ter·mi·na·lis \-,tərmə'nāləs\ *n, pl* **sulci termina·les** \-ā(,)lēz\ [NL, lit., terminal groove] **1 :** a V-shaped groove separating the anterior two thirds of the tongue from the posterior third and lodging the circumvallate papillae **2 :** a shallow groove on the outside of the right atrium of the heart

suld \ˈsəld, ˈsúd\ *archaic var of* SHOULD

sulf- *or* **sulfo-** *or* **sulph-** *or* **sulpho-** *comb form* [*sulf-, sulfo-* fr. F, fr. L *sulfur; sulph-, sulpho-* modif. (influenced by *sulphur*) of F *sulf-, sulfo-* — more at SULFUR] **:** sulfur ⟨*sulf*hydryl⟩ ⟨*sulf*one⟩ ⟨*sulf*onium⟩ ⟨*sulfo*cyanide⟩: as **a :** sulfide ⟨*sulf*arsenide⟩ ⟨*sulfo*chloride⟩ **b :** derived from sulfuric acid **:** sulfuric ⟨*sulf*amide⟩ **c** *usu* *sulfo-* **:** containing the sulfonic acid group esp. replacing hydrogen **:** sulfonic ⟨*sulfo*amino⟩ ⟨*sulfo*benzoic⟩ **d :** SULFON- 2 ⟨*sulfo*chlorinate⟩ **e :** THI- ⟨*sulfo*cyanate⟩

¹sul·fa *also* **sul·pha** \ˈsəlfə\ *adj* [short for *sulfanilamide*] **1 :** related chemically to sulfanilamide — compare SULFA- **2 :** consisting of, containing, or utilizing a sulfa drug

²sulfa *also* **sulpha** \ˈ"\ *n* -s **:** SULFA DRUG

sulfa- *or* **sulf-** *also* **sulpha-** *or* **sulph-** *comb form* [*sulfa-, sulf-* fr. *sulfanilamide; sulpha-, sulph-* alter. (influenced by *sulphur*) of *sulfa-, sulf-*] **:** derived from or otherwise closely related to sulfanilamide: as **a :** SULFANILAMIDO- ⟨*sulfa*diazine⟩ **b :** containing sulfanilyl ⟨*sulf*acetamide⟩

sul·fa·cet·a·mide *also* **sul·fa·cet·i·mide** \,səlfə'sed·ə,mīd, -məd\ *n* [*sulfacetamide* ISV *sulfa-* + *acetamide; sulfacetimide* alter. (influenced by *imide*) of *sulfacetamide*] **:** a sulfa drug $H_2NC_6H_4SO_2NHCOCH_3$ that has acid properties in solution and that is used chiefly for treating infections of the urinary tract and in the form of its sodium derivative for infections of the eye; *N*-sulfanilyl-acetamide

sul·fa·diazine \¦səlfə+\ *n* [*sulfa-* + *diazine*] **:** a sulfa drug $H_2NC_6H_4SO_2NHC_4H_3N_2$ derived from pyrimidine and sulfanilamide and used in the treatment of meningitis, pneumonia, and intestinal and other infections

sulfa drug *n* **:** any of a class of synthetic organic antibacterial usu. crystalline drugs (as sulfadiazine or sulfathiazole) that are sulfonamides closely related chemically to sulfanilamide ⟨the *sulfa drugs* are antibacterial agents, bacteriostatic rather than germicidal in action, which are used alone or in various combinations with each other or with antibiotics in the treatment of many types of infection such as those caused by *β*-hemolytic streptococci or pneumococci —M.E.Hultquist⟩

sul·fa·guanidine \ˈ"+\ *n* [*sulfa-* + *guanidine*] **:** a sulfa drug $H_2NC_6H_4SO_2NHC(=NH)NH_2$ used esp. formerly in treating intestinal infections — called also *sulfanilylguanidine*

sul·fa·mate \ˈsəlfə,māt\ *n* -s [*sulfamic* + *-ate*] **:** a salt or ester of sulfamic acid

sul·fa·mer·a·zine \,səlfə'merə,zēn, -zən\ *n* [*sulfa-* + *-mer* + *azine*] **:** a sulfa drug $C_{11}H_{12}N_4O_2S$ that is a monomethyl derivative of sulfadiazine and is similarly used and also in veterinary medicine

sul·fa·meth·a·zine \,səlfə'methə,zēn, -zən\ *n* [*sulfa-* + *meth-* + *azine*] **:** a sulfa drug $C_{12}H_{14}N_4O_2S$ that is a dimethyl derivative of sulfadiazine and is used similarly and also in veterinary medicine

sul·fa·mez·a·thine \-ezə,thēn, -,thən\ *n* -s [by alter.] *chiefly Brit* **:** SULFAMETHAZINE

sul·fam·ic acid \¦səl¦famik-\ *n* [ISV *sulf-* + *amide* + *-ic*] **1 :** a strong crystalline acid H_2NSO_3H made usu. by reaction of sulfuric acid, sulfur trioxide, and urea and used chiefly as a weed killer, in cleaning metals, and in the form of salts as a flameproofing or softening agent for paper and textiles **:** the half amide of sulfuric acid **2 :** any of a group of organic derivatives $RNHSO_3H$ or R_2NSO_3H of sulfamic acid that are stable if the R represents alkyl but unstable if one R is aryl or acyl

sulf·am·ide \,səl'fa,mīd, ˈsəlfə,m-, -,məd\ *n* [ISV *sulf-* + *amide*] **1 a :** a crystalline neutral compound $SO_2(NH_2)_2$ obtainable by treating sulfuryl chloride with ammonia **:** the amide of sulfuric acid **b :** any of several derivatives of this compound **2 :** SULFONAMIDE

sulf·a·mid·ic acid \¦səlfə¦midik-\ *n* [*sulfamide* + *-ic*] **:** SULFAMIC ACID

sul·fam·o·yl \,səl'famə,wəl\ *or* **sul·fa·myl** \ˈsəlfə,mil\ *n* -s [*sulfamic* + *-oyl or -yl*] **:** the univalent radical H_2NSO_2- of sulfamic acid

sul·fa·nil·a·mide \,səlfə'nilə,mīd, -,məd\ *n* [*sulfanilic* + *amide*] **1 :** a crystalline sulfonamide $H_2NC_6H_4SO_2NH_2$ that is made usu. by the action of ammonia and then alkali on *N*-acetyl-sulfanilyl chloride, that is the parent compound of most of the sulfa drugs, and that is used less than sulfadiazine and other sulfa drugs **:** the amide of sulfanilic acid **2 :** a derivative of sulfanilamide; *esp* **:** SULFA DRUG

sulfanilamido- *comb form* [*sulfanilamide*] **:** containing the univalent radical $H_2NC_6H_4SO_2NH$- derived from sulfanilamide ⟨2-*sulfanilamido*pyrimidine⟩

sul·fan·i·late \,səl'fanə,lāt\ *n* -s [*sulfanilic* + *-ate*] **:** a salt or ester of sulfanilic acid

sul·fa·nil·ic acid \¦səlfə¦nilik-\ *n* [ISV *sulf-* + *anilic;* prob. orig. formed as F *sulfanilique*] **:** a crystalline acid $H_2NC_6H_4SO_3H$ made by sulfonating aniline and used chiefly as a dye intermediate; *para*-amino-benzenesulfonic acid — compare METANILIC ACID, ORTHANILIC ACID

sul·fan·i·lyl \,səl'fanə,lil\ *n* -s [*sulfanilic* + *-yl*] **:** the univalent radical $H_2NC_6H_4SO_2$- of sulfanilic acid

sul·fan·i·lyl·guanidine \,=¦==,=+\ *n* [*sulfanilyl* + *guanidine*] **:** SULFAGUANIDINE

sulf·antimonide \¦səlf+\ *n* [*sulf-* + *antimonide*] **:** a compound that is both a sulfide and an antimonide

sul·fa·pyrazine \¦səlfə+\ *n* [*sulfa-* + *pyrazine*] **:** a sulfa drug $C_{10}H_{10}N_4O_2S$ derived from pyrazine and sulfanilamide and used similarly to sulfadiazine

sul·fa·pyridine \ˈ"+\ *n* [*sulfa-* + *pyridine*] **:** a sulfa drug $C_{11}H_{11}N_3O_2S$ derived from pyridine and sulfanilamide, used in small doses in the treatment of one type of dermatitis and esp. formerly against pneumococcal and gonococcal infections

sul·fa·pyrimidine \ˈ"+\ *n* [*sulfa-* + *pyrimidine*] **:** a sulfa drug derived from pyrimidine; *esp* **:** SULFADIAZINE

sul·fa·quinoxaline \ˈ"+\ *n* [*sulfa-* + *quinoxaline*] **:** a sulfa drug $C_{14}H_{12}N_4O_2S$ derived from quinoxaline and used esp. in veterinary medicine

sulf·arsenide \¦səlf+\ *n* [*sulf-* + *arsenide*] **:** a compound that is both a sulfide and an arsenide

sulf·arsphenamine \ˈ"+\ *n* [*sulf-* + *arsphenamine*] **:** an orange-yellow powder essentially $C_{12}H_{10}As_2N_2O_2(CH_2SO_3Na)_2$ that is similar to neoarsphenamine and arsphenamine in structure and uses

sulfas *pl of* SULFA

Sul·fa·sux·i·dine \,səlfə'səksə,dēn, -,dən\ *trademark* — used for succinylsulfathiazole

sul·fat·ase \ˈsəlfə,tās\ *n* -s [ISV ¹*sulfate* + *-ase*] **:** any of various esterases that accelerate the hydrolysis of sulfuric esters and that are found esp. in invertebrate and other animal tissues and in microorganisms

¹sul·fate *or* **sul·phate** \ˈsəl,fāt, *usu* -ād.+V\ *n* -s [*sulfate* fr. F, fr. L *sulfur* + F *-ate; sulphate* modif. (influenced by *sulphur*) of F *sulfate*] **:** a salt or ester of sulfuric acid of which most of the salts except those of barium, lead, strontium, and calcium are fairly soluble in water

²sulfate *or* **sulphate** \ˈ"\ *vb* -ED/-ING/-S *vt* **1 :** to treat or combine with sulfuric acid, a sulfate, or a related agent **:** convert into a sulfate; *esp* **:** to convert (an organic compound) into a sulfuric monoester containing the acid group $-OSO_2OH$ ⟨*sulfated* alcohols are important anionic detergents⟩ — compare SULFONATE **2 :** to form a deposit of a whitish scale of lead sulfate on (the plates of a storage battery) ~ *vi* **:** to become sulfated

sulfated oil *n* **:** any of numerous water-soluble oils obtained usu. by treating unsaturated or hydroxylated fatty oils (as various fish oils or castor oil) or their fatty acids with concentrated sulfuric acid so that the essential product is a sulfuric monoester — compare SULFONATED OIL

sulfate group *or* **sulfate ion** *n* **:** the bivalent group or anion SO_4 or $-OSO_2O-$ characteristic of sulfuric acid and sulfates

sulfate of potash : POTASSIUM SULFATE a — used chiefly of the fertilizer grade

sulfate paper *n* **:** unbleached or bleached paper made wholly from sulfate pulp

sulfate process *n* **:** an alkaline process for making pulp from wood chips in which the cooking liquor contains chiefly sodium hydroxide together with considerable amounts of sodium sulfide derived from the reduction of sodium sulfate added during the recovery process

sulfate pulp *n* **:** wood pulp prepared by the sulfate process

sulfate turpentine *or* **sulfate wood turpentine** *n* **:** TURPENTINE 2d

Sul·fa·thal·i·dine \,səlfə'thalə,dēn, -,dən\ *trademark* — used for phthalylsulfathiazole

sul·fa·thiazole \¦səlfə+\ *n* [*sulfa-* + *thiazole*] **:** a sulfa drug $H_2NC_6H_4SO_2NHC_3H_2NS$ derived from thiazole and sulfanilamide, seldom prescribed because of its toxicity, but formerly used esp. in the treatment of pneumococcus and staphylococcus infections

sul·fat·ic \,səl'fad·ik\ *adj* [ISV ¹*sulfate* + *-ic*] **:** of, relating to, resembling, or containing a sulfate

sul·fa·tion \,səl'fāshən\ *n* -s **:** the process of sulfating or becoming sulfated

sul·fa·tize \ˈsəlfə,tīz\ *vt* -ED/-ING/-S [ISV ¹*sulfate* + *-ize*] **:** to convert into sulfate (as sulfide ores by roasting)

sulfato- *also* **sulphato-** *comb form* [¹*sulfate*] **:** containing the sulfate group — esp. in names of coordination complexes ⟨ammonium tri-*sulfato*-cerate $(NH_4)_2[Ce(SO_4)_3]$⟩

sul·fen·ic acid \¦səl¦fenik-\ *n* [*sulf-* + *en-* + *-ic*] **:** any of a series of monobasic organic acids of sulfur having the general formula RSOH and known almost exclusively in the form of derivatives (as acid halides and amides) — compare SULFINIC ACID, SULFONIC ACID

sul·fen·yl \,səl'fenᵊl\ *n* [*sulfen*ic + *-yl*] **:** the radical of a sulfenic acid ⟨benzene-*sulfenyl* chloride C_6H_5SCl⟩

sulf·hemoglobin \¦səlf+\ *n* [ISV *sulf-* + *hemoglobin*] **:** a green pigment formed by the reaction of hemoglobin with a sulfide in the presence of oxygen or hydrogen peroxide and found in putrefied organs and cadavers

sulf·he·mo·glo·bi·ne·mia \,səlf,hēmə,glōbə'nēmēə, -,hemə,-\ *n* -s [NL, fr. ISV *sulfhemoglobin* + NL *-emia*] **:** the presence of sulfhemoglobin in the blood

sulf·hydrate \¦səlf+\ *also* **sul·phy·drate** \,səl'fī,drāt\ *n* [ISV *sulf-* + *hydrate*] **:** HYDROSULFIDE — not used systematically

sulf·hy·dryl \,səlf'hīdrəl\ *also* **sul·phy·dryl** \-l'fī-\ *n* -s [ISV *sulf-* + *hydr-* + *-yl*] **:** the mercapto group

sul·fi·da·tion \,səlfə'dāshən\ *n* -s **:** the process of sulfiding

¹sul·fide *or* **sul·phide** \ˈsəl,fīd, -lfəd\ *n* -s [ISV *sulf-* + *-ide;* prob. orig. formed as G *sulfid*] **1 :** a compound of sulfur analogous to an oxide with sulfur in place of oxygen: **a :** a binary compound of sulfur usu. with a more electropositive element **:** a salt of hydrogen sulfide ⟨~*s* of iron⟩ ⟨the metallic ~*s* except those of the alkali metals are usu. insoluble in water and occur in many cases as minerals⟩ — compare DISULFIDE 1, POLYSULFIDE **b :** a compound of sulfur with more than one element ⟨many minerals (as tetrahedrite) are double or multiple ~*s*⟩ — compare SULFOSALT **2 :** a compound of sulfur analogous to an ether with sulfur in place of oxygen **:** an ester of hydrogen sulfide ⟨ethyl ~ $(C_2H_5)_2S$⟩ — called also *organic sulfide, thioether;* compare DISULFIDE 2, MUSTARD GAS

²sulfide *or* **sulphide** \ˈ"\ *vt* -ED/-ING/-S **:** to treat with or convert into a sulfide — compare XANTHATE

sulfide dye *or* **sulfide color** *n* **:** SULFUR DYE

sulfide toning *n* **:** SULFUR TONING; *esp* **:** this process when the final bath is in a solution of sodium sulfide

sul·fid·ic \,səl¦fidik\ *adj* [ISV ¹*sulfide* + *-ic*] **:** of, relating to, or containing sulfide

sul·fi·dize \ˈsəlfə,dīz\ *vt* -ED/-ING/-S *see -ize in Explan Notes* **:** SULFIDE

sul·fil·i·mine \,səl'filə,mēn, -,mən\ *n* [*sulf-* + *-il* + *imine*] **:** any of a class of compounds containing a nitrogen-to-sulfur bond, having the general formula $R'NSR_2$, and formed by reaction of an organic sulfide with a chloramide (as chloramine-T) and alkali

sul·fi·mide \ˈsəlfə,mīd, -,məd\ *n* [ISV *sulf-* + *imide*] **:** an imide of a carboxylic-sulfonic acid; *esp* **:** SACCHARIN

sulfin- *or* **sulfino-** *comb form* [*sulfinic*] **:** containing the group $-SO_2H$ characteristic of the sulfinic acids

sul·fi·nate \ˈsəlfə,nāt\ *n* -s [*sulfin-* + *-ate*] **:** a salt or ester of a sulfinic acid

sul·fin·ic acid \¦səl¦finik-\ *n* [ISV *sulf-* + *-in* + *-ic*] **:** any of a series of monobasic organic acids of sulfur having the general formula RSO_2H and obtained by reducing the chlorides of sulfonic acids and in other ways — compare SULFOXYLIC ACID

sul·fi·nyl \ˈsəlfə,nil\ *n* -s [*sulfin-* + *-yl*] **:** the bivalent group or radical >SO occurring in sulfoxides, sulfinic acids, and derivatives of the acids **:** THIONYL — used esp. of organic compounds

sul·fi·sox·a·zole \,səlfə'säksə,zōl\ *n* [*sulfa-* + *isoxazole*] **:** a sulfa drug $C_{11}H_{13}N_3O_3S$ derived from sulfanilamide and isoxazole and used similarly to other sulfanilamide derivatives but because of its greater solubility it is less likely to produce renal damage

sul·fi·ta·tion \,səlfə'tāshən\ *n* -s [ISV *sulfite* + *-ation*] **:** the process of sulfiting

sulfitation cake *n* **:** the residue of sugarcane juice from filter presses that has been treated by sulfitation and formed into a cake containing lime and phosphorus and used for fertilizer

¹sul·fite *or* **sul·phite** \ˈsəl,fīt, *usu* -īd.+V\ *n* -s [*sulfite* fr. F, alter. (influenced by ¹*-ite*) of *sulfate; sulphite* modif. (influenced by *sulphur*) of F *sulfite*] **:** a salt or ester of sulfurous acid — **sul·fit·ic** \,səl¦fid·ik\ *adj*

²sulfite *or* **sulphite** \ˈ"\ *vt* -ED/-ING/-S **:** to treat with sulfur dioxide, sulfurous acid, or a sulfite

sulfite liquor *n* **:** the bisulfite solution used in making pulp by the sulfite process

sulfite paper *n* **:** paper made wholly from sulfite pulp

sulfite process *n* **:** an acid process for making pulp from wood in which chips are cooked at high temperature and pressure in a solution of bisulfite of calcium, magnesium, sodium, or ammonium

sulfite pulp *n* **:** wood pulp prepared by the sulfite process ⟨*sulfite pulps* are particularly useful for writing papers because of their . . . strength —J.P.Casey⟩

sulfito- *also* **sulphito-** *comb form* [¹*sulfite*] **:** containing the sulfite group SO_3 — esp. in names of coordination complexes ⟨sodium *sulfito*aurate(III) $Na[Au(SO_3)_2]$⟩

sulfo- — see SULF-

sul·fo acid \ˈsəl(,)fō-\ *n* [*sulfo* short for *sulfonic*] **1 :** THIO ACID **2 :** SULFONIC ACID

sul·fo·benzoic acid \¦səl(,)fō+. . .-\ *n* [ISV *sulf-* + *benzoic*] **:** any of three isomeric crystalline acids $HO_3SC_6H_4COOH$ that are sulfonic derivatives of benzoic acid, that are made either from benzoic acid by sulfonation in the case of the meta isomer or from the corresponding toluenesulfonic acid by oxidation in the case of the ortho or para isomer, and that are used in organic synthesis

sul·fo·bis·muth·ite \,səlfə'bizmə,thīt, -ism-, -,thīt\ *n* [*sulf-* + *bismuth* + *-ite*] **:** any of various compounds of metals with sulfur and trivalent bismuth

sul·fo·bo·rite *or* **sul·pho·bo·rite** \,səlfə'bōr,īt, -'bò,rīt\ *n* -s [G *sulfoborit,* fr. *sulf-* + *borat* borate + *-it* -ite] **:** a mineral $Mg_6H_4(BO_3)_4(SO_4)_2.7H_2O$ consisting of hydrous acid sulfate and borate of magnesium

sul·fo·chloride \¦səl(,)fō+\ *n* [ISV *sulf-* + *chloride*] **1 :** a compound with sulfur and chlorine that is analogous to an oxychloride ⟨phosphorus ~ $PSCl_3$⟩ **2 :** SULFONYL CHLORIDE

sul·fo·chlorinate \ˈ"+\ *vt* [*sulf-* + *chlorinate*] **:** to convert (as a paraffin hydrocarbon) into a sulfonyl chloride by introducing the $-SO_2Cl$ group

sul·fo·chlorination \ˈ"+\ *n* **:** conversion by sulfochlorinating

sul·fo·cyanate \ˈ"+\ *n* [ISV *sulf-* + *cyanate*] **:** THIOCYANATE — not used systematically

sul·fo·cyanide \ˈ"+\ *n* [ISV *sulf-* + *cyanide*] **:** THIOCYANATE — not used systematically

sul·fo·fi·ca·tion \,səlfəfə'kāshən\ *n* -s [*sulf-* + *-fication*] **:** a process of oxidation by which sulfur and sulfur compounds (as sulfides) are converted into sulfates esp. in soils by the agency of bacteria

sul·fo·fy \ˈsəlfə,fī\ *vt* -ED/-ING/-ES [*sulf-* + *-fy*] **:** to subject to or produce by sulfofication

sulfo group *n* [*sulfo* short for *sulfonic*] **:** the sulfonic group

sul·fo·halite *or* **sul·pho·halite** \¦səl(,)fō+\ *n* [*sulf-* + *halite*] **:** a mineral $Na_6ClF(SO_4)_2$ consisting of fluoride, chloride, and sulfate of sodium

sulfon- *also* **sulphon-** *comb form* [*sulfon-* ISV *sulfonic; sulphon-* fr. obs. E *sulphonic,* fr. *sulphone* sulfone (ISV *sulf-* + *-one*) + E *-ic*] **1 :** sulfonic ⟨*sulfon*amide⟩ **2 :** sulfonyl ⟨*sulfon*amido⟩ ⟨*sulfon*methane⟩ ⟨*sulfon*phthalein⟩

sul·fo·nal \ˈsəlfə,nal, ,=ˈ=\ *n* -s [fr. *Sulfonal,* a trademark] **:** SULFONMETHANE

sul·fon·a·mide \sal'fänə‚mīd, -fōn-, ‚salfə'na‚m-, -‚məd\ *n* [*sulfon-* + *amide*] : the amide of a sulfonic acid characterized by the grouping —SO₂N< consisting of nitrogen attached to sulfonyl (*benzene-sulfonamide* C₆H₅SO₂NH₂); *esp* : SULFA DRUG ⟨the bacteriostatic action of ~*s* is antimetabolite in nature —*U.S. Dispensatory*⟩ — see SULFANILAMIDE

¹**sul·fo·nate** \'salfə‚nāt\ *n* -s [ISV *sulfonic* + *-ate*] : a salt or ester of a sulfonic acid

²**sulfonate** *also* **sul·pho·nate** \"\ *vt* -ED/-ING/-S [*sulfonate* fr. ¹*sulfonate*; *sulphonate* fr. obs. E *sulphonate*, n., salt or ester of a sulfonic acid, fr. E *sulphon-* (fr. obs. E *sulphonic* sulfonic) + E *-ate*] : to introduce the sulfonic group into (an organic compound) : convert into a sulfonic acid or salt or halide (as by treating with concentrated sulfuric acid, oleum, or chlorosulfonic acid); *broadly* : to treat (an organic substance) with sulfuric acid or a related agent regardless of the nature of the products — compare SULFATE 1

sulfonated oil *n* : any of numerous water-soluble oils that are obtained usu. by treating various fatty oils or fatty acids with concentrated sulfuric acid or oleum by a process now considered to be essentially sulfation in most cases rather than true sulfonation and that are used chiefly as wetting and emulsifying agents, as dyeing assistants and lubricants in the textile industry, and in fat-liquoring of leather—compare SULFATED OIL, TURKEY-RED OIL

sul·fo·na·tion \‚salfə'nāshən\ *n* -s [ISV ²*sulfonate* + *-ion*] : the process of sulfonating

sul·fo·na·tor \'salfə‚nādə(r)\ *n* -s : one that sulfonates : an acid-resistant vessel used for the sulfonation of organic substances

sul·fon·chlor·amide \‚salˌfän+\ *n* [*sulfon-* + *chloramide*] : a sulfonamide in which chlorine is attached to the nitrogen atom : an *N*-chloro-sulfonamide — not used systematically; compare CHLORAMINE-T, DICHLORAMINE-T

sul·fone \'sal‚fōn\ *n* -s [ISV *sulf-* + *-one*; prob. orig. formed as G *sulfon*] : any of a class of organic compounds that are characterized by the sulfonyl group doubly united by means of its sulfur usu. with carbon (as with two hydrocarbon radicals or a single bivalent radical) and that are in general crystalline stable compounds made by oxidation of organic sulfides and in other ways; *esp* : diaminodiphenyl sulfone or a derivative or closely related compound used in medicine chiefly in the treatment of leprosy

sul·fone·phthalein *also* **sul·fon·phthalein** \‚sal‚fōn‚-fthā+\ *n* [*sulfone*, *sulfon-* + *phthalein*] : any of a group of organic compounds (as phenolsulfonephthalein or bromocresol purple) that are analogous to the phthaleins and like them are intensely colored in alkaline solution and that are made by condensation of phenols with anhydrides or acid chlorides of *ortho*-sulfobenzoic acid or its derivatives

sul·fone·eth·yl·meth·ane \‚sal‚fōⁿethal'me‚thān, -l‚fäˈ-\ *n* [*sulfon-* + *ethyl* + *methane*] : a crystalline hypnotic sulfone CH₃C(C₂H₅)(SO₂C₂H₅)₂ that is an ethyl analogue of sulfonmethane

sul·fon·ic \‚sal'fänik\ *adj* [ISV *sulfone* + *-ic*] : being, containing, or derived from the univalent acid group —SO₃H or —SO₂OH

sulfonic acid *n* : any of numerous acids that are characterized by the sulfonic group and may be regarded as derived from sulfuric acid by replacement of a hydroxyl group by either an inorganic anion or a univalent organic radical; *esp* : any of a class of organic acids (as toluenesulfonic acids or phenolsulfonic acids) that have the general formula RSO₃H when only one sulfonic group is present, that are in general stable, easily water-soluble, strong acids, that are made esp. in the case of the aromatic acids by direct sulfonation, and that are used often in the form of salts chiefly as catalysts, detergents, and intermediates (as for dyes) — compare CHLOROSULFONIC ACID, PETROLEUM SULFONATE, SULFINIC ACID

sul·fo·ni·um \‚sal'fōnēəm\ *n* -s [NL, fr. *sulf-* + *-onium*] : a univalent cation H₃S⁺ or radical H₃S analogous to oxonium with sulfur in place of oxygen and known esp. in the form of organic derivatives (as triethyl-*sulfonium* iodide) made usu. by reaction of an organic sulfide with an alkyl halide — compare -THIONIUM

sul·fon·meth·ane \‚sal‚fōn, -fäⁿ+\ *n* [*sulfon-* + *methane*] : a crystalline hypnotic sulfone (CH₃)₂C(SO₂C₂H₅)₂ made from acetone by reaction with ethyl mercaptan followed by oxidation

sul·fo·nyl \'salfə‚nil\ *n* -s [ISV *sulfon-* + *-yl*] : the bivalent group or radical >SO₂ occurring in sulfones, sulfonic acids, and derivatives of the acids : SULFURYL — used esp. of organic compounds

sulfonyl chloride *n* : the chloride of a sulfonic acid

sul·fo·salt \'salfə‚sȯlt\ *n* [ISV *sulf-* + *salt*] : a compound (as tetrahedrite) that is either a salt of an inorganic thio acid or a double or multiple sulfide

sul·fo·selenide \‚sal(‚)fō+\ *n* [*sulf-* + *selenide*] : a substance (as cadmium red) consisting of or containing both a sulfide and a selenide

sulf·ox·ide \‚sal'fäk‚sīd, -ksəd\ *n* [ISV *sulf-* + *oxide*] : any of a class of organic compounds that are characterized by the sulfinyl group doubly united by means of its sulfur with carbon (as with two hydrocarbon radicals or a single bivalent radical), that are usu. made by oxidation of organic sulfides, and that yield sulfones on further oxidation

sulf·ox·one sodium \‚sal'fäk‚sōn-\ *n* [*sulfoxone* alter. (influenced by *ox-*) of *sulfone*] : a crystalline salt SO₂(C₆H₄NHCH₂SO₃Na)₂ made by the condensation of diaminodiphenyl sulfone and sodium formaldehydesulfoxylate and used in the treatment of leprosy

sulf·ox·y·late \‚sal'fäksə‚lāt\ *n* -s [ISV *sulfoxylic* + *-ate*] : a salt or ester of sulfoxylic acid or one of its organic derivatives; *esp* : FORMALDEHYDESULFOXYLATE

sulf·ox·yl·ic acid \‚sal‚fäk'silik-\ *n* [ISV *sulf-* + *ox-* + *-yl* + *-ic*] : a hypothetical acid S(OH)₂ or HSO₂H known in the form of various organic derivatives — compare FORMALDEHYDESULFOXYLIC ACID, SULFINIC ACID

¹**sul·fur** *or* **sul·phur** \'salfə(r)\ *n* -s [ME *soufre*, *sulphre*, *sulphur* brimstone, fr. OF & L; ME *soufre* fr. OF, fr. L *sulfur*, *sulphur*; ME *sulphre*, *sulphur* fr. L *sulphur*, *sulpur*, *sulpur*, prob. fr. Oscan] **1** : a nonmetallic multivalent tasteless odorless water-insoluble element that occurs in large quantities either free esp. in yellow orthorhombic crystals or in masses often associated with limestone, gypsum, and other minerals (as in volcanic regions in Sicily and Japan and in salt domes in Louisiana and Texas) or combined esp. in sulfides (as pyrites and galena) and sulfates (as gypsum and barite), that is also a constituent of proteins and various other compounds found in animals and plants, that exists in several allotropic forms including the ordinary yellow orthorhombic alpha form stable below 95.5°C and changing successively to a pale yellow monoclinic crystalline beta form, a pale yellow mobile liquid, and a dark red to brown very viscous liquid as the temperature is raised to about 200°C, that burns in air with a blue flame forming sulfur dioxide and a trace of sulfur trioxide, that resembles oxygen chemically but is less active and more acidic, and that is used chiefly in making sulfur dioxide, sulfuric acid, carbon disulfide, and other sulfur compounds, in the pulp and paper industry, in rubber vulcanization, in metallurgy, in petroleum refining, in black powder, matches, and fireworks, in agriculture as a fungicide and insecticide, and in medicine in treating skin diseases — called also *brimstone*; symbol *S*; see FLOWERS OF SULFUR, FRASCH PROCESS, HYDROGEN SULFIDE, PLASTIC SULFUR, PRECIPITATED SULFUR, RHOMBIC SULFUR; ELEMENT table **2** *sulphur*, *archaic* : a sulfide or similar compound of sulfur **3** *sulphur* : something (as excited, inflamed, or scathing talk or language) that suggests sulfur

²**sulfur** *or* **sulphur** \"\ *adj* : of, relating to, or resembling sulfur : containing or impregnated with sulfur

³**sulfur** *or* **sulphur** \"\ *vt* -ED/-ING/-S : to treat with sulfur, with fumes of burning sulfur or sulfur dioxide, or with sulfites (as in fumigating, bleaching, or preserving) : SULFURIZE ⟨~*ing* is necessary in the preparation of most kinds of dried fruit —T.H.Jackson & Barbara Roger⟩

sul·fu·rate *or* **sul·phu·rate** \'salfyə‚rāt\ *vt* -ED/-ING/-S [LL *sulfuratus*, *sulphuratus*, past part. of L *sulfurare*, *sulphurare* to sulfurize, fr. L *sulfur*, *sulphur*] : SULFURIZE, THIONATE —

sul·fu·ra·tion \‚salfyə'rāshən\ *n* -S

sulfurated lime solution *n* : VLEMINCKX' SOLUTION

sulfurated potash *n* : a mixture composed principally of potassium polysulfides and potassium thiosulfate that is obtained by heating sublimed sulfur and potassium carbonate as liver-brown lumps changing to yellowish and decomposing in air and that is used chiefly in treating skin diseases and in producing color effects on brass and other metals — called also *liver of sulfur*

sul·fu·ra·tor \"‚rādə(r)\ *n* -s : an apparatus used in sulfuring or sulfurizing

sulfur bacterium *n* : a bacterium (as many members of the Rhodobacteriinae) possessing the power of reducing sulfur compounds

sulfur black *n*, *often cap S&B* : any of several black sulfur dyes; *esp* : one made from 2,4-dinitrophenol — see DYE table I (esp. under *Sulfur Black* 1)

sulfur chloride *n* : a chloride of sulfur: as **a** : a yellow fuming irritating corrosive toxic liquid S₂Cl₂ that is made usu. by reaction of chlorine with molten sulfur and often contains sulfur or sulfur dichloride and that is used chiefly as a chlorinating or sulfurizing agent or as both simultaneously, in making vulcanized oils, and in the cold cure of rubber; di-sulfur dichloride — called also *sulfur monochloride* **b** : SULFUR DICHLORIDE

sulfur dichloride *n* : a dark brown or reddish liquid SCl₂ that resembles the sulfur chloride (S₂Cl₂ and is used for similar purposes

sulfur dioxide *n* : a compound SO₂ that is toxic esp. to plants, that occurs in the gases from volcanoes, in many volcanic springs, and in variable amounts in the atmosphere, that is produced as a heavy colorless nonflammable gas of pungent suffocating odor usu. by burning sulfur or sulfides (as pyrite) and is present in the waste gases from many smelting and other industrial processes, that is easily condensed to a colorless liquid boiling at −10°C and is usu. sold in liquid form, and that is used chiefly in making sulfuric acid, sulfites, other sulfur compounds, and sulfite pulp, and in petroleum refining as a reducing and bleaching agent, as a preservative, disinfectant, and fumigant, and as a refrigerant — see SULFUROUS ACID

sulfur dye *or* **sulfur color** *n* : any of a class of sulfur-containing dyes that are made by heating various organic compounds (as aromatic polyamines or indophenols) with sulfur or alkali polysulfides and are used chiefly in dyeing cotton and other cellulose fibers — called also *sulfide dye*; see DYE table I

sul·fu·re·ous *or* **sul·phu·re·ous** \‚sal'fyureəs\ *adj* [L *sulfureus*, *sulphureus*, fr. *sulfur*, *sulphur*; *sulpur* sulfur + *-eus* -eous] : consisting of sulfur : having the qualities of sulfur esp. when burning : impregnated with sulfur : sulfur-colored : SULFUROUS ⟨~ gases⟩ — **sul·fu·re·ous·ly** *adv* — **sul·fu·re·ous·ness** *n* -ES

¹**sul·fu·ret** \'salf(y)ə‚ret\ *n* -s [NL *sulfuretum*, fr. L *sulfur* — more at SULFUR] : SULFIDE

²**sulfuret** \"\ *vt* **sulfureted** *or* **sulfuretted**; **sulfureting** *or* **sulfuretting**; **sulfurets** : to combine or impregnate with sulfur

sulfureted hydrogen *n* : HYDROGEN SULFIDE

sulfur family *n* : the three elements sulfur, selenium, and tellurium located in group VIA of the periodic table

sulfur flour *n* : crude or refined sulfur ground and usu. sized — called also *flour sulfur*; compare FLOWERS OF SULFUR

sulfur hexafluoride *n* : an inert gaseous compound SF₆ that has high dielectric strength and is used as an electric insulator

sul·fu·ric *or* **sul·phu·ric** \‚sal'fyurik, -rēk\ *adj* [sulfuric fr. F *sulfurique*, fr. L *sulfur* + F *-ique* -ic; *sulphuric* modif. (influenced by *sulphur*) of F *sulfurique*] **1** : of, relating to, or containing sulfur : derived from or by the use of sulfuric acid — used esp. of compounds in which this element has a higher valence as contrasted with the sulfurous compounds ⟨~ esters⟩ **2** *usu sulphuric* : SULFUROUS 2

sulfuric acid *n* **1** *obs* : SULFUR TRIOXIDE **2** : a heavy corrosive high-boiling oily liquid dibasic acid H₂SO₄ that is colorless when pure, that was made in early times by distilling green vitriol and is now made commercially from sulfur dioxide by oxidation either in the chamber process usu. giving an acid of 65 to 78 percent strength or in the contact process involving conversion of the sulfur dioxide to sulfur trioxide on contact with a catalyst (as of platinum or vanadium oxides) followed by absorption of the trioxide in strong sulfuric acid to form acid of 98 to 99 percent strength or oleum, that is a strong acid and oxidizing agent, that combines energetically with water evolving much heat and is consequently a good drying and dehydrating agent, and that is the most widely used acid in industry (as in the manufacture of superphosphate and other fertilizers, chemicals, detergents, pigments and dyes, explosives, rayon, and storage batteries and in petroleum refining and in pickling metals) — called also *oil of vitriol*; compare PYROSULFURIC ACID

sulfuric anhydride *n* : SULFUR TRIOXIDE

sulfuric ether *n* : ETHER 3a

sul·fu·ri·za·tion \‚salf(y)ərə'zāshən\ *n* -s : the process of sulfurizing

sul·fu·rize *or* **sul·phu·rize** \'salf(y)ə‚rīz\ *vt* -ED/-ING/-S see *-ize* in Explan Notes [*sulfurize* fr. F *sulfuriser*, fr. L *sulfur* + F *-iser* *-ize*; *sulphurize* modif. (influenced by *sulphur*) of F *sulfuriser*] : to combine or impregnate with sulfur or one of its compounds : SULFUR ⟨*sulfurized* lubricating and cutting oils⟩

sulfur match *n* : ³MATCH 2a

sulfur monochloride *n* : SULFUR CHLORIDE a — not used systematically

sulfur mustard *n* : MUSTARD GAS

sulfur oil *or* **sulfur olive oil** *n* : a green oil of inferior grade obtained from the expressed marc of olives by extraction with carbon disulfide and used in making soap

sul·fu·rous *or* **sul·phu·rous** \'salf(y)ərəs, *in sense 1 also* ‚sal'fyur-\ *adj* [L *sulfurosus*, *sulphurosus*, fr. *sulfur*, *sulphur* sulfur + *-osus* -ose] **1** : of, relating to, or containing sulfur : resembling or emanating from sulfur esp. when burning : SULFUREOUS ⟨~ gases⟩ — used esp. of compounds in which this element has a lower valence as contrasted with the sulfuric compounds **2** *usu sulphurous* **a** : of, relating to, or characterized by thunder : SULTRY ⟨*sulphurous* atmosphere⟩ **b** : of or heavy with the smoke of gunpowder ⟨*sulphurous* fumes⟩ **c** : of, relating to, or dealing with hellfire : INFERNAL ⟨the *sulphurous* pit —Shak.⟩ ⟨*sulphurous* sermons⟩ **d** : SCORCHING, SCATHING, VIRULENT, VITRIOLIC ⟨*sulphurous* denunciations⟩ **e** : highly profane : BLASPHEMOUS ⟨*sulphurous* language⟩ — **sul·fu·rous·ly** *adv* — **sul·fu·rous·ness** *n* -ES

sulfurous acid *n* **1** : SULFUR DIOXIDE **2** : an unstable weak dibasic acid H₂SO₃ that is known esp. in solutions of sulfur dioxide in water and in the form of its salts and that is a good reducing and bleaching agent forming sulfuric acid as it is oxidized

sulfurous anhydride *or* **sulfurous acid anhydride** *n* : SULFUR DIOXIDE

sulfur oxide *n* : any of several oxides of sulfur: as **a** : SULFUR DIOXIDE **b** : SULFUR TRIOXIDE

sulfur point *n* : the boiling point of sulfur — compare INTERNATIONAL TEMPERATURE SCALE

sulfurs *pl of* SULFUR, *pres 3d sing of* SULFUR

sulfur spring *n* : a spring whose waters contain compounds of sulfur (as hydrogen sulfide with its characteristic odor)

sulfur subchloride *n* : SULFUR CHLORIDE a

sulfur toning *n* : any of several processes in which the silver of a printing-out or developed image is caused to combine with sulfur, effecting a change in color and producing a color ranging from a yellowish to a purplish brown — compare SULFIDE TONING

sulfur trioxide *n* : a compound SO₃ that is a heavy low-boiling strongly acid corrosive liquid when first produced at ordinary temperatures but that polymerizes readily to three or more solid forms including a stable modification resembling asbestos, that is formed by the union of sulfur dioxide and oxygen (as in the contact process for making sulfuric acid) but is usu. made by distillation of strong oleum, that gives off irritating toxic fumes in air and combines violently with water evolving much heat and forming sulfuric acid, that is a powerful oxidizing agent and sets fire to materials like ex-

celsior and sawdust on contact, and that is used chiefly as a sulfonating and sulfating agent (as in making detergents)

sulfur water *n* : a natural water (as in a spring) containing combined sulfur and esp. hydrogen sulfide

sul·fu·ry \'salfərē\ *adj* [*sulfur* + *-y*] : of, relating to, or resembling sulfur : SULFUROUS, SULFUREOUS

sul·fur·yl \'salf(y)ə‚ril\ *n* -s [ISV *sulfur* + *-yl*] : the bivalent radical or cation >SO₂ of sulfuric acid : SULFONYL — used esp. in names of inorganic compounds

sulfuryl chloride *n* [ISV] : a pungent corrosive liquid SO₂Cl₂ obtained usu. by direct union of sulfur dioxide and chlorine by means of catalysts and used chiefly as a chlorinating and sulfonating agent since it dissociates when heated or in the presence of catalysts

sul·fy·drate \‚sal'fī‚drāt\ *n* -s [alter. of *sulfhydrate*] : HYDROSULFIDE — not used systematically

su·li·dae \'sülə‚dē\ *n pl*, *cap* [NL, fr. *Sula*, type genus + *-idae*] : a small family of sea birds (order Pelecaniformes) comprising the boobies and gannets

¹**sulk** \'səlk\ *vi* -ED/-ING/-S [back-formation fr. ¹*sulky*] : to be sullen or morose in mood : be moodily silent : refuse advances or intercourse with others for a time : nurse a grievance

²**sulk** \"\ *n* **1** : the state or condition of one sulking — often used in pl. **2** : a sulky mood or spell — often used in pl.

sul·ka \'salkə\ *n*, *pl* **sulka** *or* **sulkas** *usu cap* **1** : a Papuan people on New Britain Island, Bismarck Archipelago **2** : a member of the Sulka people

sulk·er \'salkə(r)\ *n* -s : one that sulks

sulk·i·ly \'salkəlē, 'sȯuk-, -əli\ *adv* : in a sulky manner

sulk·i·ness \-kēnəs, -kin-\ *n* -ES : the state of being sulky

¹**sulky** \-kē, -ki\ *adj* -ER/-EST [prob. alter. (influenced by *-y*, adj. suffix) of earlier *sulke* hard to sell, slow, sluggish, perh. back-formation fr. OE *āsolcen* lazy, sluggish, indifferent, fr. past part. of *āseolcan* to be lazy, slow; akin to MHG *selken* to drop, fall, OIr *selg* hunt, Skt *sriati* he releases, shoots, emits] **1 a** : sulking or inclined to sulk : given to spells of sulking ⟨a ~ refusal to acknowledge facts —Bertrand Russell⟩ **b** : suggestive of sulkiness : MOODY ⟨rather ~ good looks —Dorothy Sayers⟩ **2 a** : slow in movement or response : SLUGGISH, INACTIVE ⟨a ~ fire that declines to flame —Edward Sackville-West & Desmond Shawe-Taylor⟩ **b** : DULL, GLOOMY ⟨a ~ day⟩ **3** : having wheels and usu. a seat for the driver ⟨~ cultivator⟩ ⟨~ plow⟩ **syn** see SULLEN

²**sulky** \"\ *n* -ES [prob. fr. ¹*sulky*] **1** : a light 2-wheeled cart (as used for trotting races) having a seat for the driver only and usu. no body **2** : a sulky vehicle (as a plow, a lister, or a cultivator) **3** : a light stroller **4** : an arch mounted on wheels or crawler tracks and used in logging

¹**sull** \'sal\ *n* [short for *sullow*] *dial* : PLOW

²**sull** \"\ *vi* -ED/-ING/-S [back-formation fr. *sullen*] *South & Midland* : to be sullen or balky : SULK

³**sull** \"\ *n* -s [by shortening] : SULLAGE 3

sul·la \'salə\ *or* **sulla clover** *n* -s [Sp *sulla*, prob. fr. LL *sylla*, an herb] : a European herb (*Hedysarum coronarium*) valued for forage and cultivated for its pink flowers — called also *French honeysuckle*

sul·lage \'salij\ *n* -s [prob. fr. MF *souiller* to soil + E *-age* — more at SOIL] **1** : drainage or refuse esp. from a house, farmyard, or street : SEWAGE ⟨drains to remove ~ from the inhabited area —*Science & Culture*⟩ **2** : mud deposited by water : SILT **3** : scoria on molten metal in the ladle

sul·len \'salən\ *adj*, *often -ER/-EST* [earlier *sollen*, *sollein*, ME *solein*, *solain* sullen, solitary, single, prob. fr. MF *solain* (attested only in the sense of "food for a single person"), prob. fr. (assumed) VL *solanus*, fr. L *solus* alone — more at SOLE] **1 a** : ill-humoredly unsociable : gloomily or resentfully silent or repressed ⟨a ~ mood⟩ ⟨a ~ crowd⟩ ⟨the population ~ and impoverished —H.W.H.Knott⟩ **b** : relating to or indicative of a gloomy, resentful, or surly mood : suggesting a state of repressed anger ⟨began collecting the remaining things with ~ hands —Dorothy M. Richardson⟩ ⟨a ~ voluptuous mouth —Edmund Wilson⟩ **2** : OBSTINATE, REFRACTORY, INTRACTABLE ⟨~ oxen⟩ **3 a** : of a dull color : of somber hue ⟨LOWERING ⟨a ~ sky⟩ ⟨a chain of ~ clouds —Ellen Glasgow⟩ ⟨the waves were ~, heavier than usual —K.M.Dodson⟩ **b** : dull or deep of sound : of mournful tone ⟨the ~ roar of a vast cataract —William Beckford⟩ ⟨the ~ bawling of steers —Green Peyton⟩ ⟨the ~ murmur of the bees —Oscar Wilde⟩ **4** : DISMAL, SAD, MELANCHOLY ⟨rain fell with a ~ splash —Marcia Davenport⟩ **5** : moving sluggishly and resentfully or as if resentfully ⟨just a ~ line of men falling back —R.H. Newman⟩ ⟨~ rivers⟩

syn GLUM, MOROSE, SURLY, SULKY, CRABBED, SATURNINE, DOUR, GLOOMY: SULLEN applies to gloomy ill-humored refusal to be sociable or responsive ⟨her stolid exterior seemed to cloak a *sullen* resentment at the fact that she should be questioned at all —W.H.Wright⟩ ⟨sitting till three in the morning, staring at the dead fire in *sullen* apathy —G.D. Brown⟩ ⟨with *sullen*, defiant hatred still burning in their eyes —Robert Alden⟩ GLUM indicates silent dismal dispiritedness ⟨mutes at funerals could not look more *glum* than the domestics —W.M.Thackeray⟩ ⟨a *glum* guitarist who stared lifelessly into the innards of his guitar —*Time*⟩ MOROSE describes bitter, cynical, or misanthropic uncommunicative ill humor ⟨she has tempted him to drink again because he is so *morose* when he is sober that she cannot endure living with him —G.B. Shaw⟩ ⟨in the keener moments of consciousness of his loneliness, she found him *morose*, until, unable to sing or laugh with the songs and laughter of that house, he came at times to believe he was *morose* himself —E.T.Thurston⟩ SURLY applies to repelling churlish or rude sulkiness ⟨the *surly* expression of an active boy detained within walls while other boys were shouting in the park —Gertrude Atherton⟩ ⟨the family pictures glared at the spectator in the eyes like some *surly* animal, that had lost its good humor when it outlived its playfulness —Nathaniel Hawthorne⟩ SULKY may suggest a childish display of displeasure or resentment marked by sullen peevishness ⟨stared at the newcomer with a *sulky* scowl, as much as to say, Who the devil are you —W.M. Thackeray⟩ ⟨he was silent now, watching her with *sulky*, mistrustful eyes —Christine Weston⟩ CRABBED refers to accustomed, harsh, forbidding, morose crossness ⟨an old crone who knew magic and could be asked for help, but who was apt to be *crabbed* and was best left alone —W.W.Howells⟩ ⟨*crabbed* theologians involved in tenuous subtleties and disputing endlessly —V.L.Parrington⟩ SATURNINE describes heavy forbidding taciturn gloom ⟨the severe, skeptical eyes, the querulous eyebrows, the thin peevish lips, the big pedantic nose ... display a *saturnine* master bore —D.B.W.Lewis⟩ DOUR may describe uncommunicative grim obstinacy ⟨drank in silence; when deep in his cups he became more and more *dour* and taciturn —C.B.Nordhoff & J.N.Hall⟩ ⟨the pleasureloving Cavaliers were not sympathetic with the *dour* denials of enjoyment that prevailed in some of the other colonies —*Amer. Guide Series: Va.*⟩ GLOOMY describes a cheerless, sullen, or melancholy depression of spirits ⟨constitutionally *gloomy*, a congenital pessimist who always saw the doleful side of any situation —W.A.White⟩ ⟨a heart full of *gloomy* forebodings, and a brain whirling with wild fancies —Charles Kingsley⟩

sul·len·ly *adv* : in a sullen manner

sul·len·ness \-lən(n)əs\ *n* -ES : the quality or state of being sullen

sul·lens \-lənz\ *n pl* [*sullen* + *-s* (pl. suffix)] *chiefly dial* : a sullen mood : SULKS

sul·low \'sa(‚)lō, -lə\ *n* -s [ME *solow*, *suluh*, fr. OE *sulh* — more at SULCUS] *chiefly dial* : PLOW

¹**sul·ly** \'salē, -li\ *vb* -ED/-ING/-S [prob. fr. MF *souiller* to soil — more at SOIL] *vi*, *obs* : to become soiled, tarnished, or defiled — *vt* : to make soiled or tarnished : BESMIRCH, STAIN, DEFILE ⟨no cruelties *sullied* his name —Brian Fitzgerald⟩ ⟨neologisms with which I will not ~ your ears —R.W.Chapman⟩ ⟨wholesale disruption of war unsettles and *sullies* the minds of millions —R.S.Ellery⟩ ⟨charm of its houses and buildings is somewhat *sullied* by coal smoke deposits —*Amer. Guide Series: N.H.*⟩

²**sully** \"\ *n* -ES *archaic* : SOIL, TARNISH, STAIN ⟨little spots and *sullies* in his reputation —*Spectator, 1711*⟩

sulph- *or* **sulpho-** — see SULF-

sulpha *var of* SULFA

sulpha- or **sulph-** — see SULFA-
sulphate var of SULFATE
sulphate green n : a light to moderate bluish green
sulphato- — see SULFATO-
sulphide var of SULFIDE
sul·phine yellow \ˈsəl,fēn-\ n [sulphine fr. obs. E sulphine compound containing sulfur, fr. E sulf- + -ine] : a dark grayish to dark yellow that is slightly darker than pyrite yellow and very slightly lighter and stronger than bister green
sulphite var of SULFITE
sulphito- — see SULFITO-
sulphoborite var of SULFOBORITE
sulphohalite var of SULFOHALITE
sulphon- — see SULFON-
sulphonate var of SULFONATE
sul·pho rhodamine \ˈsəl(,)fō+\ n, usu cap S&R [sulpho short for obs. E sulphonic — more at SULFON-] : an acid dye — see DYE table I (under Acid Red 52)
¹**sulphur** var of SULFUR
²**sul·phur** \ˈsəlfə(r)\ or **sulphur butterfly** n -s : any of numerous butterflies of Colias and related genera (family Pieridae) usu. having the wings chiefly yellow or orange with a black border — see CLOUDED SULPHUR, CLOUDLESS SULPHUR
sulphur and molasses n : a preparation sometimes taken as a spring tonic because of the laxative influence of sulfur ⟨looks woebegone . . . as if he needed a good belt of sulphur and molasses —John McCarten⟩
¹**sulphurate** adj [L sulphuratus, sulfuratus, fr. sulphur, sulfur + -atus -ate] obs : of or relating to sulfur : SULFUROUS
²**sulphurate** var of **sulfurate**
sulphur-bottom \ˈ≈≈,≈≈\ also **sulphur-bottom whale** n [so called fr. the yellowish splotches on its belly] : BLUE WHALE
sulphur candle n : a disinfecting candle composed chiefly of sulfur and giving off fumes of sulfur dioxide when burned
sulphur-crested cockatoo \ˈ≈≈,≈≈-\ n : a large white Australian cockatoo (Kakatoe galerita) that has a showy erectile yellow crest, is often a destructive raider of grain crops, and is often kept as a pet
sulphureous var of SULFUREOUS
sulphur granule n : one of the small yellow bodies found in the pus of actinomycotic abscesses and consisting of clumps of the causative actinomycete
sulphuric var of SULFURIC
sulphurize var of SULFURIZE
sulphur ore 1 : PYRITE 2 : native sulfur
sulphurous var of SULFUROUS
sulphur plant also **sulphur flower** n [so called fr. the yellow color of some of the plants] : any of several plants of the genus Eriogonum of the western U. S.
sulphur shower or **sulphur rain** n : a shower of yellow pollen often seen in spring that is carried by the wind from conifers (as pines)
sulphur sponge n : a bright yellow sponge; esp : a boring sponge (Cliona celata)
sulphurweed also **sulphurwort** \ˈ≈≈,≈\ n : either of two European plants (Peucedanum officinale and P. palustre) the dried roots of which when burned emit a sulfurous odor
sulphur whale n : BLUE WHALE
sulphur yellow n 1 : a variable color averaging a brilliant greenish yellow that is yellower and paler than average lemon yellow (sense 1a) 2 : a light greenish yellow that is greener and deeper than Martius yellow — called also brimstone, citrus
sulphydrate var of SULFHYDRATE
sulphydryl var of SULFHYDRYL
sul·pi·cian \,səlˈpishən\ n -s usu cap [F sulpicien, fr. Compagnie de Saint-Sulpice Society of St. Sulpice (fr. Église Saint-Sulpice, church in Paris of which the founder of the Sulpicians Jean Jacques Olier †1657 was a pastor) + F -ien -ian] : a member of a Roman Catholic society of diocesan priests that was established in France in 1642 with the purpose of contributing teachers for ecclesiastical seminaries
sul pon·ti·cel·lo \,sül,päntəˈche(,)lō\ adv [It] : with the bow kept near the bridge so as to bring out the higher harmonics and thereby produce a nasal tone — used as a direction in music for a stringed instrument
sul·tam \ˈsəl,tam\ n -s [sul- + lactam] : any of a class of inner amides of amino sulfonic acids characterized by the sulfonyl-imido grouping $-SO_2NH-$ in a ring and analogous to lactams
sul·tan \ˈsəltᵊn, -tan sometimes -l,tan or -l,tän or -l,tän or sülˈtän or sülˈtän\ n [MF, fr. Ar sulṭān ruler, dominion, sultan] 1 -s : a king or ruling sovereign esp. of a Muhammadan state 2 [so called fr. its being orig. fr. Turkey] a usu cap : an obscure breed of white domestic fowls having the shanks and toes slaty blue and heavily feathered, a V-shaped comb, a crest, muffs, and five toes b -s : a bird of this breed 3 -s : CRIMSON LAKE 2
sul·tana \,səlˈtanə\ n -s [It, fem. of sultano sultan, fr. Ar sulṭān] 1 : a female member of a sultan's family; esp : a sultan's wife 2 also **sultana bird** [so called fr. its rich exotic plumage] : a purple gallinule of the genus Porphyrio 3 a : a pale yellow seedless grape grown chiefly in the Mediterranean region as a source of raisins and of a delicate white wine b : the raisin of this grape 4 : a dark red to purplish red that is less strong than plum violet and duller than neutral red
sul·tan·ate \ˈsəltᵊnət, -tənət, -tᵊn,āt, -tə,nāt, usu -d·+V\ n -s [F sultanat, fr. sultan (fr. MF) + -at -ate] 1 : the office, dignity, or power of a sultan 2 : a state or country governed by a sultan
sul·tane \,səlˈtän\ n -s [F, fr. fem. of sultan] : an elaborate gown trimmed with buttons and loops and worn around 1700
sul·tan·ess \ˈsəltᵊnəs\ n, archaic : SULTANA
sul·tan·ic \,səlˈtanik\ adj : of, relating to, or characteristic of a sultan ⟨~ splendor⟩
sul·ta·nin \ˈsəltənən\ n -s [Ar sulṭānīy royal, fr. sulṭān ruler, sultan] : an old Turkish gold coin in value somewhat less than a sequin
sul·tan·ism \ˈsəltᵊn,izəm\ n -s : a characteristic or practice of a sultan : DESPOTISM
sul·tan·ship \-,ship\ n : the office, rank, or dignity of a sultan
sul tasto \,sülˈtä(,)stō\ adv [It] : with the bow kept over the fingerboard so as to produce a soft thin tone — used as a direction in music for a stringed instrument
sul·tone \ˈsəl,tōn\ n -s [sul- + lactone] : any of a class of inner esters of hydroxy sulfonic acids characterized by the sulfonyl-oxy grouping $-OSO_2-$ in a ring and analogous to lactones
sul·tri·ly \ˈsəltrəlē, -əli\ adv : in a sultry manner
sul·tri·ness \-rēnəs, -rin-\ n -ES : the quality or state of being sultry
sul·try \-rē, -ri\ adj -ER/-EST [obs. E sulter to swelter (alter. of E ¹swelter) + E -y] 1 a : oppressively hot and humid : SWELTERING ⟨a ~ day⟩ ⟨~ weather⟩ ⟨~ islands⟩ b : burning hot : TORRID ⟨~ deserts⟩ ⟨a ~ sun⟩ 2 a : hot with passion or anger ⟨the meeting disperses with ~ mutterings —J.B. Boothroyd⟩ b : affected by, exciting, or capable of exciting strong sexual desire : PASSIONATE, SENSUAL, VOLUPTUOUS ⟨a ~ actress⟩ ⟨wish I could talk as low and throaty and ~ as she does —Calder Willingham⟩ ⟨the music was ~ —Thurston Scott⟩ b : LURID, SCABROUS ⟨~ language⟩ ⟨has a number of ~ comments to make about love —Douglas Watt⟩
¹**su·lu** \ˈsü(,)lü\ n, pl **sulu** or **sulus** usu cap [Malay Suluk, fr. Taw-Sug sulúg current] : TAW-SUG
²**sulu** \ˈ"\ n -s [Fijian] : a garment made similar to the lavalava and worn esp. by Fijians and other Melanesians
sulubba pl of SLUBBI
su·lung \ˈsü,lüŋ\ n -s [ME suling, fr. OE sulung, fr. sul, sulh plow, measure of land — more at SULCUS] : any of various old Kentish units of land area (as one of 120 acres) corresponding to the carucate and the hide
sul·van·ite \ˈsəlvə,nīt\ n -s [sul- + vanadium + -ite] : a mineral Cu_3VS_4 consisting of a sulfide of copper and vanadium that occurs in bronze-yellow masses (hardness 3.5, sp. gr. 4.0)
sul·ze \ˈzültsə\ n -s [G, calf's-foot jelly, brine, fr. OHG sulza brine; akin to OHG salz salt — more at SALT] : CALF'S-FOOT JELLY
¹**sum** \ˈsəm\ n -s [ME summe, somme, fr. OF, fr. L summa, fr. fem. of summus highest, topmost; akin to L super over — more at OVER] 1 a : an indefinite or specified amount of money ⟨received occasional ~s of money⟩ ⟨a ~ of fifty dollars⟩ ⟨are paid only a nominal ~ for their services —F.A.Ogg & P.O. Ray⟩ ⟨if all ~s for armaments were used to build libraries —Alfred Stefferud⟩ b archaic : a quantity of goods having a set value ⟨taxes assessed in ~s of tobacco⟩ 2 a : the whole amount : an existent total ⟨duty to maintain and preserve the ~ of human knowledge —H.J.J.Winter⟩ b : an aggregate of distinct usu. specified things : a discrete whole ⟨history is not merely a ~ of events⟩ ⟨possessed of such various talents in the arts . . . as in their ~ to approach genius —Osbert Sitwell⟩ 3 : the ultimate end : the utmost degree : HEIGHT, SUMMIT ⟨reached the ~ of human bliss⟩ ⟨saw the war . . . as the very crown and ~ of human folly —Rose Macaulay⟩ 4 a : a summary of the chief points or thoughts : EPITOME, SUMMATION ⟨the ~ of this criticism follows —C.W.Hendel⟩ b : the main or essential point : GIST ⟨the ~ of the evidence⟩ ⟨attempting to convey the ~ of the book in a short phrase or sentence —J.E.Miller⟩ 5 obs : NUMERAL; esp : INTEGER 6 a (1) : the aggregate of two or more numbers, magnitudes, quantities, or particulars : the result of performing an addition ⟨the ~ of 5 and 7 is 12⟩ (2) : the limit of the sum of the first n terms of an infinite series as n increases indefinitely b : numbers to be added : a column of figures : a problem in arithmetic — often used with do ⟨a child trying to do a difficult ~ in mental arithmetic —C.D.Lewis⟩ c **sums** pl : arithmetic esp. as a school subject ⟨singing is quite as important in education as ~s, spelling, or writing —George Sampson⟩ d : the result of logical addition or alternation
syn AMOUNT, AGGREGATE, TOTAL, WHOLE, NUMBER, QUANTITY: SUM may indicate the result of simple addition ⟨the sum of two and three⟩ and usu. applies to simple obvious putting together of things ⟨a personality is never a mere sum of traits and cannot be explained by the most complete inventory —H.J.Muller⟩ AMOUNT may be used of more accumulative or combinative processes ⟨the amount of snow that we usu. have in the northern United States —Richard Joseph⟩ ⟨a considerable amount of business experience —C.W.Mitman⟩ ⟨a considerable amount of unhappiness and poverty in his early youth —A.E. Wier⟩ AGGREGATE may stress the notion of separate distinct individuals or discrete particulars grouped together ⟨these larger aggregates, the enlarged family, ingroup, the tribe, the clan —Abram Kardiner⟩ ⟨not a logical unity, but an aggregate of notions of various origins —J.O.Evjen⟩ TOTAL suggests completeness comprehending inclusiveness and perhaps magnitude of result ⟨a large gold total, mostly through small, individual operations —Amer. Guide Series: Wash.⟩ ⟨a total of one million casualties⟩ WHOLE may refer to a unified or integrated totality ⟨society as a whole, acting through its laws, its schools, its publications —R.M.Weaver⟩ ⟨the history as a whole is deficient on the economic side —Allen Johnson⟩ NUMBER may suggest an aggregate of countable units, in contrast to AMOUNT, which is usu. used with uncountables ⟨the number of corpuscles in this amount of blood⟩ ⟨the number of accounts involved in this amount of trade⟩ QUANTITY is broadly used in reference to anything measurable but usu. applies to what is measured in bulk ⟨if pleasure be the sole good, the only possible criterion of pleasures is quantity of pleasure —Clive Bell⟩ ⟨farm country that produces wheat, corn, vegetables and fruit as well as quantities of poultry and milk —Amer. Guide Series: Md.⟩ ⟨a quantity of silvery-yellow hair —Elinor Wylie⟩ ⟨large quantities of silt —W.H.Dowdeswell⟩
— **in sum** adv [ME in summe, in somme, fr. MF en summe, en somme, fr. L in summa] : in short : BRIEFLY
²**sum** \ˈ"\ vb **summed**; **summed**; **summing**; **sums** [ME summen, sommen, fr. OF summer, sommer, fr. ML summare, fr. L summa sum] vt 1 : to ascertain the sum of : count or calculate the number, amount, or total of : add together : cast up ⟨~ a column of figures⟩ ⟨the costs . . . can rarely be set down in a neat row and summed —Harold Koontz & Cyril O'Donnell⟩ ⟨this term is obtained by summing the numbers in the bottom left-hand corners of the boxes —Lester Guest⟩ ⟨~ the cards on the tabulator —F.J.Gruenberger⟩ 2 : to sum up ⟨the body of thought brought to America by the immigrant Puritans . . . may be summed in a phrase as Carolinian liberalism —V.L. Parrington⟩ 3 obs : to bring to consummation or perfection : make complete : reach the goal or full development of ⟨there was the venture summed and satisfied —Christopher Marlowe⟩ ~ vi 1 : to reach a sum : AMOUNT — used with to or into ⟨benefactions that ~ into the thousands⟩ 2 : to do sums in arithmetic
sum abbr 1 [L sumat] let him take 2 [L sume, sumendus] take; to be taken 3 [L sumendum] must be taken
su·ma \ˈsümə\ n, pl **suma** or **sumas** usu cap [Sp, of AmerInd origin] 1 : a people or group of peoples of the state of Chihuahua, Mexico 2 : a member of the Suma people or peoples
su·mac or **su·mach** also **shu·mac** \ˈs(h)ü,mak sometimes -,mäk or -,mäk or ˈshü,mäk\ n -s [ME sumac, fr. MF, fr. Ar summāq] 1 a : a shrub or tree of the genus Rhus — often restricted to the innocuous members of the genus; see LAUREL SUMAC, POISON SUMAC, SQUAWBUSH, STAGHORN SUMAC; compare POISON IVY, POISON OAK b (1) : the wood of a sumac (2) : a material used in tanning and dyeing consisting of the dried and powdered leaves and panicles of various sumacs 2 : any of several shrubs and trees (as of the genera Ailanthus and Myrica) in some respect resembling though not closely related to members of the genus Rhus 3 : BUCKTHORN BROWN
sumac family n : ANACARDIACEAE
sumac wax n : JAPAN WAX
su·man \ˈsümən\ adj, usu cap [Sumo + -an] 1 : of, relating to, or characteristic of the Sumo people 2 : of, relating to, or characteristic of the Sumo language
sum and substance n : GIST ⟨the sum and substance of an argument⟩
¹**su·ma·tra** \səˈmä·trə\ adj, usu cap [fr. Sumatra, island in Indonesia] : of or from the island of Sumatra : of the kind or style prevailing in Sumatra : SUMATRAN
²**sumatra** \ˈ"\ n 1 s often cap : a violent squall common in the strait between Sumatra and the Malay peninsula 2 also **sumatra game** a usu cap S&G : an Oriental breed of long-tailed greenish black game fowls b -s usu cap S & sometimes cap G : a bird of the Sumatra breed — compare CUBALAYA
sumatra camphor n, usu cap S : BORNEO CAMPHOR
sumatra leaf n, usu cap S : a thin elastic uniformly light-colored leaf tobacco raised in Sumatra and extensively used for cigar wrappers
¹**su·ma·tran** \-trən\ adj, usu cap [Sumatra, island in Indonesia + E -an] 1 : of, relating to, or characteristic of the island of Sumatra 2 : of, relating to, or characteristic of the people of Sumatra
²**sumatran** \ˈ"\ n -s cap : a native or inhabitant of Sumatra
sumatra seed n, usu cap 1st S : Sumatra leaf tobacco grown in the U.S.
sumatra wax n, usu cap S : GONDANG WAX
sum·ba·wa·nese \süm,bäwəˈnēz, -ēs\ n, pl **sumbawanese** cap [Sumbawa Island, Indonesia + E -nese (as in Chinese)] 1 : a native or inhabitant of Sumbawa Island 2 a : an Indonesian people on Sumbawa Island b : a member of such people
sum·bul or **sam·bul** \səmˈbül\ also **sum·bal** \-ˈbäl\ n -s [Ar sunbul] 1 : the root of a muskroot (Ferula sumbul) formerly used as a tonic and antispasmodic 2 : GARDEN HELIOTROPE 1 3 : SPIKENARD 1a
sum·dum \,səmˈdəm\ n, pl **sumdum** or **sumdums** usu cap [Tlingit s'aódān] 1 : a Tlingit people at Port Houghton, Alaska 2 : a member of the Sumdum people
su·men \ˈsümən\ n -s [L, fr. sugere to suck — more at SUCK] 1 archaic : a sow's udder esp. regarded as a delicacy 2 obs : the fat of something : RICHNESS
¹**su·meri·an** \süˈmerēən, -ˈmir-\ adj, usu cap [F sumérien, fr. Sumer, ancient region of lower Babylonia + F -ien -ian] 1 : of, relating to, or characteristic of Sumer 2 : of, relating to, or characteristic of the people of Sumer
²**sumerian** \ˈ"\ n -s cap 1 : a native of Sumer 2 : the language of the Sumerian people surviving as a literary language after the rise of Akkadian ⟨Sumerian is very well known today, though archaic . . . texts still offer much difficulty to the interpreter —W.F.Albright⟩
su·mer·ic \-ˈmerik\ adj, usu cap [Sumer, ancient region of lower Babylon + E -ic] : SUMERIAN
sumero- comb form, usu cap [¹Sumerian] 1 : Sumerian ⟨Sumerology⟩ 2 : Sumerian and ⟨Sumero-Assyrian⟩
su·mero-akkadian \süˈme(,)rō, -ˈmi(,)rō+\ adj, usu cap S&A : of, relating to, or constituting the Sumerian and Akkadian languages, cultures, or peoples
su·mero-babylonian \ˈ"+\ adj, usu cap S&B : SUMERO-AKKADIAN
su·me·rol·o·gist \,süməˈräləjəst\ n -s usu cap : a specialist in Sumerology
su·me·rol·o·gy \-jē\ n -ES usu cap [Sumero- + -logy] : the study of the history, language, and archaeology of the Sumerians
su·mi \ˈsümē\ n -s [Jap] : soot of burned plants and glue made into solid cakes and used esp. by Chinese and Japanese artists for black-and-white paintings
sum·less \ˈsəmləs\ adj : UNCOUNTABLE, INCALCULABLE, INESTIMABLE ⟨the ~ tale of sorrow —A.E.Housman⟩ — **sum·less·ness** n -ES
sum·ma \ˈsümə, ˈsümə; ˈsəmə\ n, pl **sum·mae** see sense 1 \-,mī; -,mē\ [ME, fr. L — more at SUM] 1 pl also **summas** obs : SUM, SUM TOTAL 2 [ML, fr. L] a : a treatise or series of treatises covering a whole field or department of learning; esp : one of the comprehensive scholastic works (as the Summa Theologica of St. Thomas Aquinas) b : a work or series of works that is a synthesis of human knowledge c : a synthesis or summary of any subject ⟨a ~ of the principal dogmas of the Church —America⟩ ⟨a ~ of a writer's work⟩
sum·ma·bil·i·ty \,səməˈbilədē\ n : capability of being summed
sum·ma·ble \ˈsəməbəl\ adj [²sum + -able] : capable of being summed
sum·ma cum lau·de \,sùmə,kùmˈlaùdə, ,sümə,küm-, -dē, -dā; ,səmə,kəmˈlòdē\ adv (or adj) [L, with highest praise] : with highest distinction — used as a mark of meritorious achievement in the academic requirements for graduation from school or college; compare CUM LAUDE, MAGNA CUM LAUDE
summa genera pl of SUMMUM GENUS
sum·mand \ˈsə,mand, ≈ˈ≈\ n -s [ML summandus, gerundive of summare to sum — more at SUM] : a term in a summation : ADDEND
sum·mar \ˈsəmər\ adj [MF sommaire, fr. ML summarius] Scot law : SUMMARY
sum·mar·i·ly \(,)səˈmerəlē, -li also ˈsəmərəl-\ adv : in a summary manner or form ⟨was ~ relieved of his command⟩ ⟨the case was tried ~ without a jury —O.W.Holmes †1935⟩ ⟨not a theory to be dismissed ~ with raised eyebrow and shrugged shoulder —Eric Partridge⟩
sum·mar·i·ness \-rēnəs\ n -ES : the quality or state of being summary
sum·ma·rist \ˈsəmərəst\ n -s [²summary + -ist] SUMMARIZER, SUMMIST 1
sum·ma·riz·able \ˈsəmə,rīzəbəl, ≈ˈ≈≈≈\ adj : capable of being summarized ⟨a ~ story⟩
sum·ma·ri·za·tion \,səmərəˈzāshən, -mə,rīˈ-\ n -s 1 : the act of summarizing 2 : SUMMARY
sum·ma·rize \ˈsəmə,rīz\ vb -ED/-ING/-S [²summary + -ize] vt : to tell in or reduce to a summary : present briefly : sum up : RECAPITULATE ~ vi : to make or be able to make a summary
¹**sum·ma·ry** \ˈsəmərē, -ri sometimes -mr-\ adj [ME, fr. ML summarius, fr. L summa sum, whole + -arius -ary (adj. suffix) — more at SUM] 1 a : constituting or containing a summing up of points : covering the main points concisely : summarizing very briefly ⟨a ~ formulation of an enormously large situation —A.L.Kroeber⟩ ⟨check the opening and ~ sentences —S.C. Brownstein & Mitchel Weiner⟩ ⟨a ~ chapter⟩ b : lacking detailed explanation : BRIEF, TERSE ⟨a history of the Philosophic Neurosis, although that's a too ~ name —Irwin Edman⟩ 2 obs : lacking specific detail : GENERAL 3 obs : SUPREME, MAXIMUM 4 a : done or occurring without delay or formality : quickly executed ⟨violent outbursts of wrath and ~ chastisements —Margaret Mead⟩ ⟨the ~ briskness of the drawing —R.M.Coates⟩ ⟨no resentment at the ~ way in which he has been treated —R.F.Kilvert⟩ b : of, relating to, or using a summary proceeding or procedure : used in or done by summary proceeding ⟨a ~ order⟩ ⟨special ~ courts⟩ — opposed to plenary c : accomplished or performed too quickly with inadequate consideration, preparation, or space allotted ⟨the letters to him reproduced here, ~ and unimportant as many of them are —Times Lit. Supp.⟩ **syn** see CONCISE
²**summary** \ˈ"\ n -ES [L summarium, fr. summa + -arium -ary (n. suffix)] : a short restatement of the main points (as of an argument) for easier remembering, for better understanding, or for showing the relation of the points : RECAPITULATION, RÉSUMÉ, SUMMATION ⟨proceeded to give a brief ~ of the points he had covered⟩
summary court-martial n : a court-martial consisting of one commissioned officer and having authority to impose no sentence in excess of one month's confinement or forfeiture of two-thirds of one month's pay — compare GENERAL COURT-MARTIAL, SPECIAL COURT-MARTIAL
summary judgment n : a judgment granted without a formal trial when it appears on the pleadings and other showing to the court that there is no genuine issue of fact and that the moving party is entitled to judgment as a matter of law
summary jurisdiction n : the authority or power of a court to use a summary procedure
summary procedure n : the procedure followed in a summary proceeding
summary proceeding n : a civil or criminal proceeding in the nature of a trial conducted without the formalities (as indictment, pleadings, and a jury) required by the common law, authorized by statute, and used for the speedy and peremptory disposition of some minor matter
sum·mat \ˈsəmət\ dial var of SOMEWHAT
sum·mate \ˈsə,māt\ vb -ED/-ING/-S [back-formation fr. summation] : to add together : sum up
sum·ma·tion \(,)səˈmāshən\ n -s [ML summation-, summatio, fr. summatus (past part. of summare to sum) + L -ion-, -io -ion — more at SUM] 1 : the act or process of finding or forming a sum or total amount : ADDITION — symbol Σ 2 : an aggregate formed esp. by accumulation or accretion : SUM TOTAL, RESULTANT 3 : cumulative action or effect; specif : the process by which a sequence of stimuli that are individually inadequate to produce a response are cumulatively able to induce a nerve impulse 4 : SUMMING-UP ⟨writes with shiny images, spare but eloquent ~s of scenes and people —E.A. Davidson⟩; specif : a speech in court summing up the arguments in a case
sum·ma·tion·al \-shənᵊl\ adj : of or relating to a summation : produced by summation
summation tone n : a combination tone whose frequency is equal to the sum of the frequencies of the two tones generating it
sum·ma·tive \ˈsəmədiv\ adj [summation + -ive] : ADDITIVE, CUMULATIVE
sum·ma·tor \ˈsə,mād·ə(r)\ n -s : one that summates
sum·ma·to·ry \ˈsəmə,tōrē\ adj [ML summatus (past part. of summare to sum) + E -ory — more at SUM] : of, relating to, or serving as a summation ⟨his endings have that glowing ~ quality —Clifton Fadiman⟩
summed adj [ME sommed, fr. past part. of summen, sommen to sum; trans. of MF sommé — more at SUM] obs : fully developed or equipped : COMPLETED, PERFECTED, FULL-FLEDGED — used esp. of antlers or plumage
¹**sum·mer** \ˈsəm(ə)r\ n -s often attrib [ME sumer, somer, fr. OE sumor; akin to OS, OHG, & ON sumar summer, OIr sam, W haf, Av ham- summer, Skt samā year, half year, season] 1 a : the season between spring and autumn reckoned astronomically as extending from the June solstice to the September equinox b : the season comprising the months of June, July, and August c Brit : the season comprising the part of the year extending from mid-May to mid-August d : a period of warm weather or sunshine ⟨regions of everlasting ~⟩ ⟨we have had no ~ yet⟩ e : the warmer half of the year — contrasted with winter f : the dry season in the tropics g : the season reckoned astronomically in the southern hemisphere as extending from the December solstice to the March equinox 2 a : one of the years of one's life esp. when young or vigorous ⟨a girl of seventeen ~s⟩ b : early middle age : the period of maturing powers ⟨still in the ~ of one's life⟩ 3 : a character or condition suggestive of summer (as in warmth, brightness, or lushness)

2summer \"\ *vb* **summered; summered; summering** \-m(ə)riŋ\ **summers** [ME *someren,* fr. *sumer, somer,* n.] *vi* **:** to pass the summer ⟨~*ing* or wintering at vacation resorts —Graenum Berger⟩ ~ *vt* **1 :** to keep or carry through the summer **:** provide with pasture during the summer ⟨sheep and cattle are ~*ed* on the surrounding ranges in the mountains —*Amer. Guide Series: Oregon*⟩ **2 :** to infuse with summer heat or brightness **:** make summery — **summer and winter 1 :** to spend the whole year **2 :** to harbor, protect, cherish, or be loyal to always or unceasingly **3** *Scot* **:** to talk endlessly

3summer \"\ *n* -s [ME *somer, summer* packhorse, beam, fr. MF *somier,* fr. (assumed) VL *sagmarius,* fr. LL *sagma* packsaddle + L *-arius* -ary — more at SUMPTER] **:** a large horizontal beam or stone variously supported and used esp. in architecture and building: as **a :** the lintel of a door or window **:** BREASTSUMMER **b :** a stone forming the cap of a pier (as to support a lintel or arch) **c :** a principal floor timber (as a girder or lintel supporting other members) — called also *summertree* **d :** a horizontal longitudinal timber in a framing

4summer \"\ *n* -s [*2sum* + *-er*] **:** one that sums

summer beam *n* [*3summer*] **:** 3SUMMER a, c, d

summer cohosh *n* **:** a bugbane (*Cimicifuga americana*) of eastern No. American woodlands with chaffy-coated seeds

summer cress *n* **:** WATERCRESS 1

summer crookneck *n* **:** any of several crooknecks that are summer squashes and in the original and many surviving forms have typical crookneck form and bright to deep yellow warty rinds but in many improved forms have a straight neck and pale yellow smooth skins — compare WINTER CROOKNECK

summer cypress *n* **:** a densely branched Eurasian herb (*Kochia scoparia*) cultivated for its foliage which turns red in autumn

summer diarrhea *or* **summer complaint** *n* **:** diarrhea prevalent in hot weather and usu. caused by ingestion of food contaminated by various microorganisms responsible for gastrointestinal infections

summer disease *n* **:** BLUE COMB

summer duck *n* **1** *dial Eng* **:** GARGANEY **2** *dial* **:** WOOD DUCK 1

summer dwarf *n* **:** a dwarfing disease of strawberries caused by an eelworm (*Aphelenchoides besseyi*) and differing from spring dwarf esp. in occurring later in the growing season

summer egg *n* **:** a thinshelled often parthenogenetic egg that is ready for immediate development when deposited — compare WINTER EGG

summer ermine *n* **:** the tawny brown summer fur of the ermine

summer fallow *n* **1 :** land plowed and frequently tilled during the summer in preparation for a crop the next year **2 :** the practice of summer-fallowing

summer-fallow \ˈ==,==\ *vt* **:** to plow and work (land) in summer in order to prepare for sowing in the fall or the following spring **:** plow and let lie fallow

summer finch *n* **:** an American sparrow of the genus *Aimophila*; *esp* **:** a finch (*A. aestivalis*) of the southeastern U. S.

summer flounder *n* **:** a mottled greenish brown white-spotted flounder (*Paralichthys dentatus*) of the coast of the U. S. from Cape Cod to the Carolinas having the eyes and color on the left side of the body

summer forest *or* **summergreen forest** *n* **:** a deciduous forest in temperate regions as contrasted with a tropical rain forest or with northern coniferous forests

summer forget-me-not *n* **:** ANCHUSA 2

summer grape *n* **:** a wild grape (*Vitis aestivalis*) native to eastern No. America but widely cultivated in Europe that bears rather small pleasantly flavored berries and has superior powers of resisting the attacks of the phylloxera

summer grass *n* **:** any of several grasses; *esp* **:** CRABGRASS

summer hail *n* **:** hail formed by the freezing of raindrops from cumulonimbus clouds and their alternate catch of rain and snow through their oscillations in height — compare WINTER HAIL

summer haw *n* **:** MAYHAW

summer heat *n* **:** a temperature (as of 76° F) indicated on some thermometers as the approximate average temperature of summer in the temperate zone

summer heliotrope *n* **:** GARDEN HELIOTROPE 1

summer herring *n* **:** GLUT HERRING

summer house *n* [ME *somer hous*] **1 :** a country house for residence in summer **2** *usu* **summerhouse** \ˈ==,=\ **:** a rustic covered structure in a garden or park to provide a cool shady retreat in summer

summer hyacinth *n* **:** a southern African herb (*Galtonia candicans* syn. *Hyacinthus candicans*) cultivated for its spicate white bell-shaped flowers — called also *Cape hyacinth*

summerier *comparative of* SUMMERY

summeriest *superlative of* SUMMERY

sum·mer·i·ness \ˈsəmərēnəs\ *n* -ES **:** the quality or state of being summery

1summering *n* -s [ME, fr. gerund of *someren* to summer — more at SUMMER] **1 a :** the provision of pasture for livestock during the summer **b :** the pasture provided for the summering of livestock **c :** the summer regimen of livestock (as horses) **2 a :** a spending of the summer (as at a resort) **b** *archaic* **:** a summer pleasure (as an excursion)

2sum·mer·ing \ˈsəməriŋ\ *n* -s [*3summer* + *-ing*] **:** the first mass of masonry laid (as on a pier or column) esp. when it begins an arched construction

sum·mer·ish \ˈsəmərish\ *adj* **:** suggestive of or resembling summer **:** rather summerlike **:** SUMMERY ⟨~ weather⟩

sum·mer·ite \-mə,rīt\ *n* -s **:** one who summers in a place

summer kitchen *n* **:** a small building adjacent to a house and used as a kitchen in warm weather

sum·mer·less \ˈsəmə(r)ləs\ *adj* **:** having no summer

summer lightning *n* **:** HEAT LIGHTNING

summerlike \ˈ==,=\ *adj* **:** characteristic of or resembling summer ⟨~ weather⟩

summer lilac *n* **1 :** DAME'S VIOLET **2 :** BUTTERFLY BUSH **3 :** any of several California shrubs of the genus *Ceanothus*

sum·mer·li·ness \ˈsəmə(r)lēnəs\ *n* -ES **:** the quality or state of being summerly

1sum·mer·ly \-lē\ *adj* [*1summer* + *-ly*] **:** belonging to or typical of summer **:** SUMMERY ⟨~ solar radiation —*Jour. of Geol.*⟩

2summerly \"\ *adv* **:** in a summerly manner

summer mastitis *n* **:** bovine mastitis that occurs sporadically esp. in cattle on summer pasture, is caused by a pus-forming bacterium (*Corynebacterium pyogenes*), and may take an acute fatal course or one which is progressive and chronic

summer mustard *n* **:** CHARLOCK

summer oil *n* **1 :** an oil that solidifies partly or wholly in cold weather: as **a :** cottonseed oil from which the stearin has not been removed **b :** a heavy mineral lubricating oil **2 :** any of several highly refined oils used as foliage sprays to control insects (as the codling moth)

summer pumpkin *n, chiefly Brit* **:** SUMMER SQUASH

summer rape *n* **:** a rough-leaved annual rape (*Brassica napus annua*) widely grown in Europe for its seeds that are used for bird food

summer rash *n* **1 :** PRICKLY HEAT **2 :** an inflammation of the sebaceous glands and hair follicles of the skin of horses in areas rubbed by harness

summerroom \ˈ==,=\ *n, archaic* **:** SUMMERHOUSE

1summers *pl of* SUMMER, *pres 3d sing of* SUMMER

2sum·mers \ˈsəmə(r)z\ *adv* **:** during the summers ⟨has worked ~ as a news reporter —*Atlantic*⟩

summersault *var of* SOMERSAULT

summer sausage *n* **:** a sausage that has been dry-cured, smoked, and hardened and that keeps well without refrigeration ⟨cervelat is a *summer sausage*⟩ — called also *dry sausage*

summer savory *n* **:** an erect annual savory (*Satureia hortensis*) with oval leaves and pink flowers that is used for the flavoring of meats, soups, salads, or other dishes — compare WINTER SAVORY

summer school *n* **:** a school or school session conducted in summer esp. during July and August: **a :** a program of instruction offered during the summer by a school, college, or university enabling students to accelerate their progress toward a degree or make up credits lost through absence or failure **b :** a summer program offered by a college or university for professional workers (as teachers) wishing to round out their professional or general education

summer's darling *n* **:** FAREWELL-TO-SPRING

summerset *var of* SOMERSET

summer sheldrake *n* **:** HOODED MERGANSER

summer snipe *n* **:** the common European sandpiper (*Actitis hypoleucos*)

summer snowflake *n* **:** a plant (*Leucojum aestivum*) with clusters of pure white flowers borne in late spring and early summer — compare SPRING SNOWFLAKE

summer solstice *n* **1 :** the point in the sky occupied by the sun on or about June 22d when summer begins in the northern hemisphere **:** the June solstice **2 :** the time at which the sun reaches the June solstice for dwellers in the northern hemisphere or the December solstice for those in the southern hemisphere

summer sores *n pl but sing or pl in constr* **:** a skin disease of the horse caused by larval roundworms (genus *Habronema*) deposited by flies in skin wounds or abrasions where they cause intense inflammation with exudate and local necrosis followed by destruction of the parasites and gradual healing by granulation of the lesions

summer spore *n* **:** a spore (as the urediospores of the rusts) of brief vitality that germinates without resting and serves to propagate the plant during the summer — compare WINTER SPORE

summer squash *n* **:** any of various fruits of plants that are derived from a variety (*Cucurbita pepo melopepo*) and are used as a vegetable while immature and before hardening of the seeds and rind — see CYMLING, SUMMER CROOKNECK, VEGETABLE MARROW; compare PUMPKIN, SQUASH, WINTER SQUASH, ZUCCHINI

summer stock *n* **:** theatrical productions of repertory companies organized for the summer season and presented esp. in playhouses at summer resorts

summer stone *n* **:** 3SUMMER a,b

summer sweet *n* **:** a sweet pepper bush (*Clethra alnifolia*)

summer tanager *or* **summer redbird** *n* **:** a tanager (*Piranga rubra*) of the middle and southern U.S. the male of which is deep red and the female yellowish olive above and yellow beneath

summer teal *n* **1 :** BLUE-WINGED TEAL **2** *dial Eng* **:** GARGANEY

summertide \ˈ==,=\ *n* [ME *sumertid, somertid,* fr. *sumer, somer* summer + *tid* time — more at SUMMER, TIDE] **:** SUMMERTIME

summertime \ˈ==,=\ *n* [ME *somertime,* fr. *somer* summer + *time*] **:** the summer season **:** a summerlike period

summer time *n, chiefly Brit* **:** DAYLIGHT SAVING TIME

summertree \ˈ==,=\ *n* [ME *somere tree,* fr. *somer, somere* summer (beam) + *tree* — more at SUMMER, TREE] **:** 3SUMMER c

summer trout *n* **:** WEAKFISH; *esp* **:** a common weakfish (*Cynoscion regalis*)

summer truffle *n* **:** a truffle (*Tuber aestivum*)

sum·mer-up \ˈsəməˈrəp\ *n, pl* **summers-up** [*sum up* + *-er*] **:** one who sums up ⟨the *summer-up* of a literary period⟩

summer warbler *or* **summer yellowbird** *n* **:** YELLOW WARBLER 1a

summer-weight \ˈ==ˈ=\ *adj* **:** adapted in weight or texture to summer wear ⟨*summer-weight* clothes⟩ ⟨*summer-weight* shoes⟩

summerwood \ˈ==,=\ *n* **:** the portion of each annual ring of a woody plant that develops largely during the latter part of the growing season but not necessarily in the summer and that compared with the springwood is less porous, is usu. harder and heavier, consists largely of smaller and thicker-walled cells, and in softwoods is often darker — called also *latewood*

sum·mery \ˈsəmərē, -ri\ *adj, often* -ER/-EST **1 :** of, relating to, or like summer ⟨create an atmosphere of ~ somnolence and repose —R.M.Coates⟩ ⟨the fragrant ~ hay —J.H.Wheelwright⟩ **:** suggestive of summer ⟨a ~ laugh⟩ ⟨six thin, ~ girls —Truman Capote⟩ **2 :** suitable for summer **:** SUMMER-WEIGHT

summer yellowlegs *n pl but sing or pl in constr* **:** LESSER YELLOWLEGS

summing *pres part of* SUM

summing-up \ˈ==ˈ=\ *n, pl* **summings-up** [fr. gerund of *sum up*] **:** the act or statement of one who sums up **:** a conclusion in which the points made are reviewed and the conclusions set forth; *specif* **:** a lawyer's summation to a jury

sum·mist \ˈsəməst\ *n* -s [ML *summista,* fr. *summa* + L *-ista* -ist — more at SUMMA] **1 :** a writer of a summa; *specif* **:** one of the medieval philosophers who wrote a philosophical or theological summa **2** *archaic* **:** one who abridges or epitomizes

sum·mit \ˈsəmət, *usu* -əd·+V\ *n* -s *often attrib* [ME *somette,* fr. MF *somete, sommete,* fr. OF, dim. of *sum, som* top, summit, fr. L *summum,* fr. neut. of *summus* highest, topmost — more at SUM] **1 :** TOP, CREST, APEX, VERTEX ⟨the ~ of a wave⟩ ⟨the ~ of a column⟩ ⟨the ~ of a pole⟩: as **a :** the highest point, ridge, or level of a mountain or other feature **:** PEAK ⟨climb to the ~ of the mountain⟩ ⟨a range with ~s over 10,000 feet high⟩ ⟨the ~ of a plateau⟩ **b :** the point of highest elevation reached (as by a road or canal) ⟨stopped at the ~ to see the view⟩ **c :** the apex of a pyramid ⟨an octahedron with tetrahedral ~s⟩ **d** (1) **:** the highest level of officials; *esp* **:** the diplomatic level of chiefs of state or heads of government ⟨a meeting at the ~⟩ ⟨~ conference⟩ ⟨~ parley⟩ (2) **:** a conference of highest-level officials (as chiefs of state or heads of government) **2 :** the utmost height **:** the highest degree **:** PINNACLE ⟨the ~ of human fame⟩ ⟨confronting him at the ~ of his wrath —Anthony Quinton⟩

sum·mit·less \-tləs\ *adj* **:** lacking a summit

sum·mit·ry \-trē\ *n* -ES **:** the use of a summit conference for international negotiation

summity *n* -ES [ME *summite,* fr. MF *summité, sommité,* fr. LL *summitat-, summitas,* fr. L *summus* + *-itat-, -itas* -ity] **1** *obs* **:** SUMMIT **2** *obs* **:** one at the summit

summit yard *n* **:** HUMP YARD

sum·mon \ˈsəmən\ *vb* -ED/-ING/-S [ME *sumnen, somenen, somonen, somounen,* fr. OF *somondre, semondre,* fr. (assumed) VL *summonēre,* alter. of L *summonēre* to remind secretly, give a hint to, fr. *sub-* + *monēre* to remind, warn — more at MIND] *vt* **1 :** to issue a call to convene **:** CONVOKE ⟨~ a council of state⟩ ⟨~ a lodge meeting⟩ **2 :** to command by service of a summons or other statutory notice to appear in court **:** CITE ⟨~ a jury⟩ ⟨~ witnesses⟩ ⟨the same defendants were ~*ed* to court again —*Current Biog.*⟩ **3 :** to call upon for specified action ⟨~ one to be in readiness⟩ **4 :** to bid to come or go **:** command or request the presence or service of **:** send for **:** CALL ⟨~ a physician⟩ ⟨bell still ~s the parishioners to worship —*Amer. Guide Series: N.H.*⟩ **5 :** to evoke esp. by an act of the will **:** stir or bring to activity **:** call forth **:** call up **:** bring together **:** CONJURE, AROUSE ⟨~*ing* all his strength he arose to speak —S.E.Morison⟩ ⟨each conflict ~*ed* heroic effort from the nation —Dixon Wecter⟩ ⟨when tunes could not be ~*ed* by turning a knob —Nancy Mitford⟩ ⟨poetry of such pure quality cannot be ~*ed* at will —C.D.Lewis⟩ — often used with *up* ⟨endure hardship and ~ up energy for a struggle —John Dewey⟩ ⟨can ~ up arguments from businessmen themselves —H.T.Simmons⟩ ~ *vi* **:** to issue a summons

sum·mon·er \-nə(r)\ *n* -s [ME *somonour,* fr. MF *somoneur, semoneur,* fr. *somon-, semon-* (stem of *somondre, semondre* to summon) + *-eur* -or] **:** one that summons; *specif* **:** one that serves a summons or delegates another to do so

1sum·mons \ˈsəmənz\ *n, pl* **summonses** *also* **summons** [ME *somouns,* fr. OF *somonse, semonse,* fr. fem. of *somons, semons,* past part. of *somondre, semondre* to summon] **1 :** the act of summoning; *esp* **:** a call by authority or by the command of a superior to appear at a place named or to attend to some duty **2 :** a warning or citation to appear in court **:** a notice of the beginning of a particular proceeding in court and of the action to be taken therein: as **a :** the original writ by which an action was begun in old common-law practice **b :** a written notification signed by the proper officer to be served on a person warning him to appear in court at a day specified to answer to the plaintiff upon pain of judgment against the defendant for default in so doing **c :** a subpoena to appear as a witness **d :** an order to appear to answer a criminal charge usu. for a minor offense where arrest of the defendant is not regarded as appropriate or necessary **e** *Scots law* **:** a writ in the king's name to cite a defendant to appear and answer **3 :** an imperative call or a calling (as to arms or to death) **:** something (as a signal or knock) that summons ⟨were interrupted at that point by a ~ for tea —Maurice Cranston⟩

2summons \"\ *vt* -ED/-ING/-ES **:** SUMMON; *esp* **:** to take out a summons against

summons case *n, Eng law* **:** a case in which the offense is a minor one for which a police officer may without arrest notify a person to appear in court at a fixed time and place

sum·mum bo·num \ˌsüməmˈbōnəm, ˌsüməm-; ˌsəməm-\ *n* [L] **:** the supreme or highest good usu. in which all other goods are included or from which they are derived

summum ge·nus \-ˈgānəs; -ˈjēnəs\ *n, pl* **sum·ma gen·era** \ˌsüməˈgenərə, ˌsüm-; ˌsəməˈjenərə\ [NL] **:** a genus that can undergo logical division **:** a genus that cannot be classed as a species — compare TREE OF PORPHYRY

summum jus \-ˈyüs, -ˈyüs; -ˈjəs, -ˈjüs\ *n* [L, highest law] **:** strict legal right **:** exact law **:** STRICTUM JUS — distinguished from *equity*

sum·mut \ˈsəmət\ *dial var of* SOMEWHAT

sum·ner \ˈsəmnə(r)\ *archaic var of* SUMMONER

sum·ner line \ˈsəmnə(r)-\ *n, usu cap S* [after Thomas H. *Sumner,* 19th cent. Am. sea captain] **:** a line of position determined by Sumner's method

sumner's method *n, usu cap S* [after T. H. *Sumner*] **:** a method of determining one's position on the earth in which two approximate latitudes or longitudes are assumed (as from the dead reckoning), the corresponding longitudes or latitudes are calculated from an observation of a heavenly body with the point of observation being somewhere in the line joining the points so determined, and a similar line is determined from another heavenly body or from a later observation of the same body with the intersection of the two lines fixing the point of observation

1su·mo \ˈsü(,)mō\ *also* **su·mu** \-mü\ *n, pl* **sumo** *or* **sumos** *usu cap* [Sp *zuma, zumo, zumu,* of AmerInd origin] **1 a :** a people of Nicaragua **b :** a member of such people **2 :** a language of the Sumo people

2su·mo \ˈsü(,)mō\ *n* -s [Jap *sumō*] **:** a Japanese form of wrestling in which a contestant loses the match if he is forced out of the ring or if any part of his body except his feet touches the ground

1sump \ˈsəmp\ *n* -s [ME *sompe,* fr. MD *somp* morass, pool — more at SWAMP] **1** *chiefly dial* **a :** SWAMP, MORASS ⟨~s of bottomless mud, bordered by patches of coarse swamp grass and standing puddles —H.L.Davis⟩ **b :** a pool or puddle esp. of dirty water **c :** DIRT, MUD **2 :** a round clay-lined pit of stone used in metallurgy for collecting fused metal **3 :** a pit, depression, reservoir, or tank serving as a drain or a receptacle for liquids to be salvaged or further disposed of: as **a :** CESSPOOL **b :** an open drain for carrying off dripping liquids (as in factories) **c :** a depression made in a water channel to facilitate the emptying of the channel **d** *also* **sump pit :** a pit at the lowest point in a circulating or drainage system (as the oil-circulating system of an internal-combustion engine) **e** *chiefly Brit* **:** OIL PAN **4** *Brit* **:** CRANKCASE **5** [G *sumpf,* lit., marsh, fr. MHG — more at SWAMP] **a :** the portion of a mine shaft which extends below the working levels and into which the water drains **b :** an excavation smaller than and ahead of the regular work in driving a mine tunnel or sinking a mine shaft **c :** SUMPING CUT **6** *or* **sump drain :** a device by means of which deep body cavities (as the pelvis) are drained of accumulated fluids by suction

2sump \"\ *vb* -ED/-ING/-S *vt* **:** to make a sump in; *specif* **:** to depress (the bottom of a channel) ~ *vi* **:** to dig or form a sump; *specif* **:** to make a sumping cut

sump·er \-pə(r)\ *n* -s **:** one that sumps; *specif* **:** a worker who oils and greases coal-cutting machines and positions the cutter for the undercutting of the coal face

sump fuse *n* **:** a fuse used in blasting under water

sumph \ˈsəmf, ˈsümf\ *n* -s [origin unknown] *Scot & dial Eng* **:** a stupid or sulky person

sumping cut *n* **:** the preliminary undercut in a face of coal made by a continuous cutter

sumping shot *also* **sump shot** *n* **:** a shot or blast for making a sump or deepening a mine shaft

sum·pit \ˈsəmpət\ *or* **sum·pi·tan** \-pə,tan\ *n* -s [Malay, fr. *sumpit* act of shooting with a blowgun] **:** a Malaysian blowgun

sump·man \ˈsəmpmən\ *n, pl* **sumpmen :** SUMPER: **a :** a pitman's helper **b :** a worker who assists a shaft-sinking crew by putting supporting timbers in place

sump pump *n* **:** a pump to remove accumulations of water or other liquid from a sump pit

sump·si·mus \ˈsəmpsəməs\ *n* -ES [L, we have taken — more at MUMPSIMUS] **:** a strictly correct expression or usage substituted for an old popular error — compare MUMPSIMUS

sump·ter \ˈsəm(p)tə(r)\ *n* -s [ME, fr. MF *sommatier, sommetier,* fr. (assumed) VL *sagmatarius,* fr. LL *sagmat-, sagma* packsaddle (fr. Gk, covering, packsaddle) + L *-arius* -ary; prob. akin to Gk *sattein* to fill, stuff, load] **1 :** PACK, SADDLEBAG **2 :** a pack animal **:** BEAST OF BURDEN

sump·tion \ˈsəm(p)chən\ *n* -s [ME *sumpcion,* fr. ML *sumption-, sumpsio,* alter. of L *sumption-, sumptio* action of taking, fr. *sumptus* (past part. of *sumere* to take) + *-ion-, -io* -ion — more at ASSUME] **1 :** ASSUMPTION 7 **2 :** MAJOR PREMISE

sump·tu·ary \ˈsəm(p)chə,werē, -ri\ *adj* [L *sumptuarius,* fr. *sumptus* expense, cost (fr. *sumptus,* past part. of *sumere* to take, spend) + *-arius* -ary] **1 :** relating to or regulating expenditure esp. on clothes and food **:** controlling extravagance ⟨~ reforms⟩ ⟨~ edicts⟩ **2 :** of or relating to sumptuary laws

sumptuary law *n* **1 :** a law common in the 13th to 15th centuries to prevent extravagance in private life by limiting expenditure for clothing, food, and furniture **2 :** a law designed to regulate habits primarily on moral or religious grounds but regarded as justified under the police power of the state

sump·tu·os·i·ty \ˌsəm(p)chəˈwäsəd·ē\ *n* -ES [MF or LL; MF *sumptuosité,* fr. LL *sumptuositat-, sumptuositas,* fr. L *sumptuosus* + *-itat-, -itas* -ity] **:** expensive magnificence or elegance **:** lavish display **:** LUXURIOUSNESS ⟨most children like ~ —Sylvia T. Warner⟩

sump·tu·ous \ˈsəm(p)chəwəs, -)chəs, -)sh-\ *adj* [MF *sumptueux,* fr. L *sumptuosus,* fr. *sumptus* expense, cost + *-osus* -ous] **1 a :** involving large outlay or expense **:** COSTLY, LAVISH ⟨the ~ dinner given by a railroad king —Julian Maclaren-Ross⟩ ⟨a ~ piece of bookmaking —Lionel Stevenson⟩ ⟨a ~ education —O.S.J.Gogarty⟩ ⟨general effect is one of an overpowering ~ vulgarity —Arnold Bennett⟩ **b :** OPULENT, MAGNIFICENT ⟨~ furnishings⟩ **2 :** extravagantly or luxuriously dressed, fed, or housed **:** living in luxury **syn** see LUXURIOUS

sump·tu·ous·ly *adv* **:** in a sumptuous manner **:** LAVISHLY, LUXURIOUSLY, OPULENTLY ⟨a ~ furnished house⟩ ⟨a ~ illustrated book⟩

sump·tu·ous·ness *n* -ES **:** the quality or state of being sumptuous

sum·ra \ˈsəmrə\ *n, pl* **sumra** *or* **sumras** *usu cap* **:** one of an early Rajput people inhabiting the lower Sind region of West Pakistan

sums *pl of* SUM, *pres 3d sing of* SUM

sum total *n* [ME *somme total* (trans. of ML *summa totalis*), fr. *somme* sum + *total,* adj.] **1 :** an aggregate of sums **:** a total arrived at through the counting, figuring or casting up of sums ⟨the *sum total* of one's liabilities⟩ **2 a :** the aggregate amount esp. of something not calculable **:** total result **:** TOTALITY ⟨the *sum total* of the day's pleasure⟩ **b :** GIST

sumu *usu cap, var of* SUMO

sum up *vt* **1 :** to be the sum of **:** bring to a total ⟨10 victories *summed up* his record⟩ **2 :** to bring or collect into a small compass **:** state succinctly **:** SUMMARIZE, RECAPITULATE, EPITOMIZE ⟨*sum up* the evidence presented⟩ ⟨values they can *sum up* in a few simple formulas —Herbert Croly⟩ ⟨came at the end of an epoch in culture and *summed* it *up* magnificently —R.A.Hall b.1911⟩ ⟨a phrase which *sums up* the quality of the cathedral schools —R.W.Southern⟩ ~ *vi* **1 :** to present a summary or recapitulation **2 :** to be expressed or summarized ⟨it *sums up* in exactly three words —W.A.Johnston⟩

sum-up \ˈ=,=\ *n* -s [*sum up*] **:** SUMMING-UP, SUMMARY ⟨listeners who might have missed the earlier pickups were able to get a clear-cut *sum-up* —A.N.Williams b.1914⟩

1sun \ˈsən\ *n* -s *often attrib* [ME *sunne, sonne,* fr. OE *sunne;* akin to OFris *sunne* sun, OS, OHG, & ON *sunna,* Goth *sunno,* Av *xvəng* (gen.), L *sol* — more at SOLAR] **1 a** (1) **:** the luminous celestial body that in the Ptolemaic system is one of the seven planets revolving around the earth ⟨the ~ rises⟩ ⟨the ~ sets⟩ ⟨the ~ came up upon the left —S.T.Coleridge⟩ ⟨was on his way before the ~ was up —John Seago⟩ ⟨the ~ went down behind the hill⟩ (2) **:** the star around which the earth and other

planets revolve, by which they are held in their orbits, from which they receive heat and light, and which has a mean distance from earth of 93,000,000 miles, a linear diameter of 864,000 miles, a mass 332,000 times greater than earth, a mean density about one fourth that of earth, and a chemical constitution generally like that of earth but so hot that it remains completely gaseous in spite of the enormous pressure exerted by the mutual attraction of its particles **b :** a celestial body like the sun **:** a luminary center of a system **:** another star ⟨a flying rout of ~*s* and galaxies —E.M.Forster⟩ **2 :** the heat or light radiated from the sun **:** SUNSHINE ⟨standing in the full ~ in the parking lot —J.G.Cozzens⟩ ⟨so beautifully tanned by the ~⟩ ⟨the photographer has captured their . . . varying moods in ~, storm, and snow —*Brit. Bk. News*⟩ **3 :** one resembling the sun usu. in brilliance or illuminative power **:** one having a shining or radiant quality ⟨anecdotes about the man . . . , the central ~ he became for a host of surrounding satellites —Irving Kolodin⟩ **4** *usu cap* **:** SUN-GOD **5 a :** the rising or setting of the sun ⟨between ~ and ~⟩ ⟨a man works from ~ to ~ but woman's work is never done⟩ **b :** a period of daylight **:** DAY ⟨but one ~'s length off from my happiness —Elizabeth B. Browning⟩ **6 :** temperature produced by the sun; *also* **:** CLIMATE ⟨thought he would freeze there in the arctic ~⟩ **7 :** a sunlike object: as **a :** a heraldic representation of a sun surrounded with rays **b :** PARHELION **8 :** GLORY, POWER, SPLENDOR ⟨young men fresh from the wars striding . . . luminous with the ~ of conquest —Hassoldt Davis⟩ ⟨problems of the human mind over which the ~ of hope seemed to be rising —Van Wyck Brooks⟩ **9 :** an astrological hot and dry temperate masculine diurnal planet which if well aspected is fortunate, the mansion of which is Leo, the exaltation 19° Aries, the depression 19° Libra, and the orb 15° — **in the sun** *adv (or adj)* **1 :** without worry or care ⟨loves to live *in the sun* —Shak.⟩ **2 :** in the public eye ⟨too much *in the sun* —Shak.⟩ — **under the sun** *adv (or adj)* **:** in the world **:** on earth ⟨hope for decent living *under the sun* —R.J.Slavin⟩ ⟨can study almost anything *under the sun* —R.M.Hodesh⟩

²sun \"\ *vb* **sunned; sunned; sunning; suns** *vt* **1 :** to expose to or as if to the rays of the sun **:** place in the sunshine ⟨nursemaids *sunning* their charges beside the sea —D.G.Gerahty⟩ ⟨*sunned* himself . . . in the rays of his great friendships —*Amer. Guide Series: N.J.*⟩ **2 :** to shine upon **:** illumine or irradiate like the sun ⟨dandelions ~ the lawn —Philip Booth⟩ **3 :** to affect by or as if by sunlight or exposure to it ~ *vi* **1 :** to become exposed to sunlight **:** bask in the sun ⟨patchwork quilts *sunning* on the back fence —*Amer. Guide Series: N.C.*⟩ ⟨they swam and *sunned* and ate —Elizabeth Hardwick⟩ **2 :** to emit radiance **:** SHINE

sun-and-planet motion \ˌ=ˈ==ˈ==-\ *n* **:** an epicyclic train of two wheels of which the wheel on a central axis is usu. rotated by the other wheel

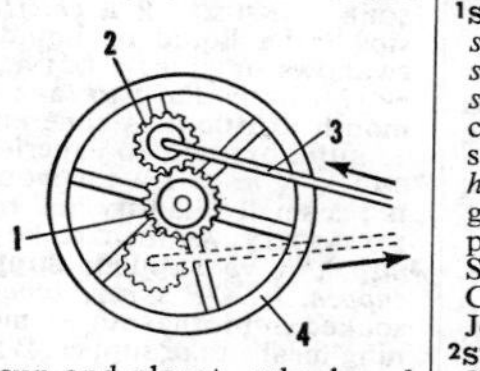

sun-and-planet wheels: *1* sun gear, *2* planet wheel, *3* connecting rod, *4* flywheel

sun animalcule *n* **:** a protozoan of the order Heliozoa; *esp* **:** a large freshwater protozoan (*Actinophrys sol*) with numerous flexible radiating axopodia

sun·a·pee trout \ˈsənə(ˌ)pē-\ *n, usu cap S* [fr. *Sunapee* Lake, N. H.] **:** a brilliantly colored char (*Salvelinus aureolus*) of Sunapee and other lakes of New Hampshire and Maine closely related to the saibling of Europe

sun arc *n* **:** a large lamp that is used in making motion pictures and that reflects light by a parabolic mirror — called also *sun lamp, sun spot*

sunback \ˈ=ˌ=\ *adj* **:** having a low-cut back for tanning and coolness — used of an article of wearing apparel ⟨sleeveless and ~ housedresses —*Women's Wear Daily*⟩ ⟨boleros make perfect cover-ups for ~ play frocks —*Springfield (Mass.) Republican*⟩

sunbaked \ˈ=ˌ=\ *adj* **1 :** baked by exposure to sunshine ⟨~ bricks⟩ **2 :** heated, parched, or compacted esp. by excessive sunlight ⟨the city had returned to its ~ quiet—Rudyard Kipling⟩

sunbath \ˈ=ˌ=\ *n* **:** exposure to sunlight or to a sunlamp

sun·bathe \ˈsənˌbāth\ *vi* [back-formation fr. *sunbather*] **:** to take a sunbath

sunbather \ˈ=ˌ==\ *n* [¹*sun* + *bather*] **:** one that takes sunbaths

sunbeam \ˈ=ˌ=\ *n* [ME *sunnebem, sonnebem*, fr. OE *sunnebēam, sunbēam*, fr. *sunne* sun + *bēam* beam — more at SUN, BEAM] **1 :** a beam or ray of light of the sun **2 a :** one that radiates happiness; *esp* **:** a bright merry child **b :** a member of a Salvationist organization for younger girls similar to Brownies **3 :** BANANA 2

sunbeam snake *n* **:** a harmless snake (*Xenopeltis unicolor*) of the family Xenopeltidae of southeastern Asia and Malaya having smooth black or brown highly iridescent scales

sunbeamy \ˈ=ˌ==\ *adj* **:** of or resembling a sunbeam **:** CHEERFUL, SHINING

sun bear *n* **:** a small bear (*Helarctos*, or *Ursus, malayanus*) of southern Asia, Java, Sumatra and Borneo that is about four feet long, has a short broad head, fine short glossy mostly black fur but brownish on the nose with a white or orange band on the chest, and is easily tamed

sun·berry \ˈsən- — *see* BERRY\ *n* **:** WONDERBERRY

sunbird \ˈ=ˌ=\ *n* **1 :** any of numerous small brilliantly colored birds of the family Nectariniidae that are native to Africa, southern Asia, the East Indies, and Australia, that in external appearance and habits somewhat resemble hummingbirds but have a curved bill and are true singing birds **2 :** SUN-GREBE

sun bittern *n* **:** SUN-GREBE

sunblasted \ˈ=ˌ==\ *adj* **:** scorched by the sun ⟨open ~ country —Marjory S. Douglas⟩

sunblind \ˈ=ˌ=\ *n, chiefly Brit* **:** AWNING

sunblink \ˈ=ˌ=\ *n, Scot* **:** a glimmer of sunlight

sun blotch *n* **:** a virus disease of avocados characterized by yellow or brownish red streaks on twigs and fruit, rough corky bark, and decumbent older stems

sunbonnet \ˈ=ˌ==\ *n* **:** a woman's bonnet worn for protection from the sun; *esp* **:** a cloth poke bonnet with or without a ruffle but usu. with a free-hanging extension at the lower edge of the back resembling a small cape

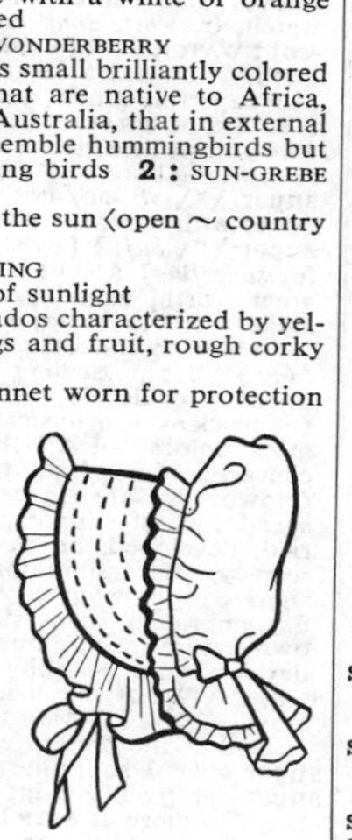

sunbonnet

sun·bow \ˈsənˌbō\ *n* **:** an arch resembling a rainbow made by the sun shining through vapor or mist

sunbreak \ˈ=ˌ=\ *n* **1 :** a breaking forth of the sun at sunrise; *also* **:** SUNBURST **2** *or* **sunbreaker** \ˈ=ˌ==\ **:** BRISE-SOLEIL

sunbright \ˈ=ˌ=\ *adj* **1 :** having a brightness that rivals the sun ⟨those other . . . ~ minds —John Mason Brown⟩ **2 :** flooded with sunshine ⟨morning is fresh and ~ —H.B. Alexander⟩

sunbrowned \ˈ=ˌ=\ *adj* **:** tanned by exposure to the sun ⟨held her hand . . . and kissed its soft ~ skin —Marcia Davenport⟩

¹sun·burn \ˈsənˌbərn, -bə̄n, -bəin\ *vb* [back-formation fr. *sunburned*] *vt* **:** to burn or discolor by the sun ~ *vi* **:** to become burned or discolored by the sun

²sunburn \"\ *n* **1 :** inflammation of the skin of variable degree caused by overexposure to sunlight — compare ERYTHEMA SOLARE **2 a :** development of chlorophyll in potato tubers that have been exposed to light **b :** SUNSCALD **c :** the discoloration of some fruits due to excessive sunlight at ripening time **3 :** FRENCH BEIGE

sunburned *or* **sunburnt** \ˈ=ˌ=\ *adj* **1 :** affected by sunburn; *specif* **:** reddened or tanned by sunburn ⟨old wrinkled ~ hands —J.C.Powys⟩ **2 :** seared by the sun ⟨a badly ~ suburban lawn —John Brooks⟩

sun burner *n* **:** a circle or cluster of gas burners formerly used in lighting large rooms

¹sunburst \ˈ=ˌ=\ *n* [¹*sun* + *burst*] **1 a :** a sudden flash of sunlight esp. through a break in the clouds ⟨off to the west the sky was pink which meant there would be a ~ —Ysabel Rennie⟩ **b :** something resembling a burst of sunlight ⟨the annual ~ of azaleas . . . that brightens the garden —*Monsanto Mag.*⟩ ⟨that brief, Renaissance ~ of the human intellect —Alan Moorehead⟩ **2 a :** a jeweled brooch representing a sun surrounded by rays ⟨a ~ in his turban —Hamlin Garland⟩ **b :** a design in the form of conventionalized rays diverging from a central point ⟨the gilt-faced clock in the ~ on the restaurant's wall —Elizabeth Bowen⟩ **3 :** the Japanese ensign bearing the device of a rising sun and rays radiating to all points in red on a white field **4 :** a moderate to strong orange that is yellower and lighter than carrot red, lighter than Mars yellow, and slightly yellower and stronger than zinc orange

²sunburst \"\ *adj* **:** pleated, tucked, or stitched in lines radiating from a circular edge ⟨blouse with a ~ yoke⟩ ⟨seven slivers of ~ fan pleats set in . . . below the hips —Lois Long⟩

sunck *also* **suncke** \ˈsəŋk\ *n* -S [of Algonquian origin; akin to Natick *sonksq* wife of a sachem, queen, fr. *soṅhquau* he prevails, overcomes + *squa* woman] *archaic* **:** a female American Indian chief — called also *sunk squaw;* compare SAGAMORE

sun-clock \ˈ=ˌ=\ *n* **:** SUNDIAL

sun compass *n* **:** a navigational compass that uses the sun and its calculated bearing to establish direction esp. in high latitudes

sun crack *n* **:** a crack due to the sun's heat esp. in dried mud **:** MUD CRACK — **sun-cracked** \ˈ=ˌ=\ *adj*

suncup \ˈ=ˌ=\ *n* **:** a yellow-flowered evening primrose (*Oenothera ovata*) found along the Pacific coast of the U.S. — called also *golden eggs*

sun-cure \ˈ=ˌ=\ *vt* [back-formation fr. *sun-cured*, fr. ¹*sun* + *cured*] **:** to cure (tobacco) by exposing the suspended leaves to the direct rays of the sun

sund *abbr* sundries

sun·dae \ˈsəndē, -di *also* -n(ˌ)dā\ *n* -S [prob. alter. of ¹*sunday*] **1 :** a portion of plain ice cream served with a topping (as crushed fruit, syrups, nuts) **2 :** a footed dish with a shallow bowl used for serving sundaes, sauces, and similar food

sun dance *n* **:** a solo or group solstice rite of American Indians: as **a :** a rite performed in Peru by a masked impersonator of the sun-god **b :** a rite performed in the area of Lake Michigan in imitation of the sun's course **c :** a rite of the Great Plains region often accompanied by votive self-torture by suspension from a pole

¹sun·da·nese \ˌsəndəˈnēz, -ēs\ *adj, usu cap* [Malay *Sunda* western Java + E *-nese* (as in *Chinese*)] **1 :** of, relating to, or belonging to the Sundanese or their language **2** [*Sunda* isles, islands of the Malay archipelago + E *-nese* (as in *Chinese*)] **:** inhabiting or native to the Sunda isles

²sundanese \"\ *n, pl* **sundanese** *usu cap* **1 :** one of the people of western Java **2 :** the Austronesian language of the Sundanese people

sun·da·ri \ˈsəndəˌrē\ *n* -S [Skt *sundarī*] **:** SUNDRI

¹sun·day \ˈsəndē, -di *also* -n(ˌ)dā\ *n* -S *usu cap* [ME *sunnenday, sonnenday, sonday, sunday*, fr. OE *sunnandæg;* akin to OFris *sunnandei* Sunday, OS *sunnundag*, OHG *sunnūn tag*, ON *sunnudagr, sunnundagr;* all fr. a prehistoric WGmc-NGmc compound formed fr. components represented by OE *sunne* sun and *dæg* day; trans. of L *dies solis*, trans. of Gk *hēmera hēliou* — more at SUN, DAY] **1 :** the first day of the week regarded by most Christians as a day for rest from secular employments and for public religious worship **:** the Christian Sabbath kept as a weekly commemoration of the day of Christ's resurrection and as the Christian analogue of the Jewish Sabbath **2 :** a newspaper circulated on Sunday

²sunday \"\ *adj, usu cap* **1 :** of, relating to, or associated with Sunday **2 :** BEST ⟨*Sunday* manners⟩ ⟨his new white *Sunday* suit —Eudora Welty⟩ **3 :** engaging in a pursuit only on Sundays or in spare time **:** AMATEUR, DILETTANTE ⟨*Sunday* painters multiply —J.D.Adams⟩ ⟨got behind a *Sunday* driver who was poking along admiring the scenery⟩

³sunday \"\ *vi* -ED/-ING/-S *usu cap* **:** to spend Sunday **:** engage in Sunday activities ⟨the religion . . . is Seventh Day Adventist and you do your *Sundaying* on Saturday —Julien Hyer⟩

sunday best *n, usu cap S* **:** clothing suitable for churchgoing; *esp* **:** one's best clothing worn on Sundays and for special occasions ⟨scrubbed behind the ears and with Eton collar and bow tie proclaiming this was *Sunday best* —K.D.Miller⟩

sunday citizen *n, usu cap S, obs* **:** a citizen in his Sunday clothes

sun·day·fied \-ˌfīd\ *adj, usu cap* [¹*Sunday* + *-fied* (past part. of *-fy*)] **:** given a character, appearance, or expression appropriate to or typical of Sunday ⟨the solemn silence and *Sundayfied* air . . . seeming to forbid any levity —F.T.Bullen⟩

sunday-go-to-meeting \ˈ=(ˌ)=ˌ=ˈ==\ *adj, usu cap S* **:** appropriate for Sunday churchgoing ⟨a *Sunday-go-to-meeting* expression⟩ ⟨had your *Sunday-go-to-meeting* garments made for you by a tailor —W.F.Harris⟩

sun·day·ish *pronunc at* SUNDAY +ish\ *adj, usu cap* **:** resembling Sunday ⟨a strange *Sundayish* hush . . . that morning —*Harper's*⟩

sun·day·ism \"+ˌizəm\ *n* -S *often cap* **:** SABBATARIANISM

sunday letter *n, usu cap S* **:** DOMINICAL LETTER

sunday punch *n, usu cap S* **1 :** a hard punishing blow; *esp* **:** a blow in boxing intended to knock out an opponent ⟨saved his *Sunday punch* for five rounds —*Time*⟩ **2 :** a tactic or maneuver resembling a Sunday punch ⟨their man was saving his *Sunday punch* for the end of the campaign —*Newsweek*⟩

sun·days \ˈsəndēz, -diz *also* -(ˌ)dāz\ *adv, usu cap* **:** on Sunday repeatedly **:** on any Sunday ⟨they would go riding *Sundays* in the park⟩

sunday school *n, usu cap 1st S & often cap 2d S* **1 :** a school held on Sunday for purposes of religious education **2 :** the pupils or teachers and pupils of a Sunday school

sunday supplement *n, usu cap 1st S* **:** the section of a Sunday newspaper consisting of material other than news and usu. including pictures, comic strips, and light often sensational reading matter

sun deck *n* **1 :** the usu. upper deck of a ship that is exposed to the most sun **2 :** a roof or terrace used for sunning

sun·der \ˈsəndə(r)\ *vb* **sundered; sundered; sundering** \-d(ə)riŋ\ **sunders** [ME *sundren, sunderen*, fr. OE *gesundrian, syndrian;* akin to MLG *sunderen* to sunder, OHG *suntarōn*, ON *sundra;* derivative fr. the root of OE *sundor* apart, OHG *suntar* aside, apart, ON *sundr* asunder, Goth *sundro* aside, apart; akin to L *sine* without, Gk *ater* without, apart from, Toch A *sne* without, Skt *sanutar* aside from, far away] *vt* **:** to break or force apart, in two, or off from a whole **:** separate usu. by rending, cutting, or breaking, or by intervening time or space **:** SEVER ⟨the Romans ~*ed* copper-bearing rock by alternately playing fire and water on it —*New Yorker*⟩ ⟨the major races are not always clearly ~*ed* by language —Edward Sapir⟩ ~ *vi* **:** to become parted, disunited, or severed ⟨pressing hands sharply for pledge of good faith, they ~*ed* —George Meredith⟩ **syn** see SEPARATE

sun·der·land \ˈsəndə(r)lənd\ *adj, usu cap* [fr. *Sunderland*, England] **:** of or from the county borough of Sunderland, England **:** of the kind or style prevalent in Sunderland

sundew \ˈ=ˌ=\ *n* [trans. of ML *ros solis*] **:** a plant of the genus *Drosera* or of the family Droseraceae — compare ALDROVANDA, DROSOPHYLLUM, RORIDULA

sundew family *n* **:** DROSERACEAE

sundial \ˈ=ˌ=\ *n* **1 :** an instrument to show the time of day by the shadow of a gnomon on a usu. horizontal plate or on a cylindrical surface **2** [so called fr. the fact that its leaves incline up to 90 degrees to follow the sun] **:** a common lupine (*Lupinus perennis*) of the eastern U.S.

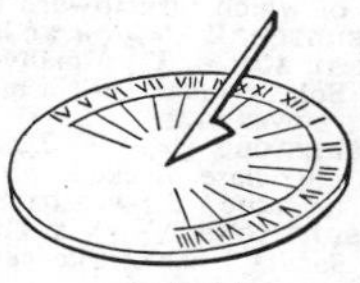

sundial 1

sundial shell *n* **:** a marine gastropod mollusk of *Architectonica* or a related genus; *also* **:** the shell of a sundial shell

sun disk *n* **:** an ancient symbol of the Near East consisting of a disk with conventionalized wings emblematic of the sun-god (as Ra in Egypt, Ashur and later Ahura-Mazda in southwestern Asia)

sun dog *n* **1 :** PARHELION **2 :** a small nearly round halo on the parhelic circle most frequently just outside the halo of 22 degrees — called also *dog, weather gall*

sun·down \ˈsənˌdau̇n\ *n* -S [prob. alter. of *sun going down*, fr. ME *sonne goyng downe*] **1 :** the time the sun disappears for the night ⟨visitors are asked to leave at ~ —Frederick Nebel⟩ ⟨they would be back . . . about ~ —Ellen Glasgow⟩ **2 :** a broad-brimmed hat for women **3 :** a light yellowish brown that is redder, lighter, and stronger than khaki or walnut brown and lighter, stronger, and slightly redder than cinnamon

sun·down·er \-nə(r)\ *n* **1** *Austral* **:** HOBO, TRAMP **2** *chiefly Brit* **:** a drink taken at sundown ⟨let's have our ~*s* back on the veranda —Stephen Longstreet⟩ **3 :** a very strict naval officer that formerly compelled midshipmen to return from shore leave at sundown **syn** see VAGABOND

sundress \ˈ=ˌ=\ *n* **:** a dress with an abbreviated bodice usu. exposing the shoulders, arms, and back

sun·dri \ˈsəndrē\ *or* **sun·dra** \-rə\ *n* -S [Skt *sundarī*] **1 :** any of several trees of the genus *Heritiera; esp* **:** an East Indian tree (*H. formes*) with a bark rather rich in tannin and a hard close-grained reddish to dark brown wood that is strong, durable, and resistant to decay and is much used locally for boat-building **2 :** the wood of a sundri

sun·dries \ˈsəndrēz, -riz\ *n pl* [¹*sundry* + *-es*] **:** miscellaneous articles, details, or items of inconsiderable size or amount individually

sun·dries·man \-zmən\ *n, pl* **sundriesmen** *chiefly Brit* **:** one that deals in sundries

sundrops \ˈ=ˌ=\ *n pl but sing or pl in constr* **:** any of several day-flowering herbs of the genus *Oenothera* (esp. *O. fruticosa*)

¹sun·dry \ˈsəndrē, -ri\ *adj* [ME *sindry, sundry, sondry*, fr. OE *syndrig;* akin to OHG *suntarīg* sundry, OE *sundor* apart — more at SUNDER] **1** *obs* **:** different or distinct for each **:** RESPECTIVE ⟨his ministers heaven's palace fill to have their ~ tasks assigned —John Wesley⟩ **2 a** *obs* **:** variously different **:** SEPARATE ⟨like to a meadow full of ~ flowers —Shak.⟩ **b :** more than one or two **:** MISCELLANEOUS, SEVERAL ⟨a guard of ~ horsemen —Charles Dickens⟩ ⟨~ sciences commonly known as social —I.A.Richards⟩ **3** *obs* **:** DIVERSE ⟨how many and how ~ are the evils wherewith our mortal state is endangered —Angel Day⟩ **4 :** of or relating to sundries ⟨a state's ~ revenue⟩

²sundry *adv* [ME *sindry, sundry, sondry*, fr. OE *syndrige*, fr. *syndrig*, adj.] *obs* **:** SEPARATELY, APART, ASUNDER

³sundry *pron, pl in constr* [ME *sindry, sundry, sondry*, fr. *sindry, sundry, sondry*, adj.] **:** an indeterminate number **:** DIVERS ⟨she danced with ~ who asked her —Donn Byrne⟩

sune \ˈsün\ *chiefly dial var of* SOON

sunfall \ˈ=ˌ=\ *n* **:** SUNSET

sunfast \ˈ=ˌ=\ *adj* **:** resistant to fading by sunlight ⟨~ dyes⟩

¹sunfish \ˈ=ˌ=\ *n* [¹*sun* + *fish*] **1 a :** OCEAN SUNFISH **b :** any of several rare related forms of the genus *Ranzania* **2 :** any of numerous American freshwater fishes constituting the family Centrarchidae and having a deep compressed body and usu. a brilliant metallic coloration — see PUMPKINSEED 1, LONGEAR SUNFISH **3 :** OPAH **4 :** a moonfish (*Vomer setipennis*) **5 :** THREADFISH 1 **6 :** BASKING SHARK 1 **7 :** a large jellyfish

²sunfish \"\ *vi, West* **:** to buck by bringing the shoulders alternately nearly to the ground and raising them ⟨the bronc . . . lunged, broke rhythm and ~*ed* —Dan Cushman⟩

sunfish·er \"+ə(r)\ *n, West* **:** a bucking horse

sunfish family *n* **:** CENTRARCHIDAE

sunflower \ˈ=ˌ==\ *n, often attrib* **1 :** a plant of the genus *Helianthus; esp* **:** COMMON SUNFLOWER **2 :** HELIOTROPE 1 **3 :** any of various plants that either bear a superficial likeness to the common sunflower or open in the sunshine: as **a :** GUMWEED **b :** POT MARIGOLD **c :** a rockrose of the genus *Helianthemum* **d :** BALSAMROOT **4 a :** a variable color averaging a strong orange yellow that is yellower and stronger than Spanish yellow and stronger and slightly yellower than average marigold **b :** SUNFLOWER YELLOW

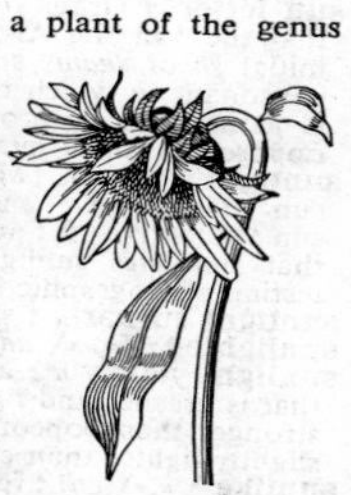

common sunflower

sunflower beetle *n* **:** a chrysomelid beetle (*Zygogramma exclamationis*) that feeds on and sometimes extensively defoliates the sunflower

sunflower chest *n* **:** CONNECTICUT CHEST

sunflower coral *n* **:** a discoid fossil of the genus *Receptaculites*

sunflower family *n* **:** COMPOSITAE

sunflower maggot *n* **:** the larva of a trypetid fly (*Strauzia longipennis*) that bores in the stems of the common sunflower

sunflower moth *n* **:** the larva of a moth (*Homoeosoma electellum*) that feeds on the developing head of the common sunflower in many parts of U.S. and Canada

sunflower oil *or* **sunflower-seed oil** *n* **:** a pale yellow semi-drying or drying fatty oil expressed from the seeds of the common sunflower and used chiefly in foods, soaps, varnishes, and paints

sunflower oil cake *n* **:** the residual cake remaining after the expression of oil from sunflower seed and used chiefly as a cattle feed

sunflower seed weevil *n* **:** any of several weevils (genus *Desmoris*) with larvae that feed and develop in sunflower seeds

sunflower star *n* **:** a large 20-rayed starfish (*Pycnopodia helianthoides*) resembling in form a conventionalized representation of a sunflower

sunflower tree *n* **:** FRINGE TREE

sunflower yellow *n* **:** a brilliant yellow — called also *balge yellow;* compare SUNFLOWER

¹sung [ME *sungen* (past pl. & past part.), fr. OE *sungon* (past pl.), *gesungen* (past part.)] *past of* SING

²sung \ˈsu̇ŋ\ *adj, usu cap* [fr. the *Sung* dynasty (960–1280), comprising 18 sovereigns of China] **:** of, relating to, or having the characteristics of the period of the Sung dynasty and esp. of the art forms developed during that period ⟨*Sung* Chinese collectors⟩ ⟨*Sung* wares⟩

¹sungar *var of* SANGAR

²sun·gar \ˈsu̇ŋˌgär, ˈsəŋ-\ *n, cap* **:** DZUNGAR

sun gear *n* **:** the gear wheel on the central axis in a sun-and-planet motion — see SUN-AND-PLANET MOTION illustration

sun gem *n* **:** a Brazilian hummingbird (*Heliactin cornuta*) that has in the male two tufts of glittering purple green and golden feathers on the head and a white breast

sun-glade \ˈ=ˌ=\ *n* **:** the bright reflection of sunlight on an expanse of water

sunglass \ˈ=ˌ=\ *adj* [back-formation fr. *sunglasses*] **:** of or relating to sunglasses ⟨a low-priced ~ lens —*Newsweek*⟩

sunglasses \ˈ=ˌ==\ *n pl* **:** glasses used to protect the eyes from the sun

sung·lo \ˈsu̇ŋˈlō\ *n* -S [fr. *Sunglo* Mt., Anhwei prov., China] **:** a green Chinese tea characterized by large loosely rolled leaves

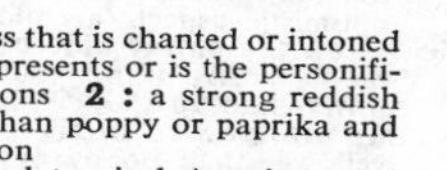

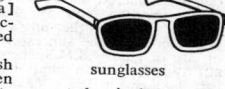

sunglasses

sunglow \ˈ=ˌ=\ *n* **:** a brownish yellow or rosy flush often seen in the sky before sunrise or after sunset that is due to solar rays scattered or diffracted from particles in the lower and upper air

sung mass *n, often cap S&M* **:** a mass that is chanted or intoned

sun-god \ˈ=ˌ=\ *n* **1 :** a god that represents or is the personification of the sun in various religions **2 :** a strong reddish orange that is yellower and paler than poppy or paprika and slightly lighter than scarlet vermilion

sun-grebe \ˈ=ˌ=\ *n* **:** any of several tropical American and African birds (family Heliornithidae) — called also *finfoot, sun bittern*

sun-grown \ˈ=ˌ=\ *adj* **:** grown in the open **:** exposed to the sun ⟨*sun-grown* tobacco⟩ — compare SHADE-GROWN

sun hat *n* **:** a broad-brimmed hat often with a high crown worn for protection from the sun

sun-heat \ˈ=ˌ=\ *n* **:** heat coming from the sun ⟨in few regions is a more regular and generous outpouring of *sun-heat* available —C.M.Longfield⟩

sun helmet *n* **:** a hat worn for protection from the sun; *esp* **:** TOPEE

sun hemp *var of* SUNN

su·ni \ˈsünē\ *n* -S [native name in southeastern Africa] **:** either of two very small delicately built antelopes (*Nesotragus moschatus* and *N. livingstonei*) of southern Africa

¹sunk \ˈsəŋk\ *adj* [fr. past part. of ¹*sink*] **1 :** SUNKEN 2 ⟨a small lean . . . man with ~ cheeks weathered to a tan

—John Masefield⟩ **2 a** : lowered or reduced esp. in status or value ⟨a depressed in spirits ⟨when he did not arrive she was rather ~⟩ **3** : SUNKEN 1 **4** : recessed rather than projected ⟨a ~ fillet⟩ **5** : absolutely finished : done for ⟨if he couldn't somehow raise the money, he was ~⟩

²**sunk** \"\ *n -s* [origin unknown] **1** *chiefly Scot* : a seat or bank of turf **2** *chiefly Scot* : a pad of straw used as a saddle or as a cushion

sunk center *n* : the portion of a watch dial that is depressed below the common surface to provide clearance for a hand

sunk cost *n* : a cost already incurred that is not subject to variation or revision and that is usu. represented by a fixed asset purchased and in use

sunk·en \ˈsəŋkən\ *adj* [fr. past part. of ¹*sink*] **1 a** : SUBMERGED; *esp* : lying at the bottom of a body of water ⟨~ treasure⟩ ⟨a ~ ship⟩ **b** : covered with a watery surface ⟨a ~ marsh⟩ **2** : fallen in : HOLLOW, RECESSED ⟨hunger gave their faces a ~ look⟩ ⟨noticed the slightly ~ cheeks underneath the trimmed beard —Joseph Conrad⟩ **3** : settled below the normal level ⟨a ~ porch gave a forlorn look to the little house⟩ ⟨that ~ avenue shaded by cypress trees —Marguerite Young⟩ **4** : SUNK **4** ⟨three bedrooms, a ~ living room —*Springfield (Mass.) Republican*⟩

sunk enamel *n* : CHAMPLEVÉ

sunken cord *or* **sunk cord** *n* : any of several cords that lie in grooves across the backbone of a hand-sewn book — compare RAISED BAND

sunken garden *also* **sunk garden** *n* : a formal garden usu. in a depression or with terraces above it

sun·ket \ˈsəŋkət, ˈsúŋ-\ *n -s* [fr. Sc *sunket* something, alter. of *somewhat*] *Scot & dial Eng* : a delicacy in food (as a fancy cake or tart)

sunk fence *n* : a ditch with a retaining wall used to divide lands without defacing a landscape — called also *ha-ha*

sunk fly *n* : WET FLY

sunk initial *n* : an initial placed to align at its top and bottom with two or more text lines

sunk key *n* : a key that fits into keyways in both the shaft and the secured member in machinery — compare SADDLE KEY

sunk panel *n* : a panel forming a shallow recess below the face of its framing or other surrounding surface

sunk relief *n* **1** : sculptural relief in which the outlines of modeled forms are incised in a plane surface beyond which the forms do not project **2** : sculpture or a sculptural form executed in sunk relief

sunk squaw *n* [*sunk* alter. of *sunck*] : SUNCK

sunk winding *n* : SLOT WINDING

sun lamp *n* **1** : SUN ARC **2** *usu* **sunlamp** \ˈ=¸=\ : an electric lamp designed to emit radiation of wavelengths from ultraviolet to infrared and used esp. for therapeutic purposes or for producing tan artificially

sun·less \ˈsənlòs\ *adj* : lacking the beneficial rays of the sun : having no sunshine : CHEERLESS, DARK ⟨ran through caverns measureless to man down to a ~ sea —S.T.Coleridge⟩

sun letter *n* [trans. of Ar *alḥurūf ashshamsīya*; fr. the fact that the *l* of the Ar definite article *al* is assimilated to the initial *sh* of *shams* sun, used as a type word] : an Arabic consonant to which the *l* of the preceding definite article *al* is assimilated in pronunciation — called also *solar letter*; opposed to *moon letter*

sun·light \ˈ=¸=\ *n* [ME *sunneliht, sonneliht*, fr. *sunne, sonne* sun + *liht* light — more at SUN, LIGHT] **1** : the light of the sun : SUNSHINE **2** : a light source and color filter combination that simulates sunlight in spectral quality and is used in testing photographic film

sunlight burner *n* : SUN BURNER

sun·light·ed \"\ *adj* : SUNLIT

sunlight yellow *n* : a variable color averaging a light yellow that is greener and lighter than jasmine, greener, lighter, and stronger than popcorn or maize, and greener, stronger, and slightly lighter than chrome lemon

sun·like \ˈ=¸=\ *adj* : resembling the sun

sun line *n* : LINE OF THE SUN

sun·lit \ˈ=¸=\ *adj* : lighted by or as if by the sun ⟨the peaceful and ~ years of the early part of this century —*Current Biog.*⟩

sun moss *n* : SUN PLANT 1

sunn \ˈsən\ *or* **sunn hemp** *or* **sun hemp** \ˈsən-\ *n -s* [*sunn*, *sun* fr. Hindi *san*, fr. Skt *śaṇa*] **1** : an East Indian plant (*Crotalaria juncea*) with slender branches, simple leaves, and yellow flowers **2** : the fiber of the sunn closely resembling that of true hemp, lighter and stronger than jute, and used for ropes and bags, and to some extent for oakum, canvas, and coarse cloth — called also *Bengal hemp, Bombay hemp, Indian hemp*

sun·na *also* **sun·nah** \ˈsùnə\ *n -s* [Ar *sunnah*] **1** *often cap* : the body of Islamic custom and practice based on Muhammad's words and deeds **2 a** : a personal or communal custom or practice ⟨follow the ~ of his ancestors⟩ **b** : a collection of such practices

sunned *past of* SUN

sun·ni \ˈsùnē\ *n -s usu cap* [Ar *sunnīy*] **1** : the Muslims comprising the larger of the two major branches of Islam that adheres to the orthodox tradition of the sunna, acknowledges the first four caliphs as rightful successors of Muhammad, and recognizes as orthodox any of four schools of jurisprudence — compare SHI'A **2** : SUNNITE **3** : the branch of Islam formed by the Sunni

sun·ni·ly \ˈsənˈlē\ *adv* : in a sunny manner ⟨she smiled ~ at him⟩

sun·ni·ness \ˈnēnòs\ *n -ES* : the quality or state of being sunny ⟨a ~ of disposition that delighted us all⟩

sunning *pres part of* SUN

sun·nism \ˈsù,nizəm\ *n -s usu cap* [*sunna* + *-ism*] : the religious system or distinctive tenets of the Sunni

sun·nite \-,nīt\ *n -s usu cap* [Ar *sunnīy* + E *-ite*] : a Muslim belonging to the Sunni branch of Islam

sunnud *var of* SANAD

¹**sun·ny** \ˈsonē, -ni\ *adj* -ER/-EST [ME *sunni*, fr. *sunne, sonne* sun + *-i, -y -y*] **1** : characterized by brilliant sunlight : full of sunshine ⟨a ~ springtime weekend —R.S.Monahan⟩ **2** : exhibiting happiness and gaiety : exceptionally cheerful and bright : MERRY, OPTIMISTIC ⟨passing suddenly from ~ moods to fits of depression —R.S.Boardman⟩ ⟨a ~ frankness and openness of spirit —J.R.Green⟩ ⟨men and women . . . forever ~ and full of virtue —Sinclair Lewis⟩ **3** : exposed to, brightened, or warmed by the sun ⟨a ~ room decorated with flowered wallpaper and potted palms —*Amer. Guide Series: N.Y. City*⟩ ⟨small lacquered leaves which . . . glisten like water in a ~ wind —Andrew Young⟩ **4** : originating with or proceeding from or as if from the sun ⟨a ~ beam danced above her head⟩ **5** : resembling the sun esp. in color or brilliance ⟨~ bushes of cup of gold —S.M.Spencer⟩

²**sunny** \"\ *n -ES* : a pumpkinseed (*Lepomis gibbosus*) ⟨angling for sunnies with flies —*Texas Game & Fish*⟩

sunny side *n* **1** : the side exposed to the sun's rays ⟨liked to walk down the *sunny side* of the street⟩ **2** : the favorable optimistic aspect ⟨a child usually sees only the *sunny side*⟩ — **on the sunny side** of : younger than ⟨perhaps she is on *the sunny side* of forty but I doubt it⟩

sunny-side up \ˈ=¸=ˈ=\ *adj, of an egg* : fried on one side only

sun orange *n* : a strong reddish orange that is paler and much yellower than poppy or paprika and yellower, lighter, and slightly stronger than fire red

sun orchid *n* : any of several chiefly Australian terrestrial orchids (genus *Thelymitra*) with showy brightly colored and sometimes fragrant flowers that are borne in terminal racemes and typically open only in bright sunlight

sun-pain \ˈ=¸=\ *n, South & Midland* : intermittent neuralgic headache

sun parlor *n* : a glass enclosed porch or living room with a sunny exposure **2** : SUN PORCH 2

sun perch *n* : SUNFISH 2

sun pillar *n* : a light pillar extending vertically above and below the sun

sun plant *n* **1** : a cultivated portulaca **2** : a plant that grows normally in a sunny habitat where it receives light of relatively high intensity — compare SHADE PLANT

sunpocket \ˈ=¸=\ *n* : SOLAR TRAP

sun porch *n* **1** : SUN PARLOR 1 **2** : a wire-floored and usu. wire-enclosed pen raised above the ground adjoining a

poultry house and used to provide fresh air and sunlight for birds with a minimum exposure to contaminated soil

sunproof \ˈ=¸=\ *adj* : impervious to the sun's rays : resistant to fading or damage by sunlight

¹**sunray** \ˈ=¸=\ *n* [¹*sun* + *ray*] **1 a** : a ray of sunlight **b** : a representation esp. in art of a sunray **2** : ANTIMONY YELLOW

²**sunray** \"\ *adj* : SUNBURST

sunrise \ˈ=¸=\ *n* [ME *sunne rise*, prob. fr. *sunne rise* (as in such phrases as *tofore the sunne rise* before the sun rises), fr. *sunne* sun + *rise*, 3d pers. pres. subj. of *risen* to rise] **1 a** : the apparent rising of the sun above the horizon : atmospheric effects that accompany the sun's appearance : the time the sun appears whether in fair or cloudy weather **b** : the time when the upper limb of the sun as affected by refraction appears above the sensible horizon as a result of the diurnal rotation of the earth **2** : the beginning or start of something ⟨in a dull condition at ~ of that century —G.M. Trevelyan⟩

sunrise clam *or* **sunrise shell** *n* : SUNSET SHELL

sunrise service *n, sometimes cap both Ss* : an Easter religious service observed at sunrise often in an outdoor setting

sunrise wall *n* : the plane of the earth's shadow in the atmosphere at sunrise or the region of changing ionization near this shadow that affects radio fading

sunrising \ˈ=¸==\ *n* [ME *sonne rising*, fr. *sonne* sun + *rising*] **1** : SUNRISE 1 **2** : the quarter in which the sun rises ⟨the winter ~⟩

sun-room \ˈ=¸=\ *n* : SUN PARLOR 1

sunrose \ˈ=¸=\ *n* **1** : HELIANTHEMUM 2 **2** : SUN PLANT 1

suns *pl of* SUN, *pres 3d sing of* SUN

sunscald \ˈ=¸=\ *n* : an injury of woody plants (as fruit or forest trees) characterized by localized death of the tissues and sometimes by cankers and caused when it occurs in the summer by the combined action of both the heat and light of the sun — see WINTER SUNSCALD

sunscreen \ˈ=¸=\ *n* : a chemical agent used in suntan preparations for filtering out ultraviolet light

¹**sunset** \ˈ=¸=\ *n* [ME *sonne set*, prob. fr. *sonne* sun + *set*] **1 a** : the apparent descent of the sun below the horizon : the atmospheric effects that accompany the sun's disappearance : the time the sun disappears **b** : the time when the upper limb of the sun as affected by refraction disappears below the sensible horizon as a result of the diurnal rotation of the earth **2** : a period of decline; *esp* : the time of old age ⟨the keynote of ~ of her life was her serene religious faith —Martha T. Stephenson⟩ ⟨the ... ~ of the secure Victorian world —DeLancey Ferguson⟩ **3** : a pale orange yellow that is redder and stronger than freestone and slightly yellower and duller than peachblow

sunset clam *n* : SUNSET SHELL

sunset gun *n* : a cannon fired at sunset or as part of the ceremony of lowering the flag at the end of a day

sunset lily *n* : a lily that is a variety (*Lilium pardalinum giganteum*) of the leopard lily and is distinguished by crimson and golden flowers thickly spotted with purple-black

sunset red *n* : a strong reddish orange that is yellower and paler than poppy, paler than paprika, and redder, slightly lighter, and stronger than fire red

sunset shell *n* **1** : any of a family (Tellinidae) of marine equivalve clams having the shell marked with bands of various colors radiating out from the umbones **2** : a similarly marked bivalve mollusk

¹**sunsetting** \ˈ=¸==\ *n* [ME *sunne settynge*, fr. *sunne* sun + *settynge, setting*, gerund of *setten* to set] **1** : SUNSET 1 **2** : the quarter in which the sun sets

sun·set·ty \ˈsən,sed-ē\ *adj* [¹*sunset* + *-y*] : of, resembling, or characteristic of sunset ⟨give the appearance of something ~ and gorgeous —Amy Lowell⟩

sunset wall *n* : the plane of the earth's shadow in the atmosphere at sunset or the region of changing ionization near this shadow that affects radio fading

sunset yellow FCF *n, usu cap S&Y* : the monoazo dye Food Yellow 3 used esp. in coloring orange drinks — compare DYE table I

sunshade \ˈ=¸=\ *n* : a shield or baffle, that deflects or redirects the sun's rays: as **a** : PARASOL **b** : AWNING **c** : BRISE-SOLEIL **d** : LENS HOOD

sun shell *n* : SUNDIAL SHELL

¹**sunshine** \ˈ=¸=\ *n* [¹*sun* + *shine*] **1 a** (1) : the sun's light : the sun's direct rays neither scattered nor reflected (2) : the sun's light when sufficiently strong to cast a shadow **b** *obs* : SUNBURST **c** : the warmth and light given by the sun's rays **d** : a spot or surface on which the sun's light shines as distinguished from surrounding shadow **2** : something resembling or suggesting the brightness of sunshine : a person, thing, condition, or influence that radiates warmth or cheer : a source of happiness ⟨last years were spent . . . in the ~ of his home circle —W.L.Worcester⟩ ⟨a good laugh is ~ in a house —W.M.Thackeray⟩

²**sunshine** \"\ *adj* **1** : SUNNY 1 **2** : radiating optimism : CHEERFUL, HAPPY ⟨a writer of the ~ type —H.J.Laski⟩ **3** : FAIR-WEATHER ⟨more than just a ~ friend⟩

sunshining \ˈ=¸==\ *adj* [¹*sun* + *shining*] : SUNSHINY ⟨that ~ June day —Robert Lowry⟩

sun-shiny \ˈsən,shīnē, -ìni\ *adj* [*sunshine* + *-y*] : bright with or as if with the rays of the sun : full of happiness : JOYOUS, RESPLENDENT ⟨a ~ day⟩ ⟨looked down at all the ~ faces⟩

sun-shot \ˈ=¸=\ *adj* : shot or permeated with sunshine ⟨in the limpid *sun-shot* air —Amy Lowell⟩

sun-shower \ˈ=¸==\ *n* : a light rain while the sun shines

sun side *n* [ME *sonne-syde*, fr. *sonne* sun + *syde*, *side* side — more at SUN, SIDE] : SUNNY SIDE 1

sun sight *n* : an observation of the altitude of the sun made for navigational purposes

sun's mean longitude *n* : the geocentric celestial longitude which the sun would have if its apparent annual motion in the ecliptic were at a uniform average or mean angular velocity

sun spider *n* : WIND SCORPION

sunspot \ˈ=¸=\ *n* **1** : FRECKLE **2** : a spot on the surface of the sun; *specif* : one of the dark spots that appear from time to time consisting commonly of a blue-black umbra with a surrounding penumbra of lighter shade and usu. visible only with the telescope **3** *usu* **sun spot** : SUN ARC

sunspot cycle *or* **sunspot period** *n* : the time between maxima in the varying numbers of sunspots averaging about 11 years but sometimes being many years shorter or longer

sunspot number *n* : an arbitrary numerical value that is used to describe the sun's spottedness, is the number of individual spots plus 10 times the number of disturbed regions, and depends upon the instrumental equipment and personal equation of the observer

sunspotted \ˈ=¸==\ *adj* : having sunspots

sunspotted·ness *n -ES* : the state of having sunspots

sunspot zone *n* : either of two zones within which nearly all sunspots occur: **a** : a zone north of the solar equator between 10 degrees and 30 degrees in solar latitude **b** : a zone correspondingly south of the solar equator

sun spurge *n* : a spurge (*Euphorbia helioscopia*) the flowers of which turn toward the sun

sunsquall \ˈ=¸=\ *n* : a large jellyfish

sun star *n* : a many-rayed starfish belonging to the family Solasteridae; *esp* : a member of the genus *Solaster* **2** : SUNFLOWER STAR

sunstone \ˈ=¸=\ *n* **1** : a brilliant variety of oligoclase flecked with minute scales of hematite **2** : AVENTURINE

sunstroke \ˈ=¸=\ *n* [trans. of F *coup de soleil*] : heatstroke caused by direct exposure to the sun

sunstruck \ˈ=¸=\ *adj* : affected or touched by the sun ⟨violet valleys and the ~ ridges —Wallace Stegner⟩

sunsuit \ˈ=¸=\ *n* : an abbreviated playsuit in one-piece or two-piece style worn usu. for sunbathing and play

sun's way *n* : the path in interstellar space along which the solar system is traveling

sunt *also* **sant** \ˈsənt\ *n -s* [Ar *sant*, fr. Copt *šonte*, fr. Egypt *šaṅa, šaṅat*] : BABUL; *esp* : the pod of the babul

sunsuit for a child

suntan \ˈ=¸=\ *n, often attrib* **1** : a browning of the skin from exposure to the rays of the sun **2 a** : a moderate orange color **b** : a light brown to light or moderate yellowish brown

suntans \ˈ=¸=\ *n pl* : a tan-colored summer uniform

sun temperature *n* : the temperature shown by a thermometer fully exposed to sunshine

sun thermometer *n* : a black-bulb thermometer used for showing sun temperatures

sun time *n* : time by the sun : APPARENT TIME

sun-trap \ˈ=¸=\ *n* : SOLAR TRAP

sun tree *n* : a showy Japanese evergreen tree (*Chamaecyparis obtusa*) that is often cultivated as an ornamental and for its fragrant weather-resistant lumber — called also *fire tree*, *hinoki*

sun trout *n, Midland & South* : GRAY TROUT 1

sunup \ˈ=¸=\ *n* [¹*sun* + *up*] : SUNRISE

sun valve *n* : a device operated by the heat and light of the sun by which beacon lights or other apparatus may be automatically turned off during the daytime

sun visor *n* : a shield usu. of green mica affixed above the windshield of an automobile

¹**sun·ward** \ˈsənwə(r)d\ *or* **sun·wards** \-dz\ *adv* [¹*sun* + *-ward, -wards*] : toward the sun ⟨hunched his shoulders ~, eager to meet it halfway —Jessamyn West⟩

²**sunward** \"\ *adj* : facing the sun ⟨the ~ side of the earth —H.N.Russell⟩

sun watch *n* : a small sundial fitted as a watch

sunweed \ˈ=¸=\ *n* : SUN SPURGE

sun wheel *n* : SUN GEAR

¹**sun·wise** \ˈsən,wīz\ *adv* [¹*sun* + *-wise*] : in the direction of the sun's apparent motion : from left to right : CLOCKWISE

²**sunwise** \"\ *adj* : moving sunwise : CLOCKWISE

sun·ya·ta \ˈshùnyə,tä\ *n* **1** *Buddhism* : the nonexistence of the fr. *śunya* empty, void] elements of things and of the self **2** : ultimate truth or reality interpreted (as in Madhyamika) as absolutely devoid of distinguishing characteristics and beyond even being and nonbeing : the transcendental void

sun yat-sen·ism \ˈsün'yät'sen,nizəm\ *n -s usu cap 1st S&Y* [Sun Yat-sen †1925 Chinese statesman and revolutionary leader + E *-ism*] : the principles propounded by Sun Yat-sen in his founding of the first Chinese republic

sun yellow *n, usu cap S&Y* : the stilbene dye Direct Yellow 11 — compare DYE table I

¹**sup** \ˈsəp\ *vb* **supped; supped; supping; sups** [ME *suppen*, fr. OE *sūpan, suppan* to swallow, sip, akin to OHG *sūfan* to drink, sip, MHG *supfen* to sip, ON *sūpa* to drink, sip, MHG *supfen* to sip — more at SUCK] *vt* **1** *obs* : ABSORB, CONSUME **2 a** *chiefly dial* : to take into the mouth in sips (as a liquid or liquid food) **b** : to take or drink in swallows or gulps : DRINK, SWALLOW — used with *off* or *up* ~ *vi, chiefly dial* : to take food and esp. liquid food into the mouth a little at a time either by drinking or with a spoon — **sup sorrow** : to experience sorrow or remorse

²**sup** \"\ *n* **1 a** : a mouthful esp. of liquor or broth : SIP **b** : a small quantity of a liquid ⟨a ~ of tea⟩ **2** *dial* : QUANTITY, AMOUNT ⟨take a good ~⟩

³**sup** \"\ *vb* **supped; supped; supping; sups** [ME *soupen, suppen*, fr. OF *soper, super, souper*, fr. *soupe* piece of bread soaked in broth, soup — more at SOUP] *vi* **1** : to eat the evening meal : take supper **2** : to make one's supper — used with *on* such prepositions as *on, upon,* or *off* ⟨~ on roast beef⟩ ~ *vt* **1** *obs* : to provide with supper : entertain at supper **2** : to feed (an animal) at night; — often used with *up*

sup *abbr* **1** superfine **2** superior **3** superlative **4** superseded **5** supine **6** supplement; supplementary **7** supply **8** support **9** [L *supra*] above **10** supreme

su·pa \ˈsüpə\ *n -s* [Tag] **1** : an Indo-Malayan tree (*Sindora supa*) of the family Leguminosae whose sap yields an oil widely used as an illuminant in the Philippines **2** : the tough durable wood of the supa

su·pa·ne·can \ˌsüpə'nekən, -näk-\ *n, pl* **supanecan** *or* **supanecans** *usu cap* [Subtiaba + Tlapanec] : a language family of the Hokan stock comprising Subtiaba of Nicaragua and Tlapanec of Mexico

su·pa·ri \sü'pärē\ *n -s* [Hindi *supārī*] : BETEL NUT

su·pawn *or* **sup·pawn** \sə'pón\ *n -s* [D *sappaen*, of Algonquian origin; akin to Massachuset *saupaun* mush, lit., softened by water] *chiefly NewEng* : HASTY PUDDING 2

supchgr *abbr* supercharger

¹**supe** \ˈsüp\ *n -s* [by shortening] **1** : SUPERNUMERARY **2** *slang* : SUPERINTENDENT

²**supe** \"\ *vi* -ED/-ING/-s : to act as a supernumerary

³**supe** \"\ *vt* -ED/-ING/-s [alter. (influenced by *supercharge*) of ²*soup*] : to soup up ⟨guided missiles — *suped*-up versions of V-2 rockets —F.V.Drake⟩

¹**su·per** \ˈsüpə(r)\ *n* **1** [short for *supernumerary, superintendent, supervisor*] **a** : SUPERNUMERARY; *esp* : a supernumerary actor **b** : one in a position of authority or superiority : SUPERINTENDENT, SUPERVISOR **2** [short for obs. *superhive*, fr. *super* + *hive*] : a removable upper story of a beehive containing sections for the storage of honey **3** [E thieves' slang, alter. of *souper*, prob. fr. *white souper* silver watch, fr. *white soup* melted silver from stolen articles + E *-er*] : WATCH 7a **4** [²*super*] **a** : a superfine or superior grade or quality : an extra large size **b** : an article of merchandise of a superfine grade, quality, or large size **5** [by shortening] : SUPERPHOSPHATE **6** [origin unknown] : a thin loosely woven open-meshed starched cotton fabric used esp. for reinforcing books **7** [by shortening] : SUPERMARKET

²**super** \"\ *vb* -ED/-ING/-s *vt* : to reinforce (as a book backbone) with super ~ *vi* : to perform as a super

³**super** \"\ *adj* **1** [by shortening] : SUPERFICIAL 1b **2** [short for *superfine*] **a** (1) : of a superfine grade or quality (2) : of great worth, value, excellence, or superiority ⟨tiered tables make ~ end tables for a small sofa —*Better Homes & Gardens*⟩ ⟨add mint to chocolate syrup for a ~ sundae sauce —*Parents' Mag.*⟩ **b** : possessing the greatest size, power, complexity, intensity, or development : being very great ⟨~ atomic bomb⟩ ⟨~ truck⟩ ⟨~ drugstore⟩ ⟨a plaster casting . . . in bilious ~ gloss colors —I.A.N.Henderson⟩ **c** (1) : exhibiting the characteristics of its type to a great or excessive degree ⟨clowns . . . are, in essence, ~ realists —John Grierson⟩; *specif* : manifesting excessive degree ⟨~ patriot⟩ **c** : carried, developed, or made use of to an excessive degree — used with *of* ⟨the assumption that safety lies in setting up verboten secrecy ⟨the assumption that safety lies in —W.E.Binkley⟩ signs . . . is what a ~ legalism leads to —W.E.Binkley⟩ **d** : embracing in its structure or authority complexes of its own nature ⟨such a business-labor-agricultural council would develop into a ~ lobby with coercive powers —*New Republic*⟩

⁴**super** \"\ *adv* **1** : VERY, EXTREMELY ⟨inclined to be ~ critical of the present era hunters —Ed Shearer⟩

super *abbr* **1** superfine **2** superheterodyne **3** superior

super- *prefix* [L, over, above, in addition, fr. *super*, adv. & prep. — more at OVER] **1 a** (1) : over and above : higher in quantity, quality, or degree : more than ⟨superstandard⟩ ⟨superconscious⟩ (2) : in addition : extra ⟨supertax⟩ (3) : of a secondary character ⟨superparasite⟩ **b** (1) : exceeding a norm ⟨superalkalinity⟩ ⟨supersecretion⟩ (2) : in excessive degree or intensity ⟨superingenous⟩ ⟨superrefined⟩ **c** : surpassing all or most others of its kind or class (as in power, size, or complexity) ⟨superbomber⟩ ⟨superweapon⟩ ⟨superstate⟩ **2 a** : situated or placed above, on, or at the top of ⟨supertower⟩ ⟨superglacial⟩; *specif* : situated on the dorsal side of ⟨supertonic⟩ **b** : next above or higher ⟨superoctave⟩ ⟨supertonic⟩ **c** : having the (specified) ingredient present in a large or unusually large proportion ⟨superoxide⟩ — compare BI- 4a, PER- 1b(1) **4** : having an additional dimension ⟨supercube⟩ ⟨supersurface⟩ **5** : constituting a more inclusive category than that specified ⟨superfamily⟩ ⟨superspecies⟩ **6** : superior in status, title, or position ⟨supersovereign⟩

su·per·a·bil·i·ty \ˌsüp(ə)rə'biləd-ē\ *n* [*superable* + *-ity*] : SUPERABLENESS

su·per·a·ble \ˈsüp(ə)rəbəl\ *adj* [L *superabilis*, fr. *superare* to go over, surmount, overcome, excel (fr. *super* over) + *-abilis* -able — more at OVER] : capable of being overcome or conquered : SURMOUNTABLE — **su·per·a·ble·ness** \-nòs\ *n -ES* — **su·per·a·bly** \-blē\ *adv*

su·per·abound \¦süpə(r)+\ *vi* [ME *superabounden*, fr. LL *superabundare*, fr. L *super-* + *abundare* to abound] **1 :** to abound or prevail in greater measure **2 :** to be very or too abundant : abound to excess or to an unusual extent ⟨~*ing* moisture⟩

su·per·abundance \"+\ *n* [ME, fr. LL *superabundantia*, fr. *superabundant-*, *superabundans* superabundant, overflowing + L *-ia* -y] **1 :** the quality or state of being superabundant : great abundance ⟨a ~ of wealth⟩ **2 :** EXCESS, SURPLUS ⟨get rid of a ~ of grain⟩

su·per·abundancy \"\ *n* -ES [LL *superabundantia*] **:** SUPERABUNDANCE

su·per·abundant \"+\ *adj* [ME, fr. LL *superabundant-*, *superabundans* overflowing, fr. pres. part. of *superabundare* to superabound] **:** abounding to a great, abnormal, or excessive degree : being considerably more than is sufficient ⟨~ zeal⟩ ⟨~ crops⟩ ⟨~ grace⟩ — **su·per·abundantly** \"+\ *adv*

su·per·acid \¦süpə(r)+\ *adj* [*super-* + *acid*] **1 :** excessively acid ⟨~ solutions of perchloric acid in acetic acid⟩ **2 :** having a pH value of 3.5–4.0 — used of a highly acid soil (as bog peat)

su·per·add \"+\ *vt* [ME *superadden*, fr. L *superaddere*, fr. *super-* + *addere* to add] **1 :** to add over and above : add in extra or superfluous amount ⟨the loss of his position was ~*ed* to the loss of his home⟩ ⟨a ~*ed* ornamentation⟩ **2 :** to make an addition; *specif* **:** to say in addition : add to what has been mentioned

su·per·addition \"+\ *n* [LL *superaddition-*, *superadditio*, fr. L *superadditus* (past part. of *superaddere* to superadd) + *-ion-*, *-io* -ion] **1 :** the act or process of superadding **2 :** something that has been superadded — **su·per·additional** \"+\ *adj*

su·per·aerodynamics \"+\ *n pl but sing in constr* [*super-* + *aerodynamics*] **:** the study of the mechanical properties of a fluid of such low density that the mean free path of its molecules is large in comparison with the dimensions of a body moving in the fluid

su·per·agency \"+\ *n* [*super-* + *agency*] **:** a large complex governmental agency esp. when set up to supervise and coordinate a group of other agencies

su·per·alimentation \"+\ *n* [*super-* + *alimentation*] **:** the action or process of overfeeding

su·per·alkaline \"+\ *adj* [*super-* + *alkaline*] **1 :** excessively alkaline **2 :** having a pH value of 10.0–10.5 — used of any of the most highly alkaline soils found in deserts

su·per·altar \"+\ *n* [ME *superaltare*, fr. ML, fr. L *super-* + *altare* altar; fr. its being used on top of an unconsecrated altar or table] **:** a portable altar consisting of a small square of precious marble : ALTAR STONE 2

su·per·al·tern \¦süpə¦röltə(r)n\ *n* -S [*super-* + *-altern* (as in *subaltern*)] **:** a universal proposition in traditional logic that is a ground for the immediate inference of a corresponding subalternate

su·per·an·nu·a·ble \‚süpə'ranyəwəbəl\ *adj* [*superannuation* + *-able*] *Brit* **:** that will entitle a person to superannuation pay on completion of a qualifying term ⟨~ position⟩

¹su·per·an·nu·ate \süpə'ranyəwət\ *adj* [ML *superannuatus*] **:** SUPERANNUATED

²superannuate \"\ *n* -S **:** one retired or disqualified on account of old age or reaching an age limit

³su·per·an·nu·ate \-‚wāt, *usu* -ād.+V\ *vb* -ED/-ING/-S [back-formation fr. *superannuated*] *vt* **1 :** to make, declare, or prove obsolete or out-of-date ⟨the press ~*s* the town crier —Helen Sullivan⟩ : disqualify or reject on account of age or antiquity **2 :** to retire and usu. pension because of old age or infirmity ~ *vi* **1 :** to become retired or ineligible because of age **2 :** to become stale by lapse of time

superannuated *adj* [ML *superannuatus* (past part. of *superannuari* to be too old, fr. L *super-* + *annus* year) + E *-ed* — more at ANNUAL] **:** rated no longer fully or passably efficient in one's job because of age : incapacitated or disqualified for active duty by advanced age

su·per·an·nu·a·tion \‚==‚==ˈwāshən\ *n* [³*superannuate* + *-ion*] **1 :** the action or process of superannuating or the state of being superannuated **2 :** an allowance to one superannuated : a retirement allowance

su·per·an·nu·i·tant \-üədənt\ *n* [blend of *superannuate* and *annuitant*] **:** a recipient of a superannuation

su·per·an·nu·i·ty \‚süpərə'n(y)üədē\ *n* [blend of *superannuate* and *annuity*] **:** SUPERANNUATION 2

su·per·au·rale \‚süpə‚rò'ra(‚)lē, -‚rò'rä(-, -‚raù'rä(-\ *n* -S [NL, prob. fr. neut. of *superauralis* of above the ear, fr. L *super-* + *auris* ear + *-alis* -al — more at EAR] **:** the highest point on the upper edge of the helix of the ear

su·perb \sü'pərb, sə'p-, -pəb,-pəib\ *adj, often* -ER/-EST [L *superbus* excellent, proud, haughty, fr. *super* over, above + *-bus* (fr. the root of *fui* I have been) — more at SUPER-, BE] **1 a :** exhibiting a majestic grace or grandeur : STATELY, LORDLY ⟨the ~ main shaft . . . rises in an almost unbroken line —*Amer. Guide Series: N. Y. City*⟩ ⟨the ~ masculinity of good Spanish dancing —Claudia Cassidy⟩ **b :** possessing or exhibiting nobility of birth, mien, position, or character : NOBLE, MAJESTIC ⟨~ as the ancient doings of the gods of old —Alice D. Estes⟩ **c** (1) **:** magnificently ornate : RICH, ELEGANT, SUMPTUOUS ⟨this coronation . . . was probably the most ~ . . . anybody now living has seen —Mollie Panter-Downes⟩ (2) **:** brilliantly colored — used chiefly of a bird **2 :** of supreme excellence, value, goodness, or beauty : of the highest quality ⟨our left has provided ~ political leadership —A.M. Schlesinger b.1917⟩ ⟨portfolios of ~ photographs —*Amer. Guide Series: N.H.*⟩ **syn** see SPLENDID

su·per·bi·ty \-bəd·ē\ *n* -ES [MF *superbité*, fr. *superbe* haughty (fr. L *superbus*) + *-ité* -ity — more at SUPERB] **:** HAUGHTINESS, ARROGANCE ⟨the vaulting ambition and ~ of youth —T.H. White b.1906⟩

su·per·block \'süpə(r)+‚-\ *n* [*super-* + *block*] **:** a very large residential or commercial block barred to through traffic, crossed by pedestrian walks and sometimes access roads, and usu. spotted with open greens or grassed malls

su·perb·ly *adv* **:** in a superb manner

su·perb·ness *n* -ES **:** the quality or state of being superb

su·per·bomb \'süpə(r)+‚-\ *n* [*super-* + *bomb*] **:** an extremely powerful bomb; *esp* **:** HYDROGEN BOMB

superb paradise bird *or* **superb bird of paradise** *n* **:** a bird of paradise (*Lophorina superba*) having in the male a large erectile fan-shaped tuft on each shoulder, a gorget of metallic green feathers on the breast, and a deep violet or nearly black color with green reflections

superb warbler *n* **:** BLUECAP 2b

¹su·per·calender \¦süpə(r)+\ *n* [*super-* + *calender*] **:** a calender stack of highly polished alternating metal and compressed paper or cotton rolls used to give an extra finish to paper — compare FRICTION CALENDER

²supercalender \"\ *vt* **:** to process (paper) in a supercalender

su·per·cargo \¦süpə(r)+\ *n, pl* **supercargos** *or* **supercargoes** [alter. (influenced by *super-*) of *supracargo*, modif. (influenced by *supra-*) of Sp *sobrecargo*, fr. *sobre-* over (fr. L *super-*) + *cargo* — more at CARGO] **1 :** an officer or person in a merchant ship whose duty is to manage the commercial concerns of the voyage **2 :** a foreign factor handling marine cargo

supercede *var of* SUPERSEDE

su·per·celestial \¦süpə(r)+\ *adj* [LL *supercaelestis* supercelestial (fr. L *super-* + *caelestis* celestial) + E *-al*] **1 :** above the heavens **2 :** higher than celestial esp. in spirituality or divinity

su·per·central \"+\ *adj* [*super-* + *central*] **:** situated above a center or central structure and esp. the central sulcus of the brain

su·per·centrifuge \"+\ *n* [*super-* + *centrifuge*] **:** a centrifuge designed to operate at higher than normal speeds to perform separations impossible in standard centrifuges — compare ULTRACENTRIFUGE

¹su·per·charge \'süpə(r)+‚-\ *vt* [*super-* + *charge*] **:** to charge greatly or excessively with vigor, energy, tension, emotion or material supplying one of these ⟨a bitter struggle for power . . . in a *supercharged* political atmosphere —Mary K. Hammond⟩ ⟨he ~*s* his ready flow of speech with slang —*English Digest*⟩ ⟨a supplementary pellet *supercharged* with vitamins and minerals —*Jour. Amer. Med. Assoc.*⟩: as **a :** to supply a charge to the intake of (an internal-combustion engine or other prime mover) at a pressure higher than that of the surrounding atmosphere **b :** PRESSURIZE 1

²supercharge \"\ *n* **:** a great or excessive charge ⟨that ~ of zest which generates gaiety in others —John Mason Brown⟩ ⟨the use of ~*s* must be avoided . . . otherwise excessive wear of the guns will result —*U. S. War Dept. Technical Manual*⟩

supercharged engine *n* [*supercharged* (past part. of ¹*supercharge*) + *engine*] **:** an internal-combustion engine equipped with or using a supercharger

su·per·charg·er \-jə(r)\ *n* [¹*supercharge* + *-er*] **:** a device (as a blower, compressor, or pump) to increase the volume air charge of an internal-combustion engine over that which would normally be drawn in through the pumping action of the pistons and to compensate for the lower density of air in altitude operation of aircraft engines or the deficiency of air charge in high-speed automotive operation; *also* **:** a similar device for increasing air pressure — see CABIN SUPERCHARGER

¹su·per·cil·i·ary \‚süpə(r)¦silē‚erē\ *adj* [irreg. (influenced by *-ary*) fr. NL *superciliaris*, fr. L *supercilium* eyebrow + *-aris* -ar] **1 :** of, relating to, or adjoining the eyebrow : SUPRAORBITAL ⟨a ~ line of color on a bird⟩ **2 :** SUPRACILIARY

²superciliary \"\ *n* -ES **:** a superciliary part or marking

superciliary ridge *or* **superciliary arch** *n* **1 :** a prominence on the frontal bone above the eye caused by the projection of the frontal air sinuses **2 :** the projecting upper part of the orbit of various animals

¹su·per·cil·ious \¦süpə(r)¦silēəs, -lyəs\ *adj* [L *superciliosus*, fr. *supercilium* eyebrow, pride, haughtiness (fr. *super-* + *-cilium* — akin to L *celare* to hide) + *-osus* -ous — more at HELL] **1 :** arrogantly superior : HAUGHTY, DISDAINFUL ⟨though elated by his rank, it did not render him ~ —Jane Austen⟩ ⟨translators . . . ~ about the possibility of using Basic English for such international conferences —Mark Starr⟩ ⟨shaggy ~ camels —L.C.Stevens⟩ **2 :** expressive of contempt : SCORNFUL, SNEERING ⟨his lip curls in a ~ smile⟩ **syn** see PROUD

²supercilious \"\ *adj* [L *supercilium* eyebrow + E *-ous*] *archaic* **:** SUPERCILIARY

su·per·cil·ious·ly *adv* **:** in a supercilious manner

su·per·cil·ious·ness *n* -ES **:** the quality or state of being supercilious

su·per·cil·i·um \‚süpə(r)'silēəm\ *n, pl* **supercil·ia** \-ēə\ [L, eyebrow, ridge, pride] **1 a :** the region of the eyebrows : EYEBROW **b :** the overhanging margin of a bony cavity (as of the acetabulum) **2 a :** a fillet surmounting the cymatium in a Roman cornice **b :** a fillet above or below the scotia of an Attic base **c :** the lintel of a door

su·per·class \'süpə(r)+‚-\ *n* [*super-* + *class*] **:** a category in taxonomy ranking between a phylum or division and a class

su·per·colossal \¦süpə(r)+\ *adj* [*super-* + *colossal*] **:** extremely colossal

su·per·columnar \"+\ *adj* [*super-* + L *columna* column + E *-ar*] **1 :** built above a column or colonnade **2 :** marked by superposition of columns

su·per·columniation \"+\ *n* [*super-* + *columniation*] **:** the superposition of one order of columns above another

su·per·commentary \"+\ *n* [*super-* + *commentary*] **:** a commentary upon a commentary

su·per·compression \"+\ *n* [*super-* + *compression*] **:** the compression of a portion of a compressed fuel-air mixture during the last stages of the compression stroke in a mixed-cycle internal-combustion engine to a much higher temperature than the remainder

su·per·conduct \"+\ *vi* [back-formation fr. *superconductivity*] **:** to exhibit superconductivity

su·per·conduction \"+\ *n* [*super-* + *conduction*] **:** electrical conduction in a superconductive substance

su·per·conductive \"+\ *adj* [prob. back-formation fr. *superconductivity*] **:** exhibiting superconductivity

su·per·conductivity \"+\ *n* [*super-* + *conductivity*] **:** abnormally high conductivity; *specif* **:** a complete disappearance of electrical resistance in a metal (as lead, mercury, vanadium, or tin) at temperatures near absolute zero — called also *supraconductivity*

su·per·conductor \"+\ *n* [*super-* + *conductor*] **:** a superconductive substance or body

¹su·per·conscious \"+\ *adj* [*super-* + *conscious*] **1 :** transcending human consciousness **2 :** of, relating to, or possessing the highest consciousness or a margin of consciousness above that within the ordinary range of attention — compare SUBCONSCIOUS — **su·per·consciousness** \"+\ *n*

²superconscious \"\ *n* **:** the superconscious part of the mind or psychic activity

su·per·contract \¦süpə(r)+\ *vi* [*super-* + *contract*] **:** to shrink irreversibly — used esp. of keratin fibers and substances (as hair or wool) containing keratin — **su·per·contraction** \"+\ *n*

super contract bridge *n* [³*super*] **:** contract bridge played with a joker added to the regular pack

su·per·cool \¦süpə(r)+\ *vt* [*super-* + *cool*] **:** to cool below the freezing point without solidification or crystallization : UNDERCOOL

su·per·cres·cence \¦süpə(r)¦kres³n(t)s\ *n* -S [fr. *supercrescent*, after such pairs as E *excrescent: excrescence*] **:** a parasitic organism

su·per·cres·cent \-nt\ *adj* [L *supercrescent-*, *supercrescens*, pres. part. of *supercrescere* to grow over, fr. *super-* + *crescere* to grow — more at CRESCENT] **:** growing on a thing : PARASITIC

su·per·critical \¦süpə(r)+\ *adj* [*super-* + *critical*] **:** capable of carrying on a chain reaction in such a manner that the rate of reaction increases — used esp. of fissionable material

su·per·crust \'süpə(r)+‚-\ *n* [*super-* + *crust*] **:** the top course of a concrete or bituminous-macadam pavement

su·per·dainty \¦süpə(r)+\ *adj* [*super-* + *dainty*] **:** extremely dainty

su·per·dominant \"+\ *n* [*super-* + *dominant*] **:** SUBMEDIANT

su·per·du·per *also* **su·per·doo·per** \¦süpə(r)¦d(y)üpə(r)\ *adj* [redupl. of ³*super*] **:** extremely super : of greatest excellence, size, complexity, intensity, or impressiveness

su·per·duty \¦süpə(r)+\ *adj* [*super-* + *duty*] **:** designed to withstand extremely hard use; *esp* **:** designed to withstand use under extreme heat ⟨~ alloys for jet engines⟩

supered *past of* SUPER

su·per·ego \¦süpə(r)+\ *n* [*super-* + *ego*] **:** a major sector of the psyche that is mostly unconscious but partly conscious, that develops out of the ego by internalization or introjection in response to advice, threats, warnings, and punishment esp. by parents but also by teachers and other authority, that reflects parental conscience and the rules of society, and that serves as an aid in character formation and as a protector for the ego against overwhelming id impulses

su·per·elevate \"+\ *vt* [prob. back-formation fr. *superelevation*] **:** BANK 1c

su·per·elevation \"+\ *n* [*super-* + *elevation*] **1 :** the vertical distance between the heights of inner and outer edges of highway pavement or railroad rails **2 :** additional elevation

su·per·eminence \"+\ *n* [LL *supereminentia*, fr. *supereminent-*, *supereminens* supereminent + L *-ia* -y] **:** the quality or state of being supereminent : distinguished eminence

su·per·eminent \¦süpə(r)+\ *adj* [LL *supereminent-*, *supereminens* rising above, prominent, fr. L, pres. part. of *supereminēre* to rise above, fr. *super-* + *eminēre* to stand out, be prominent — more at EMINENT] **1 a :** being extremely high or highest **b :** being the most distinguished in rank or esp. excellence : eminent to a conspicuous degree **2 :** of very remarkable attainments or quality **2 :** extremely conspicuous : exhibiting esp. noticeable characteristics — **su·per·eminently** \"+\ *adv*

su·per·empirical \"+\ *adj* [*super-* + *empirical*] **:** experienced or experiencing by more than empirical means : TRANSCENDENT, TRANSCENDENTAL

su·per·encipherment \"+\ *n* [*super-* + *encipherment*] **:** an enciphering of what already is a cryptogram esp. in code

su·per·endurance \"+\ *n* [*super-* + *endurance*] **:** extremely great power of endurance

su·per·er·o·gant \¦süpə¦rerəgənt\ *adj* [ML *supererogant-*, *supererogans*, pres. part. of *supererogare* to perform beyond the call of duty] **:** SUPEREROGATORY

su·per·er·o·ga·tion \‚süpə‚rerə'gāshən\ *n* -S [ML *supererogation-*, *supererogatio*, fr. *supererogatus* (past part. of *supererogare* to perform beyond the call of duty, fr. LL, to expend in addition, fr. L *super-* + *erogare* to expend money from the public treasury after asking the consent of the people, fr. *e-* + *rogare* to ask) + L *-ion-*, *-io* -ion — more at RIGHT] **1 :** the act or process or an instance of performing more than is required by duty or obligation; *specif* **:** the performance beyond what is considered by the Roman Catholic Church to be necessary for salvation of good deeds of the kind believed to have been done by the saints or to be capable of being done by men **2 :** the act or process or an instance of performing more than necessary to complete an undertaking ⟨repeating the experiment would be an act of ~⟩

su·per·erog·a·tive \¦süpərə¦rägəd·iv\ *adj* [ML *supererogatus* + E *-ive*] **:** SUPEREROGATORY

su·per·erog·a·to·ri·ly \¦==ə¦rägə¦törəlē, -tòr-, -li\ *adv* **:** in a supererogatory manner

su·per·erog·a·to·ry \-‚törē, -‚tòr-, -ri\ *adj* [ML *supererogatorius*, fr. *supererogatus* + L *-orius* -ory] **1 a :** of, relating to, or characterized by supererogation **b :** observed or performed to an extent not enjoined or required ⟨~ acts⟩ **2 :** that can be dispensed with : SUPERFLUOUS, NONESSENTIAL ⟨metaphors . . . are pleasurable accessories . . . which are ~ when one comes down to the business of understanding what is said —R.M. Weaver⟩

su·per·essential \¦süpə(r)+\ *adj* [ML *superessentialis*, fr. L *super-* + *essentia* essence + *-alis* -al] **:** having or being an essence transcending others : possessing or consisting of the supreme essence — **su·per·essentially** \"+\ *adv*

¹su·per·es·sive \¦süpə¦resiv\ *adj* [*super-* + *-essive* (as in *inessive*)] *of a grammatical case* **:** denoting position or location on or upon

²superessive \"\ *n* -S **:** the superessive case or a word in it

su·per·ette \¦süpə¦ret\ *n* -S [¹*super* + *-ette*] **:** a supermarket operating on a scale smaller than usual as measured by space occupied or volume of business

su·per·excellent \"+\ *adj* [LL *superexcellent-*, *superexcellens*, fr. pres. part. of *superexcellere* to excel greatly, fr. *super-* + *excellere* to excel] **:** extremely or supremely excellent : excellent in an uncommon degree ⟨the ~ work of professional historians —A.J.Nock⟩

su·per·existent \"+\ *adj* [*super*natural + *existent*] **:** having a supernatural existence

su·per·familial \¦süpə(r)+\ *adj* [*superfamily* + *-al*] **:** having the scope of or constituting a superfamily

su·per·family \"+\ *n* [*super-* + *family*] **:** a category of taxonomic classification ranking next above a family and being equivalent to a suborder or falling between the suborder and family

su·per·fat·ted \¦==¦fad·əd\ *adj* [*super-* + *fat* (n.) + *-ed*] **:** containing unsaponified fat ⟨~ toilet soaps⟩

su·per·fecundation \¦süpə(r)+\ *n* [*super-* + *fecundation*] **1 :** successive fertilization of two or more ova from the same ovulation esp. by different sires — compare SUPERFETATION **2 :** fertilization at one time of a number of ova excessive for the species

su·per·female \"+\ *n* [*super-* + *female*] **:** a sterile female having three X-chromosomes and two sets of autosomes — compare SUPERMALE

su·per·fetation \"+\ *n* [ML *superfetation-*, *superfetatio*, fr. L *superfetatus* (past part. of *superfetare* to conceive anew while still with young, fr. *super-* + *fetare* to bring forth young, hatch, fr. *fetus*, *foetus* act of bringing forth, young) + *-ion-*, *-io* -ion — more at FETUS] **1 :** successive fertilization of two or more ova of different ovulations resulting in the presence of embryos of unlike ages in the same uterus and occurring normally in various viviparous fishes and sometimes claimed to take place anomalously in mammals including man — compare SUPERFECUNDATION **2 :** fertilization of an ovule by two or more kinds of pollen **3 :** the process or product of the production or accretion of one thing upon another esp. in an uninterrupted superabundant cumulative development ⟨the close, technical style in which they make their discoveries known: the dense syntax and ~ of ideas —A.J.Carr⟩ ⟨a ~ of fantasies —E.M.Forster⟩

su·per·fice \'süpə(r)fəs\ *n* -S [ME, fr. MF, fr. L *superficies* top, surface — more at SUPERFICIES] **:** SUPERFICIES

¹su·per·fi·cial \¦süpə(r)¦fishəl\ *adj* [ME, fr. LL *superficialis*, fr. L *superficies* top, surface + *-alis* -al] **1 a :** of or relating to a surface : lying on, not penetrating below, occurring in, or affecting only the surface or surface layers ⟨multiple ~ wounds of the left and right thigh —Ernest Hemingway⟩ ⟨the ~ area of the wall —*Code for Dwelling Construction*⟩ ⟨the ~ layers of water through which light penetrates —R.E.Coker⟩ **b** *of a unit of measure* **:** not solid or linear : SQUARE ⟨~ foot⟩ **c :** of, relating to, or being the unconsolidated formations (as glacial drift or alluvium) that constitute most of the surface of the land : SURFICIAL **2 a** (1) **:** not penetrating beneath or farther than the easily or quickly apprehended features of a thing : concerned only with the obvious or apparent : CURSORY, HASTY, CASUAL ⟨the newspapers' ~ report . . . never gave the true picture —*Farm Jour.*⟩ ⟨current but mostly ~ explanations —Franz Alexander⟩ (2) **:** lacking in depth or substantial qualities : not profound : SHALLOW ⟨his thinking was ~ and fuzzy —W.E.Davies⟩ ⟨the religion . . . from which ~ knowledge estranges us —W.R.Inge⟩ ⟨his talents were . . . wasted in the production of ~ trash —R.A.Hall b.1911⟩ (3) **:** lacking in thoroughness of intellect, scholarship, or wisdom : not given to soundness ⟨~ research workers . . . often lack the . . . breadth of view to prevent them from giving absurd interpretations to their statistical results —M.R. Cohen⟩ ⟨children who seem to care little about learning and whose minds are definitely ~ in character —Morris Fishbein⟩ **b :** seen on the surface : EXTERNAL ⟨their ~ defect . . . cannot blind us to the sterling workmanship —W.B.Adams⟩ ⟨~ changes in costume and creed —Lewis Mumford⟩ **c :** presenting only an appearance or a semblance : not far-reaching, significant, or genuine ⟨the ~ differences of accent which are inevitable in such an international language —David Abercrombie⟩ ⟨maintaining the ~ charm of a glib intellectual —Arthur Knight⟩ — **su·per·fi·cial·ly** \-sh(ə)lē, -li\ *adv* — **su·per·fi·cial·ness** \‚==ˈfishəlnəs\ *n* -ES

²superficial \"\ *n* -S **1 :** a person or thing that is superficial **2 :** a superficial aspect, character, or quality ⟨the American novel of today is only English in ~*s* —*Times Lit. Supp.*⟩

superficial blastula *n* **:** PERIBLASTULA

superficial cleavage *n* **:** meroblastic cleavage in which a layer of cells is produced about a central mass of yolk (as in many arthropod eggs) — compare DISCOIDAL CLEAVAGE

superficial fascia *n* **:** the thin layer of loose fatty connective tissue underlying the skin and binding it to the parts beneath

su·per·fi·cial·ist \‚süpə(r)'fish(ə)ləst\ *n* -S **:** a person whose knowledge, understanding, or insight is superficial

su·per·fi·ci·al·i·ty \‚süpə(r)‚fishē'aləd·ē, -lətē, -i\ *n* -ES [¹*superficial* + *-ity*] **1 :** the quality or state of being superficial **2 :** one that is superficial

su·per·fi·cial·ize \-'fishə‚līz\ *vt* -ED/-ING/-S **:** to make superficial

superficial temporal artery *n* **:** the one of the two terminal branches of each external carotid artery that arises behind the parotid gland and passes upward between the mandibular condyle and the auditory meatus to the zygoma

¹superficiary *adj* [LL *superficiarius* built on another man's land, fr. L *superficies* surface, building on the surface of the ground + *-arius* -ary] *obs* **:** SUPERFICIAL

²su·per·fi·ci·ary \-'fishē‚erē\ *n* -ES [LL *superficiarius*, fr. *superficiarius* built on another man's land] *Rom & civil law* **:** one who has built on the soil of another usu. by agreement with him for an annual rental

su·per·fi·cies \-'fish(‚)ēz, -shē‚ēz\ *n, pl* **superficies** [L, top, surface, building on the surface of the ground, fr. *super-* + *-ficies* (fr. *facies* form, shape, face) — more at FACE] **1 a :** a depthless surface of a geometric body : the boundary or one of the boundaries of a solid or the border between two regions of space ⟨the ~ of a cube⟩ **b :** the outer surface of a body : superficial area ⟨the earth, from the ~ to an unknown depth —William Bartram⟩ **2 :** the purely external aspects, features, or characteristics of a thing : superficial appearance ⟨the audience is held by the substance of the play rather than by the ~ of the production —R.W.Speaight⟩ **3** *Roman & civil law* **a :** everything on the surface of a piece of ground or of a building so closely connected by art or nature as to constitute a part

of it (as houses or other structures, fences, trees, or vines) **b :** a real right or servitude consisting in a right in perpetuity or for a long term to enjoy the superficies of land on payment of an annual or periodic rent — compare EMPHYTEUSIS, GROUND RENT

su·per·fine \ˌ¦süpə(r)+\ *adj* [*super-* + *fine*] **1 :** very refined or delicate **:** overly nice ⟨this ~, extraordinary sort of gallantry —Jane Austen⟩ **2 :** of extremely fine size or texture ⟨~ file⟩ **3 :** very fine in quality or grade — used esp. of merchandise ⟨ornate creations, stiff with gold and silver and made of . . . ~ Flemish cloth, or of rich Italian silks —H.S.Bennett⟩

su·per·fines \ˈsüpə(r)ˌfīnz\ *n pl* **:** merchandise graded as superfine

su·per·finish \ˌ¦süpə(r)+\ *vt* [*super-* + *finish*] **:** to polish (a metal surface) to a mirrorlike finish by the use of hard abrasive stones at low pressure under a flood of lubricant of proper viscosity

su·per·fix \ˈsüpə(r)ˌfiks\ *n* [*super-* + *-fix* (as in *prefix*)] **:** a recurrent predictable pattern of stress that characterizes small stretches of speech whose constituents are parallel in relationship ⟨the ~ for *flattop* and *redhead* is \ˈ=ˌ=\⟩

su·per·flu·ent \süˈpərfləwənt\ *adj* [ME, fr. L *superfluent-*, *superfluens*, pres. part. of *superfluere* to overflow, be superfluous — more at SUPERFLUOUS] **1 :** characterized by or given to superfluity **:** SUPERFLUOUS **2 :** SUPERABUNDANT **3 :** flowing or floating above or from or on the top

su·per·fluid \ˌ¦süpə(r)+\ *n* [*super-* + *fluid*] **:** matter (as helium II) in a unique state characterized by extraordinarily large thermal conductivity and capillarity — **su·per·fluidity** \"+\ *n*

su·per·flu·i·ty \ˌsüpə(r)ˈflüəd·ē, -üətē, -i\ *n* -ES [ME *superfluitee*, fr. MF *superfluité*, fr. LL *superfluitat-*, *superfluitas*, fr. L *superfluus* superfluous + *-itat-*, *-itas* -ity] **1 a :** a superabundant excess **:** an amount greatly beyond what is sufficient, necessary, or advantageous **:** a copious oversupply ⟨this book has . . . a ~ of introductions and summaries —M.G.Singer⟩ **b :** the quality or state of being extra or superfluous **:** WASTEFULNESS ⟨there is no ~ in the means employed —C.R.Darwin⟩ **c :** a thing that is unnecessary or in excess **:** a superfluous or dispensable thing ⟨do not permit children to indulge in *superfluities* . . . until essentials are met —Mary Ines⟩ **2 :** immoderate and esp. luxurious living, habits, or desires **:** PRODIGALITY, EXTRAVAGANCE **syn** see EXCESS

su·per·flu·ous \süˈpərfləwəs, səˈp-,-pə̄f-,-pəif- *also* -fləs *or* ÷-fələs\ *adj* [ME, fr. L *superfluus* running over, superfluous, fr. *superfluere* to overflow, be in excess, fr. *super-* + *fluere* to flow — more at FLUID] **1 a :** exceeding what is sufficient, necessary, normal, or desirable **:** SUPERABUNDANT, SURPLUS, NONESSENTIAL, SUPEREROGATORY ⟨eliminating ~ words and replacing loose phrases with single words that express the thought —*N.Y. Times*⟩ ⟨armed ships allow nothing ~ to litter up the deck —Herman Melville⟩ ⟨silver plate . . . was the most suitable outlet for ~ wealth . . . when modern facilities for investment did not exist —Edwin Benson⟩ **b** *obs* (1) **:** unpleasantly excessive (2) **:** ABNORMAL ⟨a blind man, or a lame, or he that hath a flat nose, or any thing ~ —Lev 21:18 (AV)⟩ (3) **:** INORDINATE ⟨purchased at a ~ rate —Shak.⟩ **c :** exceeding the octave compass in an ecclesiastical mode **2 a** *obs* **:** WASTEFUL, EXTRAVAGANT **b :** doing something unnecessary, irrelevant, or frivolous ⟨so ~ as to demand the time of day —Shak.⟩ — **su·per·flu·ous·ly** *adv* — **su·per·flu·ous·ness** *n* -ES

su·per·flux \ˈsüpə(r)ˌfləks\ *n* [ML *superfluxus* action of overflowing, fr. L *superfluxus*, past part. of *superfluere* to overflow] **1 :** SUPERABUNDANCE, SUPERFLUITY **2 :** an excessive flowing

super foot *n* [³*super*] **1** *Austral* **:** a superficial foot **:** SQUARE FOOT **2** *Austral* **:** BOARD FOOT

su·per·frontal \ˌ¦süpə(r)+\ *n* [ML *superfrontalis*, fr. L *super-* + ML *frontale* altar frontal, fr. L, ornament for the forehead — more at FRONTAL] **:** a cloth which is placed over the top of an altar and hangs down a few inches over the frontal

superfuse *vt* [L *superfusus*, past part. of *superfundere* to pour on or over, fr. *super-* + *fundere* to pour — more at FOUND] **1** *obs* **:** POUR **2 :** SUPERCOOL

su·per·fusibility \ˌsüpə(r)+\ *n* **:** the quality, state, or condition of being superfusible

su·per·fusible \ˌ¦süpə(r)+\ *adj* [*superfuse* + *-ible*] **:** capable of being supercooled

superfusion \"+\ *n* [LL *superfusion-*, *superfusio* act of pouring on or over, fr. L *superfusus* + *-ion-*, *-io* -ion] **:** an act or instance of superfusing

su·per·galaxy \"+\ *n* [*super-* + *galaxy*] **:** an aggregation of great numbers of galaxies **:** a large cluster of galaxies

¹**su·per·gene** \ˈsüpə(r)ˌjēn\ *adj* [*super-* + *-gene* (as in *hypogene*)] **1 :** deposited or enriched by generally downward-moving solutions — used esp. of an ore deposit; opposed to *hypogene;* compare ENRICHMENT **2 :** of or relating to a process of deposition by generally downward-moving solutions

²**supergene** \"\ *n* [*super-* + *gene*] **:** a group of linked genes acting as an allelomorphic unit

su·per·generic \ˌ¦süpə(r)+\ *adj* [*super-* + *generic*] **:** of or relating to groups or characters of higher rank than generic

su·per·giant \"+\ *n* [*super-* + *giant*] **1 :** a very gigantic object **2** *or* **supergiant star :** a star of very great intrinsic luminosity and enormous size characterized by the sharpness of its spectral lines

su·per·glacial \ˌ¦süpə(r)+\ *adj* [*super-* + *glacier* + *-al*] **:** on, of, or relating to the surface of a glacier ⟨~ rivers⟩

su·per·glottic \"+\ *adj* [*super-* + *glottic*] **:** situated above the glottis

su·per·government \"+\ *n* [*super-* + *government*] **1 :** an international governing body having the power to enforce its decisions upon member nations **2 :** government by a group or body that has no authority to govern but that can force its decisions upon a legitimate government ⟨~ by private enterprise —Catherine Bauer⟩ ⟨a ~ by labor unions which may tax at will —David Lawrence⟩ **3 :** a government with extremely broad or thorough-going powers

¹**su·per·heat** \" +\ *vt* [*super-* + *heat*, v.] **1 a :** to heat (a liquid) above the boiling point without converting into vapor **b :** to heat (a vapor not in contact with its own liquid) so as to cause to remain free from suspended liquid droplets ⟨~*ed* steam⟩ **2 a :** to heat very much; *esp* **:** OVERHEAT ⟨unbuttoned his coat . . . to cool his ~*ed* blood —Josephine Pinckney⟩ **b :** to excite, intensify, or exaggerate excessively

²**su·per·heat** \ˈsüpə(r)+ˌ-\ *n* [*super-* + *heat*, n.] **1 :** the extra heat imparted to a vapor in superheating it from a dry and saturated condition; *also* **:** the corresponding rise of temperature **2 :** the difference in temperature between the lifting gas inside a balloon envelope and the outside air

su·per·heater \ˌ¦süpə(r)+\ *n* **:** one that superheats esp. steam or other gases; *esp* **:** a coil or other device through which steam from a boiler passes to be superheated

su·per·het \ˌ¦süpə(r)¦het, *usu* -ed·+V\ *n* -S [by shortening] **:** SUPERHETERODYNE

¹**su·per·heterodyne** \ˌ¦süpə(r)+\ *adj* [*super*sonic + *heterodyne*] **:** of or relating to a form of beat reception in which beats are produced of a frequency above audibility but below that of the received signals and the current of the beat frequency is then rectified, next amplified, and finally rectified again so as to reproduce the sound in a telephone receiver — compare HETERODYNE

²**superheterodyne** \"\ *n* **1 :** superheterodyne reception **2 :** a radio set which receives superheterodyne reception

³**superheterodyne** \"\ *vt* **:** to handle (radio signals) by superheterodyne methods

superhigh frequency \ˌ¦süpər+ . . . -\ *n* [*super-* + *high*] **:** a radio frequency in the next to the highest range of the radio spectrum — see RADIO FREQUENCY table

su·per·highway \ˌ¦süpə(r)+\ *n* [*super-* + *highway*] **:** a broad arterial highway (as an expressway, freeway, parkway, or turnpike) designed for high-speed traffic

su·per·historical \"+\ *adj* [*super-* + *historical*] **:** taking place or having significance outside the historical process ⟨we are now told that the fall of man is ~ —A.C.Knudson⟩

¹**su·per·human** \"+\ *adj* [*super-* + *human*] **1 :** being above the human **:** SUPERNATURAL, DIVINE ⟨~ beings⟩ ⟨~ agency⟩ **2 :** being beyond human capacity or strength **:** exceeding normal human power, size, or capability **:** EXTRAORDINARY, HERCULEAN ⟨~ courage⟩ ⟨~ effort⟩ ⟨~ tasks⟩ — **su·per·humanity** \"+\ *n* — **su·per·humanly** \"+\ *adv* — **su·per·humanness** \"+\ *n*

²**superhuman** \"+\ *n* [trans. of G *übermensch*] **:** SUPERMAN

su·per·humanize \"+\ *vt* [¹*superhuman* + *-ize*] **:** to make superhuman

su·per·humeral \"+\ *n* [LL *superhumerale*, *superumerale*, fr. L *super-* + *humerus*, *umerus* shoulder + *-ale*, neut. of *-alis* -al — more at HUMERUS] **:** something (as an ephod, pall, amice, or stole) worn or carried on the shoulders

su·per·implicant \"+\ *n* [*super-* + *implicant*] **:** SUPERALTERN

su·per·implication \"+\ *n* [*super*altern + *implication*] **:** the relation of a superaltern to a subalternate — compare OPPOSITION 2a(2)

su·per·imposable \"+\ *adj* **:** capable of being superimposed

su·per·impose \"+\ *vt* [*super-* + *impose*] **1 :** to place in a covering position **:** OVERLAY ⟨a transparent mask . . . is *superimposed* over the print —*Eastman Kodak Monthly Abstract Bull.*⟩ **2 a :** to cause to become attached, united, coexistent, or interrelated in the manner of a layer, stratum, or accretion ⟨a number of waves of different frequencies *superimposed* upon each other —F.E.Terman⟩ ⟨habits which have been *superimposed* upon other habits —J.W.M.Whiting & O.H.Mowrer⟩ ⟨laws of statutory character *superimposed* on the growing body of common law —F.A.Ogg & Harold Zink⟩ **b :** to add or impose without integrating **:** attach as an unassimilated entity ⟨his symbolism is too often something *superimposed* —E.R.Bentley⟩ ⟨*superimposed* imperatives have validity only to the extent that individuals freely assent to them —Vivian J. McGill⟩

superimposed *adj* [fr. past part. of *superimpose*] **1 :** LAYERED, STRATIFIED ⟨~ rocks⟩ **2 :** of, relating to, or being a river or a drainage system let down by erosion through the formations on which it was developed into underlying formations of different structure unconformable beneath

su·per·imposition \"+\ *n* **:** an act or instance of superimposing

su·per·imposure \ˌ¦süpə(r)+\ *n* -S [*superimpose* + *-ure*] **:** something that has been superimposed

su·per·impregnate \"+\ *vt* [*super-* + *impregnate*] **:** to subject to the process of superfetation

su·per·impregnation \"\ *n* [*super-* + *impregnation*] **:** SUPERFETATION

su·per·incumbent \"+\ *adj* [L *superincumbent-*, *superincumbens*, pres. part. of *superincumbere* to lie down on top of, fr. super- + *incumbere* to lie down on — more at INCUMBENT] **1 :** lying or resting on something else esp. so as to exert pressure ⟨~ layers of living and dead plants cut off the air and arrested decomposition —F.D.Smith & Barbara Wilcox⟩ **2 :** pressing heavily **:** BURDENSOME **3 :** *of pressure* **:** coming from above — **superincumbently** *adv*

su·per·individual \ˌ¦süpə(r)+\ *adj* [*super-* + *individual*] **:** of, relating to, or being an organism, entity, or complex of more than individual complexity or nature ⟨whenever a . . . number of individual agents carry on some relatively lasting organized cooperation . . . a ~ collectivity to which all of them belong will be found to exist —F.W.Znaniecki⟩

su·per·induce \"+\ *vt* [L *superinducere* to bring in on top of, fr. *super-* + *inducere* to lead in — more at INDUCE] **1 a :** to bring into a relationship of wife or heir so as to supplant one already established **b :** to install in a post having an incumbent **2 :** to introduce by way of addition or superimposition **:** bring in over or above that already existing **:** bring about or cause to exist as an addition or accretion ⟨a spiritual meaning *superinduced* upon the literal —*Encyc. Americana*⟩ **3 :** to draw, put, or place so as to cover or conceal — used with *over* or *upon*

su·per·inducement \"+\ *n* [*superinduce* + *-ment*] **:** SUPERINDUCTION

su·per·induction \ˌ¦süpə(r)+\ *n* [L *superinductus* + E *-ion*] **:** the act or process of superinducing or the state of being superinduced

su·per·infect \"+\ *vt* [back-formation fr. *superinfection*] **:** to cause or produce superinfection

su·per·infection \"+\ *n* [ISV *super-* + *infection*] **:** reinfection or second infection with the same type of bacteria or other parasites ⟨tuberculous ~⟩

supering *pres part of* SUPER

su·per·in·tend \ˌ¦süp(ə)rən·¦tend, -pərn·-\ *vb* -ED/-ING/-S [LL *superintendere*, fr. L *super-* + *intendere* to attend, direct attention to — more at INTEND] *vt* **:** to have or exercise the charge and oversight of **:** oversee with the power of direction **:** SUPERVISE ⟨~*ed* publication of a score of good plays —Leslie Rees⟩ ⟨a committee on finance to ~ all appropriations —Allan Nevins⟩ ~ *vi* **:** to exercise supervision **:** have charge or oversight

su·per·in·tend·ence \ˌ=(=)=·ˈtendən(t)s\ *n* -S [ML *superintendentia*, fr. LL *superintendent-*, *superintendens* (pres. part. of *superintendere* to superintend) + L *-ia* -y] **:** the act or function of superintending **:** care and oversight for the purpose of direction **:** SUPERVISION ⟨a part of good ~ to check up constantly —W.C.Voss⟩

su·per·in·tend·en·cy \-dənsē\ *n* -ES [*superintendent* + *-cy*] **1 :** the office, post, or jurisdiction of a superintendent **2 :** SUPERINTENDENCE

¹**su·per·in·tend·ent** \ˌsüp(ə)rən·ˈtendənt, -pərn·-\ *n* -S [ML *superintendent-*, *superintendens* overseer, fr. LL, pres. part. of *superintendere* to superintend] **1 a** *obs* **:** BISHOP **b :** a Protestant Christian minister charged with the general supervision of churches within a certain territory or district ⟨a Methodist ~⟩ **2 :** one who has the oversight and charge of a place, institution, department, organization, or operation with the power of direction ⟨~ of schools⟩ ⟨~ of public works⟩ ⟨~ of a railroad division⟩: as **a :** the executive head of a police department **:** a chief of police **b :** BUILDING SUPERINTENDENT

²**superintendent** \¦=(=)=¦==\ *adj* [LL *superintendent-*, *superintendens*] **:** OVERSEEING, SUPERINTENDING

superintendent general *n, pl* **superintendents general** [¹*superintendent* + *general*, adj.] **:** one exercising authority over a number of superintendents

su·per·in·tend·ent·ship \ˌ=(=)=ˈ==ˌship\ *n* [¹*superintendent* + *-ship*] **:** SUPERINTENDENCY

su·per·in·tend·er \-də(r)\ *n* -S **:** one that superintends **:** SUPERINTENDENT

¹**su·pe·ri·or** \səˈpirēə(r), -pēr- *sometimes* süˈp-\ *adj* [ME, fr. MF *superieur*, fr. L *superior*, comp. of *superus* that is above, upper, fr. *super* over, above — more at OVER] **1 :** situated higher up or farther from a bottom or base **:** HIGHER, UPPER **2 a** (1) **:** of higher degree or rank ⟨insubordinate to his ~ officer⟩ ⟨the eight ~ grades were limited to girls —Robert Lowell⟩ (2) **:** taking precedence ⟨a ~ allegiance to a foreign government —Sidney Hook⟩ ⟨certain rights are ~ to constitutions and to statute laws —Isaac Lippincott⟩ (3) **:** of high degree or rank ⟨~ classes of society⟩ **b** (1) **:** of a higher order, nature, or kind ⟨~ wisdom derived from experience —G.T.Trewartha⟩ (2) **:** not material or natural **:** SPIRITUAL, SUPERNATURAL ⟨the subtle and ~ meaning which underlay the literal meaning of Holy Writ —G.C.Sellery⟩ (3) **:** having or seeming to have a higher level of reality or existence ⟨they are more immediate than the world of friendship, nutrition, and fatigue . . . and they are frequently ~ to it —Bernard DeVoto⟩ **3 :** courageously or serenely indifferent (as to something painful, disheartening, or demoralizing) **:** staunchly unyielding in self-control or morale ⟨he is ~ to that fear —G.B.Shaw⟩ **4 a** (1) **:** of more importance, value, usefulness, or merit **:** of higher quality, accomplishment, or significance ⟨true progress is something ~ to your puffing engines and clicking telegraphs —C.B.Fairbanks⟩ ⟨a class of ~ children⟩ ⟨a smaller proportion . . . of ~ looks and a minuscule number of superlative ones —Katharine T. Kinkead⟩ (2) **:** of greater force, influence, or efficaciousness ⟨the uplifting movements proved to be far ~ to the processes of erosion —W.W.Atwood †1949⟩ ⟨overcome by a ~ opponent⟩ (3) **:** greater in quantity or amount ⟨retreated before ~ numbers⟩ ⟨nor is the tuition greatly ~ to that of the tax-supported schools —B.K.Sandwell⟩ ⟨escaped by ~ speed —Edward Breck⟩ **b** *of a railroad train* **:** having the right of way over another **c :** notably excellent of its kind **:** surpassingly good ⟨men of delicate fancy, urbane instinct and aristocratic manner — in brief, ~ men —H.L. Mencken⟩ ⟨he may have graduated to a more ~ abode —Allan Forbes & R.M.Eastman⟩ ⟨delighted in his ~ ability to memorize —*Current Biog.*⟩ ⟨the paintings on the north wall appear to be by a different and slightly ~ hand —O.Elfrida Saunders⟩ ⟨the ~ durability of parchment —G.G.Coulton⟩ **5 :** SUPERSCRIPT — used usu. postpositionally ⟨"line 57ᵇ" is read "line five seven b ~"⟩; contrasted with *inferior* **6 a** *of a part of the upright body* **:** situated above another and esp. another similar part — distinguished from *inferior* **b** *of a part of the quadrupedal body* (1) **:** situated in a more anterior position (2) **:** situated more dorsad than another and esp. another similar part **:** DORSAL **7** *of a part of a plant* **a :** situated above another organ: (1) *of a calyx* **:** attached to and apparently arising from the ovary (2) *of an ovary* **:** free from the calyx or other floral envelope **b :** ADAXIAL **c :** situated near the top of the stipe — used esp. of the annulus of a mushroom **8 :** more comprehensive ⟨a genus is ~ to a species⟩ ⟨forming a ~ unit out of diversity —Manès Sperber⟩ **9 :** affecting or assuming an air of superiority **:** SUPERCILIOUS, HAUGHTY ⟨moments when the modern audience can feel ~ and amused —Delmore Schwartz⟩

²**superior** \"\ *n* -S **1 a :** one who is above another in rank, station, or office ⟨went first to his immediate ~⟩: as (1) **:** a head of a religious house or a religious order ⟨~ of the monastery⟩ (2) **:** the lord or his heir in feudal law from whom a vassal receives a fee and to whom he owes allegiance and tribute **b :** one that surpasses another in quality, merit, or excellence **2 :** a superscript character (as in printing)

³**superior** \"\ *adv* **:** in a superior manner **:** with superiority

superior alveolar canal *n* [¹*superior*] **:** the anterior, middle, or posterior canal in the maxilla that transmits nerves and blood vessels to the teeth

superior colliculus *n* **:** either member of the anterior and higher pair of quadrigeminate bodies that together constitute a primitive center for vision

superior conjunction *n* **:** a conjunction in which a lesser or secondary celestial body passes farther from the observer than the primary body around which it revolves ⟨*superior conjunction* of Venus to the sun⟩

superior court *n* **1 :** a court of general jurisdiction intermediate between the inferior courts (as a magistrate's court, justice of the peace court, or a district court) and the higher appellate courts **2 :** a court with juries having original jurisdiction

su·pe·ri·or·ess \-rēərə̇s\ *n* -ES [²*superior* + *-ess*] **:** a superior of a religious order of women or of a convent

superior ganglion *n* [¹*superior*] **:** the upper of two ganglia on the vagus nerve at its exit through the jugular foramen — called also *jugular ganglion*

superior general *n, pl* **superiors general** [²*superior* + *general*, adj] **:** the superior of an entire religious order or congregation

su·pe·ri·or·i·ty \səˌpirēˈȯrəd·ē, -pēr-, -ˈär-, -ətē, -i *sometimes* (ˌ)süˌp-\ *n* -ES [MF *superiorité*, fr. ML *superioritat-*, *superioritas*, fr. L *superior* + *-itat-*, *-itas* -ity — more at SUPERIOR] **1** *obs* **:** the position, office, rank, dignity, authority, or jurisdiction of a superior **2 a :** the quality or state of being superior: as (1) **:** the possession or application of greater or esp. prevailing force ⟨gained the ~ over the enemy army⟩ (2) **:** the possession of superior rank, authority, or dignity ⟨men free and independent . . . amongst whom there was no natural ~ or subjection —John Locke⟩ (3) **:** the quality or state of surpassing in degree or amount ⟨immigration played an important part, in maintaining a numerical ~ of men over women —*President's Commission on Immigration & Naturalization*⟩ (4) **:** the quality or state of surpassing in virtue, merit, excellence, or worth ⟨the ~ of their equipment to the enemy's —*Current Biog.*⟩ (5) **:** the quality or state of exhibiting disdain or conceit **:** HAUGHTINESS, SUPERCILIOUSNESS ⟨had none of the condescension of the foreigner, no white man's ~ —Walter Lippmann⟩ **b :** a superior characteristic or detail ⟨the man of creative imagination pays a ghastly price for all his *superiorities* and immunities —H.L.Mencken⟩ **3 :** DOMINIUM DIRECTUM

superiority complex *n* **1 :** an exaggerated conviction of one's own superiority **2 :** an excessive striving for or pretense of superiority to compensate for supposed inferiority

su·pe·ri·or·ly *adv* [¹*superior* + *-ly*] **1 :** in or to a higher position or direction ⟨those branches of the aorta which are ~ oriented —H.T.Karsner⟩ **2 a :** in a superior manner **:** BETTER ⟨~ equipped troops⟩ **b :** in a condescending or haughty manner **:** SUPERCILIOUSLY ⟨~ puffed away . . . the absurd misgivings of women —Arnold Bennett⟩

superior nasal spine *n* [¹*superior*] **:** FRONTAL NASAL SPINE

superior oblique *n* **:** OBLIQUE 2b(1)

superior olive *n* **:** a small gray nucleus situated dorsal to the inferior olive and made up of cells in the auditory path

superior pharyngeal *n* **:** PHARYNGOBRANCHIAL

superior planet *n* **:** a planet whose orbit lies outside that of the earth

superior servant *n* **:** an employee or agent to whom the principal has delegated such control or management of a business as to make the employee or agent a vice-principal and not a fellow servant of other employees in case of injury due to negligence — compare FELLOW SERVANT

superior slope *n* **:** the slope between the banquette and the exterior crest of a fortification

superior tide *n* **:** the tide of the hemisphere having the moon above the horizon

superior vena cava *n* **:** the portion of the caval system of a vertebrate that brings blood back from the head and anterior part of the body to the heart

superior wing *n* **:** one of the anterior pair of wings of an insect

su·pe·ri·us \səˈpirēəs\ *n* -ES [ML, fr. L, neut. of *superior* higher, upper — more at SUPERIOR] **:** the highest or treble voice part in medieval music

su·per·ja·cent \ˌ¦süpə(r)¦jāsᵊnt\ *adj* [L *superjacent-*, *superjacens*, pres. part. of *superjacēre* to lie over or upon, fr. *super-* + *jacēre* to lie; akin to L *jacere* to throw — more at JET (to spout)] **:** lying above or upon **:** OVERLYING, SUPERINCUMBENT ⟨~ rocks⟩

su·per·ject \ˈsüpə(r)ˌjekt\ *n* -S [*super-* + *-ject* (as in *subject*)] **:** an individual or an actual entity that progressively emerges through feelings and the attainment of satisfactions ⟨for the philosophy of organism, a subject emerges from the world a ~ rather than a subject —A.N.Whitehead⟩ — **su·per·jec·tive** \¦==¦jektiv\ *adj*

su·per·labial \ˌ¦süpə(r)+\ *adj or n* [*super-* + *labial*] **:** SUPRALABIAL

¹**su·per·la·tive** \səˈpərləd·|iv, süˈp-, -pə̄l-,-pəil-, -lət|\ *adj* [ME *superlatif*, fr. MF, fr. LL *superlativus*, fr. L *superlatus* — suppletive past part. of *superferre* to carry over, raise high — (fr. *super-* + *latus*, suppletive past part. of *ferre* to bear, carry) + *-ivus* -ive — more at BEAR, TOLERATE] **1 :** belonging to or constituting the degree of comparison that is usu. expressed in English by placing *most* before an adjective (as *most beneficial*) or adverb (as *most fully*) or by suffixing *-est* to it (as *oldest*, *soonest*) and that typically denotes an unsurpassed or extreme level of the quality, quantity, or relation expressed by the adjective or adverb ⟨the ~ degree⟩ ⟨the irregular ~ forms *farthest* and *worst*⟩ — compare COMPARISON 3, COMPARATIVE 1, POSITIVE 2a **2 :** most eminent of its kind **:** superior to the highest degree **:** having no peers **:** surpassing all others **:** SUPREME ⟨the protection and preservation of ~ scenery —*Chronica Botanica*⟩ ⟨men of ~ talent and character —C.S. Forester⟩ **3 :** EXAGGERATED, EXCESSIVE — **su·per·la·tive·ly** \|ə̇vlē, -li\ *adv* — **su·per·la·tive·ness** \|ivnə̇s\ *n* -ES

²**superlative** \"\ *n* -S **1 a :** the superlative degree of comparison in a language **b :** a superlative form of an adjective or adverb **2 :** the superlative or utmost degree of something **:** PEAK, ACME ⟨so many highest ~*s* achieved by man —Thomas Carlyle⟩ **3 :** a superlative person or thing **:** something that is superlative or of the utmost degree in its kind **4 :** an exaggerated expression esp. of praise ⟨he spoke in ~*s* —C.B. Kelland⟩

su·per·lattice \ˌ¦süpə(r)+\ *n* [*super-* + *lattice*] **:** a space lattice of an alloy system (as a copper-gold alloy) in which each kind of atom tends to occupy definite geometrical positions instead of having a random distribution

su·per·linear \"+\ *adj* [L *super-* + *linea* line + E *-ar*] **:** SUPRALINEAR

su·per·liner \ˈsüpə(r)+ˌ-\ *n* [*super-* + *liner*] **:** an outstandingly fast, safe, and luxurious passenger liner of great size

su·per·lingua \ˌsüpə(r)+\ *n* [NL, fr. *super-* + *lingua*] **1 :** either of a pair of dorsolateral lobes arising from the hypopharynx of an insect **2 :** MAXILLULA
superlong \"+\ *adj* [*super-* + *long*] **:** OVERLONG
su·per·lunary *also* **su·per·lunar** \ˌ¦süpə(r)+\ *adj* [L *super-* + *luna* moon + E *-ary, -ar* — more at LUNAR] **:** being above the moon **:** CELESTIAL, HEAVENLY — compare SUBLUNARY
su·per·male \ˈsüpə(r)+,-\ *n* [*super-* + *male*] **:** a sterile male having one X chromosome and three or more sets of autosomes — compare SUPERFEMALE
su·per·man \ˈsüpə(r),man, -maa(ə)n\ *n, pl* **supermen** [trans. of G *übermensch*] **1 :** an ideal superior man: as **a :** one that according to the philosophy of Nietzsche has learned to discipline himself by foregoing fleeting pleasures and sublimating his baser drives to attain happiness and dominance through possessing and exercising creative power and is of a type that has appeared at rare intervals in history **b :** a future man produced in an evolutionary struggle for survival or by selective breeding **c :** one fitted to survive in an egoistic striving for mastery **2 :** a person of extraordinary power or achievements in one field or in general **:** an extraordinarily great or successful person **:** a superhuman individual ⟨social illiterates who are simultaneously scientific *supermen* —Mark Starr⟩ ⟨an omnicompetent administration by *supermen* —Roscoe Pound⟩ **3 :** a fictional hero represented as having extraordinary physical prowess or performing highly improbable feats and depicted with such scant attention to his mental and emotional makeup that he appears rather stupid ⟨when . . . the ~ of this book went down to defeat, it was more in terms of plot than actuality —J.D.Hart⟩
su·per·man·hood \-ˌhu̇d\ *n* [*superman* + *-hood*] **:** the quality or state of being a superman
su·per·man·ly \-lē\ *adj* [*superman* + *-ly*] **:** of, relating to, or characteristic of a superman
su·per·market \ˈsüpə(r)+,-\ *n* [*super-* + *market*] **:** a departmentized self-service chain or independent retail market that sells foods, convenience goods, and household merchandise arranged in open mass display
su·per·maxilla \ˌ¦süpə(r)+\ *n* [NL, fr. L *super-* + *maxilla* jaw — more at MAXILLA] **:** the upper jaw — **su·per·maxillary** \"+\ *adj*
su·per·microscope \"+\ *n* [*super-* + *microscope*] **:** a microscope having either an unusually great range of magnifying power (as in an electron microscope) or other features (as adaptability to infrared and ultraviolet) that make it superior to the ordinary microscope
su·per·microscopic \"+\ *adj* [*super-* + *microscopic*] **:** SUBMICROSCOPIC
su·per·multiplet \"+\ *n* [*super-* + *multiplet*] **:** a spectral multiplet of exceptional complexity
su·per·mundane \"+\ *adj* [LL *supermundanus*, fr. L *super-* + *mundus* world + *-anus* -an] **:** transcending the earthly **:** DIVINE, CELESTIAL, SUPERNATURAL ⟨~ idealism —A.L.Locke⟩ ⟨some ~ urge . . . for liberty, for happiness, for truth —*Biosophical Rev.*⟩
1su·per·nac·u·lum \ˌsüpərˈnakyələm\ *adv* [NL, fr. *super nagulum, super naculum* (part. trans. of G *auf den nagel*, lit., on the nail), fr. L *super* over, on + NL *nagulum, naculum* nail, fr. G *nagel* fingernail, fr. OHG *nagal*; fr. the practice of turning the emptied glass upside down on the thumbnail without emitting a drop — more at OVER, NAIL] **:** to the last drop — used chiefly in the phrase *to drink supernaculum*
2supernaculum \"\ *n* -s **:** something and specif. an alcoholic beverage of superior quality ⟨the most interesting California sherry, a ~ —S.P.Lucia⟩
su·per·nal \sůˈpərnᵊl\ *adj* [ME, fr. MF, fr. L *supernus* supernal (fr. *super* over, above) + MF *-al* — more at OVER] **1 a :** being or coming from above **:** that is or emanates from on high **:** of or from heaven — opposed to *infernal* ⟨could not help but interpret the plague as a visitation from heaven, a ~ punishment for the sins of men —E.S. Le Comte⟩ ⟨some ~ reality that had its being . . . outside the cosmos —John Dewey⟩ **b :** of a heavenly or spiritual character ⟨the beauty and the ~ happiness of a soft and quiet death —Lytton Strachey⟩; *specif* **:** ETHEREAL ⟨a ~ melody⟩ **2 a :** located in or belonging to the sky or celestial regions **:** of or from the firmament ⟨subterranean and ~ deluges —Thomas Carlyle⟩ **b :** situated at or near the top — **su·per·nal·ly** \-ᵊlē\ *adv*
1su·per·natant \ˌ¦süpə(r)+\ *adj* [L *supernatant-, supernatans*, pres. part. of *supernatare* to float, fr. *super-* + *natare* to swim — more at NOURISH] **:** floating on the surface ⟨the copra was boiled with water and the ~ fat skimmed off —T.P.Hilditch⟩
2supernatant \"\ *n* -s **:** a supernatant substance
su·per·nate \ˈsüpə(r),nāt\ *n* -s [by shortening] **:** SUPERNATANT
su·per·national \ˌ¦süpə(r)+\ *adj* [*super-* + *national*] **:** consisting of, affecting, or having jurisdiction over more than one nation ⟨modern military techniques . . . afford the most persuasive argument for ~ government —C.J.Friedrich⟩
su·per·nationalism \"+\ *n* **1** [*super-* + *nationalism*] **:** excessive pride or attachment to one's country **:** extreme nationalism or patriotism **2** [*supernational* + *-ism*] **:** advocacy of the formation of supernational organizations or governments **:** INTERNATIONALISM
su·per·nationalist \"+\ *n* [*super-* + *nationalist*] **:** an extreme nationalist ⟨the rallying point for extreme reactionary and . . . ~ leaders —E.K.Lindley⟩
1su·per·natural \"+\ *adj* [ML *supernaturalis*, fr. L *super-* + *natura* nature + *-alis* -al] **1 a :** of, belonging to, having reference to, or proceeding from an order of existence beyond the physical universe that is observable, and capable of being experienced by ordinary means **:** transcending nature in degree and in kind or concerned with what transcends nature ⟨a ~ divine order which directs history from outside and keeps man in touch with the eternal world through the Church and the sacraments —*Times Lit. Supp.*⟩ ⟨the ~ character of the soul⟩ **b :** being, having reference to, or proceeding from God or a god, demigod, spirit, or infernal being ⟨among primitive peoples today, the ~ scene is infinitely variegated —J.B.Noss⟩ ⟨inquired . . . whether the strangers were ~ beings, or men of flesh and blood —W.H.Prescott⟩ ⟨attributed to the sun and the moon ~ powers, made gods of them and worshiped them —*College English*⟩ **c :** divine as opposed to human, or spiritual as opposed to material ⟨to make students conscious of the fact that they are not merely natural men but that they have a ~ destiny —*St. John's University Cat.*⟩ ⟨man's ~ life, the life of the soul above the natural life of the body —M.W.Baldwin⟩ **2 a :** differing from the natural only in degree by being much more than natural or normal **:** SUPERHUMAN, PRETERNATURAL ⟨has come up with almost ~ speed —George Weller⟩ **b :** EXTREME, EXCESSIVE ⟨curs and mongrels . . . endowed with ~ powers of yelping —Rachel Henning⟩ **3 a :** ascribed to agencies or powers above or beyond nature or based upon such an ascription **:** initiated, effected, continued, or supported by means that transcend the laws or observed sequences of nature ⟨the ~ origin of life⟩; *esp* **:** MIRACULOUS ⟨possess the gift of second sight, and the power to wreak ~ vengeance upon those who offend them —Herman Melville⟩ ⟨did not mention the ~ events . . . for fear of encouraging skeptical laughter —Robert Graves⟩ **b :** attributable to or liable to be attributed to the action or presence of a ghost, spirit, or other invisible agent **:** EERIE, OCCULT ⟨something ~, a stirring as it were of the roots of the hair —W.B.Yeats⟩ — **su·per·naturally** \"+\ *adv* — **su·per·naturalness** \"+\ *n* -ES
2supernatural \"\ *n* **1 :** something that is supernatural **:** the supernatural order of existence **:** divine operation, influence or intervention — used with *the* ⟨the ~ is in its ultimate essence incomprehensible on our plane of existence —*Register*⟩ **2 :** something of supernatural origin **:** something miraculous or marvelous **3 :** a supernatural being, force, or essence ⟨the object itself (water, tree, or rock) which was worshiped as a ~ —W.A.L.Elmslie⟩
su·per·naturalism \ˌsüpə(r)+\ *n* [*1supernatural* + *-ism*] **1 :** the quality or state of being supernatural **2 :** belief in the supernatural; *specif* **:** a doctrine or creed that asserts the reality of an existence beyond nature and the control and guidance of nature and men by an invisible power
su·per·naturalist \"+\ *n* [*1supernatural* + *-ist*] **:** an advocate or adherent of supernaturalism
su·per·naturalistic \ˌ¦süpə(r)+\ *adj* [*supernaturalist* + *-ic*] **:** of or relating to supernaturalism
su·per·naturality \ˌsüpə(r)+\ *n* [ML *supernaturalitat-, supernaturalitas*, fr. *supernaturalis* supernatural + *-itat-, -itas* -ity] **1 :** the quality or state of being supernatural **:** SUPERNATURALISM **2 :** a supernatural event or thing
su·per·naturalize \"+\ *vt* [*1supernatural* + *-ize*] **1 :** to make supernatural **:** endow with supernatural qualities **2 :** to treat as supernatural
supernatural virtue *n* **:** THEOLOGICAL VIRTUE
su·per·nature \ˈsüpə(r)+\ *n* [*super-* + *nature*] **:** a realm or sphere of the supernatural ⟨for Plato, wisdom meant a knowledge not of nature, but of the ~ constituted by the ideas —Benjamin Farrington⟩
su·per·normal \ˌ¦süpə(r)+\ *adj* [*super-* + *normal*] **1 :** exceeding the normal or average ⟨~ employment, such as may occur in a war situation —Clark Warburton⟩ ⟨a phase of ~ excitability —C.H.Best & N.B.Taylor⟩ **2 :** being beyond natural powers esp. of man **:** not explicable naturally **:** PARANORMAL ⟨~ faculties of the mind —*Bell's Miscellany*⟩ ⟨~ manifestations⟩ ⟨a ~ experience⟩ — **su·per·normality** \"+\ *n* — **su·per·normally** \"+\ *adv*
su·per·nova \"+\ *n* [NL, fr. *super-* + *nova*] **:** one of the rarely observed nova outbursts in which the maximum intrinsic luminosity may reach 100 million times that of the sun
1su·per·nu·mer·ary \ˌ¦süpə(r)¦n(y)üməˌrerē, -ˌreri\ *adj* [LL *supernumerarius*, fr. L *super-* + *numerus* number + *-arius* -ary] **1 :** exceeding the usual, stated, or prescribed number ⟨a ~ tooth⟩ ⟨extra ribs, as well as other ~ internal parts —*Science News Letter*⟩; *specif* **:** not enumerated among the regular components of a group and esp. of a military organization or staff or of the line elements of a military organization ⟨offered the ~ position of inspector general —J.S.Roucek⟩ **2 :** exceeding what is necessary, required, or desired **:** SUPERFLUOUS ⟨the redundant subheading and ~ asterisk —*Punch*⟩ **3 :** being the more numerous ⟨in any population with an unbalanced sex composition . . . a larger number of members of the ~ sex remains in this group —*William & Mary Quarterly*⟩
2supernumerary \"\ *n, pl* **supernumeraries 1 :** a supernumerary person or thing: as **a :** a person employed not for regular service but for use in case of need **b :** an individual in excess of the number authorized for a given military or naval unit ⟨carried about two thousand men, including *supernumeraries* on a training course for sea experience —Stanley Rogers⟩ **c :** a person serving no apparent function ⟨reducing them both to the role of irrelevant *supernumeraries* —J.C. Powys⟩ **d :** an inert added member of a chromosome set **2 :** an actor employed to play a walk-on (as in a mob scene or spectacle)
supernumerary bud *n* **:** ACCESSORY BUD
supernumerary rainbow *n* **:** a faintly colored rainbow sometimes seen because of atmospheric interference next to a primary or secondary rainbow
supero- *comb form* [L *superus* upper — more at SUPERIOR] situated above ⟨*supero*anterior⟩ ⟨*supero*medial⟩
su·per·octave \ˌ¦süpə(r)+\ *n* [*super-* + *octave*] **1 :** the octave above a specific note or tone **2 :** a metal labial pipe-organ stop of 2-foot pitch
su·per·order \"+\ *n* [*super-* + *order*] **:** a taxonomic category ranking between an order and a subclass or a class when no subclass is recognized and in the latter case equivalent to a subclass
su·per·ordinal \"+\ *adj* [fr. *superorder*, after E *order: ordinal*] **:** of or relating to a superorder
su·per·ordinary \"+\ *adj* [*super-* + *ordinary*] **:** superior to or in excess of the ordinary ⟨a man of ~ probity —Jeremy Bentham⟩
1su·per·or·di·nate \ˌ¦süpə¦rȯrdᵊnət\ *adj* [*super-* + *-ordinate* (as in *subordinate*)] **1 :** superior in rank, class, or status ⟨the ~ whole may be represented for a person by a social unit —Andras Angyal⟩ ⟨two racial groups in ~ and subordinate positions —T.C.Cothran⟩ **2 :** bearing the logical relation of superordination
2superordinate \"\ *n* -s **:** a person or thing in a superordinate position
3su·per·or·di·nate \ˌ⸗⸗ˈrȯrdᵊnˌāt\ *vt* -ED/-ING/-S **:** to make superordinate ⟨the prosodic modifications which subordinate and ~ the heavy stresses in discourse —Stanley Newman⟩
su·per·or·di·na·tion \ˌ⸗⸗⸗ˈāshən\ *n* **1** [LL *superordination-, superordinatio*, fr. *superordinatus* (past part. of *superordinare* to appoint in addition, fr. L *super-* + *ordinare* to arrange, appoint) + *-ion-, -io* -ion — more at ORDAIN] **:** ordination of a person to fill a station already occupied; *esp* **:** the ordination by an ecclesiastical official of his own successor **2** [*super-* + *-ordination* (as in *subordination*)] **a :** the act or process of superordinating **:** DOMINANCE **b :** the relation of a universal proposition to a particular with the same terms
1su·per·organic \ˌ¦süpə(r)+\ *adj* [*super-* + *organic*] **:** of or relating to the sociocultural organization of a society including its language, arts, technology, and ethical and religious convictions conceived as a separate class, level, or order possessing independent properties of continuity, transmission, and capacity for change not necessarily derived from, or influenced by, organic or psychological factors ⟨culture is ~ and superindividual —A.L.Kroeber⟩
2superorganic \"\ *n* **:** the superorganic order of existence **:** the complex of superorganic phenomena — used with *the* ⟨material culture . . . is changing most rapidly and forcing the other parts of the ~, such as family life and religion, to make adjustments to it —W.F.Ogburn & M.F.Nimkoff⟩
su·per·organicism \ˌsüpə(r)+\ *n* **:** a sociological theory that asserts the reality or emphasizes the importance of superorganic phenomena
su·per·organicist \"+\ *n* **:** an advocate or adherent of superorganicism
su·per·organism \ˌ¦süpə(r)+\ *n* [*super-* + *organism*] **1 :** a huge or superior organism; *specif* **:** an organism that transcends through mind the organic or physical **2 a :** society or the state that is an integration of human beings into a whole comparable to the human organism in the diversity of its units and their mutual interdependence and in its superiority to yet limited dependence on the physically organic from which it springs **b :** a colony of social organisms (as ants) in which the members and castes are integrated in much the same way as the organs of a multicellular individual
su·per·ovulate \"+\ *vt* [back-formation fr. *superovulation*] **:** to induce excessive ovulation in (as by administration of hormones)
su·per·ovulation \"+\ *n* [*super-* + *ovulation*] **:** response to a superovulating technique; *broadly* **:** production of exceptional numbers of eggs at one time
su·per·oxide \"+\ *n* [*super-* + *oxide*] **:** a compound characterized by the univalent anion O_2^- consisting of two oxygen atoms, by paramagnetism, and by hydrolysis to hydrogen peroxide and oxygen ⟨potassium ~ KO_2⟩ — called also *hyperoxide*; compare PEROXIDE
su·per·ox·ol \ˌsüpəˈräkˌsōl, -kˌsȯl\ *n* -s [*super-* + *peroxide* + *-ol*] **:** a commercially produced hydrogen peroxide solution of 30 percent concentration
su·per·parasitism \ˌ¦süpə(r)+\ *n* **1** [*superparasite* + *-ism*] **:** HYPERPARASITISM **2** [*super-* + *parasitism*] **:** parasitization of a host by more than one parasitic individual usu. of one kind — used esp. of parasitic insects
su·per·particular \"+\ *adj* [LL *superparticularis*, fr. L *super-* + *particula* small part + *-aris* -ar — more at PARTICLE] **:** of or relating to a ratio in which the greater term exceeds the less by a unit ⟨the ratios of 4 to 3 and of 8 to 7 are ~⟩
su·per·par·ti·ent \ˌ¦süpə(r)¦pärd·ēənt\ *adj* [LL *superpartient-, superpartiens*, fr. L *super* + *partient-, partiens*, pres. part. of *partire* to divide — more at PART] **:** of or relating to a ratio in which the greater term exceeds the less by more than a unit ⟨the ratios of 5 to 3 and of 10 to 7 are ~⟩
su·per·patriot \ˌ¦süpə(r)+\ *n* [*super-* + *patriot*] **:** an excessively patriotic individual — **su·per·patriotic** \"+\ *adj*
su·per·patriotism \"+\ *n* [*superpatriot* + *-ism*] **:** excessive patriotism
su·per·personal \"+\ *adj* [*super-* + *personal*] **:** transcending the personal ⟨God's ~ being takes in and transcends all aspects of personality —Will Herberg⟩ ⟨technology . . . can be viewed as impersonal or ~ —A.L.Kroeber⟩
su·per·personality \"+\ *n* [*super-* + *personality*] **:** a deity or a collection of persons constituting a transcendent personality ⟨the people, once endowed with a will, had to be exalted into a ~ —K.R.Popper⟩
su·per·phosphate \ˌsüpə(r)+\ *n* [*super-* + *phosphate*] **:** any of various commercial phosphate fertilizers obtained as white to gray granules or powders by acidulating ground insoluble phosphate rock: as **a :** a product made by acidulating with sulfuric acid, consisting essentially of soluble primary calcium phosphate, calcium sulfate, and smaller amounts of secondary calcium phosphate, and containing usu. about 20 percent of available phosphoric acid — called also *acid phosphate, ordinary superphosphate* **b :** a product made by acidulating with phosphoric acid, consisting essentially of primary calcium phosphate, and containing usu. 40 to 50 percent of available phosphoric acid — called also *concentrated superphosphate, double superphosphate, treble superphosphate, triple superphosphate*
su·per·physical \ˌ¦süpə(r)+\ *adj* [*super-* + *physical*] **:** being above or beyond the physical world or explanation on physical principles **:** HYPERPHYSICAL, METAPHYSICAL
su·per·polyamide \ˌ¦süpə(r)+\ *n* [*super-* + *polyamide*] **:** a polyamide (as nylon) capable of forming fibers
su·per·polymer \"+\ *n* [*super-* + *polymer*] **:** a polymer (as a superpolyamide) composed of very large molecules — compare HIGH POLYMER, MACROMOLECULE
su·per·pos·able \ˌ¦süpə(r)¦pōzəbəl\ *adj* **:** capable of being superposed
su·per·pose \-ōz\ *vt* -ED/-ING/-S [prob. fr. F *superposer*, back-formation fr. *superposition*] **1 :** to place or lay over or above so as to rest or to be one of a vertical series or tier **:** superimpose with or without contact ⟨films taken on two successive days can be *superposed* —G.R.Harrison⟩ ⟨*superposed* rock strata⟩ **2 a :** to cause to occupy the same position as and coexist with another ⟨~ an electric wave upon another⟩ ⟨~ two images from different light sources⟩ **b :** to lay (a geometric figure) upon another so as to make all like parts coincide **3 :** SUPERIMPOSE ⟨~ modern industry on a backward agriculture —*Atlantic*⟩
superposed *adj* [fr. past part. of *superpose*] **1 :** growing or situated vertically over another part or organ **2** *of floral parts* **:** OPPOSITE ⟨stamens ~ to petals⟩
su·per·po·si·tion \ˌsüpə(r)pəˈzishən\ *n* [F, fr. LL *superposition-, superpositio* action of laying on, fr. L *superpositus* (past part. of *superponere* to place on top, lay on, fr. *super-* + *ponere* to place) + *-ion-, -io* -ion — more at POSITION] **:** the act or process of superposing or the state of being superposed
superposition eye *n* **:** an insect eye in which all light rays except those entering the central facet of a group of facets are intercepted — compare APPOSITION EYE
superposition principle *n* **:** a statement in physics: if two or more physical causes are vectorially additive and if the effects are proportional to the causes, the effects are vectorially additive
su·per·power \ˈsüpə(r)+,-\ *n* [*super-* + *power*] **1 :** power that is excessive, abnormal, or superior to existing power **2 a :** an extremely powerful nation; *specif* **:** one of a very few dominant states in an era when the world is divided politically into these states and their satellites **b :** an international governing body able to enforce its will upon the most powerful states **3 :** electric power developed by the coordinated utilization of all available power plants in a large area as connected parts of one system — **su·per·powered** \"+,-\ *adj*
su·per·race \ˈsüpə(r)+,-\ *n* [*super-* + *race*] **:** a race or nation of men held to be superior to others
su·per·rational \ˌ¦süpə(r)+\ *adj* [*super-* + *rational*] **:** transcending the power of reason ⟨~ intuition⟩
su·per·realism \"+\ *n* [trans. of F *surréalisme*] **:** SURREALISM
su·per·realist \"+\ *n* [trans. of F *surréaliste*] **:** SURREALIST
su·per·refractory \"+\ *n* [*super-* + *refractory*] **:** a superior pure oxide refractory
su·per·regeneration \"+\ *n* [*super-* + *regeneration*] **:** regeneration in an electronic circuit that by periodic usu. supersonic changes in the operating conditions (as a reduction of the operating voltage of a tube) prohibits free oscillation and gives the circuit a very high sensitivity to radio signals
su·per·regenerative \"+\ *adj* [*superregeneration* + *-ive*] **:** of or relating to superregeneration
supers *pl of* SUPER, *pres 3d sing of* SUPER
su·per·salesman \ˌ¦süpə(r)+\ *n* [*super-* + *salesman*] **:** an extremely successful salesman — **su·per·salesmanship** \"+\ *n*
su·per·salt \ˈsüpə(r)+,-\ *n* [*super-* + *salt*; fr. the excess of acid over base] **:** an acid salt
su·per·saturate \ˌ¦süpə(r)+\ *vt* [*super-* + *saturate*] **:** to add to beyond saturation ⟨a *supersaturated* solution⟩ ⟨*supersaturated* vapor⟩ — **su·per·saturation** \"+\ *n*
su·per·scribe \ˈsüpə(r),skrīb, ˌ⸗⸗ˈ⸗\ *vt* [L *superscribere*, fr. *super-* + *scribere* to write — more at SCRIBE] **1 :** to write or engrave on the top or surface of, outside, or directly above an object ⟨interlinear corrections . . . are often hidden by smudges or by *superscribed* Latin characters —W.H.Bennett⟩ ⟨bars *superscribed* to distinguish the numerals from words —D.E. Smith⟩ **2 :** to write or engrave on the top or surface, outside, or directly above ⟨~ each letter with a number indicating its relative order alphabetically —J.M.Wolfe⟩; *specif* **:** to write a name, title, greeting, description, or esp. an address on the outside, head, or cover of ⟨must be sent by registered post . . . and must be *superscribed* "Tenders for Agricultural Implements" —*Times of India*⟩ ⟨the epistle was *superscribed* "To the Laodicians" —T.W.Manson⟩
1su·per·script \ˈ⸗⸗,skript\ *n* [L *superscriptus*, past part. of *superscribere* to superscribe] **1** *obs* **:** an address written at the head of a letter **2** [*2superscript*] **:** a superscript character
2superscript \"\ *adj* [L *superscriptus*, past part. of *superscribere*] **1 :** of, relating to, or being a usu. smaller character printed or written directly above another character (as the tilde in ñ) **2 :** of, relating to, or being a usu. smaller character printed above and to the side of another character (as the ³ in a^3) — compare ADSCRIPT, SUBSCRIPT
su·per·scrip·tion \ˌ⸗⸗ˈskripshən\ *n* [ME, fr. MF, fr. LL *superscription-, superscriptio*, fr. L *superscriptus* (past part. of *superscribere* to superscribe) + *-ion-, -io* -ion] **1 :** something that is written or engraved on the surface of, outside, or above something else (as an address on a letter or envelope, an inscription, title, or description) ⟨letters to His Majesty the King bear the ~ "To the King's Most Excellent Majesty" —Noreen Routledge⟩ ⟨coins worn by abrasion must be accepted so long as the ~ thereon can be distinguished —*U.S. Post Office Manual*⟩ ⟨some that bear the ~ "A Psalm of David" —A.J.Feldman⟩ **2 :** the part of a pharmaceutical prescription which contains the Latin word *recipe* or the sign ℞
su·per·secret \ˌ¦süpə(r)+\ *adj* [*super-* + *secret*] **:** extremely secret
su·per·sed·able \ˌ¦süpə(r)¦sēdəbəl\ *adj* **:** capable of being superseded
su·per·sede *or* **su·per·cede** \ˌ¦süpə(r)¦sēd\ *vb* -ED/-ING/-S [MF *superseder* to refrain from, postpone, fr. L *supersedēre* to sit above, be superior to, forbear, refrain from, fr. *super-* + *sedēre* to sit — more at SIT] *vt* **1** *law* **a :** POSTPONE, DEFER **b :** to fail to proceed with **:** DISCONTINUE **c** *obs* **:** to refrain from **:** OMIT, FORBEAR **d :** to suspend the operation (of a judgment or order) by means of a supersedeas **2** *obs* **:** to omit mention of **3 a :** to make obsolete, inferior, or outmoded ⟨the lapse of time has *superseded* his astronomical system —Benjamin Farrington⟩ **b :** to make void **:** ANNUL, OVERRIDE ⟨established the principle that the welfare of a child *superseded* judgments rendered by the courts —*Current Biog.*⟩ **c :** to make superfluous or unnecessary ⟨this brief account . . . is intended to ~ the necessity of a long and minute detail —Jane Austen⟩ **4 :** to take the place of and outmode by superiority **:** supplant and make inferior by better or more efficiently serving a function ⟨the automobile began to ~ the horse —*Amer. Guide Series: Minn.*⟩ ⟨the canal never paid . . . because railroads have *superseded* it —Samuel Van Valkenburg & Ellsworth Huntington⟩ **5 a :** to cause to be supplanted in a position or function ⟨in course of time this organization would have to be *superseded* by another —Shlomo Katz⟩ **b :** to succeed to the position, office, or function of **:** take the place of ⟨the department . . . *superseded* the geologic and economic survey —*Amer. Guide Series: N.C.*⟩ ⟨~ another as chairman⟩ **6 :** to follow after in the course of time ⟨as truth prevails over error . . . goodness tends to ~ badness —Samuel Alexander⟩ **7 :** to take

precedence over ⟨the movement for adjournment ~*s* the bill under discussion⟩ ~ *vi* **:** to defer action **:** FORBEAR ⟨~ to name the many other difficulties —F.W.Newman⟩ **syn** see REPLACE

su·per·se·de·as \\ˌ⸗⸗ˈsēdēəs\\ *n, pl* **supersedeas** [ME, fr. ML, fr. L, you shall desist, 2d sing. pres. subj. of *supersedēre* to supersede; fr. the occurrence of the word in the writ] **1 a :** a common-law writ commanding a stay of legal proceedings issued under various conditions and esp. to stay an officer from proceeding under another writ **b :** an order staying proceedings esp. of an inferior court that is issued under statutory authority **2** *obs* **:** something that serves as a stay or check

superseded suretyship *n* [fr. past part. of *supersede*] **:** provision for continuity of protection when a new fidelity bond replaces one previously covering the same employees

su·per·sed·ence \\ˌ⸗⸗ˈsēdᵊn(t)s\\ *n* -S [*supersede* + *-ence*] **:** SUPERSEDURE

su·per·sed·er \\¦⸗⸗¦sēdə(r)\\ *n* -S **:** one that supersedes

su·per·se·de·re \\ˌsüpə(r)səˈdārē\\ *n* -S [L *supersedēre* to supersede] **:** a judicial order or a private agreement among creditors in Scots law granting a debtor stay of diligence

su·per·se·dure \\ˌsüpə(r)ˈsējə(r)\\ *n* -S [*supersede* + *-ure*] **:** the act or process of superseding; *specif* **:** the replacement of an old or inferior queen bee by a young or superior queen either naturally by the honeybees or artfully by the beekeeper — compare DEQUEEN

su·per·seniority \\¦süpə(r)+\\ *n* [*super-* + *seniority*] **:** seniority unrelated to length of actual service; *esp* **:** additional service sometimes credited to a union official or veteran or granted temporarily to insure a union official being employed while holding office — called also *synthetic seniority*

[1]**su·per·sensible** \\"+\\ *adj* [*super-* + *sensible*] **:** being above or beyond that which is perceivable or apparent to the senses ⟨seeks ~ goals such as eternal life, justice, both social and individual, the progress of human culture and science, the development of moral codes —Peter Dunne⟩ **:** SPIRITUAL, PSYCHICAL

[2]**supersensible** \\"\\ *n* -S **1 :** a supersensible entity **2 :** the sphere of supersensible entities ⟨his teaching that genuine knowledge is knowledge of the ~, the transcendental —G.C. Sellery⟩

su·per·sensitive \\¦süpə(r)+\\ *adj* [*super-* + *sensitive*] **1 :** HYPERSENSITIVE **2 :** that has been supersensitized ⟨a ~ emulsion⟩ **3 :** that will function on contact with a very light object — used of a fuze in an artillery shell — **su·per·sensi·tiveness** \\"+\\ *n*

su·per·sensitivity \\"+\\ *n* [*supersensitive* + *-ity*] **:** HYPERSENSITIVITY

su·per·sensitization \\"+\\ *n* **:** the act or process of supersensitizing

su·per·sensitize \\"+\\ *vt* [*supersensitive* + *-ize*] **1 :** HYPERSENSITIZE **2 a :** to increase the sensitizing effect of (a dye) by using with another dye or compound so that their combined effect is greater than the sum of their separate effects **b :** to increase the speed of (an emulsion) by means of a chemical

su·per·sensitizer \\"+\\ *n* [*supersensitize* + *-er*] **:** a dye or other compound used in photography to increase the sensitizing effect of a dye

su·per·sensory \\"+\\ *adj* [*super-* + *sensory*] **:** being above or beyond the power of the senses ⟨~ perception⟩

su·per·sensual \\"+\\ *adj* [*super-* + *sensual*] **:** transcending sense **:** SUPERSENSIBLE, IDEAL

su·per·sensuous \\"+\\ *adj* [*super-* + *sensuous*] **:** SUPERSENSUAL

su·per·septal \\"+\\ *adj* [NL *super-* + *septum* + E *-al*] **:** located above a septum

su·per·serviceable \\"+\\ *adj* [*super-* + *serviceable*] **:** doing or offering superfluous and unwanted services **:** OVEROFFICIOUS

su·per·ses·sion \\ˌsüpə(r)ˈseshən\\ *n* -S [ML *supersession-*, *supersessio*, fr. L *supersessus* (past part. of *supersedēre* to supersede) + *-ion-*, *-io* -ion] **:** the state of being superseded **:** removal and replacement **:** SUPERSEDURE ⟨the ~ of national imperialism by a genuinely international government —J.A. Hobson⟩

su·per·ses·sive \\¦⸗⸗¦sesiv\\ *adj* [L *supersessus* + E *-ive*] **:** superseding or tending to supersede

su·per·ses·sor \\-esə(r)\\ *n* -S [L *supersessus* + *-or*] **:** SUPERSEDER

su·per·size *or* **su·per·sized** \\¦süpə(r)+\\ *adj* [*super-* + *size* or *sized*] **:** of extremely large size

[1]**su·per·sonic** \\¦süpə(r)¦sänik, -nēk\\ *adj* [L *super-* + *sonus* sound + E *-ic* — more at SOUND] **1 :** having a frequency above the audibility range of the human ear or greater than about 20,000 cycles per second — used of waves and vibrations; compare INFRASONIC, SONIC **2 :** utilizing, produced by, or relating to supersonic waves or vibrations ⟨~ testing of metal⟩ ⟨~ disintegration of a chemical⟩ **3 :** of, indicating, or relating to speeds from one to five times the speed of sound in air — compare SONIC, TRANSONIC **4 :** moving, capable of moving, or utilizing air currents moving at supersonic speed ⟨~ airplane⟩ ⟨~ wind tunnel⟩ **5 :** relating to supersonic aircraft or missiles ⟨~ age⟩ **6 :** having a quality (as speed, virtue, or intensity) to an extreme degree **:** SUPER ⟨a recording of almost ~ realism — Irving Kolodin⟩ ⟨a ~ version . . . delivered breathlessly in one minute flat —Winston Brebner⟩ — **su·per·son·i·cal·ly** \\-nək(ə)lē, -nēk-, -li\\ *adv*

[2]**supersonic** \\"\\ *n* -S **:** a supersonic wave or frequency

su·per·son·ics \\ˌ⸗⸗ˈ⸗niks, -nēks\\ *n pl but usu sing in constr* [fr. [1]*supersonic*, after such pairs as E *economic: economics*] **:** the science of supersonic phenomena

supersonic velocity *n* **:** a fluid velocity relative to a body in the fluid that is greater than the local velocity of sound in the fluid

su·per·sound \\ˈsüpə(r)+ˌ-\\ *n* [*super-* + *sound*] **:** ULTRASOUND

su·per·species \\¦süpə(r)+\\ *n* [*super-* + *species*] **:** ARTENKREIS

su·per·spectacle \\"+\\ *n* [*super-* + *spectacle*] **:** something extremely spectacular

su·per·speed \\ˈsüpə(r)+ˌ-\\ *adj* [*super-* + *speed*] **:** designed to operate at exceedingly high speeds ⟨~ film⟩ ⟨~ airplane⟩

su·per·spinous \\¦süpə(r)+\\ *adj* [*super-* + *spine* + *-ous*] **:** SUPRASPINOUS

su·per·state \\ˈsüpə(r)+ˌ-\\ *n* [*super-* + *state*] **1 a :** SUPERGOVERNMENT 1 **b :** a regional group having governmental powers over a group of states **2 :** a totalitarian state **3 :** SUPERPOWER 2a

su·per·sti·tion \\ˌsüpə(r)ˈstishən\\ *n* -S [ME *supersticion*, fr. MF, fr. L *superstition-*, *superstitio*, fr. *superstit-*, *superstes* standing over (as witness, victor, or survivor) (fr. *super-* + *-stit-* — akin to *stare* to stand) + *-ion-*, *-io* -ion — more at STAND] **1 a :** a belief, conception, act, or practice resulting from ignorance, unreasoning fear of the unknown or mysterious, morbid scrupulosity, trust in magic or chance, or a false conception of causation ⟨the ~ that a black cat crossing one's path portends bad luck⟩ ⟨~*s* such as child-sacrifice, divination, soothsaying, enchantments, sorceries, charms (by magic knots, spells, or incantations), ghosts, spiritualistic mediums, necromancy —D.R.Scott⟩ **b :** an irrational abject attitude of mind toward the supernatural, nature, or God resulting from such beliefs, conceptions, or fears **2 a :** idolatrous religion **b :** IDOLATRY ⟨an alien religion whose ~*s* and ritual were regarded with abhorrence —J.H.Plumb⟩ **3 :** a fixed irrational idea **:** a notion maintained in spite of evidence to the contrary ⟨the ~ that society can only be built on a foundation of unconditional command and absolute obedience —Karl Renner⟩

su·per·sti·tion·ist \\-sh(ə)nəst\\ *n* -S **:** a person addicted to superstition

su·per·sti·tion·less \\-shənləs\\ *adj* **:** not given to superstition

su·per·sti·tious \\¦süpə(r)¦stishəs\\ *adj* [ME *supersticious*, fr. MF *supersticieux*, fr. L *superstitiosus*, fr. *superstitio* superstition + *-osus* -ous] **1 a :** of, relating to, proceeding from, characterized by, or manifesting superstition ⟨while . . . I used to ascribe the horror he felt . . . to a reasonable cause . . . I came to realize that in origin it, too, was ~ —Osbert Sitwell⟩ **b :** addicted to or swayed by superstition ⟨the darkness and the strange blue streetlights make him . . . ~ —Alexander Forbes⟩ **c :** of, relating to, or used by the adherents of a creed regarded as a superstition **2** *obs* **:** excessively or morbidly scrupulous **:** PUNCTILIOUS **3** *obs* **:** extravagant in loving **:** overly devoted — **su·per·sti·tious·ly** *adv* — **su·per·sti·tious·ness** *n* -ES

superstitious use *n, Eng law* **:** the use of a gift or bequest (as of land) for the maintenance of religious rites not tolerated by the law

superstr *abbr* superstructure

su·per·stratum \\¦süpə(r)+\\ *n* [*super-* + *-stratum* (as in *substratum*)] **1 :** an overlying stratum or layer **2 :** a language spoken for a limited time in the past in a region usu. by a dominant minority

su·per·strength \\"+\\ *n* [*super-* + *strength*] **:** extremely great strength

su·per·struct \\¦süpə(r)¦strəkt\\ *vt* -ED/-ING/-S [L *superstructus*, past part. of *superstruere* to build on or over — more at SUPERSTRUCTURE] **:** to build over or on a structure **:** erect on a foundation

su·per·structural \\¦süpə(r)+\\ *adj* **:** of, relating to, or resembling a superstructure

su·per·structure \\ˈsüpə(r)+ˌ-\\ *n* [L *superstructus* (past part. of *superstruere* to build on or over, fr. *super-* + *struere* to build) + E *-ure* — more at STRUCTURE] **1 :** a structure built on or as a vertical extension of something else **:** something that is raised on a foundation: as **a :** all of a building above the basement **b :** the structural part of a ship above the main deck **c :** the ties, rails, and fastenings of a railroad track in distinction from the roadbed **2 :** an entity, concept, or complex naturally or logically arising from or being based or imposed upon another more original or fundamental entity, concept, or complex ⟨this credit ~ rested on commodities, the collateral, rather than on the hard money —W.P.Webb⟩ ⟨a small nubbin of fact . . . used as the foundation for a ~ of inference and suspicion —Elmer Davis⟩; *specif* **:** an organization of ideas (as an ideology) or of persons (as a state bureaucracy) conceived as existing on a higher less functional level in relation to the fundamental operation of society ⟨the principle that the form of economy determines the political ~ —L.S. Feuer⟩ ⟨saying that religion is a mere ~ . . . in the class struggle —David Riesman⟩ **3 :** a regular arrangement of the atoms of a solute in the solvent crystals of an alloy that is characteristic of the solute and not of the solvent

superstructure deck *n* **:** a partial deck above a weather deck and not reaching to the sides of the vessel

su·per·substantial \\¦süpə(r)+\\ *adj* [LL *supersubstantialis*, fr. L *super-* + *substantia* substance + *-alis* -al] **:** being above material substance **:** of a transcending substance — **su·per·substantiality** \\"+\\ *n*

su·per·subtle \\"+\\ *adj* [*super-* + *subtle*] **:** extremely or excessively subtle — **su·per·subtlety** \\"+\\ *n*

su·per·system \\"+\\ *n* [*super-* + *system*] **:** a system made up of systems

su·per·tanker \\"+\\ *n* [*super-* + *tanker*] **:** an exceptionally large and fast tanker

su·per·tax \\"+ˌ-\\ *n* [*super-* + *tax*] **:** a tax in addition to the usual or normal tax: as **a :** SURTAX **b :** a graduated income tax in addition to the normal income tax imposed in the United Kingdom on the amount by which the total income of a person exceeds a certain sum

su·per·temporal \\¦süpə(r)+\\ *adj* [*super-* + *temporal*] **:** being beyond time **:** ETERNAL

su·per·ter·ra·nean \\¦süpə(r)tə¦rānēən, -ānyən\\ *also* **su·per·ter·ra·ne·ous** \\-ānēəs\\ *adj* [*super-* + *-terranean*, *-terraneous* (as in *subterranean*, *subterraneous*)] **:** lying, dwelling, or active above or on the earth's surface

su·per·ter·rene \\¦süpə(r)tə¦rēn, -te¦r-\\ *adj* [LL *superterrenus*, fr. *super-* + *terra* earth — more at TERRACE] **:** SUPERTERRANEAN

su·per·terrestrial \\¦süpə(r)+\\ *adj* [*super-* + *terrestrial*] **:** SUPERTERRANEAN

su·per·tonic \\"+\\ *n* [*super-* + *tonic*] **:** the second tone of the musical scale

su·per·tunic *or* **su·per·tunica** \\"+\\ *n* [ML *supertunica*, fr. L *super-* + *tunica* tunic] **:** a loose garment worn over a tunic; *specif* **:** a coronation robe

superv *abbr* supervision

su·per·vene \\¦süpə(r)¦vēn\\ *vb* -ED/-ING/-S [L *supervenire* to come upon, come in addition, fr. *super-* + *venire* to come — more at COME] *vi* **:** to take place after or late in the course of something else as an additional, adventitious, or unlooked-for development with intervening or countering effect ⟨what generally spoils long novels is the untimely *supervening* creative fatigue —Arnold Bennett⟩ ⟨an event *supervened* that brought disaster to my uncle's family —George Santayana⟩ ~ *vt* **:** to supervene upon **:** follow after **:** SUPERSEDE ⟨the new development is further *supervened* the following year —H.M. Muncheryan⟩ **syn** see FOLLOW

su·per·ve·nience \\ˌsüpə(r)ˈvēnyən(t)s\\ *n* -S [fr. *supervenient*, after such pairs as E *excellent: excellence*] **:** the character, condition, or fact of being supervenient

su·per·ve·nient \\¦⸗⸗¦vēnyənt\\ *adj* [L *supervenient-*, *superveniens*, pres. part. of *supervenire* to supervene] **:** coming or occurring as something additional, extraneous, or unexpected

su·per·ven·tion \\ˌsüpə(r)ˈvenchən\\ *n* -S [LL *supervention-*, *superventio*, fr. L *superventus* (past part. of *supervenire* to supervene) + *-ion-*, *-io* -ion] **:** the act, process, or an instance of supervening ⟨the ~ of an interest stronger than his practical interests —Susanne K. Langer⟩

su·per·vis·al \\¦süpə(r)¦vīzəl\\ *n* -S [[1]*supervise* + *-al*] **:** SUPERVISION ⟨~ by the central government —Thomas Carlyle⟩

[1]**su·per·vise** \\ˈsüpə(r)ˌvīz *also* ˌ⸗⸗ˈ⸗\\ *vt* -ED/-ING/-S [ML *supervisus*, past part. of *supervidēre* to look over, inspect, oversee, fr. L *super-* + *vidēre* to see — more at WIT] **1** *obs* **:** to look over in order to read **:** PERUSE, SCAN **2 :** to coordinate, direct, and inspect continuously and at first hand the accomplishment of **:** oversee with the powers of direction and decision the implementation of one's own or another's intentions **:** SUPERINTEND ⟨~ the future disposition of voting shares —*Current Biog.*⟩ ⟨~ the newspaper's own foreign and domestic correspondents —Bruce Westby⟩ ⟨*supervised* the young institution in a paternalistic way —H.E.Starr⟩

[2]**supervise** *n* -S *obs* **:** PERUSAL

supervised study *n* [fr. past part. of [1]*supervise*] **:** study or preparation of lessons by a class or group in the presence of a teacher who maintains order and may assist individual pupils in improving methods and habits of study

su·per·vis·ee \\ˌ⸗⸗¦vī¦zē\\ *n* -S [[1]*supervise* + *-ee*] **:** a person being supervised

su·per·vi·sion \\ˌsüpə(r)ˈvizhən *also* ˈ⸗⸗ˌ⸗⸗\\ *n* -S [ML *supervision-*, *supervisio*, fr. *supervisus* (past part. of *supervidere*) + L *-ion-*, *-io* -ion] **:** the act, process, or occupation of supervising **:** direction, inspection, and critical evaluation **:** OVERSIGHT, SUPERINTENDENCE ⟨under the ~ of an unbiased international commission —*Current Biog.*⟩

su·per·vi·sor \\ˈ⸗⸗ˌvīzə(r) *also* ˌ⸗⸗ˈ⸗⸗\\ *n* -S [ME, fr. ML, fr. *supervisus* + L *-or*] **1 :** one that supervises a person, group, department, organization, or operation: as **a :** such a person having authority delegated by an employer to hire, transfer, suspend, recall, promote, assign, or discharge another employee or to recommend such action **b :** the popularly elected chief administrative official of a township or other county subdivision in some states of the U.S. **c :** ROADMASTER 1 **d :** an officer of a school system who assists and supervises teachers in curriculum planning and methods of instruction or in the teaching of a special subject ⟨~ of music⟩ ⟨art ~⟩ **2** *obs* **:** ONLOOKER, SPECTATOR **3** *archaic* **:** one who reads over esp. a book for correction **:** REVISER

supervisor district *n* **:** BEAT 9a

su·per·vi·so·ri·al \\¦⸗⸗ˌvī¦zōrēəl\\ *adj* [*supervisor* + *-ial*] **:** of or relating to a supervisor

su·per·vi·sor·ship \\¦süpə(r)¦vīzə(r)ˌship\\ *n* [ME, fr. *supervisor* + *-ship*] **:** the office or function of a supervisor

su·per·vi·so·ry \\¦süpə(r)¦vīz(ə)r|ē, |i\\ *adj* [ML *supervisus* (past part. of *supervidēre* to supervise) + E *-ory*] **:** of or relating to supervision ⟨~ position⟩

su·per·voltage \\¦süpə(r)+\\ *adj* [*super-* + *voltage*] **:** of or relating to very high X-ray voltage ⟨~ radiation therapy⟩

su·per·woman \\ˈsüpə(r)+ˌ-\\ *n, pl* **superwomen** [*super-* + *woman*] **:** a superior woman **:** a strong-minded, efficient, and forceful woman

su·per·zealot \\¦süpə(r)+\\ *n* [*super-* + *zealot*] **:** an extremely earnest zealot

supes *pl of* SUPE, *pres 3d sing of* SUPE

su·pi·nate \\ˈsüpəˌnāt\\ *vb* -ED/-ING/-S [L *supinatus*, past part. of *supinare* to lay backward or on the back] *vt* **:** to cause to assume a position of supination ~ *vi* **:** to assume a position of supination

su·pi·na·tion \\ˌsüpəˈnāshən\\ *n* -S [L *supinatus* (past part. of *supinare* to lay backward or on the back, fr. *supinus* supine) + E *-ion*] **1 :** a rotation of the hand and radius around the ulna so that the palm is turned up; *also* **:** the position resulting from this movement — opposed to *pronation* **2 :** a corresponding movement of the foot and leg

su·pi·na·tor \\ˈsüpəˌnād·ə(r)\\ *n* -S [NL, fr. L *supinatus* + *-or*] **:** a muscle that produces the motion of supination; *specif* **:** a deeply situated muscle of the forearm that arises in two layers from the lateral epicondyle of the humerus and adjacent parts of the ligaments and bones of the elbow and passing over the head of the radius is inserted into its neck and the lateral surface of its shaft

[1]**su·pine** \\səˈpīn, (ˈ)sü¦p-\\ *adj* [L *supinus* lying on the back, moving backward; akin to L *sub* under, up — more at UP] **1 a :** lying on the back or with the face upward — opposed to *prone* **b :** marked by supination **2 :** manifesting mental or moral lethargy **:** indifferent to one's duty or welfare or others' needs **:** lacking stamina **:** ABJECT ⟨condition of static lethargy and ~ incuriousness —Aldous Huxley⟩ ⟨the clergy as a whole were therefore obedient and ~ —G.M.Trevelyan⟩ **3** *archaic* **:** leaning or sloping backward **:** INCLINED **syn** see INACTIVE, PRONE

[2]**su·pine** \\ˈsüˌpīn\\ *n* -S [ME *supyn*, fr. LL *supinum*, fr. L, neut. of *supinus* lying on the back] **1 :** a Latin verbal noun either in the accusative case in *-um* used after verbs of motion to denote purpose (as in *abiit piscatum* "he's gone fishing") or in the ablative in *-u* used as an ablative of specification (as in *difficile dictu* "hard to say") **2 :** an English infinitive with *to*

su·pine·ly \\səˈpīnlē, (ˈ)sü¦p-, -li\\ *adv* **:** in a supine manner ⟨called the tune to me, who ~ took it up —Jean Stafford⟩

su·pine·ness \\-īnnəs\\ *n* -ES **:** the quality or state of being supine ⟨~ and dogmatism take the place of inquiry —*Harper's*⟩

suping *pres part of* SUPE

su·pin·i·ty \\səˈpinəd·ē, süˈp-\\ *n* -ES [L *supinitat-*, *supinitas*, fr. *supinus* supine + *-itat-*, *-itas* -ity] **:** SUPINENESS ⟨Eastern government rested not so much on consent or force, as on the common ~ —T.E.Lawrence⟩

supls *abbr* supplies

supp *or* **suppl** *abbr* supplement; supplementary

suppawn *var of* SUPAWN

supped *past of* SUP

sup·pe·da·ne·um \\ˌsəpəˈdānēəm\\ *n, pl* **suppeda·nea** \\-ēə\\ [LL, footstool, fr. neut. of *suppedaneus* under the feet] **1 :** a support for the feet on a cross used for crucifixions **2 :** PREDELLA 1a

[1]**sup·per** \\ˈsəpə(r)\\ *n* -S *often attrib* [ME *soper*, *super*, *supper*, fr. OF *soper*, *super*, *souper*, fr. *soper*, *super*, *souper* to eat the evening meal — more at SUP] **1 a :** a meal taken at the close of the day; *esp* **:** the evening meal when dinner is taken at midday **b :** a social affair featuring a supper; *specif* **:** an evening social (as a box social) esp. for raising funds for charitable or other purposes ⟨church ~⟩ ⟨pie ~⟩ **c :** a usu. light evening meal ⟨have ~ after the theater⟩ **2 :** EUCHARIST 1a

[2]**supper** \\"\\ *vb* -ED/-ING/-S *vt* **1 :** to give supper to **:** entertain at supper **2 :** to feed and bed (as a horse) at night ~ *vi* **:** to eat one's supper

[3]**supper** \\"\\ *n* -S [[1]*sup* + *-er*] *Scot* **:** one that sups **:** SUCKER

supper club *n* [[1]*supper*] **:** NIGHTCLUB

sup·per·less \\ˈsəpə(r)ləs\\ *adj* [[1]*supper* + *-less*] **:** lacking supper

suppertime \\ˈ⸗⸗ˌ⸗\\ *n* [ME *soper tyme*, fr. *soper* supper + *time*, *tyme* time] **:** the time at which it is customary to eat supper

sup·ping \\ˈsəpən, ˈsu̇p-, ˈsüp-, -piŋ\\ *n* -S [ME, fr. gerund of *suppen* to sup, sip] *dial Brit* **:** soft or liquid food **:** BROTH

sup·plant \\səˈplant, -laa(ə)nt, -laint, -lånt\\ *vt* -ED/-ING/-S [ME *supplanten*, fr. MF *supplanter* fr. L *supplantare* to overthrow by tripping up, throw down, fr. *sub-* + *planta* sole of the foot — more at PLACE] **1** *obs* **:** to cause to fall **:** trip up **2** *archaic* **:** to cause the downfall of **:** bring low in estate, power, potency, or virtue **3 :** to supersede (another) esp. by force, trickery, or treachery **:** usurp the place or possessions of ⟨the pretty young wife finds herself . . . having been ~*ed* by a brisk, unlovely woman —Gerald Bullett⟩ **4 a** (1) *obs* **:** to root out **:** UPROOT (2) **:** to completely remove from a situation and replace **:** eradicate and supply a substitute for ⟨~ hysteria with common sense —Bradford Smith⟩ ⟨the attempt of an alien administration to ~ the vernacular —R.M.Lovett⟩ ⟨attempts to ~ the representational theory by a position which it considers more adequate —Hunter Mead⟩ **b :** to take the place of **:** oust from a position and serve as a substitute for esp. by reason of superior excellence or power ⟨this cheap and useful material rapidly ~*ed* the expensive iron —Tom Marvel⟩ ⟨it supplements rather than ~*s* the private agencies —*Times Lit. Supp.*⟩ **syn** see REPLACE

sup·plan·ta·tion \\(ˌ)səˌplan·ˈtāshən\\ *n* -S [ME, fr. MF, fr. LL *supplantation-*, *supplantatio*, fr. L *supplantatus* (past part. of *supplantare* to overthrow) + *-ion-*, *-io* -ion] **:** the act or process of supplanting **:** DISPOSSESSION, SUPERSESSION

sup·plant·er *pronunc at* SUPPLANT +ə(r)\\ *n* -S [ME, fr. *supplanten* to supplant + *-er*] **:** one that supplants

[1]**sup·ple** \\ˈsəpəl, ÷ˈsüp-\\ *adj, usu* **suppler** \\-p(ə)lə(r)\\ *usu* **supplest** \\-p(ə)ləst\\ [ME *souple*, fr. OF, yielding, pliant, fr. L *supplic-*, *supplex* submissive, suppliant, lit., bending under, fr. *sub-* + *-plic-* (akin to *plicare* to fold) — more at PLY] **1 a :** characterized by suggestibility, yielding compliance, or complaisance often to the point of being artfully or servilely obsequious **b :** characterized by ready adaptability to new situations, flexibility, and responsiveness ⟨the ~ spirit is hidden under an external directness and rough assertion — Hilaire Belloc⟩ **2 a :** characterized by an ability to bend, twist, or fold without creases, cracks, breaks, or other injuries **:** pliant, soft, and yielding in texture ⟨~ leather⟩ **b :** characterized by ease and readiness in bending or other actions and often by grace and agility **:** not stiff and awkward **c :** easy and fluent without stiffness, awkwardness, or turgidity ⟨sang with a lively, ~ voice —Douglas Watt⟩ ⟨his painting . . . is remarkably ~ in line and pattern —R.M.Coates⟩ **3** *Scot* **:** SLY, CUNNING

syn LIMBER, LITHE, LITHESOME, LISSOME: SUPPLE suggests easy flexibility of musculature, excellent coordination, and light, free, unlabored movement; in extended uses it suggests easy, resilient, graceful movement or flow ⟨mere manual labor stiffens the limbs, gymnastic exercises render them *supple* — Richard Jefferies⟩ ⟨in good condition, — not fat, like grass-fed cattle, but trim and *supple*, like deer —John Burroughs⟩ ⟨his use of language is always expert. Serviceable, *supple*, it is capable of a variety of effects —Dayton Kohler⟩ LIMBER may stress the fact of easy flexibility facilitating ready motion ⟨keeping his players *limber* during the off-season⟩ ⟨accustomed to mountain climbing, *limber* and agile⟩ LITHE suggests supple, slender, nimble grace ⟨the jungle and the wilderness lurked in the uplift and downput of his feet. He was cat-footed, and *lithe* —Jack London⟩ ⟨a *lithe* movement of her apparently boneless little figure —F. Tennyson Jesse⟩ LITHESOME may suggest agile vigor ⟨the warlike carriage of the men, and their strong, *lithesome*, resolute step —A.W.Kinglake⟩ LISSOME suggests light feminine graceful bearing or activity ⟨the *lissome* ladies who make their living modeling the latest French fashions —*Time*⟩ ⟨she only wanted wings to fly away, easy and light and *lissome* —J.C.Ransom⟩ **syn** see in addition FLEXIBLE

[2]**supple** \\"\\ *vb* -ED/-ING/-S [ME *souplen*, fr. *souple* supple] *vt* **1 :** to reduce the resoluteness or violence of **:** make pacific or complaisant ⟨mollify the hearts and ~ the tempers of your race —Laurence Sterne⟩ **2** *obs* **:** to soothe or alleviate by application of a salve **3 :** to make supple **:** treat so as to make flexible or pliant ⟨the rawhide was worn and *suppled* into a fair grade of dry tan leather —H.L.Davis⟩ ~ *vi, archaic* **:** to become soft, pliant, or complaisant

[1]**sup·ple·jack** \\ˈ⸗⸗ˌjak\\ *n* [[1]*supple* + *Jack*, proper name] **1 :** any of various woody climbers having tough pliant stems: as **a :** a tall-climbing glabrous woody vine (*Berchemia scandens*) of the southern and central U.S. — called also *rattan vine* **b :** any of various tropical American plants of the

genera *Paullinia* and *Serjania* from some of which canes are made **c** (1) **:** a small glabrous Australian tree (*Ventilago viminalis*) of the family Rhamnaceae with flexible sometimes twining branches (2) **:** an Australian clematis (*Clematis aristata*) **d :** a lawyer (*Rubus australis*) **2 :** a cane made from the stem of a supplejack

²supplejack \"\ *n* [*supple* + *Jack*, proper name] **:** JUMPING JACK

sup·ple·ly *also* **sup·ply** \p(ə)lē, -li\ *adv* **:** in a supple manner

¹sup·ple·ment \'səpləmənt\ *n* -s [ME, fr. L *supplementum*, fr. *supplēre* to fill up, complete, supply + *-mentum* -ment — more at SUPPLY] **1 :** something that supplies a want or makes an addition **:** something that completes, adds a finishing touch, or brings closer to completion or a desired state ⟨one of the real services of the historical novel is not that it can be a substitute for history, but that it can be . . . a ~ —T.C.Chubb⟩ ⟨the policy of apartheid is only a political supplement to an economic policy that depends on cheap native labor —Emory Ross⟩ ⟨vitamin ~⟩: as **a :** a part added to or issued as a continuation of a book or periodical to make good its deficiencies, correct its errors, bring it up to date, or provide special features not ordinarily included ⟨issued . . . in fourteen volumes and subsequently kept up to date by nine annual ~*s* —H.W.H.Knott⟩ ⟨Sunday ~⟩ ⟨magazine ~⟩ **b :** a material added to a pesticidal spray or dust to improve a physical or chemical property (as adhesiveness or wettability) — compare SPREADER 1f **c :** a feedstuff rich in protein used to balance a livestock ration **2 :** the quantity by which an arc or an angle falls short of 180 degrees

²sup·ple·ment \-,ment, -mənt — *see* ²-MENT\ *vt* -ED/-ING/-S **:** to fill up or supply by additions **:** add something to **:** fill the deficiencies of: as **a :** to serve as a supplement for ⟨the frontiersman depended for game to ~ his meager larder —R.A. Billington⟩ **b :** to supply a supplement for ⟨he signed mutual defense treaties . . . and ~*ed* many with favorable commercial agreements —R.E.Lee⟩

¹sup·ple·men·tal \,səplə'ment³l\ *adj* [¹*supplement* + *-al*] **1 :** serving to supplement **:** of the character of a supplement **:** SUPPLEMENTARY ⟨~ angle⟩ ⟨~ appropriations⟩ **2 :** of, relating to, or being an answer, bill, or plea filed or served in aid of an original one to supply some defect in the latter or to set forth new facts which cannot be added by amendment — **sup·ple·men·tal·ly** \-³lē, -³li\ *adv*

²supplemental \"\ *n* -s **:** a supplementary thing **:** SUPPLEMENT ⟨~*s* for the civilian agencies totaled more than a billion dollars —*U.S.News & World Report*⟩

supplemental air *n* **:** the air that can still be expelled from the lungs after an ordinary expiration — compare RESIDUAL AIR

supplemental irrigation *n* **:** irrigation that supplements rainfall

sup·ple·men·tar·i·ly \,səplə(,)men-'terəlē, -mən-, -rəli; -'men-trəl-, -ntərəl-\ *adv* [¹*supplementary* + *-ly*] **:** as a supplement **:** in addition

¹sup·ple·men·tary \,səplə'mentərē, -n-trē, -ri\ *adj* [¹*supplement* + *-ary*] **:** that is or is added as a supplement **:** ADDITIONAL ⟨~ income⟩ ⟨~ volume⟩ ⟨~ reading⟩

²supplementary \"\ *n* -ES **:** one that is supplementary

supplementary angles *n pl* **:** two angles or arcs whose sum is 180 degrees

supplementary cost *n* **:** the general cost of an undertaking as a whole including administration, interest, taxes, general maintenance, depreciation, and obsolescence — distinguished from *prime cost*

supplementary factor *n* **:** MODIFIER 3

supplementary proceedings *n pl* **1 :** proceedings under a code or practice act for the examination of a judgment debtor or others to discover property for payment of the judgment **2 :** proceedings ancillary to or in modification of an earlier action or suit (as a petition to modify a decree for alimony or custody of children or one to appoint a receiver)

sup·ple·men·ta·tion \,səplə(,)men-'tāshən, -,mən-\ *n* -s [²*supplement* + *-ation*] **:** the act or process or an instance of supplementing ⟨dietary ~⟩ ⟨~ of state unemployment benefits —R.A.Lester⟩

sup·ple·ment·er \'səplə,mentə(r)\ *n* -s [²*supplement* + *-er*] **:** one that supplements

sup·ple·ness \'səpəlnəs, ÷'süp-\ *n* -ES [¹*supple* + *-ness*] **:** the quality or state of being supple **:** EASE, FLEXIBILITY, ELASTICITY ⟨the ~ of youthful fingers —*Amer. Guide Series: Mich.*⟩

suppler *comparative of* SUPPLE

supples *pres 3d sing of* SUPPLE

supplest *superlative of* SUPPLE

sup·ple·tion \sə'plēshən\ *n* -s [ML *suppletion-, suppletio* act of completing, supplementing, fr. L *suppletus* (past part. of *supplēre* to fill up, complete, supply) + *-ion-, -io* -ion — more at SUPPLY] **:** the occurrence of phonemically unrelated allomorphs of the same morpheme whether that morpheme is a base (as *go*, past tense *went; bad*, comparative *worse*) or an affix (as plural ending *-es* in *boxes, -en* in *oxen*)

sup·ple·tive \sə'plēd·iv, 'səpləd-\ *adj* [LL *suppletivus* supplementary, fr. L *suppletus* + *-ivus* -ive] **:** characterized by or constituting an instance of suppletion — **sup·ple·tive·ly** \-d·əvlē\ *adv*

sup·ple·to·ry \sə'plēd·ərē, 'səplə,tōrē\ *adj* [L *suppletus* + E *-ory*] **:** supplying deficiencies **:** SUPPLEMENTARY

suppletory oath *n* **:** a restricted oath formerly administered to a party not competent as a general witness but offering documents in evidence and asked to make just and true answers to questions put by the court to prove the authenticity of the documents

suppliable *adj* [¹*supply* + *-able*] *obs* **:** capable of being supplied

¹sup·pli·ance \-īən(t)s\ *n* -s [¹*supply* + *-ance*] **:** the act or process of supplying **:** SUPPLY

²sup·pli·ance \'səplēən(t)s\ *also* **sup·pli·an·cy** \-nsē\ *n, pl* **suppliances** *also* **suppliancies** [*suppliance* fr. ²*suppliant*, after such pairs as E *benevolent: benevolence; suppliancy* fr. ²*suppliant* + *-cy*] **:** SUPPLICATION, ENTREATY ⟨bow . . . in ~ for wisdom —D.D.Eisenhower⟩

¹sup·pli·ant \'səplēənt\ *n* -s [ME, fr. MF, fr. pres. part. of *supplier* to supplicate, fr. L *supplicare* — more at SUPPLICATE] **:** one who supplicates **:** PETITIONER, BESEECHER ⟨reducing him to the position of a ~ for her favors —H.M.Parshley⟩

²suppliant \"\ *adj* [MF, pres. part. of *supplier* to supplicate] **:** marked by or expressive of supplication **:** humbly imploring ⟨does not come to the temple as a ~ sinner seeking forgiveness —O.J.Baab⟩ — **sup·pli·ant·ly** *adv*

¹sup·pli·cant \'səpləkənt, -lēk-\ *adj* [L *supplicant-, supplicans*, pres. part. of *supplicare* to supplicate] **:** asking submissively **:** SUPPLICATING, ENTREATING — **sup·pli·cant·ly** *adv*

²supplicant \"\ *n* -s **:** SUPPLIANT ⟨tapped on the door like a ~, and waited . . . with his hat in his hand —Berton Roueché⟩

sup·pli·cat \-plə,kat\ *or* **sup·pli·cate** \-kāt\ *n* -s [*supplicat* fr. L, he makes supplication, 3d sing. pres. indic. of *supplicare;* fr. the wording of the petition; *supplicate* fr. ML *supplicatus*, fr. L *supplicatus*, past part. of *supplicare*] **:** SUPPLICATION; *specif* **:** a formal written petition for a degree or for incorporation at an English university

sup·pli·cate \'səplə,kāt, *usu* -ād.+V\ *vb* -ED/-ING/-S [ME *supplicaten*, fr. L *supplicatus*, past part. of *supplicare* to supplicate, fr. *supplic-, supplex* submissive, suppliant — more at SUPPLE] *vi* **:** to make a humble entreaty **:** pray beseechingly; *specif* **:** to present a supplicat ~ *vt* **1 :** to entreat as a supplicant **:** ask humbly and earnestly of ⟨must fall on his knees and ~ the God of his fathers —S.L.Terrien⟩ **2 :** to ask for earnestly and humbly **:** entreat for in the manner of a supplicant ⟨~ a blessing⟩ **syn** see BEG

sup·pli·cat·ing·ly \'≈≈,≈≈≈, ,≈≈'≈≈≈\ *adv* [*supplicating* (pres. part. of *supplicate*) + *-ly*] **:** in a supplicating manner

sup·pli·ca·tion \,səplə'kāshən\ *n* -s [ME, fr. MF, fr. L *supplication-, supplicatio*, fr. *supplicatus* (past part. of *supplicare* to supplicate) + *-ion-, -io* -ion] **1 :** the act or process of supplicating **:** humble and earnest entreaty ⟨pained by such tender, such flattering ~ —Jane Austen⟩ **2 a** (1) *archaic* **:** a formal written petition (2) **:** SUPPLICAT **b :** a humble and earnest petition **:** ENTREATY, SOLICITATION ⟨the last ~ . . . I make of you is, that you will believe this of me —Charles Dickens⟩ **c :** a humble prayer to a deity for mercy, aid, or special blessing ⟨kneeling together on a spit of sand, with their arms raised in ~ —R.L.Stevenson⟩ **3** *obs* **:** a public religious observance of thanksgiving or religious humiliation in ancient Rome **:** a day set apart for such an observance

sup·pli·ca·tor \'≈≈,kād·ə(r), -ātə-\ *n* -s [LL, fr. L *supplicatus* + *-or*] **:** SUPPLICANT

sup·pli·ca·to·ry \'səpləkə,tōrē, -lēk-, -tór-, -ri\ *adj* [ME, fr. ML *supplicatorius*, fr. L *supplicatus* + *-orius* -ory] **:** of the nature of, containing, or expressive of supplication **:** BESEECHING

sup·pli·ca·vit \,səplə'kāvət\ *n* -s [L, he has made supplication, 3d sing. perf. indic. of *supplicare* to supplicate; fr. the opening word of the writ] **:** a writ formerly issuing out of the Court of Chancery or King's Bench for taking surety to prevent one from injuring the applicant for the writ

sup·pli·er \sə'plī(ə)r, -īə\ *n* -s **:** one that supplies: as **a :** a country or area that supplies a raw material or commodity **b :** a manufacturer that produces a part for use in the product of another part ⟨a ~ to the auto industry⟩

suppling *pres part of* SUPPLE

¹sup·ply \sə'plī\ *vb* -ED/-ING/-ES [ME *suppleen, supplien*, fr. MF *souplier, soupleier*, fr. L *supplēre* to fill up, supplement, supply, fr. *sub-* up + *plēre* to fill — more at SUB-, FULL] *vt* **1 a** *obs* **:** to make additions to by way of supplement **b :** to add (something essential or lacking) as a supplement **2 a :** to provide satisfaction or compensation for (as a need or defect) **:** make good by providing a substitute **:** fill adequately ⟨an age which *supplied* the lack of moral habits by a system of moral attitudes and poses —T.S.Eliot⟩ ⟨the laws by which the material wants of men are *supplied* —*Bull. of Bates Coll.*⟩ **b :** to satisfy a need or desire for **:** provide or furnish with **:** bring up or make available a quantity of **:** YIELD ⟨had taken to poaching as a means of ~*ing* fresh meat for the table —H.D.Quillin⟩ ⟨the millrace built to ~ power to the mission's sawmill —*Amer. Guide Series: Tenn.*⟩ ⟨the moral code of each generation . . . *supplies* a norm or standard of behavior —B.N.Cardozo⟩ ⟨a youngster in school *supplied* me the answer —Bryan MacMahon⟩ **c** (1) **:** to provide that which is required or desired by **:** satisfy the needs or wishes of **:** furnish with or as if with supplies, provisions, or equipment ⟨a contract to ~ the railroad with fuel —D.L.Graham⟩ ⟨wells were drilled to ~ the town's water system —*Amer. Guide Series: Ark.*⟩ (2) **:** to furnish (organs, tissues, or cells) with pathways for transmission or a vital element (as a nerve impulse) — used of nerves and blood vessels **3 a** (1) **:** to substitute for another in (a function) (2) **:** to occupy (a position) as a substitute; *specif* **:** to serve as a supply in (a church or pulpit) **b :** to serve instead of **:** take the place of **:** REPLACE ⟨a bold peasantry . . . when once destroyed, can never be *supplied* —Oliver Goldsmith⟩ ~ *vi* **:** to serve as a supply ⟨he *supplied* on Sundays in church pulpits of various denominations —Virginia D. Dawson & Betty D. Wilson⟩ **syn** see PROVIDE

²supply \"\ *n* -ES *often attrib* [ME *supplye*, fr. *supplien* to supply] **1** *obs* **:** ASSISTANCE, SUCCOR, AID **2 :** something that supplies or is supplied to a person or thing: **a** *obs* **:** REINFORCEMENTS — often used in pl. **b :** a clergyman that serves as a substitute for another or as a temporary or incompletely functioning pastor ⟨since the church's organization, the pulpit has been filled by *supplies* —*Presbyterian Life*⟩ **c** *obs* **:** a supplement esp. to a book **d :** the quantity or amount (as of a commodity) needed or available ⟨the state's ~ of antiquities is not alarmingly diminished —*Amer. Guide Series: Md.*⟩ ⟨the need for a ~ of symbols . . . to designate various things —Jack Guendling⟩ ⟨beer was in short ~ in that hot weather —Nevil Shute⟩ **e :** items or a quantity (as provisions, clothing, arms, or raw material) available for use, exploitation, or development or esp. set aside to be dispensed at need **:** STORES, STORE ⟨two crocodiles looking greedily . . . at this ~ of succulent beef —Francis Birtles⟩ — usu. used in pl. ⟨ensuring fresh *supplies* of managerial talent —Roy Lewis & Angus Maude⟩ **f :** an amount of money provided (as by a legislature) to meet the annual national expenditures or those not covered by other revenues — usu. used in pl. ⟨the power of giving or withholding the *supplies* at pleasure is one of absolute supremacy —T.E.May⟩ **3 :** the act, process, or an instance of filling a want or need or of providing someone or something ⟨manufacture, acquisition, provision and ~ of services and goods —*Federal Guide (Australia)*⟩ ⟨the town became a base of ~ for cowboys —*Amer. Guide Series: Texas*⟩ ⟨engaged in the ~ of raw materials to industry⟩ **4 a :** the quantities of goods or services offered for sale at various prices — compare DEMAND **b :** the desire for general purchasing power seeking its end by an offer of specific commodities or services **5 :** something that contains, delivers, maintains, or regulates a supply ⟨~ line⟩ ⟨~ depot⟩ ⟨the traces that supply one leaf constitute the leaf ~ —A.J.Eames & L.H.MacDaniels⟩

³supply *var of* SUPPLELY

supply pastor *or* **supply preacher** *n* [²*supply*] **:** SUPPLY 2b

supply price *n* **:** the lowest price at which a given amount of commodities will be offered under given conditions

¹sup·port \sə'pō(ə)r|t, -pó(ə)r|, -pōəl, -pó(ə)|, *usu* |d·+V\ *vt* -ED/-ING/-S [ME *supporten*, fr. MF *supporter*, fr. LL *supportare* to bear, endure, fr. L, to carry, convey, fr. *sub-* + *portare* to carry — more at FARE] **1 :** to endure esp. in silence or with courage **:** BEAR, SUFFER, TOLERATE ⟨wondered how he could ~ the sun, even with his helmet —Paul Bowles⟩ **2 a** (1) **:** to uphold by aid, countenance, or adherence **:** actively promote the interests or cause of ⟨the art work of the federal agencies has been ~*ed* enthusiastically —*Amer. Guide Series: Minn.*⟩ ⟨an established judicial system ~*ed* by the executive power of the state —John MacNeill⟩ (2) **:** to uphold or defend as valid, right, just, or authoritative **:** ADVOCATE ⟨would ~ the principle of arbitration —C.L.Jones⟩ ⟨the treaties . . . represent public opinion . . . and will be ~*ed* by the people —Vera M. Dean⟩ (3) **:** to argue in favor of **:** vote for ⟨difficult to ~ his political aims —Franz von Papen⟩ ⟨~*ed* increasing the base pay of servicemen —*Current Biog.*⟩; *also* **:** to advocate, endorse, vote for, or implement the policies, principles, or candidacy of ⟨he ~*ed* the administration . . . in practically all its major measures —T.P.Abernethy⟩ ⟨the state delegation . . . ~*ed* him on the first ballot —G.S.Dumke⟩ **b** (1) **:** to provide means, force, or strength that is secondary to **:** back up ⟨scattered eight hits, walked three and fanned two as his mates ~*ed* him brilliantly in the field —Deane McGowen⟩ ⟨body of . . . missionaries and businessmen, ~*ed* rather than led by a handful of politicians —D.W.Brogan⟩ (2) **:** to give assistance to (a primary battle force) by providing supplies, serving as a reserve, or furnishing additional or covering combat strength ⟨a base-building and base-stocking operation to ~ the great air and cross-channel attacks —G.A.Lincoln⟩ ⟨ahead of his main line, where they could not be ~*ed* by the rest of the troops —Tom Wintringham⟩ ⟨mortars and machine guns ~*ed* the attack⟩ (3) **:** to attend upon (a person) esp. as an assistant on a ceremonious occasion ⟨the mayor . . . will attend the old Parish Church, ~*ed* by the Council and civic bodies, in state —Austin Edwards⟩ (4) **:** to act with (a star actor) (5) **:** to provide a musical background for **:** ACCOMPANY ⟨the orchestral sound was always strong enough to ~ the voices —Irving Kolodin⟩ (6) **:** to bid in bridge so as to show support for (one's partner or his suit) **c** (1) **:** to serve as verification, corroboration, or substantiation of ⟨historic evidence ~*s* such guesses —Brewton Berry⟩; *also* **:** to provide with verification, corroboration, or substantiation ⟨his alibi that he had been home all afternoon . . . was ~*ed* by neighbors —Woody Klein⟩ (2) **:** to provide amplification or clarification of ⟨tests, keys, teachers' manuals, and the like, to ~ and supplement their textbooks —*Textbooks in Education*⟩ **3 a :** to pay the costs of **:** MAINTAIN ⟨the association is ~*ed* financially by membership dues —Helen T. Geer⟩ ⟨few graduate students ~ their studies from personal funds —M.H. Trytten⟩; *also* **:** to supply with the means of maintenance (as lodging, food or clothing) or to earn or furnish funds for maintaining ⟨~*s* his own and his brother's family⟩ **b :** to provide a basis for the existence or subsistence of **:** serve as the source of material or immaterial supply, nourishment, provender, fuel, raw material, or sustenance of ⟨the island could probably ~ three, though no more —A.B.C.Whipple⟩ ⟨the flax crop ~*s* an important linen industry —Samuel Van Valkenburg & Ellsworth Huntington⟩ ⟨to ~ study and research . . . these are . . . the outstanding collection of microfilm reproductions —*Univ. of Mich. Bull.*⟩ **c :** to have or put into circulation enough money (as from trade, wages, manufacture, or taxes) to maintain ⟨the town ~*s* a grammar school, a large high school, a movie, and two hotels —*Amer. Guide Series: Nev.*⟩ ⟨one of the large machine shops . . . that ~ the town industrially —*Amer. Guide Series: Vt.*⟩ **4 a :** to hold up or in position **:** serve as a foundation or prop for **:** bear the weight or stress of **:** keep from sinking or falling ⟨octagonal piers ~ Gothic arches along the nave —*Amer. Guide Series: Minn.*⟩ **b :** to serve as a heraldic supporter of ⟨the shield of this monarch is ~*ed* on each side by an angel habited —F.J.Grant⟩ **c :** to give one's arm to **d** *obs* **:** to be the subject or ground of (an attribute) **e :** to assume and give the appearance of having (as a character) ⟨~*ed* a general behavior in the world which could not hurt their credit or their purse —Richard Steele⟩ **f :** to maintain (a price) at a high level by purchases or loans ⟨a wool bill ~*ing* the domestic price for wool at 42 cents —F.A.Barrett⟩; *also* **:** to maintain the price of (as an agricultural commodity) by purchases or loans ⟨mandatory for the secretary to ~ six basic crops — cotton, corn, rice, peanuts, wheat and tobacco — at 90 percent of parity —Jean Begeman⟩ **5 :** to keep from fainting, sinking, yielding, or losing courage **:** COMFORT, STRENGTHEN ⟨beneath the sadness her indomitable pride ~*ed* her —Ellen Glasgow⟩ **6 :** to maintain in condition, action, or existence ⟨the fuel had not been of that substantial sort which can ~ a blaze long —Thomas Hardy⟩ ⟨~ respiration⟩ ⟨~ the fiction that the man had left in the night —*Amer. Guide Series: Tenn.*⟩

syn SUSTAIN, PROP, BOLSTER, BUTTRESS, BRACE: SUPPORT is applicable to a variety of uses with the general meaning or suggestion of carrying or leaning from or as if from below, of maintaining or holding up the weight or pressure of, and of forestalling sinking or falling back ⟨pillars *supporting* the balcony⟩ ⟨he *supports* the greater muscular tension with less evident fatigue —W.C.Brownell⟩ ⟨*support* the Constitution⟩ SUSTAIN may center attention on the fact of constantly holding up or of maintaining undiminished ⟨*sustain* the weight of office⟩ ⟨for nine years, Napoleon has been *sustained* by the people of France with a unanimity such as the United States never knew —C.B.Fairbanks⟩ ⟨this intellectual interest is great enough to *sustain* the reader through the analytical labyrinths we must search together —Hunter Mead⟩ PROP may imply a weakness, a tendency to fall, sink, or recede, a need for strengthening or reinforcing on the part of the thing being treated ⟨*propping* up the table with a packing case⟩ ⟨trying to *prop* up the decaying structures of last-century imperialism —G.L.Kirk⟩ ⟨the plot, a slim tale of vengeance, is psychologically shallow and *propped* up by unpardonable coincidences —Anthony Boucher⟩ BOLSTER blends the suggestions of SUSTAIN and PROP; it may suggest a supporting comparable to that afforded an invalid by pillows ⟨*bolster* up the falling fortunes of the East India Company —V.L.Parrington⟩ ⟨*bolster* the diminishing lumber trade within the next 75 years —*Amer. Guide Series: N. J.*⟩ ⟨assign some extra instruments to *bolster* the choir's volume of sound —P.H.Lang⟩ BUTTRESS may suggest strengthening, reinforcing, or stabilizing, sometimes massive, at a stress point, in the manner of an architectural buttress ⟨combat business slumps and to *buttress* the economy so that danger of another depression will be reduced to a minimum —*Newsweek*⟩ ⟨a code of laws *buttressed* by divine sanctions which should be unshakable —Benjamin Farrington⟩ ⟨the popular success formula is *buttressed* by evidence from the careers of an impressive minority —R.B.Morris⟩ BRACE may suggest supporting or strengthening so that the thing treated is made firm, unyielding, or rigid against pressure ⟨*brace* the shelf with an angle iron⟩ ⟨then he *braced* himself against a giant oak on his front lawn and experienced a savage kind of exaltation as the elements raged around him —Bennett Cerf⟩ ⟨the shoring up of a tottering political system, which is precisely the problem that we face in trying to *brace* the western democracies —G.W.Johnson⟩

²support \"\ *n* -s *often attrib* [ME, fr. *supporten* to support] **1 :** the act, process, or operation of supporting or the condition of being supported ⟨the ~ by society of increasingly skilled specialists —Jacquetta & Christopher Hawkes⟩ ⟨carried a large club, partly for the ~ of his weak legs —Sherwood Anderson⟩ ⟨appeared . . . to testify in ~ of universal military training —*Current Biog.*⟩: as **a :** the assistance given one military unit by another ⟨methods of ~ by machine-gun fire —*Combat Forces Jour.*⟩ ⟨the transfer of battalions between regiments . . . is done as seldom as possible in order to avoid complicating administrative ~ —M.L.Powell⟩ — see CLOSE SUPPORT **b :** acting by a company or actor that supports a star **2 :** one that supports **:** a supporting means, agency, medium, proof, or reserve **:** PROP ⟨building a steel frame as a structural ~ for the fabric of stone or brick —*Amer. Guide Series: Minn.*⟩ ⟨the first to use canvas as a ~ for painting in oil —C.W.H. Johnson⟩ ⟨one under our special supervision and the other with our cordial ~ —W.F.Brown b.1903⟩: as **a :** a means of livelihood, sustenance, or existence ⟨each son was expected to contribute to his own ~ —Carol L. Thompson⟩ ⟨the only financial ~ which a magazine could expect was from its readers —D.M.Potter⟩; *also* **:** a person or agency that furnishes support ⟨he is his family's sole ~⟩ — compare PRICE SUPPORT **b** (1) **:** one of the two primary subdivisions of an advance or rear guard: (2) **:** a military element in an outpost (3) **:** a body of troops designated to support or reinforce a unit in action (4) **:** a part of a unit held in reserve **c :** a company, actor, or actress playing with a star **d :** a supporting layer of cellulosic material, glass, or plastic on which a photographic light-sensitive layer is coated **e :** sufficient strength (as four cards of the suit or three cards including the queen or jack-ten) in a bridge suit bid by one's partner to justify raising it **f** (1) **:** SUPPORTER d (2) **:** SUSPENSORY **g :** a musical accompaniment or background **h :** corroborating or substantiating evidence, testimony, or documents ⟨the suggested hypothesis led necessarily to searching for ~ in the psychological sciences —S.J. Beck⟩ **3 :** REST 2a(3) **syn** see LIVING

sup·port·able \|d·əbəl, |təb-\ *adj* [¹*support* + *-able*] **:** capable of being supported ⟨many debtors had gone into debt up to the maximum limits ~ by boom incomes —*Defense Against Recession*⟩

sup·port·ance \|t³n(t)s\ *n* -s [ME, fr. *supporten* to support + *-ance*] **1 :** SUPPORT **2** *Scots law* **:** aid enabling a person otherwise incapable to go to kirk or market so as to validate a conveyance of heritage made within 60 days next before death

supportation *n* -s [ME *supportacion*, fr. MF, fr. ML *supportation-, supportatio*, fr. LL, endurance, bearing, fr. *supportatus* (past part. of *supportare* to endure) + L *-ion-, -io* -ion — more at SUPPORT] **1** *obs* **:** SUPPORT **2** *obs* **:** SUPPORTANCE 2

supported *past of* SUPPORT

supported joint *n* [*supported* (past part. of ¹*support*) + *joint*] **:** a rail joint in a railroad rail having a tie directly under the rail ends — compare SUSPENDED JOINT

sup·port·er \|d·ə(r), |tə-\ *n* -s [ME, fr. *supporten* to support + *-er*] **:** one that furnishes or acts as a support: as **a :** one that adheres to, advocates, or endorses a person, group, or program ⟨a firm ~ of the imperial claims to temporal domination —R.A. Hall b. 1911⟩ ⟨he was not a leader, he was an effective ~ of leaders —Charles Moore⟩ **b :** one that supports another on a ceremonious occasion ⟨his majesty proceeded to the altar attended by his ~*s* —*Whitaker's Almanack*⟩ **c :** GARTER 1 **d :** a woven or knitted band or elastic device for supporting a part ⟨a wrist ~⟩ **:** SUSPENSORY **e :** a figure (as of a man, animal, or object) placed one on each side of an escutcheon and exterior to it

supporting *pres part of* SUPPORT

supporting distance *n* [*supporting* (gerund of *support*) + *distance*] **:** the distance beyond which one military unit cannot come to the aid of another before it is defeated

sup·port·ing·ly *adv* [*supporting* (pres. part. of ¹*support*) + *-ly*] **:** so as to support

sup·port·ive \|d·iv, |tiv\ *adj* [¹*support* + *-ive*] **:** furnishing support; *specif* **:** serving to sustain the strength and condition of a patient ⟨administration of fluids, glucose, and proteins is ~ against liver failure⟩

sup·port·less \|tləs\ *adj* **:** lacking support

support mission *n* [²*support*] **:** an air attack in close support of ground forces against enemy ground forces

supports *pres 3d sing of* SUPPORT, *pl of* SUPPORT

suppos *abbr* suppository

sup·pos·able \sə'pōzəbəl\ *adj* [¹*suppose* + *-able*] **:** capable of being supposed **:** PRESUMABLE, CONCEIVABLE — **sup·pos·ably** \-blē,-bli\ *adv*

sup·pos·al \-zəl\ *n* -s [ME, fr. ¹*suppose* + *-al*] **1 :** the act or process of supposing **2 :** something supposed **:** HYPOTHESIS, CONJECTURE, SUPPOSITION; *specif* **:** a proposition in logic or the content of a proposition that is neither affirmed nor denied, neither believed nor disbelieved, but merely noted or put forward for remark

¹sup·pose \sə'pōz, *rapid often* 'spōz\ *vb* -ED/-ING/-S [ME *supposen*, fr. MF *supposer*, modif. (influenced by *poser* to put, place) of ML *supponere* to suppose, assume, fr. L, to put under, substitute (perfect stem *suppos-*), fr. *sub-* + *ponere* to put, place — more at POSITION, POSE] *vt* **1** *obs* **:** ANTICIPATE **2 a :** to lay down as a postulate or usu. a hypothesis or assumption **:** accept tentatively as true or real **:** assume as true for the sake of argument or exposition ⟨~ an epidemic of typhoid should break out —K.F.Zeisler⟩ ⟨this is the form we have *supposed* them to have in the above discussion —W.S.Sellars⟩ **b** (1) **:** to hold as belief or opinion **:** BELIEVE, THINK ⟨the new recruits *supposed* with some reason that they were advancing democratic objectives —M.W.Straight⟩ (2) **:** to think probable or in keeping with the facts **:** entertain as likely or probably true ⟨it is *supposed* that the pressure . . . may reach three hundred pounds per square inch —W.J.V.Osterhout⟩ (3) **:** to believe on slight grounds or without grounds **:** hold mistakenly or without sufficient proof **:** PRESUME ⟨the imagination feigns something unknown and invisible which it ~s to continue the same despite all variation of quality —Frank Thilly⟩ ⟨numerous pretty things, or things *supposed* to be pretty —Herbert Spencer⟩ **3 a :** to form a conception of **:** CONCEIVE, IMAGINE ⟨your mother says "Pray send my dear love". There is hardly room to add mine, but you will ~ it —William Cowper⟩ **b :** to have a notion or suspicion of **:** APPREHEND, SUSPECT **4** *obs* **:** PRETEND **5** *archaic* **:** to put in place of another **:** SUBSTITUTE **6 :** to imply as an antecedent **:** PRESUPPOSE ⟨every sound taxing system ~s such a surplus —J.A.Hobson⟩ ~ *vi* **:** CONJECTURE, THINK, OPINE

²suppose \"\ *n* -s **:** SUPPOSITION, CONJECTURE ⟨would baffle the wildest ~ —George Woodbury⟩

sup·posed \-zd *sometimes* -zəd\ *adj* [fr. past part. of ¹*suppose*] **1 a :** believed to be or accepted as such usu. on slight grounds or in error **:** erroneously imputed or ascribed ⟨the ~ necessary laws of economics —M.R.Cohen⟩; *also* **:** IMAGINED ⟨certain ~ evils which perhaps are not very real evils —A.B.Walkley⟩ **b :** EXPECTED — used in the phrase *be supposed to* ⟨the United States was ~ to present the greatest ratification difficulties —E.P.Chase⟩ **c :** UNDERSTOOD — used in the phrase *be supposed to* ⟨you will be ~ to refer to my grandaunt —G.B.Shaw⟩ **2 a :** PRETENDED — used in the phrase *be supposed to* ⟨twelve hours are ~ to elapse between Acts I and II —A.S.Sullivan⟩ **b :** ALLEGED — used in the phrase *be supposed to* ⟨we are ~ to be stable and weary and lacking new ideas —A.E.Stevenson b. 1900⟩ **3 a :** INTENDED — used in the phrase *be supposed to* ⟨it explains considerable but has to be strained beyond belief to explain all it is ~ to —H.J.Muller⟩ **b :** DESIGNED — used in the phrase *be supposed to* ⟨what's that button ~ to do⟩ **4 a :** under orders **:** REQUIRED — used in the phrase *be supposed to* ⟨the soldier . . . was ~ to furl the side flaps in the morning —Norman Mailer⟩ **b :** PERMITTED — used in the phrase *be supposed to* ⟨you're not ~ to leave the guardroom at all this morning —Robert Lowry⟩ — **sup·pos·ed·ly** \-zədlē, -li\ *adv*

sup·pos·er \-zə(r)\ *n* -s [¹*suppose* + *-er*] **:** one that supposes

supposing *conj* [fr. pres. part. of ¹*suppose*] **:** if by way of hypothesis **:** on the assumption that ⟨~ a large cube of white material to be placed on sandy ground of an orange hue —C.W.H.Johnson⟩

sup·pos·it \sə'päzət\ *n* -s [NL *suppositum*, fr. L, neuter of *suppositus*, past part. of *supponere* to place under — more at SUPPOSE] **:** an individual that is philosophically substance or subject — called also *suppositum*

sup·po·si·tion \,səpə'zishən\ *n* -s [ME, fr. LL *supposition-*, *suppositio* hypothesis, conjecture (influenced in meaning by Gk *hypothesis*, lit., act of placing under), fr. L, act of placing under, fr. *suppositus* (past part. of *supponere* to place under) + *-ion-*, *-io* -ion — more at HYPOTHESIS, SUPPOSE] **1 a :** something (as a hypothesis, conjecture, theory, or surmise) that is supposed ⟨on the ~ that . . . language so largely contributes to making us men —A.A.Hill⟩ ⟨an entirely gratuitous ~ on my part —W.F.De Morgan⟩ **b :** the act or process of supposing and esp. of assuming something tentatively, hypothetically, or for the sake of argument ⟨not the old psychology of ~, but the new psychology of practical investigation —George Sampson⟩ **c** *obs* **:** the state of being uncertain and subject to surmise ⟨he is sufficient, yet his means are in ~ —Shak.⟩ **2 :** fraudulent substitution or alteration; *specif* **:** FORGERY **3 :** one of the various connotations that a term may have in different passages

sup·po·si·tion·al \,səpə'zishən°l, -shnəl\ *adj* [*supposition* + *-al*] **:** CONJECTURAL, HYPOTHETICAL

sup·po·si·tious \-shəs\ *adj* [contr. of *supposititious*] **1 :** SUPPOSITITIOUS ⟨a ~, misguided philosophy, a pseudo science —W.W.Howells⟩ **2 :** based on supposition ⟨this . . . ~ contract between ruler and ruled in prehistoric times —V.L.Parrington⟩

sup·pos·i·ti·tious \sə,päzə'tishəs\ *adj* [L *suppositicius* substituted, spurious, fr. *suppositus* (past part. of *supponere* to place under, substitute) + *-icius* -itious; in senses 2 & 3 influenced in meaning by E *supposition*] **1 a** (1) **:** fraudulently substituted for something else (2) **:** not being what it purports to be **:** SPURIOUS, COUNTERFEIT ⟨despatched a lawyer . . . to enlarge upon the theme of his father's ~ affluence —John Kobler⟩ **b** *of a child* (1) **:** presented as a genuine heir (2) **:** ILLEGITIMATE **2 :** IMAGINARY, FABULOUS ⟨the ~ toga in which popular imagination had garbed his impressive form —S.H.Adams⟩ **3 :** of the nature of a supposition **:** HYPOTHETICAL ⟨whether the anticipation be mine or that of a ~ observer —Victor Lowe⟩ — **sup·pos·i·ti·tious·ly** *adv* — **sup·pos·i·ti·tious·ness** *n* -ES

sup·pos·i·tive \sə'päzəd·iv\ *adj* [LL *suppositivus*, fr. L *suppositus* (past part. of *supponere* to place under — influenced in meaning by Gk *hypothetikos* hypothetical) + *-ivus* -ive — more at SUPPOSE] **:** characterized by, involving, or implying supposition **:** SUPPOSED

¹sup·pos·i·to·ry \sə'päzə,tōrē, -tȯr-, -ri\ *n* -ES [ML *suppositorium*, fr. LL, neut. of *suppositorius* placed under, fr. L *suppositus* + *-orius* -ory] **:** a solid preparation made usu. of medicated cocoa butter or glycerinated gelatin in the form usu. of a cone, cylinder, or oval for introduction into a tubular body cavity (as the rectum, vagina, or urethra or the teat of a cow) where it melts at body temperature and releases the medicament it contains

²suppository \"\ *adj* [ML *suppositus* (past part. of *supponere* to suppose) + E *-ory*] **:** SUPPOSITIOUS 2

sup·pos·i·tum \sə'päzəd·əm\ *n, pl* **supposi·ta** \-d·ə\ [NL — more at SUPPOSIT] **:** SUPPOSIT

sup·press \sə'pres\ *vt* -ED/-ING/-ES [ME *suppressen*, fr. L *suppressus*, past part. of *supprimere* to press under, suppress, fr. *sub-* + *premere* to press — more at PRESS] **1 a :** to put down or out of existence by or as if by authority, force, or pressure **:** SUBDUE ⟨the incipient uprising had been completely ~*ed* —S.G.Inman⟩ **b :** to force into impotence or obscurity **c :** to extinguish by prohibiting, dissolving, or dispersing ⟨empowered the governments to ~ all opposition parties —C.E. Black & E.C.Helmreich⟩ **2 :** to keep from public knowledge: as **a :** to refrain from divulging **:** leave undisclosed ⟨a famous penal institution the name of which I prefer to ~ —Henry Miller⟩ **b :** to prohibit or interdict the publication or revelation of **:** cause to be withheld or withdrawn from circulation ⟨foreign correspondent's copy is not censored, but certain news is ~*ed* —R.H.Sollen⟩ ⟨union halls were closed, papers ~*ed* —Meridel Le Sueur⟩ **3 a :** to exclude from consciousness ⟨the satisfaction of a ~*ed* creative wish —T.S.Eliot⟩ ⟨they ought when thus . . . ~*ed* to give some sign in disorder of the conscious life —Havelock Ellis⟩ **b :** to keep from giving vent to **:** hold back ⟨it has been hard to ~ the question —*Reporter*⟩ ⟨disciplined to ~ his personal impulses —Green Peyton⟩ **4** *obs* **:** to press down **:** COMPRESS **5** *obs* **:** RAPE **6 a :** to stop or check the flow of **:** arrest the discharge of ⟨~ a cough⟩ ⟨~ a hemorrhage⟩ **b :** to inhibit the growth or development of **:** cause to become abortive or vestigial **:** STUNT ⟨growth of an apical bud usually ~*es* that of adjacent lateral buds⟩ **syn** see CRUSH

sup·press·ant \-s°nt\ *adj* [*suppress* + *-ant*] *med* **:** SUPPRESSIVE

sup·pressed \-st\ *adj* [fr. past part. of *suppress*] **1 :** subjected to, marked or affected by, or manifesting suppression ⟨~ emotion⟩ ⟨~ organ⟩ **2 :** having the crown below the main forest canopy where it receives little or no direct light and is retarded, stunted, or even killed ⟨a forest with many ~ trees⟩ — **sup·pressed·ly** \-stlē, -sədlē\ *adv*

suppressed inflation *n* **:** REPRESSED INFLATION

sup·press·ible \-səbəl\ *adj* [*suppress* + *-ible*] **:** capable of being suppressed ⟨no book . . . is ~ if the publisher and author are unashamed and unapologetic —M.L.Ernst⟩

sup·pres·sion \sə'preshən\ *n* -s [L *suppression-*, *suppressio*, fr. *suppressus* (past part. of *supprimere* to suppress) + *-ion-*, *-io* -ion] **1 a :** the action of suppressing or the state of being suppressed ⟨an excuse for slanting the news and for outright ~ of the facts —Liston Pope⟩ ⟨the ~ of rebellion⟩ **b :** an instance of suppressing **2 a :** stoppage of a bodily function or a symptom ⟨~ of urine secretion⟩ ⟨~ of a cough⟩ **b :** the failure of development of a bodily part or organ **c :** retardation or stoppage of growth in a tree or its branches caused by insufficient light or nutrition — compare SUPPRESSED 2 **3 :** the conscious intentional exclusion from consciousness of a thought or feeling — contrasted with *repression* **4 :** the control of a forest fire after its discovery **:** the extinction and limitation of the spread of a forest fire

sup·pres·sio ve·ri \sə,preshē,ō've,rī, -vā,rē\ *n* [NL] *Roman, civil, & Scots law* **:** suppression of the truth — compare DOLUS, SUGGESTIO FALSI

sup·pres·sive \sə'presiv\ *adj* [L *suppressus* + E *-ive*] **:** tending to suppress **:** effecting suppression ⟨opposed the ~ measures used by the government —S.G.Inman⟩; *specif* **:** serving to suppress activity, function, symptoms ⟨treatment of malaria by ~ but not curative drugs⟩ ⟨a ~ agent for cough⟩

sup·pres·sor \sə'presə(r)\ *n* -s [LL, fr. L *suppressus* + *-or*] **:** one that brings about suppression ⟨a noise ~ for a jet⟩: as **a :** a gene with no detectable effect other than to suppress the normal expression of another nonallelic gene when both are present — compare EPISTATIC **b :** a device (as a spark plug resistor) to suppress interfering radio signals or noise by the use of special circuits or circuit elements

suppressor grid *n* **:** a grid usu. located between the screen grid and plate of an electron or vacuum tube to prevent the passage of secondary electrons from one to the other

sup·pu·rate \'səpyə,rāt, *usu* -ād.+V\ *vb* -ED/-ING/-S [L *suppuratus*, past part. of *suppurare* to suppurate, fr. *sub-* + *pur-*, *pus* pus — more at FOUL] *vt* **:** to cause to generate pus **:** bring to a head ~ *vi* **:** to discharge pus ⟨afraid the wound will ~⟩

sup·pu·ra·tion \,==ˈrāshən\ *n* -s [L *suppuration-*, *suppuratio*, fr. *suppuratus* + *-ion-*, *-io* -ion] **:** the formation of, conversion into, or act of discharging pus ⟨an abscess is a localized area of ~⟩ ⟨~ in a wound⟩

sup·pu·ra·tive \'səpyə,rād·iv\ *adj* [L *suppuratus* (past part. of *suppurare* to suppurate) + E *-ive*] **:** attended with suppuration ⟨~ arthritis⟩

sup·pu·ta·tion \,səpyə'tāshən\ *n* -s [ME, fr. L *supputation-*, *supputatio*, fr. *supputatus* (past part. of *supputare* to count up, reckon, fr. *sub-* + *putare* to consider, think) + *-ion-*, *-io* -ion — more at PAVE] *archaic* **:** the act or process or an instance of calculating **:** COMPUTATION, RECKONING

supr *abbr* **1** superior **2** supreme

su·pra \'süprə, -ü(,)prä, -ü(,)prä\ *adv* [L] **:** ABOVE; *esp* **:** in the earlier part of this writing ⟨for additional examples see ~⟩

supra- *in pronunciations below*, '== = ¦süprə *sometimes* -ü(,)prä *or* -ü(,)prä\ *prefix* [L *supra-*, fr. *supra* above, on top, beyond, further back, earlier (adv. & prep.); akin to L *super* over — more at OVER] **1 a :** above **:** higher than ⟨*supra*-anal⟩ **b :** transcending ⟨*supra*national⟩ **2 :** situated on the dorsal or upper side of ⟨*supra*esophageal⟩ ⟨*supra*cranial⟩ **3 :** prior to ⟨*supra*lapsarian⟩

supra–angular \¦==+\ *adj* [*supra-* + *angular*] **:** of, relating to, or being a bone in the lower jaw of some vertebrates (as reptiles and birds) situated above the angular

supra–auricular \"+\ *adj* [*supra-* + *auricular*] **1 :** situated above the auricle of the ear **2** *of a feather* **:** situated above the auriculars

supra–auricular point *n* **:** a craniometric point at the top of the external auditory meatus vertically above the auricular point — see CRANIOMETRY illustration

su·pra·branchial \¦== *at* SUPRA-+\ *adj* [*supra-* + *branchial*] **:** situated over the gills — used esp. of the upper part of the pallial chamber of a bivalve mollusk

su·pra·cardinal vein \"+ . . . -\ *n* [*supra-* + *cardinal*] **:** either of two veins in the mammalian embryo and various adult lower vertebrate forms located in the thoracic and abdominal regions dorsolateral to and on either side of the descending aorta and giving rise to the azygous and hemiazygous veins and a part of the inferior vena cava

su·pra·caudal \"+\ *adj* [*supra-* + *caudal*] **:** situated above the tail — used esp. of the pygal and suprapygal bones and corresponding horny shields of a turtle's carapace

su·pra·cervical \"+\ *adj* [*supra-* + *cervical*] **:** situated or occurring above a neck or cervical process ⟨~ hysterectomy⟩

su·pra·choroid *or* **su·pra·choroidal** \"+\ *adj* [*suprachoroid* fr. NL *suprachoroideus*, fr. *supra-* + *choroides* choroid; *suprachoroidal* fr. NL *suprachoroideus* + E *-al*] **:** of, relating to, or being the layer of loose connective tissue situated between the choroid and sclerotic coats of the eyeball

su·pra·cho·roi·dea \,==kə'rȯidēə\ *n* -s [NL, fr. *lamina suprachoroidea* suprachoroid layer] **:** the suprachoroid layer of the eyeball

su·pra·ciliary \¦== *at* SUPRA- +\ *adj* [*supra-* + *ciliary*] **:** of, relating to, or being any of several small shields situated above the orbit but below the supraoculars in various lizards and snakes

su·pra·clavicle \"+\ *n* [*supra-* + *clavicle*] **:** a bone that usu. connects the clavicle with the posttemporal in the pectoral arch of a fish — called also *scapula*

su·pra·clavicular \"+\ *adj* [*supra-* + *clavicular*] **1 :** situated above the clavicle **2 :** of or relating to the supraclavicle

su·pra·commissure \"+\ *n* [*supra-* + *commissure*] **:** a small commissure anterior to the pineal body

su·pra·conductivity \"+\ *n* [*supra-* + *conductivity*] **:** SUPERCONDUCTIVITY

su·pra·conscious \"+\ *adj* [*supra-* + *conscious*] **:** existing or functioning above the level of the conscious, rational, or logical

su·pra·cor·a·coi·de·us \¦==,kȯrə'kȯidēəs\ *n* -ES [NL, fr. *supra-* + *coracoides* coracoid] **:** a muscle that is important to the body support of limbed reptiles, underlies the front part of the pectoral muscle, arises from the coracoid, and passes to the underpart of the humerus

su·pra·dental \¦== *at* SUPRA- +\ *adj* [*supra-* + *dental*] **:** ALVEOLAR 3, CEREBRAL 3a

su·pra·diaphragmatic \"+\ *adj* [*supra-* + *diaphragmatic*] **:** situated or performed from above the diaphragm ⟨~ vagotomy⟩ — **su·pra·diaphragmatically** \"+\ *adv*

su·pra·dorsal \"+\ *adj* [*supra-* + *dorsal*] **1 :** situated on the back **2 :** of, relating to, or being a series of bony or cartilaginous elements present in some vertebrates above the basidorsals and interdorsals in the primitive vertebral column

su·pra·esophageal \"+\ *adj* [*supra-* + *esophageal*] **:** situated above or over the dorsal aspect of the esophagus

supraesophageal ganglion *n* **:** the main mass of nervous tissue of the insect and some other invertebrates located in the head and dorsal to the esophagus **:** BRAIN 1b, CEREBRUM 2

su·pra·foliaceous \¦== *at* SUPRA- +\ *adj* [*supra-* + L *folium* leaf + E *-aceous* — more at BLADE] **:** inserted on the stem above a leaf

su·pra·foliar \"+\ *adj* [*supra-* + L *folium* leaf + E *-ar*] **:** growing upon a leaf

su·pra·glacial \"+\ *adj* [*supra-* + *glacier* + *-al*] **:** of, relating to, or situated or occurring at the surface of a glacier

su·pra·glottal *or* **su·pra·glottic** \"+\ *adj* [*supra-* + *glottal* or *glottic*] **1 :** situated above or anterior to the glottis — used of organs functioning in the production of sound and esp. speech **2** *of a phoneme* **:** produced by the action of supraglottal organs

su·pra·hepatic \"+\ *adj* [*supra-* + *hepatic*] **:** situated above or on the surface of the liver ⟨a ~ abscess⟩

su·pra·human \"+\ *adj* [*supra-* + *human*] **:** SUPERHUMAN

su·pra·hyoid muscle \"+ . . . -\ *n* [*supra-* + *hyoid*] **:** any of several muscles (as the mylohyoid and geniohyoid) passing upward to the jaw and face from the hyoid bone

su·pra·ilium \"+\ *n* [NL, fr. *supra-* + *ilium*] **:** a cartilaginous epiphysis at the sacral end of the ilium of some animals

¹su·pra·labial \"+\ *adj* [*supra-* + *labial*] **:** of, relating to, or situated above the upper lip — used esp. of scales bordering the upper jaw on each side of the rostral in snakes and lizards

²supralabial \"\ *n* -s **:** a supralabial scale or plate

¹su·pra·lap·sar·i·an \,== *at* SUPRA- +,lap'sa(a)rēən, -ser-\ *n* -s [*supra-* + L *lapsus* fall + E *-arian* (as in *Trinitarian*) — more at LAPSE] **:** one that adheres to the doctrine of supralapsarianism — compare INFRALAPSARIAN

²supralapsarian \¦==¦===\ *adj* **:** of or relating to the doctrine of supralapsarianism

su·pra·lap·sar·i·an·ism \,==¦===,nizəm\ *n* -s [¹*supralapsarian* + *-ism*] **:** the doctrine that God decreed both election and reprobation prior to creation and then allowed the fall of man as a means of carrying out his divine purposes — compare INFRALAPSARIANISM

su·pra·lateral \¦== *at* SUPRA- +\ *adj* [*supra-* + *lateral*] **:** situated high up on the side of the body

su·pra·liminal \"+\ *adj* [*supra-* + L *limin-*, *limen* threshold + E *-al* — more at LIMB] **:** lying above a threshold: as **a :** existing or being above the threshold of consciousness **:** CONSCIOUS **b :** exceeding the stimulus threshold or the difference threshold — **su·pra·liminally** \"+\ *adv*

su·pra·linear \"+\ *adj* [*supra-* + L *linea* line + E *-ar*] **:** situated above the regular lines of a text ⟨~ and marginal comments⟩; *usu* **:** of, relating to, or being a system of Masoretic writing in which the vowels appear immediately above the consonants

su·pra·littoral \"+\ *adj* [*supra-* + *littoral*] **:** of, relating to, constituting, or living in the marginal zone of a body of water that is above ordinary high tide mark

su·pra·loral \"+\ *adj* [*supra-* + *loral*] **:** situated above the lores

su·pra·marginal \¦== *at* SUPRA- +\ *adj* [*supra-* + *marginal*] **1 :** situated above a margin or marginal part ⟨a ~ scute⟩ **2 :** of better than marginal quality **:** SUPERIOR ⟨~ lands⟩

su·pra·mastoid \"+\ *adj* [*supra-* + *mastoid*] **:** situated above the mastoid bone — used esp. of inconstant bony ridges of the temporal and parietal bones

su·pra·maxilla \"+\ *n* [NL, fr. *supra-* + *maxilla*] **:** one of the elements forming the upper jaw of various primitive bony fishes

su·pra·maxillary \"+\ *adj* [*supra-* + *maxillary*] **1 :** of or relating to the upper jaw **2 :** extending over the lower jaw

supramaxillary nerve *n* **1 :** the marginal mandibular branch of the facial nerve extending along the lower jaw and distributed to the muscles of the lower lip and chin **2 :** the maxillary division of the trigeminal nerve

su·pra·maximal \¦== *at* SUPRA- +\ *adj* [*supra-* + *maximal*] **:** higher or greater than a corresponding maximal ⟨a ~ stimulus⟩

su·pra·meatal \"+\ *adj* [*supra-* + LL *meatus* + E *-al*] **:** situated above a meatus and esp. the external auditory meatus ⟨the ~ triangle⟩

su·pra·mental \"+\ *adj* [*supra-* + *mental* (of the chin)] **:** situated above the chin

su·pra·molecular \"+\ *adj* [*supra-* + *molecular*] **:** higher in organization or more complex than a molecule; *often* **:** composed of many molecules

su·pra·mundane \"+\ *adj* [*supra-* + *mundane*] **:** transcending the mundane **:** SPIRITUAL, CELESTIAL

¹su·pra·nasal \"+\ *adj* [*supra-* + *nasal*] **:** situated above the nose or a nasal part ⟨a ~ scale⟩

²supranasal \"\ *n* **:** a supranasal scale of a reptile

su·pra·national \¦== *at* SUPRA- +\ *adj* [*supra-* + *national*] **:** extending beyond or free of the political limitations inhering in the nation-state ⟨~ authority⟩ ⟨~ agencies⟩ ⟨~ languages⟩

su·pra·natural \"+\ *adj* [*supra-* + *natural*] **:** transcending the natural **:** SUPERNATURAL

su·pra·normal \"+\ *adj* [*supra-* + *normal*] **:** transcending the normal **:** greater than expected or usual

su·pra·nuclear \"+\ *adj* [ISV *supra-* + *nuclear*] **:** situated above a nucleus; *specif* **:** situated cortically with respect to a nucleus of the brain

¹su·pra·occipital \"+\ *adj* [*supra-* + *occipital*] **1 :** situated over or in the upper part of the occiput **2 :** of, relating to, or being a median bone of the cranium lying above the foramen magnum and forming part of the occipital bone in the adult of the higher vertebrates but distinct in the young and in lower forms

²supraoccipital \"\ *n* **:** a supraoccipital bone

¹su·pra·ocular \¦== *at* SUPRA- +\ *adj* [*supra-* + *ocular*] **:** situated above the eye **:** SUPRAORBITAL; *esp* **:** lying above the orbit and usu. in contact with the frontal of a reptile ⟨~ scales⟩

²supraocular \"\ *n* **:** a supraocular part (as a scale)

su·pra·optic \¦== *at* SUPRA- +\ *adj* [*supra-* + *optic* (*chiasma*)] **:** situated above the optic chiasma; *esp* **:** being a small nucleus of closely packed neurons overlying the optic chiasma and intimately connected with the neurohypophysis

su·pra·optimal \"+\ *adj* [*supra-* + *optimal*] **:** greater than optimal

su·pra·orbital \"+\ *adj* [NL *supraorbitalis*, fr. *supra-* + ML *orbita* orbit + L *-alis* -al] **:** situated or occurring above the orbit of the eye ⟨a ~ headache⟩ **:** SUPRAOCULAR

supraorbital artery *n* **:** a branch of the ophthalmic artery supplying the orbit and parts of the forehead

supraorbital nerve *n* **:** a branch of the frontal nerve supplying the forehead, scalp, cranial periosteum, and adjacent parts

supraorbital notch *n* **:** a notch or foramen in the bony border of the upper inner part of the orbit serving for the passage of the supraorbital nerve, artery, and vein

supraorbital point *n* **:** OPHRYON

supraorbital ridge *or* **supraorbital torus** *n* **:** SUPERCILIARY RIDGE

supraorbital vein *n* **:** a vein draining the supraorbital region and uniting with the frontal to form the angular vein

su·pra·ordinate \¦== *at* SUPRA- +\ *adj* [*supra-* + L *ordin-*, *ordo* order + E *-ate*] **:** of or concerned with higher ranks or orders ⟨~ tests in which given species are to be associated with logically proper genera⟩ — **su·pra·ordination** \"+\ *n*

su·pra·organism \"+\ *n* [*supra-* + *organism*] **:** an organized society (as of a social insect) that functions as an organic whole

su·pra·personal \"+\ *adj* [*supra-* + *personal*] **:** transcending the merely personal

su·pra·phylar \"+\ *adj* [*supra-* + *phylar*] **:** being at a level above a phylum

su·pra·position \"+\ *n* [*supra-* + *-position* (as in *superposition*)] **:** SUPERPOSITION

su·pra·protest \"+\ *n* [modif. of It *sopra protesto* upon protest] **:** an acceptance or payment of a bill by a third person for the honor of the drawer after protest for nonacceptance or nonpayment by the drawee

su·pra·pubic \"+\ *adj* [*supra-* + *pubic*] **:** situated or performed from above the pubis ⟨~ prostatectomy⟩ — **su·pra·pubically** \"+\ *or* **su·pra·pubicly** \"+\ *adv*

su·pra·pygal \"+\ *adj* [*supra-* + *pygal*] **1 :** situated above the rump **2 :** of, relating to, or being one or more median bones between the pygal bone and last neural bones or a shield between the supracaudal and last neural shields in the carapace of some turtles

su·pra·rational \"+\ *adj* [*supra-* + *rational*] **:** transcending the rational **:** based on or involving factors not to be comprehended by reason alone ⟨held that God never acts in a ~ manner —K.S.Latourette⟩

¹su·pra·renal \"+\ *adj* [NL *suprarenalis*, fr. L *supra-* + *renes* (pl.) kidneys + *-alis* -al] **:** situated above or anterior to the kidneys; *specif* **:** ADRENAL

²suprarenal \"\ *n* -s **:** a suprarenal part; *esp* **:** ADRENAL GLAND

su·pra·re·nal·ec·to·my \,süprə,rēn°l'ektəmē\ *n* -ES [ISV ²*suprarenal* + *-ectomy*] **:** ADRENALECTOMY

suprarenal gland *also* **suprarenal body** *n* **:** ADRENAL GLAND

su·pra·ren·a·lin \,süprə'ren°lən\ *n* -s [²*suprarenal* + *-in*] **:** EPINEPHRINE

su·pra·scapula \¦== *at* SUPRA- +\ *n* [NL, fr. *supra-* + *scapula*] **1 :** a cartilaginous or partly ossified plate attached to the superior end of the scapula in various amphibians and reptiles **2 :** the posttemporal of a fish

su·pra·scapular \"+\ *adj* [NL *suprascapularis*, fr. *supra-* + *scapula* + L *-aris* -ar] **1 :** situated above the scapula **2** [NL *suprascapula* + E *-ar*] **:** of, relating to, or being a suprascapula

suprascapular artery *n* **:** a branch of the thyrocervical trunk that passes obliquely from within outward across the root of the neck and over the coracoid ligament to the back of the scapula

suprascapular ligament *n* **:** CORACOID LIGAMENT

suprascapular notch *n* **:** a deep notch in the upper border of the scapula at the base of the coracoid process giving passage to a branch of the brachial plexus that supplies the supraspinatus and infraspinatus muscles

su·pra·script \'⸗⸗ *at* SUPRA- + ˌskript\ *adj or n* [L *supra-* + *scriptus*, past part. of *scribere* to write — more at SCRIBE] **:** SUPERSCRIPT

su·pra·segmental \¦⸗⸗ *at* SUPRA- +\ *adj* [*supra-* + *segment* + *-al*] **1 :** situated above or anterior to segments or segmental parts **2 :** developed in addition to segments or segmental parts: as **a :** of, relating to, or being the parts of the brain that constitute the cerebellum and cerebral cortex together with associated white matter and nuclei, are increasingly developed in higher vertebrates, and cannot be identified with specific parts of the primitive metameric chordate pattern — compare NEOPALLIUM, SEGMENTAL **b :** of or relating to significant features of pitch, stress, and juncture accompanying or superadded to vowels and consonants when the latter are assembled in succession in the construction of a speaker-to-hearer communication ⟨segmental and ~ components⟩

suprasegmental phoneme *n* **:** one of the phonemes (as pitch, stress, juncture, nasalization, voice or voicelessness in clusters) of a language that occur simultaneously with a succession of segmental phonemes — called also *prosodeme*

su·pra·sellar \¦⸗⸗ *at* SUPRA- +\ *adj* [ISV *supra-* + NL *sella* + ISV *-ar*] **:** situated or rising above the sella turcica — used chiefly of tumors of the hypophysis

su·pra·sensuous \"+\ *adj* [*supra-* + *sensuous*] **:** transcending the merely sensuous or sensory

su·pra·solar \"+\ *adj* [*supra-* + *solar*] **:** exceeding the sun in size or other characteristics

su·pra·species \"+\ *n* [*supra-* + *species*] **:** ARTENKREIS

su·pra·spinal \"+\ *adj* [*supra-* + *spinal*] **:** situated above a spine; *esp* **:** situated over the spinous process of the scapula

su·pra·spi·na·tus \ˌ⸗⸗ˌspī'nād·əs\ *n* -ES [NL, fr. *supra-* + L *spina* spine + *-atus* -ate — more at SPINE] **:** a muscle of the back of the shoulder arising from the supraspinous fossa of the scapula and inserted into the top of the greater tubercle of the humerus

su·pra·spinous \¦⸗⸗ *at* SUPRA- +\ *adj* [*supra-* + *spinous*] **1 :** SUPRASPINAL **2 :** situated above or on the dorsal side of the vertebral spines

supraspinous ligament *n* **:** a fibrous cord joining the tips of the spinous processes of the vertebrae from the seventh cervical to the sacrum and continued forward to the skull as the ligamentum nuchae

su·pra·squamosal \¦⸗⸗ *at* SUPRA- +\ *n* [*supra-* + *squamosal*] **:** SUPRATEMPORAL

su·pra·stapedial \"+\ *adj* [*supra-* + *stapedial*] **:** situated above the stapedial part of the columella of the ear

su·pra·sternal \"+\ *adj* [*supra-* + NL *stern*um + E *-al*] **:** situated above or measured from the top of the sternum ⟨~ height⟩

su·pra·ster·na·le \¦⸗⸗(ˌ)stər'na(ˌ)lē, -nā(-, -nä(-\ *n* -S [NL, fr. *supra-* + *sternum* + *-ale*, neut. of L *-alis* -al] **:** the deepest point in the hollow of the suprasternal notch lying at the middle of the anterior-superior border of the sternal manubrium

suprasternal notch *n* **:** a depression of the external surface of the neck above the sternum and between the lower ends of the sternocleidomastoid muscles

suprasternal space *n* **:** a long narrow space in the lower part of the deep cervical fascia containing areolar tissue, the sternal part of the sternocleidomastoid muscles, and the lower part of the anterior jugular veins — called also *space of Burns*

su·pra·stigmal *also* **su·pra·stigmatal** \¦⸗⸗ *at* SUPRA- +\ *adj* [*supra-* + NL *stigmat-*, *stigma* stigma + E *-al*] **:** placed or developing above a stigma and esp. a spiracle

[1]**su·pra·temporal** \"+\ *adj* [*supra-* + *temporal* (bone)] **:** situated above or relating to the upper part of the temporal bone or region

[2]**supratemporal** \"\ *n* **:** SUPRATEMPORAL BONE

[3]**supratemporal** \"\ *adj* [*supra-* + *temporal* (secular)] **:** transcending temporal affairs

supratemporal arch *n* [[1]*supratemporal*] **:** a bony arch in the skull of many reptiles bounding the supratemporal fossa below and formed typically of the postfrontal, the postorbital, and a process of the squamosal

supratemporal bone *n* **1 :** a bone of the back and side of the skull in close relation with the squamosal in many reptiles **2 :** a small bone at the back of the skull in front of and a little to the outside of the posttemporal in fishes

su·pra·tentorial \¦⸗⸗ *at* SUPRA- +\ *adj* [*supra-* + *tentorial*] **:** situated above or affecting the structures overlying the tentorium of the brain ⟨progressive ~ disease⟩

su·pra·ter·ra·ne·ous \¦⸗⸗tə¦rānēəs, -te¦r-\ *adj* [*supra-* + *-terraneous* (as in *subterraneous*)] **:** SUPERTERRANEAN

su·pra·threshold \¦⸗⸗ *at* SUPRA- +\ *adj* [*supra-* + *threshold*] **:** supramaximal for threshhold ⟨a ~ stimulus⟩

su·pra·tonsillar \"+\ *adj* [*supra-* + L *tonsillae* tonsils + E *-ar*] **:** situated above the palatine tonsil

su·pra·trochlear nerve \"+ . . . -\ *n* [*supra-* + *trochlear*] **:** a branch of the frontal nerve supplying the skin of the forehead and the upper eyelid

su·pra·ventricular \¦⸗⸗ *at* SUPRA- +\ *adj* [*supra-* + *ventricular*] **:** situated or occurring above ventricles (as of the heart); *usu* **:** AURICULAR

su·pra·ver·sion \¦süprə¦vərzhen *also* -rsh-\ *n* -S [*supra-* + *-version* (as in *retroversion*)] **:** extension of a tooth beyond the plane of occlusion

su·pra·vital \¦⸗⸗ *at* SUPRA- +\ *adj* [ISV *supra-* + L *vita* life + ISV *-al* — more at VITAL] **:** constituting or relating to the staining of living tissues or cells surviving after removal from a living body by dyes that penetrate living substance but induce more or less rapid degenerative changes — compare INTRA-VITAM — **su·pra·vitally** \"+\ *adv*

su·prem·a·cist \sə'preməsə̇st, sü'p- *sometimes* -rēm-\ *n* -S [*supremacy* + *-ist*] **:** an advocate or adherent of some concept of group supremacy; *esp* **:** WHITE SUPREMACIST

su·prem·a·cy \sə'preməsē, sü'p-, -məsi *sometimes* -rēm-\ *n* -ES [*supreme* + *-acy* (as in *primacy*)] **1 :** the quality or state of being supreme; *also* **:** supreme authority or power **2 :** the position of being accepted or established as superior to all others in some field or activity ⟨naval ~⟩ ⟨the ~ among dramatists⟩

su·prem·a·tism \-məˌtizəm\ *n* -S [*supremat*ist + *-ism*] **:** an art movement and theory originated by Kazimir Malevich in 1913 and concerned with the pictorial arrangement of austere geometric nonobjective form

su·prem·a·tist \-mətə̇st\ *n* -S [F *suprématie* supremacy (modif. of E *supremacy*) + E *-ist*] **:** an advocate or user of suprematism in art

[1]**su·preme** \sə'prēm, (')sü¦p-, *rapid sometimes* 'sp-\ *adj*, *sometimes* -ER/-EST [L *supremus*, superlative of *superus* that is above, upper, fr. *super* over, above — more at OVER] **1 :** highest in altitude **:** LOFTIEST **2 a :** highest in rank or authority (as within the state or church) **:** holding or exercising power that cannot be exceeded or overruled **:** DOMINANT **b :** of, relating to, or characteristic of one having such rank or power **3 a :** not exceeded by any other in degree, quality, or intensity **:** greatest possible ⟨~ love⟩ ⟨a ~ folly⟩ **b :** characterized by highest excellence or achievement **:** OUTSTANDING ⟨~ among musicians⟩ **4 a :** ULTIMATE, FINAL ⟨made the ~ sacrifice on the field of battle⟩ **b :** of utmost importance **:** CRUCIAL ⟨the ~ hour in our history⟩

[2]**supreme** \"\ *n* -S **:** one that is supreme: as **a** *usu cap* **:** SUPREME BEING **b :** the highest state or degree **:** HEIGHT ⟨this ~ of loveliness⟩

[3]**su·prême** \sə'prēm, sü'p-, -rām\ *n* -S [F, fr. *suprême* supreme, fr. MF, fr. L *supremus*] **1 :** a rich white sauce made of chicken stock and cream — called also *sauce suprême* **2** *also* **supreme :** a tall footed sherbet glass with a large bowl **3 a :** a made dish (as an entree) dressed with a sauce suprême ⟨a ~ of sole⟩ **b** *also* **supreme :** a dessert served in a suprême

supreme being *n* **1** *cap S & B* **:** the eternal and infinite Spirit **:** God as the creator and end of man **2 :** a god who dominates all the lesser gods and daemons of a pantheon and who is generally conceived as the creator of all **3 :** a power or being to which all else is subordinate or upon which all else is ultimately dependent

supreme court *n* **1 :** the highest judicial tribunal in a political unit (as a nation or state) ⟨the U. S. *Supreme Court* has both original and appellate jurisdiction⟩ ⟨the *Supreme Court* of Canada . . . renders decisions in disputes between the provinces and the Dominion —*Canadian Citizenship Series*⟩ — compare COURT OF CASSATION, COURT OF SESSION, HIGH COURT OF JUSTICE, SUPREME COURT OF JUDICATURE **2 :** a court of original jurisdiction in New York and formerly in New Jersey that is subordinate to a final court of appeals and constitutes the general trial court of the state

supreme court of judicature *usu cap S&C&J* **:** a consolidated system of superior courts comprising the High Court of Justice together with the Court of Appeal and the Court of Criminal Appeal and having jurisdiction in England and Wales

supreme good *n* [trans. of L *summum bonum*] **:** SUMMUM BONUM

supreme judicial court *n*, *usu cap S&J&C* **:** a judicial court of last resort (as in Maine or Massachusetts)

su·preme·ly *adv* **:** in a supreme manner **:** so as to be supreme

su·preme·ness *n* -ES **:** the quality or state of being supreme

sups *pres 3d sing of* SUP, *pl of* SUP

supsd *abbr* supersede

supt *abbr* **1** superintendent **2** support

sup·tion \'səpshən\ *n* -S [origin unknown] *dial* **:** BODY, SUBSTANCE, FLAVOR ⟨chewing tobacco until the ~ is out of it —Malcolm Cowley⟩

supv *abbr* supervise

supvr *abbr* supervisor

suq *also* **souk** *or* **suk** \'sük\ *n* -S [Ar *sūq* market] **:** a marketplace in the Muslim East

su·qua·mish \sə'kwämish, 'skw-, -wȯm-\ *n*, *pl* **suquamish** *or* **suquamishes** *usu cap* **1 a :** a Salishan people of the area directly west of Puget Sound, Washington **b :** a member of such people **2 :** a dialect related to Skagit

sur \'sər\ *prep* [F, fr. L *super* over — more at OVER] **:** ON, UPON — used chiefly in law reports and in the names of proceedings ⟨a writ of entry ~ disseisin —George Booth⟩ ⟨~ motion for a new trial —*U. S. Daily*⟩

sur- *prefix* [ME, fr. OF *sour-*, *sur-*, fr. L *super-* — more at SUPER-] **1 a :** over **:** SUPER- ⟨*sur*print⟩ ⟨*sur*revise⟩ ⟨*sur*fuse⟩ **b :** excessive ⟨*sur*cloy⟩ ⟨*sur*excitation⟩ **2 :** above **:** up ⟨*sur*anal⟩ ⟨*sur*base⟩

sur *abbr* **1** surcharged **2** surface **3** surplus **4** surrendered

[1]**su·ra** \'su̇rə\ *n* -S [Skt *surā*, lit., wine, spirituous liquor] **:** the fermented juice of various East Indian palms (as the palmyra and toddy palm)

[2]**su·ra** *also* **su·rah** \'sürə\ *n* -S [Ar *sūrah*, lit., row] **:** one of the sections or chapters of the Koran

su·ra·ba·ja *or* **soe·ra·ba·ja** *or* **su·ra·ba·ya** \¦su̇rə¦bäyə, -¦bīə\ *adj*, *usu cap* [fr. *Surabaja* or *Soerabaja* or *Surabaya*, Java] **:** of or from the city of Surabaja, on the island of Java, Indonesia **:** of the kind or style prevalent in Surabaja

su·rah \'sürə\ *n* -S [prob. alter. of [2]*surat*] **:** a soft light lustrous fabric usu. made of silk or rayon in twill weave and used for clothing (as dresses or neckties)

su·ra·kar·ta *or* **soe·ra·kar·ta** \¦su̇rə¦kärd·ə\ *adj*, *usu cap* [fr. *Surakarta* or *Soerakarta*, Java] **:** of or from the city of Surakarta, on the island of Java, Indonesia **:** of the kind or style prevalent in Surakarta

su·ral \'su̇rəl\ *adj* [NL *suralis*, fr. L *sura* calf of the leg + *-alis* -al; perh. akin to L *surus* branch — more at SURCULUS] **:** of or relating to the calf of the leg; *esp* **:** relating to branches of the popliteal artery or vein that ramify in this area

sur·a·min \'su̇rəmə̇n\ *or* **suramin sodium** *n* -S [prob. fr. *surr*a + *-am* + *-in*] **:** a trypanocidal drug $C_{51}H_{34}N_6Na_6O_{23}S_6$ obtained as a white powder and administered intravenously in the early stages of African sleeping sickness

sur·anal \¦sər+\ *adj* [*sur-* + *anal*] **:** above the anus or an anal part (as an anal fin)

suranal plate *n* **:** PYGIDIUM b

[1]**su·rat** \su̇'rat, 'sü(ˌ)rət\ *adj*, *usu cap* [fr. *Surat*, India] **:** of or from the city of Surat, India **:** of the kind or style prevalent in Surat

[2]**surat** \"\ *n* -S [fr. *Surat*, India, where it was produced] **1 :** any of several Indian cottons having coarse dark fibers **2 :** a usu. uncolored cotton cloth made from surat

sur·base \'sərˌbās\ *n* [*sur-* + *base*] **1 :** a molding immediately above the base of a wall (as of a wainscoted room) **2 :** a cornice or a series of moldings at the top of the base of a pedestal or podium — see DADO illustration

sur·based \-st\ *adj* [F *surbaissé* depressed, flattened, surbased (fr. past part. of *surbaisser* to lower from above, depress, flatten, fr. *sur-* + *baisser* to lower, fr. *bas* low, fr. MF) + E *-ed* — more at BASE] **1 :** having the curve center below the springing line of imposts ⟨~ arch⟩ ⟨~ vault⟩ **2 :** having a surbase

surbate *vb* -ED/-ING/-S [ME *surbaten*, fr. MF *surbatu*, past part. of *surbatre* to beat up, fr. *sur-* + *battre* to beat, fr. L *battuere* — more at BAT] *vt*, *obs* **:** to make footsore ~ *vi*, *obs* **:** to become footsore

[1]**sur·cease** \ˌsər'sēs, sə̄'-, səi'-\ *vb* -ED/-ING/-S [ME *surcesen*, alter. (influenced by *cesen* to cease) of *sursesen*, fr. MF *sursis*, past part. of *surseoir* to refrain, delay, fr. L *supersedēre* — more at SUPERSEDE] *vi* **1 :** to desist from or leave off some action **:** take a respite **:** discontinue a proceeding **2 :** to come to an end **:** become discontinued **:** CEASE ~ *vt* **1** *obs* **:** to put an end to **:** cause to cease **:** bring to an end **2 :** to desist or refrain from **:** give up **:** ABANDON, DISCONTINUE ⟨the hobbyhorse *surceased* his capering —Sir Walter Scott⟩

[2]**sur·cease** \'⸗ˌ⸗, ˌsər'-, sə̄'-, səi'-\ *n* -S **:** CESSATION 1; *esp* **:** a temporary suspension, intermission, or respite ⟨been in the public eye almost without ~ —Angelica Gibbs⟩ ⟨finding . . . ~ from care —*Cosmopolitan*⟩

[1]**sur·charge** \'sərˌchärj, 'sə̄ˌchȧj, 'səiˌchȧj *sometimes* ˌsər'- *or* sə̄'- *or* səi'-\ *vt* [ME *surchargen*, fr. MF *surcharger*, fr. *sur-* + *charger*, *chargier* to charge — more at CHARGE] **1 a :** to charge too much **:** subject to an excess or burdensome charge or tax **:** OVERCHARGE **b :** to charge (one) an extra or additional fee usu. for some special service **c :** to show an omission in (an account) for which credit ought to have been given **d** *Brit* **:** to charge (as one of the members) for an expense incurred outside statutory limitations by a local government body **:** charge (a public official) for monies improperly spent **2** *Brit* **:** OVERSTOCK; *esp* **:** to put more cattle into (as a common) than a person has a right to do or more than the herbage will sustain **3 a** *obs* **:** to weigh down in the manner of a physical burden **:** bear heavily upon ⟨the greatest affairs ~ him . . . not —Robert Leighton⟩ **b :** to fill to overflowing **:** OPPRESS, OVERWHELM ⟨the atmosphere . . . was *surcharged* with war hysteria —H.A.Chippendale⟩ ⟨*surcharged* with pent-up feelings, she wrote —Louis Untermeyer⟩ **c :** to fill to excess **:** OVERCROWD — usu. used in passive ⟨the hospital wards are *surcharged*⟩ **4 a :** to place an additional and usu. excessive physical weight or burden upon **:** OVERBURDEN, OVERLOAD **b** *archaic* **:** SURFEIT **c :** to impregnate to repletion **:** give an excessive charge to ⟨winds blowing from the sea are generally *surcharged* with moisture —Charles Lyell⟩ **5 a :** to add a new denomination figure to or to mark a surcharge on (a stamp) ⟨the 1*c* stamp was *surcharged* 3*c*⟩ ⟨the 2*c* stamps were *surcharged* to supply a shortage of another denomination⟩ **b :** OVERPRINT ⟨~ a stamp⟩ ⟨~ a banknote⟩ **6 :** to charge (a bearing) upon another heraldic bearing ⟨on a pointed oval shield . . . is *surcharged* a kite-shaped shield —Allan Marquand⟩

[2]**surcharge** \'⸗ˌ⸗\ *n* **1 :** the action of surcharging a common **2 a :** a charge in excess of the usual or normal amount **:** an additional tax, cost, or impost ⟨the 10 percent ~ on postal cards purchased in quantities of 50 or more —*Publishers' Weekly*⟩ **b :** an additional rate added to the usual charge in transportation ⟨a ~ for jet airplane service⟩ ⟨a sleeping car ~⟩ **c** (1) **:** an instance of surcharging an account (2) **:** a statement of such surcharging **3 :** an additional and usu. excessive charge, load, burden, or supply **4 :** the action of surcharging or the state of being surcharged **5 a** (1) **:** an overprint on a stamp; *specif* **:** one that alters the denomination (2) **:** a stamp bearing such an overprint **b :** an overprint on a currency note **6 :** the earth behind a retaining wall and above a horizontal plane at the elevation of the top of the wall

sur·cin·gle *or* **cir·cin·gle** \'sərˌsiŋgəl, 'sə̄ˌ-, 'səiˌ-\ *n* -S [ME *sursengle*, fr. MF *surcengle*, fr. *sur-* + *cengle* belt — more at CINGLE] **1 :** a belt, band, or girth passing around the body of a horse and usu. used to bind something (as a saddle or pack) fast to the horse's back **2 :** the girdle or cincture of a cassock

sur·coat \'sərˌkōt, 'sə̄ˌ-, 'səiˌ-\ *n* [ME *surcote*, fr. MF, fr. *sur-* + *cote* coat — more at COAT] **1 a** *or* **sur·cote** \"\ **:** a fitted coat or robe made in short or long styles with or without sleeves and often with a fur lining and worn by men and women in late medieval times **b** (1) **:** a sleeved or sleeveless tunic of late medieval times worn over armor and often emblazoned with heraldic devices (2) **:** a similar garment worn on formal occasions by members of various orders of knighthood **2 :** an outdoor jacket usu. hip length and belted worn chiefly by men and boys

sur·cu·lose \'sərkyəˌlōs\ *or* **sur·cu·lous** \-ˌləs\ *adj* [L *surculosus*, fr. *surculus* sucker + *-osus* -ose] **:** having numerous branches arising from near the base ⟨a ~ coral⟩ **:** producing suckers

sur·cu·lus \'sərkyələs\ *n*, *pl* **surcu·li** \-yəˌlī\ [L, dim. of *surus* branch, stake; akin to OE *swēr*, *swēor* pillar, column, MHG *swir* stake, pole, Gk *herma* prop, support, Skt *svaru* stake] **:** SUCKER 3a

[1]**surd** \'sərd, 'sə̄d, 'səid\ *adj* [L *surdus* dull-sounding, silent, deaf; akin to L *susurrus* hum, murmur — more at SWARM] **1 :** lacking sense **:** lacking reason or rationale **:** INSENSATE, IRRATIONAL ⟨the ~ mystery and the strange forces of existence —D.C.Williams⟩ **2 :** VOICELESS — used of speech sounds; opposed to *sonant*

[2]**surd** \"\ *n* -S **:** one that is surd: as **a :** an irrational radical with rational radicand ⟨$\sqrt{3}$ and $\sqrt{2/5}$ are ~*s*⟩ **b :** a surd speech sound **c :** an unknown or irrational quality ⟨the uncharted ~ at the heart of European politics —William Barrett⟩

[1]**sure** \'shu̇(ə)r, 'shu̇ə *sometimes* 'shər *or* 'shə̄, *esp South, NewEng, & Brit* 'shō(ə)r *or* 'shōə *or* 'shȯ(ə)r *or* 'shȯ(ə), *chiefly substand South* 'shō\ *adj*, *often* -ER/-EST [ME *sure*, *sur*, fr. MF *sur*, fr. L *securus* safe, secure — more at SECURE] **1** *obs* **a :** free from danger or exposure to risk **:** secure from liability to injury or destruction **b :** safely secured from doing or certain not to do some specified action ⟨make thee ~ enough from adding this lewdness to thine other abominations —Joseph Hall⟩ **c :** safely in one's possession or under one's control **:** unlikely to escape, become lost, do harm, or create disturbance; *esp* **:** DEAD ⟨cut his throat, so making him ~ —Philemon Holland⟩ **2 a :** firmly settled or established **:** unlikely to be overthrown or displaced or to yield **:** FAST, STABLE, STEADFAST, STEADY, STRONG ⟨a ~ foundation⟩ ⟨a ~ hold⟩ **b :** unfailing in character or condition **:** ENDURING, UNFALTERING ⟨a ~ faith⟩ **3 :** marked by complete dependability or reliability (as in fulfilling expectations, hopes, or trust) **:** entirely trustworthy or dependable **:** certain not to fail or disappoint expectation **:** RELIABLE ⟨a ~ messenger⟩ ⟨a ~ remedy⟩ ⟨the *surest* means to this end⟩ ⟨the English had ~ supplies of food —George Bancroft⟩ **4 a :** assured in mind **:** having no doubt or fear **:** marked by or given to feelings of confident certainty and conviction esp. of the rightness of one's judgment or intuition **:** characterized by an unwavering or unreserved certainty ⟨this same suggestion of ~ and calm conviction in some of the judgments —B.N.Cardozo⟩ ⟨did not release his bomb until he was ~ of a direct hit —F.D. Roosevelt⟩ ⟨~ that he would come⟩ ⟨always a very ~ person⟩ **b :** marked by firmness, assurance, and steadiness (as in deportment, bearing, execution, or handling) **:** characterized by a lack of wavering or hesitation ⟨~ brush strokes⟩ ⟨a ~ hand⟩ **5 :** objectively certain **:** admitting of no doubt, condition, or qualification **:** marked by unquestionable fact, verity, or substantiation **:** INDUBITABLE, INDISPUTABLE, POSITIVE ⟨the evidence is ~⟩ ⟨spoke from ~ knowledge⟩ **6** *obs* **a :** contracted or promised in marriage **:** BETROTHED **b :** bound by loyalty or an oath of allegiance (as to a person or party) ⟨made that party ~ unto him —Richard Baker⟩ **7 a :** bound to come about or to happen **:** certain to eventuate **:** ASSURED ⟨moving to ~ disaster⟩ ⟨his success is ~⟩ **b :** destined esp. by fate **:** BOUND ⟨he is ~ to win⟩

syn CERTAIN, POSITIVE, COCKSURE: SURE and CERTAIN are often interchangeable; in the few situations in which they do differ, SURE may be used with judgments or expressions that are subjective or intuitive, CERTAIN with those that rest on indubitable evidence ⟨wonderful how she managed that light note when you were *sure* she couldn't be feeling it —Mary Austin⟩ ⟨of this I am quite *sure*, that there is no inconsistency or natural repugnance between this poetical and religious faith in the same mind —William Hazlitt⟩ ⟨trust me one day more . . . without more *certain* guarantee, than this poor face you deign to praise so much —John Keats⟩ ⟨the only dependable foundation of personal liberty is the personal economic security of private property. The teaching of history is very *certain* on this point —Walter Lippmann⟩ POSITIVE intensifies sureness or certainty; it indicates conviction of one's rightness with no suggestion of doubt; it may but does not necessarily suggest an unduly strong or opinionated conviction forcefully expressed ⟨an assertive *positive* man . . . had his own notion of what a young man should be —Sherwood Anderson⟩ ⟨so much more *positive* than most of his customers, and he impressed his own convictions on them so determinedly, that he had his own way —H.E.Scudder⟩ COCKSURE almost always suggests presumptuous vanity, self-assuredness, or cocky lack of consideration of all details ⟨a people which . . . had been regarded as brash to the point of arrogance, *cocksure* to the verge of folly, and so wholly certain of its future and itself that travelers wrote books about the national assurance —Archibald MacLeish⟩ **syn** see in addition CONFIDENT

— **to be sure** *adv* **1 :** without doubt **:** CERTAINLY ⟨*to be sure* I am⟩ **2 :** it must be acknowledged **:** ADMITTEDLY — usu. used to introduce an exception or limitation ⟨they were brave, *to be sure*, but ineffectual⟩

[2]**sure** \"\ *adv* [ME, fr. *sure*, *sur*, adj.] **:** SURELY ⟨~, I'll be there⟩

[3]**sure** \"\ *n* -S **:** CERTAINTY — compare FOR SURE

sure enough *adv* **:** as one might confidently expect **:** CERTAINLY, DEFINITELY, POSITIVELY ⟨in most cases the spontaneity is there, *sure enough* —*Times Lit. Supp.*⟩

sure–enough \'⸗⸗ˌ⸗\ *adj* [*sure enough*] **:** ACTUAL, GENUINE, REAL ⟨the life for a *sure-enough* man —A.B.Guthrie⟩ ⟨upriver to look at a *sure-enough* fish wheel —*Christian Science Monitor*⟩

surefire \'⸗¦⸗\ *adj* [[1]*sure* + *fire*] **:** certain to produce a usu. specified or desired result **:** proved by experience to be reliable **:** DEPENDABLE ⟨a ~ device⟩ ⟨a ~ winner⟩ ⟨a ~ recipe⟩ ⟨made my production . . . — once an unpredictable operation — entirely ~ —*New Yorker*⟩

surefooted \'⸗¦⸗⸗\ *adj* [[1]*sure* + *footed*] **1 :** unlikely to make a slip or error (as in judgment or execution of policy) **:** proceeding surely ⟨most ~ of the statesmen who dealt with the depression —Walter Lippmann⟩ ⟨a director as ~ and experienced as this one —Aline B. Saarinen⟩ **2 :** sure of foot **:** unlikely to stumble, fall, slip, or skid **:** moving firmly and confidently on or as if on foot ⟨on ~ donkeys —M.O.Williams⟩ ⟨a ~ tractor⟩

sure·foot·ed·ness *n* -ES **:** the quality or state of being surefooted ⟨the ~ of the mountain goat⟩

sure–handed \'⸗¦⸗⸗\ *adj* **:** having or held to have hands that are sure in performing some action **:** proficient and confident in performance ⟨promising playwrights . . . *sure-handed* enough to turn out top-drawer scripts with any consistency —Henry Hewes⟩

sure·ly *adv* [ME *surly*, fr. *sur* sure + *-ly* — more at SURE] **1 :** in a sure manner: **a** *archaic* **:** SAFELY, SECURELY ⟨he that walketh uprightly walketh ~ —Prov 10:9 (AV)⟩ **b** (1) **:** with assurance or confidence ⟨people who respond immediately and ~ to works of art —Clive Bell⟩ (2) **:** without doubt **:** CERTAINLY, UNDOUBTEDLY ⟨the tremendous growth that is ~ ahead in this country —C.F.Craig⟩ **c** *obs* **:** in a faithful manner **:** LOYALLY ⟨that I may ~ keep mine oath —Shak.⟩ **2 :** ASSUREDLY,

INDEED, REALLY — often used as an interjection or intensive or to qualify a statement

sure·ness *n* -ES [ME *surnes*, fr. *sur* sure + *-nes* -ness] **:** the quality or state of being sure **:** CERTAINTY, CONFIDENCE ⟨impeccable ~ of hand —Laurence Binyon⟩ ⟨~ of purpose and steadiness of gait —O.E.Rölvaag⟩

surer *comparative of* SURE

su·res \'sü,rās\ *n pl* [Sp, pl. of *sur* south, of Gmc origin; akin to OE *sūth* south — more at SOUTH] **:** southerly winds on the coasts of Chile and Peru

sureseater \'=',==\ *n* [*sure* + *seater;* fr. there usu. being empty seats] **:** ART THEATER

sures par·dos \-'pär,dōs\ *n pl* [Sp, lit., drab sures] **:** sures accompanied by fog

surest *superlative of* SURE

¹sure thing *n* **:** something that is or is held to be certain (as to succeed or bring success) **:** something reliable in behavior or development **:** something (as a bet) upon which one allegedly cannot lose ⟨a positively *sure thing* in a race —Joel Sayre⟩ ⟨a *sure thing* does not arouse us emotionally —John Dewey⟩

²sure thing *adv* **:** CERTAINLY — often used interjectionally

su·rette \sü'ret\ *n* -S [F, sourish, dim. of *sur* sour, of Gmc origin; akin to OHG *sūr* sour — more at SOUR] **:** a tropical American tree (*Byrsonima crassifolia*) having hard dark-colored wood and edible yellow acid berries

sure·ty *R* 'shu̇r(ə)|d·|ē, |t|, |i *sometimes* 'shər-; *–R* 'shu̇ə|, 'shōə|, 'shȯ(ə)|, 'shu̇rə|, 'shōrə|, 'shȯrə| *sometimes* 'shə̄\ *n* -ES [ME *surte*, fr. MF *surté*, fr. L *securitat-*, *securitas* safety, security — more at SECURITY] **1 :** the state or condition of being sure: as **a** *obs* **:** safety or security from danger **b :** certainty of knowledge (as of a fact or an event) ⟨there is no ~ he ever reached the river —Julian Dana⟩ ⟨unable to predict a development with ~⟩ **c :** confidence and sureness in action ⟨a bit less ~ of walk —Donald Windham⟩ **2 a :** something that confirms or makes sure **:** a pledge or other formal engagement given for the fulfillment of an undertaking **:** GUARANTEE **b :** ground of confidence or security (as against loss or damage or for payment or the performance of some act) **3 a :** a person formerly given or giving himself as a gage or pledge **:** HOSTAGE **b :** one (as a sponsor at baptism or a bondsman) who makes a pledge in behalf of another and accepts certain accruing responsibilities **:** a person who is bound on an obligation from which another by the discharge of a duty should relieve him **:** one who has become legally liable for the debt, default, or failure in duty (as appearance in court or payment of a debt) of another — compare PRINCIPAL

surety bond *n* **:** a written instrument evidencing a contract of suretyship **:** a bond guaranteeing performance of a contract or obligation — compare FIDELITY BOND

surety company *n* **:** a company whose primary business is acting as a surety for the performance of obligations esp. by the issuing of surety bonds

sure·ty·ship \-,ship\ *n* **:** the state of being surety **:** the obligation of one who is surety **:** the obligation of a person to answer for the debt, default, or failure in duty of another — compare GUARANTY

sur·excitation \;sər+\ *n* [*sur-* + *excitation*] **:** excessive excitation

¹surf \'sərf, 'sə̄f, 'səif\ *n* -S *often attrib* [origin unknown] **1 a :** the swell of the sea that breaks upon the shore (as upon a sloping beach) **b :** the breaking waves or their foam, splash, and sound **2 :** something that looks like, sounds like, or otherwise is held to resemble surf ⟨a ~ of dust rising back of the carriage —Gilbert Parker⟩ ⟨a constant ~ of yells . . . from hundreds of cell windows —Jan Valtin⟩

²surf \"\ *vi* -ED/-ING/-S **1 a :** to bathe in the surf **b :** to ride the surf (as on a surfboard) **2 :** to swell, break, or otherwise behave in a manner suggesting surf ⟨the lace frill of her dress ~*ed* white in the sun —William Sansom⟩ ⟨tides of . . . commerce caught up and ~*ed* over me —Christopher Morley⟩

¹sur·face \'sərfəs, 'sə̄f-, 'səif-\ *n* -S [F, fr. *sur-* + *face*, fr. OF — more at FACE] **1 :** the exterior or outside of an object or body **:** the outermost or uppermost boundary **:** one or more of the faces of a three-dimensional thing **:** a plane of a solid ⟨the uneven ~ of the earth⟩ ⟨on the ~ of the water⟩ ⟨planks with a rough ~⟩ ⟨the octagonal ~*s* of a diamond⟩ **2 :** a two-dimensional locus of points **:** the boundary or portion of the boundary of a three-dimensional region ⟨a plane ~⟩ ⟨a spherical ~⟩ **3 :** something held to resemble the surface of an object or body: **a :** the part of something that is presented to a viewer with little or no examination **:** the outward appearance or characteristics of something **:** the external aspect ⟨the ~ of society⟩ ⟨deep beneath the ~ of the legal system —B.N.Cardozo⟩ **b :** someone or something without depth **:** a mere outside **:** one that is superficial in nature **4 :** a complete airfoil used for sustentation or control or to increase stability **5 :** the condition of a railroad track marked by vertical evenness or smoothness over short distances ⟨the track is in ~⟩ **6 a :** PRINTING SURFACE ⟨autographic works printed from ~*s* actually produced by the artist —Barnett Freedman⟩ ⟨printing done from relief ~*s*⟩ **b :** STONE 1b(11) — **on the surface** *adv* **:** to all outward appearances **:** so far as one can see ⟨the entire system was, at least *on the surface*, remarkably efficient —F.A.Ogg & Harold Zink⟩ ⟨*on the surface* there is no apparent relationship between the two books —Harrison Smith⟩

²surface \"\ *vb* -ED/-ING/-S *vt* **1 :** to give a surface to: as **a :** to plane (as lumber) or make smooth **b :** to apply the surface layer to ⟨the towers are *surfaced* with steel plates —*Amer. Guide Series: N.Y. City*⟩ ⟨~ a highway⟩ **c :** to finish (as furniture or a marble slab) esp. by polishing or varnishing **d :** to give a usu. specified surface to ⟨walls *surfaced* with cream stucco —*Amer. Guide Series: N.C.*⟩ **2 :** to bring to the surface ⟨two wells . . . ~ more than 6,000 gallons of water a minute —Gaston Burridge⟩ **~** *vi* **1 :** to work on or at the surface — used esp. of a gold digger who works the ground superficially or a tracklayer who brings the top of the rail to a true grade line **2 :** to come or rise to the surface (as of the water) ⟨a submarine *surfaced* outside the harbor⟩ ⟨a subway downtown, the line ~*s* after three miles —A.H.Brown⟩ ⟨the truth began to ~ —Robert Jackson⟩

³surface \"\ *adj* **1 a :** of, located on, or designed for use at the surface of something ⟨designing ~ instruments for the detection of oil deposits —W.J.Reilly⟩ ⟨~ forces⟩ ⟨~ vessels⟩ ⟨~ runoff of water⟩ **b :** situated on the surface of the earth rather than in the air or underground ⟨~ transportation⟩ ⟨~ communications⟩ **c** (1) **:** of or relating to surface mail ⟨~ postage⟩ (2) **:** handled as surface mail ⟨~ parcel post⟩ **2 :** acting upon or against a surface ⟨a ~ grinder⟩ **3 :** working at or near the surface ⟨~ mining⟩ **:** worked at or near the surface ⟨~ mines⟩ **4 a :** appearing on the surface only **:** lacking depth ⟨accurate ~ realism —R.A.Cordell⟩ ⟨improvements in ~ conditions but not in fundamental weaknesses⟩ **b :** SUPERFICIAL ⟨~ friendships⟩

surface–active \¦=¦==\ *adj* **:** modifying the properties of a liquid medium at a surface or interface usu. by reducing surface tension or interfacial tension ⟨all detergents are *surface-active* but not all surface-active agents are detergents —F.D.Snell⟩

surface–active agent *n* **:** a substance useful for its cleansing, wetting, dispersing, or similar powers ⟨*surface-active agents* . . . in dilute aqueous solution —Donald Price⟩ — called also *surfactant;* see DETERGENT c; compare WETTING AGENT

surface–bent \¦==¦=\ *adj* **:** bent so as to be not straight in the vertical plane ⟨a *surface-bent* railroad rail⟩

surface car *n* **:** a car (as a streetcar) for transportation on land as opposed to a subway or elevated car

surface carburetor *n* **:** a carburetor in which air is charged by being passed over the surface of gasoline

surface chemistry *n* **:** a branch of chemistry that deals with the properties of surfaces or phase boundaries and with the chemical changes occurring at a surface or interface

surface color *n* **1 a :** the color ascribed to an opaque substance or object **b :** a color extending no farther than the surface **2 :** color determined by selective reflection at the surface (as the yellow color of gold) **3 :** a color localized in the surface of an object and conforming to the orientation, configuration, and texture of that surface — compare BULKY COLOR, FILM COLOR

surface–colored paper \'==,==-\ *n* **:** a safety paper for postage stamps having color on the side which is to receive the design

surface cooler *n* **:** a tank of cold water or other liquid-cooling medium for cooling milk in cans

surface creep *n* **:** a stage in the wind erosion process in which sand grains are moved along the ground surface by impact of other grains in saltation

surfaced *adj* **:** having or provided with a usu. specified kind of surface ⟨~ roads⟩ — often used in combination ⟨a smooth-*surfaced* stone⟩

surface density *n* **:** a quantity (as mass or electricity) per unit area distributed over a surface

surface dive *n* **:** a dive made from the surface of the water to varying depths and executed headfirst in tuck or pike position or feetfirst

surfaced lumber *n* **:** lumber dressed by a planer

surface energy *n* **:** the energy associated with the intermolecular forces at the interface between two media ⟨the *surface energy* per unit area equals the surface tension⟩ — called also *free surface energy*

surface fire *n* **:** a forest fire that burns only surface litter and undergrowth

surface gauge *n* **1 :** a scriber mounted in an adjustable stand for marking off castings or testing the accuracy of plane surfaces and used with a surface plate **2 :** a gage for measuring ordinates of points on a surface of the work from a reference plane

surface gravity *n* **:** intensity of the force of gravity at the surface of the earth or a celestial body

surface harden *vt* **:** to harden the surface of (as steel) by a case hardening process or other method (as induction or flame)

surface integral *n* **:** the limit of the sum of products formed by multiplying the area of a portion of a surface by the value of a function at any point in this area, the summation covering the entire surface and the area of the largest portion approaching zero

surface layer *n* **:** a layer (as a layer of moisture) having a resistivity different from that of the body on which it is deposited

sur·face·ly *adv* **:** on the surface **:** SUPERFICIALLY ⟨aspects of life as ~ lived —Sheldon Cheney⟩

surface mail *n* **1 :** mail carried by land or sea transportation rather than by air **2 :** the postal system or services handling surface mail

sur·face·man \'==mən\ *n, pl* **surfacemen 1 :** a man who works on the surface (as on the roadbed of a railroad or the surface works of a mine) **2 :** a repairer of road surfaces

surface measure *n* **:** the surface area of a board **:** board measure when the board is one inch thick

surface noise *n* **:** a hissing sound in the background of a phonograph record reproduction produced when the needle passes along a groove of less than perfect smoothness of surface — called also *needle scratch*

surface of revolution **:** a surface held to be formed by the revolution of a plane curve about a line in its plane

surface plate *n* **:** a steel instrument of precision having a dressed flat surface or sometimes two surfaces at right angles and used as a standard of flatness

surface printing *n* **1 :** LETTERPRESS **2 :** PLANOGRAPHY

sur·fac·er \'sərfəsər; 'sə̄fəsə(r, 'səif-\ *n* -S **:** one that surfaces: as **a :** a machine for planing or dressing the surface (as of wood, metal, or stone) — compare BUZZ PLANER, CYLINDER PLANER **b :** a device used in preparing railroad ties for tie plates **c :** one that surfaces furniture **d :** an undercoat of paint used to level up inequalities of a surface **e :** a worker who grinds and polishes optical lenses **f :** SEASONER c **g :** a worker who smooths the faces of watch wheels and reduces them to the proper thickness by rubbing them on a wet emery-paper surface

surface railway *n* **:** a railway whose tracks are mainly on the surface rather than beneath it (as in a subway) or above it on a superstructure (as in an elevated railway)

surface resistance *n* **:** the electrical resistance of a surface layer to a current

surface rib *n* **:** a merely ornamental rib on the surface of a vault **:** LIERNE

surfaces *pl of* SURFACE, *pres 3d sing of* SURFACE

surface–size \'=,=\ *vt* **:** to treat the surface of (paper) with a sizing agent (as glue or starch) **:** TOP-SIZE — compare BEATER-SIZE, TUB-SIZE

surface soil *n* **:** the upper 5 to 8 inches of the soil layer **:** the portion of the soil usu. tilled

surface switch *n* **:** a snap switch designed for mounting on a plane surface and requiring no enclosing parts (as a box)

surface tension *n* **:** a condition that exists at the free surface of a body (as a liquid) by reason of intermolecular forces unsymmetrically disposed about the individual surface molecules and is manifested by properties resembling those of an elastic skin under tension; *specif* **:** the force per unit length of any straight line on the surface that the surface layers on opposite sides of the line exert upon each other

surface water *n* **:** natural water that has not penetrated much below the surface of the ground **:** drainage water — compare GROUNDWATER, RAINWATER, SPRINGWATER

surface wave *n* **:** an earthquake vibration propagated in the earth's outer shell — contrasted with *body wave*

surfacing *n* -S [fr. gerund of ²*surface*] **1 :** the action of one that surfaces: **a :** the action or process of digging gold on the surface of the ground **b :** the motion of a tool or part of a tool used in making or finishing a surface **c :** the action of bringing the top of a railroad rail to a true grade line **2 :** material forming or used to form a surface ⟨the ~ for a road⟩ ⟨wash the ~ for gold⟩ ⟨stucco ~ crudely painted to simulate black marble —H.S.Morrison⟩

surfacing machine *n* **:** SURFACER a

sur·fac·tant \,sər'faktənt\ *n* -S [*surface-active agent*] **:** SURFACE-ACTIVE AGENT

sur·facy \'sərfəsē\ *adj* [¹*surface* + *-y*] **:** characterized by surface rather than depth **:** SUPERFICIAL ⟨his music has a ~ brilliance —Irving Lowens⟩

surfbird \'=,=\ *n* [¹*surf* + *bird*] **:** a shorebird (*Aphriza virgata*) of the Pacific coasts of No. and So. America related to the turnstones but somewhat like the golden plover in form and habits and readily distinguished in all plumages by its tail which is blackish at the tip and broadly white at the base

¹surfboard \'=,=\ *n* **:** a long narrow buoyant board used in the sport of riding the surf

²surfboard \"\ *vi* **:** to ride the surf on a surfboard — **surf·board·er** \"+ə(r)\ *n*

surfboat \'=,=\ *n* **:** a boat fit for use in heavy surf; *esp* **:** one built strong and buoyant and with a marked sheer to ride the seas better

surf cast *vi* **:** to engage in surf casting

surf caster *n* **:** one that engages in surf casting

surf casting *n* **:** the technique or act of casting artificial or natural bait into the open ocean or in a bay where waves break on a beach

surf clam *n* **:** any of various typically rather large surf-dwelling edible clams constituting the family Mactridae — called also *hen clam, sea clam;* see SPISULA

surf coot *n* **:** SURF SCOTER

surf duck *n* **:** SCOTER; *esp* **:** SURF SCOTER

surfed *past of* SURF

¹sur·feit \'sərfət, 'sə̄f-, 'səif-, *usu* -əd·+V\ *n* -S [ME *surfait*, *surfet*, fr. MF *sourfait*, *seurfet*, fr. past part. of *sourfaire* to reach too high, lit., overdo, fr. *sour-*, *sur-* sur- + *faire* to make, do, fr. L *facere* — more at DO] **1 :** an overabundant supply, yield, or amount of something **:** EXCESS, SUPERFLUITY ⟨a murder with a ~ of clues and motives —*London Calling*⟩ ⟨hard to choose . . . from such a ~ of riches —Martin Levin⟩ **2 a :** an intemperate or immoderate indulgence in something (as food or drink) usu. to a degree that causes physical disorders ⟨died of a ~ of sprats —T.C.Chubb⟩ **b** *obs* **:** the amount (as of food or drink) taken intemperately or in excess ⟨his loathing stomach . . . shall cast the precious ~ up again —Richard Blackmore⟩ **3** *archaic* **:** a sickness arising from excess in eating and drinking **:** sickness caused by intemperance ⟨he died of a ~ caused by intemperance —Oliver Goldsmith⟩ **4 :** disgust caused by excess **:** SATIETY ⟨supplied abundantly and even to ~ —Edmund Burke⟩

²surfeit \"\ *vb* -ED/-ING/-S [ME *surfeten*, fr. *surfet* surfeit] *vt* **:** to feed, supply, or give to surfeit **:** disgust or sicken by excess **:** fill to satiety or repletion **:** CLOY ⟨a large and corpulent individual ~*ed* . . . with good eating —Theodore Dreiser⟩ ⟨the public was already ~*ed* with . . . histories —Edmund Wilson⟩ **~** *vi* **1** *archaic* **:** to indulge excessively or to satiety in any gratification (as of the appetite or senses) ⟨a merrier set of gourmands . . . never ~*ed* in genial diet —E.K.Kane⟩ **2 a** *obs* **:** to suffer from overindulgence **:** become sick esp. from food or drink taken in excess ⟨they are as sick that ~ with too much as they that starve with nothing —Shak.⟩ **b** *archaic* **:** to become nauseated or disgusted with an excess of something **:** become sick of something overabundant ⟨so early dost thou ~ with the wealth —H.F.Cary⟩ **syn** see SATIATE

sur·feit·er \"+ə(r)\ *n* -S *archaic* **:** one (as a glutton or libertine) that surfeits or cloys

surfeit water *n* **:** a water formerly used to cure surfeit

surf·er \'sərfər\ *n* -S **1** *dial* **:** SURF SCOTER **2 :** one that rides a surfboard

surf fish *n* **1 :** any of numerous small or medium-sized fishes that constitute the family Embiotocidae, live chiefly in shallow water along the Pacific coast of No. America, and resemble perches in form but differ from them in their anatomy and in being viviparous **2 :** any of several croakers (family Sciaenidae) of the Pacific coast of No. America **3 :** SURF SMELT

surf–fish *vi* **:** to angle along the ocean shore with tackle esp. designed to cast a natural or artificial bait up to a distance of 200 yards

surfgrass \'=,=\ *n* [¹*surf* + *grass*] **:** a grasslike aquatic plant of the genus *Phyllospadix* (family Potamogetonaceae) living on rocky ocean shores and having narrow linear basal leaves and small dioecious flowers borne on the side of a flattened spadix

surf green *n* **1 :** a light to moderate green that is yellower and less strong than Neptune **2 :** a moderate yellowish green that is yellower, lighter, and stronger than tarragon, yellower and paler than malachite green, and yellower and stronger than verdigris

sur·fi·cial \,sər¦fishəl\ *adj* [*surface* + *-icial* (as in *superficial*)] **1 :** of or relating to a surface and esp. the earth's surface — opposed to *subterranean* **2 :** SUPERFICIAL 1c

surfing *pres part of* SURF

surfle *vt* -ED/-ING/-S [perh. alter. of *sulfur*, n.] *obs* **:** to wash or tint (as the face) with a cosmetic

surf line *n* **:** a line of foam-crested waves breaking on a formation (as a shoal) near the surface

surf·man \'=mən\ *n, pl* **surfmen :** one who is skilled in handling a boat in surf; *specif* **:** one employed in the life-saving branch of the U.S. Coast Guard

surfperch \'=,=\ *n* **:** SURF FISH 1

surf plant *n* **:** a plant (as a kelp) growing where it is exposed to tidal action **:** CUMATOPHYTE

surf reel *n* **:** a free spool multiplying fishing reel used in surf-fishing

surf–riding \'=,==\ *n* **:** the sport of riding the surf esp. on a surfboard

surf rod *n* **:** a two-handed fishing rod usu. more than seven feet overall designed specif. for use with a surf reel

surfs *pl of* SURF, *pres 3d sing of* SURF

surf scoter *n* **:** a common American scoter (*Melanitta perspicillata*) of which the adult male has conspicuous white markings on the head and neck with otherwise black plumage and the female and young are grayish brown — called also *surf coot*

surf smelt *n* **:** a pale greenish smelt (*Hypomesus pretiosus*) of the coast of California and northward that spawns in the surf

surf snipe *n* **:** SANDERLING

sur·fuse \,sər'fyüz\ *vb* [*sur-* + *fuse*] **:** SUPERCOOL

sur·fu·sion \-üzhən\ *n* **:** the state of being surfused

surf whiting *n* **:** SILVER WHITING

surfy \'sərfē\ *adj* -ER/-EST [¹*surf* + *-y*] **:** of, abounding in, or resembling surf ⟨a ~ shore⟩

surg *abbr* **1** surgeon **2** surgery **3** surgical

¹surge \'sərj, 'sə̄j, 'səij\ *n* -S *often attrib* [prob. fr. MF *sourge-*, alter. (influenced by L *surgere*) of *sourj-*, stem of *sourdre* to rise, surge, fr. L *surgere* to rise, go straight up, fr. *subs-* (var. of *sub-* up) + *regere* to lead straight, rule — more at SUB-, RIGHT] **1 :** a swelling, rolling, or sweeping forward like that of an oncoming billow or series of billows **:** an onward rush **:** a violent rising and falling ⟨a ~ of interest⟩ ⟨intermittent ~*s* of enthusiasm⟩ ⟨the musketry sounded in long irregular ~*s* —Stephen Crane⟩ ⟨the ~ of the hills⟩ **2 a :** a large wave or billow **:** a great rolling swell of water ⟨the sea was rolling in immense ~*s* —R.H.Dana⟩ **b :** a series of such swells or billows **3 :** the tapered part of a windlass barrel or a capstan on which a cable surges **4 a :** a movement (as a slipping or slackening) of a rope or cable **b :** a sudden jerk or strain caused by such a movement **5 :** a barometric wave apparently independent of and unexplained by existing barometric gradients **6 :** a transient variation of current in an electrical circuit (as when a motor is started) **:** a sudden rise and fall of voltage — compare TRANSIENT CURRENT

²surge \"\ *vb* -ED/-ING/-S [MF *sourgir*, fr. OSp *surgir*, fr. L *surgere* to rise, go straight up] *vi* **1 :** to rise and fall with much motion **:** toss on the waves **:** ride atop the waves ⟨the vessel at anchor *surged* in the heavy sea⟩ **2** *obs* **:** to rise like a spring from its source or a river from underground **3 a :** to rise and move in surges, high waves, or great billows **:** swell in an agitated manner ⟨the sea . . . ~*s* on its limestone cliffs —Harrison Smith⟩ **b :** to rise in a surge **:** swell or heave with great force ⟨a wave ~*s*⟩ **4 :** to slip around a windlass, capstan, or bitts — used esp. of a rope **5 :** to rise suddenly to an excessive or abnormal value **:** rise to and fall from such a value successively — used esp. of current or voltage **6 :** to rise, heave, blow, sound, or otherwise move with a surge or in surges ⟨a great glow of . . . tenderness *surged* through him —O.E.Rölvaag⟩ ⟨the incessant traffic ~*s* past —Margaret Devlin⟩ ⟨millions of farmers . . . *surged* westward —R.A. Billington⟩ ⟨the music of the organ *surged* through the church⟩ **~** *vt* **1 :** to cause to rise or fall in surges **:** cause to move in a surge **2 :** to let go or slacken gradually (as a rope) ⟨~ a hawser to prevent its parting⟩ **syn** see RISE

surge chamber *n* **:** SURGE TANK

surge gap *n* **:** a spark gap (as in an arrester) for the discharge of surges due to lightning

surge·less \-jləs\ *adj* **:** free from surges ⟨~ seas⟩

sur·gen·cy \-jənsē\ *n* -ES [²*surge* + *-ency*] **:** a personality factor characterized by quickness and cleverness

sur·gent \'sərjənt\ *adj* [L *surgent-*, *surgens*, pres. part. of *surgere* to rise] **:** rising in a surge **:** swelling in surges or waves ⟨~ seas⟩

sur·geon \'sərjən, 'sə̄j-, 'səij-\ *n* -S [ME *surgien*, fr. AF, contr. of OF *serurgien*, *cirurgien*, fr. *serurgie*, *cirurgie* surgery + *-ien* -ian — more at SURGERY] **1 :** a medical specialist who performs surgery **:** a physician qualified to treat those diseases that are amenable to or require surgery — compare INTERNIST **2 :** the senior medical officer of a military unit **3 :** SURGEONFISH

surgeon apothecary *n, Brit* **:** a surgeon who is also an apothecary **:** a general practitioner

surgeon commander *n* **:** an officer in a medical corps (as of the British Navy) having the rank of commander

sur·geon·cy \-nsē\ *n* -ES [*surgeon* + *-cy*] *Brit* **:** the office or position of a surgeon ⟨a vacant ~⟩

surgeon dentist *n* **:** an oral surgeon

surgeonfish \'=,=\ *n* [*surgeon* + *fish;* fr. the lancelike spines suggesting a surgeon's instruments] **:** any of numerous spiny-finned fishes of the family Teuthididae that are related to the Moorish idols but are usu. less conspicuously colored and have a more elongate body, bear on each side near the base of the tail one or more movable lancelike spines, and occur in most warm seas esp. in the East Indies — called also *tang*

surgeon general *n, pl* **surgeons general 1 a :** the chief of the medical service of the U. S. Army having the rank of major general **b :** the chief of the Bureau of Medicine and Surgery in the U. S. Navy having the rank of rear admiral **c :** the chief medical officer of the U. S. Air Force **2 :** the chief medical

officer in the U. S. Bureau of Public Health or of a state public health bureau **3 :** one of the ten members of the medical staff of the British Army

surgeon major *n, pl* **surgeons major :** the ranking surgeon of a regiment in the British Army

surgeon's agaric *n* **:** a preparation in the form of a powder or thick feltlike sheets of an agaric (*Fomes fomentarius*) formerly used as a hemostatic

surgeon's knot *n* **:** any of several knots used in tying ligatures or stitches; *esp* **:** a reef knot in which the first knot has two turns

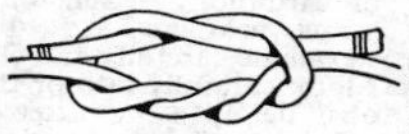

surgeon's knot

sur·gery \ˈsərj(ə)rē, ˈsə̄j-, ˈsəij-, -ri\ *n* -ES [ME *surgerie*, fr. OF, contr. of *serurgerie*, *cirurgerie*, fr. *serurgie*, *cirurgie* (fr. L *chirurgia*, fr. Gk *cheirourgia*, fr. *cheirourgos* working with the hand — fr. *cheir* hand + *-ourgos* working, fr. *-o-* + *ergon* work — + *-ia* -y) + *-erie* -ery — more at CHIR-, WORK] **1 :** a branch of medicine that is concerned with diseases and conditions requiring or amenable to operative or manual procedures ⟨orthopedic ~⟩ ⟨new techniques in brain ~⟩ **2 :** the treatment of other than human ills or diseases by methods analogous to or as drastic as those of a surgeon ⟨the agonizing ~ of revolution —John Strachey⟩ ⟨a superb piece of literary ~ —Norman Cousins⟩ — see TREE SURGERY **3 a** *Brit* **:** a room or office (as in a general practitioner's house) where a doctor sees and treats patients **b :** the room (as in a doctor's or dentist's offices) or the quarters (as in a hospital) where surgery is performed ⟨the patient walked into the doctor's ~⟩ ⟨the patient was anesthetized in ~⟩ **4 a :** the work done by a surgeon ⟨the operation was a skillful piece of bloodless ~⟩ **b :** OPERATION ⟨he had a ~ at six o'clock⟩

surges *pl of* SURGE, *pres 3d sing of* SURGE

surge tank *n* **:** a standpipe or storage reservoir at the downstream end of a closed aqueduct or feeder pipe (as for a water wheel) to absorb sudden rises of pressure and to furnish water quickly during a drop in pressure — called also *surge chamber*

sur·gi·cal \ˈsərjəkəl, ˈsə̄j-, ˈsəij-, -jēk-\ *adj* [*surgeon* + *-ical*] **1 :** of, relating to, or concerned with surgeons or surgery **2 :** requiring surgical treatment ⟨~ appendix⟩ — distinguished from *medical* **3 :** resulting from surgery ⟨~ fever⟩ **4 :** done by or used in surgery or surgical conditions ⟨~ gauze⟩ ⟨~ stocking⟩ **5 :** held to resemble medical surgery esp. in precision or incisiveness ⟨a ~ insight into character —F.A. Pottle⟩ ⟨as a tool of analysis it was ~ in its keenness —H.A. Overstreet⟩ ⟨a ~ precision⟩

surgical diathermy *n* **:** surgery by electrocoagulation

surgical knot *n* **:** SURGEON'S KNOT

sur·gi·cal·ly \-jək(ə)lē, -jēk-, -li\ *adv* **:** by or as if by means of surgery **:** in a surgical manner ⟨~ polished corridors —Alan Brien⟩ ⟨almost ~ exact work —Winthrop Sargeant⟩ ⟨~ clean⟩

surgical needle *n* **:** a needle designed to carry sutures when sewing tissues

surging *pres part of* SURGE

surgy \ˈsərjē\ *adj* [¹*surge* + *-y*] *archaic* **:** rising in or like surges or billows **:** abounding in surges ⟨over the ~ main —Alexander Pope⟩

su·ri·a·na \ˌsu̇rēˈānə\ *n, cap* [NL, fr. Joseph D. *Surian*, 18th cent. Fr. botanist] **:** a genus of tropical seashore shrubs or small trees (family Surianaceae) with narrow densely clustered leaves and small yellow flowers — see BAY CEDAR 2

su·ri·a·na·ce·ae \ˌsu̇rēəˈnāsēˌē\ *n pl, cap* [NL, fr. *Suriana*, type genus + *-aceae*] **:** a monotypic family of dicotyledonous plants (order Geraniales) — see SURIANA

su·ri·ca·ta \ˌsu̇rəˈkādˌə\ *n, cap* [NL, fr. F *surikate*] **:** a genus of mammals (family Viverridae) consisting of the suricates

su·ri·cate \ˈsu̇rəˌkāt\ *also* **su·ri·cat** \-kat\ *n* -S [F *surikate*, prob. fr. native name in southern Africa] **:** a burrowing mammal (*Suricata tetradactyla*) of southern Africa that is related to the mongooses but has only four toes, is grayish banded with black, is diurnal and social in habits and in some respects behaves like a prairie dog, and is often kept as a pet

su·ri·nam \ˈsu̇rəˌnam\ *adj, usu cap* [fr. *Surinam*, northern So. America] **:** of or from Surinam **:** of the kind or style prevalent in Surinam

surinam cabbage tree *n, usu cap S* **:** a tree (*Andira retusa*) of Guiana having bark that is used as an anthelmintic and cathartic — compare WORM BARK

surinam cherry *n, usu cap S* **1 a :** a Barbados cherry (*Malpighia glabra*) with rose to purple flowers and deep red fruits **b :** the edible aromatic fruit of this tree **2 a :** a Brazilian tree (*Eugenia uniflora*) often cultivated in California and Florida for its spicy red fruit that resembles a cherry **b :** the fruit of this tree

surinam cockroach *n, usu cap S* **:** a widely distributed dark brown tropical cockroach (*Pycnoscelus surinamensis*)

surinam disease *n, usu cap S* **:** PANAMA DISEASE

su·ri·nam·er \ˈsu̇rəˌnamə(r)\ *n, cap* [*Surinam* + E *-er*] **:** SURINAMESE

¹**su·ri·nam·ese** \ˌsu̇rəˌnaˈmēz, -ēs\ *adj, usu cap* [*Surinam* + E *-ese* (adj. suffix)] **1 :** of, relating to, or characteristic of Surinam **2 :** of, relating to, or characteristic of the people of Surinam

²**surinamese** \"\ *n, pl* **surinamese** *cap* [*Surinam* + E *-ese* (n. suffix)] **:** a native or inhabitant of Surinam

surinam quassia *n, usu cap S* **1 :** a tree (*Quassia amara*) growing in tropical America and the West Indies **2 :** the drug obtained from the Surinam quassia

surinam toad *n, usu cap S* **1 :** an aquatic aglossate toad (*Pipa pipa* syn. *P. americana*) of the Guianas and parts of Brazil of which the eggs as they are laid are distributed by the male over the back of the female where they become embedded in the skin each in a separate cavity with a lid formed from the outer capsule of the egg and within which the tadpole lives and metamorphoses **2 :** AGUA

sur les pointes \ˌsərləˈpwaⁿt, -ant\ *adv (or adj)* [F] *ballet* **:** on the tips of the toes

sur·li·ly \ˈsər|ləlē, ˈsə̄l-, ˈsəil-, -əli\ *adv* **:** in a surly manner **:** with gloomy ill nature **:** RUDELY

sur·li·ness \|lēnəs, |lin-\ *n* -ES **:** the quality or state of being surly **:** gloomy ill nature **:** surly character or manner **:** RUDENESS

¹**sur·ly** \|lē, |li\ *adj, often* -ER/-EST [alter. of obs. E *sirly*, fr. ME, fr. *sir* + *-ly* — more at SIR] **1** *obs* **:** arrogant in manner or bearing **:** DOMINEERING, HAUGHTY, IMPERIOUS ⟨be opposite with a kinsman, ~ with servants —Shak.⟩ **2 :** ill-natured, abrupt, and rude **:** churlishly cross **:** CRABBED ⟨answered in a ~ voice⟩ ⟨a ~ dog⟩ ⟨a ~ old man⟩ **3 a :** making or accompanied by threatening sounds **:** menacing, gloomy, or dismal in appearance ⟨~ weather⟩ **b :** difficult to manage **:** INTRACTABLE — used chiefly of soil **syn** see SULLEN

²**surly** \"\ *adv* **:** in a haughty or imperious manner ⟨a lion . . . went ~ by —Shak.⟩

sur·ma *or* **soor·ma** \ˈsu̇rmə\ *n* -S [Per *surma*] **:** native antimony sulfide used in India to darken the eyelids

sur·mark *or* **sir·mark** \ˈsərˌmärk\ *n* [*surmark* fr. *sur-* + *mark*; *sirmark* prob. alter. (influenced by ¹*sir*) of *surmark*] **1 :** a mark made on the molds of a ship when building to show where the frames should be beveled **2 :** a cleat temporarily placed on the side of a ship on the ways or in a ship dock to support the ribband against which the shores rest

sur·mis·able \sə(r)ˈmīzəbəl\ *adj* **:** capable of being surmised ⟨regardless of all known or ~ laws —*N. Y. Herald Tribune*⟩

¹**sur·mise** \sə(r)ˈmīz\ *vb* -ED/-ING/-S [ME *surmisen*, fr. MF *surmis*, *surmise*, masc. & fem. past part. of *surmetre* to charge, accuse, prob. fr. L *supermittere* to throw upon, fr. *super-* + *mittere* to throw — more at SMITE] *vt* **1 :** to imagine without certain knowledge **:** infer on slight grounds **:** form a notion of on slight proof **:** GUESS, SUPPOSE ⟨then she knew that what before she but *surmised* was true —John Dryden⟩ ⟨a delicate matter to ~ the thoughts of men —Emma Hawkridge⟩ ⟨he *surmised* that this was the true situation⟩ ~ *vi* **:** to make a surmise or guess **:** indulge in conjecture **syn** see CONJECTURE

²**sur·mise** \sə(r)ˈmīz; ˈsərˌm-, ˈsə̄ˌ-, ˈsəiˌ-\ *n* -S [ME, fr. MF, accusation, fr. *surmetre* to charge, accuse] **1** *archaic* **a :** SUSPICION 1 ⟨a very painful ~ arose concerning her character —Ann Radcliffe⟩ **b :** a slight trace or sign **:** SUSPICION 3 ⟨some faintest ineffectual ~ of mercy —Thomas Carlyle⟩ **2** *obs* **:** an unfounded allegation or charge **3** *obs* **:** the action of surmising or imagining **4 :** a thought or idea based on scanty evidence **:** a random conclusion **:** CONJECTURE, GUESS ⟨what he expressed as a mere ~ was transcribed by others as a positive statement —Richard Semon⟩

sur·mis·er \sərˈmīzər\ *n* -S **:** one that surmises

sur·mount \sərˈmau̇nt\ *vt* [ME *surmounten*, fr. MF *surmonter*, fr. *sour-* sur- + *monter* to rise, mount — more at MOUNT] **1 a** *obs* **:** to surpass in quality or attainment **:** EXCEL ⟨kings courts ~ poor shepherds cells —Francis Quarles⟩ **b** *archaic* **:** to exceed in amount or magnitude **:** amount to more than ⟨their increment ~s daily their decrease —Matthew Hale⟩ **2 :** to rise above or surpass in height ⟨extinct volcanic centers ~ them near the core of the plateau —*Jour. of Geol.*⟩ **3 :** to rise superior to **:** get the better of **:** prevail over **:** OVERCOME ⟨~ an obstacle⟩ ⟨~ an aversion⟩ ⟨~ a temptation⟩ **4** *obs* **:** SURPASS 3 ⟨thy thoughts of love to me ~ the power of number to recount —John Wesley⟩ **5 :** to climb over **:** get to the top of and over **:** mount and cross to the other side of ⟨~ one crag after another⟩ **6 a :** to stand or lie at the top of **:** remain on the top of **:** CROWN, TOP ⟨a cross ~s the steeple⟩ ⟨the house . . . ~s a knoll —*Amer. Guide Series: N. Y. City*⟩ **b :** to place above so as to cover partly another heraldic charge ⟨a silver crane on a gules shield, ~*ed* by a crown —M.B. Grosvenor⟩ **syn** see CONQUER

sur·mount·able \-təbəl\ *adj* **:** capable of being surmounted **:** SUPERABLE ⟨situations of measurable and ~ danger —C.P. Romulo⟩

surmounted arch *n* **:** a stilted semicircular arch

sur·mullet \ˌsər+\ *n, pl* **surmullets** *also* **surmullet** [F *surmulet*, fr. MF *sormulet*, prob. fr. *sor* reddish brown + *mulet* mullet — more at SORREL, MULLET] **:** a mullet of the family Mullidae

¹**sur·name** \ˈsərˌnām, ˈsə̄ˌ-, ˈsəiˌ-\ *n* [ME, fr. *sur-* + *name*] **1 a :** a name added onto an original or baptismal name from some pertinent or accidental circumstance (as occupation, place of residence, or physical appearance) **b** *obs* **:** a second name or an alternative title given to one (as a person, object, or place) **2 a :** the name borne in common by members of a family as distinguished from an individualizing forename **:** the inherited last name taken by children and changed only legally (as by adoption or by a woman's taking her husband's name) **b** *obs* **:** a cognomen of the ancient Romans

²**surname** \"\ *vt* **:** to give a surname to: as **a :** to give a family name to ⟨an earlier family *surnamed* from that parish —Charles Partridge⟩ **b :** to give an additional name, title, or epithet to ⟨his successor Cosmo, *surnamed* the Great —William Robertson †1793⟩ ⟨the Joan of this story is *surnamed* Regan —Ken Smith⟩ **c** *obs* **:** to call by another or additional name **:** DESIGNATE ⟨the great pyramids, *surnamed* the world's wonders —William Lithgow⟩

sur·nape *or* **sur·nap** \ˈsərˌnap\ *n* -S [ME, fr. MF *sournappe*, fr. *sour-* sur- + *nappe* tablecloth — more at NAPKIN] **:** a cloth resembling a napkin used in medieval times for washing at meals

sur·nay *or* **sur·nai** \ˈsu̇rˌnī\ *n* -S [Per *surnāī*] **:** an Oriental oboe

sur·nominal \ˌsər+\ *adj* [*sur-* + *nominal*] **:** of or relating to a surname ⟨~ forms⟩ ⟨~ characteristics⟩

sur·pass \sərˈpas, -paa(ə)s, -pais, -päs\ *vt* [MF *surpasser*, fr. *sur-* + *passer* to pass, fr. OF — more at PASS] **1 :** to become better, greater, or stronger than **:** exceed in quality, degree, or performance **:** become superior to **:** go beyond in action or achievement ⟨the reality ~*ed* all expectations⟩ ⟨he ~*ed* all his contemporaries in skill⟩ **2 :** to pass beyond **:** go over **:** OVERSTEP ⟨nor let the sea ~ his bounds —John Milton⟩ **3 :** to transcend the reach, capacity, or powers of **:** go beyond the bounds or limits of **:** become more than can be attained, achieved, or apprehended by ⟨her beauty ~*es* all description⟩ ⟨the task ~*ed* his skill⟩ **4 :** to extend beyond or above ⟨mountain masses . . . ~*ed* the level of perpetual snow —*Nature*⟩ **syn** see EXCEED

sur·pass·er \-sə(r)\ *n* **:** one that surpasses

¹**surpassing** *adj* **:** eminently excellent **:** greatly exceeding others **:** excelling something of ordinary character **:** of a very high degree ⟨the geometric pattern is of a ~ intricacy —R.H. Rovere⟩ ⟨a ~ performance⟩ ⟨a writer of ~ skill⟩

²**surpassing** *adv* **:** SURPASSINGLY ⟨a large and ~ ugly town —John Foster⟩

sur·pass·ing·ly *adv* **:** in a surpassing degree **:** EXCEEDINGLY ⟨she was a ~ beautiful woman —R.H.Davis⟩ ⟨the movie was a ~ stupid Western —T.O.Heggen⟩

¹**sur·plice** \ˈsərpləs, ˈsə̄p-, ˈsəip-\ *n* -S [ME *surplis*, fr. OF *surpliz*, fr. ML *superpellicium*, fr. L *super-* + ML *pellicium* shepherd's coat of skins, fr. L, neut. of *pellicius* made of skins, fr. *pellis* skin; fr. the fact that it was orig. worn over the fur coats customary in the churches of northern countries — more at FELL] **1 :** a loose white ecclesiastical vestment with large open sleeves that generally extends to the knees in length and that usu. is worn as a tunic over other garments by clergymen, acolytes, lay readers, and choristers in the Anglican, Roman Catholic, Moravian, and other churches **2 :** the cotta worn by Roman Catholic clergymen

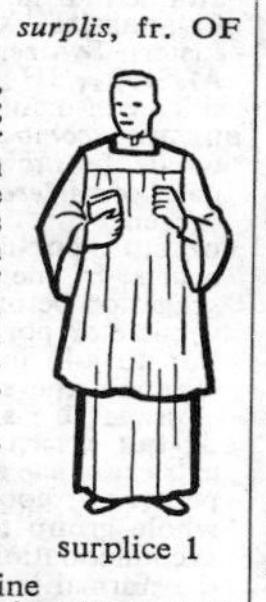

surplice 1

²**surplice** \"\ *adj* **:** having the neckline extended on each side from the shoulder often to the opposite side seam with the lines crossing in the center ⟨a ~ collar⟩ ⟨a ~ closing of a dress⟩

sur·pliced \-st\ *adj* **1 :** wearing a surplice ⟨~ priests⟩ **2 :** having a surplice collar or neckline

¹**sur·plus** \ˈsər(ˌ)pləs, ˈsə̄(-, ˈsəi(-\ *n* -ES [ME, fr. MF, fr. ML *superplus*, fr. L *super-* + *plus* more — more at PLUS] **1 a :** the amount that remains when use or need is satisfied **b :** an excess of receipts over disbursements ⟨budget ~⟩ ⟨cash ~⟩ — opposed to *deficit* **c :** an excess of the net worth of a corporation over the par or stated value of its capital stock — compare CAPITAL SURPLUS, EARNED SURPLUS, PAID-IN SURPLUS, RESERVE ACCOUNT 3, UNDIVIDED PROFITS **2** *Brit* **:** the amount remaining **:** REST **syn** see EXCESS

²**surplus** \"\ *adj* **1 :** being more than sufficient for use or need **:** constituting a surplus ⟨the steady stream of ~ population from the farms —B.K.Sandwell⟩ ⟨sales of ~ wheat to Asian countries⟩ ⟨the poem . . . heavy with ~ phrasing —William Arrowsmith⟩ **2 :** remaining after the end of a period of specific need or use; *specif* **:** designed for but not used in war usu. as a result of a cessation of hostilities ⟨~ war material⟩ ⟨~ army blankets⟩ ⟨~ jeeps⟩

sur·plus·age \-sij\ *n* -S [ME, fr. ¹*surplus* + *-age*] **1 :** SURPLUS 1a ⟨characterized by literary ~⟩ **2 a :** a quantity of material (as words or matter) that is excessive and nonessential or useless ⟨say what you have to say . . . with no ~ —Walter Pater⟩ **b** (1) **:** matter introduced in legal pleading that is not necessary or relevant to the case and may therefore be rejected **:** matter in a pleading not material to it in form or substance — distinguished from *inducement* (2) **:** a part of a verbal document that is immaterial thereto in both matter and form **syn** see EXCESS

surplus value *n* **:** the difference in Marxist theory between the value of work done or of commodities produced by labor and the usu. subsistence wages paid by the employer — compare LABOR THEORY OF VALUE

¹**sur·print** \ˈsərˌprint\ *vt* [*sur-* + *print*] **1 :** OVERPRINT 1a **2 :** to superimpose (a negative) on a resensitized film already bearing a developed negative in making a printing plate that is to contain both images ⟨a photoengraving made from a line negative with a halftone negative ~*ed* on top of it⟩

²**surprint** \"\ *n* **1 :** OVERPRINT **2 a :** a surprinted image **b :** a plate made from a surprinted negative

sur·pris·able *R* sə(r)ˈprīzəbəl; -*R* səˈ-\ *adj* **:** capable of being surprised **:** liable to surprise

sur·pris·al \-zəl\ *n* -S **:** the action of surprising **:** the state of being surprised **:** SURPRISE ⟨warfare . . . by ambush and ~ —Washington Irving⟩

¹**sur·prise** *also* **sur·prize** \-īz\ *n* -S *often attrib* [*surprise* fr. ME, fr. MF, fr. fem. of OF *surpris*, past part. of *surprendre* to take over, fr. *sur-* + *prendre* to take, fr. L *prehendere* to seize, grasp; *surprize* alter. (influenced by ⁵*prize*) of *surprise* — more at PREHENSILE] **1 a** (1) **:** the action of assailing unexpectedly or attacking without warning **:** the sudden attacking and capture of something (as a fort or body of troops) unprepared ⟨a fortified camp . . . capable of resisting ~*s* —J.A.Froude⟩ (2) **:** the action of coming upon unexpectedly or taking unawares — used esp. in the phrase *take by surprise* **b :** an instance of taking unawares **c** *obs* **:** a sudden attack of illness or emotion **2 a :** something that surprises **:** an occasion for, a cause of, or a quality arousing astonishment **:** something (as an event) unexpected or astonishing ⟨many of the psychologic ~*s* of the first flight are pleasant —H.G.Armstrong⟩ ⟨his development . . . was probably a ~ to himself —A.W.Long⟩ ⟨offering few intellectual ~*s* —Harry Levin⟩ **b :** a pie or other fancy dish with agreeably surprising contents **3 :** the emotion excited by something sudden, unexpected, or contrary to expectation: **a** *archaic* **:** terror, perplexity, or alarm caused by a sudden attack or calamity ⟨pure ~ and fear made me to quit the house —Shak.⟩ **b :** ASTONISHMENT, WONDER ⟨she never starts or shows ~ —Rose Macaulay⟩ ⟨the ~ which I felt on first learning of the award —E.C.Willatts⟩ ⟨gave a cry of delighted ~ —W.S.Maugham⟩ **4 :** the state of being mentally or emotionally surprised ⟨in his ~ he dropped the book⟩

²**surprise** *also* **surprize** \"\ *vt* -ED/-ING/-S [*surprise* fr. MF, fr. OF, fem. of *surpris*, past part. of *surprendre*; *surprize* alter. (influenced by ⁵*prize*) of *surprise*] **1** *obs* **a :** to take hold of **:** affect strongly and suddenly **:** SEIZE ⟨all on a sudden miserable pain *surpris'd* thee —John Milton⟩ ⟨*surprised* with joy at the motion —Daniel Defoe⟩ **b :** to seize and hold in one's possession **:** CAPTIVATE, OVERCOME, OVERPOWER ⟨power, like new wine, does your weak brain ~ —John Dryden⟩ **2 a :** to attack unexpectedly and without warning **:** assail suddenly **:** make an unexpected assault upon ⟨*surprised* the little garrison . . . and captured the arsenal —*Amer. Guide Series: Md.*⟩ ⟨at dawn the household was *surprised* by a sudden Indian attack —*Amer. Guide Series: N.H.*⟩ **b** (1) **:** to take suddenly by storm **:** seize or capture by a sudden and unexpected attack (2) *archaic* **:** to take possession of by force **:** make captive **:** take prisoner **:** CAPTURE, SEIZE **3 a :** to take unawares (as in an act or by an unexpected visit) **:** come upon abruptly or without warning **:** catch in the act ⟨police *surprised* the burglars leaving the store⟩ **b :** to bring out or to light by a sudden and unexpected action **:** detect, uncover, or elicit by taking (as a person) unawares ⟨*surprised* the secret of his murderous past through a stolen letter —Henri Peyre⟩ ⟨sometimes *surprised* a tragic shadow in her eyes —Willa Cather⟩ **4 a** *obs* **:** to ensnare or implicate by something (as a sudden disclosure or proposal) that takes one unawares **b :** to lead, impel, drive, or cause to do something or bring into some state in a sudden and unexpected way **:** lead on or betray into something not intended ⟨his debate . . . had *surprised* him into attacking the authority of the Pope —Stringfellow Barr⟩ ⟨*surprised* into an indiscretion⟩ **5 :** to strike with wonder or amazement because unexpected or different from what has been anticipated **:** affect with an emotion (as astonishment, awe, shock, or unexpected pleasure, disgust, or delight) ⟨the morning skies . . . *surprised* her daily as if they were uncommon things —Rebecca West⟩ ⟨his conduct *surprised* me⟩

syn ASTONISH, ASTOUND, AMAZE, FLABBERGAST: SURPRISE may indicate coming upon another suddenly and with startling effect; it may apply to any unexpected or unanticipated development bringing a degree of wonder ⟨the enemy was *surprised* —*Infantry Jour.*⟩ ⟨apt not only to be interested but also to be *surprised* by the experience life was holding in store for him —Joseph Conrad⟩ ASTONISH may indicate a surprising with the most unlikely, the unaccountable, or the incredible that virtually dazes one ⟨in the fashion of the magician who *astonishes* twice, once with the trick and again with its secret —L.J.Halle⟩ ⟨a flight that will *astonish* the world —Francis Stuart⟩ ASTOUND applies to the effect of what confounds, shocks, or stuns as unprecedented ⟨the girl was *astounded* and alarmed by the altogether unknown expression in the woman's face —Joseph Conrad⟩ ⟨*astounded* his congregation by putting up for sale a mulatto slave girl —*Amer. Guide Series: N. Y. City*⟩ AMAZE suggests astonished bewilderment or perplexity ⟨it *amazed* her that this soft little creature could be thus firm —George Meredith⟩ ⟨nothing *amazes* these people more than to see a man, apparently sane, meekly submitting to outrageous extortion —Norman Douglas⟩ FLABBERGAST may suggest thorough astonishment and often bewilderment or dismay ⟨his appointment *flabbergasted* those who knew his record⟩

surprised *past of* SURPRISE

sur·prised·ly \-zədlē, -zd-, -li\ *adv* **:** in the manner of one surprised

surprise party *n* **1 :** a party in honor of a person secretly arranged and provided for by friends as a surprise **2 :** an event or other occurrence held to resemble a surprise party in being unexpected although often of an unpleasant nature

sur·pris·er \-zə(r)\ *n* -S **:** one that surprises

surprises *pl of* SURPRISE, *pres 3d sing of* SURPRISE

surprising *adj* **1 :** of a nature to excite surprise **:** causing amazement or wonder esp. by being unexpected **:** AMAZING, ASTONISHING, UNLOOKED-FOR ⟨the commission's report shows a ~ lack of hard, factual data —*Monsanto Mag.*⟩ ⟨with ~ rapidity . . . their economic condition improved —*Amer. Guide Series: Oregon*⟩ **2** *archaic* **:** exciting admiration **:** ADMIRABLE

sur·pris·ing·ly *adv* **:** in a surprising manner or degree ⟨the casualties . . . had been ~ light —Alexander Forbes⟩ ⟨a ~ deft motion —Earle Birney⟩

surprize *var of* SURPRISE

surr *abbr* **1** surrender; surrendered **2** surrogate

sur·ra *also* **sur·rah** \ˈsu̇rə, ˈsərə\ *n* -S [Marathi *sūra* wheezing sound] **:** a severe Old World febrile and hemorrhagic disease marked by edema and anemia, caused by a flagellated protozoan (*Trypanosoma evansi*) transmitted by biting insects (as horseflies of the family Tabanidae), and commonly fatal in horses, mules, and camels although cattle and dogs often recover — compare TRYPANOSOMIASIS

sur·re·al·ism \səˈrēəˌlizəm *also* |sərˈē|r| *or* (ˈ)sē|r| *or* (ˈ)su̇(r)ˈē|r| *or* (ˈ)su̇əˈē|r| *sometimes* |ēə- *or* ˈsər| *or* ˈsərˈ| *or* ˈsu̇rˈ|\ *n* [F *surréalisme*, fr. *sur-* + *réalisme* realism, fr. *réal* real (fr. MF) + *-isme* -ism — more at REAL] **:** the principles, ideals, or practice of producing fantastic or incongruous imagery in art or literature by means of unnatural juxtapositions and combinations

¹**sur·re·al·ist** \-ləst\ *or* **sur·re·al** \ˈēəl, |ēəl\ *or* **sur·re·al·is·tic** \səˈrēəˈlistik, ˈsərˈ|, ˈsərˈ|, -tēk *also* ˈsərˈ|r| *or* (ˈ)sē|r| *or* (ˈ)su̇(r)ˈē|r| *or* (ˈ)su̇əˈē|r| *sometimes* |ēə- *or* ˈsu̇rˈ|\ *adj* [*surrealist* fr. F *surréaliste*, fr. *sur-* + *réaliste* realist; *surreal* back-formation fr. *surrealism*; *surrealistic* fr. ²*surrealist* + *-ic* — more at REALIST] **1 :** of, relating to, or having the characteristics of surrealism ⟨a ~ film⟩ ⟨~ art⟩ ⟨~ literature⟩ ⟨a ~ painter⟩ **2 :** of, relating to, or resembling mental free association

²**surrealist** \"\ *n* **:** one that adheres to, practices, or follows surrealism

sur·re·al·is·ti·cal·ly \-tək(ə)lē\ *adv* **:** in a surrealist manner ⟨the ice runs ~ riot in a phantasma of frozen sculpture —Glen Jacobsen⟩

sur·rebut \ˌsər+\ *vi* [*sur-* + *rebut*] **:** to reply by or in a surrebutter

sur·rebutter *also* **sur·rebuttal** \"+\ *n* [*sur-* + *rebutter*, *rebuttal*] **:** the reply in common law pleading of a plaintiff to a defendant's rebutter

sur·rejoin \"+\ *vi* [*sur-* + *rejoin*] **:** to reply by or in a surrejoinder

sur·rejoinder \"+\ *n* [*sur-* + *rejoinder*] **1 :** the answer in common law pleading of a plaintiff to a defendant's rejoinder **2 :** an answer (as to a rejoinder) held to resemble a surrejoinder in common law pleading

¹**sur·ren·der** \səˈrendə(r)\ *vb* **surrendered; surrendered; surrendering** \-d(ə)riŋ\ **surrenders** [ME *surrenderen*, fr. MF *surrendre*, fr. *sur-* + *rendre* to deliver, yield — more at RENDER] *vt* **1 :** to make a surrender in law of: as **a :** to give up (an estate) to the holder in remainder or reversion **b :** to relinquish (as rights or claims under a patent) to the grantor **c :** to deliver (the principal) into lawful custody **2 a :** to yield to the power, control, authority, or possession of another **:** give or deliver up possession of upon compulsion or demand **:** cease trying to retain or control and agree to yield ⟨~*ed* the fort⟩ ⟨forced to ~ the ship⟩ ⟨the continental firm ~*s* the dollars to its own bank at the official exchange rate —R.F.Mikesell⟩ **b :** to give up completely or agree to forgo esp. in favor of another **:** abandon, resign, or relinquish

possession of usu. for the sake of another **:** assent to loss of possession or exercise of or power or control over ⟨~*ed* his chair to the lady⟩ ⟨benefits bestowed by science which we are not anxious to ~ —J.W.Krutch⟩ **3 a :** to give (oneself) up into the power of another esp. as a prisoner **b :** to give (oneself) over to something (as an influence or course of action) **:** abandon or devote (as oneself) entirely to something without restraint, reservation, or further resistance ⟨the individual . . . has ~*ed* himself to destructive ideologies —F.E.Hill⟩ ⟨~*ed* his mind to more frivolous pursuits —George Meredith⟩ **~** *vi* **:** to give oneself up into the power of another **:** YIELD ⟨ordered the troops to ~⟩ ⟨the enemy must soon ~⟩ **syn** see RELINQUISH

[2]**surrender** \"\ *n* -S [ME, fr. AF, fr. MF *surrendre* to deliver, yield (taken as a n.)] **1 a :** the action of yielding one's person or giving up the possession of something into the power of another **:** ABANDONMENT, RESIGNATION ⟨complete ~ of initiative to the adversary —S.L.A.Marshall⟩ ⟨the heroine's . . . ~ to drugs, nymphomania, or catatonic dementia —Malcolm Cowley⟩ **b :** the action of yielding a particular estate to the person who has an immediate estate in remainder or reversion, merging the surrendered estate in the greater one ⟨the ~ of a lease to the landlord before its expiration⟩ ⟨the ~ of a legal tenancy in a copyhold estate to the lord of the manor⟩ — compare RELEASE, RENUNCIATION **c :** the relinquishment by a patentee of his rights or claims under a patent **d** *or* **surrender by bail :** the delivery of a principal into lawful custody by his bail **e :** the assignment of his assets to his creditors by a usu. bankrupt debtor **f :** the voluntary cancellation of the legal liability of an insurance company by the insured and beneficiary for a consideration — see SURRENDER VALUE **g :** the delivery up of a fugitive from justice by one government (as of a foreign country) to another — compare EXTRADITION 1 **2 :** an instance of surrendering

surrender charge *n* **:** a forfeit or penalty generally charged by a life insurance company against the value of a policy surrendered or allowed to lapse

sur·ren·der·ee \sə͵rendə¦rē\ *n* -S [[1]*surrender* + *-ee*] **:** one to whom a surrender (as of an estate) is made

sur·ren·der·or \sə'rendərə(r), sə͵rendə¦rȯ(ə)r\ *n* -S [[1]*surrender* + *-or*] **:** one that makes a surrender (as of an estate)

surrender value *n* **:** the cash value of an insurance policy that may be taken in cash or applied to the purchase of fractional paid-up or extended term insurance

sur·ren·dry \sə'rendrē\ *n* -ES [[1]*surrender* + *-ry*] *archaic* **:** SURRENDER

sur·rep·ti·tious \¦sər-əp¦tishəs, ¦sə-rəp-\ *adj* [ME *surrepticious*, fr. L *surrepticius, surreptitius*, fr. *surreptus* (past part. of *surripere, subripere* to snatch away, take away secretly, fr. *sub-* secretly, under + *-ripere*, fr. *rapere* to seize) + *-icius, -itius* -itious — more at SUB-, RAPID] **1 :** marked or accomplished by fraud or suppression of truth ⟨a ~ ordinance⟩ **2 a :** executed, obtained, used, done, or attended with often clever or deft circumvention of proper standards, sanction, or authority **:** enjoyed by stealth **:** CLANDESTINE ⟨a ~ removal of goods⟩ ⟨~ pleasures⟩ **b :** of fraudulent, spurious, or unauthorized issue **:** made or introduced fraudulently ⟨a ~ copy of a book⟩ **c :** acting in secret or by stealth **:** doing something clandestinely **:** SLY, STEALTHY ⟨glancing at the clock with a ~ eye —H.S. Scott⟩ **syn** see SECRET

sur·rep·ti·tious·ly *adv* **:** in a surreptitious manner ⟨publication was continued ~ during the war —*Amer. Guide Series: Va.*⟩

surreverence *obs var of* SIR-REVERENCE

[1]**sur·rey** \'sər·ē, 'sə·rē, |i\ *adj, usu cap* [fr. *Surrey*, county in southern England] **:** of or from the county of Surrey, England **:** of the kind or style prevalent in Surrey

[2]**surrey** \"\ *n* -S [fr. *Surrey (cart)*, English pleasure cart with an open spindle seat introduced into the U.S. in 1872, fr. *Surrey*, county in southern England where it was first built] **1 :** a four-wheel 2-seated pleasure carriage resembling a cabriolet but having a straight or nearly straight bottom and sometimes cut under **2 :** an early motor vehicle resembling a surrey in design

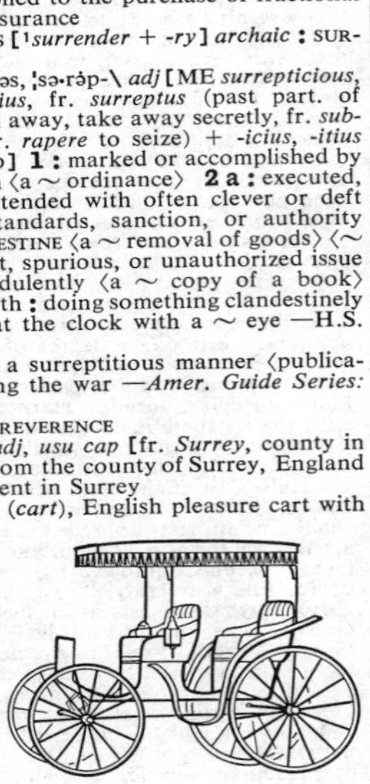
surrey

surrey green *n, often cap S* **:** a grayish yellow green to pale green that is darker than the color tea

sur·ro·ga·cy \'sərəgəsē\ *n* -ES **:** the office of surrogate

[1]**sur·ro·gate** \'sərə͵gāt, *usu* -ād·+V\ *vt* -ED/-ING/-S [L *surrogatus*, past part. of *surrogare, subrogare* to substitute, fr. *sub-* in place of, under + *rogare* to ask — more at RIGHT] **:** to put in the place of another: **a :** to appoint as successor deputy, or substitute for oneself **b :** SUBSTITUTE

[2]**sur·ro·gate** \-͵gāt, -gət, *usu* -d·+V\ *n* -S [L *surrogatus*, past part. of *surrogare, subrogare* to substitute] **1 a :** a person appointed to act in place of another **:** DELEGATE, DEPUTY, SUBSTITUTE ⟨the Lord Chief Justice . . . acted as ~ for the Earl Marshal —*Notes & Queries*⟩ ⟨college presidents or their ~*s* appealed for a revival of idealism —M.J.Adler⟩ **b :** the deputy of an ecclesiastical judge (as a bishop or a bishop's chancellor) in the Church of England; *esp* **:** one who grants marriage licenses **c :** a local judicial officer in New York and some other states who has jurisdiction over the probate of wills and testaments and the settlement of estates and often has power to appoint and supervise guardians of infants and other incompetent persons — compare PREROGATIVE COURT **2 a :** something that replaces or serves as a substitute for another ⟨the letter *y* as a ~ for *i* —Arthur Minton⟩ ⟨regard written language as only a ~ of oral communication —J.B. Carroll⟩ **b :** an artificial or synthetic product used as a substitute for a natural product **c :** a representation of a person substituted through symbolizing (as in a dream) for conscious recognition of the person ⟨persons like teachers who represent mother ~*s* —R.R.Sears⟩ **syn** see RESOURCE

[3]**surrogate** \"\ *adj* **:** constituting a surrogate **:** serving in place of or standing for something else **:** SUBSTITUTE ⟨a sort of ~ father to him —Brendan Gill⟩ ⟨introduces a native girl to offer the grieving husband a ~ satisfaction —John Barkham⟩

sur·ro·ga·tion \͵sərə'gāshən\ *n* -S [ML *surrogation-, surrogatio*, fr. L *surrogatus* (past part.) + *-ion-, -io* -ion] **1 :** the action of surrogating **:** SUBSTITUTION, SUBROGATION **2 :** an instance of surrogating

[1]**sur·round** \sə'raund\ *vb* -ED/-ING/-S [ME *surrounden* to overflow, modif. (influenced by *rounden* to round) of MF *suronder, souronder*, fr. LL *superundare*, fr. L *super-* + *undare* to rise in waves, fr. *unda* wave — more at ROUND, WATER] *vt* **1** *obs* **:** to flow over the banks of **:** FLOOD, INUNDATE, OVERFLOW, SUBMERGE **2** [influenced in meaning by [6]*round*] **:** to be situated or found around, about, or in a ring around: as **a :** to throng, press, or cluster around ⟨the crowd ~*ed* the victor⟩ **b :** to live around on all or most sides ⟨clearly distinct from the more negroid people who ~ them —C.D. Forde⟩ **c :** to form or be in the retinue, entourage, or court of ⟨flatterers who ~ the duke⟩ **d :** to be present around, about, or near in the character of an attribute, characteristic, or natural or accustomed motif ⟨we sit ~*ed* by objects which perpetually express the oddity of our own temperaments —Virginia Woolf⟩ **e :** to constitute part of the determining environment or accustomed condition of **:** ENVIRON ⟨the snow and ice which ~ the earth's polar regions —J.G.Vaeth⟩ **f :** to form a ring around **:** extend around or about the edge of **:** constitute a curving or circular boundary for **:** lie adjacent to all around or in most directions **:** ENCIRCLE ⟨woodland patches ~ the village —*Amer. Guide Series: Vt.*⟩ ⟨house ~*ed* on three sides by a wide veranda —*Amer. Guide Series: N.H.*⟩ **g** (1) **:** to envelop in or as if in a cloud or mist ⟨a fog ~*s* the ship⟩ ⟨complete secrecy ~*ed* the meeting —*Current History*⟩ ⟨the silence that ~*ed* them —Walter O'Meara⟩ (2) **:** to encase or cover like pulp around a core ⟨a hard black shell ~*ed* by a pulpy, fibrous covering —Tom Marvel⟩ **h :** to occur or be next, near, adjacent to, or before and after in a sequence or order ⟨the years that ~*ed* the American Revolution⟩ **3 :** to cause to be encompassed, encircled, or enclosed with something ⟨~*ed* himself with outstanding men —*Phoenix Flame*⟩ ⟨sought to ~ the international liquor traffic with serious restrictions —D.W.McConnell⟩ **4 a** *obs* **:** CIRCUMNAVIGATE **b** *chiefly Midland* **:** to pass or walk around **5 :** to enclose (as a city or a body of troops) so as to cut off communication or retreat **:** INVEST **~** *vi, obs* **:** to overflow the banks — used of a body of water

syn ENVIRON, ENCIRCLE, CIRCLE, RING, ENCOMPASS, COMPASS, GIRD, GIRDLE, HEM: SURROUND is a general term not esp. rich in connotation and often interchangeable with the following in situations indicating a being all around rather than a having gone all around, a traversing on a circular course ⟨the noisy, slovenly, argumentative militiamen who had *surrounded* Boston —Kenneth Roberts⟩ ⟨the unseen power which *surrounds* us —W.R.Inge⟩ ENVIRON is likely to suggest lasting situation around, as though enclosing, and forming part of an environment ⟨the passions and motives of the savage world which underlies as well as *environs* civilization —W.D. Howells⟩ ENCIRCLE may stress the idea of a circle, either a circle described by a route, march, or voyage or one enclosing something with or as if with something tangible, material, and lasting ⟨the close which *encircles* the venerable cathedral —T.B. Macaulay⟩ ⟨faster planes now *encircle* the world in a few hours⟩ CIRCLE means and connotes about the same things as ENCIRCLE; the latter may more strongly suggest completeness or perfect roundness of the figure described ⟨his eyes were darkly *circled* —Booth Tarkington⟩ ⟨the Vernon House . . . is *circled* with two rows of windows —*Amer. Guide Series: R.I.*⟩ RING is a close synonym, sometimes more vivid, for CIRCLE; it is not, however, generally used to indicate a traversing or course ⟨a septuagenarian whose few sad last grey hairs, *ringing* an otherwise completely bald head —*Irish Digest*⟩ ENCOMPASS suggests an encircling which includes, discourages entrance or exit, or ensheathes and envelops ⟨the strong fortress-walls which had long *encompassed* him —Charles Dickens⟩ ⟨whenever he moved beyond the walls . . . the drawn swords and cuirasses of his trusty bodyguard *encompassed* him thick —T.B.Macaulay⟩ ⟨nature was a presence which *encompassed* him widely —R.L.Cook⟩ COMPASS often suggests an enclosing which covers and protects or which envelops and weighs down ⟨we must be humble, for we are *compassed* by mysteries —W.R.Inge⟩ GIRD may indicate an encircling of or as if of the waist of a person, esp. with whatever arms, strengthens, or encourages ⟨Christian religious energy *girded* its loins with the cords of Francis and Dominic —H.O.Taylor⟩ GIRDLE may suggest any encirclement like that of a belt, sash, or zone ⟨the great coastal plain which *girdles* the United States —Forrest Morgan⟩ HEM, in this sense, is likely to suggest an encirclement that confines and prevents or makes difficult escape, exit, or activity ⟨the constables were *hemmed* in so closely that they could make no use of their pikes —T.B.Costain⟩ ⟨the rocky walls which, with the deep-flowing river, *hemmed* Matadi in on all sides —Tom Marvel⟩

[2]**surround** \"\ *n* -S **1 a :** a method of hunting wild animals (as the buffalo or the vicuña) by surrounding a herd and driving the animals into a circle, a ravine, or other place from which they cannot escape **b :** the action of hunting by this method **c :** the area encompassed by hunters using this method **2 :** something that surrounds: as **a** *chiefly Brit* **:** something (as a border or edging) surrounding or nearly surrounding a central object or area ⟨the brass ~ of the electric bell —Elizabeth Bowen⟩ ⟨took tea out on the paved ~ of the swimming pool —G.A.Wagner⟩ ⟨the ~ of low brown hills —Louis Allen⟩ ⟨a fireplace ~⟩ **b :** the area of illumination surrounding a test object or a motion picture or television screen ⟨the ~ should be about of equal brightness with the test field —R.S. Woodworth⟩

sur·round·er \-də(r)\ *n* -S **:** one that surrounds

surrounding *n* -S [fr. gerund of [1]*surround*] **1 surroundings** *pl* **:** the circumstances, conditions, or objects by which one is surrounded **:** ENVIRONMENT ⟨extraordinarily uninterested in his physical ~*s* —Arnold Bennett⟩ ⟨the village is . . . notable for the great beauty of its ~*s* —*Amer. Guide Series: N.H.*⟩ **2 :** ENTOURAGE — sometimes used in pl.

surrounds *pres 3d sing of* SURROUND

sur·royal \͵sər+\ *n* [ME *surryal*, fr. *sur-* + *ryal, royal* tres-tine, royal antler — more at ROYAL] **:** one of the terminal tines above the royal antler of a stag or other large deer usu. attained at the age of four years — see ANTLER illustration

sur·sass·ite \'sər'sa͵sīt\ *n* -S [*Sursass* (Oberhalbstein), eastern Switzerland, its locality + E *-ite*] **:** a mineral $Mn_4Al_4Si_5O_{21}.3H_2O$ of the epidote group consisting of a hydrous silicate of manganese and aluminum

sursum- *comb form* [L *susum, sursum* under, from below, upwards, fr. *subs-* (var. of *sub-*) + *versum*, neut. of *versus*, past part. of *vertere* to turn — more at WORTH] **:** upward ⟨*sursumvergence*⟩

sur·sum cor·da \¦sərsəm'kȯrdə, ¦su̇r-\ *n* [LL, lift up the hearts; fr. the words addressed by the celebrant to the congregation before the eucharistic preface] **1** *often cap S&C* **:** a versicle or portion of Christian liturgy inviting the congregation to join in thanksgiving to God **2 :** something held to resemble the sursum corda: **a :** an incitement to fervor or courage **b :** an exaltation of mood or spirits

sur·tax \'sər͵taks, 'sə̄,-\ *n* [*sur-* + *tax*] **:** an additional or extra tax: as **a :** a special tax levied against certain classes of persons or goods over and above the general charge upon the whole group **:** an extra charge (as on a railroad for special accommodations) **b :** a graduated income tax in addition to the normal income tax imposed on the amount by which the net income of an individual exceeds a specified sum — called also *additional tax*; compare SUPERTAX **c :** a supplementary tax added at a later date than the normal rates (as in customs duties) **d :** the charge made on a semipostal stamp above the amount required for postage

sur·ti \'sərd·ē\ *n* -S *usu cap* [native name in India] **:** MURRAH

[1]**sur·tout** \͵sər'tü, -üt\ *n* -S [F, fr. *sur* over (fr. L *super*) + *tout* all, fr. L *totus* — more at OVER] **1 :** a man's fitted coat or overcoat; *esp* **:** FROCK COAT **2 :** a woman's hood with a mantle

[2]**surtout** \"\ *adv* [F] **:** over all; *specif* **:** above other heraldic charges

sur·tur·brand \'sərd·ər͵brand\ *n* -S [Icel *surtarbrandr* jet, surturbrand, fr. *Surtr*, giant fire demon in Scandinavian legend (akin to ON *svartr* black) + Icel *brandr* firebrand, fr. ON — more at SWART, BRAND] **:** a variety of lignite in Iceland and the Faeroes occurring in seams between beds of volcanic rock

su·ru·cu·cu \¦su̇rək¦kü, -rəkü¦kü\ *n* -S [Tupi *surucucú*] **:** BUSHMASTER

surv *abbr* **1** survey; surveying; surveyor **2** surviving

sur·veil·lance \sə(r)'vālən(t)s *also* -lyən-\ *n* -S [F, fr. *surveiller* to watch over (fr. *sur-* + *veiller* to watch, fr. L *vigilare* to watch, wake, fr. *vigil* awake, watchful) + *-ance* — more at VIGIL] **1 :** close watch kept over one or more persons **:** continuous observation of a person or area (as to detect developments, movements, or activities) ⟨place a suspected person under police ~⟩ ⟨~ of air traffic by radar⟩ **2 :** close and continuous observation for the purpose of direction, supervision, or control ⟨club facilities . . . are conducted under close ~ of the U. S. Forest Service —Jean Lunzer⟩ ⟨place the disputed territory under UN ~⟩

sur·veil·lant \-nt\ *n* -S [F, fr. pres. part. of *surveiller* to watch over] **:** one that exercises surveillance over another

[1]**sur·vey** \sə(r)'vā; ͵sər'-, sə̄'-, səi'-, '≈,≈\ *vb* **surveyed; surveyed; surveying; surveys** [ME *surveyen*, fr. MF *surveer, surveeir, surveoir* to look over, survey, fr. *sur-* + *veer, veeir, veoir* to look, see — more at VIEW] *vt* **1 a :** to look over or examine with reference to condition, situation, or value **:** examine and ascertain the state of **:** APPRAISE, ESTIMATE, EVALUATE ⟨hired to ~ a manor for its extent, value, ownership, and liabilities⟩ **b :** to have oversight of **:** SUPERVISE **c :** to make a usu. statistical survey of ⟨~ population growth in the southern counties⟩ **d** (1) **:** to make an investigation and fix responsibility for destruction, loss, or damage of (as military equipment) (2) **:** to inspect (as equipment or supplies) to determine whether retention as serviceable or condemnation as unserviceable is advisable (3) **:** to retire (as men or equipment) from active duty after inspection **2 :** to determine and delineate the form, extent, and position of (as a tract of land, a coast, or a harbor) by taking linear and angular measurements and by applying the principles of geometry and trigonometry **3 a :** to view from or as if from a high place or a commanding position **:** take an inclusive or overall view of **:** consider or study comprehensively **:** examine to the whole extent ⟨silently ~*ed* the beautiful panorama below them —L.C.Douglas⟩ ⟨~ almost the whole mass of contemporary literature —S.E.Hyman⟩ **b :** make, write, or present a survey of **:** outline or describe in or as if in an overall inclusive generalized study ⟨a series of lectures which ~ the entire field of cardiology —*Bull. of Meharry Med. Coll.*⟩ **c** *obs* **:** OBSERVE, PERCEIVE, SEE **4 :** to view with a scrutinizing eye **:** examine carefully and closely the salient features or details of **:** look carefully into or through **:** inspect closely, searchingly, or in detail **:** SCRUTINIZE ⟨she . . . ~*ed* herself in the pier glass —James Joyce⟩ ⟨he ~*ed* us in a lordly way —Alan Harrington⟩ **5 :** to grade and measure (lumber) **~** *vi* **:** to make a survey **syn** see SEE

[2]**sur·vey** \'sər͵vā, 'sə̄,-, 'səi,- *sometimes* sə(r)'vā *or* ͵sər'- *or* sə̄'- *or* səi'-\ *n* -S *often attrib* **1 a** (1) **:** a critical examination or inspection often of an official character for an implied or specified purpose **:** the action of ascertaining facts regarding conditions or the condition of something to provide exact information esp. to persons responsible or interested ⟨~ of a state's roads⟩ ⟨a ~ of the schools in the area⟩ ⟨unemployment ~*s*⟩ (2) **:** an examination of a ship or a part of its cargo or equipment to determine its condition, responsibility for damage, and disposition to be made (3) **:** a study of a specified area or aggregate of units (as human beings) usu. with respect to a special condition or its prevalence or with the objective of drawing conclusions about a larger area or aggregate **:** a systematic collection and analysis of data and esp. statistical data on some aspect of an area or group ⟨a telephone ~ of major U.S. companies . . . in the atom business —Ray Cromley⟩ ⟨made a ~ . . . of farm production in the Midwest —*Current Biog.*⟩ **b :** a report, study, or document presenting the results of such an examination **2 a :** the action of looking at something from a high or commanding position **:** a general or comprehensive view ⟨resumed her ~ of the landscape —Anne D. Sedgwick⟩ **b :** a broad undetailed consideration or treatment of something **:** a history, exposition, or description presenting the outlines only ⟨competent ~*s* of the literatures of India, China, and Japan —*Times Lit. Supp.*⟩ ⟨continue his illustrated ~ of the music of southern Africa —*London Calling*⟩ — see SURVEY COURSE **3 a :** the process of surveying an area of land or water **:** the operation of finding and delineating the contour, dimensions, and position of any part of the earth's surface whether land or water ⟨a topographic and hydrographic ~ of a locality —C.H.Deetz⟩ **b :** a measured plan and description of a portion of an area or of a road or line through an area obtained by surveying **c :** an organization (as a government agency) engaged in surveying **4 :** something that is surveyed: **a** *archaic* **:** a delineation of a scene **:** VIEW **b :** PROSPECT **syn** see COMPENDIUM

sur·vey·able \(͵)sər'vāəbəl\ *adj* **:** capable of being surveyed

survey agent *n* **:** a local agent (as of a fire insurance company) who is not authorized to write policies but must send applications directly to the company

sur·vey·al \(͵)sə(r)'vā(ə)l\ *n* -S **:** the action of surveying **:** SURVEY ⟨her ~ of the room —Speed Lamkin⟩

sur·vey·ance \-āən(t)s\ *n* -S **1** *archaic* **:** SURVEY ⟨the expenses of ~ and sale —*American*⟩ **2 :** SURVEILLANCE

survey course *n* **:** a course treating briefly the chief topics of one or several allied broad fields of knowledge

surveyed *past of* SURVEY

sur·vey·ing \(͵)sər'vāiŋ, sə'-\ *n* -S [ME, fr. gerund of *surveyen* to survey] **:** the action or occupation of one that surveys; *specif* **:** a branch of applied mathematics that teaches the art of determining the area of any portion of the earth's surface, the lengths and directions of the bounding lines, and the contour of the surface and of accurately delineating the whole on paper — see GEODETIC SURVEYING, HYDROGRAPHIC SURVEYING, PLANE SURVEYING

surveying sextant *n* **:** a light sextant with a large scale used in hydrographic surveying

survey meter *n* **:** an instrument sensitive to ionizing radiations used in prospecting for radioactive deposits

survey number *n* **:** a serial number for antimalarial drugs

sur·vey·or \(͵)sər'vāər; sə(r)'vāə(r, sə̄'-, səi'-\ *n* -S [ME *surveyour*, fr. MF *surveiour*, fr. *surveer* to look over, survey + *-our* -or — more at SURVEY] **1 :** one acting as an overseer or superintendent: as **a :** a government official having the functions of superintendence, administration, or inspection over a usu. specified area of responsibility (as a department or office) ⟨~ of highways⟩ **b :** one having oversight of the lands and boundaries of an estate **2** *Brit* **:** ARCHITECT; *esp* **:** one in charge of construction — see QUANTITY SURVEYOR **3 :** one that surveys land and other surfaces **:** one that practices the art of surveying **4 :** one that takes a view and esp. a mental view of something **:** one that examines, contemplates, or beholds ⟨some recent ~*s* of the present scene —H.W.Baehr⟩ **5 a :** one that views and examines with the purpose of ascertaining the condition, quantity, or quality of something ⟨the ~ inspected the damaged ship⟩ **b** (1) **:** a customs officer who ascertains the contents of casks and the quantity of dutiable liquors **:** GAUGER (2) **:** a customs officer formerly carrying out measures for ascertaining the quantity, condition, and value of merchandise brought into a port **6 a :** one that inspects and tallies lumber in cargo lots **b :** one that marks and tallies lumber as it comes from the saw **7 :** one that makes a survey

surveyor general *n, pl* **surveyors general** *or* **surveyor generals :** a principal or superintending surveyor: as **a :** an official having general oversight (as over an area, department, or function) ⟨*surveyor general* of army purchases during World War I⟩ ⟨*surveyor general* of the king's manors⟩ **b :** a U.S. government official in charge of the survey of public lands in a particular area (as a state)

surveyor's compass *or* **surveyor's dial** *n* **:** an instrument used in surveying for measuring horizontal angles — compare CIRCUMFERENTOR 1, SEMICIRCUMFERENTOR

surveyor's cross *n* **:** a simple instrument made of two bars forming a right-angled cross with sights at each end and used in setting out right angles in surveying

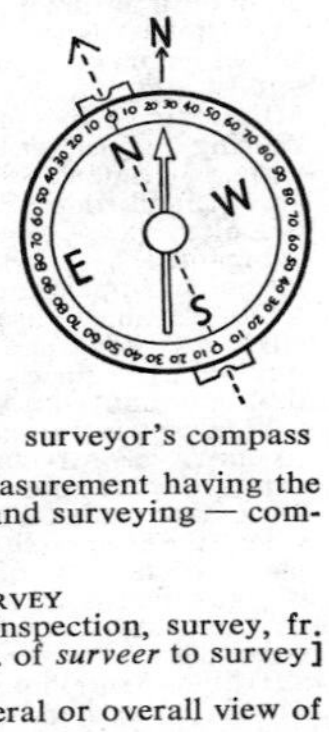

surveyor's compass

sur·vey·or·ship \-͵ship\ *n* [ME, fr. *surveyour* + *-ship*] **:** the office of surveyor

surveyor's level *n* **:** a level consisting of a telescope and a spirit level mounted on a tripod, revolving on a vertical axis, and having leveling screws provided for adjustment — compare DUMPY LEVEL, Y LEVEL

surveyor's measure *n* **:** a system of measurement having the surveyor's chain as a unit and used in land surveying — compare CHAIN 1c(1)

surveyor's rod *n* **:** LEVELING ROD

surveys *pres 3d sing of* SURVEY, *pl of* SURVEY

[1]**sur·view** \sə(r)'vyü\ *n* [ME *survewe* inspection, survey, fr. MF *surveue*, fr. fem. of *surveu*, past part. of *surveer* to survey] *archaic* **:** SURVEY

[2]**surview** \"\ *vt, archaic* **:** to take a general or overall view of **:** view as a whole

sur·vi·grous \sə(r)'vigrəs\ *adj* [*sur-* + *vigorous*] *chiefly South & Midland* **:** extremely vigorous **:** very active, enterprising, or fierce

sur·viv·abil·i·ty \sə(r)͵vīvə'biləd·ē\ *n* **:** the quality or state of being survivable

sur·viv·able \sə(r)'vīvəbəl\ *adj* **1 :** capable of surviving **2 :** resulting in or permitting survival ⟨~ accidents⟩

sur·viv·al \sə(r)'vīvəl\ *n* -S *often attrib* [*survive* + *-al*] **1 a :** the action of living longer than another person or beyond something (as a time, event, development, or condition) ⟨the wife's ~ of her husband⟩ ⟨the ~ of the soul after death⟩ **b :** the continuance of something (as a custom) after the end of the period or the cessation of the conditions in which it had significance **c :** the continuation of life or existence in the presence of or despite usu. difficult conditions ⟨the biological

needs of ~ and reproduction —Flanders Dunbar⟩ ⟨problems of ~ in arctic conditions⟩ **2 a :** one that survives or remains after others of its kind have disappeared **:** one that continues to exist after the cessation of something **:** a surviving individual or remnant ⟨~*s* of classical sculpture which . . . existed in Byzantium —O. Elfrida Saunders⟩ **b :** a culture trait remaining from former times but with diminished significance or with a function or utility meaningful only in terms of past history **c :** a linguistic feature that has escaped extinction or has resisted change

sur·viv·al·ism \-īvə,lizəm\ *n* -s **:** an attitude, policy, or practice based on the primacy of survival as a value ⟨the trend is away . . . from aggressive expansionism toward realistic ~ —Frank Gorrell⟩

survival kit *n* **:** a compact package of emergency equipment including food and other items that vary with climatic factors in the operational area for use by aircrew members who have descended in isolated or primitive territory

survival of actions : the continuance of proceedings in law despite the death of one or both of the parties involved

survival of the fittest : NATURAL SELECTION

survival value *n* **:** utility (as of one or more characters or qualities of an organism) in the struggle for existence

sur·viv·ance \sə(r)'vīvən(t)s\ *n* -s [F, fr. MF, fr. *survivant*, after such pairs as MF *abundant: abundance*] **1 :** SURVIVAL **2 :** the right of succession (as to an office or estate) of a survivor nominated before the death of the incumbent or holder

sur·viv·ant \sə(r)'vīvənt\ *adj* [MF, pres. part. of *survivre* to survive] *archaic* **:** continuing to survive **:** surviving something

sur·vive \sə(r)'vīv\ *vb* -ED/-ING/-S [ME *surviven*, fr. MF *survivre*, fr. L *supervivere*, fr. *super-* + *vivere* to live — more at QUICK] *vi* **:** to remain alive or in existence (as after another's death, or a time, event, disaster, or development, or the end of a condition) **:** live on **:** continue to exist or function ⟨pioneer methods of husbandry still ~ —E.C.Higbee⟩ ⟨men trained to ~ under severe conditions —*Boy Scout Handbk.*⟩ ⟨numerous . . . eighteenth-century houses ~ —*Amer. Guide Series: N.Y. City*⟩ **~** *vt* **1 :** to live beyond the life or existence of **:** live longer than ⟨only his son *survived* him⟩ **2 :** to continue to exist or live after (as a time or event) **:** outlast the end of (as a condition or development) ⟨other important leaders *survived* the explosion —*Current Biog.*⟩ ⟨one in a million of these childish talents ~*s* puberty —Aldous Huxley⟩ ⟨one of the few schools to ~ the 1857 panic —*Amer. Guide Series: Minn.*⟩ **3 :** to continue to exist, function, or compete despite (as a condition or development) ⟨ferries have *survived* the competition of the tunnels —*Amer. Guide Series: N.J.*⟩ ⟨one of the few Democrats . . . to ~ a Republican sweep —*Current Biog.*⟩ ⟨fishes are known to ~ conditions well below freezing-point —W.H.Dowdeswell⟩ **syn** see OUTLIVE

sur·viv·er \-īvə(r)\ *n* -s *archaic* **:** SURVIVOR

surviving *adj* **:** remaining alive or in existence ⟨some ~ friend of my youth —W.B.Yeats⟩ ⟨the only ~ frontier blockhouse in Pennsylvania —*Amer. Guide Series: Pa.*⟩

sur·vi·vor \sər'vīvər, sə'vīvə(r\ *n* -s **:** one that survives: **a :** one that outlives another **:** one remaining alive after another's death **b :** one of two or more legally designated persons (as joint tenants or holders of a joint interest) who outlives one or more of the others **c :** one living through a time, event, or development marked by the death of others ⟨interviewed ~*s* of the air raid⟩ **d :** one continuing to exist, function, or compete after others have ceased to do so ⟨~*s* of the first heat⟩ ⟨only ~ of six newspapers founded in the 19th century⟩

sur·vi·vor·ship \-,ship\ *n* **1 :** the legal right of the survivor of two or more persons having joint interests in an estate or other property to take the interest of any of the number dying ⟨when more than two survive, the survivors receive the decedent's share subject to similar ~ in those left⟩ — see PRESUMPTION OF SURVIVORSHIP **2 :** the state or condition of being a survivor **:** SURVIVAL

survivorship annuity *n* **:** an annuity payable to a designated person in the event he survives an insured person or other designated beneficiary of the annuity

sus \'səs\ *n, cap* [NL, fr. L, swine, hog — more at SOW] **:** a genus of mammals that is the type of the family Suidae and in former classifications comprised all or most of the swine but is usu. restricted to a few typical Eurasian and East Indian forms and the domestic breeds — see BEARDED PIG, CRESTED PIG, WILD BOAR

su·san \'süzᵊn\ *n* -s [*lazy susan*] **:** LAZY SUSAN

su·san·nite \sü'za,nīt\ *n* -s [modif. of G *suzannit*, fr. *Susanna* mine, Leadhills, Scotland, where it was discovered + G *-it* -ite] **:** LEADHILLITE

sus·cept \sə'sept\ *n* -s [prob. fr. ¹*susceptible*] **:** an organism upon or in which another organism is or may become parasitic — compare HOST

sus·cep·tance \sə'septən(t)s\ *n* -s [*susceptibility* + *-ance* (as in *conductance*)] **:** the ratio of the effective current to the effective electromotive force in an alternating-current circuit multiplied by the sine of the phase difference between current and electromotive force

sus·cep·ti·bil·i·ty \sə,septə'biləd·ē, -lətē, -i\ *n* -ES [ML *susceptibilitat-, susceptibilitas*, fr. LL *susceptibilis* susceptible + L *-itat-, -itas* -ity] **1 :** the quality or state of being susceptible **:** capability of or capacity for being acted upon, impressed, affected, or moved ⟨~ of a city to a submarine attack⟩ ⟨~ of a metal to corrosion⟩; *specif* **:** the state of being sensitive or predisposed (as to a pathogen, familial disease, drug) **:** SENSITIVITY, IDIOSYNCRASY 2b ⟨the ~ of a plant to a virus⟩ ⟨a test for ~ to scarlet fever⟩ — compare RESISTANCE, SPECIES SPECIFICITY **2 a :** a susceptible temperament, nature, or constitution **:** the character of being sensitive, affectible, impressionable, emotional ⟨the ~ of various social groups to Communist doctrine —Sidney Hook⟩ or esp. amorous ⟨his ~ to women interfered with his impartial judgment⟩ **b susceptibilities** *pl* **:** FEELINGS, SENSIBILITIES ⟨the mere thought of the enormity did outrage to her moral *susceptibilities* —Arnold Bennett⟩ ⟨when present at a ceremonial, the utmost care must be taken not to do or say anything to offend the *susceptibilities* of the people —*Notes & Queries on Anthropology*⟩ **3 a :** the ratio of the magnetization in a substance to the corresponding magnetizing force **b :** the ratio of the electric polarization to the electric intensity in a polarized dielectric

¹**sus·cep·ti·ble** \sə'septəbəl\ *adj* [LL *susceptibilis*, fr. L *susceptus* (past part. of *suscipere* to take up, undertake, admit, fr. *sus-* — var. of *sub-* up — + *-cipere*, fr. *capere* to take) + *-ibilis* -ible — more at SUB-, HEAVE] **1 :** of such a nature, character, or constitution as to admit or permit **:** capable of submitting successfully to an action, process, or operation — used with *of* or *to* followed by an action noun or a verbal noun ⟨a theory ~ of proof⟩ ⟨this problem is . . . ~ to solution M.V.Vishniak⟩ ⟨impulses . . . ~ of control —Abram Kardiner⟩ ⟨several . . . contributors have initials ~ of being mistaken for mine —Elinor Wylie⟩ **2 a :** having such a constitution or temperament as to be open, subject, or unresistant to some stimulus, influence, or agency **:** easily influenced or affected through some trait (as weakness, pliability, sensitiveness, naïveté, or amorousness) — usu. used with *to* ⟨the snow was damp and ~ to clear impression —W.H.Wright⟩ ⟨a city ~ to air attack⟩ ⟨he became ~ to the influences of the sea —*Times Lit. Supp.*⟩ ⟨he is still ~, but not excessively so, to the attractions of other women —Anthony Quinton⟩ ⟨the foibles of the health faddists are particularly ~ to satire —Arthur Knight⟩ ⟨even the most autocratic of industries is in some degree ~ to public opinion —S.H.Adams⟩ **b** (1) **:** having little resistance to a specific infectious disease **:** capable of being infected (2) **:** predisposed to develop a noninfectious disease ⟨~ to diabetes⟩ (3) **:** abnormally reactive to various drugs **c :** capable of affecting as being affected, of conceiving, feeling, arousing, or bringing forth ⟨the subject is hardly ~ of high poetry —Richard Garnett †1906⟩ **3 :** easily influenced, affected, or moved **:** IMPRESSIONABLE, RESPONSIVE ⟨at 32,500 feet ~ individuals may develop symptoms after a few minutes —H.G.Armstrong⟩ ⟨with all the fervency of her palpitant and ~ twelve years, she was infatuated with a man thirty years her senior —S.H.Adams⟩ ⟨landslides can be prevented by proper ditch drainage of ~ areas —*Amer. Guide Series: Tenn.*⟩ ⟨far from a rake, though of a warm and ~ temperament —C.B.Nordhoff & J.N.Hall⟩ **syn** see LIABLE

²**susceptible** \"\ *n* -s **:** one who is susceptible (as to a disease) ⟨the usual classification of persons into ~*s* and immunes is a purely artificial and inexact one —G.W.Anderson & Margaret Arnstein⟩

sus·cep·ti·ble·ness *n* -ES [¹*susceptible* + *-ness*] **:** SUSCEPTIBILITY

sus·cep·ti·bly \-blē, -li\ *adv* **:** in a susceptible manner

sus·cep·tion \sə'sepshən\ *n* -s [L *susception-, susceptio*, fr. *susceptus* (past part. of *suscipere* to take up) + *-ion-, -io* -ion — more at SUSCEPTIBLE] **:** a taking upon or to oneself **:** RECEPTION, ASSUMING, ASSUMPTION

sus·cep·tive \sə'septiv, -tēv\ *adj* [LL *susceptivus*, fr. L *susceptus* + *-ivus* -ive] **1 :** RECEPTIVE **2 :** SUSCEPTIBLE — **sus·cep·tive·ness** *n* -ES — **sus·cep·tiv·i·ty** \(,)sə,sep'tivəd·ē\ *n* -ES

sus·ci·tate \'səsə,tāt\ *vt* -ED/-ING/-S [L *suscitatus*, past part. of *suscitare* to stir up, rouse — more at RESUSCITATE] **:** EXCITE, ROUSE, ANIMATE

sus·ci·ta·tion \,==''tāshən\ *n* -s [LL *suscitation-, suscitatio*, fr. L *suscitatus* (past part. of *suscitare* to rouse, stir up) + *-ion-, -io* -ion] **:** the act of suscitating or the condition of being suscitated

¹**su·si·an** \'süzēən\ *also* **su·si·a·ni·an** \,süzē'ānēən\ *n* -s [*Susian* fr. L *Susiani* (pl.) inhabitants of Susa or of Susiana, fr. Gk *Sousianē* Susiana, province of the ancient Persian empire roughly coextensive with Elam, fr. *Sousa*, its capital; *Susianian* fr. Gk *Sousianē* + E *-ian*] **1** *cap* **:** a native or inhabitant of Susa or Susiana **2** *usu cap* **:** ELAMITE

²**susian** \"\ *also* **susianian** \"\ *adj, usu cap* **:** of, relating to, or characteristic of the ancient Persian province Susiana or to its capital Susa

sus·lik \'səslik\ *or* **sous·lik** \'süs-\ *n* -s [Russ *suslik;* akin to Bulg *sŭsel* ground squirrel, Czech *sysel*, Pol *susel;* all prob. fr. the root of OBulg *sysati* to hiss, of imit. origin] **1 :** any of several rather large short-tailed ground squirrels (genus *Citellus*) of eastern Europe or northern Asia with hairy feet and grayish black often more or less spotted pelage **2 :** the pelt or fur of a suslik

susp *abbr* suspend

¹**sus·pect** \(')sə'spekt\ *adj* [ME, fr. MF, fr. L *suspectus*, fr. past part. of *suspicere* to suspect — more at ⁴SUSPECT] **1 :** regarded with suspicion **:** DISTRUSTED, SUSPECTED ⟨the ~ drugs were removed from the market —Vivian Boardman⟩ ⟨religion has been academically ~ —George Hedley⟩ ⟨the idea of independence was ~ —E.S.Atiyah⟩ **2 :** having the nature or status of a suspicious person or thing **:** provocative or worthy of suspicion **:** SUSPICIOUS ⟨hold one ~ until his innocence is proved⟩ ⟨treat all innovation as ~ —A.T.Quiller-Couch⟩ ⟨he has been ~ to many members of his own party —*Time*⟩

²**suspect** \'=,=\ *n* -s **:** one who is suspected; *esp* **:** one suspected of a crime or of being infected ⟨question a murder ~⟩ ⟨examine a tuberculous ~⟩

³**suspect** \=''=\ *n* -s [ME, fr. ML *suspectus* act of suspecting, fr. L, act of looking up at, fr. *suspectus*, past part. of *suspicere* to look up at, suspect] *archaic* **:** the act of suspecting or the condition of being suspected **:** SUSPICION, APPREHENSION

⁴**suspect** \"\ *vb* -ED/-ING/-S [ME *suspecten*, fr. L *suspectare*, intens. of *suspicere* to look up at, regard with awe, suspect, fr. *sub-* from below, up + *specere* to look, look at — more at SUB-, SPY] *vt* **1 :** to have doubts of **:** be dubious or suspicious about **:** DISTRUST ⟨~*s* the motives of the salesman of goods or of ideas —Louis Wirth⟩ ⟨~ loud, unaccustomed noises as possible sources of danger —Elaine W. Gould⟩ **2 :** to imagine (one) to be guilty or culpable on slight evidence or without proof ⟨~ one of a theft⟩ ⟨~ one of giving false information⟩ ⟨no one had hitherto ~*ed* him of statecraft —John Buchan⟩ **3 :** to imagine to be or be true, likely, or probable **:** have a suspicion, intimation, or inkling, of **:** SURMISE ⟨we never ~ the disease because the attack amounts to nothing more than a bad headache —*Monsanto Mag.*⟩ ⟨when I know that he is honest and ~ that he is right —H.L.Mencken⟩ ⟨detective stories, which, however bad, I always enjoy since I never ~ the solution —H.J.Laski⟩ **4** *obs* **a :** to expect with dread **:** have an apprehension of **b :** RESPECT, NOTE, HEED **~** *vi* **:** to imagine something to be true or likely **:** be suspicious

sus·pect·able \sə'spektəbəl\ *adj* **:** that may be suspected

suspected *adj* [fr. past part. of ⁴*suspect*] **:** that one suspects or has a suspicion of **:** believed guilty, likely, or doubtful ⟨a ~ person⟩ ⟨a ~ infection⟩ ⟨a ~ story⟩ — **suspected·ly** *adv* — **suspected·ness** *n* -ES

sus·pect·er \sə'spektə(r)\ *n* -s **:** one that suspects

sus·pend \sə'spend\ *vb* -ED/-ING/-S [ME *suspenden*, fr. OF *suspendre* to hang up, interrupt, fr. L *suspendere*, fr. *sus-* (var. of *sub-* up) + *pendere* to cause to hang, weigh — more at SUB-, PENDANT] *vt* **1 :** to debar or cause to withdraw temporarily from any privilege, office, or function **:** subject to suspension ⟨~ a student from school for disciplinary reasons⟩ ⟨~ a member of a club⟩ ⟨was ~*ed* from the army for a year —H.E.Scudder⟩ ⟨condemned him and ~*ed* him from the ministry —A.C.McGiffert⟩ **2 a :** to cause (as an action, process, practice, use) to cease for a time **:** stop temporarily ⟨~ publication of a magazine⟩ ⟨~ bus service⟩; *sometimes* **:** to stop permanently **:** DISCONTINUE **b :** STAY ⟨~ a hearing⟩ **c :** to set aside or make temporarily inoperative ⟨ready and able to ~ their personal values for the sake of magically collective ones —E.H.Erikson⟩ ⟨credit controls were relaxed and ~*ed* —C.L.James⟩ ⟨not a detached period in which the moral standards he adheres to at home can be temporarily ~*ed* —Scott Hershey & Harry Tennant⟩ ⟨article 140 provided that the constitutional court might ~ laws which violated the constitution —C.J.Friedrich⟩ ⟨the general ~*ed* constitutional guarantees for forty-five days —*Current Biog.*⟩ **d :** to cause to be intermitted or interrupted (as in motion or execution) ⟨they ~*ed* their oars to listen⟩ **3 :** to defer till later **:** POSTPONE; *usu* **:** to withhold for a time on specified conditions ⟨~ sentence on a convicted man⟩ **4 :** to hold in an undetermined or undecided state awaiting fuller information ⟨~ judgment until further knowledge is attainable —M.R.Cohen⟩ ⟨you ~ both belief and disbelief —T.S.Eliot⟩ ⟨expression was ~*ed* as she sought his mood, to know what to conform to —Louis Auchincloss⟩ **5 a :** HANG ⟨~*ing* his linen to dry on the frame of the wagon —Van Wyck Brooks⟩ ⟨the garment of primitive man was usually a simple robe that covered the body and was ~*ed* from the shoulders —Morris Fishbein⟩ ⟨~*ed* from his neck was a medallion —R.H.Brown⟩ ⟨the exterior walls instead of supporting the roof, are ~*ed* from it —*Amer. Fabrics*⟩; *esp* **:** to hang so as to be free on all sides except at the point of support **:** cause to depend ⟨~ a ball by a thread⟩ ⟨~ a chandelier from a ceiling⟩ **b :** to cause to be upheld or to be kept from falling or sinking by some invisible support (as buoyancy) ⟨dust ~*ed* in the air⟩ ⟨particles ~*ed* in water⟩ **c :** to support (the upper part of a vehicle) on the wheels or axles by springs or other devices **6 :** to hold riveted in attention **:** keep fixed or lost (as in wonder or contemplation) ⟨man . . . is forever ~*ed* in a floating world of action and contemplation —Richard Eberhart⟩ **7 :** to keep waiting in suspense or indecision **8 :** to make contingent or dependent on or upon **:** CONDITION **9 :** to hold (a musical note or tone) over into the following chord **~** *vi* **1 :** to cease temporarily from operation or activity ⟨the magazine ~*ed*⟩ ⟨the school ~*ed* for lack of finances⟩ **2 :** to stop payment or fail to meet obligations or engagements — used of a business or a bank **3** *obs* **a :** to suspend judgment **b :** to have an apprehension or a suspicion **4 a :** HANG ⟨baleen plates ~*ing* from the upper jaw —*Alaska Sportsman*⟩ **b :** to become held in suspension ⟨fine particles that ~ readily in water⟩ **syn** see DEFER, EXCLUDE — **suspend payments :** to cease paying debts or obligations — used of a business or a bank

suspended *adj* [fr. past part. of *suspend*] **1 :** temporarily debarred, inactive, inoperative **:** held in abeyance ⟨~ officials⟩ ⟨~ construction⟩ ⟨a ~ bank⟩ **2 :** held in suspension **:** HUNG, PENDENT ⟨there are few natural waters which do not contain at least a small amount of ~ matter such as silt, mud, small plant and animal forms —*Manufacture of Bottled Carbonated Beverages*⟩ ⟨a ~ fireplace⟩

suspended animation *n* **:** temporary suspension of the vital functions (as in persons nearly drowned) ⟨each case of *suspended animation* requires certain fundamental knowledge by the physician as to different methods of resuscitation —*Medical Physics*⟩

suspended cadence *n* **:** DECEPTIVE CADENCE

suspended ceiling *n* **:** a ceiling suspended from the floor or roof construction above

suspended cymbal *n* **:** CRASH CYMBAL

suspended joint *n* **:** a rail joint coming between two railroad ties — compare SUPPORTED JOINT

sus·pend·er \sə'spendə(r)\ *n* -s **1 a :** one that suspends **b** *Scots law* **:** the party that prays the court for a suspension **2 :** a device by which something may be suspended: as **a :** one of two supporting bands of elastic, leather, or cloth, worn across the shoulders and fastened at the waistline to trousers, a skirt, or belt — usu. used in pl. and often with *pair* ⟨a pair of ~*s*⟩ **b** *Brit* **:** GARTER **c :** a support (as a hanger or hook) for an electric cable **3 :** something (as a basket of flowers) suspended

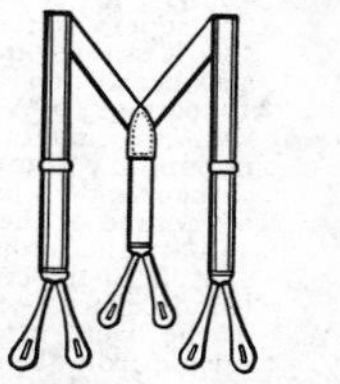

suspenders 2a

suspender belt *n, Brit* **:** GARTER BELT

sus·pend·ible \sə'spendəbəl\ *adj* **:** capable of being suspended

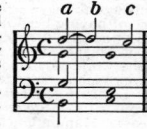

¹**sus·pense** \sə'spen(t)s\ *n* -s [ME, fr. MF, fr. fem. of *suspens* suspended, in doubt, hesitant, fr. L *suspensus*, fr. past part. of *suspendere* to suspend] **1 a :** the state of being suspended **:** temporary cessation **:** SUSPENSION ⟨asks for ~ of judgment —*Manchester Guardian Weekly*⟩ **b :** the state in which a temporary cessation of one's legal right exists **2 a :** mental uncertainty **:** ANXIETY, APPREHENSION ⟨the thought of the ~ and terror that my absence must engender in my loved ones —Elinor Wylie⟩ ⟨the ~ which was more terrible than any certainty —Ellen Glasgow⟩ **b :** pleasant excitement as to a decision or outcome ⟨a novel of ~⟩ **3 :** the state or character of being undecided, not decided, or doubtful **:** lack of certainty **:** INDECISIVENESS ⟨our next strategic move was still in ~ —Sir Winston Churchill⟩

²**suspense** \"\ *adj* [ME, fr. MF *suspens* — more at ¹SUSPENSE] **1 :** waiting for the outcome **:** held in suspension **:** SUSPENDED, WITHHELD **2 :** HESITANT, CAUTIOUS

suspense account *n* **:** an account for the temporary entry of charges or credits pending determination of their ultimate disposition — often used of doubtful accounts receivable

sus·pense·ful \-)sfəl\ *adj* **:** full of suspense **:** marked by suspense ⟨as ~ as a ghost story⟩ ⟨a ~ drama⟩ ⟨this convention has been moderately ~ —R.H.Rovere⟩ ⟨after a ~ pause, everybody stood up —F.J.Warburg⟩

sus·pen·sion \sə'spenchən\ *n* -s [LL *suspension-, suspensio*, fr. L *suspensus* (past part. of *suspendere* to suspend) + *-ion-, -io* -ion] **1 :** the act of suspending or the state or period of being suspended, interrupted, or abrogated ⟨his business duties forced the ~ of his hobbies —*Current Biog.*⟩ ⟨an actress under ~ from a moving-picture studio for failing to report to work⟩: as **a :** temporary forced withdrawal from the exercise of office, powers, prerogatives, privileges as a member or communicant ⟨~ may be employed to remove an apparently seriously objectionable boy or girl from school —H.R.Douglass⟩ ⟨a rash of police ~*s* takes place because of alleged shakedowns —R.E.Merriam⟩ **b :** temporary withholding (as of belief, decision, or judgment) **c :** temporary remission of action or execution (as of a law, regulation, or rule) **d** *Scots law* (1) **:** a judicial remedy to prevent a threatened injury or to stop an unlawful proceeding brought in the Bill Chamber before a lord ordinary who may require caution before granting emergency relief and who then hears the case on its merits — called also *suspension and interdict* (2) **:** a petition brought in the Bill Chamber by a prisoner before a lord ordinary to satisfy him that the imprisonment is illegal — called also *suspension and liberation* **e** (1) **:** the holding over of one or more musical tones of a chord into the following chord, thus producing a momentary discord and suspending the concord which the ear expects; *specif* **:** such a dissonance which resolves downward (2) **:** the tone thus held over — compare RETARDATION 5 **f :** a penalty by which a cleric is forbidden wholly or in part to exercise the power of orders or office or to enjoy the fruits of his benefice **g :** stoppage of payment of obligations or engagements **:** FAILURE — used esp. of a business or a bank **h :** a rhetorical device whereby the hearer is kept in suspense over what is to follow or over the inference or conclusion to be drawn ⟨"eye hath not seen, ear hath not heard . . ." is a ~⟩ **i :** an abbreviation (as *IHS* for ΙΗΣΟΥΣ Jesus) consisting of the first letter or the first part of a word accompanied by a special mark indicating the omission of the rest **:** an abbreviation (as *ppt* for *precipitate*) consisting of the first letter or part of a word and the first letter or part of the second or third syllable of the word **2 a :** the act of hanging or the state of being hung ⟨the simple stake was employed for the impalement as well as for the ~ of those under sentence —Victor Schultze⟩ **b** (1) **:** the state of a substance when its particles are mixed with but undissolved in a fluid or solid ⟨dust particles in ~ in air⟩ ⟨silt in ~ in water⟩ ⟨droplets in ~ in a gas⟩ (2) **:** a substance in this state ⟨a ~ of fine sand in water⟩ (3) **:** a two-phase system consisting of a finely divided solid dispersed in a solid, liquid, or gas — compare DISPERSION 4b, EMULSION 2a, SOLUTION 2b(1) **3 :** something suspended ⟨the swinging bridge, a ~ of steel cables with stone towers and a wooden walkway—*Amer. Guide Series: Minn.*⟩ **4 a :** a device by which something (as a magnetic needle) is suspended ⟨a bifilar ~⟩ **b :** the system of springs and other devices supporting the upper part of a vehicle on the axles ⟨independent front-wheel ~ has entirely replaced the rigid front axle on American cars —Joseph Heitner⟩ **c :** the act, process, or manner in which the pendulum or torsion balance of a timepiece is suspended

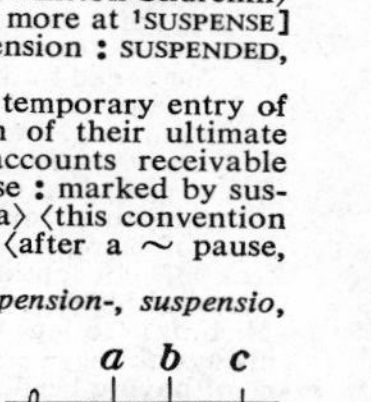

suspension 1e: *a* preparation, *b* percussion, *c* resolution

suspension bridge *n* **:** a bridge that has its roadway suspended from two or more cables usu. passing over towers and securely anchored at the ends, that has cables consisting of wire rope, eyebars, or parallel wires wrapped spirally with wire to protect them and hold them in position, and that usu. has the floor system made rigid by longitudinal stiffening trusses — see BRIDGE illustration

suspension feeder *n* **:** an animal that feeds on material (as planktonic organisms) suspended in water and that usu. has various structural modifications for straining out its food

suspension periods *or* **suspension points** *n pl* **:** usu. three spaced periods used to mark an omission of a word or group of words from a written context — compare ELLIPSIS 3

sus·pen·sive \sə'spen(t)siv, -)sēv *also* -)səv\ *adj* [ML *suspensivus*, fr. L *suspensus* (past part. of *suspendere*) + *-ivus* -ive] **1 :** stopping temporarily **:** tending or having the power to suspend **:** effecting suspension **:** SUSPENDING **2 :** characterized by suspense, suspended judgment, or indecisiveness ⟨a ~ novel⟩ **3 :** characterized by physical or rhetorical suspension **:** manifesting suspension ⟨~ sentences⟩ ⟨a ~ veto⟩

suspensive condition *n, Roman, civil, & Scots law* **:** a condition depending upon an uncertain event which must be fulfilled before an obligation arises **:** CONDITION PRECEDENT

sus·pen·sive·ly \-)səvlē, -li\ *adv* **:** in a suspensive manner

sus·pen·sive·ness \-)sivnəs\ *n* -ES **:** the quality or state of being suspensive

suspensive veto *n* **:** a veto by which a law is merely suspended until reconsidered by the legislature and becomes a law if repassed by an ordinary majority

sus·pen·soid \sə'spen(t),sȯid\ *n* -s [ISV *suspension* + *colloid*] **1 :** a colloidal system in which the dispersed particles are solid — not used scientifically; compare EMULSOID 1 **2 :** a lyophobic sol (as a gold sol)

sus·pen·sor \sə'spen(t)sə(r)\ *n* -s [NL, lit., one that suspends, fr. L *suspensus* + *-or*] **1 :** SUSPENSORIUM **2 a :** a group or chain of cells that is produced from the zygote of a heterosporous plant and serves to push the embryo which arises at its extremity deeper into the embryo sac and into contact with the food supply of the megaspore **b :** one of the two hyphae in fungi of the order Mucorales that bear gametangia at their tips and later support the zygospore

sus·pen·so·ri·al \(')sə,spen'sōrēəl\ *adj* [NL *suspensorium* + E *-al*] **:** SUSPENSORY 3

sus·pen·so·ri·um \(ˌ)səˌspenˈsōrēəm\ *n, pl* **suspenso·ria** \-ēə\ [NL, fr. LL, instrument for suspending, fr. L *suspensus* (past part. of *suspendere* to suspend) + *-orium*] **:** something that suspends a body part; *specif* **:** the bony or cartilaginous element or series of elements that in most vertebrates below mammals connects the lower jaw with the cranium

¹sus·pen·so·ry \səˈspen(t)s(ə)rē, -ri\ *adj* [L *suspensus* + E *-ory*] **1 a :** SUSPENDED **b :** fitted or serving to suspend ⟨a ~ ligament⟩ **2 :** temporarily leaving undetermined **:** SUSPENSIVE 1, SUSPENDING **3** [NL *suspensorium* (n.)] **:** belonging to a suspensorium

²suspensory \"\ *n* -ES **:** something that suspends or holds up; *specif* **:** a band or pouch for supporting a part (as the scrotum)

suspensory ligament *n* **:** a ligament or fibrous membrane suspending an organ or part: as **a :** an annular fibrous membrane of the eye continuous with the hyaloid membrane and attached to the ciliary body by its outer border and to the capsule of the crystalline lens by its inner border holding the lens in place — see EYE illustration **b :** the falciform ligament of the liver **c :** a strong ligament in the foot of the horse arising from the carpal or tarsal bones and the upper part of the cannon bone, passing down and after dividing being attached to the two sesamoid bones of the fetlock and giving off a downward prolongation on each side of the great pastern bone to unite with the border of the extensor tendon

¹sus·pi·cion \səˈspishən\ *n* -S [ME, alter. (influenced by L *suspicio-, suspicio* suspicion, fr. *suspicere* to suspect + *-ion-, -io* -ion) of *suspecion*, fr. MF *sospeçon* suspicion (influenced in meaning by L *suspicion-, suspicio*), fr. LL *suspection-, suspectio* act of looking up at, awe, fr. L *suspectus* (past part. of *suspicere* to look up at, regard with awe) + *-ion-, -io* -ion — more at SUSPECT] **1 a :** the act or an instance of suspecting **:** imagination or apprehension of something wrong or hurtful without proof or on slight evidence ⟨in the inspection and interrogation of applicants the following points should lead to a ~ of tuberculosis —H.G.Armstrong⟩ **b :** the mental uneasiness aroused in one who suspects **:** MISTRUST, DOUBT ⟨he succeeded in dispelling their ~s and won their confidence —L.R.Hafen⟩ ⟨an independent, he was regarded with ~ by both parties —W.C.Ford⟩ ⟨the intentions of other nations were viewed with great caution, if not ~ —Theodore Hsi-En Chen⟩ ⟨her weakness for peanuts was balanced by a dark ~ of certain other common vegetables —R.K.Leavitt⟩ **c :** the state of being suspected ⟨protected from ~ by her complete lack of conventional attractiveness —Gerald Bullett⟩ ⟨relieved of his post on ~ of Communist sympathies —Madaline Nichols⟩ ⟨college teams, the amateur standing of which is not always above ~ —*Amer. Guide Series: N.Y.*⟩ ⟨came under the ~ of having been implicated in the revolution —H.S.Reichle⟩ **2 :** INKLING, INTIMATION, HINT ⟨there had after all been nothing but whispered ~s, old wives' tales, fables invented by men —Sherwood Anderson⟩ ⟨not to have had the least ~ of the approaching marriage⟩ **3 :** a slight touch **:** a mere trace **:** SUGGESTION ⟨never allow even a ~ of rust to appear on or in your rifle —*Hunter's Encyclopedia*⟩ ⟨just a ~ of light in the east —Hamlin Garland⟩ ⟨without a ~ of dizziness⟩ ⟨without a ~ of scandal⟩ **syn** see UNCERTAINTY

²suspicion \"\ *vt* -ED/-ING/-S *chiefly substand* **:** SUSPECT

sus·pi·cion·al \-nᵊl\ *adj* [¹*suspicion* + *-al*] **:** of or relating to suspicion esp. the abnormal suspicion suggesting paranoid mechanisms

sus·pi·cion·less \-nləs\ *adj* **:** having or showing no suspicion

sus·pi·cious \səˈspishəs\ *adj* [ME *suspicious, suspecious*, fr. MF *suspicieus, suspecious*, fr. L *suspiciosus*, fr. *suspicion-, suspicio* suspicion + *-osus* -ous] **1 :** arousing or tending to arouse suspicion **:** QUESTIONABLE, SUSPECTED ⟨thinking the circumstances in which the watch was offered for sale somewhat ~ —Samuel Butler †1902⟩ ⟨haven't seen any *suspicious*-looking strangers around here —Lyle Saxon⟩ ⟨the patrol officer should constantly observe all ~ cars on his beat —R.L.Anderson⟩ ⟨he rises rapidly, and with almost ~ ease, to progressively important jobs —Hobe Morrison⟩ ⟨an X-ray diagnosis of a ~ tuberculous lesion was made —*Jour. of Pediatrics*⟩ ⟨have had one ~ death (suicide?) in a patient who was scheduled to start treatment —J.L.Fetterman⟩ **2 :** suspecting or inclined to suspect **:** given or prone to suspicion ⟨the unsophisticated native is often ~ of all strangers —*Notes & Queries on Anthropology*⟩ ⟨puritanism was always ~ of anything that made for physical comfort —*Amer. Guide Series: Mass.*⟩ ⟨very ~ of one who did not complain about having to doctor the numerous ailments in the manuscripts he receives —E.S.McCartney⟩ ⟨be a little bit ~ next time you hear or read some argument for keeping taxes down —K.F. Zeisler⟩ ⟨in captivity the vervet is at first very timid and ~ —James Stevenson-Hamilton⟩ **3 :** manifesting, expressing, or indicative of suspicion ⟨the countryman answered, with a ~ flash of a pair of cunning eyes —A. Conan Doyle⟩ ⟨who was now proceeding with a ~ briskness to prepare the evening meal —T.B.Costain⟩ ⟨the doors and windows were closed, and a ~ look was on everything —T.B.Thorpe⟩ ⟨no government can invite help and then adopt a prying, ~, inquisitorial attitude to those who accept the invitation —*Orient Bk. World*⟩ — **sus·pi·cious·ly** *adv* — **sus·pi·cious·ness** *n* -ES

sus·pi·ra·tion \ˌsəspəˈrāshən\ *n* -S [ME, fr. L *suspiration-, suspiratio*, fr. *suspiratus* (past part. of *suspirare* to sigh) + *-ion-, -io* -ion] **:** a long deep breath **:** SIGH ⟨little ~s of awe and astonishment —Tennessee Williams⟩

sus·pire \səˈspī(ə)r, -īə\ *vb* -ED/-ING/-S [ME *suspiren*, fr. L *suspirare* to draw a deep breath, sigh, fr. *sub-* + *spirare* to breathe — more at SPIRIT] *vi* **1 :** to draw a long breath **:** SIGH, RESPIRE ⟨the patient began to ~ —Ellery Sedgwick⟩ ⟨like two fish . . . suspended, and *suspiring* in a golden, liquid atmosphere —Hervey Allen⟩ **2 :** to long for something — used with *for* or *after* ~ *vt* **:** to utter or give forth with a breath or sigh ⟨I have caught myself *suspiring*, "Ah, those were the days!" —J.S.Redding⟩

sus·pir·i·ous \səˈspirēəs\ *adj* [L *suspiriosus*, fr. *suspirium* deep breath, sigh (fr. *suspirare*) + *-osus* -ous] **:** breathing heavily **:** SIGHING

sus·que·han·na \ˌsəskwəˈhanə\ *n, pl* **susquehanna** *or* **susquehannas** *usu cap* **1 :** an Iroquoian people of the Susquehanna River valley **2 :** a member of the Susquehanna people

susquehanna salmon *n, usu cap 1st S* [fr. the *Susquehanna* river, central New York, Pennsylvania & Maryland] **:** WALLEYE 4

¹sus·sex \ˈsəsiks\ *adj, usu cap* [fr. *Sussex*, county of southern England] **:** of or from the county of Sussex, England **:** of the kind or style prevalent in Sussex

²sussex \"\ *n* **1** *usu cap* **:** an English breed of dark red beef cattle similar to the Devon but larger and with incurving horns **2** *usu cap* **:** an English breed of domestic fowls of the meat type with single combs and usu. speckled or red plumage **3 :** SUSSEX SPANIEL **4** -ES **:** an animal of a Sussex breed

sus·sex·ite \-kˌsīt\ *n* -S [*Sussex*, county of northern New Jersey + E *-ite*] **:** a mineral $MnBO_2OH$ isomorphous with szaibelyite consisting of a borate of manganese and occurring in white fibrous veins (hardness 3, sp. gr. 3.4)

sussex spaniel *n* [ˈ*sussex*] **1** *usu cap both Ss* **:** a British breed of short-legged short-necked long-bodied spaniel of rather large size with a flat or slightly wavy golden liver coat **2** *usu cap 1st S & sometimes cap 2d S* **:** a dog of the Sussex Spaniel breed

sus·sul·ta·to·ry \səˈsəltəˌtōrē\ *adj* [It *sussultare* to leap up, heave (fr. L *subsultare*, fr. *sub-* up + *-sultare*, fr. *saltare* to leap) + E *-tory* (as in *successatory*) — more at SUB-, SALTANT] **:** characterized by up-and-down vibrations of large amplitude — used of an earthquake; compare SUCCUSSATORY

sus·sul·to·ri·al \ˌsəsəlˈtōrēəl\ *adj* [It *sussultorio* heaving, vibrating up and down (fr. *sussultare* to heave + *-orio* -ory, fr. L *-orius*) + E *-al*] **:** having the nature of or resulting from a sussultatory earthquake shock

sus·tain \səˈstān\ *vb* -ED/-ING/-S [ME *susteinen, sustenen*, fr. OF *sustenir*, fr. L *sustinēre* to hold up, sustain, fr. *sus-* (var. of *sub-* up) + *-tinēre* (fr. *tenēre* to hold) — more at SUB-, THIN] *vt* **1 :** to give support (as military support) to **:** uphold by aiding or backing up **:** furnish relief to ⟨if the director be ~*ed* in the general endeavor to make the observatory useful —Cleveland Abbe⟩ ⟨they had behind them no great organization such as that which ~*ed* French and his colleagues —F.W.Crofts⟩ ⟨the officer witnesses . . . with a record of service to their country to ~ them —H.W.Baldwin⟩ **2 :** to provide for the support or maintenance of **:** supply with sustenance **:** NOURISH ⟨plant life ~s the living world —D.C.Peattie⟩ ⟨commitment of trained men to the machines that ~ war —C.W.deKiewiet⟩ ⟨the sort of defense which our economy can ~ —W.F.Knowland⟩ ⟨settlements along the seacoast . . . are ~*ed* by the fishing trade —*Amer. Guide Series: N.J.*⟩ ⟨preached as he never preached before, ~*ing* himself with lemon juice and vegetables —*Time*⟩ **3 a :** to cause to continue (as in existence or a certain state or in force or intensity) **:** to keep up esp. without interruption, diminution, or flagging **:** MAINTAIN, PROLONG ⟨found it difficult to ~ an interest in their talk —L.C.Douglas⟩ ⟨the sort of writing which early established and has long ~*ed* his reputation —Bliss Perry⟩ ⟨policies which they said would be needed to ~ prosperity —Fritz Sternberg⟩ ⟨the civil war period was lived at a high tension that could not be ~*ed* —H.L.Matthews⟩ ⟨dissatisfaction with the work of the legislatures ~*s* the efforts of those critics —A.N.Holcombe⟩ ⟨difficult for even the most attentive and genuinely musical listener to ~ maximum attention every minute —Hunter Mead⟩ ⟨too fatigued to ~ a consecutive conversation —Lucien Price⟩ **b** (1) **:** to allow (a musical tone) to sound without dying away as long as the rhythm will permit (2) **:** to play (a musical composition or part) in legato style **4 a :** to bear up from or as if from below **:** support the weight of **:** hold up **:** PROP ⟨bones are the solid elements of structure that ~ the body —Morris Fishbein⟩ ⟨pins suitable for ~*ing* kilts —Ashley Halsey⟩ **b :** to carry or withstand (a weight or pressure) ⟨the dam . . . could not ~ the heavy head of water —*Amer. Guide Series: Minn.*⟩ ⟨beam . . . had to be much thicker in order to ~ even the same weight —S.F.Mason⟩ **5 :** to prevent (as one's mind or spirit) from sinking or giving way **:** buoy up ⟨the scientist . . . is ~*ed*, as are the religious, by a profound and unshakable faith —P.B. Sears⟩ ⟨excitement ~*ed* me —Polly Adler⟩ ⟨hope that had ~*ed* them —Frank Yerby⟩ ⟨~ the morale of the civilian population —R.D.W.Connor⟩ ⟨I read history to ~ myself in the violent confusions of these years —Ralph Bates⟩ ⟨comfort and ~ the parents —Agnes S. Turnbull⟩ **6 :** ENDURE: as **a :** to submit to without failing or yielding **:** bear up under ⟨I couldn't ~ such an act —Rex Ingamells⟩ ⟨a man bravely ~*ing* the burden of fear —*Time*⟩ ⟨he would wonder whether he could ever again ~ a year's teaching —Lucien Price⟩ **b :** to bear as an affliction **:** to bear with suffering ⟨the tremendous nervous shock which has been ~*ed* —H.G.Armstrong⟩ ⟨~*ed* a concussion of the brain —Allan Nevins⟩ **c :** SUFFER, RECEIVE, UNDERGO ⟨must be prepared to ~ heavy losses —Bruce Bliven b. 1889⟩ ⟨the walls of its building bear bullet scars ~*ed* in a riot —*Amer. Guide Series: N.Y. City*⟩ **7 a :** to support as true, legal, or just; *sometimes* **:** CONTEND **b :** to allow or admit as valid ⟨the court ~*ed* the motion⟩ **8 :** to support by adequate proof **:** ESTABLISH, CORROBORATE, CONFIRM ⟨testimony that ~*s* our contention⟩ ⟨a thesis which no one . . . could conceivably ~ —*Times Lit. Supp.*⟩ **9 :** to act the part of (a character) ⟨no reason why she should not have ~*ed* both roles —Anthony Powell⟩ ⟨directing that no letter or message be received on any occasion whatsoever from the enemy . . . but such as should be directed to them in the characters they respectively ~*ed* —H.E.Scudder⟩ ~ *vi* **:** BEAR, MAINTAIN ⟨beyond a country's capacity to ~, it recommended grants rather than loans —*Americas*⟩ **syn** see EXPERIENCE, SUPPORT

sus·tain·able \-nəbəl\ *adj* **:** capable of being sustained

sus·tained \səˈstānd\ *adj* [fr. past part. of *sustain*] **:** maintained at length without interruption, weakening, or losing in power or quality **:** PROLONGED, UNFLAGGING ⟨~ reasoning⟩ ⟨~ comedy⟩ ⟨~ flight⟩ ⟨~ performance⟩ ⟨~ verse⟩ ⟨~ piece of music⟩ — **sus·tained·ly** \-nədlē, -nd-\ *adv*

sustained yield *n* **:** a recurrent increment of a biological resource (as timber or fish) such that the portion removed by one harvest is replaced by growth or reproduction before another harvest occurs — compare SELECTION 3b

sus·tain·er \səˈstānə(r)\ *n* -S [ME *susteinere*, fr. *susteinen* to sustain + *-ere* -er] **1 :** one that sustains **2 :** SUSTAINING PROGRAM

sustaining *adj* [fr. pres. part. of *sustain*] **1 a :** serving to sustain **b :** aiding in the support of an organization through a special fee ⟨a ~ member paying $25 annually⟩ **2 :** of or relating to a sustaining program ⟨a ~ feature⟩ ⟨~ time⟩ — **sus·tain·ing·ly** *adv*

sustaining pedal *n* **1 :** DAMPER PEDAL **2 :** SOSTENUTO PEDAL

sustaining program *also* **sustaining show** *n* **:** a radio or television program that is paid for by a station or network and has no commercial sponsor

sus·tain·ment \səˈstānmənt\ *n* -S [*sustain* + *-ment*] **:** the act of sustaining **:** MAINTENANCE, SUPPORT

sus·te·nance \ˈsəstənən(t)s\ *n* -S [ME, fr. OF, fr. *sustenir* to sustain + *-ance*] **1 a :** means of support, maintenance, or subsistence **:** LIVING ⟨it is chiefly through his equipment that man acts on and reacts to the external world, draws ~ therefrom —V.G.Childe⟩ ⟨there is neither tolerance nor ~ of his intended calling —F.C.Neff⟩ **b** (1) **:** FOOD, REFRESHMENTS ⟨trooping off the ladies as soon as they had taken their ~ —George Meredith⟩ (2) **:** NOURISHMENT ⟨countries in which children are in desperate need of physical ~ to remain alive —Mark Starr⟩ **2 a :** the act of sustaining or the state of being sustained **b :** a supplying or being supplied with the necessaries of life ⟨money for ~ of the homeless⟩ **3 :** something that gives support, endurance, or strength **syn** see LIVING

sus·te·nant \-nənt\ *adj* [back-formation fr. *sustenance*] **:** SUSTAINING

sus·ten·tac·u·lar \ˌsəstənˈtakyələ(r)\ *adj* [NL *sustentaculum* + E *-ar*] **:** serving to support or sustain

sustentacular cell *n* **1 :** one of the branching connective-tissue cells of the spleen **2 :** SERTOLI CELL

sus·ten·tac·u·lum \ˌsəstənˈtakyələm\ *n, pl* **sustentacu·la** \-lə\ [NL, fr. L, prop, support, fr. *sustentare* (intens. of *sustinēre* to hold up) + *-culum*, suffix denoting an instrument — more at SUSTAIN] **:** a body part that supports or suspends another organ or part

sus·ten·ta·tion \ˌsəstənˈtāshən\ *n* -S [ME, fr. MF, fr. L *sustentation-, sustentatio* act of holding up, fr. *sustentatus* (past part. of *sustentare*) + *-ion-, -io* -ion] **1 :** the act of sustaining or the state of being sustained: as **a :** MAINTENANCE, UPKEEP ⟨taxes for the ~ of a state college⟩ **b :** PRESERVATION, CONSERVATION ⟨the ~ of peace in a nation⟩ **c :** maintenance of life, growth, courage, morale **d :** provision with sustenance ⟨gave seeds . . . and nectar of flowers for the ~ of His small birds —W.H.Hudson †1922⟩ **e :** physical support **:** a holding up or state of being held up **2 :** something that sustains or provides sustenance **:** SUPPORT

sustentation fund *n* **:** a fund of a religious body (as the Presbyterian) for the more adequate support of its ministers

sus·ten·ta·tive \ˈsəstənˌtād·iv, səˈstentəd·-\ *adj* [L *sustentatus* + E *-ive*] **1 :** serving to sustain **:** relating to or giving sustentation ⟨~ action⟩ ⟨~ food⟩ **2 :** serving to support or bind together body parts ⟨~ tissue⟩

sus·ten·tion \səˈstenchən\ *n* -S [fr. *sustain*, after such pairs as E *retain: retention*] **:** an act or instance of sustaining **:** SUSTENTATION

sus·ten·tor \səˈstentə(r)\ *n* -S [NL, fr. L *sustentus* (past. part. of *sustinere* to hold up) + *-or* — more at SUSTAIN] **:** one of two hooks on the posterior part of a butterfly pupa forming the cremaster

¹su·su \ˈsü(ˌ)sü\ *n* -S [Bengali *susuk*, fr. Skt *śiśuka*, lit., baby, baby creature, fr. *śiśu* baby, child; fr. its being confused with the crocodile and believed to eat babies; akin to Gk *kyein* to be pregnant — more at CAVE] **:** a blind cetacean (*Platanista gangetica* or *Susu gangetica*) about eight feet long resembling a dolphin, inhabiting the larger rivers of India, and having a long, slender, slightly spatulate beak, many teeth, triangular pectoral fins, and a rudimentary ridgelike dorsal fin

²susu \"\ *n, pl* **susu** *or* **susus** *usu cap* **1 a :** a West African people of the Mali and Guinea republics and the area along the northern border of Sierra Leone **b :** a member of such people **2 :** a Mande language of the Susu people

³susu \"\ *n* -S [Dobuan, lit., mother's milk; prob. akin to Malay *susu* breast, milk] **:** a Dobuan kinship group consisting of a woman, her brother, and her children but exclusive of her husband and her brother's children

su·su·hu·nan \ˌsüsüˈhüˌnän\ *n* -S *sometimes cap* [Malay, fr. Old Jav *suhun* supporting on the head] **1 :** a title of the former emperor of Java **2 :** the ruler of the principality of Surakarta in Java

su·sur·rant \səˈsərənt\ *adj* [L *susurrant-, susurrans*, pres. part. of *susurrare* to whisper, murmur, fr. *susurrus* whisper] **:** WHISPERING, MURMURING ⟨~ voices⟩

su·sur·ra·tion \ˌsüsəˈrāshən\ *n* -S [ME, fr. LL *susurration-, susurratio*, fr. L *susurratus* (past part. of *susurrare* to whisper) + *-ion-, -io* -ion] **1 :** the act of one that whispers or murmurs ⟨~ alone could not alter the proportionate emphasis of vowel over consonant —John Updike⟩ **2 :** WHISPERING, MURMUR ⟨a mild ~ was audible —G.A.Wagner⟩

su·sur·rous \səˈsərəs\ *adj* [L *susurrus*, fr. *susurrus* whisper] **:** full of whispering sounds **:** RUSTLING ⟨the night was filled with a slow, sad, ~ rustle, like the wind fingering the pines —R.P.Warren⟩

su·sur·rus \"\ *n* -ES [L, whisper, murmur, hum — more at SWARM] **:** a whispering, rustling, or muttering sound ⟨river moving with a rich ~ below the . . . pavement —Victor Canning⟩ ⟨a light ~ of conversation that seemed no more than the soughing of a faint wind —Donn Byrne⟩ ⟨the confused cries of the newspaper critics and the ~ of popular repetition that follows —T.S.Eliot⟩

su·sy-q \ˈsüzēˈkyü\ *n, usu cap S&Q* [origin unknown] **:** a dance step in which the hips and legs are swung sharply to one side while the shoulders and arms are bent forward and swung toward the opposite side with the clasped hands extended forward

su·taio \səˈtī(ˌ)ō\ *n, pl* **sutaio** *or* **sutaios** *usu cap* **1 :** an Indian people of southwestern South Dakota allied with the Cheyenne **2 :** a member of the Sutaio people

sute \ˈsüt\ *n* -S [ME, fr. *sute, siute* retinue, suite, suit — more at SUIT] **:** a flock of mallards

su·ter·berry \ˈsüd·ə(r)- — *see* BERRY\ *n* [*suter* (of unknown origin) + *berry*] **:** a prickly ash (*Zanthoxylum americanum*)

suth·er·land·shire \ˈsəthərlənd,shi(ə)r, -ˌshər\ *or* **suth·er·land** *adj, usu cap* [fr. *Sutherlandshire* or *Sutherland*, Scotland] **:** of or from the county of Sutherland, Scotland **:** of the kind or style prevalent in Sutherland

su·tile \ˈsütəl\ *adj* [L *sutilis* sewn together, fr. *sutus* (past part. of *suere* to sew) + *-ilis* -ile — more at SEW] *archaic* **:** done by stitching ⟨~ pictures which imitate tapestry —Samuel Johnson⟩

sut·ler \ˈsətlə(r)\ *n* -S [obs. D *soeteler* (now *zoetelaar*), fr. LG *suteler, sudeler* cook, sloppy cook, sloppy worker, fr. MHG *sudelen* to do sloppy work, to dirty; akin to OHG *siodan* to seethe — more at SEETHE] **:** a provisioner to an army post esp. when established in a shop on the post ⟨~ on the army post of frontier days before it had its own full-fledged quartermaster services —C.F.Kraenzel⟩

sut·lery \-lərē\ *n* -ES *archaic* **:** a sutler's occupation, stock, or shop

su·to \ˈsüd·(ˌ)ō\ *n, pl* **suto** *or* **sutos** *usu cap* **1 :** BASUTO 1 **2 :** SOTHO

su·tra \ˈsü·trə\ *also* **sut·ta** \ˈsud·ə\ *n* -S [Skt *sūtra* thread, string of rules, aphorisms; akin to Skt *sīvyati* he sews — more at SEW] **1** *Brahmanism* **:** a precept, aphorism, or collection of brief rules produced generally in the period 500–200 B.C. **2** *Buddhism* **:** one of the narrative parts of the Buddhist canonical literature; *esp* **:** the dialogues of the Buddha **3** *Jainism* **:** any of various scriptures; *esp* **:** a scripture dealing with the life of the founder of Jainism

sut·tee *or* **sa·ti** \ˌsəˈtē, ˈ=ˌ=\ *n* -S [Skt *satī*, lit., good woman, fem. of *sat, sant* existing, true, good — more at SOOTH] **1 :** the act or custom of a Hindu widow willingly cremating herself or being cremated on the funeral pile of her husband as an indication of her devotion to him **2 :** a woman cremated in this way

¹sut·tle \ˈsəd·ᵊl\ *adj* [alter. of *subtle*] *of weight* **:** remaining after the tare is deducted

²suttle \"\ *n* -S **:** the weight that remains after the tare is deducted

³suttle \"\ *vi* -ED/-ING/-S [back-formation fr. *suttler*] *archaic* **:** to act as a sutler

suttler *obs var of* SUTLER

suttlety *obs var of* SUBTLETY

su·tur·al \ˈsüchərəl\ *adj* [NL *suturalis*, fr. L *sutura* seam + *-alis* -al] **:** of, relating to, or in a suture or seam ⟨a ~ dehiscence⟩; *esp* **:** CONNECTIVE — **su·tur·al·ly** \-rəlē\ *adv*

sutural bone *n* **:** WORMIAN BONE

¹su·ture \ˈsüchə(r)\ *n* -S [MF & L; MF, fr. L *sutura* seam, suture, fr. *sutus* (past part. of *suere* to sew) + *-ura* -ure — more at SEW] **1 a** (1) **:** a strand or fiber (as of silk, nylon, cotton, catgut, wire) used to unite parts (as tissues, nerves, or blood vessels) of the human or an animal body ⟨incisions were . . . closed with stainless steel ~s —*Yr. Bk. of General Surgery*⟩ (2) **:** the material used for sutures ⟨silk is the most widely used nonabsorbable ~ at the present time —A.A.Stonehill⟩ **b :** a stitch made with a suture ⟨my right arm was bandaged to my side so as not to open the ~s —Laurence Oliphant⟩ **c :** the act or process of sewing with sutures ⟨fixation of mandibular fragments by direct bone ~ —*Internat'l Congress of Military Medicine*⟩ ⟨nerve ~ has not been the most dramatic accomplishment of this . . . metal —F.G.Slaughter⟩ **d :** a seam whereby two edges of a cut or incision in a human or animal body are brought together so that they may ultimately unite **2 a :** a uniting of parts ⟨~ with glue is convenient —John Smith †1679⟩ **b :** the seam or seamlike line along which two things or parts have been united ⟨here and there . . . we detect the ~s —J.D.Coleridge⟩ **3 a :** the line of union in an immovable articulation (as between the bones of the skull); **b :** an immovable articulation **:** SYNARTHROSIS **4 a :** the line or furrow formed at the junction of two adjacent parts; *often* **:** a line of dehiscence ⟨the ventral ~ of a legume⟩ **b :** the crease on the surface of various fruits (as the peach) **5 a :** the line at which the elytra of a beetle meet and are sometimes confluent **b :** a more or less impressed or otherwise distinguishable line of union (as between closely united sclerites of an arthropod or between the whorls of a univalve shell) **c :** the commonly more or less undulated or plicated line of junction of a septum of a cephalopod's shell with the wall of the shell — compare LOBE 2b, SADDLE 4b(2)

²suture \"\ *vt* -ED/-ING/-S **1 :** to unite the parts of by means of a suture ⟨~ a wound⟩ **2 :** to secure or fasten with sutures ⟨needles were *sutured* in place —J.B.Howell & J.M.Riddell⟩

su·tured \-(r)d\ *adj* [¹*suture* + *-ed*] **1 :** CONSERTAL ⟨grains that form the ~ mosaic —*Jour. of Geol.*⟩ **2 :** having or marked by a suture ⟨wavy septal lines that indicate the characteristically ~ Ammonites —W.E.Swinton⟩

suture needle *n* **:** SURGICAL NEEDLE

su·us et ne·ces·sa·ri·us he·res \ˈsüəˌset,nekəˈsärēəsˈhāˌrās\ *n* [L, lit., own and necessary heir] **:** a family heir including a slave in the paternal power of a decedent at the latter's death who by Roman law becomes sui juris and succeeds to the decedent's property by intestacy or by will

su·us he·res \ˌsüəsˈhāˌrās\ *n, pl* **sui here·des** \ˈsüēhāˈrāˌdās\ [L, lit., own heir] **1** *Roman law* **:** an heir (as a wife, son, daughter or slave) under the paternal power of the decedent at the latter's death **2** *Roman law* **:** an heir in the family of the decedent at his death who becomes sui juris on the decedent's property

su·wan·nee chicken \səˈwōnē-, -ˈwänē-\ *n, usu cap S* [fr. *Suwannee*, river in Georgia and Florida] **:** an edible Florida river terrapin (*Pseudemys concinna suwannensis*)

suwarro *var of* SAGUARO

su·ze·rain \ˈsüzərən, -zəˌrān *sometimes* ˈsəz-\ *n* -S [F, fr. *sus* above, up, upon (fr. L *susum, sursum* up, upwards, fr. *sub-* up + *versum*, neut. of *versus*, past part. of *vertere* to turn) + *-erain* (as in *souverain* sovereign, fr. OF *soverain*) — more at SUB-, WORTH, SOVEREIGN] **1 :** a superior lord to whom fealty is due **:** a feudal lord **:** OVERLORD **2 :** a dominant state exercising varying degrees of control over a vassal state with regard to its foreign relations but allowing it sovereign authority in its internal affairs

su·ze·rain·ship \-n,ship\ *n* -S **:** SUZERAINTY

su·ze·rain·ty \-ntē, -ti\ *n* -ES [F *suzeraineté*, fr. *suzeraine* (fem. of *suzerain*) + *-té* -ty] **:** the dominion, authority, or

relation of a suzerain with regard to the subject person or state esp. in the matter of control over the foreign affairs of such a state : OVERLORDSHIP

SV *abbr* **1** safety valve **2** sailing vessel **3** [L *Sanctitas Vestra*] Your Holiness **4** sluice valve **5** [L *spiritus vini*] spirit of wine **6** stop valve **7** *often not cap* [L *sub verbo* or *sub voce*] under the word **8** summer visitor **9** surface vessel

svab·ite \ˈsfä,bīt, ˈsvä-\ *n* -S [Sw *svabit*, fr. Anton *Svab* †1768 Swed. mining official + Sw *-it* -ite] : a mineral $Ca_5F(AsO_4)_3$ consisting of fluoride-arsenate of calcium that is at least partially isomorphous with apatite, hedyphane, and mimetite

svan *also* **svane** \ˈsfän, ˈsvän\ *or* **swan** \ˈswän\ *n, pl* **svan** *or* **svans** *usu cap* [Russ *Svan, Svanets*] **1** : one of the Kartvelian or Georgian peoples of the Caucasus dwelling on the upper course of the Ingur river **2** : a member of one of the Svan peoples

svan·berg·ite \ˈsfän,bər,gīt, ˈsvä-\ *n* -S [Sw *svanbergit*, fr. Lars F. *Svanberg* †1878 Swed. chemist + Sw *-it* -ite] : a mineral $SrAl_3(PO_4)(SO_4)(OH)_6$ consisting of a basic phosphate and sulfate of strontium and aluminum that is isomorphous with beudantite, corkite, hinsdalite, and woodhouseite

sva·ne·tian \sfäˈnēshən, svä-\ *n* -S *usu cap* [Russ *Svanets* Svan + E *-ian*] **1** : SVAN **2** : the South Caucasic language of the Svan people

¹sva·ra·bhak·ti \,sfärəˈbäktē, ,sv|, ,sw|, -ˈbak-, |ərəˈbək-, -ti\ *n* -S [Skt, lit., part of a vowel, fr. *svara* sound, vowel (fr. *svarati* he sounds, resounds) + *bhakti* division, portion, fr. *bhajati* he grants, allots — more at SWARM, BAKSHEESH] : the introduction of a vowel sound in Sanskrit esp. between *r* or *l* and a following consonant; *also* : a similar phenomenon in other languages

²svarabhakti \¦==¦==\ *also* **sva·ra·bhak·tic** \¦==¦==tik\ *adj* : of, relating to, or used in svarabhakti ⟨a ~ vowel⟩

svar·ga *or* **swar·ga** \ˈsfärgə, ˈsv|, ˈsw|, |ər-\ *n* -S [Skt *svarga*; akin to Skt *svarati* it shines — more at SWELTER] : a Hindu heaven

svastika *var of* SWASTIKA

svc *abbr* service

sve·co·fen·ni·an \¦sfekō¦fenēən, ¦svek-\ *adj, usu cap* [NL *Svecofennia* Sweden and Finland + E *-an*] : of, relating to, or constituting a division of the Precambrian — see GEOLOGIC TIME table

sved·berg \ˈsfed,bərg, ˈsve-\ *or* **svedberg unit** *n* -S *often cap S* [after The *Svedberg* b1884 Swed. chemist, its formulator] : a unit of time amounting to 10^{-13} second that serves in measuring the sedimentation velocity of a protein solution or other colloidal solution in an ultracentrifuge for use in an equation for determining the molecular weight of a protein

svelte *also* **svelt** \ˈsfelt, ˈsve-\ *adj* -ER/-EST [F, fr. It *svelto*, fr. past part. of *svellere* to pull out, stretch out, modif. (influenced by *s-*, fr. L *ex-* ¹ex-) of L *evellere* to pull out, fr. *e-* ¹ex- + *vellere* to pull — more at VULNERABLE] **1 a** : SLENDER, TRIM, LITHE ⟨her figure is ~⟩ ⟨she . . . looked . . . very ~ in a trim dark suit —Morris Gilbert⟩ ⟨a darting minnow with its ~ shadow beneath it —C.E.Craddock⟩ **b** : having clean lines : SMOOTH, SLEEK ⟨~ knitted bathing suits —*Fortune*⟩ **2** : URBANE, SOPHISTICATED, SUAVE ⟨has spoken in his usual ~ accents —Nathaniel Peffer⟩ ⟨this is cold praise . . . and if there were no more to say we should have here only another ~ artist of the deep freeze —Dudley Fitts⟩ ⟨a ~ monthly magazine . . . for Italians all over the world —Horace Sutton⟩

svelte·ly *adv* : in a svelte manner

svelte·ness *n* -ES : the quality or state of being svelte

sven·ga·li \sfenˈgälē, sve-, -ˈgal-, -li\ *n* -S *usu cap* [fr. *Svengali*, maleficent hypnotist in the novel *Trilby* (1894) by George du Maurier †1896 Brit. artist and novelist] : one who attempts usu. with evil intentions to persuade or force another to do his bidding

sverd·lovsk \ˈsferd,lō|fsk, ˈsve-, |vzk, =ˈ=, ˈ=,lə|\ *adj, usu cap* [fr. *Sverdlovsk*, U.S.S.R.] : of or from the city of Sverdlovsk, U.S.S.R. : of the kind or style prevalent in Sverdlovsk

sve·tam·ba·ra \s(h)wāˈtämbərə\ *n* -S *cap* [Skt *śvetāmbara*, lit., having white clothes, fr. *śveta* white + *ambara* garment — more at WHITE] : a major Jain sect whose members clothe themselves and their sacred images in white and in contrast to the Digambaras assert that women can attain salvation

SVP *abbr* [F *s'il vous plaît*] if you please

SVR *abbr* [L *spiritus vini rectificatus*] rectified spirit of wine

SVT *abbr* [L *spiritus vini tenuis*] proof spirit of wine

svy *abbr* survey

sw *abbr* **1** swatch **2** swell organ **3** switch

SW *abbr* **1** salt water **2** seawater **3** senior warden **4** *often not cap* sent wrong **5** shelter warden **6** shipper's weight **7** short wave **8** social work **9** southwest; southwestern **10** *often not cap* specific weight **11** stock width

¹swab *or* **swob** \ˈswäb *also* -wȯb\ *n* -S [prob. fr. obs. D *swabbe*, fr. MD; akin to LG *swabber* mop] **1 a** (1) : a mop used esp. aboard a naval vessel (2) : an absorbent bundle (as of rags) used for cleaning or for applying a substance to a surface ⟨dip the ~ . . . in clean ammonia water, and rub the carpet face hard with it —Emily Holt⟩ **b** (1) : a wad of absorbent material (as cotton) wound around one end of a small stick and used for applying medication or for removing material from an area ⟨~*s* used for applications in the treatment of . . . conditions of the nose —D.W.Maurer & V.H.Vogel⟩ (2) : a specimen taken with a swab ⟨a throat ~⟩ **c** : ¹PATCH 7b **d** : a hemp brush used in founding esp. for holding water, moistening mold joints, spraying on edges, or spreading blacking on dry-sand molds **2 a** : a useless or contemptible person ⟨considered it out of the question that a little ~ of his age could have the sense to appreciate her —*Blue Bk.*⟩ **b** : ³GOB **c** *Brit* : a naval officer's epaulet **3** : a loosely fitting plunger with an internal check valve that is run on a cable and used for lifting fluids from a drilled well

swabs 1b(1)

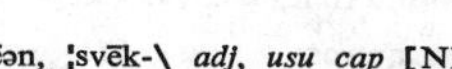

²swab *or* **swob** \"\ *vt* **swabbed** *or* **swobbed; swabbed** *or* **swobbed; swabbing** *or* **swobbing; swabs** *or* **swobs** [partly fr. ME *swabben* to sway; akin to obs. D *zwabben* to sway, LG *swabben* mop, *swabben* to splash, sway, flap; prob. all of imit. origin; partly back-formation fr. *swabber*] **1 a** : to clean with or as if with a swab : wipe up : MOP ⟨~ the decks⟩ ⟨got the towel and *swabbed* off the plates —Wallace Stegner⟩ ⟨*swabbing* down the boat's hull⟩ ⟨*swabbed* up the . . . rich beef gravy with . . . crusty French bread —H.A.Sinclair⟩ **b** : to apply medication to with a swab ⟨cleanse the wound and ~ it with iodine⟩ **c** : to use a swab in applying (medication) ⟨~ iodine over the wound⟩ **2** : to draw out (liquid) from an oil well with a swab

swab·ber \-bə(r)\ *n* -S [prob. fr. ME *swab* to sway + *-er*] **1** : one that swabs: as **a** : a worker who swabs dope onto tanned hides **b** : a worker who swabs mud from a screen at the bottom of an oil well to reestablish the flow of oil **2** : SAILOR **3** : SWAB 2a

swab·bers \-bə(r)z\ *n pl* [origin unknown] : the ace of hearts, jack of clubs, and ace and deuce of trumps formerly entitling the holder to a share of the stakes in whist

swab·bie *also* **swab·by** \-bē\ *n, pl* **swabbies** [¹*swab* + *-ie* or *-y*] *slang* : ³GOB ⟨*swabbies* who haven't seen any action —Hansford Martin⟩

swabbing *n* -S [fr. gerund of ²*swab*] : the material removed from tissue (as of a lesion) by means of a swab — usu. used in pl.

¹swa·bi·an *or* **sua·bian** \ˈswābēən\ *adj, usu cap* [*Swabia* or *Suabia* (Schwaben), duchy in medieval Germany + E *-an* (adj. suffix)] **1** : of, relating to, or characteristic of Swabia **2** : of, relating to, or characteristic of the Swabians

²swabian *or* **suabian** \"\ *n* -S [*Swabia* or *Suabia* + E *-an* (n. suffix)] **1** *cap* : a native or inhabitant of Swabia: **a** : one of a people living in the former German duchy of Swabia **b** : a native or inhabitant of the German province of Swabia **2** *usu cap* : a High German dialect of Swabia

swab stick *n* : a stick used for swabbing: as **a** : a stick with fibers frayed at one end used to clean a drill hole for a blasting charge **b** : SWAB 1b(1)

¹swack \ˈswak\ *n* -S [ME (Sc) *swak*, of imit. origin] *chiefly Scot* : a hard blow : WHACK

²swack \"\ *adj* [LG *swak* supple, pliant, weak, fr. MLG; akin to MD *swac* pliant, MLG *swacken* to rock, reel — more at SWAG] *chiefly Scot* : LITHE, NIMBLE

swacked \-kt\ *adj* [prob. fr. Sc dial. *swacked*, past part. of *swack* to drink deeply, perh. fr. ME (Sc) *swakken* to fling, dash, strike] *slang* : DRUNK, PLASTERED ⟨may come home late and be too ~ to remember —George Sklar⟩

¹swad *n* -S [prob. of Scand origin; akin to Norw dial. *svadde* big stout fellow, *sodde* slow heavy fellow] *obs* : BUMPKIN, LOUT

²swad \ˈswäd *also* -wȯd\ *n* -S [perh. back-formation fr. ²*swaddle*] *dial Eng* : POD, SHELL

³swad \"\ *n* -S [prob. fr. ¹*swad*] : SOLDIER

⁴swad \"\ *n* -S [perh. alter. of ¹*squad*] *slang* : a group of individuals : BUNCH ⟨a thick ~ of plants —*Westralian Farmers Co-Op. Gazette*⟩

¹swad·dle \ˈswädᵊl *also* -wȯd-\ *vt* **swaddled; swaddled; swaddling** \-d(ᵊ)liŋ\ **swaddles** [ME *swadelen, swathelen*, prob. alter. (influenced by *swathen* to swathe) of *swedelen, swethelen* to swaddle, fr. *swethel* swaddle, fr. OE *swethel, swæthel*; akin to MD *swadel* swaddle, OHG *swedil* swaddle, MLG *swede* bandage — more at SWATHE] **1 a** : to wrap (an infant) with swaddling clothes ⟨the baby is tightly *swaddled* in long strips of material holding its legs straight and its arms down by its sides —Patrick Mullahy⟩ **b** : to wrap completely or almost completely : SWATHE, ENVELOP ⟨had they *swaddled* the head in clothes . . . would it have ceased to bleed —Glenway Wescott⟩ ⟨an elderly lady *swaddled* in sealskin started a conversation with us —*New Yorker*⟩ **2** : to restrain protectively or in a confining manner : RESTRICT ⟨his mother ~*s* him with demure gentilities —Charles Lee⟩ ⟨liturgical style ~*s* all improprieties —Samuel Yellen⟩ **3** *archaic* : BEAT, THRASH

²swaddle \"\ *n* -S **1** : SWADDLING CLOTHES 1 **2** *archaic* : BANDAGE

swad·dler \-d(ᵊ)lə(r)\ *n* -S [²*swaddle* + *-er*; prob. fr. the frequent mention made by the preachers in their sermons to the swaddling clothes in which the infant Jesus lay (Lk 2:7)] *chiefly Irish* : a Methodist preacher; *broadly* : PROTESTANT

¹swaddling *n* -S [ME *swadeling, swatheling* act of swaddling, fr. gerund of *swadelen, swathelen* to swaddle] **1** : SWADDLING CLOTHES — usu. used in pl. ⟨changed the ~*s* on a baby —R.P. Warren⟩ **2** : BANDAGING — usu. used in pl. ⟨in case the fracture be next to the knee from below, then use no ~*s* over the knee —A.L.Fox⟩

²swaddling *adj* [¹*swaddling*; prob. fr. the frequent mention made by the preachers in their sermons to the swaddling clothes in which the infant Jesus lay (Lk 2:7)] *Brit* : PROTESTANT; *esp* : METHODIST ⟨swearing he would have none of their ~ prayers —John Wesley⟩

swaddling band *n* [ME *swadeling band*] : SWADDLING CLOTHES — usu. used in pl. ⟨the *swaddling bands* by which in darker times the human body was compressed —W.E.Channing⟩ ⟨stifled and strangled in the *swaddling bands* of mediocrity —*Nineteenth Century & After*⟩

swaddling clothes *n pl* **1 a** : narrow strips of cloth wrapped around an infant to restrict movement **b** : limitations or restrictions imposed upon the immature or inexperienced ⟨Assyrian sculpture must have freed itself from its Babylonian *swaddling clothes* —A.L.Frothingham & O.S.Tonks⟩ **2 a** : a period of immaturity ⟨I have never seen him since I was in *swaddling clothes* —G.P.R.James⟩

swad·dy \ˈswädi\ *n* -ES [³*swad* + *-y* (dim. suffix)] *Brit* : SOLDIER

swa·de·shi \swäˈdāshē, -deshē\ *n* -S *often cap* [Skt *svadeśin* native, national, fr. *sva* one's own + *deśa* country — more at SUICIDE, DESI] : a movement for national independence in India boycotting foreign goods and encouraging the use of domestic products — compare KHADDAR, SWARAJ

¹swag \ˈswag, -aa(ə)g,-aig\ *vb* **swagged; swagged; swagging; swags** [prob. of Scand origin; akin to Norw *svaga* to sway, *svagga* to walk unsteadily, ON *sveggja* to cause to sway, veer, swag; akin to MLG *swacken* to rock, reel, OHG *swingan* to swing — more at SWING] *vi* **1 a** : to sway heavily or unsteadily ⟨their shutters ~ —Joseph Mitchell⟩ **b** : to swing or tip out of line : ⁶LURCH, TILT ⟨a sudden crosscurrent caused the ship to ~⟩ ⟨trees *swagging* from constant strong winds⟩ **c** : to waver in making a decision : VACILLATE **2** : to hang heavily from or as if from weight : DROOP, SAG ⟨his heavy sensual face *swagged* —W.J.Locke⟩ ⟨the moon *swagged* in the air —Allen Tate⟩ ~ *vt* **1** : to cause to sway or lurch ⟨*swagged* the rowboat until it capsized⟩ **2** : to cause to sag ⟨the snow was starting to ~ down the old roof⟩ **3 a** : to adorn (as clothing) with swags ⟨a taffeta skirt blows out below the *swagged* hipline —*Harper's Bazaar*⟩ **b** : to arrange (as drapery) with swags ⟨the *swagged* plush curtains —Marcia Davenport⟩

²swag \"\ *n* -S **1** *obs* : a blustering person **2** : an irregular swaying movement : LURCH ⟨yawed to the deep inner ~ of the river —R.P.Warren⟩ **3** : a heavy fall : THUD **4 a** : a representation (as of urns or fruit or draperies) used to decorate furniture, walls, pewter, or brass : FESTOON ⟨the carven ~*s* of Renaissance decoration —*Britain Today*⟩ **b** : a suspended cluster (as of branches or flowers) ⟨great ~*s* of lilac and laburnum spill over ancient, weathered walls —*advt*⟩ ⟨decking his premises . . . with ~*s* of mammoth royal-purple ermine tails —Mollie Panter-Downes⟩; *esp* : a cluster of evergreen branches arranged as a decoration for a doorway and used esp. at Christmas ⟨a pine ~ . . . trimmed with kumquats and bells —Frederic Morley⟩ **c** (1) : a decorative drapery that is fastened at two points so that the middle hangs in crescent-shaped folds — compare VALANCE (2) : a decorative draped fold (as on a dress) ⟨dramatic ~*s* of draping marking the slim skirt —*advt*⟩ **d** : something resembling such a swag esp. in curved outline ⟨our rocks stand midway between two ~*s* of this uneven high-water line —Peter Mayne⟩ **5 a** : goods acquired by unlawful means : BOOTY, LOOT ⟨the ~ from this and other forms of graft —F.L.Allen⟩ **b** : valuable articles or goods ⟨will find the equitable division of the ~ . . . a problem —Horace Sutton⟩ **c** : MONEY, LUCRE ⟨any listener who may lose out on ~ being offered by another network —Saul Carson⟩ **6** : a large quantity or amount ⟨watched them putting away great ~*s* and wedges . . . of starch —Elizabeth Taylor⟩ ⟨spent a big ~ of ratepayers' money —*Sydney (Australia) Bull.*⟩ **7** : a depression in the earth often filled with water ⟨two brothers . . . were drowned while bathing in an old colliery ~ —*Pall Mall Gazette*⟩ **8** *chiefly Austral* : a pack of personal belongings carried esp. by a swagman

³swag \"\ *adj* : SAGGING, LAX ⟨men with ~ watch chains —H.E.Bates⟩ ⟨an unsuccessful poet, ~ in mind as in belly —Christopher Morley⟩

swag–bellied \ˈ=¦==\ *adj* : having a large protruding stomach ⟨a grimy, *swag-bellied* drudge —F.T.Bullen⟩

¹swage \ˈswāj\ *vb* -ED/-ING/-S [ME *swagen*, fr. OF *souagier*, fr. (assumed) VL *suaviare, -suaviare*, fr. L *suavis* sweet — more at SWEET] *vt, archaic* : ASSUAGE ⟨quench my flames, and ~ these scorching fires —Francis Quarles⟩ ~ *vi, obs* : DECREASE, ABATE ⟨would swell and ~, according to the tides —Cotton Mather⟩

²swage \", -wej\ *n* -S [ME, fr. MF *souaige, souage*] **1** *obs* : a decorative border of grooving or molding (as on a candlestick) **2** : any of several variously shaped or grooved tools: as **a** : a tool used by metalworkers to shape material to a desired form **b** : a tool used to set the teeth of a circular or band saw **c** : a tool used to form bullets **d** : a tool used to straighten damaged casing or pipe in a drilled oil well

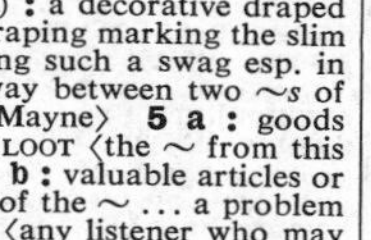

swage; *1* bottom, *2* top

³swage \"\ *vt* -ED/-ING/-S : to shape by or as if by means of a swage: as **a** : to stretch or taper (metal or plastic) by high speed hammering **b** : to form (a bullet) with a swage **c** : SWAGE-SET **d** : to shape to the form of a model, cast, or die by compressive force ⟨porcelain teeth . . . soldered to gold plates *swaged* to fit the mouth —F.L.Hise⟩ **e** : to weld by pressure or hammering ⟨bushings . . . *swaged* on preformed . . . stainless steel wire rope —*Industrial Equipment News*⟩ **f** : to fuse (a strand of suture silk) onto the end of a suture needle

swage block *n* : a perforated cast-iron or steel block with grooved sides that is used in heading bolts and swaging bars of various sizes by hand

swage bolt *n* : a bolt with indentations swaged in its body by means of which it is gripped in masonry

swag·er \ˈswājə(r), -wej-\ *n* -S [³*swage* + *-er*] **1** : one that swages **2** : SWAGE

swage-set \ˈ=,=\ *vt* [fr. *swage-set*, adj.] : to broaden the tips of (a saw tooth) to a width greater than the thickness of the saw

swagged *past of* SWAG

¹swag·ger \ˈswagə(r), -waig-\ *vb* **swaggered; swaggered; swaggering** \-g(ə)riŋ\ **swaggers** [prob. fr. ¹*swag* + *-er* (as in *batter*)] *vi* **1 a** : to conduct oneself in an arrogant or superciliously pompous manner ⟨allowed . . . to ~ and bluster and take the limelight without a word of reproach —Margaret Mead⟩; *esp* : to walk with an air of overbearing self-confidence ⟨buccaneers ~*ed* down the filthy streets —H.E.Rieseberg⟩ **b** : to move with a swinging motion ⟨three or four elephants, loaded with hay, ~*ed* down the crowded street —L.C. Stevens⟩ **c** *Scot* : STAGGER, LURCH **2** *obs* **a** : QUARREL **b** : GRUMBLE **3** : to talk in a boastful manner : BRAG ⟨talks little of his experience and I ask him why he doesn't ~ more —O.W.Holmes †1935⟩ ~ *vt* : to force by argument or threat : BULLY, BROWBEAT ⟨will strive either to cheat or to ~ you out of your money —Sir Walter Scott⟩

²swagger \"\ *n* -S **1 a** : an act or instance of swaggering ⟨his stride was majestic — just short of a ~ —Roark Bradford⟩ ⟨insisted, with a prideful ~ —Harry Hansen⟩ **b** : arrogant or conceitedly self-assured behavior ⟨the ~ of the brothers threatened further trouble —Hamlin Garland⟩ ⟨had driven to the opera with the real ~ of the aristocrat —Victoria Sackville-West⟩ **c** : ostentatious display or bravado : FANFARONADE ⟨these overtures are dazzling still for their ~ and dash —Irving Kolodin⟩ **2** : a self-confident mental or intellectual outlook : COCKINESS ⟨the throng so full of ~ and youth —Osbert Sitwell⟩ ⟨poetry with all the American ~ left in —Louise Bogan⟩

³swagger \"\ *adj* **1** : marked by elegance or showiness : FASHIONABLE, SMART, POSH ⟨~ youths in yellow gloves —Arnold Bennett⟩ ⟨a ~ wedding at eleven —Bruce Marshall⟩ **2** *of a coat* : flaring loosely and fully from the shoulder line ⟨familiar ~ trench coat —Lois Long⟩

⁴swagger *n* -S [³*swagger*] : a coat that flares loosely from the shoulder

⁵swagger \"\ *n* -S [²*swag* + *-er*] *chiefly Austral* : TRAMP

swag·ger·er \-gərə(r)\ *n* -S : one that swaggers

swaggering *adj* : of, relating to, or having the characteristics of one that swaggers ⟨a more ~ mood than usual —W.L. Shirer⟩ — **swag·ger·ing·ly** *adv*

swagger stick *n* : a short light stick typically capped at both ends with metal or covered with leather and intended for carrying in the hand (as by military officers)

swag·gie \-gē\ *n* -S [*swagman* + *-ie*] *chiefly Austral* : a traveler who carries his personal belongings in a pack

swagging *pres part of* SWAG

swaging *pres part of* SWAGE

swag·man \-gmən\ *also* **swags·man** \-gzmən\ *n, pl* **swagmen** *also* **swagsmen** [*swagman* fr. ²*swag* + *man*; *swagsman* fr. *swags* (poss. of ²*swag*) + *man*] *chiefly Austral* : VAGRANT; *esp* : one who carries a swag when traveling **syn** see VAGABOND

swa·go bass \ˈswā(,)gō-\ *n* [alter. of *Oswego bass*] : SMALLMOUTH BLACK BASS

swags *pres 3d sing of* SWAG, *pl of* SWAG

swa·hi·li \swäˈhēlē, -li\ *n, pl* **swahili** *or* **swahilis** *usu cap* [Ar *sawāḥil* (pl. of *sāḥil* coast) + *-īy* belonging to] **1 a** : a Bantu-speaking people of Zanzibar and the adjacent coast **b** : a member of such people **2** : a Bantu language of East Africa spoken orig. in Zanzibar and the adjacent coast that is a trade and governmental language over much of East Africa and in the Congo — see KINGWANA

swain \ˈswān\ *n* -S [ME *swain, swayne, swein* boy, servant, fr. ON *sveinn*; akin to OE *swān* herdsman, peasant, swain, OHG *swein* herdsman, swain, *giswīo* brother-in-law, Lith *svainė* sister-in-law, L *suus* one's own — more at SUICIDE] **1** *obs* : BOY, MAN **2** : one who lives and works in the country : RUSTIC, PEASANT ⟨the sluggish clod, which the rude ~ turns with his share —W.C.Bryant⟩; *specif* : SHEPHERD **3** : a male admirer or suitor ⟨the many ~*s* . . . besieging her from every noon to every midnight —Upton Sinclair⟩ **4** : one having a freehold within a forest

swain·ish \-nish\ *adj* : unrefined in manner or attitude : BOORISH

swainling *n* -S *obs* : a young swain

swainmote *var of* SWANIMOTE

swain·so·na \swānˈsōnə\ *n* [NL, fr. Isaac *Swainson* †1806 Eng. gardener] **1** *cap* : a genus of Australian herbs and subshrubs (family Leguminosae) having odd-pinnate leaves and racemes of small variously colored flowers with orbicular standard and twisted wings **2** -S : any plant of the genus *Swainsona* — see DARLING PEA

swain·son pea \ˈswān(t)sən-\ *n, usu cap S* [after Isaac *Swainson* †1806] : a plant of the genus *Swainsona*

swainson's hawk *also* **swainson hawk** *n* [after William *Swainson* †1855 Eng. naturalist] : a large variable but typically grayish brown to dusky brown hawk (*Buteo swainsoni*) that breeds from Alaska throughout most of western No. America, winters chiefly in the Argentine to which it migrates in large flocks, and feeds on small rodents and large insects

¹swale \ˈswā(ə)l\ *n* -S [AF *swayl*] *chiefly dial* : BOARD, PLANK, LATH; *also* : PLANKING

²swale \"\ *var of* SWEAL

³swale \"\ *n* -S [ME, shade, shady place, prob. of Scand origin; akin to ON *svalr* cool, fresh, *svala* to cool, chill; akin to OE *swelan* to burn, be burned — more at SWELTER] **1** *chiefly dial* **a** : a shady place : SHADE **b** : COOLNESS **2** : a low-lying stretch of land: as **a** : a small meadow or swamp **b** : an elongated depression in land that is at least seasonally wet or marshy, is usu. heavily vegetated, and is normally without flowing water **c** : a shallow depression in an undulating glacial moraine **d** : a low area between two ridges of a beach or sandspit

⁴swale \"\ *vi* -ED/-ING/-S [prob. fr. ¹*sway* + *-le*] : to move with a swaying motion : WAVER

swale·dale \ˈswā(ə)l,dā(ə)l\ *n* [fr. *Swaledale*, upland vale in Yorkshire, England, where it is bred] **1** *usu cap* : a British breed of hardy mutton type hill sheep producing a very long but coarse fleece **2** -S *often cap* : a sheep of the Swaledale breed

swal·ing·ly *adv* : in a swaling manner

swal·let \ˈswälət\ *n* -S [³*swallow* + *-et*] *dial Eng* : an underground stream; *also* : an opening through which a stream disappears underground

swal·lo \ˈswä(,)lō\ *n* -S [Malay (Minangkabau) *suala*] : TREPANG

¹swal·low \ˈswä(,)lō, -_lə *also* ˈswȯ(-; -ləw, -lō + V; *dial, or NE+V*, -lər\ *n* -S [ME *swalwe, swalowe*, fr. OE *swealwe, swealewe*; akin to OHG *swalawa* swallow, ON *svala* swallow, Russ *solovei* nightingale] **1** : any of numerous small long-winged passerine birds (family Hirundinidae) that are noted for their graceful flight and regular migrations, have a short bill with a wide gape, small weak feet, plumage usu. iridescent above, and often a deeply forked tail, occur in all parts of the world except New Zealand and polar regions, and feed on insects caught on the wing — see BANK SWALLOW, BARN SWALLOW, MARTIN **2** : any of several swifts (as the chimney swift) that superficially resemble swallows — see SEA SWALLOW, WOOD SWALLOW

²swallow \"\ *vb* -ED/-ING/-S [ME *swalowen, swelewen*, fr. OE *swelgan*; akin to OHG *swelgan, swelahan* to swallow, ON *svelgja*] *vt* **1 a** : to take through the esophagus into the stomach : receive into the body through the mouth and throat ⟨~*ing* pint after pint of strong old ale —G.G.Carter⟩ **b** : to eat hurriedly without careful chewing : gulp down ⟨~*ed* his lunch and rushed out⟩ **2 a** : to cause to disappear : envelop completely : ENGULF, DEVOUR ⟨admire the view before the night ~*ed* it —Claud Cockburn⟩ ⟨history is big enough to ~ us too —H.J.Muller⟩ — often used with *up* ⟨wished the floor . . . would open and ~ her up —*Fortnight*⟩ **b** : to cause to become insignificant or unnoticeable : DISPLACE ⟨in danger of being ~*ed* by the world —R.W.Southern⟩ — usu. used with *up* ⟨had been ~*ed* up by the fame of the man he later came to be —Virginia D. Dawson & Betty D. Wilson⟩ ⟨the theory of electromagnetism ~*ed* up the theory of light —A.N.White-

head⟩ **c :** to cause to become engrossed **:** occupy completely — usu. used with *up* **3 a :** to absorb eagerly or easily (as with the mind) ⟨could not ~ books like oysters —Francis Biddle⟩ **b :** to grasp fully **:** COMPREHEND ⟨her head could not ~ it —R.A.W.Hughes⟩ **c :** to seize for oneself **:** APPROPRIATE ⟨feared that his . . . neighbors . . . would ~ him and his people —A.P.Ryan⟩ — often used with *up* ⟨city after city was ~*ed* up —G.G.Coulton⟩ **4 :** to accept readily without question ⟨city fathers who couldn't quite ~ the idea of being ruled by a 17-year-old girl —C.M.L.Beuf⟩; *esp* **:** to believe implicitly and often naively ⟨~*ed* his every remark as gospel —Rex Ingamells⟩ ⟨his talks were listened to with openmouthed attention and duly ~*ed* whole —Polly Adler⟩ **5 :** to make a retraction of **:** RECANT ⟨offered the opportunity of ~*ing* their views and fading away without harsher punishment —*Time*⟩ **6 :** to put up with **:** accept submissively **:** ENDURE ⟨~*ed* an injustice which others would not have tolerated —R.G.Adams⟩ **7 :** to refrain from expressing or showing **:** REPRESS ⟨pride was ~*ed* and the government retreated —J.H.Plumb⟩ ⟨~*ed* a smile —Hamilton Basso⟩ **8 :** to utter (as words) indistinctly through failure to open the mouth wide enough ⟨~*ed* so many of his words that he might as well have been singing in Esperanto —Robert Evett⟩ ~ *vi* **1 :** to receive something into the body through the mouth and throat ⟨finished chewing and ~*ed*⟩ **2 :** to perform the action characteristic of swallowing something esp. under emotional stress ⟨~*ed* hard and turned away —F.V.W.Mason⟩ **syn** see EAT — **swallow the anchor :** to retire from life at sea ⟨*swallowed the anchor* and stayed ashore —A.E.Marten⟩

³swallow \"\ *n* -s [ME *swalowe, swelowe*, fr. OE *geswelg* gulf, abyss; akin to MHG *swalch* abyss, gullet, ON *svelgr* whirlpool, swallower, *svelgja* to swallow] **1 a** *archaic* **:** a deep opening in the earth **:** CHASM, ABYSS **b** *archaic* (1) **:** a deep body of water (2) **:** WHIRLPOOL **c** *or* **swallow hole** *chiefly Brit* **:** SINK 5 **2 a :** a passage connecting the mouth to the stomach **b :** a part (as the pharynx, throat, esophagus) of this passage **3 a :** a capacity for swallowing **:** APPETITE ⟨measures the honesty and understanding of mankind by a capaciousness of their ~ —Henry Fielding⟩ **b :** a capacity for believing ⟨he believes with the aid of those who have a bigger ~ —Leo Stein⟩ **4 a :** an instance of swallowing **:** GULP ⟨ate the canapé in one ~⟩ **b :** an amount that can be swallowed at one time ⟨took a ~ of brandy to clear his head⟩ **5 :** an aperture in a block on a ship between the sheave and frame through which the rope reeves

swal·low·able \-ləwəbəl, -lōəb-\ *adj* **:** capable of being swallowed **:** fit for swallowing

swallow bug *n* **:** any of various hairy blood-sucking bugs (genus *Oeciacus*) that are closely related to the bedbug and usu. feed on swallows and other wild birds but may also attack poultry and occas. man

swallow dive *n, chiefly Brit* **:** SWAN DIVE

swal·low·er \-ləwə(r), -lōə(-\ *n* -s **1 :** one that swallows **2 :** GLUTTON

swallow fish *n* [¹*swallow;* fr. the resemblance of its long gill-fins to a pair of long wings] **:** SAPPHIRINE GURNARD

swallow fork *n* [so called fr. its resemblance to the fork of a swallow's tail] **:** an earmark on an animal made by a triangular cut removing the tip of the ear — see EARMARK illustration

swallow hawk *n* **:** SWALLOW-TAILED KITE

swallowlike \'ˌˌ=ˌ=\ *adj* **:** resembling a swallow esp. in swiftness

swal·low·ling \-ləliŋ, -lōl-\ *n* -s **:** a young swallow

swallow plover *n* **:** PRATINCOLE

swallow roller *n* **:** a broad-billed roller of the genus *Eurystomus*

swallows *pl of* SWALLOW, *pres 3d sing of* SWALLOW

swallow shrike *also* **swallow flycatcher** *n* **:** WOOD SWALLOW

swallowtail \'ˌˌ=ˌ=\ *n* [¹*swallow* + *tail;* partly trans. of F *queue d'aronde;* partly trans. of G *schwalbenschwanz*] **1 :** a forked and tapering tail (as of a swallow) **2 :** something resembling the tail of a swallow: as **a :** BROADHEAD 2 **b :** DOVETAIL **c :** an outwork with converging sides, whose front forms a reentrant angle **d :** a pennant tapering to a double point **e** *also* **swallowtail coat :** TAILCOAT **3** *also* **swallowtail butterfly :** any of various large butterflies of *Papilio* and related genera that have the border of the hind wing produced into a taillike process and are brightly colored with black and yellow commonly predominating — see BLACK SWALLOWTAIL, TIGER SWALLOWTAIL, ZEBRA SWALLOWTAIL

swallow-tailed \ˌ=ˌ=ˌ=\ *adj* **1 :** marked by a deeply forked tail like that of a swallow ⟨a *swallow-tailed* dress suit⟩ **2 :** DOVETAILED 2

swallow-tailed duck *n* **:** OLD-SQUAW

swallow-tailed flycatcher *n* **:** SCISSORTAIL

swallow-tailed gull *n* **:** SABINE'S GULL

swallow-tailed kite *or* **swallow-tailed hawk** *n* **:** a graceful No. American kite (*Elanoides forficatus*) of the central and southern U.S. that is white with the back, wings, and deeply forked tail black

swallow-tailed moth *n* **:** a European moth (*Ourapteryx sambucaria*) having taillike lobes on the hind wings

swallow-tailed skipper *n* **:** a skipper butterfly (*Urbanus proteus*) of the eastern U.S. that is black with greenish reflections and has a long taillike process on each hind wing

swallow thorn *n* [alter. of *sallow thorn*] **:** SEA BUCKTHORN

swallow-wing \'ˌˌ=ˌ=\ *n* **:** a So. American barbet of the genus *Chelidoptera*

swallowwort \'ˌˌ=ˌ=\ *n* [¹*swallow* + *wort;* partly trans. of D *zwaluwenkruid;* partly trans. of G *schwalbenwurtz;* fr. the form of the pods suggesting a swallow with outspread wings] **1 :** CELANDINE 1 **2 :** any of several plants of the family Asclepiadaceae: as **a :** SOMA **b** (1) **:** BLACK SWALLOWWORT (2) **:** WHITE SWALLOWWORT **c :** BUTTERFLYWEED 1

swam [ME (past), fr. OE *swamm* (past)] *past and chiefly dial past part of* SWIM

swa·mi *also* **swa·my** \'swämē, -mi *also* -wȯm-\ *n, pl* **swamis** *or* **swamies** [Hindi *svāmī*, fr. Skt *svāmin* owner, lord, fr. *sva* one's own — more at SUICIDE] **1 a** *archaic* **:** a Hindu idol **b** *often cap* (1) **:** MASTER, LORD — used as a form of respectful address to a Hindu religious teacher or monk (2) **:** an initiated member of a Hindu religious order **2 :** one that resembles or emulates a swami **:** PUNDIT, SEER ⟨that modern ~, the quiz show contestant —*Shakespeare Newsletter*⟩ ⟨amateur theosophists, ~*s*, faith healers and founders of new cults in Manhattan —*Time*⟩

¹swamp \'swämp\ *adj* [ME (Sc) *swampe* distended, swollen, hollow] *chiefly Scot* **:** THIN, SLENDER

²swamp \'swämp, -wȯmp\ *n* -s *often attrib* [alter. (prob. influenced by LG *swampen* to quake & MHG *swamp* sponge, fungus) of ME *sompe* swamp, fr. MD *somp* morass, pool; akin to MHG *sumpf* marsh, OE *swamm* sponge, fungus, OHG *swamp* sponge, ON *svöppr*, Goth *swamms* sponge, Gk *somphos* spongy, porous] **1 a :** wet spongy land saturated and sometimes partially or intermittently covered with water **:** water-logged imperfectly drained land unsuitable for agriculture without artificial drainage; *esp* **:** such land supporting a natural vegetation predominantly of shrubs and trees and often intergrading into grassy marsh on the one hand and wet forest on the other — compare BOG **b :** a tract of swamp **2 :** a low spot in a coal deposit — compare SUMP

³swamp \"\ *vb* -ED/-ING/-S *vt* **1 :** to fill with or as if with water **:** INUNDATE, SUBMERGE ⟨the boat would probably be ~*ed* as soon as it hit the water —R.S.Porteous⟩ ⟨the land is completely ~*ed* by a mantle of ice —H.I.Drever & P.J. Wyllie⟩ **2 a :** to swallow up **:** overwhelm numerically or by an excess of something **:** ENGULF, FLOOD ⟨the creation of sufficient peers to ~ the opposition in the Lords —K.B. Smellie⟩ ⟨he was ~*ed* in misgivings —Marcia Davenport⟩ ⟨suddenly ~*ed* with orders —Harry Levine⟩ ⟨songs and slogans . . . ~*ed* the country —Dorothy B. Goebel⟩ **b :** to beat decisively or destroy completely **:** DEFEAT, RUIN ⟨the sailors ~*ed* the Springhill squad 13–6 —*Crowsnest*⟩ ⟨an organization of saboteurs . . . was promptly ~*ed* before it could get going —R.E.Danielson⟩ **3 a :** to clear out; *esp* **:** to open a passageway by removing underbrush or trees ⟨by oxsled in the summer of 1824, ~*ing* a road as he came —*Amer. Guide Series: N.H.*⟩ — usu. used with *out* ⟨crews . . . ~*ed* out small landing strips by hand so that larger planes could come in with grading equipment —H.W.Richardson⟩ **b :** to trim off the branches of (a felled tree) to facilitate skidding **:** LIMB ~ *vi* **1 :** to become inundated or submerged **:** FLOOD, SINK ⟨ore ships will be filled with sea water until they nearly ~ —*Newsweek*⟩ ⟨a wild-sage smell ~*s* in through doors and windows —H.W.Stoke⟩ **syn** see OVERPOWER

swamp angel *n* **1 :** a person living in or frequenting a swampy region **2 :** HERMIT THRUSH

swamp apple *n* **:** a large white or pink slightly acid edible gall on the swamp azalea caused by a fungus (*Exobasidium vaccinii*)

swamp ash *n* **:** any of several ashes usu. found in swamps: as **a :** a water ash (*Fraxinus caroliniana*) **b :** RED ASH **c :** BLACK ASH 1

swamp azalea *n* **:** a common azalea (*Rhododendron viscosum*) growing in swamps throughout the eastern U.S. and having fragrant white flowers with a clammy corolla — called also *clammy azalea, swamp honeysuckle, white honeysuckle*

swamp bay *n* **1 :** a low and often shrubby tree (*Persea pubescens*) of the southeastern U.S. with pale green lanceolate leaves and pale creamy yellow flowers followed by blackish drupes **2 :** SWEET BAY 2

swamp beggar-ticks *n pl but sing or pl in constr* **:** an American beggar-ticks (*Bidens connata*) common in wet pastures and meadows

swamp·ber·ry \'=- — *see* BERRY\ *n* **:** DWARF RASPBERRY

swamp birch *n* **1 :** YELLOW BIRCH **2 :** WESTERN PAPER BIRCH **3 :** a dwarf birch (*Betula pumila*)

swamp blackberry *n* **:** a dewberry (*Rubus hispidus*) of the eastern U.S.

swamp blackbird *n* **:** REDWING BLACKBIRD

swamp black gum *n* **:** BLACK GUM 1b

swamp blueberry *n* **:** HIGHBUSH BLUEBERRY

swamp box *n* **:** SWAMP MAHOGANY

swamp broom *n* **:** an Australian plant (*Viminaria denudata*) of the family Leguminosae resembling broom

swamp buggy *n* **:** a vehicle used to negotiate swampy terrain: as **a :** MARSH BUGGY **b :** an amphibious tractor **c** *also* **swamp glider :** a flat-bottomed boat driven by an airplane propeller

swamp bulrush *n* **:** a bulrush (*Scirpus etuberculatus*) of eastern No. America having the culm sharply 3-angled esp. above

swamp buttercup *n* **:** a common No. American perennial herb (*Ranunculus septentrionalis*) of low wet places with thick fibrous roots, elongate often trailing or spreading branches, mostly ternate leaves, and bright yellow flowers

swamp cabbage *n* **1 :** SKUNK CABBAGE 1 **2 :** CABBAGE PALMETTO

swamp candle *n* **:** a loosestrife (*Lysimachia terrestris*) with spikes of yellow flowers found in swamps or wet places — usu. used in pl.

swamp cat *n* **:** a wildcat of the Nile delta and adjacent swamps that is prob. a variety of the Kaffir cat

swamp cedar *n* **1 :** SOUTHERN WHITE CEDAR **2 :** an American arborvitae (*Thuja occidentalis*)

swamp chestnut oak *n* **:** BASKET OAK

swamp cottonwood *n* **:** a No. American poplar (*Populus heterophylla*) with resinous buds, large rounded crenate leaves, brown bark and brownish wood — called also *black cottonwood, downy poplar, swamp poplar*

swamp cypress *n* **1 :** either of two trees of the genus *Taxodium:* **a :** a bald cypress (*Taxodium distichum*) **b :** AHUEHUETE **2 :** SOUTHERN WHITE CEDAR

swamp deer *n* **:** a large yellowish brown deer (*Cervus duvaucelli*) of India having in the normal adult male six points on each antler and being in the young and sometimes also the adults spotted with white

swamp dock *n* **:** a common American dock (*Rumex verticillatus*)

swamp dogwood *n* **1 :** SILKY CORNEL **2 :** POISON SUMAC **3 :** HOP TREE **4 :** BUTTONBUSH

swamp elm *n* **:** an American elm (*Ulmus americana*)

swamp·er \'swämpə(r), -wȯm-\ *n* -s **1 :** an inhabitant of swamps or lowlands or one familiar with swampy terrain ⟨a guide, fisherman, expert on plant and animal life, crack shot — in short, a real ~ —R.E.Smallman⟩ **2 a :** one that slashes a path (as for skidding or hauling logs) or who trims the limbs and large knots from felled tree trunks — called also *busher, gutterman* **b :** GOPHERMAN **c :** BULL COOK **d :** one that works at the log deck of a woodworking establishment to trim and cut logs for the head saw **3 a :** a general assistant **:** HANDYMAN, HELPER ⟨works as a farm laborer, as a ~ on a truck, as a casual laborer around town —August Hollingshead⟩ ⟨the ~ . . . polished the brass spittoons for nothing, in exchange for the privilege of panning the sawdust in front of the bar —Klondy Nelson⟩; *esp* **:** a worker who performs heavy cleaning duties ⟨a ~ was brooming the night's debris out of Groot's saloon —H.G.Evarts⟩ **b :** a worker in a metal mine who helps load, haul, and unload ore and rock **c :** a rear brakeman

swamp evergreen *n* **:** a common club moss (*Lycopodium lucidulum*) with shining foliage and erect branches

swamp fever *n* [so called fr. its prevalence in low-lying and poorly drained areas] **1 :** LEPTOSPIROSIS **2 :** INFECTIOUS ANEMIA

swamp globeflower *n* **1 :** an American globeflower (*Trollius laxus*) **2 :** BUTTONBUSH

swamp gooseberry *n* **1 :** a No. American prickly shrub (*Ribes lacustre*) of low wet places **2 :** the reddish fruit of the swamp gooseberry

swamp grape *n* **:** FOX GRAPE

swamp gum *n* **1 :** any of various Australian gum trees (esp. *Eucalyptus regnans* and *E. ovata*) **2 :** BLACK GUM 1

swamp hare *n* **:** SWAMP RABBIT 1

swamp harrier *also* **swamp hawk** *n* **:** a harrier (*Circus approximans*) of Australia and neighboring islands that frequents open or marshy regions

swamp-haw \'ˌ=ˌ=\ *n* **:** any of several viburnums; *esp* **:** WITHE ROD

swamp hellebore *n* **:** an American hellebore (*Veratrum viride*)

swamphen \'ˌ=ˌ\ *n* **:** any of various birds (family Rallidae) that frequent swamps: as **a :** COOT 4 **b :** GALLINULE

swamp hickory *n* **1 :** BITTERNUT **2 :** WATER HICKORY

swamp honeysuckle *n* **:** SWAMP AZALEA

swamp hook *n* **:** a large hook on the end of a chain used for skidding or rolling logs

swampier *comparative of* SWAMPY

swampiest *superlative of* SWAMPY

swamp·i·ness \-pēnəs, -pin-\ *n* -ES **:** the quality or state of being swampy

swamping *n* -s [fr. gerund of ³*swamp*] **1 :** an act or instance of submerging or overwhelming ⟨numerical ~ of the natives —A.L.Kroeber⟩ ⟨the ~ of a girl's personality by the subtle influence of her parents' home —J.C.Powys⟩ **2 :** the work performed by a swamper

swamping ax *n* **:** DOUBLE-BIT AX

swampland \'ˌ=ˌ=\ *n* **:** SWAMP 1

swamp laurel *n* **1 :** a laurel (*Kalmia polifolia*) of bogs of cooler parts of No. America with pale leaves that are glaucous beneath and small purple flowers **2 :** SWEET BAY **3 :** LOBLOLLY BAY 1

swamp lily *n* **1 :** ATAMASCO LILY **2 :** a white-flowered crinum (*Crinum americanum*) of the southern U.S. **3 :** LIZARD'S-TAIL **4 :** TURK'S-CAP LILY b

swamp loosestrife *n* **:** a woody perennial marsh herb (*Decodon verticillatus*) of the family Lythraceae of eastern No. America having opposite or whorled lanceolate leaves and magenta flowers in axillary clusters — called also *swamp willow*

swamp magnolia *n* **:** SWEET BAY 2

swamp mahogany *n* **1 :** a small to medium-sized Australian eucalypt (*Eucalyptus robusta*) that grows esp. on tidal flats and yields a reddish straight-grained damp-resistant lumber **2 :** a tropical Australian tree (*Tristania suaveolens*) that yields a reddish hardwood of firm even texture that is used esp. for flooring and is highly resistant to damp and insect attack — called also *swamp box*

swamp mallow *n* **:** a rose mallow (*Hibiscus moscheutos*)

swamp maple *n* **:** any of several maples found in moist lowlands: as **a :** RED MAPLE **b :** SILVER MAPLE **c :** CALIFORNIA BOX ELDER

swamp milkweed *or* **swamp silkweed** *n* **:** a No. American milkweed (*Asclepias incarnata*) with lanceolate leaves and crimson or purple flowers

swamp moss *n* **:** SPHAGNUM

swamp oak *n* **1 :** a leafless Australian shrub (*Viminaria denudata*) of the family Leguminosae resembling broom and having small orange-yellow flowers and a one-seeded pod **2 :** a beefwood (*Casuarina glauca*) **3 :** any of several American oaks (as the pin oak, basket oak, or swamp white oak) that thrive in wet soils

swamp oat grass *n* **:** an oat grass of the genus *Trisetum*

swamp ore *n* **:** BOG IRON ORE

swamp owl *n* **:** SHORT-EARED OWL

swamp partridge *n* **:** SPRUCE GROUSE

swamp pheasant *n* **:** an Australian coucal (*Centropus phasianinus*)

swamp pine *n* **:** any of several pines that prefer or endure moist situations: as **a :** LONGLEAF PINE **b :** CARIBBEAN PINE **c :** LOBLOLLY PINE 1 **d :** BISHOP PINE

swamp pink *n* **1 a :** SWAMP AZALEA **b :** PINXTER FLOWER **2 :** a grass pink (*Calopogon pulchellus*) **3 :** a rare bog herb (*Helonias bullata*) of the eastern U.S.

swamp poplar *n* **:** SWAMP COTTONWOOD

swamp post oak *n* **:** OVERCUP OAK

swamp potato *n* **:** SWAN POTATO

swamp privet *n* **:** an American shrub (*Forestiera acuminata*) with opposite leaves and small axillary flowers

swamp quail *n* **1 :** a quail (*Coturnix ypsilophorus*) of Australia, Tasmania, and New Guinea that is reddish brown and grayish with V-shaped black bars beneath **2 :** a painted quail (*Coturnix chinensis*) of southern Asia and Australasia

swamp rabbit *n* **1 :** a large big-headed short-furred rabbit (*Sylvilagus aquaticus*) of moist lowlands in the Mississippi valley and southeastern U.S. that is closely related to but larger and darker than the cottontail — called also *canecutter, swamp hare* **2 :** MARSH HARE

swamp rattler *n* **:** MASSASAUGA a

swamp red bay *n* **:** SWAMP BAY 1

swamp robin *n* **1 :** CHEWINK **2 :** any of several thrushes; *esp* **:** WOOD THRUSH 1

swamp rose *n* **:** either of two wild roses (*Rosa carolina* and *R. palustris*) of the eastern U.S. that clamber over bushes in swamps

swamp rose mallow *n* **:** ROSE MALLOW 1

swamps *pl of* SWAMP, *pres 3d sing of* SWAMP

swamp sassafras *n* **:** SWEET BAY 2

swamp saxifrage *n* **:** a No. American saxifrage (*Saxifraga pennsylvanica*) bearing greenish flowers

swamp spanish oak *n, usu cap 2d S* **:** a pin oak (*Quercus palustris*)

swamp sparrow *n* **:** a common sparrow (*Melospiza georgiana*) of eastern No. America that lives in swampy places and is related to the song sparrow but distinguished by the absence of streaks on the underparts

swamp spleenwort *n* **:** a narrow-leaved spleenwort (*Asplenium pycnocarpon*) found in moist places in eastern No. America

swamp spruce *n* **:** BLACK SPRUCE 1

swamp squawweed *n* **:** GOLDEN RAGWORT

swamp sumac *n* **:** POISON SUMAC

swamp sunflower *n* **1 :** SNEEZEWEED 1a **2 :** a sunflower (*Helianthus angustifolius*) of eastern No. America found in wet bogs and having narrow leaves

swamp tea *n* **1 :** LABRADOR TEA a **2 :** any of several Australian or Tasmanian shrubs or trees of the genus *Melaleuca; esp* **:** a tea tree (*M. squarrosa*)

swamp thistle *n* **:** a No. American thistle (*Cirsium muticum*) with large purple flower heads

swamp tupelo *n* **:** TUPELO 1

swamp turnip *n* **:** JACK-IN-THE-PULPIT

swamp warbler *n* **:** any of several No. American warblers (as the prothonotary, the blue-winged, and the golden-winged) inhabiting swampy places

swampweed \'ˌ=ˌ=\ *n* **:** a small Australian fleshy-leaved creeping herb (*Selliera radicans*) of the family Goodeniaceae

swamp white cedar *n* **:** SOUTHERN WHITE CEDAR

swamp white oak *n* **1 :** a large flaky-barked oak (*Quercus bicolor*) of the eastern U.S. resembling white oak but having smaller leaves with fewer lobes and heavy strong wood that is used in construction **2 :** OVERCUP OAK **3 :** BASKET OAK

swamp willow *n* **1 :** a black willow (*Salix nigra*) **2 :** SWAMP LOOSESTRIFE

swamp willow herb *n* **:** a low bog herb (*Epilobium palustre*) of the north temperate zone with opposite oblong leaves, small whitish pink flowers, and long slender pods

swampwood \'ˌ=ˌ=\ *n* **1 :** LEATHERWOOD 1a **2 :** BUTTONBUSH

swampy \-pē, -pi\ *adj* -ER/-EST [²*swamp* + *-y*] **:** consisting of or resembling a swamp **:** water-logged and poorly drained

swampy cree *n, usu cap S&C* **1 :** an Algonquian people comprising the Maskegon and the Monsoni formerly inhabiting swampy regions of Manitoba and Ontario from Lake Winnipeg and Lake of the Woods to the Moose river and Hudson Bay and sometimes classed with the Cree people and sometimes with the Chippewa **2 :** a member of the Swampy Cree people

swamy *var of* SWAMI

¹swan \'swän *also* -wȯn\ *n, pl* **swans** *also* **swan** *often attrib* [ME, fr. OE; akin to MD *swane* swan, MHG *swan*, ON *svanr* swan, OE *swinsian* to make music, *swinn* music, melody; perh. fr. the legendary belief that the swan sings before it dies — more at SOUND] **1 :** any of various heavy-bodied very long-necked aquatic birds related to but larger than the geese, constituting a distinct subfamily of the family Anatidae, having usu. pure white plumage when adult, walking awkwardly, flying strongly when once started, and being graceful swimmers — see BLACK SWAN, MUTE SWAN, TRUMPETER SWAN, WHOOPER SWAN **2 a :** one that resembles or is likened to a swan ⟨the accused are all ~*s* and the blackness of guilt is thrown upon the witnesses —Miles Prance⟩ **b :** one who makes music of the melodic sweetness traditionally ascribed to the dying song of a swan **:** BARD, SINGER ⟨sweet ~ of Avon —Ben Jonson⟩

²swan \"\ *vi* **swanned; swanned; swanning; swans :** to wander aimlessly or sweep majestically **:** DALLY, SAIL ⟨such vehicles . . . would hamper operations if they started *swanning* about in the midst of a swirling, hit-and-run tank fight —Russell Hill⟩ ⟨professional delegates, *swanning* with practiced appreciation from one . . . convention to another —James Cameron⟩ ⟨aircraft equipped with loudspeakers *swanned* low over the forest with a new message —*Time*⟩

³swan \"\ *vb* **swanned; swanned; swanning; swans** [perh. euphemism for *swear*] *vi, dial* **:** DECLARE, SWEAR ⟨we're goin' to miss her, I ~ —J.C.Lincoln⟩ ~ *vt, dial* **:** SURPRISE ⟨said he'd be *swanned* . . . and took on like there was no predicting what a school education would do for a clerk —Frederick Way⟩

⁴swan *usu cap, var of* SVAN

swan animalcule *n* [¹*swan*] **:** any of various ciliate protozoans having a necklike extension of the body

swan boat *n* **:** a small pedal boat usu. for children or sightseers pedaled by an operator who sits aft in a large model of a swan ⟨*swan boats*, like those of Boston, carry visitors through the canals —Merrill Folsom⟩

swan dive *n* **:** a front dive executed with the trunk extended, head back, back arched, and arms spread sideways at shoulder height until the dive is nearly completed when they are brought together above the head to form a straight line with the body as the diver enters the water

swanflower \'ˌ=ˌ=\ *n* **:** any of several plants having flowers whose shape suggests the neck of a swan; *esp* **:** an orchid of the genus *Cycnoches* — called also *swanneck*

¹swang [ME, fr. OE] *chiefly dial past of* SWING

²swang \'swaŋ\ *n* -s [prob. blend of ²*swamp* and E dial. *wang* field (fr. ME *wang, wong*) — more at WONG] *dial Eng* **:** low wet grassy land **:** SWAMP

swan goose *n* **:** a swanlike goose; *specif* **:** CHINESE GOOSE

swanherd \'ˌ=ˌ=\ *n* [ME, fr. ¹*swan* + *herd*] **:** a herdsman of swans ⟨the royal ~ of England⟩

swan-hopper \'ˌ=ˌhäpə(r)\ *n* [by alter.] **:** SWAN-UPPER

swan-hopping \-piŋ\ *n* -s [by alter.] **:** SWAN-UPPING

swan·i·mote \'swänə,mōt\ *also* **swain·mote** \'swān,m-\ *or* **swan·mote** \'swän,m-\ *n* -s [ME *swanimote*, fr. (assumed) OE *swāngemōt*, fr. OE *swān* herdsman, peasant + *gemōt* judicial assembly, gemot — more at SWAIN, GEMOT] **:** a court formerly held before foresters, verderers, and other forest officers to try

offenses against vert and venison and to hear grievances against forest officers

¹swank \'swaŋk\ *adj* [MLG or MD *swanc* supple, pliant; akin to MHG *swank* supple, movable, swaying, OE *swancor* slender, supple, OHG *swenken* to fling, hurl, *swingan* to swing — more at SWING] *Scot* : full of life or energy : ACTIVE

²swank \"\, -waiŋk\ *vb* -ED/-ING/-S [perh. fr. MHG *swanken* to sway, swag; akin to MD *swancen* to sway, *swanc* supple, pliant] *vi* : to show off : behave ostentatiously : SWAGGER, STRUT ⟨he ~ed around . . . in white suits —Saul Bellow⟩ — often used with *it* ⟨he likes to slum and likes to ~ it too —*Newsweek*⟩ ~ *vt* 1 : to doll up ⟨the roof as a whole was ~ed and gabled to madness —F.L.Wright⟩ 2 : SNUB ⟨afraid to ~ an old acquaintance —Al Hine⟩

³swank \"\ *n* -s 1 : arrogance or ostentation of dress or manner : PRETENTIOUSNESS, SWAGGER ⟨give his wife some diamond bracelets for ~ —J.B.S.Haldane⟩ ⟨a group of Briticisms which have connotations of ~ for Americans —Thomas Pyles⟩ 2 : ELEGANCE, STYLE ⟨a prep school of considerable ~ —R.L.Taylor⟩

⁴swank \"\ *or* **swanky** \-kē,-ki\ *adj* -ER/-EST 1 : characterized by showy display : OSTENTATIOUS, PLUSHY ⟨a new sports-model car, a big ~ sky-blue job, with wire wheels —F.B. Gipson⟩ 2 : fashionably elegant : LUXURIOUS, SMART ⟨homes in the ~, well-kept Prado residential district —June W. Brown⟩ ⟨linen, nonchalant and ~ and cut with demure . . . simplicity —Lois Long⟩

swank·er \-kə(r)\ *n* -s [²swank + -er] *chiefly Brit* : one that swaggers or puts on airs

swank·i·ly \-kəlē,-li\ *adv* : in a swank manner

swank·i·ness \-kēnəs, -kin-\ *n* -ES : the quality or state of being swank

swank·ing \'swaŋkən, -kiŋ\ *adj* [¹swanky + -ing] *chiefly Scot* : STRAPPING

¹swanky *also* **swank·ie** \-ki\ *n, pl* **swankies** [of LG or D origin; akin to MLG & MD *swanc* supple, pliant — more at SWANK] *Scot* : an active alert strapping fellow

²swanky \"\ *or* **swank·ey** \"\ *n, pl* **swankies** *or* **swankeys** [*swank* of unknown origin + -y] *dial Brit* : inferior ale, beer, or cider

swanlike \'ᵊ,ᵊ\ *adj* : resembling a swan or its long neck : GRACEFUL, SINUOUS ⟨~ movement⟩ ⟨a ~ neck⟩

swan maiden *n* [trans. of G *schwanenjungfrau*] : a maiden of Germanic mythology held to be able to transform herself into a swan by the use of a magical object (as a ring or a cloak of swan feathers)

swanmark \'ᵊ,ᵊ\ *n* : a mark of ownership cut on the upper mandible of a swan

swan mussel *n* : a common European freshwater mussel (*Anodonta cygnea*)

swan-neck *also* **swan's neck** \'ᵊ,ᵊ\ *n* 1 : something (as a piece of pipe or railing) having a gooseneck or an ogee curve: as **a** : GOOSENECK **b** : a bend in a handrail of a stair consisting of a ramp terminating in a knee **c** : one of the S-shaped cornices of a scroll pediment 2 *usu* **swanneck** : SWANFLOWER — **swan-necked** \-ᵊ,ᵊ\ *adj*

swanned *past of* SWAN

swan·nery \'swänərē *also* -wòn-\ *n* -ES [¹swan + -ery] : a place where swans are bred or kept

swanning *pres part of* SWAN

swan·ny \-nē\ *adj, archaic* : SWANLIKE; *also* : full of swans

swan orchid *n* : a swanflower of the genus *Cycnoches*

swan pan *var of* SUAN PAN

swan potato *n* [alter. of *swamp potato*] : a plant of the genus *Sagittaria* having tubers used as food: as **a** : a common arrowhead (*S. latifolia*) of wetlands of the U.S. and southern Canada with starchy tubers once used extensively by the Indians **b** : a similar common Old World arrowhead (*S. sagittifolia*) that is sometimes cultivated in Japan and China

swan river daisy *n, usu cap S&R* [fr. *Swan River*, Western Australia] : an Australian annual herb (*Brachycome iberidifolia*) much cultivated for its flower heads with bluish, violet, rose, white, or variegated rays

swan river everlasting *n, usu cap S&R* [fr. *Swan River*, Western Australia] : an Australian everlasting (*Helipterum manglesii*)

swans *pl of* SWAN, *pres 3d sing of* SWAN

swans·combe man \'swänzkəm-\ *n, usu cap S* [fr. *Swanscombe*, Kent, England, where the remains were found] : a prehistoric man known from the left parietal and an occipital bone found in middle Pleistocene Thames gravels in association with Acheulean artifacts and coeval fauna and prob. representing an early form of Homo sapiens antedating Neanderthal man

swans·down \'swänz,daun *also* -wòn-\ *n* [*swan's* (gen. of ¹*swan*) + *down*] 1 : the soft downy feathers of the swan esp. when used as trimming on articles of dress ⟨she was wrapped in grey satin edged with ~ —Victoria Sackville-West⟩ 2 : a heavy cotton flannel with a thick nap on the face made with sateen weave

swan·sea \-nz̸ē, -n(t)s̸\, ¸i\ *adj, usu cap* [fr. *Swansea*, Wales] : of or from the city of Swansea, Wales : of the kind or style prevalent in Swansea

swan shot *n* : a large size of shot used in hunting wildfowl and other small game

swan·skin \-nz,kin, -n,sk-\ *n* 1 : the skin of a swan with the down or feathers on it 2 : any of various fabrics resembling flannel and having a soft nap or surface

swan song *n* [trans. of G *schwanenlied*] 1 : a song of great sweetness formerly thought to be uttered by the swan just before its death 2 : a farewell appearance or final act or pronouncement ⟨the *swan song* of a chivalry which died in the century before —*New Republic*⟩ ⟨before turning over the gavel, delivered his *swan song* as chairman of the board⟩; *specif* : the last work (as of an author or composer)

swan spectrum \-nz̸'p-, -n'sp-\ *n, usu cap 1st S* [after William *Swan* †1894 Eng. physicist] : the spectrum of the blue cone in a Bunsen burner when operating strongly caused by the excitation of carbon compounds; *also* : a similar spectrum observed in some vacuum-tube discharges

swan-upper \-,nəpə(r)\ *n* -s [*swan-upping* + -er] : an official who cuts a mark of ownership on the upper mandible of a swan

swan-upping \-,piŋ\ *n* -s 1 : the practice or process of marking young swans for the owners 2 : an annual expedition for the purpose of swan-upping on the English Thames

¹swap *also* **swop** \'swäp *also* -wòp\ *vb* **swapped** *also* **swopped**; **swapped** *also* **swopped**; **swapping** *also* **swopping**; **swaps** *also* **swops** [ME *swapen, swappen* to strike, hit, hurl, throw, of imit. origin] *vt* 1 *chiefly dial* : to cause to strike or fall against something by throwing, moving, or flinging : BANG 2 [so called fr. the practice of striking hands in closing a business deal] **a** : to give in exchange : EXCHANGE, BARTER ⟨offered to ~ 250,000 tons of rice a year for 50,000 tons of rubber —Tom Fitzsimmons⟩ ⟨~ notes on progress in their particular fields —F.L.Allen⟩ **b** *obs* : to make or agree to ⟨a bargain⟩ ~ *vi* 1 *archaic* : to move swiftly and with violent force : SWOOP, POUNCE 2 : to make an exchange : engage in trading

²swap \"\ *adv, chiefly dial* : at a blow : quickly and forcefully

³swap \"\ *n* -s [ME, fr. *swapen* to swap] 1 *chiefly dial* : BLOW, STROKE 2 : the act or process of exchanging one thing for another : EXCHANGE, BARTER, TRADE ⟨stock ~⟩

swape \'swāp\ *n* -s [ME *swipe* lever, swivel, prob. of Scand origin; akin to ON *sveipr* fold, *sveipa* to sweep, swoop — more at SWOOP] 1 *dial Eng* : a pole or bar used as a lever or swivel 2 *dial Eng* : a long steering oar used by keelmen on the Tyne

swap hook *n, dial Eng* : REAPING HOOK

swap·per \'swäpə(r), -wòp-\ *n* -s : one that swaps

swapping *adj* [ME, striking, flapping, fr. pres. part. of *swappen* to strike, throw] *dial* : very big : HUGE

swa·raj \swə'räj\ *n* -ES [Skt *svarāj* self-ruling, *svārājya* independent rule, fr. *sva* one's own + *rājya* rule — more at SUICIDE, RAJ] : political independence : national or local self-government : HOME RULE — compare KHADDAR, SWADESHI

swa·raj·ist \-jəst\ *n* -s : a member of a political party in British India advocating swaraj

¹sward \'swò(ə)rd, -ó(ə)d\ *n* -s [ME, fr. OE *sweard, swearth* skin, hide, rind; akin to OFris *swarde* scalp, MD *swaerde* skin, hide, MHG *swart* skin, hide, fur, rind, W *gweryd* sward, earth, soil, OIr *feronn, ferann* land, field, L *operire* to cover — more at WEIR] 1 *archaic* : SKIN, RIND 2 **a** (1) : the grassy surface of land : the part of the soil which is filled with the roots of grass : TURF, SOD (2) : a portion of ground covered with sward : GREENSWARD **b** : a growth or structure (as reindeer moss or a fungus) that resembles sward

²sward \"\ *vt* -ED/-ING/-S : to produce sward upon : cover with sward

sware *ME swar*, alter. of *swoor*, fr. OE *swōr*] *archaic past of* SWEAR

¹swarf \'swò(ə)rf, -wärf\ *n* [ME *swarff*, prob. of Scand origin; akin to ON *svarfa* to sweep, swerve — more at SWERVE] *Scot* : SWOON

²swarf \"\ *vi, chiefly Scot* : SWOON

³swarf \'swò(ə)rf, -ó(ə)f\ *n* -s [of Scand origin; akin to ON *svarf* file dust, *sverfa* to file — more at SWERVE] 1 : fine metallic particles removed by a cutting or grinding tool; *specif* : chippings and shavings from soft iron castings used as a reducing agent in various chemical syntheses 2 : the continuous thread of wax or lacquer produced in cutting the grooves of an original phonograph record

swarga *var of* SVARGA

¹swarm \'swò(ə)rm, -ó(ə)m\ *n* -s [ME, fr. OE *swearm*; akin to OHG *swaram* swarm, ON *svarmr* tumult; prob. akin to ON *svarra* to swarm, MLG *swirren* to whir, buzz, L *susurrus* hum, murmur, OSlav *svirati* to whistle, Skt *svarati* he sounds, resounds] 1 : a great number of honeybees emigrating together from a hive in company with a queen to start a new colony elsewhere; *also* : a colony of honeybees settled in a hive 2 **a** : a great often overwhelming number usu. in motion and esp. migratory : a dense moving crowd or throng ⟨a ~ of butterflies⟩ ⟨a ~ of meteorites⟩ ⟨a ~ of local peasants crowded around our roped-off space —Christopher Rand⟩; *specif* : a horde seeking a new home ⟨a ~ of barbarians erupted from the steppes⟩ **b** *archaic* : a group of eels **c** : an aggregation of free-floating or free-swimming unicellular organisms — usu. used of zoospores **d** : a considerable number of similar geologic features or phenomena occurring close together in space or time ⟨a ~ of dikes⟩ ⟨an earthquake ~⟩ **e** : an aggregation of molecules (as those responsible for cybotactic effects) in a liquid — compare CYBOTAXIS

²swarm \"\ *vb* -ED/-ING/-S [ME *swarmen*, fr. ¹*swarm*] *vi* 1 **a** : of bees : to collect together and depart from a hive in a body to form a new colony — compare AFTERSWARM **b** : to escape in a swarm (as from a sporangium) usu. with a typical vibrating movement 2 **a** : to move about actively previous to or following such escape **b** : to migrate, move, or assemble in a crowd : throng together **c** : to move in throngs ⟨rural population ~ed into the industrial towns —Roger Burlingame⟩ ⟨customers ~ed before the . . . meat counters —Clyde Hostetter⟩ **b** : to occur or exist in great numbers : be extremely numerous ⟨venomous species ~ed among the grass tussocks —C.L.Barrett⟩ **c** : to hover about or move irresistibly in the manner of a bee in a swarm ⟨had taken place . . . with monseigneur ~ing within a yard or two —Charles Dickens⟩ ⟨the little boy . . . just ~ing around me —William Faulkner⟩ **d** : to cover or infuse an area ⟨the exhilaration ~ing over my face —Allen Tate⟩ ⟨this tropical jungle ~s over the slopes of a mountain —Lawrence & Sylvia Martin⟩ 3 : to contain a vast number and esp. moving throngs : be alive : TEEM ⟨the big blue station wagon . . . ~ — usu. used with *with* ⟨gently rolling fields . . . ~ing with wild Canada geese —*Amer. Guide Series: Md.*⟩ ~ *vt* 1 : to fill with a swarm : cause to teem ⟨myriads of small marine insects that ~ed the ocean —H.J.Wolfe⟩ ⟨men will ~ the decks —T.O.Heggen⟩ 2 : to induce (a colony of bees) to swarm

³swarm \"\ *vb* -ED/-ING/-S [origin unknown] *vi* : to engage in climbing esp. hand over hand : SHIN ⟨two little lads . . . having a good time ~ing over the logs —Helen Eustis⟩ ⟨~ up a mast⟩ ~ *vt* : to climb up : MOUNT

swarm·er \-mə(r)\ *n* -s [²swarm + -er] 1 : one that swarms : a member of a swarm 2 : a hive of bees ready to swarm 3 : SWARM SPORE

swarming *n* -s [gerund of ²swarm] 1 : emigration or movement in a swarm 2 : a period of motility esp. in ciliate spores

swarm spore *also* **swarm cell** *n* [¹swarm] : any of various minute motile sexual or asexual spores: as **a** : ZOOSPORE **b** : PLANOGAMETE

¹swart \'swò(ə)rt\ *adj* [ME, fr. OE *sweart*; akin to OHG *swarz* black, ON *svartr*, Goth *swarts* black, L *sordes* dirt, *sordēre* to be dirty] 1 **a** : of a dark color, complexion, or cast : BLACKISH, SWARTHY **b** *archaic* : producing a swarthy complexion : causing to tan 2 : BANEFUL, MALIGNANT

swart·back \'swòrt,bak\ *n* [alter. (influenced by Norw *svartbak* swartback) of earlier *swarthback*, fr. ME *suerthbak*, fr. ON *svartbak*, fr. *svartr* black + *bak* back — more at BACK] : GREAT BLACK-BACKED GULL

¹swarth \'swò(ə)rth, -wärth\ *n* -s [ME, fr. OE *swearth* skin, hide, rind — more at SWARD] 1 *dial* : SKIN, RIND 2 : SWARD 2

²swarth \"\ *vi, chiefly dial* : to produce sward

³swarth \"\ *n* -s [alter. (influenced by ¹*swarth*) of ¹swath] *dial* : a crop of grass for hay

⁴swarth \'swò(ə)rth, -wärth\ *var of* ¹SWART

⁵swarth \'swò(ə)rth, -wärth\ *var of* SWARF

swarth·i·ness \'swò(ə)r)thēnəs, -th-, |in-\ *n* -ES : the quality or state of being swarthy

swarthy \|ē, |i\ *adj* -ER/-EST [alter. of obs. *swarty*, fr. *swart* + -y] : possessing or being a dark color, complexion, or cast ⟨having a ~ face, a straight . . . nose —John Woodburn⟩

swart·kranz ape-man *or* **swart·krans man** \'sfärt,kränz 'svä-\ *n, usu cap S* [fr. *Swartkranz or Swartkrans*, region near Johannesburg, So. Africa, where the remains were found] : a large extinct southern African australopithecine (*Paranthropus crassidens or Australopithecus crassidens*) known from skulls, teeth, and other fossil skeletal remains and having a flat face and brow with weak supraorbital crest, a well-developed sagittal crest, a distinctly manlike jaw and teeth, and a brain capacity surpassing that of any recent ape and possibly that of Java man — compare KROMDRAAI APE-MAN

swart·rut·ter \'swò(r)t,rəd.ə(r)\ *n* [alter. (influenced by D *swartrutter* black rider) of G *schwartze rotte*, lit., black gang] : a member of any of various 16th and 17th century marauding bands in the Netherlands who blackened their faces and wore black garb

swart·zia \'swò(r)tsēə\ *n, cap* [NL, fr. Olof *Swartz* †1818 Swed. botanist + NL -*ia*] : a genus of tropical trees (family Leguminosae) with racemose irregular flowers of which the corolla is often reduced to a single petal or absent — see WAMARA

swartz·ite \-t,sīt\ *n* -s [George K. *Swartz* †1949 Am. geologist + E -*ite*] : a mineral CaMg(UO₂)(CO₃)₃.12H₂O consisting of a hydrous carbonate of calcium, magnesium, and uranium and occurring as clusters of tiny prismatic green crystals

¹swash \'swäsh, -wòsh\ *n* -ES [prob. imit.] 1 **a** (1) : a body or mass of dashing splashing water (2) *or* **swash channel** : a narrow sound or channel of water lying within a sandbank or between a sandbank and the shore **b** (1) : a dashing or splashing of water against or upon something; *specif* : the rush of water up a beach from a breaking wave (2) : the sound made by the swash of water **c** : a bar over which the sea washes or an area covered by shallow seawater **d** : a slushy sloppy condition of the ground 2 **a** : one that swaggers and blusters : SWASHBUCKLER **b** : blustering noise or behavior : SWAGGER 3 : a heavy or resounding blow on or from a yielding substance

²swash \"\ *vb* -ED/-ING/-ES *vi* 1 : to act in a blustering and bullying manner : put on or present an air of swaggering bravado : SWAGGER 2 : to make a noise (as of) by clashing a sword on a sword or shield 3 : to make violent noisy movements 4 **a** : to move or wander violently or erratically ⟨whole tribes and peoples have ~ed back and forth between Europe and Asia —Waldemar Kaempffert⟩ 4 **a** of a liquid : to move or become moved back and forth or around and around with a splashing sound ⟨water ~ed throatily in a gourd —Oliver LaFarge⟩ **b** : to move within a liquid : cause a liquid to splash or become washed around or back and forth ⟨the intruder . . . ~ing through the pond —Mary McCarthy⟩ ~ *vt* 1 : to cause (a liquid) to splash about or dash upon something ⟨~ water in a pail⟩ 2 : to cause to splash

³swash \"\ *adj* [fr. obs. *swash* slanting, of unknown origin] : having one or more strokes ending in an extended flourish ⟨the ~ letters 𝒜ℛ𝒫𝒩⟩

swash-buck·le \'swäsh,bəkəl, -wósh-\ *vi* -ED/-ING/-S [back-formation fr. *swashbuckler*] 1 : to play the swashbuckler : affect in the manner of a swashbuckler 2 : to compose or consist of a tale filled with the adventures of swashbucklers

swash-buck·ler \-klə(r)\ *n* -s [²swash + *buckler*] 1 : a boasting violently active soldier, adventurer, or ruffian : a blustering daredevil : SWAGGERER, BRAVO 2 **a** : a novel, play, or esp. movie dealing with the adventures of a swashbuckling hero and usu. having a setting in a romantic past era or exotic locale **b** : a writer of or actor in a swashbuckler

swash-buck·ler·ing \-ləriŋ\ *adj* : SWASHBUCKLING

swash-buck·ling \-kliŋ, -kleŋ\ *adj* [fr. *swashbuckler*, after such pairs as E *wrestler*: *wrestling*, adj.] 1 : acting in the manner of a swashbuckler 2 : characteristic of, marked by, or done by swashbucklers **b** : rovers from all points of the compass came to the island principality ⟨~ —*Amer. Guide Series: Texas*⟩ ⟨~ historical novel⟩ ⟨gawky uncertainty and ~ juvenility —T.D.Clark⟩

swash bulkhead *n* [¹swash] : a transverse or longitudinal baffle in a tank aboard a ship to check excessive movement of liquid contents

swash·er \'swäshə(r), -wòsh-\ *n* -s [²swash + -er] : SWASHBUCKLER

swashing *adj* [fr. pres. part. of ²swash] 1 : SWASHBUCKLING 2 **a** : forcefully accompanied by a clashing sound : RESOUNDING ⟨~ blow —Shak.⟩ **b** : SPLASHING

swash mark *n* : a fine line or tiny ridge of sandy debris left on a beach by the swash at its farthest reach

swash plate *n* [fr. obs. *swash* slanting, of unknown origin] 1 : a revolving circular plate set obliquely on a shaft and acting as a cam to give a reciprocating motion to a rod in a direction parallel to the shaft 2 [³swash] : SWASH BULKHEAD

swash-turned \'ᵊ,ᵊ\ *adj* [fr. obs. *swash* slanting] : turned in a spiral pattern ⟨a *swash-turned* baluster⟩

swashway \'ᵊ,ᵊ\ *n* [¹swash + *way*] : SWASH 1a(2)

swashy \'swäshē, -wòshē\ *adj* -ER/-EST [¹swash + -y] 1 : WET, WATERY 2 : WEAK, INSIPID

swas·ti·ka *also* **svas·ti·ka** *or* **swas·ti·ca** \'swä̇stəkə, -tēkə, chiefly Brit |as-; *sometimes* -'stēkə *or* (')sf| *or* (')svi\ *n* -S [Skt *svastika*, fr. *svasti* welfare, fr. *su-* well + *asti* he is; fr. the belief that it brings good luck — more at IS] 1 : a symbol or ornament in the form of a Greek cross with the ends of the arms extended at right angles all in the same rotary direction or any of numerous variant forms of this symbol or ornament — called also *fylfot*; compare GAMMADION, HAKENKREUZ — see GAMMADION illustration 2 : a swastika with arms extended clockwise

swastika

¹swat *also* **swot** \'swät *also* -wò\; *usu* |d-+V\ *vb* **swatted**; **swatting**; **swats** [alter. of ¹*squat*] *vi* 1 *dial Eng* : SQUAT **2 a** : to hit or hit out at an object or to flail about with the arms as if attempting to strike an object ⟨an old woman with a rolled mat *swatted* at her smartly —Esther Warner⟩ ~ *vt* : to strike or hit with a quick, heavy slapping blow usu. with a club, bat, or swatter ⟨~ a person over the head with an umbrella⟩ ⟨~ a ball hard⟩ *syn* see STRIKE

²swat *also* **swot** \"\ *n* -s 1 : a vigorous or crushing blow ⟨gave him a ~ on the rear end to help him along —Shirley A. Grau⟩ 2 : a long hit in baseball; *esp* : HOME RUN

³swat \"\ [ME (past), alter. of *swatte*, fr. OE *swǣtte*; ME (past part.), fr. OE *geswǣt*] *dial past of* SWEAT

⁴swat \"\ *Brit var of* SWOT

⁵swat \"\ *also* -äd-ē, -àd-ē \ *n, pl* **swat** *or* **swats** *or* **swati** *or* **swatis** *usu cap* 1 : a Muslim people of northern West Pakistan 2 : a member of the Swat people

¹swatch \'swäch *also* -wòch\ *n* -ES [origin unknown] 1 *chiefly dial* : an owner's tally or tag attached to cloth sent to a dyer 2 **a** (1) : a sample piece or patch (as of fabric, leather, or paper) (2) : a collection of samples esp. when issued by a single manufacturer **b** : something that serves as a typical act, instance, or member : a characteristic specimen ⟨a quick glance at a ~ of dialogue . . . is usually enough to identify one of his stories —John Woodburn⟩ 3 : PATCH ⟨white ~es of hair ringing the sides and back of his head —Carson Wyatt⟩ ⟨irregular ~es of planted land —Josephine Pinckney⟩ ⟨his face . . . spotted with ~es of purple-red —Norman Mailer⟩ 4 : a small number collected or clustered together or considered as a unit ⟨impressive ~es of canceled stamps —D.S.Boyer⟩ ⟨many of my own ~ of alumni have passed away —Christopher Morley⟩

²swatch \"\ *or* **swatchway** \'ᵊ,ᵊ\ *n, pl* **swatches** *or* **swatchways** [perh. alter. of ¹*swash*] *Brit* : SWASH 1a(2)

¹swath \'swä̇th *also* -wò| *or* |th *or* **swathe** \-wā̇th\ *n, pl* **swaths** \|thz, |ths\ *or* **swathes** [ME, fr. OE *swæth, swathu* footstep, track, trace; akin to OFris *swethe* limit, boundary, MD *swat* swath, MHG *swade*] 1 **a** (1) : the whole sweep of a scythe or a machine in mowing or cradling (2) : the path or the breadth of a path cut in one course **b** : a windrow of cut grain or grass left by a scythe or mowing maching ⟨a crop or row of grass or grain ready for reaping or haying 2 : a long broad strip or belt ⟨the wide ~ of a firebreak —Victor Canning⟩ ⟨a ~ of land three blocks long —Lewis Mumford⟩ 3 : a stroke of or as if of a scythe ⟨integrating factors which have survived the ~ of time —W.W.Taylor⟩ 4 : a collection or space emptied of a collection destroyed as if by a scythe ⟨chain stores cut great ~s in the jobbing business —*Amer. Guide Series: Minn.*⟩

²swath \'swäth\ *dial Eng var of* SWARD

swathboard \'ᵊ,ᵊ\ *n* [¹swath + *board*] : a slanting board attached to the outer end of the cutter bar of a mower to force the cut grass into a narrower swath so as to leave a cleared strip for the mower wheel when cutting the next swath

¹swathe \'swä̇th *also* -wà̇th *or* -wò̇th\ *vt* -ED/-ING/-S [ME *swathen*, fr. OE *swathian*; akin to ON *svatha* to swathe, MLG *swede* dizzy; basic meaning: turn, foolish, turn] 1 : to bind, wrap, or swaddle with a swathe ⟨legs . . . *swathed* from the knee to the ankle in rough strips —Edna S. V. Millay⟩ 2 **a** : to wrap or cover tightly or thoroughly in enveloping clothing or material ⟨a figure, *swathed* in black from head to foot —T.B.Costain⟩ ⟨the barge was still *swathed* in sheets —Michael Reynolds⟩ **b** : to put clothes on or an article of clothing on ⟨*swathed* myself in the apron —Carolyn Hannay⟩ 3 : to envelop, surround, or cover over in the manner of a swathe ⟨the whole stage is *swathed* in ever-changing light —E.R.Bentley⟩ ⟨fog ~s the river⟩

²swathe \'swä̇th\ *n* -s 1 *also* ¹SWATH : a band used in wrapping or enveloping: as **a** *archaic* : SWADDLING CLOTHES — often used in pl. **b** : a surgical bandage 2 : an enveloping medium

swath·er \'swä̇thə(r), |th- *also* -wò|, *sometimes* -wà|\ *n* -s [¹swath + -er] 1 : an implement with a long cutter bar for cutting grain and seed crops and dropping them into a windrow for curing before gathering and threshing 2 : an attachment to a mower which turns the swath into a windrow behind the mower wheels

swathing band *for pronunc see* ¹SWATHE\ *n* [ME, fr. swathing (fr. gerund of *swathen* to swathe) + *band*] 1 **swathing bands** *pl* : SWADDLING CLOTHES 2 *obs* : BANDAGE

swathing clothes *or* **swathing clouts** *n pl* [ME] *obs* : SWADDLING CLOTHES

swa·tow \'swä̇taù\ *n* -s *usu cap* : the Chinese dialect of Swatow, China, and vicinity

²swatow \"\ *adj, usu cap* [fr. *Swatow*, city in southeastern China] : of or from the city of Swatow, China : of the kind or style prevalent in Swatow

swats \'swäts\ *n pl* [prob. fr. OE *swatan*, pl., beer + E -*s* (pl. suffix); perh. akin to OE *swēte* sweet — more at SWEET] *Scot* : DRINK; *esp* : new ale ⟨reaming ~ that drank divinely —Robert Burns⟩

swat·ter \'swätə(r)\ *vi* [prob. akin to G dial. *schwattern, schwadern* to splash, spill, scatter, of imit. origin] *chiefly Scot* : to splash about

²swat·ter \ˈswät|d·ə(r), |tə- *also* -wȯ|\ *n* -s [¹*swat* + *-er*] **:** one that swats: as **a :** a device for killing insects usu. consisting of a flat piece of perforated rubber or plastic or fine-meshed wire netting attached to a handle — called also *flyswatter* **b :** a heavy hitter in baseball

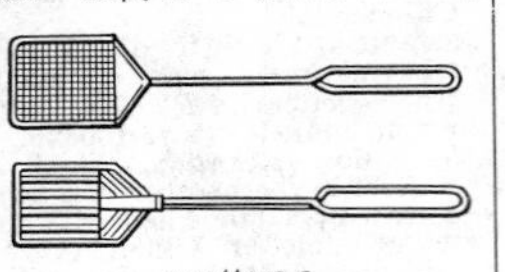
swatters a

swatting *pres part of* SWAT

s wave *n, usu cap S* **:** SHEAR WAVE

swa·ver \ˈswāvə(r)\ *vi* [ME *swaveren*, perh. of Scand origin; akin to Norw dial. *sveiva* to swing, ON *sveifla* to swing, spin, *svifa* to rove, ramble, drift — more at SWIVEL] *dial Brit* **:** STAGGER

¹**sway** \ˈswā\ *vb* -ED/-ING/-S [alter. (prob. influenced by MLG *swāien* to sway) of earlier *swey* to fall, go down, swoon, fr. ME *sweyen, sweghen* to go down, swoon, go, move, prob. of Scand origin; akin to ON *sveigja* to bow, bend, sway, *sveigr* switch (flexible twig), *svigna* to bend, give way; akin to MLG *swāien* to sway, OE *swathian* to swathe — more at SWATHE] *vi* **1 a** (1) **:** to move or become moved in usu. slow and rhythmic back and forth oscillations **:** swing esp. with suppleness or grace from or as if from a base or pivot ⟨singing to us, ~*ing* to the rhythm —O.S.J.Gogarty⟩ ⟨the redbird . . . lit on a tall white iris, making it ~ gently —Clarissa F. Cushman⟩ (2) **:** to move forward while swaying from side to side ⟨caravans of camels, ~*ing* with their padded feet across the desert —L.P.Smith⟩ **b** (1) **:** to become rocked by weight, pressure, or applied force esp. into a permanent new position ⟨the earthquake caused the wall to ~ to the right⟩ (2) **:** to move gently from an upright to a leaning position ⟨~*ed* over and actually leaned his head on her shoulder —Joseph Conrad⟩ **2 a :** to hold sway **:** act as ruler or governor **b :** to be a deciding or prevailing influence ⟨distinguish what motive actually ~*ed* with him —Abraham Tucker⟩ **3 a :** to approach with hostile intentions **b** *obs* **:** to move in a specified direction **4 :** to alternate regularly between one point, position, or opinion and another ⟨the battle has ~*ed* backwards and forwards with incredible fury —Sir Winston Churchill⟩ ⟨the industry continues to ~ between extravagancy and bankruptcy —Andrew Buchanan⟩ ~ *vt* **1 a :** to cause to sway **:** set to swinging, rocking, nodding, oscillating, or vacillating ⟨~*ed* her head from side to side with worry —Winifred Bambrick⟩ **b :** to cause to bend downward to one side ⟨the pillars were ~*ed* three inches by the blast⟩ **c :** to cause to turn aside **:** DEFLECT, DIVERT **d :** to hoist or erect esp. by throwing the weight of the body on a halyard or other rope — often used with *up* ⟨~*ed* up her topmast —Kenneth Roberts⟩ **2 a** (1) **:** to be the legitimate wielder of (a symbol of authority) ⟨reign . . . true heir, and his full scepter ~ —John Milton⟩ (2) **:** to possess or exercise authority, control, guidance, or sovereignty over **:** GOVERN, RULE ⟨with a bloody hand he ~*s* a nation —Lord Byron⟩ **b** *archaic* **:** to make use of (an implement); *also* **:** to play upon (an instrument) **3 a :** to cause (as a person or his opinions) to vacillate **b :** to exert a guiding or controlling influence upon **:** determine or help to determine a course of action, viewpoint, or decision of (as a person) or the manner or direction of (as a course of action) ⟨man's reason is imperfect, and may be ~*ed* by his physical and social environment —Herbert Agar⟩ ⟨many men are ~*ed* by nicknames and catchwords —A.W.Long⟩ ⟨a presidential aspirant should be able to ~ vast audiences with his eloquence —V.L.Albjerg⟩ **c :** to deflect from an accustomed or chosen object ⟨a determination from which he could not be ~*ed* —T.B.Costain⟩ **syn** see AFFECT, SWING

²**sway** \ˈ"\ *n* -s [alter. (influenced by ¹*sway*) of ME *sweyh, sweigh*, fr. *sweyen, sweghen* to swoon, go, move] **1 a** *obs* **:** a rotating motion about an axis **b** (1) **:** the action or an instance of swaying or of being swayed **:** an oscillating, fluctuating, swinging, nodding, or sweeping motion ⟨an easy ~ to the lurch of the ship —F.W.Crofts⟩ (2) **:** the sweep, force, or momentum of something swaying or being swayed ⟨the ~ of battle —John Milton⟩ (3) **:** an inclination or deflection caused by or as if by swaying **2 a :** a preponderating force or pressure **:** a controlling influence ⟨the personal element . . . should have little . . . ~ in determining the limits of legislative power —B.N.Cardozo⟩ ⟨scientists . . . under the ~ of a naturalistic optimism —W.R.Inge⟩ **b :** sovereign power **:** DOMINION, RULE ⟨the endeavor of the civil regime to extend its ~ to these islands —V.G.Heiser⟩ ⟨breaking down the ~ of the hereditary chiefs —Tom Marvel⟩ ⟨the region was under the ~ of great empires —David Mitrany⟩ **c :** the ability to exercise influence or authority or apply preponderating pressure **:** DOMINANCE ⟨classicism with its stateliness and promise of stability held ~ —Carl Bridenbaugh⟩ ⟨the idea once held ~ that the floor of the sea . . . was without life —R.E.Coker⟩ **3 :** grace of form, figure, carriage, or action ⟨his presence and social ~ —E.H.Collis⟩ **syn** see POWER

swayback \ˈ=ˌ=\ *n* **1 :** an abnormally hollow condition or sagging of the back found esp. in horses; *also* **:** a back so shaped — opposed to *camelback* **2 :** LORDOSIS **3 :** a copper-deficiency disease of young or newborn lambs that is marked by demyelination of the brain resulting in weakness, staggering gait, and collapse and is almost universally fatal but is readily preventable by copper supplementation of the diet of the pregnant ewe

swaybacked *also* **swayback** \ˈ=ˌ=\ *adj* **1 :** having or afflicted with swayback — opposed to *camelback* **2 a :** having or being a part with a concave center ⟨two cabins end to end . . . with a ~ roof over both —Emmett Gowen⟩ **b :** characterized by unevenness of quality, direction, or intention ⟨his performance follows a curiously ~ course —John Mason Brown⟩

sway bar *n* [²*sway*] **1 :** a bar attached to the hounds in the rear of the front axle of a wagon so as to slide on the reach as the axle is swung in turning **2 :** a steel bar placed near and parallel to an axle of an automotive vehicle to prevent excessive sway in turning

sway brace *n* **:** a brace to prevent swaying

swayed *adj* [fr. past part. of ¹*sway*] **:** SWAYBACKED

sway·er \ˈswāə(r), -we(ə)r, -weə\ *n* -s **:** one that sways

swaying *n* -s [fr. gerund of ¹*sway*] **:** a hollowing or sagging esp. as a result of swayback

sway·ing·ly *adv* **:** in a swaying manner **:** with swaying

sway·less \ˈswāləs\ *adj* **:** not capable of being swayed

sway pole *n* **:** a long pole or bar (as at a well) that can be pivoted for lifting or hanging

sways *pres 3d sing of* SWAY, *pl of* SWAY

swa·zi \ˈswäzē\ *n, pl* **swazi** *or* **swazis** *usu cap* **1 a :** a Bantu people of Swaziland **b :** a member of the Swazi people **2 :** a Bantu language of the Swazi people closely related to Zulu and Xhosa with which it forms the Ngoni group

swa·zi·land \-zēˌland\ *adj, usu cap* [fr. *Swaziland*, country in southern Africa] **:** of or from the country of Swaziland **:** of the kind or style prevalent in Swaziland

SWB *abbr* short wheelbase

swbd *abbr* switchboard

swchmn *abbr* switchman

SWD *abbr* sliding watertight door

swd *abbr* **1** sewed **2** sideward

sweal \ˈswēl, *esp before pause or consonant* -ēəl\ *vb* -ED/-ING/-S [ME *swailen, sweilen, swelen*, partly fr. OE *swelan* (vi) to burn; partly fr. OE *swǣlan* (vt) to cause to burn — more at SWELTER] *vi* **1** *chiefly dial, of a candle* **:** to melt away **:** GUTTER **2** *chiefly dial* **:** to waste away ~ *vt, chiefly dial* **:** BURN

¹**swear** \ˈswe(ə)r, ˈswa(a)(ə)r, ˈsweə, ˈswa(a)ə\ *vb* **swore** \ˈswō(ə)r, ˈswȯ(ə)r, ˈswōə, ˈswȯ(ə)\ *or archaic* **sware** *pronounced like* SWEAR\ **sworn** \ˈswō(ə)rn, ˈswȯ(ə)rn\ **swearing; swears** [ME *sweren*, fr. OE *swerian;* akin to OHG *swerien, swerren* to swear, ON *sverja* to swear, *svara* to answer, Goth *swaran* to swear, Oscan *sverrunei* (dat.) speaker, and perh. to OE *swearm* swarm — more at SWARM] *vt* **1 :** to utter or take solemnly (an oath) ⟨the queen ~*s* the oath at the high altar —*Newsweek*⟩ **2 a :** to solemnly declare or assert as true **:** affirm with an oath ⟨*swore* Monday to the banking committee he didn't yet know why he was fired —*Wall Street Jour.*⟩ ⟨a *sworn* affidavit⟩ **b :** to make a solemn promise of **:** pledge sacredly ⟨*swore* to uphold the Constitution⟩ **c :** to assert or promise emphatically or earnestly **:** ASSEVERATE ⟨~*s* that such action will cause the meat to shrivel in the cooking —*Amer. Guide Series: N.C.*⟩ ⟨*swore* to pay the money back soon⟩ **3 a :** to put to an oath **:** administer an oath to ⟨~ the witness⟩ ⟨*swore* him to secrecy⟩ **b :** to bind by a formal oath to the proper performance of a duty, function, or office esp. in connection with the law ⟨*swore* the jury⟩ ⟨two years later he was *sworn* to the bar —*Time*⟩ **4** *obs* **:** to invoke the name of (a sacred being) in an oath ⟨now by Apollo, King, thou *swear'st* thy gods in vain —Shak.⟩ **5 :** to bring into a specified or implied state by swearing ⟨*swore* himself into a fit of apoplexy⟩ ⟨*swore* his life away⟩ ~ *vi* **1 a :** to make a solemn promise or statement of intention **:** vow ⟨stay, sir, do not promise — do not ~ —Robert Browning⟩ **b :** to utter a solemn declaration with an appeal to God or a god for the truth of what is stated **:** affirm solemnly by something regarded as sacred **2 :** to give evidence or state under oath or to subscribe under the penalties of perjury **3 :** to use profane, blasphemous, or obscene language **:** CURSE ⟨not in the habit of ~*ing* even in his thoughts —LeRoy Smith⟩

syn AFFIRM, ASSEVERATE, DEPOSE, TESTIFY: to SWEAR is to give a solemn pledge, esp. before a court, often with an appeal to God or by laying one's hand on the Bible ⟨I do solemnly *swear* (or affirm) that I will faithfully execute the office of president of the United States —*U.S. Constitution*⟩ ⟨would have to make a statement and *swear* to it —Margaret Deland⟩ To AFFIRM is to state solemnly and with conviction, esp. before a court although without reference to God or like gestures ⟨must annually *affirm* his belief in a fundamentalist interpretation of the Scriptures —*Amer. Guide Series: Tenn.*⟩ ⟨the National Grange has again *affirmed* its conviction that the farmers' best hope for the future is in self-help —*Christian Science Monitor*⟩ To ASSEVERATE is to affirm earnestly and emphatically ⟨*asseverating* her innocence, and the innocence of her governess —Edith Sitwell⟩ ⟨*asseverated* that he had there become a mighty horseman —Osbert Sitwell⟩ To DEPOSE is to make a statement, as an affidavit or deposition, in writing or under oath ⟨the witness *deposed* that she had seen the man fire the shot⟩ ⟨the policeman called by the prosecutor's servant *deposed* to finding the prosecutor bruised and bleeding —Arthur Morrison⟩ To TESTIFY is to give evidence, often on the witness stand or in a deposition and usu. under oath or under penalties of perjury, or as if in such circumstances ⟨the following June he *testified* in favor of a Congressional bill providing for military advice and assistance to China —*Current Biog.*⟩ ⟨he offered affidavits from various individuals, including his parish priest, *testifying* to his good character —John Warner⟩

— **swear at 1 :** to use violent language to **:** CURSE ⟨*swore at* him for being late⟩ **2 :** to be out of harmony with **:** clash with ⟨a trailing lavender negligee that *swore at* her bright red hair —C.M.Smith⟩ — **swear by 1 :** to take an oath by ⟨*swear by* the saints⟩ ⟨*swear by* Apollo, the physician⟩ ⟨*swear by* my faith⟩ **2 :** to be sure of the existence of **:** be barely positive of — used in the phrase *enough to swear by* **3 :** to place great confidence in **:** trust implicitly ⟨the doctor has only just begun practice, but his patients *swear by* him⟩ — **swear for :** to answer for **:** GUARANTEE ⟨his friends will *swear for* his integrity⟩ — **swear off :** to vow to abstain from **:** RENOUNCE ⟨has *sworn off* drinking⟩ ⟨since his illness, he has had to *swear off* tennis⟩ — **swear the peace against :** to make oath that one is under actual fear of death or bodily harm from another in order to compel the accused to find sureties that he will keep the peace

²**swear** \ˈ"\ *n* -s **1 :** OATH ⟨do you think I would stand here and say that ~ and tell a story —Carson McCullers⟩ **2 :** a swearword or a fit of swearing ⟨finally the butler's suave voice . . . provoked a full-bodied ~ —*McClure's*⟩

swear·er \ˈswerə(r), ˈswa(a)r-\ *n* -s [ME *swerere*, fr. *sweren* to swear + *-ere* -er] **1 :** one that takes an oath **2 :** one that uses swearwords **:** one given to swearing

swearer-in \ˈ=(ˌ)=ˈ=\ *n, pl* **swearers-in** [*swear in* + *-er*] **:** one who administers an oath; *esp* **:** one who administers an oath of office

swear in *vt* **:** to induct into office by administration of an oath

swearing *pres part of* SWEAR

swear out *vt* **:** to procure (a warrant for arrest) by making a sworn accusation ⟨*swore* a warrant *out* against him⟩

swears *pres 3d sing of* SWEAR, *pl of* SWEAR

swearword \ˈ=ˌ=\ *n* **:** a profane or obscene oath or word **:** EXPLETIVE ⟨we strove after the most dreadful words we knew, and they were our father's ~*s* —Eden Phillpotts⟩

¹**sweat** \ˈswet, *usu* -ed·+V\ *vb* **sweat** \ˈ"\ *or* **sweated** \-ed·əd, -etəd\ *or dial* **swat** \ˈswät, *also* -wȯt; *usu* -äd·+V\ **sweat** *or* **sweated** *or dial* **swat; sweating; sweats** [ME *sweten*, fr. OE *swǣtan*, fr. *swāt* sweat; akin to OFris & OS *swēt* sweat, OHG *sweiz*, ON *sveiti*, L *sudor* sweat, *sudare* to sweat, Gk *hidrōs* sweat, Skt *svidyati, svedate* he sweats] *vi* **1 a :** to excrete moisture in visible quantities through the openings of the sweat glands **:** PERSPIRE **b :** to labor in such a manner as to cause perspiration **:** work hard **:** DRUDGE ⟨some can absorb knowledge, the more tardy must ~ for it —T.S.Eliot⟩ ⟨now the machines do all the ~*ing* —A.H.Raskin⟩ ⟨grunt and ~ under a weary life —Shak.⟩ **2 a** (1) **:** to emit or exude moisture ⟨green plants ~ when closely packed⟩ ⟨cheese in ripening ~*s*⟩ (2) **:** to exude oil or other liquid ⟨a varnish that ~*s*⟩ (3) **:** to exude nitroglycerin — used of dynamite in which nitroglycerin separates from its adsorbent **b :** to gather surface moisture in beads as a result of condensation ⟨stones ~ at night⟩ ⟨the glass is ~*ing*⟩ **c** (1) **:** FERMENT — used esp. of tobacco or cacao beans (2) **:** PUTREFY — used esp. of hides **3 a** *archaic* **:** to suffer an infliction or penalty **b :** to undergo anxiety or mental or emotional distress ⟨grieve and ~ to think of all the time we have let go by and fear disappointments still —O.W.Holmes †1935⟩ **4 :** to become exuded through pores or a porous surface **:** OOZE ⟨the surplus moisture will ~ out⟩ ⟨the oil coat may ~ through this varnish⟩ ~ *vt* **1 :** to emit or seem to emit from pores **:** EXUDE ⟨the flowers ~ dew⟩ **2 a :** to manipulate or move by hard physical effort ⟨two sooty men intently occupied in ~*ing* a tire on the wheel —Cliff Farrell⟩ ⟨machine gunners ~*ed* their weapons up the hill —Georg Meyers⟩ **b :** to produce by hard work or drudgery ⟨~*ed* out one novel after another⟩ ⟨stood in front of her cookstove ~*ing* up supper —P.E.Green⟩ **3 a :** to get rid of or lose by or as if by sweating or being sweated — usu. used with *away* or *off* ⟨~*ed* away three pounds in the steam room⟩ **b :** to reduce the excess weight or bulk of by or as if by sweating — used with *down* ⟨novel about the peacetime army, ~*ed* down to a fine, muscular picture —*Time*⟩ **4 :** to make wet with perspiration ⟨the white shirt and pants he had bought himself . . . were ~*ed* through —Vicki Baum⟩ **5 a :** to cause to excrete moisture from the skin ⟨his physicians ~*ed* him⟩ **b :** to drive hard **:** OVERWORK ⟨he ~*ed* his crew unmercifully, to prepare them for any emergency⟩ **c :** to exact work from at low wages and under unfair or unhealthful conditions ⟨the good employers would have either to ~ the workers like the bad ones, or else be driven out of business —G.B.Shaw⟩ **d** *slang* **:** to give the third degree to ⟨advise ~*ing* her with everything the police have got —J.M. Cain⟩ **6 :** to cause to exude or lose moisture: as **a :** to dry thoroughly (as wood in a charcoal pit) **b :** to subject to fermentation (as tobacco leaves or cacao beans) **c :** to putrefy (sheepskins or hides) by exposing to warm, humid air so as to loosen the wool or hair **7 :** to extract something valuable from by unfair or dishonest means **:** BLEED, FLEECE; *specif* **:** to remove particles of metal from (a coin) by abrasion **8 a** (1) **:** to heat (as solder) so as to melt and cause to run esp. between surfaces to unite them ⟨~ soft solder into seams⟩ (2) **:** to unite by such means ⟨~ a gold pen to an iridium point⟩ **b** (1) **:** to heat so as to extract an easily fusible constituent ⟨~ bismuth ore⟩ (2) **:** to extract (oil and low-melting material) by heating a substance ⟨~ oil out of crude paraffin wax⟩ (3) **:** to cause (as paraffin wax) to sweat ⟨scale wax that has been further ~*ed* to specific melting point ranges —J.B. Tuttle⟩ **c :** to expose (citrus fruit) to a high temperature to hasten the coloring **d :** to apply heat to **:** STEAM ⟨~ the finely chopped onions in half the butter until tender —*Food & Cookery Rev.*⟩ **9 :** to hoist, haul, or set (as a sail or rope) as flat or taut as possible — usu. used with *up* — **sweat blood :** to work or worry intensely ⟨in preparing speeches each *sweats blood* in his own way —Stewart Cockburn⟩

²**sweat** \ˈ"\ *n* -s [ME *swet, sweet*, fr. *sweten* to sweat] **1 :** hard work **:** DRUDGERY ⟨the engines . . . saved wages and they saved ~, but they killed prices —Thomas Wood †1950⟩ **2 :** the fluid excreted from the sweat glands of the skin **:** PERSPIRATION ⟨in the ~ of your face you shall eat bread —Gen 3:19 (RSV)⟩ **3 :** moisture issuing from or gathering in drops on the surface of any substance or object ⟨~ formed on the cold pitcher⟩ ⟨the ~ of hay in a stack⟩ **4 a** (1) **:** the condition of one sweating or sweated ⟨he was in a ~ from fear⟩ ⟨apples spoiled by ~⟩ (2) **:** a spell of sweating ⟨a good ~ and a cold shower to freshen you up⟩ **b :** abnormally profuse sweating in some conditions or diseases — often used in pl. ⟨soaking ~*s*⟩ **c :** an exercise given a horse before a race **5 :** something that induces or promotes perspiration **:** SUDORIFIC **6 :** a sweating process; *specif* **:** a natural fermentation that takes place during the aging of tobacco and makes it more aromatic and pliable **7 :** a state of worry or impatience ⟨the average audience is in such a ~ to learn about the future —W.L.Gresham⟩ **8 :** CHUCK-A-LUCK **9 :** SWEATBAND 1 **10** *chiefly Brit* **:** SOLDIER — used esp. in the phrase *old sweat* ⟨real old ~*s* with tattooed arms —John Masters⟩ — **no sweat** *slang* **:** with little or no difficulty **:** EASILY ⟨anybody can land on the new deck, *no sweat* —Frank Harvey⟩

sweatband \ˈ=ˌ=\ *n* **1 :** a usu. leather band used as a lining around the inner edge of a hat or cap to prevent perspiration damage **2 :** a band of material tied around the head to absorb perspiration

sweat bee *n* **:** any of numerous small short-tongued bees; *esp* **:** a bee of the genus *Halictus*

sweat board *n* **:** a strip of wood fastened to the inboard surface of a ship's frame to prevent cargo from coming in contact with the shell plating

sweatbox \ˈ=ˌ=\ *n* **1 :** a device for sweating something (as hides in tanning, dried figs, raisins) **2 :** a room, place, enclosure, or procedure in which one is made to sweat; *esp* **:** a narrow box in which a prisoner is placed for punishment

sweat cloth *n* **:** a cloth layout used for dice games by early American gamblers; *also* **:** any of several games played on such a layout

sweated *adj* **:** of, subjected to, or produced under a sweating system ⟨~ labor⟩ ⟨~ goods⟩

sweat·er \ˈswed·ə(r), -etə-\ *n* -s **1 :** one that sweats esp. as a result of exertion or hard work **2 a :** SUDORIFIC **b :** an exertion or job that causes sweating **3 a :** a heavy woolen garment worn esp. by athletes after exercise or to induce sweating **b :** a knitted or sometimes crocheted elastic jacket or pullover made in various styles and of various materials and usu. having ribbing around the neck, cuffs, and lower edge **4 :** one who operates a sweatshop or employs sweated labor **5 a :** one that brings about sweating (as of tobacco or hides) **b :** a large shallow pan or stack of such pans or a small tank in which paraffin is sweated

sweat·ered \-ə(r)d\ *adj* **:** covered with a sweater ⟨hunched his thin, ~ shoulders —Ralph Robin⟩ **:** wearing a sweater ⟨a familiar ~ figure sprawled in a lawn chair —A.J.Liebling⟩

sweater girl *n* **:** a girl with a shapely bust

sweater man *or* **sweat man** *n* **:** a petroleum worker who operates equipment for sweating oil from slack wax

sweat·ful \ˈswetfəl\ *adj* **:** accompanied by or producing sweating **:** SWEATY ⟨the ~ practice sessions which mold the mighty football teams —Al Dewlen⟩

sweat gland *n* **:** a simple tubular gland of the skin that secretes perspiration, that in man is widely distributed in nearly all parts of the skin, and that consists typically of an epithelial tube extending spirally from a minute pore which opens on the surface of the skin into the deeper layer of the dermis or into the subcutaneous tissues where it ends in a convoluted tuft

sweathouse \ˈ=ˌ=\ *n* **1 :** a hut, lodge, or cavern heated by steam from water poured on hot stones and used esp. by American Indians for ritual or therapeutic sweating **2 :** a place used for sweating (as tobacco)

sweat·i·ly \ˈswed|·ᵊlē, |tᵊl, |ᵊli, |əl-\ *adv* **:** in a sweaty manner **:** PERSPIRINGLY, LABORIOUSLY ⟨try, though not too ~, to entertain —Clifton Fadiman⟩

sweat·i·ness \|ēnəs, |in-\ *n* -ES **:** the quality or state of being sweaty

sweating *pres part of* SWEAT

sweating house *n* **:** SWEATHOUSE

sweating iron *n* **:** SWEAT SCRAPER

sweating plant *n* **:** BONESET 1

sweating sickness *n* **1 :** MILIARY FEVER **2 :** a febrile disease of southern African calves that is marked by profuse sweating, loss of hair and scaling of the skin, salivation, and more or less erosive inflammation of the mouth and that is probably due to thiamine deficiency but may represent an infective process

sweating system *n* **:** a system of employing labor (as in sweatshops) for long hours at low wages and often under unsafe or unsanitary conditions

sweat joint *n* **:** a soldered joint

sweat·less \ˈswetləs\ *adj* **:** being without sweat

sweat lodge *n* **:** SWEATHOUSE 1

sweat out *vt* **1 :** to endure, wait for, or wait through the course of (something beyond one's control) ⟨all they could do was to close their ranks, make the best speed they could, and *sweat* it *out* to the end —Nicholas Monsarrat⟩ ⟨these officers ate out of a mess kit and *sweated out* the same chow line I did —C.E.Fread⟩ **2 :** to work one's way painfully or tediously through (as a problem or situation) or to (as a solution or objective) ⟨a sprinkling of older men and women, experienced teachers, who are *sweating out* a master's degree —D.J.Lloyd⟩

sweat pants *n pl* **:** pants having a drawstring waist and elastic cuffs at the ankle that are worn esp. by athletes in warming up

sweatproof \ˈ=ˌ=\ *adj* **:** resistant to sweat

sweat room *n* **:** SWEATHOUSE 2

sweats *pres 3d sing of* SWEAT, *pl of* SWEAT

sweat scraper *n* **:** a flexible metal blade or curved rod used to sweep lather and soil from a sweating horse

sweat shirt *n* **:** a collarless long-sleeved pullover made of cotton jersey with a smooth-finished face and a heavily napped back

sweatshop \ˈ=ˌ=\ *n* **:** a usu. small manufacturing establishment employing workers under unfair and unsanitary conditions

sweat suit *n* **:** an exercise suit consisting of a sweat shirt and sweat pants

sweatweed \ˈ=ˌ=\ *n* **:** MARSHMALLOW 1a

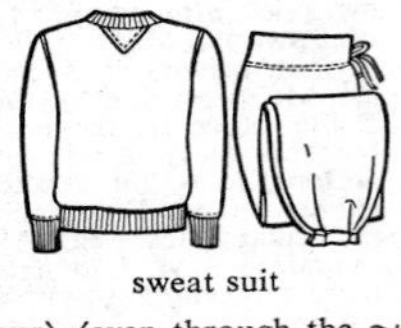
sweat suit

sweaty \ˈswed·ē, -etē, -i\ *adj* -ER/-EST [ME *swety*, fr. *swet* sweat + *-y*] **1 a :** causing sweat by extreme heat ⟨a ~ day⟩ **b :** LABORED ⟨how ~ and clumsy he can make an honest argument look —R.E.Garis⟩ **2 :** moist, stained, or odorous with sweat ⟨homesteaders clutching their ~ bills and coins —Harriot B. Barbour⟩ ⟨even through the ~ football togs . . . you could still smell the flowers —A.M. Latimer⟩

swede \ˈswēd\ *n* -s [LG *Swede* (fr. MLG *Swēde*) or D *Zweed*, fr. MD *Swede;* akin to OE *Swēon* Swedes, OSw *Svēar, Svīar*, ON *Svīar*] **1** *cap* **a :** a native or inhabitant of Sweden **b :** a person of Swedish descent **2** *or* **swede turnip** *sometimes cap S* [so called fr. its having been introduced into Scotland from Sweden] **:** RUTABAGA

swe·den \ˈswēdᵊn\ *adj, usu cap* [fr. *Sweden*, country in northwestern Europe occupying the eastern part of the Scandinavian peninsula] **:** of or from Sweden **:** of the kind or style prevalent in Sweden **:** SWEDISH

¹**swe·den·bor·gian** \ˌswēdᵊnˌbȯrj(ē)ən *also* -rgēən\ *n* -s *usu cap* [Emanuel *Swedenborg* (Svedberg) †1772 Swed. scientist, philosopher, and religious writer + E *-ian*] **:** one who holds the doctrines of the New Jerusalem Church based on the teachings of Swedenborg who claimed to have direct intercourse with the spiritual world through his spiritual senses, who affirmed that Jesus Christ as comprehending all the fullness of godhead is the one and only God, and who held that there is a spiritual or symbolic sense to the Scriptures

which God revealed through him and which enabled him to see the correspondence between natural and spiritual things

²swedenborgian \"\ *adj, usu cap* **:** of or relating to Swedenborg or his doctrines

swe·den·bor·gian·ism \-ə,nizəm\ *n* -s *usu cap* **:** the doctrines taught by Swedenborg

swe·den·bor·gite \'==,bȯr,gīt\ *n* -s [G *swedenborgit*, fr. Emanuel *Swedenborg* + G *-it* -ite] **:** a mineral $NaBe_4SbO_7$ consisting of an oxide of sodium, beryllium, and antimony found at Langban, Sweden

swedge *var of* SWAGE

¹swed·ish \'swēdish, -dēsh\ *adj, usu cap* [*Swede* + *-ish*] **1 a :** of, relating to, or characteristic of Sweden **b :** of, relating to, or characteristic of the Swedes **2 :** of, relating to, or characteristic of the Swedish language

²swedish \"\ *n* -ES *cap* **:** the North Germanic language spoken in Sweden and a portion of Finland — see INDO-EUROPEAN LANGUAGES table

swedish box *n, usu cap S* **:** a piece of gymnastic apparatus used for vaulting and consisting of a series of rectangular frames that are graded in size to fit one on top of the other

swedish clover *n, usu cap S* **:** ALSIKE CLOVER

swedish fiddle *n, usu cap S* **1** *slang* **:** CROSSCUT SAW **2** *slang* **:** a large bow saw esp. for cutting pulp

swedish fly *n, usu cap S* **:** FRIT FLY

swedish green *n, usu cap S* **:** SCHEELE'S GREEN

swedish iron *n, usu cap S* **:** wrought iron of high quality made in Sweden

swedish jib *n, usu cap S* **:** GENOA JIB

swedish juniper *n, usu cap S* **:** a columnar juniper with nodding twigs that is a horticultural variety (*Juniperus communis suecica*) of the common juniper — compare IRISH JUNIPER

swedish lilywood *n, usu cap S* **:** birch burl veneer from northern Europe

swedish massage *n, usu cap S* **:** massage together with Swedish movements

swedish movements *n pl, usu cap S* **:** a system of active and passive exercise of different muscles and joints of the body first devised in Sweden

swedish nightingale *n, usu cap S* **:** REDWING 1

swedish punsch *or* **swedish punch** \-'pȯnch\ *n, usu cap S* [*punsch* fr. Sw, punch, fr. G, fr. E ⁴*punch*] **:** a sweet yellow-colored liqueur from Sweden consisting of arrack flavored with various aromatic substances — called also *arrack punsch, caloric punsch*

swedish sumac *n, usu cap S* **:** a tanning extract prepared from the leaves of the bearberry

swedish turnip *n, usu cap S* **:** RUTABAGA

¹sweel \'swē(ə)l\ *vt* [prob. fr. ME *swedelen* — more at SWADDLE] *Scot & Irish* **:** SWADDLE

²sweel \"\ *vb* [of Scand origin; akin to Norw dial. *svela, svila* to whirl, run around] *chiefly Scot* **:** SWIRL

swee·ney layout \'swēnē, -ni-\ *n, usu cap S* [fr. the name *Sweeney*] **:** EASTERN ROLL

swee·ny *also* **swee·ney** \'swēnē, -ni\ *or* **swin·ney** \'swinē, -ni\ *n* -ES [by folk etymology fr. PaG *schwinne*, fr. *schwinne* to waste away, vanish, fr. OHG *swintan* — more at SWINDLE] **:** an atrophy of the shoulder muscles of a horse; *broadly* **:** any muscular atrophy of a horse

¹sweep \'swēp\ *vb* **swept** \'swept\ **swept; sweeping; sweeps** [ME *swepen;* akin to OE *swāpan* to sweep — more at SWOOP] *vt* **1 a :** to brush away or off **:** remove from a surface with or as if with a broom or brush ⟨sent with broom before to ~ the dust behind the door —Shak.⟩ ⟨*swept* the crumbs from the table⟩ **b :** to cut with vigorous swings (as of a sword or scythe) ⟨the grain *swept* down by the reapers⟩ **c :** to destroy completely **:** wipe out — usu. used with *away* ⟨everything she loved, everything she cherished, might be *swept* away overnight —Louis Bromfield⟩ **d :** to remove with a single continuous forceful action ⟨*swept* the books off the desk⟩ ⟨*swept* the curtains aside⟩ ⟨as the train passes the net ~*s* the pouch from the arm —F.H.Briant⟩ **:** drive or carry away forcibly ⟨*swept* him away into a far corner of the hall —W.J.Locke⟩ **e :** to drive or carry along with irresistible force ⟨the boy and the girl had been *swept* well out of his reach and were bobbing along —Charles Price⟩ ⟨a wave of protest that *swept* the opposition into office⟩ **2 a :** to clean by vigorous and continuous brushings **:** remove particles of dirt or other matter from the surface of with a broom or brush ⟨~ the floor⟩ ⟨~ the street⟩ ⟨~ out the kitchen⟩ **b :** to clear by repeated and forcible blows, strokes, or gusts **c :** COMMAND ⟨artillery placed to ~ the whole field⟩ **d :** to range over destructively or violently **:** SCOUR ⟨a darkling plain *swept* with confused alarms of struggle and flight —Matthew Arnold⟩ ⟨fire *swept* the business district —*Amer. Guide Series: Md.*⟩ ⟨bucking heavy seas that *swept* the deck —Walter Hayward⟩ **e (1) :** to achieve quick and irresistible influence or domination over ⟨a great wave of fear *swept* the country⟩ ⟨archery, croquet, roller skating and then lawn tennis *swept* the country —F.R.Dulles⟩ **(2) :** to win all the games or contests of or on ⟨the team *swept* the series⟩ ⟨the crew *swept* the river⟩ **(3) :** to win an overwhelming victory in ⟨*swept* the elections⟩ **3 :** to gather together into one heap or in one place **:** COLLECT ⟨a fine mesh net narrowing . . . to the mouth of a glass tube into which the organisms are *swept* —W.H.Dowdeswell⟩ ⟨*swept* the two groups together —Elmer Davis⟩ **:** gather in ⟨~ his winnings into his pocket⟩ **4 a :** to touch or come in contact with (a surface) as if with a brush ⟨his fingers *swept* the strings of the guitar⟩ ⟨the innkeeper bowed so that his skirt *swept* the floor —Nora Waln⟩ **b :** to move along or across with a swift continuous action **:** pass over ⟨the active areas may emit streams that ~ the earth with each rotation of the sun —C.T.Elvey⟩ ⟨broad rolling open heights, *swept* by clean mountain winds —*Amer. Guide Series: Vt.*⟩ **c :** to brush over the bottom of (a body of water) **:** DRAG ⟨*swept* the river with a dragnet⟩ **d :** to brush over the surface of (as a plant) with a net to gather insects **e :** to clear (a body of water) of mines ⟨*swept* the channel⟩ **5 a** *archaic* **:** to execute (as a curtsy) with a sweep ⟨*swept* the prettiest little curtsy ever seen —W.M.Thackeray⟩ **b :** to trace or describe the curve of (as a line or circle) **c :** to cover the entire extent of in one's field of vision or perception **:** make a broad survey of ⟨*swept* the sky with his binoculars —K.M.Dodson⟩ ⟨his keen dark eyes *swept* the room —Robert Brennan⟩ **d :** to move round or about so as to cover a wide circle or extent ⟨*swept* the binoculars slowly from right to left, from left to right —Fred Majdalany⟩ **6 a** *archaic* **:** to carry so as to brush the ground ⟨like a peacock ~ along his tail —Shak.⟩ **b :** to cause to move lightly over or along a surface ⟨*swept* his brush across the canvas⟩ ⟨*swept* her fingers over the strings of the harp⟩ **7 :** to clear away snow in front of (an advancing curling stone) **8 :** to produce (as music) by a brushing movement of the fingers along the strings of an instrument ⟨~*ing* a wail from his instrument —Katharine N. Burt⟩ **9 :** to form (a mold) by shaping the surface of the sand or loam with a template or strickle instead of using a pattern **:** STRIKE, STRICKLE — often used with *up* ~ *vi* **1 a :** to clean a surface with or as if with a broom **:** do the work of cleaning or brushing ⟨a new broom ~*s* clean⟩ **b :** to move over the surface or extent of something with swiftness, force, or devastating effect ⟨a hurricane *swept* over the island, razing all the buildings —*Amer. Guide Series: La.*⟩ ⟨a thin and watery beam of light *swept* across the dewy grass —Robertson Davies⟩ ⟨such rage and despair had *swept* over her as she had never before known —F.M.Ford⟩ **:** go, pass, or move swiftly or forcefully ⟨she *swept* to her feet like a dancer —Paul Roche⟩ ⟨when the front doors were opened, the children *swept* in —*N.Y. Times*⟩ **2 :** to move with dignity or stateliness ⟨his formidable wife *swept* past him to greet us —Maurice Cranston⟩ **3 :** TRAIL ⟨heard the trailing garments of the night ~ through her marble halls —H.W.Longfellow⟩ **4 a :** to move in a wide curve ⟨our frantic horses *swept* round an angle of the road —Thomas De Quincey⟩ ⟨when the sun ~*s* across the sky at the lowest altitude —S.M.Spencer⟩ **b :** to extend in a curve or long stretch ⟨her penciled eyebrows ~ in wide arcs over her long-lashed eyes —Jossleyn Hennessy⟩ ⟨brush-covered rangelands ~ to distant horizons —*Amer. Guide Series: Texas*⟩ **5 :** to clear the ice of snow in the path of an advancing curling stone by brushing with a broom — **sweep one off one's feet :** to gain immediate and unquestioning support, approval, or acceptance by a person ⟨his courtship *swept her off her feet*⟩ — **sweep the board** *or* **sweep the table 1 :** to win all the bets on the table **2 :** to win everything in sight **:** excel all competitors

²sweep \"\ *n* -s [ME *swepe*, fr. *swepen*, v.] **1 :** something that sweeps or works with a sweeping motion: as **a :** a hand water-raising device consisting of a long pole or timber pivoted to the top of a tall post and used to raise and lower a bucket — compare PICOTAH, SHADOOF **b :** BALLISTA **c (1) :** the lever arm of a circular horsepower machine to which a horse is hitched **(2) :** a triangular-shaped cultivator blade with a curved face that cuts off weeds under the soil surface between crop rows **(3) :** a wide heavy triangular blade used for subsurface tillage **(4) :** BUCK RAKE **d :** a windmill sail **e (1) :** a long oar used in boats or small vessels to propel or steer them **(2) :** a wire or rope stretched between two ships following parallel courses with the center of the wire being allowed to sag below the surface at set depths to drag for obstructions (as rocks, mines) **f :** STRICKLE 3 **2 a :** the act, action, or an instance of sweeping **:** a clearing out or away with or as if with a broom ⟨giving the room a good ~⟩ ⟨a clean ~ of all the holdovers from the old administration⟩ **b :** the removal from the table in one play in casino of all the cards by pairing or combining **c :** an overwhelming or decisive victory in a political contest ⟨could distinguish no landslides, no ~ in favor of either party —Christopher Serpell⟩ **d (1) :** a winning of all the games or contests in a series competition ⟨their ~ of this crucial series clinched the pennant for them⟩ **(2) :** a capture of all the prizes at stake in a contest or competition ⟨another week saw her complete a ~ of the sport's three highest titles —*Current Biog.*⟩ ⟨made a surprising clean ~ of all the delegates —*Current History*⟩ **e :** a military, naval, or air action (as a patrol, reconnaissance, or attack) ranging over a particular sector ⟨there were full-dress artillery and aerial ~*s* all day and night —Irwin Shaw⟩ ⟨patrol ships dispersed enemy small craft in inshore ~*s* —*N.Y. Times*⟩ **f :** a minesweeping operation **3 a :** a continuous and forceful forward movement (as of waves or wind) ⟨is entirely open to the unobstructed ~ of waves —P.E.James⟩ ⟨caught the full ~ of a rising southeast wind that dotted the lake with whitecaps —Joseph Millard⟩ ⟨the slow ~ of a glacier —Douglas Stewart⟩ **b :** a course, progress, or activity marked by force, drive, or continuity along a broad front ⟨the great ~*s* of western migration —Russell Lord⟩ ⟨the ~ of economic evolution seems at first sight to have passed the professions by —R.M.MacIver⟩ ⟨the symphony has passages of ~ and power⟩ **c (1) :** a usu. swift motion or movement describing an arc or a circle **:** a curving or circular course ⟨the lemon-and-white pointer went off on great ~*s* that settled the question about her running —*Newsweek*⟩ ⟨the impatient ~ of a hand —R.G.Thomas⟩ **(2) :** a systematic search of the sky with a telescope (as in a visual search for comets) **(3) :** an end run in football **d :** the compass of a sweeping movement, course, or progress **:** SCOPE ⟨the whole area lay within the ~ of the telescope⟩ ⟨was interested in the whole ~ of cultural history —R.B.West⟩ **e :** a broad unbroken area or extent often in a wide curve ⟨a vast ~ of sage and mesquite, dotted with dozens of kinds of cactus —*Amer. Guide Series: Texas*⟩ ⟨a majestic ~ of flesh on either side of a small blunt nose —William Faulkner⟩ **f :** a series of buildings or rooms **4 :** a curving or flowing line or contour ⟨the ~ of the arch⟩ ⟨the ~ of the draperies⟩: as **a (1) :** a curved wall, stairway, or section of a building ⟨the entire front is a ~ of large glass panes —*Ford Times*⟩ **(2) :** a curved section of scenery **b :** a curved driveway in front of a house or public building ⟨the driver took the gravel ~ magnificently and turned off out the gate —Elizabeth Bowen⟩ **c :** a gradual bend (as in a log or piling) **5 :** something that is swept up; *specif* **:** the sweepings of a workshop where precious metals are processed — usu. used in pl. ⟨when some walls and floors were dismantled during renovations, approximately $67,000 in gold ~*s* was recovered —F.W.Taber⟩ **6 :** CHIMNEY SWEEP 1 **7 :** SWEEPSTAKES **8 :** any of several small dark-colored Australian percoid food and game fishes of the family Scorpididae **9 a :** the radius of the curve to which a piece (as a spring leaf or fender) is shaped **b :** ARCH, CAMBER **c :** obliquity of an aeronautical member with respect to a significant reference plane as measured in degrees; *specif* **:** obliquity of a wing with reference to the plane of symmetry of an aircraft — see SWEEPBACK, SWEEPFORWARD **d :** a rapid and wide horizontal deflection of a cathode-ray beam that causes the spot to move across the screen (as in an oscilloscope or a television receiver) **syn** see RANGE

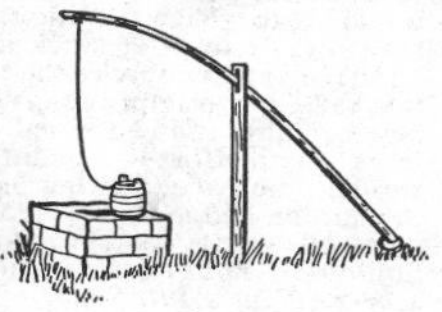
sweep 1a

³sweep \"\ *adv* **:** with a sweep

sweep·age \-pij, -pēj\ *n* -s **:** REFUSE ⟨by its strong, arched and labyrinthine roots collects the ~ of the fresh water —Marjory S. Douglas⟩

sweepback \'=,=\ *n* -s [fr. *sweep back*, v.] **:** a positive sweep in which the outer portion of an aeronautical member (as a wing) is downstream from the inner portion

sweep check *n* **:** the act or an instance of checking an opposing puck carrier in ice hockey by laying the stick flat on the ice and detaching the puck with a long, circular motion

sweep-chimney \'=;==\ *n* [¹*sweep* + *chimney*] *dial* **:** CHIMNEY SWEEP

sweep circuit *n* **:** an oscillatory circuit esp. designed to control the sweep in an oscilloscope or television cathode-ray tube

sweep cultivator *n* **:** a cultivator using sweeps to till the soil

sweep·dom \'swēpdəm\ *n* -s [²*sweep* + *-dom*] **:** the community of chimney sweeps

sweep·er \-pə(r)\ *n* -s [ME *swepare*, fr. *swepen* to sweep + *-are, -ere* -er] **1 :** a device that cleans by sweeping ⟨lawn ~⟩ **2 :** one that sweeps; *specif* **:** one whose work is cleaning an object or area by sweeping **3 :** MINE SWEEPER

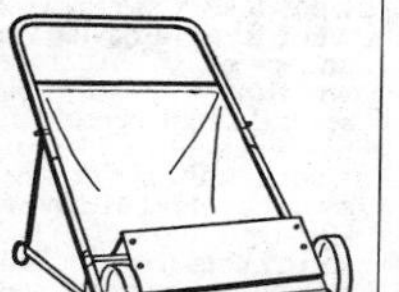
sweeper for a lawn

sweepforward \'=;==\ *n* -s [fr. *sweep forward*, v.] **:** a negative sweep in which the outer portion of an aeronautical member (as a wing) is upstream from the inner portion

sweep generator *or* **sweep oscillator** *n* **:** an oscillator or signal generator to produce sweep signals

sweep hand *n* **:** SWEEP-SECOND

¹sweep·ing \'swēpiŋ, -pēŋ\ *n* -s [ME *sweping*, fr. gerund of *swepen* to sweep] **1 :** the act or action of one that sweeps ⟨gave the room a good ~⟩ **2 sweepings** *pl* **:** things collected by sweeping **:** REFUSE, RUBBISH ⟨contaminated by ~*s*, fly, and trash —M.R.Harden⟩

²sweeping *adj* [fr. pres. part. of ¹*sweep*] **1 a :** moving or extending in a wide curve or over a wide area ⟨threw the end of the cigar, with a large ~ gesture, into the fire —Arnold Bennett⟩ ⟨has many old white houses and a ~ view of the river valley —*Amer. Guide Series: N.H.*⟩ **b :** having a curving line or form ⟨the robe lies smoothly on the upper part of the body, and falls into ~ folds below —O. Elfrida Saunders⟩ **2 a :** on a large scale **:** wide-ranging **:** EXTENSIVE ⟨voted ~ election reforms —Andrew Morsund⟩ ⟨the expense . . . had made ~ economies necessary —T.B.Costain⟩ ⟨won a ~ victory⟩ **b :** INDISCRIMINATE, WHOLESALE ⟨this condemnation of an entire age sounds even more ~ than the indictment of a nation —William Anderson⟩ ⟨~ charges⟩ ⟨~ generalizations⟩ — **sweep·ing·ly** *adv* — **sweep·ing·ness** *n* -ES

sweeping score *n* **:** a line passing through the center of the tee at right angles to the length of a curling rink — see CURLING illustration

sweep mill *n* **:** a farm feed mill actuated by a circular sweep operated by horses

sweep net *n* **1** *or* **sweep seine :** a large fishing net usually paid out around an arc of a circle from a boat and then hauled ashore **2 :** a bag-shaped net with a handle used by entomologists for catching insects by sweeping it over vegetation

sweep of the tiller : a circular frame on which the tiller of a ship travels

sweep rake *n* **:** BUCK RAKE

sweeps *pres 3d sing of* SWEEP, *pl of* SWEEP

sweep-second \'=;==\ *n* **:** a second hand on a timepiece mounted concentrically with the other hands and read on the minute dial; *also* **:** a timepiece with such a second hand — called also *center-second*

sweep smelter *n* **:** one that smelts sweeps to regain the metals

sweep·stakes \'swēp,stāks\ *n pl but usu sing in constr, also* **sweep·stake** \-āk\ [ME *swepestake* one who wins all the stakes in a game, fr. *swepen* to sweep + *stake* stake (prize) — more at SWEEP, STAKE] **1 a :** a race or contest in which the entire prize is or may be awarded to the winner; *specif* **:** a horse race in which the stakes to be distributed are made up at least in part of the entry fees or other money contributed by three or more of the owners of horses entered **b :** a race, contest, or competition ⟨the presidential ~*s*⟩ ⟨the literary ~*s*⟩ ⟨a winning entry in the spring lingerie sales ~*s* —*Lingerie Merchandising*⟩ **2 :** any of various lotteries or contests for prizes

sweepstick \'=,=\ *n* **:** the part of a loom that connects the picking arm to the picker stick

sweepswinger \'=,==\ *n* **:** a member of a racing crew **:** OARSMAN

sweepup \'=,=\ *n* -s [fr. *sweep up*, v.] **:** CLEANUP

sweepwasher \'=,==\ *n* **:** one that extracts the residuum of precious metals from gold and silver sweeps

sweepy \'swēpē, -pi\ *adj* -ER/-EST **:** sweeping in motion, line, or force ⟨a magnificent avenue of ~ Australian pines —Horace Sutton⟩

sweer \'swēr, 'swi(ə)r\ *adj* [ME *swer, swere*, fr. OE *swǣr, swǣre*, lit., heavy — more at SERIOUS] **1** *Scot & dial Eng* **:** SLOW, INDOLENT **2** *Scot & dial Eng* **:** RELUCTANT, LOATH

swee-swee \'swē,swē\ *n* -s [imit.] **:** SPOTTED SANDPIPER

¹sweet \'swēt, *usu* -ēd·+V\ *adj* -ER/-EST [ME *swete, sweete*, fr. OE *swēte;* akin to OS *swōti, suoti* sweet, OHG *suozi*, ON *sætr* sweet, L *suadis* pleasant, sweet, Gk *hēdys* sweet, Skt *svādu*] **1 a :** marked by or arising from graciousness, kindness, or sympathy ⟨not often that a mind so attractive goes with a character so ~ as his —H.J.Laski⟩ ⟨her ~ personality⟩ **b :** not intemperate or extreme **:** EVEN, MODERATE ⟨~ reasonableness —Matthew Arnold⟩ **c :** CHARMING, NICE — often used as a generalized term of approval ⟨that's very ~ of her⟩ **2 a :** pleasing to the taste **:** indicating or inducing (as by stimulation with disaccharides) the one of the four basic taste sensations that is usu. felt as pleasing and agreeable — compare BITTER, SALT, SOUR **b (1)** *of a beverage* **:** containing a perceptible quantity of sugar or other sweetening ingredient **:** not dry **(2)** *of wine* **:** retaining a portion of natural sugar often through arrested fermentation effected either by pasteurization or by the addition of grape brandy ⟨a ~ sherry⟩ **c :** CLOYING, SACCHARINE ⟨the flaw in her book is the ~ side, the Pollyanna note, that fatal emphasis on the happy ending —Rosemary Benét⟩ **d :** mildly seasoned **:** not pungent ⟨~ pickles⟩ **3 a :** pleasing to the mind or the feelings **:** arousing agreeable or delightful emotions **:** ATTRACTIVE ⟨the ~*est* privilege that any writer can ask —Irving Kolodin⟩ ⟨the pleasant smell overcame him like ~ sleep —O.E.Rölvaag⟩ **b :** pleasing to the smell **:** FRAGRANT ⟨the valleys are ~ with the fragrance of orange blossoms —*Amer. Guide Series: Ariz.*⟩ ⟨the ~ smell of new-cut boards —Sherwood Anderson⟩ **c (1) :** pleasing to the ear **:** gently harmonious **:** not raucous or disturbing **:** MELODIOUS ⟨the angelic, disembodied voices . . . were incredibly pure and ~ —John Steinbeck⟩ ⟨the bell sounds as ~ today as it ever did —*New Yorker*⟩ **(2) :** of or relating to jazz performed typically without improvisation, having a moderate and smoothly pleasing tempo, tone color, harmony, and rhythm, and often imitating the qualities of symphonic or salon music — compare HOT **d :** pleasing to the eye **:** not bold or violent in color or line **:** SOFT ⟨flower motifs and emblems, all printed in ~ colors —Charles Rosner⟩ ⟨remembered the ~ lines of her arms —Walter O'Meara⟩ **e :** PRETTY, FETCHING ⟨a ~ young thing⟩ ⟨a ~ face⟩ **4 :** much loved **:** DEAR ⟨then pardon him, ~ father, for my sake —Shak.⟩ ⟨~*est* love, I do not go, for weariness of thee —John Donne⟩ **5 a :** having the taste or odor belonging to the original sound state of something **:** not sour, rancid, decaying, or stale **:** WHOLESOME ⟨put the bottle in the stream to keep the milk ~⟩ ⟨here was the pinch of mystery that kept the legend ~ —John Rosselli⟩ **b :** not salt or salted **:** FRESH ⟨~ water⟩ ⟨a ~ spring⟩ ⟨~ butter⟩ **c** *of land* **:** suitable in composition to production of crops **:** neutral or alkaline **:** not dank or acid — opposed to *sour* **d :** free from noxious gases and odors ⟨~ crude oil⟩ ⟨~ mine air⟩ **e :** free from excess of acid, sulfur, or corrosive salts **f :** free from malodorous sulfur compounds (as hydrogen sulfide or mercaptans) — used esp. of natural gas, petroleum, and petroleum distillates ⟨gas or oil is sour or ~, but you wouldn't find the sweet as tasty as that —Harry Botsford⟩ **6 a :** easily managed **:** SMOOTH-RUNNING ⟨a ~ ship⟩ **b :** managing or acting easily and smoothly **:** SKILLFUL ⟨for a high-up man like him he was a ~ hand at weeding —Edward Sheehy⟩ ⟨a ~ pilot⟩ ⟨a ~ fielder⟩ **c** *of an archery bow* **:** easy to the hand **:** drawing smoothly and releasing without kicking **d** *of glass* **:** easily workable **7 a :** agreeable or obedient to oneself or itself alone ⟨pleaded to be allowed to descend upon a community in my own ~ way —Cornelia Parker⟩ ⟨takes its own ~ time as it rolls lackadaisically across the prairie —Green Peyton⟩ **b :** FINE, GREAT, TERRIFIC — used as an intensive ⟨it would be a ~ gag to use mass communications in order to denounce them —J.B.Priestley⟩ ⟨one ~ inferiority complex —Harvey Breit⟩

syn ENGAGING, WINNING, WINSOME, DULCET: SWEET, applied to things other than those tasted, is a term of general commendation for what pleases, attracts, or charms, usu. in a mild way ⟨twilight, *sweet* with the smell of lilac and freshly turned earth —Corey Ford⟩ ⟨pleased at this sudden return to *sweet* reasonableness —C.G.D.Roberts⟩ ⟨has been very *sweet*. He wants to help, but of course there's nothing he can do —Louis Auchincloss⟩ ENGAGING may indicate power to attract favorable attention, sometimes by intriguing or charming characteristics ⟨affectionate, cheerful, happy, his sweet and *engaging* personality drew all men's love —H.O.Taylor⟩ ⟨the most *engaging* human beings who ever harbored a sly smile —Charlton Laird⟩ WINNING may suggest power to delight, charm, placate, or enamor ⟨a quiet, self-possessed, and gracious young lady, of singularly *winning* manners, and clear and resolutely honest eyes —William Black⟩ ⟨simple as a child, with his gentle, *winning* voice and grave smile —Van Wyck Brooks⟩ WINSOME may suggest any engaging quality; it may call up notions of blended comeliness, cheer, childlike nature, and open candor ⟨remembered her childlike look, and *winsome* fanciful ways, and shy tremulous grace —Oscar Wilde⟩ DULCET may apply to something gratifying, soothing, bland, and sweet ⟨the voice . . . *dulcet* as the hum of heavy honeybees amid orange blossoms —Herman Wouk⟩

— **sweet on :** strongly attracted to **:** in love with ⟨he's been *sweet on* her for years⟩

²sweet \"\ *vt* -ED/-ING/-S [ME *sweten*, fr. OE *swētan;* akin to MLG *söten* to sweeten, MD *soeten*, OHG *suozen;* causative-denominative fr. the root of E ¹*sweet*] **:** SWEETEN

³sweet \"\ *adv* -ER/-EST [ME *swete, sweete*, fr. *swete, sweete*, adj.] **:** SWEETLY ⟨how ~ the moonlight sleeps upon this bank —Shak.⟩

⁴sweet \"\ *n* -s [ME *swete, sweete*, fr. *swete, sweete*, adj.] **1 :** something that is sweet to the taste: as **a :** a food (as a candy or preserve) having a high sugar content — usu. used in pl. ⟨filling up on candy and other ~*s* —Carl Binger⟩ ⟨can cross the street and readily buy ~*s* at a store —Jane Nickerson⟩ **b sweets** *pl, Brit* **:** sweetened wines and cordials **c** *Brit* **:** a sweet dish served at the end of a meal **:** DESSERT **d** *Brit* **:** CANDY ⟨put a large ~ in her cheek —Elizabeth Taylor⟩ ⟨this is done by swallowing, or by chewing a ~ or gum —*Before You Take Off*⟩ **e :** SWEET POTATO **2 :** a sweet taste sensation ⟨they see and smell and have their palates both for ~ and sour —Shak.⟩ **3 :** a pleasant or gratifying experience, possession, or state **:** something that delights or deeply satisfies ⟨precious ~*s* which older writers have coveted and gained —Sinclair Lewis⟩ ⟨the ~*s* of life⟩ ⟨the ~*s* of office⟩ **4 :** BELOVED, DARLING, SWEETHEART ⟨you can always talk to me, you ~ —Susan Ertz⟩ **5 a** *archaic* **:** sweet smell **:** FRAGRANCE ⟨the scent . . . makes

faint with too much ~ —P.B.Shelley⟩ **b sweets** *pl, archaic* **:** things having a sweet smell ⟨a wilderness of ~*s* —John Milton⟩
sweet acacia *n* **:** HUISACHE
sweet almond *n* **:** an almond that produces sweet edible seeds and forms a distinct variety (*Prunus amygdalus dulcis*) of the common almond; *also* **:** the edible seed of this tree — compare BITTER ALMOND
sweet almond oil *n* **:** ALMOND OIL 1a
sweet alyssum *also* **sweet alison** *n* **:** a perennial European herb (*Lobularia maritima*) having clusters of small fragrant white flowers
sweet amber *n* **:** TUTSAN
sweet-and-sour \ˈ⸗,⸗ˈ⸗\ *adj* **:** seasoned with sugar and vinegar or lemon juice ⟨*sweet-and-sour* tongue⟩
sweet anise *n* **:** a sweet cicely (*Osmorhiza longistylis*)
sweet archangel *n* **:** RED ARCHANGEL
sweet ash *n* **:** WILD CHERVIL
sweet bag *n, archaic* **:** a small bag containing a scented or aromatic substance **:** SACHET
sweet balm *n* **1 :** LEMON BALM **2 :** a Canary Island mint (*Cedronella triphylla*) with ternate leaves
sweet balsam *n* **:** a balsamweed (*Gnaphalium obtusifolium*)
sweet basil *n* **:** a common basil (*Ocimum basilicum*)
sweet bay *n* **1 :** LAUREL 1 **2 :** an American magnolia (*Magnolia virginiana*) abundant along the Atlantic coast and in the southern states that has glaucous leaves and rather small globose fragrant white flowers **3 :** RED BAY
sweet bean *n* **:** HONEY LOCUST 1
sweetbells \ˈ⸗,⸗\ *n pl* **:** an eastern No. American deciduous shrub (*Leucothoe racemosa*) with pinkish flowers in long racemes
sweet·berry \ˈ⸗- — *see* BERRY\ *n* **:** SHEEPBERRY 1
sweet betty *n, usu cap B* [*betty* fr. the name *Betty*] **:** SOAPWORT 1
sweet billy *n, usu cap B* [*billy* fr. the name *Billy*] **1 :** SWEET WILLIAM 1 **2 :** the European goldfinch
sweet birch *n* **:** a common birch (*Betula lenta*) of the eastern U.S. that has a spicy brown bark containing a volatile oil, hard dark-colored wood used for furniture and cabinetwork, and erect fruiting aments — called also *black birch, cherry birch*
sweet-birch oil \ˈ⸗,⸗-\ *n* **1 :** BIRCH OIL 2 **2 :** METHYL SALICYLATE
sweet brake *n* **:** MALE FERN
sweetbread \ˈ⸗,⸗\ *n* **1 :** the thymus of a young animal (as a calf) used for food **2 :** BEEF BREAD
sweetbrier *also* **sweetbriar** \ˈ⸗,⸗\ *n* **:** any of several closely related and similar Old World roses (esp. *Rosa eglanteria*) which have stout recurved prickles, small glandular-serrate leaves, and white to deep rosy pink single flowers followed by scarlet fruits, which are sometimes cultivated or used in hybridization, and some of which are naturalized outside their normal range (as in No. America) — called also *eglantine*
sweet broom *n* **1 :** a white-flowered fragrant shrub (*Cytisus fragrans*) of Teneriffe that is cultivated for ornament **2** *also*
sweet broomweed : BROOMWEED 1
sweet bubby *n* **:** CAROLINA ALLSPICE
sweet buckeye *n* **:** an often cultivated tall buckeye (*Aesculus octandra*) of the central U.S. that has yellow or red flowers and soft white wood
sweet bush *n* **:** SWEET FERN 2
sweet calabash *n* **:** a West Indian passionflower (*Passiflora maliformis*) with edible fruit about the size of an apple
sweet calamus *or* **sweet cane** *n* **1 :** SWEET FLAG **2 a :** SUGARCANE **b :** a grass (*Andropogon aromaticus*) of northwestern India that has leaves that are aromatic when bruised or broken
sweet cassava *n* **:** a cassava (*Manihot dulcis*) with roots that are used as a vegetable and herbage that is used for stock feed
sweet cherry *n* **1 :** a rather tall pyramidal Eurasian tree (*Prunus avium*) with reddish brown bark, white flowers, and fruits that are often small and bitter in the wild but have been developed under cultivation into large heart-shaped to globular sweet-flavored cherries — called also *gean, mazzard;* compare SOUR CHERRY **2 :** the fruit of the sweet cherry
sweet chervil *n* **:** a tall perennial sweet cicely (*Osmorhiza longistylis*) with sweet anise-flavored roots that is widely distributed in open moist woodlands of eastern and central No. America
sweet chestnut *n* **:** SPANISH CHESTNUT
sweet chocolate *n* **:** chocolate that contains added sugar
sweet cicely *n* **1 :** a European herb (*Myrrhis odorata*) having white flowers and an aromatic root **2 :** any of various herbs of an American genus (*Osmorhiza*) related to *Myrrhis* that typically have thick fleshy roots and grow in moist woodlands; *esp* **:** SWEET CHERVIL
sweet cider *n* **:** CIDER 1
sweet clover *n* **:** a tall erect annual or biennial legume of the genus *Melilotus* that is grown extensively esp. for hay and soil improvement — called also *melilot;* see WHITE SWEET CLOVER, YELLOW SWEET CLOVER
sweet clover disease *n* **:** a hemorrhagic diathesis of sheep and cattle feeding on improperly cured sweet clover containing excess quantities of dicoumarol
sweetclover weevil \ˈ⸗,⸗-\ *n* **:** a small brownish gray weevil (*Sitona cylindricollis*) that is native to Europe but now widespread in the central part of No. America and that as an adult feeds on and defoliates sweet clover while its larvae feed on the roots
sweet coltsfoot *n* **:** any of several herbs of the genus *Petasites* (as *P. fragrans* of Europe and *P. sagittatus* of No. America)
sweet corn *n* **:** an Indian corn that is grown in many horticultural varieties, is variously considered a distinct species (*Zea saccharata* or *Z. rugosa*), a subspecies (*Z. mays rugosa*), or a specific mutation of dent corn, and is distinguished esp. by kernels containing a high percentage of sugar in the milk stage when they are suitable for table use but later becoming horny, translucent, and wrinkled — compare FIELD CORN, GREEN CORN
sweet-corn wilt *n* **:** STEWART'S DISEASE
sweet cup *n* **:** any of several passionflowers or their fruits: as **a :** SWEET CALABASH **b :** JAMAICA HONEYSUCKLE
sweet-curd \ˈ⸗ˈ⸗\ *adj, of cheese* **:** made of curd formed with rennet from cow's milk set sweet and cooked rapidly to a very firm consistency
sweeted *past of* SWEET
sweet elder *n* **:** AMERICAN ELDER
sweet elm *n* **:** SLIPPERY ELM 1
sweet·en \ˈswētᵊn\ *vb* **sweetened; sweetened; sweetening** \-t(ᵊ)niŋ\ **sweetens** [¹*sweet* + *-en*] *vt* **1 a :** to add sugar or other sweetening to ⟨~ the cereal⟩ ⟨~ the coffee⟩ **b :** to make more pleasant to the ear **:** make softer or more melodious ⟨the roaring river fills all the arching way with . . . reverberating music, which is ~*ed* at times by the ouzel —John Muir †1914⟩ **c :** to make more pleasant to the smell **:** add fragrance to ⟨the piny aroma of the greenwoods, ~*ed* by the fragrance of laurel and azalea —*Amer. Guide Series: Conn.*⟩ **2 a :** to make amiable and pleasant in disposition **:** free from harshness **:** REFINE ⟨religion . . . did not ~ her old age —George Santayana⟩ **b :** to soften the mood or attitude of **:** APPEASE, MOLLIFY ⟨now they thought it was time to ~ the people, and deliver them from their burthens —Lucy Hutchinson⟩ ⟨wants to ~ up U.S. opinion —*Time*⟩ **c :** to make amenable or obliging by friendly attentions or gifts **:** soften up ⟨brought in business because he got around, and ~*ed* contacts —J.P. Marquand⟩ ⟨had to . . . ~ dealers with beer, wrangle with claims agents —Saul Bellow⟩ **3 a :** to make agreeable or delightful **:** add a pleasant quality to ⟨pastimes and sports . . . ~*ed* the voyage and prevented arguments and quarrels —David Garnett⟩ ⟨suddenly cut off from all that ~*ed* life for her —Edith Wharton⟩ **b :** to lessen the unpleasant quality or effect of **:** make less painful or trying **:** LIGHTEN ⟨the most important single function of the humor is to ~ the instruction —Rebecca P. Parkin⟩ ⟨invariably ~*ed* his violence with wit —J.J.Mallon⟩ **c :** to make soft or mellow (as a line or tint) **4 :** to make fresh and wholesome **:** CLEANSE, PURIFY ⟨all the perfumes of Arabia will not ~ this little hand —Shak.⟩ **5 :** RELIEVE, SOLACE ⟨charity which ~*s* giver and recipient in equal measure —Roy Lewis & Angus Maude⟩ **6 :** to free from a harmful or undesirable quality or substance: as **a :** to reduce the acidity of (soil) by applying lime **b :** to deprive (as sea water) of salt **c :** to neutralize acid in by the use of an alkali **d :** to treat (as gasoline) so as to remove or make inoffensive sulfur or sulfur compounds that are malodorous and corrosive **e :** to purify esp. by fumigating or filtering **7 :** to make more valuable or attractive: as **a :** to add poker chips to (a pot not won on the previous deal) prior to another deal **b** (1) **:** to place additional securities as collateral for (a loan) (2) **:** to offer stock as a bonus to the purchaser of (a bond) (3) **:** to improve the terms of (a security issue) to facilitate sale **c :** to improve (as a grade of lumber) by including a better quality than specified **d :** to add new goods to (present stock) in an effort to promote sales — often used with *up* ~ *vi* **:** to become sweet ⟨set her mother's milk pails upside down on the garden hedge to ~ —Mary Webb⟩
sweet·en·er \-t(ᵊ)nə(r)\ *n* -s **:** one that sweetens ⟨a low-calorie liquid ~ —*Time*⟩ ⟨urges concessions on minor fiscal questions as ~*s* —*Times Lit. Supp.*⟩
sweetening *n* -s **1 :** the act or process of making sweet ⟨methods for the cleaning and ~ of cider barrels⟩ **2 a :** something that sweetens **b** *South & Midland* **:** something used to sweeten food and drink ⟨poured me coffee with lots of cream and ~, just the way I like it best —Helen Eustis⟩ — see LONG SWEETENING, SHORT SWEETENING
sweeter *comparative of* SWEET
sweetest *superlative of* SWEET
sweet fennel *n* **1 :** FLORENCE FENNEL **2 :** FENNEL
sweet fern *n* **1 a :** any of several shield ferns of the genus *Dryopteris* **b :** a common polypody (*Polypodium vulgare*) **2 :** a small No. American shrub (*Comptonia peregrina*) of the family Myricaceae having sweet-scented or aromatic fernlike leaves **3** *dial Eng* **:** SWEET CICELY
sweetfish \ˈ⸗,⸗\ *n* **:** AYU
sweet flag *n* **:** a perennial marsh herb (*Acorus calamus*) having long leaves and a pungent rootstock — called also *calamus*
sweet gale *n* [*gale* fr. ME *gale, gayl* sweet gale — more at FERNGALE] **:** a bog shrub (*Myrica gale*) found throughout the north temperate zone and having bitter-tasting fragrant leaves — called also *Scotch gale*
sweet goldenrod *n* **:** BLUE MOUNTAIN TEA
sweet grass *n* **1 :** any of various grasses of sweet flavor or odor: as **a :** MANNA GRASS **b** (1) **:** a slender fragrant perennial widely distributed holy grass (*Hierochloe odorata*) that is sometimes used in basketry — called also *Seneca grass, vanilla grass* (2) **:** any of various other holy grasses **c** *southern Africa* **:** any of various grasses (as members of the genera *Panicum* and *Themeda*) that are relished by stock **2** *dial Eng* **a :** WOODRUFF **b :** EELGRASS 1 **3 :** SWEET FLAG
sweet gum *n* **1 a :** a No. American tree (*Liquidambar styraciflua*) with palmately lobed leaves, corky branches, and hard wood — see TREE illustration **b :** heartwood of the sweet gum tree or the reddish brown lumber sawed from it and sometimes used as an imitation of mahogany and Circassian walnut — called also *bilsted, gum, red gum, satin walnut* **2 :** the balsam produced by the sweet gum tree
sweet gum scale *n* **:** a scale (*Diaspidiotus liquidambaris*) that feeds on sweet gum
¹**sweetheart** \ˈ⸗,⸗\ *n* [ME *swete hert,* fr. *swete* sweet + *hert* heart — more at SWEET, HEART] **1 :** DARLING — often used as a term of endearment **2 :** one who is loved **:** LOVER ⟨she married . . . an old ~ —W. F. De Morgan⟩ ⟨saw the face of his ~, his wife —Zane Grey⟩ **3 a :** AMERICAN ORPINE **b sweethearts** *pl* **:** the cleavers (*Galium aparine*)
²**sweetheart** \"\ *vb* -ED/-ING/-S *vi* **:** to have a sweetheart **:** make love ⟨boys your age ought to be ~*ing* —Richard Church⟩ ~ *vt* **:** COURT, WOO
sweetheart agreement *or* **sweetheart contract** *n* **:** an agreement between an employer and a labor union on terms favorable to the employer and often arranged by a union official without the participation or approval of the union members
sweetheart neckline *n* **:** a neckline for women's clothing that is high in back and low in front where it is scalloped to resemble the top of a heart

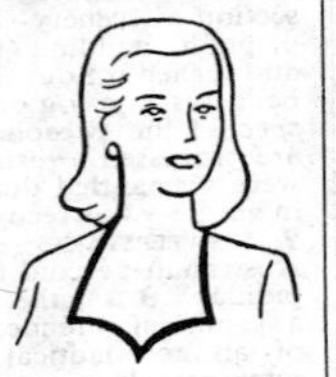
sweetheart neckline

sweetheart rose *n* **:** any of various small roses (as a polyantha rose)
sweet herb *n* **:** a fragrant herb cultivated for culinary purposes — usu. used in pl.
sweet horsemint *n* **:** DITTANY 3
sweet·ie \ˈswēd·ē, -ētē, -i\ *n* -s [¹*sweet* + *-ie*] **1** *Brit* **:** CANDY, SWEET — usu. used in pl. ⟨can't get ~*s* for all this money —Samuel Butler †1902⟩ **2 :** SWEETHEART ⟨in his wanderings he had been lucky enough to marry a true-blue ~ —James Thurber⟩
sweetie pie *n* **:** SWEETHEART
sweet·ing \ˈswēd·iŋ, -ētiŋ, -ēŋ\ *n* -s [ME *sweting,* fr. *swete* sweet + *-ing*] **1** *archaic* **:** SWEETHEART ⟨trip no further, pretty ~; journeys end in lovers meeting —Shak.⟩ **2 :** a sweet apple ⟨planted a little garden and some ~ apple trees —*Amer. Guide Series: R.I.*⟩
sweet·ish \ˈswēd·ish, -ētish, -ēsh\ *adj* **1 :** somewhat sweet ⟨emitted a ~ scent —H.G.Wells⟩ **2 :** sickeningly or unpleasantly sweet ⟨a new ~ reek that clutches horribly at your throat —John Dos Passos⟩
sweet jav·ril \-ˈjavrəl\ *also* **sweet jar·vil** \-ˈjärvəl, -ˈjáv-\ *n, pl* **sweet javrils** *also* **sweet jarvils** [*javril, jarvil* alter. of *chervil*] **:** a perennial herb (*Osmorhiza claytoni*) with aromatic roots, decompound leaves, and small white flowers in loose umbels
sweet john *n, usu cap J* [*john* fr. the name *John*] *archaic* **:** a narrow-leaved sweet william
sweetleaf \ˈ⸗,⸗\ *n* **:** a small tree (*Symplocos tinctoria*) of southern U.S. with herbage and bark that yield a yellow dye
sweetleaf family *n* **:** SYMPLOCACEAE
sweet lemon *n* **:** any of several lemons having fruit with a sweet and usu. somewhat insipid pulp
sweet·less \ˈswētləs\ *adj* **:** having no sweets or sweetening
sweet·ling \-liŋ, -lēŋ\ *n* -s **1 :** DARLING **2 :** something small and sweet
sweetlips \ˈ⸗,⸗\ *n pl but sing or pl in constr, Austral* **:** any of several small percoid fishes of the genus *Lethrinus* having a pointed snout and protrusible mouth; *specif* **:** SCAVENGER 4c
sweet locust *n* **:** HONEY LOCUST 1a(1)
¹**sweet·ly** *adv* [ME *sweteliche, swetely,* fr. *swete* sweet + *-liche -ly* -ly (adv. suffix)] **1 :** AGREEABLY, COMFORTABLY, PLEASANTLY ⟨has a ~ simple logic at first glance —Stuart Chase⟩ ⟨so golden and ~ hot it was —John Galsworthy⟩ **2 a** *archaic* **:** in a courteous or kindly manner **:** GRACIOUSLY **b :** in an affectionate or loving manner ⟨spoke ~ to him⟩ **3 :** with sweetness **:** in a manner sweet to the senses ⟨churches whose bells pealed so ~ —*Lamp*⟩ **4 :** CHARMINGLY ⟨she was indeed ~ fair —George Meredith⟩ **5 :** FINELY, GREATLY — used as an intensive ⟨will have to pay ~ for it⟩ **6 :** in an easy manner **:** SMOOTHLY ⟨the rope running ~ between us —Wynford Vaughan-Thomas⟩ ⟨the paper was coming off ~ now —Edna Ferber⟩
²**sweetly** \"\ *adj* [*sweet* + *-ly* (adj. suffix)] *archaic* **:** SWEET ⟨flowers which smelt so ~ —Thomas Hardy⟩
sweet magnolia *n* **:** SWEET BAY 2
sweet maize *n* **:** SWEET CORN
sweet marjoram *n* **:** an aromatic European herb (*Majorana hortensis*) with dense spikelike flower clusters — compare WILD MARJORAM
sweet marten *n* **:** the European pine marten
sweet mary *n, usu cap M* [*mary* fr. the name *Mary*] **1 :** a balm (*Melissa officinalis*) **2 :** OSWEGO TEA **3 :** COSTMARY 1
sweet mash *n* **:** a grain mash (as for distillation into whiskey) produced by the use of freshly developed yeast
sweetmeat \ˈ⸗,⸗\ *n* [ME *swete mete,* fr. *swete* sweet + *mete* food — more at SWEET, MEAT] **1 :** a food rich in sugar — usu. used in pl. ⟨sit down to supper at a table which is literally covered with ~*s* —*Irish Digest*⟩: as **a :** a candied or crystallized fruit **b :** CANDY, CONFECTION **2 :** the first coat of japanning or varnish applied in making patent leather **3 :** a slipper limpet (*Crepidula fornicata*) of the American coast
sweet myrtle *n* **:** SWEET FLAG
sweet·ness \ˈswētnəs\ *n* -ES [ME *swetnes, sweetnes,* fr. OE *swētnes,* fr. *swēte* sweet + *-nes* -ness — more at SWEET] **1 :** something sweet **:** a sweet substance, sound, or feeling **2 :** the quality or state of being sweet
sweetness and light *n* **1 :** a harmonious combination of beauty and intelligence ⟨declared that the ideal of culture was *sweetness and light*⟩ **2 :** mild reasonableness **:** AMIABILITY ⟨suddenly dropped his threatening tone and became all *sweetness and light*⟩
sweet niter *n* **:** ETHYL NITRITE SPIRIT
sweet oil *n* **:** a mild edible oil: as **a :** OLIVE OIL **b :** rape oil or similar oils when used as food
sweet olive *n* **:** an evergreen Asiatic shrub or small tree (*Osmanthus fragrans*) used for ornament and having leaves entire or with small teeth and the corolla divided nearly to its base
sweet orange *n* **:** an orange (*Citrus sinensis*) that is prob. native to southern China or other parts of southeastern Asia, has a fruit with a pithy central axis, and is the source of the widely cultivated table and juice oranges; *also* **:** a cultivated orange derived from this species and usu. having fruit with relatively thin skin and a sweet juicy edible pulp — compare SOUR ORANGE
sweet orange oil *n* **:** ORANGE OIL a
sweet pea *n* **:** a garden plant (*Lathyrus odoratus*) native to southern Europe but widely used as an ornamental and having slender climbing stems, pinnate leaves with narrow leaflets, and large very fragrant blue, purple, red, pink, salmon, or white flowers
sweet pepper *n* **1 :** any of various large capsicum fruits that contain little if any capsaicin, are characterized by mild flavor, usu. have distinctly thick walls, and vary in form from oblong to bell-shaped or somewhat rounded — called also *bell pepper, green pepper;* compare HOT PEPPER **2 :** the plant (*Capsicum frutescens grossum*) that bears sweet peppers
sweet pepperbush *n* **:** a plant of the genus *Clethra* (esp. *C. alnifolia*) with fragrant flowers
sweet-pickle \ˈ⸗ˈ⸗⸗\ *vt* **:** to cure (as meat) by soaking in or injecting with a solution of common salt and sugar with sometimes the addition of nitrates or spice
sweet pinesap *n* **:** a plant of the genus *Monotropsis* — called also *pygmy-pipes;* compare CAROLINA BEECHDROPS, INDIAN PIPE
sweet plum *n* **:** BURDEKIN PLUM
sweet potato *n* **1 a :** a tropical vine (*Ipomoea batatas*) widely cultivated in warm regions and in the U.S. as far north as New Jersey that is related to the morning glory and has variously shaped leaves and purplish flowers **b :** the large, thick, sweet and farinaceous tuberous root of the sweet potato vine that is cooked and eaten as a vegetable — compare YAM **2 :** OCARINA
sweet-potato beetle *n* **:** any of several tortoise beetles of the genera *Coptocycla* and *Cassida* (esp. *Cassida bivittata*) that are destructive to the leaves of the sweet potato and related plants
sweet-potato flea beetle *n* **:** a chrysomelid beetle (*Chaetocnema confinis*) that feeds on corn and other crop plants
sweet-potato hornworm *or* **sweet-potato sphinx** *n* **:** a No. American hawkmoth (*Agrius cingulatus*) whose larva feeds on sweet potato foliage
sweet-potato scurf *n* **:** a scurf disease of sweet potatoes caused by a fungus (*Moniliochaetes infuscans*)
sweet-potato weevil *or* **sweet-potato borer** *n* **:** a bluish-black weevil (*Cylas formicarius*) with a red prothorax whose larva bores in sweet-potato tubers
sweet-potato worm *n* **:** a worm that is the larva of the sweet-potato sphinx
sweet reed *n* **1 :** an Indian reed (*Cinna arundinacea*) **2** *Africa* **:** SORGO
sweet-roast \ˈ⸗ˈ⸗\ *vt* **:** DEAD-ROAST
sweet rocket *n* **:** DAME'S VIOLET
sweet roll *n* **1 :** COFFEE ROLL **2 :** ³BUN 1a
sweetroot \ˈ⸗,⸗\ *n* **1 :** LICORICE **2 :** an Australian timber tree (*Alyxia buxifolia*) of the family Apocynaceae **3 :** SWEET FLAG
sweet rush *n* **1 :** SWEET FLAG **2 :** CAMEL GRASS **3 :** a rush of the genus *Cyperus*
sweets *pres 3d sing of* SWEET, *pl of* SWEET
sweet scabious *n* **1 :** an Old World herb (*Scabiosa atropurpurea*) naturalized in America **2 :** DAISY FLEABANE **3 :** SKEVISH
sweet-scented \ˈ⸗ˈ⸗⸗\ *adj* **:** having a fragrant scent or smell — often used in vernacular names of plants to distinguish particular species or varieties ⟨*sweet-scented* cedar⟩
sweet-scented shrub *or* **sweet shrub** *n* **:** CAROLINA ALLSPICE
sweet sedge *n* **1 :** SWEET FLAG **2 :** YELLOW IRIS
sweetshop \ˈ⸗,⸗\ *n* [⁴*sweet* + *shop*] *chiefly Brit* **:** a candy store
sweetsop \ˈ⸗,⸗\ *n* **1 :** a tropical American tree (*Annona squamosa*) **2 :** the sweet pulpy fruit of the sweetsop that has a thick green scaly rind and shining black seeds — called also *anon, custard apple, sugar apple;* compare SOURSOP
sweet sorghum *n* **:** SORGO
sweet spire *n* **:** VIRGINIA WILLOW
sweet spirit of nitre *or* **sweet spirits of nitre :** ETHYL NITRITE SPIRIT
sweet sultan *n* **1 :** either of two annual Eurasian herbs (*Centaurea moschata* and *C. imperialis*) cultivated for their variously colored and fragrant flower heads **2 :** BLESSED THISTLE 1
sweet sumac *n* **:** FRAGRANT SUMAC
sweet su·san \-ˈsüzᵊn\ *n, usu cap 2d S* [*susan* fr. the name *Susan*] **:** LOBEL'S CATCHFLY
¹**sweet-sweet** \ˈ⸗ˈ⸗\ *adj* [imit.] **:** CHIRPING
²**sweet-sweet** \"\ *n* **:** a chirping sound
sweet talk *n* **:** BLANDISHMENT, SOFT SOAP ⟨was so accustomed to flattery and elaborate *sweet talk* that she would think she were being insulted if addressed with ordinary courtesy —Budd Schulberg⟩
sweet-talk \ˈ⸗ˈ⸗\ *vb* [*sweet talk*] *vt* **:** BLANDISH, CAJOLE, COAX ⟨manages somehow to *sweet-talk* the showgirl into a midnight supper at his apartment —John McCarten⟩ ~ *vi* **:** to use blandishments or flattery
sweet tangle *n* **:** a large seaweed (*Laminaria saccharina*) common along coasts and having fronds that contain a large quantity of sugar and are used in preparing a syrup
sweet thorn *n* **:** a tree (*Acacia karroo*) of southern Africa that has straight white thorns and drooping branches
sweet tooth *n* [ME *swete toth,* fr. *swete* sweet + *toth* tooth — more at SWEET, TOOTH] **:** a craving or fondness for sweet food ⟨can never get enough cake to satisfy his *sweet tooth*⟩
sweet trefoil *n* **:** BLUE MELILOT
sweet tussock *n* **:** a forage grass (*Poa bulbosa*) of Argentina
sweetveld \ˈ⸗,⸗\ *n* **:** African veld that is not markedly acid in soil reaction and is characterized by production in the presence of adequate moisture of palatable grazing of predominantly annual grasses
sweet vernal grass *n* **:** a slender European grass (*Anthoxanthum odoratum*) that is often planted with other grasses for its fragrance and has narrow spikelike panicles in early spring — called also *vernal grass*
sweet viburnum *n* **:** SHEEPBERRY 1
sweet violet *n* **:** a common cultivated violet (*Viola odorata*) of Eurasia and northern Africa that is the source of many of the commercially developed violets — called also *garden violet*
sweet walnut *n* **:** SHAGBARK HICKORY
sweet water *n* **1 :** a dilute solution of glycerol (*sweet water* from the hydrolysis of fats may contain 10 to 25 percent of glycerol) **2 :** a sugar solution; *esp* **:** one obtained by recovery of waste sugar during refining
sweet white violet *n* **:** a stemless violet (*Viola blanda*) of eastern No. America that has fragrant white flowers with purple veins
sweet william *n, sometimes cap S & often cap W* [*william* fr. the name *William*] **1 a :** a widely cultivated Eurasian pink (*Dianthus barbatus*) with small white to deep red or sometimes purple flowers that are often showily spotted, banded, or mottled and are borne in rather large flat bracteate heads at the end of erect stalks **b :** BUTTON PINK **2 :** any of several sharks of Pacific and southern seas having rank inedible flesh **3 :** a deep pink that is bluer and lighter than average coral (sense 3b), duller and less strong than fiesta, and yellower and less strong than begonia
sweet william catchfly *n, sometimes cap W* **:** LOBEL'S CATCHFLY
sweet wilson *n, usu cap W* [*wilson* fr. the name *Wilson*] **:** EARLY SAXIFRAGE
sweetwood \ˈ⸗,⸗\ *n* **1 :** a laurel (*Laurus nobilis*) **2 :** any of various chiefly tropical American trees of the family Lauraceae: as **a :** a tree of the genus *Ocotea* — compare STINKWOOD **b :** a tree of the genus *Nectandra* — compare BEBEERU **c :** a

small or medium-sized Jamaican tree (*Licaria triandra* or *Acrodiclidium jamaicense*) with easily worked greenish yellow wood **3 :** LICORICE 1,2a
sweetwood bark *n* **:** CASCARILLA
sweet woodruff *n* **:** a small European sweet-scented herb (*Asperula odorata*) sometimes used in perfumery
sweetwort \'=,=\ *n* **:** an unfermented malt infusion
sweety \'swēd·ē, -ētē, -i\ *Brit var of* SWEETIE 1
sweir \'swēr, 'swi(ə)r\ *var of* SWEER
swe·ko·man \;svākō¦män\ *n* -s *usu cap* [Sw *svekoman*, fr. *sveko-* Swedish, Sweden (fr. NL or ML *Sueco-*, fr. *Suecia* Sweden, fr. OSw *Svēar* Swedes) + *-man* maniac — more at SWEDE, FENNOMAN] **:** a Finn supporting the use of Swedish esp. as the official language against the Fennomans
¹swell \'swel\ *vb* **swelled; swelled** \-ld\ *or* **swol·len** \'swōlən *also* -ln\ **swelling; swells** [ME *swellen*, fr. OE *swellan;* akin to OS & OHG *swellan* to swell, ON *svella*, Goth uf*swalleins* inflation, conceit] *vi* **1 a :** to increase in volume **:** grow larger or bulkier **:** expand by internal pressure or growth **:** DILATE ⟨if I walked a hundred yards my ankles ~*ed* up —*Sydney* (*Austral.*) *Bull.*⟩ ⟨eight of my berries quickly disappeared, and the cheeks of the little vagabond ~*ed* —John Burroughs⟩ ⟨mucilaginous materials which ~ when water is added —Morris Fishbein⟩ **b :** to rise above or extend beyond a level, surface, or border ⟨up from the horizon ~*ed* a supernatural light —O.E.Rölvaag⟩ ⟨it is in this length of the river that it ~*s* to gigantic size —Tom Marvel⟩ **c :** to have a form that curves outward or upward **:** DISTEND, BULGE, PROTRUDE ⟨a comfortable paunch ~*ed* out beneath the buttons of his dinner jacket —Hamilton Basso⟩ ⟨the green slope ~*ed* upward to the pear orchard —Ellen Glasgow⟩ **2 a :** to become filled with pride and arrogance **:** become puffed up ⟨~*s* with pride and importance as he struts up and down —Martin Turnell⟩ **b :** to behave or speak in a pompous, blustering, self-important manner ⟨the diver crew will ~ around on the boat talking about different jobs they have been on —Richard Bissell⟩ **c :** to play the swell **:** behave as a man of fashion ⟨looked down on so much sheer ~*ing* around —*Newsweek*⟩ **3 a :** to develop and grow in the consciousness as if seeking an outlet ⟨the unseen grief that ~*s* with silence in the tortured soul —Shak.⟩ **b :** to become distended with emotion **:** become affected with a powerful feeling ⟨her heart ~*ed* with a suffocating sense of resentment —Anne D. Sedgwick⟩ **4 a :** to become augmented in force, intensity, degree, numbers, or value ⟨job opportunities ~*ed* hugely in government —Daniel Bell⟩ ⟨the credit union's capital ~*ed* to $110,000 —Frank Hamilton⟩ **b :** to become gradually louder **:** rise to a peak of loudness or sonority ⟨the cries ~*ed* and died away —John Galsworthy⟩ ⟨the organ ~*ed* to a climax⟩ ~ *vt* **1 :** to affect with a powerful or expansive emotion **:** INFLATE ⟨it ~*s* me to joyful madness —Walt Whitman⟩ ⟨he is *swollen* with pride⟩ **2 a :** to increase the volume or size of **:** cause to fill out or expand ⟨warm summer water . . . will quickly ~ the planks and so close the seams —C.D.Lane⟩ ⟨a hide . . . is put through a liming process that ~*s* it and loosens the hair —*Amer. Guide Series: Pa.*⟩ **b :** to cause (as a body of water) to become higher, wider, or more turbulent ⟨rivers *swollen* by rain⟩ ⟨ten thousand springs and creeks and a dozen lesser rivers run . . . to ~ the Sacramento —Julian Dana⟩ ⟨another little drop to ~ the flood of misery —Nevil Shute⟩ **3 a :** to increase in quantity, value, intensity, or degree **:** AUGMENT ⟨some large federal installation or project greatly ~*ed* the school population —*N.Y.Times*⟩ ⟨nobles, landed gentry, merchants . . . ~*ed* the demand for country houses —Bernard Smith⟩ **b :** to augment gradually in loudness (as a musical tone) ⟨the pealing anthem ~*s* the note of praise —Thomas Gray⟩ **syn** see EXPAND
²swell \"\ *n* -s **1 a :** the condition of being swollen **:** BULGE, PROTUBERANCE ⟨this causes too much ~ in the back of the book —Laurence Town⟩ ⟨a green bodice which fitted so snugly that the ~ of her breasts was accentuated —T.B. Costain⟩ **b** (1) **:** a rounded elevation or hill; *esp* **:** a long rounded ridge on a sea floor ⟨the mid-Atlantic ~⟩ (2) **:** a tract of rising ground (3) **:** a very broad anticlinal structure **c :** ENTASIS **d :** a local enlargement or thickening in a vein or ore deposit **e :** FLIPPER 2d **2 a :** a long relatively low wave or an unbroken series of such waves **b :** a slow rhythmic heaving or rolling action or process ⟨the thing rolls on its antique springs with a slow, disquieting ~ —Mollie Panter-Downes⟩ ⟨that sustained impressiveness, that booming ~, which becomes so intolerable —F.R.Leavis⟩ **3 a :** the act, action, or process of swelling **:** an increase in volume, size, force, or intensity ⟨a ~ in population⟩ ⟨there is little dramatic ~ into the tragic power that the end of the story demands —Edgar Johnson⟩ **b** (1) **:** a gradual increase and decrease of the loudness or volume of a musical sound; *also* **:** a sign <> indicating a swell (2) **:** a device used in a harpsichord or pipe or reed organ for governing the loudness of tones by opening or closing the cover or set of louvers over a box or chamber enclosing the sounding strings, vibrators, or pipes (3) **:** SWELL BOX (4) **:** SWELL ORGAN (5) **:** SWELL PEDAL **4 a** *archaic* **:** an impressive, pompous, or fashionable air or display **:** DASH ⟨a new necktie, nice shirts — you can imagine I cut quite a ~ —Walt Whitman⟩ **b :** a person dressed in the height of fashion **:** FASHION PLATE ⟨sketched himself as a . . . ~, in a top hat, a white silk scarf, and a chesterfield —Janet Flanner⟩ ⟨see quite a young ~ come out in the latest fashion —Patricia M. Johnson⟩ **c :** a person of high social position **:** NOB ⟨a tony street where all the ~*s* lived —J.T.Farrell⟩ **d :** a specialist or person of outstanding achievement in a particular field **:** EXPERT, MASTER ⟨a real ~ on birds —H.J.Laski⟩ ⟨an agreeable melodist and a terrific ~ at orchestration —Arnold Bennett⟩ **5 :** a small lever connected with the shuttle protector in the shuttle box of a loom
³swell \"\ *adj* -ER/-EST [²*swell* (person dressed in fashion)] **1 :** smartly dressed or turned out **:** STYLISH ⟨I am too shabby . . . only ~ people go to the park —Oscar Wilde⟩ ⟨socially prominent **:** DISTINGUISHED ⟨had a lot of ~ social connections —Wilson Collison⟩ **2 :** suitable for or characteristic of swells **:** FASHIONABLE, TIP-TOP ⟨staying at the ~*est* hotel in town⟩ **3 :** EXCELLENT, GREAT, WONDERFUL — used as a generalized term of enthusiasm or approval ⟨makes a ~ impression and is hired —W.H.Whyte⟩ ⟨she was a really ~ girl —W.F.Jenkins⟩ ⟨it's a miracle . . . I feel perfectly ~ —W.S. Maugham⟩
swellbelly \'=,=,=\ *n* **:** GLOBEFISH; *esp* **:** a common fish (*Sphoeroides maculatus*) of the Atlantic coast of No. America
swell box *n* **:** a box or chamber in an organ that contains the reeds or a set of pipes and has shutters that open or shut usu. by means of a pedal in order to regulate the volume of musical tone
swell–butted \'=¦=,=\ *adj, of a tree* **:** greatly enlarged at the base — compare KNEE 3c
swell dash *n* **:** DIAMOND DASH
swell·dom \'sweldəm\ *n* -s [²*swell* + *-dom*] **:** the world of fashion **:** high society ⟨was taken up by ~, whose practically unanimous verdict was that she was a charming addition to their circle —*Lincoln* (*Nebr.*) *Evening News*⟩
swelled *adj* **1 :** ENLARGED, INFLATED **2 :** having a bulge or curve ⟨a ~ column⟩ ⟨the ~ front of the desk⟩
swelled head *n* **1 a :** BIGHEAD 1a **b :** BIGHEAD 1c **2 :** an exaggerated opinion of oneself **:** SELF-CONCEIT ⟨risk the chance of your getting a *swelled head* and tell you what I think of your efforts —A.H.Gibbs⟩ — **swelled–headed** \'=¦=,=\ *adj* — **swelled–head·ed·ness** *n* -ES
swell·er \'swelə(r)\ *n* -s **:** one that swells
swellfish \'=,=\ *n* **:** GLOBEFISH
swell front *n* **:** a front (as of a chest of drawers or a house) rounded out in a convex curve
swellhead \'=,=\ *n* **1 a :** INFECTIOUS SINUSITIS **b :** BIGHEAD 1b **2 :** one who has a swelled head **:** a conceited person — **swellheaded** \'=¦=,=\ *adj* — **swell·head·ed·ness** *n* -ES
¹swell·ing \'sweliŋ, -lēŋ\ *n* -s [ME, fr. gerund of *swellen* to swell] **1 :** something that is swollen **:** BULGE, PROTUBERANCE; *specif* **:** an abnormal bodily protuberance or localized enlargement ⟨a neoplastic ~⟩ **2** *archaic* **:** conceited feeling or behavior **:** excessive pride **3 a** *archaic* **:** the action of rising above a level or surface **b :** the act or process of dilating or the condition of having become dilated **:** EXPANSION ⟨experienced agreeable ~*s* of virtue —Mary Austin⟩
²swelling \"\ *adj* [fr. pres. part. of *swellen* to swell] **1 :** increasing in volume, amount, or force **:** filling out **:** ENLARGING, RISING ⟨the ~ bubble⟩ ⟨the ~ sails⟩ ⟨the ~ tide⟩ ⟨the ~ roar of the crowd⟩ **2 :** having a bulging or curving form; *specif* **:** having a gently rising contour ⟨eastward rise the ~ foothills —*Amer. Guide Series: Oregon*⟩ **3 a :** inflated with conceit **:** OVERWEENING ⟨prizefighters — ~ in triumph —Bergen Evans⟩ **b :** marked by intensity of feeling **:** EXPANSIVE ⟨the ~ sense of great things impending —F. Tennyson Jesse⟩ **c :** inflated in style or manner **:** BOMBASTIC, POMPOUS ⟨a ~ speech⟩ ⟨a ~ scene⟩ — **swell·ing·ly** *adv*
swell·ish \'swelish, -lēsh\ *adj* [²*swell* + *-ish*] **:** STYLISH, SWELL — **swell·ish·ness** *n* -ES
swell mob *n* [²*swell*] *Brit* **:** a group of criminals who dress fashionably and act with seeming respectability
swell–mobsman \'=¦=,=\ *n, Brit* **:** a criminal (as a pickpocket) who dresses fashionably and conducts himself with seeming respectability for professional purposes
swell organ *n* **:** a division in a pipe organ in which the pipes are enclosed in a swell box
swell pedal *n* **:** a pedal that operates an organ swell usu. by working a balanced lever mechanism that opens or shuts the louvers of the swell box
swell piece *n* **:** a flat piece (as of wood) with a convex outer face
swells *pres 3d sing of* SWELL, *pl of* SWELL
swell shark *n* **:** any of several short, wide-bodied sharks of the family Scyliorhinidae that take in air when caught and swell up; *esp* **:** a shark (*Cephaloscyllium uter*) of the California coast
swelltoad \'=,=\ *n* **:** GLOBEFISH
swelt \'swelt\ *vb* -ED/-ING/-S [ME *swelten* — more at SWELTER] *vi* **1** *dial* **a :** DIE, PERISH **b :** FAINT, SWOON **2** *dial* **:** to become oppressed by heat **:** SWELTER, SUFFOCATE ~ *vt* **1** *dial* **:** to cause to die **2** *dial* **:** to overpower with or as if with heat **:** BROIL, SCORCH
¹swel·ter \'sweltə(r)\ *vb* **sweltered; sweltered; sweltering** \-ltəriŋ, -l·triŋ\ **swelters** [ME *sweltren, swelteren*, freq. of *swelten* to die, faint, be overcome by heat, fr. OE *sweltan* to die, perish; akin to OS *sweltan* to die, OHG *swelzan* to burn up (with passion), ON *svelta* to die, starve, be hungry, Goth *swiltan* to die, and prob. to OE *swelan* to burn, MLG *swelen* to smolder, Gk *heilē, eilē, helē* heat of the sun, sunshine, Lith *svilti* to singe, Skt *svarati* it lights up, shines] *vi* **1 a :** to be faint from heat **:** become oppressed or excessively uncomfortable with heat **:** perspire profusely **:** SWEAT ⟨an explorer who has ~*ed* in the jungle and frozen in the far north⟩ **b :** to become exposed to excessive heat ⟨a land that ~*s* for most of the year⟩ **2** *archaic* **:** WALLOW, WELTER **3** *archaic* **:** to become exuded ~ *vt* **1 :** to oppress with heat **:** make faint with heat **:** cause to sweat profusely ⟨amphitheater which sheltered and ~*ed* the last . . . convention —Phyllis Battelle⟩ **2** *archaic* **:** EXUDE ⟨~*ed* venom —Shak.⟩
²swelter \"\ *n* -s **1 :** a state of oppressive heat ⟨the officers ate in a ~, sweat dripping from their hands and faces —Norman Mailer⟩ **2 :** WELTER ⟨the immense sweeps and ~*s* of the whirl —E.A.Poe⟩ **3 :** an excited or overwrought state of mind **:** SWEAT ⟨for all the bitter cold and my thin gown and us being far from the fire, I was all in a ~ —Mary Webb⟩
¹sweltering *adj* **:** oppressively hot **:** causing or marked by excessive sweating or faintness ⟨a ~ day⟩ ⟨a ~ room⟩ ⟨watch the players battle their ~ way through matches lasting a couple of hours —Mollie Panter-Downes⟩
²sweltering *adv* **:** SWELTERINGLY
swel·ter·ing·ly *adv* **:** to a sweltering degree ⟨the sun came ~ in on us through the glass roof —Robert Lynd⟩
swel·try \'swel·trē, -ri\ *adj* -ER/-EST [¹*swelter* + *-y*] **:** SWELTERING, SULTRY
swept *adj* [fr. past part. of ¹*sweep*] **:** possessing sweep ⟨the ~ wing of the airplane⟩
swept–back \'=¦=\ *adj* [fr. past part. of *sweep back*, v.] **:** possessing sweepback
swept–forward \'=¦=,=\ *adj* [fr. past part. of *sweep forward*, v.] **:** possessing sweepforward
sweptwing \'=¦=\ *adj* **:** having swept wings; *specif* **:** having swept-back wings
swer·tia \'swərsh(ē)ə, -rd·ēə\ *n, cap* [NL, fr. Emanuel *Swert* (Sweert), 17th cent. Du. botanist + NL *-ia*] **:** a small genus of herbs (family Gentianaceae) found chiefly in the western U.S. and having thick, bitter roots, opposite or whorled leaves, and dull-colored flowers — see GREEN GENTIAN
¹swerve \'swərv, 'swəv, 'swəiv\ *vb* -ED/-ING/-S [ME *swerven*, fr. OE *sweorfan* to file away, polish, wipe, rub, scour; akin to OFris *swerva* to creep, OS *swerban* to wipe off, OHG *swerban* to wipe off, ON *sverfa* to file, *svarfa* to sweep, swerve, Goth af*swairban* to wipe off, W *chwerfu* to whirl, turn around, Gk *syrein* to drag, Russ *sverbet'* to itch; basic meaning: to turn] *vi* **1 :** to move from a straight line or course **:** turn aside **:** become deflected **:** DEVIATE ⟨*swerving* to avoid two errand boys on bicycles —Robert Graves⟩ ⟨the bull *swerved* to meet this new opponent —Francis Birtles⟩ ⟨the highway ~*s* south —*Amer. Guide Series: Fla.*⟩ **2 :** to become deflected from a fixed or right course of action, conduct, or belief **:** shift one's position or allegiance **:** WAVER ⟨had never *swerved* from what she conceived to be her duty —A.J.Kennedy⟩ **3** *archaic* **:** to give way **:** YIELD, TOTTER ~ *vt* **:** to turn aside **:** cause to turn from a straight course **:** cause to deviate ⟨~ the car⟩ ⟨~ a ball⟩ ⟨do not let your apprehension of what the judges may say ~ you from saying what you think —C.P. Curtis⟩
syn SWERVE, VEER, DEVIATE, DEPART, DIGRESS, and DIVERGE can mean, in common, to turn aside from a straight line or a defined course. SWERVE may suggest a physical, mental, or moral turning from a given course, usu. by an abrupt shift of direction ⟨the highway now skirts the lake shore . . . and again *swerves* inland —*Amer. Guide Series: Vt.*⟩ ⟨the driver of the motorcar *swerved* the other way but could not avoid the cab —Eric Linklater⟩ ⟨*swerved* and veered like a gull —John Dos Passos⟩ ⟨not to *swerve* from the path of duty or righteousness⟩ VEER, applying commonly to the change in the course of a wind or ship and often suggesting frequent turning or a series of turnings in the same direction, implies a change or a series of changes of direction or course under an external influence comparable to the wind ⟨the wind suddenly *veered* and drove the waters of the Gulf in mountainous waves upon them —*Amer. Guide Series: La.*⟩ ⟨his thought, *veering* and tacking as the winds blew —V.L.Parrington⟩ ⟨drift with every current of opinion and *veer* like a weathercock with every breeze of fashion —S.J.Brown⟩ ⟨literary men *veer* between the extremes of a contempt for the masses and a glorification of the people —H.J.Muller⟩ DEVIATE implies a turning aside from a customary, allotted, or prescribed course, suggesting a swerving from what is the norm, the law, the standard, or the proper procedure or course ⟨if he diminishes his speed by a fraction of a second or *deviates* a hair's breadth from the prescribed and never-changing movements of his hands —C.H.Grandgent⟩ ⟨anyone who *deviates* from that faith —V.M.Hancher⟩ ⟨has never *deviated* from the belief that the basis of a good cartoon is caricature —*Current Biog.*⟩ DEPART usu. signifies little more than leaving a given path, usu. figurative ⟨one point in which the definition of virtue and vice given above *departs* from tradition and from common practice —Bertrand Russell⟩ ⟨the design of the center departs somewhat from that of the newer buildings —*Amer. Guide Series: Minn.*⟩ ⟨forced by circumstances to *depart* from the principles of his own logic —W.P.Webb⟩ DIGRESS implies a departure from the subject of one's discourse whether intentional or from general lack of a sense of coherence ⟨*digress* a moment from a main point of discussion to consider a pressing tangential problem⟩ ⟨an irritating habit of *digressing* and never getting back to the main point of a story⟩ DIVERGE, often used in the sense of DEPART, usu., however, suggests a separation of one, usu. a main, path into two or more leading in different directions ⟨the absolute prohibition of all ideas that *diverge* in the slightest from the accepted platitudes —H.L.Mencken⟩ ⟨*diverged* from the path, and got before them on the left flank —George Meredith⟩ ⟨proceeded along the road together till they reached the town, and their paths *diverged* —Thomas Hardy⟩ ⟨a year later the careers of the brothers, so far linked together, *diverged* —*Current Biog.*⟩
²swerve \"\ *n* -s **1 :** the act, process, or an instance of swerving ⟨with a dexterous ~ he rounded the yawl about —Frederick Way⟩ **2 :** side-to-side curve of a bowled cricket ball before it pitches; *esp* **:** such curve induced by finger spin
swerved *past of* SWERVE
swerve·less \'=ləs\ *adj* **:** UNSWERVING
swerv·er \'swərvər, 'swəvə(r, 'swəivə(r\ *n* -s **:** one that swerves
swerves *pres 3d sing of* SWERVE
swerving *pres part of* SWERVE
swev·en \'swevən\ *n* -s [ME, fr. OE *swefn* sleep, dream, vision — more at SOMNOLENT] *archaic* **:** DREAM, VISION
swg *abbr* switching
SWG *abbr* standard wire gauge
swich \'swich\ *chiefly dial var of* SUCH
swid·den \'swidᵊn\ *n* -s [E dial., burned clearing, prob. fr. ON *svithinn*, past part. of *svītha* to burn, singe] **:** an impermanent agricultural plot produced by cutting back and burning off vegetative cover — called also *kaingin;* compare MILPA
swie·te·nia \swē'tēnēə\ *n, cap* [NL, fr. Gerard van *Swieten* †1772 Du. botanist and physician in Austria + NL *-ia*] **:** a small genus of tropical trees (family Meliaceae) having seeds winged above and anthers borne between the teeth of the stamen tube — see MAHOGANY
¹swift \'swift\ *adj* -ER/-EST [ME, fr. OE; akin to OE *swīfan* to revolve, wend, sweep — more at SWIVEL] **1 :** moving or capable of moving with great speed **:** characterized by rapidity of motion **:** rapidly running, flying, flowing ⟨the ~ flight of an arrow⟩ ⟨making . . . a man a ~ runner, a nimble climber, a strong swimmer —J.G.Frazer⟩ ⟨the river's too deep to ford and too ~ to swim —Willa Cather⟩ **2 a :** taking place, done, or concluded within a very short time ⟨northers sometimes bring a ~ change from sunshine to howling blizzards —*Amer. Guide Series: Texas*⟩ ⟨shot a ~ smile toward him in that instant⟩ ⟨the ~ achievement of goals in half the projected time⟩ **b :** changing abruptly in character **:** SUDDEN ⟨the plains end, and with a ~ dramatic uprise the world of the mountains begins —Wynford Vaughan-Thomas⟩ **3 a :** quick in execution or accomplishment **:** speedy in action or performance ⟨better to be ~ and casual than to be slow and thorough —Ellen Glasgow⟩ ⟨must not search for penetrating or subtle characterization but rather for ~ and arresting caricature —William Peden⟩ **b :** quick to respond **:** READY, ALERT, PROMPT ⟨in her youth and prime . . . ~ in affection, and ~*er* still for vengeance —William Baucke⟩ ⟨afraid of rousing his ~ and terrible anger⟩ ⟨I will be a ~ witness against the sorcerers —Mal 3:5 (RSV)⟩ **syn** see FAST
²swift \"\ *adv* -ER/-EST [ME, fr. ¹*swift*] **:** SWIFTLY ⟨~ to its close ebbs out life's little day —Henry Lyte⟩ — often used in combination ⟨*swift*-flowing⟩
³swift \"\ *n* -s [¹*swift*] **1 :** one that is swift: as **a :** any of several lizards (as the pine lizard and others of the genus *Sceloporus*) that run swiftly **b :** the rapid current of a stream **2 a :** a reel for winding yarn or thread usu. collapsible for removal or application of the skein **b :** one of the large cylinders covered with card cloth that carry forward the material in a carding machine; *also* **:** a similar cylinder in other machines **c :** a tapering reel revolved on a vertical spindle and used for uncoiling wire **3 :** any of numerous small plainly colored birds constituting the family Apodidae that are related to the hummingbirds and goatsuckers but superficially much resemble swallows, that have very long narrow wings, weak feet, and a short bill with a wide gape, that spend most of their time on the wing and when they alight usu. cling to some vertical surface, that feed on insects taken on the wing, and that have nests cemented together with their sticky saliva and often attached by saliva to some vertical surface (as the inside of a hollow tree or the wall of a building, cave, or cliff); *specif* **:** a common European bird (*Apus apus* syn. *Micropus apus*) noted for its shrieking notes, having a somewhat forked tail, and nesting chiefly in crevices about the eaves of buildings or on cliffs — compare CHIMNEY SWIFT, SWIFTLET **4 :** the sail of a windmill **5** *or* **swift moth :** GHOST MOTH **6** *also* **swift fox :** KIT FOX
⁴swift \"\ *vt* -ED/-ING/-S [ME *swiften*, prob. of Scand origin; akin to ON *svipta* to sweep off, reef, *svífa* to ramble, turn, drift — more at SWIVEL] *Brit* **:** SWIFTER
swift·en \'swiftən\ *vi* -ED/-ING/-S [¹*swift* + *-en*] **:** to move swiftly or more swiftly **:** HASTEN
¹swift·er \'swiftə(r)\ *n* -s [⁴*swift* + *-er*] **1 :** the forward or after shroud of a lower mast — see SHIP illustration **2 :** a rope confining the capstan bars in their sockets while the capstan is being turned **3 :** a rope encircling a boat or ship longitudinally to strengthen or protect the sides
²swifter \"\ *vt* **swiftered; swiftered; swiftering** \-t(ə)riŋ\ **swifters :** to tauten, secure, or protect with a swifter or other line; *specif* **:** to tauten (slack standing rigging) by bringing the shrouds closer together with a swiftering line — often used with *in* ⟨~ in the shrouds⟩
³swifter \"\ *n* -s [³*swift* + *-er*] **:** a worker at a swift (sense 2); *esp* **:** WINDER
swiftering line *n* [*swiftering* (gerund of ²*swifter*) + *line*] **:** a line used to swifter in rigging
swiftest *superlative of* SWIFT
swiftfoot \'=,=\ *n, pl* **swiftfoots** [¹*swift* + *foot*] **:** a European courser (*Cursorius cursor*)
swift·i·an \'swiftēən\ *adj, usu cap* [Jonathan *Swift* †1745 Eng. satirist + E *-ian*] **:** of, relating to, or characteristic of Jonathan Swift or his writings; *specif* **:** satirizing with bitter often savage irony the weakness and corruption of the human race ⟨a *Swiftian* satire⟩ ⟨*Swiftian* morality⟩
swift·let \'=lət\ *n* -s [³*swift* + *-let*] **:** a swift of the genus *Collocalia; specif* **:** a swift (*C. inexpectata*) of eastern Asia that produces the edible bird's nest
swift·ly \'swiftlē, -li\ *adv, sometimes* -ER/-EST [ME, fr. OE *swiftlīce*, fr. ¹*swift* + *-līce* -ly] **:** in a swift manner ⟨early novels had ~ established him as an important new figure —*London Calling*⟩
swift·ness \-f(t)nəs\ *n* -ES [ME *swiftnes*, fr. OE, fr. ¹*swift* + *-nes* -ness] **1 :** the quality or state of being swift **:** SPEED, CELERITY ⟨the ~ of a lizard catching a fly —Vicki Baum⟩ **2 :** the fact of being swift ⟨when ~ of action was indispensable to surprise⟩
¹swig \'swig\ *n* -s [origin unknown] **1 :** LIQUOR **2 :** a quantity drunk at one time **:** DRAFT, DRINK, PULL ⟨many ~*s* out of his father's decanter of whiskey —Hamilton Basso⟩
²swig \"\ *vb* **swigged; swigged; swigging; swigs** *vt* **:** to drink in long drafts **:** GULP ⟨fancy *swigging* a liqueur like beer —C.D.Lewis⟩ ~ *vi* **:** to take a swig **:** DRINK — **swig·ger** \-gə(r)\ *n* -s
³swig \"\ *vb* **swigged; swigged; swigging; swigs** [origin unknown] *vi* **1 :** to pull at right angles on the bight of a tackle or rope fast at one end to a weight to be raised and at the other passing through a block or around something and then to let go quickly and simultaneously take in the slack — usu. used with *off* **2 :** SWAY, ROCK; *also* **:** SWASH ~ *vt* **1 :** to hoist or set up taut (as a sail) by swigging off on a halyard or tackle — usu. used with *up* ⟨~ up a racing mainsail⟩ **2 :** to haul taut (as a rope, tackle) by swigging off on
⁴swig \"\ *n* -s **1 :** a tackle whose ropes run at a considerable angle **2 :** an act of swigging off on a tackle
swig·gle \'swigəl\ *vb* -ED/-ING/-S [by alter.] *dial* **:** SWIG
swile \'swīl\ *n* -s [origin unknown] **:** ¹SEAL
¹swill \'swil\ *vb* -ED/-ING/-S [ME *swilen*, fr. OE *swillan*, *swilian* to wash out, rinse, gargle; perh. akin to OE *swelgan* to swallow — more at SWALLOW] *vt* **1 :** WASH, DRENCH, RINSE ⟨~*ed* my hands in the enamel bowl on the washhouse table —E.L.Thomas⟩; *esp* **:** to wash by flushing with water ⟨the amount of water used for ~*ing* cowsheds and pigsties should not be more than is necessary —C.B.Palmer⟩ ⟨a pint of bitter would ~ the dryness of the barley off his lips —G.A.Wagner⟩ **2 :** to supply abundantly or fill with (as an intoxicant) ⟨~*ing* themselves with ale —George Eliot⟩ **3 a :** to drink great drafts of **:** GUZZLE ⟨were ~*ing* down gin . . . and talking with loud jocosity —Bruce Marshall⟩ **b :** to devour greedily ⟨dogs who ~ their food from the ground —Norman Kelman⟩ **4 :** to pour (a liquid) freely ⟨~ out drinks⟩ **5 :** to cause

(liquid) to swish in a container — used with *about* or *around* ⟨~s a little hot water around in the pot before steeping the tea⟩ **6** [²*swill*] : to feed (as a pig) with swill ~ *vi* **1** : to drink or eat freely, greedily, or to excess; *esp* : to drink liquor in large drafts or to excess ⟨as bad as the rest of them ... ~ing in taverns ... in planting time —Clements Ripley⟩ **2** : to flow in a free, forcible, or turbulent manner : SWASH ⟨a wave ~ed along the steps —Haldane Macfall⟩

²**swill** \"\ *n* -s **1 a** (1) : a semiliquid food for animals (as swine) composed of the animal or vegetable refuse of kitchens, markets, or stores, mixed with water or skimmed or sour milk : SLOP, WASH (2) : a hog ration made of distillery slop **b** : food refuse : GARBAGE **2** : something suggestive of slop or garbage : something evoking disgust : HOGWASH, REFUSE ⟨dismissed the whole literary production of his rival as ~⟩ **3** : an act or instance of swilling : as **a** : a draft of liquor **b** : the swash of a liquid ⟨heard the ~ of the flood waters⟩

³**swill** \"\ *n* -s [¹*swill* + *bowl*] : DRUNKARD

swill·er \'swilə(r)\ *n* -s : one that swills

swill·ing *n* -s [fr. gerund of ¹*swill*] **1** : the act or process of one that swills **2** *obs* : swill for hogs **3** *swillings pl* : dirty liquid from washing

swill milk *n* [¹*swill*] : milk given by cows fed on swill (as from a distillery)

¹**swim** \'swim\ *vb* **swam** \'swam, -aa(ə)m\ *also chiefly dial* **swimmed** \'swimd\ *or* **swum** \'swəm\ *swum also chiefly dial* **swam** *or* **swimmed**; **swimming**; **swims** [ME *swimmen*, fr. OE *swimman*; akin to OHG *swimman* to swim, ON *svimma*, Goth *swumfsl* swimming pool] *vi* **1** : to propel oneself progressively in water by natural means (as by strokes of the hands and feet or by movements of the fins, flippers, or tail) **2** : to move with a motion like that of swimming : slip or glide smoothly and quietly : FLOAT ⟨a cloud *swam* slowly across the moon⟩ **3 a** : to float on the surface of or rise to the top of a liquid : not sink ⟨oil ~s on water⟩ **b** : to overcome or surmount difficulties : not go under ⟨sink or ~, live or die, survive or perish —Daniel Webster⟩ **4** : to become immersed or flooded : become surrounded or covered or filled with or as if with a liquid ⟨the meat ~s in gravy⟩ ⟨his heart *swam* with joy⟩ ⟨he ~s in riches⟩ **5** : to appear to move unsteadily before the eyes : REEL ⟨sat down again as the room began to ~ crazily around her⟩ **6** : to be dizzy : have an unsteady or reeling sensation ⟨feels faint and his head ~s⟩ — *vt* **1 a** : to move over, cover, or cross by propelling oneself through water ⟨~ a stream⟩ ⟨~ a mile⟩ **b** : to execute (a stroke) in swimming **2 a** : to cause or compel to swim or float ⟨a horse across a river⟩ **b** : to make float or permit floating of in or on the surface of a liquid ⟨immerse the eggs in enough water to ~ the light ones⟩ **3** : to subject (one) to ordeal by water **4** : to bring to a specified state by swimming **5** : to compete with in a swimming match — **swim against the stream** : to move counter to or work against the prevailing or popular current (as in religion or politics)

²**swim** \"\ *n* -s **1** : a smooth gliding motion : SWIM BLADDER **3** : an act or period of swimming ⟨took a ~ in the bay⟩ ⟨back from his early morning ~⟩ **4** : a temporary forgetfulness, dizziness, or unconsciousness : SWOON **5 a** : a part of a stream or other water frequented by fish **b** : the current trend of affairs ⟨that manufacturers slow to make the design change would be out of the ~⟩ : the thick of fashionable activity — usu. used in the phrase *in the swim* ⟨spent his vacation at a popular resort to be in the ~⟩ **6** : a square flat overhanging bow on a barge (as used formerly in the east of England)

³**swim** \"\ *adj* : of, concerned with, or used in or for swimming ⟨~ lessons⟩ ⟨~ show⟩ ⟨~ trunks⟩

swim bladder *n* : the air bladder of a fish

swim fin *n* : FLIPPER 1b

swim·able \'swiməbəl\ *adj* : that can be swum

swim·mer \-mə(r)\ *n* -s [ME, fr. *swimmen* to swim + *-er*] **1** : one that swims **2** : a body part (as a specialized appendage) used in swimming

swim·mer·et *also* **swim·mer·ette** \'swimə'ret\ *n* -s [*swimmer* + *-et*, *-ette*] : one of a series of small unspecialized appendages under the abdomen of many crustaceans that are best developed in some decapods and are used in some cases for swimming but usu. for carrying eggs

swimmer's itch *n* : SCHISTOSOME DERMATITIS

swim·mi·ly \'swiməlē, -li\ *adv* : in a swimmy manner

swim·mi·ness \-mēnəs, -min-\ *n* -es : the quality or state of being swimmy

¹**swim·ming** \'swimiŋ, -mēŋ\ *n* -s [ME, fr. gerund of *swimmen* to swim] **1** : the act, art, or sport of swimming and diving **2 a** : VERTIGO, DIZZINESS **b** : blurred or dazzled vision (as in dizziness)

²**swimming** *adj* [fr. pres. part. of ¹*swim*] **1 a** : that swims : capable of or habituated to swimming ⟨a ~ bird⟩ **b** [¹*swimming*] : adapted to or used in or for swimming ⟨a ~ stroke⟩ ⟨a ~ lash⟩ **2** : filled or flooded with or as if with water ⟨~ eyes⟩ **3** : being in or affected by a state of vertigo or dizziness ⟨~ brain⟩

swimming bath *n*, *Brit* : SWIMMING POOL

swimming bell *n* : a bell-shaped swimming organ in some siphonophores composed of a greatly modified zooid without mouth or tentacles and serving to propel the colony by its rhythmical contractions : NECTOPHORE, NECTOCALYX

swimming bladder *n* **1** : the air bladder of a fish **2** : PNEUMATOCYST

swimming crab *n* : any of numerous marine crabs esp. of the family Portunidae that have some of the joints of one or more pairs of legs flattened and fringed so as to serve as fins

swimming funnel *n* : a large forwardly directed tube in cephalopods opening just behind and below the neck through which the water from the mantle cavity is discharged with the animal being able to swim backward by suddenly expelling water through it

swimming hole *n* : a comparatively deep place in a stream locally used for swimming

swim·ming·ly *adv* [*swimming* (pres. part. of ¹*swim*) + *-ly*] : in the easy, smooth, or steadily progressive manner of one swimming; *esp* : PROSPEROUSLY, SUCCESSFULLY ⟨in spite of one or two minor mishaps everything was going ~ —P.L.Fermor⟩

swimming plate *n* : one of the platelike rows of fused cilia forming the combs of a ctenophore

swimming pool *also* **swim pool** *n* : a pool suitable for swimming; *esp* : a tank (as of concrete or plastic) made for swimming

swimming sandpiper *n* : PHALAROPE

swimming stone *n* : FLOATSTONE 1

swim·my \'swimē, -mi\ *adj* -ER/-EST [¹*swim* + *-y*] **1** : verging on, causing, or affected by dizziness or giddiness : tending toward vertigo ⟨~ with the local cider —Clemence Dane⟩ **2** : of vision : BLURRED, UNSTEADY ⟨had red patches on his cheeks and his eyes were ~ —Greville Texidor⟩

swim ring *n* : an inflated ring of rubber or plastic material that a person may take into the water and hold onto for buoyancy

swimsuit \'swim‚süt\ *n* -s : BATHING SUIT; *esp* : MAILLOT

swin·burn·ian \swin'bərnēən, -bən-‚bȯiə-, -nyən\ *adj*, *usu cap* [*Algernon Charles Swinburne* †1909 Eng. poet + *-ian*] : of, relating to, or having the characteristics of Swinburne or his writings ⟨*Swinburnian* rhythms⟩

¹**swin·dle** \'swin'd°l\ *vb* **swindled**; **swindled**; **swindling** \-d(ə)liŋ\ **swindles** [back-formation fr. *swindler*] *vt* : to obtain money or property from one by fraud or deceit : practice imposture or deceit for gain — *vt* : to deprive of money or property by fraud or deceit : cheat ⟨~ the unwary with fakes⟩ **syn** see CHEAT

²**swindle** \"\ *n* -s **1** : the act or process of swindling or defrauding **2** : an instance of swindling : FRAUD

swin·dle·able \-d(ə)ləbəl\ *adj* : that can be swindled : GULLIBLE

swin·dler \-d(ə)lə(r)\ *n* -s [G *schwindler* giddy person,

fantastic schemer, fr. *schwindeln* to be dizzy, fr. OHG *swintilōn*, freq. of *swintan* to diminish, vanish, become unconscious; akin to OE *swindan* to languish, vanish, OIr *a-sennad* finally] : one that swindles : CHEAT, SHARPER

swindle sheet *n*, *slang* : EXPENSE ACCOUNT

swin·dling·ly *adv* [*swindling* (pres. part. of ¹*swindle*) + *-ly*] : in a swindling manner

¹**swine** \'swīn\ *n*, *pl* **swine** *often attrib* [ME, fr. OE *swīn*; akin to OHG *swin* swine, ON *svín*, Goth *swein*, L *suinus* of swine, *sus* swine, hog— more at sow] **1** : any of various animals that constitute the family Suidae and comprise stout-bodied short-legged omnivorous mammals with a thick skin usu. covered with coarse bristles, a rather long mobile snout, small tail, and two functional and except in peccaries two nonfunctional hoofed digits; *specif* : a domesticated member of the species (*Sus scrofa*) that includes the European wild boar — usu. used collectively **2** : a contemptible person

swine back *n* : HOGBACK

swine-backed \'‚‚\ *adj* [*swine back* + *-ed*] **1** : having a hog-back **2** : convexly curved ⟨a *swine-backed* bow⟩

swine belt *n* : an area in the north-central U.S. in which hog raising is a major farm enterprise and which is more or less coextensive with the corn belt

swine-chopped \'‚‚\ *adj*, *of a dog* : having an overshot jaw

swine cress *or* **swine's-cress** \'swīnz‚‚\ *n*, *pl* **swine's-cresses** : a cress of the genus *Coronopus* — called also wart cress

swine dysentery *n* : an acute infectious hemorrhagic dysentery of swine that is possibly a severe form of necrotic enteritis

swine erysipelas *n* : a destructive contagious disease of various mammals and birds that is caused by a bacterium (*Erysipelothrix rhusiopathiae*) that may occur in an acute highly fatal septicemic form or take a chronic course marked by endocarditis, arthritis, or urticaria, and that is of esp. economic importance in swine and domesticated turkeys — called also *erysipelas*; see DIAMOND SKIN DISEASE, ERYSIPELOID

swine fever *n* : HOG CHOLERA

swineherd \'‚‚‚\ *n* [ME, fr. OE *swȳnhyrde*, fr. *swīn* swine + *hyrde* herd] : one who tends swine

swineherd's disease \'‚‚‚-\ *also* **swineherder's disease** \'‚‚‚-\ *n* : LEPTOSPIROSIS

swine influenza *n* : an acute contagious febrile disease of swine marked by severe coughing and inflammation of the upper respiratory tract, sometimes passing into bronchopneumonia but rarely fatal, and caused by interaction of a specific virus introduced by the swine lungworm and a bacterium (*Hemophilus suis*) related to that of human influenza

swinelike \'‚‚‚\ *adj* : resembling swine

swine-man \'‚man\ *n*, *pl* **swinemen** : one in charge of or specializing in the raising of swine

swinepipe \'‚‚‚\ *n* : REDWING 1

swine plague *n* : hemorrhagic septicemia of swine with symptoms resembling those of hog cholera but commonly complicated by pneumonia

swine pox *n* **1** *obs* : CHICKENPOX ⟨found her up and merry as it did not prove the smallpox but the *swine pox* —Samuel Pepys⟩ **2** : a mild virus disease of young pigs marked by fever, loss of appetite, dullness, and production of skin lesions suggestive of those of smallpox and caused by either of two unrelated viruses, one of which is related to the viruses of smallpox and cowpox

swin·ery \'swīn(ə)rē, -ri\ *n* -ES [*swine* + *-ery*] **1 a** : a place where swine are kept **2** : a swinish condition or action **3 a** : group of swine

swine's-feather \'‚‚‚‚\ *also* **swine's-pike** \'‚‚‚\ *n*, *pl* **swine's-feathers** *also* **swine's-pikes** [trans. of G *schweinsfeder*; so called fr. its being originally used as a hunting weapon] : a stake or spear resembling a bayonet formerly fixed in a musket rest or placed in the ground to hinder cavalry

swine's-grass \'‚‚‚\ *n*, *pl* **swine's-grasses** : KNOTGRASS 1

swine's-succory \'‚‚‚‚\ *n*, *pl* **swine's-succories** **1** : CHICORY **2** : LAMB SUCCORY

swinestone \'‚‚‚\ *n* [trans. of G *schweinstein*; so called fr. its unpleasant odor] : a black bituminous limestone that usu. emits a fetid smell when rubbed

swinesty \'‚‚‚\ *n* : PIGSTY

swine typhoid *n* : NECROTIC ENTERITIS

¹**swing** \'swiŋ\ *vb* **swung** \'swəŋ\ *also chiefly dial* **swang** \'swaŋ, -aiŋ\ **swung; swinging; swings** [ME *swingen* to strike, beat, fling, hurl, rush, fr. OE *swingan* to strike, beat, fling oneself, rush; akin to OHG *swingan* to fling, rush, Goth *afswaggwjan* to make doubtful; basic meaning: to move with a rotating motion] *vt* **1 a** : to cause (something grasped or attached at one point) to move vigorously through a wide circle or arc : wield with a sweep or flourish ⟨charged the rival gang ~ing clubs and knives⟩ ⟨~ an axe⟩ ⟨~ a bat⟩ ⟨~ a scythe⟩ ⟨went for each other ~ing their fists⟩ ⟨jumped aside when the porcupine *swung* his tail⟩ **b** (1) : to cause (something suspended) to sway to and fro ⟨troops that marched and *swung* their arms in time with their song⟩ (2) : to give (a person) a ride in something (as a swing, hammock) that sways to and fro **c** (1) : to cause to turn on an axis : make rotate or pivot ⟨a gust that *swung* the door to⟩ (2) : to cause to face or move in another direction ⟨grasp him by the shoulder and ~ him around⟩ ⟨~ the gun towards them and fire⟩ ⟨~ the car into a side road⟩ (3) : to execute a swing with (a square dance partner) ⟨~ your partner once around⟩ **d** (1) : to turn (a ship or airplane) to successive compass points (as the cardinal and quadrantal points) in order to ascertain and correct or record magnetic compass deviations by comparing on each heading the compass bearing of an object (as a distant landmark, the sun, a mark on an airport swinging base) with its known true magnetic bearing ⟨a tabulation of the deviation on different headings as made from the data obtained by ~ing ship —*Bluejackets' Manual*⟩ (2) : to ascertain the deviation of (an airplane compass) by so swinging the airplane usu. on a swinging base **2** : to attach (as from an overhead support or by hinges) so as to permit swaying or turning : cause to hang : SUSPEND ⟨~ a hammock between nearby trees⟩ **3** : to convey by suspension from a support ⟨huge cranes that ~ cargo up over the ship's side and into the hold⟩ **4** *of a lathe or lathe centers* : to be capable of holding for turning ⟨a lathe that ~s 12 inches⟩ **5 a** (1) : to exercise a determining influence on : influence decisively ⟨whether the labor vote will ~ the presidential election⟩ ⟨a lobby that ~s a lot of votes in the legislature⟩ (2) : to cause to change in attitude, loyalty, or outcome ⟨~ a bat-hater from fear and disgust to avid interest —R.K.Plumb⟩ (3) : to cause to rally or conform ⟨~ 20,000 workers behind the party line —C.H.Arke⟩ **b** : to succeed in doing, making, or having : bring about : MANAGE, ACCOMPLISH ⟨whether he is man enough to ~ the job⟩ ⟨the sale by entertaining the customer⟩ ⟨sure he can ~ a new car on his income⟩ **c** : to exert or be able to exert — used with *weight* ⟨got the job through a friend who ~s a lot of weight in city politics⟩ **6** [²*swing*] : to play or sing (as a melody) in the style of swing music ⟨~ a folk song⟩ — *vi* **1** : to move freely to and fro (as in suspension from an overhead support) ⟨the pendulum ~s with great regularity⟩ ⟨a basket ~s from her arm⟩ **b** : to ride in a swing **2 a** : to die by hanging ⟨was caught spying and made to ~ for it⟩ **b** : to hang freely from a support : be in suspension ⟨gray Spanish moss, ~ing from live oak and cypress —*Amer. Guide Series: La.*⟩ **3** : to turn on or as if on an axis : move in or describe a circle or arc: as **a** : to move with the wind or tide around a single anchor or mooring ⟨a ship *swung* in the roadstead, awaiting cargo —Carleton Mitchell⟩ **b** : to go in a swinging curve ⟨~s around the corner with a squeal of tires⟩ ⟨a plane that *swung* low over the field and nosed up again⟩ ⟨the highway ~s north around the end of the mountain —G.R.Stewart⟩ **c** : to turn on a hinge or pivot ⟨doors that ~ open automatically⟩ **d** : to turn in place : face a different direction : WHEEL ⟨she *swung* on a high heel and walked away —Wilson Collison⟩ **e** : to convey oneself from one point to another by swaying or pivoting on a fixed support ⟨~ aboard the train as it pulls out⟩ ⟨put one foot in the stirrup and ~ up into the saddle⟩ ⟨monkeys that ~ from limb to limb through the jungle⟩ **1** : to turn about with a partner in dancing : execute a swing ⟨gents ~ in and ladies ~ out⟩ **4 a** : to sound with or have a steady pulsing rhythm ⟨likes verses that ~⟩ **b** [²*swing*] : to play or sing with a lively compelling rhythm ⟨pomps ... of life chronicled in ~ing

hymnbook rhythms —*Brit. Bk. News*⟩; *specif* : to play swing music ⟨this band ~s more than anything since the bop era began —W.C.Herman⟩ **c** : to dance in swing or jazz style **5** : to shift or fluctuate from one condition, form, position, or object of attention or favor to another (as an opposite) ⟨constantly from optimism to pessimism and back —Sinclair Lewis⟩ ⟨leading newspapers ... *swung* against him —S.P. Brewer⟩ **6 a** : to move along with free, swaying movements ⟨a cocky, swaggering bunch of Americans *swung* along the jungle trail —Dave Richardson⟩ ⟨long Pacific rollers ~ing in rank after rank —Thomas Wood †1950⟩ **b** : to start up in a smooth vigorous manner ⟨minutemen who were ready to ~ into action against the British at a moment's notice —*Amer. Guide Series: Mass.*⟩ ⟨heard the musicians ~ into their first tune —Earl Hammer⟩ ⟨haul up the prisoning anchor, ~ out upon the tide —Bertha Runkle⟩ **7** : to hit or aim at something with a sweeping arm movement ⟨a fast ball that the batter *swung* at and missed⟩ ⟨told the boxer to go to the ring *swinging* at and missed⟩ ⟨thinking I was being held up, I *swung* on him with all I had —H.A.Chippendale⟩ ⟨mounts his gun to his shoulder quickly but smoothly, ~s on the target ... touches the trigger while the gun is still in motion —*Amer. Rifleman*⟩ **8** : to ascertain the deviation of a magnetic ship or airplane compass by swinging the ship or plane **9** : to make a circuit : take a side trip ⟨promised to ~ by and pick them up⟩ : take a tour ⟨*swung* through his district campaigning⟩ **10** : to change direction in skiing by a swing

syn SWAY, OSCILLATE, VIBRATE, FLUCTUATE, PENDULATE, WAVER, UNDULATE: SWING implies a movement back and forth or in one direction of something attached at one side or one end ⟨swing like a pendulum⟩ ⟨the door *swung* open⟩ ⟨*swing* a lasso around your head⟩ SWAY implies a back and forward or teetering movement, usu. of an upright object esp. flexible or unsteady ⟨the bamboos at the corner of the house *swayed* slowly under a gentle night wind —Pearl Buck⟩ ⟨*sway* to the rhythm of the music⟩ ⟨the chimney *swayed* under the shock of the explosion⟩ OSCILLATE suggests the swinging of a pendulum, implying a movement, usu. rapid, between two points, poles, or conditions ⟨an *oscillating* reed⟩ ⟨it is clear that Bohemianism has continuously *oscillated* between the poles of escape and revolt —Harry Levin⟩ ⟨*oscillating* between humility and hatred —Francis Golffing⟩ VIBRATE, sometimes interchangeable with OSCILLATE, usu. implies a motion like the pulsating of a string on a musical instrument when plucked or struck or a periodic motion in alternating directions ⟨a car *vibrating* with the irregularity of the motor's explosions⟩ ⟨the ultrasonic, or high frequency, waves *vibrate* so fast they can't be heard by the human ear —Boyd Wright⟩ ⟨on summer evenings when the air *vibrated* with the song of insects —Sherwood Anderson⟩ FLUCTUATE implies constant irregular alternations suggestive of the movements of waves ⟨food prices *fluctuate* according to the law of supply and demand⟩ ⟨a handsome, confused and narcissistic woman who continually *fluctuates* between coldness and torturing kindness —Jean Garrigue⟩ ⟨causes the respiration, pulse, and blood pressure of the test subject to *fluctuate* widely from the normal —H.G.Armstrong⟩ PENDULATE, rare, is close to OSCILLATE, suggesting a swinging between two extremes or a similar constant change ⟨*pendulated* between extremes —John Cournos⟩ WAVER stresses an unsteady or uncertain swinging ⟨a reed *wavering* in the wind⟩ ⟨*waver* between love and hate⟩ UNDULATE suggests a steady gentle fluctuation as of a continuous rolling or rippling sea ⟨the great serpent drew back like a flash, and turning, *undulated* slowly away —William Beebe⟩ ⟨the country round with its *undulating* meadows —S.P.B.Mais⟩ ⟨blue hills, *undulating* like waves — *Amer. Guide Series: Ark.*⟩

syn WAVE, FLOURISH, BRANDISH, SHAKE, THRASH: SWING indicates regular oscillation back and forth or continuous rotation around ⟨*swinging* his arms as he walked⟩ ⟨*swinging* the pail over his head⟩ WAVE implies undulating, fluttering, or streaming motion without rhythmical regularity, as in signaling, warning, or greeting ⟨*wave* to an acquaintance⟩ ⟨*waved* a flag⟩ ⟨the guard laughed and *waved* him through the gate —A.W.Long⟩ ⟨you cannot *wave* a wand over the country and say "Let there be Socialism": at least nothing will happen if you do —G.B.Shaw⟩ FLOURISH may imply triumph, bravado, or ostentation in waving or swinging ⟨rushed into my room *flourishing* a handsome volume —M.R.Cohen⟩ ⟨*flourishing* his cane as he strolled along⟩ SHAKE may but does not always imply forceful or violent motion or movement ⟨*shake* a rug⟩ ⟨*shake* a tree to bring down the fruit⟩ ⟨*shake* your fist in another's face⟩ BRANDISH usu. involves a shaking or waving with menace or threat ⟨*brandishing* their swords⟩ ⟨striking what appeared to them to be most belligerent attitudes, *brandishing* his machete —Thomas Barbour⟩ THRASH suggests the action of a flail in threshing grain; it may apply to any vigorous swinging or beating ⟨on a blanket on the nursery floor and watched him proudly while he *thrashed* his sturdy arms and legs —Marcia Davenport⟩ **syn** see in addition HANDLE

— **swing round the circle 1** : to cover all points of a topical outline **2** : to hold in turn all the various positions or conflicting beliefs ⟨had *swung round the circle* of theories and systems ... without finding relief —A.V.G.Allen⟩ **3** : to make a tour of a constituency to deliver speeches and explain one's policies —used of a political candidate — **swing the lead** [fr. the feeling that the task of sounding with the lead is a comparatively light assignment for a sailor] *Brit* : MALINGER

²**swing** \"\ *n* -s **1** : an act or instance of swinging : swinging movement: as **a** (1) : a stroke or blow delivered with a sweeping arm movement (the basic techniques of golf — stance, grip, and ~ —*Official Sports Guide*⟩ ⟨a batter with a powerful ~⟩; *specif* : a round-arm blow in boxing ⟨knocked out ... with a right ~ —P.J.Cunningham⟩ (2) : a sweeping or rhythmic movement of the body or a bodily part ⟨dismounted with an easy ~⟩ ⟨the machinelike ~ of the bodies of the plant setters —Sherwood Anderson⟩ (3) : a square dance figure variously executed in which two dancers join arms or hands and dance around a point between them — see WALTZ SWING (4) : jazz dancing in moderate tempo with a peculiar lilting syncopation — see JITTERBUG (5) : a skiing turn executed by a rhythmical crouch-spring-crouch succession of movements combined with a simultaneous turn and inward leaning of the body and a turning of both skis (6) : a gymnastic movement in which the body describes an arc forward or backward around the point of support **b** (1) : the regular movement of a freely suspended object (as a pendulum) along an arc and back : the action of swinging to and fro from a fixed point or on a fixed axis (2) : steady movement to and fro between wide limits : back and forth sweep ⟨the ~ of the tides⟩ ⟨the rains follow the sun in its annual ~ north and south —Tom Marvel⟩ (3) : the horizontal motion of a boom or shovel — compare CROWD, HOIST **c** (1) : steady pulsing rhythm (as in poetry or music) ⟨a perfect metrical ~ of the modern kind should have been attained by one poet —George Saintsbury⟩ (2) : a steady vigorous movement characterizing an activity or creative work ⟨his ~ and gusto, his abundant detail, and the swift excitement of his narrative —*Times Lit. Supp.*⟩ — often used in the phrase *go with a swing* (the small, informal evening party will go with a ~ —Agnes M. Miall⟩ (3) : a trend toward a high or low point in a fluctuating cycle of interest rates, prices, or any business activity ⟨industrialized nations have been subject to periodic ~s of prosperity and depression —Asher Achinstein⟩ (2) : an often periodic shift from one condition, form, position, or object of attention or favor to another (as an opposite) ⟨manic depressive ~s⟩ ⟨in a wave of ... straining for novelty, with constant ~s of style from one extreme to the other —Thomas Munro⟩ ⟨the ~ to diesels on U.S. railroads—*Time*⟩ **2** *obs* : an impulsion from within : natural bent or bias : INCLINATION (2) : a swinging ⟨letting youth have its ~⟩ (3) : liberty of action : free scope ⟨LICENSE, REIN ⟨given full ~ in the conduct of the business⟩ **b** *archaic* : controlling au-

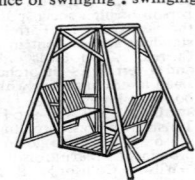

lawn swing 5a

thority : ruling power **c** (1) : the driving power of something swung or hurled ⟨the ~ of a battering ram against a wall⟩ (2) : steady vigorous advance : driving speed ⟨a train approaching at full ~⟩ **3 a** : the progression of an activity, process, or phase of existence : COURSE, PROGRESS — usu. used in the phrase *in full swing* ⟨when the work is in full ~ this summer some fifteen thousand men . . . will be engaged on the highway —Harold Griffin⟩ **b** : the normal round or pace of activities ⟨will take you a couple of days . . . to get into the ~ of things —Richard Joseph⟩ **c** : a state of vigorous activity ⟨got production into full ~ after a slow start⟩ — usu. used in the phrase *in full swing* ⟨animated conversation was still in full ~ in the small hours —Enid McLeod⟩ **4 a** : the arc or range through which something swings : the distance between the outer limits to which something swings ⟨a pendulum with a 3-inch ~⟩ **b** : the capacity of a turning lathe measured in the U.S. by the diameter of the largest object that can be turned on it and in England by half this measurement **5** : any of various objects that swing freely from or on a support: as **a** : an apparatus for recreation consisting of a seat suspended from a support (as by a looped rope or two chains) **b** : an amusement park ride in which the rider is mechanically revolved on a vertical or oblique plane in a suspended seat or compartment **c** : the movable part of a swing bridge **d** : the swingable part of a logging boom by means of which the boom is opened or closed **e** : SWINGBACK **6** : a curving course or outline: as **a** : a course from and back to a point or place : a circular tour (as of a political candidate) **b** : the curvature of the outer side of a shoe sole **7** : the lateral margins of a herd of cattle being driven : the sides of a trail herd; *also* : SWINGMEN **8** *or* **swing music** : music usu. modified and arranged for a large commercial dance band characterized by a lively insistent rhythm, a basic melody often submerged in improvisation, and a collective use of syncopated rhythms — compare JAZZ **9** : a score in contract bridge resulting from a swing hand **10** : an interval in a continuous work period during which a regular worker or shift takes a recess and a relief worker or alternate shift carries on : BREAK — **swing around the circle** : a tour about the country for political campaigning (as by a presidential candidate) ⟨whistle-stopped in 43 of the 50 states in his *swing around the circle*⟩

³**swing** \"\ *adj* [in sense 1, fr. ¹*swing;* in other senses, fr. ²*swing*] **1 a** : hinged or pivoted so as to permit swinging into a desired position or in either direction ⟨a ~ handle⟩ ⟨a ~ sash⟩ **b** : HANGING, SUSPENDED ⟨a ~ lamp⟩ **2** : of, belonging to, or used as a swing ⟨a ~ rope⟩ **3** : of, performing, or performed in the style of musical swing ⟨~ fans⟩ ⟨~ musicians⟩ ⟨~ tunes⟩ **4** : that may swing often decisively either way on an issue or in an election ⟨the candidate's need to attract the ~ vote⟩ ⟨the court's ~ man — whose vote is often decisive in close cases —*Newsweek*⟩ **5** : relieving other workers as needed : RELIEF ⟨a ~ chef⟩

swing·able \ˈswiŋəbəl\ *adj* : that can be swung — **swing·ably** \-blē\ *adv*

¹**swingback** \ˈ=,=\ *n* [³*swing* + *back*, n.] **1** : a pivoting back for some cameras that allows the film or plateholder to be tilted for correcting or distorting the perspective in a photograph or for shifting the focal plane so as to bring oblique objects into focus **2** : swayback of lambs

²**swingback** \"\ *n* -S [fr. the phrase *swing back*, fr. ¹*swing* + *back*, adv.] : a movement of reaction (as a return to favor or influence of a political party)

swing bar *n* [³*swing*] : a pivoted or hinged bar (as a whippletree)

swing beam *also* **swing bolster** *n* : a crosspiece sustaining a railroad-car body so suspended that it may have an independent lateral motion

swingboat \ˈ=,=\ *n* : one of a group of boat-shaped commercial amusement swings (as at a British fair) having facing seats and propelled by the riders

swing bolt *n* : EYEBOLT

swing bridge *also* **swing drawbridge** *n* : a drawbridge that

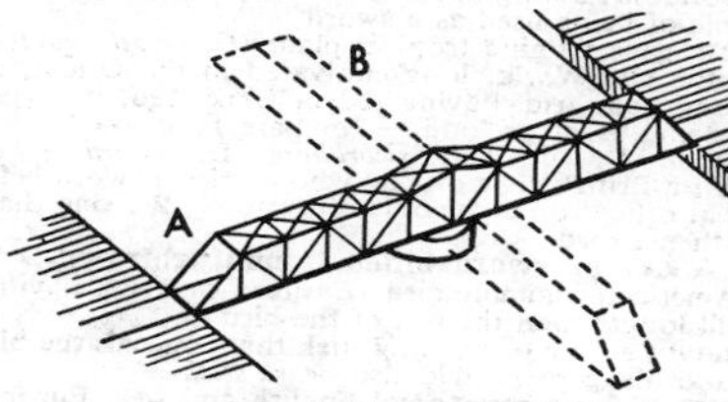

swing bridge: *A* closed; *B* open

opens and closes to river craft by rotating around a central pier — called also *swivel bridge;* compare LIFT BRIDGE

swing credit *n* : a credit provided for in the terms of an international trade agreement permitting trade to be unbalanced to a stated extent in either direction without settlement during the term of the agreement

swingdevil \ˈ=,==\ *n* : a common European swift

swing door *or* **swinging door** *n* : a door that can be pushed open from either side and that swings to when released ⟨the *swing door* between the pantry and dining room⟩ ⟨push through the *swinging doors* of a waterfront dive⟩

¹**swinge** \ˈswinj\ *vt* **swinged; swinged; swingeing; swinges** [ME *swengen* to shake, move violently, fr. OE *swengan;* akin to OE *swingan* to beat, fling oneself, rush — more at SWING] **1** *chiefly dial* : BEAT, SCOURGE, THRASH ⟨the young dogs — ~ them to the labor —Robert Burns⟩ **2** *obs* : REVOLVE, WHIRL **3** *obs* : to swing (a tail) violently : LASH

²**swinge** *n* -S **1** *obs* : POWER, AUTHORITY **2** *obs* : freedom of action : SWING 2a(3) **3** *obs* : driving power : IMPETUS

³**swinge** \ˈswinj\ *vt* **swinged; swinged; swingeing; swinges** [alter. of *singe*] *dial* : SINGE, SCORCH ⟨a-*swingeing* the pinfeathers off that gobbler — Frances Gaither⟩

¹**swinge·ing** *or* **swing·ing** \-njiŋ, -jēŋ\ *adj* [fr. pres. part. of ¹*swinge*] *chiefly Brit* : superlative in size, amount, or character : very large or good : WHOPPING, CAPITAL ⟨the ~ penalty . . . though dropped to half to secure payment, stopped the trade for a time —John Craig⟩ ⟨Parliament asserted its "Loyal Devotion to his Royal Person" in ~ terms —Nicholas Monsarrat⟩

²**swingeing** *or* **swinging** \"\ *adv, chiefly Brit* : to a swingeing degree : SUPERLATIVELY, VERY ⟨we reckon the time's coming when we'll want it ~ bad —P.L.Ford⟩

¹**swing·er** \ˈswiŋə(r)\ *n* -S [¹*swing* + *-er*] : one that swings

²**swing·er** \ˈswinjə(r)\ *n* -S [¹*swinge* + *-er*] **1** : one that swinges **2** : a swingeing example or instance : WHOPPER

swing ferry *n* [³*swing*] : a ferryboat operated by a cable and the river current

swing front *n* : a pivoting front for some cameras that allows the lens to be tilted with respect to the camera axis for correcting or distorting the perspective in a photograph

swing gate *n* : a gate that swings in either direction and closes when released

swing-glass \ˈ=,=\ *n* : CHEVAL GLASS

swing hammer crusher *n* : HAMMER MILL 2

swing hand *n* : a deal in a contract bridge tournament in which a choice of bids or plays results or may result in a large gain (as 500 points or more) for one side

swingier *comparative of* SWINGY

swingiest *superlative of* SWINGY

¹**swing·ing** \ˈswiŋiŋ, -ēŋ\ *n* -S [fr. gerund of ¹*swing*] **1** : the action or act of one that swings **2 a** : variation in frequency of a transmitted radio wave that may be observed either as a variation in the beat frequency in beat reception or as a variation in received signal intensity **b** : FADING

²**swinging** \"\ *adj* [fr. pres. part. of ¹*swing*] **1** : that swings : characterized by swing or a swing ⟨a ~ flower basket⟩ ⟨a ~ pace⟩ **2** *of a livestock brand* : suspended from a horizontal quarter circle — see BRAND illustration

swinging bar *n* [²*swinging*] : SWING BAR

swinging base *n* : a permanent circular turntable at an airplane factory or airport marked with the cardinal and quadrantal points of the compass for swinging an airplane to ascertain compass deviation

swinging boom *n* : LOWER BOOM

swinging buoy *n* [¹*swinging*] : one of a group of buoys used in swinging ship

¹**swing·ing·ly** \ˈswinjiŋlē, -jēŋ-, -li\ *adv* [¹*swingeing, swinging* + *-ly*] *chiefly Brit* : SWINGEING

²**swing·ing·ly** \ˈswiŋiŋlē, -li\ *adv* [²*swinging* + *-ly*] : in a swinging manner : with a swinging movement

swinging play *n* : a game similar to a dance in which participants swing each other by the hands or waist to the music of ballad-singing — see PLAY-PARTY

swinging post *n* [²*swinging*] : GATEPOST

swinging ring *n* : a gymnastic ring usu. made of metal covered with leather or rubber and suspended so as to swing freely at the end of a rope

swing jack *n* [³*swing*] : TRAVERSING SCREW JACK

swing joint *n* : a pipe joint so constructed that the parts joined are movable either so that one of the parts may be rotated relative to the other or so that one of the parts in addition to being rotatable relative to the other may be moved about its own axis — called also respectively *single swing joint, double swing joint*

swing knife *n* : SWINGLE 1

¹**swin·gle** \ˈswiŋgəl\ *n* -S [ME *swingel, swengil,* fr. MD *swinghel, swenghel* instrument for beating flax, swipe; akin to OE *swingell* whip, rod, blow, *swingan* to strike, beat — more at SWING] **1** : a wooden instrument like a large knife that is about two feet long, has one thin edge, and is used for beating and cleaning flax : SCUTCHER **2 a** : the swiple of a flail **b** : a cudgel resembling a flail **3** : a lever resembling a spoke and used for turning the barrel in wire drawing or the roller of a plate press

²**swingle** \"\ *vt* **swingled; swingled; swingling** \-g(ə)liŋ\ **swingles** [ME *swinglen,* fr. MD *swinghelen,* fr. *swinghel* swingle] : to clean by beating with a swingle : separate away the coarse and woody parts of : SCUTCH

swing leaf *n* [³*swing*] : one of two swinging doors or casements of a double door or window

swinglebar \ˈ=,=,=\ *n* [¹*swingle* + *bar*] *Brit* : WHIFFLETREE

swing leg *n* [³*swing*] : a hinged leg without stretcher that supports the drop leaf of a table

swingle staff *n* : SWINGLE 1

swingletail \ˈ=,=,=\ *or* **swingletail shark** *n* : THRESHER SHARK

swin·gle·tree \ˈswiŋgəl·(,)trē, -l·tri\ *n* [¹*swingle* + *tree*] : WHIFFLETREE

swingling tow *also* **swingle tow** *n* [*swingling tow* fr. *swingling* (gerund of ²*swingle*) + *tow; swingle tow* fr. ²*swingle*] : coarse flax separated by swingling and hatcheling

swing·man \ˈ=mən\ *n, pl* **swingmen** [in sense 1, fr. ²*swing;* in other senses, fr. ³*swing*] **1** *or* **swing rider** : one of usu. two cowboys riding at each side of a trail herd behind the point men and ahead of the flank riders or the tail riders to prevent straying and keep other cattle out **2** : ROUNDSMAN 3 **3** : a superintendent of a dairy route

swing music *n* : SWING 8

swing-over \ˈ=,=,=\ *n* -S [fr. the phrase *swing over,* fr. ¹*swing* + *over*] : a marked shift of opinion or favor ⟨the *swing-over* to conservatism displayed in the four recent by-elections —*Economist*⟩

swing pipe *n* [³*swing*] : a discharge pipe on a tank the extended intake end of which can be raised (as to drain only a floating layer)

swing plate *n* : a plate that may be swung about a pivot and clamped

swing plow *n* **1** : a plow without a fore wheel under the beam **2** : SWIVEL PLOW

swing port *n* : a port with a hinged cover in the gunwale of a ship

swing room *n* [²*swing*] : a room in which postal employees temporarily off duty may spend their time

swings *pres 3d sing of* SWING, *pl of* SWING

swing saw *n* [³*swing*] : a circular saw on a swinging frame

swing shift *n* **1 a** : the shift usu. from 4 p.m. to midnight **b** : the workers working the swing shift between the day and night shifts in a factory operating 24 hours a day **2** : a group of workers in a factory operating seven days a week that mans the place as needed to permit the regular shift workers to have one or more free days per week

swing shifter *n* [*swing shift* + *-er*] : a worker on a swing shift

swing sickness *n* [²*swing*] : MOTION SICKNESS

swing-stock \ˈswiŋ+,-\ *n* [²*swingle* + *stock*] : a timber against the blunt top edge of which flax is laid to be swingled

swing-swang \ˈswiŋ,swaŋ, -aiŋ\ *n* -S [redupl. of ²*swing*] : a swing backward and forward (as of a pendulum)

swing team *n* : the middle pair of a 6-mule or 6-horse team — compare LEADER, WHEELHORSE

swing tool *n* [³*swing*] : a device swung on centers so as to yield to unequal pressure in which delicate work (as parts of a watch) is held to be polished

swingy \ˈswiŋē, -iŋi\ *adj* -ER/-EST [¹*swing* + *-y*] **1** : marked by swing : SWINGING **2** : offering more resistance to a sliding stone — used of ice in curling

swin·ish \ˈswīnish, -nēsh\ *adj* [*swine* + *-ish*] : of, suggesting, or befitting swine; *esp* : characterized by grossness or gluttony : BEASTLY, SENSUAL ⟨the aristocratic contempt of the Federalists for that same ~ multitude —V.L.Parrington⟩ — **swin·ish·ly** \-nəshlē, -nēsh-, -li\ *adv* — **swin·ish·ness** \-nishnəs, -nēsh-\ *n* -ES

¹**swink** \ˈswiŋk\ *vi* -ED/-ING/-S [ME *swinken,* fr. OE *swincan;* akin to OE *swingan* to fling oneself, rush — more at SWING] *archaic* : LABOR, TOIL, SLAVE

²**swink** \"\ *n* -S [ME, labor, trouble, affliction, fr. OE *swinc,* fr. *swincan* to swink] *archaic* : LABOR, DRUDGERY

swinney *var of* SWEENY

swi·no·mish \swəˈnōmish\ *n, pl* **swinomish** *or* **swinomishes** *usu cap* **1 a** : a Salishan people of Whidbey island and the lower Skagit river valley, Washington **b** : a member of such people **2** : a dialect related to Skagit

swint *var of* SUINT

¹**swipe** \ˈswīp\ *n* -S [prob. alter. of ²*sweep*] **1** *dial chiefly Brit* : a pole or bar used as a lever or swivel : SWAPE: as **a** : SWEEP 1a **b** : a starting lever for a portable engine **2** : a strong sweeping blow or stroke (as with a bat or club or paw of an animal) **3** : a long drink : DRAFT **4** : one who takes care of horses : GROOM **5** : a progression of two or more chords sung (as by a barbershop quartet) on a single syllable **6** : resource material (as clippings, tear sheets, brochures) from outside sources filed for use in advertising or fashion design

²**swipe** \"\ *vb* -ED/-ING/-S [partly alter. of ¹*sweep;* partly fr. ¹*swipe*] *vi* **1** : to cut, strike, or hit with a sweeping motion — often used with *at* ⟨~*s* away at the punching bag —Gertrude Samuels⟩ **2** : to drink a mug of liquor at one draft ~ *vt* **1** : to give a swipe to : strike or wipe with a sweeping motion ⟨an upper wing tore loose and *swiped* the cockpit going past —L.S.Jamieson⟩ **2** : SNATCH, PILFER ⟨caught *swiping* watermelons from a farmer's patch⟩ **syn** see STEAL

swip·er \-pə(r)\ *n* -S : one that swipes

swipes \ˈswīps\ *n pl* [origin unknown] *Brit* : poor, thin, or spoiled beer : small beer; *also* : BEER

swi·ple *or* **swip·ple** \ˈswipəl\ *n* -S [ME *swepyl, swipylle,* fr. *swepen* to sweep] : the part of a flail that strikes the grain in threshing : SWINGLE

¹**swirl** \ˈswərl, *esp before pause or consonant* ˈswər·əl; ˈswəl, ˈswəil\ *n* -S [ME (Sc); prob. of imit. origin] **1 a** : a whirling mass or motion (as of water, air, dust) : EDDY, VORTEX **b** : a state of whirling confusion ⟨a ~ of voices⟩ ⟨~ of events⟩ **2** : a spiraling shape or mark (as on fur or in the grain of wood) suggesting an eddy : CONVOLUTION ⟨icing . . . spread in rich creamy ~*s* —Patricia Benn⟩ **3** : an act or instance of swirling ⟨filled my glass . . . and gave it a gentle ~ to spread the bouquet —Joseph Wechsberg⟩ ⟨the ~ and splash of pickerel —*Amer. Guide Series: Maine*⟩

²**swirl** \"\ *vb* -ED/-ING/-S *vi* **1 a** : to move with an eddying or whirling motion ⟨water that heaved and ~*ed* and gurgled as the ferries slid in and out —Thomas Wood †1950⟩ **b** : to flow turbulently as if in eddies : pass in whirling confusion ⟨a topic about which there has ~*ed* much talk and few facts —C.R.Rogers⟩ **2** : to have a twist or convolution ⟨prefers back hair . . . luxuriant enough to ~ snugly across the back —Lois Long⟩ ~ *vt* : to cause to swirl ⟨~*ed* the brandy around in the huge goblet —J.B.Benefield⟩ **syn** see TURN

swirl·er \ˈswərlər; ˈswələ(r, ˈswəil-\ *n* -S : one that swirls

swirl·ing·ly *adv* [swirling (pres. part. of ²*swirl*) + *-ly*] : in a swirling manner

swirly \ˈswərlē, ˈswəl-, ˈswəil-, -li\ *adj* -ER/-EST [¹*swirl* + *-y*] **1** *Scot* : KNOTTED, TWISTED **2** : having a swirling motion, shape, or marking ⟨a ~ full skirt for country dancing⟩ : full of eddies ⟨the ~ water of the rapids⟩

¹**swish** \ˈswish\ *vb* -ED/-ING/-ES [imit.] *vi* : to move, pass, swing, or whirl with the sound of a swish : make the sound of a swish ⟨~*ed* before me in a tight dress —Raymond Chandler⟩ ⟨could hear cars ~*ing* past on the main road —Elizabeth Taylor⟩ ⟨windshield wipers ~*ing* —John McCarten⟩ ~ *vt* **1** : to move, pass, swing, or agitate with or as if with the sound of a swish : WHISK ⟨the saddled horse ~*ing* its tail —James Courage⟩ ⟨sipping water and ~*ing* it about in the mouth —F.A.Geldard⟩ **2** : to cut or remove with or as if with a swish — used with *off* ⟨~ off the tops of weeds with a sickle⟩ **3** : to strike or lash with a swish : FLOG

²**swish** \"\ *n* -ES [imit.] **1** *also* **swish-swish** \ˈ=ˈ=\ **a** : a prolonged hissing sound (as produced by a whip rapidly cutting the air) ⟨the slow, steady ~ of scythes —S.H.Holbrook⟩ ⟨a far-off ~ of surf —S.E.Morison⟩ ⟨~ of tires —William Faulkner⟩ ⟨poplars swayed and tossed with a roaring ~ —Harvey Breit⟩ **b** : a light sweeping or brushing sound (as of a long or full silk skirt in motion) ⟨the ~ of drawing paper being unrolled —Angus McGugan⟩ ⟨the ~ of a mop —Virginia Woolf⟩ **2** : a movement accompanied by the sound of a swish ⟨tails swung rhythmically except for occasional sudden ~*es* at flies —Elizabeth Janeway⟩ **3** : a flogging birch or cane : SWITCH ⟨smarting under recent applications of the ~ —George Meredith⟩ **4** [⁵*swish*] : SMARTNESS, FASHIONABLENESS **5** [¹*swish;* fr. his effeminate gait and gestures] *slang* : HOMOSEXUAL; *esp* : a male homosexual

³**swish** \"\ *adv* [imit.] : with a swish ⟨one day when the foliage all went ~ with autumn —Robert Frost⟩

⁴**swish** \"\ *n* -ES [origin unknown] : sun-dried earth used in West Africa as a building material

⁵**swish** \"\ *adj* [E dial., of unknown origin] : SMART, FASHIONABLE ⟨a ~ gown⟩ ⟨a ~ automobile⟩

swish·er \-shə(r)\ *n* -S : one that swishes : FLOGGER

swish·ing·ly *adv* [*swishing* (pres. part. of ¹*swish*) + *-ly*] : in a swishing manner or with a swishing sound

swishy \ˈswishē, -shi\ *adj* -ER/-EST [²*swish* + *-y*] **1** : producing a swishing sound : characterized by swishing sounds or movements ⟨~ fabrics⟩ **2** *slang* : characterized by or inclined to homosexuality

¹**swiss** \ˈswis\ *n* -ES *see sense 1* [in sense 1, fr. MF *Suisse,* fr. MHG *Swizer* — more at SWITZER; in other senses fr. ²*swiss*] **1** *pl* **swiss** *cap* **a** : a native or inhabitant of Switzerland **b** : one that is of Swiss descent **2** *often cap* : any of various fine sheer fabrics of cotton made in Switzerland; *esp* : DOTTED SWISS **3** *or* **swiss cheese** *usu cap S* : a hard cheese characterized by elastic texture, mild nutlike flavor, and large holes that form during ripening

²**swiss** \"\ *adj, usu cap* **1** : of, relating to, or characteristic of Switzerland **2** : of, relating to, or characteristic of the people of Switzerland

swiss blue *n, often cap S* : a grayish blue that is redder and less strong than electric, redder and duller than copenhagen, and redder and deeper than Gobelin

swiss catchfly *n, usu cap S* : a rare catchfly (*Silene vallesia*) of the European Alps with long-peduncled white flowers

swiss chard *n, usu cap S* : CHARD

swiss cheese plant *n, usu cap S* [so called fr. the sometimes perforated leaves] : CERIMAN

swisser *n* -S *cap* [modif. (influenced by ¹*swiss*) of MHG *Swizer* — more at SWITZER] *obs* : SWISS

swiss guard *n, usu cap S* [so called fr. the fact that each member must be a native Swiss] : one of a small body of soldiers serving as a bodyguard for the pope of the Roman Catholic Church

swiss·ing \ˈswisiŋ, -sēŋ\ *n* -S [origin unknown] : a calendering process for cotton fabrics that produces a smooth compact texture

swiss mountain pine *n, usu cap S* : a prostrate shrub or low pyramidal tree (*Pinus mugo*) of central Europe with short bright green leaves

swiss pine *also* **swiss stone pine** *n, usu cap 1st S* : a tall Eurasian pine (*Pinus cembra*) having dark green leaves in bundles of five, short spreading branches, and cones usu. less than four inches in length and yielding cedar nuts and a resinous exudate

swiss roll *n, usu cap S* : JELLY ROLL

swiss steak *n, usu cap 1st S* : a slice of round steak into which flour is pounded on both sides and which is then browned in fat and smothered in onions, tomatoes, and other vegetables and seasonings

swiss tea *n, usu cap S* : an infusion of the herbage of any of several plants of the genus *Achillea* (as *A. atrata, A. moschata,* or *A. nobilis*)

¹**switch** \ˈswich\ *n* -ES [perh. fr. MD *swijch* bough, branch, twig] **1** : a slender flexible whip, rod, or twig ⟨a riding ~⟩ **2** [²*switch*] : an act of switching : the action or office of one who switches: as **a** : a blow with a switch **b** : a turn of a switch **c** : a changing or switching from one (as an investment) to another **d** : a reversal or distinct variation of a familiar or usual mode or situation : a decided or unexpected change from the usual **e** : a shift to another suit than that previously led by one's side in bridge **3** : a tuft of long hairs at the end of the tail of an animal (as a cow or ox) — see COW illustration **4 a** : a device made usu. of two movable rails, necessary connections, and operating parts and designed to turn a locomotive or train from a track on which it is running to another track **b** : a railroad sidetrack **5** : a device for making, breaking, or changing the connections in an electrical circuit **6** : a heavy strand of usu. long cut hair fastened at one end and used in addition to a person's own hair for some hairdresses

²**switch** \"\ *vb* -ED/-ING/-ES *vt* **1 a** : to strike, beat, whip, or flog with or as if with a switch ⟨lower branches of the hornbeam ~*ing* the back of his head —J.C.Powys⟩ **b** : to stir up, drive away, or spur on with or as if with a switch ⟨horses contentedly ~*ing* flies —B.A.Williams⟩ **2 a** : SWING, WHISK, LASH ⟨~ a cane⟩ ⟨horse ~*es* his tail⟩ **b** : to jerk or pull with a jerk ⟨the rope may be ~*ed* out of your hand⟩ **3 a** : to turn aside : DIVERT, SHIFT, CHANGE ⟨~ methods⟩ ⟨~ places⟩ ⟨~ one's vote⟩ ⟨~ the talk to another subject⟩ **b** : to dispose of (one issue of securities) and invest the proceeds in another **c** *of a produce exchange* : to transfer a futures contract from one month to another **4 a** : to turn from one railroad track to another : transfer by a switch : SHUNT **b** : to move (cars) to different positions on the same track within terminal areas **5 a** : to shift to another electrical circuit by means of a switch **b** : to operate an electrical switch so as to turn off or on ⟨~ off a current⟩ ⟨~ on a light⟩ ~ *vi* **1** : to move by or as if by being swung or lashed from side to side ⟨the cat's tail ~*ing*⟩ ⟨her black hair in a long thick braid ~*ing* to the speed of the . . . hoofs —Edna Ferber⟩ **2** : to move off on or as if on a spur track **3 a** : to change or shift things, places, methods, actions, or directions **b** : to lead a suit other than that which one's side previously led in a card game

switch angle *n* : the angle formed by the switch and stock rails of a railroad track at the point of juncture as measured between the gage lines

¹**switchback** \ˈ=,=\ *n* -S [²*switch* + *back* (adv.)] **1** : a zigzag road or trail in a mountainous region ⟨roads which today's tourists climb in easy ~*s* —*Ford Times*⟩; *specif* : an arrangement of zigzag railroad tracks for surmounting the grade of a steep hill **2** *or* **switchback railway** *Brit* : ROLLER COASTER

²**switchback** \ˈ=,=\ *adj* **1** : of or relating to a switchback : attained by means of switchbacks ⟨~ curves⟩ ⟨a long ~ descent —Stephen Bone⟩ **2** : resembling a switchback (as in shape or variety of levels) ⟨accident . . . explains his hero's career —*Information Please Almanac*⟩

³**switchback** \ˈ=,=\ *vi* : to ride on or move as if on a switchback : zigzag in ascending or descending ⟨a trail that ~*ed* through rock and pine —Dan Cushman⟩ — **switchbacker** \ˈ=,==\ *n* -S

switchblade knife \'ˌ=ˌ=-\ *or* **switchblade** *n* **:** a pocketknife having the blade spring-operated so that pressure on a release catch causes it to fly open

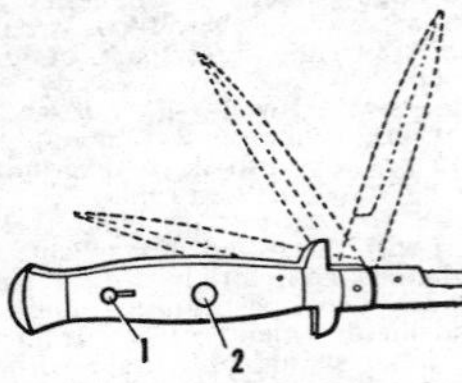

switchblade knife: *1* lock, *2* catch release

switchboard \'ˌ=ˌ=\ *n* **:** an apparatus consisting of a panel, an assembly of panels, or a frame on which are mounted insulated switching, measuring, controlling, and protective devices with buses and connections so arranged that a number of circuits may be connected, combined, controlled, measured, and protected
switch box *n* **:** a metal box containing the working parts of an electrical switch
switch cane *n* **:** a grass (*Arundinaria tecta*) of watery or moist locations esp. in the southern U. S.
switched *adj* [fr. past part. of ²*switch*] **:** CONFOUNDED, DASHED — used in mild imprecation or exclamation of surprise ⟨I'll be ~⟩
switch·el \'swichəl\ *n* -s [origin unknown] **:** a drink made of molasses or sometimes honey or maple syrup, water, and sometimes rum and usu. flavored with ginger and vinegar
switch engine *n* **:** a railroad engine usu. of the total-adhesion type that is used for switching — compare ROAD ENGINE
switch·er \'swichə(r)\ *n* -s **:** one that switches: as **a :** SWITCHMAN **b :** SWITCH ENGINE **c :** a petroleum worker who controls the flow of oil from wells to tanks to pipelines according to proration — called also *switchman* **d :** a television technician who operates the equipment that cuts, fades, or dissolves from one picture to another and regulates the brightness of the image
switch·er·oo \ˌswichəˈrü\ *n* -s [alter. of ¹*switch*] *slang* **:** a reversal or surprising variation of a familiar or expected action or manner **:** SWITCH ⟨would work one ~ on the traditional presentation —W.L.Gresham⟩ ⟨life keeps pulling hilarious ~*s* on his fiction-bred expectations —Anthony Boucher⟩
switches *pl of* SWITCH, *pres 3d sing of* SWITCH
switchgear \'ˌ=ˌ=\ *also* **switcher gear** *n* **:** the aggregate of switching facilities for a power station or transforming station
switch grass *n* [alter. of *quitch grass*] **:** a panic grass (*Panicum virgatum*) of the western U. S. that is used for hay
switch-hit \'ˌ=ˌ=\ *vi* [back-formation fr. *switch-hitter*] **:** to bat right-handed against a left-hander and left-handed against a right-handed pitcher in baseball
switch-hitter \'ˌ=ˌ=ˌ=\ *n* **:** a baseball player who can bat either left-handed or right-handed
switch hook *n* **:** a hook provided with an insulating handle for opening and closing disconnecting switches
switch-horn \'ˌ=ˌ=\ *n* **1 :** a simple unbranched horn on a stag **2 :** a stag bearing switch-horns
switching *pres part of* SWITCH
switching limits *n pl* [*switching* (gerund of ²*switch*) + *limits*] **:** boundaries for a railroad terminal area
switching yard *n* **:** YARD 3c
switch-ivy \'ˌ=ˌ==\ *n* [¹*switch*] **:** DOG LAUREL
switchkeeper \'ˌ=ˌ=ˌ=\ *n* **:** SWITCH TENDER
switch key *n* **:** a key used for locking or unlocking manually operated railroad switches
switch knife *n* **:** SWITCHBLADE KNIFE
switch lamp *n* **:** a lamp for indicating by the color of its light whether a railroad switch is open or closed
switch line *or* **switch position** *n* **:** a defensive military position that is oblique to the front, connects other positions of a defensive system, and is designed to prevent hostile penetrations from being exploited to the flanks
switch lock *n* **:** a manual or automatic locking device for assuring that a switch remains in proper position prior to and during the passage of a train
switch·man \'=mən\ *n, pl* **switchmen 1 :** one who tends a switch **:** one employed in switching (as in a classification yard) **2 :** one who tests and repairs telephone or telegraph central-office equipment **3 :** SWITCHER c
switchover \'ˌ=ˌ==\ *n* -s [²*switch* + *over*] **:** CHANGEOVER
switch plant *n* [¹*switch*] **:** a plant (as a broom) lacking true foliage leaves but with green twigs replacing them functionally
switch plate *n* **:** the metal plate in front of an electrical switch box through which the plugs or tumblers protrude
switch plug *n* **:** a combination of a switch and a plug attached to a flexible cord for use with an electric appliance (as an electric iron)
switch point *or* **switch rail** *n* **:** POINT RAIL

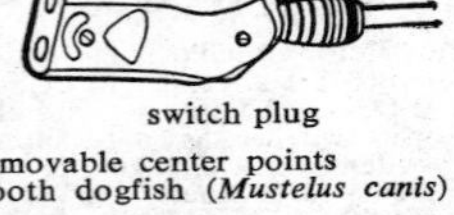
switch plug

switch sorrel *n, Jamaica* **:** AKEAKE 1
switch stand *n* **:** a stand near a railroad track to which is pivoted a lever for the manual operation of switches or of movable center points
switchtail \'ˌ=ˌ=\ *n* **1 :** a smooth dogfish (*Mustelus canis*) **2 :** SHOVELNOSE STURGEON
switch tender *n* **:** one that tends and operates a railroad switch; *esp* **:** a railroad yardman who throws track switches
switch tie *n* **:** a railroad crosstie of extra length for use at turnouts or crossovers
switch tower *n* **:** a small tower containing the controls for working railroad switches and signals
switchyard \'ˌ=ˌ=\ *n* **1 :** a place where railroad cars are switched from one track to another and where trains are made up **2 :** an area that is usu. enclosed by fence and that embraces the gear of a switching station of a power system
swith *or* **swithe** \'swith\ *adv* [ME, strongly, very much, quickly, fr. OE *swīthe* strongly, very much, fr. *swīth* strong; akin to MHG *swinde* strong, quick, ON *svinnr* quick, wise, Goth *swinths* strong, healthy — more at SOUND] *chiefly dial* **:** INSTANTLY, QUICKLY
¹**swith·er** \'swithə(r)\ *vi* [origin unknown] *dial chiefly Brit* **:** DOUBT, WAVER, HESITATE
²**swither** \"\ *n* **1** *dial chiefly Brit* **:** INDECISION, DOUBT **2** *dial chiefly Brit* **:** FLURRY, PANIC
³**swither** \"\ *vi* [imit.] *dial chiefly Brit* **:** WHIZ, RUSH
switz·er \'switsə(r)\ *n* -s *cap* [MHG *Swizer*, fr. *Swīz* Switzerland] **:** SWISS
switz·er·land \'switsə(r)lənd\ *adj, usu cap* [fr. *Switzerland*, federal republic in central Europe] **:** of or from Switzerland **:** of the kind or style prevalent in Switzerland **:** SWISS
swive \'swīv\ *vb* -ED/-ING/-S [ME *swiven*, fr. OE *swīfan* to revolve, wend, sweep — more at SWIVEL] *vt, archaic* **:** to copulate with ~ *vi, archaic* **:** COPULATE
¹**swiv·el** \'swivəl\ *n* -s *often attrib* [ME *swivel, swevill;* akin to OE *swīfan* to revolve, wend, sweep, OHG *sweibōn*, *swebēn* to move freely, MHG *swibelen* to reel, waver, ON *svīfa* to ramble, drift, turn, *sveifla* to swing in a circle, MLG *swāien* to sway — more at SWAY]

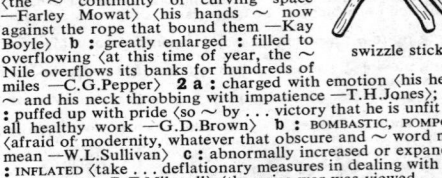

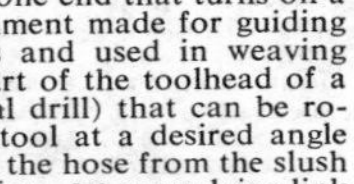
swivel 1a in a chain

1 : a part that pivots freely on or as if on a headed bolt or pin: as **a :** a compound chain link having one end that turns on a headed bolt or pin **b :** a loom attachment made for guiding additional shuttles over limited areas and used in weaving small spot designs, esp. dots **c :** a part of the toolhead of a machine (as a planer, shaper, or radial drill) that can be rotated and clamped so as to hold the tool at a desired angle **d :** a swivel connection placed between the hose from the slush pumps and the drill stem in rotary drilling **e :** a revolving link used on terminal tackle to prevent twisting of a fishing line **2 :** SWIVEL GUN
²**swivel** \"\ *vb* **swiveled** *or* **swivelled; swiveled** *or* **swivelled; swiveling** *or* **swivelling** \-v(ə)liŋ\ **swivels** *vt* **1 :** to turn on or as if on a swivel ⟨~ one's eyes in various directions⟩ **2 :** to provide with or secure by a swivel ~ *vi* **:** to swing or turn on or as if on a swivel ⟨~*ed* around in his chair to face the door⟩ ⟨an odd gust ~*ed* around the corner —Liam O'Flaherty⟩
swivel bridge *n* **:** SWING BRIDGE
swivel chain *n* **:** a chain having a swivel attached to or linked into it
swivel chair *n* **:** a chair that swivels on its base
swivel gun *n* **:** a usu. small gun fixed on a swivel (as on a stanchion or a wall) so that it can be rotated horizontally and vertically
swivel-hip \'ˌ=ˌ=ˌ=\ *vi* [back-formation fr. *swivel-hipped*] **:** to move or turn with a twisting motion of the hips ⟨the crowd *swivel-hipped* out of the way at the last moment, and the car sliced through the narrow corridor —H.W.Young⟩ ⟨the brunette came *swivel-hipping* out to the curb —Ray Brennan⟩
swivel-hipped \ˌ=ˌ=ˌ=\ *adj* **:** moving with or characterized by movement with a twisting motion of the hips
swivel hips *n pl but sing in constr* **:** a trampoline stunt consisting of a seat drop followed by a ½ twist to another seat drop
swivel hook *n* **:** a hook secured by means of a swivel
swivel joint *n* **:** a joint with packed swivel to permit rotational motion of one part relative to another
swivel plow *n* **:** a plow having a reversible moldboard making the plow capable of throwing the furrow either to the right or to the left
swivel saw *n* **:** a pruning saw so made that the blade can be loosened, turned at an angle, and tightened in this position
swivel table *n* **:** a table of a machine tool that may be swiveled to and clamped in any of various positions
swivel union *n* **:** a union for connecting machine parts that permits relative rotation of the connected parts
swivel vise *n* **:** a vise that can be swiveled in one plane — compare UNIVERSAL VISE
swivel weaving *n* **:** weaving on a loom provided with a swivel
swiv·et *also* **swiv·vet** \'swivət, *usu* -əd·+V\ *n* -s [origin unknown] **:** a state of extreme agitation **:** TIZZY, FRENZY, SWEAT — usu. used in phrase *in a swivet*
swiz *or* **swizz** \'swiz\ *n, pl* **swizzes** [origin unknown] *Brit* **:** SWINDLE
¹**swiz·zle** \'swizəl\ *n* -s [origin unknown] **:** a cocktail consisting of a spirituous liquor, lime or lemon juice, bitters, and sugar churned in ice in a pitcher until the surface is frothed and served strained ⟨rum ~⟩ ⟨gin ~⟩
²**swizzle** \"\ *vb* **swizzled; swizzled; swizzling** \-z(ə)liŋ\ **swizzles** *vi* **:** to drink esp. to excess **:** GUZZLE ~ *vt* **:** to mix or stir with or as if with a swizzle stick
swiz·zler \-z(ə)lə(r)\ *n* -s **:** one that swizzles; *specif* **:** SWIZZLE STICK
swizzle stick *n* **1 :** a pronged stick made of wood, metal, or plastic and used to stir mixed drinks **2 :** a round or thin flat stick without prongs used to stir mixed drinks

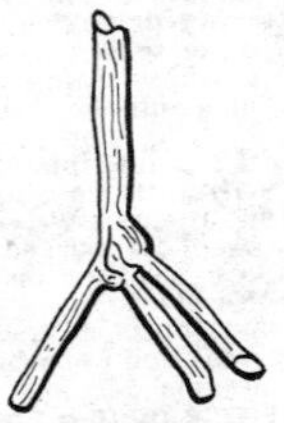
swizzle stick

SWL *abbr* **1** short wave listener **2** sulfite waste liquor
swob *var of* SWAB
swol·len \'swōlən *also* -ln\ *adj* [ME, fr. past part. of *swellen* to swell] **1 a :** protuberant or abnormally distended (as by injury or disease) **:** BULGING, PUFFY ⟨elongate in shape, small, flat or ~, usually with smooth shells —Joyce Allan⟩ ⟨the ~ continuity of curving space —Farley Mowat⟩ ⟨his hands ~ now against the rope that bound them —Kay Boyle⟩ **b :** greatly enlarged **:** filled to overflowing ⟨at this time of year, the ~ Nile overflows its banks for hundreds of miles —C.G.Pepper⟩ **2 a :** charged with emotion ⟨his heart ~ and his neck throbbing with impatience —T.H.Jones⟩; *esp* **:** puffed up with pride ⟨so ~ by . . . victory that he is unfit for all healthy work —G.D.Brown⟩ **b :** BOMBASTIC, POMPOUS ⟨afraid of modernity, whatever that obscure and ~ word may mean —W.L.Sullivan⟩ **c :** abnormally increased or expanded **:** INFLATED ⟨take . . . deflationary measures in dealing with her ~ currency —R.F.Mikesell⟩ ⟨the price war was viewed . . . as primarily a method of cleaning out ~ inventories —*Publishers' Weekly*⟩ ⟨the turgid, ~ city, with its acute job shortages —Frances Keene⟩
swollen-headed \ˌ=ˌ=ˌ=\ *adj* **:** having a swelled head **:** ARROGANT, CONCEITED
swollen shoot *or* **swollen shoot disease** *n* **:** a virus disease of cacao characterized by mosaic and shedding of leaves, dwarfing and mottling of pods, and esp. by shortening and swelling of the internodes of the stem and of the roots
¹**swoon** \'swün\ *vb* -ED/-ING/-S [ME *swowenen, swounen*, prob. back-formation fr. *swowening, swouning* swoon — more at SWOONING] *vi* **1 a :** to suffer partial or total loss of consciousness **:** FAINT ⟨perhaps he fell asleep, perhaps he ~*ed* . . . who could say —Upton Sinclair⟩ **b :** to become enraptured **:** go into ecstasies ⟨the ladies were ~*ing* with joy —Frederick Way⟩ ⟨a man . . . whose mind ~*ed* with apocalyptic splendors —Bernard De Voto⟩ **2 :** to drift languidly or die away **:** FLOAT, FADE ⟨soar and swoop and ~ and glide again —Robert Gibbings⟩ ⟨the noise ~*ed* away, the trees were shrouded in a midnight hush —Gwyn Jones⟩ ~ *vt* **:** to cause to swoon
²**swoon** \"\ *n* -s [ME *swoune, swoun* fr. *swounen* to swoon] **1 a :** a partial or total loss of consciousness **:** SYNCOPE ⟨when I wakened from the ~ —Sheridan Le Fanu⟩ **b :** a state of bewilderment or ecstasy **:** DAZE, RAPTURE ⟨sat in a floating ~ of . . . erotic longing —William Faulkner⟩ **2 a :** a state of suspended animation **:** TORPOR ⟨left the author . . . in a kind of moral and intellectual ~ —*Times Lit. Supp.*⟩ **b** *obs* **:** a deep sleep **3 :** a languorous drift ⟨the orchestra goes Neapolitan in a ~ of strings —Claudia Cassidy⟩
swoon·er \-nə(r)\ *n* -s **:** one that swoons or causes swooning
¹**swoon·ing** \-niŋ, -nēŋ\ *n* -s [ME *swowening, swouning*, fr. *iswowen, swoun* being in a swoon (fr. OE *geswōgen* in a swoon, lifeless) + *-ing*] *archaic* **:** SWOON ⟨even disagreeable smells will sometimes occasion ~*s* —William Buchan⟩
²**swooning** *adj* [fr. pres. part. of ¹*swoon*] **:** characterized by languor or loss of consciousness — **swoon·ing·ly** *adv*
¹**swoop** \'swüp\ *vb* -ED/-ING/-S [alter. of ME *swopen* to sweep, fr. OE *swāpan* to sweep, swing, drive, rush; akin to OHG *sweifan* to swing around, coil, ON *sveipa* to sweep, swoop, wrap up, *swatha* to swathe — more at SWATHE] *vi* **1 a** *obs* **:** to move haughtily esp. in trailing robes **b :** to move rapidly or graze in passing **:** BRUSH, SWEEP ⟨~*ed* by the table and glanced at the papers that lay there —John Steinbeck⟩ ⟨the wind will be ~*ing* up . . . from the lake —J.J.Godwin⟩ **2 a :** to make a sudden attack **:** DESCEND, POUNCE ⟨arming and preparing to ~ —Dorothy Thompson⟩ — usu. used with *down* ⟨wind and snow ~*ed* down upon him —Robert Murphy⟩ ⟨fixed newcomers with an eagle eye, ~*ed* down upon them and demanded their names —*Amer. Guide Series: R.I.*⟩ **b :** to plunge suddenly or move in a sweeping arc **:** DIP, VEER ⟨seagulls and cranes wheel and ~ —*Geog. School Bull.*⟩ ⟨ladies in tights . . . ~*ing* through the air over our heads —Mary Deasy⟩ ⟨boat ~*ed* to the rise and fall of the waves —R.S.Porteous⟩ **c :** to come down **:** ALIGHT, DROP ⟨~*ed* down before the fire —F.C.Burnand⟩ ⟨in little more than an hour one may ~ down from winter to summer —John Muir †1914⟩ ~ *vt* **1 a :** to dislodge or remove abruptly **:** carry off **:** SWEEP ⟨the whirlwind's blast . . . ~*s* the haycocks off the lea —William Tennant⟩ ⟨British Intelligence . . . ~*ed* him off to London —J.P.O'Donnell⟩ **b :** to seize or capture unexpectedly **:** CATCH, SNATCH ⟨~*ed* her off the swing into his arms —Helen Howe⟩ **c :** to draw in **:** SWALLOW, SUCK ⟨~*ed* in a hot swallow, then aired his mouth —Helen Rich⟩ **2 :** to describe a sweeping arc with ⟨storks ~ white streaks . . . against the luminous blue —Claudia Cassidy⟩
²**swoop** \"\ *n* -s **:** an act or instance of swooping: as **a :** the swift plummeting of a bird on its prey **:** POUNCE, STOOP ⟨even as the fish's head fell from the crocodile's munching mouth there was a ~ of white wings —Francis Birtles⟩ **b :** a concentrated effort or attack **:** EXERTION, STROKE ⟨baggage can . . . be pushed off onto the pier in one ~ —*N.Y.Times*⟩ ⟨all my pretty chickens and their dam at one fell ~ —Shak.⟩ **c :** a sudden incursion **:** DESCENT, GRAB ⟨a ~ of security officers on a Communist espionage ring —Whittaker Chambers⟩ ⟨bring evacuees out to . . . ships in as few ~*s* as possible —*Time*⟩ **d :** an undulating line or movement **:** DIP, FESTOON ⟨swallows . . . fluttered in graceful ~*s* in and out —Nora Waln⟩ ⟨the ~ and curl of the road up . . . from the plain —John Connell⟩
swoop·er \-pə(r)\ *n* -s **:** one that swoops
swoopstake *adv* [irreg. (influenced by ¹*swoop*) fr. *sweepstake*] *obs* **:** in the manner of a sweepstake **:** INDISCRIMINATELY
¹**swoosh** \'swüsh\ *vb* -ED/-ING/-ES [imit.] *vi* **1 :** to make a rushing sound ⟨something ~*ed*, and six sprinklers sent up watery bouquets —Ellery Queen⟩ **2 a :** to move with a rushing or rustling sound ⟨a car ~*ed* by . . . in a sucking swirl of dust —Gordon Woodward⟩ ⟨his date ~*ed* down the stairway in a taffeta evening gown⟩ **b :** to gush out **:** EDDY, SWIRL ⟨water ~*ing* from the town pump —Willie S. Ethridge⟩ ⟨the ~*ing* cloud of powder shown at right —*Life*⟩ ~ *vt* **:** to discharge or transport with a rushing sound ⟨the experimental rocket ship . . . expected to ~ a man into space —*Springfield (Mass.) Union*⟩
²**swoosh** \"\ *n* -ES **1 :** an act or instance of swooshing **:** GUSH ⟨spectacular flashes and ~*es* from the new weapons —*Newsweek*⟩ ⟨skirt fullness is concentrated in a ~ at the back —*Women's Wear Daily*⟩; *specif* **:** a rushing sound ⟨multiple jet engines audible as a sibilant ~ . . . gone almost as quickly as the planes themselves —H.E.Salisbury⟩ **2 :** almost a swift movement accompanied by a rushing sound ⟨first jet airliner to span the North Atlantic in a nonstop ~ —Frederick Graham⟩ ⟨whipped out a razor and made a violent ~ in the neighborhood of the other's neck —Alan Barth⟩
swop *var of* SWAP
swope \'swōp\ *archaic var of* SWOOP
¹**sword** \'sō(ə)rd, -ō(ə)rd, -ōəd, -ō(ə)d\ *n* -s *often attrib* [ME *swerd, sword*, fr. OE *sweord;* akin to OHG *swert* sword, ON *sverth*, Av *xvara* wound; basic meaning: to cut, stab] **1 a :** a weapon with a long blade for cutting or thrusting set in a hilt usu. terminating in a pommel and often having a tang or a protective guard where the blade joins the handle — see BROADSWORD, CUTLASS, ÉPÉE, ESTOC, RAPIER, SABER, SMALLSWORD; compare BAYONET, DAGGER, FOIL, KNIFE, SCIMITAR **b :** a sword worn as one of the side arms of ceremonial regalia or displayed as a symbol of honor or authority ⟨a ceremonial ~ with the Queen's cipher on the blade and hilt —René Lecler⟩ ⟨had the diamonds removed from the ~ of honor . . . and made into a necklace —R.A.H.N.Hood⟩ **2 a** (1) **:** an instrument of destruction **:** a militant force ⟨avarice . . . hath been the ~ of our slain kings —Shak.⟩ ⟨tempering . . . conscience until it should become a ~ with which to do effective battle against the vicious majority —Roy Lewis & Angus Maude⟩ (2) **:** a combative spirit **:** struggle as a means of achieving a worthwhile objective ⟨I have not come to bring peace, but a ~ —Mt 10:34 (RSV)⟩ ⟨this younger senator, whose ~ is not yet sheathed in pragmatism —Marya Mannes⟩ **b :** military prowess **:** war esp. as a means of settling disputes ⟨hireling combatants sold their ~*s* . . . to the best bidder —Sir Walter Scott⟩ ⟨the pen is mightier than the ~ —E.G.Bulwer-Lytton⟩ **3 :** coercive power or jurisdiction ⟨the magistrate . . . bears the ~ of justice by the consent of the whole community —William Blackstone⟩ ⟨to the Church belong both ~*s*, the spiritual and . . . the temporal —C.H.McIlwain⟩ **4 :** something that resembles a sword: as **a :** SWINGLE 1 **b :** the beak of the swordfish **c :** one of the end bars by which the lay of a handloom is suspended, or one of the uprights supporting the lay of a power loom — **at swords' points** *adv* **:** displaying mutual hostility **:** ready to fight **:** ANTAGONISTIC ⟨at the height of the quarrel when the two groups were *at swords' points*⟩
²**sword** \"\ *vt* -ED/-ING/-S **1 :** to arm with a sword **2 :** to wound or kill with or as if with a sword
sword-and-buckler *adj* \ˌ=ˌ=ˌ=\ *archaic* **:** marked by or suggestive of braggadocio **:** SWASHBUCKLING ⟨lived in a ruffling time, so he loved *sword-and-buckler* men —Robert Naunton⟩
sword arm *n* [so called fr. its being the arm that wields the sword] **:** the right arm
sword bayonet *n* **:** a long bayonet formerly worn as a side arm and capable of being used as a sword
sword bean *n* **:** a twining tropical plant (*Canavalia gladiata*) native to the Old World, long cultivated in the Orient, and bearing long pods usu. having red or pink seed, both pods and seed being used for food — compare JACK BEAN
sword-bearer \'ˌ=ˌ=\ *n* [ME *swordberer*, fr. ¹*sword* + *berer* bearer] **1 :** a British civic official who carries a sword before a municipal officer on ceremonial occasions **2 :** one that is armed with a sword
swordbill \'ˌ=ˌ=\ *or* **sword-billed hummingbird** \'ˌ=ˌ=-\ *n* **:** a So. American hummingbird (*Ensifera ensifera*) having a slender bill longer than the rest of the bird
sword cane *n* **:** a cane or walking stick that conceals the blade of a sword or dagger — called also *sword stick*
sword dance *n* **1 :** a ceremonial English and west European folk dance executed by men in a ring by performing evolutions with a sword in the right hand and the tip of a neighbor's sword in the left and joining in figures in which the swords are brandished **2 :** a dance performed over or around swords without touching them; *esp* **:** the Scottish Highland solo dance performed in the angles formed by two swords or a sword and scabbard crossed on the ground **3 :** any male solo dance performed with the flourishing of a sword or saber
sword dancer *n* **:** one that performs or participates in a sword dance
sword dollar *n* **:** the Scottish silver ryal of James VI having a sword on the reverse
sword·er \'sōrdər, 'sȯr-, 'sōədə, 'sō(ə)də\ *n* -s [¹*sword* + *-er*] *archaic* **:** SWORDSMAN, CUTTHROAT
sword fern *n* **:** any of several ferns with long narrow more or less sword-shaped fronds: as **a :** a tropical fern (*Nephrolepis exaltata*) from which the Boston fern has been developed **b :** GIANT HOLLY FERN
swordfish \'ˌ=ˌ=\ *n* [ME *swerd fyssh*, fr. *swerd* sword + *fyssh*, *fish* fish] **1 a :** a very large and widely distributed oceanic fish (*Xiphias gladius*) that constitutes the family Xiphiidae, has the bones of the upper jaw consolidated into a long rigid swordlike beak, the dorsal fin high and without distinct spines, the ventral fins absent, and the adult destitute of teeth, sometimes attains a weight of 600 pounds, and is highly valued as a food and sport fish — called also *broadbill, espada, espadon* **b** (1) **:** MARLIN (2) **:** SAILFISH **2 :** a synchronized swimming stunt executed from a prone position with the back arched and the head and one foot above water and the other knee bent in which the head is submerged and the hands propel the body toward the feet while the extended leg is raised above the water until the body is overbalanced onto the back after which the bent leg is straightened
swordfisherman \'ˌ=ˌ=ˌ=\ *n* [blend of *swordfish* and *fisherman*] **:** one that is engaged in swordfishing
swordfishing \'ˌ=ˌ=\ *n* [blend of *swordfish* and *fishing*] **:** fishing for swordfish
sword grass *n* **1 :** any of various grasses or sedges having leaves with a sharp or toothed edge: as **a** *Austral* **:** CUTTING GRASS **b :** any of several other Australian grasses of the genus *Cladium* **2 :** a plant having more or less sword-shaped leaves: as **a :** REED CANARY GRASS **b :** the common bulrush **3 :** a European spurry (*Spergulavia segetalis*)
sword knot *n* **1 :** a leather thong attaching the hilt of a sword to the wrist to prevent its loss if forced out of the hand **2 :** an ornamental cord or tassel tied to the hilt
sword·less \'ˌ=ləs\ *adj* **:** lacking a sword
swordlike \'ˌ=ˌ=\ *adj* **:** resembling a sword
sword lily *n* **:** GLADIOLUS
swordman *n, pl* **swordmen** [ME *swerdman*, fr. *swerd* sword + *man*] **1** *obs* **:** SWORDSMAN 1 **2** *obs* **a :** a soldier armed with a sword **b :** a military man **:** WARRIOR ⟨worthy fellows, and like to prove most sinewy *swordmen* —Shak.⟩
sword mat *n* [so called fr. the wooden sword used in weaving it] **:** a mat of closely woven rope yarns used as chafing gear on a ship
sword of dam·o·cles \-'daməˌklēz\ *often cap S & usu cap D* [so called fr. the sword suspended by a single hair over the head of Damocles, guest at a sumptuous banquet given by Dionysius the Elder †367 B.C. Greek tyrant of Syracuse, as a reminder of the insecurity of a tyrant's happiness] **:** an impending disaster ⟨unaware of the *Sword of Damocles* hanging

over her, she pursued her own way . . . casually and cheerfully —Olive H. Prouty⟩

sword-plant \ˈ=,=\ *n* **:** any of several plants of the genus *Sagittaria*

swordplay \ˈ=,=\ *n* **1 a :** the art or skill of wielding a sword esp. in fencing **b :** an exhibition of swordsmanship **2 :** something that resembles a fencing duel ⟨some very pretty diplomatic ~ —*Economist*⟩

swordplayer \ˈ=,==\ *n* [*swordplay* + *-er*] *archaic* **:** one skilled in swordplay

swords *pl of* SWORD, *pres 3d sing of* SWORD

sword sedge *n* **:** an Australian sedge (*Lepidosperma gladiatum*) that is important as a sand binder and yields a paper material similar to papyrus

sword service *n* **:** military service owed to a liege lord by his vassal

sword side *n* **:** the father's side of a family — compare DISTAFF

swords·man \-dzmən\ *n, pl* **swordsmen** [*swords-* (fr. genitive of ¹*sword*) + *man*] **1 :** one skilled in swordplay; *esp* **:** a saber fencer **2** *archaic* **:** a military man; *specif* **:** a soldier armed with a sword

swordsman·ship \ˈ==,ship\ *n* [*swordsman* + *-ship*] **:** SWORDPLAY 1

sword stick *n* **:** SWORD CANE

sword sucker *n* **:** a vigorous shoot arising from the rootstock of a banana plant and frequently used for replanting

sword-swallower \ˈ=,===\ *n* **:** a performer who pretends to swallow a sword or some other rigid object — **sword-swallowing** \ˈ=,===\ *n*

swordswoman \ˈ=,==\ *n, pl* **swordswomen** [*swords-* (fr. genitive of ¹*sword*) + *woman*] **:** a woman fencer

swordtail \ˈ=,=\ *n* **1 :** KING CRAB 1 **2 a :** any of various bugs (genus *Uroxiphus*) found on forest trees **b :** a long-horned grasshopper (genus *Conocephalus*) having a long swordlike ovipositor **3 :** any of several small Central American topminnows (genus *Xiphophorus*): as **a :** a fish (*X. helleri*) in which the lower lobe of the tail of the male is greatly prolonged and brightly colored and which is often kept in the tropical aquarium and is bred in many color varieties **b :** HELLERI 2

swordweed \ˈ=,=\ *n* [so called fr. its sword-shaped pods] **:** a senna (*Cassia occidentalis*)

swore [ME *swoor*, fr. OE *swōr*] *past of* SWEAR

sworl \ˈswȯr(-ə)l\ *chiefly dial var of* SWIRL

sworn \ˈswō(ə)rn, ˈswȯ(ə)n\ *adj* [ME *sworen, sworn*, fr. past part. of *sweren* to swear] **1 a :** bound by an oath **:** AVOWED ⟨now my ~ friend, and then mine enemy —Shak.⟩; *specif* **:** pledged by an oath of chivalry to share each other's fortunes, good or bad — used formerly of companions in arms ⟨according to an early tradition became his ~ brother —F.M.Stenton⟩ **b :** serving under an official oath of office ⟨~ jury⟩ ⟨all loads of gravel . . . are to be accompanied by weight slips signed by ~ weighers —*Springfield (Mass.) Union*⟩ **c :** certified under oath **:** ATTESTED ⟨~ evidence⟩ ⟨the ~ outlay . . . was $128,300 —S.H.Adams⟩ **2 :** as firmly established as if bound by oath **:** CONFIRMED, INVETERATE ⟨a ~ conservative⟩

¹**swot** \ˈswät *also* -wȯt; *usu* \|d·+V\ *n* -s [alter. of ²*sweat*] **1** *Brit* **:** one given to swotting **:** a student who has few interests besides studying **:** GRIND **2** *Brit* **:** hard work

²**swot** \"\ *vi* **swotted; swotted; swotting; swots** *Brit* **:** to study hard and constantly **:** GRIND — compare BONE

³**swot** *var of* SWAT

swot·ter \|d·ə(r), |tə-\ *n* -s *Brit* **:** ¹SWOT 1

¹**swound** \ˈswaund, ˈswünd\ *n* -s [ME, alter. of *swoun* swoon] *archaic* **:** SWOON

²**swound** \"\ *vi* -ED/-ING/-S *archaic* **:** SWOON

¹**swow** \ˈswau\ *dial var of* SOUGH

²**swow** \"\ *vi* [prob. fr. *swear* + *vow*] *dial* **:** SWEAR — usu. used in the phrase *I swow* as a mild oath

SWP *abbr* safe working pressure

s wrench *n, cap S* **:** a wrench with an S-shaped handle

swtg *abbr* switching

swum [ME *swummen* (past pl. & past part.), fr. OE *swummon* (past pl.), *geswummen* (past part.)] *past part. & chiefly dial past of* SWIM

S wrench

swung [ME *swungen* (past pl. & past part.), fr. OE *swungon* (past pl.), *geswungen* (past part.)] *past of* SWING

swung dash *n* [*swung* + *dash*; fr. its reversal of direction] **:** a character ~ used in printing to conserve space by representing part or all of a previously spelled-out word

swy \ˈswī\ *n* -s [modif. of G *zwei* two, fr. OHG — more at TWO] *Austral* **:** TWO-UP

sx *abbr* **1** sacks **2** simplex

sxn *abbr* section

sy \ˈsī\ *n* -s [by shortening & alter.] *chiefly dial* **:** SCYTHE

-sy \sē, si\ *n suffix* -ES [¹-*s* + -*y*] **:** small one **:** one affectionately regarded ⟨mop*sy*⟩ ⟨pop*sy*⟩

sy *abbr* **1** sticky **2** supply

SY *abbr* square yard

sya·gush \ˈsyä,güsh\ *n* -ES [Per *siyāh-gōsh*, lit., black ear, fr. *siyāh* black (fr. MPer) + *gōsh* ear, fr. OPer *gausha-*; akin to Av *gaosha-* ear, Skt *ghoṣa* noise] **:** CARACAL

syb·a·rite \ˈsibə,rīt, *usu* -īd·+V\ *n* -s [L *Sybarita*, fr. Gk *Sybaritēs*, fr. *Sybaris*, ancient Greek city in southern Italy + Gk *-itēs* -ite] **1** *cap* **:** a native or resident of the ancient city of Sybaris noted for its love of luxury and pleasure **2** *often cap* **:** a person devoted to luxury and pleasure **:** VOLUPTUARY ⟨laid aside this Spartan temperance for the ostentatious luxury of a *Sybarite* —T.B.Macaulay⟩

syb·a·rit·ic \ˌ==ˈrid·ik, -itik, -ēk\ *adj* [L *Sybariticus*, fr. Gk *Sybaritikos*, fr. *Sybaritēs* + *-ikos* -ic] **1** *usu cap* **a :** of, relating to, or characteristic of ancient Sybaris **b :** of, relating to, or characteristic of the people of Sybaris **2 :** marked by or given to luxury or voluptuous living ⟨take his rest in ~ grandeur that eclipses the splendor of a sultan's harem —Green Peyton⟩ ⟨the . . . basically ~ boy became a strong, aggressive, Spartan adult —G.W.Johnson⟩ **syn** see SENSUOUS

syb·a·rit·i·cal \-ə̇kəl\ *adj, often cap* [L *Sybariticus* + E *-al*] **:** SYBARITIC

syb·a·rit·i·cal·ly \-k(ə)lē\ *adv* **:** in a sybaritic manner **:** with sybaritic luxury

syb·a·rit·ish \-ˌrīd·ish\ *adj, often cap* **:** SYBARITIC

syb·a·rit·ism \ˈ===,rīd,izəm, -rī,tiz-\ *n* -s **:** the quality or state of being sybaritic ⟨lapsed into the ~ of sheer sensation —T.R.Weiss⟩ ⟨sensual to the point of ~ —R.R. Von Abele⟩

sybil *often cap, var of* SIBYL

sy·bo *or* **sy·bow** \ˈsī,bō\ *Scot var of* CIBOL

syc·a·mine \ˈsikə,min, -,mən\ *n* -s [L *sycaminus*, fr. Gk *sykaminos*, of Sem origin; akin to Heb *shiqmāh* mulberry tree, sycamore] **:** MULBERRY 1a

syc·a·more *also* **syc·o·more** \ˈsikə,mō(ə)r, -mȯ(ə)r, -ōə, -ȯ(ə)\ *n* -s [ME *sicamour, sicomour*, fr. MF *sicamor*, fr. L *sycomorus*, fr. Gk *sykomoros*, prob. modif. (influenced by Gk *sykon* fig & *moron* mulberry) of a Sem word akin to Heb *shiqmāh* sycamore — more at MULBERRY] **1** *or* **sycamore fig** *also* **sycomore fig :** a tree (*Ficus sycomorus*) of Egypt and Asia Minor that is the sycamore of Scripture, is useful as a shade tree, and has sweet and edible fruit similar but inferior to the common fig and leaves resembling those of the mulberry — called also *mulberry fig* **2 :** a Eurasian maple (*Acer pseudoplatanus*) having long racemes of showy yellow flowers that is widely planted as a shade tree **3 a :** ²PLANE; *esp* **:** a very large spreading tree (*Platanus occidentalis*) of eastern and central No. America with 3- to 5-lobed broadly ovate leaves — see TREE illustration **b :** the variably colored and sometimes variegated hard tough elastic wood of a sycamore — called also *lacewood*

sycamore anthracnose *n* **:** a disease of the sycamore caused by an ascomycetous fungus (*Gnomonia veneta*) and characterized by leaf and twig blight

sycamore lace bug *n* **:** a tingid bug (*Corythucha ciliata*) that is a serious pest on sycamores in No. America

sycamore maple *n* **:** SYCAMORE 2

syce \ˈsīs\ *n* -s [Hindi *sā'is*, fr. Ar *sā'is* (colloq. *sāyis*)] **:** a groom or attendant esp. in India

sy·cee \ˈsīˈsē\ *n* -s [Chin (Cant) *sai sz*, lit., fine threads, fine silk] **:** silver money formerly used in China and made in the form of ingots measured by weight and usu. stamped — see SHOE

sy·cet·ta \sə̇ˈsed·ə\ *n, cap* [NL, fr. *Sycon* + It *-etta*, dim. suffix (fr. LL *-ita*, fem. of *-itus*)] **:** a genus (the type of the family Sycettidae) of primitive sycon sponges with the flagellated chambers opening directly into the paragaster

sy·cet·ti·dae \sə̇ˈsed·ə,dē\ *n pl, cap* [NL, fr. *Sycetta*, type genus + *-idae*] **:** a widely distributed family of calcareous sycon sponges — see SYCETTA, SYCON

sych·no·car·pous \ˌsiknəˈkärpəs\ *adj* [Gk *sychnos* plentiful, frequent + E *-carpous*] *of a plant* **:** able to produce fruit repeatedly **:** PERENNIAL

sy·con \ˈsī,kän\ *n* [NL, fr. Gk *sykon* fig — more at FIG] **1** *cap* **:** a genus of calcareous sponges (family Sycettidae) having typical sycon structure **2** -s **a :** any sponge of the genus *Sycon* **b :** a sponge or sponge larva in which the flagellated layer is restricted to more or less tubular outpouchings of the paragastric wall that are indirectly connected with the incurrent canals through lateral pores — compare ASCON, LEUCON — **sy·co·noid** \ˈsīkə,nȯid\ *adj or n*

sy·co·nes \sīˈkō(,)nēz\ *n pl, cap* [NL, fr. pl. of *Sycon*] *in some classifications* **:** a group comprising the sycon sponges: **a :** a group coextensive with Syconosa **b :** a suborder of Syconosa

sy·co·ni·um \-ˈnēəm\ *n, pl* **syco·nia** \-ēə\ [NL, fr. Gk *sykon* fig + NL *-ium*] **:** a collective fleshy fruit in which the ovaries are borne within an enlarged succulent concave or hollow receptacle (as in the fig)

sy·co·no·sa \ˌsīkəˈnōsə, -ōzə\ *n pl, cap* [NL, fr. *Sycon* + L *-osa* (neut. pl. of *-osus* -ous)] **:** an order of Calcispongiae comprising simple syconoid sponges and others derived from this type

syco·phan·cy \ˈsikəfənsē, -nsi *sometimes* ˈsīk-\ *n* -ES [L *sycophantia*, fr. Gk *sykophantia*, fr. *sykophantēs* + *-ia* -y] **1 :** the spreading of slanderous accusations **:** DEFAMATION; *esp* **:** the informing practiced in ancient Athens **2 a :** base or obsequious flattery **:** TOADYING ⟨as deplorable as the bootlicking ~ which they displayed —R.L.Riggs⟩ ⟨there has ever been and ever will be found ~ on the side of power —F.W. Robertson⟩ **b :** the characteristic of a servile flatterer or toady ⟨had seen the straightforwardness of many boys from the bush turn into whining ~ when they came to the coast —Esther Warner⟩

¹**syco·phant** \-fənt *sometimes* -,fant *or* -,faa(ə)nt\ *n* -s [L *sycophanta*, fr. Gk *sykophantēs*, fr. *sykon* fig + *-phantēs* (fr. *phainein* to reveal, show, make known); perh. fr. the use of the gesture of the fig in denouncing a culprit — more at FANCY] **1 :** a slandering accuser **:** DEFAMER; *esp* **:** one of a group of talebearers of ancient Athens **2 :** a base or servilely attentive flatterer and self-seeker **:** TOADY ⟨the ~s were gone, for the outgoing president had nothing to give —W.A.White⟩ ⟨her children entrusted to the care of court ~s —Ann F. Wolfe⟩ ⟨is surrounded by a group of arrogant military ~s —*New Republic*⟩ **3** *obs* **:** LIAR, DECEIVER **syn** see PARASITE

²**sycophant** \"\ *vb* -ED/-ING/-S *vt, obs* **:** to traduce or flatter in the manner of a sycophant ~ *vi, obs* **:** to act the sycophant

³**sycophant** \"\ *adj* **:** SYCOPHANTIC

syco·phan·tic \ˌ==ˈfantik, -faan-, -tēk\ *adj* [Gk *sykophantikos*, fr. *sykophantēs* + *-ikos* -ic] **:** of, relating to, or characteristic of a sycophant: **a :** FAWNING, OBSEQUIOUS ⟨some . . . have been chosen rather for their ~ talents than for their intellectual acumen —Ezra Pound⟩ ⟨creeps his ~ way along the bureaucratic path to knighthood —C.J.Rolo⟩ ⟨peacocking about on the lawn, among an imported bevy of ~ females —Osbert Sitwell⟩ **b :** SLANDEROUS, DEFAMATORY

syco·phan·ti·cal \-tə̇kəl, -tēk-\ *adj* [Gk *sykophantikos* + E *-al*] **:** SYCOPHANTIC

syco·phan·ti·cal·ly \-k(ə)lē, -li\ *adv* **:** in a sycophantic manner **:** by or with sycophancy

syco·phant·ish \ˈ==,fantish, -,faan-, ˈ==fən-\ *adj* **:** SYCOPHANTIC — **syco·phant·ish·ly** *adv*

syco·phant·ism \ˈ==fən,tizəm, -,fan-, -,faan-\ *n* -s **:** SYCOPHANCY

syco·phant·ize \ˈ==(,)=,tīz\ *vi* -ED/-ING/-S [¹*sycophant* + *-ize*] *archaic* **:** to play the sycophant

syco·phant·ly *adv* [³*sycophant* + *-ly*] **:** SYCOPHANTICALLY

sy·co·sis \sīˈkōsə̇s\ *n, pl* **syco·ses** \-ō,sēz\ [NL, fr. Gk *sykōsis*, fr. *sykon* fig + *-ōsis* -osis] **:** a chronic inflammatory disease involving the hair follicles esp. of the bearded part of the face and marked by papules, pustules, and tubercles perforated by hairs with crusting

sycr *abbr* **1** synchronize **2** synchronizer

syden·ham's chorea \ˈsidᵊnəmz-, ˈsidᵊn,hamz-\ *n, usu cap S* [after Thomas *Sydenham* †1689 Eng. physician] **:** chorea following infection (as rheumatic fever) and occurring usu. in children and adolescents

sydenham's laudanum *n, usu cap S* [after T. *Sydenham*] **:** either of two opium preparations: **a :** WINE OF OPIUM **b :** tincture of opium with saffron

syd·ney \ˈsidnē, -ni\ *adj, usu cap* [fr. *Sydney*, New So. Wales, Australia] **:** of or from Sydney, the capital of New So. Wales **:** of the kind or style prevalent in Sydney

sydney blue gum *n, usu cap S* **:** a large Australian gum tree (*Eucalyptus saligna*) having bark with a bluish cast

sydney golden wattle *n, usu cap S* **:** a golden wattle (*Acacia longifolia*) with willowy branches

syd·ney·ite \ˈsidnē,īt\ *n* -s *cap* [*Sydney*, Australia + E *-ite*] **:** a native or resident of Sydney, Australia

sydney peppermint *n, usu cap S* **:** a peppermint gum (*Eucalyptus piperita*)

syd·none \ˈsid,nōn\ *n* -s [*Sydney*, Australia (where this type of compound was discovered) + E *-one*] **:** any of a class of heterocyclic compounds that contain a ring composed of two carbon atoms, two nitrogen atoms, and a fifth atom (as oxygen) and have an oxo or similar group, that are resonance hybrids of several ionic states and have large dipole moments, and that are obtainable in various ways (as by dehydration of *N*-nitroso-*N*-phenyl-glycine by acetic anhydride)

¹**sye** *var of* SIE

²**sye** *vi* [ME *syen*, fr. OE *sīgan*; akin to OS & OHG *sīgan* to sink, fall, ON *sīga* to sink, slide, *sía* to strain, filter — more at SACK (wine)] *obs* **:** SINK, FALL, DESCEND

sye *var of* SY

sy·e·nite \ˈsīə,nīt\ *n* -s [L *Syenites* (*lapis*), fr. *Syenites* of Syene (fr. Syene, ancient city in Egypt + L *-ites* -ite) + *lapis* stone] **1** *archaic* **:** a variety of granite anciently quarried at Syene in Upper Egypt in which biotite is substituted for or accompanied by hornblende **2 :** a phanerocrystalline intrusive igneous rock composed of dominant alkaline feldspar with or without subordinate plagioclase and without notable quartz or nepheline

sy·e·nit·ic \ˌ==ˈnid·ik\ *adj* **:** of, relating to, or containing syenite

sy·e·no·diorite \ˌsīə,nō+\ *n* [*syenite* + *-o-* + *diorite*] **:** a plutonic rock composed of acid plagioclase, less orthoclase, and a ferromagnesian mineral — compare GRANODIORITE

sy·e·no·gabbro \"+\ *n* [*syenite* + *-o-* + *gabbro*] **:** a plutonic rock composed of basic plagioclase, less orthoclase, and a dark mineral (as augite)

¹**syke** *var of* SIKE

²**syke** \ˈsīk\ *n* -s [ME (northern dial.), small stream, rill, fr. OE *sīc* — more at SIKE] **:** FOUNTAIN 4

syl *or* **syll** *abbr* syllable

syl·la·ba an·ceps \ˌsiləbəˈäŋ,keps, -aŋ,ke-, -an,se-\ *n* [L, lit., doubtful syllable] **:** a syllable occurring at the end of a sentence or verse in a metrical scheme whose short or long quantity is obscured by the terminal pause; *specif* **:** such a syllable occurring in the rhythms of ancient verse wherever there is a diaeresis or serving as a terminal demarcation at the end of a verse or between asynartetic cola

syl·la·bar·i·um \ˌsiləˈba(a)rēəm, -ber-, -bär-\ *n, pl* **syl·labar·ia** \-rēə\ [NL] **:** SYLLABARY

syl·la·bary \ˈsilə,berē, -ri\ *n* -ES [NL *syllabarium*, fr. L *syllaba* syllable + *-arium* -ary — more at SYLLABLE] **:** a table or listing of syllables; *specif* **:** a series or set of written characters each one of which is used to represent a syllable — distinguished from ALPHABET; compare CUNEIFORM, KANA

syllabi *pl of* SYLLABUS

¹**syl·lab·ic** \sə̇ˈlabik, -bēk\ *adj* [LL *syllabicus*, fr. Gk *syllabikos*, fr. *syllabē* syllable + *-ikos* -ic — more at SYLLABLE] **1 :** of, relating to, or denoting syllables ⟨~ accent⟩ ⟨~ characters⟩ **2 :** constituting a syllable or the nucleus of a syllable: **a** *of a consonant* **:** not accompanied in the same syllable by a vowel ⟨\n\ is ~ in \ˈbätᵊnē\ *botany*, nonsyllabic in \ˈbätnē\⟩ **b** *of a vowel* **:** having vowel quality more prominent than that of another vowel in the syllable ⟨the first vowel of a falling diphthong, as \ȯ\ in \ȯi\, is ~⟩ **3 :** consisting of or using syllabic characters or a syllabary ⟨the Eskimos of the eastern arctic have a system of ~ writing —*Sat. Eve. Post*⟩ **4 :** characterized by distinct enunciation or separation of syllables ⟨~ utterance⟩ ⟨~ tunes⟩ — see SYLLABIC MELODY **5 :** forming or comprising a type of verse distinguished primarily by count of syllables rather than by rhythmical arrangement of accents or quantities — compare QUANTITATIVE

²**syllabic** \"\ *n* -s **1 :** a syllabic sign or character ⟨some signs . . . were used in the sense of an alphabet; some signs were employed as ~s; others were ideographic —Stanley Wernyss⟩ **2 :** a syllabic sound or utterance ⟨when two or more ~s occur . . . one can clearly hear different degrees of articulatory force —Stanley Newman⟩

-syl·lab·ic \sə̇ˌlabik, -bēk\ *adj comb form* [F *-syllabique*, fr. *-syllabe* -syllabic (fr. L *-syllabus*, fr. Gk *-syllabos*, fr. *syllabē* syllable) + *-ique* -ic — more at SYLLABLE] **:** having or relating to syllables of a (specified) kind or number ⟨ambi*syllabic*⟩ ⟨hepta*syllabic*⟩ ⟨impari*syllabic*⟩

syl·lab·i·cal \sə̇ˈlabə̇kəl, -bēk-\ *adj* [LL *syllabicus* + E *-al*] *archaic* **:** SYLLABIC

syl·lab·i·cal·ly \-k(ə)lē, -li\ *adv* **:** in, with, or by syllables

syl·lab·i·cate \sə̇ˈlabə,kāt, *usu* -ād·+V\ *vt* -ED/-ING/-S [back-formation fr. *syllabication*] **:** SYLLABIFY

syl·lab·i·ca·tion \=,==ˈkāshən\ *n* -s [ML *syllabication-, syllabicatio*, fr. *syllabicatus* (past part. of *syllabicare* to form into syllables, fr. LL *syllabicus* syllabic) + L *-ion-, -io* -ion] **:** the act, process, or method of forming or dividing words into syllables

syl·la·bic·i·ty \ˌsiləˈbisəd·ē\ *n* -ES **:** the state of being or the power of forming a syllable ⟨~ determined also by manner of articulation —Leonard Bloomfield⟩ ⟨the patterns of ~ are significant in determining the morpheme boundaries and junctures —E.A.Nida⟩

syllabic melody *or* **syllabic song** *n* **:** a song (as a Gregorian chant) in which each syllable has but one note — compare MELISMATIC

syl·lab·ic·ness \sə̇ˈlabiknə̇s, -bēk-\ *n* -ES **:** SYLLABICITY

syl·lab·i·fi·ca·tion \sə̇,labəfə̇ˈkāshən\ *n* -s [L *syllaba* syllable + E *-i-* + *-fication*] **:** SYLLABICATION

syl·lab·i·fy \ˈ=ˈ=bə,fī\ *vt* -ED/-ING/-ES [L *syllaba* + E *-ify*] **:** to form or divide into syllables

syl·la·bism \ˈsilə,bizəm\ *n* -s [ISV *syllab-* (fr. L *syllaba* syllable) + *-ism*] **1 :** the use or development of syllabic characters ⟨a polysyllabic language did not lend itself so readily as the Chinese monosyllabic to ~ —Edward Clodd⟩ **2 :** SYLLABICATION

syl·la·bize \-,bīz\ *vt* -ED/-ING/-S [ML *syllabizare*, fr. Gk *syllabizein*, fr. *syllabē* syllable + *-izein* -ize] **1 :** SYLLABIFY **2 :** to utter (as verse) with distinct articulation of separate syllables

¹**syl·la·ble** \ˈsiləbəl\ *n* -s [ME *sillable*, fr. MF *sillabe*, fr. L *syllaba*, fr. Gk *syllabē*, fr. *syllambanein* to gather together, put together, combine in pronunciation, fr. *syn-* + *lambanein* to take, grasp — more at LATCH] **1 :** a unit of spoken language that is next bigger than a speech sound and consists of one or more vowel sounds alone (as \ī\ and \ə\ in \ īleftində\ *I left India*) or of a syllabic consonant alone (as \ᵊn\ in \wīdᵊn\ *widen*) or of either accompanied by one or more consonant sounds preceding or following (as \stāt\ in \stātmənt\ *statement* or \ᵊnd\ in \wīdᵊnd\ *widened* **2 :** one or more letters (as *syl*, *la*, and *ble*) in a word (as *syl·la·ble*) usu. set off from the rest of the word by a centered dot or a hyphen and roughly but often not exactly corresponding to the syllables of spoken language and treated as helps to the ascertainment of pronunciation or as markers of places where a word may be hyphenated at the end of a written or printed line **3 :** a monosyllabic word considered with reference to its meaning ⟨those awful ~s, hell, death, and sin —William Cowper⟩ **4 :** the smallest conceivable expression or unit of something **:** JOT ⟨kept a diary for years, but never entered in it a ~ that had to do with his official life —H.G.Dwight⟩ ⟨towns of gold can never countervail the least sentence or ~ of wit —R.W.Emerson⟩ ⟨as if the past had resolved itself into this tiny esoteric pattern and that I could grasp it in an instant of time, and interpret its every single ~ as briefly —Walter de la Mare⟩ **5 a :** SYLLABLE NAME **b :** SOL-FA SYLLABLES ⟨to sing by ~⟩

²**syllable** \"\ *vt* **syllabled; syllabled; syllabling** \-b(ə)liŋ\ **syllables 1 :** to give a number or arrangement of syllables to (a word or verse) ⟨some uncouth poet scarcely able to ~ his words —Virginia Woolf⟩ ⟨long unbroken sentences . . . filled with poly*syllabled* abstract nouns —*Times Lit. Supp.*⟩ **2 :** to express or utter in or as if in syllables ⟨tongues that ~ men's names —John Milton⟩ ⟨where the birds talked with words too sad and strange to ~ —J.C.Ransom⟩

syllable name *n* **:** the name of a given musical tone in solmization — compare SOL-FA SYLLABLES

syl·la·bub *or* **sil·la·bub** \ˈsilə,bəb\ *n* -s [origin unknown] **1 :** a drink or dessert made by curdling milk or cream with wine or other acid **2 :** a dessert that is made by beating to a froth sweetened milk or cream sometimes with added whites of eggs, is flavored with wine or liquor, and is served as a drink when thin or when thick is often poured over cake or fruit — compare WHIP

syl·la·bus \-,bəs\ *n, pl* **sylla·bi** \-,bī\ *or* **syllabuses** [LL, alter. (influenced by Gk *syllambanein*) of L *sillybus* label for a book, fr. Gk *sillybos*] **1 :** a compendium or summary outline of a discourse, treatise, course of study, or examination requirements **:** a series of abstracts **:** ABSTRACT, EPITOME ⟨drew up in consultation a definite scheme or ~ of the intended course —Edward Jenks⟩ ⟨preparing a complete historical and geographic ~ for each tour —*Current Biog.*⟩ **2 :** HEADNOTE 2 **3** *or* **syllabus of errors :** a collection of propositions condemned as erroneous by the Roman Catholic Church **syn** see COMPENDIUM

syl·lep·sis \sə̇ˈlepsə̇s\ *n, pl* **syllep·ses** \-p,sēz\ [L, fr. Gk *syllēpsis*, fr. the stem of *syllambanein* to gather together, put together + *-sis* — more at SYLLABLE] **1 :** the use of a word (as an adjective or verb) in grammatical agreement with only one of two nouns by which it is governed ⟨the verb in "I remain well and my wife also" is an example of ~⟩ **2 :** the use of a word in the same grammatical relation to two adjacent words in its literal sense with one and a metaphorical sense with the other ⟨"the tank fired, and the bridge and many hopes sank" is an example of ~⟩ — compare ZEUGMA

syl·lep·tic \-ptik\ *also* **syl·lep·ti·cal** \-tə̇kəl\ *adj* [fr. *syllepsis*, after such pairs as E *prolepsis*: *proleptic*, *proleptical*] **:** of, relating to, or involving a syllepsis — **syl·lep·ti·cal·ly** \-k(ə)lē\ *adv*

¹**syl·lid** \ˈsilə̇d\ *or* **syl·lid·i·an** \sə̇ˈlidēən\ *adj* [*syllid* fr. NL *Syllidae*; *syllidian* fr. NL *Syllidae* + E *-ian*] **:** of or relating to the Syllidae

²**syllid** \"\ *or* **syllidian** \"\ *n* -s **:** a worm of the family Syllidae

syl·li·dae \ˈsilə,dē\ *n pl, cap* [NL, fr. *Syllis*, type genus + *-idae*] **:** a large family of small free-swimming polychaete worms related to the Nereidae but usu. reproducing by asexual budding

syl·lis \ˈsilə̇s\ *n* [NL] **1** *cap* **:** the type genus of Syllidae **2** -ES **:** any worm of the genus *Syllis*

syl·lo·ge \ˈsilə(,)jē\ *n* -s [Gk *syllogē*, fr. *syllegein* to collect, fr. *syn-* + *legein* to collect, gather — more at LEGEND] **:** COLLECTION, COMPENDIUM

syl·lo·gism \-,jizəm\ *n* -s [ME *silogisme*, fr. MF, fr. L *syllogismus*, fr. Gk *syllogismos*, fr. *syllogizesthai* to infer, syllogize, fr. *syn-* + *logizesthai* to calculate — more at ANTILOGISM] **1 :** a deductive logical scheme or analysis of a formal argument that consists of a major premise, a minor premise, and a conclusion and that may be used either to prove a conclusion by showing that it follows from known premises or to test the truth of premises by showing what follows from them (as in "every virtue is laudable; kindness is a virtue; therefore kindness is laudable") — compare FIGURE table **2 :** explication of the relations of ideas esp. in accordance with

syllogistic principles : DEDUCTIVE METHOD ⟨a man knows first, and then he is able to prove syllogistically; so that ~ comes after knowledge —John Locke⟩ — compare INDUCTION 2 **3 :** a subtle, specious, or crafty argument, piece of reasoning, or method of attaining one's end ⟨blithely accepts the perilous ~ that the end justifies the means —C.B.Davis⟩

syl·lo·gist \-jəst\ n -s [fr. syllogism, after such pairs as E atheism: atheist] : one who applies or is skilled in syllogistic reasoning

1syl·lo·gis·tic \¦==¦jistik, -tēk\ adj [L syllogisticus, fr. Gk syllogistikos, fr. (assumed) syllogistos (verbal of syllogizesthai) + -ikos -ic] : of, relating to, or consisting of syllogism ⟨~ reasoning⟩

2syllogistic \"\ n, pl **syl·lo·gis·tics** \-ks\ sometimes sing in constr **1 :** the branch of logic dealing with the syllogism **2 :** syllogistic reasoning ⟨views on abstraction . . . and his ~s —E.W.Beth⟩ ⟨knowledge was to be a ~, or at least rational and jointed —H.O.Taylor⟩

syl·lo·gis·ti·cal \¦==¦jistəkəl, -tēk-\ adj [L syllogisticus + E -al] **1 :** SYLLOGISTIC **2 :** given to reasoning by or depending on syllogisms — **syl·lo·gis·ti·cal·ly** \-k(ə)lē, -li\ adv

syl·lo·gi·za·tion \,siləjə'zāshən, -,jī'z-\ n -s [ML syllogization-, syllogizatio, fr. LL syllogizatus (past part. of syllogizare) + L -ion-, -io -ion] : the act or process of syllogizing

syl·lo·gize \'silə,jīz\ vb -ED/-ING/-S [ME sylogysen, fr. LL syllogizare, fr. Gk syllogizesthai to infer, syllogize — more at SYLLOGISM] vi : to reason or infer by means of syllogisms : argue deductively ⟨can scarcely be said to ~; whatever he knows he knows all at once —Frank Thilly⟩ ⟨this thinking and syllogizing . . . this running over and over of hypothesis and surmise and supposition —L.P.Smith⟩ ~ vt : to deduce (something) by syllogism ⟨~s his moral laws⟩

sylph \'silf\ n -s [NL sylphus] **1 :** an imaginary or elemental being inhabiting the air and being mortal but soulless — compare UNDINE **2 :** a slender woman or girl of light and graceful carriage **3 :** any of several brilliant So. American hummingbirds (as Aglaiocercus kingi) having a long forked tail

sylph·ic \-fik\ adj : of, relating to, or resembling a sylph

1sylph·id \-fəd\ n -s [F sylphide, fr. sylphe sylph (fr. NL sylphus) + -ide -id] : a young or diminutive sylph

2sylphid \"\ adj : SYLPHIC

sylphlike \'=,=\ adj : resembling a sylph : SYLPHIC

Syl·phon \'sil,fän\ trademark — used for a thin-walled tubular bellows used in temperature and pressure regulators, bellows seals, and expansion joints

syl·va \'silvə\ n -s [L silva, sylva forest, grove] **1 :** SILVA **2** archaic : a collection of poems, anecdotes, or literary pieces — used chiefly as a title

1syl·van or **sil·van** \'silvən\ n -s [L silvanus, sylvanus, fr. Silvanus, Sylvanus, god of woods and trees, fr. silva, sylva forest + -anus -an (n. suffix)] **1 :** a deity or spirit frequenting groves or woods **2 :** a person, animal, or bird living in or frequenting the woods or forest

2sylvan also **silvan** \"\ adj [ML silvanus, sylvanus, fr. L silva, sylva + -anus -an (adj. suffix)] **1 a :** living or located in the woods or forest ⟨a group of ~ beings —J.G.Frazer⟩ ⟨still others, swamp and ~ types mainly, never leave their native haunts —V.M.Ehlers & E.W.Steel⟩ **b :** of, relating to, or characteristic of the woods or forest ⟨owned the whole mountain, led a ~ life there —Vincent Sheean⟩ ⟨some such ~ instrument of music —Nathaniel Hawthorne⟩ **2 a :** made, shaped, or formed of woods or trees ⟨living in a ~ bower⟩ ⟨an unbroken expanse of ~ vegetation⟩ **b :** abounding in woods, groves, or trees : WOODY, WOODED ⟨through which wind ~ drives and paths edged with laurel —Amer. Guide Series: Conn.⟩ ⟨a ~ setting for the Singing Tower —Amer. Guide Series: Fla.⟩

3sylvan var of SILVAN

syl·vaner \sil'vänər, -van-\ n -s usu cap [G sylvaner, silvaner, prob. fr. L Sylvanus, Silvanus, god of woods and trees + G -er] **1 a :** a German white wine grape **b :** a Rhine wine made from such grapes **2 a :** a California wine grape resembling the German Sylvaner **b :** a wine made from such grapes

syl·van·ite also **sil·van·ite** \'silvə,nīt\ n -s [F sylvanite, fr. sylvane sylvanite (fr. Transylvania, its locality) + -ite] : a mineral $(Au,Ag)Te_2$ consisting of a gold silver telluride, having a steel gray, silver white, or brass yellow color, and often occurring in implanted crystals resembling written characters (hardness 1.5–2 sp. gr. 7.9–8.3) — called also graphic tellurium — **syl·van·it·ic** \¦==¦nid·ik\ adj

syl·vat·ic \(')sil¦vad·ik\ adj [L silvaticus, sylvaticus — more at SAVAGE] **1 :** SYLVAN ⟨the ~ Indians who occupied the extreme western parts of the provinces —J.A.Cosculluela⟩ **2 :** occurring in wild animals ⟨in its ~ form it is endemic among wild rodents on the west coast —Jour. Amer. Med. Assoc.⟩ ⟨~ yellow fever —Ecology⟩

sylvatic plague n : a plague of which wild rodents and their fleas are the reservoirs and vectors and which is widely distributed in western No. and So. America though rarely affecting man

syl·ves·trene \sil've,strēn\ n -s [ISV sylvestr- (fr. NL sylvestris — specific epithet of Pinus sylvestris, the species of pine from which it is derived —, fr. L, sylvan) + -ene] : a liquid terpene hydrocarbon $C_{10}H_{16}$ or mixture of two isomeric terpenes occurring in dextrorotatory, levorotatory, and inactive racemic forms and obtained as the dihydrochloride of the dextrorotatory form by treating either of the carenes or oil fractions containing them with hydrogen chloride; 1, 8- or 6,8-meta-menthadiene

syl·ves·tri·an \(')sil¦vestrēən\ adj [L silvestris, sylvestris sylvan (fr. silva, sylva forest, fro) + E -an] : SYLVAN ⟨~ gods —John Gay⟩

syl·via \'silvēə\ n [NL, fr. the name Sylvia, often used as a nickname for a robin] **1** cap : the type genus of warblers of the formerly extensive family Sylviidae restricted to the European whitethroat, the blackcap, and related forms **2** -s : any warbler of the genus Sylvia

syl·vi·an aqueduct \'silvēən-\ n, usu cap S [sylvian fr. Sylvius (Jacques Dubois) †1555 Fr. anatomist + E -an] : AQUEDUCT OF SYLVIUS

sylvian fissure n, usu cap S : LATERAL FISSURE

syl·vi·col·i·dae \,silvē'kälə,dē\ [NL, fr. Sylvicola, type genus (fr. L, adj., inhabiting the forest, fr. silvi-, sylvi- — fr. silva, sylva forest — + -cola inhabitant) + -idae — more at -COLOUS] syn of PARULIDAE

1syl·vic·o·line \sil'vikə,līn, -lən\ adj [NL Sylvicola + E -ine] : of or relating to the Parulidae

2sylvicoline \"\ n -s : a warbler of the family Parulidae

sylvics var of SILVICS

sylviculture var of SILVICULTURE

syl·vid \'silvəd\ n -s usu cap [L silva, sylva forest + E -id] : an early American Indian of a physical type characterized by marked dolichocephaly and found esp. in the forested eastern part of No. America — compare CENTRALID, PACIFID

1syl·vi·id \'silvēəd, -ē,id\ adj [NL Sylviidae] : of or relating to the Sylviidae

2sylviid \"\ n -s : a bird of the family Sylviidae

syl·vi·i·dae \sil'vīə,dē\ n pl, cap [NL, fr. Sylvia, type genus + -idae] : a family of small 10-primaried oscine passerine birds related to the thrushes and consisting of the Old World or true warblers and the kinglets and gnatcatchers of America

syl·vil·a·gus \sil'viləgəs\ n [L silvi-, sylvi- (fr. silva, sylva woods) + Gk lagōs hare] **1** cap : a genus of mammals (family Leporidae) comprising the cottontail and related New World rabbits **2** -s : any rabbit of the genus Sylvilagus

syl·vin·ite \'silvə,nīt\ n -s [sylvin + -ite] : rock that contains chiefly potassium chloride though in an impure state

syl·vite \'sil,vīt\ also **syl·vin** \-vən\ or **syl·vine** \,-vən, -,vēn\ n -s [sylvite alter. of sylvine; sylvin, sylvine fr. F sylvine, fr. NL (sal digestivus) Sylvii, lit., digestive salt of Sylvius + F -ine] : a mineral KCl consisting of native potassium chloride and occurring in colorless cubes or crystalline masses like rock salt but having a sharper taste (hardness 2, sp. gr. 1.98)

1sym- — see SYN-

2sym- or **s-** comb form [symmetrical] usu ital : symmetrical — in names of organic compounds ⟨sym-dichloro-ethylene⟩ ⟨s-dichloro-ethylene⟩

sym abbr **1** symbol; symbolic **2** symmetrical **3** symphony

sym–allylene \'sim+\ n [2sym- + allylene] : ALLENE 1

symar var of SIMAR

sym·bal·lo·phone \sim'bōlə,fōn\ n [Gk symballein to throw together, compare + E -o- + -phone — more at SYMBOL] : a double stethoscope having two chest pieces for the comparison of sounds in the body heard through the earpieces

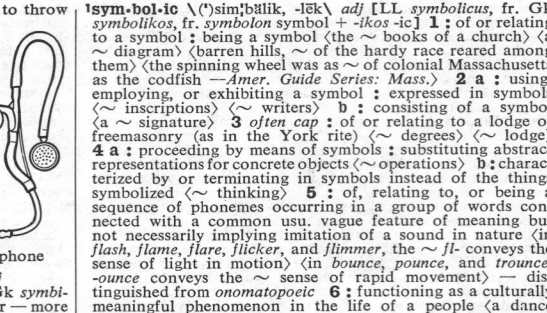

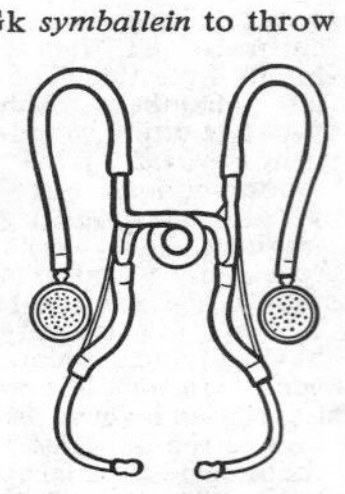
symballophone

sym·bat·ic \(')sim¦bad·ik\ adj [ISV, fr. Gk symbatikos tending or leading to agreement, fr. symbat- (verbal stem of symbainein to come to an agreement, fr. syn- + bainein to walk, come) + -ikos -ic — more at COME] of two related variables : increasing or decreasing together though not necessarily in direct proportion

sym·bi·on \'simbī,än, -bē,-\ n -s [NL, fr. Gk symbiōn (pres. part. of symbioun) or fr. Gk symbion, neut. of symbios living together — more at SYMBIOSIS] : SYMBIONT — **sym·bi·on·ic** \¦==¦änik\ adj

sym·bi·ont \'==,änt\ n -s [prob. fr. G, modif. of Gk symbiount-, symbiōn, pres. part. of symbioun to live together — more at SYMBIOSIS] : an organism living in symbiosis; usu : the smaller member of a symbiotic pair of dissimilar size as opposed to the larger host — **sym·bi·on·tic** \¦==¦äntik\ adj

sym·bi·on·ti·cism \,=='äntə,sizəm\ n -s [symbiontic + -ism] : SYMBIOSIS

sym·bi·ose \'simbī,ōs, -bē,-\ vi -ED/-ING/-S [back-formation fr. NL symbiosis] : to associate symbiotically

sym·bi·o·sis \,simbī'ōsəs, -bē'-\ n, pl **symbio·ses** \-'ō,sēz\ [NL, modif. (influenced by Gk symbiōsis) of G symbiose, fr. Gk symbiōsis state of living together, fr. symbioun to live together, fr. symbios living together, fr. syn- + bios life, mode of life — more at QUICK] **1 a :** the living together in more or less intimate association or even close union of two dissimilar organisms (as in parasitism, mutualism, or commensalism) — compare HELOTISM **b :** the intimate living together of two dissimilar organisms in any of various mutually beneficial relationships; often : MUTUALISM **2 :** mutual cooperation between persons and groups in a society esp. when mutual interdependence is involved

sym·bi·ote \'simbī,ōt, -bē,-\ also **sym·bi·ot** \-,ät\ n -s [F symbiote, fr. Gk symbiōtēs companion, partner, fr. symbioun to live together] : SYMBIONT

sym·bi·ot·ic \¦==¦äd·|ik, ät|, |ēk\ also **sym·bi·ot·i·cal** \|əkəl\ adj [symbiotic fr. NL symbiosis + ISV -otic; symbiotical fr. symbiotic + -al] : relating to, characterized by, living in, or resulting from a state of symbiosis — compare FREE-LIVING, PARASITIC — **sym·bi·ot·i·cal·ly** \|ək(ə)lē\ adv

sym·bi·ot·ics \,=='äd·iks\ n pl but sing in constr [fr. symbiotic, after such pairs as E economic: economics] : a field of study dealing with symbiosis

symbiotic saprophytism n : the association of a saprophytic plant with a symbiotic fungus (as a mycorrhiza)

sym·bi·o·tism \'simbīə,tizəm, -bēə,-\ n -s [symbiotic + -ism] : SYMBIOSIS

sym·bleph·a·ron \sim'blefə,rän\ n -s [NL, fr. syn- + Gk blepharon eyelid] : adhesion between an eyelid and the eyeball (as from a burn)

1sym·bol \'simbəl\ n -s [in sense 1, fr. LL symbolum baptismal creed, fr. LGk symbolon, lit., token, sign, fr. Gk; in other senses, fr. L symbolus, symbolum token, sign, fr. Gk symbolon token of identity (verified by comparing its other half), sign, symbol, fr. symballein to throw together, compare, contribute, fr. syn- + ballein to throw — more at DEVIL] **1 :** an authoritative summary of faith or doctrine : a creedal formulary : CREED **2 :** something that stands for or suggests something else by reason of relationship, association, convention, or accidental but not intentional resemblance; esp : a visible sign of something (as a concept or an institution) that is invisible ⟨the lion is the ~ of courage⟩ ⟨the cross was always one of the ~s of Christianity —E.S.Holden⟩ ⟨a flock of sheep is not the ~ of a free people —New Republic⟩ ⟨shop windows are full of festive ~s: cats and candles, witches and brooms, pumpkins and grotesque masks —Lucy Embury⟩ ⟨a heritage is at any moment a selection of ~s out of the past —Max Lerner⟩ **3 :** an arbitrary or conventional sign (as a character, a diagram, a letter, or an abbreviation) used in writing or printing relating to a particular field (as mathematics, physics, chemistry, music, or phonetics) to represent operations, quantities, spatial position, valence, direction, elements, relations, qualities, sounds, or other ideas or qualities : SIGN ⟨the usual ~s for crossroads, stores, and churches on rural maps —Amer. Guide Series: Minn.⟩ **4 a** (1) : a formal unit of expression (as a term, proposition, or formal argument) that represents an abstract thought capable of being dealt with as a unit (2) : a conventionally adopted character in logic **b :** a conventional or nonnatural sign depending for its meaning on an interpretant — contrasted with icon and index **5 :** an object or act that represents a repressed complex through unconscious association rather than through objective resemblance or conscious substitution **6 :** an act, sound, or material object having cultural significance and the capacity to excite or objectify a response ⟨there must be some ~s around which interaction can be organized —W.F.Whyte⟩

syn SYMBOL, EMBLEM, ATTRIBUTE, TYPE can signify, in common, a visible thing that stands for or suggests something invisible or intangible. SYMBOL and EMBLEM are often used interchangeably but may be distinguished by the fact that SYMBOL can apply to anything that serves as an outward sign of something else, usu. spiritual or immaterial ⟨the key symbols are the lilac which stands for the new birth in the spring of the year, the drooping star which stands for death, and the bird whose song embraces birth and death indifferently, and so inspires the poet that he becomes the bird —J.C.Ransom⟩ ⟨the present law is spiteful, and . . . has become a symbol of dissension and bitterness —A.E.Stevenson †1965⟩ ⟨"Dr. Livingstone, I presume", a phrase whose casualness made it a symbol everywhere of British aplomb —Amer. Guide Series: Ark.⟩ ⟨language consists of symbols⟩ EMBLEM usu. applies to pictorial representation or to something standing as a pictorial or picturelike symbol and is often used of a pictorial device found on a shield or banner intended to serve as a chosen symbol of the character or history of the nation, royal line, or organization that has adopted it ⟨the national emblem of the Future Farmers of America is significant and meaningful in every detail . . . made up of five symbols: the owl, the plow, and the rising sun, within the cross section of an ear of corn which is surmounted by the American eagle —Future Farmers of America⟩ ⟨his emblem was a butterfly with a sting in its tail — a sting he attempted to keep in constant use —Time⟩ ⟨the American eagle, emblem of the U.S.⟩ ⟨the emblem of the U.S.S.R., the sickle around an arm and hammer⟩ ⟨the cold teapot, the emptied cups, emblems of hospitality —Joseph Conrad⟩ ATTRIBUTE, a term in painting and sculpture, applies to an object usu. associated with a representation of a character or personified abstraction and serving to identify it ⟨the attribute of Fortune, a turning wheel⟩ ⟨the scales and blindfold, the attribute of Justice⟩ TYPE, in this connection occurring chiefly in theological use, applies to a person or thing prefiguring or foreshadowing something or someone to come and serving as his or its symbol until the reality appears, often implying a divine dispensation whereby a person, event, or experience prefigures a spiritual or immaterial reality ⟨allegory was also called on to justify, as against educated pagans, certain acts of that heroic but peccant type of Christ, David, the son of Jesse —H.O.Taylor⟩ **syn** see in addition CHARACTER

2symbol \"\ vb **symboled** or **symbolled**; **symboled** or **symbolled**; **symboling** or **symbolling** \-b(ə)liŋ\ **symbols** vt : to visualize by means of a symbol : SYMBOLIZE ~ vi : to employ symbols ⟨man has the power to ~⟩

3symbol \"\ n -s [L symbola, fr. Gk symbolē, fr. symballein to throw together, contribute] : something that is thrown into a common fund : CONTRIBUTION

sym·bol·gram \-l,gram\ n [1symbol + -gram] **1 :** an artistic combination of symbols usu. of American Indian origin that expresses the ambitions and desires of its designer **2 :** a personally symbolic design (as of a camp fire girl)

1sym·bol·ic \(')sim¦bälik, -lēk\ adj [LL symbolicus, fr. Gk symbolikos, fr. symbolon symbol + -ikos -ic] **1 :** of or relating to a symbol : being a symbol ⟨the ~ books of a church⟩ ⟨a ~ diagram⟩ ⟨barren hills, ~ of the hardy race reared among them⟩ ⟨the spinning wheel was as ~ of colonial Massachusetts as the codfish —Amer. Guide Series: Mass.⟩ **2 a :** using, employing, or exhibiting a symbol : expressed in symbols ⟨~ inscriptions⟩ ⟨~ writers⟩ **b :** consisting of a symbol ⟨a ~ signature⟩ **3** often cap : of or relating to a lodge of freemasonry (as in the York rite) ⟨~ degrees⟩ ⟨~ lodge⟩ **4 a :** proceeding by means of symbols : substituting abstract representations for concrete objects ⟨~ operations⟩ **b :** characterized by or terminating in symbols instead of the things symbolized ⟨~ thinking⟩ **5 :** of, relating to, or being a sequence of phonemes occurring in a group of words connected with a common usu. vague feature of meaning but not necessarily implying imitation of a sound in nature ⟨in flash, flame, flare, flicker, and flimmer, the ~ fl- conveys the sense of light in motion⟩ ⟨in bounce, pounce, and trounce, -ounce conveys the ~ sense of rapid movement⟩ — distinguished from onomatopoeic **6 :** functioning as a culturally meaningful phenomenon in the life of a people ⟨a dance ritual with ~ rather than abstract, mimetic, or purely personal importance⟩

2symbolic \"\ n -s **1 :** something that is symbolic — usu. used with the ⟨the ~ may lose itself in unintelligibility —John Dewey⟩ **2** [G symbolik, fr. symbol creed (fr. LL symbolum) + -ik -ics, fr. Gk -ikē, fem. of -ikos -ic] : SYMBOLICS 1

sym·bol·i·cal \-ləkəl, -lēk-\ adj [LL symbolicus of a symbol + E -al] : marked by symbolism : SYMBOLIC, ALLEGORICAL, EMBLEMATIC ⟨~ language⟩ ⟨whether art is ~, poetic or imitative —Herbert Read⟩

sym·bol·i·cal·ly \-älək(ə)lē, -ālēk-, -)li\ adv [symbolical + -ly] : in a symbolic manner : ALLEGORICALLY, EMBLEMATICALLY ⟨the primitive was alleged not to think logically, but mystically and ~ —W.E.Moore⟩

sym·bol·i·cal·ness n -ES [symbolical + -ness] : the quality or state of being symbolic ⟨the ~ of an act⟩

symbolic books or **symbolical books** n pl, often cap S&B : books containing creeds or confessions of faith of a church ⟨the Symbolic Books of Orthodoxy⟩

symbolic delivery n : the delivery of property by means of a token (as a key or a bankbook)

symbolic equation n : a mathematical equation declaring the equivalence of a group of operations

symbolic language n : a language that employs symbols either extensively or exclusively; esp : one that has been artificially constructed for the purpose of precise formulations (as in symbolic logic, mathematics, or chemistry) — compare CALCULUS 3

symbolic logic n : a science of developing and representing logical principles by means of symbols for the purpose of providing an exact canon of deduction based on primitives, postulates, and formation and transformation rules — called also mathematical logic; see ALGEBRA OF CLASSES, ALGEBRA OF RELATIONS, CALCULUS OF INDIVIDUALS, COMBINATORY LOGIC, FUNCTIONAL CALCULUS, PROPOSITIONAL CALCULUS

sym·bol·ic·ly adv [1symbolic + -ly] : SYMBOLICALLY

sym·bol·ics \sim'bäliks\ n pl but sing in constr [1symbolic + -ics] **1 :** historical theology dealing with Christian creeds and confessions of faith : SYMBOLISM **2 :** the study of ancient symbols and ceremonies

symbolic theology n [symbolics] : a branch of theology that deals with the doctrinal differences of churches as found in creeds

sym·bol·ism \'simbə,lizəm\ n -s [1symbol + -ism] **1 :** the practice or art of using symbols esp. by investing things with a symbolic meaning or by expressing the invisible, intangible, or spiritual, by means of visible or sensuous representations: as **a :** the use of conventional or traditional signs (as the nimbus) in the representation esp. of divine beings and spirits in order to indicate qualities, powers, degrees, or other attributes **b :** artistic imitation or invention that is not an end in itself but a method of revealing or suggesting immaterial, ideal, or otherwise intangible truth or states and ranges in form from the allegorization of nature or life to the presentation of ideas, emotions, or states of mind through concatenations of sound (as in music or poetry), arrangements of lines and planes (as in painting and sculpture), or contrasts or blendings of color (as in painting) — compare IMAGISM **2 :** the theological study of religious creeds and confessions of faith : SYMBOLICS **3 :** a system of symbols or representations

1sym·bol·ist \-ləst\ n -s [1symbol + -ist] **1 a** often cap : one who regards the elements of the Eucharist as symbols and not as the body and blood of Christ **b :** one who advocates or employs symbolism in religious worship **2 :** one who employs symbols or symbolism **3 :** one skilled in the interpretation or explication of symbols **4** [F symboliste, fr. symbole symbol (fr. L symbolus, symbolum) + -iste -ist] usu cap : one of a group of writers and artists (as in France after 1880) who are reactionists against realism and the theories and practices of the Parnassians and who concern themselves with general truths instead of actualities, exalt the metaphysical and the mysterious, and aim to unify and blend the arts and the functions of the senses — compare DECADENT 2 **5 :** a logician who advocates or employs symbolic logic

2symbolist \"\ adj : of, relating to, or characteristic of symbolists

sym·bol·is·tic \¦simbə¦listik, -tēk\ adj [symbolist + -ic] : of, relating to, or characteristic of symbolists : executed by or in the manner of a symbolist : employing or marked by symbolism : SYMBOLIC ⟨~ poetry⟩ ⟨~ methods⟩ — **sym·bol·is·ti·cal·ly** \-tək(ə)lē\ adv

sym·bol·iza·tion \,simbələ'zāshən, -bə,lī'-\ n -s **1 :** the act or process of symbolizing : symbolical representation or an instance of it : SYMBOLISM **2 :** symbolic representation of a repressed complex (as in dreams) **3 :** the capacity of man in distinction to infrahuman beings to develop a system of meaningful symbols

sym·bol·ize \'simbə,līz\ vb -ED/-ING/-S see -ize in Explan Notes, vi **1** [MF symboliser, fr. ML symbolizare to express by a symbol, to be alike in quality, fr. L symbolus, symbolum symbol + LL -izare -ize] archaic : to be alike (as in qualities, properties, or principles) : become united : HARMONIZE, AGREE, CONCUR **2** [1symbol + -ize] : to use symbols or symbolism ⟨the Middle Ages, with their constant tendency to ~ —Lewis Mumford⟩ ~ vt [ML symbolizare to express by a symbol] **1 :** to serve as a symbol of : stand for : TYPIFY ⟨the wedding ring ~s unending love⟩ **2 :** to represent, express, or identify by a symbol ⟨streets of a populated place need not be symbolized —Topographic Surveying⟩ ⟨talking ~s experience —Stuart Chase⟩

sym·bol·iz·er \-zə(r)\ n -s : one that symbolizes : SYMBOLIST

symbolled past of SYMBOL

symbolo- comb form [Gk symbolon] : sign : symbol ⟨symbololatry⟩

sym·bo·log·i·cal \¦simbə¦läjəkəl\ adj : of, relating to, or characteristic of symbology — **sym·bo·log·i·cal·ly** \-jək(ə)lē\ adv

sym·bol·o·gist \sim'bäləjəst\ n -s : a specialist in symbology

sym·bol·o·gy \-jē, -ji\ n -ES [symbolo- + -logy] **1 :** the art of expression by symbols **2 :** the study or interpretation of symbols

sym·bo·lo·phobia \¦simbə(,)lō+\ n [NL, fr. symbolo- + phobia] : fear that one's acts or speech may contain symbolic meanings

symbols pl of SYMBOL, pres 3d sing of SYMBOL

symbol train n : MANIFEST 4

sym·branch \'sim,braŋk\ n -s [NL Symbranchii] : a fish of the order Symbranchii

sym·bran·chia \sim'braŋkēə\ [NL, fr. sym- + -branchia] syn of SYMBRANCHII

1sym·bran·chi·ate \-ēət, -ē,āt\ adj [NL Symbranchia + E -ate] : of or relating to the Symbranchii

2symbranchiate \"\ n -s : SYMBRANCH

sym·bran·chi·dae \sim'braŋkə,dē\ [NL, alter. of Synbranchidae] syn of SYNBRANCHIDAE

sym·bran·chii \sim'braŋkē,ī\ n pl, cap [NL, alter. of Synbranchia] : an order of teleost tropical fishes resembling the true eels (order Apodes) but having the maxillaries and

premaxillaries well developed and the pectoral arch joined to or near the skull

sym·bran·choid \sim'braŋ,kȯid\ *adj* [NL *Symbranchus* (syn. of *Synbranchus*, type genus of the Synbranchidae, fr. *syn-* + L *branchia* gill) + E *-oid* — more at BRANCHIA] **:** resembling or related to the Synbranchidae

sym·me·lus \'siməlәs\ *n, pl* **symme·li** \-mə,lī\ [NL, fr. *syn-* + *-melus*] **:** SIRENOMELUS

sym·metallic \¦sim+\ *adj* [*syn-* + *-metallic* (as in *bimetallic*)] **:** of or relating to symmetallism ⟨~ coins⟩

sym·met·al·lism \(')sim¦med·ᵊl,izəm\ *n* -s [*syn-* + *-metallism* (as in *bimetallism*)] **:** a system of coinage in which the unit of currency consists of a particular weight of an amalgam of two or more metals (as gold and silver)

sym·met·ri·cal \sə'me·trəkəl, -rēk-\ *or* **sym·met·ric** \-rik, -rēk\ *adj* [*symmetry* + *-ical* or *-ic*] **1 :** having or involving symmetry **:** exhibiting symmetry **:** exhibiting correspondence in size and shape of parts **:** BALANCED, REGULAR ⟨the human body is ~⟩ ⟨crystals are often ~⟩ ⟨a ~ garden⟩ ⟨a ~ grouping⟩ **2 :** having corresponding points whose connecting lines are bisected by a given point or perpendicularly bisected by a given line or plane — used of geometrical figures **3 a :** being of such nature that the terms may be interchanged without altering the value, character, or truth — used esp. of mathematical relations, functions, and equations ⟨$c=f(a+b)$ is ~ with respect to *a* and *b* but not generally with respect to *a* and *c*⟩ **b :** COMMENSURABLE **4 a** *of a shoot or other plant part* **:** capable of division by a longitudinal plane into similar halves — compare ACTINOMORPHIC, ZYGOMORPHIC **b** *of a flower* **:** having the same number of members in each whorl of floral leaves — compare REGULAR 2c **5 :** affecting corresponding parts simultaneously and similarly ⟨~ gangrene of the legs⟩ **6 :** exhibiting symmetry in the structural formula; *esp* **:** relating to derivatives in which groups are substituted symmetrically in the molecule ⟨~ dichloro-ethylene ClCH=CHCl⟩ ⟨~ or 1,3,5-trinitro-benzene⟩

symmetrical diphenyl-urea *n* **:** CARBANILIDE

symmetrical lens *n* **:** a simple or compound lens whose optical properties are unaltered when the axis is rotated through 180 degrees

sym·met·ri·cal·ly \-rək(ə)lē, -rēk-, -li\ *adv* [*symmetry* + *-ically* (as in *geometrically*)] **:** in a symmetrical manner ⟨~ placed windows⟩ ⟨highly cultivated and ~ developed persons —C.W.Eliot⟩

sym·met·ri·cal·ness *n* -ES **:** the quality or state of being symmetrical **:** SYMMETRY

sym·me·tri·za·tion \,simə·trə'zāshən\ *n* -s [*symmetrize* + *-ation*] **:** the action of making symmetrical

sym·me·trize \'simə,trīz\ *vt* -ED/-ING/-S [*symmetry* + *-ize*] **:** to make symmetrical **:** reduce to symmetry

sym·me·tro·phobia \,simə·trə'fōbēə\ *n* [NL, fr. E *symmetry* + NL *-o-* + *phobia*] **:** a characteristic asymmetry (as in ancient Egyptian architecture and in Japanese design) implying an aversion to symmetry

sym·me·try \'simə·trē, -ri\ *n* -ES [L *symmetria*, fr. Gk, commensurability, proportion, symmetry, fr. *symmetros* commensurate, suitable, symmetrical (fr. *syn-* + *metron* measure) + *-ia* -y — more at MEASURE] **1 a** *obs* **:** mutual relationship of parts (as in size, arrangement, or measurements) **:** PROPORTION **b :** due or balanced proportions **:** beauty of form or arrangement arising from balanced proportions ⟨with order, ~, and taste unblest —Robert Burns⟩ **2 :** correspondence in size, shape, and relative position of parts that are on opposite sides of a dividing line or median plane or that are distributed about a center or axis **:** an arrangement or external form (as in a body, a design, or a grouping) marked by bilateral conformity or geometrical regularity — see BILATERAL SYMMETRY, RADIAL SYMMETRY **3 :** the property of being symmetrical **4 :** the property of a crystal of having two or more directions that are alike in physical and crystallographic respects because of identity of atomic structure in the directions concerned or mirror-image relations along such directions

sym·minct \'simiŋkt\ *adj* [modif. of Gk *symmeiktos*, *symmiktos* mixed together, fr. *symmeignynai*, *symmignynai* to mix together, fr. *syn-* + *meignynai*, *mignynai* to mix — more at MIX] **:** composed of material that has not been segregated into separate layers of fine and coarse particles ⟨~ clay⟩ ⟨~ varve⟩

sym·pa·thec·to·mize \,simpə'thektə,mīz\ *vt* -ED/-ING/-S **:** to perform a sympathectomy on

sym·pa·thec·to·my \-təmē\ *n* -ES [ISV *sympath-* (fr. ²*sympathetic*) + *-ectomy*] **:** the surgical interruption (as by resection of a ganglion or plexus) of sympathetic nerve pathways

¹**sym·pa·thet·ic** \¦simpə¦thed·¦ik, -et|, |ēk\ *adj* [NL *sympatheticus*, fr. Gk *sympatheia* sympathy + *-ētikos* (as in *pathētikos* pathetic)] **1 :** existing or operating through a real or assumed affinity, interdependence, or mutual association in which the condition of one thing influences sometimes in an occult way that of a separate unrelated thing ⟨cut hair and nails are supposed by primitive man to remain in a ~ relation with their original owner —J.G. Frazer⟩ ⟨the ~ exhilaration of so many people's cheerfulness —Nathaniel Hawthorne⟩ **2 a :** of such nature or character that coexistence, accord, or association is feasible or satisfying **:** not discordant or antagonistic ⟨antipathetic to the law of community living, but ~ to the law of survival —Agnes N. Keith⟩ ⟨~ to slum-clearance programs⟩ **b :** appropriate to one's mood, inclinations, or disposition **:** having qualities leading to kindly acceptance, gratification, appreciation, or pleasurable association ⟨meekness was not a quality that she found ~ —Helen Howe⟩ ⟨found a ~ medium in wood engraving —Herbert Read⟩ **c :** marked by kindly or pleased appreciation ⟨in general the treatment of the subject is ~ rather than hostile —W.L.Sperry⟩ **3 :** given to, marked by, or arising from sympathy, compassion, friendly fellow feelings, and sensitivity to others' emotions ⟨when you are cold and critical, instead of ~ —Nathaniel Hawthorne⟩ ⟨a ~ gesture⟩ **4 :** favorably inclined **:** showing attitudes or preferences in harmony **:** APPROVING, FAVORING ⟨those more ~ to your ways or views —M.R.Cohen⟩ ⟨not ~ to the idea of a sales tax⟩ **5 :** showing empathy **:** exhibiting ready comprehension of others' mental states **:** led by disposition or intuition to a warm friendly appreciative interest in others ⟨though some considered her arrogant and forbidding, I found her personality ~ —Edmund Wilson⟩ **6 a :** of or relating to the sympathetic nervous system **b :** mediated by or acting on the sympathetic nerves **7 :** relating to musical tones produced by means of sympathetic vibration (as from a resonator or resonance cavity) ⟨~ tones⟩ or so tuned as to sound by sympathetic vibration rather than by being struck, plucked, or bowed ⟨~ string⟩ **syn** see CONSONANT, TENDER

²**sympathetic** \"\ *n* -s **:** a sympathetic structure; *esp* **:** SYMPATHETIC NERVOUS SYSTEM

sym·pa·thet·i·cal \|əkəl\ *adj* [NL *sympatheticus* + E *-al*] *archaic* **:** SYMPATHETIC

sym·pa·thet·i·cal·ly \|ək(ə)lē, |ēk-, -li\ *adv* [*sympathetical* + *-ly*] **:** in a sympathetic manner or mood **:** by reason of sympathy esp. through counteraction, consonance, or interdependence ⟨write ~⟩ ⟨the crisis must ~ affect all nations⟩ ⟨the characters are brilliantly observed but not ~ understood —M.R.Ridley⟩

sympathetic chain *n* **:** either of the ganglionated longitudinal cords of the sympathetic nervous system

sympathetic clock *n* **:** a clock synchronized from a master clock

sympathetic ink *n* **:** SECRET INK

sympathetic magic *n* **:** magic based on the assumption that a person or thing can be supernaturally affected through its name or an object (as a nail paring, image, or dancer) representing it **:** CONTAGIOUS MAGIC — compare IMITATIVE MAGIC

sympathetic nerve *n* **:** a nerve of the sympathetic nervous system

sympathetic nervous system *n* **1** *archaic* **:** AUTONOMIC NERVOUS SYSTEM **2 :** the part of the autonomic nervous system that contains chiefly adrenergic fibers and tends to depress secretion, decrease the tone and contractility of smooth muscle, and cause the contraction of blood vessels and that consists essentially of preganglionic fibers arising in the thoracic and upper lumbar parts of the spinal cord and passing through delicate white rami communicantes to ganglia located in a pair of ganglionated cords situated one on each side of the vertebral column or to more peripheral ganglia or ganglionated plexuses and postganglionic fibers passing typically through gray rami communicantes to spinal nerves with which they are distributed to various end organs — compare PARASYMPATHETIC NERVOUS SYSTEM

sym·pa·thet·ic·ness *n* -ES **:** the quality of being sympathetic

sympathetico- *comb form* [*sympathetic* (*nervous system*)] **1 :** sympathetic ⟨*sympathetico*mimetic⟩ **2 :** sympathetic and ⟨*sympathetico*adrenal⟩

sym·pa·thet·i·co·adrenal \¦simpə¦thed·ə(,)kō+\ *adj* [*sympathetico-* + *adrenal*] **:** of, relating to, or made up of sympathetic nervous and adrenal elements ⟨~ system⟩

sym·pa·thet·i·co·lyt·ic \¦simpə¦thed·əkə¦lid·ik\ *adj* [*sympathetico-* + *-lytic*] **:** SYMPATHOLYTIC

sym·pa·thet·i·co·mimetic \¦simpə¦thed·ə(,)kō+\ *adj or n* [*sympathetico-* + *mimetic*] **:** SYMPATHOMIMETIC

sympathetic ophthalmia *n* **:** inflammation in an uninjured eye as a result of injury and inflammation of the other

sym·pa·thet·i·co·to·nia \,simpə,thed·əkə'tōnēə\ *n* -S [NL, fr. *sympathetico-* + *-tonia*] **:** SYMPATHICOTONIA — **sym·pa·thet·i·co·ton·ic** \¦==¦==¦tänik\ *adj*

sympathetic powder *n* **:** a powder held by alchemists to be a sovereign cure for a wound even if applied merely to blood from it or to the weapon inflicting it

sympathetic strike *n* **:** a strike in which the strikers make no demands on their own employers but try to bring pressure against the employers of other workers on strike — called also *sympathy strike*

sympathetic system *n* **:** SYMPATHETIC NERVOUS SYSTEM

sympathetic vibration *n* **:** a vibration produced in one body by the vibrations of exactly the same period in a neighboring body

sym·pa·thet·o·blast \,simpə'thed·ə,blast\ *n* [*sympathetic* + *-o-* + *-blast*] **:** a cell destined to become a sympathetic neuron

sympathico- *comb form* [NL *sympathicus*, fr. *sympathia* sympathy + *-icus* -ic] **:** sympathetic ⟨*sympathico*tonia⟩

sym·path·i·co·blast \sim¦pathəkō,blast\ *n* [ISV *sympathico-* + *-blast*] **:** SYMPATHETOBLAST

sym·path·i·co·lyt·ic \sim¦pathəkō¦lid·ik\ *adj* [ISV *sympathico-* + *-lytic*] **:** SYMPATHOLYTIC

sym·path·i·co·mimetic \sim¦pathə(,)kō+\ *adj* [ISV *sympathico-* + *mimetic*] **:** SYMPATHOMIMETIC

sym·path·i·co·to·nia \sim,pathəkō'tōnēə\ *n* -S [NL, fr. *sympathico-* + *-tonia*] **:** a condition characterized by domination of body functioning by the sympathetic nervous system and characterized by gooseflesh, vascular spasm, and abnormally high blood pressure — **sym·path·i·co·ton·ic** \¦=¦==¦tänik\ *adj*

sym·path·i·co·trop·ic cell \sim¦pathəkō·¦träpik-\ *n* [ISV *sympathico-* + *-tropic*] **:** any of various large epithelioid cells found in intimate association with unmyelinated nerve fibers in the ovary and testis esp. of the fetus

sym·pa·thin \'simpəthən\ *n* -s [ISV *sympath-* (fr. ¹*sympathetic*) + *-in*] **:** a neurohormone secreted by the sympathetic nerve endings and acting as chemical mediator to the various nerve organs ⟨noradrenaline . . . and adrenaline . . . were identified with the ~s —*U.S. Dispensatory*⟩

sym·pa·thism \'simpə,thizəm\ *n* -s [*sympathy* + *-ism*] **:** the presence of like sensations or emotions in two or more persons

sym·pa·thize \'simpə,thīz\ *vb* -ED/-ING/-S *see -ize in Explan Notes* [MF *sympathiser*, fr. *sympathie* sympathy (fr. L *sympathia*) + *-iser* -ize] *vi* **1** *obs* **:** to experience in common **2** *obs* **:** to answer to **:** correspond to **:** MATCH **3** *obs* **:** to represent, express, conceive, or contrive with sympathetic imagination or art **~** *vi* **1 :** to suffer or be affected (as through affinity, association, or interdependence) **:** react or respond in sympathy ⟨a good eye often ~s with the diseased eye⟩ **2 :** to be in keeping, accord, harmony, or agreement **:** be like **:** resemble in nature or disposition **3 a :** to share in suffering or grief **:** experience compassion or pity **:** COMMISERATE — often used with *with* ⟨~ with a friend in trouble⟩ **b :** to express such sympathy — often used with *with* **4 :** to be in sympathy intellectually **:** understand through fellow feeling **:** be favorably impressed ⟨~ with one's insurgency⟩ ⟨~ with a proposal⟩

sym·pa·thiz·er \-zə(r)\ *n* -s **:** one that sympathizes **:** one that acts or reacts in sympathy ⟨strikers and their ~s⟩

sym·pa·thiz·ing·ly *adv* [*sympathizing* (pres. part. of *sympathize*) + *-ly*] **:** in a sympathizing manner

sympatho- *comb form* [NL *sympathicus* — more at SYMPATHICO-] **:** sympathetic ⟨*sympatho*lytic⟩

sym·pa·tho·blast \'simpəthō,blast\ *n* [ISV *sympatho-* + *-blast*] **:** SYMPATHETOBLAST

sym·pa·tho·lyt·ic \¦simpəthō¦lid·ik\ *adj* [ISV *sympatho-* + *-lytic*] **:** tending to oppose the physiological results of sympathetic nervous activity or of sympathomimetic drugs — used chiefly of chemical substances and their effects; compare PARASYMPATHOLYTIC, SYMPATHOMIMETIC

sym·pa·tho·mimetic \¦simpə(,)thō+\ *adj* [ISV *sympatho-* + *mimetic*] **:** simulating sympathetic nervous action in physiological effect **:** ADRENERGIC 2 — used esp. of various amines related to adrenaline or of their effects; compare PARASYMPATHOMIMETIC, SYMPATHOLYTIC

sym·pa·thy \'simpəthē, -thi\ *n* -ES [L *sympathia* state of feeling in common, fr. Gk *sympatheia*, fr. *sympathēs* having common feelings, sympathetic (fr. *syn-* + *pathos* feelings, emotion, experience) + *-ia* -y — more at PATHOS] **1** *archaic* **:** correspondence in qualities, properties, or disposition **:** mutual suitability **:** CONCORD ⟨you are not young, no more am I; go to then, there's ~ —Shak.⟩ **2 a :** an affinity, association, or relationship between persons or things or between persons and things wherein whatever affects one similarly affects the other ⟨steel prices have advanced in this district in ~ with rising prices elsewhere⟩ ⟨the magical ~ . . . supposed to exist between a man and any severed portion of his person, as his hair or nails —J.G.Frazer⟩ **b :** mutual or parallel susceptibility or a condition brought about by it ⟨there is a purely physical ~: a very young child will cry because a brother or sister is crying —Bertrand Russell⟩ **c :** unity or harmony in action or effect ⟨the most felicitous unity of general design . . . for every part is in complete ~ with the scheme as a whole —Edwin Benson⟩ **3 a :** inclination to think or feel alike **:** emotional or intellectual accord ⟨~ is as essential as love in marriage⟩ ⟨though not a member of the Society of Friends, I am in ~ with their aims⟩ **b :** feeling of loyalty **:** tendency to favor or support **:** active interest ⟨always identified in ~ with the laboring classes —E.S. Bates⟩ — often used in pl. ⟨radical *sympathies*⟩ ⟨republican *sympathies*⟩ ⟨they were Philadelphians, Quaker in their religious *sympathies* —Lucien Price⟩ **4 a :** the act or capacity of entering into or sharing the feelings or interests of another **:** the character or fact of being sensitive to or affected by another's emotions, experiences, or esp. sorrows **b :** the feeling or mental state brought about by such sensitivity **:** the expression or demonstration of this feeling ⟨have ~ for the poor⟩ ⟨seek ~ from a friend⟩ ⟨a boy goes for ~ and companionship to his mother and sisters, not often to his father —A.C.Benson⟩ **5 :** the correlation existing between bodies capable of communicating their vibrational energy to one another through some medium

syn PITY, COMPASSION, COMMISERATION, CONDOLENCE, RUTH, EMPATHY: SYMPATHY is the most general term, ranging in meaning from friendly interest or agreement in taste or opinion to emotional identification, often accompanied by deep tenderness ⟨in immediate *sympathy* with my desire to increase my . . . knowledge —David Fairchild⟩ ⟨*sympathies* were . . . with the Roman Stoics —Havelock Ellis⟩ ⟨satire had its roots not in hatred but in *sympathy* —Bliss Perry⟩ PITY has the strongest emotional connotation; the emotion may be one of tenderness, love, or respect induced by the magnitude of another's suffering or of fellowship with the sufferer ⟨*pity* is the feeling which arrests the mind in the presence of whatsoever is grave and constant in human sufferings and unites it with the human sufferer —James Joyce⟩ ⟨*pity* that made you cry . . . not for this person or that person who is suffering, but . . . for the very nature of things . . . out of *pity* comes the balm which heals —William Saroyan⟩ PITY may suggest a tinge of contempt for one who is inferior whether because of suffering or from inherent weakness; there is also a frequent suggestion that the effect if not the purpose of pity is to keep the object in a weak or inferior state ⟨*pity* for the man who could think of nothing better —T.S.Eliot⟩ ⟨the parents of a crippled child should give him understanding and challenge rather than *pity*⟩ COMPASSION orig. meant fellowship in suffering between equals; now it denotes imaginative or emotional sharing of the distress or misfortune of another or others who are considered or treated as equals; it implies tenderness and understanding as well as an urgent desire to aid and spare ⟨one of his neighbor women cooked a chicken and brought it in to him out of pure *compassion* —Willa Cather⟩ ⟨with understanding, with *compassion* (so different from pity) she shows the sordid impact . . . on the lives of the natives —Sarah Campion⟩ ⟨when Jesus came in his gentleness with his divine *compassion* —Robert Bridges †1930⟩ but while COMPASSION suggests a greater dignity in the object than PITY often does, it also implies a greater detachment in the subject ⟨as a priest he regards all history from that eminence of spiritual objectivity which is called *compassion* —W.F.Albright⟩ COMMISERATION and CONDOLENCE agree in placing the emphasis on expression of a feeling for another's affliction, rather than on the feeling itself. COMMISERATION denotes a spontaneous and vocal expression, often one made in public or by a crowd ⟨there was a murmur of *commiseration* as Charles Darnay crossed the room . . . the soft and compassionate voices of women —Charles Dickens⟩ CONDOLENCE denotes a formal expression of sympathy esp. for the loss of a relative through death and refers strictly to an observance of etiquette without any implication as to the underlying feeling ⟨a *condolence* call⟩ ⟨they received many *condolences*⟩ RUTH denotes softening of a stern or indifferent disposition ⟨look homeward, Angel, now, and melt with *ruth* —John Milton⟩ EMPATHY, of all the terms here represented, has the least emotional content; it describes a gift, often a cultivated gift, for vicarious feeling, but the feeling need not be one of sorrow; thus EMPATHY is often used as a synonym for some senses of SYMPATHY as well as in distinction from SYMPATHY ⟨what he lacks is not *sympathy* but *empathy*, the ability to put himself in the other fellow's place —G.W. Johnson⟩ EMPATHY is frequently employed with reference to a nonhuman object (as a literary character, an idea, culture, or work of art) ⟨a fundamental component of the aesthetic attitude is *sympathy*, or — more accurately — *empathy*. In the presence of any work of art . . . the recipient . . . must surrender his independent and outstanding personality, to identify himself with the form or action presented by the artist —Herbert Read⟩

sympathy strike *n* **:** SYMPATHETIC STRIKE

sym·pat·ric \(')sim¦pa·trik, -pā-\ *adj* [*syn-* + Gk *patra* fatherland (fr. *patēr* father) + E *-ic* — more at FATHER] **:** occupying or taking place in the same area ⟨a ~ distribution of two species⟩; *specif* **:** capable of occupying the same range without loss of identity due to interbreeding ⟨~ species kept apart by physiologic isolation⟩ — compare ALLOPATRIC — **sym·pat·ri·cal·ly** \-rək(ə)lē\ *adv* — **sym·pa·try** \'simpə·trē\ *n* -ES

sym·pet·a·lae \sim'ped·ᵊl,ē\ [NL, fr. *syn-* + *-petalae*] *syn of* METACHLAMYDEAE

sym·pet·a·lous \(')sim¦ped·ᵊləs\ *adj* [*syn-* + *-petalous*] **1 :** GAMOPETALOUS **2 :** characteristic of the Metachlamydeae — **sym·pet·a·ly** \sim'ped·ᵊlē\ *n* -ES

sym·pha·lan·gus \,sim(p)fə'laŋgəs\ *n, cap* [NL, fr. *syn-* + *phalang-*, *phalanx*] **:** a genus of gibbons comprising the siamang

sym·phile \'sim,fīl\ *n* -s [prob. back-formation fr. *symphily*] **:** an insect (as any of various beetles) living as a guest in the nest of a social insect (as an ant or termite) by which it is fed and guarded for its secretions which are used as food — called also *myrmecoxene*, *true guest*

sym·phil·ic \(')sim¦filik\ *adj* [*symphily* + *-ic*] **:** of, relating to, or characterized by symphily

¹**sym·phi·lid** *also* **sym·phy·lid** \'sim(p)fələd\ *adj* [NL *Symphyla* + E *-id*] **:** of or relating to the Symphyla

²**symphilid** *also* **symphylid** \"\ *n* -s **:** an arthropod of the class Symphyla and esp. of the genus *Scutigerella* — see GARDEN CENTIPEDE

sym·phi·lism \'sim(p)fə,lizəm\ *n* -s [*symphily* + *-ism*] **:** SYMPHILY

sym·phi·lous \'sim(p)fələs\ *adj* [*symphily* + *-ous*] **:** SYMPHILIC

sym·phi·ly \-lē\ *n* -ES [G *symphilie*, fr. Gk *symphilia* mutual friendship, fr. *syn-* + *philia* friendship — more at PHILIA] **:** commensalism with mutual benefit or attraction (as between some ants or termites and various guest insects that live in their nests) — compare SYNECHTHRY, SYNOECY

sym·phog·e·nous \(')sim¦fäjənəs\ *adj* [Gk *symphy*esthai to grow together + E *-o-* + *-genous* — more at SYMPHYSIS] **:** arising through the interweaving and compacting of hyphal branches (as in the development of some pycnidia) — compare MERISTOGENOUS

sym·pho·nette \¦sim(p)fə¦net\ *n* -s [*symphony* + *-ette*] **:** a symphony orchestra reduced in personnel and typically playing ensemble and salon music in addition to the standard orchestral literature

sym·pho·nia \sim'fōnēə\ *n* -s [L — more at SYMPHONY] **1 :** concord of sounds; *esp* **:** musical harmony **2** [LL, a kind of musical instrument, fr. L, concord of sounds] **:** any of various musical instruments (as the bagpipe and hurdy-gurdy) of the medieval period **3 :** SYMPHONY 2a, 2d, 2e

sym·phon·ic \(')sim¦fänik, -nēk\ *adj* [*symphony* + *-ic*] **1 :** relating to harmony of sound **:** HARMONIOUS, SYMPHONIOUS ⟨the ~ hum of a million insects —Jack Kerouac⟩ **2 :** relating to or characteristic of a symphony or symphony orchestra ⟨~ form⟩ ⟨~ music⟩ **3 :** suggestive of a symphony esp. in form, interweaving of themes, or harmonious arrangement ⟨a ~ drama⟩ ⟨a ~ novel⟩ ⟨a ~ flower arrangement⟩

sym·phon·i·cal·ly \-nək(ə)lē, -nēk-, -li\ *adv* [obs. *symphonical* (fr. *symphony* + *-ical*) + *-ly*] **:** in a symphonic form, style, or manner

symphonic ballet *n* **:** ballet emphasizing patterns rather than story

symphonic poem *n* [trans. of G *symphonische dichtung*] **:** an extended musical composition for a symphony orchestra differing from a symphony in being less restricted in form and based on a definite literary subject or a program, being usu. in one continuous movement, and having one or more principal themes

sym·pho·ni·ous \(')sim¦fōnēəs, -nyəs\ *adj* [*symphony* + *-ous*] **:** agreeing esp. in sound **:** producing harmonies **:** ACCORDANT, HARMONIOUS — **sym·pho·ni·ous·ly** *adv*

sym·pho·nist \'sim(p)fənəst\ *n* -s [*symphony* + *-ist*] **:** a composer of symphonies

sym·pho·nize \-fə,nīz\ *vi* -ED/-ING/-S *see -ize in Explan Notes* [*symphony* + *-ize*] **:** to play or sound together in or as if in a symphony **:** ACCORD, AGREE, HARMONIZE

sym·pho·ny \'sim(p)fənē, -ni\ *n* -ES [ME *symphonie*, fr. OF, fr. L *symphonia*, fr. Gk *symphōnia*, fr. *symphōnos* agreeing in sound, concordant (fr. *syn-* + *phōnē* voice, sound) + *-ia* -y — more at BAN] **1 :** a consonance or harmony of sounds ⟨night was a ~ of sounds —Guy Fowler⟩ **2 a :** an instrumental musical passage in a vocal composition **b :** SINFONIA 1 **c :** an instrumental movement in a choral work ⟨the Pastoral *Symphony* in Handel's *Messiah*⟩ **d :** an elaborate instrumental composition usu. in sonata form for full orchestra **e :** a work of similar proportions for organ **f :** SYMPHONY ORCHESTRA **3 a :** consonance or harmony of color (as in a painting) **b :** a pictorial composition or other arrangement marked by consonance or harmony of color **4 :** something that in its harmonious complexity or variety suggests a symphonic composition ⟨barren wastelands burst out in a fleeting ~ of wild flowers —Gladwin Hill⟩

symphony band *n* **:** CONCERT BAND

symphony orchestra *n* **:** a large orchestra with well-proportioned instrumentation presenting musical programs usu. made up of symphonic works and other compositions of serious artistic worth

sym·pho·ri·car·pos \,sim(p)fərə'kär,päs\ *n* [NL, fr. Gk *symphora* act of gathering or collecting (fr. *sympherein* to bring together, fr. *syn-* + *pherein* to bear, carry) + NL *-i-* + Gk *karpos* fruit; fr. the clustering of the fruit — more at BEAR, HARVEST] **1** *cap* **:** a small genus of No. American shrubs (family Caprifoliaceae) having bell-shaped flowers in axillary

racemes succeeded by fleshy white or red 2-seeded berries — see CORALBERRY, SNOWBERRY **2** *pl* **symphoricarpos** : any plant of the genus *Symphoricarpos*

sym·phy·la \'sim(p)fələ\ *n pl, cap* [NL, fr. *syn-* + Gk *phylē* kind, species, tribe; fr. their combining characteristics of both insects and myriopods — more at PHYL-] : a small class of minute progoneate arthropods that with the exception of the garden centipede are rarely seen and of no economic importance

sym·phy·lan \-lən\ *adj or n* [NL *Symphyla* + E *-an*] : SYMPHILID

symphylid *var of* SYMPHILID

sym·phy·note \'sim(p)fə,nōt\ *adj* [Gk *symphyēs* grown together (fr. *symphyesthai* to grow together) + *nōton* back — more at SYMPHYSIS] : having the valves cemented together at the back ⟨the ~ shells of some freshwater mussels⟩

sym·phy·ple·o·na \,sim(p)fə'plēənə\ *n pl, cap* [NL *symphy-* (fr. Gk *symphyēs* grown together) + *-pleona* (fr. Gk *plein* to swim) — more at FLOW] : a suborder of Collembola comprising collembolans with a nearly spherical body in which the segmentation is obscure or lacking — compare ARTHROPLEONA

sym·phys·e·al *also* **sym·phys·i·al** \(')sim¦fizēəl\ *adj* [*symphysial* fr. NL *symphysis* + E *-al*; *symphyseal*, alter. (influenced by Gk *symphyseōs*, gen. of *symphysis*) of *symphysial*] **1** : of or relating to symphysis **2** : having or relating to a mesial position between elements commonly in symphysis

symphyseal height *n* : the distance from the gnathion to a point between the two middle incisors of the lower jaw

sym·phys·i·on \sim'fizē,än\ *n* -s [NL, fr. *symphysis* + *-ion* (as in *gnathion*)] **1** : the upper end of the symphysis of the jaw at the outer surface — see CRANIOMETRY illustration **2** : the middle point in the upper border of the pubic arch

sym·phy·si·ot·o·my \,sim(p)fəzē'ädəmē\ *n* -ES [NL *symphysis* + E *-o-* + *-tomy*] : the operation of dividing the pubic symphysis to facilitate childbirth

sym·phy·sis \'sim(p)fəsəs\ *n, pl* **sym·phy·ses** \-fə,sēz\ [NL, fr. Gk, state of growing together, symphysis, fr. *symphyesthai* to grow together, middle of *symphyein* to make grow together, fr. *syn-* + *phyein* to make grow, bring forth — more at BE] **1** : an immovable or more or less movable articulation of various bones in the median plane of the body — see PUBIC SYMPHYSIS, SYMPHYSIS MENTI **2** : a symphysis (as of a joint between the bodies of vertebrae) in which the bony surfaces are connected by pads of fibrocartilage without a synovial membrane

symphysis menti *n* [NL, lit., symphysis of the chin] : the median articulation of the two bones of the lower jaw

symphysis pubis *n* [NL, lit., symphysis of the pubes] : PUBIC SYMPHYSIS

sym·phy·so·dac·tyl·ia \,sim(p)fəsōdak'tilēə\ *n* -s [NL, fr. *symphysis* + *-o-* + *-dactylia*] : fusion of two or more fingers or toes

sym·phy·ta \'sim(p)fədə\ [NL, fr. Gk, neut. pl. of *symphytos* grown together] *syn of* CHALASTROGASTRA

sym·phyt·ic \(')sim¦fid·ik\ *adj* [Gk *symphytos* grown together (fr. *symphyein* to make grow together) + E *-ic* — more at SYMPHYSIS] : formed by fusion : being a symphysis — **sym·phyt·i·cal·ly** \-d·ək(ə)lē\ *adv*

sym·phy·tum \'sim(p)fədəm\ *n, cap* [NL, fr. Gk *symphyton*, neut. of *symphytos* grown together] : a genus of Old World perennial herbs (family Boraginaceae) having coarse hairy entire leaves, yellow, blue, or purple flowers in one-sided racemes, and four obliquely ovoid nutlets — see COMFREY

sym·plasm \'sim,plazəm\ *n* [ISV *syn-* + *-plasm*] **1** : COENOCYTE **2** : an amorphous mass made up of numerous intimately fused bacteria — **sym·plas·mic** \(')sim¦plazmik\ *adj*

sym·plast \'sim,plast\ *n* -s [ISV *syn-* + *-plast*] : COENOCYTE — **sym·plas·tic** \(')sim¦plastik\ *adj*

symplastic growth *n* : growth in a group of cells without either movement of the cells or new contacts between them and accompanied by mutual adjustment between all the cells — compare GLIDING GROWTH, INTRUSIVE GROWTH

¹sym·plec·tic \(')sim¦plektik\ *adj* [Gk *symplektikos* of intertwining, fr. *symplektos* (verbal of *symplekein* to plait together, intertwine, fr. *syn-* + *plekein* to plait) + *-ikos* -ic — more at PLY] **1** : relating to or being an intergrowth of two different minerals (as in ophicalcite, myrmekite, or micropegmatite) **2** : relating to or being a bone between the hyomandibular and the quadrate in the mandibular suspensorium of many fishes that unites the other bones of the suspensorium

²symplectic \"\ *n* -s : the symplectic bone

sym·ple·site \'simplə,sīt\ *n* -s [G *symplesit*, fr. Gk *syn-* + *plēsiazein* to bring near, come near, associate with (fr. *plēsios* near) + G *-it* -ite; fr. its being found in association with other minerals — more at PLESI-] : a mineral $Fe_3(AsO_4)_2.8H_2O$ consisting of a hydrous iron arsenate and occurring in small blue to bluish-green monoclinic crystals and in radiated aggregates (hardness 2.5, sp. gr. 3)

sym·plo·ca·ceae \,simplə'kāsē,ē\ *n pl, cap* [NL *Symplocos*, type genus + *-aceae*] *in some classifications* : a family coextensive with the genus *Symplocos*

sym·plo·cos \'simplə,käs\ *n* [NL, fr. LGk *symplokos* entwined, fr. *symplekein* to plait together — more at SYMPLECTIC] **1** *cap* : a large genus of trees and shrubs (family Styracaceae) having flowers with the calyx tube adnate to the 5-celled ovary which becomes a fleshy indehiscent fruit and numerous stamens inserted on the corolla and being widely distributed in all continents except Europe and Africa — see SWEETLEAF; SYMPLOCACEAE **2** *pl* **symplocos** *also* **symplocoses** : any plant of the genus *Symplocos*

sym·po·di·al \(')sim¦pōdēəl\ *adj* [NL *sympodium* + E *-al*] **1 a** : characteristic of or simulating a sympodium **b** : CYMOSE **2** : shifting in line of direction or development in the manner of a sympodium — used esp. of social phenomena — **sym·po·di·al·ly** \-əlē\ *adv*

sym·po·dite \'simpə,dīt\ *n* -s [*syn-* + *-podite*; fr. its more or less consolidated segments] : PROTOPODITE

sym·po·di·um \sim'pōdēəm\ *n, pl* **sympo·dia** \-ēə\ [NL, fr. *syn-* + Gk *podion* small foot, base — more at PEW] : an apparent main axis (as in the grapevine) not developed from a terminal bud but made up of successive secondary axes each of which represents one fork of a dichotomy the other fork of which is of weaker growth or suppressed entirely — compare MONOPODIUM

¹sym·po·si·ac \sim'pōzē,ak\ *n* -s [back-formation fr. obs. *symposiacs* (pl.) table conversation, fr. L *Symposiaca* (title given to the *Symposium* of Plutarch †*ab*120 A.D. Greek writer), fr. neut. pl. of *symposiacus* of a symposium] *archaic* : SYMPOSIUM

²symposiac \"\ *adj* [L *symposiacus*, fr. Gk *symposiakos*, fr. *symposion* symposium] : of, relating to, or similar to a symposium

sym·po·si·arch \sim'pōzē,ärk\ *n* -s [Gk *symposiarchos*, fr. *symposion* symposium + *archos* leader — more at ARCHI-] : one who presides over a symposium

sym·po·si·ast \-,ast\ *n* -s [Gk *symposiazein* to take part in a symposium, fr. *symposion* symposium; after such pairs as Gk *enthousiazein* to be inspired: E *enthusiast* — more at ENTHUSIASM] **1** : BANQUETER **2** : one who contributes to a symposium

sym·po·si·um \sim'pōzēəm *sometimes* -ōzh(ē)əm\ *n, pl* **sympo·sia** \-zēə, -zh(ē)ə\ *or* **symposiums** [L, fr. Gk *symposion*, fr. *sympinein* to drink together, fr. *syn-* + *pinein* to drink — more at POTABLE] **1 a** : a drinking party; *esp* : one following a banquet and providing music, singing, and conversation **b** : a banquet or other social gathering at which there is free interchange of ideas **2 a** : a meeting at which several speakers deliver short addresses on related topics or on various aspects of the same topic **b** : a collection of opinions on a subject; *esp* : one assembled and published by a periodical **c** : DISCUSSION

symp·tom \'sim(p)təm\ *n* -s [LL *symptomat-, symptoma*, fr. Gk *symptōmat-, symptōma* chance occurrence, property that goes with something, symptom, fr. *sympiptein* to fall together, meet with, occur by chance, fr. *syn-* + *piptein* to fall — more at FEATHER] **1 a** : subjective evidence of disease or physical disturbance observed by the patient ⟨headache is a ~ of many diseases⟩ ⟨visual disturbances may be a ~ of retinal arteriosclerosis⟩ — contrasted with *sign* **b** : an evident reaction to a pathogen by a plant — contrasted with *sign* **2 a** : something that indicates the existence of something else ⟨volcanoes . . . are ~s of some kind of internal disorder in the earth —Howel Williams⟩ ⟨sedition is often the ~ and not the cause of serious unrest —Zechariah Chafee⟩ ⟨describe the ~s which accompany a maladjustment between people and the land —P.E. James⟩ **b** : a slight indication : TRACE ⟨not a ~ of a draught disturbs the air —Thomas Hardy⟩ **syn** see SIGN

symp·to·mat·ic \¦sim(p)tə¦mad·¦ik, -atl, ¦ēk\ *adj* [LL *symptomat-, symptoma* symptom + E *-ic*] **1 a** : being a symptom of a disease ⟨gummas ~ of syphilis⟩ ⟨excessive drinking ~ of a psychiatric disturbance⟩ **b** : having the characteristics of a particular disease but arising from another cause ⟨~ epilepsy resulting from brain injury⟩ — opposed to *idiopathic* or *essential* **2** : according to, concerned with, or affecting symptoms ⟨~ treatment⟩ **3** : CHARACTERISTIC, INDICATIVE ⟨his behavior was ~ of his character⟩ ⟨changes in the vegetation were ~ of greater geographical changes —W.E.Swinton⟩ ⟨personality formation is ~ of both individual and social institutions —Abram Kardiner⟩ — **symp·to·mat·i·cal·ly** \|ək(ə)lē, |ēk-, -li\ *adv*

symptomatic anthrax *n* : BLACKLEG 1

symp·tom·a·tize \'sim(p)təmə,tīz\ *vt* -ED/-ING/-S *see -ize in Explan Notes* [Gk *symptōmat-, symptōma* symptom + E *-ize*] : to be symptomatic of

symp·to·mat·o·log·ic \¦sim(p)tə¦mad·ᵊl¦äjik\ *or* **symp·to·mat·o·log·i·cal** \-jəkəl\ *adj* [*symptomatology* + *-ic* or *-ical*] : SYMPTOMATIC — **symp·to·mat·o·log·i·cal·ly** \-jək(ə)lē\ *adv*

symp·tom·a·tol·o·gy \,sim(p)təmə'täləjē, -ji\ *n* -ES [NL *symptomatologia*, fr. Gk *symptōmat-, symptōma* symptom + *-o-* + L *-logia* -logy] **1** : a branch of medical science that treats of symptoms of diseases **2** : the symptoms of a disease in a given case taken as a whole

symptom complex *n* : a group of symptoms occurring together and characterizing a particular disease : SYNDROME

symp·tom·ize \'sim(p)tə,mīz\ *vt* -ED/-ING/-S *see -ize in Explan Notes* [*symptom* + *-ize*] : SYMPTOMATIZE

symp·tom·less \'sim(p)təmləs\ *adj* : exhibiting no symptoms ⟨a ~ infection⟩

symp·to·mol·o·gy \,sim(p)tə'mäləjē, -ji\ *n* -ES [*symptom* + *-o-* + *-logy*] : SYMPTOMATOLOGY

sym·pus \'simpəs\ *n* -ES [NL, fr. Gk *sympous* with feet together, fr. *syn-* + *pous* foot — more at FOOT] : SIRENOMELUS

syn \'sin\ *adj* [*syn-*] : CIS — opposed to *anti*; compare SYN- 3

syn- *or* **sym-** *prefix* [*syn-* fr. ME *sin-, syn-*, fr. OF, fr. L *syn-*, fr. Gk, fr. *syn* with, together with, by means of, at the same time as, alter. of *xyn*; *sym-* fr. ME *sim-, sym-*, fr. MF, fr. L *sym-*, fr. Gk, fr. *syn*] **1** : with : along with : together ⟨*syn*cline⟩ ⟨*syn*genesis⟩ **2** : at the same time ⟨*syn*anthesis⟩ **3** *syn-* : CIS- 3 — used esp. of chemical structures in which the atoms or groups on the same side of the molecule are attached to carbon-to-nitrogen or nitrogen-to-nitrogen double bonds ⟨sodium *syn*-benzene-diazoate⟩; opposed to *anti-* (sense 7); see BENZALDOXIME **4** : like : associated ⟨*syn*type⟩

syn *abbr* **1** synchronize; synchronized; synchronizing **2** synergist **3** synonym; synonymous **4** synthetic

syn·a·del·phite \,sinə'del,fīt\ *n* -s [G *synadelphit*, fr. Gk *synadelphos* one that has a brother or sister (fr. *syn-* + *adelphos* brother) + G *-it* -ite — more at -ADELPHOUS] : a mineral $(Mn,Mg,Ca,Pb)(AsO_4)(OH)_5$ composed of a basic arsenate of manganese often with other elements (as magnesium, calcium, lead) and occurring in black prismatic crystals and grains (hardness 4.5, sp. gr. 3.5)

synaeresis *var of* SYNERESIS

synaesthesia *var of* SYNESTHESIA

syn·aes·the·sis \,sinəs'thēsəs\ *n* -ES [Gk *synaisthēsis* joint sensation, joint perception, fr. the stem of *synaisthanesthai* to perceive simultaneously, to share in perception (fr. *syn-* + *aisthanesthai* to perceive) + *-sis* — more at AUDIBLE] : harmony of different or opposing impulses produced by a work of art ⟨~ of thought and feeling in philosophical poetry⟩ ⟨~ of anxiety and calmness in a tragedy⟩ — compare SYNESTHESIA

synaesthetic *var of* SYNESTHETIC

syn·a·gog·al \¦sinə¦gägəl, -nē¦g- *sometimes* -¦gōg- *or* **syn·a·gog·i·cal** \-¦gäjəkəl, -¦gägə- *sometimes* -¦gōgə-\ *also* **syn·a·gogu·al** *like* SYNAGOGAL\ *adj* : of, relating to, or performed in a synagogue ⟨~ ritual⟩ ⟨~ music⟩ ⟨~ worship⟩

syn·a·gogue *or* **syn·a·gog** \'=ə,gäg *sometimes* -,gōg\ *n* -s [ME *synagoge*, fr. OF, fr. LL *synagoga*, fr. Gk *synagōgē* assembly, place of assembly, synagogue, fr. *synagein* to bring together, draw together, fr. *syn-* + *agein* to lead, drive — more at AGENT] **1 a** (1) : a Jewish local community under religious and more or less civil jurisdiction (2) : a local assembly of Jews organized chiefly for public worship **b** : the building or place of assembly used by Jewish communities primarily for religious worship **2** : the Jewish religion or communion

syn·al·lag·mat·ic *or* **sin·a·lag·mat·ic** \¦sinə¦lag¦mad·ik, sə¦naləg-\ *adj* [Gk *synallagmatikos* of a contract, fr. *synallagmat-, synallagma* contract, covenant (fr. *synallassein* to enter into a contract, fr. *syn-* + *allassein* to change, exchange, barter, fr. *allos* other) + *-ikos* -ic — more at ELSE] : imposing reciprocal obligations and characterized by mutual rights and duties : BILATERAL ⟨~ contract⟩ — sometimes distinguished from *commutative*; compare COMMUTATIVE CONTRACT

syn·a·loe·pha *or* **syn·a·le·pha** \,sinə'lēfə\ *n* -s [NL, fr. Gk *synaloiphē, synaliphē*, fr. *synaleiphein* to clog up, coalesce, unite two syllables into one, fr. *syn-* + *aleiphein* to anoint, besmear; akin to Gk *lipos* fat — more at LEAVE] : the blending into one syllable of two vowels of adjacent syllables (as by crasis, synaeresis, synizesis, elision); *esp* : a contraction of syllables by obscuring or suppressing a vowel or diphthong at the end of a word before another vowel or diphthong (as in *th' army*, for *the army*)

syn·anastomosis \¦sin, sən+\ *n* [NL, fr. *syn-* + *anastomosis*] : an anastomosis involving several vessels

syn·an·ce·ja \,sinən'sējə\ *n, cap* [NL, irreg. fr. Gk *synankeia* place where two glens meet, meeting of waters, fr. *syn-* + *ankos* bend, glen + *-eia* -y — more at ANGLE] : a genus (the type of the family Synancejidae) of scorpion fishes comprising the stonefishes

syn·an·gial \sə'nanj(ē)əl\ *adj* [NL *synangium* + E *-al*] : of, relating to, or being a synangium

syn·an·gi·um \-jēəm\ *n, pl* **synan·gia** \-j(ē)ə\ [NL, fr. *syn-* + *-angium*] **1** : the peripheral part of an arterial trunk from which the branches arise in a lower vertebrate — compare PYLANGIUM **2** : a sorus (as in ferns of the family Marattiaceae) made up of sporangia variously united or cohered into a compound structure

syn·an·tec·tic \¦sinən-¦tektik, -i,nan-\ *or* **syn·an·tet·ic** \-ed·ik\ *adj* [*synantectic* alter. of *synantetic*; *synantetic* fr. (assumed) Gk *synantetos* (verbal of Gk *synantan* to meet, encounter, fr. *syn-* + *antan* to meet face to face, fr. *anta* opposite) + E *-ic*; akin to Gk *anti* against — more at END] : formed by the reaction of two other minerals — compare CORONA 2h

syn·an·thae \sə'nan(t)(,)thē\ [NL, fr. Gk *synanthein* to bloom together, fr. *syn-* + *anthein* to bloom, fr. *anthos* flower — more at ANTHOLOGY] *syn of* CYCLANTHALES

syn·an·thous \sə'nan(t)thəs\ *adj* [in sense 1, fr. *syn-* + *-anthous*; in sense 2, fr. Gk *synanthein* + E *-ous*] **1** : exhibiting synanthy **2** : having flowers and leaves which appear at the same time

syn·an·thy \'si,nan(t)thē, sə'na-\ *n* -ES [*syn-* + *-anthy*] : coalescence of normally separate flowers

syn-anti isomerism \(')=¦=(,)=-\ *n* [*syn-* + *anti-*] : cis-trans isomerism in compounds (as oximes, diazoates, and azo compounds) containing one or more carbon-to-nitrogen or nitrogen-to-nitrogen double bonds — compare BENZALDOXIME

syn·a·phea \,sinə'fēə\ *also* **syn·a·pheia** \-fē(y)ə, -fīə\ *n* -s [Gk *synapheia*, lit., combination, union, fr. *synaphēs* united, connected (fr. *syn-* + *-aphēs*, fr. *haptein* to fasten) + *-ia* -y — more at APSIS] : continuous metrical regularity (as in a group of anapestic verses) such that syllables at the end of one line may form part of a foot completed by syllables at the beginning of the next line

syn·aposematic \¦sin, sən+\ *adj* [*syn-* + *aposematic*] : relating to protective mimicry in which defenseless species resemble others having special means of defense

syn·ap·o·sem·a·tism \,si,napə'sēmə,tizəm, sə,n-, -'sem-\ *n* -s : the occurrence or possession of synaposematic mimicry

¹syn·apse \'si,naps, sə'n-\ *n, pl* **synaps·es** \-psəz\ [NL *synapsis*, fr. Gk, contact, point of juncture, fr. *synaptein* to join together (fr. *syn-* + *haptein* to fasten) + *-sis* — more at APSIS] **1 a** : the locus at which the nervous impulse passes from the axon of one neuron to the dendrites of another having the form of an actual boundary between the two nerve fibers or possibly only a surface of contact and constituting the polarizing and selective element typical of most of the nervous systems of the higher animals **b** : the function of affording such communication between neuron processes **2** : SYNAPSIS 1

²synapse \"\ *vi* -ED/-ING/-S : to form a synapse or come together in synapsis ⟨nerve endings ~ in the ganglia⟩

¹syn·ap·sid \sə'napsəd\ *adj* [NL *Synapsida*] : of or relating to the Synapsida

²synapsid \"\ *n* -s : a reptile or fossil of the subclass Synapsida

syn·ap·si·da \-psədə\ *n pl, cap* [NL, fr. *synapsis* + *-ida*] : a subclass of Reptilia comprising extinct reptiles of the Pennsylvanian, Permian, and Triassic, having a single pair of lateral temporal openings in the skull, and usu. held to be ancestral to the true mammals — compare ICTIDOSAURIA, THERAPSIDA

syn·ap·sis \-psəs\ *n, pl* **synap·ses** \-p(,)sēz\ [NL — more at SYNAPSE] **1** : the process of association of homologous chromosomes with chiasma formation that is characteristic of the first meiotic prophase and that provides the mechanism for crossing-over **2** : SYNAPSE 1

syn·ap·te \sē,näp'tē\ *n, pl* **synap·tai** \-tā\ [MGk *synaptē*, fr. fem. of *synaptos*] : a series of supplicatory prayers in the Eastern Orthodox Church that are in the form of a litany

syn·ap·tic \sə'naptik\ *also* **syn·ap·ti·cal** \-təkəl\ *adj* [fr. NL *synapsis*, after such pairs as E *prolepsis: proleptic, proleptical*] : of, relating to, or communicated by a synapse or synapsis ⟨~ transmission⟩ ⟨~ delay⟩ — **synaptically** *adv*

synaptic nervous system *n* : a nervous system in which functional contact is through synapses — distinguished from *nerve net*

syn·ap·tic·u·la \,si,nap'tikyələ, sə,n-\ *n, pl* **synapticu·lae** \-,lē, -,lī\ [NL, fr. Gk *synaptos* joined together (fr. *synaptein* to join together) + NL *-i-* + L *-cula*, fem. dim. suffix — more at SYNAPSE] : SYNAPTICULUM

syn·ap·tic·u·lar \¦si,nap¦tikyələ(r), sə¦n-\ *or* **syn·ap·tic·u·late** \-lət\ *adj* [NL *synapticulum* + E *-ar* or *-ate*] : of, relating to, or constituting a synapticulum

syn·ap·tic·u·lum \,si,nap'tikyələm, sə,n-\ *n, pl* **synapticu·la** \-lə\ [NL, fr. Gk *synaptos* + NL *-i-* + L *-culum*, neut. dim. suffix] : one of numerous conical or cylindrical calcareous processes that extend between and unite the adjacent septa of some corals

¹syn·ap·tid \sə'naptəd\ *adj* [NL *Synaptidae*] : of or relating to the Synaptidae

²synaptid \"\ *n* -s : a sea cucumber of the family Synaptidae

syn·ap·ti·dae \-tə,dē\ *n pl, cap* [NL, fr. *Synapta*, type genus (fr. Gk *synaptē*, fem. of *synaptos* joined together) + *-idae*] : a widely distributed family (order Apoda) of sea cucumbers lacking a respiratory tree, having the water-vascular system greatly reduced, and being mostly littoral but including some forms found in very deep waters

syn·ap·tol·o·gy \,si,nap'täləjē, sə,n-\ *n* -ES [Gk *synaptos* joined together + E *-o-* + *-logy*] : the scientific study of neural synapses

syn·ap·to·sau·ria \sə,naptə'sȯrēə\ *n pl, cap* [NL, fr. Gk *synaptos* + NL *-sauria*] : a subclass of Reptilia comprising Permian and Mesozoic typically aquatic or amphibious reptiles with temporal openings high on the roof of the skull and including the orders Protorosauria and Sauropterygia — **syn·ap·to·sau·ri·an** \=¦=¦=rēən\ *adj*

syn·aptychus \¦sin, sən+\ *n* [NL, fr. *syn-* + *aptychus*] : an operculum of two parts united in the median line (as in some ammonites)

synarchism *usu cap, var of* SINARQUISM

syn·ar·chy \'sinərkē, -,närkē\ *n* -ES [Gk *synarchia*, fr. *synarchein* to rule jointly with (fr. *syn-* + *archein* to rule, begin) + *-ia* -y — more at ARCHI-] : joint rule : joint sovereignty

syn·ar·tet·ic \¦si,när¦ted·ik, -,nər-\ *adj* [fr. (assumed) Gk *synartētos* (verbal of *synartan* to join together) + E *-ic* — more at ASYNARTETIC] : consisting of or relating to a succession of cola not separated by diaeresis : metrically continuous — opposed to *asynartetic*

syn·ar·thro·dia \,si,när'thrōdēə\ *n* -s [NL, fr. *syn-* + *arthrodia*] : SYNARTHROSIS

syn·ar·thro·di·al \-ēəl\ *adj* [NL *synarthrodia* + E *-al*] : of, relating to, or being a synarthrosis — **syn·ar·thro·di·al·ly** \-ēəlē\ *adv*

syn·ar·thro·sis \-ōsəs\ *n, pl* **synarthro·ses** \-ō,sēz\ [NL, fr. Gk *synarthrōsis*, fr. *syn-* + *arthrōsis* arthrosis — more at ARTHROSIS] : an immovable articulation in which the bones are united by intervening fibrous connective tissues

syn·as·try \sə'nastrē, ,si,nas-, 'sinəs-\ *n* -ES [LL *synastria*, fr. Gk, fr. *syn-* + *astr-* + *-ia* -y] : concurrence of starry position or influence upon two persons : similarity of condition or fortune prefigured by astrology

syn·ax·a·rion \,se,näk'sär(,)yō(n), ,si,nak'sa(a)rēən\ *or* **syn·ax·a·ry** \sə'naksərē\ *or* **syn·ax·a·ri·um** \,si,nak'sa(a)rēəm\ *n, pl* **synaxa·ria** \-är(,)yä, -äryə, -a(a)rēə\ *or* **synaxaries** [*synaxarion* fr. MGk, fr. *synaxis* + *-arion* -ary (fr. L *-arium*); *synaxary, synaxarium* fr. ML *synaxarium*, fr. MGk *synaxarion*] : a short narrative of the life of a saint or exposition of a feast included in the Menaion and read in religious services of the Eastern Orthodox Church; *also* : a liturgical book containing such narratives

syn·ax·a·rist \sə'naksərəst\ *n* -s [*synaxarion* + *-ist*] : the author of a synaxarion

syn·ax·is \sə'naksəs *or esp in sense 2* 'sēnək(,)sēs\ *n, pl* **synax·es** \-ak(,)sēz, -ək(,)sēs\ [LL, fr. LGk, fr. Gk *synagein* to bring together, draw together + *-sis* — more at SYNAGOGUE] **1** : an assembly met for worship; *esp* : a congregation in the early Church gathered for a liturgical service **2** : an early part of the divine liturgy of the Eastern Orthodox Church

syn·branch \'sin,braŋk\ *adj* [NL *Synbranchus*] : of or relating to Synbranchidae

syn·bran·chi·dae \sin'braŋkə,dē\ *n pl, cap* [NL, fr. *Synbranchus*, type genus (fr. *syn-* + L *branchia* gill) + *-idae*] : a family (suborder Synbranchoidea) of tropical freshwater and brackish water elongated fishes

syn·bran·chii \-kē,ī\ [NL, fr. *Synbranchus*] *syn of* SYMBRANCHII

syn·bran·choi·dea \,sin,braŋ'kȯidēə\ *n pl, cap* [NL, fr. *Synbranchus*, genus of synbranch fishes + *-oidea*] : a suborder of Symbranchii coextensive with the family Synbranchidae

¹sync *also* **synch** \'siŋk\ *n* -s [by shortening] : SYNCHRONIZATION, SYNCHRONISM ⟨sound track out of ~ with the actors' lips⟩

²sync \"\ *vb* **synced** \-ŋkt\ **synced** \"\ **syncing** \-ŋkiŋ\ **syncs** [by shortening] : SYNCHRONIZE ⟨each changeover should be noted on the film . . . for convenience in later playback ~*ing* —*Cinematographer*⟩

³sync \"\ *adj* [*sync*] : relating to or having to do with synchronization : SYNCHRO

sync *abbr* synchronism; synchronizing; synchronous

syn·carida \(')sin, -iŋ+\ *n pl, cap* [NL, fr. *syn-* + *Carida*] : a division of Malacostraca coextensive with Anaspidacea

syn·car·pous \(')sin¦kärpəs, -iŋ¦k-\ *adj* [*syn-* + *-carpous*] : having the carpels of the gynoecium united in a compound ovary — opposed to *apocarpous*

syn·car·py \'=,=pē\ *n* -ES [*syncarpous* + *-y*] : a syncarpous state or quality

syncaryon *var of* SYNKARYON

¹syn·categorematic \¦si|n, sə|, |ŋ+\ *adj* [LL *syncategoremat-, syncategorema* + E *-ic*] : not capable of standing alone as a term in a proposition : having significance only in conjunction with another expression ⟨*left* and *up* are ~ terms⟩ ⟨punctuation marks are ~ signs⟩ — opposed to *categorematic* — **syn·categorematically** \"+\ *adv*

²syncategorematic \"\ *n* -s : a syncategorematic word or sign

syn·cat·e·go·reme \sən'kad·əgə,rēm, səŋ'k-; ,sinkə'tegə,rēm, ,siŋk-\ *n, pl* **syncatego·rema·ta** \=,==='remədə, ,==,==-'rēm-\ [LL *syncategorema*, fr. LGk *synkatēgorēma*, fr. Gk *synkatēgorein* to predicate jointly, fr. *syn-* + *katēgorein* to predicate — more at CATEGORY] : a syncategorematic term

syn·cel·lus \sən'seləs\ *n, pl* **syncel·li** \-e,lī\ [ML, fr. MGk *synkellos*, fr. LGk, cell mate, fr. Gk *syn-* + LGk *kella* cell, fr. L *cella* — more at CELL] : a diocesan official in the Eastern Church serving usu. as the secretary and chaplain of a bishop or metropolitan

syn·ceph·a·lus \sənˈsefələs\ *n, pl* **syncepha·li** \-fəˌlī\ [NL, fr. *syn-* + *-cephalus*] **:** a twin fetus having the two heads fused
syn·cerebral \(ˈ)sin, sən+\ *adj* [NL *syncerebrum* + E *-al*] **:** relating to or having a syncerebrum
syn·cerebrum \"+\ *n* [NL, fr. *syn-* + *cerebrum*] **:** a brain (as of an insect) consisting of several segments
synch *abbr* synchronize; synchronized; synchronizing
syn·chi·site \ˈsiŋkəˌsīt, -inkˌ-\ *n* -s [irreg. fr. Gk *synchysis* mixture, confusion (fr. *synchein* to pour together, confound, confuse — fr. *syn-* + *chein* to pour — + *-sis*) + E *-ite* — more at FOUND] **:** a mineral $(Ce,La)Ca(CO_3)_2F$ related to parisite and consisting of a fluoride and carbonate of calcium, cerium, and lanthanum
syn·chon·dro·sial \ˌsinˌkänˈdrōzh(ē)əl, -iŋˌk-\ *adj* [NL *synchondrosis* + E *-al*] **:** of, relating to, or being a synchondrosis — **syn·chon·dro·sial·ly** \-əlē\ *adv*
syn·chon·dro·sis \ˌ=ˌ=ˈdrōsəs\ *n, pl* **synchondro·ses** \-ōˌsēz\ [NL, fr. Gk *synchondrōsis*, fr. *syn-* + *chondr-* + *-ōsis* -osis] **:** an immovable skeletal articulation in which the union is cartilaginous
syn·chon·drot·o·my \-ˈdräd·əmē\ *n* -ES [ISV *synchondro-* (fr. NL *synchondrosis*) + *-tomy*] **:** SYMPHYSIOTOMY
syn·chorial \(ˈ)sin, sən, |iŋ+\ *adj* [*syn-* + *chorial*] **:** having a common placenta — used of twin or multiple fetuses
¹**syn·chro** \ˈsin(ˌ)krō, ˈiŋ(-\ *n* -s [*synchronous*] **:** SELSYN
²**synchro** \"\ *adj* [*synchro-*] **:** adapted to synchronization ⟨~ camera shutter⟩; *specif* **:** SYNCHROMESH
synchro- *comb form* [*synchronized* & *synchronous*] **:** synchronized **:** synchronous ⟨*synchroflash*⟩ ⟨*synchromesh*⟩
synchro-cyclotron \ˌ=(ˌ)=+\ *n* [*synchro-* + *cyclotron*] **:** a modified cyclotron that achieves greater energies for the charged particles by compensating for the variation in mass that the particles experience with increasing velocity
synchroflash \ˈ==ˌ=\ *adj* [*synchro-* + *flash*] **:** employing or produced with a synchronizing mechanism that fires a flash lamp the instant the camera shutter opens ⟨~ photography⟩
¹**synchromesh** \ˈ==ˌ=\ *adj* [*synchro-* + *mesh*] **:** designed for effecting synchronized shifting of gears ⟨~ automobile transmission⟩ ⟨~ construction⟩
²**synchromesh** \"\ *n* **:** a synchromesh gear or gear system
syn·chro·nal \ˈsiŋkrənᵊl, -inkˌ-\ *adj* [LL *synchronus* synchronous + E *-al* — more at SYNCHRONOUS] **:** SYNCHRONOUS
syn·chro·ne·ity \ˌ==nəˈnēəd·ē\ *n* -ES [*synchronous* + *-eity* (as in *spontaneity*)] **:** the state of being synchronous **:** SYNCHRONISM ⟨theory of glacial ~ over the northern hemisphere —S.A.Cain⟩
syn·chron·ic \(ˈ)si|n|ˈkränik, sə|n|ˈk-, |iŋ|, -ˈänēk\ *also* **syn·chron·i·cal** \-ənəkəl, -ˈänēk-\ *adj* [LL *synchronos* synchronous + E *-ic*, *-ical*] **1 :** SYNCHRONOUS **2 a** [F *synchronique*, fr. LL *synchronos* + F *-ique* -ic, -ical] **:** DESCRIPTIVE 4 ⟨~ grammar⟩ — contrasted with *diachronic* **b :** concerned with the complex of events existing in a limited time period (as the present) and ignoring historical antecedents ⟨the functionalist emphasis upon institutional interrelationships has resulted in a ~ view of society⟩ — contrasted with *diachronic* **3** *of taxa* **:** occurring in the same segment of geologic time **:** CONTEMPORANEOUS — compare ALLOCHRONIC — **syn·chron·i·cal·ly** \-ənək(ə)lē, -ˈänēk-, -lī\ *adv*
syn·chro·nic·i·ty \ˌsiŋkrəˈnisəd·ē, -inkˌ-\ *n* -ES **:** SYNCHRONISM 1
syn·chro·nism \ˈsiŋkrəˌnizəm, ˈsink-\ *n* -s [LL *synchronos* synchronous + E *-ism*] **1 :** the quality or fact of being synchronous or simultaneous **:** concurrence of acts, events, or developments in time **:** coincident movement or existence **:** SIMULTANEOUSNESS ⟨find a general ~ in the secular and religious phases of lyric growth —H.O.Taylor⟩ **2 :** chronological arrangement of historical events and personages so as to indicate coincidence or coexistence; *also* **:** a table showing such concurrences ⟨in that book were . . . ~s of the kings of Ireland with the kings and emperors of the world —*Irish Digest*⟩ **3 a :** a representation in the same picture of two or more events which occurred at different times **b :** historical accuracy in detail in period architecture or interior decoration **4 a :** the state of having the same period or the same period and phase **b :** the condition of excessive rolling obtaining when a ship's rolling period is equal to the wave period or to one half the wave period **5 :** the concurrence in time of the picture image and the corresponding sound during projection on a motion-picture or television screen
syn·chro·nis·tic \ˌ==ˈnistik\ *adj* [LL *synchronos* + E *-istic*] **:** relating to, manifesting, or involving synchronism **:** SYNCHRONOUS — **syn·chro·nis·ti·cal** \-tәkəl\ *adj* — **syn·chro·nis·ti·cal·ly** \-tək(ə)lē\ *adv*
syn·chro·ni·za·tion \ˌ==nəˈzāshən, -ˌnīˈ-\ *n* -s **:** the act or result of synchronizing **:** concurrence of events or motions in respect to time
syn·chro·nize \ˈ==ˌnīz\ *vb* -ED/-ING/-S *see -ize in Explan Notes* [LL *synchronos* synchronous + E *-ize*] *vi* **1 :** to happen or take place at the same time **:** be synchronous ⟨the voyages of discovery *synchronized* with the emergence of a capitalist economy —H.J.Laski⟩ ⟨action and sound must ~ perfectly⟩ ~ *vt* **1 :** to represent or arrange (events) so as to indicate coincidence or coexistence ⟨~ events of biblical and classical history⟩ **2 :** to cause to agree in time ⟨~ two watches⟩ **:** make synchronous in operation ⟨~ troop movements and artillery fire⟩ ⟨~ factory operations⟩ **3 a :** to make (dialogue, music, or sound effects) exactly simultaneous with the action shown in a motion picture **b :** to maintain a time interlock throughout (a television system) so that the scanning beams in the studio and the receiver move together **c :** to adjust (a camera shutter) so that a flashbulb fires at the instant the shutter opens
synchronized shifting *n* **:** a changing from one speed gear to another in a motor vehicle through a transmission employing a device by which both gears are brought to the same speed before the shift can be made
synchronized swimming *n* **:** exhibition swimming in which the movements of one or more swimmers are synchronized with a musical accompaniment so as to form changing patterns in the manner of dancers
syn·chro·niz·er \-zə(r)\ *n* -s **:** one that synchronizes **:** a device to indicate, produce, or maintain synchronous motion: as **a :** a regulator for a system of clocks **b :** a device for synchronizing the firing of a flashbulb with the opening of the camera shutter
syn·chron·o·graph \sinˈkränəˌgraf, siŋˈk-, -gräf\ *n* [*synchronous* + *-o-* + *-graph*] **:** an automatic telegraph in which the alternating current which transmits the signals is regulated by a perforated paper ribbon traveling in synchronism with the generator
syn·chronological \(ˈ)si|n, sə|, |iŋ+\ *adj* **:** showing simultaneous occurrence or existence ⟨~ table of historical events⟩
syn·chronology \ˈsin, ˈsiŋ+\ *n* [*syn-* + *chronology*] **:** systematic arrangement of synchronous events
syn·chron·o·scope \sənˈkränəˌskōp, səŋˈk-\ *n* [*synchronous* + *-o-* + *-scope*] **:** SYNCHROSCOPE
syn·chro·nous \ˈsiŋkrənəs, -inkˌ-\ *adj* [LL *synchronos*, fr. Gk, fr. *syn-* + *chronos* time] **1 :** happening, existing, or arising at the same time ⟨having their beginning at different times, although their endings were ~ —*Encyc. Americana*⟩ ⟨recovery was ~ with therapy —*Jour. Amer. Med. Assoc.*⟩ **2 :** recurring or operating at exactly the same periods **:** marked by strict and exact coincidence in time, rate, or rhythm ⟨the ~ action of a bird's wings in flight⟩ ⟨~ set of clocks⟩ **3 :** involving or indicating synchronism ⟨~ account of World War II⟩ **4 :** having the same period; *also* **:** having the same period and phase ⟨~ vibrations⟩ ⟨~ oscillations⟩ **syn** see CONTEMPORARY
synchronous clock *n* **:** ELECTRIC CLOCK e
synchronous condenser *n* **:** a synchronous phase advancer; *usu* **:** an overexcited synchronous motor equipped with damper windings to facilitate starting and to prevent surging and hunting — called also *rotary condenser*
synchronous converter *n* **:** a synchronous machine that converts from alternating to direct current or vice versa — called also *rotary converter*
syn·chro·nous·ly *adv* **1 :** at the same time **:** SIMULTANEOUSLY, CONTEMPORANEOUSLY **2 :** at the same speed or frequency
synchronous machine *n* **:** a dynamoelectric machine (as a generator or motor) that has a constant magnetic field and an armature which receives or delivers alternating current in synchronism with the motion of the machine and at a frequency equal to the product of the number of pairs of poles and the speed of the machine in revolutions per second — compare ALTERNATOR, CONVERTER b, MOTOR 4, RECTIFIER 3, SYNCHRONOUS CONVERTER
synchronous motor *n* **:** an electric motor having a speed that is strictly proportional to the frequency of the operating current
synchronous speed *n* **:** a definite speed for an alternating-current machine that is dependent on the frequency of the supply circuit because the rotating member passes one pair of poles for each alternation of the alternating current
synchronous telegraph *n* **:** MULTIPLE SYNCHRONOUS TELEGRAPH
syn·chro·ny \ˈsiŋkrənē, -inkˌ-\ *n* -ES [*synchronous* + *-y*] **1 :** synchronous or simultaneous occurrence **2 :** synchronistic arrangement or treatment; *specif* **:** synchronic linguistics — contrasted with *diachrony*
synchros *pl of* SYNCHRO
syn·chro·scope \-rəˌskōp\ *n* [*synchro-* + *-scope*] **:** any of several devices for showing whether two associated machines or moving parts are operating in synchronism with each other or for giving an indication of their relative phase; *esp* **:** an instrument that permits the pilot of a multiengine airplane to synchronize the engines so as to prevent disagreeable beats and vibration
synchro-shutter \ˈsin(ˌ)krō, -iŋ(-+\ *n* [*synchro-* + *shutter*] **:** a camera shutter containing an electrical switching device to fire a flashbulb at the instant the shutter opens
synchro-sunlight \"+\ *adj* [*synchro-* + *sunlight*] **:** relating to the use of flash lamps as a supplement to daylight exposure
syn·chro·tron \ˈsiŋkrə-ˌträn, -inkˌ-\ *n* -s [*synchro-* + *-tron*] **:** an apparatus for imparting very high speeds to charged particles (as electrons, protons) by means of a combination of a high-frequency electric field (as in the cyclotron) and a low-frequency magnetic field (as in the betatron)
synchs *pl of* SYNC
syn·chyt·ri·um \sənˈki·trēəm, səŋˈk-\ *n, cap* [NL, fr. *syn-* + Gk *chytrion* small earthen pot, dim. of *chytra* earthen pot — more at CHYTRA] **:** a genus (the type of the family Synchytriaceae of the order Chytridiales) of simple parasitic fungi having no mycelium but a unicellular thallus that at maturity functions either as single resting sporangia or as a sorus of sporangia surrounded by a common membrane — see POTATO WART
syncing *pres part of* SYNC
syn·clastic \(ˈ)si|n, sə|, |iŋ+\ *adj* [*syn-* + Gk *klastos* broken + E *-ic* — more at CLASTIC] **:** curved toward the same side in all directions — used of a surface (as of a sphere) that in all directions around any point bends away from a tangent plane toward the same side; opposed to *anticlastic*
¹**syn·cli·nal** \(ˈ)si|n|ˈklīnᵊl, sə|n|ˈk-, |iŋ|\ *adj* [*syn-* + Gk *klinein* to lean + E *-al* — more at LEAN] **1 :** inclined down from opposite directions so as to meet **2 :** having or relating to a folded rock structure in which the sides or limbs dip toward a common line or plane ⟨~ fold⟩ ⟨~ axis⟩ — opposed to *anticlinal* — **syn·cli·nal·ly** \-ᵊlē\ *adv*
²**synclinal** \"\ *n* -s **:** SYNCLINE
synclinal valley *n* **:** a valley produced by or coinciding in position with a synclinal fold
syn·cline \ˈsinˌklīn, ˈsiŋˌk-\ *n* -s [back-formation fr. ¹*synclinal*] **:** a trough of stratified rock in which the beds dip toward each other from either side — compare ANTICLINE
syn·clin·i·cal \-ˈklinəkəl\ *adj* [*syncline* + *-ical*] **:** SYNCLINAL
syn·cli·nore \ˈsiŋkləˌnō(ə)r, -inkˌ-\ *n* -s [NL *synclinorium*] **:** SYNCLINORIUM
syn·cli·no·ri·al \ˌ==ˈnōrēəl\ *or* **syn·cli·no·ri·an** \-ēən\ *adj* [NL *synclinorium* + E *-al* or *-an*] **:** relating to or resembling a synclinorium
syn·cli·no·ri·um \ˌ==ˈrēəm\ *n, pl* **synclino·ria** \-ēə\ [NL, fr. ISV *syncline* + NL *-orium*] **:** a compound flexure of the earth's crust having the form of an inverted anticlinorium
syn·clit·ic \(ˈ)si|n|ˈklid·ik, sə|n|ˈk-, |iŋ|\ *adj* [fr. (assumed) Gk *synklitos* (verbal of Gk *synklinein* to lean together, fr. *syn-* + *klinein* to lean) + E *-ic* — more at LEAN] **:** parallel to the axis of the pelvis — used of the planes of the fetal head in labor; compare ENCLITIC
syn·co·pal \ˈsiŋkəpəl, -inkˌ-\ *adj* [*syncope* + *-al*] **:** of, relating to, or characterized by syncope ⟨~ attack⟩
syn·co·pate \ˈsiŋkəˌpāt, -inkˌ-, *usu* -ād·+V\ *vt* -ED/-ING/-S [ML *syncopatus*, past part. of *syncopare*, fr. LL *syncope*, *syncopa*] **1 a :** to shorten by syncope ⟨~ *suppose* to *s'pose*⟩ **:** produce by syncope ⟨*bewild'ring* is *syncopated* from *bewildering*⟩ **b :** to omit (a sound or letter) in the interior of a word ⟨~ the *o* of *policeman*⟩ **c :** to cut short **:** CLIP, ABBREVIATE **2 :** to modify or affect (musical rhythm) by syncopation
syncopated *adj* [ML *syncopatus* + E *-ed*] **1 :** marked by or exhibiting syncopation ⟨~ rhythm⟩ ⟨~ melody⟩ ⟨poetry using many ~ forms of words⟩ **2 :** cut short **:** ABBREVIATED, ABRIDGED ⟨correct the ~ calendar of memory —Dixon Wecter⟩ ⟨cleared his throat . . . producing a small, ~ noise —Dorothy Parker⟩
syncopated counterpoint *n* **:** counterpoint in which one note is added to each note of the cantus firmus after a fixed rhythmic interval
syncopated perforation *n* **:** INTERRUPTED PERFORATION
syn·co·pa·tion \ˌ==ˈpāshən\ *n* -s [ML *syncopation-*, *syncopatio*, fr. *syncopatus* + L *-ion-*, *-io* -ion] **1 :** SYNCOPE 2 **2 a :** a temporary displacement or shifting of the regular metrical accent in a musical composition occurring typically when a tone is begun on an unaccented beat and continued through the following accented beat or when a tone begins after the commencement of a beat and is continued into the following beat **3 :** a rhythm or dance step in syncopated time ⟨shoes scuffing ~s on the cement sidewalk —Booth Tarkington⟩

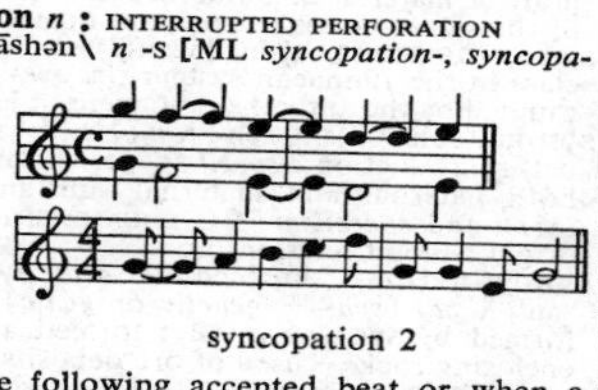

syncopation 2

syn·co·pa·tive \ˈ==ˌpād·iv\ *adj* **:** relating to syncopation ⟨all sorts of ~ subtleties that are quite foreign to European music —Aaron Copland⟩
syn·co·pa·tor \-ād·ə(r)\ *n* -s **:** one that uses syncopation; *esp* **:** a player of jazz music
syn·co·pe \ˈsiŋkə(ˌ)pē, -inkˌ-, -ˌpi\ *n* -s [LL, fr. Gk *synkopē*, fr. *synkoptein* to chop up, cut short, fr. *syn-* + *koptein* to strike, cut off — more at CAPON] **1 :** a partial or complete temporary suspension of respiration and circulation due to cerebral ischemia and characterized by sudden pallor, coldness of the skin, and partial or complete unconsciousness **:** FAINT, SWOON **2 a :** the loss of one or more sounds or letters in the interior of a word (as in *di'mond* for *diamond* or *fo'c'sle* for *forecastle*) — compare APHAERESIS, APOCOPE, CONTRACTION, HYPHAERESIS **b :** a form resulting from such a loss of sounds or letters **3 :** suppression or omission of a short syllable within a metrical foot or measure usu. with compensating protraction of an adjacent long **4** *obs* **:** SYNCOPATION 2
syn·craniate \(ˈ)si|n, sə|, |iŋ+\ *adj* [*syn-* + *craniate*] **:** relating to or having a skull with which certain vertebral elements are fused ⟨the skulls of amniotes are considered to be ~⟩ — opposed to *archaecraniate*
syn·cranium \"+\ *n* [NL, fr. *syn-* + *cranium*] **:** a syncraniate skull
syn·cran·te·ri·an \ˌsinˌkranˈtirēən, ˌsiŋˌk-\ *also* **syn·cran·ter·ic** \-ˈterik\ *adj* [*syn-* + Gk *krantēres* wisdom teeth + E *-ian* or *-ic*] **:** having the teeth in a continuous row — compare DIACRANTERIAN
syn·cret·ic \(ˈ)si|n|ˈkred·ik, sə|n|ˈk-, |iŋ|\ *adj* [*syncretism* + *-ic*] **1 :** characterized or brought about by syncretism **:** aiming at or making for syncretism **:** SYNCRETISTIC ⟨~ religious sect⟩ **2 :** having absorbed the functions of one or more other grammatical cases ⟨the Latin ablative is a ~ case⟩
syn·cre·tion \sənˈkrēshən, səŋˈk-\ *n* -s [*syncretic* + *-ion*] **:** an instance of syncretism **:** act of syncretizing
syn·cre·tism \ˈsiŋkrəˌtizəm, ˈsink-\ *n* -s [NL *syncretismus*, fr. Gk *synkrētismos* federation of Cretan cities, fr. *synkrētizein* to unite against a common enemy] **1 :** the reconciliation or union of conflicting (as religious) beliefs or an effort intending such; *specif* **:** a movement of a Lutheran party in the 17th century led by George Calixtus seeking the union of Protestant sects with each other and with the Roman Catholic Church **2 :** flagrant compromise in religion or philosophy **:** eclecticism that is illogical or leads to inconsistency **:** uncritical acceptance of conflicting or divergent beliefs or principles **3 :** the developmental process of historical growth within a religion by accretion and coalescence of different and often orig. conflicting forms of belief and practice through the interaction with or supersession of other religions **4 :** the union or fusion into one of two or more orig. different inflectional forms
¹**syn·cre·tist** \-rəd·əst\ *n* -s [fr. *syncretism*, after such pairs as E *fatalism: fatalist*] **:** one who advocates or promotes syncretism
²**syncretist** \"\ *adj* **:** SYNCRETISTIC
syn·cre·tis·tic \ˌ=krəˈtistik\ *adj* **:** of or relating to syncretism ⟨~ writings⟩ ⟨~ adaptation of faith⟩
syn·cre·tize \ˈ==ˌtīz\ *vb* -ED/-ING/-S [NL *syncretizare*, fr. Gk *synkrētizein* to unite against a common enemy as did the Cretans), fr. *syn-* + *Krēt*, *Krēs* Cretan + *-izein* -ize] *vi* **1 :** to become fused or united **2 :** to favor or practice syncretism ~ *vt* **:** to attempt to unite and harmonize (as conflicting principles) esp. without critical examination or real logical unity
syncrisis *n* [LL, fr. Gk, combination, comparison, fr. *synkrinein* to combine, compare (fr. *syn-* + *krinein* to separate, judge) + *-sis* — more at RIDDLE] *obs* **:** comparison of contraries or opposites
syn·cryp·ta \sinˈkriptə, siŋˈk-\ *n, cap* [NL, fr. *syn-* + Gk *kryptē*, fem. of *kryptos* hidden — more at CRYPT] **:** a genus of biflagellate free-swimming flagellates (order Chrysomonadina) occurring as spheroidal colonies and sometimes causing in water supplies odors suggestive of overripe cucumbers
syn·cryp·tic \(ˈ)=ˈkriptik\ *adj* [*syn-* + *cryptic*] **:** of, relating to, or being a protective resemblance in appearance in which basically unlike organisms are similar (as in color) often through a common adaptation to their environment; *also* **:** exhibiting such resemblance ⟨~ species⟩ — compare SYNTECHNIC
syncs *pl of* SYNC, *pres 3d sing of* SYNC
syn·cyte \ˈsinˌsīt\ *n* -s [NL *syncytium*] **:** SYNCYTIUM
syn·cy·tial \(ˈ)sinˈsishəl, sənˈs-\ *adj* [NL *syncytium* + E *-al*] **:** of, relating to, or constituting syncytium ⟨~ tissue⟩
syn·cy·tio·trophoblast \sənˈsishē(ˌ)ō+\ *n* [NL *syncitium* + *-o-* + E *trophoblast*] **:** SYNTROPHOBLAST
syn·cy·tium \sənˈsish(ē)əm\ *n, pl* **syncy·tia** \-ə\ [NL, fr. *syn-* + *cyt-* + *-ium*] **1 :** a multinucleate mass of protoplasm resulting from fusion of cells (as in the plasmodium of a slime mold) **2 :** COENOCYTE 1
syn·cy·toid \ˈsinsəˌtȯid\ *adj* [NL *syncytium* + E *-oid*] **:** of, relating to, or resembling a syncytium
synd *abbr* syndicate
¹**syn·dac·tyl** *or* **syn·dac·tyle** \(ˈ)sinˈdaktᵊl, sənˈd-\ *adj* [F *syndactyle*, fr. *syn-* + Gk *daktylos* finger] **:** having two or more digits wholly or partly united — see SYNDACTYLISM
²**syndactyl** *or* **syndactyle** \"\ *n* -s **:** a syndactyl bird or mammal
syn·dac·ty·la \ˌ=ˈdaktələ\ *n pl, cap* [NL, fr. *syn-* + *-dactyla* (fr. Gk *daktylos* finger)] *in some classifications* **:** a primary division of Marsupialia comprising forms in which the second and third pedal digits are bound together into a single double-nailed toe and being approximately equal to Diprotodontia
syn·dac·tyl·ia \-ˌsinˌdakˈtilēə\ *n* -s [NL, fr. ISV ¹*syndactyl* + NL *-ia*] **:** SYNDACTYLISM
syn·dac·tyl·ic \ˌsinˌdakˈtilik\ *or* **syn·dac·ty·lous** \(ˈ)sinˈdaktələs, sənˈd-\ *adj* [F *syndactyle* + E *-ic*, *-ous*] **:** SYNDACTYL
syn·dac·ty·lism \-ˈdaktəˌlizəm\ *n* -s **:** the state of being syndactyl **:** a union of two or more digits that is normal in many birds (as kingfishers, motmots, bee eaters, or hornbills) in which some of the toes are united and in some mammals (as the kangaroos and some other marsupials) and occurs in man as a familial anomaly marked by webbing of two or more fingers or toes
syn·dac·ty·ly \(ˈ)sinˈdaktəlē, sənˈd-\ *n* -ES **:** SYNDACTYLISM
syn·de·re·sis \ˌsindəˈrēsəs\ *or* **syn·te·re·sis** \-ntə-\ *n* -ES [ML, fr. Gk *syntērēsis* preservation, fr. *syntērein* to preserve (fr. *syn-* + *tērein* to guard, observe) + *-sis*; akin to Gk *tinein* to pay — more at PAIN] **1 :** inborn knowledge of the primary principles of moral action — distinguished from *syneidesis* **2 :** the essence, ground, or center of the soul that enters into communion with God **:** the spark or emanation of divinity in the soul
syn·de·sis \ˈsindəsəs\ *n* -ES [NL, fr. Gk, action of binding together, fr. *syndein* to bind together + *-sis* — more at ASYNDETON] **:** SYNAPSIS 1
syndesm- *or* **syndesmo-** *comb form* [Gk *syndesmos*, fr. *syndein* to bind together] **:** ligament ⟨*syndesmosis*⟩ **:** connection **:** contact ⟨*syndesmochorial*⟩
syn·des·mo·chorial \(ˌ)sinˌdezmə+\ *adj* [*syndesm-* + *chorial*] *of a placenta* **:** having fetal epithelium in contact with maternal submucosa (as in ruminants) — compare ENDOTHELIOCHORIAL, EPITHELIOCHORIAL, HEMOCHORIAL
syn·des·mo·sis \ˌsinˌdezˈmōsəs\ *n, pl* **syndesmo·ses** \-ōˌsēz\ [NL, fr. *syndesm-* + *-osis*] **:** an articulation in which the contiguous surfaces of the bones are rough and are bound together by an interosseous ligament
syn·des·mot·ic \ˌ=ˌ=ˈmäd·ik\ *adj* [fr. NL *syndesmosis*, after such pairs as NL *hypnosis*: E *hypnotic*] **:** relating to or marked by syndesmosis
syn·det \ˈsinˌdet\ *n* -s [*syn*thetic *det*ergent] **:** DETERGENT c
syn·det·ic \(ˈ)sinˈded·ik, sənˈde-\ *adj* [Gk *syndetikos*, fr. *syndetos* bound together + *-ikos* -ic — more at ASYNDETON] **:** CONNECTING, CONNECTIVE, INTERCONNECTED ⟨~ pronoun⟩; *also* **:** marked by a conjunctive ⟨~ relative clause⟩ — **syn·det·i·cal·ly** \-ed·ək(ə)lē\ *adv*
syn·dic \ˈsindik, -dēk\ *n* -s [F, fr. LL *syndicus*, fr. Gk *syndikos* court assistant, advocate, fr. *syn-* + *dikē* right, judgment — more at DICTION] **1 :** an officer of government invested with different powers (as magisterial or mayoral) in different countries **2 :** an agent of a corporation (as a university) or of a body of men engaged in a business enterprise **3 a :** an advocate, agent, or attorney for a city, university, or corporate body **b :** one appointed to manage an estate as a trustee **c** *Louisiana* **:** the assignee of a bankrupt **4 :** one of various officials in cities of ancient Greece having duties similar to those of a judge or advocate
syn·di·cal \-dəkəl, -dēk-\ *adj* [F, fr. *syndic* + *-al*] **1 :** of or relating to a syndic or to a committee that assumes the powers of a syndic **2 :** of or relating to syndicalism ⟨~ organization of capital and labor⟩
syn·di·cal·ism \-kəˌlizəm\ *n* -s [F *syndicalisme*, fr. (*chambre*) *syndicale* trade union (fr. *chambre* chamber + *syndicale*, fem. of *syndical*) + *-isme* -ism] **1 :** a revolutionary political movement that aims by the general strike and direct action of labor unions to overthrow parliamentary democracy and establish a corporate society with general control in the hands of trade unions and workers' cooperatives — called also *anarcho-syndicalism*; compare CRIMINAL SYNDICALISM, MARXISM **2 :** TRADE UNIONISM
¹**syn·di·cal·ist** \-ləst\ *n* -s [F *syndicaliste*, fr. (*chambre*) *syndicale* + *-iste* -ist] **:** an advocate or adherent of syndicalism
²**syndicalist** \"\ *or* **syn·di·cal·is·tic** \ˌ==kəˈlistik, -tēk\ *adj* **:** relating to or advocating syndicalism
¹**syn·di·cate** \ˈsindəˌkāt, *usu* -ād·+V\ *vb* -ED/-ING/-S [in sense 1, fr. ML *syndicatus*, past part. of *syndicare*, fr. LL *syndicus* syndic; in other senses, fr. ²*syndicate* — more at SYNDIC] *vt* **1** *obs* **:** CENSURE, JUDGE **2 :** to subject to or bring under the control of a syndicate ⟨~ a mining enterprise⟩ ⟨~ a bond issue⟩ **:** combine into or manage as a syndicate ⟨~ a number of newspapers⟩ **3 a :** to sell (as an article or a cartoon) for publication through a syndicate ⟨a *syndicated* feature in the Sunday supplement⟩ **b :** to sell (as an article or a cartoon) for publication in many newspapers or periodicals at once ⟨never able to ~ his column widely —G.S.Perry⟩ ~ *vi* **:** to unite to form a syndicate — **syn·di·ca·tion** \ˌ==ˈkāshən\ *n* -s
²**syn·di·cate** \ˈsindəkət, -dēk-, *usu* -kəd·+V\ *n* -s [F *syndicat*, fr. *syndic* + *-at* -ate] **1 a :** the office or jurisdiction of a syndic **b :** a council, committee, or body of syndics **2 :** an association of persons officially authorized to undertake some duty or to negotiate some business **3 a :** a group of persons or concerns who combine under a usu. temporary agreement to carry out a particular transaction ⟨~ of investment houses for under-

writing a bond issue⟩ ⟨~ of real estate men formed to buy an office building⟩ **b** : CARTEL 4 **c** : a loose association of racketeers in control of organized crime (as the policy racket, bookmaking, prostitution) **4** : a business concern that sells to the press materials (as special articles, photographs, or comic strips) for publication in a number of newspapers or periodicals simultaneously **5** : a group of newspapers under one management : a newspaper chain

syn·di·ca·tor \-də,kād·ə(r), -ātə-\ *n* -s : one that syndicates : one that manages or operates a syndicate

syn·diploidy \(ˈ)sin, sən+\ *n* [*syn-* + *diploidy*] : doubling of the gametic chromosome number by reassociation of the daughter groups of meiotic chromosomes at any time after the first meiotic metaphase

syn·drome \ˈsin,drōm *sometimes* -,drəm *or* -drə(,)mē *or* -drəmi\ *n* -s [NL, fr. Gk *syndromē* act of running together, combination, syndrome, fr. *syn-* + *-dromē* (fr. *dramein* to run) — more at DROMEDARY] **1** : a group of symptoms or signs typical of a disease, disturbance, condition, or lesion in animals or plants ⟨shoulder-arm ~⟩ ⟨~ of genetic abnormalities⟩ ⟨starvation ~⟩ ⟨schizophrenia . . . is a ~ related to a variety of etiological factors —Leopold Bellak & Elizabeth Willson⟩ **2** : a set of concurrent things : CONCURRENCE ⟨a word possesses a ~ of meanings —*English Jour.*⟩ — **syn·drom·ic** \(ˈ)sinˈdrōmik, -räm-, -mēk\ *adj*

syn·dy·oc·er·as \,sindēˈäsərəs\ *n, cap* [NL, fr. Gk *syndyo* two together (fr. *syn-* + *dyo* two) + NL *-ceras* — more at TWO] : a genus of extinct ungulates from the Miocene of Nebraska related to *Protoceras* and having a skull with two pairs of horns curving toward each other

syn·dyo·tac·tic *or* **syn·dio·tac·tic** \ˈsindēō¦taktik, sən¦dīə¦t-\ *adj* [ISV *syndyo* (fr. Gk) + *-tactic*] : having or relating to a regular alternation of differences in stereochemical structure in the repeating units of a polymer — compare ISOTACTIC

¹syne \(ˈ)sīn\ *adv* [ME (northern dial.) *syne, seyne*, prob. fr. ON *sīthan*, fr. *sīth* since — more at SINCE] **1** *chiefly Scot* : NEXT, THEN **2** *chiefly Scot* : LATER **3** *chiefly Scot* : since then : AGO ⟨got a shot at me two days ~ —John Buchan⟩

²syne \"\ *conj* [ME (northern dial.) *syne, seyne*, fr. *syne, seyne*, adv.] *Scot* : SINCE

³syne \"\ *prep* [¹*syne*] *Scot* : SINCE

syn·ec·do·che \səˈnekdə(,)kē\ *n* -s [L, fr. Gk *synekdochē*, fr. *syn-* + *ekdochē* interpretation, fr. *ekdechesthai* to receive from another, understand in a certain way, fr. *ek, ex* out of, from + *dechesthai* to take, accept, receive; akin to Gk *dokein* to seem good — more at EX-, DECENT] : a figure of speech by which a part is put for the whole (as *fifty sail* for *fifty ships*), the whole for a part (as *the smiling year* for *spring*), the species for the genus (as *cutthroat* for *assassin*), the genus for the species (as *a creature* for *a man*), or the name of the material for the thing made (as *willow* for *bat*) — compare METONYMY

syn·ec·doch·ic \¦si,nek¦däkik, sə¦n-\ *or* **syn·ec·doch·i·cal** \-ˈäkəkəl\ *adj* [Gk *synekdochikos*, fr. *synekdochē* + *-ikos* -ic, -ical] : expressed by or implying a synecdoche — **syn·ec·doch·i·cal·ly** \-ˈäkək(ə)lē\ *adv*

syn·ec·do·chism \səˈnekdə,kizəm\ *n* -s [*synecdoche* + *-ism*] **1** : the use of synecdoche : an instance of such use **2** : the use in sympathetic magic of a part of an object as representing the whole — compare MAGIC 1a

syn·echia \səˈnekēə, -ˈnēk-; ,sinəˈkīə\ *n, pl* **synechiae** \-kē,ē, -ˈkī,ē\ [NL, fr. Gk *synecheia* continuity, coherence, fr. *synechēs* holding together, continuous (fr. *synechein* to hold together, fr. *syn-* + *echein* to have, hold) + *-ia* -y — more at SCHEME] : an adhesion of parts; *specif* : a disease of the eye in which the iris adheres to the cornea or to the capsule of the crystalline lens

syn·e·chism \ˈsinə,kizəm\ *n* -s [Gk *synechismos* continuity, fr. *synechizein* to make continuous, fr. *synechēs* continuous + *-izein* -ize] : a principle in philosophy holding continuity (as of hypotheses) to be of prime importance

syn·ech·thran \səˈnekthrən\ *n* -s [*synechthry* + *-an*] : an insect (as a beetle) living as an unwelcome guest among other insects (as ants)

syn·ech·thry *or* **syn·ec·thry** \ˈsi,nekthrē, səˈn-\ *n* -ES [*syn-* + Gk *echthros* enemy + E *-y*; perh. akin to Gk *ex* from, out of — more at EX-] : hostile commensalism — compare SYMPHILY, SYNOECY

syn·ecologic *or* **syn·ecological** \(ˈ)sin+\ *adj* : of, relating to, or involving synecology — **syn·ecologically** \"+\ *adv*

syn·ecology \ˈsin+\ *n* [G *synökologie*, fr. *syn-* + *ökologie* ecology] : a branch of ecology that deals with the structure, development, and distribution of ecological communities in relation to environment — compare AUTECOLOGY

syn·ec·pho·ne·sis \,si,nekfəˈnēsəs, sə,n-\ *n, pl* **synecphoneses** \-ē,sēz\ [NL, fr. Gk *synekphōnēsis*, fr. *synekphōnein* to utter together (fr. *syn-* + *ekphōnein* to utter, pronounce, fr. *ek*, *ex* out of, from + *phōnein* to speak, utter, fr. *phōnē* sound, voice) + *-sis* — more at EX-, BAN] : contraction of two syllables into one : SYNIZESIS, SYNAERESIS

syn·edra \səˈnēdrə, səˈned-, ˈsinəd-\ *n, cap* [NL, fr. Gk *synedros* sitting together, fr. *syn-* + *-edros* (fr. *hedra* seat) — more at SIT] : a large genus related to *Fragilaria* and comprising elongated linear or commonly needle-shaped solitary or loosely colonial diatoms that may cause earthy odors in water supplies

syn·edri·al *or* **syn·edri·an** \səˈnēdrēəl, -ned-\ *adj* [*synedrion* + *-al, -an*] : of or relating to the Sanhedrin

syn·edri·on \-rēən\ *or* **syn·edri·um** \-rēəm\ *n, pl* **syn·edria** \-rēə\ *usu cap* [Gk *synedrion* — more at SANHEDRIN] : SANHEDRIN

syn·ei·de·sis \,si,nīˈdēsəs\ *n, pl* **syneide·ses** \-ē,sēz\ [ML, fr. Gk *syneidēsis*, lit., consciousness, awareness, fr. *syneidenai* to have knowledge of something, be aware of something (fr. *syn-* + *eidenai* to know) + *-sis* — more at WIT] : the capacity to apply general principles of moral judgment to particular cases — distinguished from *synderesis*

sy·ne·ma \səˈnēmə\ *n, pl* **sy·nema·ta** \-nēməd·ə, -nem-\ [NL, irreg. fr. *syn-* + Gk *nēma* thread — more at NEEDLE] : the column of united filaments in a monadelphous flower

syn·ener·gy \səˈnenərjē, ˈsinə,nər-\ *n* [*syn-* + *energy*] *archaic* : SYNERGY

syn·en·tog·nath \ˈsinən·ˈtäg,nath, səˈnentəg-\ *n* -s [NL *Synentognathi*] : a fish of the order Synentognathi

syn·en·tog·na·thi \,sinənˈtägnə,thī\ *n pl, cap* [NL, fr. *syn-* + *ent-* + *-gnathi* (fr. Gk *gnathos* jaw) — more at GNATH-] : an order of fishes having spineless fins, united lower pharyngeal bones, and the lateral line forming a ridge along the lower lateral part of the body that includes the needlefishes, sauries, flying fishes, and halfbeaks — **syn·en·tog·na·thous** \¦=;=¦=-thəs\ *adj*

syn·eph·rine \səˈnefrən, -,frēn\ *n* -s [*syn-* + *epinephrine*] : a crystalline sympathomimetic amine $C_9H_{13}NO_2$ isomeric with phenylephrine

syn·er·e·sis *or* **syn·aer·e·sis** \səˈnerəsəs, -nir-, *esp in sense 2* ÷ ,sinəˈrēsəs\ *n, pl* **synere·ses** *or* **synaere·ses** \-ə,sēz, -ē,sēz\ [LL *synaeresis*, fr. Gk *synairesis*, lit., contraction, fr. *synairein* to seize and bring together, shorten, contract (fr. *syn-* + *hairein* to seize, take) + *-sis* — more at HERESY] **1 a** : the union or drawing together into one syllable of two vowels ordinarily separated in pronunciation (as \ˈsēst\ for \ˈsē·əst\ *seest*) — opposed to *diaeresis* **b** : SYNIZESIS 1 **2** : the separation of liquid from a gel caused by contraction ⟨~ if carried further . . . results in coagulation —J.W.McBain⟩ — compare COAGULATION 1, IMBIBITION 2a

syn·er·get·ic \¦sinər¦jed·ik\ *adj* [Gk *synergētikos*, fr. (assumed) *synergētos* (verbal of *synergein* to work with, cooperate, fr. *synergos* working together, fr. *syn-* + *ergon* work) + *-ikos* -ic — more at WORK] : SYNERGIC

syn·er·gia \səˈnərj(ē)ə\ *n* -s [NL — more at SYNERGY] : SYNERGY, SYNERGISM

syn·er·gic \səˈnərjik, (ˈ)si¦n-\ *also* **syn·er·gi·cal** \-jəkəl\ *adj* [NL *synergicus*, fr. *synergia* + L *-icus* -ic, -ical] : working together : COOPERATING, COOPERATIVE ⟨~ muscles⟩ — **syn·er·gi·cal·ly** \-jək(ə)lē\ *adv*

syn·er·gid \səˈnərjəd, ˈsinər-\ *n* -s [NL *synergida*, fr. Gk *synergein* to work together, cooperate + NL *-ida* (fr. L *-ides*, patronymic suffix)] : one of the two small cells lying near the micropylar end of the embryo sac in seed plants constituting with the egg the egg apparatus — **syn·er·gi·dal** \səˈnərjədᵊl\ *adj*

syn·er·gi·da \səˈnərjədə\ *n, pl* **synergi·dae** \-,dē\ [NL] : SYNERGID

syn·er·gism \ˈsinər,jizəm\ *n* -s [NL *synergismus*, fr. Gk *synergos* working together + L *-ismus* -ism] **1** : an ancient theological doctrine holding that in regeneration there is cooperation of divine grace and human activity ⟨this form of ~ is technically known as semi-Pelagianism, but it is much older than the semi-Pelagians, being essentially the view of the Church, both east and west, ever since Irenaeus —A.C. McGiffert⟩ — compare MONERGISM **2** : cooperative action of discrete agencies (as drugs or muscles) such that the total effect is greater than the sum of the two or more effects taken independently — opposed to *antagonism*

syn·er·gist \-jəst\ *n* -s [NL *synergista*, fr. Gk *synergos* + L *-ista* -ist] **1** : one who holds the doctrine of synergism **2** : an agent that increases the effectiveness of another agent when combined with it: as **a** : a drug that acts in synergism with another **b** : a substance (as piperonyl butoxide) that increases the effectiveness of an insecticide or other pesticide **c** : a substance that increases the activity of an antioxidant; *esp* : such a substance (as phosphoric acid) that is not an antioxidant by itself **3** : an organ (as a muscle) that acts in concert with another to enhance its effect — compare AGONIST

syn·er·gis·tic \¦sinər¦jistik\ *also* **syn·er·gis·ti·cal** \-təkəl\ *adj* **1** : of or relating to the doctrine of synergism ⟨~ controversy⟩ **2 a** : having the capacity to act in synergism ⟨~ drug⟩ ⟨~ muscle⟩ ⟨~ action⟩ — compare INCOMPATIBLE **b** : of, relating to, or resembling synergism ⟨a ~ reaction⟩ ⟨a ~ effect⟩ — **syn·er·gis·ti·cal·ly** \-tək(ə)lē\ *adv*

syn·er·gize \ˈsinər,jīz\ *vb* -ED/-ING/-S [*synergy* + *-ize*] *vi* : to act as synergists : exhibit synergism : COOPERATE, COORDINATE ~ *vt* : to increase the activity of (a substance)

syn·er·gy \ˈsinərjē\ *n* -ES [NL *synergia*, fr. Gk *synergos* working together + L *-ia* -y — more at SYNERGETIC] : combined action or operation (as of muscles or nerves); *specif* : SYNERGISM 2

syn·er·ize \ˈsinə,rīz\ *vi* -ED/-ING/-S [*syneresis* + *-ize*] : to undergo syneresis ⟨clots of another type . . . ~ readily, become dense with loss of fluid —E.J.Cohn⟩

syn·esis \ˈsinəsəs\ *n* -ES [NL, fr. Gk, union, intelligence, fr. *synienai* to bring together, perceive, understand (fr. *syn-* + *hienai* to send) + *-sis* — more at JET] : a construction in which one or more forms make agreement or reference not according to the requirements of syntax but according to the sense of the passage (as *anyone* and *them* in "if anyone calls, tell them I am out")

syn·es·the·sia *or* **syn·aes·the·sia** \,sinəsˈthēzh(ē)ə\ *n* [NL, fr. *syn-* + *-esthesia, -aesthesia* (as in *anesthesia, anaesthesia*)] : a concomitant sensation; *esp* : a subjective sensation or image of a sense (as of color) other than the one (as of sound) being stimulated — compare CHROMESTHESIA, PHONISM, PHOTISM

syn·es·thete \ˈsinəs,thēt, səˈnes-\ *n* -s [back-formation fr. *synesthetic*] : one who experiences synesthesia ⟨no two ~s agree on the correspondence between the colors and the pitches —R.J.Williams⟩

syn·es·thet·ic *or* **syn·aes·thet·ic** \¦sinəs¦thed·ik\ *adj* [fr. NL *synesthesia, synaesthesia*, after such pairs as NL *anesthesia*: E *anesthetic, anaesthetic*] : relating to or experiencing synesthesia ⟨~ response to music⟩ : involving more than one of the senses ⟨~ metaphor⟩

synezesis *var of* SYNIZESIS

syn·game·on \sinˈgamēən, siŋˈg-, -gām-\ *n* -s [NL, fr. Gk *syngameon, syngamoun*, neut. of *syngameōn, syngamōn*, pres. part. of *syngamein* to marry together, fr. *syngamos* united in wedlock, connected by marriage] : the members of a population capable of exchanging genes directly or indirectly

syn·ga·mi·a·sis \,siŋgəˈmīəsəs, ,sing-\ *or* **syn·ga·mo·sis** \-ˈmōsəs\ *n, pl* **syngamia·ses** \-ə,sēz\ *or* **syngamo·ses** \-ō,sēz\ [NL, fr. *Syngamus* + *-iasis* or *-osis*] : infestation with or disease caused by roundworms of the genus *Syngamus* : GAPES

syn·gam·ic \(ˈ)si¦n¦gamik, sə¦n¦g-, ¦ŋ¦\ *adj* [Gk *syngamos* + E *-ic*] : relating to or involving sexual reproduction

¹syn·gam·id \sənˈgaməd, səŋˈg-; ˈsiŋgəm-, -ing-\ *adj* [NL *Syngamidae* family of nematode worms, fr. *Syngamus*, type genus + *-idae*] : of or relating to the genus *Syngamus* or family Syngamidae

²syngamid \"\ *n* -s : a nematode of the genus *Syngamus* or family Syngamidae

syn·ga·mus \ˈsiŋgəməs, -ing-\ *n, cap* [NL, fr. Gk *syngamos* united in wedlock, connected by marriage, fr. *syn-* + *-gamos* -gamous] : a genus (coextensive with the strongyloid family Syngamidae) of nematode worms parasitic in the trachea or esophagus of various birds and mammals — see GAPEWORM, GULLET WORM

syn·ga·my \-mē\ *n* -ES [ISV *syn-* + *-gamy*] : sexual reproduction by union of gametes — compare HOLOGAMY

syn·ge·ne·sio·transplantation \,sinjə¦nēzē(,)ō+\ *n* [irreg. fr. Gk *syngenēs* inborn, related, cognate (fr. *syn-* + *-genēs*, fr. *gignesthai* to be born) + E *transplantation* — more at KIN] : a graft of material or tissue between closely related individuals of the same species — compare HOMOGRAFT

syn·ge·ne·sious \¦sinjə¦nēzh(ē)əs\ *adj* [NL *Syngenesia*, a class in the Linnaean system (fr. *syn-* + *-genesia*) + E *-ous*] : united by the anthers ⟨~ stamens⟩ : having stamens so united

syn·genesis \(ˈ)sin, sən+\ *n* [NL, fr. *syn-* + *genesis*] **1** : sexual reproduction; *specif* : derivation of the zygote from both paternal and maternal substance — contrasted with *ovism* and *spermism* **2** : ENCASEMENT 1b **3** : community of origin : blood relationship

syn·ge·net·ic \¦sinjə¦ned·ik\ *also* **syn·gen·ic** \(ˈ)sin¦jenik, sən¦j-\ *adj* [*syn-* + *genetic* or *genic*] **1** : of, relating to, or formed by syngenesis **2** : formed at the same time as the enclosing rock — used of ore deposits; compare EPIGENETIC

syn·ge·nite \ˈsinjə,nīt\ *n* -s [G *syngenit*, fr. Gk *syngenēs* related + G *-it* -ite; fr. its relationship to polyhalite] : a mineral $K_2Ca(SO_4)_2.H_2O$ consisting of a hydrous calcium potassium sulfate and occurring in colorless or white tabular crystals (hardness 2.5, sp. gr. 2.6)

syng·natha \ˈsiŋnəthə\ [NL, fr. *syn-* + *-gnatha*] *syn of* CHILOPODA

syng·na·thid \-thəd\ *n* -s [NL *Syngnathidae*] : a fish of the family Syngnathidae

syng·nath·i·dae \siŋˈnathə,dē\ *n pl, cap* [NL, fr. *Syngnathus*, type genus + *-idae*] : a family of fishes (order Solenichthyes) having an elongate tubular snout, lacking the pelvic and first dorsal fins, and comprising the sea horse and pipefishes

¹syng·na·thoid \ˈsiŋnə,thȯid\ *adj* [NL *Syngnathus* + E *-oid*] : resembling or related to the Syngnathidae

²syngnathoid \"\ *n* -s : a syngnathoid fish

syng·na·thous \ˈsiŋnəthəs\ *adj* [in sense 1, fr. *syn-* + *-gnathous*; in sense 2, fr. NL *Syngnathus* + E *-ous*] **1** : having the jaws drawn out into a tubular snout **2** : of or relating to the Syngnathidae

syng·na·thus \"\ *n, cap* [NL, fr. *syn-* + *-gnathus*] : the type genus of Syngnathidae comprising various typical pipefishes

syn·go·ni·um \sinˈgōnēəm, siŋˈg-\ *n, cap* [NL, fr. *syn-* + *gon-* + *-ium*] : a genus of climbing shrubs (family Araceae) native to Central and So. America and used as ornamental house plants esp. for their velvety foliage

syn·graph \ˈsin,graf, -iŋ,g-, -ráf\ *n* [L *syngraphus*, fr. Gk *syngraphos* something written down, decree, contract, fr. *syngraphein* to write down, draw up a contract, fr. *syn-* + *graphein* to write — more at CARVE] : a written statement or contract signed and often sealed by all the parties thereto; *specif* : an indenture corresponding to the chirograph of common law

syn·hexyl \(ˈ)sin, sən+\ *n* [*syn-* + *hexyl*] : a compound derived from dibenzo-pyran that is said to have a euphoriant action more powerful than that of cannabis and is used experimentally in the treatment of depressive mental states

syn·i·ze·sis \,sinəˈzēsəs\ *n* -ES [in sense 1, fr. LL, fr. Gk *synizēsis*, lit., collapse, fr. *synizein* to collapse (fr. *syn-* + *hizein* to sit, sit down) + *-sis*; akin to Gk *hezesthai* to sit; in sense 2, NL, fr. Gk *synizēsis* — more at SIT] **1** : contraction of two syllables into one by uniting in pronunciation two adjacent vowels (as when the *ee* of *eleemosynary* is pronounced as one syllable) or by making a high vowel before another vowel consonantal (as in \ˈrōmyō\ for \ˈrōmē,ō\ *Romeo*) : SYNECPHONESIS — compare SYNERESIS 1a **2** *or* **syn·eze·sis** \"\ **a** : the massing of the chromatin in the nucleus preceding the maturation division **b** : SYNAPSIS — not used technically

syn·kary·on *also* **syn·kari·on** *or* **syn·cary·on** \(ˈ)si¦n¦-ˈkarē,än, -ēən, sə¦n¦k-, ¦ŋ¦\ *n* -s [NL, fr. *syn-* + Gk *karyon* nut — more at CAREEN] : a cell nucleus formed by the fusion of two preexisting nuclei : a zygote nucleus — compare FERTILIZATION, PRONUCLEUS — **syn·kar·y·on·ic** \(¦)=¦==¦änik\ *adj*

syn·ka·tath·e·sis \,sinkəˈtathəsəs, -iŋk-\ *n* -ES [Gk, lit., approval, assent, fr. the stem of *synkatatithenai* to agree entirely with (fr. *syn-* + *katatithenai* to put down, put an end to, settle, fr. *kata-* cata- + *tithenai* to put, place) + *-sis* — more at DO] : acceptance or endorsement of a presentation or idea as true or valid — used of a Stoic doctrine analogous to the modern view of judgment

syn·ki·ne·sia \,sin,kīˈnēzh(ē)ə, -iŋ,k-, -kə¦n-\ *n* -s [NL, fr. *syn-* + *-kinesia*] : SYNKINESIS

syn·ki·ne·sis \-¦nēsəs\ *n* [NL, fr. *syn-* + *kinesis*] : involuntary movement in one part when another part is moved : an associated movement

syn·ki·net·ic \-¦ned·ik\ *adj* [*syn-* + *kinetic*] : relating to or involving synkinesis

syn·les·ti·dae \sənˈlestə,dē\ *n pl, cap* [NL, fr. *Synlestes*, type genus (irreg. fr. *syn-* + Gk *lēistēs* robber) + *-idae* — more at LESTOBIOSIS] : a family of primitive mostly tropical damselflies

syn·ne·ma \səˈnēmə\ *n, pl* **syn·nema·ta** \-nēməd·ə, -nem-\ [NL, fr. *syn-* + Gk *nēma* thread — more at NEEDLE] : a coremium having tightly compacted hyphae

syn·neu·ro·sis \,sinyə¦rōsəs, ,sinn(y)ə-\ *n* [NL, fr. Gk *synneurōsis*, fr. *syn-* + *neuron* sinew + *-osis* — more at NERVE] : SYNDESMOSIS

syn·od \ˈsinəd\ *n* -s [ME, fr. LL *synodus* synod, conjunction of heavenly bodies, fr. LGk & Gk; LGk *synodos* synod, fr. Gk, assembly, meeting, conjunction of heavenly bodies, fr. *syn-* + *hodos* way, journey — more at CEDE] **1** : an ecclesiastical council : a formal meeting to consult and decide on church matters **2** : a church governing or advisory body: as **a** : an official meeting of clerical and lay deputies from the dioceses within a province of the Protestant Episcopal Church **b** : a Presbyterian judicatory ranking in authority above a presbytery but below the general governing body and composed of the members of or delegates from all the presbyteries within its bounds **c** : any of the courts above the classes in various Reformed Churches **d** : a denominational body of clerical and lay delegates representing the congregations within a region ⟨each of the 33 synods of the Evangelical and Reformed Church⟩ **e** : the entire body of a church or denomination — see GENERAL SYNOD, HOLY SYNOD **3** : the ecclesiastical district governed by a synod ⟨commended to all churches within the bounds of that ~⟩ **4 a** : COUNCIL, ASSEMBLY **b** : CONVENTION, MEETING

¹syn·od·al \-dᵊl\ *adj* [ME *synodall*, fr. LL *synodalis*, fr. *synodus* + L *-alis* -al] : of, relating to, of the nature of, or constituting a synod — **syn·od·al·ly** \-ᵊlē\ *adv*

²synodal \"\ *n, pl* **synodals** \-ᵊlz\ *or* **syn·o·da·lia** \,sinəˈdālyə\ [ML *synodale*, fr. LL, decree made by a synod, fr. neut. of *synodalis*] **1** : a constitution made in a provincial or diocesan synod **2** : a tribute in money formerly paid to the bishop or archdeacon at the time of his visitation by every parish priest of the Church of England

syn·od·al·ist \ˈsinədᵊləst\ *n* -s : a member of a synod

¹syn·od·i·cal \səˈnädəkəl, (ˈ)si¦n-\ *or* **syn·od·ic** \-dik\ *adj* [LL *synodicus*, fr. LGk & Gk; LGk *synodikos* of a synod, fr. Gk, of a meeting, of a conjunction, fr. *synodos* + *-ikos* -ic, -ical] **1** : SYNODAL **2** : relating to conjunction; *esp* : relating to the period between two successive conjunctions of the same celestial bodies (as the moon and the sun) — **syn·od·i·cal·ly** \-dək(ə)lē\ *adv*

²synodical \"\ *n* -s *usu cap* : a women's auxiliary organization associated with a synod and composed of delegates from the presbyterials within its bounds

synodic month *also* **synodical month** *n* : the average period of recurrence of the phases of the moon (as from new moon to new moon) equal to 29 days, 12 hours, 44 minutes, and 2.8 seconds of mean solar time — called also *lunar month*

syn·odi·con \səˈnädə,kän, sēnōˈthēˈkōn\ *n* -s [LGk *synodikon*, fr. neut. of *synodikos*] : a letter, decree, or other document emanating from a synod in the Eastern Orthodox Church; *specif* : an instrument of appointment to a high ecclesiastical office (as of a bishop)

synodic period *n* : the time between two successive conjunctions of a planet with the sun

syn·od·ist \ˈsinədəst\ *n* -s [*synod* + *-ist*] : one who supports a synod or council; *esp* : one who upholds the jurisdiction of a synod in preference to that of a pope or patriarch

syn·odon·ti·dae \,sinəˈdäntə,dē\ *n pl, cap* [NL, fr. *Synodont-*, *Synodus*, type genus (fr. *syn-* + *-odont-*, *-odus*) + *-idae*] : a family of fishes (order Iniomi) comprising the lizard fishes

syn·ods·man \ˈsinədzmən\ *n, pl* **synodsmen** **1** : a lay member of a synod **2** : a churchwarden's assistant : SIDESMAN

syn·oe·cete \səˈnē,sēt\ *or* **syn·oe·kete** \-nē,kēt\ *n* -s [Gk *synoiketēs* fellow lodger, fr. *synoikein* to live together (fr. *synoikos* dwelling in the same house, fr. *syn-* + *oikos* house) + *-tēs*, agent suffix — more at VICINITY] : an ant or termite guest tolerated with indifference by the host

syn·oe·cious \səˈnēshəs\ *adj* [in sense 1, fr. *syn-* + *-oecious* (as in *dioecious*); in sense 2, fr. *synoecy* + *-ous*] **1** : exhibiting monoecism **2** : exhibiting or relating to synoecy — **syn·oe·cious·ly** *adv* — **syn·oe·cious·ness** *n* -ES

syn·oe·cism \səˈnē,sizəm\ *also* **syn·oi·cism** \-nȯi,kizəm, -nȯi,si-\ *n* -s [Gk *synoikismos* wedlock, act of combining into one city-state, fr. *synoikizein*] **1** : a joining together : UNION; *specif* : a uniting of several towns or villages into one community (as in ancient Greece) **2** : the condition of being synoecious

syn·oe·cize \-nē,sīz\ *vt* -ED/-ING/-S [Gk *synoikizein* to give in wedlock, combine into one city-state, unite, fr. *synoikos* dwelling in the same house + *-izein* -ize] : to join (diverse things) together; *esp* : to form into a large community by synoecism

syn·oe·cy \səˈnēsē, si,n-\ *also* **syn·oe·ky** \-nēkē\ *n* -ES [Gk *synoikia* body of people living together, community, fr. *synoikos* dwelling together + *-ia* -y] : SYNOECISM: **a** : commensalism in which the guests are indifferently tolerated by their hosts — compare SYMPHILY, SYNECHTHRY **b** : association between two species benefiting the one without harm to the other **c** : MONOECISM

syn·oi·cous \səˈnȯikəs\ *adj* [Gk *synoikos* dwelling together] : having archegonia and antheridia in the same involucre ⟨~ moss⟩ — compare AUTOICOUS, DIOICOUS, MONOICOUS, PAROICOUS, SYNOECIOUS

syn·o·nym \ˈsinə,nim\ *n* -s [ME *sinonyme*, fr. L *synonymum*, fr. Gk *synōnymon*, fr. neut. of *synōnymos* synonymous — more at SYNONYMOUS] **1** : a word having the same meaning as another word: as **a** : one of two or more words of the same language and grammatical category having the same or nearly the same essential or generic meaning and differing only in connotation, application, or idiomatic use : one of two or more words having essentially identical definitions ⟨nonscientific writers are free to use a variety of ~s to express the same idea in subtly different ways —Aldous Huxley⟩ ⟨a determined repetition of the same word, where it occurred often in a passage, instead of hunting about for a ~ or periphrasis —Robert Graves⟩ — compare ANTONYM **b** : one of two or more words that have one or more senses in common **c** : one of two or more expressions any one of which can in accordance with the rules of the language be substituted in a statement for each of the others without changing the meaning of the statement **2** : a name that suggests another through real or supposed association : a symbolic or figurative name : METONYM ⟨the name of the street was . . . the local ~ for poverty —Nadine Gordimer⟩ **3** : one of two or more names for the same thing in different languages or localities ⟨whose name, Minerva, suggested the Greek ~, Athena —*Amer. Guide Series: Vt.*⟩ **4** : a taxonomic name (as of a species or genus) rejected as being incorrectly applied or incorrect in form or spelling or rejected in favor of another because of evidence of the priority of that other or evidence establishing a more natural genetic classification — compare HOMONYM, NOMENCLATURE

syn·o·nym·at·ic \ˌsinəˌniˈmad·ik\ *adj* [*synonym* + *-atic* (as in *idiomatic*)] **:** of or relating to synonymy
syn·o·nyme \ˈsinəˌnim\ *archaic var of* SYNONYM
syn·o·nym·ic \ˌsinəˈnimik\ *or* **syn·o·nym·i·cal** \-mə̇kəl\ *adj* [*synonym* + *-ic, -ical*] **:** of, relating to, composed of, or characterized by synonyms ⟨~ relations between classical and other words in English —W.K.Wimsatt⟩
syn·o·nym·i·con \ˌsinəˈniməˌkän\ *n* -s [*synonym* + *-icon* (as in *lexicon*)] **:** a lexicon of synonyms
syn·o·nym·ics \ˌ==ˈ=miks\ *n pl but usu sing in constr* **:** the scientific or theoretical treatment of synonyms **:** SYNONYMY
syn·on·y·mist \sə̇ˈnänəmə̇st\ *n* -s **:** one who lists, studies, or discriminates synonyms
syn·o·nym·i·ty \ˌsinəˈniməd·ē\ *n* -ES **:** the quality or fact of being synonymous **:** identity of meaning or significance ⟨commonly assumed ~ of homelessness, vagrancy (and all equivalent terms) with alcoholic addiction —Robert Straus & R.G.McCarthy⟩
syn·on·y·mize \sə̇ˈnänəˌmīz\ *vb* -ED/-ING/-S *vt* **1 :** to give or analyze synonyms of (a word) **:** provide (as a dictionary) with synonymies **2 :** to demonstrate (a taxonomic name) to be a synonym **:** place in synonymy ~ *vi* **:** to use synonyms **:** express an idea variously by means of synonyms
syn·on·y·mous \sə̇ˈnänəməs\ *adj* [ML *synonymus*, fr. Gk *synōnymos*, fr. *syn-* + *onyma, onoma* name — more at NAME] **1 :** having the character of a synonym **:** alike or nearly alike in meaning ⟨*glad* is ~ with *joyful*⟩ **:** capable of being substituted for another word or expression in a statement without essentially changing the statement's meaning **2 :** having the same connotations, implications, or reference **:** suggesting the same thing — usu. used with *with* ⟨Newark has become virtually ~ in the public mind with long-distance air travel —*Amer. Guide Series: N.J.*⟩ ⟨believed that lack of knowledge of English is ~ with stupidity —C.S.Stine⟩ — **syn·on·y·mous·ly** *adv* — **syn·on·y·mous·ness** *n* -ES
syn·on·y·my \-mē,-mi\ *n* -ES [*synonym* + *-y*] **1 a :** the study or discrimination of synonyms or of words which may be confused in meaning **b :** a list or collection of synonyms or words of similar meaning often defined and discriminated from each other **2 :** the scientific names that have been used in different publications to designate a species or other taxonomic group; *also* **:** a list of these names specifying by date the books and authors employing them **3** [LL *synonymia* synonym, synonymousness, fr. Gk *synōnymia* synonym, fr. *synōnymos* synonymous + *-ia* -y] **:** the quality or fact of being synonymous **:** SYNONYMOUSNESS, SYNONYMITY
syn·op·sis \sə̇ˈnäpsə̇s\ *n, pl* **synop·ses** \-pˌsēz\ [LL, fr. Gk, general view, estimate, synopsis, fr. *synopsesthai* to be going to have a general view, be going to comprehend (fr. *syn-* + *opsesthai* to be going to see) + *-sis* — more at OPTIC] **1 :** a brief orderly outline affording a quick general view (of a treatise or narrative) **:** a condensed statement **:** ABSTRACT ⟨~ of a scientific report⟩ ⟨~ of the week's news⟩ **2 a :** a brief outline summarizing the action of a proposed screen play or television script **b :** a summary of a completed film (as for cataloging in a film library) **3 :** a conjugation by one person and number **syn** see ABRIDGMENT
sy·nop·size \-pˌsīz\ *vt* -ED/-ING/-S [LGk *synopsizein*, fr. Gk *synopsis* + *-izein* -ize] **1 :** to make a synopsis of **:** give the essential points of **:** summarize briefly ⟨~ a novel⟩ **2 :** EPITOMIZE ⟨this changing taste of Americans is *synopsized* in the advertisements of bookstores —J.D.Hart⟩
¹syn·op·tic \-ptik,-ptēk\ *also* **syn·op·ti·cal** \-ptə̇kəl, -ptēk-\ *adj* [Gk *synoptikos*, fr. *synoptos* (verbal of *synopsesthai*) + *-ikos* -ic, -ical] **1 :** affording a general view of a whole ⟨~ presentation of a physical theory⟩ **2 :** manifesting or characterized by comprehensiveness or breadth of view ⟨~ genius of Shakespeare⟩ **3 a :** affording, presenting, or taking the same or common view **b** *often cap* **:** of or relating to the first three Gospels of the New Testament as being distinguished from the fourth by their many agreements in subject, order, and language ⟨the *synoptic* Gospels⟩ ⟨*synoptic* sayings⟩ **4 :** relating to or displaying atmospheric and weather conditions as they exist simultaneously over a broad area ⟨~ study of polar air masses⟩ ⟨~ chart⟩ — **syn·op·ti·cal·ly** \-ptə̇k(ə)lē, -ptēk-, -li\ *adv*
²syn·op·tic \"\ *n* -s *often cap* **:** any of the synoptic Gospels
synoptic meteorology *n* **:** a branch of meteorology that uses synoptic weather observations and charts for the diagnosis, study, and forecasting of weather
syn·op·tist \sə̇ˈnäptə̇st\ *n* -s *often cap* [²*synoptic* + *-ist*] **:** an author of one of the synoptic Gospels
syn·op·to·phore \-təˌfō(ə)r\ *n* -s [Gk *synoptos* + E *-phore*] **:** an instrument for diagnosing imbalance of eye muscles and treating them by orthoptic methods
syn·or·chism \sə̇ˈnȯ(r)ˌkizəm, ˈsi,n-\ *also* **syn·or·chi·dism** \-ˌkəˌdizəm\ *n* -s [*syn-* + *-orchism* or *-orchidism*] **:** partial or complete fusion of the testes
syn·orogenic \(ˌ)sin, sən+\ *adj* [*syn-* + *orogenic*] **:** formed or occurring during an orogenic movement ⟨~ plutonism⟩
syn·os·tose \ˈsinəˌstōs, -ˌnäˌs-, -ōz, sə̇ˈnäˌs-\ *vt* -ED/-ING/-S [back-formation fr. *synostosis*] **:** to unite by synostosis
syn·os·to·sis \ˌsiˌnäˈstōsə̇s\ *also* **syn·os·te·osis** \(ˌ)siˌnästēˈōsə̇s, səˌn-\ *n, pl* **synosto·ses** *also* **synoste·oses** \-ōˌsēz\ [*synostosis*, NL, fr. *syn-* + *-ostosis*; *synosteosis*, NL, fr. *syn-* + *oste-* + *-osis*] **:** union of two or more separate bones to form a single bone; *also* **:** the union so formed (as at an epiphyseal line) — compare ANKYLOSIS
syn·os·tot·ic \ˌsiˌnäˈstäd·ik\ *adj* [fr. NL *synostosis*, after such pairs as NL *hypnosis*: E *hypnotic*] **:** of, affected by, or marked by synostosis — **syn·os·tot·i·cal·ly** \-d·ə̇k(ə)lē\ *adv*
syn·o·vec·to·my \ˌsinəˈvektəmē\ *n* -ES [ISV *synov-* (fr. *synovial membrane*) + *-ectomy*; orig. formed as F *synovectomie*] **:** surgical removal of a synovial membrane
syn·ovia \sə̇ˈnōvēə\ *n* -s [NL] **:** a transparent viscid lubricating fluid that contains a substance resembling mucin and is secreted by the synovial membranes of articulations, bursae, and tendon sheaths
syn·ovi·al \-ēəl\ *adj* [NL *synovia* + E *-al*] **1 :** of or relating to synovia **:** secreting synovia **2 :** occurring in or affected by synovitis — **syn·ovi·al·ly** \-ēəlē\ *adv*
synovial capsule *n* **:** the completely closed cavity containing synovia formed by the smooth cartilages covering the articular surfaces of the bones and the surrounding capsular ligament in freely movable joints
synovial fluid *n* **:** SYNOVIA
synovial joint *n* **:** DIARTHROSIS
synovial ligament *n* **:** one of the folds of the synovial membrane resembling ligaments and occurring in various joints (as the knee)
synovial membrane *n* **:** the dense connective-tissue membrane often produced into folds or villi and partially covered with patches of flattened cells that lines the ligamentous surfaces of articular capsules, sheaths of tendons where free movement is necessary, and bursae and that secretes the synovia
syn·ovi·o·ma \sə̇ˌnōvēˈōmə\ *n, pl* **synoviomas** *or* **synovio·ma·ta** \-məd·ə\ [NL, fr. *synovia* + *-oma*] **:** a tumor of a synovial membrane
syn·ovi·tis \ˌsinəˈvīd·ə̇s\ *n* -ES [NL, fr. *synovia* + *-itis*] **:** inflammation of a synovial membrane usu. with pain and swelling of the joint
syn·pel·mous \(ˈ)sinˈpelməs, sənˈp-\ *adj* [irreg. fr. *syn-* + Gk *pelma* sole of the foot + E *-ous* — more at FELL] **:** having the two main flexor tendons of the toes blended above the divisions which go to each digit ⟨~ foot of a bird⟩
syn·rhabdosome \(ˈ)sin, sən+\ *n* [irreg. fr. *syn-* + *rhabdosome*] **:** a colony of graptolites made up of rhabdosomes
syn·sacrum \"+\ *n* [NL, fr. *syn-* + *sacrum*] **:** a solidly fused series of vertebrae in the pelvic region in birds, dinosaurs, and pterosaurs comprising usu. the last rib-bearing or thoracic vertebra, the two sacral vertebrae, and a varying number of caudal vertebrae — compare SACRUM
synscp *abbr* synchroscope
syn·semantic \ˌsin+\ *adj* [*syn-* + *semantic*] **:** AUXILIARY, DEPENDENT, INCOMPLETE, SYNCATEGOREMATIC ⟨a ~ expression⟩ ⟨~ sign⟩
syn·sepalous \(ˈ)sin, sən+\ *adj* [*syn-* + *-sepalous*] **:** GAMOSEPALOUS
syn·tac·tic \(ˈ)sinˈtaktik, sənˈt-, -aktēk\ *or* **syn·tac·ti·cal** \-aktə̇kəl, -tēk-\ *adj* [NL *syntacticus*, fr. Gk *syntaktikos* putting together, composing, fr. *syntaktos* (verbal of *syntassein* to put in order, arrange, fr. *syn-* + *tassein* to put in order, arrange) + *-ikos* -ic, -ical — more at TACTICS] **:** of, relating to, or according to the rules of syntax or syntactics — **syn·tac·ti·cal·ly** \-tə̇k(ə)lē, -tēk-, -li\ *adv*
syntactical aphasia *n* **:** the loss of power to form grammatical constructions
syntactic construction *n* **:** a grammatical construction having only free forms as immediate constituents and having no formal characteristics identifying it as a compound (as "he went to school") — compare MORPHOLOGICAL CONSTRUCTION
syntactic definition *n* **:** DEFINITION 4b(1)
syn·tac·ti·cian \ˌsinˌtakˈtishən\ *n* -s **:** a grammarian who specializes in syntax **:** an authority on syntax
syn·tac·tics \sənˈtaktiks, -aktēks\ *n pl but sing or pl in constr* **:** a theory that deals with the formal relations between signs or expressions in abstraction from their signification and their interpreters — compare PRAGMATICS, SEMIOTIC
syn·tagm \ˈsinˌtam\ *or* **syn·tag·ma** \sənˈtagmə\ *n, pl* **syn·tagms** \-amz\ *or* **syntag·mas** \-gməz\ *or* **syntag·ma·ta** \-gməd·ə\ [Gk *syntagma*, fr. *syntassein* to put in order, arrange — more at SYNTACTIC] **1 :** a systematic collection of writings **2 :** a syntactic unit **:** a word or phrase that has syntactic relation
syn·tag·mat·ic \ˌsinˌtagˈmad·ik\ *adj* [Gk *syntagmatikos*, fr. *syntagmat-, syntagma* + *-ikos* -ic] **1 :** relating to or being a syntagm **2 :** SYNTACTIC
syn·tal·i·ty \sənˈtaləd·ē\ *n* -ES [*syn-* + *-tality* (as in *mentality*)] **:** the inferred behavioral tendencies of a group acting as a group that correspond to personality in an individual
syn·tan \ˈsinˌtan\ *n* [*synthetic* + *tan*] **:** any of a class of synthetic tanning materials that are sulfonated condensation products of aromatic compounds with formaldehyde or some other aldehyde
syn·tax \ˈsinˌtaks\ *n* -ES [F or LL; F *syntaxe*, fr. LL *syntaxis*, fr. Gk, fr. the stem of *syntassein* to put in order, arrange + *-sis* — more at SYNTACTIC] **1 :** connected system or order **:** orderly arrangement **:** harmonious adjustment of parts or elements **2 a :** sentence structure **:** the arrangement of word forms to show their mutual relations in the sentence **b :** the part of grammar that treats of the expression of predicative, qualifying, and other word relations according to established usage in the language under study — compare MORPHOLOGY **3 a :** SYNTACTICS **b :** the area of syntactics dealing specifically with the formal properties of languages or calculi — called also *logical syntax*
syn·tax·ic \sənˈtaksik\ *adj* [*syn-* + *-taxic* (as in *parataxic*)] **:** characterized by or relating to a mode of experience or symbolic behavior that relates symbols and referents, speech and action, subject and object in a sequentially logical and interpersonally or publicly verifiable manner — compare PROTOTAXIC
syn·tax·is \sənˈtaksə̇s\ *n* [LL] **1** *archaic* **:** SYNTAX **2** [NL, fr. Gk, arrangement, syntax] **:** ARTICULATION 2a
syntax language *n* **:** a metalanguage used to refer to the syntactic properties of a language under study
syn·technic \(ˈ)sin, sən+\ *adj* [*syn-* + *technic*] **:** of, relating to, or being a similarity in behavior of unlike organisms due to adaptation to a common environment; *also* **:** exhibiting such similarity — compare SYNCRYPTIC
syn·tec·tic \(ˈ)sinˈtektik, sənˈt-\ *also* **syn·tec·ti·cal** \-ektə̇kəl\ *adj* [Gk *syntēktikos* able to liquefy, liquefactive, fr. *syntēktos* (verbal of *syntēkein* to dissolve, liquefy, fr. *syn-* + *tēkein* to melt) + *-ikos* -ic, -ical — more at THAW] **:** of, relating to, or produced by syntexis **:** melting or wasting away
syn·telome \(ˈ)sin, sən+\ *n* [*syn-* + *telome*] **:** a group of fused telomes
syn·te·no·sis \ˌsinˌtəˈnōsə̇s\ *n* -ES [NL, fr. *syn-* + *teno-* + *-sis*] **:** articulation by tendons
synteresis *var of* SYNDERESIS
syn·tex·is \sənˈteksə̇s\ *n* -ES [Gk *syntēxis* liquefaction, fr. *syntēkein* to dissolve, liquefy + *-sis*] **:** the generation and augmentation of magma by melting and assimilation of crustal rocks
syn·ther·mal \(ˈ)sin, sən+\ *adj* [*syn-* + *thermal*] **:** maintained at equal temperatures — used of two or more bodies whose temperatures may or may not be varying
syn·the·sis \ˈsin(t)thəsə̇s\ *n, pl* **synthe·ses** \-thəˌsēz\ [L, fr. Gk, lit., action of putting together, fr. the stem of *syntithenai* to put together (fr. *syn-* + *tithenai* to put, place) + *-sis* — more at DO] **1 :** a loose garment of ancient Rome sometimes worn in place of the more formal toga **2 a :** composition or combination of parts or elements so as to form a whole ⟨~ of those arts . . . completely blended to achieve . . . performance at its finest —Miles Kastendieck⟩ **b :** the production of a chemical compound by the union of elements or simpler compounds or by the degradation of a complex compound esp. by laboratory or industrial methods ⟨~ of water from hydrogen and oxygen⟩ ⟨~ of ascorbic acid from glucose⟩ ⟨~ of phthalic anhydride by oxidation of naphthalene⟩; *broadly* **:** the artificial production of a substance — contrasted with *analysis;* compare BIOSYNTHESIS, PHOTOSYNTHESIS, REACTION **c :** the combining of often varied and diverse ideas, forces, or factors into one coherent or consistent complex; *also* **:** the complex so formed ⟨a summa is a ~ of the philosophy of an age⟩ ⟨only political parties can produce the ~ or compromise of interest necessary to make representative government work —D.D.McKean⟩ **3 a :** deductive reasoning from general principles or causes to particular instances or effects **b :** the combination of separate elements of sensation or thought into a whole (as of simple into complex conceptions or of species into genera) **c** *Hegelianism* **:** the combination of the partial truths of a thesis and its antithesis into a higher stage of truth — compare DIALECTIC **4 :** the combination of radical and modifying elements into single words (as Latin *patri* to the father) **:** frequent and systematic use of inflected grammatical forms — contrasted with *analysis;* compare POLYSYNTHESISM
synthesis gas *n* **:** a gas used in synthesis; *esp* **:** a mixture composed essentially of hydrogen and carbon monoxide often in a ratio of 2 to 1, produced by various methods (as by the action of steam with or without oxygen on coal or lignite, by the action of steam or oxygen on methane or natural gas, or by enrichment of blue gas with hydrogen), and used chiefly in the synthesis of methanol and ammonia, in the Fischer-Tropsch process, and in the oxo process — compare PRODUCER GAS
syn·the·sist \-thəsə̇st\ *n* -s [blend of *synthesis* and *-ist*] **:** one who employs synthesis or follows synthetic methods **:** SYNTHESIZER
syn·the·size \-thəˌsīz\ *vb* -ED/-ING/-S *see -ize in Explan Notes* [blend of *synthesis* and *-ize*] *vt* **1 :** to combine or put together by synthesis **:** form into a whole **:** deal with synthetically ⟨*synthesizing* the teachings of modern dynamic psychiatry and religion —*advt*⟩ ⟨does not examine one aspect of the war but attempts to ~ the whole situation —Peter Ritner⟩ **2 :** to produce by synthesis ⟨~ alizarin⟩ ~ *vi* **:** to make a synthesis **:** proceed or function synthetically ⟨*synthesizing* tradition of masculine reason —J.C.Powys⟩
syn·the·siz·er \-zə(r)\ *n* -s **:** one that synthesizes ⟨~ of scattered results of investigations⟩; *esp* **:** an instrument used in scientific synthesis ⟨electronic ~ for reproducing speech sounds⟩
syn·the·tase \ˈsin(t)thəˌtās, -āz\ *n* -s [¹*synthetic* + *-ase*] **:** an enzyme that catalyzes the union of two molecules with concurrent breakdown of a pyrophosphate bond in a triphosphate (as ATP) ⟨glutamine ~⟩
¹syn·thet·ic \(ˈ)sinˈthed·|ik, sənˈth-, -et|, |ēk\ *also* **syn·thet·i·cal** \|ə̇kəl, |ēk-\ *adj* [Gk *synthetikos* skilled in putting together, component, fr. *synthetos* put together, compounded, composed (fr. *syntithenai* to put together) + *-ikos* -ic, -ical — more at SYNTHESIS] **1 a :** relating to or involving synthesis ⟨limnology is essentially a ~ science composed of elements . . . which extend well beyond the limits of biology —P.S.Welch⟩ **b :** not analytic ⟨the ~ aspects of a philosophy⟩ **2 a :** attributing to a subject a predicate that is not contained in the essence of that subject **b :** having the truth determined by observation or the facts of experience **c :** not resulting in a contradiction upon being negated **3** *of a language* **:** characterized by synthesis **:** INFLECTIONAL ⟨Sanskrit, Greek, Latin, and Turkish are ~ languages⟩ — contrasted with *analytic* **4 a :** of, relating to, or being a taxonomic category retained for reasons of convenience but not regarded as constituting a natural unit **b :** of, relating to, or being a group deliberately produced by combining genes in a manner unlikely to occur in nature ⟨a ~ tetraploid variety produced by colchicine⟩ **5** *of an organ stop* **:** composed of two or more pipes for each tone ⟨~ clarinet⟩ **6 a :** produced by artificial processes either from relatively simple substances or from naturally occurring sometimes complex substances **:** MAN-MADE ⟨~ quartz⟩ ⟨~ indigo⟩ ⟨natural and ~ dyes⟩ ⟨~ plastics⟩ — compare SEMISYNTHETIC **b :** devised, arranged, or fabricated for special situations to imitate or replace usual realities ⟨~ diet⟩ ⟨~ mock-up for pilots' ground training⟩ **:** employing or concerning such devices or fabrications instead of actualities ⟨~ flight instruction⟩ **c :** patently produced or maintained by special effort and therefore often forced, constrained, distorted, or simulated **:** not natural or spontaneous **:** SPURIOUS, FACTITIOUS ⟨no comfort I could have offered that wouldn't have sounded ~ —Norman Cousins⟩ ⟨producing ~ books to suit fancied trends —John Farrar⟩ **7** *of cubist art* **:** involving the composing of pictorial objects without the restrictions of natural appearances or relations — opposed to *analytical;* compare CUBISM **syn** see ARTIFICIAL
²synthetic \"\ *n* -s **:** something produced by synthesis rather than natural growth; *esp* **:** a yarn or fabric (as nylon) made by chemical synthesis usu. of hydrocarbons
syn·thet·i·cal·ly \|ə̇k(ə)lē, |ēk-, -li\ *adv* **:** in a synthetic manner ⟨what followed is so confused in my memory, so transposed and foreshortened, that I can only describe it ~ —Christopher Isherwood⟩ **:** by synthetic means or methods ⟨producing drugs ~⟩
synthetic ammonia process *n* **:** any of several processes (as the Haber process or the Claude process) for the manufacture of ammonia from nitrogen and hydrogen under conditions of high temperature and pressure in the presence of a catalyst (as a promoted iron catalyst) — compare NITROGEN FIXATION 1
synthetic a priori *n* **:** a synthetic judgment or proposition that is known to be true on a priori grounds; *specif* **:** one that is factual but universally and necessarily true ⟨the Kantian conception that the basic propositions of geometry and physics are *synthetic a priori*⟩
synthetic detergent *n* **:** DETERGENT c
synthetic fiber *n* **:** any of various man-made textile fibers including usu. those made from natural materials (as rayon and acetate from cellulose or regenerated protein fibers from zein or casein) as well as fully synthetic fibers (as nylon or acrylic fibers) — compare POLYMER
synthetic geometry *n* **:** elementary or projective geometry as distinguished from analytic geometry
synthetic iron oxide *n* **:** a pigment that is produced from an iron salt (as copperas) by precipitation or calcination under controlled conditions and is often purer than natural iron oxides
syn·thet·i·cism \sə̇nˈthed·əˌsizəm, -etə,-\ *n* -s **:** synthetic principles or method
synthetic judgment *n* **:** a judgment that attributes to a subject a predicate not contained in the essence or connotation of that subject — compare ANALYTIC JUDGMENT
synthetic medium *n* **:** a culture medium consisting only of known mixtures of chemical compounds (as salts, sugars)
synthetic philosophy *n* **:** SPENCERIANISM
synthetic photograph *n* **:** a combination picture in which a photograph of a staged scene is combined with other photographs to represent a scene unavailable for direct photography — called also *composograph*
synthetic resin *n* **:** a resinlike product made by polymerization or condensation **:** RESIN 2a; *sometimes* **:** a resinlike product made by chemical modification of a natural substance **:** RESIN 2b — distinguished from *natural resin*
synthetic rubber *n* **:** any of various products (as GR-S, neoprene, butyl rubber, or nitrile rubber) that resemble natural rubber more or less closely esp. in physical properties and ability to be vulcanized, that are made usu. by polymerization of butadiene, isoprene, or similar unsaturated hydrocarbons or by copolymerization of such hydrocarbons with styrene, isobutylene, acrylonitrile, or other polymerizable compounds, and that have uses similar to those of natural rubber but are superior for some applications and inferior for others and are often used in combination with natural rubber **:** RUBBER 2b — compare ELASTOMER
synthetic seniority *n* **:** SUPERSENIORITY
syn·the·tism \ˈsin(t)thəˌtizəm\ *n* -s *often cap* [Gk *synthetos* put together, composed + E *-ism* — more at SYNTHETIC] **:** an art theory current in France about 1890 that a painting is to be considered a formal arrangement of color on a flat surface before it is a particular representation — compare NABI
syn·the·tist \-ˌtəst\ *n* -s [¹*synthetic* + *-ist*] **1 :** SYNTHESIST **2** *often cap* **:** an advocate of synthetism
syn·the·tize \-ˌtīz\ *vt* -ED/-ING/-S *see -ize in Explan Notes* [¹*synthetic* + *-ize*] **:** SYNTHESIZE
syn·thol \ˈsinˌthōl, -thȯl\ *n* -s [¹*synthetic* + *-ol*] **:** a synthetic motor fuel made by heating water gas or synthesis gas under pressure in the presence of a catalyst and containing chiefly alcohols, fatty acids, and ketones or chiefly hydrocarbons — compare FISCHER-TROPSCH PROCESS
syn·thro·non \ˈsin(t)thrəˌnän, ˈsenthrōnōn\ *or* **syn·thro·nus** \ˈsin(t)thrənəs\ *or* **syn·thro·nos** \ˈsin(t)thrəˌnäs, ˈsenthrōnōs\ *n, pl* **synthro·ni** \ˈsin(t)thrəˌnī\ *also* **synthro·noi** \ˈsin(t)thrəˌnȯi, ˈsenthrənē\ [MGk *synthronon, synthronos*, fr. Gk *syn-* + *thronos* throne — more at FIRM] **:** a structure in a church combining the bishop's throne and clergy stalls placed behind the altar against the east wall and now found chiefly in Eastern churches
syn·tone \ˈsinˌtōn\ *n* -s [back-formation fr. *syntonic*] **:** a person of syntonic constitution or temperament
syn·ton·ic \(ˈ)sinˈtänik, sənˈt-\ *adj* [Gk *syntonos* being in harmony with + E *-ic*] **1 :** possessing a temperament normally responsive and adaptive to one's social or interpersonal environment — compare CYCLOTHYMIC **2 :** of or relating to resonance; *esp* **:** having the same resonant frequency — **syn·ton·i·cal·ly** \-ə̇nə̇k(ə)lē\ *adv*
syntonic comma *n* **:** the difference in pitch between two tones respectively four perfect fifths and two octaves plus a major third from a given tone represented by the ratio of 81:80 — called also *comma syntonum*
syn·to·ni·za·tion \ˌsintənə̇ˈzāshən, -ˌnīˈz-\ *n* -s **:** the act or result of syntonizing
syn·to·nize \ˈsintəˌnīz\ *vt* -ED/-ING/-S [*syntony* + *-ize*] **:** to put (two or more radio instruments or systems) in resonance **:** TUNE
syn·to·nous \ˈsintənəs\ *adj* [Gk *syntonos* being in harmony] **:** SYNTONIC
syn·to·ny \-nē\ *n* -ES [Gk *syntonia* agreement, fr. *syntonos* being in harmony (fr. *syn-* + *tonos* voice, pitch) + *-ia* -y — more at TONE] **1 :** the state of being normally responsive to and in harmony with the environment **2 :** RESONANCE 1b(2)
syn·trope \ˈsinˌtrōp\ *n* -s [*syn-* + *-trope*] **:** a syntropic part or appendage — opposed to *antitrope*
syn·troph·ic \(ˈ)sinˈträfik, sənˈt-\ *adj* [ISV *syn-* + *-trophic*] **:** associated or mutually dependent upon one another with reference to food supply ⟨~ cells⟩
syn·tro·phism \ˈsintrəˌfizəm\ *n* [*syntrophic* + *-ism*] **:** mutual dependence (as of different strains of bacteria) for the satisfaction of nutritional needs **:** syntrophic state
syn·trophoblast \(ˈ)sin, sən+\ *n* [*syn-* + *trophoblast*] **:** the outer syncytial layer of the trophoblast that actively invades the uterine wall forming the outermost fetal component of the placenta — **syn·trophoblastic** \(ˈ)sin, sən+\ *adj*
syn·trop·ic \(ˈ)sin, sən+\ *adj* [*syn-* + *-tropic*] **:** repeated symmetrically without being reversed ⟨~ ribs⟩ — opposed to *antitropic*
syn·tro·py \ˈsintrəpē\ *n* -ES [*syn-* + *-tropy*] **:** the quality or state of being syntropic
syn·type \ˈsinˌtīp\ *n* [*syn-* + *type*] **1 :** a member of a taxonomic type series when no holotype is designated **2 :** PARATYPE 1, ISOTYPE 1b(1) — **syn·typ·ic** \(ˈ)sinˈtipik, sənˈt-\ *adj*
syn·ura \sə̇ˈn(y)u̇rə\ *n, cap* [NL, fr. *syn-* + *-ura*] **:** a genus of biflagellate free-swimming flagellates (order Chrysomona-

dina) occurring in spheroidal colonies and producing odors and sometimes oily fishy flavors in water supplies

syn·usia \sə'n(y)üzh(ē)ə, -zēə\ *n, pl* **syn·usi·ae** \-z(h)ē,ē\ [NL, fr. Gk *synousia* social intercourse, society, company, fr. *synous-* (part. stem of *syneinai* to come together, assemble, gather, fr. *syn-* + *einai* to be) + *-ia* -y — more at IS] **:** a structural unit of a major ecological community characterized by relative uniformity of life-form or of height and usu. constituting a particular stratum of that community ⟨the herbaceous ~ of open forest⟩ — **synusial** *adj*

syph \'sif\ *n* -s [by shortening] **:** SYPHILIS

sy·pha·cia \sī'fāshēə\ *n, cap* [NL, irreg. fr. L *sipho, siphon* tube, pipe + *-acea*, fem. of *-aceus* -aceous — more at SIPHON] **:** a genus of nematode worms (family Oxyuridae) including a species (*S. obvelata*) normally parasitic in the cecum and colon of rodents and rarely in man

syphil- *or* **syphilo-** *comb form* [NL, fr. *syphilis*] **:** syphilis ⟨*syphil*ology⟩ ⟨*syphil*oma⟩

syph·i·lid \'sifələd\ *n* -s [NL *syphilides*, fr. *syphilis* + *-ides* -id] **:** a syphilitic id

syph·i·lis \'sif(ə)ləs\ *n* -ES [NL, after *Syphilus*, the supposed first sufferer from the disease and the hero of the poem *Syphilis sive Morbus Gallicus* (1530), by Girolamo Fracastoro †1553 Ital. physician, astronomer, and poet] **:** a chronic, contagious, usu. venereal, and often congenital disease caused by a spirochete (*Treponema pallidum*) and characterized by a clinical course in three stages continued over many years and lesions that may involve many organs and tissues of the body — see PRIMARY SYPHILIS, SECONDARY SYPHILIS, TERTIARY SYPHILIS

¹syph·i·lit·ic \ˌsifə¦lid·|ik, -lit|, |ēk\ *adj* [NL *syphiliticus*, fr. *syphilis* + L *-iticus* -itic] **:** of, relating to, or infected with syphilis

²syphilitic \"\ *n* -s **:** a person infected with syphilis

syph·i·li·za·tion \ˌsifələ'zāshən\ *n* -s [F *syphilisation*, fr. *syphiliser* + *-ation*] **1 :** the condition of being infected with syphilis **2 :** the act or process of inoculating with the spirochete (*Treponema pallidum*)

syph·i·lize \'sifə,līz\ *vt* -ED/-ING/-S [F *syphiliser*, fr. *syphil-* + *-iser* -ize] **1 :** to inoculate with syphilis **2 :** to introduce syphilis among

syph·i·lo·derm \'sifəlō,dərm\ *or* **syph·i·lo·der·ma** \ˌ≈≈≈'dərmə\ *n, pl* **syphiloderms** \-mz\ *or* **syphiloder·ma·ta** \ˌ≈≈≈'dərməd·ə\ [NL *syphiloderma*, fr. *syphil-* + *-derma*] **:** SYPHILID

syph·i·log·ra·pher \ˌsifə'lägrəfə(r)\ *n* -s [*syphilography* + *-er*] **:** one who writes scientifically about syphilis

syph·i·log·ra·phy \-fē\ *n* -ES [*syphil-* + *-graphy*] **:** the scientific description of syphilis

syph·i·loid \'sifə,lȯid\ *adj* [*syphil-* + *-oid*] **:** resembling syphilis ⟨~ infection⟩

syph·i·lo·log·ic \ˌsifəlō¦läjik\ *adj* **:** relating to or concerning syphilis ⟨~ practice⟩

syph·i·lol·o·gist \ˌsifə'läləjəst\ *n* -s **:** a physician who specializes in the diagnosis and treatment of syphilis

syph·i·lol·o·gy \-jē\ *n* -ES [*syphil-* + *-logy*] **:** a branch of medicine that deals with syphilis

syph·i·lo·ma \ˌsifə'lōmə\ *n, pl* **syphilomas** *or* **syphilomata** [NL, fr. *syphil-* + *-oma*] **:** a syphilitic tumor **:** GUMMA — **syph·i·lom·a·tous** \ˌ≈≈¦lämədəs, -¦lōm-\ *adj*

syph·i·lo·phobe \'sifəlō,fōb\ *n* -s [NL, fr. *syphil-* + *-phobe*] **:** one afflicted with syphilophobia

syph·i·lo·phobia \ˌsifə(ˌ)lō+\ *n* [NL, fr. *syphil-* + *phobia*] **:** abnormal dread of syphilis or fear of being infected with it

syph·i·lo·psychosis \"+\ *n* [NL, fr. *syphil-* + *psychosis*] **:** a mental disorder resulting from syphilis of the brain

syph·i·lo·therapy \"+\ *n* [*syphil-* + *therapy*] **:** the treatment of syphilis ⟨~ with penicillin⟩

syphon *var of* SIPHON

syr *abbr* syrup

¹syr·a·cu·san \ˌsirə¦kyüzᵊn, -üsᵊn\ *also* **syr·a·cu·si·an** \-üzēən, -üsēən, -üzhən, -üshən\ *adj, usu cap* [*Syracuse*, Sicily & *Syracuse*, N.Y. + E *-an*, *-ian*] **:** of or belonging to the ancient city of Syracuse, Sicily, or to the city of Syracuse, N.Y.

²syracusan \"\ *also* **syracusian** \"\ *n* -s *cap* **:** a native or resident of Syracuse, Sicily, or Syracuse, N.Y.

syr·a·cuse \'≈≈,kyüs (*usual local pronunc*), -üz, *locally also* 'ser-\ *adj, usu cap* [fr. *Syracuse*, N.Y.] **:** of or from the city of Syracuse, N.Y. ⟨a *Syracuse* industry⟩ **:** of the kind or style prevalent in Syracuse

syracuse watch glass *or* **syracuse dish** *n, usu cap S* **:** a small circular flat-bottomed dish of thick glass with a shallow depression used in biology (as for staining, culturing, and various phases of microtechnic)

sy·ren \'sīrən\ *chiefly Brit var of* SIREN

Syr·ette \sə'ret\ *trademark* — used for an injection unit comprising a small collapsible tube fitted with a hypodermic needle and containing a single dose of a medicinal agent

syr·ia \'sirēə\ *adj, usu cap* [fr. *Syria*, country in southwestern Asia] **:** of or from Syria **:** of the kind or style prevalent in Syria **:** SYRIAN

¹syr·i·ac \'sirē,ak\ *adj, usu cap* [L *syriacus* Syrian, fr. Gk *syriakos*, fr. *Syria*] **1 :** of, relating to, or written in Syriac **2 :** using or versed in Syriac

²syriac \"\ *n* -s *cap* **1 :** ARAMAIC **2 a :** a literary language based on an eastern Aramaic dialect and used as the literary and liturgical language by several Eastern churches **b :** a form of Aramaic spoken by eastern Christian communities

syriac alphabet *n, usu cap S* **:** an alphabet of Aramaic origin used for writing Syriac

syr·i·a·cism \'sirēə,sizəm\ *n* -s *usu cap* **:** a form of expression peculiar to Syriac

¹syr·i·an \'sirēən\ *n* -s [ME *sirien*, fr. MF, fr. *Syrie* Syria + MF *-en* -an] *usu cap* **1 :** a native or inhabitant of Syria **2 a :** a member of a Syrian church

²syrian \"\ *adj, usu cap* **1 a :** of or relating to ancient Syria **b :** of or relating to the territory now included in Syria and Lebanon **c :** of or relating to the Republic of Syria or the Syrian Region of the United Arab Republic **2 :** of, relating to, or being one of the Eastern churches originating in Byzantine or Persian Syria, using Syriac liturgies, and including the Jacobite church and the Nestorian church

syrian bear *n, usu cap S* **:** a silvery or yellowish gray Syrian brown bear (*Ursus arctos syriacus*)

syrian grass *n, usu cap S* **:** JOHNSON GRASS

syrian hamster *n, usu cap S* **:** GOLDEN HAMSTER

syrian hyrax *n, usu cap S* **:** the common hyrax (*Procavia syriaca*) of Asia Minor that is the cony of the Old Testament

syrian juniper *n, usu cap S* **:** an evergreen tree (*Juniperus drupacea*) of Greece and Asia Minor with a brownish or bluish edible fruit covered with a bloom

syrian rue *n, usu cap S* **:** AFRICAN RUE

syrian tobacco *n, usu cap S* **:** a wild tobacco (*Nicotiana rustica*) formerly supposed to yield the tobacco produced in Syria

syrian wild ass *n, usu cap S* **:** HEMIPPE

syr·i·asm \'sirē,azəm\ *n* -s *usu cap* [Syriac + *-asm* (as in *enthusiasm*)] **:** SYRIACISM

syring- *or* **syringo-** *comb form* [Gk, panpipe, fistula, tube, fr. *syring-, syrinx* — more at SYRINGE] **:** tube **:** fistula ⟨*syring*adenous⟩

sy·rin·ga \sə'riŋgə\ *n* [NL, fr. Gk *syring-, syrinx*] **1** *cap* **:** a genus of Old World shrubs or low trees (family Oleaceae) having purple, white, or sometimes pink flowers with a cylindrical tube and four spreading lobes that are borne in terminal usu. thyrsoid panicles and are followed by winged seeds and comprising the widely cultivated lilacs **2** -s **:** MOCK ORANGE 1

syr·ing·ad·e·nous \ˌsiriŋ¦adᵊnəs\ *adj* [*syring-* + *aden-* + *-ous*] **:** of or relating to the sweat glands

¹sy·ringe \sə'rinj *also* 'sirənj *or* 'si,rinj, *in rapid speech often* 'srinj\ *n* -s [ME *syring*, fr. ML *syringa, siringa*, fr. LL, injection, fr. Gk *syring-, syrinx* panpipe, fistula, tube; akin to Gk *sōlēn* channel, pipe, OSlav *tulŭ* quiver, Skt *tūṇa, tūṇī* quiver, *tūṇava* flute] **1 :** a device used to inject fluids into or withdraw them from the body or its cavities: as **a :** a device consisting of a nozzle of varying length and a compressible rubber bulb and used for injection or irrigation ⟨ear ~⟩ ⟨vaginal ~⟩ **b :** an instrument that consists of a glass barrel fitted with a plunger and a hollow needle and is used for the injection of medicines or for aspiration of fluid from body cavities ⟨hypodermic ~⟩ **c :** a device that operates by gravity, consists of a reservoir of rubber, glass, or enamelware fitted with a long rubber tube ending with an exchangeable nozzle, and is used for irrigation of the vagina or bowel — called also *fountain syringe* **2 :** SYRINGIUM

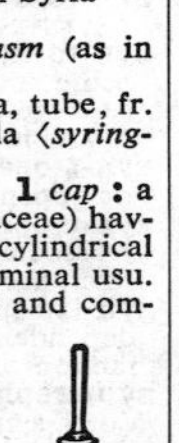

sy-ringe 1a

²syringe \"\ *vb* -ED/-ING/-S *vt* **1 :** to irrigate (a part of the body) by means of a syringe **2 a :** to spray (plants) with a fine powerful spray of water usu. directed at the lower surface of the foliage to dislodge insects **b :** to spray (a greenhouse) with a fine mist of water usu. from an overhead spray system primarily to help maintain humidity ~ *vi* **1 :** to use a syringe **2 :** to spray a plant or greenhouse with water

sy·rin·ge·al \sə'rinjēəl\ *adj* [NL *syring-, syrinx* + E *-eal* (as in *laryngeal*)] **:** of or relating to the syrinx ⟨~ muscles⟩

sy·ringe·ful *pronunc at* SYRINGE +,fu̇l\ *n* -s **:** the amount a syringe can hold

sy·rin·gic acid \sə'rinjik-\ *n* [ISV *syringin* + *-ic*] **:** a crystalline phenolic acid $HO(CH_3O)_2C_6H_2COOH$ obtained by decomposition esp. of syringin and prepared by acid hydrolysis of the trimethyl ether of gallic acid

sy·rin·gin \-jən\ *n* -s [F *syringine*, fr. NL *Syringa* (generic name of *Syringa vulgaris*) + F *-ine*] **:** a crystalline glucoside $C_{17}H_{24}O_9$ found esp. in the bark of a lilac (*Syringa vulgaris*) and of privets that on hydrolysis yields glucose and methoxyconiferyl alcohol

sy·rin·gi·um \sə'rinjēəm\ *n* -s [NL, fr. *syring-* + *-ium*] **1 :** a muscular tubular organ connected with the mouth parts of hemipterous insects and used for the ejection of a poisonous salivary secretion **2 :** a tubular organ on the body of some insect larvae from which an offensive fluid can be ejected

sy·rin·go·bul·bia \sə,riŋgō'bəlbēə\ *n* -s [NL, fr. *syring-* + L *bulbus* onion, bulb + NL *-ia* — more at BULB] **:** the presence of abnormal cavities in the medulla oblongata

sy·rin·go·my·e·lia \sə,riŋgō,mī'ēlēə\ *n* -s [NL, fr. *syring-* + *-myelia*] **:** a chronic progressive disease of the spinal cord characterized by the presence of long cavities in the substance of the spinal cord with sensory disturbances, muscle atrophy, and spasticity — **sy·rin·go·my·el·ic** \≈¦≈≈,≈¦elik\ *adj*

syr·in·goph·i·lus \ˌsiriŋ'gäfələs\ *n, cap* [NL, fr. *syring-* + *-philus*] **:** a genus of parasitic mites that live inside the quills of bird feathers in Europe and No. America

syr·inx \'siriŋks, -rēŋks\ *n, pl* **sy·rin·ges** \sə'rin,jēz\ *or* **syrinxes** [in sense 1a, fr. Gk; in sense 2, fr. LL, fr. Gk; in other senses, fr. NL, fr. Gk — more at SYRINGE] **1 a :** PANPIPE **b :** a mouthpiece attached to the aulos **2 :** a tunnel-shaped rock-cut passage of ancient Egypt esp. when in a burial vault **3 :** the vocal organ of birds that is a special modification of the lower part of the trachea or of the bronchi or of both — called also *lower larynx* **4 :** a tube formed from modified deltidial plates and surrounding the pedicle in some extinct brachiopods

syr·i·ol·o·gist \ˌsirē'äləjəst\ *n* -s *usu cap* [*Syria* + E *-o-* + *-logy* + *-ist*] **:** an archaeologist specializing in Syrian remains

syr·ma \'sərmə\ *n, pl* **syrmas** \-məz\ *or* **syrma·ta** \-məd·ə\ [Gk, fr. *syrein* to drag — more at SWERVE] **:** a trailing robe worn by tragic actors of ancient Greece

syr·ni·um \'sərnēəm\ [NL, fr. Gk *syrnion*, a bird of ill omen] *syn of* STRIX b

syro- *comb form, usu cap* [L, fr. Gk, fr. *Syros* Syrian] **1 :** Syria or Syrians ⟨*Syro*phile⟩ **2 :** Syrian and ⟨*Syro*-Egyptian⟩ ⟨*Syro*-Iraqi⟩ **3 :** Syriac and ⟨*Syro*-Aramaic⟩

sy·ro-aramaic \ˌsī(ˌ)rō, ˌsi(ˌ)rō+\ *n* -s *cap S&A* [*Syro-* + *Aramaic*] **:** Syriac and Aramaic considered as a single language

sy·ro-hittite \"+\ *adj, usu cap S&H* [*Syro-* + *Hittite*] **:** of or relating to the esp. glyptic art and the archaeological remains characteristic of northern Syria and eastern Asia Minor

¹sy·ro·phoenician \"+\ *adj, usu cap* [*Syrophoenicia*, ancient Roman province in southwestern Asia + E *-an*] **1 :** of or relating to the Roman province of Syrophoenicia **2 :** of or relating to Syrophoenicians

²syrophoenician \"\ *n* -s *cap* **:** a native or inhabitant of Syrophoenicia

¹syr·phid \'sərfəd\ *adj* [NL *Syrphidae*] **:** of or relating to the Syrphidae

²syrphid \"\ *n* -s **:** a fly of the family Syrphidae **:** SYRPHUS FLY

syr·phi·dae \-fə,dē\ *n pl, cap* [NL, fr. *Syrphus*, type genus + *-idae*] **:** a large and widely distributed family of cyclorrhaphous dipterans — see SYRPHUS FLY

syr·phus fly \'sərfəs-\ *or* **syrphid fly** *n* [*syrphus* fr. NL *Syrphus* genus of dipterous flies, fr. Gk *syrphos* gnat] **:** any of numerous active day-flying flies that constitute the family Syrphidae, frequent flowers and feed on nectar, vary greatly in form and coloration but generally have a spurious longitudinal vein near the middle of each wing, often mimic bees or wasps and have the abdomen banded with yellow, and produce larvae which feed on decaying organic matter or are predaceous on plant lice — called also *flowerfly*; compare HOVER FLY, RAT-TAILED LARVA

syr·tis \'sərd·əs\ *or* **syrt** \'sərt\ *n, pl* **syr·tes** \-rd·(ˌ)ēz, -r,tēz\ *or* **syrts** [L *Syrtis* (fr. Gk), either of two inlets of the Mediterranean sea on the coast of northern Africa (Gulf of Gabès and Gulf of Sidra), known in classical times for their quicksands] *archaic* **:** QUICKSAND, BOG

¹syr·up *or* **sir·up** \'sər·əp, 'sirəp *sometimes* 'sə·rəp *or* 'serəp *or rapid* 'sərp\ *n* -s [ME *sirop, sirup*, fr. MF *sirop*, fr. ML *syrupus, sirupus*, fr. Ar *sharāb* drink, wine, coffee, syrup, fr. *shariba* to drink] **1 a :** a thick sticky liquid consisting of a concentrated solution of sugar and water with or without the addition of a flavoring agent ⟨lemon ~⟩ ⟨chocolate ~⟩ or medicinal substance ⟨~ of codeine⟩ or of sugar and juice of a fruit or herb — compare CORN SYRUP **b :** the concentrated juice of a fruit or plant ⟨apple ~⟩; *specif* **:** the evaporated juice of the sugar cane as it occurs just prior to crystallization of the sugar in the process of manufacturing cane sugar — compare MAPLE SYRUP, SORGHUM 2 **2 :** cloying sweetness or sentimentality ⟨fancy blended with ~ and eroticism and having almost nothing to do with facts —Iris Barry⟩ ⟨children's theater . . . production . . . was, for sophisticated adults at least, pretty much tricks and ~ —Henry Hewes⟩ **3 :** a light to moderate olive brown — called also *antique* **4 :** a synthetic resin or plastic in the form of a liquid or solution ⟨partially polymerized casting ~⟩

²syrup *or* **sirup** \"\ *vt* -ED/-ING/-S **:** to add syrup to (as fruit in canning)

syr·up·er *or* **sir·up·er** \-pə(r)\ *n* -s **1 :** one that bottles syrup or that places a fixed amount of syrup in a bottle prior to the addition of plain or carbonated water **2 :** one that fills containers of canned goods with syrup

syrup pan *n* **:** a large evaporating pan usu. containing a series of alternating baffles in which the juice of sugar cane or sorghum is boiled into syrup

syr·upy *or* **sir·upy** \-pē, -pi\ *adj* **1 :** resembling syrup in appearance or quality ⟨~ color⟩ ⟨coffee . . . thick and ~ —Hugh MacLennan⟩ **2 :** cloyingly sweet or sentimental ⟨promptly cover the taste of defeat with ~ new daydreams —Katharine Scherman⟩ ⟨when a ~ mood is on him and his wife, they spend a deplorable amount of time clutching at and kissing each other —John McCarten⟩; *esp* **:** excessively sweet and melodious **:** DULCET ⟨theater organ music, ~ sweet —Rumer Godden⟩ ⟨slender fingers would draw out the ~ music from the strings —Osbert Sitwell⟩

syr·ye·ni·an \sər'yēnēən\ *also* **syr·yan** \'sir,yan, + sər'y-\ *n, pl* **syryenian** *or* **syryenians** *cap* [*Syryenian* irreg. fr. Russ *Zyryanin* Zyrian + E *-an*; *Syryan* modif. of Russ *Zyryanin*] **:** ZYRIAN

sys *pl of* SY

sys *abbr* system

sys·sar·co·sis \ˌsisär'kōsəs\ *n, pl* **syssarco·ses** \-ō,sēz\ [NL, fr. Gk *syssarkōsis* fact of being overgrown with flesh, fr. *syssarkousthai* to be overgrown with flesh also (fr. *syn-* + *sarkousthai*, passive of *sarkoun* to make fleshy, grow fleshy, fr. *sark-, sarx* flesh) + *-sis* — more at SARCASM] **:** the junction of two or more bones by means of attached muscles (as the scapula with the thorax or the hyoid with the mandible and sternum)

sys·sel \'sisəl\ *n* -s [Dan, fr. Icel *sȳsla* business, work, activity, syssel, fr. ON; akin to OE *sūsl* misery, torment, torture, *sēoslig* afflicted, ON *sȳsl* eager, painstaking, *sjūkr* sick — more at SICK] **:** an Icelandic administrative district

syst *abbr* system

sys·tal·tic \sə'stȯltik, -tal-\ *adj* [Gk *systaltos* (verbal of *systellein* to contract) + E *-ic* — more at SYSTOLE] **:** marked by regular contraction and dilatation **:** PULSING ⟨the ~ action of the heart⟩ ⟨flux and reflux of ~ tides —V.P.Watkins⟩

sys·tem \'sistəm\ *n* -s [LL *systema*, fr. Gk *systēma*, fr. *synistanai* to bring together, combine, fr. *syn-* + *histanai* to cause to stand — more at STAND] **1 a :** a complex unity formed of many often diverse parts subject to a common plan or serving a common purpose **b :** an aggregation or assemblage of objects joined in regular interaction or interdependence **:** a set of units combined by nature or art to form an integral, organic, or organized whole **:** an orderly working totality **:** a coherent unification ⟨the notion implicit in the word *universe* expresses an act of faith, for it projects ~ far beyond the evidence⟩ **c :** a group of bodies (as the solar system) moving together in an interrelated pattern or under the influence of related forces or attractions **d :** the related body organs that cooperate in performing one of the fundamental vital functions **e :** a group of related natural objects or forces ⟨a weather ~⟩ ⟨rivers of the continental drainage ~⟩ **f :** a group of devices or artificial objects forming a network or used for a common purpose ⟨a nationwide dial telephone ~⟩ ⟨an express highway ~⟩ ⟨a ~ of public parks⟩ ⟨a hot air heating ~⟩ ⟨the electrical ~*s* of automobiles grew steadily more elaborate⟩ **g :** a major division of rocks usu. larger than a series and including all formations deposited or otherwise formed during a period or an era ⟨the Silurian ~⟩ **h :** a group of freight or passenger transportation lines or services operating under common management and usu. covering several routes ⟨a national airfreight ~⟩ **2 a :** the body considered as a functional unit ⟨toxins from a focal lesion pervading the whole ~⟩ **b :** one's whole affective being ⟨a few hard knocks will get that cockiness out of his ~⟩ **3 a :** the structure or whole formed by the essential principles or facts of a science or branch of knowledge or thought **:** an organized or methodically arranged set of ideas, theories, or speculations **b** (1) **:** the content of laws, doctrines, ideas, or principles belonging to a philosophy, a religion, or a form of government **:** an orderly scheme of thought or constitutions **(2) :** a particular philosophy, religion, or political order ⟨a positivistic ~⟩ ⟨a collectivist ~⟩ ⟨the capitalist ~⟩ (3) **:** a form of social, economic, or other organization or practice ⟨a tenant farmer ~⟩ ⟨a managed currency ~⟩ **c :** HYPOTHESIS **d :** TREATISE **e :** coherent or harmonious arrangement, pattern, or form **:** ORDERLINESS, REGULARITY ⟨began to plan how she would . . . bring ~ out of confusion —Ellen Glasgow⟩ **f :** a particular classification, notation, or other formal arrangement or scheme ⟨a biological taxonomic ~⟩ ⟨a ~ of musical notation⟩ ⟨a Vigenère ~ of cryptography⟩ **4** *Eng law* **:** method or design as shown by other acts of a defendant similar to that charged of which evidence is admissible to rebut or negative a defense of accident, mistake, or ignorance or to prove a course of conduct **5 a :** a sequence of syllables, feet, cola, periods, lines, or strophes so related together as to present a relatively discrete and bounded rhythmic pattern or figure **b :** a series with fixed limits in classical prosody: (1) **:** a group of two or more periods (2) **:** a group of verses in the same measure **6 a :** a musical interval in ancient Greek music regarded as a compound of two lesser ones **b :** a classified series of tones (as a mode or scale) **c :** the collection of staffs which form a full score **7 :** a group of zooids in a compound ascidian arranged about a cloacal cavity which serve for them in common and into which the atrial orifices of all open **8 :** an assemblage of substances that is in or tends toward equilibrium, that may be homogeneous or heterogeneous and if the latter may be classed by the number of phases, and that may also be classed by the number of components or the number of variables ⟨a two-phase ternary ~⟩ ⟨univariant and bivariant ~*s*⟩ — see PHASE RULE **9 :** an organized or established procedure or method or the set of materials or appliances used to carry it out ⟨a business office ~⟩ **10 :** an organization or network for the collection and distribution of information, news, or entertainment **:** a communications industry ⟨a financial news ~⟩ ⟨a radio broadcasting ~⟩ ⟨a telephone ~⟩ **11 :** either of the two sets of four rows of squares that extend across the checkerboard from the black squares in the king row **12 :** an organized society or social situation regarded as hampering, stifling, or stultifying ⟨had always loved that effort to beat the ~ —J.P.Marquand⟩ ⟨it's the ~, and I'm caught —Morley Callaghan⟩ **13 :** a method or scheme of betting by which a gambler tries to assure himself of greater winnings than luck or chance would afford ⟨invented a new ~ at roulette —D.G.Gerahty⟩

syn SCHEME, NETWORK, COMPLEX, ORGANISM, ECONOMY: SYSTEM may imply that the component units of an aggregate exist and operate in unison or concord according to a coherent plan for smooth functioning ⟨amid a *system* where the classic principles of capitalism still work successfully —H.J.Laski⟩ ⟨comprehend all experience in a closed *system* —W.R.Inge⟩ ⟨it does not form an independent *system*, like the universe: it exists as an element in human culture —Lewis Mumford⟩ SCHEME may stress an overall design for the interrelation of components, often a design carefully calculated ⟨the cheerful, sanguine, courageous *scheme* of life, which was in part natural to her and in part slowly built up —Havelock Ellis⟩ ⟨our complex system, presenting the rare and difficult *scheme* of one general government, whose action extends over the whole —John Marshall⟩ ⟨the Newtonian *scheme* of the universe does not banish God from the universe —*Times Lit. Supp.*⟩ NETWORK suggests a system with interconnection or intercrossing at salient points sometimes involved but susceptible to analysis or control ⟨a *network* of abandoned narrow-gage logging roads penetrates the wooded areas —*Amer. Guide Series: Mich.*⟩ ⟨even the lowliest savages live in a social world characterized by a complex *network* of traditionally conserved habits, usages, and attitudes —Edward Sapir⟩ COMPLEX stresses an elaborate interweaving, interconnection and interrelationship of components difficult to trace ⟨for these ancestors of ours, in one half of their thoughts and acts, were still guided by a *complex* of intellectual, ethical, and social assumptions of which only medieval scholars can today comprehend the true purport —G.M. Trevelyan⟩ ⟨this *complex* of conditions which taxes the terms upon which human beings associate and live together is summed up in the word *culture* —John Dewey⟩ ⟨modern science, with infinite effort, has discovered and announced that man is a bewildering *complex* of energies —Henry Adams⟩ ORGANISM literally applies only to systems having life; figuratively, it suggests analogies to biological systems ⟨not because of an interest in the individual himself as a matured and single *organism* of ideas but in his assumed typicality for the community as a whole —Edward Sapir⟩ ⟨the Church grew, like any other *organism*, by responding to its environment —W.R.Inge⟩ ECONOMY implies a system concerned with needs and their regulation and fulfillment by individual, species, household, business, or government ⟨the plantation *economy*, with its base in slavery, was not conducive to the growth of industrial enterprise —*Amer. Guide Series: N.C.*⟩ ⟨the principle may operate successfully in the close *economy* of a good family, or even within a small religious community —J.A.Hobson⟩ **syn** see in addition METHOD

sys·tem·at·ic \ˌsistə¦mad·|ik, -at|, |ēk\ *also* **sys·tem·at·i·cal** \|əkəl, |ēk-\ *adj* [*systematic* fr. LL *systematicus*, fr. Gk *systēmatikos*, fr. *systemat-, systēma* system + *-ikos* -ic; *systematical* fr. LL *systematicus* + E *-al*] **1 a :** expounding a subject or covering a field thoroughly according to an orderly scheme or plan ⟨~ study of market movements and consumer demand —F.H.Boland⟩ ⟨a ~ treatise⟩ ⟨a ~ scholar⟩ **b :** reduced to or presented or formulated as a coherent body of ideas or principles **:** offering or constituting a complete scheme, outline, or classification ⟨~ philosophical thought⟩ **c :** marked by or manifesting system, method, or orderly procedure **:** following or observing a plan **:** METHODICAL, REGULAR ⟨~ examination of the terrain was begun —*Amer. Guide Series: Pa.*⟩ ⟨a ~ workman he was ~⟩ **2 :** of or relating to classification esp. in the sciences ⟨the ~ name of a chemical⟩ **:** TAXONOMIC ⟨~ botany⟩ **3 :** SYSTEMIC **4 a :** of, relating to, or constituting a group of two or more periods in classical prosody **b :** of, relating to, or constituting a group of verses in the same classical measure **syn** see ORDERLY

sys·tem·at·i·cal·ly \|ək(ə)lē, |ēk-, -li\ *adv* **:** in a systematic manner

systematic error *n* : a statistical error that persists and cannot be considered as due entirely to chance — opposed to *random error*

sys·tem·a·ti·cian \,sistə́mə'tishən\ *n* -s : SYSTEMATIST ⟨hence the word *theology* is not to be defined solely as the ~s do —G.E.Wright⟩

sys·tem·at·ic·ness *n* -ES : the quality or state of being systematic

sys·tem·at·ics \,sistə́'mad·|iks, -at|, |ēks\ *n pl but sing in constr* **1** : the science of classification : classificatory method : ORGANIZATION ⟨his genius was not for ~ but for penetrating fragments —Maurice Natanson⟩ **2** : a system of classification; *usu* : the classification and study of organisms with regard to their natural relationships : TAXONOMY — compare BIOSYSTEMATY **3** : an organizational scheme or structure : FORM, HIERARCHY, PLAN ⟨a highly theoretical assumption about the ~ of a culture —Abraham Edel⟩

systematic theology *n* : constructive theology : a branch of theology that attempts to reduce all religious truth to statements forming a self-consistent and organized whole

sys·tem·a·tism \'sistə,tizəm\ *n* -s [fr. *systematize*, after such pairs as *organize: organism*] : the practice of systembuilding or an addiction to it

sys·tem·a·tist \'sistámad·əst\ *n* -s [LL *systemat-*, *systema* system + E *-ist*] **1** : a maker or follower of a system **2** : a classifying scientist : TAXONOMIST

sys·tem·a·ti·za·tion \,sistə́məd·ə́'zāshən, -mə́tə́'-, -mə,tī'-\ *n* -S : the act or practice of systematizing

sys·tem·a·tize \'sistə́mə,tīz\ *vb* -ED/-ING/-S *see -ize in Explan Notes* [LL *systemat-*, *systema* system + E *-ize*] *vt* : to make into a system : arrange methodically : reduce to order : CLASSIFY, METHODIZE, ORGANIZE ⟨the great historic efforts to ~ the law⟩ ~ *vi* : to form a system : ORGANIZE ⟨cultures differ in their ability to ~ —A.L.Kroeber⟩ **syn** *see* ORDER

sys·tem·a·tiz·er \-zə(r)\ *n* -s : one that systematizes ⟨he was a ~ and an innovator of methods resulting in great economies —W.J.Ghent⟩

sys·tem·a·ty \sə́'stemad·ē\ *n* -ES [*systematic* + *-y*] : systematic classification : TAXONOMY

sys·temed \'sistəmd\ *adj* : operating as or made into a system : ordered systematically

sys·tem·ic \sə́'stemik, -mēk\ *adj* [*system* + *-ic*] : of, relating to, or common to a system: as **a** : affecting the body generally distinguished from *local* ⟨~ death⟩ ⟨~ wilt in plants⟩ **b** : supplying those parts of the body that receive blood through the aorta rather than the pulmonary artery **c** : absorbed into and effective throughout a plant body ⟨~ insecticides that make the whole plant toxic to pests⟩

sys·tem·i·cal·ly \-mək(ə)lē, -mēk-, -li\ *adv* : in a manner affecting the body as a whole

systemic arch *n* : any branchial arch that persists in the adult : AORTIC ARCH

systemic circulation *n* : the passage of arterial blood from the left auricle of the heart through the left ventricle, the systemic arteries, and the capillaries to the organs and tissues that receive much of its oxygen in exchange for carbon dioxide and its return via the systemic veins to enter the right auricle and participate in the pulmonary circulation — used of man and other animals with a complete double circulation

systemic heart *n* : the part of the heart propelling blood through the systemic circulation; *specif* : the left auricle and ventricle of higher vertebrates — compare PULMONARY HEART

systemic insecticide *also* **systemic** *n* -S : a substance (as schradan) that as used is harmless to a plant or higher animal but is absorbed into the sap stream or blood stream and kills aphids and other sucking insects, red spider and other mites, and cattle grubs

sys·tem·ist \'sistámóst\ *n* -s [*system* + *-ist*] : SYSTEMATIST

sys·tem·iza·tion \,sistámə'zāshən, -tə,mī'-\ *n* -s : SYSTEMATIZATION

sys·tem·ize \'sistə́,mīz\ *vt* -ED/-ING/-s [*system* + *-ize*] : to reduce to system : SYSTEMATIZE

sys·tem·less \'sistómlós\ *adj* : devoid of system, order, or structure

systems *pl of* SYSTEM

sys·to·le \'sistə(,)lē, -li\ *n* -S [Gk *systolē*, lit., contraction, fr. *systellein* to contract, fr. *syn-* + *stellein* to set up, place, send — more at STALL] **1** *obs* : the shortening in verse of a syllable naturally or by position long (as for metrical convenience) — opposed to *ectasis*, *diastole* **2** [NL, fr. Gk *systolē*] : a rhythmically recurrent contraction: as **a** : the contraction of the heart by which the blood is forced onward and the circulation kept up **b** : the contraction of a rhythmically pulsating contractile vacuole — **sys·tol·ic** \sə́'stäl,lik, -lēk\ *adj*

systolic pressure *n* [*systole* + *-ic*] : the highest arterial blood pressure of a cardiac cycle occurring immediately after systole of the left ventricle of the heart — compare DIASTOLIC PRESSURE

sys·tyle \'si,stīl\ *n* -s [L *systylos*, fr. Gk, having columns close together, fr. *syn-* + *stylos* column, pillar — more at STEER] : an intercolumniation of two diameters — see INTERCOLUMNIATION ILLUSTRATION

syz·y·get·ic \,sizə,jed·ik\ *adj* [*syzygy* + *-etic*] : of, relating to, or constituting a syzygy : SYZYGIAL — **syz·y·get·i·cal·ly** \-d·ə́k(ə)lē\ *adv*

sy·zyg·i·al \sə́'zijēəl\ *adj* [*syzygy* + *-al*] : of or relating to a syzygy

sy·zyg·i·um \-ēəm\ *n, pl* **syzyg·ia** \-ēə\ [NL, alter. of LL *syzygia*] : SYZYGY

syz·y·gy \'sizəjē, -ji\ *n* -ES [LL *syzygia*, fr. Gk, lit., state of being yoked together, fr. *syzygos* yoked together, united (fr. *syn-* + *zygon* yoke) + *-ia* -y — more at YOKE] **1** : the nearly straight-line configuration of three celestial bodies (as the sun, moon, and earth during a solar or lunar eclipse) in a gravitational system **2** : a group of two coupled feet in Greek or Latin prosody: **a** : DIPODY **b** (1) : a combination of two differing feet (2) : a foot of four syllables **3** : a pair of correlatives, opposites, or otherwise related things; *esp* : a pair of gnostic aeons male and female (the ~ of Man and Church) **4 a** (1) : the immovable union and partial concrescence of two joints of an arm of a crinoid to form a single segment (2) : the segment so formed **b** : temporary end-to-end union of gregarines — compare PRIMITE, SATELLITE

szai·bel·yite \sä'bel,yīt\ *n* -s [G *szajbelyit*, fr. Stephan *Szailbely* †1855 Hungarian mine surveyor + G *-it* -ite] : a mineral MgBO₂OH consisting of a magnesium borate that occurs in nodular masses of white acicular crystals

szcze·cin \'shchetsēn\ *adj, usu cap* [fr. *Szczecin*, Poland] : of or from the city of Szczecin, Poland : of the kind or style prevalent in Szczecin

sze·ged \'se,ged\ *adj, usu cap* [fr. *Szeged*, Hungary] : of or from the city of Szeged, Hungary : of the kind or style prevalent in Szeged

szek·ler \'seklə(r)\ *or* **szek·el** \'sekəl\ *n* -s *cap* [*szekler* fr. G, fr. Hung *Székely*, fr. *székel* to reside; *szekel* fr. Hung *Székely*] **1** : a member of the Transylvanian branch of the Magyar race **2** : the Hungarian dialect of the Szeklers written in its own runic alphabet

szi \'sē\ *n, pl* **szi** *or* **szis** *usu cap* : a member of a people found mainly in the Sadon area of the Burma-China frontier and closely related to or identical with the Maru

szmik·ite \'smi,kīt\ *n* -s [G *szmikit*, fr. Ignaz *Szmik*, 19th cent. Hung. mining official + G *-it* -ite] : a mineral MnSO₄.H₂O consisting of a hydrous manganese sulfate isomorphous with kieserite and szomolnokite

szo·mol·nok·ite \sə'mälnə,kīt\ *n* -S [G *szomolnokit*, fr. *Szomolnok* (Smolnik), Czechoslovakia + G *-it* -ite] : a mineral FeSO₄.H₂O consisting of a hydrous ferrous sulfate isomorphous with kieserite and szmikite

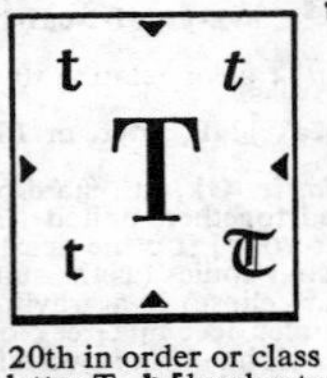

¹t \'tē\ *n, pl* **t's** *or* **ts** \'tēz\ *often cap, often attrib* **1 a :** the 20th letter of the English alphabet **b :** an instance of this letter printed, written, or otherwise represented **c :** a speech counterpart of orthographic *t* (as *t* in *tie, sty, bat, hatpin, later,* or French *tu*) **2 :** a printer's type, a stamp, or some other instrument for reproducing the letter *t* **3 :** someone or something arbitrarily or conveniently designated *t* esp. as the 19th or when j is used for the 10th the 20th in order or class **4 a :** something having the shape of the letter T **b** [by shortening] **:** T FORMATION — **to a T** *adv* [short for *to a tittle*] **:** to perfection ⟨suits me *to a T*⟩

²t *abbr, often cap* **1** table **2** [It *tace*] be silent **3** tackle **4** taken **5** taper **6** tare **7** target **8** teaspoon **9** technical; technician **10** telephone **11** teletype **12** temperature **13** tempo **14** temporal **15** temporary **16** [L *tempore*] in the time of **17** tenor **18** tense **19** tension **20** tensor **21** terminal; termination **22** territorial; territory **23** tertiary **24** testament **25** thickness **26** thief **27** thread **28** tied **29** time; times **30** toe **31** tome **32** [L *tomus*] volume **33** ton **34** tooth **35** top **36** town; township **37** trace **38** trainer **39** transcription **40** transformer **41** transit **42** transition; transitional **43** transitive **44** tread **45** triangle **46** trillo **47** [LL *Trinitas*] the Trinity **48** triple **49** tropical **50** trotter **51** troy **52** true **53** tun **54** Turkish **55** tutti

³t *symbol* **1** *cap* absolute temperature **2** *ital* meridian angle **3** *cap* octodecimo **4** *cap* tritium **5** *usu ital* triton

t- \¦tərt\ *abbr, usu ital* [*tertiary*] tertiary — esp. in names of organic chemical radicals ⟨*t*-butyl⟩

¹t' \tə\ *prep* [by contr.] **:** TO ⟨*t'* abandon⟩ ⟨*t'* engrave⟩

²t' \tə *before a consonant,* t *before a vowel*\ *definite article* [by contr.] *dial* **:** THE ⟨*t'* other⟩ ⟨*t'* bottle⟩ ⟨*t'* heart⟩

't \t\ *pron* [by contr.] **:** IT ⟨'twill do⟩ — not often in formal use

¹ta \'tä\ *dial var of* TAKE

²ta \'tə\ *chiefly dial var of* TO

³ta \"\ *pron* [by alter.] **:** THOU, YOU ⟨what was ~ doin in theer —Alfred Ollivant⟩

⁴ta \'tä\ *n* [baby talk] *dial Brit* **:** THANKS

⁵ta \tə\ *definite article* [by alter.] *dial chiefly Scot* **:** THE

TA *abbr* **1** table of allowances **2** target area **3** tax agent **4** telegraphic address **5** territorial army **6** *often not cap* [L *testantibus actis*] as the acts show **7** toxin-antitoxin **8** traffic agent; traffic auditor **9** transit authority

Ta *symbol* tantalum

taaffe·ite \'tä,fīt\ *n* -s [Count Edward Charles Richard *Taaffe* b1898 Irish gemmologist born in Bohemia who first found it as a faceted gem + E *-ite*] **:** a rare mineral $BeMgAl_4O_{16}$ consisting of oxide of beryllium, magnesium, and aluminum and resembling mauve-colored spinel

taal \'täl\ *n, cap* [Afrik, fr. D, speech, language, fr. MD *tale;* akin to OE *talu* speech — more at TALE] **:** AFRIKAANS — usu. used with *the*

ta·a·nith es·ther *or* **ta·a·nit esther** \,tä'ə'nēt(h)e'ster\ *n, pl* **taanith esthers** *or* **taanit esthers** *usu cap T&E* [Heb *ta'ănīth esthēr*] **:** FAST OF ESTHER

¹tab \'tab, -aa(ə)b\ *n* -s *often attrib* [origin unknown] **1 a :** a short flap, loop, or other device projecting from an object to facilitate its identification or grasping: as (1) **:** the piece of leather with which a saddle girth is secured (2) *dial Eng* **:** the tip of a shoelace (3) **:** a small hand grip ⟨swung the musette around front and pulled open the ~s on it —R.O. Bowen⟩; *specif* **:** PULL STRAP (4) **:** a small lettered guide affixed to the bottom of the notch of a thumb index or projecting from the edge of a page (5) **:** a projection from a card used as an aid in filing (6) **:** a margin on a stamp or sheet of stamps bearing an ornamentation or a descriptive or advertising inscription **b** (1) **:** the collar insignia of a British army officer (2) *Brit* **:** STAFF OFFICER **c** (1) **:** *dial chiefly Eng* **:** a shoe latchet (2) **:** a small strap or flap fastening (as for a coat) stitched to a garment at one end and buttoned at the loose end (3) **:** a projecting metal strip or a key fitting into a slot (as for securing a roller to its mandrel) **d :** a small insert, addition, or remnant ⟨license plate ~⟩ ⟨shoe . . . reinforced at the toe and heel by metal ~s —William Duber⟩ **e** *dial Eng* **:** DAB ⟨boys, as they followed the path above, could toss ~s of turf down her chimney —A.T. Quiller-Couch⟩ **f :** APPENDAGE, EXTENSION: as (1) **:** a small pendant or projecting part of a garment ⟨~s . . . are favorite trimmings, used at necklines —*Women's Wear Daily*⟩; *esp* **:** one of a series of pendants forming a decorative border or edge (2) *or* **tab·leau** \'ta,blō, =ˈ=\ [*tableau* fr. ¹*tableau*] **:** a narrow framed or unframed drop used (as for masking offstage spaces (3) **:** TAG 3d(1) **g :** a piece of leather with two finger holes and a slot for the arrow shaft worn by an archer to protect the drawing fingers **h :** a small auxiliary airfoil hinged to a control surface (as to the trailing edge of an aileron, rudder, or elevator) to help stabilize an airplane in flight — called also *trim tab* **2** [partly short for ¹*table;* partly fr. sense 1] **a :** an itemized account or close surveillance **:** TALLY, WATCH ⟨keep close ~s on both American and British publications —Bennett Cerf⟩ ⟨difficult to keep a ~ on the nefarious activities of these people —R.G.Menzies⟩ ⟨a color styling service . . . keeps ~s on mass-market trends in color —*Dun's Rev.*⟩ **b :** a creditor's statement **:** BILL, CHECK ⟨few merchants could afford to throw out all their fixtures and foot the ~ for a . . . new floor setup —E.B.Weiss⟩ ⟨big spending, which includes . . . picking up the ~, as well as big tipping —John Bainbridge⟩ **c :** an incurred expense or market value **:** COST, PRICE ⟨45 cents a pound, the ~ at which the industry . . . hope butter will move quickly onto dinner tables —*Wall Street Jour.*⟩ ⟨the ~ for superhighways may run as high as 3 million dollars a mile —*Changing Times*⟩ **3** [by shortening] **a :** TABLOID ⟨farm ~s that sometimes go out with larger dailies —Lois M. Miller⟩ ⟨~ show, specializing in brief revues —R.L.Taylor⟩ **b :** TABULATOR ⟨for typing tables, first set ~s to space the columns evenly⟩ ⟨run data cards through a ~⟩ **c :** TABLET ⟨two boxes of heat ~s —Paul Gallico⟩

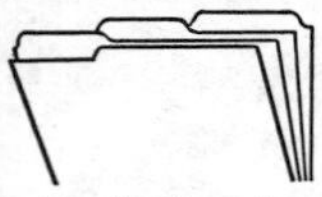
tabs 1a(5) cut in thirds

²tab \"\ *vt* **tabbed; tabbed; tabbing; tabs 1 :** to furnish or ornament with tabs ⟨when these cards are removed from the active list, they are *tabbed* according to group —*Amer. Business*⟩ ⟨cuffed neckline is looped and *tabbed* at the side —*Fashion Digest*⟩ **2 :** to single out **:** NAME, DESIGNATE, IDENTIFY ⟨the $14 million *tabbed* . . . for aid to school districts —*Fortnight*⟩ ⟨listeners have her *tabbed* as a chanteuse of the whispering school —*Los Angeles (Calif.) Times*⟩ ⟨someone once *tabbed* me the critic's critic —Ralph de Toledano⟩ **3** [by shortening] **:** TABULATE ⟨*tabbing* up ballots —*Time*⟩ ⟨~ all lines except the first . . . and double-space —H.H.Smith & A.C.Lloyd⟩

tab *abbr* **1** [NL *tabella*] lozenge **2** table **3** tabulate; tabulated

ta·baco *also* **ta·bac·co** \tə'ba(,)kō\ *archaic var of* TOBACCO

ta·ba·li·an \tə'bālēən\ *n* -s *usu cap* [*Tabal* the Tabalians + E *-an*] **:** a member of a Hittite cultural group living north of the Taurus mountains in southern Turkey and comprising 24 kingdoms in the second millennium B.C.

¹ta·ba·nid \'tabənəd\ *adj* [NL *Tabanidae*] **:** of or relating to the Tabanidae

²tabanid \"\ *n* -s **:** a fly of the family Tabanidae

ta·ban·i·dae \tə'banə,dē\ *n pl, cap* [NL, fr. *Tabanus,* type genus + *-idae*] **:** a very large and important family of Diptera comprising the horseflies and deerflies whose females suck blood and sometimes transmit disease (as loaiasis) to human beings

ta·ba·nu·co *or* **ta·bo·nu·co** \,täbə'nü(,)kō\ *n* -s [AmerSp, prob. fr. Taino] **:** CANDLEWOOD 1e

ta·ba·nus \tə'bānəs\ *n, cap* [NL, fr. L, horsefly] **:** the type genus of Tabanidae comprising various horseflies and green-bottle flies

tab·ard \'tabə(r)d\ *n* -s [ME, fr. OF *tabart*] **1 :** a tunic with or without short sleeves worn by a knight over his armor and emblazoned with his arms **2 a :** the official cape or coat of a herald made with or without short sleeves and emblazoned with his lord's arms **b :** the official surcoat of an officer of arms emblazoned with the royal arms ⟨dressed as heralds, with ~ and trumpet, looking for all the world like the knaves in a pack of cards —Victoria Sackville-West⟩ **3 :** a rectangular silk pendant bearing special emblems and attached to the bugles or trumpets of a military organization

tab·ard·ed \-dəd\ *adj* **:** wearing a tabard

Ta·bas·co \tə'ba(,)skō\ *trademark* — used for a pungent condiment sauce made from capsicum berries

tabasco mahogany *n, usu cap T* [fr. *Tabasco,* state in Mexico] **:** HONDURAS MAHOGANY

tab·a·sheer *also* **tab·a·shir** \,tabə'shi(ə)r\ *n* -s [Hindi *tabāshīr,* fr. Per] **:** a siliceous concretion in the joints of the bamboo valued in the East Indies as a medicine

¹tab·ber \'tabə(r)\ *dial Eng var of* TABOR

²tabber \"\ *n* -s [²*tab* + *-er*] **:** one that tabs; *specif* **:** a worker who makes or attaches tabs (as for identification, strengthening, or ornament)

tabbinet *var of* TABINET

¹tab·by \'tabē, -bi\ *n* -ES [F *tabis,* fr. MF *atabis,* fr. ML *attabi,* fr. Ar *'attābī,* fr. *Al-'Attābīya,* quarter in Baghdad where it was orig. made] **1 a** *archaic* (1) **:** a plain silk taffeta esp. with a moiré finish (2) **:** a dress of this fabric **b** (1) **:** PLAIN WEAVE ⟨~ is used for more purposes than any other weave —Harriette Brown⟩ (2) **:** a fabric in plain weave **2** [²*tabby*] **a :** a domestic cat having a gray or tawny coat striped and mottled with black and with the individual hairs variously banded and barred **b :** a domestic cat; *esp* **:** a female cat ⟨*tabbies* and toms⟩ **3 a :** a prying woman **:** BUSYBODY, GOSSIP ⟨some old *tabbies* would begin asking questions —Helen Eustis⟩ **b** *chiefly Brit* **:** SPINSTER 3

²tabby \"\ *adj* **1 a :** made of tabby ⟨a ~ waistcoat⟩ **b :** of or relating to tabby ⟨~ weave⟩ **2 a :** striped and mottled with black or with another color darker than the ground color **:** BRINDLED ⟨a ~ cat⟩ ⟨white with a ~ saddle on his back —Ngaio Marsh⟩ — compare MACKEREL **b :** DOMESTIC ⟨turn a ~ cat into a tiger —*Newsweek*⟩

³tabby \"\ *n* -ES [Gullah *'tabi,* of African origin; akin to Wolof *tabax* wall of a house made of sand, lime, or mud, Hausa *ta'bo* mud, Kongo *ntaba* muddy place] **:** a cement made of lime, sand or gravel, and oyster shells and used chiefly along the coast of Georgia and So. Carolina in the 17th and 18th centuries — compare TABIA, TAPIA

ta·be·bu·ia \,tabē'büyə\ *n, cap* [NL, fr. Tupi *tabebuya,* a tree, fr. *tacyba* ant + *bebuya* wood] **:** a large genus of tropical American shrubs and trees (family Bignoniaceae) having the calyx at first closed and differing from *Tecoma* chiefly in having digitate instead of pinnate leaves

ta·bel·la \tə'belə\ *n, pl* **tabel·lae** \-e,lē\ [NL, fr. L, tablet] **:** a medicated lozenge or tablet

tab·el·lar·ia \,tabə'la(a)rēə\ *n, usu cap* [NL, fr. fem. of L *tabellarius* relating to tablets, fr. *tabella* tablet + *-arius* -ary] **:** a genus of pinnate diatoms (family Tabellariaceae) united in zigzag often fixed colonies and often causing in water odors suggestive of fish or geraniums

ta·bel·lion \tə'belyən\ *n* -s [LL *tabellion-, tabellio,* fr. L *tabella* tablet, writing, document, dim. of *tabula* board — more at TABLE] **1 :** a scrivener under the Roman Empire with some notarial powers **2 :** an official scribe or notary public esp. in England and New England in the 17th and 18th centuries

¹tab·er·na·cle \'tabə(r),nakəl\ *n* -s [ME, fr. OF, fr. LL *tabernaculum* (trans. of Heb *ōhel mō'ēd*), fr. L, tent, dim. of *taberna* hut — more at TAVERN] **1 a** *often cap* **:** a portable sanctuary consisting of a rectangular wooden framework covered with curtains and carried by the Israelites during their wanderings of the Exodus as a holy dwelling place for their God and as a place for worship — called also *tent of meeting* **b :** a dwelling place **:** HABITATION — used formerly of the body as the temporary abode of the soul ⟨true image of the Father . . . enshrined in fleshly ~ —John Milton⟩ **c** *archaic* **:** a temporary shelter **:** HUT, TENT ⟨a place wherein to pitch their ~ and pursue their fortune —J.H.Burton⟩ **2 a :** a canopied niche or recess usu. framed by columns or pilasters and having a corbel or bracket (as for a statue) — compare BALDACHIN **b :** an ecclesiastical receptacle for the consecrated elements of the Eucharist; *esp* **:** an ornamental locked box resting on the middle of the altar and containing the pyx **3 a :** a temporary place of worship **:** one not conforming to traditional church architecture; *esp* **:** a meetinghouse with a large assembly hall ⟨Mormon ~⟩ **b :** a building or shelter used predominantly for evangelistic services ⟨the camp meeting is held each year . . . under a big open-air ~ —Green Peyton⟩ **4 a :** a boxlike support above deck in which the heel of a mast is stepped and pivoted so that it can be lowered to rest on the deck (as for negotiating a low bridge) **b :** a similar device in an open boat fitted from keel to thwart

²tabernacle \"\ *vb* **tabernacled; tabernacled; tabernacling** \-k(ə)liŋ\ **tabernacles** [ML *tabernaculare* (trans. of Gk *skēnoun* to pitch tent, encamp), fr. LL & L *tabernaculum*] *vi* **:** to take up temporary residence **:** SOJOURN; *esp* **:** to inhabit a physical body ⟨the Logos has become flesh, and has *tabernacled* among men —S.A.Cook⟩ ~ *vt, archaic* **:** to deposit in a tabernacle **:** ENSHRINE

tabernacle mirror *n* **:** CONSTITUTION MIRROR

tabernacle work *n* **1 :** ornamental usu. pierced tracery (as in the carved canopies over niches or stalls in churches) **2 :** architectural design characterized by the use of tabernacles

tab·er·nac·u·lar \¦tabə(r)¦nakyələ(r)\ *adj* [LL *tabernaculum* + E *-ar*] **:** of or characterized by tabernacle work ⟨cloisters . . . fronted with ~ or open work —Thomas Warton †1790⟩

ta·ber·nae·mon·ta·na \tə,bərnəmän'tānə\ *n* [NL, fr. J. T. *Tabernaemontanus* (Latin name of J. T. Müller) †1590 Ger. botanist] **1** *cap* **:** a large genus of tropical trees and shrubs (family Apocynaceae) having cymose flowers and a fleshy fruit **2** -s **:** any plant of the genus *Tabernaemontana*

ta·ber·nan·thine \,tabə(r)'nan(t),thēn, -,thən\ *n* -s [NL *Tabernanthe* (genus name of the plant *Tabernanthe iboga*) — fr. a native name in central Africa — + E *-ine*] **:** a bitter crystalline alkaloid $C_{20}H_{26}N_2O$ isomeric with ibogaine and occurring with it

ta·bes \'tā,bēz\ *n, pl* **tabes** [L — more at THAW] **1 :** wasting accompanying a chronic disease **2** [NL, fr. L] **:** TABES DORSALIS — **ta·bes·cent** \tə'bes°nt\ *adj*

tabes dorsalis *n* [NL, dorsal tabes] **:** syphilis involving the posterior columns of the spinal cord and sensory nerve trunks, characterized by wasting, and marked by paroxysmal attacks of pain, functional disturbances of organs (as the stomach or larynx), incoordination of voluntary movements, loss of reflexes, and disorders of sensation, nutrition, and vision — called also *locomotor ataxia*

ta·bet \'tabət\ *n* -s [origin unknown] *Scot* **:** sense of feeling **:** SENSATION — often used in pl.

¹ta·bet·ic \tə'bed·ik\ *adj* [ISV *tab-* (fr. NL *tabes*) + *-etic*] **:** resembling, having the nature of, or affected with tabes dorsalis

²tabetic \"\ *n* -s **:** one who is affected with tabes dorsalis

tabetic crisis *n* **:** a paroxysmal attack of pain occurring in tabes dorsalis

ta·bet·i·sol \tə'bed·ə,sōl, -sȧl\ *n* -s [L *tabēre* to melt + E connective *-t-* + *-isol* (as in *pergelisol*)] **:** unfrozen ground above, within, or below the pergelisol

ta·bet·less \'tabətləs\ *adj* [*tabet* + *-less*] **1** *Scot* **:** NUMB ⟨~ fingers had to be thawed —James Colville⟩ **2** *Scot* **:** SENSELESS, FOOLISH

ta·bia \'täbyə\ *n* -s [prob. alter. of *tapia*] **:** a building material composed of earth, lime, and pebbles rammed into place between forms and found very durable in rainless areas and esp. in building the castles of the northern Sahara — compare ³TABBY

tab·id \'tabəd\ *adj* [L *tabidus,* fr. *tabēre* to waste away, melt — more at THAW] *archaic* **:** TABETIC

tab index *n* **:** an index consisting of projecting tabs — compare STEP INDEX

tab·i·net *or* **tab·bi·net** \'tabə,net\ *n* -s [*tabinet* fr. obs. E *tabine,* a fabric, prob. tabby (prob. fr. ¹*tabby* + *-ine*) + E *-et; tabbinet* alter. (influenced by ¹*tabby*) of *tabinet*] **:** a silk and worsted fabric similar to poplin and usu. given a moiré finish

tab·la·ture \'tablə,chü(ə)r, -,chüə, -,chə(r)\ *n* -s [MF, prob. fr. (assumed) NL *tabulatura,* fr. ML *tabulatus* tablet, fr. L *tabula* record, document, writing tablet + *-atus* -ate] **1 a :** an early instrumental musical notation indicating by letters and other signs the string, fret, key, or finger to be used instead of the tone to be sounded **b :** tonic sol-fa notation **c :** TABULATUR 1 **2** *archaic* **a :** a tablet (as a gravestone) bearing an inscription **b :** a work of art **:** PAINTING, PICTURE **c :** pictorial representation **d :** a verbal image **:** DESCRIPTION **3 :** division into plates or tables with intervening spaces ⟨the ~ of the cranial bones⟩

¹ta·ble \'tābəl\ *n* -s [ME, fr. OE *tabule* & OF *table;* both fr. ML & L; ML *tabula* table, fr. L, board, tablet, writing tablet, record, document, list; perh. akin to OHG *dili, dilla* plank, plank floor — more at THILL] **1 a** *obs* **:** a flat slab (as of wood or stone) ⟨the inner part of the temple is . . . covered with great ~s of porphyry —Thomas Washington⟩ **b** (1) **:** TABLET 1a(1) ⟨leave a ~ in the middle of the panel —Fiske Kimball⟩ ⟨write the vision, and make it plain upon ~s, that he may run that readeth it —Hab 2:2 (AV)⟩ (2) **:** a set of laws inscribed on tablets ⟨the Twelve *Tables* of Roman law⟩ ⟨~s of the decalogue⟩ **c** *obs* (1) **:** TABLET 1b ⟨asked for a writing ~, and wrote . . . his name —Lk 1:63 (AV)⟩ (2) **:** an indelible record ⟨the everlasting ~s of right reason —Richard Bentley †1742⟩ **2 a** (1) **tables** *pl* **:** BACKGAMMON (2) **:** one of the two leaves of a backgammon board or either half of a leaf ⟨white's inner ~ is opposite black's inner ~⟩ ⟨play into the home ~⟩ **b :** a game board **3 a** (1) **:** a piece of furniture consisting of a smooth flat slab fixed on legs or other support and variously used (as for eating, writing, working, or playing games) (2) **:** an operating or examining table ⟨put the patient on the ~⟩ (3) **:** an official bench or rostrum ⟨the original of the letter . . . must be delivered at the ~ by the member who makes the complaint —T.E.May⟩ **b** (1) **:** a supply or regular source of food or the manner of its preparation **:** BOARD, FARE ⟨their farms were better and their ~s more bountiful than most —R.H.Shryock⟩ ⟨spent his teens . . . as a poor relation at the ~ of his mother's family —*Amer. Guide Series: N.Y.*⟩ ⟨the ~ the landlady set was really something special and we ate all we could hold —Emmett Kelly⟩ (2) **:** an act or instance of assembling to eat **:** MEAL, SITTING ⟨sit down to ~ with an ambassador —Agnes M. Miall⟩ ⟨if visitors can see into the kitchen while at ~, no doubt they will offer to help with the washing up —G.F.Lawson⟩ ⟨still hoping . . . he'll get to eat at the first ~ —F.B.Gipson⟩ **c** (1) **:** a group of people (as diners, committeemen, or players in a game) assembled at or as if at a table ⟨the ~ then spoke of . . . how bracing the air was —James Joyce⟩ ⟨a ~ of aldermen⟩ ⟨a ~ of bridge⟩ ⟨a famous poker ~, which challenged all comers —Harvey Fergusson⟩ (2) **:** a legislative or negotiating session ⟨an ill-armed victor lacks power at the peace ~ —F.E.Hill⟩ **4 a :** the altar or altar rail at which communicants receive Holy Communion **b :** EUCHARIST 1a **5 a :** a flat usu. raised band or projecting ledge on a wall **:** STRINGCOURSE, WATER TABLE **b** *archaic* **:** PANEL 3b(2) **6 a :** a tabular arrangement of data ⟨results of this survey are given in ~s in the appendix⟩; *specif* **:** a systematic arrangement (as of numerical values) usu. in parallel rows or columns for ready reference ⟨~ of weights and measures⟩ ⟨~ of logarithms⟩ ⟨multiplication ~⟩ **b :** a condensed enumeration **:** LIST, SYNOPSIS ⟨~ of contents⟩ ⟨~ of organization⟩ ⟨offer his little ~ of oppositions and . . . let it stand —Carlos Baker⟩ **7 :** something that resembles a table esp. in having a plane surface: as **a** (1) **:** the principal facet at the top of a brilliant — see BRILLIANT illustration (2) **:** TABLE DIAMOND **b** (1) **:** TABLELAND (2) **:** LEVEL — see WATER TABLE **c** *obs* (1) **:** PICTURE (2) **:** the surface on which a picture is painted (3) **:** a plane of perspective **d** (1) **:** the external or internal layer of compact bone of the skull separated by cancellous diploe (2) **:** the flat worn upper surface of a tooth (as of a horse) **e** *archaic* **:** a large round sheet of crown glass **f :** a flat or short prismatic crystal **g** (1) **:** a flat plate in a machine tool that is often movable and is usu. provided with T slots on its upper surfaces to which work can be fastened while it is being processed (2) **:** a concentrating table (as for washing or screening coal ore) **:** settling trough **:** RUN **h :** a long flat-bottomed slightly inclined trough down which a slurry of starch and gluten flows slowly so that the heavier starch particles settle out while the gluten runs off **i :** BELLY 5f — **on the table** *adv* **:** in plain sight **:** in a fully revealed position ⟨put your cards *on the table*⟩ ⟨the editors do an excellent job in putting both sides *on the table* —Benjamin Fine⟩ — **under the table** *adv* **1 :** into a stupor ⟨drink a man *under the table*⟩ ⟨five minutes' serious thought about the eruption of eternity into time puts me *under the table* —Stuart Chase⟩ **2 :** under the counter **:** SECRETLY ⟨buy your liquor *under the table* —J.H. Allen⟩ ⟨strategic requirements for tin will be the major consideration *under the table* during the coming negotiations —*Economist*⟩

²table \"\ *adj* [ME, fr. ¹*table*] **1** *obs* **:** of or relating to backgammon ⟨your ~ players, and other gamesters —James Mabbe⟩ **2 a :** of, relating to, or used on a table ⟨~ mat⟩ ⟨~ lamp⟩ ⟨~ model⟩ ⟨gambling-license holders must pay a ~ tax to the state —J.F.McDonald⟩ **b :** raised or processed for table use **:** suitable for human consumption ⟨~ bird⟩ **3 :** resembling a table **:** having a plane surface ⟨~ rock⟩ ⟨~ reef⟩ ⟨*table*-jawed tweezers⟩ **4 :** TABULAR ⟨~ matter⟩ ⟨~ work⟩ **5 :** of, relating to, or mounted on the table of a machine ⟨~ vise⟩ ⟨tool has more teeth in cutters allowing for increased ~ feed per minute —*Steel*⟩

³table \"\ *vb* **tabled; tabled; tabling** \-b(ə)liŋ\ **tables** [ME *tablen,* fr. ¹*table*] *vt* **1 :** to enter on a table **:** TABULATE ⟨quarterly distribution . . . is as *tabled* below —T.J.Grayson⟩ **2 :** to provide with food **:** FEED ⟨*tabled* in midmorning they ate sour pickles —Thomas Wolfe⟩ **3 a** *Brit* **:** to place on the agenda **:** submit for discussion ⟨research groups prepare the draft bills *tabled* by . . . parliamentary representatives —Barbara & Robert North⟩ **b :** to lay on the table ⟨the hydroelectric project has been *tabled,* revived, *tabled* again —E.W. Smith⟩ **c :** to put on a table ⟨ale, for which he too used to ~ his twopence —Thomas Carlyle⟩ ⟨florists *tabled* a large . . assortment of cut flowers —*Gardeners' Chronicle*⟩ **4 a** *archaic* **:** ⁴SCARF 1 **b :** to strengthen (a sail) by making a broad hem on the edges attached to the boltrope **5 :** to wash or screen on a table ⟨~ ground ore⟩ **6 :** to sediment (starch) by use of a table ~ *vi, archaic* **:** to take food **:** BOARD, EAT

¹tab·leau \'ta,blō, =ˈ=\ *n, pl* **tab·leaux** \-ō(z)\ *also* **tableaus** \-ōz\ [F, fr. MF *tablel,* dim. of *table*] **1 a :** a graphic description or visualization **:** IMAGE, PICTURE ⟨a popular writer . . . presenting winsome *tableaux* of old-fashioned literary days and ways —J.D.Hart⟩ ⟨thirteen *tableaux* . . . using one permanent frame —*Spectator*⟩ **b :** a striking effect or artistic grouping **:** ARRANGEMENT, SCENE ⟨the whole house party grouped in a welcoming ~ —Osbert Lancaster⟩ ⟨a series of window *tableaux* planned and executed by . . . interior designers —*Antiques*⟩ **c** *or* **tableau vi·vant** \-vē'väⁿ\ *pl* **tableaux vivants** \"\ [F, lit., living picture] **:** a sustained pose **:** a static depiction usu. presented on a stage with participants in appropriate costume ⟨a series of *tableaux* called "Grecian Statues", accompanied by explanatory song —*Amer. Guide Series: Wash.*⟩ ⟨stood with outstretched hand . . . in what seemed an endlessly-held ~ —Hartley Howard⟩ **2 a** *archaic* **:** an official list **:** TABLE ⟨official *tableaux* of rank —*Harper's*⟩ **b :** a large alphabet square in cryptography **3 :** the part of a solitaire layout on which building is usu. done

²tableau *var of* TAB

tableau curtain *n* **:** a stage curtain that opens in the center and has its sections drawn upward as well as to the side in order to produce a draped effect

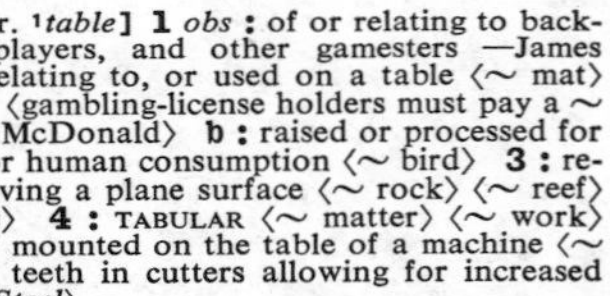
tableau curtain

table-board \'==,=\ *n* **1 :** a gaming table **2** *chiefly dial* **a :** TABLE 3a(1) **b :** TABLETOP **3 :** board without room ⟨often find *table-board* at some of the neighboring houses —W.D.Howells⟩

table book *n* **1** *archaic* **:** TABLET 1c ⟨found in the dead man's

pocket a *table book,* wherein were entered . . . names —Samuel Pepys⟩ **2 :** a book customarily displayed on a table ⟨this was the age of . . . lavish and heavy *table books* —J.M.Wells⟩
table chair *n* **:** CHAIR TABLE
table clock *n* **:** an early mainspring-driven clock with a horizontal dial
tablecloth \'==,=\ *n* [ME, fr. *table* + *cloth*] **1 :** a covering spread over a dining table before the places are set **2** *archaic* **:** an ornamental cover for a table — compare SCARF 3
table-cut \'=¦=\ *adj* **1 :** cut with a table — used of a gem **2 :** cut individually **:** CUSTOM-MADE — used of gloves
table cut *n* **:** a style of cutting gems in which the table is wider than the culet and joins the girdle in beveled edges — compare STEP CUT; see CUT illustration
ta·ble d'hôte \,täbəl'dōt, ,tab-, ,tab-\ *n, pl* **table d'hôtes** \-'dōt(s)\ [F, lit., host's table] **1 :** a meal (as in a hotel) served to all guests at a stated hour and a fixed price **2 :** a complete meal of several courses (as appetizer, entrée, dessert, and beverage) offered at a fixed price — compare À LA CARTE
table diamond *n* **:** a relatively flat diamond of table cut
table dormant *n* [ME, dormant table, fr. MF] **:** the first permanent type of table to replace the movable board on trestles in the medieval period
ta·ble·ful \'tābəl,fu̇l\ *n, pl* **tablefuls** *or* **tablesful** \-l,fu̇lz, -lz,fu̇l\ **:** as much or as many as a table can hold or accommodate ⟨a ~ of dishes⟩ ⟨a ~ of guests⟩
table garden *n* [so called fr. its supplying vegetables to the owner's table] **:** KITCHEN GARDEN
table-hop \'==,=\ *vi* **:** to move from table to table (as in a restaurant) visiting with friends ⟨customers *table-hopped,* called out greetings from across the room —*Omnibook*⟩
table jelly *n, chiefly Brit* **:** JELLO
ta·ble·land \'tābəl,(l)and\ *n* **:** a broad level elevated area **:** PLATEAU, MESA
table linen *n* **:** linen (as tablecloths and napkins) for use at the table
ta·ble·man \'tābəlmən\ *n, pl* **tablemen** [ME] **1** *obs* **:** a piece used in playing backgammon **2 :** one who works at or tends a table: as **a :** a worker who lays out and marks marble slabs for cutting **b :** an operator of a machine for cutting bricks or tiles from a column of moist clay **c :** one who tends the tables where ore is concentrated
table mountain *n* **:** a mountain with a flat top
table-mountain pine *n* **:** a pine (*Pinus pungens*) distinguished by spine-tipped knobby cone scales — called also *hickory pine, prickly pine, yellow pine*
table rapping *or* **table tapping** *n* **:** SPIRIT RAPPING
table roll *n* **:** any of a series of small rolls that support and hold level the wire of a fourdrinier machine
tables *pl of* TABLE, *pres 3d sing of* TABLE
table salt *n* **:** salt for use at the table and in cooking; *esp* **:** SALT 1a
table settle *n* **:** a settle having a back hinged so that it can be let down on the arms
tablespoon \'==,=\ *n* **1 :** a spoon of a size convenient for serving rather than eating food — see SPOON illustration **2 :** TABLESPOONFUL
ta·ble·spoon·ful \'==¦spün,fu̇l *sometimes* -pu̇n-\ *n, pl* **tablespoonfuls** *also* **tablespoonsful** \-n,fu̇lz, -nz,fu̇l\ **1 :** an amount equal to the capacity of one tablespoon **:** enough to fill a tablespoon **2 :** a unit of measure used esp. in cookery equal to one level tablespoonful or 4 fluidrams
table stake *n* **1 :** a stake that a player places on the table at the start of a poker game or deal as the amount he is willing to bet and that may not be changed after the deal begins **2 table stakes** *pl* **:** poker in which the betting limit for a player is the amount remaining in his table stake
table stone *n* **:** DOLMEN
¹tab·let \'tablət, *usu* -əd·+V\ *n* -s [ME *tablett, tablette,* fr. MF *tablete,* dim. of *table* — more at TABLE] **1 a (1) :** a flat surface, slab, or plaque suited for or bearing an inscription ⟨cuneiform ~s⟩ ⟨~s . . . range in size from small nameplates and directional signs to large memorials and honor rolls —*Sweet's Catalog Service*⟩ (2) *archaic* **:** a relatively thin flat panel containing a picture or engraving ⟨knew not when to take his hand from the ~ which he was painting —Vicesimus Knox⟩ **b :** a thin slab (as of clay) or one of a set of portable leaves or sheets (as of ivory or wax-coated wood) used for writing ⟨behind the throne stood . . . the scribe, inscribing the judgments with a pointed tool on ~s of clay —Nora B. Kubie⟩ ⟨two ~s fastened together with string . . . could form a closed letter which the recipient, after smoothing over the wax, could return with his answer —F.G.Kenyon⟩ **c :** a collection of sheets of paper usu. of the same size laid together and glued at one edge and usu. having a front cover — compare PAD 7 **d :** something that resembles a tablet: as (1) **:** a flat piece of an inflexible material (as an ornamental tile for a fireplace) (2) **:** PANEL 3f(3) (3) **:** a key controlling a stop on an electronic organ ⟨by . . . depressing any one of the stop ~s a tonal combination is set up —R.L.Eby⟩ **2 a :** a compressed or molded block of a solid material **:** CAKE, BAR ⟨a ~ of soap⟩ **b :** a small mass of medicated material usu. in the shape of a disk or flat square ⟨aspirin ~⟩ — compare PILL **c** *chiefly Brit* **:** a small patty or lozenge of candy ⟨almond ~⟩ ⟨lemon ~⟩ **3 a :** a table-cut gem **b :** a tabular crystal **4 a :** a horizontal coping stone **b :** TABLE 5a
²tablet \"\ *vt* **tableted** *or* **tabletted; tableted** *or* **tabletted; tableting** *or* **tabletting; tablets 1 a :** to provide or mark with a tablet **b :** to inscribe on a tablet **2 :** to form into a tablet
table talk *n* **:** informal conversation at or as if at a dining table; *esp* **:** the social conversation of a celebrity recorded for publication
tablet-arm chair *also* **tablet chair** *n* **:** a chair with the right arm broadened to serve as a writing surface

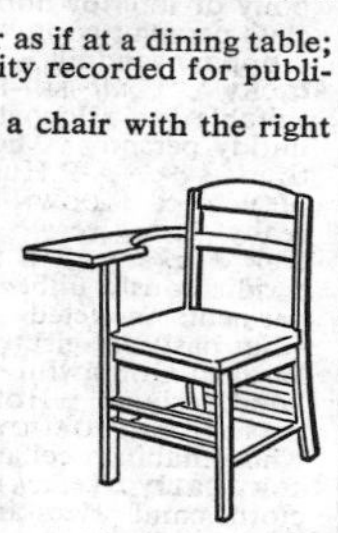
tablet-arm chair

table tennis *n* **:** a table game resembling lawn tennis played with wooden paddles and a small hollow celluloid or plastic ball — see RACKET illustration
table tipping *or* **table tilting** *or* **table turning** *n* **:** the lifting or manipulation of a table during a séance attributed to the agency of spirits
¹tabletop \'==,=\ *n* **1 :** the top of or as if of a table ⟨the ~ of a road vehicle is about 3′6″ above the ground —*Materials Handling in the Wool Industry*⟩ **2 :** a photograph of small objects or a miniature scene arranged on a table ⟨~s are popular for Christmas cards —*Amer. Photography*⟩ — distinguished from *still life*
²tabletop \"\ *adj* **1 :** forming or designed for use on a flat working surface ⟨~ water heater⟩ ⟨~ can opener⟩ **2 :** of or relating to small models in a miniature setting ⟨~ photography⟩
tablet tea *n* **1 :** a small brick of choice tea **2 :** tea dust pressed into a small tablet for making one cup or into smaller tablets so that several are needed to infuse a cup of tea — compare BRICK TEA
tablet triturate *n* **:** a small tablet made by molding fine moistened powder containing a medicinal and a diluent (as a sugar)
table viewer *n* [so called fr. being small enough to operate on a table] **:** a small projector incorporating its own rear projection screen, optics, and illumination for viewing transparencies (as 35mm slides)
tableware \'==,=\ *n* **:** china, glassware, silver, and other utensils used for setting a table or serving food and drink — compare FLATWARE, HOLLOW WARE
table wine *n* **:** a still wine of not more than 14 percent alcohol by volume that is red (as Burgundy and claret) or white (as sauterne and Rhine wine) and usu. served with food — called also *light wine, natural wine;* compare DESSERT WINE, SPARKLING WINE
tabling *n* -s [ME, fr. gerund of *tablen* to table — more at TABLE] **1** *archaic* **:** TABULATION **2 a :** ¹COPING **b :** TABLE 5a **c :** the formation of a horizontal joint by placing various stones in a course so they will extend into the next course to prevent slippage **3** *archaic* **:** BOARD 4c **4 :** a broad hem along the edges of a sail to which the boltrope is sewed
tab·li·num \ta'blīnəm\ *n, pl* **tabli·na** \-nə\ [L, contr. of *tabulinum,* fr. *tabula* record, writing tablet, tablet, board + *-inum* (neut. of *-inus* -ine) — more at TABLE] **:** a room or alcove between the atrium and the peristyle of a Roman house for storing the family records on tablets
ta·bli·ta \tä'blēd·ə\ *n* -s [AmerSp, dim. of Sp *tabla* tablet, board, fr. L *tabula*] **:** a headdress in the form of a colored panel or plaque decorated with feathers and symbolic designs and worn by Pueblo Indian women in ceremonial dances
¹tab·loid \'ta,blȯid\ *adj* [fr. *Tabloid,* a trademark applied to a concentrated form of drugs and chemicals] **1 a :** greatly condensed or shortened **:** CAPSULE ⟨provides in ~ form the evolution of the orchestra by families of instruments —William Schuman⟩ **b :** consisting of abbreviated episodes ⟨~ musical⟩ **2 a :** characterized by sensationalism **:** LURID, VULGAR ⟨the sensation-mongering ~ press —Robert Eisler⟩ ⟨feeding its ~ hungers . . . on more local horrors —John Mason Brown⟩ **b :** of, relating to, or resembling a tabloid (as in size or format) ⟨a ~ machine . . . takes the double 32-page signatures, gives then the final fold —P.R.Russell⟩ ⟨conservative-appearing ~ newspapers . . . published weekly in small towns —T.F. Barnhart⟩
²tabloid \"\ *n* -s **1 :** a short item or episode **:** BRIEF, SYNOPSIS ⟨provides in the form of a . . . ~ the concentrated essence of science —*Saturday Rev.*⟩ **2 a :** a newspaper of small format usu. presenting the news in concise form ⟨there is about these American ~s a terseness and finality which leave nothing to be said —Eric Partridge⟩; *esp* **:** a small profusely illustrated newspaper characterized by sensationalism ⟨it was a ~, and the headlines were a mixture of war news, recent murders, and scandals —Caroline Slade⟩ **b :** a publication resembling a tabloid in size or format ⟨most company ~s, like company magazines, are monthly —K.C.Pratt⟩ **c :** DIGEST, SUMMARY ⟨a 28-page ~ containing complete texts of all . . . regulations, interpretations, and directions issued through November —*Jour. of Accountancy*⟩
tab·loid·ism \-ȯi,dizəm\ *n* -s **:** the journalistic style and characteristics of a tabloid newspaper ⟨to astound the world with the new is the very essence of ~ —Oscar Cargill⟩
tabo- *comb form* [NL, fr. L *tabes* — more at THAW] **:** progressive wasting **:** tabes ⟨*tabo*phobia⟩
tabonuco *var of* TABANUCO
¹ta·boo *or* **ta·bu** \tə'bü, ta'- *sometimes* 'ta¦bü\ *adj* [Tongan *tabu*] **1 :** set apart as venerable or as charged with a dangerous supernatural power **:** forbidden to profane use or contact **:** SACRED, INVIOLABLE ⟨the sacred or ~ animal of a neighboring people —L.E.Fuller⟩ ⟨~ grounds — the home only of spirit hosts awaiting the return of the ancient worship —I.L.Idriess⟩ ⟨the person of the tribal chief is ~⟩ **2 :** banned on grounds of morality or taste or as constituting a risk **:** outlawed by common consent **:** DISAPPROVED, PROSCRIBED ⟨many obscene and sacred words are ~ because the name is regarded as the equivalent of the object —Daniel Katz⟩ ⟨a ~ list containing 300,000 songs —Leonard Allen⟩ ⟨many of the cows are tubercular, so fresh milk is strictly ~ —*Infantry Jour.*⟩
²taboo *or* **tabu** \"\ *n* -s [Tongan *tabu*] **1 a :** a prohibition instituted for the protection of a cultural group or as a safeguard against supernatural reprisal ⟨~ on using . . . a dead person's name —J.B.Casagrande⟩ ⟨Great Spirit set the whirlwinds blowing . . . as a punishment to those who, breaking the ~, had taught the white men how to snare salmon —*Amer. Guide Series: Oregon*⟩ — called also *kapu, tapu* **b (1) :** an act or object avoided as sacrosanct (2) **:** the quality or state of being taboo ⟨fishes are spread out on the floor . . . until the women pour water over them to free them from ~ —Margaret Mead⟩ **2 :** a prohibition imposed by social usage or as a protective measure **:** BAN, RESTRAINT ⟨subject to all the conventional ~s of her age, her sex and her pleasant place in the Victorian sun —Florence Bullock⟩ ⟨control of behavior by the inner ~s of moral sense —R.L.Jenkins⟩ ⟨rigid ~s about older men doing heavy work —*N. Y. State Legislative Committee on Problems of the Aging*⟩ **3 :** belief in or observance of taboos **:** CONVENTION, SUPERSTITION ⟨the man of the tribe, ruled by totem and ~ —Dorothy Thompson⟩ ⟨social repressions lead to . . . folklore, religion, and ~ —Thomas Munro⟩
³taboo *or* **tabu** \"\ *vt* **tabooed** *or* **tabued; tabooed** *or* **tabued; tabooing** *or* **tabuing; taboos** *or* **tabus 1 a :** to set apart as sacrosanct esp. by marking with a ritualistic symbol **:** exclude from profane use or contact ⟨names of sacred chiefs and gods are ~*ed,* and may not be spoken —J.G.Frazer⟩ **b :** to avoid or ban on grounds of morality or taste or as constituting a danger **:** PROSCRIBE, SHUN ⟨you will do, or ~, what your culture calls for —L.A.White⟩ ⟨provoke . . . wrath by discussing ~*ed* subjects —Lucy M. Montgomery⟩ **2** *archaic* **:** to curtail the use of **:** put off limits ⟨that sacred enclosure of respectability was ~*ed* to us —J.R.Lowell⟩ ⟨splendid couches ~*ed* against the reception of wearied feet —T.E.Hook⟩
ta·bo·paralysis \¦tā(,)bō+\ *n* [NL, fr. *tabo-* + *paralysis*] **:** TABOPARESIS
ta·bo·paresis \"\ *n* [NL, fr. *tabo-* + *paresis*] **:** paresis occurring with tabes, and esp. tabes dorsalis
¹ta·bor *also* **ta·bour** \'tābə(r)\ *n* -s [ME *tabor,* fr. OF *tabor,* perh. modif. of Per *tabīr* drum] **:** a small drum with one head of soft calfskin used as an accompaniment to a pipe or fife, both being played by the same person — compare TABRET, TAMBOURINE
²tabor *also* **tabour** \"\ *vb* -ED/-ING/-S [ME *tabouren,* fr. *tabor, tabour*] *vi, dial* **:** to beat on or as if on a drum ~ *vt, archaic* **:** to strike or tap repeatedly
ta·bor·er *also* **ta·bour·er** \-bərə(r)\ *n* -s [ME *tabourer,* fr. *tabor, tabour* + *-er*] **:** one that plays on the tabor
tab·o·ret *or* **tab·ou·ret** \¦tabə¦ret, 'tabərət\ *n* -s [F *tabouret,* lit., small drum, fr. MF, dim. of *tabour* drum, tabor, fr. OF *tabor*] **1 a :** a cylindrical seat or stool without arms or back **b :** a small portable stand (as for holding a potted plant) **2 :** a small cabinet often on casters for making supplies readily available in a working area

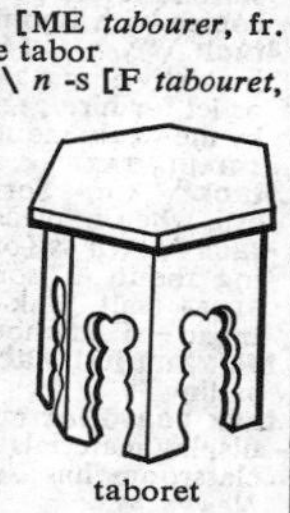
taboret

tab·o·rin \'tabərən\ *also* **tab·o·rine** \¦tabə¦rēn\ *n* -s [MF *tabourin,* fr. OF *tabor* + *-in* -ine] **:** TABRET
ta·bor·ite \'tābə,rīt\ *n* -s *usu cap* [*Tábor,* town south of Prague in the former kingdom of Bohemia (now a province of western Czechoslovakia) founded in 1420 as a Taborite stronghold by Jan Ziska †1424 Bohemian Hussite leader + E *-ite*] **:** a member of the radical wing of the Hussites rejecting everything without direct biblical warrant except war (as waged fiercely under Ziska)
tabor pipe *n* **:** PIPE 1a(1)
tab·ret \'tabrət\ *n* -s [ME *taberet,* fr. *tabor, tabour* + *-et*] **:** a small tabor — called also *taborin*
¹ta·briz \tə'brēz\ *adj, usu cap* [fr. *Tabriz,* Iran] **:** of or from the city of Tabriz, Iran **:** of the kind or style prevalent in Tabriz
²tabriz \"\ *n, pl* **tabriz** *usu cap* [fr. *Tabriz,* city in northwestern Iran] **:** a Persian rug usu. having a cotton warp, firm wool pile, medallion design and usu. tied with a Sehna knot
tabs *pl of* TAB, *pres 3d sing of* TAB
tabucki grass *var of* TAMBOOKIE GRASS
tab·u·la \'tabyələ\ *n, pl* **tabu·lae** \-yə,lē\ [NL, fr. L, board, tablet] **:** one of the transverse septa found in the calyculi of various corals and hydroids
tab·u·la·ble \'tabyələbəl\ *adj* [¹*tabulate* + *-able*] **:** capable of being tabulated
tab·u·lar \'tabyələ(r)\ *adj* [L *tabularis* relating to boards, fr. *tabula* board + *-aris* -ar] **1 a :** having a plane surface **:** resembling a slab **:** FLAT, LAMINAR ⟨a ~ root system⟩ ⟨~ plateaus, cliff-bound mesas —C.O.Dunbar⟩ ⟨~ deposits . . . of magnetite and hematite —A.M.Bateman⟩ **b (1) :** having two parallel faces that predominate — used of a crystal (2) **:** composed of thin platelike crystals ⟨a ~ mineral⟩ **2 a (1) :** of, relating to, or arranged in a table ⟨~ logarithms⟩ ⟨data summarized in ~ form⟩; *specif* **:** set up in rows and columns ⟨printers' rates for ~ work⟩ (2) **:** used in setting up a table ⟨~ key⟩ **b :** derived from or computed by means of a table ⟨~ value⟩ — **tab·u·lar·ly** *adv*
tabula ra·sa \-'räsə, -'rāsə\ *n, pl* **tabulae ra·sae** \-'rä,sī, -'rā,sē\ [L] **:** a smoothed tablet or blank slate — used esp. of the mind before receiving outside impressions; see LOCKEANISM
tabular berg *or* **tabular iceberg** *n* **:** BARRIER BERG
tabular difference *n* **:** the difference between two consecutive numbers in a table sometimes printed in the table (as in the last column of a table of logarithms)
tabular spar *n* [so called fr. appearing sometimes in tabular twinned crystals] **:** WOLLASTONITE
tabular standard *n* **:** a sliding scale to regulate the amount of money to be paid in discharge of a debt designed to assure the creditor of a definite amount of purchasing power rather than a fixed sum in currency that may have changed in value — compare INDEX NUMBER
tab·u·la·ta \,tabyə'lād·ə\ *n pl, cap* [NL, fr. neut. pl. of *tabulatus* tabulate] *in some classifications* **:** an artificial group of stony corals (as of the genus *Favosites*) including those having tubular calicles divided into chambers by transverse septa
¹tab·u·late \'tabyə,lāt, *usu* -ād·+V\ *vb* -ED/-ING/-S [L *tabula* board, tablet + E *-ate* — more at TABLE] *vt* **1 :** to put into tabular or summary form ⟨~ the results of a poll⟩ ~ *vi* **1 :** CONDENSE, SUMMARIZE **2** [back-formation fr. *tabulator*] **a :** to set a tabulator stop **b :** to move the carriage of a typewriter to a designated point by depressing the tabulator bar or key
²tab·u·late \-yələt, -yə,lāt\ *adj* [NL *tabulatus,* fr. *tabula* + L *-atus* -ate] **:** having tabulae
tab·u·lat·ed \-yə,lād·əd\ *adj* [in sense 1, fr. L *tabulatus* boarded (fr. *tabula* board + *-atus* -ate) + E *-ed;* in sense 2, fr. past part. of ¹*tabulate*] **1** *archaic* **:** TABULAR 1 **2 a :** reduced to tabular or synoptic form ⟨~ statistics⟩ **b :** derived from a table ⟨~ altitude⟩
tabulating machine *n* **:** TABULATOR b
tab·u·la·tion \,tabyə'lāshən\ *n* -s [¹*tabulate* + *-ion*] **1 :** the act or process of tabulating ⟨the ~ of results⟩ **2 :** a result of tabulating **:** TABLE ⟨his aim was to gain international acceptance for this ~ —Roger Burlingame⟩
tab·u·la·tor \'tabyə,lād·ə(r), -ātə-\ *n* -s [¹*tabulate* + *-or*] **:** one that tabulates: as **a :** a typist or clerk who makes tabulations **b :** a business machine for tabulating data; *esp* **:** one that sorts and selects information from a series of marked or perforated cards fed into it — compare PUNCH CARD **c :** a device on an office machine (as a typewriter or biller) having stops that can be set for tabular work
ta·bu·la·tur \,täbəla'tu̇(ə)r\ *n* -s *usu cap* [G, prob. fr. (assumed) NL *tabulatura* musical notation — more at TABLATURE] **1 :** the system of rules for poetic and musical composition established by the Meistersinger **2 :** TABLATURE 1a
ta·bun \'tä,bün\ *n* -s *often cap* [G] **:** a liquid organic phosphorus ester $(CH_3)_2NP(CN)O(OC_2H_5)$ that acts as a nerve gas
ta·bun man \tä'bün-\ *n, usu cap T* [fr. *Tabun,* cave at the mouth of the Wadi Mughara on the slopes of Mt. Carmel in northwestern Palestine, where the remains were found] **:** a fundamentally Neanderthaloid strain of Palestine man known from a female skeleton and a large male mandible with well-developed chin
tabus *pl of* TABU, *pres 3d sing of* TABU
ta·but \tä'büt\ *n* -s [Ar *tābūt*] **:** a bier or tomb found in Muslim countries
tac *abbr* tactical
tac·a·ma·hac \'tak(ə)mə,hak\ *also* **tac·a·ma·haca** \,=(=)=-'hakə, -'häkə\ *or* **tac·ma·hack** \'tak(ə)mə,hak\ *or* **tak·a·maka** \,takə'makə\ *n* -s [Sp *tacamahaca, tacamaca,* fr. Nahuatl *tecamaca*] **1 :** an aromatic oleoresin used in ointments and plasters and for incense: as **a :** the product of any of several tropical trees of the genera *Protium* (esp. *P. heptaphyllum* and *P. altissimum*) and *Bursera* — compare ELEMI b **b :** the product of either of two East Indian trees (*Calophyllum inophyllum* and *C. tacamahaca*) **c :** the resinous exudate of the balsam poplar **d :** GALIPOT **2 :** a tree yielding tacamahac; *esp* **:** BALSAM POPLAR
ta·ca·na \tə'känə\ *n, pl* **tacana** *or* **tacanas** *usu cap* [Sp, of AmerInd origin] **1 a :** a group of peoples of Bolivia, Brazil, and Peru **b :** a member of any of such peoples **2 :** the language family of the Tacana peoples — **ta·ca·nan** \-nən\ *adj, usu cap*
tac·ca \'takə\ *n, cap* [NL, fr. Malay *takah,* lit., notched] **:** a small genus (the type of the family Taccaceae) of tropical herbs having creeping rootstocks, basal compound leaves, and small umbellate flowers — see PIA
tac·ca·ce·ae \ta'kāsē,ē\ *n pl, cap* [NL, fr. *Tacca,* type genus + *-aceae*] **:** a family of tropical herbs (order Liliales) comprising only *Tacca* and the monotypic genus *Schizocapsa* and having regular flowers with six stamens and a one-celled ovary — **tac·ca·ceous** \(')ta¦kāshəs\ *adj*
t account *n, cap T* **:** a simplified form of account usu. for demonstration or instruction that consists of a horizontal line for the heading and a vertical line separating debits and credits and forms a T shape
tace *var of* TASSE
ta·cet \'tä,ket, 'tāsət\ *v imper* [L, 3d pers. sing. pres. indic. of *tacēre* to be silent — more at TACIT] **:** be silent — used as a direction in music for a part to be silent through a movement or a section
tachanun *var of* TAHANUN
ta·char·dia \tə'shärdēə\ [NL, fr. Gui *Tachard* †1712 Fr. Jesuit missionary in East Indies and Siam + NL *-ia*] *syn of* LACCIFER
¹tache \'tash\ *n* -s [ME *teche, tache,* fr. MF, stain, spot, of Gmc origin; akin to OS *tēkan* sign — more at TOKEN] *chiefly Scot* **:** STAIN, BLEMISH
²tache \"\ *vt* -ED/-ING/-S [ME *tassen, tatchen,* fr. MF *tacher,* fr. OF *techier, tachier,* fr. *teche, tache* stain, spot] *chiefly Scot* **:** to stain, blemish, or tarnish esp. with respect to character and reputation
³tache \'tach\ *also* **tach** \"\ *n, pl* **taches** [ME, fr. MF *tache* nail, fastening, of Gmc origin; akin to MD *tac* pointed instrument, sharp point — more at TACK] **:** BUCKLE, CLASP ⟨couple the curtains together with the ~s —Exod 26:6 (AV)⟩
tache noire \(')tash¦nwär, ¦=,nə¦w-\ *n, pl* **taches noires** \-r(z)\ [F, lit., black spot] **:** a small dark-centered ulcer that appears at the site of a tick bite and is the primary lesion of boutonneuse fever
tach·e·om·e·ter \,takē'ämәd·ə(r)\ *n* [F *tachéomètre,* irreg. fr. Gk *tachys* swift (gen. masc. sing. *tacheos*) + F *-mètre* -meter — more at TACHY-] **:** TACHYMETER
tach·i·na fly \'takənə-\ *n* [NL *Tachina,* genus of flies — more at TACHINIDAE] **:** any of numerous bristly usu. grayish or black flies comprising the family Tachinidae
tach·i·nar·ia \,takə'na(a)rēə\ *n pl, cap* [NL, fr. *Tachina* + *-aria*] *in some classifications* **:** a group coextensive with the family Tachinidae
¹tach·i·nid \'takənəd\ *adj* [NL *Tachinidae*] **:** of or relating to the Tachinidae
²tachinid \"\ *n* -s **:** a fly of the family Tachinidae
ta·chin·i·dae \ta'kinə,dē, tə'k-\ *n pl, cap* [NL, fr. *Tachina,* type genus (fr. Gk *tachinos* swift, fleet, fr. *tachos* speed + *-inos* -ine) + *-idae* — more at TACHO-] **:** a large family of specialized two-winged flies that have bare aristae, are active flyers, and produce larvae which are parasitic in caterpillars and other insects and are important factors in the natural control of various noxious insects — see TACHINA FLY
ta·chis·to·scope \tə'kistə,skōp\ *n* [ISV *tachisto-* (fr. Gk *tachistos,* superl. of *tachys* swift) + *-scope;* orig. formed as G *tachistoskop*] **:** an apparatus for the brief exposure of visual stimuli that is used in the study of learning, attention, and perception ⟨worked with a ~ to accelerate the pupils' reading⟩
ta·chis·to·scop·ic \=¦=;=¦skäpik\ *adj* **:** of, relating to, or conducted by a tachistoscope ⟨~ work⟩ ⟨~ training⟩ ⟨~ presentation⟩
ta·chis·to·scop·i·cal·ly \-pək(ə)lē\ *adv* **:** by means of a tachistoscope ⟨exposed ~⟩
tacho- *comb form* [ISV, fr. Gk *tachos* speed; akin to Gk *tachys* swift — more at TACHY-] **:** speed ⟨*tacho*gram⟩
tach·o·gram \'takə,gram\ *n* [ISV *tacho-* + *-gram*] **:** an autographic record of a registering tachometer
tach·o·graph \-raf,-räf\ *n* [ISV *tacho-* + *-graph*] **1 :** a recording or registering tachometer **2 :** TACHOGRAM
ta·chom·e·ter \ta'kämәd·ə(r), tə'k-\ *n* [*tacho-* + *-meter*] **1 :** a device for indicating speed of rotation **2 :** a part of a chronograph dial that gives the speed of an object
tach·o·met·ri·cal·ly \,takə¦me·trək(ə)lē\ *adv* [fr. *tachometer,* after such pairs as E *meter: metrically*] **:** by means of a tachometer

ta·chom·e·try \ta'kämə·trē, tə'k-\ *n* -ES [*tacho-* + *-metry*] **:** measurement with a tachometer

tachy- *comb form* [Gk, fr. *tachys;* perh. akin to OIr *daingen* strong, firm, OSlav *degŭ* strength] **:** swift **:** rapid **:** accelerated ⟨*tachy*cardia⟩ ⟨*tachy*genesis⟩ ⟨*tachy*lyte⟩ ⟨*tachy*meter⟩

tachy·auxesis \¦takē+\ *n* [NL, fr. *tachy-* + *auxesis*] **:** allometric growth characterized by acceleration of a part in comparison with the body as a whole — compare BRADYAUXESIS — **tachy·auxetic** \"+\ *adj*

tachy·car·dia \¦takə¦kärdēə\ *n* -S [NL, fr. *tachy-* + *-cardia*] **:** relatively rapid heart action whether physiological (as after exercise) or pathological — compare PAROXYSMAL TACHYCARDIA

tachy·genesis \¦takə+\ *n* [NL, fr. *tachy-* + L *genesis*] **1 :** acceleration of development by the shortening of ancestral stages during embryonic development — compare BRADYGENESIS, LIPOGENESIS **2 :** SALTATORY EVOLUTION

tachy·genetic \"+\ *or* **tachy·gen·ic** \"+¦jenik\ *adj* [*tachy-* + *-genetic* or *-genic*] **:** of, relating to, or exhibiting tachygenesis

tachy·glos·sal \¦takə¦gläsəl, -lös-\ *or* **tachy·glos·sate** \-sət, -,sāt\ *adj* [NL *Tachyglossus* + E *-al* or *-ate*] **:** TACHYGLOSSID

¹tachy·glos·sid \-,säd\ *adj* [NL *Tachyglossidae*] **:** of or relating to the Tachyglossidae

²tachyglossid \"\ *n* -S **:** a mammal of the family Tachyglossidae **:** ECHIDNA

tachy·glos·si·dae \,==ˈsə,dē\ *n pl, cap* [NL, fr. *Tachyglossus*, type genus + *-idae*] **:** a family of mammals (order Monotremata) consisting of the genera *Tachyglossus* and *Zaglossus* and comprising the echidnas

tachy·glos·sus \-səs\ *n, cap* [NL, fr. *tachy-* + Gk *glōssa* tongue — more at GLOSS] **:** the type genus of Tachyglossidae including all the Australian echidnas — compare ZAGLOSSUS

tachy·graph \'takə,graf, -rȧf\ *n* [F *tachygraphe*, fr. Gk *tachygraphos*, fr. *tachy-* + *-graphos* (fr. *graphein* to write) — more at CARVE] **1 :** TACHYGRAPHER **2 :** a tachygraphic writing

ta·chyg·ra·pher \ta'kigrəfə(r), tə'k-\ *or* **ta·chyg·ra·phist** \-fəst\ *n* -S [*tachygraphy* + *-er* or *-ist*] **:** one skilled in tachygraphy **:** STENOGRAPHER; *esp* **:** an ancient Greek or Roman notary

tachy·graph·ic \¦takə¦grafik\ *or* **tachy·graph·i·cal** \-fəkəl\ *adj* [*tachygraphy* + *-ic* or *-ical*] **:** of or relating to tachygraphy

tachy·graph·i·cal·ly \-fək(ə)lē\ *adv* **:** in a tachygraphic manner **:** by means of tachygraphy

tachy·graph·om·e·ter \,==gra'fämə·tə(r), -rȧ'f-\ *n* [blend of *tachymeter* and *grapho-*] **:** a tachymeter with alidade for surveying

tachy·graph·om·e·try \-mə·trē\ *n* -ES [blend of *tachymetry* and *grapho-*] **:** measurement with a tachygraphometer

ta·chyg·ra·phy \ta'kigrəfē, tə'k-\ *n* -ES [Gk *tachygraphein* to write shorthand (fr. *tachygraphos* tachygrapher) + E *-y* — more at TACHYGRAPH] **1 :** the art or practice of rapid writing **:** SHORTHAND, STENOGRAPHY; *esp* **:** the rapid writing or shorthand of the ancient Greeks and Romans **2 a :** cursive writing **b :** the abbreviated form of Greek and Latin used in the Middle Ages

tachy·hy·drite \¦takə'hī,drīt\ *also* **tach·y·drite** \'takə,drīt\ *n* -S [modif. of G *tachhydrit*, blend of *tachy-* and *hydr-* + *-it* -ite] **:** a mineral $CaMg_2Cl_6.12H_2O$ consisting of a hydrous chloride of calcium and magnesium

tachy·lyte *also* **tachy·lite** \'takə,līt\ *n* -S [*tachylyte* fr. G *tachylyt*, fr. *tachy-* + Gk *lytos* soluble, fr. *lyein* to unbind, release, dissolve; *tachylite* alter. (influenced by *-lite*) of *tachylyte* — more at LOSE] **:** BASALT GLASS

ta·chym·e·ter \ta'kimədə(r), tə'k-\ *n* [ISV *tachy-* + *-meter*] **1 :** an instrument for determining quickly the distances, bearings, and elevations of distant objects in surveying; *esp* **:** a transit or theodolite with stadia hairs **2 :** a speed indicator

tachy·met·ric \¦takə¦me·trik\ *adj* **:** of, relating to, or determined by tachymetry

ta·chym·e·try \ta'kimə·trē, tə'k-\ *n* -ES [F *tachymétrie*, fr. *tachy-* + *-métrie* -metry] **:** measurement with the tachymeter

tachy·phy·lac·tic \¦takəfə¦laktik\ *adj* [fr. NL *tachyphylaxis*, after such pairs as NL *prophylaxis:* E *prophylactic*] **:** of or relating to tachyphylaxis

tachy·phy·lax·is \,===ˈlaksəs\ *n, pl* **tachyphylax·es** \-k,sēz\ [NL, fr. *tachy-* + *-phylaxis* (as in *prophylaxis*)] **:** diminished response to later increments in a sequence of applications of a physiologically active substance (as the diminished pressor response that follows repeated injections of renin)

tachy·pnea *also* **tachy·pnoea** \,takə(p)'nēə\ *n* -S [NL, fr. *tachy-* + *-pnea*, *-pnoea*] **:** increased rate of respiration — **tachy·pne·ic** \,==¦nēik\ *adj*

tachy·scope \'takə,skōp\ *n* [ISV *tachy-* + *-scope;* orig. formed as G *tachyskop*] **:** an early animated-picture machine in which glass photographic transparencies mounted on the periphery of a large rotating wheel are viewed through an aperture with a flashing light source serving as the illuminant

ta·chys·ter·ol \ta'kistə,rōl, tə'k-, -rōl\ *n* [*tachy-* + *sterol*] **:** an oily liquid alcohol $C_{28}H_{43}OH$ isomeric with ergosterol that is formed by ultraviolet irradiation of ergosterol or lumisterol and that on further irradiation yields vitamin D_2 — compare DIHYDROTACHYSTEROL

tachy·tel·ic \¦takə¦telik\ *adj* **:** of or relating to tachytely

tachy·tely \'=,=,telē\ *n* -ES [*tachy-* + Gk *telos* end, consummation, degree of completion, state of maturity + E *-y* — more at WHEEL] **:** evolution at a relatively rapid rate tending to result in speedy differentiation and fixation of new types — compare BRADYTELY, HOROTELY

tac·it \'tasət, *usu* -əd·+V\ *adj* [F or L; F *tacite*, fr. L *tacitus* silent, fr. past part. of *tacēre* to be silent, to pass over in silence; akin to OS *thagon, thagian* to be silent, OHG *dagēn*, ON *thegja*, Goth *thahan* to be silent, and perh. to W *tagu* to choke, OIr *tachtaid* he chokes] **1 a** *archaic* **:** not speaking **:** SILENT ⟨a man rather ~ than discursive —Thomas Carlyle⟩ **b :** expressed or carried on without words or speech **:** UNSPOKEN, WORDLESS ⟨the blush was a ~ answer —Bram Stoker⟩ ⟨wooed her with ~ patient worship —George Eliot⟩ ⟨occasioned ~ rejoicing among the men —A.J.Liebling⟩ **2 a :** implied or indicated but not actually expressed **:** IMPLICIT ⟨~ consent⟩ ⟨a ~ assumption⟩ ⟨a ~ warning⟩ ⟨notions . . . some ~, some openly expressed —Fred Rodell⟩ ⟨enjoys the ~ support . . . of the inhabitants —*New Statesman & Nation*⟩ **b** (1) **:** arising without express contract or agreement — compare CONVENTIONAL 1a (2) **:** arising by operation of law ⟨a ~ mortgage⟩ — compare LEGAL

tac·i·te·an \¦tasə¦tēən, ta'sid·ē·\ *adj, usu cap* [fr. Cornelius *Tacitus* † *ab* A.D.117 Rom. statesman and historian + E *-ean*] **:** of or relating to the historian Tacitus or resembling his style or writings (as in terseness or studied lack of parallelism) ⟨his discourse . . . was couched on this occasion in *Tacitean* brevity —Norman Douglas⟩

tacit hypothec *or* **tacit hypothecation** *n* **:** MARITIME LIEN

tac·it·ly *adv* **:** in a tacit manner: as **a :** without speaking **:** SILENTLY ⟨held his look, ~ assuring him that she valued it fully —Helen Howe⟩ **b :** by unexpressed agreement, allowance, or understanding **:** IMPLICITLY, ACQUIESCENTLY ⟨~ consenting to whatever violence must be done —K.K.Darrow⟩ ⟨~ permitted by the judges to practise —H.D.Hazeltine⟩ ⟨phenomena . . . ~ recognized since time immemorial —Ralph Linton⟩ **c :** without acknowledgment ⟨borrowed extensively but ~ from these . . . volumes —J.T.Krumpelmann⟩

tac·it·ness *n* -ES **:** the quality or state of being tacit **:** SILENCE, QUIET ⟨inward ~ of mind —Walter Pater⟩

tacit relocation *n, civil & Scots law* **:** a renewal of a lease arising by operation of law from a failure of both landlord and tenant to discover properly their intention to have the lease dissolved at the expiration of its term

tac·i·turn \'tasə,tərn, -,tōn, -,təin\ *adj* [F or L; F *taciturne*, fr. L *taciturnus*, fr. *tacitus*] **1 :** habitually silent **:** temperamentally disinclined or reluctant to talk or converse **:** LACONIC, RETICENT ⟨a brooding and ~ man, he said nothing till others had their say —G.D.Brown⟩ **2 :** marked by a lack of expressiveness or amiability **:** DOUR ⟨from self-revealing sociability to ~ misanthropy —Aldous Huxley⟩ ⟨a ~ and iron-bound visage —Charles Dickens⟩ **syn** see SILENT

tac·i·tur·ni·ty \,==ˈtərnəd·ē, -ətē, -i\ *n* -ES [ME *taciturnite*, fr. MF or L; MF *taciturnité*, fr. L *taciturnitat-, taciturnitas*, fr. *taciturnus* + *-itat-, -itas* -ity] **1 :** the quality or state of being taciturn: **a :** inclination to spare, curt, or laconic speech **:** RETICENCE ⟨the ~ and the short answers which gave so much offense —T.B.Macaulay⟩ **b :** lack of expressiveness **:** RESERVE ⟨tight-lipped they endure their fates and we are the losers from their numb ~ —Anthony Quinton⟩ **2** *Scots law* **a :** such failure to assert a legal right as implies that there has been satisfaction or abandonment of it **b :** the plea of mora and taciturnity setting up such failure

tac·i·turn·ly *adv* **:** in a taciturn manner: as **a :** RETICENTLY **b :** SILENTLY

¹tack \'tak\ *n* -S *often attrib* [ME *tak;* akin to MLG *tacke* pointed instrument, sharp point, MD *tac*] **1 a** *obs* **:** a small hooked, knobbed, or pointed device of metal for fastening one thing to another: as (1) **:** BUCKLE (2) **:** a hook fitting into an eye (3) **:** NAIL **b :** a small short sharp-pointed nail usu. having a broad flat head; *esp* **:** one for affixing a light object or material to a solid surface ⟨a carpet ~⟩ ⟨a thumb ~⟩ **c :** a strip binding stalks (as to a wall) in gardening **d :** an ear on a pipe for fastening it (as to a wall) **2** *chiefly dial* **:** the ability to hold on, last, or endure **:** STABILITY, ENDURANCE **3 a :** a rope to hold in place the forward lower corner of a course on a sailing ship — compare SHEET **b :** a rope for hauling the outer lower corner of a studding sail to the lower end of the boom **c :** the lower forward corner of a fore-and-aft sail **d :** the corner of a sail to which a tack is fastened (as the weather clew of a square sail) **4 a :** the direction of a ship with respect to the trim of her sails ⟨the starboard ~⟩ ⟨the port ~⟩ **b :** the run of a sailing ship on one tack ⟨the ship sailed well on that last ~⟩ **c :** a change when close-hauled from the starboard to the port tack or vice versa ⟨made two ~*s* in rounding the point⟩ **d :** a zigzag movement on land ⟨watched for openings and got through the dense crowd in a series of ~*s*⟩ **e :** a course or method of action; *esp* **:** one sharply divergent from that previously taken or followed ⟨go off on the wrong ~⟩ ⟨try a new ~⟩ ⟨kept changing the ~ of your questions —B.V.Dryer⟩ **5 a :** a tying or fastening esp. of a temporary kind **b :** any of various usu. temporary stitches: as (1) **:** TAILOR'S TACK (2) **:** BAR TACK **c** *Brit* **:** a supplement or rider esp. to a parliamentary bill **d :** a short deposit for holding the sections of a joint in place in welding **6 a :** the quality or state of sticking or adhering **:** ADHESIVENESS, STICKINESS ⟨the ~ of a paint⟩ ⟨the ~ of ink⟩ ⟨tape with good ~⟩ **b :** the property of raw rubber or compounded rubber stock of adhering firmly when layers are pressed together **7 :** stable gear

²tack \"\ *vb* -ED/-ING/-S [ME *takken*, fr. *tak*, n.] *vt* **1 a :** to cause to join or hold together **:** ATTACH ⟨~ on a fragment of black cloth for an eye —*Farmer's Weekly (So. Africa)*⟩; *esp* **:** to nail, pin, or affix with tacks ⟨~*ing* down a stairway carpet⟩ ⟨~ a notice on a bulletin board⟩ ⟨~*ing* upholstery⟩ **b** *archaic* **:** to join in matrimony **:** HITCH 2c ⟨~ me first; my love is waiting —R.B.Sheridan⟩ **c :** to join (things that are separated) by a linking part **:** CONNECT ⟨islands ~*ed* together by . . . bridges —John Evelyn⟩ ⟨at this common point . . . the two routes may be ~*ed* —S.H.Lynne⟩ **2 :** to attach or join slightly or only at separated points for a temporary purpose: as **a :** to join (two pieces of metal) by drops of solder **b :** to stitch together lightly (two pieces of cloth) **:** BASTE ⟨~ the pleat in position at the hemline⟩ **3 a :** to add, attach, or join as a usu. inappropriate or arbitrary complement **:** LINK, TIE ⟨themes loosely and rather aimlessly ~*ed* together⟩ — usu. used with *to* or *on* ⟨a weak, spotty piece of music ~*ed* to an absurd, garish drama —Alfred Frankenstein⟩ ⟨~*ed* on to escape a banal conclusion —Anthony Quinton⟩ **b** (1) **:** to add or attach to as a supplement **:** ANNEX — usu. used with *on* or *onto* ⟨~*ed* it on as an afterthought⟩ ⟨~ an extra dollar onto the price⟩ ⟨one large studio with three . . . little rooms ~*ed* onto it —Aldous Huxley⟩ (2) **:** to add (a rider) to a parliamentary bill **:** APPEND — usu. used with *to, on,* or *onto* ⟨a provision . . . ~*ed* to a supply bill —T.E.May⟩ ⟨get the measure through the legislature by ~*ing* it onto an appropriation bill⟩ **4 a** *Eng law* **:** to unite or join (securities given at different times) so as to prevent a person having intermediate securities or rights from claiming a title to redeem or otherwise discharge one or more prior ones without also redeeming or discharging one or more subsequent ones united to the prior ones **b :** to add on (a period of disability or adverse possession by one person to that of another immediately preceding or following and in privity with him) **5 a :** to change the direction of (a sailing ship) when sailing close-hauled by putting the helm alee and shifting the sails so that it will come up into the wind and then fall off on the other side until it proceeds at about the same angle to the wind as before **b :** to navigate (a sailing ship) by a series of tacks ⟨often he had ~*ed* a monstrous ship of the line in heavy weather —C.S. Forester⟩ — compare WEAR ~ *vi* **1 a :** to change the direction of a sailing ship **b :** *of a sailing ship* **:** to move in a different direction through the shifting of the helm to leeward so that the wind strikes the sails from the other side ⟨~*ed* along smoothly with the onshore breeze —H.H.Martin⟩ **2 a :** to follow a zigzag course **:** ⁵ANGLE 2 ⟨rode scornfully on, ~*ing* from side to side —Angela Thirkell⟩ **b :** to modify abruptly (as a policy or an attitude) esp. for reasons of expediency **:** SHIFT ⟨~*ing* temporarily in her aggressive designs but hoping to push on directly again later⟩ **3 :** to associate oneself with or follow closely after a person **:** tag along ⟨thought you wouldn't mind my ~*ing* on to you —C.S.Lewis⟩ — **tack down wind :** to sail before the wind in a series of alternate reaches to starboard and port with sheets in instead of in a direct straight course with boom off and spinnaker set

³tack \"\ *n* -S [ME *tak*, fr. *taken* to take — more at TAKE] **1** *chiefly Scot* **:** a contract by which the use of something is set or let for hire **:** LEASE **2** *chiefly Scot* **:** pasture land hired usu. by the week, month, or quarter **3** *chiefly Scot* **:** a catch of fish **:** HAUL, TAKE

⁴tack \"\ *n* -S [origin unknown] *dial Eng* **:** a distinctive flavor esp. when unpleasant

⁵tack \"\ *n* -S [origin unknown] **:** STUFF ⟨we should be jawing about . . . some such ~ —D.H.Lawrence⟩; *esp* **:** FOODSTUFF ⟨salt junk and weevily ~ give way to soggy baker's bread —E.J.Schoettle⟩

tack and half tack *n* **:** a long tack followed by a short one in sailing

tack board *n* **:** a usu. cork board for tacking up notices and display materials (as charts or maps) **:** BULLETIN BOARD ⟨each classroom has . . . *tack boards* —*Springfield (Mass.) Daily News*⟩

tack bumpkin *n* **:** BUMPKIN a

tack claw *n* **:** a small hand tool with a handle and slightly bent bifurcated end for removing tacks

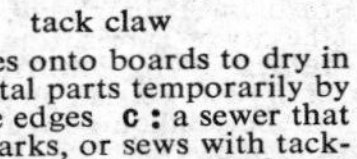
tack claw

tack duty *n* [³*tack*] *Scots law* **:** rent under a lease

tack·er \'takə(r)\ *n* -S [²*tack* + *-er*] **1 :** one that tacks: as **a :** one that fastens wet hides onto boards to dry in leather working **b :** one that joins metal parts temporarily by welding at a number of spots along the edges **c :** a sewer that makes bar tacks **d :** one that joins, marks, or sews with tacking stitches **e :** one that staples or sews padding to the innersprings of mattresses **f :** a device incorporating a strong spring made tense and then released by a trigger and used for the rapid driving of staples fed from a reservoir chamber **2** *Brit* **:** one seeking to secure passage of a legislative measure by appending it to a money bill

¹tack·et \'takət\ *n* -S [ME *taket*, fr. *tak* tack + *-et*] *dial Brit* **:** HOBNAIL

²tacket \"\ *vt* -ED/-ING/-S *dial Brit* **:** to strengthen or fasten with tackets

tacketing gut *n, Brit* **:** bookbinder's gut

tack·ety \-ətī\ *adj, chiefly Scot* **:** HOBNAILED ⟨~ boots⟩

tack·ey *var of* ³TACKY

tack hammer *n* **:** a lightweight hammer that has usu. one magnetized face and is used for holding and driving tacks

tackier *comparative of* TACKY

tackies *pl of* TACKY

tackiest *superlative of* TACKY

tack·i·fi·er \'takə,fī(ə)r\ *n* -S **:** a tackifying agent

tack·i·fy \-fī\ *vt* -ED/-ING/-ES [*tacky* + *-fy*] **:** to improve the tack of (as rubber) **:** make tacky

tack·i·ness \'takēnəs, -kin-\ *n* -ES **:** the quality or state of being tacky **:** STICKINESS, ADHESIVENESS ⟨the ~ of unvulcanized rubber⟩

tacking *pres part of* TACK

¹tack·le \'takəl, *by seamen often* 'tāk-\ *n* -S *often attrib* [ME *takel;* akin to MLG & MD *takel* ship's rigging, and perh. to E ¹*tack*] **1 :** a collection, set, or complement of the equipment, apparatus, or materials designed for use in a particular activity **:** PARAPHERNALIA, GEAR ⟨sports ~ was rationed —Tom Clarke⟩ ⟨so undignified, using father's shaving ~ —Dodie Smith⟩: as **a :** equipment for fishing **b :** an archer's equipment **c :** harness for a horse **2 a :** a ship's rigging; *specif* **:** a ship's purchase (as an arrangement of lines and blocks) in which the line runs through more than one block **b :** an assemblage of ropes and pulleys arranged to gain mechanical advantage for hoisting and pulling **:** PURCHASE 4a(2) — compare BURTON 1; see PULLEY illustration **3** [²*tackle*] **a :** the act or an instance of tackling ⟨he made key ~*s* and ran to several first downs —*N.Y.Times*⟩ **b :** one of two players on each side of the center and between guard and end in the line in football ⟨played as right ~ early in the season and left ~ in later games⟩ **syn** see EQUIPMENT

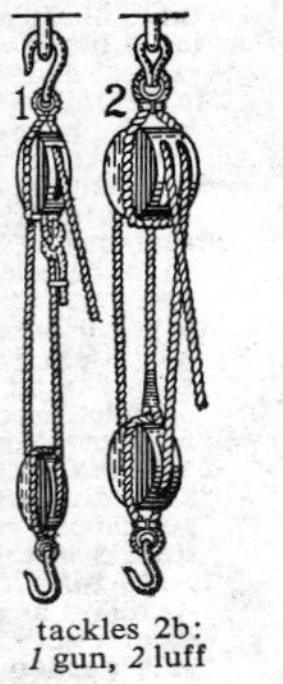

tackles 2b: *1* gun, *2* luff

²tackle \"\ *vb* **tackled; tackled; tackling** \-k(ə)liŋ\ **tackles** *vt* **1 a :** to attach or secure with or as if with tackle; *specif* **:** HARNESS — often used with *up* ⟨~ the horse up for plowing⟩ **b :** to harness a horse to (as a coach) **2 a :** to seize, take hold of, or grapple with esp. with the intention of stopping or subduing ⟨a wrestler ~*s* his opponent⟩ ⟨dive in and ~ the creature —*Amer. Guide Series: Fla.*⟩ **b :** to seize and throw down or stop (an opposing player with the ball) in U.S. or rugby football ⟨*tackled* the ball carrier and brought him down a yard from the goal line⟩ **c :** to obstruct or interfere with (an opponent dribbling or playing the ball) so as to bring about loss of possession of the ball (as in soccer or field hockey) **3 a :** to set about dealing with (as a difficult problem or a formidable task) **:** come to grips with **:** take on ⟨~ the problem of disarmament —Gordon Dean⟩ ⟨~ a steep ascent that lay before me —R.L.Stevenson⟩ **b :** to approach (a person) esp. with the expectation of encountering hostility or resistance ⟨planned to ~ the boss for a raise⟩ ⟨proceeded to ~ him on the subject —*Irish Digest*⟩ **c :** to attack (food) ⟨the most elaborate dinner I ever *tackled* —W.A.White⟩ ~ *vi* **:** to tackle an opposing player (as in football)

tackle block *n* **:** BLOCK 4a

tackle board *or* **tackle post** *n* **:** a board, post, or frame at the end of a rope walk that supports the spindles or whirls for twisting the yarns

tack·led \'takəld, 'tāk-\ *adj* [¹*tackle* + *-ed*] **:** made of tackle or ropes ⟨cords made like a ~ stair —Shak.⟩

tackle fall *n* **:** the rope or cable of a tackle to which force is applied

tackle-house \'==,=\ *n* **:** a house or building having a tackle used in lading or unlading ships

tack·ler \-k(ə)lə(r)\ *n* -S **:** one that tackles: as **a** *Brit* **:** LOOMFIXER **b** *Brit* **:** an attendant of a machine for making paper bags **c :** one that tackles an opponent in a sport (as wrestling or football) ⟨shook off half a dozen ~*s* to crash over the goal line —*N.Y.Times*⟩

tackline \'=,=\ *n* **:** a short piece of line used to separate flags in a signal hoist

tack·ling \'tak(ə)liŋ, 'tāk-\ *n* -S [ME *takling*, fr. gerund of *taklen* to furnish with tackle, fr. *takel*, n.] **1 :** furniture of the masts and yards of a ship (as rigging or cordage) **:** TACKLE 2a **2 a :** a collection of equipment or apparatus used in a particular activity **:** TACKLE 1 ⟨fishing ~⟩ **b :** the harness of a draft animal **3 a :** the act or skill of making a tackle in football **b :** the act or skill of taking or attempting to take possession of the ball from an opponent in soccer or field hockey

tack pin *n* **:** BELAYING PIN

tack rag *n* **:** a cloth for picking up dust before painting

tack rivet *n* **:** a temporary rivet for securing pieces during riveting

tack room *n* **:** a room in or attached to a stable for the storage and maintenance of riding tack (as saddles and bridle) and often of stud records or for the display of prizes or other honors of the stable

tacks *pl of* TACK, *pres 3d sing of* TACK

tacks·man \'taksmən\ *n, pl* **tacksmen** [fr. poss. of ³*tack* + *man*] *Scots law* **:** LESSEE

tackweed \'=,=\ *n* **:** PUNCTURE VINE

tack-weld \'=,=\ *vt* [back-formation fr. *tack welding*] **:** to fasten (two pieces of metal) together by welding them at various isolated points

tack weld *n* [*tack-weld*] **1 :** a joint or fastening secured by tack welding **2 :** one of the small welded points in a joint that has been tack-welded

¹tacky \'takē, -ki\ *adj* -ER/-EST [²*tack* + *-y*] **:** barely sticky to the touch **:** ADHESIVE: as **a :** having a quality of adhering, clinging, or binding ⟨~ varnish⟩ ⟨~ ink⟩ ⟨keeps rubber rollers and blankets ~ —*Graphic Arts Monthly*⟩ **b :** characterized by tack

²tacky \"\ *n* -ES *chiefly Brit* **:** SNEAKER, TENNIS SHOE — usu. used in pl.

³tacky \"\ *n* -ES [origin unknown] **1** *chiefly South* **:** a small pony or inferior horse **2** *chiefly South* **:** an inferior or low-class person **:** POOR WHITE ⟨the ditch-edge child of some sharecropping sandhill ~ —William Humphrey⟩

⁴tacky \"\ *adj* -ER/-EST **1 a :** having the characteristics of or suitable for a low-class person **:** COMMON ⟨a poor-white and untidy person . . . he in short, was ~ —J.B.Cabell⟩ ⟨stigmatized as ~ —A.P.Hudson⟩ **b :** marked by shabbiness or signs of neglect **:** DOWN-AT-HEEL, SEEDY ⟨the neighborhood was really getting very ~ —Walter Karig⟩ ⟨a ~ boardinghouse —*New Yorker*⟩ **2 a :** marked by lack of style or good taste **:** ridiculously unbecoming **:** OUTMODED, DOWDY ⟨~ knitted garments modeled on dumpy hausfrau types —*Newsweek*⟩ ⟨that pasty fat girl with those ~ pigtails —Carson McCullers⟩ ⟨looked God-awful ~ for a woman who was supposed to be a good designer —Hollis Alpert⟩ **b :** marked by cheap showiness **:** FLASHY, GAUDY ⟨a ~ costume⟩ ⟨sumptuously ~ countess who inhabits a cellar —*Time*⟩

tacky party *n* [⁴*tacky*] **:** a party at which the guests wear tacky clothes and prizes are awarded for the tackiest costume

tacmahack *var of* TACAMAHAC

ta·co \'tä(,)kō\ *n* -S [MexSp, fr. Sp, bung, drink of wine, snack, perh. of Gmc origin; akin to E ¹*tack*] **:** a sandwich made of a tortilla rolled up with or folded over a filling and usu. fried

ta·co·ma \tə'kōmə\ *adj, usu cap* [fr. *Tacoma*, Wash.] **:** of or from the city of Tacoma, Wash. **:** of the kind or style prevalent in Tacoma

ta·co·man \-mən\ *n* -S *cap* [*Tacoma*, Wash. + E *-an*] **:** a native or resident of Tacoma, Wash.

ta·con·ic \tə'känik\ *adj, usu cap* [fr. *Taconic* range, mountains in northeastern U.S.] **:** of or relating to mountain-making movements in northeastern No. America near the close of the Ordovician period — see GEOLOGIC TIME table

tac·o·nite \'takə,nīt\ *n* -S [*Taconic* range + E *-ite*] **:** a flintlike rock containing granules of iron oxide; *specif* **:** this rock when high enough in iron content to become commercially valuable as an ore

tact \'takt\ *n* -S [F, fr. L *tactus* sense of touch, fr. *tactus*, past part. of *tangere* to touch — more at TANGENT] **1 a** *archaic* **:** the sense of touch **:** FEELING ⟨sight is a very refined ~ —Joseph Le Conte⟩ **b :** a sensitive touch **:** SKILL ⟨must not be set to do work of a practical nature until he has shown ~ —Katharine S. Woods⟩ **2 :** sensitive mental or aesthetic perception **:** a nice feeling for refinements or subtle values **:** SENSITIVITY, TASTE ⟨the Venetians as a school were from the first endowed with exquisite ~ in their use of color —Bernhard Berenson⟩ ⟨precision and ~ of interpretation —Martin Price⟩ **3 :** a keen sense of what to do or say in a difficult or delicate situation in order to maintain good relations with others or avoid offense **:** CONSIDERATENESS, DIPLOMACY, DELICACY ⟨without the ~ to perceive when remarks were untimely —Thomas Hardy⟩ ⟨~ is an inestimable quality in a secretary —Harold

Croft⟩ ⟨his editing is a marvel of unobtrusive ~ —*N. Y. Herald Tribune Bk. Rev.*⟩

syn ADDRESS, POISE, SAVOIR FAIRE: TACT implies both skill and considerateness in dealings with others and esp. delicacy or sympathetic understanding in observing the feelings of others ⟨his vicar, who had so much *tact* with the natives, so much sympathy with all their shortcomings —Willa Cather⟩ ⟨hoping however that the matter would be handled with sufficient delicacy and *tact* to avoid breaking up the committee —A.L.Funk⟩ ⟨more than sufficient *tact* never to discuss either whiskeys or sermons in the wrong place —Arnold Bennett⟩ ADDRESS is more general than TACT in suggesting a general command, stressing the skill involved in creating a good impression when meeting strangers or in handling new or difficult situations, often implying adroitness or suavity ⟨tall, well formed, of remarkably fine *address*, ready in decision and prompt in action, a gentleman of heart and intellect whom both teachers and children respected —H.N.Sherwood⟩ ⟨if he expresses his judgments cogently and aims them with sufficient *address* at the critical conscience —F.R.Leavis⟩ POISE suggests a self-possession or equanimity that is preserved even under the stress of embarrassing or upsetting situations ⟨the appearance of self-possession or *poise* that comes from an habitual attention to what is graceful and becoming —D.C.Hodges⟩ ⟨recovers its dignity and *poise* and becomes once more a stately avenue of a waterborne commerce —Tom Marvel⟩ SAVOIR FAIRE carries the idea of a worldly experience that gives the skilled ability to handle all situations with tact and poise ⟨to her relief he took it with the *savoir faire* of a man of the world —*MacLean's Mag.*⟩ ⟨its technical know-how needs to be supplemented in the political field by some European *savoir faire* —Percy Winner⟩

tact·ful \ˈtaktfəl\ *adj* **:** showing tact: as **a :** marked by considerateness and appreciation of the feelings of others **:** DIPLOMATIC ⟨his ~ skill in negotiations —Vera M. Dean⟩ ⟨a ~ verdict . . . which awarded each claimant a similar amount —*Amer. Guide Series: Mass.*⟩ **b :** unobtrusively sympathetic and perceptive **:** SENSITIVE ⟨a ~ editor⟩ **c :** skillfully appropriate **:** FITTING ⟨the action in relation to the camera is always ~ —Parker Tyler⟩

tact·ful·ly \-fəlē, -li\ *adv* **:** in a tactful manner: as **a :** CONSIDERATELY, DIPLOMATICALLY ⟨terminate the acquaintance ~ —Agnes M. Miall⟩ **b :** with skillful appropriateness **:** ADROITLY ⟨an almost slangy everyday speech, ~ used to relieve the modern ear —Leslie Rees⟩

tact·ful·ness \-fəlnəs\ *n* -ES **:** the quality or state of being tactful **:** DIPLOMACY, SENSITIVITY ⟨the ~ demanded of a labor-management mediator⟩

¹tac·tic \ˈtaktik, -aktēk\ *adj* [NL *tacticus*, fr. Gk *taktikos* of order, of tactics, fit for arrangement — more at TACTICS] **1** *archaic* **:** of or relating to military or naval tactics **:** TACTICAL **2 a :** of or relating to arrangement or order **b :** regular in structure of repeating units in a polymer **3** [Gk *taktikos*] **:** of, relating to, or showing biological taxis

²tactic \"\ *n* -S [NL *tactica*, fr. Gk *taktikē*, fr. fem. of *taktikos*] **1 :** TACTICS **2 a :** a method of employing troops, ships, or aircraft in combat ⟨for taking such heavily fortified centers, encirclement is the customary ~ —Anna L. Strong⟩ **b :** a device or expedient for accomplishing an end **:** MANEUVER ⟨a delaying ~⟩ ⟨using the ~ of surprise⟩ ⟨a ~ for splitting the opposition⟩ ⟨set up a row of straw men and then knock them down . . . a standard ~ of the doctrinaire —Roderick Stephens⟩ ⟨think up six ~*s* to get that person to change the habit —Bennett Cerf⟩ ⟨the politician's ~*s* are determined by the way that your vote may be won —Volta Torrey⟩

³tactic \"\ *adj* [*tact* + *-ic*] **:** of or relating to touch **:** TACTUAL

-tac·tic \ˌtaktik, -aktēk\ *adj comb form* [Gk *taktikos*] **1 :** having an arrangement or pattern of ⟨chaeto*tactic*⟩ **2 :** showing orientation or movement directed by a (specified) force or agent ⟨geo*tactic*⟩ ⟨photo*tactic*⟩ **3 :** having an arrangement or pattern of a (specified) kind ⟨homo*tactic*⟩

tac·ti·cal \ˈtaktəkəl, -aktēk-\ *adj* [Gk *taktikos* + E *-al*] **1 :** of or relating to military tactics (as of air, sea, or ground forces): as **a :** involving actions or means (as equipment or plans) that are distinguished from those of strategy by being of less importance to the outcome of a war or of less magnitude or by taking place or going into effect at a shorter distance from a base of operations **b** *of an air force* (1) **:** designed for use in the battle area including air-to-air and air-to-surface action (2) **:** of or relating to air attack on the enemy in the battle line in support of friendly ground forces **c :** of or relating to combat functions or units as distinguished from those concerned with support or administration **d :** of or relating to the activities concerned with military drill as distinguished from the technical activities on a training base **2 a :** of or relating to tactics generally **:** designed to achieve a given purpose ⟨made a ~ error⟩ ⟨regard such negotiations as ~ maneuvers —R.H.S.Crossman⟩: as (1) **:** of or relating to the planning or execution of small-scale actions as part of a larger purpose ⟨the big gains . . . count, not the little ~ advances —*Nation's Business*⟩ ⟨played excellent ~ tennis⟩ (2) **:** made or carried out with only a limited or immediate end in view **:** designed to gain a temporary advantage **:** SHORT-RANGE, OPPORTUNISTIC ⟨~ decisions⟩ ⟨think . . . they are merely forming a ~ alliance —Edmond Taylor⟩ ⟨~, makeshift policies —Joel Carmichael⟩ (3) **:** designed as a necessary or prudent temporary adjustment to unfavorable conditions **:** EXPEDIENT ⟨has only made a ~ withdrawal, not given up —Claire Sterling⟩ **b :** marked by skill in tactics **:** adroit in planning or maneuvering to accomplish a purpose **:** POLITIC ⟨a ~ statesman⟩ ⟨their ~ treatment of American politics —D.W.Brogan⟩ **3 :** of or relating to tactics, tagmemes, or taxemes in linguistics

tactical diameter *n* **:** the perpendicular distance between a ship's course when the helm is put hard over and its course when she has turned through 180 degrees

tac·ti·cal·ly \-aktək(ə)lē, -tēk-, -li\ *adv* **1 :** in a tactical manner ⟨handled his Army Corps ~ —*Current History*⟩ **2 :** in terms of or with regard to tactics ⟨finds it ~ convenient to encourage the spread of this belief —G.F.Hudson⟩ **3 :** with regard to the study of tactics in linguistics ⟨~ equivalent to two or more morphemic categories —W.L.Wonderly⟩

tactical radius *n* **:** the distance an aircraft can fly and return to its base with its load under existing weather conditions and fill other operating requirements of a particular mission

tactical range *n* **:** the distance that an aircraft can fly in one general direction under combat conditions — compare RANGE

tactical unit *n* **:** an organization of troops designed to function as a single unit in combat; *specif* **:** the organizational unit (as an infantry battalion or a cavalry squadron) in any arm of the service upon which the tactical instruction of that particular arm is based

tac·ti·cian \takˈtishən\ *n* -S [F *tacticien*, fr. *tactique* tactics, after such pairs as F *mathématique* mathematics: *mathématicien* mathematician] **:** one versed in tactics **:** a skillful maneuverer ⟨the wily ~, with a keen eye for electioneering advantage —Alexander Brady⟩; *specif* **:** one skilled in military tactics ⟨a brilliant ~ in armored warfare with a poor grasp of the grand strategy⟩

tac·tic·i·ty \takˈtisəd·ē\ *n* -ES **:** the quality or state of being stereochemically tactic

tac·tics \ˈtaktiks, -aktēks\ *n pl* [NL *tactica*, pl., fr. Gk *taktika*, fr. neut. pl. of *taktikos* of order, of tactics, fit for arranging, fr. *taktos* (verbal of *tassein*, *tattein* to arrange, order, place in battle formation) + *-ikos* -ic; akin to TochA *tāṣṣi* commanders, Lith *patogus* comfortable, respectable, Latvian *patāgs* comfortable; basic meaning: to arrange] **1** *usu sing in constr* **a :** the science and art of disposing and maneuvering troops, ships, or aircraft in relation to each other and the enemy and of employing them in combat ⟨strategy wins wars; ~ wins battles —*Plane Talk*⟩ ⟨~ . . . requires concentration of troops —S.O.Fuqua⟩ **b :** the art or skill of employing available forces with an end in view ⟨devising . . . a ~ of power —John Buchan⟩ **2** *usu pl in constr* **:** a system or mode of procedure **:** METHOD ⟨the bullying ~ of the prosecuting attorney⟩ ⟨their ~ demoralize the industry —*N.Y.Times*⟩ **3** *sing or pl in constr* **:** the study of the grammatical relations within a language including morphology and syntax; *esp* **:** the study of the structure of combinations of morphemes into larger constructions as to order, selection of allomorphs, agreement, and concurrent stress, pitch, and rhythm patterns

¹tac·tile \ˈtaktᵊl, -k,tīl, -k(,)til\ *adj* [F or L; F, fr. L *tactilis*, fr. *tactus* (past part. of *tangere* to touch) + *-ilis* -ile — more at TANGENT] **1 :** perceptible by the touch **:** capable of being felt or touched **:** TANGIBLE ⟨~ qualities⟩ ⟨slide rule for sightless individuals employs ~ symbols —*Scientific Monthly*⟩ **2 a :** of or relating to the sense of touch **:** TACTUAL ⟨~ sensitivity⟩ ⟨~ sensuality⟩ ⟨the ~ sensations he gets manipulating the controls —Herbert Mitgang⟩ **b :** having the sense of touch **:** used in touching ⟨fingers ~ as antennae —Marcia Davenport⟩ ⟨~ organs⟩ **c :** affecting the sense of touch ⟨~ anesthesia⟩ **3 :** depending on the sense of touch (as for orientation) ⟨corals and sea anemones have an almost purely ~ contact with their environment⟩ **4 :** appealing by synesthesia to the sense of touch ⟨how extraordinarily ~ the verses are —Dudley Fitts⟩

²tactile \"\ *n* -S **:** one whose prevailing mental imagery is tactile rather than visual, auditory, or motor — compare AUDILE, MOTILE, VISUALIZER

tactile cell *n* **:** one of the oval nucleated cells that are situated in close contact with the expanded ends of nerve fibers in the deeper layers of the epidermis and dermis of some parts of the body and prob. serve a tactile function

tactile corpuscle *n* **:** one of the numerous minute bodies in the skin and some mucous membranes that usu. consist of a group of cells enclosed in a capsule, contain nerve terminations, and are held to be end organs of touch

tactile disk *n* **:** MERKEL'S CELL

tactile hair *n* **:** a hair or hairlike structure sensitive to touch occurring in various groups of animals

tactile receptor *n* **:** an end organ that responds to light touch

tac·til·ist \ˈtaktələst, -k,tīl-\ *n* -S **:** a painter emphasizing tactile values

tac·til·i·ty \takˈtiləd·ē, -lətē, -i\ *n* -ES **:** the quality or state of being tactile: as **a :** the capability of being felt or touched **:** TANGIBILITY **b :** responsiveness to stimulation of the sense of touch **:** tactile sensitivity

tac·tion \ˈtakshən\ *n* -S [L *taction-*, *tactio*, fr. *tactus* (past part. of *tangere* to touch) + *-ion-*, *-io* -ion — more at TANGENT] **:** the act of touching **:** TOUCH, CONTACT ⟨being roused by some external ~ upon the organs of speech and hearing —Jonathan Swift⟩

tac·tism \ˈtak,tizəm\ *n* -S [ISV *tact-* (fr. Gk *taktos*, verbal of *tassein*, *tattein* to arrange, order) + *-ism* — more at TACTICS] **:** TAXIS 2

tac·tite \ˈtak,tīt\ *n* -S [L *tactus* (past part. of *tangere* to touch) + E *-ite* — more at TANGENT] **:** a contact-metamorphosed carbonate rock (as limestone) containing crystalline silicate minerals (as garnet, diopside, or vesuvianite)

tact·less \ˈtak(t)ləs\ *adj* **:** marked by a lack of tact: as **a :** INCONSIDERATE, UNDIPLOMATIC ⟨~, forever lugging in disagreeable truths —V.L.Parrington⟩ **b :** BLUNT ⟨the canals are sewers and, in ~ truth, they smell —Claudia Cassidy⟩ **c :** INEPT ⟨their ~ handling of the situation —E.E.Shipton⟩

tact·less·ly *adv* **:** in a tactless manner

tact·less·ness *n* -ES **:** the quality or state of being tactless

tac·toid \ˈtak,tȯid\ *n* -S [ISV *tact-* (fr. Gk *taktos*, verbal of *tassein*, *tattein* to arrange, order) + *-oid* — more at TACTICS] **:** an elongated particle (as in vanadium pentoxide sol, tobacco mosaic virus, myosin, or fibrin) that appears as a spindle-shaped body under the polarizing microscope and occurs in a tactosol — compare COACERVATE

tac·tom·e·ter \takˈtäməd·ə(r)\ *n* [L *tactus* sense of touch + E *-o-* + *-meter* — more at TACT] **:** an instrument for testing and measuring the acuteness of the sense of touch

tac·tor \ˈtaktə(r)\ *n* -S [NL, fr. LL, one that touches, fr. L *tactus* (past part. of *tangere* to touch) + *-or* — more at TANGENT] **:** a tactile organ (as an antenna or a tactile corpuscle)

tac·to·receptor \ˌtak(,)tō+\ *n* [L *tactus* sense of touch + E *-o-* + *receptor*] **:** TACTILE RECEPTOR

tac·to·sol \ˈtaktə,sōl, -sȯl\ *n* -S [ISV *tacto-* (fr. Gk *taktos*) + *sol*; orig. formed as G *taktosol*] **:** a sol containing tactoids arranged spontaneously on aging in parallel order

tacts *pl of* TACT

tac·tual \ˈtakchəwəl, -ksh-\ *adj* [L *tactus* sense of touch + E *-al*] **:** of or relating to the sense or the organs of touch **:** derived from or producing the sensation of touch **:** TACTILE ⟨a ~ sense⟩ ⟨~ tests⟩ ⟨the ~ luxury of stroking human hair —F.R. Leavis⟩

tac·tu·al·ly \-wəlē\ *adv* **:** in a tactual manner **:** by means of touch ⟨test a fabric ~⟩

ta·cu·ba·ya \ˌtäküˈbīə\ *adj, usu cap* [fr. *Tacubaya*, Mexico] **:** of or from the city of Tacubaya, Mexico **:** of the kind or style prevalent in Tacubaya

tad \ˈtad\ *n* -S [prob. fr. E dial., toad, fr. ME *tade*, *tadde*, *tode* — more at TOAD] **:** BOY ⟨film . . . that will give any ~ his fill of action —John McCarten⟩

ta·dar·i·da \təˈdarədə\ *n, cap* [NL] **:** a nearly cosmopolitan genus of small brown free-tailed bats of the family Molossidae — see POCKETED BAT

tad·dick \ˈtadik\ *South var of* TODDICK 2

tadjik *usu cap, var of* TAJIK

tad·pole \ˈtad,pōl\ *n* -S [ME *taddepol*, fr. *tade*, *tadde*, *tode* toad + *pol* head — more at TOAD, POLL] **1 :** a larval amphibian; *specif* **:** a frog or toad larva that at hatching has a rounded body with a long fin-bordered tail and external gills soon replaced by internal gills and that subsequently undergoes a metamorphosis in which limbs and lungs are developed, adult body proportions are attained, and the tail and gills are lost **2 :** a minute tadpole-shaped larva of an ascidian **3** *usu cap* **:** MISSISSIPPIAN — used as a nickname

tadpole madtom *n* **:** a common widely distributed madtom (*Schilbeodes mollis*)

tadpole shrimp *n* **:** a notostracan crustacean esp. of the genus *Triops*

tadzhik *usu cap, var of* TAJIK

¹tae \tə, (ˈ)tā\ *Scot var of* TO

²tae \ˈtā\ *Scot var of* TOE

taedium *var of* TEDIUM

tae·di·um vi·tae \ˌtēdēəmˈvī,tē, -mˈwē,tī; ˌtīdēəmˈwē,tī\ *n* [L] **:** weariness or loathing of life **:** intense discontent

tae·gu \(ˈ)taˌgü, (ˈ)tāˈgü\ *adj, usu cap* [fr. *Taegu*, Korea] **:** of or from the city of Taegu, Korea **:** of the kind or style prevalent in Taegu

tae·jon \(ˈ)taˌjän, (ˈ)tāˌj-\ *adj, usu cap* [fr. *Taejon*, Korea] **:** of or from the city of Taejon, Korea **:** of the kind or style prevalent in Taejon

tael *or* **tale** \ˈtā(ə)l\ *n* -S [Pg *tael*, fr. Malay *tahil*, a weight, tael, prob. fr. Hindi *tolā* weight of a sicca rupee, fr. Skt *tulā* balance, scale, weight — more at TOLERATE] **1 :** any of various units of weight of eastern Asia; *esp* **:** LIANG **2 :** any of various Chinese units of value based on the value of a tael weight of silver — see HAIKWAN TAEL, KUPING TAEL

taen- *or* **taeni-** *or* **taenio-** *comb form* [L *taenia*] **1 :** ribbon **:** fillet ⟨*taeni*ate⟩ ⟨*taenio*donta⟩ **2 :** tapeworm ⟨*taeni*asis⟩ ⟨*taeni*cide⟩ ⟨*taeni*fuge⟩

tae·nia \ˈtēnēə, -nyə\ *n* [L, fr. Gk *tainia*; akin to Gk *teinein* to stretch — more at THIN] **1** *pl* **taenias :** an ancient Greek fillet **2** *also* **te·nia** \ˈtēnēə, -nyə\ *pl* **taeni·ae** \-nē,ē\ *or* **taenias** *also* **tenias :** a band on a Doric order separating the frieze from the architrave **3** *also* **tenia** *pl* **taeniae** *or* **taenias** *also* **tenias** [NL, fr. L] **:** a band of nervous tissue or muscle **4 a** *also* **tenia** *pl* **taenias** *also* **tenias :** TAPEWORM **b** *cap* [NL, fr. L] **:** a genus (the type of the family Taeniidae) of cyclophyllidean tapeworms including the common beef and pork tapeworms of man and numerous other forms usu. occurring as adults in the intestines of carnivores and as larvae in various ruminants

tae·nia·ci·dal *also* **te·nia·ci·dal** \ˌtēnēəˈsīdᵊl, -nyə-\ *adj* [*taeniacide*, *teniacide* + *-al*] **1 :** destroying tapeworms **2 :** of, relating to, or being a taeniacide

tae·nia·cide *also* **te·nia·cide** \ˈtēnēə,sīd, -nyə-\ *n* -S [*taeniacide* fr. *taenia* + *-cide*; *teniacide* alter. of *taeniacide*] **:** an agent that destroys tapeworms

taenia co·li \-ˈkō,lī\ *n, pl* **taeniae coli** [NL, lit., band of the colon] **:** any of three external longitudinal muscle bands of the large intestine

tae·ni·a·da \tēˈnīədə; ˌtēnēˈädə, -ˈādə\ [NL, irreg. fr. *Taenia* + *-ida*] *syn of* CESTOIDEA

tae·ni·a·dea \ˌtēnēˈādēə\ [NL, irreg. fr. *Taenia* + *-idea*] *syn of* CYCLOPHYLLIDEA

tae·nia·fuge *also* **te·nia·fuge** \ˈtēnēə,fyüj, -nyə-\ *n* -S [*taeniafuge* fr. *taenia* + *-fuge*; *teniafuge* alter. of *taeniafuge*] **:** a tapeworm expellant

tae·nia·rhyn·chus \ˌ==ˈriŋkəs\ *n, cap* [NL, fr. *Taenia* + *-rhynchus*] *in some classifications* **:** a genus of tapeworms comprising the beef tapeworm of man

tae·ni·a·sis *also* **te·ni·a·sis** \tēˈnīəsəs\ *n* -ES [NL, fr. *taen-* + *-iasis*] **:** infestation with or disease caused by tapeworms

tae·ni·ate \ˈtēnē,āt, -nēət\ *adj* [*taen-* + *-ate*] **:** longitudinally striped

tae·nid·i·al \tēˈnidēəl\ *adj* [NL *taenidium* + E *-al*] **:** of, relating to, or having the characteristics of a taenidium ⟨~ ridges⟩

tae·nid·i·um \-dēəm\ *n, pl* **taenid·ia** \-dēə\ [NL, fr. Gk *tainidion* small ribbon, dim. of *tainia*] **:** a spiral sclerotized fiber that stiffens the walls of the tracheae of insects

¹tae·ni·id \ˈtēnēəd\ *adj* [NL *Taeniidae*] **:** of or relating to the Taeniidae

²taeniid \"\ *n* -S **:** a tapeworm of the family Taeniidae

tae·ni·idae \tēˈnīə,dē\ *n pl, cap* [NL, fr. *Taenia*, type genus + *-idae*] **:** a large family of tapeworms (order Cyclophyllidea) including numerous worms of medical or veterinary importance — see TAENIA 4b

taenio- — see TAEN-

tae·nio·bran·chia \ˌtēnēōˈbraŋkēə\ [NL, fr. *taen-* + *-branchia*] *syn of* THALIACEA

tae·ni·odont \ˈtēnēə,dänt\ *n* -S [NL *Taeniodonta*] **:** a mammal or fossil of the order Taeniodonta

tae·ni·odon·ta \ˌ===ˈdäntə\ *n pl, cap* [NL, fr. *taen-* + *-odonta*] **:** an order of No. American Paleocene and Eocene mammals related to the edentates but distinguished by molars with roots and enamel

tae·ni·odon·tia \-ˈdänch(ē)ə\ [NL, fr. *taen-* + *-odontia* (irreg. fr. *odont-*, *odōn* tooth) — more at TOOTH] *syn of* TAENIODONTA

tae·nio·glos·sa \ˌtenēōˈgläsə, -lȯsə\ *n pl, cap* [NL, fr. *taen-* + *-glossa*] **:** a large suborder of Pectinibranchia comprising marine and freshwater gastropod mollusks in which the odontophore is long and narrow and usu. bears seven teeth in each transverse row — compare HETEROPODA, PLATYPODA — **tae·nio·glos·sate** \-sət, -ˌsāt\ *adj or n*

tae·ni·oid \ˈtēnē,ȯid\ *adj* [*taen-* + *-oid*] **:** resembling or related to the Taeniidae

tae·ni·o·in·ei \ˌtēnēōˈinē,ī\ [NL, fr. *Taenia*] *syn of* ¹CESTOIDEA

tae·ni·op·ter·is \ˌtēnēˈäptərəs\ *n, cap* [NL, fr. *taen-* + *-pteris*] **:** a genus of fossil ferns or cycad ferns found in Mesozoic or Late Paleozoic strata and characterized by ribbon-shaped pinnae and usu. pinnately arranged veins or veinlike structures

tae·nio·some \ˈtēnēə,sōm\ *n* -S [NL *Taeniosomi*] **:** a fish of the suborder Taeniosomi

tae·nio·so·mi \ˌ===ˈsō,mī\ *n pl, cap* [NL, fr. *taen-* + *-somi* (fr. Gk *sōma* body) — more at -SOMA] *in some classifications* **:** a suborder of Allotriognathi containing the oarfishes and dealfishes

tae·nio·so·mous \ˌ===ˈsōməs\ *adj* [NL *Taeniosomi* + E *-ous*] **:** of, relating to, or resembling the Taeniosomi

tae·nio·thrips \ˈtēnēə,thrips\ *n, cap* [NL, fr. *taen-* + *thrips*] **:** a widely distributed genus of thrips — see GLADIOLUS THRIPS, PEAR THRIPS

tae·nite \ˈtē,nīt\ *n* -S [G *tänit*, fr. *tän-* taen- + *-it* -ite] **:** a mineral consisting of a nickel-iron alloy that forms with kamacite the mass of most meteoric iron

taen·sa \ˈten,sȯ, tä'en-\ *n, pl* **taensa** *or* **taensas** *usu cap* [fr. *Taensas*, a village of the Taensa people] *cap* **1 a :** a Natchesan people of northeastern Louisiana **b :** a member of such people **2 :** the language of the Taensa people

TAF *abbr* tactical air force

taf·fe·ta \ˈtafəd·|ə, -fət|\ *also* **taf·fe·ty** \|ē, |i\ *or* **taf·fa·ta** \|ə\ *n, pl* **taffetas** *also* **taffeties** *or* **taffatas** [ME, *taffeta*, *taffata*, fr. MF *taffetas*, fr. OIt *taffettà*, fr. Turk *tafta*, fr. Per *tāftah* woven, spun, fr. *tāftan* to spin] **1 :** a crisp plain-woven fabric with a fine cross rib and a smooth lustrous surface on both sides that is woven of various fibers (as silk, linen, rayon) and used esp. for women's clothing **2 :** a yellow greaseproof film of cellulose used as a covering (as for greased areas or moist surgical dressings)

taffeta weave *n* **:** PLAIN WEAVE

taf·fe·tized \-fə,tīzd\ *adj, of cloth* **:** having a crisp finish ⟨standout value among ~ cottons —*Women's Wear Daily*⟩

taff·rail \ˈtafrəl; ˈta,frāl, ˈtai,f-\ *also* **taf·fer·el** \ˈtaf(ə)rəl\ *n* -S [*taffrail* alter. (influenced by *rail*) of *tafferel*; *tafferel* fr. D *tafereel*, fr. MD, picture, fr. OF *tablel* picture, tableau — more at TABLEAU] **1 :** the upper flat part of the stern of a wooden ship often ornamented with carvings **2 :** a rail around the stern of a ship

taffrail log *n* **:** a log that is mounted on the taffrail of a ship and consists of a rotator, log line, and recording device — compare HARPOON LOG

¹taf·fy \ˈtafē, ˈtaif-, -fi *also* ˈtaaf-\ *n* -ES [origin unknown] **1 :** a candy made usu. of molasses or brown sugar boiled until caramelized and pulled until porous and light-colored **2 :** insincere flattery or wheedling ⟨just giving him ~ . . . but he did not know —G.H.Devol⟩ **3 :** WALNUT BROWN

²taffy \"\ *n* -ES *usu cap* [modif. of W *Dafydd* David, a common Welsh Christian name] *slang* **:** WELSHMAN

taffy pull *n* **:** a social gathering at which taffy is made

taf·ia \ˈtafēə\ *n* -S [F, fr. West Indian Creole, alter. of *ratafia*] **:** an inferior rum made esp. from distilled sugarcane juice in the West Indies

¹tag \ˈtag, -aa(ə)-, -ai-\ *n* -S [ME *tagge*, prob. of Scand. origin; akin to Sw & Norw *tagg* barb, prickle; perh. akin to MLG *tacke* pointed instrument, sharp point — more at TACK] **1 :** a loose hanging piece of cloth **:** TATTER, RAG **2 :** a metal or plastic ferrule on an end of a shoelace for facilitating passage through an eyelet **3 :** a piece of material hanging from or attached to something: as **a :** a loop, knot, or tassel on a garment ⟨their long-plumed hats and . . . endless ~*s* and aiglets and rosettes —Austin Dobson⟩ **b :** a large lock of soiled and matted wool **c :** a strip of parchment attached to a deed for bearing a seal **d** (1) **:** a shred of flesh or muscle (2) **:** a small abnormal projecting piece of tissue esp. when potentially or actually neoplastic in character **e :** a shred of metal adhering to a casting **4 :** the tip of an animal's tail; *specif* **:** the white tip of a fox's tail **5 a :** material added as ornamentation or explanation to something written or spoken ⟨~*s* provided a moral framework for the play —Muriel C. Bradbrook⟩ **b** (1) **:** a brief quotation used for rhetorical emphasis or sententious effect ⟨in the great days of . . . empire building, Latin ~*s* were on the lips of the builders —D.W.Brogan⟩ ⟨dotes on . . . spellbinding oratory stuffed with big words . . . and Latin ~*s* —*Newsweek*⟩ ⟨famous Popian ~ —Donald Davie⟩ (2) **:** a hackneyed saying or quotation **:** CLICHÉ, SAW ⟨the trite ~ . . . that wars are declared by the wicked and fought by the virtuous —Herbert Agar⟩ ⟨could hardly open his mouth without using one or other of his ~*s* —Samuel Butler †1902⟩ **c :** TAGLINE 1 **d :** a rhyming end of a line of verse **e :** a closing usu. improvised phrase in a jazz piece — compare CODA **f :** a recurrent characteristic verbal expression ⟨characters with mannerisms and ~*s* of speech parade through the novel —E.R. Davis⟩ **g :** a word or phrase acting as an interrogative increment to a question ⟨the ~ *isn't it* in "it's fine, isn't it?"⟩ **6 a** (1) **:** a marker made usu. of cardboard, plastic, or metal and used for identification or classification ⟨a ~ pinned to his lapel, bearing his name and destination —*Current Biog.*⟩ ⟨a string shipping ~ slipped through a loop in the handle is used instead of the gummed label —Elizabeth Golterman⟩ — see DOG TAG, LICENSE PLATE, PRICE TAG (2) **:** TAGBOARD **b :** a word or phrase used as an often superficial description or identification **:** LABEL, EPITHET ⟨to the name of murderess would be added the ~ of ingrate —Grace Metalious⟩ ⟨*social behaviorist* is the ~ that has remained on him —Maurice Natanson⟩ **7 :** a small piece of tinsel or other bright material encircling the shank of the hook at the end of the body of an artificial fly — see FLY illustration **8 :** a detached fragmentary piece of something **:** VESTIGE ⟨the few ~*s* and oddments I was able to hold on to, and treasure up in memory —Thomas Wood †1950⟩ **9 :** a document notifying an automobile

owner of having committed a traffic violation **:** TICKET ⟨been putting ~*s* on the car at twenty-minute intervals —Erle Stanley Gardner⟩ **10 :** LABEL 9

²tag \"\ *vb* **tagged; tagged; tagging; tags** [ME *taggen*, fr. *tagge*, n.] *vt* **1 :** to provide or mark with or as if with a tag: as **a :** to supply with an identifying marker ⟨took a week to ~ every item in the store⟩ **b** (1) **:** to provide with a verbal tag ⟨~*s* his speeches with poetry —*Examiner*⟩ (2) **:** to provide with a name or epithet **:** LABEL, IDENTIFY, BRAND ⟨one might ~ this book traditional —William Nicoll⟩ ⟨the trick is always to ~ the other fellow as . . . left-wing —T.H.White b. 1915⟩ ⟨study of what have perhaps been loosely *tagged* as guilt patterns —Abraham Edel⟩ ⟨~ with an unfavorable word the pursuit of human desires —F.L.Mott⟩ **c :** to put a ticket on for a traffic violation ⟨cars *tagged* for obstructing traffic —J.C.Ingraham⟩ **2 a** *obs* **:** to fasten together **:** CONJOIN **b :** to link together esp. with rhymes **3 :** to attach as an addition **:** JOIN, APPEND ⟨*tagged* to our name all the opprobrious epithets the English language supplies —Thomas Campbell⟩ ⟨the general theory . . . *tagged* on at the end seems a little forced —Rayner Heppenstall⟩ **4 :** to clear (a sheep) of tags of wool **5 :** to follow closely and persistently **:** DOG, TAIL, TRAIL ⟨~*s* his big brothers around —John Bird⟩ ⟨a huge hammerhead shark . . . was *tagging* me —H.A.Chippendale⟩ **6 :** to hold responsible for something **:** SADDLE ⟨is *tagged* with the . . . defeat —Gordon Harrison⟩: as **a :** to charge with a violation of the law ⟨was *tagged* by . . . Michigan cops for driving through a stop signal —*Best True Fact Detective*⟩ ⟨was *tagged* for . . . assault —Burt Woolis⟩ **b :** to charge (a pitcher) with defeat in baseball ⟨made two more runs in the eighth to ~ him with his first setback of the season⟩ **7 :** to fix the price of ⟨decided to ~ the picture at $100⟩ **8 a :** LABEL 2 ⟨~ penicillin molecules with radioactive sulfur as tracer⟩ **b :** to distinguish (as a part of a living organism or the organism as a whole) by introducing a labeled atom ⟨the donors' red cells became *tagged* by the radioactive iron atoms in the hemoglobin molecules of the red cells —R.D. Evans⟩ **~** *vi* **:** to keep close **:** stay close at hand ⟨first honeymoon I ever knew where a mother-in-law *tagged* —W.A. White⟩ ⟨*tagged* after her, glancing over her shoulder —Hamilton Basso⟩ ⟨inclined to crash parties or ~ onto older groups —Elizabeth Bowen⟩ ⟨two unarmed launches *tagged* behind —Joseph Millard⟩ ⟨a spaniel *tagging* at their heels —Corey Ford⟩ **syn** see FOLLOW

³tag \"\ *n* -s [origin unknown] **1 :** a game in which one player chases the others and tries to touch one to make him it **2 :** an act or instance of tagging a runner in baseball ⟨put the ~ on him as he slid into third⟩

⁴tag \"\ *vt* **tagged; tagged; tagging; tags 1 a :** to touch in or as if in a game of tag ⟨runs . . . around the outside of the circle and ~*s* another as he goes —Ruth McIntire⟩ **b :** to put out (a runner in baseball) by a touch with the ball or the gloved hand in which the ball is held — often used with *out* ⟨*tagged* him out on a steal of home⟩ **2 a :** to hit solidly **:** STRIKE ⟨*tagged* his opponent on the jaw twice in the first round⟩ ⟨was almost *tagged* by passing cars —James Thurber⟩ **b :** to hit (a baseball) with a bat **3 :** to choose esp. for a special purpose **:** SELECT, PICK ⟨peacetime equipment . . . would be *tagged* for civil defense use —R.W.Stokley⟩ ⟨two years at the forestry school . . . before the Army *tagged* him —Nard Jones⟩ **4 :** to make a hit or a run off (a pitcher) in baseball ⟨*tagged* him for three runs in the second inning⟩

TAG *abbr* the adjutant general

ta·ga·bi·li \ˌtägəˈbēlē\ *n, pl* **tagabili** *or* **tagabilis** *usu cap* [Cebuan, fr. Tagabili *Tabili*] **1 a :** a people of southern Mindanao in the Philippines **b :** a member of such people **2 :** an Austronesian language of the Tagabili people

ta·ga·kao·lo \ˌtägəˈkau̇(ˌ)lō\ *n, pl* **tagakaolo** *or* **tagakaolos** *usu cap* **1 a :** a people of southwestern Mindanao in the Philippines **b :** a member of such people **2 :** an Austronesian language of the Tagakaolo people

ta·gal \təˈgäl\ *n* -s [prob. fr. Sp *tagalo* Tagalog] **:** a straw braid made from Manila hemp and used for hats

ta·ga·la \təˈgälə\ *n* -s *usu cap* [Sp, fem. of *tagalo* Tagalog, fr. Tag *Tagalog*] **:** a subgroup of Austronesian languages of the Philippines — used in former classifications

tag alder *n* [¹*tag*] **:** any of several American alders: as **a :** SPECKLED ALDER **b :** RED ALDER 1

ta·ga·log \təˈgäləg, -gȧl-, -ˌlȯg, -ˌläg\ *n, pl* **tagalog** *or* **tagalogs** *usu cap* [Tag] **1 a :** a people of central Luzon in the Philippines **b :** a member of such people **2 :** an Austronesian language of the Tagalog people that is the official national language of the Republic of the Philippines — called also *Filipino language*

tag along *vi* [²*tag*] **:** to follow another's lead **:** go in company with another ⟨the biggest first and the smallest *tagging along* frantically in the rear —Alan Moorehead⟩ ⟨got in by *tagging along* with the assistant D.A. and posing as his aide —*Current Biog.*⟩

tagalong \ˈ≈ₑ≈\ *n* -s [*tag along*] **:** one that persistently and often annoyingly follows the lead of another ⟨felt honored to be a ~ tolerated by the older boys —Jay Edwards⟩

tag and rag *n* **:** RAG, TAG, AND BOBTAIL ⟨shout of *tag and rag*, and march of rank and file —Robert Southey⟩

ta·gan·rog \ˈtaganˌräg, ˈtäg-, -rȯg\ |k, ˌ≈≈ˈ≈\ *adj, usu cap* [fr. *Taganrog*, U.S.S.R.] **:** of or from the city of Taganrog, U.S.S.R. **:** of the kind or style prevalent in Taganrog

ta·ga·sas·te \ˌtägəˈsästē\ *n* -s [Sp] **:** a shrub (*Cytisus proliferus*) of the Canary islands that yields cattle fodder

tag·a·tose \ˈtagəˌtōs *also* -ōz\ *n* -s [alter. of *galactose*] **:** a crystalline sugar $C_6H_{12}O_6$ of the ketohexose class found naturally in the D-form (as in gum from a West African tree *Sterculia setigera*) and also obtainable from galactose by treatment with dilute alkali

ta·gaur \təˈgau̇(ə)r\ *n, pl* **tagaur** *or* **tagaurs** *usu cap* **1 :** an Indo-European people living in the central Caucasus and speaking an Ossetic dialect **2 :** a member of the Tagaur people

tag·ba·nu·wa \ˌtäg(ˌ)bänəˈwä\ *also* **tag·ba·nua** *n, pl* **tagbanuwa** *or* **tagbanuwas** *also* **tagbanua** *or* **tagbanuas** *usu cap* **1 a :** a people of Palawan in the Philippines **b :** a member of such people **2 :** an Austronesian language of the Tagbanuwa people

tagboard \ˈ≈ₑ≈\ *n* [¹*tag* + *board*] **:** strong cardboard used esp. for making tags

tag dance *n* [³*tag*] **:** a ballroom dance in which a man may cut in on a couple by touching the other man on the shoulder

tag day *n* [¹*tag*] **:** a day on which contributions are solicited (as for a charity) and small tags are given in return

tag end *n* [¹*tag*] **1 :** the last part of something **:** TAIL END ⟨born at the *tag end* of the eighteenth century —S.H.Adams⟩ ⟨at the *tag end* of nearly every long . . . party —John Cheever⟩ **2 :** a miscellaneous or random fragment of something — usu. used in pl. ⟨*tag ends* of memories bob up unexpectedly —*Dial*⟩

tage·tes \ˈtajəˌtēz, təˈjed·(ˌ)ēz\ *n* [NL, prob. after *Tages*, an ancient Etruscan deity] **1** *cap* **:** a genus of strong-scented tropical American herbs (family Compositae) having opposite pinnatifid leaves and showy heads of flowers with yellow or orange rays — see MARIGOLD 1b **2** *pl* **tagetes** \"\ any plant of the genus *Tagetes*

tag·e·tone \ˈtajəˌtōn\ *n* -s [NL *Tagetes* (genus name of *Tagetes minuta*) + E *-one*] **:** a pale yellow oily unsaturated ketone $C_{10}H_{16}O$ obtained from a So. American marigold (*Tagetes minuta*)

tagged \ˈtagd, -aa(ə)-,-ai-\ *adj* [ME, fr. *tagge* tag + *-ed* — more at TAG] **:** having, bearing, or marked with a tag or label; *esp* **:** matted into tags (as of wool)

tagged atom *n* **:** a radioactive isotope or isotope of unusual mass useful as a tracer

tag·ger \-gə(r)\ *n* -s **:** one that tags

tagging *pres part of* TAG

tag·gy \-gē,-gi\ *adj* -ER/-EST [¹*tag* + *-y*] **:** full of or matted into tags (as of wool)

tagh·lik \ˈtäglik\ *n, pl* **taghlik** *or* **taghliks** *usu cap* **1 :** a people of western Tibet **2 :** a member of the Taghlik people

tag·i·lite \ˈtagəˌlīt, təˈgi,l-\ *n* -s [G *tagilith*, fr. (*Nizhni*) *Tagil*, Sverdlovsk region, U.S.S.R., its locality + G *-lith* -lite] **:** a mineral $Cu_2(PO_4)(OH).H_2O$ consisting of a hydrous basic copper phosphate and occurring in bright green reniform masses (hardness 3–4, sp. gr. 4.1)

ta·gish \təˈgash\ *n, pl* **tagish** *or* **tagishes** *usu cap* [fr. *Tagish* lake, B.C., Canada] **1 a :** an Athapascan people of Yukon Territory and British Columbia **b :** a member of such people **2 :** a language of the Tagish people

ta·glia·ri·ni \ˌtalyəˈrēnē\ *n* -s [It, fr. *tagliare* to cut (fr. LL *taliare*) + *-ini* (pl. of *-ino* -ine, fr. L *-inus*) — more at TAILOR] **:** an alimentary paste in flat ribbon form

tag line *n* [¹*tag*] **1 a :** a final line (as in a play, story, joke); *esp* **:** one that serves to clarify a point or create a dramatic effect ⟨always hesitated before delivering the *tag line* that stunned the audience⟩ **b :** a reiterated phrase identified with an individual, group, or product **:** SLOGAN, CATCHWORD ⟨song lyrics, jokes . . . and performers' *tag lines* became . . . part of the whole country's stock of knowledge —Joe Laurie⟩ ⟨never wrote a *tag line* that didn't sell⟩ **2 :** a cable running from a crane boom to a bucket for steadying the bucket

ta·gli·o·ni \talˈyōnē\ *n* -s [after Filippo *Taglioni* †1871 Ital. ballet master] **:** an overcoat worn in the early 19th century

taglock \ˈ≈ₑ≈\ *n* [¹*tag* + *lock*] **:** a matted or tangled lock of hair or wool **:** DAGLOCK

tag·ma \ˈtagmə\ *n, pl* **tagma·ta** \-məd·ə\ [NL, fr. Gk *tagma* arrangement, order, row, fr. *tassein, tattein* to arrange — more at TACTICS] **:** a compound body section of an arthropod resulting from embryonic fusion of two or more somites (as the cephalothorax of a spider) or consisting of two or more distinguishable segments (as the thorax of an insect)

tag·man \ˈtagˌman, -ˌmən\ *n, pl* **tagmen** [¹*tag* + *man*] **:** a construction worker who handles the guide lines on loads to be hoisted or lowered

tag match *n* [³*tag*] **:** a wrestling match between two tag teams

tag·meme \ˈtagˌmēm, ˈtaig-\ *n* -s [Gk *tagma* arrangement, order, row + E *-eme*] **1 :** a constituent of a meaningful grammatical relation that cannot be analyzed into smaller meaningful features and that may be marked by features of word order, selection of allomorphs, agreement with finite verb forms, and elaboration by preceding adjectival modifiers **2 :** the class of grammatical forms that function in a particular grammatical relation

tag·mo·sis \tagˈmōsəs\ *n, pl* **tagmo·ses** \-ōˌsēz\ [NL, irreg. fr. *tagma* + *-osis*] **:** division of the arthropod body into tagmata

¹tagrag \ˈ≈ₑ≈\ *n* [¹*tag* + *rag*] **1 :** RAGTAG **2 :** a loosely connected tag

²tagrag \"\ *adj* **:** SHABBY ⟨clad in the ~ garb of democracy —William Taylor †1836⟩

³tagrag *adv, obs* **:** in a mob **:** HELTER-SKELTER

tag, rag, and bobtail *or* **tagrag and bobtail** *n* **:** a motley group **:** RABBLE, CANAILLE ⟨all the *tagrag and bobtail* of the town —J.G.Frazer⟩

tag·rag·gery \ˈtaˌgragərē\ *n* -ES [¹*tagrag* + *-ery*] **:** a heterogeneous collection of people or things

tags *pl of* TAG, *pres 3d sing of* TAG

tag team *n* [³*tag*] **:** a team composed of two professional wrestlers who spell one another during a match

ta·gua \ˈtägwə\ *n* -s [AmerSp, fr. Araucan] **1 :** IVORY PALM **2 :** IVORY NUT 1

ta·guan \ˈtäˌgwän\ *n* -s [native name in Philippines] **:** a large East Indian flying squirrel (*Petaurista petaurista*)

tag up *vi* [⁴*tag*] **:** to touch a base in baseball before running after a fly ball is caught ⟨*tagged up* and scored after an outfield fly⟩

ta·ha \ˈtä(ˌ)hä\ *n* -s [Zulu *taka*] **:** a So. African weaverbird (esp. *Euplectes taha*) with black and yellow plumage in the male

ta·ha·nun *or* **ta·cha·nun** \ˈtäk̟ˌnün\ *n, pl* **tahanu·nim** *or* **tachanu·nim** \ˌtäk̟(ˌ)nüˈnēm\ *usu cap* [LHeb *taḥănūn*, fr. Heb *ḥannēn* to beg for grace, fr. *ḥēn* grace] **:** a prayer for grace recited in the daily morning and afternoon synagogue service

ta·ha·rah \täˈhärä\ *n, pl* **taha·roth** *or* **taha·rot** \tähäˈrōt(h), -ōs\ [Heb *ṭāhărāh*, lit., purification, fr. *ṭāhēr* to be clean, be pure] **:** a ceremony in the Jewish religion of washing a corpse before burial

¹ta·hi·tian \təˈhēshən *also* täˈh- *or* täˈh- *or* -ēd·ēən *or* -et|iən\ *adj, usu cap* [fr. *Tahiti*, island in the southern Pacific + E *-an*] **1 a :** of, relating to, or characteristic of Tahiti **b :** of, relating to, or characteristic of the Tahitians **2 :** of, relating to, or characteristic of the Tahitian language

²tahitian \"\ *n* -s *cap* **1 :** a native or inhabitant of Tahiti **2 :** the Polynesian language of the Tahitian people

ta·hi·ti orange *or* **tahiti lime** \-hēd·ē-, -hēt|, |i-\ *n, usu cap T* [fr. *Tahiti*, island in the southern Pacific] **:** PERSIAN LIME

tahl·tan \ˈtältən\ *n, pl* **tahltan** *or* **tahltans** *usu cap* **1 a :** an Athapaskan people of northwestern British Columbia and southern Alaska **b :** a member of such people **2 :** a language of the Tahltan people

ta·hoe trout \ˈtäˌhō-, ˈtāˌhō-\ *n, usu cap 1st T* [fr. Lake *Tahoe* on the California-Nevada boundary] **:** a large cutthroat trout (*Salmo clarkii henshawi*) found in Lake Tahoe and neighboring regions

ta·ho·ka daisy \təˈhōkə-\ *n, usu cap T* [fr. *Tahoka*, Texas] **:** an aster (*Aster tanacetifolius*) of the southern U.S. and Mexico that has pinnatifid leaves and flower heads with lavender-blue rays and golden-yellow centers and is widely cultivated as an ornamental

ta·ho·na \təˈhōnə\ *n* -s [Sp, fr. Ar *ṭāḥūna* mill] **:** ARRASTRA

tahr *or* **thar** \ˈtär\ *n* -s [Nepali *thār*] **:** a Himalayan beardless wild goat (*Hemitragus jemlaicus*) having short thick recurving horns and a dark reddish brown mane; *also* **:** a closely related and similar goat (*H. hylocrius*)

tah·sil \täˈsē(ə)l\ *n* -s [Hindi *tahsīl*, fr. Ar, collection of revenue] **:** a district administration or revenue subdivision in India

tah·sil·dar \ˈtäsēlˈdär\ *n* -s [Hindi *tahsīldār*, fr. Per, fr. Ar *taḥṣīl* + Per *-dār* having] **:** a revenue officer in India

¹tai \ˈtī\ *n, pl* **tai** *usu cap* **:** a widespread group of peoples in south China and southeast Asia associated ethnically with valley paddy-rice culture and including various groups (as the Burma Shan, the Chinese Chungchia, the valley dwellers of Laos, and the dominant people of Thailand) — compare THAI

²tai \"\ *n, pl* **tai** [Jap] **:** any of several Pacific porgies of *Pagrus* or a related genus; *esp* **:** RED TAI

ta·i·a·ha \ˈtīəˌhä\ *n* -s [Maori] **:** a long light staff or club adorned with a band of red feathers or dog's hair that is carried by Maori chiefs as a sign of authority and used as a two-handed striking weapon

tai–chinese \ˈ≈¦≈¦≈\ *adj, usu cap T&C* **:** of or relating to the Tai and Chinese language groups jointly

tai·chung \ˈtīˈchu̇ŋ\ *adj, usu cap* [fr. *Taichung*, Formosa] **:** of or from Taichung, Formosa **:** of the kind or style prevalent in Taichung

tai·ga \tīˈgä, -ˈgȧ, ˈtīgə\ *n* -s [Russ *taĭga*, of Turkic origin; akin to Teleut *taiga* rocky, mountainous terrain, Turk *dağ* mountain] **1 :** swampy coniferous forest of Siberia beginning where the tundra ends **2 :** moist subarctic forest of Europe and No. America dominated by spruces and firs

taiglach *var of* TEIGLACH

tai·gle \ˈtāgəl\ *vb* [ME *tagilen, tangilen* — more at TANGLE] **1** *Scot & dial Eng* **:** CATCH, ENTRAP **2** *Scot & dial Eng* **:** DELAY, HINDER, FATIGUE **3** *Scot & dial Eng* **:** DRAG, TRAIL, LOITER

¹tail \ˈtāl, *esp before pause or consonant* -āəl\ *n* -s *often attrib* [ME, fr. OE *tægel, tægl*; akin to OHG *zagal* tail, ON *tagl* horse's tail, Goth *tagl* hair, OIr *dúal* lock of hair, and perh. to Skt *daśā* fringe of a garment, wick] **1 a :** the part of the vertebrate body posterior to the portion containing the body cavity: (1) **:** a rather slender more or less elongated process that arises from the trunk of many mammals immediately above the anus, contains the caudal vertebrae, and is often variously modified as a support, a balancer, or a grasping organ — see COCCYX; see COW illustration (2) **:** the uropygium of a bird with its attached feathers; *sometimes* **:** the feathers alone of this part ⟨the peacock spreads his splendid ~⟩ — see BIRD illustration (3) **:** the caudal fin and caudal peduncle of a fish; *sometimes* **:** CAUDAL FIN (4) **:** the portion of the body of a limbless reptile behind the vent **b :** any of various backwardly directed and usu. posterior processes on the body of an invertebrate animal **2 :** something resembling an animal's tail in shape or position **:** a hindmost part or something that trails behind **:** a terminal appendage or rear end: as **a :** the luminous train of a comet **b :** a stroke or loop at the bottom of a letter (as *g* or *y*) of the alphabet usu. extending below the line **c :** one of the narrow prolongations of the hind wings of some butterflies and moths **d :** one of the slender stringy tips of some swollen roots (as of beets or turnips) **e :** a rudder or vane that turns a windmill to face the wind **f :** a braid of hair or a long switch or pigtail ⟨her woolly hair was braided in sundry little ~*s* —Harriet B. Stowe⟩ **3 :** a train or company of attendants **:** RETINUE **4 tails** *pl* **a :** TAILCOAT **b :** full evening dress for men ⟨came downstairs resplendent in ~*s* and white tie —Joseph Wechsberg⟩ **c :** the skirt, hem, or train of a gown or other long garment ⟨his raincoat . . . kept slipping and he trod on its ~ —John Buchan⟩ **5 a :** BUTTOCKS ⟨sits on his ~ at a desk —Frances & Richard Lockridge⟩ ⟨warm their little ~*s* —Thomas Wolfe⟩ **b** *slang* **:** ⁴ASS 3 **6 a :** something that trails or follows in time or place **:** the back, last, lower, or inferior part of something **:** the part opposed to the head, superior part, front, or beginning **:** END, EXTREMITY, REAR, CONCLUSION **b :** the concluding part of a word, sentence, or discourse ⟨at the ~ of their conversation —Harriet Martineau⟩ **c :** a part that occurs or appears last ⟨seemed to tire toward the ~ of the evening⟩ **d :** the rear of a vehicle or of a traveling mechanism or implement ⟨tumbled out at the ~ of the cart —Roger Fry⟩ ⟨in the private cabin in the ~ of the ship —W.L.Worden⟩ **e :** the rear end of a procession (as a marching army) **f :** the reverse of a coin — see HEAD OR TAIL **g :** the part of a millrace downstream from the wheel **:** the downstream section of a pool or river **h :** the outermost or underwater part of a projecting bank or bar **i :** one end of a molecule regarded as opposite to the head — used esp. of monomers as they are joined in polymers **7 a :** the residuum or refuse part left after a process (as milling, ore dressing, or distilling) **:** DREGS, TAILINGS **b :** the lowest grade of flour derived in milling from a final treatment of the impure stocks **8 :** a sprout of barley **9 a :** the group standing hindmost in accomplishment, value, or skill (as in a political party, a society, a team, or in a herd or flock) **b** *also* **tail end :** the members of a cricket team who are not played primarily as batsmen and who go in to bat towards the end of the innings **10 :** a horsetail formerly used in Turkey as a mark of rank ⟨a pasha of two ~*s*⟩ **11 :** any of various parts of bodily structures that are terminal: as **a :** the distal tendon of a muscle **b :** the slender left end of the human pancreas **c :** the common convoluted tube that forms the lower part of the epididymis **12 :** the stem of a written or printed musical note **13 :** a police or other spy who follows or keeps watch on someone **:** DETECTIVE, INVESTIGATOR, OPERATIVE, SHADOW ⟨his ~ might be anything from a private dick to a G-man —Erle Stanley Gardner⟩ **14 a :** the exposed lower end of a slate, tile, or rafter **b :** TAILING 4 **15** *naut* **:** a rope spliced around a block with long ends by which it may be lashed to something **16 :** an augment (as the additional lines of a tailed sonnet) added to a recognized prosodic form — see TAIL RHYME **17 :** TAIL FLY **18 a :** the blank space below the printed part of a page or the corresponding part of the form from which the page is printed **b :** FOOT 9d **19 :** ⁶JET 3 **20** *or* **tail unit** *or* **tail group :** the rear part of an airplane consisting of horizontal and vertical stabilizing surfaces to which are attached movable surfaces for longitudinal and directional control **:** EMPENNAGE **21 :** the trail left by one who is going forward in or as if in flight ⟨let the guy pass me to get him off my ~⟩ ⟨had a posse on his ~⟩

²tail \"\ *vb* -ED/-ING/-S *vt* **1 :** to fasten by or at the tail, stern, or rear **:** connect end to end **:** string out ⟨~*ed* weak words endlessly one to another⟩ **2 :** to drag, grasp, or pull by the tail ⟨~*ed* a badger that the dog had drawn out⟩ **3 a :** to remove the tail of (an animal) **:** DOCK **b :** to cut off the stringy ends of ⟨top and ~ the green beans —Dione Lucas⟩ **4 a :** to make or furnish with a tail ⟨~*ed* a kite for his young son⟩ **b :** to follow or be drawn behind like a tail ⟨~*ed* the champion to take second place⟩ **5 :** to fasten an end of (a tile, brick, or timber) into a wall or other support **6** *Austral* **:** to act as herdsman of (sheep or cattle) **:** DRIVE, HERD **7 :** to follow (someone) for purposes of surveillance **:** keep under observation **:** TRAIL, WATCH ⟨all the afternoon, the detectives ~*ed* the two men —Joel Sayre⟩ **~** *vi* **1 :** to ground stern first — used with *aground* **2 :** to form or move in a straggling line **:** stretch out in a loose, irregular, or widely spaced column or file ⟨with some hundred more ~*ing* out in single file to join them —N.J.Berrill⟩ **3 a :** to diminish gradually **:** grow progressively smaller, fainter, or more scattered **:** approach an end **:** SUBSIDE ⟨her voice ~*ed* off into hesitant silence⟩ ⟨the airy rain had ~*ed* away into the soft, moist blackness —Mervyn Wall⟩ **b :** to blend or merge gradually ⟨a beach ~*ed* out into the shallows —Nelson Hayes⟩ **4 :** to break the surface of water with the tail while feeding on the bottom or in weeds **5 :** to become built into a wall or other support so as to be held by the end — used of a timber, tile, or brick **6 :** to swing or lie with the stern in a named direction — used of a ship at anchor ⟨the ship ~*ed* into the wind⟩ ⟨a liner ~*ed* downriver⟩ **7 :** to follow or mix closely with **:** TAG ⟨found it pleasanter to ~ along with the crowd he knew⟩ **syn** see FOLLOW

³tail \"\ *adj* [ME *taille, tayle*, fr. AF *taylé*, fr. OF *taillié*, past part. of *taillier* to cut, shape, fix, limit — more at TAILOR] **:** limited as to tenure **:** ABRIDGED, CURTAILED, ENTAILED, REDUCED — compare ESTATE TAIL, FEE TAIL

⁴tail \"\ *vt* -ED/-ING/-S [ME *taylen, taillen*, fr. AF *tayler*, fr. OF *taillier* to cut, shape, limit] **:** to limit or encumber with an entail **:** grant in tail

⁵tail \"\ *n* -s [ME *tayle, taille*, fr. MF *taille*, fr. OF, fr. *taillier*] **1** *obs* **:** TALLY 1a **2 :** the state or condition of entailment **:** LIMITATION, ABRIDGMENT

tailback \ˈ≈ₑ≈\ *n* **:** the offensive football back who lines up farthest from the line of scrimmage

tailband \ˈ≈ₑ≈\ *n* **:** FOOTBAND

tail barley *n* **:** brewer's screenings of barley

tail bay *n* **1 a :** the bay of a framed floor or roof which is next to the end wall so that its joists rest one end on the wall and the other on a girder **b :** the space between a wall and the nearest girder of a floor — compare CASE BAY **2 :** the part of a canal lock below the lower gates

tail beam *n* **:** TAILPIECE 4

tail block *n* **:** a pulley block with a loose tail of rope for attaching it

tailboard \ˈ≈ₑ≈\ *n* **:** the tail gate esp. of a wagon — called also *endgate*

tailbone \ˈ≈ₑ≈\ *n* **1 :** a caudal vertebra **2 :** COCCYX ⟨walking bent over, one hand on his ~ like an old man —Shelby Foote⟩

tail boom *n* **:** ²BOOM 7

tail bud *n* **:** a knob of embryonic tissue not divided into germ layers that arises at the primitive knot and contributes to the formation of the posterior part of the vertebrate body

tailcoat *n* **:** a coat with tails; *esp* **:** a man's full-dress coat with satin-faced lapels, waist-length fronts that do not close, and two long tapering skirts at the back resembling the tail of a swallow — called also *claw hammer*; compare EVENING DRESS

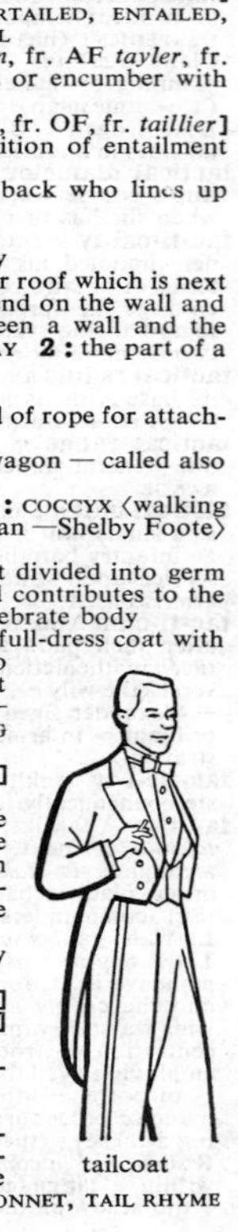

tailcoat

tail·coat·ed \ˈ≈ˌkōd·əd\ *adj* [*tailcoat* + *-ed*] **:** wearing a tailcoat ⟨~ headwaiters⟩

tail cone *n* **:** the exhaust tube of a jet engine

tail coverts *n pl* **:** the feathers that cover the bases of the tail quills — see BIRD illustration

tailcup lupine *n* **:** a lupine (*Lupinus caudatus*) of the northwestern U.S. having the calyx lobes reflexed

tail down *vt* **:** to roll (logs) down a skidway (as for loading)

tailed \ˈtā(ə)ld\ *adj* [ME, fr. *tail* + *-ed*] **1 :** having a tail **2** [fr. past part. of ²*tail*] **:** deprived of a tail

tailed pepper *n* **1 :** CUBEB 1a **2 :** JAVA PEPPER

tailed rhyme *var of* TAIL RHYME

tailed sonnet *n* **:** a sonnet augmented by additional lines that are arranged systematically and are often shorter than the basic line of the sonnet proper — compare CURTAL SONNET, TAIL RHYME

tail end *n* [ME *tailende*, fr. *tail* + *ende* end — more at END] **1 :** RUMP, BEHIND, BUTTOCKS ⟨sitting around the house on his *tail end* —Shirley A. Grau⟩ **2 :** the hindmost end **:** the part opposite to the head or inferior to the rest ⟨watched the *tail end* of the company move out —James Jones⟩ **3 :** the concluding period ⟨the *tail end* of a cabinet meeting —A.M.Schlesinger b. 1917⟩ **4 :** TAIL 9b

tail·end·er \'ˌ'endə(r)\ *n* -s [*tail end* + *-er*] **:** one at the tail end (as in a competition)

[1]**tail·er** \'tālə(r)\ *n* -s [[2]*tail* + *-er*] **1 :** one that tails: as **a :** SHADOW 10b ⟨combined all the attributes of a successful ~ — iron legs and arches, the considerable acting ability a man must have to make himself unnoteworthy, and a sixth sense of anticipation —Joel Sayre⟩ **b :** one that follows; *esp* **:** one that rounds up or drives on the stragglers of a herd **c :** one that removes products from the discharge end of a machine (as a lathe, wrapping machine, or wet machine) **2 a :** a fish that tails **b :** a device that closes a metal loop around the tail of a fish (as a salmon) and is used in landing it

[2]**tailer** \"\ *n* -s [alter. of [1]*tailor*] **:** BLUEFISH 1

tailer–down \'ˌˌ'ˌ\ *n* -s [*tail down*, v. + *-er*] **:** TAILER-IN

tailer–in \'ˌˌ'ˌ\ *n* -s [*tail in*, v. + *-er*] **:** a worker who rolls logs with cant hook or peavey to a place convenient for loading or stacking

tail fan *n* **:** the fanlike swimming organ formed by the last pair of pleopods and the telson in some decapod crustaceans

tail–female \'ˌ'ˌ\ *n* [[5]*tail* (limitation) + *female* (adj.)] **:** the maternal ancestral line esp. of a thoroughbred horse

tail fin *n* **1 :** CAUDAL FIN **2 :** FIN 2c(3)

tailfirst \'ˌ'ˌ\ *adv* **:** with the hinder part foremost **:** BACKWARD ⟨a coon comes down a tree headfirst for most of the way . . . then finishes the descent ~ —E.B.White⟩

tailflower \'ˌˌ\ *n* **:** an aroid of the genus *Anthurium*

tail fly *n* **:** the fly at the end of a fishline leader — called also *end fly*

tailforemost \'ˌ'ˌ\ *adv* **:** TAILFIRST

[1]**tailgate** \'ˌˌ\ *n* **1 :** a gate at the rear: as **a :** the lower gate of a canal lock **b :** a board or gate at the rear end of a vehicle that can be removed or let down for convenience in loading **c :** a heavy wooden panel pivoted to the end of a railroad freight car to form an incline from the car bottom to the rails that is used in loading **2** [so called fr. the custom of seating trombonists at the rear end of trucks carrying jazz bands in parades] **:** a style of jazz trombone playing (as the playing of Dixieland in ensemble) characterized by slides to and from long sustained tones, smears and glissandi, and the playing of improvised countermelodies and rhythms often in a nonlegato manner extending through the entire range of the instrument

[2]**tailgate** *vi* **:** to drive too close to another vehicle for safety ~ *vt* **:** to follow (another vehicle) too close for safety

tail grape *n* **:** any of various tropical woody vines constituting a genus (*Artabotrys*) of the family Annonaceae and having solitary or clustered flowers borne on a woody often hooked peduncle that functions as a tendril; *esp* **:** an eastern Asian vine (*A. odoratissimus* or *A. uncinatus*) that is sometimes cultivated for its very fragrant inconspicuous reddish brown flowers and showy inedible golden yellow pear-shaped fruits

tail group *n* **:** TAIL 20

tailhead \'ˌˌ\ *n* **:** the base of an animal's tail — see COW illustration

tail–heavy \'ˌˌˌ\ *adj* **:** having a nose that tends to rise when the longitudinal control is released in level flight ⟨a *tail-heavy* airplane⟩ — compare NOSE-HEAVY

tail house *n* **1 :** a housing for the tension carriage in an endless-rope mine hoisting system **2 :** a building in which are placed the discharge ends of the condensing apparatus used in petroleum distillation

tailing *n* -s [fr. gerund of [2]*tail*] **1 :** the act of one that tails ⟨the ~ of people is a normal part of detective and intelligence work⟩ **2 :** inferior or refuse material separated as residue in processing — usu. used in pl.: as **a :** stones that tail over the largest openings of the screen of a stone crusher **b :** the lighter inferior coffee berries floated away in washing **c :** the gangue and other refuse material resulting from the washing, concentration, or treatment of ground ore ⟨the ~s of the silver mines of those times are being worked over for the tin that was then discarded —Marrion Wilcox⟩ — compare CONCENTRATE, HEAD, MIDDLING **3 :** the last part of something **4 :** the part of a projecting stone or brick inserted in a wall **5 :** a blur or other break in impression in textile printing **6 tailings** *pl* **:** the lighter and coarser particles (as bran or fibrous or flaked endosperm) that tail over the sieves of a purifier while the heavier middlings pass through **7 tailings** *pl* **:** GRUFFS **8 tailings** *pl* **:** the parts (as of crude spirit) that come over last in fractional distillation **:** FOOTS **9 :** a reused tanning liquor **10 :** short lengths of yarn or fabric — usu. used in pl.

tail joist *n* **:** TAILPIECE 4

tail–kidney \'ˌ'ˌˌ\ *n* **:** METANEPHROS

tail lamp *n* **:** TAILLIGHT

tail·le \'tī, 'tā(ə)l\ *n* -s [F, fr. OF, fr. *taillier* to cut, shape, fix, limit, tax — more at TAILOR] **1 a :** an imposition or tax formerly levied by a French king or seigneur on his subjects or on lands held of or under him **b :** a royal or a national tax in 15th century France from which the lords and later the clergy and others were exempt — compare CORVÉE, GABELLE, TALLAGE **2** *obs* **:** the shape of the bust **:** BUILD, FIGURE, FORM **3 a :** a middle voice or tenor in early choral music **b :** a part to be performed on the tenor viol, the viola, or the English horn

tail·less \'tā(ə)lləs\ *adj* **:** having no tail — **tail·less·ly** *adv* — **tail·less·ness** *n* -ES

tailless airplane *n* **:** an aircraft consisting of a single wing without conventional fuselage or tail, housing cargo and personnel within the wing structure, and achieving stability and control by means of vertical external surfaces mounted on the wing tips or booms attached to the wing

tailless whip scorpion *n* **:** an arachnid of the family Tarantulidae

tail·leur \R tä'yər, tal'-, +V -'yər-; -R -'yə, + *vowel in a word following without pause* -'yər- *or* -'yə *also* 'yər\ *n* -s [F, lit., cutter, tailor, fr. OF] **1 :** the dealer in a card game **2 :** a woman's tailored costume; *esp* **:** a suit for town wear

tail·lie \'tāli\ *n* -s [ME — more at TAILZIE] *Scots law* **:** TAILZIE

taillight \'ˌˌ\ *n* **:** a usu. red light mounted at the rear esp. of an automotive vehicle as a warning to following traffic

taillike \'ˌˌ\ *adj* **:** resembling a tail

tail louse *n* **:** a widely distributed sucking louse (*Haematopinus quadripertusus*) that is an ectoparasite on cattle on the tail of which the adults congregate

tail–male \'ˌ'ˌ\ *n* [[5]*tail* (limitation) + *male* (adj.)] **:** the paternal ancestral line esp. of a thoroughbred horse

tail of the eye : the outer corner of the eye ⟨out of the *tail of his eye*, he glanced at his only passengers —Agnes S. Turnbull⟩

[1]**tai·lor** \'tālə(r)\ *n* -s [ME *tailour*, fr. OF *tailleur*, lit., one that cuts, fr. *taillier* to cut (fr. LL *taliare*, fr. L *talea* twig, stick, cutting) + *-eur* -or; akin to Gk *talis* marriageable girl, *tēlis* fenugreek, Lith *attolas, atolas* rowen, and perh. to ON *thöll* young pine tree; basic meaning: growing thing] **1 :** one whose occupation or business is making or altering men's or women's outerwear (as suits and coats) **2 a** *or* **tailor herring :** FALL HERRING **b** (1) **:** BLUEFISH 1 (2) **:** a closely related Australian fish

[2]**tailor** \"\ *vb* -ED/-ING/-S *vi* **1 :** to do the job or carry on the business of a tailor **2 :** to adapt to tailoring ⟨a material that ~s well⟩ ~ *vt* **1 a :** to make or fashion as the work of a tailor ⟨~*ed* him several suits⟩ **b :** to make or adapt to suit a special need or purpose ⟨this striking force that can ~ its power to meet the demands of the moment —H.H.Martin⟩ ⟨~*ed* a new cartridge to the new gun —W.W.Stout⟩ ⟨failed to ~ the manners of his ego to those prevailing in the environment he invaded —Thomas Sugrue⟩ **2 :** to fit with clothes **:** make clothes for ⟨the best tailors ~*ed* him⟩ **3 :** to fit or style (women's garments or items of interior decor) with trim, straight lines and finished handwork like that of a tailor's work on men's garments

[3]**tailor** \"\ *n* -s [by folk etymology] **:** [1]TELLER 2b

tailorbird \'ˌˌˌ\ *n* **:** any of numerous Asiatic, East Indian, and African warblers (family Sylviidae) that stitch leaves together to support and hide their nests; *esp* **:** a common garden-frequenting bird (*Orthotomus sutorius*) of southern and eastern Asia that is yellowish green above and white below and has a long tapering tail

tai·lor·dom \-(r)dəm\ *n* -s **1 :** tailors as an occupational group **:** the trade or domain of tailors **2 :** TAILORING

tailored *adj* **1 :** made by a tailor **2 a :** fashioned or fitted to resemble a tailor's work **b :** having trim, simple, straight lines ⟨~ curtains⟩ **3 :** MADE-TO-ORDER **4 a :** having the look of one fitted by a custom tailor **:** well turned out ⟨she has the ~ look —John Mason Brown⟩ **b :** appearing well cared for **:** STYLISH, TRIM ⟨a well-*tailored* neighborhood —*Time*⟩

tailored gardenia *n* **:** a gardenia removed from the peduncle, wired, and supported by a collar of stapled foliage

tai·lor·ess \'tālərəs\ *n* -ES **:** a woman tailor

tailor–fashion \'ˌˌ'ˌˌ\ *adv* (*or adj*) **:** CROSS-LEGGED 1 ⟨sat down *tailor-fashion* in a place of honor —F.G.Slaughter⟩

tailoring *n* -s **1 a :** the business or occupation of a tailor **b :** the work or workmanship of a tailor ⟨the kind of ~ which goes by the name of ready-made —Irving Kolodin⟩ **2 :** the making or adapting of something to suit a particular purpose ⟨the ~ of history books to fit the party line of the moment had for some time been an established practice —Sergius Yakobson⟩ **3 :** a rounding off of the corners of grooved rolls of iron and steel to prevent fins from forming on the bars in rolling

tai·lor·ism \'tālə,rizəm\ *n* -s **1 :** the labor, employment, or product of a tailor **2 :** a tailor's mannerism

tai·lor·ize \-,rīz\ *vb* -ED/-ING/-S *vi* **:** to do the work of a tailor **:** behave as a tailor ~ *vt* **:** to reduce to a tailor's status **:** treat as a tailor **:** DEGRADE, DEMORALIZE

[1]**tailor–made** \'ˌˌ'ˌ\ *adj* [[1]*tailor* + *made*] **1 a :** made by a tailor or with a tailor's care and style ⟨a *tailor-made* suit⟩ **b :** marked by trimness of fit, simplicity of line and ornament, and fine finish — used of women's garments **c :** having the appearance of one turned out by a good tailor ⟨a *tailor-made* man⟩ **2 :** made or fitted esp. to a particular use or purpose **:** MADE-TO-ORDER ⟨the wage provisions of its agreement are *tailor-made* for that company's circumstances —R.A.Lester⟩ ⟨his music is *tailor-made* to the requirements and conditions of a specific time and place —Abraham Veinus⟩ ⟨a *tailor-made* fuel with special characteristics —*Ethyl News*⟩ **3 :** factory-made rather than hand-rolled — used of cigarettes

[2]**tailor–made** \"\ *n* -s **1 :** a woman's tailor-made garment **2 :** a factory-made cigarette

tailor–make \'ˌˌ'ˌ\ *vt* [back-formation fr. [1]*tailor-made*] **:** to make or adapt to a particular use or purpose or to the needs of an individual — opposed to *mass-produce*

tailor muscle *also* **tailor's muscle** *n* **:** SARTORIUS

tailor's chair *n* **:** a seat with back rest but no legs used by tailors at work

tailor's chalk *n* **:** a thin flat piece of hard chalk or soapstone used by tailors and seamstresses for making temporary marks on cloth

tailor's cushion *n* **:** a tailor's ham

tai·lor·ship \'tālə(r),ship\ *n* **:** the trade or work of a tailor **:** TAILORING

tailor's tack *n* **:** a basting stitch taken with a double thread through two pieces of fabric and then cut apart with large loops being left in each piece for marking seam lines and perforations

tailor warbler *n* **:** a tailorbird (*Orthotomus sutorius*)

tai·lory \'tālərē\ *n* -ES [ME *taillourie*, fr. *taillour* tailor + *-ie* -y — more at TAILOR] **1 :** the work or business of a tailor **2 :** clothing made by a tailor

tail over *vt* **:** to pass (material that will not go through) over a sieve in milling

tailpiece \'ˌˌ\ *n* **1 :** a subsidiary part at the lower or rear end **:** a piece added on at the end **:** APPENDAGE ⟨the ~ of a crustacean⟩ ⟨the ~ of a musical composition⟩ **2 :** a triangular piece (as of ebony) between which and the pegs the strings of a stringed musical instrument are stretched **3 :** the part of a telescope containing the adjusting device for the eyepiece **4 :** a relatively shorter beam or rafter tailed in a wall and supported by a header **5 :** a piece for transmitting motion from the hub of a lock to the latch bolt **6 :** an ornament placed below the text matter of a page (as at the end of a chapter) — compare HEADPIECE

tailpin \'ˌˌ\ *n* **1 :** the tailstock center in a lathe **2 :** a pin projecting from the body of a large stringed musical instrument (as a cello) to raise it off the floor when being played

tailpipe \'ˌˌ\ *vt* **:** to tie a tin can to the tail of (a dog)

tail pipe *n* **1 :** the suction pipe of a pump **2 :** the pipe discharging into the atmosphere the exhaust gases from the muffler of an automotive engine **3 :** the part of a jet engine that carries the exhaust gases rearward and discharges them through a nozzle

tail–pipe burner *n* **:** AFTERBURNER

tail plane *n* **:** the horizontal tail surfaces of an airplane including the stabilizer and the elevator

tail print *n* **:** a core print carried to the top of a foundry mold so that the pattern may be molded in one box

tailrace \'ˌˌ\ *n* **1 :** a race for conveying water away from a point of industrial application (as a waterwheel or turbine) after use — called also *afterbay;* compare HEADRACE, MILLRACE **2 :** the channel in which mine tailings are floated off

tail rhyme *also* **tailed rhyme** *n* **:** a verse form in which rhymed lines (as couplets or triplets) are followed by a line of different usu. shorter length which does not rhyme with the couplet or triplet

tail–rhyme stanza *also* **tail–rhymed stanza** \'ˌ-ˌ\ *n* **:** a stanza consisting of rhymed couplets or triplets with tails that rhyme with each other

tail rider *n* **:** one of usu. two cowboys who keep a herd of cattle moving from the rear **:** one that rides drag — compare SWING-MAN

tail rod *n* **:** a continuation of a piston rod or valve rod through the back cylinder cover or valve chest (as of a steam engine or an air compressor)

tail rope *n* **:** a rope attached to the rear part or end of something: as **a :** a rope fastened to the tail of a mine car or train to haul it back empty after unloading or to brake its speed on a downgrade **b :** the rope beneath either of two counterbalancing cages in a mine shaft

tails *pl of* TAIL, *pres 3d sing of* TAIL

tail set *n* **:** a device used to hold the tail of a gaited saddlehorse in the desired cocked position

tail shaft *n* **:** the after section of a ship's propeller shaft extending through the stern tube

tail sheet *n* **:** a strip of larger-mesh bolting cloth used at the tail end of a sieve to sift out coarser stock in milling

tail skid *n* **:** a yielding support on which the tail of an airplane rests when on the ground

tail slide *n* **:** the tailfirst slide rearward and downward that some airplanes may be made to take after being brought into a stalling position by a steep climb

tailspin \'ˌˌ\ *n* **1 :** [2]SPIN 2a ⟨the airplane went into a ~⟩ **2 :** a collapse into mental or emotional depression or confusion ⟨the sight of it had nearly sent him into a ~ —Jean Stafford⟩ **3 :** a state of disordered or depressed activity **:** CHAOS, DEMORALIZATION ⟨an abrupt falling off in foreign trade may send the economy into a ~ —*Atlantic*⟩

tail spindle *n* **:** the tailstock spindle in a lathe

tailstock \'ˌˌ\ *n* **:** the adjustable or sliding head of a lathe containing the dead center

tail surface *n* **:** a stabilizing surface or a control surface in the tail of an airplane

tail tackle *n* **1 :** WATCH TACKLE **2 :** LUFF TACKLE

tail tree *n* **:** the spar tree farthest from the power source in a cable logging rig

tail trimmer *n* **:** a trimmer placed along a wall to receive the ends of joists

tail twisting *n* **1 :** the twisting of an animal's tail usu. as a means of torture **2 :** HARASSMENT, ABUSE

tail unit *n* **:** TAIL 20

tail up *vt* [[1]*tail*] *West* **:** to lift (an animal) out of a bog by the tail; *also* **:** to twist the tail as a means of forcing (a benumbed animal) to rise

tail–wagging \'ˌˌˌ\ *n* **:** TEMPO TURN

[1]**tail·ward** \'tā(ə)lwə(r)d\ *adj* [[1]*tail* + *-ward*] **:** located at or directed toward the rear **:** REARWARD

[2]**tailward** \" *or* **tail·wards** \-dz\ *adv* **:** to the rear **:** REARWARD

tail water *n* **1 :** water in a tailrace **2 :** water below a dam or waterpower development

tail wheel *n* **:** an auxiliary wheel on which the rear of an airplane rests or taxis on the ground

tail wind *n* **:** a wind having the same general direction as the course of an airplane or a ship in motion ⟨a stout *tail wind* was giving a friendly boost —W.D.Patterson⟩

[1]**tail·zie** \'tāl(y)i\ *n* [alter. (ʒ being taken as *z*) of earlier *tailʒie*, fr. ME *taillie*, *tailyie*, *tailʒie*, fr. MF *tailliee*, fr. fem. of *taillié*, past part. of *taillier* to cut, shape, fix, limit — more at TAILOR] *Scots law* **:** ENTAIL

[2]**tailzie** \"\ *vt* -ED/-ING/-S *Scots law* **:** ENTAIL

tai·men \'tī,men\ *n* -s [Russ *taĭmen'*, fr. Finn *taimen*] **:** a giant trout (*Salmo taimen* or *S. fluviatilis*) of the rivers of northern Asia

[1]**tai·nan** \'tīnən\ *adj, usu cap* [*Taino* + *-an*] **:** of or relating to the Taino or their language

[2]**tai·nan** \'tī'nän\ *adj, usu cap* [fr. *Tainan*, Formosa] **:** of or from the city of Tainan on the island of Formosa, China **:** of the kind or style prevalent in Tainan

tai·ni·o·lite \'tīnēō,līt\ *n* -s [*tainio-* (fr. Gk *tainia* band) + *-lite;* akin to Gk *teinein* to stretch — more at THIN] **:** a mineral $KLiMg_2Si_4O_{10}F_2$ consisting of a silicate and fluoride of potassium, lithium, and magnesium of the mica group

tai·no \'tī(,)nō\ *n, pl* **taino** *or* **tainos** *usu cap* [Sp, of AmerInd origin] **1 a :** an extinct aboriginal Arawakan people of the Greater Antilles and the Bahamas, esp. of Hispaniola **b :** a member of such people **2 :** the language of the Taino people

[1]**taint** \'tānt\ *vb* -ED/-ING/-S [ME *taynten*, fr. AF *teinter*, fr. MF *teint*, past part. of *teindre* to color, dye, fr. L *tingere* — more at TINGE] *vt* **1** *obs* **:** to touch with color **:** TINGE, TINT **2** *obs* **:** to apply balm or ointment to (a wound or sore spot) **:** ANOINT **3** [influenced in meaning by obs. *taint* to attaint, fr. ME *taynten*, fr. MF *ataint*, past part. of *ataindre* to accuse, convict, attain — more at ATTAIN] **a :** to touch or affect slightly with something bad or undesirable ⟨to aid openly would be to . . . ~ his memory —S.H.Adams⟩ ⟨directed toward the purge from the public service rolls of those ~*ed* with fascism —Taylor Cole⟩ **b :** to affect with putrefaction **:** make noxious or poisonous **:** ROT ⟨the meat was ~*ed*⟩ **c :** to contaminate morally **:** CORRUPT, DEFILE, DEPRAVE, STAIN ⟨all the lighter kinds of literature were deeply ~*ed* by the prevailing licentiousness —T.B.Macaulay⟩ ~ *vi* [influenced in meaning by obs. *taint* to attaint] **1** *obs* **:** to become weak **:** lose courage ⟨I cannot ~ with fear —Shak.⟩ **2** *archaic* **:** to become affected with putrefaction or corruption **:** ROT **syn** see CONTAMINATE

[2]**taint** \"\ *n* -s [MF *teint*, fr. past part. of *teindre*] **1** *obs* **:** COLOR, HUE, TINGE **2** [influenced in meaning by [3]*taint*] **a :** a spot or stain of something bad (as of dishonor or disgrace) **:** BLEMISH ⟨some ineradicable ~ of impropriety attached in their minds to any association with the stage —Mary Austin⟩ ⟨the river that I know washes from all ~ of sin —Rudyard Kipling⟩ **b :** a germ, source, or cause of corruption **:** a contaminating influence **:** a rotting or depraving force ⟨remembered his bouts with the bottle and were afraid that the ~ had been passed on to me —Hamilton Basso⟩

[3]**taint** \"\ *n* -s [MF *atainte* — more at ATTAINT] **:** ATTAINT 1

tain·ter gate *or* **tain·tor gate** \'tāntə(r)-\ *n* [after Jeremiah B. *Tainter*, 19th cent. Am. inventor] **:** RADIAL GATE

taint·less \'tāntləs\ *adj* [[2]*taint* + *-less*] **:** having no taint **:** CLEAN, IMMACULATE, PURE — **taint·less·ly** *adv* — **taint·less·ness** *n* -ES

tain·ture \'tānchə(r)\ *n* -s [MF *teinture*, fr. L *tinctura* — more at TINCTURE] **:** DEFILEMENT, STAIN, TAINT

taintworm \'ˌˌ\ *n* [[2]*taint* + *worm*] **:** a worm or larva parasitic on mammals

tai nua \'tīnü'ä\ *n, pl* **tai nua** *or* **tai nuas** *usu cap T&N* **1 :** a Tai people closely related to the Laotians of Laos **2 :** a member of the Tai Nua people

[1]**tai·pan** \'tī,pan\ *n* -s [Chin (Pek) *tai⁴ pan¹*] **:** the head of a foreign house of business in China **:** a great merchant

[2]**taipan** \"\ *n* -s [native name in Australia] **:** an exceedingly venomous elapid snake (*Oxyuranus scutellatus*) of northern Australia and the Pacific islands

tai·pei *or* **tai·peh** \'tī'pā, -'bā\ *adj, usu cap* [fr. *Taipei*, Formosa] **:** of or from Taipei, the capital of Formosa, China **:** of the kind or style prevalent in Taipeh

tai·ping \'tī'piŋ\ *n* -s *usu cap* [Chin (Pek) *t'ai⁴ p'ing²* peaceful] **:** a Chinese insurgent taking part in a rebellion (1848–65) against the Manchu dynasty

ta·i·po \'tīə,pō\ *n* -s [Maori *taepo*] *NewZeal* **:** a demon, devil, or other specter appearing at night

taira *var of* TAYRA

ta·i·ro·na \,tīə'rōnə\ *n, pl* **tairona** *or* **taironas** *usu cap* [Sp, of AmerInd origin] **1 :** an extinct Chibchan people of northern Colombia **2 :** a member of the Tairona people

taisch \'tāsh, 'tīsh\ *n* -ES [ScGael *taibhis*, *taibhse;* akin to IrGael *taidhbhse* ghost, OIr *taidbsiu* to show] *Scot* **:** an apparition of a person about to die

[1]**tait** \'tāt\ *var of* TATE

[2]**tait** \"\ *n* -s [native name in Australia] **:** HONEY POSSUM

[1]**tai·ver** \'tāvər\ *var of* TAVER

[2]**taiver** \"\ *n* -s [prob. of Scand origin; akin to Norw & Dan dial. *tave* rag; akin to ON *thefja* to stir, *thōf* act of beating cloth, Gk *tapeinos* low, humble, abject] *Scot* **:** SHRED, TATTER — usu. used in pl.

tai·vert \-rt\ *var of* TAVERT

tai·wan \(')tī'wän\ *adj, usu cap* [fr. *Taiwan* (Formosa), island in the China Sea] **:** FORMOSA

[1]**tai·wan·ese** \(,)tī,wä'nēz, -ēs\ *adj, usu cap* [*Taiwan* + E *-ese*] **1 :** of, relating to, or characteristic of the island of Taiwan **2 :** of, relating to, or characteristic of the people of Taiwan

[2]**taiwanese** \"\ *n, pl* **taiwanese** *cap* **:** a native or inhabitant of Taiwan

tai·wa·nia \tī'wänēə\ *n, cap* [NL, fr. *Taiwan* + NL *-ia*] **:** a genus of coniferous trees (family Pinaceae) having leathery triangular leaves that are incurved at the apex

tai·yu·an \'tīyü'än\ *adj, usu cap* [fr. *Taiyuan*, China] **:** of or from the city of Taiyuan, China **:** of the kind or style prevalent in Taiyuan

taj \'täzh, 'täj\ *n* -ES [Ar *tāj*, fr. Per, crown, crest, cap] **:** a cap worn in Muslim countries; *esp* **:** a tall cone-shaped cap worn by dervishes

ta·jik *or* **ta·djik** *or* **ta·dzhik** \tä'jik, -'jēk\ *n, pl* **tajik** *or* **tajiks** *or* **tadjik** *or* **tadjiks** *or* **tadzhik** *or* **tadzhiks** *usu cap* **:** a member of a people of old Iranian blood and speech bearing resemblance to Europeans and dispersed among the populations of Afghanistan and Turkistan

ta·jiki \-kē\ *n* -s *usu cap* **:** the Iranian language of the Tajik people

ta·jin \tä'hēn\ *adj, usu cap* [MexSp *Tajín*, a pyramidal monument found near Papantla, Vera Cruz, Mexico, constructed by the Totonacs, fr. Nahuatl, thunder] **:** of or relating to the extinct culture of the Totonacs near the present state of Vera Cruz, Mexico, and characterized by the use of double outlines in design and of stone ax blades shaped like human faces

tak·able *or* **take·able** \'tākəbəl\ *adj* **:** capable of being taken ⟨would take . . . whatever was ~ —*Harper's*⟩

Taka–Diastase \'takə, 'täkə+\ *trademark* — used for an enzyme preparation obtained usu. as a yellowish white hygroscopic powder by growing a mold (*Aspergillus oryzae*) on wheat bran and used chiefly as a starch digestant

ta·ka·he \tə'kī\ *n* -s [Maori] **:** NOTORNIS 2

TAKAMAHAC

ta·ka·mat·su \,täkə,mät(,)sü\ *adj, usu cap* [fr. *Takamatsu*, city of Shikoku Island, Japan] **:** of or from the city of Takamatsu, Japan **:** of the kind or style prevalent in Takamatsu

ta·ka·oka \'tä'käōkə, -'kaükə\ *adj, usu cap* [fr. *Takaoka*, city of central Japan] **:** of or from the city of Takaoka, Japan **:** of the kind or style prevalent in Takaoka

[1]**take** \'tāk\ *vb* **took** \'tu̇k, *dial* 'tək\ *or dial* **tak·en** \'tākən *sometimes* -kᵊn\ **taken** \" *or dial* **took** *or chiefly Scot* **tane** \'tān\ **taking; takes** [ME *taken*, fr. OE *tacan*, fr. ON *taka;* akin to MD *taken* to take, Goth *tekan* to touch] *vt* **1 :** to get into one's hands or into one's possession, power, or control by force or stratagem: as **a :** to seize or capture physically (as men, munitions, works, or territory in war, a person charged with an offense, or a piece of property by legal process) ⟨*took* 300 of the enemy's men and a dozen of his cannon⟩ ⟨believed they could ~ the fort in about three days⟩ ⟨was *taken* by the police within three hours of the crime⟩ ⟨*took* the town and

carried off what wine and oil it contained —C.L.Jones⟩ **b** (1) **:** to get possession of (as fish or game) by killing or capturing ⟨eighty percent of the whales today are *taken* in the Antarctic —Mary H. Vorse⟩ ⟨the nets by which the bats were to be *taken* —R.L.Ditmars & A.M.Greenhall⟩ ⟨*took* many nice fish —Alexander MacDonald⟩ ⟨had never more than three or four pellets in them . . . for he *took* them upon the very edge of the shot pattern —William Humphrey⟩ ⟨proclamation governing the *taking* of upland game birds and deer —*N. Dak. Hunting Regulations*⟩ — sometimes used to include acts in attempt to kill or capture ⟨the word ~ as used in this Act means hunt, shoot, pursue, lure, kill, destroy, capture, trap or ensnare, or to attempt so to do —*Illinois Game & Fish Codes*⟩ (2) **:** to seize as prey ⟨tales of children *taken* by tigers⟩ **c :** to capture or secure (as an opponent's piece in chess or card in bridge) in order to remove from play ⟨*took* his opponent's queen on the fourth move⟩; *also* **:** to serve to capture ⟨planned to let his rook ~ the knight⟩ ⟨ace ~*s* the king⟩ **d :** to seize or destroy (property) for public purposes **:** acquire title by eminent domain **:** CONFISCATE **e** (1) **:** to catch or field (as a batted ball) in baseball or cricket ⟨~ it on the fly⟩ ⟨*took* it on the first hop⟩ (2) **:** to catch (a batsman) out in cricket ⟨was *taken* in the slips⟩ **2 a :** to lay or get hold of with arms, hands, or fingers or with a hand or an instrument **:** GRASP, GRIP ⟨~ the ax by the handle⟩ ⟨~ the book in your right hand⟩ ⟨always *took* his hand when they crossed the street⟩ ⟨*took* his sleeve to guide him⟩ ⟨*took* him by the shoulders and shook him soundly⟩ ⟨dentist *took* the tooth in his forceps⟩ ⟨*took* the child in her arms to comfort it⟩ ⟨~ the railing as you go down⟩ **b :** to catch hold upon (as by contact or adhesion) ⟨sound of a ship *taking* the ground⟩ ⟨oars rhythmically *taking* the water⟩ **3 a :** to catch, seize, or attack through the effect of a sudden force or influence: as (1) **:** to seize or attack so as to have an effect upon ⟨was *taken* with a fit of laughing⟩ ⟨was suddenly *taken* with a need for companionship⟩ ⟨liked to work as the humor *took* him⟩ ⟨toward morning he was *taken* with frenzy and leaped from bed —J.A.Michener⟩ ⟨seemed to be *taken* with a great restlessness —S.H.Holbrook⟩ (2) **:** to strike or affect so as to cause to be in a particular condition ⟨was *taken* ill⟩ ⟨found himself *taken* hoarse⟩ ⟨was *taken* down with pneumonia⟩ (3) **:** to attack through magical or supernatural forces **:** cast a spell on **:** use malign influence over ⟨blasts the tree and ~*s* the cattle —Shak.⟩ **b :** to catch or come upon (as a person) in a particular situation or action ⟨question *took* him unprepared⟩ ⟨was *taken* unawares⟩ ⟨tried to ~ him napping⟩ ⟨*took* him in the very act⟩ **c :** to strike or hit (as a person) usu. in or on a specified part ⟨a straight left-hander that *took* him on the broad chin —Arthur Morrison⟩ ⟨*took* the boy a smart box on the ear⟩ **d** (1) **:** to capture or gain the approval or liking of **:** CAPTIVATE, CHARM, DELIGHT ⟨performance that seemed to have *taken* the fancy of the crowd⟩ — usu. used with *with* ⟨was much *taken* with him at their first meeting⟩ ⟨so *taken* with the decorations that she decided to copy them⟩ or sometimes with *by* ⟨quite *taken* by their concern for his comfort⟩ (2) **:** to catch and hold (as the attention, interest, regard) often for only a short time ⟨*took* his attention momentarily⟩ ⟨kind of thing that ~*s* one's eye⟩ **4 a :** to get into one's hand or one's hold or possession by a physical act of simple transference ⟨I ~ my pen in hand⟩ ⟨*took* his hat and coat and left⟩ ⟨reached over and *took* a piece of bread⟩ ⟨*took* a cigar and lit it⟩ ⟨*took* the youngster on her lap⟩ ⟨*took* a stake and pounded it in the ground⟩ **b** (1) **:** to introduce or receive into one's body (as by eating, drinking, or inhaling) ⟨had *taken* no food for three days⟩ ⟨~ a glass of water⟩ ⟨~ snuff⟩ ⟨~*s* the smoke into his lungs⟩ ⟨~ one tablet after each meal⟩ ⟨*took* poison⟩ ⟨killed himself by *taking* gas⟩ ⟨communed with spirits while *taking* tobacco and a narcotic herb —J.H.Steward⟩ ⟨label reading "this medicine is not to be *taken* internally"⟩ ⟨*took* his bottle well and had gained back to birth weight —E.F.Patton⟩ (2) **:** to expose oneself to (as sun or air) for pleasure or for physical benefit ⟨*taking* the sun on the beach before the little teahouse —Hamilton Basso⟩ ⟨piers . . . where families in the neighborhood could ~ the river air in warm weather —Brooks Atkinson⟩ (3) **:** to partake of (as a meal) **:** EAT, DRINK ⟨the audience would ~ tea there —Virginia Woolf⟩ ⟨*took* supper with an English earl —F.B.Gipson⟩ ⟨residents are required to ~ their meals in the houses —*Official Register of Harvard Univ.*⟩ ⟨~*s* dinner about six⟩ **5 a** (1) **:** to bring or receive into a relation or connection ⟨*took* his son into the firm⟩ ⟨wouldn't ~ me into his confidence⟩ ⟨~*s* a few private pupils⟩ ⟨was reduced to *taking* lodgers⟩ ⟨time he *took* a wife⟩ ⟨the stupid bride he means to ~ —Carl Van Doren⟩ ⟨*took* a squaw to wife —Burges Johnson⟩ ⟨serve you right if she *took* a lover —Guy McCrone⟩ (2) **:** to receive into one's household for provision and care or to adopt ⟨*took* her dead brother's youngest child⟩ ⟨married children arranged to ~ their father a month at a time⟩ ⟨agreed to ~ a war orphan⟩ **b :** to copulate with **6 :** to transfer into one's own keeping **:** enter into or arrange for possession, ownership, or use of: **a :** APPROPRIATE ⟨*took* the umbrella to keep it from being lost or stolen⟩ ⟨if nobody wants this, I'll ~ it⟩ ⟨found that somebody had *taken* his hat⟩ ⟨accused me of *taking* his camera⟩ ⟨had been *taking* money out of the till for months⟩ **b** (1) **:** to obtain or secure for use (as by lease, subscription, or contract) ⟨~ a cottage for the summer⟩ ⟨~ a box at the opera⟩ ⟨family ~*s* several magazines⟩ ⟨~ two quarts of milk every other day⟩ (2) **:** to obtain by purchasing **:** BUY ⟨spent an hour looking around but didn't ~ anything⟩ ⟨finally decided to ~ a blue serge suit⟩ ⟨wanted to ~ the ranch house but his wife wouldn't agree⟩ ⟨salesman tried to persuade him to ~ the convertible⟩ **7 :** to adopt or lay hold of for oneself or as one's own **:** ASSUME: as **a** (1) **:** to invest oneself with (as a property or an attribute) ⟨butter often ~*s* the flavor of substances near it⟩ ⟨fog *took* ghostly shapes⟩ ⟨ancient Greek gods often *took* the likeness of a human being⟩ ⟨unconsciously he *took* color from his environment —V.L.Parrington⟩ ⟨~ different shapes on different occasions —Curtis Bok⟩; *also* **:** to assume a property or attribute of ⟨the plaster *took* the mold in perfect detail⟩ (2) **:** to assume as a badge or symbol (as of a function or an office) ⟨~ the veil of a nun⟩ ⟨asked him to ~ the gavel⟩ ⟨had *taken* the throne at twenty⟩ **b :** to charge oneself with (as a duty, obligation, or task) **:** UNDERTAKE ⟨~ office⟩ ⟨~ service under a foreign flag⟩ ⟨~ the responsibility for keeping order⟩ ⟨each teacher must ~ the study hall once every week⟩; *specif* **:** to assume responsibility for checking the effectiveness of (a player on an opposing team) on a given play ⟨our right end ~*s* defensive fullback —A.E. Neale⟩ **c** (1) **:** to subject oneself to **:** bind oneself by ⟨~ a vow⟩ ⟨~ a pledge⟩ ⟨~ my oath he hasn't grown an inch —*New Yorker*⟩ ⟨*took* oath as president on December 1st —Virginia Prewett⟩ (2) *obs* **:** to make oneself responsible for the truth of (as a statement) **:** AFFIRM, SWEAR — used with *it* ⟨*took*'t upon mine honor thou hadst it not —Shak.⟩ **d** (1) **:** to undertake and perform or exercise ⟨~ the role of the villain⟩ ⟨*took* an important part in the negotiations⟩ ⟨the teacher who *took* the third grade last year⟩ ⟨~ soprano⟩ ⟨had to ~ three sections of freshman English⟩ ⟨curate *took* the early morning service⟩ (2) **:** to give or impose upon oneself (as special or added responsibility) as part of or in the course of something undertaken or done — used chiefly in the phrase *take pains* or *take the trouble* ⟨man who is willing to ~ the trouble to do good work⟩ ⟨have *taken* pains with the documentation —Van Wyck Brooks⟩ ⟨*took* no pains to soften their footsteps —Jean Stafford⟩ ⟨few of our statesmen can have *taken* so little pains to keep themselves in the public eye —G.M. Young⟩ **e :** to adopt (as another's part or side) as one's own **:** align or ally oneself with ⟨knew that his mother would ~ his side⟩ — often used in the phrase *take sides* ⟨members *take* sides against each other in all public affairs —A.C.Whitehead⟩ **f :** to adopt or advance as one's fundamental point of argument or defense ⟨a point well *taken*⟩ ⟨*took* his stand on judicial incorruptibility⟩ **g :** to assume as if rightfully one's own or as if granted **:** arrogate to oneself ⟨~ the credit⟩ ⟨~ the liberty of disagreeing⟩ ⟨*took* my consent for granted⟩ ⟨~ leave to protest⟩ **h :** to have or assume as a proper part of or accompaniment to itself **:** be formed or used with ⟨~*s* an accent on the last syllable⟩ ⟨~*s* an *s* in the plural⟩ ⟨transitive verbs ~ an object⟩ ⟨~*s* the objective case⟩ ⟨plural noun ~*s* a plural verb⟩ **8 a :** to secure by winning in competition **:** WIN ⟨*took* six tricks in a row⟩ ⟨*took* the fight by a knockout⟩ ⟨*took* first place in the broad jump⟩ ⟨*took* the Latin prize for two years⟩ ⟨was lucky to ~ one game out of four⟩ ⟨*took* first-class honors in history —*Current Biog.*⟩ ⟨*took* ribbons for his vegetables —*Lamp*⟩ **b :** to win over (as an opponent) **:** BEAT, DEFEAT ⟨*took* him in straight sets⟩ ⟨bragged that he could ~ the new marshal —J.W.Schaefer⟩ **9 :** to pick out **:** CHOOSE, SELECT ⟨was told to ~ the road bearing left at the fork⟩ ⟨always *took* the middle course if there was one⟩ ⟨let him ~ his pick⟩ ⟨~ any number from one to ten⟩ **10 :** to adopt, choose, or avail oneself of for use **:** have recourse to and use ⟨~ the first opportunity⟩ ⟨*took* every means he could think of⟩ ⟨was forced to ~ severe measures⟩: as **a :** to have recourse to as an instrument for doing something ⟨had *taken* his belt to the disobedient boy⟩ ⟨nothing to do with the weeds but ~ a scythe to them⟩ **b :** to use as a means of transportation or progression ⟨could ~ the subway to work⟩ ⟨*took* a freighter to Europe⟩ ⟨usually *took* the car⟩ ⟨he ~*s* airplanes, but his wife won't fly —Philip Hamburger⟩ ⟨insisted on *taking* a taxi all the way —Christopher Isherwood⟩; *also* **:** to go aboard or mount (as something providing such transportation) **:** BOARD ⟨always *took* the train at the main station⟩ ⟨had *taken* horse and ridden into the fields —J.H.Wheelwright⟩ ⟨just before I *took* ship at New York for Sweden —Sinclair Lewis⟩ ⟨~*s* the train every morning at 6:45⟩ **c :** to have recourse to (as a place) esp. for safety or refuge ⟨~ shelter⟩ ⟨~ sanctuary⟩ ⟨~ harbor⟩ ⟨had one look at the bear and then *took* the nearest tree⟩ ⟨could often ~ refuge from his humiliation in a sort of dignity —Elizabeth Bowen⟩ ⟨~ cover behind prejudices and theories —Roger Fry⟩ **d :** to enter upon or into in order to go along or through ⟨wished he could ~ a paved road⟩ ⟨every single plane . . . fit to ~ the air —Ira Wolfert⟩ ⟨readying the boat to ~ the water⟩ **e** (1) **:** to proceed to occupy (as a place or position) ⟨~ a seat in the rear⟩ ⟨*took* the nearest chair⟩ ⟨*took* his place in the procession⟩ ⟨was unwilling to ~ the center of the stage⟩ ⟨always ready to ~ the spotlight⟩ ⟨*took* the chair in the absence of the regular chairman⟩ (2) **:** to use up (as space by filling or time by consuming) ⟨~ enough time to be sure⟩ ⟨doesn't ~ much room⟩ ⟨*took* a long time to dry out⟩ (3) **:** NEED, REQUIRE ⟨~*s* a size nine shoe⟩ ⟨job *took* more attention than he could give⟩ ⟨*took* two men to keep the tub filled —H.A.Chippendale⟩ ⟨a good long letter (*took* two postage stamps) —Walt Whitman⟩ ⟨*took* the baroque age to invent, and to respect, the . . . periwig —Gilbert Highet⟩ ⟨getting to the right place at the right time . . . ~*s* a bit of doing —Nevil Shute⟩ **11 a :** to obtain by deriving from a source **:** DRAW ⟨~*s* its title from the name of the hero⟩ ⟨family probably *took* its name from the place where it lived⟩ ⟨*took* his design from natural rock formations⟩ ⟨~*s* his good looks from his mother⟩ ⟨*took* his text from the Old Testament⟩ ⟨*took* his subject from his own experience⟩: as (1) **:** to extract and use over again (as for quoting or adapting) **:** BORROW ⟨*took* his plot from an old folk tale⟩ ⟨retorted with a line *taken* verbatim from Shakespeare⟩ ⟨our habit of *taking* words from other languages —Thomas Pyles⟩ (2) **:** to obtain from a natural source ⟨coal used is imported . . . while the limestone is *taken* from the company's own quarries —N.R. Heiden⟩ **b** (1) **:** to obtain as the result of a special procedure (as of observation, examination, or inquiry) **:** ASCERTAIN ⟨~ the temperature⟩ ⟨~ the dimensions of a room⟩ ⟨tailor *took* his measurements⟩ ⟨~ a census⟩ ⟨*took* the opinion of the group⟩; *also* **:** to carry out (a procedure yielding such a result) **:** CONDUCT ⟨~ an observation of the sun⟩ ⟨~ a test of its efficiency⟩ ⟨~ a poll⟩ ⟨~ a vote⟩ (2) **:** to get in writing **:** write down ⟨~ notes⟩ ⟨~ the attendance⟩ ⟨~ minutes of a meeting⟩ ⟨~ an inventory⟩ ⟨~ a copy of a will⟩ — often used with *down* ⟨~ down a speech in shorthand⟩ ⟨*took* down the principal points⟩ ⟨sent for a stenographer to ~ down his confession⟩ (3) **:** to get by drawing or painting or esp. by photography **:** make or execute a picture of **:** represent or portray in any artistic form; *esp* **:** to make a photograph of **:** PHOTOGRAPH ⟨likes to ~ pictures⟩ ⟨~ a snapshot⟩ ⟨*took* the children in their party clothes⟩ (4) **:** to get by transference from one surface to another (as by means of ink) ⟨~ a proof⟩ ⟨~ a person's fingerprints⟩ ⟨~ rubbings of ancient brasses⟩ ⟨worked out a way of *taking* the carved impression from the stone —Roger Burlingame⟩ **12 :** to receive or accept whether willingly or reluctantly (as something given, offered, proposed, or administered) ⟨wouldn't ~ my hand when I offered it⟩ ⟨taught her not to ~ candy from strangers⟩ ⟨*took* the present but didn't seem pleased with it⟩ ⟨wouldn't ~ no for an answer⟩ ⟨~ a bribe⟩ ⟨~ a bet⟩ ⟨was told to ~ it or leave it⟩ ⟨shipped it through the Canal and I *took* delivery on it here this afternoon —Robert Carson⟩: as **a :** to receive when bestowed or tendered (as an office, an honor, a degree, a prize) ⟨was on hand to ~ an honorary doctorate⟩ ⟨has been trained to ~ salutes on state occasions —*Star Weekly*⟩ **b** (1) **:** to submit to **:** ENDURE, UNDERGO ⟨*took* his punishment like a man⟩ ⟨~ a blow without flinching⟩ ⟨is *taking* treatments⟩ ⟨physician told him he ought to stay for six months and ~ the cure —*College English*⟩ ⟨the mauling his corps *took* in the peach orchard —R.M.Lovett⟩ ⟨seeing men die and *taking* three wounds in his own body —Dixon Wecter⟩ **:** put up with ⟨don't have to ~ anything from him, or to stand his bad manners —Willa Cather⟩ ⟨after *taking* twenty years of living in these cramped quarters —Henry Hewes⟩ — often used with *it* ⟨for people who can ~ it like pioneers, here is a new frontier —W.P.Webb⟩ ⟨she deserved the accolade of the modern generation — she could ~ it —*New Republic*⟩ (2) **:** to undergo without yielding **:** resist successfully **:** WITHSTAND ⟨~*s* hard usage⟩ ⟨specifications may require the glass . . . to ~ an impact blow of 6 to 9 ft. lbs. —E.B.Shand⟩ ⟨~*s* extremes of weather beautifully⟩ **c** (1) **:** to accept as true **:** BELIEVE ⟨had to ~ his word for it⟩ ⟨you can ~ it from me that he is not here⟩ (2) **:** to accept for guidance **:** FOLLOW ⟨~ a warning⟩ ⟨~ a hint⟩ ⟨~ a suggestion⟩ ⟨please ~ my advice⟩ (3) **:** to accept with the mind in a specified way ⟨~ a situation calmly⟩ ⟨*took* the joke in earnest⟩ ⟨*took* it ill of them⟩ ⟨would ~ it kindly if we could answer at once⟩ (4) **:** to accept without objection or opposition ⟨~ things as they come⟩ ⟨ready to ~ the consequences of his act⟩ ⟨~ the bad along with the good⟩ **d :** to indulge in and enjoy ⟨was *taking* his ease on the porch⟩ ⟨hoped to be able to ~ a brief vacation⟩ ⟨*took* a five-minute break for coffee⟩ ⟨time to ~ a rest⟩ **e :** to receive or accept as a return (as in payment, compensation, or reparation) ⟨agreed to ~ a thousand dollars in complete settlement of the claim⟩ ⟨wouldn't ~ less than a hundred a week⟩ ⟨wants more but would probably ~ less⟩ **f** (1) *obs* **:** to exact (as a promise or an oath) of another (2) **:** to accept the tender of (as a promise or an oath) (3) **:** to accept (as an oath, an affidavit, or a deposition) in a legal capacity (as by administering or witnessing) **g :** to admit (a male animal) in copulation **:** be covered by **h :** to respond to (bait or a lure) by seizing ⟨bonefish will ~ a fly during a strong wind —R.R.Camp⟩ ⟨*taking* feathered lures and spinning stuff —*Sports Illustrated*⟩ **i :** to accept a bet offered by ⟨ready to ~ all comers⟩ **j :** to deliberately make no attempt to hit (a pitched ball) ⟨manager signaled him to ~ the next pitch⟩ **13 a** (1) **:** to permit to enter **:** let in **:** ADMIT ⟨liable to ~ a great deal of water over the bow in bad weather —D.W. Pye⟩ ⟨seams had opened and the boat was ~*ing* water fast⟩ (2) **:** to have room for **:** ACCOMMODATE ⟨shelf just ~*s* the books⟩ ⟨harbor is so badly silted it can ~ only small craft —Christopher Rand⟩ ⟨suitcase wouldn't ~ another thing⟩ ⟨runway . . . long enough to ~ any of the biggest airliners of tomorrow —A.J.Cathrein⟩ ⟨largest canals ~ barges of more than a thousand tons —Alice Mutton⟩ **b :** to be affected injuriously by (as a disease) **:** CATCH, CONTRACT ⟨~ cold⟩ ⟨*took* the measles⟩ ⟨one of the sorrels *took* colic and died —J.F.Dobie⟩ ⟨their liability to ~ the blight —H.E.Laffer⟩ **:** be seized by ⟨~ a fit⟩ ⟨~ fright⟩ **c :** to absorb or become impregnated with (as dye) **:** be affected by (as polish) ⟨cloth that ~*s* dye well⟩ ⟨surface will not ~ paint⟩ ⟨granite ~*s* a high polish⟩ ⟨won't ~ a shine, no matter how long you wear it —Clarence Woodbury⟩ **d :** to receive into itself: (1) *obs* **:** CONTAIN, INCLUDE (2) *Scot* **:** to close in upon and submerge ⟨giantess who was so big the Sound of Mull *took* her only knee-deep —Alastair Borthwick⟩ **14 a** (1) **:** to receive into the mind **:** APPREHEND, COMPREHEND, UNDERSTAND ⟨his hearers were slow to ~ his meaning⟩ ⟨object of the writer will be . . . to make the reader ~ his meaning readily and precisely —Ernest Gowers⟩ ⟨event was so unusual and unexpected that we did not know how to ~ it —R.M.Lovett⟩ ⟨~ a remark as it was intended⟩ (2) **:** to apprehend the meaning of (a person) ⟨if I ~ you correctly⟩ ⟨in the other scenes we have no difficulty in *taking* him as we are meant to ~ him —F.R.Leavis⟩ **b :** to regard or look upon **:** CONSIDER, SUPPOSE ⟨we ~ this to be your final offer⟩ ⟨~ it as settled⟩ ⟨I ~ it that you approve⟩ ⟨hoped he would not be *taken* as absolutely committed⟩ ⟨does not wish people to ~ his fictions as novels —Carlos Lynes⟩ ⟨the type *taken* as normal in English political writing —D.W. Brogan⟩ ⟨canon law may be *taken* to include theology —H.O. Taylor⟩ ⟨do not ~ me as urging that it ought to be done —F.S. Mitchell⟩ **c :** to accept, consider, or reckon as being or as equal to ⟨*taking* a stride at the usual 30 inches⟩ ⟨reports by . . . untrained observers are all *taken* at a hundred percent of their face value —M.R.Cohen⟩ **d :** to feel or begin to feel or experience (as a state of mind) ⟨~ pleasure⟩ ⟨*took* delight in perversity —G.W.Brace⟩ ⟨*took* an immediate dislike to the newcomer⟩ ⟨saw no reason to ~ offense⟩ ⟨~ a little reasonable umbrage —C.E.Montague⟩ ⟨~*s* satisfaction in inertly orthodox generalities —F.R.Leavis⟩ ⟨*took* pride in his work⟩ ⟨nurse their griefs . . . seem, in fact, almost to ~ a delight in brooding over them —H.A.Overstreet⟩ **e** (1) **:** to form and adopt in the mind or with the will ⟨~ a resolution⟩ ⟨~ a grave view of a situation⟩ ⟨was here that the real decisions on policy were *taken* —J.H.Plumb⟩ ⟨whenever he *took* a notion he wanted something, he bought it —Margaret Cousins⟩ ⟨*taking* harsh judgments of his contemporaries —S.L.A.Marshall⟩ (2) **:** to form with the mind or will and exercise or display in action ⟨~*s* pity on all suffering creatures⟩ ⟨had *taken* no further heed of her existence —W.J.Locke⟩ **15 a :** to convey, lead, carry, remove, or cause to go along to another place, the direction of movement being away from the place from which the action is regarded: as (1) **:** to cause (as a person) to go along with one to a place ⟨~ the baby to the park⟩ ⟨*took* his girl to the prom⟩ ⟨promised to ~ the whole family to dinner⟩ ⟨this bus will ~ you into town⟩; *also* **:** LEAD ⟨this line ~*s* us directly to the city⟩ ⟨fine road ~*s* you through the forest —Tom Marvel⟩ ⟨to climb it would ~ us in the wrong direction —D.L.Busk⟩ (2) **:** to bear with one to a place or person ⟨~ your father's slippers to him⟩ ⟨~ the dishes to the kitchen⟩ ⟨*took* a plentiful lunch with them but brought most of it back⟩ (3) **:** to require or induce to go ⟨business *took* him west⟩ ⟨an appointment that *took* him into town⟩ ⟨neighbor whose employment ~*s* him on periodic trips across the country —Sidney Alexander⟩ **b :** to lead, convey, or remove in thought or mind ⟨seeking interests that would ~ him out of himself⟩ ⟨journey *took* his mind away from his troubles⟩ **c :** to convey to a higher or lower degree ⟨last-minute touchdown *took* the score to 57⟩ ⟨heavy selling in the afternoon *took* the list lower⟩ **d** *archaic* **:** to give (oneself) up or over **:** BETAKE, COMMIT, DEVOTE **16 a :** to remove or obtain by removing **:** ABSTRACT ⟨~ eggs from a nest⟩ ⟨~ the cream off the milk⟩ ⟨you can ~ a cork out of one of those bottles⟩ **b** (1) **:** to put an end to (as life or one's life) ⟨the right of the state to ~ human life⟩ ⟨*took* his own life in a fit of despondency⟩ (2) **:** to remove by death **:** deprive of life **:** cause to die ⟨was *taken* in his prime⟩ ⟨those who have been *taken* hence⟩ ⟨a mother whose only child had recently been *taken*⟩ ⟨a cruel fate *took* him from us⟩ **c** (1) **:** DEDUCT, SUBTRACT ⟨~ two from four⟩ ⟨*took* ten percent off the bill for cash⟩ ⟨celebrates his fiftieth birthday, give or ~ a few months, with this selection —Carlos Baker⟩ (2) **:** to carry away **:** WITHDRAW ⟨never *took* his eyes from hers⟩ ⟨gave him kicks that *took* the laugh off his face —Claud Cockburn⟩ **17 :** to undertake and make (as a movement) or do or perform (as an act or an action) ⟨~ a walk⟩ ⟨~ a look⟩ ⟨~ aim⟩ ⟨~ a trip⟩ ⟨~ a turn around the block⟩ ⟨~ two steps forward⟩ ⟨stopped two or three times to ~ a sounding —Nevil Shute⟩ ⟨able to ~ such action by air, naval, or land forces as may be necessary —Vera M. Dean⟩: as **a :** to direct and make a specified motion (as a blow) ⟨*took* a swing at a policeman⟩ ⟨tested the pillow by *taking* a poke at it⟩ **b :** to set in motion (as a lawsuit) **:** INSTITUTE ⟨~ proceedings⟩ ⟨~ legal action⟩ **c :** to put or set forth **:** RAISE ⟨~ an objection⟩ ⟨be fired . . . if an important reader or advertiser *took* exception to something he said —*Phoenix Flame*⟩ ⟨might ~ exception to his representative having a meal with casteless persons —Dillon Ripley⟩ **d :** BID, SAY ⟨~ adieu⟩ ⟨~ a last farewell⟩ **18** *archaic* **:** to assume or resume (as a discourse) at a point of leaving off **19 a :** to apply oneself to and treat or deal with ⟨~ first things first⟩ ⟨doctor was sure he had *taken* the disease in time⟩ ⟨~ the problems one by one⟩ ⟨next let us ~ the Peloponnesian War⟩ ⟨if he be summoned to court, his case is *taken* in a language he does not understand —Stuart Cloete⟩ **b** (1) **:** to deal with, consider, or view in a particular relation ⟨*taken* together, the details were quite significant⟩ ⟨*taking* one thing with another, decided they had not done badly⟩ (2) **:** to consider as an instance ⟨to illustrate, ~ ancient Greece⟩ **c :** to apply oneself to the study of or the acquisition of skill in ⟨~ fancy dancing⟩ ⟨~ music lessons⟩; *specif* **:** to study (as a subject or course) at an educational institution ⟨*took* English 21 last year⟩ ⟨is *taking* both French and German⟩ **20 :** to apply oneself to getting through or past or to surmounting (as a hedge or a hurdle) **:** succeed in clearing (as a difficulty or an obstacle) ⟨~ two stairs at a time⟩ ⟨*took* the corner on two wheels⟩ ⟨was *taking* fences at the age of six⟩ ⟨*took* the puddle in an easy leap⟩ ⟨*took* an exit at three times the posted limit —Hugh Sherwood⟩ ⟨sort of hill which any car can ~ with ease —F.G. Kay⟩ **21 :** to impose upon **:** CHEAT, SWINDLE ⟨how can the amateur collector be sure he isn't being *taken* —*New Orleans (La.) Times-Picayune*⟩ ⟨*taken* for over a hundred thousand dollars on shakedowns alone —F.B.Gipson⟩ ⟨girl who would ~ me for a lot of money —Merle Miller⟩ **~** *vi* **1 :** to obtain possession: as **a :** CAPTURE ⟨the queen in chess ~*s* at any distance in a straight line⟩ ⟨the symbol *x*, read "~*s*", indicates a capture —*New Complete Hoyle*⟩ **b :** to receive property under law as one's own **:** receive the title to property ⟨he ~*s* as heir⟩ ⟨was entitled, as a society with a lawful object, to ~ under a charitable bequest —Eduard Jenks⟩ **c** *of a fish* **:** to seize a lure or bait **:** rise to bait **:** BITE ⟨salmon *took* that morning, though halfheartedly —B.A.Williams⟩ ⟨will ~ in clear water⟩ ⟨tench, who stop *taking* soon after breakfast —T.H. White b. 1906⟩ **2 :** to lay hold **:** CATCH, ENGAGE, HOLD ⟨high-velocity harpoon is fired. If this strikes and ~*s*, an explosive charge goes off inside the animal's rib cage —I.T.Sanderson⟩ **3 a :** to establish a take esp. by uniting or growing — used of living things (as plant or surgical grafts) ⟨with an experienced surgeon some 90 percent of the grafts ~ —*Lancet*⟩ **b :** STRIKE 17a **4 a** (1) **:** to betake oneself **:** strike out **:** set out **:** GO, PROCEED ⟨~ after a purse snatcher⟩ ⟨~ down the street and around the corner⟩ ⟨~ across a field⟩ ⟨~ over the hill⟩ (2) *chiefly dial* **:** to take its course or run or lead (as of a road or river) ⟨road turns here and ~*s* over the hill⟩ **b** *chiefly dial* — used as an intensifier or often simply redundantly with a following verb ⟨*took* and swung at the ball but missed⟩ ⟨*took* and grabbed his hat and ran⟩ ⟨*took* and cried everytime anybody looked at her⟩; compare GO **5 a :** to have the natural or intended effect or action **:** take effect **:** ACT, OPERATE ⟨an expensive lesson in caution; it could only be hoped that it would ~⟩: as (1) **:** to catch hold **:** get hold ⟨wick was dry and the sparks didn't ~⟩ (2) *of a plan* **:** to work out or turn out successfully **:** SUCCEED ⟨fanciful schemes without a chance of *taking*⟩ ⟨where retirements are often announced but seldom ~ —*Springfield (Mass.) Union*⟩ (3) *of a vaccine or vaccination* **:** to produce a take **b :** to show the natural or intended effect (as of fire or cold) **:** become affected (as by adherence or absorption) in the expected or desired way ⟨dry fuel ~*s* readily⟩ ⟨had never *taken* after his first vaccination⟩ **6 :** CHARM, CAPTIVATE: **a :** to exert a spell ⟨no planets strike, no fairy ~*s*, nor witch hath power to charm —Shak.⟩ **b :** to prove taking or attractive **:** gain a favorable reception **:** win popular favor ⟨the play *took* greatly and was still drawing big audiences —W.A.Darlington⟩ ⟨book had not yet *taken* with the general reader⟩ **7 :** DETRACT — used with *from* ⟨a few minor irritations that *took* only slightly from their general satisfaction⟩ **8 :** to be or admit of being affected: as **a :** to be seized or attacked in a specified way **:** BECOME, FALL ⟨died suddenly in 1820, *taking* ill on his way home —Isobel Hutchison⟩ ⟨*took* sick⟩ ⟨*took* pretty surly —*Punch*⟩ **b :** to be capable of being moved in a specified way **:** COME ⟨top ~*s* off⟩ ⟨toy clock with varicolored plastic works that ~ apart for reassembly by the child⟩ ⟨table ~*s* apart for packing⟩ ⟨gadget ~*s* to pieces for cleaning⟩ **c :** to adhere or become absorbed ⟨ink

that ~*s* well on cloth⟩ **d :** to admit of being photographed ⟨colors that ~ well⟩ ⟨~*s* best highlighted against a dark background⟩

syn SEIZE, GRASP, CLUTCH, SNATCH, GRAB: TAKE is a general term without very specific connotation and applicable to the notion of coming to hold or possess, momentarily or longer, by physical action of the hand or in any other way ⟨*take* the book from the shelf⟩ ⟨a city *taken* by the enemy⟩ ⟨*take* a cottage for the summer⟩ SEIZE suggests sudden and forcible taking, often the taking or apprehending of something elusive or difficult by quick, opportune action ⟨they *seize* all the cattle and other property left behind by the fugitives in their haste —J.G.Frazer⟩ ⟨the Breton *seized* more than he could hold; the Norman took less than he would have liked —Henry Adams⟩ ⟨the character . . . is difficult to *seize*, for it comprised qualities hardly ever combined in one man —Hilaire Belloc⟩ GRASP implies a firm quick laying hold and tightening fingers around, a taking or seizing likened to such an action, or a similar effective comprehension ⟨she *grasped* him by the arm, driving her fingers deep into the flesh —R.P.Warren⟩ ⟨determined to *grasp* all they could for Pennsylvania, Colonial officials tricked the Indians —*Amer. Guide Series: Pa.*⟩ ⟨understood the words I heard, but couldn't seem to *grasp* their meaning —Kenneth Roberts⟩ CLUTCH may suggest increased suddenness, force, or firmness in taking hold, apprehending, or attempting to take hold ⟨with an agonized cry, she *clutches* his shoulders and drags herself to her feet —G.B. Shaw⟩ ⟨straws were straws, and the frailer they were the harder she *clutched* them —George Meredith⟩ ⟨flung himself forward with the others, desperately *clutching* at the precious escaping fish —A.J.Cronin⟩ SNATCH stresses suddenness of motion without indicating a forceful retention and may suggest stealthy or ready promptness in action ⟨many too are killed by their stronger companions in their desperate attempts to *snatch* their share of food —James Stevenson-Hamilton⟩ ⟨tried to keep hold of the plate which the school teacher tried to *snatch* away and for a few minutes they struggled laughing —Sherwood Anderson⟩ GRAB typically suggests rude rough forceful action, often in indifference to or violation of the rights of others ⟨could apparently *grab* Silesia by force of arms —Stringfellow Barr⟩ ⟨the more adventurous hastened to California with a pocketful of paper to *grab* rich mineral and timber lands —*Amer. Guide Series: Minn.*⟩ **syn** see in addition ATTRACT, RECEIVE

— **take a bow 1 :** to bow in acknowledging applause (as in a theater) **2 :** to accept credit or recognition (as for an accomplishment) ⟨high time we *took a bow* for what we have been able to do well —Nard Jones⟩ ⟨*take the bows* with the burdens —J.S.Dickey⟩ — **take account of :** to take into account — **take a chance** *or* **take one's chances :** to leave an outcome entirely to chance **:** trust one's fortunes in a particular venture to mere chance ⟨*take a chance* on the weather remaining fair⟩ ⟨Pilgrims . . . preferred to *take their chances* with the Indians —Leslie Thomas⟩ — **take a dare 1 :** to be dared to do something and attempt it **2 :** to be dared to do something and not to attempt it — **take a dive** *of a boxer* **:** to pretend to be knocked out esp. in a fixed fight — **take advantage of 1 :** to make use of for one's own benefit **:** use to advantage **:** profit by ⟨extends his examination . . . to *take advantage of* modern methods of diagnosis —Morris Fishbein⟩ ⟨feels we are not *taking* proper *advantage of* our opportunity —R.A.Smith⟩ **2 :** impose upon **:** ABUSE, EXPLOIT ⟨was always good to people . . . and there was those that *took advantage of* him —Nigel Balchin⟩ ⟨not above *taking advantage of* another's weakness⟩ — **take after 1 :** to take as an example **:** FOLLOW ⟨she is going to *take after* her grandmother —Elizabeth Taylor⟩ **2 :** to resemble in features, build, character, or disposition ⟨*takes after* his mother's side of the family⟩ ⟨*takes after* his father in everything except his eyes⟩ ⟨sons all *took after* him, if only at a distance —G.G.Coulton⟩ — **take against** *chiefly Brit* **:** take sides against **:** OPPOSE **:** feel dislike for or disapproval of ⟨nodded to the unknown guest; *took against* him —Virginia Woolf⟩ ⟨whether I was right or wrong, I *took* faintly *against* him —William Plomer⟩ — **take a joke :** to endure a joke at one's own expense — **take alarm 1 :** to heed a warning of danger **2 :** to become alarmed — **take amiss :** to impute a wrong motive or a bad meaning or intention to **:** take offense at ⟨afraid a refusal will be *taken amiss* —Dorothy Barclay⟩ ⟨don't *take* it *amiss* if his counsels are not pleasant —Richard Ginder⟩ — **take apart 1 :** to separate part from part or into parts **:** DISASSEMBLE, DISMANTLE, DISMEMBER **:** treat as if to dismember by force **:** rough up ⟨*take* a town *apart*⟩ **2 :** to analyze or dissect esp. in order to discover or reveal a weakness, flaw, or fallacy ⟨dislikes the dictum . . . and in this small book he *takes* it *apart* skillfully and ruthlessly —G.W.Johnson⟩ ⟨specialists in sports who *take* the various games and sponsors *apart*, but seldom bother to reassemble them —*Phoenix Flame*⟩ ⟨*takes* the ordinary American citizen *apart* in a most callous fashion —G.W. Johnson⟩ **3 a :** to subject to treatment intended to disorganize ⟨chances are that some opposing congressman will . . . *take* the witness *apart* —J.R.Fitzpatrick⟩ **b :** to treat roughly or harshly in any way **:** tear into ⟨isn't like an ordinary election campaign where you can *take* your opponent *apart* —*Time*⟩ ⟨*took* wives *apart* for the way they play poker —T.S. Geisel⟩ — **take a powder** *or* **take a runout powder** *slang* **:** to leave hurriedly **:** skip out **:** DECAMP, FLEE ⟨not likely to cross you up or *take a powder* on you —W.L.Gresham⟩ ⟨*taking a powder* and leaving everything up in the air —George Sklar⟩ ⟨*took a powder* for Paris accompanied by a beautiful blond mistress —Mike Stern⟩ ⟨*took a runout powder* this morning —Clayton Rawson⟩ — **take a reef 1 :** to reduce sail by reefing **2 :** to proceed more cautiously (as by curtailing expenses or activities) — **take arms :** to commence war or hostilities — **take breath :** to stop (as from working) in order to rest — **take care :** to be careful **:** exercise caution or prudence ⟨difference between *taking* due *care* and striking blindly in a wave of hysteria —Vannevar Bush⟩ **:** be watchful ⟨shall *take care* that the laws be faithfully executed —*U. S. Constitution*⟩ or provident or solicitous ⟨have *taken care* to assemble a good cast —Edward Sackville-West & Desmond Shawe-Taylor⟩ ⟨life *takes care* that we all learn the lesson thoroughly —Roger Fry⟩ — **take care of 1 a :** to attend to the needs, operation, or treatment of ⟨*takes care of* a ten-room house without help⟩ ⟨is home *taking care of* a sick child⟩ ⟨each operator can *take care of* three machines⟩ ⟨family doctor who had been *taking care of* them for 20 years⟩ **b :** to provide for ⟨five dollars should *take care of* unavoidable tips⟩ ⟨has his aged parents to *take care of*⟩ ⟨little steamers *take care of* transportation —Samuel Van Valkenburg & Ellsworth Huntington⟩ **2 a :** to deal with ⟨a change in the draft law to *take care of* draftees who refuse to answer loyalty questions —*Newsweek*⟩ ⟨a clerk *takes care of* routine inquiries⟩ **b :** to dispose of ⟨*take care of* the rubbish⟩ ⟨ordinary ventilation will automatically *take care of* the excess carbon dioxide —H.G. Armstrong⟩ ⟨the "longest lake entirely within New England" (that *takes care of* Lake Champlain) —R.S.Monahan⟩ **c** (1) **:** FIX ⟨could be counted on to *take care of* a traffic ticket⟩ ⟨the cops were well *taken care of*; the joint was running wide open —W.L.Gresham⟩ (2) **:** KILL ⟨they take another inmate . . . and they tell him to *take care of* and they'll take good care of him for it —*Workers Defense Bull.*⟩ — **take charge 1 :** to assume care, custody, command, or control ⟨*take charge* of an office⟩ ⟨*take charge* of a neighbor's children⟩ ⟨*took charge* of operations in the western sector⟩ ⟨was sent to the new division to *take charge*⟩ **2 a :** to get out of control ⟨anchor chain *took charge* and ran out⟩ ⟨should a ladder which is being raised or lowered *take charge* —*Fire Service Drill Bk.*⟩ **b** *of a ship* **:** to come up into the wind in spite of the helmsman — **take counsel :** CONSULT, DELIBERATE ⟨when a student decides to become a musician, let him first *take counsel* with himself —S.A.Koussevitzky⟩ ⟨*taking counsel* of his own thought, not overtolerant of those who differed with him —V.L. Parrington⟩ ⟨you have *taken counsel* of your ambition —Abraham Lincoln⟩ — **take croquet :** to croquet a ball — **take effect 1 :** to become operative ⟨any alteration of the charter . . . shall *take effect* when ratified —Vera M. Dean⟩ — compare EFFECT 10 **2 :** to produce a result esp. as expected or intended **:** be effective ⟨fired four shots, all *taking effect* —D.D.Martin⟩ — **take example :** to use as an example or warning — **take fire :** to catch fire ⟨sulfur and quicklime, which *took fire* when exposed to moisture —Tom Wintringham⟩ ⟨small number of students *take fire* from these courses —*New Republic*⟩ ⟨immense crowds of people *took fire* and came alive under their leadership —John Reed⟩ — **take five** *or* **take ten :** to take a five or ten minute intermission (as in a rehearsal of actors or musicians or on a march or work detail) **:** take a short break — **take for :** to suppose to be; *esp* **:** to suppose mistakenly to be **:** mistake for ⟨was often *taken for* a German because of his fair hair⟩ ⟨a car which could be *taken for* a custom sports model —*Lamp*⟩ ⟨strangers often *took* her *for* her own daughter⟩ ⟨naturally disliked being *taken for* a fool⟩ — **take from the table :** to call up (as a parliamentary report or motion) for consideration from the table of the presiding officer — **take guard :** to place the bat at guard in cricket — **take heart :** to gain courage or confidence **:** become encouraged — **take hold 1 a :** GRASP, GRIP, SEIZE ⟨*take hold* of a railing⟩ ⟨*took hold* and hung on tight⟩ **b :** to establish a hold on or over ⟨felt hate *take hold* of my whole body —Edita Morris⟩ ⟨a second conviction *took hold* of him —T.B.Costain⟩ ⟨story . . . *takes hold* of a reader from the first —Walter Havighurst⟩ **c :** to assume management or control **:** take in hand and deal with **:** take charge ⟨there was a new overseer . . . and he was *taking hold*, fast —Laura Krey⟩ ⟨women who *take hold* of things and aren't afraid of work —Ellen Glasgow⟩ ⟨administration fails to *take hold* of and solve the big problems —F.D.Roosevelt⟩ **2** [ME *taken hold*, fr. *taken* to take + *hold*] **:** to become attached or established ⟨once the glue dries and *takes* firm *hold* —Emily Holt⟩ **:** take effect **:** catch on ⟨theory *took hold* because the future was with it —W.P.Webb⟩ ⟨idea . . . does not seem to have *taken hold* very widely —Elmer Davis⟩ — **take into account** *or* **take into consideration :** to make allowance for (as in passing judgment) ⟨judge *took* the boy's age *into account*⟩ — **take into camp :** take in **:** DECEIVE, DUPE, TRICK ⟨straightforward, modest manner *took into camp* everybody he met —Bennett Cerf⟩ — **take into one's head :** to conceive as a sudden notion **:** be seized with an idea or form a sudden resolve ⟨*took it into his head* to open a small shop of his own⟩ — **take in vain** [ME *taken in vain*] **:** to use (a name) profanely or without proper respect — **take issue :** to adopt an opposed or contrary view or position **:** take up the opposite side **:** join issue **:** DISPUTE ⟨*took issue* with reports which charged the army with laxness —*Current Biog.*⟩ — **take it in snuff :** to become angry or offended — **take it on the chin :** to undergo complete defeat, failure, or frustration **:** endure punishment, abuse, or suffering — **take it or leave it :** accept or reject unconditionally — **take it out of :** to exact satisfaction or a penalty from ⟨threatened to *take it out of* the boy's hide⟩ **:** take the energy out of ⟨hot summer *took it out of* him as never before⟩ — **take kindly to :** to feel a natural attraction toward or an inclination or willingness to accept or adopt — **take lying down :** to endure (as an injury, an affront) passively or submissively — **take notice :** to look about one with attention ⟨as we approach, the black ducks begin to *take notice* —Wyman Richardson⟩ — **take notice of 1 :** to perceive especially **:** observe or treat with special attention ⟨isn't likely she'd ever *take* any *notice of* me —J.D. Beresford⟩ **2 :** to comment or remark upon ⟨papers *took notice of* his promotion⟩ — **take oath :** to swear with solemnity or in a judicial manner — **take one at one's word :** to understand and accept one's statement as literally true ⟨when he said he wanted to be left alone, we *took him at his word* and went away⟩ — **take one's death :** to expose oneself to death (as by catching cold or a disease) — **take one's life in one's hands :** to risk one's life deliberately — **take one's medicine :** to submit to punishment **:** accept unpleasant consequences of one's acts — **take one's time** *or* **take one's own time :** to be leisurely about doing something — **take order** *archaic* **:** to take suitable measures **:** make arrangements ⟨whiles I *take order* for mine own affairs —Shak.⟩ — **take orders 1 :** to receive directions or commands **2 :** to enter the Christian ministry by ordination (as to the priesthood) — **take or leave 1 :** to accept or reject solely according to one's judgment or inclination often of the moment ⟨a singer I can *take or leave* —Charles Miller⟩ ⟨imply that peace is something we Americans can *take or leave* —R.J.Bunche⟩ **2 :** to give or take ⟨left an estate of $100,000,000, *take or leave* a few dollars —Lucius Beebe⟩ — **take part** [ME *taken part*] **:** JOIN, PARTICIPATE, SHARE ⟨able to play games and *take part* in conversation —R.A.Hall b. 1911⟩ ⟨opportunity to *take part* in a practical solution of the social problem —R.M.Lovett⟩ — **take place :** HAPPEN, OCCUR ⟨died before the marriage could *take place* —O. Elfrida Saunders⟩ ⟨music *takes place* in time and painting in space —C.W.H. Johnson⟩ ⟨heard a conversation *taking place* in the next room⟩ — **take possession :** to get into one's possession by an act of one's own **:** enter into possession ⟨*take possession* of a new house⟩ ⟨doing the Lord's work by *taking possession* of the Promised Land —A.J.Toynbee⟩ ⟨had bought a car but hadn't yet *taken possession*⟩ **:** affect, sway, or dominate to the exclusion of all else ⟨idiotic slogan . . . *took possession* of his brain —Dorothy Sayers⟩ — **take root 1 :** to send forth roots **:** become rooted **2 :** to become fixed or established as if by sending forth roots ⟨colony has *taken root* and become a city —Tom Marvel⟩ ⟨free public education had been slow to *take root* —Jerome Ellison⟩ ⟨expectation *takes root* that American military forces will be available against any aggressor —A.O.Wolfers⟩ ⟨the price . . . of never having been allowed to *take root* in any community —F.R.Leavis⟩ — **take shape :** to assume a definite or distinctive form ⟨idea which was *taking shape* almost frightened him by its novelty —Marcia Davenport⟩ ⟨vision of a railway network covering the whole country was beginning to *take shape* —O.S.Nock⟩ ⟨our American universities . . . had not really *taken shape* much before 1910 —Harlan Hatcher⟩ — **take silk** *Brit* **:** to become a king's or queen's counsel — **take stage** *or* **take the stage :** to center attention upon oneself (as by moving to an important position on the stage) — **take the bull by the horns :** to face up to and grapple with a difficulty — **take the cake :** to carry off the prize orig. in a cakewalk **:** rank first ⟨*takes the cake* for sheer weight of national holidays — twenty-seven —*New Yorker*⟩ ⟨for . . . pure cheek that *takes the cake* —*Sydney (Australia) Bull.*⟩ — **take the count 1** *of a boxer* **:** to remain down while the referee completes a count of ten seconds **:** be counted out **2 :** to go down in defeat ⟨always had the willingness to *take the count* if I'm wrong —Hollis Alpert⟩ — **take the cross** [ME *taken the croice*, fr. *taken* to take + *the* + *croice, cros* cross] **:** to take a vow to fight the enemies of Christianity (as by entering upon a crusade) — **take the field 1 :** to go upon the playing field (as of a football team) **2 :** to enter upon a military campaign — **take the floor 1 :** to rise (as in a meeting or a legislative assembly) to make a more or less formal address, to make a motion, or for some similar purpose **2 :** to stand up to dance — **take the road :** to begin traveling; *specif* **:** to engage on a round of theatrical performances from town to town — **take the rue** *Scot* **:** REPENT — **take the wind out of one's sails 1 :** to sail to windward of a sailing vessel and so cut off the wind **2 :** to frustrate by anticipating (as in argument) or by forestalling (as in action or movement) — **take the word** *also* **take up the word :** to begin to speak — **take the words out of one's mouth :** to utter the exact words about to be used by another — **take time by the forelock :** to make prompt use of something **:** not let slip an opportunity — **take to** [ME *taken to*] **1 :** to take in hand **:** take charge of **:** care for ⟨charladies who *take to* their gentlemen —F.A.Swinnerton⟩ ⟨long to make pets of them all, but . . . their mothers *take to* them —Rachel Henning⟩ **2 :** to betake oneself to **:** have recourse to (as a place or a means of progression) ⟨*take to* the lifeboats⟩ ⟨bird *took to* flight⟩ ⟨*take to* the woods⟩ ⟨*took to* the parlor sofa and let everyone wait on her —Rosemary Benét⟩ **3 :** to begin to apply or devote oneself to (as a practice, habit, occupation) ⟨*take to* begging⟩ ⟨*take to* drink⟩ ⟨women who seem to *take to* the dressmaking and millinery trades by instinct —Mary Austin⟩ ⟨develop howls or *take to* biting visitors —Robert Littell⟩ **4 :** to adapt oneself to **:** respond to ⟨*took* so well *to* animal bait —Richard Semon⟩ ⟨never been milked by a woman . . . don't know how they'll *take to* it —Ellen Glasgow⟩ ⟨young stock *took* most readily *to* the concentrates —*Sydney (Australia) Bull.*⟩ ⟨home rulers would not *take* kindly *to* any suggestion of a centralized state —V.L.Parrington⟩ **5 :** to conceive a liking for ⟨*took to* the stranger at first sight⟩ ⟨nice to anybody she happens to *take to* —Kenneth Roberts⟩ — **take to one's heels :** to run away **:** FLEE — **take to task 1** *obs* **:** to undertake as one's special work **:** challenge to a feat **:** deal with **2 :** to call to account for a shortcoming **:** REPROVE ⟨is right in *taking to task* the historians for slighting this important development —C.V.Woodward⟩ — **take wake :** to let one's boat fall into the wake of another — **take water 1 :** to enter the water — used of a waterfowl **2 :** to ship water (as in a rough sea) — **take with** [ME *taken with* to accept, fr. OE *tacan with*, fr. *tacan* to take + *with*] **1** *Scot* **a :** to be pleased with **:** LIKE **b :** to put up with **2** *Scot* **:** ADMIT, CONFESS, ACKNOWLEDGE **3** *archaic* **:** to take the part or side of **:** agree with **:** side with **4** *dial* **:** to become affected by (as fire or water)

²**take** \ˈtāk\ *n* -S **1 :** an act or the action of taking (as by seizing, accepting, or otherwise coming into possession): as **a :** an act or the action of killing, capturing, or catching (as game or fish) ⟨the hunting ~ and other causes of mortality to pheasant eggs —*Sports Illustrated*⟩ **b** *chiefly Brit* **:** the action of leasing land (as for farming or mining) **c :** an action of accepting something (as by way of compromise) — compare GIVE-AND-TAKE **d** (1) **:** the capture of a chessman (2) **:** a position in which capture can be made — used with *on* ⟨White has left his queen on ~⟩ **e** (1) **:** the uninterrupted photographing or televising of a single scene or part of a scene (2) **:** the making of a sound recording ⟨session opened with the second ~ of the first part of the concerto —Murray Schumach⟩ **2 :** something that is taken: **a :** the amount of money received (as from a business venture, a sale, an admission charge, an enforced contribution): as (1) **:** the sum total taken in esp. from particular sources ⟨was fixing to increase the state's ~ on mutuel betting —J.G. Forrest⟩ ⟨the farmer's ~ last year⟩ ⟨the tax ~⟩ ⟨~ has lagged behind the increased outgo —Harlow Shapley⟩ ⟨a box-office ~ which yearly declined —Kaspar Monahan⟩ ⟨the 1956 ~ from tourism —*Newsweek*⟩ ⟨crowds became larger, and the ~ greater —Carey McWilliams⟩ (2) **:** a percentage of total receipts deducted or reserved (as the amount of a racing bet deducted by the state and the track owners) **:** CUT ⟨gambling ~ helps pay for the state's roads —Jack Goodman⟩ ⟨2.17 percent, the syndicate's net ~ on the issue —John Brooks⟩ (3) **:** a criminal's haul **b :** the number or quantity (as of animals, fish, or pelts) taken at one time **:** CATCH, HAUL ⟨a catch of four cows and an oil ~ of more than a hundred barrels —H.A.Chippendale⟩ ⟨yearly ~ of cottontail rabbits . . . runs into the millions —*Amer. Guide Series: Mich.*⟩ **c** (1) *chiefly Brit* **:** a piece of land taken by lease **:** HOLDING (2) **:** oil taken or bought from a lease **d** (1) **:** an installment of copy given to a compositor for typesetting; *esp* **:** a section of a running newspaper or wire service story sent to the pressroom in sections (2) **:** the type set from such copy **e** (1) **:** a passage to be taken down or an amount taken down at one time (as in shorthand) or transcribed (as on a typewriter) ⟨the high-speed ~*s* in this course have been taken from the *Congressional Record* —C.I.Blanchard & C.E.Zoubek⟩ (2) **:** a section or installment (as of an article, a speech) arbitrarily chosen (as for convenience in reading, recording, translation) ⟨prepared speech, translated in short ~*s* —W.V.Shannon⟩ ⟨an informal anthology in short ~*s* —William Miller⟩ ⟨might be wisest to read them in short ~*s* —*New Yorker*⟩ **f** (1) **:** a scene or part of a scene filmed or televised at one time without stopping the camera and with or without a sound recording ⟨usually a cutter receives hundreds of ~*s* of scenes —Andrew Buchanan⟩; *also* **:** the photography of a scene sequence identified by photographing a scene number on a take board (2) **:** a sound recording made during a single recording period usu. seven or eight minutes in length ⟨hundreds of feet of tape contain dozens of ~*s* —*N.Y. Times*⟩; *often* **:** a trial recording **3 a :** something that takes effect: as (1) *obs* **:** a magic spell (2) **:** taking quality **:** CHARM **b :** something (as a play or song) that becomes popular **4 :** an action or a result of taking effect: **a :** reaction of vaccinia indicating successful introduction of virus into the skin and its multiplication ⟨should be vaccinated again and again, if necessary, until there is a ~ —Benjamin Spock⟩ **b :** a successful union (as of a graft) ⟨skin grafting . . . resulted in a complete ~ —*Science News Letter*⟩ **5 :** an act or the action of taking something in mentally (as by a show of understanding) **:** REACTION, RESPONSE ⟨gave my name to the uniformed maid — whose ~, as I announced myself, was something to behold —Polly Adler⟩ ⟨the lovable baby with the big feet and the slow ~ —Robert Hatch⟩ ⟨no stage gasp or actor's ~ —Otis Ferguson⟩ ⟨would strike the committee, in a giant delayed ~ —Russell Maloney⟩ — compare DOUBLE TAKE — **on the take** *adv (or adj)* **:** alert to, in search of, or in pursuit of an opportunity to take or take advantage of another ⟨the big fish will be *on the take* in the water —Alec Robertson⟩

takeable *var of* TAKABLE

take about *vt* **:** to escort publicly to various places (as of entertainment)

take-all \ˈ=,=\ *n* -S **:** a destructive disease of cereal grasses caused by a fungus (*Ophiobolus graminis*) and characterized by foot rot and partially filled or empty heads and by bleaching of stalks, leaves, and heads — called also *whiteheads*

take-apart \ˈ=,=\ *adj* [*take apart*] **:** constructed so as to be readily taken apart and reassembled **:** TAKEDOWN ⟨*take-apart* toys⟩

take away *vb* [ME *taken away*, fr. *taken* to take + *away*] *vt* **1 :** to bear off to another place **:** carry away ⟨drop in . . . and *take away* an armful of their publications —Richard Joseph⟩ ⟨would allow foreign investors . . . to *take away* their capital gains —W.B.Preston⟩ **2 a :** REMOVE, SEPARATE ⟨*took* geometry *away* from its subject matter of lengths, areas, and volumes —S.F.Mason⟩ ⟨improved the house by *taking* the front porch *away*⟩ **b :** SUBTRACT ⟨*take away* six from nine⟩ **3 a :** to cause deprivation of ⟨*take* the right to vote *away*⟩ ⟨if support is suddenly *taken away* from an infant —H.A.Overstreet⟩ **b :** DETRACT ⟨without desiring to *take away* anything from the . . . production showing —*Securities Outlook*⟩ ~ *vi* **1 :** to clear away a meal from the table ⟨younger children had the task of *taking away*⟩ **2 :** to derogate or detract (as from merit or effect) often to a specified extent **:** lessen reputation ⟨these new elements have constantly *taken away* from the sea . . . until little but mediocrity remains —E.J.Schoettle⟩ — **take it away** — used as a cue or signal to begin a radio or television broadcast and equivalent to *you're on the air* — **take one's breath away :** to make one breathless from excitement or emotion or from astonishment or amazement

take back *vt* **1 :** RETURN ⟨*take* that jar *back* and get the right brand —*Phoenix Flame*⟩ **2 :** to resume possession of: **a :** to accept the return of ⟨store willingly *takes back* anything it sells⟩ **b :** REPOSSESS ⟨stories of . . . furniture *taken back* because of failure to meet payments —E.S.Hoyt⟩ **3 :** to permit to come back ⟨had been fired twice and both times *taken back*⟩ **4 :** RETRACT, WITHDRAW ⟨would neither apologize nor *take back* what he had said⟩ **5 :** to lead or draw back in thought to an earlier time ⟨*took* me *back* to when I was about twenty —Walter de la Mare⟩ ⟨there's nothing like music for *taking* you *back* —Mary Deasy⟩

take board *n* **:** SLATE 3b

take down *vb* [ME *taken down*, fr. *taken* to take + *down*] *vt* **1 a :** to pull down or to pieces (as a building, a scaffold) **:** cut down (as a tree) **b** (1) **:** to take apart or to pieces (as a motor) **:** DISASSEMBLE ⟨*take* a rifle *down*⟩ (2) **:** DISTRIBUTE ⟨*take* standing type *down*⟩ **2 :** to take from a higher to a lower place or level: as **a** (1) **:** SWALLOW ⟨*took* the dose *down* with a grimace⟩ (2) **:** SUBMERGE ⟨*take* a submarine *down* in a practice dive⟩ **b :** to conduct or escort to a place on a lower level ⟨*take* a lady *down* to dinner⟩ **c** (1) **:** to lower the spirit or vanity of **:** ABASE, HUMBLE ⟨had two methods of *taking* men *down*: babying them and harping on their faults —Edmund Wilson⟩ ⟨whippersnapper needs to be *taken down* a bit⟩ (2) **:** to reduce in strength **:** lay low ⟨was *taken down* with fever⟩ (3) *dial Eng* **:** to reduce in flesh **:** EMACIATE **d :** to reduce (as light or sound) in intensity ⟨signals the electrician to *take* the houselights *down* —Henning Nelms⟩ **3 :** to remove from a shelf or a hook ⟨*took down* his navy blue suit from the wardrobe —D.M.Davin⟩ ⟨*took* the family Bible *down*⟩ **4 a :** to write down ⟨notes *taken down* in shorthand⟩ ⟨no stenographers in Athens to *take down* what Demosthenes said —Max Eastman⟩ ⟨*take* a name *down*⟩ **b :** to record by mechanical means ⟨a wire recorder that was *taking down* the bebop music —Chandler Brossard⟩ ⟨this particular performance . . . was

taken down in the Rome Opera House —Douglas Watt⟩ ~ *vi* **1 :** to become seized or attacked esp. by illness ⟨*took down* with typhoid fever⟩ ⟨man . . . who was bearing most of the fitting-out expense *took down* sick —J.F.Dobie⟩ ⟨youngsters always *took down* with notions —H.L.Davis⟩ **2 :** to admit of being taken down ⟨hospital could set up in four hours and *take down* in two, they boasted —A.J.Liebling⟩ ⟨doubles *take down* into a shorter package than most pumps —Warren Page⟩

1**takedown** \ˈ=ˌ=\ *adj* [*take down*] **:** constructed so as to be readily taken apart ⟨a ~ rifle⟩ ⟨~ style⟩

2**takedown** \"\ *n* -s [*take down*] **1 :** the action or an act of taking down: as **a :** the action of humiliating esp. by deceiving **b :** DISASSEMBLY ⟨~ of an engine⟩ ⟨easy ~ for cleaning and oiling⟩ **c :** the act of bringing one's opponent in amateur wrestling under control to the mat from a standing position for a score of 2 points — compare ESCAPE, REVERSAL **2 :** one that takes down or humiliates (as by deception) **3 :** something (as a rifle or shotgun) having takedown construction

take-home pay *also* **take-home** \ˈ=ˌ=-\ *n* -s **:** the remainder of a person's gross salary or wages after deduction usu. at the source of salary payment of such items as income tax withholding, retirement insurance payments, and union dues

take in *vb* [ME *taken in*, fr. *taken* to take + *-in*] *vt* **1 a :** to allow to enter **:** ADMIT ⟨ship was *taking* water *in*⟩ **b :** to bring or draw in from outside ⟨air compressor . . . is used to *take in* atmospheric air, compress it, and force it into the cabin —H.G. Armstrong⟩ ⟨tankers . . . *taking in* cargoes of finished oil products —Martin Chisholm⟩ **2 a :** to carry or conduct within doors or into a room; *specif* **:** to escort (a lady) from a drawing room into dinner **b :** to take into custody **:** take to a police station as a prisoner ⟨going to have to *take* you *in* for attempted homicide —Ellery Queen⟩ **3 :** to draw into a smaller compass **:** reduce the extent of (as by shortening or tightening) ⟨*take in* a slack line⟩: **a :** FURL ⟨*take* a sail *in*⟩ **b :** to make (a garment) smaller by making seams, darts, and tucks larger ⟨dress needed to be *taken in* a bit⟩ **4 a :** to receive as a guest or inmate ⟨inn gladly *takes in* children⟩ ⟨widow had started *taking* a few lodgers *in*⟩ **b :** to give shelter to ⟨*take in* a stray dog⟩ **5 :** to receive in payment or as proceeds of a venture ⟨store *takes* a lot of money *in* each day⟩ ⟨compare notes on how much each has *taken in* on his pitch —W.L.Gresham⟩ **6 a** *chiefly Brit* **:** to receive (as a periodical) regularly ⟨*takes in* four daily papers —Christopher Isherwood⟩ **b :** to receive (work) into one's house to be done for pay ⟨*take in* washing⟩ ⟨sisters *took* a little plain sewing *in*⟩ ⟨*take in* typing jobs⟩ **7 :** to take (land) into possession **:** ANNEX, ENCLOSE, FENCE; *also* **:** to take under cultivation ⟨soil was usually exhausted in two or three years, when fresh land was *taken in* —Mary Tew⟩ **8 a :** to encompass within its limits **:** COMPRISE, EMBRACE, INCLUDE ⟨that expansiveness of view which *takes in* all the discrepant factors —H.A.Overstreet⟩ ⟨ban will *take in* fifty-eight miles of curb space —*N.Y.Times*⟩ ⟨in this day of the guided missile . . . the real world we live in *takes in* the whole earth —Herbert Bracker⟩ **b** (1) **:** to include in an itinerary or visit **:** explore or visit in seeing the sights ⟨can also *take in* some of the notable architectural monuments —Paul Henissart⟩ ⟨is *taking in* the sights of the World's Fair —*Newsweek*⟩ (2) **:** ATTEND ⟨*take in* a movie⟩ ⟨read more history or *take in* more plays —W.H.Whyte⟩ **9 a :** to receive into the mind **:** COMPREHEND, UNDERSTAND ⟨paused a few seconds to *take* the situation *in* —Rex Ingamells⟩ ⟨was pleased at the . . . way his mind was *taking in* impressions and interpreting them —Irwin Shaw⟩ ⟨stood motionless as though trying to *take in* the meaning of her words —Agnes S. Turnbull⟩ ⟨cannot easily *take in* new ideas —*Atlantic*⟩ **b :** to take note of ⟨in the second before she spoke . . . she had *taken in* the expensive hat and coat —Ruth Park⟩ **:** observe keenly ⟨seemed to *take* him all *in* anew before answering —S.H.Adams⟩ **:** PERCEIVE ⟨*took in* the special possibilities open to a monarch for extortion —Francis Hackett⟩ **10 :** to impose upon **:** CHEAT, DECEIVE, TRICK ⟨prides himself . . . that he will not be *taken in* by anybody —Louis Wirth⟩ ⟨*taken in* by a spurious document —G.C.Sellery⟩ ⟨couldn't lie convincingly enough to *take* a child *in*⟩ ⟨even the most experienced eye may be *taken in* on certain occasions —Henry Wynmalen⟩ ~ *vi* **:** COMMENCE, OPEN ⟨school *takes in* at nine and lets out at three⟩ — **take in with** *obs* **:** to take sides with **:** agree with **:** make terms with

take-in \ˈ=ˌ=\ *n* -s [*take in*] **1 :** an act of taking in (as by cheating or deceiving someone or by bringing something in) **2 :** one that takes in someone; *esp* **:** FRAUD **3 :** a number or quantity taken in

ta·kel·ma \təˈkelmə\ *n, pl* **takelma** *or* **takelmas** *usu cap* **1 a :** an Indian people of southwestern Oregon **b :** a member of such people **2 :** a Takilman language of the Takelma people

1**taken** [ME (past part.)] *past part or dial past of* TAKE

2**ta·ken** \ˈtākən *sometimes* -kᵊŋ\ *dial var of* TOKEN

take off *vb* [ME *taken of*, fr. *taken* to take + *of* off] *vt* **1 :** to remove from a position on something or the condition of being attached to or part of something (as by lifting, pulling, cutting, or breaking off or by subtracting or deducting) ⟨*took* his shoes *off* and put on his slippers⟩ ⟨chinook winds . . . *took off* as much as a foot of snow in 24 hours —E.B.Crane⟩ ⟨gave up trying to drive a car after *taking off* a fender —T.P.Whitney⟩ ⟨preparation *takes* paint *off* in one application⟩ ⟨system for *taking off* honey —Guy Diemer⟩: as **a :** RELEASE ⟨*take* the brake *off*⟩ **b :** DISCONTINUE, WITHDRAW ⟨play was *taken off* after three performances⟩ ⟨company announced that it would *take* two evening trains *off*⟩ **c :** to pick up and take along (as from a ship or an island) ⟨put in to *take* some stranded seamen *off*⟩ ⟨steamer calls once a week to *take off* mail⟩ **d** (1) **:** to take or allow as a discount ⟨*take* 10 percent *off* for cash⟩ (2) **:** to except, omit, or withhold from service owed or from time being spent or usu. spent in a particular way (as at one's occupation) ⟨looking for any excuse to *take* an hour *off* —Lillian Hellman⟩ ⟨*took* two weeks *off* in August⟩ ⟨usually played golf on Sunday but decided to *take* that Sunday *off*⟩ ⟨*took* a few minutes *off* to rest⟩ **2 :** to remove the burden of ⟨*take off* a tax⟩ ⟨promised to *take* the restrictions *off*⟩ **3 :** to put an end to **:** do away with ⟨turn up the furnace long enough to *take* the chill *off*⟩ ⟨poured in a small jug of raw cream — this, as they said, *took off* the greasiness —Paul Jennings⟩ **4 :** to take the life of ⟨disease appeared . . . and without respect of persons or neighborhoods, *took off* young and old —*Amer. Guide Series: Del.*⟩ ⟨pneumonia *took* him *off* in his prime⟩ **5 :** to drink down ⟨*took* a pint of beer *off* without lowering his glass⟩ **6 a :** to copy from an original **:** REPRODUCE ⟨*take off* a hundred copies⟩ **b :** to make a likeness of **:** PORTRAY ⟨*took off* his head and shoulders in charcoal⟩ **c :** to imitate esp. so as to parody or burlesque **:** MIMIC ⟨mannerisms that his critics delighted in *taking off*⟩ **d :** to take down from a receiving apparatus ⟨*take off* a telegram⟩ **7 a :** to measure off or estimate in determining requirements (as of materials in building) ⟨in *taking off* glass . . . even inches are used to describe the sizes —*Building, Estimating & Contracting*⟩ **b :** to calculate (as a quantity) with a calculating machine ⟨*take off* a total⟩ **c :** PREPARE ⟨*take off* a trial balance⟩ **8 a :** to lead away ⟨was *taken off* by the police⟩ **b :** to betake (oneself) from a place ⟨*takes* himself *off*, then telegraphs home for money —Elizabeth Bowen⟩ ~ *vi* **1 a :** to cause lessening or subtraction (as from the value of something) **:** DETRACT **:** take away **b** *of a tide, storm, or wind* **:** to grow less **:** ABATE, DECREASE **2 a :** to start off or away often suddenly **:** set out **:** DEPART, LEAVE ⟨*took off* in a radio command car —Bill Davidson⟩ ⟨*took off* without comment, stamping down the steps —R.O.Case⟩ ⟨*took off* downriver —Bernard De Voto⟩ **b** (1) **:** to branch off (as from a main stream or stem) ⟨pike *taking off* straight east is the Ramona Freeway —Ralph Friedman⟩ ⟨occasionally . . . *takes off* from reality, and then he is at his best —*Time*⟩ (2) **:** to take or have origin **:** DERIVE, ORIGINATE, STEM ⟨*takes off* from something observed or remembered —David Daiches⟩ **c** *of a jumper, hurdler, or vaulter* **:** to begin a leap or spring **d** *of an airplane, rocket, or bird* **:** to leave the surface of the land or water **:** begin flight **e :** to play a solo in jazz music that is characterized by wild improvisation and usu. a fast rhythmic beat **f :** to take a narcotic drug ⟨ritual of *taking off* was over and the drug was in his head —Hal Ellson⟩ **3 :** to be removable ⟨top *takes off* easily⟩

takeoff \ˈ=ˌ=\ *n* -s *often attrib* [*take off*] **1 :** something that detracts **:** DRAWBACK **2 :** an imitation esp. in the way of caricature **:** the action or an instance of mimicking **:** BURLESQUE, PARODY ⟨one of his ~*s* is on a young Southern novelist —Hollis Alpert⟩ ⟨a ~ on the conventional college song —Stewart Alsop⟩ ⟨musical comedy ~ on the Westerns —Arthur Knight⟩ ⟨competition started as a ~ on the traditional races —*Buick Mag.*⟩ **3 a :** a rise or leap esp. from the ground in making a jump or flight **:** a start in leaping or hurdling, in making an ascent in an aircraft, or in the launching of a rocket ⟨~ was done without any of your springboards —Edward Bass⟩ ⟨other birds need a long ~ run —*Time*⟩ ⟨had been test-fired twice . . . and that in each case it had blown up, or been detonated, soon after ~ —John Brooks⟩; *specif* **:** an action of beginning flight in which an aircraft is accelerated from rest to the condition of normal flight ⟨~ had been normal⟩ ⟨~ distance⟩ ⟨it was the ~ and the landing which he loved best —Louis Bromfield⟩ ⟨~ time⟩ **b :** an action of starting out or setting out ⟨everybody made a scram ~ for a foxhole —Ira Wolfert⟩ ⟨~ hour for the armored cars —Joseph Alsop⟩ ⟨severity with which you drive your car (sudden stops, quick ~*s*, fast cornering) —Walt Woron⟩ ⟨book . . . has a long, slow ~, although the materials are interesting —Edmund Fuller⟩ ⟨statesmen are elderly and slow on the ~ —Upton Sinclair⟩ **4 a :** a spot at which one takes off or may take off ⟨cars are arriving at the ~ —Bert Pierce⟩ ⟨can be climbed onto and used as a ~ for a higher leap —A.L.Kroeber⟩; *specif* **:** the spot or an object (as a rubber or board) from which a jumper, vaulter, or hurdler rises in leaping ⟨sketch of their pit showing two high jump ~*s* —*Athletic Jour.*⟩ ⟨~ board⟩ **b :** a starting point **:** point of departure **:** base of operations ⟨the ~ point of the real revolution of industrialization —H.R.Lieberman⟩ ⟨study of filter cigarettes published nearly seven months ago . . . became the ~ for a new campaign this week —*Advertising Age*⟩ **5 :** an action of removing something ⟨package is positioned horizontally to allow a better ~ —S.B.Bradley⟩ ⟨chemical and physical treatments of rayon, from the ~ at the spinning machine to the final product —F.C.Hahn⟩; *specif* **:** the skinning process in leather manufacturing **6 :** the action of estimating or measuring an amount of material needed (as in building) **:** quantity survey ⟨plumbing ~⟩ ⟨~ man⟩ **7 :** a device, mechanism, or part by means of which something is led or drawn off (as to another place, for another purpose) ⟨~*s* to houses are loops that return to the mains —W.R.Moore⟩; *specif* **:** a mechanism for transmission through which the power of an engine or vehicle may be taken off to operate some other mechanism ⟨two power ~*s* at the front of the motor —Bernard Gladstone⟩ ⟨rear ~ can provide either a belt drive . . . or a shaft drive —*Country Life*⟩ ⟨~ power from his tractor —*Ethyl News*⟩

take on *vb* [ME *taken on*, fr. *taken* to take + *on*] *vt* **1 a :** to invest or clothe oneself with **:** DON ⟨dry facts of history *take on* flesh and blood —V.L.Parrington⟩ **b :** ADD ⟨had been *taking* flesh *on*⟩ ⟨*took on* five pounds in one month⟩ **c :** to take aboard ⟨train stops only to *take on* through passengers⟩ ⟨put in to *take* water and provisions *on*⟩ **:** LOAD ⟨*take* cargo *on*⟩ **2 a :** to begin to perform or deal with **:** UNDERTAKE ⟨*take* a new job *on*⟩ ⟨didn't realize what a responsibility he had *taken on* —L.C.Douglas⟩ ⟨was *taking on* quite a contract —Russell Lord⟩ ⟨I'd just *taken on* a dealership for milking machines —C.A.Lindbergh b. 1902⟩ **b :** to undertake or engage with as or as if an opponent **:** accept the challenge of ⟨*taking on* the powerful in behalf of the poor and the weak —P.H.Douglas⟩ ⟨*took on* the wild boar, the water buffalo, the rhinoceros . . . and he conquered them all —James Thurber⟩ ⟨she and two sister subs *took on* a seventeen-ship convoy —E.L.Beach⟩ ⟨funks riding the black colt but *takes* it *on* to please his dad —Leslie Rees⟩ ⟨*took on* all comers in the boxing booth attached to the circus —G.E.Odd⟩ **3 a :** ENGAGE, HIRE ⟨company was *taking* workmen *on*⟩ ⟨*take on* a bookkeeper⟩ **b :** to accept in a relationship ⟨doctor was not *taking on* any new patients⟩ ⟨talked him into *taking* me *on* as a client⟩ ⟨wife . . . worked in a war plant but *took on* one man after another —W.L.Gresham⟩ **4 a :** to assume or acquire (as an appearance or quality) as or as if one's own ⟨can act . . . in the old-fashioned sense of *taking on* the complete being and personality of a wide variety of characters —Faubion Bowers⟩ ⟨green through all the winter, it now *takes on* every shade of color —Norman Douglas⟩ ⟨had begun to *take on* that wasted appearance which is characteristic of unused muscles —Grace Reiten⟩ ⟨*taking on* the slowness of a tidal stream —Julian Dana⟩ ⟨riddle of church and state has *taken on* fresh urgency —W.L.Sperry⟩ ⟨disease *took on* epidemic character —C.L. Jones⟩ ⟨familiar features . . . appear in a different perspective, *take on* another meaning —W.P.Webb⟩ **b :** ADOPT ⟨foreign dynasties in China have always submitted to the superior culture of the Chinese and have *taken on* their language —Edward Sapir⟩ ⟨threw in with the Indians, *taking on* their dress and manners —F.B.Gipson⟩ ⟨soon *took on* new ways of life —Kemp Malone⟩ **5** *Scot* **:** to get into debt for **:** obtain on credit ~ *vi* **1 a :** to show one's feelings esp. of grief or anger in a demonstrative way **:** behave or talk excitedly or extravagantly **:** make a great fuss ⟨*took on* about it as though he had lost a child —Sherwood Anderson⟩ ⟨dressed as an old lady and they cried and *took on* something terrible until I removed my wig —Bob Hope⟩ **b :** to put on airs **:** behave in a proud or haughty manner **2 a :** to engage oneself for service esp. by enlisting or reenlisting in military service **b :** to begin to associate or consort **:** take up **3 :** to find acceptance; *esp* **:** to become popular **:** make a hit **:** catch on ⟨song *took on* overnight⟩ ⟨idea somehow failed to *take on*⟩

take out *vb* [ME *taken out*, fr. *taken* to take + *out*] *vt* **1 :** to remove from within (as from a receptacle, a place, enclosing bounds or limits, a set or composite) ⟨had his tonsils *taken out*⟩ ⟨*took* his pen *out* and signed on the spot⟩ ⟨*took* the melodrama *out* of the rescue scenes and substituted pathos —M.W.Fishwick⟩ ⟨nurse *took out* the supper trays and the lights in the ward were turned off —Carson McCullers⟩: as **a** (1) **:** DEDUCT, SEPARATE ⟨*took* his commission *out* before turning over the proceeds⟩ (2) **:** EXCEPT, EXCLUDE, OMIT ⟨21 working days, *taking out* weekends and holidays⟩ (3) **:** WITHDRAW, WITHHOLD ⟨some land will be *taken out* of spring wheat and flaxseed —*Successful Farming*⟩ **b :** to draw out by cleansing ⟨a preparation for *taking* stains *out*⟩ **c :** to find release for **:** give vent to **:** EXPEND — usu. used with *on* ⟨*take out* their resentments on one another —J.W.Aldridge⟩ ⟨*take out* their wanderlust on geographic magazines —T.H.Robsjohn-Gibbings⟩ **d :** to get rid of or put an end to (as an obstacle, an opponent) **:** ELIMINATE ⟨second ball *takes out* all the remaining pins —*Beginning Bowling*⟩ ⟨main job was to *take out* enemy airfields —Walter Millis⟩ ⟨needed to have some of the conceit *taken out* of him⟩ **2** *obs* **:** COPY **3 :** to lead or carry forth (as into the open air, from a private to a public place, into society) ⟨*took* the dog *out* for a run⟩ ⟨mother liked to be *taken out* for dinner occasionally⟩ ⟨perfect weather for *taking* the baby *out*⟩ ⟨prettiest girl he had ever *taken out* on the dance floor⟩: as **a :** ESCORT ⟨not a puzzle to her that men seldom wanted to *take* her *out* —Aurelia Levi⟩ **b :** CONDUCT ⟨the next year he *took out* his first road company —W.B.Shaw⟩ **4 :** to take as an equivalent **:** obtain or receive the value of in another form — used with *in* ⟨part of the mill-workers' pay is *taken out* in houses —Sinclair Lewis⟩ ⟨*took* what remained of the debt *out* in goods⟩ **5 a :** to obtain (as by application) from the proper authority ⟨*take out* a summons⟩ ⟨*take out* a charter⟩ ⟨forgot to *take* a new dog license *out*⟩ ⟨new Socialist peers have followed tradition and *taken out* coats of arms —*N. Y. Herald Tribune*⟩ ⟨applied to *take out* citizenship⟩ **b :** to arrange for (insurance) ⟨your age at the time you *take out* your annuity —*advt*⟩ **6 :** to overcall (as one's bridge partner or his bid) in a denomination that is different or to bid over (as a double or redouble by partner) when the intervening opponent has passed, doubled, or redoubled ~ *vi* **:** to start on a course **:** set out **:** strike out ⟨wagons were *taking out*, some of them to face . . . miles of country road —William Faulkner⟩ ⟨saw the tracers of his machine guns *taking out* after them —Ira Wolfert⟩ ⟨trail *took out* across a long undulating grass prairie —H.L.Davis⟩ ⟨*take out* for home⟩ — **take it out on :** to expend anger, vexation, or frustration in harassment of ⟨*taking it out on* one another because of their hopeless dissatisfaction —Leslie Rees⟩

takeout \ˈ=ˌ=\ *n* -s [*take out*] **1 :** the action or an act of taking out; *specif* **:** a bridge bid that takes a partner out of a bid, double, or redouble after the intervening opponent has passed ⟨a forcing ~⟩ **2 :** a usu. automatic device for taking something out (as a finished article from a press or mold) **3 :** something taken out ⟨the state's ~ from racetrack receipts⟩ or prepared for taking out ⟨restaurant did a brisk trade in ~*s*⟩: as **a :** the minimal number or value of poker chips a player may buy from the banker at one time or the usual number or value of such chips **:** STACK **b :** a special article (as a biographical sketch, a background study) printed to fill completely successive pages or columns for easy removal ⟨a huge (39-page) and handsome Mexican ~ —*Time*⟩ ⟨a meaty ~ on the profitable doings of the famous five-and-tens —*Fortune*⟩

takeout double *n* **:** INFORMATORY DOUBLE

take over *vt* **:** to assume control or possession of esp. from or after another **:** succeed to the management of **:** assume charge of or responsibility for ⟨officers . . . preparing to *take over* the administration of occupied territories —Bernard Bloch⟩ ⟨a perfect handbook . . . on how to *take over* and use an honest nationalist government —R.A.Smith⟩ ⟨*took* the family business *over* when he was thirty⟩ ⟨automation is *taking* us *over* —John Lear⟩ ⟨*took over* the furniture of the previous tenant⟩ **:** ADOPT, BORROW ⟨Christianity *took over* this aspect of Platonism —Bertrand Russell⟩ ⟨Romans continued to *take over* from the Greeks not only their philosophy but their more practical arts —Benjamin Farrington⟩ ~ *vi* **1 :** to assume control or possession esp. by succeeding or supplanting another **:** take charge ⟨told his assistant to *take over* for him⟩ ⟨placed two loaded pistols on the president's desk and told all who had tarried to listen that he was *taking over* —*New Republic*⟩ **2 :** to displace another **:** become dominant ⟨saw a new point of view *taking over* —W.H.Hale⟩ ⟨the home is vanishing and the business office is *taking over* —Eric Sevareid⟩ ⟨the late twenties, when the movies *took over* —Arthur Miller⟩ ⟨now his emotional nature *took over* —H.A.McHugh⟩ ⟨transplanted tropical flowers and plants *take over* completely —Steve Trumbull⟩

take-over \ˈ=ˌ==\ *n* -s [*take over*] **:** the action or an act of taking over **:** assumption of management, control, ownership, or possession ⟨Communist Party here aims for a gradual legal *take-over* of the democratic machinery —George Weller⟩ ⟨have been preparing the ground for the *take-over* —*Atlantic*⟩ ⟨best, perhaps only, hope for blocking a Red *take-over* —*Newsweek*⟩ ⟨the presidential *take-over* —Drew Pearson⟩

tak·er \ˈtākə(r)\ *n* -s [ME, fr. *taken* to take + *-er*] **:** one that takes (as by seizing, removing, accepting, receiving) ⟨our ~*s* of the West were nomads of fixed and gentle habits —Russell Lord⟩ ⟨United States was a heavy ~ of copper —R.G.Woolbert⟩ ⟨fish . . . are often free ~*s* there —J.E.Hutton⟩: **a :** one that captures or seizes **:** CATCHER, CAPTOR ⟨these natives were the fur ~*s* —Julian Dana⟩ **b** *obs* **:** one that takes wrongfully **:** PILFERER, ROBBER, THIEF **c** (1) **:** one that takes possession esp. of land (2) **:** one that takes a lease of property **:** LESSEE, TENANT **d :** one that takes by collecting, receiving, removing, or recording ⟨ticket ~⟩ ⟨assiduous ~*s* of notes⟩ ⟨a ~ of dictation, maker of appointments, mailer of reminders —Helen Waterman⟩ ⟨one inventory ~ counts the units and a second puts down the count —H.S.Noble⟩; *specif* **:** a worker who carries or moves leather from one place or process to another in the hide house, beamhouse, or tan house **e :** one that accepts something offered (as a bet, a dare or challenge, merchandise, assistance, an opportunity) ⟨odds were five to three with no ~*s*⟩ ⟨if he was hunting a feud, he had no ~*s* who dared to quip about his kilt —Ashley Halsey⟩ ⟨call money offered at 2⅝ percent without attracting ~*s* —*Financial Times (London)*⟩ ⟨a creative mathematician . . . peddling lessons to no ~*s* —E.T. Bell⟩ ⟨section of the table given over to tea and raisin cakes had had no ~*s* —*New Yorker*⟩

taker-down \ˌ==ˌ=\ *n* -s **:** one that takes something down esp. as a part of the process of manufacture; *specif* **:** a worker who takes down galvanized sheets from the cooling racks for sorting and sending — called also *drier-down*

taker-in \ˌ==ˌ=\ *n* -s **:** one that takes in: as **a :** CHEAT, DECEIVER, SWINDLER **b :** LICKER-IN **c :** a boy (as an apprentice) who carries articles of glassware to the annealing oven

taker-off \ˌ==ˌ=\ *n* -s **:** one that takes something off esp. in withdrawing or carrying away as part of a process (as of manufacture) ⟨worked as a *taker-off* in a brickyard⟩ ⟨attachment . . . saves labor, by dispensing with the work of the *taker-off* —John Southward⟩

takes *pres 3d sing of* TAKE, *pl of* TAKE

take up *vb* [ME *taken up*, fr. *taken* to take + *up*] *vt* **1 a :** to pick up ⟨*took up* the morning paper and left the room⟩ ⟨*take up* longhandled nets and go forth into the salt marshes —Hugh Cave⟩ **:** LIFT, RAISE ⟨*take* her *up* tenderly —Thomas Hood †1845⟩ **b :** to remove by lifting or pulling up from a settled position ⟨*took* the carpets *up* each spring⟩ ⟨city was *taking* the old streetcar tracks *up*⟩ ⟨noise of workers *taking up* the street⟩ **c :** to pick up with the intention of using ⟨first time he had *taken up* his pen in days⟩ ⟨private gentlemen who had *taken up* arms against the king —H.E.Scudder⟩ ⟨*take up* the life of some eminent public man . . . often an autobiography —G.M. Young⟩ **d :** to allow to mount **:** take aboard ⟨train stops on signal to *take up* passengers⟩ **2 :** to carry or conduct to a higher place **3 :** to take into possession **:** assume possession of ⟨chartered or, as they then called it, *taken up* for the voyage —*Manchester Guardian Weekly*⟩ ⟨told that all available accommodation was *taken up* —*Farmer's Weekly (So. Africa)*⟩: as **a :** to begin to occupy (land) ⟨new industries to start . . . and new land to *take up* —F.D.Roosevelt⟩ ⟨have *taken up* the fertile plains and valleys —A.L.Kroeber⟩ ⟨first *taken up* for sheep in 1882, it was abandoned twenty years later —George Farwell⟩ **b :** to buy up ⟨scalpers *took* all available tickets *up*⟩ **c :** to borrow at interest ⟨arranged to *take up* a new loan⟩ **d :** to pay the amount of (as a note or loan) **:** pay in full for (as stock bought on a margin) **e :** to gather in ⟨*take up* a collection⟩ ⟨*take up* contributions⟩ **f :** to remove from the possession of another **:** take away ⟨has his license *taken up* by the policeman who issues the summons —*N.Y.Times*⟩ ⟨authorization from the attorney general to *take up* the alien's border-crossing identification card —*U.S.Code*⟩ **4 :** to receive, accept, or adopt for the purpose of assisting **:** lend one's favor or support to **:** proceed to patronize ⟨is *taken up* by the daughter of the college's athletic director —K.S.Davis⟩ ⟨rabble-rousing broadcaster . . . who was *taken up* by rich men and conservative politicians —Elmer Davis⟩ ⟨amazed at the suddenness with which you will be *taken up* by the best people —*New Republic*⟩ ⟨the universities were *taking* him *up* —*Times Lit. Supp.*⟩ **5 a :** to take or accept as one's own (as a belief, idea, practice) **:** come to use, do, or believe in **:** ADOPT ⟨*took up* the practice of walking to work⟩ ⟨*took up* the use of toothbrush, nail file, clothes brush —Dixon Wecter⟩ ⟨outline style also was *taken up* and modified by the Court artists —O.Elfrida Saunders⟩ ⟨Latin accentual verse did not *take up* the principle of regularity —H.O.Taylor⟩ **b :** to invest oneself with **:** take on oneself **:** ASSUME ⟨ready to *take up* an active and aggressive attitude to any . . . problem —J.H.Plumb⟩ ⟨no suggestion in his work . . . that corruption is an affectation *taken up* in order to astonish the bourgeoisie —Roger Fry⟩ **c :** to receive into itself or upon its surface and hold **:** SORB ⟨the elastic roller thus *takes up* the color from the pores of the wood —*Scribner's*⟩ ⟨plants generally *take up* nitrogen as nitrates —C.B. Palmer⟩ ⟨invading yeast was *taken up* by the phagocytic cells —*Immunity*⟩ **6 a :** to enter upon (as a business, profession, subject of study) ⟨*took up* his father's trade⟩ ⟨disliked the subject and wished he had not *taken* it *up*⟩ ⟨is thinking of *taking up* the violin⟩ ⟨town . . . has *taken up* art in its old age —S.T.Williamson⟩ **:** engage in ⟨passengers streamed off . . . to *take up* their daily chores —H.A.Smith⟩ **b :** to take in hand **:** proceed to deal with ⟨effect is to compel Congress to *take up* one industrial situation at a time —T.W.Arnold⟩ ⟨expected his case to be *taken up* at the next session⟩ **c :** concern oneself or itself with ⟨his next lecture would *take up* early Christian art⟩ ⟨*takes up* again a situation he dealt with . . . more than forty years —Paul Pickrel⟩ **d :** to make (as a cause) one's own concern **:** ESPOUSE, SUPPORT ⟨a reputation for *taking up* unpopular causes⟩ **7 :** to check or interrupt by dissent or reproof **:** REBUKE, REPRIMAND ⟨author should not *take up* his reviewer on matters of judgment —Patric Dickinson⟩ ⟨before she could *take* him *up* for it the door . . . opened —H.L.Davis⟩ **8 a :** to proceed to occupy (as a place or position) **:** establish oneself in ⟨restored emperor *took up* his residence at the "eastern capital" —F.A.Ogg & Harold Zink⟩ ⟨was invited to *take up* his abode in the town —*Amer. Guide Series: R.I.*⟩ ⟨*took up*

quarters in an abandoned schoolhouse⟩ ⟨studied in Italy, returning to *take up* a canonry —S.F.Mason⟩ ⟨would return ready and equipped to *take up* jobs —*Lamp*⟩ **b :** to occupy (as space, time) entirely or exclusively and often so as to obstruct **:** fill up ⟨only exit was *taken up* with two bicycles and a baby carriage⟩ ⟨spoken programs . . . *take up* more than 70 percent of our radio time —*Americas*⟩ ⟨afternoons that are not *taken up* with baptisms or visits —Frank Hamilton⟩ ⟨darkness . . . which *takes up* the largest area in his pictures —C.W.H. Johnson⟩ **c :** to engage (as a person, the mind, the attention) fully **:** ENGROSS, EMPLOY ⟨had been reading it to himself, and . . . seemed all *taken up* with it —Dorothy C. Fisher⟩ ⟨ideas, interests, and occupations that *take up* the attention of the community —Edward Sapir⟩ ⟨is too much *taken up* with the children —Rachel Henning⟩ **9 a :** to constrict (as an artery) by tying up **b :** to pull up or pull in (as by drawing or winding) so as to tighten or to shorten ⟨*take up* the slack in a rope⟩ ⟨*take up* stirrup leathers⟩ ⟨*take* a brake cable *up*⟩ **c :** to gather or pull together and make fast ⟨*take* a dropped stitch *up*⟩ **d :** to remove looseness from (as by adjustment of parts) ⟨*take up* lost motion in a machine bearing⟩ **10 :** to take into custody **:** ARREST, SEIZE ⟨had been *taken up* for crap shooting —R.M. Lovett⟩ ⟨Jews were also *taken up* in the streets and trams —*Manchester Guardian Weekly*⟩ **11 :** ACCEPT; *esp* **:** to respond favorably to (as a bet, challenge, proposal or the one offering it) ⟨men threaten a strike and . . . he invites them to try running the company . . . they *take* him *up* —Robert Hatch⟩ ⟨bragging kid who made a pass at me . . . was scared half to death when I *took* him *up* on it —James Jones⟩ **12 :** to begin again (as something left off) or take over from another ⟨your turn to *take up* the tale —John Buchan⟩ ⟨another band *took up* the tune —Elsie Singmaster⟩ ⟨secretary had now joined us and *took up* the discussion —Oscar Handlin⟩ **:** RESUME ⟨*took* the story *up* again where she had left off⟩ ⟨should *take up* life vigorously again —H.A.Overstreet⟩ **13** *Scot* **:** COMPREHEND, UNDERSTAND **:** to get the point of (as a joke, an allusion) **:** APPRECIATE **~** *vi* **1** *dial* **:** to come to a stop **:** restrain oneself; *esp* **:** to stop short in some bad practice **2** *of weather* **:** CLEAR **3 a :** to make a beginning esp. where another has left off ⟨practitioner is often required to *take up* where the theorist . . . is obliged to leave off —K.W.Thompson⟩ **b** *of a school* **:** to begin a session **4 a :** to become shortened **:** draw together **:** SHRINK **b :** to close up of itself (as of a leak) — **take up for :** take the part or side of **:** stand up for **:** side with ⟨had nobody to *take up for* him⟩ — **take up the cudgels :** to engage vigorously in a defense (as of a person, a principle) esp. in argument or debate — usu. used with *for* ⟨will gladly *take up the cudgels* for you, if you'll just send in your arguments —*Wilson Library Bull.*⟩ — **take up the hatchet :** to make or declare war **:** begin warlike activity ⟨induce the Indians to *take up the hatchet* for England —R.C.Downes⟩ — **take up with 1 :** to become interested or absorbed in ⟨*taking up with* forbidden science, listening to forbidden propaganda —H.A.Overstreet⟩ **2 :** to begin to associate with ⟨found myself *taking up with* someone who turned out to be more plausible than trustworthy —*Harper's*⟩; *esp* **:** to begin to keep company with **:** CONSORT ⟨a nice girl who *takes up with* a not so nice boy —F.H.Bennett⟩ ⟨*takes up with* many sorts of women —*Newsweek*⟩ **3 a :** to assent to **:** agree with **:** ADOPT, ESPOUSE ⟨not one to *take up* readily *with* new ideas —L.C.Douglas⟩ **b** *obs* **:** to receive or accept without opposition **:** put up with

take–up \ˈ=,=\ *n* -s [*take up*] **1 :** the action or an act of taking up (as by gathering or contraction, reeling in, absorption, compensation or adjustment) ⟨bottom edge should be slightly curved and wider than the top to allow for *take-up* in draping —Mary B. Picken⟩ ⟨liner plate reversible and adjustable for wear *take-up* —*Jaeger Dewatering Pumps*⟩ ⟨nylon fibers and fabrics have a very low water *take-up* —R.S.Horsfall & L.G. Lawrie⟩ ⟨selenium — soil and plant *take-up* of, from spraying orange groves —*Jour. of Amer. Pharmaceutical Assoc.*⟩ **2 :** UPTAKE 2a **3 :** any of various devices for tightening or drawing in: as **a :** a device in a sewing machine for drawing up the slack thread as the needle rises in completing a stitch **b :** a sometimes automatic device for taking up slack in the belt of an elevator or belt conveyor **c** *or* **take–up motion :** an automatic motion in a loom for rolling up the cloth as it is woven **d :** a device for winding photographic film upon a reel, core, or spool **e :** a device or piece of equipment used in shopwork to take up slack or to remove looseness (as from wear of parts) ⟨screw *take-up*⟩ ⟨brake cable *take-up*⟩ **4 a :** decrease in length of yarns when twisted or plied **b :** decrease in length of warp yarn in a cloth compared with original length of yarn on the beam

tak·haar \ˈtak,här, ˈta,kär, ˈtä-\ *n* -s [Afrik, lit., unkempt person, fr. *tak* branch, bough (fr. MD *tac* sharp point, branch) + *haar* hair, fr. MD *haer;* akin to OE *hǣr* hair — more at TACK, HAIR] *southern Africa* **:** a backveld Boer

takh·ta·djy \täkˈtäjē\ *n, pl* **takhtadjy** *or* **takhtadjies** *usu cap* **1 :** a Turkish-speaking and mostly Muslim people of the Anatolian plateau **2 :** a member of the Takhtadjy people

ta·kil·man \təˈkilmən\ *n* -s *usu cap* [irreg. fr. *takelma* + *-an*] **:** a language family of the Penutian phylum in Oregon comprising only the Takelma language

ta·kin \təˈkēn, ˈtä,k-\ *n* -s [Mishmi] **:** a large heavily built goat antelope (*Budorcas taxicolor*) of Tibet related to the musk-ox

¹taking *n* -s [ME, fr. gerund of *taken* to take] **1 a :** SEIZURE ⟨had a ~, which he took calmly, simply bidding us hold him upside down by his ankles —J.J.Chapman⟩ **b** *obs* **:** a seizure or attack from a malevolent influence **:** BLIGHT **2 a** *chiefly Scot* **:** an unfavorable state or condition **:** PLIGHT ⟨his head and his stomach were in a very sad ~ —C.E.Abernethy⟩ **b :** a state of violent agitation and distress ⟨put him in a great ~ . . . grew as white as a napkin —John Buchan⟩ **3 :** something taken or received: as **a takings** *pl* **:** receipts esp. of money ⟨in those days the ~*s* of a popular play were much less —W.S.Maugham⟩ ⟨~*s* did not cover expenses⟩ ⟨gross ~*s*⟩ **b :** a catch or take of fish or animals **c :** a holding of land for mining

²taking *adj* [fr. pres. part. of ¹*take*] **1 :** that takes the fancy **:** ALLURING, ATTRACTIVE, CAPTIVATING, PLEASING ⟨book has a very ~ period flavor —*Times Lit. Supp.*⟩ ⟨knew she would be a ~ girl; how lovely, I did not guess —George Meredith⟩ ⟨smiling inexpressibly ~ in his manner —Douglas Jerrold⟩ **2 :** CONTAGIOUS, INFECTIOUS, CATCHING

tak·ing·ly *adv* **:** in a taking manner **:** ATTRACTIVELY, ENGAGINGLY

tak·ing·ness *n* -ES **:** the quality of being taking **:** ATTRACTIVENESS

taki–taki \ˌtäkēˈtäkē\ *n* -s *usu cap both Ts* [Taki-Taki, by modif. & redupl., fr. E ²*talk*] **:** an English-based pidgin language of Surinam — called also *Ningre-Tongo*

tak·ka·nah \täˈkä(,)nä\ *n, pl* **takka·noth** *or* **takka·not** \-,nōs; ,=ˈnōt(h), -ōs\ [LHeb *taqqānāh*] **:** a rabbinic ordinance initiating a practice not directly based on biblical authority or oral tradition and promulgated to meet the needs of the times or circumstances

ta·ko·sis \təˈkōsəs, taˈk-\ *n* -ES [NL, fr. Gk *tak-* (akin to Gk *tēkein* to melt) + NL *-osis* — more at THAW] **:** a bacterial wasting disease of goats that is marked by diarrhea, pneumonic symptoms, and emaciation and is often fatal

ta·krou·ri \təˈkrürē\ *n* -s [origin unknown] **:** the chopped tops of cannabis used by addicts for smoking

takt \ˈtäkt\ *n* -s [G, time in music, measure, fr. L *tactus* touch, sense of touch — more at TACT] **1 :** a beat or pulse in music **2 :** MEASURE 4c(1) **3 :** TEMPO

taku \ˈtä(,)kü, ˈtä(-\ *n, pl* **taku** *or* **takus** *usu cap* **1 :** a Tlingit people on Taku river and inlet, Stevens Channel, and Gastineau Channel, Alaska **2 :** a member of the Taku people

¹ta·la \ˈtälə\ *n* -s [Sp, fr. Quiche *tara*] **:** a timber tree (*Celtis tala*) of Argentina; *also* **:** the yellowish gray hard wood of this tree

²tala \ˈ"\ *n* -s [Mongolian, open country] **:** a broad structural basin formed by subsidence or upwarp

ta·laing \täˈlīŋ\ *n* -s *usu cap* [Burmese] **:** ³MON

talaisim *pl of* TALIS

ta·la·je \təˈlähā\ *n* -s [AmerSp, fr. Nahuatl *tlalaxin*] **:** a tick (*Ornithodoros talaje*) of the American tropics that infests horses, man, and other mammals

ta·lak \təˈläk\ *n* -s [Ar *ṭalāq*] **:** a Muhammadan divorce that is effected by the simple act of the husband's rejecting the wife

ta·la·man·ca \ˌtäləˈmäŋkə\ *n, pl* **talamanca** *or* **talamancas** *usu cap* **1 a :** a Chibchan people of central Costa Rica **b :** a member of such people **2 :** a language of the Talamanca people

tal·a·poin \ˈtalə,pȯin, -pwan\ *n* -s [F, Buddhist monk, talapoin (fr. its fancied resemblance to a Buddhist monk), fr. Pg *talapão* (pl. *talapões*) Buddhist monk, fr. Mon *tala poi* our lord (title of respect)] **:** a western African monkey (*Cercopithecus talapoin*) that is the smallest of the guenons and is olivaceous above and whitish beneath with a black face and yellowish whiskers

ta·la·ri \ˈtälərē\ *n* -s [Ar *ṭalari*, fr. G *taler* taler — more at DOLLAR] **:** an old silver coin of Ethiopia last minted in 1904

ta·lar·ia \təˈla(a)rēə\ *n pl* [L, fr. neut. pl. of *talaris*, fr. *talus* ankle, heel + *-aris* -ar] **:** winged shoes fastened to the ankles and chiefly used as an attribute of the god Hermes or Mercury of classical mythology

tala·ve·ra \ˌtaləˈverə\ *n* -s *usu cap* [fr. *Talavera* de la Reina, commune of central Spain where it originated] **:** colorful glazed and decorated earthenware of Spanish or Spanish colonial origin

ta·la·yot \təˈlä,yōt\ *n* -s [Catalan, fr. Ar *ṭalā'i'* advance guard] **:** one of the prehistoric corbelled stone towers of the Balearic islands resembling the nuraghe of Sardinia

tal·bot \ˈtȯlbət, ˈtal-\ *also* **talbot dog** *or* **talbot hound** *n* -s *usu cap T* [prob. fr. *Talbot*, name of a Norman family in England] **:** a large heavy mostly white hound with pendulous ears and drooping flews that is thought to be ancestral to the bloodhound and some other modern breeds; *also* **:** a figure representing such a dog esp. as a heraldic device

talbot's law *n, usu cap T* [prob. after W. H. F. *Talbot* †1877] **:** a principle in optics: when two or more colors or degrees of brightness are alternately presented (as on a rotating sector disk) to the eye, there is a frequency of recurrence beyond which flicker ceases and the color or impression appears to be uniform

tal·bo·type \ˈtȯlbə,tīp, ˈtal-\ *n* [W. H. F. *Talbot* †1877 Eng. pioneer in photography + E *type*] **:** CALOTYPE

talc \ˈtalk, ˈtau̇k\ *n* -s [MF *talc* or ML *talcum*, fr. Ar *ṭalq*] **1 :** mica of muscovite; *also* **:** a thin sheet of such mineral **2 a :** a mineral $Mg_3Si_4O_{10}(OH)_2$ consisting of a basic magnesium tetrasilicate that is usu. whitish, greenish, or grayish with a soapy feel and occurs in foliated, granular, or fibrous masses (hardness 1, sp. gr. 2.6–2.9) — compare STEATITE **b :** TALCUM POWDER

tal·ca gum \ˈtalkə-\ *or* **tal·co gum** \-l(,)kō-\ *n* [by alter.] **:** TALHA GUM

talc·er \-kə(r)\ *n* -s [*talc* + *-er*] **:** SOAPSTONER

talcky \-kē\ *adj* [*talc* + *-y*] **:** TALCOSE

talc- *comb form* [*talcum*] **:** talc and ⟨*talc*ochlorite⟩ **:** talcose and ⟨*talc*omicaceous⟩

talc·ose \ˈtal,kōs\ *adj* [*talcum* + *-ose*] **:** of, relating to, or containing talc

talc·ous \ˈtalkəs, ˈtau̇k-\ *adj* [*talc* + *-ous*] **:** composed of or resembling talc

tal·cum \-kəm\ *n* -s [ML, fr. Ar *ṭalq*] **:** TALC 2

talcum powder *n* **1 :** powdered talc **2 :** a toilet powder composed of perfumed talc or talc and some mild antiseptic

¹tale \ˈtāl, *esp before pause or consonant* -āəl\ *n* -s [ME, talk, narrative, list, fr. OE *talu;* akin to OHG *zala* number, ON *tala* talk, number, Goth *talzjan* to instruct, and prob. to L *dolus* guile, deceit, Gk *dolos*] **1** *obs* **:** RELATION, DISCOURSE, TALK **2 a :** a series of related events or facts told or presented usu. to justify or clarify something **:** explanatory statement **:** ACCOUNT ⟨this error was due to a ~ of misfortunes piling up simultaneously —Frank Debenham⟩ ⟨a similar ~ of lack of communication between administrators and students —M.J. Herskovits⟩ ⟨multiple-factor analysis has much the same ~ to tell —William Stephenson⟩ ⟨thereby hangs a ~ —Shak.⟩ **b** (1) **:** a report of a secret or confidential matter — often used in pl. ⟨dead men tell no ~*s*⟩ ⟨telling ~*s* out of school⟩ (2) **:** idle talk or rumor **:** SLANDER ⟨the person who listens to gossip makes no free and generous effort to understand . . . the person about whom the ~ is told —H.A.Overstreet⟩ **c :** an account, enumeration, or category common to two or more persons or things ⟨the disputants ultimately found themselves in the same ~⟩ **3 a :** a narrative of some event or sequence of actual, legendary, or fictitious events usu. imaginatively composed with intent to entertain or amuse **:** STORY ⟨~*s* based on folklore, legends of great men and small —Jane G. Mahler⟩ ⟨it is essential . . . to know whether a given ~ is regarded as historical fact or fiction —W.R.Bascom⟩ ⟨the ~ goes back to the time when he was still a buck private —Marion Hargrove⟩ **b :** an untrue or inaccurate relation of events, incidents, or facts **:** FALSEHOOD ⟨the prince of literary rogues, who always preferred the ~ to the truth —Sir Winston Churchill⟩ ⟨sheer tall ~*s* spun by a moralist who was also a comic poet —Margaret Marshall⟩ **4 a :** a reckoning or enumeration by numbers **:** COUNT, TALLY ⟨as he admitted them to the fold . . . cast away one pebble at a time from his pile until the ~ was complete —J.A.N.Friend⟩ ⟨when the short ~ of English dead is rendered —L.G.Pine⟩ **b :** a number of things taken in the aggregate **:** SUM, TOTAL ⟨find pride, impatience, unreasonableness . . . all the unpleasant if effective ~ of traits of the successful technician of revolution —Crane Brinton⟩ **c :** a recorded accounting or declaration ⟨repaired to the treasury where each handed over his ~ of 70 pieces —John Craig⟩

²tale \ˈ"\ *vt* -ED/-ING/-s **:** to count, enumerate, or tell out (something) by number

³tale *var of* TAEL

talebearer \ˈ=,==\ *n* [¹*tale* + *bearer*] **:** one that officiously or maliciously spreads gossip, scandal, or idle rumors **:** GOSSIP

¹talebearing \ˈ=,==\ *n* **:** the act or habit of spreading gossip ⟨a reputation for ~⟩

²talebearing \ˈ"\ *adj* **:** given to talebearing ⟨my ~ neighbor⟩

taleisim *pl of* TALIS

tal·ent \ˈtalənt\ *n* -s [ME *talent, talente;* in sense 1, fr. OE *talente*, fr. L *talenta*, pl. of *talentum* unit of weight or money, fr. Gk *talanton* balance, pair of scales, unit of weight or money; akin to L *tollere* to lift up — more at TOLERATE; in sense 2, fr. OF *talent* inclination, desire, disposition, fr. ML *talentum*, perh. fr. L, unit of weight or money; in remaining senses fr. ME, unit of money; fr. the parable of the talents in Mt 25: 14–30] **1 a :** any of several ancient units of weight (as a Babylonian unit equal to 3600 shekels, a unit equal to 3000 shekels used in Palestine and Syria, and a Greek unit equal to 6000 drachmas) **b :** a unit of value equal to the value of a talent of gold or silver **c** *obs* **:** WEALTH, RICHES, ABUNDANCE **2 a** *archaic* **:** a characteristic feature, aptitude, or disposition of a person or animal **b** *obs* **:** an evil disposition or attitude **:** PASSION, ANGER **3 :** the abilities, powers, and gifts bestowed upon a man **:** natural endowments ⟨the stewardship of your time, ~, and treasure⟩ ⟨the ~*s* which God has given you as a divine trust⟩ **4 a :** a special innate or developed aptitude for an expressed or implied activity usu. of a creative or artistic nature ⟨the possessor of rare ~ as a pianist —Arthur Krock⟩ ⟨mental characteristics . . . connected with mathematical ~ —C.R.Fish⟩ ⟨the American mind with its great ~ for satire —J.B.Priestley⟩ ⟨credits the ladies . . . with a great ~ for intrigue —A.M.Young⟩ ⟨has no ~ for metaphysical speculation —J.W.Beach⟩ ⟨a man with a ~ for ingratitude and unsociability —T.S.Eliot⟩ ⟨man's industrious and senseless ~ for involving himself in the superfluous —James Boyd⟩ — often used in pl. ⟨students with ~*s* in music find both recreation and training —*Bull. of Bates Coll.*⟩ ⟨opportunity for the exercise of his political ~*s* —C.L.Becker⟩ **b :** general intelligence or mental power **:** ABILITY ⟨the labors of many scholars of ~, and some few of genius, had brought new technique to lexicography —R.W.Chapman⟩ ⟨~ is a wishy-washy thing unless . . . solidly founded on honest hard work —E.G. Coleman⟩ ⟨this task calls for . . . sheer imaginative ~ —R.D. Altick⟩ **5 a :** a person of talent usu. in a specific branch of activity ⟨he was a minor ~, but authentic —Malcolm Cowley⟩ ⟨the most . . . significant ~*s* in contemporary writing —Richard Watts⟩ ⟨younger ~*s* came to the fore —Hans Kohn⟩; *collectively* **:** a number of persons of talent in a usu. specified field or activity ⟨argued with an immense array of legal ~ —D.W. Brogan⟩ ⟨competing . . . for top-grade scientific ~ —Vannevar Bush⟩ ⟨methods of recruiting athletic ~ —Robert Rice⟩ **b :** one that is talented or skilled in a performing art ⟨one of Hollywood's most luminous ~*s* —Seymour Peck⟩ ⟨one of our big spontaneous musical ~*s* —Arthur Berger⟩; *collectively* **:** those engaged in a performing art ⟨the succession of new, worthwhile ~ was augmented by . . . a young baritone —Irving Kolodin⟩ ⟨the young ~ . . . caromed off to Hollywood —W.I. Nichols⟩ ⟨staging the show with local ~⟩ **syn** see GIFT

tal·ent·ed \-təd\ *adj* [*talent* + *-ed*] **:** having talent **:** possessing special aptitude **:** mentally gifted **:** ACCOMPLISHED ⟨a ~ musician⟩ ⟨our most ~ and successful chronicler of the upper middle class —Taliaferro Boatwright⟩ ⟨~ young actors⟩

tal·ent·less \-tləs\ *adj* **:** lacking talent

talent scout *n* **:** a person engaged in discovering and recruiting people of talent for a specialized field or activity ⟨a *talent scout* . . . saw him in the leading role —*Current Biog.*⟩ ⟨acting as a *talent scout* who brings into the firm many new authors —Hellmut Lehmann-Haupt⟩ ⟨oil firms have *talent scouts* constantly out searching for new dealers —W.C.Oursler⟩ ⟨is a full-time player *talent scout* for the Lions —Tommy Devine⟩

talent show *n* **:** a show or entertainment consisting of a series of individual performances (as singing, playing, dancing) by amateur or aspirant performers who may be selected for special recognition or advancement as performing talent ⟨the winners . . . compete in the intercollegiate *talent show* —*Springfield (Mass.) Daily News*⟩ ⟨annual all-community *talent show* —*Future*⟩

ta·ler *also* **tha·ler** \ˈtälə(r)\ *n* -s [G — more at DOLLAR] **:** any one of numerous large silver coins issued by various German states from the 15th to the 19th centuries and varying considerably in weight and fineness **:** a German dollar

¹tales *pl of* TALE, *pres 3d sing of* TALE

²ta·les \ˈtā(,)lēz\ *n, pl* **tales** [ME, fr. the ML phrase *tales de circumstantibus* such (persons) of the bystanders; fr. the use of the phrase in the writ summoning them] **1** *tales pl* **:** persons added to a jury usu. from those in or about the courthouse to make up a deficiency in the available number of jurors regularly summoned **2 :** a judge's writ or order summoning the tales

tales·man \ˈtālzmən, ˈtā(,)lēz-\ *n, pl* **talesmen** [*tales* + *man*] **:** a person summoned as one of the tales added to a jury

tale–teller \ˈ=,==\ *n* **1 :** one who tells tales or stories **2 :** TALEBEARER, TELLTALE

tal·ha gum \ˈtalhə-\ *or* **talh gum** \ˈtal-\ *n* [fr. native name of *Acacia stenocarpa* in Sudan] **:** a brittle commercial gum arabic obtained from two north African acacias (*Acacia stenocarpa* and *A. seyal*) — called also *Suakin gum, talca gum*

¹tali *pl of* TALUS

²ta·li \ˈtälē\ *n* -s [Tamil *tāli*] **:** a gold piece tied about a bride's neck by the bridegroom in India and worn during his life

³tali \ˈ"\ *n* -s [origin unknown] **:** SISSOO

tal·i·era \ˌtaləˈerə\ *n* -s [Bengali *tāliera*, fr. Skt *tālī*, fr. *tāla* palmyra palm, of Dravidian origin; akin to Kanarese *tār* palm] **:** BOOK PALM

tal·i·grade \ˈtalə,grād\ *adj* [L *talus* ankle, ankle bone + E *-i-* + *-grade*] **:** bearing the weight on the outer side of the foot in walking

taling *pres part of* TALE

ta·li·num \təˈlīnəm\ *n, cap* [NL, fr. native name of one species in Senegal] **:** a genus of chiefly American herbs (family Portulacaceae) having ephemeral variously clustered flowers with 2 sepals and 10 stamens — see ROCK PINK

tal·i·on \ˈtalēən\ *n* -s [ME *talioun* legal retaliation, punishment in kind, fr. L *talion-, talio;* prob. akin to MIr *taile* pay, W *tal*] **:** LEX TALIONIS

tal·i·pes \ˈtalə,pēz\ *n* [NL *taliped-, talipes*, fr. L *talus* ankle, ankle bone + *ped-, pes* foot — more at FOOT] **:** CLUBFOOT 1a

tal·i·pot \ˈtalə,pät\ *n* -s [Bengali *tālipōt* palm leaf, fr. Skt *tāli* book palm + *pattra* feather, leaf; akin to Skt *patati* he flies — more at TALIERA, FEATHER] **1** *or* **talipot palm :** a showy fan palm (*Corypha umbraculifera*) of Ceylon, the Philippines, and the Malabar coast having a trunk 60 to 100 feet high and bearing a crown of gigantic fan-shaped leaves that are used as umbrellas and fans and when cut into strips as a substitute for writing paper — see BUNTAL, OLLA **2 :** a starch obtained from the talipot palm

ta·li·say \təˈlē,sī\ *n* -s [Tag] **:** JAVA ALMOND

ta·lishi \təˈlishē\ *n* -s *usu cap* **:** one of the Caspian languages

tal·is·man \ˈtaləsmən, -əzm-\ *n, pl* **talismans** [F *talisman* or Sp *talismán* or It *talismano*, fr. Ar *ṭilsam*, fr. MGk *telesma*, fr. Gk, consecration, fr. *telein* to complete, initiate into the mysteries, fr. *telos* end — more at WHEEL] **1 :** an object cut or engraved with a sign or character under various superstitious observances or influences of the heavens and thought to act as a charm to avert evil and bring good fortune ⟨the stone had become a . . . ~ on which the fertility of their crops depended —Edward Clodd⟩ **2 :** something that produces extraordinary or apparently magical or miraculous effects ⟨truth is a ~ of which the charm never fails —Arnold Bennett⟩ ⟨her pride . . . as the sort of ~ that would save her from every kind of ill —Hugh Walpole⟩ ⟨representative government is . . . not in itself a ~ —W.C.Brownell⟩

tal·is·man·ic \ˌtaləˈsmanik, -əzˈm-, -nēk\ *or* **tal·is·man·i·cal** \-nəkəl, -nēk-\ *adj* **:** of, relating to, or having the properties of a talisman **:** MAGICAL ⟨~ signs⟩ ⟨the ~ power of driving away snakes —Norman Lewis⟩ ⟨the book turns out to have a ~ effect on the fortunes of the family —Robert Lynd⟩ — **tal·is·man·i·cal·ly** \-nək(ə)lē\ *adv*

talith *or* **talit** *or* **talis** *var of* TALLITH

tal·i·tol \ˈtalə,tȯl, -tōl\ *n* -s [*talose* + *-itol*] **:** a crystalline polyhydroxy alcohol $C_6H_{14}O_6$ formed by reduction of talose

¹talk \ˈtȯk\ *vb* -ED/-ING/-s [ME *talken;* akin to Fris *talken* to talk, OE *talu* tale — more at TALE] *vt* **1 :** to deliver or express in speech **:** SAY, UTTER ⟨to say that . . . is to ~ very little sense —Charlton Laird⟩ ⟨the vice-president ~*ed* what . . . was sensible enough —O.W.Holmes †1935⟩ **2 a :** to make the subject of conversation or discourse **:** CONSIDER, DISCUSS ⟨~*ed* books till the small hours —H.J.Laski⟩ ⟨~ the day's news —Paul Engle⟩ ⟨never . . . ~*s* personalities —Elmer Davis⟩ — often used with *over* ⟨~*ed* it over with his family —W.L.Gresham⟩ ⟨suggest . . . that the three of us ~ the situation over —H.B. Safford⟩ **b :** to speak confidently or boastfully of without matching the words with performance ⟨~*s* a good, enlightened prolabor line which . . . turns out to be window dressing —*New Republic*⟩ ⟨they don't just ~ a good game, they play it —Charles Price⟩ **3 :** to use (a language) for conversing or communicating **:** SPEAK ⟨to ~ the language well is still the indispensable accomplishment of a gentleman —E.G.Bulwer-Lytton⟩ ⟨the peculiar French patois that he ~*ed* —Aaron Copland⟩ ⟨~*ed* Italian fluently and French like a Frenchman —G.M.Trevelyan⟩ **4 a :** to bring to a specified state by talking ⟨~*ed* herself hoarse answering queries over the phone —Jane Woodfin⟩ ⟨~*ed* him deaf, dumb, and blind⟩ ⟨~ the economy into a recession —*New Republic*⟩ **b :** to persuade, influence, or affect by talking ⟨could ~ the university into giving me money enough —Oliver LaFarge⟩ ⟨his own weak effort to ~ himself out of what he had already decided to do —W.F.Davis⟩ **~** *vi* **1 a :** to express, communicate, or exchange ideas or thoughts by means of spoken words **:** CONVERSE ⟨had supper and ~*ed* until very late —Bruce Siberts & W.D.Wyman⟩ ⟨stood outside . . . in little groups ~*ing* —Louis Bromfield⟩ — often used with *to* or *with* ⟨~*s* to the children when they come to see him⟩ ⟨out ~*ing* with the neighbors⟩ **b :** to convey information or communicate with signs or with sounds made as if by talking ⟨30 deaf mutes, their faces alight . . . when they ~ —W.F.McDermott⟩ ⟨ahead of him two flickers were ~*ing* —Steve Frazee⟩ ⟨a rawhide drum started ~*ing* in measured beats —F.B.Gipson⟩ ⟨on the flying bridge . . . the light began to ~ to us —Vincent McHugh⟩ ⟨how to choose the book that's going to ~ to him in a way he finds enjoyable —Horace Sutton⟩ **c :** to make sounds or noises that are suggestive of talking ⟨a bracing wind . . . ~*s* menacingly of storm and stress and shipwreck —Alfred Buchanan⟩ ⟨a gun was ~*ing* . . . filling the night with battle uproar —Alan LeMay⟩ **2 a :** to use the faculty of speech **:** utter or make the sound of words ⟨~ in human language better than many a parrot —Morris Gilbert⟩ ⟨most hard-of-hearing people . . . ~ very loud —Eleanor B. Simmons⟩ ⟨this is a microphone . . . you ~ straight into it —Jane Woodfin⟩ **b :** to speak idly or incessantly to no purpose **:** PRATE, CHATTER ⟨all the while she ~*ed*, saying trivial, idiotic things —Louis Bromfield⟩ ⟨foolish and perverse,

banal, intolerably ~*ing* on and on —H.O.Taylor⟩ ⟨and Congress ~*ed* —*Economist*⟩ **c :** to speak to the point **:** say something worthwhile ⟨now you're ~*ing*⟩ **:** carry weight ⟨money ~*s*⟩ **3 a :** to transmit a speculation or rumor usu. about another **:** GOSSIP — often used with *about* ⟨she does not ~ about others behind their backs⟩ **b :** to reveal secret or confidential information usu. concerning unlawful acts or practices ⟨he ~*ed* and revealed much valuable information to the F.B.I. —J.M.Wolfe⟩ ⟨cash-on-the-side payments . . . are oftentimes difficult to ascertain unless the buyer ~*s* —M.B.Clinard⟩ **4 :** to give a talk **:** LECTURE ⟨he ~*s* on the radio and to community groups⟩ **syn** see SPEAK — **talk at :** to speak to (a person) urgently or unremittingly ⟨goes into company not to contradict but to *talk at* you —William Hazlitt⟩ ⟨whenever she could get me into a corner, she *talked at* me —Gladys Schmitt⟩ — **talk big :** to talk boastfully or bombastically ⟨here was an unknown . . . who *talked big* but could he deliver —Neal Stanford⟩ ⟨people have come to country towns, *talked big* or tried to organize fantastic schemes —P.E.Curtiss⟩ — **talk of** *or* **talk about :** to refer to or deliberate (something) **:** PONDER, CONTEMPLATE ⟨*talk of* the devil and he'll appear⟩ ⟨a $20 million office structure the state *talks of* building —*New Englander*⟩ ⟨it is *about* the bet on yourself that I want to *talk* —J.S.Dickey⟩ ⟨the stability statesmen *talk about* would be possible —E.M.Forster⟩ — **talk one's head off :** to talk to one volubly and unremittingly ⟨are shy at first, but once they get to know you, they'll *talk your head off*⟩ — **talk one's way :** to obtain passage through or in a restricted place by talking or persuasion ⟨would *talk his way* into monasteries, ask to see the library —Gilbert Highet⟩ ⟨once *talking his way* past a detective who stopped him —Al Spiers⟩ — **talk sense :** to voice rational, logical, or sensible thoughts or ideas ⟨at a time for greatness . . . we owe it to the people to *talk sense* —A.E. Stevenson †1965⟩ — **talk through one's hat :** to voice irrational, illogical, or erroneous statements ⟨unless we test it, our talk of . . . economic aid and government propaganda will be *talking through our hats* —*Wall Street Jour.*⟩ — **talk to Midland :** COURT, WOO — **talk to death :** to prevent passage of (a legislative bill) by unlimited discussion or filibuster ⟨rule 22 . . . allows . . . senators to *talk to death* any civil rights measure —*Economist*⟩ ⟨reports persisted today that friends . . . might try to *talk to death* a resolution proposing his censure, on which the Senate opens formal debate tomorrow —*Springfield (Mass.) Daily News*⟩

²**talk** \"\ *n* -s [ME, fr. *talken* to talk] **1 a :** the act of talking **:** SPEECH, CONVERSATION ⟨an opportunity to . . . enjoy a bit of ~ —Margaret Jones⟩ ⟨asked the question . . . with apparent intention only of keeping ~ going —Gilbert Parker⟩ **b :** an instance or period of such speech or conversation ⟨expects to have a long ~ with his old friend⟩ ⟨stops to have ~*s* with people he knows⟩ **2 a :** the utterance of words **:** ARTICULATION ⟨writers . . . whose ear for the vernacular is so accurate that they can bring a whole stratum of society to life by the ~ of their characters —Amy Loveman⟩ ⟨it is difficult to understand them because of their strange ~⟩ **b :** pointless or fruitless discussion **:** VERBIAGE, CHATTER ⟨meeting produced little but ~ —*Time*⟩ ⟨a man who has had his dinner is never a revolutionist: his politics are all ~ —G.B.Shaw⟩ ⟨the drowning of one's mental disturbances in brave ~ —W.J.Reilly⟩ **3 :** a formal or prearranged discussion, negotiation, or exchange of views usu. of a political nature **:** CONFERENCE, MEETING ⟨latest bid for Big Four ~*s* on a . . . peace treaty —*Current History*⟩ ⟨sent word to . . . come in for ~*s* at Fort King —Marjory S. Douglas⟩ **4 a :** the making of often speculative statements or comment **:** MENTION, REPORT ⟨much ~ of the atomic bomb —C.G.McAleer⟩ ⟨~ of acquiring a large amount of surplus war material —A.H.Lybyer⟩ ⟨all the ~ we hear about quality being adversely affected —Bruce Payne⟩ **b :** RUMOR, GOSSIP ⟨only telling you the ~ in our neighborhood —Mary R. Rinehart⟩ ⟨a lot too much ~ going on —S.H.Adams⟩ **5 :** the topic of interested comment, conversation, or gossip ⟨it was the ~ not only of the town but of the country —Edward Bok⟩ ⟨by evening of that day the project had become the ~ . . . of the whole community —L.B.Salomon⟩ ⟨a pert young daughter . . . whose adventures were common ~ —L.C.Douglas⟩ **6 a :** an analysis or discussion formally prepared for public presentation **:** SPEECH, LECTURE ⟨at the first American Writers' Congress . . . he gave a ~ on "The Tradition of American Literature" —C.I.Glicksberg⟩ ⟨broadcasts a weekly inspirational ~ called "The Art of Living" —Bernard Kalb⟩ **b :** written analysis or discussion presented in an informal or conversational manner ⟨here is timeless old England . . . given in such lists and such ~ as only this writer can command —*N. Y. Herald Tribune Bk. Rev.*⟩ ⟨wrote a book called *Talks to Teachers*⟩ **7 :** communicative sounds or signs resembling or functioning as talk ⟨heard a scuffle and then a good deal of pheasant ~ up a hill among some huge boulders —Dillon Ripley⟩ ⟨lake ships use a whistle ~ that consists of 450 different signals —H.F.Unger⟩ ⟨occasional slang signs with which a deaf person . . . intersperses his ~ —J.S.Long⟩

talk·abil·i·ty \ˌtȯkəˈbiləd·ē\ *n* **:** the quality or state of being talkable

talk·able \ˈtȯkəbəl\ *adj* **1 :** capable of being talked about ⟨fishing is always a ~ subject⟩ **2 :** disposed to friendly conversation ⟨a ~ person has the gift . . . of being interesting, charming, delightful, in the most offhand and various modes of utterance —Henry Van Dyke⟩

talk around *vt* **:** to talk over ⟨*talked* most of them *around* . . . and kept the wagon train moving down the trail —A.M. Schlesinger b. 1917⟩

talk·a·thon \ˈtȯkəˌthän\ *n* -s [¹*talk* + -*athon* (as in *marathon*)] **:** a protracted session of public discussion or speech-making: as **a :** FILIBUSTER 2a ⟨had not yet decided whether they would conduct a ~ against the bill —*Wall Street Jour.*⟩ **b :** a campaigning device in which a candidate answers telephoned queries on radio or television for a period of many hours ⟨waged one of the most vigorous campaigns . . . through his radio ~*s* —Graham Hovey⟩

talk·a·tive \ˈtȯkəd·|iv, -ət|\ *adj* [¹*talk* + -*ative*] **:** given to or filled with talking **:** LOQUACIOUS, GARRULOUS ⟨was now, especially when fortified with liquor, as ~ as might be —W.M. Thackeray⟩ ⟨this is a ~ town and you are the last person it will spare —O.S.J.Gogarty⟩ ⟨for the first time in all these ~ weeks, people appeared to have nothing much to say, whether they approved of the decision or not —Mollie Panter-Downes⟩ ⟨a ~ book⟩

syn TALKATIVE, LOQUACIOUS, GARRULOUS, and VOLUBLE all apply to one given to talking; TALKATIVE usu. stresses only a readiness to engage in talk but may suggest a disposition to enjoy conversation ⟨told a number of his best Indian stories; for he was extremely *talkative* in man's society —W.M. Thackeray⟩ ⟨his wife was considerably younger . . . and *talkative* where he was monosyllabic —Dorothy Sayers⟩ LOQUACIOUS commonly implies fluency and ease in speech or an unusual talkativeness ⟨talks in a rapid and persuasive fashion (he is described as *loquacious* and good-natured) —*Current Biog.*⟩ ⟨the briskness of the mountain atmosphere, or some other cause, made everybody so *loquacious* —Nathaniel Hawthorne⟩ GARRULOUS usu. stresses an unchecked, rambling, often foolish, sometimes tedious, talkativeness ⟨this delightfully *garrulous* volume of memoirs —*Books of the Month*⟩ ⟨the Italian quarter, noisy, *garrulous*, good-natured, and vital —*Amer. Guide Series: Mass.*⟩ ⟨did most of the talking: he was a *garrulous* young man —T.O.Heggen⟩ ⟨the glories of silent appreciation were shattered by *garrulous* nothings —William Beebe⟩ ⟨a *garrulous* old man⟩ VOLUBLE suggests a free, easy, often seemingly endless loquacity ⟨a *voluble* man, given to telling anecdotes —Jean Stafford⟩ ⟨was to placate *voluble* voters who came in to complain —Sinclair Lewis⟩ ⟨was very *voluble*, repeating, with increased circumlocutory detail and reference to what he had said to Dick and Dick to him, the account he had originally given to the police —Dorothy Sayers⟩

talk·a·tive·ly \|əvlē\ *adv* **:** in a talkative manner **:** with much talking

talk·a·tive·ness \|ivnəs\ *n* -ES **:** the quality or state of being talkative

talk away *vt* **:** to consume or pass (as time) in talking ⟨*talking* the long night hours *away*⟩

talk back *vi* [¹*talk* + *back*, adv.] **:** to speak in answer usu. to a command or admonishment in a flippant or impertinent manner — usu. used with *to* ⟨her children *talk back* to her —*Saturday Rev.*⟩ ⟨a young man should not *talk back* to his superiors⟩ ⟨soldiers are taught not to *talk back* to superior officers⟩

talk–back \ˈ⸗,⸗\ *n* -s [fr. the phrase *talk back*, fr. ¹*talk* + *back*, adv.] **:** a two-way radio system providing esp. for one receiving instructions or directions to speak back to the instructor; *esp* **:** such a system set up between a broadcasting studio and its control room

talk down *vt* **1 :** to overcome or silence by superior argument or by loud and insistent talking ⟨burst out with attacks on the play . . . but they had their facts wrong and were *talked down* —Elmer Davis⟩ ⟨tries to argue back but his opponent vociferously *talks* him *down*⟩ **2 :** to disparage or belittle by talking ⟨endeavored to interrupt and then to *talk down* all hymns —Haldane Macfall⟩ ⟨in boosting his own products he never *talks* theirs *down*⟩ **3 :** to bring an airplane in for a blind landing by means of instructions radioed to the pilot by a ground observer who watches the approach of the craft by means of radar ⟨the ground control radar operator *talked* the . . . pilot *down* the landing approach to the runway —A.M. Johnston⟩ ~ *vi* **:** to speak in a condescending or oversimplified fashion with the false assumption that the listener is altogether ignorant of the matter involved — usu. used with *to* ⟨tired of being *talked down* to and are rightly insulted by being treated most of the time as . . . morons —John Mason Brown⟩ ⟨in teaching him he never *talked down* to him, indulged or flattered him; he treated him as a man and an equal —Elizabeth Goudge⟩

talked *past of* TALK

talk·ee–talk·ee \ˈtȯkēˈtȯkē\ *n* -s [West Indies Pidgin E, by modif. & redupl. fr. E ²*talk*] **1 :** broken speech; *esp* **:** corruption of speech due to unfamiliarity with its words, idioms, or pronunciation **2 :** idle chatter **:** PRATTLE

talk·er \ˈtȯkə(r)\ *n* -s [ME, fr. *talken* + -*er*] **:** one that talks; *specif* **:** a man trained and equipped to transmit orders or communications to the crew of a naval vessel by telephone or the PA

talkfest \ˈ⸗,⸗\ *n* -s [²*talk* + -*fest*] **1 :** an informal gathering for general talk or discussion **2 :** a protracted discussion or debate of a matter of public concern ⟨new ~*s* may break out in Congress over the measure to set up a private atomic industry —*Wall Street Jour.*⟩ ⟨the village branches of all these . . . organizations were called together for endless ~*s* —Joseph Alsop⟩

talk·ie \ˈtȯkē, -ki\ *n* -s [¹*talk* + *movie*] **:** a sound motion picture

talk in *vt* [¹*talk* + *in*] **:** to talk down (sense 3) ⟨had to *talk* me *in* when the . . . windshield iced over on one of my early rocket flights —Arthur Murray⟩

talking *pres part of* TALK

talking book *n* **:** a phonograph recording of a reading of a book or magazine that is designed chiefly for the use of the blind

talking chief *n* **:** a Polynesian and esp. a Samoan noble or title-holder who speaks and acts for a high chief in official, social, and economic matters

talking film *also* **talking picture** *n* **:** TALKIE

talking machine *n* **:** PHONOGRAPH

talking point *n* [*talking* (fr. gerund of ¹*talk*) + *point*] **1 :** a point, fact, or development that lends support for an argument or proposal ⟨provided the Revolutionary leaders in Philadelphia with a *talking point* in urging the establishment of a navy —*Amer. Guide Series: Maine*⟩ ⟨one of the greatest *talking points* in the argument —*Jour. of the History of Ideas*⟩ **2 :** a feature or argument of use in selling ⟨yarns . . . are the *talking points* of some interesting new fabrics —*Women's Wear Daily*⟩

talking–to \ˈ⸗⸗,⸗\ *n* -s **:** DRESSING DOWN, LECTURE ⟨came down and gave me a tremendous *talking-to* —Rebecca West⟩ ⟨thought I would give him a *talking-to* in a nice way —Mary S. Watts⟩

talk out *vt* **1 :** FILIBUSTER ⟨the arguments by which it has been *talked out* of existence —Stephen Spender⟩ **2 :** to clarify or settle (as a problem) by oral expression or discussion ⟨meet . . . to discuss knotty problems and *talk* them *out* to a point of mutual understanding —C.E.Wilson⟩ ⟨the caseworker . . . encourages her to *talk out* her anxieties which have been critically restricting —Gertrude Samuels⟩

talk over *vt* **:** to change the mind or opinion of (a person) by talking ⟨is very good at *talking* opponents *over* to his viewpoint⟩

talks *pres 3d sing of* TALK, *pl of* TALK

talk up *vt* **:** to discuss in a favorable fashion **:** COMMEND, PROMOTE, ADVOCATE ⟨enthusiast had been *talking up* the game —F.S.Blanchard⟩ ⟨organizing crews to ring doorbells and *talk up* loans —N.M.Clark⟩ ⟨sponsoring and . . . *talking up* a so-called right-to-work bill —P.F.Healy⟩ ~ *vi* **:** to speak up plainly or directly ⟨if you do not talk down to a child, it will assuredly *talk up* to you —Wilson Follett⟩ ⟨*talks up* in the evening . . . talking bolder than he sometimes feels —Meridel Le Sueur⟩

talky \ˈtȯkē, -ki\ *adj* -ER/-EST [¹*talk* + -*y*] **1 :** given to talking **:** TALKATIVE ⟨a rather ~ lawyer . . . who likes to dilate upon the distinction between business and the professions —*New Yorker*⟩ **2 :** abounding in or containing too much talk **:** reaching a level no higher than talk ⟨when a play is ~, the talk must be purposeful, or it will be dull —M.M.Smith⟩ ⟨his book is bold and ~ and generally fuzzy, an excellent example of the axiom that good intentions are not enough —Walter Bernstein⟩

talky–talky \ˈ⸗⸗ˈ⸗⸗\ *adj* **:** TALKY 2 ⟨a rather loose, flat, *talky-talky* idiom —Dorothy Van Ghent⟩

¹**tall** \ˈtȯl\ *adj* -ER/-EST [ME, ready, handsome, brave, prob. fr. OE *getæl* quick, ready; akin to OHG *gizal* quick, Goth *untals* disobedient, uninstructed, *talzjan* to instruct — more at TALE] **1** *obs* **:** BRAVE, BOLD, COURAGEOUS ⟨spoke like a ~ fellow that respects his reputation —Shak.⟩ **2** *obs* **:** comely of feature **:** HANDSOME **3** *obs* **:** READY, QUICK, DEXTEROUS ⟨swear to the prince thou art a ~ fellow of thy hands —Shak.⟩ **4 a :** high in stature **:** of greater than average height among others of a kind or class ⟨was ~ — about six feet in height —H.N.Fowler⟩ ⟨the giraffe, ~*est* of animals⟩ **b :** of a specified stature or height ⟨stands five feet one inch ~ and weighs 97 pounds —*Current Biog.*⟩ **5 a :** of a considerable or great height **:** elevated above the ground **:** LOFTY ⟨the shade of the ~ young pines —Corey Ford⟩ ⟨the ~ clouds of deep July —C.G.Glover⟩ ⟨command of a ~ and gallant ship —S.E. Morison⟩ ⟨a ~ cavernous room —Ben Hecht⟩ ⟨hit a ~ fly to the outfield⟩ ⟨a ~ hill⟩ ⟨climbing a ~ fence⟩ **b :** of unusual length from bottom to top **:** LONG ⟨wears ~ hats to add to her height —*Current Biog.*⟩ ⟨a ~, cool lemonade —Ray Bradbury⟩ ⟨unusual page sizes, including ~ books —*Publishers' Weekly*⟩ **c :** of a distinctly higher growing variety or species of plant ⟨two types of lima beans — dwarf and ~ —*New Zealand Jour. of Agric.*⟩ **6 a :** large or formidable in amount, extent, or degree ⟨think £10,000 rather a ~ price —M.V.Reidy⟩ ⟨saving anything is a ~ order today —*advt*⟩ ⟨got to . . . do some ~ growing —*Adult Leadership*⟩ ⟨will have some ~ explaining to do —*New Republic*⟩ ⟨had to do some ~ riding to keep 'em together —Will James⟩ ⟨a ~ problem that has been a long time growing —H.R.Isaacs⟩ **b :** grandiloquent, high-flown, or affected in style or subject matter ⟨indulging in ~ talk about the vast mysteries of life —W.A.White⟩ ⟨~ talk, empty talk, the stuff dreams are made of —H.G.Evarts⟩ ⟨placing a number of ~, opaque words . . . betwixt your own and the reader's conception —Laurence Sterne⟩ **c :** outside of the usual, ordinary, or fanciful in conception or invention **:** IMPROBABLE ⟨~ tales they are . . . the man who shot five bears with one bullet —*Amer. Guide Series: Maine*⟩ ⟨the talk grew ~, and it only took a few makings to roll up a good story —Meridel Le Sueur⟩ ⟨spin ~ yarns about frontier life —E.S.Clifton⟩ **syn** see HIGH

²**tall** \"\ *adv* **:** in a tall manner ⟨the entrance makes you walk ~ —Claudia Cassidy⟩ ⟨renewing faith, we shall stand ~ again —Isabel Tudeen⟩ ⟨two books about fighting — rather savage persons talking ~ in both — but how different in manners —O.W.Holmes †1935⟩

tal·lage \ˈtalij\ *n* -s [ME *taillage, taliage, tallage*, fr. OF *taillage*, fr. *taillier* to cut, limit, tax + -*age* — more at TAILOR] **1 :** a toll, fee, or render paid by a feudal tenant to his lord apparently in commutation of a render in kind or services **2 :** an impost or due levied by a lord upon his tenants sometimes of definite amount according to local custom or the terms of tenure; *specif* **:** a tax or compulsory aid levied occas. by the Norman kings on their demesne lands and royal boroughs or cities

tal·la·has·see \ˌtaləˈhasē, -si\ *adj, usu cap* [fr. *Tallahassee*, capital of Florida] **:** of or from Tallahassee, the capital of Florida **:** of the kind or style prevalent in Tallahassee

tall·ate \ˈtäˌlāt\ *n* -s [*tall (oil)* + -*ate*] **:** a metallic soap made from tall oil

tall bellflower *n* **:** an annual or biennial herb (*Campanula americana*) of eastern No. America bearing long leafy spikes of blue or white flowers

tall blueberry *or* **tall bilberry** *n* **:** HIGHBUSH BLUEBERRY

tall blue lettuce *n* **:** a No. American annual or biennial herb (*Lactuca spicata*) bearing mostly pinnatifid leaves and small blue or white flower heads in large clusters

tallboy \ˈ⸗,⸗\ *n* [¹*tall* + *boy*] **1 :** a tall-stemmed drinking glass **2 a :** HIGHBOY **b :** CHEST-ON-CHEST **c** *Brit* **:** CLOTHESPRESS

tall buttercup *or* **tall crowfoot** *or* **tall field buttercup** *n* **:** a perennial European buttercup (*Ranunculus acris*) widely naturalized esp. in eastern No. America and having a short thick rootstock and long petioled rosette leaves that are 5- to 7-parted with linear toothed segments

tall case clock *n* **:** a tall narrow floor clock equipped with a pendulum, striking mechanism, chimes, and sometimes a device for showing the month, day, and phases of the moon — compare GRANDFATHER CLOCK

tall clock *n* **:** GRANDFATHER CLOCK

tall coneflower *n* **:** a No. American herb (*Rudbeckia laciniata*) from which the golden glow is derived

tall copy *n* **:** an esp. good copy of a book with ample margins at the tops and bottoms of the pages

tall cupflower *n* **:** a shrubby Chilean herb (*Nierembergia frutescens*) used as an ornamental and having bluish white tubular flowers

tall drink : a mixed drink served in a tall glass

tal·le·ga·lane \ˈtaləgəˌlān\ *or* **tal·le·ga·lene** \-ˌlēn\ *or* **tal·ly·ga·lone** \-ˌlōn\ *n* -s [fr. native name in Australia] **:** a sand mullet (*Myxus elongatus*) or a related Australian fish

taller *comparative of* TALL

tallest *superlative of* TALL

tal·let \ˈtalət\ *n* -s [W *taflawd* loft, roof, fr. ML *tabulata* boarded platform, flooring, fr. fem. of L *tabulatus* floored, boarded, fr. *tabula* board, tablet + -*atus* -ate] **1** *dial Eng* **:** HAYLOFT **2** *dial Eng* **:** ATTIC

tall fescue *or* **tall fescue grass** *n* **:** MEADOW FESCUE

tall grama *n* **:** a No. American grama grass (*Bouteloua curtipendula*) having flower spikes arranged in slender one-sided racemes

tallgrass \ˈ⸗,⸗\ *n* **:** any of various grasses (as members of the genus *Andropogon*) that are characterized by tall stature and are prominent chiefly in periods and areas of abundant moisture — compare SHORTGRASS

tallied *past of* TALLY

tallies *pl of* TALLY, *pres 3d sing of* TALLY

tal·lin *or* **tal·linn** \ˈtälən, ˈtäl-\ *adj, usu cap* [fr. *Tallin* or *Tallinn*, capital of Estonia] **:** of or from Tallin, the capital of Estonia **:** of the kind or style prevalent in Tallin

tall·ish \ˈtȯlish, -lēsh\ *adj* **:** somewhat or rather tall

tal·lith *or* **tal·it** *or* **tal·lis** *also* **ta·lith** *or* **ta·lit** *or* **ta·lis** \ˈtäləs, ˈtäl-, ˈtal-, -ət(h)\ *n, pl* **tal·li·thim** *or* **tal·li·tim** *or* **tal·li·sim** \ˌtäləˈsēm, -ˈt(h)ēm\ *or* **tal·lei·sim** \täˈlāsəm\ *also* **ta·li·thim** *or* **ta·li·tim** *or* **ta·li·sim** \ˌtäləˈsēm, -ˈt(h)ēm\ *or* **ta·lei·sim** *or* **ta·lai·sim** \täˈlāsəm\ [Heb *ṭallīth* cover, sheet, cloak, fr. Aram. *ṭĕlal* to cover] **:** a woolen or silk rectangular or square shawl with fringes at the 4 corners and black or blue stripes at the ends that is worn over the head or round the shoulders by orthodox and conservative Jewish men and boys over 13 usu. during morning prayers — called also *prayer scarf*; see ZIZITH; compare ARBA KANFOTH

tall larkspur *n* **:** a slender herb (*Delphinium exaltatum*) of the central U.S. bearing a dense raceme of blue or purple flowers

tall meadow rue *n* **:** a meadow rue (*Thalictrum polygamum*) bearing white or purplish flowers

tall·ness *n* -ES **:** the quality or state of being tall

tall oat grass *or* **tall meadow oat** *n* **:** a perennial Eurasian grass (*Arrhenatherum elatius*) resembling the oat and introduced into No. America for use as forage esp. in moist soils

tall oil \ˈtäl-\ *n* [part trans. of G *tallöl*, part trans. of Sw *tallolja*, fr. *tall* pine (akin to ON *thöll* young pine tree) + *olja* oil — more at TAILOR] **:** a by-product from the manufacture of chemical pulp that is obtained from the black liquor as a dark odorous liquid before refining, that contains principally resin acids and fatty acids (as oleic acid and linoleic acid) with some sterols and other nonacid compounds, and that is used chiefly in making paint, varnish, and other coatings, driers and drying oils, emulsions, lubricants, and soaps

tal·lo·te \täˈl(l)yōd·ē\ *n* -s [Sp *talayote*, a kind of gourd, fr. Nahuatl *tlalayōtli*, fr. *thalli* earth + *ayotli* gourd] **:** CHAYOTE

¹**tal·low** \ˈta(ˌ)lō, -lə; -ləw *or* -lō+V\ *n* -s *often attrib* [ME *talgh, talow*; akin to MD *talch* tallow, ON *tōlgr*] **1 :** animal fat **:** SUET **2 a :** the rendered fat of cattle and sheep that is white and almost tasteless when pure, that is in general harder than grease with a titer of above 40°C, that is composed of glycerides of fatty acids containing a large proportion of palmitic acid and stearic acid, and that is used chiefly in making soap, glycerol, margarine, candles, and lubricants **b :** any of various fats (as from other animals or from plants) resembling beef and mutton tallow — compare WAX MYRTLE

²**tallow** \"\ *vb* -ED/-ING/-S [ME *taloghen, talowen*, fr. *talgh, talow* tallow] *vt* **:** to grease or smear with tallow ~ *vi* **:** to produce or yield tallow

tallow bayberry *or* **tallow shrub** *n* **:** WAX MYRTLE

tallow drop *n* **:** a style of cutting a precious stone so that one or both sides are dome-shaped

tallow–faced \ˈ⸗⸗,⸗\ *adj* **:** having a sickly pale or yellow complexion

tal·low·i·ness \ˈtaləw|ēnəs, -lō|, |in-\ *n* -ES **:** the quality or state of being tallowy

tallow nut *n* **1 :** FALSE SANDALWOOD **2 :** the fruit or seed of the false sandalwood

tallow oil *n* **:** an animal oil obtained by pressing tallow and used chiefly as a lubricant esp. when mixed with minerals oils — compare OLEO OIL, OLEOSTEARIN

tallow pot *n* **:** a locomotive fireman

tallow–top \ˈ⸗⸗,⸗\ *n* **:** a precious stone cut rounded in front and flat in the back — **tallow–topped** \ˈ⸗⸗,⸗\ *adj*

tallow tree *n* **1 :** CHINESE TALLOW TREE **2 :** CANDLENUT 2

tallowweed \ˈ⸗⸗,⸗\ *n* **:** an annual herb (*Actinea linearifolia*) of the family Compositae used to fatten cattle in the southwestern U.S.

tallowwood \ˈ⸗⸗,⸗\ *n* **1 a :** an Australian gum tree (*Eucalyptus microcorys*) having stringy bark and hard wood and containing an oily principle and a gum rich in tannin **b :** a related tree (*E. affinis*) **2 :** FALSE SANDALWOOD

tal·lowy \ˈtaləw|ē, -lō|, |i\ *adj* [ME *talwy*, fr. *talow* tallow + -*y*] **1 :** of the nature of or like the substance of tallow **:** SEBACEOUS **2 :** similar to tallow in color or complexion ⟨the moon . . . throwing its ~ light along the lawns —Richard Church⟩ ⟨behind his ~ mask and goggle eyes —F.M.Ford⟩ **3 :** CAPPY

tall redtop *n* **:** a No. American perennial grass (*Triodia flava*) with spreading purplish panicles

tall sisymbrium *n* **:** TUMBLE MUSTARD

tall speedwell *n* **:** CULVER'S ROOT

tall thistle *n* **:** a coarse prickly herb (*Cirsium altissimum*) of the eastern U.S. with large usu. solitary heads of purplish flowers

tall timber *n* **:** the rural or sparsely settled districts **:** BACKWOODS ⟨a prize contest that seemed very corny to sophisticates but . . . wowed booklovers in the *tall timber* —Bennett Cerf⟩

tall wheatgrass *n* **:** a European grass (*Agropyron elongatum*) introduced into the U.S. as a pasture and forage crop

tall white lettuce *n* **:** a tall perennial herb (*Prenanthes alba*) with large panicles of drooping greenish yellow or yellowish white flower heads

tallwood *var of* TALWOOD

¹**tal·ly** \ˈtalē, -li\ *n* -ES [ME *taly, talye*, fr. ML *talea, tallia*, fr. L *talea* stick, twig, cutting — more at TAILOR] **1 :** a visible

device for recording or accounting esp. business transactions: as **a :** a usu. square wooden rod or stick notched with marks representing numbers and split lengthwise through the notches so that each of two bargaining parties may have a record of a transaction and of the amount of money due or paid; *specif* **:** such a cloven stick formerly used by the English Exchequer as a record of government transactions **b :** any of various primitive devices or wooden sticks used for marking or counting **c :** any of various bookkeeping forms or sheets serving to record or check accounts, sales, or shipments **d :** a mechanical counter held in the hand and operated with a button or lever **e :** a tag or label used to mark or classify plants, trees, or goods **f :** a card or folder that designates a bridge player's starting position and provides space for recording his score **2 a :** a reckoning or recorded account of something ⟨a daily ~ of accidents should be kept —Theodore Loveless⟩ ⟨game warden keeps ~ on the creel —*Amer. Guide Series: Conn.*⟩ ⟨been out on the range . . . helping with the fall ~ —W.V.T. Clark⟩ ⟨a ~ of mixed blessings —Dixon Wecter⟩ **b :** a score or point made (as in a game) ⟨a record ~ of 263 for 72 holes —*Current Biog.*⟩ ⟨drove in the first . . . ~ in the opening inning —*N.Y.Times*⟩ ⟨the ~ coming on a 15-yard pass —*N.Y.Times*⟩ **c :** a record of the number of pieces and the grades of lumber **3 a :** a half, part, or entity that agrees or corresponds to an opposite or companion member **:** COMPLEMENT, COUNTERPART ⟨one twin is the ~ of the other⟩ **b :** the state or fact of correspondence or agreement ⟨will find again the ~ between proportion and thought —*Edinburgh Rev.*⟩ **4 a :** a usu. specified number or lot taken as a whole **:** TOTE **b :** a number or division used as a unit of computation **c :** the last of a specified unit or number **5** *dial Eng* **:** COMPANIONATE MARRIAGE 2

²tally \"\ *vb* -ED/-ING/-ES *vt* **1 a :** to mark (as a number) on or as if on a tally **:** TABULATE, RECORD ⟨~ the election returns as they are reported⟩ ⟨*tallied* a deficit of . . . $1000 —*Future*⟩ ⟨*tallies* some 10,000 automobile miles a year —*Time*⟩ ⟨ideas and methods . . . impossible to ~ on a balance sheet —*Nation's Business*⟩ **b :** to list or check off (a cargo, load, or shipment) by items ⟨the mates supervising the loading and ~*ing* the cargo⟩ **c :** to supply (a bale or shipment) with a label or distinguishing mark **d :** to grade and record the number of pieces (as of lumber) **e :** to register or cause to be registered (a point or score) in a game or contest ⟨some means of ~*ing* the scores —C.J.Erasmus⟩ ⟨~*ing* 269 for 72 holes and prize money —*Current Biog.*⟩ ⟨*tallied* five TD's and two field goals —Eddie Beachler⟩ **2 :** to make a count of (something) **:** RECKON, TOTAL ⟨~ your expenses for the day —Winston Brebner⟩ ⟨can ~ among his followers . . . three or four democratic senators —R.L.Neuberger⟩ ⟨those men are waiting to ~ . . . cattle —S.E.White⟩ ⟨try to ~ the bloody price exacted for this crime —O.T.Lanham⟩ — sometimes used with *out* or *up* ⟨when we *tallied* out the herd, every cow was counted —S.E.Fletcher⟩ ⟨~ up the *for* and *against* —C.C.Furnas⟩ ⟨when the intelligence reports were finally *tallied* up —Lou Stoumen⟩ **3 :** to cause to correspond or complement **:** MATCH ⟨the far-fetched imagery, the insistent anecdote . . . are *tallied* by an equal amount of pains and forethought —Sacheverell Sitwell⟩ ~ *vi* **1 a :** to make a tally by or as if by tabulating a number or record ⟨if an error is made in ~*ing*, the results of computations will be wrong —Lester Guest⟩ ⟨at that time they *tallied* close to $110 billion —W.H.Anderson⟩ ⟨the quarterly and annual ~*ing* of payrolls —A.J.Caruso⟩ **b :** to register a point or score in a game or contest ⟨*tallied* on a 34-yard burst through tackle —*N.Y.Times*⟩ ⟨the first time . . . over a five-year span that they had not *tallied* —Louis Effrat⟩ **2 :** to balance or correspond in complementary fashion ⟨calculated values of the centripetal force and the gravitational force did not ~ —S.F.Mason⟩ ⟨so completely did the two ghosts . . . ~ in their particularity —Sacheverell Sitwell⟩ — often used with *with* ⟨representation must ~ with thing represented —R.M.Weaver⟩ ⟨this family doctrine *tallied* so little with the manifest circumstances —H.G.Wells⟩ **syn** see AGREE

³tally \"\ *vt* -ED/-ING/-ES [origin unknown] **:** to haul aft (as a sheet)

tally board *n* **1 :** a board used as a tally sheet **2 :** a board attached to the tail block of a rope sent out to a ship in distress containing instructions for using the apparatus

tally clerk *n* **:** TALLYMAN

tallygalone *var of* TALLEGALANE

¹tal·ly·ho \ˌtalēˈhō\ *n* -S [prob. fr. F *taïaut*, cry used to excite hounds in deer hunting, fr. OF *taho, tielau*] **1 a :** the cry sounded by hunters upon sighting the fox as it breaks from cover — usu. used interjectionally **b :** a call transmitted by radio by a fighter pilot upon sighting an enemy plane — usu. used interjectionally **2** [after the *Tally-ho*, name of a coach formerly plying between London and Birmingham] **:** a four-in-hand coach **3 :** a dark grayish yellowish brown that is very slightly deeper than lama or bison and slightly lighter than Congo

²tallyho \"\ *vi* -ED/-ING/-S **:** to utter the cry *tallyho* ⟨our combat patrols ~*ed* on the 200 . . . planes —Fletcher Pratt⟩

tal·ly·man \ˈtalēmən, -lim-\ *n, pl* **tallymen** [¹*tally* + *man*] **1** *Brit* **:** one who keeps a tally shop or sells goods on the installment plan **2 :** one who tallies, checks, or keeps an account or record; *esp* **:** a worker who keeps a tally of information (as of quantity or weight) needed for records concerning production, shipping, or receipt of goods

tally sheet *also* **tally card** *n* **:** a sheet on which a tally or account is kept often in tabular form

tal·ly·wag \ˈtalēˌwag\ *n* -S [origin unknown] **:** a sea bass (*Centropristes striatus*) of the Atlantic coast

tal·ma \ˈtalmə\ *n* -S [after François-Joseph *Talma* †1826 Fr. actor] **:** a large cape or short full cloak of the 19th century

tal·mi gold \ˈtalmē-\ *n* [G *talmigold*] **:** a brass made to resemble gold and sometimes gold-plated and used for trinkets or costume jewelry

tal·mouse \talˈmüs\ *n, pl* **talmous·es** \-üs(əz)\ [F] **:** a pastry shell with a filling of cheese

tal·mud \ˈtälˌmu̇d, ˈtalməd\ *n* -S *usu cap* [LHeb *talmūdh*, lit., instruction, fr. Heb *lāmadh* to learn] **:** the authoritative body of Jewish law and tradition developed on the basis of the scriptural law after the closing of the Pentateuchal text about 400 B.C., incorporated in the Hebrew Mishnah and the Aramaic Gemara, and represented in one edition completed in Palestine in the 4th century A.D. and another longer and more authoritative edition completed in Babylon in the 5th century A.D. — see AMORA, SABORA; compare HAGGADA, HALAKAH

tal·mud·ic \(ˈ)talˈm(y)üdik, (ˈ)täl-, (ˈ)məd-, -dēk\ *also* **tal·mud·i·cal** \-dəkəl, -dēk-\ *adj, often cap* **1 :** of, relating to, or characteristic of the Talmud ⟨~ literature⟩ ⟨~ studies⟩ ⟨~ lore⟩ **2 :** of or relating to the period in which the Talmud was compiled ⟨the ~ age⟩ ⟨~ sages⟩

tal·mud·ism \ˈtälˌmu̇dˌizəm, ˈtalməˌd-\ *n* -S *often cap* [*talmud* + *-ism*] **:** the teachings of the Talmud; *also* **:** adherence to such teachings

tal·mud·ist \-ˌdəst\ *n* -S *often cap* [*talmud* + *-ist*] **1 :** one of the compilers of the Talmud **2 :** one who is versed in, accepts, or practices the teachings and law of the Talmud

talmud torah *n, pl* **talmud torahs** *usu cap both Ts* [NHeb *talmūdh tōrāh*, lit., study of or instruction in the Torah] **:** a communal religious school for instruction of children in Hebrew, Scriptures, Talmud, and Jewish history —compare ²HEDER

ta·lo \ˈtä(ˌ)lō\ *n* -S [Samoan; akin to Tahitian *taro*] **:** TARO

talo- *comb form* [L *talus* ankle, anklebone] **:** astragalar and ⟨*talo*fibular⟩ ⟨*talo*tibial⟩

tal·on \ˈtalən\ *n* -S [ME, fr. MF, heel, spur, fr. (assumed) VL *talon-, talo*, fr. L *talus* ankle, anklebone, heel] **1 a** *obs* **:** the hinder part of a hoof **b :** the claw of an animal; *esp* **:** the claw of a bird of prey — usu. used in pl. ⟨the hawk seizes its prey in its sharp ~*s*⟩ **c :** a finger of the human hand ⟨led . . . around the contorted wrist to a sinewy ~ that had been a thumb —Earle Birney⟩ **2 :** a part or object shaped like or suggestive of a heel or claw: as **a :** an ogee molding — see INVERTED TALON **b :** the shoulder of the bolt of a lock on which the key acts to shoot the bolt **c :** the crushing region of the crown of an upper molar posterior to the trigon — compare TRITUBERCULY **3 a :** cards laid aside in a pile in a game of solitaire that may or may not be used again in the game **b :** STOCK 17a **4 :** a certificate attached to various bonds and exchangeable for an extra set of coupons

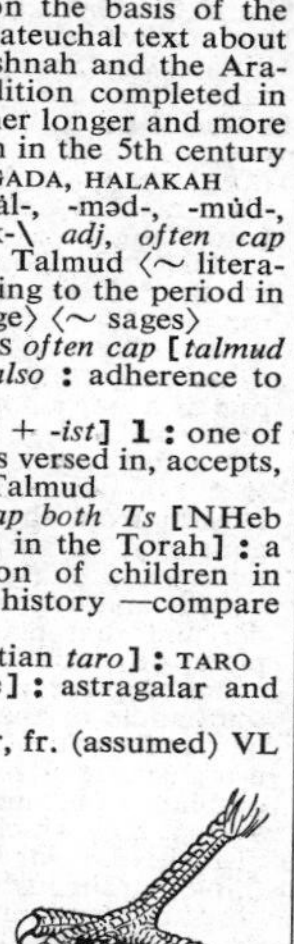

talon 1b of a hawk

ta·lo·navicular \ˌtā(ˌ)lō+\ *adj* [*talo-* + *navicular*] **:** of or relating to the talus and the navicular of the tarsus

tal·oned \-nd\ *adj* [*talon* + *-ed*] **:** having or provided with talons ⟨these creatures with ~ fingers fought —Hugh Walpole⟩

ta·lon·ic acid \təˈlänik-\ *n* [ISV *talon-* (irreg. fr. *galactonic acid*) + *-ic*; orig. formed as G *talonsäure*] **:** a crystalline acid $HOCH_2(CHOH)_4COOH$ formed by oxidation of talose but more readily obtained by heating galactonic acid with pyridine

tal·on·id \ˈtalənəd\ *n* -S [*talon* + *-id* (structural element)] **:** the crushing region of a lower molar tooth usu. better developed than the corresponding talon

tal·ose \ˈtaˌlōs\ *n* -S [ISV *tal-* (in *talonic acid*) + *-ose*] **:** a rare sugar $C_6H_{12}O_6$ of the aldohexose class obtained indirectly from galactose or formed by reduction of talonic acid

tal·pa \ˈtalpə\ *n, cap* [NL, fr. L, mole] **:** a genus (the type of the family Talpidae) that comprises the common Old World moles

tal·pa·co·ti \ˌtalpəˈkōd·ē\ *n* -S [NL, of AmerInd origin] **:** a So. American ground dove (*Columbigallina talpacoti*)

tal·pa·ta·te *or* **tal·pe·ta·te** \ˌtälpəˈtäd·ē\ *n* -S [AmerSp *tepetate, talpetate*, fr. Nahuatl *tepetatl*, fr. *tetl* stone + *petatl* mat] **1 :** a rock of superficial origin formed by the cementing action of calcium carbonate on sand, soil, or volcanic ash and equivalent in part to caliche or calcrete **2 :** rather poor thin soil consisting of partly decomposed volcanic ash more or less consolidated

talpi- *comb form* [L *talpa*] **:** mole ⟨*talpi*form⟩

¹tal·pid \ˈtalpəd\ *adj* [NL *Talpidae*] **:** of or relating to the Talpidae

²talpid \"\ *n* -S **:** a mole of the family Talpidae

tal·pi·dae \ˈtalpəˌdē\ *n pl, cap* [NL, fr. *Talpa*, type genus + *-idae*] **:** a family of insectivores (superfamily Soricoidea) including all moles except the golden and marsupial moles — see TALPA

tal·poid \ˈtalˌpȯid\ *adj* [NL *Talpa* + E *-oid*] **:** like or related to the Talpidae

tal qual \ˈtälˈkwäl\ *abbr* [L *talis qualis* such as] just as they come

tal·tush·tun·tu·de \ˌtältu̇shtünˈtüdā\ *n, pl* **taltushtuntude** *or* **taltushtuntudes** *usu cap* **1 :** an Athapaskan people on Galise creek, a tributary of the Rogue river in southwestern Oregon **2 :** a member of the Taltushtuntude people

ta·luk \täˈlük\ *or* **ta·lu·ka** *also* **ta·loo·ka** \-kə\ *n* -S [Urdu *ta'alluq* estate, fr. Ar] **1 :** an hereditary estate in India **2 :** a collectorate or administrative subdivision comprising an Indian revenue district

¹ta·lus \ˈtāləs\ *n* -ES [F, fr. L *talutium* slope indicating presence of gold under the soil, prob. of Iberian origin] **1 :** a slope formed esp. by an accumulation of rock debris **2 :** rock debris at the base of a cliff or slope chiefly as the result of gravitational roll or slide; *also* **:** a mass of such debris

²talus \"\ *n, pl* **ta·li** \-ˌlī\ [NL, fr. L, ankle, anklebone, heel] **1 :** the astragalus of man bearing the weight of the body and with the tibia and fibula forming the ankle joint **2 a :** the entire ankle esp. of man **b :** a part in birds and insects corresponding to the ankle

talus glacier *n* [¹*talus*] **:** ROCK STREAM

tal·wood *or* **tall·wood** \ˈtōlˌwu̇d\ *n* [ME, part trans., part modif. of OF *bois de tail*] **:** wood cut up for firewood

ta·lysh·in \təˈlishən\ *or* **ta·lyshe** \-shē\ *n, pl* **talyshin** *or* **talyshins** *or* **talyshe** *or* **talyshes** *usu cap* **1 a :** a people of the region around Lenkoran, Azerbaidzhan **b :** a member of such people **2 :** a dialect related to Talishi

tam \ˈtam, -aa(ə)m\ *n* -S [by shortening] **:** TAM-O'-SHANTER

tam·abil·i·ty *or* **tame·abil·i·ty** \ˌtāməˈbiləd·ē\ *n* **:** capacity for being tamed

tam·able *or* **tame·able** \ˈtāməbəl\ *adj* **:** capable of being tamed — **tam·able·ness** *n* -ES

tamachek *usu cap, var of* TAMASHEK

ta·ma·le \təˈmälē, -mal-, -li\ *n* -S [MexSp *tamales*, pl. of *tamal* tamale, fr. Nahuatl *tamalli*] **:** ground meat seasoned with chili or other filling, rolled up in cornmeal dough, wrapped in corn husks, and steamed

ta·man·dua \təˈmandəˌwä, -njə-, ˌ==ˈwə\ *n* [Pg *tamanduá*, fr. Tupi, lit., ant-catcher, fr. *taixi* ant + *mondê* to catch] **1** -S **a :** a prehensile-tailed arboreal anteater (*Tamandua tetradactyla*) of Central and So. America that is smaller than the ant bear and much more variable in marking, being sometimes gray striped with black and sometimes straw-colored and unstriped **b :** an edentate anteater **2** *cap* [NL, fr. Pg *tamanduá*] **:** a genus comprising the tamandua

ta·ma·noir \ˌtamənˈwär\ *n* -S [F, of Cariban origin; akin to Galibi *tamanoa* ant bear, Acawai *tamanowa;* akin to Tupi *tamanduá* tamandua] **:** ANT BEAR

ta·ma·nu \təˈmä(ˌ)nü\ *n* -S [Tahitian & Samoan] **1 :** POON **2 :** a heavy green resin derived from the poon

tam·ar \ˈtamə(r)\ *adj* [Ar *tamr* dried date] **:** of, relating to, or constituting the last of four recognized stages in the ripening of the date in which it is dried sufficiently to prevent spoiling — compare KHALAL, KIMRI, RUTAB

ta·ma·ra \təˈmärə\ *n* -S [origin unknown] **:** a powdered mixture of cinnamon, cloves, and coriander, anise, and fennel seeds used as a condiment esp. in Italy

tam·a·rack \ˈtaməˌrak\ *n* -S [origin unknown] **1 a** (1) **:** any of several American larches; *esp* **:** a larch (*Larix laricina*) of northern U.S., Canada, and Alaska — called also *American larch, black larch* (2) **:** the wood of the tamarack **b** *or* **tamarack pine :** LODGEPOLE PINE **2 :** MUMMY BROWN 2b

ta·ma·rau \ˌtaməˈrau̇\ *or* **tim·a·rau** \ˌtim-\ *also* **tam·a·rao** \ˌtaməˈrau̇\ *n* -S [Tag *tamaráw, timaraw*] **:** a small dark hairy water buffalo (*Bubalus mindorensis* or *Anoa mindorensis*) of the Philippine island of Mindora

tam·a·ri·ca·ce·ae \ˌtaməˈrəˈkāsēˌē\ *n pl, cap* [NL, fr. *Tamaric-, Tamarix*, type genus + *-aceae*] **:** a family of chiefly desert and often heathlike shrubs or trees (order Parietales) widely distributed in warm regions and having narrow entire leaves and flowers with five stamens and a one-celled ovary — **tam·a·ri·ca·ceous** \ˌ===ˈkāshəs\ *adj*

tam·a·rin \ˈtamərən, -ˌran\ *n* -S [F, fr. Galibi] **:** any of numerous small So. American marmosets of the genus *Leontocebus* having elongate canine teeth, silky fur, and long nonprehensile tail, and running about like squirrels rather than leaping from branch to branch — see PINCHE, SILKY TAMARIN

tam·a·rind \ˈtamərənd, -ˌrind\ *also* **tam·a·rin·do** \ˌ==ˈrin-(ˌ)dō\ *n* -S [Sp & Pg *tamarindo*, fr. Ar *tamr hindī*, lit., Indian date, fr. *tamr* dried date + *hindī* of India, fr. *Hind* India; akin to OPers *Hindu* India — more at INDIA] **1 a :** a widely cultivated tropical tree (*Tamarindus indica*) of the family Leguminosae with hard yellowish wood that is used in turnery and pinnate leaves and red-striped yellow flowers that are eaten in India and are also used as mordants in dyeing **b :** the fruit of the tamarind tree that has an acid pulp used for preserves and made into a cooling laxative drink and seeds that are cooked and also ground into meal **2 :** any of various trees resembling the tamarind ⟨bastard ~⟩ ⟨native ~⟩

tam·a·risk \ˈtamərəsk, -ˌrisk\ *n* -S [ME *tamarisc*, fr. LL *tamariscus*, fr. L *tamaric-, tamarix*] **:** a shrub or tree of the genus *Tamarix*

tamarisk family *n* **:** TAMARICACEAE

tamarisk gall *n* **:** a gall that is formed on a tamarisk (*Tamarix articulata*) and yields tannin

tam·a·rix \ˈtaməˌ(r)iks\ *n* [NL, fr. L, tamarisk] **1** *cap* **:** a large genus (the type of the family Tamaricaceae) of shrubs or small trees that are natives of the eastern Mediterranean region and tropical Asia and have minute scalelike leaves and feathery racemes of small white or pinkish flowers with free stamens and 3 to 4 styles **2** -ES **:** any shrub or tree of the genus *Tamarix*

tamarix family *n* **:** TAMARICACEAE

ta·ma·ru·gite \ˌtaməˈrüˌgīt\ *n* -S [G *tamarugit*, fr. *tamarug-* (fr. Pampa del *Tamarugal*, desert plateau in northern Chile, its locality) + *-it* -ite] **:** a mineral $NaAl(SO_4)_2.6H_2O$ that is a hydrous sulfate of sodium and aluminum isostructural with amarillite

ta·mas \ˈtəməs\ *n* -ES [Skt, darkness — more at TEMERITY] **:** the inertia or dullness that constitutes one of the three gunas of Sankhya philosophy — compare RAJAS, SATTVA

tam·a·shek *also* **tam·a·chek** \ˈtaməˌshek\ *n* -S *usu cap* **:** the Berber language of the Tuareg people spoken in the central and southern Sahara

ta·mau·li·pec \təˈmau̇ləˌpek\ *n, pl* **tamaulipec** *or* **tamaulipecs** *usu cap* **1 a :** an Indian people of northeastern Mexico **b :** a member of such people **2 :** a Coahuiltecan language of the Tamaulipec people

tambac *var of* TOMBAC

tam·ber \ˈtambə(r), ˈtaam-\ *n* -S [by alter.] **:** TIMBRE

¹tam·bo \ˈtam(ˌ)bō\ *n* -S *often cap* [short for ¹*tambourine*] **:** an end man in a minstrel show who often plays the tambourine — compare BONES

²tam·bo \", ˈtäm-\ *n* -S [AmerSp, fr. Quechua *tánpu* army camp, storehouse, inn] **1 :** an Inca inn or way station on the highroads of ancient Peru **2 :** a wayside tavern in modern Peru, Ecuador, and Bolivia

tam·boo·kie \tamˈbükē, -bükē\ *also* **tambookie thorn** *n* -S [Afrik *tamboekie*, fr. *Tamboekie* Kaffir of the Tembu tribe, prob. fr. *Tamboe* Tembu + *-kie* (fr. D *-kje*, dim. suffix)] **1 :** a southern African shrub or small tree (*Erythrina acanthocarpa*) with spiny fruit **2 :** the extremely light wood of the tambookie

tambookie grass \"-\ *or* **ta·bucki grass** \təˈbükē-\ *n, usu cap T* [trans. of Afrik *tamboekiegras*] **:** any of several southern African grasses; *esp* **:** a grass (*Sorghum verticilliflorum*) growing to a height of six or eight feet and used for thatching and in making paper

tam·bor \ˈtamˌbȯ(ə)r, ==\ *n* -S [Sp, drum, fr. Ar *tanbūr*] **1 :** any of several puffers **2 :** a red rockfish (*Sebastodes ruberrimus*) of the Pacific coast

tam·bo·ri·to \ˌtämbəˈrēd·(ˌ)ō\ *n* -S [AmerSp, lit., little drum, fr. Sp, dim. of *tambor* drum] **:** a modern Panamanian couple dance with intricate footwork

¹tam·bour \ˈtamˌbu̇(ə)r, ==\ *n* -S *often attrib* [F, drum, fr. MF, fr. Ar *tanbūr*, modif. (influenced by *ṭunbūr*, a lute) of Per *tabīr*] **1** *also* **tam·bor** \-bȯ(ə)r\ **a :** ¹DRUM 1 **b :** DRUMMER 1 **2 a :** ¹DRUM 4a(1) **b :** ¹BELL 5e **c :** a circular wall (as one supporting a dome) **d :** a sloping buttress or projection (as in court tennis or fives) for deflecting a ball that strikes it **3 a :** an embroidery frame; *esp* **:** a set of two interlocking hoops between which cloth is stretched before stitching **b :** the embroidery made on a tambour frame; *esp* **:** embroidery consisting of looped stitches similar to chain stitch and worked with a fine hook **c :** TAMBOUR LACE **4 :** a shallow metallic cup or drum with a thin elastic membrane supporting a writing lever used singly or in groups to transmit and register arterial pulsations, blood pressure, respiratory movements, peristaltic contractions, and other slight motions (as of speech) **5 :** a rolling top or front (as of a desk) composed of narrow half-round strips of wood glued on canvas

²tambour \"\ *vb* -ED/-ING/-S *vt* **:** to embroider (cloth) with tambour ~ *vi* **:** to work at a tambour frame — **tam·bour·er** \-ürə(r)\ *n* -S

tam·bou·ra *or* **tam·bu·ra** \tamˈbu̇rə\ *n* -S [Per *ṭambūra*] **:** an Asiatic musical instrument of the lute type but without frets used only to produce a drone accompaniment to singing

tambour clock *n* **:** a clock enclosed in an upright drum-shaped case with an extended base

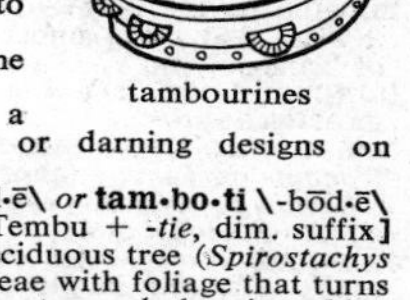

tambour clock

tambour de basque \-dəˈ=\ *n* [F, lit., Basque drum] **:** TAMBOURIN 1a

tam·bou·rin \ˈtambərən, ˌ==ˈran\ *n* -S [Prov, dim. of *tambour* drum, fr. Ar *ṭanbūr*] **1 a :** a long narrow drum used in Provence **b :** an Egyptian bottle-shaped drum **2 a :** a lively old Provençal dance orig. with tambourin accompaniment **b :** music written for or in the quick duple measure of a tambourin dance usu. with a drone bass on the tonic or dominant

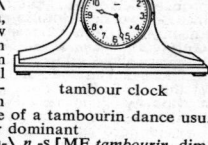

¹tam·bou·rine \ˌtambəˈrēn, ˌtaam-\ *n* -S [MF *tambourin*, dim. of *tambour* drum — more at TAMBOUR] **1 :** a small drum; *esp* **:** a shallow one-headed drum with loose metallic disks or jingles at the sides that is played by shaking, striking with the hand, or rubbing with the thumb **:** TIMBREL **2 :** a mostly white African wild dove (*Tympanistria tympanistria*) whose wings and tail are black-tipped and which has a distinctive resonant note

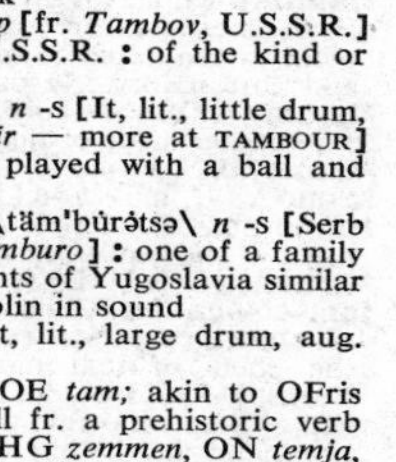

tambourines

²tambourine \"\ *vi* -ED/-ING/-S **:** to play on the tambourine

tam·bou·rin·ist \-nəst\ *n* -S **:** one who plays on the tambourine

tambour lace *n* **:** a lace made in a tambour frame by embroidering or darning designs on machine-made net

tam·bou·ti *also* **tam·bu·ti** \tamˈbüd·ē\ *or* **tam·bo·ti** \-bōd·ē\ *n* -S [Afrik *tamboetie*, fr. *Tamboe* Tembu + *-tie*, dim. suffix] **:** a southern and eastern African deciduous tree (*Spirostachys africanus*) of the family Euphorbiaceae with foliage that turns red in fall and hard slightly fragrant wood that is golden yellow in the sapwood and black in the heartwood and is used locally for furniture and cabinetwork

tam·bov \(ˈ)tämˈbȯf, -ȯv\ *adj, usu cap* [fr. *Tambov*, U.S.S.R.] **:** of or from the city of Tambov, U.S.S.R. **:** of the kind or style prevalent in Tambov

tam·bu·rel·lo \ˌtämbəˈre(ˌ)lō, ˌtam-\ *n* -S [It, lit., little drum, dim. of *tamburo* drum, fr. Ar *ṭanbūr* — more at TAMBOUR] **:** a modification of pallone that is played with a ball and rackets like battledores

tam·bu·rit·za *also* **tam·bou·rit·za** \tämˈbu̇rətsə\ *n* -S [Serb *tamburitza*, fr. *tambur* drum, fr. It *tamburo*] **:** one of a family of plucked stringed musical instruments of Yugoslavia similar to the guitar in shape and the mandolin in sound

tam·bu·ro·ne \ˌtämbəˈrōnē\ *n* -S [It, lit., large drum, aug. of *tamburo* drum] **:** BASS DRUM

¹tame \ˈtām\ *adj* -ER/-EST [ME, fr. OE *tam;* akin to OFris *tam* tame, OHG *zam*, ON *tamr;* all fr. a prehistoric verb represented by OE *temian* to tame, OHG *zemmen*, ON *temja*, Goth *gatamjan*, L *domare*, Gk *damnanai* to tame, Skt *damayati* he tames] **1 a :** reduced from a state of native wildness **:** made tractable and useful to man **:** DOMESTICATED ⟨~ cattle gone wild —Hart Stilwell⟩ **b :** maintained or displayed to serve the purposes of another **:** permitted to exist as a harmless specimen of its kind ⟨our ~ firebrand —Dorothy Sayers⟩ ⟨the new ~ sultan —Janet Flanner⟩ **c :** brought under control **:** HARNESSED ⟨on the day the control structures are completed . . . the mighty Mississippi should be a pretty ~ and useful river —A.W.Baum⟩ **2 a :** not having or showing the qualities (as ferocity or shyness) characteristic of a wild state ⟨the chipmunks . . . are so ~ they beg for food —*Amer. Guide Series: Calif.*⟩ **b :** made docile and submissive **:** MEEK, SUBDUED ⟨no colt will bear it, or he's a ~ beast —George Meredith⟩ **3 :** CULTIVATED ⟨the yield of ~ blueberries runs from 150 to 1200 quarts per acre —J.M.White⟩ **4 :** lacking in spirit, zest, or interest **:** DULL, MILD, INSIPID ⟨struck out for himself and refused to live the ~ easy life —Frank Sargeson⟩ ⟨a little ~ wood which rambled up from the village —Audrey Barker⟩ ⟨a ~ book⟩ ⟨a ~ campaign⟩

syn SUBDUED, SUBMISSIVE: TAME, in relation to persons and their actions and utterances, suggests domination by others, often with voluntary surrender, or a marked docility and timidity, and lack of independence, assertiveness, exuberance, or wildness ⟨the *tamest*, the most abject creatures that we can possibly imagine: mild, peaceable, and tractable, they seem to have no will or power to act but as directed by their masters —William Bartram⟩ ⟨*tame* acquiescence in tradition and routine —Irving Babbitt⟩ SUBDUED generally implies a loss of vehemence, intensity, or force; in reference to people it suggests the quietness or meekness of one dependent, chastised, broken, or timorous ⟨*subdued* voices⟩ ⟨there were seamen going about routine duties, but they performed them in a *subdued*, soundless manner as though they were officiating at church —C.B.Nordhoff & J.N.Hall⟩ ⟨their next meeting displayed her quieter: *subdued* as one who had been set thinking

—George Meredith⟩ SUBMISSIVE implies deferring to the will of another and yielding and humbly obeying ⟨a people, gentle, *submissive*, prompt to obey, and accustomed, as were the Egyptians, to the inexorable demands of tyranny —Agnes Repplier⟩ ⟨in the *submissive* way of one long accustomed to obey under coercion, he ate and drank what they gave him —Charles Dickens⟩

²tame \"\ *vb* -ED/-ING/-S [ME *tamen*, fr. *tame*, adj.] *vt* **1 a :** to reduce from a wild to a domestic state **:** make gentle or tractable **:** DOMESTICATE ⟨~ a lion⟩ **b :** to subject to cultivation ⟨small valleys and plains that have been *tamed* and worked into precise patterns by generations of farmers —Patrick O'Donovan⟩ **c :** to bring under control **:** make manageable or usable ⟨roads blasted in the solid rock, wild streams dammed and *tamed* —John Muir †1914⟩ ⟨~ the atom⟩ ⟨the sources have been *tamed* in a masterly fashion —M.M. Postan⟩ **2 :** to deprive of spirit, courage, or resistance **:** HUMBLE, SUBDUE ⟨*tamed* the populace with shiploads of . . . wheat —T.H.Fielding⟩ **3 :** to tone down **:** SOFTEN ⟨in revising the play, he has *tamed* it⟩ ~ *vi* **:** to become tame ⟨the manatees *tamed* quickly —*Natural History*⟩ ⟨a roughneck frontiersman who ~*s* down at the end —Walter Havighurst⟩

³tame \"\ *vt* -ED/-ING/-S [ME *tamen*, short for *atamen*, fr. MF *atamer* to attack, fr. LL *attaminare*, fr. L *ad-* + *taminare* to violate (akin to L *tangere* to touch) — more at TANGENT] **1** *dial Eng* **:** to cut into **:** PIERCE; *esp* **:** BROACH **2** *dial Eng* **:** PRUNE

tameable *var of* TAMABLE

tame cat *n* **:** one who allows himself to be used or controlled by another **:** a person completely subordinate to another

tame hay *n* **:** hay cut from cultivated grasses

ta·mein \tə'mīn, -mān\ *n* -S [Burmese *thameiṅ*] **:** a draped skirt worn by Burmese women

tame·less \'tāmləs\ *adj* **:** not tamed or not capable of being tamed ⟨~ and swift and proud —P.B.Shelley⟩ — **tame·less·ly** *adv* — **tame·less·ness** *n* -ES

tame·ly *adv* **:** in a tame manner **:** MEEKLY ⟨people who ~ allow slavery to be imposed on them —Kenneth Roberts⟩

tame·ness *n* -ES **:** the quality or state of being tame

tame pasture *n* **:** pasture land sown to cultivated grasses or legumes

tam·er \'tāmə(r)\ *n* -S **:** one that tames

tamest *superlative of* TAME

tami·as \'tāmēəs, 'tam-\ *n, cap* [NL, fr. Gk, dispenser, steward; akin to Gk *temnein* to cut — more at TOME] **:** a genus of ground squirrels comprising the chipmunks of eastern No. America and sometimes extended to include the western No. American and the Old World chipmunks commonly placed in *Eutamias*

tam·il \'tamәl, 'təm-,'täm-\ *n, pl* **tamil** *or* **tamils** *usu cap* **1 :** a Dravidian language of Madras state in southern India and of northern and eastern Ceylon **2 :** a Tamil-speaking person or a descendant of Tamil-speaking ancestors **3 :** a script customarily used for writing Tamil

¹ta·mil·ian \tə'milēən\ *also* **ta·mil·ic** \-lik\ *adj, usu cap* **1 :** of or relating to Tamil or the Tamils **2 :** DRAVIDIAN

²tamilian \"\ *n* -S *usu cap* **1 :** TAMIL **2 :** DRAVIDIAN

tami·ops \'tamē,äps, 'tam-\ *n, cap* [NL, fr. *Tamias* + *-ops*] **:** a genus of striped arboreal squirrels of southeastern Asia resembling the chipmunks but having tufted ears and a short slender thinly-haired tail

tam·is \'tamē, məs\ *n, pl* **tam·ises** \-mēz,-məsəz\ [F, fr. OF, prob. of Celt origin; akin to Bret *tamouez* strainer] **:** a strainer made of worsted cloth in a plain open weave

tam·mann's rule \'tamənz-, 'tä,mänz-\ *n, usu cap T* [after Gustav *Tammann* †1938 Ger. chemist] **:** a rule in metallurgy: in binary alloys a less fusible metal dissolves more of a more fusible metal in the solid phase than the more fusible does of the less fusible

tam·ma·ny \'tamənē, -ni\ *adj, usu cap* [fr. *Tammany* Hall, headquarters of the Tammany Society, a political organization orig. founded as a fraternal society in New York City that between 1865 and 1871 under the political boss William M. Tweed †1878 obtained control of the city and plundered it of millions of dollars, fr. *Tammany* Society, after *Tamanend fl* 1682–1700 Delaware Indian chief] **:** of, relating to, or constituting a group or organization exercising or seeking municipal political control by methods often associated with corruption and bossism

tam·ma·ny·ism \-nē,izəm, -ni,iz-\ *n* -S *usu cap* [*Tammany* Hall + E *-ism*] **:** the political principles or practices attributed to or associated with Tammany Hall

tam·ma·ny·ite \-,īt\ *n* -S *usu cap* [*Tammany* Hall + E *-ite*] **:** an adherent of Tammany Hall or of Tammanyism

tam·ma·ny·ize \-,īz\ *vt* -ED/-ING/-S *often cap* [*Tammany* Hall + *-ize*] **:** to bring under Tammany rule or the domination of Tammanyism

tam·mar \'tamə(r)\ *n* -S [native name in Australia] **:** DAMA PADEMELON

tam·mie no·rie *or* **tam·my norie** \,tamī'nōri\ *n* [prob. fr. *Tammie* or *Tammy* (alter. of *Tommy*, nickname for the name *Thomas*) + *Norie*, prob. dim. of the feminine name *Nora*, short for *Honora*] *Scot* **:** PUFFIN 1

tam·muz *also* **ta·muz** \'tä(,)müz\ *n* -ES *usu cap* [Heb *Tammūz*] **:** the 10th month of the civil year or the 4th month of the ecclesiastical year in the Jewish calendar — see MONTH table

¹tam·my \'tamē\ *n* -ES [prob. by shortening and alter. fr. obs. E *tamin* estamin, fr. obs. F *estamine* — more at ESTAMIN] **:** a plain-woven often glazed cloth of fine worsted or woolen and cotton formerly used for dresses, curtains, and linings

²tammy \"\ *n* -ES [prob. by shortening and alter. fr. *tamis*] **:** a strainer made of tammy cloth

³tammy \"\ *vt* -ED/-ING/-ES **:** to strain through a tammy

ta·mo \'tä(,)mō\ *n* -S [Jap] **:** JAPANESE ASH 2

¹tamo·nea \tə'mōnēə, ,tamə'nēə\ *n* -S [NL] **:** a flower or plant of the genus *Miconia*

²tamonea \"\ [NL] *syn of* MICONIA

tam-o'-shanter \'tamə,shantə(r), -shaan-, ,==\'==\ *n, pl* **tam-o'-shanters** [after *Tam o' Shanter*, hero of the poem of that name (1789) by Robert Burns †1796 Scot. national poet] **:** a woolen cap of Scottish origin that is made with a tight headband and a very wide flat circular crown usu. with a pompon in the center — compare BONNET

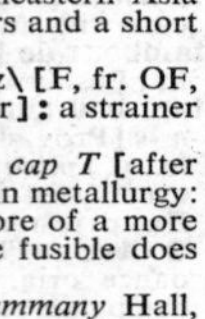

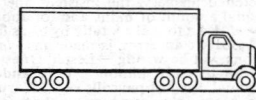

tam-o'-shanter

¹tamp \'tamp, -aa(ə)-,-ai-\ *vb* -ED/-ING/-S [prob. fr. F *tamponner* to stop up, plug, fr. MF, fr. *tampon*, *tapon* plug, fr. (assumed) OF *taper* to stop up, of Gmc origin; akin to OE *tæppa* tap — more at TAP] *vt* **1 :** to fill up (a drill hole) above a blasting charge with material (as clay, earth, sand) **2** [partly fr. E *tamponner* to stop up; partly fr. F *étamper* to punch, strike, stamp, fr. OF *estamper*, of Gmc origin; akin to OHG *stampfōn* to stamp — more at STAMP] **a :** to drive in or down by a succession of light or medium blows **:** COMPACT ⟨~*ed* some more tobacco into my pipe —H.G. Evarts⟩ ⟨~*ed* the earth⟩ ⟨~*ed* the wet concrete⟩ **b :** to put a cover on ⟨these rivalries are usually ~*ed* down by the code that has governed the army —T.H.White b. 1915⟩ **3 :** to fill in or pack round tightly ⟨took out his pipe and began to ~ it —Dilys Laing⟩ ~ *vi* **:** to pack or consolidate loose material by ramming **syn** see PACK

²tamp \"\ *n* -S **:** a tool for tamping ⟨a pipe-smoker's knife, complete with a reamer, a ~, and a regular blade —*New Yorker*⟩

tam·pa \'tampə, -aam-,-aim-\ *adj, usu cap* [fr. *Tampa*, Fla.] **:** of or from the city of Tampa, Fla. ⟨a *Tampa* cigar⟩ **:** of the kind or style prevalent in Tampa

tam·pala \tam'palə\ *n* -S [native name in India] **:** an annual potherb (*Amaranthus tricolor*) native to the Orient that is cultivated for its tender stems and for its often variegated leaves which resemble spinach in taste — see JOSEPH'S COAT

¹tam·pan \'tam,pan\ *n* -S [native name in southern Africa] **:** any of various argasid ticks; *esp* **:** CHICKEN TICK

²tam·pan \'tampən, -aam-,-aim-\ *n* -S *cap* [*Tampa*, Fla. + E *-an*] **:** a native or resident of Tampa, Fla.

tam·pa·ni·an \(')tam'pānēən\ *adj, usu cap* [Kota *Tampan*, locality in northern Malaya where the tools were found + E *-an*] **:** of or belonging to a Lower Paleolithic cultural development in Malaya characterized by choppers flaked on one surface only

¹tam·per \'tampə(r), -aam-,-aim-\ *vb* **tampered; tampered; tampering** \-p(ə)riŋ\ **tampers** [prob. fr. MF *temprer* to mix, meddle, blend, temper — more at TEMPER] *vi* **1 :** to deal secretly **:** carry on underhand or improper negotiations **:** bring improper influence to bear (as by bribery or intimidation) — used with *with* ⟨charged that the defense attorney had ~*ed* with the witnesses⟩ **2 a :** to interfere so as to weaken or change for the worse — used with *with* ⟨as old customers themselves, they would not ~ with the place's traditions or staff —*Newsweek*⟩ ⟨could not easily ~ with the privileges of the nobility —D.W.Brogan⟩ **b :** to busy oneself rashly **:** try foolish or dangerous experiments — used with *with* ⟨is far from innocent in her own ~*ing* with his sensibilities —James Gray⟩ **3** *archaic* **:** to work secretly for some end **:** PLOT, SCHEME ~ *vt* **:** to alter for an improper purpose or in an improper way ⟨here, perhaps, is the most objectionable aspect of . . . ~*ing* the texts: his bland presumption —Richard Hanser⟩ **syn** see MEDDLE

²tamp·er \"\ *n* -S [¹*tamp* + *-er*] **:** one that tamps: as **a :** one that prepares for blasting by filling the hole in which the charge has been placed **b :** a round wooden stick or metal bar used to pack tamping in a drill hole **c :** a tool or machine for compacting concrete by tamping **d :** a mass of material used to delay a nuclear reaction and prevent the escape of neutrons

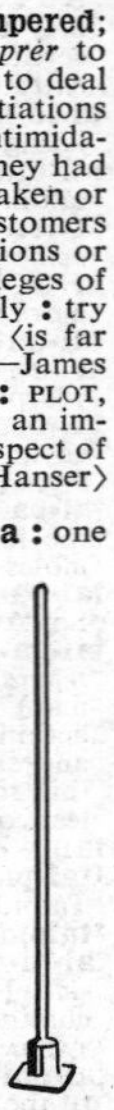

tamper c

tam·pe·re \'tampərə, 'täm-\ *adj, usu cap* [fr. *Tampere*, Finland] **:** of or from the city of Tampere, Finland **:** of the kind or style prevalent in Tampere

tam·per·er \'tampərə(r), -aam-,-aim-\ *n* -S **:** one that tampers

tam·pi·can \tam'pēkən, taam-\ *n* -S *cap* [*Tampico*, seaport in eastern Mexico + E *-an*] **:** a native or resident of Tampico, Mexico

tam·pi·co fiber *also* **tampico hemp** \-pē(,)kō-\ *n, usu cap T* [fr. *Tampico*, Mexico] **:** ISTLE b

tampico jalap *n, usu cap T* [fr. *Tampico*, Mexico] **:** the dried root of a Mexican morning glory (*Ipomoea simulans*) or the powdered drug containing a resin prepared from it

tamping *n* -S [fr. gerund of ¹*tamp*] **1 :** the act or an instance of tamping; *specif* **:** the act of filling up a hole preparatory to blasting **2 :** the material used in tamping

tamping bar *n* **:** a long-handled metal bar with a wide flat head for tamping the ballast under railroad ties

tamping pick *n* **:** a pick built with a wide flat head on one end for driving ballast under railroad ties

tam·pi·on \'tampēən, 'täm-\ *or* **tom·pi·on** \'täm-\ *n* -S [ME *tampion*, *tampine*, *tampon*, fr. MF *tampon*, *tapon* — more at TAMP] **:** something that stops an opening **:** PLUG: as **a** *archaic* **:** a wooden plug used as wadding for a gun **b :** a wooden plug used to close the muzzle of a gun not in use **c :** a metal or canvas cover for the muzzle of a gun

¹tam·pon \'tam,pän, -,pən\ *n* -S [F, fr. MF *tampon*, *tapon* plug] **1 :** a plug of cotton or other material introduced into a natural or artificial body cavity to arrest hemorrhage, absorb secretions, or fill a defect **2 :** an ink dabber sometimes used in gravure **3 :** a 2-headed drumstick sometimes used in playing the bass drum

²tampon \"\ *vt* -ED/-ING/-S [prob. fr. F *tamponner* — more at TAMP] **:** to plug with a tampon

tam·pon·ade \,tampə'nād\ *or* **tam·pon·age** \'==,nij\ *n* -S [²*tampon* + *-ade* or *-age*] **1 :** the use of tampons to stop bleeding **2 :** CARDIAC TAMPONADE

tamps *pres 3d sing of* TAMP, *pl of* TAMP

tamrac pine *var of* TAMARACK PINE

tam-tam \'tam,tam, 'təm,təm\ *n* -S [Hindi *ṭamṭam*] **1 :** TOM-TOM **2 :** GONG; *esp* **:** one of a tuned set as used in a gamelan orchestra

ta·mu·re \tə'mürē\ *n* -S [Maori] **:** ³SNAPPER 3c

ta·mus \'tāməs\ *n, cap* [NL, prob. fr. L *tamnus*, a vine] **:** a genus of tuberous-rooted vines (family Dioscoreaceae) with twining stems, cordate leaves, and flowers in axillary racemes

tamuz *usu cap, var of* TAMMUZ

tam·worth \'tam(,)wərth\ *n* [fr. *Tamworth*, borough in Staffordshire, England, where the breed was developed] **1** *usu cap* **:** a breed of large long-bodied red swine of the bacon type originated in Ireland but largely developed in England **2** -S *often cap* **:** an animal of the Tamworth breed — called also *Irish grazier*

¹tan \'tan, -aa(ə)n\ *vb* **tanned; tanned; tanning; tans** [ME *tannen*, fr. MF *tanner*, fr. ML *tannare*, fr. *tannum*, *tanum* tanbark, prob. of Celt origin; akin to Ir *tana* thin, Corn *tanow*] *vt* **1 a** (1) **:** to convert (skin) into leather by impregnation with an infusion of tree bark, mineral salts, or some other form of tannin or a substitute (2) **:** to convert (collagen or other protein) to leather or a similar product **b :** to apply a mixture (as of oak bark and coloring matter) to (as a sail) for preservative or hardening purposes **2 :** to make tan or brown (as by exposure to the rays of the sun) ⟨~ the skin⟩ **3 :** to thrash soundly **:** BEAT, WHIP ⟨would have *tanned* my hide if they had caught me rambling around —Louis Armstrong⟩ **4 :** to make (the gelatin layer of a photographic material) selectively insoluble in water by chemical treatment or by the action of light ~ *vi* **:** to get or become tanned ⟨a man's skin ~*s* more deeply —J.F.Stanwell-Fletcher⟩

²tan \"\ *n* -S [F, fr. OF, fr. ML *tanum*] **1 :** TANBARK 1 **2 a :** a tanning material **b :** the active tanning agent (as tannin) in such a material **3 :** a brown color imparted to the skin by exposure to the sun or weather ⟨hands covered with ~⟩ **4 a :** a variable color averaging a light yellowish brown that is redder, lighter, and stronger than khaki, deeper and slightly yellower than walnut brown, and yellower and slightly paler than cinnamon **b :** LEATHER 4 **5 tans** *pl* **:** tan-colored articles of clothing; *esp* **:** SHOES ⟨school superintendents were freshening their ~*s* . . . and looking up timetables —*Newsweek*⟩

³tan \"\ *adj, sometimes* **tanner**; *sometimes* **tannest 1 :** of, relating to, or used for tan or tanning **2 :** of the color tan

⁴tan \'dän\ *n, pl* **tan** [Chin (Pek) *tan*¹] **:** a Chinese unit of weight **:** PICUL

⁵tan \'tän\ *n, pl* **tan** [Jap] **:** a Japanese unit of land area equal to ¼ acre

⁶tan \'dän\ *n, pl* **tan** *or* **tans** *usu cap* [short for *tanka*] **:** one of a boat-dwelling people distantly related to the Li whose boats form compact colonies in the river esp. at Canton and Foochow, China — called also *Tanka*

tan *abbr* tangent

ta·na \'tänə\ *n, cap* [Malay (*tupai*) *tanah* ground shrew, fr. *tupai* shrew, squirrel + *tanah* ground] **:** a small genus of Bornean and Sumatran tree shrews with a long muzzle bearing an extended nose pad

²tana *often cap, var of* TANNA

tan·a·ce·tin \,tanə'sētᵊn\ *n* -S [ISV *tanacet-* (fr. NL *Tanacetum*, genus name of the tansy *Tanacetum vulgare*) + *-in*] **:** the bitter principle $C_{11}H_{16}O_4$ of the common tansy

tan·a·ce·tum \-ēd·əm\ *n, cap* [NL, fr. ML, tansy] **:** a genus of chiefly Old World strong-scented herbs (family Compositae) having usu. dissected foliage and small discoid flower heads in flat-topped corymbs — see TANSY 1a

ta·nach \tä'näk\ *n, cap* [MHeb *tnk*, abbr. of Heb *tōrāh*, *nĕbhī'īm*, *kĕthūbhīm* Pentateuch, Prophets, Hagiographa] **:** the Hebrew Scriptures

tan·a·ger \'tanəjə(r), -nēj-\ *n* -S [NL *tanagra*, fr. Pg *tangará*, fr. Tupi] **:** any of numerous American passerine birds (family Thraupidae) having brightly colored males, being mainly unmusical, and chiefly inhabiting woodlands — see SCARLET TANAGER, WESTERN TANAGER

¹tan·a·gra \'tanəgrə, tə'nagrə\ *n, cap* [NL] **:** a genus of small fruit-eating tropical American tanagers having variegated coloring and short tails and broad gapes — see EUPHONIA

²tanagra \"\ *n* -S [fr. *Tanagra*, town in the ancient republic of Boeotia, east central Greece] **1** *or* **tanagra figurine** *usu cap T* **:** one of many small terra-cotta statuettes often representing people of fashion discovered in ancient tombs principally in Boeotia and highly prized by collectors **2** *often cap* **:** CASTILIAN BROWN

ta·nag·ri·dae \tə'nagrə,dē\ [NL, fr. *Tanagra* + *-idae*] *syn of* THRAUPIDAE

tan·a·ida·cea \,tanēə'dāshēə\ *n pl, cap* [NL, fr. *Tanaid-*, *Tanais*, genus of crustaceans (fr. L *Tanais* the river Don, fr. Gk *Tanaïs*) + *-acea*] **:** a small order of malacostracan crustaceans (division Peracarida) often included in the Isopoda and intermediate in character between that order and the Cumacea

tanaim *pl of* ²TANA

ta·nai·na \tə'nīnə\ *n, pl* **tanaina** *or* **tanainas** *usu cap* **1 a :** an Athapaskan people of the area around Cook Inlet, southern Alaska **b :** a member of such people **2 :** the language of the Tanaina people

ta·na·la \tə'nälə\ *n, pl* **tanala** *or* **tanalas** *usu cap* **:** one of a forest people in southeastern Madagascar prob. more directly descended from the aboriginal inhabitants than are the bulk of the island's peoples

tan·a·na \'tanə,nō\ *n, pl* **tanana** *or* **tananas** *usu cap* **1 a :** an Athapaskan people of the Tanana and Yukon river valleys, Alaska, near their confluence **b :** a member of such people **2 :** the language of the Tanana people

ta·nan·a·rive \tə'nanə,rēv\ *adj, usu cap* [fr. *Tananarive*, capital of the Malagasy Republic] **:** of or from Tananarive, the capital of the Malagasy Republic **:** of the kind or style prevalent in Tananarive

tanbark \'=,=\ *n* [²*tan* + *bark*] **1 a :** a bark rich in tannin bruised or cut into small pieces and used in tanning **b** (1) **:** spent tanbark used as a covering (as for a circus ring or racetrack) (2) **:** a surface covered with tanbark **2 :** a light to moderate brown that is slightly redder than suede and very slightly redder than mocha bisque — called also *Algerian*

tanbark beetle *n* **1 :** the adult of the tanbark borer **2 :** a small black boring beetle (*Stephanopachys substriatus*) that infests hemlock tanbark

tanbark borer *n* **:** a borer that is the larva of a cerambycid beetle (*Phymatodes testaceus*) and feeds beneath the bark of various trees

tanbark oak *n* **:** an oak that yields tanbark: as **a :** an evergreen oak (*Lithocarpus densiflora*) of the Pacific coast area differing from the typical oaks esp. in having erect staminate catkins **b :** CHESTNUT OAK c **c :** a black oak (*Quercus velutina*)

tanbark tree *n* **:** HEMLOCK 2a

tan bay *n* **:** LOBLOLLY BAY 1

tan·bur \'tan,bu̇(ə)r, =\'=\ *n* -S [Per *tambūr*] **:** TAMBOURA

¹tan·chel·mi·an \(')taŋ'kelmēən, -aŋ,k-\ *adj, usu cap* [*Tanchelm* †1115? Flemish heretic + E *-an*] **:** of or relating to Tanchelm who denounced the church and the sacraments and led an armed revolt

²tanchelmian \"\ *n, usu cap* **:** a follower of Tanchelm

T and A *abbr* tonsillectomy and adenoidectomy

tan·dan \'tandən\ *n* -S [native name in Australia] **:** an Australian freshwater catfish (*Tandanus tandanus*)

tan·da·va \'tändəvə\ *n* -S [Skt *tāṇḍava*] **:** the energetic and virile dance type of India — contrasted with *lasya*

¹tan·dem \'tandəm, -aan-\ *n* -S [L, at length, at last (taken to mean "lengthwise"), fr. *tam* so, so much, as (akin to Gk *to* that) + *-dem* (demonstrative suff.) — more at THAT] **1 a** (1) **:** a 2-seated carriage drawn by horses harnessed one before the other (2) **:** a team harnessed in this manner **b :** TANDEM BICYCLE **c :** TANDEM AIRPLANE **d :** a vehicle (as a trailer or truck) having close-coupled pairs of axles **2 :** a group of two or more arranged or following one behind the other **:** two or more used or acting in conjunction ⟨a more persuasive . . . ~ could not be found, nor two men with more sincerity —Darrell Berrigan⟩ — **in tandem** *adv* **1 :** in a tandem arrangement ⟨tugging two supply-laden sleds *in tandem* —*Time*⟩ **2 :** in partnership ⟨the majority party will be functioning *in tandem* with the minority party —Elmo Roper⟩

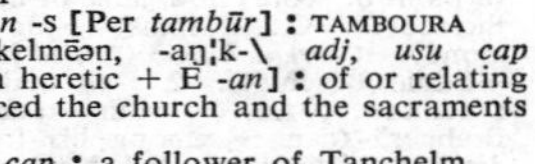

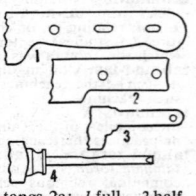

tandem 1d

²tandem \"\ *adv* [L, adv., at length] **:** one after or behind another ⟨horses driven ~⟩

³tandem \"\ *adj* **:** consisting of two arranged one behind the other ⟨a ~ arrangement of engine cylinders⟩

tandem airplane *n* **:** an airplane having two or more sets of wings of about the same area placed one in front of the other on the same level

tandem bicycle *n* **:** a bicycle for two or more persons on which the riders sit one behind another

tandem cart *n* **:** a 2-wheeled vehicle having seats back to back with the front one somewhat elevated

tandem compound *n* **:** a tandem compound steam engine or turbine

tandem engine *n* **:** a steam engine having two or more steam cylinders in line with a common piston rod

tandem hitch *n* **:** a hitch in which two or more animals are placed in line tail to head or two rows of several animals abreast are placed one row ahead of the other

tandem method *n* **:** a method of improving livestock by breeding animals selected for excellence in one quality (as milk production) and neglecting other qualities until that chosen is considered adequately fixed in the strain when another quality may be selected and bred into the strain — compare TOTAL SCORE METHOD

tandem mill *n* **:** a rolling mill with several stands in succession

tandem office *n* **:** a telephone central office or switchboard used entirely for the interconnection of telephone exchanges that reduces the number of trunk circuits

tandem roller *n* **:** a steam or gasoline driven roller in which the weight is divided between two heavy iron rolls one behind the other

T and G *abbr* **1** tongue and groove **2** tongued and grooved

tan disease *n* [²*tan*; fr. the brownish patches] **:** a condition of roots or woody stems caused by excessive moisture in which brownish or white granular or woolly patches consisting of dead cells form on the surface

T and O *abbr* taken and offered

tandour *var of* TENDOUR

¹tane *chiefly Scot past part of* TAKE

²tane \'tān\ *Scot & dial Eng var of* ¹TONE

ta·ne·ka·ha \,tänə'kä(,)hä\ *n* -S [Maori] **:** CELERY-TOPPED PINE

¹tang \'taŋ, -aiŋ\ *n* -S [ME *tang*, *tange*, of Scand origin; akin to ON *tangi* point, spit of land, tang of a knife; perh. akin to ON *tunga* tongue — more at TONGUE] **1 a** *dial* (1) **:** a serpent's tongue (2) **:** STING, PANG **b** *Scot & dial Eng* **:** something having a sharp projecting point: as (1) **:** a tine of a stag's horn (2) **:** a prong of a fork (3) **:** a buckle tongue (4) **:** the tongue of a Jew's harp **2 a :** a piece that forms an extension from the blade or analogous part of an instrument (as a table knife or fork, file, chisel, or sword) and connects with the handle and that may be a thin flat plate on each side of which a rounded piece is secured to form the handle or that may be a tapered piece inserted into the haft or handle — see FILE illustration **b :** a butt and stem of a prehistoric arrowhead made to fit into a shaft **c :** the strip or plate sometimes extending from the receiver or frame of a firearm by which it is secured to the stock **3 a** (1) **:** a sharp distinctive flavor that lingers on the tongue **:** a taste of something extraneous to the thing itself that may produce an unpleasant response ⟨a cheese with the ~ of garlic⟩ ⟨cider with the ~ of the cask⟩ ⟨meals . . . retain the unmistakable ~ of country cooking —*Amer. Guide Series: Ind.*⟩ (2) **:** a particularly pungent odor ⟨the ~ of peat fires —*Holiday*⟩ ⟨an afternoon full of . . . the ~ of mown grass —J.C.Trewin⟩ **b :** something having the effect of a sharp taste in the mouth or a pungent odor ⟨treated murder as a joke with a ~ to it —Graham Greene⟩ ⟨her prose is a cidery flowing of sweetness

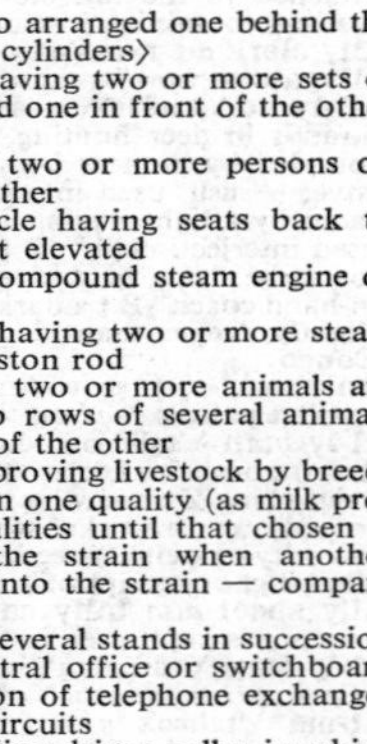

tangs 2a: *1* full, *2* half, *3* flat or push, *4* round or rattail

and ~ —Charles Lee⟩ **4 a :** a faint suggestion **:** noticeable trace **:** SMATTERING — usu. used with *of* ⟨kindness is seasoned with the ~ of humor —Elliott Dobson⟩ ⟨will find himself getting a ~ of enjoyment out of it —S.C.Pepper⟩ **b :** a distinguishing characteristic that sets apart or gives a special individuality ⟨nothing in contemporary England quite to match . . . the American ~ —Howard M. Jones⟩ ⟨give the place a definite grass-roots ~ —D.F.Malcolm⟩ **5 :** SURGEONFISH **6** *Scot & dial Eng* **:** a low projecting cape or narrow strip of land **7 :** JET 3 **8 :** a ship's mast fitting to which stays and shrouds are attached **9 :** a diamond cutter's stand for holding the dop in constant position with reference to the surface of the skeif so as to cut and polish the stone **syn** see TASTE

²**tang** \"\ *vt* -ED/-ING/-S [ME *tangen,* fr. *tang, tange,* n.] **1** *dial Eng* **:** STING **2 :** to furnish with a tang **3 :** to affect with or as if with a tang ⟨evergreen forests ~*ed* with salt air —*Amer. Guide Series: Oregon*⟩ ⟨breeze blows . . . ~*ed* with flowers —Amy Lowell⟩

³**tang** \"\ *n* -S [of Scand origin; akin to Dan & Norw *tang* seaweed, ON *thang* kelp, tangleweed] **:** any of various large coarse seaweeds; *esp* **:** a rockweed of the genus *Fucus* — compare BLADDER WRACK 1; see PRICKLY TANG

⁴**tang** \"\ *vb* -ED/-ING/-S [imit.] *vt* **1 :** to cause to ring or sound loudly ⟨~*ing* the spoon on the shovel —Flora Thompson⟩ **2 :** to utter with a tang ⟨let thy tongue ~ arguments of state —Shak.⟩ ~ *vi* **:** to make a harsh ringing sound

⁵**tang** \"\ *n* -S [imit.] **:** a sharp twanging sound (as of a single stroke on metal or of the plucking of a string) **:** TWANG

⁶**tang** \'täŋ\ *adj, usu cap* [*Tang, T'ang,* Chin. dynasty (A.D. 618–907), fr. Chin (Pek) *t'ang²*] **:** of, relating to, or having the characteristics of the period of the Tang dynasty and esp. of the art forms developed during that period ⟨*Tang* pottery⟩

tan·ga *also* **tang·ka** *or* **tan·ka** *or* **tan·kah** \təŋ'gä, -ŋ'kä\ *n* -S [Hindi *taṅgā*] **:** any of various Eastern coins: as **a :** a former silver coin of India corresponding to the rupee **b :** an old debased silver coin of Tibet **c :** a bronze coin of Portuguese India and corresponding unit of value equal to ¹⁄₁₆ rupia

tan·ga·le \täŋ'gälē\ *n, pl* **tangale** *or* **tangales** *usu cap* **1 :** a people of the Bauchi district of northern Nigeria **2 :** the language of the Tangale people

tan·ga·lung \təŋ'gälaŋ\ *n* -S [Malay *tĕnggalong*] **:** a long-muzzled civet (*Viverra tangalunga*) that is dark gray with longitudinal black stripes more or less broken into spots and is widely distributed in the East Indies

tang·an·tang·an \ˌtaŋ,än'taŋ,än\ *n* -S [Tag] **:** CASTOR-OIL PLANT

tan·gan·yi·ka \ˌtaŋgən¦yēkə, ¦taŋg-, ¦taiŋg-, -gə¦nē-\ *adj, usu cap* [fr. *Tanganyika,* territory in eastern Africa] **:** of or from Tanganyika **:** of the kind or style prevalent in Tanganyika

¹**tan·gan·yi·kan** \-ēkən\ *adj, usu cap* [*Tanganyika,* eastern Africa + E *-an*] **1 :** of, relating to, or characteristic of Tanganyika **2 :** of, relating to, or characteristic of the people of Tanganyika

²**tanganyikan** \"\ *n* -S *cap* [*Tanganyika* + E *-an* (n. suffix)] **:** a native or inhabitant of Tanganyika

tan·gar·i·dae \tan'garə,dē, taŋ'g-\ [NL, fr. Pg *tangará* tanager + NL *-idae* — more at TANAGER] *syn of* THRAUPIDAE

tanga·ro·an \ˌtäŋ(g)ə'rōən, ˌtaŋ-\ *n* -S *usu cap* [*Tangaroa,* Polynesian deity + E *-an*] **:** one of an ethnic group or late wave of conquering Polynesians

tang chisel *n* [¹*tang*] **:** a chisel in which the shank tapers to a point and is driven into a handle

tanged \'taŋd, -aiŋd\ *adj* **:** having or equipped with a tang ⟨~ flint daggers⟩

tan·ge·lo \'tanjə,lō\ *n* -S [blend of *tangerine* and *pomelo*] **1 :** a hybrid between a tangerine or mandarin orange and either a grapefruit or shaddock **2 :** the fruit of the tangelo

tan·gem·on \tan'jemən\ *n* -S [blend of *tangerine* and *lemon*] **1 :** a hybrid between the tangerine and the lemon **2 :** the fruit of the tangemon

tan·gen·cy \'tanjənsē, 'taan-, -si\ *n* -ES **:** the quality or state of being tangent

tang end *n* **:** a projection on the end of a rod used to strengthen the joint between the rod and a pipe

¹**tan·gent** \'tanjənt, 'taan-\ *adj* [L *tangent-, tangens,* pres. part. of *tangere* to touch; akin to Gk *tetagōn* having seized, OE *thaccian* to stroke, touch gently] **1 a :** touching at a single point **:** TOUCHING ⟨a straight line ~ to a curve⟩ **b** (1) **:** having a common tangent line at a point — used of two curves in a plane, two space curves, or a surface and a space curve (2) **:** having a common tangent plane at a point — used of two surfaces **2 a :** diverging from an original purpose or course **:** ERRATIC ⟨much of his work is chaotic and distorted by ~ obsessions —Tennessee Williams⟩ **b :** CONTIGUOUS **:** being in agreement ⟨subject matter ~ to the country's growth in those years —G.F.Milton⟩

²**tangent** \"\ *n* -S [NL *tangent-, tangens,* fr. L, pres. part. of *tangere* to touch] **1 a :** TANGENT LINE **b :** the ordinate of any point on the terminal side of an angle divided by the nonzero abscissa of this point with the vertex coinciding with the origin of a plane rectangular coordinate system and the initial side of the angle coinciding with the positive x-axis — abbr. *tan* **2 :** a course abruptly deviating from that previously pursued **:** DIGRESSION, IRRELEVANCY ⟨avoid wandering off on ~*s* —J.F.Wharton⟩ ⟨his critics . . . went off at a ~ —Saul Carson⟩ **3 :** a small upright flat-ended metal pin at the inner end of a clavichord key that strikes the string to produce the musical tone and fixes the pitch by damping the string **4 :** a piece of straight railroad track

tan·gen·tal \'tanjənt°l, (')tan¦jen-\ *adj* **:** TANGENTIAL

tangent arc *n* **:** a halo that touches a circular halo

tangent-cut \¦==¦=\ *adj* **:** TANGENT-SAWED

tangent galvanometer *n* **:** a galvanometer consisting of a very small magnetic needle in the center of a large vertical circular coil of wire through which electric current is passed and whose plane is in the magnetic meridian with the intensity of the current being proportional to the tangent of the angle of deflection of the needle

tan·gen·tial \(')tan¦jenchəl, -aan¦-\ *adj* **1 :** of, relating to, or of the nature of a tangent **:** being in the direction of a tangent **2 a :** acting along or lying in a tangent **b :** arranged or having parts arranged like tangents **3 a :** deviating widely and sometimes erratically **:** DIVERGENT ⟨the discussion method . . . is time-consuming and alarmingly ~ —R.C.Snyder⟩ **b :** touching lightly or in the most tenuous way **:** INCIDENTAL ⟨no place . . . for political controversy save in occasional ~ comment —W.R.Benét⟩

tangential creep *n* **:** slow horizontal movement of material composing the earth's crust

tangential force *n* **:** a force that acts on a moving body in the direction of a tangent to the curved path of the body

tan·gen·tial·ly \-chəlē, -li\ *adv* **:** in a tangential manner **:** at a tangent ⟨the vapors enter the trap ~ —*Modern Chem. Processes*⟩ ⟨a few of the times great figures come into the story, but only ~ —Jean S. Untermeyer⟩

tangential motion *n* **:** proper motion of a star corrected for the effect of distance and expressed in linear units usu. kilometers per second and being that component of the star's motion with respect to the solar system that is at right angles to the line of sight

tangential stress *n* **:** a force acting in a generally horizontal direction; *esp* **:** a force that produces mountain folding and overthrusting

tangent line *n* [trans. of NL *linea tangens*] **:** a line at a fixed point *P* of a curve that is the limit approached by the secant *PQ* as *Q* approaches *P* along the curve

tan·gent·ly \'tanjəntlē\ *adv* **:** TANGENTIALLY

tangent plane *n* **:** the plane through a point of a surface that contains the tangent lines to all the curves on the surface through the same point

tangent-saw \¦==¦=\ *vt* **:** to saw (a log) lengthwise by parallel cuts in regular succession — compare QUARTERSAW

tangent screw *n* **1 :** a worm that works tangentially on a worm wheel to which it imparts an endless motion **2 :** a very fine screw giving a tangential movement for making the final adjustment to an instrument of precision (as a surveyor's transit)

tangent sight *n* **:** a rear sight for a firearm that has the graduations corresponding to the tangents of the angles of elevation and that is usu. graduated to read in yards of range

tangent spoke *n* **:** a tension spoke of a bicycle or similar wheel secured tangentially to the hub

tan·ger·e·tin \ˌtanjə'rēt°n\ *n* -S [²*tangerine* + *-etin* (as in *fisetin*)] **:** a crystalline flavone $C_{20}H_{20}O_7$ obtained from the peel of tangerines

¹**tan·ger·ine** \ˌtanjə¦rēn, ˌtaan-\ *adj, usu cap* [*Tanger* (Tangier), seaport in Morocco + E *-ine*] **:** of, relating to, or from Tangier

²**tangerine** \"\ *n* -S [*Tanger* (Tangier), Morocco + E *-ine* (n. suffix)] **1** *cap* **:** a native or inhabitant of Tangier **2 a** (1) **:** any of various cultivated citrus fruits that have deep orange to almost scarlet skin and pulp and are the only mandarins grown on a large scale in the U.S. and southern Africa — distinguished from *mandarin* (2) **:** MANDARIN 4b(1) **b :** a tree producing tangerines **:** MANDARIN 4a **3 a :** a variable color ranging from moderate reddish orange to vivid or strong orange **b :** *of textiles* **:** a strong reddish orange

tangfish \'=,=\ *n* [³*tang* + *fish*] *dial Brit* **:** HARBOR SEAL

tanghan *var of* TANGUN

tan·ghin \'taŋgən\ *n* -S [F, fr. Malagasy (*voa*) *tanging*] **1 :** a virulent poison derived from the kernels of the ordeal tree of Madagascar **2 :** ORDEAL TREE 1

tan·ghin·ia \tan'ginēə, taŋ'g-\ *n, cap* [NL, fr. Malagasy *tanging* + NL *-ia*] **:** a genus of Madagascan trees (family Apocynaceae) having evergreen oblanceolate leaves clustered at the ends of the branches and terminal cymes of small white flowers — see ORDEAL TREE 1

tan·ghin·in \tan'ginən, taŋ'g-; 'taŋgənən\ *n* -S [ISV *tanghin-* (fr. NL *Tanghinia,* genus name of the ordeal tree *Tanghinia venenifera*) + *-in*] **:** a poisonous bitter crystalline compound constituting the active principle of the ordeal tree

¹**tangi** \'taŋē, 'täŋē\ *n* -S [Maori, lit., to mourn, cry] **:** a Maori funeral rite; *also* **:** a lamentation or dirge that accompanies it

²**tan·gi** \(')tän¦gē\ *n* -S [Per *tangī* narrowness, fr. *tang* narrow] *India* **:** a narrow gorge

tan·gi·bil·i·ty \ˌtanjə'bilǝd·ē, ˌtaan-, -lətē, -i\ *n* -ES **:** the quality or state of being tangible

¹**tan·gi·ble** \'tanjəbəl, 'taan-\ *adj* [LL *tangibilis,* fr. L *tangere* to touch + *-ibilis* -ible — more at TANGENT] **1 a :** capable of being touched **:** able to be perceived as materially existent esp. by the sense of touch **:** PALPABLE, TACTILE ⟨a ~ separable thing, like . . . salt or bread —Sinclair Lewis⟩ ⟨wished he had had a ~ reward for his efforts⟩ **b :** substantially real **:** MATERIAL ⟨the conquest of a territory meant a ~ advantage to the conqueror —Norman Angell⟩ ⟨a ~ gain in money —Wessie Connell⟩ **2 :** capable of being realized by the mind **:** conceived or thought of as definable or measurable ⟨I have never been in a community where happiness was so ~ —Arthur Langford⟩ ⟨the motives of action are quite ~ and the tales reflect actual situations —H.O.Taylor⟩ **3 :** constituting or consisting of a corporeal item capable of being appraised at an actual or approximate value ⟨~ assets⟩ **syn** see PERCEPTIBLE

²**tangible** \"\ *n* -S **:** something that is tangible: as **a :** a tangible asset **b :** a piece of tangible property

tan·gi·ble·ness *n* -ES **:** TANGIBILITY

tangible property *n* **:** property (as real estate) having physical substance apparent to the senses; *sometimes* **:** intangible property (as stocks, bonds, notes) involved in a government's exercise of its police or taxing power

tan·gi·bly \'tanjəblē, 'taan-, -bli\ *adv* **:** in a tangible manner ⟨virtue is ~ rewarded —J.D.Hart⟩

¹**tan·gier** \(')tan¦ji(ə)r, -aan-, -iə\ *also* **tan·giers** \-i(ə)rz, -iəz\ *adj, usu cap* [fr. *Tangier, Tangiers,* Morocco] **:** of or from the city of Tangier, Morocco **:** of the kind or style prevalent in Tangier **:** TANGERINE

²**tangier** \"\ *n, often cap* [fr. *Tangier, Tangiers,* seaport in Morocco] **:** OCHER ORANGE

³**tangier** *comparative of* TANGY

tangier pea *also* **tangier peavine** *n, usu cap T* **:** a wild pea (*Lathyrus tingitanus*) of northern Africa resembling the sweet pea and having showy but odorless flowers and pods without wings

tangiest *superlative of* TANGY

tangile *var of* TANGUILE

tan·gil·in \tan'gilən\ *n* -S [Malay *tĕnggiling,* fr. *giling* roll; fr. its characteristic of rolling itself into a ball] **:** an East Indian pangolin (*Manis javanica*)

tanging *pres part of* TANG

tan·gi·pa·hoa \ˌtanjəpə¦hō, ¦tanchp-\ *n, pl* **tangipahoa** *or* **tangipahoas** *usu cap* **1 :** an extinct Muskhogean people of southeastern Louisiana **2 :** a member of the Tangipahoa people

tangka *var of* TANGA

tang·khul \'taŋ,kül\ *n, pl* **tangkhul** *or* **tangkhuls** *usu cap* **:** one of a Naga people on the eastern slopes of the Manipur hills

¹**tan·gle** \'taŋgəl, 'taiŋ-\ *vb* **tangled**; **tangled**; **tangling** \-g(ə)liŋ\ **tangles** [ME *tangilen, tagilen,* prob. of Scand origin; akin to Sw dial. *taggla* to disarrange, tangle] *vt* **1 :** to involve so as to hamper, obstruct, or embarrass ⟨lost in a growing institutionalism, and *tangled* in a hopeless controversy —F.K.Stamm⟩ **2 :** to seize and hold in or as if in a snare **:** ENTRAP ⟨he was *tangled* by his own lies⟩ **3 a :** to unite or knit together in confusion **:** interweave or interlock in a manner almost impossible to unravel **b :** to mix intricately ⟨economics and literature had become so . . . *tangled* —May L. Becker⟩ ⟨father's business affairs are greatly *tangled* —P.B.Kyne⟩ ~ *vi* **1 :** to engage in conflict **:** become involved in argument or altercation **:** have a set-to ⟨opposing lawyers *tangled* heatedly over . . . constitutional guarantees —*N.Y. Times*⟩ ⟨only a few planes dared to . . . ~ with the allied fleets —*Newsweek*⟩ **2 :** to become entangled **:** INTERTWINE

²**tangle** \"\ *n* -S **1 a :** a tangled twisted condition or mass **:** a knot of threads or something similar (as hairs, branches, vines) united confusedly or so interwoven as not to be easily disengaged **:** RAVEL, SNARL ⟨a stretch of back road that . . . now is a ~ of weeds and wild grasses —A.W.Turnbull⟩ **b :** something resembling a tangle in appearance ⟨became lost in the ~ of streets along the waterfront⟩ ⟨an interminable ~ of waterless ravines —S.H.Howard⟩ ⟨the old wharf with its ~ of sails and boats and people —Vicki Baum⟩ **2 a :** a complicated jumbled aggregation **:** a highly involved often confused state or condition ⟨in a hopeless ~ of conflicting allegiances —Gordon Merrick⟩ ⟨the formerly open . . . border is now a ~ of red tape —J.S.Roucek⟩ ⟨works amid a forbidding ~ of technical regulations and restrictions —*Lamp*⟩ **b :** a state of perplexity or complete bewilderment ⟨his brain got all in a ~ and he could make a beginning nowhere —Liam O'Flaherty⟩ **3 :** a bar or frame to which short lengths of chain bearing bundles of various material (as frayed rope or cotton waste) are attached and which is dragged over the sea bottom to entangle and catch animals (as starfish) **4 :** a serious altercation **:** ARGUMENT, CONFLICT ⟨felt she was not to blame for the ~ with her neighbor⟩ ⟨unwillingness . . . to trust an armed Germany has been a factor in every European political ~ for several hundred years —G.W.Johnson⟩

³**tangle** \"\ *also* **tangleweed** \'==,=\ *n* -S [*tangle* of Scand origin; akin to Norw *tongull* tangle, ON *thöngull* tangle, Dan *tang* seaweed — more at TANG] **:** a large seaweed; *esp* **:** either of two seaweeds (*Laminaria saccharina* or *L. digitata*)

⁴**tangle** \"\ *n* -S [prob. fr. ²*tangle;* influenced in meaning by ¹*dangle*] **:** something that is pendulous: as **a** *Scot* **:** a hanging icicle **b** *Scot* **:** a lock of hair

tangleberry \'==- — *see* BERRY\ *n* [⁴*tangle* + *berry*] **:** DANGLEBERRY

tanglebush \'==,=\ *n* [²*tangle* + *bush*] **:** a spiny branching spreading forestiera (*Forestiera neomexicana*) of the western and southwestern U.S.

tangled *adj* [fr. past part. of ¹*tangle*] **1 :** existing in or giving the appearance of a state of utter disorder **:** JUMBLED, SNARLED **:** thickly intertwined ⟨the ~ path which led beneath the ruined walls —Sheila Rowlands⟩ ⟨around us loom the ~ masses of peaks —P.A.Moore⟩ ⟨twenty miles of ~ traffic —Claudia Cassidy⟩ **2 :** exceedingly complex **:** very involved ⟨laws had failed to resolve the ~ case —*N.Y. Times*⟩ ⟨a simplification of ~ customs rules —*Newsweek*⟩

tanglefish \'==,=\ *n* [⁴*tangle* + *fish;* fr. its lean slender shape] **:** a pipefish (*Syngnathus acus*) of Europe

tanglefoot \'==,=\ *n, pl* **tanglefoots** [¹*tangle* + *foot*] **1 :** strong drink; *esp* **:** a cheap whiskey **2 a :** HEATH ASTER **b :** DEERWEED

tanglehead \'==,=\ *n* **:** a perennial grass (*Heteropogon contortus*) of worldwide distribution that is used as a forage grass in the southwestern U.S. and has long tangled flexuous awns

tangle-legs \'==,=\ *n pl but sing or pl in constr* **:** HOBBLEBUSH

tan·gle·ment \'taŋgəlmənt, 'taiŋ-\ *n* -S **:** a tangled condition **:** a state of being embroiled or confused ⟨great issues in our drama . . . serve as the background for individual human ~*s* —S.L.Weaver⟩

tangle net *n* **:** GILL NET

tangleroot \'==,=\ *n* **:** an abnormal condition of the pineapple in which the main roots wind around the rootstock instead of growing out into the soil

tangle-tail \'==,=\ *n* **:** a stonecrop (*Sedum acre*)

tanglewrack \'==,=\ *n* [³*tangle* + *wrack*] **:** ³TANGLE

tan·gly \'taŋg(ə)lē, 'taiŋ-, -li\ *adj* -ER/-EST **:** full of tangles or knots **:** ENTANGLED, INTRICATE, SNARLY

¹**tan·go** \'taŋ(,)gō, 'taiŋ-\ *n* -S [AmerSp, Negro drum dance, Negro dance and festival, tango, prob. of Niger-Congo origin; akin to Ibibio *tamgu* to dance] **1 a :** a ballroom dance of Spanish-American origin in ²⁄₄ time characterized by posturing, frequent pointing positions, and a great variety of steps **b :** the music for the tango or a composition marked by similar syncopation shown typically as a dotted eighth note, sixteenth note, and two eighth notes **2 :** a variety of bingo

²**tango** \"\ *vi* -ED/-ING/-S **:** to dance the tango

³**tango** \"\ *usu cap* — a communications code word for the letter *t*

tan·gor \'tan,jȯ(ə)r, 'taŋ,gȯ-\ *n* -S [blend of *tangerine* and *orange*] **1 :** a hybrid between the mandarin orange and the sweet orange usu. having large deeply colored and easily peeled fruit ⟨temple oranges are usu. considered to be ~*s*⟩ **2 :** the fruit of a tangor

tan·go·receptor \ˌtaŋ(,)gō+\ *n* [*tango-* (fr. L *tangere* to touch) + *receptor* — more at TANGENT] **:** a receptor for the sense of touch

tang peep *n* **:** a peep sight mounted on the tang of the receiver of a gun

tan·gram \'taŋgrəm, -ang-, -an,gram\ *n* [perh. fr. Chin (Pek) *t'ang²* Chinese + E *-gram*] **:** a Chinese puzzle made by cutting a square of thin material into five triangles, a square, and a rhomboid which are capable of recombination in many different figures

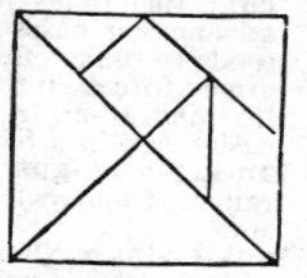

tangram

¹**tangs** \'taŋz\ *Scot & dial Eng var of* TONGS

²**tangs** *pl of* TANG, *pres 3d sing of* TANG

tangue \'taŋ\ *n* -S [Malagasy *tàndeke*] **:** TENREC

tang·ui·le *or* **tang·i·le** \'täŋəlē\ *n* -S [Tag *tangili*] **1 :** a Philippine mahogany (*Shorea polysperma*) with reddish brown wood **2 :** the wood of tanguile — called also *red lauan*

tang·uing·ue \täŋ'iŋē\ *also* **tang·ui·gue** \täŋ'ēgē\ *n* -S [Tag *tanguingi*] **:** SPANISH MACKEREL 1c

tan·guis cotton \'täŋ,gwēs-\ *n, usu cap T* [AmerSp *tangüis*] **:** a white-fibered Peruvian cotton with a staple length of 1 to 1¼ inches

tan·gun \'täŋgən\ *or* **tan·gum** \-gəm\ *also* **tan·ghan** \-gən\ *n* -S [Hindi *ṭāgan, ṭāghan*] **:** a small strong usu. piebald pony of Tibet and Bhutan

tan·gut \(')tän¦güt\ *n* -S *usu cap* [fr. *Tangut,* ancient region in northwestern China] **:** a Tibetan esp. of the west central province of Tsinghai in China

tangy \'taŋē, 'taiŋ-, -ŋi\ *adj, sometimes* -ER/-EST [¹*tang* + *-y*] **:** having or suggestive of a tang ⟨the rich ~ scent of pine needles —Ysabel Rennie⟩ ⟨told in ~ 18th century English —Bernardine Kielty⟩

tanh *abbr* hyperbolic tangent

tan·ha \'tən(,)hä\ *n* -S [Pali *taṇhā,* fr. Skt *tṛṣṇā* thirst, desire, fr. *tṛṣyati* he thirsts — more at THIRST] *Buddhism* **:** an intense desire for life

tan house *n* [ME *tanhous,* fr. *tannen* to tan + *hous* house — more at TAN, HOUSE] **:** a tannery building for tanning vats or drums

tan·ia *or* **tan·ier** *or* **tan·nia** *or* **tan·nier** *or* **tan·ya** *also* **tan·yah** \'tanēə(r), -nyə(r)\ *n* -S [F *tannie,* perh. modif. (influenced by *tanaisie* tansy, fr. OF *tanesie*) of a word of Arawakan, Cariban, or Tupian origin; akin to Arawak *taya* taro, Calinago *táia,* Tupi *taiá* — more at TANSY] **:** any of several aroids having edible farinaceous roots: as **a :** TARO 1 **b :** YAUTIA a

ta·ni·ko \'tänə(,)kō\ *n* -S [Maori] **1 :** a Maori ornamental border of a mat **2 :** a type of weaving with colored yarns used commonly for headdresses and bodices worn in Maori dances and for belts

tan·ist \'tanəst, 'thȯn-\ *n* -S [IrGael *tānaiste* second, second person in rank, tanist] **:** the lord or proprietor elected under the system of tanistry

tan·ist·ry \-trē\ *or* **tan·is·tria** \ta'nistrēə, thȯ'n-\ *n, pl* **tanistries** *or* **tanistrias** [*tanistry* fr. *tanist* + *-ry;* *tanistria* fr. NL, fr. *tanista* tanist (fr. IrGael *tānaiste*), after E *tanistry*] **:** an early Irish law of succession by which the heir or successor of a chief or king is appointed during the lifetime of the reigning chief, is not necessarily his oldest son, is generally the worthiest and wisest of the male relatives of the chief, and is elected by the people from among the eligible candidates but because of resultant bloody wars and feuds between families declared illegal by a decision of the Anglo-Irish judges in the first year of James I

ta·nite \'tä,nīt\ *adj, usu cap* [*Tanis,* ancient city in the Nile delta, Lower Egypt + E *-ite*] **:** of or relating to ancient Tanis in Egypt or the kings of the XXIst and XXIIId dynasties making it their capital

tan·jong \'tän,jȯŋ\ *n* -S [Malay, cape, headland, promontory] **:** CAPE, POINT

¹**tank** \'taŋk, -aiŋk\ *n* -S [Pg *tanque,* short for *estanque,* fr. *estancar* to stop a flow, dam, stanch, fr. (assumed) VL *stanticare* to cause to stand, stanch — more at STANCH] **1 a** *India* **:** a pool of water **:** LAKE, RESERVOIR **b** *dial* **:** a small lake **:** POND, POOL; *esp* **:** a pond built as a water supply **c :** a basin where experimental models of ships are tested ⟨submarine ~⟩ **2 a :** a usu. large artificial receptacle used for holding, transporting, or storing liquids ⟨gasoline ~⟩ ⟨fish ~⟩ ⟨oil ~⟩ **b :** a compartment in a ship for holding water, oil, or liquids **c :** a container in or attached to an airplane for carrying fuel; *esp* **:** one that is auxiliary or droppable and used to increase range or to carry napalm **3** [so called fr. the fact that during its orig. secret manufacture in England the hull was referred to as a water tank] **:** a full-track enclosed armored vehicle that usu. mounts a cannon and automatic weapons and has excellent cross-country mobility, armor protection, fire power, and the capability of shock action — compare ARMORED CAR **4 :** TANK FURNACE **5 :** a container for a photographic solution **6 :** a congregate prison cell or enclosure used esp. for receiving prisoners

²**tank** \"\ *vt* -ED/-ING/-S **1 :** to subject to some operation in a tank; *specif* **:** to treat (as animal refuse) in a closed tank with steam and hot water to extract fat **2 :** to cause to flow into a tank **:** store in a tank

³**tank** \"\ *n* -S [imit.] *dial chiefly Eng* **:** KNOCK, HIT, BANG

⁴**tank** \'täŋk\ *n, pl* **tank** [Hindi *ṭāk,* fr. Skt *ṭaṅka* stamped coin] **:** an Indian unit of weight for pearls equal to about 0.15 ounce

¹**tan·ka** \'dän'gä\ *n, pl* **tanka** *or* **tankas** *usu cap* [Chin (Cant) *taānka,* lit., egg people] **:** ⁶TAN

²**tanka** *or* **tankah** *var of* TANGA

³**tan·ka** \'täŋkə\ *n* -S [Jap] **:** a Japanese fixed form of verse of five lines the first and third of which have five syllables and the others seven — compare HOKKU

⁴**tanka** \"\ *n* -S [Tibetan *thaṅka*] **:** a Tibetan religious painting mounted on brocade for use as a processional banner

tank·age \ˈtaŋkij, -aiŋ-, -kēj\ *n* -s **1 :** the capacity or contents of a tank **2 :** a by-product of slaughterhouses or rendering plants that consists of animal residues (as meat scrap, blood, and bone) cooked and usu. freed of fat and gelatine and dried and that is used in feeds and fertilizers — see DIGESTER TANKAGE, GARBAGE TANKAGE **3 a :** the act or process of putting or storing in tanks **b :** fees charged for storage in tanks
tan·kard \-ŋkə(r)d\ *n* -s [ME] **1 :** a tall one-handled drinking vessel; *esp* **:** a mug of silver or pewter with a lid **2 :** a drink served in a tankard ⟨we can give you cold meat and a ~ —Charles Lamb⟩
tank barge *n* **:** a barge equipped with tanks for transporting liquids
tank car *n* **:** a railroad car for transporting liquids or gases in bulk
tank circuit *n* **1 :** an oscillatory radio circuit associated with the output circuit of a tube generator which absorbs the generator ouput in the form of energy impulses of high value and short duration and in turn delivers its output to an antenna **2 :** a tuned circuit connected in the plate circuit of a tube generator **3 :** an absorption circuit

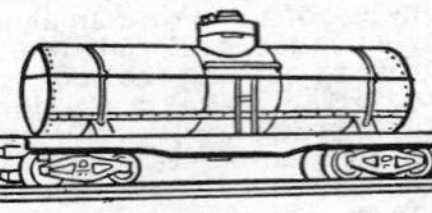
tank car

tank destroyer *n* **:** a highly mobile lightly armored vehicle that is usu. constructed on a half track or a tank chassis and mounts a cannon
tank dome *n* **:** the vertical chamber on the top of a tank car
tank·doz·er \ˈ=,dōzə(r)\ *n* [¹*tank* + bull*dozer*] **:** a tank with a bulldozer blade attached
tank drama *n* **1 :** a melodrama having as its chief sensation the use of a tank of water usu. in representing a rescue from drowning **2 :** a spectacular sensational play; *esp* **:** one with cheap or claptrap effects **3 :** drama suitable for or played in tank towns
tanked *adj* [fr. past part. of *tank* (in *tank up*)] **:** DRUNK
tank engine *n* **:** TANK LOCOMOTIVE
tank·er \ˈtaŋkə(r), -aiŋ-\ *n* -s **1 a :** a steel cargo boat fitted with tanks for the carrying of oil, molasses, or other liquid in bulk **b :** a vehicle on which a tank is mounted to carry liquids (as water, gasoline, milk, chemicals) — see TANK TRAILER, TANK TRUCK, TANK WAGON **c :** a cargo airplane fitted with large fuel tanks inside its fuselage for transporting fuel to advance air bases or for use in aerial refueling **2 :** one that tends to tanks **3 a :** a member of the armored branch of the armed forces **b :** a member of a military tank crew **4** [prob. fr. ¹*tank* + *-er;* fr. his taking a dive] **:** a boxer who goes down easily esp. in a fixed fight
tan·ker·a·bo·gus \ˌtaŋkərəˈbōgəs\ *n* -ES [prob. fr. *tanker* (alter. of *tantara*) + *bogus*, alter. of *bogey*] *dial Eng* **:** BOOGEYMAN
tank·er·man \ˈtaŋkə(r)mən, ˈtaiŋ-\ *n, pl* **tankermen :** a seaman who is a qualified member of a crew of a tanker
tank·ette \(ˈ)taŋ¦ket\ *n* -s [¹*tank* + *-ette*] **:** a small military tank
tank farm *n* **:** a continuous area used exclusively for the field storage of oil in tanks; *esp* **:** such an area with all of the tanks and equipment
tank farming *n* **:** HYDROPONICS
tank furnace *n* **:** a hearth or basin into one end of which a batch is shoveled and from the other end of which melted glass is drawn
tanking *pres part of* TANK
tank iron *n* **:** plate iron thinner than boiler plate and thicker than sheet iron or stovepipe iron
tan·kle \ˈtaŋkəl\ *n* -s [short for *tinkle-tankle*, redupl. of *tinkle*] **:** a sound louder and less acute than a tinkle
tank locomotive *n* **:** a locomotive having compartments for carrying its own fuel and water and not needing a tender
tank·man \ˈtaŋkmən, ˈtaiŋ-\ *n, pl* **tankmen 1 :** a worker who tends tanks or vats in which an industrial operation is carried out **2 :** TANKER 3 **3 :** an attendant in an aquarium who takes care of the fish and aquatic plants and their tanks
tank runner *n* **:** PHEASANT-TAILED JACANA
tanks *pl of* TANK, *pres 3d sing of* TANK
tankship \ˈ=,=\ *n* **:** TANKER 1
tank-stock \ˈ=,=\ *n* **:** lumber from heartwood of California redwood, western red cedar, and other trees that has close grain and high decay resistance and is well suited for wood= tank construction
tank table *n* **:** a table that has a tank-shaped top and is suitable for collecting oil cast in it
tank top *n* **:** INNER BOTTOM
tank town *n* **1 :** a town at which trains stop for water **2 :** an insignificant small town ⟨a kind of tent show playing the *tank towns* —Thomas Pyles⟩
tank trailer *n* **:** a truck-drawn trailer equipped and used as a tanker
tank trap *n* **:** a natural or artificial obstacle of sufficient width and depth and with steep sides to stop military tanks
tank truck *n* **:** a truck equipped and used as a tanker
tank up *vi* **:** to stuff oneself with food or drink ⟨*tank up* on breakfast —G.S.Perry⟩ ⟨*tanked up* on beer —J.V.Fox⟩; *esp* **:** to drink liquor to excess
tank wagon *n* **:** a horse-drawn wagon equipped and used as a tanker
tan·ling \ˈtanliŋ\ *n* -s [³*tan* + *-ling*] **:** one tanned by the sun
tann- *or* **tanno-** *comb form* [F, fr. *tannin*, *tanin* — more at TANNIN] **:** tan **:** tannin **:** tanning substance ⟨*tanno*gen⟩ ⟨*tann*ase⟩ ⟨*tanno*meter⟩
tan·na *also* **ta·na** \ˈtä(,)nä\ *n, pl* **tanna·im** *also* **tana·im** \ˌtänäˈim, -näˈēm\ *often cap* [Heb *tannā* teacher, tanna, fr. Aram *tĕnā* to repeat, teach] **:** one of the rabbis of Palestine during the first two centuries A.D. whose interpretations of biblical law and Hebrew oral tradition are recorded in the Mishnah, Tosephta, and other works together with their parables and homiletic comments on Scripture — compare AMORA, SABORA
tan·nage \ˈtanij\ *n* -s [¹*tan* + *-age*] **:** the act, process, or result of tanning
tan·na·ite \ˈtänə,īt\ *n* -s *often cap* [Heb *tannā* + E *-ite*] **:** TANNA
tan·na·it·ic \¦tänə¦id·ik\ *also* **tan·na·ic** \täˈnä,ik\ *adj, often cap* [*tannaitic* fr. *tannaite* + *-ic; tannaic* fr. *tanna* + *-ic*] **:** of or relating to the tannaim
tan·nase \ˈta,nās, -āz\ *n* -s [ISV *tann-* + *-ase*] **:** an enzyme that accelerates the hydrolysis of a tannin
tan·nate \-nāt\ *n* -s [F, fr. *tann-* (fr. *tannin, tanin*) + *-ate*] **:** a compound (as a salt) of a tannin
tanned *adj* [ME, partly fr. past part. of *tannen* to tan hides & partly fr. OE *getanned*, fr. past part. of *tannian* to tan hides, prob. fr. ML *tannare* — more at TAN] **1 :** treated or colored by tanning **2 :** made tawny or brown by exposure to the sun **:** covered with tan
¹tan·ner \ˈtanə(r), ˈtaan-\ *n* -s [ME, fr. OE *tannere*, fr. *tannian* to tan hides + *-ere* -er] **:** one that tans hides
²tanner *comparative of* TAN
³tan·ner \ˈtanə(r)\ *n* -s [origin unknown] *Brit* **:** SIXPENCE
tanner's bark *n* **:** TANBARK
tanner's sumac *or* **tanning sumac** *n* **:** a European sumac (*Rhus coriaria*) widely grown in Sicily for use in tanning and dyeing
tanner's wool *n* **:** ²SLIPE
tan·nery \ˈtanərē, ˈtaan-, -ri\ *n* -ES **1 :** a place where the work of tanning is carried on **2 :** the art or process of tanning
tannery fungus *n* **:** a slime mold (*Fuligo septica*) common on tanbark
tannest *superlative of* TAN
tannia *or* **tannier** *var of* TANIA
tan·nic \ˈtanik, -nēk\ *adj* [F *tannique*, fr. *tann-* + *-ique* -ic] **:** of or relating to tan **:** derived from or resembling tan or tannin
tannic acid *n* **1 :** GALLOTANNIN **2 :** TANNIN 1b
tan·nide \ˈta,nīd, -,nəd\ *n* -s [*tann-* + *-ide*] **:** a substance that whether it is a tannin or not gives microchemical tannin reactions and that may occur in the same plant cells with alkaloids sometimes combined with them
tan·nif·er·ous \(ˈ)ta¦nif(ə)rəs\ *adj* [*tann-* + *-iferous*] **:** yielding or containing tannin
tan·nin \ˈtanən\ *n* -s [F *tannin, tanin*, fr. *tanner* to tan hides (fr. MF) + *-in* — more at TAN] **1 a :** GALLOTANNIN **b :** any of a group of soluble astringent complex phenolic substances including gallotannin that are widely distributed in plants and are obtained commercially from various sources (as powdered gallnuts, shredded tara, quebracho wood, chestnut wood, wattle, sumac, valonia), that precipitate gelatin and albumin from solution and tan skin and hides, that also precipitate many alkaloids and most basic dyes, that form bluish black or greenish black colors or precipitates with ferric salts, that have been classified on the basis of behavior with acids or enzymes as either hydrolyzable to water-soluble products or as condensed yielding phlobaphenes, and that are used chiefly in tanning, dyeing, and making ink and in medicine as astringents and formerly in the treatment of burns — compare ELLAGITANNIN, TEA TANNIN **2 :** a substance that has a tanning effect as determined by its adsorption by hide powder **:** TAN 2b
tan·nined \-ənd\ *adj* **:** impregnated or treated with tannin
tanning *n* -s [ME, fr. gerund of *tannen* to tan] **1 :** the art or process by which a skin is tanned **2 :** a browning esp. of the skin by exposure to sun **3 :** a usu. severe whipping ⟨when his father got home he'd get a good ~⟩
tanning drum *n* **:** a revolving wood or metal container used for tumbling hides in the tanning process
tanning extract *n* **:** an extract that may be liquid, semisolid, or solid and that is made from tanniferous material (as oak bark, sumac leaves and twigs, or quebracho wood) for use in tanning
tan·nish \ˈtanish\ *adj* [³*tan* + *-ish*] **:** somewhat tan
tanno- — see TANN-
¹tan·noid \ˈta,nȯid\ *adj* [*tann-* + *-oid*] **:** resembling the tannins
²tannoid \"\ *n* -s **:** a tannoid substance
tan·nom·e·ter \taˈnäməd·ə(r)\ *n* [*tann-* + *-meter*] **1 :** an apparatus for determining the strength of a tanning liquor by drawing it through hide and measuring its resulting loss in density **2 :** BARKOMETER
tannu-tuvan \ˌtanüˈtüvən\ *n* -s *cap both Ts* [*Tannu-Tuva*, former name of the Tuva Autonomous Region + E *-an*] **:** a native or inhabitant of the Tuva Autonomous Region, U.S.S.R. — called also *Tuvinian*
ta·no \ˈtä(,)nō\ *n* -s *usu cap* **1 :** a group of former pueblos lying south of Santa Fe, New Mexico **2 :** an Indian of any of the Tano pueblos
ta·noa \təˈnōə\ *n* -s [Samoan, Tongan, & Fijian] **:** a bowl used in western Polynesia and Fiji for kava
tan oak *n* **:** TANBARK OAK a
¹ta·no·an \ˈtänəwən\ *adj, usu cap* [*tano* + E *-an* (adj. suffix)] **1 :** of or relating to the Tanos **2 :** of or relating to Tanoan
²tanoan \"\ *n* -s *usu cap* [*tano* + E *-an*] **:** a language family of New Mexico including Tewa, Tiwa, and Towa
tan pit *n* **:** TAN VAT
tan·que·lin·i·an \ˌtäŋkəˈlinēən, ˌtaŋ-\ *n* -s *usu cap* [*Tanquelin* (Tanchelm) †1115? Flemish heretic + E *-an*] **:** TANCHELMIAN
tanrec *var of* TENREC
tan ride *n* **:** a riding track covered with tan
tan rot *n* **:** a disease of strawberries caused by a fungus (*Pezizella lythri*) and characterized by somewhat sunken tan-colored areas in the fruit that lift out readily
tans *pres 3d sing of* TAN, *pl of* TAN
tan spud *n* **:** a spud used for stripping bark from trees
tan·sy *also* **tan·sey** \ˈtanzē, ˈtaan-, -zi\ *n, pl* **tansies** *or* **tanseys** [ME *tansy, tanesey*, fr. OF *tanesie*, fr. ML *athanasia* medicine to prolong life, tansy, fr. Gk, immortality, fr. *a-* ²*a-* + *-thanasia* (fr. *thanatos* death) — more at THANAT-] **1 a :** a plant of the genus *Tanacetum; esp* **:** a common herb (*T. vulgare*) with a strong aromatic odor and a very bitter taste **b :** any of various other plants: as (1) **:** SILVERWEED a (1) (2) **:** TANSY RAGWORT **2 :** a tansy-flavored cake or pudding
tansy mustard *n* **:** an herb of the genus *Descurainia; esp* **:** a No. American herb (*D. pinnata*) that resembles a cress but has leaves like those of a tansy
tansy oil *n* **:** a yellow poisonous essential oil obtained from the leaves and tops of the common tansy
tansy ragwort *n* **:** a common ragwort (*Senecio jacobaea*) with pinnatifid leaves and compact clusters of yellow flower heads that is native to Europe, No. Africa, and western Asia but has been introduced in No. America, New Zealand, and Australia and in some areas is a dangerous and aggressive weed and toxic to cattle when consumed in quantity
tan·ta \ˈtäntə\ *adj, usu cap* [fr. *Tanta*, Egypt] **:** of or from the city of Tanta, Egypt **:** of the kind or style prevalent in Tanta
tantal- *or* **tantalo-** *also* **tantali-** *comb form* [Sw, fr. NL *tantalum*] **:** tantalum ⟨*tantali*ferous⟩
tan·ta·late \ˈtantᵊl,āt, -ᵊlət\ *n* -s [ISV *tantalic* + *-ate*] **:** a salt of a tantalic acid
tan·ta·le·an \¦tantᵊl¦ēən, (ˈ)tan·¦tālē-\ *or* **tan·ta·li·an** \(ˈ)tan¦tālē-\ *adj, usu cap* [L *tantale*us of or relating to Tantalus (fr. *Tantalus*, mythical king) + E *-an*] **:** of or relating to Tantalus **:** ELUSIVE, TANTALIZING
tan·tal·ic \(ˈ)tan·¦talik\ *adj* [ISV *tantal-* + *-ic*] **:** of, relating to, or derived from tantalum
tantalic acid *n* **:** any of several weakly acidic hydrated forms $Ta_2O_5.nH_2O$ of tantalum pentoxide that react with alkalies to yield salts
tan·ta·lite \ˈtantᵊl,īt\ *n* -s [Sw *tantalit*, fr. NL *tantalum* + Sw *-it* -ite] **:** a mineral $(FeMn)(TaCb)_2O_6$ consisting of a heavy iron-black oxide of iron, manganese, tantalum, and columbium that is isomorphous with columbite (hardness 6, sp. gr. up to 7.3)
tan·ta·li·za·tion \ˌtantᵊlə̇ˈzāshən, ˌtaan-, -ᵊl,īˈz-\ *n* -s **:** the act or process of tantalizing ⟨a girl with an infinite capacity for ~ —H.T.Moore⟩
tan·ta·lize \ˈtantᵊl,īz, ˈtaan-\ *vb* -ED/-ING/-S *see -ize in Explan Notes* [*Tantalus*, in Greco-Roman mythology the king of Phrygia who for his sins was condemned to stand in Tartarus up to his chin in water that receded whenever he stooped to drink and under some branches of fruit that likewise receded whenever he tried to grasp them (fr. L, fr. Gk *Tantalos*) + E *-ize*] *vt* **:** to tease or torment by presenting something to the view and exciting desire but continually frustrating the expectations by keeping it out of reach ⟨anchors, dots, and arrows on the rocks . . . have long *tantalized* treasure hunters —*Amer. Guide Series: Oregon*⟩ ⟨*tantalized* by dreams of being . . . his country's savior —John Buchan⟩ ⟨~ their publishers by submitting synopses that sparkle —Bennett Cerf⟩ **~** *vi, obs* **:** to suffer in a manner resembling Tantalus **syn** see WORRY
tan·ta·liz·er \-zə(r)\ *n* -s **:** one that tantalizes
tantalizing *adj* **:** possessing a quality that arouses or stimulates desire or interest **:** mockingly or enticingly out of reach **:** teasingly provocative ⟨for me it remained a ~ puzzle —Herbert Passin⟩ ⟨smiled his lazy ~ smile —P.B.Kyne⟩ ⟨thick shrubs make it impossible to get more than a ~ glimpse of this beautiful house —S.P.B.Mais⟩
tan·ta·liz·ing·ly \ˈ=,==,==, ,=ˈ===,==\ *adv* **:** in a tantalizing manner ⟨a ~ slim chance of survival in the courts —Wenzell Brown⟩ ⟨illuminate an era of human life and of nature so ~ recent and so utterly destroyed —John Collier b.1884⟩
tan·ta·lum \ˈtantᵊləm\ *n* -s [NL, fr. *Tantalus*, mythical king condemned to stand up to his chin in water that receded whenever he stooped to drink; fr. its incapacity to absorb acid] **:** a lustrous platinum-gray hard ductile metallic element that has a very high melting point, that is chiefly pentavalent and is resistant to attack by most chemicals except hydrofluoric acid, that occurs combined in tantalite, columbite, and other rare minerals almost always associated with niobium, that is extracted usu. by the formation and reduction of a complex potassium tantalum fluoride, and that is used chiefly in making corrosion-resistant chemical apparatus and processing equipment, in electrolytic capacitors and rectifiers, in surgery as suture wire and bone-repair plates, and in alloys — symbol *Ta;* see ELEMENT table
tantalum carbide *n* **:** a very high-melting heavy dark yellow or brown crystalline compound TaC that is one of the hardest substances known, that is made by heating carbon with tantalum or tantalum pentoxide at high temperatures, and that is used in the cutting edges of high-speed tools, in dies, and in wear-resisting parts
tantalum gauze *or* **tantalum mesh** *n* **:** a flexible netting of tantalum wire used esp. in the repair of large hernias and other body defects
tantalum lamp *n* **:** an incandescent lamp with tantalum filament
tantalum oxide *n* **:** an oxide of tantalum; *esp* **:** the crystalline pentoxide Ta_2O_5 obtained by igniting tantalum in air or oxygen and used in making optical glass and tantalum carbide
¹tan·ta·lus \ˈtantᵊləs, ˈtaan-\ [NL, fr. *Tantalus*, mythical king] *syn of* MYCTERIA
²tantalus \"\ *n* -ES [after *Tantalus* — more at TANTALIZE] **:** a locked case or cellaret for wines and liquors having the contents visible but not obtainable without a key

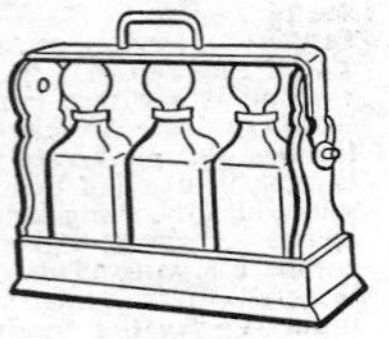
tantalus

tantamount \ˈtantə,maůnt\ *adj* [obs. E *tantamount*, n., something equivalent, fr. *tant amount*, v., to amount to as much, fr. AF *tant amunter*, fr. OF *tant* so much, as much (fr. L *tantum*, fr. neut. of *tantus* so great, fr. *tam* so, so much, as) + *amounter* to ascend, add up to; akin to Skt *tat*, neut. demonstrative pron. — more at THAT, AMOUNT] **:** equivalent in value, significance, or effect ⟨refusal to prolong the truce . . . would be ~ to a threat —*Current Biog.*⟩ **syn** see SAME
tan·tara \tanˈtarə, -ˈtärə; ˈtantərə\ *also* **tan·ta·rara** \ˌtantəˈrarə, -ˈrärə\ *or* **tar·an·tara** \ˌtarənˈtarə, ˌtärən-, -nˈtärə; təˈrantərə\ *or* **tar·a·tan·tara** \ˌtarə,tanˈtarə, ˌtärə,t-, -ˈtärə; ˌ==ˈtantərə\ *n* -s [*tantara, tantarara, tarantara* by shortening & alter. fr. L *taratantara*, of imit. origin] **1 a :** the blare of a trumpet or horn **b :** FANFARE **2 :** a sound resembling a trumpet call ⟨the ~ of growing winds —Gene Fowler⟩
tan·ta·ra·bo·bus \ˌtantərəˈbōbəs\ *n* -ES [prob. fr. *tantara* + *bobus*, alter. of *bogey*] *dial Eng* **:** BOOGEYMAN
tan·ti \ˈtantē\ *n* -s [Skt, weaver, fr. *tanoti* he stretches, weaves — more at THIN] **:** one of a Hindu caste of weavers of Assam and Bengal
tan·tième \tänˈtyem\ *n* -s [F, fr. *tant* so much + *-ème* thing, unit, -eme] **:** a percentage or proportional share esp. of profits or earnings; *also* **:** BONUS
¹tan·tivy \(ˈ)tan·ˈtivē\ *adv* [origin unknown] **:** in a headlong dash **:** at a gallop ⟨for three weeks U. S. tabloids went ~ after her . . . diary —*Time*⟩
²tantivy \"\ *n* -ES **1 :** a rapid gallop or ride **:** rushing movement **:** impetuous rush **2** *usu cap* [so called fr. a cartoon published in 1680–81 in England that depicted a number of Tory clergymen mounted upon the Church of England and riding tantivy to Rome behind the duke of York] **:** an English Royalist or Tory esp. of the last quarter of the 17th century **3 :** the blare of a horn ⟨the fanfare and ~ of the bugles were stilled —Frank Sullivan⟩
³tantivy \"\ *adj* [²*tantivy*] **:** having the demeanor of a Tantivy
tan·to \ˈtän·(,)tō\ *adv* [It, fr. L *tantum* — more at TANTAMOUNT] **:** MUCH **:** so much ⟨allegro non ~ (brisk, but not too much so)⟩
tan·tra \ˈtən·trə\ *n* -s *often cap* [Skt, lit., warp, essential part, doctrine, fr. *tanoti* he stretches, weaves — more at THIN] **1 :** a Hindu religious writing of the less ancient fourth class of shastras containing mystical teachings (as that the natural processes of creation and destruction rather than being illusory manifest the active conscious energy of divine spirit to be worshiped as a goddess wife of a Vedic god who attains his highest power in union with her) and ritual instructions including magical incantations, gestures, and diagrams (as for healing illness, averting evil), largely supplanting the Vedas, and forming esp. the scriptures of the Shakta sects **2 :** one of a body of related Buddhist treatises of similar character
tan·tric *or* **tan·trik** \-rik\ *adj, often cap* [Skt *tāntrika*, fr. *tantra* + *-ika*, adj. suffix — more at -Y] **1 :** of or relating to the tantras or Tantrism ⟨the gross *Tantric* rites connected with the worship of Kali —A.C.Bouquet⟩ **2 :** having the character of a tantra or Tantrism ⟨~ Buddhism⟩
tan·trism \ˈtən,trizəm\ *n* -s *usu cap* [*tantra* + *-ism*] **1 :** SHAKTISM **2 :** a school of Mahayana Buddhism originating in northern India and formative in Lamaism and Shingon that incorporates Hindu and pagan elements (as pantheistic mysticism, spells, the worship of female divinities) and teaches that the individual can realize his essential Buddhahood and obtain earthly benefits by theurgic practices (as mantra, mudra, erotic rites)
tan·trist \ˈtən·trə̇st\ *n* -s *usu cap* **:** a follower of Tantrism
tan·trum \ˈtan·trəm, ˈtaan-,ˈtain-\ *n* -s [origin unknown] **:** a burst of ill humor **:** a fit of bad temper ⟨a brief outburst of ~s at a children's tea party —Richard Joseph⟩ ⟨~s that used to flare up after the chimpanzees had made the wrong choice and had been denied food —G.W.Gray b.1886⟩
tan vat *n* **:** a vat in which hides steep in liquor with tan
tanwood \ˈ=,=\ *n* **:** wood yielding a tanning extract
tany- *comb form* [NL, fr. Gk, long, stretched out — more at THIN] **:** stretched out ⟨*Tany*stomata⟩ ⟨*Tany*gnathus⟩
tanya *also* **tanyah** *var of* TANIA
tanyard \ˈ=,=\ *n* [³*tan* + *yard*] **:** the section or portion of a tannery housing tanning vats
tany·lo·bous \¦tanə¦lōbəs\ *adj* [NL, fr. *tany-* + *lobus*] **:** having or being an elongated prostomium set off by a groove and overlapping the first true segments in the form of a tonguelike process ⟨an annelid worm with a ~ prostomium⟩
tan·yo·sho pine \tänˈyō(,)shō-\ *n* [*tanyosho* fr. Jap. umbrella pine] **:** a low-growing broad-headed ornamental pine that is a variety (*Pinus densiflora umbraculifera*) of the Japanese red pine — called also *umbrella pine*
tany·sto·ma·ta \ˌtanəˈstōməd·ə\ *n pl, cap* [NL, fr. *tany-* + *-stomata*] *in some classifications* **:** a division of dipterous insects in which the proboscis is large and contains lancelike mandibles and maxillae — compare HORSEFLY, ROBBER FLY
tany·stoma·tous \¦==ˈstäməd·əs, -tōm-\ *adj* [NL *Tanystomata* + E *-ous*] **:** of or relating to the Tanystomata
tany·stome \ˈ==,stōm\ *n* -s [F, fr. *tany-* + *-stome*] **:** an insect of the division Tanystomata
tan·za·nia \¦tanzə¦nēə\ *adj, usu cap* [fr. *Tanzania*, country in eastern Africa] **:** of or from the country of Tanzania **:** of the kind or style prevalent in Tanzania
tan·za·ni·an \-ēən\ *n* -s *cap* [*Tanzania*, Africa + E *-an*] **:** a native or inhabitant of Tanzania — **tanzanian** *adj, usu cap*
¹tao \ˈtaů, ˈdaů\ *n* -s [Chin (Pek) *tao*⁴, lit., way] **1** *Taoism* **a :** the unitary first principle from which all existence and all change in the universe spring **:** the unconditioned unnameable source of all reality that transcends being and nonbeing by standing above and beyond all distinctions **b :** the eternal order of the universe **2** *Confucianism* **a :** the right way of life **:** the path of virtuous conduct **b :** the principles that govern each separate category of existence **c :** the universal criterion of right and wrong **:** TRUTH **d :** the ultimate principle of universal reality **:** cosmic reason
²tao \ˈtaů\ *n* -s [Tag, person, man] *Philippines* **:** MAN, PEASANT
taoi·seach \ˈthēshək\ *n* -s [IrGael, lit., leader, chief] *Irish* **:** PRIME MINISTER
tao·ism \ˈtaů,izəm, ˈdaů-\ *n* -s *cap* [¹*tao* + *-ism*] **:** a religion and philosophy of China traditionally founded by Lao-tzu in the 6th century B.C. and orig. teaching conformity to the Tao by unassertive action and retirement from the world for a pristine simplicity but later becoming a highly syncretistic religion greatly concerned with obtaining longevity and immortality often by magical means
¹tao·ist \-əst\ *or* **tao·is·tic** \(ˈ)=¦istik\ *adj, usu cap* [¹*tao* + *-ist* or *-istic*] **:** of or relating to Taoism
²taoist \"\ *n* -s *cap* [¹*tao* + *-ist*] **:** an adherent of Taoism
taos \ˈtaůs\ *n, pl* **taos** *usu cap* **1 a :** a Tanoan people occupying a pueblo in New Mexico **b :** a member of such people **2 :** the language of the Taos people
tao-ti·eh \ˈtaůtē¦ā\ *n* -s [Chin (Pek) *t'ao*¹- *t'ieh*⁴] **:** an often conventionalized figure of a mythical animal's face appearing as a decorative motive on very ancient objects of Chinese art and possibly intended as a warning against gluttony

[1]tap \ˈtap\ *n* -s [ME *tappe*, fr. OE *tæppa*; akin to MD *tappe* tap, OHG *zapho*, ON *tappi* tap, OE *ātimplian* to provide with nails, MLG *timpe* tip and prob. to OHG *zumpfo* penis, Av *duma* tail] **1 a :** a plug for stopping a hole (as in a cask) **:** SPIGOT **b :** a device consisting of a spout and valve that is attached to the end of a pipe to control the flow of a liquid or gas **:** FAUCET, COCK ⟨turn on the ~ of a hydrant⟩ **c :** CORPORATION COCK **2 a** (1) **:** liquor drawn through a tap (2) *archaic* **:** a particular kind or quality of liquor ⟨liquor of the same ~⟩ **b :** a quantity of a liquid (as molten metal from a furnace) run out at one time **c :** the procedure of removing fluid (as from a body cavity) ⟨a spinal ~⟩ **3** [by shortening] **:** TAPROOM **4** [by shortening] **:** TAPHOLE **5 a :** a tool for forming an internal screw thread (as in a nut) consisting of a hardened tool-steel male screw grooved longitudinally so as to have cutting edges — see BOTTOMING TAP, HAND TAP, MACHINE TAP, PIPE TAP **b :** NUT 3 **6** *slang* **:** a request for a loan or gift **7 a :** a connection to an electric coil making it possible to place only part of the coil in circuit **b :** a wire brought from a winding to which connections may be made **c :** a current tap **d :** an intermediate point where an electrical connection may be made **8 :** the action or an instance of wiretapping ⟨put a ~ on the suspect's telephone —Joel Sayre⟩ — **on tap 1 :** ready to be drawn ⟨ale *on tap*⟩ **2 :** broached or furnished with a tap **3 :** on hand **:** AVAILABLE ⟨other sports and entertainment facilities are *on tap* —Richard Joseph⟩ ⟨doesn't have to think: the newspapers are always *on tap* —Henry Miller⟩ **4 :** offered for sale continuously and not limited as to amount that can be purchased — used esp. of government securities ⟨savings bonds are sold *on tap*⟩

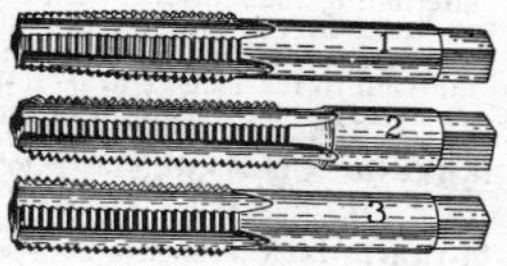

taps 5a: *1* taper, *2* second, *3* bottoming

[2]tap \"\ *vb* **tapped; tapped; tapping; taps** [ME *tappen*, fr. OE *tæppian*; akin to MD *tappen* to draw off, tap, OHG *zepfo*; denominative fr. the root of E [1]*tap*] *vt* **1 :** to furnish with a tap ⟨~ a bolt⟩ **2 :** to let out or cause to flow by piercing or by drawing a plug from the containing vessel ⟨~ a liquor⟩ **3 a :** to pierce so as to let out or draw off a fluid **:** draw off or drain off fluid or gas from ⟨~ a cask⟩ ⟨~ the abdomen⟩ ⟨~ a rubber tree⟩ ⟨~ a blast furnace⟩ **b :** to open up (anything) so as to extract something **:** draw from ⟨several railways ~ the region —C.L.White & G.T.Renner⟩ ⟨~ new sources of energy⟩ **4 :** to remove the taproot from **5 :** to form a female screw in by means of a tap ⟨~ a nut⟩ — distinguished from *thread* **6 :** to get money from as a loan or gift **7 :** to connect (a street gas or water main) with a local supply (as at a house) by a corporation cock **8 a :** to connect or cut in (an electrical circuit) on another circuit **b :** to cut in on (a telephone or telegraph wire) to get messages, information, or evidence **9 :** to bet in a game of poker played for table stakes all the money in the possession of (oneself) or an amount equaling all the money in the possession of (an opponent) whichever is the lesser amount **~** *vi* **:** to tap oneself or an opponent in game of poker played for table stakes

[3]tap \"\ *adj* [fr. the phrase (*on*) *tap*] **:** offered for sale continuously and not in a fixed total amount ⟨a ~ issue of government bonds⟩ — see TAP BOND

[4]tap \"\ *vb* **tapped; tapped; tapping; taps** [ME *tappen*; partly fr. MF *taper* to strike with the flat of the hand, of Gmc origin; akin to MHG *tāpe* paw, blow dealt with the paw; partly of Scand origin; akin to Sw dial. *täpa* to tap, ON *tæpta*; akin to MLG *tappen* to tug, pluck, ON *tapa* to lose, bring to an end, destroy and prob. to OHG *teilen* to divide, Skt *dayate* he apportions — more at DEAL, TIDE] *vt* **1 :** to strike lightly esp. with a slight sound **:** rap lightly and repeatedly ⟨*tapped* a typewriter all morning⟩ ⟨*tapped* me on the shoulder with his forefinger⟩ ⟨~ a bell with a hammer⟩ ⟨~ a brick into place⟩ ⟨had *tapped* him to sleep with a blackjack —Erle Stanley Gardner⟩ **2 :** to give one or more light usu. audible blows with ⟨~ a pencil on the table⟩ **3 :** to produce by striking repeatedly with light blows ⟨a woodpecker *tapped* a hole in the tree⟩ — often used with *out* ⟨~ out a telegraph message⟩ ⟨~ out a paragraph on a typewriter⟩ **4 :** to repair by putting a tap on ⟨~ shoes⟩ **5 :** SELECT, DESIGNATE ⟨was *tapped* for police commissioner⟩; *specif* **:** to elect to membership in a particular organization (as a fraternity) **6 :** to divert (a basketball) to a player of one's own side or into the basket by a tap with the fingertips **:** TIP **~** *vi* **1 :** to strike lightly but audibly **:** RAP ⟨moths *tapped* and blurred at the window screen —R.P.Warren⟩ **2** *of a hare or rabbit* **:** to drum with the feet **3 :** to walk with light but audible steps ⟨*tapped* off on nonchalant heels —LaSelle Gilman⟩ **4 :** TAP-DANCE

[5]tap \"\ *n* -s [ME *tape*, *tappe*, fr. *tappen* to tap] **1 a :** a light usu. audible blow **:** a light rap **b :** the sound of a light blow ⟨the ~ of ivy on the pane —Virginia Woolf⟩ **c :** one of several drumbeats on a snare drum played usu. at a rapid speed **d :** a striking of the ball with the fingertips in basketball ⟨gained the opening ~⟩ **e :** FLAP 6 **2 :** a partial sole put on over the worn sole of a shoe **:** HALF SOLE — called also *tap sole* **3 :** a slight amount ⟨didn't do a ~ of work⟩ ⟨without a ~ of work or fuss by your client —*Empire State Architect*⟩ **4 taps** \ˈtaps\ *pl* **a :** a small metal plate for attaching to the sole or heel of a shoe esp. to make a clicking sound (as in tap dancing) — compare CLEAT 2a **b :** TAP SHOE **c :** a step (as in tap dancing) in which the ball or the toes of one foot are touched lightly to the floor so as to make a sound **d :** TAP DANCE ⟨~ lessons⟩ **5 :** a solid hit in the pocket that leaves a lone bowling pin standing

[6]tap \ˈtəp\ *n* -s [Hindi, fr. Skt *tapa* heat, fr. *tapati* it gives out heat — more at TEPID] **1** *India* **:** HEAT **2** *India* **:** MALARIAL FEVER 1 **3** *India* **:** PENANCE

[7]tap \ˈtap\ *n* -s [by shortening] **:** TAPADERO

[1]ta·pa *also* **tap·pa** \ˈtäpə\ *n* -s [Marquesan & Tahitian *tapa*] **1 :** the bark of the paper mulberry or of an Hawaiian tree (*Pipturus albidus*) **2** *or* **tapa cloth :** a coarse cloth made in the Pacific islands from the pounded bark of the paper mulberry, breadfruit, and other plants, usu. decorated with geometric patterns, and still used as clothing and covering in isolated islands but elsewhere worn only on festive occasions, exchanged ceremonially, used as a house ornament, or sold to foreigners

[2]tapa \"\ *n* -s [Sp, fr. *tapar* to stop up, cover, fr. *tapa* cover, lid, of Gmc origin; akin to OE *tæppa* tap — more at TAP] **:** SNACK

ta·pa·chu·la \ˌtäpəˈchülə\ *or* **ta·pa·chul·tec** \-ˈchül,tek\ *n*, *pl* **tapachula** *or* **tapachulas** *or* **tapachultec** *or* **tapachultecs** *usu cap* [MexSp, fr. Nahuatl] **1 a :** a Zoquean people of the Mexico-Guatemala border region **b :** a member of such people **2 :** the language of the Tapachula people

tap·a·co·lo \ˌtapəˈkō(,)lō\ *or* **tap·a·cu·lo** \-ˈkü(,)lō\ *n* -s [AmerSp *tapaculo*, lit., one that covers its backside, fr. Sp *tapar* to cover + *culo* backside, fr. L *culus* — more at CULET] **1 :** a small plainly colored clamatorial terrestrial bird (*Scelorchilus albicollis*) of the family Rhinocryptidae of Chile and Argentina having short rounded wings and short tail carried erect **2 :** any of several birds related to the tapacolo — see TURCO

tap·a·de·ro \ˌtapəˈde(,)rō\ *or* **tap·a·de·ra** \-rə\ *n* -s [AmerSp, fr. Sp, cover, plug, fr. *tapar* to cover, stop up] *West* **:** a leather hood covering the stirrup of a stock saddle and used esp. to protect the boot when riding through brush

tap bolt *n* **:** a headed bolt used without a nut for screwing into a hole — called also *cap screw*, *tap screw*; see BOLT illustration

tap bond *n* **:** a government security of an issue unlimited in total amount and offered for sale for an unspecified period — called also *tap issue*

tap borer *n* **:** an implement for boring tapholes

tap box *n* **1 :** CHINESE TEMPLE BLOCK **2 :** JUNCTION BOX **3 :** an enclosure for a corporation cock

tap changer *n* **:** an apparatus or accessory for usu. automatically changing transformer taps to regulate system voltage

tap dance *n* **:** a step dance esp. in a difficult syncopated rhythm that is tapped out audibly with the feet or parts of the feet (as the toes or heels) often by means of clogs or of specially made hard-soled shoes

tap-dance \ˈ=,=\ *vi* [*tap dance*] **:** to perform a tap dance

tap dancer *n* **:** one that performs a tap dance **:** one proficient in tap dancing

tap drill *n* **:** a drill for drilling a hole of exact diameter for tapping

[1]tape \ˈtāp\ *n* -s [ME *tape*, *tappe*, fr. OE *tæppe* narrow strip of cloth; prob. akin to OFris *tapia* to tug, unravel, pluck, MLG *tappen* — more at TAP (touch)] **1 a :** a narrow fabric of natural or artificial fibers usu. woven singly in plain or twill weaves esp. in widths of less than 8 inches and used esp. for string, binding esp. on clothing and carpets, wicks, and with or without special finishes for medical and industrial purposes **b :** any of the woven cotton bands sewn across the backbone of a book and attached to the covers **c :** the narrow belt that turns each of the spindles on a ring spinner **d :** one of the endless flexible fabric bands on which sheets travel (as in the delivery of some cylinder presses and in some folding machines) **e :** ADHESIVE TAPE **f :** FRICTION TAPE **2 :** RED TAPE **3 :** a piece of light string stretched breast-high above the finishing line to aid the judges in determining the winner of a race **4 :** a narrow limp or flexible strip or band (as of paper, plastic, or metal): as **a :** TICKER TAPE **b :** MASKING TAPE **c :** MAGNETIC TAPE ⟨record a program on ~⟩ **5 a :** a graduated steel ribbon used by surveyors in place of a chain **b :** TAPE MEASURE **c :** a specially calibrated flexible rule for measuring the circumference and diameter of railroad-car wheels **6** [Ly shortening] **:** TAPEWORM **7 :** TAPE RECORDING

[2]tape \"\ *vb* -ED/-ING/-S *vt* **1 :** to furnish with tape **:** fasten, tie, bind, cover, or support with tape (as adhesive tape or friction tape) ⟨the sprain cases had all been *taped* up —Earle Birney⟩: as **a :** to bind or finish (an edge) with tape ⟨~ the seams of a leather jacket⟩ **b :** to join the sections of (a book) with tape **2 a :** to measure with a tape **b :** GIRTH 3 **3 :** to widen (a pelt) by leathering — compare LET OUT **4** *chiefly Brit* **:** to size up **:** figure out **:** CLASSIFY ⟨you had this world all *taped* —Ernest Hemingway⟩ ⟨afraid you've got all this *tapea* out wrong —Agatha Christie⟩ **5 :** to record on magnetic tape ⟨~ a TV program⟩ ⟨a *taped* interview⟩ **~** *vi* **1 :** MEASURE **2 :** to stick threads together during the slashing operation in textile manufacture

tape condenser *n* **:** a device that receives the wide fiber web from a woolen card, divides it, and rubs each section into a sliver

tape grass *n* **:** a submerged aquatic plant (*Vallisneria spiralis*) with long ribbonlike leaves — called also *celery*, *eelgrass*, *water celery*, *wild celery*

tape-grass family \ˈ=,=-\ *n* **:** VALLISNERIACEAE

tape guide *n* **:** a rod of sapphire, glass, or hardened steel in a magnetic recorder that is used to force the tape to move in a precisely defined path

ta·pei·no·ce·phal·ic \tə¦pīnōsəˈfalik, -pān-\ *adj* [F *tapinocéphale* (fr. Gk *tapeinos* low + F *-céphale* -cephalic) + E *-ic*] **:** having a low skull with a breadth-height index of less than 79 due to synostosis of the great wings of the sphenoid with the frontal bone — **ta·pei·no·ceph·a·lism** *n* -s — **ta·pei·no·ceph·a·ly** \-lē\ *n* -ES

ta·pei·no·cra·nic \=¦==ˈkränik\ *adj* [G *tapeinokran* (fr. Gk *tapeinos* low + *kranion* cranium) + E *-ic*] **:** having a low skull flattened in front with a cranial breadth-height index of less than 92 — **ta·pei·no·cra·ny** \=ˈ==,krānē\ *n* -ES

tape·less \ˈtāplə̇s\ *adj* **:** being without tape **:** operated or done without the use of tape

tapeline \ˈ=,=\ *n* [[1]*tape* + *line*] **:** TAPE MEASURE

tape machine *n* **1** *Brit* **:** TICKER b **2 :** TAPE RECORDER

tape·man \ˈtāpmən\ *n*, *pl* **tapemen :** CHAINMAN 4

tape measure *n* **:** a narrow strip of a strong but limp or flexible material (as cloth or steel) that is marked off in units of length (as inches or centimeters) for measuring

tape primer *n* **:** a primer for some percussion locks consisting of bits of priming compound sealed in a paper tape

tape punch *n* **:** a device for recording symbols in tape by perforating individual holes or combinations of holes

[1]ta·per \ˈtāpə(r)\ *n* -s [ME *taper*, *tapre*, fr. OE *taper*, *tapor*] **1 a :** a usu. slender wax candle **b :** a long waxed wick used esp. as a spill **c :** any feeble light or source of light **2 a :** a tapering form or figure (as a spire) **b :** gradual diminution of thickness, diameter, or width in an elongated object often expressed in inches per foot, inches per inch, or by numbers ⟨the ~ of a tree trunk⟩ ⟨glass tubing with extremely accurate ~ —C.J.Phillips⟩ ⟨the ~ of a file⟩ **c :** a gradual decrease **3 :** a trowel used by molders in founding **4 :** DRAFT 17a,b **5 :** a taper wire used esp. to splice electric cables

[2]taper \"\ *adj* [ME *tapre*, fr. *taper*, *tapre*, n.] **1 :** regularly narrowed toward a point **:** CONICAL, PYRAMIDAL ⟨~ fingers⟩ — see LEG illustration **2 :** GRADUATED, SCALED ⟨~ freight rates⟩

[3]taper \"\ *vb* **tapered; tapered; tapering** \-p(ə)riŋ\ **tapers** [[1]*taper*] *vi* **1 :** to become gradually smaller toward one end ⟨a stick that ~*s* to a point⟩ ⟨a wall ~*ing* from a thickness of three feet at the bottom to two feet at the top⟩ **2 :** to grow gradually less **:** DIMINISH ⟨as ... defense demands ~*ed*, prices started down —*Time*⟩ ⟨sparse subarctic forest which ~*s* northward to the treeless tundra —Jim Wright⟩ — often used with *down* ⟨the way that a news story is written — beginning with the most important and ~*ing* down to the least important —T.F.Barnhart⟩; see TAPER OFF **~** *vt* **1 :** to make or cause to taper ⟨~ a stick to a point⟩ **2 :** to cut and thin (the hair) so that the ends are invisibly blended

[4]tap·er \ˈtāpə(r)\ *n* -s [[1]*tape* + *-er*] **1 :** a worker who applies tape (as to seal, label, protect, decorate, or strengthen objects) by hand or by machine **2 :** a device for dispensing or applying tape

tape reading *n* **:** the study and interpretation of transactions as printed on the ticker tape for indications of price trends

tape-record \ˈ==,=\ *vt* [back-formation fr. *tape recording*] **:** to make a tape recording of ⟨*tape-record* a speech⟩

tape recorder *n* **:** a magnetic recorder using magnetic tape

tape recording *n* **:** magnetic recording on magnetic tape; *also* **:** a recording made by this process

tapered *adj* [fr. past part. of [3]*taper*] **:** TAPER

ta·per·er \ˈtāp(ə)rə(r)\ *n* -s [ME, fr. [1]*taper* + *-er*] **1 :** one who bears a candle (as in a religious procession) **2 :** one that tapers

taper file *n* **:** a file with converging edges — distinguished from *blunt file*

ta·per·ing·ly *adv* **:** in a tapering fashion

ta·per·ness \ˈtāpə(r)nə̇s\ *n* -ES **:** the quality or state of being taper

taper off *vi* **1 :** to become taper **:** TAPER **2 :** to stop gradually **:** cease little by little ⟨the organization *tapered off* in about a year —G.B.Oxnam⟩ **~** *vt* **:** to make or cause to taper **:** decrease gradually ⟨if not retire, at least *taper off* the amount of time given to work —Lynn White⟩ ⟨use in *tapering off* morphine and opium addicts —D.W.Maurer & V.H.Vogel⟩

taper pin *n* **:** a tapered rod of metal or hardwood used as a dowel to locate one part with reference to another or to secure two parts together by driving into a tapered hole passing through both parts

taper pipe thread *n* **:** pipe thread formed with a slightly tapering diameter to secure a firm and leakproof joint

taper reducer sleeve *or* **taper sleeve** *n* **:** a sleeve that is tapered both externally (as to fit a specified socket) and internally (as to receive the tapered shank of a drill) — called also *reducer sleeve*, *shell socket*

taperstick \ˈ==,=\ *n* [[1]*taper* + *stick*] **:** a candlestick for holding small tapers

taper tool *n* **:** TURRET TAPER TOOL

tapes *pl of* TAPE, *pres 3d sing of* TAPE

tap·es·tried \ˈtapəstrēd, -rid\ *adj* [*tapestry* + *-ed*] **1 :** covered or decorated with or as if with tapestry ⟨chairs with wooden backs and arms and ~ seats —Sally Benson⟩ ⟨terraces of limestone, ~ with velvet moss —*Amer. Guide Series: Oregon*⟩ **2 :** woven or depicted in tapestry ⟨~ scenes from legend⟩

tap·es·try \-trē, -tri\ *n* -ES [ME *tapistry*, *tapstery*, modif. of MF *tapisserie*, fr. *tapisser* to furnish with a carpet, cover with tapestry (fr. OF *tapis*, *tapiz* carpet, carpeting, fr. Gk *tapēt-*, *tapēs* carpet, rug, prob. of Iranian origin) + *-ie* -y; akin to Per *tābīdan* to turn, spin; akin to Lith *tempti* to stretch — more at TEMPORAL] **1 a :** a heavy handwoven textile for hangings, curtains, and upholstery made either by the low-warp or high-warp method and usu. with a wool, linen, or cotton warp and with wool, silk, and metal threads in the weft with the warp threads set out on the loom for the width of the fabric and the weft threads loosely inserted by hand over and under the warp threads and pressed down to cover the warp threads completely and characterized by complicated pictorial designs that are the same on both sides except for the ends of threads showing on the back as a result of the weft threads being used not from selvage to selvage but only in the limited area of each separate color and being joined to other weft threads by interlocking or dovetailing or left unjoined leaving a slit — see GOBELIN **b :** a nonreversible conventionalized imitation of tapestry made usu. of wool, cotton, and rayon on a jacquard loom and used chiefly for upholstery **c :** embroidery on canvas resembling the woven tapestry ⟨needlepoint ~⟩ **2 :** TAPESTRY CARPET

tapestry beetle *n* **:** CARPET BEETLE b

tapestry brussels *n*, *usu cap B* **:** BRUSSELS CARPET 2

tapestry carpet *n* **:** a carpet (as tapestry Brussels or tapestry velvet) in which the designs are printed in colors on the threads before the fabric is woven; *esp* **:** a carpet the threads of which are printed before even the warp is formed and which is often used in place of real tapestry for hangings

tapestry moth *n* **:** CARPET MOTH

tapestry needle *n* **:** a short needle with a long eye and a blunt point

tapestry red *n* **:** a dark red that is yellower, less strong, and slightly darker than cranberry and yellower and paler than average garnet or average wine

tapestry velvet carpet *n* **:** a velvet carpet made like tapestry Brussels but having the pile longer and cut so that the surface resembles that of Wilton carpet

tapestry weave *n* **1 :** a weave used for handmade tapestry **2 :** a machine method of weaving tapestry having weft threads running from selvage to selvage **3 :** a hand or machine weave for rugs that have warp threads completely covered by weft threads

tapestry-woven \ˈ===ˌ==\ *adj* **:** having a tapestry weave

ta·pe·tal \təˈpēdᵊl\ *adj* [NL *tapetum* + E *-al*] **:** of or relating to a tapetum

ta·pe·te \təˈpēdē\ *n* -s [NL, fr. L, carpet, tapestry] **:** TAPETUM 1

tape thermometer *n* **:** a small thermometer attached temporarily to a steel measuring tape for the purpose of indicating the temperature of the tape

tap·e·ti *or* **tap·i·ti** \ˈtapədē\ *n* -s [Tupi] **:** a small So. American rabbit (*Sylvilagus braziliensis*)

ta·pe·to·retinal \tə¦pēd·ō+\ *adj* [NL *tapetum* + E *-o-* + *retinal*] **:** of, relating to, or involving both tapetum and retina

ta·pe·tum \təˈpēdəm\ *n*, *pl* **tape·ta** \-də\ [NL, fr. L *tapete* carpet, tapestry, fr. Gk *tapēt-*, *tapēs* carpet, rug — more at TAPESTRY] **1 :** the layer of nutritive cells that invests the sporogenous tissue in the sporangium of higher plants and that is broken down and digested during development of the spores **2 a :** any of various membranous layers or areas esp. of the choroid and retina of the eye; *specif* **:** a layer in the choroid chiefly of nocturnal mammals that reflects light and is made up of several layers of flattened cells covered by a zone of doubly refracting crystals **b :** a layer of nerve fibers derived from the corpus callosum and forming part of the roof of each lateral ventricle of the brain — called also *tapetum lu·ci·dum* \-ˈlüsədəm\

tapeworm \ˈ=,=\ *n* [[1]*tape* + *worm*] **:** a worm (subclass Cestoda) that is parasitic as an adult in the alimentary tract of vertebrates including man and as larva in a great variety of vertebrates and invertebrates, that typically consists of an attachment organ usu. with suckers, grooves, hooks, or other devices for adhering to the host's intestine followed by an undifferentiated growth region from which buds off a chain of segments of which the anterior members are little more than blocks of tissue, the median members have fully developed organs of both sexes, and the posterior members are degenerated to egg-filled sacs, that has no digestive system and absorbs food through the body wall, and that has a nervous system consisting of ganglia and commissures in the scolex and longitudinal cords extending the length of the strobila — see BEEF TAPEWORM, FISH TAPEWORM, PORK TAPEWORM; compare ECHINOCOCCUS

tapeworm plant *n* **:** CENTIPEDE PLANT

taph·e·pho·bia \ˌtafēˈfōbēə\ *n* [NL, fr. Gk *taphē* burial, grave (akin to Gk *thaptein* to inter, bury) + NL *phobia* — more at EPITAPH] **:** fear of being buried alive

tap holder *n* **:** a device (as a chuck or grip) for holding or floating a tap (as in a screw machine or turret lathe) when tapping holes

taphole \ˈ=,=\ *n* **:** a hole for a tap; *specif* **:** a hole at or near the bottom of a furnace or ladle through which molten metal, matte, or slag can be tapped

taph·ria \ˈtafrēə\ [NL, fr. Gk *taphrē* trench, ditch + NL *-ia*] *syn of* TAPHRINA

ta·phri·na \təˈfrīnə, təˈf-, -rēnə\ *n*, *cap* [NL, fr. Gk *taphrē* trench, ditch (akin to Gk *taphos* tomb) + NL *-ina* — more at EPITAPH] **:** a genus (the type of the family Taphrinaceae) of parasitic fungi that produce asci in a superficial hymenium having an indeterminate margin and cause leaf curling and malformations like blisters on various vascular plants — see LEAF CURL, PLUM POCKET

taph·ri·na·ce·ae \ˌtafrəˈnāsēˌē\ *n pl*, *cap* [NL, fr. *Taphrina*, type genus + *-aceae*] **:** a small family of ascomycetous fungi (order Taphrinales) with thin-walled chlamydospores — see TAPHRINA — **taph·ri·na·ceous** \¦==ˈnāshəs\ *adj*

taph·ri·na·les \-ˈnā(,)lēz\ *n pl*, *cap* [NL *Taphrina* + *-ales*] **:** an order of parasitic fungi (subclass Hemiascomycetes) in which chlamydospores produced from the hyphae each germinate to form a single ascus

ta·pia \ˈtäpyə\ *n* -s [Sp] **:** a building material made chiefly of clay or earth; *esp* **:** puddled adobe — compare PISÉ, TABBY

ta·pi·eté \ˌtäpēäˈtā\ *n*, *pl* **tapieté** *or* **tapietés** *usu cap* [Sp, fr. Guarani] **1 :** a Guaranian people of Bolivia **2 :** a member of the Tapieté people

tap-in \ˈ=,=\ *n* -s [fr. *tap in*, v.] **:** TIP-IN

taping *pres part of* TAPE

tap·i·no·ma \ˌtapəˈnōmə\ *n*, *cap* [NL, fr. Gk *tapeinos* low, humble + NL *-oma*] **:** a genus of small ants with a noticeably pungent odor

tap·i·o·ca \ˌtapēˈōkə\ *n* -s [Pg & Sp, fr. Tupi *typyóca*, fr. *ty* juice + *pýa* heart, pith + *ocó* to be removed] **1 :** a preparation of cassava starch processed into granular, flake, pellet, or flour form and used as a food in bread or as a thickening agent in liquid foods, as puddings, soups, or juicy pies, or industrially as a size or adhesive **2** *or* **tapioca plant :** CASSAVA 1

tapioca fish *n* **:** ESCOLAR

tap·i·o·lite \ˈtapēə,līt\ *n* -s [Sw *tapiolit*, fr. *Tapio*, Finnish god of the forests + Sw *-lit* -lite; fr. its being found in the village of Sukula in Finland] **:** a mineral $FeTa_2O_6$ that consists of oxide of iron and tantalum and is isomorphous with mossite and polymorphous with tantalite

ta·pir \ˈtāpə(r)\ *sometimes* təˈpi(ə)r *or* -iə *or* ˈtä,pi-\ *n*, *pl* **tapir** *or* **tapirs** [Tupi *tapiira*] **:** any of several large perissodactyl ungulates (family Tapiridae) that inhabit So. and Central America, Malaya, and Sumatra, have a heavy sparsely hairy body, the snout prolonged into a short mobile proboscis, a rudimentary tail, stout legs, and four front and three hind toes, are chiefly nocturnal, shy, and gentle, and frequent heavy forests in the vicinity of water — see INDIAN TAPIR

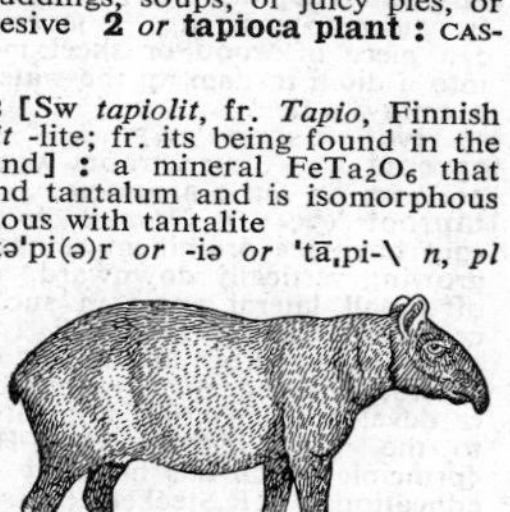
tapir (Malayan)

ta·pi·ra·na \ˌtäpəˈränə\ *n, pl* **tapirana** [Pg, fr. *tapir*, fr. Tupi *tapiíra*] : ³ANTA 1a

ta·pi·ra·pé \ˈtäpərəˌpä\ *n, pl* **tapirapé** *or* **tapirapés** *usu cap* [Sp, fr. Guarani] **1 a** : a Guaranian people of the northeastern part of Mato Grosso state, Brazil **b** : a member of such people **2** : the language of the Tapirapé people

ta·pir·id \ˈtäpərəd, təˈpirəd\ *adj* [NL *Tapiridae*] : of or relating to the Tapiridae

²tapirid \"\ *n -s* : an ungulate of the family Tapiridae

ta·pir·i·dae \təˈpirəˌdē\ *n pl, cap* [NL, fr. *Tapirus*, type genus + *-idae*] : a family of ungulate mammals (suborder Ceratomorpha) that comprises the tapirs and extinct related forms

ta·pir·id·i·an \ˌtäpəˈridēən\ *adj or n* [NL *Tapiridae* + E *-an*] : TAPIRID

ta·pir·ine \ˈtäpəˌrīn, təˈpiˌr-, -rən\ *adj* [NL *Tapirus* + *-ine*] : of or relating to the genus *Tapirus*

ta·pi·ro \təˈpi(ˌ)rō\ *n, pl* **tapiro** *or* **tapiros** *usu cap* **1** : a Negrito people inhabiting the northern part of Netherlands New Guinea **2** : a member of the Tapiro people

¹ta·pir·oid \ˈtäpəˌroid, təˈpiˌr-\ *adj* [NL *Tapiroidea*] : of or relating to the Tapiroidea

²tapiroid \"\ *n -s* : a tapiroid mammal

ta·pi·roi·dea \ˌtäpəˈroidēə\ *n pl, cap* [NL, fr. *Tapirus* + *-oidea*] *in some classifications* : a superfamily of perissodactyl mammals comprising the tapirs and extinct related forms — compare CERATOMORPHA

tap·i·rus \ˈtäpərəs\ *n, cap* [NL, fr. Tupi *tapiíra* tapir] : a genus (the type of the family Tapiridae) of ungulates comprising the tapirs

tap·is \-ES [MF, fr. OF *tapis, tapiz* carpet, carpeting — more at TAPESTRY] *obs* : tapestry or a similar material used esp. for hangings, floor coverings, and tablecloths — **on the tapis** \(ˈ)taˌpē, (ˈ)taˌpēs, ˈtapəs, taˈpēs\ *adv (or adj)* [trans. of F *sur le tapis*] archaic : under consideration

ta·pis·se·rie \ˈtäpēsˌrē\ *n, pl* **ta·pis·se·ries** \"\ [ME, fr. MF — more at TAPESTRY] : TAPESTRY 1

ta·pis·sier \ˌtäpēˈsyā\ *n, pl* **ta·pis·siers** \"\ [F, fr. OF, fr. *tapis, tapiz* carpet + *-ier -er*] : a dealer in or maker of tapestries

tap issue *n* : TAP BOND

tapiti *var of* TAPETI

taplash \ˈ-ˌ-\ *n* [¹*tap* + *lash* (onslaught of water)] **1** *dial* : the washings or dregs of a cask or glass of liquor **2** *dial* : poor or weak liquor; *esp* : weak or stale beer

tap·let \ˈtaplət\ *n -s* [¹*tap* + *-let*] : a small tap; *specif* : an insulating block usu. of porcelain provided with screw terminals for connection of electrical circuits

tap line *n* [¹*tap*] : INDUSTRIAL RAILROAD

tap·man \ˈ-mən\ *n, pl* **tapmen** **1** : one who taps a blast furnace **2** : TAPPER-OUT 2

ta·poa \təˈpōə\ *n -s* [native name in New South Wales, Australia] : a Tasmanian phalanger (*Trichosurus fuliginosus*)

tap off *vi* : to start a play in basketball from the center circle by tapping a jump ball toward a player of one's own side

tap-off \ˈ-ˌ-, ˌ-ˈ-\ *n* [*tap off*] : TIP-OFF

ta·po·sa \təˈpōsə\ *n, pl* **taposa** *or* **taposas** *usu cap* **1** : an extinct Muskogean people of the Yazoo river valley, Mississippi **2** : a member of the Taposa people

ta·pote·ment \təˈpōtmənt\ *n -s* [F, fr. *tapoter* to tap (fr. *taper* to strike with the flat of the hand) + *-ment*] : percussion in massage

tap out *vi* : to bet all one has

tappa *var of* TAPA

tap·pable \ˈtapəbəl\ *adj* [²*tap* + *-able*] : capable of being tapped : fit for tapping — **tap·pable·ness** *n -ES*

tapped *past of* TAP

¹tap·per \ˈtap·(ə)r\ *n -s* [⁴*tap* + *-er*] : one that makes a sound of tapping or that performs an operation by lightly striking

²tapper \"\ *n -s* [²*tap* + *-er*] : one that applies or makes taps or draws by tapping

tapper-out \ˌ-ˌ-ˈ-\ *n, pl* **tappers-out** **1** : one that taps something out **2** : an iron or steel worker who keeps clean the slag lining of a furnace

tapper tap *n* : a tap designed primarily for use in a nut-tapping machine

¹tap·pet \ˈtapət, *usu* -əd-+V\ *n -s* [⁴*tap* + *-et*] **1** : a lever or projection moved by some other piece

tappet motion *n* : a valve motion (as in a steam pump) worked by tappets

tappet rod *n* : a rod carrying or actuating a tappet

tappet wrench *n* : a wrench with an open-end jaw at each end of a long thin handle

tap·pie-too·rie \ˈtapiˌtüri\ *n -s* [*tappie* (dim. of *tap*, var. of ¹*top*) + *toorie*] *Scot & Irish* : TOORIE

tapping *n -s* [fr. gerund of ²*tap*] **1** : the act, process, or means by which something is tapped **2** : PARACENTESIS

tapping drill *n* **1** : TAP DRILL **2** : a machine for tapping nuts

tapping hole *n* : a hole made smaller than the nominal size of a screw or pipe to allow for tapping

tapping key *n* : a light flexible metallic strip provided with contacts

tapping screw *n* : a hardened screw that cuts threads in the pieces it secures

¹tap·pit hen \ˈtapət-\ *n* [*tappit* fr. *tap* (var. of ¹*top*) + *-it*] **1** *Scot* : a crested hen **2** *Scot* : a drinking vessel with a knob on the lid

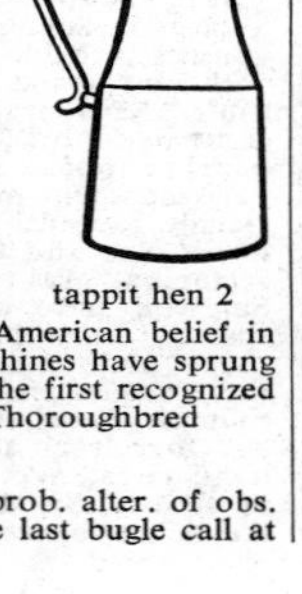

tap·poon \taˈpün\ *n -s* [Sp *tapón* stopper, fr. *tapar* to stop up — more at TAPA] : a piece of wood or sheet metal fitted into a ditch to dam up the water

tap rivet *n* : SCREW RIVET

taproom \ˈ-ˌ-, ˈ-ˌ-\ *n* : a room where liquors are kept on tap : BARROOM

¹taproot \ˈ-ˌ-, ˈ-ˌ-\ *n* [¹*tap* + *root*] **1 a** : a root having a prominent central portion, growing vertically downward

²taproot *vi* : to put forth a taproot

¹taps *pl of* TAP, *pres 3d sing of* TAP

²taps \ˈtaps\ *n pl but usu sing in constr* [prob. alter. of obs. *taptoo* tattoo — more at TATTOO] **1** : the last bugle call at

tappit hen 2

night blown as a signal that all unauthorized lights are to be put out **2** : a similar call blown as part of the final honors at military funerals

tapsal–teerie \ˌtapsəlˈtēri\ *adv* [by alter.] *Scot* : TOPSY-TURVY

tap screw *n* : TAP BOLT

tap shoe *n* : a shoe worn esp. for tap-dancing

tap sole *n* : ⁵TAP 2

tap·ster \ˈtapstə(r)\ *n -s* [ME, fr. OE *tæppestre* female tapster] : one employed to dispense liquors in a barroom

¹tap-tap \ˈ-ˌ-\ *n* [redupl. of ⁵*tap*] : a series of taps or their sound

²tap-tap \"\ *vi* : to make a sound of repeated tapping

ta·pu \ˈtäˌpü\ *n -s* [Maori] : TABOO

ta·pu·ya \təˈpüyə\ *n, pl* **tapuya** *or* **tapuyas** *usu cap* [Pg, fr. Tupi, savage, Tapuya] : a non-Tupi Amerind people

tap water *n* : ordinary water from a tap or faucet

tap wrench *n* : a wrench for turning a tap

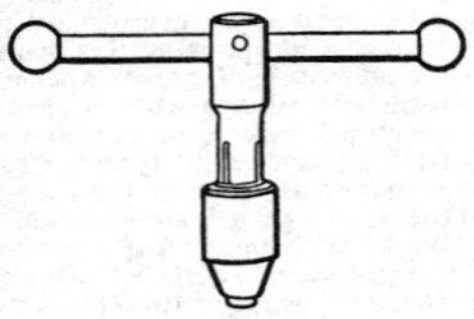

ta·qi·ya *or* **ta·qi·yah** \taˈkēyə\ *n -s* [Ar *taqīyah*, lit., self-protection] : the principle of practicing the dissimulation of outward conformity permitted Muslims

taq·lid \taˈklēd\ *n -s* [Ar *taqlīd*, lit., winding round] *Islam* : uncritical and unqualified acceptance of a traditional orthodoxy

tap wrench

¹tar \ˈtär, ˈtȧ(r)\ *n -s* [ME *tarr, terr*, fr. OE *teoru*] **1 a** : any of various dark brown or black bituminous usu. odorous viscous liquids or semiliquids obtained by the destructive distillation of wood, coal, peat, shale, and other organic materials — see COAL TAR, WATER-GAS TAR, WOOD TAR **b** : a substance resembling tar **2** [short for *tarpaulin*] : SEAMAN, SAILOR

²tar \"\ *or* **tarre** \"\ *vt* **tarred; tarred; tarring; tars** *or* **tarres** [ME *terren, tarren*, fr. OE *tyrwan, tirgan* to irritate] : to urge into action : INCITE

³tar \"\ *vt* **tarred; tarred; tarring; tars** [ME *tarren, terren*, fr. *tarr, terr* tar] **1** : to cover or overspread with tar **2** : to smear or defile as if with tar : TAINT, STAIN — **tar and feather** : to smear a person with tar and cover with feathers — **tar with the same brush** : to mark or stain with the same fault

⁴tar \"\ *n -s* [Per] : an oriental lute

¹tara *var of* TARO

²tara \ˈtärə, ˈtarə\ *n -s* [AmerSp, fr. Quechua *tára*] : any of various plants of the genus *Caesalpinia*

ta·ra·boo·ka \ˌtärəˈbükə, ˌtarə-\ *n -s* [Ar *darābukkah*] : DARABUKKA

¹tara·ca·hi·tian \ˌtärəkəˈhēshən\ *adj, usu cap* [*Tarahumara* + *Cahita* + E *-an*] : of, relating to, or characteristic of the Taracahitian peoples

²taracahitian \"\ *n -s usu cap* [*Tarahumara* + *Cahita* + E *-an*] **1 a** : a group of peoples of Mexico

tar acid *n* : any of the phenols (as phenol, cresols, xylenols) obtained from tar and esp. coal tar — compare CRESYLIC ACID

tar-acid oil *n* : an oil containing usu. 10 to 55 percent of tar acids — compare CARBOLIC OIL

tar-a-did-dle *also* **tar-ra-did-dle** \ˈtarəˌdidᵊl\ *n -s* [origin unknown] **1** : a minor falsehood : FIB **2** : pretentious nonsense

tar·a·hu·ma·ra \ˌtärəˈhü·märə\ *also* **tar·a·hu·ma·re** \-ārē\ *or* **tar·a·hu·mar** \ˌ-ˌ-ˈmär\ *n, pl* **tarahumara** *or* **tarahumaras** *also* **tarahumare** *or* **tarahumares** *or* **tarahumar** *or* **tarahumars** *usu cap* **1 a** : a Taracahitian people of southern Sonora and Chihuahua, Mexico **b** : a member of such people **2** : the language of the Tarahumara

ta·rai·re *also* **ta·rai·ri** \təˈrīrē\ *n -s* [Maori] **1** : a New Zealand timber tree (*Beilschmiedia tarairi*) of the family Lauraceae

tar·a·ki·hi \ˌtärəˈkēˌhē\ *or* **ter·a·ki·hi** \ˌter-\ *n -s* [Maori] : a morwong (*Dactylopagrus macropterus*)

tar·a·mel·lite \ˌtärəˈmeˌlīt\ *n -s* [It, fr. Torquato *Taramelli* †1922 Ital. geologist + It *-ite*] : a mineral BaFe₅Si₁₀O₃₁

tar·a·na·ki \ˌtärəˈnäkē\ *adj, usu cap* [*Taranaki*, New Zealand] : of or from the provincial district of Taranaki, New Zealand

tar·a·na·kite \ˌ-ˌ-ˈ-ˌkīt\ *n -s* [*Taranaki*, provincial district in New Zealand] : a mineral K₂Al₆(PO₄)₆(OH)₂·18H₂O(?)

ta·ran·chi \təˈränchē\ *n, pl* **taranchi** *or* **taranchis** *usu cap* [Jagatai *Taranči*, lit., farmer] : a Turkic people of mixed Iranian origin living in Kazakh Soviet S.S.R.

tarantara *var of* TANTARA

ta·ran·tass \ˌtärənˈtäs\ *n -ES* [Russ *tarantas*, fr. Kazan Tatar *tarÿntas*] : a low four-wheeled carriage used in Russia

tar·an·tel·la \ˌtarənˈtelə\ *or* **tar·en·telle** \-ˈtel\ *n -s* [*tarantella*, fr. It, fr. *Taranto*, seaport in southern Italy + It *-ella*] : a vivacious folk dance

sextuple measure usu. alternating suddenly between the major and the minor modes

tar·an·tism \ˈtarənˌtizəm\ *n -s* [NL *tarantismus*, fr. *Taranto*, seaport in southern Italy where tarantism was common from the 15th to the 17th cent. + L *-ismus* -ism] : a dancing mania or malady of late medieval Europe

ta·ran·to \təˈranˌtō, -ˈtär-; təˈran·(ˌ)tō\ *adj, usu cap* [fr. *Taranto*, Italy] : of or from the city of Taranto, Italy

ta·ran·tu·la \təˈranch(ə)lə, -raan-, -ntᵊlə\ *n* [ML, fr. OIt *tarantola*, fr. *Taranto*, seaport in southern Italy] **1** *pl* **tarantulas** \-ləz\ *or* **ta·rantu·lae** \-chə,lē, -tᵊl,ē\ : a European wolf spider (*Lycosa tarentula*) regarded as the cause of tarantism **2** *pl* **tarantulas** *also* **tarantulae a** : a spider of the suborder Mygalomorphae; *esp* : any of various large hairy spiders of the family Theraphosidae **b** : a large spider — not used technically **3** *cap* [NL, fr. ML] : a genus (the type of the family Tarantulidae) of whip scorpions

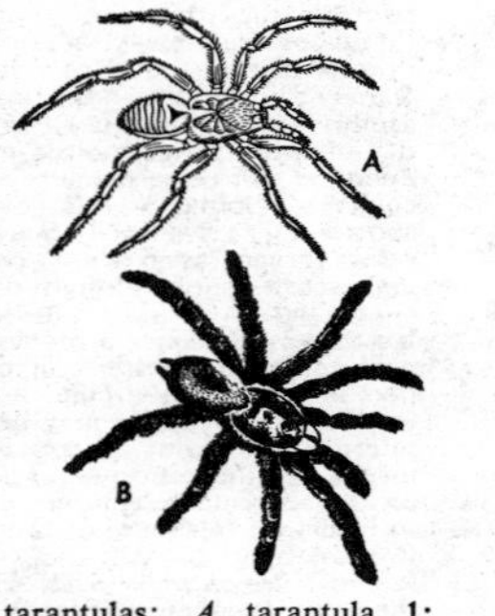

tarantulas: *A* tarantula 1; *B* an American tarantula 2a

tarantula hawk *or* **tarantula killer** *n* : a large wasp of the genus *Pepsis* (family Pompilidae); *esp* : any of several solitary wasps of the southwestern U.S. that capture tarantulas as food for their young

¹ta·ran·tu·lid \-ch(ə)ləd, -tᵊləd\ *adj* [NL *Tarantulidae*] : of or relating to the Tarantulidae

²tarantulid \"\ *n -s* : a scorpion of the family Tarantulidae

tar·an·tu·li·dae \ˌtarənˈt(y)ülə,dē\ *n pl, cap* [NL, fr. *Tarantula*, type genus + *-idae*] : a family of whip scorpions (order Pedipalpida)

tar·a·pa·ca·ite \ˌtärəpəˈkäˌīt\ *n -s* [Sp *tarapacaita*, fr. *Tarapacá*, province in northern Chile, its locality + Sp *-ita* *-ite*] : a mineral consisting of a native potassium chromate

ta·ras·can \təˈraskən, -räs-\ *n -s usu cap* [Sp *Tarasco* + E *-an*] **1** : TARASCO **2** : a language family of the state of Michoacán, Mexico

ta·ras·co \-(ˌ)skō\ *n, pl* **tarasco** *or* **tarascos** *usu cap* [Sp] **1 a** : a people of the state of Michoacán, Mexico **b** : a member of such people **2** : the language of the Tarasco people

ta·ra·ta *also* **ta·ra·tah** \təˈräd-ə\ *n -s* [Maori *tarata*] : a small evergreen tree (*Pittosporum eugenioides*) of New Zealand — called also *white mapau*

tara vine \ˈtärə-, ˈtarə-\ *n* [*tara* fr. Jap] : BOWER ACTINIDIA

ta·rax·a·cum \təˈraksəkəm\ *n* [NL, fr. Ar *tarakhshaqūn* wild chicory] **1** *cap* : a genus of chiefly weedy nearly cosmopolitan scapose perennial herbs (family Compositae) — see DANDELION, KOKSAGHYZ **2** *-s* : the dried rhizome and roots of the dandelion (*T. officinale*) used as a bitter and laxative

ta·rax·e·in \təˈraksēən\ *n -s* [Gk *taraxis* confusion (fr. *tarassein* to trouble, confuse) + E *-ein* (as in protein)] : a substance isolable from the blood of schizophrenic persons

tar·ba·gan \ˈtärbəˌgan\ *n -s* [Russ, fr. Teleut] : a pale or reddish gregarious bobac inhabiting the grassy steppes of central Asia

tar base *n* : any of the organic bases (as aniline, pyridine, or quinoline) obtained esp. from coal tar or ammonia liquor — compare PYRIDINE BASE

tar·boosh *also* **tar·bush** *or* **tar·boush** \(ˈ)tärˈbüsh, -búsh\ *n -ES* [Ar *ṭarbūsh*] : a red hat similar to the fez used alone or as part of a turban

tar·bou·ka \tärˈbükə\ *n -s* [Ar *darbūkkah*] : DARABUKKA

tarbrush \ˈ-ˌ-, ˌ-ˈ-\ *n* [¹*tar* + *brush*] **1** : a brush for applying tar **2** : colored or Negro blood

tar·bush \ˈ-ˌ-\ *n* [¹*tar* + *bush*] **1** : YERBA SANTA **2** : any of several California shrubs of the genus *Chamaebatia* **3** : a sticky shrub (*Flourensia cernua*) of the family Compositae native to the southwestern U.S. and Mexico

tarbrush

tar·but·tite \ˈtärbəˌtīt\ *n -s* [Percy C. *Tarbutt*, 20th cent. Australian mine director + E *-ite*] : a basic zinc phosphate Zn₂PO₄(OH) in clusters of colorless or pale yellow, brown, red, or green triclinic crystals

tar·da·men·te \ˌtärdəˈmentē\ *adv* [It, fr. *tardo* slow, fr. L *tardus* slow — more at TARDY] : SLOWLY — used as a direction in music

tar·dan·do \tärˈdändō\ *adv (or adj)* [It, fr. L *tardandum*, gerund of *tardare* to delay] : RITARDANDO

tar·de·noi·sian \ˌtärdᵊˈnoizhən, -ˈoizēən, -ˈwäzēən\ *adj, usu cap* [Fère-en-*Tardenois*, town in northeastern France] : of or belonging to an early Mesolithic culture characterized by small flint implements of geometrical form

tar·di·gra·da \tärˈdigrədə, ˌtärdəˈgrädə\ *n pl, cap* [NL, neut. pl. of L *tardigradus* slow-moving] **1** *in former classifications* : an order of mammals equivalent to the Bradypodidae **2** : a division of Arthropoda comprising microscopic creatures that live in water or damp moss

¹tar·di·grade \ˈtärdəˌgrād\ *adj* [F, fr. L *tardigradus*, fr. *tardus* slow + *gradus* step — more at TARDY, GRADE] **1** : moving or stepping slowly : SLOW-PACED, SLUGGISH **2** [NL *Tardigrada*] : of or relating to the Tardigrada

²tardigrade \"\ *or* **tar·di·grad** \-ˌgrad\ *n -s* [NL *Tardigrada*] : an arthropod of the division Tardigrada

tar·di·ly \ˈtärdᵊlē, -ˌtäd-, -dᵊli, ˌli\ *adv* **1** : in an unhurried manner : at a slack pace : SLOWLY **2** : after the expected, hoped for, or proper time : LATE

tar·di·ness \-dēnəs, -din-\ *n -ES* : the quality or state of being tardy

tar distillate *n* : a fraction in petroleum refining containing heavy oils and paraffin

tar·dive \ˈtärdiv\ *adj* [F, fem. of *tardif*, fr. MF, tardy] : tending to or characterized by lateness in development or maturity

tar·do \'tär(,)dō\ *adj* [It, fr. L *tardus*] **:** SLOW — used as a direction in music

tar drum *n* **:** a separator used in petroleum distilling for condensing the heavier vapors

¹**tar·dy** \'tärdē, 'tȧd-, -di\ *adj* -ER/-EST [alter. (influenced by *-y*, adj. suffix) of earlier *tardif*, fr. MF, fr. (assumed) VL *tardivus*, fr. L *tardus* slow + *-ivus* -ive; prob. akin to Gk *terēn* soft, tender — more at TENDER] **1 a :** moving with slow pace, motion, or progress **:** SLUGGISH ⟨she could not wait for the ~ operations of her ambassadress —W.M.Thackeray⟩ ⟨where the vulgar dialects were *tardiest* in taking distinctive form —H.O. Taylor⟩ ⟨ten years is a long . . . courtship, and she summons courage to spur her ~ swain —Seamus Kelly⟩ **b :** acting, occurring, or developing after the expected, hoped for, or proper time **:** DELAYED, DILATORY, LATE ⟨is often an hour ~ at school⟩ ⟨~ in recognizing that the barbiturates are just as dangerous as the opiates —D.W.Maurer & V.H.Vogel⟩ ⟨the intellectuals were somewhat ~ . . . what they discovered was what the public everywhere had long known —John Mason Brown⟩ **2** *obs* **:** off guard **:** UNPREPARED, REMISS

syn LATE, BEHINDHAND, OVERDUE: TARDY applies to failure to arrive at a time set, sometimes through lack of punctuality, negligence, or tendency to dawdle, sometimes through unavoidable delay ⟨*tardy* arrivals at the play slowing down the first act⟩ ⟨a number of *tardy* children rebuked by the principal⟩ LATE centers attention on the fact of not arriving on time; it may or may not imply blame ⟨*late* for school⟩ ⟨persons coming *late* were seated in the balcony⟩ ⟨docked for being *late*⟩ BEHINDHAND applies to the situation of persons who have fallen into arrears or whose development, progress or action is slower than normal ⟨*behindhand* in his mortgage payments⟩ ⟨in a big house . . . one is always *behindhand*. The days aren't long enough —George Moore⟩ OVERDUE may refer to what has been due and left unpaid or undone, to what has been expected or scheduled but lacks arrival or completion, or to what might logically or suitably have occurred or appeared a long time before ⟨an *overdue* bill⟩ ⟨an *overdue* library book⟩ ⟨small chance of search planes even though we were a week *overdue* —L.A.Viereck⟩ ⟨the valuable work of this branch of chemistry received long *overdue* recognition —J.H.Kuney⟩ ⟨legislative reforms are long *overdue*⟩

²**tardy** *adv, archaic* **:** TARDILY ⟨too swift arrives as ~ as too slow —Shak.⟩

¹**tare** \'ta(a)(ə)r, 'te(, |ə\ *n* -S [ME; prob. akin to MD *tarwe* wheat, Gaulish *dravoca* darnel, Gk *daratos*, a bread, Lith *dirva* field, Skt *dūrvā* panic grass, OE *teran* to tear — more at TEAR] **1 a :** the seed of a vetch **b :** any of several vetches (esp. *Vicia sativa* and *V. hirsuta*) **2 tares** *pl* **:** an injurious weed of grainfields esp. of Biblical times that is usu. held to be the darnel ⟨while men slept, his enemy came and sowed ~*s* among the wheat —Mt 13:25(AV)⟩ **3 tares** *pl* **:** a bad or undesirable element or growth that endangers the well-being of what is good or desirable ⟨though . . . generally condemned by the Church . . . these ~*s* did manage at all times to flourish amidst the orthodox wheat —G.G.Coulton⟩ ⟨the bitter ~*s* of the past were exorcised —Sylvia Berkman⟩ ⟨the critic . . . should endeavor to discipline his personal prejudices and cranks — ~*s* to which we are all subject —F.R.Leavis⟩

²**tare** \"\ *n* -S [ME, fr. MF, fr. OIt *tara*, fr. Ar *ṭarḥa* that which is removed, fr. *ṭaraḥa* to remove, reject] **1 a :** the weight of a container or vehicle that is deducted from the gross weight to obtain the net weight — see ACTUAL TARE **b :** a deduction from the gross weight of a substance and its container made in allowance for the weight of the container — see AVERAGE TARE; compare TARE WEIGHT **2 a :** COUNTERWEIGHT; *esp* **:** an empty receptacle similar to one being used as a container used to counterpoise any change in weight of the container due to temperature, moisture, or other conditions ⟨the best ~ is made of the same material as the apparatus —A.A.Benedetti-Pichler⟩ **b :** the weight of a container used as a deduction esp. in laboratory weighing operations **3 :** soil or similar waste material adhering to sugar beets ⟨the percentage of ~ for a load is estimated from a sample⟩

³**tare** \"\ *vt* -ED/-ING/-S **:** to ascertain or mark the tare of **:** weigh so as to determine the tare ⟨the weight on one beam being used to ~ the bottle or jar while the other weight is left free —E.F.Cook & E.W.Martin⟩ ⟨allow the mercury to flow into a *tared* vessel and divide the net weight —*Science*⟩

⁴**tare** \"\ *usu cap* — a communications code word for the letter *t*

tare grass *n* **1 :** TARE 2 **2 :** TUFTED VETCH **3 :** DARNEL

tarekat *var of* TARIQA

tare man *n* **1 :** a worker who estimates the percentage of tare in a load of sugar beets by weighing a sample before and after cleaning **2 :** a textile worker who handles wool and identifies the types

ta·rente \tə'ränt\ *n* -S [F, fr. *Tarente* Taranto, seaport in southern Italy] **:** a gecko (*Tarentola mauritanica*) of southern Europe and adjacent regions that is found esp. among old ruins

tarentelle *var of* TARANTELLA

¹**tar·en·tine** \'tarən,tīn, -,tēn; tə'rentᵊn\ *adj, usu cap* [L *tarentinus*, fr. *Tarentum* Taranto (fr. Gk *Tarant-*, *Taras*) + *-inus* -ine] **1 :** of, relating to, or characteristic of Tarentum, a Greek city of ancient Italy **2 :** of, relating to, or characteristic of the people of Tarentum

²**tarentine** \"\ *n* -S *cap* **:** a native or inhabitant of Tarentum

ta·ren·to·la \tə'rentᵊlə\ *n* [NL, fr. It dial. *tarantola* salamander, fr. OIt, tarantula, fr. *Taranto*, seaport in southern Italy] **1** -S **:** TARENTE **2** *cap* **:** a widely distributed genus of Old and New World geckos including the tarente

tares *pl of* TARE, *pres 3d sing of* TARE

tare vetch *n* **:** ¹TARE 1

tare weight *n* **:** the officially accepted weight of an empty car, vehicle, or container that when subtracted from gross weight yields the net weight of cargo or shipment upon which charges can be calculated — compare ²TARE

tarflower \'ˌ=,=\ *n* [¹*tar* + *flower*] **:** an evergreen undershrub (*Bejaria racemosa*) of the family Ericaceae of the southern U.S. bearing pinkish white racemose flowers and bristly hairy twigs

¹**targe** \'tärj\ *n* -S [ME, fr. OF — more at TARGET] *archaic* **:** a light shield or buckler carried esp. by footmen and archers

²**targe** \'tärj\ *vt* -ED/-ING/-S [origin unknown] **1** *chiefly Scot* **:** to question in some detail **:** INTERROGATE **2** *chiefly Scot* **:** to keep in order or under strict watch **3** *chiefly Scot* **:** BEAT, SCOLD

¹**tar·get** \'tärgət\ *n* -S *often attrib* [ME, fr. MF *targette*, dim. of OF *targe* light shield, of Gmc origin; akin to OHG *zarga* frame, border, ON *targa* shield; prob. akin to MIr *dremm* group of people, Bret *dramm* bundle, Arm *trcak* bundle of wood, and perh. to Gk *drassesthai* to grasp] **1 a :** a small circular shield or buckler **b :** such a target or its replica used as a heraldic device **2 a :** a butt or mark to shoot at in practice or competition or for testing the accuracy of a firearm or the force of a projectile: as (1) **:** a series of concentric circles of specified size marked on a paper or wooden surface with a bull's-eye at the center (2) **:** a circular mat of straw four feet in diameter covered by a canvas face painted with five concentric circles and mounted on a tripodal stand for use in archery — see PRINCE'S RECKONING **b** (1) **:** a target marked or penetrated by the shots fired at it to make a score (2) **:** the score made in target shooting ⟨shot the high ~ for the day⟩ (3) **:** CLAY PIGEON (4) **:** the section or part of a person or animal regarded as the object to be hit (as in hunting or fencing) **c :** something (as an airplane or ship, installation or area) that is or may be fired at as a military objective ⟨directly over the ~ . . . gave the order to drop the ash cans and a floating flare to mark the point of attack —John Hersey⟩ ⟨must be used to obtain the required results upon hostile ~*s* —H.P.Rand⟩ **3 :** something that is or may be aimed at: as **a :** a person or thing that is made the object of derogatory remarks or critical comment ⟨the colonists . . . made him their chief ~ of scorn —Stanley Pargellis⟩ ⟨was making herself a ~ for ridicule —Virginia Woolf⟩ ⟨in some ways the textbook makes an even more satisfactory ~ than the teacher —V.M. Rogers⟩ ⟨his social criticism . . . remains primarily moral — its principal ~ is human nature —C.J.Rolo⟩ **b :** a person or thing that is made the object of an action, political movement, or other development designed usu. to affect or change ⟨investors . . . might become a favored ~ for unfair action on the part of foreign governments —M.A.Heilperin⟩ ⟨might direct such investigations to ~*s* like corruption or inefficiency — Christopher Serpell⟩ ⟨this area was the constant ~ of enemy propaganda —H.I.Poleman⟩ ⟨the peninsula . . . is not an easy ~ for economic development —Marion Wilhelm⟩ **c :** a goal (as a date, figure, production level, or quota) set or proposed for achievement ⟨with the ~ for land collection set at 50 million acres by 1957 —Vera M. Dean⟩ ⟨the ~ of the air route . . . was 85,000 tons per month —G.C.Marshall⟩ ⟨the week-end adjournment ~ was abandoned —J.D.Morris⟩ ⟨officers whose initial ~ was the rapid establishment of law and order — *Current History*⟩ **4 :** a visible signal or device used to mark or identify something: as **a :** a railroad day signal attached to a switch stand that indicates by its position, shape, color, or shape and color combined whether the switch is open or closed **b :** the vane or sliding sight on a surveyor's leveling staff **c :** an indicator to show that an electrical relay has functioned — compare DROP 3f **5 a :** the metallic surface usu. of a platinum or tungsten anode upon which the stream of cathode rays within an X-ray tube is focused **b :** a body, surface, or substance bombarded with nuclear particles **c :** the fluorescent material on which the desired patterns or pictures are produced in television, radar, and other electronic devices **6 :** the standard or original object or thought that is to be recognized or affected through psychokinesis, telepathy, or clairvoyance **:** STIMULUS-OBJECT

²**target** \"\ *vt* -ED/-ING/-S **1 a :** to make a target of ⟨is already ~*ed* as the first victim —*Newsweek*⟩ ⟨the fires were smothered to keep . . . planes from ~*ing* the oil fields —*Nat'l Geographic*⟩ **b :** to set forth or determine as a goal or mark to be achieved ⟨coal production . . . was ~*ed* for 100 million tons in 1955 — *Newsweek*⟩ ⟨if zooming costs had not prevented . . . the bargain price originally ~*ed* —*Forbes*⟩ **2 :** to signal (as the position of a railroad switch) by means of a target **3 :** to determine by experiment the firing data necessary for aiming and firing (a firearm) accurately ⟨traded rifles . . . and I ~*ed* the thing —W.C.Tuttle⟩ **4 :** to direct toward a target

target cell *or* **target corpuscle** *n* **:** an atypical red blood cell with a peripheral ring and central mass of hemoglobin-containing cytoplasm separated by a relatively hemoglobin-free ring

target date *n* **:** the date set for an event or for the completion of a project, goal, or quota ⟨the *target date* for the invasion . . . was set —F.D.Roosevelt⟩ ⟨would not set a *target date* for accomplishment of the plan —Stanley Levey⟩ ⟨here and there the *target dates* may have to be changed —Van McDougall⟩

tar·ge·teer *also* **tar·ge·tier** \,tärgə'ti(ə)r\ *n* -S **1 :** one armed with a target or shield **2 :** SIGHTER 1

target gland *or* **target organ** *n* **:** an endocrine organ of which the functional activity is controlled by a tropic fraction of the pituitary secretion

target lamp *or* **target lantern** *n* **:** a lamp or lantern for use at a railroad switch target

tar·get·man \'tärgət,man\ *n, pl* **targetmen :** one who uses a railroad target in signaling

target of opportunity : a military target on which fire or attack is unplanned and which is attacked upon favorable presentation or unexpected discovery or appearance — usu. used in pl. ⟨was permitted to engage any *targets of opportunity* which I might see —*Coast Artillery Jour.*⟩ ⟨this company was held in reserve for . . . attacking *targets of opportunity* — *Infantry Jour.*⟩

target pistol *n* **:** a pistol made esp. for target shooting

target practice *n* **:** practice in shooting at targets

target range *n* **:** RANGE 5a(3)

target rifle *n* **:** a rifle made esp. for target shooting

target rod *n* **:** a leveling rod that has an adjustable target

target spot *n* **1 :** a disease (as early blight of tomato and potato) characterized by lesions having concentric markings resembling a target **2 :** a target-spot lesion

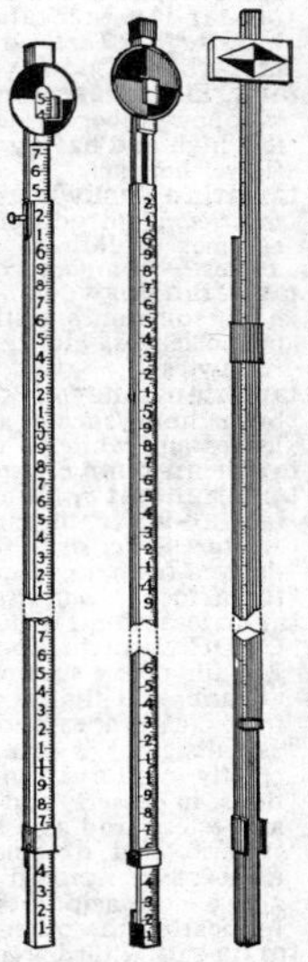

target rods

tar·ghee \'tär(,)gē\ *n* [fr. *Targhee* Pass, southwestern Montana, near Dubois, Idaho, where the breed originated] **1** *usu cap* **:** an American breed of sheep developed by intercrossing Lincolns and Rambouillets to produce a hardy range sheep with good mutton conformation and a heavy fleece of moderately fine wool **2** -S *often cap* **:** a sheep of the Targhee breed

targing *pres part of* TARGE

tar·gum \'tär,güm, -güm\ *n, pl* **targums** \-mz\ *or* **targu·mim** \,==='mēm\ *usu cap* [LHeb *targūm*, fr. Aram, translation, interpretation] **:** an Aramaic translation or paraphrase of a portion of the Old Testament

tar·gum·ic \(')=¦=ik\ *adj, often cap* **:** of or relating to the Targums

tar·gum·ist \'=,=əst\ *n* -S *usu cap* **1 :** the writer or translator of a Targum **2 :** a specialist in the Targums

tarheel \'=,=\ *also* **tar·heel·er** \"ə(r)\ *n* -S *usu cap* [*tarheel* fr. ¹*tar* + *heel*; *tarheeler* fr. *Tarheel* State, nickname for North Carolina + E *-er*] **:** a North Carolinian — a nickname

ta·ri \(')tä¦rē\ *n* -S [It *tarì*] **:** a small medieval coin struck in Italy, Sicily, and Malta; *also* **:** a corresponding unit of value

tar·i·ana \,tarē'ānə, -'änə\ *n, pl* **tariana** *or* **tarianas** *usu cap* **1 a :** an Arawakan people of northwestern Brazil **b :** a member of such people **2 :** the language of the Tariana people

tar·iff \'tarəf *also* 'ter-\ *n* -S [It *tariffa*, fr. Ar *ta'rīfa*, *ta'rīf*, fr. *'arifa* to inform, make known] **1** *also* **ta·rif·fa** \tə'rifə, -rēfə\ *archaic* **:** an arithmetic or multiplication table **2 :** a schedule, system, or scheme of duties imposed by a government on imported or exported goods for the production of revenue, for the artificial fostering of home industries, or as a means of coercing foreign governments to grant reciprocity privileges — compare PROTECTION, FREE TRADE **3 :** a listing or scale of rates or charges for a business or a public utility: as **a :** a published schedule of rates, ratings, or charges with associated rules, regulations, routes, and information issued by carriers or their agents and filed with a public regulatory agency **b :** a schedule of rates or charges of a hotel, motel, or lodging house ⟨rooms and meals at ~*s* well below comparable accommodations elsewhere —Lucius Beebe⟩ **c :** a schedule of postal rates or charges ⟨the flat rate principles on which the postal ~ is based —A.J.Bruwer⟩ **4 :** the duty or rate of duty imposed in a tariff ⟨the ~ on wool⟩ ⟨a ~ of two cents a pound⟩ **5 :** a charge or fee set as the cost of goods or service **:** PRICE ⟨creating a market in shells . . . and modifying the ~ according to the supply —Arnold Bennett⟩ ⟨excellent workmanship at not too high a ~ —*Fashion Digest*⟩ ⟨the stiff ~ of 15 bucks that the fraternity was charging —Martin Dibner⟩ ⟨keep the tickets on a par with the ~ in the unofficial stands —Horace Sutton⟩

²**tariff** \"\ *vt* -ED/-ING/-S **:** to levy a tariff or set a price on (goods or service)

tar·iff·less \'tarəfləs *also* 'ter-\ *adj* **:** being without or not subject to a tariff ⟨wants a single, ~ European market —F.R. Kuh⟩

tariff wall *n* **:** a rate or scale of custom duties designed to check the flow of imports

ta·rin *also* **te·rin** \tə'ran\ *n* -S [F, prob. of imit. origin] **:** the European siskin

taring *pres part of* TARE

ta·ri·qa *also* **ta·ri·qah** \tə'rēkə\ *or* **ta·ri·qat** \-kət\ *n* -S [Ar *ṭarīqah*, *ṭarīqat*, lit., way] **1 :** the Sufi path of spiritual development involving stages of meditation and contemplation leading to intimate communion with the deity **2** *or* **ta·re·kat** \-kət\ **:** a Muslim religious brotherhood; *esp* **:** a religious fraternity of Muslim mystics

ta·rir·ic acid \tə'ririk-\ *n* [ISV *tariri-* (fr. NL *Tariri*, fr. AmerSp *tariri*, a plant of the genus *Picramnia*, of AmerInd origin) + *-ic*] **:** a crystalline acetylenic fatty acid $CH_3(CH_2)_{10}C{\equiv}C(CH_2)_4COOH$ that is isomeric with linoleic acid and occurs as a glyceride in the oil of the seeds of several plants of the genus *Picramnia*

tar·ka·ni \tär'känē\ *also* **tar·ka·la·ni** \,tärkə'länē\ *n, pl* **tarkani** *or* **tarkanis** *also* **tarkalani** *or* **tarkalanis** *usu cap* **1 :** one of a group of Pathan hill people of Durani descent that live west of the Panjkora river in northern West Pakistan **2 :** a member of the Tarkani people

tar·khan \'tär,kän\ *n* -S [Osmanli & Jagatai *Tarchan*, fr. OTurk *Tarkan*, a privileged class] **:** a member of a low Muslim caste of artisans of Upper India

tar·la·tan \'tärlətᵊn, -lətən\ *also* **tarle·ton** \", -ltən\ *n* -S [F *tarlatane*, *tarnatane*] **:** a sheer cotton fabric in open plain weave usu. heavily sized for stiffness and used for dresses, costumes, dust covers, trimmings, and some industrial purposes

tar·mac \'tär,mak\ *n* -S [short for *tarmacadam*] **:** a tarmacadam road, apron, or runway

Tar·mac \"\ *trademark* — used for a bituminous binder for surfacing roads

tarmacadam \¦==¦==\ *n* [¹*tar* + *macadam*] **1 :** a pavement constructed by spraying or pouring a tar binder over courses of crushed stone in situ and then consolidating with a power roller **2 :** a material of tar and aggregates mixed in a plant and shaped on the roadway

tarn \'tärn\ *n* -S [ME *tarne*, *terne*, of Scand origin; akin to ON *tjǫrn* small lake; akin to Skt *dara* hole in the ground, OE *teran* to tear — more at TEAR] **:** a small steep-banked mountain lake or pool; *specif* **:** one in a basin produced by glacial erosion or deposition

tar·nal \'tärnᵊl, 'tȧn-\ *adv* (*or adj*) [alter. of *eternal*] *dial* **:** DAMNED — used as a mild imprecation ⟨paid a ~ high price for it —C.G.Loomis⟩ ⟨fire is a cruel, ~ thing —Conrad Richter⟩ — **tar·nal·ly** \-ᵊlē, -ᵊli\ *adv, dial*

¹**tar·na·tion** \(')tär¦nāshən, (')tȧ|n-\ *adv* (*or adj*) [alter. (influenced by *tarnal*) of *darnation*] *dial* **:** DAMNED — used as a mild imprecation ⟨so ~ still there you began listening for something —Esther Forbes⟩ ⟨so ~ old —Josephine Y. Case⟩ ⟨some ~ fool'll be going over —Della Lutes⟩

²**tarnation** \"\ *n* -S *dial* **:** DAMNATION — used as a mild imprecation ⟨where in ~ is she at —Frederick Way⟩ ⟨what in ~'s pemmican —F.V.W.Mason⟩

¹**tar·nish** \'tärnish, 'tȧn-, -nēsh, *esp in pres part* '-nəsh\ *vb* -ED/-ING/-S [MF *terniss-*, stem of *ternir* to tarnish, prob. of Gmc origin; akin to OHG *ternen*, *tarnen* to hide — more at DERN] *vt* **1 :** to diminish, dull, or destroy the luster of esp. by or as if by air, dust, or dirt **:** SOIL, STAIN ⟨polishing the ~*ed* spoons⟩ ⟨the mist settling down and ~*ing* the great plaque of silver —William Beebe⟩ ⟨a ~*ed* tidewater creek —Berton Roueché⟩ ⟨~*ed* marigold stalks —J.C.Powys⟩ **2 a :** to detract from the good or desirable quality of **:** VITIATE, SPOIL ⟨the brightest of its ideas grow ~*ed* —H.V.Gregory⟩ ⟨reciting some plain facts . . . which somewhat ~*ed* the latter's eulogies —V.L.Parrington⟩ ⟨had ~*ed* himself, filled his mind with corruption —Oscar Wilde⟩ **b :** to bring disgrace or cast doubt upon (one's name or reputation) **:** TAINT, SULLY ⟨am not worried that the . . . name will be ~*ed* by my association with the governor —F.D.Roosevelt⟩ ⟨the belief that some uranium stocks . . . could ~ the reputation of American business — *Wall Street Jour.*⟩ ~ *vi* **1 :** to become dull, discolored, or stained in appearance ⟨silver ~*es* quickly if left uncared-for⟩ **2 a :** to undergo a lowering in quality **:** DISSIPATE, DETERIORATE ⟨the bright hopes of the Liberation have ~*ed* rapidly —Stanley Karnow⟩ ⟨in contact with the seamy realities . . . the dream soon ~*es* —L.C.Stevens⟩ **b :** to grow less in prestige or esteem **:** DIMINISH ⟨his reputation may have ~*ed* somewhat among . . . the population —J.H.Huizinga⟩ ⟨have allowed his justly bright fame . . . to ~ —C.R.Anderson⟩ ⟨lacks the visionary gleam without which . . . poetic repute ~*es* —*Times Lit. Supp.*⟩

²**tarnish** \"\ *n* -ES **1 a :** the condition of being tarnished **:** STAIN, SOIL, BLEMISH ⟨~ on silver⟩ **b :** the altered luster or surface color of a mineral or metal caused either by slight alteration or a thin film of deposition **2 :** the condition of being lowered in quality, worth, or esteem **:** DEBASEMENT, DETERIORATION ⟨time and circumstance brought a ~ to the glory —R. T. La Piere⟩ ⟨bright as that reputation long was, it is beginning to show ~ —V.L.Parrington⟩

tar·nish·able \-shəbəl\ *adj* **:** likely to undergo tarnishing

tarnished plant bug *n* **:** a common and widespread mirid bug (*Lygus lineolaris*) that is destructive to many kinds of plants by sucking the sap from buds, leaves, and fruits and causing decline and disfigurement (as catfacing of peaches) and by carrying diseases (as fire blight of pears) — see STOPBACK

tarnishproof \¦==¦=\ *adj* **:** incapable of tarnishing ⟨the most ~ preconceived picture of Paris —P.E.Deutschman⟩

taro \'tä(,)rō, 'ta(a)(,)-, 'te(,)-, 'tȧ(,)-\ *also* **tara** \-rə\ *n* -S [Tahitian & Maori *taro*] **1 :** an aroid (*Colocasia esculenta*) of the Pacific islands that is grown throughout the tropics for its edible starchy tuberous rootstocks and in temperate regions for ornament — called also *dalo*; compare ELEPHANT'S EAR **2 :** the rootstock of the taro plant that serves as a food staple in the tropics — called also *eddo*; see POI

ta·ro·ga·to \'tärōgə,tō\ *n* -S [Hung *tárogató*] **:** a Hungarian musical instrument consisting of a wooden pipe with a clarinet reed at the mouthpiece and a globular bell similar to that of an English horn

tar oil *n* **:** any of various oils obtained from tar (as coal tar or pine tar) usu. by distillation

ta·rok *also* **ta·roc** *or* **ta·rock** \tə'räk\ *n* -S [obs. It *tarocco* (now *tarocchi*, pl. of obs. *tarocco*), fr. OIt] **:** an old and popular card game of central Europe played with a pack containing the 22 tarots plus 40, 52, or 56 cards equivalent to modern playing cards

ta·rot \(')ta¦rō\ *n, pl* **tarots** \-ō(z)\ [MF, fr. OIt *tarocco*] **1 :** any of a set of 22 pictorial playing cards used for fortune-telling and serving as trumps in tarok **2 tarots** *pl* **:** TAROK

tarp \'tärp, 'tȧp\ *n* -S [by shortening] **:** TARPAULIN

tar·pan \(')tär¦pan\ *n* -S [Russ, fr. Kirghiz] **:** a small swift dun-colored wild horse of the steppes of central Asia

tar paper *n* **:** a heavy paper coated or impregnated with tar for use esp. in building

¹**tar·pau·lin** \tär'pȯlən, tȧ'p-, '=,pələn, *chiefly in substand speech* ='pōlyən *or* -ōlēən\ *n* -S [earlier *tarpauling*, *tarpawling*, prob. fr. ¹*tar* + *-pauling*, *-pawling* covering, fr. *paule*, *pawl*, *pall* cloth, covering, fr. ME *pall* — more at PALL] **1 :** a piece or sheet of waterproofed canvas or other waterproof material used for covering or protecting goods, vehicles, athletic fields, or other exposed objects **2 :** SAILOR

²**tarpaulin** \"\ *vt* -ED/-ING/-S **:** to cover with a tarpaulin ⟨the ~*ed* shelter which housed the car and the truck —Jon Godden⟩

tarpaulin muster *n* [so called fr. its being formerly collected by having the crew toss their money into a tarpaulin] **:** a pooling of funds for common use esp. by seamen

tar·pe·ian \(')tär¦pē(y)ən\ *adj, usu cap* [L *tarpeius* (fr. *Tarpeius*, cliff or rock on the Capitoline hill, prob. fr. *Tarpeia*, legendary Roman maiden) + E *-an*] **:** of, relating to, or designating a cliff or rock of the Capitoline hill in Rome used in ancient times for hurling condemned criminals to their deaths

tar·pon \'tärpən, 'tȧp- *sometimes* -,pän\ *n, pl* **tarpon** *or* **tarpons** [origin unknown] **1 a :** a marine fish (*Tarpon atlanticus* or *Megalops atlanticus*) that is closely related to the tenpounder, is common in the Gulf of Mexico off the coast of Florida, has an elongate and compressed body with large scales brilliantly silvery on the sides and belly, reaches a length of about six feet and a weight of 200 pounds, and is noted as a sport fish **b :** a smaller related fish (*Megalops cyprinoides*) of the Indo-Pacific area — called also *oxeye* **2** *southern Africa* **:** the common bonefish (*Albula vulpes*)

tar·pum \-pəm, -pᵊm\ *n* -S [by alter.] **:** TARPON 1

tar putty *n* **:** a mixture of tar and lampblack

tar·quin·i·an \(')tär¦kwinēən\ *adj, usu cap* [L *tarquinius* (fr. *Tarquinius* Tarquin, any one of a succession of legendary Roman kings of the 6th and 5th centuries B.C., prob. fr. *Tarquinii* Tarquinia, ancient Roman town in central Italy that was the birthplace of the first Tarquin king) + E *-an*] **:** of or relating to the legendary Tarquin kings of ancient Rome noted esp. for their tyranny

tarradiddle *var of* TARADIDDLE

tar·ra·gon \ˈtarəˌgän, -ˌgən\ *n* -s [earlier *taragon*, fr. MF *targon*, fr. ML *tarcon, tarchon*, fr. Ar *ṭarkhūn*] **1 :** a small European perennial wormwood (*Artemisia dracunculus*) grown for its pungent aromatic foliage that is used in making pickles and vinegar **2 :** the foliage of tarragon **3 :** a moderate yellowish green that is yellower and stronger than average almond green and yellower and duller than malachite green or verdigris

tar·ra·go·na \ˌtarəˈgōnə\ *n* -s [fr. *Tarragona*, Spanish port-like wine, fr. *Tarragona*, region in northeastern Spain where it is produced] **:** IRON-OXIDE RED

tarragon oil *n* **:** an aromatic essential oil obtained from tarragon and used chiefly as a flavoring material — called also *estragon oil*

tarras *var of* TRASS

tar·ra·tine *also* **tar·ra·teen** \ˈtarəˌtēn\ *n* -s *usu cap* **:** ABNAKI

tarre *var of* TAR

tarred *past of* TAR

tar·ri·ance \ˈtarēən(t)s *also* ˈter-\ *n* -s **1 :** the act of tarrying **:** PUTTING OFF, DELAY ⟨the day was too far advanced to admit of further ~ —Susan E. Ferrier⟩ **2 :** a temporary stay in a place **:** SOJOURN ⟨after two days ~ there, returned —Alfred Tennyson⟩ **3** *obs* **:** the act of waiting usu. in anticipation

tar·ri·etia \ˌtarēˈēsh(ē)ə\ *n*, *cap* [NL, fr. native name in Java] **:** a small genus of chiefly eastern Asian and Australian timber trees (family Sterculiaceae)

tar·ri·ness \ˈtärēnəs, ˈtär-, -rin-\ *n* -ES **:** the quality or state of being tarry

tarring *pres part of* TAR

[1]**tar·ry** \ˈtarē, -ri *also* ˈter-\ *vb* -ED/-ING/-ES [ME *tarien*] *vt* **1** *obs* **:** to cause (as a person) to stay or wait **:** DELAY, HINDER **2 :** to wait for or in expectation of ⟨sitting down to ~ their return⟩ ~ *vi* **1 a :** to delay or be tardy in acting or doing **:** PROCRASTINATE, DAWDLE ⟨the men ~ about marriage —Jack Lusby⟩ ⟨we could not ~ if we wanted to be there on time⟩ **b :** to stay or linger in expectation of a person or an event **:** WAIT ⟨not ~*ing* long before the door is opened⟩ **2 a** *archaic* **:** to remain or continue in a state or condition **b :** to abide or stay in or at a place **:** SOJOURN ⟨no reason to ~ in this town —Elmer Davis⟩ ⟨over the island a horrid stillness *tarried* —Jean Stafford⟩ **syn** see STAY

[2]**tarry** \ˈ"\ *n* -ES [ME *tary*, fr. *tarien*] **:** STAY, SOJOURN ⟨make some little ~ in this town —J.G.Whittier⟩

[3]**tar·ry** \ˈtärē, ˈtär-, -ri\ *adj* -ER/-EST [[1]*tar* + *-y*] **1 :** of, resembling, or having the characteristics of tar ⟨the room had a ~, stuffy odor from the fire —Kenneth Roberts⟩ **2 :** consisting of or covered with or as if with tar **:** TARRED ⟨~ deposits are found in the cylinders —Malcolm McLaren⟩

tarrying irons *n pl* **:** TIRING IRONS

tarry stool *n* **:** an evacuation from the bowels having the color of tar caused by hemorrhage in the stomach or upper intestines or by drugs (as iron or bismuth)

tars *pl of* TAR, *pres 3d sing of* TAR

tars- *or* **tarso-** *comb form* [NL, fr. *tarsus*] **1** *usu tarso-* **:** tarsus ⟨*tarso*phyma⟩ ⟨*tars*algia⟩ ⟨*tars*ectomy⟩ **2** *usu tarso-* **:** tarsal and ⟨*tarso*orbital⟩ ⟨*tarso*tibial⟩

[1]**tar·sal** \ˈtärsəl, ˈtás-\ *adj* [NL *tarsalis*, fr. *tarsus* + L *-alis* -al] **1 :** of or relating to the tarsus **2 :** being or relating to plates of dense connective tissue that serve to stiffen the eyelids of man and many animals

[2]**tarsal** \ˈ"\ *n* -s **:** a tarsal part (as a bone or cartilage)

tarsal arch *n* **:** either of two arterial loops: **a :** a superior loop near the free margin of the upper or lower eyelid **b :** an inferior loop in this region

tar·sale \tärˈsā(ˌ)lē, -sä(, -sā(-\ *n*, *pl* **tarsa·lia** \-lēə\ [NL, fr. neut. sing. of *tarsalis*] **:** one of the bones or cartilages of the tarsus; *esp* **:** one of those articulating with the metatarsals

tarsal gland *n* **:** MEIBOMIAN GLAND

tarsal pad *n* **:** a flat pad on the tarsus of an insect

tar sand *n* **:** a natural impregnation of sand or sandstone with petroleum from which the lighter portions have escaped

tarsi *pl of* TARSUS

tar·sia \ˈtärsēə, ˌ=ˈ==\ *n* -s [It, fr. Ar *tarṣī'*] **:** INTARSIA 1

tar·si·er \ˈtärsēˌā, -ēər\ *n* -s [F, fr. *tarse* tarsus (fr. NL *tarsus*) + *-ier* -er] **:** any of several closely related nocturnal arboreal mammals of the genus *Tarsius* of the East Indies that are related to the lemurs, that are about the size of a small squirrel with soft grayish brown fur, slender legs, a tufted tail, and very large goggle eyes, and that have adhesive disks on the fingers and toes and very long proximal tarsal bones

tar·si·idae \tärˈsīəˌdē\ *n pl*, *cap* [NL, fr. *Tarsius*, type genus + *-idae*] **:** a family of lower primates (suborder Prosimii) that is coextensive with the genus *Tarsius*

tar·si·i·for·mes \ˌtärsēəˈfȯr(ˌ)mēz\ *n pl*, *cap* [NL, fr. *Tarsius* + *-iformes*] **:** a subgroup of Prosimii equivalent to Tarsioidea

[1]**tar·si·oid** \ˈtärsēˌȯid\ *adj* [in sense 1, fr. NL *Tarsioidea*; in sense 2, fr. *tarsier* + *-oid*] **1 :** of or relating to the Tarsioidea ⟨a ~ prosimian⟩ **2 :** resembling or resembling that of a tarsier ⟨a ~ foot⟩ ⟨a ~ stage of development⟩

[2]**tarsioid** \ˈ"\ *n* -s **:** a tarsioid primate **:** TARSIER

tar·si·oi·dea \ˌtärsēˈȯidēə\ *n pl*, *cap* [NL, fr. *Tarsius* + *-oidea*] *in some classifications* **:** a suborder or lesser division of primate mammals comprising the tarsier and extinct related mammals that are often placed with the lemurs in Prosimii

tar·si·pes \ˈtärsəˌpēz\ *n* [NL *Tarsiped-*, *Tarsipes*, fr. *tarsus* + L *ped-*, *pes* foot — more at FOOT] **:** a genus of marsupial mammals (family Phalangeridae) consisting of the honey possum

tar·si·us \ˈtärsēəs\ *n*, *cap* [NL, fr. *tarsus*; fr. the length of the tarsal bones] **:** a genus (the type of the family Tarsiidae) comprising the tarsiers

tarso- — see TARS-

tar·so·mere \ˈtärsəˌmi(ə)r\ *n* -s [*tars-* + *-mere*] **:** one of the movable subsegments of the insect tarsus

tar·so·metatarsal \ˌtär(ˌ)sō+ˌ==ˈ==\ *adj* [in sense 1, fr. *tars-* + *metatarsal*; in sense 2, fr. NL *tarsometatarsus* + E *-al*] **1 :** of or relating to the tarsus and metatarsus ⟨~ articulations⟩ **2 :** of or relating to the tarsometatarsus

tar·so·metatarsus \ˈ"+ˌ==ˈ==\ *n* [NL, fr. *tars-* + *metatarsus*] **:** the large bone of the shank of a bird consisting of the fused metatarsal bones united with the end of the distal tarsal elements; *also* **:** the segment of the limb this structure supports

[1]**tar·so·ne·mid** \ˌtärsəˈnēməd\ *adj* [NL *Tarsonemidae*] **:** of or relating to the Tarsonemidae

[2]**tarsonemid** \ˈ"\ *n* -s **:** a mite of the family Tarsonemidae

tar·so·nemi·dae \ˌtärsəˈneməˌdē, -nēm-\ *n pl*, *cap* [NL, fr. *Tarsonemus*, type genus + *-idae*] **:** a family of small soft-bodied usu. pale-colored mites including some that suck the juices of plants and others that are predaceous on insects and other minute animals

tar·so·ne·mus \-nēməs\ *n*, *cap* [NL, fr. *tars-* + *-nemus* (fr. Gk *nēma* thread) — more at NEEDLE] **:** the type genus of Tarsonemidae

tar·sor·rha·phy \tärˈsȯrəfē\ *n* -ES [*tars-* + *-rrhaphy*] **:** the operation of suturing the eyelids together entirely or in part

tar spot *n* [[1]*tar*] **1 a :** a leaf-blotch disease of maple, willow, or oak caused by fungi of the genus *Rhytisma* that produce raised black stromatic cushions on the foliage **b :** one of the spots produced **2 :** a disease of many grasses caused by a fungus (*Phyllacora graminis*) and resembling the tar spot of trees

tar still *n* **:** a still in which tar or similar material is distilled: as **a :** a still in which the heavy residuum from the first distillation in petroleum refining is rectified — compare CRUDE STILL **b :** an apparatus for testing esp. tars and asphalt

tar·sus \ˈtärsəs\ *n*, *pl* **tar·si** \-ˌsī, -(ˌ)sē\ [NL, fr. Gk *tarsos* frame of a wickerwork, flat basket, flat of the foot, ankle, flat edge of the eyelid; akin to Gk *tersesthai* to become dry — more at THIRST] **1 a :** the part of the foot of a vertebrate between the metatarsus and the leg **:** ANKLE **b :** the small bones that support this part of the limb **2 :** TARSOMETATARSUS **3 :** the distal part of the limb of an arthropod: **a :** the part of the limb of an insect distal to the tibia and usu. consisting of four or five segments and bearing two claws often with a pulvillus at the end **b :** the distal segment of the foot of a spider **4 :** the plate of strong dense fibrous connective tissue that forms the supporting structure of the eyelid

[1]**tart** \ˈtär|t, ˈtá|, *usu* |d.+V\ *adj* -ER/-EST [ME, fr. OE *teart* sharp, severe; akin to MHG *traz, truz* spite, hostility, stubbornness, MD *torten* to defy, challenge and prob. to OE *teran* to tear — more at TEAR] **1 a :** agreeably acid, sharp, or piquant to the taste **:** ACIDULOUS, PUNGENT ⟨a ~, fiery applejack —*N. Y. Times*⟩ ⟨soup ~ with quantities of fresh watercress —*Amer. Guide Series: N. Y. City*⟩ **b :** possessing a sharp or mildly acrid odor ⟨the ~ smell of rainy grass —V.S.Pritchett⟩ **2 :** marked by a biting, acrimonious, or cutting quality **:** CAUSTIC ⟨his ~ deflations of the more boastful accounts —H.A.Larrabee⟩ ⟨insert ~ rejoinders to the opposition's noisy interjections —Guy Eden⟩ ⟨a short, ~, scathing laugh —Mary McCarthy⟩ ⟨a sort of ~ but not sour cheerfulness —Arnold Bennett⟩ ⟨was decidedly ~ in his admonitions —A.T. Quiller-Couch⟩ **syn** see SOUR

[2]**tart** \ˈ"\ *n* -s [ME *tarte*, fr. MF] **1 :** a small pie or shell of pastry containing jelly, custard, or fruit and often having no top crust **2 :** a wanton or loose girl or woman; *esp* **:** PROSTITUTE ⟨morals was what kept you out of going to bed . . . with some ~ or other —Richard Llewellyn⟩

tart *abbr* **1** tartar **2** tartaric

tar·ta·go \ˈtärd·əˌgō\ *n* -s [Sp *tártago*] **:** PHYSIC NUT

[1]**tar·tan** \ˈtärtᵊn, ˈtát-\ *n* -s [prob. fr. MF *tiretaine* linsey-woolsey] **1 :** a plaid textile design of Scottish origin consisting of stripes of varying width and color against a solid ground and usu. patterned to designate a distinctive clan **2 a :** a twilled woolen fabric with a tartan design **b :** any of various imitative fabrics in other fibers with woven or printed designs **3 :** a garment of cloth with a tartan design ⟨the ~ was thrown over the shoulder —*Botany Call O' The Clans*⟩

[2]**tartan** \ˈ"\ *also* **tar·tana** \ˌ=ˈtanə, =ˈtänə\ *or* **tartane** \(ˈ)=¦tan\ *n* -s [F *tartane*, fr. It *tartana*] **:** a coasting vessel having one mast carrying a large lateen sail and a bowsprit with stay-sail or jib and used in the Mediterranean

[1]**tar·tar** \ˈtär|d·ər, ˈtá|d·ə(r, |tə-\ *n* -s [ME *tartre, tartar*, fr. MF & ML; MF *tartre*, fr. ML *tartarum*] **1 :** a substance consisting essentially of cream of tartar found in the juice of grapes and deposited in wine casks together with yeast and other suspended matters as a pale or dark reddish crust or sediment; *esp* **:** a recrystallized product yielding cream of tartar on further purification — compare [1]ARGOL, [3]LEE **2 a :** an incrustation deposited from a liquid **b :** an incrustation on the teeth consisting of salivary secretion, food residue, and various salts (as calcium carbonate or phosphate)

[2]**tartar** \ˈ"\ *n* -s [ME *Tartre*, fr. MF *Tartare*, prob. fr. ML *Tartarus*, modif. (influenced by L *Tartarus* the infernal regions) of Per *Tātār* — more at TATAR] **1** *cap* **:** a native or inhabitant of Tatary of Mongolic or Turkic origin **2** *usu cap* **:** TATAR 2 **3** *often cap* **:** a person of irritable, violent, or intractable temper **4 :** a person or thing that when grasped or tackled proves unexpectedly formidable ⟨had caught a ~, a fish too heavy even for his strength —Bud Jackson⟩ ⟨raillery seems to be a proper rod . . . but great caution and skill are necessary in the use of it or you may happen to catch a ~ —Earl of Chesterfield⟩

[3]**tartar** \ˈ"\ *adj*, *usu cap* **1 :** of, relating to, or characteristic of the region of Tatary extending indefinitely from the Sea of Japan to the Dnieper river **2 :** of, relating to, or characteristic of the Tartars

tartarated *var of* TARTRATED

tar·tar·ean \(ˈ)tär¦ta(a)rēən\ *adj*, *usu cap* [L *tartareus* (fr. Gk *tartareios*, fr. *Tartaros* Tartarus) + E *-an*] **:** of or relating to Tartarus **:** INFERNAL ⟨the *Tartarean* gloom in which he found himself —Edith Sitwell⟩

tartar emetic *n* **:** a poisonous efflorescent crystalline salt that has a sweetish metallic taste and is used chiefly in dyeing as a mordant, in poisoned baits as an insecticide, and in medicine as an expectorant and in the treatment of tropical diseases and formerly as an emetic — called also *antimony potassium tartrate*

tar·tar·e·ous \-ēəs\ *adj* [NL *tartareus*, fr. ML *tartarum* tartar + L *-eus* -eous] **:** consisting of or resembling tartar

tartar horse *n*, *usu cap T* [[3]*tartar*] **:** TARPAN

[1]**tar·tar·ian** \tärˈta(a)rēən\ *n* -s *usu cap* [ME *Tartarien*, fr. MF, fr. ML *Tartarus* + MF *-ien* -ian] *archaic* **:** TARTAR 1

[2]**tartarian** \(ˈ)=¦==\ *adj*, *usu cap* **:** TARTAR

tartarian aster *n*, *usu cap T* **:** a commonly cultivated late-blooming Siberian herb (*Aster tataricus*) often growing seven feet high and having very long basal leaves and blue to purple flower heads

tartarian buckwheat *n*, *usu cap T* **:** a buckwheat (*Fagopyrum tataricum*) introduced from Asia and distinguished by slender racemes of flowers and fruit with obtuse often corrugated angles — compare COMMON BUCKWHEAT

tartarian dogwood *n*, *usu cap T* **:** a tall Asiatic shrub (*Cornus alba*) sometimes cultivated as an ornamental and having opposite leaves, bluish white or whitish fruit, and often bright red twigs

tartarian honeysuckle *n*, *usu cap T* **:** a widely cultivated Asiatic bush honeysuckle (*Lonicera tatarica*) with cordate-ovate leaves and white to pink flowers

tartarian lamb *n*, *usu cap T* **:** SCYTHIAN LAMB

tartarian oat *n*, *usu cap T* **:** SIDE OAT

[1]**tar·tar·ic** \(ˈ)tär¦tarik (ˈ)tá¦t-, -arēk *also* -¦ter-\ *adj* [ISV [1]*tartar* + *-ic*; orig. formed as F *tartarique*] **:** of, relating to, derived from, or resembling tartar or tartaric acid

[2]**tartaric** \ˈ"\ *adj*, *usu cap* [[2]*tartar* + *-ic*] **:** TARTAR

tartaric acid *n* **:** a strong dicarboxylic acid HOOC(CHOH)₂COOH occurring in four optically isomeric crystalline forms; 2,3-dihydroxy-succinic acid: **a :** a dextrorotatory or D(+)-tartaric acid that is widely distributed in plants and esp. in fruits (as grapes and mountainash) both free and combined as salts, that is usu. obtained from tartar, and that is used chiefly in effervescent beverages and pharmaceutical preparations, in desserts and candies, in photography, in making salts and esters, and as a sequestrant **b :** a levorotatory or L(−)-tartaric acid obtained usu. by resolving the racemic acid **c :** RACEMIC ACID **d :** an internally compensated optically inactive meso acid obtained usu. as the crystalline monohydrate by heating the other forms with alkali

tar·ta·rin \ˈtärd·ərən\ *n* -s [F, prob. fr. *Tartarie* Tatary, indefinite region in Asia and Europe inhabited by Tatars (fr. ML *Tartaria*) + F *-in*] **:** SACRED BABOON

tar·tar·ish \ˈtärd·ərish\ *adj* **:** tending to form a tartar

tar·tar·ize \ˈtärd·əˌrīz\ *vt* -ED/-ING/-S **1 :** to impregnate or combine with tartar **:** subject to the action of tartar **2 :** to rectify with cream of tartar

tartarized antimony *n* **:** TARTAR EMETIC

tar·tar·ly \ˈtärd·ərlē\ *adj* **:** of, relating to, or resembling the manner of a Tartar **:** FEROCIOUS, ROUGH ⟨literature . . . needs the savage and ~ note, even the astringence of insult —Clifton Fadiman⟩

tar·tar·ous \ˈtärd·ərəs\ *adj* **:** containing, consisting of, or resembling tartar **:** due to or derived from tartar

tar·tar sauce *or* **tar·tare sauce** \ˌtär|d·|ər-, ˌtá|d·|ə-, |t|\ *n* [F *sauce tartare*] **:** a sauce made of mayonnaise dressing with chopped pickles, olives, capers, and parsley and usu. served with fish

tar·ta·rus \-rəs\ *n* -ES *usu cap* [L, fr. Gk *Tartaros*] **1 :** the infernal regions of ancient mythology — compare ELYSIUM, HADES **2 :** a place suggestive of Tartarus **:** HELL

tar·ta·ry buckwheat \ˈtärd·ərē-\ *n*, *usu cap T* [*tartary* fr. *Tartary* (Tatary), indefinite region in Asia and Europe inhabited by Tatars, fr. ME *Tartarie*, fr. MF, fr. ML *Tartaria*] **:** TARTARIAN BUCKWHEAT

tartar yeast *n* **:** a deposit of yeast cells, tartar, and other substances formed during the fermentation of grape juice in wine manufacture

tartemorion *var of* TETARTEMORION

tarter *comparative of* TART

[1]**tar·tes·sian** \tärˈteshən, -eshən\ *adj*, *usu cap* [L *tartessius* (fr. *Tartessus*, ancient kingdom on the southwestern coast of Spain) + E *-an* (adj. suffix)] **1 :** of, relating to, or characteristic of ancient Tartessus, Spain **2 :** of, relating to, or characteristic of the people of Tartessus

[2]**tartessian** \ˈ"\ *n* -s *cap* [L *Tartessii* the inhabitants of Tartessus + E *-an* (n. suffix)] **:** a native or inhabitant of ancient Tartessus

tartest *superlative of* TART

tar·tine \(ˈ)tär¦tēn\ *n* -s [F, fr. *tarte* tart, fr. MF] **:** a slice of bread spread with butter and usu. preserves or jam

tar·ti·ni's tone \tärˈtēnēz-\ *n*, *usu cap 1st T* [after Giuseppe *Tartini* †1770 Ital. violinist and composer] **:** COMBINATION TONE

tart·ish \ˈtärd·ish\ *adj* **:** somewhat tart ⟨a ~ taste⟩ — **tart·ish·ly** *adv*

tart·let \ˈtärtlət\ *n* -s **:** a small tart

tart·ly *adv* **:** in a tart manner; *esp* **:** with asperity ⟨was ~ called to account by . . . party spokesmen —F.A.Ogg & Harold Zink⟩

tart·ness *n* -ES **:** the quality or state of being tart ⟨behind her ~ lay a large tolerant humor —John Buchan⟩

tartr- *or* **tartro-** *comb form* [F, fr. *tartre* tartar, fr. MF — more at TARTAR] **:** tartar **:** tartaric acid ⟨*tartr*amide⟩

tar·tram·ic acid \(ˈ)tär¦tramik-\ *n* [ISV *tartr-* + *-am* + *-ic*] **:** a syrupy acid HOOC(CHOH)₂CONH₂ made by the action of aqueous ammonia on a tartaric ester **:** the half amide of tartaric acid

tar·tra·mide \ˈtär·trəˌmīd, -ˌməd\ *n* [ISV *tartr-* + *amide*] **:** a crystalline compound H₂NCO(CHOH)₂CONH₂ made by the action of alcoholic ammonia on a tartaric ester **:** the amide of tartaric acid

tar·trate \ˈtär·ˌtrāt\ *n* -s [ISV *tartr-* + *-ate*] **:** a salt or ester of tartaric acid

tar·trat·ed \-ˌād·əd\ *also* **tar·tar·at·ed** \ˈtärd·əˌrā-\ *adj* [*tartr-* or [1]*tartar* + *-ate* + *-ed*] **1 :** containing tartar **2 :** derived from tartar **3 :** combined with tartaric acid

tartrated antimony *n* **:** TARTAR EMETIC

tar·tra·zine \ˈtär·trəˌzēn, -ˌzən\ *n* [ISV *tartr-* + *azine*] **:** a yellow pyrazolone acid dye used chiefly in dyeing wool and silk, in making organic pigments, and in coloring foods and drugs — see DYE table I (under *Acid Yellow 23*)

tar·tron·ic acid \(ˈ)tär¦tränik-\ *n* [F *tartronique*, fr. *tartr-* + *-onique* (as in *malonique* malonic)] **:** a crystalline hydroxy acid HOCH(COOH)₂ obtained by reducing mesoxalic acid and by hydrolysis of bromo-malonic acid; hydroxy-malonic acid

tarts *pl of* TART

tar·tuffe *or* **tar·tufe** \(ˈ)tär¦tüf, -¦tüf\ *n* -s *usu cap* [F, fr. *Tartufe*, hypocritical hero of the play *Tartufe* (1669) by Molière (Jean Baptiste Poquelin) †1673 Fr. playwright] **:** a hypocritical pretender to religion; *broadly* **:** HYPOCRITE

tar·tuf·fery *or* **tar·tuf·fer·ie** \=ˈ=ərē\ *n*, *pl* **tartufferies** *usu cap* [F *tartufferie*, fr. *tartuffe* + *-rie* -ry] **:** the character or behavior of a Tartuffe **:** HYPOCRISY ⟨his chronicle of evasions, face-saving absurdities, and bureaucratic *Tartufferies* —Anthony West⟩

tar·tuf·fism \=ˈ=ˌizəm\ *n* -s *usu cap* **:** TARTUFFERY

tar·u·má \ˌtarəˈmä\ *n*, *pl* **tarumá** *or* **tarumas** *usu cap* **1 a :** an Arawakan people of southern British Guiana **b :** a member of such people **2 :** the language of the Tarumá people

Tar·via \ˈtärvēə\ *trademark* — used for a viscid surfacing and binding material for roads that is made from coal tar

tar–water \ˈ=ˌ==\ *n* **:** a cold infusion of tar in water formerly regarded as a cure-all

tarweed \ˈ=ˌ=\ *n* [[1]*tar* + *weed*; fr. their stickiness and heavy smell] **1 :** any of various California resinous glandular plants esp. of the genera *Madia* and *Grindelia* **2 :** MOUNTAIN MISERY **3 :** FIDDLE-NECK 2

tar·whine \ˈtär(ˌh)wīn\ *n* -s [origin unknown] *Austral* **:** either of two sea breams (family Sparidae): **a :** SILVER BREAM 1 **b :** a closely related fish (*Rhabdosargus australis*)

tarwood \ˈ=ˌ=\ *n* [[1]*tar* + *wood*] **:** a New Zealand silver pine (*Dacrydium colensoi*) of conical habit with long slender flexuous branches

tar·zan \ˈtärzᵊn, ˈtáz- *also* -ˌzan *or* -ˌzaa(ə)n\ *n* -s *usu cap* [fr. *Tarzan*, hero of the adventure stories of Edgar Rice Burroughs †1950 Am. writer] **:** a strong agile person of heroic proportions and bearing ⟨a chimpanzee can easily run away . . . and once in the trees, no human *Tarzan* is half a match for it —Weston La Barre⟩

TAS *abbr* true air speed

ta·sa·ji·llo \ˌtäsəˈhē(ˌ)(y)ō\ *n* -s [MexSp, dim. of *tasajo*] **:** an arborescent prickly pear (*Opuntia leptocaulis*) of the southwestern U. S. and Mexico with slender cylindrical joints and greenish yellow flowers

ta·sa·jo *also* **tas·sa·jo** \təˈsä(ˌ)hō\ *n* -s [Sp *tasajo*, fr. OSp, piece of meat; akin to Pg *tossalho* large piece of something to eat] **1 :** jerked meat; *esp* **:** jerked beef **2** [MexSp, fr. Sp] **:** any of several cacti of the southwestern U. S. and Mexico; *esp* **:** CHOLLA

tas·bih \ˈtäzˌbē\ *n* -s [Ar] **:** a Muslim rosary or set of 33, 66, or 99 prayer beads used in reciting the 99 titles of Allah and in meditation

tas-de-charge \ˌtädəˈshärzh\ *n* -s [F *tas de charge*, lit., pile for the burden] **:** the portion of a group of vault ribs that occurs just above the spring where the ribs are still joined together

tash *var of* TACHE

ta·shi lama \ˈtäshē-\ *or* **te·shu lama** \ˈtā(ˌ)shü-\ *n*, *usu cap T&L* [*tashi*, *teshu* fr. *Tashi* (*Lunpo*), *Teshu* (*Lunpo*), monastery in Tibet presided over by the Panchen Lamas] **:** PANCHEN LAMA

tash·kent *or* **tash·kend** \(ˈ)täsh¦kent, (ˈ)tash-\ *adj*, *usu cap* [fr. *Tashkent* (*Tashkend*), U. S. S. R.] **:** of or from the city of Tashkent, U. S. S. R. **:** of the kind or style prevalent in Tashkent

tash·lik *or* **tash·lich** \ˈtäshlik\ *n* -s [Heb *tashlīkh* thou will cast (as in Mic 7:19), 2d sing. imperf. of *hishlīkh* to cast] **:** a symbolic propitiatory rite that is celebrated by Orthodox Jews traditionally on the afternoon of Rosh Hashanah and that consists in assembling along the banks of a running stream, reciting Micah 7:18–20 and penitential prayers, and shaking one's garments as if casting one's sins into the water to be washed or swept away

[1]**ta·si·an** \ˈtäsēən\ *adj*, *usu cap* [(*Deir*) *Tasa*, village in Upper Egypt, type site of the Tasian culture + E *-ian*] **:** of or relating to a predynastic neolithic culture of Upper Egypt earlier than the Badarian

[2]**tasian** \ˈ"\ *n* -s *usu cap* **:** one of the ancient Egyptian people who produced the Tasian culture

[1]**task** \ˈtask, ˈtaa(ə)sk, ˈtaisk, ˈtásk\ *n* -s [ME *taske*, *tasque*, fr. ONF *tasque*, fr. (assumed) VL *tasca* task, remuneration, alter. of *taxa*, fr. L *taxare* to touch, feel, rate, compute — more at TAX] **1 a :** a specific piece or amount of work usu. assigned by another and often required or expected to be finished within a certain time ⟨the ~s that were set for chemistry at last year's examination for the school-leaving certificate of the high schools —*Jour. of Chem. Education*⟩ ⟨a novel . . . I had once read as a school holiday ~ —Adrian Bell⟩ **b :** something that has to be done or needs to be done and usu. involves some difficulty or problem ⟨Greece . . . passed on to Macedon and thence to Rome that ~ of reconciling the individual and the class with the whole —G.L.Dickinson⟩ **:** something hard or unpleasant to do ⟨deciphering some people's handwriting is quite a ~⟩ **c :** the job allotted to someone as his duty or to some inanimate thing as its proper function ⟨forecasting is . . . one of the most important ~s of the statistician in business —M.K.Adler⟩ ⟨every inch of material . . . from crypt to vault . . . had its ~ —Henry Adams⟩ **2** *obs* **:** TAX, IMPOST **3 :** subjection to adverse criticism **:** REPRIMAND — used in the expressions *to take*, *call*, or *bring one to task* **4 :** the performance that is required of the subject in a psychological experiment or test and that is usu. made known to a human subject by verbal instructions **5 :** a definite usu. operational objective assigned to a unit or group of units in the armed forces **6 :** a set of actions performed to accomplish a specific purpose whose accomplishment is one of the duties though usu. not the only duty of an employee holding a particular position

syn DUTY, ASSIGNMENT, JOB, STINT, CHORE: TASK refers to a specific piece of work or service usu. imposed by authority or circumstance, sometimes undertaken voluntarily ⟨some person or some organization whose *task* it is to realize the daydreams of the masses —Aldous Huxley⟩ ⟨the spirit in which judge or advocate is to look upon his *task* —B.N.Cardozo⟩ DUTY is likely to indicate work, service, or conduct enjoined on a person because of his rank, status, occupation, or affiliation; it is likely in most uses to suggest obligation, often moral ⟨it is emphatically the province and *duty* of the judicial department to say what the law is —John Marshall⟩ ⟨some of the military branches having a preferred status . . . had higher pay scales for less dangerous *duties* —Kingsley Davis⟩ ASSIGNMENT suggests a specific amount of work or sort of service assigned authoritatively ⟨it is not our *assignment* to settle specific ques-

tions of territories —H.S.Truman⟩ JOB is a general term wide in suggestion ranging from voluntary undertaking of some signal service down to an assigned bit of menial work ⟨a job that suffers from some relative poverty in charm, such as totting up endless small sums at a desk or feeding coal in at the door of a furnace —C.E.Montague⟩ STINT stresses carefully or equitably measured or timed apportionment of work ⟨took to doing "German Romance" as my daily work, ten pages daily my stint —Thomas Carlyle⟩ CHORE is likely to suggest minor routine activity necessary for continuing satisfactory operating, as of farm or office ⟨leisure after the chores and happy meeting places where the farmer and his family might play —Roger Burlingame⟩

²**task** \"\ vt -ED/-ING/-S [ME tasken, fr. taske, tasque, n.] **1** obs : TAX **2** : to impose a task upon : assign a definite amount of business, labor, or duty to ⟨there ~ thy maids, and exercise the loom —John Dryden⟩ **3 a** obs : REPRIMAND **b** archaic : ACCUSE, CHARGE — often used with with ⟨too impudent to ~ me with those errors —Francis Beaumont & John Fletcher⟩ **4 a** : to oppress with great labor : keep busy at or as if at a task : BURDEN ⟨~s his mind with details⟩ **b** : to test as by the imposition of a burden

task-and-bonus system \'ˌ�=ˌ=-ˌ=\ n : a system of incentive wage payment whereby a worker receives a guaranteed hourly rate and for accomplishing or bettering a set task a bonus that is a percentage of his hourly rate for the time allowed for the task

task·er \-kə(r)\ n [ME, fr. taske, tasque, n. + -er] **1** chiefly dial : one that performs a task; specif : a laborer (as a thresher or reaper) at piecework **2** : one that imposes a task : TASK-MASTER

task force n **1** : a temporary grouping of armed forces units under one commander for the purpose of accomplishing a definite usu. operational objective ⟨as taking an island from an enemy⟩ ⟨a task force of over 50 naval vessels⟩ ⟨a small task force that might, say, ... blow up an atomic stockpile —New Yorker⟩ ⟨a task force to test military equipment under polar conditions —Frank Illingworth⟩ **2 a** : a group of persons with various specialties that is charged with investigating a particular problem (as in industry or government) and with formulating proposals for its solution and that frequently is part of a larger group dealing with a complex of related problems ⟨the commission promptly secured the service of three hundred experts, who were assigned to twenty-four research committees called task forces —B.D.L.Nash & Cornelius Lynde⟩ **b** : any group of persons charged with the accomplishment of a definite objective ⟨a courtroom task force that tore the state's case to shreds —G.A.Morran⟩

task group n **1** : a part of a naval task force **2** : TASK FORCE 2

taskmaster \'ˌ=ˌ==\ n : one that imposes a task or burdens another with labor : one whose duty is to assign tasks : OVER-SEER

task·mas·ter·ship \'ˌ=ˌ==ˌship\ n : the status or position of a taskmaster

taskmistress \'ˌ=ˌ==\ n : a female taskmaster

tasks pl of TASK, pres 3d sing of TASK

tasksetter \'ˌ=ˌ==\ n : one that sets a task: **a** : one that sets the tasks of workers by designating the output to be attained or the time to be consumed and that also usu. determines the pay rate when an incentive plan is used **b** : a worker whose rate of output on a specified task is used as a standard for other workers

tasksetting \'ˌ=ˌ==\ n : performance of the duties of a task-setter

task time n : the time set in an incentive wage system as proper for the performance of an industrial operation by a worker

task unit n : a part of a naval task group

taskwork \'ˌ=ˌ=\ n [ME taske werke] **1** : PIECEWORK **2** : hard work

tas·let \'tasˌlet\ n [tasse + -let] : TASSE

tas·ma·nia \taz'mānē, -nyə\ adj, usu cap [fr. Tasmania, island in the southern Pacific] **:** of or from the island or the state of Tasmania : of the kind or style prevalent in Tasmania : TASMANIAN

¹**tas·ma·ni·an** \-ən\ n -s cap [Tasmania + E -an] **1** : a native or inhabitant of Tasmania; specif : one of the extinct aborigines of Tasmania **2** : any of several languages of the Tasmanian aborigines

²**tasmanian** \"\ adj, usu cap : of or belonging to Tasmania

tasmanian blue gum n, usu cap T : a blue gum (Eucalyptus globulus)

tasmanian devil n, usu cap T : a powerful carnivorous burrowing marsupial (Sarcophilus harrisii) formerly widely distributed in Australia but now limited to the wilder parts of Tasmania that is about the size of a large cat or badger, has a black coat marked with white on the chest, and in many of its habits resembles the raccoon

tasmanian dodge n, usu cap T : a device used to cast fraudulent ballots in an election that usu. involves the theft of an unmarked ballot by one voter, its delivery to the person buying votes for marking outside the polling place, and its deposit in the ballot box by another voter who in turn steals a new ballot to continue the process

tasmanian myrtle n, usu cap T : an Australian evergreen tree (Nothofagus cunninghamii)

tasmanian oak n, usu cap T : any of several Australian trees of the genus Eucalyptus (esp. E. obliqua)

tasmanian sassafras n, usu cap T : SASSAFRAS 3a(1)

tasmanian wolf also **tasmanian tiger** n, usu cap 1st T : a carnivorous dasyurid marsupial (Thylacinus cynocephalus) formerly common in Australia but now limited to the remoter parts of Tasmania that is doglike in appearance and somewhat larger than a fox and has a smooth grayish brown pelt conspicuously cross-striped with black on the hinder half of the back and the base of the tapering tail

tas·ma·nite \'tazmə̇ˌnīt\ n -s [Tasmania, its locality + E -ite] **1** : a compound of carbon, hydrogen, oxygen, and sulfur in minute reddish brown scales in shale **2** : a light-colored shaly coal that is composed largely of the compound tasmanite and yields a large quantity of petroleum on dry distillation — called also combustible shale

tas·ma·noid \'tazmə̇ˌnȯid\ adj, usu cap [Tasmania + E -oid] : of, belonging to, or constituting an ethnic group of northern Queensland that is characterized by pygmy build, round skulls, and curly hair

tass \'tas\ n -ES [ME tasse, fr. Ar tass, tasseh, fr. Per tast] **1** chiefly Scot : a drinking cup or bowl **2** chiefly Scot : a small drink esp. of liquor

tassajo var of TASAJO

tasse \'tas\ or **tace** \"\, 'tās\ n -s [perh. fr. MF tasse purse, pouch, fr. MHG tasche pouch, pocket, fr. OHG tasca; akin to OS dasga pouch, MD tassche, tessche; all fr. (assumed) VL tasca task, remuneration, money pouch — more at TASK] : one of a series of overlapping metal plates in a suit of armor that form a short skirt covering the part of the body just below the waist — see ARMOR illustration

¹**tas·sel** \'tasȯl, 'taas-, 'tais-, 'täs- also 'tȯs- or 'tȯs-\ n -s [ME, clasp, tassel, fr. OF, fr. (assumed) VL taxillus small die, alter. of L taxillus small die, dim. of (assumed) OL taxlus (whence L talus ankle, anklebone, die)] **1** : a pendent ornament used on clothing, curtains, and other articles that is made by laying parallel a bunch of cords or threads of even length and fastening the bunch at one end **2** : something resembling or felt to resemble a tassel: as **a** : the male inflorescence of some plants esp. at the top of a stalk of corn — compare SILK **b** : the beard of a male turkey **3 a** : a pendant of woolen yarn worn on an archer's wrist and used for wiping arrows

tassel 1

²**tassel** \"\ vb tasseled or tasselled; tasseling or tasselling \-s(ə)liŋ\ tassels [ME tasselen, fr. tassel, n.] vt : to adorn with or as if with tassels : attach tassels to ~ vi : to put forth inflorescences ⟨when the corn begins to ~⟩ — often used with out

³**tassel** var of TIERCEL

⁴**tassel** var of TORSEL

tassel bush n **1** : a shrub (Garrya elliptica) of the Pacific coast of the U.S. **2** : BEAR BRUSH

tas·sel·er \-s(ə)lə(r)\ n -s : a worker who makes tassels

tasselfish \'˻=ˌ=\ n **1** : any of several threadfins **2** Africa : any of several croakers of the family Sciaenidae

tassel flower n **1** : a tropical Asiatic annual herb (Emilia sagittata) sometimes cultivated for its small tassel-shaped heads of scarlet flowers **2** : PRAIRIE CLOVER **3** : any of several plants of the genus Brickellia; esp : a perennial herb (B. umbellata) of the western U.S. **4** : LOVE-LIES-BLEEDING 1

tassel-gentle var of TERCEL GENTLE

tassel grass n : an aquatic herb of the genus Ruppia; esp : TASSEL PONDWEED

tassel hyacinth n : a grape hyacinth (Muscari comosum monstrosum) that bears only sterile flowers which are bluish violet with a fringed corolla and are borne in loose clusters on a branched scape

tasselled crab n : a small dull brown or gray hairy crab (Pilumnus fissilfrons) common on Australian seashores

tassel plant n : BAY CEDAR 2

tassel pondweed n : a marine tassel grass (Ruppia maritima)

tas·sely or **tas·sel·ly** \-s(ə)lē\ adj : decorated with tassels : resembling a tassel

tas·set \'tasȯt\ n -s [tasse + -et] : TASSE

tas·sie \'tasi\ n -s [tass + -ie] chiefly Scot : a small cup

tastable var of TASTEABLE

¹**taste** \'tāst\ vb -ED/-ING/-s [ME tasten to touch, examine by touch, test, feel, taste, fr. OF taster, fr. (assumed) VL tastare, alter. of taxitare, freq. of L taxare to touch — more at TAX] vt **1** obs : TOUCH **b** : TEST **2** : to become acquainted with by experience : gain firsthand knowledge of : FEEL, UNDERGO ⟨~ ... the privations of modern warfare —Earle Birney⟩ ⟨tasted the sweet delights of office —J.H.Plumb⟩ **3 a** : to ascertain the flavor of by taking a small quantity into the mouth ⟨tasted the tea and then added more sugar; specif : to test the quality of (a food or drink) by the taste ⟨~ wine⟩ **b** : to test the quality of as if by tasting ⟨the rare ability to ~ a sentence before he writes or utters it —E.R.Murrow⟩ **4 a** (1) : to eat or drink esp. in small quantities ⟨the first food he has tasted since yesterday morning⟩ (2) : to experience to a slight extent ⟨have at least tasted these evils —J.C.Powys⟩ **b** : to consume a sample of (food or drink prepared for another) in order to test whether poison is present **5** : to perceive, recognize, or experience by or as if by the sense of taste **6** : to impart a flavor to : FLAVOR **7** chiefly dial : to make a pleasant taste in (the mouth) : please (a person) by an agreeable taste **8** archaic : LIKE, APPRECIATE, ENJOY **9** obs : to copulate with **10** : SMELL **1a** ~ vi **1** : to exercise the sense of taste : distinguish flavors **2 a** (1) : to eat or drink a part : eat or drink a little : eat or drink even a little — often used with of ⟨~ of these conserves —Shak.⟩ ⟨food whereof we wretched seldom ~ —John Milton⟩ (2) : to have a limited experience or portion — often used with of ⟨age but ~s of pleasures, youth devours —John Dryden⟩ **b** : to consume a sample of food or drink prepared for another and thereby test whether poison is present **3** : to ascertain the flavor or quality of something by or as if by taking a small quantity into the mouth — often used with of **4** : to have perception, experience, or enjoyment : PARTAKE — often used with of ⟨~ of nature's bounty⟩ ⟨the valiant never ~ of death but once —Shak.⟩ **5 a** : to have a certain flavor when applied to the taste organs : excite a particular sensation by which the specific quality or flavor is distinguished ⟨the milk ~s sour⟩ ⟨a liquid that ~s like vinegar⟩ ⟨the salad ~s of garlic⟩ **b** : to have a particular quality that is perceived as if by taste ⟨when will life ~ clean again —Laurence Binyon⟩ — **taste blood** : to experience a new and keen pleasure esp. as a result of defeating an opponent

²**taste** \"\ n -s [ME tast touch, action of touching, testing, testing, taste, fr. OF, fr. taster] **1** obs : TEST **2 a** obs : the act of tasting with or as if with the mouth **b** : a small amount tasted or eaten **c** : a small or tiny amount : BIT, SAMPLE; esp : a small sample of an experience ⟨a ~ of high life —Robert Westerby⟩ **3 a** : the power of perceiving flavor : gustatory sensation or the capacity for it **b** : the one of the special senses that is concerned with the perception and distinguishing of the sweet, sour, bitter, or salty quality of a dissolved substance, is mediated through the taste buds of the tongue, is conducted centrally by the glossopharyngeal and lingual nerves, and is coordinated esp. by centers in the posteroventral nuclei of the thalamus **4** : the objective sweet, sour, bitter, or salty quality of a dissolved substance as perceived by the sense of taste **5 a** : a sensation produced by the stimulation of the sense of taste : the total blend of sensations that is obtained from a substance in the mouth and that typically consists not only of sensations produced by stimulating the sense of taste but also esp. the sense of smell : FLAVOR ⟨the ~ of an orange⟩ **b** : the distinctive quality of an experience esp. with reference to the emotion that it consist of or arouses ⟨the flat ~ of another disillusionment —C.J.Rolo⟩ — often used with in one's mouth ⟨his attempt to cheat me left a bad ~ in my mouth⟩ **6 a** : individual preference : LIKING, RELISH, FONDNESS, INCLINATION ⟨a ~ for music⟩ ⟨the note of sadness ... which the poets were to find so much more to their ~ than the note of gladness —Henry Adams⟩ ⟨expensive ~s⟩ ⟨walking too fast for my ~⟩ ⟨all ~s are legitimate, and it is not necessary to account for them —Virgil Thomson⟩ ⟨not a historian by training or ~ —D.W.Brogan⟩ **b** : preference or liking in food or drink ⟨a ~ for rare beef⟩ ⟨season to ~⟩ **7 a** : the power or practice of discerning and enjoying whatever constitutes excellence esp. in the fine arts and belles lettres : critical judgment, discernment, or appreciation ⟨~ is nothing but sensibility to the different degrees and kinds of excellence in the works of art or nature —William Hazlitt⟩ ⟨establishing sound canons of literary ~ —Encyc. Americana⟩ ⟨the laws of ~ differ ... widely in different nations —W.H.Prescott⟩ ⟨a well developed and cultivated ... musical ~ —P.H.Lang⟩ **b** : manner indicative of such discernment or appreciation : aesthetic quality : style of artistic production or of any behavior capable of being judged on an aesthetic basis ⟨a pleasant room upstairs, Victorian in its ~ —R.M.Stern⟩ ⟨the chapters on ... courtship and conquest are thoroughly engrossing and written with ~ —J.M.Flagler⟩ ⟨her book is a minor miracle of ... good ~ —Lon Tinkle⟩ ⟨people who mock educational deficiencies of others show bad ~ —David Minsberg⟩

syn TASTE, SAPIDITY, FLAVOR, SAVOR, TANG, RELISH, and SMACK can signify in common that property of a substance that makes it perceptible to the gustatory sense; TASTE merely indicates the property ⟨the taste of cherries⟩ ⟨the taste of castor oil⟩ ⟨there was the cold taste of fear in his mouth —Gordon Merrick⟩ SAPIDITY implies a highly perceptible taste as opposed to blandness ⟨cook all sapidity out of the food⟩ FLAVOR suggests both taste and smell acting together ⟨the flavor of coffee⟩ ⟨the tart flavor of quinces⟩ ⟨the strong flavor of ripe muskmelons⟩ SAVOR usu. stresses a sensitivity of palate in detection of flavor, esp. delicate or pervasive ⟨the savor of roast pheasant and a good dry wine⟩ ⟨the savor of aristocracy about a man⟩ TANG applies chiefly to a sharp, penetrating, often pungent, savor, flavor, or odor ⟨the tang of outdoor cooking⟩ ⟨the tang of saltwater spray —Frank Waters⟩ RELISH and SMACK are close to SAVOR and usu. connote enjoyment, SMACK often suggesting a flavor that is added to or different from one characteristic of a substance ⟨the relish of wine —David Hume †1776⟩ ⟨a smack of pepper in a stew⟩

³**taste** \"\ n -s [origin unknown] : a narrow thin silk ribbon

taste·able also **tast·able** \-təbəl\ adj : capable of being tasted

taste bud also **taste bulb** or **taste goblet** n : an end organ mediating the sensation of taste, lying chiefly in the epithelium of the tongue and esp. in the walls of the vallate papillae, and consisting of a conical or flask-shaped mass made up partly of supporting cells and partly of neuroepithelial sensory cells that terminate peripherally in short hairlike processes which project into the pore in the overlying epithelium and by which communication with the mouth cavity is effected

taste cell n : a neuroepithelial cell that is located in a taste bud and is the actual receptor of the sensation of taste — called also gustatory cell

taste cup n : a sensillum in insects that has a gustatory function

tasted \'tāstə̇d\ adj : having such a taste — used in combinations ⟨pleasant-tasted⟩ ⟨sweet-tasted⟩

taste·ful \'tāstfəl\ adj **1** : TASTY 1a **2** : having, exhibiting, or conforming to good taste ⟨~ simplicity⟩ ⟨~ furniture⟩ ⟨a ~ artisan⟩ — **taste·ful·ly** \-fəlē, -li\ adv — **taste·ful·ness** \-nə̇s\ n -ES

taste hair n : the hairlike termination of a neuroepithelial cell in a taste bud

taste·less \'tāstlə̇s\ adj **1** : having no sense of taste : unable to distinguish flavors **2 a** : having no taste : INSIPID ⟨~ vegetables⟩ **b** : arousing no interest : DULL, UNINTERESTING ⟨the tale comes to a flat and ~ end, despite some tension in the last chapters —R.C.Carpenter⟩ **3** : not having or not exhibiting good taste : lacking in critical discernment : not being in good taste ⟨coarse and ~ luxury —F.W.Farrar⟩ — **taste·less·ly** adv — **taste·less·ness** n -ES

taste panel n : a group of persons having the joint duty to taste a product in order to determine factors relating to its flavor

tast·er \'tāstə(r)\ n -s [ME, fr. tasten to taste + -er] **1** : one that tastes: as **a** : a person that has the duty of tasting food or drink prepared for another person (as a king) and thereby testing whether poison is present **b** : a person employed to sample a food product or beverage to determine its quality and taste appeal before it is offered for sale to the public **2** : a person able to taste the chemical phenylthiourea **2** : a device used in tasting or sampling something: as **a** : a shallow metal cup used in tasting wine **b** : a fluted tool for taking a sample of cheese or butter **3 a** : a small amount esp. of food or drink taken as a sample : TASTE **b** Brit : a serving of ice cream in a shallow glass dish

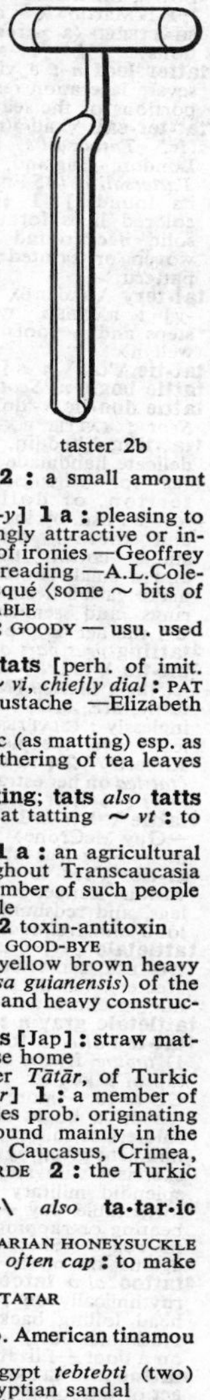

taster 2b

tastes pres 3d sing of TASTE, pl of TASTE

tast·i·ly \'tāstə̇lē, -li\ adv **1** : in a tasteful manner ⟨~ decorated⟩ **2** : in a tasty manner ⟨~ cooked⟩

tast·i·ness \-tēnə̇s, -tin-\ n -ES **1** : the quality or state of being tasteful **2** : the quality or state of being tasty

tasting n -s [ME, fr. gerund of tasten to taste] **1** : the act of one that tastes **2** : a small amount : SAMPLE

¹**tasty** \'tāstē, -ti\ adj -ER/-EST [²taste + -y] **1 a** : pleasing to the taste : SAVORY ⟨a ~ pie⟩ **b** : strikingly attractive or interesting ⟨the tastiest irony in a book full of ironies —Geoffrey Moore⟩ ⟨gusto and detail that make ~ reading —A.L.Coleman; esp : arousing interest by being risqué ⟨some ~ bits of gossip⟩ **2** : TASTEFUL 2 syn see PALATABLE

²**tasty** \"\ n -ES : something good to eat : GOODY — usu. used in pl.

¹**tat** \'tat\ vb tatted; tatted; tatting; tats [perh. of imit. origin] vt, chiefly dial : to touch lightly ~ vi, chiefly dial : PAT ⟨he stood, frowned, tatted at his moustache —Elizabeth Bowen⟩

²**tat** \'tät\ n -s [Hindi tāṭ] : a coarse fabric (as matting) esp. as stretched on a frame and used for the withering of tea leaves

³**tat** \'tat\ n -s [by shortening] : ⁵TATTOO

⁴**tat** also **tatt** \"\ vb tatted; tatted; tatting; tats also tatts [back-formation fr. tatting] vi : to work at tatting ~ vt : to make by tatting

⁵**tat** \'tät\ n -s usu cap [Russ, fr. Turk] **1 a** : an agricultural people living in scattered groups throughout Transcaucasia and possibly allied to the Tajiks **b** : a member of such people **2** : the Iranian language of the Tat people

TAT abbr **1** thematic apperception test **2** toxin-antitoxin

ta-ta \(')tä¦tä\ interj [origin unknown] : GOOD-BYE

ta·ta·ju·ba \ˌtätə'zhübə\ n -s [Pg] : the yellow brown heavy durable wood of a Brazilian tree (Bagassa guianensis) of the family Moraceae that is used for furniture and heavy construction

ta·ta·mi \tə'tämē\ n, pl tatami or tatamis [Jap] : straw matting used as a floor covering in a Japanese home

ta·tar \'tädə(r), -ätə-\ n -s usu cap [Per Tātār, of Turkic origin; akin to Kazan Tatar & Turk Tatar] **1** : a member of one of the numerous chiefly Turkic peoples prob. originating in Manchuria and Mongolia and now found mainly in the Tatar republic of the U.S.S.R., the north Caucasus, Crimea, and sections of Siberia — see GOLDEN HORDE **2** : the Turkic language of any of the Tatar peoples

ta·tar·i·an \tä'ta(a)rēən, -ter-, -tär-\ also **ta·tar·ic** \-'tarik\ adj, usu cap : TURKIC

tatarian honeysuckle n, usu cap T : TARTARIAN HONEYSUCKLE

ta·tar·ize \'tädə̇ˌrīz, -ätə-\ vt -ED/-ING/-S often cap : to make Tatarian

tatar of the volga usu cap T&V : KAZAN TATAR

tatar sable n, usu cap T : KOLINSKY 1b

ta·tau·pa \tä'tȯpə\ n -s [Pg, fr. Tupi] : a So. American tinamou (Crypturellus tataupa)

tat·beb \'tatˌbeb\ n -s [F, modif. of Egypt tebtebti (two) sandals, soles of the feet] : an ancient Egyptian sandal

tate \'tāt\ n -s [perh. of Scand origin; akin to Icel tæta tuft, tatter, fiber; akin to ON tō tuft of grass, tuft of wool — more at TOW] **1** dial Brit : a small piece (as of wool or hay) **2** dial Brit : a lock of hair

ta·ter \'tādə(r)\ n -s [by shortening & alter.] dial : POTATO

ta·tha·ga·ta \tə̇ˌtägə'tä\ n -s [Skt tathāgata, fr. tathā thus + gata gone, come, arrived, fr. gamati he goes — more at COME] Buddhism : an enlightened one : a finder of truth : one who has attained perfection

ta·tha·ga·ta·gar·bha \tə̇ˌtägə̇təˈgərbə\ n -s [Skt tathāgatagarbha, fr. tathāgata + garbha womb — more at DOLPHIN] Buddhism : the eternal and immutable matrix of all reality : the womb of the absolute and the essence of Buddhahood

ta·tha·ta \'tädə̇ˌtä\ n -s [Pali tathatā, fr. tathā thus, fr. Skt; akin to Skt tad, neut. demonstrative pron. — more at THAT] : SUCHNESS 2

ta·tian·ist \'tāsh(ē)ənə̇st\ n -s usu cap [Tatian, 2d cent. A.D. Christian writer + E -ist] : ENCRATITE

ta·tie \'tādē\ n -s [by shortening & alter.] dial : POTATO

tatoo var of TATTOO

ta·tou also **ta·tu** \tə'tü\ n -s [F tatou & Pg tatú, tatu, fr. Tupi & Guarani tatú, tatu] : ARMADILLO; esp : GIANT ARMADILLO

tat·ou·ay \'tatü̇ˌā, ˌätü̇'ī\ n -s [Sp tatuay, fr. Guarani tatu aí, lit., worthless armadillo; fr. the inedibility of the flesh] : a large armadillo (Cabassous unicinctus) of tropical So. America that has 12 or 13 movable bands or plates around the body

tatou peba n : PEBA

tat·pur·u·sha \tat'pu̇rəshə, ˌtət-\ n -s [Skt tatpuruṣa, lit., his servant (a compound of this type), fr. tad-, tat- that one (fr. tad, neut. demonstrative pron.) + puruṣa man, servant] **1** : a class of compound words having as first constituent a noun or noun stem that modifies the second constituent by standing in the relation to it of possessor (as in sheepskin), thing possessed (as in motorboat), object of action (as in shoemaker), location or habitat (as in tree toad), agent (as in man-made), instrument (as in landlocked), or any of numerous other relations **2** — see ¹DEPENDENT 2f

¹**tats** \'tats\ n pl [origin unknown] slang : DICE; esp : false dice

²**tats** pres 3d sing of TAT, pl of TAT

tatt var of TAT

tat-tat \(')tat'tat\ also **tat-tat-tat** \'tatˌtat'tat\ n -s [imit.] : RAT-A-TAT

tatted past of TAT

¹**tat·ter** \'tadə(r), -ätə-\ n -s [ME tater, tatter, of Scand origin; akin to ON tǫturr tatter, rag; akin to OE tætteca rag, tatter, OHG zotta matted hair, tuft — more at TOD] **1 a** : a part torn and left hanging : RAG, SHRED ⟨tear a passion to ~s —Shak.⟩ ⟨a stand of ragged gums that drip their ~s of gray bark on the gravelly paths —T.A.G.Hungerford⟩ **b** tatters pl : tattered clothing : RAGS ⟨the tramp was dressed in ~s⟩ **2** archaic : TATTERDEMALION ⟨a scarecrow ~ of a man —William Goyen⟩ **3** also **tat·ter·er** \-ərə(r)\ : one that collects waste with a cart or barrow : a rag gatherer

²**tatter** \"\ vb -ED/-ING/-S vt : to tear into shreds : to make ragged ⟨~ a flag⟩ ~ vi : to become ragged

³**tat·ter** \'tatə(r)\ vi -ED/-ING/-S [imit.] dial Brit : BUSTLE, HURRY

⁴**tat·ter** \'tadə(r)\ n -s [⁴tat + -er] : one that makes tatting

¹**tat·ter·de·ma·lion** \ˌtadə(r)də̇'mālyən, -ətə(-, -dē-, -'mal-, -lēən\ n -s [¹tatter + -demalion, of unknown origin] : a person

dressed in ragged clothing : one who is disreputable in appearance : RAGAMUFFIN, SCARECROW

2tatterdemalion \"\ *adj* **1 a :** ragged or disreputable in dress or appearance ⟨~ and careless in dress, with unpolished boots, baggy trousers, and shapeless cloth cap —Vernon Leonard⟩ **b :** being in a decayed state or condition : BROKEN-DOWN, DILAPIDATED ⟨the old ~ farmhouse —Theodore Dreiser⟩ **2 :** BEGGARLY, DISREPUTABLE ⟨the most ~ party ever seen in American politics —H.L.Mencken⟩

tat·tered \'tad·ə(r)d, -atə-\ *adj* [ME *tatered*, fr. *tater* + *-ed*] **1 :** wearing ragged clothes ⟨a ~ barefoot boy⟩ **2 :** torn in shreds : RAGGED ⟨going about in shirts which have become ~ shreds in their struggles —E.H.Spicer⟩ ⟨a ~ book⟩ **3 a :** BROKEN-DOWN, DILAPIDATED ⟨decaying houses along ~ paved streets —P.B.Martin⟩ ⟨~ cottages —Jane Austen⟩ **b :** DISRUPTED, SHATTERED ⟨a ~ remnant of its former strength⟩ ⟨~ conventions⟩

tatter leaf *n* **:** a virus disease of sweet cherries marked by severe laceration resulting from the dropping out of necrotic portions of the leaves

tat·ter·sall \'tad·ə(r),sȯl, -atə-, -,səl\ *or* **tattersall check** *n* -s [fr. *Tattersall's* horse market, London, England, after Richard *Tattersall* †1795 English horseman, its founder] **1 :** a pattern of colored lines forming squares of solid background **2 :** a fabric woven or printed in a tattersall pattern

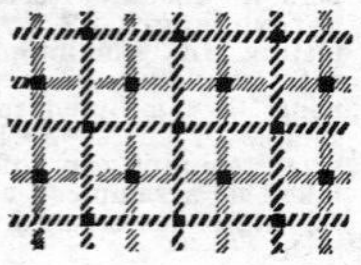
tattersall 1

tat·tery \'tad·ərē\ *adj* [1*tatter* + *-y*] **:** RAGGED, TATTERED ⟨worn steps and ~ roofs —Richard Llewellyn⟩

tat·tie \'tati\ *n* -s [by shortening & alter.] *Scot* **:** POTATO

tattie bogle *n*, *Scot* **:** a scarecrow in a potato field

tattie doo·lie \-'düli\ *n* [Sc *doolie* scarecrow, of imit. origin] *Scot* **:** TATTIE BOGLE

1tat·ting \'tad·|iŋ, -at|, |ēŋ\ *n* -s [origin unknown] **1 :** a delicate handmade lace (as for edgings, insertion, or doilies) formed usu. by looping and knotting with a single cotton thread and a small shuttle to make varied designs of rings and semicircles **2 :** the act or process of making tatting

tatting 1

2tatting *pres part of* TAT

1tat·tle \'tad·ᵊl, -atᵊl\ *vb* **tattled; tattled; tattling** \-d·ᵊliŋ, -t(ᵊ)liŋ\ **tattles** [MD *tatelen*; akin to MLG *tatelen* to babble, tattle, ME, MD, & MLG *tateren*] *vi* **1 :** to talk idly or meaninglessly : CHATTER, PRATE ⟨the voice of the boy *tattled* endlessly over the piece he was learning to say —Elizabeth M. Roberts⟩ **2 :** to tell tales or secrets : be a talebearer : BLAB ⟨*tattled* on her estranged husband —*Springfield (Mass.) Union*⟩ ~ *vt* **:** to utter or disclose in gossip or chatter ⟨~ tales⟩

2tattle \"\ *n* -s **1 :** idle talk : CHATTER ⟨endless ~ about dress —Guy McCrone⟩ **2 :** GOSSIP, TALEBEARING ⟨snaps his fingers at ~ —George Meredith⟩

tat·tler \'tad·ᵊlə(r), -at(ᵊ)lə-\ *n* -s **1 :** TATTLETALE **2 :** any of various slender long-legged shorebirds (as the willet, yellowlegs, and redshank) of the family Scolopacidae that have a loud and frequently uttered call

tattletale \'=,=\ *n* [1*tattle* + *tale*] **:** one that tattles : INFORMER, TATTLER, TELLTALE ⟨the inescapable odium of the ~ —Dixon Wecter⟩ ⟨small things like these are often big ~s about human character —Laura Z. Hobson⟩

tattletale gray *n* **:** a grayish white : OFF-WHITE

1tat·too *also* **ta·too** \(')ta¦tü\ *n* -s [alter. of earlier *taptoo*, fr. D *taptoe*, fr. the imperative phrase *tap toe!* taps shut!, fr. *tap* tap of a keg (fr. MD *tappe*) + *toe* to, shut, fr. MD; akin to OE *tō* to — more at TAP, TO] **1 a :** a call or signal sounded (as on a bugle or drum) shortly before taps as notice to soldiers or sailors to repair to quarters **b :** an evening entertainment given by troops usu. in the form of outdoor military exercises with music ⟨the evening was not yet over, for the splendid military ~ and massed bands rounded out an unforgettable day —J.W.Davies⟩ **2 :** a usu. rapid rhythmic beating or rapping ⟨the hoofs of his horse beat a soft ~ on the roads —Sherwood Anderson⟩ ⟨the running gear beat a ~ against the masts —H.A.Chippendale⟩ — see DEVIL'S TATTOO

2tattoo *also* **tatoo** \"\ *vb* -ED/-ING/-S *vt* **:** to beat or rap rhythmically on : drum on ⟨dragged him out, face up, his head lolling back, his slack heels ~*ing* the pavement —Nathaniel Burt⟩ ~ *vi* **:** to give a series of rhythmic taps ⟨~*ed* on a door —Elizabeth Bowen⟩

3tattoo *also* **tatoo** \"\ *n* -s [modif. of Tahitian *tatau*] **1 :** the act of tattooing or the fact of being tattooed ⟨~ . . . consists of pricking pigment into the skin —*Notes & Queries on Anthropology*⟩ ⟨facial ~ with conspicuous curvilinear patterns . . . was common —R.H.Lowie⟩ **2 :** an indelible mark or figure fixed upon the surface of the body by the insertion of pigment under the skin or by the production of scars

4tattoo *also* **tatoo** \"\ *vt* -ED/-ING/-S **1 a :** to mark or color (the skin) by pricking in coloring matter so as to form indelible marks or figures or by production of scars **b :** to mark the skin with (a tattoo) ⟨~*ed* a flag on his chest⟩ **2 :** to mark permanently ⟨his entire body is ~*ed* with souvenirs of the first bomb —W.M.Hitzig⟩

5tat·too \'ta(,)tü, 'tə(-\ *n* -s [Hindi *ṭaṭṭū*] **:** a native-bred pony of India

tat·too·er \(')ta'tüə(r)\ *or* **tat·too·ist** \-üəst\ *n* -s **:** one that makes a business of forming or removing tattoos

tattooing *n* -s **1 :** the act or practice of marking the skin with tattoos **2 :** a tattoo or a set of tattoos

tatts *pres 3d sing of* TATT

1tat·ty \'tad·|ē, -at|, |i\ *adj* [perh. akin to OE *tætteca* rag, tatter — more at TATTER] **1** *dial Brit* **:** SHAGGY **2 :** CHEAP, INFERIOR — used as a generalized term of disapproval ⟨the street . . . seemed immensely long and wide, but rather dirty and ~ —Geoffrey Cotterell⟩ ⟨the ~ climax . . . seems an inexcusable last resort —*Time*⟩

2tatty *also* **tattie** *n*, *pl* **tatties** [Hindi *ṭaṭṭī*] *India* **:** a mat or screen of fibers in a door or window kept wet to cool the air

1tatu *var of* TATOU

2ta·tu \'tä(,)tü\ [NL, fr. Pg *tatú*, *tatu* armadillo — more at TATOU] *syn of* DASYPUS

3ta·tu \'tä(,)tü\ *n*, *pl* **tatu** *or* **tatus** *usu cap* [Pomo] **:** HUCHNOM

ta·tu·a·su \tə,tüə'sü\ *n* -s [Pg *tatuaçu*, *tatuaçú*, fr. Tupi *tatú asú*, lit., giant armadillo] **:** GIANT ARMADILLO

ta·tu·ki·ra \,tätü'kērə\ *n* -s [Pg *tatuquira*] **:** a small So. American biting fly of the genus *Phlebotomus* that is believed to carry leishmaniasis

ta·tu·sia \tə'tüzēə, -üsēə\ [NL, modif. of Tupi *tatú* armadillo] *syn of* DASYPUS

tau \'taü, 'tȯ\ *n* -s [Gk, of Sem origin; akin to Heb *tāw* sign, cross, taw (letter)] **1 a :** the 19th letter of the Greek alphabet — symbol T or τ; see ALPHABET table **b :** 4TAW **2 :** a T-shaped mark or object (as a St. Anthony's cross, a pastoral staff, or an ankh)

tau·ba·da \taü'bädə\ *n* -s [Papuan] *Austral* **:** MASTER

tau cross *n* **1 :** a T-shaped cross sometimes having expanded ends and foot : SAINT ANTHONY'S CROSS 1 **2 :** CRUX COMMISSA 1

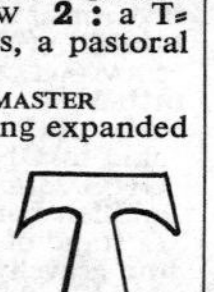
tau cross

tau·fer \'toifə(r)\ *n* -s *usu cap* [G *täufer* one that baptizes, fr. OHG *toufāri*, fr. *toufen* to baptize + *-āri* -er — more at DOPE] **:** DUNKER

1taught \'tȯt, *usu* -ȯd·+V\ [ME *taghte*, *taughte* (past), *taght*, *taught*, *ytaght*, *ytaught* (past part.), fr. OE *tǣhte*, *tāhte* (past), *tǣht*, *tāht*, *getǣht*, *getāht* (past part.) — more at TEACH] *past of* TEACH

2taught \"\ *adj* [ME *taght*, *taught*, fr. *taght*, *taught*, past part.] **1 :** INSTRUCTED ⟨he is badly ~⟩ **2 :** conveyed by instruction ⟨a ~ tradition of hewing to principles —*Nation's Business*⟩

tauhid *var of* TAWHID

tau·la \'taülə\ *n* -s [Catal, lit., table, fr. ML *tabula* — more at TABLE] **:** an ancient massive crude stone structure of unknown use but suggesting a table, platform, or altar that is found esp. in the Balearic islands

taung·thu \'taüŋ,tü\ *n*, *pl* **taungthu** *or* **taungthus** *usu cap* **1 a :** a Karen people of eastern Burma **b :** a member of such people **2 :** the Karen language of the Taungthu people

1taunt \'tȯnt, 'tänt, 'tant\ *vb* -ED/-ING/-S [fr. obs. E *taunt* to tease, perh. fr. MF *tenter*, *tanter* to try, tempt — more at TEMPT] *vt* **1 a :** to reproach in a mocking or insulting manner : jeer at : UPBRAID ⟨at last he ~*ed* me beyond endurance —G.B.Shaw⟩ ⟨took no part in the revivals and usually teased and ~*ed* those who did —J.M.Hunt⟩ **b** *obs* **:** to make the subject of censure or reproach : cast in one's teeth ⟨~ my faults —Shak.⟩ **2 :** to drive or accomplish by taunting : PROVOKE ⟨~*ed* him into losing his temper⟩ ~ *vi* **:** to utter taunts ⟨~ away —Robert Browning⟩ **syn** see RIDICULE

2taunt \"\ *n* -s **1 :** a bitter or sarcastic reproach, insult, or challenge ⟨calmly ignored the ~s of his enemy⟩ **2** *archaic* **:** one who is taunted : an object of scornful reproach ⟨will make them . . . a reproach, a byword, a ~, and a curse —Jer 24:9 (RSV)⟩

3taunt \"\ *adj* [origin unknown] **:** very tall — used esp. of the masts of a ship

taunt·er \-tə(r)\ *n* -s **:** one that taunts

taunt·ing·ly *adv* **:** in a taunting manner

taun·ton turkey \'täntᵊn-, 'tȯntᵊn-, 'tántᵊn-, 'tantᵊn-\ *n*, *usu cap 1st T* [fr. *Taunton*, Mass.] **:** 2ALEWIFE 1a

taupe \'tōp\ *n* -s [F, lit., mole, fr. L *talpa*] **1 :** a brownish gray that is paler and slightly yellower than chocolate, duller and slightly redder than mouse gray, and duller and slightly redder than castor **2 :** MOLE 4a

taupe brown *n* **:** a variable color averaging a grayish reddish brown that is yellower and paler than liver brown

taupe gray *n* **:** a dark purplish gray that is redder and lighter than slate, redder, lighter, and stronger than charcoal, and bluer and darker than pigeon

taupe rose *n* **:** ROSE TAUPE

tau·pou *also* **tau·po** \taü'pō\ *n* -s [Samoan *taupo*] **:** a ceremonial hostess selected by a high chief of a Samoan village from the young girls of his household, elevated to a high rank, and charged with the formal reception and entertainment of visitors

taur- *or* **tauri-** *or* **tauro-** *comb form* [*taur-*, *tauri-* fr. L, fr. *taurus*; *tauro-* fr. LL, fr. Gk, fr. *tauros* — more at STEER] **1 :** bull ⟨*tauro*dont⟩ ⟨*tauri*cide⟩ ⟨*tauro*morphic⟩ **2 :** taurine ⟨*tauro*cholic⟩

tau·ra·co \'taůrə,kō\ *n*, *cap* [NL, alter. of *Touraco*, fr. F *touraco*] **:** a genus of touracos including those with feathered nostrils

tau·ran·ga \taü'räŋgə\ *n* -s [Maori] *NewZeal* **:** BUSH SICKNESS

tau·re·an *or* **tau·ri·an** \'tȯrēən\ *adj* [*taurean* fr. L *taureus* taurine (fr. *taurus* bull) + E *-an*; *taurine* fr. *taur-* + *-ine*] **:** TAURINE

tau·ri \'tȯ,rī\ *n pl*, *usu cap* [L, fr. Gk *Tauroi*] **:** an ancient people of the southern Crimea

tau·ric \'tȯrik\ *adj* [*taur-* + *-ic*] **:** TAURINE

1tau·rine \'tȯ,rīn, -ȯrən\ *adj* [L *taurinus*, fr. *taur-* + *-inus* -ine] **1 :** of or relating to a bull : BOVINE **2 :** of or relating to the common ox (*Bos taurus*) as distinguished from the zebu (*B. indicus*)

2tau·rine \'tȯ,rēn, -ȯrən\ *n* -s [ISV *taur-* + *-ine*; fr. its having been discovered in the bile of cattle] **:** a crystalline compound $H_2NCH_2CH_2SO_3H$ of neutral reaction that occurs esp. in invertebrates (as in the juices of muscles) that is obtained by the hydrolysis of taurocholic acid or the decarboxylation of cysteic acid, that is synthesized usu. by reaction of sodium isethionate and aqueous ammonia under heat and pressure, and that is used in making various surface-active agents; 2-amino-ethanesulfonic acid

tau·ris·cite \'tȯrə,sīt\ *n* -s [G *tauriszit*, fr. L (*Pagus*) *Tauriscorum* Canton Uri, Switzerland, its locality + G *-it* -ite] **:** a mineral $FeSO_4.7H_2O$ that is a hydrous ferrous sulfate sometimes considered isomorphous with epsomite

tau·ro·bo·li·um \,tȯrə'bōlēəm\ *also* **tau·rob·o·ly** \tȯ'räbəlē\ *n*, *pl* **taurobolia** \-'bōlēə\ *also* **taurobolies** [LL *taurobolium*, fr. Gk *taurobolion*, fr. *tauros* bull + *-bolion* (fr. *ballein* to throw) — more at STEER, DEVIL] **:** a ceremony in the cult of certain Mediterranean deities (as Cybele and Mithras) in which worshipers were baptized with the blood of a sacrificed bull — compare CRIOBOLIUM

tau·ro·cho·late \,tȯrə'kō,lāt, -'kä,-\ *n* -s [ISV *taurocholic* + *-ate*] **:** a salt or ester of taurocholic acid

tau·ro·cho·lic acid \¦==¦kōlik-, -¦kälik-\ *n* [ISV *taur-* + *cholic acid*] **:** a deliquescent crystalline acid $(HO)_3C_{23}H_{36}CONHCH_2CH_2SO_3H$ that occurs in the form of the sodium salt in the bile of man, of carnivorous animals, and of the ox and a few other herbivorous animals and that on hydrolysis yields taurine and cholic acid

tau·ro·dont \'tȯrə,dänt\ *adj* [*taur-* + *-odont*] **:** having the pulp cavities of the teeth very large and the roots reduced — used esp. of a primitive fossil man

tau·ro·dont·ism \-nt,izəm, -n-,ti-\ *n* -s **:** a dental condition marked by the enlargement of the pulp cavities and the reduction of the roots

tau·ro·ka·thap·sia \,tȯrəkə'thapsēə\ *n pl but sing in constr* [Gk, fr. *tauros* + *kathaptos* (verbal of *kathaptein* to fasten upon, attack, fr. *kata-* cata- + *haptein* to fasten) + *-ia* -y — more at APSIS] **:** an ancient Cretan sport in which a performer grasps the horns of a bull and somersaults over him

tau·ro·ma·chi·an \,tȯrə'mākēən\ *or* **tau·ro·mach·ic** \-¦mak·ik\ *adj* [*tauromachian* fr. *tauromachy* + *-an*; *tauromachic* fr. Sp *tauromáquico*, fr. *tauromaquia* + *-ico* -ic (fr. L *-icus*)] **:** of or relating to tauromachy

tau·rom·a·chy \tȯ'räməkē\ *n* -ES [Sp *tauromaquia*, fr. Gk *tauromachia*, fr. *taurus* + *-machia* -machy] **1 :** the art or practice of bullfighting **2 :** BULLFIGHT

tau·ro·ma·quia \,taůrō'mäkēə\ *n* -s [Sp] **:** TAUROMACHY

tau·ro·mor·phic \¦tȯrə¦mȯrfik\ *adj* [*taur-* + *-morphic*] **:** shaped in the form of a bull : resembling a bull ⟨the ~ vases of the Minoan culture⟩

tau·rot·ra·gus \tȯ'rä·trəgəs\ *n*, *cap* [NL, fr. *taur-* + Gk *tragos* he-goat] **:** a genus of large African antelopes consisting of the elands

1tau·rus \'tȯrəs\ *n* -ES *usu cap* [ME, fr. L, lit., bull — more at STEER] **:** the second sign of the zodiac — see SIGN table; ZODIAC illustration

2taurus \"\ [NL, fr. L, bull] *syn of* BOS

tau·ryl \'tȯrəl\ *n* -s [*taur-* + *-yl*] **:** the univalent acid radical $H_2NCH_2CH_2SO_2-$ of taurine

tau-sa·ghyz \'taůsə'gēz\ *n* -ES [Russ *tau-sagyz*, fr. Turki *tau-sagïz*, fr. *tau* mountain + *sagïz* gum, rubber] **:** a perennial yellow-headed herb (*Scorzonera tau-saghyz*) of the family Compositae that is native to the Kazakh republic of the U. S. S. R., bears leafy rosettes, and is cultivated for its rubber-containing roots

1taut \'tȯt, *usu* -ȯd·+V\ *adj* -ER/-EST [ME *tought*; prob. akin to OE *togian* to draw, drag — more at TOW] **1 a :** tightly drawn : tensely stretched : not slack ⟨the flesh seemed smoothed back, even painfully ~ —R.P.Warren⟩ ⟨a piece of strong fabric about one yard square, kept ~ by a wooden frame —W.H.Dowdeswell⟩ **b :** HIGH-STRUNG, TENSE ⟨her nerves were ~ as bowstrings —O.E.Rölvaag⟩ ⟨strain our already ~ nerves a little further —W.F.Hambly⟩ **2 :** SEVERE, STRICT ⟨is reputed to drive pretty ~ bargains —G.S.Perry⟩ **3 a :** kept in proper order or condition : well disciplined ⟨sailormen prefer a happy ship to a ~ ship, where strict discipline is the only diet —A.R.Griffin⟩ ⟨each team had brought a small but ~ cheering section of its own —A.J.Liebling⟩ **b :** not loose or flabby : FIRM, TRIM ⟨a figure that was slender, ~, and graceful —Aline B. Saarinen⟩ ⟨the ~, economical style contains more than meets the casual eye —*Time*⟩ **syn** see TIGHT

2taut \'tät\ *vt* -ED/-ING/-S [origin unknown] *Scot* **:** TANGLE

taut *abbr* tautological; tautology

taut- *or* **tauto-** *comb form* [LL, fr. Gk, fr. *tautos* identical, fr. *to auto* the same, fr. *to*, neut. definite article + *auto* (neut. of *autos*) same — more at THAT, AUT-] **:** same ⟨*taut*omerism⟩ ⟨*tauto*nym⟩

taut·en \'tȯtᵊn\ *vb* -ED/-ING/-S [1*taut* + *-en*] *vt* **:** to make taut ⟨~ your canvas again and resume your cruise —*All Hands*⟩ ~ *vi* **:** to become taut ⟨the skin of her cheeks ~*ed* —G.A. Wagner⟩

taut helm *n* **:** WEATHER HELM

taut·ly *adv* **:** in a taut manner

taut·ness *n* -ES **:** the quality or state of being taut

tau·to·chrone \'tȯd·ə,krōn\ *n* -s [F, fr. *taut-* + Gk *chronos* time] **:** a curve which is a cycloid under a horizontal base and down which the time of descent under gravity from every point to the lowest point is the same

tau·tog *or* **tau·taug** \'tȯ'tȯg, -'täg\ *n* -s [Narraganset *tautauog*, pl. of *taut*, *tautau*] **:** a common food and sport fish (*Tautoga onitis*) of the family Labridae that is found along the Atlantic coast of the U. S. and in the adult is black with greenish gray blotches — called also *blackfish*, *oysterfish*

tau·to·log·i·cal \¦tȯd·ᵊl¦äjəkəl, -ȯtᵊl-, -jēk-\ *also* **tau·to·log·ic** \-jik, -jēk\ *adj* **:** of, relating to, or marked by tautology : TAUTOLOGOUS — **tau·to·log·i·cal·ly** \-jək(ə)lē, -jēk-, -li\ *adv*

tau·tol·o·gism \tȯ'tälə,jizəm\ *n* -s **:** the use or an instance of tautology

tau·tol·o·gist \-,jəst\ *n* -s **:** one who uses tautology

tau·tol·o·gize \-lə,jīz\ *vi* -ED/-ING/-S **:** to practice tautology

tau·tol·o·gous \-ləgəs\ *adj* [Gk *tautologos*, fr. *taut-* + *logos* word, speech — more at LEGEND] **1 :** TAUTOLOGICAL **2 a :** ANALYTIC **b :** true in terms of the sentential connectives of a truth table **c :** true purely by virtue of the meanings of component terms — **tau·tol·o·gous·ly** *adv*

tau·tol·o·gy \tȯ'täləjē, -ji\ *n* -ES [LL *tautologia*, fr. Gk, fr. *tautologos* + *-ia* -y] **1 a (1) :** needless or meaningless repetition in close succession of an idea, statement, or word : PLEONASM, REDUNDANCY ⟨a certain ~ in describing any act of society as social —*Foreign Affairs*⟩ **(2) :** an instance of such repetition ⟨the phrase "a beginner who has just started" is a ~⟩ ⟨a speech full of *tautologies*⟩ **b :** a tautologous statement **2 :** repetition of an act or experience ⟨the ~ of two drunken brawls in the same scene⟩

tau·to·mer \'tȯd·əmə(r)\ *n* -s [ISV *taut-* + *-mer*] **:** one of the forms of a tautomeric compound

tau·to·mer·ic \¦tȯd·ə¦merik\ *adj* [ISV *taut-* + *-meric*] **1 :** characterized by or relating to tautomerism ⟨~ equilibrium⟩ **2 :** taking part in tautomerization ⟨the enolic or the ~ hydrogen atom —G.W.Wheland⟩

tau·tom·er·ism \tȯ'tämə,rizəm\ *n* -s [*taut-* + *-merism*] **:** the phenomenon shown by a compound of behaving in chemical reactions as though the atoms in its molecule were arranged in more than one way expressible by different structural formulas, the two or more interconvertible isomeric forms not necessarily being isolable — called also *dynamic isomerism*; see ANIONOTROPY, CATIONOTROPY, DESMOTROPISM, KETO-ENOL TAUTOMERISM; compare ISOMERISM, RESONANCE 5

tau·tom·er·iza·tion \tȯ,tämərə'zāshən\ *n* -s **:** the process of tautomerizing

tau·tom·er·ize \tȯ'tämə,rīz\ *vb* -ED/-ING/-S [*tautomer* + *-ize*] *vi* **:** to become changed into a tautomeric form ~ *vt* **:** to cause to change into a tautomeric form

tau·tom·ery \-mərē\ *n* -ES [ISV *taut-* + *-mery*] **:** TAUTOMERISM

tau·to·met·ric \¦tȯd·ə¦me·trik\ *also* **tau·to·met·ri·cal** \-rəkəl\ *adj* [*taut-* + *metric*, *metrical*] **:** equal or identical in metrical structure, arrangement, or position

tau·to·nym \'tȯd·ə,nim, -ȯtə-, -ȯtᵊn,im\ *n* -s [*taut-* + *-onym*] **:** a taxonomic binomial in which the generic name and specific epithet are alike and which is in common use in zoology esp. to designate a common or typical form but is forbidden to botanical taxonomists under the International Code of Botanical Nomenclature ⟨*Mephitis mephitis* is a ~ designating a common No. American skunk⟩ — **tau·to·nym·ic** \¦==¦nimik, ¦==¦imik\ *or* **tau·ton·y·mous** \(')tȯ¦tänəməs\ *adj* — **tau·ton·y·my** \tȯ'tänəmē\ *n* -ES

tau·toph·o·ny \tȯ'täfənē\ *n* -ES [MGk *tautophōnia*, fr. *tautophōnos* sounding identical, fr. Gk *taut-* + *-phōnos* (fr *phōnein* to sound, fr. *phōnē* voice, sound) + *-ia* -y — more at BAN] **:** repetition of the same sound

tau·to·syllabic \¦tȯd·(,)ō+\ *adj* [*taut-* + *syllabic*] **:** belonging to the same syllable

tau·to·zonal \"+\ *adj* [*taut-* + *zonal*] **:** belonging to the same zone — **tau·to·zonality** \"+\ *n*

tave \'tāv\ *vi* [ME *taven*, prob. of Scand origin; akin to Norw *tava* to toil fruitlessly] *dial Brit* **:** to thrash or toss wildly : STRUGGLE

ta·ver \'tāvər\ *vi* [freq. of *tave*] **1** *Scot* **:** ROAM, WANDER **2** *Scot* **:** to talk foolishly : BABBLE

1tav·ern \'tavə(r)n\ *n* -s *often attrib* [ME *taverne*, fr. OF, fr. L *taberna* hut, booth, shop, inn, tavern, alter. of (assumed) *traberna*, fr. *trabs*, *trabes* beam, roof — more at THORP] **1 a** *obs* **:** a shop for selling and drinking wine **b :** an establishment where alcoholic liquors are sold to be drunk on the premises **2 :** a house where travelers or other transient guests are accommodated with rooms and meals : INN

2tavern \"\ *vi* -ED/-ING/-S **:** to frequent a tavern

tavern car *n* **:** LOUNGE CAR

tav·ern·er \-nə(r)\ *n* -s [ME *tavernere*, fr. MF *tavernier*, fr. OF, fr. *taverne* + *-ier*] **1 :** one that keeps a tavern **2** *obs* **:** one that frequents taverns

tav·ern·less \-nləs\ *adj* **:** having no tavern

tavern table *n* **:** a type of small table with oval or rectangular top and four turned legs used as a service table in the taproom of 18th century taverns

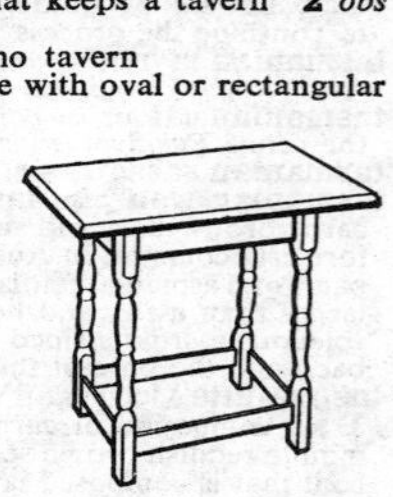
tavern table

tavern token *n* **:** a token issued as change by a tavern keeper

ta·vert \'tāvərt\ *adj* [Sc *tavert*, past part. of *taver*] **1** *Scot* **:** TIRED, FATIGUED **2** *Scot* **:** CONFUSED, STUPID

tav·gi \täv'gē\ *n*, *pl* **tavgi** *cap* **1 :** NGANASANI **2 :** the Uralic language of the Nganasani people — see URALIC LANGUAGES table

tav·is·tock·ite \'tavə,stä,kīt\ *n* -s [*Tavistock*, Devonshire, England + E *-ite*] **:** a mineral $Ca_3Al_2(PO_4)_3(OH)_3$ consisting of a basic calcium aluminum phosphate and occurring in minute white crystals

1taw \'tȯ\ *vt* -ED/-ING/-S [ME *tawen*, fr. OE *tawian*; akin to OHG *zouwen* to prepare, ON *tæja*, *tȳja* to help, Goth *taujan* to do, make, L *bonus* good — more at BOUNTY] **1** *archaic* **:** to prepare or dress (as hemp by beating) for use **2 :** to convert (skin) into white leather (as for gloves) by mineral tanning with alum, salt, and other agents (as an emulsion of egg yolk) **3** *archaic* **:** BEAT, SCOURGE

2taw \"\ *n* -s [origin unknown] **1 a :** a marble to be used as a shooter **b :** RINGTAW **2 a** *also* **tawline** \'=,=\ **:** the line from which players shoot at marbles **b :** the starting line in any game or sport (as racing) **3 :** a square-dance partner **4 :** a sum of money invested : STAKE

3taw \"\ *vi* -ED/-ING/-S **:** to shoot a marble

4taw *or* **tav** \'tä|f, 'tȯ|, |v\ *also* **thau** \'t(h)aů\ *n* -s [Heb *tāw*, lit., sign, cross] **1 :** the 23d letter of the Hebrew alphabet — symbol ת; see ALPHABET table **2 :** the letter of the Phoenician or of any of various other Semitic alphabets corresponding to Hebrew taw

TAW *abbr*, *often not cap* twice a week

ta·wa \'täwə, 'taůə\ *n* -s [Maori] **:** a New Zealand evergreen tree (*Beilschmiedia tawa*) of the family Lauraceae with slender branches and graceful foliage resembling that of the willow and white straight-grained wood used chiefly for rough work (as clothespins)

ta·wa·sa \tə'wäsə\ *n*, *pl* **tawasa** *usu cap* **1 a :** a Muskogean people of northwestern Florida **b :** a member of such people **2 :** the language of the Tawasa people — compare MUSKOGEE

taw·dri·ly \'tȯdrəlē, 'täd-\ *adv* **:** in a tawdry manner : so as to be tawdry ⟨a ~ papered room⟩ ⟨~ dressed⟩

taw·dri·ness \-rēnəs, -rin-\ *n* -ES **:** the quality or state of being tawdry

1taw·dry \-rē, -ri\ *n* -ES [*tawdry (lace)*] **:** cheap showy finery

2tawdry \"\ *adj* -ER/-EST **:** cheap and gaudy in appearance or quality : tastelessly showy ⟨she was festooned with flags, but she appeared rather ~ . . . for her white hull was streaked with rust and she had a general air of dishevelment —*New Yorker*⟩ **syn** see GAUDY

tawdry lace *n* [alter. of earlier *St. Audrey's lace*, after *St. Audrey* (Etheldreda or Æthelthrȳth) †679 queen of Northumbria who founded an abbey at Ely; fr. the tradition that she died of a throat tumor inflicted as a punishment for her fondness for necklaces] *obs* : a woman's tie of lace worn about the neck

¹taw·er \'tó(ə)r, 'tóə\ *n* -s [ME, fr. *tawen* to taw + *-er*] : one that taws skins : a dresser of white leather

²tawer \"\ *n* [³*taw* + *-er*] : one that shoots marbles

taw·ery \'tó(ə)rē\ *n* -ES [¹*taw* + *-ery*] : a place where skins are tawed

ta·whai \'tä,hwī\ *n* -s [Maori] : RED BIRCH 3

taw·hid *or* **tau·hid** \tō'hēd\ *n* [Ar *tawhīd* unity] **1** : the Muslim doctrine of the radical unity of God **2** *Sufism* : the union of the individual soul with God

taw·ie \'tó·i\ *adj* [prob. fr. ¹*taw* + *-ie* (alter. of *-y*)] *Scot* : TRACTABLE

taw·kee \'tókē\ *also* **taw·kin** \-kən\ *n* -s [of Algonquian origin; akin to Delaware *p'tuckquen* it is round, Natick *pĕtŭkqui*] **1** : GOLDEN CLUB **2** : an arrow arum (*Peltandra virginica*)

tawn·i·ly \'tónᵊlē, 'tän-, -nəl-\ *adv* : in a tawny shade

tawn·i·ness \-nēnəs\ *n* -ES : the quality or state of being tawny

¹tawny \-nē, -ni\ *adj* -ER/-EST [ME *taune, tawny,* fr. MF *tanné,* past part. of *tanner* to tan — more at TAN] : of the color tawny ⟨walking along the ~ sands⟩ ⟨~ squares of ripened grain —*Amer. Guide Series: Oregon*⟩ ⟨~ lion⟩ ⟨black . . . dog with ~ points —Irving Bacheller⟩

²tawny \"\ *n* -ES [ME *taune, tawny,* fr. *taune, tawny,* adj.] **1** : a brownish orange to light brown that is slightly redder than sorrel — compare TENNÉ **2** : a tawny-colored cloth or garment **3** *archaic* **a** : a brown-skinned person **b** : AMERICAN INDIAN

tawny birch *n* : SANDSTONE 2

tawny bunting *n* : SNOW BUNTING

tawny-coat *n, obs* : an ecclesiastical apparitor

tawny eagle *n* **1** : a brownish eagle (*Aquila rapax*) with varied purplish and rufous feathers on the back found in Africa and parts of Asia and rarely in Europe **2** : an eagle of the Indian peninsula that is smaller than but usu. considered a variety (*Aquila rapax vindiana*) of the African tawny eagle

tawny-moor \'≈≈,≈\ *n, archaic* : a dark-skinned native of a non-European land

tawny owl *n* **1** : a common owl (*Strix aluco* syn. *Syrnium aluco*) of Europe and northern Africa related to the barred owl of America and having no ear tufts, the upper parts reddish brown with blackish vermiculations, and the underparts buffy, streaked, and barred with brown **2** *usu cap T&O* : an assistant adult leader of a pack of brownie scouts in the Girl Guide movement in Britain, Canada, and various other countries and formerly in the U.S.

tawny port *n* **1** : a port wine consisting of a blend of several vintages matured in wood so that it loses some of its original color and acquires a brownish tinge **2** : a wine lighter in color and body than standard port and made from grapes not as rich in color

tawny thrush *n* : VEERY

¹taw·pie *or* **taw·py** \'tōpē, -pi\ *n, pl* **tawpies** [of Scand origin; akin to Norw *tåpe* simpleton, Dan *tåbe,* Sw *tåp;* akin to ON *tæpta* to tap — more at TAP] *chiefly Scot* : a foolish or awkward young person

²tawpie *or* **tawpy** \"\ *adj* : FOOLISH, SENSELESS

taws *also* **tawse** \'tóz\ *n pl but sing or pl in constr* [prob. fr. pl. of obs. *taw* tawed leather, thong, fr. ¹*taw*] *Brit* : a whip consisting of a strap or thong of leather slit into two or more strips at the end

taw-sug \'tō'süg\ *n, pl* **taw-sug** *or* **taw-sugs** *usu cap T&S* [Taw-Sug, fr. *taw* person + *sug, sulúg* current] **1 a** : a Moro people of the Sulu Archipelago **b** : a member of such people **2** : an Austronesian language of the Taw-Sug people

tawt \'tät\ *Scot var of* ²TAUT

¹tax \'taks\ *vt* -ED/-ING/-ES [ME *taxen,* fr. MF & ML; MF *taxer,* fr. ML *taxare* to tax, assess, fr. L, to touch, feel, rate, compute, censure, freq. of *tangere* to touch — more at TANGENT] **1 a** *archaic* : to place a value upon : estimate the worth of or fix the price of **b** : to assess, fix, or determine judicially the amount of ⟨~ the costs of an action in court⟩ **2** : to make subject to the payment of a tax : levy a charge on; *esp* : to exact money from for the support of government **3** *obs* : to enter in a list ⟨a decree . . . that all the world should be ~ed —Lk 2:1 (AV)⟩ **4 a** : to call to account : take to task : CHARGE, ACCUSE ⟨ran to grandfather and ~ed him with his falsehoods —W.H.Hudson †1922⟩ **b** : CENSURE ⟨~es science for being unable . . . to give us moral directives —Bernard Rosenberg⟩ — usu. used with *with* **5** : to place under onerous and rigorous demands ⟨every muscle is ~ed, and every nerve strained —John Burroughs⟩ ⟨it may ~ the highest wisdom of the race to preserve civilization at all —F.N.Robinson⟩

syn see BURDEN

²tax \"\ *n* -ES *often attrib* [ME, fr. *taxen,* v.] **1 a** (1) : a usu. pecuniary charge imposed by legislative or other public authority upon persons or property for public purposes : a forced contribution of wealth to meet the public needs of a government — compare CUSTOM 3, DEATH TAX, EXCISE, INCOME TAX, INDIRECT TAX, INHERITANCE TAX, SINGLE TAX (2) : DIRECT TAX ⟨the Congress shall have the power to lay and collect ~es, duties, imposts, and excises —*U.S. Constitution*⟩ (3) *Brit* : a levy (as on income) paid to the national government — compare RATE 3b (5) **b** : a sum levied on the members of an organization to defray its expenses **2** : a heavy charge or demand exacted : BURDEN, STRAIN ⟨the grinding duties of this position . . . proved too great a ~ on the strength of even so robust a man —A.W.Long⟩

tax- *or* **taxo-** *also* **taxi-** *comb form* [tax- fr. Gk *taxis;* taxo- fr. F, fr. Gk *taxis;* taxi- fr. F, fr. Gk, fr. *taxis* — more at TAXIS] : arrangement ⟨*taxaspidean*⟩ ⟨*taxeme*⟩ ⟨*taxidermy*⟩ ⟨*taxology*⟩

taxa *pl of* TAXON

tax·abil·i·ty \,taksə'biləd·ē\ *n* : the quality or state of being taxable

¹tax·able \'taksəbəl\ *adj* [ME, fr. *taxen* to tax + *-able*] **1** : capable of being taxed : liable by law to the assessment of taxes **2** : that may be legally charged by a court against the plaintiff or defendant in a suit ⟨~ costs⟩ **3** *obs* : CENSURABLE **4** : used as the basis of a tax computation ⟨the ~ year⟩ ⟨~ horsepower⟩ — **tax·able·ness** *n* -ES — **tax·a·bly** \-blē, -li\ *adv*

²taxable \"\ *n* -s : one that is liable to a tax : a subject for taxation, whether property, person, corporation, or other legal entity

tax·a·ce·ae \tak'sāsē,ē\ *n pl, cap* [NL, fr. *Taxus,* type genus + *-aceae*] : a family of mostly evergreen trees and shrubs (order Coniferales) distinguished from the Pinaceae by dioecious flowers, commonly fleshy fruit, and an embryo with but two cotyledons — **tax·a·ceous** \(')tak'sāshəs\ *adj*

tax·ad \'tak,sad\ *n* -s [NL *Taxus* + E *-ad*] : a tree or shrub of the family Taxaceae

tax·am·e·ter \tak'samad·ə(r)\ *n* [G, irreg. fr. ML *taxa* charge, assessment, tax (fr. *taxare* to assess, tax) + G *-meter* — more at TAX] : TAXIMETER

tax·as·pid·e·an \,taksa'spidēən\ *adj* [tax- + aspid- + -ean] : having or being a tarsus of a bird with the scales of its hind side rectangular and arranged in regular rows

tax·a·tion \tak'sāshən\ *n* -s [ME *taxacioun,* fr. MF *taxation,* fr. ML *taxation-, taxatio,* fr. L, evaluation, appraisal fr. *taxatus* (past part. of *taxare*) + *-ion-, -io* -ion] **1** : the action of taxing: as **a** : the imposing of taxes on the subjects of a state by government or on the members of a corporation or company by the proper authority **b** : the act of assessing judicially (as a bill of costs) **2** : an amount assessed or obtained by taxation : TAX **3** : a system of raising revenue by the imposition of compulsory contributions — see DOUBLE TAXATION

tax·a·tion·al \-shənᵊl\ *adj* : of or relating to taxation

tax·a·tor \tak'sād·ə(r)\ *n* -s [ME *taxatour,* fr. ML *taxator,* fr. *taxatus* (past part. of *taxare* to tax, assess) + L *-or* — more at TAX] : TAXOR

tax bond *n* : a government bond made receivable in payment of taxes

tax book *n* : TAX LIST

tax cart *or* **taxed cart** *n* : a spring cart formerly subject to a small tax in England

tax certificate *n* : the certificate issued to the purchaser of land at a tax sale certifying to the sale and the payment of the consideration therefor and entitling the purchaser upon certain conditions and at a certain time thereafter to a deed or instrument of conveyance of the land to be executed by the proper officer

tax deed *n* : a deed in the form required by statute evidencing the statutory rights and title acquired by the grantee as purchaser of the property described at its sale for nonpayment of a tax — compare TAX CERTIFICATE, TAX SALE, TAX TITLE

taxeater \'≈,≈≈\ *n* : a person deriving support from public funds

taxed *past of* TAX

tax·eme \'tak,sēm\ *n* -s [*tax-* + *-eme*] : a minimum grammatical feature of selection (as the occurrence of the noun *actor* before *-ess* in *actress*), of order (as the fact that *actr-* precedes *-ess* in *actress*), of stress (as the occurrence of one main stress on the first syllable in *actress*), of pitch (as the interrogative final pitch when *Actress?* is an entire utterance constituting a question), or of phonetic modification (as the change of *actor* to *actr-* before *-ess*) — **tax·e·mic** \(')tak'sēmik\ *adj*

tax·e·op·o·da \,taksē'äpədə\ *n pl, cap* [NL, fr. Gk *taxis* arrangement, order, regularity (gen. *taxeōs*) + NL *-poda*] *in former classifications* : an order of chiefly taxeopodous mammals comprising the Proboscidea, Condylarthra, Hyracoidea, and sometimes others

tax·e·op·o·dous \;≈≈;äpədəs\ *adj* [irreg. fr. Gk *taxis* + E *-podous*] : having each or most of the tarsal or carpal bones of one row articulating with only one bone of the other row — used esp. of an ungulate mammal; opposed to *diplarthrous*

tax·er \'taksə(r)\ *n* -s [¹*tax* + *-er*] : one that taxes

taxes *pl of* TAXIS *or of* TAX, *pres 3d sing of* TAX

-taxes *pl of* -TAXIS

¹tax-exempt \;≈;≈\ *adj* [²*tax* + *exempt*] **1** : exempted from a tax **2** : bearing interest free from a federal or state income tax ⟨*tax-exempt* securities⟩

²tax-exempt \"\ *n* -s : a tax-exempt bond

tax-free \'≈;≈\ *adj* : TAX-EXEMPT

¹taxi \'taksē, -si\ *n, pl* **taxis** *also* **taxies** [short for *taxicab*] **1** : TAXICAB **2** : a similarly operated boat or airplane

²taxi \"\ *vb* **taxied; taxied; taxiing** *or* **taxying; taxis** *or* **taxies** *vi* **1** : to ride in a taxicab : go by taxicab **2 a** *of an airplane* : to go at low speed along the surface of the ground or water (as when maneuvering into position for takeoff or parking) ⟨the plane comes in and ~s up to its place —C.B. Palmer b. 1910⟩ **b** : to operate an airplane on the ground under its own power ⟨a pilot ~s to the warmup apron and holds there for several minutes before taking off —*Civil Air Regulations*⟩ **~** *vt* **1** : to transport by or as if by taxi ⟨the last visiting novelist has been safely ~ed to his . . . hotel —*Saturday Rev.*⟩ **2** : to cause (an airplane) to taxi ⟨the aircraft captain . . . ~s the plane . . . across the airport to the terminal — Richard Thruelsen⟩

³taxi \"\ *n* -s [²*taxi*] : an act or action of taxiing

taxi- — see TAX-

-tax·ia \'taksēə\ *n comb form* -s [NL, fr. Gk — more at -TAXY] : -TAXIS 1 ⟨hetero*taxia*⟩

tax·i·arch \'taksē,ärk\ *n* -s [Gk *taxiarchos, taxiarchēs,* fr. *taxis* + *archos, -archēs* -arch] : a commander of an ancient Greek taxis

tax·ic \'taksik\ *adj* [NL *taxis* + E *-ic*] : of, relating to, or involving a taxis

taxi·cab \'taksē,kab, -si,-, -kaa(ə)b\ *n* [*taximeter cab*] : a chauffeur-driven automobile available on call to carry a passenger between any two points (as within a city) for a fare determined by a taximeter, zone system, or flat rate

taxi dance hall *n* : a dance hall catering to men and providing taxi dancers as partners

taxi dancer *n* [¹*taxi;* fr. the fact that such dancers are hired like taxis for a short period of time] : a girl employed by a dance hall, café, or cabaret to dance with patrons who pay a certain amount for each dance or period of time

tax·id·ea \tak'sidēə\ *n, cap* [NL, fr. ML *taxus* badger (of Gmc origin; akin to OHG *dahs* badger) + NL *-idea* — more at TECHNICAL] : a genus of mammals (family Mustelidae) consisting of the American badger

tax·i·der·mic \'taksə;dərmik, -dəm-, -dəim- -mēk\ *also* **tax·i·der·mal** \-məl\ *adj* : of or relating to taxidermy

tax·i·der·mist \'≈≈,≈məst\ *n* -s : one who practices taxidermy

tax·i·der·my \-mē, -mi\ *n* -ES [*tax-* + *derm-* + *-y*] : the art of preparing lifelike representations of animals by stuffing the skin or usu. by fashioning a wooden or plaster model on which the skin of the specimen (as a bird or mammal) is mounted or by molding and painting a plastic replica of the specimen (as a fish or reptile)

-taxies *pl of* -TAXY

tax·i·fo·lin \,taksə'fōlən\ *n* [NL *taxifolia* (specific epithet of *Pseudotsuga taxifolia,* fr. *tax-* + *-folia,* fr. L *folium* leaf) + E *-in* — more at BLADE] : a crystalline pentahydroxy flavanone $C_{15}H_7O_2(OH)_5$ that occurs naturally esp. in the heartwood of Douglas fir, may be prepared from quercetin by reduction with sodium hydrosulfite, and yields quercetin on oxidation; dihydro-quercetin

taximan \'≈≈mən\ *n, pl* **taximen** [¹*taxi* + *man*] *chiefly Brit* : the operator of a taxi : taxi driver

taxi·me·ter \'taksē,mēd·ə(r), -si,- -ētə-\ *n* [F *taximètre,* modif. of G *taxameter* — more at TAXAMETER] : an instrument for use in a hired vehicle (as a taxicab) for automatically showing the fare due

tax·ine \'tak,sēn, -ksən\ *n* -s [ISV *tax-* (fr. NL *Taxus*) + *-ine*] : a bitter poisonous alkaloid $C_{37}H_{51}NO_{10}$ obtained as an amorphous powder from the leaves, shoots, and seeds of the English yew

taxing *adj* [fr. pres. part. of ¹*tax*] : that taxes : ONEROUS, WEARING — **tax·ing·ly** *adv*

tax in kind : a tax payable in goods or services instead of money

tax·in·o·my \tak'sinəmē\ *n* -ES [by alter.] : TAXONOMY

taxiplane \'≈≈,≈\ *n* [¹*taxi* + *plane*] : an airplane used as a public vehicle for hire

¹tax·is \'taksəs\ *n, pl* **tax·es** \-k,sēz\ [Gk, lit., arrangement, order, fr. *taktos* (verbal of *tassein* to arrange, order) + *-sis* — more at TACTICS] **1** : the manual restoration of a displaced body part; *specif* : the reduction of a hernia manually **2** [NL, fr. *-taxis*] **a** : reflex movement by a freely motile and usu. simple organism that is translational or sometimes merely orientational and that constitutes a positive or negative response to a source of stimulation (as a light or a temperature or chemical gradient) — compare KINESIS, TROPISM **b** : a reflex reaction involving such movement **3** : a unit (as a company, battalion) of varying size in an ancient Greek army

²taxis *pl of* TAXI, *pres 3d sing of* TAXI

-tax·is \'taksəs\ *n comb form, pl* **-tax·es** \-k,sēz\ [NL, fr. Gk *taxis*] **1** : arrangement : order ⟨homo*taxis*⟩ **2** : taxis (sense 2) ⟨chemo*taxis*⟩ ⟨helio*taxis*⟩ ⟨thermo*taxis*⟩

taxi stand *n* : a place where taxis may park awaiting hire : CABSTAND

taxi strip *n* : TAXIWAY

tax·ite \'tak,sīt\ *n* -s [G *taxit,* fr. *tax-* + *-it* -ite] : volcanic rock of clastic or schlieric appearance due to the aggregation of flows of different colors, textures, granularity, or mineral composition : EUTAXITE, ATAXITE — **tax·it·ic** \(')tak'sid·ik\ *adj*

taxi track *n, Brit* : TAXIWAY

taxiway \'≈≈,≈\ *n* : a usu. paved strip for taxiing (as from the terminal to the end of the runway) at an airport

tax·less \'taksləs\ *adj* : free from taxation : UNTAXED — **tax·less·ly** *adv* — **tax·less·ness** *n* -ES

tax lien *n* : a statutory charge on property for taxes due giving the taxing authority a security interest therein

tax list *or* **tax roll** *n* : a document maintained by a public officer (as an assessor) listing taxable persons or property or both within a taxing district and often also the tax assessed on each — called also *tax book*

taxo- — see TAX-

tax·o·di·a·ce·ae \tak,sōdē'āsē,ē\ *n pl, cap* [NL, fr. *Taxodium,* type genus + *-aceae*] : a family of coniferous trees or rarely shrubs that are sometimes included in Pinaceae but are distinguished by flat or peltate cone scales lacking bracts and each producing 2 to 9 seeds and by dimorphic leaves or none — **tax·o·di·a·ceous** \;≈;≈;āshəs\ *adj*

tax·o·di·ine \tak'sōdē,īn\ *or* **tax·o·di·oid** \-ē,ȯid\ *adj* [NL *Taxodium* + E *-ine* or *-oid*] : of or relating to *Taxodium* or the Taxodiaceae

tax·o·di·um \-ōdēəm\ *n* [NL, fr. *Taxus* + *-odium* (fr. Gk *-odos* -ode)] **1** *cap* : a small genus of tall deciduous trees (family Taxodiaceae) having drooping branches, spirally arranged linear leaves, and globose cones with thick woody scales — see AHUEHUETE, BALD CYPRESS **2** -s : any tree of the genus *Taxodium*

¹tax·o·dont \'taksə,dänt\ *adj* [NL *Taxodonta*] : of or relating to the Taxodonta

²taxodont \"\ *n* -s : a mollusk of the order Taxodonta

tax·o·don·ta \,≈≈'däntə\ *n pl, cap* [NL, fr. *tax-* + *-odonta*] *in some classifications* : an order of Lamellibranchia comprising bivalve mollusks with the hinge teeth numerous and unspecialized and the adductor muscles both present and equally developed

tax·ol·o·gy \tak'säləjē\ *n* -ES [*tax-* + *-logy*] : TAXONOMY 1

tax·on \'tak,sän\ *n, pl* **taxa** \-ksə\ *also* **taxons** [ISV, backformation (influence of *etymon*) fr. *taxonomy*] **1** : a taxonomic group or entity **2** : the name applied to a taxonomic group in a formal system of nomenclature

tax·o·nom·ic \;taksə;nämik, -mēk\ *also* **tax·o·nom·i·cal** \-məkəl, -mēk-\ *adj* : of or relating to or having the character of taxonomy

tax·o·nom·i·cal·ly \-mək(ə)lē\ *adv* : from a taxonomic standpoint : with regard to taxonomy

tax·on·o·mist \tak'sänəmə̇st\ *n* -s : a specialist in taxonomy

tax·on·o·my \-mē, -mi\ *n* -ES [F *taxonomie,* fr. *tax-* + *-nomie* -nomy] **1** : the study of the general principles of scientific classification : SYSTEMATICS **2** : the systematic distinguishing, ordering, and naming of type groups within a subject field : CLASSIFICATION; *specif* : orderly classification of plants and animals according to their presumed natural relationships forming a basic biological discipline involving during its Linnaean period the firm establishment of binomial nomenclature and acceptance of the static concept of fixity of the species, during its Darwinian period the dynamic concept of speciation by natural selection, and during its modern Mendelian epoch an expansion to include study of the mechanisms underlying speciation and related processes (as raciation, variation) — compare BIOSYSTEMATY, CYTOTAXONOMY, DETERMINE 5b

tax·or \'taksə(r)\ *n* -s [ME *taxour* assessor, fr. AF, fr. OF *taxer* to tax + AF *-our* -or — more at TAX] : one of two former officers at the older British universities empowered to regulate the prices of students' lodgings and food

taxpayer \'≈,≈≈\ *n* **1** : one that pays or is liable to pay a tax **2** : a temporary building erected to earn something to meet the taxes on the land

tax sale *n* : a sale (as at public auction) conducted by an officer of the taxing authority of specific property for nonpayment of a tax due from its owner and granting to the purchaser a tax title

tax stamp *n* **1** : a stamp marked on or affixed to a taxable item as evidence that the tax has been paid **2** : POSTAL TAX STAMP

tax title *n* : the right or title acquired by a purchaser of property at a tax sale being subject to redemption by the delinquent owner for a specified time, sometimes granting immediate possession and the title that the owner had, sometimes granting only the right upon compliance with statutory requirements to acquire that owner's title or a new paramount title in fee simple absolute, and often requiring confirmation by a court decree

tax·us \'taksəs\ *n* [NL, fr. L, yew] **1** *cap* : a small genus (the type of the family Taxaceae) comprising the yews and including ornamental trees and shrubs having stiff somewhat petioled linear leaves spirally arranged, a fruit consisting of a fleshy aril enclosing a hard seed, and poisonous juice — see GROUND HEMLOCK, JAPANESE YEW **2** *pl* **taxus** : any plant of the genus *Taxus*

taxwise \'≈,≈\ *adv* [²*tax* + *-wise*] : with respect to a tax or taxation

-taxy \'taksē, -si\ *n comb form* -ES [Gk *-taxia,* fr. *taktos* (verbal of *tassein* to arrange, order) + *-ia* -y — more at TACTICS] : -TAXIS ⟨epi*taxy*⟩ ⟨pleio*taxy*⟩

taying *pres part of* TAY

tay \'tā\ *dial var of* **tea**

ta·ya·ci·an \tə'yāsēən\ *adj, usu cap* [F *tayacien,* fr. *Tayac,* its type site near Les Eyzies in southwestern France + F *-ien* -ian] : of or belonging to a stage of culture intermediate between the Clactonian and the Mousterian characterized by poorly made planoconvex flake tools

ta·yal \tə'yäl\ *also* **ata·yal** \,äd·ə'yäl\ *n, pl* **tayal** *or* **tayals** *usu cap* **1** : a Malaysian people on Formosa **2** : a member of the Tayal people

ta·yas·su \tə'ya(,)sü\ *n, cap* [NL, fr. Pg *taiaçu, taiaçú* white-lipped peccary, fr. Tupi] : a genus (the type of the family Tayassuidae) of American wild swine comprising the living peccaries and having a complex stomach, a gland on the back, and three toes on the hind feet — compare SUIDAE

¹ta·yas·su·id \-asəwəd\ *adj* [NL *Tayassuidae,* family of wild swine, fr. *Tayassu,* type genus + *-idae*] : of or relating to the genus *Tayassu* or family Tayassuidae

²tayassuid \"\ *n* -s : a swine of the genus *Tayassu* or family Tayassuidae : PECCARY

tay·lor·ism \'tālə,rizəm\ *n* -s *usu cap* [Frederick W. *Taylor* †1915 Am. engineer + E *-ism*] **1** : the methods of factory management first developed and advocated by Frederick W. Taylor **2** : SCIENTIFIC MANAGEMENT

tay·lor·ite \'tālə,rīt\ *n* -s [W. J. *Taylor* †1864 Am. mineral chemist + E *-ite*] : a mineral $(K,NH_4)_2SO_4$ consisting of a potassium ammonium sulfate and occurring in compact white lumps in the guano beds of the Chincha islands, Peru

tay·lor system *also* **taylor plan** \'tālə(r)-\ *n, usu cap T* [after F. W. *Taylor*] : TAYLORISM 1; *specif* : DIFFERENTIAL PIECE-RATE SYSTEM

taylor-white process \'≈≈(h)wīt-\ *n* [after F. W. *Taylor* & Maunsel B. *White* †1912 Am. engineers] : a process invented about 1899 for heat-treating high-speed steels

tay·ra *also* **tai·ra** \'tīrə\ *n* -s [Pg *taira* & Sp *taira, tayra,* fr. Tupi] : a long-tailed mustelid mammal (*Galera barbara*) of So. and Central America that resembles the No. American fisher in size but has short fur and is black with a grayish head

taz·et·tine \'tazə,tēn, -zətən\ *n* -s [NL *tazetta* (specific epithet of *Narcissus tazetta*) + E *-ine*] : a crystalline alkaloid $C_{18}H_{21}NO_5$ obtained chiefly from the bulbs of the polyanthus narcissus

taze·well \'taz,wel, -,wəl\ *n* -s *usu cap* [fr. *Tazewell,* county in Ill.] : a substage of the Wisconsin glacial stage; *also* : the drift of such substage

ta·zia \tə'zēə\ *n* -s [Ar *ta'zīyah,* lit., mourning for the dead] **1** : a Muslim passion play celebrated by the Shi'a in Muharram **2** : a replica of the tomb of Husain the martyred son of Muhammad carried in processions during the Shi'ite festival of Muharram

taz·za \'tätsə\ *n* -s [It, cup, mug, basin, fr. Ar *tass, tassah* — more at TASS] : an ornamental receptacle (as a cup or vase) with a large flat shallow bowl resting on a pedestal or pillar and often having handles

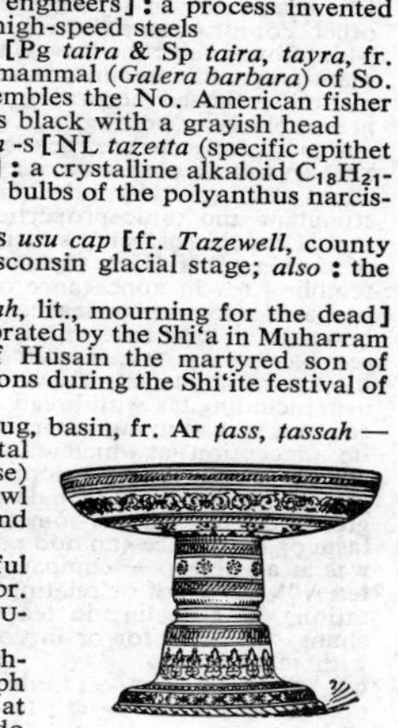
tazza

tb *abbr* tablespoon; tablespoonful

TB \'tē'bē\ *n* -s [fr. *TB,* abbr. for *tubercle bacillus*] : TUBERCULOSIS

TB *abbr* **1** tariff bureau **2** technical bulletin **3** telegraph bureau **4** time base **5** times at bat **6** torpedo boat **7** torpedo bomber **8** total bases **9** traffic bureau **10** trial balance **11** tubercle bacillus

Tb *symbol* terbium

TBA *abbr* **1** table of basic allowances **2** tires, batteries, and accessories **3** to be announced

t bandage *n, cap T* : a bandage shaped like the letter T and used chiefly about the waist or perineum to hold a dressing in place

TB and S *abbr* top, bottom, and sides

t bar *or* **t beam** *cap T, or* **tee bar** *or* **tee beam** *n* **:** a metal bar or beam having a cross section of the form of the letter T

t–bar lift \ˈ≈,≈-\ *or* **t–bar** *n, cap T* **:** a ski lift in which two skiers at a time lean against a bar suspended in the center while being pulled uphill

TBB *abbr* tenor, baritone, bass

t–beam bridge \ˈ≈,≈-\ *n, cap T* **:** a reinforced-concrete bridge consisting of a floor slab monolithic with the supporting beams so that a cross section resembles a series of T beams

t bevel *n, cap T* **:** BEVEL 2

TBL *abbr* through bill of lading

tblspn *abbr* tablespoon; tablespoonful

TBM *abbr* temporary bench mark

t bolt *cap T, also* **tee bolt** *n* **1 :** a bolt having a crosspiece for a head **2 :** a bolt with a head of square or rectangular shape intended to fit a T slot

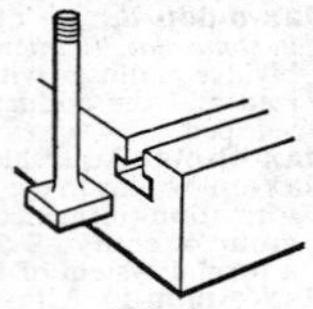

T bolt

t–bone \ˈ≈,≈\ *also* **t–bone steak** *n, cap T* **:** a small beefsteak from the thin end of the short loin containing a T-shaped bone and a small piece of tenderloin — compare PORTERHOUSE; see BEEF illustration

TB–1 *or* **TB 1–698** *n* [G, fr. *TB* + *1–698*, its laboratory code number; fr. its use in the treatment of tuberculosis] **:** THIACETAZONE

TBP *abbr* true boiling point

tbr *abbr* timber

tbs *abbr* tablespoon; tablespoonful

TBS \ˌtē,bēˈes\ *abbr or n* -s [*t*alk *b*etween *s*hips] **:** a short range radio system for communication within task forces

tbsp *abbr* tablespoon; tablespoonful

t–budding \ˈ≈,≈≈\ *n, cap T* **:** SHIELD BUDDING

TBW *abbr* to be withheld

tc *abbr* **1** tical **2** tierce

TC *abbr* **1** tank corps **2** tariff circular; tariff commission **3** teachers college **4** technical college **5** temporary constable **6** tennis club **7** terra-cotta **8** thermocouple **9** till countermanded **10** top of column **11** total chances **12** touring club **13** town clerk; town councillor **14** traffic commissioner; traffic consultant **15** training center; training circular **16** transportation corps **17** turret captain

Tc *symbol* technetium

TCA *abbr or n* -s [*t*ri*c*hloro*a*cetic acid] **:** trichloroacetic acid or one of its derivatives (as the sodium salt)

t cart *n, cap T* **:** an open 2-seated wagon with T-shaped body

tce *abbr* terrace

tcham·bu·li \chämˈbülē\ *n, pl* **tchambuli** *or* **tchambulis** *usu cap* **1 :** a people of the Sepik district, Territory of New Guinea **2 :** a member of the Tchambuli people

tcha·viche \chəˈvēsh\ *n* -s [F, fr. NL *tschawytscha* (specific epithet of *Onchorhyncus tschawytscha*), fr. Russ *chavycha*] **:** KING SALMON

tche·by·cheff inequality \chəbəˈshôf-\ *n, usu cap T* [after Pafrutii L. *Tchebycheff* †1894 Russ. mathematician] **:** an inequality that gives an upper limit to the probability that a variable will assume a value more than a specified number of standard deviations away from its mean

tche·func·te \chəˈfüŋktə\ *adj, usu cap* [fr. *Tchefuncte* State Park, La.] **:** of or relating to a culture of Louisiana of about A.D. 500–900 characterized by conical burial mounds, circular structures, and coiled pottery with linear punctate ornamentation

tcher·vo·nets *or* **tcher·vo·netz** \chərˈvónəts\ *var of* CHERVONETS

tchet·vert \ˈchetvə(r)t\ *var of* CHETVERT

tchi *usu cap, var of* TWI

tchr *abbr* teacher

t connection *n, cap T* **:** a connection of two coils (as of a transformer) diagrammatically as a letter T chiefly used for transforming two-phase systems into three-phase systems and vice versa — called also *Scott connection;* compare DELTA CONNECTION

t connector *n, cap T* **:** an electrical binding post consisting of three posts forming the three arms of a letter T

TCP *abbr or n* -s **1** [*t*ri*c*hloro*p*henoxyacetic acid] trichlorophenoxyacetic acid **2** [*t*ri*c*resyl *p*hosphate] tricresyl phosphate

TCP *abbr* traffic control post

tcr *abbr* tracer

TCS *abbr* traffic control station

t–cushion \ˈ≈,≈≈\ *n, cap T* **:** a square cushion for an upholstered chair having front extensions to fit around the arms in T shape

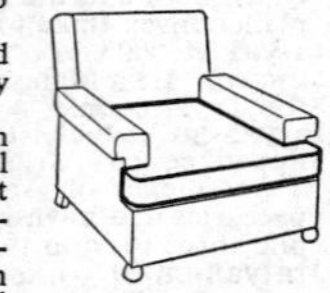

T-cushion

TD \ˈtēˈdē\ *n* -s [fr. *TD*, initials stamped on a common make of clay pipe] **:** a clay pipe

TD *abbr or n* -s [*t*ouch*d*own] touchdown

TD *abbr* **1** tank destroyer **2** [IrGael *Teachta Dala*] member of parliament **3** telegraph department **4** telephone department **5** temporary disability; temporary duty **6** territorial decoration **7** time deposit **8** tons per day **9** total depth **10** tractor-drawn **11** traffic director **12** treasury decision; treasury department

TDE \ˌtē,dēˈē\ *abbr or n* -s [*t*etrachloro-*d*iphenyl-*e*thane] **:** DDD

tdm *abbr* tandem

TDN *abbr* total digestible nutrients

TDS *abbr* **1** *often not cap* [L *ter die sumendum*] to be taken three times a day **2** time, distance, speed

TDY *abbr or n* -s temporary duty

te *var of* TEE

TE *abbr* **1** table of equipment **2** topographical engineer **3** trailing edge

Te *symbol* tellurium

¹tea \ˈtē\ *n* -s [Chin (Amoy) *tʻe;* akin to Chin (Pek) *chʻa²* tea] **1 a :** a shrub (*Camellia sinensis*) cultivated from antiquity in China and now in Japan, India, Ceylon, Sumatra, Java, and other countries and having lanceolate leaves and fragrant white flowers **b :** the leaves, leaf buds, and internodes of this plant prepared and cured for the market by several recognized methods, classed according to method of manufacture (as green, black, or oolong) and graded according to leaf size (as congou, orange pekoe, pekoe, souchong) — see GUNPOWDER TEA, HYSON **c :** an aromatic beverage that is prepared from cured tea leaves by infusion with boiling water, has mild stimulant and tonic properties due to the alkaloid caffeine, and is capable of being strongly astringent from the presence of tannin **2 a** (1) **:** any of numerous plants somewhat resembling tea in appearance or properties (2) **:** an infusion prepared from their leaves and used medicinally or as a beverage — used usu. with qualifying adjective or attributive; see ABYSSINIAN TEA, BREAST TEA, LABRADOR TEA, SAGE TEA **b :** TEA ROSE **c** *slang* **:** MARIHUANA **3 a :** light refreshments usu. including tea with bread and butter sandwiches, crackers, cookies, served in late afternoon **b :** a formal social occasion (as a reception) at which tea and other refreshments are served **c** *Brit* **:** a light late afternoon or evening meal **:** SUPPER **4 :** a grayish yellow green to pale green that is lighter than Surrey green **5** *chiefly Brit* **:** something or someone that suits one's taste or preference ⟨an odd pair, I shouldn't have thought she was at all his ~⟩ — compare CUP OF TEA

²tea \ˈ"\ *adj* **1 :** of or relating to tea or the tea plant ⟨~ plantation⟩ **2 :** dealing in tea ⟨~ merchant⟩ **3 :** used for or in connection with tea ⟨~ urn⟩

³tea \ˈ"\ *vi* -ED/-ING/-S **:** to drink tea or take a light meal ~ *vt* **:** to entertain with a tea

tea bag *n* **:** a cloth or filler paper bag holding a measured amount of tea for making an individual serving of tea

tea ball *n* **:** a perforated metal ball for making tea in cups or in a teapot

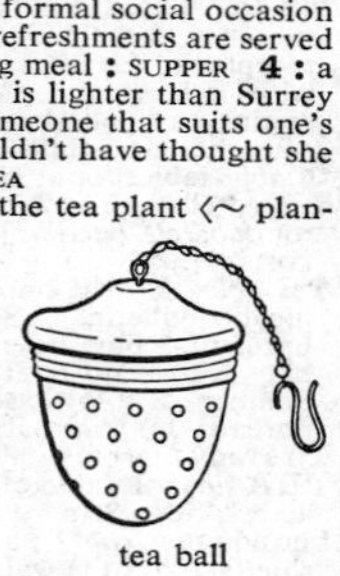

tea ball

tea basket *n, Brit* **:** a lunch basket or picnic hamper

tea·berry \ˈtē- — *see* BERRY\ *n* [¹*tea* + *berry;* fr. the use of its dried leaves to make a substitute for tea] **1 :** CHECKERBERRY 1a **2 :** CREEPING SNOWBERRY

tea biscuit *n, Brit* **:** a short or sweet biscuit served with afternoon tea **:** CRACKER, COOKIE

teaboard \ˈ≈,≈\ *n* **:** a tray for serving tea

tea borer *n* **:** a borer that is the larva of a moth (*Zeuzera coffeae*) of the family Cossidae and bores into the stems and branches of coffee, tea, and sandal

teabowl \ˈ≈,≈\ *n* **:** a teacup having no handle

tea·boy \ˈtē,bȯi\ *n, Irish* **:** MANSERVANT

tea bread *n* **:** sweetened bread or buns to be eaten with tea

tea broom *n* **:** an Australian tea tree (*Leptospermum scoparium*)

tea caddy *n* **:** CADDY 1a

tea cake *n* **1** *Brit* **:** a light flat cake **2 :** COOKIE

tea cart *n* **:** a dinner wagon used in serving tea or light refreshments

teach \ˈtēch\ *vb* **taught** \ˈtȯt, *usu* -ȯd.+V\ **taught; teaching; teaches** [ME *techen*, fr. OE *tǣcan* to show, instruct; akin to OE *tācen, tācn* sign, token — more at TOKEN] *vt* **1** *obs* **:** SHOW, GUIDE, DIRECT **2 a :** to cause to know a subject ⟨all children are *taught* the three R's⟩ ⟨*taught* his sons a trade⟩ **b :** to cause to know how to do something **:** show how ⟨my father is ~*ing* me to drive⟩ **c :** to accustom to some action or attitude ⟨should ~ students to think for themselves⟩ ⟨have been *taught* respect for the self-made man⟩ **d :** to make (one) know the disagreeable consequences of some action ⟨I'll ~ you to come home late⟩ **3 :** to direct as an instructor **:** guide the studies of **:** conduct through a course of studies **:** give instruction to ⟨the most active mind that I have ever *taught*⟩ **4 a :** to impart the knowledge of ⟨~ algebra⟩ **b :** to present in a classroom lecture or discussion ⟨have *taught Hamlet* many times⟩ **c :** to instruct in the rules, principles, or practice of ⟨~ music⟩ ⟨~ dancing⟩ **5 a :** to direct, instruct, or train by precept, example, or experience ⟨that same prayer does ~ us all to render the deeds of mercy —Shak.⟩ ⟨had *taught* himself to view the war as one of God's processes —R.M.Weaver⟩ **b :** to seek to make known and accepted **:** IMPLANT, PREACH ⟨the philosopher *taught* purity, moderation, and self-containment⟩ ⟨the culture which *taught* despising of the body —H.A.Overstreet⟩ ⟨experience ~*es* us that our powers are limited⟩ **6 :** to conduct instruction regularly in ⟨*taught* school for several years before her marriage⟩ ~ *vi* **1 a :** to provide instruction, guidance, or discipline **:** act or become employed as a teacher **b :** to propound a doctrine **:** demonstrate a lesson or moral ⟨Freudianism ~*es* the importance of the unconscious mind⟩ ⟨history ~*es* that poverty favors the rise of communism⟩ **2 :** to be capable of exposition or explanation ⟨a book that ~*es* easily⟩

syn INSTRUCT, EDUCATE, TRAIN, DISCIPLINE, SCHOOL, COACH, TUTOR: TEACH is a general term for causing one to acquire knowledge or skill, usu. with the imparting of necessary incidental information and the giving of incidental help and encouragement ⟨*teach* a child to read⟩ ⟨*teaching* him algebra⟩ ⟨*taught* the boys how to swim⟩ INSTRUCT may suggest methodical, continuing, or formal teaching ⟨*instruct* the men in safety procedures⟩ ⟨*instructing* students in military drill⟩ EDUCATE may apply to more pretentious processes of teaching and instruction designed to ensure full development of the capacities of a more intelligent person ⟨a school designed to *educate* candidates for the ministry⟩ ⟨a program to *educate* the leaders of tomorrow⟩ TRAIN may suggest methodical, thorough instruction and guidance with a specific end in mind until rapid and successful execution of duties and tasks is assured ⟨a *trained* anesthetist⟩ ⟨officers' *training* schools⟩ ⟨a *trained* radio actress⟩ DISCIPLINE calls attention to subordination to a master or subjection to control, sometimes one's own ⟨well-*disciplined* cadets⟩ ⟨*disciplined* party workers⟩ ⟨one must not let one's thoughts run on like this: one must *discipline* one's mind —Victoria Sackville-West⟩ SCHOOL, often interchangeable with others in this set, perhaps more often has suggestions of TRAIN although it lacks the specificity of this latter word ⟨the growing demand by industry for able people *schooled* in engineering and business administration —*Report of General Motors Corp.*⟩ ⟨with division, corps, and Army staffs *schooled* in the same language, practices, and techniques —W.P. Corderman⟩ ⟨*schooled* himself to accept her will, in this as in other matters, as absolute and unquestionable —Thomas Hardy⟩ COACH is likely to refer to training with demonstration and practice in some specialized, often extracurricular activity ⟨*coaching* football⟩ ⟨was *coaching* the school play⟩ TUTOR usu. applies to teaching on an individual basis in some specialized subject ⟨*tutoring* him in mathematics⟩ ⟨special *tutoring* sessions for those deficient⟩ ⟨the enemies of this faith know no god but force, no devotion but its use. They *tutor* men in treason —D. D.Eisenhower⟩

teach·abil·i·ty \ˌtēchəˈbiləd.ē\ *n* **1 :** suitability for use in teaching ⟨illustrations increase the ~ of a textbook⟩ **2 :** ability to learn by instruction **:** TEACHABLENESS

teach·able \ˈtēchəbəl\ *adj* **1 a :** capable of being taught ⟨whether virtue was ~ or not⟩ **b :** apt and willing to learn **:** DOCILE ⟨a ~ pupil⟩ ⟨the ~ humility essential to learning —G.B.Oxnam⟩ **2 :** favorable to teaching **:** making for easy teaching ⟨choosing the ~ moment⟩ ⟨a ~ text⟩ — **teach·able·ness** *n* -ES — **teach·ably** \-blē\ *adv*

teach·er \ˈtēchə(r)\ *n* -s [ME *techer*, fr. *techen* to teach + *-er*] **1 :** one that teaches or instructs ⟨nature was his only ~⟩; *esp* **:** one whose occupation is to instruct ⟨a ~ at the local high school⟩ ⟨a driving ~⟩ **2 a :** a religious instructor or preacher often not regularly ordained in a Congregational church **b :** a member of the Aaronic priesthood of the Mormon Church of the grade between deacon and priest

teach·er·age \-chərij\ *n* -s [*teacher* + *-age* (as in *parsonage*)] **:** a residence provided for teachers

teacher bird *also* **teacher** *n* [imit.] **1 :** OVENBIRD 2 **2 :** RED-EYED VIREO

teach·er·less \-chə(r)ləs\ *adj* **:** lacking a teacher

teachers college *n* **:** a college for the training of teachers usu. offering a full four-year course and granting a bachelor's degree — compare NORMAL SCHOOL

teachers' council *n* **:** a representative assembly chosen from the teaching staff of a school system that makes recommendations to the superintendent of schools and to the board of education

teach·er·ship \-(r),ship\ *n* [*teacher* + *-ship*] **:** a teaching position

teacher's pet *n* **1 :** a pupil who has won his teacher's special favor **2 :** one who has ingratiated himself with an authority **:** FAVORITE

teach·ery \-chərē\ *adj* [*teacher* + *-y*] **:** suggestive of a teacher

tea chest *n* **1 :** CADDY 1a **2 :** a square wooden case usu. lined with sheet lead or tin and used for exporting tea

¹teaching *n* -s [ME *teching*, fr. gerund of *techen* to teach] **1 :** the act, practice, or profession of teaching ⟨~ requires intelligence, maturity, and devotion⟩ ⟨many young people will go into ~⟩ **2 :** something that is taught **:** INSTRUCTION, DOCTRINE ⟨you have had excellent ~⟩ ⟨the ~*s* of Confucius⟩

²teaching *adj* [fr. pres. part. of *teach*] **:** that teaches ⟨~ profession⟩ ⟨~ doctor⟩

teaching aid *n* [¹*teaching*] **:** printed material (as a picture or map) or other device (as a record player or gyroscope) used by a teacher to fortify or enliven classroom instruction ⟨audio-visual *teaching aids*⟩

teaching elder *n* [²*teaching*] **:** a minister in the Presbyterian Church — compare ELDER 4b

teaching fellow *n* **:** a resident student at a graduate school who is granted free tuition and maintenance in return for assisting with teaching or laboratory duties

teaching hospital *n* [¹*teaching*] **:** a hospital that is affiliated with a university medical school and provides the means for medical education to students, interns, and residents and sometimes postgraduates

teachy \ˈtēchē\ *adj* [*teach* + *-y*] **:** DIDACTIC, SCHOOLMASTERISH

tea clipper *n* **:** a clipper built for tea trade (as from China to London)

tea cloth *n* **:** a small tablecloth

tea cozy *n* **:** a cozy for keeping tea warm

tea crab *n* **:** an Asiatic crab tree (*Malus hupehensis*) used as an ornamental and having branches growing wide in a fan shape and pink flowers that turn to white

teacup \ˈ≈,≈\ *n* **:** a cup with a handle and usu. of less than 8-oz. capacity used commonly with a saucer for hot beverages

tea·cup·ful \ˈ≈,≈,fu̇l\ *n, pl* **teacupfuls** *or* **teacupsful** \-p,fu̇lz, -ps,fu̇l\ [*teacup* + *-ful*] **:** as much as a teacup can hold **:** enough to fill a teacup

tea dance *n* **:** a dance held in the late afternoon

tea dust glaze *n* **:** a greenish opaque glaze on Chinese porcelain

teaed *past of* TEA

tea·ette \(ˈ)tēˌet\ *n* -s [¹*tea* + *-ette*] **:** TEA MAKER

tea family *n* **:** THEACEAE

tea fight *n* **:** TEA PARTY

tea garden *n* **1 :** a public garden where tea and other refreshments are served **2 :** a tea plantation

tea gown *n* **:** a semiformal gown of fine materials in graceful flowing lines worn esp. for afternoon for entertaining at home

tea green *n* **:** a grayish yellow green that is yellower and paler than average sage green and yellower and lighter than palmetto — called also *Queen Anne green*

tea hound *n* **:** a man who frequents teas ⟨assumption that . . . every diplomat is a *tea hound* —*Wall Street Jour.*⟩

teahouse \ˈ≈,≈\ *n* **:** a public house or restaurant where tea and light refreshments are sold

teaing *pres part of* TEA

¹teak \ˈtēk\ *n* -s [Pg *teca*, fr. Malayalam *tēkka*] **1 a :** a tall East Indian timber tree (*Tectona grandis*) of the family Verbenaceae now planted in West Africa and tropical America for its wood **b :** the hard strong durable yellowish brown wood of teak that is highly resistant to insect attack and to warping and is used esp. for shipbuilding **2 :** any of several trees resembling teak or having wood used in place of teakwood: as **a** (1) **:** AUSTRALIAN TEAK a (2) **:** FLINDOSA **b :** an Australian timber tree (*Dissiliaria baloghioides*) of the family Euphorbiaceae **c :** AFRICAN OAK 1 **d** *NewZeal* **:** PURIRI **e :** IROKO **f :** RHODESIAN MAHOGANY **3 a :** EBONY 4 **b** *or* **teak brown :** SIENNA BROWN

²teak \ˈ"\ *adj* **:** of or relating to teak **:** made of teakwood

teakettle \ˈ≈,≈≈\ *n* **:** a covered kettle with a fixed handle or bail and spout for boiling water

tea knife *n* **:** a small table knife used esp. for pastry

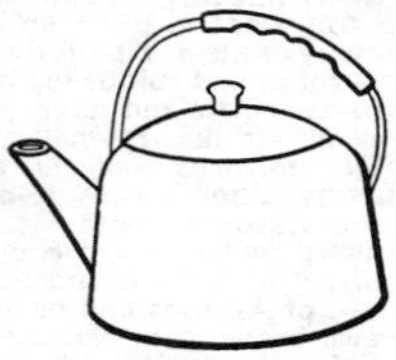

teakettle

teakwood \ˈ≈,≈\ *n* **1 :** TEAK 1b **2 :** SOOT BROWN

teal \ˈtēl, *esp before pause or consonant* -ēəl\ *n, pl* **teal** *or* **teals** [ME *tele;* akin to MD *teling, teelingh* teal] **1 a :** any of several small short-necked river ducks of Europe and America belonging to the genus *Anas* or esp. formerly placed in *Nettion* and *Querquedula* and including the garganey and related birds and the blue-winged and cinnamon teals which both have a light blue area on the forepart of the wing — compare GREENWING **b :** any of several other small wild ducks (as *Aythya novae-seelandiae* and *Stictonetta naevosa*) of New Zealand and Australia **2 :** a variable color averaging a dark greenish blue that is greener, lighter, and stronger than teal duck or teal blue and greener and less strong than drake

teal blue *n* **:** a variable color averaging a dark greenish blue that is bluer and duller than average teal, duller and slightly greener than drake, and greener, lighter, and stronger than teal duck

teal duck *n* **1 :** TEAL **2 :** a dark greenish blue that is bluer and duller than average teal, averaging teal blue, drake, or duckling

tea lead *n* **:** a metal alloy used to line tea chests

tea·less \ˈtēləs\ *adj* [¹*tea* + *-less*] **:** lacking or deprived of tea

tealgrass \ˈ≈,≈\ *n* [*teal* + *grass;* fr. its being considered an important food for teal] **:** a love grass (*Eragrostis hypnoides*) of the central U. S.

teal gray *n* **:** a dark bluish gray that is greener and lighter than smoke blue

teal green *n* **:** a variable color averaging a dark bluish green that is bluer, lighter, and stronger than invisible green (sense 2) or pine tree

teall·ite \ˈtē,līt\ *n* -s [J. J. Harris *Teall* †1924 Eng. geologist + E *-ite*] **:** a mineral $PbSnS_2$ consisting of a sulfide of tin and lead and occurring in black metallic flexible folia (hardness 1–2, sp. gr 6.4)

¹team \ˈtēm\ *n* -s [ME *teme, tem*, fr. OE *tēam* offspring, lineage, group of draft animals; akin to OFris *tām* bridle, progeny, lineage, OHG *zoum* rein, bridle, ON *taumr*, OE *tēon* to draw, pull — more at TOW] **1** *obs* **:** LINEAGE, RACE **2 :** a group of animals having something in common: as **a :** a brood of young animals (as pigs or ducks) **b :** a number of animals moving together **c :** a flock of birds flying together **d :** a matched group of animals for exhibition **e** *Austral* **:** a group of rams used together on a flock of ewes **3 a :** two or more horses, oxen, or other draft animals harnessed to the same vehicle (as a coach, wagon, sled) or to the same plow or other implement **b** (1) **:** draft animals with their harness and attached vehicle (2) **:** a single animal used for labor and service often with harness and vehicle **c :** a wagon, carriage, or other drawn vehicle ⟨a horse and ~⟩ **4 :** a number of persons associated together in work or activity: as **a :** a number of persons selected to contend on one side in a match (as in cricket, football, rowing, or a debate) **b :** a group of workmen each completing one of a set of operations **:** CREW, GANG ⟨~ of riveters⟩ ⟨~ of divers⟩ **c :** a group of specialists or scientists functioning as a collaborative unit ⟨the diagnostic ~ of psychiatrist, clinician, and social worker in a child guidance clinic⟩ **5 :** a person of extraordinary ability or energy ⟨he's a whole ~ by himself⟩ **6** *old Eng law* **a :** an action to authenticate a claim (as to purchased goods) by summoning a seller to court **b :** a right or franchise of holding a court into which persons out of the jurisdiction may be vouched as warrantors (as where a purchaser vouches his seller as warrantor to prove that goods were not stolen) — used usu. in the phrase *toll and team*

²team \ˈ"\ *vb* -ED/-ING/-S *vt* **1 :** to yoke or join in a team ⟨one horse and one cow which were ~*ed* to a crude plow —R. A.Billington⟩ **2 :** to convey or haul with a team ⟨~ lumber⟩ ⟨~*ing* grain to market⟩ ~ *vi* **1 :** to drive a team or motortruck **:** be a teamster **2 :** to form a team **:** join forces or efforts ⟨~*ed* together in a defensive alliance⟩ — often used with *up* ⟨Communist tactics of ~*ing* up with hot-blooded nationalism —Tillman Durdin⟩

³team \ˈ"\ *adj* **:** of, belonging to, or performed by a team ⟨~ horse⟩ ⟨~ game⟩ ⟨~ effort⟩

tea maker *n* **:** a covered spoon with perforations for holding tea used in brewing tea in a cup

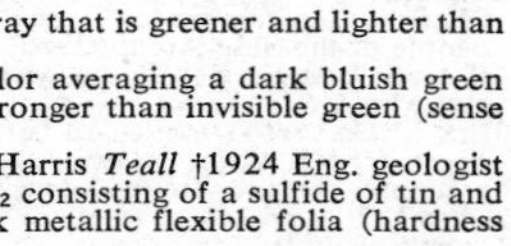

tea maker

tea·man \ˈtēmən\ *n, pl* **teamen :** a dealer in tea; *esp* **:** a tea buyer

team boat *n* **:** a paddle boat propelled by horses

team·er \ˈtēmə(r)\ *n* -s [¹*team* + *-er*] **:** TEAMSTER

tea mite *n* **:** any of several mites that infest and injure the tea plant

teamland \ˈ≈,≈\ *n* [ME *teme lond*, fr. *teme* team + *lond* land] *Old Eng law* **:** PLOWLAND 1

team·man \ˈtēmmən\ *n, pl* **teammen :** TEAMSTER

teammate \ˈ≈,≈\ *n* **:** a fellow member of a team **:** PARTNER

team of four : four bridge players in two partnerships entered as a unit in a tournament or other contest

tea mosquito *n* **:** a capsid bug of the genus *Helopeltis* (esp. *H. theivora*) that feeds on the tea plant and causes a stem canker resembling a fungus disease

team play *n* **1 :** collective play with mutual assistance of team members ⟨skillful *team play* in hockey⟩ **2 :** cooperative effort ⟨need for *team play* in time of war —Christopher La Farge⟩

teams·man \ˈtēmzmən\ *n, pl* **teamsmen** [*teams-* (fr. genitive of ¹*team*) + *man*] **:** TEAMSTER

team·ster \ˈtēmztə(r), -m(p)st-\ *n* -s [¹*team* + *-ster*] **:** one who drives a team or motortruck esp. as an occupation

team track *n* **:** a siding with public access on which freight cars are placed for loading or unloading by shippers and consignees

teamwork \ˈ≈,≈\ *n* **:** work done by a number of associates with usu. each doing a clearly defined portion but all sub-

ordinating personal prominence to the efficiency of the whole ⟨~ of a football eleven⟩ ⟨the smoothly coordinated ~ of a crack gun crew⟩
team yard *n* **:** a railroad yard having team tracks
tea oil *n* **1 :** a fragrant essential oil obtained from black tea **2 :** TEA-SEED OIL
tea oil tree *n* **:** SASANQUA
tea olive *n* **:** any of several cultivated Asiatic shrubs of the genus *Osmanthus*
tea party *n* [³*tea* + *party*] **1 :** an afternoon social gathering at which tea is served **2** [so called fr. the Boston Tea Party, name facetiously applied to the occasion in 1773 when a group of citizens threw a shipment of tea into Boston harbor in protest against the tax on imports] **:** an exciting disturbance or proceeding **:** SKIRMISH
teapot \ˈ=,=\ *n* **:** a vessel with a spout in which tea is brewed and from which it is served
tea·poy *or* **te·poy** \ˈtē,pȯi\ *n* -S [Hindi *tipāī*, fr. Skt *tri* three + *pāda* foot; akin to Skt *pad* foot — more at THREE, FOOT] **1 :** an ornamental stand with three legs **2 :** a stand for a tea service **:** TEA TABLE

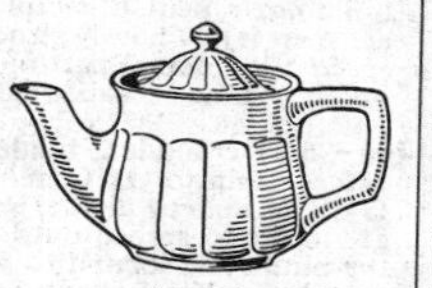
teapot

¹**tear** \ˈti(ə)r, ˈtiə\ *n* -S [ME *ter, tere, tear*, fr. OE *tēar, tæhher, teagor*; akin to OHG *zahar* tear, ON *tār*, Goth *tagr*, OL *dacruma*, L *lacrima*, Gk *dakry*] **1 a :** a drop of the clear saline fluid secreted normally in small amount by the lacrimal gland, diffused between the eye and the eyelids to moisten the parts and facilitate their motion, and passed ordinarily through the nasolacrimal duct into the nose **b tears** *pl* **:** a secretion of profuse tears that overflow the eyelids and dampen the face **2 tears** *pl* **a :** an act of weeping ⟨break into ~*s*⟩ ⟨found the child in ~*s* over her broken doll⟩ **b :** an act of grieving **3 a :** a transparent drop of fluid or hardened fluid matter (as resin) **b :** RUPERT'S DROP **4 :** undissolved material or a partially vitrified bit of clay in glass
²**tear** \"\ *vb* -ED/-ING/-S [ME *teren*, fr. *ter, tere*, tear] *vi* **:** to fill with tears **:** shed tears ⟨eyes ~*ing* in the November wind —Saul Bellow⟩ ~ *vt* **:** to cause to flow or fill with tears ⟨sudden pity ~*ed* his sight⟩
³**tear** \ˈta(a)(ə)r, ˈte(, \ə\ *vb* **tore** \ˈtō(ə)r, ˈtȯ(ə)r, -ōə, -ō(ə)\ *or archaic* **tare** \ˈta(a)(ə)r, ˈte(, \ə\ **torn** \ˈtō(ə)rn, ˈtȯ(ə)rn, -ōən, -ō(ə)n\ *or archaic* **tare; tearing; tears** [ME *teren*, fr. OE *teran*; akin to OHG *zeran* to destroy, Goth *gatairan* to tear, destroy, Gk *derein* to skin, flay, Skt *dṛṇāti* he tears, bursts] *vt* **1 a :** to divide (as a piece of fabric or paper) forcefully or violently into parts ⟨~ a letter in half⟩ **b :** to make a rent in ⟨~ a coat on a nail⟩ **c :** to wound by slashing or lacerating ⟨~ the skin⟩ **d :** to shatter or destroy usu. as if by tearing ⟨~ the place apart⟩ ⟨the explosion *tore* the town to pieces⟩ **2 a :** to split or disrupt emotionally and violently by presenting with a compulsory choice between unacceptable or equally pressing alternatives ⟨*torn* between love and hate⟩ ⟨*torn* by conflicting loyalties⟩ **b :** disrupt or throw into confusion by violent oppositions as between parties or factions ⟨*torn* by factional disputes and religious dissension⟩ **c :** to affect violently as if by lacerating ⟨*torn* by doubts⟩ ⟨*torn* by anarchy⟩ ⟨thunderbolt *tore* the heavens⟩ **3 a :** to pull, wrench, or remove by force or violent means ⟨~ a weapon from the agent's grasp⟩ ⟨~ a glove away from a dog⟩ ⟨*tore* out his hair by the roots⟩ ⟨~ some pages out of a book⟩ ⟨~ a cover off a box⟩ **b :** to force as if by pulling or wrenching ⟨tried to ~ his eyes from the scene⟩ ⟨try to ~ your thoughts from the past⟩ ⟨a reply *torn* from the heart⟩ **4 :** to cut (a hole, a path) by violent means ⟨~ a hole in the wall⟩ ⟨the flood *tore* a . . . gorge through the township —*Amer. Guide Series: Vt.*⟩ ~ *vi* **1 :** to divide, separate, or develop breaks or rents on being subjected to pulling, laceration, snagging ⟨this cloth ~*s* easily⟩ ⟨the stocking *tore* when it caught on the nail⟩ **2 :** to run, move, or act with great speed, impetus, or force or without restraint or check ⟨automobiles . . . in which the rich could ~ noisily along —F.L.Allen⟩ ⟨*tore* up the stairs two steps at a time⟩
syn RIP, REND, SPLIT, CLEAVE, RIVE: TEAR implies a forcible, somewhat crude, pulling or wrenching part from part, as of a fabric, or pulling or wrenching away, usu. so that ragged or irregular edges result ⟨*tear* a newspaper in half⟩ ⟨a Roman citizen was *torn* to pieces by the infuriated populace of Thebes —Agnes Repplier⟩ ⟨*tear* a photograph out of an album⟩ RIP implies a less crude, often purposeful, pulling part from part, as of a fabric in a rapid, uninterrupted action often along a straight line, grain, or seam or so that more or less straight edges result ⟨the woman *ripped* the pages out of the book, neatly, one by one⟩ REND is more rhetorical than RIP or TEAR and suggests greater violence than either ⟨*rend* your hearts and not your garments —Joel 2:13 (RSV)⟩ ⟨the black volume of clouds . . . *rent* asunder by flashes of lightning —Washington Irving⟩ CLEAVE implies very forceful, often violent, cutting into or separation of part from part, as of a substance more solid than fabric ⟨struck the final blow, *cleaving* the archbishop's skull —E.V.Lucas⟩ ⟨Norse vessels *cleaving* the channel with high and figured prows —Will Durant⟩ SPLIT suggests a more precise though forceful cutting or separation of part from part than CLEAVE, usu. along a grain or seam or between layers ⟨*split* a log for firewood⟩ ⟨mines opened, forests planted, and racks *split* —William Wordsworth⟩ RIVE suggests an action similar to SPLIT or CLEAVE but rougher, more violent ⟨the oak was struck and *riven* by lightning —George Santayana⟩ ⟨even in the days of the *riven* atom —Vannevar Bush⟩ **syn** see in addition RUSH
—tear at : LACERATE ⟨the sight of her grief *tore at* his heart⟩ **—tear into :** to attack without caution or restraint ⟨*tore into* his opponent with head down and fists flying⟩ ⟨*tore into him* with a fearful tongue-lashing⟩ **—tear it** *chiefly Brit* **:** to bring an end (as to one's hopes or expectations) **:** make continuation impossible ⟨discovered that I bored her to tears, which *tore it* for me —H.A.Vachell⟩ **—tear one's hair :** to pull or pluck one's hair as an expression of grief, rage, frustration, desperation, anxiety; *also* **:** to feel or display such an emotion ⟨*tearing his hair* over a pile of bills⟩
⁴**tear** \"\ *n* -S **1 :** the act of tearing **:** damage from being torn — used chiefly in the phrase *wear and tear* **2 a :** a hole or flaw made by tearing **:** RENT ⟨mending a ~ in her skirt⟩ **b :** a crack in a casting **3 a :** a tearing pace **:** violent rush **:** FLURRY ⟨the train went by at a ~⟩ **b :** a state of headlong urgency or eagerness **:** great hurry ⟨why are you in such a ~ to get home⟩ **c :** SPREE ⟨go on a ~⟩
⁵**tear** \"\ *adj* [ME *tere, tere, ter*, fr. MD *teder*, *teer* tender, delicate; akin to OE *tieder* weak, delicate] *obs* **:** DELICATE, DAINTY, FINE
⁶**tear** \"\ *n* -S [ME *teer*, fr. *teer* delicate, fine] **1** *archaic* **:** something (as flax or hemp) of the finest quality **2 :** the proportion of top to noil in combing wool
tear·able \ˈta(a)rəbəl, ˈter-\ *adj* [³*tear* + *-able*] **:** capable of being torn **:** readily torn — **tear·able·ness** *n* -ES
tear·age \-rij\ *n* -S [⁶*tear* + *-age*] **:** amount of or allowance for removal of short fiber in wool combing
tear around *vi* **1 :** to go about in excited or angry haste **2 :** to lead a wild or disorderly life ⟨when is he going to stop *tearing around* and settle down⟩
tear away *vt* [³*tear*] **:** to remove (as oneself) reluctantly ⟨several hours before he could *tear* himself *away* from the party⟩
tearaway \ˈ=,=,=\ *n* -S [*tear away*] *chiefly Brit* **:** one that acts or moves with impetuosity or speed ⟨at his best, man is a patchy dead old ~ —Bryan MacMahon⟩ ⟨a great ~ chestnut horse —T.E.Hook⟩
tear bag *n* [¹*tear*] **:** TEARPIT
tear–blanket \ˈ=,=\ *n* [³*tear* + *blanket*] **:** HERCULES'-CLUB
tear bomb *n* [¹*tear*] **:** a bomb charged with tear gas
tear bottle *n* **:** LACHRYMATORY
tear–coat \ˈ=,=\ *n* [³*tear* + *coat*] **:** HERCULES'-CLUB
tear down *vt* **1 a :** to cause to decompose or disintegrate **:** DESTROY **b :** VILIFY, DENIGRATE ⟨*tear* down a reputation⟩ **2 :** to take apart **:** DISASSEMBLE ⟨*tear* an engine *down* for overhaul⟩
teardown \ˈ=,=\ *n* -S [*tear down*] **:** DISASSEMBLY

¹**teardrop** \ˈ=,=\ *n* [¹*tear* + *drop*] **1 :** ¹TEAR 1a **2 :** something shaped like a dropping tear; *specif* **:** a pendent gem on an earring or necklace

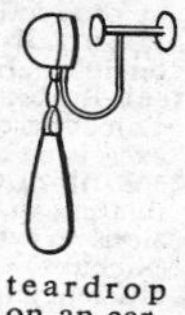
teardrop on an earring

²**teardrop** \"\ *adj* **:** PEAR-DROP
tear duct *n* **:** LACRIMAL DUCT
teared *past of* TEAR
tear·er \ˈta(a)rə(r), ˈter-\ *n* -S [³*tear* + *-er*] **1 :** one that tears or rends; *specif* **:** one who tears cloth from bolts for the making of handkerchiefs, sheets, or other specified articles **2 :** one that rushes or blusters **:** something that violently attracts attention ⟨that storm was a ~⟩
tear fault *n* [⁴*tear*] **:** a fault occurring in the rocks above a low-angle thrust fault and striking approximately at right angles to the strike of the thrust fault
tear·ful \ˈtirfəl, ˈtiəf-\ *adj* [¹*tear* + *-ful*] **1 :** flowing with or accompanied by tears **:** WEEPING ⟨~ entreaties⟩ **2 :** causing tears ⟨fine sense of the grim and the ~ —T.L.Peacock⟩ — **tear·ful·ly** \-f(ə)lē, -li\ *adv* — **tear·ful·ness** *n* -ES
tear gas *n* **:** a solid, liquid, or gaseous substance that on dispersion in the atmosphere blinds the eyes with tears but does not damage them and that is used chiefly in dispelling mobs — called also *lacrimator*
tear gland *n* **:** LACRIMAL GLAND
tear grass *n* **:** JOB'S TEARS 2
tear·i·ly \ˈtirəlē\ *adv* **:** in a teary manner **:** with tears or weeping
¹**tearing** *adj* [fr. pres. part. of ³*tear*] **1 :** causing continuing or repeated pain or distress **:** HARROWING ⟨~ headache⟩ ⟨~ cough⟩ **2 :** HASTY, VIOLENT, FURIOUS ⟨~ hurry⟩ ⟨~ rage⟩ **3** *chiefly Brit* **:** SPLENDID, IMPRESSIVE ⟨~ success⟩
²**tearing** *n* -S [fr. gerund of ²*tear*] **:** abnormal watering of the eyes occurring as a reaction to local conditions (as conjunctivitis) or because of obstruction of the lacrimal passages ⟨~ from the eye and nose-blowing —M.F.A.Montagu⟩
tea ring *n* [²*tea*] **:** a yeast-raised coffeecake baked in ring form
tearing strength *n* [*tearing* (gerund of ³*tear*) + *strength*] **:** the property of paper or fabric that is measured by the force required to tear it
tearjerker \ˈ=,=,=\ *n* [¹*tear* + *jerker*] **:** an extravagantly pathetic story, play, film, or radio or television program
tear–jerking \ˈ=,=,=\ *adj* [¹*tear* + *jerking*] **:** excessively or deliberately pathetic **:** SENTIMENTAL ⟨*tear-jerking* plot⟩ ⟨*tear-jerking* appeals for donations⟩
tear·less \ˈtirləs, ˈtiəl-\ *adj* [¹*tear* + *-less*] **:** shedding no tears **:** free from tears — **tear·less·ly** *adv* — **tear·less·ness** *n* -ES
tear–off \ˈ=,=\ *n* -S [fr. the phrase *tear off*] **:** part of a piece of paper intended to be removed by tearing usu. along a marked line (as a row of dashes)
tear off *vt* [³*tear*] **:** to compose rapidly ⟨*tore off* a whole play in three weeks⟩ ⟨just time to *tear off* a letter home⟩
tea·room \ˈtē,rüm, -rum\ *n* **:** a public dining room or small restaurant with service and decor designed primarily for a feminine clientele — **tea·roomy** \-mē\ *adj*
tea rose *n* **1 :** any of numerous tender or half-hardy hybrid garden bush roses descended chiefly from a Chinese rose (*Rosa odorata*) and valued esp. for their abundant large usu. tea-scented blossoms — see HYBRID TEA **2** *or* **tea–rose pink a :** a variable color averaging a light yellowish pink that is yellower and stronger than average shell pink (sense 1) and yellower and slightly lighter than average baby pink **b** *of textiles* **:** a strong yellowish pink that is redder and paler than average salmon
tearpit \ˈ=,=\ *n* [¹*tear* + *pit*] **:** a sebaceous gland that opens beneath the lower eyelid of most deer and antelope, that can be controlled in its opening voluntarily, and that secretes a waxy odorous substance — called also *lacrimal sinus*
tears *pl of* TEAR, *pres 3d sing of* TEAR
tear sac *n* **:** TEARPIT
tear sheet *n* [³*tear*] **:** a sheet torn from a publication usu. to send as proof of insertion to an advertiser whose advertisement appears on it
tear shell *n* [¹*tear*] **:** an artillery shell charged with tear gas
tearstain \ˈ=,=\ *n* **1 :** a spot or streak left by tears **2 :** a reddish or reddish green streaking of citrus fruits that occurs in some diseases (as anthracnose or melanose) or is caused by attacks of the rust mite
tear streak *n* **:** TEARSTAIN 2
tear strip *n* [³*tear*] **:** the scored band in a can or added narrow ribbon in a wrapper or on a fiber box that provides an easy and defined way of opening
¹**teart** \ˈti(ə)rt\ *adj* [alter. of *tart*] **1** *dial Eng* **:** TART, SOUR **2** *of soil or herbage* **:** containing excessive quantities of molybdenum — **teart·ness** *n* -ES
²**teart** \"\ *n* -S **:** scouring of cattle on pastures in parts of England containing excess molybdenum
tear tape *n* [³*tear*] **:** a strong tape glued to the inside of a shipping container with one end protruding so that the container is readily opened by pulling out the tape
tearthumb \ˈ=,=\ *n* [³*tear* + *thumb*; fr. the minute prickles on the stem] **:** any of several plants of the genus *Polygonum* having prickly stems
tear up *vt* [³*tear*] **1 :** to damage, remove, or effect an opening in (as a floor surface) ⟨*tear* the street *up* to repair a sewer⟩ **2 :** destroy by tearing **:** tear to pieces ⟨*tear* a letter *up*⟩ ⟨*tear up* an agreement⟩
teary \ˈtirē, -ri\ *adj* -ER/-EST [ME *tery*, fr. *ter* tear + *-y*] **1 a :** wet or stained with tears **:** TEARFUL **b :** consisting of tears or drops like tears **2 :** provocative of tears **:** PATHETIC ⟨~ story⟩
teas *pl of* TEA, *pres 3d sing of* TEA
teas·able \ˈtēzəbəl\ *adj* **:** capable of being teased — **teas·able·ness** *n* -ES
tea scrub *n* **:** a scrub formed by the Australian tea tree; *also* **:** the tree itself
¹**tease** *also* **teaze** \ˈtēz\ *vb* -ED/-ING/-S [ME *tesen, teesen*, fr. OE *tǣsan*; akin to OHG *zeisan* to pluck, tease] *vt* **1 a :** to disentangle and lay parallel by combing or carding ⟨~ wool⟩ **b :** to scratch (cloth) so as to raise a nap **:** TEASEL **2 :** to tear in pieces; *esp* **:** to separate (a tissue or specimen) into minute shreds for microscopic examination **3 :** ³RUFF 3 **4 a :** to disturb or annoy by persistent irritating or provoking action ⟨an unpleasant thought seemed to ~ him like a wasp: he moved his head slightly to avoid it —Christopher Isherwood⟩ — or tantalizing elusiveness ⟨curiosity to know more about living things . . . has *teased* man's mind for centuries —Joel Turner⟩ **b :** to attempt to provoke anger, resentment, or confusion in esp. for sport **:** GOAD, TORMENT ⟨a cheap cleverness put on to worry and ~ the simple philistine —J.C.Powys⟩ **c :** to annoy or disturb with petty persistent requests **:** PESTER, IMPORTUNE ⟨the children have been *teasing* me all day to be allowed to go out⟩; *also* **:** to obtain by repeated coaxing **d :** to coax or persuade into acquiescence esp. by persistent small efforts ⟨relieved to be in a house where the family did not ~ him to break the promise —Dorothy C. Fisher⟩ **5 :** to tantalize or baffle by arousing desire in without the intention of satisfying it; *specif* **:** to determine the presence of estrus in (a female domestic animal) by approach to or contact with a male ~ *vi* **:** to engage in tormenting, tantalizing, provoking, or importuning **syn** see WORRY
²**tease** *also* **teaze** \"\ *n* -S **1 :** act of teasing or state of being teased ⟨most parodies are little more than literary ~*s* —Michael Swan⟩ **2 :** one that teases or torments ⟨a cruel ~ when the comic spirit was riding him —J.W.Beach⟩ **3** *slang* **:** MONEY ⟨a mere national dearth of ~ may have seemed a redundant misfortune —A.J.Liebling⟩
³**tease** \"\ *vt* -ED/-ING/-S [alter. (influenced by ¹*tease*) of ME *taysen, teisen*] *archaic* **:** to urge on **:** DRIVE, ROUSE ⟨did ~ their horses homeward with convulsed spur —John Keats⟩
⁴**tease** *also* **teaze** \"\ *vt* -ED/-ING/-S [F *tiser*, short for *attiser* to feed or stir up (a fire), fr. (assumed) VL *attitiare*, fr. L *ad-* + *titio* firebrand] **:** to operate or stoke (a glass-melting furnace)
tea–seed oil *n* **:** a fatty oil resembling olive oil obtained from the seeds of the sasanqua and used chiefly as an edible oil, as a hair oil, and in soap — called also *tea oil*
teasehole \ˈ=,=\ *n* [⁴*tease* + *hole*] **:** the opening in a glass-making furnace for fuel
¹**tea·sel** *also* **tea·sle** *or* **tea·zel** *or* **tea·zle** \ˈtēzəl\ *n* -S [ME *tesel, tasel*, fr. OE *tǣsel*; akin to OHG *zeisila* teasel, OE *tǣsan* to tease — more at TEASE] **1 :** a plant of the genus *Dipsacus* (esp. *D. fullonum* and *D. sylvestris*) — see FULLER'S TEASEL, WILD TEASEL **2 a :** a flower head of the fuller's teasel covered with firm finely hooked bracts and used when dried to raise a nap on woolen cloth **b :** a wire substitute for the fuller's teasel
²**teasel** \"\ *vt* **teaseled** *or* **teaselled; teaseled** *or* **teaselled; teaseling** *or* **teaselling** \-z(ə)liŋ\ **teasels :** to nap (cloth) with teasels
tea·sel·er *also* **tea·sel·ler** \-z(ə)lə(r)\ *n* -S [ME *teselere*, fr. *tesel* teasel + *-ere* -er] **:** GIGGER
teasel family *n* **:** DIPSACACEAE
teasel gourd *n* **:** HEDGEHOG GOURD
teaselwort \ˈ=,=,=\ *n* **:** a plant of the family Dipsacaceae
tease·ment \ˈtēzmənt\ *n* -S [¹*tease* + *-ment*] **:** an act of teasing
tease out *vt* [¹*tease*] **:** to obtain by disentangling or freeing with or as if with a pointed instrument ⟨isolated striated muscle fibers can be *teased out* from muscles —*Medical Physics*⟩ ⟨delicately *teasing out* the embryos from a little deer mouse —D.C.Peattie⟩
¹**teas·er** \ˈtēzə(r)\ *n* -S [ME *teser*, fr. *tesen* to tease + *-er*] **1 :** a textile worker or a textile machine that teases fiber or cloth **2 :** something difficult to dispose of, solve, or decide about **:** something not easily either grasped or dismissed ⟨whether to accept the offer was a ~⟩ ⟨riddles, conundrums, ~*s*⟩ **3 a :** one that annoys, torments, or tantalizes **b :** a woman who provokes or encourages sexual advances but evades or refuses intercourse **c :** a male animal used for identifying females in heat; *also* **:** a cow in heat used to stimulate a bull for semen collection for artificial insemination **d :** STRIPTEASER **4 a :** an object without hooks towed astern of a boat to attract fish **b :** an advertisement meant to arouse curiosity sometimes by withholding part of the material information **5** [so called fr. its habit of chasing other birds and forcing them to disgorge their prey] **:** JAEGER **6 :** a border, curtain, or canvas-covered framework suspended parallel to and just behind the proscenium arch in order to establish the height of the actual proscenium opening and to conceal the upper part of the stage **7 :** one of two coils or transformers forming a T connection
²**teaser** *also* **teaz·er** \"\ *n* -S [F *tiseur*, fr. *tiser* to tease — more at TEASE (stoke)] **:** an operator or fireman of a glass-melting furnace
tea service *n* **:** a set of china or metalware for service at table: **a :** a set of china consisting of a teapot, sugar bowl, creamer, sometimes a coffeepot, and usu. plates, cups, and saucers — compare COFFEE SERVICE **b :** a set of metalware consisting of a teapot, sugar bowl, creamer, sometimes a coffeepot, and usu. waste bowl, kettle, and tray

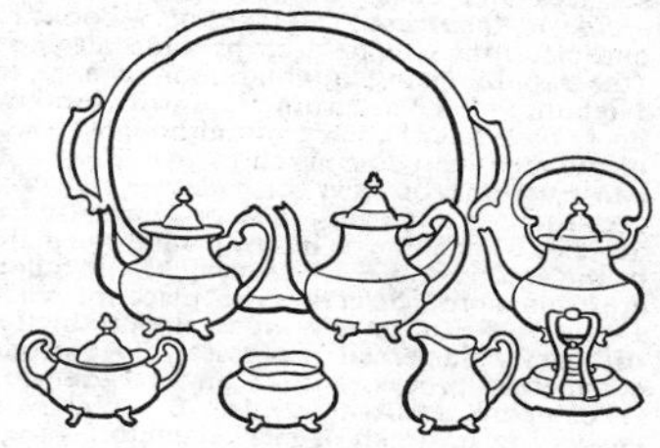
tea service

tea set *n* **1 :** TEA SERVICE **2 :** a china set consisting of teapot, sugar bowl, creamer, cups and saucers, and dessert plates
tease up *vt* [¹*tease*] **:** to improve or bring into being by small changes or touches ⟨*tease up* a picture⟩
tea shop *n* **1** *chiefly Brit* **:** TEAROOM **2** *Brit* **:** LUNCHROOM, CAFÉ
teas·ing·ly *adv* [*teasing* (pres. part. of ¹*tease*) + *-ly*] **:** in a teasing manner ⟨threatened ~ to throw her in the pond⟩ **:** ANNOYINGLY, NAGGINGLY ⟨~ elusive significance in his remarks⟩
teasing needle *n* [*teasing* (gerund of ¹*tease*) + *needle*] **:** a tapering needle mounted in a handle and used for teasing tissues or other objects for microscopic examination
teaspoon \ˈ=,=\ *n* **1 :** a small commonly silver spoon suitable for stirring and sipping tea or coffee and having a standard capacity of one third of a tablespoon — see SPOON illustration **2 :** TEASPOONFUL
tea·spoon·ful \ˈ=,spün,fu̇l *sometimes* -pu̇n-\ *n, pl* **teaspoonfuls** *or* **teaspoonsful** \-n,fu̇lz, -nz,fu̇l\ [*teaspoon* + *-ful*] **1 :** as much as one teaspoon can hold **:** enough to fill a teaspoon **2 :** a unit of measure used esp. in cookery and pharmacy equal to one level teaspoonful or 1⅓ fluid drams
teasy \ˈtēzē\ *adj* -ER/-EST [¹*tease* + *-y*] **:** inclined to tease **:** IRRITATING, ANNOYING
teat \ˈtit, ˈtēt, *usu* |d·+V\ *n* -S [ME *tete, tet*, fr. OF *tete, tette*, of Gmc origin; akin to OE *tit, titt* teat, MHG *zitze*] **1 :** the protuberance through which milk is drawn from the udder or breast of a mammal **:** NIPPLE, MAMMILLA, DUG — see COW illustration **2** *Brit* **:** NIPPLE 2a **3 a :** a small projecting part on a countersink or counterbore to guide it in a drilled hole **b :** a nib or projection on a leaf spring
tea table *n* **1 :** a table used or spread for tea; *specif* **:** a small table for serving afternoon tea **2 :** the place of gathering or company at tea ⟨favorite topics at the *tea table*⟩
tea tannin *n* **:** a tannin found in green tea leaves and in green tea and in oxidized form in black tea
teataster \ˈ=,=,=\ *n* **:** an expert who judges or grades tea by tasting a standard brew
teat canal *n* **:** the channel in a teat through which milk passes
teat cup *n* **:** the part of a milking machine that covers the teat of a cow
teat·ed \|d·əd\ *adj* [*teat* + *-ed*] **:** having teats; *often* **:** having functional teats ⟨a three-*teated* cow⟩
teatfish \ˈ=,=\ *n* [so called fr. the shape of the tentacles] **:** TREPANG
tea–things \ˈ=,=\ *n pl* **:** articles used for serving tea
teatime \ˈ=,=\ *n* **:** the customary time for tea **:** late afternoon or early evening ⟨long past ~⟩ ⟨traffic at ~ was heavy⟩
tea tortrix *n* **:** a small Indian moth (*Homona coffearia*) whose larva feeds on the leaves of tea, coffee, and other plants
tea towel *n* **:** DISH TOWEL
tea tray *n* **:** a tray that accommodates a tea service
tea tree *n* [¹*tea* + *tree*] **1 :** TEA 1a **2** [so called fr. the use of their leaves as a substitute for tea] **a :** any of various Australian shrubs or trees of the genus *Leptospermum* (esp. *L. scoparium*) or the genus *Melaleuca* (esp. *M. squarrosa*) forming dense thickets **b :** AFRICAN TEA TREE
tea–tree oil *n* **:** an essential oil obtained fr. the leaves and terminal branches of various tea trees (sense 2a); *esp* **:** a light yellow oil obtained from an Australian tree (*Melaleuca alternifolia*) and used as a germicide
tea trolley *n, chiefly Brit* **:** TEA WAGON
tea wagon *n* **:** a small table on wheels used in serving tea and light refreshments
tea yellows *n pl but usu sing in constr* **:** a sulfur deficiency disease of tea characterized by chlorosis of the leaves

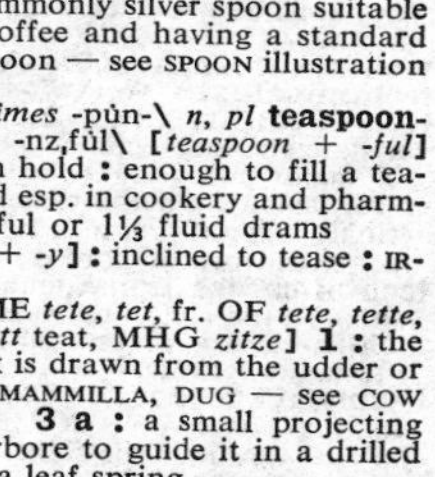
tea wagon

teaze *var of* TEASE
teazel *or* **teazle** *var of* TEASEL
teb·bad \ˈte,bad\ *n* -S [perh. fr. Per *tab* fever + *bād* wind, fr. MPer *vāt*; akin to Av *vāta-* wind, Skt *vāta* — more at WIND] **:** a sandstorm
teb·bit \ˈtebət\ *var of* TABET
te·bel·di \təˈbeldē\ *n* -S [Ar dial. *tabaldi*; prob. of Berber origin] **:** BAOBAB
te·bet *also* **te·beth** *or* **te·vet** *or* **te·veth** \tāˈvāth, ˈtā,ves\ *n* -S *usu cap* [Heb *Ṭēbhēth*] **:** the 4th month of the civil year or the 10th month of the ecclesiastical year in the Jewish calendar — see MONTH table
tebu *usu cap, var of* TIBBU
tec \ˈtek\ *n* -S [by shortening] *slang* **:** DETECTIVE
tec *abbr* technical; technician; technology

te·ca·li \ˌtäkäˈlē\ *n* -s [Sp *tecali,* fr. *Tecali,* village in Puebla, Mexico] : ALABASTER 1
tech *or* **techn** *abbr* technical; technically; technician; technology
teched *or* **tetched** \ˈtecht\ *adj* [alter. of *touched*] : mentally unbalanced : somewhat deranged
techiness *var of* TETCHINESS
techinnah *var of* TEHINNAH
tech·ne \ˈteknē\ *n* -s [Gk *technē* — more at TECHNICAL] : ART, SKILL; *esp* : the principles or methods employed in making something or attaining an objective — compare UNDERSTANDING
tech·ne·ti·um \tekˈnēshēəm\ *n* -s [NL, fr. Gk *technētos* artificial (fr. *technasthai* to devise by art, fr. *technē* art) + NL *-ium* — more at TECHNICAL] : a crystalline radioactive metallic element that resembles rhenium and manganese chemically and that was obtained as the first synthetic element by bombarding molybdenum with deuterons or neutrons and later as one of the fission products of uranium — symbol *Tc;* see ELEMENT table
¹tech·nic \ˈteknik, -nēk\ *adj* [Gk *technikos*] : TECHNICAL
²technic \"*, in sense 2 also* (ˈ)tekˈnēk\ *n* -s **1** : a technical term or detail : TECHNICALITY **2** [trans. of F *technique*] **a** : TECHNIQUE 1 ⟨glaring defects both in sonority and recording ~ —*Scribner's*⟩ — often used in pl. but sing. or pl. in constr. ⟨literary ~*s* . . . depends on reproducing experiments from life —*Contemporary Rev.*⟩ **b** : TECHNIQUE 2a ⟨various ~*s* have been developed for increasing the consumption of oxygen —Morris Fishbein⟩ **3 technics** *pl but sing or pl in constr* : TECHNOLOGY 2a, 2b(1) ⟨modern ~*s* is giving man a sense of power —Bertrand Russell⟩
¹tech·ni·cal \ˈteknəkəl, -nēk-\ *adj* [Gk *technikos* of art, skillful, practical (fr. *technē* art, craft, practical skill + *-ikos* -ic) + E *-al;* akin to Gk *tektōn* carpenter, builder, Skt *takṣan* carpenter, *takṣati* he forms, constructs, L *texere* to weave, construct, OHG *dehsa* hatchet, *dahs* badger] **1 a** : having special usu. practical knowledge esp. of a mechanical or scientific subject ⟨the construction of the thermonuclear weapon was a great challenge to the ~ people of this country —Edward Teller⟩ **b** : marked by or characteristic of specialization ⟨highly ~ matters hardly suitable for popular lecturing —William James⟩ ⟨~ language⟩ **2** : of or relating to a particular subject ⟨outlined his ~ qualifications for the office of comptroller⟩; *esp* : of or relating to a practical subject that is organized on modern scientific principles ⟨is a college of liberal arts and sciences and does not undertake to provide a ~ training —*Encyc. Americana*⟩ ⟨all types of ~ books ranging from radio and electronics to field crops and dairying —*Saturday Rev.*⟩ ⟨the rapidly changing conditions of a ~ society —Reinhold Niebuhr⟩ **3 a** : according to a strict legal interpretation ⟨had no knowledge of the crimes although he was in ~ command of the men who committed them —*Time*⟩ **b** : created by the constructions of laws or rules — see TECHNICAL FELONY, TECHNICAL KNOCKOUT **4** : of or relating to technique ⟨the absence of genuine ~ innovation in the majority of the novels of the second war —J.W.Aldridge⟩ ⟨no amount of ~ skill and craftsmanship can take the place of vital interest —John Dewey⟩ **5** : of or relating to the production of chemicals by ordinary commercial processes; *esp* : produced by ordinary commercial processes often on a large scale ⟨~ sulfuric acid⟩ — compare COMMERCIAL 1e **6** : chiefly resulting from or depending on internal market factors (as price changes and volume) rather than fundamental economic considerations ⟨the late burst of demand . . . yesterday was interpreted by most analysts as confirming their forecasts that the market is due for a ~ rally —C.J.Elia⟩ — **tech·ni·cal·ly** \-nək(ə)lē, -nēk-, -li\ *adv* —**tech·ni·cal·ness** *n* -ES
²technical \"\ *n* -s : TECHNIC 1
technical estoppel *n* : an estoppel by record or by deed : a common law or legal estoppel
technical felony *n* : a felony that usu. results in imprisonment for life or for an indeterminate sentence when an offender has been convicted of designated serious offenses for three or some other specified number of times
technical foul *n* **1** : a foul in basketball caused by one who is not playing **2 a** : a player foul in basketball that involves no contact with an opponent **b** : a player foul that involves unsportsmanlike contact with an opponent when the ball is not in play
tech·ni·cal·ism \-kəˌlizəm\ *n* -s : addiction to technicality
tech·ni·cal·ist \-ləst\ *n* -s : one addicted to technicality
tech·ni·cal·i·ty \ˌteknəˈkaləd·ē, -latē, -i\ *n* -ES **1** : the quality or state of being technical ⟨~ in the presentation would defeat the major purpose —R.E.Coker⟩ **2** : something that is technical: as **a** : a detail that has meaning only for the specialist ⟨finally caught him in a legal ~ —Dorothy C. Fisher⟩ **b** : a technical word or phrase
tech·ni·cal·iza·tion \ˌteknəkələˈzāshən\ *n* -s [*technicalize* + *-ation*] : the action of making technical
tech·ni·cal·ize \ˈteknəkəˌlīz\ *vt* -ED/-ING/-S [¹*technical* + *-ize*] : to make technical
technical knockout *n* : a knockout ruled by the referee when a boxer is unable or is declared to be unable (as because of injury) to continue the fight
technical sergeant *n* : a noncommissioned officer in the air force just below a master sergeant and above a staff sergeant
technical traverse *n* : a legal traverse preceded by an inducement
tech·ni·cian \tekˈnishən\ *n* -s [¹*technic* + *-ician*] **1** : a specialist in the technical details of a subject: as **a** : a technical expert ⟨a scholarly ~ . . . who is of service to the management side of industry but not of it —Alfred Kazin⟩ **b** : one who has learned the practical technical details and special techniques of an occupation ⟨skilled electrical ~*s* are needed to keep this equipment in good running condition —*Best True Fact Detective*⟩ **2** : one who has acquired the technique of an art or other area of specialization ⟨a superb ~ and a musician of integrity —Irving Kolodin⟩ ⟨the ~ had finally become the artist —*Newsweek*⟩ ⟨an excellent ~ at every level of politics —T.H.White b. 1915⟩
tech·ni·cist \ˈteknəsəst\ *n* -s [¹*technic* + *-ist*] : TECHNICIAN
tech·ni·cize \ˈteknəˌsīz\ *vt* -ED/-ING/-S [¹*technic* + *-ize*] : TECHNICALIZE
tech·ni·col·o·gy \ˌteknəˈkäləjē\ *n* -ES [Gk *technikos* + E *-logy*] : TECHNOLOGY
technics *pl of* TECHNIC
tech·ni·cum *or* **tech·ni·kum** \ˈteknəkəm\ *n* -s [Russ or G; Russ *tekhnikum,* fr. G *technikum,* fr. Gk *technikon,* neut. of *technikos* technical] : a technical school esp. in the U.S.S.R.
tech·nique \(ˈ)tekˈnēk\ *n* -s [F, fr. *technique* technical, fr. Gk *technikos* — more at TECHNICAL] **1** : the way in which technical details are treated: as **a** : the manner in which a creative artist (as a writer or painter) uses the technical elements of his art to express himself ⟨where ~ is deficient, characterization cannot but suffer —E.R.Bentley⟩ **b** (1) : the manner in which a musician, dancer, or athlete uses basic physical movements in performance ⟨will specialize in ~ and improvisation for teenage and professional dancers —*Dance Observer*⟩ (2) : the ability of a musician, dancer, or athlete to use basic physical movements effectively ⟨a clarinetist of very limited ~ —John Hammond⟩ **c** (1) : a body of technical methods; *esp* : a body of technical methods used in scientific research ⟨every science has its own special ~ a considerable part of which serves chiefly to prevent error —R.W.Murray⟩ (2) : the ability to use such methods effectively **2 a** : a technical method of accomplishing a desired aim ⟨the ~ of establishing linguistic families . . . is too difficult to be gone into here —Edward Sapir⟩; *esp* : a particular technical method ⟨used a ~ involving radioactive carbon to measure photosynthesis —E.F.Thompson⟩ **b** : METHOD, WAY, MANNER ⟨the usual fishing ~ is to loll around quietly in a small boat —*Buick Mag.*⟩ ⟨young women whose ~ is faulty are prone to meet failure and disillusionment —C.W.Cunnington⟩
techno- *comb form* [Gk, fr. *technē* — more at TECHNICAL] **1** : art : craft ⟨*techno*graphy⟩ **2** : technical : technological ⟨*techno*cracy⟩ ⟨*techno*culture⟩ **3** : applied ⟨*techno*psychology⟩
tech·noc·ra·cy \tekˈnäkrəsē, -si\ *n* -ES [*techno-* + *-cracy*] **1** : government by technicians; *specif* : management of society by technical experts **2** *often cap* : a movement flourishing in the early 1930s and advocating replacement of the capitalist price system as the basis of industrial production and distribution by a system of control by technicians aiming primarily at production to the limit of industrial capacity **3** : TECHNOLOGY 2b ⟨the ~ of destruction has become greater and more terrible —E.L.Beach⟩
tech·no·crat \ˈteknəˌkrat\ *n* -s [*techno-* + *-crat*] **1** *often cap* : an adherent of technocracy **2** : a technical expert; *esp* : one exercising managerial authority
tech·no·crat·ic \ˌteknəˈkrad·ik\ *adj* [*techno-* + *-cratic*] : of, relating to, or having the characteristics of technocracy ⟨illusions to which a ~ culture is already too prone —Reinhold Niebuhr⟩ ⟨under a ~ as under a capitalist arrangement, the efficiency of machines as well as of human beings would have economic significance only in terms of production of values —A.L.Harris⟩
tech·nog·ra·phy \tekˈnägrəfē\ *n* -ES [ISV *techno-* + *-graphy*] : the description of arts and crafts esp. with reference to their ethnic distribution and historical development
tech·no·log·ic \ˌteknəˈläjik\ *adj* [*technology* + *-ic*] : TECHNOLOGICAL ⟨inject an element of ~ unemployment in an industry —*Science News Letter*⟩
tech·no·log·i·cal \-jəkəl, -jēk-\ *adj* [*technology* + *-ical*] **1** : of, relating to, or characterized by technology ⟨~ advances⟩ ⟨~ reasons⟩ ⟨a ~ civilization⟩ **2** : resulting from improvement in technical processes that increases the productivity of machines and eliminates manual operations or the operations done by older machines ⟨~ unemployment⟩ — **tech·no·log·i·cal·ly** \-jək(ə)lē, -jēk-, -li\ *adv*
tech·nol·o·gist \tekˈnäləjəst\ *n* -s [*technology* + *-ist*] : a specialist in technology
tech·nol·o·gy \-jē, -ji\ *n* -ES [Gk *technologia* systematic treatment, fr. *techno-* + *-logia* -logy] **1** : the terminology of a particular subject : technical language **2 a** : the science of the application of knowledge to practical purposes : applied science ⟨the great American achievement has been . . . less in science itself than in ~ and engineering —Max Lerner⟩ **b** (1) : the application of scientific knowledge to practical purposes in a particular field ⟨studies are also made of polymeric materials to dental ~ —*Report: Nat'l Bureau of Standards*⟩ (2) : a technical method of achieving a practical purpose ⟨a ~ for extracting petroleum from shale⟩ **3** : the totality of the means employed by a people to provide itself with the objects of material culture
-tech·ny \ˌteknē, -ni\ *n comb form* -ES [F *-technie,* fr. Gk *technē* art, craft + F *-ie* -y — more at TECHNICAL] : technical specialization ⟨hydro*techny*⟩ ⟨metallo*techny*⟩
techy *var of* TETCHY
tecno- *comb form* [Gk *tekno-,* fr. *teknon* — more at THANE] : child ⟨*tecno*logy⟩ ⟨*tecno*genesis⟩
te·co \ˈtā(ˌ)kō\ *n, pl* **teco** *or* **tecos** *usu cap* [Sp cuitla*teco* cuitlatec] : CUITLATEC
te·coma \təˈkōmə\ *n* [NL, fr. MexSp *tecomasuchil,* fr. Nahuatl *tecomaxochitl,* fr. *tecomatl* clay pot + *xochitl* flower] **1** *cap* : a genus of tropical American shrubs and trees (family Bignoniaceae) having large showy flowers with a 5-toothed calyx, a nearly regular corolla, and four perfect stamens **2** -s : any plant of the genus *Tecoma* or the related genus *Campsis; esp* : TRUMPET CREEPER
tecs *pl of* TEC
tecta *pl of* TECTUM
tec·tal \ˈtektəl\ *adj* [NL *tectum* + E *-al*] : of or relating to the tectum
¹tec·ti·branch \ˈtektəˌbraŋk\ *adj* [NL *Tectibranchia*] : of or relating to the Tectibranchia
²tectibranch \"\ *n* -s : a mollusk of the suborder Tectibranchia
tec·ti·bran·chia \ˌ==ˈbraŋkēə\ *n pl, cap* [NL, fr. L *tectus* covered (fr. past part. of *tegere* to cover) + NL *-i-* + *-branchia* — more at THATCH] : a suborder of Opisthobranchia comprising gastropod mollusks (as bubble shells and sea hares) in which the gill is usu. situated on one side of the back and protected by a fold of the mantle — compare PTEROPODA — **tec·ti·bran·chi·an** \ˌ==ˈbraŋkēən\ *adj or n* — **tec·ti·bran·chi·ate** \-ēət, -ēˌāt\ *adj or n*
tec·ti·bran·chi·a·ta \ˌ==ˌbraŋkēˈād·ə\ [NL, fr. L *tectus* + NL *-i-* + *branchi-* + *-ata*] *syn of* TECTIBRANCHIA
¹tec·ti·form \ˈtektəˌfȯrm\ *adj* [NL *tectiformis,* fr. L *tectum* roof + *-iformis* -iform — more at TECTUM] : shaped like a roof
²tectiform \"\ *n* -s : a design found (as at Font-de-Gaume, Dordogne, France) in the cave art of paleolithic man assumed to represent a dwelling
tec·to·fu·gal \(ˈ)tekˈtäfyəgəl\ *adj* [NL *tectum* + *-o-* + E *-fugal*] : passing out of the tectum
tec·to·gene \ˈtektəˌjēn\ *n* -s [ISV *tecto-* (fr. Gk *tektainein* to frame, build, fr. *tektōn* carpenter, builder) + *-gene* — more at TECHNICAL] : a long narrow downward fold of the earth's crust that is postulated as an early phase in the process of the formation of a mountain range or an island arc — **tec·to·gen·ic** \ˌ==ˈjenik\ *adj*
tec·to·na \tekˈtōnə\ *n, cap* [NL, perh. fr. Gk *tektōn* carpenter; fr. its use in carpentry] : a small genus of trees (family Verbenaceae) of India, Malaysia, and the Philippines having entire woolly leaves and paniculate cymes of small white or bluish flowers — see TEAK
tec·ton·ic \(ˈ)tekˈtänik\ *adj* [LL *tectonicus,* fr. Gk *tektonikos* of a builder or carpenter, skilled in building, fr. *tektōn* carpenter, builder + *-ikos* -ic — more at TECHNICAL] : of or relating to tectonics: as **a** : ARCHITECTURAL, ARCHITECTONIC **b** : of or relating to the deformation of the earth's crust, the forces involved in or producing such deformation, and the resulting rock structures and external forms — **tec·ton·i·cal·ly** \-nək(ə)lē\ *adv*
tec·ton·ics \tekˈtäniks\ *n pl but usu sing in constr* [fr. *tectonic,* after such pairs as *economic: economics*] **1** : the science or art of construction (as of a building) both in relation to use and to artistic design : ARCHITECTONICS **2 a** : geological structural features as a whole **b** : a branch of geology concerned with structure esp. with folding and faulting **c** : DIASTROPHISM
tec·ton·ism \ˈtektəˌnizəm\ *n* -s [ISV *tecton-* (fr. *tectonic*) + *-ism*] : DIASTROPHISM
tec·ton·ite \-ˌnīt\ *n* -s [ISV *tecton-* + *-ite*] : a rock that has undergone differential movement of its component parts and in consequence still retains a coherent fabric
tec·tono·physicist \tekˈtä(ˌ)nō, ˈtektə(ˌ)nō + \ *n* : a specialist in tectonophysics
tec·tono·physics \"+\ *n pl but sing in constr* [*tectonic* + *-o-* + *physics*] : a branch of geophysics that deals with the forces responsible for movements in and deformation of the earth's crust
tec·tono·sphere \tekˈtänəˌsfi(ə)r, ˈtektənō,-\ *n* [ISV *tectonic* + *-o-* + *sphere*] : the zone within the earth in which crustal movements originate
tec·to·ri·al \(ˈ)tekˈtōrēəl, -tȯr-\ *adj* [L *tectorius* (fr. *tectus* — past part. of *tegere* to cover — + *-orius* -ory) + E *-al* — more at THATCH] : forming a covering : resembling a roof
tectorial membrane *n* [NL *tectorium* + E *-al*] : MEMBRANE OF CORTI
tec·to·ri·din \tekˈtōrədən\ *n* -s [*tectorum* (specific epithet of *Iris tectorum*) (fr. L, gen. pl. of *tectum* roof, house, building) + *-idin* — more at TECTUM] : a crystalline isoflavone glucoside $C_{22}H_{22}O_{11}$ found esp. in the rhizomes of an Asiatic iris (*Iris tectorum*)
tectorigenin *n* -s [*tectoridin* + *-genin*] : a crystalline phenolic isoflavone $CH_3OC_{15}H_6O_2(OH)_3$ obtained by hydrolysis of tectoridin
tec·to·ri·um \tekˈtōrēəm, -tȯr-\ *n, pl* **tecto·ria** \-ēə\ [NL, fr. L, cover, covering, fr. neut. of *tectorius* of or forming a covering] : MEMBRANE OF CORTI
tec·to·silicate \ˈtek(ˌ)tō+\ *n* [L *tectum* roof, building + E *-o-* + *silicate* — more at TECTUM] : a polymeric silicate in which the silicon-oxygen tetrahedral groups are linked by sharing all of their oxygen atoms with other such groups so as to form a three-dimensional structure or network — compare CYCLOSILICATE
tec·to·sphere \ˈtektəˌsfi(ə)r\ *n* [Gk *tēktos* molten (fr. *tēkein* to melt) + E *sphere* — more at THAW] : ASTHENOSPHERE
tec·to·spinal \ˈtek(ˌ)tō+\ *adj* [NL *tectum* + E *-o-* + *spinal*] : extending from the tectum of the midbrain to the spinal cord — used esp. of a tract of nerve fibers connecting these parts
tec·to·spon·dy·li \ˌtektōˈspändəˌlī\ *n pl, cap* [NL, prob. fr. L *tectum* roof + NL *-o-* + *-spondyli*] *in some classifications* : an order or other division of elasmobranch fishes typically having tectospondylic vertebrae and comprising the spiny dogfishes and related forms and the angelfish (genus *Squatina*) and formerly also the rays and sawfishes — compare BATOIDEI, CYCLOSPONDYLI
tec·to·spon·dyl·ic \ˌtektōˌspänˈdilik\ *also* **tec·to·spon·dy·lous** \-ndələs\ *adj* [NL *Tectospondyli* + E *-ic, -ous*] : having more than one calcified cylinder surrounding the notochord in each vertebral centrum ⟨~ sharks⟩ — see TECTOSPONDYLI; compare CYCLOSPONDYLIC
tec·tri·cial \(ˈ)tekˈtrishəl\ *adj* [NL *tectric-, tectrix* + E *-ial*] : of or relating to a tectrix
tec·trix \ˈtektriks\ *n, pl* **tectri·ces** \-rəˌsēz, tekˈtrīˌsēz\ [NL *tectric-, tectrix,* fem. of L *tector* one that covers, fr. *tectus* (past part. of *tegere* to cover) + *-or*] : COVERT 3
tec·tum \ˈtektəm\ *n, pl* **tec·ta** \-tə\ [NL, fr. L, roof, dwelling, building, fr. neut. of *tectus,* past part. of *tegere* to cover — more at THATCH] : a bodily structure resembling or serving as a roof; *specif* : the dorsal part of the midbrain including the corpora quadrigemina — called also *tectum me·sen·ceph·a·li* \-ˌmesᵊnˈsefəˌlī\
ted \ˈted\ *vt* **tedded; tedded; tedding; teds** [fr. (assumed) ME *tedden;* akin to OHG *zetten* to spread, ON *tethja* to manure, Gk *dateisthai* to divide, *daiesthai* to divide, distribute — more at TIDE] : to spread out in order to dry : SCATTER ⟨where are the blithe and jocund to ~ the hay? —John Betjeman⟩
te·da \ˈtādə\ *n, pl* **teda** *or* **tedas** *usu cap* : TIBBU
ted·der \ˈtedə(r)\ *n* -s : one that teds; *specif* : a machine for stirring and spreading hay to hasten drying and curing
ted·dy \ˈtedē, -di\ *n, pl* **teddies** *sometimes sing in constr* [origin unknown] : CHEMISE 2
teddy bear *n, sometimes cap T* [fr. *Teddy,* nickname of Theodore Roosevelt †1919 26th U. S. president; fr. a cartoon depicting the president sparing the life of a bear cub while hunting] : a stuffed toy bear

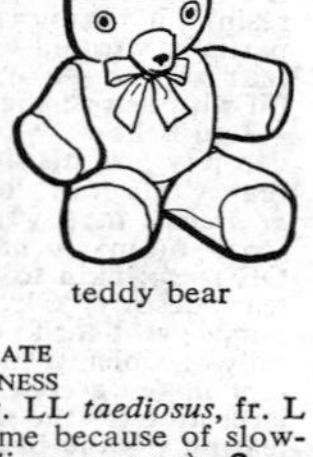

teddy bear

teddy boy *n, usu cap T & often cap B* [fr. *Teddy,* nickname for Edward] : a young British hoodlum who affects Edwardian dress
te de·um \(ˈ)tāˈdāəm, (ˈ)tēˈdēəm\ *n, pl* **te deums** *usu cap T&D* [ME, fr. LL *te deum laudamus* thee, God, we praise, the opening words of the hymn] **1 a** : a hymn of thanksgiving and praise to God **b** : an expression of praise or thanksgiving **2** : a religious service that consists chiefly of a hymn of praise and thanksgiving
tedge \ˈtej\ *n* -s [origin unknown] : ²INGATE
tediosity *n* [*tedious* + *-ity*] *obs* : TEDIOUSNESS
te·di·ous \ˈtēdēəs *also* ˈtējəs\ *adj* [ME, fr. LL *taediosus,* fr. L *taedium* tedium + *-osus* -ous] **1** : tiresome because of slowness, continuance, or prolixity ⟨a ~ public ceremony⟩ **2** *archaic* : SLOW, DILATORY **3** : tiresome because of dullness ⟨rather ~ fellows who substituted fustian for creative thought —V.L.Parrington⟩
te·di·ous·ly *adv* : in a tedious manner ⟨lengthily and ~ interrogated —Glenway Wescott⟩
te·di·ous·ness *n* -ES : the quality or state of being tedious
te·di·ou·some \ˈtēdēəsəm, ˈted-\ *adj* [*tedious* + *-some*] *chiefly Scot* : TEDIOUS
te·di·um *also* **tae·di·um** \ˈtēdēəm\ *n* -s [L *taedium* irksomeness, disgust, fr. *taedēre* to disgust, weary] **1** : the quality or state of being tedious : TEDIOUSNESS ⟨incessant recurrence without variety breeds ~ —J.L.Lowes⟩ **2** : a tedious period of time ⟨long ~*s* of strained anxiety —H.G.Wells⟩
¹tee \ˈtē\ *n* -s [ME] **1** *also* **te** \"\ : the letter *t* **2** : something that is shaped like a capital T: as **a** : a short piece of pipe that has a lateral outlet and is used to connect a line of pipe with a pipe at a right angle to the line — see BRANCH illustration **b** : a short piece of iron fastened at its middle to the end of a chain, passed through a hole, and turned crosswise to secure the chain **c** : T BAR **d** : WIND TEE **3** : the mark aimed at in various games (as curling) — see CURLING illustration **4** : a lattice weave in basketry in which upright and horizontal rods are twined together — **to a tee** *adv* : PRECISELY, EXACTLY ⟨suits me *to a tee*⟩

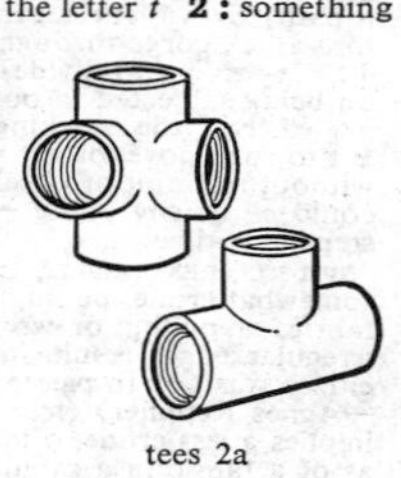

tees 2a

²tee \"\ *vt* **teed; teed; teeing; tees** : to connect or secure by means of a tee
³tee \"\ *n* -s [back-formation fr. earlier *teaz* (taken as pl.), of unknown origin] **1 a** (1) : a small artificial elevation of dirt on which a golf ball is placed before being struck at the beginning of play on a hole (2) : a peg with a concave top used to raise a golf ball before striking it at the beginning of play on a hole **b** : a device for holding a football in position so that it can be kicked off the ground **2** : the area from which a golf ball is struck at the beginning of play on a hole
⁴tee \"\ *vt* **teed; teed; teeing; tees 1** : to place (as a ball) on or as if on a tee — often used with *up* **2** : PREPARE, ARRANGE — usu. used with *up* ⟨an offensive was being *teed* up —Fred Majdalany⟩
tee bar *var of* T BAR
tee beam *var of* T BEAM
tee bolt *var of* T BOLT
tee–bulb \ˈ=ˌ=\ *adj* [¹*tee* + *bulb*] : BULB-TEE
tee·dle \ˈtēdᵊl\ *vb* [prob. imit.] *Scot* : to sing by humming
teed off *adj* [prob. fr. past part. of *tee off*] : ANNOYED, ANGRY ⟨was *teed off* because the chief had me type his spares inventory —N.T.Kenney⟩
tee–hee *var of* TEHEE
tee hinge *var of* T HINGE
tee–hole \ˈ=ˌ=\ *n* [origin unknown] *dial Eng* : the entrance to a beehive
teeing ground *n* [fr. gerund of ⁴*tee*] : ³TEE 2
tee iron *var of* T IRON
tee joint *also* **tee connection** *n* [¹*tee*] : an electrical connection used for joining a branch conductor to a main conductor where the main conductor continues beyond the branch
teel *var of* TIL
teel oil *n* : SESAME OIL
¹teem \ˈtēm\ *vb* -ED/-ING/-S [ME *temen, teamen,* fr. OE *tīeman, tēman, tȳman;* akin to OE *tēam* offspring — more at TEAM] *vt, archaic* : to bring forth : give birth to : PRODUCE ⟨the even mead . . . conceives by idleness and nothing ~*s* but hateful docks —Shak.⟩ ~ *vi* **1** *obs* **a** : to bring forth offspring : give birth **b** : to become pregnant : CONCEIVE ⟨if that the earth could ~ with woman's tears, each drop she falls would prove a crocodile —Shak.⟩ **2 a** : to be marked by fertility : become filled to overflowing : ABOUND, SWARM — usu. used with *with* ⟨the inland lakes ~ with pike —*Amer. Guide Series: Mich.*⟩ ⟨this sprawling boisterous capital which ~*s* with color and historic interest —A.J.Mathers⟩ **b** : to be present in such large quantity as to cause overflowing ⟨a score of plans were ~*ing* in his mind —Edna Ferber⟩
²teem \"\ *vb* -ED/-ING/-S [ME *temen,* fr. ON *tœma;* akin to OE *tōm* empty, OHG *zuomīg,* ON *tōmr*] *vt* **1** *archaic* : EMPTY **2** : POUR; *specif* : to pour (molten metal) into a mold ~ *vi* : POUR; *esp* : to rain in torrents
teem·er \-mə(r)\ *n* -s : one that teems; *specif* : a workman who controls the rate at which stainless steel is poured into molds
teem·ful \-mfəl\ *adj* [¹*teem* + *-ful*] : PRODUCTIVE, FRUITFUL — **teem·ful·ness** *n* -ES
teem·ing·ly *adv* [*teeming* (pres. part. of ¹*teem*) + *-ly*] : in a teeming manner
teem·ing·ness *n* -ES : the state or quality of being teeming
teemless *adj* [¹*teem* + *-less*] *obs* : BARREN
teems \ˈtēmz\ *n pl* [pl. of E dial. *teem* large quantity, fr. ¹*teem*] *dial Brit* : LOT 9
¹teen \ˈtēn\ *n* -s [ME *tene,* fr. OE *tēona* injury, anger, grief; akin to OFris *tiona* injury, OS *tiono,* ON *tjōn,* and perh. to Gk *daiein* to kindle, burn up, Skt *dunoti* he burns, distresses] **1** *obs* : INJURY, DAMAGE, HURT **2** *chiefly Scot* : IRRITATION,

ANGER **3** *archaic* **:** GRIEF, MISERY, AFFLICTION ⟨with public toil and private ~ thou sank'st alone —Matthew Arnold⟩
²teen \"\ *var of* TIND
³teen \"\ *adj* [-*teen* (as in *thirteen*)] **:** TEENAGE ⟨about the beginning of the ~ period —John Ruskin⟩
teen·age \ˈ=,=\ *adj* [-*teen* (as in *thirteen*) + *age*] **:** of, being, or relating to people in their teens
teen-aged \ˈ=,=\ *adj* [-*teen* (as in *thirteen*) + *aged*] **:** TEENAGE
teen-ag·er \ˈtē,nājə(r)\ *n* -s [*teenage* + -*er*] **:** a person in his teens
teename *var of* TO-NAME
teen·er \ˈtēnə(r)\ *n* -s [-*teen* (as in *thirteen*) + -*er*] **:** TEENAGER
teens \ˈtēnz\ *n pl* [-*teen* (as in *thirteen*)] **1 :** the numbers 13 to 19 inclusive; *specif* **:** the years 13 to 19 in a lifetime ⟨in his ~⟩ or in a particular century **2 :** TEENAGERS ⟨the ~ want fun and glamour —*Parents' Mag.*⟩
teens·ter \ˈtēnztə(r), -n(t)st-\ *n* -s [*teens* + -*ster*] **:** TEENAGER
teen·sy *also* **teent·sy** \ˈtēn(t)sē\ *adj* -ER/-EST [alter. of *teeny*] **:** TINY ⟨just a ~ keg of whiskey —A.B.Guthrie⟩
teen·sy-ween·sy *also* **teent·sy-weent·sy** *or* **teen·sie-ween·sie** \ˌtēn(t)sēˈwēn(t)sē\ *adj* [alter. of *teeny-weeny*] **:** TINY ⟨another *teensy-weensy* martini —Merle Miller⟩
teen·ty \ˈtēntē\ *adj* -ER/-EST [alter. of *teeny*] **:** TINY ⟨the least little ~ hands —Mary S. Watts⟩
tee·ny \ˈtēnē, -ni\ *adj* -ER/-EST [alter. (influenced by *weeny*) of *tiny*] **:** TINY ⟨cheated just a ~ bit⟩ **syn** see SMALL
tee·ny-wee·ny *also* **tee·nie-wee·nie** \ˌtēnēˈwēnē\ *adj* [*teeny* + *weeny*] **:** TINY ⟨even a pair of *teeny-weeny* rubber gloves in the kitchen —V.V.Nabokov⟩
tee off *vi* [⁴*tee*] **1 :** to drive from a tee **2 :** BEGIN, START ⟨the book *tees off* with a discussion of bitterness —*Holiday*⟩ **3 :** to hit hard ⟨*teed off* on the new pitcher's first delivery and sent it over the center-field wall —Bennett Cerf⟩ **4 :** to make an angry denunciation **:** SCOLD — often used with *on* ⟨*teed off* on the selection committee in an ill-tempered article —*Time*⟩
teepee *var of* TEPEE
tee·ple·ite \ˈtēpə,līt\ *n* -s [John E. *Teeple* †1931 Am. chemist + E -*ite*] **:** a mineral $NaBO_2Cl.2H_2O$ consisting of hydrous chloride and borate of sodium
tees *pl of* TEE, *pres 3d sing of* TEE
tee shirt *var of* T-SHIRT
tee slot *var of* T SLOT
tee square *var of* T SQUARE
teest \ˈtēst\ *n* -s [origin unknown] **:** a small anvil
tees·water \ˈtēz+,-\ *n* [*Tees*, river of northern England + *water*] **1** *usu cap* **:** an extinct British breed of cattle believed to have been the principal stock from which the Shorthorns are derived **2** -s *often cap* **:** an animal of the Teeswater breed
teetee *var of* TITI
¹tee·ter \ˈtēd·ə(r), -ētə-\ *vb* -ED/-ING/-S [alter. of earlier *titter*, fr. ME *titeren* to totter, reel, sway; akin to OHG *zittarōn* to shiver, shake, ON *titra* to twinkle, shiver, Gk *apodidraskein* to run away, *dramein* to run, Skt *drāti* he runs — more at DROMEDARY] *vi* **1 a :** to move unsteadily: as (1) **:** to progress (as by walking) unsteadily ⟨~*ed* across the half-finished bridge —Burgess Scott⟩ (2) **:** to move unsteadily before or as if before falling **:** WOBBLE ⟨stood on chairs and ~*ed* on stepladders —John Dos Passos⟩ **b** (1) **:** to waver precariously **:** show signs of possible impending failure ⟨for the next few days the attack would ~ from enemy counterattacks —Norman Mailer⟩ — often used with *on* ⟨is always ~*ing* on the edge of catastrophe —Charles Hamblett⟩ (2) **:** to oscillate unsteadily esp. in a dangerous position ⟨a passive type who ~*s* between conformity and revolt —R.N.Denney⟩ **2 :** SEESAW ⟨took the little girl to the park so that she could ~⟩ ~ *vt* **:** SEESAW ⟨~*ed* his chair and sighed —G.A.Chamberlain⟩
²teeter \"\ *n* -s **1** [so called fr. the teetering movements of its tail] **:** SPOTTED SANDPIPER **2 :** an act of teetering **3 :** SEESAW 2b **4 :** a transverse rolling or rocking in a spring suspension **:** UNDULATION
teeterboard \ˈ==,=\ *n* [¹*teeter* + *board*] **1** *also* **teetering board :** SEESAW 2b **2 :** a board placed on a raised support in such a way that a person standing on one end of the board is thrown into the air if another person jumps on the opposite end
teetertail \ˈ==,=\ *n* [¹*teeter* + *tail*] **:** SPOTTED SANDPIPER
¹tee·ter-tot·ter \ˈtēd·ə(r),tädə(r), ˈtētə(r),tätə(r)\ *vi* [alter. of E dial. *titter-totter*, game of seesawing, fr. obs. *titter* to teeter + *totter* — more at TEETER] **:** SEESAW
²teeter-totter \"\ *n* -s **:** SEESAW
tee·tery \ˈtēd·ərē\ *adj* [¹*teeter* + -*y*] **:** TOTTERY
teeth *pl of* TOOTH
teethe \ˈtēth\ *vb* -ED/-ING/-S [back-formation fr. *teething*] *vi* **:** to cut one's teeth **:** grow teeth ~ *or* **teeth** \ˈtēth\ *vt, chiefly Scot* **:** to provide (as a comb or harrow) with teeth
teeth·er \-thə(r)\ *n* -s [*teethe* + -*er*] **:** an object (as a teething ring) designed for a baby to chew on safely during teething
teeth·i·ly \ˈtēthəlē\ *adv* [¹*teethy* + -*ly*] *chiefly Scot* **:** IRRITABLY, CROSSLY
teeth·ing \ˈtēthiŋ, -thēn\ *n* -s [*teeth* + -*ing*] **1 :** the first growth of teeth **2 :** the phenomena accompanying the growth of teeth through the gums

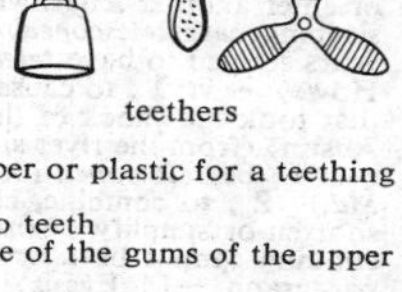

teethers

teething ring *n* **:** a ring usu. of rubber or plastic for a teething infant to bite on
teeth·less \ˈtēthləs\ *adj* **:** having no teeth
teethridge \ˈ=,=\ *n* **:** the inner surface of the gums of the upper front teeth
¹teethy \ˈtēthi\ *adj* [ME *tethee*, perh. fr. *tethen* to teethe (fr. *teth*, *teeth* teeth) + -*ee* -y; fr. the irritability of teething infants] *chiefly Scot* **:** IRRITABLE, CROSS
²teethy \ˈtēthē, ˈtēthē\ *adj* -ER/-EST [*teeth* + -*y*] **:** TOOTHY
¹tee·to·tal \ˈtēˈtōd·ᵊl, -ōtᵊl\ *adj* [*total* + *total* (*abstinence*)] **1 a :** of or relating to total abstinence from alcoholic drinks ⟨the ~ movement was strong in the state capital —S.H.Adams⟩ **b :** totally abstaining from alcoholic drinks ⟨the stale joke of a ~ spinster getting drunk and amorous —E.R.Bentley⟩ **2 :** TOTAL, COMPLETE, ABSOLUTE ⟨rest in ~ peace —Della Lutes⟩ — **tee·to·tal·ly** \-ᵊlē\ *adv*
²teetotal \"\ *vi* **:** to advocate or practice teetotalism
tee·to·tal·er *or* **tee·to·tal·ler** \-ᵊlə(r)\ *n* -s **:** one that practices or advocates total abstinence from alcoholic drinks
tee·to·tal·ism \-ᵊl,izəm\ *n* -s [¹*teetotal* + -*ism*] **:** the principle or the practice of complete abstinence from alcoholic drinks
tee·to·tal·ist \-ᵊləst\ *n* -s [¹*teetotal* + -*ist*] **:** one who advocates or practices teetotalism
¹tee·to·tum \(ˈ)tēˈtōd·əm, -ōtəm\ *n* -s [¹*tee* + L *totum* all, the whole, fr. neut. of *totus* whole, entire; fr. the letter *T* inscribed on one side as an abbr. of *totum* (take) all] **1 a :** a small top inscribed with letters and used in playing put-and-take; *also* **:** PUT-AND-TAKE **2 :** a small top
²teetotum \"\ *vi* -ED/-ING/-S **:** to spin like a teetotum
tee·vee \ˈtēˈvē\ *n* -s [¹*tee* + *vee*; fr. the abbr. *TV*] **:** TELEVISION
teff \ˈtef\ *also* **teff grass** *n* -s [Amharic *tēf*] **:** an economically important African cereal grass (*Eragrostis abyssinica*) used for its grain which yields a white flour of good quality and as a forage and hay crop
te·fil·lin *or* **te·phil·lin** *also* **tfil·lin** \təˈfilən *also* -ləm\ *n pl but sometimes sing in constr* [LHeb *tĕphillīn*, fr. Aram, attachments; akin to Heb *tāphēl* whitewash, mortar] **:** the phylacteries worn by Jews
teg *also* **tegg** \ˈteg\ *n* -s [origin unknown] **1 :** a doe in its second year **2 a** *chiefly Brit* **:** a sheep in its second year **b :** the fleece cut from a sheep in its second year
TEG *abbr, often not cap* top edges gilt
teg·e·nar·ia \,tejəˈna(a)rēə\ *n, cap* [NL] **:** a genus of spiders related to *Agalena*
teg·e·tic·u·la \,tejəˈtikyələ\ *n, cap* [NL, fr. L, little mat, dim. of *teget-*, *teges* covering, mat, fr. *tegere* to cover — more at THATCH] **:** a genus of moths (family Tineidae) that includes the yucca moth
teg·men \ˈtegmən\ *n, pl* **teg·mi·na** \-mənə\ [NL, fr. L *tegmen*, *tegumen*, covering, cover, fr. *tegere* to cover] **:** INTEGUMENT, COVERING: as **a :** ENDOPLEURA **b** (1) **:** one of the elytra of a beetle (2) **:** one of the thickened forewings of various orthopterans **c** *or* **tegmen tympani :** a thin plate of bone that covers the middle ear and separates it from the cranial cavity
teg·men·tal \(ˈ)tegˈmentᵊl\ *adj* [L & NL *tegmentum* + E -*al*] **1 :** of or relating to an integument **2 :** of, relating to, or associated with a tegmentum esp. of the brain
teg·men·tum \tegˈmentəm\ *or* **teg·u·men·tum** \-gyə'-\ *n, pl* **tegmen·ta** *or* **tegumen·ta** \-tə\ [NL, fr. L, covering, integument — more at TEGUMENT] **:** COVERING: as **a :** the part of the cerebral peduncles above the substantia nigra formed of longitudinal white fibers with arched transverse fibers and gray matter **b** (1) **:** the outer covering of scales on a leaf bud (2) **:** one of these scales **c :** the outer layer of a plate of a chiton — compare ARTICULAMENTUM
tegu *var of* TEJU
te·gua \ˈtāgwə\ *n* -s [Keresan] **:** an ankle-high rawhide moccasin of the southwestern U. S. and Mexico
te·gu·ci·gal·pa \tə,güsəˈgalpə\ *adj, usu cap* [fr. *Tegucigalpa*, capital of Honduras] **:** of or from Tegucigalpa, the capital of Honduras **:** of the kind or style prevalent in Tegucigalpa
te·guex·in \təˈgweksən\ *n* -s [NL *teguixin* (specific epithet of *Tupin-ambis teguixin*, genus of lizards), fr. Nahuatl *tecoixin*, *tecuixin*] **:** a bluish black teju (*Tupinambis teguixin*) with pale or whitish yellow spots on the back
teg·u·la \ˈtegyələ\ *n* [NL, fr. L, tile — more at THATCH] **1** *pl* **teg·u·lae** \-yə,lē\ **a :** one of a pair of small scalelike sclerites of the mesothorax of some insects (as of the orders Hymenoptera and Lepidoptera) that cover the bases of the forewings **b :** a patagium of a lepidopterous insect **c :** the alula of a dipterous insect **2** *cap* **:** a widely distributed genus of turban shells sometimes used for food
teg·u·lar \-yələ(r)\ *adj* [L & NL *tegula* + E -*ar*] **1 :** of, relating to, or resembling a tile **2 :** of or relating to a tegula — **teg·u·lar·ly** *adv*
teg·u·ment \ˈtegyəmənt\ *n* -s [ME, fr. L *tegmentum*, *tegumentum*, fr. *tegere* to cover + -*mentum*, -ment — more at THATCH] **:** INTEGUMENT — **teg·u·men·tal** \ˌtegyəˈmentᵊl\ *adj*
teg·u·men·tary \ˌ==ˈmentərē, -ri\ *adj* [*tegument* + -*ary*] **:** of, relating to, or consisting of an integument **:** serving as a covering ⟨the reduction of the ~ tissues goes very far in some seeds —A.J.Eames & L.H.MacDaniels⟩
te·gu·ri·um *or* **tu·gu·ri·um** \təˈgyu̇rēəm\ *n, pl* **teguria** *or* **tuguria** [LL, covering, shrine, fr. L, hut, cottage, perh. fr. *tegere* to cover] **:** a roof over an altar or a sarcophagus usu. supported by light columns and often pointed
¹te-hee *or* **tee-hee** \tēˈhē\ *n* -s [ME *te he*, of imit. origin] **:** a laugh in a high voice — often used interjectionally
²tehee *or* **tee-hee** \"\ *vi* **teheed** *or* **tee-heed; teheed** *or* **tee-heed; teheeing** *or* **tee-heeing; tehees** *or* **tee-hees :** to laugh in a high voice esp. in superficial amusement or derision **:** TITTER
te·hin·nah *or* **te·chin·nah** \təˈkinə\ *n, pl* **tehin·noth** *or* **tehin·not** *or* **techin·noth** *or* **techin·not** \təkiˈnōt(h)\ [Yiddish *tekhine*, fr. LHeb *tāḥanūn* prayer for grace — more at TAHANUN] **1 :** a prayer in Yiddish used by Jewish women only **2 :** a book of tehinnoth
teh·ran *or* **te·he·ran** \ˌtāˈran, ˌteə-, -ˈrän *sometimes* təˈran *or* tā'- *or* -ˈrän\ *adj, usu cap* [fr. *Tehran*, *Teheran*, capital of Iran] **:** of or from Tehran, the capital of Iran **:** of the kind or style prevalent in Tehran
te·huan·te·pec·er \təˈwäntə,pekə(r)\ *n* -s *usu cap* [Gulf of *Tehuantepec*, inlet of the Pacific, southeastern Mexico + E -*er*] **:** a violent north wind that brings an inflow of cold air to Central America and esp. to regions around the Gulf of Tehuantepec
te·huel·che \təˈwelchē\ *n, pl* **tehuelche** *or* **tehuelches** *usu cap* [Araucanian, lit., people of the southeast] **1 a :** a Chonan people of southern Argentina **b :** a member of such people **2 :** the language of the Tehuelche people — **te·huel·che·an** \-ēən\ *adj, usu cap*
teian \ˈtē(y)ən\ *adj, usu cap* [L *teius* (fr. Gk *tēios*, *Tēos*, *Teōs* Teos, ancient Greek city of Asia Minor) + E -*an*] **:** of or relating to Teos ⟨produce his dainty translations of the *Teian* bard —Thomas Walsh⟩
teich·mann's crystal \ˈtīkmənz-\ *n, usu cap T* [after L. K. *Teichmann*-Stawiarski †1895 Ger. anatomist] **:** one of the crystals of hemin obtainable from hemoglobin and useful as a test for blood **:** BLOOD CRYSTAL
teig·lach *also* **taig·lach** *or* **teig·lech** \ˈtāgläk, ˈtīg-\ *n pl but sing or pl in constr* [Yiddish *teyglekh*, dim. of *teyg* dough, fr. MHG *teig*, *teic*, fr. OHG *teic* — more at DOUGH] **:** small pieces of dough boiled in honey
¹teiid \ˈtē(y)əd\ *adj* [NL *Teiidae*] **:** of or relating to the Teiidae
²teiid \"\ *n* -s **:** a lizard of the family Teiidae
teiidae \ˈtē(y)ə,dē\ *n pl, cap* [NL, fr. *Teius*, type genus (fr. Pg *tejú*, *teiú* teju) + -*idae* — more at TEJU] **:** a family of mostly tropical American lizards (as the tejus of So. America and the race runner of the western U. S.) having a flat elongate scaly tongue that ends in two long smooth points
teil tree \ˈtē(ə)l-\ *also* **teil** *n* -s [F dial. *teil*, fr. OF, fr. L *tilia*] **:** LINDEN 1a
teind \ˈtēnd\ *n* -s [ME *tend*, *teind*, fr. *tende*, *tend*, *teind* tenth; akin to OHG *zehanto* tenth, ON *tīundi*; Goth *taihunda*, Gk *dekatos*; all fr. a prehistoric IE adjective fr. the source of OE *tien* ten] **1** *chiefly Scot* **:** TITHE **2 :** the part of the estates of the Scottish laity that can be assessed for the stipend of the clergy of the established church
teind·able \-dəbəl\ *adj* [Sc *teind* to assess tithes (fr. ME *tenden*, *teinden*, fr. *teind*) + -*able*] *Scot* **:** TITHABLE
teind boll *n, Scot* **:** a boll of grain accepted as tithe
teind court *n, usu cap T&C* **:** a court for the control of teinds consisting of the judges of the Court of Session
tein·ite \ˈtā,nīt\ *n* -s [*Teine*, name of a mine in Hokkaido, Japan + E -*ite*] **:** a mineral $Cu_{13}(SO_4)_3(TeO_4)_{10}.26H_2O$ consisting of hydrous sulfate and tellurate of copper
teist·ie \ˈtīsti, ˈtēs-\ *Scot var of* TYSTIE
teize \ˈtēz\ *archaic var of* TEASE
te·ja·no \tāˈhä(,)nō\ *n* -s [Sp, fr. *Tejas* Texas + -*ano* -an, fr. L -*anus*] *Southwest* **:** TEXAN
te·ji·dae \ˈtējə,dē, ˈtej-\ [NL, fr. *Tejus*, genus of lizards (fr. Pg *tejú*, *teiú* teju) + -*idae*] *syn of* TEIIDAE
te·ju \təˈzhü\ *also* **te·gu** \-ˈgü\ *n* -s [Pg *tejú*, *teiú*, fr. Tupi & Guarani *tejú*, *teyú*] **:** any of several large blackish So. American lizards of the genus *Tupinambis* (family Teiidae) that have yellow or white bands across the back, grow to a length of about three feet, often raid hen roosts, and are hunted as pests and for their flesh which is regarded as a delicacy
te·ki·ah \təˈkēə\ *n, pl* **teki·oth** *or* **teki·ot** \təkēˈōt(h)\ *or* **tekiahs** [Heb *teqī'āh*] **:** one of the long deep calls sounded on the shofar as prescribed in the Jewish ritual for Rosh Hashanah and Yom Kippur — compare TERUAH
te·kint·si \təˈkin(t)sē\ *n, pl* **tekintsi** *or* **tekintsis** *usu cap* **:** TEKKE
¹tek·ke \ˈtek,kē\ *n, pl* **tekke** *or* **tekkes** *usu cap* **1 :** a Turkoman people living on the frontiers of Iran, Afghanistan, and the Turkmen S.S.R. **2 :** a member of the Tekke people
²tekke *n, pl* **tekkes** *also* **tekke** [Turk] **:** a dervish monastery
tek·non·y·mous \(ˈ)tekˈnänəməs\ *adj* **:** of or relating to teknonymy — **tek·non·y·mous·ly** *adv*
tek·non·y·my \tekˈnänəmē\ *n* -ES [Gk *teknon* child + E -*onymy* — more at THANE] **:** the custom of naming the parent after the child
tek·tite \ˈtek,tīt\ *n* -s [ISV *tekt-* (fr. Gk *tēktos* molten, fr. *tēkein* to melt) + -*ite* — more at THAW] **:** a glassy body of probably meteoritic origin and of rounded but indefinite shape found esp. in Czechoslovakia, Indonesia, and Australia
¹tel- *or* **tele-** *also* **telo-** *comb form* [NL & ISV, fr. Gk *tēl-*, *tēle-* far, far off, distant, fr. *tēle* — more at PALE-] **1 :** distant **:** at a distance **:** over a distance ⟨*tel*egnosis⟩ ⟨*tele*kinesis⟩ ⟨*tele*sthesia⟩ ⟨*tele*vision⟩ ⟨*telo*dynamic⟩ **2 a :** telegraph ⟨*tele*tape⟩ ⟨*tele*typewriter⟩ **b :** television ⟨*tele*camera⟩ **c :** telephoto ⟨*tel*elens⟩ **d :** telecommunication ⟨*tele*man⟩
²tel- *or* **telo-** *also* **tele-** *comb form* [ISV, fr. Gk *tel-*, *telo-*, fr. *telos* end, consummation, completeness — more at WHEEL] **1 :** end ⟨*tel*angiectasia⟩ ⟨*telo*blast⟩ ⟨*tele*metacarpal⟩ **2 :** complete **:** mature ⟨*Tel*anthera⟩ ⟨*Tel*anthropus⟩
tel *abbr* **1** telegram **2** telegraph; telegraphic; telegraphy **3** telephone; telephony
TEL *abbr* tetraethyl lead
te·la \ˈtēlə\ *n, pl* **te·lae** \-,lē\ [NL, fr. L, web — more at TOIL] **:** an anatomical tissue or layer of tissue: as **a :** a fold of pia mater roofing a ventricle of the brain **b :** a layer of loose connective tissue separating layers of other tissues — **te·lar** \-lə(r)\ *adj*
telaesthesia *var of* TELESTHESIA
telaesthetic *var of* TELESTHETIC
te·la·ku·cha \təˈläkə,chä\ *n* -s [Bengali *telākucā*] **:** IVY GOURD
tel·a·mon \ˈtelə,män, -,mən\ *n, pl* **telamo·nes** \ˌ==ˈmō(,)nēz\ [L, fr. Gk *telamōn* bearer, supporter, fr. the stem of *tlēnai* to bear — more at TOLERATE] **1 :** a male figure used like a caryatid as a supporting column or pilaster **:** ATLAS 4 **2** [NL, fr. L] **:** an accessory outgrowth of the cloacal wall forming part of the copulatory apparatus of various male nematode worms
tel·ang \ˈte,lanj\ *adj* [by shortening] **:** TELANGIECTATIC ⟨a ~ bovine liver⟩
tel·an·gi·ectasia *or* **tel·an·gi·ec·ta·sis** \tə,lanjē, teˌl-+\ *n, pl* **telangiectasias** *or* **telangiectases** [NL, fr. ²*tel-* + *angi-* + *ectasia* or *ectasis*] **1 :** an abnormal dilatation of capillary vessels and arterioles that often forms an angioma; *specif* **:** a pathological state of the bovine liver in which dilated capillaries form small angiomas and there is excessive storage of vitamin A **2 :** a hereditary abnormality inherited as a simple dominant and characterized by bleeding into the tissues and mucous surfaces because of the abnormal fragility of the capillaries — **tel·an·gi·ec·tat·ic** \"+\ *adj*
tel·an·thera \təˈlan(t)thərə, teˈl-\ *n* [NL, fr. ²*tel-* + -*anthera*] **1** *cap* **:** a genus of tropical herbs or shrubs (family Amaranthaceae) that is commonly included in the genus *Alternanthera* from which it may be distinguished by the presence of five stamens and five staminodia united into a tube and that comprises plants with inconspicuous whitish flowers and showy brightly colored foliage which are often used for carpet bedding **2** -s **:** ALTERNANTHERA 2
tel·an·thro·pus \təˈlan(t)thrəpəs, teˈl-; ,te,lanˈthrōp-\ *n, cap* [NL, fr. ²*tel-* + -*anthropus*] **:** a genus of southern African fossil hominids that is based on an incomplete lower jaw and associated teeth and is held to comprise forms intermediate in some respects between the australopithecines and true man
tel·au·to·gram \teˈlȯd·ə,gram\ *n* [ISV *telautograph* + -*gram*] **:** a message or other facsimile transmitted and recorded by a TelAutograph device
Tel·Au·to·graph \-raf, -räf\ *trademark* — used for a facsimile telegraph for reproducing graphic matter by means of a transmitter in which the motions of a pencil are communicated by levers to two rotary shafts that produce variations in current in two separate circuits and by means of a receiver in which these variations are utilized by electromagnetic devices and levers to move a pen as the pencil moves
tel aviv \ˌteləˈvēv\ *adj, usu cap T&A* [fr. *Tel Aviv*, Israel] **:** of or from the city of Tel Aviv, Israel **:** of the kind or style prevalent in Tel Aviv
tel aviv·ian \ˌteləˈvēvēən, -vēvyən\ *n* -s *cap T&A* [*Tel Aviv*, Israel + E -*ian*] **:** a native or resident of Tel Aviv, Israel
¹tele \ˈtelē\ *n* -s [Gk *tēle* far, far off, distant — more at PALE-] **:** mutual feeling or psychic affinity between two or more people
²tele \ˈtelē, -lə\ *n* -s [by shortening] **:** TELEVISION
¹tele- — see ¹TEL-
²tele- *or* **teleo-** *comb form* [NL, fr. Gk *teleio-*, *teleo-*, fr. *teleios*, *teleos*, fr. *telos* end, consummation, completeness — more at WHEEL] **:** complete **:** perfect ⟨*tele*odont⟩ ⟨*Teleo*cephali⟩
³tele- — see ²TEL-
tele·binocular \ˈtelə+\ *n* [¹*tel-* + *binocular*] **:** a stereoscopic instrument for determining various eye defects, measuring visual acuity or fusion of images, and conducting orthoptic training
tel·e·blem \ˈtelə,blem\ *n* -s [¹*tel-* + -*blem* (as in *periblem*)] **:** UNIVERSAL VEIL
tele·camera \ˈtelə +\ *n* [¹*tel-* + *camera*] **:** a television camera
¹tele·cast \ˈtelə+,-\ *n* -s [¹*tel-* + broad*cast*] **:** a broadcasting or a program broadcast by television
²telecast \"\ *vb* **telecast** *also* **telecasted; telecast** *also* **telecasted; telecasting; telecasts :** to broadcast by television
tele·cast·er \"ə(r)\ *n* -s **:** a television broadcaster
tele·cen·tric \ˌteləˈsen·trik\ *adj* [¹*tel-* + -*centric*] **:** of or relating to a telecentric lens
telecentric lens *n* **:** a lens system in which either the entrance pupil or the exit pupil is at infinity and which is used in optical measuring devices to eliminate parallax between an image and the scale for its measurement
tele·cine \ˌteləˈsinē\ *n* [¹*tel-* + *cine*] **:** a televised motion picture ⟨~ equipment⟩ ⟨a ~ program⟩ ⟨~ transmission⟩
tele·communication \ˈtelə+\ *n* [ISV ¹*tel-* + *communication*] **1 :** communication at a distance (as by cable, radio, telegraph, telephone, or television) **2 :** the science that deals with telecommunication ⟨study ~⟩ — usu. used in pl.
tele·control \"+\ *n* [¹*tel-* + *control*] **:** remote control utilizing radio, wire transmission line, or sound waves
tele·course \ˈtelə+,-\ *n* [¹*tel-* + *course*] **:** a course of study conducted over television
teledendron *var of* TELODENDRION
tel·e·du \ˈtelə,dü\ *n* -s [Malay *tēledu*] **:** a small carnivorous mammal (*Mydaus meliceps*) of the mountains of Java and Sumatra resembling the badger and like the skunk secreting an offensive fluid which it can expel a short distance and being blackish brown with a yellowish white stripe down the back — called also *Javanese skunk*
tel·e·fer·ic \ˌteləˈferik\ *also* **tel·e·fé·rique** \ˌteləfəˈrēk\ *n* -s [*teleferic* fr. It *teleferica*, fr. fem. of *teleferico* of telpherage, fr. F *téléphérique*, fr. *téléphérage* telpherage (alter. of *telpherage*, fr. E *telpherage*) + -*ique* -ic; *teleferique* fr. F *téléférique*, fr. It *teleferica*] **:** TELPHER
tele·film \ˈtelə+,-\ *n* [¹*tel-* + *film*] **:** a motion picture produced for televising
teleg *abbr* **1** telegram **2** telegraph; telegraphic; telegraphy
te·le·ga \təˈlegə, təlˈye-\ *n* -s [Russ] **:** a 4-wheeled springless wagon used by the Russians
tel·e·gen·ic \ˌteləˈjenik\ *adj* [¹*tel-* + -*genic*] **:** eminently suitable for broadcast by television; *esp* **:** having an appearance and manner that are markedly attractive to television viewers — **tel·e·gen·i·cal·ly** \-nək(ə)lē\ *adv*
tel·eg·no·sis \ˌteləˈnōsəs, ,te,legˈn-\ *n* -ES [NL, fr. ¹*tel-* + -*gnosis*] **:** knowledge of distant happenings obtained by occult or unknown means **:** CLAIRVOYANCE — **tel·eg·nos·tic** \ˌ=(,)=ˈnästik\ *adj*
te·leg·o·ny \təˈlegənē\ *n* -ES [ISV ¹*tel-* + -*gony*] **:** the supposed carrying over of the influence of a sire to the offspring of subsequent matings of the dam with other males — compare SATURATION
¹tel·e·gram \ˈtelə,gram, -raa(ə)m, *South also* -,grəm\ *n* [¹*tel-* + -*gram*] **:** a message by telegraph; *esp* **:** one sent at the regular daytime rate
²telegram \"\ *vb* **telegrammed; telegrammed; telegramming; telegrams :** TELEGRAPH
tel·e·gram·mat·ic \ˌteləgrəˈmad·ik, -,graˈm-, -at|, |ēk\ *adj* [*telegram* + -*atic* (as in *epigrammatic*)] **:** TELEGRAMMIC
tel·e·gram·mic \-,gramik\ *adj* **:** relating to or resembling a telegram **:** LACONIC, BRIEF ⟨scribbled her ~ poems on torn-off newspaper margins and old envelopes —J.T.Winterich⟩
¹tel·e·graph \ˈtelə,graf, -raa(ə)f, -raif, -räf\ *n, often attrib* [F *télégraphe*, fr. *télé-* ¹tel- + -*graphe* -graph] **1 a :** an apparatus for communication at a distance by means of preconcerted signals; *broadly* **:** an apparatus, system, or process for communication at a distance other than the ordinary ones of speech and letter writing — compare SEMAPHORE **b :** an electrical apparatus consisting essentially of a wire that forms a complete circuit, a source of current, a transmitter by which the circuit can be made or broken at will, and a receiver that is affected by every make and break so that an audible or visual indication is given (as by deflection of a pointer, marks made on a moving tape, or sharp clicks) — compare PRINTER 2b **c :** an electrical or mechanical apparatus that is used on a ship for issuing or repeating orders from and to the bridge **2 :** TELEGRAM **3 :** a device (as an elevated board or frame-

work) on which information can be displayed (as for the benefit of spectators at a game or race) **4** : an inclined trough, chute, or similar device through which coal or other material slides to a lower level **5** : TELEGRAPH STAMP
²**telegraph** \"\ vb -ED/-ING/-s vt **1 a** : to send or communicate by or as if by telegraph ⟨~ news⟩ ⟨~ congratulations⟩ ⟨sensory nerves which immediately ~ to the brain the sensations experienced by them —T.D.Buchanan⟩ ⟨the kiss from her full, pouty lips ~ed itself to his toes —T.W.Duncan⟩ **b** : to send a telegram to **c** : to send (as flowers or money) by means of a telegraphic order **2** : to display (as a score) on a telegraph board **3** a : to make known by signs : SIGNAL ⟨a look about him which ~ed bad news —Niven Busch⟩ ⟨a jaw that ~ed to every movie villain that here was a man who would take no foolishness —Emmett Kelly⟩ **b** : to reveal unknowingly and in advance the intention with respect to (as a blow, move, or pitch) ⟨swung, but he ~ed it and the other ducked easily —G.A.Wagner⟩ ~ vi **1** : to send a telegram : communicate or signal by telegraph **2** : to telegraph something
telegraph block n : a block with many small sheaves used in making nautical flag signals
telegraph blue n : a grayish purple that is bluer and darker than mauve gray, bluer and duller than average orchid gray, and bluer and paler than average rose mauve
telegraph board n : TELEGRAPH 3
telegraph cable n : a telegraphic cable of several conducting wires enclosed in an insulating and protecting material so as to bring the wires into compact compass for use on poles or to form a strong cable impervious to water to be laid under ground or under water
telegraph editor n : an editor who handles the copy that comes into a newspaper or news periodical office by wire
te·leg·ra·pher \tə'legrəfə(r); 'telə,grafə(r), -raəf-,-raif-,-rȧf-\ n -s [¹telegraph + -er] : one that sends and receives telegraphic messages : telegraphic operator
tel·e·graph·ese \,telə,gra'fēz, -raə'f-, -rai'f-, -rȧ'f-, -ēs\ n -s [¹telegraph + -ese] : language characterized by the terseness and elliptical expressions that are common in telegrams ⟨~ style ... is distinguished by its omission of articles, relatives, connectives, personal, demonstrative and other pronouns, and auxiliary verbs —Richard Hoggart⟩ ⟨in vivid ~ which combined pithy comment with a tart humor —Notes & Queries⟩
tel·e·graph·ic \,telə'grafik, -fēk\ adj [¹telegraph + -ic] **1** : of or relating to the telegraph ⟨a ~ machine⟩ : made or communicated by a telegraph ⟨a ~ report⟩ ⟨~ news⟩ **2** : communicated over a distance as if by telegraph ⟨stopped in answer to a ~ glance from his companion⟩ **3** : having the style of a telegram; esp : SHORT, CONCISE, TERSE ⟨with economy of words —F.S.Mitchell⟩ ⟨the author's ~ style with its verbless sentences and one-lined paragraphs —Grace Frank⟩ **4** : being a place for the receipt of telegrams ⟨my ~ address while I am away from home⟩ — **tel·e·graph·i·cal·ly** \-fə̇k(ə)lē, -fēk-, -li\ adv
telegraphic transfer n, chiefly Brit : CABLE TRANSFER
te·leg·ra·phist \tə'legrəfə̇st; 'telə,grafə̇st, -raəf-, -raif-, -rȧf-\ n -s [F télégraphiste, fr. télégraphe + -iste -ist] : one skilled in telegraphy : TELEGRAPHER
te·leg·ra·phone \tə'legrə,fōn\ n [Dan telegrafon, fr. tele- ¹telo- + -grafon (blend of graf- graph- and -fon -phone)] : an early magnetic recorder
tel·e·graph·o·scope \'telə'grafə,skōp\ n [¹telegraph + -o- + -scope] : an early device for transmitting pictures over a telegraph circuit
telegraph plant n : an East Indian tick trefoil (Desmodium gyrans) whose lateral leaflets jerk up and down like the arms of a semaphore and also rotate on their axes
telegraph stamp n : a stamp for use as evidence that charges on a telegram have been paid
te·leg·ra·phy \tə'legrəfē, -fi\ n -ES [¹tel- + -graphy] **1 a** : the use or operation of a telegraph apparatus or system esp. of the electric telegraph for transmitting or receiving communications **b** : the occupation of one who specializes in such use or operation ⟨railroad ~⟩ **c** : a system of communication by telegraph and esp. electric telegraph **2** : the transmission of intelligence or information over a distance as if by telegraph ⟨mental ~⟩
telegu usu cap, var of TELUGU
tel·ei \'te(,)lī\ n, pl telei or teleis usu cap **1 a** : a Papuan people on Bougainville, Solomon islands **b** : a member of such people **2** : the language of the Telei people
tele·ki·ne·sis \,teləkə̇'nēsə̇s, -,kī-\ n, pl telekine·ses \-ē,sēz\ [NL, fr. ¹tel- + -kinesis] : the apparent production of motion in objects (as by a spiritualistic medium) without contact or other physical means — **tele·ki·net·ic** \-'ned-ik\ adj
tele·lens \'telə+,-\ n [¹tel- + lens] : a telephoto lens
tele·man \'telə,man\ n, pl telemen [¹tel- + man] : a petty officer (as in the U.S. Navy) who performs clerical, coding, and communications duties
tel·e·mark \'telə,märk\ n -s sometimes cap [Norw, fr. Telemark, region in southern Norway] : a turn in which the ski that is to be on the outside of the turn is advanced considerably ahead of the other ski and then turned inward at a steadily widening angle until the actual turn
tele·mechanic \'telə+\ adj [ISV ¹tel- + mechanic] : being or relating to a device for operating mechanisms at a distance — **tele·mechanically** \'telə+\ adv
tele·metacarpal \'+\ adj [²tel- + metacarpal] : having the terminal parts of the first and fifth metacarpals vestigial (as various deers)
tele·meteorograph \'telə+\ n [ISV ¹tel- + meteorograph; prob. orig. formed as F télémétéorographe] : an apparatus recording meteorological phenomena at a distance from the measuring apparatus (as by electricity or compressed air); esp : an apparatus recording conditions at many distant stations at a central office — **tele·meteorographic** \'+\ adj — **tele·meteorography** \'+\ n -ES
¹**tele·me·ter** \'telə,mēd·ə(r)\ n [ISV ¹tel- + -meter] **1** : an instrument (as a telescope with a micrometer for measuring the apparent diameter of an object whose dimensions are known or a telescope with stadia hairs) for measuring the distance of an object from an observer : RANGE FINDER **2** : an electrical apparatus for measuring a quantity (as pressure, radiation intensity, speed, temperature), transmitting the result to a distant station, and there indicating or recording the quantity measured : an automatic radio transmitter (as in a rocket) that broadcasts measurements of such quantities — **tele·met·ric** \tə'metrik, te-\ also **tele·met·ri·cal** \-rə̇k(ə)lē\ adv — **te·lem·e·try** \tə'lemə,trē\ n -ES
²**telemeter** \"\ vb -ED/-ING/-s vt : to transmit (the measurement of a quantity) by telemeter ⟨rocket-powered research models ~ heating data obtained on flights through the atmosphere —Report: Nat'l Advisory Committee for Aeronautics⟩ ~ vi : to telemeter the measurement of a quantity ⟨a new ~ing device was developed for transmitting scientific and operating information from high-flying rockets back to ground observation stations —G.R.Henninger⟩
tele·microscope \,telə+\ n [NL telemicroscopium, fr. ¹tel- + microscopium] — more at MICROSCOPE] : a microscope with a long-focus objective that may be used either as a low-power microscope or as a reading telescope
tele·mor·phic \,telə'mȯrfik\ adj [¹tel- + -morphic] : having an effect at a distance from its point of origin or location ⟨~ plant hormones⟩
tele·mo·tor \'telə+,-\ n [ISV ¹tel- + motor] : a hydraulic device by which the movement of the wheel on a ship's bridge operates the steering gear at the stern
tel·en·ce·phal·ic \(')tel[in]sə'falik\ adj [NL telencephalon + E -ic] : of or relating to the telencephalon
tel·encephalon \'tel+\ n [NL, fr. ²tel- + encephalon] : the anterior subdivision of the forebrain comprising the cerebral hemispheres and associated structures
te·len·get also **te·len·git** \tə'leŋgə̇t\ n, usu cap : TELEUT
te·len·o·mus \tə'lenəməs\ n, cap [NL] : a large and widespread genus of minute serphoid wasps (family Scelionidae) having larvae that are parasitic in the eggs of various insects
teleo- — see TELE-
tele·objective \,telē+\ n [ISV ¹tel- + objective] : a telephoto lens
tel·eo·ceph·a·li \,telēō'sefə,lī sometimes ,tel-\ n pl, cap [NL, fr. ²tele- + -cephali] in some classifications : a division of

teleost fishes including those having the typical number of cranial and opercular bones, separate anterior vertebrae, and no mesocoracoid (as the perches and pike) — **tel·eo·ceph·a·lous** \,-\ adj
tel·e·oc·er·as \,telē'äsərəs\ n, cap [NL, fr. ²tele- + -ceras] : a genus of short-legged rhinoceroses from the American Upper Miocene and Lower Pliocene having a small nasal horn
tel·eo·des·ma·cea \,telēō,dez'māshēə\ n pl, cap [NL, fr. ²tele- + desm- + -acea] in some classifications : a large group comprising bivalve mollusks with well-developed cardinal teeth in the hinge and being nearly equivalent to the order Eulamellibranchia — **tel·eo·des·ma·cean** \,mash'ən\ adj or n — **tel·eo·des·ma·ceous** \-shəs\ adj
tele·odont \,telēə,dänt sometimes -\ adj [²tele- + -odont] : having large mandibles — used (as of an insect (as various stag beetles)) compare PRIODONT
tel·e·o·log·i·cal \,telē'läjē̇kəl, -jēk-\ or **tele·o·log·ic** \-jik, -jēk-\ adj [teleology + -ic, -ical] : of or relating to teleology; specif : having the nature of or relating to, design, purpose, final intention, or cause — **tel·e·o·log·i·cal·ly** \-jə̇k(ə)lē, -li\ adv
teleological argument n : ARGUMENT FROM DESIGN
teleological ethics n pl but sing or pl in constr : a theory of ethics (as utilitarianism or ethical egoism) according to which the rightness of an act is determined by its end
teleological idealism n : an idealistic philosophy that endeavors to reconcile the ethicoreligious idealism of Fichte with the stricter critical idealism of Kant
tel·e·ol·o·gism \,telē'älə,jizəm\ n -s [teleology + -ism] : belief in or acceptance of teleology
tel·e·ol·o·gist \-,jə̇st\ n -s [teleology + -ist] **1** : one that specializes in or believes in the actuality of teleology **2** : an advocate of a doctrine of teleology
te·le·ol·o·gy \-jē,-ji\ n -ES [NL teleologia, fr. teleo- (irreg. fr. Gk telos end) + L -logia -logy — more at WHEEL] **1 a** : the philosophical study of evidences of design in nature — compare MECHANISM **b** : the doctrine or belief that ends are immanent in nature (as in vitalism and holism) **c** : a metaphysical doctrine explaining phenomena and events by final causes **2** : the fact or the character of being directed toward an end or shaped by a purpose — used of natural processes or of nature as a whole conceived as determined by final causes or by the design of a divine Providence and opposed to purely mechanical determinism or causation exclusively by what is temporally antecedent **3** : the use of design, purpose, or utility as an explanation of any natural phenomenon **4** : ENTELECHY
tel·eo·mitosis \,telēō+\ n, pl teleomitoses [NL, fr. ²tele- + mitosis] : KARYOKINESIS
tele·op·tile \,telē'äptəl, -,tīl\ n -s [²tele- + -ptile] : a mature feather — compare NEOSSOPTILE
tel·eo·roentgenogram \,telēō sometimes ,tel-\ also **tele·roentgenogram** \-lə+\ n [ISV ²tele- + roentgenogram] : an X-ray photograph taken at a distance of usu. six feet with resultant practical parallelism of the rays and production of shadows of natural size
tel·eo·roentgenography \"+\ also **tele·roentgenography** \"+\ n [ISV ²tele- + roentgenography] : the act, science, or practice of making teleoroentgenograms
tel·eo·saur \'telēə,sȯ(ə)r sometimes 'tel-\ n -s [NL Teleosaurus] : a teleosaurian reptile
tel·eo·sau·ri·an \,telēə'sȯrēən\ adj [NL Teleosaurus + E -ian] : of or relating to the genus Teleosaurus or family Teleosauridae
²**teleosaurian** \"\ n -s : TELEOSAUR
tel·eo·sau·rus \,telēə'sȯrəs\ n, cap [NL, fr. ²tele- + -saurus] : a genus (the type of the family Teleosauridae) of crocodilian reptiles of the Jurassic having a long and slender snout like a gavial and platyceious vertebrae
tel·e·ost \'telē,äst sometimes 'tel-\ adj [NL Teleostei] : relating to or having the characteristics of the Teleostei
²**teleost** \"\ n -s : one of the Teleostei
tel·e·os·te·an \,telē'ästēən\ adj or n [NL Teleostei + E -an] : TELEOST
tel·e·os·tei \,telē'ästē,ī\ n pl, cap [NL, fr. ²tele- + -ostei (fr. Gk osteon bone) — more at OSSEOUS] in some classifications : a subclass or other division of fishes nearly or exactly equivalent to Teleostomi
tel·e·os·to·mate \,telē'ästəmāt\ adj [NL Teleostomi + E -ate] : TELEOSTOMOUS
tel·e·os·tome \'telēə,stōm\ n -s [NL Teleostomi] : one of the Teleostomi : a true fish
tel·e·os·to·mi \,telē'ästə,mī\ n pl, cap [NL, fr. ²tele- + -stomi] : a class or sometimes a subclass that contains all existing jawed fishes (as the Chondrichthyes or sometimes the Chondrichthyes and Choanichthyes, that is characterized by membrane bones developed in connection with and entering into the structure of the jaws, cranium, pectoral arch, and opercular apparatus, gill arches bearing filamentous gills, and no claspers on the ventral fins, and that includes the ganoids and teleosts and is further characterized by the hyostylic suspensorium, bony fin rays, and lack of cerebral hemispheres
tel·e·os·to·mi·an \,telē'ästōmēən\ or **tel·e·os·tom·ic** \,stä'mik\ or **tel·e·os·to·mous** \,telē'ästəməs\ adj
tel·e·ot·ro·cha \,telē'ätrəkə sometimes ,tel-\ n [NL, fr. ²tele- -trocha] var of TELOTROCHA
¹**tele·path** \'telə,path\ vb -ED/-ING/-s [back-formation fr. telepathy] vt : to communicate by telepathy ~ vi : to practice telepathy
²**telepath** \"\ n -s [back-formation fr. telepathy] : TELEPATHIST
tel·e·path·ic \,telə'pathik, -thēk\ adj [telepathy + -ic] : of or relating to telepathy : supposedly transferred or communicated by telepathy — **telepathically** \-thə̇k(ə)lē, -thēk-, -li\ adv
te·lep·a·thist \tə'lepəthə̇st\ n -s [telepathy + -ist] **1** : a believer in telepathy **2** : one supposedly having telepathic power
te·lep·a·thize \-,thīz\ vb -ED/-ING/-s [telepathy + -ize] vt : to affect telepathically ~ vi : to practice telepathy
te·lep·a·thy \-thē, -thi\ n -ES [¹tel- + -pathy] : apparent communication from one mind to another other than through the channels of sense : THOUGHT TRANSFERENCE
¹**tele·phone** \'telə,fōn\ n [¹tel- + -phone] **1** : an instrument for reproducing sounds esp. articulate speech at a distance: as **a** : a device in which the voice or sound causes in a thin diaphragm vibrations that are directly transmitted along a wire or string connecting it to a similar diaphragm thus reproducing the sound **b** : an apparatus consisting of a transmitter (as a microphone) for converting sound

telephones 1

esp. of the human voice into electrical impulses or varying electrical current for transmission by wire, a receiver for reproducing the original sounds from such transmitted varying electrical current, and usu. a switch and a signaling device **2** : any of various devices (as a sound-signaling device or a speaking tube) resembling or suggesting the telephone
²**telephone** \"\ vi : to communicate by telephone : call on the telephone ~ vt **1** : to send (as a message) by telephone **2** : to speak to (a person) by telephone : call on the telephone
telephone book n : a book listing names, addresses, and telephone numbers of telephone subscribers
telephone booth n : an enclosure (as for a public or widely-used telephone) intended to insure privacy for one telephoning
telephone box n, Brit : a public telephone booth
telephone exchange n : a central office in which the wires of telephones may be connected to permit conversation
telephone number n : a number assigned to a telephone instrument and used by a person to call that telephone
tel·e·phon·er \-nə(r)\ n -s : one that telephones

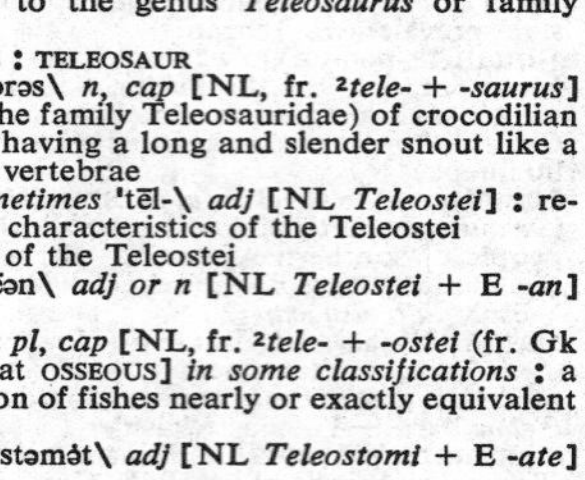

telephone receiver n : a device (as in a telephone) for converting electric impulses or varying current into sound
telephone theory n : a theory in physiology: the perception of pitch depends on the frequency of the nerve impulses induced by sounds of different pitch — compare PLACE THEORY
telephone transmitter n : TRANSMITTER a(1)
tel·e·phon·ic \,telə'fänik, -nēk\ adj [¹tel- + phonic] **1** : conveying sound to a distance **2** [telephone + -ic] : of or relating to the telephone : carried or conveyed by telephone — **tel·e·phon·i·cal·ly** \-nə̇k(ə)lē, -nēk-, -li\ adv
tel·e·phon·ist \,telə'fōnə̇st, tə'lefən-\ n -s [¹telephone + -ist] : one who uses or operates a telephone; specif : a switchboard operator in a telephone exchange
tel·e·phon·itis \,telə,fō'nīdə̇s\ n -ES [¹telephone + -itis] : marked fondness for or obsession with telephoning ⟨afflicted with the ~ ... common to all teen-agers —J.S.Qualey⟩
te·leph·o·ny \tə'lefənē, 'telə,fōnē\ n -ES [ISV ¹tel- + -phony] : the use or operation of an apparatus for transmission of sounds between widely removed points; specif : the use of a telephone employing electrical variations or a system of such telephones for such transmission with or without connecting wires — compare RADIOTELEPHONY
¹**tele·photo** \,telə+\ adj [by shortening] : TELEPHOTOGRAPHIC ⟨a ~effect⟩; specif : designating a camera lens system designed to give a usu. large image of a distant object
²**telephoto** \"\ n : a telephoto lens
Telephoto \"\ trademark — used for an apparatus for transmitting photographs electrically or for a photograph so transmitted
tele·photograph \,telə+\ n [¹tel- + photograph] : a photograph taken with a camera having a telephoto lens
tele·photographic \"+\ adj [ISV ¹tel- + photographic] : of, relating to, or being the process of telephotography
telephotographic lens n : a telephoto lens
tele·photography \,telə+\ n [ISV ¹tel- + photography] **1** : PHOTOTELEGRAPHY **2** : the photography of distant objects in more enlarged form than is possible by the ordinary means usu. by a camera provided with a telephoto lens or mounted in place of the eyepiece of a telescope so that the real or a magnified image falls on the sensitive plate
tele·photometer \"+\ n [¹tel- + photometer] : a photometer used to measure the illumination of distant objects
tele·plasm \'telə+,-\ n [ISV ¹tel- + -plasm] : ECTOPLASM — **tele·plasmic** \,telə+,-\ n [¹tel- + play] : a play written for or presented on television
tele·play \'telə+,-\ n [¹tel- + play] : a play written for or presented on television
tele·port \"+-\ vt [¹tel- + port (to carry)] : to move (an object or person) without physical contact by psychokinesis — **tele·por·ta·tion** \,+,pȯr'tāshən, -pȯr-, par-\ n -s
tele·printer \'telə+\ n [¹tel- + printer] : TELETYPEWRITER
Tele·Promp·Ter \"+\ trademark — used for a device for unrolling a magnified script in front of a speaker on television
tel·e·ran \'telə,ran\ n -s [television-radar navigation] : a system of aerial navigation in which ground radar scans the area about an airport and the results are televised so that the pilot of an airplane sees the positions of all craft in the vicinity superimposed upon a map of the area
tel·er·gic \(')telˈȯrjik\ or **tel·er·gi·cal** \-jəkəl\ adj : of or relating to telergy — **tel·er·gi·cal·ly** \-jə̇k(ə)lē\ adv
tel·er·gy \'te(,)lȯrjē\ n -ES [¹tel- + -ergy] : a hypothetical action of one person's thought and desire upon the brain of another person by the transmission of some unknown form of energy
teles pl of TELE
¹**tel·e·scope** \'telə,skōp\ n, often attrib [NL telescopium, fr. Gk tēleskopos far-seeing (fr. tēle- ¹tel- + skopos watcher) + -ium — more at SCOPE] **1 a** : an optical instrument usu. tubular in shape for viewing distant objects by means of the refraction of light rays through a lens or the reflection of light rays by a concave mirror so that the rays enter an opening and converge to form an image seen through a magnifying eyepiece — compare CASSEGRAINIAN TELESCOPE, GALILEAN TELESCOPE, HERSCHELIAN TELESCOPE, REFLECTOR, REFRACTOR, TERRESTRIAL TELESCOPE **b** : TELESCOPE SIGHT **c** : any of various tubular magnifying optical instruments (as for reading the scale on a galvanometer or for use in a bronchoscope) ⟨a bronchoscopic ~⟩ ⟨a cystoscopic ~⟩ **d** : RADIO TELESCOPE **2** or **telescope bag** : a traveling bag consisting of two parts of which the larger fits over the smaller **3** : TELESCOPE GOLDFISH **4** : something that telescopes or that is telescoped ⟨rigged the ~ steel bait rod first —Hugh Fosburgh⟩

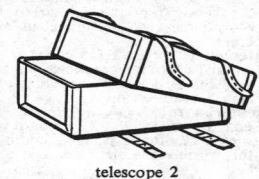

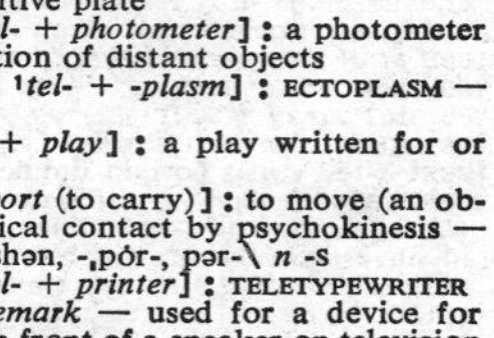

telescope 2

²**telescope** \"\ vb -ED/-ING/-s vi **1** : to slide or pass one within another like the cylindrical sections of a hand telescope ⟨a two-piece knockdown support, designed for the tent and made of telescoping aluminum tubes —Sheila Hibben⟩ ⟨both rods ~ to extend to exact size —Spiegel's Catalog⟩ : force a way into or enter another lengthwise as the result of collision ⟨the two sleeping cars telescoped⟩ **2** : to become telescoped ⟨those years seemed to have telescoped, like time in a dream —Helen Howe⟩ ~ vt **1** : to cause to telescope ⟨the front and end cars that took the shock of the impact were telescoped —Howard Austin⟩ ⟨from the river side the three parts of the building appear to be telescoped into each other —Amer. Guide Series: Md.⟩ **2** : to combine, coalesce, or run together in order to shorten or simplify : COMPRESS, CONDENSE ⟨the rules of good cooking cannot be telescoped into a single sentence or even paragraph —J.L.Evans⟩ ⟨the book arbitrarily ~s time and space, and as arbitrarily extends them —Phoebe Adams⟩ ⟨~ a century of industrial history into a decade —G.L.Arnold⟩ ⟨telescoped into a brief span experiences that represented chronologically many times that number of years —Stella Center⟩ ⟨if an evolutionary development may be verbally telescoped into an event —A.L.Kroeber⟩ ⟨one can ~ the seasons and witness four weeks of spring's advance in the space of seven days —I.R.Barnes⟩; specif : to combine (words) by omitting part of one or more of the components ⟨~ two words (like infanticipate, from infant and anticipate) —Word Study⟩ : form (as a word or title) by such combining
telescope box n : a two-piece box in which the sides of one part fit over those of the other
telescope eye n : an eye on a retractile stalk (as in land snails)
telescope fly n : any of various acalyptrate two-winged flies with eyes on very long stalks that constitute Diopsis and a few related genera of Africa and Asia
telescope goldfish n : a goldfish of a breed characterized by a very short thick body, a large and double tail fin, and protuberant eyes — see CELESTIAL TELESCOPE
telescope jack n : a lifting jack whose male screw is a telescope screw in which another male screw works with the two screws having threads of unequal pitch or opposite direction so that the effect is similar to that produced by a differential screw
telescope sight or **telescopic sight** n : a telescope on a firearm for use as a sight
telescope table n : EXTENSION TABLE
telescope word n : BLEND d
tel·e·scop·ic \,telə'skäpik, -pēk\ also **tel·e·scop·i·cal** \-pə̇kəl, -pēk-\ adj [¹telescope + -ic, -ical] **1 a** : of or relating to a telescope ⟨the ~ tube⟩; specif : performed by a telescope ⟨a ~ observation⟩ **b** : suitable for magnifying distant objects : used in a telescope ⟨a ~ lens⟩ **2** : seen or discoverable only by a telescope ⟨~ stars⟩ **3** : able to discern objects at a distance : FARSEEING, FAR-REACHING ⟨a ~ eye⟩ ⟨~ vision⟩ ⟨a historian with a ~ view of the vagaries of man throughout civilization —Harper's⟩ **4** : having the power of moment (as extension) by joints sliding one within another like the tube of a hand telescope ⟨~ shock absorbers⟩ ⟨a ~ vertical antenna⟩ ⟨a ~ landing gear⟩; esp : constructed of concentric tubes or other parts that fit one within another ⟨a ~ drinking cup⟩ ⟨a ~ box⟩ — **tel·e·scop·i·cal·ly** \-pə̇k(ə)lē, -pēk-, -li\ adv
tele·screen \'telə+,-\ n [¹tel- + screen] : the screen of a television receiver

tele·seism \'telə,sīzəm\ *n* -s [¹*tel-* + *-seism*] **:** an earth tremor caused by an earthquake in a part of the world remote from the recording station — **tele·seis·mic** \¦telə+\ *adj*

tele·seismology \"+\ *n* [¹*tel-* + *seismology*] **:** seismology dealing with records obtained at long distances — compare ENGYSSEISMOLOGY

tel·e·sis \'teləsəs\ *n, pl* **tele·ses** \-lə,sēz\ [NL, fr. Gk, event, fulfillment, fr. *telein* to complete, fulfill (fr. *telos* end) + *-sis* — more at WHEEL] **:** progress intelligently planned and directed **:** the attainment of desired ends by the application of intelligent human effort to the means

tel·es·mat·ic \¦teləz¦mad·ik\ *or* **tel·es·mat·i·cal** \-d·əkəl\ *adj* [MGk *telesmat-, telesma* + E *-ic*] *archaic* **:** TALISMANIC — **tel·es·mat·i·cal·ly** \-d·ək(ə)lē\ *adv, archaic*

tel·esme \'te,lezəm\ *n* -s [MGk *telesma* — more at TALISMAN] *archaic* **:** TALISMAN

tel·es·ta·cea \,telə'stāshēə\ *n pl, cap* [NL, fr. *Telesto*, genus of Coelenterata (fr. Gk *telestos* fulfilled, fr. *telein* to fulfill) + *-acea*] **:** a small order of alcyonarian coelenterates sometimes included in the Alcyonacea and having colonies that consist of long axial polyps with lateral polyps as side branches

tele·stereoscope \¦telə+\ *n* [ISV ¹*tel-* + *stereoscope*; orig. formed as G *telestereoskop*] **:** a binocular telescope; *esp* **:** one in which the distance between the objectives is greater than the interocular distance and which is used to obtain enhanced impressions of relief in distant objects

tel·esthesia *or* **tel·aesthesia** \¦tel+\ *n* [NL, fr. ¹*tel-* + *esthesia, aesthesia*] **:** an impression similar to a sense impression and supposedly received at a distance without the normal operation of the organs of sense — **tel·esthetic** *or* **telaesthetic** \"+\ *adj*

te·les·tial glory \tə'les(h)chəl, (')te¦l, -stēəl\ *n* [*telestial* fr. ¹*tel-* + *-estial* (as in *celestial*)] **:** the lowest of three Mormon degrees or kingdoms of glory attainable in heaven — compare CELESTIAL GLORY, TERRESTRIAL GLORY

te·les·tic \tə'lestik\ *adj* [Gk *telestikos*, fr. *telestos* (verbal of *telein* to fulfill, initiate into mysteries or sacred rites) + *-ikos* -ic] **:** MYSTICAL

te·les·tich \tə'lestik, 'telə,s-\ *n* -s [²*tel-* + Gk *stichos* line — more at STICH] **:** a poem in which the consecutive final letters of the lines spell a name — compare ACROSTIC 1a

tele·tape \'telə+,-\ *n* [¹*tel-* + *tape*] **:** a tape perforated in accordance with the telegraph code by a special typewriter and run through a telegraph transmitter to obtain a higher speed of transmission

tele·therapy \¦telə+\ *n* [¹*tel-* + *therapy*] **:** the treatment of diseased tissue with high-intensity radiation (as gamma rays from radioactive cobalt)

tele·thermometer \"+\ *n* [ISV ¹*tel-* + *thermometer*] **:** an apparatus for indicating the temperature of a distant point (as by a thermoelectric circuit and a galvanometer) — **tele·thermometry** \"+\ *n*

tele·thermoscope \"+\ *n* [¹*tel-* + *thermoscope*] **:** TELETHERMOMETER

tel·e·thon \'telə,thän\ *n* -s [¹*tel-* + *-thon* (as in *marathon*)] **:** a television program lasting several hours; *esp* **:** one for soliciting money for a specific fund

tele·transcription \¦telə+\ *n* [¹*tel-* + *transcription*] **:** KINESCOPE 2

Tele·type \'telə+,-\ *trademark* **1** — used for a teletypewriter **2 :** a message sent by a Teletype machine

Tele·typesetter \¦telə+\ *trademark* — used for an apparatus for the automatic operation of a keyboard slugcasting machine consisting essentially of a separate keyboard that perforates a tape which is fed either into an attachment to the slugcasting machine or into a sender that transmits electrical impulses telegraphically to any number of reperforators with the perforated tape causing the slugcasting machine to set type by automatic operation of the keyboard

tele·typesetting \"+\ *n* **:** the process of setting type with a Teletypesetter apparatus

tele·typewriter \"+\ *n* [¹*tel-* + *typewriter*] **:** a printing telegraph recording like a typewriter and capable of being used over practically any telephonic communication system

tele·typist \"+\ *n* [*tel-* + *typist*] **:** one that operates a teletypewriter

tel·e·ut \'telē,üt, ,==ˈ=\ *n, pl* **teleut** *or* **teleuts** *usu cap* **1 a :** a group of nomadic Altaic Tatar peoples of the Altai plateau, West Siberia Region, that are Mongolian in type and Buddhist in religion — called also *Telenget* **b :** a member of any of such peoples **2 :** the Turkic language of the Teleut peoples

teleut- *or* **teleuto-** *comb form* [Gk *teleutē*, fr. *telos* end — more at WHEEL] **:** completion ⟨*teleuto*spore⟩

te·leu·to·sorus \tə¦lüd·ə, təl¦yü·+\ *n, pl* **teleutosori** [NL, fr. *teleut-* + *-sorus*] **:** TELIUM

te·leu·to·spore \=ˈ==+\ *n* [ISV *teleut-* + *-spore*] **:** TELIOSPORE — **te·leu·to·spor·ic** \=¦==+¦spōrik\ *or* **te·leu·to·sporiferous** \=¦==+\ *adj*

tele·view \'telə+,-\ *vi* [¹*tel-* + *view*] **:** to observe or watch by means of a television receiver — **tele·viewer** \" + ,-\ *n*

tel·e·vise \'telə,vīz\ *vb* -ED/-ING/-S [back-formation fr. *television*] *vt* **:** to pick up and usu. to broadcast (as a baseball game, meeting, movie, news event, scene, or speaker) by television ~ *vi* **:** to broadcast by television

tel·e·vi·sion \'telə,vizhən *sometimes* ,==ˈ==\ *n* [F *télévision*, fr. *télé-* ¹*tel-* + *vision*] **1 :** the transmission and reproduction of transient images of fixed or moving objects; *specif* **:** an electronic system of transmitting such images together with sound over a wire or through space by apparatus that converts light and sound into electrical waves and reconverts them into visible light rays and audible sound **2 :** a television receiving set **3 a :** the television broadcasting industry **b :** television as a medium of communication — **tel·e·vi·sion·al·ly** \¦==¦vizhən³lē, -zhnəlē\ *adv* — **tel·e·vi·sion·ary** \-zhə,nerē\ *adj*

television receiver *or* **television set** *n* **:** a television receiving set

television transmitter *n* **:** a television transmitting set

television tube *n* **:** KINESCOPE 1

tel·e·vi·sor \'==,vīzə(r) *sometimes* ,==ˈ==\ *n* -s [*televise* + *-or*] **1 :** a television transmitting or receiving apparatus **2 a :** a television broadcaster **b :** one that uses a television receiver

tele·visual \¦telə+\ *adj* [fr. *television*, after such pairs as E *vision: visual*] **1 :** of or relating to television **2 :** TELEGENIC

tele·writer \'telə+,-\ *n* [¹*tel-* + *writer*] *chiefly Brit* **:** a Tel-Autograph device

tel·fair·ia \tel'fa(a)rēə\ *n, cap* [NL, fr. Charles *Telfair* †1833 Ir. naturalist + NL *-ia*] **:** a genus of tropical African vines (family Cucurbitaceae) having very long shoots which may exceed 45 feet, purplish flowers, and immense gourds — see OYSTER NUT

telfer *var of* TELPHER

¹**tel·ford** \'telfə(r)d\ *adj* [after Thomas *Telford* †1834 Scot. civil engineer] **:** being or relating to a road pavement having a surface of small stone rolled hard and smooth and distinguished from macadam road by its firm foundation of large stones with fragments of stone wedged tightly in the interstices

²**telford** \"\ *n* -s **:** a telford road

tel·ford·ize \-fə(r),dīz\ *vt* -ED/-ING/-S [¹*telford* + *-ize*] **:** to furnish (a road) with a telford pavement

telg *abbr* telegram

tel·harmonium \¦tel+\ *n* [NL, fr. ¹*tel-* + *harmonium*] **:** an instrument for producing music at a distant point via telephone wire by means of alternating currents of electricity controlled by an operator who plays on a keyboard

te·li \'tālē\ *n, pl* **teli** *or* **telis** [Hindi *telī* oilmaker, fr. Skt *taila* sesame oil, fr. *tila* sesame] **:** a member of a low Hindu caste of characteristically oil makers and merchants

te·lial \'tēlēəl, -lyəl\ *adj* [NL *telium* + E *-al*] **:** of or relating to a telium

telic \'telik, 'tēl-\ *adj* [Gk *telikos* final, fr. *tel-* ²*tel-* + *-ikos* -ic] **1 :** tending toward an end **:** PURPOSIVE, TELEOLOGICAL ⟨the writing is always ~, never a mere stream of consciousness —R.D.Ellmann⟩ ⟨the mind . . . becomes ~, thus enabling mankind to pass from passive to active evolutionary processes, and from natural to human or social evolution —J.Q.Dealey⟩ ⟨a linguistic change is not ~: it does not work for the benefit of the system; on the contrary it disrupts it —R.S.Wells⟩ **2 :** PERFECTIVE 2 — contrasted with *atelic* — **teli·cal** \-ləkəl\ *adj* — **teli·cal·ly** \-lək(ə)lē\ *adv*

te·lin·ga \tə'liŋgə\ *n* -s *usu cap* [of Dravidian origin; akin to Tamil *teliṅkam* Telugu country; fr. the employment of Telugus as sepoys] **:** SEPOY

telinga potato *n, usu cap T* **:** YAM

te·lio·sorus \¦tēlēə+\ *n, pl* **teliosori** [NL, fr. *telium* + *-o-* + *-sorus*] **:** TELIUM

te·lio·spore \'===+,-\ *n* [*telium* + *-o-* + *spore*] **:** one of the thick-walled one or more-celled chlamydospores developed in the final stage in the life cycle of rust fungi and within which nuclear fusion occurs prior to development of the promycelium — see TELIUM — **te·lio·spor·ic** \¦===¦spōrik\ *adj*

te·lio·spo·re·ae \,===ˈspōrē,ē\ *n pl, cap* [NL, fr. ISV *teliospore*] *in some classifications* **:** a subclass of fungi (class Basidiomycetes) including the rusts and smuts (orders Uredinales and Ustilaginales) and characterized by the production of a teliospore or a comparable body in which the diploid nucleus is produced — compare EUBASIDIAE, HETEROBASIDIAE

te·li·um \'tēlēəm\ *n, pl* **te·lia** \-lēə\ [NL, fr. ²*tel-* + *-ium*] **:** an aggregation of teliospores often stalked and either forming a subcuticular or subepidermal cushion or rupturing the host tissue to form an open sorus — compare AECIUM

¹**tell** \'tel\ *vb* **told** \'tōld\ **told; telling; tells** [ME *tellen* (past *tolde*, past part. *told*), fr. OE *tellan* (past — northern & Midland dial. — *talde*, past part. — northern & Midland dial. — *getald*); akin to OHG *zellen* to count, tell (past *zalta*, past part. *gizalt*), ON *telja* (past *talthi*, past part. *talithr*); causative-denominative fr. the root of E ¹*tale*] *vt* **1 :** to mention one by one or piece by piece **:** COUNT, NUMBER, RECKON ⟨~ the stars, if thou be able to number them —Gen 15:5 (AV)⟩ ⟨walked round the walls and *told* the towers —Rose Macaulay⟩ ⟨all *told* there were 27 public schools —C.L.Jones⟩: as **a :** to count in keeping track of decades of rosary prayers — used in the phrase *to tell one's beads* **b** *obs* **:** to calculate the total amount or value of **2 a :** to relate in detail **:** NARRATE, RECOUNT ⟨one of her recipes . . . ~*s* how to make maple syrup dumplings —Rose Feld⟩ ⟨~*ing* a boastful story —J.V. Allen⟩ ⟨dancers *told* ancient legends with tradition's rhythms and gestures —*Nat'l Geographic*⟩ **b :** SAY, UTTER ⟨to ~ you the truth, I don't really remember —Lenard Kaufman⟩ ⟨a man in high position utters an accusation or ~*s* a lie —Gilbert Seldes⟩ ⟨give me a chance to ~ Kit good-by —Hamilton Basso⟩ **3 a :** to make known **:** DISCLOSE, DIVULGE ⟨~ the news⟩ ⟨~ your name⟩ **:** REVEAL, MANIFEST ⟨fossils ~ much about the past⟩ ⟨more than words, his movements, gestures *told* his evident delight in ballet —Cyril Cusack⟩ ⟨followed suit with an ungainly stiffness which *told* how much at sea he felt —T.B.Costain⟩ **b :** to express in words ⟨cannot ~ how sorry I am⟩ **4 a :** to give information to **:** report to **:** INFORM ⟨I'll ~ him as soon as he comes⟩ ⟨~ executives and employees of our policies and plans —Milton Hall⟩ ⟨*told* his listeners about his vacation —*Current Biog.*⟩ **b :** to give information on **:** REPORT ⟨he said all of it in a flat, business voice that *told* you nothing more or less than the words said —Wirt Williams⟩ ⟨no book could really ~ you what a hell of a feeling it was —Gwyn Thomas⟩ ⟨nobody could ~ her anything —Edith Sitwell⟩ ⟨the victim's subconscious generally ~*s* him something is wrong as soon as the prowler enters —Rufus Jarman⟩ ⟨his eyes *told* him that the walls were festooned with flowers —T.B.Costain⟩ **c :** to inform positively **:** assure emphatically ⟨he did not do it, I ~ you⟩ ⟨we are distinctly *told* that he did not buy it —Douglas Carruthers⟩ **5 :** ORDER, REQUEST, DIRECT ⟨*told* her to wait⟩ **6 :** to discern so as to report **:** ascertain by observing **:** find out **:** DECIDE, RECOGNIZE ⟨how if it is unpublished can you ~ that it is a masterpiece —John Barkham⟩ ⟨the patrol officer can ~ whether things are normal or abnormal —R.L.Anderson⟩ ⟨usually one couldn't ~ much about the writer from the letter of a not very well-educated woman —Elizabeth Goudge⟩ ⟨management can ~, by its own observation, whether a man is capable of leadership —Bruce Payne⟩ ~ *vi* **1 :** to give an account **:** make a report ⟨wrote an article ~*ing* of his experiences⟩ ⟨the twelve contributors ~ of modern man —F.E.Hill⟩ **2 :** to state positively **:** decide definitely **:** SAY ⟨who can ~⟩ ⟨you can't ~ about drunks —S.H.Holbrook⟩ **3 :** to act as a talebearer **:** INFORM — usu. used with *on* or *of* ⟨the sister *told* on him, though he tried to shush her —John Dollard⟩ ⟨never *told* on each other, no matter what happened —C.T.Jackson⟩ ⟨I'll get even with you if you ever ~ on me —*Inside Detective*⟩ **4** *dial Eng* **:** TALK, CHAT **5 :** to take effect **:** have a marked effect **:** be of account ⟨events of the past two or three weeks were beginning to ~ on her nerves —Edna Ferber⟩ ⟨the influence of the school had begun to ~ —Robert Littell⟩ ⟨a great many garments of the highest quality and all designed for overseas markets where quality ~*s* —D.E.Keir⟩ ⟨the long hours, the close confinement, and the strain of having to stand behind a counter from eight o'clock in the morning till eight o'clock at night was beginning to ~ upon her —J.C.Snaith⟩ **6 :** to serve as evidence or indication **:** be significant — usu used with *of* ⟨the calculating look in his eyes that *told* of his Norman blood —T.B.Costain⟩ ⟨the arid sands that ~ of desert days will still show angled stones that forgotten winds have carved —W.E.Swinton⟩ **7 :** to stand forth clearly **:** become apparent, evident, or known ⟨evidence that you were riding at a race-meeting will ~ strongly against you in the subsequent police proceedings —*Punch*⟩ ⟨he remains so disfigured that appearances will always ~ against him —Dixon Wecter⟩ **syn** see COUNT, REVEAL

²**tell** \"\ *n* -s *dial* **:** something that is told **:** TALK, TALE, ACCOUNT ⟨have a ~ with you —Eden Phillpotts⟩

³**tell** \"\ *n* -s [Ar *tall*] **:** HILL, MOUND; *specif* **:** an ancient mound in the Middle East composed of remains of successive settlements — compare TEPE

tell down *vt, Scot* **:** to pay down

tel·len \'telən\ *n* -s [modif. of NL *Tellina*] **:** TELLIN

¹**tell·er** \'telə(r)\ *n* -s [ME, fr. *tellen* to tell + *-er*] **1 :** one that relates or communicates **:** INFORMER, NARRATOR, DESCRIBER ⟨a story based on the ~'s actual experiences⟩ **2 a :** a device or apparatus that announces **:** ANNUNCIATOR **b** *dial Eng* **:** one of the strokes made by a church bell in tolling for a death **3 :** one that reckons or counts: as **a :** one appointed to count votes (as in a legislative body, public meeting, assembly) ⟨those for and those against a motion pass between ~*s*, and the affirmative and negative vote is counted separately —Alice F. Sturgis⟩ **b :** a member of a bank's staff concerned with the direct handling of money received by or paid out by the institution ⟨a paying ~⟩ ⟨a receiving ~⟩ ⟨a savings ~⟩

²**tel·ler** \"\ *dial Eng var of* TILLER

tel·li·cher·ry bark \'telə,cherē-\ *n, usu cap T* [fr. *Tellicherry*, seaport in Madras state, India] **:** the bitter bark of any of several East Indian or African trees of the family Apocynaceae (as *Wrightia zeylanica*, *Holarrhena antidysenterica* or *H. africana*) used esp. in folk medicine as a remedy for dysentery

tellicherry pepper *n, usu cap T* **:** a superior grade of Indian pepper characterized by exceptional richness of body and fullness of flavor

tellies *pl of* TELLY

tel·li·ma \'teləmə\ *n, cap* [NL, anagram of *Mitella*, genus of plants allied to *Tellima*, fr. L, headband, dim. of *mitra* headband, turban — more at MITER] **:** a genus of hardy herbaceous perennials (family Saxifragaceae) of western No. America that have palmately lobed leaves and long racemes of small nodding 5-petaled flowers — see FALSE ALUMROOT

tel·lin \'telən\ *n* -s [NL *Tellina*] **:** a mollusk of the family Tellinidae **:** SUNSET SHELL

tel·li·na \tə'līnə, -lēnə\ *n* [NL, fr. Gk *tellinē*, a shellfish] **1** *cap* **:** a genus (the type of the family Tellinidae) of marine bivalve mollusks having the siphons long and separate, the foot and labial palpi very large, and the shell thin, delicate, and often showily colored **2** -s **:** any mollusk of the genus *Tellina* **:** SUNSET SHELL

tel·li·na·cea \,telə'nāshēə\ *n pl, cap* [NL, fr. *Tellina* + *-acea*] **:** a suborder or other division of Eulamellibranchia comprising usu. rather small and bottom-dwelling mollusks with separate siphons, a large strong foot, and often brightly colored shells and including the sunset shells, surf clams, and wedge shells

telling *adj* [fr. pres. part. of *tell*] **1 :** producing a marked effect **:** EFFECTIVE, IMPRESSIVE, STRIKING ⟨a ~ attack, made with skill and shrewd insight —V.L.Parrington⟩ ⟨delivered ~ blows in the interests of toleration and freedom —M.R. Cohen⟩ ⟨describes in her deft and ~ phrases the teacher-town relationship —E.A.Weeks⟩ ⟨paragraphs, packed with ~ detail —Benjamin Farrington⟩ ⟨a ~ piece of satire —A.L.Vogelback⟩ ⟨advocated with ~ effect better measures for the equipment of the soldiers —C.A.Duniway⟩ ⟨he made a ~ picture standing alert —John Muir †1914⟩ **2 :** REVEALING, EXPRESSIVE ⟨many of the most ~ pages in her story —E.K.Brown⟩ ⟨a ~ study of the corrosive effects of snobbery and ostracism on the human spirit —Paul Pickrel⟩ **syn** see VALID

tell·ing·ly *adv* **:** in a telling manner

tel·lin·i·dae \tə'linə,dē\ *n pl, cap* [NL, fr. *Tellina*, type genus + *-idae*] **:** a family of marine bivalve mollusks (suborder Tellinacea) comprising the sunset shells

tell off *vt* **1 :** to number and set apart; *esp* **:** to detail for special duty **:** count off **:** ASSIGN ⟨*told off* a detail and put them to opening a trench —J.F.Dobie⟩ ⟨men were *told off* for household duties —*Amer. Guide Series: Mich.*⟩ ⟨trains *told off* for the use of British soldiers —Robert Keable⟩ ⟨*told off* to make a speech —A.P.Herbert⟩ **2 :** to reprove severely **:** DENOUNCE, REPRIMAND, SCOLD ⟨when she increases her nagging, I lose patience and *tell* her *off* quite brutally —Rex Ingamells⟩ ⟨his growing disgust boils over, he *tells off* the boss —Hobe Morrison⟩ ⟨in a mood to be *told off*, and they embraced most warmly the writers who scolded hardest —J.H. Jackson⟩

tells *pres 3d sing of* TELL, *pl of* TELL

¹**telltale** \'=,=\ *n* [¹*tell* + *tale* (after the phrase *tell tales*)] **1 :** one who officiously gives information of the private concerns of others **:** one who tells what should be withheld **:** TALEBEARER, INFORMER **2 :** something that serves to disclose something else or give information **:** HINT, INDICATION **3 :** a device for indicating or recording something: as **a :** a device for keeping a check on employees (as factory hands, drivers, check takers); *esp* **:** TIME CLOCK **b** (1) **:** a mechanical attachment to a ship's steering wheel that shows the position of the helm or rudder (2) **:** a compass in the cabin where the captain can see it (3) **:** a wind direction indicator in the form of a ribbon or similar piece of material **c :** a small overflow pipe that indicates by dripping when a tank is full **d :** a strip of metal on the front wall of a racquets or squash court to a height of from 2 to 2½ feet above the ground over which the ball must be hit **e :** a device serving as a warning on a railroad: as (1) **:** a row of long strips (as of rope) hung from a bar over the tracks to warn freight brakemen of their approach to a low overhead bridge (2) **:** a low fender placed near a hole in the permanent way to warn trackwalkers and others **4 :** TATTLER 2

²**telltale** \"\ *adj* **1 :** officiously telling what one should hold secret or in confidence **:** INFORMING, TALEBEARING **2 :** disclosing or indicating something often of a private or secret nature **:** BETRAYING, REVEALING ⟨there was only that ~ patch of oil on the water to mark where he had disappeared —*Oxford Bk. of English Talk*⟩ ⟨scanning each vein of rock for the ~ glint of yellow metal —R.A.Billington⟩ ⟨a hair-brush can be a ~ thing when a fellow begins to lose his hair —Valentine Williams⟩ ⟨months of ~ psychological preparation must precede an aggressive war —M.W.Straight⟩ **3 a :** being any of various devices for giving warning or keeping a watch or record ⟨a ~ indicator in the bureau, calling attention of the management only in case a bell has rung —J.R.Stuart⟩ ⟨a ~ panel of lights indicating everything from motor heat to whether the stewardess shut the door —H.G.Armstrong⟩ **b :** being a process or operation by which such a device warns or records ⟨a ~ operation⟩ — **tell·tale·ly** *adv*

³**telltale** \"\ *vt* -ED/-ING/-S [²*telltale*] **:** to perform a telltale operation on ⟨~ forgings to determine whether there is sufficient stock for finishing⟩

telltruth \'=,=\ *n* [¹*tell* + *truth* (after the phrase *tell the truth*)] **:** one who tells the truth **:** a frank and honest person

tellur- *or* **telluri-** *or* **telluro-** *comb form* [L *tellur-, tellus* earth — more at THILL] **1 :** earth ⟨*tellur*ian⟩ ⟨*telluro*meter⟩ **2 :** tellurium ⟨*tellur*ic⟩ ⟨*telluri*ferous⟩ ⟨*telluro*bismuthite⟩ **3** *usu* *telluro-* **:** containing bivalent tellurium usu. in place of oxygen ⟨*telluro*cyanic acid HTeCN⟩ — compare THI-

tel·lu·rate \'telyə,rāt\ *n* -s [*tellur-* + *-ate*] **:** a salt or ester of telluric acid

¹**tel·lu·ri·an** \tə'lu̇rēən, te¦, ¦l'yu̇-\ *adj* [*tellur-* + *-ian*] **:** of, relating to, or characteristic of the earth ⟨the newly discovered ~ genus —T.H.Huxley⟩ ⟨great collective forces of instinct, resentment and ~ inspiration —Jacques Maritain⟩

²**tellurian** \"\ *n* -s **:** a dweller on the earth

³**tellurian** \"\ *or* **tel·lu·ri·on** \"\ *n* -s [*tellurian* modif. of NL *tellurion*; *tellurion*, NL, fr. *tellur-* + Gk *-ion*, dim. suffix] **:** an apparatus to illustrate the causation of day and night by the rotation of the earth on its axis and the dependence of the seasons on the sun's declination

tel·lu·ric \-rik\ *adj* [*tellur-* + *-ic*] **1 :** of, relating to, or containing tellurium — used esp. of compounds in which this element has a higher valence than in tellurous compounds **2 :** of or relating to the earth **:** proceeding from the earth **:** TERRESTRIAL ⟨we have lived too long in the ~ cavern —Eugene Jolas⟩ ⟨an apology for men enmeshed in the ~ forces —Roger Bastide⟩ ⟨how are we, as ~ clods, to know what you are talking about —Herbert Mirschel⟩

telluric acid *n* **:** an acid containing hexavalent tellurium: as **a :** a very weak acid H_6TeO_6 that is a good oxidizing agent and is obtainable in two crystalline forms and as a tetrahydrate by oxidizing tellurium or tellurium dioxide — called also *orthotelluric acid* **b :** a polymerized acid $(H_2TeO_4)_n$ obtainable in a syrupy mixture by heating orthotelluric acid; poly-meta-telluric acid — called also *allo-telluric acid*

telluric line *n* **:** any of the absorption lines or bands added to the spectrum of a heavenly body by various substances in the earth's atmosphere ⟨the *telluric lines* of nitrogen, oxygen, water vapor⟩

tel·lu·ride \'telyə,rīd\ *n* -s [ISV *tellur-* + *-ide*] **:** a binary compound of tellurium usu. with a more electropositive element or radical ⟨metal ~*s* are sometimes regarded as alloys⟩

tel·lu·rif·er·ous \¦telyə¦rif(ə)rəs\ *adj* [ISV *tellur-* + *-ferous*] **:** containing or yielding tellurium

tel·lu·rite \'telyə,rīt\ *n* -s [*tellur-* + *-ite*] **1 :** a salt of tellurous acid **2 :** a mineral TeO_2 that consists of tellurium dioxide and occurs sparingly in tufts of white or yellowish crystals

tel·lu·ri·um \tə'lu̇rēəm, te¦, ¦l'yu̇-\ *n* -s [NL, fr. *tellur-* + *-ium*] **1 :** a semimetallic element that is related to selenium and sulfur and resembles them chemically, that is known either in a silvery white brittle crystalline form having a metallic luster but conducting electricity poorly or in a dark amorphous form of variable properties, that burns in air with a greenish blue flame to yield the crystalline dioxide, that is found native but more often combined esp. with metals in tellurides (as sylvanite) associated with sulfides and selenides, that is obtained usu. as a by-product in the electrolytic refining of copper and also as a fission product of uranium, and that is used chiefly in the rubber industry as a secondary vulcanizing agent and in metallurgy in iron castings and in copper, lead, and other alloys — symbol *Te*; see ELEMENT table **2 :** a place for the care and exhibition of selected flora and fauna (as in a school for instruction purposes)

tel·lu·rized \'telyə,rīzd\ *adj* [*tellur-* + *-ize* + *-ed*] **:** combined with or containing tellurium

tel·lu·ro·bismuthite \¦telyə(,)rō, tə¦lu̇(,)rō, te¦, ¦l'yu̇-+\ *n* [*tellur-* + *bismuthite*] **:** a mineral Bi_2Te_3 consisting of bismuth telluride and found as irregular plates or foliated masses

tel·lu·rom·e·ter \,telyə'rämad·ə(r)\ *n* [*tellur-* + *-meter*] **:** a device that measures distance by means of a modulated continuous-wave radio signal

tel·lu·ro·ni·um \,telyə'rōnēəm\ *n* -s [NL, fr. *tellur-* + *-onium* (as in *sulfonium*)] **:** a univalent cation $TeH_3{}^+$ or radical H_3Te analogous to sulfonium

tel·lu·rous \'telyərəs; tə¦'lu̇r-, te¦, ¦l'yu̇-\ *adj* [ISV *tellur-* + *-ous*] **:** of, relating to, or containing tellurium — used esp. of compounds in which this element has a lower valence than in telluric compounds

tellurous acid *n* **:** a very weak unstable acid H_2TeO_3 containing tetravalent tellurium and known in solution and in the form of salts

tel·ly \'telī\ *n* -ES [by shortening & alter.] *chiefly Brit* : TELEVISION: as **a** : television considered as a source of entertainment — usu. used with *the* ⟨a merciful relief from the mediocre twaddle on the ~ —*The People*⟩ **b** : a television receiver ⟨in the ~ on —William Sansom⟩

tel·ma·tol·o·gy \,telmə'täləjē\ *n* -ES [Gk *telmat-, telma* stagnant water, marsh + E *-o-* + *-logy*; akin to Gk *stalassein* to let drop, drip — more at STALE] : a branch of physiography treating of wet lands (as peat bogs or swamps)

¹telo- — see ²TEL-

²telo- — see ¹TEL-

telo·blast \'telə,blast, 'tel-\ *n* -S [ISV ²*tel-* + *-blast*] : one of the large cells that produce lines of smaller cells at the growing end of many embryos (as of most annelids) — **telo·blas·tic** \¦==¦blastik\ *adj*

¹telo·cen·tric \¦==¦sen·trik\ *adj* [ISV ²*tel-* + *-centric*] : having the form of a straight rod due to the terminal position of the centromere ⟨a ~ chromosome⟩ — compare METACENTRIC

²telocentric \"\ *n* : a telocentric chromosome

telo·den·dri·on \,==ˈdendrēən\ *also* **tele·den·dron** *or* **telo·den·dron** \,==ˈdendrən\ *n, pl* **telo·den·dria** \-rēə\ [*telodendrion*, NL, fr. ²*tel-* + Gk *dendrion* small tree, dim. of *dendron* tree; *teledendron, telodendron*, NL, fr. ²*tel-* + *-dendron* — more at DENDR-] : the terminal arborization of a nerve fiber — used orig. of dendrites but now esp. of the main arborization of an axon

telo·dynamic \¦telō, ¦telō+\ *adj* [ISV ¹*tel-* + *dynamic*] : relating to the transmission of power to a distance esp. by a system of ropes or cables and pulleys

telo·go·nia \,=ə'gōnēə\ *n pl, cap* [NL, fr. ²*tel-* + *-gonia* (fr. Gk *gonos* offspring, procreation, genitals) — more at GON-] *in some classifications* : an order of Nematoda comprising forms in which new germ cells originate only at the distal end of the gonad — compare HOLOGONIA — **telo·gonic** \¦==¦gänik -¦gōn-\ *adj*

telo·lecithal \¦telō, ¦telō+\ *adj* [²*tel-* + Gk *lekithos* yolk of an egg + E *-al*] : having the yolk large in amount and concentrated at one pole — used of an egg; compare CENTROLECITHAL

telome \'tē,lōm *also* 'te,l-\ *n* -S [ISV ²*tel-* + *-ome*; orig. formed as G *telom*] : a basic unit of structure in vascular plants: **a** : a terminal branchlet having a distal sporangium and a vascular supply **b** : the simplest most fundamental unit of the plant body whether terminal or not — compare MESOME — **te·lomic** \tē'lōmik, te'l-, -lām-\ *adj*

tel·o·mer \'teləmə(r)\ *n* -S [²*tel-* + *-mer*] : the product of telomerization

telo·mere \'telə,mi(ə)r, 'tel-\ *n* -S [ISV ²*tel-* + *-mere*] : a chromosome end regarded as a specialized self-perpetuating structure

tel·o·mer·iza·tion \,teləmərə'zāshən, -,rī'z-\ *n* -S [*telomer* + *-ize* + *-ation*] : a chemical reaction involving addition of fragments of one molecule (as of an alcohol, acetal, or chloroform) to the ends of a polymerizing olefin system ⟨~ of carbon tetrachloride with styrene in the presence of acetyl peroxide forms the telomer $Cl[CH(C_6H_5)CH_2]_nCCl_3$⟩

telome theory *n* : a theory in botany: the entire plant body can be interpreted in terms of telomes whether single, with or without sporangia, or variously modified (as in being fused to serve as leaves or other organs)

telo·mit·ic \¦==¦mid·ik\ *adj* [²*tel-* + *mit-* + *-ic*] : TELOCENTRIC

teloogoo *usu cap, var of* TELUGU

te·lo·pea \tə'lōpēə\ *n, cap* [NL, fr. Gk *tēlōpos* seen from afar, fr. *tēl-* ¹tel- + *-ōpos* (akin to Gk *ōps* eye, face) — more at EYE] : a genus of Australian shrubs and trees (family Proteaceae) notable for their showy scarlet tetramerous flowers which have a common involucre at the base of the clusters and which are followed by capsules with winged seeds — see WARATAH

telo·phase \'telə, 'telə+,-\ *n* [ISV ²*tel-* + *phase*; orig. formed in G] : the final stage of mitosis in which the new nuclei are differentiated and which is usu. accompanied by cytoplasmic division to form new daughter cells — **telo·phasic** \¦==+\ *adj*

telo·phragma \,==+\ *n, pl* **telophragmata** [NL, fr. ²*tel-* + Gk *phragma* fence — more at PHRAGMA] : KRAUSE'S MEMBRANE

te·lop·o·dite \tə'läpə,dīt\ *n* -S [²*tel-* + *-podite*] : the part of the arthropod limb distal to the coxa

te·los \'te,läs, 'te,l-\ *n, pl* -ES [Gk — more at WHEEL] : an ultimate end or object

telo·spo·rid·ia \,telōspə'ridēə, ,tel-\ *n pl, cap* [NL, fr. ²*tel-* + *-sporidia*] : a subclass of Sporozoa comprising parasitic protozoans that form spores without polar capsules or filaments which contain one or more infective sporozoites and including the orders Gregarinida, Coccidia, and Haemosporidia — **telo·spo·rid·i·an** \¦==¦dēən\ *adj or n*

telo·syn·ap·sis \¦==sə'napsəs\ *n* [NL, fr. ²*tel-* + *synapsis*] : end-to-end union of chromosomes in synapsis — compare PARASYNAPSIS — **telo·syn·ap·tic** \-ptik\ *adj* — **telo·syn·ap·tist** \-ptəst\ *n*

telo·syndesis \¦telō, ¦telō+\ *n* [NL, fr. ²*tel-* + *syndesis*] : TELOSYNAPSIS

telo·taxis \"+\ *n* [NL, fr. ²*tel-* + *taxis*] : a taxis in which an organism orients itself in respect to a stimulus (as a light source) as though that were the only stimulus acting on it

telo·trema·ta \,==ˈtremədə, -rēm-\ *n pl, cap* [NL, fr. ²*tel-* + Gk *trēmata*, pl. of *trēma* hole — more at THROW] : an order of brachiopods having the opening for the peduncle shared by both valves in earlier stages but usu. confined to one in later stages and more or less limited below by a pair of deltidial plates and having spiral arms that are supported by calcareous bars, loops, or spirals — **telo·tremate** \,==ˈmāt\ *n* -S — **telo·trema·tous** \¦==¦məd·əs\ *adj*

telo·troch \'==,träk\ *n* -S [NL *telotrocha*] **1 a** : the preanal tuft of cilia in a trochophore larva **b** : a ciliated girdle at the hinder end of an actinotrocha or of the tornaria of hemichordates **2** : TELOTROCHA

te·lot·ro·cha \tə'lä·trəkə\ *n, pl* **telotro·chae** \-,kē\ [NL, fr. ²*tel-* + *-trocha*] : a larva of various annelids having a preoral and a posterior circlet or tuft of cilia — **te·lot·ro·chal** \-kəl\ *adj* — **te·lot·ro·chous** \-kəs\ *adj*

telo·troph \'telə,träf, 'tel-, -rōf\ *n* -S [²*tel-* + Gk *trophos* feeder — more at TROPH-] : a growing vegetative form of some sporozoans that does not engage in schizogony

telo·troph·ic \¦==¦träfik\ *adj* : ACROTROPHIC

telo·type \'telə,tīp, 'tel-\ *n* [¹*tel-* + *-type*] **1** : a printing telegraph **2** : an automatically printed telegram

tel·pher *also* **tel·fer** \'telfə(r)\ *n* -S [*telpher* irreg. fr. ¹*tel-* + Gk *pherein* to bear; *telfer* alter. of *telpher* — more at BEAR] : a light car suspended from and running on aerial cables; *esp* : one automatically propelled by electricity

tel·pher·age *also* **tel·fer·age** \-f(ə)rij\ *n* -S **1** : a system of automatic electric transportation; *esp* : an automatic electric system in which the cars are hung from and run on wire cables suspended in the air **2** : a telpher system operated by other than electric power

telpher carrier *n* : the carriage, car, bucket, or other unit container used in a telpher conveyor system

tel·pher·man \'telfə(r)mən\ *n, pl* **telphermen** : a telpher operator

tel·puch·cal·li \,tel,püch'kälē\ *n, pl* **telpuchcalli** [Sp *telpuchcalli, telpuchcalli*, fr. Nahuatl *telpuchcalli*] : an Aztec school for boys giving instruction in civil and military arts including crafts, history, and religious practices — distinguished from *calmecac*

tel·son \'telsən, -,sän\ *n* -S [NL, fr. Gk, boundary, limit, prob. fr. *telos* end — more at WHEEL] : the terminal segment of the body of an arthropod or segmented worm or of a crustacean (as the lobster) where it forms the middle lobe of the tail — **tel·son·ic** \(')tel¦sänik\ *adj*

tel·u·gu *or* **tel·e·gu** *also* **tel·oo·goo** \'telə,gü\ *n, pl* **telugu** *or* **telugus** *or* **telegu** *or* **telegus** *also* **teloogoo** *or* **teloogoos** *usu cap* **1 a** : the largest group of people in Andhra, India **b** : a member of such people **2 a** : the Dravidian language of the Telugu people **b** : the script usu. employed in writing this language

telvsn *abbr* television

tel·yn \'telən\ *n* -S [W, fr. MW; akin to OCorn *telein* harp, Bret *telenn*] : an old Celtic harp

TEM \¦tē,ē¦em\ *abbr or n* -S : TRIETHYLENEMELAMINE

te·ma \'tāmə\ *n* -S [It, theme (in general), fr. L *thema* — more at THEME] : THEME 4a

te·ma·cha \'tāmə,chä, tā'māchə\ *n* -S [Per *tamākhra* joke, humor] : a Persian comic or farcical interlude performed by traveling players

te·ma·dau \,temə'daü\ *n, pl* **temadau** *or* **temadaus** [native name in Borneo] : a Bornean banteng

te·ma·la·ca·tl \,tāmələ'käd·ᵊl\ *n* -S [Nahuatl, lit., spindle stone, fr. *tetl* stone + *malacatl* spindle] : a spindle-shaped stone in Aztec sacrificial rites to which an inadequately armed captive was attached while allowed ostensibly to defend himself against his executioners — called also *spindle stone*

tem·be \'tembē\ *n, pl* **tembe** *or* **tembes** *usu cap* **1** : a people that is a northern Malay branch of the Sakai **2** : a member of the Tembe people

tem·blor \'temblə(r), 'tem,blō(ə)r, -ó(ə)\ *or* **trem·blor** \'trem-\ *or* **trem·bler** \-mblə(r)\ *n* -S [*temblor* fr. Sp, tremblor, earthquake, fr. *temblar* to tremble, quiver, fr. ML *tremulare*; *tremblor* alter. of *temblor*; *trembler* modif. (influenced by E *tremble*) of Sp. *temblor* — more at TREMBLE] : EARTHQUAKE ⟨deposits of sand and mud . . . periodically dislodged by submarine ~s —F.J.Pettijohn⟩

tem·bu \'tem(,)bü\ *n, pl* **tembu** *or* **tembus** *usu cap* **1** : a Bantu-speaking people of Tembuland in southern Africa **2** : a member of the Tembu people

tem·e·nos \'temə,näs\ *n, pl* **teme·ne** \-,nē\ [Gk, piece of land cut off as an official or sacred domain, temenos, fr. *temnein* to cut — more at TOME] : a temple enclosure or court in ancient Greece : a sacred precinct

tem·er·ar·i·ous \¦temə¦ra(a)rēəs, -¦rer-\ *adj* [L *temerarius*, fr. *temere* by chance, rashly + *-arius* -ary — more at TEMERITY] **1** : marked by temerity : rashly or presumptuously daring : RECKLESS, BRASH ⟨how often we have been cowardly and hung back, or ~ and rushed unwisely in —R.L.Stevenson⟩ **2** *archaic* : happening by chance : FORTUITOUS ⟨principles . . . not merely casual and ~ —James Harris⟩ **syn** see ADVENTUROUS

tem·er·ar·i·ous·ly *adv* : in a temerarious manner : RASHLY, FOOLHARDILY ⟨~ criticized the board chairman in open meeting⟩

tem·er·ar·i·ous·ness *n* -ES : the quality or state of being temerarious : TEMERITY

te·mer·i·ty \tə'merəd·ē, -rətē, -i\ *n* -ES [ME *temeryte*, fr. L *temeritas*, fr. *temere* by chance, rashly + *-itas* -ity; akin to OS *thim* dark, OHG *demar* darkness, *dinstar* dark, ON *thām* mugginess, OIr *temel* darkness, L *tenebrae*, Skt *tamas*; basic meaning: dark] : unreasonable or foolhardy contempt of danger or opposition : reckless and often presumptuous boldness : rash venturesomeness ⟨a private with the ~ to speak up against the sergeant's bullying⟩ ⟨the author's intellectual ~ is colossal —Rubin Gotesky⟩

syn HARDIHOOD, AUDACITY, NERVE, EFFRONTERY, CHEEK, GALL: TEMERITY suggests a boldness or courage in forward action or gesture arising from contempt of danger or from lack of due consideration of chances of failure, rebuff, or defeat ⟨he impetuously brushed aside the legalistic twaddle of the lawyers . . . and they frowned on such *temerity* —C.G. Bowers⟩ ⟨tenth-rate critics and compilers, for whom any violent shock to the public taste would be a *temerity* not to be risked —Matthew Arnold⟩ HARDIHOOD indicates a determined resolution or self-confidence in bold steps that may involve defiance or insolence ⟨glowering in sullen suspense between *hardihood* and fear —John Galsworthy⟩ ⟨the reviewers . . . were staggered by my *hardihood* in offering a woman of forty as a subject of serious interest —Arnold Bennett⟩ AUDACITY suggests a daring boldness with an openly expressed disdain of prudence, restraint, convention, or authority ⟨the supreme *audacity* of looking into her soul —Victoria Sackville-West⟩ ⟨the *audacity* . . . in offering battle against forces ten times his own⟩ NERVE indicates an assured, cool boldness which may offend by being presumptuous ⟨you had the *nerve* to ask me to marry you —Barnaby Conrad⟩ EFFRONTERY suggests flagrant or flaunted insolence that is rude and presumptuous ⟨had the *effrontery* to pose as the avenger of outraged morality —G.B.Shaw⟩ ⟨unable to endure the cool *effrontery* of a Yankee schoolmaster's dabbling in affairs peculiarly English —H.R.Warfel⟩ CHEEK suggests impudent or insolently flaunted self-assurance ⟨I've never allowed anyone to talk to me as you do . . . you have the *cheek* of the devil himself —Hartley Howard⟩ GALL is most extreme in suggesting a brazen boldness likely to irritate or enrage ⟨some have only one attribute, a colossal *gall* —Stanley Walker⟩

tem·es·cal *or* **tem·as·cal** \,temə'skal\ *n* -S [MexSp *temascal*, fr. Nahuatl *temazcalli*, fr. *tema* to bathe + *calli* house] : a sweathouse of Mexican or Central American Indians

tem·minck's stint \'temiŋks-\ *n, usu cap T* [after Conrad J. *Temminck* †1858 Du. naturalist] : a very small Old World sandpiper (*Pisobia temminckii* or *Calidris temminckii*) that is largely gray with sparse white markings on wings and tail

tem·ne \'temnē\ *or* **tim·ne** \'tim-\ *n, pl* **temne** *or* **temnes** *or* **timne** *or* **timnes** *usu cap* **1 a** : a people of the interior of Sierra Leone in western Africa **b** : a member of the Temne people **2** : a West-Atlantic language of the Temne people

tem·no·spon·dy·li \,temnō'spändə,lī\ *n pl, cap* [NL, fr. Gk *temnein* to cut + NL *-o-* + *-spondyli* — more at TOME] *in some classifications* : a suborder of Stegocephalia including parts of the orders Embolomeri and Rhachitomi and sometimes the Stereospondyli

tem·no·spon·dy·lous \¦==¦spändələs\ *adj* [NL *Temnospondyli* + E *-ous*] **1** : RHACHITOMOUS — opposed to *stereospondylous* **2** : of or relating to the Temnospondyli

tem·o·ra \'temərə\ *n, cap* [NL] : a genus of marine copepods important as fish food in northern waters

temp \'temp\ *n* -S [by shortening] **1** : TEMPERATURE **2** : TEMPO

temp *abbr* **1** temperance **2** template **3** temporal **4** temporary **5** [L *tempore*] in the time of

tem·pe \'tempē\ *n* -S *usu cap* [L, fr. *Tempe*, a beautiful valley in ancient Thessaly, fr. Gk *Tempē*] : a place (as a valley, glen, or rustic retreat) of great natural beauty and charm

tem·pe·an \-ēən\ *adj* : of, relating to, or resembling a Tempe

¹tem·per \'tempə(r)\ *vb* **tempered; tempered; tempering** \-p(ə)riŋ\ **tempers** [ME *temperen, tempren*, fr. OE & OF; OE *temprian* & OF *temprer*, fr. L *temperare* to mix, blend, regulate, restrain oneself, abstain, prob. fr. *tempor-, tempus* period of time, fitting time, season, time (in general) — more at TEMPORAL] *vt* **1 a** : to dilute, qualify, or soften (as something strong, harsh, or excessive) by the addition or influence of something else : make temperate : MODERATE, SEASON ⟨~ wine with water⟩ ⟨~ justice with mercy⟩ ⟨enthusiasm ~*ed* with a touch of skepticism⟩ ⟨~*s* the wind . . . to the shorn lamb —Laurence Sterne⟩ ⟨the breeze . . . ~*ed* the August sun —Arnold Bennett⟩ ⟨his firmness must always be ~*ed* with tact and shrewdness —R.M.Dawson⟩ **b** : to make suitable for : adapt to : ADJUST, MODIFY — usu. used with *to* ⟨officers . . . ~ their actions to outside political whimsy —T.H.White b. 1915⟩ ⟨stick to these few principles and ~ them to suit your taste —Betty Fisk⟩ **c** *archaic* : to mix (ingredients) in suitable proportions : prepare by combining : COMPOUND, BLEND ⟨a confection after the art of the apothecary, ~*ed* together —Exod 30:35 (AV)⟩ ⟨importuned me to ~ poisons for her —Shak.⟩ **2** *archaic* **a** : to exercise control over : GOVERN, RESTRAIN ⟨Jove ~*s* the fates of human race above —Alexander Pope⟩ **b** : to cause to be well disposed : MOLLIFY ⟨~*ed* and reconciled them both —Richard Steele⟩ **3** : to bring (a substance or material) to a suitable state (as of consistency or workability) by mixing in or adding a usu. liquid ingredient: as **a** (1) : to mix (clay) with water and knead to a uniform texture (2) : to add an aplastic material (as grog or sand) to (clay) **b** : to mix oil with (colors) in making paint ready for use **c** : to moisten (as sand for molding) to a proper consistency and stir thoroughly **d** : to dampen or remove moisture from (grain) to secure the best grinding **e** : to make (leather) uniformly moist and soft for further processing **4 a** (1) : to soften (hardened steel or cast iron) by reheating at a temperature well below that from which previous quenching for hardening was done (2) : to harden and reheat (steel or cast iron) or to harden alone esp. in oil — not used technically **b** : to anneal or toughen (glass) by a process of gradually heating and cooling **5** : to make stronger and more resilient through hardship : TOUGHEN ⟨the hammerblows of fate seemed not to weaken but to ~ her strength —John Buchan⟩ **6 a** : to put in tune with : ATTUNE ⟨to which the birds ~*ed* their matin lay —P.B.Shelley⟩ ⟨our ears are ~*ed* to harsh sounds —Ronald Bottrall⟩ **b** : to adjust the pitch of (a note, chord, instrument) to a temperament ~ *vi* : to produce satisfactory temper — used of metallic alloys which can be treated to give the desired physical properties **syn** see MODERATE

²temper \"\ *n* -S [ME *tempre*, fr. *tempren*, v.] **1 a** *archaic* : the state of any compound substance resulting from the mixture of ingredients; *esp* : a suitable proportion or balance of qualities : a middle state between extremes : MEAN, MEDIUM ⟨virtue is . . . a just ~ between propensities any one of which, if indulged to excess, becomes vice —T.B.Macaulay⟩ **b** *archaic* : a particular mixture of elements or characteristics : CHARACTER, QUALITY ⟨the ~ of the land you design to sow —John Mortimer⟩ ⟨a man of such a feeble ~ —Shak.⟩ **c** : characteristic tone : TREND, TENDENCY ⟨the ~ of the times⟩ ⟨the general ~ of his view —Alan Gewirth⟩ ⟨literary circles which foster certain modes and ~*s* of form and emotion —W.S.B.Braithwaite⟩ ⟨the ~ of English literature at the turn of the century —*Times Lit. Supp.*⟩ **d** : high quality of mind or spirit : COURAGE, METTLE ⟨no trumpet calls . . . to keep our ~ at its keenest —R.W.Livingstone⟩ ⟨not of the ~ of which martyrs are made —Ellen Glasgow⟩ **2** : the state of a substance with respect to certain desired qualities (as hardness, elasticity, or workability): as **a** (1) : the degree of hardness or resiliency given steel by tempering (2) : the color of steel after tempering : TEMPER COLOR **b** : the condition of relative dryness (as of grain) proper for treatment in processing **c** : the feel and relative solidity of leather **3** : a substance added to or mixed with something else to modify the properties of the latter: as **a** : any of various mixtures of metals added to another metal in making an alloy **b** : the carbon content of steel that affects its hardening properties **c** : the moisture content of foundry sand **d** : aplastic material (as grog or sand) added to clay to reduce shrinkage upon drying and firing **4 a** *obs* : atmospheric conditions : CLIMATE ⟨the changeful ~ of the skies —John Dryden⟩ **b** *archaic* : TEMPERATURE **5 a** : a characteristic or habitual cast of mind or state of feeling : DISPOSITION ⟨a calm ~⟩ ⟨a sunny ~⟩ ⟨an occupation that suited his ~⟩ ⟨the man of mercurial ~ —William McDougall⟩ ⟨that reverence towards fact which constitutes . . . the scientific ~ —Bertrand Russell⟩ **b** : calmness of mind : COMPOSURE, EQUANIMITY ⟨keep me in ~; I would not be mad —Shak.⟩ — used esp. in the expressions *keep one's temper*, *lose one's temper*, and *out of temper* ⟨kept his ~ despite the provocation⟩ ⟨failed to get the witness to lose her ~⟩ ⟨are you out of ~ because you let those men put something over on you —Ellen Glasgow⟩ **c** : state of feeling or frame of mind at a particular time : HUMOR, MOOD ⟨had they been in a ~ to judge fairly —T.B. Macaulay⟩ ⟨keep the populace . . . in good ~ —R.M.French⟩ ⟨she was . . . in a gay, frolicsome ~ —W.H.Hudson †1922⟩ **d** : heat of mind or emotion : proneness to anger : PASSION ⟨a man with a ~ to beware of⟩ ⟨a display of ~⟩ ⟨as the strike dragged on, ~*s* flared on all sides —Mary K. Hammond⟩ ⟨threw down the cloth in a ~ —*Irish Digest*⟩ **syn** see DISPOSITION, MOOD

tem·pera *also* **tem·po·ra** \'tempərə\ *n* -S *often attrib* [It *tempera* temper (of metals), distemper (in music), tempera, fr. *temperare* to temper, fr. L — more at TEMPER] : a process of painting in which an albuminous or colloidal medium is employed as a vehicle instead of oil — compare ⁴DISTEMPER

tem·per·able \'temp(ə)rəbəl\ *adj* [ME, fr. *tempren, temperen* to temper + *-able*] : capable of being tempered

temperality *n* -ES *obs* : physical condition ⟨now you are in an excellent good ~ —Shak.⟩

tem·per·a·ment \'temp(ə)rəmənt, -pərm-\ *n* -S [ME, fr. L *temperamentum*, fr. *temperare* to mix, blend, regulate + *-mentum* -ment — more at TEMPER] **1** *obs* **a** : the state (as of a substance, body, or organism) with respect to the mixture or balance in due proportions of its elements, qualities, or parts : CONSTITUTION, MAKEUP ⟨the best founded commonwealths . . . have aimed at a certain mixture or ~, partaking the several virtues of each other state —John Milton⟩ **b** : COMPLEXION 1b **2 a** : the peculiar or distinguishing mental or physical character of a person as determined according to medieval physiology by the relative proportions of the humors in his body — compare ¹HUMOR 1b ⟨the choleric, melancholic, phlegmatic, and sanguine ~*s*⟩ **b** : characteristic or habitual inclination, frame of mind, or mode of emotional response ⟨a nervous ~⟩ ⟨the artistic ~⟩ ⟨the poetic ~⟩ ⟨buoyant and expansive in ~⟩ ⟨the mind of a dreamer joined to the ~ of a soldier —John Buchan⟩ ⟨the ~ of an animal shown by its gait and carriage⟩ **c** : extremely high sensibility; *esp* : excessive sensitiveness or irritability often accompanied by impatience or lack of restraint : TEMPER ⟨always having ~ and making trouble —*This Week Mag.*⟩ ⟨dropped his racket during a rare display of ~ —Harry Gordon⟩ **3** *archaic* **a** : CLIMATE **b** : TEMPERATURE 5 **4** *archaic* **a** : the act or process of tempering or modifying : ADJUSTMENT, COMPROMISE ⟨any ~ that can be found in things . . . so disputable —John Milton⟩ **b** : middle course : MEAN ⟨a judicious ~, which the reformers would have done well to adopt —Henry Hallam⟩ **5 a** : the system or process of slightly modifying the musical intervals of the pure scale to produce a set of compromise tones consisting of 12 fixed tones to the octave and thus permit modulations without the use of an inconveniently large number of distinctions in pitch **b** : the adjustment so made **syn** see DISPOSITION

tem·per·a·men·tal \¦temp(ə)rə¦mentᵊl, -pər¦-\ *adj* **1** : of, relating to, or arising from temperament : CONSTITUTIONAL ⟨~ peculiarities⟩ ⟨~ indifference to neatness and order —G. W.Johnson⟩ **2 a** : marked by excessive sensitivity and sudden impulsive and often explosive changes of mood : HIGH-STRUNG, EXCITABLE ⟨a ~ opera singer⟩ ⟨~, argumentative and full of rowdy spirits —Stanley Walker⟩ **b** : marked by erratic, unpredictable behavior : CAPRICIOUS, FICKLE ⟨this parasite . . . proved to be a most ~ performer; sometimes it would and sometimes it would not —C.C.Furnas⟩ ⟨that beautiful, but ~ instrument, the flute —Osbert Lancaster⟩

tem·per·a·men·tal·ly \-ᵊlē, -ᵊli\ *adv* : in, by, or according to temperament : in nature or disposition : CONSTITUTIONALLY ⟨~ a conservative⟩ ⟨~ unable to appreciate irony⟩ ⟨a time that was ~ unfriendly to . . . historical criticism —R.E.Spiller⟩

tem·per·ance \'temp(ə)rən(t)s, -pərn-\ *n* -S *often attrib* [ME *temperaunce*, fr. L *temperantia*, fr. *temperant-, temperans* (pres. part. of *temperare* to mix, blend, regulate, restrain oneself, abstain) + *-ia* -y — more at TEMPER] **1 a** : moderation in action, thought, or feeling : RESTRAINT ⟨the cardinal virtues of prudence, justice, ~, and fortitude⟩ ⟨public opinion . . . its ~ or caprice —A.E.Stevenson †1965⟩ ⟨compositions marked by ~, serious reflection, and expert writing —*New Yorker*⟩ **b** : habitual moderation in the indulgence of the appetites or passions : SELF-CONTROL ⟨preaches ~ in the enjoyment of the pleasures of bed and table⟩ ⟨his own . . . perfect ~ had in it a fascinating power —Walter Pater⟩; *specif* : moderation in or abstinence from the use of intoxicating drink : SOBRIETY ⟨~ in those days was generally understood to mean total abstinence —John Lardner⟩ **2 a** *obs* : the proper mixture or proportion of elements or qualities; *esp* : the combination producing the desired state of a substance : CONSISTENCY ⟨boiled until they come unto a soft ~ —Edward Topsell⟩ **b** : mildness of weather or climate : TEMPERATENESS ⟨this island . . . must needs be of subtle, tender, and delicate ~ —Shak.⟩

tem·per·ate \'temp(ə)rət, *usu* -əd+V\ *adj* [ME *temperat*, fr. L *temperatus*, fr. past part. of *temperare*] **1** : marked by moderation : keeping or existing in the middle ground between extremes: as **a** : keeping or held within limits : not extreme or excessive : MILD ⟨expressing ~ satisfaction with his results —R.W.Firth⟩ **b** : moderate in indulgence of appetite or desire : SELF-CONTROLLED, CONTINENT ⟨singularly ~ . . . noted for his scant indulgence in meat, drink, or sleep —J.R.Green⟩ **c** : moderate in or abstemious from the use of intoxicating liquors ⟨not as ~ as he might have been but never a drunkard⟩ **d** : marked by an absence or avoidance of extravagance, violence, or extreme partisanship : RESTRAINED, DISPASSIONATE ⟨~ language⟩ ⟨rare indeed is such ~ and rational discussion of crucial problems —C.A.Baylis⟩ **e** : having duly limited power : CONSTITUTIONAL — used of a monarchy or ruler ⟨our loyal passion for our ~ kings —Alfred Tennyson⟩ **f** : existing as a prophage in infected cells and rarely causing lysis ⟨~ bacteriophages⟩ **2 a** : having a moderate climate ⟨a ~ region⟩ ⟨the ~ zones⟩ **b** : found in or associated with a

moderate climate ⟨a ~ plant⟩ ⟨~ insects⟩ **c :** of or relating to a point (as the 66° F reading on a thermometer) marking a moderate temperature **3 :** TEMPERED — used of a musical interval or scale **syn** see SOBER

tem·per·ate·ly *adv* [ME *temperatly*, fr. *temperat* + *-ly*] **:** in a temperate manner: as **a :** without extravagance **:** DISPASSIONATELY ⟨these preferences are ~ . . . stated —Agnes Repplier⟩ **b :** with restraint ⟨~ used the privileges of his office —A.T. Quiller-Couch⟩ **c :** without overindulgence **:** ABSTEMIOUSLY ⟨indulge ~ in cocktails⟩

tem·per·ate·ness *n* -ES [ME *temperatnes*, fr. *temperat* + *-nes* -ness] **:** the quality or state of being temperate **:** MODERATION: as **a** *obs* **:** TEMPERANCE 1b **b :** SELF-RESTRAINT ⟨an effective ~ in debate⟩ **c :** mildness of climate ⟨the ~ of the weather⟩

temperate rain forest *n* **:** woodland of temperate but usu. rather mild climatic areas with heavy rainfall usu. including numerous kinds of trees and being distinguished from tropical rain forest by the presence of a dominant tree (as the podocarpus forests of New Zealand)

temperate zone *n, often cap T&Z* **:** the area or region between the tropic of Cancer and the arctic circle or between the tropic of Capricorn and the antarctic circle

tem·per·a·ture *R* 'tempə(r)\|,chů(ə)r, -p(ə)rə\|, \|chər *sometimes* \|·,tyů(ə)r *or* \|,tů(ə)r *or* 'tem(p)chər; *–R* 'tempə(r)\|,chůə, -p(ə)rə\|, \|chə *sometimes* \|·,tyůə *or* \|,tůə *or* 'tem(p)chə\\ *n* -S *often attrib* [L *temperatura*, fr. *temperatus* (past part. of *temperare* to mix, blend, regulate, restrain oneself, abstain) + *-ura* -ure — more at TEMPER] **1** *archaic* **:** a mixture or blending of elements **:** COMPOSITION, CONSTITUTION ⟨beings of our make and ~ —John Bonnycastle⟩ **2** *obs* **a :** a proper middle course **:** a mean between extremes **:** COMPROMISE, MODERATION **b :** mildness of climate **:** TEMPERATENESS **3** *archaic* **a :** COMPLEXION 1b **b :** TEMPERAMENT 2a **c :** TEMPERAMENT 2b **4 :** TEMPER 2a **5 a :** degree of hotness or coldness measured on one of several arbitrary scales based on some observable phenomenon (as the expansion of mercury) **:** the degree of a material substance that is a linear function of the kinetic energy of the random motion of its molecules **:** the degree of a vacuum that depends upon the density of the radiant energy within it — compare ABSOLUTE ZERO, HEAT **b :** the degree of heat that is natural to the body of a living being, that in invertebrates and cold-blooded vertebrates approximates that of the environment, and that in warm-blooded vertebrates fluctuates in a narrow range characteristic of the kind of animal and largely independent of the environment ⟨man's normal oral ~ of about 98.6° F⟩ **c :** abnormally high body heat ⟨running a ~⟩ **:** a feverish condition ⟨had a ~ for three days⟩ **d :** relative state of emotional warmth **:** level of interest **:** INTENSITY ⟨aware of a change in the ~ of our friendship —Christopher Isherwood⟩ ⟨the low ~ of competition —V.O. Key⟩

temperature coefficient *n* **:** a numerical value indicating the relation between a change in temperature and a simultaneous change in some other property (as solubility); *specif* **:** the factor a in the equation $R_t = R_o(1+at)$ in which R_t equals the resistance of a conductor at t° centigrade and R_o equals its resistance at 0° centigrade

temperature curve *n* **:** a graph recording changes in temperature over given periods of time

temperature gradient *n* **:** the rate of change of temperature with displacement in a given direction (as with increase of height) — compare LAPSE RATE

temperature inversion *n* **:** an increase of temperature with height through a layer of air

temperature scale *n* **1 :** the scale of degrees on a thermometer **2 :** a system of reckoning temperature ⟨the centigrade *temperature scale*⟩ ⟨the Kelvin *temperature scale*⟩ ⟨the international *temperature scale*⟩

temperature sensation *n* **:** a sensation of warmth or cold mediated respectively by warm spots and cold spots of the skin

temperature sense *n* **:** the largely cutaneous sense that responds to stimulation by warmth and cold

temperature spot *n* **:** one of many points on the skin that are selectively sensitive either to warmth or to cold

temperature wave *n* **:** a wave in which the propagated disturbance is a variation of temperature and of which the velocity is ordinarily very small except in the case of liquid helium II where the wave speed approaches that of sound — compare SECOND SOUND

temper color *n* **:** any of the colors varying from very pale yellow to very dark blue that are assumed by a smooth surface of steel as a result of reheating, are due to thin films of oxide, and correspond to definite temperatures

tem·pered \\¦tempə(r)d\\ *adj* [ME *tempred, tempered,* fr. past part. of *tempren, temperen* to temper — more at TEMPER] **1 a :** having the elements or qualities mixed in proper or satisfying proportions **:** TEMPERATE ⟨this finely ~ air —G.B.Shaw⟩ ⟨has a wonderfully ~ mind —H.J.Laski⟩ **b :** qualified, lessened, or diluted by the mixture or influence of an additional ingredient **:** MODERATED ⟨a pale gleam of ~ sunlight fell through the leaves —W.H.Hudson †1922⟩ ⟨plea . . . for a guided and ~ experimentalism —P.H.Douglas⟩ **2 :** treated by tempering **:** brought to the desired state (as of hardness, flexibility, or resiliency) ⟨~ steel⟩ ⟨~ glass⟩ **3 :** having a specified temper — used in combination ⟨bad-*tempered*⟩ ⟨ill-*tempered*⟩ ⟨short-*tempered*⟩ ⟨even-*tempered*⟩ **4 :** conformed to esp. equal temperament — used of a musical interval, intonation, semitone, or scale

tem·per·er \\'tempərə(r)\\ *n* -S [1*temper* + *-er*] **:** one that tempers: as **a :** one who mitigates or soothes **b :** one whose work is tempering (as metal, leather, chocolate) **c :** a machine in which materials (as lime or cement) are mixed with water

tempering *pres part of* TEMPER

tem·per·ish \\-rish\\ *adj* [2*temper* + *-ish*] **:** inclined to show temper **:** easily angered **:** IRASCIBLE ⟨a beefy, ~ customer, stubborn and cocksure —Arthur Mayse⟩

temper pin *n, chiefly Scot* **:** the regulating pin of a spinning wheel

tempers *pres 3d sing of* TEMPER, *pl of* TEMPER

temper screw *n* **1 :** a screw link to which the rope of a rope-drilling apparatus is attached so that the drill may be fed and slightly turned at each stroke **2 :** a setscrew used for adjusting

tem·per·some \\-pə(r)səm\\ *adj* [2*temper* + *-some*] **:** marked by displays of temper **:** HOTHEADED ⟨used to humoring a ~ man —Mary Webb⟩

tem·pery \\-pərē\\ *adj* [2*temper* + *-y*] **:** marked by quick temper or irritability **:** TOUCHY ⟨she had ~ ways —H.E.Giles⟩

tempes *pl of* TEMPE

1tem·pest \\'tempəst\\ *n* -S [ME *tempeste, tempest,* fr. OF *tempeste,* fr. (assumed) VL *tempesta,* alter. of L *tempestas* period of time, season, weather, storm, fr. *tempus* time — more at TEMPORAL] **1 a :** an extensive violent wind; *esp* **:** one accompanied by rain, hail, or snow **:** a furious storm ⟨a real ~ blowing that had been rising for two or three days —Mary Webb⟩ **b** *dial* **:** THUNDERSTORM **2 :** a violent commotion or agitation **:** TUMULT, UPROAR ⟨a ~ of applause⟩ ⟨a ~ of tears⟩ ⟨a political ~⟩ ⟨raised a ~ of derision —T.B.Macaulay⟩ ⟨seek frantically for anchors amid the ~*s* of our time —Ben Bradford⟩ **3** *archaic* **a :** a noisy confused throng **b :** a fashionable assembly or reception **:** 2ROUT 4

2tempest \\"\\ *vb* -ED/-ING/-S [ME *tempesten,* fr. MF *tempester,* fr. *tempeste,* n.] *vt* **1 :** to raise commotion in **:** stir up **:** AGITATE ⟨the huge dolphin ~*ing* the main —Alexander Pope⟩ **2** *archaic* **:** to disturb by emotional outbursts **:** UPSET ⟨his house is ~*ed* by female eloquence —Thomas Campbell⟩ ~ *vi* **:** to cause a commotion like a tempest **:** RAGE, STORM ⟨she ~*ed* out —W.D.Howells⟩

tem·pes·ti·cal \\(')tem¦pestəkəl\\ *adj* [1*tempest* + *-ical*] *dial* **:** STORMY

tempest in a teapot : a great commotion about a matter of small importance ⟨her anger was unreasonable, a *tempest in a teapot* —E.A.McCourt⟩

tem·pes·tive \\(')tem¦pestiv\\ *adj* [L *tempestivus,* fr. *tempestus* period of time, season (fr. *tempus* time) + *-ivus* -ive — more at TEMPORAL] *archaic* **:** occurring at a proper time or season **:** OPPORTUNE, TIMELY

tempest-tossed *or* **tempest-tost** \\¦==¦=\\ *adj* **:** tossed about or agitated violently **:** thrown into confusion **:** OVERWHELMED ⟨when upon life's billows you are *tempest-tossed* —Johnson Oatman⟩ ⟨send these, the homeless, *tempest-tossed,* to me —Emma Lazarus⟩

tem·pes·tu·ous \\(')tem¦pes(h)chəwəs\\ *adj* [L *tempestuosus,* fr. *tempestus* + *-osus* -ous] **1 :** of, involving, or resembling a tempest **:** WINDY, WILD ⟨~ weather⟩ ⟨~ seas⟩ ⟨a wild, ~ evening, when the wind screamed and rattled against the windows —A. Conan Doyle⟩ **2 :** marked by violent disturbance **:** TURBULENT, STORMY ⟨an actress of ~ disposition⟩ ⟨a ~ debate⟩ ⟨~ ovations⟩ ⟨their ~ life together —Al Hine⟩ ⟨the rapidity of his ~ thoughts —Liam O'Flaherty⟩

tem·pes·tu·ous·ly *adv* **:** in a tempestuous manner **:** VIOLENTLY, STORMILY ⟨stirring the atmosphere ~⟩ ⟨those ~ beautiful moments which once had been so freely theirs —B.A.Williams⟩

tem·pes·tu·ous·ness *n* -ES **:** the quality or state of being tempestuous **:** STORMINESS, WILDNESS ⟨the ~ of the sea⟩ ⟨a time of violence and ~⟩

tempi *pl of* TEMPO

1tem·plar \\'templə(r)\\ *n* -S [ME *templere, templer,* fr. OF *templier,* fr. ML *templarius,* fr. L *templum* temple + *-arius* -ary — more at TEMPLE] **1** *usu cap* **:** a member of a religious military order established about 1118 in Jerusalem, widespread in Europe, and suppressed by the Council of Vienne in 1312 **2 :** a barrister or student of law having chambers in the Temple, London **3** *usu cap* **:** KNIGHT TEMPLAR 2 **4** *sometimes cap* **:** GOOD TEMPLAR

2templar \\"\\ *adj* [L *templaris,* fr. *templum* + *-aris* -ar] **:** of or relating to a temple

tem·plary \\-lərē\\ *n* -ES *usu cap* [ME *templarie,* fr. ML *templarius*] **1** *obs* **:** 1TEMPLAR 1 **2** [1*templar* + *-y*] **:** the membership or realm of an organization of Templars

1tem·plate *or* **tem·plet** \\'templət, *usu* -əd·+V\\ *n* -S [*template* alter. (influenced by *plate*) of *templet; templet* prob. fr. F, temple (device in a loom), dim. of *temple*] **1 :** a short piece placed horizontally in a wall under a girder or other beam to distribute its weight or pressure (as over a door or window frame) **2 :** a pattern or guide of any of various kinds used in manufacturing: as **a :** a usu. thin metal pattern used in laying out and scribing a work piece **b :** a metal pattern followed by the tracer of an automatic machine in guiding the cutting tool to produce a desired profile **c :** a chart showing the standard form against which machined parts are checked in an optical comparator **d :** any of various locating devices (as for placing rivets or applying airplane trim) **e :** a full-size wooden mold or paper pattern used in making ship hull parts of steel plate or wood **f :** a gage or pattern for checking dimensions, locations, or contours (as on castings) **g :** a pattern used in lettering **h :** a pattern used by a tailor or dressmaker in cutting a part to shape or in locating buttonholes **i :** 2OVERLAY 2f **3** *usu templet* **:** a bezel in a cut gem **4 :** 5LUTE 2 **5 :** a framed workbench for making theatrical flats

2template *also* **templet** \\"\\ *vt* -ED/-ING/-S **:** to mark or lay off the pattern or position of with a template ⟨he *templated* the rivet holes⟩

template excavator *n* **:** an excavator in which a small scoop moves back and forth along the underside of a vertical steel template having the form of the cross section of the ditch to be excavated

1tem·ple \\'tempəl\\ *n* -S *often attrib* [ME, fr. OE & OF; OE *templ, tempel* & OF *temple,* fr. L *templum* space for observation marked out by the augur, consecrated place, shrine, temple; prob. akin to L *tempus* period of time — more at TEMPORAL] **1 :** an edifice dedicated to the worship of a deity **:** an edifice held to be a residing place of a deity **2** *often cap* **:** one of three successive buildings for Hebrew worship in ancient Jerusalem built respectively by Solomon, Zerubbabel, and Herod the Great **3 :** a usu. large imposing edifice for public worship **4 :** a place in which the divine presence specially resides ⟨the ~ of his body —Jn 2:21(RSV)⟩ ⟨you are God's ~ —1 Cor 3:16(RSV)⟩ **5 :** a building constructed, dedicated, and used for the administration of Mormon sacred ordinances to and for the living and to the living in behalf of the dead (as baptism for the dead, the endowment, and sealing in marriage) **6 :** SYNAGOGUE **7 a :** a local lodge of any of various fraternal orders or the building housing it **b :** a building housing labor organizations **8 a :** a building devoted to a particular purpose or focusing on activity of a special kind ⟨movie ~*s*⟩ ⟨financial ~*s*⟩ **b :** the structure of thought, value, or belief that enshrines the spirit or essence of something ⟨a belief that is the cornerstone of the ~ of Christian faith⟩ ⟨the ~ of man's historic achievement⟩ **c :** the center or focus of something prized or valued ⟨a ~ of domesticity⟩

2temple \\"\\ *vt* -ED/-ING/-S **:** to build or devote a temple to **:** provide with a temple

3temple \\"\\ *n* -S [ME, fr. MF, fr. (assumed) VL *tempula,* alter. (influenced by L *-ula,* fem. dim. suffix) of L *tempora,* pl. of *tempus* temple; prob. akin to L *tempus* period of time — more at TEMPORAL] **1 :** the area on each side of the head of man and some other mammals back of the eye and forehead, above the zygomatic arch, and in front of the ear **2 :** one of the side supports of a pair of glasses jointed to the bows and passing on each side of the head **3 :** the posterior or upper part of the gena of an insect

4temple \\"\\ *n* -S [ME *tempylle,* fr. MF *temple,* prob. fr. L *templum* temple (sanctuary), small timber] **:** a device (as a flat wooden bar with small pins at each end or nippers through which selvage must pass) in a loom for keeping the web stretched transversely

templed \\-ld\\ *adj* [1*temple* + *-ed*] **1 :** supplied with temples or churches **2 :** enclosed in a temple

templelike \\'==,=\\ *adj* **:** resembling a temple

1temple mound *n* **1 :** a mound forming the foundation of a temple (as in Mayan and Aztec architecture) — compare TEOCALLI **2 :** a truncated American Indian mound believed to have been the site of an altar or rude temple

2temple mound *adj, usu cap T&M* [1*temple mound*] **:** of or belonging to a culture of the southern and southeastern U. S. about 1300–1700 characterized by pyramidal mounds built as platforms for temples and by village-states, shell-tempered polychrome pottery, and intensive hoe agriculture

1templet *var of* TEMPLATE

2tem·plet \\'templət\\ *n* -S [F — more at TEMPLATE] **:** 4TEMPLE

3templet \\"\\ *n* -S [1*temple* + *-et*] **:** a small temple

tem·ple·to·nia \\,tempəl'tōnēə\\ *n, cap* [NL, fr. John *Templeton* †1825 Irish botanist + NL *-ia*] **:** a genus of Australian shrubs (family Leguminosae) having simple leaves and red or yellow flowers with a reflexed standard and narrow wings — see CORALBUSH

temple tree *n* **:** a tree grown in temple gardens; *esp* **:** PAGODA TREE c(1)

1tem·po \\'tem(,)pō\\ *n, pl* **tem·pi** \\-pē\\ *or* **tempos** [It, time, tempo, fr. L *tempus* time — more at TEMPORAL] **1 :** rate of rhythmic recurrence or movement; *specif* **:** the rate of speed of a musical piece or passage indicated by one of a series of directions associated conventionally with speed (as largo, presto, allegro) and often by an exact metronome marking ⟨the symphonies were set forth very authoritatively and occasionally in ~*s* more deliberate than some I have heard —Winthrop Sargeant⟩ **2 :** rate of motion or activity **:** PACE ⟨the campaign ~ stepped up —*Newsweek*⟩ ⟨staccato dance *tempi*⟩ ⟨increased sales and production ~ —*Wall Street Jour.*⟩ ⟨after dawn the ~ of the town slowed down —H.E.Rieseberg⟩ **3 :** a turn to move in chess in relation to one's opponent's turns ⟨gain a ~ when the opponent makes a useless move⟩

2tempo \\"\\ *n* -S [Jap] **:** an old oval bronze coin of Japan having a square hole in the center coined in the first half of the 19th century

1tempora *pl of* TEMPUS

2tempora *var of* TEMPERA

1tem·po·ral \\'temp(ə)rəl\\ *adj* [ME, fr. L *temporalis,* fr. *tempor-, tempus* period of time, fitting time, season, time (in general) + *-alis* -al; akin to ON *thambr* swollen, thick, Lith *tempti* to stretch, and prob. to L *tendere* to stretch — more at THIN] **1 a :** of or relating to time as opposed to eternity **:** TEMPORARY, TRANSITORY ⟨~ matters of but fleeting moment —F.D.Roosevelt⟩ **b :** of or relating to earthly life as contrasted with heavenly **:** TERRESTRIAL ⟨the same actual, prosaic, uninspired regard which he turned upon ~ matters —Hilaire Belloc⟩ **c** [ME, fr. ML *temporalis,* fr. L] **:** of or relating to lay or secular concerns as opposed to clerical or sacred **:** CIVIL, POLITICAL ⟨~ courts⟩ ⟨~ power⟩ — see LORD TEMPORAL **2 a :** of or relating to the quantity of syllables (as in Greek and Latin verse) **b :** of or relating to grammatical tense **:** expressive of a distinction of time **3 :** of or relating to time as distinguished from space or to a particular time **:** CHRONOLOGICAL ⟨music is a ~ art —Hunter Mead⟩ ⟨all the external events of which we are aware are recorded as spatial and ~ patterns of excitation in the sense organs —E.D.Adrian⟩ **syn** see PROFANE

2temporal \\"\\ *n* -S [ME, fr. *temporal,* adj.] **:** something temporal, secular, or material **:** TEMPORALITY — usu. used in pl. ⟨its ~*s* provided the church's revenue⟩

3temporal \\"\\ *n* -S [MF, fr. *temporal,* adj.] **:** a temporal part (as a bone, muscle, or scale)

4temporal \\"\\ *adj* [MF, fr. LL *temporalis,* fr. L *tempor-, tempus* temple (of the head) + *-alis* -al — more at TEMPLE] **1 :** of or relating to the temples or the sides of the skull behind the orbits **2 :** of or relating to the temporal bone **3** *of a scale of a reptile* **:** lying behind the postoculars and between the parietals and supralabials

temporal arch *n* [4*temporal*] **:** a bony bar extending from the upper jaw to the quadrate in some turtles

temporal artery *n* [4*temporal*] **:** any of several arteries supplying the sides of the head: **a :** any of the branches of the internal maxillary artery that supplies the temporal muscle — called also *deep temporal artery* **b :** SUPERFICIAL TEMPORAL ARTERY **c :** any of three branches of the superficial temporal artery — called also respectively *anterior temporal artery, middle temporal artery, posterior temporal artery*

temporal augment *n* [1*temporal*] **:** the lengthening of an initial vowel in past tenses of Greek and Sanskrit verbs

temporal bone *n* [4*temporal*] **:** a compound bone of the side of the human skull whose four principal parts are the squamous, petrous, and tympanic portions and the mastoid process

temporal convolution *or* **temporal gyrus** *n* [4*temporal*] **:** any of three major convolutions of the external surface of the temporal lobe of the cerebrum that are ordered approximately horizontally as a superior, a middle, and an inferior convolution

tem·po·ra·le \\,tempə'rā(,)lē\\ *n* -S [ML, fr. L, neut. of *temporalis* temporal (of time) — more at TEMPORAL] **:** a part of the breviary and missal that contains the daily offices of the ecclesiastical year — compare SANCTORALE

temporal fascia *n* [4*temporal*] **:** a broad fascia covering the temporal muscle and attached below to the zygomatic arch

temporal fossa *n* [4*temporal*] **:** one of the broad fossae on the sides of the skull of higher vertebrates behind the orbit lodging muscles for raising the lower jaw that in man is separated from the orbit by the zygomatic bone and greater wing of the sphenoid lying mostly above the zygomatic arch and is occupied by the temporal muscle

tem·po·ral·is \\,tempə'raləs, -'rāl-, -'räl-\\ *n* -ES [NL, fr. LL, temporal (of the temple) — more at TEMPORAL] **:** TEMPORAL MUSCLE

tem·po·ral·ism \\'temp(ə)rə,lizəm\\ *n* -S [1*temporal* + *-ism*] **:** a philosophical doctrine that emphasizes the ultimate reality of time and temporal things as contrasted with doctrines which reduce the temporal to a manifestation of the eternal — compare ETERNALISM

tem·po·ral·ist \\-ləst\\ *n* -S [1*temporal* + *-ist*] **1 :** an adherent of the doctrine of temporalism **2 :** one who emphasizes the temporal element in analyzing the rhythmic structures of verse

tem·po·ral·is·tic \\¦temp(ə)rə¦listik\\ *adj* **:** of or relating to temporalism or temporalists

tem·po·ral·i·ty \\,tempə'raləd·ē, -lətē, -i\\ *n* -ES [in sense 1, fr. ME *temporalite,* fr. ML *temporalitas,* fr. *temporalis* temporal (secular) + L *-itas* -ity; in sense 2, fr. LL *temporalitas,* fr. L *temporalis* temporal (of time) + *-itas* -ity — more at TEMPORAL] **1 a :** civil or political as distinguished from spiritual or ecclesiastical power or authority **b :** ecclesiastical properties or revenues — often used in pl. **2 a :** temporary or transitory quality **:** relation to time and the world rather than to eternity, transcendence, or spirit ⟨we cannot afford to be too self-conscious about the ~ of our attitudes —H.J.Muller⟩ **b :** concern with time, process, and overt mundane events as more real or significant than timeless or eternal forms, structures, or patterns (as ideas or institutions) **:** emphasis on change rather than permanence **c :** position, extension, or duration in time — distinguished from *spatiality*

tem·po·ral·ize \\'temp(ə)rə,līz\\ *vt* -ED/-ING/-S [1*temporal* + *-ize*] **1 :** to place or define in time relations **2 :** SECULARIZE

temporal lobe *n* [4*temporal*] **:** a large lobe of each cerebral hemisphere situated below the lateral fissure and in front of the occipital lobe and containing the middle cornu of the lateral ventricle

tem·po·ral·ly \\-rəlē, -li\\ *adv* [ME, fr. 1*temporal* + *-ly*] **1 :** in regard to or with concern for temporal things **:** in earthly life **2 :** with regard to time

temporal muscle *n* [4*temporal*] **:** a large muscle in the temporal fossa serving to raise the lower jaw and in man being composed of fibers that arise from the surface of the temporal fossa and converge to an aponeurosis which contracts into a thick flat tendon inserted into the coronoid process of the mandible

temporal nerve *n* [4*temporal*] **:** any of several nerves derived from the facial and mandibular nerves and supplying the structures of the temporal region

tem·po·ral·ness *n* -ES [1*temporal* + *-ness*] **:** the quality or state of being temporal

temporal pattern *n* [1*temporal*] **:** the unitary impression produced by a succession of stimuli (as in a melody or rhythm)

temporal punishment *n* **:** a punishment for sin that according to Roman Catholic doctrine may be expiated in this world or if not sufficiently expiated here will be exacted in full in purgatory

temporal ridge *or* **temporal line** *n* [4*temporal*] **:** any of four nearly parallel curved ridges or lines situated two on each side of the skull and chiefly on the parietal bone

temporals *pl of* TEMPORAL

temporal sign *n* [1*temporal*] **:** an indicator of the position or relations in time of something perceived

temporal sulcus *n* [4*temporal*] **:** any of the sulci between temporal convolutions

tem·po·ral·ty \\'temp(ə)rəltē, -ti\\ *n* -ES [ME *temporalte,* fr. MF *temporalité,* fr. ML *temporalitat-, temporalitas* — more at TEMPORALITY] **1 a** *obs* **:** TEMPORALITY 1a **b :** TEMPORALITY 1b **2 :** lay persons (as lords temporal and commons) **:** LAITY — distinguished from *spirituality*

temporal vein *n* [4*temporal*] **:** any of several veins draining the temporal region: as **a :** a large vein on each side of the head formed by anterior and posterior tributaries from the scalp and adjacent parts receiving a middle tributary from the temporal muscle and uniting with the internal maxillary vein to form the posterior facial vein — called also *superficial temporal vein* **b :** one of the veins arising from behind the temporal muscle and emptying into the pterygoid plexus — called also *deep temporal vein*

tem·po·rar·i·ly \\¦tempə¦rerəlē, -li\\ *adv* **1 :** for a brief period **:** during a limited time **:** BRIEFLY ⟨a power failure ~ darkened the town⟩ **2 :** in time **:** in relation to time **:** TEMPORALLY ⟨a ~ punctiform occurrence . . . must necessarily be counted as one event —H.A.C.Dobbs⟩

tem·po·rar·i·ness \\'==,rerēnəs, -,rerin-\\ *n* -ES **:** the quality or state of being temporary

1tem·po·rary \\-,rerē, -reri\\ *adj* [L *temporarius,* fr. *tempor-, tempus* period of time, fitting time, season, time (in general) + *-arius* -ary — more at TEMPORAL] **1 a :** lasting for a time only **:** existing or continuing for a limited time **:** IMPERMANENT, TRANSITORY ⟨insisted on the entirely ~ quality of any victory over nature —David Riesman⟩ **b** *obs* **:** bearing the marks of a particular time **:** deriving interest from or having relation to a restricted period or special era **:** DATED, EPHEMERAL — distinguished from *universal* **2** *obs* **a :** of or relating to man's present life on earth **:** MUNDANE, TEMPORAL **b :** occurring in or related to time rather than eternity

2temporary \\"\\ *n* -ES **:** someone or something serving for a limited time only ⟨the others were *temporaries* like me —Tom Weir⟩ ⟨the wartime *temporaries* . . . will be replaced by 75 permanent homes —*Springfield* (*Mass.*) *Union*⟩

temporary alimony *n* **:** ALIMONY PENDENTE LITE

temporary annuity *n* **:** an annuity payable for a limited time only; *usu* **:** TEMPORARY LIFE ANNUITY

temporary chairman *n* **:** the chairman chosen by the national committee of a political party to preside at the opening of a national convention
temporary duty *n* **:** military service away from one's assigned organization usu. for a limited period of time
temporary hardness *n* **:** the portion of the total hardness of water that is removable by boiling whereby the soluble bicarbonates of calcium and magnesium are converted into the corresponding insoluble carbonates and are precipitated — distinguished from *permanent hardness*
temporary life annuity *n* **:** an annuity payable for a life not extending beyond a specified date
temporary partial disability *n* **:** disability resulting from an injury that temporarily impairs a worker's earning capacity
temporary star *n* **:** NOVA
temporary total disability *n* **:** disability resulting from an injury that temporarily destroys a worker's earning capacity
temporary wilting *n* **:** wilting from which a plant will recover by reduction of the transpiration rate and without addition of water to the soil
tem·po·ri·za·tion \ˌtempərəˈzāshən, -pəˌrī-\ *n* -s **:** the act, policy, or practice of temporizing
tem·po·rize \ˈtempəˌrīz\ *vb* -ED/-ING/-s *see -ize in Explan Notes* [MF *temporiser,* fr. ML *temporizare* to pass the time, fr. L *tempor-, tempus* time + *-izare* -ize — more at TEMPORAL] *vi* **1 :** to act to suit the time or occasion **:** adapt to a situation **:** bow to practical necessities **2 :** to make terms or work out a compromise with someone or between parties **3 :** to draw out discussions or negotiations so as to gain time **:** put off decisive action ⟨you'd have to ~ until you found out how she wanted to be advised —Mary Austin⟩ **~** *vt* **:** EXTEMPORIZE
tem·po·riz·er \-zə(r)\ *n* -s **:** one that temporizes **:** TRIMMER, TIMESERVER
tem·po·riz·ing·ly *adv* **:** in a temporizing manner
temporo- *comb form* [⁴*temporal*] **:** temporal and ⟨*temporo*maxillary⟩ ⟨*temporo*frontal⟩
tem·po·ro·mandibular \ˌtempə(ˌ)rō+\ *adj* [*temporo-* + *mandibular*] **:** relating to or joining the temporal bone and the mandible
tem·po·ro·maxillary \"+\ *adj* [*temporo-* + *maxillary*] **:** relating to or situated in the region of the temporal bone or area and the upper jaw
tem·po·ro·spatial \"+\ *adj* [*temporo-* + *spatial*] **:** of, relating to, or occurring in both time and space
tempos *pl of* TEMPO
tempo turn *n* **:** a parallel-ski turn of wide radius executed without breaking speed — called also *high-speed turn, parallel turn, tail-wagging*
¹**temps** \ˈtäⁿ\ *n, pl* **temps** \"\ [F, lit., time, fr. L *tempus* — more at TEMPORAL] **:** a ballet movement or part of a step without change of weight
²**temps** *pl of* TEMP
tempt \ˈtem(p)t\ *vt* -ED/-ING/-s [ME *tempten,* fr. OF *tempter, tenter,* fr. L *temptare, tentare* to touch, feel, attack, attempt, urge, excite, tempt; *temptare* akin to L *tempus* time; *tentare* fr. *tentus,* past part. of *tendere* to stretch, strive, try — more at TEMPORAL, THIN] **1 :** to entice to do wrong by promise of pleasure or gain **:** allure into evil **:** SEDUCE **2 a** *obs* **:** to put to the test **:** make trial of **:** PROVE ⟨God did ~ Abraham —Gen 22:1 (AV)⟩ **b :** to make presumptuous trial of **:** PROVOKE ⟨you have agreed together to ~ the Spirit of the Lord —Acts 5:9 (RSV)⟩ ⟨*~ed* Providence by driving at excessive speed⟩ **c :** to risk the disfavor of (fate or fortune) **:** incur the chance of loss or injury from (adverse fortune) **3 :** to induce to do something **:** attract or allure to an act **:** INCITE, PERSUADE, PROMPT ⟨laughter that I should be *~ed* to call ironic —E.K. Brown⟩ ⟨*~s* him to forget the obvious —A.L.Kroeber⟩ ⟨*~ed* thousands of new commuters into the state —*Amer. Guide Series: N. J.*⟩ ⟨*~ed* the young man into kissing her —Sherwood Anderson⟩ **4 :** to venture on **:** risk the dangers of ⟨*~ed* the hardships of a strange land⟩ **syn** see LURE
tempt·able \-təbəl\ *adj* **:** capable of being tempted
temp·ta·tion \tem(p)ˈtāshən\ *n* -s [ME *temptacioun,* fr. OF *temptation, tentation,* fr. LL *temptation-, temptatio, tentation-, tentatio,* fr. L *temptatus, tentatus* (past part. of *temptare, tentare*) + *-ion-, -io* -ion] **1 a :** the act of tempting or the state of being tempted esp. to evil **:** ALLUREMENT, ENTICEMENT, SEDUCTION ⟨it is a ~ to abandon hopes of which the realization seems distant and difficult —Bertrand Russell⟩ **b :** something tempting **:** a cause or occasion of enticement ⟨view it, and lay the bright ~ down —John Dryden⟩ **2 :** TESTING, TRIAL **3** *obs* **:** a severely trying experience **:** a painful affliction
temp·ta·tion·al \(ˈ)tem(p)¦tāshən³l\ *adj* **:** of, relating to, or offering temptation **:** ALLURING
tempt·er \ˈtem(p)tə(r)\ *n* -s [ME, fr. *tempten* to tempt + *-er*] **1 :** one that tempts or entices **2** *often cap* **:** DEVIL 1 ⟨when he was on his knees, the *Tempter* would come —R.H.Bainton⟩
tempting *adj* [ME, fr. pres. part. of *tempten* to tempt] **:** ALLURING, ENTICING — **tempt·ing·ly** *adv* — **tempt·ing·ness** *n* -ES
tempt·ress \-trəs\ *n* -ES **:** a female tempter
tem·pu·ra \ˌtempəˈrä\ *n* -s [Jap, fried food] **:** fritters of sea food and vegetables fried in deep fat
tem·pus \ˈtempəs\ *n, pl* **tempo·ra** \-pərə\ [L, time — more at TEMPORAL] **:** the unit of time in mensural music
tem·pus de·li·be·ran·di \ˈtempəsdəˌlibəˈrandē, -nˌdī\ *n* [L, time for deliberating] *Roman, civil, & Scots law* **:** the time formerly permitted to an heir to decide whether to accept an inheritance — compare JUS DELIBERANDI
TEMs *pl of* TEM
¹**temse** \ˈtemz\ *n* -s [ME *temse,* fr. OE *temes;* akin to MLG *tēmes, tēmse* sieve, MD *teems,* G dial *zims* sieve, OHG *zimissa* bran] *dial chiefly Brit* **:** SIEVE
²**temse** \"\ *vb* -ED/-ING/-s [ME *temsen,* fr. OE *temsian, temesian,* fr. *temes,* n.] *dial chiefly Brit* **:** SIFT
temsebread \ˈ⸗,⸗\ *n, dial Eng* **:** bread made of sifted flour
¹**ten** \ˈten\ *adj* [ME, fr. OE *tien, tӯn, tēn;* akin to OHG *zehan* ten, ON *tīu,* Goth *taihun,* L *decem,* Gk *deka,* Skt *daśa*] **:** being one more than nine in number ⟨~ years⟩ — see NUMBER table
²**ten** \"\ *pron, pl in constr* [ME *tene, ten,* fr. OE *tīene, tӯne tēne,* pl. *tien, tӯn, tēn,* adj.] **:** ten countable persons or things not specified but under consideration and being enumerated ⟨~ are here⟩ ⟨~ were found⟩
³**ten** \"\ *n* -s [ME *tene, ten,* fr. OE *tīene, tӯne, tēne,* fr. *tīene, tӯne tēne,* pron.] **1 :** twice five **:** five times two **2 a :** ten units or objects ⟨a total of ~⟩ **b :** a group or set of ten ⟨arranged by *~s*⟩ **3 a :** the numerable quantity symbolized by the arabic numerals 10 **b :** the letter X **4 :** 10 o'clock — compare BELL table, TIME illustration **5 :** the tenth in a set or series: as **a :** a playing card marked to show that it is tenth in a suit **b :** an article of clothing of the tenth size ⟨wears a ~⟩ **6 :** something having as an essential feature ten units or members **7 a :** a ten-shilling note **b :** a ten-pound note **c :** a ten-dollar bill **8 :** the number occupying the position two to the left of the decimal point in the arabic notation (as 6 in the number 2968) — usu. used in pl. **9 a :** a short rest period (as of ten minutes) **:** BREAK ⟨the captain halted the company and ordered them to take ~⟩
ten *abbr* **1** tenement **2** tenor **3** tenuto
ten'a \ˈtenə\ *n, pl* **ten'a** *usu cap* **:** KOYUKON
ten·a·bil·i·ty \ˌtenəˈbilәd·ē *chiefly Brit* -ətē, *also* ˌtēn-, -i\ *n* **:** the quality or state of being tenable
ten·a·ble \ˈtenəbəl *chiefly Brit also* ˈtēn-\ *adj* [F, capable of being held, fr. OF, fr. *tenir* to hold (fr. L *tenēre*) + *-able* — more at THIN] **1 a :** capable of being defended against attack **:** DEFENSIBLE ⟨their position was no longer ~ and they retreated to the main line of defense⟩ **b :** capable of being maintained against argument or objection **:** REASONABLE ⟨a ~ assumption⟩ ⟨a ~ theory⟩ ⟨a ~ guess⟩ **2** *archaic* **:** capable of being retained or kept under control ⟨if you have hitherto concealed this sight, let it be ~ in your silence still —Shak.⟩ **3 :** capable of being occupied or used ⟨has been appointed . . . to the chair of public health, ~ at the London School of Hygiene and Tropical Medicine —*Science*⟩ ⟨the scholarships will be ~ for a full, four-year college course —*College English*⟩ — **ten·a·ble·ness** \-bəlnəs\ *n* -ES — **ten·a·bly** \-blē, -li\ *adv*
ten·ace \ˈteˌnās, teˈnās, ˈtenəs\ *n* -s [modif. (influenced by F *tenace* tenacious, fr. L *tenac-, tenax*) of Sp *tenaza,* lit., forceps, pincers, prob. fr. L *tenacia,* neut. pl. of *tenac-, tenax* tenacious] **:** a combination in one hand in bridge and other card games of two high or relatively high cards once separated in rank (as ace and queen) with an opponent holding the intervening card — see MAJOR TENACE, MINOR TENACE
te·na·cious \təˈnāshəs *also* teˈn-\ *adj* [L *tenac-, tenax* tending to hold fast (fr. *tenēre* to hold) + E *-ious* — more at THIN] **1 a :** having parts or elements strongly adhering to each other **:** not easily pulled apart **:** COHESIVE, TOUGH ⟨her ships provided a slender, but very ~, link between East and West —R.W. Southern⟩ ⟨a ~ metal⟩ **b :** tending to adhere to another substance **:** ADHESIVE, STICKY, VISCOUS ⟨slippers stuck fast in the ~ yellow clay and were nearly dragged off my feet —Mary S. Broome⟩ ⟨~ sputum⟩ **2 a :** holding fast or tending to hold fast **:** persistent in maintaining or adhering to something valued or habitual (as an opinion, purpose, way of life) ⟨a mind not gifted to discover truth but ~ to hold it —T.S. Eliot⟩ ⟨here . . . men are slow of speech, ~ of opinion, and averse . . . to innovation of any sort —C.B.Nordhoff & J.N. Hall⟩ **b :** RETENTIVE ⟨combined an encyclopedic knowledge with a ~ memory —C.M.Fuess⟩ **3 :** not yielding **:** OBSTINATE, STUBBORN ⟨men are more ~ dieters than women —*Newsweek*⟩ ⟨the transition to a new theory is seldom easy; old ideas are apt to be ~ —J.B.Conant⟩ **syn** see STRONG
te·na·cious·ly *adv* **:** in a tenacious manner
te·na·cious·ness *n* -ES **:** the quality or state of being tenacious **:** TENACITY
te·nac·i·ty \⸗ˈnasəd·ē, -ətē, -i\ *n* -ES [L *tenacitat-, tenacitas,* fr. *tenac-, tenax* tenacious + *-itat-, -itas* -ity] **1 a :** the quality or state of holding fast **:** DETERMINATION, FIRMNESS, PERSISTENCE ⟨the stubborn ~ with which its landowners have clung to their homes —*Amer. Guide Series: La.*⟩ ⟨maintained this conviction with a fearless ~ —Russell Kirk⟩ **b :** PERSISTENCY, RETENTIVENESS ⟨~ of memory⟩ ⟨the chief distinguishing feature is their ~ of life —C.R.A.Martin⟩ **2 a :** the quality or state of being cohesive **:** tensile strength **:** COHESIVENESS: as (1) **:** resistance of a mineral to deformation (as breaking, crushing, bending) (2) **:** resistance of a textile fiber, filament, or yarn to strain or breaks **:** BREAKING STRENGTH **b :** ADHESIVENESS, GLUTINOUSNESS ⟨clay of the most extraordinary ~ —O.S.Nock⟩ **syn** see COURAGE
ten·a·cle \ˈtenəkəl\ *n* -s [LL *tenaculum* instrument for holding] **1** *obs* **:** a stalk of a plant **2 tenacles** *pl* **:** the tentacles by which some plants (as ivies) attach themselves in climbing
te·nac·u·lum \təˈnakyələm\ *n, pl* **tenacu·la** \-lə\ *or* **tenaculums** [NL, fr. LL, instrument for holding, fr. L *tenēre* to hold + *-aculum,* suffix denoting instrument] **1 :** a slender sharp-pointed hook attached to a handle and used mainly in surgery for seizing and holding parts (as arteries) **2 :** an adhesive structure: as **a :** a pair of partially fused appendages on the third abdominal segment of a collembolan which holds the furcula in place **b :** the claspers of a shark or a chimaera

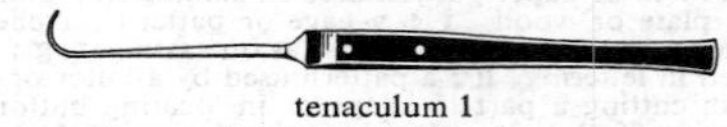

tenaculum 1

te·naille \təˈnā(y)əl, -nī\ *n* -s [MF, lit., forceps, pincers, fr. LL *tenacula,* pl. of *tenaculum* instrument for holding] **:** an outwork in the main ditch between two bastions of a fortification
te·nail·lon \tənālyōⁿ\ *n, pl* **tenaillons** \-ōⁿ(z)\ [F, fr. *tenaille*] **:** a work constructed on each side of a ravelin to increase its strength, procure additional ground beyond the ditch, or cover the shoulders of the bastions
te·na·im *or* **tna·im** \təˈnä(y)əm, -ēm; təˌnäˈēm\ *also* **tnoy·im** \təˈnȯi(y)əm, -ēm\ *n pl but sing or pl in constr* [Yiddish *tnoyim,* fr. LHeb *tĕnā'īm,* fr. pl. of *tĕnā'ī* agreement] **1 :** formal prenuptial conditions or agreement made at a Jewish betrothal ceremony **2 :** a Jewish social function announcing an engagement
ten·an·cy \ˈtenənsē, -si\ *n* -ES [*tenant* + *-cy*] **1 a :** a holding of an estate or a mode of holding an estate **:** the temporary possession of something that belongs to another **:** TENURE; *specif* **:** a temporary occupancy (as of land, a house, an office) usu. for a specified period under the terms of a lease **b :** the period of a tenant's occupancy or possession **2 :** the possession or occupation of a position or place ⟨the ~ of a university lectureship —Yakov Malkiel⟩ ⟨a minuscule jail now in ~ of spiders —Idwal Jones⟩
tenancy at sufferance : a tenancy that arises in an estate when a tenant under a lawful demise holds over after his estate is ended — compare ESTATE AT SUFFERANCE
tenancy at will : a tenancy of an estate that is terminable at the will of either party and that may be created by oral declaration or by deed — compare ESTATE AT WILL
tenancy by the entirety *or* **tenancy by entireties :** a tenancy in which husband and wife are seized of the whole estate but without power of severing — compare JOINT TENANCY
tenancy by the rod *or* **tenancy by the verge :** COPYHOLD
tenancy from year to year : a tenancy in which the property is held for a year and upon the condition that the tenancy cannot be determined by either party alone except at the end of any number of entire years from the time of its beginning
tenancy in common : the tenancy of those who hold lands or other property in common — compare JOINT TENANCY
¹**ten·ant** \ˈtenənt\ *n* -s [ME *tenaunt, tenant,* fr. MF *tenant,* fr. pres. part. of *tenir* to hold — more at TENABLE] **1 a :** one who holds or possesses real estate or sometimes personal property (as an annuity) by any kind of right (as in fee simple, in common, in severalty, for life, for years, or at will) **b :** one who has the occupation or temporary possession of lands or tenements the title of which is in another; *specif* **:** one who rents or leases (as land or a house) from a landlord **2 :** one that has possession of a place **:** DWELLER, INHABITANT, OCCUPANT ⟨it is the *~s* of this upper gallery who . . . make all the noise and uproar —Eugene Burr⟩ ⟨grass is the best possible ~ for our far-spread domain of retired and resting lands —C.E.Wilson⟩
²**tenant** \"\ *vb* -ED/-ING/-s *vt* **:** to hold, occupy, or possess as a tenant **:** INHABIT ⟨won some measure of relief by being allowed to ~ the bogs —*Irish Digest*⟩ ⟨broad and pleasant meadow . . . *~ed* by the summer camps of the shepherds —Douglas Carruthers⟩ **~** *vi* **:** to occupy a place as a tenant
ten·ant·able \-təbəl\ *adj* **:** capable of being tenanted
tenant at sufferance : one who has a tenancy at sufferance
tenant at will : one who has a tenancy at will
tenant by copy of court roll *or* **tenant by the verge :** COPYHOLDER
tenant by curtesy initiate : a husband who holds a potential interest in an estate by curtesy initiate
tenant by the entirety : one who has a tenancy by the entirety
tenant farmer *n* **:** a farmer who works land owned by another and pays rent either in cash or in shares of produce — compare MÉTAYER
tenant hair *var of* TENENT HAIR
tenant in capite *or* **tenant in chief :** a feudal tenant holding immediately of his lord and esp. of the crown
tenant in common : one who has a tenancy in common
tenant·less \ˈ⸗⸗ləs\ *adj* **:** having no tenants **:** UNOCCUPIED, UNTENANTED
tenantlike \ˈ⸗⸗,⸗\ *adj* [¹*tenant* + *like*] **:** conforming to the rights and obligations of a tenant
tenant right *n, Brit* **:** the beneficial interest that remains in the tenant after the expiration of his lease and that includes various legal and customary rights (as the right to claim compensation for improvements not exhausted at the expiration of the lease, the right to claim fixity of tenure on condition of paying the former rent or some rent not arbitrarily fixed by the landlord)
ten·ant·ry \ˈtenəntrē, -ri\ *n* -ES [ME, fr. ¹*tenant* + *-ry*] **1 :** property rented out to tenants ⟨made . . . a neat village of brick buildings . . . for his own appropriate little ~ with rents at a guinea a year —G.E.Fussell⟩ **2 a :** the condition or state of occupying as a tenant **:** TENANCY ⟨ended his ~ of the estate⟩ **b :** the condition, state, or system of being occupied by a tenant ⟨survey his . . . lands for ~ —J.C.Fitzpatrick⟩ **3 :** the body of tenants ⟨urban mechanics and laborers, the ~ of New York —S.E.Morison & H.S.Commager⟩ ⟨the empty shacks perched upon them rot and tumble about their ~ of field rats and spiders —Edward Kimbrough⟩
tenant·ship \ˈ⸗⸗,ship\ *n* [¹*tenant* + *-ship*] **:** TENANCY
ten–cent \(ˈ)⸗¦⸗\ *adj* [*ten* + *cent*] **:** CHEAP, CONTEMPTIBLE, SORRY ⟨what a cheap, insecure, *ten-cent* snob —Hamilton Basso⟩
ten–cent store *n* [*ten* + *cent* + *store*] **:** FIVE-AND-TEN
tench \ˈtench\ *n, pl* **tench** *or* **tenches** [ME, fr. MF *tenche,* fr. LL *tinca*] **:** a European and western Asiatic freshwater cyprinoid fish (*Tinca tinca*) that is related to the dace and ide, is noted for its ability to survive for some time outside its normal watery environment, sometimes approaches a weight of eight pounds, and is a locally important table fish
¹**tend** \ˈtend\ *vb* -ED/-ING/-s [ME *tenden,* short for *attenden* to attend] *vi* **1** *archaic* **:** to give ear **:** LISTEN ⟨~ to the master's whistle —Shak.⟩ **2 :** to pay attention **:** apply oneself ⟨you mind your business, and I'll ~ to mine —Evelyn Barkins⟩ **3 :** to act as an attendant or servant **:** SERVE, WAIT ⟨never closed an eye watching and *~ing* in his house —Walter Macken⟩ **4** *obs* **:** to be waiting **:** AWAIT ⟨the time invites you, go, your servants ~ —Shak.⟩ **~** *vt* **1** *archaic* **:** to attend as a servant **:** accompany in order to render service ⟨had I not four or five women once that *~ed* me —Shak.⟩ **2** *chiefly dial* **:** to be present at **:** ATTEND **3 a :** to apply oneself to the care of **:** care for the wants of **:** minister to **:** watch over ⟨*~ed* him and ministered to his wants like an angel —C.B.Fairbanks⟩ ⟨*~ing* the destitute mothers and children —Winston Churchill⟩ **b :** to have or take charge of as a caretaker or overseer ⟨a likely little citizen who . . . *~s* the family sheep —Irene Smith⟩ **c :** CULTIVATE, FOSTER ⟨rice which has been specially planted and *~ed* —J.G.Frazer⟩ **d :** to manage the operations of or do the necessary work connected with **:** MIND ⟨*~ed* his textile mills —T.D.Parrish⟩ ⟨quit to ~ an open hearth —*Time*⟩ ⟨~ store⟩ ⟨~ bar⟩ ⟨~ the fire⟩ **4** *archaic* **:** be attentive to **:** listen to ⟨the stars that ~ thy bidding —John Keats⟩ — **tend out on** *dial* **:** to attend on or attend to
²**tend** \"\ *vi* -ED/-ING/-s [ME *tenden,* short for *intenden, entenden* to intend] *dial* **:** INTEND, PURPOSE
³**tend** \"\ *vb* -ED/-ING/-s [ME *tenden,* fr. MF *tendre* to stretch, stretch out, direct oneself toward a place, tend, fr. L *tendere* — more at THIN] *vi* **1 a :** to direct one's course or become moved in a particular direction ⟨saw far in the north the misty outlines of the shore towards which they were *~ing* —William Black⟩ **b :** to undergo change or development in a particular direction or toward a particular goal ⟨the ideal toward which evolution continually *~ed* —Roscoe Pound⟩ ⟨the symptoms — where they were *~ing,* where they were bound to end — disturbed him —J.G.Cozzens⟩ **c :** to extend in a certain direction ⟨the foot of each sail is *~ing* aft at quite an angle —*All Hands*⟩ **2 a :** to have an inclination to a particular quality, aspect, or state ⟨modern hive design *~s* to simplicity —F.D.Smith & Barbara Wilcox⟩ ⟨many marine invertebrates ~ towards transparency or a bluish coloration —W.H.Dowdeswell⟩ **b :** to have an inclination toward a particular belief, feeling, or attitude ⟨he *~s* to deny the moral content in human affairs —Norman Cousins⟩ ⟨painters ~ to rejoice in the commonplace —David Sylvester⟩ **3 :** to exert activity or influence in a particular direction **:** serve as a means **:** CONDUCE ⟨the reduction of reserve requirements will ~ to ease business borrowing —*Nation's Business*⟩ ⟨not true that any advance in the scale of culture inevitably *~s* to the preservation of society —A.N.Whitehead⟩ **4** *of a ship* **:** to swing with the tide or wind while anchored **~** *vt* **1 :** to manage (an anchored vessel) so as to prevent fouling of the cable **2 :** to stand by (as a rope) in readiness to prevent fouling or other mischance ⟨has a lifeline round him which is *~ed* inboard —*Manual of Seamanship*⟩
⁴**tend** \"\ *n* -s **:** the angle made by the line of a ship's keel and the direction of the anchor cable when the ship is swinging at anchor ⟨signaling with a flashlight the ~ of the chain to the bridge —Chesley Wilson⟩
ten–dai \ˈten¦dī\ *n* -s *cap* [Jap, fr. Chin (Pek) *t'ien¹ t'ai²* t'ien t'ai, fr. *T'ien¹ T'ai²,* mountain in Chekiang province, eastern China, where the doctrine was first formulated] **:** a Japanese Buddhist sect founded in the 9th century A.D. by Dengyo Daishi that is the doctrinal equivalent of the Chinese T'ien T'ai sect
tend·ance \ˈtendən(t)s\ *n* -s [short for *attendance*] **1 a :** the act of looking after someone or something **:** the giving of attention **:** watchful care **:** MINISTRATION ⟨fidelity and patience and unselfish ~ gently rendered by a domestic angel —A.C. Benson⟩ **b :** service done to gain favor **:** service or homage to the gods for divine favor ⟨needs and values associated with rites of ~ —H.E.Barnes & H.P.Becker⟩ **2** *archaic* **:** persons in attendance **:** RETINUE
tend·ant \-dənt\ *adj* [by shortening] *archaic* **:** ATTENDANT
ten–day fern *n* **:** a widely distributed tropical fern (*Polystichum adiantiforme*) in which the ultimate pinnae of the large fronds resemble those of the maidenhair
tend·ence \-dən(t)s\ *n* -s [ML *tendentia*] **:** TENDENCY ⟨the sedan developed a ~ to overheat —N.F.Busch⟩
tendencious *var of* TENDENTIOUS
tend·en·cy \ˈtendənsē, -si\ *n* -ES [ML *tendentia,* fr. L *tendent-, tendens* (pres. part. of *tendere* to tend) + *-ia* -y] **1 a :** direction or course toward a place, object, effect, or result **:** BIAS, INCLINATION ⟨regarded political economy as a science of *tendencies* only —R.H.Hutton⟩ ⟨that ~ in art which has been called abstract —Herbert Read⟩ **b :** a proneness to or readiness for a particular kind of thought or action **:** DRIVE, PROPENSITY, SET ⟨disliked the ~ of amateur diplomats to burst into print —H.G.Dwight⟩ ⟨my instinctive ~ has always been to temperance —Havelock Ellis⟩ **c :** a presumptive course of future behavior in continuation of observed acts and attitudes **2 a :** the designed and purposeful trend of something written or said **:** AIM ⟨an evident ~ on the part of the writers to enlarge on the blessings of nature —R.H.Brown⟩ **b :** deliberate but indirect advocacy (as in speech or writing) of a particular point of view ⟨a policy at once plausible and insidious, temporizing and yet thick with ~ —Francis Hackett⟩
syn TENDENCY, TREND, DRIFT, TENOR, CURRENT can mean a movement in a particular direction or of a particular character or the direction or character of such a movement. TENDENCY usu. implies an inherent or acquired inclination to move in a given direction, literally or figuratively, sometimes suggesting something opposable and alterable with great difficulty in the long run ⟨the whole *tendency* of evolution is towards a diminishing birthrate —Havelock Ellis⟩ ⟨a *tendency* toward lower prices for some equipment —*Nation's Business*⟩ ⟨the revolutionary oil is designed to decrease the *tendency* of engines to knock —*Report: Union Oil Co. of Calif.*⟩ ⟨has not escaped that *tendency* to violence —G.B.Shaw⟩ ⟨the *tendency* to moralize —Bliss Perry⟩ TREND is a general direction maintained despite minor deviations, differing from TENDENCY in usu. implying a direction more subject to change ⟨by *trend* is meant a persistent general movement in the direction of some distant goal as yet undefined or only vaguely held —C.A.Dawson & W.E. Gettys⟩ ⟨the national *trend* toward corporate control and mass production —*Amer. Guide Series: Ind.*⟩ ⟨a *trend* toward a favorable balance of trade —R.E.Scott⟩ ⟨the *trend* of his mind was historical —H.N.Fowler⟩ DRIFT adds to TREND the idea of a slowness and seeming indirection, often a meandering or uncertain quality, often a direction the objective of which is not overt or obvious to a quick view ⟨a more general process of internal migration that involved both regional shifts and a *drift* to the cities —Oscar Handlin⟩ ⟨vigorous protest against the *drift* toward revolution —H.J.Thornton⟩ ⟨saw the *drift* of the fellow's intentions —Rafael Sabatini⟩ ⟨the *drift* and meaning of the story —Gilbert Parker⟩ TENOR is very close to DRIFT but applies more commonly and specif. to the import of statements or documents and suggests more certainty and clearness ⟨the whole *tenor* of the teaching of Jesus —W.F.Hambly⟩ ⟨the general *tenor* or direction of the talks —Bernard Smith⟩ ⟨one frightening aspect of the *tenor* of the times —V.M.Rogers⟩ CURRENT implies a movement or course more clearly defined and of more distinct identity and some substance ⟨the *current* of opinion and the whole drift of feeling —W.C.Brownell⟩ ⟨the very central *current* of the evolution of medieval Latin poetry —H.O.Taylor⟩ ⟨he has not . . . changed the *current* of our constitutional law —M.R.Cohen⟩
tend·ent \-dənt\ *adj* [alter. (influenced by L *tendent-, tendens,* pres. part. of *tendere* to tend) of earlier *tendant,* fr. ME, fr. MF, pres. part. of *tendre* to tend] **:** DIRECTED, INCLINED

ten·den·tial \ten'denchəl\ *adj* [ML *tendentia* tendency + E *-al*] : TENDENTIOUS — **ten·den·tial·ly** \-chəlē, -li\ *adv*

ten·den·tious *also* **ten·den·cious** \ten'denchəs\ *adj* [ML *tendentia* tendency + E *-ous*] **1** : marked by a tendency in favor of a particular point of view : motivated by an intent to promote a particular cause : BIASED ‹under the cloak of objective reporting the reporter can be as ~ as the writer who openly expresses his own opinion —*Times Lit. Supp.*› **2** : having or conforming to a particular tendency ‹the most recalcitrant, ~, and subtly variable of all animal species —Melville Jacobs & B.J.Stern› — **ten·den·tious·ly** *adv* — **ten·den·tious·ness** *n* -ES

ten·denz \ten'dents\ *n, pl* **tendenz·en** \-ntsən\ [G, lit., tendency, fr. ML *tendentia*] : a dominating point of view or purpose influencing the structure and content of a literary work : BIAS, MESSAGE ‹scarcely a week went by without a new magazine of some unearthly ~ or other appearing on the stands —H.L.Mencken›

1**ten·der** \'tendə(r)\ *adj* -ER/-EST [ME, fr. OF *tendre*, fr. L *tener* tender, young; prob. akin to Sabine *tereno-* soft, Gk *terēn* soft, tender, *teru* weak, delicate, Skt *taruṇa* tender, young] **1 a** : having a soft or yielding texture : easily broken, cut, or damaged : not hard or tough : not resistant : DELICATE, FRAGILE ‹that remarkable ~ limestone which is the island's chief treasure —J.P.O'Donnell› ‹the ruthless flint doth cut my ~ feet —Shak.› ‹its eggs are extremely frail and ~ —Richard Semon› **b** : easily chewed : SUCCULENT ‹small buttered ears of the ~*est* white corn —Mary McCarthy› **c** *of wool* : having a weak staple lacking in tensile strength **2 a** : physically weak : not able to endure hardship ‹they're a thought too young and ~ for the work at hand . . . it's bitter cold up at the front now —Rudyard Kipling› **b** : not fully developed or grown : IMMATURE, YOUNG ‹blight so agreeable a myth in its ~ stage —V.L.Parrington› ‹children of ~ years› **c** : incapable of resisting cold : not hardy ‹as the climate grows more severe toward the interior of the continent, many of the more ~ species drop out —*Boy Scout Handbk.*› **d** *dial chiefly Brit* : in feeble health **3** : marked by, responding to, or expressing the softer emotions : FOND, LOVING ‹the security that goes with a ~ relationship —Abram Kardiner› ‹for the moment she was ~ with regrets —Sherwood Anderson› ‹the sweet things of life, the fastidious and ~ things, the gentle approaches —Richard Church› **4 a** : showing care or thoughtful consideration : careful to keep from harm or injury : SOLICITOUS ‹a ~ and consistent regard for the rights of states —C.A. & Mary Beard› ‹a ~ and far-reaching solicitude could not always save the Egyptian cat from harm —Agnes Repplier› **b** : highly susceptible to impressions or emotions : IMPRESSIONABLE ‹thinking to quiet your ~ conscience with this pitiful stratagem —T.L.Peacock› **c** : showing care to avoid or prevent : CAUTIOUS, WARY ‹did not want to take blame to herself, and was most ~ of throwing any on her husband —Jane Austen› **5 a** : soft in action or movement ‹a ~ wind stirred the water —Elinor Wylie› **b** : appropriate or conducive to a delicate or sensitive constitution or character : not rough, harsh, or severe : GENTLE, MILD ‹~ breeding› ‹~ irony› **c** : delicate or soft in quality or tone ‹looked out on the long and ~ dawn of the flatlands —Meridel Le Sueur› ‹sounds of many contrasting kinds: harsh as well as mellow, brilliant as well as ~ —Robert Donington› **6** *obs* : DEAR, PRECIOUS ‹whose life's as ~ to me as my soul —Shak.› **7 a** : sensitive to the touch ‹a ~ scar› : painful on palpation ‹a ~ palpable kidney› ‹a ~ spleen› **b** : sensitive to injury or insult : easily offended : TOUCHY ‹a peerage was protection for ~ pride —J.M. Barzun› **c** : demanding careful and sensitive handling : TICKLISH ‹they both felt that the situation was extremely ~ and critical —W.M.Thackeray› **d** *of a ship* : inclined to heel over easily under sail : somewhat crank ‹the bricks were not good ballast because they were too light and the boat was very ~ —H.A.Calahan›

syn RESPONSIVE, COMPASSIONATE, SYMPATHETIC, WARM, WARMHEARTED: TENDER may indicate an inclination to gentle emotions like love or kindliness or cherishing, affectionate, or gentle solicitude ‹his mother was very *tender* with him —D.H. Lawrence› ‹a *tender* laugh of benevolence —W.M.Thackeray› RESPONSIVE indicates a ready inclination to respond or react impressionably to others' emotions, esp. warmer ones, or to conditions or circumstances facing one ‹she took up life, and became alert to the world again, *responsive*, like a ship in full sail, to every wind that blew —Rose Macaulay› COMPASSIONATE describes a disposition easily moved to pity, mercy, or tolerance of others ‹one who cherishes the ideal of tolerance may enfold Fascists in the mantle of *compassionate* understanding —H.J.Muller› ‹love was unfailing in *compassionate* word and deed —H.O.Taylor› SYMPATHETIC is somewhat wider than *compassionate* in indicating a disposition to share another's emotions, esp. his sorrows, but also his interests and ways of thought ‹cynicism found no echo in the large and *sympathetic* temper —J.R.Green› ‹the sailors themselves were *sympathetic* . . . but the masters (the hunters and the captain) were heartlessly indifferent —Jack London› ‹a temper so *sympathetic* and responsive was immensely influenced by others as well as inclined to influence them —Gamaliel Bradford› WARM indicates a ready capacity for love, affection, or interest, with more heartiness, cordiality, or fervor, and less softness and gentleness than indicated by TENDER ‹a perfect gentleman, unaffected, *warm*, and obliging —Jane Austen› ‹the *warm* courage of national unity —F.D.Roosevelt› WARMHEARTED may describe a warm personality oriented toward well-wishing, generosity, or sympathy ‹Arizonans are *warmhearted* and hospitable —*Amer. Guide Series: Ariz.*› ‹the idea of sharing poverty and privation in company with the beloved object is . . . far from being disagreeable to a *warmhearted* woman —W.M.Thackeray›

2**tender** \"\ *vb* **tendered; tendered; tendering** \-(ə)riŋ\ **tenders** [ME *tendren*, fr. 1*tender*] *vt* **1** : to make tender : SOFTEN, WEAKEN ‹the ~*ed* areas to which leaks are due —*Manual of Firemanship (Gt. Brit.)*› **2** *archaic* : to regard or treat with tenderness ‹which name I ~ as dearly as my own —Shak.› **3** : to weaken (textile fibers or fabrics) esp. in the process of bleaching, dyeing, or printing ~ *vi* : to become tender ‹the dyed cotton is liable to ~ on prolonged storage —C.M.Whittaker & C.C.Wilcock›

3**tender** *n* -S [1*tender*] *obs* : CONSIDERATION, REGARD

4**tend·er** \'tendə(r)\ *n* -S [ME, fr. *tenden* to tend, attend to + *-er*] : one that tends : one that takes care of a person or thing: as **a** (1) : a ship employed to attend other ships (as to supply them with provisions and other stores, to transport catches of fish to the market) (2) : a boat or small steamer for communication between shore and a larger vessel (3) : a warship that provides logistic support ‹a destroyer ~› ‹seaplane ~› **b** : a vehicle attached to a locomotive for carrying a supply of fuel and water **c** *or* **tender truck** : an auxiliary fire-fighting vehicle; *esp* : one carrying hose and special equipment

5**ten·der** \'tendə(r)\ *vb* **tendered; tendered; tendering** \-d(ə)riŋ\ **tenders** [MF *tendre* to stretch out, offer — more at TEND] *vt* **1** : to offer in payment, satisfaction, or performance of a demand or obligation and in order to save a penalty or forfeiture : make a tender of ‹~ the amount of rent› **2 a** : to present for acceptance : offer freely : PROFFER ‹~*ed* his resignation› ‹~*ed* his advice› ‹~*ed* a banquet to their colleague on retirement› **b** : to offer for sale ‹~ stock› ~ *vi* : to make a tender for a contract : make a bid — often used with *for* ‹contractors who propose ~*ing* for this scheme —*Scotsman*› **syn** see OFFER

6**tender** \"\ *n* -S **1** : an unconditional offer of money to pay a debt or of service to be performed in satisfaction of a debt or obligation that is made in order to save a penalty or forfeiture that would be incurred by nonpayment or nonperformance **2** : an offer or proposal made for acceptance ‹honored him by the ~ of some important appointment —J.D.Hicks›: as **a** : an offer of a bid for a contract ‹became as exhilarated as if his ~ for building a mansion had been accepted —Flora Thompson› **b** : an offering of securities for bidding **c** *Scots law* : an offer of compromise settlement made during litigation **3** : something that may be offered in payment; *specif* : MONEY ‹no State shall . . . make any thing but gold and silver coin a ~ in payment of debts —*U.S.Constitution*›

ten·der·abil·i·ty \,tend(ə)rə'biləd-ē, -ətē, -i\ *n* : the quality or state of being tenderable

ten·der·able \'tend(ə)rəbəl\ *adj* [5*tender* + *-able*] : capable of being tendered; *specif* : of a quality or grade acceptable for delivery in settlement of a futures contract

tender annual *n* [1*tender*] : an annual (as the tomato or squash) not able to withstand cold and injured by the first frost — compare HARDY ANNUAL

ten·der·er \'tend(ə)rə(r)\ *n* -S [5*tender* + *-er*] : one that tenders

tenderest *superlative of* TENDER

tenderfoot \'==,=\ *n, pl* **tenderfeet** *also* **tenderfoots** *often attrib* [1*tender* + *foot*] **1 a** : a newcomer in a comparatively rough or newly settled region; *esp* : one not hardened to frontier or outdoor life **b** : an inexperienced beginner : NEOPHYTE ‹political ~› ‹business ~› **2** : the first rank in the rising scale of ranks in the Boy Scouts of America or the Girl Scouts of America — compare FIRST CLASS, SECOND CLASS

tenderfooted \'==,==\ *adj* [1*tender* + *footed*] : TIMID

tendergreen \'==,=\ *n* [1*tender*] : a mustard (*Brassica perviridis*) prob. of eastern Asiatic origin that is used as a vegetable for its swollen root crown and edible foliage — called also *spinach mustard*

tenderhearted \'==,==\ *adj* [1*tender* + *hearted*] : easily moved to love, pity, or sorrow : susceptible to the softer emotions : COMPASSIONATE, IMPRESSIONABLE ‹a noble ~ creature, who sympathizes with all the human race —W.M.Thackeray› — **tenderheartedly** \'==,===\ *adv* — **tenderheartedness** \'==,===\ *n* -ES

tender-heft·ed \'==,heftəd\ *adj* [1*tender* + *heft* (alter. of *haft* handle) + *-ed*] *archaic* : TENDERHEARTED ‹thy *tender-hefted* nature shall not give thee o'er to harshness —Shak.›

tendering *n* -S [fr. gerund of 2*tender*] : a lessening of the strength of cloth or yarn; *esp* : a weakening caused by acids during manufacture

ten·der·iza·tion \,tendərə'zāshən, -,rī'z-\ *n* -S : the process of tenderizing

ten·der·ize \'==,rīz\ *vt* -ED/-ING/-S [1*tender* + *-ize*] : to make tender; *specif* : to make (meat or meat products) tender by applying any process or substance that breaks down connective tissue without impairment of flavor or nutritive quality

ten·der·iz·er \-zə(r)\ *n* -S : a device or substance that tenderizes — compare PAPAIN

ten·der·ling \'tendə(r)liŋ, -lēŋ\ *n* -S [1*tender* + *-ling*] **1** *archaic* **a** : one who has been coddled : one who is weak or effeminate **b** : a little child **2** : one of the budding antlers of a deer

tenderloin \'==,=\ *n* [1*tender* + *loin*] **1** : a strip of tender meat consisting of the psoas muscle on each side of the vertebral column : a fillet of beef or pork — compare CHATEAUBRIAND, FILET MIGNON, TOURNEDOS **2** [so called fr. its making possible a luxurious diet for a corrupt policeman] : a district of a city largely devoted to vice and other forms of lawbreaking that encourage political or police corruption ‹the dives and shady ~*s* of the underworld —H.E.Barnes & N.K.Teeters›

ten·der·ly *adv* [ME, fr. 1*tender* + *-ly*] : in a tender manner

tender-minded \'==,==\ *adj* [*tender* + *minded*] : tending toward or characterized by idealism, optimism, and dogmatism; *esp* : reluctant to face unpleasant facts or to test assumptions by observation and experience

ten·der·ness \'tendə(r)nəs\ *n* -ES [ME *tendernes*, fr. 1*tender* + *-nes* -ness] : the quality or state of being tender

tender-nosed \'==,=\ *adj* [*tender* + *nosed*] : KEEN-SCENTED ‹only the most persistent and *tender-nosed* hounds can make anything of scent on these occasions —Muriel Bowen›

tender of amends [6*tender*] : an offer of satisfaction for a wrong or breach of contract that serves when sufficient to stop the further accruing of interest and to impose on the plaintiff liability for subsequent costs in the action

tender of issue : a form of words in a pleading by which a party offers to refer the question raised upon it to the appropriate mode of decision

tenders *pres 3d sing of* TENDER, *pl of* TENDER

ten·di·do \ten'dē(,)dō, -ē(,)thō\ *n* -S [Sp, fr. past part. of *tender* to stretch out, fr. L *tendere* — more at THIN] : one of several tiers of seats at a bullring that are located above the ringside rows — compare BARRERA

tending *pres part of* TEND

ten·di·ni·tis \,tendə'nīdəs\ *n* -ES [NL, fr. *tendin-*, *tendo* tendon + *-itis*] : inflammation of a tendon

ten·di·nous \'tendənəs\ *adj* [NL *tendinosus*, fr. *tendin-*, *tendo* tendon + L *-osus* -ous] **1 a** : relating to a tendon **b** : like or resembling a tendon **2** : consisting of tendons : SINEWY

tendinous arch *n* : a thickened fascial arch through which pass vessels or nerves or both; *esp* : one in the pelvic fascia giving origin to fibers of muscles of the pelvic opening

tendinous ring of zinn \-'zin, -tsin\ *usu cap Z* [after Johann G. *Zinn* †1759 Ger. physician and botanist] : a fibrous membrane surrounding the optic foramen and serving as a common origin for the rectus muscles of the eye

ten·di·ped·id \'tendə'pedəd\ *adj or n* [NL *Tendipedidae*] : CHIRONOMID

ten·di·ped·i·dae \,==='pedə,dē\ [NL, fr. *Tendiped-*, *Tendipes*, genus of two-winged flies (fr. L *tendere* to stretch + *-i-* + *-ped-*, *-pes* -ped) + *-idae* — more at THIN] *syn of* CHIRONOMIDAE

ten·do \'ten,dō\ *n, pl* **tendi·nes** \-,də,nēz\ [NL *tendin-*, *tendo*, alter. of ML *tendon-*, *tendo*] : TENDON 1

ten·don \'tendən\ *n* -S [ML *tendon-*, *tendo*, fr. L *tendere* to stretch — more at THIN] **1** : a tough cord or band of dense specialized regularly arranged white fibrous connective tissue that unites a muscle with some other part, transmits the force which the muscle exerts, and is continuous with the connective-tissue epimysium and perimysium of the muscle and when inserted into a bone with the periosteum of the bone — see APONEUROSIS **2** : FRENULUM 2

tendon of achilles *usu cap A* [modif. (influenced by *tendon*, *Achilles*) of NL *tendo Achillis* Achilles' tendon] : ACHILLES' TENDON

ten·don·ous \'tendənəs\ *adj* [*tendon* + *-ous*] : TENDINOUS

tendon reflex *n* : a reflex act (as a knee jerk) in which a muscle is made to contract by a blow upon its tendon

tendon sense *n* : a sense adjunct to the muscle sense and mediated by receptors on or near the tendons

tendon spindle *n* : a sensory end organ in a tendon

ten·dour *also* **tan·dour** *or* **ten·door** \(')ten'dü(ə)r, (')tan-\ *n* -S [Turk *tandur*, fr. Ar *tannūr*, fr. Aram *tannūra*, fr. Akkadian *tinūru*] : a table or seat with a brazier of coals under it that is used for warmth in some countries of southwestern Asia

ten·do·vaginal \'tendō+\ *adj* [NL *tendovaginalis*, fr. *tendo* tendon + L *vagina* sheath + *-alis* -al — more at VAGINA] : of or relating to a tendon and its synovial sheath

ten·dre \'tändrə\ *n* -S [F, fr. *tendre*, adj., tender — more at TENDER] *archaic* : a tender regard : LOVE

ten·dresse \tän'dres\ *n, pl* **tendresses** \"\ [F, fr. MF, fr. *tendre* tender] **1** : tender feeling : FONDNESS ‹suppose I have some ~ for hidden weakness —Anthony West› **2** : LOVE ‹it was a strange ~ . . . I was never once alone with her —Alec Waugh›

1**ten·dril** \'tendrəl\ *n* -S [perh. modif. of MF *tendron* tendril, alter. (influenced by *tendron* tender bud, cartilage) of *tendon* tendon, tendril, fr. ML *tendon-*, *tendo* tendon] **1** : a portion or the whole of a leaf, stipule, or stem that is modified into a slender spirally coiling sensitive organ serving to attach a plant (as a peavine or grapevine) to its support and to assist it in climbing **2 a** : something resembling a tendril ‹her hair hung in loose, vivid ~*s* around her face —Laura Krey› ‹~*s* of mist were curling over the edges of the meadow —P.A. Brodeur› **b** : something that clings like a tendril ‹was aware of each ~ of her being seeking some substance to which it might cling —Helen Howe›

2**tendril** \"\ *adj* **1** : of, relating to, or like a tendril **2** : TENDRILED

ten·driled *or* **ten·drilled** \-ld\ *adj* [1*tendril* + *-ed*] : having tendrils

ten·dril·if·er·ous \'tendrə'lif(ə)rəs\ *adj* [1*tendril* + *-iferous*] : bearing tendrils

ten·dril·lar \'tendrələ(r)\ *adj* [1*tendril* + *-ar*] : TENDRILOUS

ten·dril·ly \-lē\ *adj* [1*tendril* + *-y*] : TENDRILOUS

ten·dril·ous \-drələs\ *adj* [1*tendril* + *-ous*] **1** : TENDRILED **2** : like a tendril

ten·dron \'tendrən\ *n* -S [ME, fr. MF, fr. OF *tendre* tender, soft] **1** *archaic* : a young shoot, sprout, or bud **2** **tendrons** *pl*, *archaic* : pieces of tender cartilage from the bones situated at the extremity of a breast of veal

tends *pres 3d sing of* TEND, *pl of* TEND

ten·du \tä'dü\ *adj* [F, fr. past part. of *tendre* to stretch, stretch out, fr. MF — more at TENDER (to offer)] : extended in a taut manner — used of a leg in ballet

-tene \,tēn\ *n comb form* -S [L or Gk; L *taenia* ribbon, band, fr. Gk *tainia* — more at TAENIA] : synaptic stage characterized by (such) a chromosome filament ‹diplo*tene*› ‹pachy*tene*› ‹zygo*tene*›

ten·e·brae \'tenə,brā, -,brī, -(,)brē\ *n pl but sing or pl in constr*, *often cap* [ML, fr. L, darkness — more at TEMERITY] : a church service observed during the final part of Holy Week in commemoration of the sufferings and death of Christ with the public chanting of psalms and the progressive extinguishing of all candles until only one remains burning behind or under the altar

ten·e·bres·cence \,=='bresᵊn(t)s\ *n* -S [L *tenebrae* darkness + E *-escence*] : an absorption of light (as induced in a crystal by irradiation with X rays) that is not intrinsic to the material involved

ten·e·brif·ic \'=='brifik\ *adj* [L *tenebrae* + E *-i-* + *-fic*] **1** : GLOOMY ‹it brightens the ~ scene —Robert Burns› **2** : causing gloom or darkness ‹a ~ time —Robert Browning›

1**te·neb·ri·o·nid** \tə'nebrēənəd\ *adj* [NL *Tenebrionidae*] : of or relating to the Tenebrionidae

2**tenebrionid** \"\ *n* -S : a beetle of the family Tenebrionidae

te·neb·ri·on·i·dae \,==='änə,dē\ *n pl, cap* [NL, fr. *Tenebrion-*, *Tenebrio*, type genus (fr. L, one who shuns light, fr. *tenebrae* darkness) + *-idae*] : a large family of heteromerous firm-bodied mostly dark-colored vegetable-feeding beetles esp. characteristic of arid regions and often with the hind wings vestigial and functionless and with larvae that are usu. hard cylindrical worms — see DARKLING BEETLE, MEALWORM

te·neb·ri·ous \='=rēəs\ *adj* [by alter.] : TENEBROUS

ten·e·brism \'tenə,brizəm\ *n* -S *often cap* [L *tenebrae* darkness + E *-ism*] : a style of painting typically associated with the Italian painter Caravaggio and his followers of the late 16th and early 17th centuries that submerges most of the forms depicted in shadow but dramatically illuminates the remaining forms by a concentrated beam of light usu. coming from an identifiable source

1**ten·e·brist** \-,brəst\ *n* -S *often cap* [L *tenebrae* + E *-ist*] : one who adheres to or uses tenebrism

2**tenebrist** \"\ *adj* : marked by, using, or constituting tenebrism ‹perhaps the glare in his ~ canvases is a bit too strong —Stuart Preston›

ten·e·brose \-,brōs\ *adj* [L *tenebrosus* — more at TENEBROUS] : TENEBROUS

ten·e·bros·i·ty \,=='bräsəd-ē, -sətē, -i\ *n* -ES [ML *tenebrositat-*, *tenebrositas*, fr. L *tenebrosus* dark + *-itat-*, *-itas* ity] : DARKNESS ‹switches off the light, calls for the first slide, and talks for three quarters of an hour in Stygian ~ —*Lancet*›

ten·e·bro·so \,tenə'brō(,)sō, -)zō\ *adj* [It, lit., dark, fr. L *tenebrosus*] : TENEBRIST; *specif* : of or relating to the painting of Caravaggio and his immediate followers

ten·e·brous \'tenəbrəs\ *adj* [ME, fr. MF *tenebreus*, fr. L *tenebrosus*, fr. *tenebrae* (pl.) darkness + *-osus* -ous — more at TEMERITY] **1 a** : shut off from the light : DARK, MURKY ‹a ~ cave› ‹a ~ forest› **b** : TENEBRIST **2** : hard to understand : MYSTERIOUS, OBSCURE ‹a ~ affair› ‹a ~ theory› **3** : GLOOMY ‹moderates our ~ and fantastical imaginations —Rose Macaulay› — **ten·e·brous·ness** *n* -ES

1080 *also* **ten-eighty** \(')te'nād-ē, -ātē, -ā|, |i\ *n, pl* **1080s** *also* **ten-eighties** [so called fr. its laboratory serial number] : SODIUM FLUOROACETATE

ten·e·ment \'tenəmənt\ *n* -S [ME, fr. MF, fr. ML *tenementum*, fr. L *tenēre* to hold + *-mentum* -ment — more at THIN] **1 a** : something that is held by tenure : land or any of various forms of incorporeal property (as an inheritable estate, an estate for life, or an estate for years) treated like land that is held by a person of another or as owner : HOLDING **b** : a freehold estate in a corporeal or an incorporeal hereditament as distinguished from a less estate (as an estate for a term of years) **2 a** : a house used as a dwelling : RESIDENCE **b** : a single room or set of rooms for use by one tenant or family : APARTMENT, FLAT ‹a vacant second-floor ~ —*Springfield (Mass.) Union*› **c** *Scot* : an edifice of several houses separately tenanted **d** : TENEMENT HOUSE ‹the bare flat at the top of an ugly ~ —Marjorie Earl› **3 a** : DWELLING, HABITATION ‹whole roads and ~*s* of experience poorly mapped —C.D.Lewis› **b** : a human body in which the soul is held to have a temporary dwelling place ‹beholds man trapped in the ~ of flesh —C.I. Glicksberg›

ten·e·men·tal \'=='mentᵊl\ *adj* : of or relating to a tenement : held by or leased to tenants

ten·e·men·ta·ry \'=='mentərē, -n·trē, -ri\ *adj* [*tenement* + *-ary*] : consisting of tenements : TENEMENTAL

ten·e·ment·ed \'tenəməntəd\ *adj* [*tenement* + *-ed*] **1** : leased to tenants : containing separate dwelling units ‹~ houses› **2** : consisting of tenement houses ‹born in the teeming and ~ . . . section —*Reporter*›

tenement house *n* : a dwelling house divided into separate apartments for rent to families : APARTMENT BUILDING; *esp* : one meeting minimum standards of sanitation, safety, and comfort and occupied by poorer families usu. in a large city

te·nen·das \tə'nen,das\ *n* -ES [L, accus. pl. fem. of *tenendus*; fr. *tenendas praedictas terras* the aforesaid lands to be held, a phrase of the clause] *Scots law* : TENENDUM

te·nen·dum \-ndəm\ *n* -S [L, to be held, neut. of *tenendus*, gerundive of *tenēre* to hold; fr. the first word of the clause — more at THIN] : a clause formerly used in a deed to designate the kind of tenure vested in the grantee — compare HABENDUM

tenent *n* -S [L, they hold, 3d sing. pres. indic. of *tenēre* to hold] *obs* : TENET

tenent hair *or* **tenant hair** *n* [L *tenent-*, *tenens*, pres. part. of *tenēre* to hold] : a hair much more swollen at the tip than the base, sometimes secreting an adhesive fluid, growing in tufts on the feet of many spiders and insects, and enabling them to move freely on smooth or vertical surfaces

ten·er·al \'tenərəl\ *adj* [L *tener* tender, young + E *-al* — more at TENDER] : of, relating to, or constituting a state of the imago of an insect immediately after molting during which it is soft and immature in coloring

ten·er·a·men·te \,tenərə'mentē, -men·(,)tā\ *adv* [It, fr. *tenero* tender, fr. L *tener*] : TENDERLY — used as a direction in music

ten·er·iffe lace \'tenə,rif-, -rēf-\ *n, usu cap T* [fr. *Teneriffe*, *Tenerife*, one of the Canary islands] : a handmade or machine-made lace with spider-web designs that is used for insertion and edging

te·nes·mus \tə'nezməs *also* -nes-\ *n* -ES [L, fr. Gk *teinesmos*, fr. *teinein* to stretch, strain — more at THIN] : a painful and distressing but ineffectual urge to evacuate the rectum or urinary bladder

ten·et \'tenət *Brit often* 'tēn-; *usu* -əd·+V\ *n* -S [L, he holds, 3d sing. pres. indic. of *tenēre* to hold; fr. its use in NL to introduce an account of the opinion of an individual or sect — more at THIN] **1** : a principle, dogma, belief, or doctrine generally held to be true; *esp* : one held in common by members of an organization, group, movement, or profession ‹the two great ~*s* of the physical sciences, observation and deduction —M.A.Pei› ‹rare to find a design so boldly original in conception transgressing so few architectural ~*s* —W.M. Emery› **2** *archaic* : a personal opinion **syn** see DOCTRINE

te·ne·te·hara \,tenətə'härə, -harə\ *n, pl* **tenetehara** *or* **teneteharas** *usu cap* **1 a** : a Tupian people of the state of Maranhão, Brazil **b** : a member of such people **2** : the language of the Tenetehara people

1**ten·fold** \'=¦fōld\ *adj* [ME, fr. 1*ten* + *-fold*] **1** : having 10 parts or aspects **2** : being 10 times as large, as great, or as many as some understood size, degree, or amount ‹a ~ increase›

2**tenfold** \"\ *adv* : to 10 times as much or as many : by ten times ‹increased ~›

ten-foot·er \'=¦füd·ə(r)\ *n* [1*ten* + *foot* + *-er*] : a small building or ell ten feet square; *specif* : one formerly used for shoemaking on some New England farms

ten-gallon hat \'=¦==-\ *n* [so called fr. its great size] : COWBOY HAT

teng·ger·ese \ˌteŋgəˈrēz, -ēs\ *n, pl* **tenggerese** *or* **tenggereses** *usu cap* [Jav *Těnggěr* Tenggerese (fr. *těnggěr* high-level land, plateau) + E *-ese*] **1 :** an Indonesian people inhabiting the mountain regions of eastern Java **2 :** a member of the Tenggerese people

tenia *var of* TAENIA

teniacide *var of* TAENIACIDE

teniafuge *var of* TAENIAFUGE

teniasis *var of* TAENIASIS

te·nien·te \tən'yentē\ *n* -s [Sp, fr. L *tenent-, tenens,* pres. part. of *tenēre* to hold — more at THIN] **:** a local official in Latin America and the Philippines

te·ni·no \tə'nē,nō\ *n, pl* **tenino** *or* **teninos** *usu cap* **1 :** a Shahaptian people of the Columbia river valley of northern Oregon **2 :** a member of the Tenino people

ten–in–one ration \ˌ=ˌ=ˌ=-\ *n* **:** a packaged field ration (as of the U. S. Army) intended to feed ten men for one day

te·nio \tə'nē,ō\ *n* -s [Sp *teniu*] **1 :** a timber tree (*Weinmannia trichosperma*) of southern So. America **2 :** the rosy-brown wood of the tenio that resembles that of the sweet birch

Ten·ite \'te,nīt\ *trademark* — used for any of various thermoplastic molding compositions made from a cellulose ester

ten·nant·ite \'tenən‚tīt\ *n* -s [Smithson *Tennant* †1815 Eng. chemist + E *-ite*] **:** a mineral $(Cu,Fe)_{12}As_4S_{13}$ that consists of a blackish lead-gray sulfide of iron, copper, arsenic, and sulfur and is isomorphous with tetrahedrite

ten·ne \'tenē\ *n* -s [MF *tenné,* alter. of *tanné,* past part. of *tanner* to tan — more at TAN] **1** *also* **tenney** *or* **tenny** \"\ **:** the heraldic color orange or orange-tawny **2 :** TAWNY

ten·ner \'tenə(r)\ *n* -s [¹*ten* + *-er*] **1 :** a ten-pound note **2 :** a ten-dollar bill

¹**ten·nes·se·an** *or* **ten·nes·see·an** \ˌtenəˈsēən\ *adj, usu cap* [*Tennessee,* state of U.S.A. + E *-an*] **1 :** of, relating to, or characteristic of the state of Tennessee **2 :** of, relating to, or characteristic of the people of Tennessee

²**tennessean** *or* **tennesseean** \"\ *n, cap* **:** a native or resident of Tennessee

ten·nes·see \ˌtenəˈsē\ *adj, usu cap* [fr. *Tennessee,* southeast central state of U.S.A., fr. the *Tennessee* river, fr. Cherokee *Tanasi,* name of a village] **:** of or from the state of Tennessee ‹a *Tennessee* county› **:** of the kind or style prevalent in Tennessee **:** TENNESSEAN

tennessee walker *n, usu cap T&W* **:** TENNESSEE WALKING HORSE

tennessee walking horse *n* **1** *usu cap T&W&H* **:** an American breed of large easy-gaited saddle horses that is largely of Standardbred and Morgan ancestry **2** *usu cap T & sometimes cap W&H* **:** a horse of the Tennessee Walking Horse breed — called also *Plantation walking horse*

tennessee warbler *n, usu cap T* **:** a small olive-green white-breasted warbler (*Vermivora peregrina*) of No. America that nests in Canada and winters in northern So. America

ten·nis \'tenəs\ *n* -ES *often attrib* [ME *tenys, teneys, tenetz,*

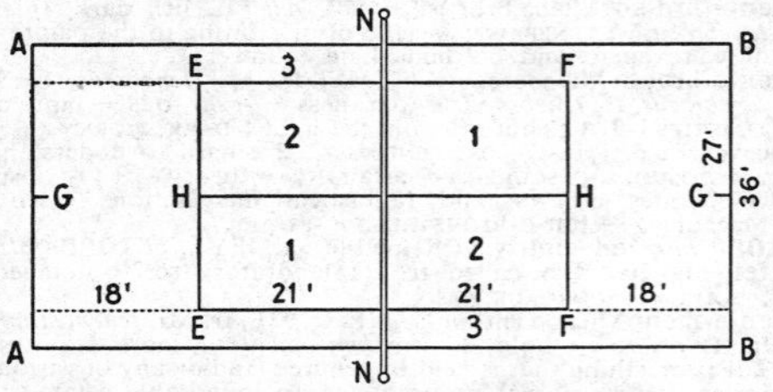

tennis court laid out for doubles: base lines *AA, BB;* sidelines *AB, AB;* service lines *EE, FF;* service sidelines *EF, EF;* center marks *G, G;* center service lines or half-court lines *HH;* net *NN; 1, 1,* right service courts; *2, 2,* left service courts; *3, 3* alleys

prob. fr. AF *tenetz,* 2d pers. pl. imper. of *tenir* to hold — more at TENABLE] **1 :** COURT TENNIS **2 :** a typically outdoor game that is played with rackets and a light elastic ball by two players or pairs of players on a level court divided by a low net and that is scored in points, games, and sets — called also *lawn tennis;* see RACKET illustration

tennis ball *n* **:** a ball used in tennis that is made of rubber covered with felt and weighs about two ounces

tennis elbow *n* **:** inflammation and pain over the outer side of the elbow involving the lateral epicondyle of the humerus and usu. resulting from excessive or violent twisting movements of the hand

tennis shoe *n* **:** a light shoe worn esp. in playing tennis and generally made of canvas with a rubber sole — compare SNEAKER

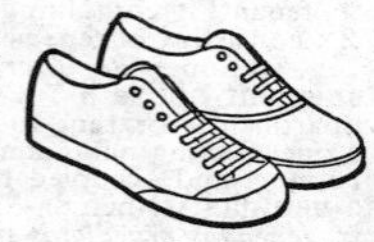
tennis shoes

ten·nisy \'tenəsē\ *adj* [*tennis* + *-y*] **:** devoted to tennis

ten·no \'te(‚)nō, =ˈ=\ *n, pl* **tenno** *or* **tennos** *often cap* [Jap *tennō*] **:** an emperor of Japan who is a religious leader and held to be an incarnation of the divine — compare MIKADO

ten·ny·so·nian \ˌtenəˈsōnēən, -nyən\ *adj, usu cap* [Alfred, Lord *Tennyson* †1892 Eng. poet + E *-ian*] **:** of, relating to, or having the characteristics of the poet Tennyson or his writings ‹it had been produced specifically as an exercise in *Tennysonian* art —*Atlantic*›

teno- *comb form* [irreg. fr. Gk *tenont-, tenōn* tendon; akin to Gk *teinein* to stretch — more at THIN] **:** tendon ‹*teno*plasty› ‹*tenotomy*›

te·noch·ca \tə'nächkə\ *n, pl* **tenochca** *or* **tenochcas** *usu cap* [MexSp, fr. *Tenochtitlán,* ancient name of Mexico City] **:** AZTEC 1

ten·o·de·sis \ˌtenəˈdēsəs, -'des-; tə'nädəsəs\ *n, pl* **tenode·ses** \-‚sēz\ [NL, fr. *teno-* + *-desis*] **:** the operation of suturing the end of a tendon to a bone ‹*tenodeses* or transplantations of the tendons alone —*Jour. Amer. Med. Assoc.*›

¹**ten·on** \'tenən\ *n* -s [ME, fr. OF, fr. *tenir* to hold — more at TENABLE] **:** a projecting member in a piece of wood or other material for insertion into a mortise to make a joint; *esp* **:** one passing entirely through the piece in which a mortise is cut — compare TUSK TENON; see LEWIS illustration

²**tenon** \"\ *vb* -ED/-ING/-S *vt* **1 :** to unite or hold in place by or as if by a tenon **2 :** to cut or fit for insertion in a mortise ~ *vi* **:** to become fixed in place by means of a tenon

ten·on·er \-nə(r)\ *n* -s **:** one that tenons

tenon's capsule \tə'nōⁿz-, 'tenənz-\ *n, usu cap T* [after Jacques-René *Tenon* †1816 Fr. anatomist] **:** a thin connective-tissue membrane ensheathing the eyeball behind the conjunctiva

tenon's space *n, usu cap T* [after Jacques-René *Tenon*] **:** a lymph space between Tenon's capsule and the sclerotic coat of the eye that is traversed by strands of reticular tissue and by the optic nerve and ocular muscles

tenon tooth *n* **:** a fine saw tooth for cutting tenons

¹**ten·or** \'tenə(r)\ *n* -s [ME *tenour, tenor,* fr. OF, fr. L *tenor,* act of holding on, uninterrupted course, fr. *tenēre* to hold — more at THIN] **1 a :** the course of thought that is held to through a discourse, speech, or piece of writing **:** the general drift of something spoken or written **:** INTENT, PURPORT, SUBSTANCE ‹the ~ of the book is expressed in the introduction —J.B.Griffin› **b :** an exact copy of a writing set forth in the words and figures of it **:** TRANSCRIPT **c :** the concept, object, or person meant in a metaphor **:** the latent aspect of a metaphorical statement — compare VEHICLE 2b **2 a (1) :** a melodic line that usu. forms the cantus firmus in medieval polyphony **(2) :** the voice part next to the lowest in four-part harmony **b :** the highest natural adult male voice **c :** a person who sings the tenor part or an instrument that plays it **d :** the main reciting note in plainsong psalmody **e :** the lowest of a set of church bells used in change ringing **3 :** a continuance in a course, movement, or activity **:** PROCEDURE, TREND ‹kept the noiseless ~ of their way —Thomas Gray› ‹earth and sun will continue the even ~ of their ways for an inconceivably long period —K.F.Mather› **4 :** habitual condition **:** CHARACTER, NATURE, STAMP ‹this success would look like chance, if it were not perpetual, and always of the same ~ —John Dryden› **5 :** the time between the date of issue or acceptance of a note or draft and the maturity date — compare USANCE **6 :** the percentage or average amount of metal or mineral in an ore **syn** see TENDENCY

²**tenor** \"\ *adj* **:** of or relating to the tenor or the tenor part in music ‹~ singer› ‹~ quality›

tenor clef *n* [so called fr. the fact that such a staff is most convenient for writing notes within the tenor voice range] **:** the C clef when it is on the fourth line of the staff — see CLEF illustration

te·no·re \tā'nōr(‚)ā, -ō(‚)rā\ *n, pl* **teno·ri** \-ōr(‚)ē, -ō(‚)rē\ [It, fr. L *tenor* act of holding, uninterrupted course — more at TENOR] **:** TENOR

ten·or·ist \'tenərəst\ *n* -s [*tenor* + *-ist*] **:** one who sings tenor or plays a tenor instrument

ten·o·rite \'tenə‚rīt\ *n* -s [It *tenorite,* fr. M. *Tenore* †1861 Ital. botanist + It *-ite*] **:** a mineral CuO that is a native cupric oxide occurring in minute steel-gray or iron-gray scales or black earthy masses — compare MELACONITE

tenor·less \'==‚ləs\ *adj* **:** having no tenor **:** lacking intent or substance

ten·or·man \'==‚man, -‚mən\ *n, pl* **tenormen :** one who plays the tenor saxophone

ten·or·oon \ˌtenəˈrün\ *n* -s [²*tenor* + *bassoon*] **1 :** a tenor bassoon that is pitched a fifth higher than the standard bassoon **2 :** an incomplete stop found in an old pipe organ

tenor violin *n* **1 :** VIOLA **2 :** any of several instruments intermediate between the viola and the violoncello; *specif* **:** VIOLOTTA

ten·o·synovitis \ˌtenō+\ *n* [NL, fr. *teno-* + *synovitis*] **:** inflammation of a tendon sheath that is usu. a result of trauma or infection

ten·o·tome \'tenə‚tōm\ *n* -s [*teno-* + *-tome*] **:** a slender narrow-bladed surgical instrument mounted on a handle

te·not·o·mist \tə'nädəməst\ *n* -s [*tenotomy* + *-ist*] **:** one who performs a tenotomy

te·not·o·mize \-‚mīz\ *vt* -ED/-ING/-S [*tenotomy* + *-ize*] **:** to perform a tenotomy on

te·not·o·my \-‚mē\ *n* -ES [*teno-* + *-tomy*] **:** surgical division of a tendon

ten·our \'tenə(r)\ *chiefly Brit var of* TENOR

ten·pence *Brit* 'tenpən(t)s, *US* " *or* '=‚pen-\ *n, pl* **tenpence** *or* **tenpences** [¹*ten* + *pence*] **1 :** the sum of ten usu. British pennies **2 :** a token representing ten pennies or a coin worth ten pennies

¹**ten·pen·ny** \-pənē, -ni; -‚penē\ *adj* [¹*ten* + *penny*] **:** amounting to, worth, or costing tenpence

²**tenpenny** \"\ *n* **1 :** a tenpenny token or coin **2** *Scot* **:** a child's reader formerly costing tenpence

tenpenny nail *n* [so called fr. its original price per hundred] **:** a nail 3 inches long

ten–percent·er \'tenpə(r)'sentə(r)\ *n* -s [*ten percent* + *-er;* fr. the rate of his commission] *slang* **:** an actor's agent

tenpin \'=‚=\ *n* **1 :** a bottle-shaped bowling pin 15 inches high **2 tenpins** *pl but sing in constr* **:** a bowling game using ten tenpins and a large ball 27 inches in circumference and allowing each player to bowl two balls in each of ten frames — compare CANDLEPINS, DUCKPINS

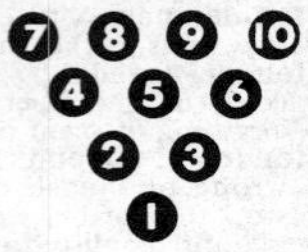

arrangement of pins in tenpins

ten·pound·er \'='paündə(r)\ *n* [*ten pounds* + *-er*] **1 :** a large silvery food and sport fish (*Elops saurus*) that has a somewhat compressed body resembling that of a herring, is closely related to the tarpon, and is prob. cosmopolitan in warm seas **2** *Brit* **:** a voter occupying property valued at ten pounds' annual income

ten·rec \'ten‚rek\ *n* [F *tanrac, tanrec, tenrec,* fr. Malagasy *tràndraka, tàndraka*] **1** *also* **tanrec** \'tan‚-\ -s **:** any of numerous small often spiny insectivorous mammals of the family Tenrecidae of Madagascar; *esp* **:** a tailless insectivore (*Tenrec ecaudatus*) that breeds prolifically and feeds chiefly on earthworms — compare RICE TENREC **2** *cap* [NL, fr. F *tenrec*] **:** the type genus of the family Tenrecidae

ten·rec·i·dae \ten'resə‚dē\ *n pl, cap* [NL *Tenrec,* type genus + *-idae*] **:** a family of insectivores comprising the tenrecs and with the West African otter shrew, the West Indian alamiqui, and extinct related forms often constituting a distinct superfamily of Insectivora

ten–ring \'=‚=\ *n* [so called fr. its value in scoring] **:** the center ring of a paper target used in small-bore riflery

tens *pl of* TEN

¹**tense** \'ten(t)s\ *n* -s [ME *tens, tense* time, tense, fr. MF *tens,* fr. L *tempor-, tempus* — more at TEMPORAL] **1 :** a distinction of form in a verb to express past, present, or future time or duration of the action or state it denotes **2 a :** a set of inflectional forms of a verb that express distinctions of time — see PAST TENSE, PRESENT TENSE **b :** a particular inflectional form of a verb expressing a specific time distinction ‹used the wrong ~ of the verb in this sentence› **3 :** the part of the meaning of a verb form that consists of the expression of a time distinction **4 :** a verb phrase that includes a tense auxiliary

²**tense** \"\ *vt* -ED/-ING/-S **:** to provide with a tense ‹a *tensed* statement›

³**tense** \"\ *adj* -ER/-EST [L *tensus,* fr. past part. of *tendere* to stretch — more at THIN] **1 :** stretched tight **:** made taut **:** RIGID ‹the skeletal musculature involuntarily becomes ~ —H.G.Armstrong› **2 a :** feeling or showing nervous tension **:** under mental or emotional strain **:** HIGH-STRUNG, JITTERY ‹~, taciturn, sensitive, given to worry —A.L.Kroeber› **b :** causing strain **:** inducing tension ‹the riffles get rougher and navigating is a bit ~ —*Buick Mag.*› ‹no game is *tenser* than solemn tournament billiards: cold-blooded concentration and steady nerves are demanded —*Time*› **c :** charged with tension **:** marked by strain or suspense ‹the air was ~ with complaint and constraint —L.C.Douglas› ‹the first eleven pages . . . have a ~ and gripping power —A.H.MacCormick› **3** *of a speech sound* **:** produced with the muscles involved in a relatively tense state ‹the vowels \ē\ and \ü\ in contrast with the vowels \i\ and \ú\ are ~› — compare LAX **syn** see STIFF, TIGHT

⁴**tense** \"\ *vb* -ED/-ING/-S *vt* **:** to make tense ‹held my mouth open to ~ my eardrums —Christopher Morley› ~ *vi* **:** to become tense ‹*tensed* like a coiled rattler —Jack McLarn› ‹*tensed* as he heard it slow down —Earle Birney› — often used with *up*

tense auxiliary *n* [¹*tense*] **:** an auxiliary verb (as *be, have*) used to form a compound tense of another verb

tense·less \'=‚ləs\ *adj* **:** not having a tense or tenses — **tense·less·ly** *adv* — **tense·less·ness** *n* -ES

tense·ly *adv* [³*tense* + *-ly*] **:** in a tense manner ‹the sound we had been waiting ~ to hear —H.L.Merillat› ‹stretched ~ over the drumhead›

tense·ness *n* -ES **:** the quality or state of being tense

ten·ser *or* **ten·sor** \'ten(t)sə(r)\ *n* -s [ME *tenser,* fr. MF *tense, tence* protection (fr. OF, fr. *tenser, tencer* to defend, protect) + ME *-er*] **:** a noncitizen resident of an English city formerly required to pay for license to trade in the city

ten·si·bil·i·ty \‚ten(t)sə'biləd·ē\ *n* -ES **:** the quality or state of being tensible ‹the nonelastic nature of the arthropod cuticula gives the body wall but little ~ —R.E.Snodgrass›

ten·si·ble \'ten(t)səbəl\ *adj* [LL *tensibilis,* fr. L *tensus* (past part. of *tendere*) + *-ibilis* -ible] **:** capable of being extended — **ten·si·ble·ness** \-bəlnəs\ *n* -ES — **ten·si·bly** \-blē\ *adv*

ten·sile \'ten(t)səl, -n‚sīl, -n(‚)sil\ *adj* [NL *tensilis,* fr. L *tensus* (past part. of *tendere* to stretch) + *-ilis* -ile — more at THIN] **1 :** capable of tension **:** DUCTILE ‹is made of highly ~ steel alloy —Sam Pollock› **2 :** of or relating to tension ‹~ pull› ‹~ stress› — **ten·sile·ly** \-əl(l)ē, -ill, -il(l)l, |i\ *adv* — **ten·sile·ness** \-əlnəs, -īln-, -iln-\ *n* -ES — **ten·sil·i·ty** \ten'siləd·ē, -lətē, -i\ *n* -ES

tensile strength *n* **:** resistance to rupture under tension **:** BREAKING STRENGTH, COHESIVENESS; *specif* **:** the greatest longitudinal stress (as pounds per square inch) a substance can bear without tearing apart — compare COMPRESSIVE STRENGTH

ten·sim·e·ter \ten'siməd·ə(r)\ *n* [*tension* + *-meter*] **:** an instrument for measuring gas or vapor pressure **:** MANOMETER

Ten·si·om·e·ter \‚ten(t)sē'äməd·ə(r)\ *trademark* — used for an instrument for measuring the surface tension of liquids

¹**ten·sion** \'tenchən\ *n* -s *often attrib* [MF or L; MF *tension,* fr. L *tension-, tensio,* fr. *tensus* (past part. of *tendere* to stretch) + *-ion-, -io* -ion — more at THIN] **1 a :** the act or action of stretching or the condition or degree of being stretched to stiffness **:** TAUTNESS ‹to install the belt, slip it over the pulleys and adjust its ~ —H.F.Blanchard & Ralph Ritchen› **b :** STRESS ‹arterial ~› ‹muscular ~› **c :** a momentary state of muscular tautness in dance technique that inevitably resolves into relaxation **2 a :** either of two balancing forces causing or tending to cause extension **b :** the stress resulting from the elongation of an elastic body — contrasted with *compressive stress* **c** *archaic* **:** PRESSURE **3 a :** inner unrest, striving, or imbalance **:** a feeling of psychological stress often manifested by increased muscular tonus and by other physiological indicators of emotion ‹went back to bed and dropped asleep suddenly with the release of ~ —Mary Austin› ‹~s distort personality —Bruce Bliven b. 1889› **b :** a state of latent hostility or opposition between individuals or groups (as classes, races, nations) ‹there is bitter ~ between them —Bernard De Voto› ‹a lessening of minority-group ~s —J.A.Morris b. 1904› ‹mob insanity explodes when ~ reaches the flash point —*New Republic*› **c :** a balance maintained in an artistic work (as a poem, painting, musical composition) between opposing forces or elements **:** a controlled dramatic or dynamic quality ‹the ~ which makes his sonata . . . so compelling —Stephen Spender› ‹the poetry of Dryden and Pope is characterized by the ~ between its constituent elements —F.W.Bateson› **4 :** ELECTRIC POTENTIAL **5 :** any of various devices in textile manufacturing machines or sewing machines that are used to control the tautness and movement of thread or material passing through **syn** see BALANCE, STRESS

²**tension** \"\ *vt* **tensioned; tensioned; tensioning** \-ch(ə)niŋ\ **tensions :** to subject to tension **:** tighten to a desired degree **:** TAUTEN ‹this must be heavily ~*ed,* almost to the breaking point —Albert Thompson & Sigfrid Bick› ‹cut the wire off and ~*ed* and dead-ended it —W.W.Haines›

ten·sion·al \-chənᵊl, -chnəl\ *adj* **:** of, relating to, or resulting from tension ‹manufacturers and distributors of ~ steel —*Economist*› ‹is not religion essentially a ~ relation between God and man —Georges Florovsky›

tension element *n* **:** a flexible link (as an endless belt with its pulleys) for transmitting tension only — compare PRESSURE ELEMENT

ten·sion·er \-ch(ə)nə(r)\ *n* -s [²*tension* + *-er*] **:** ¹TENSION 5

tension·less \'==‚ləs\ *adj* **:** free from tension

tension man *n* **:** a worker who keeps newsprint feeding through a web press at the proper tension

tension pulley *n* **:** a pulley over which a belt is caused to pass in order to keep it taut

tension rod *n* **:** a metal rod used as a tension member

tension wood *n* **:** a reaction wood formed on the upper side of tree branches and leaning trunks and characterized by narrower and thinner walled wood and fiber elements, excessive longitudinal shrinkage, and tendency to collapse on drying — compare COMPRESSION WOOD

tension zone *n* **:** ECOTONE

ten·si·ty \'ten(t)səd·ē, -sətē, -i\ *n* -ES [ML *tensitat-, tensitas,* fr. L *tensus* tense + *-itat-, -itas* -ity] **:** TENSENESS ‹with a sudden ~ of which he had never suspected her —A.J.Cronin›

ten·sive \'ten(t)siv, -sēv *also* -səv\ *adj* [F *tensif,* fr. MF, fr. L *tensus* (past part. of *tendere* to stretch) + MF *-if* -ive] **:** of, relating to, or causing tension

ten·son \'ten(t)sən\ *also* **ten·so** \-n‚sō\ *or* **ten·zon** \-nzən\ *n* -s [*tenson* fr. F, fr. MF *tençon, tenson,* fr. Prov *tensoun; tenzon* fr. It *tenzone,* fr. Prov *tensoun; tenso* fr. Prov *tensoun, tenso* quarrel, contest, tenson, fr. L *tension-, tensio* tension — more at TENSION] **:** a lyric poem of dispute composed by Provençal troubadours in which two opponents speak alternate stanzas, lines, or groups of lines usu. identical in structure — compare DÉBAT, PARTIMEN

¹**ten·sor** \'ten(t)sə(r), -n‚sō(ə)r\ *n* -s [NL, fr. L *tensus* (past part of *tendere* to stretch) + *-or* — more at THIN] **1** *or* **tensor muscle :** a muscle that stretches a part or makes it tense **2 :** an invariant that is specified by N^c components in each of two coordinate systems such that the components of one system may be transformed to those of the other by a specified set of N^c equations involving partial derivatives

²**tensor** *var of* TENSER

ten·so·ri·al \(')tenˈsōrēəl, -sȯr-\ *adj* [NL *tensor* + E *-al*] **:** of, relating to, or characteristic of a tensor

ten–spot \'=‚=\ *n* [¹*ten* + *spot*] **1 :** a ten-dollar bill **2 :** a playing card with ten spots

ten–strike \'=‚=\ *n* **1 :** a strike in tenpins **2 :** a highly successful stroke or achievement **:** a smashing success ‹three months ago I thought that at last I had written a *ten-strike* —Bernard De Voto›

¹**tent** \'tent\ *n* -s *often attrib* [ME *tente, tent,* fr. OF *tente,* fr. L *tenta,* fem. of *tentus,* past part. of *tendere* to stretch — more at THIN] **1 :** a collapsible shelter of canvas or other material stretched and sustained by poles, usu. made fast by ropes attached to pegs hammered into the ground, and used for camping outdoors (as by soldiers or vacationers) or as a temporary building (as for a theatrical performance) — see FLY TENT, PUP TENT, SIBLEY TENT, WALL TENT **2 :** ABODE, DWELLING, HABITATION ‹others among the great who are admissible into the ~s of the mighty —J.T.Farrell› ‹moved with the smart clientele, pitching his ~ in the resorts during the proper seasons —E.O.Hauser› **3 :** something that resembles a tent or that serves as a shelter ‹the pale, silky-looking ~s of the . . . mountains —Cid R. Sumner› ‹the ~ of free enterprise —*Wall Street Jour.*›: as **a** *Scot* **:** a wooden pulpit for open-air preaching **b :** HUT, SHACK **c :** a local organization of the Rechabites **d :** the web of a tent caterpillar **e :** a canopy or airtight chamber placed over the head and shoulders of a patient to retain vapors or oxygen during administration

²**tent** \"\ *vb* -ED/-ING/-S *vi* **1 :** to reside for the time being **:** make a temporary abode **:** LODGE ‹the blue skies with the leisurely clouds ~*ing* among them —J.H.Wheelwright› **2 :** to live in a tent ‹~*ed* in the state park for a week› ~ *vt* **1 :** to cover with or as if with a tent ‹the rich brocade in which she was ~*ed* —John Mason Brown› ‹~*ed* his head with his hands —Warren Eyster› **2 :** to lodge in tents ‹~*ed* his men on top of the hill›

³**tent** \"\ *n* -s [ME, short for *attent* attention, intention, expectation, fr. OF *attente,* fr. L *attenta,* fem. of *attentus,* past part. of *attendere* to attend] *dial chiefly Brit* **:** ATTENTION, HEED, CARE

⁴**tent** \"\ *vt* -ED/-ING/-S [ME *tenten,* fr. ³*tent*] **1** *chiefly Scot* **:** to pay attention to **:** HEED **2** *chiefly Scot* **:** to attend to **:** care for **:** watch over **:** TEND **3** *chiefly Scot* **:** OBSERVE, WATCH

⁵**tent** \"\ *n* -s [ME *tent, tente,* fr. MF *tente,* fr. OF, fr. *tenter* to try, tempt, test, probe — more at TEMPT] **1** *obs* **:** a probe for searching a wound ‹the ~ that searches to the bottom of the worst —Shak.› **2 :** a roll of lint or linen or a conical or cylindrical piece of sponge or other absorbent formerly used chiefly to dilate a natural canal, to keep open the orifice of a wound, or to absorb discharges

⁶**tent** \"\ *vt* -ED/-ING/-S **1** *obs* **:** PROBE ‹~ him to the quick —Shak.› **2** *archaic* **:** to keep open or treat with a surgical tent

⁷**tent** \"\ *n* -s [Sp *tinto,* fr. *tinto* dark red, fr. L *tinctus,* past part. of *tingere* to wet, dye — more at TINGE] **:** a very dark red sweet Spanish wine

tent·a·bil·i·ty \‚tentə'biləd·ē\ *n* [irreg. fr. *temptable* + *-ity*] **:** the quality or state of being temptable

ten·ta·cle \'tentəkəl, -tēk-\ *n* -s [NL *tentaculum,* fr. L *tentare* to touch, feel, attempt + *-culum,* suffix denoting an instrument — more at TEMPT] **1 :** any of various elongate flexible simple or branched processes that are usu. tactile or prehensile or both in function but sometimes have other functions (as respiration or locomotion) and that are borne by animals chiefly on the head or about the mouth: as **a :** one of the arms of a cephalopod, crinoid, or polyp **b :** one of the fleshy processes sometimes bearing eyes on the head of a gastropod mollusk or many worms — see SNAIL illustration **c :** one of the

threadlike processes bearing stinging cells that depend from the margin of the umbrella of many jellyfishes **d :** one of the tubular suctorial processes of a suctorian **e :** one of the numerous small ciliated processes borne on the arms of a brachiopod or the lophophore of a bryozoan **2 a :** something that acts like a tentacle in grasping or feeling out **:** FEELER, TENDRIL ⟨these ~s of organized crime and corruption —R.E.Merriam⟩ ⟨in every experience we touch the world through some particular ~ —John Dewey⟩ **b :** a sensitive hair or emergence (as one of the gland-tipped insect-catching hairs on the leaves of the sundew)

ten·ta·cled \-kəld\ *adj* [*tentacle* + *-ed*] **:** having tentacles ⟨influences which reach . . . like ~ weeds —*Newsweek*⟩

ten·tac·u·lar \(ˈ)ten·ˈtakyələ(r)\ *adj* [NL *tentaculum* + E *-ar*] **1 :** of, relating to, or resembling tentacles ⟨matted beards that seemed ~ as the arms of an octopus —Osbert Sitwell⟩ **2 :** equipped with tentacles **:** acting by means of tentacles ⟨his ~ mind poking into everything —Amy Lowell⟩ ⟨the ~ organization of modern society —*Times Lit. Supp.*⟩

ten·tac·u·la·ta \ten,takyəˈlād·ə, -lad·ə\ *n pl, cap* [NL, fr. neut. pl. of *tentaculatus* tentaculate] **:** a class of Ctenophora comprising forms with tentacles that are retractile into sheaths and that may be long and pinnate (as in members of the orders Cydippida and Platyctenea), small and unbranched (as in members of the order Cestida), or present only in the immature stage (as in members of the order Lobata)

ten·tac·u·late \-ˈ==lət\ *adj* [NL *tentaculatus*, fr. *tentaculum* + L *-atus* -ate] **1 :** having tentacles **2 :** of or relating to the Tentaculata

ten·tac·u·lat·ed \-,lād·əd\ *adj* [NL *tentaculatus* + E *-ed*] **:** TENTACLED

ten·tac·u·lif·era \=,==ˈlif(ə)rə\ [NL, fr. *tentaculum* + *-i-* + L *-fera*, neut. pl. of *-fer*] *syn of* SUCTORIA

ten·tac·u·lif·er·ous \=ˈ==ˈlif(ə)rəs\ *adj* [NL *tentaculum* + E *-iferous*] **:** bearing tentacles

ten·tac·u·lite \=ˈ==,līt\ *n* -S [NL *Tentaculites*] **:** a fossil or individual of the genus *Tentaculites* or family Tentaculitidae

ten·tac·u·li·tes \=,==ˈlīd·(,)ēz\ *n, cap* [NL, fr. *tentaculum* + *-ites*] **:** a genus of small conical fossil shells found abundantly in some Paleozoic rocks and often made the type of the family Tentaculitidae

ten·tac·u·lit·i·dae \-ˈlid·ə,dē\ *n pl, cap* [NL, fr. *Tentaculites*, type genus + *-idae*] **:** a family of shelled Paleozoic invertebrates (group Conulariida) — see TENTACULITES

ten·tac·u·lo·cyst \=ˈ==,lō+\ *n* [NL *tentaculum* + *-o-* + E *cyst*] **:** one of the sense organs situated on the margin of the umbrella of many jellyfishes, consisting of a greatly modified and reduced tentacle containing a cavity with lithites, and often being sunk in a pit or enclosed in a pouch

ten·tac·u·loid \-,lȯid\ *adj* [NL *tentaculum* + E *-oid*] **:** resembling a tentacle

ten·tac·u·lo·zooid \=ˈ==lō+\ *n* [NL *tentaculum* + *-o-* + E *zooid*] **:** a zooid of a colonial polyp that is adapted to act as a tentacle

ten·tac·u·lum \=ˈ=ˈ=ləm\ *n, pl* **tentacu·la** \-lə\ [NL — more at TENTACLE] **1 a :** TENTACLE 1 **b :** VIBRISSA **2 :** HAPTERON, HOLDFAST

ten·ta·dero \,tentəˈde(,)rō\ *n* -S [Sp, corral where young bulls are tested, fr. *tentado* (past part. of *tentar* to touch, feel, try, fr. L *tentare*), fr. L *tentatus*, past part. of *tentare* — more at TEMPT] **:** TIENTA

tent·age \ˈtentij, -tēj\ *n* -S [¹*tent* + *-age*] **:** a collection or supply of tents **:** tent facilities or equipment ⟨are equipped with sufficient ~ for sheltering patients —C.M.Walson⟩

ten·ta·tion \ten·ˈtāshən\ *n* -S [L *tentation-*, *tentatio*, fr. *tentatus* (past part. of *tentare* to feel, attempt, tempt) + *-ion-*, *-io* -ion] **1** *archaic* **:** TEMPTATION **2 :** a mode of adjusting or operating by successive steps, trials, or experiments

¹**ten·ta·tive** \ˈtentəd·iv, -ətiv\ *adj* [ML *tentativus*, fr. L *tentatus* (past part. of *tentare* to feel, attempt tempt) + *-ivus* -ive — more at TEMPT] **1 a :** of the nature of an experiment or hypothesis **:** offered, undertaken, or arrived at as a first step **:** PROVISIONAL ⟨for him all questions are open, all assumptions ~ —Walter Moberly⟩ **b :** offered or given for the time being **:** subject to change or withdrawal **:** not final ⟨a ~ program⟩ ⟨a ~ acceptance⟩ ⟨a ~ refusal⟩ **2 :** HESITANT, UNCERTAIN ⟨a sort of ~, almost apologetic smile —R.P. Warren⟩ ⟨made his voice ~ —Jean Stafford⟩ ⟨his speech is jerky and ~ —Walter Bernstein⟩ — **ten·ta·tive·ly** \-əvlē, -li\ *adv* — **ten·ta·tive·ness** \-ivnəs\ *n* -ES

²**tentative** \"\ *n* -S **:** a tentative undertaking, experiment, or offer ⟨the few surviving scraps of notes . . . are crammed with story ~s —Jay Leyda⟩

tent bed *n* [¹*tent*] **:** FIELD BED

tent caterpillar *n* **:** any of several gregarious caterpillars that construct on trees large silken webs into which they retreat when at rest — see EASTERN TENT CATERPILLAR, FOREST TENT CATERPILLAR; compare FALL WEBWORM, WEBWORM

tent club *n* **:** a club devoted to the sport of pigsticking

tent·ed \ˈtentəd\ *adj* [¹*tent* + *-ed*] **1 a :** covered with tents **:** containing tents ⟨the ~ field⟩ **b :** sheltered by or provided with a tent ⟨the ~ soldiers⟩ **2 :** shaped like a tent ⟨~ arch⟩ ⟨~ ice⟩

tented wagon *n* **:** COVERED WAGON

¹**ten·ter** \ˈtentə(r)\ *n* -S [ME *teyntur*, *tayntour*, *taynter*, perh. modif. (influenced by MF *teindre* to dye) of ML *tentura*, fr. L *tentus* (past part. of *tendere* to stretch) + *-ura* -ure — more at THIN] **1 :** a frame or endless track with hooks or clips along two sides that is used for drying and stretching cloth **2** *archaic* **:** TENTERHOOK — **on the tenters** *archaic* **:** on tenterhooks ⟨I have seen him stretched *on the tenters* to keep thee in countenance —Samuel Richardson⟩

²**tenter** \"\ *vt* -ED/-ING/-S [ME *teynteren*, fr. *teyntur*, *taynter* tenter] **:** to hang or stretch on or as if on a tenter

³**tent·er** \ˈtentə(r)\ *n* -S [⁴*tent* + *-er*] **1** *Brit* **:** one that has charge of something; *specif* **:** one that tends a machine in a factory **2** *Brit* **:** HELPER 2

⁴**tenter** \"\ *n* -S [²*tent* + *-er*] **:** one that lives in or occupies a tent ⟨they slept in better style than ~s —Gordon Webber⟩

ten·ter·er \ˈtentərə(r)\ *n* -S [²*tenter* + *-er*] **:** one that tenters (as cloth)

tenterhook \ˈ==,=\ *n* [ME *tentourhok*, *tayntyrhok*, fr. *taynter*, *tayntour* tenter + *hok* hook] **1 :** a sharp hooked nail used esp. for fastening cloth on a tenter **2 :** something that serves as a means or device for stretching or straining — **on tenterhooks** **:** in a state of uneasiness, strain, or suspense ⟨the new men are frankly *on tenterhooks*, for they have a career at stake —Roy Lewis & Angus Maude⟩ ⟨puts his readers right *on tenterhooks* —W.G.Rogers⟩

¹**tenth** \ˈten(t)th\ *adj* [ME *tenthe*, alter. (influenced by *ten*) of *tethe*, fr. OE *tēotha*; akin to OS *tegotho* tenth, MLG *tegede*; all fr. a prehistoric WGmc ordinal whose first element is the source of OE *tīen*, *tȳn*, *tēn* ten and whose second element is the source of OE *-otha*, *-tha* -th — more at TEN, -TH] **1 :** being number 10 in a countable series ⟨the ~ day⟩ — see NUMBER table **2 :** being one of 10 equal parts into which something is divisible ⟨a ~ share of the money⟩

²**tenth** \"\ *n, pl* **tenths** \-n(t)s, -n(t)ths\ [ME *tenthe*, fr. *tenthe*, adj.] **1 :** number 10 in a countable series ⟨the ~ of the month⟩ **2 :** the quotient of a unit divided by 10 **:** one of 10 equal parts of something ⟨one ~ of the total⟩ **3 a :** a tax of one tenth levied on the personal property of a subject and granted to the English sovereign from 1272 to 1624 **b :** a tenth part of the annual profit of every Anglican benefice paid from 1534 to 1703 to the crown and after 1703 into a special fund to aid needy churches or augment church livings **4 a :** a musical interval embracing an octave and a third **b :** a note or tone at this interval **c :** an organ stop sounding a tenth above the normal pitch of the digitals played upon **5 :** a unit of capacity for wine equal to one tenth of a U.S. gallon; *also* **:** a bottle holding this quantity of wine

³**tenth** \"\ *adv* [¹*tenth*] **1 :** in the tenth place **2 :** with nine exceptions ⟨the nation's ~ largest city⟩

tenth card *n* **:** a card in cribbage (as a face card or a ten) counting ten points

tenth cranial nerve *or* **tenth nerve** *n* **:** VAGUS NERVE

tenth·ly *adv* [¹*tenth* + *-ly*] **:** in the tenth place

tenthmeter \ˈ=,==\ *n* [²*tenth* + *meter* (unit)] **1 :** a metric unit of length equal to one ten millionth of a millimeter ⟨one meter equals 10^{10} ~s⟩ **2 :** ANGSTROM a

tenth-rate \ˈ=ˈ=\ *adj* **:** most inferior **:** of the lowest character or quality ⟨the way he had done his research, his lack of critical sense, his taking his professor's evidence — that wasn't even second-rate, it was *tenth-rate* —C.P.Snow⟩

¹**ten·thred·i·nid** \tenˈthredənəd\ *adj* [NL *Tenthredinidae*] **:** of or relating to the Tenthredinidae

²**tenthredinid** \"\ *n* -S **:** a sawfly of the family Tenthredinidae

ten·thre·din·i·dae \,ten(t)thrəˈdinə,dē\ *n pl, cap* [NL *Tenthredin-*, *Tenthredo*, type genus (fr. Gk *tenthrēdōn*, a kind of wasp) + *-idae*] **:** a family of Hymenoptera comprising all the sawflies or now more commonly including various typical sawflies — see TENTHREDINOIDEA

ten·thre·di·noi·dea \,ten(t)thrədəˈnȯidēə\ *n pl, cap* [NL, fr. *Tenthredin-*, *Tenthredo* + *-oidea*] **:** a superfamily (suborder Chalastogastra) of hymenopterous insects comprising the sawflies and being coextensive with Tenthredinidae in its broadest use

tent·i·form \ˈtentə,fȯrm\ *adj* [¹*tent* + *-iform*] **:** resembling or building a nest that resembles a tent in form ⟨~ leaf miners⟩

ten·til·lum \ten·ˈtiləm\ *n, pl* **tentil·la** \-lə\ [NL, fr. L *tentare* to feel + *-illum*, dim. suffix — more at TEMPT] **:** a branch of a tentacle; *esp* **:** one of the contractile branches that are rich in nematocysts and that occur on the tentacles of various siphonophores

tenting *pres part of* TENT

¹**tent·less** \ˈ=ləs\ *adj* [³*tent* + *-less*] *Scot* **:** CARELESS, HEEDLESS

²**tentless** \"\ *adj* [¹*tent* + *-less*] **:** having no tent **:** being without means of shelter

tentmaker \ˈ=,==\ *n* **1 :** one that makes tents **2 :** any of numerous moths whose gregarious larvae spin communal nests usu. in trees

tentmate \ˈ=,=\ *n* **:** one that occupies the same tent

tent of meeting : TABERNACLE 1a

ten·to·ri·al \(ˈ)ten·ˈtōrēəl, -tȯr-\ *adj* [NL *tentorium* + E *-al*] **:** of, relating to, or involving the tentorium

tentorial ridge *n* **:** a bony ridge on the inner surface of the skull that marks the attachment of the tentorium

tentorial sinus *n* **:** STRAIGHT SINUS

ten·to·ri·um \ten·ˈtōrēəm\ *n, pl* **tento·ria** \-rēə\ [NL, fr. L, tent, fr. *tentus* (past part. of *tendere* to stretch) + *-orium*] **1** *or* **tentorium ce·re·bel·li** \-,serəˈbe,lī\ [*tentorium cerebelli*, fr. NL, lit., tentorium of the cerebellum] **:** an arched fold of dura mater covering the upper surface of the cerebellum, supporting the occipital lobes of the cerebrum, having its posterior and lateral border attached to the skull and its anterior border free, and in some forms (as the cat) being completely ossified **2 :** the internal chitinous skeleton of an insect's head formed usu. of two or three paired apodemes arising from the chitinous head capsule

tent pegging *n* [*tent peg* + *-ing*] **:** a sport originating in India of riding a horse at a charging pace and endeavoring to uproot on the point of a lance a tent peg in the ground

tents *pl of* TENT, *pres 3d sing of* TENT

tent shell *n* **:** LIMPET

tent slide *or* **tent slip** *n* **:** a device used to adjust the tension of a guy rope of a tent — called also *rope key*

tent stitch *n* **:** a short stitch slanting to the right that is used in embroidery and canvas work to form even lines of solid background — compare GROS POINT, PETIT POINT

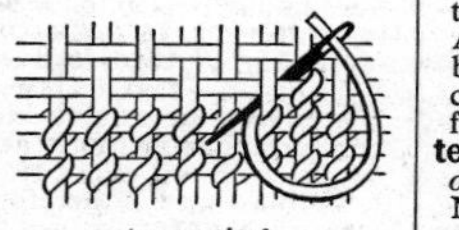

tent stitch

ten–twenty–thirty \ˈ=ˈ==ˈ==\ *or* **ten–twent–thirt** \ˈ=ˈtwentˈthərt\ *n* [so called fr. the prices in cents of seats] **:** a cheap and typically melodramatic theatrical entertainment; *also* **:** a theater or touring company offering such entertainment

tent worm *n* **:** TENT CATERPILLAR

tenty *also* **tent·ie** \ˈtenti\ *adj* [³*tent* + *-y*] *Scot* **:** ATTENTIVE, CAREFUL, WATCHFUL

te·nue \tənˈü\ *n, pl* **tenues** \"\ [F, fr. fem. of *tenu*, past part. of *tenir* to hold, fr. OF — more at TENABLE] **1 :** BEARING, CARRIAGE, DEPORTMENT ⟨the sacrifices made in the sacred name of ~ . . . the smiles amiably exchanged in public between mortal enemies —Victoria Sackville-West⟩ **2 :** mode of dress ⟨the long black coat with the lavender trousers and mauve vest that must have been his ~ when he married his first wife —*Young's Mag.*⟩

ten·u·i·ros·ter \,tenyəwēˈrästə(r)\ *n* -S [NL, sing. of *Tenuirostres*] **:** a bird of the Tenuirostres

ten·u·i·ros·tres \-ä,strēz\ *n pl, cap* [NL, fr. L *tenuis* thin + *rostrum* beak — more at THIN, ROSTRUM] *in former classifications* **:** an unnatural group of mostly passerine birds (as hummingbirds, sunbirds, honey eaters, nuthatches) having slender bills

ten·u·is \ˈtenyəwə̇s\ *n, pl* **ten·u·es** \-ə,wēz\ [ML, lit., thin, slight, trans. of Gk *psilos* bare, unaspirated — more at PSIL-] **:** an unaspirated voiceless stop

te·nu·i·ty \teˈn(y)üəd·ē, təˈn-, -üətē, -i\ *n* -ES [L *tenuitat-*, *tenuitas*, fr. *tenuis* thin, slight + *-itat-*, *-itas* -ity] **1 :** lack of substance **:** MEAGERNESS, POVERTY ⟨as far as the ~ of my understanding would hold out —Laurence Sterne⟩ **2 :** lack of thickness **:** SLENDERNESS, THINNESS ⟨the ~ of a hair⟩ **3 :** lack of density **:** rarefied quality or state **:** RARITY ⟨in studying the upper atmospheric region it is helpful to bear in mind its high ~ —S.K.Mitra⟩ **4 :** lack of intensity or vigor **:** FAINTNESS, FEEBLENESS ⟨speak with a shrill yet sweet ~ of voice —Nathaniel Hawthorne⟩

ten·u·lin \ˈtenyələn\ *n* -S [NL *tenuifolium* (specific epithet of *Helenium tenuifolium*) (fr. L *tenuis* thin + *folium* leaf) + *-lin* (as in *helenalin*) — more at BLADE] **:** a crystalline sesquiterpenoid lactone $C_{17}H_{22}O_5$ obtained from plants of the genus *Helenium* (as *H. tenuifolium*)

ten·u·ous \ˈtenyəwəs\ *adj* [L *tenuis* thin, slight, tenuous — more at THIN] **1 :** not dense **:** having a thin consistency **:** RARE ⟨as ~ as a comet's trail —A.M.Young⟩ **2 :** not thick **:** SLENDER, SLIM ⟨lowering himself down rocky ravines with a ~ nylon rope —*Sydney (Australia) Bull.*⟩ ⟨write it in ~, trailing letters —P.M.Hollister⟩ **3 a :** having little substance or strength **:** FLIMSY, INSIGNIFICANT, WEAK ⟨a ~ idealism lost touch with reality —Laurence Binyon⟩ ⟨the ~ character of his physical strength —E.H.Blashfield⟩ **b :** not firmly based or supported ⟨the seeds sprout slowly, and take ~ root —Fred Rodell⟩ ⟨~ growth that will wither beneath the hot winds of summer —George Farwell⟩ **c :** not definite, sharp, or clear-cut **:** HAZY, VAGUE ⟨impossible to analyze all the ~ influences at work —*Amer. Guide Series: Mich.*⟩ **syn** see THIN

ten·u·ous·ly *adv* **:** in a tenuous manner

ten·u·ous·ness *n* -ES **:** the quality or state of being tenuous

¹**ten·ure** \ˈtenyə(r) *also* -,nyů(ə)r *or* -üə\ *n* -S [ME, fr. OF *teneüre*, *tenure*, fr. ML *tenitura*, fr. (assumed) VL *tenitus* (past part. of L *tenēre* to hold) + L *-ura* -ure — more at THIN] **1 a** (1) **:** the act or right of holding property esp. real estate ⟨land ~ is a leading political issue in many parts of the world⟩ (2) *Eng law* **:** the holding of an estate of a superior **b :** the manner of holding property **:** the title and conditions by which property is held ⟨~ by knight service⟩ ⟨~ by fee simple absolute⟩ **2 :** ESTATE, HOLDING ⟨like most Old English leaseholds, the ~s . . . created were limited to three lives —F.M.Stenton⟩ **3 a :** the act, action, or a means of holding something **:** GRASP, HOLD ⟨the uncertain ~ which mere military demonstrations in force gave her over a proud people —John Buchan⟩ ⟨hope that you will hold your place in company by a nobler ~ —Earl of Chesterfield⟩ ⟨trousers held, apparently, by a very insecure ~ —Rachel Henning⟩ **b :** manner, condition, or term of holding something ⟨the great limitations just indicated affect the ~ of this power —C.H.McIlwain⟩ ⟨spends his ~ of office fighting for time to assess facts and to think —Dorothy Fosdick⟩ **c :** a status granted usu. after a probationary period to one holding a position esp. as a teacher and protecting him from dismissal except for serious misconduct or incompetence determined by formal hearings or trial **:** permanent tenure

²**ten·ure** \ˈtenyə(r)\ [ME, alter. of *tenour* tenor] *archaic var of* TENOR

tenure by free alms : FRANKALMOIGN

tenure in chivalry : tenure by knight service

ten·u·ri·al \teˈnyůrēəl, təˈn-\ *adj* [¹*tenure* + *-ial*] **:** of or relating to tenure ⟨this ~ revolution never degenerated into a scramble for land —F.M.Stenton⟩ — **ten·u·ri·al·ly** \-əlē\ *adv*

te·nu·to \təˈnüd·(,)ō\ *adv (or adj)* [It, fr. past part. of *tenere* to hold, fr. L *tenēre* — more at THIN] **:** in a manner so as to hold a tone or chord firmly to its full value — used as a direction in music; compare STACCATO

ten–week stock \ˈ=ˈ=-\ *n* **:** any of several garden stocks that constitute a variety (*Matthiola incana annua*) of the common stock and that bloom from seed during the summer and fall of their first season of growth — compare BRAMPTON STOCK

tenzon *var of* TENSON

te·o·cal·li \,tēəˈkalē, ,tāəˈkälē\ *n* -S [Nahuatl, fr. *teotl* god + *calli* house] **:** an ancient temple of Mexico or Central America usu. built upon the summit of a truncated pyramidal mound; *also* **:** the mound itself

te·o·pan \ˈtāə,pän, ,==ˈ=\ *n* -S [Nahuatl, fr. *teotl* god + *pan* place] **:** the precincts of an ancient temple of Mexico **:** a walled enclosure containing a teocalli and other buildings devoted to religious uses

te·o·sin·te \,tāəˈsintē\ *also* **te·o·cen·tli** \-sentlē\ *or* **te·o·cin·tle** \-sintlē\ *n* -S [Nahuatl *teocentli*, fr. *teotl* god + *centli* ear of corn] **:** a large annual grass (*Euchlaena mexicana*) that is native to Mexico and Central America, is sometimes regarded as the progenitor of Indian corn, and is grown esp. for fodder in many warm countries

te·o·ti·hua·can \,tāə,tēwəˈkän\ *adj, usu cap* [fr. *Teotihuacán*, town of central Mexico noted for its Toltec ruins] **:** of or belonging to the Toltec period of Nahuatl culture in Mexico characterized by temple building and the establishment of gods such as Tlaloc and Quetzalcoatl

te·pa \ˈtāpə\ *n* -S [fr. native name in Chile] **1 :** a So. American timber tree (*Laurelia serrata*) of the family Monimiaceae **2 :** the wood of the tepa

te·pa·che \təˈpächē\ *n* -S [Sp, fr. Nahuatl *tepiatl*, fr. *tepitl* a kind of corn + *atl* water] **:** any of several Mexican drinks; *specif* **:** an intoxicating beverage made from pulque and coarse sugar with timbe used to retard fermentation

tepal \ˈtepəl, ˈtep-\ *n* -S [F *tépale*, alter. (influenced by *sépale* sepal, fr. NL *sepalum*) of *pétale* petal, fr. NL *petalum* — more at SEPAL, PETAL] **:** any of the modified leaves making up a perianth

tep·a·nec \,tepəˈnek\ *or* **tep·a·neca** \,==ˈnekə\ *n, pl* **tepanec** *or* **tepanecs** *or* **tepaneca** *or* **tepanecas** *usu cap* **1 :** a Nahuatl people of the Valley of Mexico **2 :** a member of the Tepanec people

tep·a·ry bean \ˈtepərē-\ *n* [origin unknown] **:** an annual twining bean (*Phaseolus acutifolius latifolius*) native to southwestern U.S. and Mexico but cultivated for its resistance to drought and heat and having roundish white, yellow, brown, or bluish black edible seeds

te·pe \ˈtepē\ *n* -S [Turk, hill, summit] **:** an artificial mound — used in place names; compare ³TELL

tep·e·ca·no \,tepəˈkä(,)nō\ *n, pl* **tepecano** *or* **tepecanos** *usu cap* [MexSp, fr. Nahuatl *tepetl* mountain + *aco* on top of] **1 a :** a Piman people of the northern part of the state of Jalisco, Mexico **b :** a member of such people **2 :** the language of the Tepecano people

te·pee *or* **ti·pi** *also* **tee·pee** \ˈtē(,)pē, -,pi\ *n* -S [Dakota *tipi* tent, fr. *ti* to dwell + *pi* to use for] **:** an American Indian conical tent used esp. by the Plains tribes and consisting of a covering usu. of skins spread over a frame of poles — compare LODGE 8a

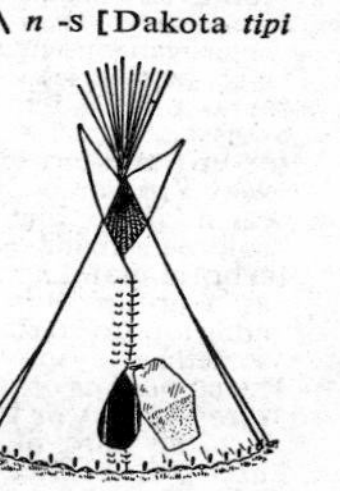

tepee

te·pe·hua \təˈpā(,)wä\ *n, pl* **tepehua** *or* **tepehuas** *usu cap* [MexSp, prob. fr. Nahuatl *Tepehuan*] **1 a :** a Totonac people of southeastern Mexico **b :** a member of such people **2 :** the language of the Tepehua people

te·pe·huan \,tepəˈwän\ *or* **te·pe·hua·ne** \,==ˈwänē\ *n, pl* **tepehuan** *or* **tepehuans** *or* **tepehuane** *or* **tepehuanes** *usu cap* [MexSp *Tepehuán*, *Tepehuane*, fr. Nahuatl *Tepehuan*, fr. *tepetl* mountain + *huan* at the junction of] **1 a :** a Piman people of Durango and adjacent states in northwestern Mexico **b :** a member of such people **2 :** the language of the Tepehuan people

tep·e·ta·te \,tepəˈtäd·ē\ *n* -S [MexSp, fr. Nahuatl *tepetatl*, fr. *tetl* stone + *petatl* matting] **:** CALICHE

te·pex·pán man \,tepəˈspän-\ *n, usu cap T* [fr. *Tepexpán*, village of central Mexico] **:** an extinct man that is known from a fossilized skeleton found in the Valley of Mexico and attributed to the late Pleistocene and that was probably coeval with Folsom man

tephillin *var of* TEFILLIN

te·phrit·i·dae \təˈfridə,dē\ [NL, fr. *Tephritis*, genus of two-winged flies (fr. Gk *tephros* ash gray) + *-idae*] *syn of* TRYPETIDAE

teph·ro·ite \ˈtefrō,īt\ *n* -S [G *tephroit*, fr. Gk *tephros* ash gray + G *-it* -ite] **:** a mineral Mn_2SiO_4 that consists of Manganese silicate and is isomorphous with olivine

te·phro·sia \təˈfrōzh(ē)ə, teˈf-\ *n, cap* [NL, fr. Gk *tephros* ash gray, fr. *tephra* ashes; fr. the appearance of its foliage — more at DAY] **:** a genus of herbs or undershrubs (family Leguminosae) having odd-pinnate leaves, white or purplish flowers, and flat legumes

teph·ro·sin \ˈtefrəsən\ *n* -S [NL *Tephrosia* + ISV *-in*] **:** a crystalline compound $C_{23}H_{22}O_7$ that is obtained from the leaves of a leguminous plant (*Tephrosia vogelii*) and from the roots of derris and cube and that is isomeric with toxicarol; hydroxy-deguelin

tep·id \ˈtepəd\ *adj* [L *tepidus*, fr. *tepēre* to be moderately warm; akin to Skt *tapati* it gives out heat, *tapas* heat, OIr *tess* heat] **1 :** moderately warm **:** LUKEWARM ⟨a ~ bath⟩ ⟨a ~ pool⟩ **2 a :** lacking in passion, force, or animation **:** DULL, LIFELESS ⟨grave and precise in manner, courteous and ~ —Arnold Bennett⟩ ⟨was so ~ and had so few resources and so little initiative —George Santayana⟩ **b :** marked by an absence of enthusiasm or conviction **:** HALFHEARTED ⟨had only a ~ interest in public health —A.W.Long⟩ ⟨still enjoys a measure of ~ praise —T.S.Eliot⟩ — **tep·id·ly** *adv* — **tep·id·ness** *n* -ES

tep·i·dar·i·um \,tepəˈda(a)rēəm\ *n, pl* **tepidar·ia** \-rēə\ [L, fr. L *tepidus* tepid + *-arium*] **:** a warm room of the ancient Roman thermae used to sit in

te·pid·i·ty \təˈpidəd·ē, -dətē, -i\ *n* -ES [LL *tepiditat-*, *tepiditas*, fr. L *tepidus* tepid + *-itat-*, *-itas* -ity] **:** the quality or state of being tepid **:** LUKEWARMNESS

tep·o·nax·tle *or* **tep·o·nax·tli** \,tepəˈnästlē\ *n* -S [MexSp & Nahuatl; MexSp *teponaxtle*, fr. Nahuatl *teponaztli*] **:** a Mexican slit-drum of Aztec origin

tepoy *var of* TEAPOY

TEPP \,tē,ē,pēˈpē\ *abbr or n* -S [*tetraethyl pyrophosphate*] **:** TETRAETHYL PYROPHOSPHATE

tep·ti·ar \ˈteptē,är\ *n, pl* **teptiar** *or* **teptiars** *usu cap* **1 :** a Tatar people of central Asia related to the Kazaks and Bashkirs **2 :** a member of the Teptiar people

te·qui·la \təˈkēlə\ *n* -S [Sp, fr. *Tequila*, district of Jalisco state, west central Mexico] **1 :** a Mexican century plant (*Agave tequilana*) much cultivated as one of the chief sources of mescal **2** *also* **te·quil·la** \"\ **a :** a Mexican liquor made by redistilling mescal — compare SOTOL **b :** MESCAL

te·quis·tla·tec \təˈkistlə,tek\ *n, pl* **tequistlatec** *or* **tequistlatecs** *usu cap* **1 a :** an Indian people of southern Oaxaca, Mexico **b :** a member of such people **2 :** the Tequistlatecan language of the Tequistlatec people — called also *Chontal*

te·quis·tla·tec·an \ˈ=,==ˈ==ən\ *n, pl* **tequistlatecan** *or* **tequistlatecans** *usu cap* [*tequistlatec* + *-an*] **:** a language family of the Hokan stock in Mexico comprising only the Tequistlatec language

ter- *comb form* [L, fr. *ter* three times; akin to Gk & Skt *tris* three times, L *tres* three — more at THREE] **1 :** three times, threefold, thrice, three ⟨*ter*centenary⟩ **2 :** TRI- 4 — esp. in names of organic compounds to denote tripling of a radical or molecule ⟨*ter*phenyl⟩

ter *abbr* **1** terrace **2** terrazzo **3** territory **4** tertiary

ter·a·con·ic acid \,terəˈkänik-\ *n* [ISV *terebic* + *itaconic*] **:** a crystalline dicarboxylic acid $C_7H_{10}O_4$ that is obtainable by the

distillation of terebic acid and that is a dimethyl homologue of itaconic acid; isopropylidene-succinic acid

ter·a·cryl·ic acid \ˌterəˌkrilik-\ *n* [ISV *terpenylic* + *acrylic*] **:** an unsaturated liquid acid $C_7H_{12}O_2$ obtained by distillation of terpenylic acid; 3,4-dimethyl-3-penten-oic acid

ter·a·glin \ˈterəglən\ *n* -S [fr. native name in Australia] **:** GEELBEC 2

te·rai \təˈrī\ *also* **terai hat** *n* -S [fr. *Tarai* a swampy lowland belt of northeastern India] **:** a double felt sun hat with wide turned brim worn esp. in subtropical regions

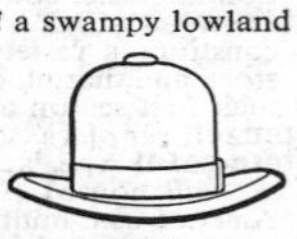

terai

terakihi *var of* TARAKIHI

te·rap \təˈrap\ *n* -S [Malay *tĕrap*] **1 :** a tall Malayan tree (*Artocarpus kunstleri*) **2 :** a coarse fiber from the bark of the terap

ter·aph \ˈterəf\ *n, pl* **tera·phim** \ˈterəˌfim *also* -fēm *sometimes* ˌ==ˈ=\ [Heb *tĕrāphīm* (pl. in form but sing. in meaning)] **:** an image representing a primitive household god among the ancient Jews and other Semitic peoples and later used in divination and as a talismanic figure

ter·as \ˈterəs\ *n, pl* **tera·ta** \-rəd·ə\ [NL *terat-, teras*, fr. Gk, marvel, monster] **:** an organism (as a fetus) that is grossly abnormal in structure due to genetic or developmental causes **:** MONSTER

terat *abbr* teratology

terat- *or* **terato-** *comb form* [Gk, fr. *terat-, teras* marvel, portent, monster; akin to Lith *keras* enchantment, Skt *kṛtyā* action, enchantment, *karoti* he does, acts, and perh. to ON *skars* monster, *skyrsi* portent, Skt *āścarya* marvelous — more at KARMA] **:** monster ⟨*teratism*⟩ ⟨*teratology*⟩

ter·a·tism \ˈterəˌtizəm\ *n* -S [*terat-* + *-ism*] **1 :** anomaly of organic form and structure **:** MONSTROSITY **2 :** love of the marvelous **:** worship of monsters ⟨man's pathetic struggle up from ~ through animism and taboo and magic to our present day —*Saturday Rev.*⟩

ter·a·to·genesis \ˌterətō+\ *n* [NL, fr. *terat-* + L *genesis*] **:** production of monstrous growths or fetuses

ter·a·to·genetic \ˌterə(ˌ)tōjəˈned·ik\ *or* **ter·a·to·gen·ic** \-ˌtōˈjenik\ *adj* [ISV *terat-* + *-genetic* or *-genic*] **:** relating to teratogenesis **:** tending to cause monstrosity ⟨~ agent⟩

¹ter·a·toid \ˈterəˌtȯid\ *adj* [ISV *terat-* + *-oid*] **1 :** abnormal in formation ⟨~ tumor⟩ **2 :** characteristic of a teratoma

²teratoid \ˈ"\ *n* -S **:** TERATOMA

ter·a·to·log·i·cal \ˌterətəˈläjəkəl, -rəd·ᵊlˈä-\ *adj* [*teratology* + *-ical*] **:** relating to abnormality of organic growth or structure ⟨~ specimen⟩ **:** belonging to teratology ⟨~ publications⟩

ter·a·tol·o·gist \ˌterəˈtäləjəst\ *n* -S [ISV *teratology* + *-ist*] **:** a student of teratology

ter·a·tol·o·gy \-jē\ *n* -ES [Gk *teratologia*, fr. *terat-* + *-logia* -logy] **1 a :** fantastic mythmaking or storytelling in which prodigies and monsters play a large part **b :** a collection of such stories **2** [ISV *terat-* + *-logy*] **:** the study of malformations, monstrosities, or serious deviations from the normal type in growing organisms **:** study of the nature and origin of terata

ter·a·to·ma \ˌterəˈtōmə\ *n, pl* **teratomas** \-məz\ *or* **tera·toma·ta** \-məd·ə\ [NL, fr. *terat-* + *-oma*] **:** a tumor derived from more than one embryonic layer and made up of a heterogeneous mixture of tissues (as epithelium, bone, cartilage, or muscle)

ter·a·to·sis \ˌterəˈtōsəs\ *n* -ES [NL, fr. *terat-* + *-osis*] **:** TERATISM

ter·bi·um \ˈtərbēəm\ *n* -S [NL, fr. *Ytterby*, village of southwest Sweden + NL *-ium*] **:** a metallic element of the rare-earth group that is usu. trivalent but is tetravalent in its colored dioxide — symbol *Tb*; see ELEMENT table

terbium metal *n* **:** any of a group of rare-earth metals separable as a group from other metals occurring with them and in addition to terbium including europium, gadolinium, and sometimes dysprosium — compare YTTRIUM METAL

¹terce *obs var of* TIERCE

²terce \ˈtərs\ *or* **tierce** \ˈti(ə)rs\ *n* -S [ME — more at TIERCE] **1 :** the third of the canonical hours beginning at 9 a.m.; *also* **:** the service or office for that hour **2** *Scots law* **:** the widow's right corresponding to the common-law dower

tercel *var of* TIERCEL

terce·let \ˈtərslət\ *n* -S [ME, fr. MF, fr. *tercel* tiercel + *-et* — more at TIERCEL] **:** TIERCEL

tercel gentle *or* **tassel-gentle** \ˈ==ˈ==\ *n* [ME *tercel gentil*, fr. *tercel* tiercel + *gentil* gentle] **:** a trained male falcon

¹ter·centenary \(ˈ)tər, ˈtə, ˌtə+\ *adj* [*ter-* + *centenary*] **:** relating to a 300th anniversary or its celebration

²tercentenary \ˈ"\ *n* **:** a 300th anniversary or its celebration

ter·centennial \ˈtər, ˈtə+\ *adj or n* [*ter-* + *centennial*] **:** TERCENTENARY

ter·centesimal \ˈ"+\ *adj* [*ter-* + *centesimal*] **:** based on the number 300 ⟨~ scale⟩

terc·er \ˈtərsər\ *n* -S [*²terce* + *-er*] *Scots law* **:** a widow entitled to terce

ter·ce·ron \ˈtərsəˌrōn\ *n* -S [AmSp *tercerón*, fr. Sp *tercero* third, fr. L *tertiarius* containing a third part; fr. his being third in descent from a Negro — more at TERTIARY] **:** QUADROON

ter·cet \ˈtərsət\ *or* **tier·cet** \ˈtirsət\ *n* -S [It *terzetto* tercet, terzetto, fr. dim. of *terzo* third, fr. L *tertius* — more at THIRD] **:** a unit or group of three lines of verse: **a :** one of the three-line stanzas linked by rhyme in terza rima **b :** one of the two groups of three lines forming the sestet in an Italian sonnet

ter·chloride \ˈtər+\ *n* [*ter-* + *chloride*] **:** TRICHLORIDE

ter·cio \ˈtersēˌō\ *or* **ter·cia** \-ēə\ *n* -S [Sp *tercio*, fr. *tercio* third (adj.), fr. L *tertius* — more at THIRD] **:** a Spanish or Italian infantry regiment of the 16th and 17th centuries

ter·diurnal \ˈtər+\ *adj* [*ter-* + *diurnal*] **:** occurring three times per day ⟨~ variation of atmospheric pressure⟩

ter·e·bel·la \ˌterəˈbelə\ *n, cap* [NL, fr. dim. of L *terebra* borer, gimlet — more at TEREBRA] **:** a genus of tube-forming marine polychaete worms with horseshoe-shaped preoral lobe, many filamentous tentacles, several pairs of segmental gills, and reduced parapodia that is type of a family Terebellidae of nearly cosmopolitan distribution — **ter·e·bel·lid** \ˌ==ˈ==ləd\ *adj or n* — **ter·e·bel·loid** \-ˌlȯid\ *adj or n*

ter·e·bel·li·dae \ˌ==ˈbeləˌdē\ *n pl, cap* [NL, fr. *Terebella*, type genus + *-idae*] **:** a large family of marine burrowing or tube-forming polychaete worms with often showy filamentous anterior gills and usu. a long thick body

ter·e·bene \ˈterəˌbēn\ *n* -S [F *térébène*, fr. *térébinthe* terebinth (fr. MF) + *-ène* -ene] **:** a liquid mixture of terpenes that is formed by the action of sulfuric acid on turpentine (sense 2) and distillation with steam, that consists chiefly of dipentene and terpinenes, that resinifies on exposure to air and light, and that is used chiefly as an expectorant

ter·e·ben·thene \ˌ==ˈbenˌthēn\ *n* -S [F *térébenthène*, irreg. (influenced by *térébenthine* turpentine, fr. MF *terebentine*) fr. L *terebinthus* terebinth + F *-ène* -ene — more at TURPENTINE] **:** levorotatory alpha-pinene

te·rebic acid \təˈrebik-, -rēbik-\ *n* [L *terebinthus* terebinth + E *-ic*] **:** a crystalline lactonic acid $C_7H_{10}O_4$ obtained esp. by the oxidation of turpentine oil; dimethyl-paraconic acid

ter·e·binth \ˈterəˌbin(t)th\ *n* -S [ME *therebinthe, terebynt*, fr. MF *therebinte, terebinthe*, fr. L *terebinthus* — more at TURPENTINE] **1** *or* **terebinth tree :** a small European tree (*Pistacia terebinthus*) yielding Chian turpentine **2** *obs* **:** the resin yielded by the terebinth

ter·e·bin·tha·ce·ae \ˌterəbənˈthāsēˌē\ *n pl, cap* [NL, fr. *Terebinthus*, type genus (fr. L, terebinth) + *-aceae*] *in some classifications* **:** a family of plants coextensive with the Anacardiaceae

ter·e·bin·thi·nate \ˌterəˈbin(t)thəˌnāt\ *adj* [NL *terebinthinatus*, fr. *terebinthina* turpentine, fr. L, fem. of *terebinthinus* of the terebinth — more at TURPENTINE] **:** relating to, containing, or resembling turpentine (as in odor)

ter·e·bin·thine \ˈterəˈbin(t)thən\ *adj* [L *terebinthinus* of the terebinth] **:** TEREBINTHINATE

tere·bra \təˈrēbrə, ˈterəb-\ *n* [L, borer, gimlet, fr. *terere* to rub, grind + *-bra*, suffix denoting an instrument — more at THROW] **1** *pl* **terebras** \-brəz\ *or* **terebrae** \-ˌē(ˌ)brē, -ə(ˌ)brē, -əˌbrī\ **:** a device used by the ancient Romans for starting a breach in a fortified wall **2** [NL, fr. L, borer] **a :** the boring ovipositor of a hymenopterous insect **b** *cap* **:** a genus of marine gastropods (suborder Stenoglossa) having a long tapering spire and being the type of a family Terebridae comprising the auger shells **c** -S **:** AUGER SHELL — **tere·bral** \təˈrēbrəl, ˈterəb-\ *adj*

¹tere·brant \təˈrēbrənt, ˈterəb-\ *adj* [NL *Terebrantia*] **:** of or relating to the Terebrantia

²terebrant \ˈ"\ *n* -S **:** an insect of the suborder Terebrantia

ter·e·bran·tia \ˌterəˈbranchēə\ *n pl, cap* [NL, fr. L, neut. pl. of *terebrant-, terebrans*, pres. part. of *terebrare* to bore, fr. *terebra* borer, gimlet] **1 :** a suborder or other division of Hymenoptera including insects (as sawflies, horntails, and various parasitic hymenoptera) that have a boring ovipositor — compare ACULEATA **2 :** a suborder of hairy-winged Thysanoptera in which the females have a serrated ovipositor

tere·bra·tel·la \təˌrēbrəˈtelə, ˌterəb-\ *n, cap* [NL, fr. L *terebratus* (past part. of *terebrare* to bore) + *-ella*] **:** a cosmopolitan genus of articulate brachiopods (family Terebratulidae) that includes a common species (*T. transversa*) of the western coast of No. America

ter·e·brat·u·la \ˌterəˈbrachələ\ *n* [NL, fr. L *terebratus* + *-ula*] **1** *cap* **:** a genus of articulate brachiopods with arms borne by a calcareous loop and a short peduncle projecting through the shell that is type of a family Terebratulidae **2** *pl* **terebratulas** \-ləz\ *or* **terebratu·lae** \-ˌlē\ **:** a brachiopod of the genus *Terebratula* **:** LAMP SHELL — **ter·e·brat·u·lar** \ˌ==ˈ==lə(r)\ *adj* — **ter·e·brat·u·line** \-ˌlīn, -lən\ *adj*

¹ter·e·brat·u·lid \ˌ==ˈ==ləd\ *adj* [NL *Terebratulidae*] **:** of or relating to the Terebratulidae

²terebratulid \ˈ"\ *n* -S **:** a brachiopod or fossil of the family Terebratulidae

ter·e·bra·tu·li·dae \ˌterəbrəˈtüləˌdē, -brəˈtyü-\ *n pl, cap* [NL *Terebratula*, type genus + *-idae*] **:** a large family of living and extinct brachiopods usu. placed with a few related forms in a distinct superfamily or suborder of the order Telotremata — see TEREBRATULA

¹ter·e·brat·u·loid \-ˌlȯid\ *adj* [NL *Terebratula* + E *-oid*] **:** related to or resembling the Terebratulidae

²terebratuloid \ˈ"\ *n* -S **:** a terebratuloid brachiopod or fossil

te·reb·ri·dae \təˈrebrəˌdē\ *n pl, cap* [NL, fr. *Terebra*, type genus + *-idae*] **:** a family of chiefly tropical marine snails (group Toxoglossa) with slender tall-spired shells of many whorls — see AUGER SHELL

¹ter·e·din·id \ˌterəˈdinəd, təˈredᵊn-\ *adj* [NL *Teredinidae*] **:** of or relating to the Teredinidae

²teredinid \ˈ"\ *n* -S **:** a mollusk of the family Teredinidae **:** SHIPWORM

ter·e·din·i·dae \ˌterəˈdinəˌdē\ *n pl, cap* [NL, fr. *Teredin-, Teredo*, type genus + *-idae*] **:** a family of marine bivalve mollusks (order Eulamellibranchia) that live in burrows (as in wood or clay) which they rasp out with their small trilobed shells and line with a calcareous secretion, are very destructive to marine wooden constructions (as ships and wharves), and are vermiform with very long siphons united through most of their length — see BANKIA, SHIPWORM, TEREDO; compare PHOLAS

te·re·do \təˈrē(ˌ)dō\ *n* [L *teredin-, teredo* worm that bores wood, fr. Gk *terēdon-, terēdōn*; akin to Gk *tetrainein* to bore through, pierce — more at THROW] **1** *pl* **teredos** \-ōz\ *or* **te·red·i·nes** \-redᵊnˌēz\ **:** SHIPWORM **2** *cap* [NL *Teredin-, Teredo*, fr. L, worm that bores wood] **:** a genus of mollusks that contains the typical shipworms and is type of a family Teredinidae — compare BANKIA

¹te·re·fah *or* **te·re·fa** *or* **tre·fah** *or* **tre·fa** \təˈrāfə, ˈtrā-, -(ˌ)fä\ *n, pl* **tere·foth** *or* **tere·fot** *or* **tre·foth** *or* **tre·fot** \-(ˌ)fōt(h), -ˌfəs\ [Heb *ṭĕrēphāh*, fr. *ṭāraph* to tear, rend] **1 :** the meat of animals killed accidentally or by beasts of prey and forbidden to the Israelites as food **2 :** a food, food product, utensil that is not ritually clean or prepared according to Jewish law and is therefore prohibited as unfit for Jewish use

²terefah *or* **terefa** *var of* TREF

ter·ek \ˈterək\ *n* -S [fr. *Terek*, river of southeast Soviet Russia, Europe] **:** a sandpiper (*Xenus cinerea*) of the Old World breeding in the far north of eastern Europe and Asia and migrating to southern Africa and Australia and frequenting rivers

te·re·na \təˈrānə\ *also* **te·re·no** \-(ˌ)nō\ *n, pl* **terena** *or* **tereno** *usu cap* **1 a :** an Arawakan people of southern Mato Grosso, Brazil **b :** a member of such people **2 :** the language of the Terena people

te·ren·tian \təˈrenchən, teˈr-\ *adj, usu cap* [L *Terentianus*, fr. P. *Terentius* Afer (Terence) †159 B.C. Roman playwright + L *-anus* -an] **:** of or relating to Terence or having qualities (as refinement and poetic finish) like those of his comedies

ter·eph·thal·ate \ˌteˌrefˈthaˌlāt, -lət; təˈrefthəˌlāt\ *n* -S [ISV *terephthalic* + *-ate*] **:** a salt or ester of terephthalic acid

ter·eph·thal·ic acid \ˈteˌrelfˈthalik-, ˈterəl\ *n* [ISV *terebene* + *phthalic*] **:** a crystalline dicarboxylic acid $C_6H_4(COOH)_2$ that is much less soluble and much higher melting than phthalic acid, that has been obtained by oxidation of turpentine but is usu. made by oxidation of *para*-xylene, and that is used chiefly in the synthesis of polyesters for textile fibers or film by reaction with ethylene glycol; *para*-benzene-dicarboxylic acid

teres \ˈtiˌrēz, ˈteˌr-\ *n, pl* **ter·e·tes** \ˈterəˌtēz\ [NL *teret-, teres*, fr. L, smooth, rounded — more at TERETE] **:** an elongated cylindrical anatomical structure; *usu* **:** either of two muscles arising from the scapula and inserting on the humerus, one arising chiefly from the lower third of the axillary border and inserting on the bicipital groove, the other chiefly from the upper two thirds of the same border and passing behind the long head of the triceps to insert on the great tubercle of the humerus — called also respectively *teres major, teres minor*

te·re·sian \təˈrēzhən\ *n* -S *usu cap* [*Teresa, Theresa* †1582 Span. saint + E *-ian*] **:** a barefooted Carmelite of the reformed order established in the 16th century by St. Teresa of Avila

terete \təˈrēt, (ˈ)teˈr-\ *adj* [L *teret-, teres* smooth, well turned, rounded; akin to L *terere* to rub — more at THROW] **:** approximately cylindrical but usu. tapering at one or both ends ⟨a ~ seedpod⟩

ter·fez \tə(r)ˈfez\ *n, pl* **terfez** [F, fr. NL *Terfezia*] **:** the edible fruit of a fungus (genus *Terfezia*) of the desert regions of Africa, Asia, and southern Europe

ter·fez·ia \-zēə\ *n, cap* [NL, fr. Tuareg *tarfest, tĕrfest* (fr. Ar *tirfās, tirfāsh* truffle) + NL *-ia*] **:** a genus of fungi (family Tuberaceae) resembling truffles and having subterranean tuberous ascocarps and in some classifications comprising a distinct family

ter·gal \ˈtərgəl\ *adj* [L *tergum* back + E *-al*] **:** relating to a tergum; *sometimes* **:** DORSAL

ter·gant \ˈtərgənt\ *also* **ter·gi·ant** \-rjēənt\ *adj* [L *tergum* back + E *-ant* (as in *rampant*)] **:** showing the back ⟨arms showing an eagle ~⟩

ter·gif·er·ous \(ˌ)tərˈjif(ə)rəs\ *adj* [L *tergum* + E *-iferous*] **:** DORSIFEROUS

ter·gite \ˈtərˌjīt\ *n* -S [ISV *terg-* (fr. L *tergum*) + *-ite*] **:** the dorsal plate or dorsal portion of the covering of a metameric segment of an articulate animal; *esp* **:** one on the abdomen — compare NOTUM

¹ter·gi·ver·sant \ˈtərjəˈvərsᵊnt, (ˌ)tərˈjiv- *sometimes* (ˌ)tərˈgi-\ *adj* [L *tergiversant-, tergiversans*, pres. part. of *tergiversari* to tergiversate] **:** TERGIVERSATING

²tergiversant \ˈ"\ *n* -S **:** TERGIVERSATOR

ter·giver·sate \ˈtərjəvərˌsāt, ˌ==ˈ=ˌ=; (ˌ)tərˈjivər-, *sometimes* (ˌ)tərˈgi-\ *vi* -ED/-ING/-S [L *tergiversatus*, past part. of *tergiversari* to turn the back, shuffle, shift, evade, fr. *tergum* back + *versare* to turn, freq. of *vertere* to turn — more at WORTH] **1 :** to practice tergiversation **:** become a renegade **:** APOSTATIZE **2 :** to use subterfuges **:** SHUFFLE, EQUIVOCATE

ter·gi·ver·sa·tion \ˌtərjə(ˌ)vərˈsāshən; (ˌ)tərˌjivə- *sometimes* (ˌ)tərˌgi-\ *n* -S [L *tergiversation-, tergiversatio* evasion, fr. *tergiversatus* + *-ion-, -io* -ion] **1 :** desertion of a cause, party, or religious faith **:** reversal of opinion or policy ⟨a policy of utility is apt to fluctuate, and between 1868 and 1875 there were some extraordinary ~*s* —A.M.Young⟩ **2 :** evasion of straightforward action or clearcut statement of position **:** EQUIVOCATION, AMBIGUITY ⟨while we trust the human mind I think we have carefully to scrutinize its ~*s* —H.J.Laski⟩ ⟨humanism depends very heavily . . . on the ~*s* of the word *human* —T.S.Eliot⟩ ⟨the vacillations and ~*s* of the experts —I.A.Richards⟩

ter·gi·ver·sa·tor \ˈtərjə(ˌ)vərˌsād·ər, ˌ==ˈ=ˌ==; (ˌ)tərˈjivər- *sometimes* (ˌ)tərˈgi-\ *n* -S [L, fr. *tergiversatus* + *-or*] **:** one that tergiversates **:** TURNCOAT, RENEGADE

ter·gi·ver·sa·to·ry \ˈtərjə(ˌ)vərsəˌtōrē; (ˌ)tərˈjivər- *sometimes* (ˌ)tərˈgi-\ *adj* [LL *tergiversatorius*, fr. L *tergiversatus* + *-orius* -ory] **:** displaying or practicing tergiversation ⟨~ political career⟩

ter·gi·verse \ˈtərjəˌvərs\ *vi* -ED/-ING/-S [L *tergiversari*] **:** TERGIVERSATE

ter·gum \ˈtərgəm\ *n, pl* **ter·ga** \-gə\ [L; in senses 2 & 3 fr. NL, fr. L, back] **1 :** the back of an animal **2 :** TERGITE, NOTUM **3 :** one of the dorsal plates of the operculum of a barnacle

-te·ria \ˈtirēə\ *n comb form* -S [*cafeteria*] **:** place having self-service ⟨*groceteria*⟩

terin *var of* TARIN

ter·lin·gua·ite \(ˌ)tərˈliŋgwəˌīt\ *n* -S [*Terlingua*, Brewster co., Texas + E *-ite*] **:** a mineral Hg_2ClO consisting of a mercuric oxychloride and occurring in yellow monoclinic crystals (hardness 2–3, sp. gr. 8.7)

¹term \ˈtərm, ˈtəm, ˈtəim\ *n* -S [ME *terme*, fr. OF, fr. L *terminus* boundary, limit, end; akin to Gk *termōn* boundary, end, *termat-, terma* boundary, end, turning post, Skt *tarati* he crosses over, overcomes, and perh. to Gk *tormos* hole, socket, pivot] **1 a** *archaic* **:** a bound or limit in space **b :** END, TERMINATION ⟨the age of liberalism had reached its ~, and had been replaced by a totalitarian regime —*Times Lit. Supp.*⟩ **2 a :** a limited or definite extent of time **:** the time for which something lasts **:** DURATION, TENURE ⟨~ of five years in prison⟩ ⟨during the ~ of an insurance policy⟩ ⟨president's second ~⟩ ⟨borrowing for a long ~⟩ **b (1) terms** *pl, obs* **:** MENSTRUATION **(2) :** parturition at the normal period **:** time at which a pregnancy of normal length terminates ⟨continued to develop to ~ but was stillborn⟩ — often used with *full* ⟨a healthy calf born at full ~⟩ **3 a :** a time or date fixed or agreed upon for an action or as a boundary between periods **b :** a time fixed for the payment of rents or interest — compare QUARTER DAY **c :** the day on which a working period ends **d (1) :** the whole period for which an estate is granted **(2) :** the estate or interest held by one for a term **e :** a space of time granted to a debtor for discharging his obligation **f :** the time for which a court is held or is open for the trial of cases and during which the powers of the court incidental to actual settings for the hearing of cases may be validly exercised — see EASTER TERM, HILARY TERM, MICHAELMAS TERM, TRINITY TERM **4 :** one of several divisions of the year in a school, college, or university representing a continuous period during which instruction is regularly given to students — compare QUARTER 4b, SEMESTER 2; see CANDLEMAS TERM, HILARY TERM, MARTINMAS TERM, MICHAELMAS TERM, TRINITY TERM, WHITSUN TERM **5 :** one of the unequal divisions of the 30 degrees of a sign allocated in astrology to each of the planets as an essential dignity **6 a :** a member of an expression connected with another member by a plus or minus sign **b :** any of the members composing a ratio or proportion **c :** any or each of a series or sequence ⟨~*s* of a geometrical progression⟩ **d :** one of a set of frequencies assigned one for each state to an atomic system such that the frequencies of the light emitted are differences between the members of the set **7 :** a substantive word or phrase used as the subject or predicate of a proposition or standing as one member of a relation; *esp* **:** one of the three substantive elements of a syllogism each of which appears twice — see MAJOR TERM, MIDDLE TERM, MINOR TERM **8 a :** a word or expression that has a precisely limited meaning in some uses or is peculiar to a science, art, profession, trade, or special subject ⟨technical ~⟩ ⟨legal ~⟩ **b terms** *pl* **:** diction of a specified kind ⟨described in glowing ~*s*⟩ ⟨praised in the highest ~*s*⟩ ⟨talking of marriage in vague ~*s*, not actually proposing⟩ **9 terms** *pl* **:** propositions, limitations, or provisions stated or offered for the acceptance of another and determining (as in a contract) the nature and scope of the agreement **:** CONDITIONS ⟨~*s* of a sale⟩ ⟨credit granted on liberal ~*s* of repayment⟩ ⟨~*s* of a will⟩ **10 terms** *pl* **a :** mutual relationship **:** relative position **:** FOOTING — usu. used with *on* or *upon* ⟨remained on good ~*s* with his neighbors⟩ ⟨fight on even ~*s*⟩ **b :** AGREEMENT, CONCORD ⟨came to ~*s* after long bargaining⟩ **11 :** a boundary post or stone; *esp* **:** a quadrangular pillar often tapering downward and adorned on the top with the figure of a head or upper part of the body — called also *terminal figure*; compare HERM, TERMINUS 2b **syn** see CONDITION, WORD — **at term** *adv* **:** at the end of a definite or stipulated period of time — **in terms of** *prep* **:** with respect to, in relation to, or in ways of thought belonging to (a particular category) **:** in comparison with ⟨a conception of nature *in terms of* human politics —William Empson⟩ ⟨tends to think of everything *in terms of* money⟩

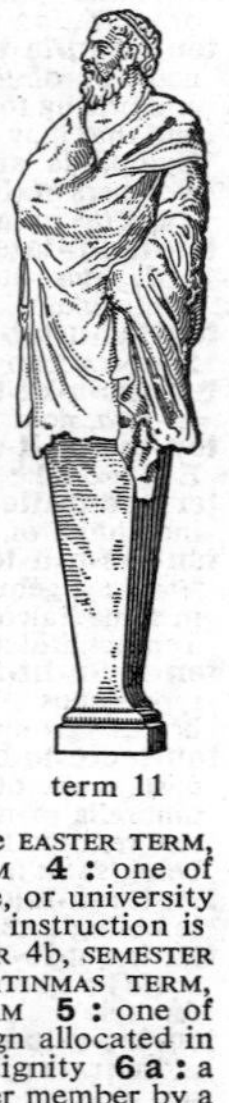

term 11

²term \ˈ"\ *vt* -ED/-ING/-S **1** *obs* **:** EXPRESS, STATE, PHRASE **2 :** to apply a term to **:** CALL, NAME ⟨determined to overcome what she ~*ed* her own selfishness —Agnes S. Turnbull⟩ ⟨normal collector who in some circles would be ~*ed* naive —Reginald Kell⟩

term *abbr* **1** terminal **2** termination

ter·ma·gan·cy \ˈtərməgənsē, ˈtəm-, ˈtəim-, -si\ *n* -ES [*termagant* + *-cy*] **:** the quality or state of being termagant **:** habitual bad temper **:** scolding disposition

¹ter·ma·gant \-gənt *sometimes* -ˌgant *or* -gaa(ə)nt\ *n* -S [ME *Tervagant, Termagant*, imaginary Muslim deity represented in medieval mystery plays as a boisterous character] **1** *obs* **:** a brawling boisterous turbulent person **2 :** an overbearing, quarrelsome, scolding, or nagging woman **:** SHREW, VIRAGO ⟨matrimonial adventures of an extremely rich and bullying ~ —*Saturday Rev.*⟩

²termagant \ˈ"\ *adj* **:** TUMULTUOUS, TURBULENT, BOISTEROUS ⟨life . . . wrecked by a ~ mother —*Newsweek*⟩ — **ter·ma·gant·ly** *adv*

ter·ma·gant·ish \-ˌgantish, -ˌgaan-, -gən-, -tēsh\ *adj* [¹*termagant* + *-ish*] **:** resembling a termagant **:** SHREWISH

term attendant *n* [¹*term* + *attendant*, adj.] **:** ATTENDANT TERM

term day *n* [ME *terme day*, fr. *terme* term + *day*] **1 :** a day that is set as a term (as a Scottish quarter day) or is a day in a term (as of the sitting of a court) **2 :** one of a series of special days designated by scientists for making synoptic magnetic, meteorological, or other physical observations

ter·men \ˈtərmən\ *n, pl* **termi·na** \-mənə\ [NL *termin-, termen*, fr. L, end, boundary; akin to L *terminus* end, boundary — more at TERM] **:** the outer margin of a triangularly shaped wing of an insect

term·er \ˈtərmər; ˈtəmə(r, ˈtəimə(r\ *n* -S [¹*term* + *-er*] **1** *obs* **:** one resorting to London only during the law term or fashionable season **2 :** a person serving for a specified term (as in prison) ⟨first ~⟩ ⟨life ~⟩

ter·mes \ˈtər(ˌ)mēz\ *n, cap* [NL *Termit-, Termes*, fr. L *termit-, termes, tarmit-, tarmes* worm that eats wood; akin to Gk *tetrainein* to bore through, pierce — more at THROW] **:** the type genus of the family Termitidae

term fee *n* **:** a fee by the term chargeable to a suitor or by law fixed and taxable in the costs of a case for each or any term it is in court

ter·mi·na·bil·i·ty \ˌtərmənəˈbiləd·ē, ˌtəm-, ˌtəim-, -lət, -i\ *n* -ES **:** the quality or state of being terminable ⟨~ of an annuity at the death of an annuitant⟩

ter·mi·na·ble \ˈ===bəl\ *adj* [ME, fr. *terminen* to termine + *-able*] **:** capable of being terminated or bounded **:** discontinuing after a definite period **:** subject to termination ⟨institutions . . . to fit the fact that marriage is a ~ institution —Margaret Mead⟩ ⟨~ bond⟩ — **ter·mi·na·ble·ness** \-nəs\ *n* -ES — **ter·mi·na·bly** \-blē, -bli\ *adv*

¹ter·mi·nal \ˈtərmənᵊl, ˈtəm-, ˈtəim-, -mnəl\ *adj* [L *terminalis*, fr. *terminus* boundary, end + *-alis* -al — more at TERM] **1 a :** of or relating to an end, extremity, boundary, or terminus ⟨~ pillar⟩ **b :** growing at the end of a branch or stem ⟨~ bud⟩ — compare LATERAL **c :** of or relating to either end of a transport line ⟨~ airport⟩ ⟨freight pickup is a ~ service⟩ ⟨~ charge⟩ **2 a :** of or relating to a fixed period of time **:** occurring in a term or each term ⟨~ examinations⟩ ⟨~ payments⟩ **b :** relating to or constituting a term in a proposition or equation ⟨~ quantity⟩ **c :** occurring at or contributing to the end of life

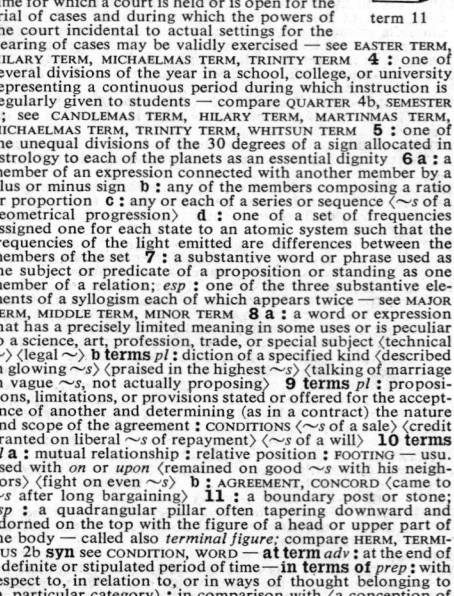

⟨~ pneumonia⟩ ⟨~ cancer⟩ **3 a :** occurring at or constituting the end of a closed series : CONCLUDING, FINAL ⟨~ syllable⟩ : ULTIMATE ⟨~ problems⟩ **b** *of an educational institution or program* : constituting an entity that is limited but complete : leading to an end which may but need not be a step to further education ⟨the modern junior college, besides preparing some of its students for the four-year college, has a ~ curriculum⟩ **c :** at or near the end of a chain of atoms constituting a molecule ⟨a ~ hydroxyl group⟩ ⟨~ bonds⟩ **syn** see LAST

2terminal \"\ *n* -s **1 :** a part that forms the end : END, EXTREMITY, TERMINATION **2 :** a letter, sound, syllable, or word, forming a termination **3 :** a terminating and usu. ornamental detail : FINIAL **4 :** a device attached to the end of a wire or cable or to a piece of electrical apparatus for convenience in making connections — see LIGHTNING ARRESTER illustration **5 :** an apical growth on a plant **6 a :** either end of a carrier line (as a railroad, trucking or shipping line, or airline) with classifying yards, dock and lighterage facilities, management offices, storage sheds, and freight and passenger stations **b :** a freight or passenger station that is central to a considerable area or serves as a junction at any point with other lines **c :** a town or city at the end of a carrier line : TERMINUS

terminal arborization *n* : a multiple branching at the end of a nerve fiber

terminal board *n* : an insulating slab (as on a switchboard) on which electric terminals are mounted

terminal company *n* : a company or organization whose business is the operation of a railroad terminal

terminal cutting *n* : a stem cutting consisting of a portion of a stem or branch with a terminal bud

terminal figure *or* **terminal statue** *n* : TERM 11

terminal filament *n* : the distal part of an insect ovariole

1ter·mi·na·lia \ˌtərməˈnālēə, -lyə\ *n, cap* [NL, fr. L *terminalis* terminal + NL *-ia*] : a large genus of tropical trees and shrubs (family Combretaceae) having entire leaves clustered at the ends of the branches and small apetalous flowers in loose spikes — see MALABAR ALMOND, MYROBALAN 1

2terminalia \"\ *n pl* [NL, fr. L, neut. pl. of *terminalis* terminal] : the terminal elements of a part; *esp* : the final segments of the insect abdomen modified to form the external genitalia

ter·mi·na·li·a·ce·ae \ˌtərməˌnālēˈāsēˌē\ [NL, fr. *Terminalia* + *-aceae*] *syn of* COMBRETACEAE

ter·mi·nal·iza·tion \ˌtərmənᵊlə̇ˈzāshən, -ᵊlˌīˈz-\ *n* -s [*1terminal* + *-ization*] : the movement of transverse bonds between paired chromosomes in meiosis from their points of origin toward the ends of the chromosomes

terminal juncture *n* : an intonation pattern signaling the end of an utterance or a break between utterances

terminal leave *n* : a final leave consisting of accumulated unused leave granted to a member of the armed forces just prior to his separation or discharge from service

ter·mi·nal·ly \ˈtərmənᵊlē, ˈtə̄m-,ˈtəim-, -mnəl|, |i\ *adv* [*1terminal* + *-ly*] **1 :** at each term: by the term ⟨rent to be paid ~⟩ **2 :** at the end ⟨bear leaves laterally or ~⟩

terminal market *n* : a central marketing place for a farm product (as grain, livestock) received from scattered or outlying shipping points and sold through a public exchange

terminal moraine *n* : a moraine deposited by a glacier at its end when the ice is at its maximum extent — compare END MORAINE

terminal parenchyma *n* : parenchyma occurring as a more or less continuous layer at the outer boundary of a growth ring

terminal pedestal *n* : GAINE

terminal reserve *n* : the reserve for an insurance policy at the close of a year after net premiums for the year have been received and death claims paid

terminal sclereid *n* : any of various diversely branched or lobed sclereids found singly or in groups esp. at the ends of veinlets in leaves

terminal shoe *n* : an appliance for permitting the transfer of a telpher carrier from a track to the cable without jar or impact

terminal side *n* : the straight line that is revolved about a point on another straight line in forming a trigonometric figure

terminal sinus *n* : a circular blood sinus bordering the area vasculosa of the vertebrate embryo

terminal velocity *n* : the limiting uniform velocity attained by a falling body when the resistance of the air has become equal to the force of gravity

terminal voltage *n* : the voltage at the terminals of an electrical device (as a battery or a generator)

1ter·mi·nate \ˈtərməˌnāt, ˈtə̄m-,ˈtəim-, *usu* -ād.+V\ *vb* -ED/-ING/-S [L *terminatus*, past part. of *terminare* to set bounds, limit, fr. *terminus* boundary, limit, end — more at TERM] *vt* **1 a :** to bring to an ending or cessation in time, sequence, or continuity : CLOSE ⟨~ a conference⟩ ⟨benediction *terminated* the service⟩ **b :** to form the ending or conclusion of ⟨his acceptance *terminated* the interview⟩ **c :** to end formally and definitely (as a pact, agreement, contract) ⟨his employment with the company was *terminated*⟩ ⟨the age at which the youth of each nation ~*s* full-time education —J.B.Conant⟩ **d :** to bring or deliver (a passenger, a freight shipment) to destination **e :** to discontinue the employment of : DISCHARGE **2 :** to set a limit to in space : serve as an ending, boundary, limit, dividing line ⟨the gallery was *terminated* by folding doors —Jane Austen⟩ **3 a** *archaic* : to perfect with finishing touches **b** *archaic* : to express or describe in terms ⟨censuring or rather *terminating* my own soul —R.W.Emerson⟩ **c** *obs* : to direct or destine to something as object or end ~ *vi* **1 a :** to come to an end in space or extent : extend only to a point, line, surface, or other limit **b :** to find or reach a terminus ⟨a railroad line *terminating* at a seaport⟩ **2 a :** to come to an end in time : cease to be ⟨the coalition . . . *terminated* with the danger from which it had sprung —T.B.Macaulay⟩ **b :** to become nil or void after reaching a term or limit : EXPIRE ⟨Italian sovereignty over Trieste *terminated* upon the coming into force of the Treaty of Peace —*Amer. Jour. of Internat. Law*⟩ **3 a :** to form an ending or final part ⟨words that properly ~ in an obscure vowel —C.H. Grandgent⟩ ⟨chair legs *terminating* in ball-and-claw feet⟩ ⟨the two imposing towers at the facade ~ in pale blue tile domes —*Amer. Guide Series: Mich.*⟩ ⟨his thoughts always *terminated* in regret⟩ **b :** to have an indicated outcome or result ⟨the fight *terminated* with the champion winning⟩ **syn** see CLOSE

2ter·mi·nate \-nə̇t, *usu* -əd.+V\ *adj* [L *terminatus*, past part. of *terminare*] **1 :** coming to an end or capable of ending : LIMITED, LIMITABLE **2 :** expressed or expressible in a finite number of figures ⟨~ decimal⟩ ⟨~ number⟩ **3 :** indicating an action as a whole ⟨~ aspect of a verb⟩

terminating building and loan association *or* **terminating society** *n* : a savings and loan association whose members have provided by their articles of association that upon their shares all attaining the value specified in the articles that value shall be paid to the shareholders and the society dissolved

terminating decimal *n* [*terminating* (pres. part. of *1terminate*) + *decimal*] : a terminate decimal

ter·mi·na·tion \ˌtərməˈnāshən, ˌtə̄m-, ˌtəim-\ *n* -s [ME, fr. L *termination-, terminatio* act of setting bounds, determining, fr. *terminatus* (past part. of *terminare* to set bounds, determine) + *-ion-, -io* -ion — more at TERMINATE] **1** *obs* : the act of determining : DECISION **2** *obs* : WORD, TERM **3 a :** end in time or existence : CLOSE, CESSATION, CONCLUSION ⟨~ of life⟩ ⟨~ of the middle ages⟩ **b :** a limit in space or extent : BOUND, EXTREMITY ⟨~ of a route⟩ ⟨~ of a cave⟩ ⟨~ of a journey⟩ **c :** the ending of a word : a final syllable or letter; *esp* : the part added to a stem in inflection : ENDING, SUFFIX **4 :** the act of terminating : act of setting bounds or bringing to an end or concluding ⟨after the ~ of hostilities⟩ ⟨voluntary ~ of an agreement⟩ **5 :** OUTCOME, RESULT ⟨a dispute brought to a satisfactory ~⟩ **syn** see END

ter·mi·na·tion·al \ˌ≈≈ˈnāshənᵊl, -shnəl\ *adj* [*termination* + *-al*] **1 :** of, relating to, or forming a termination ⟨~ accentuation⟩ **2 :** formed by inflectional suffixes ⟨~ comparison of adjectives⟩ — compare PERIPHRASTIC

1ter·mi·na·tive \ˈtərməˌnād·|iv, ˈtə̄m-,ˈtəim-, -m(ə)nəl, |t|, |ēv *also* |əv\ *adj* [ME, fr. ML *terminativus*, fr. L *terminatus* + *-ivus* -ive] **1 a :** tending or serving to put an end to or set a limit to something **b :** coming to an end : ENDING ⟨contracts ~ with the cessation of hostilities⟩ **2 a :** relating to a verb or a verbal form which expresses the action as complete or denotes the end or completion of the action — compare PERFECTIVE 2 **b :** denoting direction toward ⟨~ case of a noun⟩ — **ter·mi·na·tive·ly** \|əvlē, -li\ *adv*

2terminative \"\ *n* -s : the terminative case or a form in the terminative case

ter·mi·na·tor \-məˌnād·ə(r), -ātə-\ *n* -s [LL, fr. L *terminatus* + *-or*] **1 :** one that terminates **2 :** the dividing line between the illuminated and the unilluminated part of the moon's or a planet's disk : the dividing line between day and night as observed from a distance

ter·mi·na·to·ry \-m(ə)nəˌtōrē\ *adj* [L *terminatus* + E *-ory*] : TERMINAL, TERMINATING

ter·mine \ˈtərmən\ *vb* -ED/-ING/-S [ME *terminen*, fr. OF *terminer*, fr. L *terminare* — more at TERMINATE] **1** *obs* : BOUND, LIMIT, TERMINATE **2 :** DETERMINE

terming *pres part of* TERM

ter·mi·nism \ˈtərməˌnizəm\ *n* -s [*terminist* + *-ism*] : the doctrine of the terminists; *specif* : OCKHAMISM

ter·mi·nist \-nə̇st\ *n* -s [NL *terminista*, fr. ML *terminus* term, period + L *-ista* -ist] **1 :** one who maintains that God has fixed a certain term for the probation of individual persons during which period and no longer they have the offer of grace **2 :** OCKHAMIST — **ter·mi·nis·tic** \ˌ≈≈ˈnistik\ *adj*

ter·mi·nize \ˈtərməˌnīz\ *vt* -ED/-ING/-S [ML *terminus* term + E *-ize*] : to supply (as a science) with nomenclature ⟨conceptions that owe their present definiteness . . . to felicitous *terminizing* —*Popular Science Monthly*⟩ ⟨the industrious *terminizing* of a cherished colleague —C.F.Talman⟩

ter·mi·no·log·i·cal \ˌtərmənᵊlˈäjə̇kəl, ¦tə̄m-, ¦təim-, -mnə¦lä-, -jēk-\ *adj* : relating to terminology ⟨~ convenience⟩ ⟨pure ~ dispute⟩ — **ter·mi·no·log·i·cal·ly** \-k(ə)lē, -li\ *adv*

terminological platonism *n, often cap P* : PLATONISM 5

ter·mi·nol·o·gy \ˌtərməˈnäləjē, -ji\ *n* -ES [ML *terminus* term, expression, word (fr. L, boundary, limit, end) + E *-o-* + *-logy* — more at TERM] **1 :** the technical or special terms or expressions used in a business, art, science, or special subject **2 :** nomenclature as a field of study

term insurance *n* : insurance for a specified period providing for no payment to the insured except upon losses during the period and becoming void upon its expiration

ter·mi·nus \ˈtərmənəs, ˈtə̄m-,ˈtəim-\ *n, pl* **termi·ni** \-ˌnī, -ˌnē\ *or* **terminuses** [L — more at TERM] **1 :** final goal of a journey or an endeavor : finishing point : END; *also* : starting point ⟨obligation to be born separately, and to die separately, and, owing to these unavoidable *termini* —E.M.Forster⟩ **2 a :** TERM 11 **b :** a post or stone marking a boundary **3 a :** either end of a transportation line, travel route, pipe line, tunnel, canal **b :** the station or the town or city at such a place : TERMINAL **4 :** EXTREMITY, TIP ⟨~ of a glacier⟩ ⟨~ of a peninsula⟩ **5 :** that end of a line representing a vector quantity which indicates the sense of the vector and is commonly identified by an arrowhead : the end of a vector that is not the origin **syn** see END

terminus ad quem \-ˌadˈkwem\ *n* [NL, lit., limit to which] **1 :** a goal, object, or course of action, motion, or purpose : DESTINATION, END, PURPOSE **2** *also* **terminus an·te quem** \-ˌantē-\ [*terminus ante quem* fr. NL, lit., limit before which] : a time or date established or chosen as the end of a time period : the later of two limiting points in time

terminus a quo \-ˌäˈkwō\ *n* [NL, lit., limit from which] **1 :** starting point of line of action or of a journey : point of origin **2** *also* **terminus post quem** \-ˌpōst-\ [*terminus post quem* fr. NL, lit., limit after which] : a time or date established or chosen as the beginning of a time period : the earlier of two limiting points in time

ter·mi·tar·i·um \ˌtərməˈterēəm\ *n, pl* **termitar·ia** \-ēə\ [NL, fr. *Termit-, Termes* genus of termites + L *-arium*] : a termites' nest

ter·mi·tary \ˈtərməˌterē\ *n* -ES [*termite* + *-ary*] : TERMITARIUM

ter·mite \ˈtərˌmīt, ˈtə̄ˌm-, ˈtəiˌm-, *usu* -īd.+V\ *n* -s [NL *Termit-, Termes* genus of termites — more at TERMES] : any of numerous pale-colored soft-bodied social insects of the order Isoptera that live in colonies each consisting of distinct forms (as queen, male, wingless sterile workers and soldiers) that show incomplete metamorphosis, build or tunnel out large nests, and feed on wood and that include some (as *Reticulitermes flanipes* in U.S. and *R. lucifugus* in Europe) which are very destructive to wooden structures and trees

termite–proof \ˈ≈ˌ≈ˈ≈\ *adj* [*termite* + *proof*] : constructed or treated so as to prevent entrance of termites

ter·mit·ic \ˌtərˈmid·ik\ *or* **ter·mit·al** \ˈ≈ˌmīd·ᵊl\ *adj* [*termite* + *-ic* or *-al*] : of, relating to, or produced by termites

1ter·mi·tid \ˈtərməd·əd, -ˌmīd·əd\ *adj* [NL *Termitidae*] : of or relating to the Termitidae

2termitid \"\ *n* -s : a termite of the family Termitidae

ter·mit·i·dae \ˌtərˈmid·əˌdē\ *n pl, cap* [NL, fr. *Termit-, Termes*, type genus + *-idae*] : a family of termites including the most highly specialized forms characterized by having 4-jointed tarsi and a simple radial vein in the wings

termito- *comb form* [NL *Termit-, Termes*] : termite ⟨*termitophagous*⟩

ter·mi·tol·o·gist \ˌtərməˈtälə̇jə̇st, ˌtərˌmīd·ˈä-\ *n* -s [*termito-* + *-logist*] : one who studies termites

ter·mi·to·phile \ˌtərˈmīd·əˌfīl\ *n* -s [ISV *termito-* + *-phile*] : an insect normally living in association with termites in their nests — **ter·mitoph·i·lous** \ˌtərməˈtäfələs, -ˌmīd·ˈä-\ *adj*

term·less \ˈtərmlə̇s\ *adj* **1 :** having no term or end : BOUNDLESS, UNENDING ⟨~ grief⟩ **2 :** UNCONDITIONED, UNCONDITIONAL ⟨~ peace⟩

term loan *n* : a loan extended by banks or insurance companies to corporations with provision for serial repayment generally for a period of from 5 to 15 years

1term·ly \ˈtərmlē\ *adv* [ME *termely*, fr. *terme* term + *-ly*] *archaic* : by the term : PERIODICALLY

2termly \"\ *adj* [*1term* + *-ly*] *archaic* : occurring every term

term of art *archaic* : a word or phrase having a specific signification in a particular art, craft, or department of knowledge : a technical term

term of reference *chiefly Brit* : a defined or assigned task or field of activity or inquiry ⟨numerous royal commissions . . . whose *terms of reference* concerned farming and farm workers —G.E.Fussell⟩

ter·molecular \ˌtər+\ *adj* [*ter-* + *molecule* + *-ar*] : TRIMOLECULAR ⟨~ reaction⟩

ter·mon \ˈtərmən\ *n* -s [MIr *termonn* church lands, sanctuary, fr. L *terminus* boundary — more at TERM] : land belonging to a religious house in Ireland : church land exempt from secular taxation

ter·mone \ˈtərˌmōn\ *n* -s [de*termining* + *hormone*] : a sex-determining hormone or chemical substance

ter·mor \ˈtərmər\ *n* -s [ME *termurre*, fr. AF *termer*, fr. OF *terme* term + AF *-er*] : one who has an estate for a term of years or for life

term paper *n* : a major written assignment in a school or college course representative of a student's achievement during a term

term policy *n* : a property insurance policy issued for a period of usu. three to five years at a reduced rate

term rate *n* : the reduced rate that applies to a term policy

terms *pl of* TERM, *pres 3d sing of* TERM

term settlement *n* : a reckoning (as on the London stock exchange) between buyers and sellers occurring periodically instead of daily

terms of trade : the ratio between the prices of two countries participating in international trade

termtime \ˈ≈ˌ≈\ *n* [ME *terme tyme*, fr. *terme* term + *tyme* time] **1 :** the time during a university, college, school, or legal term **2** *chiefly Scot* : TERM 3a

term–trotter \ˈ≈ˌ≈\ *n, Brit* : one who attends a college or a law court for an occasional term but not regularly

1tern \ˈtərn, ˈtə̄n, ˈtəin\ *n* -s [of Scand origin; akin to ON *therna* tern, and prob. to OE *stearn*, a bird, prob. tern — more at STARLING] : any of numerous sea birds of *Sterna* and related genera that are smaller and slenderer in body and bill than typical gulls, have narrower wings and often forked tails, and are more graceful and dashing in flight — called also *sea swallow*

2tern \"\ *adj* [L *terni* (pl.) three each; akin to L *tres* three — more at THREE] : TERNATE

3tern \"\ *n* -s **1 :** something that consists of three things or numbers together : TRIO, TRIPLET **2** *also* **tern schooner** [F *terne*, fr. L *terni* three each] : a 3-masted schooner

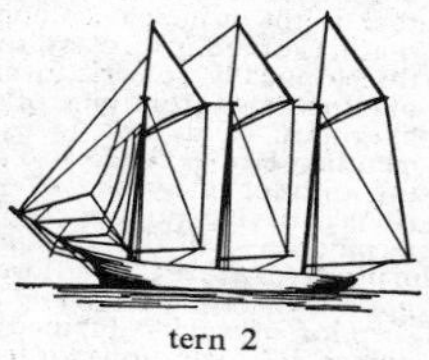

tern 2

ter·na \ˈtərnə, ˈtər-\ *n* -s [NL, fr. L, neut. pl. of *terni* three each] : a list of three nominees for institution into a Roman Catholic benefice or bishopric presented to the pope or other authority

ter·nar *or* **ter·ner** \ˈtərnər\ *n* -s [L *ternarius* ternary] : a university student assigned to the third and lowest social rank and required to pay the lowest fees — compare SECONDER

1ter·na·ry \ˈtərnərē\ *adj* [ME, fr. L *ternarius*, fr. *terni* three each + *-arius* -ary] **1 a :** consisting of or based on three : proceeding by threes ⟨~ method of counting⟩ **b :** having three elements, parts, or divisions : THREEFOLD, TRIPLE **c :** arranged in threes ⟨~ petals⟩ **2 a :** using three as the base ⟨~ numeration⟩ ⟨~ logarithm⟩ **b :** involving three variables ⟨~ form⟩ **3 :** consisting of an alloy of three elements **4 :** containing, consisting of, or relating to three different parts (as elements, atoms, radicals or components) ⟨sulfuric acid is a ~ acid⟩ ⟨~ liquid mixtures⟩ **5 :** relating or belonging to a crystal system in which 3-sided forms occur **6 :** third in series, order, or rank

2ternary *n* -ES [ME, fr. *1ternary*] *obs* : a set or group of three

ternary form *n* **1 :** a musical form (as a rondo) in which the principal subject appears three or more times **2 :** a song form in which the third part is a repetition of the first with a contrasting section in the middle

ternary steel *n* : a steel of iron and carbon alloyed with one other metal

ternary system *n* : a physical-chemical system having three components

ter·nate \ˈtərˌnāt, -nə̇t\ *adj* [NL *ternatus*, fr. ML, past part. of *ternare* to treble, fr. L *terni* three each — more at TERN] **1 :** arranged in threes ⟨~ leaves⟩ **2 :** composed of three leaflets or subdivisions ⟨a compound ~ leaf⟩ — **ter·nate·ly** *adv*

ternati- *comb form* [NL *ternatus* ternate] : ternately ⟨*ternati*pinnate⟩

1terne \ˈtərn\ *also* **terneplate** \ˈ≈ˌ≈\ *n* -s [*terne*, short for *terneplate*, prob. fr. F *terne* dull (fr. MF, fr. *ternir* to tarnish) + E *plate* — more at TARNISH] : sheet iron or steel coated with an alloy of about 4 parts lead to 1 part tin

2terne \"\ *vt* -ED/-ING/-S : to coat with an alloy of tin and lead ⟨*terned* steel plates⟩

terner *var of* TERNAR

tern·ery \ˈtərnərē\ *n* -ES [*1tern* + *-ery*] : a place where terns breed gregariously

tern foot *n* [*2tern*] : a foot (as of a chair) formed of three scrolls or carved lines

ter·ni·dens \ˈtərnəˌdenz\ *n, cap* [NL, fr. L *terni* three each + *dens* tooth — more at TERN, TOOTH] : a genus of nematode worms (family Strongylidae) parasitic in the intestine of various African apes and monkeys and occas. in man

ter·ni·on \ˈtərnēən, -ēˌän\ *n* -s [L *ternion-, ternio*, fr. *terni* three each] *archaic* : a set or group of three : TRIAD, TRIO

tern·let \ˈtərnlə̇t\ *n* -s [*1tern* + *-let*] : any of various small terns

ter·nov·skite \tərˈnȯfˌskīt, -nȯvz,k-\ *n* -s [Russ *ternovskit*, fr. *Ternovskiĭ*, name of a mine in Krivoi Rog, southeast central Ukraine, U.S.S.R. + Russ *-it* -ite] : a mineral $Na_2(Mg,Fe)_3Fe_2Si_8O_{22}(OH)_2$ consisting of a basic silicate of sodium, magnesium, and iron of the amphibole group

tern schooner *var of* TERN

tern·stroe·mia \ˌtərnˈstrēmēə, -strōm-\ *n, cap* [NL, fr. Christopher *Ternström* †1746 Swed. botanist + NL *-ia*] : a large genus of chiefly tropical American trees and shrubs (family Theaceae) having bracteate flowers with free sepals and petals slightly coherent at the base

tern·stroe·mi·a·ce·ae \ˌ≈ˌ≈≈ˈāsēˌē\ [NL, fr. *Ternstroemia* + *-aceae*] *syn of* THEACEAE

terp \ˈte(ə)rp\ *n, pl* **terps** \-ps\ *or* **terpen** \ˈterpən\ [Fris, fr. OFris, village; akin to OE *thorp* village — more at THORP] : a large artificial mound in the Netherlands (as in Friesland) providing a site or refuge for a prehistoric settlement in a seasonally flooded area

ter·pa·di·ene \ˌtərpəˈdīˌēn\ *n* -s [*terpane* + *-diene*] : MENTHADIENE

ter·pane \ˈtərˌpān\ *n* -s [ISV *terp-* (fr. G *terpentin*) + *-ane*] : MENTHANE; *esp* : the para isomer

ter·pene \-ˌpēn\ *n* -s [ISV *terp-* (fr. G *terpentin* turpentine, fr. ML *terbentina*) + *-ene* — more at TURPENTINE] **1 a :** any of a class of isomeric hydrocarbons $C_{10}H_{16}$ (as myrcene, limonene, or pinene) that are found in many essential oils esp. from conifers, that have also been synthesized in many cases, that are usu. classified according to the absence or presence of one or more rings in the molecule as acyclic, monocyclic, bicyclic, or tricyclic, and that are used chiefly as solvents and as intermediates in organic synthesis : MONOTERPENE ⟨~s and sesquiterpenes⟩ **b :** any of a large class of hydrocarbons $(C_5H_8)_n$ including the monoterpenes and also hemiterpenes, sesquiterpenes, diterpenes, triterpenes, and polyterpenes that are found esp. in essential oils, resins, and balsams, that are regarded in general as structurally constituted of branched five-carbon units (as in isoprene and 2-methyl-butane), and that are also classifiable according to the absence or presence of rings in the molecule **2 :** any of various compounds derived from terpene hydrocarbons or closely related to them; *esp* : a naturally occurring oxygenated derivative (as geraniol, citral, camphor, or abietic acid) — compare TERPENOID

ter·pene·less \ˈtərˌpēnlə̇s\ *adj* : free or relatively free from terpenes and esp. monoterpenes usu. as a result of processing (as extraction with solvents or distillation in a vacuum) ⟨~ essential oils⟩

terpene resin *n* : any of various pale amber transparent thermoplastic polyterpene resins

ter·pe·nic \ˌtərˈpēnik\ *adj* [*terpene* + *-ic*] : relating to, containing, or derived from a terpene

1ter·pe·noid \ˈtərpəˌnȯid\ *adj* [*terpene* + *-oid*] : resembling a terpene in molecular structure

2terpenoid \"\ *n* -s : any of a class of compounds that are characterized by an isoprenoid structure like that of the terpene hydrocarbons and that often include these hydrocarbons as well as oxygenated derivatives (as alcohols, aldehydes, ketones, or acids) and hydrogenated derivatives (as menthane) — compare CAROTENOID, STEROID, TERPENE 2

ter·pe·nyl·ic acid \ˌtərpəˈnilik-\ *n* [ISV *terpene* + *-yl* + *-ic*] : a crystalline lactonic acid $C_8H_{12}O_4$ obtained esp. by the oxidation of turpentine (sense 2)

ter·phenyl \ˌtər+\ *n* [ISV *ter-* + *phenyl*] : any of three isomeric crystalline hydrocarbons $C_6H_5C_6H_4C_6H_5$ that contain three benzene rings linked in ortho, meta, and para positions, that are obtained usu. along with biphenyl from benzene, and that are used chiefly as industrial heat transfer media; *also* : a mixture of two or all three of these hydrocarbons

ter·pin \ˈtərpə̇n\ *n* -s [ISV *terpene* + *-in*] : a crystalline saturated terpenoid glycol $C_{10}H_{18}(OH)_2$ that is known in cis and trans forms and is obtained readily in the form of terpin hydrate — called also *1,8-terpin*

ter·pi·nene \-pəˌnēn\ *n* -s [ISV *terpin* + *-ene*] : any of three liquid isomeric monocyclic terpene hydrocarbons $C_{10}H_{16}$ obtained usu. in mixtures of the alpha and gamma isomers (as by isomerization of pinene, alpha-phellandrene, or dipentene with sulfuric acid): as **a :** the isomer that has an odor like that of lemons and is the principal component of the mixtures and that occurs in coriander oil, chenopodium oil, and other essential oils; 1,3-*para*-mentha-diene — called also *alpha-terpinene* **b :** the isomer that occurs in coriander oil, lemon oil, and other essential oils; 1,4-*para*-menthadiene — called also *crithmene, gamma-terpinene*

ter·pin·e·ol \ˌtərˈpinēˌōl, -ˌōl\ *n* -s [ISV *terpine, terpin* + *-ol*] : any of three fragrant isomeric unsaturated low-melting crystalline terpenoid alcohols $C_{10}H_{17}OH$ or a viscous liquid commercial mixture containing them obtained from terpin or

terpin hydrate by dehydration and used chiefly in perfumes, in soap, in denaturing alcohol, and as a solvent: **a :** the isomer that is the principal component of the commercial mixture, that has an odor of lilacs, that occurs in many essential oils in three optically isomeric forms and in the form of esters, that is obtained also from pine oil by distillation or from pinene by hydration, and that is used chiefly in perfumes; 1-*para*-menthen-8-ol — called also *alpha-terpineol* **b :** an isomer having an odor of hyacinths — called also *beta-terpineol* **c :** an isomer having an odor of lilacs similar to that of alpha-terpineol — called also *gamma-terpineol*

terpin hydrate *n* **:** an efflorescent crystalline or powdery compound $C_{10}H_{18}(OH)_2.H_2O$ formed from *cis*-terpene by absorption of water, obtained usu. from turpentine oil or alpha-pinene by hydration with dilute acids or from pine oil by steaming the residual rosin, and used as an expectorant for a cough and as an intermediate in making terpineol

ter·pi·nol \ˈtərpə,nȯl, -nōl\ *n* -s [ISV *terpin* + *-ol*] **1 :** TERPIN **2 :** TERPINEOL; *esp* **:** the commercial liquid mixture

ter·pin·o·lene \,tərˈpinᵊl,ēn\ *n* -s [ISV *terpinol* + *-ene*] **:** a liquid monocyclic terpene hydrocarbon $C_{10}H_{16}$ reported in a few essential oils and obtained synthetically (as in the manufacture of terpineol); 1,4(8)-*para*-menthadiene

ter·pi·nyl \ˈtərpənᵊl, -,nil\ *n* -s [ISV *terpin* + *-yl*] **:** a univalent radical $C_{10}H_{17}$ derived from terpineol and esp. alpha-terpineol

terpinyl acetate *n* **:** a fragrant liquid ester $CH_3COOC_{10}H_{17}$ found in several essential oils, made synthetically (as by reaction of alpha-terpineol or alpha-pinene with acetic anhydride), and used in perfumes and soaps

ter·polymer \ˌtər+\ *n* [*ter-* + *polymer*] **:** a product of the polymerization of three different polymerizing substances — compare COPOLYMER

terp·sich·o·re \,tərpˈsikə(,)rē, tə̄p-,təip-, -kəri\ *n* -s [after *Terpsichore*, the muse of choral dance and song] **:** DANCING, CHOREOGRAPHY — **terp·si·cho·re·an** \ˌ=,sikəˈrēən, ˌ=-səkəˈr-, ˌ=səˈkōr-\ *adj*

terr *abbr* **1** terrace **2** territorial; territory

ter·ra al·ba \,terəˈalbə, -rəˈȯl-\ *n* [NL, lit., white earth] **:** any of several white mineral substances: as **a :** gypsum ground for a pigment **b :** kaolin used esp. as an adulterant of paints **c :** BURNT ALUM **d :** MAGNESIA 3a **e :** BLANC FIXE

terra car·i·o·sa \ˌ==,karēˈōsə, -ōzə\ *n* [L, lit., rotten earth] **:** ROTTENSTONE

¹ter·race \ˈterəs\ *n* -s [MF *terrasse, terrace* pile of earth, platform, terrace, fr. OProv *terrassa*, fr. *terra* earth, fr. L, earth, land, country; akin to OIr *tír* territory, *tir* dry, L *torrēre* to dry, parch — more at THIRST] **1 a :** a colonnaded porch or promenade **:** GALLERY, PORTICO ⟨shops in arcade and along a covered ~ —*Architectural Rev.*⟩ **b :** a flat roof or open platform **:** BALCONY, DECK ⟨the dining ~ looks out upon the tumbling, rushing waters —*Ford Times*⟩ **c :** a relatively level paved or planted area adjoining a building and in formal settings often surrounded by a balustrade ⟨the court side . . . shelters a formal English ~ and garden —*Amer. Guide Series: Mich.*⟩ **2 a :** a raised embankment with the top leveled for walking **b :** a horizontal or gently sloping ridge or offset made in a hillside to conserve moisture or to minimize erosion ⟨built his ~s with a moldboard plow; uses them as guides for his contour rows —*Farm Journal*⟩ — compare STEP TERRACE **c :** something that resembles a terrace ⟨the pyramid . . . had five ~s —E.H.Short⟩ ⟨stood on a status ~ with some below and others above him —John Dollard⟩ **3 a :** a level and ordinarily rather narrow plain usu. with a steep front bordering a river, a lake, or the sea **:** a topographic bench — compare ALLUVIAL TERRACE, KAME TERRACE, MARINE TERRACE, ROCK TERRACE, STREAM TERRACE **b :** STRUCTURAL TERRACE **4 a :** a row of houses or apartments situated on raised ground or a sloping site **b :** a group of row houses ⟨street after street exactly alike, lined with . . . ~s —Talbot Hamlin⟩ **c :** MEDIAN STRIP **d :** STREET

²terrace \"\ *vb* -ED/-ING/-S *vt* **1 :** to make into a terrace or supply with terraces ⟨farms long ago *terraced* by the Inca Indians —Russell Lord⟩ ⟨planted and *terraced* the . . . estate —Alva Johnston⟩ **2 :** to provide (a building) with a terrace; *esp* **:** to design (a structure) with offsets ~ *vi* **:** to occupy a terrace ⟨olive trees *terracing* in steps dug out of rock —Richard Llewellyn⟩

³terrace \"\ *adj* **1 :** of or relating to a terrace ⟨~ roof⟩ ⟨~ farmer⟩ ⟨depositional ~ plains —H.N.Fisk⟩ **2 :** having or forming a terrace ⟨~ apartment⟩

⁴terrace *var of* TRASS

ter·raced \ˈterəst\ *adj* [partly fr. ¹*terrace* + *-ed*; partly fr. past part. of ²*terrace*] **:** formed into or provided with or as if with a terrace

ter·ra·ceous \(ˈ)teˈrāshəs\ *adj* [L *terra* earth + E *-aceous*] **:** EARTHEN

ter·rac·er \ˈterəsə(r)\ *n* -s [²*terrace* + *-er*] **:** a machine used for constructing terraces or wide channels for surface drainage

ter·rac·ette \,terəˈset\ *n* -s [¹*terrace* + *-ette*] **:** CATSTEP

ter·rac·i·form \teˈrasə,fȯrm, ˈterəs-\ *adj* [¹*terrace* + *-iform*] **:** having the form of a terrace

terracing *n* -s [fr. gerund of ²*terrace*] **1 :** a terraced structure or contour ⟨there are more miles of ~ in Georgia and Alabama today than in any other states —Louis Bromfield⟩ **2 :** the formation of terraces ⟨~ occurs . . . as a result of shrinkage of the glacier —R.F.Flint⟩ ⟨wind and soil erosion . . . should be checked by ~ —Welles Hangen⟩

terra-cotta \,terəˈkädə, -ätə\ *n, pl* **terra-cottas** [It *terra cotta*, lit., baked earth] **1 a :** a usu. low-fired and typically reddish unglazed ceramic material (as the earthenware of many primitive potters); *also* **:** an object (as a bowl or figurine) of such material ⟨Greek *terra-cottas*⟩ **b :** a usu. hard-fired glazed or unglazed ceramic architectural material often pressed or cast in ornamental forms and used esp. for decorative facing and tiles **2 a :** a brownish orange that is redder and deeper than spice, leather, or gold pheasant **b** *of textiles* **:** a moderate to strong reddish brown

terra-cotta lumber *n* **:** a very porous earthenware that is easy to pierce or cut and will hold nails driven into it

ter·ra dam·na·ta \,terə,damˈnädə\ *n* [ML, lit., condemned earth] **:** CAPUT MORTUUM 1

ter·rae fil·i·us \te(,)rēˈfilēəs, -rīˈf-\ *n, pl* **terrae fil·ii** \-ēˈfilē,ī, -īˈfilē,ē\ [L, lit., son of the earth] **1** *archaic* **:** a person of lowly birth **2 :** a student (as at Oxford University) formerly appointed to deliver a satirical oration — compare PREVARICATOR 4

ter·ra fir·ma \,terəˈfərmə, -fōmə,-fəimə\ *n* [NL, lit., solid land] **1 a** *obs* **:** CONTINENT, MAINLAND **b** *archaic* **:** Italian peninsular territories formerly controlled by Venice **2 :** dry land **:** solid ground

¹ter·rain \təˈrān *also* (ˈ)teˈr-\ *n* -s [F, land, ground, modif. of L *terrenum* — more at TERRENE] **1** *archaic* **:** a geographical location **:** SPOT **2 a** (1) **:** a geographical area **:** REGION, TERRITORY ⟨explosions . . . spread a large amount of ash over the surrounding ~ —*Report: Smithsonian Institution*⟩ (2) **:** a piece of earth **:** GROUND ⟨bump along the ~ right up to the clubhouse —W.B.Furlong⟩ **b :** the physical features of a tract of land **:** CONTOUR, TOPOGRAPHY ⟨analysis of ~ in aerial photos in different seasons —Ragnar Thoren⟩ **c :** a physical environment of various kinds ⟨a ~ of water that covered almost four million square miles —Wirt Williams⟩ **d :** an area devoted to a specified activity ⟨the entire Union became a racing and breeding ~ —John Hervey⟩ **3 :** TERRANE 1 **4 a :** a defined range of subject matter **:** field of knowledge ⟨travel lightly but skillfully over the whole ~ of economics —S.E.Harris⟩ **b :** a sphere of action **:** ARENA ⟨transferred the ~ of theological controversy from the learned tractate to the popular pamphlet —Helen Sullivan⟩

²terrain \"\ *adj* [alter. (influenced by ¹*terrain*) of ¹*terrene*] **:** TERRESTRIAL, TOPOGRAPHIC

ter·ra in·cog·ni·ta \÷ˈ;terə,inˌkägˈnēdə *also* ˌ==ənˈkägnəd·ə\ *n, pl* **ter·rae incogni·tae** \ˈte,rī . . . nē,tī, -nə,tī\ [L] **:** unknown territory **:** an unexplored country or field of knowledge

ter·ra ja·pon·i·ca \,terəjəˈpänəkə\ *n* [NL, lit., Japanese earth] **1 :** GAMBIER **2 :** CATECHU

ter·ral \teˈräl\ *n* -s [Sp, fr. *tierra* earth, land (fr. L *terra*) + *-al* (fr. L *-alis*) — more at TERRACE] **:** a land breeze

ter·ra lem·nia \,terəˈlemnēə\ *n* [L, lit., Lemnian earth] **1** *usu cap L* **:** LEMNIAN BOLE **2** *often cap L* **:** BOLE 3

ter·ra·ma·ra \,terəˈmärə\ *n, pl* **terrama·re** \-ärē\ [It, mound of crumbling earth (such as found in terramara settlements), terramara, prob. fr. *terra* earth (fr. L) + It dial. *mara* marl, alter. of It *marna*, fr. OF *marne*, alter. of *marle* — more at TERRACE, MARL] **:** a late Neolithic or early Bronze Age lake dwelling or settlement of northern Italy known from remains found in mounds of the Po valley

ter·ra mi·rac·u·lo·sa \ˌterəmə,rakyəˈlōsə\ *n* [NL, lit., miraculous earth] **:** ²BOLE 1

Ter·ra·my·cin \,terəˈmīsᵊn\ *trademark* — used for oxytetracycline

ter·rane \təˈrān, (ˈ)teˈr-\ *n* -s [alter. of ¹*terrain*] **1 a :** a rock formation or group of formations **b :** the area or surface over which a particular rock or group of rocks is prevalent **2 :** TERRAIN 2a

ter·ra·nean \təˈrānēən, teˈr-, -ānyən\ *adj* [L *terra* earth + E *-anean* (as in *subterranean*)] **:** of or relating to the earth

ter·ra·neous \-ēəs,-yəs\ *adj* [L *terra* + E *-aneous* (as in *subterraneous*) — more at TERRACE] **:** TERRESTRIAL, TERRANEAN

terra nul·li·us \,terənəˈlēəs, -ˈnůlē-\ *n* [NL, lit., nobody's land] **:** territory not annexed by any nation ⟨the greater portion of Antarctica . . . is still *terra nullius* —L.M.Gould⟩

ter·ra or·el·la·na \,terə,ȯrəˈlänə, -ȯrə(l)ˈyä-\ *n* [NL, lit., earth of Orellana (Francisco de Orellana †1549 Span. soldier and explorer)] **:** ANNATTO 2a

ter·ra·pe·ne \,terəˈpēnē\ *n, cap* [NL, fr. obs. E *terrapine, terrapene* terrapin] **:** a genus comprising the box tortoises

ter·ra·pin \ˈterəpən, ˈtar-\ *n* -s [obs. E *terrapine*, of Algonquian origin; akin to Delaware *torope* turtle] **1 a :** any of various edible No. American turtles of the family Testudinidae living in fresh or brackish water; *esp* **:** DIAMONDBACK TERRAPIN — see RED-BELLIED TERRAPIN, YELLOW-BELLIED TERRAPIN **b :** any of various other esp. freshwater turtles **2 :** a moderate brown that is redder, lighter, and stronger than coffee, lighter, stronger, and slightly redder than chestnut brown, and yellower, lighter, and stronger than auburn — called also *feuille* **3** *usu cap* **:** a Marylander — used as a nickname

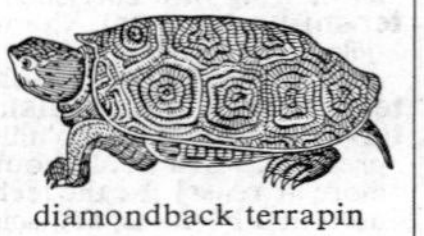

diamondback terrapin

terrapin scale *n* **:** a small brownish convex soft scale (*Lecanium nigrofasciatum*) that is very destructive to several cultivated trees (as peach, plum, and apple) — called also *peach lecanium*

ter·ra pon·der·o·sa \ˌterə,pändəˈrōsə\ *n* [NL, lit., heavy earth] *archaic* **:** BARITE

terra poz·zu·o·li \-,pätsəˈwȯlē\ *n* [It *terra* earth (fr. L) + *Pozzuoli*, commune of Campania, southern Italy] **:** BOLE 3

terra pu·tu·ra \,==,pəˈtůrə, -pyəˈtyůrə\ *n* [NL] *Old Eng law* **:** land subject to puture

terr·aqueous \(ˈ)ter, ˌtər +\ *adj* [L *terra* earth + E *aqueous* — more at TERRACE] **:** consisting of land and water ⟨cover . . . more than half of the ~ globe —Malcolm Cowley⟩

ter·rar \ˈterər, -e,rär\ *n* -s [ML *terrarius*, fr. L *terra* land + *-arius* -ary; fr. his handling the income from and disbursements for the lands belonging to the house] **:** a bursar of a religious house

ter·rar·i·um \təˈrerēəm\ *n, pl* **terrar·ia** \-ēə\ *or* **terrariums** [NL, fr. L *terra* earth + *-arium* (as in *aquarium*)] **1 :** a vivarium for terrestrial animals **2 :** a fully enclosed wholly or predominantly glass container (as a Wardian case) for the indoor cultivation of moisture-loving plants; *also* **:** a planting in such a container **:** GLASS GARDEN

ter·ra ro·sa \,terəˈrōzə, -ōsə\ *n* [NL, lit., gnawed earth] **:** RED OCHER

terra ros·sa \-ˈrōsə, -ˈräsə\ *n* [It, lit., red earth] **:** red shallow residual clayey soils formed from hard limestone and occurring in the Mediterranean climate and in limited areas in southern Australia

terra si·en·na \,==,sēˈenə\ *n* [modif. of It *terra di Siena*] **:** RAW SIENNA 2

terra sig·il·la·ta \ˌ==,sigəˈlädə, -,sijəˈlād·ə\ *n* [ML, lit., stamped earth] **1 :** BOLE 3 **2 :** ancient Roman pottery of red or occas. black body adorned with figures; *esp* **:** ARRETINE WARE

ter·rasse \teˈräs\ *n* -s [F, fr. MF] **:** TERRACE

ter·ra ver·de \,terəˈver(,)dā\ *n* [It, lit., green earth] **:** TERRE VERTE

ter·raz·zo \təˈra\|(,)zō, -räl, \|t(,)sō, \|_zə, \|tsə\ *n* -s [It, terrace, terrazzo, perh. fr. OProv *terrassa* terrace — more at TERRACE] **1 :** a mosaic flooring made by embedding small pieces of marble or granite in freshly placed mortar and after hardening grinding and polishing the surface **2 :** a surface (as a border or counter top) of mosaic and mortar either precast or cast-in-place

terre à terre \,terə,te(ə)r\ *adj* [F, lit., earth to earth] **1 a :** performed on or close to the ground or floor **:** performed with little elevation ⟨*terre à terre* dancing⟩ **b :** performing with the feet close to the ground ⟨*terre à terre* dancer⟩ **2 :** lacking in imagination **:** MATTER-OF-FACT, PROSAIC

ter·rel·la \təˈrelə\ *n* -s [NL, small earth or planet, spherical magnet, fr. L *terra* earth + *-ella* — more at TERRACE] **:** a spherical magnet used to simulate the magnetic properties of the earth

ter·rell grass \ˈterəl-\ *n, usu cap T* [fr. the proper name *Terrell*] **:** a coarse American lyme grass (*Elymus virginicus*) used in some districts for pasturage

¹ter·rene \(ˈ)teˈrēn, təˈr-\ *adj* [ME, fr. L *terrenus* of earth, of the earth, fr. *terra* earth — more at TERRACE] **1 :** of or relating to this world or life **:** MUNDANE ⟨by what devotion call down the notice of these eyes to so ~ a being as himself —R.L. Stevenson⟩ **2** *archaic* **a :** consisting of or resembling earth **:** EARTHY **b :** encountered on land rather than water **:** TERRESTRIAL **syn** see EARTHLY

²terrene \"\ *n* -s [L *terrenum* land, ground, fr. neut. of *terrenus* of earth] **:** a land area **:** EARTH, TERRAIN

ter·rene·ly *adv* **:** in an earthly manner **:** MUNDANELY

terre·plein \ˈterə,plān\ *n* -s [MF, fr. OIt *terrapieno*, fr. ML *terraplenum*, fr. the phrase *terrā plenus* filled with earth, full of earth, fr. L *terrā* (abl. sing. of *terra* earth) + *plenus* full — more at TERRACE, FULL] **1 a :** the level space behind the parapet of a rampart where guns are mounted **b :** the level at which a battery is placed whether above or below ground **2 :** an embankment of earth with a broad level top

¹ter·res·tri·al \təˈrestrēəl, teˈr-, *prob by* r-*dissimilation or/and on the analogy of* "*celestial*" ÷-es(h)chəl *or* -estēəl\ *adj* [ME, fr. L *terrestris* of the earth, of land (fr. *terra* earth, land) + ME *-al* — more at TERRACE] **1 a :** of or relating to the earth or its inhabitants **:** EARTHLY, GLOBAL ⟨the nearest thing to an angelic being that treads this ~ ball —J.B.Martin⟩ ⟨funneling an inadequate supply of U. S. dollars into the large ~ dollar deficit —*Economist*⟩ **b :** mundane in scope or character **:** EARTHBOUND, PROSAIC ⟨that philosophy is essentially ~, not . . . cosmic —J.L.Lowes⟩ ⟨self-taught from childhood, he developed an immense ~ practicality —Alfred Kreymborg⟩ **2** *obs* **:** consisting of or resembling soil **:** EARTHY **3 a :** of or relating to land as distinct from air or water ⟨~ transportation⟩ ⟨sedimentary material of ~ origin —*Jour. of Geol.*⟩ **b** (1) **:** living on or in or growing from the land ⟨~ plants⟩ ⟨~ birds⟩ — distinguished from *amphibious, aquatic, arboreal, epiphytic* (2) **:** of or relating to terrestrial organisms ⟨~ habits⟩ **4** *astron* **:** belonging to the same class with the earth **syn** see EARTHLY

²terrestrial \"\ *n* -s **:** an inhabitant of land or of the earth ⟨this orchid is one of the ~s⟩

terrestrial deposit *n* **1 :** a sedimentary deposit made on land above tidal reach as a result of the activity of glaciers, wind, rainwash, and streams **2 :** a sedimentary deposit formed by springs or by underground water in cavities of rocks

terrestrial equator *n* **:** EQUATOR 2

terrestrial glory *n* **:** the second of three Mormon degrees or kingdoms of glory attainable in heaven — compare CELESTIAL GLORY, TELESTIAL GLORY

terrestrial latitude *n* **:** latitude on the earth — compare ASTRONOMICAL LATITUDE, GEOCENTRIC LATITUDE, GEOGRAPHICAL LATITUDE

terrestrial longitude *n* **:** longitude on the earth

ter·res·tri·al·ly \-ēəlē, -li\ *adv* [¹*terrestrial* + *-ly*] **1 :** in an earthly manner **:** MUNDANELY, TEMPORALLY ⟨~ transient⟩ **2 :** to a land environment ⟨~ adapted⟩ **3 :** by contact with the earth or its atmosphere ⟨a ~ oxidized meteor⟩

terrestrial magnetism *n* **1 :** the magnetism of the earth **2 :** a branch of geophysics that deals with the phenomena of the earth's magnetic condition

terrestrial meridian *n* **:** MERIDIAN 4a

terrestrial planet *n* **:** one of the four inner planets of the solar system ⟨Mercury, Venus, Earth, and Mars are the *terrestrial planets*⟩ — compare MAJOR PLANET

terrestrial pole *n* **:** ⁴POLE 1b

terrestrial telescope *n* **:** a refracting telescope for viewing terrestrial objects through an eyepiece that consists of three or four lenses so arranged that the final image is right side up — compare ASTRONOMICAL TELESCOPE, FIELD GLASS, SPYGLASS

ter·ret *also* **ter·rit** \ˈterət\ *n* -s [ME *toret, teret*, fr. MF *toret*, fr. OF, dim. of *tor* circuit] **:** one of the rings on the top of a harness pad through which the reins pass

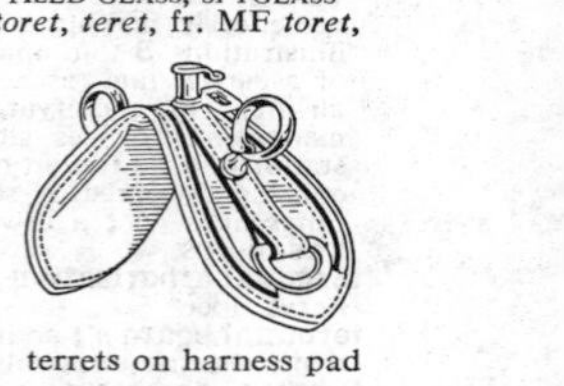

terrets on harness pad

terre-tenant *or* **ter·ten·ant** \ˈter-,tenənt, ˈtər-\ *n* [ME *teretenaunt*, fr. AF *terre tenaunt*, fr. OF *terre* land (fr. L *terra*) + *tenant* holding, fr. pres. part. of *tenir* to hold, fr. L *tenēre* — more at TERRACE, THIN] **:** one who has the actual possession of land **:** the occupant of land; *often* **:** one other than a judgment debtor owning an interest in the debtor's land after the lien of the judgment creditor attached thereto

terre verte \(ˈ)terˈve(ə)rt\ *n* [F, lit., green earth] **1 :** GREEN EARTH 2 **2 :** the variable color of terre verte pigment, which averages a grayish green that is bluer, lighter, and stronger than slate green, bluer and duller than average reseda (sense 2a), and yellower and duller than average blue spruce (sense 2a) — called also *Bohemian earth, cyprian earth, green earth, green ocher, holy green, Italian green, permanent green, Tyrol green, Verona green*

ter·ri·bi·li·ta \,terə,bēləˈtä\ *n* -s [It *terribilità*, lit., terribleness, fr. LL *terribilitat-, terribilitas*, fr. L *terribilis* terrible + *-itat-, -itas* -ity] **:** an effect or expression of powerful will and immense angry force (as in the work of Michelangelo)

¹ter·ri·ble \ˈterəbəl\ *adj* [ME, fr. MF, fr. L *terribilis*, fr. *terrēre* to frighten + *-ibilis* -ible — more at TERROR] **1 a :** exciting extreme alarm **:** FRIGHTENING, TERRIFYING ⟨the instantly cataclysmic effect of these ~ new weapons —J.C. Slessor⟩ ⟨the ~ powers of the Inquisition —J.H.Randall⟩ **b :** overwhelmingly tragic ⟨a human being devoid of hope is the most ~ object in the world —Victor Heiser⟩ **c :** formidable in nature **:** commanding respect **:** AWESOME, IMPOSING ⟨courage of those sailors . . . made the flag of England ~ on the seas —T.B.Macaulay⟩ ⟨a choice . . . which affected so many other lives was a ~ responsibility —John Mason Brown⟩ **d :** requiring extreme effort or fortitude **:** DIFFICULT, LABORIOUS ⟨a ~ ordeal⟩ ⟨a ~ task⟩ **2 :** extreme in degree **:** GREAT, INTENSE ⟨~ anxiety⟩ ⟨the artist's ~ and all-consuming dedication to his work —David Sylvester⟩ **3 a :** defective or injurious in nature **:** BAD, DESTRUCTIVE ⟨the road got bumpier . . . and the land on either side of it was in ~ shape —Emily Hahn⟩ ⟨the rainy season finds its ~ climax . . . in the crashing impact of a hurricane —Marjory S. Douglas⟩ **b :** strongly repulsive **:** DISREPUTABLE, OBNOXIOUS ⟨people . . . live in that ~ old shack —Peggy Bennett⟩ ⟨musk . . . smells simply ~ by itself —D.W.Dresden⟩ **4 a :** tending to appall **:** DREADFUL, SHOCKING ⟨blend of ~ sentimentality and brassy sophistication —Wolcott Gibbs⟩ ⟨gave the beggar . . . my own quarter, so what's so ~ —Mary Barrett⟩ **b :** of very poor quality **:** AWFUL, PUNK ⟨Italian painting, when it is bad, can be really ~ —R.M. Coates⟩ ⟨bought a drink of ~ whiskey —Herbert Asbury⟩ **syn** see FEARFUL

²terrible \"\ *adv* **:** to an extreme degree **:** VERY, TERRIBLY ⟨a ~ brave man —John Buchan⟩ ⟨a ~ cold night⟩

³terrible \"\ *n* -s **:** a terrible person or thing

ter·ri·ble·ness *n* -ES **:** the quality or state of being terrible

ter·ri·bly \-blē,-bli\ *adv* [¹*terrible* + *-ly*] **1 :** in a formidable or frightening manner **:** AWESOMELY, TERRIFYINGLY ⟨the ~ glittering advance of a tidal wave⟩ ⟨the fear is ~ mutual —Hal Lehrman⟩ **2 a :** to a superlative degree **:** EXTREMELY, INTENSELY ⟨it is ~ difficult to translate poetry —Gilbert Highet⟩ ⟨the reaction of a ~ sincere spirit to something . . . sham and sophisticated —Herbert Read⟩ ⟨an eighty-five cent dinner that was ~ good and quick —Mary McCarthy⟩ **b :** to an excruciating or shocking extent **:** APPALLINGLY ⟨wars . . . aggravated matters ~ —E.B.George⟩ ⟨the story is ~ involved —Roger Fry⟩ ⟨played pinochle, and . . . cheated ~ —Edita Morris⟩

ter·ric·o·lae \teˈrikə,lē, təˈr-, -,lī\ *n pl, cap* [NL, fr. L, pl. of *terricola* earth dweller, fr. *terri-* (fr. *terra* earth) + *-cola*] *in some esp former classifications* **:** a group of Oligochaeta comprising mainly the more terrestrial oligochaete worms — compare LIMICOLAE, NEOLIGOCHAETA

ter·ric·o·lous \-ləs\ *or* **ter·ri·cole** \ˈterə,kōl\ *also* **ter·ric·o·line** \teˈrikə,līn, təˈr-, -,lən\ *adj* [*terricole* fr. L *terricola* earth dweller; *terricolous, terricoline* fr. L *terricola* + E *-ous* or *-ine*] **:** TERRESTRIAL 3b

¹ter·ri·er \ˈterēə(r), *chiefly dial* ˈtar-\ *n* -s [F, fr. MF, fr. ML (*liber*) *terrarius*, lit., book relating to land, fr. L *liber* book + ML *terrarius* of earth, of land — more at LEAF] **1 :** a register (as in a book or roll) of English real property: **a :** one listing the names of vassals or tenants with details of their holdings, services, and rents **:** RENT-ROLL **b :** one in which the lands of a private person or of a corporation are described by site, boundaries, and acreage; *esp* **:** one detailing the real property of a parish church **2** *obs* **:** an inventory of property or goods

²terrier \"\ *n* -s [F (*chien*) *terrier*, lit., earth dog, fr. *chien* dog (fr. L *canis*) + *terrier* of earth, fr. ML *terrarius* of earth, of land, fr. L *terra* earth, land + *-arius* -ary — more at HOUND, TERRACE] **:** any of various usu. small and rather low-built dogs (as an airedale, fox terrier, schnauzer) kept chiefly as pets but orig. used by hunters to dig for small furred game and engage the quarry underground or drive it out of its hole — compare BULLTERRIER; see FOX TERRIER illustration

terries *pl of* TERRY

ter·rif·ic \təˈrifik, -fēk\ *adj* [L *terrificus*, fr. *terrēre* to frighten + *-i-* + *-ficus* -fic — more at TERROR] **1 a :** exciting fear or awe **:** TERRIBLE, TERRIFYING ⟨the ~ destruction . . . visited upon the country —I.M.Price⟩ ⟨~, serrated outcrops of naked rock —Douglas Carruthers⟩ **b :** very bad **:** AWFUL, FRIGHTFUL ⟨might well have passed at three hearts . . . with this ~ distribution —*Springfield (Mass.) Daily News*⟩ ⟨covering up a ~ literary scandal for one of his clients —Robert Cantwell⟩ **2 a :** of an extraordinary nature **:** ASTOUNDING, TREMENDOUS ⟨can read the most involved books at the ~ rate of 600 pages a day —Bernard Eaton⟩ ⟨the ~ heat exploded ammunition in the wing guns —O.O.Jensen⟩ **b :** exceptionally strong or violent **:** POWERFUL, SEVERE ⟨punched him . . . in the stomach, short ~ jabs —Raymond Chandler⟩ ⟨sad to see . . . the damage done by this ~ winter —Georgina Grahame⟩ ⟨the impact of thirty million aliens is a ~ test of any culture —G.W. Johnson⟩ **3 :** unusually fine or gratifying **:** exciting admiration or enthusiasm **:** MAGNIFICENT, MARVELOUS ⟨a ~ view . . . all the way to the Black Mountains of Wales, some fifty miles distant —Richard Joseph⟩ ⟨told him that the piece would be a great success in the concert hall and ~ on records —Moses Smith⟩ **syn** see FEARFUL

ter·rif·i·cal·ly \-fək(ə)lē, -fēk-, -li\ *adv* [*terrific* + *-ally*] **:** to a terrific degree or extent

terrified *adj* [fr. past part. of *terrify*] **1 :** filled with intense fear or apprehension ⟨the men were ~ . . . and wanted to retreat out of harm's way —C.S.Forester⟩ **2 :** filled with anxiety or worry ⟨has no faith in her powers of attraction, and she's ~ of being thought ridiculous —Constance Walsh⟩ **syn** see AFRAID

ter·ri·fy \ˈterə,fī\ *vt* -ED/-ING/-ES [L *terrificare*, fr. *terrificus* terrific] **1 a :** to fill with terror **:** frighten greatly ⟨sermons . . . providing a sanction for other men to ~ the imaginations of ill-balanced persons —V.L.Parrington⟩ ⟨the prospect of nuclear warfare *terrifies* the population⟩ **b :** to drive or impel by menacing **:** SCARE ⟨the gunman's threats ~ her into handing over the money⟩ **c :** DETER, INTIMIDATE ⟨book . . . so technical as to ~ the average reader —Anthony Boucher⟩ ⟨museums

and galleries ~ us —Clive Bell⟩ **2** *dial Brit* **:** to cause trouble to **:** HARASS, TORMENT **syn** see FRIGHTEN
terrifying *adj* [fr. pres. part. of *terrify*] **1 :** causing terror or apprehension **:** FRIGHTENING ⟨the most ~ things he met on his travels were the marching ants of Tanganyika —*Irish Digest*⟩ ⟨ascent of a ~ icefall —Raymond Holden⟩ ⟨his ~ insistence upon appalling and merciless retribution —W.L.Sullivan⟩ **2 :** of a formidable nature **:** AWESOME, TREMENDOUS ⟨the ~ formality . . . of the great drawing rooms of Paris —Elinor Wylie⟩ ⟨a ~ and voracious erudition —Morris Watnick⟩ ⟨take a ~ leap to the unimaginable range of temperatures . . . in the universe —Gerard Piel⟩ — **ter·ri·fy·ing·ly** \ˈ==,===, ,=ˈ===\ *adv*
ter·rig·e·nous \təˈrijənəs, teˈr-\ *adj* [L *terrigena* earthborn (fr. *terri-* — fr. *terra* earth — + *-gena* — akin to L *gignere* to beget) + E *-ous* — more at TERRACE, KIN] **:** formed by the erosive action of rivers, tides, and currents — used of an ocean bottom ⟨~ deposits drape the continental shelves . . . and trail downward to the abysses —F.C.Lane⟩
ter·rine \təˈrēn, (ˈ)teˈr-\ *n* -s [F — more at TUREEN] **1 a :** TUREEN **b :** a usu. earthenware dish (as a casserole) in which foods are cooked and served **2 :** an earthenware jar containing a table delicacy (as goose liver) and sold with its contents
territ *var of* TERRET
¹ter·ri·to·ri·al \ˌterəˈtōrēəl, -ōr-\ *adj* [L *territorialis* of a territory, fr. *territorium* territory + *-alis* -al] **1 a :** of or relating to the immediate vicinity **:** LOCAL **b :** serving outlying areas **:** REGIONAL ⟨the ~ minister and the district worker —W. G.Blaikie⟩ **2 a :** of or relating to a territory ⟨~ government⟩ ⟨~ regiment⟩ ⟨~ delegate⟩ ⟨protested violations of its ~ air by planes of a foreign power —*Springfield (Mass.) Union*⟩ ⟨two states have been admitted to the Union without having passed through the ~ stage —J.E.Stoner⟩ **b :** of or relating to private property ⟨the soil of Italy was fast passing into the hands of a few ~ magnates —J.A.Froude⟩ **3 a :** of or relating to an assigned or preempted area ⟨the line of . . . command extends, in its simplest terms, from general to chief of the staff to ~ commanders —Don Pitt⟩ ⟨although some animals appear to have no discernible ~ demands, most . . . are territory-conscious —L.W.Wing⟩ **b :** exhibiting territoriality ⟨a ~ species⟩ ⟨strongly ~ birds⟩ — **ter·ri·to·ri·al·ly** \-ēəlē, -li\ *adv*
²territorial \"\ *n* -s **1 :** a territorial military unit; *esp* **:** HOME RESERVE **2 :** a member of a territorial military unit
territorial gold *n* **:** PRIVATE GOLD
ter·ri·to·ri·al·ism \ˌ==ˈ===,lizəm\ *n* -s [¹*territorial* + *-ism*] **1 :** LANDLORDISM 2 **2 :** the principle established by the Peace of Augsburg in 1555 providing for compulsory conformity of all the inhabitants of a territory of the Holy Roman Empire to the Lutheranism or Roman Catholicism established by their ruler or for their emigration **3** *often cap* **:** a doctrine, theory, or movement among the Jews seeking to establish the settlement of the Jews on an autonomous basis in any suitable and available part of the world — compare ZIONISM **4 :** TERRITORIALITY 2
ter·ri·to·ri·al·ist \-ləst\ *n* -s [¹*territorial* + *-ist*] **:** one that practices or advocates territorialism
ter·ri·to·ri·al·i·ty \ˌ==,==ˈaləd·ē, -ətē, -i\ *n* -ES [¹*territorial* + *-ity*] **1 :** territorial status **2 a :** persistent attachment to a specific territory **b :** the pattern of behavior associated with the defense of a male animal's territory
ter·ri·to·ri·al·iza·tion \ˌ==,===ləˈzāshən, -ə,līˈz-\ *n* -s [*territorialize* + *-ation*] **:** the act or process of organizing into territories
ter·ri·to·ri·al·ize \ˌterəˈtōrēə,līz, -ˈtȯr-\ *vt* -ED/-ING/-S *see -ize in Explan Notes* **:** to reduce to the status of a territory **:** organize on a territorial basis
territorial jurisdiction *n* **:** the sovereign jurisdiction that a state has over the land within its boundary limits, over its inland and territorial waters and to a reasonable extent over the airspace above and subsoil below in such land and waters, and over all persons and things within those areas subject to its control (as on its vessels on or aircraft over the high seas) — compare EXTRATERRITORIALITY
territorial law *n* **:** law applying alike to all persons regardless of their nationality or citizenship within a given territory — distinguished from *personal law*
territorial reserve *n* **:** HOME RESERVE
territorial sea *n* **:** the part of territorial waters subject to the jurisdiction of a coastal state usu. extending from mean low water mark on the shore or from the seaward limit of a bay or mouth of a river a marine league or 3 geographical miles outward to the open sea — compare INLAND WATER
territorial style *n, usu cap T* **:** the architectural style resulting from the influences of eastern U. S. settlers on the Indian and Spanish building techniques of New Mexico
territorial waters *n pl* **:** the waters under the territorial jurisdiction of a nation or state including both inland waters and marginal sea as measured from mean low-water mark or from the seaward limit of a bay or river mouth
ter·ri·to·ri·an \ˌ==ˈ==ēən\ *n* -s *usu cap* [*territory* + *-an*] **:** an inhabitant of the Northern Territory of Australia
ter·ri·to·ry \ˈterə,tōrē, -ōri, -ȯr-\ *n* -ES [ME, fr. L *territorium* land around a town, district, territory, prob. fr. *terri-* (fr. *terra* land) + *-torium* (as in *praetorium*) — more at TERRACE] **1 a :** a geographical area belonging to or under the jurisdiction of a political authority ⟨defeated the German armies on their home ~ —C.E.Black & E.C.Helmreich⟩ ⟨out-of-town police . . . questioned him about several similar murders in their *territories* —E.D.Radin⟩ **b :** an administrative subdivision of a country ⟨the 15 republics of the U. S. S. R. are divided into 128 *territories* and regions⟩ **c :** an organized portion of a country not yet admitted to statehood ⟨Minnesota became a ~ in 1849 —*Amer. Guide Series: Minn.*⟩ ⟨Mexico is divided into 29 states, 1 federal district . . . and 2 *territories* —*Statesman's Yr. Bk.*⟩ **d :** a geographical area (as a colonial possession) dependent upon an external government but having some degree of autonomy ⟨the status of France's third North African ~ will be challenged —Mario Rossi⟩ — compare TRUST TERRITORY **e** *Scots law* **:** the district subject to the jurisdiction of a court or judge **:** JURISDICTION **2 a** (1) **:** a geographical area of indeterminate extent **:** REGION, TRACT ⟨in Virginia . . . there were large *territories* of unsettled lands —R.B.Taney⟩ (2) **:** LAND, TERRAIN ⟨without their mustangs Texas cowboys could never have covered so much ~ —S.E. Fletcher⟩ (3) **:** an area of specified potential ⟨some of the state's best fish and game ~ —*Amer. Guide Series: Vt.*⟩ ⟨huge accumulations of . . . clouds that made perfect ambush ~ for pilots —Ira Wolfert⟩ **b :** an area of knowledge or special interest **:** FIELD, GROUND ⟨the large adjoining *territories* of social and economic history —Franz Philipp⟩ ⟨that question covers a lot of ~ —*Magazine of Wall Street*⟩ **c :** a specified area (as of the body) ⟨stuck soda straws up each nostril . . . while we poured plaster over his surrounding facial ~ —Beverly Smith⟩ **3 :** an assigned or preempted area: as **a :** the area defended by an athletic team ⟨a brilliant 52-yard dash . . . moved Ohio State from deep in its own ~ into striking position —*N. Y. Times*⟩ **b :** a geographic area to which a salesman or distributor confines his commercial activities **c :** the largest administrative unit of the Salvation Army usu. comprising a country or group of countries **d :** an area usu. including the nesting or denning site and a variable foraging range that is preempted by an individual male (as a bird or mammal) and defended against the intrusion of rival individuals — compare HOME RANGE **syn** see FIELD
territory wool *n* [so called fr. the former territorial status of the states in which it was produced] **:** wool produced esp. in Montana, Wyoming, Idaho, Utah, Nevada, Colorado, and Washington
ter·ron \təˈrōn\ *n, pl* **terro·nes** \-ˈnēz\ [MexSp *terrón*, fr. Sp, clod, lump of earth, fr. *tierra* earth, fr. L *terra*] **:** a block of sun-dried sod used as a construction brick in the Rio Grande valley ⟨heavy clay with abundant fine grass roots makes the best ~*es* —A.A.Lindsey⟩
¹ter·ror \ˈterə(r)\ *n* -s *often attrib* [ME *terrour*, fr. MF *terreur*, fr. L *terror*, fr. *terrēre* to frighten; akin to Gk *trein* to flee from fear, be afraid, Skt *trasati* he trembles, is afraid] **1 a :** a state of intense fright or apprehension **:** stark fear ⟨disquietude had developed into fright; fright . . . into ~ —Emile Gaboriau⟩ ⟨every beast . . . jarred out of tranquillity into ~, was spending its strength in flight —F.D.Davison⟩ **b :** TERRIBLENESS ⟨the dramatic, apocalyptic ~ of concentrated bombing attacks —Anthony West⟩ ⟨the blizzard broke in all its ~ —O.E.Rolvaag⟩ **2 a :** one that inspires fear **:** THREAT, SCOURGE ⟨horse thieves and murdering ruffians who were the ~ of the border —E.V.Buckholder⟩ **b :** a frightening aspect ⟨while withdrawal from opiates is never a pleasant experience, its ~*s* have probably been exaggerated —D.W.Maurer & V.H. Vogel⟩ **c :** a cause of anxiety **:** WORRY ⟨it was the ~ of my life that he might catch a chill —Ernest Beaglehole⟩ **d :** an appalling person or thing; *esp* **:** ²BRAT 2 ⟨a little ~ at two and a half —May Sherwin⟩ **3 :** REIGN OF TERROR ⟨reports that the Germans are increasing their ~ in occupied regions —Walter Bernstein⟩ **syn** see FEAR
²terror \"\ *vt* -ED/-ING/-S **:** FRIGHTEN
ter·ror·ful \-fəl\ *adj* **:** full of terror **:** TERRIFYING
ter·ror·ism \ˈterə,rizəm\ *n* -s [F *terrorisme*, fr. L *terror* + F *-isme* -ism] **1 :** the systematic use of terror as a means of coercion ⟨the opening stage of a well-planned campaign of political ~ —Heinz Eulan⟩ — compare REIGN OF TERROR **2 :** an atmosphere of threat or violence ⟨study the effects on children of ~ in TV shows⟩
ter·ror·ist \ˈterərəst\ *n* -s [F *terroriste*, fr. L *terror* + F *-iste* -ist] **1 :** an advocate or practitioner of terror as a means of coercion; *esp* **:** JACOBIN 2a **2 :** one who panics or causes anxiety **:** ALARMIST — **ter·ror·is·tic** \ˌterəˈristik\ *adj*
ter·ror·iza·tion \ˌterərəˈzāshən, -erə,rīˈz-\ *n* -s **:** the act or process of terrorizing
ter·ror·ize \ˈterə,rīz\ *vb* -ED/-ING/-S *see -ize in Explan Notes* [¹*terror* + *-ize*] *vt* **1 :** to fill with terror or anxiety **:** SCARE **2 :** to coerce by threat or violence ⟨~ the members of that union into helpless submission —T.W.Arnold⟩ ~ *vi* **:** to excite fear **:** rule by intimidation **syn** see FRIGHTEN
ter·ror·less \ˈterə(r)ləs\ *adj* **:** holding no terrors
ter·rour *n* [ME] *archaic* **:** TERROR
ter·ry \ˈterē, -ri\ *n* -ES *often attrib* [perh. modif. of F *tiré*, past part. of *tirer* to draw, fr. OF — more at TIRADE] **1 :** the loop forming the pile in uncut pile fabrics — compare ⁸PILE 2 **2** *or* **terry cloth :** a soft absorbent usu. cotton fabric characterized by loops in allover or pattern effects on one or both sides and made in various weights (as for towels, bathrobes, sportswear, spreads)
ter·ry clock \ˈterē-, -ri-\ *n, usu cap T* [after Eli *Terry* †1852 Am. clock manufacturer] **:** PILLAR AND SCROLL
ter·sanctus \ˈtər, ˈter+\ *n* -ES *often cap* [NL, lit., thrice holy (trans. of LGk *trisagios*), fr. L *ter* three times + *sanctus* holy — more at TER-, SAINT] **1 :** SANCTUS **2** *often cap* **:** any hymn or invocation praising God as the thrice-holy deity
terse \ˈtərs, ˈtəs, ˈtəis\ *adj* [L *tersus* clean, neat, fr. past part. of *tergēre* to rub off, wipe; akin to Goth *thairko* hole, Gk *trōgein* to gnaw, *trōglē* hole, cave, L *terere* to rub — more at THROW] **1 a** *archaic* **:** freed of debris or roughness **:** CLEAN, BURNISHED ⟨enamored of this street . . . 'tis so polite and ~ —Ben Jonson⟩ **b :** smoothly elegant **:** POLISHED, REFINED ⟨clinging, with a true instinct for style, to what is ~ and elliptic —C.E.Montague⟩ ⟨the more lapidary and ~ this subject the better it is suited for symphonic elaboration —P.H.Lang⟩ **2 :** devoid of superfluity **:** BRIEF, CONCISE ⟨his answers were very clipped and ~ —Raymond Boyle⟩ ⟨occasional ~ volleys of rifle fire —H.E.Bates⟩ ⟨keep the copy short, ~ and easy to read —*Printers' Ink*⟩ **syn** see CONCISE
terse·ly *adv* **:** in a terse manner **:** BRIEFLY
terse·ness *n* -ES **:** the quality or state of being terse **:** BREVITY, POLISH
ter·sulfide \ˈtər+\ *n* [*ter-* + *sulfide*] **:** TRISULFIDE
tert- \ˈtərt\ *comb form, usu ital* [*tertiary*] **:** tertiary — esp. in names of organic chemical radicals ⟨*tert*-butyl⟩
tertenant *var of* TERRE-TENANT
tertia *var of* TERCIO
¹ter·tial \ˈtərshəl\ *adj* [L *tertius* third + E *-al*; fr. the fact that tertials form the third row of feathers] **1 :** of, relating to, or constituting the flight feathers borne on the basal joint of a bird's wing — compare PRIMARY 2c **2 :** of, relating to, or constituting some of the innermost secondaries when different from the others or the scapular feathers — not used technically
²tertial \"\ *n* -s **:** a tertial feather
¹ter·tian \ˈtərshən\ *adj* [in sense 1, fr. ME *tercian (fever)* tertian fever, part trans. of L *tertiana febris*, fr. *tertiana* (fem. of *tertianus* of the third) + *febris* fever; fr. its recurring every third day; in other senses fr. L *tertianus* of the third, fr. *tertius* third + *-anus* -an — more at THIRD] **1 :** recurring at approximately 48-hour intervals — used chiefly of vivax malaria — compare QUARTAN **2 :** of or relating to a tertiary or to tertianship **3 :** relating to the mean tone system of musical temperament in which the major thirds are perfectly in tune
²tertian \"\ *n* -s [L *tertianus* of the third] **1** [ME *tercian*, fr. L *tertiana*, fr. *tertiana febris*] **:** a tertian fever; *specif* **:** VIVAX MALARIA **2** [ME *tercian*, fr. L *tertianus* of the third] **:** an old unit of liquid capacity equal to ⅓ tun **3 :** a third-year student in arts (as at Aberdeen University) **4** *or* **tertian father** *usu cap T&F* **:** a Jesuit during tertianship **5 :** a compound organ stop composed of two ranks of open metal pipes tuned a major third apart
ter·tian·ship \-,ship\ *n* [²*tertian* + *-ship*] **:** a third period of novitiate or training undertaken by a Jesuit after ordination
¹ter·tiary \ˈtərshē,erē, ˈtəsh-,ˈtəish-, -eri *also* -shər-\ *n* -ES [in sense 1, fr. ML *tertiarius*, fr. L, of or containing a third; in other senses fr. ²*tertiary*] **1 :** a member of a monastic third order after the first order of monks and the second order of nuns composed of men and women of the laity who take no more than simple vows, who may remain outside of a monastery and hold property, and yet who follow to some degree a portion of a monastic rule ⟨Franciscan and Dominican *tertiaries*⟩ **2 :** a tertial feather **3** *usu cap* **:** the Tertiary period or system of rocks **4 :** TERTIARY COLOR **5 a :** a lesion of tertiary syphilis **b :** TERTIAN 1
²tertiary \"\ *adj* [L *tertiarius* of or containing a third, fr. *tertius* third + *-arius* -ary — more at THIRD] **1 a :** third in order or importance **:** preceded by two others ⟨a ~ characteristic⟩ ⟨a few transformers are provided . . . with a ~ winding —J.B.Gibbs⟩ ⟨a ~ cambium develops around a number of the secondary elements —Ernst Artschwager⟩ **b :** of or relating to a monastic third order **c :** of or relating to education following the secondary level whether at a college or university or at an intermediate institution **d :** of or relating to the service industries (as distribution, transportation, domestic service) compared with agriculture or manufacturing **e :** of, relating to, or constituting the third strongest of the three or four degrees of stress recognized by most linguists ⟨the third syllable in *basketball's fun* carries the ~ stress⟩ **f :** TERTIAL **2** *usu cap* **:** of or relating to the time interval between the close of the Mesozoic era and the beginning of the Quaternary period during which the Alps, Caucasus, Himalayas, and other high mountains were formed, the Cordilleran system from Alaska to Cape Horn was developing, and the dominant land life was mammalian — see GEOLOGIC TIME table **3 :** characterized by replacement in the third degree **:** resulting from the substitution of three atoms or groups in a molecule ⟨a ~ salt⟩ ⟨~ phosphates⟩; *esp* **:** being or characterized by a carbon atom united by three valences to chain or ring members ⟨~ butyl $(CH_3)_3C$⟩ — compare PRIMARY 5, SECONDARY 2e **4 :** occurring or being in the third stage ⟨~ lesions of syphilis⟩
tertiary alcohol *n* **:** an alcohol characterized by the group $\equiv$COH consisting of a carbon atom holding the hydroxyl group and attached by its other three valences to other carbon atoms in a chain or ring
tertiary amine *n* **:** an amine (as trimethylamine, dimethylaniline, or nicotine) having three organic substituents attached to the nitrogen atom
tertiary amyl alcohol *n* **:** a secondary pentyl alcohol $CH_3CH_2C(OH)(CH_3)_2$ having a camphoraceous odor, a burning taste, and hypnotic properties that can be made by hydrating amylene (sense a) and that is used chiefly as a solvent; 2-methyl-2-butanol — called also *amylene hydrate*
tertiary color *n* **:** a color produced by mixing two secondary colors
tertiary quality *n* **:** the quality of a thing as an object of evaluation — compare PRIMARY QUALITY, SECONDARY QUALITY
tertiary syphilis *n* **:** the third stage of syphilis developing soon or late after the disappearance of the secondary symptoms and marked by ulcers in and gummas under the skin and commonly involvement of the skeletal, cardiovascular, and nervous systems
ter·ti·um quid \ˌtərshēəmˈkwid, ˌtərd·ē-, ˌterd·ē-\ *n* [LL, lit., third something, trans. of Gk *triton ti*] **1 :** a middle course or intermediate component **:** something that escapes classification with either of two mutually exclusive and supposedly exhaustive categories but shares elements of both ⟨God occupies merely an external relation, as a *tertium quid*, to mind and matter —James Martineau⟩ ⟨where there are two systems of law and two orders of courts, there must obviously be some *tertium quid* to deal with conflicts of law and jurisdiction —Ernest Baker⟩ **2 :** a third party of ambiguous status ⟨once upon a time there was a man and his wife and a *tertium quid* —Rudyard Kipling⟩
ter·tul·lian·ist \(,)tərˈtəlēənəst, -ˈtül-, -lyən-\ *n* -s *usu cap* [*Tertullian* †A.D.230? Latin ecclesiastical writer + E *-ist*] **:** a follower of Tertullian of Carthage
te·ru·ah \təˈrüə, -ü(,)ä\ *n, pl* **teru·oth** *or* **teru·ot** \-ü,ōt(h), -ōs\ *or* **teruahs** [Heb *tĕrū'āh* shout or blast of war, fr. *rūa'* to raise a shout, give a blast] **:** one of the calls composed of a series of staccato blasts followed by a longer high note and blown on the shofar as prescribed in the Jewish ritual on certain festivals and at certain ceremonies — compare TEKIAH
te·ru·tero \ˌterüˈte(,)rō\ *or* **ter·u·teru** \-(,)rü\ *n* -s [Sp, fr. Guarani *teruteru*, of imit. origin] **:** a So. American lapwing (*Belonopterus chilensis cayennensis*) similar to the common lapwing but having a shorter hind toe and a spur on the bend of the wing
ter·valence *also* **ter·valency** \ˈtər+\ *n* [*ter-* + *valence, valency*] **:** TRIVALENCE
ter·valent \"+\ *adj* [*ter-* + *valent*] **:** TRIVALENT
ter·za ri·ma \ˌtertsəˈrēmə\ *n* [It, lit., third rhyme] **:** a verse form consisting of tercets usu. in iambic pentameter in English poetry in which the second line of each rhymes with the first and third lines of the next ⟨Dante's *Divina Commedia* is written in *terza rima*⟩
ter·zet·to \tertˈsed·(,)ō\ *or* **ter·zet** \(ˈ)tertˈset\ *n, pl* **terzet·tos** \-d·(,)ōz\ *or* **terzets** \-ts\ *also* **terzet·ti** \-d·(,)ē\ [It *terzetto* — more at TERCET] **:** a musical composition for three voices **:** TRIO
ter·zi·na \tertˈsēnə\ *n, pl* **terzinas** \-nəz\ *or* **terzi·ne** \-nā\ [It] **:** TRIPLET 1
tes *pl of* TE
tesch·e·mach·er·ite \ˈteshə,makə,rīt\ *n* -s [Frederick E. *Teschemacher* †1863 Eng. chemist + E *-ite*] **:** a mineral consisting of an acid ammonium carbonate occurring in yellowish to white crystals in beds of guano (hardness 1.5, sp. gr. 1.4)
te·schen disease \ˈteshən-\ *n, usu cap T* [fr. *Teschen* (Cieszyn), region on the border of Poland and Czechoslovakia where it was first recognized] **:** a severe virus encephalomyelitis of swine marked by lesions of the central nervous system and by varying degrees of systemic paralysis and in many respects resembling human poliomyelitis but prob. not closely related etiologically
te·shu·bah *or* **te·shu·vah** \ˈchüvə, təˈshüvə, -(,)vä\ *n* [LHeb *tĕshūbhāh*, fr. Heb, return] **:** REPENTANCE
teshu lama *usu cap T&L, var of* TASHI LAMA
tes·la coil \ˈteslə-\ *or* **tesla transformer** *n, usu cap T* [after Nikola *Tesla* †1943 Am. electrician and inventor] **:** an air-core transformer for high-frequency alternating or oscillating electrical currents
tesla current *n, usu cap T* [after Nikola *Tesla* †1943] **:** a high-frequency oscillating current of medium voltage used in therapeutic treatment
te·so \ˈtā(,)sō\ *n, pl* **teso** *or* **tesos** *usu cap* **1 a :** a Nilo-Hamite people of eastern Uganda **b :** a member of such people **2 :** a Nilotic language of the Teso people
te·so·ta \təˈsōd·ə\ *n* -s [NL (specific epithet of *Olneya tesota*), fr. AmerSp, ironwood] **:** DESERT IRONWOOD 1
tessara- *or* **tessera-** *also* **tessar-** *comb form* [L, fr. Gk *tessara, tessera*, neut. of *tessares, tesseres, tettares* four — more at FOUR] **:** four ⟨*tessara*glot⟩ ⟨*tessera*decade⟩
tes·sa·ra·ce \ˈtesərə,sē\ *n* -s [*tessara-* + *-ace*] **:** a tetrahedral summit
tes·sa·ra·con·ter \ˌtesərəˈkäntə(r)\ *n* -s [Gk *tessarakontērēs*, fr. *tessarakonta, tesserakonta* forty, fr. *tessara-* + *-konta* (akin to L *-ginti* in *viginti* twenty) — more at VICENARY] **:** a galley with forty banks of oars
tes·sa·ra·glot \ˈ===,glät\ *adj* [*tessara-* + *-glot*] **:** using or containing four languages
tes·sel·la \təˈselə\ *n* -s [L, small die, dim. of *tessera*] **:** TESSERA 2a
tes·sel·lar \ˈtesələ(r)\ *adj* **:** formed of or resembling tesserae
tes·sel·la·ta \ˌtesəˈläd·ə, -ād·ə\ [NL, fr. L, neut. pl. of *tessellatus* checkered, tessellated] *syn of* PALAEOCRINOIDEA
¹tes·sel·late *also* **tes·se·late** \ˈtesə,lāt, *usu* -ād·+V\ *vt* -ED/-ING/-S [LL *tessellatus*, past part. of *tessellare* to pave with tiles, fr. L *tessella* small die] **1 :** to decorate with or as if with tesserae **:** make a mosaic of ⟨~ a floor⟩ **2** *archaic* **:** to fit into or as if into a mosaic ⟨this meaning is vague . . . impossible to ~ into any formal scheme —F.W.Farrar⟩
²tes·sel·late *also* **tes·se·late** \-ələt, -ə,lāt, *usu* -d·+V\ *adj* [L *tessellatus*, fr. *tessella* + *-atus* -ate] **:** TESSELLATED
tes·sel·lat·ed *also* **tes·se·lat·ed** \-,lād·əd\ *adj* [L *tessellatus* + E *-ed*] **1 :** of, relating to, or resembling mosaic ⟨a ~ pavement⟩ **2 :** having a checkered appearance **:** MOTTLED, RETICULATED
tessellated epithelium *n* **:** PAVEMENT EPITHELIUM
tessellated scale *n* **:** a soft flattened dark brown scale (*Eucalymnatus tessellatus*) marked with pale lines that infests a variety of tropical plants and that occurs commonly in greenhouses
tes·sel·la·tion \ˌtesəˈlāshən\ *n* -s [LL *tessellatus* (past part. of *tessellare* to pave with tiles) + E *-ion*] **1 :** an act or instance of tessellating **:** state of being tessellated ⟨~ of a counter top⟩ ⟨~ of a leaf blade⟩ **2 :** a careful juxtaposition of elements into a coherent pattern **:** MOSAIC ⟨a ~ of important sentences from this book —D.A.Stauffer⟩
tes·sera \ˈtesərə\ *n, pl* **tesser·ae** \-ə,rē, -rī\ [L, perh. fr. Gk *tessares, tesseres, tettares* four; fr. its being four-cornered — more at FOUR] **1 a :** a small tablet or die (as of wood, bone, or ivory) used by the ancient Romans as a ticket, tally, voucher, or means of identification ⟨*tesserae* . . . served as tokens for the distribution of corn —R.L.Poole⟩ **b :** an identifying card or password ⟨showed him the ~ with photograph and identification —Ernest Hemingway⟩ **2 a :** a small piece (as of marble, glass, or tile) cut usu. with a square or rectangular face and used in mosaic work ⟨inlaid with shining *tesserae* of blue glass —Norman Douglas⟩ **b :** something that is likened to a piece of mosaic ⟨*tesserae* cemented together with brief comment and explanation —*Times Lit. Supp.*⟩ **3 :** a small rectangular plate of bone (as in the carapace of the armadillo)
tes·ser·act \ˈtesə,rakt\ *n* -s [Gk *tesseres* four + *aktis* ray — more at ACTIN-] **:** the four-dimensional analogue of a cube
tes·ser·al \-sərəl\ *also* **tes·su·lar** \-syələ(r)\ *adj* [*tesseral* fr. *tessera* + *-al*; *tessular* fr. (assumed) NL *tessula* (dim. of L *tessera*) + E *-ar*] **1 :** of, relating to, or resembling a tessera **:** TESSELLAR **2 :** having or constituting an isometric system **:** REGULAR ⟨a ~ crystal⟩
tes·ser·ate \-ərət, -,rāt *usu* -d·+V\ *also* **tes·ser·at·ed** \-,rād·əd\ *adj, archaic* **:** TESSELLATED
tes·si·tu·ra \ˌtesəˈtu̇rə\ *n* -s [It, lit., texture, fr. L *textura* — more at TEXTURE] **:** the general range of a melody or voice part; *specif* **:** the part of the register in which most of the tones of a melody or voice part lie ⟨wrote always with the colors and ~*s* of instruments and voices clear in his mind —*Times Lit. Supp.*⟩
¹test \ˈtest\ *n* -s [ME, vessel in which metals were assayed, cupel, fr. MF, fr. L *testum* earthen vessel; akin to L *testa* piece of burned clay, earthen pot, shell, Av *tashta* cup, L *texere* to construct, weave — more at TECHNICAL] **1 a** *chiefly Brit* **:** CUPEL **b** (1) **:** an act or process that reveals inherent qualities (as of character) **:** TRIAL ⟨needs to put his thinking to the ~ of research experience —*Jour. of Social Studies*⟩ ⟨a fiberless man disintegrating before ~ —Leslie Rees⟩ (2) **:** the procedure of submitting an empirical statement to observational or experimental conditions designed either to negate or confirm it (3) **:** the procedure of submitting an analytical statement to such either generally recognized or specifically stipulated

operations as will either prove or disprove it — compare PROOF (4) **:** something that serves as a basis for evaluation **:** CRITERION, TOUCHSTONE ⟨insisted that the correct ~ of any social system . . . was the type of man it tended to produce —H.D.Gideonse⟩ ⟨the best ~ of a travel book is a place the reader has also been —Gerald Sykes⟩ **c :** an ordeal or oath required as proof of conformity with a set of beliefs ⟨no religious ~ shall ever be required as a qualification to any office or public trust under the United States —*U.S.Constitution*⟩ **2 a :** a procedure or reaction used to identify or characterize a substance or constituent ⟨the iodine ~ for starch⟩ — compare ¹ASSAY 1d(1) **b :** the reagent used in such a test **c :** a positive result obtained in such a test **d :** a procedure for determining the performance characteristics (as of a product or machine) ⟨abrasion ~⟩ ⟨shakedown ~⟩ **e :** a diagnostic procedure for determining the nature of a condition or disease or for revealing a change in a function ⟨eye ~⟩ **f :** an instance or result of testing: as (1) **:** TEST MATCH (2) **:** an oil well drilled to test the possibilities of an undeveloped area (3) **:** AUDITION, SCREEN TEST (4) **:** minimum tensile strength as determined by test ⟨a fishing line of 20 pound ~⟩ **3 a :** a technique for measuring objectively an individual's personal characteristics, potentialities, or accomplishments esp. by comparing his behavior in response to standard stimuli or situations with the behavior of others against whom the particular technique is said to have been standardized — compare BATTERY 7a(1), INTELLIGENCE TEST, INVENTORY 5, ⁷SCALE 8 **b :** an examination to determine factual knowledge or mental proficiency esp. given to students during the course of a school term and covering a limited part of the year's work — compare ACHIEVEMENT TEST

²**test** \"\ *vb* -ED/-ING/-S *vt* **1 a** *chiefly Brit* **:** to subject (as gold or silver) to cupellation **:** ASSAY **b :** to put to the proof **:** TRY, VALIDATE ⟨a strategy of restraint would . . . ~ the patience and self-control of Americans —H.W.Baldwin⟩ ⟨the constant ~*ing* of hypotheses by empirical data —*Amer. Polit. Sci. Rev.*⟩ ⟨~ a court ruling by appeal to a higher court⟩ — often used with *out* ⟨~ out a formula⟩ **c :** to require a doctrinal oath of ⟨you shall not ~ or examine any prophet who speaks in the spirit —E.J.Goodspeed⟩ **2 a :** to examine or analyze (a substance) by the use of a reagent ⟨~ a solution with litmus paper⟩; *esp* **:** to examine for the presence of a substance ⟨~ a salt for calcium⟩ **b :** to determine the attributes or performance characteristics of ⟨enough samples must be ~*ed* to show how the product performs —*Mech. Engineering*⟩ **c :** to examine for disease or physical defect ⟨~ a tumor⟩ ⟨~ the reflexes⟩ **3 :** to explore the aptitudes, attitudes, knowledge, or skills of (as a student or a job applicant) by means of tests ⟨they have been trade ~*ed* by the adjutant, who . . . interviewed each —H.H.Arnold & I.C.Eaker⟩ ~ *vi* **1 a :** to undergo a test ⟨actors . . . best suited to the roles for which they ~*ed* —*Christian Herald*⟩ ⟨the great turboprop . . . was still ~*ing* —*Newsweek*⟩ **b :** to achieve a rating on the basis of tests ⟨the eyesight of different peoples may ~ the same —Ruth Benedict⟩ ⟨this same group when seniors . . . ~*ed* to a median of 70 —Angell Mathewson⟩ **2 :** to apply a test as a means of analysis or diagnosis — used with *for* ⟨use colored blocks to ~ for mechanical aptitude⟩ ⟨use the scratch technique in ~*ing* for allergies⟩ **syn** see PROVE

³**test** \"\ *adj* **1 :** of, relating to, or constituting a trial, proof, or criterion **2 a :** subjected to, used for, or revealed by testing ⟨~ group⟩ ⟨summaries of ~ data⟩ ⟨twelve medium-sized, geographically scattered ~ cities are trying to discover ways of coordinating and expanding adult education —F.M.Hechinger⟩ **b :** employed in determining attributes or performance characteristics (as of a product or machine) ⟨~ dive⟩ ⟨~ apparatus⟩ ⟨questions . . . carefully prepared and given a ~ run with a selected guinea-pig group —R.D.Haun & Leo Herbert⟩

⁴**test** \"\ *n* -S [ME, fr. L *testis* — more at TESTAMENT] **1** *obs* **:** EVIDENCE, WITNESS **2** *Scot* **:** WILL, TESTAMENT

⁵**test** \"\ *vb* -ED/-ING/-S [L *testari,* fr. *testis* witness] *vi, Scot* **:** to make a will ~ *vt* **1** *archaic* **:** to date and sign (as a writ) **:** ATTEST **2** *Scot* **:** to bear witness to **:** AUTHENTICATE

⁶**test** \"\ *n* -S [L *testa* shell — more at TEST (trial)] **:** the external shell or other hard or firm covering of many invertebrates (as foraminiferans, mollusks, many echinoderms, and crustaceans); *esp* **:** the thick outer covering of the body of a tunicate secreted by the mantle but containing cells which have emigrated into it, varying in consistency in different forms from leathery or cartilaginous to soft and gelatinous, and in compound ascidians usu. forming a solid mass in which the zooids are embedded

test *abbr* **1** testament; testamentary **2** testator

tes·ta \ˈtestə\ *n, pl* **tes·tae** \-eˌstē, -stī\ *also* **testa** [NL, fr. L, shell — more at TEST]: the hard external coating or integument of a seed — called also *episperm*

test·abil·i·ty \ˌtestəˈbiləd·ē, -ətē, -i\ *n* **:** susceptibility to testing

¹**test·able** \ˈtestəbəl\ *adj* [L *testabilis,* fr. *testari* to be a witness, make a will + *-abilis* -able] **1 :** qualified (as by being legally capable) to bear witness or make a will **2 :** disposable by will

²**testable** \"\ *adj* [²*test* + *-able*] **:** capable of being tested **:** CONFIRMABLE

tes·ta·cea \teˈstāsh(ē)ə\ *n pl, cap* [NL, fr. L, neut. pl. of *testaceus* covered with a shell] **:** an order of Rhizopoda containing forms (as of the genera *Arcella* and *Difflugia*) with an external test — **tes·ta·cean** \(ˈ)=ˈ=shən\ *adj or n*

tes·ta·ceous \(ˈ)=ˈ=shəs\ *adj* [L *testaceus* consisting of bricks, covered with a shell, fr. *testa* piece of burned clay, brick, shell + *-aceus* -aceous] **1** *obs* **:** of, relating to, or made of earthenware **2 a :** having a shell ⟨a ~ protozoan⟩ **b :** consisting of shell or calcareous material ⟨stone . . . of a pale reddish brick color, and a ~ composition —Mark Van Doren⟩ **3 :** of any of the several light colors of bricks, averaging the color pheasant

tes·ta·cy \ˈtestəsē, -si\ *n* -ES [¹*testate* + *-cy*] **:** the state or circumstance of being testate

tes·ta·ment \ˈtestəmənt\ *n* -S [ME, fr. LL & L; LL *testamentum* covenant, Scripture (trans. of Gk *diathēkē* covenant), fr. L, last will, fr. *testari* to be a witness, make a will (fr. *testis* witness) + *-mentum* -ment; L *testis* akin to Oscan *trstus* witnesses; both fr. a prehistoric Italic compound whose first and second constituents respectively are akin to L *tres* three and to L *stare* to stand; fr. the witness standing by as a third party in a litigation — more at THREE, STAND] **1 a :** the written record of a compact **:** COVENANT, SCRIPTURE ⟨ancient ikons and ~*s* —A.R.Williams⟩ **b** *usu cap* **:** either of two main divisions of the Bible (~s discuss the measure of unity between the *Testaments* —*British Book News*⟩ **2 a :** a tangible proof or tribute **:** EVIDENCE, WITNESS ⟨this capital teems with ~*s* to the tragic miscalculations . . . of U.S. policy —John Osborne⟩ ⟨a ~ to the skilled men who have penetrated the ocean of air —J.A.Michener⟩ **b :** an expression of conviction **:** AFFIRMATION, CREDO ⟨the ~ of a man in a high state of indignation —E.B. White⟩ ⟨works . . . published as a political ~ —S.E.Morison⟩ **3 :** an instrument in writing by which a person declares his intent as to the disposal of his estate and effects after his death **:** WILL

tes·ta·men·tal \ˌ==ˈment³l\ *adj* [LL *testamentalis,* fr. L *testamentum* will + *-alis* -al] **:** of or relating to a testament **:** TESTAMENTARY

tes·ta·men·ta·ry \ˌtestəˈmentərē, -n·trē, -ri\ *adj* [ME, fr. LL *testamentarius,* fr. L *testamentum* will + *-arius* -ary] **1 :** of or relating to a will or testament or the administration of a will ⟨letters ~⟩ ⟨~ witnesses⟩ **2 :** bequeathed by will **:** given by or expressed in a testament ⟨~ heirlooms⟩ **3 :** done or appointed by or founded on a testament or will ⟨a ~ donation⟩

testamentary capacity *n* **:** the mental competence necessary for making a will

testamentary guardian *n* **1** *Brit* **:** a person appointed by deed or will by a father to act as guardian of his minor child **:** a guardian by statute **2 :** a person named in a will to serve as guardian **:** STATUTORY GUARDIAN

testamentary succession *n* **:** succession determined in accordance with the provisions of a lawful will and the applicable rules of law

testamentary trust *n* **:** a trust created by the terms of a will — compare LIVING TRUST

testament dative *n, pl* **testaments dative** *Scots law* **:** confirmation by the sheriff of one's right upon giving security to execute a will when not designated executor in the will

tes·ta·men·tum \ˌtestəˈmentəm\ *n, pl* **testamen·ta** \-ntə\ [L] **:** TESTAMENT

tes·ta·mur \teˈstāmə(r)\ *n* -S [L, we are witnesses, 1st pers. pl. pres. indic. of *testari* to be a witness; fr. the opening phrase of the certificate] *Brit* **:** a certificate that an examination held esp. by a university has been passed

¹**tes·tate** \ˈteˌstā|t, -ˌstə|, *usu* |d.+V\ *adj* [ME, fr. L *testatus,* past part. of *testari* to be a witness, make a will] **1 :** having made and left a will ⟨a person dying ~⟩ — opposed to *intestate* **2 :** disposed of in a will ⟨~ property⟩

²**testate** \"\ *n* -S [L *testatus,* past part. of *testari*] **1** *obs* **:** WITNESS, TESTIMONY **2 :** a testate person **:** TESTATOR

³**testate** \"\ *adj* [⁶*test* or *testa* + *-ate,* adj. suffix] **:** having a firm external covering **:** covered with a test or testa

tes·ta·tion \teˈstāshən\ *n* -S [L *testation-, testatio,* fr. L *testatus* (past part.) + *-ion-, -io* -ion] **1** *obs* **:** AFFIRMATION, TESTAMENT **2 :** the act or power of disposing of property by testament or will

tes·ta·tor \ˈteˌstād·ə(r), -ātə-, =ˈ==\ *n* -S [ME *testatour,* fr. AF, fr. LL *testator,* fr. L *testatus* (past part. of *testari* to be a witness, make a will) + *-or* — more at TESTAMENT] **1 :** a person who leaves a will or testament in force at his death **2** *obs* **:** one that testifies **:** WITNESS

tes·ta·trix \teˈstāˌtriks, ˈ=ˌ==\ *n, pl* **testatri·ces** \teˈstāˌtrəˌsēz, ˌtestəˈtrī(ˌ)sēz\ [LL, fem. of *testator* — more at -TRIX] **:** a female testator

tes·ta·tum \teˈstād·əm, -ātəm\ *n, pl* **testa·ta** \-ād·ə, -ātə\ [NL, fr. neut. of L *testatus,* past part. of *testari*] **1 :** the portion of the ordinary purchase deed that contains the statement of the consideration, the words incorporating covenants for title, and the operative words **2 :** TESTATUM CAPIAS

testatum ca·pi·as \-ˈkāpēəs\ *or* **testatum capias ad satis·fa·ci·en·dum** \-ˌadˌsad·əˌsfāshēˈendəm\ *n* [NL, lit., take the writ (for satisfying)] **:** a supplementary writ sometimes issued by a court of one county to the sheriff of another when an ordinary capias has been returned without action

test–bed \ˈ=ˌ=\ *n* **:** a support often in or on a vehicle (as an airplane or submarine) for an engine while it is being tested

test board *n* **:** a paperboard for shipping containers that must test up to specific requirements (as for resistance to puncture)

test case *n* **1 :** a representative case whose outcome is likely to serve as a precedent for decisions in future or pending cases involving similar points of law **2 :** a proceeding usu. in the form of a suit for injunction brought by agreement or on an understanding of the parties to obtain a decision as to the constitutionality of a statute

¹**test check** *n* **:** an auditing procedure based on selective and systematic sampling

²**test check** *vt* **:** to verify by means of a test check

¹**testcross** \ˈ=ˌ=\ *n* [³*test* + *cross*] **:** a cross between a recessive homozygote and the corresponding dominant to determine whether the latter is heterozygous or homozygous

²**testcross** \"\ *vt* **:** to subject to a testcross

tes·te \ˈte(ˌ)stē\ *n* -S [L, abl. of *testis* witness — more at TESTAMENT] **1 :** the witnessing or concluding clause of a writ or other precept **2 :** WITNESS — often used to indicate that what immediately follows is named as authority for what precedes

¹**tested** *adj* [fr. past part. of ²*test*] **1 :** subjected to test **:** TRIED, PROVEN ⟨a ~ combat veteran⟩ ⟨time-*tested* principles⟩ **2 :** certified by examination; *esp* **:** pronounced free of disease as a result of testing ⟨tuberculin-*tested* cattle⟩

²**tes·ted** \ˈte(ˌ)stēd\ *adj* [*teste* + *-ed*] **:** having the teste duly attached — used of a legal precept (as a writ or deed)

test·ee \(ˈ)teˈstē\ *n* -S [¹*test* + *-ee*] **:** one who takes an examination

¹**tes·ter** \ˈtestə(r), ˈtēs-\ *n* -S [ME *testere* headpiece, tester, fr. MF *testiere* headpiece, head covering, fr. *teste* head (fr. LL *testa* skull, fr. L, shell) + *-iere* -er — more at TEST (trial)] **1 a :** the frame on which the canopy of a bed rests **b :** the canopy of a bed including the frame and its hangings **2 :** BALDACHIN; *esp* **:** a canopy suspended from the ceiling over an altar or pulpit

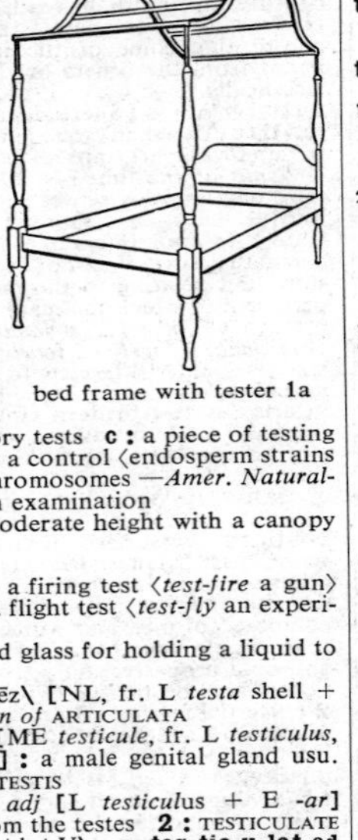

bed frame with tester 1a

²**tes·ter** \ˈtestə(r)\ *n* -S [modif. (influenced by *-er*) of MF *testart* teston, fr. *teston* + *-art* -ard — more at TESTON] **:** TESTON C

³**test·er** \ˈtestə(r)\ *n* -S [²*test* + *-er*] **:** one that tests: as **a :** ASSAYER **b :** one whose work is testing the quality and conformance to specifications of products by visual examination, by means of testing instruments, or through laboratory tests **c :** a piece of testing apparatus **d :** one that serves as a control ⟨endosperm strains crossed with . . . ~*s* for all 10 chromosomes —*Amer. Naturalist*⟩ **e :** one who administers an examination

tester bed *n* **:** a four-poster of moderate height with a canopy supported on a frame

testes *pl of* TESTIS

test–fire \ˈ=ˌ=\ *vt* **:** to subject to a firing test ⟨*test-fire* a gun⟩

test–fly \ˈ=ˌ=\ *vt* **:** to subject to a flight test ⟨*test-fly* an experimental plane⟩

test glass *n* **:** a small often footed glass for holding a liquid to be tested

tes·ti·car·di·nes \ˌtestəˈkärdᵊnˌēz\ [NL, fr. L *testa* shell + NL *cardines* — more at TEST] *syn of* ARTICULATA

tes·ti·cle \ˈtestəkəl, -tēk-\ *n* -S [ME *testicle,* fr. L *testiculus,* dim. of *testis* — more at TESTIS] **:** a male genital gland usu. with its enclosing membranes **:** TESTIS

tes·tic·u·lar \(ˈ)teˈstikyələ(r)\ *adj* [L *testiculus* + E *-ar*] **1 :** of, relating to, or derived from the testes **2 :** TESTICULATE

tes·tic·u·late \-lə|t, -ˌlā|, *usu* |d.+V\ *or* **tes·tic·u·lat·ed** \-ˌlād·əd, -ātəd\ *adj* [*testiculate* fr. NL *testiculatus,* fr. L *testiculus* testicle + *-atus* -ate; *testiculated* fr. NL *testiculatus* + E *-ed*] **1 :** resembling a testis **:** ovate and solid **2 :** having two tubers shaped like testes — used of an orchid

testier *comparative of* TESTY

testiest *superlative of* TESTY

tes·ti·fi·er \ˈtestəˌfī(ə)r, -īə\ *n* -S **:** one that testifies **:** WITNESS; *esp* **:** a religious proselyte

tes·ti·fy \-ˌfī\ *vb* -ED/-ING/-ES [ME *testifien,* fr. L *testificari,* fr. *testis* witness + *-ficare* -fy — more at TESTAMENT] *vi* **1 a :** to make a statement based on personal knowledge or belief **:** bear witness ⟨I can ~ as to the vital influences that reading had upon our thinking —C.R.Woodward⟩ ⟨of such enormous importance was the birth of a child in the imperial family that there must be many witnesses . . . to ~ to having seen the birth —P.I.Wellman⟩ ⟨the Quakers had long been ~*ing* against the abuses —H.S.Canby⟩ **b :** to serve as evidence **:** constitute a proof ⟨renaissance of the trade fair *testifies* to the rapid recovery of European economies —*Modern Industry*⟩ ⟨shattered gateways . . . ~ to the existence of a population at this remote spot —Norman Douglas⟩ ⟨two major works . . . ~ to his industry as well as to his high standards of scholarship —L.P.Kirwan⟩ **2 :** to express a personal conviction ⟨suffered the worst and emerged to ~ without rancor to the dignity of the spirit —Gordon Harrison⟩; *esp* **:** to affirm one's regeneration by the grace of God ⟨hear reformed sinners ~ —Green Peyton⟩ **3 :** to make a solemn declaration under oath for the purpose of establishing a fact (as in a court) **:** give testimony according to the law of legal procedure ⟨a neighbor *testified* against the accused man —B.L.K.Henderson⟩ ⟨called to ~ before a congressional fact-finding committee⟩ ~ *vt* **1 a :** to support the truth of (a statement) **:** bear witness to (a fact) **:** ATTEST ⟨everyone who has ever worked in the editorial sanctum will ~ that her story . . . has the true ring of experience —*Atlantic*⟩ ⟨the college demands a letter ~*ing* that the student is of good moral character —W.A.Lunden⟩ **b :** to serve as evidence of **:** PROVE ⟨thy breath shall ~ thou livest —Shak.⟩ ⟨that it is of no recent date is *testified* by the age of the tree whose roots penetrate it —*Amer. Guide Series: Minn.*⟩ **2** *archaic* **a :** to make known (a personal conviction) **:** AFFIRM, PROFESS ⟨~ their faith therein openly and aloud —P.E.F.W.Smythe⟩ **b :** to give evidence of **:** SHOW ⟨could not better ~ my respect for your sister —Charles Dickens⟩ **3 :** to declare under oath before a tribunal or officially constituted public body **syn** see SWEAR

tes·ti·ly \ˈtestəlē, -li\ *adv* **:** in a testy manner

¹**tes·ti·mo·nial** \ˌtestəˈmōnēəl, -nyəl\ *adj* [ME, fr. LL *testimonialis,* fr. L *testimonium* witness, evidence + *-alis* -al] **1 :** of, relating to, or constituting testimony ⟨a ~ letter from a satisfied customer⟩ **2 :** expressive of appreciation or esteem ⟨~ dinner⟩

²**testimonial** \"\ *n* -S [ME, fr. LL *testimonialis* of testimony] **1 :** something that serves as evidence **:** PROOF, TESTIMONY ⟨it is a remarkable ~ to the truth of these statistics that . . . the percentages should agree so closely —G.G.Coulton⟩ ⟨the layout . . . is a ~ to the designers' ingenuity in mastering a difficult site —*Amer. Guide Series: N.Y. City*⟩ **2 a :** a certified statement **:** AFFIDAVIT, WARRANT; *specif* **:** an endorsement of a product or service usu. solicited from a celebrity by the supplier for advertising purposes **b :** a character reference **:** letter of recommendation ⟨selected what seemed to me from the ~*s* to be the two best men —F.W.Crofts⟩ **c :** a public profession of the healing or uplifting effect of religious experience upon the life of an individual ⟨numerous ~*s* were offered during the revival meeting⟩ **3 :** an expression of appreciation **:** token of esteem **:** TRIBUTE ⟨a ~ planned in his honor —*Springfield (Mass.) Daily News*⟩ ⟨as a ~ to his war service, he was . . . made the recipient of a sword of superb workmanship —C.D.Rhodes⟩

tes·ti·mo·nial·ize \-əˌlīz\ *vt* -ED/-ING/-S **:** to honor with a testimonial

testimonial of the great seal : the quarter seal of Scotland

tes·ti·mo·ni·um \ˌtestəˈmōnēəm\ *n, pl* **testimoniums** \-ēəmz\ *or* **testimo·nia** \-ēə\ [L, witness, evidence] **1** *archaic* **:** TESTIMONIAL 2b **2 :** the final or authenticating clause of an instrument that typically begins "In witness whereof" and furnishes such information as when it was signed and before what witnesses

tes·ti·mo·ny \ˈtestəˌmōnē, -ni, *US also & Brit usu* -mən-\ *n* -ES [ME, fr. LL & L; LL *testimonium* Decalogue, tablets of the Decalogue (trans. of Heb *ʿēdūth,* lit., witness, testimony), fr. L, witness, evidence, fr. *testis* witness — more at TESTAMENT] **1 a :** the tablets inscribed with the Mosaic law or the ark containing them ⟨you shall put into the ark the ~ which I shall give you —Exod 25:16 (RSV)⟩ ⟨encamp around the tabernacle of the ~ —Num 1:53 (RSV)⟩ **b :** the word of God as contained in the Scriptures ⟨enriched the book with a number of *testimonies* from the Old Testament —*Interpreter's Bible*⟩ **2 a :** firsthand authentication of a fact **:** EVIDENCE, WITNESS ⟨that he was impressive in bearing was . . . the common ~ of all who met him —W.J.Ghent⟩ ⟨the ~ of the great geologist . . . confirmed the new thesis —R.W.Murray⟩ ⟨eruptions . . . bear vivid ~ to this upward concentration of gas in a magma column —Howel Williams⟩ **b :** something that serves as an outward sign **:** PROOF, SYMBOL ⟨how unpretentious clarity is . . . ~ to his discipline —Irwin Edman⟩ ⟨the new library, which he hopes will remain a ~ to his brief career as acting president —F.J.Hoffman⟩ **c :** a solemn declaration usu. made orally by a witness under oath in response to interrogation by a lawyer or authorized public official ⟨power to administer oaths and take ~ —*Harvard Law Rev.*⟩ ⟨~ before a grand jury is secret —Brian Gilbert⟩ **3 a :** an open acknowledgement **:** PROFESSION; *specif* **:** TESTIMONIAL 2c ⟨there is no ordained ministry; services consist of prayer, ~, and readings —F.S.Mead⟩ **b** *archaic* **:** an expression of disapproval **:** PROTEST ⟨uplifting her voice in many a ~ against it —Elizabeth C. Gaskell⟩ **4 :** a written attestation **:** CERTIFICATE

testimony meeting *n* **:** EXPERIENCE MEETING ⟨telling in a *testimony meeting* about her husband's conversion —*Sunday School Times*⟩

test indicator *n* **:** a sensitive gauge (as a dial gauge) combined with an adjustable mount for testing the accuracy of machined work

tes·ti·ness \ˈtestēnəs, -tin-\ *n* -ES **:** the quality or state of being testy

¹**testing** *n* -S [fr. gerund of ²*test*] **:** an act or process of subjecting to test **:** EXAMINATION, TRIAL ⟨the ~ of 50 million children . . . for tuberculosis —Paul Harris⟩ ⟨laboratories concerned . . . with commercial ~ —*Science*⟩

²**testing** *adj* [fr. pres. past. of ²*test*] **1 :** of, relating to, or used for demonstration or experiment ⟨~ procedure⟩ ⟨~ ground⟩ **2 :** requiring maximum effort or ability ⟨confronted with a most difficult and ~ problem —Ernest Bevin⟩ ⟨felt out of practice for severe rock climbing and wanted something less ~ —Tom Weir⟩ — **test·ing·ly** *adv*

testing clause *n, Scots law* **:** TESTIMONIUM 2

tes·tis \ˈtestəs\ *n, pl* **tes·tes** \-eˌstēz\ [L, witness, testis; perh. fr. its being evidence of maleness — more at TESTAMENT] **1 :** a male reproductive gland that usu. consists largely of convoluted tubules from the epithelium of which spermatozoa develop, that corresponds to the ovary of the female and in craniate vertebrates is usu. paired and developed from the genital ridges of the embryo, and that in most mammals descends into the scrotum before the attainment of sexual maturity and in many cases before birth **2 :** either of the inferior corpora quadrigemina

test lamp *n* **:** a portable lamp in socket with free leads to connect to various points of a faulty circuit to locate a defect (as a blown fuse)

test lead *n* **:** lead free from silver and often finely granulated for use in a metallurgical process (as cupellation)

test match *n* **1 :** any of a series of championship cricket matches played between teams representing Australia and England — compare ³ASH 6 **2 :** a championship game or series (as of cricket or rugby) played between teams representing different countries

test meal *n* **:** a meal of definite composition and quantity given to excite gastric secretion and so furnish material to withdraw for examination

tes·to \ˈte(ˌ)stō\ *n* -S [It, lit., text, fr. L *textus* — more at TEXT] **1 :** the libretto of a musical composition **2 :** a narrator or soloist in a musical performance

test oath *n* **:** an oath required of an applicant or candidate for public employment or political office to determine his fitness

tes·ton \ˈtestən, -ˌstän\ *or* **tes·toon** \(ˈ)teˈstün\ *n* -S [MF *teston,* fr. OIt *testone,* aug. of *testa* head, fr. LL, skull; fr. the fact that the obverse type on the testone was a head — more at TESTER] **:** any of several old European coins: as **a :** TESTONE 1 **b :** a French silver coin of the 16th century worth between 10 and 14½ sous **c :** a shilling of Henry VII of England decreasing in value to ninepence, then to sixpence in Shakespeare's time **d :** TOSTÃO

tes·to·ne \teˈstō(ˌ)nā\ *n* -S [OIt] **1 :** an Italian silver coin of the 15th and 16th centuries **2 :** TOSTÃO

tes·tos·ter·one \teˈstästəˌrōn\ *n* -S [*testis* + *-o-* + *sterol* + *-one*] **:** an androgenic hormone that is a crystalline hydroxy steroid ketone $C_{19}H_{28}O_2$, is obtained esp. from the testes of bulls or synthetically (as from cholesterol or diosgenin), and is used in medicine chiefly in the form of esters (as the propionate)

test paper *n* **1 :** paper (as litmus paper) cut usu. in strips and saturated with an indicator or other reagent that changes color in testing for various substances **2 :** a writing admitted as a standard for comparison of handwriting

test pattern *n* **:** a fixed picture broadcast by a television station to assist viewers in adjusting their receivers

test pilot *n* **:** a pilot who specializes in putting new or experimental airplanes through maneuvers designed to test them (as for strength or controllability) by producing strains in excess of normal

test pit *n* **:** a shallow shaft sunk in ore or overburden to determine the existence, grade, or extent of a mineral deposit

test record *n* **:** a phonograph record containing recordings of various tones of accurately controlled frequency and intensity and used for testing phonographs and pickups

tests *pl of* TEST, *pres 3d sing of* TEST

test solution *n* **:** a solution used in chemical testing

test tube *n* **:** a tube for simple tests that is usu. a plain tube of thin glass closed at one end but sometimes has a foot, bulb, graduated scale, or other modification

test-tube \(')=,=\ *adj* [*test tube*] **1 :** developed or produced in or as if in a test tube ⟨*test-tube* fabrics⟩ **2 :** produced by artificial insemination ⟨a *test-tube* calf⟩ ⟨testimony . . . that there were about 20,000 *test-tube* babies in the United States —Morris Ploscowe⟩
test type *n* **:** any of the printed letters or characters on an eye chart ⟨a typeface carefully chosen for use as *test type*⟩

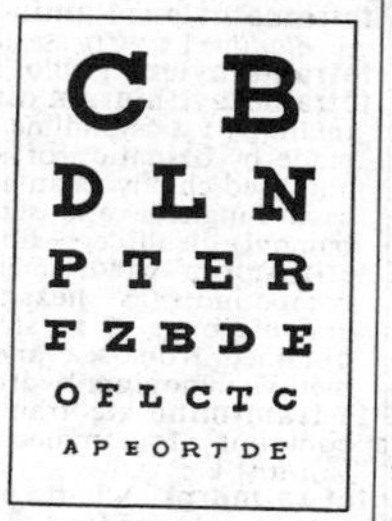

test type

tes·tu·di·nal \(')te¦st(y)üdᵊnəl\ *or* **tes·tu·di·nar·i·ous** \(¦)te-¦st(y)üdᵊn¦a(a)rēəs\ *adj* [*testudinal* fr. L *testudin-, testudo* tortoise + E *-al; testudinarious* fr. L *testudin-, testudo* + E *-arious* (as in *arbitrarious*)] **:** of, relating to, or resembling a tortoise or tortoise shell
tes·tu·di·nar·ia \(,)=,==ˈa(a)rēə\ *n, cap* [NL, fr. L *testudin-, testudo* tortoise + NL *-aria;* fr. the surface of the rootstock often becoming cracked into pieces resembling tortoise shells] *in some classifications* **:** a small genus of southern African desert vines that is characterized by huge edible rootstocks growing partly above ground and by seeds winged only at the apex and that is usu. included in the genus *Dioscorea*
tes·tu·di·na·ta \(,)=,==ˈäd·ə, -ˈād·ə\ *n pl, cap* [NL, fr. *Testudin-, Testudo* + *-ata*] **:** an order or other division of Reptilia comprising the turtles and tortoises and being distinguished by a trunk more or less enclosed in a shell of bony dermal plates that is usu. covered externally with horny shields and in nearly all cases firmly united with some of the vertebrae, ribs, and sternum, and by jaws that are toothless and sheathed
¹tes·tu·di·nate \(')=¦=ˈ=ət, -,āt\ *adj* [NL *Testudinata*] **:** of or relating to the Testudinata
²testudinate \"\ *n* -s **:** a reptile of the order Testudinata
tes·tu·di·nes \teˈst(y)üdᵊn,ēz\ [NL, pl. of *Testudin-, Testudo*] *syn of* TESTUDINATA
tes·tu·din·i·dae \,test(y)üˈdinə,dē\ *n pl, cap* [NL, fr. *Testudin-, Testudo,* type genus + *-idae*] **:** a family of turtles comprising carnivorous freshwater and herbivorous terrestrial forms that usu. have a strong thick convex carapace, broad plastron, and club-shaped feet in which the toes are firmly bound together so that the claws alone are evident — compare EUROPEAN TORTOISE, PAINTED TURTLE
tes·tu·do \teˈstü(,)dō\ *n* [NL, fr. L, tortoise, tortoise shell, vault; akin to L *testa* shell — more at TEST (trial)] **1** *cap* **:** a genus (the type of the family Testudinidae) of turtles comprising the typical land tortoises but formerly including all turtles — compare GIANT TORTOISE **2** -s **:** a protective screen (as a cover of overlapping shields held overhead or a shed wheeled up to a wall) used by an attacking force in ancient Rome **3** -s **:** an ancient Greek lyre believed to have been made of a tortoise shell **4** -s **:** an arched ceiling or vault esp. when surbased
tes·ty \ˈtestē, -ti\ *adj* -ER/-EST [ME *testif,* fr. AF, heady, headstrong, fr. OF *teste* head (fr. LL *testa* skull) + *-if* -ive — more at TESTER] **1 :** having a quick temper **:** easily annoyed **:** IRRITABLE, WASPISH ⟨a ~ man, given to incalculable fits of temper —Adrienne Koch⟩ ⟨became ~ when a long-winded doctor of divinity overprayed the time allotted to him on a commencement program —A.W.Long⟩ **2 :** marked by or indicative of impatience or ill humor **:** CAUSTIC, EXASPERATED ⟨a somewhat ~ emphasis on contemporary barbarians —H. A.Finch⟩ ⟨made ~ noises with her tongue —Nigel Dennis⟩ **syn** see IRASCIBLE
te·su·que \təˈsükē\ *n, pl* **tesuque** *or* **tesuques** *usu cap* **1 :** a Tanoan people occupying a pueblo in New Mexico **2 :** a member of the Tesuque people
tet *var of* TETH
tetan- *or* **tetano-** *comb form* [NL, fr. Gk, fr. *tetanos* — more at TETANUS] **:** tetanus ⟨*tetanogenic*⟩ ⟨*tetaniform*⟩
tet·a·nal \ˈtetᵊnəl *sometimes* -tnəl\ *adj* [*tetan-* + *-al*] **:** relating to or derived from tetanus ⟨~ antitoxin⟩
te·tan·ic \teˈtanik\ *adj* [NL *tetanicus,* fr. Gk *tetanikos* suffering from tetanus, fr. *tetanos* tetanus + *-ikos* -ic] **1 :** of or relating to tetanus or tetany ⟨a ~ condition⟩ **:** constituting tetanus or tetany ⟨~ contraction⟩ **2 :** producing or tending to produce tetanus or tetany ⟨~ toxin⟩ — **te·tan·i·cal·ly** \-nək(ə)lē\ *adv*
te·tan·i·form \-nə,fȯrm\ *adj* [ISV *tetan-* + *-iform;* orig. formed as F *tétaniforme*] **:** resembling tetanus or tetany
tet·a·ni·za·tion \,tetᵊnəˈzāshən, -ᵊn,īˈz-\ *n* -s [ISV *tetanize* + *-ation*] **:** the induction of muscular tetanus; *also* **:** tetanized condition of muscle
tet·a·nize \ˈtetᵊn,īz\ *vt* -ED/-ING/-S [ISV *tetan-* + *-ize*] **:** to induce tetanus in ⟨~ a muscle⟩
tet·a·no·gen·ic \¦tetᵊnə¦jenik\ *adj* [*tetan-* + *-genic*] **:** producing tetanus
tet·a·noid \ˈtetᵊn,ȯid\ *adj* [ISV *tetan-* + *-oid*] **:** resembling tetanus or tetany ⟨~ spasms⟩
tet·a·no·lysin \¦tetᵊnō+\ *n* [ISV *tetan-* + *lysin*] **:** a hemolytic toxin produced by the tetanus bacillus
tet·a·no·spas·min \,===ˈspazmən\ *n* -s [ISV *tetan-* + *spasm* + *-in*] **:** TETANUS TOXIN
tet·a·nus \ˈtetᵊnəs *sometimes* -tnəs\ *n* -ES [ME, fr. L, fr. Gk *tetanos,* fr. *tetanos* rigid, stretched, fr. *teinein* to stretch — more at THIN] **1 a :** an acute infectious disease characterized by tonic spasm of voluntary muscles and esp. of the muscles of the jaw and caused by the specific toxin produced by the tetanus bacillus which is usu. introduced through a wound — see LOCKJAW **b** *or* **tetanus bacillus :** the bacterium (*Clostridium tetani*) that causes tetanus **2 :** prolonged contraction of a muscle resulting from a series of motor impulses following one another too rapidly to permit intervening relaxation of the muscle — compare CONTRACTURE
tetanus toxin *or* **tetanal toxin** *n* **:** a crystalline unstable neurotoxin produced by the tetanus bacillus and held to be the cause of the tetanic convulsions of tetanus — called also *tetanospasmin*
tet·a·ny \ˈtet(ᵊ)nē, -ni\ *n* -ES [ISV *tetan-* + *-y;* prob. orig. formed as F *tétanie*] **:** a condition of physiologic mineral imbalance (as abnormal calcium metabolism) characterized by intermittent tonic spasm of the voluntary muscles and associated with deficiencies of parathyroid secretion or other disturbances
tetart- *or* **tetarto-** *comb form* [ISV, fr. Gk, fr. *tetartos;* akin to Gk *tettares, tessares* four — more at FOUR] **:** one fourth ⟨*tetartohedral*⟩
te·tar·te·mo·ri·on \tə,tärd·əˈmōrē,än, -ēən\ *also* **tar·te·mo·ri·on** \,tärd·əˈ-\ *n* -s [*tetartemorion* fr. Gk *tetartēmorion,* fr. *tetartē* one fourth (fr. fem. of *tetartos*) + *morion* part, portion, dim. of *moros* part (akin to Gk *meros* part); *tartemorion* fr. Gk *tartēmorion,* short for *tetartēmorion* — more at MERIT] **:** a small coin struck in Athens and several small city-states of the Greeks **:** a quarter obol
te·tar·to·cone \təˈtärd·ə,kōn\ *also* **tet·ar·cone** \ˈted·ə(r)-,kōn\ *n* [*tetartocone* fr. *tetart-* + *cone; tetarcone* contr. of *tetartocone*] **:** the posterior medial cusp of an upper molar tooth
te·tar·to·co·nid \tə,tärd·əˈkōnəd\ *also* **tet·ar·co·nid** \,ted·ə(r)ˈkōnəd\ *n* [*tetartocone, tetarcone* + *-id*] **:** the posterior medial cusp of a lower molar tooth
te·tar·to·he·dral \tə¦tärd·ō¦hēdrəl\ *adj* [*tetart-* + *-hedral*] **1** *of a crystal* **:** having one fourth the number of planes required by complete symmetry — compare HOLOHEDRAL **2 :** having the symmetry appropriate to a tetartohedral form — **te·tar·to·he·dral·ly** \-drəlē, -li\ *adv*
te·tar·to·he·drism \-ˈhē,drizəm\ *n* -s [*tetartohedral* + *-ism*] **:** the quality of crystallizing tetartohedrally
te·tar·to·he·dron \-drən\ *n, pl* **tetartohe·drons** \-drənz\ *or* **tetartohe·dra** \-drə\ [NL, fr. *tetart-* + *-hedron*] **:** a tetartohedral form
te·tar·toid \təˈtär,tȯid\ *n* -s [*tetart-* + *-oid*] **:** a 12-faced solid belonging to the tetartohedral group of the isometric system and having faces corresponding to one fourth of those of the hexoctahedron
te·tar·toi·dal \,te,tärˈtȯidᵊl, tə¦tä-\ *adj, of a crystal* **:** having symmetry that produces a tetartoid **:** having three inverse tetrad axes and four triad axes of symmetry
tetched *var of* TECHED
tetch·i·ly \ˈtechəlē, -li\ *adv* **:** in a tetchy manner
tetch·i·ness *also* **tech·i·ness** \-chēnəs, -chin-\ *n* -ES **:** the quality or state of being tetchy
tetchy *or* **techy** \ˈtechē, -chi\ *adj* -ER/-EST [perh. fr. obs. E *tetch* habit, quality, bad habit (fr. ME *tecche, tache,* fr. MF *teche, tache* stain, spot, fr. OF) + E *-y* (adj. suffix) — more at TACHE] **:** irritably or peevishly sensitive **:** TOUCHY ⟨the ~ manner of two women living in the same house —Elizabeth Taylor⟩ ⟨a ~ traveler at best —*New Yorker*⟩ ⟨a ~ situation⟩ ⟨a ~ question⟩ **syn** see IRASCIBLE
tête \ˈtāt\ *n* -s [F, head, fr. MF *teste* — more at TESTER (canopy)] **:** a high elaborately ornamented style of woman's hairdress or wig worn esp. in the latter half of the 18th century
¹tête-à-tête \¦tād·ə¦tāt, ¦tātə- (+V *usu* -ə¦tād·), ÷-ə¦tā *sometimes* ¦tēd·ə¦tēt, ¦tetə- (+V *usu* -ə¦tēd·)\ *n, pl* **tête-à-têtes** \-āts,-āz,-ēts\ *also* **têtes-à-têtes** \"\ [F, lit., head to head] **1 :** a private conversation or familiar interview between two persons without the presence of a third person **2 :** a short sofa or other piece of furniture intended to seat two persons esp. so that they face each other **:** CONVERSATION CHAIR 2
²tête-à-tête \"\ *adv* [F] **:** FACE-TO-FACE, PRIVATELY, FAMILIARLY
³tête-à-tête \"\ *adj* **:** being face-to-face ⟨find yourself *tête-à-tête* with one member of the assembly —Agnes M. Miall⟩ **:** PRIVATE ⟨a *tête-à-tête* home dinner —*New Yorker*⟩
tête-bêche \(')tet¦bash\ *adj* [F, n., pair of inverted stamps, fr. *tête* head + *bêche,* short for obs. F *bechevet* double bedhead, fr. F *bes-* (fr. L *bis*) + *chevet* bedhead, chevet — more at CHEVET] **:** of or relating to a pair of stamps inverted in relation to one another either as the result of an error in printing or intentionally so printed ⟨a set of bicolor *tête-bêche* triangular stamps —A.H.Murphey⟩
teth *also* **tet** \ˈtāt, -āth, -ās, -et, -eth, -es\ *n* -s [Heb *ṭēth*] **1 :** the 9th letter of the Hebrew alphabet — symbol ט; see ALPHABET table **2 :** the letter of the Phoenician or of any of various other Semitic alphabets corresponding to Hebrew teth
¹teth·er \ˈte*th*ə(r)\ *n* -s [ME *tethir, tedir,* prob. of Scand origin; akin to ON *tjōthr* tether, Sw *tjuder;* akin to MD *tuder* tether, OHG *zeotar* pole of a wagon and perh. to OHG *zogōn* to pull — more at TOW] **1 :** something (as a rope or chain) by which an animal is fastened so that it can range or feed only within the radius allowed **2 :** something (as a rope or cable) used in a way suggesting a tether **3 :** the limit of one's strength or resources **:** SCOPE ⟨poverty-stricken farmer is at his last ~ —Leslie Rees⟩ — used esp. in the phrase *the end of one's tether*
²tether \"\ *vt* **tethered; tethered; tethering** \-*th*(ə)riŋ\ **tethers** [ME *tediren,* fr. *tethir, tedir* tether] **1 a :** to fasten or restrain (an animal) with a rope or chain ⟨~ a cow to graze⟩ ⟨grove was full of ~*ed* teams —William Faulkner⟩ **b :** to fasten so as to allow a short radius of movement ⟨~ a boat⟩ ⟨toddlers, ~*ed* for safety —*Nat'l Geographic*⟩ ⟨balloon was ~*ed* by a string to the doorknob —Joseph Mitchell⟩ ⟨threads should be firmly ~*ed* at one end —Peggy Tearle⟩ **2 :** to limit the effectiveness or activity of **:** BIND ⟨~ one's plans to one's resources⟩
tetherball \ˈ==,=\ *n* **:** a game which is played by two contestants with rackets and a ball suspended by a string from an upright pole and in which the object of each contestant is to wrap the string around the pole by striking the ball in a direction opposite to the other
tether-devil \ˈ==¦==\ *n* **:** a bittersweet (*Solanum dulcamara*)
¹teth·y·id \ˈtethēəd\ *adj* [NL *Tethyidae*] **:** of or relating to the Tethyidae
²tethyid \"\ *n* -s **:** an ascidian or a mollusk of the family Tethyidae
te·thy·i·dae \təˈthīə,dē\ *n pl, cap* [NL; in sense 1, fr. *Tethyum,* type genus + *-idae;* in sense 2, fr. *Tethys,* type genus + *-idae*] **1 :** a family of simple ascidians with tough leathery often brightly colored tests, large branchial sacs, and several lateral longitudinal folds — see TETHYUM **2 :** a family of mollusks (suborder Tectibranchia) including the sea hares — see TETHYS
te·thys \ˈtēthəs\ *n, cap* [NL, fr. L *Tethys,* wife of Oceanus and mother of sea nymphs and deities, fr. Gk *Tēthys*] **:** a genus (the type of the family Tethyidae) of large often conspicuously colored sluglike marine mollusks having a pair of lateral swimming lobes on the foot and four tentacles, occurring chiefly in the warmer seas, and including forms that emit a purple fluid when disturbed — see SEA HARE
te·thy·um \ˈtethēəm\ *n, cap* [NL, fr. Gk *tēthyon* sea squirt, fr. *Tēthys,* wife of Oceanus] **:** a genus (the type of the family Tethyidae) of large muscular simple ascidians sometimes used for food
te·ti·o·thal·ein sodium \¦tetē¦ō¦thalēən-, -āl-, -,lēn-\ *n* [*tetiothalein* fr. *tetraiodophenolphthalein,* fr. *tetra-* + *-iod-* + *phenol* + *phthalein*] **:** the disodium salt of iodophthalein
te·ton \ˈtē,tän, -,tᵊn\ *n, pl* **teton** *or* **tetons** *usu cap* **1 a :** a western division of the Dakota peoples — see BRULÉ, MINICONJOU, OGLALA, SIHASAPA, TWO KETTLE **b :** a member of such division **2 :** a dialect of Dakota
tet·ra \ˈte·trə\ *n* -s [short for NL *Tetragonopterus,* genus of tetras in former classifications, fr. LL *tetragonum* square + NL *-pterus* — more at TETRAGONAL] **:** any of numerous small brightly colored So. American characin fishes often bred in the tropical aquarium — see NEON TETRA
tetra- *or* **tetr-** *comb form* [ME, fr. LL, fr. Gk; akin to Gk *tettares, tessares* four — more at FOUR] **1 :** four **:** having four **:** having four parts ⟨*tetra*carpellary⟩ ⟨*tetra*partite⟩ ⟨*tetr*atomic⟩ **2 :** containing four atoms, radicals, or groups (of a specified kind) ⟨*tetra*boric⟩ ⟨*tetr*acid⟩
tet·ra·acetate \¦te·trə+\ *n* [*tetra-* + *acetate*] **:** an acetate containing four acetate groups
tetraacid *var of* TETRACID
tet·ra·basic \¦te·trə+\ *adj* [ISV *tetra-* + *basic*] **1 :** having four hydrogen atoms capable of replacement by basic atoms or radicals — used of acids (as hypophosphoric acid) **2 :** containing four atoms of a univalent metal or their equivalent — used of salts **3 :** having four basic hydroxyl groups **:** able to react with four molecules of a monoacid — used of bases and basic salts — **tet·ra·basicity** \"+\ *n* -ES
tet·ra·borate \"+\ *n* [ISV *tetrabor-* (in *tetraboric acid*) + *-ate*] **:** a salt or ester of tetraboric acid
tet·ra·boric acid \"+-\ *n* [ISV *tetra-* + *boric*] **:** a dibasic acid $H_2B_4O_7$ containing four atoms of boron in the molecule, formed by heating ordinary boric acid, and known esp. in the form of salts (as borax)
tet·ra·brach \ˈte·trə,brak\ *n* -s [Gk *tetrabrachys,* fr. *tetra-* + *brachys* short — more at BRIEF] **:** a word or foot of four short syllables in classical prosody
¹tet·ra·branch \ˈte·trə,braŋk, -aiŋk\ *adj* [NL *Tetrabranchia*] **:** of or relating to the Tetrabranchia
²tetrabranch \"\ *n* -s **:** a tetrabranch mollusk or fossil **:** NAUTILOID
tet·ra·bran·chia \¦==ˈbraŋkēə, -aiŋ-\ *n pl, cap* [NL, fr. *tetra-* + *-branchia*] **:** a subclass or order of Cephalopoda including among existing forms only the genus *Nautilus,* differing from the remaining existing cephalopods in having four gills, four auricles to the heart, and a large chambered external shell, and including many extinct forms — see AMMONOIDEA, NAUTILOIDEA; compare DIBRANCHIA
tet·ra·branchiata \"+\ [NL, fr. *tetra-* + *branchiata*] *syn of* TETRABRANCHIA
tet·ra·branchiate \¦==+\ *adj or n* [NL *Tetrabranchiata*] **:** TETRABRANCH
tetrabrom- *or* **tetrabromo-** *comb form* [ISV *tetra-* + *brom-*] **:** containing four atoms of bromine — in names of chemical compounds ⟨*tetrabromo*ethylene⟩; compare BROM-
tet·ra·bromide \¦te·trə+\ *n* [*tetrabrom-* + *-ide*] **:** a bromide containing four atoms of bromine
tet·ra·bro·mo \¦te·trə¦brō(,)mō\ *adj* [*tetrabrom-*] **:** containing four atoms of bromine
tet·ra·bro·mo·ethane \¦==¦=(,)ō+\ *n* [ISV *tetrabrom-* + *ethane*] **:** either of two isomeric heavy liquid compounds $C_2H_2Br_4$; *esp* **:** the heavy yellowish liquid symmetrical isomer $CHBr_2CHBr_2$ used chiefly in separating minerals and as a solvent
tet·ra·bro·mo·phenolphthalein \"+\ *n* [*tetrabrom-* + *phenolphthalein*] **:** a dye $C_{20}H_{10}Br_4O_4$ used in the form of its disodium salt in X-ray examination esp. of the gall bladder
tet·ra·caine \ˈte·trə,kān\ *n* -s [*tetra-* + *procaine*] **:** a crystalline basic ester $C_{15}H_{24}N_2O_2$ closely related chemically to procaine and used chiefly in the form of its hydrochloride as a local anesthetic
tet·ra·carbonyl \¦te·trə+\ *n* [*tetra-* + *carbonyl*] **:** a compound containing four carbonyl groups combined with a metal
tet·ra·carboxylic \"+\ *adj* [*tetra-* + *carboxylic*] **:** containing four carboxyl groups in the molecule
tet·ra·cene \ˈte·trə,sēn\ *n* -s [alter. of *tetrazene*] **:** a yellow solid compound $(H_3N_2C)NHNHN{=}N(CN_2H_2)NHNO$ made by reaction of amino-guanidine and nitrous acid and used as an explosive in priming compositions for cartridges and in combination with lead azide to reduce the flash point of the latter — called also *tetrazene*
te·trac·er·us \təˈtrasərəs\ *n, cap* [NL, fr. *tetra-* + *-cerus*] **:** a genus of Asiatic ruminant mammals consisting of the four-horned antelope of India
tetrachlor- *or* **tetrachloro-** *comb form* [ISV *tetra-* + *chlor-*] **:** containing four atoms of chlorine — in names of chemical compounds; compare CHLOR- ⟨*tetrachloro*phthalic anhydride⟩
tet·ra·chloride \¦te·trə+\ *n* [*tetrachlor-* + *-ide*] **:** a chloride (as carbon tetrachloride) containing four atoms of chlorine
tet·ra·chlo·ro \¦te·trə¦klōr(,)ō, -ȯ(,)ō\ *adj* [*tetrachlor-*] **:** containing four atoms of chlorine
tet·ra·chlo·ro·ethane \"+\ *also* **tet·ra·chlor·ethane** \¦==-klōr+\ *n* [ISV *tetrachlor-* + *ethane*] **:** either of two isomeric heavy liquid compounds $C_2H_2Cl_4$; *esp* **:** the symmetrical isomer $CHCl_2CHCl_2$ that forms toxic vapors with an odor similar to that of chloroform, that is made from acetylene and chlorine, and that is used chiefly as a nonflammable solvent of medium volatility and in making trichloroethylene and tetrachloroethylene
tet·ra·chlo·ro·ethylene \¦te·trə¦klōr(,)ō, -ȯ(,)rō+\ *n* [ISV *tetrachlor-* + *ethylene*] **:** a heavy mobile nonflammable liquid compound $CCl_2{=}CCl_2$ made in various ways (as by treating penta-chloro-ethane with lime or by heating carbon tetrachloride) and used chiefly in dry cleaning and dry-cleaning soaps, in degreasing metals, as a solvent for rubber, tar, and other organic materials, and as an anthelmintic — called also *perchloroethylene*
tet·ra·chlo·ro·methane \"+\ *n* [ISV *tetrachlor-* + *methane*] **:** CARBON TETRACHLORIDE
tet·ra·chord \ˈte·trə,kȯrd, -ō(ə)d\ *n* [Gk *tetrachordon* unit of four tones, fr. neut. of *tetrachordos* four-stringed, fr. *tetra-* + *-chordos* stringed (fr. *chordē* string) — more at YARN] **1 :** a musical instrument with four strings **2 :** the basic unit of analysis in ancient Greek music consisting of a diatonic or disjunct series of four notes or tones with an interval of a perfect fourth between the first and last and distinguished by the relative position of the half step or steps or quarter tone or tones in the series **3 :** the musical interval of a perfect fourth
tet·ra·cho·ric \¦te·trə¦kȯrik\ *adj* [*tetra-* + *chori-* + *-ic;* fr. the correlation involving a fourfold table] **:** of, relating to, or being a method of statistical correlation between variables that do not admit of exact measurement
tet·ra·chot·o·mous \¦==ˈkäd·əməs\ *adj* [Gk *tetracha* in four parts (fr. *tetra-* + *-cha,* as in *dicha* in two) + E *-tomous* (as in *dichotomous*) — more at DICH-] **:** regularly dividing by fours **:** having a quadruple arrangement ⟨~ peduncles⟩
tet·ra·chromatic \"+\ *adj* [*tetra-* + *chromatic*] **1 :** having four colors **2 :** dependent upon or sensitive to four primary colors
te·trach·ro·nous \təˈtrakrənəs\ *adj* [Gk *tetrachronos,* fr. *tetra-* + *-chronos* -chronous] **:** TETRASEMIC
¹te·trac·id \təˈtrasəd\ *also* **tet·ra·acid** \¦te·trə+\ *adj* [*tetra-* + *acid* (adj.)] **1 :** able to react with four molecules of a monobasic acid or two of a dibasic acid to form a salt or ester — used esp. of bases **2** [*²tetracid*] **:** containing four hydrogen atoms replaceable by basic atoms or radicals — used esp. of acid salts
²tetracid \"\ *also* **tetraacid** \"\ *n* [*tetra-* + *acid* (n.)] **:** an acid having four acid hydrogen atoms
¹tet·ra·coc·cus \,te·trəˈkäkəs\ *n* [NL, fr. *tetra-* + *-coccus*] **:** a micrococcus occurring in square groups of four
²tetracoccus \"\ [NL] *syn of* GAFFKYA
³tetracoccus \"\ [NL] *syn of* MICROCOCCUS
tet·ra·co·lon \,te·trəˈkōlən, -,län\ *n* [L, fr. Gk *tetrakōlon,* neut. of *tetrakōlos* of four members, of four limbs, fr. *tetra-* + *-kōlos* limbed (fr. *kōlon* limb) — more at CALK] **:** a period of four cola in classical prosody
tet·ra·cor·al \,==ˈkȯrəl, -kär-\ *n* [NL *Tetracoralla*] **:** one of the Tetracoralla
tet·ra·co·ral·la \,==kəˈralə\ *n pl, cap* [NL, fr. *tetra-* + L *coralla*] *in some classifications* **:** a subclass or other group of Paleozoic corals in which the septa when present are usu. in multiples of four and of which many are solitary and cornucopia-shaped and sometimes attain large size
tet·ra·coralline \¦==+\ *adj* [NL *Tetracoralla* + E *-ine*] **:** of or relating to the Tetracoralla
tet·ra·co·sane \ˈte·trəkə,sān\ *n* -s [*tetra-* + *eicosane*] **:** a solid paraffin hydrocarbon $C_{24}H_{50}$; *esp* **:** the normal hydrocarbon $CH_3(CH_2)_{22}CH_3$ obtained from coal tar
tet·ra·co·sa·no·ic acid \¦==¦kōsə¦nōik-\ *n* [*tetracosanoic* fr. *tetracosane* + *-oic*] **:** LIGNOCERIC ACID
tet·ra·covalent \¦==+\ *adj* [*tetra-* + *covalent*] **:** sharing four covalent bonds with other atoms or characterized by such sharing ⟨~ nitrogen⟩
¹tet·ract \ˈte,trakt\ *adj* [*tetra-* + *-act*] *of a sponge spicule* **:** having four rays
²tetract \"\ *n* -s **:** a 4-rayed sponge spicule
te·trac·tine \təˈtrak,tīn, -,tən\ *n* -s [*tetra* + *-actine*] **:** TETRACT
¹te·trac·ti·nel·lid \tə¦traktə¦neləd\ *also* **te·trac·ti·nel·li·dan** \-lədən\ *adj* [*tetractinellid* fr. NL *Tetractinellida; tetractinellidan* fr. NL *Tetractinellida* + E *-an*] **:** of or relating to the Tetractinellida
²tetractinellid \"\ *n* -s **:** a sponge of the subclass Tetractinellida
te·trac·ti·nel·li·da \=,==ˈnelədə\ *n pl, cap* [NL, fr. *Tetractina,* a division of sponges in some classifications (fr. *tetra-* + *-actina* -actine) + *-ella* + *-ida*] *in some classifications* **:** a subclass or other division of Demospongiae comprising sponges with siliceous 4-rayed spicules or sometimes with desmas or without spicules
te·trac·ti·nel·line \=¦=¦ne,līn, -,lən\ *adj* [NL *Tetractinellida* + E *-ine*] **:** TETRACTINELLID
tet·ra·cyanoauric acid \¦te·trə+-\ *n* [*tetra-* + *cyanoauric*] **:** CYANOAURIC ACID
tet·ra·cyclic \¦==+\ *adj* [ISV *tetra-* + *cyclic*] **1** *of a flower* **:** having four whorls of floral organs **2 :** containing four usu. fused rings in the molecular structure
tet·ra·cy·cline \,te·trəˈsī,klīn, -,klən\ *n* -s [ISV *tetracyclic* + *-ine*] **1 :** a yellow crystalline broad-spectrum antibiotic $C_{22}H_{24}N_2O_8$ derived from an octa-hydro-naphthacene, produced by a soil actinomycete (*Streptomyces viridifaciens*), or prepared from chlortetracycline by catalytic reduction, and administered usu. in the form of its hydrochloride **2 :** any of various derivatives of tetracycline (as chlortetracycline or oxytetracycline)
¹tet·rad \ˈte,trad\ *n* -s [Gk *tetrad-, tetras* group of four, four; akin to Gk *tettares, tessares* four — more at FOUR] **1 :** a group or arrangement of four **:** something composed of four parts **:** QUATERNION: as **a :** a tetravalent element, atom, or radical **b :** a group of four cells arranged usu. in the form of a tetrahedron and produced by the successive divisions of a mother cell — compare SPORE MOTHER CELL **c :** an arrangement of chromosomes by fours in the first meiotic prophase due to precocious longitudinal splitting of paired homologous chromosomes **2 :** TETRALOGY 3
²tetrad \"\ *adj* **:** FOURFOLD — used esp. of an axis of symmetry ⟨a ~ axis requires that every aspect of the crystal be repeated at 90 degree intervals during rotation about the axis⟩
tet·ra·dactyl \¦te·trə+\ *adj* [Gk *tetradaktylos*] **:** TETRADACTYLOUS — **tet·ra·dac·tyl·i·ty** \,==,dakˈtiləd·ē\ *n* -ES — **tet·ra·dactyly** \¦==+\ *n* -ES
²tetradactyl \"\ *n* -s **:** a tetradactylous animal
tet·ra·dac·ty·lous \¦==¦daktələs\ *adj* [Gk *tetradaktylos,* fr. *tetra-* + *daktylos* finger, toe] **:** having four digits ⟨a ~ animal⟩

tet·ra·decane \"+\ n [ISV tetra- + decane] : a paraffin hydrocarbon $C_{14}H_{30}$; esp : the normal liquid hydrocarbon $CH_3(CH_2)_{12}CH_3$ that is a liquid of high boiling point and freezes at 5°C

tet·ra·de·canoic acid \"+-\ n [tetradecane + -oic] : MYRISTIC ACID

tet·ra·de·cap·o·da \ˌ�⸱dəˈkapədə\ [NL, fr. tetra- + deca- + -poda] syn of ARTHROSTRACA

tet·ra·decyl \"+\ n [ISV tetra- + decyl] : an alkyl radical $C_{14}H_{29}$ derived from a tetradecane; esp : the normal radical $CH_3(CH_2)_{12}CH_2-$

tetradecyl alcohol n : a higher aliphatic alcohol $C_{14}H_{29}OH$; esp : the normal waxy alcohol $CH_3(CH_2)_{12}CH_2OH$ obtained from spermaceti or made by hydrogenation of myristic acid or one of its esters

tet·ra·dic \təˈtradik\ adj [Gk tetradikos, fr. tetrad-, tetras tetrad, four + -ikos -ic] : of or relating to a tetrad : taking the form of a tetrad

tet·rad·ite \ˈtetrəˌdīt\ n -s usu cap [NL Tetradites, fr. LGk Tetradītēs, a heretic, fr. Gk tetrad-, tetras tetrad, four + -itēs -ite] : one holding that there are four persons in God ⟨the epithet of Tetradite has historically been applied to Nestorians and Origenists among others⟩

tet·ra·drachm \ˈtetrəˌdram, -aa(ə)m\ also **tet·ra·drach·ma** \ˌtetrəˈdrakmə\ n [tetradrachm fr. Gk tetradrachmon, fr. tetra- + drachmē drachma; tetradrachma alter. (influenced by L drachma) of L tetradrachmum, fr. Gk tetradrachmon — more at DRACHMA, DRAM] : an ancient Greek silver coin worth four drachmas — **tet·ra·drach·mal** \ˈdrakməl\ adj

tet·ra·drach·mon \ˈdrakˌmän\ n, pl **tetradrach·ma** \-kmə\ [Gk] : TETRADRACHM

tet·ra·dym·ia \ˌtetrəˈdimēə\ n, cap [NL, fr. tetra- + -dymia] : a genus of low rigid tomentose shrubs (family Compositae) having alternate entire leaves, head with concave overlapping bracts, and terete achenes

te·trad·y·mite \təˈtradəˌmīt\ n -s [LGk tetradymos fourfold, fr. Gk tetra- + didymos twin; fr. its occurrence in compound twin crystals — more at -DYMUS] : a mineral Bi_2Te_3 consisting of a telluride and sulfide of bismuth, sometimes containing selenium, being pale steel gray in color and of a metallic luster, and occurring usu. in foliated masses (hardness 1.5–2, sp. gr. 7.2–7.6)

tet·ra·dy·nam·ia \ˌtetrəˌdīˈnamēə, -də⸱-, -nām-\ n, pl cap [NL, fr. tetra- + Gk dynamis power + NL -ia — more at DYNAMIC] in former classifications : a class of higher plants comprising all plants having tetradynamous stamens

tet·ra·dy·nam·i·an \ˈdīˌnamēən\ adj [NL Tetradynamia + E -an] : of or relating to the Tetradynamia

tet·ra·dy·nam·i·ous \-mēəs\ adj [NL Tetradynamia + E -ous] : TETRADYNAMIAN

tet·ra·dy·na·mous \ˌtetrəˈdīnəməs, -din-\ adj [fr. tetradynam- (fr. tetra- + Gk dynamis power) + -ous] : having six stamens four of which are longer than the others ⟨the Cruciferae are ~⟩

tet·ra·eth·oxy·silane \ˈtetrəˌethˌäksēˈthăksēⁱ+\ n [tetra- + eth- + oxy- + silane] : ETHYL SILICATE

tet·ra·ethyl \ˈtetrə+\ adj [ISV tetra- + ethyl] : containing four ethyl groups in the molecule

tetraethylammonium \ˌtetrəˌ⸙\ n [tetraethyl + ammonium] : the quaternary ammonium ion $(C_2H_5)_4N^+$, containing four ethyl groups; also : a salt of this ion (as the deliquescent crystalline chloride used as a ganglionic blocking agent)

tetraethyl lead n : a heavy oily poisonous liquid compound $Pb(C_2H_5)_4$ that is insoluble in water but soluble in gasoline and other organic solvents, that is made usu. by the action of ethyl chloride on a sodium-lead alloy, and that is used as an antiknock agent — abbr. TEL

tetraethyl orthosilicate n : ETHYL SILICATE

tetraethyl pyrophosphate n : a mobile hygroscopic corrosive liquid ester $(C_2H_5)_4P_2O_7$ that is a powerful anticholinesterase agent and is used as an insecticide and parasympathomimetic agent — abbr. TEPP; compare HEXAETHYL TETRAPHOSPHATE

tetraethylthiuram disulfide n : a cream-colored crystalline compound $[(C_2H_5)_2NCS]_2S_2$ used in the treatment of alcoholism and in the vulcanization of rubber; bis-(diethyl-thiocarbamoyl) disulfide — called also disulfiram

tet·ra·fluoride \ˈtetrə+\ n [tetra- + fluoride] : a fluoride containing four atoms of fluorine

tet·ra·flu·or·o·ethylene \ˈtetrəˌflüərō⸱+\ n [tetra- + fluor- + ethylene] : a flammable gaseous fluorocarbon $CF_2=CF_2$ used in making polytetrafluoroethylene resins — abbr. TFE

tet·ra·fossate \"+\ adj [tetra- + fossate] of a tapeworm : having four bothridia

te·trag·e·nous \təˈtrajənəs\ adj [tetra- + -genous] : growing in square groups of four ⟨~ bacteria⟩

te·trag·o·nal \təˈtragən'l, -raig-\ adj [LL tetragonalis, fr. tetragonum square, quadrangle (fr. Gk tetragōnon, fr. neut. of tetragōnos tetragonal, fr. tetra- + -gōnos -cornered, -angled, fr. gōnia corner, angle) + L -alis -al — more at -GON] 1 : having four angles or sides ⟨the parallelogram, square, and rhombus are ~ figures⟩ — see SCALENOHEDRON illustration 2 : of, relating to, or characteristic of the tetragonal system — **te·trag·o·nal·ly** \-n'lē, -'li\ adv — **te·trag·o·nal·ness** n -ES

tetragonal system n : a crystal system (as in the right square prism) characterized by three axes at right angles of which only the two lateral axes are equal — compare RHOMBOHEDRAL SYSTEM; see CRYSTAL SYSTEM illustration

tetragonal tristetrahedron n : DELTOHEDRON

tet·ra·go·nia \ˌtetrəˈgōnēə\ n, cap [NL, fr. Gk tetragōnia four-angled fruit, fr. tetragōnos tetragonal + -ia -y] : a genus of spindle tree, fr. tetragōnos tetragonal + -ia -y] : a genus of fleshy herbs or undershrubs (family Aizoaceae) of wide distribution having yellow or reddish apetalous flowers and a winged or quadrangular nut or drupe — see NEW ZEALAND SPINACH

tet·ra·go·ni·a·ce·ae \ˌ⸙ˈˌgōnēˌāsēˌē\ n pl, cap [NL, fr. Tetragonia -aceae] syn of AIZOACEAE

tet·ra·gram \ˈtetrəˌgram, -raa⸱m\ n [MGk tetragrammon, fr. neut. of Gk tetragrammos having four letters, fr. Gk tetra- + -grammos (fr. gramma letter)] : a word of four letters — TETRAGRAMMATON

tet·ra·gram·ma·ton \ˌtetrəˈgraməˌtän, -ad-ən, -ət²n also -ə,tlin\ n, pl **tetragramma·ta** \-mətə, -ətə\ sometimes -ə,tä or -ə,tä\ often cap [ME Tetragramaton, fr. Gk tetragrammaton, fr. neut. of tetragrammatos having four letters, fr. tetra- + grammat-, gramma letter — more at GRAM] : the Hebrew word of the four letters יהוה constituting a divine proper name which the Jews out of reverence or for fear of desecration ceased to pronounce about four centuries B.C. and for which they substituted Adonai or Elohim and being variously transliterated without indication of the vocalization usu. by YHWH, YHVH, JHVH, JHWH, or IHVH and with vowels usu. by Jehovah, Yahweh, Jahveh, Jahweh, Yahveh, Jahve, Jahwe, Yahvè, or Yahwe — compare BLASPHEMY

tet·ra·graph \ˈtetrəˌgraf\ n [tetra- + -graph] : a cluster of four successive letters in cryptography — **tet·ra·graph·ic** \ˌ⸙ˈgrafik\ adj

tet·ra·gyn·ia \-ˈjinēə\ n pl, cap [NL, fr. tetra- + -gynia] in former classifications : a class of higher plants comprising those with four styles or pistils

tet·ra·gyn·i·an \-ˈjinēən\ adj [NL Tetragynia + E -an] : of or relating to the Tetragynia

tet·ra·gy·nous \ˈtetrəˌjinəs, -ˌgī-\ adj [tetra- + -gynous] : having four pistils or carpels

tet·ra·he·dral \ˌtetrəˈhēdrəl\ adj [tetrahedron + E -al] 1 : of or relating to a tetrahedron : having or made up of four sides 2 a : having the form of the regular tetrahedron b : relating to a tetrahedron or the system of hemihedral forms to which the tetrahedron belongs c : having the symmetry of a tetrahedron — **tet·ra·he·dral·ly** \-drəlē, -li\ adv

tetrahedral angle n : a polyhedral angle of four faces

tetrahedral coordination n : the state of being surrounded by four atoms whose centers are at the corners of a tetrahedron

tetrahedral hypothesis n : a hypothesis in geology: the earth's assumed original spherical form giving a minimum surface for a given volume tended as the earth shrank to develop into a tetrahedron giving a maximum surface for a given volume with the continents as the edges and the ocean basins as the sides

tetrahedral kite n : a kite shaped like a tetrahedron

tet·ra·he·drite \ˈtetrəˌhēˌdrīt\ n -s [G tetraëdrit, fr. LGk tetraedros having four faces + G -it -ite] : a fine-grained gray mineral $(Cu,Fe)_{12}Sb_4S_{13}$ that is isomorphous with tennantite, consists of a sulfide of copper, iron, and antimony and often also contains zinc, lead, mercury, or silver, occurs in characteristic tetrahedral crystals and also in massive form, and is often a valuable ore of silver and is also worked for copper (hardness 3–4, sp. gr. 4.4–5.1)

tet·ra·he·dron \ˌtetrəˈhēdrən sometimes \drän or chiefly Brit ˈhē\ n, pl **tetrahedrons** or **tetrahe·dra** \-drə\ [NL, fr. LGk tetraedron, neut. of tetraedros having four faces, fr. Gk tetra- + hedra seat, face — more at SIT] 1 : a polyhedron of four faces 2 : an object having the form of or suggesting a tetrahedron: as a : CALTROP 2a b : three logs or lengths of steel bolted or lashed together and used as an obstacle c : a large concrete block of tetrahedral shape used esp. in constructing or strengthening revetments — compare TETRAPOD 3 d : a large wind-indicating device used on airfields and consisting of a frame covered with airplane cloth and pivoted so that the pointed end indicates the wind direction

tet·ra·hex·a·he·dral \ˈtetrə+\ adj [NL tetrahexahedron + -al] : of, relating to, or being a tetrahexahedron

tet·ra·hexahedron \ˈtetrə+\ n [NL, fr. tetra- + hexahedron] : a form of the isometric system bounded by 24 congruent isosceles-triangular faces with four to each face of the cube

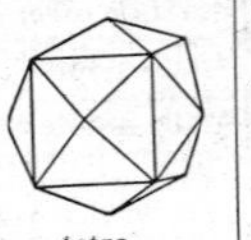

tetrahexahedron

tetrahydr- or **tetrahydro-** comb form [ISV tetra- + hydr-] : combined with four atoms of hydrogen — in names of chemical compounds ⟨tetrahydride⟩ ⟨tetrahydronaphthalene⟩

tet·ra·hydrate \ˌ⸙+\ n [tetra- + hydrate] : a chemical compound with four molecules of water — **tet·ra·hydrated** \"+\ adj

tet·ra·hy·dric \ˌ⸙ˈhīdrik\ adj [ISV tetra- + -hydric] : TETRAHYDROXY — used esp. of alcohols and phenols

tet·ra·hy·dride \ˌ⸙ˈhīˌdrīd, -drəd\ n [tetrahydr- + -ide] : a binary compound of an element or radical with four atoms of hydrogen

tet·ra·hy·dri·do·borate \ˌ⸙ˈhīdrədō⸱+\ n [tetrahydride + -o- + borate] : BOROHYDRIDE — used in the system of nomenclature adopted by the International Union of Pure and Applied Chemistry

tet·ra·hy·dro \ˈtetrəˈhīˌdrō\ adj [tetrahydr-] : combined with four atoms of hydrogen

tet·ra·hy·dro·benzene \ˌ⸙ˈ⸙+\ n [tetrahydr- + benzene] : CYCLOHEXENE

tet·ra·hy·dro·borate \"+\ n [tetrahydr- + borate] : BOROHYDRIDE

tet·ra·hy·dro·furan \"+\ n [ISV tetrahydr- + furan] : a flammable liquid heterocyclic ether C_4H_8O resembling ethyl ether that is made by hydrogenation of furan and is used as a solvent and as an intermediate in the manufacture of nylon

tet·ra·hy·dro·furfuryl alcohol \"+-\ n [tetrahydr- + furfuryl] : a high-boiling liquid $(C_4H_7O)_2CH_2OH$ made by catalytic hydrogenation of furfural and used as a solvent and in the preparation of esters

tet·ra·hy·dro·naphthalene \"+\ n [ISV tetrahydr- + naphthalene] : an oily liquid hydrocarbon $C_{10}H_{12}$ obtained by partial hydrogenation of naphthalene in the presence of a catalyst and used chiefly as a solvent (as for paints and lacquers) — called also 1,2,3,4-tetrahydronaphthalene

tet·ra·hy·droxy \ˌ⸙ˈhīˌdräksē\ adj [tetrahydroxy-] : containing four hydroxyl groups in the molecule

tetrahydroxy- comb form [ISV tetra- + hydroxy-] : containing four hydroxyl groups — in names of chemical compounds ⟨tetrahydroxyanthraquinone⟩

tetraiod- or **tetraiodo-** comb form [tetra- + iod-] : containing four atoms of iodine — in names of chemical compounds ⟨tetraiodofluorescein⟩; compare IOD-

tet·ra·iodide \ˌ⸙+\ or **te·tri·odide** \təˈtrīəˌdīd, -dəd\ n [tetra- + iodide] : an iodide containing four atoms of iodine

tet·ra·iodo \ˈtetrəˈī)dō, ˈīə,dō\ adj [tetraiod-] : containing four atoms of iodine in the molecule

tet·ra·iodo·phenolphthalein \ˈ⸙ˈ(,)⸱+, ˌ⸙,⸱+\ n [ISV tetraiod- + phenolphthalein] : IODOPHTHALEIN

tet·ra·kai·dec·a·he·dron \ˌtetrəˌkīˌdekəˈhēdrən\ n [NL, fr. LGk tetrakaidekaedron, fr. Gk tetrakaideka fourteen (fr. tetra- + kai and + deka ten) + -edron -hedron — more at TEN] : a 14-sided figure having 6 quadrilateral and 8 hexagonal faces

tetrakis- comb form [Gk, fr. tetrakis; akin to Gk tettares, tessares four — more at FOUR] : four times ⟨quadrivalent — esp. in complex chemical expressions ⟨tetrakis-(2-hydroxyethyl)⟩ ammonium chloride $(HOCH_2CH_2)_4NCl⟩$

tet·ra·kis·azo \ˈtetrəkəsˈazō\ adj [tetrakis- + azo] : containing four azo groups in the molecule ⟨~ dyes⟩

tet·ra·kis·hexahedron \"+\ n [NL, fr. tetrakis- + hexahedron] : TETRAHEXAHEDRON

tet·ra·lem·ma \ˌtetrəˈlemə\ n -s [tetra- + dilemma] : an argument analogous to a dilemma but presenting four alternatives in the premises

Tet·ra·lin \ˈtetrələn\ trademark — used for tetrahydronaphthalene

te·tral·o·gy \teˈtraləjē, ˈtral-, -ji\ n -ES [Gk tetralogia, fr. tetra- + -logia -logy] 1 : a group of four dramatic pieces including three tragedies and one satyric piece or sometimes four tragedies represented consecutively on the Attic stage at the Dionysiac festival 2 : a series of four connected works (as dramas, operas, or novels) 3 : a group of four symptoms that are characteristic of a disease ⟨~ of Fallot⟩ : TETRALOGY OF FALLOT

tetralogy of Fallot \-('fä,lō\ usu cap F [after E. L. A. Fallot †1911 Fr. physician who orig. described it] : a congenital abnormality of the heart characterized by pulmonic stenosis, an opening in the interventricular septum, malposition of the aorta over both ventricles, and hypertrophy of the right ventricle

tet·ra·lone \ˈtetrəˌlōn\ n -s [ISV tetralin + -one] : either of two ketones $C_{10}H_{10}O$ derived from tetrahydronaphthalene

tet·ra·loph·odon \ˌtetrəˈläfəˌdän\ n, cap [NL, fr. tetra- + loph- + -odon] : a genus of Pliocene mastodons having a very short lower jaw and long straight upper tusks

¹tet·ra·lophodont \ˈtetrə+\ adj [ISV tetra- + lophodont] 1 of a molar tooth : having four crests or ridges 2 : having tetralophodont molars

²tetralophodont \"\ adj [NL Tetralophodont, Tetralophodon] : of or relating to the genus Tetralophodon

³tetralophodont \"\ n : a mastodon of the genus Tetralophodon

tet·ra·mer \ˈtetrəmə(r), -ə⸱-\ n -s [tetra- + -mer] : a polymer formed from four molecules of a monomer

te·tram·era \teˈtramərə\ n, pl, cap [NL, fr. neut. pl. of tetramerus tetramerous] syn of PSEUDOTETRAMERA

te·tram·er·al \-mərəl\ also **tet·ra·mer·ic** \ˌtetrəˈmerik\ adj [NL tetramerus tetramerous + E -al] : TETRAMEROUS

te·tram·er·es \teˈtramə,rēz\ n, cap [NL, fr. tetra- + -meres having four parts] : a genus of nematode worms (family Spiruridae) parasitic in the proventriculus of gallinaceous birds including domestic fowls

te·tram·er·ism \-ə,rizəm\ n -s : the quality or state of being tetramerous

te·tram·er·ous \-əs\ adj [NL tetramerus, fr. Gk tetramerēs, fr. tetra- + -merēs (fr. meros part) — more at MERIT] : having or characterized by the presence of four parts: a of a flower : having the parts arranged in sets of four or multiples of four — often written 4-merous b : having four or apparently only four joints in each of the tarsi ⟨~ beetles⟩

tet·ra·metaphosphate \ˌ⸙+\ n [tetra- + metaphosphate] : a cyclic tetrameric metaphosphate [as sodium tetrametaphosphate $(NaPO_3)_4$]

¹te·tram·e·ter \teˈtramədə(r), -ətə-\ n [Gk tetrametron, fr. neut. of tetrametros of four measures] : a line of four measures consisting either of four dipodies (as in classical iambic, trochaic, and anapaestic verse) or four feet (as in modern English verse)

²tetrameter \"\ adj [LL, fr. Gk tetrametros, fr. tetra- + -metros (akin to Gk metron measure, meter) — more at MEASURE] : consisting of four dipodies or four metrical feet

tet·ra·methyl \ˈtetrə+\ adj [ISV tetra- + methyl] : containing four methyl groups in the molecule

tetramethylammonium \ˌ⸙+\ n [tetramethyl + ammonium] : the quaternary ammonium ion $(CH_3)_4N^+$ containing four methyl groups — see TETRAMINE 2

tet·ra·methylene \"+\ n [ISV tetra- + methylene] 1 : a bivalent radical $-CH_2CH_2CH_2CH_2-$ containing four methylene groups 2 : CYCLOBUTANE

tetramethylene cyanide or **tetramethylene dicyanide** n : ADIPONITRILE

tetramethylenediamine \ˌ⸙,⸱⸱⸱+\ n [ISV tetramethylene + diamine] : PUTRESCINE

tetramethylene glycol n : BUTANEDIOL b

tetramethylthiuram disulfide \ˌ⸙+\ n [tetramethyl + thiuram] : a crystalline irritating compound $[(CH_3)_2NCS]_2S_2$ made by oxidation of a salt of dimethyl-dithiocarbamic acid and used chiefly as an accelerator of rubber vulcanization and as a fungicide and seed disinfectant; bis-(dimethyl-thiocarbamoyl) disulfide — abbr. TMTD; called also thiram

tet·ra·mine \ˈtetrəˌmēn, -mən\ n [tetra- + amine] 1 : a compound (as hexamethylenetetramine) containing four amino groups 2 : a strong toxic unstable base $(C_2H_5)_4NOH$ obtained from sea anemones or made synthetically; tetraethylammonium hydroxide

te·tram·mine \teˈtramən\ n [tetra- + ammine] : an ammine containing four molecules of ammonia — compare CUPRAMMONIUM 1

tet·ra·morph \ˈtetrəˌmorf\ n [Gk tetramorphon, neut. of tetramorphos of four shapes, fr. tetra- + -morphos -morphous] : a representation of the four attributes of the Evangelists in a winged figure standing on winged fiery wheels with the wings covered with eyes — **tet·ra·mor·phic** \ˌ⸙ˈmorfik\ adj

tet·ra·mor·phism \ˌ⸙ˈmor,fizəm\ n -s [tetra- + -morphism] : the property of crystallizing in four distinct forms — compare POLYMORPHISM

tet·ra·mor·phous \ˌ⸙ˈmorfəs\ adj [tetra- + -morphous] : relating to or characterized by tetramorphism

te·tran·dria \teˈtrandrēə\ n pl, cap [NL, fr. tetra- + -andria] in former classifications : a class of higher plants comprising those with four stamens

te·tran·dri·an \-drēən\ adj [NL Tetrandria + E -an] : of or relating to the Tetrandria

te·tran·drous \-drəs\ adj [ISV tetra- + -androus] : having four stamens

tet·ra·nitrate \ˈtetrə+\ n [tetra- + nitrate] : a chemical compound containing four nitrate groups

tetranitro- comb form [ISV tetra- + nitr-] : containing four nitro groups — in names of chemical compounds

tet·ra·ni·tro·aniline \ˌ⸙ˈnī,trō⸱+\ n [tetranitro- + aniline] : a powerful explosive $C_6H(NO_2)_4NH_2$ obtained as a yellow crystalline solid by nitrating aniline

tet·ra·ni·tro·methane \"+\ n [ISV tetranitro- + methane] : a volatile toxic liquid compound $C(NO_2)_4$ made usu. by the action of nitric acid on acetic anhydride and used chiefly in very powerful liquid explosive mixtures

tet·ra·nuclear \ˌ⸙+\ adj [tetra- + nuclear] : containing four nuclei ⟨~ cyanine dyes⟩ — compare TETRACYCLIC 2

tet·ra·nucleotide \"+\ n [tetra- + nucleotide] : a nucleotide consisting of four mononucleotides in combination

¹te·tran·y·chid \teˈtranəkid, ˈtetrəˌnī⸱-\ adj [NL Tetranychidae] : of or relating to the Tetranychidae

²tetranychid \"\ n -s : a mite of the family Tetranychidae

tet·ra·nych·i·dae \ˌtetrəˈnikəˌdē\ n pl, cap [NL, fr. Tetranychus, type genus + -idae] : a family of medium-sized soft-bodied mites that have the movable chela of each chelicera modified into a long piercing organ, tenent hairs on the claws, and no genital suckers, that feed on plants and usu. spin silken webs over the foliage, and that comprise the economically important red spiders

te·tran·y·chus \teˈtranəkəs\ n, cap [NL, fr. tetra- + Gk -onychos -clawed (fr. onych-, onyx claw) — more at NAIL] : a genus (the type of the family Tetranychidae) of mites — see PACIFIC MITE

tet·rao \ˈtetrəˌō, -rēˌō\ n, cap [NL, fr. L heath cock, moorfowl, fr. Gk tetraōn — more at TURTLE (turtledove)] : a genus (the type of the family Tetraonidae) of grouses now restricted to the capercaillie and closely related forms

te·tra·odon \ˈtetrəˌodän\ n, cap [NL, fr. tetra- + -odon] : a genus (the type of the family Tetraodontidae) of tropical marine fishes

¹te·tra·odont \-,dänt\ adj [NL Tetraodontidae] : of or relating to the Tetraodontidae

²tetraodont \"\ n -s : a fish of the family Tetraodontidae

tet·ra·odon·ti·dae \ˌtetrəōˈdäntəˌdē, -rēō-\ n pl, cap [NL, fr. Tetraodont-, Tetraodon, type genus + -idae] : a family of tropical marine fishes comprising the puffers and with the ocean sunfishes and a few other related forms constituting a distinct suborder of the Plectognathi — see GLOBEFISH

tetraodontoxin var of TETRODOTOXIN

tet·ra·on·i·dae \ˌtetrəˈänəˌdē, -rēˌō-\ n pl, cap [NL, fr. Tetraon-, Tetrao, type genus + -idae] : a variously limited family of birds (order Galliformes) that is usu. restricted to those grouses which have the tarsi and nostrils feathered

tet·ra·phosphate \ˈtetrə+\ n [ISV tetra- + phosphate] 1 : a substance similar to a metaphosphate glass — used chiefly commercially 2 : a fertilizer made by heating ground phosphate rock principally with carbonates of calcium, magnesium, and sodium carbonates

¹tet·ra·phyl·lid \ˈtetrəˈfiləd\ adj [NL Tetraphyllidea] : of or relating to the Tetraphyllidea

²tetraphyllid \"\ n -s : a tapeworm of the order Tetraphyllidea

tet·ra·phyl·lid·ea \ˌtetrəfəˈlidēə\ n pl, cap [NL, fr. tetra- + phyll- + -idea] : an order of Cestoda comprising tapeworms parasitic in elasmobranch fishes and distinguished by a scolex having four bothridia and sometimes also hooks or suckers for attachment to the host

tet·ra·phyl·lid·e·an \ˌ⸙fəˈlidēən\ adj [NL Tetraphyllidea + E -an] : TETRAPHYLLID

tet·ra·pla \ˈtetrəplə\ n -s often cap [NL, fr. neut. pl. of Gk tetraplous, tetraploos fourfold, fr. tetra- + -plous, -ploos -fold (as in diploos twofold, double) — more at DOUBLE] : a polyglot book with four texts in parallel columns — compare HEXAPLA, OCTAPLA

tet·ra·ple·gia \ˌ⸙ˈplēj(ē)ə\ n -s [NL, fr. tetra- + -plegia] : QUADRIPLEGIA

¹tet·ra·ploid \ˈtetrəˌploid\ adj [ISV tetra- + -ploid] : fourfold in appearance or arrangement; specif : having or being a chromosome number that is four times the monoploid number ⟨a ~ cell⟩ — compare POLYPLOID — **tet·ra·ploi·dic** \ˌ⸙ˈploiˌdik\ adj

²tetraploid \"\ n -s : a tetraploid individual

tet·ra·ploi·dy \ˌ⸙ˈploidē\ n -ES [ISV ¹tetraploid + -y] : the condition of being tetraploid

tet·ra·pod \ˈtetrəˌpäd\ n -s [NL tetrapodus, fr. Gk tetrapod-, tetrapous four-footed] 1 : a four-footed animal : QUADRUPED — used chiefly of higher terrestrial vertebrates 2 : a four-footed bottom section (as of a pedestal table) 3 : a large reinforced concrete object having four arms and used esp. for protecting breakwaters from wave damage — compare TETRAHEDRON 2c

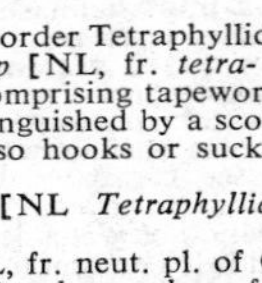

tetrapod 2

²tetrapod \"\ also **te·trap·o·dous** \teˈtrapədəs\ adj [tetrapod fr. tetrapod-, tetrapous, fr. tetra- + pod-, pous foot; tetrapodous fr. Gk tetrapod-, tetrapous + E -ous — more at FOOT] : having four feet or walking appendages

¹te·trap·o·da \teˈtrapədə\ n pl, cap [NL, fr. neut. pl. of Gk tetrapodos four-footed, fr. tetrapod-, tetrapous] : a division of tetrapod butterflies including those with only two pairs of perfect legs

²tetrapoda \"\ n pl, cap [NL, fr. Gk, neut. pl.] in former classifications : a division of vertebrates including all forms above fishes

te·trap·o·dal \-d'l\ adj [¹tetrapod + -al] 1 : TETRAPOD ⟨~ reptiles⟩ 2 : constituting one of four supporting legs ⟨pottery consisting of vessels with ~ supports⟩

te·trap·o·dy \teˈtrapədē\ n -ES [NL tetrapodia, fr. tetrapod-, tetrapous four-footed + -ia -y] : a unit of four metrical feet

tet·ra·polar \ˈtetrə+\ adj [tetra- + polar] : having four poles ⟨certain abnormal mitotic figures are ~⟩ — **tet·ra·polarity**

te·trap·ter·an \te·'traptərən\ *adj* [Gk *tetrapteros* + E *-an*] *of an insect* **:** having four wings

te·trap·ter·on \-ə,rän\ *n* -s [NL, fr. neut. of Gk *tetrapteros* having four wings] **:** a four-winged insect

te·trap·ter·ous \-,rəs\ *adj* [Gk *tetrapteros,* fr. *tetra-* + *-pteros* -pterous] **:** TETRAPTERAN

tet·rap·tu·rus \,te,trap't(y)ürəs\ *n, cap* [NL, fr. *tetra-* + *pter-* + *-urus*] **:** a genus of large vigorous marine fishes (family Istiophoridae) comprising the spearfishes (sense 1)

te·trap·tych \te·'traptik\ *n* -s [Gk *tetraptychon,* neut. of *tetraptychos* fourfold, fr. *tetra-* + *-ptychos* (akin to Gk *ptychē* fold, layer)] **:** an arrangement of pictures in four parts (as for an altarpiece)

tet·ra·py·lon \¦te·trə+\ *n, pl* **tetrapyla** [Gk, fr. *tetra-* + *pylōn* gateway — more at PYLON] **:** an edifice having four gates or portals (as one marking the intersection of two thoroughfares in an ancient Roman city)

tet·ra·radiate \¦te·trə+\ *adj* [*tetra-* + *radiate,* adj.] **:** having four principal radii of symmetry ⟨a ~ sponge spicule⟩

¹tetrarch \'te,trärk, 'tē,-\ *n* -s [ME, fr. LL *tetrarcha,* fr. L *tetrarches,* fr. Gk *tetrarchēs,* fr. *tetra-* (akin to Gk *tettares, tessares* four) + *-archēs* ¹-arch — more at FOUR] **1 :** a governor of the fourth part of an ancient province (as in the Roman Empire) **2 :** a subordinate prince or petty king **3 :** any of four officials or directors jointly in control

²tetrarch \"\ *adj* [*tetra-* + *-arch*] **:** having four xylem groups — used of a stele

tetrarch·ate \-r,kāt\ *n* -s [¹*tetrarch* + *-ate*] **:** TETRARCHY

te·trar·chic \(')te·¦trärkik, (')tē¦t-, tə't-\ *also* **te·trar·chi·cal** \-rkəkəl\ *adj* [*tetrarchic* fr. Gk *tetrarchikos* of a tetrarch, fr. *tetrarchēs* tetrarch + *-ikos* -ic; *tetrarchical* fr. Gk *tetrarchikos* + E *-al*] **:** of or relating to a tetrarchy or a tetrarch

¹tetrarchy \'te,trärkē, 'tē,-\ *n* -ES [ME *tetrarchie,* fr. L *tetrarchia,* fr. Gk, fr. *tetrarchēs* tetrarch + *-ia* -y] **1 :** the district, office, or jurisdiction of a tetrarch **2 a :** rule by four persons jointly **b :** the four rulers of a tetrarchy

²tetrarchy \"\ *n* -ES [²*tetrarch* + *-y*] **:** the state of having four xylem strands or groups

tet·ra·rhyn·chi·dea \,te·trə(,)riŋ'kidēə\ *or* **tet·ra·rhyn·choi·dea** \-'kȯidēə\ [NL, fr. *Tetrarhynchus,* genus of tapeworms (fr. *tetra-* + *-rhynchus*) + *-idea* or *-oidea*] *syn of* TRYPANORHYNCHA

tet·ra·rhyn·chid·e·an \¦==(,)=¦kidēən\ *or* **tet·ra·rhyn·choid** \¦==¦riŋ,kȯid\ *adj or n* [*tetrarhynchidean* fr. NL *Tetrarhynchidea* + E *-an; tetrarhynchoid* fr. NL *Tetrarhynchoidea*] **:** TRYPANORHYNCHAN

tet·ra·saccharide \¦te·trə+\ *n* [ISV *tetra-* + *saccharide*] **:** any of a class of carbohydrates (as stachyose) that yield on complete hydrolysis four monosaccharide molecules

tet·ra·selenodont \"+\ *adj* [*tetra-* + *selenodont*] **:** relating to or having molar teeth with four crescentic crests or ridges

tet·ra·seme \'te·trə,sēm\ *n* -s [back-formation fr. *tetrasemic*] **:** a tetrasemic foot (as a tetrabrach or a spondee)

tet·ra·se·mic \¦==¦sēmik\ *or* **tet·ra·seme** \'==,sēm\ *adj* [*tetrasemic* fr. Gk *tetrasēmos* of four time units (fr. *tetra-* + *-sēmos,* fr. *sēmeion* unit of time, mark, sign, fr. *sēma* sign) + E *-ic; tetraseme* fr. Gk *tetrasēmos* — more at SEMANTICS] **:** consisting of or of the length of four morae in classical prosody

tet·ra·silicate \¦te·trə+\ *n* [ISV *tetra-* + *silicate*] **:** a silicate (as talc) containing four atoms of silicon in the molecule

tet·ra·skele *also* **tet·ra·scele** \'te·trə,skēl\ *n* -s [NL, fr. Gk *tetraskelēs* four-legged, fr. *tetra-* + *-skelēs* (fr. *skelos* leg) — more at CYLINDER] **:** TETRASKELION

tet·ra·skel·i·on \,te·trə'skelēən, -ē,än\ *n, pl* **tetraskelions** \-nz\ *or* **tetraskel·ia** \-ēə\ [NL, dim. of *tetraskele*] **:** a figure (as the swastika) composed of four arms radiating from a center and bent in the same direction — compare TRISKELION

tet·ra·sodium pyrophosphate \¦te·trə+-\ *n* [*tetra-* + *sodium*] **:** SODIUM PYROPHOSPHATE b

tet·ra·so·mat·ic \¦==sō¦mad·ik\ *adj* [*tetrasomaty* + *-ic*] **:** of or relating to tetrasomaty

tet·ra·som·a·ty \¦==¦sōmad·ē\ *n* -ES [*tetra-* + *somat-* + *-y*] **:** polysomatic octoploidy — compare POLYSOMATY

tet·ra·some \'==,sōm\ *n* -s [*tetra-* + *-some*] **:** an association (as in a polyploid) of four homologous chromosomes in the meiotic prophase — compare BIVALENT, TETRAD

¹tet·ra·so·mic \¦==¦sōmik\ *adj* [*tetra-* + *-somic*] **:** having one or a few chromosomes tetraploid in otherwise diploid nuclei due to nondisjunction — **tet·ra·so·my** \'==,sōmē\ *n* -ES

²tetrasomic \"\ *n* -s **:** a tetrasomic individual

tet·ra·spo·ra·les \,==spə'rā(,)lēz\ *n pl, cap* [NL, fr. *Tetraspora,* genus of green algae (fr. *tetra-* + *-spora*) + *-ales*] **:** an order of green algae having vegetative cells that are immobile but capable of changing temporarily into a motile stage and that form colonies that are not filamentous and are often amorphous

tet·ra·spo·ran·gi·ate \¦===¦ranjēət, -ē,āt\ *adj* [NL *tetrasporangium* + E *-ate*] **:** of, relating to, or being a tetrasporangium

tet·ra·sporangium \"+\ *n* [NL, fr. *tetra-* (in ISV *tetraspore*) + *sporangium*] **:** a sporangium producing tetraspores

tet·ra·spore \'==,spō(ə)r\ *n* [ISV *tetra-* + *spore*] **:** one of the haploid asexual spores in the red algae developed meiotically and commonly in groups of four from the diploid tetrasporangia and germinating to produce the haploid gametophytic plants — compare CARPOSPORE — **tet·ra·spor·ic** \¦==¦spōrik\ *adj* — **tet·ra·spor·ous** \¦==¦spōrəs, tə'trasparəs\ *adj*

tet·ra·spo·rif·er·ous \¦==,spə¦rif(ə)rəs\ *adj* [*tetraspore* + *-iferous*] **:** bearing tetraspores

tet·ra·spo·ro·phyte \,=='spōrə,fīt\ *n* [*tetraspore* + *-o-* + *-phyte*] **:** a plant bearing tetraspores

tet·ras·ter \(')te¦trastə(r)\ *n* -s [NL, fr. *tetra-* + *-aster*] **:** a mitotic figure characterized by four astral poles instead of the more usual two and in an embryo usu. resulting from abnormal polyspermy

tet·ra·stich \'te·trə,stik\ *n* -s [L *tetrastichon,* fr. Gk, neut. of *tetrastichos* of four lines, fr. *tetra-* + *stichos* line, verse — more at STICH] **:** a prosodic unit or stanza of four lines — **te·tras·ti·chal** \tə'trastəkəl\ *adj* — **tet·ra·stich·ic** \¦te·trə¦stikik\ *adj*

te·tras·ti·chous \te·'trastəkəs\ *adj* [LL *tetrastichus* of four lines, of four rows, fr. Gk *tetrastichos*] **1 :** ranked by fours **2 :** arranged in four vertical rows — used esp. of the inflorescence of a grass or of its constituent parts

te·tras·ti·chus \-kəs\ *n, cap* [NL, fr. Gk *tetrastichos* of four lines] **:** a genus of minute chalcid flies that contains numerous hyperparasites and is sometimes made the type of a distinct family

tet·ra·sto·on \,te·trə'stō,än, te·'trastə,wän\ *n, pl* **tetra·stoa** \-stōə, -stəwə\ [Gk, fr. neut. of *tetrastoos* having four porticoes, fr. *tetra-* + *stoa* portico — more at STOIC] **:** a courtyard enclosed by four porticoes

¹tet·ra·style \'te·trə,stīl\ *n* [LL *tetrastylon,* fr. L, neut. of *tetrastylos* having four pillars, fr. Gk, fr. *tetra-* + *stylos* pillar — more at STEER] **:** a building or portico having four columns in front — **tet·ra·styl·ic** \¦==¦stilik\ *or* **tet·ra·sty·lous** \¦==¦stīləs\ *adj*

²tetrastyle \"\ *adj* **:** marked by columniation with four columns across the front — compare DISTYLE

tet·ra·substituted \¦==+\ *adj* [*tetra-* + *substituted*] **:** having four substituent atoms or groups in the molecule

tet·ra·sulfide \"+\ *n* [*tetra-* + *sulfide*] **:** a binary compound of an element or radical with four atoms of sulfur

tet·ra·syllabic \¦==+\ *or* **tet·ra·syllabical** \"+\ *adj* [Gk *tetrasyllabos* (fr. *tetra-* + *-syllabos,* fr. *syllabē* syllable) + E *-ic* or *-ical* — more at SYLLABLE] **:** having four syllables

tet·ra·the·ism \¦==(,)thē,izəm\ *n* [*tetra-* + *-theism*] **:** a doctrine that there are three persons in the Godhead and a divine essence constituting their common origin and that is interpreted as being a belief in four Gods

tet·ra·thi·o·nate \,=='thīə,nāt\ *n* [ISV *tetrathion-* (in *tetrathionic acid*) + *-ate*] **:** a salt of tetrathionic acid

tet·ra·thionic acid \¦==+-\ *n* [ISV *tetra-* + *thionic;* orig. formed as F *tétrathionique*] **:** the thionic acid $H_2S_4O_6$ containing four atoms of sulfur in the molecule

tet·ra·thyridium \"+\ *n* [NL, fr. *tetra-* + *thyridium*] **:** a modified cysticercus resembling an elongated plerocercoid with a scolex invaginated at one end

tet·ra·tom·ic \¦te·trə'tämik\ *adj* [ISV *tetra-* + *atomic*] **1 :** consisting of four atoms **:** having four atoms in the molecule **2 :** having four replaceable atoms or radicals

tet·ra·ton·ic \¦==¦tänik\ *adj* [Gk *tetratonos* having four tones (fr. *tetra-* + *tonos* tone) + E *-ic* — more at TONE] **1 :** consisting of four musical tones ⟨~ scale⟩ **2 :** relating to the tetratonic scale

tet·ra·valence \¦te·trə+\ *or* **tet·ra·valency** \"+\ *n* [*tetravalence* ISV, fr. *tetravalent,* after such pairs as E *present: presence; tetravalency* fr. *tetravalent,* after such pairs as E *president: presidency*] **:** the quality or state of being tetravalent ⟨the ~ of the carbon atom⟩

¹tet·ra·valent \"+\ *adj* [ISV *tetra-* + *valent*] **1 :** having a valence of four **2 :** QUADRUPLE — used of homologous chromosomes when four are present and associate in synapsis

²tetravalent \"\ *n* -s **:** a tetravalent chromosome group

te·trax·i·al \te·'traksēəl\ *also* **te·trax·ile** \-k,sīl\ *adj* [*tetra-* + *axial* or *axile*] **:** having four axes

te·trax·on \te·'traksän\ *n* -s [*tetra-* + Gk *axōn* axle, axis — more at AXIS] **:** a tetraxial sponge spicule

tet·rax·o·nia \,te,trak'sōnēə\ [NL, fr. *tetra-* + *axonia*] *syn of* DEMOSPONGIAE

te·trax·o·nid \te·'traksənəd, -,nid\ *adj or n* [NL *Tetraxonida*] **:** TETRACTINELLID

tet·rax·on·i·da \,te,trak'sänədə\ [NL, fr. *tetra-* + Gk *axōn* axis + NL *-ida*] *syn of* TETRACTINELLIDA

tetraz- *or* **tetrazo-** *comb form* [ISV *tetra-* + *az-*] **:** containing four atoms of nitrogen — in names of chemical compounds ⟨*tetrazole*⟩

tet·ra·zene \'te·trə,zēn\ *n* -s [ISV *tetraz-* + *-ene*] **1 :** either of two hypothetical isomeric hydrides of nitrogen HN=NNH-NH_2 or $H_2NN=NNH_2$ known in the form of organic derivatives (as tetracene) **2 :** TETRACENE

tet·ra·zine \'te·trə,zēn, -,zən\ *n* -s [ISV *tetraz-* + *-ine*] **1 :** any of three isomeric parent compounds $C_2H_2N_4$ that may be regarded as benzene with four methylidyne groups replaced by nitrogen atoms; *esp* **:** the symmetrical or 1,2,4,5-isomer forming very volatile unstable purple-red crystals **2 :** any of various derivatives of the tetrazines

tet·ra·zo \-,zō\ *adj* [*tetraz-*] **1 :** containing four atoms of nitrogen in the molecule; *esp* **:** DISAZO **2 :** TETRAKISAZO

tet·ra·zole \'te·trə,zōl\ *n* -s [ISV *tetraz-* + *-ole*] **:** a crystalline acidic parent compound CH_2N_4 containing a ring composed of one carbon atom and four nitrogen atoms; *also* **:** any of various derivatives of this compound — compare PENTYLENETETRAZOL

tet·ra·zo·li·um \,=='zōlēəm\ *n* -s [NL, fr. ISV *tetrazole* + NL *-ium*] **:** a univalent ion $CH_3N_4^+$ or radical CH_3N_4 analogous to ammonium and derived from tetrazole; *also* **:** any of various derivatives of this ion ⟨~ salts are redox indicators —*Science*⟩ — compare FORMAZAN

tetrazolium chloride *n* **1 :** the hydrochloride of tetrazole **2 :** TRIPHENYLTETRAZOLIUM CHLORIDE

te·traz·o·lyl \te·'trazə,lil\ *n* -s [*tetrazole* + *-yl*] **:** the univalent radical CHN_4 derived from tetrazole

tet·ra·zooid \¦te·trə+\ *n* [*tetra-* + *zooid*] **:** one of the first four blastozooids formed from the precocious stolon of the cyathozooid of a member of the genus *Pyrosoma*

te·traz·o·ti·za·tion \te·,trazəd·ə'zāshən, -zə,tī'z-\ *n* -s **:** the process of tetrazotizing

te·traz·o·tize \=¦==,tīz\ *vt* -ED/-ING/-S [*tetra-* + *-azotize* (as in *diazotize*)] **:** to diazotize doubly **:** convert (as an aromatic diamine) into a disazo compound ⟨benzidine is *tetrazotized* for making a benzidine disazo dye⟩

¹te·trig·id \te·'trijəd\ *adj* [NL *Tetrigidae*] **:** of or relating to the Tetrigidae

²tetrigid \"\ *n* -s **:** an insect of the family Tetrigidae

te·trig·i·dae \-jə,dē\ *n pl, cap* [NL, fr. *Tetrig-, Tetrix,* type genus + *-idae*] **:** a family of saltatorial insects (order Orthoptera) comprising the grouse locusts and having the pronotum greatly lengthened

tetriodide *var of* TETRAIODIDE

tet·ri·tol \'te·trə,tȯl, -tōl\ *n* -s [*tetrose* + *-itol*] **:** any of the tetrahydroxy alcohols $HOCH_2(CHOH)_2CH_2OH$ (as erythritol) obtainable by reducing the corresponding tetrose

tet·rix \'te·triks\ *n, cap* [NL, modif. (influenced by Gk *tetrix,* a bird, perh. pipit) of Gk *tettix* cicada, of imit. origin — more at TURTLE (turtledove)] **:** a genus of small very active usu. dark-colored grouse locusts

te·trobol \te·'träbəl, -rōb-\ *also* **te·trob·o·lon** \-rābəlän\ *n, pl* **tetrobols** \-bəlz\ *also* **tetrobo·la** \-bələ\ [Gk *tetrōbolon* fr. neut. of *tetrōbolos* of four obols, fr. *tetra-* + *obolos* obol — more at OBOL] **:** a silver coin of ancient Greece worth four obols

tet·rode \'te,trōd\ *n* -s [*tetra-* + *-ode*] **:** a vacuum tube with four electrodes, a cathode, an anode, a control grid, and an additional grid or other electrode

tet·rodon \'te·trə,dän\ [NL, fr. *tetra-* + *-odon*] *syn of* TETRAODON

tet·ro·dont \-nt\ *adj or n* [NL *Tetrodontidae*] **:** TETRAODONT

tet·ro·don·ti·dae \,=='däntə,dē\ [NL, fr. *Tetrodont-, Tetrodon* + *-idae*] *syn of* TETRAODONTIDAE

tet·ro·do·toxin \¦te·trədō+\ *or* **tet·ra·odon·toxin** \¦te·trō-,dän+\ *n* [*tetrodotoxin* ISV *tetrodo-* (fr. NL *Tetrodon*) + *toxin; tetraodontoxin* fr. NL *Tetraodon* + *toxin*] **:** a poisonous compound $C_{16}H_{31}NO_{16}$(?) obtained from Japanese fugus

te·trolic acid \te·'trälik-, -trōl-\ *n* [ISV *tetra-* + *-ol* + *-ic*] **:** a crystalline acetylenic acid $CH_3C{\equiv}CCOOH$ obtained synthetically; methyl-propiolic acid

te·tron·ic acid \te·'tränik-\ *n* [ISV *tetron-* (fr. *tetra-* + connective *-on-*) + *-ic*] **:** a crystalline enolic lactone $C_4H_4O_3$ that has acidic properties and is the parent compound of acidic compounds obtained by the fermenting action of a mold (*Penicillium charlesii*) from spoiled corn

tet·rose \'te,trōs *also* -ōz\ *n* -s [ISV *tetra-* + *-ose*] **:** any of a class of monosaccharides $C_4H_8O_4$ (as erythrose or threose) containing four carbon atoms

te·trox·a·late \te·'träksə,lāt\ *n* [*tetra-* + *oxalate*] **:** a complex acid oxalate (as potassium tetroxalate) made by adding one equivalent of base to four equivalents of oxalic acid

te·trox·ide \-k,sīd\ *n* [ISV *tetra-* + *oxide*] **:** an oxide containing four atoms of oxygen

tet·ryl \'te·trəl\ *n* -s [ISV *tetra-* + *-yl*] **:** a pale yellow crystalline explosive $(NO_2)_3C_6H_2N(CH_3)NO_2$ obtainable by nitrating dimethylaniline or methylaniline and used esp. as a detonator; methyl-picryl-nitramide — called also *trinitrophenylmethylnitramine*

tet·ter \'ted·ə(r), -etə-\ *n* -s [ME *tetere,* fr. OE *teter* — more at DARTROSE] **1 :** any of various vesicular skin diseases (as ringworm, eczema, and herpes) **2** *dial* **:** PIMPLE, PUSTULE, BLISTER, ULCER

tetterwort \'==,=\ *n* [ME *teterwort,* fr. *tetere* tetter + *wort*] **:** a plant used to treat tetter: as **a** *Eng* **:** CELANDINE **b :** BLOODROOT

tet·ti·gel·li·dae \,ted·ə'jelə,dē\ *n pl, cap* [NL, fr. *Tettigella,* type genus (fr. Gk *tettig-, tettix* cicada + L *-ella*) + *-idae*] **:** a family of insects (suborder Homoptera) consisting of the true leafhoppers — compare JASSIDAE

tet·tig·i·dae \te'tijə,dē\ [NL, fr. *Tettig-, Tettix* + *-idae*] *syn of* TETRIGIDAE

¹tet·ti·go·ni·id \¦ted·ə¦gōnēəd\ *adj* [NL *Tettigoniidae*] **:** of or relating to the Tettigoniidae

²tettigoniid \"\ *n* -s **:** an insect of the family Tettigoniidae **:** LONG-HORNED GRASSHOPPER

tet·ti·go·ni·idae \,== gə'nīə,dē\ *n pl, cap* [NL, fr. *Tettigonia,* type genus (fr. L *tettigonia* leafhopper, fr. Gk *tettigonion,* dim. of *tettig-, tettix* cicada) + *-idae*] **:** a large family of insects (order Orthoptera) having long slender antennae and four-segmented tarsi and comprising the long-horned grasshoppers

tet·tix \'te·tiks\ [NL, fr. Gk, cicada, of imit. origin] *syn of* TETRIX

teu·cri·um \'t(y)ükrēəm\ *n, cap* [NL, fr. Gk *teukrion* germander, perh. fr. *Teukros* Teucer, first king of Troy] **:** a large widely distributed genus of herbs (family Labiatae) having flowers with four exserted stamens, a short corolla tube, and a prominent lower lip — see GERMANDER 1

teuk \'t(y)ük\ *n* -s [imit.] *dial Eng* **:** REDSHANK 1

teu·thid·i·dae \t(y)ü'thidə,dē\ *n pl, cap* [NL, fr. *Teuthid-, Teuthis,* type genus + *-idae*] **:** a family of marine fishes comprising the surgeonfishes that are distinguished by a bony plate or spine on the side of the tail, teeth resembling incisors, and fine scales resembling shagreen and with the Moorish idols constituting a distinct suborder of Percomorphi

teu·this \'t(y)üthəs\ *n, cap* [NL, fr. LL, squid, fr. Gk] **:** the type genus of Teuthididae

teu·ton \'t(y)üt°n\ *n* -s *cap* [L *Teutoni, Teutones,* pl.] **1 :** a member of an ancient prob. Germanic or Celtic people first appearing in history as allies of the Cimbri **2 :** a member of one of the peoples speaking a language of the Germanic branch of the Indo-European family of languages; *esp* **:** GERMAN

¹teu·ton·ic \t(y)ü¦tänik, -nēk\ *adj, usu cap* [L *teutonicus,* fr. *Teutoni, Teutones* Teutons + *-icus* -ic] **:** of, relating to, or having the characteristics of the Teutons; *esp* **:** ¹GERMANIC 1 ⟨formidable volumes, *Teutonic* in their thoroughness —*Times Lit. Supp.*⟩ — **teu·ton·i·cal·ly** \-nək(ə)lē, -nēk-, -li\ *adv, usu cap*

²teutonic \"\ *n* -s *cap* **:** GERMANIC

teutonic knight *n, usu cap T&K* **:** a knight of a powerful religious military order founded at Acre in 1190 as a brotherhood of German crusaders

teu·ton·ism \'t(y)üt°n,izəm\ *n, usu cap* [NL *teutonismus,* fr. L *Teutoni* + *-ismus* -ism] **:** GERMANISM ⟨the style is stilted and marred by *Teutonisms* —John Layard⟩ ⟨prejudice in favor of *Teutonism* —W.Z.Ripley⟩

teu·ton·ist \-°nəst\ *n* -s *usu cap* **:** GERMANIST

teu·ton·ization \,t(y)üt°nə'zāshən, -°n,ī'z-\ *n* -s *often cap* **:** GERMANIZATION

teu·ton·ize \'t(y)üt°n,īz\ *vt* -ED/-ING/-S *often cap* **:** GERMANIZE ⟨keep their eyes . . . on a *Teutonized* Europe —*Blackwood's*⟩ ⟨~s his phrases for a scholarly effect⟩

tevet *or* **teveth** *usu cap, var of* TEBET

¹tew \'t(y)ü\ *vb* -ED/-ING/-S [ME *tewen,* alter. of *tawen* — more at TAW] *vt* **1** *obs* **:** to work (leather) by beating or kneading **2** *obs* **:** to prepare for some purpose **3** *obs* **:** BEAT, BELABOR ~ *vi* **1** *chiefly dial* **:** to work hard **2** *dial* **:** FUSS, WORRY

²tew \"\ *n* -s *chiefly dial* **:** a state of worried agitation or excitement **:** STEW ⟨my wife was always in a ~ about the danger —W.D.Howells⟩

³tew *vt* -ED/-ING/-S [prob. alter. of ¹*tow*] *obs* **:** PULL, HAUL

te·wa \'tāwə, 'tēwə\ *n, pl* **tewa** *or* **tewas** *usu cap* **1 a :** any of several Tanoan peoples of New Mexico and northeastern Arizona **b :** a member of any of such peoples **2 :** a language of the Tewa peoples

tew·el \'t(y)üəl\ *n* -s [ME, shaft, vent, tewel, fr. MF *tuel, tuyau* pipe, tube, prob. of Gmc origin; akin to MD & MLG *tute* pipe, tube] *archaic* **:** ANUS, RECTUM — used chiefly of a horse

¹tex·an \'teksən\ *also* **tex·i·an** \-sēən\ *adj, usu cap* [*Texas* state + E *-an* (adj. suffix)] **1 :** of, relating to, or characteristic of Texas **2 :** of, relating to, or characteristic of Texans

²texan \"\ *also* **texian** \"\ *n* -s *cap* [*Texas* state + E *-an* (n. suffix)] **:** a native or resident of the state of Texas

¹tex·as \'teksəs, *esp by Texans* -əz\ *adj, usu cap* [fr. *Texas,* state in the southwestern U.S., fr. AmerSp, a confederation of Indians allied against the Apache, fr. Caddo *techas* allies] **:** of or from the state of Texas ⟨a *Texas* ranch⟩ **:** of the kind or style prevalent in Texas **:** TEXAN

²texas \"\ *n, pl* **texas** *or* **texases** [AmerSp, a confederation of Indians, prob. Hasinai] **1** *usu cap* **:** HASINAI **2** [fr. *Texas* state; fr. the practice on Mississippi steamboats of naming the cabins after the states, the officers' cabins being the largest] **:** a structure on the awning deck of a steamer containing the officers' cabins and having the pilothouse in front or on top

texas adelia *n, usu cap T* **:** SWAMP PRIVET

texas bedbug *n, usu cap T* **:** CONENOSE

texas bluegrass *n, usu cap T* **:** a vigorous forage grass (*Poa arachnifera*) of the southern U.S. that resembles Kentucky bluegrass but has stems that are less flattened

texas brown-eyed susan *n, usu cap T&S* **:** a bristly annual herb (*Rudbeckia bicolor*) of the southern U.S. that has ray flowers darker toward the center of the head

texas buckeye *or* **texan buckeye** *n, usu cap T* **:** SPANISH BUCKEYE

texas buckthorn *n, usu cap T* **:** LOTE

texas catclaw *n, usu cap T* **:** a tall shrub or small to large tree (*Acacia wrightii*) with many short spines and dense foliage that yields firewood and is a locally important honey plant in parts of the southwestern U.S. — called also *tree cat's-claw*

texas fever *or* **texas cattle fever** *n, usu cap T* **:** an infectious disease of cattle transmitted by the cattle tick and caused by a protozoan (*Babesia bigemina*) that multiplies in the blood and destroys the red blood cells — called also *blackwater, splenetic fever;* see RED WATER 1a; compare ICTEROHEMATURIA

texas fever tick *n, usu cap T* **:** a cattle tick (*Boophilus annulatus*)

texas fly *n, usu cap T* **:** HORN FLY

texas independence day *n, usu cap T&I&D* **:** March 2 that is observed as the anniversary of the declaration of independence of Texas from Mexico in 1836 and also as the birthday of Sam Houston

texas leaf-cutting ant *n, usu cap T* **:** a leaf-cutting ant (*Atta texana*) that is sometimes a destructive defoliator in Texas and Louisiana

texas leaguer *n* [*Texas* (baseball) *League* + E *-er*] **:** a fly in baseball that falls too far out to be caught by an infielder and too close in to be caught by an outfielder

texas longhorn *n, usu cap T* **:** LONGHORN 2b

texas millet *n, usu cap T* **:** an annual weedy grass (*Panicum texanum*) used for hay

texas nighthawk *n, usu cap T* **:** a largely gray black-striped goatsucker (*Chordeiles acutipennis texensis*) of the southwestern U. S. and parts of Mexico

texas palmetto *n, usu cap T* **:** a tall palm (*Sabal texana*) of southern Texas and Mexico whose leaves are used for thatching and chair seats

texas pea *n, usu cap T* **:** a perennial bushy herb (*Astragalus nuttallianus*) of the southwestern U. S. that yields forage

texas plume *n, usu cap T* **:** STANDING CYPRESS

texas ranger *n, usu cap T&R* **:** a member of a mounted police force in Texas

texas red oak *also* **texas oak** *n, usu cap T* **:** a usu. small to medium-sized oak (*Quercus texana*) of dry Texas uplands having a reddish brown bark, deeply lobed leaves, and usu. solitary short-stalked biennial acorns

texas root rot *n, usu cap T* **:** COTTON ROOT ROT

texas sage *n, usu cap T* **:** a perennial herb (*Salviastrum texanum*) of the family Labiatae having tufted hairy stems and blue flowers in close panicles

texas snakeroot *n, usu cap T* **:** a birthwort (*Aristolochia reticulata*) of the southwestern U. S. that resembles the Virginia snakeroot in its medicinal properties

texas sparrow *n, usu cap T* **:** a finch (*Arremonops rufivirgatus*) of southern Texas and Mexico that is olive green above with inconspicuous rufous stripes on the head and yellow on the wings

texas star *n, usu cap T* **1 :** an annual Texan herb (*Lindheimera texana*) of the family Compositae sometimes cultivated for its rather showy radiate yellow heads **2 :** PRAIRIE SABBATIA

texas steer *n, usu cap T* **:** a small side-branded steer hide

texas tender *n* **:** a waiter in the texas of a steamboat

texas thistle *n, usu cap 1st T* **1 :** BASKET FLOWER 1 **2** *or* **texas nettle :** BUFFALO BUR

texas tower *n, usu cap 1st T* [²*texas*] **:** a radar-equipped platform supported on caissons sunk in the ocean floor and forming part of an offshore warning system against air attack

texas umbrella tree *n, usu cap 1st T* **:** an ornamental tree that has a crowded often flattened crown and is a horticultural variety (*Melia azedarach umbraculiformis*) of the china tree

¹text \'tekst\ *n* -s [ME, fr. MF *texte,* fr. ML *textus* text, passage, Scripture, fr. L, texture, tissue, structure, context, fr. past part. of *texere* to construct, weave — more at TECHNICAL] **1 a** (1) **:** the original written or printed words and form of a literary work ⟨apologize for . . . methods of softening or otherwise changing the ~ of the letters —J.S. Bassett⟩ ⟨no room to print full ~s of important speeches in Congress —Herbert Agar⟩ (2) **:** an edited or emended copy of the wording of an original work ⟨the ~ that was printed showed the results of an editor's blue pencil⟩ ⟨prepared a new ~ of the Shakespearean comedies⟩ **b :** a work containing such text ⟨pleased with the autographed ~ the young poet had given him⟩ ⟨~s did not sell as well as its predecessor⟩ **2 a :** the main body of printed or written matter

on a page exclusive of headings, running title, footnotes, illustrations, or margins **b :** the principal part of a book exclusive of the front and back matter ⟨use roman numerals in preliminary pages, arabic in ~⟩ **c :** the printed score of a musical composition ⟨strictly observed the ~ of the preludes and fugues and resisted individual interpretation⟩ **3 a** (1) **:** a verse or passage of Scripture chosen esp. for the subject of a sermon or for authoritative support (as in a question of doctrine) ⟨these outlines . . . and Scriptural ~*s* will be excellent supplementary material in the preparation of sermons —*Lenten & Easter Cat.*⟩ ⟨then, mustering ~*s* to justify his course . . . proceeded to baptize himself —George Willison⟩ (2) **:** a passage from an authoritative source providing an introduction or basis (as for an essay, speech, or lecture) ⟨one brief phrase which might form the ~ to an exhaustive treatise —Bernard Groom⟩ ⟨uses that ~ . . . as the point of departure —A.T.Weaver⟩ **b :** something providing a chief source of information or authority ⟨my ~ for this chapter is . . . any good daily newspaper —Weston La Barre⟩ ⟨Confucianism provided, in the main, the ~ for the cultivation of feudal loyalty —A.M.Young⟩ **c :** TEXTBOOK ⟨a ~ in chemistry, designed for use in a high school —*Chemistry at Work*⟩ ⟨included three Greek plays on the list of ~*s* for his humanities course⟩ **4 a :** TEXT HAND **b :** a type considered suitable for printing running text **5 a :** a subject on which one writes or speaks **:** THEME, TOPIC ⟨writers who hold forth glibly on that ~ —Douglas Bush⟩ **b :** the form and substance of something written or spoken ⟨the ~ of the appeal was a closely reasoned, eloquent and occasionally rhetorical argument against slavery —Martha Gruening⟩ ⟨the ~ of their conversation consists . . . of a recital of the exact order of action which is habitual on such an expedition —E.D.Chapple & C.S.Coon⟩ **6 :** the words of something (as a poem, libretto, scriptural passage, folktale) set to music ⟨in all vocal compositions a complete ~ for every voice part is given in the music —Carl Parrish & J.F.Ohl⟩ ⟨many hundred ~*s* and tunes of English-Canadian folk songs —*Report: (Canadian) Royal Commission on Nat'l Development*⟩

²**text** *vt, obs* **:** to write in large letters

text bible *n, usu cap B* **:** an edition of the Bible published with an unannotated text

textbook \ˈ=,=\ *n, often attrib* **:** a book used in the study of a subject: as **a :** a book containing a usu. systematic presentation of the principles and vocabulary of a subject ⟨preparing a comprehensive ~ on geomorphology⟩ **b :** a book recording the historical development of a subject ⟨criticized an art history ~ for its sketchy treatment of the Florentine artists⟩ **c :** a collection of writings by various authors dealing with a specific subject ⟨a ~ of literary criticism by contemporary British and American authors⟩ **d :** a literary work relevant to the study of a subject ⟨among the suggested ~*s* were several novels written during the period⟩

textbookish \ˈ=,==\ *adj* **:** of, relating to, or having the characteristics of a textbook ⟨has tied all the strands of his plot together in a slightly ~ fashion —*Amer. Scholar*⟩ ⟨except for a few all too brief interludes, the style is heavy and ~ —*Nation*⟩

text-critical \ˈ=¦===\ *adj* **:** of, relating to, or having the characteristics of textual criticism esp. of the Scriptures ⟨*text-critical* study . . . makes it clear that the Hebrew text has suffered little corruption —Robert Gordis⟩

text edition *n* **:** an edition prepared for use esp. in schools and colleges — compare TRADE EDITION

text hand *n* **:** a style of handwriting marked by the use of large letters

tex·tile \ˈtek,stīl, -kst°l, -k(,)stil\ *n* -s *often attrib* [L, fr. neut. of *textilis* woven, fr. *textus* (past part.) + *-ilis* -ile] **1 :** CLOTH 1a; *esp* **:** a woven or knit cloth **2 :** a fiber, filament, or yarn used in the making of cloth

textile cone *n* **:** a showy but extremely venomous cone shell (*Conus textile* or *Darioconus textile*) having a cylindrical ovate shell that is pearly white blotched and reticulated with orange brown and marked with wavy dark brown tracery — called also *cloth-of-gold cone*

textile red WR-263 *n, usu cap T&R* **:** an organic pigment — see DYE table I (under *Pigment Red 23*)

textile screw pine *n* **:** a Polynesian screw pine (*Pandanus tectorius*) — called also *lauhala*

textile tissue *n* **:** TWISTING PAPER

text letter *n, obs* **:** a large calligraphic letter

tex·tu·al \ˈtekschəwəl, -chəl\ *adj* [ME *textuel*, fr. AF, fr. OF *texte* text + *-el* -al — more at TEXT] **:** of, relating to, or based on the text of something ⟨his management of ~ questions in his own edition of Shakespeare —Elizabeth Morrow⟩ ⟨the ~ image, the rose, appears and reappears —Austin Warren⟩ ⟨sought to extract a meaning from the ~ reading⟩

textual critic *n* **:** a practitioner of textual criticism

textual criticism *n* **1 :** the study of a literary work that aims to establish the original text ⟨those . . . who have given themselves to the *textual criticism* of the New Testament —B.W. Bacon⟩ ⟨*textual criticism* of Shakespearean tragedies⟩ — compare LOWER CRITICISM **2 :** a critical study of literature emphasizing a close reading and analysis of the text ⟨subjected several modern poems to concentrated *textual criticism*⟩ — compare NEW CRITICISM

tex·tu·al·ism \-ə,lizəm\ *n* -s **:** rigid adherence to a text of the Scriptures

tex·tu·al·ist \-ləst\ *n* -s **:** one who is a close student of the text of the Scriptures

tex·tu·al·ly \-ch(əw)əlē, -li\ *adv* **1 :** in or with regard to the text of something ⟨references implied but not expressed ~⟩ ⟨unacquainted with the Koran ~ —J.E.Merrill⟩ **2 :** VERBATIM ⟨rules . . . which reproduce ~ provisions of the charter —*U.N. General Assembly Rules of Procedure*⟩

¹**tex·tu·ary** \-chə,werē\ *n* -ES [ML *textus* + E *-ary* (n. suffix)] **:** one who is well informed on the Bible or in biblical scholarship

²**textuary** \"\ *adj* [ML *textus* + E *-ary* (adj. suffix)] **:** TEXTUAL

tex·tur·al \ˈtekschərəl\ *adj* **:** of, relating to, or marked by texture ⟨based upon the ~ and physical characteristics . . . of the rock fragments —*Jour. of Geology*⟩ ⟨her skin had undergone a ~ change —Thomas Hardy⟩

¹**tex·ture** \ˈtekschə(r)\ *n* -s [L *textura* web, texture, fr. *textus* (past part. of *texere* to weave) + *-ura* -ure — more at TECHNICAL] **1 a :** something composed of closely interwoven elements ⟨nor the spider entangle the heedless fly in his ~ —Abraham Tucker⟩; *specif* **:** a woven cloth ⟨took up from the couch the great purple-and-gold ~ that covered it —Oscar Wilde⟩ **b :** the structure formed by the threads of a fabric ⟨the open ~ of mesh⟩ **2 a :** the essential part of something **:** SUBSTANCE, NATURE ⟨not a mere exercise in metaphysics: for him it is . . . the very ~ of action —Irving Howe⟩ ⟨musical theater, American in its quality and ~ —Rouben Mamoulian⟩ **b :** an identifying quality **:** CHARACTER ⟨the distinctive ~ of Mediterranean culture —Morris Watnick⟩ ⟨by the cigars they smoke, and the composers they love, ye shall know the ~ of men's souls —John Galsworthy⟩ **3 a :** the size and organization of small constituent parts of a body or substance ⟨cellular ~ of a plant stem⟩ ⟨a soil is fine or coarse in ~ according to the relative proportions of fine and coarse particles present —C.F.Marbut⟩ **b :** the visual or tactile surface characteristics and appearance of something ⟨the ~*s* and shapes of people's well-kept-up places showed cold-washed and brilliant —Edmund Wilson⟩ ⟨nubby ~ of tweed⟩ ⟨a photography that transmutes the ~*s* of earth and water, woods, and grasses —Arthur Knight⟩ ⟨scrawl calligraphic convolutions over the painted surface . . . to give it ~ —David Sylvester⟩ **c :** the characteristic consistency esp. of a liquid or semiliquid ⟨thinning baby's cereal with formula . . . makes the ~ more familiar —*advt*⟩ ⟨the finished product, made of glue and glycerin, has a rubbery ~ —*Saturday Rev.*⟩ **d :** GRAIN 6a ⟨the ~ varies with different woods and rate of growth —Thomas Corkhill⟩ **4 a :** the smaller features of a rock that depend on the size, shape, arrangement, and distribution of the component minerals ⟨the ~ of the unaltered rock varies, ranging from porphyritic . . . to seriate —*Economic Geology*⟩ — compare STRUCTURE **b :** a composite of the elements of prose or poetry ⟨all these words . . . meet violently to form a ~ impressive and exciting —John Berryman⟩ ⟨the ~ of the internal monologue derives its richness and stiffness from a continuous thread of quotation —Harry Levin⟩ **c :** a pattern of musical sound created by tones or lines played or sung together ⟨the harmonic ~ constantly suggested tonality to my ear —Irving Kolodin⟩ ⟨is sung by each voice in turn so that another parallel melodic line is added to the ~ —Norman Demuth⟩ **5 a :** a basic scheme or structure **:** FABRIC ⟨closely inwoven with the ~ of rational experience —W.R.Inge⟩ ⟨believed that character was the pervasive ~ of personality —Doris F. Bernays⟩ **b :** the overall structure of something incorporating all or most of its parts **:** BODY ⟨lessons . . . yet to become absorbed into the ~ of contemporary society —F. H.A.Micklewright⟩ ⟨once a theme . . . assumes importance it tends to recur and become integrated into the ~ of the play —E.A.Armstrong⟩

²**texture** \"\ *vt* -ED/-ING/-S **1 :** to make by or as if by weaving ⟨a bright faultless vision *textured* out of mere sunbeams —Jane W. Carlyle⟩ **2 a :** to form with a texture ⟨walled with opaque glass . . . *textured* into little cubes —Lewis Mumford⟩ **b :** to give a texture to ⟨carpets *textured* with patterns in high and low pile⟩

texture·less \ˈ==ləs\ *adj* **:** lacking a texture

texture paint *n* **:** a paint of heavy consistency and coarse grain consisting usu. of gypsum and sand with water-thinned binder and used for creating a rough patterned effect on a wall

tex·tus \ˈtekstəs\ *n, pl* **textus** [ML & L — more at TEXT] **1 :** a text of the Bible **2 :** TISSUE

textus re·cep·tus \-rəˈseptəs, -rē'-\ *n* [NL, lit., received text] **:** the generally accepted text of a literary work (as the Greek New Testament)

text writer *n* **:** one who writes textbooks relating esp. to law

TF *abbr* **1** task force **2** territorial force **3** *often not cap* till forbidden **4** *often not cap* to fill **5** *often not cap* to follow

TFE *abbr or n* -s tetrafluoroethylene

tfillin *var of* TEFILLIN

t formation *n, cap T* **:** an offensive football formation in which the fullback lines up behind the center and quarterback and one halfback is stationed on each side of the fullback

tfr *abbr* transfer

tg *abbr* **1** telegram **2** telegraph

TG *abbr* **1** task group **2** tollgate **3** *often not cap* type genus

TGB *abbr, often not cap* tongued, grooved, and beaded

tgl *abbr* toggle

tgt *abbr* target

¹**-th** — see ¹-ETH

²**-th** \th\, *usu with preceding epenthetic* t *after some consonants and in eighth; often* t *after some consonants or/and before the plural ending* s, *as in* sixth(s), ninths\ *or* **-eth** \əth\ *adj suffix* [ME *-the, -te, -ethe*, fr. OE *-tha, -ta, -otha, -etha*; akin to OHG *-do, -to* -th, ON *-di, -ti*, Goth *-da, -ta*, L *-tus*, Gk *-tos*, Skt *-tha*] — used in forming ordinal numbers ⟨ten*th*⟩ ⟨twentie*th*⟩

³**-th** \th\, *usu with preceding epenthetic* p, t, *or* k *after some consonants; often* t *before the plural ending* s, *as in* widths\ *n suffix* -s [ME *-the, -th*, fr. OE *-thu, -th*; akin to OHG *-ida*, suffix forming abstract nouns, ON *-th*, Goth *-itha*, L *-ta*, Gk *-tē*, Skt *-tā*] **1 :** act or process ⟨spil*th*⟩ **2 :** state or condition ⟨bread*th*⟩ ⟨green*th*⟩ ⟨wid*th*⟩

th *abbr* **1** thoroughbred **2** threshold

-th *symbol* [²-th] — used after figures (as 4, 5, 6, 7, 8, 9) to indicate ordinal numbers ⟨May 4*th*⟩ ⟨44*th* Street⟩

TH *abbr* **1** true heading **2** two hands

Th *symbol* thorium

th' \th\ *definite article* [ME, short for *the*] **:** THE — used sometimes before words beginning with a vowel sound

¹**tha** \thə\ *dial var of* THEE

²**tha** \"\ *dial var of* THOU

³**tha** \"\ *dial var of* THY

thack *also* **thak** \ˈthak\ *dial var of* THATCH

thack·er \-kə(r)\ *dial var of* THATCHER

¹**thack·er·ay·an** \ˈthakərēən\ *adj, usu cap* [William M. *Thackeray* †1863 Eng. novelist + E *-an* (adj. suffix)] **:** of, relating to, or characteristic of W.M.Thackeray or his writings ⟨digressing in obsolete *Thackerayan* fashion —J.B.Cabell⟩ ⟨*Thackerayan* asides —H.L.Mencken⟩

²**thackerayan** \"\ *n* -s *usu cap* [William M. *Thackeray* †1863 + E *-an* (n. suffix)] **:** an authority on or devotee of Thackeray

¹**thae** \ˈthā\ *chiefly Scot var of* THOSE

²**thae** \"\ *chiefly Scot var of* THESE

thai \ˈtī\ *n, pl* **thai** *or* **thais** *cap* **1** *or* **thai·land·er** \ˈtī-,landə(r)\ -s **:** a native or inhabitant of Thailand or one of his descendants **2 :** the language of the Thai **:** the official language of Thailand — called also *Siamese* **3 :** a group of languages including Thai, Lao, Shan, Khamti, and Ahom and considered by some to belong to the Sino-Tibetan language group

thai·land \ˈtī,land *sometimes* -,lənd\ *adj, usu cap* [fr. *Thailand*, country in southeast Asia] **:** of or from Thailand **:** of the kind or style prevalent in Thailand **:** SIAMESE

thairm \ˈthārm\ *n* -s [ME *therm, tharm* gut, fr. OE *thearm* — more at DERMA (beef casing)] *dial chiefly Scot* **:** CATGUT; *esp* **:** a fiddle string

tha·is \ˈthāəs\ *n, cap* [NL, after *Thais*, 4th cent. B.C. Greek hetaera, fr. L, fr. Gk *Thais*] **:** a widely distributed genus that comprises marine snails with a rough thick shell sometimes ornamented with tubercles and is sometimes made the type of a distinct family but is usu. placed in Muricidae — see DOG WHELK, PURPURA

tha·kur \ˈtä,kù(ə)r\ *n* -s *usu cap* [Hindi *thākur*, fr. Skt *ṭhakkura*] **:** a member of the Kshatriya caste among the Hindus

thalam- *or* **thalamo-** *comb form* [NL, fr. *thalamus*] **1 :** thalamus ⟨*thalam*encephalon⟩ ⟨*thalamo*fugal⟩ **2 :** thalamic and ⟨*thalamo*cortical⟩

thal·a·men·ce·phal·ic \¦thalə¦mensəˈfalik\ *adj* [NL *thalamencephalon* + E *-ic*] **:** DIENCEPHALIC

thal·a·men·ceph·a·lon \,thaləˌmenˈsefə,län\ *n* -s [NL, fr. *thalam-* + *encephalon*] **:** DIENCEPHALON

tha·lam·ic \thəˈlamik, -mēk\ *adj* [NL *thalamicus*, fr. *thalamus* + L *-icus* -ic] **:** of, relating to, or involving the thalamus — **tha·lam·i·cal·ly** \-mək(ə)lē\ *adv*

thalamic radiation *n* **:** any of several large bundles of nerve fibers connecting the thalamus with the cerebral cortex by way of the internal capsule

thal·a·mite \ˈthalə,mīt\ *n* -s [Gk *thalamitēs*, fr. *thalamos* chamber, hold of a ship + *-itēs* -ite] **:** the outermost of the three rowers to a bench on a trireme sitting somewhat in advance and below the other two — compare THRANITE, ZYGITE

thal·a·mo·cele *or* **thal·a·mo·coele** \ˈthaləmō,sēl\ *n* -s [*thalam-* + *-cele, -coele*] **:** the third ventricle of the brain

thal·a·mo·cortical \¦thalə(,)mō+\ *adj* [*thalam-* + *cortical*] **:** of, relating to, or connecting the thalamus and the cerebral cortex

thal·a·mof·u·gal \,thaləˈmäfyəgəl\ *adj* [*thalam-* + *-fugal*] **:** passing out of the thalamus

thal·a·mo-olivary \¦thalə(,)mō+\ *adj* [*thalam-* + *olivary*] **:** relating to or connecting the thalamus and the inferior olivary body

thal·a·moph·o·ra \,thaləˈmäfərə\ [NL, fr. Gk *thalamos* chamber + NL *-phora*] *syn of* FORAMINIFERA

thal·a·mot·o·my \,thaləˈmädəmē\ *n* -ES [*thalam-* + *-tomy*] **:** a surgical operation involving electrocoagulation of areas of the thalamus and thereby interrupting pathways of nervous transmission through the thalamus for relief of certain mental disorders

thal·a·mus \ˈthaləməs\ *n, pl* **thal·a·mi** \-lə,mī\ [NL, fr. Gk *thalamos* room, woman's apartment, bridal chamber; perh. akin to Gk *tholos* rotunda — more at DALE] **1 :** the largest subdivision of the diencephalon consisting chiefly of an ovoid mass of nuclei in each lateral wall of the third ventricle and being divisible into an anterior and medial group of nuclei that constitutes the paleothalamus, is concerned with primitive correlations in connection with the corpus striatum but not the cerebral cortex, and is a center for the crude perception of pain and the affective qualities of other sensations and a lateral group of nuclei that constitutes the neothalamus and serves as the great relay station of somatic sensory and optic paths to the cerebral cortex with which it is connected by the thalamic radiation **2 :** RECEPTACLE 3b **3** *or* **tha·la·mi·um** \thəˈlāmēəm\ -s [*thalamus* fr. L, fr. Gk *thalamos*; *thalamium*, NL, dim. of L *thalamus*] **:** an inner room or bower in classic architecture usu. for the women of the family

thal·arc·tos \thaˈlärk,täs\ *n, cap* [NL, irreg. fr. Gk *thalassa* sea + *arktos* bear — more at ARCTIC] **:** a genus of bears consisting of the polar bear — compare URSUS

thalass- *or* **thalasso-** *comb form* [Gk, fr. *thalassa, thalatta*] **:** sea ⟨*thalass*emia⟩ ⟨*thalasso*meter⟩

tha·las·sal \thəˈlasəl\ *adj* [*thalass-* + *-al*] **:** THALASSIC

thal·as·sarc·tos \,thaləˈsärk,täs\ [NL, fr. *thalass-* + Gk *arktos* bear] *syn of* THALARCTOS

thal·as·se·mia \,thaləˈsēmēə\ *also* **thal·ass·anemia** \¦thaləs+\ *n* -s [NL, fr. *thalass-* + *-emia* or *anemia*] **:** a familial hypochromic anemia characterized by microcytic anemia, splenomegaly, and changes in the bones and skin and occurring esp. in children of Mediterranean parents

tha·las·si·an \thəˈlasēən\ *n* -s [*thalass-* + *-ian*] **:** SEA TURTLE

tha·las·sic \thəˈlasik, -sēk\ *adj* [F *thalassique*, fr. *thalass-* + *-ique* -ic] **1 :** of or relating to the sea or ocean **2 :** of or relating to seas or gulfs as distinguished from oceans ⟨deposits of sediment in gulfs and seas rather than in the oceans proper are known as ~ deposits —*Scientific Monthly*⟩

¹**tha·las·si·nid** \thəˈlasənəd\ *adj* [NL *Thalassinidea*] **:** of or relating to the Thalassinidea

²**thalassinid** \"\ *n* -s **:** a crustacean of the subtribe Thalassinidea

tha·las·si·nid·ea \thə,lasəˈnidēə\ *n pl, cap* [NL, fr. *Thalassina*, genus of crustaceans (fr. *thalass-* + *-ina*) + *-idea*] **:** a subtribe of Anomura including small crustaceans with a thin flexible carapace, long soft abdomen, and unsymmetrical chelae that burrow in sand or mud along seashores — compare GHOST SHRIMP — **tha·las·si·nid·e·an** \=¦==¦nidēən\ *n or adj* — **tha·las·si·noid** \thəˈlasə,nȯid\ *adj*

thal·as·soch·e·lys \,thaləˈsäkələs\ [NL, fr. *thalass-* + Gk *chelys* tortoise — more at CHELYS] *syn of* CARETTA

thal·as·soc·ra·cy \,thaləˈsäkrəsē\ *n* -ES [Gk *thalassokratia*, fr. *thalass-* + *-kratia* -cracy] **:** maritime supremacy ⟨insecurity of the seas . . . which followed the collapse of the Mycenaean ~ —*Interpreter's Bible*⟩

tha·las·so·crat \thəˈlasə,krat\ *n* -s [fr. *thalassocracy*, after such pairs as E *democracy: democrat*] **:** one who has maritime supremacy

thal·as·sog·ra·pher \,thaləˈsägrəfə(r)\ *n* -s [*thalassography* + *-er*] **:** a specialist in thalassography

tha·las·so·graph·ic \thə¦lasə¦grafik\ *or* **tha·las·so·graph·i·cal** \-fəkəl\ *adj* **:** of or relating to thalassography

thal·as·sog·ra·phy \,thaləˈsägrəfē\ *n* -ES [ISV *thalass-* + *-graphy*] **:** oceanography esp. relating to seas and gulfs

thal·as·som·e·ter \,thaləˈsämad·ə(r)\ *n* [ISV *thalass-* + *-meter*] **:** TIDE GAGE

thale-cress \ˈthā(ə)lˈkres\ *n* [after Johann *Thal* †1583 Ger. physician] **:** MOUSE-EAR CRESS

tha·len·ite \ˈthälə,nīt\ *n* -s [F *thalénite*, fr. T. R. *Thalén* †1905 Sw. physicist + F *-ite*] **:** a mineral $Y_2Si_2O_7$ or $2Y_2Si_2O_7.H_2O$ consisting of an yttrium silicate and occurring in flesh-red monoclinic crystals possibly isomorphous with thortveitite (hardness 6.5, sp. gr. 4.2)

thaler *var of* TALER

tha·le·sian \thāˈlēzhən\ *adj, usu cap* [*Thales* †546 B.C. Gk philosopher and scientist + E *-ian*] **:** of, relating to, or typical of the Grecian Thales or his nature philosophy according to which water is the basic stuff of the physical universe — compare MILESIAN

tha·lia \ˈthālēə\ *n, cap* [NL, fr. Gk, abundance, fr. the stem of *thallein* to sprout, grow, thrive + *-ia* -y; akin to Arm *dalar* green, fresh, Alb *dal* I come forth, and perh. to W *dail* leaves, MIr *duille;* basic meaning: to blossom, bloom] **1 :** a small genus of American mostly aquatic herbs (family Marantaceae) with broad long-stalked basal leaves, terminal panicles of bracted purple flowers, and globose capsules **2 :** a genus of pelagic tunicates commonly regarded as a subgenus of *Salpa*

tha·li·a·cea \,thālēˈāshēə\ *n pl, cap* [NL, fr. *Thalia* + *-acea*] **:** a small order of tunicates consisting of various aberrant free-swimming pelagic forms (as of the genera *Salpa* and *Doliolum*) — **tha·li·a·cean** \¦==¦āshən\ *n or adj*

tha·li·an \thəˈlīən\ *adj, sometimes cap* [*Thalia*, ancient Greek Muse of comedy (fr. L, fr. Gk *Thaleia*) + E *-an*] **:** of or relating to comedy **:** COMIC

tha·lic·trum \thəˈliktrəm\ *n* [NL, fr. L, meadow rue, fr. Gk *thaliktron*] **1** *cap* **:** a large widely distributed genus of herbs (family Ranunculaceae) comprising the meadow rues and having ternately decompound leaves, small polygamous or unisexual apetalous flowers, and fruit consisting of several achenes **2** -s **:** any plant of the genus *Thalictrum*

thall- *or* **thalli-** *or* **thallo-** *comb form* [NL, fr. Gk *thall-, thallo-*, fr. *thallos* — more at THALLUS] **1 :** a young shoot **:** thallus ⟨*Thallo*phyta⟩ ⟨*thall*ium⟩ ⟨*thalli*form⟩ **2 :** thallium ⟨*thall*ic⟩

thal·lic \ˈthalik\ *adj* [ISV *thall-* + *-ic*] **:** of, relating to, or containing thallium — used esp. of compounds in which this element is trivalent; compare THALLOUS

thal·lif·er·ous \thəˈlif(ə)rəs\ *adj* [*thall-* + *-ferous*] **:** containing or yielding thallium

thal·li·form \ˈthalə,fȯrm\ *adj* [*thall-* + *-form*] **:** having the form of a thallus

¹**thal·line** \ˈtha,līn, -alən\ *adj* [*thall-* + *-ine*] **:** consisting of or constituting a thallus

²**thal·line** \ˈtha,lēn, -alən\ *n* -s [ISV *thall-* + *-ine*; fr. the green color it forms with oxidizing agents] **:** a crystalline base $CH_3OC_9H_9NH$ derived from quinoline, forming a green color with oxidizing agents, and formerly used in the form of salts as an antipyretic

thal·li·um \ˈthalēəm\ *n* -s [NL, fr. *thall-* + *-ium*; fr. the bright green line in its spectrum] **:** a sparsely but widely distributed metallic element that resembles tin in appearance but on exposure to air readily forms a gray and then brownish-black coating of oxide, that is malleable like lead but a little softer, that occurs combined in a few minerals (as crookesite and lorandite) and in smaller amounts in various other minerals and in plants, that is usu. obtained from flue dusts from pyrites burners or from lead and zinc smelters and refiners, that is very poisonous and principally univalent but sometimes trivalent in its compounds, and that forms alloys but is used chiefly in the form of compounds (as the sulfide in photoelectric cells) — symbol *Tl*; see ACTINIUM SERIES, THORIUM SERIES, URANIUM SERIES; ELEMENT table

thallium sulfate *n* **:** a poisonous crystalline salt Tl_2SO_4 used chiefly as a rodenticide and insecticide — called also *thallous sulfate*

thal·lo·gen \ˈthaləjən\ *n* -s [*thall-* + *-gen*] **:** a plant in which growth is not restricted to an apical growing point **:** THALLOPHYTE — compare ACROGEN — **thal·lo·gen·ic** \¦thalə¦jenik\ *or* **thal·log·e·nous** \thəˈläjənəs\ *adj*

thal·loid \ˈtha,lȯid\ *adj* [*thall-* + *-oid*] **:** of, relating to, resembling, or consisting of a thallus

thal·loph·y·ta \thəˈläfəd·ə\ *n pl, cap* [NL, fr. *thall-* + *-phyta*] *in some classifications* **:** a primary division of the plant kingdom that consists of plants with single-celled sex organs or with many-celled sex organs of which all cells give rise to gametes, that is now commonly considered to be a heterogeneous assemblage, and that when recognized comprises the Algae and Fungi — compare EUMYCETES

thal·lo·phyte \ˈthalə,fīt\ *n* -s [NL *Thallophyta*] **:** a plant belonging to the Thallophyta — **thal·lo·phyt·ic** \¦==¦fid·ik\ *adj*

thal·lose \ˈtha,lōs\ *adj* [*thall-* + *-ose*] **:** THALLOID

thal·lo·spore \ˈthalə,spō(ə)r, -pȯ(ə)r\ *n* [ISV *thall-* + *-spore*] **:** a spore not abstricted from a conidiophore; *esp* **:** a spore (as a blastospore) developing by septation or budding of hyphal cells

thal·lous \ˈthaləs\ *adj* [*thall-* + *-ous*] **:** of, relating to, or containing thallium — used esp. of compounds in which this element is univalent; compare THALLIC

thallous sulfate *n* **:** THALLIUM SULFATE

thal·lus \ˈthaləs\ *n, pl* **thal·li** \-a,lī\ *or* **thalluses** [NL, fr. L, young shoot, green stalk, fr. Gk *thallos*, fr. *thallein* to sprout — more at THALIA] **:** a plant body that is characteristic of the thallophytes, that does not grow from an apical point, shows no differentiation into distinct tissue systems (as vascular tissue) or members (as stems, leaves, or roots) or is composed of members resembling and performing many of the functions of but not homologous with those of the higher plants, and that may be simple or branched, may consist of filaments or plates of cells, and may vary widely in form and

size from microscopic one-celled plants to complex foliated or arborescent forms (as in some of the larger marine algae)

thal·po·sis \thal'pōsəs\ *n, pl* **thalpo·ses** \-ō,sēz\ [NL, fr. Gk *thalpos* heat, warmth (fr. *thalpein* to heat) + NL *-osis*; perh. akin to *thallein* to sprout — more at THALIA] **:** the warmth sense **:** warmth sensation

thal·pot·ic \(')thal¦päd·ik\ *adj* **:** of, relating to, or having a sense of warmth

thal·weg \'täl,veg, -väk\ *n* -s [G *talweg* (formerly spelled *thalweg*), fr. *tal* valley (fr. OHG) + *weg* way, path, fr. OHG — more at DALE, WAY] **1 a :** a line following the lowest part of a valley whether under water or not **b :** the line of continuous maximum descent from any point on a land surface or one crossing all contour lines at right angles **c :** subsurface water percolating beneath and in the same direction as a surface stream course **2 :** the middle of the chief navigable channel of a waterway which constitutes a boundary line between states

tha·ma·kau \'thämə¦kaù\ *n* -s [Fiji] **:** a large outrigger canoe used in the Fiji islands

thames barge \'temz-\ *n, usu cap T* [fr. the *Thames* river, England] **:** a round-bowed transom-sterned broad-beamed freight boat usu. having a sprit mainsail and small gaff mizzen that can be lowered to pass under bridges and plying the coast and rivers of southern England

thames measurement *n, usu cap T* **:** a British measurement of tonnage esp. for yachts ⟨small vessel of . . . 36 tons *Thames measurement* —*Times Lit. Supp.*⟩

tha·min \'thä,min\ *also* **tha·meng** \-meŋ\ *n* -s [Burmese *thamin, thamaṅ*] **:** a deer (*Cervus eldi*) of Burma, Siam, and the Malay peninsula having antlers with long curved brow tines

thamn- *or* **thamno-** *comb form* [Gk, fr. *thamnos*; akin to Gk *thama* frequent, often, *tithenai* to place, put — more at DO] **:** bush **:** shrub ⟨*thamnophile*⟩

tham·nid·i·um \tham'nidēəm\ *n, cap* [NL, fr. *thamn-* + *-idium*] **:** a genus (the type of the family Thamnidiaceae) of molds related to the typical bread molds and characterized by branched sporangiophores and sporangia consisting of a large terminal one with a columella and smaller lateral sporangioles without columella — compare WHISKER 2c

tham·ni·um \'thamnēəm\ *n* -s [NL, fr. Gk *thamnion* small bush, dim. of *thamnos* bush] **:** the branched or fruticose thallus of various lichens (as of the genus *Cladonia*)

tham·no·phile \'thamnə,fīl\ *n* -s [NL *Thamnophilus*] **:** ANT-SHRIKE

tham·noph·i·line \tham'näfə,līn\ *adj* [NL *Thamnophilus* + E *-ine*] **:** of or relating to the genus *Thamnophilus*

tham·noph·i·lus \-fələs\ *n, cap* [NL, fr. *thamn-* + *-philus*] **:** a genus of Neotropical hook-billed antbirds (family Formicariidae) consisting of the antshrikes

tham·no·phis \'thamnəfəs\ *n, cap* [NL, fr. *thamn-* + *-ophis*] **:** a genus of American colubrid snakes comprising the garter snake

tham·no·tet·tix \,thamnō'ted·iks\ *n, cap* [NL, fr. *thamn-* + Gk *tettix* cicada, of imit. origin] **:** a genus of leafhoppers including some that transmit virus diseases (as yellows) to many plants

¹tha·mu·dic \thə'müdik\ *adj, usu cap* [*Thamud*, an ancient people of Arabia (fr. Ar *Thamūd*) + E *-ic*] **:** of or relating to various old Semitic inscriptions in characters resembling the Sabaean

²thamudic \"\ *n* -s *usu cap* **:** a form of North Arabic that is known from inscriptions from the fifth century B.C. to the fourth century A.D.

¹than \thən, then, (,)than, *rapid sometimes* ən *or* ᵊn (*after* t, d, s, *or* z) *or* n (*as in one pronunciation*, ,bed·ə(r)ⁿnəthə(r)z, *of* "better than others")\ *conj* [ME *thanne, than, thenne, then*, fr. OE *thanne, thonne, thænne*; akin to OFris *than*, OS *thanna, thanne*, than, OHG *thanne, thanna, denne*; all fr. a prehistoric WGmc conj. derived fr. an adv. represented by OE *thanne, thonne, thænne* then — more at THEN] **1 a** — used as a function word to indicate that what immediately follows is the second member or the member taken as point of departure in a comparison expressive of inequality; used with comparative adjectives and comparative adverbs ⟨he is older ~ I⟩ ⟨deer can run faster ~ cows⟩ ⟨easier said ~ done⟩ ⟨arrived earlier ~ usual⟩ ⟨paid more ~ necessary⟩ ⟨knows better ~ to start a quarrel⟩ ⟨I regard him more highly ~ to suspect him⟩ ⟨has more ~ doubled his output⟩ ⟨he deceived us worse ~ if he had told us an outright lie⟩ ⟨he resolved, rather ~ yield, to die with honor —Samuel Butler †1680⟩ ⟨lemurs . . . are nearly related to the true monkeys, ~ which they are a more primitive type —James Stevenson-Hamilton⟩ **b** — used as a function word to indicate difference of kind, manner, or identity; used with some adjectives and adverbs that express diversity and with some words derived from them ⟨other woe ~ ours —John Keats⟩ ⟨anywhere else ~ at home⟩ ⟨he could hardly have behaved otherwise ~ he did⟩ ⟨others ~ the four who hold the . . . center of his stage —Carl Van Doren⟩ ⟨the task of education is not different for gifted children ~ for others —Elise Martens⟩; sometimes considered substandard except with *other, else*, and their derivatives, though use with *different* and *differently* is of long standing and found in many reputable authors; compare ¹DIFFERENT 1 **2 :** rather than — usu. used only after *prefer, preferable*, and *preferably*, and sometimes considered substandard even there ⟨I preferred to be called a coward ~ fight —John Reed⟩ **3 :** other than ⟨we have no alternative ~ to follow the sense of our own experience —K.L. Patton⟩ **4 :** WHEN ⟨had barely left the lift at the bottom ~ the lift bell started to ring —David Masters⟩ — used esp. after *scarcely* and *hardly* ⟨hardly had the birds dropped ~ she jumped into the water and retrieved them —G.G.Carter⟩

²than \"\ *prep* **:** in comparison with **:** by way of superiority or inferiority to — used by speakers on all educational levels and by many reputable writers with the objective case form of the following pronoun when the first term in the comparison is the subject of a verb or the predicative complement after a copulative verb though disapproved by some grammarians except in the phrase *than whom* ⟨they were both somewhat taller ~ her —Anthony Trollope⟩ ⟨man, ~ whom nothing can be more miserable —Jeremy Taylor⟩

tha·na \'tänə\ *n* -s [Hindi *thānā*, fr. Skt *sthāna* place, fr. *tiṣṭhati* he stands — more at STAND] **1 :** a military post in India during the British occupation **2 :** an Indian police station **:** police division serving as a unit of Indian local administration

tha·na·dar \,tänə'där\ *n* -s [Hindi *thānādār*, fr. *thānā* + Per *-dār* having] **:** the chief officer of a thana

than·age \'thānij\ *n* -s [ME, fr. ML *thanagium, thenagium*, fr. ME *theyn, thayn* + ML *-agium* (fr. OF *-age*) — more at THANE] **1 :** the land held by a thane **2 :** the rank or office of a thane

thanat- *or* **thanato-** *comb form* [Gk, fr. *thanatos*; akin to Skt *adhvanīt* it vanished and prob. to L *fumus* smoke — more at FUME] **:** death ⟨*thanatoid*⟩ ⟨*thanatology*⟩

than·a·to·coe·nose \,thanətō'sē,nōs\ *or* **than·a·to·coe·no·sis** \-tōsə'nōsəs\ *n, pl* **thanatocoeno·ses** \-sə'nō,sēz\ [NL *thanatocoenosis*, fr. *thanat-* + Gk *koinōsis* sharing — more at BIOCENOSE] **:** an assemblage of organisms or their parts brought together (as by deposition from flowing water) in nature after death

than·a·toid \'thanə,tȯid\ *adj* [*thanat-* + *-oid*] **:** resembling death **:** DEATHLY

than·a·to·log·i·cal \¦thanətə¦läjəkəl\ *adj* **:** of or belonging to thanatology

than·a·tol·o·gy \,thanə'täləjē\ *n* -ES [*thanat-* + *-logy*] **:** the description or study of the phenomena of somatic death

than·a·to·mania \¦thanə(,)tō+\ *n* [NL, fr. *thanat-* + *mania*] **1 :** suicidal mania **2 :** death by autosuggestion

than·a·to·phid·ia \,thanətə'fidēə\ *n pl* [NL, fr. *thanat-* + *Ophidia*] **:** venomous snakes

than·a·to·pho·bia \,thanətə'fōbēə\ *n* [NL, fr. *thanat-* + *phobia*] **:** fear of death ⟨thus he showed how Epicurus tried to rid the mind of ~ —O.S.J.Gogarty⟩

than·a·tos \'thanə,täs\ *n* -ES *usu cap* [Gk, death — more at THANAT-] **:** instinctual destructiveness **:** DEATH INSTINCT — contrasted with *Eros*

than·a·to·sis \,thanə'tōsəs\ *n* -ES [NL, fr. *thanat-* + *-osis*] **:** a state that in some respects resembles shock, is characterized by cessation of all voluntary activity and usu. by assumption of a posture suggestive of death, and occurs in various insects (as beetles) when disturbed

than·a·tot·ic \¦==¦täd·ik\ *adj* [*Thanatos* + *-otic*] **:** of or belonging to Thanatos

thane *or* **thegn** \'thān\ *n* -s [*thane* fr. ME *theyn, thayn*, fr. OE *thegn*; *thegn* fr. OE; akin to OS & OHG *thegan* warrior, freeman, thane, ON *thegn* freeman, thane, Gk *teknon* child, *tiktein* to give birth to, beget, Skt *takman* offspring, child; basic meaning: to beget, bear] **1 :** a retainer or free servant of a lord; *specif* **:** one holding lands from the king or other superior in Anglo-Saxon England and performing military and various other governmental services **2 a :** one holding land of a Scottish king **b :** the chief of a Scottish clan **c :** a Scots peer or noble

thane·dom *or* **thegn·dom** \-ndəm\ *n* -s [ME *thayndom*, fr. *theyn, thayn* thane + *-dom*] **:** THANAGE

thane·hood *or* **thegn·hood** \-n,hùd\ *n* **1 :** thanes as a class **2 :** the rank or office of a thane

thane·land *or* **thegn·land** \-n,land, -nlənd\ *n* **:** land granted to a thane by his feudal superior

thane·ship *or* **thegn·ship** \-n,ship\ *n* **:** THANAGE

than·ess \-nəs\ *n* -ES [*thane* + *-ess*] **:** the wife of a Scottish thane

¹thank \'thaŋk, 'thaiŋk\ *n* -s [ME *thank, thonk*, fr. OE *thanc, thonc* thought, will, mercy, favor, pleasure, gratitude; akin to OHG *thank, dank* memory, thought, gratitude, ON *thökk* gratitude, Goth *thanks* gratitude, L *tongēre* to know, Alb *tângë* resentment, Toch A *tuṅk-* love, Toch B *taṅkw*; basic meaning: to think, feel] **1 thanks** *pl* **:** kindly or grateful thoughts **:** GRATITUDE ⟨express my ~*s*⟩ **2** *obs* **:** worthiness to be thanked **:** MERIT, CREDIT ⟨if ye do good to them which do good to you, what ~ have ye? —Lk 6:33 (AV)⟩ **3 a :** an expression of gratitude **:** acknowledgment esp. by words of a benefit received from or offered by another ⟨never a ~ was accorded any for always battling . . . the foemen —W.B. Smith & Walter Miller⟩ — usu. used in pl.; often used in pl. in an utterance containing no verb and serving as an ordinarily courteous and somewhat informal expression of gratitude ⟨~*s*⟩ ⟨many ~*s*⟩ ⟨~*s* a lot⟩ ⟨~*s* for helping me⟩ ⟨no, ~*s*⟩ **b thanks** *pl* **:** an expression of gratitude to God in the form of a short prayer before or after a meal — used esp. in the phrases *give thanks* and *return thanks* — **no thanks to :** not as a result of any benefit conferred by ⟨I am feeling better now, *no thanks to* you⟩ — **thanks to :** with the help of ⟨*thanks to* his stepmother . . . he secured a good education —W.A.Robinson⟩ **:** owing to ⟨it took us a couple of days to get there, *thanks to* fog —D.B. Putnam⟩

²thank \"\ *vb* -ED/-ING/-S [ME *thanken, thonken*, fr. OE *thancian, thoncian*; akin to OHG *thankōn, danchōn* to thank, ON *thakka*; denominative fr. the root of E ¹*thank*] *vt* **1 a :** to express gratitude to **:** acknowledge esp. by words a benefit received from or offered by ⟨~*ed* her uncle for the birthday present⟩ — used in the phrase *thank you* with a first person subject or without any subject as the most polite formula for expressing gratitude on the part of the speaker or writer or the group to which he belongs ⟨~ you very much for the loan⟩ ⟨I ~ you for your music —Shak.⟩; used in such phrases as *thank God, thank goodness, thank heaven* usu. without any subject to express gratitude or more often only pleasure or satisfaction on the part of the speaker or writer ⟨~ God nobody was killed in the wreck⟩ ⟨the beds are all made, ~ goodness⟩ **b :** to hold responsible **:** give the credit or blame to ⟨whether we eat the food directly as the plant stored it or indirectly after some animal has converted it into meat or milk, we still have to ~ the plant for it —J.B.Robson⟩ ⟨had only his inexperience to ~ for his failure to get ahead⟩ **c :** REQUEST — used esp. after *will* or *'ll* to imply forced courtesy or barely veiled hostility ⟨I'll ~ you to open the window⟩ ⟨I will ~ you to mind your own business⟩ **d :** to feel gratitude to ⟨a textbook that thousands of teachers will ~ the author for writing⟩ **2 :** to express gratitude for ⟨ten thousandfold the favor I shall ~ —Robert Browning⟩ ~ *vi* **:** to express gratitude — **thank one's stars** *or* **thank one's lucky stars :** to congratulate oneself on one's good fortune **:** consider oneself fortunate

thank·ee *or* **thanky** \-kē\ *also* **thank·ye** \-kyē\ *interj* [alter. of *thank you*] — used to express gratitude

thank·er \-kə(r)\ *n* -s **:** one that thanks

thank·ful \-kfəl\ *adj, sometimes* **thankfuller**; *sometimes* **thankfullest** [ME, fr. OE *thancful* thoughtful, contented, thankful, fr. *thanc* thought, pleasure, gratitude + *-ful*] **1 :** conscious of benefit received and kindly disposed toward the benefactor **:** GRATEFUL ⟨a ~ heart⟩ **2 :** expressive of thanks or gratitude ⟨a ~ service⟩ **3 :** well pleased **:** GLAD ⟨I was ~ they could not see my face, for I was blushing —Paul Roche⟩ — **thank·ful·ly** \-fəlē, -li\ *adv* — **thank·ful·ness** *n* -ES

thank·less \-kləs\ *adj* **1 :** not expressing or feeling gratitude **:** UNGRATEFUL ⟨how sharper than a serpent's tooth it is to have a ~ child —Shak.⟩ **2 :** not obtaining thanks **:** not likely to obtain thanks **:** UNAPPRECIATED ⟨a ~ task⟩ — **thank·less·ly** *adv* — **thank·less·ness** *n* -ES

thank offering *n* **:** an offering made as an expression of thanks

thanks *pl of* THANK, *pres 3d sing of* THANK

thanksgiver \'=,=\ *n* **:** one that gives thanks

thanksgiving \(')=¦==\ *n* **1 :** the act of giving thanks **:** acknowledgment of favors or benefits ⟨hymns of high ~ —John Keble⟩ **2 :** an utterance (as a prayer) that is often in a set form of words and that expresses gratitude esp. for divine mercies ⟨in the ~ before meat —Shak.⟩ **3 a :** a public acknowledgment or celebration of divine goodness and mercies **b** *usu cap* **:** a day appointed for such celebration: as (1) **:** THANKSGIVING DAY a (2) **:** THANKSGIVING DAY b

thanksgiving day *n, usu cap T&D* **:** a day appointed for giving thanks for divine goodness and mercies: as **a :** the fourth Thursday in November observed as a legal holiday in the U.S. **b :** the second Monday in October observed as a legal holiday in Canada

thankworthy \'=,==\ *adj* [ME, fr. *thank* + *worthy*] **:** worthy of thanks or gratitude **:** MERITORIOUS

thank-you \'=,=\ *n* -s [fr. the phrase *thank you*] **:** a polite expression of one's gratitude as by saying "thank you"

thank-you-ma'am \'==,=\ *n* -s [prob. so called fr. the fact that such rough spots cause a passenger in a vehicle to double over in a way reminiscent of the bow formerly prescribed as an adjunct of an expression of thanks to a woman] **:** a bump or depression in a road; *specif* **:** a small ridge or hollow made across a road esp. on a hillside to cause water to run off

thap·sia \'thapsēə\ *n* [NL, fr. L, a poisonous plant, fr. Gk, fr. *Thapsos*, town and peninsula in Sicily] **1** -s **:** a plant of the genus *Thapsia*; *esp* **:** DEADLY CARROT **2** *cap* **:** a small genus of herbs (family Umbelliferae) of the Mediterranean region having the flowers in compound umbels without involucres and the fruit broadly winged

thap·sic acid \'thapsik-\ *n* [NL *Thapsia* (genus name of the deadly carrot *Thapsia garganica*) + E *-ic*] **:** a crystalline dicarboxylic acid $HOOC(CH_2)_{14}COOH$ found in the roots of the deadly carrot and the wax of a juniper (*Juniperus sabina*); hexadecane-dioic acid

¹thar \'thär\ *dial var of* THERE

²thar *var of* TAHR

tharf \'thärf\ *adj* [ME *therf, tharf* unleavened, fr. OE *theorf*; akin to OHG *derb* unleavened, ON *thjarfr* unleavened, insipid, OE *starian* to stare — more at STARE] *dial Brit* **:** HEAVY, STIFF, UNBENDING

tharf·cake \'thärf,kāk\ *n* [ME *therfcake*, fr. *therf* unleavened + *cake*] *dial Eng* **:** a cake made of unleavened flour or meal dough rolled thin and baked

thar·ge·lia \thär'gelēə, -'jēl-\ *n* -s *usu cap* [Gk *Thargēlia*, pl.] **:** an ancient Athenian and Ionian festival celebrated in May in honor of Apollo

thar·par·kar \(')tär¦pärkər\ *n* [fr. *Thar (and) Parkar*, district in Pakistan] **1** *usu cap* **:** an Indian breed of pale gray humped dairy cattle with lyrate horns **2** -s *often cap* **:** an animal of the Tharparkar breed

tha·ru \'tä(,)rü\ *n* -s *usu cap* **:** a member of a valley-dwelling people of Mongol origin in Nepal

¹tha·si·an \'thash(ē)ən\ *n* -s *cap* [*Thasos*, island in Aegean sea + E *-ian*] **:** a native or inhabitant of the island of Thasos in the Aegean sea

²thasian \"\ *adj, usu cap* **:** of or relating to Thasos

thas·pi·um \'thaspēəm\ *n, cap* [NL, irreg. fr. *Thapsia*] **:** a small genus of herbs (family Umbelliferae) found in eastern No. America that have yellow flowers and have fruit with all the ribs prominently winged

¹that \'that, *usu* -ad·+V\ *pron, pl* **those** \'thōz\ [ME, fr. OE *thæt*, neut. demonstrative pron. & definite article; akin to OHG *thaz, daz*, neut. demonstrative pron. & definite article, ON *that*, neut. demonstrative pron., Goth *thata*, neut. demonstrative pron. & definite article, L *istud*, neut. demonstrative pron., Gk *to*, neut. demonstrative pron. & definite article, Skt *tad*, neut. demonstrative pron. & adj.] **1 a :** the person, thing, or idea pointed to, mentioned, or understood from the situation **:** the one indicated ⟨who is ~?⟩ ⟨~ is my father⟩ ⟨what kind of tree is ~?⟩ ⟨~ is a maple⟩ ⟨*those* are my sisters talking to the man in the corner⟩ ⟨*those* are violets⟩ ⟨he wanted to become a professional writer but ~ was no easy matter⟩ — often used as subject of a form of the verb *be*, usu. the contracted third person singular present indicative *'s*, in expressions indicating or implying that the person mentioned in the predicate is following or is expected shortly to follow an approved course of action ⟨hold the pen like this, ~*'s* a good girl⟩ ⟨take your medicine, ~*'s* a good boy⟩ ⟨~*'s* the boy⟩; sometimes used disparagingly of a person who has been mentioned by name or otherwise circumstantially identified ⟨the boy who sits across from my daughter in history class offered to take her to the football game but she refused him and told her friends she wouldn't be seen in public with ~⟩ **b** *Scot* **:** the following thing — used to point forward to a noun clause occurring later in the sentence **c :** the time just mentioned **:** the action or event just mentioned viewed with reference to the time of its occurrence — used after any of various prepositions ⟨he will not be there until eleven o'clock, and I expect to get there before ~⟩ ⟨read to the end of the chapter, and after ~ he went to bed⟩ **d :** the one specified as follows **:** the kind specified as follows **:** the thing specified as follows — used before a modifying expression other than a clause, esp. a prepositional phrase or a participle with or without a modifier or an adjective with or without a modifier ⟨one of the first major tasks confronting the pioneer was ~ of clearing some land —W.M.Kollmorgen⟩ ⟨the symptoms of the disease . . . sounded a good deal like *those* of polio —*Time*⟩ ⟨the purest water is ~ produced by distillation⟩ ⟨the organism that causes Malta fever . . . is closely related to ~ responsible for brucellosis —S.A.Waksman⟩ **e :** the blow just being dealt **:** the insult or injury just being inflicted — used in the expression *take that* **f :** a settled matter **:** something about which no further action can be taken — used in the predicate after a form of the verb *be* with *that* (sense 1a) as subject ⟨I won't sell it for less than fifty dollars and that is ~⟩ **g :** a person, thing, idea, or group of the indicated kind **:** such a one **:** such ones **:** such a thing ⟨when you want something you can't have it, and by the time you can have it you've stopped wanting it, but ~*'s* life⟩ ⟨wily and destructive —~*'s* foxes for you⟩ **2 a** (1) **:** the one farther away **:** the one less immediately under observation or discussion ⟨*those* are elm trees and these are maples⟩ ⟨~ is porcelain and this is plastic⟩ — contrasted with *this* (2) **:** the former ⟨two principles in human nature reign; self-love, to urge, and reason, to restrain; nor this a good, nor ~ a bad we call —Alexander Pope⟩ — contrasted with *this* **b :** another thing — sometimes contrasted with *this* ⟨talking about this and ~⟩; sometimes used as second member of a three-part series with *this* as the first member and *the other* as the third ⟨buying this, ~, or the other⟩ **3 a** — used as a function word after *and* to indicate emphatic repetition of the idea expressed by a previous word or phrase which is not necessarily a noun or noun equivalent ⟨he shall pay . . . , and ~ soundly —Shak.⟩ ⟨he was helpful, and ~ to an unusual degree⟩ **b** — used as a function word immediately before or immediately after a word group consisting of either a verbal auxiliary or a form of the verb *be* preceded by either *there* or a personal pronoun subject to indicate emphatic repetition of the idea expressed by a previous verb or predicate noun or predicate adjective ⟨is he capable? He is ~⟩ ⟨he told the whole truth; ~ he did⟩ **4 a :** the one **:** the thing **:** the kind **:** SOMETHING, ANYTHING — used as antecedent to a relative pronoun ⟨recognize the truth of ~ which is true⟩ ⟨one of *those* who introduced into the United States the results of foreign . . . scholarship —H.N.Fowler⟩ or in a like function with reference to a relative adverb ⟨the senses are ~ whereby we experience the material world⟩ or to a relative clause containing no relative pronoun or relative adverb ⟨what's ~ you say⟩ **b** *those pl* **:** some persons — used as antecedent to a relative pronoun ⟨there are *those* who think that the time has now come for a further step —*Report: (Canadian) Royal Commission on Nat'l Development*⟩ — **all that 1 a :** everything of the kind indicated ⟨tact, discretion, and *all that*⟩ ⟨he made an eloquent speech, but his hearers were unconvinced for *all that*⟩ **b :** more things of the same kind ⟨a store where you can get cabbage and carrots and *all that*⟩ **2 :** the extreme degree or quantity that has been indicated or implied — used in negative comparisons after *as* ⟨not as cold as *all that*⟩ — **and that :** and more things of the same kind **:** and so forth ⟨blow all their money on tarts and cards, on getting tight *and that* —Robert Westerby⟩ — **at that 1 :** in spite of what has been said or implied **:** taking everything into consideration ⟨we might be worse off *at that*⟩ **2 :** in addition to what has already been said **:** into the bargain **:** BESIDES ⟨a bridge built on stilts, and weak stilts *at that* —O.S.Nock⟩ **3 :** in the state or form indicated ⟨we left it *at that*⟩ — **that is** *or* **that is to say :** the following or immediately preceding word or word group may express the intended meaning more understandably or more accurately than a previous word or word group — used to introduce or accompany an explanation or correction

²that \"\ *adj, pl* **those** \"\ [ME, fr. OE *thæt*, neut. demonstrative pron. & definite article — more at ¹THAT] **1 a :** being the person, thing, or idea pointed to, mentioned, or understood from the situation **:** being the one indicated ⟨~ dog⟩ ⟨*those* houses⟩ **b :** being the one specified or singled out — used interchangeably with the definite article *the* but usu. expressing slightly greater emphasis; used almost exclusively before nouns having a following modifier (as a phrase or clause) ⟨three o'clock in the afternoon, ~ last moment when the sun's intensity may be felt —A.N.Lytle⟩ ⟨a little understood . . . subject of bird migration —F.C.Lincoln⟩ ⟨*those* topics that lie outside the scope of this book —Fred Hoyle⟩ **c :** the well known **:** being the one about whom or about which further comment is unnecessary ⟨*those* little steamers that are Venice's street cars —Claudia Cassidy⟩ ⟨one of *those* election bets⟩ — often used disparagingly ⟨*those* feet of his⟩ ⟨~ brother of yours⟩ **d :** SUCH **:** such a **:** so great a ⟨~ gentleness . . . as I was wont to have —Shak.⟩ ⟨perplexed his mind to ~ degree that he was fain . . . to scratch his head —Charles Dickens⟩ **2 a :** the farther away **:** the less immediately under observation or discussion ⟨this chair or ~ one⟩ — contrasted with *this* **b :** the other **:** ANOTHER — sometimes contrasted with *this* ⟨we argued it this way and we argued it ~ way —Lilian Balch⟩; sometimes used as second member of a three-part series with *this* as the first member and *the other* as the third ⟨this, ~, and the other way⟩ — **that way 1 :** in the manner indicated **:** as indicated ⟨what makes him act *that way*⟩ **2 a :** in or into the condition indicated ⟨a very successful man and it is easy to see how he got *that way*⟩ **b :** in a lovesick condition ⟨those two are *that way* about each other⟩ ⟨Texans are *that way* about quarter horses —*Time*⟩

³that \thəlt, (,)tha| *sometimes* _the|, *usu* |d·+V\ *conj* [ME, fr. OE *thæt*, fr. *thæt*, neut. demonstrative pron. — more at ¹THAT] **1 a** (1) — used as a function word to introduce a subordinate clause that is a noun equivalent, esp. the subject or object of a verb, the predicate nominative after a copulative verb, or the substantive expression anticipated by the expletive *it* occurring as grammatical subject or object of a verb ⟨~ many historic houses . . . are rapidly disappearing for lack of care has been emphasized by several organizations —*Report: (Canadian) Royal Commission on Nat'l Development*⟩ ⟨courts declare ~ they have nothing to do with theoretic economics —M.R. Cohen⟩ ⟨the idea is ~, without ruining the sport, you want to protect the participants —Charles Oldfather⟩ ⟨it is interesting ~ so many of the books which have really stirred things up . . . have been small books —A.J.Nock⟩ ⟨he made it clear ~ he did not agree⟩ (2) — used as a function word to introduce a subordinate clause anticipated by the expletive *it* occurring

as subject of a form of the copulative verb *be* when what follows the copulative verb is an adverb or adverbial phrase logically modifying the verb of the clause introduced by *that* ⟨it was there ~ I first met her⟩ ⟨it was almost as if in entreaty or reproach ~ she put her next question —Walter de la Mare⟩ (3) — used as a function word to introduce a subordinate clause that is joined as complement or modifier to a noun or adjective or is in apposition with a noun ⟨we are certain ~ this is true⟩ ⟨the certainty ~ this is true⟩ ⟨the fear ~ something unpleasant may happen⟩ ⟨the fact ~ you are here⟩ **b** (1) — used as a function word to introduce a subordinate clause that is the object of a preposition; usu. interpreted as being joined with the preposition to form a compound subordinating conjunction; used currently and frequently in only a few combinations, esp. *but that, except that, in that, notwithstanding that,* and *save that,* and occurring as an archaism in a few others, esp. *after that, before that, for that, till that,* and *until that* ⟨some of his earlier writings . . . have become classics in ~ they are read by most students professionally interested in anthropology —D.G.Mandelbaum⟩ ⟨if we sin wilfully after ~ we have received the knowledge of the truth —Heb 10:26 (AV)⟩ (2) — used as a function word to introduce a subordinate clause that is in absolute construction with a participle; often interpreted as being joined with the participle to form a compound subordinating conjunction ⟨men and women . . . could yet live in an ideal society provided ~ they were governed by a hard-living intellectual minority —Maurice Cranston⟩ **c** — used as a function word to introduce an exclamatory clause expressing a strong emotion esp. of surprise or sorrow or indignation; sometimes preceded by an interjection or other short exclamation ⟨oh Lord! ~ ever I lived to see this day⟩ ⟨~ it should come to this!⟩ ⟨alas! ~ all we loved of him should be . . . as if it had not been —P.B. Shelley⟩ **2 a** — used as a function word to introduce a subordinate clause expressing purpose or desired result ⟨cutting down expenses ~ her son might inherit an unencumbered estate —W.B.Yeats⟩; often preceded by *so* or *in order* and sometimes by *to the end* **b** — used as a function word to introduce an exclamatory clause expressing a wish; sometimes preceded by an interjection or other short exclamation ⟨oh, ~ the world could be persuaded of the truth of that maxim —W.S.Gilbert⟩ **3 a** — used as a function word to introduce a subordinate clause expressing a reason or cause ⟨rejoice ~ you are lightened of a load —Robert Browning⟩; often used with *should* in the clause which it introduces ⟨I am sorry ~ you should think so⟩ **b** — used as a function word after *not* to introduce a clause making a statement that is understood to be not true and therefore impossible to be taken as the reason or basis for an immediately preceding or following statement ⟨she ignored my suggestion — not ~ I care⟩ ⟨not ~ it matters, but the shirts aren't back from the laundry yet⟩ **4 a** — used as a function word to introduce a subordinate clause expressing consequence, result, or effect ⟨are of sufficient importance ~ they cannot be neglected —Hannah Wormington⟩; often preceded by *so* or *such* ⟨he gazed so long ~ both his eyes were dazzled —Alfred Tennyson⟩ **b** — used as a function word after a question or negative statement to introduce a clause expressing an appropriate consequence of what is being questioned or denied ⟨am I a dog, ~ you come to me with sticks —1 Sam 17:43 (RSV)⟩ ⟨I am not a doormat, ~ you should walk all over me⟩ **c** — used as a function word to introduce a negative subordinate clause after a negative main clause and to indicate that what is denied in the subordinate clause is the inevitable result or invariable accompaniment of what is denied in the main clause ⟨I can't speak, ~ you don't try to insult me —Douglas Jerrold⟩ **5** *archaic* — used as a function word at the beginning of the second of two subordinate clauses in parallel construction to replace the conjunction which introduces the first such clause ⟨when he had carried Rome and ~ we looked for no less spoil than glory —Shak.⟩ **6** — used as a function word after a subordinating conjunction without modifying its meaning ⟨if ~ thy bent of love be honorable —Shak.⟩; used currently and frequently in only a few combinations, esp. *now that* **7 a** — used as a function word to introduce a subordinate clause modifying an adverb or adverbial expression ⟨will go anywhere ~ he is invited⟩ ⟨the more ~ doubts assailed me . . . the louder I apologized —Eugene Lyons⟩ **b** *obs* — used as a function word to introduce a subordinate clause that is the equivalent of a sentence adverb modifying the entire main clause ⟨thou hast well done ~ thou art come —Acts 10:33 (AV)⟩ — **for all that** *conj* : in spite of the fact that : ALTHOUGH ⟨I don't trust him, *for all that* so many people consider him reliable⟩

⁴**that** \"\ *pron* [ME, fr. OE *thæt,* neut. relative pron., fr. *thæt,* neut. demonstrative pron. — more at ¹THAT] **1 a** — used as a function word to introduce a restrictive relative clause and to serve as a substitute within that clause for the substantive modified by that clause; used in any grammatical relation within the relative clause except that of a possessive or the object of a preceding preposition ⟨a court jester ~ fell in love with a queen —M.I.Seiden⟩ ⟨the cow ~ started the Chicago fire —L.A.White⟩ ⟨another conclusion ~ emerges clearly from this . . . statement —*Times Lit. Supp.*⟩ ⟨this ideal theater . . . ~ he discerns —Stark Young⟩ ⟨those beliefs ~ demonstrate they are trustworthy —J.L.Childs⟩ ⟨the responsibilities ~ literature owes to itself —Harry Levin⟩ ⟨a subject ~ most Americans probably think nothing need be said about —J.W.Clark b. 1907⟩ ⟨thoughtful journalist and conscientious citizen ~ he was, he did not look with any satisfaction on that little story —F.L.Mott⟩; sometimes used after *so* or *such* with the implication that the action or state expressed in the clause introduced by *that* is a real or appropriate consequence of what is expressed by the phrase containing *so* or *such* ⟨who is here so base ~ would be a bondman —Shak.⟩ **b** — used as a function word to introduce a nonrestrictive relative clause and to serve as a substitute within that clause for the substantive modified by that clause; used in any grammatical relation within the relative clause except that of a possessive or the object of a preceding preposition ⟨out of the forty thousand who were within the walls eight hundred only, ~ had fled at the first sound of the attack, made their way to the camp —J.A.Froude⟩ ⟨it was his specialty, ~ he never liked to do when there was a crowd —James Jones⟩ **2 a** : at which : in which : on which : by which : with which : to which — used not only to serve within its restrictive relative clause as a substitute for the substantive modified by that clause but also additionally to express a relation of conformity, agreement, or identity esp. in reference to time ⟨each year ~ the lectures were given⟩ ⟨I will drink no more of the fruit of the vine, until that day ~ I drink it new in the kingdom of God —Mk 14:25 (AV)⟩ ⟨work in the arts is significant in the measure ~ it has submitted to discipline —*General Education in a Free Society*⟩ ⟨this author has never been neglected to the same extent ~ some of his contemporaries have been⟩ ⟨treated with the same respect ~ others are⟩ **b** : according to what : to the extent of what — used after a negative ⟨has never been here ~ I know of⟩ ⟨have never met him ~ I can recall⟩ **3 a** *archaic* : that which — used to introduce a relative clause with no expressed antecedent ⟨~ thou doest, do quickly —Jn 13:27 (AV)⟩ **b** *obs* : the person who : persons who — used to introduce a relative clause with no expressed antecedent ⟨I am ~ I am —Exod 3:14 (AV)⟩ ⟨'tis he ~ can rule Naples as well as he —Shak.⟩

⁵**that** \ˈthat, *usu* -ad.+V\ *adv* [ME, fr. *that,* adj.] **1** *dial* : to such an extent — used as modifier of a following adjective or adverb followed in turn by a clause that completes the meaning ⟨I'm ~ tired I can hardly walk⟩ **2 a** : to the extent that has already been indicated ⟨it is a hot day . . . when boys devote themselves principally to conversation and this day was ~ hot —Booth Tarkington⟩ **b** : to the extent that is being indicated by some nonlinguistic reference (as a gesture) ⟨a nail about ~ long⟩ **3** *dial* : EXTREMELY ⟨she'll be ~ pleased when I tell her the news⟩

⁶**that** \"\ *n* -s [¹*that*] **1** : one of the members and usu. the second of a pair or series ⟨civilization, they agree, faces an inexorable alternative, either this or that; but their thises are irreconcilable and even their ~s are not the same —*Saturday Rev.*⟩ — sometimes used with an initial capital to stand for a proper name which is not mentioned ⟨Squire This and Farmer *That* whom he had known since boyhood —Max Peacock⟩; contrasted with *this* **2** : an existent thing apart from whatever may be known or stated about it : the substratum of an entity in abstraction from all its qualities — compare ⁴WHAT 2b

that·away \ˈthad·ə,wā, -atə,-\ *adv* [alter. of the phrase *that way*] **1** *dial* : in that direction **2** *dial* : in that manner : like that

¹**thatch** \ˈthach\ *vb* -ED/-ING/-ES [ME *thecchen, thacchen,* fr. OE *theccan* to cover, conceal; akin to OE *thæc* roof, OHG *dah* roof, *decchen, decken* to cover, ON *thak* roof, thatch, *thekja* to cover, L *tegere* to cover, *tegula* tile, Gk *stegein* to cover, shelter, *stegos, tegos,* roof, Skt *sthagati* he covers] *vt* : to roof or cover with or as if with thatch : make of thatch ~ *vi* : to cover something with thatch : make something (as a roof) of thatch

²**thatch** \"\ *n* -ES [ME *thacche,* fr. *thecchen, thacchen* to thatch] **1 a** : a plant material (as rushes, reeds, palm leaves, or esp. straw) arranged in a thick mat with the individual parts parallel and sloping so as to shed water and used as a sheltering cover esp. of a house ⟨a house with a roof of ~ —Fiske Kimball⟩ ⟨we all went about in thatched-straw raincoats and peaked ~ hats —Nora Waln⟩ **b** : a sheltering cover (as a house roof) made of such material **2** : something resembling the thatch of a house ⟨the cool spring that flowed out from under a bank into a ~ of dark watercress —Willa Cather⟩; *esp* : the hair of one's head ⟨a man with a cap on his white ~ —Eudora Welty⟩ **3** : THATCH PALM

thatch·er \-chə(r)\ *n* -s [ME *thaccher,* fr. *thacchen, thecchen* to thatch + *-er*] : one that thatches

thatch grass *n* : any of various usu. tall coarse grasses or occas. other plants that are used or suitable for use in thatching; *esp* : any of several southern African grasses of the genus *Hyparrhenia*

thatch·ing \-chiŋ\ *n* -s [ME *thecchyng,* fr. gerund of *thecchen, thacchen* to thatch] **1** : the act or art of covering with thatch **2** [²*thatch* + *-ing*] : THATCH 1a

thatch palm *also* **thatch tree** *n* : any of various palms (as the nipa) whose leaves are used in thatching; *esp* : any of several tropical American palms esp. of the genera *Thrinax, Sabal,* or *Inodes* — see SILVER THATCH

¹**that'n** \-thatᵊn\ *adv* [irreg. fr. ¹*that*] *dial chiefly Eng* : in that way

²**that'n** \"\ [by alter.] *dial* : that one

that·ness *n* -ES [¹*that* + *-ness*] **1** : the condition of being an existent thing apart from whatever may be known or stated about that thing **2** : resemblance to or affinity with one of the members and usu. the second of a pair or series ⟨metaphor . . . brings out the thisness of a that, or the ~ of a this —K.D. Burke⟩

thau *var of* TAW

thau·ma·site \ˈthȯmə,sīt\ *n* -s [ISV *thaumas-* (fr. Gk *thaumasios* wondrous, fr. *thauma* miracle, wonder) + *-ite* — more at THEATER] : a white mineral $Ca_4Al_6Si_6O_{24}(SO_4,CO_3,Cl_2)$ consisting of a basic silicate, carbonate, and sulfate of calcium (hardness 3.5, sp. gr. 1.88)

thau·ma·tol·o·gy \,thȯməˈtäləjē\ *n* -ES [ISV *thaumato-* (fr. Gk, fr. *thaumat-, thauma* miracle, wonder) + *-logy* — more at THEATER] : doctrine, discussion, or study of the performing of miracles

thau·ma·trope \ˈthȯmə,trōp\ *n* -s [Gk *thauma* miracle, wonder + E *-trope*] : an optical instrument or toy that shows the persistence of an impression upon the eye and that consists of a card having on its opposite faces different designs that appear to the eye combined in a single picture when the card is whirled rapidly round a diameter by the strings that hold it — **thau·ma·trop·i·cal** \ˌ==ˈträpəkəl\ *adj*

thau·ma·turge \ˈthȯmə,tərj, -təj, -təij\ *also* **thau·ma·turg** \-rg\ *n* -s [F & NL; F *thaumaturge,* fr. NL *thaumaturgus,* fr. Gk *thaumatourgos* working miracles, fr. *thaumat-, thauma* miracle + *-ourgos* working (akin to Gk *ergon* work) — more at THEATER, WORK] : a performer of miracles (as a saint or magician)

thau·ma·tur·gic \ˌ==ˈtərjik, -təj-, -təij-\ *also* **thau·ma·tur·gi·cal** \-jəkəl, -jēk-\ *adj* [NL *thaumaturgicus,* fr. *thaumaturgus* + L *-icus* -ic, -ical] **1** : performing miracles **2** : of, connected with, or dependent on thaumaturgy

thau·ma·tur·gist \ˈ==,tərjəst, -təj-, -təij-\ *n* -s : a performer of miracles; *esp* : MAGICIAN

thau·ma·tur·gus \ˌ==ˈtərgəs\ *n, pl* **thaumatur·gi** \-r,jī\ [NL] : a performer of miracles

thau·ma·tur·gy \ˈ==,tərjē, -təj-, -təij-, -ji\ *n* -ES [Gk *thaumatourgia,* fr. *thaumatourgos* + *-ia* -y] **1** : the performance of miracles **2** : HOCUS-POCUS 3 ⟨any metaphysics which portrays reality as something strangely unfamiliar or beyond the ordinary grasp, stamps itself as ~ —C.I.Lewis⟩ **syn** see MAGIC

thau·me·to·poea \,thȯmətōˈpēə\ *n, cap* [NL, prob. irreg. fr. *thaumat-, thauma* miracle + *-o-* + *-poiia* (fr. *poiein* to make) — more at POET] : a genus of chiefly palaearctic notodontid moths comprising the processionary moths

¹**thaw** \ˈthȯ\ *vb* **thawed** *or dial* **thew** \ˈthü\ **thawed** \-ȯd\ *also archaic* **thawn** \-ȯn\ **thawing; thaws** [ME *thawen,* fr. OE *thawian;* akin to MD *dooyen, douwen* to thaw, OHG *douwen, dōan, dewen,* ON *theyja* to thaw, L *tabes* wasting disease, *tabēre* to waste away, melt, *tabescere* to melt gradually, decay, Gk *tēkein* to melt, Ossetic *thayun* to thaw, melt, Arm *tʻanam* I moisten; basic meaning: to melt] *vt* **1 a** : to cause (something frozen) to go into a liquid state ⟨~*ing* the ice⟩ **b** : to rid of stiffness, hardness, numbness, ice, or other effect of cold by warming ⟨held his hands close to the fire to ~ them out⟩ ⟨~*ing* frozen vegetables⟩ **2** : to rid of cold aloofness or hostility : cause to grow gentle or genial ⟨the convivial crowd soon ~*ed* him out⟩ **3** : to nullify or cause to disappear as if by melting ⟨she can unlock the clasping charm, and ~ the numbing spell —John Milton⟩ **4** : to bring into a condition in which adjustments, adaptations, or modifications are possible ⟨broke through the static repose of the Aristotelian system, and, so to speak, ~*ed* its frozen logic —P.E.More⟩ **5** : to activate or change in a manner that reverses the effect of a legislative, administrative, or economic freeze ⟨~*ing* out the frozen assets⟩ ~ *vi* **1 a** : to go from a frozen to a liquid state (as of ice or snow) : MELT **b** : to become free of stiffness, hardness, numbness, ice, or other effect of cold as a result of being warmed ⟨the ground has ~*ed* out⟩ **2** : to be warm enough to melt ice and snow — used with *it* in reference to the weather ⟨it is ~*ing* today⟩ **3** : to abandon aloofness, reserve, or hostility : grow gentle or genial : UNBEND **4** : to become mobile, active, or susceptible to change ⟨in medieval times property and people were all frozen, but with the opening of the Great Frontier both ~*ed* out and began to flow and mingle —W.P.Webb⟩

²**thaw** \"\ *n* -s [ME *thawe,* fr. *thawen, v.*] **1 a** : the action, fact, or process of thawing **b** : a warmth of weather sufficient to thaw ice or snow : period when the weather is so warm as to thaw ice or snow ⟨a January ~⟩ **2** : the action or process of becoming less aloof, less hostile, or more genial **3** : reversal, weakening, or termination of a legislative, administrative, or economic freeze

thaw house *also* **thawing house** *n* : a small building fitted and equipped for thawing frozen dynamite

thaw·less \-ōləs\ *adj* : never thawing

thawy \-ōi, -ōē\ *adj* -ER/-EST : characterized by thawing : tending to thaw

ThD *abbr or n* -s [NL *theologiae doctor*] : a doctor of theology

thd *abbr* **1** thread **2** thunderhead

thdr *abbr* thunder

¹**the** *before consonants & esp South before vowels also* thə, *before vowels* thē *or* thi, *in sense 1r often* ˈthē\ *definite article* [ME, fr. OE *thē,* masc. demonstrative pron. & definite article, alter. (influenced by the oblique cases — as *thæs,* gen., & *thǣm,* dat. — & by *thæt,* neut. demonstrative pron. & definite article) of *sē;* akin to ON *sā,* masc. demonstrative pron. & adj., Goth *sa,* masc. demonstrative pron. & definite article, Gk *ho,* masc. demonstrative pron. & definite article, Skt *sa,* masc. demonstrative pron. & adj. — more at THAT] **1 a** — used as a function word to indicate that a following noun or noun equivalent refers to someone or something previously mentioned or clearly understood from the context or the situation ⟨if anyone offers you a dollar for that picture, take ~ dollar⟩ ⟨put ~ cat out⟩ ⟨this is a good shirt but ~ sleeves are too long⟩; sometimes used archaically before the relative pronoun *which* ⟨a foolish quest, ~ which to gain and keep he sacrificed all rest —Lord Byron⟩; found in obsolete usage as recently as the 17th century before the relative pronoun *whom* ⟨your mistress, from ~ whom I see there's no disjunction to be made —Shak.⟩ **b** — used as a function word before an abstract noun; obsolete except with a very few nouns with which it appears in certain set constructions, in some of which it has some particularizing force ⟨a fight to ~ finish⟩ ⟨portrayed to ~ life⟩ ⟨~ truth is that I was absent⟩ ⟨that's ~ truth⟩ ⟨that's ~ bunk⟩ ⟨to keep ~ peace⟩ **c** — used as a function word to indicate that a following noun or noun equivalent refers to someone or something that is unique or is thought of as unique or exists as only one at a time ⟨~ Lord⟩ ⟨~ Messiah⟩ ⟨~ devil⟩ ⟨~ sun⟩ ⟨~ earth⟩ ⟨~ universe⟩ ⟨~ Pope⟩ ⟨~ Dalai Lama⟩; often used with some kinds of geographical names, esp. of rivers ⟨~ Hudson⟩, oceans ⟨~ Atlantic⟩, seas ⟨~ Adriatic⟩, and groups (as of islands or mountains) that have a plural name but a distinctive identity ⟨~ Azores⟩ ⟨~ Alps⟩; often used with names of literary or artistic works ⟨~ *Paradise Lost*⟩ ⟨~ Mona Lisa⟩ ⟨~ Moonlight Sonata⟩ **d** — used as a function word before nouns that designate natural phenomena or points of the compass ⟨~ night is cold⟩ ⟨~ heat is intense⟩ ⟨~ wind came from ~ east⟩ ⟨~ clouds look threatening⟩ **e** — used as a function word before some esp. rather old-fashioned or nontechnical names of diseases ⟨~ palsy⟩ ⟨~ measles⟩ ⟨~ piles⟩ ⟨~ flu⟩ ⟨~ pox⟩ **f** — used as a function word before a title or a class name to designate the particular holder of that title or the particular member of that class that is most familiar to the speaker or writer by reason of the nation or culture of which he is a member ⟨~ President⟩ ⟨~ Congress⟩ ⟨~ Civil War⟩ ⟨~ west coast⟩ ⟨~ Renaissance⟩ **g** (1) *Brit* — used as a function word before the name of a day of the week to indicate reference to the next ensuing day so named in the period immediately under consideration ⟨five days later, on ~ Sunday —David Masters⟩ (2) — used as a function word before a noun denoting time to indicate reference to that which is present or immediate or is under consideration ⟨news of ~ hour⟩ ⟨best movie of ~ week⟩ ⟨he was at a loss for ~ moment⟩ ⟨in ~ future⟩ (3) *chiefly Scot* — used as a function word immediately before any of several nouns denoting divisions of time, esp. *day, night, morn,* and *year,* to form phrases with an adverbial function corresponding in meaning to standard English *today, tonight, tomorrow, this year* **h** — used as a function word before names of some parts of the body or of the clothing as an equivalent of a possessive adjective indicating that the part in question belongs to a person previously mentioned ⟨led her by ~ hand⟩ ⟨grabbed him by ~ collar⟩ or to the speaker or writer or the person addressed ⟨how's ~ arm today⟩ ⟨~ ankle is better today, thanks⟩; sometimes used in a similar way before nouns denoting a family, a member of a family, an ailment from which the speaker or writer or the person addressed is known to have been suffering, or some other aspect of an individual person's situation in life ⟨he's going on a trip and taking ~ family along⟩ ⟨I suppose you'll have to consult ~ wife⟩ ⟨how's ~ cough⟩ ⟨~ headache is better, thanks⟩ ⟨you've been lucky enough to rate a four-week vacation from ~ job —Richard Joseph⟩ **i** (1) — used as a function word before a title or a personal name to designate a person of eminence or widespread reputation, esp. as a man of high rank, a figure of great historical importance, a singer, an actress, or a courtesan ⟨Robert ~ Bruce⟩ ⟨~ Siddons⟩ ⟨~ Duse⟩ ⟨~ Pompadour⟩; sometimes used somewhat disparagingly in reference to a person of only very local or restricted prominence (2) — used as a function word before the surname of an Irish or Scottish clan to indicate reference to the chief of the clan ⟨~ Mackintosh⟩ **j** — used as a function word before the name of an art, artistic movement, craft, branch of learning, profession, sport, or other branch of human endeavor or proficiency; used in standard English only in a very limited number of such combinations ⟨~ opera⟩ ⟨~ cinema⟩ ⟨~ rococo⟩ ⟨~ calculus⟩ ⟨~ law⟩ ⟨~ ministry⟩ ⟨~ turf⟩ **k** (1) : in, to, or for each : for every : ²A 5 ⟨twenty cents ~ copy⟩ ⟨a dollar ~ bottle⟩ (2) : EACH, EVERY — used after prepositions ⟨about eighty crackers to ~ package⟩ (3) — used as a function word in prepositional phrases esp. with *by* to indicate that the noun in the phrase serves as a basis for computation ⟨sold by ~ dozen⟩ ⟨rented by ~ month⟩ ⟨dying by ~ hundreds⟩ **l** — used as a function word before the proper name of a ship or a well-known building (as a theater or movie house well known at least in the city where it is located) ⟨~ Mayflower⟩ ⟨~ Bijou⟩ **m** — used as a function word before the name of a language; obsolete except in contexts that indicate translation from an original language ⟨translated from ~ German⟩ **n** — used as a function word before a gerundial verbal noun to indicate reference to an immediate instance ⟨will cause the meat to shrivel in ~ cooking —*Amer. Guide Series: N.C.*⟩ **o** — used as a function word before a noun derived without affixation from a verb expressing an action or state that has duration in time and after the preposition *upon* or usu. *on* to indicate a single continuous involvement in such an action or state ⟨on ~ move⟩ ⟨on ~ prowl⟩ or the temporal point of termination of such involvement ⟨caught the ball on ~ fly⟩ **p** (1) — used as a function word before a date consisting only of a numeral denoting a year; obsolete except before *1715* or its contraction *'15* in reference to the Jacobite uprising of that year or to the year itself as marked by that uprising and before *1745* or its contraction *'45* in reference to the Jacobite uprising of that year or to the year itself as marked by that uprising ⟨he was not out in ~ 1715 —W.M.Parker⟩ ⟨the commencement of the rising of ~ '15 —Leslie Smith⟩ (2) — used as a function word before the plural form of a numeral that is a multiple of ten to denote a particular decade of a century or of a person's life ⟨American life in ~ twenties⟩ ⟨a man somewhere in ~ sixties⟩ **q** — used as a function word before the name of a commodity or any familiar appurtenance of daily life to indicate reference to the individual thing, part, or supply thought of as at hand ⟨too fond of ~ booze⟩ ⟨looking out of ~ window⟩ ⟨talked to him on ~ telephone⟩ **r** — used as a function word to designate one of a class as the best, most typical, or most worth singling out ⟨this is ~ life⟩ ⟨an author who even in his own lifetime was widely regarded as ~ novelist⟩; sometimes used before a personal name to denote the most prominent bearer of that name ⟨became acquainted with a mathematician who was named Einstein but was not ~ Einstein⟩; sometimes used with the plural form of a family name to denote the most prominent branch of the family ⟨on his father's side he was, to be sure, a Guzmán but not one of ~ Guzmáns —D.C.Peattie⟩; often marked in speech by full stress or in writing by special typography (as italics) **s** : ENOUGH ⟨I would have liked to write a letter instead of a postcard, but I didn't have ~ time⟩ **t** (1) — used as a function word before a proper name denoting a particular character in a dramatic work or before a common noun denoting a particular role in a dramatic work to refer to the one playing that character or filling that role ⟨in this performance a singer who has not appeared here before was ~ Figaro⟩ ⟨threw rotten eggs at ~ villain⟩ (2) — used as a function word before a noun denoting a particular role in a real-life situation to refer to the one filling that role ⟨I'm no fool; you're ~ fool⟩ ⟨in 1914, by contrast with 1898, England and France were ~ belligerents and America was ~ neutral⟩ **2 a** (1) — used as a function word with a noun modified by an adjective or by an attributive noun to limit the application of the modified noun to that specified by the adjective or by the attributive noun ⟨~ right answer⟩ ⟨~ privileged classes⟩ ⟨~ third time⟩ ⟨~ English language⟩ ⟨~ greatest difficulty⟩ ⟨~ Boston road⟩ ⟨~ seafood industry⟩; sometimes used with the adjective following the article-noun combination and itself either unmodified or more often modified ⟨~ church militant⟩ ⟨~ man sitting behind that desk⟩; often used in conventional epithets ⟨~ Venerable Bede⟩ ⟨~ White House⟩ including some in which the article and the adjective both follow the noun ⟨Peter ~ Great⟩ ⟨Elizabeth ~ Second⟩; used also in constructions containing an additional modifier (as a subordinate clause, prepositional phrase, or infinitive phrase) as well as an adjective or an attributive noun ⟨~ usual excuses that everybody gives⟩ ⟨~ seafood industry of this country⟩ ⟨~ wrong way to do it⟩ (2) — used as a function word before an absolute adjective that is equivalent in meaning to a noun modified by an adjective, including virtually all absolute occurrences of superlative adjectives or ordinal numbers ⟨use

the white buttons and not ~ black⟩ ⟨he and she are both very intelligent, but her responses are ~ quicker⟩ ⟨nothing but ~ best⟩ ⟨he is to arrive on ~ sixth⟩ **b** : used as a function word before a noun to limit its application to that specified by a noun esp. a proper name in apposition ⟨~ poet Wordsworth⟩; often used before a title consisting of a generic term followed by a limiting appositive ⟨~ Lord Chief Justice⟩; sometimes used with the limiting term first esp. in conventional epithets ⟨William ~ Conqueror⟩ **c** : used as a function word before a noun to limit its application to that specified by a succeeding element in the sentence, esp. a subordinate clause, prepositional phrase, or infinitive phrase ⟨~ flowers that bloom⟩ ⟨~ days of our youth⟩ ⟨~ man in the iron mask⟩ ⟨~ London of Elizabeth I⟩ ⟨~ right to vote⟩; often used before a title consisting of a generic term followed by a limiting prepositional phrase ⟨~ Duke of York⟩ **3 a (1)** : used as a function word before a singular noun denoting a human being, an animal, a plant, or a precious stone to indicate that the noun is to be understood generically and not individually ⟨helpful hints for ~ beginner⟩ ⟨courtesy distinguishes ~ gentleman⟩ ⟨~ dog was domesticated in prehistoric times⟩ ⟨hunt ~ wild ox⟩ ⟨cultivation of ~ potato⟩ ⟨~ diamond is a form of carbon⟩; used with man or woman only in explicit contrast with another noun denoting a human being ⟨the child is father of ~ man —William Wordsworth⟩ ⟨when man or woman is the object of the verb act or play; used also with a noun other than man or woman occurring as object of the verb act or play ⟨play ~ knave⟩ ⟨play ~ martyr⟩ ⟨act ~ fool⟩ **(2)** : used as a function word before a singular substantivized adjective denoting a human being to indicate generic rather than individual application ⟨let ~ wicked forsake his way —Isa 55:7 (RSV)⟩ **b** : used as a function word before a noun denoting the body, the mind, the soul, or any part, attribute, or function of any of them, to indicate generic rather than individual application ⟨mind is clearest when ~ body is in good health⟩ ⟨good for ~ soul⟩ ⟨~ hand is quicker than ~ eye⟩ ⟨pleasing to ~ appetite⟩ ⟨a product of ~ imagination⟩ **c** : used as a function word before a noun denoting an object (as an implement, weapon, or musical instrument) to indicate generic rather than individual application ⟨invention of ~ wheel⟩ ⟨users of ~ bow and arrow⟩ ⟨playing ~ piano⟩ ⟨the writing is close, analytic, sharply focused on ~ significant detail —William Barrett⟩ **d** archaic : used as a function word before the name of a day of the week to indicate reference to that day as one that recurs week after week ⟨on ~ Sunday he goes perhaps to church —T.B.Macaulay⟩ **e** : used as a function word before a singular substantivized adjective to indicate an abstract idea ⟨an essay on ~ sublime⟩ ⟨to recognize and enjoy ~ beautiful⟩ **4 a** : used as a function word before a singular noun denoting a group to indicate reference to the group as a whole ⟨~ elite⟩ ⟨~ aristocracy⟩ ⟨~ rabble⟩ **b** : used as a function word before a plural substantivized adjective to indicate inclusive reference to a group so characterized ⟨blessed are ~ merciful —Mt 5:7 (AV)⟩ ⟨the land of ~ free — F.S.Key⟩ **c** : used as a function word before a plural noun denoting a group to indicate reference to the group as a whole ⟨~ Greeks⟩ ⟨~ newspapers⟩

²**the** \before consonants & esp South before vowels also thə, before vowels thē or thi\ adv [ME, the, thi, fr. OE thē, thȳ by that, because of that, instrumental of thæt, neut. demonstrative pron.—more at THAT] **1** : than before : than otherwise — used before a comparative ⟨I am none ~ wiser for attending that lecture⟩ ⟨instead of quieting down, they talked all ~ louder⟩ ⟨pulled his cot alongside the window, ~ better to lean his chin on the sill —Ethel Anderson⟩ **2 a** : by how much : to what extent — used before a comparative as one of the members, usu. the first member, of the correlative pair the . . . the . . . ⟨~ sooner the better⟩ ⟨~ harder you work, the sooner you will finish⟩ **b** : by that much : to that extent — used before a comparative as one of the members, usu. the second member, of the correlative pair the . . . the . . . ⟨the sooner ~ better⟩ **3** : so as to exceed all others — used before a superlative ⟨of all my books I like this ~ best —Charles Dickens⟩

the- or **theo-** comb form [ME theo-, fr. LL, fr. L, fr. Gk the-, theo- god, fr. theos; perh. akin to MHG getwâs ghost, Lith dvasia spirit, dvasas spirit, breath — more at DUST] **1 a** : God ⟨theism⟩ ⟨theocentric⟩ **b** : god ⟨theomancy⟩ **2 a** : theological and ⟨theoastrological⟩ **b** : theology and ⟨theomythology⟩

thea \'thēə\ n, cap [NL, fr. thea tea, fr. the source of E ¹tea] in some classifications : a genus comprising evergreen shrubs with pediceled flowers and persistent sepals that are now usu. placed in the genus Camellia and include the tea plant of commerce

the·a·ce·ae \thē'āsē,ē\ n pl, cap [NL, fr. Thea, type genus + -aceae] : a family of trees and shrubs (order Parietales) having alternate undivided leaves, large regular pentamerous flowers, and a fleshy or capsular fruit and being mainly tropical but widely distributed — compare ¹CAMELLIA, ²GORDONIA, STEWARTIA

the·a·ce·ous \-'āshəs\ adj [NL Theaceae + E -ous] : of or relating to the Theaceae

t-head \'⸱⸱\ adj, cap T **1** : having the intake and exhaust valves in compartments of the block on opposite sides of the cylinder ⟨a T-head gasoline engine⟩ **2** : having a cross member at the head end of a longitudinal one ⟨a T-head pier⟩ ⟨a T-head bolt⟩

t-head toggle n, cap T : a toggle (as a rod or screw) with a piece pivoted near its end that turns transversely and prevents withdrawal after the toggle has been inserted through a hole

the·an·dric \thē'andrik\ adj [LGk theandrikos, fr. theandros God-man (fr. Gk the- + -andros -androus) + Gk -ikos -ic] : of or relating to the divine and human or their union or joint operation ⟨affirmed that there was but one and the same Christ, working both the divine and the human actions by one ~ operation —B.J.Kidd⟩

the·an·throp·ic \,thēən'thräpik, -pēk\ adj [theanthropos + -ic] **1 a** : believed to incarnate or to be a god in man **b** : being both divine and human ⟨Jesus Christ's ~ nature⟩ **2** : partaking of the natures of a god and of man — used as a sacrificial victim

the·an·thro·pism \thē'an(t)thrə,pizəm\ n -s [theanthropos + -ism] **1** : a state of being God and man; esp : the union of the divine and human natures in Christ **2 a** : the ascription of human attributes to the Deity, or to a polytheistic deity : ANTHROPOMORPHISM **b** : belief in the incarnation of deity in human form or in the divinity of a manhood

the·an·thro·pist \-pəst\ n -s [theanthropos + -ist] : a defender of theanthropism or believer in it

the·an·throp·ol·o·gy \thē,an(t)thrə'päləjē\ n -ES [theanthropos + -logy] : THEANTHROPISM

the·an·thro·poph·a·gy \-äfəjē\ n -ES [theanthropos + -phagy] : the practice of eating a god-man

the·an·thro·pos \thē'an(t)thrə,päs\ n [LGk theanthrōpos, fr. Gk the- + anthrōpos man — more at ANTHROP-] : God incarnating or believed to incarnate God or a god : GOD-MAN

the·an·thro·pos·o·phy \thē,an(t)thrə'päsəfē\ n -ES [theanthropos + -sophy] : a system of belief concerning theanthropism

the·an·thro·py \thē'an(t)thrəpē\ n -ES [theanthropos + -y] : THEANTHROPISM

the·arch·ic \thē'ärkik\ adj [LGk thearchikos, fr. thearchia + Gk -ikos -ic] **1** : of or relating to the rule of God : divinely sovereign or supreme : THEOCRATIC **2** : of or relating to a system of deities

the·ar·chy \'thē,ärkē\ n -ES [LGk thearchia, fr. Gk the- + -archia -archy] **1** : a political system based on government of men by God : divine sovereignty : THEOCRACY ⟨in the Hindu ~ there are two powerful and rival goddesses among manifold others —Rumer Godden⟩ **2** : a system or hierarchy of deities

theat abbr theater; theatrical

the·a·ter or the·a·tre \'thēəd·ə(r), 'thiə\, |tə sometimes 'thē,ā| or thē'ā\ n -S [ME theatre, fr. MF, fr. L theatrum, fr. Gk theatron, fr. theasthai to see, view (fr. thea action of seeing, sight) + -tron, suffix denoting means, instrument, or place; akin to Gk thauma wonder, miracle — more at -TRON] **1 a** : an outdoor structure for dramatic performances or spectacles in ancient Greece and Rome including a stage with associated rooms and usu. semicircular tiers of unroofed

---

seats **b** : a building for dramatic performances in modern

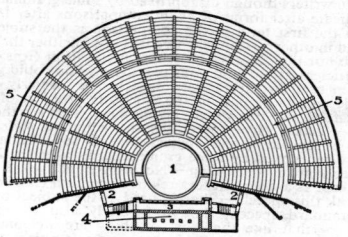

theater 1a: plan of Greek theater: *1* orchestra, *2* parodos, *3* proscenium, *4* skene, *5* diazoma

times usu. including a stage with side wings and flies and with dressing rooms for actors and an auditorium often with balconies and boxes : PLAYHOUSE **c** obs : a theater stage **d** : a theater audience : HOUSE ⟨the ~ applauded him warmly⟩ **e** : a building for the showing of motion pictures **2** : something resembling a theater in form or use: as **a** : a place rising by steps or gradations ⟨shade above shade, a woody ~ of stateliest view —John Milton⟩ **b** : a room often with rising tiers of seats for lectures, surgical demonstrations, or other assemblies or exhibitions ⟨the hospital has . . . a clinic or student instruction —Amer. Guide Series: Md.⟩ usu theatre, Brit : a hospital operating room **3** obs : a comprehensive outline or view : CONSPECTUS — used chiefly in book titles **4 a** : a place or sphere that is the scene of dramatic events or significant action ⟨the ~ of public life⟩ ⟨this was the ~ of . . . the most stupendous financial fiasco in the history of the world —F.J.Haskin⟩ **b** : the scene of a public ceremony (as a temporary platform) ⟨the cathedral crossing became the ~ for the coronation⟩ **5** obs : EXAMPLE, EXHIBITION, SPECTACLE **6 a** : written dramatic literature : PLAYS ⟨the ~ of Eugene O'Neill⟩ ⟨the ~ of 19th century France⟩ **b** : dramatic performance or representation : drama as an active art ⟨naïveté was the keynote to the American ~ —Otis Skinner⟩ **c** : dramatic aptitude or effectiveness : skillful depiction of character or of the conflict or interplay of persons ⟨this is pure ~ —Cecile Starr⟩ ⟨the play makes lively ~⟩ ⟨the weakest ~ in the play⟩

the·a·ter·go·er \-,gō(ə)r, -ȯə\ n : an habitual attendant at theaters : PLAYGOER

the·a·ter·go·ing \-,ōiŋ\ n : attendance at theaters

theater-in-the-round \'ʒʒʒʒʒ'ʒ\ n : ARENA THEATER

theater of operations : the part of a theater of war in which active operations are conducted including a combat zone and a communications zone

theater of war : the entire land, sea, and air area that is or may become involved directly in war operations and includes the theater of operations and the zone of the interior

the·a·tine \'thēə,tīn\ n -s usu cap [NL Theatinus, fr. L Teatinus inhabitant of Chieti, fr. Teate Chieti, Italy + -inus -ine; fr. the fact that one of the founders of the congregation was Giovanni P. Caraffa †1559 Ital. prelate, archbishop of Chieti and later Pope Paul IV] : a member of a Roman Catholic congregation of regular clerics established in 1524 in Italy to elevate clerical and lay morality and to combat Lutheranism

the·a·tral \'thēə,trol\ adj [F théâtral, fr. L theatralis, fr. theatrum + -alis -al] : of or relating to theater or drama

theatre sister n, Brit : an operating-room nurse

the·at·ric \thē'a,trik, thi'-\ adj [LL theatricus] : THEATRICAL

¹**the·at·ri·cal** \thē'a,trəkəl, thi'- -rēk-\ adj [LL theatricus (fr. Gk theatrikos, fr. theatron theater + -ikos -ic) + E -al —more at THEATER] **1** : of or relating to the theater or to the acting or presentation of plays ⟨a ~ jack-of-all-trades —Claudia Cassidy⟩ ⟨made no objection to his son's ~ ambitions —Collier's Yr. Bk.⟩ **2** : marked by pretense or artificiality : not genuine : UNREAL ⟨a ~ evangelist whose staged confessions and railings against sin are . . . hypocritical —Nona B. Brown⟩ **3 a** : having the qualities of a stage play or of an actor's performance : DRAMATIC, HISTRIONIC ⟨active virtue . . . is therefore ~, consciously dramatic, the wearing of a mask —W.B. Yeats⟩ **b** : marked by extravagant display or exhibitionism : SHOWY, SPECTACULAR ⟨a ~ bow —Michael McLaverty⟩ ⟨one of the most ~ figures in public life —J.K.Howard⟩

²**theatrical** \"\ n -ES [²theatrical] **1** : the performance and presentation of plays ⟨forbid ~s and other secular amusements in churches and churchyards —K.S.Latourette⟩ ⟨amateur ~s⟩ ⟨student ~s⟩ **2** theatricals n pl : the arts of acting and stagecraft : DRAMATICS **b** : theater properties or memorabilia **3** : a professional actor ⟨an eminent ~ —Times Lit. Supp.⟩ **4** theatricals pl : showy or extravagant gestures or actions ⟨the addition of exaggerated ~s continued the steady deterioration of this ancient and once popular sport —Collier's Yr. Bk.⟩

theatrical gauze n : a transparent open-mesh gauze of cotton or linen with a stiff finish for use in theatrical costumes and scenery and in curtains

the·at·ri·cal·ism \-kə,lizəm\ n -s : stage mannerisms, methods, or practices : EXHIBITIONISM, SHOWINESS, STAGINESS ⟨a display of moody ~ —Bosley Crowther⟩

the·at·ri·cal·i·ty \thē,a·trə'kaləd·ē\ n : the quality or state of being theatrical (as in action, appearance, or style) ⟨a gesture of large ~ and little meaning —Frederic Morton⟩

the·at·ri·cal·i·za·tion \thē,a·trəkələ'zāshən\ n : the act of theatricalizing or the state of being theatricalized

the·at·ri·cal·ize \thē'a·trəkə,līz\ vt -ED/-ING/-S [¹theatrical + -ize] **1** : to adapt to the theater : make theatrical : DRAMATIZE **2** : to display in showy fashion : make flashy

the·at·ri·cal·ly \thē'a·trək(ə)lē, thi'- -rēk-, -li\ adv : in a theatrical manner ⟨~ talented students⟩ ⟨its green-lit fumes rose ~ against the enormous cheap-gaudy nightscape —Christopher Isherwood⟩

the·at·ri·cal·ness \-nəs\ n -ES : the quality or state of being theatrical

the·a·tri·cian \,thēə'trishən\ n -s : a specialist or technician in theater arts

the·at·ri·cism \thē'a·trə,sizəm\ n -s : THEATRICALISM

the·at·rics \thē'a·triks, thi'-, -rēks\ n pl [theatric + -s] **1** : ²THEATRICAL 1 ⟨amateur ~⟩ **2** : staged or contrived effects ⟨a tale of high adventure — heightened not by studio ~ but by one's sense of being an immediate participant —Arthur Knight⟩

theatro- comb form [Gk, fr. theatron — more at THEATER] : theater ⟨theatromania⟩

the·a·troc·ra·cy \,thēə'träkrəsē\ n -ES [Gk theatrokratia, fr. theatro- + -kratia -cracy] : government by the people assembled in their theater (as in the Athenian democracy)

the·a·tro·graph \thē'a·trə,graf, -ráf\ n [theatro- + -graph] : an early motion picture projector

theave \'thēv, 'thāv\ n -s [ME theyve] dial Eng : a young ewe; esp : one that has not yeaned

¹**the·ba·ic** \thə'bāik\ adj, usu cap [L Thebaicus, fr. Gk Thēbaikos, fr. Thēbai, Thēbē Thebes, ancient city in Upper Egypt + -ikos -ic] : of or relating to Thebes in Egypt

²**thebaic** \"\ n -s : SAHIDIC

the·ba·ine \'thēbə,ēn, thə'bāin, -āēn\ n -s [NL thebaia Egyptian opium produced at Thebes (fr. L Thebae Thebes, fr. Gk Thēbai) + E -ine] : a poisonous crystalline alkaloid $C_{19}H_{21}NO_3$ found in opium in small quantities, related chemically to morphine and codeine, and possessing a sharp astringent taste and a tetanic action like strychnine

¹**the·ban** \'thēbən\ adj, usu cap [ME, fr. L Thebanus adj. & n., fr. Thebae Thebes, city in ancient Greece and in Upper Egypt (fr. Gk Thēbai) + -anus -an] : of or relating to ancient Thebes, Egypt, or Thebes, Greece

²**theban** \"\ n -s cap [ME, fr. L Thebanus] : a native or inhabitant of Thebes

the·be·sian vessel also **thebesian vein** or **thebesian channel** \thə'bēzhən-\, sometimes cap T [fr. Adam C. Thebesius †1732 Ger. anatomist + E -an] : any of the minute veins of the heart wall that drain directly into the cavity of the heart

thec- or **theci-** or **theco-** comb form [NL, fr. theca] : theca ⟨theciferous⟩ ⟨thecitis⟩ ⟨Thecosomata⟩

---

the·ca \'thēkə\ n, pl **the·cae** \-ē,(,)sē\ [NL, fr. L, case, cover — more at TICK] **1** : SAC, CAPSULE, SPORE CASE: as **a** : the capsule of a moss **b** : the pollen sac of an anther **2** : an enveloping sheath or case: as **a** : the cuticular case of an insect larva **b** : the sheath of dura mater enclosing the spinal cord **c** : the layer of dense stroma surrounding a Graafian follicle **d** : HYDROTHECA **e** : the calcareous wall of a coral calyculus **f** : the test of a testate protozoan or rotifer **g** : the dorsal cup of the calyx of a crinoid

-theca \"\ n comb form, pl **-thecae** \"\ [NL, fr. L theca] : sheath or covering of a (specified) type ⟨gonotheca⟩ ⟨myxotheca⟩

the·cal \'thēkəl\ adj [thec- + -al] : of or relating to a theca

the·ca·moe·bae \,thēkə'mē(,)bē\ or **the·cam·oe·baea** \thə,kamē'bēə\ n pl [NL, fr. L pl. of Thecamoeba genus of Rhizopoda, fr. thec- + Amoeba] syn of TESTACEA

the·ca·ta \thə'kād·ə\ n [NL, fr. thec- + -ata] syn of LEPTOMEDUSAE

the·cate \'thē,kāt\ adj [thec- + -ate] : having a theca : TESTATE

the·cial \'thēsh(ē)əl, -sēəl\ adj [NL thecium + E -al] : of or relating to a thecium

the·ci·um \'thēs(h)ēəm\ n, pl **the·cia** \-)sēə\ [NL, fr. Gk thēkion small case, small chest, dim. of thēkē case, chest — more at TICK] : HYMENIUM

-thecium \"\ n comb form, pl **-thecia** \"\ [NL, fr. Gk thēkion small case, small chest] : small containing structure ⟨endothecium⟩

thec·la \'theklə\ n [NL, prob. fr. the name Thecla] syn of STRYMON

¹**the·co·dont** \'thēkə,dänt\ adj [thec- + -odont] : having the teeth inserted in sockets in the alveoli

²**thecodont** \"\ n -s : a thecodont animal; esp : a thecodont reptile

the·co·don·tia \,thēkə'dänchə\ n pl, cap [NL, fr. thec- + -odontia] : an order of Reptilia comprising various generalized diapsid Triassic forms presumably on the common ancestral line of the dinosaurs, crocodiles, and birds

the·coid \'thē,kȯid\ adj or n [NL Thecoidea] : EDRIOASTEROID

the·coi·dea \thə'kȯidēə\ n pl, cap [NL, fr. thec- + -oidea] syn of EDRIOASTEROIDEA

¹**the·coph·o·ra** \thə'käf(ə)rə\ n [NL, fr. thec- + -phora] syn of LEPTOMEDUSAE

²**thecophora** \"\ n pl, cap [NL, fr. thec- + -phora] in some classifications : a suborder of Testudinata including all recent turtles except the leatherback — **the·coph·o·ran** \-rən\ adj or n

the·coph·o·roi·dea \thə,käfə'rȯidēə\ n pl, cap [NL, fr. Thecophora + -oidea] syn of THECOPHORA

the·co·so·ma·ta \,thēkə'sōməd·ə\ n pl, cap [NL, fr. thec- + -somata] in some classifications : a division of Pteropoda comprising pteropods with a shell — compare GYMNOSOMATA — **thecosomatous** adj

thé dansant \tādäⁿsäⁿ\ n, pl **thés dansants** \"\ [F] : TEA DANCE

¹**thee** \(')thē, thi\ pron, objective case of THOU [ME, fr. OE thē — more at THOU] **1** : ¹THOU: **a** archaic — used esp. in biblical, ecclesiastical, solemn, or poetical language, and to some extent in the speech of Friends esp. among themselves, in contexts where the objective case form of an inflected pronoun is the one to be expected esp. as indirect object of a verb ⟨the land . . . which he sware unto thy fathers to give ~ —Exod 13: 5 (AV)⟩ or as personal object of an impersonal verb ⟨do what seemeth ~ good —1 Sam 1: 23 (AV)⟩ or as object of a preposition ⟨sweet land of liberty, of ~ I sing —Samuel Francis Smith⟩ or as direct object of a verb ⟨I take ~ at thy word —Shak.⟩ **b** — used by reputable writers occas. from the 14th to the 17th centuries, in many British dialects down to the present day, and in the prevailing usage of the speech of Friends esp. among themselves, in contexts where the nominative case form of an inflected pronoun is the one to be expected esp. as subject of a verb ⟨don't think I am afraid of such a fellow as ~ art —Henry Fielding⟩ or in the predicate after a form of the verb be ⟨proud . . . that I am not ~ —Shak.⟩; in the usage of Friends and in many British dialects usu. accompanied by the third person singular form of a verb of which it is the subject ⟨~ still thinks of going to Canada —Harriet B. Stowe⟩ **2** archaic : THYSELF — used reflexively as indirect object of a verb ⟨get ~ a sword —Shak.⟩ or object of a preposition ⟨when Thou tookest upon Thee to deliver man —Te Deum Laudamus⟩ or direct object of a verb ⟨thou bearest ~ like a king —Shak.⟩

²**thee** \'thē\ n -s : ³THOU

³**thee** \'thē\ vb **thee'd**; **thee'd**; **thee·ing**; **thees** vt : to address as thee — vi : to use thee in address

⁴**thee** vi [ME theen, fr. OE thēon; akin to OHG dīhan to thrive, Goth theihan to increase, progress — more at TIGHT] obs : THRIVE, PROSPER ⟨well more ye ~ —Edmund Spenser⟩

theek \'thēk\ vt -ED/-ING/-S [ME theken, perh. of Scand origin; akin to ON thekja to cover, thatch — more at THATCH] Scot : THATCH, COVER

thee·lin \'thēlin\ n -s [irreg. fr. Gk thēlys female + E -in — more at FEMININE] : ESTRONE

thee·lol \-,lȯl, -,lōl\ n -s [ISV theelin + -ol] : ESTRIOL

theet·see \'thēt,sē\ n -s [Burmese thitse] : BLACK-VARNISH TREE

thee·zan tea \'thē'z⁽ʰ⁾n-\ n -s [fr. Sageretia theezans (specific epithet of Sageretia theezans), prob. fr. NL Thea] : a Chinese shrub with edible fruit and leaves that are often used in place of tea

theft \'theft\ n -s [ME thiefthe, thefthe, thefte, thifte, fr. OE thiefth, thēofth, thȳfth; akin to OFris thiûvethe, thiûfthe theft, OS thiubda, ON thȳfth theft; derivative fr. the stem of E thief] **1 a** : the act of stealing; specif : the felonious taking and removing of personal property with intent to deprive the rightful owner of it **b** : an instance of such an act **2** : the taking of property unlawfully (as by robbery, embezzlement, fraud) (has just ruled that . . . from a spouse is possible —Jour. of the Amer. Judicature Society) **3** obs : something that is stolen (if the ~ be certainly found in his hand alive . . . he shall restore double —Exod 22: 4 (AV))

theft-bote \'theft,bōt\ n -s [alter. of theftbote, fr. ME, fr. thef thief + bote compensation — more at THIEF, BOOT (help)] old Eng & Scots law : the offense of agreeing to receive stolen goods or a compensation from a thief whether by the owner by way of composition or by a judge as an inducement for conniving at the escape of the thief from punishment

theft insurance n : insurance against loss or damage caused by the unlawful taking of property

theftproof \'⸱,⸱\ adj : safe from theft : resistant to thieves ⟨~ strongbox⟩ ⟨~ lock⟩

thef·tu·ous \'thefchəwəs\ adj [alter. (influenced by -uous) of ME thiftwis, fr. thifte theft + -wis, wise wise —more at THEFT, WISE] : THIEVISH — **thef·tu·ous·ly** adv

the·gith·er \thə'gith̲ər\ adv [trans. of OE thegnlic] : TOGETHER

thegn var of THANE

thegn·ly adj [trans. of OE thegnlic] : of, relating to, or befitting a thane

thei·le·ria \thī'lirēə\ n [NL, fr. Sir Arnold Theiler †1936 Eng. veterinary bacteriologist born in Switzerland + NL -ia] **1** cap : a genus of parasitic protozoans (family Babesiidae) that includes the parasite of east coast fever of cattle and is sometimes variously treated either as a subgenus of Babesia or under a separate family **2** pl **thei·le·ri·ae** \-ē,ē\ also **theilerias** : any organism of the genus Theileria — **thei·le·ri·al** \-ēəl\ adj

thei·le·ri·a·sis \,thīlə'rīəsəs\ n or **thei·le·ri·o·sis** \-,thī',lirē-'ōsəs\ n -ES [NL, fr. Theileria + -iasis or -osis] : infection with or disease caused by a theileria; esp : EAST COAST FEVER

the·ine \'thē,ēn, 'thēən\ n -s [NL theina, fr. thea tea + -ina -ine; fr. its occurrence in tea — more at THEA] : CAFFEINE

¹**their** [ME, fr. ON theirra, theira, gen. pl. demonstrative & personal pron.; akin to ON that, neut. demonstrative pron.—more at THAT] obs possessive of ²THEY

²**their** \thər, (')the(ə)r, (')tha(ə)r\ adj [ME, fr. their, pron.] **1 a** : of or belonging to them or themselves esp. as possessors, agents, or objects of an action ⟨~ furniture⟩ ⟨~ rights⟩ ⟨~ neighbors⟩ : due to them : inherent in them : associated or connected with them ⟨~ furniture⟩ ⟨~ rights⟩ ⟨~ neighbors⟩ : of or relating to them or themselves as authors, doers, givers, or agents, effected by them : experienced by them as subject : that they are capable of ⟨~ verses⟩ ⟨~ confidence in you⟩ ⟨responsible for ~ being here⟩ ⟨doing ~ utmost⟩ : of or relating to them or

themselves as object of an action : experienced by them as object ⟨~ defeat⟩ ⟨~ being seen⟩ **d** : that they have to do with or are supposed to possess or to have knowledge or a share of or some special interest in ⟨they know ~ algebra⟩ ⟨they like ~ leisure⟩ **e** : that is esp. significant for them : that brings them good fortune or prominence — used with *day* or sometimes with other words indicating a division of time ⟨the twins had a wonderful birthday party; this certainly was ~ day⟩ **2** : his or her : HIS, HER — used with a singular antecedent that is indefinite or that does not specify gender ⟨anyone in ~ senses —W.H.Auden⟩ ⟨we shall be pleased to send a free specimen copy . . . to a friend or relative on receipt of ~ address —*London Calling*⟩ **3** *obs* — used after a plural or collective noun or a group of two or more nouns to indicate a possessive case relation ⟨in the father, mother, and governess *their* absence —*The Lives of Women Saints*⟩ **4** *archaic* : of those — used esp. as antecedent to a relative pronoun ⟨nor better was ~ lot who fled —Sir Walter Scott⟩

theirn \'the(ə)rn, 'tha(ə)l, |ən\ *pron* [by alter. (influence of *mine, thine, hisn*)] *dial* : THEIRS

¹theirs \'the(ə)rz, 'tha(ə)l, |əz\ *pron* [ME *theirs, theires,* fr. *their* + *-s, -es* -'s] **1** : their one : their ones — used without a following noun as a pronoun equivalent in meaning to the adjective *their* ⟨bought his car the same day his neighbors bought ~⟩ ⟨our customs are not like ~⟩; often used after *of* to single out one or more members of a class belonging to or connected with certain persons not including the one speaking or writing nor the one being addressed ⟨a friend of ~⟩ ⟨some shrubs of ~⟩ or merely to identify something or someone as belonging to or connected with certain persons not including the one speaking or writing nor the one being addressed without any implication of membership in a more extensive class ⟨that dog of ~⟩ ⟨those flashy clothes of ~⟩ **2** : something belonging to them : what belongs to them ⟨they are determined to get ~⟩ **3** : his or hers : HIS, HERS — used with a singular antecedent that is indefinite or that does not specify gender ⟨I will do my part if everybody else will do ~⟩

²theirs *adj, obs* : ²THEIR 1 — used as the first of two possessive adjectives modifying the same noun

their·selves \thər'selvz, ther-, tha(ə)r-, -euvz\ *pron* [obs. E *theirself* themselves (fr. ME *their* + *self*) + E *-es*] *substand* : THEMSELVES

the·ism \'thē,izəm\ *n* -s [*the-* + *-ism*] **1** : belief in the existence of a god or gods; *specif* : belief in the existence of one God who is viewed as the creative source of man, the world, and value and who transcends and yet is immanent in the world ⟨Christian ~⟩ — opposed to *atheism;* distinguished from *pantheism* and *polytheism* **2** : a system of thought founded on the belief in one or more gods ⟨these philosophies, which are usually called ~*s*, view all of life as a divinely ordered sequence —J.R. Everett⟩

-the·ism *when immediately preceded by stress* thē,izəm *or* 'th-, *when immediately preceded by nonstress* (,)th- *or* 'th-\ *n comb form* -s [MF *-théisme*, fr. *thé-* the- + *-isme* -ism] : belief in (such) a god or (such or so many) gods ⟨*pantheism*⟩ ⟨*zootheism*⟩

the·ist \'thēəst\ *n* -s [*the-* + *-ist*] : a believer in theism

-the·ist *when immediately preceded by stress* thēəst *or* 'th-, *when immediately preceded by nonstress* (,)th- *or* 'th-\ *n comb form* -s [MF *-théiste*, fr. *thé-* the- + *-iste* -ist] : one that believes in (such) a god or (such or so many) gods ⟨*hylotheist*⟩ ⟨*monotheist*⟩ — **-the·is·tic** \thē'istik, -tēk\ *adj comb form*

the·is·tic \thē'istik, -tēk\ *also* **the·is·ti·cal** \-tәkəl, -tēk-\ *adj* : of, relating to, or characterized by theism : believing in theism — **the·is·ti·cal·ly** \-tәk(ə)lē, -tēk-, -li\ *adv*

theistic naturalism *n* : PROCESS PHILOSOPHY

theistic naturalist *n* : an advocate of religious naturalism; *specif* : a Protestant Christian theologian who utilizes process philosophy as a framework for interpreting the Christian faith

the·la·zia \thə'lāzēə\ *n, cap* [NL, fr. Gk *thēlazein* to suckle, suck (fr. *thēlē* nipple) + NL *-ia* — more at FEMININE] : a genus of nematode worms that comprises various eye worms and is the type of the family Thelaziidae

thel·a·zi·a·sis \,thelə'zīəsəs\ *n* -ES [NL, fr. *Thelazia* + *-iasis*] : infestation with or disease caused by roundworms of the genus *Thelazia*

thel·a·zi·idae \,thelə'zīə,dē\ *n pl, cap* [NL, fr. *Thelazia*, type genus + *-idae*] : a family of spiruroid nematode worms containing various forms of medical or veterinary importance — see THELAZIA

thel·em·ite \'thelə,mīt\ *n* -s [F *thélémite*, fr. Abbaye de *Thélème*, imaginary abbey with the motto "Do as you please" in *Gargantua* (1535) by François Rabelais †1553 Fr. satirist + F *-ite*] : one who does as he pleases; *esp* : LIBERTINE

thel·e·pho·ra·ce·ae \,theləfə'rāsē,ē\ *n pl, cap* [NL, fr. *Thelephora*, type genus (fr. Gk *thēlē* teat, nipple + NL *-phora*) + *-aceae* — more at FEMININE] : a family of fungi (order Agaricales) having leathery or membranous sporophores with smooth or corrugated basidial surfaces

the·lig·o·num *also* **the·lyg·o·num** \thə'ligənəm\ [NL, fr. L *thelygonon*, any of several plants of the genera *Mercurialis* and *Crucianella*, fr. Gk *thēlygonon*, fr. *thēlys* female + *-gonon* (fr. the stem of *gignesthai* to be born) — more at FEMININE, KIN] *syn of* CYNOCRAMBE

the·li·on \'thēlē,än\ *n* -s [NL, fr. Gk *thēlē* nipple, teat + NL *-ion*, dim. suffix] : the central point of the nipple

thel·o·don·ti·dae \,thelə'däntə,dē\ *n pl, cap* [NL, fr. *Thelodont-, Thelodus*, type genus + *-idae*] : a family of Devonian and Silurian ostracoderms that is included among the Heterostraci or isolated in the order Coelolepida

thel·o·dus \'theladəs\ *n, cap* [NL, fr. Gk *thēlē* nipple + NL *-odus*] : a genus of Silurian and Devonian ostracoderms (family Thelodontidae) that have small dermal tubercles consisting of dentin and enamel

thel·phu·sa \thel'fyüsə\ *n, cap* [NL] : a genus (the type of the family Thelphusidae) of freshwater crabs living in or on river banks in warm countries — **thel·phu·si·an** \(')thel¦fyüsēən, -üshən\ *adj or n*

thely- *comb form* [Gk *thēly-*, fr. *thēlys* — more at FEMININE] : female ⟨*thelygenic*⟩

thel·y·gen·ic \,thelə¦jenik\ *adj* [*thely-* + *-genic*] : producing female offspring solely or predominantly

¹the·lyph·o·nid \thə'lifənəd\ *adj* [NL *Thelyphonidae*] : of or relating to the Thelyphonidae

²thelyphonid \"\ *n* -s : a whip scorpion of the family Thelyphonidae

thel·y·phon·i·dae \,thelə'fänə,dē\ *n pl, cap* [NL, fr. *Thelyphonus*, type genus (fr. *thely-* + Gk *phonos* murder) + *-idae* — more at PHOENICIAN] : a widely distributed family of tailed whip scorpions

thel·y·to·cia \,thelē'tōshēə\ *n* -s [NL, fr. Gk *thēlytokia* condition of bearing females] : THELYTOKY

the·lyt·o·kous \thə'lidəkəs\ *also* **thel·y·ot·o·kous** \,thelē'ädəkəs\ *adj* [Gk *thēlytokos* bearing females] : producing only females ⟨~ parthenogenesis⟩

the·lyt·o·ky \-kē\ *also* **thel·y·ot·o·ky** \,==¦ädəkē\ *n* -ES [Gk *thēlytokia* condition of bearing females, fr. *thēlytokos* bearing females (fr. *thely-* thely- + *-tokos*, fr. *tiktein* to bear) + *-ia* -y — more at THANE] : parthenogenesis in which only female offspring are produced — compare ARRHENOTOKY

¹them \(th)əm, 'm, (')them\ *pron, objective case of* THEY [ME *them;* partly fr. *tham*, fr. OE *thǣm, thām*, dat. pl. demonstrative pron. & definite article; partly fr. *theim*, fr. ON, dat. pl. demonstrative & personal pron.; akin to OE *thæt*, neut. demonstrative pron. & definite article — more at THAT] **1** : ¹THEY 1, 3; **a** — used as indirect object of a verb ⟨men . . . who, as the fields and woods have given ~ birth, will build their savage fortunes only there —William Wordsworth⟩ **b** — used as object of a preposition ⟨to provide for organizing, arming, and disciplining the militia, and for governing such part of ~ as may be employed in the service of the United States —*U.S.Constitution*⟩ **c** — used as direct object of a verb ⟨you do not have to understand someone in order to love ~ —Lawrence Durrell⟩ ⟨they say things are going from bad to worse, but for my part, let ~ say what they like⟩ **d** — used in comparisons after *than* and *as* when the first term in the comparison is the direct or indirect object of a verb or the object of a preposition ⟨would hurt us as much as ~⟩ ⟨giving you better terms than ~⟩ ⟨easier for you than ~⟩ **e** — used in absolute constructions esp. together with a prepositional phrase, adjective, or participle ⟨~ being my friends, I did as they asked⟩ **f** — used by speakers on all educational levels and by many reputable writers though disapproved by some grammarians in the predicate after forms of *be*, in comparisons after *than* and *as* when the first term in the comparison is the subject of a verb, and in other positions where it is itself neither the subject of a verb nor the object of a verb or preposition ⟨it is ~⟩ ⟨we are as efficient as ~⟩ ⟨did your parents say you could go? Not ~⟩ **g** — used in substandard speech and formerly also by reputable writers as part of the compound subject of a verb ⟨your safety, for the which myself and ~ bend their best studies —Shak.⟩ **h** — used like the adjective *their* with a gerund by speakers and writers on all educational levels though disapproved by some grammarians ⟨whether there are any objections to ~ smoking —Noreen Routledge⟩ **2** : THOSE — used esp. as antecedent to a relative pronoun ⟨the best of ~ that speak this speech —Shak.⟩; used as the subject of a verb in substandard speech, though formerly also by reputable writers ⟨~ that like that sort of thing are welcome to it⟩ **3** : THEMSELVES — used reflexively as indirect object of a verb ⟨a folk that had founded ~ homes round wintry Dodona —W. B.Smith & Walter Miller⟩ or object of a preposition ⟨people that have their wits about ~⟩ or archaically as direct object of a verb ⟨like bride and groom devesting ~ for bed —Shak.⟩

²them \'them\ *adj, substand* : THOSE ⟨take ~ dirty boots off —Helen Eustis⟩ ⟨~ box pleats . . . is the latest thing —Ellen Glasgow⟩

the·ma \'thēmə\ *n, pl* **the·ma·ta** \-mədə\ [L — more at THEME] **1** : a topic or subject of discourse or of a written dissertation : THESIS **2** : THEME 6 **3** : THEME 4

the·mat·ic \(')thē¦mad·ik, thə'-, -at|, |ēk\ *adj* [Gk *thematikos*, fr. *themat-, thema* theme + *-ikos* -ic] **1 a** : of or relating to the stem of a word **b** *of a vowel* : being the last part of a word stem before an inflectional ending **2** : of or relating to a melodic subject ⟨~ development⟩ ⟨~ catalog of a composer's works⟩ **3** : of, relating to, or constituting a topic of discourse or a subject of artistic or cultural expression ⟨~ analysis of a poem⟩ ⟨~ approach to the study of a primitive society⟩ — **the·mat·i·cal·ly** \-ək(ə)lē, |ēk-, -li\ *adv*

thematic apperception test *n* : a projective technique widely used in clinical psychology wherein personality, psychodynamic, and diagnostic assessments are based on the subject's verbal responses to a series of black-and-white pictures — abbr. *TAT*

thematic verb *n* : a verb whose present tense stem ends in the varying thematic vowel *e:o*, (as Latin *seque, sequo*)

thematic vowel *n* : a vowel ending the stem of a noun or verb but not belonging to the root; *esp* : the varying *e:o* (as in Latin nominative *servos*, vocative *serve* slave) — compare GRADE 4

the·ma·tist \'thēmədəst\ *n* -s [L *themat-, thema* + E *-ist*] : one who composes themes

¹theme \'thēm\ *n* -s [ME *teme, theme*, fr. OF & L; OF *teme*, fr. L *thema*, fr. Gk, lit., something laid down, that which is laid down, fr. *tithenai* to place, set, lay down — more at DO] **1 a** : a subject or topic on which one speaks or writes ⟨~ of rags to riches⟩ ⟨economic ~*s*⟩ **b** : a proposition for discussion or argument ⟨stressed the ~ of equal rights for all⟩ **c** : a subject of fictional or artistic representation ⟨waterfalls are from very early times a favorite ~ for the painter —Laurence Binyon⟩ ⟨guilt and its punishment is the constant ~ of the dramas of Aeschylus —G.L.Dickinson⟩ **d** : an idea, ideal, or orienting principle that is dominant or persistent in a popular or tribal culture and often effective in controlling and activating belief and conduct in a specific direction — compare ETHOS, GESTALT **2** : STEM 4a **3** : a written exercise required of a student commonly at frequent regular intervals in a composition course ⟨weekly ~⟩ ⟨research ~⟩ **4 a** : a melodic subject of a musical composition or movement **b** : a short melody constituting the basis of variation, development, or other repetition with modification **c** : a visual motif or figure that forms by repetition, contrast, or variation a component of design in any of the graphic or plastic arts **5** : HOROSCOPE **6** : an administrative division of the Byzantine Empire **7** : SIGNATURE 9

²theme \"\ *vt* -ED/-ING/-S : to give a topic, subject, or text to : furnish with or direct toward a theme — used chiefly in past part. ⟨*themed* to making things out of wood, the book is written in clear, simple terms —*Toys and Novelties*⟩

theme and variations *n* : a standard form of musical composition consisting of a simple usu. harmonized melody presented first in its original unadorned form then repeated several or many times with varied treatment so based on the theme that at least some semblance of its general melodic or harmonic form is evident

theme·less \-mləs\ *adj* : lacking a theme

them·er \-mə(r)\ *n* -s : one that sets or provides a theme

theme song *n* **1** : a melody recurring so often in a musical or dramatic performance that it characterizes the production or one of its principal characters **2** : an assertion or complaint repeated so often as to be regarded as characteristic of its user **3** : SIGNATURE 9

the·mis·tian \thə'mis(h)chən\ *n* -s *usu cap* [*Themistius*, 6th cent. deacon of Alexandria, founder of the sect + E *-an*] : AGNOETE

them·selves \thəm'selvz, them-, -euvz, *South often* -e(ə)vz\ *pron pl* [obs. E *themself* themselves (fr. ME *thamself, theimself, themself*, fr. *tham, theim, them* them + *self*) + E *-es*] **1** : those identical ones that are they : the ones that belong to them : the selves that are theirs — used (1) reflexively as object of a preposition or direct or indirect object of a verb ⟨they keep their plans to ~⟩ ⟨nations that govern ~⟩ ⟨they are getting ~ an incinerator⟩; (2) for emphasis in apposition with *they, who, which, that*, or a noun ⟨they ~ were surprised⟩ ⟨some who were very busy nevertheless took the time to help others⟩ ⟨postcards which ~ supply the skeleton of the message —Randall Jarrell⟩ ⟨people that enjoy a game of bridge ~⟩ ⟨the teachers ~ were as glad as the pupils when the school year ended⟩; (3) for emphasis instead of nonreflexive *them* as object of a preposition or direct or indirect object of a verb ⟨their combined salaries support their children and ~⟩; (4) for emphasis instead of *they* or instead of *they themselves* as predicate nominative ⟨there is someone they can always depend on and that is ~⟩ or in comparisons after *than* or *as* ⟨they envied us though we were as poor as ~⟩ or as part of a compound subject ⟨to get their education as ~ or their neglectful government might see fit —S.A.Allibone⟩ or archaically or dialectally as only subject of a verb ⟨some . . . can render no ill services, in recompense for what ~ required —William Wordsworth⟩; (5) in absolute constructions ⟨~ bankrupt morally and economically, the landowners have sought to prevent and retard government intervention —Mario Einaudi⟩ **2** : their normal, healthy, or sane condition ⟨both persons involved in the accident were in a state of shock for a time but soon came to ~⟩ : their normal, healthy, or sane selves ⟨after a good night's rest they were ~ again⟩ **3** : HIMSELF, HERSELF — used with a singular antecedent that is indefinite or that does not specify gender ⟨nobody can call ~ oppressed —Leonard Wibberley⟩

¹then \(')then *sometimes* thən\ *adv* [ME *thanne, than, thenne, then*, fr. OE *thanne, thonne, thænne;* akin to OHG *thanne, thanna, denne* then, ON *thā*, Goth *than* then, OE *thæt*, neut. demonstrative pron. & definite article — more at THAT] **1** : at that time : at the time mentioned or specified ⟨the situation as it ~ was⟩ ⟨science as it was ~ taught⟩ **2** : soon after that : immediately after that : next in order of time ⟨walked to the door, ~ turned⟩ ⟨first left, ~ right⟩ ⟨~ came the thunder⟩ — used often to imply a causal or other relation to the preceding ⟨come closer, ~ I won't have to shout⟩ **3 a** : following next after this in order of position, narration, enumeration ⟨a hill, ~ a river valley, ~ another hill⟩ **b** : in addition : BESIDES ⟨and ~ there is the interest to be paid⟩ **4 a** : in that case : under those circumstances ⟨keep it, ~, if you want to⟩ ⟨if he didn't take it, ~ who did⟩ ⟨hurry, ~, if you're coming with us⟩ ⟨what if there should be a fire, what ~⟩ — used after *but* to qualify or offset a preceding statement ⟨it's true he lost the race, but ~ he never really expected to win it⟩ **b** : according to that : as may be inferred ⟨you did go, ~, after all⟩ ⟨your mind is made up, ~⟩ **c** : by way of summing up : as it appears ⟨these, ~, are the things you must do⟩ ⟨the cause of the accident, ~, seems to be established⟩ **d** : as a necessary or logical consequence : CONSEQUENTLY ⟨if the angles are equal, ~ their complements are equal⟩ — **and then some** : with much more in addition : at the very least ⟨would need all his luck *and then some*⟩

²then *conj* [ME *thanne, than, thenne, then*, fr. *thanne, than, thenne, then*, adv.] *obs* : at the time that : WHEN

³then \'then\ *n* -s [ME *thanne, than, thenne, then*, fr. *thanne, than, thenne, then*, adv.] : that time : that moment ⟨till ~, who knew the force of those dire arms —John Milton⟩ ⟨we should get there long before ~⟩ ⟨they were friends from ~ on⟩

⁴then \"\ *adj* [¹*then*] : existing, acting at, or belonging to the time mentioned ⟨the ~ current of opinion⟩ ⟨the ~ secretary of state⟩

⁵then \thən, (')then\ *dial var of* THAN

then·a·bouts \'thenə,baüts\ *adv* [¹*then* + *-abouts* (as in *thereabouts*)] : near that time : about then

then·a·days \-,dāz\ *adv* [¹*then* + *-adays* (as in *nowadays*)] : at that time : in those days

then and there *adv* : on the spot : IMMEDIATELY ⟨decided *then and there* to give up the trip and go home⟩

¹the·nar \'thē,när, -nə(r)\ *n* -s [NL, fr. Gk; akin to OHG *tenar* palm of the hand — more at DEN] **1 a** *or* **thenar eminence** : the ball of the thumb **b** *or* **thenar muscle** : the intrinsic musculature of the thumb **2** : PALM 2a; *sometimes* : ¹SOLE 1a

²thenar \"\ *also* **the·nal** \-ēnᵊl\ *adj* [*thenar* fr. NL *thenar; thenal* fr. NL *thenar* + E *-al*] : of, relating to, involving, or constituting the thenar ⟨~ neuritis⟩

the·nard·ite \thə'närdīt\ *n* -s [F *thénardite*, fr. Baron Louis J. *Thénard* †1857 French chemist + F *-ite*] : a mineral Na_2SO_4 consisting of native anhydrous sodium sulfate and occurring in white or brownish crystals, masses, or crusts often in connection with salt lakes

the·nard's blue \thə'närdz-\ *n, usu cap T* [after Baron L. J. *Thénard*] **1** : COBALT BLUE 1a **2** : COBALT BLUE 2

thence \'then(t)s *also* 'the-\ *adv* [ME *thannes, thennes*, fr. *thanene, thonene, thenene, thanne, thenne* from that place (fr. OE *thanon, thonan, thonon*) + *-s*, adv. suffix; akin to OFris *thana* from that place, OS & OHG *thanana, thanana*, ON *thanan* from that place, *thā* then — more at THEN] **1** : from that place ⟨proceeding ~ directly to college⟩ — often used with *from* ⟨timed . . . the farther walk from ~ to the entrance to the docks —F.W.Crofts⟩ **2 a** *archaic* : not there : ELSEWHERE **b** : away from there — used chiefly in statements of distance ⟨the church stood two miles ~⟩ **3** *archaic* : from that time : THENCEFORTH **4** : from that fact or circumstance : THEREFROM ⟨atomic formulas and all compounds ~ constructible —W.V.Quine⟩ ⟨a natural conclusion follows ~⟩

thenceafter \(')=¦==\ *adv* : after that time : AFTERWARD

thenceforth \(')=¦=\ *adv* [ME *thennes forth*] : from that time forward : THEREAFTER ⟨in the island which was ~ to be their home —Kemp Malone⟩

thenceforward *also* **thenceforwards** \(')=¦==\ *adv* [ME *thens forward*] : onward from that place or time : THENCEFORTH

thencefrom \(')=¦=\ *adv, archaic* : from that place : THENCE

then–clause \'=,=\ *n* : the conclusional clause of a conditional sentence — compare IF-CLAUSE

then·ness \'thennəs\ *n* -ES : the quality or state of having existence in past time ⟨feel a difference between nowness and ~⟩ or a specified past time ⟨thereness and ~ of a particular event⟩

the·no·ic acid \thə'nōik-\ *n* [*thiophene* + *-o-* + *-ic*] : either of two isomeric crystalline acids C_4H_3SCOOH made from thiophene; thiophene-carboxylic acid

then·o·yl \'thenə,wil\ *n* -s [*thenoic* (*acid*) + *-yl*] : either of the two radicals C_4H_3SCO- of the thenoic acids

then·yl \'thenᵊl\ *n* -s [*thiophene* + *-yl*] : the radical $C_4H_3SCH_2-$ derived from methyl-thiophene by removal of a hydrogen atom from the methyl group — compare BENZYL, THIENYL

theo- — see THE-

theo *abbr* **1** theology **2** theoretical

the·o·bro·ma \,thēə'brōmə\ *n, cap* [NL, fr. *the-* + Gk *brōma* food, fr. *bibrōskein* to devour — more at VORACIOUS] : a genus of tropical American trees (family Sterculiaceae) having large simple leaves, small flowers with inflexed petals borne on the old wood, and large fleshy fruits — see CACAO

theobroma oil *n* : COCOA BUTTER

the·o·bro·mine \-ō,mēn, -ōmən\ *n* -s [NL *Theobroma* + ISV *-ine*] : a feebly basic bitter crystalline compound $C_7H_8N_4O_2$ that is the principal base of cacao beans and chocolate, is found in small amounts elsewhere (as in kola nuts and tea), and is also made synthetically, that is isomeric with theophylline and is closely related to caffeine, and that is used in the form of salts and other derivatives as a diuretic, myocardial stimulant, and vasodilator; 3,7-dimethyl-xanthine

the·o·cen·tric \,thēə¦sen·trik\ *adj* [*the-* + *-centric*] : assuming God as the center : having God as the central interest and ultimate concern ⟨a ~ view of the world⟩ — **the·o·cen·tric·i·ty** \,==sen·'trisəd·ē\ *n*

the·o·cen·trism \,==¦sen,trizəm\ *or* **the·o·cen·tri·cism** \-rə,sizəm\ *n* -s : theocentric beliefs

the·oc·ra·cy \thē'äkrəsē, -si\ *n* -ES [Gk *theokratia*, fr. *the-* + *-kratia* -cracy] **1 a** : government of a state by the immediate direction or administration of God **b** : government or political rule by priests or clergy as representatives of God **2** : a state governed by God or by religious officials

the·oc·ra·sy \"\ *or* **the·o·cra·sia** *also* **the·o·kra·sia** \,thēə'krāz(h)ēə\ *n, pl* **theocrasies** *or* **theocrasias** [LGk *theokrasia*, fr. Gk *the-* + *-krasia* (fr. *kras-* — stem of *kerannynai* to mix — + *-ia* -y) — more at CRATER] **1** : a fusion or mixture of different deities in the minds of worshipers ⟨the ~ of divinities of East and West⟩; *also* : the identification of formerly separate deities ⟨the ~ of Zeus and Helios in the invocation of Zeus-Helios as one god⟩ **2** : an intimate union of the soul with the One or God in contemplation

the·o·crat \'thēə,krat\ *n* -s [*the-* + *-crat*] **1** : one who rules in or lives under a theocratic form of government **2** : one who favors a theocratic form of government

the·o·crat·ic \¦==krad·ik, -at|, |ēk\ *adj* : of, relating to, or being a theocracy ⟨a ~ state⟩ — **the·o·crat·i·cal·ly** \|ək(ə)lē, |ēk-, -li\ *adv*

the·oc·ri·te·an \thē,äkrə¦tēən\ *also* **the·oc·ri·tan** \thē'äkrətən\ *adj, usu cap* [*Theocritus*, 3d cent. B.C. Greek pastoral poet + E *-ean, -an*] : of, relating to, or in the manner of the poet Theocritus : IDYLLIC, PASTORAL, BUCOLIC ⟨a *Theocritean* idyl⟩ ⟨*Theocritean* simplicity⟩

theo·democracy \¦thē(,)ō+\ *n* [*the-* + *democracy*] : a community governed by the people according to the revealed will of deity

the·od·i·ce·an \thē,ädə¦sēən\ *adj* **1** : of or relating to theodicy **2** : having the character of a theodicy

the·od·i·cy \thē'ädəsē\ *n* -ES [modif. of F *théodicée*, fr. *théo-* the- + Gk *dikē* right, judgment — more at DICTION] **1** : vindication of the justice of God esp. in ordaining or permitting natural and moral evil **2** : an area of philosophy that treats of the nature and government of God and the destiny of the soul — NATURAL THEOLOGY

the·od·o·lite \thē'ädᵊl,īt\ *n* -s [NL *theodelitus*, perh. modif. of E *the alidade* — more at ALIDADE] : a surveyor's instrument for measuring horizontal and usu. also vertical angles that consists of a telescope mounted so as to swivel vertically in supports secured to a revolvable table carrying a vernier for reading horizontal angles and usu. includes also a graduated arc or circle for altitudes and a horizontal compass — compare TRANSIT 4 — **the·od·o·lit·ic** \=¦==¦id·ik\ *adj*

the·o·dore \'thēə,dō(ə)r, -dō(ə)r\ *n* -s [by folk etymology fr. Sp *fiador*] : FIADOR

¹the·o·do·sian \,thēə¦dōsh(ē)ən\ *adj, usu cap* **1** [*Theodosius* I †395 A.D. Roman emperor + E *-an*, adj. suffix] : of or relating to Theodosius the Great under whom the Roman state undertook to enforce Christianity and orthodoxy **2** [*Theodosius* II †450 A.D. Eastern Roman emperor + E *-an*, adj. suffix] : of or relating to Theodosius II or the Theodosian Code promulgated during his reign codifying imperial constitutions issued since the reign of Constantine I and including laws banning paganism and penalizing heresy

²theodosian \"\ *n* -s *usu cap* **1** [*Theodosius* †*ab* 538 A.D. patriarch of Alexandria + E *-an*, n. suffix] : a follower of Theodosius of Alexandria the leader of the Monophysites in the 6th century **2** [*Theodosius*, 16th cent. Russ. monk + E *-an*, n. suffix] : a follower of the Russian monk Theodosius

who preached in Lithuania in 1525 against idolatry and founded a sect practicing prayer for purification of articles acquired from unbelievers

the·o·do·tian \ˌthēəˈdōshən\ *n* -s *usu cap* [*Theodotus fl* 190 A.D. Byzantine tanner and religious teacher who founded dynamic monarchianism + E *-ian*] **:** a follower of Theodotus of Constantinople

the·o·dy \ˈthēədē\ *n* -ES [modif. (influenced by *the-*) of It *teodia*, fr. *te-* the- (fr. LL *theo-*) + *-odia* (as in *melodia* melody, fr. LL) — more at MELODY] **:** a hymn praising God

the·o·gon·ic \ˌthēəˈgänik\ *adj* **:** of or relating to theogony

the·og·o·nist \thēˈägənəst\ *n* -s **:** an authority on theogony

the·og·o·ny \-nē, -ni\ *n* -ES [Gk *theogonia*, fr. *the-* + *-gonia* (fr. the stem of *gignesthai* to be born + *-ia* -y) — more at KIN] **:** the generation or genealogy of the gods **:** a branch of theology or mythology that deals with the origin and descent of the deities

the·ol·a·try \thēˈälətrē\ *n* -ES [*the-* + *-latry*] **:** worship of a god

the·ol·o·gas·ter \thēˈäləˌgastə(r), ˌ=ˌ==ˈ==\ *n* -s [NL, fr. L *theologus* theologue + *-aster*] **:** a shallow theologian; *esp* **:** one who pretends to possess great theological knowledge

the·ol·o·gate \thēˈäləgət, -ləˌgāt\ *n* -s [*theologue* + *-ate*] **:** SEMINARY 2b(2)

the·ol·o·ger \thēˈäləjə(r)\ *n* -s [*theology* + *-er*] **:** THEOLOGIAN

the·o·lo·gian \ˌthēəˈlōjən *sometimes* -jēən\ *n* -s [MF *theologien*, fr. *theologie* theology (fr. LL *theologia*) + *-en* -an — more at THEOLOGY] **1 :** a specialist in theology **:** a professor of or writer on theology or divinity **2 :** a candidate for Roman Catholic priesthood engaged in his theological course of study

the·o·log·i·cal \ˌthēəˈläjəkəl, -jēk-\ *also* **the·o·log·ic** \-jik, -jēk\ *adj* [*theological* fr. MF *theologique* or LL *theologicus* + E *-al*; *theologic* fr. MF *theologique*, fr. LL *theologicus*, fr. *theologia* + L *-icus* -ic] **1 :** of, relating to, or emphasizing theology ⟨~ principles⟩ ⟨~ systems⟩ ⟨a religious outlook more ~ than devotional⟩ **2 :** preparing for a religious vocation (as for the ministry, priesthood, or rabbinate or for religious education in church and school) ⟨~ students⟩ ⟨~ education⟩ ⟨a ~ school⟩

the·o·log·i·cal·ly \-jək(ə)lē, -jēk-, -li\ *adv* **1 :** in a theological manner ⟨dealt with the problem of evil ~ rather than philosophically⟩ **2 :** from the standpoint of theology **:** as regards theology ⟨examined the ministerial candidate and found him ~ sound⟩

theological virtue *n* **:** one of the three basic spiritual graces faith, hope, and charity often held in Christian ethics to be created by God in the redeemed man and to perfect the natural virtues by giving them harmony and fulfillment in the service of God — called also *supernatural virtue*

theologico- *comb form* [NL, fr. LL *theologicus*] **:** theological and ⟨*theologico*philosophical⟩ ⟨*theologico*political⟩

the·ol·o·gism \thēˈäləˌjizəm\ *n* -s [fr. *theologize*, after such pairs as E *criticize: criticism*] **1 :** theological speculation **2 :** the act or process of subsuming other disciplines under theology **:** excessive extension of theological presuppositions or authority

the·ol·o·gist \-jəst\ *n* -s [NL *theologista*, fr. LL *theologia* theology + L *-ista* -ist] **:** THEOLOGIAN 1

the·ol·o·gize \-ləˌjīz\ *vb* -ED/-ING/-S [ML *theologizare*, fr. LL *theologia* + *-izare* -ize] *vi* **:** to theorize or speculate on theological subjects ⟨~ from a biblical basis⟩ ~ *vt* **:** to make theological **:** treat in a theological manner **:** give a religious character or theological significance to ⟨~ wit and good humor⟩ ⟨~ astrology⟩

the·o·lo·gou·me·non \ˌthēəlōˈgüməˌnän\ *or* **the·o·lo·gu·me·non** *n, pl* **theologoumena** *or* **theologumena** \-mənə\ [NL, fr. Gk *theologoumenon*, neut. of *theologoumenos*, pres. passive part. of *theologein* to discourse on the gods, talk about God, fr. *theologos* theologue] **:** a theological statement or concept in the area of individual opinion rather than of authoritative doctrine

the·o·logue \ˈthēəˌlȯg *also* -läg\ *n* -s [L *theologus*, fr. Gk *theologos*, fr. *the-* + *-logos* (fr. *legein* to speak) — more at LEGEND] **1 :** THEOLOGIAN **2** *or* **the·o·log** \"\ **:** a student preparing for full-time work in religion **:** a theological student

the·ol·o·gy \thēˈäləjē, -ji\ *n* -ES [ME *theologie*, fr. LL *theologia*, fr. L, study of the heathen gods, fr. Gk, fr. *the-* + *-logia* -logy] **1 :** rational interpretation of religious faith, practice, and experience: as **a :** the analysis, application, and presentation of the traditional doctrines of a religion or religious group — see APOLOGETICS, DOGMATIC THEOLOGY, NATURAL THEOLOGY, SYSTEMATIC THEOLOGY; compare PRACTICAL THEOLOGY **b :** the study of God and his relation to man and the world **:** a branch of systematic theology dealing with the arguments for the existence of God, the divine nature and attributes, and the doctrines of the Trinity, creation, and Providence — compare CHRISTOLOGY, ESCHATOLOGY, SOTERIOLOGY **c** (1) **:** the analytical and historical study of religious beliefs ⟨historical ~⟩ ⟨exegetical ~⟩ ⟨comparative ~⟩ — compare PATROLOGY, SYMBOLICS (2) **:** descriptive study of concepts relating to matters of ultimate concern ⟨a ~ of culture⟩ **d :** the interpretation of religious beliefs in relation to contemporary thought and life **e :** an inquiry that seeks an adequate interpretation of matters of ultimate concern **2 a :** a coherent body of theological doctrine **:** a theological theory or system ⟨a ~ of atonement⟩ ⟨the normative status of Thomist ~⟩; *specif* **:** the doctrine of God **b** (1) **:** a body of theological opinion distinguished by some characteristic emphasis, method, or association ⟨the ~ of the Word of God⟩ ⟨the ~ of paradox⟩ ⟨Calvinist ~⟩ (2) **:** the group of theologians sharing such a viewpoint ⟨the task of present-day liberal ~⟩ **c :** the sum of the beliefs held by an individual or group regarding matters of religious faith or of ultimate concern **:** the ideational element in religion ⟨the vagueness of the average man's ~⟩ **3 :** a course of Roman Catholic seminary study usu. requiring four years and including Scripture, church history, homiletics, canon law, moral and dogmatic theology

the·om·a·chist \thēˈäməkəst\ *n* -s [*theomachy* + *-ist*] **:** one who resists God or the gods or the divine will

the·om·a·chy \-kē\ *n* -ES [LL *theomachia*, fr. Gk, fr. *the-* + *-machia* -machy] **1** *obs* **:** opposition to God or the gods or the divine will **2 :** a battle or strife among the gods

the·o·man·cy \ˈthēəˌman(t)sē\ *n* -ES [*the-* + *-mancy*] **:** divination by the responses of oracles supposed to be divinely inspired

theo·mania \ˌthē(ˌ)ō+\ *n* [NL, fr. *the-* + *mania*] **:** religious madness in which the patient believes that he is the Deity or is inspired — **theo·maniac** \"+\ *n*

theo·monism \"+\ *n* [*the-* + *monism*] **:** metaphysical monism holding that one divine spirit governs the universe **:** theistic spiritualism

the·o·mor·phic \ˌthēəˈmȯrfik\ *adj* [Gk *theomorphos* (fr. *the-* + *morphē* form) + E *-ic* — more at FORM] **:** having divine form **:** formed in the image of deity **:** endued with a divine aspect ⟨the Christian emphasis on the ~ conception of man rather than the anthropomorphic conception of God⟩

the·o·mor·phism \ˌthēəˈmȯ(r)ˌfizəm\ *n* -s [*the-* + *-morphism*] **:** representation or conception of something or someone in the form of deity **:** the condition of being formed in the image of God

the·on·o·mous \thēˈänəməs\ *adj* [*the-* + *-nomous* (as in *autonomous*)] **:** governed by God **:** subject to God's authority — compare AUTONOMOUS, HETERONOMOUS — **the·on·o·mous·ly** *adv*

the·on·o·my \-mē\ *n* -ES [G *theonomie*, fr. *theo-* the- + *-nomie* -nomy] **:** government by God **:** divine rule; *also* **:** the state of being subject to God's authority and rule ⟨are told . . . to re-turn to Christianity, to ~ —R.K.Bultmann⟩

the·o·pan·tism \ˌthēəˈpanˌtizəm\ *n* -s [*the-* + Gk *pant-*, *pas* all, every + E *-ism* — more at PAN-] **:** the mystical doctrine that God is the sole reality — compare PANTHEISM

the·o·pas·chite \ˌthēəˈpaˌskīt\ *n* -s *usu cap* [ML *theopaschita*, fr. LGk *theopaschitēs*, fr. Gk *the-* + *paschein* to experience, suffer + *-itēs* -ite — more at PATHOS] **:** one holding that in Christ's passion God suffered; *specif* **:** an adherent of a sixth century sect of Monophysites — compare PATRIPASSIAN

theo·pathetic \ˌthē(ˌ)ō+\ *or* **the·o·path·ic** \ˌthēəˈpathik\ *adj* [*the-* + *pathetic* or *-pathic*] **:** of or relating to theopathy; *esp* **:** of, relating to, or associated with intense absorption in religious devotion

the·op·a·thy \thēˈäpəthē\ *n* -ES [*the-* + *-pathy*] **:** experience or capacity for experience of the divine illumination; *esp* **:** intense absorption in religious devotion

the·oph·a·gous \thēˈäfəgəs\ *also* **the·o·phag·ic** \ˌthēəˈfajik\ *adj* [*theophagous* fr. *the-* + *-phagous*; *theophagic* fr. *theophagy* + *-ic*] **:** of, relating to, or practicing theophagy

the·oph·a·gy \thēˈäfəjē\ *n* -ES [*the-* + *-phagy*] **:** the sacramental eating of a god typically in the form of an animal, image, or other symbol as a part of a religious ritual and commonly for the purpose of communion with or the receiving of power from the god

the·o·phan·ic \ˌthēəˈfanik\ *also* **the·oph·a·nous** \thēˈäfənəs\ *adj* [*theophany* + *-ic* or *-ous*] **1 :** of, relating to, or characterized by theophany **2 :** that constitutes a theophany

¹the·oph·a·ny \thēˈäfənē\ *n* -ES [ML *theophania*, fr. LGk *theophaneia*, fr. Gk *the-* + *-phaneia* (as in *epiphaneia* appearance, manifestation) — more at EPIPHANY] **1 :** a physical presentation or personal manifestation of a deity to an individual **:** a brief appearance of Deity ⟨the glorious ~ in which Jehovah will avenge himself of his adversaries —R.H.Pfeiffer⟩ **2 :** something manifesting or revealing deity ⟨in earlier Hebrew traditions angels had often been direct *theophanies* —George Santayana⟩ ⟨an enchanted world where every living thing was a ~ —Evelyn Underhill⟩

²theophany \"\ *n* -ES [LL *theophania*, fr. Gk, pl., fr. *the-* + *-phania* (fr. the stem of *phainein* to show + *-ia*, neut. pl. of *-ios*, adj. suffix) — more at FANCY] *Eastern Church* **:** EPIPHANY

the·o·phil·an·throp·ic \ˌthēōˌfilənˈthräpik\ *adj* [F *théophilanthropique*, fr. *théophilanthropie* + *-ique* -ic] **:** of or relating to theophilanthropism or the theophilanthropists

theo·phi·lan·thro·pism \ˌthēōfəˈlan(t)thrəˌpizəm\ *n* [F *théophilanthropisme*, fr. *théophilanthropie* + *-isme* -ism] **:** the doctrines or tenets of the theophilanthropists

the·o·phi·lan·thro·pist \-pəst\ *n* [*theophilanthropy* + *-ist*] **:** a member of a deistic society established in Paris during the period of the Directory aiming to institute in place of Christianity, which had been officially abolished, a new religion affirming belief in the existence of God, in the immortality of the soul, and in virtue

the·o·phi·lan·thro·py \-pē\ *n* [F *théophilanthropie*, fr. *théo-* the- + *philanthopie* philanthropy, fr. LL *philanthropia*] **:** THEOPHILANTHROPISM

theo·phobia \ˌthē(ˌ)ō+\ *n* [NL, fr. *the-* + *phobia*] **1 :** dread of the wrath of God **2 :** a phobia of which God is the object

the·o·phor·ic \ˌthēəˈfȯrik, -fär-\ *or* **the·oph·o·rous** \thēˈäf(ə)rəs\ *adj* [*theophoric* fr. Gk *theophoros* theophoric (fr. *the-* + *-phoros* -phorous) + E *-ic*; *theophorous* fr. Gk *theophoros*] **:** derived from or bearing the name of a god

the·o·phras·ta·ce·ae \ˌthēəˌfrasˈtāsēˌē\ *n pl, cap* [NL, fr. *Theophrasta*, type genus (after *Theophrastus*, who wrote treatises on botany) + *-aceae*] **:** a family of mainly tropical trees and shrubs (order Primulales) distinguished from Myrsinaceae mainly by staminodia in the flowers — **the·o·phras·ta·ceous** \ˌ=ˌ==ˈstāshəs\ *adj*

the·o·phras·tian \ˌthēəˈfras(h)chən\ *adj, usu cap* [*Theophrastus* †*ab* 287 B.C. Greek philosopher and scientist + E *-ian*] **1 :** of or relating to the philosopher Theophrastus or his writings on natural philosophy **2 :** treated in the manner of Theophrastus in his sketches of character types ⟨*Theophrastian* characters⟩

the·o·phyl·line \ˌthēəˈfiˌlēn, -lən\ *n* -s [ISV *theo*bromine + *phyll-* + *-ine*] **:** a feebly basic bitter crystalline compound $C_7H_8N_4O_2$ that is extracted from tea leaves but is usu. made synthetically, that is isomeric with theobromine and closely related to caffeine, and that is used in medicine often in the form of derivatives or combinations with other drugs chiefly as a muscle relaxant in asthma, as a vasodilator, and as a diuretic; 1,3-dimethyl-xanthine

theophylline ethylenediamine *n* **:** AMINOPHYLLINE

the·op·neust \ˈthēäpˌn(y)üst\ *or* **the·op·neus·tic** \ˌ=ˌ=ˈn(y)üstik\ *adj* [*theopneust* fr. Gk *theopneustos*, fr. *the-* + (assumed) *pneustos*, verbal of *pnein* to breathe; *theopneustic* fr. Gk *theopneustos* + E *-ic* — more at SNEEZE] **:** given by inspiration of the Spirit of God **:** divinely inspired

theor *abbr* theorem

the·or·bist \thēˈȯrbəst\ *n* -s **:** a player on a theorbo

the·or·bo \-r(ˌ)bō\ *n* -s [modif. of It *tiorba*, *teorba*, prob. fr. Venetian dial. *tiorba*, *tuorba* traveling bag, fr. Slovenian *torba*, fr. Turk, bag; fr. its having been carried by wandering mendicants] **:** an obsolete 17th century musical instrument like a large lute but having two necks with two sets of pegs, the upper carrying long bass strings used for open tones **:** ARCHLUTE

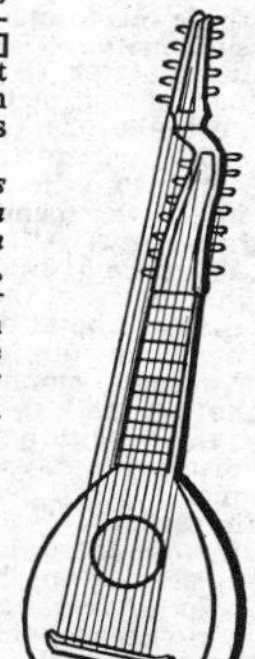

theorbo

the·o·rem \ˈthēərəm, ˈthi(ə)r- *sometimes* ˈthēr-\ *n* -s [LL *theorema*, fr. Gk *theōrēma* sight, spectacle, theory, theorem, fr. *theōrein* to look at, behold, contemplate, consider, fr. *theōros* spectator, fr. *thea* sight, view — more at THEATER] **1 a :** a statement in mathematics that has been proved or whose truth has been conjectured **b :** a rule or statement of relations (as the binomial theorem) expressed in a formula or by symbols **c :** a formula, proposition, or statement in logic deduced from a set of axioms **2 :** an idea accepted or proposed as a demonstrable truth and often forming part of a general theory **:** PROPOSITION, THEORY ⟨an arms policy based on the ~ that the best defense is offense⟩ ⟨test the ~s that make up his theory of social structure⟩ **syn** see PRINCIPLE

the·o·re·mat·ic \ˌthēərəˈmad·ik\ *adj* [Gk *theōrēmatikos*, fr. *theōrēmat-*, *theōrēma* + *-ikos* -ic] **1 :** of, relating to, or comprised in a theorem **2 :** consisting of theorems — **the·o·re·mat·i·cal·ly** \-d·ək(ə)lē\ *adv*

theorem of py·thag·o·ras \-pəˈthagərəs, -pī-, -thaig-\ *usu cap P* [after *Pythagoras*, 6th cent. B.C. philosopher and mathematician] **:** PYTHAGOREAN PROPOSITION

the·o·ret·ic \ˌthēəˈred·ik\ *or* **the·o·ret·ics** \-ks\ *n, pl* **theoretics** [LL *theoretica*, fr. fem. of *theoreticus*] **:** the speculative part of an art or science **:** THEORY

the·o·ret·i·cal \ˌ=ˌ=ˈred· əkəl, -et|, |ēk-\ *also* **the·o·ret·ic** \|ik, |ēk\ *adj* [LL *theoreticus*, fr. Gk *theōrētikos*, fr. *theōrētos* (verbal of *theōrein* to look at, behold, contemplate, consider) + *-ikos* -ic, -ical — more at THEOREM] **1 a :** of, relating to, or having the character of theory — compare APPLIED, PRACTICAL **b :** depending on or confined to theory **:** terminating in theory or speculation **:** SPECULATIVE ⟨~ learning⟩ ⟨~ mechanics⟩ — compare DESCRIPTIVE **2 :** addicted to speculative thought **:** given to theorizing; *also* **:** having the ability to theorize **3 :** of or relating to abstract knowledge as contrasted with practical knowledge (as moral intuitions or religious beliefs) **:** CONTEMPLATIVE, INTELLECTUAL — compare PRACTICAL REASON **4 :** existing only in theory **:** HYPOTHETICAL, FICTITIOUS

the·o·ret·i·cal·ly \|ək(ə)lē, |ēk-, -li\ *adv* **1 :** with reference to theory ⟨the most conservative ~ of the . . . British chemists —S.F.Mason⟩ **:** in a theoretical way ⟨it is quite possible to enjoy flowers . . . without knowing anything about plants ~ —John Dewey⟩ **2 :** according to an ideal or assumed set of facts or principles **:** in theory **:** HYPOTHETICALLY ⟨the absolute . . . vacuum ~ involves an area in which no atomic particles are present —T.A.Dickinson⟩ ⟨a task that would ~ take a man equipped with pencil and paper 800 years —Robert Bendiner⟩

theoretical reason *n* **:** reason leading to cognition **:** the capacity to grasp the universal in the particular — contrasted with *practical reason*

the·o·re·ti·cian \ˌthēərəˈtishən\ *n* -s **1 :** THEORIST ⟨attracted foreign scientists, chiefly young ~s —F.D.Rasetti⟩ ⟨dismiss professors as eggheads and ivory-domed ~s —L.L.Snyder⟩ **2 :** one who bases practice on theory ⟨his emphasis upon the craft of composition places him among the ~s —Norman Demuth⟩

theoretico- *comb form* [*theoretical*] **:** theoretical and ⟨*theoretico*practical⟩

theoretic virtue *n*, *Aristotelianism* **:** one of the intellectual virtues of understanding, science, and wisdom

¹the·o·ric \ˈthēərik\ *or* **the·o·rique** \ˌthēəˈrēk\ *n* -s [ME *theorique*, fr. MF, fr. LL *theorice*, fr. fem. of *theoricus*] **1** *archaic* **:** SPECULATION, THEORY — sometimes used in pl. **2 :** a device used in early modern astronomy for calculating positions of bodies

²the·o·ric \thēˈȯrik, -ˈärik\ *or* **the·or·i·cal** \-rəkəl\ *adj* [MF *theorique*, fr. LL *theoricus*, fr. *theoria* theory + L *-icus* -ic, -ical] **1** *obs* **:** THEORETICAL **2** [Gk *theōrikos*, fr. *theōria* act of viewing + E *-ic*] **:** of or relating to an ancient Greek public spectacle — **the·or·i·cal·ly** \-rək(ə)lē\ *adv*

the·o·ri·cian \ˌthēəˈrishən\ *n* -s [F *théoricien*, fr. *théorique*, after such pairs as F *mathématique* mathematic: *mathématicien* mathematician] **:** THEORIST

the·o·rist \ˈthēərəst, ˈthi(ə)r- *sometimes* ˈthēr-\ *n* -s [*theory* + *-ist*] **:** one who theorizes **:** a person given to speculative thought **:** one who formulates theories (as to account for perceived phenomena)

the·o·ri·za·tion \ˌthēərəˈzāshən\ *n* -s **:** an act or product of theorizing **:** formation of a theory **:** SPECULATION

the·o·rize \ˈthēəˌrīz\ *vb* -ED/-ING/-S *see -ize in Explan Notes* [ML *theorizare*, fr. LL *theoria* + *-izare* -ize] *vi* **:** to form a theory or theories **:** form opinions solely by theory ~ *vt* **1 :** to formulate a theory about **2 :** to postulate (something stated) as a step in the formulation of a theory

the·o·riz·er \-zə(r)\ *n* -s **:** one that theorizes

the·o·ry \ˈthēərē, ˈthi(ə)r-, -ri *sometimes* ˈthēr-\ *n* -ES [LL *theoria*, fr. Gk *theōria* act of viewing, contemplation, consideration, theory, fr. *theōrein* to look at, behold, contemplate, consider + *-ia* -y — more at THEOREM] **1** *archaic* **:** imaginative contemplation of reality **:** direct intellectual apprehension **:** INSIGHT ⟨nor can I think I have the true ~ of death when I contemplate a skull —Sir Thomas Browne⟩ **2 a :** a belief, policy, or procedure proposed or followed as the basis of action **:** a principle or plan of action ⟨educational system, based on the ~ that men learn better from actual experience than from books —*Amer. Guide Series: Mich.*⟩ ⟨wanted to kill him, presumably on the ~ that dead men tell no tales —D.D.Martin⟩ ⟨the hedonistic ~ of ethics⟩ **b :** an ideal or hypothetical set of facts, principles, or circumstances ⟨the days when law and order was more of a ~ than a fact —Seth Agnew⟩ — often used in the phrase *in theory* ⟨the failure in practice of what looked so promising in ~⟩ **3 a** (1) **:** the body of generalizations and principles developed in association with practice in a field of activity (as medicine, music) and forming its content as an intellectual discipline **:** pure as distinguished from applied art or science ⟨spent two years . . . in the study of ~ and piano —W.T.Upton⟩ ⟨made a distinct contribution to museum ~ and practice —R.F.Bach⟩ (2) **:** the coherent set of hypothetical, conceptual, and pragmatic principles forming the general frame of reference for a field of inquiry (as for deducing principles, formulating hypotheses for testing, undertaking actions) ⟨the ~ of monetary calculation . . . is a part of the general theory of praxeology —Ludwig Von Mises⟩ ⟨controversies over the ~ of morals⟩ ⟨contributions to the ~ of knowledge⟩ (3) **:** a body of mathematical theorems presenting a clear, rounded, and systematic view of a subject ⟨~ of equations⟩ ⟨~ of probability⟩ — see THEORY OF NUMBERS **b :** abstract knowledge ⟨necessary . . . in designing retaining walls to be guided by experience rather than by ~ —G.T.Snelling⟩ ⟨the period of transition from ~ to practice in the study of shorthand —J.R.Gregg⟩ **c** (1) **:** a field of intellectual inquiry ⟨literary critics badly need the sort of foundation that such . . . inquiries as ~ of signs and ~ of value could give them —P.B.Rice⟩ (2) **:** a systematic analysis, elucidation, or definition of a concept ⟨study the philosophers' conflicting *theories* of right⟩ — see COHERENCE THEORY **4 :** a judgment, conception, proposition, or formula (as relating to the nature, action, cause, or origin of a phenomenon or group of phenomena) formed by speculation or deduction or by abstraction and generalization from facts ⟨her ~ of the relationship of order to disorder in the language of poetry —Archibald MacLeish⟩ ⟨the wave ~ of light⟩ ⟨the ~ that the individual recapitulates the development of the race⟩ ⟨the gesture ~ of the origin of language⟩ ⟨the emotive ~ of value judgments⟩: as **a :** a hypothetical entity or structure explaining or relating an observed set of facts ⟨the Freudian ~ of the superego⟩ ⟨the Greek ~ of the atom⟩ **b :** a working hypothesis given probability by experimental evidence or by factual or conceptual analysis but not conclusively established or accepted as a law ⟨the ~ of relativity⟩ ⟨the ~ that compounds in dilute solutions obey the same laws that apply to gases⟩ ⟨the ~ of radioactive decay⟩ ⟨a ~ of exchange rates which is merely a special case of the general theory of exchange and markets —K.E.Boulding⟩ **5 :** an unproved assumption **:** CONJECTURE, SPECULATION, SUPPOSITION ⟨her ~ that the house was once occupied by spies⟩

theory of epigenesis : a theory in biology: development involves differentiation of an initially undifferentiated entity

theory of exchange : a theory in physics: when thermal radiation occurs from one body to another, it also takes place in the opposite direction, and therefore the question as to whether or not the temperature of either body will change depends upon whether the body gains more energy than it loses or loses more than it gains

theory of games : a method of applying mathematical logic to determine which of several available strategies is likely to maximize one's gain or to minimize one's loss in a game, a business situation, or a military problem in which one's opponent or opponents also can choose between several strategies — called also *game theory*

theory of internal relations : the doctrine that all relations are internal and every part of reality is intrinsically related to every other part

theory of numbers : a theory dealing with properties of integers

theory of signs : SEMIOTIC

theory of types : a rule in symbolic logic: the arguments for which a propositional function is significant are restricted by type

the·o·soph \ˈthēəˌsäf\ *n* -s [F *théosophe*, fr. ML *theosophus*] **:** THEOSOPHIST 1

the·os·o·pher \thēˈäsəfə(r)\ *n* -s [ML *theosophus* (fr. LGk *theosophos*, fr. Gk *the-* + *sophos* clever, wise, skilled) + E *-er*] **:** THEOSOPHIST

the·o·soph·i·cal \ˌthēəˈsäfəkəl, -fēk-\ *also* **the·o·soph·ic** \-fik, -fēk\ *adj* **:** of or relating to theosophy — **the·o·soph·i·cal·ly** \-fək(ə)lē, -fēk-, -li\ *adv*

the·os·o·phism \thēˈäsəˌfizəm\ *n* -s [*theosophy* + *-ism*] **:** belief in theosophy

the·os·o·phist \-fəst\ *n* -s [*theosophy* + *-ist*] **1 :** an adherent of theosophy **2** *usu cap* **:** a member of a theosophical society

the·os·o·phis·tic \thēˌäsəˈfistik\ *also* **the·os·o·phis·ti·cal** \-təkəl\ *adj* **:** THEOSOPHICAL

the·os·o·phize \thēˈäsəˌfīz\ *vi* -ED/-ING/-S [*theosophy* + *-ize*] **:** to speculate theosophically

the·os·o·phy \-əfē, -fi\ *n* -ES [ML *theosophia*, fr. LGk, fr. Gk *the-* + *sophia* wisdom — more at -SOPHY] **1 :** a body of doctrine relating to deity, cosmos, and self and held to rest on direct intuitions of supersensible reality by preternaturally perceptive individuals and to give a wisdom superior to that of historical religion or empirical philosophy or science by which the initiate can master nature and guide his destiny **:** a system of often occult and esoteric thought presented as a means of individual salvation and sometimes associated with mysticism, pantheism, or magic — compare BOEHMENISM, GNOSTICISM, NEOPLATONISM, SWEDENBORGIANISM **2** *usu cap* **:** a syncretistic system of theosophy following chiefly Hindu philosophies and associated with a movement originating in the U.S. in 1875, aiming to serve through its societies as the nucleus of a universal brotherhood of man and to guide the individual toward perfect wisdom through the study of world literature on the laws of the universe and through the development under the esoteric teachings of mahatmas of his latent inner senses responsive to the invisible cosmos, and teaching physical and spiritual evolution (as of the soul through reincarnations); *also* **:** the modern movement promulgating this theosophy

the·o·to·kion \ˌthēōˈtōˌkyȯn, -tōˈkēˌȯn\ *n, pl* **theoto·kia** \-(ˌ)kyä, -ˈkē(ˌ)ä\ [MGk, fr. LGk *theotokos* bearer of God (epithet of the Virgin Mary), fr. Gk *the-* + *-tokos* (fr. *tiktein* to bear, beget) — more at THANE] **:** a hymn of the Eastern Church ascribing praise to the Virgin Mary as the Mother of God and forming the final troparion of a canonical ode

the·ow \ˈthā(,)ō\ *n* -s [OE *thēow;* akin to OHG *thiomuoti* servant's disposition, humility, *thionōn* to serve, ON *thjōna* to serve, Goth *thius* servant, and perh. to OIr *techid* he flees, Skt *takti* he hurries; basic meaning: to run] **:** a British slave of Anglo-Saxon times

ther- *or* **thero-** *comb form* [Gk *thēr-, thēro-,* fr. *thēr* — more at FIERCE] **:** wild beast ⟨*Ther*omorpha⟩ ⟨*thero*dont⟩

ther·a·peu·sis \,therəˈpyüsə̇s\ *n, pl* **therapeu·ses** \-ü,sēz\ [NL, fr. Gk, treatment, fr. *therapeuein* to attend, treat] **:** therapeutic treatment **:** THERAPEUTICS ⟨high pressure oxygen as a means of ~ in CO poisoning —*Science*⟩ ⟨isolation of vitamin K . . . an important advance in ~ —*Surgery, Gynecology & Obstetrics*⟩

ther·a·peu·tae \,therəˈpyü(,)tē\ *n pl, cap* [NL, fr. Gk *therapeutai,* pl. of *therapeutēs* attendant, worshiper, medical attendant, fr. *therapeuein* to attend] **:** ascetics of both sexes held to have dwelt anciently near Alexandria and described by Philo as devoted to contemplation and meditation

ther·a·peu·tant \-üt³nt\ *n* -s [¹*therapeutic* + *-ant*] **:** a healing or curative agent or medicine ⟨plant ~*s*⟩ ⟨spraying ~*s* on elms is much easier and cheaper —*Agric. Chemicals*⟩

¹**ther·a·peu·tic** \,therəˈpyüd·ik, -üt\, \ēk\ *also* **ther·a·peu·ti·cal** \ə̇kəl, \ēk-\ *adj* [*therapeutic* fr. Gk *therapeutikos,* fr. *therapeutos* (verbal of *therapeuein* to attend, worship, treat medically, fr. *theraps* attendant) + *-ikos* -ic; *therapeutical* fr. Gk *therapeutikos* + E *-al*] **:** of or relating to the treatment of disease or disorders by remedial agents or methods **:** CURATIVE, MEDICINAL ⟨~ diet⟩ ⟨~ dose⟩ ⟨~ approach to criminality⟩ — **ther·a·peu·ti·cal·ly** \ə̇k(ə)lē, \ēk-, -li\ *adv*

²**therapeutic** \"\ *n, usu cap* [NL *therapeutae* + E *-ic*] **:** one of the Therapeutae

therapeutic abortion *n* **:** abortion induced when pregnancy constitutes a threat to the mother's life

therapeutic nihilism *n* **:** skepticism regarding the worth of therapeutic agents esp. in a particular disease

therapeutic positivism *n* **:** positivism that undertakes to remedy the ambiguities, paradoxes, and perplexities of traditional philosophical and esp. metaphysical problems by employing logical analysis to disclose the linguistic confusions that give rise to them

ther·a·peu·tics \,therəˈpyüd·iks, -üt, \ēks\ *n pl but sing or pl in constr* [trans. of LL *therapeutica,* fr. Gk *therapeutika,* fr. neut pl. of *therapeutikos* therapeutic] **:** a branch of medical science that treats of the application of remedies for diseases **:** THERAPY — often used in combination ⟨electro*therapeutics*⟩

therapeutic shock *n* **:** SHOCK THERAPY

therapeutic test *n* **:** a test to aid in diagnosis of an undiagnosed disease by giving the specific remedy for the disease suspected ⟨use of liver extract as a *therapeutic test* for suspected pernicious anemia⟩

ther·a·peu·tist \,therəˈpyüd·əst, -ütə-\ *n* -s [*therapeutic* + *-ist*] **:** THERAPIST

ther·a·pho·sa \,therəˈfōsə, -ōzə\ *n, cap* [NL, fr. Gk *theraphion,* dim. of *thēr,* *thērion* wild beast, animal, monster — more at FIERCE] **:** the type genus of the family Theraphosidae including a rare African spider (*T. blondi*) that is the largest of spiders with a body length of over three inches and a leg span of nearly 10 inches

ther·a·phose \ˈtherə,fōs, -ōz\ *n* -s [NL *Theraphosa*] **:** a spider of the genus *Theraphosa*

¹**ther·a·pho·sid** \,therəˈfōsə̇d, -ōzə̇d\ *adj* [NL *Theraphosidae*] **:** of or relating to the Theraphosidae

²**theraphosid** \"\ *n* -s **:** a spider of the family Theraphosidae **:** BIRD SPIDER

ther·a·pho·si·dae \,therəˈfōsə,dē, -ōzə-\ *n pl, cap* [NL, fr. *Theraphosa,* type genus + *-idae*] **:** a family of very large chiefly tropical spiders with four spinnerets and the eight eyes in a compact group — see BIRD SPIDER, EURYPELMA, TARANTULA, THERAPHOSA

ther·a·pist \ˈtherəpə̇st\ *n* -s [*therapy* + *-ist*] **1 :** a physician concerned with treatment of disease **2 :** one trained in applying occupational or physical measures in the treatment or rehabilitation of patients ⟨occupational ~⟩

ther·a·pon \ˈtherə,pän\ *n* [NL, fr. Gk *therapont-, therapōn* attendant; akin to Gk *theraps* attendant] **1** *cap* **:** a genus of small silvery Indo-Pacific percoid fishes — see SILVER PERCH **2** -s **:** any fish of the genus *Therapon*

¹**the·rap·sid** \thəˈrapsə̇d\ *adj* [NL *Therapsida*] **:** of or relating to the Therapsida

²**therapsid** \"\ *n* -s **:** a reptile of the order Therapsida

the·rap·si·da \-sədə\ *n pl, cap* [NL, fr. Gk *theraps* attendant + NL *-ida*] **:** an order of Reptilia comprising Permian and Triassic reptiles (subclass Synapsida) with upright-walking rather than crawling habits and including the ancestors of the mammals

ther·a·py \ˈtherəpē, -pi\ *n* -ES [NL *therapia,* fr. Gk *therapeia* attendance, medical treatment, fr. *therapeuein* to attend, treat + *-ia* -y — more at THERAPEUTIC] **1 :** treatment of disease in animals or plants by therapeutic means ⟨specific ~⟩ ⟨surgical ~⟩ ⟨dance ~⟩ — often used in combination ⟨chemo*therapy*⟩ ⟨syphilo*therapy*⟩ ⟨hydro*therapy*⟩ **2 :** PSYCHOTHERAPY **3 a :** treatment of the maladjusted (as prisoners, social agency clients) through a program of clinical, custodial, or casework services in order to further their restoration to society **b :** a force working to relieve a social tension ⟨recreation activities provide a form of community ~⟩ ⟨a human relations program as ~ for workers⟩

ther·a·va·da \,therəˈvädə\ *n* -s *usu cap* [Pali *theravāda,* lit., doctrine of the elders, fr. *thera* elder (fr. *thera* old, venerable, fr. Skt *sthavira* stout, old, venerable) + *vāda* speech, doctrine, fr. Skt, fr. *vadati* he speaks — more at STEER] **:** HINAYANA

ther·a·va·din \-dᵊn\ *n* -s *usu cap* [Pali *theravādin,* fr. *theravāda* Hinayana] **:** an adherent of Hinayana

ther·blig \ˈthər(,)blig\ *n* -s [anagram, after Frank B. *Gilbreth* †1924 Am. engineer] **1 :** one of the manual, visual, or mental elements into which an industrial manual operation may be analyzed in time and motion study **2 :** a symbol devised for representing a therblig in writing or notation

¹**there** \(ˈ)tha(a)(ə)r, (ˈ)the\, \ə\ *adv* [ME *ther, there, thar, thare,* fr. OE *thǣr, thēr, thār;* akin to OHG *dār* there, ON & Goth *thar,* Skt *tarhi* then, OE *thæt* that — more at THAT] **1 a :** in or at that place **:** in or at a place other than that of the speaker — opposed to *here* ⟨stand over ~ until I call you⟩ ⟨put it ~ on that table⟩ ⟨please go home and stay ~⟩ **b :** in or at a place indicated, referred or pointed to, described, or qualified ⟨~, where the roads meet⟩ ⟨for where your treasure is, ~ will your heart be also —Mt 6:21 (AV)⟩ — used to call attention to something ⟨~ goes the dinner bell⟩ ⟨~ he comes now⟩ or point to with approval ⟨~'s glory for you⟩; often used interjectionally ⟨~, look at that⟩ ⟨~, that must be his car now stopping outside⟩ **2 :** to or into that place **:** THITHER — used after verbs of motion or direction ⟨time to go ~ and back⟩ ⟨seldom go ~ any more⟩ ⟨when she got ~ the cupboard was bare —*Mother Goose*⟩ **3 :** at that point of time in a continuing action or progress ⟨stop right ~ before you say any more⟩ **4 :** in that matter **:** in that respect **:** in relation to that ⟨to sleep, perchance to dream: aye, ~'s the rub —Shak.⟩ ⟨just ~ is where I disagree with you⟩ **5** — used interjectionally to express satisfaction ⟨~, that's finished at last⟩ ⟨~, I told you so⟩ or approval ⟨~, that should be enough scrubbing⟩ or encouragement or sympathy ⟨~ now, it's not really that bad, is it⟩ or spitefulness or defiance ⟨I'm not sorry I said it, so ~⟩ — **have been there :** to achieve one's object **:** SUCCEED — **have been there :** to know at first hand ⟨her hold on actuality is everywhere firm. She *has been there* — she knows —L.O.Coxe⟩ — **in there :** continuing the fight or the struggle **:** not quitting or flagging in effort ⟨plain people . . . will be *in there* fighting for peace and freedom —G.P.Musselman⟩ ⟨a revue that . . . involved the services of a bunch of people who were always *in there* trying —Wolcott Gibbs⟩

²**there** \(,)tha(a)r, (,)the\, \ə, *in sense 1 often* thə(r)\ *pron* [ME *ther, thar,* fr. OE *thǣr,* fr. *thǣr,* adv.] **1** — used as a function word to introduce a sentence or clause esp. when the verb has no complement ⟨~ shall come a time⟩ ⟨~ shall be weeping and gnashing of teeth —Lk 13:28 (AV)⟩ ⟨~ are many things to be considered⟩ ⟨~ is no telling when he'll be home⟩ **2** — used as an indefinite substitute for a name ⟨hi ~⟩ ⟨well, hello ~⟩

³**there** *like* ¹THERE\ *n* -s [¹*there*] **1 :** that place or position — opposed to *here* ⟨there is no here and no ~ . . . in pure space —James Ward⟩ **2 :** that point ⟨I'll get everything ready and you take it from ~⟩

⁴**there** \"\ *adj* [¹*there*] **1 a** — used for emphasis esp. after a demonstrative pronoun ⟨I'd rather take those ~⟩ or after a noun modified by a demonstrative adjective ⟨those men ~ can tell you⟩ **b** *substand* — used for emphasis after a demonstrative adjective but before the noun modified ⟨I wouldn't vote for that ~ fellow for anything⟩ **2 :** EXISTENT, PRESENT ⟨nothing is more imperiously ~ for observation and study than the tactics —K.D.Burke⟩ ⟨prosperity was ~ and almost every civilian shared in it —*Time*⟩ ⟨the pain was still ~ when he woke up⟩ **3 a :** DEPENDABLE, RELIABLE ⟨he's always right ~ when you need him⟩ **b :** fully conscious **:** fully aware ⟨an hour that I lay there . . . I was ~ in the head by that time —J.M. Cain⟩

there·abouts \ˈ=ə,bau̇ts, ,==ˈ=\ *also* **there·about** \-t\ *adv* [*thereabout* fr. ME *ther aboute,* fr. OE *thǣr abūtan,* fr. *thǣr* there + *abūtan* about; *thereabouts* fr. ME *ther aboutes,* fr. *ther aboute* + *-s* (as in *dayes* days)] **1 :** near that place **:** in the neighborhood ⟨film set in the Mojave desert and the mountains *thereabout* —*Sydney (Australia) Bull.*⟩ ⟨stayed there or ~ for several days⟩ **2 a :** near that time or date ⟨got home at six o'clock or ~⟩ ⟨vignettes seen through the French illustrations of the 1850's or ~ —Irving Kolodin⟩ **b :** near that number **:** near that degree **:** near that quantity ⟨living in Wessex, off and on, for thirty years or *thereabout* —H.M.Tomlinson⟩ **3** *usu thereabout, archaic* **:** about that **:** in connection with that ⟨they were much perplexed *thereabout* —Lk 24:4 (AV)⟩

there·af·ter \(ˈ)=ˈ==\ *adv* [ME *therafter,* fr. OE *thǣr æfter,* fr. *thǣr* there + *æfter* after] **1 :** after that ⟨died that year, and his wife died soon ~⟩ **:** from then on **:** THENCEFORTH ⟨he wrote only occasionally⟩ **2** *archaic* **:** according to that **:** ACCORDINGLY

thereagainst \ˌ==ˈ=\ *adv* [ME *there agenst,* fr. ¹*there* + *agenst* against] **:** against that **:** against it **:** on the contrary

thereamong \ˌ==ˈ=\ *adv* [ME, fr. ¹*there* + *among*] **:** among them **:** among that

thereanent \ˌ==ˈ=\ *adv* [¹*there* + *anent*] **:** with reference to that matter, subject, or affair

thereat \(ˈ)=ˈ=\ *adv* [ME, fr. OE *thǣr æt,* fr. *thǣr* there + *æt* at] **1 :** at that place or point ⟨wide is the gate, and many there be which go in ~ —Mt 7:13 (AV)⟩ **2 :** at that occurrence or event **:** upon that **:** on that account ⟨ridiculously soon at his ease, and much astonished ~ —Donn Byrne⟩

thereaway \ˈ==ˌ=\ *adv* [ME *there away,* fr. ¹*there* + *away*] *chiefly dial* **:** APPROXIMATELY, THEREABOUTS

therebeside \ˌ==ˈ=\ *adv* [ME *there beside,* fr. ¹*there* + *beside*] *archaic* **:** by the side of that

therebetween \ˌ==ˈ=\ *adv* [¹*there* + *between*] **:** in the space between

thereby \(ˈ)=ˈ=\ *adv* [ME *therby,* fr. OE *thǣrbī,* fr. *thǣr* there + *bī* by] **1 :** by that ⟨judges in every state shall be bound ~ —*U.S.Constitution*⟩ **:** by that means **:** in consequence of that ⟨paid cash, ~ avoiding interest charges⟩ **2 :** connected with that **:** with reference to that ⟨~ hangs a tale —Shak.⟩ **3** *chiefly Scot* **:** beside that **:** near by **:** about that **:** BESIDE, THEREABOUTS

therefor \(ˈ)=ˈ=\ *adv* [ME *therfor, therfore, therefor, therefore* fr. ¹*ther, there* there + *for, fore* for] **1 :** for that **:** in return for that ⟨reasons ~⟩ ⟨issued bonds ~⟩ ⟨when the need ~ no longer exists⟩ ⟨substituting ~ a more general term⟩ **2 :** THEREFORE

¹**there·fore** *R* ˈtha(a)r,fō(ə)r, ˈther,f-, -fȯ(ə)r; *–R* ˈtha(a)ə-,fōə, ˈtheə,f-, ˈtha(a),f-, -fȯ(ə), + V " *or* -fō(ə)r *or* -fȯ(ə)r; *sometimes* -,fə(r)\ *adv* [ME *therfor, therfore, therefor, therefore* for that, for that reason] **1** *obs* **:** THEREFOR **2** *archaic* **:** THEN, ACCORDINGLY ⟨hear ye ~ the parable of the sower —Mt 13:18 (AV)⟩ **3 :** for that reason **:** because of that **:** on that ground **:** to that end **:** CONSEQUENTLY, HENCE ⟨lost the wager; ~ they must pay⟩ ⟨A is greater than B, and B is greater than C, ~ A is greater than C⟩

²**therefore** \"\ *n* -s **:** a proved proposition **:** an argumentative conclusion **:** a logical implication

therefrom \(ˈ)=ˈ=\ *adv* [ME *therfrom,* fr. *ther* there + *from*] **:** from that **:** from it ⟨public opinion and a policy . . . deriving ~ —Frank Gorrell⟩

therein \(ˈ)=ˈ=\ *adv* [ME *therin,* fr. OE *thǣrin,* fr. *thǣr* there + *in*] **1 :** in or into that place **:** in or into that thing ⟨the box and the jewels found ~⟩ **2 :** in that particular **:** in that respect **:** in such matter ⟨~ our letters do not well agree —Shak.⟩

thereinafter \ˌ==ˈ==\ *adv* [*therein* + *after*] **:** in the following part of that matter (as writing, document, or speech)

thereinbefore \ˌ=(,)=ˈ=\ *adv* [*therein* + *before*] **:** in the preceding part of that matter (as writing, document, or book)

thereinto \(ˌ)=ˈ=+\ *adv* [¹*there* + *into*] *archaic* **:** into that or into it ⟨let them not enter ~ —Lk 21:21 (AV)⟩

ther·e·min \ˈtherəmə̇n *sometimes* ˈter-\ *n* -s [after Leo *Theremin* b1896 Russ. engineer & inventor] **:** a purely melodic instrument of the electronic family typically played by moving the right hand between two projecting electrodes with the left hand controlling dynamics and articulation — **ther·e·min·ist** \-mənə̇st, -,min-\ *n* -s

there·ness \ˈtha(a)(ə)rnə̇s, ˈthe\, \ən-\ *n* -ES [¹*there* + *-ness*] **:** the condition of being there in position **:** presence in a place distinguishably there not here; *also* **:** real existence ⟨things are really there . . . capture the ~ of them —Charles Hopkinson⟩

thereof \(ˈ)=ˈ= *sometimes* -ˈäf\ *adv* [ME *therof,* fr. OE *thǣrof,* fr. *thǣr* there + *of*] **1 :** of that **:** of it ⟨in the day that thou eatest ~, thou shalt . . . die —Gen 2:17 (AV)⟩ ⟨problem and the solution ~⟩ **2 :** from that cause **:** from that particular **:** THEREFROM ⟨more good ~ shall spring —John Milton⟩

thereon \(ˈ)=ˈ=\ *adv* [ME *theron,* fr. OE *thǣron,* fr. *thǣr* there + *on*] **1 :** on that **:** on it ⟨text and commentary ~⟩ **2** *archaic* **:** after or as a result of some specified thing **:** THEREUPON

thereout \(ˈ)=ˈ=\ *adv* [ME *theroute,* fr. OE *thǣrūt,* fr. *thǣr* there + *ūt* out] *archaic* **:** out of that **:** THEREFROM

thereover \(ˈ)=ˈ==\ *adv* [ME *ther over,* fr. OE *thǣrofer,* fr. *thǣr* there + *ofer* over] **:** over that **:** ABOVE **:** in a superior position over

there·right \(ˈ)=ˈrīt\ *adv* [ME *ther riht,* fr. OE *thǣr rihte,* fr. *thǣr* there + *rihte* right] *dial Eng* **:** FORTHWITH, STRAIGHTWAY

theres *pl of* THERE

therethrough \(ˈ)=ˈ=\ *adv* [ME *ther thurh,* fr. *ther* there + *thurh* through] **1 :** through that **:** in or through a specified opening **2 :** in consequence of that **:** THEREBY, BECAUSE

thereto \(ˈ)=ˈ=\ *adv* [ME *therto,* fr. OE *thǣrtō,* fr. *thǣr* there + *tō* to] **1 :** to that ⟨with all the appurtenances fitting ~⟩ **2** *archaic* **:** BESIDES, MOREOVER, ALSO

there·to·fore \ˈtha(a)(r)d·ə,fō(ə)r, ˈthe\, \ə\, \tə, -fȯ(ə)r, -fōə, -fȯ(ə), ,==ˈ=\ *adv* [ME *ther tofore,* fr. *ther* there + *tofore* before — more at HERETOFORE] **:** up to that time **:** until then **:** before then ⟨~ obscure community —Robert Rice⟩

there·toward \(ˌ)=+\ *adv* [ME *thertoward,* fr. *ther* there + *toward*] **:** toward it

thereunder \(ˈ)=ˈ==\ *adv* [ME *therunder,* fr. OE *thǣrunder,* fr. *thǣr* there + *under*] **:** under that ⟨heading and the items listed ~⟩ ⟨acreage with . . . mineral wealth lying ~ —*U.S.Code*⟩

there·until \(ˌ)=+\ *adv* [¹*there* + *until*] **:** up to that time **:** THERETOFORE

there·unto \"+\ *adv* [ME *therunto,* fr. *ther* + *unto*] **1** *archaic* **:** unto that **:** THERETO, BESIDES **2** *obs* **:** in addition to that **:** BESIDES

thereupon \ˈ==ˌ=, ,==ˈ=\ *adv* [ME *ther upon,* fr. *ther* there + *upon*] **1 :** upon that **:** on that matter **:** THEREON **2 :** on account of or in consequence of that **:** THEREFORE **3 :** immediately after that **:** at once **:** without delay

¹**the·rev·id** \thəˈrevə̇d, ˈtherəv-\ *adj* [NL *Therevidae*] **:** of or relating to the Therevidae

²**therevid** \"\ *n* -s **:** a two-winged fly of the family Therevidae **:** STILETTO FLY

the·rev·i·dae \thəˈrevə,dē\ *n pl, cap* [NL, fr. *Thereva,* type genus (fr. Gk *thēreuein* to hunt, fr. *thēr* wild animal) + *-idae* — more at FIERCE] **:** a family of chiefly holarctic brachycerous two-winged flies constituted by the stiletto flies

therewhile *also* **therewhilst** \(ˈ)=ˈ=\ *adv* [*therewhile* fr. ME *ther whyle,* prob. fr. OE *thǣre hwīle* in that time, fr. *thǣre* (dat. sing. fem. of *sē, sēo, thæt* that) + *hwīle,* dat. sing. of *hwīl* while, time; *therewhilst* alter. (influenced by *whilst*) of *therewhile* — more at THAT] *obs* **:** in the meantime **:** WHILST

therewith \(ˈ)=ˈ=\ *adv* [ME *therwith,* fr. OE *thǣrwith,* fr. *thǣr* there + *with*] **1 :** with that ⟨I have learned in whatsoever state I am, ~ to be content —Phil 4:11(AV)⟩ **2** *archaic* **:** THEREUPON, FORTHWITH

there·with·al \ˈ=wə̇,thȯl, -,thȯl, ,==ˈ=\ *adv* [ME *ther withal,* fr. *ther* there + *withal*] **1** *archaic* **:** BESIDES, MOREOVER **2 :** with that **:** at the same time **:** THEREWITH ⟨thy slanders I forgive; and ~ remit thy other forfeits —Shak.⟩ **3 :** at the same time **:** THEREUPON

therewithin \ˌ==ˈ=\ *adv* [ME *ther within,* fr. *ther* there + *within*] *archaic* **:** within that

the·ria \ˈthirēə, ˈthēr-\ *n pl, cap* [NL, fr. Gk *thēria,* pl. of *thērion* wild animal — more at TREACLE] *in some classifications* **:** a subclass of Mammalia comprising the higher mammals and including the Pantotheria, Metatheria, and Eutheria and excluding the Prototheria and Allotheria — **the·ri·an** \-ēən\ *n or adj*

-theria \"\ *n comb form* [NL, fr. Gk *thēria,* pl. of *thērion*] **:** beasts **:** animals — in names of higher taxa of mammalian forms ⟨Proto*theria*⟩

¹**the·ri·ac** \ˈthirē,ak\ *n* -s [NL *theriaca*] **1 :** THERIACA **2 :** CURE-ALL

²**theriac** \"\ *also* **the·ri·a·cal** \thəˈrīəkəl\ *adj* **:** ANTIDOTAL, MEDICINAL

the·ri·a·ca \thəˈrīəkə\ *n* -s [NL, fr. L, antidote against poison — more at TREACLE] **1** *or* **theriaca andromachi** *usu cap A* [*theriaca Andromachi* fr. NL, lit., antidote of Andromachus (Greek physician of the emperor Nero)] **:** an antidote to poison consisting typically of about 70 drugs pulverized and reduced with honey to an electuary — called also *Venice treacle* **2** *Brit* **:** TREACLE, MOLASSES

the·ri·an·throp·ic \,thirē,anˈthräpik\ *adj* [Gk *therianthrōpos* beast-man (fr. *thēri-* therio- + *anthrōpos* man, human being) + E *-ic* — more at ANTHROP-] **1 :** combining human and animal form ⟨~ deity⟩ **2 :** relating to religions in which the deities worshiped are partly human and partly animal in form

the·ri·an·thro·pism \,==ˈan(t)thrə,pizəm\ *n* -s [*therianthropic* + *-ism*] **:** the conception of or belief in therianthropic deities

the·ri·at·rics \,thirēˈa·triks\ *n pl but sing or pl in constr* [*ther-* + *-iatrics*] **:** the science of veterinary medicine

the·rid·i·id \thəˈridēə̇d, ˌtherəˈdīə̇d\ *adj* [NL *Theridiidae*] **:** of or relating to the Theridiidae

²**theridiid** \"\ *n* -s **:** a spider of the family Theridiidae

ther·i·di·idae \,therəˈdīə,dē\ *n pl, cap* [NL, fr. *Theridion,* type genus (fr. Gk *thēridion,* dim. of *thēr* wild beast) + *-idae* — more at FIERCE] **:** a family of spiders that spin netlike webs and have usu. a small globose body and slender legs

-the·ri·idae \thəˈrīə,dē\ *n comb form* [NL, fr. Gk *thērion* wild beast, animal + NL *-idae*] **:** beasts **:** animals — in names of families of chiefly extinct mammalian forms ⟨Mega*theriidae*⟩

therio- *comb form* [Gk *thērio-, thēri-,* fr. *thērion* — more at TREACLE] **:** wild animal **:** beast ⟨*therio*latry⟩ ⟨*therio*mimicry⟩

the·ri·odont \ˈthirēə,dänt\ *n* -s [NL *Theriodontia*] **:** a reptile of the suborder Theriodontia

¹**the·ri·o·don·tia** \,thirēəˈdänch(ē)ə\ *n pl, cap* [NL, fr. Gk *thēri-* therio- + NL *-odontia*] **:** a suborder of Therapsida or other group of extinct reptiles having teeth differentiated into incisors, prominent canines, and molars with numerous cusps and being mostly known from skulls found in the Permian and Triassic formations of southern Africa

²**theriodontia** \"\ *or* **the·ri·odon·ta** \,thirēəˈdäntə\ [NL, fr. Gk *thēri-* therio- + NL *-odontia* or *-odonta*] *syn of* PELYCOSAURIA

the·ri·ol·a·try \,thirēˈälə·trē\ *n* -ES [*therio-* + *-latry*] **:** worship of animals or theriomorphic divinities

the·rio·morph \ˈthirēə,mȯrf\ *n* [Gk *thēriomorphos* shaped like an animal, fr. *thērio-* therio + *morphē* shape, form — more at FORM] **:** an artifact or object (as a vase) shaped in animal form

the·rio·mor·phic \,===ˈmȯrfik\ *adj* [Gk *thēriomorphos* + E *-ic*] **:** having an animal form ⟨~ gods⟩ ⟨~ stage in the development of the divinity —*Modern Language Rev.*⟩

the·rio·mor·phism \,===ˈmȯr,fizəm\ *n* -s [Gk *thēriomorphos* + E *-ism*] **1 :** the conception or representation of deity in animal form **2 :** ascription of animal characteristics to man — compare ANTHROPOMORPHISM

the·rio·mor·phize \,===ˈ=,fīz\ *vt* -ED/-ING/-S [Gk *thēriomorphos* + E *-ize*] **:** to represent or conceptualize (something) in animal form ⟨in Assyrian history the forces of nature were *theriomorphized* —*Times Lit. Supp.*⟩

-the·ri·um \ˈthirēəm, ˈthēr-\ *n comb form* [NL, fr. Gk *thērion* — more at TREACLE] **:** beast **:** animal — in generic names of extinct mammalian forms ⟨Mega*therium*⟩ ⟨Titano*therium*⟩

therm \ˈthərm, ˈthəm, ˈthəim\ *n* -s **1** [MF *thermes* (pl.), fr. L *thermae* hot springs, public baths, fr. Gk *thermai,* fr. pl. of *thermē* heat, fr. *thermos* hot — more at WARM] *archaic* **:** a public bathing establishment **2** [Gk *thermos* hot, or *thermē* heat] **:** any of several units of quantity of heat: as **a :** CALORIE b(1) **b :** CALORIE a **c :** 1000 kilogram calories **d :** 100,000 British thermal units

therm- *or* **thermo-** *comb form* [Gk, fr. *thermē* heat] **1 :** heat ⟨*thermo*acoustic⟩ ⟨*thermo*chemistry⟩ **2 :** thermoelectric ⟨*thermo*pile⟩

-therm \,=\ *n comb form* -s [Gk *thermē* heat, fr. *thermos* hot] **1** [prob. fr. F *-therme,* fr. Gk *thermē* heat] **a :** plant accustomed to a (specified) type of heat ⟨mega*therm*⟩ ⟨micro*therm*⟩ ⟨xero*therm*⟩ **b :** animal having a (specified) body temperature ⟨ecto*therm*⟩ ⟨endo*therm*⟩ ⟨poikilo*therm*⟩ **2 :** thermic line ⟨isobathy*therm*⟩

therm *abbr* thermometer

ther·mae \ˈthər,mē\ *n pl* [L — more at THERM] **:** a public bathing establishment esp. in ancient Greece or Rome

¹**ther·mal** \ˈthərməl, ˈthəm-, ˈthəim-\ *adj* [Gk *thermē* heat + E *-al*] **1** [L *thermae* hot springs + E *-al* — more at THERM] **:** of or relating to hot springs or geysers ⟨~ regions⟩ ⟨health resort with natural ~ waters —*advt*⟩ **2 :** of, relating to, or caused by heat **:** WARM, HOT ⟨~ requirements of a room —Herman Nelson⟩ ⟨~ burns⟩ **3 :** of or relating to a state of matter that depends upon its temperature alone ⟨the ~ agitation of the molecules⟩ ⟨~ equilibrium⟩ **4 :** having translational speeds and energies of the order of those due to thermal agitation ⟨~ neutrons⟩

²**thermal** \"\ *n* -s **:** a rising body of warm air

thermal agitation *n* **:** the ceaseless random motion of molecules or other small component particles of a substance that is associated with heat

thermal ammeter *n* **:** a hot-wire ammeter

thermal analysis *n* **:** the study of transition processes (as from one allotropic form to another) or of chemical changes in a substance as indicated by abrupt evolution or absorption of heat accompanying such processes

thermal barrier *n* **:** a limit to unlimited increase in airplane or rocket speeds imposed by aerodynamic heating that without adequate provisions for cooling the exposed surfaces will result in loss of strength and eventual melting of the metal skin — called also *heat barrier*

thermal belt *n* **:** a well-defined zone on the sides of many valleys where frost damage is at a minimum that is due to the adiabatic compression and consequent heating of the cold air flowing down the hill or mountain sides into the valley

thermal black *n* **:** a carbon black made by thermal decomposition of hydrocarbons (as natural gas and acetylene) in preheated furnaces — called also *furnace thermal black;* compare ACETYLENE BLACK

thermal capacity *n* **:** HEAT CAPACITY

thermal conduction *n* **:** the transmission of heat energy by conduction (as through the bottom of a kettle)

thermal conductivity *n* **1 :** capability of conducting heat **2 :** the quantity of heat that passes in unit time through a unit area of plate whose thickness is unity when its opposite faces differ in temperature by one degree

thermal converter *n* **:** a thermoelectric hot-wire alternating-current ammeter

thermal cracking *n* **:** cracking of petroleum or similar oils by means of heat and pressure alone — distinguished from *catalytic cracking;* compare PYROLYSIS

thermal cutout *n* **:** a protective device for automatically opening an overloaded electrical circuit because of excessive rise of temperature

thermal death point *n* **:** the temperature at which all organisms of a culture will be killed by heat either instantaneously or within an arbitrary brief finite period

thermal diffusion *n* **:** an effect wherein a temperature gradient in a gaseous or liquid mixture tends to cause a separation of the heavy components from the light
thermal diffusivity *n* **:** DIFFUSIVITY 2
thermal efficiency *n* **:** the ratio of the heat utilized by a heat engine to the total heat units in the fuel consumed
thermal electromotive force *n* **:** THERMOELECTROMOTIVE FORCE
thermal energy *n* **:** energy in the form of heat
thermal equator *n* **1 :** the region of the earth enclosed within the annual isotherms of 80° including the northern part of So. America and the greater part of Africa and India **2 :** the middle line of the thermal equator belt
thermal equilibrium *n* **:** a state of a system in which all parts are at the same temperature
thermal expansion *n* **:** increase in linear dimensions of a solid or in volume of a fluid because of rise in temperature
thermal head *n* **:** temperature difference responsible for a flow of heat or for convection
thermal inertia *n* **:** the degree of slowness with which the temperature of a body approaches that of its surroundings and which is dependent upon its absorptivity, its specific heat, its thermal conductivity, its dimensions, and other factors
thermal insulation *n* **1 :** the process of insulating against transmission of heat **2 :** material of relatively low heat conductivity used to shield a volume against loss or entrance of heat by radiation, convection, or conduction
thermal ionization *n* **:** ionization of a gas or vapor produced by subjecting it to a high temperature
ther·mal·iza·tion \ˌthərmələ'zāshən, -ˌlī'z-\ *n* -S **:** the action or process of thermalizing
ther·mal·ize \'==ˌlīz\ *vt* -ED/-ING/-S [¹*thermal* + *-ize*] **:** to change the effective speed of (a particle) to a thermal value ⟨~ a neutron⟩
ther·mal·ly \'thərməlē, 'thəm-, 'thəim-, -li\ *adv* **:** in a thermal manner **:** by means of heat **:** with respect to thermal qualities
thermal metamorphism *n* **:** THERMOMETAMORPHISM
thermal noise *n* **:** radio-receiver or amplifier noise due to thermal agitation of the free electrons in the circuit and the tubes — called also *Johnson noise;* compare SHOT EFFECT
thermal radiation *n* **:** quantized electromagnetic radiation excited by thermal agitation of molecules or atoms and having a range including infrared, visible light, and ultraviolet
thermal resistance *n* **:** the resistance of a body to the flow of heat
thermals *pl of* THERMAL
thermal shock *n* **:** a large and rapid change of temperature considered esp. with respect to its effects upon living organisms or structural parts
thermal spring *n* **:** a spring whose water issues at a temperature higher than the mean temperature of the locality where the spring is situated — compare HOT SPRING
thermal stress *n* **:** stress in a body or structure due to inequalities of temperature
thermal transpiration *or* **thermal effusion** *n* **:** transpiration of gas through a capillary tube between enclosures orig. at the same pressure but at different temperatures wherein the movement is from the cooler to the warmer chamber
thermal unit *n* **:** a unit for the comparison or calculation of quantities of heat — see BRITISH THERMAL UNIT; compare CALORIE
therm·antidote \ˌthərm+\ *n* [*therm-* + *antidote*] **:** a device used in India for circulating and cooling the air and consisting essentially of a kind of rotating wheel fitted in a window and encased in wet tatties
ther·mate \'thərˌmāt\ *n* -S [fr. *Thermit,* a trademark + E *-ate*] **:** a mixture of aluminum powder, powdered iron oxide, and other substances (as barium nitrate) to accelerate burning that forms the standard filling for incendiary bombs
therm·el \'thərˌmel\ *n* -S [*therm-* + *electric*] **:** a thermoelectric thermometer
therm foot \'thərmˌ=\ *n* [fr. obs. E *therm* pillar with tapering rectangular base, alter. (influenced by *herm*) of E ¹*term*] **:** SPADE FOOT
-ther·mia \'thərmēə, 'thəm-, 'thəim-\ *or* **-ther·my** \ˌ=mē, -mi\ *n comb form, pl* **-thermias** *or* **-thermies** [NL *-thermia,* fr. Gk *thermē* heat + L *-ia* -y — more at THERM] **:** state of heat **:** generation of heat ⟨dia*thermy*⟩ ⟨hypo*thermia*⟩
ther·mic \'thərmik\ *adj* [Gk *thermē* heat + E *-ic*] **:** of or relating to heat **:** due to heat **:** THERMAL ⟨~ energy⟩ ⟨~ reaction⟩ — **ther·mi·cal·ly** \-mək(ə)lē\ *adv*
thermic anomaly *n* **:** the difference of the mean temperature of a place from the normal temperature of its latitude
thermic fever *n* **:** fever caused by heatstroke
ther·mi·dor \'thərməˌdȯ(ə)r; 'thəməˌdȯ(ə), 'thəim-, + V " *or* -dȯ(ə)r\ *n* -S *usu cap* [F *Thermidor,* month of the Fr. revolutionary calendar beginning July 19; fr. the overthrow of Robespierre which took place in that month in 1794] **:** a moderate counterrevolutionary stage following an extremist stage of a revolution and usu. characterized often through the medium of a dictatorship by an emphasis on the restoration of order, a relaxation of tensions, and some return to patterns of life held to be normal
ther·mi·do·re·an *also* **ther·mi·do·ri·an** \¦==¦dōrēən, -¦dȯr-\ *adj, usu cap* [F *thermidorien,* fr. *Thermidor* + *-ien* -ian] **:** of, relating to, or having the characteristics of a Thermidor
therm·ion \'thərm +\ *n* -S [ISV *therm-* + *ion*] **:** an electrically charged particle emitted by an incandescent substance
therm·ion·ic \¦thərˌmī¦änik, -ˌmē¦ä-\ *adj* [ISV *thermion* + *-ic*] **:** of, relating to, or characteristic of thermions ⟨~ cathode⟩ ⟨~ properties⟩ — **therm·ion·i·cal·ly** \-nək(ə)lē\ *adv*
thermionic current *n* **:** an electric current due to the directed movements of thermions (as in the electric discharge through a vacuum tube with the cathode incandescent)
thermionic emission *n* **:** emission of particles (as electrons) from materials at high temperatures due to the heat energy imparted to them — compare FIELD EMISSION, PHOTOEMISSION
therm·ion·ics \ˌ=(ˌ)='äniks\ *n pl but usu sing in constr* [fr. *thermionic,* after such pairs as E *economic: economics*] **:** a branch of physics dealing with thermionic phenomena and devices
thermionic tube *n* **:** an electron tube in which electron emission is produced by the heating of an electrode
therm·is·tor \(¦)thər'mistər\ *n* -S [*thermal resistor*] **:** an electrical resistor made of a material whose resistance varies sharply in a known manner with the temperature
Ther·mit \-ˌmət\ *trademark* — used for a mixture of aluminum powder and powdered iron oxide that when caused to react by strong heating evolves a great deal of heat and yields alumina and a white-hot molten mass of metallic iron and that is used in welding and in incendiary bombs
therm leg \'thərmˌ=\ *n* [fr. obs. E *therm* pillar with tapering rectangular base — more at THERM FOOT] **:** a tapered furniture leg that is square in section
thermo- — see THERM-
ther·mo·ammeter \¦thər(ˌ)mō+\ *n* [*therm-* + *ammeter*] **:** a thermoelement in circuit with a sensitive voltmeter for measuring small currents
ther·mo·analysis \"+\ *n* [*therm-* + *analysis*] **:** THERMAL ANALYSIS
ther·mo·bacterium \"+\ *n* [NL, fr. *therm-* + *bacterium*] **:** any of various thermoduric lactobacilli often considered to constitute a subgenus (*Thermobacterium*) of the genus *Lactobacillus*
ther·mo·balance \"+\ *n* [*therm-* + *balance*] **:** a balance designed esp. for weighing bodies at high temperatures
ther·mo·barograph \"+\ *n* [ISV *therm-* + *barograph*] **:** an instrument for recording simultaneously the pressure and temperature of a gas **:** a combined thermograph and barograph
ther·mo·barometer \"+\ *n* [ISV *therm-* + *barometer*] **1 :** HYPSOMETER **2 :** a siphon barometer adapted to be used also as a thermometer
ther·mo·cautery \"+\ *n* [ISV *therm-* + *cautery*] **:** ACTUAL CAUTERY
ther·mo·chemical \"+\ *adj* [*thermo*chemistry + *-ical*] **:** of, relating to, or obtained by thermochemistry — **ther·mo·chemically** \"+\ *adv*
ther·mo·chemist \"+\ *n* [back-formation fr. *thermochemistry*] **:** one trained in or engaged in thermochemistry
ther·mo·chemistry \"+\ *n* [*therm-* + *chemistry*] **1 :** a branch of chemistry that deals with the relations existing between heat and chemical reaction or physical changes of state — compare ENDOTHERMIC, EXOTHERMIC, HEAT OF REACTION **2 :** the thermochemical properties of a substance ⟨~ of rocket propellants —G.P.Sutton⟩
ther·mo·chro·mic \¦thərmə¦krōmik\ *adj* [*thermochrom*ism + *-ic*] **:** of, relating to, or exhibiting thermochromism
ther·mo·chro·mism \¦thərməˌkrōˌmizəm\ *n* [*therm-* + *chrom-* + *-ism*] **:** the phenomenon of reversible change of color of a substance with change of temperature (as the change of mercuric oxide from nearly colorless on being cooled by liquid air to red at room temperature and to black on being heated)
ther·mo·clin·al \¦thərmə¦klīnᵊl\ *adj* **:** of, relating to, or constituting a thermocline
ther·mo·cline \'==ˌklīn\ *n* -S [*therm-* + *-cline*] **1 :** a temperature gradient; *esp* **:** one marking sharp change **2 :** a layer of water in a thermally stratified lake or other body of water separating an upper warmer lighter oxygen-rich zone from a lower colder heavier oxygen-poor zone; *specif* **:** a stratum in which temperature declines at least one degree centigrade with each meter increase in depth
ther·mo·coagulation \¦thər(ˌ)mō+\ *n* [*therm-* + *coagulation*] **:** surgical coagulation of tissue by the application of heat (as from a high-frequency current)
ther·mo·couple \'thərmə +ˌ-\ *n* [*therm-* + *couple*] **:** a device for measuring temperature in which two electrical conductors of dissimilar metals (as copper and iron) are joined at the point where heat is to be applied and the free ends are connected to an electrical measuring instrument (as an ammeter) which by registering the amount of thermoelectric current being produced at the juncture of the dissimilar conductors indicates the temperature at that point
ther·mo·current \¦thərmō+\ *n* [*therm-* + *current*] **:** a thermoelectric current
ther·mo development \¦thər(ˌ)mō-\ *n* [*therm-* + *development*] **:** TIME AND TEMPERATURE METHOD
ther·mo·diffusion \¦thər(ˌ)mō+\ *n* [ISV *therm-* + *diffusion*] **:** THERMAL DIFFUSION
¹**ther·mo·du·ric** \¦thərmō¦d(y)u̇rik\ *adj* [*therm-* + L *durare* to last + E *-ic* — more at DURE] **:** able to survive high temperatures; *specif* **:** able to survive pasteurization — used of microorganisms ⟨determination of ~ organisms in rinses of dairy equipment —*Chem. Abstracts*⟩
²**thermoduric** \"\ *n* -S **:** a thermoduric microorganism
ther·mo·dynamic *also* **ther·mo·dynamical** \¦thərmə+\ *adj* [*therm-* + *dynamic, dynamical*] **:** of or relating to thermodynamics **:** caused or operated by force due to the application of heat ⟨~ principles⟩ — **ther·mo·dynamically** \"+\ *adv*
thermodynamic cycle *n* **:** a succession of processes in a substance which involve changes esp. in temperature, pressure, density, and entropy, which result in the return of the substance to its original condition, and in which the substance acts in general as a means of transformation of energy — compare CARNOT CYCLE
thermodynamic efficiency *n* **:** the ratio of work output to heat-energy input in a heat-engine cycle or of heat energy removal to work input in a refrigeration cycle
thermodynamic equilibrium *n* **:** a state of a physical system in which it is in mechanical, chemical, and thermal equilibrium and in which there is therefore no tendency for spontaneous change
ther·mo·dy·nam·i·cist \ˌthərmōˌdī'naməsəst *sometimes* -ˌdə-'n-\ *n* -S **:** a specialist in thermodynamics
thermodynamic potential *n* **:** a quantity of energy that along with other defining quantities determines the condition of a thermodynamic medium
ther·mo·dynamics \¦thərmə +\ *n pl but sing or pl in constr* [*therm-* + *dynamics*] **1 :** a branch of physics that deals with the mechanical action or relations of heat **2 :** thermodynamic processes and phenomena
thermodynamic scale *n* **:** the Kelvin scale
thermodynamic system *n* **:** an aggregation of atoms, molecules, colloidal particles, or larger bodies that constitute an isolated group
ther·mo·elastic \¦thər(ˌ)mō+\ *adj* [*therm-* + *elastic*] **:** of or relating to a thermodynamic aspect of elastic deformation ⟨anomalous ~ behavior of rubber —William Seifriz⟩
ther·mo·electric \"+\ *adj* [*therm-* + *electric*] **:** of or relating to a class of phenomena involving relations between the temperature and the electrical condition in a metal or in contacting metals
thermoelectric constant *n* **:** either of two constants characteristic of any metal that enter into the expressions for the thermoelectric power of the metal and for the electromotive forces of thermocouples utilizing it
thermoelectric inversion *n* **:** reversal in direction of a current produced by a thermocouple when the difference of temperature is increased beyond a neutral point
ther·mo·electricity \¦thər(ˌ)mō+\ *n* [*therm-* + *electricity*] **:** electricity involved in thermoelectric phenomena; *specif* **:** electricity accumulated or put in motion by thermoelectric action
thermoelectric power *n* **:** rate of change of the thermoelectromotive force of a thermocouple with temperature ⟨the *thermoelectric power* of a given metal is that of a couple formed of that metal with lead, the *thermoelectric power* of lead being taken arbitrarily as zero⟩
thermoelectric series *n* **:** a series of conductors arranged in the order of their thermoelectric powers
ther·mo·electromotive force \¦thər(ˌ)mō+. . .-\ *n* [*therm-* + *electromotive force*] **:** electromotive force in a circuit composed of dissimilar conductors that is produced because of its not being at a uniform temperature throughout — compare PELTIER EFFECT, THOMSON EFFECT
ther·mo·electron \¦thər(ˌ)mō+\ *n* [*therm-* + *electron*] **:** an electron released in thermionic emission — **ther·mo·electronic** \"+\ *adj*
ther·mo·element \"+\ *n* [*thermo*couple + *element*] **:** a device for measuring small currents consisting of a wire heating element and a thermocouple in electrical contact with it — compare THERMOAMMETER
ther·mo·for process \'thərməˌfȯ(ə)r-\ *n, often cap T* [*therm-* + *reforming*] **:** a catalytic cracking process in which the catalyst is passed by gravity through the oil or oil vapors in a tall reactor
ther·mo·galvanometer \¦thər(ˌ)mō+\ *n* [*thermo*element + *galvanometer*] **:** a thermoammeter for small currents usu. consisting of a thermoelement and a direct-current galvanometer
ther·mo·genesis \¦thərmō+\ *n* [NL, fr. *therm-* + *genesis*] **:** the production of heat esp. in the body (as by oxidation)
ther·mo·gen·ic \¦thərmə¦jenik\ *adj* [*therm-* + *-genic*] **:** of or relating to the production of heat **:** producing heat
ther·mo·gram \'thərməˌgram\ *n* [*therm-* + *-gram*] **:** the trace or record made by a thermograph
¹**ther·mo·graph** \-ˌgraf,-ˌgrȧf\ *n* [ISV *therm-* + *-graph*] **:** a self-recording thermometer
²**thermograph** \"\ *vt* [back-formation fr. *thermography*] **:** to produce by thermography ⟨a ~*ed* business card⟩
ther·mog·ra·pher \(ˌ)thər'mägrəfər\ *n* -S **:** one that thermographs **:** one engaged in thermography
ther·mo·graph·ic \¦thərmə¦grafik\ *adj* **1 :** relating to, obtained by, or used in a thermograph ⟨a ~ process⟩ ⟨~ paper⟩ **2 :** of or used in thermography ⟨a ~ process⟩ ⟨~ inks⟩ — **ther·mo·graph·i·cal·ly** \-fək(ə)lē\ *adv*
ther·mog·ra·phy \(ˌ)thər'mägrəfē\ *n* -ES [*therm-* + *-graphy*] **:** a process of writing or printing involving the use of heat: as **a :** the conversion of a temperature pattern by contrast into an image for viewing or recording (as by photography) **b :** a raised-printing process in which matter printed by letterpress is dusted with powder while the ink is still wet and heated to make the lettering rise above the surface of the paper
ther·mo·hardening \¦thər(ˌ)mō+\ *adj* [*therm-* + *hardening*] **:** THERMOSETTING
ther·mo·hydrometer \¦thər(ˌ)mō+\ *n* [*therm-* + *hydrometer*] **:** a hydrometer enclosing a thermometer to indicate the temperature of the liquid under test
ther·mo·junction \¦thərmō+\ *n* [*therm-* + *junction*] **:** a junction of two dissimilar conductors used to produce a thermoelectric current **:** one junction of a thermocouple
ther·mo·labile \"+\ *adj* [ISV *therm-* + *labile*] **:** unstable when heated; *specif* **:** subject to loss of characteristic properties on being heated to or above 55° C — used esp. of immune bodies, enzymes, and vitamins; opposed to *thermostable*
ther·mo·lability \¦thər(ˌ)mō+\ *n* **:** the quality or state of being thermolabile
ther·mo·luminescence \"+\ *n* [ISV *therm-* + *luminescence;* orig. formed as G *thermolumineszenz*] **:** phosphorescence developed in a previously excited substance (as quartz) upon gentle heating — called also *thermophosphorescence* — **ther·mo·luminescent** \"+\ *adj*
ther·mol·y·sis \(ˌ)thər'mäləsəs\ *n* [ISV *therm-* + *-lysis;* orig. formed as G *thermolyse*] **:** the dissipation of heat from the living body
ther·mo·lyt·ic \¦thərmə¦lid·ik\ *adj* [fr. *thermolysis,* after such pairs as E *analysis: analytic*] **:** of or relating to thermolysis ⟨~ mechanisms of the body⟩
ther·mo·magnetic \¦thər(ˌ)mō+\ *adj* [*therm-* + *magnetic*] **1 :** of or relating to the effects of heat upon the magnetic properties of substances **2 :** of or relating to the effects of a magnetic field upon thermal conduction (as in the Righi-Leduc effect)
ther·mo·mechanical \"+\ *adj* [*therm-* + *mechanical*] **:** designed for or relating to the transformation of heat energy into mechanical work
ther·mo·metamorphic \"+\ *adj* [*therm-* + *metamorphic*] **:** of or relating to thermometamorphism
ther·mo·metamorphism \"+\ *n* [*therm-* + *metamorphism*] **:** metamorphism in rocks due to heat but not the result of dynamic action or volcanic emanations
ther·mom·e·ter *R* thə(r)'mäməd·ər, -ämətər, −*R* thə'mäməd·ə(r, -ämətə(r\ *n* [F *thermomètre,* fr. Gk *thermē* heat + F *-o-* + *-mètre* -meter — more at THERM] **1 :** an instrument for determining temperature usu. by means of a scale graduated directly in temperature units and consisting typically of (1) a device having a bimetallic element whose expansion or contraction indicates a change in temperature or (2) a glass bulb attached to a fine tube of glass with a numbered scale etched on or fastened to it and containing a liquid (as mercury or colored alcohol) that is sealed in and rises and falls with changes of temperature and that indicates the temperature by the number corresponding to the top of the column of liquid — see DRY-BULB THERMOMETER, GAS THERMOMETER, RESISTANCE THERMOMETER, REVERSING THERMOMETER, WET-BULB THERMOMETER **2 :** one that serves as a precise indicator of a position on a scale ⟨retail sales as a business ~⟩ ⟨letters to the editor — a ~ of public opinion⟩

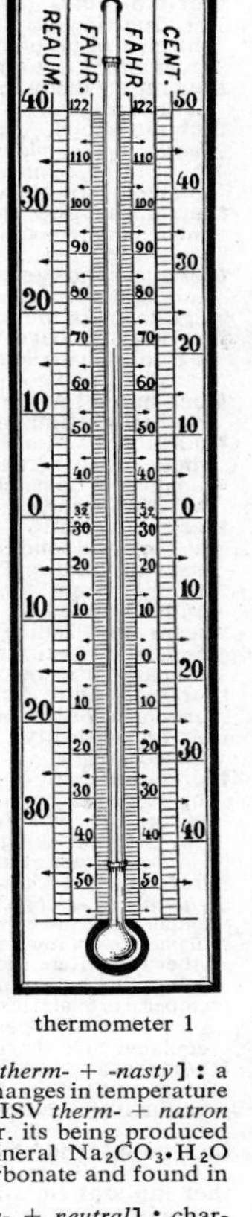

thermometer 1

thermometer screen *or* **thermometer shelter** *n* **:** a structure that shelters a thermometer from direct sunlight and other conditions that would cause the thermometer to give erroneous readings of the free air temperature
ther·mo·met·ric \¦thərmə¦me·trik, ¦thōm-, ¦thəim, -·trēk\ *adj* [*thermometer* + *-ic*] **:** of or relating to a thermometer or thermometry **:** made or ascertained by means of a thermometer — **ther·mo·met·ri·cal·ly** \-trək(ə)lē, -rēk-, -li\ *adv*
ther·mo·met·ro·graph \ˌthərmə'me·trəˌgraf, -ˌrȧf\ *n* [*therm-* + Gk *metron* measure + E *-graph* — more at METER] **:** THERMOGRAPH
ther·mom·e·try \thə(r)'mämə·trē, -·tri\ *n* -ES [ISV *therm-* + *-metry*] **:** the measurement of temperature
ther·mo·molecular pressure \¦thər(ˌ)mō+. . .-\ *n* [*therm-* + *molecular*] **:** the pressure difference developed due to thermal transpiration
ther·mo·motive \¦thərmə +\ *adj* [*therm-* + *motive*] **:** of or relating to the production of motion by heat — used esp. of a hot-air engine
ther·mo·motor \"+\ *n* [*therm-* + *motor*] **:** HEAT ENGINE, HOT-AIR ENGINE
ther·mo·nas·tic \¦thərmə¦nastik\ *adj* [*thermonasty* + *-ic*] **:** of, relating to, or caused by thermonasty — **ther·mo·nas·ti·cal·ly** \-stək(ə)lē\ *adv*
ther·mo·nas·ty \'==ˌnastē\ *n* -ES [ISV *therm-* + *-nasty*] **:** a nastic movement that is associated with changes in temperature
ther·mo·na·trite \ˌthərmə'nāˌtrīt\ *n* -S [ISV *therm-* + *natron* + *-ite;* orig. formed as G *thermonatrit;* fr. its being produced by the action of heat on natron] **:** a mineral $Na_2CO_3 \cdot H_2O$ consisting of native hydrous sodium carbonate and found in some lakes and alkali soils
ther·mo·neutral \¦thərmō+\ *adj* [*therm-* + *neutral*] **:** characterized by thermoneutrality ⟨a ~ environment⟩ **:** not tending to alter thermal relationships (as of an organism)
ther·mo·neutrality \¦thər(ˌ)mō+\ *n* [*therm-* + *neutrality*] **:** a state of thermal balance between an organism and its environments such that bodily thermoregulatory mechanisms are inactive
ther·mo·nuclear \"+\ *adj* [ISV *therm-* + *nuclear*] **1 :** of or relating to the transformations in the nucleus of atoms of low atomic weight (as hydrogen) that require an extraordinarily high temperature for their inception — used of the fusion of elements of low atomic weight into elements of higher atomic weight (as in the hydrogen bomb or in the sun) ⟨~ reaction⟩ ⟨~ weapon⟩ **2 :** of, utilizing, or relating to a thermonuclear bomb ⟨~ explosion⟩ ⟨~ war⟩ ⟨~ attack⟩
ther·mo·period \¦thərmō+\ *n* [*therm-* + *period*] **:** the period of exposure of a plant to a particular temperature; *specif* **:** the period characteristic of the diurnal alternation of day and night temperature when both period and temperature are at or near the optimum for the induction of various activities (as growth or flowering) — compare PHOTOPERIOD — **ther·mo·periodic** \¦thər(ˌ)mō+\ *adj*
ther·mo·pe·ri·od·ism \ˌthərmō'pirēəˌdizəm\ *also* **ther·mo·pe·ri·o·dic·i·ty** \-ˌpirēə'disəd·ē\ *n* [*thermoperiodism* fr. *thermoperiod* + *-ism; thermoperiodicity* fr. *thermoperiodic* + *-ity*] **:** the sum of the responses of an organism to appropriately fluctuating temperatures — compare PHOTOPERIODISM
¹**ther·mo·phile** \'thərməˌfīl\ *also* **ther·mo·phil** \-ˌfil\ *adj* [ISV *therm-* + *-phil*] **:** of, relating to, or being a thermophile
²**thermophile** \"\ *also* **thermophil** \"\ *n* -S **:** an organism growing at a high temperature (as various bacteria that thrive at 122–131° F) — compare PSYCHROPHILE
ther·mo·phil·ic \¦thərmə¦filik\ *or* **ther·moph·i·lous** \(ˌ)thər'mäfələs\ *adj* [*therm-* + *-philic* or *-philous*] **:** THERMOPHILE
ther·moph·i·ly \(ˌ)thər'mäfəlē\ *n* -ES [ISV *therm-* + *-phily*] **:** the ability of an organism to grow at a high temperature
ther·mo·phone \'thərməˌfōn\ *n* [ISV *therm-* + *telephone*] **1 :** a portable telethermometer using a telephone in connection with a differential thermometer **2 :** a telephone involving heat effects (as changes in temperature) due to pulsations of the line current in a fine wire connected with the receiver diaphragm
ther·mo·phosphor \¦thərmə+\ *n* [*therm-* + *phosphor*] **:** a substance that exhibits thermoluminescence
ther·mo·phosphorescence \¦thər(ˌ)mō+\ *n* [*therm-* + *phosphorescence*] **:** THERMOLUMINESCENCE
ther·mo·phyte \'thərməˌfīt\ *n* -S [*therm-* + *-phyte*] **:** a plant that requires or thrives best at elevated temperatures
ther·mo·pile \-ˌpīl\ *n* [*therm-* + *pile* (heap)] **:** an apparatus consisting of a number of thermoelectric couples (as of antimony and bismuth or of copper sulfide and German silver) combined so as to multiply the effect and used to generate electric currents for various purposes and also in a very sensitive form for determining intensities of radiation due esp. to its heating effect
¹**ther·mo·plas·tic** \¦thərmə¦plastik\ *adj* [*therm-* + *plastic*] **:** having the property of softening or fusing when heated and of hardening and becoming rigid again when cooled ⟨~

synthetic resins) ⟨~ materials can be remelted and cooled time after time without undergoing any appreciable chemical change —J.S.Campbell⟩ — distinguished from *thermoset* and *thermosetting* — **ther·mo·plas·tic·i·ty** \ˌ==ˌplaˈstisəd-ē\ *n*

²thermoplastic \"\ *n* **:** a thermoplastic material (as gutta-percha, cellulose acetate, or polyethylene)

ther·mo·polymerization \ˈthər(ˌ)mō+\ *n* [*therm-* + *polymerization*] **:** polymerization effected with heat

ther·mo·prene \ˈthərməˌprēn\ *n* [*therm-* + *-prene* (as in *neoprene*)] **:** any of various tough thermoplastic cyclized rubbers

ther·mop·sis \(ˌ)thərˈmäpsəs\ *n, cap* [NL, fr. Gk *thermos* lupine + NL *-opsis*] **:** a genus of American and Asiatic showy herbs (family Leguminosae) having trifoliolate stipulate leaves and yellow or purple racemose flowers — see BUSH PEA

ther·mo·radiography \ˈthər(ˌ)mō+\ *n* [*therm-* + *radiography*] **:** conversion of a pattern of radiant heat into an image for viewing or recording (as by photography)

ther·mo·receptor \ˈthərmō+\ *n* [*therm-* + *receptor*] **:** a sensory end organ that is stimulated by heat or cold

ther·mo·reduction \"+\ *n* [*therm-* + *reduction*] **:** reduction at high temperatures

ther·mo·regulation \"+\ *n* [ISV *therm-* + *regulation*] **1 :** the maintenance or regulation of temperature; *specif* **:** the maintenance of a particular temperature of the living body **2 :** the physiological mechanisms concerned with the maintenance of steady body temperature in an environment with a fluctuating temperature

ther·mo·regulator \"+\ *n* [ISV *therm-* + *regulator*] **:** a device for the regulation of temperature **:** THERMOSTAT

ther·mo·regulatory \"+\ *adj* [*therm-* + *regulatory*] **:** serving to maintain a body at a particular temperature whatever its environmental temperature ⟨the ~ mechanisms of warm-blooded vertebrates⟩

ther·mo·relay \ˈthər(ˌ)mō+\ *n* [*therm-* + *relay*] **:** a device for detecting very small optical-lever deflections in which a reflected beam of radiation falls on a sensitive thermocouple so arranged as to measure very small deflections

ther·mos \ˈthərməs, ˈthəm-, ˈthəim-\ *n* -ES [fr. *Thermos*, a trademark] **:** VACUUM BOTTLE

ther·mo·scope \ˈthərməˌskōp\ *n* [NL *thermoscopium*, fr. *therm-* + *-scopium* -scope] **:** an instrument for indicating changes of temperature by the accompanying changes in volume of some material (as a gas)

ther·mo·scop·ic \ˌ==ˈskäpik\ *adj* [*thermoscope* + *-ic*] **:** distinguishing temperature differences — **ther·mo·scop·i·cal·ly** \-pək(ə)lē\ *adv*

ther·mo·senescence \ˈthərmō+\ *n* [*therm-* + *senescence*] **:** an aging process consisting of prolonged maintenance at a high temperature

ther·mo·sensitive \"+\ *adj* [*therm-* + *sensitive*] **:** relating to or being a material that is in one or more ways sensitive to heat ⟨~ adhesives⟩ ⟨~ papers⟩

¹ther·mo·set \ˈthərməˌset\ *n* [*therm-* + *set* (become solid)] **:** a thermosetting material before or after curing

²thermoset \"\ *adj* **:** relatively incapable of softening or fusing when heated **:** THERMOSETTING ⟨a truly ~ material may decompose at some elevated temperature but will not soften —R.R.McGregor⟩ — compare THERMOPLASTIC

ther·mo·set·ting \-ed·iŋ\ *adj* [*therm-* + *setting*, pres. part. of *set* (become solid)] **:** having the property of becoming permanently hard and rigid when heated or cured **:** capable of changing from a plastic or fusible state to an infusible or insoluble state by a chemical reaction effected by heat or other means and leading to a complex high polymer ⟨the phenol resins and plastics were the original synthetic ~ materials⟩ — compare THERMOPLASTIC

ther·mo·siphon \ˈthərmō+\ *n* [*therm-* + *siphon*] **:** an arrangement of siphon tubes for assisting circulation in a liquid

ther·mo·stability \ˈthərmō+\ *n* **:** the quality of being thermostable

ther·mo·stable \"+\ *adj* [*therm-* + *stable*] **:** stable when heated — used esp. of a substance (as an immune substance, enzyme, or vitamin) that does not lose its characteristic properties on being heated to moderate temperatures ⟨are ~ and do not act as antigens —*Science*⟩

¹ther·mo·stat \ˈthərməˌstat, ˈthəm-, ˈthəim-, *usu* -ad·+V\ *n* -S [*therm-* + *-stat*] **1 a :** an automatic device for regulating temperature (as by opening or closing the damper of a heating furnace or by regulating supply of gas) and commonly utilizing either the differential expansion of solids or the vapor pressure of liquids **b :** a similar device esp. for actuating fire or low-temperature alarms or for controlling automatic sprinklers **2 :** a piece of apparatus (as a constant-temperature chamber) regulated by a thermostat

²thermostat \"\ *vt* **thermostated** *or* **thermostatted; thermostated** *or* **thermostatted; thermostating** *or* **thermostatting; thermostats :** to provide with or control by a thermostat ⟨a ~ed heating system⟩

ther·mo·stat·ic \ˌ==ˈstad·|ik, -at|, |ēk\ *adj* [*thermostat* + *-ic*] **:** of or relating to a thermostat **:** controlled by a thermostat

ther·mo·stat·i·cal·ly \|ək(ə)lē, |ēk-, -li\ *adv* **:** by means of a thermostat ⟨recorded by a glass dilatometer placed in a ~ controlled high-pressure vessel —D.W.van Krevelen & Johannes Schuyer⟩

ther·mo·stimulation \ˈthər(ˌ)mō+\ *n* [*therm-* + *stimulation*] **:** stimulation (as of a nerve) by means of heat

ther·mo·stromuhr \ˈthərmə+\ *n* [ISV *therm-* + *stromuhr*] **:** a stromuhr that measures the rate of blood flow in an intact blood vessel by determining the amount of heating of the blood as indicated by a sensitive galvanometer when a radio-frequency current is passed through the vessel between thermocouples so that the amount of heating is inversely proportional to the rate of flow

ther·mo·tactic \ˈthərmōˈtaktik\ *adj* [*therm-* + *-tactic*] **:** characterized by or exhibiting thermotaxis **:** of or relating to thermotaxis

ther·mo·tax·is \-aksəs\ *n* [NL, fr. *therm-* + *-taxis*] **1 :** a taxis in which a temperature gradient constitutes the directive factor **2 :** the regulation of body temperature

ther·mo·therapy \ˈthərmō+\ *n* [ISV *therm-* + *therapy*] **:** treatment of disease by heat (as by hot air, hot baths, or diathermy)

ther·mo·tolerant \"+\ *adj* [*therm-* + *tolerant*] **:** THERMODURIC

ther·mo·trop·ic \ˈthərməˈträpik\ *adj* [ISV *therm-* + *-tropic*] **:** manifesting thermotropism **:** characterized by thermotropism

ther·mot·ro·pism \(ˌ)thərˈmä·trəˌpizəm\ *n* [ISV *therm-* + *-tropism*] **:** a tropism in which a temperature gradient determines the orientation

-ther·mous \ˈthərməs, -ˈthəm-, -ˈthəim-\ *adj comb form* [Gk *-thermos*, fr. *thermē* heat — more at THERM] **:** having (such) heat ⟨homo*thermous*⟩ ⟨xero*thermous*⟩

ther·mo·well \ˈthərmō+,-\ *n* [*thermometer* + *well*] **:** a tube or tubular opening provided expressly for the insertion of a thermometer

therms *pl of* THERM

-therms *pl of* -THERM

-thermy — see -THERMIA

thero- — see THER-

the·ro·dont \ˈthirəˌdänt\ *n* -S [*ther-* + *-odont*] **:** THERIODONT

the·rol·o·gy \thiˈräləjē\ *n* -ES [NL *therologia*, fr. *ther-* + *-logia* -logy] **:** MAMMALOGY

the·ro·morph \ˈthirəˌmȯrf\ *n* [NL *Theromorpha*] **:** PELYCOSAUR

the·ro·mor·pha \ˌthirəˈmȯrfə\ [NL, fr. *ther-* + *-morpha*] *syn of* PELYCOSAURIA

the·ro·phyte \ˈthirəˌfīt\ *n* -S [ISV *thero-* (fr. Gk *theros* summer) + *-phyte;* akin to Gk *thermos* hot — more at WARM] **:** an annual plant that overwinters as a seed

¹the·ro·pod \-ˌpäd\ *adj* [NL *Theropoda*] **:** of or relating to the Theropoda

²theropod \"\ *n* -S [NL *Theropoda*] **:** a dinosaur of the suborder Theropoda

the·rop·o·da \thiˈräpədə\ *n pl, cap* [NL, fr. *ther-* + *-poda*] **:** a suborder of Saurischia that comprises carnivorous digitigrade dinosaurs having premaxillary teeth, small forelimbs, and simple slender pubic bones meeting in a symphysis and walking on their hind legs — see COMPSOGNATHUS, MEGALOSAURUS

the·rop·o·dous \-dəs\ *adj* [NL *Theropoda* + E *-ous*] **:** THEROPOD

thesaurer *n* -S [ME, fr. LL *thesaurarius*, fr. L, of treasure, fr. *thesaurus* treasure + *-arius* -ary] *obs* **:** TREASURER

the·sau·rus \thəˈsȯrəs\ *n, pl* **thesau·ri** \-ˌrī\ *or* **thesau·ruses** [NL, fr. L, treasure, store, collection, fr. Gk *thēsauros*] **1 a :** a book containing a store of words or of information about a particular field or set of concepts; *specif* **:** a dictionary of synonyms **b :** a collection of concepts or words constituting the contents of a thesaurus ⟨must employ only the ~ of Chinese rhetoric —H.H.Hart⟩ ⟨indicated by . . . use of such terms as *ostensible, emulative, conspicuous*, and the rest of his beautifully ironic ~ —David Riesman⟩ **2 :** TREASURY, STOREHOUSE

these [ME *these, thes* (pl. of *this*, pron. & adj.), fr. OE *thǣs* (pl. of *thes*, pron. & adj., this) — more at THIS] *pl of* THIS

the·sis \ˈthēsəs, *in sense 3* " *or* ˈthes-\ *n, pl* **the·ses** \-(ˌ)sēz\ [L, fr. Gk, act of placing, act of laying down, position, proposition, downbeat of the foot in keeping time, fr. *tithenai* to put, place, lay down — more at DO] **1 a :** a claim put forward **:** STATEMENT, PROPOSITION; *specif* **:** a position or proposition that a person (as a candidate for scholastic honors) advances and maintains or offers to maintain by argument **b :** an affirmation or proposition to be proved or one advanced without proof esp. in contrast with a negation: as (1) **:** the proposition or point of view defended by an argument (2) **:** ASSUMPTION, POSTULATE (3) **:** the consequent of a hypothetical proposition (4) *Kantianism* **:** the affirmative member of one of the antinomies or paradoxes of reason (5) *Hegelianism* **:** the proposition or conception representing the first and least adequate stage of developing thought — compare ANTITHESIS, SYNTHESIS **2 :** a dissertation embodying results of original research and esp. substantiating a specific view: as **a :** a substantial paper written by a candidate for an academic degree under the individual direction of a professor **b :** a paper written by an undergraduate desirous of achieving honors or distinction **3 a** (1) [LL, fr. Gk, act of placing; fr. the lowering of the voice] **:** the lighter or unstressed part of a poetic foot esp. in accentual verse (2) **:** the heavier or longer part of a poetic foot esp. in quantitative verse **b :** the accented part of a musical measure **:** DOWNBEAT — compare ARSIS **syn** see DISCOURSE

thesis novel *n* **:** a novel that advances, illustrates, or defends a thesis ⟨a *thesis novel* directed against the corruption of the clergy —E. G. Du Cal⟩

thesis play *n* **:** a play that advances, illustrates, or defends a thesis

the·si·um \ˈthēsēəm, thəˈsīəm\ *n, cap* [NL, fr. L *thesium, thesion* bastard toad flax, fr. Gk *thēseion*, prob. fr. neut. of *thēseios* of Theseus, fr. *Thēseus* Theseus, mythological Greek hero] **:** a large genus of Old World root-parasitic herbs of the family Santalaceae with small linear or scalelike leaves and diclinous flowers — see BASTARD TOADFLAX

thes·mo·pho·ria \ˌthezməˈfōrēə\ *n* -S *usu cap* [L (pl.), fr. Gk, fr. *thesmophoros* giving laws (epithet of Demeter), fr. *thesmos* law, ordinance (fr. *tithenai* to put, lay down) + *-phoros* -phore — more at DO] **:** a festival of Demeter as Thesmophoros or of Demeter and Kore celebrated by women and having as its essential ceremony the casting of pigs into chasms of the earth and the bringing up of their decaying flesh to be mixed with seed to insure fertility — **thes·mo·pho·ri·an** \ˌ==ˈ==ēən\ *adj, usu cap* — **thes·mo·phor·ic** \ˌ==ˈfōrik\ *adj, usu cap*

thes·mo·thete \ˈthezməˌthēt\ *n* -S [Gk *thesmothetēs*, fr. *thesmos* law + *thetēs* one who sets, lays down, fr. *tithenai* to put, lay down] **:** LAWGIVER, LEGISLATOR; *specif* **:** one of the six ancient Athenian junior archons

thes·o·cyte \ˈthesəˌsīt\ *n* -S [Gk *thesis* act of laying down, deposit + E *-o-* + *-cyte* — more at THESIS] **:** an amoebocyte containing ergastic inclusions

thes·pe·sia \theˈspēzh(ē)ə\ *n, cap* [NL, fr. Gk, fem. of *thespesios* marvelous, divine, lit., told by a god; akin to Gk *theos* god and to *enepein, ennepein* to tell, speak — more at THE-] **:** a small genus of tropical trees (family Malvaceae) having undivided leaves and large bracted flowers with a nearly simple style and 5-celled ovary — see PORTIA TREE

thes·pe·sius \-zh(ē)əs\ *n, cap* [NL, fr. Gk *thespesios* marvelous] **:** a genus of Upper Cretaceous No. American ornithischian dinosaurs related to *Hadrosaurus*

¹thes·pi·an \ˈthespēən\ *adj* [*Thespis*, 6th cent. B.C. Greek poet and reputed originator of the actor's role in drama + E *-an*, adj. suffix] **1** *usu cap* **:** of or relating to Thespis **2** *often cap* **:** relating to the drama **:** DRAMATIC ⟨a movie director getting excellent ~ cooperation —H.E.Clurman⟩

²thespian \"\ *n* -S *sometimes cap* [*Thespis* + E *-an*, n. suffix] **:** ACTOR

¹thes·sa·lian \theˈsālēən, -lyən\ *adj, usu cap* [L *Thessalius* of Thessaly, fr. *Thessalia* Thessaly, district of east central Greece + E *-an*] **1 :** of or relating to Thessaly **2 :** of or relating to the people of Thessaly

²thessalian \"\ *n* -S *cap* **1 :** a native or inhabitant of Thessaly **2 :** an Aeolic dialect of ancient Greek used by the Thessalians

¹thes·sa·lo·nian \ˌthesəˈlōnyən, -ōnēən\ *adj, usu cap* [irreg. fr. *Thessalonica*, seaport city of west central Macedonia (now *Salonika*) + E *-an*] **:** of or relating to ancient Thessalonica, Macedonia

²thessalonian \"\ *n* -S *cap* **:** a native or resident of Thessalonica

the·ta \ˈthād·ə, -ātə *also* ˈthē-\ *n* -S [Gk *thēta*, of Sem origin; akin to Heb *ṭēth* teth] **:** the eighth letter of the Greek alphabet — symbol Θ or θ; see ALPHABET table

thet·ic \ˈthed·ik\ *adj* [Gk *thetikos* fit for placing, of a thesis, positive, fr. *thetos* (verbal of *tithenai* to put, place, lay down) + *-ikos* -ic — more at DO] **1** *or* **thet·i·cal** \-d·əkəl\ **:** laid down **:** PRESCRIBED, POSITIVE, ARBITRARY **2 a :** constituting a poetic thesis ⟨a ~ syllable⟩ **b :** beginning with a thesis ⟨~ line⟩ ⟨~ measure⟩ — **thet·i·cal·ly** \-d·ək(ə)lē\ *adv*

the·tin \ˈthētᵊn\ *also* **the·tine** \", -ēˌtēn\ *n* -S [*thio-* + *betaine*] **:** any one of a class of sulfonium carboxylates that are analogous to the betaines ⟨dimethyl-*thetin*, $(CH_3)_2S^{+}CH_2COO^{-}$⟩

the·ur·gic \(ˈ)thēˈərjik\ *or* **the·ur·gi·cal** \-jəkəl\ *adj* [*theurgic* fr. LL *theurgicus*, fr. LGk *theourgikos*, fr. *theourgos* wonder-worker, divine worker (fr. Gk *the-* + *-ourgos* worker, fr. *-o-* + *ergon* work) + Gk *-ikos* -ic; *theurgical* fr. LL *theurgicus* + E *-al* — more at WORK] **:** of or relating to theurgy **:** MAGICAL

the·ur·gist \ˈthē(ˌ)ərjəst\ *n* -S [*theurgy* + *-ist*] **:** WONDER-WORKER, MAGICIAN

the·ur·gy \-jē\ *n* ES [LL *theurgia*, fr. LGk *theourgia*, fr. *theourgos* wonder-worker + Gk *-ia* -y] **1 a :** the art or science of compelling or persuading a god or beneficent supernatural power to do or refrain from doing something; *specif* **:** an occult art in which the operator by means of self-purification and discipline, sacred rites, and knowledge of divine signatures in nature is held to be capable of evoking or utilizing the aid of divine and beneficent spirits **b :** a human act, process, power, or state of supernatural efficacy or origin; *also* **:** theurgic acts **2 :** a divine work **:** MIRACLE

the·ve·tia \thəˈvēsh(ē)ə\ *n, cap* [NL, fr. André *Thévet* †1592 Fr. traveler and author + NL *-ia*] **:** a genus of tropical American trees and shrubs (family Apocynaceae) having alternate entire leaves and large cymose flowers with a campanulate corolla that has overlapping lobes

the·ve·tin \thəˈvētᵊn, ˈthevətən\ *n* -S [NL *Thevetia* + ISV *-in*] **:** a poisonous crystalline cardiac glycoside $C_{42}H_{66}O_{18}$ obtained esp. from the seeds of the yellow oleander that yields on hydrolysis glucose, digitalose, and a sterol — compare DIGITOXIN

¹thew \ˈth(y)ü\ *n* -S [ME, custom, habit, personal quality, virtue, fr. OE *thēaw;* akin to OS *thau* custom, habit, OHG *kathau* discipline, and prob. to L *tuēri* to observe, protect — more at TUITION] **1 thews** *pl, archaic* **:** mental or moral qualities, traits, or customs **2 a :** MUSCLE, SINEW ⟨broad of shoulder and great of ~ —Frank Yerby⟩ — usu. used in pl. **b** (1) **:** muscular power or development (2) **:** STRENGTH, VITALITY ⟨the naked ~ and sinew of the English language —G.M.Hopkins⟩

²thew *dial past of* THAW

thewed \ˈth(y)üd\ *adj* [ME, fr. ¹*thew* + *-ed*] **1** *obs* **:** MANNERED, BEHAVED **2 :** furnished with thews ⟨buxom, deep-breasted, strong-*thewed*, fit to be mates and mothers of big men — Bernard DeVoto⟩

thew·less \ˈth(y)üləs\ *var of* THOWLESS

¹they \(ˈ)thā, *before* "re" *or* "are" *usu* (ˌ)the\ *pron, pl in constr* [ME, fr. ON *their*, masc. pl. demonstrative & personal pron.; akin to ON *that*, neut. demonstrative pron. — more at THAT] **1 a :** those ones — used as nominative third person pronoun serving as the plural of *he*, the plural of *she*, or the plural of *it*, or referring to a group of two or more individuals that are not all of the same sex ⟨your sons are popular because ~ dance well⟩ ⟨ask your wife and daughter what ~ think about it⟩ ⟨we are so used to matches that we can hardly imagine what life was like before ~ were invented⟩ ⟨today is my neighbors' wedding anniversary but I don't know what presents ~ are giving each other⟩; often used with an antecedent that is singular in form but collective in meaning ⟨even if the unofficial minority voted solidly against a government measure — a rare circumstance because ~ were divided by mutual jealousies —W.T. Stace⟩ ⟨if industry is to do this important job ~ must understand not only what the men think —E.R.Smith⟩; sometimes in poetry and in substandard speech used pleonastically together with a noun or group of nouns as subject of a verb ⟨the olives ~ were not blind to Him —Sidney Lanier⟩ ⟨my father and mother ~ told me not to do it⟩; compare HE, IT, SHE **b :** he or she **:** ¹HE 2 — used with an indefinite singular antecedent ⟨everyone tries to make the person ~ love just like themselves —H.D.Skidmore⟩ ⟨no person has a right to any coat of arms (or crest) unless ~ are the "heir-male" for the time being —Thomas Innes⟩ ⟨the liability for damages lies against whoever is knowingly involved in such sale whether or not ~ receive any part of the consideration —*U.S.Code*⟩ **2 :** THOSE — used esp. as antecedent to a relative pronoun ⟨blessed are ~ that mourn —Mt 5:4 (AV)⟩ ⟨the mothers who kept score did a fine job but ~ who did the umpiring left much to be desired —*Deerfield (Wisc.) Independent*⟩ **3 :** ¹PEOPLE 1a **:** unspecified persons and esp. those responsible for a particular act, practice, or decision ⟨curiosity killed a cat, ~ say⟩ ⟨~ are going to hold the commencement exercises outdoors if the weather permits⟩ ⟨he's as lazy as ~ come⟩ ⟨at Nedroma ~ think they can make a prodigious crop rise from the earth by inviting the tallest worker to stretch himself at full length in the first furrow —J.G.Frazer⟩ **4** *dial chiefly Eng* **:** THEM — used emphatically as object of a verb or preposition ⟨good enough for the likes of ~⟩

²they \"\ *adj* [ME, fr. *they*, pron.] *dial Eng* **:** THOSE ⟨its ~ deserters that commit half the crimes —Rose Macaulay⟩ ⟨if you fetches out ~ hedges, master . . . I'll not work for 'ee no more —C.G.Glover⟩

³they \"\ *n* -S [¹*they*] **:** a group of unspecified persons or forces of which the speaker or writer is not a member; *esp* **:** such a group held to be responsible for acts or decisions that impose unwelcome restrictions on the speaker or writer ⟨the same ~ we always mean, . . . authority, the gods, fate, circumstances — Ralph Ellison⟩

⁴they \"\ *pron* [by alter.] *substand* **:** ²THERE 1 ⟨~'s music in the twitter of the bluebird and the jay —J.W.Riley⟩ ⟨~ wasn't a house nowhere in sight —Helen Eustis⟩

⁵they \"\ *adj* [by alter.] *substand* **:** ²THEIR ⟨the kids was sleeping all together in ~ bed over in the corner —Ralph Ellison⟩

thi- *or* **thio-** *comb form* [ISV, fr. Gk *thei-, theio-* sulfur, brimstone, fr. *theion;* prob. akin to Gk *thyein* to rage, seethe — more at DUST] **:** containing sulfur ⟨*thiamine*⟩; *esp* **:** containing bivalent sulfur usu. in place of oxygen ⟨*thiocyanic*⟩ ⟨*thioether*⟩ — compare SULF- c

THI *abbr* time handed in

¹thia- *or* **thi-** *comb form* [ISV, fr. *thi-* + *-a-*] **:** containing sulfur in place of carbon or regarded as in place of carbon usu. in place of the methylene group $-CH_2-$ ⟨*thia*cyclohexane⟩ ⟨*thia*diazole⟩ ⟨*thiazole*⟩ — compare AZA-, OXA-

²thia- *comb form* **:** THI- ⟨*thia*chroman⟩

thi·acet·azone \ˌthīəˈsed·əˌzōn\ *n* -S [*thi-* + *acet-* + *az-* + *-one*] **:** a bitter pale yellow crystalline tuberculostatic drug $C_{10}H_{12}N_4OS$; *para*-acetamido-benzaldehyde thiosemicarbazone

thia·diazole \ˈthīə+\ *n* [*thia-* + *diazole*] **:** any of four isomeric heterocyclic parent compounds $C_2H_2N_2S$ containing a ring composed of two carbon atoms, two nitrogen atoms, and one sulfur atom; *also* **:** a derivative of any of these

thi·al \ˈthīˌal\ *n* -S [ISV *thi-* + *-al*] **:** THIOALDEHYDE

thi·al·dine \thīˈalˌdēn, -ˌdən\ *n* [ISV *thi-* + *ald-* + *-ine*] **:** a crystalline heterocyclic compound $CH_3CH{=}(SCHCH_3)_2{=}NH$ formed by action of ammonia and hydrogen sulfide on acetaldehyde; *broadly* **:** a compound similarly derived from another aldehyde

thi·ami·nase \thīˈaməˌnās, ˈthīəm-, -āz\ *n* [ISV *thiamine* + *-ase*] **:** an enzyme or any of a group of enzymes that promote the destruction of thiamine in the body and are found esp. in raw freshwater fish and in raw clams, crustaceans, and starfish

thi·amine \thīˈamən; ˈthīəˌmēn, -mən\ *also* **thi·amin** \-ˌmən\ *n* [*thiamine* alter. (influenced by *amine*) of *thiamin*, fr. *thi-* + *-amin* (as in *vitamin*)] **1** *also* **thiamine chloride :** the antineuritic member of the vitamin B complex that is an amino hydroxy quaternary ammonium water-soluble salt $[C_{12}H_{17}N_4OS]Cl$ containing a thiazole ring and a pyrimidine ring, that occurs widely both free (as in the germs of cereals and hulls of grain) and combined (as in yeast and in animal tissues like liver, kidneys, and heart) but is usu. synthesized commercially, that functions in the body as cocarboxylase and is essential for conversion of carbohydrate to fat and for normal nervous action and that is used in nutrition (as in vitamin preparations and in enriching flour and bread) and in medicine in treating thiamine deficiency — called also *vitamin B_1* **2** *or* **thiamine base :** the cation $[C_{12}H_{17}N_4OS]^{+}$ of thiamine chloride ⟨~ mononitrate is used similarly to thiamine hydrochloride⟩

thia·naph·thene \ˈthīəˈnafˌthēn, ÷ -apˌth-\ *n* -S [¹*thia-* + *naphth-* + *-ene*] **:** a crystalline heterocyclic compound C_8H_6S that has an odor like that of naphthalene and is found in lignite tar — called also *benzothiophene*

thi·an shan sheep \tēˈänˌshän-\ *n, usu cap T & 1st S* [*Thian Shan* (Tien Shan), mountain chain in central Asia] **:** MARCO POLO SHEEP

thian shan stag *n, usu cap T & 1st S* **:** a very large deer (*Cervus eustephanus*) of the Tien Shan mountains of western China related to the maral and the American wapiti

thi·an·threne \thīˈanˌthrēn\ *n* -S [ISV *thi-* + *-anthrene*] **:** a crystalline heterocyclic parent compound $C_{12}H_8S_2$ that is regarded as anthracene in which the two middle methylidyne groups are replaced by sulfur atoms and that is made by the action of sulfur chloride on benzene in the presence of aluminum chloride and in other ways

thi·ara \thīˈa(a)rə\ *n, cap* [NL] **:** a genus of freshwater snails that is the type of the family Thiaridae and that includes several forms which are intermediate hosts of medically important trematodes

thi·ar·i·dae \-ˈarəˌdē\ *n pl, cap* [NL, fr. *Thiara*, type genus + *-idae*] **:** a family of Old World operculate freshwater snails (suborder Taenioglossa) — see HUA, SEMISULCOSPIRA, THIARA

thi·a·sine \ˈthīəˌsēn, -sən\ *n* -S [irreg. fr. *thi-*] **:** ERGOTHIONEINE

thi·a·zine \ˈthīəˌzēn, -zən\ *n* [ISV *thi-* + *azine*] **:** any of several parent compounds C_4H_5NS or their derivatives containing a ring composed of four carbon atoms, one sulfur atom, and one nitrogen atom; *also* **:** any of various derivatives of them — see AZINE 1; compare PHENOTHIAZINE

Thiazine \"\ *trademark* — used for a dyestuff; see DYE table I (under *Direct Red 45*)

thi·a·zole \ˈthīəˌzōl\ *n* [ISV *thi-* + *azole*] **1 :** a basic liquid parent compound C_3H_3NS that has an odor resembling that of pyridine and that is analogous in structure to oxazole with sulfur in place of oxygen — compare STRUCTURAL FORMULA **2 :** any of various derivatives of thiazole or benzothiazole

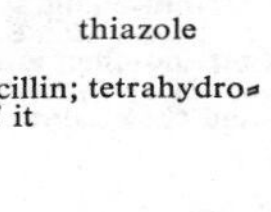

thiazole

thi·a·zol·idine \ˌthīəˈzōləˌdēn, -zäl-, -dən\ *n* -S [ISV *thiazole* + *-idine*] **:** a basic liquid saturated heterocyclic compound C_3H_7NS whose ring is present in the structure of penicillin; tetrahydrothiazole; *also* **:** any of various derivatives of it

thi·az·o·line \thī'azə,lēn, -,lən\ n -s [ISV thiazole + -ine] : any of three basic heterocyclic compounds C_3H_5NS; dihydro-thiazole; also : any of various derivatives of them
thi·a·zol·sul·fone \thīə,zōl'səl,fōn, -zōl-\ n [prob. irreg. fr. thiazole + sulfone] : a crystalline antibacterial drug $C_9H_9N_3O_2S_2$ used orally in treating leprosy; 2-amino-5-sulfanilyl-thiazole
¹thibet usu cap, var of TIBET
²thi·bet also **ti·bet** \tə'bet, usu -ed·+V\ n -s [Thibet (Tibet), country in central Asia where the wool was originally produced] **1** : a fine woolen fabric formerly used for dresses **2** : a suiting and coating fabric usu. of wool and finished with a soft smooth heavily-felted face
thi·ble \'thībəl, 'thib-\ var of THIVEL
¹thick \'thik\ adj -ER/-EST [ME thikke, fr. OE thicce; akin to OHG dicki thick, ON thykkr, OIr tiug] **1 a** : having or being of relatively great depth or extent from one surface to its opposite ⟨a ~ plank⟩ ⟨a ~ neck⟩ ⟨a ~ book⟩ **b** : heavily built : BURLY, THICKSET ⟨that ~ man . . . is as fine as a needle —Joseph Conrad⟩ ⟨a slow, closemouthed man, ~ in the shoulders and muscled like a bull —H.G.Evarts⟩ **2 a** : close-packed with units or individuals : densely massed or tightly filled : CRAMMED, CROWDED ⟨the air was ~ with snow⟩ ⟨a ~ forest⟩ ⟨libel suits were ~ in the air —Dorothy C. Fisher⟩ **b** : occurring in large numbers in a limited area or in close succession : NUMEROUS, FREQUENT ⟨in that canyon the fossils were particularly ~ —D.B.Putnam⟩ **c** : holding much solid matter in suspension or solution : dense or viscous in consistency ⟨a ~ syrup⟩ **d** : foul or heavy with fumes : heavy with dust or other foreign matter : CLOSE 6, IMPURE, STUFFY — used of the air **e** : dense with particles : having drops or specks close together ⟨~ fog⟩ ⟨~ smoke⟩ **f** : marked by haze, fog, or mist enough to obstruct or reduce vision ⟨~ weather⟩ ⟨a ~ day⟩ **g** : impenetrable to the eye : GROSS, PROFOUND — used of night or darkness **h** : showing massive concentration : UNRELIEVED ⟨serves in place of a slower and ~er naturalism —N.Y.Times⟩ ⟨one of the ~est concentrations of heavy industry in the world —Sam Pollock⟩ **i** : extreme in intensity : SHEER, UTTER ⟨~ silence⟩ **3** : measuring in thickness ⟨a log 12 inches ~⟩ ⟨a coin 1 mm. ~⟩ **4 a** : marked by huskiness or hoarseness : imperfectly articulated : INDISTINCT, MUFFLED, GUTTURAL, ROUGH ⟨plays his part with a ~ accent —Henry Hewes⟩ **b** : marked by rich and close harmony esp. in the lower register — used of a musical score **5 a** : dull of hearing or sight **b** : dull or slow of mind or apprehension : not acute or keen : OBTUSE, STUPID ⟨you're obtuse, that's all; just plain ~ —Jean Kerr⟩ **6** obs : lined up one behind another : DEEP ⟨a guard of spies ten ~ —Ben Jonson⟩ **7** : associated on close or familiar terms : INTIMATE ⟨the two were ~ as thieves for months⟩ **8** : exceeding bounds of propriety or fitness : past toleration or endurance : EXCESSIVE, EXTRAVAGANT, EXTREME, GROSS ⟨called it a bit ~ to be fired out of hand in that way⟩ ⟨laid his flattery on ~⟩ **syn** see CLOSE, FAMILIAR, STOCKY
²thick \"\ n -s [ME thikke, fr. thikke, adj.] **1** : the most crowded or most fully occupied part : the densest concentration ⟨we came around a turn into the ~ of a mob of yelling people —Mollie Panter-Downes⟩ ⟨wide-reaching branches and a ~ of leaves —Padraic Colum⟩ **2** : the most intense or most active part or stage ⟨the ~ of battle⟩ ⟨major producers . . . are in the ~ of this trend —Wall Street Jour.⟩ **3 a** : the part of greatest thickness ⟨the ~ of the thumb⟩ **b** : THICKET **c** : a dense or stupid person ⟨you must think I'm a right ~ —Brendan Behan⟩
³thick \"\ adv -ER/-EST [ME thicke, fr. OE thicce; akin to OHG dicco often; both fr. a prehistoric WGmc adv. fr. the root of OE thicce, adj. — more at ¹THICK] : THICKLY ⟨misfortunes came ~ and fast⟩ — often used in combination ⟨thick-starred⟩ ⟨thick-swarming⟩
⁴thick \"\ vb -ED/-ING/-S [ME thikken, fr. OE thiccian, fr. thicce, adj.] archaic : to make, be, or become thick : THICKEN
thick and thin n [ME thikke and thinne, fr. thikke, n., thick + and + thinne, n., thin] : every difficulty and obstacle : all hindrances and obstructions — used esp. in the phrase through thick and thin ⟨stand by her shoulder to shoulder through thick and thin —Gustave Weigel⟩ ⟨had been his friend through thick and thin⟩
thick-and-thin \ˌ≈≈'≈\ adj [thick and thin] **1** : having one sheave thicker than the other and taking two ropes of differing size — used of a tackle block; compare FIDDLE BLOCK **2** : ready to go through thick and thin : unreservedly or blindly loyal or devoted ⟨a thick-and-thin friend⟩ **3** : having regularly or irregularly spaced sections thicker than the rest — used of yarns
thick and threefold adv (or adj) : in rapid succession : THICKLY, CONTINUOUSLY, FREQUENTLY
thick-billed murre or **thick-billed guillemot** \'≈,≈-\ n : a widely distributed murre (Uria lomvia) with a rather short distinctly thick bill
thick-billed parrot n : a parrot (Rhynchopsitta pachyrhyncha) of northern Mexico and southwestern U. S. that is green marked with red
thick china n [perh. so called fr. the resemblance of the coating to the glaze of chinaware] : a coated paperboard similar to railroad board but lighter in weight
thick·en \'thikən\ vb **thickened; thickened; thickening** \-k(ə)niŋ\ **thickens** [ME thiknen, fr. thikke, adj., thick + -nen -en] vt **1 a** : to make thick, dense, or viscous in consistency ⟨~s gravy with flour⟩ **b** : to make close or compact : fill up the openings or interstices of ⟨~ platoon fires and turn back any enemy counterattack —Combat Forces Jour.⟩ **2** : to make stronger : CONFIRM, INTENSIFY ⟨this may help to ~ other proofs —Shak.⟩ **3 a** : to increase the thickness of : add to the depth or diameter of ⟨the years had ~ed the man's figure⟩ **b** : BROADEN ⟨the strokes m and n are halved and ~ed to indicate a following d —Pitman Shorthand⟩ **4** : BLUR, OBSCURE ⟨alcohol had ~ed his speech⟩ ~ vi **1 a** : to become dense (as in consistency or texture) : grow thick or compact ⟨the mist ~ed⟩ **b** : to become concentrated in numbers, mass, or frequency : gather in a crowd or dense aggregation ⟨the Indians . . . were ~ing in Kentucky again —Rebecca Caudill⟩ ⟨all through the café the groups of players had ~ed —Winifred Bambrick⟩ **2** : to grow blurred, obscure, or dark : become foggy or misty ⟨his speech ~ed as he drank on⟩ ⟨the weather ~ed⟩ **3** : to increase in mass or measurement : grow broader or bulkier ⟨her tall straight figure had ~ed —Ellen Glasgow⟩ **4** : to become more profound, intense, or intricate : grow complicated or complex ⟨the plot ~s⟩
thick·en·er \-k(ə)nə(r)\ n -s : one that thickens: as **a** : an apparatus for the sedimentation and collection of suspended solids in industrial liquids **b** : a mechanical device for removing part of the water from slush pulp
thickening n -s **1** : the act of making or becoming thick ⟨underwent a gradual ~⟩ **2** : something used to thicken (as flour in a gravy) **3** : a thickened part or place
thicker comparative of THICK
thickest superlative of THICK
thick·et \'thikət, usu -əd·+V\ n -s [fr. (assumed) ME thikket, fr. OE thiccet, fr. thicce, adj., thick] **1** : a dense and usu. circumscribed growth of shrubbery or small trees : COPPICE ⟨~s of sumac, blackberries, and poison ivy —Nathaniel Burt⟩ **2** : something likened to a thicket for density or impenetrability : TANGLE ⟨the myriad ~s and morasses of superstition —Alan Gregg⟩ ⟨ghost-written sources have built an impenetrable ~ around the truth —E.R.May⟩
thick·et·ed \-əd·əd, -ətəd\ adj : dotted or covered with thickets : abounding in thickets ⟨~ hills⟩
thick·ety \-əd·ē, -ət|, |i\ adj : full of thickets
thickhead \'≈,≈\ n **1 a** : WHISTLER 1b(1) **b** : a thick-knee (Burhinus capensis) of southern Africa **2** : a stupid person : BLOCKHEAD **3** : BLUETONGUE 1
thickheaded \'≈'≈≈\ adj **1** : having a thick head — used esp. in names of animals **2** : dull of intellect : STUPID — **thick·head·ed·ly** adv — **thick·head·ed·ness** n -ES
thickheaded fly n : any of various flies comprising the family Conopidae, having a more or less elongate and sometimes pedicellate abdomen and a large head broader than the thorax, and being parasitic as larvae on other insects (as wasps)
thick·ish \'thikish, -kēsh\ adj : rather thick
thick-knee \'≈,≈\ n : STONE CURLEW 1; esp : a stone curlew of the genus Burhinus
thick lead n : a printer's lead of 3 points thickness
thicklips \'≈,≈\ n pl but sing in constr : one with thick lips
thick·ly adv [ME thikkely, fr. thikke, adj., thick + -ly] : in a thick manner
thickneck \"\ n : SCALLION 3
¹thick·ness n -ES [ME thiknesse, fr. OE thicnes, fr. thicce, adj., thick + -nes -ness] **1** : the quality or state of being thick **2** : the smallest of three dimensions ⟨the length, width, and ~ of a sheet of paper⟩ ⟨the length, height, and ~ of a wall⟩ ⟨the length, circumference, and ~ of a log⟩ **3 a** : viscous consistency ⟨boiled to the ~ of honey⟩ **b** : the condition of being smoky, foul, or foggy — used of the air **4 a** : roughness or harshness of breathing **b** : dullness of hearing **c** : a blurring or indistinctness of speech **5** : the thick part of something ⟨this winding stair had been constructed in the ~ of the castle wall —Sax Rohmer⟩ **6** : density of aggregation : CONCENTRATION ⟨the relative ~ of population in any given area —Edward Sapir⟩ **7** : dullness of mind or perception : STUPIDITY ⟨made up my mind to forgive your ~ —Anne Green⟩ **8** : LAYER, PLY, SHEET ⟨the number of ~es of boxboard was reduced from 244 to 60 —Paper Trade Jour.⟩ ⟨a single ~ of canvas⟩ **9** : fullness of content or meaning : FIRMNESS, SOLIDITY, VOLUMINOUSNESS ⟨that forgotten moral ~ for which so many of us were sick —Herbert Gold⟩
²thickness \"\ vt -ED/-ING/-ES **1** : to make uniform in thickness (as flooring planks) **2** : to cover or coat in thicknessing
thickness gage n : FEELER 3
thicknessing n -s **1** : a method of making a mold for a plaster cast or a metal casting in which a temporary thickness of wax or other material is put on the pattern or part of the unfinished mold and run out by heat or otherwise removed after it has been used to complete the mold **2** : the thickness of wax or other material used in thicknessing
thickness piece n : a board or narrow flat used to outline a door or window in theatrical scenery and suggest the thickness of a wall
thickness ratio n : the ratio of the maximum thickness of an airfoil to the chord at that station
thick register n : CHEST REGISTER
thicks pl of THICK, pres 3d sing of THICK
¹thickset \'≈,≈\ adj [ME thikke sette, fr. thikke, adv., thick + sette, sett, adj., set] **1** : closely placed : densely planted : growing thickly ⟨a ~ wood⟩ **2** : set or studded thickly or abundantly ⟨~ trees⟩ **3** : having a thick body : BURLY **syn** see STOCKY
²thickset \"\ n : something thickset: as **a** : a cotton fabric with a short dense pile; esp : a durable corduroy for working clothes **b** : THICKET
thick shellbark n : BIG SHELLBARK
thickskin \'≈,≈\ adj : THICK-SKINNED
thick-skinned \'≈'≈\ adj **1** : having a thick skin : PACHYDERMATOUS **2** : CALLOUS, INSENSITIVE ⟨there was a force in him that . . . subdued even a thick-skinned, conceited boy —Virginia Woolf⟩ ⟨being a thick-skinned man, he had no conception of how galling such remarks could be —C.B.Nordhoff & J.N. Hall⟩
thickskull \'≈,≈\ n : a dull-witted person : BLOCKHEAD
thickskulled \'≈'≈\ adj **1** : having a thick skull **2** : dull of apprehension : slow to learn : INSENSITIVE, STUPID
thick-sown \'≈'≈\ adj : sown closely together : thickly set : STUDDED ⟨speech thick-sown with French phrases⟩
thick space n : THREE-EM SPACE
thick stuff n : sided ship's timber more than 4 inches thick and less than 12
thick-tailed ray \'≈,≈-\ n : a ray of the suborder Sarcura
thick wind \'≈,≈\ n : a chronic defect of respiration in the horse due to obstruction of the respiratory passages (as by nasal polyps or deformed bones) — compare ROARING 2 — **thick-wind·ed** \'≈'windəd\ adj
thick-witted \'≈'≈\ adj : dull or slow of mind : DENSE, STUPID — **thick-wit·ted·ly** adv — **thick-wit·ted·ness** n -ES
thief \'thēf\ n, pl **thieves** \-ēvz\ [ME theef, fr. OE thēof; akin to OHG diob thief, ON thjōfr, Goth thiubs thief, Lith tupėti to squat, crouch] **1 a** : one who steals esp. stealthily or secretly : one who commits theft or larceny **b** archaic : FREEBOOTER, ROBBER **c** dial Brit : SCOUNDREL, RASCAL, SCAMP **2** : something that takes possession by stealth ⟨procrastination is the ~ of time⟩ **3** also **thief tube** : a device for taking a sample esp. of a liquid from a receptacle at any specified depth below the surface
thief ant n : any of several minute ants (esp. Solenopsis molesta) that nest near the galleries of other ants from which they steal food
thief·dom \'thēfdəm, -ftəm\ or **thieve·dom** \-ēvdəm\ n -s **1** : THIEVES **2** : the domain of thieves
thieftaker \'≈,≈\ n, Brit : a person who apprehends thieves or highwaymen
thief vault n : a vault over a piece of gymnastic apparatus executed from a one-foot takeoff in which both feet are thrust forward and over and the hands are placed on the apparatus as the body passes over it
thie·la·via \thē'lāvēə\ n, cap [NL, fr. F. von Thielaw, 19th cent. Ger. botanist + NL -ia] : a genus of fungi of the family Aspergillaceae but sometimes placed in the family Perisporiaceae having spherical brown perithecia and conidia that are endogenous and conidia that are borne in chains — see ROOT ROT
thie·la·vi·op·sis \(,)thē,lāvē'äpsəs\ n, cap [NL, fr. Thielavia + -opsis] : a form genus of fungi (family Aspergillaceae) having conidia dark in color, borne in chains, and arising both endogenously and exogenously
thi·enyl \'thīə,nil\ n -s [ISV thiophene + -yl] : either of two univalent isomeric radicals C_4H_3S derived from thiophene by removal of a hydrogen atom from either the alpha or 2-position or the beta or 3-position
thieve \'thēv\ vb -ED/-ING/-S [fr. thief, after such pairs as E grief: grieve] vi : to practice or engage in theft : steal something : subsist by theft ~ vt **1** : to take by theft : STEAL **2** or **thief** : to extract by means of a thief ⟨~ a sample of oil⟩ **syn** see ROB
thieve·less \'thēvləs\ adj [perh. alter. of thowless] Scot **1** : LISTLESS **2** : cold of manner or demeanor
thiev·ery \'thēv(ə)rē, -ri\ n -ES **1** : the act, practice, or an instance of stealing : THEFT **2** archaic : something stolen
thieves' kitchen n, Brit : a slum or other area harboring thieves where children are easily led into crime
thieves' latin n, usu cap L : the cant of thieves
thiev·ing·ly adv [thieving (pres. part. of thieve) + -ly] : by means of theft
thiev·ish \'thēvish, -vēsh\ adj [ME thevysch, thefyisch, fr. thef, theef thief + -ysch, -ish -ish] **1** obs : infested by thieves ⟨bid me . . . walk in ~ ways —Shak.⟩ **2 a** : given to stealing ⟨~ magpies⟩ **b** : of, relating to, or characteristic of a thief : STEALTHY, SLY — **thiev·ish·ly** adv — **thiev·ish·ness** n -ES
thig \'thig\ vb **thigged; thigged; thigging; thigs** [ME thiggen, of Scand origin; akin to OSw thiggia to beg; akin to OE thicgan to accept, receive, OHG diggen to ask for, W teg beautiful, Lith tèkti to extend, suffice] Scot : BEG
thig·ger \-gə(r)\ n -s [ME(Sc) thiggar, fr. ME thiggen to beg + -ar, -er, -ere -er] Scot : BEGGAR
thigh \'thī\ n -s [ME thigh, thie, fr. OE thēoh, thīoh; akin to OHG dioh thigh, ON thjō buttock, MIr tōn buttocks, OSlav tukŭ fat, Skt tavīti he is strong — more at THUMB] **1 a** : the proximal segment of the vertebrate hind limb extending from the hip to the knee and supported by a single large bone — compare FEMUR **b** : the segment of the leg immediately distal to the thigh in a bird or in a quadruped in which the true thigh is obscured by skin or feathers or by its position in relation to the trunk — see COW illustration **c** : the femur of the leg of an insect **2** : something resembling or covering a thigh ⟨the ground . . . fell back from the ~ of his moldboard —Stuart Cloete⟩ ⟨rubbed his oily hands on the ~s of his pants —Thomas Anderson⟩
thighbone \'≈,≈\ n [ME the bane, fr. the, thigh, thie thigh + bane, boon, bon bone] : FEMUR
thigh boot n : a boot whose upper part covers the thigh
thigmo- comb form [NL, fr. Gk thigma touch (fr. thinganein to touch, handle) + NL -o-; akin to L fingere to shape — more at DOUGH] : touch ⟨thigmoreceptor⟩
thig·mo·cyte \'thigmə,sīt\ n -s [thigmo- + -cyte] : a blood cell of a crustacean that plays an important role in blood clotting
thig·mo·receptor \ˌthig(,)mō+\ n [thigmo- + receptor] : a sensory end organ responding to simple touch
thig·mo·tac·tic \ˌthigmə¦taktik\ adj [fr. NL thigmotaxis, after such pairs as NL hypotaxis: E hypotactic] : STEREOTACTIC
thig·mo·tax·is \-¦taksəs\ n [NL, fr. thigmo- + -taxis] : STEREOTAXIS
thig·mo·trop·ic \ˌthigmə¦träpik\ adj [thigmo- + -tropic] : STEREOTROPIC
thig·mot·ro·pism \thig'mä trə,pizəm\ n [ISV thigmo- + -tropism] : STEREOTROPISM
thik \(ˌ)thik\ pron [ME thike, alter. of thilke] dial Brit : that same : THIS, THAT
thilk \(ˌ)thilk\ pron [ME thilke, fr. ¹the + ilk, ilke same — more at ILK] obs : that same : THIS, THAT
¹thill \'thil\ n -s [ME thille, perh. fr. OE thille, plank, thin board; akin to OHG dili, dilla plank, plank floor, ON thili plank, wainscot, thilja plank, planking, L tellus earth, Gk tēlia table, board, Skt tala surface, level] : the shaft of a vehicle
²thill \"\ n -s [ME, fireclay] **1** dial Brit : the floor of a coal mine **2** dial Brit : a thin stratum of fireclay
thill·er \'thilə(r)\ n -s : THILL HORSE
thill horse n [ME thil horse, fr. thil, thille thill + hors, horse horse] : a horse that goes between the shafts and supports them
thim·ble \'thimbəl\ n -s [ME thymbyl, prob. alter. of OE thȳmel thumb-stall, fr. thūma thumb — more at THUMB] **1** : a cuplike cover made usu. of metal or plastic with a pitted surface and used to protect the end of a finger when pushing a needle through material **2** : a more or less thimble-shaped apparatus, appendage, or fixture: as **a** : a tubular distance piece through which a bolt or pin passes (as a socket in a door-lock escutcheon plate to receive the knob spindle) **b** : a fixed or movable ring, tube, or lining **c** : a tubular cone for expanding a flue tube **d** : a circular wall box **e** : a metal socket for fixing a lead pipe to stoneware **f** : a ring of thin metal formed with a grooved outer edge so as to fit within an eye (as in a rope, sail, or rope splice) and protect it from chafing **g** : a short section of metal tubing fastened to the underside of a muzzle-loader for holding a ramrod **h** : a small tapering cup with a projecting arm used as a support for plates during firing in a kiln **i** : a thimble-shaped cup or shell (as of filter paper or fritted glass) for containing material to be extracted by solvents esp. in chemical analysis ⟨extraction ~s⟩ **3** : THIMBLEFUL **4 a** : a foxglove (Digitalis purpurea) **b thimbles** pl : HAREBELL 1

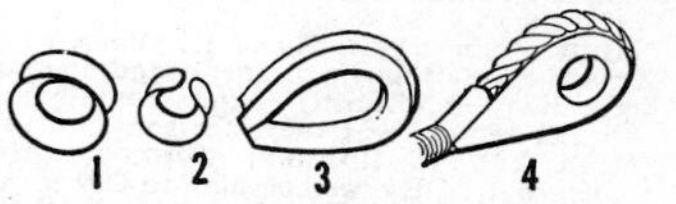

thimbles 2f: *1* round welded, *2* round open, *3* heart-shaped open, *4* solid

thimble and pea n, Brit : THIMBLERIG 1
thim·ble·berry \'thimbəl-— see BERRY\ n : any of several American raspberries or blackberries having thimble-shaped fruit (esp. Rubus occidentalis, R. parviflorus, and R. argutus)
thimble chamber n [so called fr. its shape and size] : an ionization chamber for measuring roentgens
thimble-eye \'≈≈,≈\ n **1** : CHUB MACKEREL **2** : an eye in a plate used esp. as a deadeye
thimbleflower \'≈≈,≈\ n **1** : a self-heal (Prunella vulgaris) **2** : a foxglove (Digitalis purpurea) **3** : a gilia (Gilia capitata) with lavender blue flowers in dense heads
thim·ble·ful \'thimbəl,fu̇l\ n -s : as much as a thimble will hold : a very small quantity
thimble lily n **1** : an Australian plant (Blandfordia nobilis) cultivated for its ornamental racemose flowers **2** : a lily (Lilium bolanderi) of western U.S. that is used as an ornamental and has whorled leaves and red-purple flowers with darker spots
¹thim·ble·rig \'thimbəl,rig\ n **1** : a sleight-of-hand trick that is often practiced as a swindling operation (as at a fair) and that is played with three small cups shaped like thimbles and a small ball or pea that is so quickly shifted from under one cup to under another that the person watching is often misled — compare SHELL GAME **2** : THIMBLERIGGER
²thimblerig \"\ vt **1** : to swindle by thimblerig **2** : to cheat by trickery — **thim·ble·rig·ger** \-gə(r)\ n
thimbleweed \'≈≈,≈\ n [so called fr. the conical receptacle] **1** : CONEFLOWER a **2** : any of various anemones: as **a** : WOOD ANEMONE a **b** : a common No. American anemone (Anemone cylindrica) with silky leathery sepals and crimson styles **c** : a similar plant (A. riparia) of northern No. America with white to red petaloid sepals **d** : an anemone (A. virginiana) of the eastern and central U.S. with variable often pubescent leathery or petaloid green to reddish or pure white sepals **3** : PRAIRIE CLOVER
thi·mero·sal \thī'mərə,sal, -'mer-\ n -s [prob. fr. thi- + mercury + -o- + salicylate] : a cream-colored crystalline organic mercurial $C_9H_9HgNaO_2S$ used in medicine and surgery as an antiseptic and germicide and also as a biological preservative; sodium (ethyl-mercuri)-thio-salicylate
¹thin \'thin\ adj **thinner; thinnest** [ME thinne, fr. OE thynne; akin to OHG dunni thin, ON thunnr, L tenuis thin, Gk tanylong, stretched out, Skt tanu thin, OE thennan to stretch out, OHG dennen to stretch, ON thenja, Goth ufthanjan, L tendere to stretch, tenēre to hold, Gk teinein to stretch, Skt tanoti he stretches] **1 a** : having little extent from one surface to its opposite ⟨~ paper⟩ ⟨~ layer of paint⟩ ⟨~ slice of meat⟩ ⟨~ coin⟩ **b** : measuring little in cross section or diameter ⟨~ rope⟩ ⟨~ rod⟩ **2** : not dense in arrangement or distribution : not compactly set or disposed ⟨~ stand of trees⟩ ⟨a ~ rain was falling⟩ ⟨his hair was ~ and lank⟩ **3** : not well fleshed : not filled out : not plump or fat : SPARE, LEAN, SKINNY ⟨~ lips⟩ ⟨long ~ figure⟩ **4 a** : more fluid or rarefied than usual, normal, or average ⟨~ syrup⟩ ⟨~ batter⟩ ⟨~ air of the high mountains⟩ **b** : having less than the usual number of persons ⟨~ congregation⟩ ⟨~ attendance at a meeting⟩ **c** : few in number : not abundant : SCARCE **d** : scantily occupied, supplied, or provided ⟨~ assortment of goods on the counter⟩ ⟨~ ranks of volunteers⟩ **e** of a market : characterized by a paucity of bids or offerings so that transactions tend to be few and difficult to effect **5 a** : wanting substance, strength, or richness from lack of a usual constituent : WEAK, UNSATISFYING ⟨~ broth⟩ ⟨~ wine⟩ ⟨~ diet⟩ **b** of soil : POOR, INFERTILE **6 a** : lacking in solidity, substance, or force : UNSUBSTANTIAL, INADEQUATE ⟨novel with a ~ plot⟩ **b** : UNBELIEVABLE, UNCONVINCING ⟨~ excuse⟩ **c** : not up to expectations : disappointingly poor or hard ⟨have a ~ time of it⟩ **7 a** of a voice : wanting in fullness and resonance : somewhat feeble and shrill ⟨nearly soundless laughter ~ as a bat's cry —Elinor Wylie⟩ **b** of harmony : lacking richness of texture **c** of reproduced sound (1) : having prominent treble and weak bass tones (2) : having a narrow range of overtones **d** of a speech sound : FRONT 2 **8 a** of light : wanting in radiance ⟨~ winter sunshine⟩ **b** of a color : lacking in intensity or brilliance : DULL **9 a** : easily seen through or penetrated : TRANSPARENT, FLIMSY ⟨~ pretext⟩ ⟨~ disguise⟩ **b** : ready to snap or give way ⟨his patience was wearing ~⟩ **10** of a photographic negative or print : lacking sufficient density or contrast ⟨overexposure produces ~ images —E.F.Brewer⟩
syn THIN, SLENDER, SLIM, SLIGHT, TENUOUS, and RARE can mean, in common, not broad, thick, abundant, or dense. THIN implies comparatively little extension between two surfaces ⟨a thin board⟩ ⟨a thin layer of frosting⟩ or a comparatively small diameter of a cylindrical or roughly cylindrical object in proportion to its length ⟨a thin pole⟩ ⟨a thin wire⟩ and it implies also a comparative lack of flesh or substance giving a thing fullness, richness, or density ⟨a thin face⟩ ⟨a thin soup⟩ ⟨thin hair⟩ ⟨a play that is pretty thin in plot⟩ SLENDER chiefly implies leanness or spareness without suggesting gauntness or lankiness, usu. connoting gracefulness and good proportions ⟨slender hands⟩ ⟨a slender figure⟩ and is similar to THIN though implying, not strongly, a meagerness or scantiness ⟨slender success in an enterprise⟩ ⟨slender advice⟩ ⟨a slender chance of success⟩ SLIM is much like SLENDER when applied to persons or animals, though suggesting more fragility, gauntness, or lack of flesh than grace or good proportion ⟨very slim children⟩ and it is like SLENDER in extended meaning, though stressing meagerness and scantiness more strongly ⟨a slim chance of

recovery⟩ ⟨a *slim* pay envelope⟩ SLIGHT stresses smallness rather than thinness, seldom suggesting height or length as do SLENDER and, sometimes, SLIM ⟨a *slight* woman of very small frame⟩ and in application to things, it is often derogatory, applying to what is inappreciable or inadequate ⟨a *slight* difference in age between two men⟩ ⟨a very *slight* imaginative quality in a book⟩ ⟨a *slight* compensation for great effort⟩ TENUOUS implies extreme thinness ⟨a *tenuous* thread⟩ ⟨the *tenuous* filament of a spider's web⟩ or sheerness ⟨a *tenuous* and almost fully transparent fabric⟩ and its most common extended use implies an extreme lack of density, solidity, or substance ⟨*tenuous* mists along the road⟩ ⟨a mind given to *tenuous* ideas⟩ ⟨a *tenuous* grasp of a difficult subject⟩ RARE is applied chiefly to air or gases and implies tenuousness or lack of density ⟨the extremely *rare* atmosphere of the stratosphere⟩
— **into thin air** *adv* : without a trace : UTTERLY, COMPLETELY ⟨his whole fortune suddenly vanished *into thin air*⟩ — **on thin ice** *adv* (*or adj*) : in a position or situation requiring wariness, dexterity, or tact if trouble or embarrassment is to be avoided : on dangerous ground — **out of thin air** : out of nothing : without substantial basis, precedent, or evidence ⟨create stories *out of thin air*⟩ ⟨arbitrary authority which sets up standards *out of thin air* —A.T.Weaver⟩

[2]thin \"\ *adv* **thinner; thinnest** [ME *thinne*, fr. *thinne*, adj., thin] : THINLY — used esp. in combinations ⟨*thin*-clad⟩ ⟨*thin*-flowing⟩

[3]thin \"\ *n* -s [ME *thinne*, fr. *thinne*, adj., thin] : a thin part : something thin or thinner ⟨sandpipers running in the ~ of the tide —F.M.Ford⟩ ⟨letters embodying sharply contrasted thicks and ~s —Stanley Morison⟩

[4]thin \"\ *vb* **thinned; thinned; thinning; thins** [ME *thinnen*, fr. OE *thynnian;* akin to ON *thynna* to thin; causative fr. the root of E [1]*thin*] *vt* **1 a** : to reduce in thickness or depth : ATTENUATE **b** : to make less dense or viscous : make more fluid : RAREFY ⟨~ glue with alcohol⟩ **c** : to make less strong or less rich : make weak : cause to lose vigor, force, or effectiveness : DILUTE ⟨~ wine with water⟩ ⟨the ballad, with its old religious, military, or tragic contents, was *thinned* out into the sentimental popular song —Lewis Mumford⟩ **d** : to make lean or slender : cause to lose flesh ⟨*thinned* by weeks of privation⟩ **e** : to make less crowded or less populated — used often with *out* **f** : to remove surplus plants or trees from (a bed, nursery, woodland) so as to improve the growth of the rest; *also* : to take out (as superfluous buds or shoots) : PRUNE **g** : to reduce the bulk of (hair) by spaced cutting with specially notched shears ~ *vi* **1** : to grow or become thin or thinner : become less thick, dense, or crowded ⟨his hair is *thinning*⟩ — used often with *down* or *out* or *off* ⟨the limestone layer *thinned* out and soon came to an end⟩ ⟨toward the city limits the houses began to ~ out⟩ ⟨the stream had *thinned* down to a mere trickle⟩ **2** : to become weak, ineffective, or less urgent ⟨this desire ~s out —M.L.Anshen⟩

syn ATTENUATE, EXTENUATE, DILUTE, RAREFY: THIN is a general term indicating reduction in thickness, density, weight, intensity, strength, or concentration ⟨*thinning* paint⟩ ⟨*thinning* the trees in a woodlot⟩ ⟨the crowd *thinned* a little⟩ ⟨the *thinning* ranks of true cowboys —*Amer. Guide Series: Texas*⟩ ⟨the lines of magnetic and electric force *thinned* out geometrically with the square of the distance from their origin —S.F.Mason⟩ ATTENUATE may indicate thinning by mechanical or chemical means or thinning accompanied by enervation, enfeeblement, or other weakening ⟨*attenuate* wire by drawing it out⟩ ⟨the powerful frame *attenuated* by spare living —Charles Dickens⟩ ⟨the apparent brightness of the stars as we see them, with their light *attenuated* by distance and the cosmic haze —G.W.Gray b. 1886⟩ ⟨illusions which science can *attenuate* or destroy —J.W.Krutch⟩ EXTENUATE may sometimes mean to emaciate; it usu. suggests a diminution of significance and effect ⟨the whole tendency of modern thought and modern opinion and modern manners is to *extenuate* the responsibility of human nature —Compton Mackenzie⟩ DILUTE indicates a weakening of concentration by addition of a weakening, neutralizing, or counteracting agency ⟨*dilute* the paint with turpentine⟩ ⟨acid *diluted* with water⟩ ⟨explosives in nuclear weapons, when *diluted*, provide the fuel required for most peaceful atom products —*New Republic*⟩ ⟨the strength of passionate emotion is *diluted* to the languor of interminable sentimentality —R.A. Hall b. 1911⟩ ⟨the pioneer spirit has been *diluted* by new race mixtures, its confidence shaken by new social trends —*Amer. Guide Series: Minn.*⟩ RAREFY indicates a thinning in density, sometimes, with reference to matters intellectual or emotional, by refining and eliminating all dross or by imparting a tenuous or even nebulous quality ⟨*rarefied* mountain air⟩ ⟨these claims are argued in the *rarefied* atmosphere of academic discussion —M.S.Handler⟩ ⟨a civilization so *rarefied* that it is almost decadent —Santha Rama Rau⟩

thin–boiling starch \'=,==-\ *n* : SOLUBLE STARCH

[1]thine [ME *thin*, fr. OE *thīn*, gen. of *thū*, *thu* thou; akin to OHG *dīn* (gen. of *dū*, *du* thou), ON *thīn* (gen. of *thū* thou), Goth *theina* (gen. of *thu* thou) — more at THOU] *obs possessive of* [1]THOU

[2]thine \'thīn\ *adj* [ME *thin*, fr. OE *thīn* — more at THY] *archaic* : THY — used esp. before a word beginning with a vowel or *h* ⟨give every man ~ ear, but few thy voice —Shak.⟩ ⟨a true report which I heard . . . of ~ acts —2 Chron 9:5 (AV)⟩ ⟨be ready to ~ helpers —1 Chron 12:18 (AV)⟩

[3]thine \"\ *pron, sing or pl in constr* [ME *thin*, fr. OE *thīn*, fr. *thīn*, adj., thy — more at THY] : something belonging to thee ⟨all that I have is ~ —Lk 15:31 (AV)⟩ : thy one or thy ones — used without a following noun as a pronoun equivalent in meaning to the adjective *thy* ⟨not my will, but ~, be done —Lk 22:42 (AV)⟩ ⟨mine eyes, even sociable to the show of ~, fall fellowly drops —Shak.⟩; often used after *of* to single out one or more members of a class belonging to or connected with the one that is being addressed ⟨thou too, desert stream! no pool of ~ . . . did e'er reflect the stately virgin's robe —S.T.Coleridge⟩ or merely to identify something or someone as belonging to or connected with the one that is being addressed without any implication of membership in a more extensive class ⟨what means that hand upon that breast of ~ —Shak.⟩ ⟨those linen cheeks of ~ —Shak.⟩; used archaically esp. in biblical, ecclesiastical, solemn, or poetic language and still surviving to some extent in ordinary usage in the speech of Friends esp. among themselves; compare YOURS

[1]thing \'thiŋ\ *n* -s [ME, fr. OE, thing, assembly, reason; akin to OHG *ding* thing, assembly, reason, ON *thing* object of value, assembly, parliament, Goth *theihs* time, and prob. to Gk *teinein* to stretch — more at THIN] **1 a** : a matter of concern : AFFAIR ⟨let's get this ~ over with quickly⟩ ⟨several ~s to attend to⟩ **b things** *pl* : state of affairs in general or within a specified or implied sphere ⟨~s are getting better⟩ ⟨that wouldn't change ~s between us⟩ ⟨how are ~s going at the office⟩ **c** : a particular state of affairs : SITUATION, COMPLICATION ⟨try to look at this ~ from another viewpoint⟩ **d** : EVENT, CIRCUMSTANCE ⟨that shooting was a terrible ~⟩ ⟨a lucky ~ no one was lost in the fire⟩ **2 a** : DEED, ACT, ACCOMPLISHMENT — used commonly as cognate object of *do* ⟨expects to do great ~s⟩ ⟨that was a mean ~ to do to your brother⟩ ⟨a ~ worth doing is worth doing well⟩ **b** : a product of work or activity ⟨likes to make ~s with his hands⟩ **c** : the end or aim of effort or activity ⟨the ~ is now to get well⟩ ⟨liked to put first ~s first⟩ **3 a** : whatever exists or is conceived to exist as a separate entity or as a distinct and individual quality, fact, or idea : a separable or distinguishable object of thought ⟨there is a name for every ~⟩ **b** : the real or actual essence or substance as distinguished from its appearances or from a name, word, or symbol that stands for it : REALITY ⟨in talking of *its* appearances we appear to distinguish the ~ from the appearances —A.J.Ayer⟩ ⟨a philosopher who deals with words and not ~s⟩ — compare THING-IN-ITSELF **4 a** : an entity that can be apprehended or known as having existence in space or time as distinguished from what is purely an object of thought ⟨virtue is not a ~, but an attribute of a ~⟩ **b** : an inanimate object as distinguished from a living being **c things** *pl* : POSSESSIONS, GOODS ⟨assemble the inhabitants, their cattle, and their ~s⟩ **d** : whatever may be possessed or owned or be the object of a right — distinguished from *person* **e** : an article of clothing ⟨haven't a ~ to wear to the party⟩ ⟨some new ~s for Easter⟩ ⟨time to put on your ~s and come to dinner⟩ ⟨get your outdoor ~s⟩ **f things** *pl* : equipment or utensils esp. for a particular purpose ⟨bring in the tea ~s⟩ **g things** *pl* : personal belongings : EFFECTS ⟨packed his ~s and left⟩ ⟨his ~s are always lying around⟩ **5** : an object or entity that cannot or need not be precisely designated ⟨what's that ~ in your left hand⟩ ⟨do you ever use this ~⟩ ⟨what does that round ~ on the end of the motor do⟩ ⟨churches . . . turned into mosques . . . or used for army stores and ~s —Rose Macaulay⟩ **6 a** : DETAIL, QUALITY, POINT, PARTICULAR ⟨worrying over every little ~⟩ ⟨the ~ I don't like about this plan⟩ ⟨the important ~ to remember in night driving⟩ **b** : a material or substance (as food, drink, medicine) of a specified kind ⟨avoid sweet or starchy ~s⟩ **7** : something that is said, told, or thought ⟨say the right ~⟩ ⟨think hard ~s of a person⟩: **a** : a written or spoken discourse ⟨that any ~ of mine is fit to live —P.B.Shelley⟩ **b** : a witty retort or story : JEST ⟨got off some good ~s in his speech⟩ : IDEA, NOTION ⟨says the first ~ that comes into his head⟩ **c** : a piece of news or information ⟨couldn't get a ~ out of him⟩ ⟨refused to tell me a ~ about what he was doing⟩ **8** : BEING, INDIVIDUAL ⟨not a living ~ was to be seen on that rocky expanse⟩ — used often in pity ⟨poor little ~⟩ or contempt ⟨how could you ever speak to that vile ~⟩ or reproach ⟨you selfish ~, you⟩ or affection ⟨she's a pretty little ~⟩ **9** : an artistic composition (as a piece of music) ⟨has written many popular ~s for small bands⟩ **10 a** : way of acting or behaving ⟨always tried to do the decent ~⟩; *esp* : the proper, right, desirable, required, or fashionable way of behaving, talking, dressing — used with *the* ⟨rolled-up blue jeans were the ~ then among the teen-agers⟩ **b** *chiefly Brit* : one in normal health and good spirits — used with *the* ⟨you've seemed nervous and not quite the ~ ever since the reception —Margery Allingham⟩ **11** : an irrational fear of or strong prejudice concerning something : a mild obsession or phobia ⟨she has this ~, lately, about driving at night⟩ — **a thing or two** : something worth knowing or telling : something proving equality or superiority in knowledge ⟨knows *a thing or two* about finance⟩; *also* : words of blunt advice or reproach ⟨if he does it again I'll certainly tell him *a thing or two*⟩ — **first thing** *adv* : before anything else : right away : IMMEDIATELY ⟨I'll get that letter off *first thing*⟩ ⟨promised to call *first thing* in the morning⟩ — **good thing** : a profitable investment, enterprise, or transaction ⟨made a *good thing* out of stamp collecting⟩ ⟨put him onto a *good thing* in the stock market⟩; *also* : information leading to such a transaction — **of all things** *adv* : least appropriately : with the least degree of logical justification : most surprisingly ⟨people still call it, *of all things*, a system of free, individual initiative —Max Ascoli⟩ — **sure thing** : something safe to wager on : something certain to take place : a contestant certain to win

[2]thing \'thiŋ(g), -ŋk\ *also* **ting** \'tiŋ\ *n* -s *usu cap* [*thing* fr. ON & Icel; Icel *thing* assembly, parliament, fr. ON; *ting* fr. Norw, Dan, & Sw, fr. or akin to ON *thing* — more at [1]THING] : a legislative or judicial assembly in Iceland and other Scandinavian countries

thing·a·bob \'thiŋə,bäb\ *or* **thing·a·ma·bob** \'thiŋəm(ə)-,bäb\ *n* -s [by alter.] : THINGUMBOB

t hinge *cap T, or* **tee hinge** *n* : a hinge having the appearance of a letter T when opened : a strap hinge of which one leaf is replaced by a butt

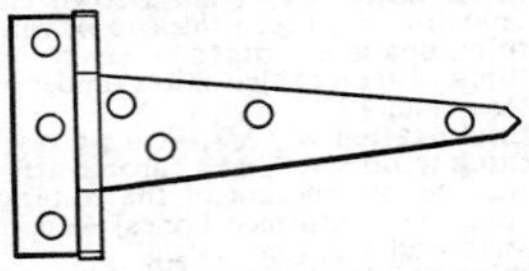
T hinge

thing·hood \'thiŋ,hu̇d\ *n* **1** : the quality or state of being a thing : objective existence : THINGNESS ⟨reducing human life to ~ —C.J. Rolo⟩ **2** : something that constitutes a thing as such ⟨~ must also include objective change —C.I.Lewis⟩

thing in action : CHOSE IN ACTION

thing·i·ness \-ŋēnəs\ *n* -ES : the quality or state of being thingy

thing-in-itself \'=,==='=\ *n, pl* **things-in-themselves** [trans. of G *ding an sich*] : an ultimate reality unqualified by the subjective modes of human perception and thought : a metaphysical reality — compare NOUMENON, PHENOMENON 2a(4)

thing·ish \'thiŋish\ *adj* : THINGY

thing-language \'=,==\ *n* : a language whose terms refer to spatiotemporal things and events and their physical attributes — contrasted with *sense-datum language;* compare PHYSICAL LANGUAGE

thinglike \'=,=\ *adj* : like a physical object : lacking consciousness or will — **thing·like·ness** *n*

thing·man \'thiŋmən\ *n, pl* **thingmen** [trans. of ON *thingmathr*] : a member of a Scandinavian legislative or judicial assembly; *specif* : HOUSECARL

thing·ness \'thiŋnəs\ *n* -ES : the fact, quality, or condition of objective existence : objective reality

things personal *n pl* : PERSONAL PROPERTY

thing·stead \'thiŋz,ted, -ŋ,st-\ *n* [[2]*thing* + *stead*] : the place where a Scandinavian assembly is held

thing·um \'thiŋəm\ *n* -s [irreg. fr. [1]*thing*] : THINGUMBOB

thing·um·a·jig *or* **thing·a·ma·jig** \'thiŋəmə,jig\ *n* -s [irreg. fr. *thingum*] : something which is hard to classify or whose name is not known ⟨a patented ~ that prevents salt from caking —Sheila Hibben⟩

thing·um·bob *or* **thing·um·a·bob** \'thiŋəm(ə),bäb\ *n* -s [irreg. fr. *thingum*] : something whose specific name or designation has been forgotten or is not known ⟨mysterious electrical ~s that go off with a bang —*Literary Rev.*⟩

thing·um·my \'thiŋəmē\ *n* -ES [irreg. fr. *thingum*] : THINGUMBOB, THINGUMAJIG ⟨promise . . . that you will not . . . not invent anything other than a silent burglar ~ —A.J.Coutts⟩

thingy \'thiŋē\ *adj* [[1]*thing* + *-y*] **1** : of, relating to, or having the characteristics of things : REAL, MATERIAL **2** : concerned with or devoted to real things or practical matters

thinite \'thī,nīt, 'thi,n-\ *adj, usu cap* [*Thinis* (This), ancient city in central Upper Egypt + E *-ite*, n. suffix] : of or relating to the period of culture in Egypt during the First and Second Dynasties from 3000 B.C. to 2778 B.C., characterized by the stereotyping of forms and relative dimensions of statues and reliefs

[1]think *vi* **thought; thought; thinking; thinks** [ME *thinken* (past *thoughte*), fr. OE *thyncan* (past *thūhte*, past part. *gethūht*); akin to OHG *dunken* to seem (past *dūhta*, past part. *gidūht*), ON *thykkja* (past *thōtti*, past part. *thōtt*), Goth *thunkjan* (past *thūhta*), L *tongēre* to know] *obs* : SEEM, APPEAR — usu. used impersonally ⟨him *thought* that in his depth of sleep he saw a soldier armed —Thomas Heywood⟩; compare METHINKS

[2]think \'thiŋk\ *vb* **thought** \'thȯt, *usu* -ȯd·+V\ *or dial* **thunk** \'thəŋk\ **thought** *or dial* **thunk; thinking; thinks** [ME *thenken* (past *thoughte*, past part. *thought*, *ythought*), fr. OE *thencan* (past *thōhte*, past part. *gethōht*); akin to OHG *denken* to think (past *dāhta*, past part. *gidāht*), ON *thekkja* to perceive (past *thātti*), Goth *thankjan* to deliberate (past *thāhta*), L *tongēre* to know — more at THANK] *vt* **1 a** : to form or have (as a thought) in the mind ⟨few people think accurately — and ~ things not words —O.W.Holmes †1935⟩ ⟨"an evil bird," he *thought* —Louis Bromfield⟩ ⟨ashamed to ~ how easily we capitulate —R.W.Emerson⟩ **b** *dial chiefly Brit* : FEEL 2b ⟨men should ~ shame to be less heroic —Gilbert Highet⟩ **2** : to have in one's mind as an intention or desire : INTEND, HOPE ⟨*thought* to return early⟩ ⟨yet manhood remained to act the thing I *thought* —P.B.Shelley⟩ **3 a** (1) : to have as an opinion : BELIEVE ⟨*thought* the question might arise —F.J. Haskin⟩ ⟨a fine performance, he *thought*⟩ (2) : to have as an opinion without sufficient basis in fact ⟨comes to ~ that the prison is the world —J.B.Priestley⟩ ⟨we know, or ~ we know, . . . the critical method —T.S.Eliot⟩ ⟨was first *thought* to have drowned —*Time*⟩ **b** : to regard as : take for : CONSIDER ⟨may adjourn them to such time as he shall ~ proper —*U.S. Constitution*⟩ ⟨~ it not unfair to suggest —Virgil Thomson⟩ ⟨put a copy on order . . . if you ~ it your kind of book —*Times Lit. Supp.*⟩ **4 a** : to reflect on : PONDER ⟨these deeds must not be *thought* after these ways —Shak.⟩ ⟨~ what their children would be —E.T.Thurston⟩ — often used with *over* ⟨said he would ~ the matter over⟩ **b** : to determine by reflecting ⟨was ~*ing* what to do next⟩ — often used with *out* ⟨parents must ~ out for themselves what this means to their own young —Dorothy Barclay⟩ **5** : to call to mind : REMEMBER ⟨*thought* to ask him the trick of it —Anne S. Mehdevi⟩ **6** : to create or devise by thinking ⟨the Almighty . . . *thought* the archetypes of all things and devised their variations —William James⟩ — usu. used with *out* or *up* ⟨remain calm and ~ out a solution —James Hewitt⟩ ⟨*thought* up a caption that exactly covered the whole idea —William Murrell⟩ **7 a** *obs* : SUSPECT ⟨he, ~*ing* no harm, agreed —Daniel Defoe⟩ **b** : EXPECT ⟨*thought* to find him at home⟩ **8** : to believe to exist ⟨there be who ~ not God at all —John Milton⟩ **9** : to bring (as into a specified position or condition) by thinking ⟨a novelist has *thought* . . . characters into existence —Bernard DeVoto⟩ ⟨learned to ~ his feelings by way of French symbolism —Harold Rosenberg⟩ **10 a** (1) : to center one's thoughts on : have one's mind full of ⟨talks and ~s nothing but airplanes⟩ (2) : to be imbued with the thoughts and the ways of thinking that are characteristic of a people or a group ⟨many white men . . . were ~*ing* black and advocating absolute equality between the two races —*Cape Times*⟩ **b** : to bring before one's mind clearly (as by imagining or recalling) : form a mental picture of ⟨found it difficult to ~ infinity⟩ **11** : to subject to the processes of logical thought esp. in order to reach a conclusion — usu. used with *out* or *through* ⟨wanted to be left alone to ~ things out —Victoria Sackville-West⟩ ⟨always ~s the problems through before acting⟩ ~ *vi* **1 a** : to exercise the powers of judgment, conception, or inference as distinguished from simple sense perception ⟨it is the power to ~ which makes us human —Vicki Baum⟩ **b** (1) : to exercise the powers of thought with regard to a particular matter ⟨would do well to ~ again —J.F. Golay⟩ ⟨will ~ twice before he risks another defeat —L.C. Douglas⟩ — often used with a preposition (as *about, of,* or *on*) ⟨the American child is taught to ~ about each situation as it comes up —Margaret Mead⟩ (2) : to call an idea (as of a possible solution or a device) to mind by mental effort — usu. used with *of* ⟨the best plan they could ~ of was to leave⟩ **2 a** : to have the mind engaged in reflection : MEDITATE — usu. used with a preposition (as *about, of, on,* or *upon*) ⟨enabled me to ~ with tender affection upon her loyalty and devotion —*Nashville Tennessean*⟩ **b** (1) : to have something (as a plan) in the mind — usu. used with *of* or *about* ⟨the department is ~*ing* of opening new message centers —Armand Schwab⟩ (2) : to consider the suitability (as of a person under consideration for a vacant position) — usu. used with *of* ⟨*thought* of him for the presidential nomination⟩ **3 a** (1) : to have a thought in the mind : have a thought come into the mind — usu. used with *of* ⟨*thought* of his old home when he saw the house⟩ (2) : to have or form a particular idea : REGARD — usu. used with *of* and *as* ⟨will ~ of himself as a painter —Thomas Munro⟩ ⟨was to ~ of nothing as being his own —K.S.Latourette⟩ **b** : to have an opinion — usu. used with *of* and an adverb or an adverbial phrase that indicates the kind of opinion ⟨*thought* well of him —Carol L. Thompson⟩ ⟨~s a great deal of his physician —Walt Whitman⟩ ⟨~s nothing of his brother⟩ **4** : to have consideration, regard, or concern — usu. used with *of* ⟨a man must ~ of his family, his realm, his empire —Francis Hackett⟩ **5** : to be aware (as of the future) : EXPECT, SUSPECT ⟨may strike when you least ~⟩ — sometimes used with *for* ⟨will get along better than he ~s for —Walt Whitman⟩

syn SPECULATE, REFLECT, REASON, DELIBERATE, COGITATE: THINK is a general term, nearly always capable of being substituted for any of the following terms. SPECULATE is often used in reference to thought, logical and analytic or not, on that on which certainty is impossible or unlikely ⟨what caused the Mound Builder culture . . . to die out? We can only *speculate* —R.W.Murray⟩ ⟨in times of peace the specialists of war . . . may only *speculate* about the effect of new weapons —S.L.A. Marshall⟩ REFLECT is likely to suggest an unhurried contemplative consideration involving recall and reexamination ⟨she could *reflect* in long, sane meditations above the uneasy sea of her pain —Arnold Bennett⟩ ⟨the standpoint of the man who did not criticize or *reflect*, but accepted simply —G.L.Dickinson⟩ REASON indicates careful attention to rational or logical thought sequences, to orderly thought processes from evidence or premise to conclusion ⟨Lincoln's way with any problem was to examine it from all sides and *reason* it out intellectually —Ruth P. Randall⟩ ⟨perhaps a close study of the behavior of very young children . . . may provide some valuable hints, but it seems dangerous to *reason* from such experiments —Edward Sapir⟩ ⟨found himself *reasoning* in a circle⟩ DELIBERATE implies a pondering with careful thought, unhurried procedure, and fair consideration of various aspects ⟨a nationwide representative assembly, with power to *deliberate* although not actually to make laws —F.A.Ogg & Harold Zink⟩ ⟨the future relations of the two countries could now be *deliberated* on with a hope of settlement —J.A.Froude⟩ COGITATE indicates deep, intent, sometimes labored thinking ⟨*cogitating* over the problem for hours⟩ ⟨*cogitated* about the question a noticeable time before answering⟩

syn CONCEIVE, IMAGINE, FANCY, REALIZE, ENVISAGE, ENVISION: THINK, often general and not specific, may indicate merely the mental harboring of an idea; it may imply conscious mental effort to achieve a definite picture or clear impression ⟨helpful to *think* of two economic systems operating simultaneously throughout rural parts of the Northeast —P.E.James⟩ ⟨found church a very good place for *thinking* her love affairs into their right proportion —Sheila Kaye-Smith⟩ CONCEIVE may imply forming an idea and nurturing and developing it to serviceable fullness as a concept ⟨for the poem Coleridge *conceived* in theory as well as evolved in practice a quantitative metric —W.R. Parker⟩ ⟨now *conceived* a plan of returning to France and obtaining a force to conquer Canada —J.C.Fitzpatrick⟩ IMAGINE may imply the process of free mental visualization or pictorialization that is often vivid, relatively unguided, and unchecked by rationality ⟨a marvelously *imagined* description of the state of blessed souls —H.O.Taylor⟩ ⟨by burning or otherwise destroying the image he *imagines* that he kills his foe —J.G.Frazer⟩ ⟨could *imagine* easily original plots for stories or plays, but never received any impulse to write them —G.W.Russell⟩ FANCY, often interchangeable with IMAGINE, may imply a dreamy, indulgent fondness for unguided contemplation of the unreal ⟨*fancied* he saw them take each other's hands and dance a strange and monstrous dance, the dance of the Annihilation of All Life —J.C.Powys⟩ ⟨who *fancied* she had been transferred to a fairy palace —William Black⟩ REALIZE suggests a vividness of conception or imagination whereby a grasp is attained of the significance of the matter being thought about ⟨saw a tin lamp burning kerosene, and *realized* its possibilities —Allan Nevins⟩ ⟨burning with the passion of infinitely *realized* and therefore eternally restless love —W.L.Sullivan⟩ ENVISAGE and ENVISION may imply a clarity of conception or imagination with clear-cut detail ⟨had a flair for *envisaging* the possible molecular structures of compounds —S.F.Mason⟩ ⟨*envisaged* the flat land beyond the Alps in Lombardy as he later *envisaged* Catalonia beyond the Pyrenees and the right bank of the Middle Rhine, not as country to be conquered but as a belt of protection beyond a frontier —Hilaire Belloc⟩ ⟨includes the territories *envisioned* by the tsarist planners of 1914–16 as part of the Russian empire —D.J.Dallin⟩ ⟨the approaching truck driver tramped down hard; brakes squealed; the photographer momentarily *envisioned* a smashed truck and mangled driver —G.R.Stewart⟩ ⟨those early predictors who *envisioned* great ports in the shores of Lake Pontchartrain —*Amer. Guide Series: La.*⟩
— **think better of** : to reconsider and make a better decision ⟨started to protest but *thought better of* it —Irwin Shaw⟩ — **think long** *dial Brit* : LONG, YEARN — **think much** *obs* : to consider serious or burdensome ⟨*thought* not *much* to clothe his enemies —John Milton⟩

[3]think \"\ *n* -s **1** : an act of thinking ⟨has to make up his mind in a deep hard ~ —Jerome Ellison⟩ ⟨if he thinks he can fool me, he has another ~ coming⟩ **2** : something (as an idea or opinion) that is thought ⟨let's exchange ~s⟩

[4]think \"\ *adj* **1** : of or relating to thinking: as **a** : used for thinking **b** : appealing to the mind ⟨a new ~ film⟩ **2** : of or relating to think pieces ⟨a frequently quoted ~ columnist⟩

[1]think·able \'thiŋkəbəl\ *adj* **1** : capable of being thought about ⟨concepts that are easy enough to be ~⟩ **2** : capable of being made actual : conceivably possible ⟨nationalism was at

this time scarcely ~ —*Times Lit. Supp.*⟩ — **think·able·ness**
\-nəs\ *n* -ES — **think·ably** \-blē-bli\ *adv*
²**thinkable** \"\ *n* -s : one that is thinkable ⟨wants to discover if there are any intuitively presented ~s —Norman Malcolm⟩
think·er \'thiŋkə(r)\ *n* -s [ME *thenkere*, fr. *thenken* to think + -*are*, -*er*, -*ere* -er — more at THINK] : one that thinks: as **a** : one that thinks in a specified way ⟨a superficial ~⟩ **b** : one that has special capacity for thinking : one that devotes himself to study and thought rather than to action : PHILOSOPHER ⟨widely known as an original ~ and a distinguished teacher —R.G.Cole⟩ *syn* **c** : MIND, BRAIN
¹**thinking** *n* -s [ME *thenkinge*, fr. gerund of *thenken* to think] **1** : the action of using one's mind to produce thoughts ⟨~ is mainly . . . performed with words and other symbols —J.B.S. Haldane⟩ ⟨plain living and high ~⟩ **2 thinkings** *pl* : THOUGHTS, MEDITATIONS ⟨full of ~s about his people at home —Mark Twain⟩ ⟨speak to me as to thy ~s —Shak.⟩ **3 a** : OPINION, JUDGMENT ⟨is to my ~ the highest point that poetry has ever reached —T.S.Eliot⟩ **b** : the kind of thought that belongs (as to a period, group, or person) in modern ~ the emotion is viewed as a response —J.E.Anderson⟩ ⟨the traditions of economic ~⟩
²**thinking** *adj* [fr. pres. part. of ²*think*] **1** : having or using the ability to think ⟨admires his high-*thinking* offspring —*Newsweek*⟩ **2** : marked by use of the intellect : THOUGHTFUL, RATIONAL ⟨~ people throughout the country were concerned with social justice —Mary H. Vorse⟩ — **think·ing·ness** *n* -ES
thinking cap *n* : a state or mood in which one thinks ⟨put on your *thinking* caps —Zane Grey⟩
think·ing·ly *adv* : in a thinking manner; *esp* : with awareness ⟨~ abandoned the dog⟩
thinking-machine \'═══,══\ *n* : COMPUTER a
thinking part *n* : a theatrical role that has no lines to be spoken : silent part
think piece *n* : a news article consisting chiefly of background material, generalized observations, and personal opinion and analysis as distinguished from direct factual news reporting — compare DOPE STORY
thinks *pres part of* THINK, *pl of* THINK
think-so \'═,═\ *n* -s [fr. the phrase *think so*] : an unsupported opinion
thin lead *n* : a 1-point or 1½-point printer's lead
thin·ly *adv* [ME *thynnelich*, fr. *thynne*, *thinne* thin + -*lich*, -*liche* -ly] : in a thin manner : INSUFFICIENTLY ⟨~ disguised⟩ SPARSELY ⟨~ clad⟩ ⟨~ settled⟩
thinned *past of* THIN
¹**thinner** *comparative of* THIN
²**thin·ner** \'thinə(r)\ *n* -s [¹*thin* + -*er*] : one that thins: as **a** : a volatile liquid (as turpentine) used esp. to thin paint, lacquer, and cement to the desired consistency — compare DILUENT a **b** : one that adds thinners and driers to paste mixtures to make liquid paint or varnish **c** : one that pulls out superfluous plants or picks off superfluous buds or fruit to improve the crop
thin·ness \'thinnəs\ *n* -ES [ME *thinnesse*, fr. OE *thynnes*, fr. *thynne* thin + -*nes* -ness] : the quality or state of being thin
thinnest *superlative of* THIN
thinning *pres part of* THIN
thinning shears *n pl* : shears with a serrate blade for thinning hair
thin·nish \'thinish, -nēsh\ *adj* : somewhat thin : inclined to thinness ⟨~ arms⟩ ⟨~ humor⟩
thino·cor·i·dae \,thinə-'korə,dē, -ə\ *n pl, cap* [NL, fr. *Thinocorus*, type genus + -*idae*] : a family of So. American birds (suborder Charadrii) comprising the seed snipes
thi·noc·o·rus \thə'näkərəs, thī'n-\ *n, cap* [NL, fr. Gk *thin-*, *this* shore, sandbank + NL -*o-* + -*corus* (irreg. fr. Gk *korys* helmet); perh. akin to Gk *thyein* to rage, seethe — more at DUST, CORYTHOSAURUS] : the type genus of the family Thinocoridae
thin register *n* : HEAD REGISTER
thin rind *n, usu cap T&R* [prob. so called fr. its use as a bacon breed] : HAMPSHIRE 1
thins *pl of* THIN, *pres 3rd sing of* THIN
thin section *n* : a section of rock 0.02 to 0.03 millimeters thick cemented for study between clear glass plates
thin-shell concrete *n* : thin reinforced usu. precast concrete forming arched or domed roofs esp. over large unpartitioned areas
thin-skinned \'═,═\ *adj* **1** : having a thin skin or rind ⟨*thin-skinned* orange⟩ **2** : readily or unduly susceptible to criticism or insult : SENSITIVE, TOUCHY
thin-skinned-ness \'═'skin(d)nəs\ *n* -ES : the quality or state of being thin-skinned
thin space *n* **1** : FOUR-EM SPACE **2** : FIVE-EM SPACE
thin stroke *n* : HAIRLINE 2c(1)
thin-wall conduit *n* : light steel tubing for enclosing electric wiring — compare RIGID CONDUIT
thio \'thī(,)ō\ *adj* [*thi-*] : relating to or containing sulfur esp. in place of oxygen
thio- *see* THI-
thio·acetal \'thī(,)ō+\ *n* [*thi-* + *acetal*] : MERCAPTAL
thio·acetic acid \"+...-\ *n* [*thioacetic* ISV *thi-* + *acetic*] : a pungent liquid acid CH₃COSH made by heating acetic acid with phosphorus pentasulfide and used as a chemical reagent
thio acid *n* [ISV *thio* + *acid*] : an acid in which oxygen is partly or wholly replaced by sulfur
thio·alcohol \'thī(,)ō+\ *n* [ISV *thi-* + *alcohol*] : an aliphatic mercaptan (as ethyl mercaptan)
thio·aldehyde \"+\ *n* [ISV *thi-* + *aldehyde*] : a compound having the general formula RCHS that is an aldehyde in which oxygen is replaced by sulfur and that in general is readily polymerizable — called also *thial*
thio·amide \"+\ *n* [ISV *thi-* + *amide*] : an amide of a thio acid; *esp* : an amide having the general formula RCSNH₂ and made usu. by the reaction of an amide of a carboxylic acid with phosphorus pentasulfide or by addition of hydrogen sulfide to a nitrile
thio·antimonate *also* **thio-antimoniate** \"+\ *n* [ISV *thi-* + *antimonate*, *antimoniate*] : a salt or ester containing pentavalent antimony and sulfur in the acid portion of the molecule — see SCHLIPPE'S SALT
thio·an·ti·mo·nite \thī(,)ō'antəmə,nīt\ *n* [*thi-* + *antimony* + -*ite*] : a salt or ester containing trivalent antimony and sulfur in the acid portion of the molecule — see CROCUS OF ANTIMONY
thio·arsenate \'thī(,)ō+\ *n* [ISV *thi-* + *arsenate*] : a salt (as sodium thioarsenate Na₃AsS₄) or ester containing pentavalent arsenic and sulfur in the acid portion of the molecule and obtainable from arsenic pentasulfide
thio·arsenite \"+\ *n* [NL, fr. *thi-* + *arsenite*] : a salt (as sodium thioarsenite Na₃AsS₃) or ester containing trivalent arsenic and sulfur in the acid portion of the molecule and obtainable in the case of the salts from arsenic trisulfide
thio·bacillus \"+\ *n, cap* [NL, fr. *thi-* + *bacillus*] **1** *cap* : a genus of small rod-shaped bacteria (family Thiobacteriaceae) that live in water, sewage, and soils, derive energy from oxidation of sulfides, thiosulfates, or elemental sulfur, and obtain carbon from carbon dioxide, bicarbonates, or carbonates in solution **2** *pl* **thiobacilli** : any member of the genus *Thiobacillus*
thio·bacteriaceae \"+\ *n pl, cap* [NL, fr. *Thiobacterium*, genus of sulfur bacteria in some classifications + -*aceae*] : a family of coccoid to rod-shaped free-living bacteria (order Pseudomonadales) that oxidize sulfur compounds as a source of energy usu. with the deposit of free sulfur and that may not require an organic source of carbon — see THIOBACILLUS; compare NITROBACTERIACEAE
thio·bacteriales \"+\ *n pl, cap* [NL, fr. *Thiobacterium* + -*ales*] *in some classifications* : an order of bacteria of various shapes usu. containing either sulfur granules or bacteriopurpurin or both, usu. thriving best in the presence of hydrogen sulfide, and comprising the families Achromatiaceae, Beggiatoaceae, and Rhodobacteriaceae

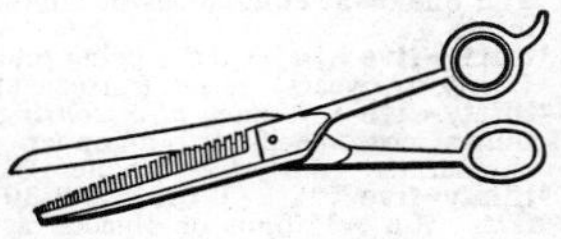

thio·bacterium \"+\ *n, pl* **thiobacteria** *often cap* [NL, fr. *thi-* + *bacterium*] : SULFUR BACTERIUM
thio·carbamide \,thī(,)ō+\ *n* [ISV *thi-* + *carbamide*] : THIOUREA
thio·carbamoyl *or* **thio-carbamyl** \"+\ *n* [ISV *thi-* + *carbamoyl*, *carbamyl*] : the univalent radical NH₂CS— that is carbamoyl in which oxygen is replaced by sulfur — called also *thiuram*
thio·carbanilide \"+\ *n* [ISV *thi-* + *carbanilide*] : a crystalline compound CS(NHC₆H₅)₂ made by reaction of aniline and carbon disulfide and used chiefly as an accelerator for the vulcanization of rubber and as an intermediate in organic synthesis — called also *diphenylthiourea*
thio·carbimide \"\ *n* [*thi-* + *carbimide*] : ISOTHIOCYANATE, MUSTARD OIL 2b
thio·carbonate \"+\ *n* [*thi-* + *carbonate*] : a salt or ester of a thiocarbonic acid
thio·carbonic acid \"+...-\ *n* [*thiocarbonic* ISV *thi-* + *carbonic*] : an acid derived from carbonic acid by replacement of oxygen by sulfur: as **a** : TRITHIOCARBONIC ACID **b** : XANTHIC ACID 2
thio·carbonyl \"+\ *n* [ISV *thi-* + *carbonyl*] : the bivalent radical >CS that is carbonyl in which oxygen is replaced by sulfur
thiochem sulfur yellow R \'thīō,kem-\ *n, usu cap T&S&Y* [*thiochem* fr. *thi-* + -*chem* (prob. fr. *chemical*)] : a sulfur dye — see DYE table I (under *Sulfur Yellow 1*)
thio·chrome \'thīə,krōm\ *n* [ISV *thiamine* + -*o-* + -*chrome*] : a yellow crystalline tricyclic alcohol C₁₂H₁₄N₄OS found in yeast, formed by oxidation of thiamine, and giving a blue fluorescence under ultraviolet light that serves as the basis of a method of determining thiamine
thi·oc·tic acid \(')thī,äktik-\ *n* [*thioctic* fr. *thi-* + *octa-* + -*ic*] : alpha or oxidized lipoic acid — called also *6,8-thioctic acid*
thiocyan- *or* **thiocyano-** *comb form* [ISV *thi-* + *cyan-*] : thiocyanogen : containing the thiocyanogen radical — esp. in names of organic compounds; compare ISOTHIOCYAN-
¹**thio·cyanate** \thī,ō+\ *n* [ISV *thiocyan-* + -*ate*, n. suffix] : a salt or ester of thiocyanic acid
²**thiocyanate** \"\ *vt* -ED/-ING/-S [*thiocyan-* + -*ate*, v. suffix] : to introduce the thiocyanogen radical into (a chemical compound) esp. with replacement of hydrogen — **thio·cy·a·na·tion** \,══,sīə'nāshən\ *n* -s
thiocyanato- *comb form* [¹*thiocyanate* + -*o-*] : THIOCYAN- — esp. in names of inorganic acids and salts and of coordination complexes ⟨potassium *thiocyanato*chromate K₃Cr(SCN)₆⟩
thio·cyanic acid \,thī,ō+...-\ *n* [*thiocyanic* ISV *thi-* + *cyanic*] : an unstable liquid acid HSCN or HNCS of strong odor that is usu. obtained by distilling a thiocyanate salt with dilute sulfuric acid and that polymerizes readily — see ISOTHIOCYANIC ACID
thio·cyanide \,thī,ō+\ *n* [*thiocyan-* + -*ide*] : THIOCYANATE
thio·cyano \,thī,ō+\ *adj* [*thiocyan-*] : relating to, containing, or being the thiocyanogen radical — used esp. of organic compounds
thio·cyanogen \"+\ *n* [*thi-* + *cyanogen*] **1** : a univalent radical —SCN present in thiocyanic acid and other simple and complex thiocyanates **2** : an unstable liquid compound (SCN)₂ that is obtained by the action of halogens on thiocyanates and that polymerizes readily (as to a red or an orange solid)
thiocyanogen value *or* **thiocyanogen number** *n* : a measure of unsaturation (as of an oil or fat) expressed usu. as the number of grams or percentage of iodine equivalent to the thiocyanogen absorbed by 100 grams of the substance and serving as a supplement to the iodine number because thiocyanogen adds to double bonds to a different extent from the usual reagents for determining iodine number ⟨the *thiocyanogen value* . . . is thus different from the ordinary iodine value in that it differentiates between oleic, linoleic, and linolenic groups —T.P.Hilditch⟩
thio·diglycol \,thīō+\ *n* [ISV *thi-* + *diglycol*] : a hygroscopic liquid glycol (HOCH₂CH₂)₂S that is made from ethylene oxide and hydrogen sulfide, that yields mustard gas on reaction with hydrochloric acid, and that is used as a solvent esp. for dyes; bis-(2-hydroxyethyl) sulfide
thio·diphenylamine \,thī(,)ō+\ *n* [ISV *thi-* + *diphenylamine*] : PHENOTHIAZINE
thio·ether \'thīō+\ *n* [ISV *thi-* + *ether*] : SULFIDE 2
thio·flavine *also* **thio·flavin** \"+\ *n*, *often cap T* [ISV *thi-* + *flavin*, *flavine*] : either of two yellow thiazole dyes used as biological stains as well as in dyeing or making organic pigments — see DYE table I (under *Basic Yellow 1* and *Direct Yellow 7*)
thio·gly·colate \,thīō+\ *also* **thio·gly·col·late** \,thī'ō'glīkə,lāt, -,glī'kälət\ *n* [ISV *thioglycol-*, *thioglycoll-* (fr. *thioglycolic acid*, *thioglycollic acid*) + -*ate*] : a salt or ester of thioglycolic acid : a mercapto-acetate
thio·glycolic acid *also* **thio·glycollic acid** \,thīō+...-\ *n* [*thioglycolic*, *thioglycollic* ISV *thi-* + *glycolic*, *glycollic* (in *glycolic acid*, *glycollic acid*)] : an ill-smelling liquid mercapto acid HSCH₂COOH analogous to the hydroxy acid glycolic acid that is made usu. by reaction of chloroacetic acid and hydrogen sulfide, that is a sensitive reagent for ferric iron (as by the formation of an intense red color in ammoniacal solution), and that is used chiefly in the form of its ammonium salt in setting cold waves and in the form of the calcium and other alkaline salts as depilating agents — called also *mercaptoacetic acid*; not used systematically
-thio·ic \,thī(,)ōik-\ *adj comb form* [ISV *thi-* + -*ic*] : containing one atom of sulfur replacing one oxygen atom in the molecule of an acid ⟨phosphoro*thioic* acid⟩ ⟨octane*thioic* acid C₇H₁₅COSH⟩
thio·indigo \,thī(,)ō+\ *n* [ISV *thi-* + *indigo*] **1** : a red vat dye C₁₆H₈O₂S₂ like indigo in chemical structure except for replacement of both imino groups by sulfur atoms — see DYE table I (under *Vat Blue 41*) **2** : any of several vat dyes derived from thioindigo — see DYE table I
thio·indigoid \"+\ *adj* [*thioindigo* + -*oid*] : related to or resembling thioindigo esp. in chemical structure and dyeing properties
thioindigoid dye *also* **thioindigoid** *n* : any of a class of vat dyes characterized by the same chromophore as indigo (sense 1b) but with sulfur instead of an imino group as an auxochrome — compare INDIGOID DYE
thioindigo red B *n, usu cap T&R* : THIOINDIGO 1
thio·ketone \,thī(,)ō+\ *n* [*thi-* + *ketone*] : a compound that is a ketone in which oxygen is replaced by sulfur and which in general is readily polymerizable (as in the general formula RCSR) — called also *thione*
Thi·o·kol \'thīə,kol, -kol\ *trademark* — used for any of a series of polysulfide rubbers or closely related liquid polymers or water-dispersed latices
thi·ol \'thī,ol, -,ol\ *n* -s [ISV *thi-* + -*ol*] **1** : MERCAPTAN **2** : the mercapto group — **thi·ol·ic** \(')═'ik\ *adj*
thiolic acid *n* [*thiolic* fr. *thiol* + -*ic*] : a thio acid in which the mercapto group is present — compare THIONIC ACID 2
¹**thion-** *comb form* [ISV, fr. Gk *theion* — more at THI-] : sulfur
²**thion-** *or* **thiono-** *comb form* [*thion-* ISV, fr. Gk *theion* sulfur; *thiono-* fr. Gk *theion* + ISV -*o-*] : containing sulfur doubly bound to another atom (as in the thiocarbonyl group) ⟨*thiono*thiolic⟩
thionic acid *n* [*thionic* ISV ¹*thion-* + -*ic*] **1** : any of a series of unstable acids of the general formula H₂S_xO₆ in which the number of atoms of sulfur in the molecule varies from 2 to 6 — compare DITHIONIC ACID, POLYTHIONIC ACID **2** [*thionic* ISV ²*thion-* + -*ic*] : a thio acid in which sulfur doubly re-

another atom (as in the thiocarbonyl group) is present — compare THIOLIC ACID
Thi·o·nine \'thīə,nēn, -,nən\ *trademark* — used for a dark crystalline basic dye of the thiazine class that is the parent compound of methylene blue and is used chiefly as a biological stain
thi·o·ni·um \thī'ōnēəm\ *n* -s [NL, fr. *thi-* + -*onium*] : SULFONIUM
-thionium \"\ *n comb form* -s [NL, fr. *thi-* + -*onium*] : onium compound containing sulfur and usu. another element (as nitrogen) besides carbon in a ring ⟨phenaza*thionium*⟩
thi·o·nyl \'thīən°l, -,nil\ *n* -s [ISV ¹*thion-* + -*yl*; orig. formed in G] : the bivalent radical or cation >SO of sulfurous acid : SULFINYL — used esp. in names of inorganic compounds
thionyl chloride *n* : a volatile fuming corrosive liquid compound SOCl₂ usu. made commercially by oxidation of sulfur dichloride with sulfur trioxide or sulfuryl chloride and used chiefly in making acyl chlorides from carboxylic acids and alkyl chlorides or alkyl sulfites from alcohols
thio·pen·tal \,thīō'pen,tal, -,tol\ *n* -s [*thi-* + *penta-* + -*al*] : a barbiturate C₁₁H₁₈N₂O₂S that is a sulfur analogue of pentobarbital and is used in the form of its yellowish white powdery sodium derivative as an intravenous anesthetic of short duration and also in psychotherapy
thio·pen·tone \,══'══, -,tōn\ *n* [*thi-* + *penta-* + -*one*] *Brit* : THIOPENTAL
thi·o·phen \'thīəfən, -,fen\ *chiefly Brit var of* THIOPHENE
thi·o·phene \'thīə,fēn\ *n* -s [ISV *thi-* + *phene*] : a liquid compound C₄H₄S that is analogous to furan and pyrrole in its heterocyclic structure and resembles benzene both physically and chemically except for its greater reactivity, that is found in small amounts (as up to 0.5 percent by weight) in benzene from coal tar unless it has been removed by treatment with sulfuric acid, that is usu. made commercially from butane and sulfur at high temperature, and that is used chiefly in organic synthesis (as of antihistaminic drugs) — see INDOPHENIN; compare STRUCTURAL FORMULA

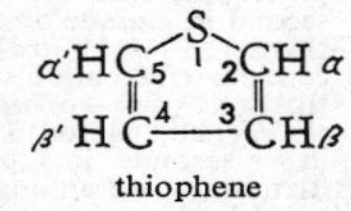

[chemical structure diagram]
α'HC—═C—CH α
β'HC═C—CHβ
S at top, 5, 2, 4, 3 positions
thiophene

thi·oph·e·nine \thī'äfə,nēn, thīə'fēn-\ *n* -s [ISV *thiophene* + -*ine*] : either of two amines (C₄H₃S)NH₂ structurally resembling aniline but stable only when acidified to form salts; amino-thiophene
thio·phenol \,thīō+\ *n* [ISV *thi-* + *phenol*] **1** : a mobile liquid mercaptan C₆H₅SH with a smell like garlic and with acid properties somewhat stronger than those of phenol that may be formed by the action of phosphorus pentasulfide on phenol but that is better synthesized by reduction of benzenesulfonyl chloride — called also *phenyl mercaptan* **2** : an aromatic mercaptan (as thiophenol)
thio·phosgene \,thīō+\ *n* [ISV *thi-* + *phosgene*] : a red ill-smelling liquid compound CSCl₂ obtainable (as by reaction with hydrogen sulfide at high temperature) from carbon tetrachloride; thiocarbonyl chloride
thio·phosphate \"+\ *n* [ISV *thi-* + *phosphate*] : a salt or ester of a thiophosphoric acid
thio·phosphite \"+\ *n* [*thi-* + *phosphite*] : a salt or ester of a thiophosphorous acid
thio·phosphoric acid \"+...-\ *n* [*thiophosphoric* fr. *thi-* + *phosphoric*] : any of a series of acids derived from the phosphoric acids by replacement of one or more atoms of oxygen with sulfur; *esp* : the mono-thio orthophosphoric acid H₃PO₃S obtained as a concentrated solution at low temperature or in the form of salts and esters
thio·phosphorous acid \"+...-\ *n* [*thiophosphorous* fr. *thi-* + *phosphorous*] : any of a series of acids derived from the phosphorous acids by replacement of one or more atoms of oxygen with sulfur
thio·phosphoryl \"+\ *n* [*thi-* + *phosphoryl*] : the usu. trivalent radical PS that is phosphoryl in which oxygen is replaced by sulfur — compare SULFOCHLORIDE 1
thi·o·plast \'thīə,plast\ *n* -s [ISV *thi-* + -*plast*] : any of various rubberlike materials made from an alkali polysulfide and an organic dihalide : POLYSULFIDE RUBBER
thio·rho·da·ce·ae \,thīərō'dāsē,ē, -ə,i\ *n pl, cap* [NL, fr. *thi-* + *rhod-* + -*aceae*] : a family of purple sulfur bacteria (suborder Rhodobacteriinae) using hydrogen sulfide as a hydrogen donor in their metabolism and accumulating molecular sulfur as a metabolic by-product
thio·semicarbazide \,thī(,)ō+\ *n* [*thi-* + *semicarbazide*] : a crystalline compound H₂NCSNHNH₂ that is the analogue of semicarbazide in which oxygen is replaced by sulfur
thio·semicarbazone \"+\ *n* [*thi-* + *semicarbazone*] : any of a class of compounds analogous to semicarbazones and formed by the action of thiosemicarbazide on an aldehyde or ketone; *esp* : THIACETAZONE
thio·sin·amine \,thīōsə'namēn, -ō'sinə,mēn\ *n* -s [ISV *thi-* + *sin-* (fr. L *sinapis* mustard) + *amine* — more at SINAPIS] : ALLYLTHIOUREA
thio·spirillum \,thīō+\ *n* [NL, fr. *thi-* + *Spirillum*] **1** *cap* : a genus of spiral purple sulfur bacteria (family Thiorhodaceae) motile by means of polar flagella and common in mud and stagnant water **2** *pl* **thiospirilla** : any bacterium of the genus *Thiospirillum*
thio·sulfate \'thīə+\ *n* [ISV *thi-* + *sulfate*] : a salt or ester of thiosulfuric acid; *esp* : SODIUM THIOSULFATE
thiosulfato- *comb form* [*thiosulfate* + -*o-*] : containing the bivalent radical S₂O₃ characteristic of thiosulfates — esp. in names of coordination complexes ⟨sodium *thiosulfato*aurate (I) Na₃Au(S₂O₃)₂⟩
thio·sulfonic acid \,thīə +...-\ *n* [*thiosulfonic* fr. *thi-* + *sulfonic*] : any of a series of unstable acids of the general formula RSO₂SH derived from sulfonic acids by replacement of oxygen by sulfur and known only in the form of salts and esters
thio·sulfuric acid \"+...-\ *n* [*thiosulfuric* fr. *thi-* + *sulfuric*] : an unstable acid H₂S₂O₃ derived from sulfuric acid by replacement of one oxygen atom by sulfur and known only in solution or in the form of salts and esters
thio·thrix \'thīə,thriks\ *n, cap* [NL, fr. *thi-* + -*thrix*] : a genus of bacteria (family Beggiatoaceae) consisting of nonmotile ensheathed attached filaments differentiated into a base and a tip
thio·uracil \'thīō+\ *n* [ISV *thi-* + *uracil*] : a bitter crystalline compound C₄H₄N₂OS that depresses the function of the thyroid gland; 2-mercapto-pyrimidin-4-ol; *also* : any of several of its derivatives (as methylthiouracil or propylthiouracil)
thio·urea \"+\ *n* [ISV *thi-* + *urea*] : a bitter crystalline compound CS(NH₂)₂ that is analogous to urea with the oxygen replaced by sulfur and resembles urea in chemical properties, that is obtained by heating ammonium thiocyanate or by adding hydrogen sulfide to cyanamide, and that is used chiefly in the separation of hydrocarbons (as various liquid normal paraffin hydrocarbons from branched-chain hydrocarbons), in organic synthesis, and esp. formerly in synthetic resins
thiouronium *var of* THIURONIUM
thio·xanthone \,thīō+\ *n* [ISV *thi-* + *xanthone*] : a yellow crystalline ketone C₆H₄(CO)(S)C₆H₄ that is the sulfur analogue of xanthone
thir \,thər, (')thir, (')thü(ə)r\ *pron* [ME (northern dial.), perh. irreg. fr. ME ¹*this*] *dial Brit* : THESE ⟨~ breeks o' mine, my only pair —Robert Burns⟩
thi·ram \'thī,ram\ *n* -s [prob. alter. of *thiuram*] : TETRAMETHYLTHIURAM DISULFIDE — used of the fungicide and seed disinfectant
¹**third** \'thərd, 'thǝd, 'thǝid\ *adj* [ME *thirde*, *thridde*, fr. OE *thridda*, *thridda*; akin to OHG *dritto* third, ON *thrithi*, Goth *thridja*, L *tertius*, Gk *tritos*; Skt *tṛtiya*; derivative fr. the root of OE *thrie*, *threo* three — more at THREE] **1 a** : being three in a countable series ⟨the ~ day⟩ — abbr. 3d or 3rd; see NUMBER table **b** (1) : being next to the second in place or time ⟨~ in line for promotion⟩ (2) : ranking next to the second of a series or degree in authority or precedence ⟨~ mate⟩ **c** : being a type of grammatical declension or conjugation conventionally placed third in a standard arrangement of the types **d** : being the forward speed or gear next higher than second in an automotive vehicle **2 a** : being one of three equal parts into which anything is divisible ⟨a ~ share of the money⟩

b : being the last in each group of three in a series — often preceded by *every* ⟨take out every ~ card⟩ **3 :** other than the two known, mentioned, or participating ⟨there cannot be a ~ person in a secret⟩ **4 :** being between 2.51 and 3.50 on the magnitude scale — used of the magnitude of a star

²**third** \"\ *n* -s [ME *thridde,* fr. *thirde, thridde,* adj.] **1 :** number three in a countable series ⟨the ~ of the month⟩ **2 :** the quotient of a unit divided by three : one of three equal parts of something ⟨one ~ of the total⟩ **3 thirds** *pl* **a :** the third part of the personal estate of a deceased husband which by the common-law statute of distribution and by some local statutes goes after various conditions have been fulfilled absolutely to the widow upon the husband's dying intestate and leaving a child or descendant **b :** a widow's dower **c :** a widow's statutory right to share in her deceased husband's estate and esp. in his personalty **d** *Scots law* **:** the third part of the revenues of the ecclesiastical benefices taken in 1562 and 1567 and later by the king into his hands and appropriated to the support of the acting clergy **4 a :** a musical interval embracing three diatonic degrees **b :** a tone at this interval; *specif* **:** the third note or tone of a scale **:** MEDIANT **c :** the harmonic combination of two tones a third apart **5 :** an article of merchandise (as coarse flour) of a third grade or quality or inferior to seconds — usu. used in pl. **6 :** the price formerly paid by a student entering a British university for the furniture in his rooms being commonly two thirds of that paid by the previous tenant **7 :** THIRD BASE **8 :** the third gear or speed of an automotive vehicle **9 :** TIERCE 4 **10 :** one having authority or precedence next below that of a person (as a mate) ranking second in a grade or degree

³**third** \"\ *adv* [¹*third*] **1 :** in the third place **2 :** with two exceptions ⟨the nation's ~ largest city⟩

⁴**third** \"\ *vt* -ED/-ING/-S [ME(Sc) *thridden,* fr. ME *thirde, thridde,* adj., third] **1 :** to divide into three parts **2 :** to follow a seconder in supporting (as a motion)

third angle *n* **:** an angle of the Great Triangle formed on the palm by the intersection of the lines of Head and Mercury that when clear, well-pointed, and even is usu. held by palmists to indicate quickness of intellect, individuality, and good health — called also *middle angle;* compare FIRST ANGLE, SECOND ANGLE

third base *n* **1 :** the base that must be touched third by a base runner in baseball **2 :** the player position for defending the area of the infield around third base

third baseman *n* **:** the baseball player stationed at the third-base position — see BASEBALL illustration

third-best \ˈ=ˈ=\ *adj* [ME(Sc) *thrid best,* fr. ME *thirde, thridde, thrid* third + *best*] **:** next to second-best in quality or excellence

third·borough \ˈthərd,=(,)=\ *n* [ME *thridborro,* prob. by folk etymology (influence of ME *thirde, thridde, thrid* third) fr. *frithborg* frankpledge — more at FRITHBORH] **:** a former English peace officer esp. of a tithing

third class *n* **:** the third and usu. next below the second class in a classification: as **a :** a class of U.S. mail comprising printed matter exclusive of regularly issued periodicals and merchandise less than 16 ounces in weight and not sealed against inspection; *also* **:** a similar class of Canadian mail with different weight limits **b :** the least expensive class of accommodations (as on a railroad train) — compare TOURIST CLASS

¹**third-class** \ˈ=ˈ=\ *adj* [*third class*] **:** of or relating to a class, rank, or grade next below the second

²**third-class** \ˈ=ˈ=\ *adv* **:** by a third-class conveyance **:** with third-class accommodations ⟨travel *third-class*⟩

third cranial nerve *or* **third nerve** *n* **:** OCULOMOTOR NERVE

third day *n, usu cap T* **:** TUESDAY — used chiefly by the Friends

third deck *n* **:** LOWER DECK 1b — see DECK illustration

third degree *n* **1 :** MASTER MASON 2a **2 :** the subjection of a prisoner to mental torture (as continuous questioning over excessively long periods) or physical torture (as restriction to a meager diet or deprivation of sleep) in an effort to wring a confession from him

¹**third-degree** \ˌ==ˈ=\ *adj* [fr. the phrase *third degree*] **:** of a degree next to the second; *specif* **:** of a degree of criminal culpability or seriousness second after first-degree ⟨*third-degree* arson⟩

²**third-degree** \"\ *vt* [*third degree*] **:** to administer the third degree to ⟨the police beat prisoners and *third-degree* them —*Newsweek*⟩

third-degree burn *n* **:** a burn characterized by destruction of the skin through the depth of the derma and possibly into underlying tissues, loss of fluid, and sometimes shock if the burned area is extensive

third dimension *n* **1 :** thickness or depth esp. when it is the quality that confers solidity on an object ⟨the image on the paper seems to have a *third dimension*⟩ **2 :** a quality that confers reality or lifelikeness ⟨night sounds that stick in the mind and give a *third dimension* to the memory —Adie Suehsdorf⟩ — **third-dimensional** *adj*

third estate *n* **:** the third of the traditional political orders; *specif* **:** the commons

third eyelid *n* **:** NICTITATING MEMBRANE

third floor *n* **:** THIRD STORY

third force *n* **:** a grouping (as of political parties or nations) intermediate between two opposing political forces

third-generation \ˌ=,==ˈ==\ *adj* [fr. the phrase *third generation*] **1 :** being a member of the third generation of a family to be born in the U.S. ⟨a *third-generation* American⟩ **2 :** being a member of the second generation of a family to be born in the U.S.

third hand *n* **1 :** the third person to own or sell a used article **2 :** a thirdhand source (as of information) **3 :** the third player to have the right to bid in bridge **:** the third player to play to any trick **4 a :** a workman who helps the backtender at the dry end of a paper machine **b :** one who under the direction of a second hand supervises a section of workers in a textile mill **c :** a factory worker who assists operators or fixers of machines

¹**thirdhand** \ˈ=ˈ=\ *adj* [*third hand*] **1 :** received from or through two intermediaries ⟨~ information⟩ **2 a :** used or worn by two previous owners **:** bought or acquired after being used by two others ⟨a ~ stove⟩ **b :** dealing in thirdhand merchandise

²**thirdhand** \"\ *adv* **:** at third hand

third house *n* [so called fr. its relation to the two houses of which many legislatures are composed] **:** a legislative lobby

third·ings \ˈthərdiŋz\ *n pl* [*thirding* (gerund of ⁴*third*) + -s, n. pl. suffix] **:** a heriot consisting of the third part of the corn or grain growing on the ground at the tenant's death

third inversion *n* **:** a seventh chord with the seventh in the bass — see SEVENTH CHORD illustration

third law of thermodynamics : LAW OF THERMODYNAMICS 3

third·ly *adv* **:** in the third place

third man *n* **1 :** an off side fielding position in cricket usu. near the boundary and roughly in line with third slip and the striker; *also* **:** a player fielding in this position — see CRICKET illustration **2** [trans. of Gk *tritos anthrōpos*] **:** a logical paradox in which the attempt to pass from one thing to another or to relate one conception to another reveals the necessity of a third and intervening thing or conception and hence leads to an infinite regress

third mortgage *n* **:** a mortgage given or recorded after two others have been previously given on the same property with a lien subordinate to the first two given or recorded

third·ness *n* -ES **:** a fundamental category in Peircean philosophy consisting of the connecting bond between firstness and secondness and expressive of law, generality, purpose, and habit

third order *n* [trans. of ML *tertius ordo;* fr. the partial resemblance to an order of monks or an order of nuns] **:** a group affiliated with a Roman Catholic religious order and comprising men and women devoted to a special rule of pious living usu. without vows

third-order reaction *n* [*third-order* fr. the phrase *third order*] **:** a chemical reaction in which the rate of reaction is proportional to the concentration of each of three reacting molecules — compare ORDER OF A REACTION

third party *n* **1 :** a person other than the principals ⟨a *third party* to a divorce proceeding⟩ ⟨insurance against injury to *third parties*⟩ **2 a :** a major political party operating over a limited period of time in addition to two other major parties in a political unit (as a nation or state) normally characterized by a two-party system **b :** MINOR PARTY

third-party \ˈ=ˈ=\ *adj* [*third party*] **:** of, involving, or referring to a third party ⟨*third-party* insurance⟩ ⟨the *third-party* vote⟩

third person *n* **1 a :** a set of linguistic forms (as verb forms, pronouns, and inflectional affixes) referring to someone or something that is neither the speaker or writer of the utterance in which they occur nor the one to whom that utterance is addressed ⟨Latin *videt* "he sees" is in the *third person* singular⟩ ⟨English *they* is a nominative plural pronoun of the *third person*⟩ **b :** a linguistic form belonging to such a set ⟨English *is* and *goes* are *third person*⟩ **2 :** reference of a linguistic form to someone or something that is neither the speaker or writer of the utterance in which it occurs nor the one to whom that utterance is addressed ⟨the Latin verb ending *-t* that marks the *third person*⟩

third personal *adj* **:** of or belonging to the third person ⟨a *third personal* pronoun⟩

third rail *n* **:** a metal rail through which current is led to the motors of an electric locomotive — compare RUNNING RAIL

third-rate \ˈ=ˈ=\ *adj* [fr. the phrase *third rate*] **:** of third quality or value **:** less than second rate in excellence or worth

third-rat·er \ˈ=ˈrād·ə(r), -ātə-\ *n* **:** one that is third-rate

third reading *n* **1 :** the stage in the British legislative process following the report stage and usu. providing for debate on the reported text of a bill before a vote on its final disposition **2 :** the stage in the U.S. legislative process which follows the second reading and in which an engrossed bill is read usu. by title only before a vote on its final disposition

thirds *pl of* THIRD, *pres 3d sing of* THIRD

third sex *n* **:** HOMOSEXUALS

third slip *n* **:** a fielding position in cricket near to and on the off side of second slip; *also* **:** a player fielding in this position

third story *n* **1 :** the second story above the ground floor **2** *Brit* **:** the third story above the ground floor

third ventricle *n* **:** the median unpaired ventricle of the brain bounded by parts of the telencephalon and diencephalon — see BRAIN illustration

third water *n* **:** the quality or luster next below second water — used of a gem (as a diamond or pearl)

third way *n* **:** economic and political development distinct from or esp. midway between the paths proposed by two extremes

¹**thirl** \ˈthər(ə)l\ *n* -s [ME, fr. OE *thyrel,* fr. *thurh* through — more at THROUGH] *dial* **:** HOLE, PERFORATION, OPENING

²**thirl** \"\ *vt* -ED/-ING/-S [ME *thirlen,* fr. OE *thyrlian,* fr. *thyrel,* n.] **1** *dial Brit* **:** PIERCE, PERFORATE, DRILL **2** *dial Brit* **:** to pierce with emotion **:** THRILL

³**thirl** \"\ *vt* -ED/-ING/-S [alter. of Sc *thrill,* fr. ME (Sc) *thrillen* to subject to thirlage, enslave, fr. *thril* thrall, alter. of ME *thral* — more at THRALL] **1** *Scots & old Eng law* **:** to subject to thirlage **2** *chiefly Brit* **:** to tie down **:** confine in course of action **:** RESTRICT

⁴**thirl** \"\ *n* -s **1** *Scot* **:** THIRLAGE **2** *Scot* **:** SUCKEN

thirl·age \ˈthərlij\ *n* -s [alter. of Sc *thrillage* thralldom, fr. ME (Sc), fr. *thril* thrall + ME *-age*] **:** a feudal servitude, right, or service binding the tenants of a sucken to carry the grain produced there to a particular mill for grinding and to pay the agreed or customary dues; *also* **:** the dues so exacted — compare OUTSUCKEN

thirl·ing \-liŋ\ *n* -s [fr. gerund of ²*thirl*] **:** a cross hole or short passage between breasts or headings in a coal mine usu. for ventilation

¹**thirst** \ˈthərst, ˈthəst, ˈthəist\ *n* -s [ME, alter. (prob. influenced by *thirsten* to thirst) of *thurst,* fr. OE; akin to OHG *durst* thirst, ON *thorsti,* Goth *thaurstei* thirst, L *torrēre* to dry, parch, Gk *tersesthai* to become dry, Skt *tṛṣyati* he thirsts] **1 a :** a sensation of dryness in the mouth and throat associated with a desire for liquids; *also* **:** the bodily condition (as of dehydration) that induces this sensation **b :** a desire for potable liquids or to drink **2 :** an ardent desire **:** CRAVING, LONGING ⟨the home folks' ~ for news of its armies —Bruce Catton⟩ ⟨the ~ for new and up-to-date vehicles —F.L.Allen⟩ **3** *or* **thirstland** \ˈ=,=\ **:** a waterless tract (as a desert)

²**thirst** \"\ *vi* -ED/-ING/-S [ME *thirsten,* fr. OE *thyrstan;* akin to OHG *dursten* to thirst, ON *thyrsta;* denominative fr. the root of OE *thurst,* n., thirst] **1 :** to feel thirsty **:** suffer thirst **2 :** to have a vehement desire **:** CRAVE ⟨a savage, unprincipled brute who ~*ed* to overturn a society . . . not to his advantage —J.H.Plumb⟩ ⟨adventurers ~*ing* for excitement —Waldemar Kaempffert⟩ ⟨~ after every conceivable form of achievement —Ernest Nagel⟩ **syn** see LONG

thirst·er \-stə(r)\ *n* -s [ME *thristere,* fr. *thristen, thirsten* to thirst + *-ere* -er] **:** one that is thirsty

thirst·i·ly \-stəlē, -li\ *adv* **:** with thirst **:** on account of thirst ⟨drink ~⟩ ⟨we wait ~ for each new poem —Kenneth Clark⟩

thirst·i·ness \-stēnəs, -stin-\ *n* -ES **:** the quality or state of being thirsty

thirsting *n* -s **:** the sensation of thirst; *also* **:** CRAVING, LONGING

thirst·less \-stləs\ *adj* **:** having no thirst

thirst·less·ness *n* -ES **:** the quality or state of being thirstless

thirst out *vt* **:** to conquer, expel, or gain control of by causing to thirst ⟨will turn off the water . . . with their dams and *thirst us out* —Mary Lindsay⟩

thirsty \ˈthərstē, ˈthəs-,ˈthəis-, -sti\ *adj* -ER/-EST [ME, fr. OE *thyrstig, thurstig;* akin to OHG *durstag* thirsty; both fr. a prehistoric WGmc adjective whose first constituent is represented by OE *thurst* thirst and whose second constituent is represented by OE *-ig* -y] **1 a :** feeling thirst **:** experiencing a desire for drink **b :** deficient in moisture **:** DRY, PARCHED, ARID ⟨a dry and ~ land, where no water is —Ps 63:1 (AV)⟩ **c :** able to take in large quantities of liquid or moisture **:** highly absorbent ⟨the water sinks rapidly into the ~ ground —P.E. James⟩ **2 :** having a strong desire **:** LONGING, AVID ⟨~ for some contact with the natural world —Fairfield Osborn⟩

¹**thir·teen** \(ˈ)thər(t)ˈtēn, (ˈ)thə̄, (ˈ)thəi| *sometimes* |d-ˈtēn\ *adj* [ME *thirttene, thrette ne,* fr. OE *thrēotīne, thrēotȳne, thrēotēne* (akin to OHG *drizehan,* ON *threttān*), fr. *thrīe, thrēo* three + *-tīne, -tȳne, -tēne* (fr. *tīen, tȳn, tēn* ten) — more at THREE, TEN] **:** being one more than 12 in number ⟨~ years⟩ — see NUMBER table

²**thirteen** \"\ *pron, pl in constr* [ME *threttene,* fr. OE *thrēotȳne,* fr. *thrēotīne, thrēotȳne, thrēotēne,* adj.] **:** thirteen countable persons or things not specified but under consideration and being enumerated ⟨~ are here⟩ ⟨~ were found⟩

³**thirteen** \"\ *n* -s [ME *thrittene,* fr. *thirttene, threttene, thrittene,* adj.] **1 :** 10 and three **2 a :** 13 units or objects ⟨a total of ~⟩ **b :** a group or set of 13 **3 :** the numerable quantity symbolized by the arabic numerals 13 **4** [so called fr. the fact that it was once worth thirteen copper pence in Irish money] *chiefly Irish* **:** an English shilling **5 :** the 13th in a set or series; *esp* **:** an article of clothing of the 13th size

thir·teen·er \-nə(r)\ *n* -s **1 :** THIRTEEN 4 **2 :** the card of a suit left after 12 are played

thirteen-lined ground squirrel *also* **thirteen-lined gopher** \ˌ=,=ˌ=-\ *n* **:** a widely distributed western No. American burrowing squirrel (*Citellus tridecemlineatus*) that is grayish brown and marked with a series of longitudinal white lines more or less broken into discrete spots — called also *leopard squirrel, striped ground squirrel*

¹**thir·teenth** \-n(t)th\ *adj* [ME *threttenthe,* alter. (influenced by *threttene* thirteen) of *threttethe,* fr. OE *thrēotēotha* (akin to ON *threttāndi* thirteenth), fr. *thrēotīne, thrēotȳne, thrēotēne* thirteen + *-otha, -tha* -th] **1 :** being number 13 in a countable series ⟨the ~ day⟩ — see NUMBER table **2 :** being one of 13 equal parts into which anything is divisible ⟨a ~ share of the money⟩

²**thirteenth** \"\ *n, pl* **thirteenths** \-n(t)s, -n(t)ths\ **1 :** number 13 in a countable series ⟨the ~ of the month⟩ **2 :** the quotient of a unit divided by 13 **:** one of 13 equal parts of anything ⟨one ~ of the total⟩ **3 :** a tax in medieval England comprising the 13th part of the value of movables or of an annual rent **4 a :** the musical interval comprising an octave and a sixth **b :** a note or tone at this interval

¹**thir·ti·eth** \ˈthər|d·|ēəth, ˈthə̄|, ˈthəi|, |t|, |iəth\ *adj* [ME *thrittithe,* fr. OE *thrītigotha* (akin to ON *thritugandi*), fr. *thrītig* thirty + *-otha, -tha* -th] **1 :** being number 30 in a countable series ⟨the ~ day⟩ — see NUMBER table **2 :** being one of 30 equal parts into which anything is divisible ⟨a ~ share of the money⟩

²**thirtieth** \"\ *n* -s **1 :** number 30 in a countable series ⟨the ~ of the month⟩ **2 :** the quotient of a unit divided by 30 **:** one of 30 equal parts of anything ⟨one ~ of the total⟩

thirt·over \ˈthər,tōvər, ˈth-\ *var of* THWARTOVER

¹**thir·ty** \ˈthər|d·|ē, ˈthə̄|, ˈthəi|, |t|, |i\ *adj* [ME *thirty, thritty,* fr. OE *thrītig,* fr. *thrītig,* n., group of 30, fr. *thrīe, thrēo* three + *-tig* group of 10 — more at THREE, EIGHTY] **:** being one more than 29 in number ⟨~ years⟩ — see NUMBER table

²**thirty** \"\ *pron, pl in constr* [ME *thirty, thritty,* fr. OE *thrītig,* fr. *thrītig,* n. & adj.] **:** 30 countable persons or things not specified but under consideration and being enumerated ⟨~ are here⟩ ⟨~ were found⟩

³**thirty** \"\ *n* -ES [ME *thritty,* fr. OE *thrītig,* fr. *thrītig,* adj.] **1 :** three tens **:** twice 15 **:** five times six **:** six fives **2 a :** 30 units or objects ⟨a total of ~⟩ **b :** a group or set of 30 ⟨arranged by *thirties*⟩ **3 :** the numerable quantity symbolized by the arabic numerals 30 **4 thirties** *pl* **a :** the numbers 30 to 39 inclusive ⟨a score in the *thirties*⟩ ⟨low grades in the *thirties*⟩ **b :** the members of a series or set of successive numbers that end in 30 to 39 inclusive ⟨the *thirties* of the preceding century⟩ ⟨lives in the *thirties* in the next block⟩ **c :** the portion of a continuum lying between 30 and 40 on a scale of measurement or segmentation ⟨temperatures in the *thirties* tomorrow⟩ ⟨a man in his *thirties*⟩ ⟨dresses selling in the *thirties*⟩ ⟨in the latitude of the *thirties*⟩ **5 :** the 30th in a set or series; *esp* **:** an article of clothing of the 30th size ⟨wears a ~⟩ **6 :** something having as an essential feature 30 units or members **7 a :** a mark or sign of completion ⟨"Thank you, Mr. President" the traditional ~ closing press conferences —*Ethyl News*⟩ **b :** END, CONCLUSION ⟨had ~ written on their earthly life —*Trade Compositor*⟩ **8 :** the second point scored by a side in tennis **9 :** a 30 caliber machine gun — usu. written .30

¹**thirty-eight** \ˌ==ˈ=\ *adj* **:** being one more than 37 in number ⟨*thirty-eight* years⟩ — see NUMBER table

²**thirty-eight** \"\ *pron, pl in constr* **:** 38 countable persons or things not specified but under consideration and being enumerated ⟨*thirty-eight* are here⟩ ⟨*thirty-eight* were found⟩

³**thirty-eight** \"\ *n* **1 :** eight and 30 **:** 19 times two **2 a :** 38 units or objects ⟨a total of *thirty-eight*⟩ **b :** a group or set of 38 **3 :** the numerable quantity symbolized by the arabic numerals 38 **4 :** the 38th in a set or series **5 :** a 38 caliber pistol — usu. written .38

¹**thirty-eighth** \ˌ==ˈ=\ *adj* **1 :** being number 38 in a countable series ⟨the *thirty-eighth* day⟩ — see NUMBER table **2 :** being one of 38 equal parts into which anything is divisible ⟨a *thirty-eighth* share of the money⟩

²**thirty-eighth** \"\ *n* **1 :** number 38 in a countable series **2 :** the quotient of a unit divided by 38 **:** one of 38 equal parts of anything ⟨one *thirty-eighth* of the total⟩

¹**thirty-fifth** \ˌ==ˈ=\ *adj* **1 :** being number 35 in a countable series ⟨the *thirty-fifth* day⟩ — see NUMBER table **2 :** being one of 35 equal parts into which anything is divisible ⟨a *thirty-fifth* share of the money⟩

²**thirty-fifth** \"\ *n* **1 :** number 35 in a countable series **2 :** the quotient of a unit divided by 35 **:** one of 35 equal parts of anything ⟨one *thirty-fifth* of the total⟩

¹**thirty-first** \ˌ==ˈ=\ *adj* **1 :** being number 31 in a countable series ⟨the *thirty-first* day⟩ — see NUMBER table **2 :** being one of 31 equal parts into which anything is divisible ⟨a *thirty-first* share of the money⟩

²**thirty-first** \"\ *n* **1 :** number 31 in a countable series ⟨the *thirty-first* of the month⟩ **2 :** the quotient of a unit divided by 31 **:** one of 31 equal parts of anything ⟨one *thirty-first* of the total⟩

¹**thirty-five** \ˌ==ˈ=\ *adj* **:** being one more than 34 in number ⟨*thirty-five* years⟩ — see NUMBER table

²**thirty-five** \"\ *pron, pl in constr* **:** 35 countable persons or things not specified but under consideration and being enumerated ⟨*thirty-five* are here⟩ ⟨*thirty-five* were found⟩

³**thirty-five** \"\ *n* **1 :** five and 30 **:** five times seven **:** seven fives **2 a :** 35 units or objects ⟨a total of *thirty-five*⟩ **b :** a group or set of 35 **3 :** the numerable quantity symbolized by the arabic numerals 35 **4 :** a gambling game for from two to five players in which the pot is won by the player who holds cards of the same suit totaling 35 or more points in value

¹**thir·ty·fold** \ˌ==ˈfōld\ *adj* [ME *thrittifold,* fr. OE *thrītigfeald,* fr. *thrītig* thirty + *-feald* -fold] **1 :** having 30 parts or aspects **2 :** being 30 times as large, as great, or as many as some understood size, degree, or amount ⟨a ~ increase⟩

²**thirtyfold** \"\ *adv* **:** to 30 times as much or as many **:** by 30 times ⟨brought forth fruit, some an hundredfold, some sixtyfold, some ~ —Mt 13:8 (AV)⟩

¹**thirty-four** \ˌ==ˈ=\ *adj* **:** being one more than 33 in number ⟨*thirty-four* years⟩ — see NUMBER table

²**thirty-four** \"\ *pron, pl in constr* **:** 34 countable persons or things not specified but under consideration and being enumerated ⟨*thirty-four* are here⟩ ⟨*thirty-four* were found⟩

³**thirty-four** \"\ *n* **1 :** four and 30 **:** 17 times two **2 a :** 34 units or objects ⟨a total of *thirty-four*⟩ **b :** a group or set of 34 **3 :** the numerable quantity symbolized by the arabic numerals 34

¹**thirty-fourth** \ˌ==ˈ=\ *adj* **1 :** being number 34 in a countable series ⟨the *thirty-fourth* day⟩ — see NUMBER table **2 :** being one of 34 equal parts into which anything is divisible ⟨a *thirty-fourth* share of the money⟩

²**thirty-fourth** \"\ *n* **1 :** number 34 in a countable series **2 :** the quotient of a unit divided by 34 **:** one of 34 equal parts of anything ⟨one *thirty-fourth* of the total⟩

thir·ty·ish \ˈ==ish\ *adj* **:** approaching or being about 30 years old

¹**thirty-nine** \ˌ==ˈ=\ *adj* **:** being one more than 38 in number ⟨*thirty-nine* years⟩ — see NUMBER table

²**thirty-nine** \"\ *pron, pl in constr* **:** 39 countable persons or things not specified but under consideration and being enumerated ⟨*thirty-nine* are here⟩ ⟨*thirty-nine* were found⟩

³**thirty-nine** \"\ *n* **1 :** nine and 30 **:** three times 13 **2 a :** 39 units or objects ⟨a total of *thirty-nine*⟩ **b :** a group or set of 39 **3 :** the numerable quantity symbolized by the arabic numerals 39

¹**thirty-ninth** \ˌ==ˈ=\ *adj* **1 :** being number 39 in a countable series ⟨the *thirty-ninth* day⟩ — see NUMBER table **2 :** being one of 39 equal parts into which anything is divisible ⟨a thirty-ninth share of the money⟩

²**thirty-ninth** \"\ *n* **1 :** number 39 in a countable series **2 :** the quotient of a unit divided by 39 **:** one of 39 equal parts of anything ⟨one *thirty-ninth* of the total⟩

¹**thirty-one** \ˌ==ˈ=\ *adj* **:** being one more than 30 in number ⟨*thirty-one* years⟩ — see NUMBER table

²**thirty-one** \"\ *pron, pl in constr* **:** 31 countable persons or things not specified but under consideration and being enumerated ⟨*thirty-one* are here⟩ ⟨*thirty-one* were found⟩

³**thirty-one** \"\ *n* **1 :** one and 30 **2 a :** 31 units or objects ⟨a total of *thirty-one*⟩ **b :** a group or set of 31 **3 :** the numerable quantity symbolized by the arabic numerals 31 **4** [trans. of F *trente et un*] **:** any of various games played with cards, dice, or numbers in which the winner is the player whose score equals or most nearly approaches 31

thirty-one order *n* **:** a train order for which the engineer or other member of a train crew must sign — compare *nineteen order*

¹**thirty-second** \ˌ==ˈ=\ *adj* **1 :** being number 32 in a countable series ⟨the *thirty-second* day⟩ — see NUMBER table **2 :** being one of 32 equal parts into which anything is divisible ⟨a *thirty-second* share of the money⟩

²**thirty-second** \"\ *n* **1 :** number 32 in a countable series **2 :** the quotient of a unit divided by 32 **:** one of 32 equal parts of anything ⟨one *thirty-second* of the total⟩

thirty-second note *n* **:** a musical note with a three-flagged stem having the time value of one thirty-second of a whole note — called also *demisemiquaver*

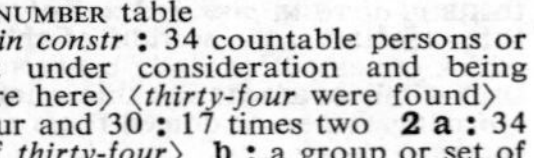

thirty-second notes

thirty-second rest *n* **:** a rest equal in time value to a thirty-second note

¹**thirty-seven** \ˌ==ˈ=\ *adj* **:** being one more than 36 in number ⟨*thirty-seven* years⟩ — see NUMBER table

²**thirty-seven** \"\ *pron, pl in constr* **:** 37 countable persons or things not specified but under consideration and being enumerated ⟨*thirty-seven* are here⟩ ⟨*thirty-seven* were found⟩

³**thirty-seven** \"\ *n* **1 :** seven and 30 **2 a :** 37 units or objects ⟨a total of *thirty-seven*⟩ **b :** a group or set of 37

3 : the numerable quantity symbolized by the arabic numerals 37

¹thirty-seventh \ˌ==ˈ==\ *adj* **1** : being number 37 in a countable series ⟨the *thirty-seventh* day⟩ — see NUMBER table **2** : being one of 37 equal parts into which anything is divisible ⟨a *thirty-seventh* share of the money⟩

²thirty-seventh \"\ *n* **1** : number 37 in a countable series **2** : the quotient of a unit divided by 37 : one of 37 equal parts of anything ⟨one *thirty-seventh* of the total⟩

¹thirty-six \ˌ==ˈ=\ *adj* : being one more than 35 in number ⟨*thirty-six* years⟩ — see NUMBER table

²thirty-six \"\ *pron, pl in constr* : 36 countable persons or things not specified but under consideration and being enumerated ⟨*thirty-six* are here⟩ ⟨*thirty-six* were found⟩

³thirty-six \"\ *n* **1** : six and 30 : three times 12 : four times nine : three dozen : six sixes : the square of six **2 a** : 36 units or objects ⟨a total of *thirty-six*⟩ **b** : a group or set of 36 **3** : the numerable quantity symbolized by the arabic numerals 36 **4** : the 36th in a set or series; *esp* : an article of clothing of the 36th size ⟨wears a *thirty-six*⟩

¹thirty-sixth \ˌ==ˈ=\ *adj* **1** : being number 36 in a countable series ⟨the *thirty-sixth* day⟩ — see NUMBER table **2** : being one of 36 equal parts into which anything is divisible ⟨a *thirty-sixth* share of the money⟩

²thirty-sixth \"\ *n* **1** : number 36 in a countable series **2** : the quotient of a unit divided by 36 : one of 36 equal parts of anything ⟨one *thirty-sixth* of the total⟩

¹thirty-third \ˌ==ˈ=\ *adj* **1** : being number 33 in a countable series ⟨the *thirty-third* day⟩ — see NUMBER table **2** : being one of 33 equal parts into which anything is divisible ⟨a *thirty-third* share of the money⟩

²thirty-third \"\ *n* **1** : number 33 in a countable series **2** : the quotient of a unit divided by 33 : one of 33 equal parts of anything ⟨one *thirty-third* of the total⟩

thirty-thirty \ˌ==ˈ==\ *n* : a rifle that fires a 30 caliber cartridge having a 30 grain powder charge — usu. written .30-30

¹thirty-three \ˌ==ˈ=\ *adj* : being one more than 32 in number ⟨*thirty-three* years⟩ — see NUMBER table

²thirty-three \"\ *pron, pl in constr* : 33 countable persons or things not specified but under consideration and being enumerated ⟨*thirty-three* are here⟩ ⟨*thirty-three* were found⟩

³thirty-three \"\ *n* **1** : three and 30 : three times 11 **2 a** : 33 units or objects ⟨a total of *thirty-three*⟩ **b** : a group or set of 33 **3** : the numerable quantity symbolized by the arabic numerals 33 **4** : a microgroove phonograph record designed to be played at 33⅓ revolutions per minute — usu. written 33

¹thirty-two \ˌ==ˈ=\ *adj* : being one more than 31 in number ⟨*thirty-two* years⟩ — see NUMBER table

²thirty-two \"\ *pron, pl in constr* : 32 countable persons or things not specified but under consideration and being enumerated ⟨*thirty-two* are here⟩ ⟨*thirty-two* were found⟩

³thirty-two \"\ *n* **1** : two and 30 : four times eight **2 a** : 32 units or objects ⟨a total of *thirty-two*⟩ **b** : a group or set of 32 **3** : the numerable quantity symbolized by the arabic numerals 32 **4** : the 32d in a set or series; *esp* : an article of clothing of the 32d size ⟨wears a *thirty-two*⟩ **5** : a 32 caliber pistol — usu. written .32

thirty-two-foot octave \ˌ==ˌ=ˈ=-\ *n* : SUBCONTRAOCTAVE

thirty-two-foot pitch *n* : the pitch of a 32-foot stop on a pipe organ

thirty-two-foot stop *n* : a pipe-organ stop sounding pitches two octaves lower than the notes indicate — compare EIGHT-FOOT STOP

thirty-two-mo \ˌ==ˈ=ˌmō\ *n* [*thirty-two* + *-mo*] : the size of a piece of paper cut 32 from a sheet; *also* : paper or a page of this size — abbr. *32mo*; symbol *32°*; see BOOK tables

thirty-year man *n* : an enlisted man who plans to complete thirty years of military service

¹this \(ˈ)t͟his, t͟həs\ *pron, pl* **these** \(ˈ)t͟hēz\ [ME *this*, pron. & adj. (pl. *thes, these, thos, those*), fr. OE *thes* (masc.), *thēos* (fem.), *this* (neut.), pron. & adj. (pl. *thās, thās*); akin to OHG *dese, desēr* this, ON *thessi*; all fr. a prehistoric NGmc-WGmc pronoun whose first constituent is akin to OE *thæt* (neut. demonstrative pron. & definite article) and whose second constituent is prob. akin to OE *sē* (masc. demonstrative pron. & definite article) — more at THAT, THE] **1 a** (1) : the person, thing, or idea that is present or near in place, time, or thought, or that has just been mentioned ⟨~ is the twelfth of August⟩ ⟨*these* are my hands⟩ ⟨~ is a warmer welcome than I was expecting⟩ ⟨the plan has only two faults, but *these* are so serious that they may outweigh its merits⟩ — often used with a general reference to something stated or implied in the previous context but without particular reference to a noun or noun equivalent in that context ⟨in so far as those habits did change gradually over the century, ~ was thought to be due to a thing called progress —Christopher Hollis⟩ ⟨what he had to teach is far from clear, and ~ despite the fact that his prose style is extolled . . . for its marvelous simplicity —Irving Kristol⟩; often used in reference to a person as subject of a form of the verb *be* esp. in performing an introduction ⟨~ is my sister⟩ ⟨*these* are my sons⟩ (2) : what is stated in the following or the not yet completed phrase, clause, or discourse ⟨let me tell you ~: I have had feeling of my cousin's wrongs —Shak.⟩ ⟨a queer problem ~, of causing a character . . . to step out of the page —*Countryman*⟩ ⟨the demonstratives may, and ~ in most languages . . . hold up their nouns to censure or to blame —M.E.B.Charnley⟩ **b** : the present time : this time ⟨expected him to return before ~⟩ ⟨the time 'twixt ~ and supper —Shak.⟩ **c** : this place ⟨take yourself from ~, young fellow, or I'll maybe add a murder to my deeds today —J.M. Synge⟩ **2 a** (1) : the nearer one : the one more immediately under observation or discussion ⟨~ is iron and that is tin⟩ ⟨*these* are sparrows and those are robins⟩ — contrasted with *that* (2) : the latter — contrasted with *that* **b** : one thing — sometimes contrasted with *that;* sometimes used as first member of a 3-part series with *that* as the second member and *the other* as the third

²this \"\ *adj, pl* **these** [ME, fr. OE *thes, thēos, this*] **1 a** : being the person, thing, or idea that is present or near in place, time, or thought, or that has just been mentioned ⟨~ man sitting beside me is the one who made the highest bid⟩ ⟨~ book is mine⟩ ⟨~ moment⟩ ⟨entertaining a great deal *these* days⟩ ⟨one of the most memorable experiences I had in Europe ~ summer⟩ ⟨he is to enter college ~ fall⟩ ⟨*these* United States⟩ — used before a noun denoting a part of a day to indicate reference to the present day ⟨got up early ~ morning⟩ ⟨expecting to dine out with some friends ~ evening⟩; used before a noun denoting a day of the week to indicate reference to the next ensuing day so named ⟨going to make a business trip ~ Monday⟩; sometimes used before a noun denoting a person to form a phrase referring to the writer or speaker ⟨~ reviewer⟩ ⟨~ commentator⟩; sometimes used archaically before a combination of possessive adjective plus noun ⟨in ~ our country⟩, where the standard and fully current construction instead has the noun followed by *of* plus the corresponding possessive pronoun ⟨in ~ country of ours⟩ **b** : constituting the immediately following part of the present utterance or writing ⟨~ commandment we have from him, that he who loves God should love his brother also —1 Jn 4:21 (RSV)⟩ **c** : that is well known or much talked about esp. as being recent or in vogue ⟨~ existentialism⟩ ⟨*these* satellites⟩ — sometimes used disparagingly **d** : constituting the immediate past or the immediate future — used with expressions denoting a length of time ⟨after being friends all *these* years⟩ ⟨dinner has been waiting ~ half hour⟩ ⟨may your husband live *these* fifty years —R.B.Sheridan⟩ **e** (1) *these pl, obs* : SUCH ⟨under *these* hard conditions as this time is like to lay on us —Shak.⟩ (2) *these pl* : constituting such a number — used in the same construction with *many* ⟨the products of a technically adequate adjustment to reality constitute *these* many proofs of human potency —Weston La Barre⟩ **f** : being one not previously mentioned ⟨I was waiting for the bus and ~ old man came along and asked me for a dime⟩ ⟨gave me a light from ~ big lighter off the table —J.D.Salinger⟩ **2 a** : the nearer at hand : the more immediately under observation or discussion ⟨~ car or that one⟩ — contrasted with *that* **b** : a certain : ONE, SOME — sometimes contrasted with *that* ⟨turn his ship ~ way and that —C.S.Forester⟩; sometimes used as first member of a 3-part series with *that* as the second member and *the other* as the third ⟨~, that, or the other business —F.D.Roosevelt⟩

³this \"\ *adv* [ME, fr. ¹*this*] **1** *obs* : in this way : THUS **2** : to the degree or extent indicated by something immediately present : as this ⟨didn't expect to have to wait ~ long⟩ ⟨the fact that a novel about present-day Formosa could be quite ~ interesting seems odd —Margaret Parton⟩

⁴this \ˈthis\ *n, pl* **thises** *or* **thisses** [¹*this*] : one of the members and usu. the first of a pair or series — sometimes used with an initial capital to stand for a proper name which is not mentioned ⟨Lady *This* running an antique shop, and Madam That selling hats —*Spectator*⟩; contrasted with *that*

this and that *n* **1** : one thing and another ⟨weighing *this and that* —*New Yorker*⟩ **2** : a number of heterogeneous or pertinent things ⟨filling with cheese and a little chopped *this and that* —Anne Parrish⟩

this·a·way \ˈt͟hisəˌwā\ *adv* [alter. of the phrase *this way*] *dial* : in this manner or direction

this·ness \ˈt͟hisnəs\ *n* -ES [trans. of ML *haecceitas*] : the quality in a thing of being here and now or such as it is : the concrete objective reality of a thing : HAECCEITY

this·sen \ˈt͟hisᵊn\ *adv* [irreg. fr. ¹*this*] *dial Eng* : in this way : SO — sometimes used in the phrase *a thissen*

this·tle \ˈthisəl\ *n* -S [ME *thistel*, fr. OE; akin to OHG *distil* thistle, ON *thistill*, and perh. to Skt *tejate* it is sharp — more at STICK] **1 a** (1) : any of various prickly plants of the family Compositae and esp. of the genera *Carduus, Circium*, and *Onopordon* that are often segregated in the separate family Carduaceae — see SCOTCH THISTLE (2) : any of various similar plants of other sections of the family Compositae — see SOW THISTLE **b** : any of various prickly plants of families other than Compositae — usu. used with a qualifying adjective; see RUSSIAN THISTLE **2** *usu cap* : membership in the Scottish Order of the Thistle **3** : COBALT VIOLET 2

thistle

thistlebird \ˈ==ˌ=\ *n* : GOLDFINCH

thistle butterfly *n* : a showy butterfly (*Vanessa cardui*) whose larva eats thistles

thistle crown *n* : a gold coin of four shillings issued 1604 to 1612 by James I of England and having a Scotch thistle on the obverse

thistle cup *n* : a metal cup made esp. in 17th century Scotland and shaped somewhat like a thistle

thistle dollar *n* : a Scottish coin of the reign of James VI worth two marks and having a thistle on the reverse

thistledown \ˈ==ˌ=\ *n* : the pappus from the ripe flower head of a thistle

thistle family *n* : CARDUACEAE, COMPOSITAE

thistle finch *n* : GOLDFINCH 1

thistlelike \ˈ==ˌ=\ *adj* : resembling a thistle

thistle poppy *n* : PRICKLY POPPY

thistle saffron *n* : SAFFLOWER 1

thistle sage *n* : an annual woolly herb (*Salvia carduacea*) of the western U. S. yielding considerable honey

thistle-shaped \ˈ==ˌ=\ *adj* : suggesting the rounded swollen base of a typical flower head of a thistle

thistle tube *n* : a funnel tube usu. of glass with a bulging top and flaring mouth

this·tly \ˈthis(ə)lē\ *adj* **1** : resembling a thistle : PRICKLY, THORNY ⟨the contemplation of various ~ matters —John Woodburn⟩ **2** : consisting of or abounding in thistles

this world *n* [ME, fr. OE *thēos worold*] : the world known to living men; the world of here and now — compare OTHER-WORLD

this-world·li·ness \ˈ=ˈ===\ *n* [*this-worldly* + *-ness*] : interest in, concern with, or devotion to things of this world

this-world·ly \ˈ=ˈ==\ *adj* [*this world* + *-ly*] : characterized by or manifesting this-worldliness ⟨the struggle between *this-worldly* and otherworldly values —George Orwell⟩

¹thith·er \ˈthit͟hə(r) *also* ˈt͟hi-\ *adv* [ME *thither, thider*, fr. OE *thider*, prob. alter. (influenced by *hider* hither) of *thæder;* akin to ON *thathra* there, Skt *tatra* there, to that place; all fr. a prehistoric IE adverb whose first constituent is akin to OE *thæt* (neut. demonstrative pron. & definite article) and whose second constituent is represented by OE *-der* (in *hider*) — more at THAT, HITHER] **1** : to that place : THERE ⟨I shall go ~ to claim my reward —Allen Upward⟩ ⟨in transit ~ —W.P.Webb⟩ — compare HITHER **2** *obs* : to that end

²thither \"\ *adj* : being on the other and farther side more remote : FARTHER ⟨the ~ bank of a stream⟩ ⟨on the ~ side of forty⟩ — compare HITHER

thitherto \ˌ==ˈtü\ *adv* [ME *thider to*, fr. *thider* thither + *to*] : until that time : up to a past time specified or implied ⟨an approach to ~ unknown truth —G.W.Johnson⟩

thith·er·ward \ˈ== wə(r)d\ *also* **thith·er·wards** \-dz\ *adv* [*thitherward* fr. ME *thiderward*, fr. OE *thiderweard*, fr. *thider* thither + *-weard* -ward; *thitherwards* fr. ME *thiderwardes*, fr. OE *thiderweardes*, fr. *thiderweard* + *-es* -s] : toward that place : THITHER

thit·ka \ˈthitkə\ *n* -S [native name in Burma] : BURMA MAHOGANY

thi·u·ram \thīˈyůrəm, ˈthīyəˌram\ *n* -S [perh. irreg. fr. *thiourea* + *-amyl* (as in *carbamyl*)] **1 a** : THIOCARBAMOYL — used esp. in names of sulfides **b** : any of several organic derivatives of this radical R_2NCS— **2** : any of several thiuram sulfides (as tetraethylthiuram disulfide and tetramethylthiuram disulfide)

thi·u·ro·ni·um \ˌthīyəˈrōnēəm\ *also* **thio·uro·ni·um** \ˌthīōyəˈr-\ *n* -S [*thiur-* (as in *thiuram*) or *thiour-* (as in *thiourea*) + *-onium*] : the cation $[HSC(NH_2)_2]^+$ resulting from addition of a proton to thiourea; *esp* : any of its derivatives formed by adding organic halides to thiourea

thivel \ˈthīvəl, ˈthiv-, ˈthēv-\ *n* -S [ME *thyvelle*] *dial Brit* : a stick or spatula for stirring porridge or other food

thixo·trop·ic \ˌthiksəˈträpik\ *adj* : of, relating to, or exhibiting thixotropy ⟨~ ink⟩ ⟨mayonnaise, a good example of a ~ fluid —*Technical News Bull.*⟩

thix·ot·ro·py \thikˈsä·trəpē\ *n* -ES [ISV *thix-* (fr. Gk *thixis* action of touching, fr. *thinganein* to touch, handle) + *-o-* + *-tropy;* akin to L *fingere* to shape — more at DOUGH] : the property exhibited by various gels (as bentonite or paint containing pigment) of becoming fluid when shaken, stirred, or otherwise disturbed and of setting again to a gel when allowed to stand : a reversible gel-sol transformation under isothermal shearing stress followed by rest — compare FALSE BODY, RHEOPEXY

thk *abbr* thick

thlas·pi \ˈthlaˌspī, -ˌspē\ *n, cap* [NL, fr. L, shepherd's purse, fr. Gk] : a genus of herbs (family Cruciferae) native to temperate regions and distinguished by the sessile often orbicular pod with two or more seeds in each cell — see PENNYCRESS

thling·cha·din·ne \ˌthlinchəˈdinə, -nē\ *n, pl* **thlingchadinne** *or* **thlingchadinnes** *usu cap* [*Dēnē*, lit., dog flank] : DOGRIB

¹tho *var of* THOUGH

²tho \ˈtō\ *n, pl* **tho** *or* **thos** *usu cap* **1** : a Tai people of northern Tonkin and adjoining parts of the Chinese provinces of Yunnan and Kwangsi **2** : a member of the Tho people

thocht \ˈthäkt\ *chiefly Scot var of* THOUGHT

¹thoft \ˈthäft\ *n* -S [ME *thofte*, fr. OE; akin to MLG *ducht* rower's bench, OHG *dofta*, ON *thopta* rower's bench, and prob. to Lith *tupėti* to squat, crouch — more at THIEF] *dial Brit* : a rower's bench

²thoft \"\ *dial Eng var of* THOUGHT

¹thole \ˈthōl\ *vb* -ED/-ING/-S [ME *tholen*, fr. OE *tholian* — more at TOLERATE] *chiefly dial* : to endure esp. with patience or in silence : SUFFER, BEAR

²thole \"\ *also* **thow·el** \ˈthōəl\ *n* -S [ME *tholle* peg, fr. OE *thol* peg, thole for an oar; akin to MLG *dolle* thole for an oar, ON *thollr* peg, Gk *tylos* callus, knob, Skt *tavīti* he is strong — more at THUMB] : PEG, PIN; *specif* : a wooden or metal pin set in pairs in the gunwale of a boat to serve in place of an oarlock

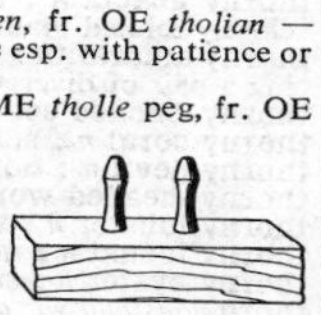
tholes

tholepin \ˈ=ˌ=\ *n* : a thole for an oar

thol·o·bate \ˈthäləˌbāt\ *n* -S [Gk *tholos* rotunda + *-batēs* one that goes — more at DALE, -BATES] : the base of a dome

tho·loid \ˈthōˌlȯid\ *n* -S [Gk *tholos* + E *-oid*, n. suffix] : a rounded dome-shaped mass of lava rising above the surface of a lava flow or crater floor

tho·los \ˈthōˌläs\ *or* **tho·lus** \-ōləs\ *n, pl* **tho·loi** \-ōˌlȯi\ *or* **tho·li** \-ōˌlī\ [Gk & L; L *tholus* rotunda, tholos, fr. Gk *tholos*] **1** : a round building of classical Greek date and style **2** : a circular tomb of beehive shape approached by a horizontal passage in the side of a hill

tho·mae·an *or* **tho·me·an** \tōˈmēən, thō-\ *n* -S [prob. fr. (assumed) NL *thomaeus* of or belonging to Thomas (fr. LL *Thomas* Thomas, one of Jesus' twelve apostles) + E *-an*] *usu cap* : a member of the Mar Thoma Church in southwestern India that claims the apostle Thomas as its founder

thom·as \ˈtäməs\ *n* -ES *usu cap* : DOUBTING THOMAS

thom·as-gil·christ process \ˈtäməsˈgilkrəst-\ *or* **thomas process** *n, usu cap T&G* [after Sidney G. *Thomas* †1885 and Percy C. *Gilchrist* †1935 Eng. metallurgists who invented it] : the basic Bessemer process

thom·as·ing \ˈtäməsiŋ\ *n* -S [*Thomas*, one of Jesus' twelve apostles + E *-ing*] *Brit* : begging from house to house on St. Thomas' Day, Dec. 21

thom·as·ite \ˈtäməˌsīt\ *n* -S *usu cap* [John *Thomas* †1871 Am. physician and religious leader + E *-ite*] : CHRISTADELPHIAN

thomas meal *n, usu cap T* [after Sidney G. *Thomas* †1885 Eng. metallurgist] : basic slag ground for use as a fertilizer

thomas precession *n, usu cap T* [after L. H. *Thomas b*1903 Am. physicist (born in England) who discovered it] : a precessional motion of the spin axis of an orbital electron caused by the interaction between the electron spin and the electric field of the nucleus

thomas slag *or* **thomas phosphate** *n, usu cap T* [after Sidney G. *Thomas* †1885 Eng. metallurgist] : BASIC SLAG

thomas splint *n, usu cap T* [after Hugh Owen *Thomas* †1891 Eng. surgeon] : a metal splint for fractures of the arm or leg that consists of a ring at one end to fit around the upper arm or leg and two metal shafts extending down the sides of the limb in a long U with a crosspiece at the bottom where traction is applied

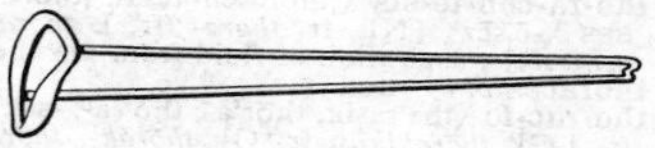
Thomas splint

¹tho·mi·sid \ˈthōməsəd\ *adj* [NL *Thomisidae*] : of or relating to the Thomisidae

²thomisid \"\ *n* -S [NL *Thomisidae*] : a crab spider of the family Thomisidae

tho·mis·i·dae \thōˈmisəˌdē\ *n pl, cap* [NL, fr. *Thomisus*, type genus (irreg. fr. Gk *thōminx* cord, string) + *-idae*; fr. their drawing single threads — more at FUNICULUS] : a widely distributed family of spiders that spin no webs, usu. have the first two pairs of legs much longer than the last two pairs, and comprise the crab spiders

tho·mism \ˈtōˌmizəm *sometimes* ˈtä,-\ *n* -S *usu cap* [prob. fr. (assumed) NL *thomismus*, fr. *Thomas* Aquinas †1274 Ital. scholastic philosopher + L *-ismus* -ism] **1** : the system of Thomas Aquinas teaching that philosophy and theology have separate spheres with one seeking truth through the agency of reason and the other through that of revelation but reaching conclusions that support each other, that all knowledge begins with sense perception from the data of which the intellect abstracts universals and on the basis of these proceeds through deduction and induction to science or knowledge of things in their causes and thence to knowledge of ultimate causality and the conclusion that the universe is the creation of an infinite uncreated Being, that everything in nature is composed of matter and form with the potentiality of the former being brought to actuality by the latter, that everything that is natural is good in itself and a cause of evil only when used for ends other than those for which it was created or beyond the limits prescribed by sound reason or divine law, and that because of his rational nature man is compelled by necessity to seek the highest good **2** : a theological theory deriving from Thomas Aquinas that explains the relation between efficacious grace and free will as a free determination of the will accomplished by virtue of a divine physical premotion — compare MOLINISM

¹tho·mist \-məst\ *n* -S *usu cap* [ML *thomista*, fr. *Thomas* Aquinas + L *-ista* -ist] : an adherent of Thomas Aquinas or of Thomism

²thomist \"\ *or* **tho·mis·tic** \tōˈmistik\ *adj, usu cap* [*thomist* fr. ¹*thomist; thomistic* fr. NL *thomisticus*, fr. ML *thomista* + L *-icus* -ic] : of or relating to Thomism or Thomists

tho·mite \ˈtōˌmīt, ˈthō-\ *n* -S *usu cap* [*Thomas*, one of Jesus' twelve apostles + E *-ite*] : THOMAEAN

tho·mo·mys \ˈthōməˌmis\ *n, cap* [NL, fr. Gk *thōmos* heap + NL *-mys;* fr. the heaps of earth thrown out along the burrows; akin to Gk *tithenai* to place, set — more at DO] : a genus of rodents (family Geomyidae) comprising the pocket gophers of western No. America

thomp·son \ˈtäm(p)sən\ *n, pl* **thompson** *or* **thompsons** *usu cap* [*Thompson* river, southern British Columbia, Canada] **1 a** : a Salishan people of the Fraser river valley, British Columbia **b** : a member of such people **2** : the language of the Thompson people

thompson river indian *n, usu cap T&R&I* : THOMPSON 1b

thompson submachine gun *n, usu cap T* [after John T. *Thompson* †1940 Am. army officer who invented it in collaboration with John Blish †1921 Am. naval officer] : a light portable automatic weapon fed from a magazine or drum and provided with a pistol grip and a buttstock for firing from the shoulder

thom·sen·o·lite \ˈtäm(p)sənəˌlīt\ *n* -S [Julius *Thomsen* †1909 Dan. chemist + E *-o-* + *-lite*] : a mineral $NaCaAlF_6.H_2O$ consisting of a hydrous fluoride of aluminum, calcium, and sodium and occurring in small white prismatic monoclinic crystals on cryolite

thom·son coefficient \ˈtäm(p)sən-\ *n, usu cap T* [after William *Thomson* (Baron Kelvin) †1907 Brit. mathematician and physicist] : the Thomson electromotive force per degree of temperature

thomson effect *or* **thomson heat** *n, usu cap T* : a redistribution of temperature differences along an otherwise homogeneous strip of metal due to an electric current passing through it — called also *Kelvin effect* — see THOMSON ELECTROMOTIVE FORCE

thomson electromotive force *n, usu cap T* : a difference of electric potential associated with difference of temperature between different parts of an otherwise homogeneous strip of metal arising from the Thomson effect

thom·so·ni·an \tämˈsōnēən\ *adj, usu cap* [James *Thomson* †1748 Scot. poet + E *-an*] : of, relating to, or having the characteristics of James Thomson or his writings ⟨*Thomsonian* blank verse⟩

thom·son·ite \ˈtäm(p)səˌnīt\ *n* -S [Thomas *Thomson* †1852 Scot. chemist + E *-ite*] : a mineral $NaCa_2Al_5Si_5O_{20}.6H_2O$ of the zeolite family consisting of a hydrous silicate of aluminum, calcium, and sodium, occurring generally in masses of a radiated structure or rarely in distinct orthorhombic crystals, and being snow-white when pure (hardness 5–5.5)

thomson process *n, usu cap T* [after Elihu *Thomson* †1937 Am. electrician and inventor] : a process of electric welding in which heat is developed by a large current passing through the metal

thomson's gazelle *n, usu cap T* [after Joseph *Thomson* †1895 Scot. explorer] : an East African gazelle (*Gazella thomsoni*) that is the smallest of the gazelles

thomson's hypothesis *n, usu cap T* [after Sir George Paget *Thomson b*1892 Eng. physicist] : a theory in physics: an atom consists of a large number of electrons held together by a mass with a positive charge equal to the sum of the negative charges of the electrons

¹thon \ˈthän\ *pron* [alter. (influenced by ¹*this* and ¹*that*) of *yon*, pron.] *chiefly Scot* : the one yonder : ¹THAT

²thon \"\ *adj, chiefly Scot* : being the one yonder : ²THAT

thon·der \ˈthändə(r)\ *adv or adj* [by alter. (influenced by *thon*)] *chiefly Scot* : YONDER

thon·draki \thänˈdrakī\ *n* -S *also* **thon·drak·i·ans** \-akēənz\ *or* **thon·dra·cians** \-rāshənz\ *n pl, cap* [*thondraki* prob. fr. (assumed) MGk *thondrakoi*, fr. *Thondrak*, town in Armenia that was the headquarters of Smbat, 9th cent. Armenian theologian;

thondrakians, thondracians fr. *Thondrak* + E *-ans* (pl. of *-an*, n. suffix)] **:** a group of Armenian Paulicians founded by Smbat of Thondrak in the 9th century

¹thong \'thȯŋ *also* 'thäŋ\ *n* -s [ME *thong, thwong, thwang,* fr. OE *thwang, thwong;* akin to MLG *dwenge* ferrule, ON *thvengr* thong, latchet, OE *gethwinglod* fastened up, OHG *dwingan* to oppress, overcome, compel, ON *thvinga* to oppress, burden, Av *thwązjaiti* he becomes distressed] **1 a :** a strap or strip of leather or hide used as a whiplash or a rein **b :** a strip of leather or hide used for fastening something (as a snowshoe or sandal) **2 :** a root cutting

²thong \"\ *vt* -ED/-ING/-S [ME *thongen,* fr. *thong,* n.] **1 :** to furnish or fasten with a thong **2 :** to lash with a thong

thon·ga \'täŋgə\ *n, pl* **thonga** *or* **thongas** *usu cap* **:** RONGA

thong seal *n* [so called fr. the use of its hide for leather lines] **:** BEARDED SEAL

thon·nier \tō'nyā\ *n* -s [F, fr. *thon* tuna — more at TUNNY] **:** a Breton sailing boat used in fishing for tuna

thon·zyl·a·mine \thän'zilə,mēn, -,mən\ *n* [prob. fr. *methoxy-* + *benzyl* + *amine*] **:** an antihistaminic drug $C_{16}H_{22}N_4O$ derived from pyrimidine and used in the form of its crystalline hydrochloride

¹tho·oid \'thō,ȯid\ *adj* [Gk *thōs* jackal + E *-oid;* akin to L *faunus* faun — more at FAUN] **:** resembling a wolf — used of a wolf, dog, or jackal as distinguished from the foxes or alopecoid members of the genus *Canis*

²thooid \"\ *n* -s **:** a thooid canine

thorac- *or* **thoraci-** *or* **thoraco-** *comb form* [F *thorac-,* fr. LGk *thōrak-,* fr. Gk *thōrak-, thōrako-,* corslet, fr. *thōrak-, thōrax* corslet, chest — more at THORAX] **1 :** chest **:** thorax ⟨*thoracodynia*⟩ ⟨*thoracoplasty*⟩ **2 :** thoracic and ⟨*thoracispinal*⟩ ⟨*thoracolumbar*⟩

tho·ra·cen·te·sis \,thōrəsen'tēsə̇s, ,thȯr-\ *n, pl* **thoracenteses** \-ē,sēz\ [NL, fr. *thora-* (fr. L *thorax* chest, thorax) + *centesis*] **:** aspiration of fluid from the chest (as in empyema)

thoraces *pl of* THORAX

tho·rac·ic \thə'rasik, thȯr'a-, thō'ra-, -sēk\ *adj* [F *thoracique,* fr. LGk *thōrakikos,* fr. Gk *thōrak-, thōrax* corslet, chest + *-ikos* -ic] **1 :** of, relating to, located within, or involving the thorax **2** *of a pelvic fin* **:** placed under the corresponding pectoral fin and connected with the pectoral girdle

tho·rac·i·ca \-sə̇kə\ *n pl, cap* [NL, fr. *thoracica,* neut. pl. of *thoracicus* thoracic, fr. LGk *thōrakikos*] **:** a division of Cirripedia including barnacles that have six thoracic segments usu. bearing six pairs of cirri

tho·rac·i·cal \-kəl\ *adj* [*thoracic* + *-al*] *archaic* **:** THORACIC

thoracic aorta *n* **:** the part of the aorta extending beyond the arch and lying in the thorax

thoracic artery *n* **:** any of several branches of the axillary artery supplying the pectoral muscles, walls of the thorax, axilla, and adjacent parts

thoracic cage *n* **:** RIB CAGE

thoracic cavity *n* **:** the division of the body cavity of a warm-blooded vertebrate lying anterior to or above the diaphragm, bounded peripherally by the wall of the chest, and containing the heart and lungs

thoracic choke *n* **:** obstruction of the thoracic part of the esophagus of horses or cattle resulting in choking or asphyxia due to pressure on the trachea

thoracic duct *n* **:** the main trunk of the system of lymphatic vessels lying along the front of the spinal column, extending from a dilatation behind the aorta and opposite the second lumbar vertebra up through the thorax where it turns to the left and opens into the left subclavian vein, and receiving chyle from the intestine and lymph from the abdomen, the lower limbs, and the entire left side of the body

thoracic nerve *n* **1 :** any of several nerves arising from the brachial plexus and supplying chiefly muscles of the walls of the thorax **2 :** a spinal nerve emerging just below a thoracic vertebra

tho·rac·i·co·acromial \thə,rasə̇(,)kō+\ *adj* [*thoracic* + *-o-* + *acromial*] **:** of, relating to, or lying between the thorax and the acromial process of the scapula

thoracicoacromial artery *n* **:** a short branch of the axillary artery supplying the deltoid, pectoral, and serratus anterior muscles

tho·rac·i·co·lumbar \"+\ *or* **tho·ra·co·lumbar** \;thōrə(,)kō, ;thȯrə(,)kō+\ *adj* [*thoracicolumbar* fr. *thoracic* + *-o-* + *lumbar; thoracolumbar* fr. *thorac-* + *lumbar*] **:** of, relating to, arising in, or involving the thoracic and lumbar regions; *often* **:** SYMPATHETIC ⟨~ nerve fibers⟩

thoracic vertebra *n* **:** any of the vertebrae dorsal to the thoracic region and characterized by articulation with the ribs ⟨there are 12 *thoracic vertebrae* in man⟩ — called also *dorsal vertebra*

tho·raci·spinal \thə,rasə̇+\ *adj* [*thorac-* + *spinal*] **:** of or relating to the thoracic part of the spinal column or cord

tho·ra·co·dorsal \;thōrə(,)kō, ;thȯrə(,)kō+\ *adj* [*thorac-* + *dorsal*] **:** of, relating to, or lying in the dorsal aspect of the thorax

tho·ra·co·dyn·ia \,thōrəkə'dinēə, ,thȯr-\ *n* -s [NL, fr. *thorac-* + *-odynia*] **:** pain in the chest

tho·ra·cop·a·gus \,thōrə'käpəgəs, ,thȯr-\ *n, pl* **thoracopaguses** \-səz\ *or* **thoracopa·gi** \-pə,jī\ [NL, fr. *thorac-* + *-pagus*] **:** Siamese twins joined at the thorax

tho·ra·co·plas·ty \'thōrəkō,plastē, 'thȯr-\ *n* -ES [ISV *thorac-* + *-plasty*] **:** the surgical operation of removing or resecting one or more ribs so as to obliterate the pleural space and collapse a diseased lung (as to accomplish immobilization) — compare COLLAPSE THERAPY

tho·ra·co·scope \thə'rakə,skōp, -'rak-\ *n* [ISV *thorac-* + *-scope*] **:** an instrument fitted with a lighting system and telescopic attachment, designed to permit visual inspection within the chest cavity and treatment under visual control, and inserted through a puncture in the chest wall in an intercostal space — **tho·ra·co·scop·ic** \;=;=;skäpik\ *adj*

tho·ra·cos·tei \,thōrə'kästē,ī, ,thȯr-\ *n pl, cap* [NL, fr. *thorac-* + *-ostei* (fr. Gk *osteon* bone) — more at OSSEOUS] *in some classifications* **:** an order comprising fishes with the body more or less completely covered by bony plates and the pharyngeal bones and other structures about the head more or less undeveloped and including the sticklebacks, pipefishes, and sea horses

tho·ra·cos·to·my \,thōrə'kästəmē, ,thȯr-\ *n* -ES [ISV *thorac-* + *-stomy*] **:** surgical opening of the chest (as for drainage)

tho·ra·cos·tra·ca \,thōrə'kästrəkə, ,thȯr-\ [NL, fr. *thorac-* + *-ostraca*] *syn of* PODOPHTHALMIA

tho·ra·cot·o·my \,thōrə'kädəmē, ,thȯr-\ *n* -ES [ISV *thorac-* + *-tomy*] **:** surgical incision of the chest wall

tho·rax \'thōr,aks, -ȯr-\ *n, pl* **thoraxes** \-səz\ *or* **tho·ra·ces** \'thōrə,sēz, -ȯr *also* thə'rā,s-\ [NL, fr. L, corslet, chest, fr. Gk *thōrax;* perh. akin to Skt *dhārayati* he holds, carries, keeps — more at FIRM] **1 :** the part of the body of man and other mammals situated between the neck and the abdomen and supported by the ribs, costal cartilages, and sternum; *also* **:** THORACIC CAVITY **2** [NL, fr. L] **a :** a portion of the insect body that is the middle of the three chief divisions of the body and that consists of three segments each commonly bearing a pair of legs and the last two each usu. bearing a pair of wings in the adult **b :** the corresponding part of a crustacean or arachnid usu. fused with the head to form a cephalothorax **c :** the anterior division of the body of a zooid of a compound ascidian comprising the branchial sac and surrounding atrium **d :** an anterior differentiated part of the body behind the head of many tubicolous polychaete worms **3 :** BREASTPLATE, CUIRASS, CORSLET; *esp* **:** the breastplate worn by the ancient Greeks

tho·reau·lite \'thōrō,līt\ *n* -s [F, fr. Jacques *Thoreau* b1886 Belg. mineralogist + F *-lite*] **:** a mineral $SnTa_2O_7$ consisting of an oxide of tin and tantalum

tho·reau·vi·an \thə'rōvēən\ *adj, usu cap* [Henry David *Thoreau* †1862 Am. writer + E *-v-* (as in *peruvian*) + *-an*] **:** of, relating to, or having the characteristics of Thoreau or his writings ⟨often wanted to go and live a *Thoreauvian* life —Charles Poore⟩

tho·ria \'thōrēə\ *n* -s [NL, fr. *thorium* + *-a*] **:** THORIUM OXIDE

tho·ri·a·nite \-ēə,nīt\ *n* -s [*thoria* + connective *-n-* + *-ite*] **:** a strongly radioactive mineral ThO_2 that is an oxide of thorium isomorphous with uraninite and often contains rare-earth metals

tho·ri·ate \-ē,āt\ *vt* -ED/-ING/-S [*thoria* + *-ate*] **:** to impregnate (an electron-tube cathode) with thoria in order to increase the thermionic emission

thor·ic \'thȯrik, 'thär-, 'thōr-\ *adj* [ISV *thor-* (fr. NL *thorium*) + *-ic*] **:** of, relating to, or containing thorium

tho·rif·er·ous \thə'rif(ə)rəs\ *adj* [*thorium* + *-iferous*] **:** containing or yielding thorium

tho·rite \'thōr,īt\ *n* -s [Sw *thorit,* fr. NL *thorium* + Sw *-it* -ite] **:** a rare mineral $ThSiO_4$ that is a brown to black or sometimes orange-yellow thorium silicate resembling zircon but usu. metamict (sp. gr. 4.5–5.4)

tho·ri·um \'thōrēəm, 'thȯr-\ *n* -s [NL, fr. *Thor,* Norse god of thunder + NL *-ium*] **:** a radioactive tetravalent metallic element that occurs combined in minerals (as monazite and thorite) and usu. associated with rare earths and principally as the isotope of mass number 232 having a half-life of 1.39×10^{10} years and emitting alpha particles to form mesothorium 1, that is obtained by reduction of its compounds as a pyrophoric gray powder or a heavy malleable metal changing from silvery white to dark gray or black in air, and that is used chiefly with tungsten or nickel electrodes in gas-discharge lamps and for conversion to fissionable uranium of mass number 233 by the absorption of neutrons and gamma rays — symbol *Th;* see ACTINIUM SERIES, THORIUM SERIES, URANIUM SERIES; ELEMENT table

thorium emanation *n* **:** THORON

thorium nitrate *n* **:** an oxidizing salt $Th(NO_3)_4$ obtained as a deliquescent crystalline mass by extraction of monazite sand in a series of steps and used chiefly in producing thorium oxide by ignition in the manufacture of incandescent gas mantles

thorium oxide *or* **thorium dioxide** *n* **:** a refractory crystalline compound ThO_2 obtained usu. as a dense white powder by igniting thorium nitrate and used chiefly in incandescent gas mantles, in crucibles and refractories, in silica-free optical glass, and in catalysts — called also *thoria*

thorium series *n* **:** a radioactive series beginning with thorium of mass number 232 and ending with thorium D which is the nonradioactive isotope of lead of mass number 208: thorium, at. no. 90 → mesothorium 1, at. no. 88 (syn. radium 228) → mesothorium 2, at. no. 89 (syn. actinium 228) → radiothorium, at. no. 90 (syn. thorium 228) → thorium X, at. no. 88, (syn. radium 224) → thoron, at. no. 86 (syn radon 220) → thorium A, at. no. 84 (syn. polonium 216) → thorium B, at. no. 82 (syn. lead 212) [or astatine 216] → thorium C, at. no. 83 (syn. bismuth 212) → thorium C′, at. no. 84 (syn. polonium 212) [or thorium C″, at. no. 81 (syn. thallium 208)] → thorium D, at. no. 82 (syn. lead 208)

¹thorn \'thȯ(ə)rn, -ȯ(ə)n\ *n* -s *often attrib* [ME, fr. OE; akin to OHG *dorn* thorn, ON *thorn,* Goth *thaurnus* thorn, Skt *tṛṇa* grass, blade of grass] **1 a :** a woody plant bearing briers, prickles, spines, or other sharp impeding process **b :** a plant of the genus *Crataegus:* as (1) **:** HAWTHORN (2) **:** PEAR HAW **c :** the wood of a thorn; *esp* **:** the tough hard wood of a hawthorn or blackthorn **d :** a growth or thicket of thorn **2 a :** a sharp rigid process on a plant; *specif* **:** a short, indurated, sharp-pointed, and leafless branch developed from a bud in a manner typical to a leafy branch — compare PRICKLE, SPINE **b :** any of various sharp spinose structures on an animal (as the spines of a sea urchin's test) **c :** something that affects like a thorn (as by pricking, stinging, or hurting) **:** a cause of irritation or source of distress ⟨had been a nagging ~ to her husband through 40 years of marriage⟩ **3** [ME, runic letter þ, thorn (plant), thorn (process on a plant), fr. OE] **:** the runic letter þ used in Old English and Middle English for either of the sounds of Modern English *th* (as in *thin, then*) and in Icelandic in early use for either of the same two sounds but in modern use only for *th* as in *thin* — see ANGLO-SAXON ALPHABET; compare EDH

²thorn \"\ *vt* -ED/-ING/-S [ME *thornen,* fr. *thorn,* n.] **1 :** to cause to be thorny; *esp* **:** to provide (as a newly set hedge) with a protection of thorny brush **2 :** to prick with or as if with a thorn **:** ANNOY, IRRITATE, HARASS

thorn apple *n* **1 a :** the fruit of a hawthorn **:** HAW **b :** a plant that produces thorn apples **2 :** a plant of the genus *Datura; esp* **:** JIMSONWEED

thornback \'=,=\ *n* [ME *thornebakk,* fr. *thorne, thorn* thorn + *bakk, bak* back] **1 a :** any of various rays having spines on the back **b :** THREE-SPINED STICKLEBACK **2 :** a large European spider crab (*Maja squinado*) **3** *archaic* **:** SPINSTER 3

thornback ray *n* **:** a common European ray (*Raja clavata*) having several large curved spines on the back and tail

thornbill \'=,=\ *n* **1 :** any of several small brilliant So. American hummingbirds of the genera *Ramphomicron* and *Chalcostigma* that have a long slender sharp bill and feed on honey, insects, and the juice of sugarcane **2 :** any of several small Australian warblers of the genus *Acanthiza*

thornbush \'=,=\ *n* [ME *thorn busk,* fr. ¹*thorn* + *bush, busk* bush] **1 :** any of various spiny or thorny shrubs or small trees: as **a :** ¹THORN 1b **b :** WHITETHORN 3 **c :** any of various shrubby and thorny African or Australian acacias **2 :** a low growth of thorny shrubs esp. of dry tropical regions (as in southern Africa and parts of Brazil) — compare THORN FOREST

thorned \-nd\ *adj* **:** having or abounding in thorns or thornbushes **:** THORNY

thorn forest *n* **:** a tropical xerophytic savanna woodland commonly dominated by small thorny trees

thorn-headed worm \'=,=-\ *n* **:** ACANTHOCEPHALAN

thorn hedge *n* **:** a hedge of thornbushes; *esp* **:** a hawthorn hedge — **thorn-hedged** \'=,=\ *adj*

thorn·i·ly \'thȯ(r)nᵊlē, -n'lī, -nəl-\ *adv* **:** so as to be thorny **:** in the manner of a thorn

thorn·i·ness \-nēnə̇s, -nin-\ *n* -ES **:** the quality or state of being thorny

thorn·less \'thȯrnlə̇s\ *adj* **:** free from thorns — **thorn·less·ness** *n* -ES

thorn·let \-lə̇t\ *n* -s **:** a minute thorn

thornlike \'=,=\ *adj* **:** resembling a thorn esp. in sharpness or irritating quality

thorn locust *n* **:** HONEY LOCUST

thorn needle *n* **:** a phonograph needle made of cactus spine

thorn oyster *n* **:** SPINY OYSTER

thorn palm *n* **:** any of various palms (as of the genera *Bactris, Acrocomia,* and *Astrocaryum*) with spiny trunks; *also* **:** any of various hook climbers (as of the genera *Desmoncus* and *Calamus*)

thorn plum *n* **1 :** THORN APPLE 1 **2 :** a rough or spiny American wild plum

thorn poppy *n* **:** PRICKLY POPPY

thorntail \'=,=\ *n* **:** any of several Neotropical hummingbirds of the genus *Popelairia; esp* **:** a hummingbird (*P. conversii*) whose tail is deeply forked with the outer feathers slender and pointed

thorn tree *n* [ME *thorne tree,* fr. *thorne, thorn* thorn + *tree*] **:** any of various thorny or spiny trees: as **a :** HAWTHORN **b :** HONEY LOCUST **c** *Africa* **:** a spiny arborescent acacia

thorny \'thȯrnē, -ȯ(ə)n-, -ni\ *adj* -ER/-EST [ME, fr. OE *thornig,* fr. ¹*thorn* + *-ig* -y] **1 :** full of thorns or spines or thornbushes **:** rough or thick with thorns **:** SPINY, BRAMBLY ⟨a ~ bush⟩ ⟨~ ground⟩ **2 a :** beset with trials, vexations, obstacles, or other difficulties ⟨the steep and ~ way to heaven —Shak.⟩ **b :** sharp as a thorn **:** keenly distressing **:** STABBING ⟨~ cares⟩ **c :** as difficult to handle as a thorny branch or a thornbush **:** bristling with perplexities, points of controversy, or other conflicting elements ⟨the ~ question of states' rights⟩

thorny acacia *n* **:** any of various notably thorny acacias or closely related plants (as a honey locust)

thorny amaranth *n* **:** an amaranth (*Amaranthus spinosus*) having a pair of divergent spines at most of its leaf nodes

thorny-backed eel \'=,=-\ *n* **:** SPINY EEL

thorny coral *n* **:** BLACK CORAL

thorny devil *n* **:** MOLOCH 2b

thorny-headed worm \'=,=-\ *n* **:** ACANTHOCEPHALAN

thorny lobster *n* **:** SPINY LOBSTER

thorny locust *n* **:** HONEY LOCUST

thorny oyster *n* **:** SPINY OYSTER

thoro *nonstand var of* THOROUGH

tho·ro·gummite \,thōrə'gə,mīt, ,thȯr-\ *n* [*thorium* + *-o-* + *gummite*] **:** a decomposition mineral approximately $Th_2(UO_2)Si_3O_{11}.3H_2O$ that is a hydrous silicate of thorium and uranium

tho·ron \'thō,rän, 'thȯ,rän\ *n* -s [NL, fr. *thor-* (fr. *thorium*) + *-on*] **:** a heavy radioactive gaseous isotope of the group of inert gases that is isotopic with radon and actinon, is formed by disintegration of thorium, emits alpha rays, and has a half-life of less than a minute (mass number 220) — called also *thorium emanation;* see THORIUM SERIES

Tho·ro·trast \'thōrə,trast\ *trademark* — used for a suspension of thorium oxide used as a radiopaque medium

¹thor·ough \'thər·(,)ō, 'thər·ə, 'thə·(,)rō, 'thə·rə *sometimes* 'thō(,)rō *or* -,rō; -rəw *or* -·rəw *or* -,rō +V\ *prep* [ME *thorugh, thorw, thorow,* fr. OE *thuruh, thurh,* prep. & adv. — more at THROUGH] *archaic* **:** THROUGH ⟨~ the fog it came —S.T. Coleridge⟩

²thorough \"\ *adv* [ME *thorugh, thorw, thorow,* fr. OE *thuruh, thurh,* prep. & adv.] **1** *archaic* **:** THROUGH ⟨the plowshare drawn ~ —A.C.Swinburne⟩ **2** *dial chiefly Brit* **:** THOROUGHLY ⟨a ~ good sort —Virginia Woolf⟩

³thorough \"\ *adj, sometimes* -ER/-EST [ME *thorow,* fr. *thorugh, thorw, thorow,* adv.] **1 :** marked by completeness: as **a** (1) **:** carried through to completion esp. with full attention to details **:** COMPLETE ⟨a ~ search⟩ ⟨drastic ~ intensive reform —J.G. Harrison⟩ (2) **:** marked by attention to many details ⟨the very ~ description of the country —G.F.Hudson⟩; *esp* **:** marked by sound systematic attention to all aspects and details ⟨completed ~ courses in mathematics —H.H.Arnold & I.C.Eaker⟩ ⟨his ~ grasp of economic matters —Alexander Brady⟩ (3) **:** complete in all respects ⟨the performance is a ~ delight —Brooks Atkinson⟩ **b** (1) **:** characterized by mastery (as of a profession or an art) ⟨a ~ musician⟩ (2) **:** having all the typical qualities ⟨were both ~ children of the Renaissance —Gamaliel Bradford⟩ (3) **:** careful about all details ⟨is not brilliant but he is very ~ —O.W.Holmes †1935⟩ **2 :** passing through — **thor·ough·ly** \-r·lē -·rə-, -li\ *adv* — **thor·ough·ness** *n* -ES

⁴thorough \"\ *n* -s *usu cap* **:** a thorough policy or action; *esp* **:** a thorough and tyrannical political policy (as in 17th century England)

thorough-band \'=,=,=\ *n* **:** PERPEND 1

thorough bass *n* **:** CONTINUO

thorough-bind \'=,=,=\ *vt* **:** to bind with a perpend

thor·ough·brace \-r·ə,brās, -·rə,-\ *n* **1 :** one of several leather straps supporting the body of a carriage and serving as springs **2 :** a vehicle (as a stagecoach) that is supported on thoroughbraces

¹thor·ough·bred \-,bred\ *adj* **1 a :** thoroughly trained or skilled ⟨a ~ soldier who weighs all contingencies⟩ **b :** THOROUGH, COMPLETE, GENUINE ⟨a ~ sailor —Herman Melville⟩ **2 :** bred from the best blood through a long line **:** PUREBLOOD, PUREBRED — used of domestic animals **3** [²*thoroughbred*] **a** *usu cap* **:** of, relating to, or being a member of the breed of horses called Thoroughbred **b** (1) **:** having characteristics resembling those of a Thoroughbred **:** GRACEFUL, ELEGANT, CULTIVATED, ARISTOCRATIC ⟨more ~ or fairer fingers —Lord Byron⟩ ⟨a beautifully . . . ~ piece of work moving with . . . conscious but quiet assurance —M.R.Ridley⟩ (2) **:** FIRST-CLASS ⟨the stability and accuracy of the ~ sports car —*Country Life*⟩ — **thor·ough·bred·ness** *n* -ES

²thoroughbred \"\ *n* **1** *usu cap* **a :** an English breed of light speedy horses kept chiefly for racing and originating from crosses between English mares of uncertain ancestry and Arabian stallions imported about the end of the 17th century **b** -s **:** a horse of this breed **2** -s **:** a purebred or pedigreed animal **3** -s **:** one that has characteristics resembling those of a Thoroughbred: as **a :** a thoroughbred person **b :** a first-class vehicle

¹thor·ough·fare \-,fa(a)(ə)r, -,fe|, |ə\ *n* [ME *thoruhfare,* fr. *thoruh, thorugh, thorw, thorow* through + *fare* passage — more at THOROUGH, FARE] **1 :** a way or place through which there is passing: as **a** *archaic* **:** a town through which considerable traffic passes **b** (1) **:** a street that goes through from one street to another (2) **:** an unobstructed way open to the public (3) **:** an important street or highway **c** (1) **:** a waterway (as a river or strait) used for travel or shipping (2) **:** a waterway usu. without flowage between two bodies of water (as lakes) **2 a :** the action of passing through **:** PASSAGE, TRANSIT ⟨hell and this world, one realm, one continent of easy ~ —John Milton⟩ **b :** the conditions necessary for passing through ⟨a streetcar came, jerked to a stop just at the bumper, and clanged for ~ —Margaret Avison⟩

²thoroughfare \"\ *vt* **:** to pass through ⟨those slits that *thoroughfared* the older town —J.R.Lowell⟩

thoroughfoot \'=,=,=\ *vt* -ED/-ING/-S **:** to straighten (twisted rope) by coiling

thoroughgoing \;=;=;=\ *adj* **:** marked by thoroughness or zeal **:** going the full length **:** THOROUGH, EXTREME ⟨the most ~ democrat of his generation —V.L.Parrington⟩ ⟨reconstruction will require ~ cooperation between industry and labor —F.D. Roosevelt⟩ — **thor·ough·go·ing·ly** *adv* — **thor·ough·go·ing·ness** *n* -ES

thorough light *n* **1 thorough lights** *pl, archaic* **:** windows on opposite sides of a room **2** *archaic* **:** a light that passes through

thorough-paced \;=;=;=\ *adj* **1 :** thoroughly trained **:** ACCOMPLISHED ⟨a *thorough-paced* politician⟩ **2 :** THOROUGH, COMPLETE ⟨only a *thorough-paced* rotter would have made such a suggestion —Margaret Kennedy⟩ ⟨his reforms were too *thorough-paced* —*Times Lit. Supp.*⟩

thoroughpin \'=,=,=\ *n* [so called fr. the appearance of the swelling as if a peg were sticking through the leg and causing the skin to bulge on each side] **:** a synovial dilatation just above the hock of the horse on both sides of the leg and slightly anterior to the hamstring tendon that is often associated with lameness

thoroughsped \;=;=;=\ *adj* **:** THOROUGH-PACED

thoroughstem \'=,=,=\ *n* **:** a boneset (*Eupatorium perfoliatum*)

¹thorough-stitch \'=,=,=\ *adv* [prob. fr. the phrase *thorough stitch* fr. ¹*thorough* + *stitch,* n.] *archaic* **:** all the way through ⟨obliged to go *thorough-stitch* with it —Bernard Mandeville⟩

²thorough-stitch \"\ *or* **thorough-stitched** \'=,=,=\ *adj* [*thorough-stitch* fr. ¹*thorough-stitch; thorough-stitched* fr. ¹*thorough-stitch* + *-ed*] *archaic* **:** THOROUGHGOING ⟨his book may properly be considered . . . a *thorough-stitched* digest and regular institute —Laurence Sterne⟩

thoroughwax \'=,=,=\ *n* [²*thorough* + *wax,* v.; trans. of G *durchwachs;* fr. the fact that the stem appears as if growing through the leaves] **1 :** HARE'S-EAR 1 **2 :** a boneset (*Eupatorium perfoliatum*)

thoroughwort \'=,=,=\ *n* -s **:** BONESET 1

thorp *also* **thorpe** \'thȯrp\ *n* -s [ME *thorp, throp,* fr. OE; akin to OHG *dorf* village, ON *thorp* village, Goth *thaurp* landed property, L *trabs, trabes* beam, timber, roof, Gk *teramna* house, Latvian *trāba* building] *archaic* **:** VILLAGE, HAMLET

thort·veit·ite \(')tȯ(r)t'vī,tīt, (')thȯ-\ *n* -s [G *thortveitit,* fr. Olaus *Thortveit,* 20th cent. Norw. mineralogist + G *-it* -ite] **:** a mineral $(Sc,Y)_2Si_2O_7$ consisting of scandium yttrium silicate and occurring in slender grayish-green orthorhombic crystals (hardness 6–7, sp. gr. 3.6)

thor·y·bes \'thȯrə,bēz\ *n, cap* [NL] **:** a genus of skipper butterflies with broad wings

¹thos \'thäs\ *n, cap* [NL, fr. L, jackal, fr. Gk *thōs;* akin to L *faunus* faun — more at FAUN] *in some classifications* **:** a genus that is now usu. considered a subgenus of *Canis* and that includes the Asiatic and African jackals and sometimes the American coyotes

²thos *pl of* THO

those [ME *thos, those,* fr. *thos, those* these (pl. of *this,* pron. & adj.), fr. OE *thās* (pl. of *thes,* pron. & adj., this) — more at THIS] *pl of* THAT

¹thou \'thau̇\ *pron* [ME, fr. OE *thū, thu* (dat. & acc. *thē*); akin to OHG *dū, du* thou (dat. *dir,* acc. *dih*), ON *thū* (dat. *thēr,* acc. *thik*), Goth *thu* (dat. *thus,* acc. *thuk*), L *tu* (dat. *tibi,* acc. *te*), Gk *sy* (dat. *soi,* acc. *se*), Skt *tvam* (dat. *te,* acc. *tvā*)] *archaic* **:** the one that is being addressed — used as a nominative pronoun of the second person singular esp. in biblical, ecclesiastical, solemn, or poetic language ⟨~ shalt have no other gods before me —Exod 20:3 (AV)⟩ ⟨be ~ our guide while life shall last —Isaac Watts⟩ ⟨~ wast not born for death, immortal bird —John Keats⟩; used in Middle English and in early modern English at least into the 17th century as the appropriate form of address to an intimate friend or a person of lower social status than the speaker and hence adopted by the early Friends as the universal form of address to one person

in accordance with their belief in the equality of all persons before God; compare THEE, THINE, THY, YE, YOU

²thou *vb* -ED/-ING/-S [ME *thouen*, fr. *thou*, pron.] *vt* : to address as *thou* ~ *vi* : to use *thou* in address

³thou \"\ *n* -S [¹*thou*] : the person or self of the one that is being addressed ‹in thinking I am related to general truth, to ideas, not to the ~ of my neighbor —Emil Brunner›

⁴thou \'thau̇\ *n, pl* **thou** *or* **thous** [short for ¹*thousand*] : a thousand of anything: as **a** : a thousand pounds **b** : a thousand dollars

thou *abbr* thousand

¹though *also* **tho** \'thō\ *adv* [ME *though, thogh*, adv. & conj., of Scand origin; akin to ON *thō* nevertheless, yet; akin to OE *thēah* nevertheless, yet, though, OHG *doh* nevertheless, yet, though, Goth *thauh* then as a result] : HOWEVER, NEVERTHELESS — used at the end or in the middle of a sentence ‹continued to eat at the hotel ~ —Sloan Wilson›

²though *also* **tho** \(')thō\ *conj* [ME *though, thogh*, adv. & conj.] **1 a** : in spite of the fact that : WHILE ‹~ they know the war is lost, they continue to fight —Bruce Bliven b. 1889› ‹the earliest fishes, ~ remarkable, have close resemblances to some modern forms —W.E.Swinton› **b** : in spite of the possibility that : even if ‹~ he slay me, yet will I trust in him —Job 13:15 (AV)› ‹~ they may all ultimately fail, they do try —Harry Roskolenko› **2** *obs* : THAT, IF ‹no marvel, my lord, ~ it affrighted you —Shak.› ‹this book, ~ only forty pages, is quite difficult to read›

¹thought [partly fr. ME *thoughte* (past of *thinken* to seem, (assumed) ME *ythought* (past part. of ME *thinken*), fr. OE *thūhte* (past of *thyncan*), *gethūht* (past part. of *thyncan*); akin to OHG *dūhta* seemed (past of *dunken*), *gidūht* seemed (past part. of *dunken*), ON *thōtti* (past of *thykkja*), *thōtt* (past part. of *thykkja*), Goth *thūhta* (past of *thunkjan*); partly fr. ME *thoughte* (past of *thenke* to think), *thought*, *ythought* (past part. of *thenken*), fr. OE *thōhte* (past of *thencan*), *gethōht* (past part. of *thencan*); akin to OHG *dāhta* thought (past of *denken*), *gidāht* thought (past part. of *denken*), ON *thātti* perceived (past of *thekkja*), Goth *thāhta* deliberated (past of *thankjan*)] *past of* THINK

²thought \'thȯt, *usu* -ȯd·+V\ *n* -S [ME, fr. OE *thōht*, *gethōht*; OE *thōht* akin to MHG *dāht* thought; derivative fr. the root of OE *thencan* to think; OE *gethōht* akin to MD *gedacht* thought; both fr. a prehistoric WGmc word whose first constituent is represented by OE *ge-* (perfective, associative, and collective prefix) and whose second constituent is derived fr. the root of OE *thencan* — more at CO-, THINK] **1 a** (1) : the action or process of thinking : mental concentration on ideas as distinguished from sense perceptions or emotions : the arranging of ideas in the mind ‹a philosophy of life filled with deep ~ —William Clark› ‹there must be ~ and care even in such a task as the delivery of milk —William Feather› (2) : MEDITATION, REFLECTION ‹a very necessary off day with only swimming and lazy ~ —Elyne Mitchell› **b** : serious consideration : ATTENTION, CARE, REGARD ‹gave no ~ at all to the opportunities the river landing offered —*Amer. Guide Series: Minn.*› ‹built with some ~ for the officers and crew —Alan Dixon› **c** : RECOLLECTION, MIND ‹I and my brother are not known; yourself so out of ~ . . . cannot be questioned —Shak.› **2 a** (1) : the faculty or power of thinking; *esp* : the ability to think logically ‹the course will deal . . . with ~ directed toward problems of human relations —*Official Register of Harvard Univ.*› (2) : such use of the ability to think logically ‹a situation that calls for swift sure ~ —*N.Y. Herald Tribune Bk. Rev.*› **b** : the power to conceive or realize : CONCEPTION, IMAGINATION ‹beauty beyond ~› **3** : something that is thought: as **a** (1) : an individual product of thinking : IDEA ‹have to wait for the occasional genius or the occasional lucky ~ —A.N.Whitehead› ‹the central ~ of the paragraph› (2) : an individual act of thinking ‹too familiar to give a ~ to —John Buchan› ‹a fearful person needs . . . ~s of courage —W.J.Reilly› (3) : an idea that stimulates thinking or supplies material for reflection ‹concluded his sermon with what he called a ~ for the day› (4) : a more or less clearly defined intention or plan ‹the ~ behind the campaign is to win decisively› — often used in negative constructions ‹had no ~ of becoming a minister —H.E.Starr› (5) : HOPE, EXPECTATION ‹beset by lung trouble, he gave up ~ of a college education —L.A.Weigle› ‹an experiment undertaken . . . without ~ of a strict financial return —W.B.Fisher› (6) : OPINION, BELIEF ‹a change has been made . . . but with tests, in the ~ of many, too mechanical and absolute —B.N.Cardozo› **b** (1) : whatever is in one's mind : IDEAS, OPINIONS ‹if he disliked anything one said or did, he spoke all his ~ —W.B. Yeats› (2) : the product of careful and reasoned consideration ‹those of us who like . . . more ~ in our music —Virgil Thomson› (3) : the intellectual product or the organized views and principles (as of a particular period, place, group, or individual) : PHILOSOPHY ‹it is only in criticism that the ~ of an era becomes articulate —C.I.Glicksberg› ‹modern scientific ~› **4** *archaic* : SORROW, GRIEF, TROUBLE **5** : ³BIT 3c — used only in the adverbial phrase *a thought* ‹slapped him a ~ too heartily on the back —Noel Coward› **syn** see IDEA

thought control *n* **1** : the practice by a totalitarian government of attempting (as by propaganda) to prevent subversive and other undesired ideas from being received and competing in the minds of the people with the official ideology and policies **2** : the use by a group or institution of authoritarian techniques similar in nature and purpose to governmental thought control

thought·ed \'thȯd·əd, -ȯtəd\ *adj* : having thoughts — usu. used in combination ‹high-*thoughted*›

thoughten *adj* [irreg. fr. ¹*thought*] *obs* : having specified thoughts ‹be you ~ that I came with no ill intent —Shak.›

thought experiment *n* [prob. trans. of G *gedankenexperiment*] : an imaginary experiment worked through with ideal apparatus under ideal conditions but with no violation of the basic laws of physics : GEDANKENEXPERIMENT

thought·ful \'thȯtfəl\ *adj* [ME, fr. ²*thought* + *-ful*] **1** : marked by thought: as **a** : absorbed in calm reflective thought : MEDITATIVE ‹looked ~ for a moment and went away —Dashiell Hammett› **b** : characterized by careful reasoned thinking ‹a ~ person, slow to act, who enjoys analyzing, interpreting, and patiently summarizing —W.J.Reilly› ‹a ~ book on a serious subject —L.E.Seltzer› **c** : having thoughts : MINDFUL, HEEDFUL ‹became ~ about his personal religion and joined the church —H.K.Rowe› **d** : marked by consideration for others : CONSIDERATE ‹a ~ generous man› **2** *obs* : suffering from anxiety or sorrow : SAD, MELANCHOLY — **thought·ful·ly** \-fəlē, -li\ *adv* — **thought·ful·ness** *n* -ES

thought·less \'thȯtləs\ *adj* **1** : marked by absence of thought: as **a** : marked by failure to think before acting : CARELESS, RASH ‹the ~ victim of an unnecessary accident› **b** : marked by failure to keep in mind : HEEDLESS ‹easy to fault them, to call them . . . ~ of tomorrow and God —A.B.Guthrie› **c** (1) : marked by a deficiency of thought : showing lack of intelligence : STUPID ‹a ~ housing boom which contains the seeds of its own undoing —*New Republic*› (2) : devoid of thought : INSENSATE ‹the ~ forces of nature —Bertrand Russell› **d** : marked by lack of consideration for others : INCONSIDERATE ‹is horribly ~ and seems to take a real delight in giving me pain —Oscar Wilde› **2** *archaic* : free from trouble or care ‹every ~ nest —William Blake› — **thought·less·ly** *adv* — **thought·less·ness** *n* -ES

thought·let \-lət\ *n* -S : a small or inconsequential thought

thought-out \'=,=\ *adj* [fr. *thought out*, past part. of the phrase *think out*] : produced or arrived at through careful and thorough consideration ‹a coherent and deeply *thought-out* philosophy of life —E.V.Rostow›

thought-read \'=,=\ *vt* **1** : to determine the unspoken thoughts of (a person) by observation of facial expressions or by telepathy ‹easily *thought-read* his friend› **2** : to determine (the unspoken thoughts) of a person by observation of facial expressions or by telepathy ‹*thought-read* the commander's plans› — **thought-reader** \'=,==\ *n*

thought transference *n* : the transference of thought from one mind to another; *specif* : TELEPATHY ‹every sort of psychical investigation . . . conducting experiments in *thought transference* —W.H.Salter›

thoughtway \'=,=\ *n* : a way of thinking that is characteristic of a particular group (as a profession or social class), time, or culture ‹a society dominated by scientific ~s —Ralph Pieris›

thoughty \'thȯd·ē\ *adj* [ME, fr. ²*thought* + *-y*] *chiefly dial* : THOUGHTFUL

thouing *pres part of* THOU

thou·let solution \(')thü¦lā\ *n, usu cap T* [after J. Thoulet, 19th cent. Fr. chemist] : SONSTADT SOLUTION

thous *pl of* THOU, *pres 3d sing of* THOU

¹thou·sand \'thau̇z³n(d)\ *n, pl* **thousands** *or* **thousand** [ME, fr. OE *thūsend*; akin to OHG *dūsunt* thousand, ON *thūsund*, Goth *thūsundi*; all fr. a prehistoric Gmc compound whose first constituent is akin to the first part of Lith *tūkstantis* thousand and of Russ *tysyacha* thousand and to Skt *tavas* strong, *taviti* he is strong, and whose second constituent is akin to OE *hund* hundred — more at THUMB, HUNDRED] **1** : 10 hundred; 100 times 10 — see NUMBER table **2 a** : 1000 units or objects ‹a total of a ~› ‹a total of four ~› **b** : a group or set of 1000 **3 a** : the numerable quantity symbolized by the arabic numerals 1000 **b** : the letter M **4** : the number occupying the position four to the left of the decimal point in the Arabic notation (as 2 in the number 2968) — usu. used in pl. **5** : a very large number ‹had ~s of things to do before the guests arrived› **6 a** : typeset matter equivalent to 1000 ems ‹he keyboards five ~ an hour› ‹a piecework rate of $1 a ~› **b** *Brit* : typeset matter equivalent to 1000 ens — **by the thousand** *or* **by the thousands** : in great numbers

²thousand \"\ *adj* [ME, fr. OE *thūsend*, fr. *thūsend*, n.] **1** : being 1000 in number ‹a ~ years› — usu. preceded by *a* or a numeral (as *one, four*) **2** : being very great in number ‹a ~ questions› — usu. preceded by *a* or a numeral (as *one, four*) **3** *obs* : THOUSANDTH

¹thou·sand·fold \'==,fōld\ *adv* [ME, fr. ¹*thousand* + *-fold*] : by 1000 times — usu. preceded by *a* or a numeral ‹increased a ~› ‹the small sum spent upon his scientific genius would be returned to the nation ten ~ —*World's Work*›

²thousandfold \"\ *adj* [ME, fr. OE *thūsendfeald*, fr. *thūsend* thousand + *-feald* -fold] : being 1000 times as large, as great, or as many as some understood size, degree, or amount : very great — usu. preceded by *a* or a numeral (as *one, four*) ‹and with a ~ reverberation —S.T.Coleridge› ‹a ~ increase› — **thou·sand·fold·ly** *adv*

thousand-headed cabbage \'==,==-\ *n* : BRUSSELS SPROUTS

thousand-headed kale *also* **thousand-head kale** *n* : a tall many-branched leafy kale (*Brassica oleracea fruticosa*) that is used as green feed for cattle and poultry

thousand island dressing *n, usu cap T&I* [prob. fr. *Thousand Islands*, group of islands in the St. Lawrence river partly in New York state and partly in Ontario, Canada] : mayonnaise with various added seasoning and flavoring ingredients (as chili sauce, chopped green peppers, pickles, olives, and cream)

thousand-leaf \'==,=\ *n* : YARROW

thousand-legger \'==,legə(r)\ *n* -S [*thousand-legger* fr. ²*thousand* + *leg* + *-er*; *thousand-legged worm* fr. *thousand-legged* (fr. ²*thousand* + *legged*) + *worm*] : MILLIPEDE ‹as if a *thousand-legger* had scurried over his skin —Gladys Schmitt›

thousand-legs \'==,=\ *n pl but sing or pl in constr* : MILLIPEDE

thousand-miler \'==,mīlə(r)\ *n* [²*thousand* + *mile* + *-er*] : a dark shirt (as worn by railroad men) that does not show dirt

thousand mothers *n pl but sing or pl in constr* : PICKABACK PLANT

¹thou·sandth \'thau̇z³n(t)th\ *adj* **1** : being number 1000 in a countable series — see NUMBER table **2** : being one of 1000 equal parts into which anything is divisible

²thousandth \"\ *n* -S \-³n(t)s, -³n(t)ths\ **1** : number 1000 in a countable series **2** : the quotient of a unit divided by 1000 : one of 1000 equal parts of anything

thousandweight \'==,=\ *n* : a unit equal to 1000 pounds

thow *or* **thowe** \'thō\ *chiefly Scot var of* THAW

thowel *var of* THOLE

thow·less \'thau̇ləs\ *adj* [ME *thowles, thewles* immoral, dissolute, fr. *thew* custom, moral quality + *-les* -less — more at THEW] *Scot* : FEEBLE, LAZY, SPIRITLESS

thowt \'thōt\ *dial Eng var of* THOUGHT

THP *abbr, often not cap* thrust horsepower

thr *abbr* **1** their **2** there **3** through

¹thra·cian \'thrāshən\ *n* -S *cap* [L *thracius*, adj., Thracian (fr. Gk *thraikios*, fr. *Thraikē* Thrace, region of the eastern Balkan peninsula, southeast Europe) + E *-an*, n. suffix] **1** : a native or inhabitant of Thrace **2** : the language of the Thracians generally assumed to be Indo-European but of uncertain position within the family

²thracian \"\ *adj, usu cap* [L *thracius*, adj., Thracian + E *-an*, adj. suffix] : of or relating to Thrace or the Thracians

thra·co-illyrian \¦thrā(,)kō+\ *adj, usu cap T&I* [*thraco-* (fr. Gk *thraiko-*, fr. *Thraikē* Thrace + Gk *-o-*) + *illyrian*] : of, relating to, or constituting a supposed subfamily of Indo-European languages comprising Thracian, Illyrian, and Albanian

thraco-phrygian \"+\ *adj, usu cap T&P* [*thraco-* + *phrygian*] : of, relating to, or constituting a tentative branch of the Indo-European language family to which are sometimes assigned various languages of the Balkans and Asia Minor not otherwise assignable

¹thrall \'thrȯl\ *n* -S [ME *thral*, fr. OE *thrǣl*, fr. ON *thræll*; prob. akin to OHG *drigil* servant, OE *thrāg* time, *thrǣgan* to run, Goth *thragjan* to run, OIr *traig* foot] **1 a** : a member of the lowest social class of ancient northern and esp. Scandinavian Europe existing either as an accident of birth or as a result of capture in a state of slavery to a master or lord : a servant slave : BONDMAN; *sometimes* : SERF **b** *archaic* : a person (as a captive held for ransom) deprived of liberty **c** : a person in moral or mental servitude : a person intangibly bound (as by a habit) **2** : the condition of a thrall: **a** : a state of complete absorption or servitude : SLAVERY ‹the summer mountains could hold me in ~ with a subtle attraction of their own —Elyne Mitchell› ‹in the ~ of a habit› **b** *archaic* : OPPRESSION, SUFFERING

²thrall \"\ *vt* -ED/-ING/-S [ME *thrallen*, fr. *thral*, n.] *archaic* : ENTHRALL, ENSLAVE

³thrall \"\ *adj* [ME *thral*, fr. *thral*, n.] *archaic* : ENSLAVED, SUBJUGATED, SUBJECT

⁴thrall \"\ *n* [origin unknown] *dial Eng* : a stand for barrels, milk pans, or cans

thrallborn \'=,=\ *adj* : born in thralldom

thrall·dom *or* **thral·dom** \'thrȯldəm\ *n* -S [ME *thraldom*, fr. *thral* thrall + *-dom*] : the condition of a thrall : SLAVERY, BONDAGE ‹from this world's ~ to the joys of heaven —Shak.›

thra·neen \thrə'nēn\ *var of* TRANEEN

¹thrang \'thraŋ\ *chiefly Scot var of* ³THRONG

²thrang \"\ *adv* [ME *thrange*, fr. *thrang* throng, adj.] *Scot* : BUSILY

thra·nite \'thrā,nīt\ *n* -S [Gk *thranitēs*, fr. *thranos* bench + *-itēs* -ite; akin to Gk *thrēsasthai* to sit down — more at FIRM] : the rower highest and farthest back on a bench of three rowers on a trireme — compare THALAMITE

thrap \'thrap\ *vt* **thrapped; thrapped; thrapping; thraps** [by alter.] *chiefly dial* : FRAP 2

thrap·ple \'thrapəl\ *n* -S [alter. of *thropple*] *Scot* : THROAT, WINDPIPE — used esp. of the horse

¹thrash \'thrash, -raa(ə)sh, -raish, *dial* -räsh\ *vb* -ED/-ING/-ES [alter. of *thresh*] *vt* **1** : to separate the grain of (as a cereal grass) from the husks and straw by beating : THRESH 1 **2 a** : to beat soundly with or as if with a stick or whip : strike repeatedly : POUND, FLOG, DRUB ‹~ed him well› **b** : to defeat decisively or with severe losses : VANQUISH ‹~ the visiting team› **3** : to swing, beat, or strike in the manner of a rapidly moving flail ‹~ing his arms from side to side› ‹~ed the water futilely with his oars› **4** : to go over (as a problem) repeatedly usu. in search of a plan of action — usu. used with *over* but sometimes with *about* ‹~ed the matter over once more without reaching a conclusion›; compare THRASH OUT **5** : to sail (a ship) to windward in a lively sea ~ *vi* **1** : to thresh grain **2** : to deal blows or strokes in the manner of one using a flail or whip ‹~ at a hedge with his cane› **3** : to move or stir about violently : toss about ‹~ in bed with a high fever› ‹the ship ~ed against her anchor› — compare THRESH **4** : to sail to windward in a fresh breeze **syn** see BEAT, SWING

²thrash \"\ *n* -ES : an act of thrashing: as **a** : an act of sailing to windward in a fresh breeze and a lively sea **b** : a method of moving the legs employed in the crawl and the backstroke

³thrash \'thrash\ *n* -ES [alter. of ⁵*rash*] *Scot* : RUSH

⁴thrash \"\ *dial var of* TRASH

¹thrash·er \'thrashə(r), -raash-, -raish-\ *n* -S [alter. of *thresher*] **1** : one that threshes something and esp. grain **2** : THRESHER 2 **3** : one that thrashes

²thrasher \"\ *n* -S [prob. alter. (influenced by ¹*thrasher*) of *thrush*] : any of numerous long-tailed birds of the American family Mimidae and esp. of the genus *Toxostoma* that resemble thrushes, are closely related to the mockingbird, and include notable singers and mimics — see BROWN THRASHER, CALIFORNIA THRASHER, CRISSAL THRASHER, CURVE-BILLED THRASHER, SAGE THRASHER

thrasherman *var of* THRESHERMAN

thrasher shark *n* : THRESHER 2

thrasher whale *n* : KILLER 3

thrashing *n* -S **1** : the act of one that thrashes **2** : a result of thrashing: as **a** : a batch of thrashed grain **b** : a severe or vicious beating : DRUBBING

thrashing machine *n* : THRESHING MACHINE

thrash out *vt* : to go over (as a problem or a disputed point) in detail with careful exploration of diverse views and possibilities for solution usu. in an attempt to reach an agreement between conflicting interests ‹you'll have to *thrash out* that question among yourselves›

thra·son·i·cal \thrā'sänəkəl\ *also* **thra·son·ic** \-nik\ *adj* [L *Thrason-, Thraso* Thraso, braggart soldier in the comedy *Eunuchus* by Terence †159 B.C. Roman playwright + E *-ical* or *-ic*] : of, relating to, like, or characteristic of Thraso : BRAGGING, BOASTFUL ‹Caesar's ~ brag of "I came, saw, and overcame" —Shak.› — **thra·son·i·cal·ly** \-nək(ə)lē\ *adv*

thrau·pi·dae \'thrȯpə,dē\ *n pl, cap* [NL, fr. *Thraupis*, type genus (fr. Gk *thraupis*, a small bird) + *-idae*] : a family of passerine birds comprising the tanagers and closely related to Fringillidae

thrave \'thrāv\ *n* -S [ME *thrave, threve*, fr. OE *threfe*, of Scand origin; akin to ON *threfi* thrave, OSw *thravi*] **1** : any of various units of measure for unthreshed grain used locally in Great Britain; *esp* : a unit equal to 24 sheaves **2** : a goodly quantity or number

¹thraw \'thrȯ\ *vb* -ED/-ING/-S [ME *thrawen*, fr. OE *thrāwan*] *vt* **1** *chiefly Scot* : to cause to twist or turn **2** *chiefly Scot* : CROSS, THWART ~ *vi* **1** *chiefly Scot* : TWIST, TURN **2** *chiefly Scot* : to be in disagreement

²thraw \"\ *n* -S **1** *chiefly Scot* : TWIST, TURN **2** *chiefly Scot* : ILL HUMOR, ANGER

thra·wart \'thräwərt\ *adj* [ME (Sc), alter. of ME *froward* — more at FROWARD] **1** *chiefly Scot* : habitually disposed to opposition : STUBBORN, PERVERSE **2** *Scot* : CROOKED, TWISTED

thrawn \'thrän\ *adj* [ME (Sc) *thrawin*, fr. past part. of ME *thrawen* to cause to twist or turn] *chiefly Scot* : lacking in pleasing or attractive qualities: as **a** : PERVERSE, RECALCITRANT **b** : CROOKED, MISSHAPEN **c** : SULLEN, GLOOMY — **thrawn·ly** *adv, chiefly Scot*

thre- *or* **threo-** *comb form* [ISV, fr. *threose*] **1** : threose ‹*thre*itol› **2** *threo-, usu ital* : having the same stereochemical arrangement of two asymmetric carbon atoms as that found in threose ‹*threo*-3-chloro-2-butanol›

¹thread \'thred\ *n* -S [ME *thred, threed*, fr. OE *thrǣd*; akin to OHG *drāt* wire, ON *thrāthr* thread; derivative fr. the root of OE *thrāwan* to cause to twist or turn — more at THROW] **1 a** : a filament, a group of filaments twisted together, or a filamentous length formed by spinning and twisting short textile fibers into a continuous strand **b** : a fine continuous strand made by plying two or more of these filament groups or lengths either with a tight twist and smooth finish (as for sewing or lace) or with a loose twist (as for embroidery) — compare CORD, ROPE **c** : a piece of thread; *esp* : a length for hand sewing **d** : YARN; *esp* : a warp or weft yarn in a woven fabric **2** : something felt to resemble a textile thread: as **a** : any of various natural filaments ‹the ~s of a spider web› ‹byssus ~s› **b** : a slender stream (as of water) **c** : the middle of a river **d** : a narrow line or streak (as of light or color) ‹a ~ of lamplight escaped under the edge of the shade› ‹a quartz sparkling with fine ~s of gold› **e** : SCREW THREAD **f** (1) : any of various manufactured filaments (as of glass, plastic, rubber, metal) (2) : a filament removed in the course of some process (as the cutting of the grooves of an original disc recording) **g** : the filament that forms when sugar boiled to 240° F is poured from a spoon **3** : something felt as drawn out or spun out or blended together like the filaments forming a textile thread: as **a** : the continuing course of a life : THREAD OF LIFE **b** : an ordered course (as that linking the elements of a discourse) : a line of reasoning, sequence of ideas, or train of thought ‹lost the ~ of his argument› **c** : CLEW 2b **d** : a continuing element that colors and modifies a whole ‹a ~ of poetry marked all his writing› **4** : a tenuous or feeble support that offers no real security : an extremely uncertain and problematical turn of events ‹a life hanging by a ~› **5** *obs* : KIND, QUALITY, NATURE **6** : a measure for cotton yarn that is equal to 1⁄80 lea or 1½ yards or 1.37 meters

²thread \"\ *vb* -ED/-ING/-S [ME *threden*, fr. *thred*, *threed*, n.] *vt* **1 a** : to pass a thread through the eye of (a needle) **b** : to arrange a thread, yarn, or lead-in piece in working position for use in (a particular machine or device) ‹~ a bobbin› ‹~ the sewing machine› **c** : to feed (an exposing or a projecting mechanism) with film : feed film into (a camera) **2 a** : to pass through in the manner of a thread ‹~ a pipe with wire› ‹~ tubing in a vein› ‹streamlets ~ing the valley floor› **b** : PIERCE, PENETRATE **c** : to make one's way through or between (as a narrow way or obstacles) ‹peddlers ~ing the narrow alleys›; *also* : to make (one's way) usu. cautiously through a hazardous place or situation ‹~ed his way through the legal entanglements› **3** : to put or bring together by or as if by passing a thread through ‹~ beads› ‹~ed several casual ideas into a charming essay› **4 a** : to interweave with or as if with threads : INTERSPERSE ‹dark hair ~ed with silver› **b** : to cover with threads or a network of threads : screen with overlapping threads ‹~ plants to protect them from destructive birds› **5** : to form a screw thread or threads on or in; *specif* : to form an external thread on — distinguished from *tap* **6** : to carry (a web) from point to point through a papermaking machine ~ *vi* **1** : to thread or wind a way — usu. used with *through* ‹~ing through narrow passages› ‹able to ~ but slowly through the intricate report› **2** *of a boiling syrup* : to reach the thread stage : form a thread when poured from a spoon

³thread \"\ *adj* [¹*thread*] : relating to, made of, or resembling thread ‹~ stockings› ‹*thread*-shaped›

thread angle *n* : ANGLE OF THREAD

thread bacterium *n* : ACTINOMYCETE

thread bar *n* : a threaded bar or rod

threadbare \'=,=\ *adj, sometimes* -ER/-EST [ME *thredbare*, fr. *thred* thread + *bare*] **1 a** : worn to the point that the thread is visible : having the nap wholly or partly worn off ‹~ clothes› **b** : clad in threadbare clothing : SHABBY ‹a neat but ~ clerk› **2** : suggesting a threadbare fabric (as in poverty of invention, meanness, or shabbiness) : SCANTY, BARREN ‹a ~ history› **3** : having lost its freshness or bloom : lacking in novelty or interest : TRITE, HACKNEYED **syn** see TRITE

thread·bare·ness *n* -ES : the quality or state of being threadbare

thread blight *n* : a disease of cocoa, tea, citrus, and other woody plants in semitropical and tropical countries caused by basidiomycetous fungi of the genera *Pellicularia* and *Marasmius* that form filamentous strands of mycelium over the surface of leaves and twigs

thread cell *n* : NEMATOCYST

thread chaser *n* : a multiple point tool used typically as one of a set of four in a die head for cutting a screw thread

thread count *n* : COUNT 8b

thread·dle \'thred³l\ *var of* THREADLE

thread·ed \'thredəd\ *adj* : furnished with a thread ‹a ~ needle› — usu. used in combination ‹double-*threaded*›

threaded glass *or* **thread glass** *n* : glass with a surface decoration of fine applied threads often of contrasting color or a surface appearance of being made up of fine threads

thread eel *n* : SNIPE EEL

thread·en \'thred³n\ *adj* [ME *threden*, fr. *thred* thread + *-en*] : made of thread

thread·er \'thredə(r)\ *n* -s **:** one that threads: as **a :** a worker who threads material into a machine or sets up a machine by threading **b** (1) **:** a device for threading a needle (2) **:** any of various devices for drawing a line through one or more narrow openings or channels **c :** a device for cutting a screw thread ⟨bolt and pipe ~s⟩

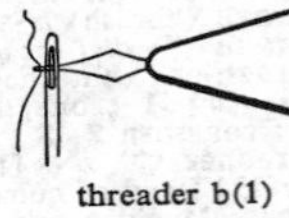

threader b(1)

thread escutcheon *n* **:** a small plate outlining an opening (as a keyhole)

threadfin \'⸗,⸗\ *n* [so called fr. the filaments of the pectoral fin] **1 :** a fish of the family Polynemidae **2 :** a fish of the genus *Polymixia*

threadfish \'⸗,⸗\ *n, pl* **threadfish** *or* **threadfishes 1 :** a small compressed deep-bodied carangid fish (*Alectis ciliaris*) having long filamentous streamers depending from its fins and being nearly cosmopolitan in warm seas **2 :** THREADFIN 1

threadflower \'⸗,⸗\ *n* **1 :** any of various plants of the genus *Nematanthus* (family Gesneriaceae) having long slender peduncles to the crimson flowers **2 :** a plant of the genus *Poinciana*

threadfoot \'⸗,⸗\ *n* [so called fr. its threadlike leaves] **:** RIVERWEED

thread fungus *n* **:** a fungus causing dermatomycosis

thread gage *n* **:** a gage for measuring screw threads or for checking or determining the pitch, thread angle, or diameter of a screw thread

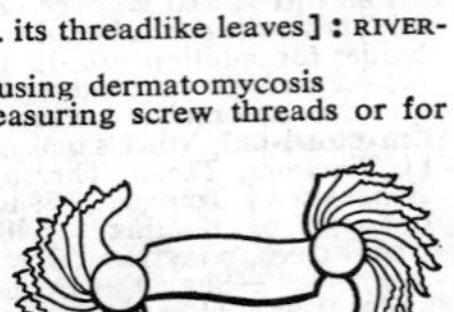

thread gage

thread generator *n* **:** a machine in which screw threads (as of a worm) are produced by a cutter in the form of a helical pinion

thread herring *n* **1 :** GIZZARD SHAD **2 :** either of two herrings: **a :** a herring (*Opisthonema oglinum*) of the West Indies and east coast of the U. S. having the last ray of the dorsal fin long and slender **b :** a very similar fish (*O. libertate*) of the west coast of tropical America

thread·i·ness \'thredēnəs\ *n* -ES **:** the quality or state of being thready

threading *n* -s [fr. gerund of ²*thread*] **:** DRAWING-IN

threading lathe *n* **:** a screw-cutting lathe having a control shaft that operates mechanisms which remove the tool from the work at the end of the cut and set it for the next operation

threading machine *n* **:** THREADER c

threading tool *n* **:** a tool for cutting screw threads

thread lace *n* **:** lace made of linen thread

threa·dle \'thred³l\ *vt* -ED/-ING/-S *dial Eng* **:** THREAD

threadleaf *also* **threadleaved** \'⸗,⸗\ *adj* **:** having long slender leaves

threadleaf sedge *also* **threadleaved sedge** *n* **:** a sedge (*Carex filifolia*) of No. America with filiform or acicular leaves

thread-legged bug \'⸗,⸗(ə)-\ *n* **:** SPIDER BUG

thread·less \'thredləs\ *adj* **:** lacking thread or a thread ⟨a rambling ~ story⟩ ⟨a ~ connection between pipes⟩

thread·let \-lət\ *n* -s **:** a small thread **:** a delicate filament

threadlike \'⸗,⸗\ *adj* **:** slender and elongated like a thread **:** FILAMENTOUS

thread-line fishing *n* **:** SPINNING

thread lungworm *n* **:** a slender widely distributed nematode worm (*Dictyocaulus filaria*) that parasitizes the air passages of the lungs of sheep

thread miller *n* **:** a milling machine on which screw threads are milled with a formed cutter or a hob

¹**thread-needle** \'⸗,⸗\ *also* **thread-the-needle** \'⸗⸗'⸗⸗\ *n* [*thread-needle* fr. ²*thread* + *needle*, n.; *thread-the-needle* fr. the phrase *thread the needle*] **1 :** a children's game in which all join hands and the leader followed by the other players passes under the arched arms of those at the other end **2 :** a country dance figure resembling the procession of the thread-needle game

²**thread-needle** \"\ *vi* **1 :** to play or move as if playing thread-needle **2 :** to execute the thread-needle figure in dancing

thread of life : the course of individual existence esp. as fabled in ancient times to be spun and cut by the Fates

thread paper *n* **1 :** a strip of folded paper serving to hold skeins of thread in its divisions **2 :** something and esp. a person as long and narrow as a thread paper

thread roller *n* **:** a roller designed to make threads (as on a screw)

threads *pl of* THREAD, *pres 3d sing of* THREAD

thread-waisted wasp \'⸗,⸗⸗-\ *n* **:** any of numerous wasps of the family Sphecidae having a very slender abdominal petiole

threadway \'⸗,⸗\ *n* **:** a way (as in a nut) for a thread

threadworm \'⸗,⸗\ *n* **:** a long slender nematode worm

thread-worn \'⸗,⸗\ *adj* **1 :** THREADBARE **2 :** worn in the thread ⟨a *thread-worn* sock⟩

thready \'thredē, -di\ *adj* -ER/-EST [ME *thredy*, fr. *thred* thread + *-y*] **1 :** consisting of or bearing fibers or threadlike elements ⟨a coarse ~ bark⟩ **2 a :** having the form or appearance of a thread **:** slenderly elongate **:** FILAMENTOUS ⟨~ prolongations of the lobes⟩ **b :** tending to form threads or to draw out into somewhat elastic strands **:** ROPY ⟨a thick ~ solution⟩; *also* **:** marked by such a tendency ⟨a ~ condition of the urine⟩ **3 :** lacking in strength or fullness **:** deficient in body or vigor **:** THIN, SLIGHT ⟨a ~ voice⟩ — see THREADY PULSE **4** *of a fabric* **:** having a clear finish that allows all threads to be seen

thready pulse *n* **:** a scarcely perceptible and commonly rapid pulse that feels like a fine mobile thread under the palpating finger

¹**threap** \'thrēp\ *vb* -ED/-ING/-S [ME *threpen*, fr. OE *thrēapian*] *vt* **1** *chiefly Scot* **:** SCOLD, CHIDE **2** *chiefly Scot* **:** to assert to be **:** affirm or maintain persistently **3** *obs* **:** to urge the acceptance of **:** PRESS ~ *vi, chiefly Scot* **:** to talk contentiously **:** DISPUTE, WRANGLE

²**threap** \"\ *n* -s [ME *threp*, fr. *threpen*, v.] **1** *chiefly Scot* **:** the act of one who threaps **:** ACCUSATION **2** *chiefly Scot* **:** a debatable account **:** TRADITION, LEGEND, REPORT

threap down *vt, chiefly Scot* **:** to reduce to silence by vigorous or repeated assertion

threap·er \-pər\ *n* -s *chiefly Scot* **:** one that asserts or argues pertinaciously

¹**threat** \'thret, *usu* -ed·+V\ *n* -s [ME *thret* threat, coercion, troop, fr. OE *thrēat* coercion, troop; akin to OE *thrēotan* to annoy, MHG *drōz* annoyance, OHG *driozan* to annoy, ON *thraut* hard task, *thrjōta* to fail, lack, Goth *usthriutan* to harass, persecute, L *trudere* to push, thrust, Russ *trud* labor] **1 :** an indication of something impending and usu. undesirable or unpleasant ⟨the air held a ~ of rain⟩: as **a :** an expression of an intention to inflict evil, injury, or damage on another usu. as retribution or punishment for something done or left undone ⟨quieted at once on the teacher's ~ to keep them in after school⟩ **b :** expression of an intention to inflict loss or harm on another by illegal means and esp. by means involving coercion or duress of the person threatened ⟨~s inducing fear of bodily harm are often cause for legal action even in the absence of overt violence⟩ **2 :** something that by its very nature or relation to another threatens the welfare of the latter ⟨the crumbling cliff was a constant ~ to the village below⟩ ⟨economic depressions constitute a major ~ to party hegemony —C.A.M.Ewing⟩

²**threat** \"\ *vb* -ED/-ING/-S [ME *threten*, fr. OE *thrēatian*, fr. *thrēat*, n.] *vt* **1** *obs* **:** to exert pressure upon **:** URGE, PRESS **2** *archaic* **:** THREATEN ~ *vi, archaic* **:** THREATEN

threat·en \'thret³n\ *vb* **threatened; threatened; threatening** \-t(³)niŋ\ **threatens** [ME *thretnen, thretenen*, fr. OE *thrēatnian* to force, fr. *thrēat* coercion + *-nian* -en] *vt* **1 :** to utter threats against **:** promise punishment, reprisal, or other distress to ⟨~ trespassers with arrest⟩ **2** *archaic* **:** to charge under pain of punishment **:** WARN ⟨let us straitly ~ them, that they speak henceforth to no man in this name —Acts 4:17 (AV)⟩ **3 :** to promise as a threat **:** hold out by way of menace or warning ⟨~ punishment to all trespassers⟩ **4 a :** to give signs of the approach of (something evil or unpleasant) **:** indicate as impending **:** PORTEND ⟨the sky ~s a storm⟩ **b :** to hang over as a threat **:** MENACE ⟨famine ~s the city⟩ **5 :** to announce as intended or possible ⟨~ to buy a car⟩ ~ *vi* **1 :** to utter or use threats or menaces **2 :** to have a menacing appearance **:** portend evil ⟨though the seas ~ they are merciful —Shak.⟩

syn MENACE: THREATEN applies to the probable visitation of some evil or affliction; it may be used of attempts to dissuade by promising punishment or retribution ⟨most of them lived on the margin of survival, constantly *threatened* by famine and disease —Arthur Geddes⟩ ⟨another form of lying, which is extremely bad for the young, is to *threaten* punishments you do not mean to inflict —Bertrand Russell⟩ ⟨discredit completely all other forms of Christianity, denying any efficacy to their rites, and *threatening* all their members with eternal damnation —W.R.Inge⟩ MENACE may connote more deeply a dire, malignant, hostile, or fearful character or aspect ⟨the devastating weapons which are at present being developed may *menace* every part of the world —Clement Attlee⟩ ⟨the conviction that it was foreigners who *menaced* the American Way —Oscar Handlin⟩

threat·en·er \-t(ə)nə(r)\ *n* -s **:** one that threatens

threat·en·ing·ly *adv* **:** in a threatening manner **:** so as to provide or constitute a threat

threat·ful \'thretfəl\ *adj* **:** full of threats **:** THREATENING, MENACING — **threat·ful·ly** \-fəlē\ *adv*

threats action *n, Brit* **:** an action for damages and an injunction against one threatening without justification to sue for alleged infringement of patent rights

¹**three** \'thrē\ *adj* [ME *three, thre*, fr. OE *thrīe* (masc.), *thrēo* (fem. & neut.); akin to OHG *drī* (masc.) three, *drīo* (fem.), *driu* (neut.), ON *thrīr* (masc.), *thrjār* (fem.) *thrjū* (neut.), Goth *thrija* (neut.), L *tres* (masc. & fem.), *tria* (neut.), Gk *treis* (masc. & fem.), *tria* (neut.), Skt *tri*] **:** being one more than two in number ⟨~ years⟩ — see NUMBER table

²**three** \"\ *pron, pl in constr* [ME *three, thre*, fr. *three, thre*, adj.] **:** three countable persons or things not specified but under consideration and being enumerated ⟨~ are here⟩ ⟨~ were found⟩

³**three** \"\ *n* -s [ME *three, thre*, fr. *three, thre*, adj.] **1 :** one more than two **2 a :** three units or objects ⟨a total of ~⟩ **b :** a group or set of three ⟨arranged by ~s⟩ **3 a :** the number-able quantity symbolized by the arabic numeral 3 **b :** the figure 3 **4 :** three o'clock — compare BELL table, TIME illustration **5 :** the third in a set or series: as **a :** a playing card marked to show that it is third in a suit **b :** a domino with three spots on one of its halves **c :** a die with three spots on the side uppermost **d :** an article of clothing of the third size

three-arm protractor *or* **three-armed protractor** \'⸗,⸗-\ *n* **:** STATION POINTER

three-awn \'⸗,⸗\ *also* **three-awn grass** *n* **:** a grass of the genus *Aristida*

three-ball \'⸗,⸗\ *n* **:** STRAIGHT RAIL

three-ball match *n* **:** a golf match in which three players compete against one another with each playing his own ball

three-banded armadillo \'⸗,⸗⸗-\ *n* **:** an armadillo with a shell having three bands; *esp* **:** APAR

three-base hit \'⸗,⸗-\ *or* **three-bag·ger** \'⸗'bagə(r), -'baag-, -'baig-\ *n* **:** a base hit that enables a batter to reach third base safely — called also *triple*

three birds *n pl but sing or pl in constr* [so called fr. the suggested resemblance of the shape of flower to three birds perched on the spur] **1 :** a perennial toadflax (*Linaria triornithophora*) of Spain cultivated for its showy purple and yellow flowers **2 :** NODDING CAP

three-card monte *n* **:** a gambling game in which the dealer shows three cards, then manipulates them by sleight-of-hand, throws them face down on a table, and invites persons to bet they can identify the location of a particular card

three-card poker *n* **:** poker in which each player's hand contains only three cards and the hands rank downward in the order three of a kind, three cards of the same suit in sequence, three cards of the same suit, three cards in sequence, pair, and high card

three-centered arch \'⸗,⸗⸗-\ *n* **:** an arch whose intrados curve is described from three centers

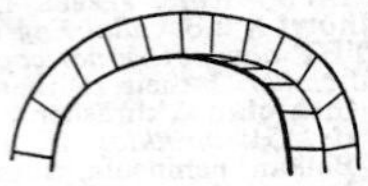

three-centered arch

three-cent piece *n* **:** a silver coin worth three cents issued in the U. S. 1851–1873 or a nickel coin issued 1865–1889

three-charge rate *n* **:** a two-charge rate to which has been added a service charge

three-circuit switch *n* **:** THREE-WAY SWITCH

three-color \'⸗'⸗⸗\ *adj, of process printing* **:** using inks of 3 different colors

three-color photography *or* **three-color process** *n* **:** any of various processes of color photography wherein three primary colors (as blue-violet, green, and red in the additive process or magenta, yellow, and blue-green in the subtractive process) are used to produce the color of the subject photographed

three-color theory *n* **:** a theory of color vision that assumes three psychologically primary colors

three-corner \'⸗'⸗⸗\ *adj* **:** THREE-CORNERED

three-cornered \'⸗'⸗⸗\ *adj* [ME, fr. *three, thre* three + *cornered*] **1 :** having three corners ⟨a *three-cornered* hat⟩ — see COCKED HAT **2 :** involving a group or set of three ⟨the race ended in a *three-cornered* tie⟩

three-cornered constituency *n* **:** a constituency with three members to be returned at one election with each voter voting for only two candidates

three-cushion billiards *also* **three cushions** *n pl but usu sing in constr* **:** carom billiards in which the cue ball must touch one or more cushions three different times plus the two object balls to score a count

three-cushion carom *n* **:** THREE-CUSHION BILLIARDS

threed \'thrēd\ *dial Brit var of* THREAD

¹**3-D** \'thrē'dē\ *adj* [*D* abbr. of *dimensional*] **:** THREE-DIMENSIONAL

²**3-D** \'⸗'⸗\ *n* **:** the three-dimensional form or a picture produced in it

three-day fever *n* **:** a fever or febrile state lasting three days: as **a :** PHLEBOTOMUS FEVER **b :** DENGUE **c** *or* **three-day sickness :** an infectious disease of cattle esp. in Africa marked by fever, muscular rigidity, conjunctivitis, and nasal discharge, and usu. subsiding within two or three days — called also *ephemeral fever*

three-deck *or* **three-decked** \'⸗'⸗\ *adj* **:** having three decks

three-decker \'⸗'⸗⸗\ *n* [*three-deck* + *-er*] **1 a :** a warship carrying guns on three decks **b :** a cargo or passenger ship with three full decks **2 a :** a structure having three floors, stories, or tiers: as (1) **:** the clerk's desk, reading desk, and pulpit proper arranged one above the other on three separate levels in some churches (2) **:** a sandwich made of three slices of bread and two fillings **b :** a book and esp. a novel in three volumes; *broadly* **:** an unusually long novel **3 :** a thing of great importance, size, or eminence

three-dimensional \'⸗⸗'⸗(ə)⸗\ *adj* **1 :** of or involving three dimensions ⟨*three-dimensional* space⟩ **2 :** giving the illusion of depth or varying distances — used of a pictorial representation (as a photograph or a motion picture in which this illusion is enhanced by stereoscopic or other means) — compare TWO-DIMENSIONAL **3 :** describing or being described in well-rounded completeness ⟨a *three-dimensional* analysis of multiple historical processes —L.L.Snyder⟩; *esp* **:** LIFELIKE ⟨the only book of the batch . . . that has *three-dimensional* characters —David Dempsey⟩ **4 :** of, relating to, or involving military operations in three spheres (as land, sea, and air)

three-eighths blood *n* **:** a grade of wool next below half blood in a descending scale of fineness — compare BLOOD 7, HALF BLOOD 3

three-em space *n* **:** a space in printing that is ⅓ of an em in thickness

three farthings *n pl but sing or pl in constr* **:** an Elizabethan silver coin worth ¾ of an English penny

three-field system *or* **three-course system** *n* **:** a system of land cultivation under which the common land is divided into three parts of which one or two in rotation lie fallow in each year and the rest are cultivated

¹**three-fold** \'thrē,fōld\ *adj* [ME *threfold*, fr. OE *thrēofeald*, fr. *thrie, thrēo* three + *-feald* -fold] **1 :** having three parts or aspects **:** TRIPLE ⟨a ~ purpose⟩ ⟨a ~ meaning⟩ **2 :** being three times as large, as great, or as many as some understood size, degree, or amount ⟨a ~ increase⟩

²**threefold** \"\ *adv* [ME *threfolde*, fr. OE *thrēofealde*, fr. *thrēofeald*, adj.] **:** to three times as much or as many **:** THRICE ⟨by three times ⟨increased ~⟩

threefold purchase *or* **threefold tackle** *n* **:** a tackle of two treble blocks

three-four \'⸗'⸗\ *or* **three-four time** *n* **:** the rhythmic content per measure as indicated ¾ in a musical composition consisting of three quarter notes or tones or their equivalent

three-fourths value clause *n* **:** an insurance policy provision limiting the insurer's liability to an amount not greater than three fourths of the cash value of the insured property but not exceeding the face of the policy often used to cause the insured to safeguard the property

three-gaited \'⸗'⸗⸗\ *adj, of a horse* **:** trained to use the walk, trot, and canter

three-halfpence \'⸗'⸗⸗\ *n, pl* **three-halfpence** *or* **three-halfpences** [ME *threhalpenys*, fr. *three, thre* three + *halpenys, halfpenys*, pl. of *halpeny, halfpeny* halfpenny] **1 :** the sum of three halfpence **:** one penny halfpenny **2 :** a small English silver coin of Queen Elizabeth I worth 1½ pennies; *also* **:** a silver coin struck under William IV and Queen Victoria for the colonies

three-halfpenny \'⸗'⸗(⸗)⸗\ *adj* **:** worth or costing three-halfpence

three-handed \'⸗'⸗⸗\ *also* **three-hand** \'⸗'⸗\ *adj* **:** played or to be played by three players

three-high \'⸗'⸗\ *adj* **:** of or relating to a train of three rolls in a rolling mill set one above another

three-hol·er \'thrē,hōlə(r)\ *n* [¹*three* + *hole* + *-er*] **:** a privy with three openings

three-hooped *adj, obs* **:** bound with three hoops

three-in-hand \'⸗⸗,⸗\ *n* **1 :** a team of three horses driven by one person **2 :** a vehicle drawn by a three-in-hand team

three in one *cap T&O* **:** TRINITY 1a(1)

three island ship *n* **:** a ship with a raised forecastle, midship structure, and poop

three jump *n* **:** a leap in figure skating from a forward outside edge of one foot to an outside back edge of the opposite foot with a one-half turn of the body in the air — called also *waltz jump*

three kings' day *n, usu cap T&K&D* [so called fr. the wise men (traditionally kings and three in number) that brought gifts to the infant Jesus (Mt 2:1–12)] **:** EPIPHANY

three-leaved arum \'⸗,⸗-\ *n* **:** JACK-IN-THE-PULPIT

three-leaved hop tree *n* **:** HOP TREE

three-leaved indian turnip *n, usu cap I* **:** JACK-IN-THE-PULPIT

three-leaved ivy *n* **:** POISON IVY

three-leaved maple *n* **:** BOX ELDER

three-leaved stonecrop *n* **:** WILD STONECROP

three-legged \'⸗'⸗(⸗)\ *adj* **:** having three legs ⟨a *three-legged* stool⟩

three-legged race *n* **:** a race between contestants who run in pairs having the proximate legs bound together

three-lined potato beetle \'⸗,⸗-\ *n* **:** a small yellow leaf beetle (*Lema trilineata*) with three black lines on each elytron whose larva feeds on the potato plant

three-line octave *n* [so called fr. the three accent marks of the symbol C‴ representing the second C above middle C] **:** the musical octave that begins on the second C above middle C — see PITCH illustration

three·ling \'thrēliŋ\ *n* -s [³*three* + *-ling*] **:** TRILLING

three-master \'⸗'⸗⸗\ *n* -s [obs. E *three-mast*, adj., having three masts (fr. E ¹*three* + *mast*, n.) + E *-er*] **:** a 3-masted ship

three-men-in-a-boat \'⸗,⸗⸗⸗'⸗\ *n* **:** OYSTER PLANT 3

three-mile limit *n* **:** a limit of the marine belt of three miles included in the territorial waters of a state

three-minute glass *n* **:** a device similar to an hourglass used to measure 3-minute intervals and esp. to time the boiling of eggs

three of a kind : three cards of the same rank — see POKER illustration

three old cat \,thrē,ōlkat, ,thrē,ōl'k-\ *or* **three o'cat** \,thrēə'k-\ *n* **:** one old cat played with three batters

threep \'thrēp\ *var of* THREAP

three-part form *n* **:** TERNARY FORM

three·pence *Brit* 'thripən(t)s *or* -rəp- *or* -rep- *or* -rûp-, *US* " *or* -rē,pen-\ *n, pl* **threepence** *or* **threepences 1 :** the sum of three usu. British pennies **2 :** a coin worth three pennies

three·pen·ny \-nē, -ni, -,pnē, -pni\ *adj* [ME *threpeny*, fr. *three, thre* three + *peny* penny] **1 :** costing or worth threepence **2 :** worth little **:** POOR, MEAN

threepenny bit *or* **threepenny piece** *n* **:** THREEPENCE 2

threepenny nail *n* [so called fr. the former price per hundred] **:** a nail 1⅛ inches long

three·pen·ny·worth \(')thrē'penē(,)wərth, -nərth\ *n* **:** the amount that a threepence buys

three-phase \'⸗'⸗\ *adj* **:** of, relating to, or operating by means of a combination of three circuits energized by alternating electromotive forces that differ in phase by one third of a cycle

¹**three-piece** \'⸗'⸗\ *adj* **:** consisting of or made in three pieces ⟨*three-piece* living room set⟩ ⟨a woman's *three-piece* suit⟩

²**three-piece** \'⸗'⸗\ *n* **:** a three-piece outfit

three-piled *or* **three-pile** \'⸗'⸗\ *adj* **1 :** having a pile of treble thickness **2** *obs* **:** of high rank, quality, or excellence

three-plier \'⸗'plī(ə)r\ *n* [*three-ply* + *-er*] **:** a three-ply rivet

three-ply \'⸗'⸗\ *adj* **1 :** consisting of three distinct parts: as **a :** having three strands ⟨*three-ply* yarn⟩ **b :** having three layers interwoven ⟨*three-ply* cloth⟩ **c :** consisting of three veneers glued together with opposing grains **2 :** passing through three thicknesses ⟨*three-ply* rivet⟩

three-point landing *n* **:** an airplane landing in which the two main wheels of the landing gear and the tail wheel or skid or nose wheel touch the ground simultaneously

three-point perspective *n* **:** linear perspective in which parallel lines along the width of an object meet at two separate points on the horizon and vertical lines on the object meet at a point on the perpendicular bisector of the horizon line

three-point problem *n* **:** the problem of locating the point of observation from the observed angles subtended by three known sides of a triangle either by mathematical calculation or by plotting with a station pointer

three-point switch *n* **:** THREE-WAY SWITCH

¹**three-quarter** *or* **three-quarters** \'⸗'⸗⸗\ *adj* **1 a :** of, relating to, or being a painted portrait measuring 30 by 25 inches or one showing the figure down to the hips only **b :** of, relating to, or being a photographic portrait showing the figure about to the knees **2 :** extending to three-quarters of the normal full length ⟨*three-quarter* coat⟩ ⟨*three-quarter* sleeve⟩

²**three-quarter** \"\ *n* **1 a :** a three-quarter-length portrait **b :** a three-quarter-face portrait **c :** three-quarter lighting of a face or figure **2** *or* **three-quarter back :** a player in rugby whose regular position is between the standoff half and the fullback

three-quarter binding *n* **:** a book binding in which the material (as leather) of the backbone and the corners is different from that of the sides and the material of the backbone extends upon the boards for one third of their width — compare FULL BINDING, HALF BINDING, QUARTER BINDING

three-quarter-bound *adj, of a book* **:** having a three-quarter binding

three-quarter-bred \'⸗'⸗⸗,⸗\ *adj* **:** having three grandparents of the pure blood of one breed — used of a domestic animal

three-quarter-floating axle \'⸗'⸗⸗'⸗⸗-\ *n* **:** a live axle in which the outer ends of the axle shaft are supported by wheels forming a rigid unit with the shaft and depending on it for alignment

three-quarter nelson *n* **:** a wrestling hold in which a wrestler kneeling beside a prone opponent passes his far arm under the opponent's corresponding arm and behind his neck and grasps the wrist of his own near arm passed under his opponent's body from the near side — compare FULL NELSON, HALF NELSON, QUARTER NELSON

three-quarter time *n* **:** THREE-FOUR

three-quarter vamp *n* **:** a vamp extending from the inner side of the shank around the toe to the backseam

three-quarter view *n* **:** a representation of a head or figure posed about halfway between front and profile views

three-ridge \'=,=\ *n* [so called fr. the three ridges on the shell] **:** a freshwater clam (*Amblema costata* syn. *Quadrula plicata*) of the Mississippi drainage system

three-ring circus *or* **three-ringed circus** \'=,=-\ *n* **1 :** a circus with simultaneous performances in three rings **2 :** something wild, confusing, engrossing, or entertaining ‹what a *three-ringed circus* that fellow is —Dorothy C. Fisher›

three r's *n pl, usu cap R* [so called fr. the facetiously used phrase *reading, 'riting, and 'rithmetic*] **1 :** the fundamentals taught in elementary school; *esp* **:** reading and writing and arithmetic **2 :** the fundamental skills in a field of endeavor

threes *pl of* THREE

threescore \'=\'=\ *adj* [ME *thre scoor,* fr. *three, thre* three + *scoor, scor* score] **:** being 60 in number

three-seeded mercury \'=,=-\ *n* **:** a weedy herb of the genus *Acalypha* (esp. *A. virginica* of eastern No. America)

¹three·some \'thrēsəm\ *n* -s [ME(Sc) *thresum,* fr. ME *three, thre* three + ME (northern dial.) *-sum* -some] **1 :** a group of three **:** TRIO **2 :** a golf match in which one person plays his ball against the ball of two others playing each stroke alternately

²threesome \"\ *adj* **:** performed or engaged in by three persons ‹a ~ dance›

three-spined stickleback \'=,=-\ *n* **:** a stickleback (*Gasterosteus aculeatus*) of fresh or brackish waters typically with three dorsal spines

three-spot \'=,=\ *n* **:** a three in cards or dice

three-spot gourami *n* [so called fr. the spot at the body center, the spot at the caudal base, and the prominent eye] **:** a small gourami (*Trichogaster trichopterus*) of southeastern Asia introduced into other countries as an aquarium fish

¹three-square \'=\'=\ *adj* [ME *thre sqware* having three equal sides, fr. *three, thre* three + *sqware, square* square] **:** having an equilateral triangular cross section — used esp. of a file

²three-square \'=,=\ *n* **1** *also* **three-square rush** [so called fr. the triangular stems] **:** any of various rushes of the genus *Scirpus; esp* **:** CHAIRMAKER'S RUSH **2 :** a three-square file

three-step \'=,=\ *n* **1 :** a dance characterized esp. by three steps in each movement **2 :** a skiing maneuver to attain speed on level ground consisting of two short steps followed by a glide

three-striper \'=\'=\ *n* **:** a commander in the U.S. Navy

three-syllable law *n* **:** a statement in grammar: in some languages (as Latin) the primary accent is limited to one of the last three syllables of a word

three-tailed porgy \'=,=-\ *n* **:** a spadefish (*Chaetodipterus faber*)

three thorn acacia *also* **three-thorned acacia** \'=,=-\ *n* **:** HONEY LOCUST

three-throw \'=,=\ *adj* **1 :** THREE-WAY **2 :** having three cranks on the same shaft

three times three : three cheers repeated three times

three-toed plover \'=,=-\ *n* **:** GOLDEN PLOVER

three-toed sloth *n* **:** a sloth of the genus *Bradypus* having three claws on each front foot

three-toed woodpecker *n* **:** any of several boreal woodpeckers of the genus *Picoides* in which the inner digit is lacking or vestigial

three-toes \'=,=\ *n pl but sing or pl in constr* **:** GOLDEN PLOVER

three-toothed cinquefoil \'=,=-\ *n* **:** CRYSTAL TEA 1

three-valued \'=\'==\ *adj* [trans. of G *dreiwertig,* trans. of Pol *trójwartościowej*] **:** possessing three truth values instead of the customary two of truth and falsehood

three-vol·um·er \'='välyəmə(r)\ *n* -s [¹*three* + *volume* + *-er*] *Brit* **:** a 3-volume novel

three-way \'=\'=\ *adj* **1 :** allowing passage in any of three directions ‹*three-way* intersection› ‹*three-way* valve› **2 :** involving three participants ‹a *three-way* profit split› ‹a *three-way* play-off›

three-way bulb *n* **:** an electric light bulb having two filaments of different wattage that can be lighted separately or together to give three levels of illumination

three-way cross *n* **:** the first generation obtained by crossing a simple hybrid with a third form

three-way lamp *n* **:** a lamp using a three-way bulb

three-way switch *n* **:** an electric switch having three terminals used to control a circuit from two different points

three-wheel·er \'=\(h)wēlə(r)\ *n* [¹*three* + *wheel* + *-er*] **:** a vehicle with three wheels: as **a :** TRICYCLE **b :** a motorcycle with a side car; *also* **:** a motorcycle with one front wheel and two rear wheels **c :** a 3-wheeled automobile

three-wire generator *n* **:** a direct-current generator with both slip rings and a commutator used for supplying current to a direct-current three-wire system whose neutral wire is connected to the center point of a high-reactance winding connected across the slip rings and whose two main conductors are connected to the commutator brushes

three-wire system *n* **:** a constant potential system of electric distribution in which lamps or other receiving devices are connected between either one of two main conductors and a third wire and motors and heavy duty appliances are usu. connected across the main conductors

thre·i·tol \'thrēə,tōl, -,tōl\ *n* -s [*thre-* + *-itol*] **:** a sweet crystalline tetrahydroxy alcohol $HOCH_2(CHOH)_2CH_2OH$ known in three optically isomeric forms and formed by reduction of threose

threm·ma·tol·o·gy \,thremə'täləjē\ *n* -ES [Gk *thremmat-, thremma* nursling + E *-o-* + *-logy* — more at ATROPHY] **:** the science of breeding animals and plants under domestication

thre·node \'thrē,nōd, 'thre,-\ *n* -s [by alter. (influenced by *ode*)] **:** THRENODY — **thre·nod·ic** \thrə'nädik\ *adj*

thren·o·dist \'threnədəst\ *n* -s [*threnody* + *-ist*] **:** a writer of threnodies

thren·o·dy \-dē, -di\ *n* -ES [Gk *thrēnōidia,* fr. *thrēnos* threnody, dirge + *-ōidia* (fr. *aeidein* to sing); akin to Skt *dhranati* it sounds — more at DRONE, ODE] **:** a song, poem, composition, or speech of lamentation esp. for someone dead or something regarded as dead **:** DIRGE, ELEGY

thre·nos \'thrē,näs\ *also* **thre·nus** \-ēnəs\ *n, pl* **thre·noi** \-ē,nȯi\ *also* **thre·ni** \-ē,nī\ [*threnos* fr. Gk *thrēnos; threnus* fr. LL, fr. Gk *thrēnos*] **:** THRENODY; *esp* **:** a lyrical lament over a victim of the catastrophe in a tragedy

threo- — see THRE-

thre·on·ic acid \thrē'änik-\ *n* [*threonic* ISV *thre-* + *-onic*] **:** a syrupy or crystalline trihydroxy acid $HOCH_2(CHOH)_2COOH$ formed by oxidation of threose

thre·o·nine \'thrēə,nēn, -,nən\ *n* -s [prob. fr. *threon-* (as in *threonic acid*) + *-ine*] **:** a crystalline alpha-amino acid $CH_3CHOHCH(NH_2)COOH$ known in six optically isomeric forms; 2-amino-3-hydroxy-butyric acid; *esp* **:** the levorotatory L-form related to D-threose that is obtained by hydrolysis of various proteins (as casein and egg proteins) and is essential to normal nutrition

thre·ose \'thrē,ōs\ *n* -s [ISV *thre-* (prob. anagram of part of *erythr-*) + *-ose*] **:** a syrupy synthetic aldo-tetrose sugar $CH_2OH(CHOH)_2CHO$ that is the epimer of erythrose and is known in three optically isomeric forms

threpe \'thrēp\ *dial var of* THREAP

threp·tic \'threptik\ *adj* [Gk *threptikos* able to feed, fr. *threptos* (verbal of *trephein* to nourish, feed) + *-ikos* -ic — more at ATROPHY] **:** of or relating to the feeding or rearing of offspring esp. among ants or other social insects

¹thresh \'thrash, -raa(ə)sh, -raish, -resh\ *vb* -ED/-ING/-ES [ME *threshen,* fr. OE *threscan, therscan;* akin to OHG *dreskan* to thresh, ON *threskja,* Goth *thriskan* to thresh, L *terere* to rub — more at THROW] *vt* **1 a :** to beat out grain or seed from (as wheat stalks) by treading, rubbing, striking with a flail, or by a threshing machine **b :** to beat off (as kernels of grain) **2 :** to go over (as a problem) again and again — often used with *over* ‹~*ing* over the systems of the past —John Dewey› ‹continued to ~ the matter over in his mind —T.B.Costain› **3 :** to strike repeatedly **:** THRASH ‹the paddles . . . ~*ing* the black water —F. Tennyson Jesse› ~ *vi* **1 :** to thresh grain **:** operate a flail or threshing machine **2** *of grain* **:** to undergo the threshing process **3 :** to strike with or as if with a flail or whip **4 :** to toss about — compare THRASH **syn** see BEAT

²thresh \"\ *n* -ES **1 :** the act of threshing grain **2 :** THRASH

³thresh \'thresh\ *n* -ES [alter. of ²*resh*] *Scot* **:** ¹RUSH

thresh·er \'thrashə(r), -raash-, -raish-, -resh-\ *n* -s [ME *thressher,* fr. *thresshen* to thresh + *-er, -ere* -er] **1 :** one that threshes **:** a threshing machine or a person tending or operating a flail or a threshing machine **2** *also* **thresher shark :** a large shark (*Alopias vulpinus*) nearly cosmopolitan in distribution that is distinguished by the greatly elongated curved upper lobe of its tail with which it is said to thresh the water to round up the fish on which it feeds and that is highly regarded as a sport fish and in some areas used as food — called also *fox shark*

thresh·er·man *also* **thrash·er·man** \'==mən\ *n, pl* **threshermen** *also* **thrashermen** [*thresher* or ¹*thrasher* + *man*] **:** one who makes a business of custom threshing

thresher whale *n* **:** KILLER 3

threshing floor *n* [ME *thresschinge flor,* fr. *thresschinge, thresshinge* (gerund of *thresschen, thresshen* to thresh) + *flor* floor] **:** ground or floor space for threshing or treading out grain

threshing machine *n* **:** a machine for separating grain or seeds from straw

¹thresh·old \'thresh,(h)ōld\ *n* -s [ME *threshwold, thresshold,* fr. OE *threscwald, threscold;* akin to ON *threskjöldr* threshold, OE *threscan, therscan* to thresh] **1 :** the plank, stone, or piece of timber or metal that lies under a door; *esp* **:** SILL **2 a :** GATE, DOOR **b** (1) **:** END, BOUNDARY; *specif* **:** the end of a runway (2) **:** the place or point of entering or beginning **:** ENTRANCE, OUTSET ‹the ~ of an era of scientific and technological development —A.L.Nickerson› ‹on the ~ of adulthood —Frances Keene› ‹a hamlet on the ~ of a narrow valley —*Amer. Guide Series: Oregon*› **3** [trans. of G *schwelle*] **:** the point at which a physiological or psychological effect begins to be produced (as the degree of stimulation of a nerve or nerve center which just produces a response or the concentration of sugar in the blood at which sugar just begins to pass the barrier of the kidneys and enter the urine) ‹below the ~ of consciousness› ‹the ~ of pain› ‹a high renal clearance ~› ‹with an alteration of the physical environment some ecological ~*s* of the ecosystem or of certain of its components may be crossed and the system disrupted —J.R.Beerbower›

²threshold \"\ *adj* **1 :** resembling a threshold; *also* **:** suggesting a threshold in nature, use, or function **2 :** that constitutes a threshold ‹a ~ voltage› ‹~ levels of sugar›

threshold exposure *n* **:** the least photographic exposure whose effect is discernible on development

threshold frequency *n* **:** the minimum frequency of radiation that will produce a photoelectric effect

thresh out *vt* **:** to thrash out

thres·ki·or·nith·i·dae \,threskē,ȯ(r)'nithə,dē\ *n pl, cap* [NL, fr. *Threskiornith-, Threskiornis,* type genus (fr. Gk *thrēskeia* religion, worship + NL *-ornith-, -ornis* -ornis) + *-idae;* prob. akin to Skt *dhārayati* he holds, carries, keeps — more at FIRM] **:** a family of birds (order Ciconiiformes) consisting of the ibises and spoonbills or restricted to the former

threw *past of* THROW

¹thrib·ble \'thribəl\ *adj* [¹*three* + *-ble* (as in *double*)] *dial* **:** TRIPLE

²thribble \"\ *n* -s **:** a unit of pipe for drilling oil consisting of three lengths coupled together — compare FOURBLE

thrice \'thrīs\ *adv* [ME *thries,* fr. *thrie* three times (fr. OE *thriga, thriwa*) + *-es,* gen. sing. ending of nouns (functioning adverbially, as in *nedes* needs); akin to OFris *thria* three times, OS *thriio, thriwo;* derivative fr. the root of OE *thrīe* three — more at THREE, -s] **1 :** three times ‹a cleaning woman ~ weekly should do —Waldo Frank› ‹bells . . . which ~ daily chime the Angelus —*Amer. Guide Series: Calif.*› **2 a :** in a threefold manner or degree **b :** to a high degree **:** FULLY, REPEATEDLY — used as an intensive ‹~ is he armed that hath his quarrel just —Shak.›

thrice-accented octave \'=\'=,==-\ *n* **:** THREE-LINE OCTAVE

thricecock \'=,=\ *n* [prob. alter. of *thrush cock*] *dial Eng* **:** MISTLE THRUSH

thrid \'thrid\ *vb* **thridded** *also* **thrid; thridded** \-dəd\ *also* **thridden** \-dᵊn\ **thridding; thrids** [alter. of ²*thread*] *vt* **:** THREAD ‹woodpeckers . . . ~ the wildwood branches —Robinson Jeffers› ~ *vi* **:** THREAD ‹we ~ all the way among shoals —R.L.Stevenson›

thrift \'thrift\ *n* -s *often attrib* [ME, fr. ON, success, prosperity, fr. *thrīfask* to thrive — more at THRIVE] **1 :** healthy and vigorous growth ‹the first things noticed about infested sheep are dullness and lack of ~ —J.T.Lucker & A.O.Foster› **2 :** good fortune **:** SUCCESS ‹with excellent ~ he fixed his young affections upon the only child of a wealthy merchant —V.L.Parrington› **3 :** savings accumulated through frugality **:** acquired or hoarded wealth **4 a :** careful management esp. of financial affairs **:** good husbandry **:** wise frugality in expenditure ‹children should early be trained to value ~› **b :** STINGINESS, MISERLINESS ‹showed his ~ by refusing his daughter a college education› **5** *chiefly Scot* **:** gainful occupation **:** useful employment **6 :** a plant of the genus *Armeria; esp* **:** a tufted scapose herb (*A. maritima*) of the seacoasts and mountains of the north temperate zone having heads of pink or white flowers — called also *cliff rose*

thrift account *n* **:** a savings account esp. in a commercial bank

thrift·i·ly \-tᵊlē, -tᵊli, -təl-\ *adv* [ME, fr. *thrifty* + *-ly*] **1** *obs* **:** in a proper or worthy manner ‹hast sung well and ~ —Philip Sidney› **2 :** with particular attention to the cost **:** ECONOMICALLY ‹the houses are ~ built —William Petersen›

thrift·i·ness \-tēnəs, -tin-\ *n* -ES **:** the quality or state of being thrifty

thrift·less \-tləs\ *adj* [ME *thriftles* unsuccessful, not prosperous, fr. *thrift* + *-les* -less] **1 :** lacking usefulness or worth ‹what ~ sighs —Shak.› **2 :** incapable of frugal management **:** wasteful of money or resources **:** IMPROVIDENT ‹a ~ character who never knew where his next meal was coming from› — **thrift·less·ly** *adv*

thrift·less·ness *n* -ES **:** the quality or state of being thriftless ‹blame their difficulties on their ~ —Bruno Lasker›

thrift society *n* **:** a voluntary association usu. unincorporated to promote thrift and for the collective investment of the savings of the members

thrifty \-tē, -ti\ *adj, sometimes* -ER/-EST [ME, fr. *thrift* + *-y*] **1 :** thriving by industry and frugality **:** increasing in wealth ‹this is a ~ modern-looking town —Elihu Burritt› **2 :** growing vigorously **:** THRIVING ‹my flock is *thriftier* looking than a year ago —E.B.White› ‹the bean plants stood erect in ~ order —Pearl Buck› **3 a :** given to or evincing thrift **:** characterized by economy and good management **:** PROVIDENT ‹she had been a prudent and ~ wife to him —W.M.Thackeray› ‹~ farmers whose hard work made the limestone region . . . a huge wheat granary —Allan Nevins & H.S.Commager› **b :** overly frugal **:** SAVING, SPARSE ‹ginger cookies with which she was not too ~ when little girls passed by —Nancy Hale› ‹only to be regretted that the references to literature are so very ~ —*Philosophic Abstracts*› **syn** see SPARING

¹thrill \'thril\ *vb* -ED/-ING/-S [ME *thrillen,* alter. of *thirlen* to pierce — more at THIRL] *vt* **1** *obs* **a :** to perforate or penetrate with or as if with a pointed instrument **b :** to hurl (as a lance, spear) with strength **2 :** to cause to have a shivering or tingling sensation **:** produce excitement in **:** affect emotionally ‹a spectacle which has ~*ed* and fascinated the human race —Barbara Buchman› ‹new gold rushes continued to ~ the prospectors —R.A.Billington› **3 :** to cause to vibrate **:** affect so as to produce vibrations or quivering ‹an earthquake ~*s* the land› ~ *vi* **1** *obs* **:** PIERCE — usu. used with *through* **2 a :** to act, move, or pass in such a manner as to provoke a sudden wave of emotion ‹a faint cold fear ~*s* through my veins —Shak.› **b :** to experience an unexpected emotional reaction **:** feel a tingling or shivering sensation ‹people ~ to gay and beautiful music —*London Calling*› ‹you'll ~ at seeing sights reminiscent of life two centuries ago —*advt*› ‹the humblest peasant can ~ with pride —M.R.Cohen› **3 :** to move or act tremulously **:** seem to tremble **:** VIBRATE ‹very rocks seem to ~ with life —John Muir †1914› ‹though a very old town . . . it ~*s* and reverberates with the romance of machinery —Arnold Bennett›

²thrill \"\ *n* -s **1 :** an instantaneous excitement **:** a tingling of or as if of the nerves produced by a sudden emotional reaction ‹the pungent ~ of hate —M.R.Cohen› ‹her laughter contained a ~ of joy —Ellen Glasgow› ‹a ~ of anticipation —Guy Priest› ‹a little ~ of horror —W.S.Maugham› **2 :** a tangible vibration or tremor (as of the land during an earthquake) **:** THROBBING **3 :** an abnormal fine tremor or vibration in the respiratory or circulatory systems felt on palpation **4 a :** a stirring, sensational, or exciting quality or element ‹stories . . . that for sheer ~*s* rival gold prospecting —Ruth & Leonard Greenup› **b :** THRILLER

³thrill *var of* TRILL

thrill·er \'thrilə(r)\ *also* **thriller-dil·ler** \'==\'dilə(r)\ *n* -s [*thriller* fr. ¹*thrill* + *-er; thriller-diller* fr. *thriller* + *-diller* (as in *killer-diller*)] **:** one that produces thrills; *esp* **:** a work of fiction or drama designed to hold the interest by the use of a high degree of action, intrigue, adventure, or suspense

thrill·ful \'thrilfəl\ *adj* **:** full of thrills or excitement ‹a small ~ boy, prepared to follow . . . the band —Stephen Crane›

thrilling *adj* **1 a** *obs* **:** PIERCING **b :** penetrating with cold **:** inducing shivering and shaking ‹a ~ wind blew off the frozen lake› **2 :** causing an instantaneous surge of emotion **:** producing tremulous excitement **:** deeply moving ‹gave ~ hints of an unknown world —W.H.Downes› ‹~ narratives of Indian captivities became a favorite form of literature —A.F.Harlow› ‹a postcard . . . gave me ~ news —Christopher Morley› **3 :** THROBBING, VIBRATING

thrill·ing·ly *adv* **:** in a thrilling manner

thrilly \-lē\ *adj* [²*thrill* + *-y*] **:** providing thrills **:** SENSATIONAL

¹thrim·ble \'thrimbəl\ *vt* -ED/-ING/-S [origin unknown] *chiefly Brit* **:** to finger (as money) in a hesitating way

²thrimble \"\ *dial Eng var of* TREMBLE

thrin \'thrin\ *n* -s [alter. (influenced by *three*) of *twin*] *dial* **:** one of triplets **:** one of three

thri·nax \'thrī,naks\ *n, cap* [NL, fr. Gk, trident, three-pronged fork; fr. the shape of the leaves] **:** a genus of No. American fan palms with orbicular leaves cleft into many induplicate segments, smooth petioles, and monoecious flowers succeeded by small globose fruits — see THATCH PALM

thring \'thriŋ\ *vi* [ME *thringen,* fr. OE *thringan* — more at THRONG] *chiefly Scot* **:** to press or push ahead in or as if in a throng

¹thrin·ter \'thrintə(r)\ *n* -s [¹*three* + *winter*] *dial Brit* **:** a three-year-old sheep

²thrinter \"\ *adj, dial Brit* **:** being three years old

¹thrip \'thrip\ *vt* **thripped; thripped; thripping; thrips** [imit.] **1** *obs* **:** to snap (the fingers) softly **2 :** to twitch slightly

²thrip \"\ *n, pl* **thrips** *or* **thrip** [back-formation] *chiefly Brit* **:** THRIPS

¹thrip·id \'thripəd\ *adj* [NL *Thripidae*] **:** of or relating to the family Thripidae

²thripid \"\ *n* -s [NL *Thripidae*] **:** an insect of the family Thripidae **:** THRIPS

thrip·i·dae \'thripə,dē\ *n pl, cap* [NL, fr. *Thrip-, Thrips,* type genus + *-idae*] **:** a family of insects (order Thysanoptera) comprising the thrips

thrip·pence *like* THREEPENCE\ *also* **thrip** \'thrip\ *n* [*thrippence* alter. of *threepence; thrip* by shortening & alter. fr. *threepence*] **:** THREEPENCE

thrip·ple \'thripəl\ *n* -s [ME *therrepyll*] *Eng* **:** an extension frame or rail used on a vehicle usu. for hay

thrips \'thrips\ *n* [NL *Thrip-, Thrips,* fr. L *thrip-, thrips* woodworm, fr. Gk] **1 a** *cap* **:** a genus of insects that is the type of the family Thripidae **b** *pl* **thrips :** any of numerous insects (family Thripidae) that are of small often minute size, that have narrow broadly fringed wings with rudimentary nervures, asymmetrical mouth parts used for sucking, and tarsi ending in a peculiar bladderlike structure, and that feed mostly on plant juices and are often destructive pests — see ONION THRIPS, TOBACCO THRIPS **2** *pl* **thrips :** any of various small injurious insects; *esp* **:** GRAPE LEAFHOPPER

¹thrist \'thrist\ *dial Brit var of* THIRST

²thrist \"\ *dial Brit var of* THRUST

this·tle *or* **thris·sel** \'thrisəl\ *chiefly Scot var of* THISTLE

thrive \'thrīv\ *vi* **throve** \-rōv\ *or* **thrived** \-rīvd\ **thriv·en** \-rivən\ *also* **thrived; thriving; thrives** [ME *thriven,* fr. ON *thrīfask,* prob. reflexive of *thrīfa* to clutch, grasp] **1 :** to grow vigorously **:** become increasingly larger and healthier **:** physically improve ‹sheep and goats ~ on uplands and rough, eroded regions —*Amer. Guide Series: Texas*› ‹the sparrow *thrived* under her care —Thomas Foster› ‹children seem to ~ even in city streets› **2 :** to prosper outstandingly **:** gain in wealth or material possessions **:** advance successfully ‹industry has never *thriven* under restrictions —L.D.Stamp› ‹the region *thrived* as steel and aircraft . . . establishments built up —Oscar Handlin› **3 :** to achieve growth or progress toward one's own goal **:** flourish despite or because of circumstances or conditions ‹creating an atmosphere in which injustice finds it harder to ~ —Lionel Trilling› ‹she ~*s* on the attention —Bradford Smith› ‹he *thrived* on opposition —*Sydney (Australia) Bull.*› **syn** see SUCCEED

thrive·less \'thrīvləs\ *adj* **:** being without advantage **:** UNSUCCESSFUL

thriving *adj* **:** characterized by prosperity **:** successfully engaged in achieving a goal ‹the city is now a ~ tourist center —Sam Pollock› ‹floral booths did a ~ business in orchids —Dorothy Kahn› — **thriv·ing·ly** *adv*

-thrix \(,)thriks\ *n comb form* [NL *-trich-, -thrix,* fr. Gk *trich-, thrix* hair — more at TRICHINA] **1 :** one having (such) hair or hairlike filaments — in generic names of plants and animals ‹Lago*thrix*› ‹Strepto*thrix*› **2** *pl* **-tri·ches** \(,)trə,kēz\ *or* **-thrixes :** pathological condition of having (such) hair ‹lepo*thrix*› ‹monile*thrix*›

thro \'thrü\ *prep* [ME *thro,* short for *throgh, through*] *archaic* **:** THROUGH ‹stares ~ the window at a scrawl of boughs —Constance Carrier›

¹throat \'thrōt, *usu* -ōd·+V\ *n* -s *often attrib* [ME *throte,* fr. OE *throte, throtu;* akin to OHG *drozza* throat, ON *throti* swelling, *thrūtna* to swell, OE *thrūtian*] **1 a** (1) **:** the part of the neck in front of the spinal column (2) **:** the passage through it to the stomach and lungs containing the pharynx and upper part of the esophagus, the larynx, and the trachea **b :** voice or the seat of the voice ‹the nightingale poured out his ~ in song› **2 :** something felt to resemble the throat esp. in being an entrance, a passageway, a constriction, or a narrowed part ‹the ~ of a vase› ‹the narrow ~ of a stream›: as **a :** the part of a chimney (as of a house) between the portion of the funnel that contracts in ascending (as above a hearth) and the flue proper; *also* **:** a similar part of an industrial flue system (as of a metallurgical furnace) **b :** a groove or channel on the underside of a projection (as a stringcourse or coping) that prevents water from running back into the wall **c** (1) **:** the inside of a timber knee of a ship — compare BREECH (2) **:** the end of a gaff next to the mast (3) **:** the upper fore corner of a staysail or of a fore-and-aft sail (4) **:** the curved part of an anchor's arm where it joins the shank — see ANCHOR illustration **d :** the orifice of a tubular organ esp. of a plant; *usu* **:** the spreading upper part of the tube of a gamopetalous corolla or calyx **e :** a gullet or clearance space at the bottom of a sawtooth **f** (1) **:** the narrowest place between the wing rails of a railroad frog (2) **:** the curved space between the flange and tread of a car wheel (3) **:** the point at which a railroad line enters or leaves a yard and from which the yard tracks branch out — called also *choke point* **g :** a gap in the frame behind the tool in a punching, shearing, vertical-boring, or similar machine the depth of which limits the size of the work taken **h :** a short tube connecting larger tubes or a contracted section of a tube between expanded portions **i :** the opening in the vamp of a shoe at the instep — see SHOE illustration **j :** the part of a tennis racket between the head and the handle **k :** the minimum distance from the root of a fusion weld to its face **3** *obs* **:** a center of or capacity for destructive action **:** JAWS, MOUTH

²throat \"\ *vt* -ED/-ING/-S **1 a :** to utter in the throat **:** MUTTER ‹~ threats› **b :** to sing or enunciate in a throaty voice ‹~*ing* her words huskily› **2 :** to make or provide with a throat ‹~ the underside of a stringcourse›

throatband \'=,=\ *n* **1 :** THROATLATCH **2 :** NECKBAND

throat botfly *n* **:** a rusty reddish hairy botfly (*Gasterophilus nasalis*) that lays its eggs on the hairs about the mouth of the horse whence the larvae on hatching migrate and attach themselves to the walls of the stomach and intestine — called also *chin fly*

throat brail *n* **:** a brail running through a block at the throat of a gaff

throat·ed \'thrōd·əd, -ōtəd\ *adj* [ME *throted,* fr. *throte* throat + *-ed*] **:** having a throat — usu. used in combination ‹choke-*throated*› ‹deep-*throated*› ‹white-*throated*›

throat halyard *n* **:** a line used to hoist the throat of a gaff

throat·i·ly \'thrōd·ᵊlē, -ōt|, |ᵊli, |əl-\ *adv* [*throaty* + *-ly*] **:** in a throaty manner **:** with a peculiar tonal quality caused by oral utterance with the throat constricted **:** GUTTURALLY ⟨wiped her red old eyes . . . and clucked ~ —Rudyard Kipling⟩
throat·i·ness \|ēnəs, |in-\ *n* -ES **:** the quality or state of being throaty
throat·ing \'thrōd·iŋ\ *n* -S [¹*throat* + *-ing*] **:** a throated structure or area (as the throat beneath a stringcourse)
throatlash \'⸗,⸗\ *n* [¹*throat* + *lash*, alter. of ²*latch*] **:** THROATLATCH
throatlatch \'⸗,⸗\ *n* **1 :** a strap of a bridle or halter passing under a horse's throat — see BRIDLE illustration **2 a :** the portion of a horse's throat around which the throatlatch passes — see HORSE illustration **b :** a corresponding region on another animal ⟨the ~ of a fish⟩
throat·less \'thrōtləs\ *adj* **:** having no throat
throat microphone *n* **:** a small contact microphone or pickup held or fastened against the speaker's throat and actuated directly by the vibration of the larynx
throat plate *n* **1 :** THROAT SHEET **2 :** a flat plate holding the feed dog of a sewing machine
throat register *n* **:** a middle register of the clarinet extending from the written G above middle C to and including the B flat immediately above it
throatroot \'⸗,⸗\ *n* **1 :** a bennet (*Geum virginianum*) **2 :** WATER AVENS
throats *pl of* THROAT, *pres 3d sing of* THROAT
throat seizing *n* **:** a seizing in which the parts of a rope cross each other
throat sheet *n* **:** a boiler plate on a steam locomotive flanged to connect the cylindrical part of the boiler with the side sheets of the firebox or on some models with both the side and roof sheets
throatstrap \'⸗,⸗\ *n* **:** THROATLATCH 1
throat sweetbread *n* **:** THYMUS
throat track *n* **:** a track connecting ladder tracks with main tracks at a railway yard or station
throatwort \'⸗,⸗\ *n* **1 :** any of several bellflowers; *esp* **:** a European herb (*Campanula trachelium*) formerly used to treat sore throat **2 :** FOXGLOVE 1 **3 :** any of various figworts (as *Scrophularia nodosa* of Europe or *S. marylandica* of America) **4 :** a button snakeroot (*Liatris spicata*)
throaty \'thrōd·|ē, -ōt|, |i\ *adj* -ER/-EST [¹*throat* + *-y*] **1 a :** uttered with a hard quality caused by the sound coming from the throat rather than from the mouth **:** GUTTURAL **b :** relatively heavy, thick, and deep as if emitted from low in the throat ⟨an entrancing ~ laugh⟩ ⟨a rich ~ voice⟩ ⟨~ from her cold⟩ ⟨a cat's little ~ meow⟩ **2 :** having a large loose-hanging throat — used esp. of cattle or dogs
¹**throb** \'thräb\ *vi* **throbbed; throbbed; throbbing; throbs** [ME *throbben*, prob. of imit. origin] **1 a :** to pulsate with abnormal force or rapidity (as from fright, pain, or agitation) **:** PALPITATE ⟨her heart *throbbed* with sudden shock⟩ ⟨a finger *throbbing* from an infected cut⟩ **b :** to pulsate, vibrate, or beat in a normal rhythmic manner ⟨pulse *throbbing* steadily⟩ ⟨the engines *throbbed* quietly beneath the deck⟩ **2 :** to become moved strongly by or as if by emotion ⟨a spirit *throbbing* with desire⟩ ⟨the child *throbbed* with loneliness⟩ **syn** see PULSATE
²**throb** \"\ *n* -S **1 :** a single pulse of a pulsating movement or sensation (as of pain or violent emotion) ⟨a sudden ~ of pain⟩ ⟨each ~ of her heart⟩ **2 :** a rhythmic pulsation or beating ⟨a pulsating rhythm, like the ~ of . . . many machines in a big factory —W.T.C.King⟩
throb·ber \-bə(r)\ *n* -S **:** one that throbs; *esp* **:** one that is unduly emotional
throb·bing·ly *adv* [*throbbing* (pres. part. of ¹*throb*) + *-ly*] **:** in a throbbing manner **:** with a throb
throb·less \-bləs\ *adj* **:** free from throbs or throbbing **:** STATIC, QUIET, PLACID, UNEXCITING
¹**throe** \'thrō\ *n* -S [ME *throwe*, alter. (influenced by *throwen* to suffer, fr. OE *thrōwian* — akin to OE *thrāwu* threat, pang) of *thrawe*, fr. OE *thrāwu*, *thrēa* threat, punishment, pang; akin to OHG *drawa*, *drōa* threat, ON *thrā* pang, longing, Gk *trauma* wound, *tryein* to wear out, distress] **1 a throes** *pl* **:** the physical struggle and anguish accompanying parturition **:** labor pains **b :** the struggle and anguish immediately preceding death **:** a death struggle — usu. used in pl. **c :** a sudden spasm or pang (as of pain or emotion) ⟨forced from love's exultant ~ —James McAuley⟩ **2 throes** *pl* **:** a condition of struggle, anguish, disorder, or confusion characteristic of a transitional period (as the active phase of creation of some new thing) ⟨a state in the ~*s* of revolution⟩ ⟨a college . . . in the ~*s* of selecting a new president —W.S.Carlson⟩ ⟨air commerce is in the ~*s* of an essential transition —*Current Biog.*⟩ **syn** see PAIN
²**throe** \"\ *vb* -ED/-ING/-S *vt*, *obs* **:** to put in agony **:** cause to suffer ~ *vi* **:** to struggle in distress **:** be in agony
thromb- *or* **thrombo-** *comb form* [Gk *thrombos* lump, clot of blood, curd — more at ATROPHY] **1 a :** blood clot ⟨*thrombo*cyst⟩ **b :** associated with the clotting of blood ⟨*thromb*in⟩ ⟨*thrombo*stasis⟩ **2 :** marked by or associated with thrombosis ⟨*thrombo*angiitis⟩
throm·base \'thräm,bās\ *n* -S [ISV *thromb-* + *-ase*] **:** THROMBIN
throm·bas·the·nia \,thrämbəs'thēnēə\ *n* [NL, fr. *thromb-* + *asthenia*] **:** PSEUDOHEMOPHILIA
thrombi *pl of* THROMBUS
throm·bin \'thrämbən\ *n* -S [ISV *thromb-* + *-in*] **:** a proteolytic enzyme that is formed from prothrombin (as in blood plasma as needed), that facilitates the clotting of blood by promoting conversion of fibrinogen to fibrin, and that is used as a local hemostatic for capillary bleeding and also in binding tissues together after surgery — compare ANTITHROMBIN, FIBRIN FOAM
throm·bo·angiitis \¦thräm(,)bō+\ *n* [NL, fr. *thromb-* + *angiitis*] **:** inflammation of the lining of a blood vessel with thrombus formation
thromboangiitis ob·lit·er·ans \-ə'blid·ə,ranz\ *n* [NL, lit., obliterating thromboangiitis] **:** thromboangiitis of the small arteries and veins of the extremities and esp. the feet resulting in occlusion, ischemia, and gangrene — called also *Buerger's disease*
throm·bo·arteritis \¦thräm(,)bō+\ *n* [NL, fr. *thromb-* + *arteritis*] **:** inflammation of an artery with thrombus formation
throm·bo·blast \'thrämbə,blast\ *n* [*thromb-* + *-blast*] **:** an immature thrombocyte
throm·bo·cyte \-,sīt\ *n* -S [ISV *thromb-* + *-cyte*] **:** BLOOD PLATELET; *also* **:** a cell having a similar function in clotting (as a spindle cell of some lower vertebrates) — **throm·bo·cyt·ic** \¦⸗⸗¦sid·ik\ *adj*
throm·bo·cy·to·pe·nia \,thrämbō,sīd·ō'pēnēə\ *n* -S [NL, fr. ISV *thrombocyte* + *-o-* + NL *-penia*] **:** persistent decrease in the number of blood platelets usu. associated with hemorrhagic conditions — compare PURPURA 1 — **throm·bo·cy·to·pe·nic** \¦⸗⸗⸗⸗¦pēnik\ *adj*
thrombocytopenic purpura *n* **:** PURPURA HEMORRHAGICA 1
throm·bo·cy·to·poi·e·sis \,⸗⸗,⸗⸗,pȯi'ēsəs\ *n* [NL, fr. ISV *thrombocyte* + *-o-* + NL *-poiesis*] **:** the production of blood platelets from megakaryocytes typically in the bone marrow
throm·bo·cy·to·sis \,thrämbō,sī'tōsəs\ *n*, *pl* **thrombocytoses** \-'tō,sēz\ [NL, fr. ISV *thrombocyte* + NL *-osis*] **:** increase and esp. abnormal increase in the number of blood platelets
throm·bo·em·bol·ic \¦thrämbōem¦bälik\ *adj* [ISV *thromb-* + *embol-* + *-ic*] **:** marked by or associated with thromboembolism ⟨~ disease⟩ ⟨a ~ syndrome⟩
throm·bo·embolism \¦thräm(,)bō+\ *n* [*thromb-* + *embolism*] **:** the blocking of a blood vessel by an embolus that has broken away from a thrombus at its site of formation
throm·bo·gen \'thrämbəjən\ *n* -S [ISV *thromb-* + *-gen*] **:** PROTHROMBIN
throm·bo·gen·ic \¦thrämbə¦jenik\ *adj* [ISV *thromb-* + *-genic*] **:** tending to produce a thrombus
throm·bo·kinase \¦thräm(,)bō+\ *n* [ISV *thromb-* + *kinase*] **:** THROMBOPLASTIN
throm·bon \'thrämbən\ *n* -S [*thrombocyte* + *-on* (as in *plankton*)] **:** the entire body of blood platelets and their precursors that constitute a distinct organ of the body
throm·bo·pe·nia \,thrämbō'pēnēə\ *n* -S [NL, fr. *thromb-* + *-penia*] **:** THROMBOCYTOPENIA — **throm·bo·pe·nic** \¦⸗⸗¦pēnik\ *adj*
throm·bo·phlebitis \¦thräm(,)bō+\ *n* [NL, fr. *thromb-* + *phlebitis*] **:** inflammation of a vein with formation or presence of a thrombus and esp. one that is firmly attached to the vessel wall — compare PHLEBOTHROMBOSIS
throm·bo·plas·tic \¦thrämbō¦plastik\ *adj* [ISV *thromb-* + *-plastic*] **1 :** initiating or accelerating the clotting of blood usu. by converting prothrombin to thrombin **2 :** of, relating to, or constituting thromboplastin — **throm·bo·plas·ti·cal·ly** \-tək(ə)lē\ *adv*
throm·bo·plas·tin \,⸗⸗'plastən\ *n* -S [ISV *thromboplastic* + *-in*] **:** a complex substance that contains chiefly protein and various phosphatides, that is found in brain, lung, and other tissues and esp. in blood platelets, and that when released from disintegrating cells participates in the clotting of blood by promoting the conversion of prothrombin to thrombin; *also* **:** a tissue extract rich in this substance sometimes used as a local hemostatic
throm·bose \'thräm,bōz, -ōs\ *vb* -ED/-ING/-S [back-formation fr. *thrombosis*] *vt* **:** to affect with thrombosis ~ *vi* **:** to undergo thrombosis
throm·bo·sis \thräm'bōsəs\ *n*, *pl* **thrombo·ses** \-ō,sēz\ [NL, fr. Gk *thrombōsis* coagulation, clotting, fr. *thrombousthai* to become clotted, fr. *thrombos* clot] **1 :** the formation or presence of a blood clot within a blood vessel during life **2 :** a plant disease in which water conduction is interfered with by the growth of a parasite (as in wilt diseases)
throm·bot·ic \(')thräm¦bäd·|ik, -bät|, |ēk\ *adj* [fr. NL *thrombosis*, after such pairs as NL *narcosis*: E *narcotic*] **:** of, relating to, involving, or affected with thrombosis ⟨a ~ disorder⟩ ⟨~ changes⟩ ⟨a ~ patient⟩
throm·bus \'thrämbəs\ *n*, *pl* **throm·bi** \-m,bī\ [NL, fr. Gk *thrombos* lump, clot of blood, curd — more at ATROPHY] **:** a clot of blood formed within a blood vessel and remaining attached to its place of origin — compare EMBOLUS
¹**throne** \'thrōn\ *n* -S [ME, alter. (influenced by L *thronus*) of *trone*, fr. OF, fr. L *thronus*, fr. Gk *thronos* chair, throne — more at FIRM] **1 a :** a chair of state: as **(1) :** a royal seat on a dais with a canopy **(2) :** the ceremonial seat of a prince, bishop, or other high dignitary — see CATHEDRA **(3) :** the seat of a deity or superhuman power ⟨Satan's dark ~⟩ **b :** an elevated seat provided by an artist for his model **c** *slang* **:** TOILET SEAT **2 a :** sovereign or sometimes episcopal power and dignity **:** supreme rank or position **:** SOVEREIGNTY **b :** the one invested therewith **:** an exalted or dignified personage **3 thrones** *pl* **:** a high order of angels — see CELESTIAL HIERARCHY **4** *Eastern Church* **:** SANCTUARY 1b
²**throne** \"\ *vb* -ED/-ING/-S [ME *tronen*, *thronen*, fr. *trone*, *throne* throne] *vt* **:** to exalt to a throne **:** give sovereignty or dominion to **:** ENTHRONE ~ *vi* **:** to be in or to sit on a throne **:** be in power as if on a throne ⟨a kind of sanctuary in which she *throned* among his secret thoughts and longings —Edith Wharton⟩
throne·less \-nləs\ *adj* **:** lacking a throne
throne·let \-lət\ *n* -S **:** a little throne **:** an insignificant dominion
throne name *n* **:** the official name taken by a ruler and esp. an ancient Egyptian pharaoh on ascending the throne
throne room *n* **1 :** a formal audience room in which stands the throne of a sovereign **2 :** a place in which authority is actually centered
throne·ward \-nwə(r)d\ *adv* [¹*throne* + *-ward*] **:** toward a throne
¹**throng** \'thrȯŋ *also* 'thräŋ\ *n* -S [ME *thrang*, *throng*, fr. OE *gethrang*, *thrang*; akin to OE *thringan* to press, crowd, push ahead, OHG *dringan*, ON *thröngva*, Goth *threihan* to press, squeeze, Lith *trenkti* to jolt] **1 a :** a multitude of persons congregated into a close assemblage **b :** a goodly number assembled in fact or concept **:** HOST ⟨~*s* of ants joined the picnic⟩ ⟨a ~ of confused notions cluttering her brain⟩ **2 a :** a crowding together of many persons **b :** a pressing of activity (as in seasonal work) **:** PRESSURE ⟨this ~ of business —S.R.Crockett⟩ **3** *chiefly Scot* **:** DISTRESS, HARDSHIP **syn** see CROWD
²**throng** \"\ *vb* -ED/-ING/-S [ME *thrangen*, *throngen*, fr. *thrang*, *throng* throng] *vt* **1 a** *obs* **:** to press closely together or as if between opposing forces **:** COMPRESS, SQUEEZE **b** *archaic* **:** to gather together in one place **:** CROWD **2 :** to gather about and press upon so as to crush or jostle ⟨much people followed him, and ~*ed* him —Mk 5:24 (AV)⟩ **3 :** to fill closely by forcing or pressing into **:** PACK, JAM ⟨shoppers ~*ing* the streets⟩ ~ *vi* **1 :** to crowd together in great numbers **:** move, pass, go, or advance in multitudes ⟨commuters ~*ing* towards the station⟩ **2** *obs* **:** to press one's way against difficulties (as in forcing a way through a crowd)
³**throng** \'thräŋ\ *adj* [ME *thrang*, *throng*; akin to OE *thringan* to press, crowd] **1** *chiefly Scot* **:** closely packed **:** CROWDED **2** *chiefly Scot* **:** filled with or fully engaged in work **:** BUSY **3** *chiefly Scot* **:** closely associated **:** INTIMATE
¹**throp·ple** \'thräpəl\ *n* -S [ME *throppill*] *chiefly dial* **:** THROAT, WINDPIPE — used esp. of a horse; compare THROATLATCH
²**thropple** \"\ *vt* -ED/-ING/-S [alter. (influenced by ¹*thropple*) of ¹*throttle*] *chiefly Scot* **:** THROTTLE
thros·tle \'thräsəl\ *n* -S [ME *throstle*, *throstil*, fr. OE *throstle* — more at THRUSH] **1 :** ¹THRUSH 1; *specif* **:** SONG THRUSH **2 a :** an outmoded frame for spinning cotton from roving **b** *Brit* **:** a worsted spinning frame
throstle cock *n* [ME *throstilcok*, fr. *throstil* throstle + *cok* cock] **1 :** SONG THRUSH **2 :** MISTLE THRUSH
throt \'thrät\ *chiefly Scot var of* THROAT
¹**throt·tle** \'thräd·ᵊl, -ät·ᵊl\ *vb* **throttled; throttled; throttling** \-d·ᵊl·, -t(ᵊ)liŋ\ **throttles** [ME *throtelen*, *throtlen*, fr. *throte* throat] *vt* **1 a (1) :** to seize and compress the throat of so as to impede or check breathing; *broadly* **:** to impede or check the breathing of by any means **:** CHOKE **(2) :** to kill by such action **b :** to suppress or prevent or hinder expression, expansion, or other activity of by choking constriction **:** bring under severe check or control ⟨might not such regulation ~ the freedom of science —John Dewey⟩ **2** *obs* **:** to utter brokenly as if half suffocated **3 a :** to obstruct the flow of (as steam to an engine) esp. by a throttle valve **b :** to reduce the speed of (as an engine) by such means — often used with *down* ⟨*throttled* the car down to 20 miles an hour⟩ — compare GOVERN 2b ~ *vi* **:** to have the throat obstructed so as to be in danger of suffocation **:** CHOKE **syn** see SUFFOCATE
²**throttle** \"\ *n* -S [perh. alter. (influenced by ¹*throttle*) of ¹*thropple*] **1 a :** THROAT 1 **b :** TRACHEA 1 **2** [*throttle valve*] **a :** THROTTLE VALVE **b :** THROTTLE LEVER — **at full throttle :** with the throttle valve set at its widest opening **:** at full speed
throttlebottom \'⸗⸗,⸗⸗\ *n*, *usu cap* [after Alexander *Throttlebottom*, character in the musical comedy *Of Thee I Sing* (1932) by George S. Kaufman *b*1899 & Morris Ryskind *b*1895 Am. playwrights] **:** an innocuously inept and futile person in public office
throttlehold \'⸗⸗,⸗\ *n* [¹*throttle* + *hold*] **:** a vicious, strangling, or stultifying control ⟨a ~ on the daily press⟩
throttle lever *n* **:** a pedal or lever that controls a throttle valve
throt·tle·man \'⸗⸗mən\ *n*, *pl* **throttlemen** [²*throttle* + *man*] **:** one stationed at or in immediate control of a throttle valve
throt·tler \'thräd·ᵊlə(r)\ *n* -S **:** one that throttles
throttle valve *n* [¹*throttle* + *valve*] **:** a valve designed to regulate the supply of a fluid (as steam or gas and air) to an engine and operated by a handwheel, a lever, or automatically by a governor; *esp* **:** the valve in an internal-combustion engine incorporated in or just outside the carburetor and controlling the volume of vaporized fuel charge delivered to the cylinders
throttling bar *n* [*throttling* (fr. pres. part. of ¹*throttle*) + *bar*] **:** a bar of varying cross section that controls the flow of the liquid past the piston in some types of hydraulic recoil brakes
throttling governor *n* **:** an automatic governor on a throttle valve
¹**through** *also* **thru** \'thrü\ *prep* [ME *thurgh*, *thurh*, *thruh*, *through*, fr. OE *thuruh*, *thurh*; akin to OHG *durh*, *duruh* through, Goth *thairh*, L *trans* across, beyond, Skt *tiras* through, across, *tarati* he crosses over — more at TERM] **1 a (1) —** used as a function word to indicate penetration of or passage within, along, or across an object, substance, or space usu. from one side or surface to the opposite one ⟨sawed ~ the board⟩ ⟨put a bullet ~ his hat⟩ ⟨the oars cut ~ the water⟩ **(2) —** used as a function word to indicate passage from one side to another of an object by means of an opening or openings ⟨the party encountered the wire, and again crawled ~ it —P.W.Thompson⟩ ⟨walked ~ the gate⟩ **(3) —** used as a function word to indicate extension from one end or boundary (as of a place or area) to another ⟨a road ~ the desert⟩ ⟨a path ~ the woods⟩ **b —** used as a function word to indicate passage into and out of some treatment, handling, or process ⟨had probably been ~ half a dozen men's hands by now —C.S.Forester⟩ **c (1) —** used as a function word to indicate the transmission of light or vision by some opening or medium ⟨must conduct its observations ~ the restless, dust-filled, and moisture-laden atmosphere —J.G.Vaeth⟩ ⟨learned to look at trees ~ the eyes of a craftsman —W.F.Hambly⟩ ⟨looked ~ the window⟩ ⟨looked ~ the telescope⟩ **(2) —** used as a function word to indicate movement by way of a specified channel or passage ⟨went out ~ the kitchen⟩ ⟨walk across the platform, wait until a train pulls in, walk ~ this train to the next platform —A.C.Spectorsky⟩ **d —** used as a function word to indicate passage between or among the separate or separable units of something ⟨a broad highway ~ overhanging palms —Rex Moorfoot⟩ ⟨a big "whew" went ~ the audience —Dart Smith⟩ **e (1) —** used as a function word to indicate passage around or past an obstacle or impeding force ⟨took the shock of the man's shoulder without breaking stride, ran right ~ him —Irwin Shaw⟩ **(2) :** without stopping for **:** in disregard of **:** PAST ⟨drove ~ a red light⟩ ⟨went ~ a stop sign⟩ **f —** used as a function word to indicate the change in the quality of certain speech sounds consequent on the opening of the nasal passages ⟨speaks ~ the nose⟩ **g —** used as a function word to indicate the penetration of one sound by a fainter or more distant sound ⟨the radio whined so loud that it was a job to talk ~ it —Rose Macaulay⟩ **2 a (1) :** by means of **:** by the help or agency of ⟨the educated himself ~ correspondence courses —*Current Biog.*⟩ ⟨this idea is somewhat more difficult to present ~ statistics —N.R.Heiden⟩ **(2) :** by the intermediary of **:** in the person of ⟨speaking ~ the chairman of its committee on economic policy —*Collier's Yr. Bk.*⟩ ⟨speaking ~ an interpreter⟩ **(3) —** used as a function word to indicate passage by an intermediary or transmission at second hand ⟨a conception of politics derived ~ books⟩ ⟨has gotten his knowledge of the country ~ the reports of travelers⟩ **(4) —** used as a function word to indicate descent from or relationship by means of a specified individual or group of individuals ⟨the principal lines . . . are those ~ four celebrated stallions —Dennis Craig⟩ ⟨are related ~ their grandfather⟩ **b :** by reason of **:** on the basis of **:** because of ⟨farmers at first refused to use it ~ fear that it might poison the soil —*Amer. Guide Series: N.J.*⟩ **c :** as a result of ⟨now extinct ~ disease —R.N.Rudmose-Brown⟩ ⟨~ illness, he lost the use of his feet —Louise P. Kellogg⟩ **3 a :** along the entire expanse of **:** THROUGHOUT ⟨landmarks scattered ~ the pastoral countryside —Budd Schulberg⟩ **b —** used as a function word to indicate movement from point to point within a broad expanse or area ⟨felt the earth wheeling ~ infinity —F.M.Ford⟩ ⟨he'd fly ~ the air with the greatest of ease, this handsome young man on the flying trapeze —George Leybourne⟩ **c —** used as a function word to indicate movement within a specified environment or exposure to a specified set of conditions ⟨the drive . . . was ~ a radiant summer morning —Lucien Price⟩ ⟨didn't you know that she'd try to get it out of me, putting me ~ hell —Hamilton Basso⟩ **4 a :** during the entire period of ⟨all ~ the year⟩ ⟨~ life⟩ — sometimes used postpositively ⟨study the whole summer ~⟩ **b :** from the first to the last of (as an event, action, process) ⟨remained standing ~ the earthquake⟩ ⟨never rested ~ the entire campaign⟩ ⟨put him ~ his paces⟩ **c :** to and including ⟨estimated to cost $425 million for 1954 ~ 1957 —*Wall Street Jour.*⟩ **d —** used as a function word to indicate extension (as of an action or process) into and to the end of a specified period ⟨has decided to prolong his visit ~ the weekend⟩ ⟨will continue construction ~ the winter months⟩ **5 a —** used as a function word to indicate completion or exhaustion of something ⟨a rapid reader who has been known to go ~ three books in a morning —*Current Biog.*⟩ ⟨went straight ~ the brandy and even then had not had enough to drink —Jean Stafford⟩ ⟨went ~ a fortune in one year⟩ **b (1) —** used as a function word to indicate completion of a stage in a process or course of development ⟨passing ~ nature to eternity —Shak.⟩ ⟨many things only just ~ the prototype stage —Bertram Mycock⟩ **(2) —** used as a function word to indicate a specified quantity, extent, or angle of change or movement ⟨the heat required to raise one pound of water ~ 1° F. —S.F.Mason⟩ ⟨the airplane would roll or pitch very slowly ~ several degrees of rotation —H.G.Armstrong⟩ **c —** used as a function word to indicate achievement of a desired or successful outcome or result of a process, activity, or experience ⟨got ~ his final examinations⟩ ⟨got ~ the ordeal of his speech⟩ **d —** used as a function word to indicate satisfaction or completion of the requirements for acceptance or approval by a group or official body ⟨got his application ~ the committee⟩ ⟨got the bill ~ the legislature⟩
²**through** *also* **thru** \"\ *adv* [ME *thurgh*, *thurh*, *thruh*, *through*, fr. OE *thuruh*, *thurh*, prep.] **1 a :** from one end or side to the other by passing into the inner part or space ⟨jealousy pierced her ~⟩ **b :** over the whole distance **:** all the way to a destination ⟨always buy ~ to your farthest destination —Richard Joseph⟩ ⟨the next train goes ~ to New York⟩ **c :** in diameter ⟨a tree measuring twelve inches ~⟩ **2 a :** from beginning to end **:** along the whole of a planned or required course or process ⟨do you read books ~ —Samuel Johnson⟩ ⟨heard the speech ~ without interrupting⟩ **b :** to the very end **:** to completion, conclusion, or accomplishment ⟨were determined to see it ~ at whatever cost —D.W.Brogan⟩ ⟨think it ~⟩ ⟨follow ~⟩ **3 :** to the core **:** COMPLETELY, THOROUGHLY — used only following an adjective or participle ⟨the rain is over, but I am soaked ~ —Ellen Glasgow⟩ ⟨returned to the house chilled ~ by the exposure —H.E.Scudder⟩ ⟨wet ~⟩ **4 :** into the open **:** into perception ⟨when the strong emotion did actually break ~ —H.A.Overstreet⟩
³**through** *also* **thru** \"\ *adj* **1 a :** extending or passing from one end or surface to another ⟨a ~ mortise⟩ ⟨~ ventilation⟩ **b (1) :** admitting free or continuous passage **:** not interrupted or obstructed **:** DIRECT ⟨a ~ road⟩ ⟨a ~ route⟩ **(2) :** affording right of way **c :** at a point of issuance from a substance or channel ⟨that rain pepped things up . . . corn and beans are ~ —H.R.O'Brien⟩ **2 a :** going from point of origin to destination without change or reshipment and often involving more than one carrier ⟨~ train⟩ ⟨~ trailer⟩ **b :** of or relating to such movement ⟨a ~ rate⟩ ⟨a ~ bill of lading⟩ ⟨a ~ ticket⟩ **3 a :** arrived at completion or accomplishment ⟨the patient receives his treatment and then is ~ except for follow-up —*Jour. Amer. Med. Assoc.*⟩ ⟨is almost ~ with his studies⟩ **b :** having no further value, strength, or resources **:** no longer useful or wanted **:** done for **:** FINISHED ⟨nor can you ever be quite sure when a man is ~ —Elmer Davis⟩ ⟨you are ~, you're finished, your nerves are shot —Barnaby Conrad⟩ **c :** having no further concern **:** DONE ⟨he was ~ with school and he was ~ with family —John Dos Passos⟩ ⟨~ with gambling⟩ ⟨~ with drinking⟩
⁴**through** \"\ *n* -S [³*through*] **1 :** PERPEND 1 **2 throughs** *pl* **:** material that falls through something (as a screen or sieve); *specif* **:** the material that passes through a sieve during the process of milling flour
⁵**through** \'thrük\ *n* -S [ME *thrughe*, *throgh*, *through* coffin, through stone, fr. OE *thrūh* pipe, trough, coffin; akin to ON *thrō* trough] *chiefly Scot* **:** ¹THROUGH STONE
¹**through and through** *prep* [ME] **:** repeatedly through **:** in at one side and out the other side of ⟨thy slander hath gone *through and through* her heart —Shak.⟩
²**through and through** *adv* [ME] **1 :** in every possible way or aspect **:** to the fullest extent **:** THOROUGHLY ⟨was *through and through* a liberal, a democrat, and a republican —Oscar Handlin⟩ **2 :** all the way through **:** from one end to the other ⟨a thunderstorm that drenched them *through and through*⟩
through-and-through coal \'⸗⸗'⸗-\ *n*, *Brit* **:** RUN OF MINE
through arch *n* **:** an arch through a heavy wall
through bolt *n* **:** a bolt passing through all the thicknesses or layers which it binds or in which it is fixed and made fast by a nut at the end opposite the head
through bond *n* **:** a transverse bond formed by a member that extends crosswise through the wall

through bridge *n* **1 :** a bridge in which the roadway or track passes between the supporting elements (as trusses, girders, or arches) — compare DECK BRIDGE **2 :** BOTTOM-ROAD BRIDGE
through check *n* **:** a check in a piece of timber extending all the way through from surface to surface
through–composed \'=,=\ *adj* [trans. of G *durchkomponiert*] **:** having an individual musical setting for each stanza or strophe — used of a song or aria; compare STROPHIC
through cut *n* **:** a cut with excavated slopes on both sides of the roadway
throughfall \'=,=\ *n* **:** rainfall in a forest area that is not intercepted by the crown canopy and reaches the forest floor
throughfare *n* [by contr.] *obs* **:** THOROUGHFARE
through girder bridge *n* **:** a girder bridge in which the traffic passes between the girders
¹throughgoing \'=,==\ *n* [²*through* + *going*, gerund of *go*] **1** *archaic* **:** EXAMINATION, OVERHAULING **2** *archaic* **:** REPRIMAND
²throughgoing \"\ *adj* [²*through* + *going*, pres. part. of *go*] **1 :** passing or extending all the way through **2** *archaic* **:** ENERGETIC
¹through·ith·er \'thrü,ithə(r)\ *or* **through·oth·er** \-,əthə(r)\ *adv* [¹*through* + *other*] *chiefly Scot* **:** in confusion **:** PROMISCUOUSLY
²throughither \"\ *or* **throughother** \"\ *adj, chiefly Scot* **:** CONFUSED, DISORDERLY, SCATTERBRAINED ⟨would turn out scientific, and him such a *throughither* laddie —John Buchan⟩
through·ly *adv* [ME, fr. ²*through* + *-ly*] **1** *archaic* **:** THOROUGHLY ⟨I'll be revenged most ~ for my father —Shak.⟩ **2** *archaic* **:** THROUGH AND THROUGH ⟨take this book; peruse it ~ —Christopher Marlowe⟩
¹throughout \'=,=\ *adv* [ME *thurhout, throughout,* fr. *thurh, through* through (adv.) + *out*] **1 a :** in or to every part **:** from one end to the other **:** EVERYWHERE ⟨the second variety . . . is a light pink ~, with flecks of red —*Amer. Guide Series: Tenn.*⟩ **b :** as far as the edges or extremities of a heraldic field **2** *archaic* **:** right through to the end **:** COMPLETELY ⟨you may read a book ~ —L.R.McCalvin⟩ **3 :** during the whole time or action **:** from beginning to end ⟨the survey has ~ aimed at carrying out a large scientific program —G.deQ.Robin⟩
²throughout \"\ *prep* [ME *thurhout, throughout,* fr. *thurh, through* through (prep.) + *out*] **1 :** all the way from one end to the other of **:** in or to every part of ⟨all duties, imposts, and excises shall be uniform ~ the United States —*U.S.Constitution*⟩ **2 :** during the whole course or period of ⟨receiving a wound in one of his arms that troubled him ~ life —E.W. Parks⟩
³throughout \"\ *adj* [ME, fr. ¹*throughout*] **:** extending to the edges of a heraldic field **:** ENTIRE — used postpositively ⟨a lozenge ~⟩
throughput \'=,=\ *n* **:** an amount of raw material put through processing or finishing operations in a specific time ⟨its initial daily ~ of 110,000 barrels —*Lamp*⟩ ⟨a ~ of about 500,000 birds a year —*Country Life*⟩
through rate *n* **1 :** a single transportation rate on an interline haul made up of two or more separately established rates **2 :** JOINT RATE
through retort *n* **:** a retort (as used for the distillation of mercury from cinnabar or for producing coal gas) with doors or mouthpieces at both ends that are closed during distillation
throughs *pl of* THROUGH
through shake *n* **:** a crack or fissure in timber that extends from side to side, edge to edge, or side to edge
through–shine \'=,=\ *adj* [ME, fr. OE *thurhscīne,* fr. *thurh* through + *scīnan* to shine — more at SHINE] **:** TRANSPARENT ⟨a *through-shine* glow of boyish vanity —George Biddle⟩
through station *n* **:** a railroad station whose tracks do not terminate at the station building but extend past it — compare STUB STATION
¹through stone *n* [ME *throgh stone,* fr. *throgh* through + *stone* — more at THROUGH ⟨through stone⟩] *chiefly Scot* **:** a flat tombstone
²through stone *n* [³*through* + *stone*] **:** PERPEND 1
through street *n* **:** a street on which the through movement of traffic is given preference; *specif* **:** one at which traffic on all intersecting streets is required by law to stop or yield before entering or crossing except where traffic signal or officer control is employed
through switch *n* **:** a snap switch installed in a length of flexible cord
through traffic *n* **:** traffic initiated at and destined for points outside a local zone
through train *n* **:** a train usu. making a limited number of stops on which passengers may travel to a scheduled destination without changing to another train
through valley *n* **:** a depression or channel eroded across a divide by glacial ice or meltwater
throughway \'=,=\ *n* **1 :** THROUGH STREET **2 :** EXPRESSWAY
throve *past of* THRIVE
¹throw \'thrō\ *vb* **threw** \'thrü\ *or dial* **throwed** \'thrōd\ *or* **trun** \'trən\ **thrown** \'thrōn\ *or dial* **throwed; throwing; throws** [ME *thrawen, throwen* to cause to twist, throw, fr. OE *thrāwan* to cause to twist or turn; akin to MD *draeyen* to cause to twist or turn, OHG *drāen,* L *terere* to rub, grind, *terebra* borer, gimlet, Gk *tetrainein* to bore through, pierce, *trēmat-, trēma* hole, *teirein* to oppress, distress, *tribein* to rub, grind; basic meaning: to rub with a twisting motion, bore] *vt* **1 a (1) :** to propel through the air by a forward motion of the hand and arm ⟨~ a baseball⟩ ⟨have no intention of ~*ing* bombs —J.B.Priestley⟩ **(2) :** to propel through the air with the hand and arm in an attempt to surpass competitors in an athletic contest ⟨~ the discus⟩ ⟨~ the javelin⟩ **b :** to propel through the air in any manner ⟨heavy rifles . . . able to ~ a bullet about five miles —Mari Sandoz⟩ ⟨a fire engine ~*ing* a stream of water⟩ ⟨satellite will be *thrown* into space —Courtney Sheldon⟩ **c :** to cast (a net, line hook, bait) in fishing **2 a (1) :** to cause to fall ⟨the wrestler easily *threw* his opponent⟩ **(2) :** to tackle (a ballcarrier) behind the line of scrimmage ⟨sometimes save our passer from being *thrown* for a loss —Norman Geske⟩ **(3) :** WEDGE 5 **b :** to cause to fall off **:** UNSEAT ⟨the horse *threw* his rider⟩ **c :** to get the better of **:** OVERCOME ⟨it was too formidable an enterprise for her but it didn't ~ her entirely —Douglas Watt⟩ **3 a :** to fling (oneself) in a precipitate manner ⟨just had time to ~ myself behind a small sofa —Patrick Campbell⟩ ⟨*threw* himself down on his knees like a miser who has found a . . . treasure —O.E.Rölvaag⟩ **b :** to drive or impel in a violent manner **:** DASH ⟨the ship was *thrown* on a reef⟩ **4 a (1) :** to cause to be in a particular position, condition, or situation **:** PUT ⟨*thrown* upon his own resources at the age of fifteen —D.E.Smith⟩ ⟨~*s* a subject out of balance with other ideas —C.E.Kellogg⟩ ⟨wage earners were *thrown* out of employment —W.J.Ghent⟩ ⟨a lot of yak-yak ~*s* me off my game —Willard Temple⟩ ⟨~*ing* her body backward at the shoulders like a young cadet —Scott Fitzgerald⟩ ⟨prepared to ~ open another room —David Garnett⟩ ⟨turned to ~ her arms round him —C.W.H.Johnson⟩ **(2) :** to put on hastily or carelessly **:** DON ⟨*threw* a coat over her shoulders and ran into the yard⟩ **(3) :** to put forcefully or roughly ⟨*threw* the chiefs of the opposition into prison —T.B.Macaulay⟩ **(4) :** to place or propel as if by a throw ⟨is not intended to . . . ~ any slur whatever on your firm —F.W.Crofts⟩ ⟨wants to ~ into a word every trace of meaning that it can hold —C.S.Kilby⟩ **b :** to move quickly **:** ADVANCE ⟨resolved to ~ his army across the river —J.W.Pratt⟩ **c :** to bring to bear **:** EXERT ⟨her influence was *thrown* upon the side of . . . the students —D.C.Peattie⟩ ⟨*threw* the weight of his paper against the movement —Broadus Mitchell⟩ **d :** to change into another form **:** CONVERT ⟨stories which they *threw* into crude stanzas —W.A.Neilson⟩ ⟨the necessity of ~*ing* confidential correspondence into cipher —Fletcher Pratt⟩ **e :** BUILD, CONSTRUCT ⟨the two concrete dams they *threw* across the stream bed to create reservoirs —F.J.Taylor⟩ ⟨*threw* his pontoon bridge across the river near this spot —*Amer. Guide Series: Tenn.*⟩ **f :** to bring into association ⟨his inclinations . . . naturally *threw* him into companionship with geologists —G.P.Merrill⟩ ⟨found himself *thrown* less with his queen and her sober intimates —Francis Hackett⟩ **g :** TIE ⟨~ a diamond hitch⟩ **5 a :** to form or shape on a potter's wheel ⟨smudging their smocks as they ~ the wet spinning clay —*Time*⟩ ⟨used the rotating wheel to ~ his pottery —*Times Lit. Supp.*⟩ **b :** to fashion or frame in a particular shape or manner **:** FORM ⟨*threw* his opinion into a neatly turned phrase⟩ **c :** CAST 4a (1) ⟨~ a bullet⟩ **d :** to form by digging or plowing ⟨plows . . . set for ~*ing* a ridge . . . 18 in. high —*Farmer's Weekly (So. Africa)*⟩ **6 a :** to deliver (a blow) in or as if in boxing ⟨*threw* . . . a tentative right to the expansive midriff of his towering opponent —L. W.T.Dovale⟩ **b :** to give (a salute) in a jaunty manner ⟨*threw* the marine on guard a nifty salute —J.A.Michener⟩ **7 a :** to twist two or more filaments of (as silk, rayon) into a thread or yarn **b :** to double and twist (singles) in the making of plied yarns **8 a :** to direct orally ⟨~*ing* a cheerful greeting to his secretary —Max Peacock⟩ ⟨paused for a moment and then *threw* an abrupt question at him —T.B.Costain⟩ **b :** to direct (as a look) in a hurried or cursory manner ⟨a glance that I had seen her ~ over her shoulder —Lord Dunsany⟩ ⟨*threw* a slight, easy look at his men and . . . walked out on the platform —Owen Wister⟩ **9 a (1) :** to make a cast of (dice) **(2) :** to make (a cast) at dice **b :** to play (a card) in a card game; *esp* **:** DISCARD **10 a :** to get rid of **:** divest or strip oneself of **:** cast off ⟨the snake ~*s* her enameled skin —Shak.⟩ ⟨his horse had *thrown* a shoe and he came up to the barn to draw out the nails —Erskine Caldwell⟩ ⟨one tank *threw* a track on a coconut log and went out of action —*Infantry Jour.*⟩ **b :** to free oneself from **:** DISLODGE, EJECT ⟨the fish leaps clear of the water trying to ~ the hook —Carlos Baker⟩ **c :** to give up as if by throwing away **:** ABANDON ⟨*threw* prudence to the wind and eloped —DeLancey Ferguson⟩ ⟨~*ing* all her moral teachings and inhibitions overboard —Ruth Park⟩ **11 a :** to send forth **:** PROJECT ⟨men . . . ~*ing* two burly shadows across the rocking chair —William Wiser⟩ ⟨fog ~*ing* the light back into his eyes —Harry Sylvester⟩ ⟨their effort ~*s* light on how the brain itself operates —Stuart Chase⟩ ⟨the light it ~*s* on the art movements of the time —O. Elfrida Saunders⟩ **b :** to give off **:** EMIT ⟨one of the planes began to ~ smoke⟩ **12 :** to make (oneself) dependent **:** commit (oneself) for help, support, or protection ⟨had *thrown* herself on their good nature —Ida A. R. Wylie⟩ ⟨you can . . . ~ yourselves on his mercy —John Buchan⟩ **13 a :** to cause to move or turn ⟨~ your mind back to the time when you saw melodrama of the now unfashionable kind —Daniel George⟩ **b :** to turn in a sudden or forceful manner ⟨was obliged to ~ his craft violently to avoid a collision —Walter O'Meara⟩ **14 a :** to give oneself up to unrestrainedly **:** give way to ⟨others ~ temper tantrums or pick fights —M.M. Hunt⟩ ⟨was able to get off the bus without ~*ing* a fit —J.D. Sheridan⟩ **b :** to apply freely or fully **:** DEVOTE ⟨dancing . . . with all the force and energy they could ~ into it —Meridel Le Sueur⟩ ⟨*threw* his whole physique into his conducting —Warwick Braithwaite⟩ **c :** to busy (oneself) in a zealous earnest manner ⟨*threw* themselves heartily into the preparations —Agnes S. Turnbull⟩ ⟨~*s* himself into his painting with furious energy —C.C.Walcutt⟩ **15 a :** to cast (a vote) in an election ⟨presidential votes . . . *thrown* for the Democratic candidate —James Bryce⟩ **b :** to send (an election) for final decision ⟨through lack of a popular majority the election was *thrown* into the legislature —W.A.Robinson⟩ **16 a (1) :** to give birth to **:** bring forth ⟨a fat sow . . . will not ~ large farrows —E.W.Lloyd⟩ **(2) :** SIRE, ENGENDER ⟨this ram is ~*ing* good stock —F.C.Stone⟩ **b :** PRODUCE, BEAR ⟨a field that ~*s* a good crop⟩ **17 :** to allow an opponent to win **:** lose intentionally or deliberately ⟨basketball players convicted of ~*ing* games —*Christian Science Monitor*⟩ ⟨~ a case . . . by remarks in court which will lay grounds for mistrials —D.D.McKean⟩ **18 a :** to move (a lever) so as to connect or disconnect parts of a clutch, machine, or switch **b :** to connect or disconnect (as a clutch, switch) by moving a lever **19 a :** to draw and aim (as a firearm) ⟨his finger was tight on the trigger as he *threw* the gun —R.J.Hogan⟩ — often used with *down* **b :** to make use of in a military attack ⟨*threw* everything they had against her: high-level bombs, dive bombers, and suicidal torpedo bombers —T.W.Lawson⟩ **20 :** to move (a typewriter carriage) to the left on completing a line by striking the line space lever **21 :** to give by way of entertainment **:** serve as host at ⟨had *thrown* one of his tremendous parties for the circus people —Alva Johnston⟩ **22 :** to engage in (as aimless talk) often as a means of passing the time ⟨sat around most of the afternoon ~*ing* the bull⟩ **23 :** to demand or obtain an advantage over a person by the assertion of (as superiority) ⟨sergeant . . . I have got to ~ rank at you —Bill Mauldin⟩ **24 :** to weigh out (a charge of powder) ~ *vi* **1 a :** to propel something through the air ⟨are taught the proper way to . . . field a ball and ~ —*Scholastic Coach*⟩ **b :** to have the capacity of propelling a missile ⟨the bazooka would have to ~ about eighty yards to reach the tank —Irwin Shaw⟩ **2 :** to fling oneself forcefully or violently **:** SPRING ⟨the black dog . . . *threw* at her —J.C.Atkinson⟩ **3 :** to cast dice **:** play at dice
syn TOSS, CAST, SLING, PITCH, HURL, FLING: THROW is the general term in this set and is very often interchangeable with the others; typically it indicates propelling through the air by distinctive movement of the bent arm followed by release of the object involved. TOSS may suggest less force, occasional aimlessness or lack of purpose, and an upward outward motion of the arm ⟨she rested on a log and *tossed* the fresh chips —Robert Frost⟩ In extended uses it may indicate light, easy throwing ⟨prevented Americans from *tossing* aside their global burdens —E.D.Canham⟩ CAST is a close synonym for *throw* but has been supplanted by the latter except in various special uses ⟨*cast* a net⟩ ⟨*casting* dice⟩ ⟨*cast* seed⟩ SLING may imply quick, sudden propulsion well aimed, as though accomplished with a sling ⟨*slung* an inkwell at a fellow senator in a congressional free-for-all —*Time*⟩ PITCH may suggest a definite, purposive aim to a specific spot or area ⟨*pitching* matchbooks at a crack for tomorrow's ration . . . was the favorite sport —James Jones⟩ ⟨possible for whole companies of grenadiers to run up to their enemy's lines and roll, bowl, or *pitch* their grenades among the legs of their opponents —Tom Wintringham⟩ HURL implies forceful impetus in the propulsion ⟨the wind picked the sand off the flinty, rolling ridges and *hurled* it in malicious bursts at you —Irwin Shaw⟩ ⟨electrons are *hurled* between cloud and cloud or between cloud and earth in long, branching flashes —Waldemar Kaempffert⟩ FLING stresses a certain force in throwing and may suggest unnecessary violence or random aimlessness brought about by strong emotion ⟨then he loathed his own beauty, and, *flinging* the mirror on the floor, crushed it into silver splinters beneath his heel —Oscar Wilde⟩ ⟨came racing up the path on his bicycle, *flung* it down in the yard and rushed straight into the farmhouse —George Orwell⟩
— **throw one's weight around** *or* **throw one's weight about :** to exercise influence or authority esp. to an excessive degree or in an objectionable manner ⟨began *throwing her weight around* the moment she was installed in her job —Bennett Cerf⟩ ⟨prickly with vanity and *throwing his weight about* as a young lieutenant —V.S.Pritchett⟩ — **throw together 1 :** to put together in a hurried and usu. careless manner ⟨an obviously profitable move to *throw together* six excerpts for a third suite —Arthur Berger⟩ **2 :** to bring into casual association ⟨were *thrown together* necessarily by a common interest —R.M.Lovett⟩
²throw \"\ *n* -S **1 a :** an act or instance of throwing, hurling, or flinging ⟨the catcher's ~ was high and the runner slid safely into second⟩ ⟨an underhand ~⟩ **b (1) :** an act of throwing dice **(2) :** the number or aggregate thrown ⟨a ~ of 7 or 11⟩ **c :** a method of throwing an opponent in wrestling or judo ⟨scissor-jump ~⟩ ⟨straight thigh ~⟩ **d** *chiefly Brit* **(1) :** an act of felling timber **(2) :** the quantity of trees felled **2 :** the distance that a missile is or may be thrown ⟨lived within a stone's ~ of the school⟩ **3 :** an undertaking that involves chance or danger **:** RISK, VENTURE ⟨has been marked by . . . a reckless ~ that failed —T.R.Ybarra⟩ **4 :** an instrument (as a potter's wheel) for turning **5 a :** the amount of vertical displacement up or down produced by a fault — compare DOWNTHROW, UPTHROW **b :** DISLOCATION b **6 a :** the extreme movement given or available to a pivoted or reciprocating piece by a cam, crank, or eccentric **:** TRAVEL, STROKE ⟨the ~ of a switch⟩ **b (1) :** the length of the radius of a crank or the virtual crank radius of an eccentric or cam **(2) :** CRANK WEB **7 a :** a lightweight flat cover (as a bedspread or afghan) that is casually draped or laid over something **b :** a woman's scarf or light wrap **8 :** the instantaneous deflection of a galvanometer needle or suspension when the instrument is used as a ballistic galvanometer **9 a :** the distance between a projector lens and the screen surface upon which an image is focused **b :** the distance between a loudspeaker and its audience **10 :** an object or individual regarded as a distinct member of a kind or class **:** UNIT, PIECE ⟨copies are to be sold at $5 a ~ —Harvey Breit⟩ **11 a :** ²SLING 2 **b :** the stipulated number of shots in a round of darts **12 :** a lever by means of which the binding of a ski is tightened
throw about *vi* **:** to go in a different direction **:** TACK
throw away *vt* **1 a :** to get rid of as worthless or unnecessary ⟨*threw away* a pair of old shoes⟩ **b :** DISCARD 1b **2 a :** to use in a foolish or wasteful manner **:** SQUANDER ⟨worked too hard for this money to *throw it away* —Kenneth Roberts⟩ **b :** to fail to take advantage of **:** WASTE ⟨the chance for a successful stand . . . was *thrown away* —Herbert Agar⟩ **3 :** to de-emphasize (as a line in a play) by casual delivery ⟨knows when to move upstage, when to modulate his voice, when to *throw away* a line —Harriet Van Horne⟩
throwaway \'=,=\ *n* -S [*throw away*] **:** something that is or is designed to be thrown away: as **a :** a handbill, pamphlet, advertising circular, newspaper, or shopping guide distributed free **b :** a line or segment of dialogue (as in a play) de-emphasized by casual delivery
throw back *vt* **1 :** to delay the progress or advance of **:** CHECK ⟨armies concentrated to . . . *throw back* the British striking forces —Tom Wintringham⟩ **2 :** to cause to rely **:** make dependent ⟨the Boston mind, *thrown back* upon itself, resumed its old colonial allegiance —Van Wyck Brooks⟩ **3 :** REFLECT ⟨pavements *throw back* the lights in wavy lines —Thomas Wood †1950⟩ ~ *vi* **:** to revert to an earlier type or phase; *specif* **:** to exhibit atavism ⟨the tendency of all varieties of pigeons to *throw back* —*Amer. Pigeon Jour.*⟩
throwback \'=,=\ *n* -S [*throw back*] **1 :** a reversal or backward deviation from a path or course **2 a :** reversion to an earlier type or phase; *specif* **:** ATAVISM **b :** an instance or product of such reversion ⟨have eliminated the sports and ~*s* and are getting a definite, consistent, and predictable type —*Fortune*⟩ ⟨a ~ to the heroic drama of Shakespearean times —Leslie Rees⟩ ⟨an aristocrat of the old line, a ~ to another century —W.A.White⟩ **3 :** FLASHBACK ⟨makes clever use of multiple-scene ~*s* and is . . . in every way a first-rate drama —*N.Y. Herald Tribune Bk. Rev.*⟩
throw by *vt* **:** to put aside **:** discard as worthless or unnecessary
throw–crook \'=,=\ *n* [¹*throw* + *crook*] *chiefly Scot* **:** an instrument used for twisting rope from hay, straw, or hair
throw down *vt* [ME *throwen doun,* fr. *throwen* to throw + *doun* down] **1 :** to cause to fall **:** OVERTHROW ⟨if a tree is *thrown down* in a storm —J.G.Frazer⟩ **2 :** PRECIPITATE **3 :** to cast off **:** DISCARD, REJECT ⟨her beau's gone and *thrown* her *down* —William Faulkner⟩
throwdown \'=,=\ *n* -S [*throw down*] **:** an act or instance of a referee's putting a soccer ball in play by dropping it to the ground between two opposing players
throwed *dial past of* THROW
throw·er \'thrō(ə)r, -ōə\ *n* -S **:** one that throws: as **a :** a worker who forms pottery on a potter's wheel **b :** THROWSTER
throw in *vt* **1 :** to add as a gratuity or supplement ⟨compromised in the end by *throwing in* a cheap clock —Arthur Morrison⟩ **2 :** to introduce or interject in the course of something **:** CONTRIBUTE ⟨not a word wasted, not a sentiment capriciously *thrown in* —Matthew Arnold⟩ **3 :** DISTRIBUTE 3b(1) **4 a :** to cause (as gears) to mesh **b :** ENGAGE ⟨*throw in* the clutch⟩ ~ *vi* **1 :** to enter into association or partnership **:** JOIN ⟨agrees to *throw in* with a crooked ex-cop —*Newsweek*⟩ **2 :** DROP 2b(6) — **throw in one's hand 1 :** to signify withdrawal from the current hand of a card game by putting one's cards into the discard **2 :** to give up the struggle or contest **:** SURRENDER — **throw in one's lot with :** to join as an associate **:** share the fate of ⟨reluctant to *throw in their lot with* a new society —*Farmer's Weekly (So. Africa)*⟩ — **throw in the sponge** *or* **throw up the sponge** *or* **throw in the towel** [fr. the practice of a boxer's second of throwing a sponge or towel into the ring for his fighter to wipe his face, this being taken as an admission that they were no longer willing to continue the bout] **:** to abandon the struggle **:** acknowledge defeat **:** give up ⟨*throwing in the sponge* and failing to accomplish our mission —Glen Jacobsen⟩ ⟨when so many had *thrown up the sponge* and surrendered all faith in humanity —Van Wyck Brooks⟩ ⟨when the chaplain *throws in the towel* over your problem —*All Hands*⟩
throw–in \'=,=\ *n* -S [*throw in*] **1 :** an act or instance of throwing a ball in: as **a :** a throw made from the touchline in soccer to put the ball back in play after it has gone into touch **b :** a throw made by an outfielder in baseball to the infield **c :** a throw between the opposing ranks of players in polo with each team being on its own side of the line of the throw **d :** a throw made from outside the boundaries in basketball to put the ball back in play after it has gone out of bounds **2 :** an end play in bridge in which an opponent is forced to win a trick at a time when he must next make a lead disadvantageous to his side
throwing *pres part of* THROW
throwing–knife \'==,=(=)\ *or* **throwing–iron** \'==,=(=)\ *n* [*throwing* (gerund of ¹*throw*) + *knife* or *iron*] **:** a knifelike weapon often with several blades set at different angles that is used by some central African people for casting at an enemy or animal
throwing power *n* **:** the ability to deposit a plating of uniform depth on a surface of irregular shape
throwing–spear \'==,=\ *n* **:** a spear or spear-shaped object that is propelled with or without the help of a mechanical device
throwing–stick \'==,=\ *n* **1** *or* **throwing–board** \'==,=\ **:** a device for throwing a spear or dart consisting of a rod or board with a groove on the upper surface and a hook, thong, or projection at the rear end to hold the weapon in place until its release — called also *dart thrower, spear-thrower* **2 :** a wooden weapon in the form of a simple club or of an S-shaped, angular, or curved stick that is thrown by hand — compare WAR CLUB
throw lathe *n* **:** a small hand lathe
throw line *n* **1 :** a handline for fishing **2 :** a line indicating the throw of a crank or eccentric
thrown \'thrōn\ *adj* [fr. past part. of ¹*throw*] *of a violin stroke* **:** performed with a loose grip so that the upper part of the bow is free to fall and rebound on the strings by its own weight ⟨~ staccato⟩
thrown–out \'=,=\ *adj* **:** inserted as a throw-out ⟨*thrown-out* maps⟩
thrown silk *n* **:** reeled silk that has been twisted or doubled and twisted into yarns
throw off *vt* **1 a :** to free oneself from **:** get rid of ⟨his only chance of *throwing off* the evil spell —Bill Beatty⟩ ⟨*threw off* his political masters and start a revolution —T.P.Whitney⟩ **b :** to cast off often in a hurried or vigorous manner **:** ABANDON, DISCARD ⟨*threw off* his coat and went to work⟩ ⟨*threw off* all sense of restraint⟩ **c :** to shake off **:** DIVERT ⟨wasn't to be *thrown off* by a false scent —*Blackwood's*⟩ **2 :** to make a start with in a hunt ⟨*throw off* thy ready pack —William Somerville⟩ **3 :** to give off **:** EMIT, EJECT ⟨mills *throwing off* . . . greenish clouds of smoke —*Amer. Guide Series: Conn.*⟩ **4 :** to produce in or as if in an offhand manner **:** execute with speed or facility ⟨some little scrap of tune that the composer had *thrown off* —James Hilton⟩ ⟨can *throw off* a criticism of eighteenth-century architecture or of the fad for whole-meal bread —*Times Lit. Supp.*⟩ **5 :** to remove (a man) from the backgammon board after all the men are home **6 a :** to cause to depart from an expected or desired course ⟨hidden assumptions *threw* the Newtonian calculations *off* just the smallest bit —T.H.Littlefield⟩ ⟨violation of form had *thrown* the whole story *off* —Alec Rackowe⟩ **b :** to cause to make a mistake or form a wrong impression **:** MISLEAD ⟨it had been her thick accent that had *thrown* me *off* —Richard Wright⟩ ~ *vi* **1 :** to begin hunting **2 :** to make derogatory comments **:** cast aspersions ⟨was constantly *throwing off* on the neighbors⟩
throw–off \'=,=\ *n* -S [*throw off*] **1 :** an act or instance of throwing off; *specif* **:** the start of a hunt **2 :** something that is thrown off **3 :** something that throws off: as **a (1) :** a device

in a printing press for suspending impression without stopping the machine (2) : an automatic device in a machine tool to stop the feed **b** : DERAIL **4** : the amount of cash generated by the operation of a business

throw out *vt* **1 a** : to remove from a place, office, or employment usu. in a sudden or unexpected manner ⟨your grooms . . . could perhaps *throw* me *out* —S.H.Adams⟩ ⟨be *thrown out* again as a result of some fresh change in the political landscape —A.J.Toynbee⟩ **b** : to get rid of as worthless or unnecessary ⟨people . . . won't *throw out* things fast enough to create new needs —K.D.Burke⟩ **2** : to give expression to : UTTER ⟨*threw out* a remark . . . that utterly confounded him —Jean Stafford⟩ ⟨merely *throw out* these considerations to the House —Sir Winston Churchill⟩ **3** : to dismiss from acceptance or consideration : REJECT ⟨a coerced confession . . . is sure to be *thrown out* —Charles Oldfather⟩ ⟨had *thrown out* certain specked ballots —E.F.Humphrey⟩ **4** : to make visible or manifest : DISPLAY ⟨the signal was *thrown out* for the . . . fleet to prepare for action —Archibald Duncan⟩ **5** : to leave behind : OUTDISTANCE ⟨had been unluckily *thrown out* and was riding fast to be in my place —Sir Walter Scott⟩ **6** : to give forth from or as if from within : EMIT ⟨the radio *throwing out* a good tune —Anton Vogt⟩ ⟨an apple tree . . . *threw out* a sharp scent —Edith Sitwell⟩ **7 a** : to send out ⟨urged the general to *throw out* . . . Indian scouts into the woods —H.E.Scudder⟩ **b** : to cause to project : EXTEND ⟨this whitish house with . . . the wing *thrown out* at right angles —Virginia Woolf⟩ **8** : to put out : CONFUSE, DISCONCERT ⟨automobiles in line blocking the road . . . *threw* the whole schedule *out* —F.D.Roosevelt⟩ ⟨anyone boorish . . . *threw* him *out* a little —Elizabeth Taylor⟩ **9** : to cause to stand out : make prominent or clear ⟨the figures of . . . its greater men are *thrown out* plainly by their written works —H.O.Taylor⟩ **10 a** : to run out (a cricket batsman) by breaking the wicket with a direct throw of a fielded ball **b** : to make a throw that enables a teammate in baseball to put out (a base runner) **11** : DISENGAGE ⟨*throw out* the clutch⟩

throw–out \ˈ⸗,⸗\ *n* -s [*throw out*] **1** : an act or instance of throwing out **2** : one that is rejected or discarded ⟨the attack on the government was led by envious *throw-outs* —George Orwell⟩ ⟨the *throw-outs* of ten generations, household rubbish made romantic by time —Richard Church⟩ **3 a** : a device for throwing a machine out of gear **b** : the mechanism or assemblage of mechanisms by which the driven and driving plates of a clutch in an automotive vehicle are separated **4** : a book insert made in such a way that when unfolded its printed content is outside the edges of the book **5** : BREAK 4f

throw over *vt* **1** : to forsake despite bonds of attachment or duty : ABANDON ⟨*threw* her *over* for a girl from a wealthy family —Polly Adler⟩ **2** : to refuse to accept : REJECT ⟨in his chapter on accent . . . *throws over* the ancient rules —H.O. Taylor⟩ ⟨carefully planned campaign to *throw over* the treaty —F.D.Roosevelt⟩

throw rug *n* : SCATTER RUG

throws *pres 3d sing of* THROW, *pl of* THROW

throw·ster \ˈthrōstə(r)\ *n* -s [ME *throwester*, fr. *throwen* to throw, twist + *-ster*] : one who throws silk or synthetic filaments

throw stick *n* : THROWING-STICK

throw up *vb* [ME *throwen up*, fr. *throwen* to throw + *up*] *vt* **1** : to raise quickly or unexpectedly ⟨*throw up* the window⟩ **2** : to give up : QUIT, RELINQUISH ⟨*threw up* a good job to devote his whole time to art —Herbert Read⟩ ⟨*throw* the whole thing *up* and do exactly what he wanted to do —Mary Deasy⟩ **3** : to build in or as if in a hurried manner : construct hastily ⟨makeshift dwellings . . . were *thrown up* almost overnight —*Amer. Guide Series: N.Y. City*⟩ ⟨a breastwork was *thrown up* around the outskirts —*Amer. Guide Series: Minn.*⟩ **4** : VOMIT ⟨if they are swallowed whole they may be *thrown up* —H.H.Miller⟩ **5** : to bring forth : PRODUCE ⟨proves that Parliament can *throw up* leaders —Ernest Barker⟩ ⟨all the voluminous information *thrown up* by successive . . . investigations —S.F.Bemis⟩ **6** : to make prominent or distinct esp. by contrast : cause to stand out ⟨white and yellow . . . help to *throw up* the other colors in the garden —Stuart Ogg⟩ **7** : to mention repeatedly by way of reproach ⟨don't want that *thrown up* to me when I'm old and gray —Hamilton Basso⟩ ~ *vi* **1** : VOMIT ⟨it was pretty hot . . . and she got sick and *threw up* —Don Ludlow⟩ **2** *of a hound* : to raise the head on losing the scent — **throw up one's hands** : to admit defeat ⟨the average conductor, faced with such a score, *throws up his hands* —Deems Taylor⟩

thru *var of* THROUGH

¹thrum \ˈthrəm\ *n* -s [ME, fr. OE *-thrum* (as in *tungethrum* ligament of the tongue); akin to OS *thrumi* end part of a spear, OHG *drum* end part, fragment, ON *thrömr* edge, verge, brim, Gk *tramis* perineum, *termōn* boundary, end — more at TERM] **1 a** (1) : a fringe of warp threads left on the loom after the cloth has been removed (2) : one of these warp threads **b** : loom waste consisting of warp ends and test fabric pieces **c** : a short soft thread or tuft of threads **d** : a tuft or short piece of rope yarn used in thrumming canvas — usu. used in pl. **e** : something held to resemble a thrum : BIT, PARTICLE, SCRAP **2 a** : a hair, fiber, or threadlike leaf on a plant that resembles or is held to resemble a thrum **b** : a tuft, bundle, fringe, or other mass of such structures **3** *obs* : a ragged beggarly lout **4** *Brit* : THREEPENCE : a threepenny piece

²thrum \"\ *vt* **thrummed; thrummed; thrumming; thrums** **1 a** : to furnish with thrums **b** : to cover with tufts or pile **2** *obs* : to attire with or as if with a covering or fringe : CLOTHE, FRINGE **3** : to insert short pieces of rope yarn or spun yarn in (a piece of canvas) to make a rough surface or a mat which can be wrapped about rigging to prevent chafing or used to stop a leak — **thrum caps** *obs* : to waste time in an idle or foolish occupation

³thrum \"\ *adj* : made of or woven from thrum ⟨in his ~ nightcap —Laurence Sterne⟩

⁴thrum \"\ *vb* **thrummed; thrummed; thrumming; thrums** [imit.] *vi* **1** : to play idly on or as if on a stringed musical instrument by plucking or strumming with the fingers or by keys ⟨at night, with guitars, we *thrummed* and sang —Eve Langley⟩ ⟨~ on a mandolin⟩ ⟨~ on a table⟩ **2 a** : to sound with a repeated and often monotonous hum like a string or an instrument when strummed ⟨the blood *thrummed* in my ears —Rumer Godden⟩ **b** : to move accompanied by such a sound ⟨the wire ~*s* out steadily —*Science*⟩ **3** : to repeat something over and over : to speak or read aloud monotonously ~ *vt* **1** : to play (as a stringed musical instrument) in an idle or relaxed manner ⟨~*s* a preliminary chord or two —P.B.Kyne⟩ ⟨~ a guitar⟩ **2** : to recite monotonously : repeat in a singsong voice **3** : to strike with the fingers as if playing on a musical instrument : drum on ⟨~ the table⟩

⁵thrum \"\ *n* -s **1** : an often monotonous sound made by thrumming ⟨across the plaza came the ~ of guitars —*Atlantic*⟩ ⟨~ of hoofs from the paddock —Elizabeth Bowen⟩ ⟨the ~ of the mighty engines⟩ **2** : the purring of a cat

thrum·ble \ˈthrəm(b)əl, -rüm-\ *var of* THRIMBLE

thrum–eyed \ˈ⸗,⸗\ *adj* : having the anthers exserted and visible at the throat of the corolla ⟨*thrum-eyed* flowers of various primulas⟩ — compare PIN-EYED

thrum·mer \ˈthrəmə(r)\ *n* -s [⁴*thrum* + *-er*] : one that thrums an instrument; *esp* : a strolling player

thrum·ming \ˈthrəmiŋ, -mēŋ\ *n* -s [¹*thrum* + *-ing*] : a mass of tufts or short pieces of rope yarn used in thrumming canvas

thrum·my \-mē, -mi\ *adj* [¹*thrum* + *-y*] **1** : made of or with thrums ⟨a ~ cap⟩ **2** : having a shaggy or downy surface ⟨~ flowers⟩

thrump \ˈthrəmp\ *n* -s [imit.] : a heavy and usu. repeated sound (as of motors, artillery, or marching men)

thrumwort \ˈ⸗,⸗\ *n* [¹*thrum* + *wort*] **1** : a love-lies-bleeding (*Amaranthus caudatus*) **2** : STARFRUIT **3** : a water plantain (*Alisma plantago-aquatica*)

¹thrush \ˈthrəsh\ *n* -ES [ME *thrusche, thrusch*, fr. OE *thrysce*; akin to OE *throstle* thrush, OS *throsla*, OHG *droscala*, ON *thröstr*, L *turdus*, Russ *drozd*] **1** : any of numerous small or medium sized passerine birds that constitute the widely distributed family Turdidae, include many excellent singers, are mostly of a plain color although many have spotted underparts and the young have the entire plumage spotted, have 10 primaries of which the first is spurious and booted tarsi, and feed esp. on worms and insect larvae or on fruits — see BLACKBIRD, FIELDFARE, GRAY-CHEEKED THRUSH, HERMIT THRUSH, MISTLE THRUSH, OLIVE-BACKED THRUSH, REDWING, ROBIN, SONG THRUSH, VARIED THRUSH, VEERY, WOOD THRUSH; BILL illustration **2** : any of numerous birds of families other than Turdidae that are felt to resemble the true thrushes — usu. used with qualifier; see SHRIKE THRUSH, WATER THRUSH **3** : CANARY 4 **4** *or* **thrush brown** : a grayish to moderate yellowish brown — called also *shagbark*

²thrush \"\ *n* -ES [prob. of Scand origin; akin to Dan & Norw *trøske* thrush, Sw *torsk*, Sw dial. *trosk* thrush; prob. akin to Sw dial. *trosk* growth, Norw dial. *trausk, trosk*] **1 a** : a mycotic disease of the upper digestive tract characterized by the formation of white plaques within the oral cavity often coalescing in a false membrane, occurring esp. in debilitated children and adults and in birds, and caused by infection with a fungus (*Candida albicans*) **b** : any of several oral disorders (as sore mouth of sheep) more or less resembling this mycotic disease **2** : an inflammatory and suppurative affection of the feet in various animals; *specif* : a purulent degenerative state of the frog in the horse

thrush blackbird *n* : RUSTY BLACKBIRD

thrush fungus *n* [²*thrush*] : a fungus (*Candida albicans*) causing thrush

thrush lichen *or* **thrush moss** *n* [²*thrush*] : a lichen (*Peltigera apthosa*) held to cure thrush

thrushlike \ˈ⸗,⸗\ *adj* : resembling a thrush (as in song or appearance)

thrush nightingale *n* : a large nightingale (*Luscinia luscinia*) of eastern Europe

thrushy \ˈthrəshē, -shi\ *adj* -ER/-EST [²*thrush* + *-y*] : having or affected with thrush

¹thrust \ˈthrəst\ *vb* **thrust; thrust; thrusting; thrusts** [ME *thrusten, thristen*, fr. ON *thrȳsta* to thrust, press; prob. akin to ON *thrjōta* to fail, lack — more at THREAT] *vt* **1 a** : to push or drive with physical force : exert force upon or against so as to move in a desired direction : DRIVE, FORCE, IMPEL, SHOVE ⟨~ his hand into his pocket⟩ ⟨~ the chair forward⟩ ⟨~ me suddenly from her —Kenneth Roberts⟩ ⟨a hen having medicine ~ down its throat —Andrew Buchanan⟩ **b** : to push, drive, or impel as if with physical force ⟨he ~ aside all precautionary advice⟩ ⟨poetry ~*s* the great passions of men before us —C.S.Kilby⟩ ⟨into his churning mind . . . one single idea ~ itself —Walter O'Meara⟩ **2** : to cause to enter, pierce, or penetrate something or some place by or as if by pushing ⟨~ a dagger into her heart⟩ **3** : to push forth into some place : extend in some direction : throw out in or as if in the process of growth : SPREAD ⟨a poplar ~*s* its rootlets far and wide⟩ ⟨mountains which ~ an arm eastward into the Great Plains —R.A.Billington⟩ ⟨prosperous cities had . . . ~ out suburbs —G.M.Trevelyan⟩ **4** *archaic* : to stab or pierce with a pointed weapon **5 a** : to put (as a person who is unwilling) forcibly into some course of action or position ⟨he was ~ into the leadership —*Irish Digest*⟩ ⟨~ into an atmosphere of superinduced excitement —R.M.Weaver⟩ **b** : to introduce often improperly or irrelevantly into some position : INTERPOLATE **6 a** : to intrude (as a person) into a position or upon one or more other persons : INTERPOSE **b** : to press, force, or impose the acceptance of (something) upon someone ⟨~ new responsibilities upon him⟩ ⟨some have greatness ~ upon 'em —Shak.⟩ ~ *vi* **1 a** : to push in : force an entrance or passage **b** (1) : to push forward : press onward or into a place ⟨railroads began to ~ into the buffalo country —C.C.Rister⟩ ⟨the determination of the United Nations forces . . . to ~ beyond the 38th parallel —*Current Biog.*⟩ ⟨with a whoop . . . the Indian ~ ashore —*McClure's*⟩ (2) : to ride forward of the field in hunting : ride too close to the hounds **c** : to push upward ⟨a rock said to ~ 200 feet above the water⟩ **2** : to make a thrust, stab, or lunge with or as if with a pointed weapon ⟨~ at her with a knife⟩ **syn** see PUSH

²thrust \"\ *n* -s *often attrib* **1** *obs* : a crowd of people : PRESS, THRONG **2 a** (1) : an action of forcibly moving a pointed weapon (as a sword or dagger) in the direction of its length and usu. toward an objective : LUNGE (2) : the result of such an action : a stab made with a pointed weapon or an instrument of any kind ⟨a bayonet ~ in the . . . abdomen —Raymond Boyle⟩ **b** : an action held to resemble such a movement: as (1) : a verbal attack of greater or lesser intensity ⟨enliven their editorials with barbed ~*s* at their neighbors —*Amer. Guide Series: Minn.*⟩ ⟨hilarious . . . ~*s* at our sentimentality —John Mason Brown⟩ (2) : an attack or assault by military forces ⟨the enemy made a ~ deep into our position⟩ ⟨withstanding a sudden ~ by . . . 100 to 150 divisions —Patrick McMahon⟩ **3** : a pushing or driving force: as **a** : a force causing breakdown of a mine-gallery roof under its superincumbent weight **b** : the sideways force or pressure of one part of a structure against another part; *esp* : a horizontal or diagonal outward pressure (as of an arch against an abutment or any member of the upper chord of a truss against its terminal joints) **c** (1) : the force that is exerted endwise through a propeller shaft (as of a ship or airplane) due to reaction of the water or air on the revolving blades or vanes of the propeller and that serves to drive the craft ahead (2) : the forwardly directed reaction force produced by a high-speed jet of fluid discharged rearwards from a nozzle or orifice (as in a jet airplane or a rocket) — called also *jet thrust* **d** : a compressive tangential stress in the earth's crust or the effect of such stress : THRUST FAULT **4 a** : the action of pushing, driving, or otherwise moving something by the exertion of physical force ⟨the glide of birch canoes and the ~ of . . . paddles —*Amer. Guide Series: Vt.*⟩ **b** : an instance of such movement by the exertion of force **5 a** (1) : an action of pushing forward into some place or in some direction ⟨helps him in his ~ for higher office —*Saturday Rev.*⟩ ⟨forward ~*s* in history have not always been the product of universal assent —*Saturday Rev.*⟩ (2) : a movement (as by a group of people) in a usu. specified direction ⟨the most westerly ~ of the English toward the Dutch settlement —*Amer. Guide Series: Conn.*⟩ **b** : an instance of pushing upward ⟨the upward ~ of the . . . skyscrapers —*Amer. Guide Series: N.Y. City*⟩ **c** : a quality marked by usu. forceful movement forward or upward ⟨Japanese walkers are silent, less full of ~ —Santha Rama Rau⟩ ⟨his performance has a ~ . . . that none of the other violinists brings to the music —H.C.Schonberg⟩ **d** : something (as a projection) that is thrust out or up ⟨~*s* . . . extrude at almost every section of the frontiers —Herbert Feis⟩ ⟨the most easterly ~ of the mountain range⟩ **6** : a percussive movement of striking or shoving in modern dance **syn** see STRESS

thrust augmentation *n* : a process by which the thrust produced by a jet-propulsion engine may be increased temporarily over its normal value by some secondary means (as the burning of additional fuel in the tail pipe, or the injection of water into the engine inlet and the combustion chambers) which increases the mass flow, the velocity, or both

thrust augmentor *n* : AUGMENTOR

thrust bearing *or* **thrust block** *n* : a bearing to resist end thrust; *specif* : one provided with collars or horseshoe-shaped pieces or rollers which bear against corresponding collars on the shaft journal

thrust block *n* : a segment of the earth's crust moved along a thrust fault esp. at a low angle

thrust coefficient *n* : the thrust force of a jet-propulsion engine per unit of frontal area per unit of incompressible dynamic pressure

thrust·er \ˈthrəstə(r)\ *n* -s [¹*thrust* + *-er*] : one that thrusts: as **a** : one that rides too close to the hounds in fox hunting **b** : one that intrudes himself or pushes himself forward : PUSHER ⟨a crude and awkward social ~⟩

thrust face *n* : BLADE FACE

thrust fault *n* : a reverse fault in which the angle between the horizontal and the plane is small — called also OVERTHRUST FAULT

thrust·ful \ˈ⸗fəl\ *adj*, *Brit* : characterized by thrusting or an ability to thrust : FORCEFUL, AGGRESSIVE

thrust·ful·ness *n* -ES *Brit* : the quality or state of being thrustful

thrust hoe *n* : SCUFFLE HOE

thrust horsepower *n* **1** : the actual horsepower delivered by the engine-propeller unit in an airplane and found less than brake horsepower because the propeller is never 100 percent efficient **2** : the thrust of a jet engine or a rocket expressed in horsepower and found by multiplying thrust in pounds by speed of aircraft and dividing by 375

thrusting *pres part of* THRUST

thrust key *n* : PUSH KEY

thrust line *n* : a line located on a map by two points or one point and a direction and from which any point can be identified by giving a distance along the line from the base point and a perpendicular distance to the thrust line

Thrus·tor \ˈthrəstə(r)\ *trademark* — used for a hydraulic operating mechanism actuated by an electric motor

thrust plane *n* : the surface that is never strictly a plane along which dislocation has taken place in the case of a reverse or thrust fault

thrust plate *or* **thrust sheet** *n* : a geologic thrust block of great lateral extent

thrusts *pres 3d sing of* THRUST, *pl of* THRUST

thrust shaft *n* : the length of a propeller shaft provided with collars for resisting the end thrust of the propeller and held by the thrust bearing

thrust spoiler *n* : a device intended to reduce the thrust of a jet engine (as by deflecting the jet of exhaust gases)

thruway *var of* THROUGHWAY

thrym·sa \ˈthrimzə, -msə\ *n* -s [OE *thrymsa, thrimsa*, gen. pl., alter. (influenced by *thrīe* three) of *trymesa, trimesa*, gen. pl. of *trymes, trimes*, fr. LL *tremis*, a coin, fr. L *tres* three + *-mis* (as in *semis*) — more at THREE, SEMIS (coin)] : a 7th century gold coin and corresponding unit of value of Anglo-Saxon England

¹thry·on·o·my·id \thrīˌänəˈmīəd\ *adj* [NL *Thryonomyidae*, family of rodents, fr. *Thryonomys*, type genus + *-idae*] : of or relating to the genus *Thryonomys* or to the family Thryonomyidae

²thryonomyid \"\ *n* -s : a thryonomyid rodent

thry·on·o·mys \thrīˈänəməs\ *n*, *cap* [NL, fr. Gk *thryon* reed, rush + NL *-o-* + *-mys*] : a genus (coextensive with the family Thryonomyidae) of hystricomorph rodents comprising the African ground pigs

thsd *abbr* thousand

thu·cho·lite \ˈth(y)ükəˌlīt\ *n* -s [*Th* (symbol for *thorium*) + *U* (symbol for *uranium*) + *C* (symbol for *carbon*) + *H* (symbol for *hydrogen*) + *O* (symbol for *oxygen*) + *-lite*] : a bitumen containing uranium and thorium

thu·cyd·i·de·an \(ˌ)th(y)üˌsidəˈdēən\ *adj*, *usu cap* [*Thucydides* †ab 400 B.C. Greek historian + E *-an*] **1** : of, relating to, or characteristic of the Greek historian Thucydides (as in compactness and precision of expression, historical accuracy, or philosophical breadth of view) **2** : of, relating to, or resembling the device of putting appropriate speeches into the mouths of persons who appear in a history

¹thud \ˈthəd\ *vi* **thudded; thudded; thudding; thuds** [prob. fr. ME *thudden* to thrust, push, fr. OE *thyddan*] : to move or strike so as to make a thud ⟨an uppercut that *thudded* like a mallet on wood —Donn Byrne⟩

²thud \"\ *n* -s **1** *Scot* : a tempest or gust of wind : WINDSTORM **2 a** : a blow or a series of repeated blows **b** : a dull sound like that produced by striking with or against a somewhat soft substance : THUMP ⟨the whistle and ~ of the bullets —Hanama Tasaki⟩ ⟨fell with the dull ~ of a sack of sand —Green Peyton⟩

thud·ding·ly *adv* : with thuds ⟨~ galloped across the floor —Sinclair Lewis⟩

thug \ˈthəg\ *n* -s [Hindi *ṭhag*, lit., thief, fr. Skt *sthaga* rogue, fr. *sthagati* he covers, conceals — more at THATCH] **1** *often cap* : one of a group of professional robbers and murderers in India characteristically strangling their victims **2** : a person inclined or hired to treat another roughly, brutally, or murderously : GANGSTER, KILLER

thu·ga \ˈth(y)ügə\ *also* **thu·ya** \-üyə\ *n* -s [modif. of NL *thuja*] : THYINE WOOD

thug·gee \ˈthəgē\ *n* -s [Hindi *ṭhagī* robbery, fr. *ṭhag* thief — more at THUG] : murder and robbery by thugs

thug·gery \ˈthəgərē, -ri\ *n* -ES [*thug* + *-ery*] **1** : THUGGEE **2** : the behavior of a thug

thu·id·i·um \th(y)üˈidēəm\ *n*, *cap* [NL, fr. ML *thuia* + NL *-idium*] : a widely distributed genus of mosses (order Hypnobryales) with fernlike leaves — see FERN MOSS

thu·ja \ˈth(y)üjə\ *n* [NL, fr. ML *thuia*, a kind of cedar, fr. Gk *thyia*] **1 a** *cap* : a genus of evergreen shrubs and trees (family Pinaceae) having flat distichous branches and scalelike closely imbricated or compressed leaves **b** -s : any tree of the genus *Thuja*; *esp* : ARBORVITAE **2** -s : THUGA

thu·jane \-ˌjān\ *n* -s [ISV *thuj-* (fr. NL *Thuja*) + *-ane*] : a saturated bicyclic terpene hydrocarbon $C_{10}H_{18}$ that is the parent compound of thujene and thujone — called also *sabinane*

thuja oil *n* : a fragrant essential oil obtained from the leaves and twigs of arborvitae and used chiefly in scenting shoe polishes, floor waxes, and other technical preparations — called also *cedarleaf oil*

thu·ja·pli·cin \-ˈplīsᵊn\ *n* -s [NL *Thuja plicata* species of red cedar + E *-in*] : any of three isomeric crystalline compounds $C_3H_7C_7H_5O_2$ that are obtained esp. from the heartwood of the canoe cedar and possess the fungicidal properties that preserve this wood against decay : isopropyl-tropolone

thu·jene \ˈth(y)üˌjēn\ *n* -s [ISV *thuj-* (fr. NL *Thuja*) + *-ene*] : any of several unsaturated bicyclic terpene hydrocarbons $C_{10}H_{16}$ related to thujane: as **a** : an oily liquid obtained from various essential oils — called also *alpha-thujene, 3-thujene* **b** : SABINENE

thu·jic acid \ˈth(y)üjik-\ *n* [NL *Thuja* + E *-ic*] : a crystalline unsaturated acid $C_9H_{11}COOH$ containing a 7-membered ring and found in the heartwood of the canoe cedar

thu·jone \-ˌjōn\ *n* -s [ISV *Thuj-* (fr. NL *Thuja*) + *-one*] : a fragrant oily ketone $C_{10}H_{16}O$ derived from thujane, occurring in mixtures of dextrorotatory and levorotatory stereoisomeric forms in various essential oils (as thuja oil, wormwood oil, tansy oil), and used in making synthetic essential oils

thu·jop·sis \th(y)əˈjäpsəs\ *n*, *cap* [NL, fr. *Thuja* + *-opsis*] : a genus of Japanese evergreen trees (family Pinaceae) with irregular or whorled horizontal branches and leaves glossy green above and marked with a white band beneath — see HIBA ARBORVITAE

thu·jyl \ˈth(y)üjəl\ *n* -s [ISV *thujone* + *-yl*] : a univalent radical $C_{10}H_{17}$ derived from thujyl alcohol

thujyl alcohol *n* : an alcohol $C_{10}H_{17}OH$ known in several stereoisomeric usu. syrupy liquid forms, found free or combined as esters in various essential oils (as wormwood oil), and formed by reduction of thujone

¹thu·le \ˈth(y)ülē, -li\ *n* -s [fr. L *Thule, Thyle* (fr. Gk *Thoulē, Thylē*), a land represented as being six days' sail north of Britain and considered to be the northernmost part of the habitable world] **1** *usu cap* : the northernmost part of the habitable world **2** *often cap* **a** : a very distant mysterious or mythical region **b** : a remote goal or end

²thu·le \ˈtülē, -li\ *adj*, *usu cap* [fr. *Thule*, settlement in Greenland] : of or belonging to the Eskimo culture extending over arctic lands from Alaska to Greenland about A.D. 500–1400, characterized by the hunting of sea mammals and esp. of whales, winter semisubterranean houses of whalebone or wood, stone, and earth and summer tents, stone or earthenware lamps and pots, ground slate tools, and use of dog sleds

thu·lite \ˈth(y)üˌlīt\ *n* -s [L *Thule*, northernmost part of the habitable world + E *-ite*] : a mineral consisting of a rose-red variety of zoisite found in Tellemarken, Norway, and elsewhere and occas. cut for use in jewelry

thulite pink *n*, *often cap T* : a dark to deep purplish pink

thu·li·um \-lēəm\ *n* -s [NL, fr. *Thule* + *-ium*] : a trivalent metallic element of the rare-earth group that occurs combined in rare minerals associated with granite or pegmatite veins and that forms pale green compounds resembling those of erbium, ytterbium, and lutetium in solubility — symbol *Tm*; see ELEMENT table

thu·luth \ˈthüləth\ *n* -s [Ar] : one of the chief forms of Arabic and Persian script

¹thumb \ˈthəm\ *n* -s *often attrib* [ME *thoume, thoumbe, thombe*, fr. OE *thūma*; akin to OS & OHG *thūmo* thumb, ON *thumall* thumb of a glove, L *tumēre* to swell, Gk *saos, sōs* whole, sound, Skt *taviti* he is strong; basic meaning: to swell] **1 a** : the short and thick first or most preaxial digit of the human hand differing from the other fingers in having but two phalanges and in having greater freedom of movement

and being opposable to the other fingers : POLLEX **b** : the corresponding digit in any of various animals — see BAT illustration **2** : the width of the thumb usu. equated with one inch **3** : something resembling or suggesting a thumb (as in appearance, place, or function): as **a** : a thumb-shaped projection from a plant or tree **b** : a thumb-shaped pinnacle of rock **4** : the part of a glove or mitten that covers the thumb — see GLOVE illustration **5** : a convex molding : OVOLO **6** : the large fixed branch of an arthropod's chela — **all thumbs** : extremely awkward or clumsy ⟨as an example of playwriting, it is *all thumbs*, echoes, and foolishness —John Mason Brown⟩ — **under the thumb of** *or* **under one's thumb** : under the influence of : in a state of subservience to ⟨is *under the thumb of* an excellent but stern mother —V.S.Pritchett⟩ ⟨had only to bring *under his thumb* the existing control points —*Wall Street Jour.*⟩

²**thumb** \"\ *vb* -ED/-ING/-S *vt* **1** : to play (a musical instrument) with or as if with the thumbs **2 a** : to examine, feel, press, point at, attack, or sort by means of the thumb ⟨~*ed* the front door release —*Newsweek*⟩ ⟨~*ed* him in the eye⟩ **b** : to bring into a specified state by gesturing with or applying the thumb ⟨~*ed* a match afire on the packet —Thurston Scott⟩ ⟨~*ed* his hat off his forehead —Luke Short⟩ ⟨only twice have umpires ~*ed* him out of a game —*Newsweek*⟩ **3 a** : to leaf through (as a book or periodical) rapidly as in searching or examining ⟨~*ing* his billfold —Jerome Ellison⟩ ⟨anyone who has even ~*ed* leaves in that book will have noticed it —Albert Hofstadter⟩ **b** : to read often, regularly, or repeatedly : REREAD ⟨I shall prize it and continue to ~ it —L.F.Ward⟩ **c** : to soil or wear by or as if by frequent or repeated thumbing ⟨a badly ~*ed* law book⟩ **4** : to retard the speed of (a fishing reel) by pressure of the thumb on the line wound on the spool or by a mechanical device esp. in order to prevent a backlash **5 a** : to request or obtain (a ride) in a passing automobile by signaling with the thumb in the desired direction **b** : to signal (an approaching vehicle) with the thumb in asking a ride ⟨~*ed* the big trucks that started rolling —Jack Kerouac⟩ **c** : to make (one's way) by thumbing rides ~ *vi* **1** : to turn over pages in searching or perusal ⟨~ through volumes . . . hunting for the answer —*Mech. Engineering*⟩ **2** : to travel or make a trip by thumbing rides — **thumb one's nose 1** : to point at with extended fingers and the thumb at one's nose as a gesture of derision, scorn, or defiance **2** : to treat or regard with disdain ⟨*thumb their noses* at the collective wisdom of the ages —C.I.Glicksberg⟩

thumb–and–finger rule \ˌ=ˈ=ˌ=-\ *n* : either of two statements in electromagnetism: when the fingers of the right hand are bent so that the thumb points in the direction of the decrease in flux in a magnetic circuit, the fingers will point in the direction of the induced voltage in the electric circuit linked with the magnetic circuit; and when the fingers of the right hand are bent so that they follow the direction of the flow of current through a helical or coil conductor, the thumb will point in the direction of the flux through the helix or coil — compare LEFT-HAND RULE, RIGHT-HAND RULE

thumb–bolt \ˈ=ˌ=\ *n* : a lock operated by a thumb turn

thumb bottle *n* : PHIAL

thumb box *n* : a small box that contains painting materials, a panel for mixing colors, and a small canvas or board and has a thumb hole or other device by which it can be held upon the thumb like a palette to make a small sketch usu. in oil

thumb cleat *n* : a small cleat with but one horn used on a yard or boom

thumb cut *n* : THUMB NOTCH 2

thumb down *vt* : to turn thumbs down on : REJECT ⟨*thumbed down* one request that it print the whole Bible, chapter by chapter —*Newsweek*⟩

thumb·er \ˈthəmə(r)\ *n* -S **1** : one that thumbs rides : HITCHHIKER **2** : a worker who sews thumbs in gloves or mittens

thumb flint *n* : a prehistoric often tiny flint tool shaped like a thumb and thought to be a scraper

¹**thumbhole** \ˈ=ˌ=\ *n* [¹*thumb* + *hole*] **1** : an opening in which to insert the thumb; *specif* : a semicircular cut in the sides or ends of a container to facilitate lifting the cover **2** : a hole in a wind musical instrument opened or closed by the thumb

²**thumbhole** \"\ *vt* : to provide with a thumbhole

thumb·hol·er \-lə(r)\ *n* : a worker who makes thumbholes

thumbier *comparative of* THUMBY

thumbiest *superlative of* THUMBY

thumb index *n* : an index consisting of rounded thumb notches cut symmetrically on the fore edge of a book and tabs denoting the letters (as in a dictionary) or sections referred to beginning on the page that faces or forms the base of each notch

thumb–index \ˈ=ˌ=ˌ=\ *vt* [*thumb index*] : to equip (a book) with a thumb index ⟨the main part of the book is a *thumb-indexed* directory listing ministries —*Times Lit. Supp.*⟩

thumbing *pres part of* THUMB

thumb knot *n* : OVERHAND KNOT; *also* : a loop knot made with an overhand knot

thumb·less \ˈ=ləs\ *adj* **1** : having no thumb **2** : CLUMSY

thumb·ling \ˈthəmliŋ, -lēŋ\ *n* -S [¹*thumb* + -*ling*] : a very tiny thumb-sized person : MANIKIN

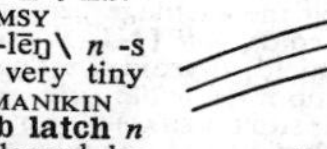

thumb knot

thumb lock *also* **thumb latch** *n* : a lock that can be released by pressure with the thumb

¹**thumbmark** \ˈ=ˌ=\ *n* [¹*thumb* + *mark*] **1** : an impression left by a thumb esp. when used as a mark of identification **2** : a depression in the sides of a single comb of a fowl that is a defect in show birds

²**thumbmark** \"\ *vt* : to mark with the thumb; *also* : to take a thumbmark of (as for identification)

thumb mold *or* **thumb molding** *n* : a narrow convex molding on furniture having a profile in a flattened curve

¹**thumbnail** \ˈ=ˌ=, ˌ=ˈ=\ *n, often attrib* [¹*thumb* + *nail*] **1** : the nail of the thumb **2** : something small, brief, or concise ⟨a ~ sketch⟩

²**thumbnail** \ˈ=ˌ=\ *vt* : to make a thumbnail sketch of ⟨the minor characters have been methodically ~*ed* in conventional types —J.S.Shrike⟩ ⟨practically everybody anybody ever heard of is cited, ~*ed*, keelhauled, cuddled —*Time*⟩

thumb notch *n* **1** : a notch of a size to admit the tip of a thumb cut in the outer edges of the pages of a book for the insertion of index letters or headings — compare THUMB INDEX **2** : a half-moon cut in the sides of a slipcase to facilitate removal of the book — called also *thumb cut*

thumb nut *n* : a nut designed to be turned by thumb and finger: as **a** : WING NUT **b** : a nut with a knurled edge

thumb pad *n* : a fleshy pad over the inner metacarpal bone of various frogs and esp. of males in breeding condition

thumbpiece \ˈ=ˌ=\ *n* **1** : an appendage to a handle (as of a vessel) to afford a hold for the thumb **2** : a part designed to be operated by the thumb or thumb and fingers: as **a** : a small inside knob for a night latch **b** : a small knob or button to operate a catch (as on a bracelet) **3** *dial* : a small amount of food

thumb pin *n* : THUMBTACK

thumb piston *n* : COMBINATION PISTON

thumb plane *n* : a very small carpenter's plane for use in a somewhat inaccessible place

thumb pot *n* : a flowerpot of the smallest size used esp. for starting seedlings (as of orchids)

¹**thumbprint** \ˈ=ˌ=\ *n* [¹*thumb* + *print*] : an impression made by the thumb; *esp* : a print made by the inside of the first joint and showing its characteristic lineation — compare FINGERPRINT

²**thumbprint** \"\ *vt* : to take a thumbprint of

thumb ring *n* **1** : a ring worn on the thumb **2** : a ring (as on a bow or a sword guard) to receive or protect the thumb

thumbrope \ˈ=ˌ=\ *n, dial Brit* : a rope made by twisting hay or straw round the thumb

thumb rule *n* : RULE OF THUMB

thumbs *pl of* THUMB, *pres 3d sing of* THUMB

¹**thumbscrew** \ˈ=ˌ=\ *vt* [¹*thumb* + *screw*, v.] : to torture by use of the thumbscrew; *also* : to coerce by or as if by such torture

²**thumbscrew** \"\ *n* [¹*thumb* + *screw*, n.] **1** : a screw whose head is flattened at the side or knurled so that the screw may be turned by the thumb and forefinger — see SPOKESHAVE illustration **2** : an instrument of torture for compressing the thumb by a screw

thumbs–down \ˈ=ˈ=\ *n* -S [fr. the imperative phrase *thumbs down*] : the act, process, or an instance of rejection, disapproval, or condemnation ⟨the government *thumbs-down* on penicillin for endocarditis was published —Paul de Kruif⟩

thumbstall \ˈ=ˌ=\ *n* [¹*thumb* + *stall*] : a protective covering for the thumb; *also* : any of various similar devices for other purposes (as a rubber cover for the thumb to aid in sorting mail)

thumb–sucker \ˈ=ˌ==\ *n* : an infant or young child that habitually sucks a thumb

thumb–sucking \ˈ=ˌ=\ *n* -S : the habit of sucking a thumb beyond the period of physiologic need

thumbs up *interj* — used to raise one's spirits or to express a hope of good fortune

¹**thumbtack** \ˈ=ˌ=\ *n* [¹*thumb* + *tack*] : a short steel point with a broad flat head for pressing into a board by the thumb and used for temporary or quick securing of a light thin object (as a sheet of drawing paper)

²**thumbtack** \"\ *vt* : to fasten with a thumbtack

thumb turn *n* : a part designed to be turned by the thumb and finger

thumby \ˈthəmē\ *adj* -ER/-EST [¹*thumb* + -*y*] : AWKWARD, CLUMSY

¹**thump** \ˈthəmp\ *vb* -ED/-ING/-S [imit.] *vt* **1 a** : to strike or beat with or as if with something thick or heavy or so as to cause a dull sound ⟨his tail ~*ed* the ground —John & Ward Hawkins⟩ ⟨~*ing* the counter with his fist —Rearden Conner⟩ **b** : POUND, KNOCK, HAMMER **c** : CUDGEL, THRASH, WHIP ⟨~*ed* the indoctrination officer who tried to stop him —*Springfield (Mass.) Union*⟩ **2** : to force or drive by repeatedly thumping **3** : to defeat decisively **4** : to strike against an object with a dull sound ⟨the old man ~*ed* his glass down on the bar and stalked out —G.G.Carter⟩ **5** : to produce (music) mechanically or in a mechanical manner by means of repeated thumps — usu. used with *out* ⟨~ out a tune on the piano⟩ ~ *vi* **1 a** : to inflict or emit a thump : fall or hit so as to produce a dull sound ⟨the gorilla is just as likely to ~ upon the upper chest with his fists —Weston La Barre⟩ ⟨the drums ~*ed* and rolled again —Kenneth Roberts⟩ **b** : to move with heavy pounding sounds ⟨down the steps ~*ed* a crush of cheerful boys —Wilfred Goatman⟩ ⟨the convoy of trucks ~*ed* along for about thirty miles —Earle Birney⟩ **c** : to beat heavily ⟨his heart ~*ed* at the sight of her —T.B.Costain⟩ ⟨the radiators began to ~ —Berton Roueché⟩ **2** : to vigorously advocate, endorse, or advertise a program, policy, candidate, or product ⟨got a couple of United States senators to ~ for him —*N.Y. Herald Tribune*⟩

²**thump** \"\ *n* -S **1** : a blow or knock with or as if with something blunt or heavy ⟨the ~*s* and bumps of factory and warehouse activity —*Modern Industry*⟩; *also* : the sound made by such a blow ⟨the smooth rumble of wheels over rails broke into a series of rattling ~*s* —John Dos Passos⟩ **2 thumps** *pl but sing in constr* **a** : a dyspneic breathing that is marked by throbbing movements of the sides of the chest due to spasmodic contractions of the diaphragm analogous to those of hiccups in man, is esp. common in young pigs, and is associated with deficiency anemia or the passage of larval ascarid worms through the lungs **b** : a disease (as a nutritional anemia or verminous pneumonia) of young pigs of which thumps is a symptom **3** : interference in a telephone circuit caused by the operation of telegraph or signaling circuits esp. if the interfering circuits are using the same lines

thump·er \ˈthəmpə(r)\ *n* -S **1** : one that thumps **2** : something extra large or great

thumping *adj* [fr. pres. part. of ¹*thump*] : impressively large, great, or excellent ⟨passed by a ~ seven-to-one majority —*Wall Street Jour.*⟩ ⟨the short story became a ~ two-volume novel —Thomas Mann⟩

thump·ing·ly *adv* **1** : with a thump **2** : in a thumping manner : IMPRESSIVELY, RESOUNDINGLY ⟨~ lost the national election —Philip Hamburger⟩

thun·ber·gia \ˌthənˈbərj(ē)ə\ *n* [NL, fr. Carl P. *Thunberg* †1828 Swed. botanist + NL -*ia*] **1** *cap* : a genus of herbs or twining woody vines (family Acanthaceae) native to the tropics of the Old World and having opposite leaves and large flowers succeeded by beaked capsules — see BLACK-EYED SUSAN 3, CLOCK VINE **2** -S : any plant of the genus *Thunbergia*

thun·berg lespedeza \ˈthən,bərg-\ *n* [after Carl P. *Thunberg*] : an Asiatic lespedeza (*Lespedeza thunbergii*) with long slender racemes of purple flowers that is used as an ornamental and is often found as an escape from cultivation in No. America

¹**thun·der** \ˈthəndə(r)\ *n* -S [ME *thoner, thonder, thunder*, fr. OE *thunor;* akin to OS *thunar* thunder, OHG *thonar* thunder, ON *Thōrr* god of thunder, L *tonare* to thunder, Gk *stenein* to moan, groan, Skt *stanati, stanīti, stanayati* it thunders, *tanyati* it resounds, roars] **1 a** : the loud and at a distance often rolling sound that follows a flash of lightning due to the sudden expansion of the air in the path of the discharge **b** *archaic* : a discharge of lightning : THUNDERBOLT ⟨six the ~ has smitten —P.B.Shelley⟩ **c** *archaic* : a peal of thunder : THUNDERCLAP ⟨a sullen ~ is rolled —Alfred Tennyson⟩ **d** *dial* : THUNDERSTORM **2 a** : a usu. threatening declamation or utterance whether bombastic or eloquent ⟨hurled his ~ over the terrified heads of mortals who had spoken in error —C.R.Tracy⟩ ⟨legal maneuvers, editorial ~, and political speech —J.B.Martin⟩ — often used in pl. **b** : great force, strength, violence, or energy ⟨their carefully cultivated air of benevolence . . . shattered by the ~ of a purge —*N. Y. Times*⟩ **3** : a loud or noisy sound likened to thunder : BANG, RUMBLE ⟨the roaring ~ of big guns —*Amer. Guide Series: Vt.*⟩ ⟨the ~ of horses' hooves⟩ **4** — used often interjectionally as a mild oath ⟨who in ~ are you⟩ ⟨by ~, I'll show you who's master —Max Peacock⟩

²**thunder** \"\ *vb* **thundered; thundered; thundering** \-d(ə)riŋ\ **thunders** [ME *thoneren, thonderen, thunderen*, fr. OE *thunrian*, fr. *thunor*, n.] *vi* **1 a** : to produce thunder : sound, rattle, or roar as the effect of a discharge of atmospheric electricity — usu. used impersonally ⟨it ~*ed* loudly⟩ **b** : to give forth a sound likened to thunder ⟨clarion notes of the trumpet ~*ed* through five expansive movements —*Lutheran Quarterly*⟩ **c** : to move, go, or progress with the accompaniment of loud reverberations suggesting thunder ⟨a huge white horse came ~*ing* into the yard —Zane Grey⟩ ⟨a mighty cataract ~*ed* into the ravine —*Amer. Guide Series: Minn.*⟩ **d** : to strike an object so as to produce a loud sound ⟨the general's fist ~*ed* on the table —Kenneth Roberts⟩ **2** : to utter violent, loud, bombastic, or impressively phrased denunciation, warning, or threat ⟨~*ed* day in and day out on the "manifest destiny" of the United States —*Amer. Guide Series: Nev.*⟩ ⟨the preacher ~*ed* from the pulpit against corruption⟩ ~ *vt* **1 a** : to utter in or as if in a loud thundering tone esp. as a threat or warning ⟨"woe unto you" he ~*ed* at these blind leaders —W.F.Hambly⟩ ⟨~*ed* out the words: "Seekest thou great things for thyself" —*Current Biog.*⟩ **b** : to express (as an emotion) in or as if in a loud thundering tone ⟨preachers had ~*ed* hatred of the South —Dixon Wecter⟩ **2** : to strike so as to cause a sound likened to thunder

thunder–and–lightning \ˈ==ˈ==\ *adj, of apparel* : of strongly contrasting colors : of a startling color

thun·der·a·tion \ˌthəndəˈrāshən\ *interj* [*thunder* + -*ation*] — used as a mild oath

thunderball \ˈ=ˌ=\ *n* : THUNDERBOLT 1b

thunderbird \ˈ=ˌ=\ *n* **1** : an Australian whistler (*Pachycephala pectoralis*) that in the male is marked with black and yellow and has a black crescent on the breast **2 a** : a mythical bird believed by American Indians to cause lightning and thunder that is frequently a supernatural eagle conceived as the spirit or god of thunder and rain **b** : a figure of a bird with outstretched wings common in aboriginal No. American art

thunder–blasted \ˈ==ˈ==\ *adj, archaic* : struck by lightning

¹**thun·der·bolt** \ˈthəndə(r),bōlt\ *n* [ME *thonder-bolte*] **1 a** : a single discharge of lightning with the accompanying thunder **b** (1) : an imaginary elongated mass cast as a missile to earth in the lightning flash (2) : a stone or stone implement (as a hatchet or arrowhead) thought to be the material part of lightning; *broadly* : THUNDERSTONE 2 **2 a** : a person or thing likened to lightning in suddenness, effectiveness, or destructive power ⟨nuclear subs may hide under the polar ice cap, awaiting only a signal . . . to fire their ~*s* —*Newsweek*⟩ **b** : vehement threatening or censure : FULMINATION ⟨hurling ~*s* at the newspapers —E.D.Canham⟩ **3** : a conventionalized representation of a thunderbolt; *specif* : a twisted bar with inflamed ends between two wings and with four jagged darts issuant from its center — used in heraldry

²**thunderbolt** \"\ *vt* -ED/-ING/-S *dial Brit* : to strike with a thunderbolt

thunderclap \ˈ=ˌ=\ *n* [ME *thonder clappe*] **1** : a clap of thunder **2** : something likened to or suggesting a clap of thunder (as in suddenness, sound, or effect) ⟨a ~ of applause —*New Yorker*⟩

thundercloud \ˈ=ˌ=\ *n* **1** : a cloud charged with electricity and producing lightning and thunder **2** : something threatening, gloomy, or expressive of anger ⟨turned a ~ face toward the struggling prisoners —Frank Yerby⟩

thundercrack \ˈ=ˌ=\ *n* [ME *thunder-crakke*] : THUNDERCLAP

thunder egg *n* : chalcedony in rounded concretionary nodules

thun·der·er \ˈthənd(ə)rə(r)\ *n* -S [ME *thonderere*, fr. *thonderen* to thunder + -*ere* -er] : one that thunders ⟨a continuous editorial ~ against stream pollution —K.S.Dixon⟩

thunderfish \ˈ=ˌ=\ *n* **1** : WEATHERFISH; *esp* : a European fish (*Misgurnus fossilis*) **2** : ELECTRIC CATFISH

thunderflower \ˈ=ˌ=\ *n* **1** *dial Eng* : STITCHWORT **2** *dial Eng* : CORN POPPY **3** *dial Eng* : WHITE CAMPION A

thun·der·ful \ˈthəndə(r)fəl\ *adj* : charged or resounding with thunder

thunder god vine *n* : a perennial Chinese vine (*Tripterygium wilfordii*) of the family Celastraceae introduced into the U.S. for its possible use as a source of an insecticide

thunder–gust \ˈ=ˌ=\ *n* : a thunderstorm with wind

thunderhead \ˈ=ˌ=\ *n* : a rounded mass of cumulus cloud with shining white edges often appearing before a thunderstorm

¹**thun·der·ing** \ˈthənd(ə)riŋ, -rēŋ\ *n* -S [ME *thondring*, fr. OE *thunring*, fr. *thunrian* to thunder + -*ing*] : THUNDER

²**thundering** *adj* [fr. pres. part. of ²*thunder*] : awesome in virtue of impressive greatness, magnitude, or unusualness ⟨the ~ silence of what was left unsaid —A.E.Stevenson b. 1900⟩ ⟨a ~ success as a salesman —R.H.Rovere⟩ — **thun·der·ing·ly** *adv*

thun·der·less \ˈ==ləs\ *adj* : being without accompanying thunder

thunder lizard *n* : BRONTOSAUR

thunder mug *n, dial* : CHAMBER POT

thun·der·ous \ˈthənd(ə)rəs\ *adj* [¹*thunder* + -*ous*] **1** : producing thunder; *also* : making or accompanied by a noise like thunder **2** : extremely remarkable or great esp. in ominousness ⟨world events of ~ import —F.D.Roosevelt⟩ — **thun·der·ous·ly** *adv*

thunderpeal \ˈ=ˌ=\ *n* : THUNDERCLAP

thunder pumper *or* **thunderpump** \ˈ=ˌ=\ *n* **1** : AMERICAN BITTERN **2** : FRESHWATER DRUM

thunders *pl of* THUNDER, *pres 3d sing of* THUNDER

thunder sheet *n* : a large galvanized iron sheet suspended from a rope in a theater and shaken or hit to produce a sound representing thunder, artillery, or explosions

thundershower \ˈ=ˌ=\ *n* : a shower accompanied by lightning and thunder

thunder snake *n* **1** : MILK SNAKE; *also* : any of various closely related snakes **2** : a reddish colubrid ground snake (*Carphophis amoena*) of the eastern U.S.

thundersquall \ˈ=ˌ=\ *n* : a squall attended with lightning and thunder

thunderstick \ˈ=ˌ=\ *n* : BULL-ROARER

thunderstone \ˈ=ˌ=\ *n* **1** *archaic* : THUNDERBOLT 1b(1) **2** : any of various somewhat cylindrical or tapering stones (as a fossil belemnite shell, prehistoric stone implement, natural concretion, or meteorite) supposed to be a thunderbolt — compare FAIRY ARROW, THUNDERBOLT 1b(2)

thunderstorm \ˈ=ˌ=\ *n* : a storm accompanied by lightning and thunder

thunderstorm cirrus *n* : FALSE CIRRUS

thunderstrike \ˈ=ˌ=\ *vt* **1** *archaic* : to strike, blast, or injure by or as if by lightning **2** : to strike dumb with or as if with something terrible : ASTONISH ⟨readers will be *thunderstruck* to learn —*Current Biog.*⟩

thunderstroke \ˈ=ˌ=\ *n* : a stroke by or as if by lightning with the attendant thunder

thunderwood \ˈ=ˌ=\ *n* : POISON SUMAC

thunderworm \ˈ=ˌ=\ *n* [so called fr. its habit of leaving its burrows after thundershowers] : a small burrowing limbless lizard (*Rhineura floridana*) that resembles a worm and is native to Florida

thun·dery \ˈthənd(ə)rē, -ri\ *adj* **1** : accompanied with or indicating thunder : THUNDEROUS **2** : OMINOUS, THREATENING

thunge \ˈthənj, ˈthůnj\ *n* -S [imit.] *dial Brit* : a loud hollow sound; *also* : a blow causing such a sound

¹**thunk** \ˈthəŋk\ *dial past of* THINK

²**thunk** \"\ *n* -S [imit.] : a flat hollow sound ⟨heard the dull ~ of wood against wood —Brian Harwin⟩

thun·nus \ˈthənəs\ *n, cap* [NL, fr. L, tunny — more at TUNNY] : a genus of large marine fishes that comprises the typical tunas and is sometimes made the type of a separate family but is usu. included among the Scombridae

thur·be·ria \ˌthərˈbirēə\ *n* [NL, fr. George *Thurber* †1890 Am. botanist + NL -*ia*] **1** *cap, in some classifications* : a genus of shrubby herbs that are characterized by a 3-celled capsule and are usu. included in *Gossypium* **2** -S : WILD COTTON 2a

thurberia weevil *n, sometimes cap T* : a boll weevil (*Anthonomus grandis thurberiae*) that is native to Arizona and adjacent Mexico, feeds on a wild cotton (*Gossypium thurberi*), and also attacks cultivated cotton in that region

thu·ri·ble \ˈth(y)ůrəbəl, ˈthərə-\ *n* -S [ME *turrible*, fr. MF *thurible*, fr. L *thuribulum, turibulum*, fr. *thur-, thus, tur-, tus* incense (fr. Gk *thyos* incense, sacrifice, fr. *thyein* to sacrifice) + -*i-* + -*bulum*, suffix denoting an instrument — more at THYME] : a censer used in religious services

thu·ri·fer \-rəfə(r)\ *n* -S [NL, fr. L *thurifer, turifer*, adj., incense-burning, fr. *thur-, thus, tur-, tus* + -*ifer* -iferous] : one who carries a censer in an ecclesiastical rite

thu·rif·er·ous \th(y)əˈrif(ə)rəs\ *adj* [L *thurifer* + E -*ous*] : producing frankincense

thu·ri·fi·ca·tion \ˌth(y)ůrəfəˈkāshən, ˌthərə-\ *n* -S [ME *thurybcacyon*, fr. MF *thurification*, fr. ML *thurification-, thurificatio*, fr. LL *thurificatus* (past part. of *thurificare*) + L -*ion-*, -*io* -ion] : the act, process, or an instance of censing

thu·ri·fy \ˈ=ˌ=ˌfī\ *vt* -ED/-ING/-ES [ME *thurifien*, fr. MF *thurifier*, fr. LL *thurificare*, fr. L *thur-, thus, tur-, tus* incense + -*ificare* -ify] : CENSE

thü·rin·ger \ˈth(y)ůrəŋə(r), ˈthərə-, ˈthirə-; ˈtiriŋə-, ˈtēriŋə-\ *also* **thüringer sausage** *n, usu cap T* [*thüringer* fr. G *Thüringer*wurst, fr. *Thüringer* Thuringian (fr. *Thüringen* Thuringia) + *wurst* sausage; *thüringer sausage* part trans. of G *Thüringerwurst*] : a mildly seasoned fresh or smoked summer sausage

¹**thu·rin·gian** \th(y)əˈrinj(ē)ən\ *n* -S *cap* [in sense 1, fr. L *Thuringi*, a Germanic people living in central Germany in ancient times + E -*an*; in sense 2, fr. *Thuringia*, region in Central Germany + E -*an*] **1** : a member of an ancient Germanic people established in a kingdom near the center of Germany and overthrown by the Franks in the 6th century **2** : a native or inhabitant of the kingdom, principality, region, or state of Thuringia

²**thuringian** \"\ *adj, usu cap* **1** : of or relating to Thuringia or the Thuringians **2** : of or relating to the Franconian dialect of the German language spoken in Thuringia

thu·rin·gite \th(y)əˈrin,jīt\ *n* -S [G *thuringit*, fr. *Thuringia* + G -*it* -ite] : a mineral $Fe_3(Si,Al)_2O_5(OH)_4$ of the chlorite family consisting of a basic aluminum iron silicate and occurring as an aggregation of minute scales with an olive-green color and pearly luster

¹**thurl** \ˈthər(-ə)l\ *dial Eng var of* THIRL

²**thurl** \"\ *n* -S [perh. fr. E dial. *thirl, thurl* gaunt] : the hip joint in cattle — see COW illustration

thurm \ˈthərm\ *vt* -ED/-ING/-S [origin unknown] : to work (as a table leg or molding) with saw and chisel across the grain so as to produce patterns like those produced by turning

thur·nia \ˈthərnēə\ *n, cap* [NL, fr. Sir Everard F. Im *Thurn* †1932 Eng. botanist & explorer] : a small genus of herbs (family Juncaceae) related to and resembling the typical rushes

and having heads of flowers on 3-angled stalks with long bracts and perianth parts that are all similar

thurs·day \'thərzdē, -ōz-, -əiz-, -di *also* -z(,)dā\ *n* -S *usu cap* [ME *thuresday, thursday*, fr. OE *thuresdæg, thursdæg*, fr. ON *thōrsdagr;* akin to OE *thunresdæg* Thursday, OHG *Donares tag;* all fr. a prehistoric NGmc-WGmc compound formed fr. constituents represented by OHG *Donar*, the Germanic god of the sky (fr. *thonar, donar* thunder) and by OHG *tag* day; trans. of L *Jovis dies*, lit., day of Jupiter (the ancient Roman god of the sky and the planet Jupiter) — more at THUNDER, DAY] **:** the fifth day of the week **:** the day following Wednesday

thurs·days \-z\ *adv, usu cap* **:** on Thursday repeatedly **:** on any Thursday

¹**thus** \'thəs\ *adv* [ME, fr. OE; akin to OS & OFris *thus*, MD *dus, dos* thus, OE *thæt*, neut. demonstrative pron. & definite article — more at THAT] **1 :** in this or that manner or way ⟨had lain exposed . . . and ~ had become extremely fragile —R.D. Altick⟩ ⟨I picture the process ~ —Anthony Harris⟩ **2 :** to this degree or extent **:** so ⟨~ wise⟩ ⟨~ far⟩ **3 :** because of this or that **:** for this or that reason or cause **:** CONSEQUENTLY, HENCE ⟨there had been no coordinated building program; ~ examples of the worst and the best . . . will be found —*Amer. Guide Series: Minn.*⟩ **4 :** as an example ⟨~, a man . . . may simply mean —A.J.Aydr⟩

²**thus** \'thəs\ *n* -ES [ME, fr. L, incense — more at THURIBLE] **:** GUM THUS 2

¹**thus and thus** *or* **thus and so** *adv* [*thus and thus* fr. ME] **:** in the manner explained esp. in detail **:** in this or that way

²**thus and thus** *or* **thus and so** *n* **:** an unspecified member of a group usu. not of persons **:** any one of several or of several possibilities

thu·shi \'tüshē\ *n, pl* **thushi** *or* **thushis** *usu cap* **1 :** a people of the Chechen group **2 :** a member of the Thushi people

thus·ly \'thəslē, -li\ *adv* **:** in this manner **:** to this degree **:** THUS ⟨he summoned his counselors and spoke ~ to them —*Congressional Record*⟩

thus·ness *n* -ES **1 :** the condition of being thus **2 :** SUCHNESS 2

thus·wise \'≈,wīz\ *adv* [ME *thus wise*] **:** THUS, SO

thut·ter \'thəd·ə(r), -ətə-\ *vi* -ED/-ING/-S [imit.] **:** to make a dull, throbbing, or sputtering sound ⟨a light machine gun ~*ed* briefly —J.M.Moore b. 1890⟩

¹**thu·ya** \'thüyə\ *syn of* THUJA

²**thuya** *var of* THUGA

thu·yop·sis \thü'yäpsəs\ *syn of* THUJOPSIS

¹**thwack** \'thwak\ *vb* -ED/-ING/-S [imit.] *vt* **1 a** (1) **:** to strike with or as if with something flat or heavy **:** BANG, WHACK (2) **:** to beat (a half-dried pantile) into shape **b :** to bring into a specified state by thwacking ⟨to modulate the voice was ~*ed* into them by a generation of firm-handed mothers —J.H. Wheelwright⟩ **2** *obs* **:** to fill to overflowing **:** PACK **3 :** to administer a stinging defeat, punishment, or rebuke to; *also* **:** to satirize severely ~ *vi* **:** to strike with a thwack ⟨her head ~*ed* against the sidewalk —Jonas Bayer⟩

²**thwack** \"\ *n* -S **:** a heavy blow with or as if with something flat or heavy **:** WHACK ⟨hitting the floor with a ~ that would have broken every bone in an adult's body —Mary Lasswell⟩; *also* **:** the sound of a thwack ⟨the crews worked silently except for the ~ of axhead against trees —R.G.Lillard⟩

thwack·er \-kə(r)\ *n* -S **:** one that thwacks; *specif* **:** a wooden implement with which a half-dried pantile is beaten to take out any warping

¹**thwaite** \'thwāt\ *n* -S [of Scand origin; akin to ON *thveit* parcel of land; akin to OE *thwītan* to cut, cut off — more at WHITTLE] *dial* **:** a piece of land used as a meadow, field, or pasture; *specif* **:** forest land cleared and converted to tillage

²**thwaite** *or* **thwaite shad** *var of* TWAITE

¹**thwart** \'thwȯ(ə)r|t, -ȯ(ə)|, *nautical often* 'thȯ-; *usu* |d·+V\ *adv* [ME *thwert, thwart*, fr. ON *thvert*, fr. neut. of *thverr* transverse, oblique; akin to OE *thweorh* transverse, crooked, angry, OHG *dwerah, twerh* transverse, oblique, Goth *thwairhs* angry, L *torquēre* to twist — more at TORTURE] **:** THWARTLY, ATHWART

²**thwart** \"\ *adj* [ME *thwert, thwart*, fr. *thwert, thwart*, adv.] **1 :** situated or placed across something else **:** TRANSVERSE, OBLIQUE **2 :** PERVERSE, STUBBORN, INTRACTABLE ⟨reasoning that defies ~ time —*Times Lit. Supp.*⟩ — **thwartly** *adv*

³**thwart** \"\ *vb* -ED/-ING/-S [ME *thwerten, thwarten*, fr. *thwert, thwart*, adv.] *vt* **1 a :** to run counter to **:** OPPOSE, BAFFLE, CONTRAVENE ⟨I did not like to ~ her in her present mood —Rose Macaulay⟩ **b :** to oppose successfully: (1) **:** to defeat the hopes, aspirations or plans of ⟨attempted to seize the governorship . . . and was ~*ed* by the State Supreme Court —*New Republic*⟩ ⟨religious taboos have not succeeded in ~*ing* lovers —Waldemar Kaempffert⟩ (2) **:** to block or check the occurrence, performance, or completion of **:** prevent the development or fulfillment of ⟨to prohibit children from reaching them would be to ~ the reading habit —Eamon Ryan⟩ ⟨hesitated to ~ the whims of the king —J.H.Plumb⟩ **2 a** (1) **:** to move or pass through or across (2) *archaic* **:** to cross the path of **b** (1) *obs* **:** to lay across an object (2) *archaic* **:** to cause to be crossed by or as if by an overlying mark **c :** to place an obstruction across (as a passage) ~ *vi* **1 :** to be in opposition **:** CLASH, QUARREL **2** *archaic* **:** to go or extend in an oblique manner **syn** see FRUSTRATE

⁴**thwart** \"\ *prep* [ME, fr. *thwert, thwart*, adv.] *archaic* **:** ACROSS, ATHWART

⁵**thwart** \"\ *n* -S [³*thwart*] **1 :** OPPOSITION, OBSTRUCTION **2 a :** a rower's seat extending athwart a boat or canoe **b :** one of the short crosspieces secured to one or two of the uprights erected alongside a ship in process of construction to support the stages

thwart·ed·ly *adv* **:** in a thwarted manner

thwart·er \-ȯr|d·|ər, -ȯ(ə)|, |t|\ *n* -S **:** one that thwarts

thwartover \'≈¦≈≈\ *adj* [ME *thwertover, thwartover*, fr. *thwert, thwart*, adv. + *over*, adv.] *dial chiefly Eng* **:** CONTRARY

thwartsaw *n* [ME *thwertsawe, thwartsawe*, fr. *thwert, thwart*, adj. + *sawe* saw] *obs* **:** CROSSCUT SAW

thwartship \'≈¦≈\ *adj* [⁴*thwart* + *ship* (n.)] **:** lying or leading athwartship ⟨a ~ spar⟩

thwart·ships \-ps\ *adv* [⁴*thwart* + *ship* + *-s*] **:** ATHWARTSHIPS

thwartwise \'≈,≈\ *adv (or adj)* [²*thwart* + *-wise*] **:** in a transverse manner **:** CROSSWISE

thwit·tle \'thwid·ᵊl, -itᵊl\ *n* -S [ME *thwitel* — more at WHITTLE] *Brit* **:** KNIFE

thy \'thī\ *adj* [ME *thy, thi, thin*, fr. OE *thīn*, gen. of *thū* thou — more at THINE] *archaic* **:** of, belonging to, or connected with thee or thyself as possessor, as author, doer, giver, or agent or as object of an action ⟨stretch out ~ rod —Exod 8:16(AV)⟩ ⟨~ slanders I forgive —Shak.⟩ ⟨so thou be chastened by ~ banishment —Alfred Tennyson⟩ — used esp. in biblical, ecclesiastical, solemn, or poetic language, and to some extent in the speech of Friends esp. among themselves; compare ¹THEE, ¹THOU, YOUR

thy·es·te·an \(')thī¦estēən\ *adj, usu cap* [*Thyestes*, ancient Greek legendary character who at a banquet unwittingly ate the flesh of his own sons (fr. L, fr. Gk *Thyestēs*) + E *-an*] **:** of or relating to the eating of human flesh **:** CANNIBAL

thy·iad \'thī,(y)ad, -(y)əd\ *n, pl* **thyiads** \-dz\ *or* **thy·ia·des** \thī(y)ə,dēz, thī'īə,d-\ *usu cap* [L *Thyiad-, Thyias*, fr. Gk, fr. *thyein* to rage, seethe; akin to Gk *thymos* spirit, mind, courage — more at FUME] **:** a member of a group of ancient Greek women devoted to the orgiastic worship of Dionysus esp. as practiced on Mount Parnassus

thy·ine wood \'thī(y)ən-\ *n* [ME *tyyin, thyine, thina*, fr. LL *thyinus* of citron wood, fr. Gk *thyinos*, fr. *thyon, thya* thyine≈ wood] **:** the fragrant and ornamental wood of the sandarac tree (sense 1)

thy·la·cine \'thīlə,sīn, -,sən\ *n* -S [NL *Thylacinus*] **:** TASMANIAN WOLF

thy·la·ci·nus \,thīlə'sīnəs\ *n, cap* [NL, fr. Gk *thylakos* sack, pouch + L *-inus* -ine] **:** a genus of marsupial mammals (family Dasyuridae) consisting of the Tasmanian wolf

thy·la·co·leo \,thīlə'kōlē,ō\ *n, cap* [NL, fr. Gk *thylakos* sack + L *leo* lion — more at LION] **:** a genus (coextensive with the family Thylacoleontidae) of Pleistocene Australian marsupial mammals having a skull about the size of that of a lion, large tusks, and crushing molars

thy·lac·o·mys \thī'lakəməs\ *n, cap* [NL, fr. Gk *thylakos* sack + NL *-mys*] **:** a genus of Australian marsupial mammals (family Peramelidae) comprising the rabbit bandicoots

thy·la·cy·nus \,thīlə'sīnəs\ *syn of* THYLACINUS

thy·la·ken·trin \,thīlə'ken·trən\ *n* -S [*thylakentr-* (blend of Gk *thylakē* scrotum and *kentron* sharp point, good) + *-in* — more at CENTER] **:** FOLLICLE-STIMULATING HORMONE

thy·log·a·le \thī'lägə(,)lē\ *n, cap* [NL, irreg. fr. Gk *thylakos* sack, pouch + *galeē, galē* weasel, ferret — more at GALEA] **:** a genus of marsupial mammals (family Macropodidae) comprising the scrub wallabies and pademelons

¹**thym-** *or* **thymo-** *comb form* [ISV, fr. L *thymum* — more at THYME] **1 :** thyme ⟨*thym*ol⟩ **2 :** thymol ⟨*thymo*quinone $CH_3C_6H_2(C_3H_7)O_2$⟩

²**thym-** *or* **thymo-** *comb form* [NL *thymus*] **:** thymus **:** of the thymus ⟨*thymo*privic⟩ ⟨*thym*ectomize⟩

³**thym-** *or* **thymo-** *comb form* [NL, fr. Gk, fr. *thymos* spirit, soul, mind — more at FUME] **:** soul **:** spirit **:** emotion ⟨*thymo*genic⟩ ⟨*thymo*tactic⟩

thy·mal·li·dae \thī'malə,dē\ *n pl, cap* [NL, fr. *Thymallus*, type genus (fr. Gk *thymallos*, a salmonoid fish, prob. fr. *thymon* thyme; fr. the odor) + *-idae*] **:** a family of salmonoid fishes constituted by the graylings

¹**thyme** \'tīm *sometimes* 'thīm\ *n* -S [ME *thyme, tyme*, fr. MF *thym, tym*, fr. L *thymum*, fr. Gk *thymon*, fr. *thyein* to make a burnt offering, sacrifice; akin to L *fumus* smoke — more at FUME] **1 a :** a mint of the genus *Thymus*; *esp* **:** a common garden herb (*T. vulgaris*) used in seasoning and esp. formerly in medicine **b :** any of several other pungent aromatic herbs chiefly of the family Labiatae — usu. used with a qualifying term; see BASIL THYME **2 :** PITCH PINE 2

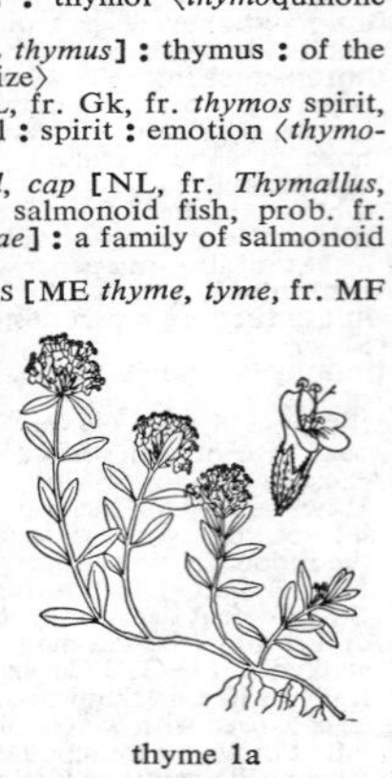

thyme 1a

²**thyme** \"\ *vt* -ED/-ING/-S **:** to cover or scent with thyme ⟨*thymed* breezes⟩

thyme camphor *n* **:** THYMOL

thy·mec·to·my \thī'mektəmē\ *n* -ES [ISV ²*thym-* + *-ectomy*] **:** excision of the thymus

thyme dodder *n* **:** CLOVER DODDER

thyme·laea \,thīmə'lēə, ,thim-\ *n, cap* [NL, fr. L, any of several plants of the genus *Daphne*, fr. Gk *thymelaia*, fr. *thymos* thyme + *elaia* olive] **:** a genus of European and Asiatic herbs and undershrubs (family Thymelaeaceae) having small sessile apetalous flowers with a calyx that has a spreading border and is usu. persistent

thyme·lae·a·ce·ae \,≈≈≈'āsē,ē\ *n pl, cap* [NL, fr. *Thymelaea*, type genus + *-aceae*] **:** a family of tough-barked trees, shrubs, and herbs (order Myrtales) that are native to temperate climates chiefly of the Old World and have entire leaves, capitate apetalous flowers, and drupaceous or capsular fruits

thyme·lae·a·les \-ā(,)lēz\ [NL, fr. *Thymelaea* + *-ales*] *syn of* MYRTALES

thym·e·le \'thimə(,)lē\ *n* -S [LL *thymele, thymela*, fr. Gk *thymelē*, fr. *thycin* to make a burnt offering — more at THYME] **:** an ancient Greek altar; *esp* **:** a small altar of Dionysus standing in the middle of the orchestra of a theater — **thy·mel·ic** \(')thī¦melik, thə'm-\ *or* **thy·mel·i·cal** \-ləkəl\ *adj*

thyme-leaved sandwort \'≈¦≈-\ *n* **:** a Eurasian annual sprawling weed (*Arenaria serpyllifolia*) naturalized throughout No. America and having opposite entire leaves and paniculate small white flowers

thyme-leaved speedwell *n* **:** a perennial decumbent herb (*Veronica serpyllifolia*) found throughout Eurasia and the New World and having small opposite leaves and blue flowers in short narrow racemes

thy·mel·i·ci \(')thī'melə,sī\ *n pl* [L, fr. Gk *thymelikoi*, fr. pl. of *thymelikos* of a thymele, fr. *thymelē* + *-ikos* -ic] **:** a chorus that dances around the thymele in an ancient Greek theater

thyme oil *n* **:** a fragrant essential oil containing thymol and carvacrol that is obtained from various thymes and is used chiefly as an antiseptic in pharmaceutical and dental preparations, as a perfume esp. in soaps, and as a flavor in foods — compare ORIGANUM OIL

thymes *pl of* THYME, *pres 3d sing of* THYME

thymey *var of* THYMY

thymi *pl of* THYMUS

-thy·mia \'thīmēə\ *n comb form* -S [NL, fr. Gk, fr. *thymos* spirit, mind, courage + *-ia* — more at FUME] **:** (such) a condition of mind and will ⟨schizo*thymia*⟩

thy·mi·a·te·ri·on \,thīmēə'tirēən\ *n* -S [Gk *thymiatērion*, fr. *thymian* to smoke, burn incense, fr. (assumed) Gk *thymos* smoke (whence Gk *thymos* spirit) — more at FUME] **:** a vessel for burning incense esp. as used by the ancient Greeks

¹**thy·mic** \'tīmik, 'thī-\ *adj* [ISV ¹*thym-* + *-ic*] **:** relating to or derived from thyme

²**thy·mic** \'thīmik\ *adj* [²*thym-* + *-ic*] **:** of, relating to, or involving the thymus

³**thy·mic** \'thīmik\ *adj* [³*thym-* + *-ic*] **:** of or relating to emotion or emotional lability

thy·mi·dine \'thīmə,dēn, -,dən\ *n* -S [blend of *thymine* and *-id*] **:** a crystalline nucleoside $C_{10}H_{14}N_2O_5$ that is obtained by partial hydrolysis of deoxyribonucleic acid, yields on hydrolysis thymine and deoxyribose, and is a growth factor esp. for lactobacilli

thy·mi·dyl·ic acid \,thīmə¦dilik-\ *n* [*thymidine* + *-yl* + *-ic*] **:** either of two isomeric crystalline nucleotides $C_{10}H_{15}N_2O_8P$ obtained by partial hydrolysis of deoxyribonucleic acid **:** an ester of thymidine and orthophosphoric acid

thy·mine \'thī,mēn, -mən\ *n* -S [G *thymin*, fr. *thym-* ²thym- + *-in* -ine] **:** a crystalline pyrimidine base $C_5H_6N_2O_2$ obtained by hydrolysis of deoxyribonucleic acid and from spermatozoa of fishes; 5-methyl-uracil

thymo- — see THYM-

thy·mo·centric \¦thīmə¦sen·trik\ *adj* [³*thym-* + *-centric*] **:** oriented toward feeling and emotion rather than toward intellect and morality

thy·mo·cyte \'≈≈,sīt\ *n* -S [ISV ²*thym-* + *-cyte*] **:** a cell of the thymus; *esp* **:** a thymic lymphocyte

thy·mol \'thī,mȯl, -mōl\ *n* -S [ISV ¹*thym-* + *-ol*] **:** a crystalline phenol $CH_3C_6H_3(C_3H_7)OH$ that has a pleasant aromatic odor and antiseptic properties, occurs naturally in thyme oil and other essential oils or is made synthetically (as from *meta*≈cresol and isopropyl alcohol or propylene), and is used chiefly as a fungicide and preservative and in pharmaceutical, dental, and toilet preparations; 5-methyl-2-isopropyl-phenol — compare CARVACROL

thymol blue *n* **:** a greenish crystalline compound $C_{27}H_{30}O_5S$ of the sulfonephthalein series derived from thymol and used as an acid-base indicator

thymolphthalein \¦≈≈¦≈≈≈\ *n* [ISV *thymol* + *phthalein*] **:** a crystalline compound $C_{28}H_{30}O_4$ analogous to phenolphthalein and likewise used as an acid-base indicator

thy·mo·ma \thī'mōmə\ *n, pl* **thymo·mas** \-məz\ *or* **thy·moma·ta** \-məd·ə\ [NL, fr. ²*thym-* + *-oma*] **:** a tumor that arises from the tissue elements of the thymus

thy·mo·nucleic acid \¦thī,mō+-\ *also* **thymus nucleic acid** *n* [ISV ²*thym-* + *nucleic*] **:** DEOXYRIBONUCLEIC ACID

¹**thy·mus** \'thīməs\ *also* **thymus gland** *n, pl* **thymus·es** \-məsəz\ *or* **thy·mi** \-,mī\ *often attrib* [NL, fr. Gk *thymos* warty excrescence, thymus gland] **:** a glandular structure largely of lymphoid tissue that is present in the young of most vertebrates, arises from the epithelium of one or more embryonic branchial clefts, lies typically in the upper anterior part of the chest or at the base of the neck, tends to become vestigial in the adult, and is held to play a major role in cellular immunological responses — see SWEETBREAD

²**thymus** \"\ *n, cap* [NL, fr. Gk *thymos, thymon* thyme — more at THYME] **:** a large genus of Old World mints having small entire leaves and clustered purple 2-lipped flowers — see THYME

thymy *also* **thymey** \'tīmē, 'thī-, -mi\ *adj* **thym·i·er**; **thym·i·est :** constituting or resembling thyme **:** abounding in or fragrant with thyme

thy·myl \'thīməl\ *n* -S [ISV ¹*thym-* + *-yl*] **:** a univalent radical $C_{10}H_{13}$ derived from thymol

¹**thyn·nid** \'thinəd\ *adj* [NL *Thynnidae*] **:** of or relating to the Thynnidae

²**thynnid** \"\ *n* -S **:** an insect of the family Thynnidae

thyn·ni·dae \-nə,dē\ *n pl, cap* [NL, fr. *Thynnus*, type genus (fr. L *thynnus, thunnus* tunny) + *-idae* — more at TUNNY] **:** a family of aculeate hymenopterans confined mainly to Australia and having the females wingless and much smaller than the winged males

thyr- *or* **thyro-** *comb form* [*thyroid*] **1 :** thyroid ⟨*thyr*asthenia⟩ **2 :** thyroid and ⟨*thyro*arytenoid⟩

thy·ra·tron \'thīrə,trän\ *n* -S [fr. *Thyratron*, a trademark] **:** a gas-filled 3-element hot cathode tube in which the grid controls only the start of a continuous current thus giving the tube a trigger effect

thyreo- *comb form* [ISV, fr. Gk *thyreoeidēs* — more at THYROID] **1 :** thyroid ⟨*thyreo*tomy⟩ **2 :** thyroid and ⟨*thyreo*cervical⟩

thy·re·o·cor·i·dae \,thīrēō'kȯrə,dē\ *n pl, cap* [NL, fr. *Thyreocoris*, type genus (fr. Gk *thyreos* oblong shield + *koris* bug) + *-idae*; akin to Gk *keirein* to cut — more at THYROID, SHEAR] **:** a family of true bugs including the negro bugs

thy·re·oid \'thīrē,ȯid\ *adj or n* [ISV, fr. Gk *thyreoeidēs* — more at THYROID] **:** THYROID

thy·re·o·trop·ic \¦≈≈ə¦träpik\ *adj* [*thyreo-* + *-tropic*] **:** THYROTROPHIC

thy·rid·i·al \thī'ridēəl\ *adj* [NL *thyridium* + E *-al*] **:** of, relating to, or being a thyridium

thy·rid·i·dae \-də,dē\ *n pl, cap* [NL, fr. *Thyrid-, Thyris*, type genus (fr. Gk *thyrid-, thyris* window, dim. of *thyra* door) + *-idae* — more at DOOR] **:** a family of small moths having the wings marked with translucent spots

thy·rid·i·um \-dēəm\ *n, pl* **thyrid·ia** \-ēə\ [NL, fr. Gk *thyridion* window, dim. of *thyra* door] **1 :** a pale spot in the wing vein of some insects esp. of the orders Hymenoptera and Trichoptera **2 :** one of a pair of oval pits on the second abdominal tergite of some hymenopterans

thy·ri·o·the·ci·um \,thīrēō'thēs(h)ēəm\ *n, pl* **thyriothe·cia** \-s(h)ēə\ [NL, irreg. fr. Gk *thyreos* oblong shield + NL *-thecium* — more at THYROID] **:** an ascocarp so inverted that the generative hyphae are dependent

Thy·rite \'thī,rīt\ *trademark* — used for an electrical resistance material consisting primarily of silicon carbide, having low resistance at high currents and high resistance at low currents, and used esp. in lightning arresters

thyro- — see THYR-

thy·ro·active \¦thīrō+\ *adj* [*thyr-* + *active*] **1 :** capable of entering into the thyroid metabolism and of being incorporated into the thyroid hormone ⟨~ iodine⟩ **2 :** simulating the action of the thyroid hormone ⟨~ iodocasein⟩

thy·ro·arytenoid \"+\ *adj* [NL *thyroarytenoides*, fr. *thyr-* + *arytenoides* arytenoid — more at ARYTENOID] **:** connecting the thyroid and arytenoid cartilages of the larynx

thy·ro·ar·y·te·noi·de·us \,thīrō,arəd·ə'nȯidēəs\ *also* **thy·ro·arytenoid** \¦thīrō+\ *n* [NL *thyroarytenoideus*, fr. *thyroarytenoides*] **:** a muscle extending between the thyroid and arytenoid cartilages and serving to relax and shorten the vocal cords

thyroarytenoid fold *or* **thyroarytenoid ligament** *n* **:** any of four elastic ligaments of the larynx that are covered by folds of mucous membrane and arranged in a superior pair constituting the false vocal cords and an inferior pair forming the true vocal cords

thyroarytenoid muscle *n* **:** THYROARYTENOIDEUS

thy·ro·cervical \¦≈≈+\ *adj* [*thyr-* + *cervical*] **:** of or relating to the neck and the thyroid gland

thy·ro·colloid \"+\ *n* [*thyr-* + *colloid*] **:** the colloid substance within the vesicles of the thyroid gland

thy·ro·epiglottic \"+\ *adj* [ISV *thyr-* + *epiglottic*] **:** connecting the thyroid cartilage and epiglottis

thy·ro·genic \¦thīrə¦jenik\ *or* **thy·rog·e·nous** \thī'räjənəs\ *adj* [*thyr-* + *-genic* or *-genous*] **:** originating in or caused by activity of the thyroid

thy·ro·globulin \¦thīrō+\ *n* [ISV *thyr-* + *globulin*] **:** an iodine≈containing protein that exhibits the general properties of the globulins, is obtained from the thyroid gland, and yields on hydrolysis thyroxine, diiodotyrosine, and related iodo amino acids in addition to amino acids found as constituents of most proteins

thy·ro·glossal \"+\ *adj* [*thyr-* + *glossal*] **:** of, relating to, or connecting the tongue and thyroid gland

thy·ro·hy·al \-¦hīəl\ *n* -S [*thyr-* + *hy-* + *-al*] **:** the greater cornu of the hyoid bone; *also* **:** an embryonic skeletal element that becomes the greater cornu or in lower forms remains as a separate bone or cartilage

¹**thy·ro·hyoid** \¦thīrō+\ *also* **thy·ro·hyoidean** \"+\ *adj* [*thyr-* + *hyoid* or *hyoid* + *-an*, adj. suffix] **1 a :** connecting the thyroid cartilage of the larynx and the hyoid bone **b :** of, relating to, or associated with the thyrohyoid muscle **2 :** of, relating to, or being the first branchial arch of the vertebrate embryo

²**thyrohyoid** \"\ *n* **:** a thyrohyoid part (as a muscle or a nerve)

thyrohyoid arch *n* **:** the third branchial arch of the vertebrate embryo of which the cartilage persists as the thyrohyal

¹**thy·roid** \'thī,rȯid\ *adj* [NL *thyroides*, fr. Gk *thyreoeidēs* shaped like a shield, thyroid, fr. *thyreos* shield shaped like a door (fr. *thyra* door) + *-eidēs* -oid — more at DOOR] **1** *of an anatomical part* **:** SHIELD-SHAPED — used almost exclusively of a cartilage in the larynx and an endocrine gland **2 a :** of, relating to, involving, or caused or produced by the thyroid gland ⟨a severe ~ insufficiency⟩ **b :** suggestive of a disordered and esp. a hyperactive thyroid ⟨~ eyes⟩ ⟨a tense ~ personality⟩ ⟨a somewhat ~ spinster —*Time*⟩

²**thyroid** \"\ *n* -S [NL *thyroides*, fr. *thyroides*, adj.] **1 a** *or* **thyroid gland :** a large endocrine gland of craniate vertebrates that arises as a median ventral outgrowth of the pharynx, lies in the base of the neck or anterior ventral part of the thorax, is often accompanied by lateral accessory glands sometimes more or less fused with the main mass, produces an iodine-containing hormone having a profound influence on growth and development and specifically stimulating the metabolic rate, and has complex interrelations with the pituitary and adrenal and possibly other endocrine glands — see CRETINISM, GOITER, HYPERTHYROIDISM, HYPOTHYROIDISM, THYROXINE; compare MYXEDEMA **b :** a body part (as an artery or nerve) associated with the thyroid gland or cartilage **2 :** a preparation of the thyroid gland of various food animals containing approximately ¹⁄₁₀ percent of iodine combined in thyroxine and used in treating thyroid disorders

thy·roi·dal \(')thī¦rȯidᵊl\ *adj* [²*thyroid* + *-al*] **1 :** THYROID 2 **2 :** resembling that of the thyroid hormone

thyroid artery *n* **:** either of two arteries supplying not only the thyroid gland but many muscles and other structures of the front of the neck

thyroid cartilage *n* **:** the chief cartilage of the larynx

thy·roid·ec·to·mize \,thī,rȯi'dektə,mīz\ *vt* -ED/-ING/-S [*thyroidectomy* + *-ize*] **:** to subject to thyroidectomy

thy·roid·ec·to·my \-mē, -mi\ *n* -ES [ISV *thyroid* + *-ectomy*] **:** partial or complete excision of the thyroid gland

thyroid ganglion *n* **:** the middle of the three cervical ganglia of the sympathetic system of each side

thyroid hormone *n* **:** thyroxine or other closely related metabolically active compound (as triiodothyronine) that is stored in the thyroid gland in the form of thyroglobulin or circulates in the blood apparently bound to plasma protein

thy·roid·i·tis \,thī,rȯi'dīd·əs\ *n* [NL, fr. *thyroides* thyroid + *-itis*] **:** inflammation of the thyroid gland

thyroid vein *n* **:** any of several small paired veins carrying blood from the thyroid gland and other structures of the front of the neck

thy·ro·lac·tin \,thīrə'laktən\ *n* [*thyr-* + *lact-* + *-in*] **:** IODINATED CASEIN

thy·ro·nine \'thīrə,nēn, -,nən\ *n* -S [*thyr-* + *-on* + *-ine*] **:** a phenolic amino acid $HOC_6H_4OC_6H_4CH_2CH(NH_2)COOH$ of which thyroxine is a tetraiodo derivative; the *para*-hydroxy≈phenyl ether of tyrosine

thy·ro·protein \¦thīrō+\ *n* [*thyr-* + *protein*] **:** any of various preparations made by iodinating proteins and having physiological activity similar to that of thyroxine and related iodinated protein constituents from the thyroid gland; *esp* **:** IODINATED CASEIN

thy·ros·tra·ca \thī'rästrəkə\ *n pl, cap* [NL, fr. *thyro-* (fr. Gk *thyra* door, opening) + Gk *ostraka*, pl. of *ostrakon* shell —

more at DOOR, OYSTER〉 *in some esp. former classifications* : a subclass of Crustacea coextensive with Cirripedia — **thy·ros·tra·can** \(')\ *adj or n*

thy·ro·toxic \'thīrō,täksik\ *adj* [*thyr-* + *-toxic*] : of, relating to, or affected with hyperthyroidism — **thy·ro·toxicity** \"..\ *n*

thy·ro·toxi·cosis \"+\ *n* [NL, fr. *thyr-* + *toxicosis*] : HYPERTHYROIDISM

thy·ro·trophic \,thīrə'träfik, -tröf-\ *or* **thy·ro·trop·ic** \-'träp-\ *adj* [*thyr-* + *-trophic* or *-tropic*] : exerting or characterized by a direct influence on the secretory activity of the thyroid gland 〈the ~ hormone of the anterior pituitary〉 — **thy·ro·trophi·cal·ly** \-fək(ə)lē\ *adv*

thy·ro·tro·phin \thī'rä(ə)trəfən, ,thīrə'trō\ *or* **thy·ro·tro·pin** \-pən\ *n* -s [*thyrotrophic, thyrotropic* + *-in*] : a hormone secreted by the anterior lobe of the pituitary body that regulates the formation and secretion of thyroid hormone and is used chiefly in the treatment of hypothyroidism due to pituitary deficiency

thy·rox·ine \thī'räk,sēn, -sən\ *also* **thy·rox·in** \-sən\ *n* -s [ISV *thyr-* + *ox-* + *-ine, -in*] : a crystalline iodine-containing phenolic amino acid $C_{15}H_{11}I_4NO_4$ that is the chief active principle of the thyroid gland, occurs there in the levorotatory L-form combined in thyroglobulin and in the blood apparently bound to plasma protein, is also made synthetically (as from diiodotyrosine), and is used esp. in the form of its soluble sodium salt in the treatment of hypothyroidism; tetraiodothyronine — compare THYROID HORMONE, TRIIODOTHYRONINE

thyrse \'thərs, -ōs, -ois\ *n* -s [NL *thyrsus*] : an inflorescence as in the lilac and horse chestnut in which the main axis is racemose and the secondary and later axes are cymose

thyr·soid \'thər,sòid\ *adj* [NL *thyrsus* + E *-oid*] : having somewhat the form of a thyrse 〈a ~ panicle〉

thyr·sus \-.səs\, *pl* **thyr·si** \-,sī\ *n* [L, fr. Gk *thyrsos*] **1** : a staff surmounted by a pine cone or by a bunch of vine or ivy leaves with grapes or berries that is carried by Bacchus and by satyrs and others engaging in Bacchic rites **2** [NL, fr. L] : THYRSE

thysan- *or* **thysano-** *comb form* [NL, fr. Gk, fr. *thysanos*] : tassel : fringe 〈*Thysanoptera*〉 〈*Thysanura*〉

thysa·no·car·pus \,thīsənō'kärpəs, ,this-\ *n, cap* [NL, fr. *thysan-* + *-carpus*] : a small genus of slender annual herbs (family Cruciferae) that have pinnatifid basal leaves, entire stem leaves, small white flowers, and an ovate or orbicular one-seeded winged silicle and are widely distributed in dry upland areas of the Pacific coast of No. America — see FRINGEPOD

thysa·nop·ter \,thīsə'näptə(r), ,this-\ *n* -s [NL *Thysanoptera*] : THYSANOPTERON

thysa·nop·tera \-tərə\ *n pl, cap* [NL, fr. *thysan-* + *-ptera*] : an order of insects comprising the thrips and including various important plant pests — **thysa·nop·ter·an** \',ə-'terən\ *adj or n* — **thysa·nop·ter·ous** \-t(ə)rəs\ *adj*

thysa·nop·ter·ist \,',ə-'tərəst\ *n* -s [NL *Thysanoptera* + E *-ist*] : a specialist in the Thysanoptera

thysa·nop·ter·on \-tə,rän, ,-\ *n, pl* **thysanop·tera** \-tərə\ [NL, back-formation fr. *Thysanoptera*] : one of the Thysanoptera : THRIPS

thysa·no·so·ma \,ə-nō'sōmə\ *n, cap* [NL, fr. *thysan-* + *-soma*] : a genus of tapeworms (family Anoplocephalidae) including the common fringed tapeworm of ruminants

thysa·nu·ra \,ə-'n(y)ùrə\ *n pl, cap* [NL, fr. *thysan-* + *-ura*] : an order of wingless insects having setiform caudal appendages projecting as bristles and comprising the bristletails — **thysa·nu·ran** \,'ə-'rən\ *adj or n* — **thysa·nu·rous** \,ə-'rəs\ *adj*

thysa·nu·ri·form \,'ə-'rə,fòrm\ *adj* [NL *Thysanura* + E *-iform*] : CAMPODEIFORM

thy·self \thī'self\ *pron* [ME, alter. (influenced by *thy* & *herself*) of *theeself*, fr. OE *thē selfum* & *thē selfne*, dat. & acc. respectively of *thū self* thou thyself — more at THOU, THEE, SELF] *archaic* : YOURSELF 〈thou to ~ wast cruel —John Milton〉 〈physician, heal ~ —Lk 4:23 (AV)〉 〈do ~ no harm —Acts 16:28 (AV)〉 〈thou ~ hast . . . shed a gleam —William Wordsworth〉 〈thou hadst power ~ to keep this vow —Robert Herrick †1674〉 〈he whom next ~ of all the world I loved —Shak.〉 〈as if it were ~ that's here —William Wordsworth〉 〈me than ~ more miserable —John Milton〉 〈~ and thy belongings are not thine own —Shak.〉 〈~ should govern Rome and me —Shak.〉 〈thou . . . standest smiling in thy future grave, . . . ~ thy monument —Sidney Lanier〉 — used esp. in biblical, ecclesiastical, solemn, or poetical language, and to some extent in the speech of Friends esp. among themselves — **thy·sen** \-'sen\ *pron* [by alter.] *dial Eng* : THYSELF

thy·sen \-'sen\ *pron* [by alter.] *dial Eng* : THYSELF

¹ti \'tē\ *n* -s [Tahitian, Marquesan, Samoan, & Maori] **1** *or* **ki** \'kē\ : any of several Asiatic and Pacific trees or shrubs of the genus *Cordyline*: as **a** : a medium-sized New Zealand tree (*C. australis*) having either a single trunk with a terminal tuft of elongated often varicolored leaves or a branching trunk with each branch similarly crowned and having very large panicles of tiny creamy white or bluish globose berries **b** : a variable woody plant (*C. terminalis*) with terminal tufts of elongated leaves that are used locally for thatching, clothing, and food wrappers and thick sweet roots that are used as food or as the base of an intoxicating beverage **2** [by shortening & alter.] : TEA TREE 2a

²ti \"\ *n* -s [alter. of *si*] : the seventh tone of the diatonic scale in solmization

³ti \"\ *n, pl* **ti** *or* **tis** *usu cap* **1** : an early Tatar people related to the Hsiung-Nu **2** : a member of the Ti people

Ti *symbol* titanium

¹ti·a·hua·na·can \,tēəwə'näkən\ *adj, usu cap* [*Tiahuanaco*, Bolivia + E *-an*, adj. suffix] : TIAHUANACO

²tiahuanacan \"\ *n* -s *usu cap* [*Tiahuanaco*, Bolivia + E *-an*, n. suffix] : one of the prehistoric peoples of Peru and Bolivia who produced the Tiahuanaco culture

ti·a·hua·na·co \-ä(,)hä'kō\ *adj, usu cap* [fr. *Tiahuanaco*, village in western Bolivia where remains of the culture were found] : of or relating to a culture of Peru, Bolivia, and contiguous areas from about 100 B.C. to A.D. 900 characterized by fine stone masonry and carving in stone, polychrome pottery, textiles (as tapestry) and bronze ornaments, weapons, and tools; *also* : of the stiff angular but dignified style of design found on these artifacts having as central motif an anthropomorphized demon figure often carrying a throwing-stick

ti·a·hua·na·coid \-ä,kòid\ *adj, usu cap* [*Tiahuanaco*, Bolivia + E *-oid*] **1** : EPIGONAL **2** : resembling the style and symbols of Tiahuanaco textile and pottery designs

ti·ang \'(')tē,an\ *n* -s [Dinka] : TOPI; *esp* : a rather small purplish red black-marked Senegalese topi (*Damaliscus korrigum tiang*)

tiao \'dē'aù\ *n* -s [Chin (Pek) *tiao²*] : a string of former Chinese cash or a unit of value equivalent to it varying in amount in different times and localities and the cash often being units of account rather than actual coins

tiaong \'tē'aòn\ *n* -s [native name in [the Philippines] : RED LAUAN

ti·ar \'tī(ə)r\ *n* *archaic var of* TIARA

ti·ara \tē'a(ə)rə, -'erə, -'ärə, -'árə *sometimes* tī'a(ə)- *or* tī'ä-\ *n* -s [L, fr. Gk *tiara, tiaras*] **1 a** : a headdress worn by the ancient Persians; *specif* : a high and erect royal tiara encircled with a diadem **b** : the pope's triple crown **2** : a decorative band or semicircular ornament for the head often made of flowers, fabric, or metal for wear by women on formal occasions **3 a** *also* **ti·are** \'tēa(ə)r, -'e\ ; \tiare *tr. F tiare*, fr. L *tiara*] : any of several fragrant-flowered shrubs of the genus *Gardenia* found in Pacific islands **b** : MITER 3

ti·a·rel·la \,tēə'relə, ,tīə-\ *n, cap* [NL, fr. L *tiara* + *-ella*] : a small genus of NL. American herbs (family Saxifragaceae) having mostly basal palmately lobed or divided leaves with long petioles and a slender raceme of delicate white flowers with a one-celled ovary and basal placentae — see FALSE MITERWORT

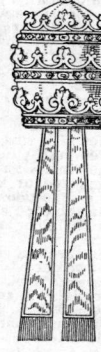

tiara 1b

ti·ar·is \tē'a(a)ròs\ *n, cap* [NL, fr. L *tiara*] : a genus of tropical American finches (family Fringillidae) often with bright yellow markings about the head — see GRASSQUIT

tib \'tib\ *n* -s [origin unknown] **1** [prob. fr. *Tib*, nickname fr. the feminine name *Isabel*] *obs* : GIRL, LASS; *also* : PROSTITUTE **2** : the ace of trumps in gleek

tib·a·re·ni \,tibə'rānē\ *n pl, usu cap* : one of numerous ancient peoples associated with iron making in the Armenian plateau

tib·bit \'tibət\ *var of* TABET

tib·bu *or* **tibu** \'ti(,)bü\ *n, pl* **tibbu** *or* **tibbus** *or* **tibu** *or* **tibus** *usu cap* **1** : a Negroid people of the area around and in the Tibesti mountains northeast of Lake Chad in Africa **2** : a member of the Tibbu people

ti·ber green \'tībə(r)-\ *n, often cap T* [fr. *Tiber*, river in central Italy] : a light yellowish green that is yellower and paler than apple green (sense 2), lighter and stronger than pistachio, and yellower and stronger than crayon green

ti·be·ri·an \(')tī'birēən, -ber-\ *adj, usu cap* [L *tiberianus*, fr. *Tiberius* †A.D. 37 second emperor of Rome + *-anus -an*] **1** : of, relating to, or resembling the Roman emperor Tiberius or his policies **2** [*Tiberias*, northern Palestine + E *-an*] : of or relating to the ancient city of Tiberias

¹tibet *var of* THIBET

²ti·bet *also* **thi·bet** \tə'bet, *usu* -ed-+V\ *adj, usu cap* [fr. *Tibet* (Thibet), country in central Asia] : of or from Tibet : of the kind or style prevalent in Tibet : TIBETAN

¹ti·bet·an \tə'bet'n\ *adj, usu cap* [*Tibet*, country in central Asia + E *-an*, adj. suffix] **1** : of, relating to, or characteristic of Tibet **2** : of, relating to, or characteristic of the people of Tibet

²tibetan \"\ *n, pl* **tibetans** *cap* [*Tibet* + E *-an*, n. suffix] **1 a** : a member of the Mongoloid native race of Tibet that is modified in the west and south by intermixture with Indian peoples and in the east with Chinese typically being about five feet five inches in height and brachycephalic and having wavy hair, brown or hazel eyes, skin tawny brown to white, the beard scant, and the nose either flat or prominent **b** : a native or inhabitant of Tibet **2** : the Tibeto-Burman language of the Tibetan people

tibetan mastiff *n, usu cap T* : a very large powerful roughcoated dog with small drooping ears, bushy tail, and black or black-and-tan hair that is native to central Asia

tibetan terrier *n, usu cap both Ts* [so called fr. its being found in parts of Asia, esp. India and China] : a breed of medium-sized terrier much resembling the old English sheepdog but having a curled, well-feathered tail; *also* : a dog of this breed — called also *chrysanthemum dog*

tibeto- *comb form, usu cap* [²*tibet* + *-o-*] : Tibetan and 〈*Tibeto-Chinese*〉 〈*Tibeto-Himalayan*〉

¹tibeto-burman \tə'bed-(,)ō+\ *n, cap T&B* **1** : a language family of Asia including Tibetan, Garo, Bodo, Lushei, Kachin, Burmese, by some included in Sino-Tibetan **2** : a member of a people speaking a Tibeto-Burman language

²tibeto-burman \"\ *adj, usu cap T&B* **1** : of, relating to, or being Tibeto-Burman or a language belonging to Tibeto-Burman **2** : of, relating to, or being Tibeto-Burmans

tibeto-burmese \tə'bed-(,)ō+\ *n, cap T&B* : TIBETO-BURMAN

ti·bey \tə'bā\ *n* -s [AmerSp] : any of several plants of the genus *Isotoma* (family Lobeliaceae) the foliage of which is poisonous to cattle

tib·ia \'tibēə\ *n, pl* **tibi·ae** \-bē,ē, -bē,ī\ *also* **tibias** [L, shinbone, pipe, flute — more at SIPHON] **1 a** : the preaxial and in the usual position of the limb the inner and usu. the larger of the two bones of the vertebrate leg or hind limb between the knee and ankle articulating above with the femur and below with the talus and in many forms more or less fused with the accompanying fibula **b** : the fourth joint counting from the base of the leg of an insect that lies between the femur and tarsus **2** : an ancient flute orig. fashioned from an animal's leg bone — used esp. in names of various labial wood pipe organ stops 〈~ clausa〉 〈~ plena〉

tib·i·al \-bēəl\ *adj* [L *tibialis*, fr. *tibia* + *-alis -al*] : of, relating to, or located near a tibia

tibial artery *n* : either of the arteries of the lower leg formed by the bifurcation of the popliteal artery being a larger posterior that divides between the medial malleolus and heel into the two plantar arteries and a smaller anterior that passes forward between the bones

tib·i·ale \,tibē'ā,(,)lē, -'ä'(-, -'ä(-\ *n, pl* **tibi·alia** \-,lēə\ [NL, fr. neut. of L *tibialis* tibial] : the most preaxial element of the proximal row of bones of the tarsus and in man prob. a part of the talus

²tibiale \"\ *n, pl* **tibialia** [NL] : TIBIAL POINT

tib·i·alis \-,lis\ *n, pl* **tibia·les** \-,(,)lēz\ [NL; in sense a, short for *tibialis anticus* anterior tibial (muscle), fr. *tibialis* tibial muscle (fr. L, tibial) + *anticus* anterior; in sense b, short for *tibialis posticus* posterior tibial (muscle), fr. *tibialis* + *posticus* posterior — more at ANTICUS, POSTICOUS] : either of two muscles of the calf of the leg: **a** : a muscle arising chiefly from the outer tuberosity and part of the shaft of the tibia and inserted by a long tendon into the first cuneiform and first metatarsal bones — called also *tibialis anterior, tibialis anticus* **b** : a deeply situated muscle arising from the tibia and fibula, interosseous membrane, and intermuscular septa and inserted by a tendon passing under the medial malleolus into the navicular and first cuneiform bones — called also *tibialis posterior, tibialis posticus*

tibial nerve *n* : the large nerve in the back of the leg that is a continuation of the sciatic and terminates at the medial malleolus in the lateral and medial plantar nerves

tibial pad *n* : a flexible pad on the tibia in some insects

tibial point *n* : the upper margin and edge of the interior prominence of the head of the tibia

tibial spur *n* : a spine or one of several spines borne on the distal end of the tibia of many insects : CALCAR

tibial vein *n* : either the anterior vein or the posterior vein accompanying the corresponding tibial arteries

tibio- *comb form* [NL, fr. L *tibia* shinbone — more at SIPHON] **1** : fused tibia and 〈*tibiotarsus*〉 **2** : tibial and 〈*tibiocalcaneal*〉 〈*tibiofemoral*〉

tib·io·fib·u·la \,tibēō'+\ *n* [NL, fr. *tibio-* + *fibula*] : a bone resulting from fusion of the tibia and the fibula (as in the tailless amphibia) — **tib·io·fib·u·lar** \"+\ *adj*

Ti·bi·one \,tē(,)bē'wän\ *trademark* — used for thiacetazone

tib·io·tar·sal \,tibēō'+\ *adj* [NL *tibiotarsus* + E *-al*] : of or relating to the tibiotarsus

tibio·tar·sus \"+\ *n* [NL, fr. *tibio-* + *tarsus*]: some of the tarsal elements being fused into its lower end : the tibia of a bird

tib·ou·chi·na \,tibə'kīnə, -kēnə\ *n* [NL, fr. *tibouch* (fr. native name in Guiana) + *-ina*] : a large genus of So. American shrubs or rarely herbs (family Melastomaceae) having entire 5- to 7-nerved leaves and trichotomous panicles of large purple flowers with a hairy calyx, 10 stamens, and a 5-celled ovary — see GLORY-BUSH, SPIDERFLOWER 2 -s : any plant of the genus *Tibouchina*

ti·bour·bou \,tibə'bü\ *n* -s [F, fr. Galibi] : a tropical American tree (*Apeiba tibourbou*) of the family Tiliaceae with yellowish flowers in lateral cymes, bark that yields jangada fiber, and an extraordinarily light wood that is used along the coast of Brazil for making jangadas

tibs *pl of* TIB

tibu *usu cap, var of* TIBBU

ti·bu·ron \,tibə'rän, -rōn\ *n, pl* **tiburo·nes** \,rə'rō(,)nēz\ [Sp *tiburón*, fr. Pg *tubarão*, prob. fr. Tupi *tubarām*] : any of various large voracious sharks of the West Indies and Central

ti·bur·tine \'tibə(r),tīn\ *adj, usu cap* [ME, fr. L *tiburtinus*, fr. *tiburt-, tiburs* of Tibur (fr. *Tibur*, region in ancient Latium corresponding to Tivoli, commune in central Italy) + *-inus -ine*] : of or relating to Tivoli 〈the *Tiburtine* sibyl〉

tic \'tik\ *n* -s [F] **1** : a convulsive motion of some muscles esp. of the face usu. resulting from nervous habit : TWITCHING **2** : OBSESSION, FIXATION

ti·cal \ti'käl\ *n, pl* **tical, tikal, 'tēkəl\ *n, pl* **ticals** *or* **tical** [Thai, fr. Malay *tikal*, a monetary unit] **1 a** : an old Thai monetary unit orig. used in designation of the value of uncoined silver **b** : an old Thai silver coin containing 15 grams

of silver 0.900 fine **2** : the basic monetary unit of modern Thailand : BAHT

tic dou·lou·reux \,tikdülə'rü, -dül-, -'rər(-), -'rə, -'rö\ *n* [F, painful twitch] : TRIGEMINAL NEURALGIA

ti·chod·ro·ma \tī'kädrəmə, tə'k-\ *n, cap* [NL, fr. Gk *teichos* wall + *dromos* act of running, racecourse — more at DOUGH, -DROM] : a genus of birds (family Certhiidae) consisting of the wall creeper

ticho·drome \'tikə,drōm, 'tik-\ *n* -s [NL *Tichodroma*] : WALL CREEPER

tichor·rhine \'tikə,rīn, 'tik-\ *n* [*tichorhinus* (specific epithet of the woolly rhinoceros *Rhinoceros tichorhinus*, fr. Gk *teichos* wall + NL *-rhinus*; fr. the vertical bony septum forming a supporting wall for the nose] : WOOLLY RHINOCEROS

¹ti·ci·nese \,ticha'nēz, -ēs\ *adj, usu cap* [*Ticino*, canton in the Lepontine Alps, Switzerland + E *-ese*, adj. suffix] : of, relating to, or characteristic of the canton of Ticino **2** : of, relating to, or characteristic of the people of Ticino

²ticinese \"\ *n, pl* **ticinese** *cap* [*Ticino, Switzerland* + E *-ese*, n. suffix] : a native or inhabitant of Ticino

¹tick \'tik\ *n* -s [ME *tyke, tike*; akin to OE *ticia* tick, MHG *zeche* tick, MIr *dega* stag beetle, Arm *tiz* tick] **1** : any of numerous arachnids that constitute the acarine superfamily Ixodoidea, are much larger than the closely related mites, are bloodsuckers which attach themselves to warm-blooded vertebrates to feed, are chiefly important as vectors of various infectious diseases of man and lower animals, and although the immature larva has but six legs, may be readily distinguished from an insect by the complete lack of external segmentation **2** : any of various usu. wingless parasitic dipterous insects (as a bird tick, sheep ked, or bat fly)

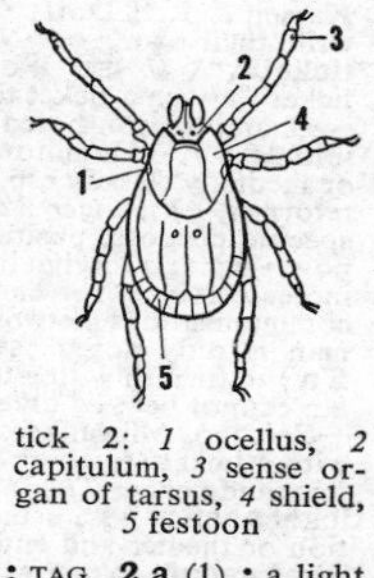

tick 2: *1* ocellus, *2* capitulum, *3* sense organ of tarsus, *4* shield, *5* festoon

²tick \"\ *n* -s [ME *tek*; akin to MHG *zic* light push, tick, Norw dial. *tikka* to push lightly, touch lightly and prob. to ME *teke* tick (arachnid)] **1 a** *obs* : a light touch : TAP **b** *Brit* : TAG **2 a** (1) : a light quick distinct audible tapping sound esp. in a rhythmic series 〈the beating of the metronome . . . at 120 ~s per minute —R.S. Woodworth〉; *also* : a series of such ticks 〈the breathless ~ of the clock —Berton Roueché〉 (2) : a pulsation or series of pulsations likened to the tick of a clock 〈his heart gave a ~ —Marguerite Steen〉 **b** *chiefly Brit* : the time taken or indicated by the tick of a clock : a very small interval of time : MOMENT, SECOND 〈we'll be ready in a couple of ~s —Richard Llewellyn〉 **3 a** : a dot, speck, dash, or check used to direct attention to something, to mark off an item (as on a list) as having been examined, to represent a point on a scale, or as a symbolic abbreviation 〈making ~s in a small-order catalogue on her lap with a pencil stub —Arthur Mayse〉 〈had to start all over again, using the same letters with ~s to signify higher decimal orders —Lancelot Hogben〉 〈the intervals on the scale are marked off by lines and ~s —C.F.Schmid〉 **b** : a small spot of a different color on a furred or feathered creature — **on the tick** *or* **to the tick** *adv, chiefly Brit* : at a precise moment : exactly on the tick 〈arrived at my destination *on the tick* —Adrian Bell〉

³tick \"\ *vb* -ED/-ING/-S *vi* **1 a** : to make the sound of a tick or a continuous series of ticks 〈listening to the clock ~〉 **b** : to make a muted oscillating somewhat regular rumbling noise — used of an idling internal-combustion engine; *also* : IDLE 2 — usu. used with *over* **2** : to take place in or as a measured or regular esp. temporal sequence 〈meantime life in the ward ~ed away as usual —Earle Birney〉 〈the telephone poles ~ing past —Harper's〉 **3** : to take place, come into existence, or arrive to the accompaniment of ticks 〈the sports news has been ~ing in from places of which few Americans have ever heard —Horace Sutton〉 **4** : to act in or manifest an often unusual or inexplicable character : operate or function by or as if by a hidden clockwork mechanism 〈persons who are ~ing along fine on one kidney —*Time*〉 〈his mind kept ~ing on steadily —Ira Wolfert〉 — often used in such phrases as *what makes one tick* 〈knowledge about my fellow citizens and what makes them ~ —*Survey Graphic*〉 〈shows what makes totalitarian society ~ —W.H.Chamberlin〉 〈find out how and why a modern poet ~ed —Mary Barrett〉 ~ *vt* **1** : to mark with or as if with a written tick : CHECK 〈~ing away in his mind the yards yet separating her from the onrushing . . . destroyer —E.L.Beach〉 — usu. used with *off* 〈dashing up and down with lists and ~ing off names —Anthony Carson〉 〈~ing off small numbers with his fingers —J.A.N. Friend〉 **2** : to mark, note, count, give forth, measure, or announce by or as if by repeated ticking beats 〈~ing off heroic couplets —H.R.Warfel〉 〈his taxicab outside, ominously ~ing out the pence and minutes —Osbert Sitwell〉 〈clockwork that ~s off the years and their changes —Rose Feld〉 **3** : to touch with a momentary sharp or glancing blow 〈determining if the ball ~s the net on the serve —J.W.Bunn〉 〈~ed the cat under the chin —Raymond Chandler〉

⁴tick \"\ *n* -s [ME *tike, teke*, prob. fr. MD; akin to OHG *ziahha* pillowcase, tick; both fr. a prehistoric WGmc word borrowed fr. L *theca* cover, sheath, fr. Gk *thēkē*; akin to Gk *tithenai* to put, set — more at DO] **1** : the fabric case usu. of ticking of a mattress, pillow, or bolster; *also* : a mattress consisting of a tick and its resilient filling **2** : TICKING

⁵tick \"\ *n* -s [short for ¹*ticket*] : CREDIT, TRUST; *also* : a credit account 〈ordered a suit of clothes on ~ —W.A.White〉

⁶tick *vi* -ED/-ING/-S *obs* : to buy or sell on credit

tickbean \'~,~\ *n* [¹*tick* + *bean*] : any of various horsebeans having small seeds shaped like a tick

tickbird \'~,~\ *n* [¹*tick* + *bird*] : a bird (as the oxpecker or ani) that eats ticks infesting quadrupeds

tick-bite fever *n* : TICK FEVER

tick-borne *adj* : capable of being transmitted by the bites of ticks 〈Rocky Mountain spotted fever is a *tick-borne disease*〉

tick-borne fever *n* : a mild rickettsial disease of sheep transmitted by a tick (genus *Ixodes*), marked by fever, listlessness, and loss of condition, and persisting for about ten days

tick clover *n* : TICK TREFOIL

tickeater \'~,~\ *n* : TICKBIRD

ticked \'tikt\ *adj* [¹*tick* + *-ed*] **1** : marked or variegated with ticks **2** *of a hair* : banded with two or more colors

tick·en \'tikən\ *n* -s [alter. (influenced by *-en* as in *woolen*) of ¹*ticking*] *Brit* : TICKING

¹tick·er \'tikə(r)\ *n* -s [³*tick* + *-er*] : something that ticks or produces a ticking sound: as **a** : WATCH **b** : a telegraphic receiving instrument that automatically prints off stock quotations or news on a paper ribbon **c** : HEART 〈I'm feeling better, but the old ~'s not so good —*Newsweek*〉

²ticker *var of* TIKKER

tick·er·man \'tikə(r)mən, -,man\ *n, pl* **tickermen** : a worker who installs and repairs telegraphic tickers

ticker tape *n* **1** : the paper ribbon on which a telegraphic ticker prints off its information **2** : paper streamers (as ticker tape) and scraps (as confetti) thrown from upper-story windows usu. over a passing parade in honor of a celebrity

¹tick·et \'tikət, *usu* -əd-+V\ *n* -s *often attrib* [obs. F *etiquet* (now *étiquette*), fr. MF *etiquet, estiquet*, fr. *estiquer, estiquier* to attach, stick, fr. MD *steken* to stick; akin to OHG *stehhan* to stick — more at STICK] **1 a** *obs* : a short note or document in writing 〈if your ~ had overtaken me . . . I had certainly returned —Richard Baker〉 **b** : a document that serves as a certificate, license, or permit; *specif* : a master's, captain's, mate's, pilot's, or airman's certificate **c** : a written, typed, printed, stamped, or engraved notice, record, memorandum, or token: as (1) : a paper or card on an item giving information (as of its owner, identity, maker, or price) : TAG, LABEL 〈tagged with a ~ giving the number of the machine, the operator, and the lot —Werner Von Bergen & H.R.Mauersberger〉 〈examined the price on the ~〉 (2) *obs* : PROMISSORY NOTE (3) *Brit* : VISITING CARD (4) : a summons or warning issued to an offender esp. of a traffic regulation 〈parking ~〉 **d** (1) : a certificate, evidence, or token of a right (as of admission to a place of assembly, of passage in a public conveyance,

of debt, or of a chance) ⟨a theater ~⟩ ⟨a railroad ~⟩ ⟨a lottery ~⟩ ⟨a pawn ~⟩ (2) *Brit* : a library borrower's card **e** (1) : SLATE 4b ⟨the power of a popular president to carry his whole ~ to victory with him —W.H.Hessler⟩ ⟨some individuals vote the party ~ —L.W.Doob⟩ — see SPLIT TICKET, STRAIGHT TICKET (2) : a sheet of paper bearing the names of candidates for office (as of a political party or faction) and usu. used as a ballot ⟨the voter received the party ~ outside the polling place —H.R.Penniman⟩ **f** : a slip or card with ruled spaces on which is written a record of a transaction or undertaking or detailed instructions (as an order for specific repairs on some equipment) ⟨deposit ~⟩ ⟨sales ~⟩ ⟨the driver is required to make an entry on his trip ~ at each stop⟩ — compare DEPOSIT SLIP **2** : a sealed bid for ore to be sold **3 a** : a means to something desirable ⟨a used car is the ~ out of the bad living conditions —Warner Bloomberg⟩ ⟨good manners . . . are your ~ to popularity —*Girl Scout Handbk.*⟩ **4** : the suitable, correct, or desirable thing ⟨quick action, that's the ~ —T.B. Costain⟩ ⟨a little trip'll be just the ~ for you —Maritta Wolff⟩ **5** : a program or plan for a project, career, or intended course of life used esp. in such phrases as *write one's own ticket* ⟨engineering graduates . . . are writing their own job ~*s* —Ira Kamen & R.H.Dorf⟩ ⟨committees make their own rules and write their own ~*s* —*New Yorker*⟩

²ticket \"\ *vb* -ED/-ING/-S *vt* **1 a** : to classify or mark by a ticket : attach a ticket to : LABEL ⟨things in their proper place, ~*ed* and pigeon-holed —W.M.Dixon⟩ ⟨~*ed* only with the initials *A.J.* —Hamilton Basso⟩ **b** : to describe, characterize, or mentally classify esp. in a set phrase ⟨he's ~*ed* as a zealous reformer —*Kiplinger Washington Letter*⟩ **c** : to designate for a specific purpose, position, or destination ⟨a defense contract now ~*ed* for a foreign factory —G.E.Cruikshank⟩ ⟨most of the increase is ~*ed* for earthbound assets like bases, radar, and communications networks —*Newsweek*⟩ ⟨a promising young man is duly noted . . . and ~*ed* for future office —*Time*⟩ **2 a** : to furnish with a ticket : BOOK ⟨children . . . under twelve . . . cannot be ~*ed* unless accompanied by parent or guardian —Chicago, Milwaukee, St. Paul & Pacific RR⟩ **b** : to serve with a ticket ⟨~*ed* for backing out of a parking space into an oncoming car —*Time*⟩ ~ *vi* : to issue or check tickets

ticket agency *n* : a usu. independent agency selling transportation or theater and entertainment tickets

ticket agent *n* : one who acts as an agent of a transportation company to sell tickets for travel by train, boat, airplane, or bus; *also* : one who sells theater and entertainment tickets

ticket book *n* : a book having tickets authorizing a specified amount of travel or a specified number of trips between designated points esp. for commuter travel

ticket day *n, Brit* : NAME DAY 2

tick·et·er \ˈtikəd·ə(r), -ətə-\ *n* -S : a worker who prepares labeling tickets or attaches them to goods

ticket gate *n, Brit* : an exit on a railway platform where passengers issuing from a train surrender their tickets

tick·et·less \ˈtikətləs\ *adj* : lacking a ticket : not requiring a ticket

ticket office *n* : an office of a transportation company, theatrical or entertainment enterprise, or ticket agency where tickets are sold and reservations made

ticket-of-leave \ˌ==ˈ=\ *n, pl* **tickets-of-leave** *n* : a license or permit formerly given in the United Kingdom and the British Commonwealth to a convict under imprisonment to go at large and to labor for himself subject to certain specific conditions

ticket porter *n* : a licensed porter in the city of London

tickets *pl of* TICKET, *pres 3d sing of* TICKET

tickety-boo \ˌtikəti͵bü\ *adj* [¹*ticket* (sense 4) + *-y* + ¹*boo*] *Brit* : FINE, OKAY ⟨everything is going to be *tickety-boo* eventually —A.J.Liebling⟩

tick·ey *also* **tick·ie** *or* **ticky** \ˈtikē\ *n* -S [Afrik, prob. modif. of Pg *pataca* & F *patac* pataca (fr. Pg)] *Africa* : THREEPENCE

tick farcy *n* : EPIZOOTIC LYMPHANGITIS

tick fever *n* **1** : a febrile disease (as Rocky Mountain spotted fever) transmitted by the bites of ticks **2** : TEXAS FEVER

tick·i·ci·dal \ˌtikəˈsīdᵊl\ *adj* **1** : destroying or controlling ticks ⟨~ drugs⟩ **2** : of or relating to a tickicide

tick·i·cide \ˈtikə͵sīd\ *n* -S [¹*tick* + *-i-* + *-cide*] : an agent used to kill ticks

tickier *comparative of* TICKY

tickiest *superlative of* TICKY

¹tick·ing \ˈtikiŋ, -kēŋ\ *n* -S [⁴*tick* + *-ing*] : a strong firm fabric of cotton or linen usu. twilled and striped used for upholstering, covering mattresses, pillows, or box springs, and in lighter weights for clothing

²ticking \"\ *n* -S [fr. gerund of ³*tick*] : ticks made by a clock, telegraph sounder, or other device ⟨telegraphic ~ is virtually a pure example of referential symbolism —Edward Sapir⟩

³ticking \"\ *n* -S [²*tick* + *-ing*] **1** : minute distinct color marks on a bird or mammal esp. on the tips of feathers — compare LACING **2** : the presence of longer guard hairs of a color unlike the body fur scattered throughout a fur **3** : the condition of having the individual hairs marked with several bands of distinct color usu. with the tip black — compare AGOUTI

¹tick·le \ˈtikəl\ *vb* **tickled; tickled; tickling** \-k(ə)liŋ\ **tickles** [ME *tikelen;* akin to OE *tinclian* to tickle and prob. to OE *citelian* to tickle, OHG *kizzilōn, kuzzilōn,* ON *kitla*] *vi* **1** *obs* : to feel excitement, tingling, or titillation : tingle or thrill with or as if with pleasure ⟨he with secret joy therefore did ~ inwardly in every vein —Edmund Spenser⟩ **2** : to have a tingling or restless sensation ⟨my back ~*s*⟩ **3** : to excite the surface nerves : cause a tickle ⟨that feather ~*s*⟩ ~ *vt* **1 a** (1) : to excite or stir up agreeably : awaken a sensation of pleasure in : furnish with esp. sensual gratification ⟨a piece of music . . . does more than ~ our sense of rhythm or color —Edward Sapir⟩ ⟨it ~*s* the sense of vicarious adventure —John Dolman⟩ ⟨intentional cheapening of her work to ~ the banal reader —Sinclair Lewis⟩ (2) : to excite or arouse from dormancy or to a higher degree : STIMULATE, ANNOY, PROVOKE ⟨it *tickled* all that is evil in me —O.W.Holmes †1935⟩ ⟨the self-esteem of the selected candidates was immensely *tickled* —Tom Marvel⟩ ⟨men have to be . . . *tickled* up by propaganda before they'll fight —Aldous Huxley⟩ **b** (1) : to excite amusement or merriment in : arouse the sense of humor of : AMUSE ⟨so excessively *tickled* by the jest that he couldn't forget it —Charles Dickens⟩ (2) : to provide with pleasure or enjoyment : make pleased ⟨how *tickled* they were . . . because they still had time to sell our rooms to four royalists —Christopher Morley⟩ **2 a** (1) : to touch (as a person or a part of the body) lightly with or as if with the fingers so as to excite the surface nerves and to cause uneasiness, laughter, or spasmodic movements ⟨the physical spasm which seizes children when they are *tickled* —Willa Cather⟩ (2) : to tease, torment, or pet by or as if by tickling ⟨the sound of the wrapping paper being torn away *tickled* his ears —N.A.Wasserman⟩ (3) : to bring into a specified state by or as if by tickling ⟨be *tickled* to death to see you⟩ ⟨all were *tickled* pink to be on land again⟩ **b** : to touch or stir gently ⟨the piano player *tickled* the keys⟩ **c** : to capture (a fish) by groping for it with the hands and sliding the fingers into its gills **3** : WHIP, CHASTISE, BEAT **syn** see PLEASE — **tickle it** *obs* : to bring to a desired end : complete successfully — **tickle the palm of** *or* **tickle in the palm 1** : BRIBE **2** : TIP

²tickle \"\ *n* -S **1** : something (as a touch) that tickles **2** : a tickling sensation **3** : the act or process of tickling

tickle grass *n* **1** : any of several grasses of the genus *Agrostis; esp* : ROUGH BENT **2** : WITCHGRASS 2

tick·len·burg \ˈtiklən͵bərg\ *n* -S [fr. *Ticklenburg* (Tecklenburg), locality in northwestern Germany where it was orig. manufactured] : a coarse linen fabric

tick·ler \ˈtik(ə)lə(r)\ *n* -S **1** : a person or device that tickles ⟨tormented passersby with water pistols and ~*s*⟩ **2** : a device for jogging the memory; *specif* : a book, file, or set of memoranda kept as a reminder esp. by a business firm ⟨sales ~⟩ **3** *or* **tickler coil** : a feedback coil

tickler file *n* : a file that serves as a reminder and is arranged to bring matters to timely attention

tickles *pres 3d sing of* TICKLE, *pl of* TICKLE

tickleweed \ˈ==͵=\ *n* : AMERICAN HELLEBORE

tickling *pres part of* TICKLE

¹tick·lish \ˈtik(ə)lish, -lēsh\ *adj* [³*tickle* + *-ish*] **1** : sensitive to tickling **2 a** : easily disturbed emotionally : TOUCHY, OVERSENSITIVE ⟨employed to scare the dickens out of anyone who is ~ about atomic energy —*Newsweek*⟩ **b** : easily overturned or unbalanced : not affording security or support : UNSTEADY, UNSTABLE ⟨a canoe is the most ~ of navigable things —Herman Melville⟩ **3** : requiring delicate handling : DELICATE, NICE, CRITICAL ⟨hesitates to be explicit on so ~ a subject —*Publ's Mod. Lang. Assoc. of Amer.*⟩ ⟨the takeoff is twice as ~ as the landing —T.H.Fielding⟩ **4** : UNCERTAIN, UNRELIABLE, CHANGEABLE ⟨~ weather⟩ — **tick·lish·ly** *adv* — **tick·lish·ness** *n* -ES

²ticklish \"\ *adv* : TICKLISHLY

tick·ly \-k(ə)lē, -li\ *adj* -ER/-EST : TICKLISH

tick off *vt* **1** : to read off (an item in a list) : RECITE, ENUMERATE ⟨the commission *ticked off* six specific causes for the price spiral —*Wall Street Jour.*⟩ ⟨*ticking off* the appetizing aspects of summer —Jane Nickerson⟩ **2** : REPRIMAND, REBUKE ⟨wanted to *tick* him *off* a bit for letting me in for all this —P.G.Wodehouse⟩ **3** : to describe with succinct accuracy ⟨a period which it would be so difficult to *tick off* in a phrase —*Times Lit. Supp.*⟩

tick over *vi* : to come near to failure : FALTER ⟨when they have nothing to say their music *ticks over* dopingly —Charles Reid⟩

tick paralysis *n* : an ascending paralysis in man or lower animals caused by a neurotoxin secreted by some ticks (as *Dermocentor andersoni*) and injected into the host during feeding

tick pyemia *n* : staphylococcal pyemia of lambs due to bacteria introduced by tick bite

ticks *pl of* TICK, *pres 3d sing of* TICK

tickseed \ˈ=͵=\ *n* [¹*tick* + *seed;* fr. the shape of the seeds] **1** : COREOPSIS **2** : TICK TREFOIL

tickseed sunflower *n* : any of various large-rayed No. American plants of the genus *Bidens* (esp. *B. coronata* and *B. trichosperma*)

¹tick·tack *or* **tic·tac** \ˈtik͵tak\ *n* -S [imit.] **1 a** : a repeated ticking or tapping noise like that made by a clock or watch ⟨the ~ of sleet on frosted windowpanes —Merle Crowell⟩ **b** : a contrivance to make a tapping or rattling sound (as on a window or door) operated from a distance esp. as a practical joke ⟨hold ~*s* up against their windows —John O'Hara⟩ **2** [modif. of MF *trictrac*] *obs* : TRICTRAC **3** *Brit* : secret signaling between bookmakers at a race

²ticktack *or* **tictac** \"\ *vb* -ED/-ING/-S **1** : to move or sound with a ticktack **2** *Brit* : to signal by ticktack

tick·tack·toe \ˌtik͵takˈtō\ *also* **tick·tack·too** \-akˈtü\ *or* **tic-tac-toe** \-akˈtō\ *also* **tit-tat-toe** \ˌti(t)͵ta-\ *n* -S [fr. *tic-tac-toe* game formerly played in which the players with the eyes shut brought a pencil down on a slate marked with numbers and scored the number hit, fr. *tictac* + *toe*] : a game in which two players alternately put crosses and ciphers in compartments of a figure formed by two vertical lines crossing two horizontal lines and try to get a row of three crosses or three ciphers before the opponent does — called also *noughts-and-crosses*

tick·tick \ˈtik͵tik\ *n* [redupl. of ²*tick*] : a repeated ticking sound

¹tick·tock *also* **tic·toc** \ˈtikˈtäk\ *n*-S [imit.] : a ticking sound made esp. by a large clock

²ticktock *also* **tictoc** \"\ *vi* -ED/-ING/-S : to make a sound like a ticktock

tick trefoil *n* [¹*tick;* fr. the sticky loments that adhere to clothing and the hair of animals] : any of various plants (genus *Desmodium*) characterized by trifoliolate leaves and rough sticky loments

tick typhus *n* : a disease that occurs in widely separated areas in Asia, Australia, Africa, Siberia, and Europe and is caused by the bite of a tick

tickweed \ˈ=͵=\ *n* **1** : PENNYROYAL 2 **2** : COREOPSIS

tick-worry \ˈ=͵==\ *n* : a generalized state of unease and irritability of cattle severely infested with ticks often leading to serious loss of energy and condition

¹ticky \ˈtikē, -ki\ *adj* -ER/-EST : affected or infested with or full of ticks

²ticky *var of* TICKEY

tic-polonga \͵tikpəˈlȯŋgə\ *n* -S [Sinhalese *tikpolangā,* fr. *tik* spot + *polangā* viper] : RUSSELL'S VIPER

tics *pl of* TIC

ticul \tēˈkəl, ˈtik-, ˈtēk-\ *n, pl* **ticul** *or* **ticuls** [by alter.] : TICAL

¹tid \ˈtid\ *n* -S [alter. of ¹*tide*] **1** *chiefly Scot* : a right time or season esp. for an agricultural activity **2** *chiefly Scot* : MOOD, HUMOR

²tid \"\ *n* -S [by alter.] : a girl or young woman

TID *abbr, often not cap* [L *ter in die*] three times a day

tid·al \ˈtīdᵊl\ *adj* [¹*tide* + *-al*] **1** : of or relating to tides : caused by tides : having tides : periodically rising and falling or flowing and ebbing ⟨~ waters⟩ **2** : moved or actuated by tides ⟨a ~ motor⟩ **3** : dependent (as in regard to the time of arrival or departure) upon the state of the tide ⟨a ~ steamer⟩ ⟨a ~ train run in connection with a tidal steamer⟩; *also* : navigable only at high tide ⟨a ~ harbor⟩ **4** : of, relating to, or constituting tidal air ⟨the ~ volume exhaled⟩ — **tid·al·ly** \-dᵊlē, -li\ *adv*

tidal air *n* : the air that passes in and out of the lungs in an ordinary breath and averages 500 cubic centimeters in human adults

tidal amplitude *n* : the elevation of tidal high water above mean sea level

tidal basin *n* : a dock or basin communicating with tidal water usu. through lock gates or locks

tidal bore *n* : ⁴BORE

tidal box *n* : a hatching box used in fish culture with an automatic siphon that causes the level of the water in the box to rise and fall alternately

tidal breeze *n* : a light breeze (as in the Gulf of St. Lawrence) attributed to tidal action

tidal clock *n* : a clock showing the times of high and low water and the state of the tides at any time of day

tidal constant *n* : either of the two factors that when combined completely specify a simple tide and include the tidal amplitude and the tidal epoch

tidal current *n* : a current produced by tidal forces

tidal day *n* : TIDE DAY

tidal epoch *n* : the tidal constant that represents the time elapsing between the moon's meridian passage and the ensuing high tide

tidal flat *n* : essentially horizontal and commonly muddy or marshy land that is covered and uncovered by the rise and fall of tides

tidal friction *n* : the frictional effect of the tidal wave esp. in shallow waters lengthening the tidal epoch and tending to retard the rotational velocity of the earth and so increase very slowly the length of the day

tidal load *n* : variation of pressure in the earth due to the movement of the water caused by the tide or due to the stresses produced by the changing positions of the moon and sun relative to the earth

tidal marsh *n* : wet land regularly inundated by the backing up of adjoining streams through tidal action — compare TIDAL FLAT

tidal pool *n* : TIDE POOL

tidal river *n* : a river up the course of which the tides are noticeable for a considerable distance

tidal stream *n* **1** : TIDAL RIVER **2** *Brit* : TIDAL CURRENT

tidal theory *n* **1** : a theory of the evolution of a celestial body that is based on the action of tidal forces; *specif* : such a theory explaining the moon's evolution **2** : the theory of the present ocean tides

tidal watch *n* : a watch functioning like a tidal clock

tidal water *n* : TIDEWATER 1

tidal wave *n* **1** : TIDE WAVE **2 a** : an unusually high sea wave that sometimes follows an earthquake : SEISMIC SEA WAVE **b** : an unusual rise of water alongshore due to exceptionally strong winds **3** : an unexpected and intense reaction (as an overwhelming impulse, a burst of feeling, or a heavy majority vote)

tid·bit *or* **tit·bit** \ˈtid͵bit, ˈtit͵b-, *usu* -bid+V\ *n* [perh. fr. *tit-* (as in *titmouse*) + *bit*] **1** : a delicate piece of anything eatable : a choice morsel of food **2** : a small and pleasing, interesting, or spicy bit (as of news or information)

tid·dle \ˈtidᵊl\ *vb* **tiddled; tiddled; tiddling** \-d(ᵊ)liŋ\ **tiddles** [origin unknown] *vi* **1** : POTTER, FIDGET **2** *chiefly NewEng* : SEESAW, TEETER ~ *vt, dial chiefly Eng* : to rear or care for with excessive solicitude : COSSET, PAMPER

tid·dle·dies \ˈtidᵊldēz, -diz\ *n pl* [origin unknown] : soft flexible ice or chunks of floating ice

tid·dle·dy·wink \ˈtidᵊl(d)ē͵wiŋk, ˈtidlē-, ͵=(=)=ˈ=\ *n* [alter. of *tiddlywink*] **1 tiddledywinks** *pl but sing in constr* : a game the object of which is to snap small disks from a flat surface into a small container **2** : ⁴WINK

tid·dler \ˈtid(ᵊ)lə(r)\ *n* -S [prob. fr. E dial. *tiddly* little + *-er*] **1** *Brit* **a** : a small fish; *esp* : STICKLEBACK **b** *slang* : a small 4-man submarine used by the British in World War II **2** *Brit* : a small child **3** : a player at tiddledywinks

¹tid·dly *or* **tid·dley** \ˈtid(ᵊ)li\ *n, pl* **tiddlies** *or* **tiddleys** [prob. fr. E dial. *tiddly* little, alter. of *little*] *Brit* : an alcoholic drink

²tiddly *or* **tiddley** \"\ *adj* **1** *chiefly Brit* : somewhat intoxicated : DRUNK ⟨will make me ~ if I drink it all —Nathaniel Benchley⟩ **2** *chiefly Brit* : precisely arrayed and ordered : dressed up : SMART ⟨quite a busy time getting the ship ~ —*Crowsnest*⟩

tid·dly·wink \ˈtid(ᵊ)lē͵wiŋk\ *n* [prob. fr. E dial. *tiddly* little + *wink*] **1** *dial Eng* : an unlicensed public house : BEERHOUSE **2** *or* **tid·dley·wink** \"\ : TIDDLEDYWINK

tid·dy \ˈtidē, -di\ *adj* [prob. alter. of *little*] *chiefly Brit* : TINY, TRIVIAL

¹tide \ˈtīd\ *n* -S *often attrib* [ME *tyde, tide* time, fr. OE *tīd;* akin to OFris & OS *tīd* time, OHG *zīt,* ON *tīthr* time, Gk *daiesthai* to distribute, divide, Skt *dayate* he apportions, *dāti* he cuts, divides, mows; basic meaning: to divide] **1 a** *obs* : a space of time : WHILE, PERIOD **b** *archaic* : a particular point in time : a definite moment : OCCASION **c** : fit or opportune time : OPPORTUNITY **d** (1) : an ecclesiastical anniversary or religious festival (2) : HOLIDAY; *also* : a holiday season as distinguished from the specific day on which the holiday is celebrated (3) *Brit* : a fair or merrymaking on a parish feast day **e** : a space of time (as between two high tides or during the height of a flood tide) at sea when the water level permits a particular activity to be carried out **2 a** (1) : the alternate rising and falling of the surface of the ocean and of gulfs, bays, estuaries, and other water bodies connected with the ocean that occurs twice a day over most of the earth and is caused by the gravitational attraction of the sun and moon occurring unequally on different parts of the earth — see DIRECT TIDE, EBB TIDE, FLOOD TIDE, NEAP TIDE, OPPOSITE TIDE, SPRING TIDE (2) : a similar but less marked rising and falling of an inland body of water (3) : EARTH TIDE (4) : ATMOSPHERIC TIDE **b** (1) : FLOOD TIDE ⟨the ship departed on the ~⟩ (2) : a specific instance of tide ⟨there was a ~ at 9:53 p.m.⟩ **c** : the mass of water moving in a tide ⟨sand castles covered by the ~⟩; *also* : TIDEMARK ⟨animals living between the ~*s*⟩ **3 a** : something that may turn, rise and fall, or decrease or increase like the tides of the sea ⟨a waning ~ of popular interest⟩ **b** : an extreme condition usu. of excellence or badness ⟨how our fortunes ever got to such a ~⟩ **4** : mobile water: as **a** : a flowing stream : CURRENT **b** : the waters of the ocean **c** : flood waters : the overflow of a flooding stream **syn** see FLOW

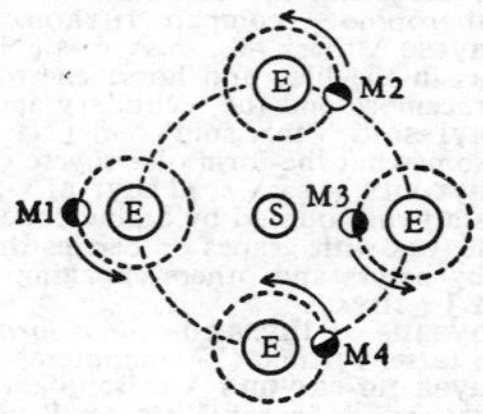

tides 2a(1): *M1* and *M3* position of moon at spring tides; *M2* and *M4* moon at neap tides

²tide \"\ *vb* -ED/-ING/-S *vi* **1** : to flow as or in a tide : surge to and fro : pour forth **2 a** : to drift with the tide esp. in navigating a ship into or out of an anchorage, harbor, or river **b** : to become carried : drift as if with a tide — usu. used with *on* or *onward* or *over* ⟨*tiding* on toward an uncertain fate⟩ ~ *vt* **1** : to transport or cause to float with or as if with the tide ⟨the sea *tiding* debris back to shore⟩ **2** : to proceed along (one's way) by taking advantage of tides

³tide \"\ *vi* [ME *tiden,* fr. OE *tīdan;* akin to OFris *tīdia* to proceed to, MD *tiden* to go, come, MLG *tiden* to hurry, strive, ON *titha* to long for, wish, *tīthr* time — more at ¹TIDE] *archaic* : BETIDE, HAPPEN, BEFALL

tide boat *n* : a small craft plying with the tides

tide crack *n* : a crack caused by the tide and separating the ice foot and sea ice along a frigid shore

tid·ed \ˈtīdəd\ *adj* [¹*tide* + *-ed*] : affected by or having tides ⟨~ waters⟩

tide day *n* : an interval occurring between the arrival of any two consecutive high waters of the direct tide or of the opposite tide at any given place and averaging 24 hours 51 minutes

tideflat \ˈ=͵=\ *n* : TIDAL FLAT

tide·ful \-fəl\ *adj* [ME, fr. *tyde, tide* + *-ful*] : flooded by the tide

tide gage *or* **tide register** *n* : a gage for showing the height of the tide; *esp* : one for registering its state continuously

tide gate *n* **1** : an opening through which water may flow freely when the tide sets in one direction but which closes automatically and prevents the water from flowing in the other direction **2** : a place where the tide runs with great velocity as if through a gate : TIDEWAY

tidehead \ˈ=͵=\ *n* : the inland limit of the tide

tide·land \ˈ=͵land, -͵laa(ə)nd, -͵lənd\ *n* **1** : littoral land that is overflowed by the tide but exposed by low water **2** : land underlying the ocean, lying beyond the low tidemark, but being within a nation's territorial waters — often used in pl.

tideland spruce *n* : SITKA SPRUCE

tide·less \ˈtīdləs\ *adj* : having no tides ⟨a ~ sea⟩ — **tide·less·ness** *n* -ES

tide line *n* : TIDEMARK

tide lock *n* : a lock situated between an enclosed basin or a canal and the tidewater of a harbor or river when they are on different levels so that craft can pass either way at all times of the tide

tidemark \ˈ=͵=\ *n* **1** : a high-water or sometimes low-water mark left by tidal water or a flood ⟨between the ~*s*⟩; *also* : a mark placed to indicate this point **2** : the point to which something has attained or below which it has receded

tide mill *n* **1** : a mill operated by the tidal currents **2** : a mill for clearing lands from tidewater

tide over *vt* [²*tide*] **1** : to carry through or help along in the manner of a boat floated on a high tide ⟨food enough to *tide* us *over* until spring⟩ **2** : to provide money or supplies to ⟨willing to *tide over* his sister a little longer⟩

tide pool *n* : a pool left (as in a rock basin) by an ebbing tide — compare BEACH POOL

tide predictor *n* : a mechanical device for predicting the times of high and low tide

tide race *n* : a strong tidal current

tide rip *n* **1** : a rip due to opposing tides **2** : a swift tidal current

tide-rode \ˈ=ˌ=\ *adj* [¹*tide* + *rode,* chiefly dial. past part. of *ride*] : swung by the tide regardless of the wind when at anchor — opposed to *wind-rode*

tides *pl of* TIDE, *pres 3d sing of* TIDE

tides·man \ˈtīdzmən\ *n, pl* **tidesmen** : TIDEWAITER

tide staff *n* : a vertical graduated rod used as a tide gage

tidesurveyor \ˈ=(͵)=ˌ==\ *n* : an executive customs officer in charge of tidewaiters

tide table *n* : a table that indicates the height of the tide in a given harbor at different times of the day and night throughout one year

tide through *vt* [²*tide*] : to tide over (sense 1)

tidewaiter \ˈ=͵==\ *n* **1 a** : an officer in various preventive customs services who boards ships and watches the landing of goods **b** : any customs inspector working at dockside or aboard ships **2** : an English dock laborer who tows or warps ships in or out at full tide

tidewater \ˈ=͵==\ *n* **1** : water overflowing land at flood tide; *also* : water (as rivers and streams) affected by the ebb and flow of the tide **2** : land traversed by tidewater streams : low-lying coastal land ⟨the forests of ~ Virginia⟩

tidewater glacier *n* **:** a glacier that descends to the sea and usu. breaks off into icebergs

tide wave *n* **:** a rise and fall of water as the tide moves about the earth

tideway \ˈ=,=\ *n* **1 :** a channel in which the tide runs; *also* **:** a rush of tidal water through a channel or stream **2 :** a course or onrush suggestive of a tideway ⟨one of the remaining great ~*s* of urban retail business⟩

tide wheel *n* **:** a waterwheel operated by the tides

ti·di·ly \ˈtīdəlē, -li\ *adv* [ME, fr. *tidy* + *-ly*] **:** in a tidy manner **:** NEATLY

ti·di·ness \-dēnəs, -din-\ *n* -ES **:** the quality or state of being tidy

¹tid·ing \ˈtīdiŋ, -dēŋ\ *n* -S [ME, fr. OE *tīdung*, fr. *tīdan* to happen + *-ung* -ing — more at TIDE] **1** *archaic* **:** EVENT, HAPPENING **2 :** an account of an event hitherto unknown or unreported **:** a piece of news **:** MESSAGE, NEWS, INTELLIGENCE — usu. used in pl. ⟨good ~*s*⟩

²tid·ing \ˈtīdiŋ, -dēŋ\ *n* -S [¹*tide* + *-ing*] **:** a tidal flow or ebb; *also* **:** a progressing or drifting with the tide

tid·ley \ˈtid(ᵊ)li\ *n* -S [prob. fr. E dial. *tiddly* little — more at TIDDLY] *dial Eng* **:** WREN

tid·ol·o·gy \tīˈdäləjē, -ji\ *n* -ES [¹*tide* + *-o-* + *-logy*] **:** the science or theory of tides

tids *pl of* TID

¹ti·dy \ˈtīdē, -di\ *adj* -ER/-EST [ME, fr. *tyde*, *tide* time + *-y* — more at TIDE] **1 :** properly filled out **:** PLUMP, COMELY, HEALTHY ⟨a sleek, ~ beauty —*Current Biog.*⟩ **2 a** *obs* **:** DILIGENT, UPRIGHT, WORTHY, SKILLFUL **b :** adequately satisfactory **:** sufficiently good or pleasing to be acceptable **:** DECENT, FAIR ⟨a convenient and sufficiently ~ arrangement —*Times Lit. Supp.*⟩ ⟨got a ~ price for the property⟩ **c :** clever usu. to the point of being somewhat crafty **:** SHREWD ⟨hoped to play him some ~ little tricks —F.M.Ford⟩ **3** *obs* **:** occurring at a suitable time **:** TIMELY, SEASONABLE **4 a :** neat and orderly in appearance or habits **:** kept in good trim **:** well ordered and cared for ⟨a ~ person⟩ ⟨~ white houses⟩ **b :** maintaining neatness and order in things under one's charge ⟨a ~ housekeeper⟩ **c :** characterized by inherent neatness and order (as in formulation or function) **:** free from irregularity or slovenliness and often from any marked individuality **:** PRECISE ⟨a ~ handwriting⟩ ⟨~ thinking⟩ ⟨a ~ mind⟩ **5 :** not small in worth **:** comfortably large or valuable ⟨came into a ~ estate⟩ ⟨must have paid a ~ sum⟩ **syn** see NEAT

²tidy \"\ *vb* -ED/-ING/-ES *vt* **:** to put in proper order **:** make neat or tidy — often used with *up* ⟨~ up a room⟩ ~ *vi* **:** to make things tidy — usu. used with *up* ⟨~*ing* up after supper⟩

³tidy \"\ *n* -ES **:** any of various articles or devices intended to promote neatness or order: as **a :** a piece of fancywork used to protect the back, arms, or headrest of a chair or sofa from wear or soil **b :** a receptacle with pockets or compartments in which sewing materials, toilet articles, or odds and ends can be kept in order **c :** a perforated receptacle for draining small garbage at a sink

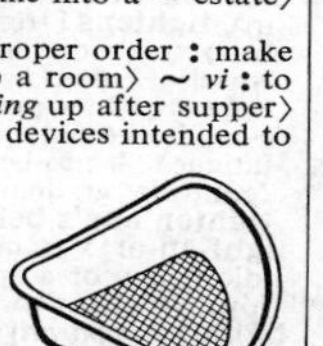
tidy c

⁴tidy \"\ *adv, chiefly dial* **:** TIDILY

tidytips \ˈ=,=\ *n pl but sing or pl in constr* **:** an annual California herb (*Layia platyglossa*) having yellow-rayed flower heads often tipped with white

¹tie \ˈtī\ *n* -S [ME *teg, tey, tye*, fr. OE *tēag;* akin to ON *taug* rope, string, OE *tēon* to pull — more at TOW] **1 a :** something (as a line, chain, ribbon) in the form of a cord used for fastening, uniting, or drawing closed some material thing ⟨dainty pink ~*s* down the front of her robe⟩ ⟨ordered six cattle ~*s*⟩ ⟨the mouth of the sack was closed by a ~⟩: as (1) **:** SHOELACE (2) **:** ⁴TYE (3) **:** STOP 4c(1) **b :** a structural element that serves to link other elements and usu. to reinforce the structure of which it is a part: as (1) **:** a beam, rod, or angle iron holding two pieces together **:** a tension member in a construction — compare STRUT (2) **:** one of the transverse supports to which railroad rails are fastened to keep them to line, gage, and grade and to cushion, distribute, and transmit the stresses of traffic through the ballast to the roadbed — called also *crosstie, sleeper* (3) **:** KEY 12a (4) **:** a fastening strip of leather, cord, or fabric attached to a book cover at its fore edge or to the open end of a portfolio (5) **:** a narrow strip left in the open part of a stencil to stiffen or hold together the design **2 :** something that serves as a connecting link usu. between discrete elements: as **a** (1) **:** a moral or legal obligation to someone or something typically constituting a restraining power, influence, or duty **:** a bond that constrains or restrains ⟨pledged by the ~*s* of common purpose⟩ ⟨unwilling to accept the ~*s* and responsibilities of family life⟩ (2) **:** a linking force that tends to unify **:** a shared and unifying relationship ⟨the ~*s* of race⟩ ⟨the strong ~ of community of interests⟩ ⟨there may or may not be a determinable ~ between race and language⟩ **b** (1) **:** a curved line that joins two musical notes indicating the same pitch and that is used to denote a single tone sustained through the time value of the two **:** BIND — compare SLUR 2a (2) **:** a connecting line in stroked notes **c** *Brit* **:** the obligation of a tied house to purchase its goods of a particular firm **d :** a connection between electric power systems by means of which each can interchange power with the other **3 a :** an equality in number (as of votes or scores) **b :** equality in a contest (as a race, election, or competition); *also* **:** a match or contest that ends in a draw **c** *Brit* **:** a deciding match played by those who tied in previous competition **d :** a match in a sports tournament in which the contestants are paired off two by two and the losers drop out until only one contestant is left as winner **4 :** a method or style of tying or knotting: as **a :** a method of connecting the harness cords in a jacquard loom to produce a desired pattern; *also* **:** the arrangement of cords thus produced **b :** an arrangement (as of loops or eyelets) for the lacing of a shoe **5 :** something that is knotted or is to be knotted when worn: as **a :** TIEWIG **b** *archaic* **:** a knot of hair **c :** NECKTIE **d :** a low laced shoe commonly without a tongue and with three or fewer pairs of eyelets — compare OXFORD **6 :** a depression over the spine near the middle of the back of developed cattle where the skin is bound down by connective tissue

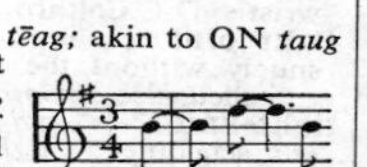
ties 2b(1)

²tie \"\ *vb* **tied** *or archaic* **tight**; **tied** *or archaic* **tight**; **tying** *or* **tieing**; **ties** [ME *tegen, teyen, tyen*, fr. OE *tīegan, tīgan;* akin to ON *teygja* to stretch out, draw; causative-denominative fr. the root of E ¹*tie*] *vt* **1 a :** to fasten, attach, bring together, close, or restrain by means of a tie (as a line, chain, ribbon) ⟨~ your horse to the tree⟩ ⟨her bonnet was *tied* on⟩ ⟨*tied* his bathrobe and went to the door⟩ ⟨vicious dogs should be *tied*⟩ ⟨~ off a bleeding artery⟩ ⟨~ a bundle⟩ **b** (1) **:** to form a knot or bow in (as a line) ⟨~ your scarf⟩ (2) **:** to form (as a knot) in the course of tying something ⟨wished she could ~ such a neat bow⟩ ⟨learned to ~ a square knot⟩ (3) **:** to make by tying constituent elements ⟨*tied* a daisy wreath⟩; *esp* **:** to make (artificial angling flies) by securing feathers, tinsel, and other parts to the shank of a fishhook **2 :** to bring together firmly as if tied by a rope **:** unite in some manner into a functional whole ⟨*tied* the addition into the older building⟩: as **a :** to unite in marriage **b :** to unite (as musical notes) by a tie **c :** to fix (a railroad track) in position with supporting ties; *also* **:** to provide (as a railroad line) with ties **d :** to join electrically (two power systems) in order that power may be interchanged **3 :** to restrain from independence or freedom of action or choice as if tied by a rope ⟨illness *tied* him to his bed⟩: as **a :** to constrain by or as if by authority, influence, agreement, or obligation ⟨*tied* to his job by a contract⟩ ⟨responsibilities that ~ one down⟩ **b** *obs* **:** to reduce to bondage **:** ENSLAVE **c :** to bind by gratitude for past favors **:** put under obligation **d** *obs* **:** to make (as a treaty) binding usu. by some formal act or attestation **4 a :** to make or have an equal score with in a contest or competition ⟨the home team *tied* the visitors⟩ **b :** to come up with something equal to or better than **:** EQUAL, BEAT ⟨can you ~ that⟩ **5 :** to cancel (a postage stamp) so that both cover and stamp receive a firm imprint giving the stamp added philatelic value on cover and making the cover proof against falsification as a philatelic item ⟨~ a stamp with a slogan cancellation⟩ ⟨a stamp *tied* to cover with a first-day cancellation⟩ ~ *vi* **1 :** to make a tie: as **a :** to make a bond or connection **b :** to make an equal score **:** EQUAL **c :** to pair one's vote **d :** ATTACH ⟨his answer ~*s* logically to the earlier discussion⟩ **e :** to close by means of a tie ⟨a wraparound that ~*s* at the waist⟩ **2 :** to stipulate in a loan contract between two countries that the borrowing country expend all or part of the loan on goods of the lending country — **tie a can to** *slang* **:** to get rid of — **tie by the leg :** to restrain as if by physical bonds **:** SHACKLE — **tie into 1 :** to attack with vigor ⟨*tied into* the job and was soon finished⟩: as **a** *slang* **:** to reprimand with severity ⟨the old lady really *tied into* me⟩ **b :** to consume voraciously ⟨*tied into* his dinner as if he hadn't eaten in a week⟩ **c :** to hit a pitched baseball hard ⟨*tied into* the ball for a home run⟩ **d :** to hit a baseball pitcher for a series of hits ⟨*tied into* him in the ninth for four runs⟩ **2 :** to get into one's possession **:** CATCH ⟨hoped to *tie into* a few good bass⟩ — **tie one on** *slang* **:** to get drunk — **tie one's hands :** to make one unable to act or to proceed in an action ⟨her secrecy *tied his hands*⟩ — **tie one's tongue :** to compel one to remain silent **:** constrain one to secrecy — **tie the knot :** to perform a marriage ceremony; *also* **:** to get married — **tie to :** to become associated with so as to depend on (as for protection or care) ⟨a man to *tie to*⟩

tie-and-dye \ˌ=ˈ=ˈ=\ *also* **tie-dye** \ˈ=,=\ *n* **:** a hand method of textile printing characterized by tying portions of the fabric or yarn so that they will not absorb the dye — **tied-and-dyed** \ˌ=ˈ=ˈ=\ *also* **tie-dyed** \ˈ=ˈ=\ *adj*

tieback \ˈ=,=\ *n* [fr. *tie back*, v.] **1 :** a decorative strip or device of cloth, cord, or metal for draping a curtain to the side of a window **2 :** a curtain with a tieback — usu. used in pl.

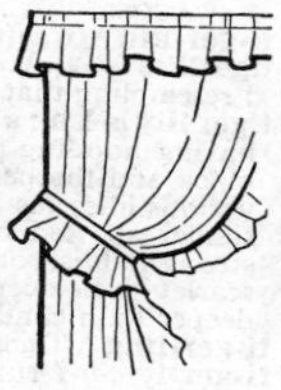
tieback 2

tie ball *n* **:** HELD BALL

tie bar *n* **1 :** a bar used as a tie rod **2 :** a rod between two railway switch rails to hold them to gage

tie beam *n* **:** a beam acting as a tie (as in a roof) — see ROOF illustration

tie breaker *n* **1 :** a circuit breaker placed on a tie line **2 :** a contest of exceptional difficulty used to select a winner from among contestants with tied scores in a previous contest

tie conductor *n* **:** a conductor used to join two power systems electrically

tied cottage *n, Brit* **:** a cottage maintained by an employer (as a farmer) for occupancy by an employee

tied house *n* **1** *Brit* **:** a business house that is under contract to buy of a particular firm; *esp* **:** a public house rented from or mortgaged to a brewery with or through whom the local proprietor is pledged to do all his liquor buying **2** *Brit* **:** TIED COTTAGE

tied image *n* **:** a memory image blended with and completing a sensory impression

tied island *n* **:** an island connected with the mainland by a tombolo

tied letters *n pl* **:** two or more characters constituting a ligature

tie-down \ˈ=,=\ *n* -S [fr. *tie down*, v.] **1 :** a fitting or a system of lines and fitting used to tie something (as an airplane, a horse's head, or a load of cargo) down in a desired position **2 :** the act of tying something down

tie dyeing *n* **:** TIE-AND-DYE

tie hack *n* **:** a faller and hewer of crossties

tie in *vt* **:** to bring into connection with something relevant **:** join in a unified whole ⟨*tie* a generating station *in* with a power system⟩: as **a :** to make the final connection of ⟨*tied in* the new branch pipeline⟩ **b :** to coordinate in such a manner as to produce balance and unity ⟨the illustrations were cleverly *tied in* with the text⟩ ⟨*tied in* his arguments to the previous discussion⟩ **c :** to use as a tie-in esp. in advertising ~ *vi* **1 :** to become tied in — usu. used with *with* or *to* **2 :** to join warp threads of one series to another **:** pull a new set of warp threads through the reed

¹tie-in \ˈ=,=\ *n* -S [*tie in*] **:** something that ties in: as **a** (1) **:** an advertisement by a retail dealer that is placed near or coordinated with a related advertisement by a manufacturer (2) **:** an advertisement that is coordinated with some topical matter (as a specific holiday) (3) **:** an advertisement that fixes attention on an idea by presentation of two or more of its aspects (as by punning allusion) (4) **:** comment uniting in one advertisement two otherwise separate advertising items; *also* **:** similar comment in other than advertising writing **b :** the electrical joining of two power systems so that each can furnish power to the other **c :** an article or right to purchase that is only available under a tie-in arrangement **d :** an obscure or secret relation ⟨there is evidently some *tie-in* between delinquency and divorce⟩ ⟨suspected a *tie-in* between his assistant and the opposition⟩

²tie-in \ˈ=,=\ *adj* [*tie in*] **:** allowed by a seller only on condition of attendant purchase of another product or fulfillment of an attendant agreement ⟨a *tie-in* sale⟩; *also* **:** involving the use of tie-in sales ⟨*tie-in* merchandising⟩

tieing *pres part of* TIE

tie line *n* **1 :** a string used for lining one end of track ties before laying rails when building a railroad track **2 :** a line measured on the ground to connect some object to a survey **3 :** a line connecting two power systems for interchange of power **4 :** a telephone line that directly connects two or more private branch exchanges **5 :** a straight horizontal line drawn on a phase diagram to join two points on curves giving the compositions of phases in equilibrium

tie·mann·ite \ˈtēmə,nīt\ *n* -S [G *tiemannit*, fr. W. *Tiemann*, 19th cent. Ger. scientist who discovered it + G *-it* -ite] **:** a mineral HgSe that is a native mercuric selenide and occurs commonly in dark gray or nearly black masses of metallic luster (sp. gr. 8.2–8.5)

tie mill *n* **:** a machine with four circular saws arranged to cut from a log two slabs, two boards, and a cant or a tie in a single operation

t'ien \tēˈen, ˈtyen\ *n* -S *usu cap* [Chin (Pek) *t'ien*¹] **1 :** the physical heaven **:** SKY **2 :** a controlling principle **:** DIVINITY

tiend \ˈtēnd\ *Brit var of* TEIND

tien·da \tēˈendə\ *n* -S [Sp, tent, awning, shop, fr. (assumed) VL *tenda*, alter. of L *tenta*, fem. of *tentus*, past part. of *tendere* to stretch — more at THIN] *chiefly Southwest* **:** a booth or shop where goods are sold **:** STORE

tien·ta \tēˈentə\ *n* -S [Sp, lit., test, probe, fr. *tentar* to touch, test, probe, fr. L *temptare, tentare* to touch, feel, attempt, tempt — more at TEMPT] **:** a test of the spirit and keenness of young bulls and heifers to determine their fitness for the ring or for breeding — called also *tentadero*

t'ien t'ai \tēˈenˈtī, ˈtyenˈtī\ *n, usu cap 1st T & often cap 2d T* [Chin (Pek) *t'ien*¹ *t'ai*² — more at TENDAI] **:** a Chinese Buddhist sect founded in the 6th century A.D. that teaches a comprehensive doctrine of salvation for all based on sutras and the principle of the ultimate harmony of three levels of truth

tien·to \tēˈen·(,)tō\ *n* -S [Sp, lit., touch, fr. *tentar*] **:** a 16th century Spanish pipe-organ composition having strict imitative counterpoint and resembling the ricercar

tien·tsin \ˈtē·en(t)ˈsin, ˈtin(t)-\ *adj, usu cap* [fr. *Tientsin*, China] **:** of or from the city of Tientsin, China **:** of the kind or style prevalent in Tientsin

tientsin jute *n* **:** CHINGMA

tie off *vt* **1 :** to close by means of an encircling or enveloping tie ⟨*tie off* a bleeding vessel⟩ **2 :** to fasten (a fly line) to a pinrail in adjusting theatrical scenery

tie-on \ˈ=,=\ *adj* [fr. *tie on*, v.] **:** fastened with ties or by tying on **:** designed to be used or worn tied on or over something else ⟨variations of a striped playsuit and a *tie-on* overskirt —*Women's Wear Daily*⟩

tie-out \ˈ=,=\ *n* -S [fr. *tie out*, v.] **1 :** a rope or cable anchorage **2 :** a batch of mail bundled and tied for dispatch to the post office that will deliver it

tiepin \ˈ=,=\ *n* **:** an ornamental straight pin often with a jeweled head and a sheath for the point that is used to hold the ends of a necktie in place

tie plate *n* **1 :** one of several narrow plates to space and strengthen deck beams of a ship — see SHIP illustration **2 :** a plate to distribute the pressure of a tie (as on a supporting beam) **3 :** a metal plate between a railroad rail and tie to assist in holding the rail to line and to protect the tie from mechanical wear

tie-plate \ˈ=,=\ *vt* [*tie plate*] **:** to furnish (as a railroad track) with tie plates

tie plug *n* **:** a small section of wood shaped like a spike and used for plugging a hole in a railroad tie left when a spike has been withdrawn

¹tier \ˈti(ə)r, -iə\ *n* -S [MF *tire* order, rank, row — more at ATTIRE] **1 :** a row, rank, or layer of articles; *esp* **:** one of two or more rows arranged one above another ⟨~ upon ~ of huge casks⟩ ⟨built up neat ~*s* of firewood⟩ ⟨a window curtained with three ~*s* of ruffled net⟩ **2 a :** a row of guns or gun portholes (as in a warship or fort) **b** (1) **:** the ranges of the windings of a coiled cable; *also* **:** a layer of anchor chain (2) **:** the hollow space enclosed by a coil of cable (3) **:** CABLE TIER **c :** a row of moored or anchored ships **d :** a vertical layer of brickwork whose thickness is the width of a brick — called also *withe* **e** *Austral* **:** a mountain range **f :** a group of political or geographical divisions (as counties or states) that form a row across the map **g :** an antenna array consisting of rows of antenna elements placed one above another **3 a :** CLASS, CATEGORY ⟨the lowest ~ of society⟩ **b :** RANK 9

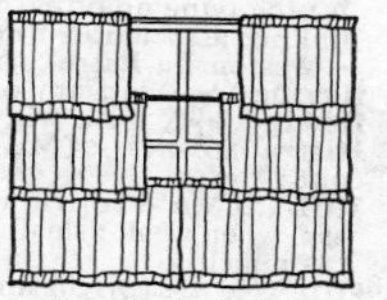
tiers 1 of window curtains

²tier \"\ *vb* -ED/-ING/-S *vt* **:** to place or arrange in tiers ~ *vi* **:** to rise in tiers ⟨cliffs ~*ing* along the margin of the valley⟩

³ti·er *also* **ty·er** \ˈtī(ə)r, -īə\ *n* -S [²*tie* + *-er*] **1 :** one that ties; *esp* **:** a worker that closes openings or binds articles by tying **2** *NewEng* **:** a child's pinafore fastened with ties

tier *abbr* tierce

tier·able \ˈtirəbəl\ *adj* [²*tier* + *-able*] **:** suitable for stacking ⟨~ goods⟩

¹tierce *var of* TERCE

²tierce \ˈti(ə)rs\ *n* -S [ME *terce, tierce*, fr. MF, fr. fem. of *terz, ters, tiers*, adj., third, fr. L *tertius* — more at THIRD] **1** *obs* **:** THIRD 1 **2 a :** any of various units of liquid capacity equal to ⅓ pipe; *esp* **:** a unit equal to 42 wine gallons **b :** a cask of tierce capacity for wine or other commodities (as salted meat) **3 :** a sequence of three playing cards of the same suit **4 :** a fencing parry or guard position which defends the upper outside target and in which the hand is in a position of pronation at chest height and the tip of the blade is directed toward the opponent's eyes — compare SIXTE **5 a :** THIRD 4 **b :** the tone two octaves and a major third above a given tone **c :** an organ stop giving tones at this interval from the normal pitch of the digitals

³tier·cé \ˈtirˈsā\ *adj* [F, fr. *tierce* third] **:** TIERCED

tierced \ˈti(ə)rst, ˈtiəst\ *adj* [F *tiercé* + E *-ed*] *heraldry* **:** divided into three parts of different tinctures or bearing different coats of arms — followed usu. by an indication of the direction of the lines of partition ⟨~ in bend⟩ ⟨~ in fess⟩ ⟨~ bendwise⟩

tierce de pic·ar·die \,tirsdəˈpikärdē\ *n, pl* **tierces de picardie** *usu cap P* [F] **:** PICARDY THIRD

tier·cel \ˈtirsəl\ *or* **ter·cel** \ˈtərs-\ *or* **tas·sel** \ˈtas-\ *n* -S [ME *tercel, tassel*, fr. MF *tercel, tiercel*, fr. (assumed) VL *tertiolus*, fr. dim. of L *tertius* third; perh. fr. the belief that every third egg in the nest produced a male — more at THIRD] **:** a male of various hawks (as the peregrine falcon and the goshawk)

tier·ce·ron \ˈtirsərən\ *n* -S [F, fr. MF, fr. *tierce* third] **:** one of the minor or intermediate ribs in Gothic vaulting that spring from the pier on each side of the main diagonal rib and therefore do not pass through the center of the vault

tiercet *var of* TERCET

tiered \ˈti(ə)rd, -iəd\ *adj* [¹*tier* + *-ed*] **:** having or arranged in tiers, rows, or layers — used chiefly in combination ⟨triple-tiered⟩

tier·er \ˈtirə(r)\ *n* -S **:** one that tiers; *specif* **:** one of the sailors stationed in the cable tier of a ship to stow the chain or cable as it comes in

tier-in \ˌtīəˈrin\ *n, pl* **tiers-in** [*tie in*, v. + *-er*] **:** a textile worker who ties in new warp threads

tiering *pres part of* TIER

tie rod *n* **1 :** a rod used as a connecting member or brace **:** TIE BAR — see BUCKSTAY illustration **2 :** a rod in the steering system of an automotive vehicle connecting one of the arms of each steering knuckle to the corresponding arm of the other

tier pole *n* **:** a horizontal pole in a tobacco barn on which the tobacco sticks are hung

tier·ra ca·lien·te \tēˌerə,kalēˈentē\ *n, pl* **tierras calientes** [Sp, lit., hot land] **:** a region or zone of hot climate; *esp* **:** low-lying tropical land usu. below 2000 feet with continuous hot weather

tierra fría \ˌ=,==ˈfrēə\ *n, pl* **tierras frí·as** [Sp, lit., cold land] **:** a region or zone of cold climate; *esp* **:** tropical land of usu. above 6000 foot elevation in which the temperature is sharply modified by the elevation

tier ranger *n, Brit* **:** a waterfront thief

tier·ras \tēˈerəz\ *n pl* [Sp, pl. of *tierra* earth, land, fr. L *terra* — more at TERRACE] **:** fine material of earth or rock mixed with quicksilver ore

tierra tem·pla·da \-temˈplädə\ *n, pl* **tierras templadas** [Sp, lit., temperate land] **:** a region or zone of temperate climate; *esp* **:** tropical land of usu. from 2000 to 6000 foot elevation in which the temperature is modified by the elevation

tiers *pl of* TIER, *pres 3d sing of* TIER

tiers-argent \tēˌerˈzärˈzhäⁿ\ *n* [F, fr. *tiers* third + *argent* silver — more at TIERCE, ARGENT] **:** a silver alloy containing approximately one third of its weight of silver usu. alloyed with aluminum or German silver

tier shot *n* **:** grapeshot having the shot arranged in regular tiers separated by plates

tiers·man \ˈti(ə)rzmən, ˈtiəz-\ *n, pl* **tiersmen 1 :** one who arranges articles (as casks) in tiers **2** *Austral* **:** MOUNTAINEER

tier table *n* **:** a small table or stand with two or more usu. round tops arranged one above another

ties *pl of* TIE, *pres 3d sing of* TIE

ti-es \(ˈ)tēˈes\ *n* [Haitian Creole] **:** CANISTEL

-ties *pl of* -TY

tie scoring machine *n* **:** a portable power-operated machine provided with two circular saws designed to saw the face of railroad track ties to uniform width and depth as a guide for hand adz work to provide a proper bearing for rail or tie plates in relay track work

tie silk *n* **:** a usu. twilled silk fabric of firm resilient pliable texture and in solid color or with typically small stylized and bright design that is suitable for neckties and much used for blouses and accessories; *also* **:** a similar fabric of a material other than silk

tie tack *n* **:** an ornamented pin whose point holds a necktie to a shirt and fits into a receiving button or snap underneath

tie·tick \ˈtētək\ *n* -S [imit.] *dial Brit* **:** MEADOW PIPIT; *also* **:** ROCK PIPIT

tie-tie \ˈ=,=\ *n* **:** one of several cords on a nautical hammock by which it may be tied in a roll; *broadly* **:** any of various lines or cords

tie up *vt* **1 :** to fasten or restrain with or as if with a tie **2 :** to cause to be in a hindered, impaired, or inoperative condition ⟨all week long . . . filibustering and Communist clamoring *tied up* the assembly —*Time*⟩ ⟨a strike that would *tie up* the port —C.P.Curtis⟩ **3 a :** to put in such a place or invest in such a manner as to make unavailable for other purposes ⟨*tie* your money *up* in stocks⟩ **b :** to subject (property) to such restrictions or bring into such condition that alienation or sale is impossible ⟨the will *tied up* the estate⟩ **4 :** to connect closely **:** LINK ⟨a striking window display *tied up* with an autographing party —*Publishers' Weekly*⟩ **5 a :** to keep busy **:** PREOCCUPY ⟨*tied up* in conference all day⟩ **b :** to preempt the use of ⟨*tied up* the phone for an hour⟩ ~ *vi* **1 a :** to make a boat secure ⟨we *tied up* . . . twenty-six hours after leaving —W.O.Douglas⟩ **b :** DOCK ⟨warships . . . *tie up* together —*N. Y. Herald Tribune*⟩ **2 a :** to establish a close relationship ⟨Christian counsels . . . *tie up* integrally with the civil law —Mary W. Hess⟩ **b :** to enter into a partnership ⟨*tie up* with other advertisers⟩

tie-up \'⸗(,)⸗\ *n* -s [*tie up*] **1 :** something that is tied up or used in tying up: as **a** *obs* **:** TIEWIG **b :** TIE 4a **c :** a mooring place for a boat **d :** a cow stable esp. when forming an extension of a larger barn; *also* **:** a space for a single cow in a stable **2 :** the act or fact of tying up or the state of being tied up: as **a** (1) **:** a suspension of traffic or business (as by a strike or lockout of employees or a breakdown of machinery) (2) **:** enforced idleness of a train crew because of a rule or statutory provision on the maximum number of hours' work **b :** the tying up of harnesses in a plain or dobby loom **c :** a linking association **:** CONNECTION ⟨the close brain-eye *tie-up* —Weston La Barre⟩ ⟨political *tie-up* with gangsters⟩
tievine \'⸗,⸗\ *n* **:** any of several bindweeds
tiewig \'⸗,⸗\ *n* **:** a wig having the back hair tied with ribbon
¹tiff *vt* -ED/-ING/-S [ME *tiffen*, fr. OF *tifer, tiffer*] *obs* **:** to deck out **:** DRESS
²tiff \'tif\ *n* -s [origin unknown] **1** *archaic* **:** alcoholic liquor esp. when weak **:** small beer **2** *archaic* **:** a small draft of liquor (as punch)
³tiff \"\ *n* -s [origin unknown] **:** a slight fit of anger **:** an outburst of temper or spite **:** a petty quarrel ⟨in tizzies over ~*s* with boyfriends —Stanley Frank⟩ **syn** see QUARREL
⁴tiff \"\ *vi* **:** to be in a tiff or pet **:** quarrel in a small way **:** be peevish — usu. used with *with* ⟨~*ed* with friends and foes alike⟩
⁵tiff \"\ *vi* [back-formation fr. *tiffin*] *India* **:** to take tiffin **:** LUNCH
⁶tiff \"\ *n* [origin unknown] *chiefly Midland* **:** BARITE
¹tif·fa·ny \'tifənē, -ni\ *n* -ES [prob. fr. obs. F *tiphanie* Epiphany, fr. LL *theophania* — more at THEOPHANY] **1 :** any of several very thin transparent textiles: as **a :** a sheer silk gauze formerly used for clothing and trimmings **b :** a plain-weave open-mesh cotton fabric (as cheesecloth) **2 :** an article (as a sieve) made of tiffany
²tiffany \"\ *adj* **:** DELICATE, FILMY, FRAGILE ⟨a *tiffany*-winged fly⟩
³tiffany \"\ *adj, usu cap* [after Charles L. *Tiffany* †1902 Am. jeweler] *of a jewelry setting* **:** having long prongs to hold a gem
⁴tiffany \"\ *adj, usu cap* [after Louis C. *Tiffany* †1933 Am. artist] **:** exhibiting or characterized by irregular areas of translucent blended color due to the use of a glazing liquid over a suitably painted surface (as of a wall) ⟨a *Tiffany* effect⟩ ⟨the popularity of *Tiffany* finishes⟩ — compare SCUMBLE
tiffany glass *n, usu cap T* [after L. C. *Tiffany*] **:** American glassware made in the late 19th and early 20th century and often characterized by an iridescent surface
¹tif·fin \'tifən\ *n* -s [prob. alter. of *tiffing*, gerund of obs. *tiff* to drink, eat between meals, fr. ²*tiff*] **1 :** a midday meal **:** LUNCHEON **2 :** a moderate yellowish brown that is very slightly redder and deeper than mummy, redder and very slightly darker than Bismarck brown, and darker and slightly redder than maple sugar — called also *condor*
²tiffin \"\ *vi* -ED/-ING/-S **:** to take tiffin **:** LUNCH
ti·fi·nagh \tə'fē,näg\ *also* **ti·fi·nar** \-är\ *adj* [Tuareg *tifinagh* writing, writings] **:** of, relating to, or constituting a Libyan alphabet that is apparently descended from the Old Libyan or Numidian characters derived from the Punic cursive script and is still used by the Tuaregs
ti·flis \'tifləs *sometimes* tə'flēs\ *adj, usu cap* [fr. *Tiflis*, U.S.S.R.] **:** of or from the city of Tiflis, U.S.S.R. **:** of the kind or style prevalent in Tiflis
¹tift \'tift\ *vt* -ED/-ING/-S [ME *tiften*, perh. fr. *tift*, past part. of *tiffen* to tiff (deck out) — more at TIFF] *chiefly dial* **:** to put in order **:** make ready or array properly **:** ARRANGE
²tift \"\ *n* -s *chiefly Scot* **:** a particular state, condition, or mood
³tift \"\ *chiefly dial var of* TIFF
⁴tift \"\ *n* -s [prob. of imit. origin] *chiefly Scot* **:** a puff or gust of wind
¹tig \'tig\ *vb* **tigged; tigged; tigging; tigs** [ME *tiggen*] *vi* **1** *chiefly Scot* **a :** to poke or pat one in a playful manner **b :** to have dealings **:** MEDDLE, TAMPER — used with *with* **2** *dial* **:** ANNOY, TEASE, PESTER ~ *vi* **1 :** ⁴TAG **2** *Austral* **:** to touch for a loan
²tig \"\ *n* -s **1** *chiefly Scot* **:** a noticeable but not violent touch **:** PAT, POKE **2 :** the game of tag
tige \'tēzh\ *n* -s [F, stem, shaft, rod, pin, fr. L *tibia* shinbone, pipe, flute — more at SIPHON] **:** a steel pin in the breech of an early rifle against which the ball is hammered by the ramrod and expanded to fit the grooves
ti·gel·la \tə'jelə\ *or* **ti·gelle** \-'jel\ *n* -s [*tigella*, NL, fr. F *tigelle; tigelle* fr. F, dim. of *tige* stem, stalk] **:** a short or rudimentary stem; *specif* **:** the hypocotyl sometimes together with the plumule — **ti·gel·late** \-lət\ *adj*
ti·ger \'tīgə(r)\ *n, pl* **tigers** *also* **tiger** [ME *tigre*, fr. OE *tiger* & OF *tigre*, both fr. L *tigris*, fr. Gk, of Iranian origin; akin to Av *tighri-* arrow, *tighra-* pointed; akin to Skt *tejate* it is sharp — more at STICK] **1 a :** a large Asiatic carnivorous mammal (*Felis tigris*) having a tawny coat transversely striped with black, a long unfutted tail that is ringed with black, underparts that are mostly white, and no mane, being typically slightly larger than the lion with a total length usu. of 9 to 10 feet but sometimes of more than 12 feet, living usu. on the ground, feeding mostly on larger mammals (as cattle), in some cases including man, and ranging from Persia across Asia to the Malay peninsula, Sumatra, and Java and northward to southern Siberia and Manchuria — compare BENGAL TIGER, SABER-TOOTHED TIGER **b :** any of several large felid mammals: as (1) *Africa* **:** LEOPARD (2) **:** JAGUAR (3) **:** COUGAR **c :** a domestic cat with a striped pattern **:** TIGER CAT **d** *Austral* **:** TASMANIAN WOLF **e :** TIGER SNAKE **f :** any of several strong vigorous aggressive fishes: as (1) **:** TIGER SHARK (2) *Africa* **:** a large grunt (*Pomadasys operculare*) of the Indian ocean that is highly esteemed as a sport and food fish (3) **:** a fish that is a hybrid between the muskellunge and pike **2 a :** a representation of a tiger usu. as a symbol or badge (as of an organization) **b** *often cap* **:** any of several organizations having a tiger as recognized emblem; *also* **:** a member of such an organization **3 a :** a person or sometimes an animal of fierce and bloodthirsty ways **b :** fierce tigerish quality or aspect ⟨aroused the ~ in his nature⟩ **c :** a person vigorously aggressive and usu. highly skilled in some activity (as a sport or military combat) **4** *Brit* **a :** a groom in livery; *esp* **:** a young or small groom who rides usu. standing on a platform at the rear of a vehicle (as a dogcart) driven by the person on whom he is in attendance **b :** a dissolute or vulgar fellow **:** SWAGGERER, BULLY, RAKE **5 a** (1) **:** BIG CAT (2) **:** LITTLE CAT **b** (1) **:** FARO (2) **:** FARO BANK **6 :** a loud cry often of the word *tiger* that terminates a round of enthusiastic cheering (as at a political or sports rally) **7** *slang* **:** BLIND TIGER

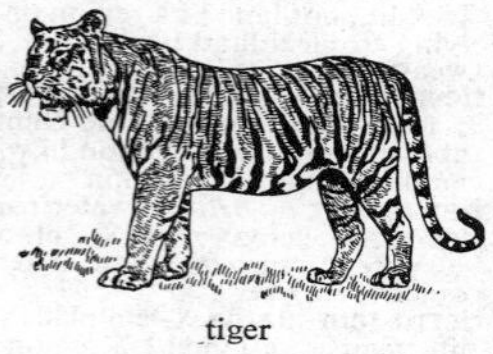

tiger

tiger barb *n* **:** a small vigorous eastern Asian barb (*Barbus sumatranus* or *B. tetragona*) sometimes kept in the tropical aquarium
tiger bass *n* **:** SMALLMOUTH BLACK BASS
tiger beetle *n* **:** any of numerous active rapid-flying carnivorous beetles constituting the family Cicindelidae and having larvae that live in tunnels in the soil
tiger bittern *n* **:** any of several So. and Central American herons of the genus *Tigrisoma* having plumage with much buff or chestnut vermiculated with black
tiger butterfly *n* **:** TIGER SWALLOWTAIL
tiger cat *n* **1 a :** any of various wildcats of moderate size and variegated coloration: as (1) **:** CLOUDED LEOPARD (2) **:** MARBLED CAT (3) **:** SERVAL (4) **:** OCELOT (5) **:** MARGAY **b** *Austral* **:** NATIVE CAT; *esp* **:** a large native cat (*Dasyurus maculatus*) with a white-spotted tail that is now largely restricted to Tasmania **2 :** a domestic cat with markings suggesting those of a tiger **:** a striped or sometimes blotched tabby cat
tiger cocoa *n* **:** PATASHTE
tiger cowry *n* **:** a large abundant cowry (*Cypraea tigris*) having a shell mottled and blotched with brown on an ivory or pale brown ground or sometimes with green on a paler green ground
ti·gered \'tīgə(r)d\ *adj* **:** striped or blotched usu. with a darker color
tigereye \'⸗⸗,⸗\ *n* -s **1** *also* **tiger's-eye** \'⸗⸗,⸗\ *pl* **tiger's-eyes** **:** a usu. yellow-brown chatoyant stone that is much used for ornament and is a silicified crocidolite in which the fibers embedded in quartz are changed to oxide of iron — compare HAWK'S-EYE **2 :** a ceramic glaze resembling in appearance the tigereye
tiger finch *n* **:** AVADAVAT
tiger fish *n* **:** any of various fishes that suggest a tiger usu. either in being extremely voracious or in being marked with black: as **a :** any of several vigorous predaceous freshwater sport fishes (genus *Hydrocyon*) widely distributed in African rivers **b :** CARIBE **c** *Africa* **:** a black-striped Indo-Pacific sea perch (*Therapon jarbua*)
tiger flathead *n* **:** a large vigorous flathead (*Neoplatycephalus macrodon*) of deep waters off the eastern coast of Australia that is an important market fish and is usu. taken by trawling
tigerflower \'⸗⸗,⸗\ *n* **:** a plant or flower of the genus *Tigridia*
tiger frog *n* **1 :** LEOPARD FROG **2 :** a large frog (*Rama tigrina*) of India and Malaysia
tiger heart *n* **:** a heart on the inside of which stripes of yellowish or white myocardium caused by fatty degeneration alternate with stripes of normal color so that tiger skin is simulated
ti·ger·ish \'tīg(ə)rish, -rēsh\ *adj* **:** of or relating to tigers **:** resembling a tiger usu. in sleek grace, voracity, ferocity, or vigorous intensity of action ⟨~ grace⟩ ⟨a ~ appetite⟩ ⟨a ~ fury⟩ ⟨worked with ~ concentration⟩ — **ti·ger·ish·ly** *adv* — **ti·ger·ish·ness** *n* -ES
ti·ger·ism \-gə,rizəm\ *n* -s *archaic* **:** showy ostentation **:** SWAGGER
ti·ger·kin \'tīgə(r)kən\ *n* -s **:** a little tiger
tigerlike \'⸗⸗,⸗\ *adj* **:** having the ways or appearance of a tiger **:** resembling that of a tiger ⟨a ~ grace⟩
tiger lily *n* **1 a :** a common Asiatic garden lily (*Lilium tigrinum*) having nodding orange-colored flowers densely spotted with black and the perianth segment strongly reflexed **b :** any of various lilies (as *L. pardalinum* and *L. philadelphicum*) having similar spotted flowers **2** *usu* **tigerlily a :** a moderate to strong reddish orange that is redder and lighter than chrome scarlet **b :** a deep yellowish pink of a textile that is redder and deeper than candy pink
ti·ger·ling \'tīgə(r)liŋ, -lēŋ\ *n* -s **:** a little tiger
ti·ger·ly *adj* **:** TIGERISH, TIGERLIKE
tiger maple *n* **:** maple lumber with a distinct irregularly striped pattern resembling but bolder than curly maple
tiger mosquito *n* **:** YELLOW-FEVER MOSQUITO
tiger moth *n* **:** any of various stout-bodied long-winged moths (family Arctiidae) that are usu. of moderate size with bright or richly colored wings often intricately patterned and with larvae that are hairy caterpillars — compare WOOLLY BEAR
tigernut \'⸗⸗(,)⸗\ *n* **:** CHUFA
tiger pear *n* **:** a much-branched very spiny prickly pear (*Opuntia aurantiaca*) that is a troublesome weed esp. in Australia
tiger python *n* **:** INDIAN PYTHON
tiger rattlesnake *n* **:** a rather small yellow or tawny rattlesnake (*Crotalus tigris*) that is narrowly striped with black and occurs in mountainous deserts of western No. America
tiger salamander *n* **:** a widely distributed No. American salamander (*Ambystoma tigrinum*) that is brown or black above with vertical yellowish lateral blotches often running together ventrally
tiger's-claw \'⸗⸗,⸗\ *n, pl* **tiger's-claws** **:** a boring rod or rifling rod in which the tool is sheathed on entering the bore and is automatically thrust outward on the cutting stroke
tiger's-eye \'⸗⸗,⸗\ *var of* TIGEREYE
tiger shark *n* **:** a large very voracious gray or brown stocky-bodied shark that is often a man-eater, is nearly cosmopolitan esp. in warm seas, and is commonly held to constitute a single species (*Galeocerdo arcticus* or *G. cuvieri*) but is sometimes separated into two or more species
tiger shell *n* **:** TIGER COWRY
tiger's-jaw \'⸗⸗,⸗\ *n, pl* **tiger's-jaws** **:** a southern African fig marigold (*Faucaria tigrinum* syn. *Mesembryanthemum tigrinum*) having long ciliate teeth on the upturned leaf margins — compare CAT-CHOP
tiger's-mouth \'⸗⸗,⸗\ *n, pl* **tiger's-mouths** **:** any of several plants of the family Scrophulariaceae (as the foxglove, snapdragon, and toadflax)
tiger snake *n* **1 :** a widely distributed extremely venomous elapid snake (*Notechis scutatus*) of Australia and Tasmania that is predominantly brown with dark crossbars **2 :** an African boigid snake (*Tarbophis semiannulatus*)
tiger's-tail spruce \'⸗⸗,⸗-\ *or* **tigertail spruce** \'⸗⸗,⸗-\ *n* **:** a Japanese evergreen tree (*Picea polita*) that has rigid spiny leaves and is often cultivated for ornament
tiger swallowtail *n* **:** a widely distributed swallowtail butterfly (*Papilio glaucus*) of eastern No. America
tigerware \'⸗⸗,⸗\ *n* **:** stoneware characterized by a mottled glaze somewhat resembling the coat of a tiger and orig. produced in the Rhine valley
tiger weasel *n* **:** any of several heavily built Old World weasels closely related to the polecats but usu. held to comprise a separate genus (*Vormela*)
tiger wolf *n* **1 :** SPOTTED HYENA **2 :** TASMANIAN WOLF
tigerwood \'⸗⸗,⸗\ *n* **:** any of several showy striped or black-marked woods used in cabinetwork; *esp* **:** AFRICAN WALNUT
tigged *past of* TIG
tigging *pres part of* TIG
¹tight \'tīt, *usu* -īd·+V\ *adj* -ER/-EST [ME, alter. of *thight*, of Scand origin; akin to ON *théttr* tight, close; akin to OE *metethīht* thick with food, MLG & MHG *dīhte* close, thick, Goth *theihan* to increase, progress, MIr *tēcht* coagulated, Skt *tanakti* it causes to coagulate; basic meaning: thick, thicken] **1 :** of firm compact texture **:** DENSE, SOLID **2 :** so close in structure as not to permit passage of a liquid or gas **:** not slack or leaky **:** firm or solid in condition ⟨a ~ roof⟩: as **a :** proof or proofed against the entry or exit of something expressed or implied ⟨the ship was sound and ~⟩ ⟨as ~ as a cask⟩ — usu. used in combination ⟨gas*tight* fitting⟩ ⟨an air*tight* cover⟩ **b** (1) **:** impervious to moisture **:** WATERTIGHT (2) **:** not giving free passage to water ⟨~ clay soils are often wet and sour⟩ **c :** WET 11 **d :** impervious to the activity or effect of ⟨a hog-*tight* fence⟩ **3 a :** fixed firmly or securely in place so as to be difficult to move ⟨loosen a ~ jar cover⟩ ⟨a ~ sticking door⟩ ⟨the roots are very long and ~⟩ **b :** FAITHFUL, CONSTANT **4 :** not slack or loose: as **a :** firmly stretched, drawn, or set **:** TAUT ⟨a ~ drumhead⟩ ⟨the rope was ~ and firm⟩ **b :** fitting closely and usu. too closely (as for comfort or good taste) ⟨a ~ dress⟩ ⟨a painfully ~ shoe⟩ **c** *of the respiratory passages* **:** congested, constricted, or sometimes dehydrated so as to be partially occluded ⟨her throat was ~ with fear⟩ ⟨the ~ clogged nose of a bad head cold⟩ **d :** having the participants in close touch with one another ⟨a ~ formation in football⟩ **e :** excessively precise without breadth of treatment ⟨a work of art that is unduly harsh and ~ in treatment⟩ **5** *chiefly dial* **a :** marked by energetic competence **:** CAPABLE, ALERT, READY **b :** marked by shapely graceful form **:** COMELY **c** (1) **:** trim and tidy in dress (2) **:** neat and orderly in arrangement or design **:** SNUG **6 :** difficult to get through or out of **:** not readily coped with or circumvented **:** TRYING, EXACTING ⟨in a ~ corner for money⟩ ⟨a good man in a ~ situation⟩: as **a :** firm in control **:** designed to master and maintain order ⟨kept a ~ hand on all his affairs⟩ **b :** unwilling to part with money or other possessions **:** MISERLY; *often* **:** difficult to do business with because of this tendency ⟨perfectly honest but ~ in all his dealings⟩ **c :** evenly contested **:** CLOSE ⟨a ~ tennis match⟩ ⟨~ play in a game⟩ **7 :** packed or compressed to the limit **:** entirely full ⟨a ~ bale⟩: as **a :** full of liquor **:** INTOXICATED, DRUNKEN **b** *of language* **:** highly condensed and often to the point of loss of fluency ⟨a ~ literary style⟩ **c** *of printed matter* (1) **:** closely spaced ⟨a ~ line⟩ (2) **:** so full as to make insertion of additional matter difficult ⟨a ~ page⟩ (3) *of a line* **:** set to full measure and safe to lift **d :** having little space available for news usu. because of large volume of advertising to be accommodated ⟨a ~ edition of a newspaper⟩ **e :** FULL 12a **8 a :** scantily supplied or obtainable in proportion to demand **:** available only in inadequate amounts to meet existent needs ⟨~ money is delaying construction⟩ ⟨steel is very ~ just now⟩ — compare EASY 2f(2) **b :** characterized by such a scarcity ⟨a ~ labor market⟩ **9** *of lumber* **:** sound in every way and free from ring shakes and checks ⟨logs with ~ hearts⟩
syn TAUT, TENSE: TIGHT is likely to describe a snug binding together, a close drawing together of all parts, a confining constriction, or a cornering or squeezing together ⟨a *tight* coat⟩ ⟨forming *tight* ranks⟩ ⟨a *tight* roof⟩ ⟨shoelaces that were too *tight*⟩ ⟨in a *tight* position⟩ TAUT applies to what has been stretched or drawn out to the limit; in reference to persons TAUT may describe the effects of strain making a drain on nervous energy ⟨pulling the ropes *taut*⟩ ⟨her sails are loose, her tackles hanging, waiting men to seize and haul them *taut* —Amy Lowell⟩ ⟨their look of horror as they stared up at me, eyes and mouths open and faces *taut* —Norman Cousins⟩ TENSE calls attention strongly to a keyed-up, intent condition or to tension and strain ⟨signalman, *tense* and alert, awaited the word to flash out orders by blinker —Alexander Forbes⟩ ⟨yet she was, as always after a concert, *tense* and nervous, filled with a terrible energy which would not let her sleep until dawn —Louis Bromfield⟩ ⟨he is *tense*, jittery — a mass of jangled nerves — his fingers tremble as he lights one cigarette after another —S.N.Behrman⟩ **syn** see in addition DRUNK, STINGY
²tight \"\ *vt* -ED/-ING/-S **1** *obs* **:** to make tight and esp. watertight **2** *chiefly dial* **:** to put in order **:** TIDY — used with *up*
³tight \"\ *adv* -ER/-EST **1 :** TIGHTLY, FIRMLY, HARD ⟨holding ~ to the rail⟩ ⟨the door was shut ~⟩ **2** *chiefly dial* **:** SOUNDLY, VIGOROUSLY, THOROUGHLY ⟨fell ~ asleep⟩
⁴tight \"\ *n* -s **:** something that is tight: as **a** *slang* **:** a difficult or trying situation **:** a tight place ⟨pulled him out of a ~ —F. B.Gipson⟩ **b :** close forward play in rugby — often used with *the;* contrasted with *loose* ⟨packs which could hold their own with any, whether in the ~ or loose —O.L.Owen⟩ **c** (1) **:** a radio or television program that is barely held within time limits (2) **:** a television close shot made with a narrow angle lens
⁵tight *archaic past of* TIE
tight backbone *or* **tight back** *n* **:** a book backbone adhered solidly to the cover — compare HOLLOW BACK; see SPINE illustration
tight-cut *adj* **:** having little or no evident checking — used esp. of thin-cut veneer
tight·en \'tīt°n\ *vb* **tightened; tightened; tightening** \-t(°)niŋ\ **tightens** [¹*tight* + *-en*] *vt* **:** to make tight or tighter ⟨~ a belt⟩ ⟨~ economic controls⟩ ⟨~*s* his hand on a steering wheel⟩ — often used with *up* ⟨~ up a bolt⟩ ~ *vi* **:** to become tight or tighter ⟨money ~*ed* after the war⟩ ⟨the drying rawhide ~*ing* in the sun⟩: as **a :** to become tense ⟨muscles ~*ing* with fatigue⟩ **b :** to become more complete or adequate **:** IMPROVE ⟨controls gradually ~*ed*⟩ ⟨his act ~*ed* considerably⟩ — **tighten one's belt :** to practice rigid economy
tight·en·er \-t(°)nə(r)\ *n* -s **:** one that tightens; *often* **:** an idle pulley or a sprocket wheel pressed against a belt, band, rope, or chain to tighten it — called also *tightening pulley*
tighter *comparative of* TIGHT
tightest *superlative of* TIGHT
tightfisted \'⸗;⸗⸗\ *adj* **:** reluctant to part with money **:** wary about expenditures ⟨must be eagle-eyed and ~ about these expenditures —A.E.Stevenson †1965⟩ **syn** see STINGY
tight·ish \'tīd·|ish, 'tīt|, |ēsh\ *adj* [¹*tight* + *-ish*] **1 :** somewhat tight **:** CLOSE-FITTING ⟨~ long sleeves pushed back over the wrist —D.C.Calthrop⟩ **2 :** somewhat difficult
tight joint *n* **:** a book joint against which the cover board is set snugly without the space or depression of the open joint — called also *smooth joint*
tight-knit \'⸗;⸗\ *adj* **:** closely and firmly integrated ⟨a *tight-knit* schedule⟩ ⟨a *tight-knit* organization⟩
tight-laced \'⸗;⸗\ *adj* **:** STRAITLACED
tight-leg *vi* **:** to grip a horse firmly with the legs without using the spurs in riding
tightlining \'⸗,⸗⸗\ *n* **:** a method of high-line logging in which the logs are lifted over obstructions by tightening on the haul-back
tight-lipped \'⸗;⸗\ *adj* **1 :** having the lips and mouth closed tight through determination or suppression of emotion ⟨*tight-lipped* throughout her ordeal⟩ **2 :** marked by accustomed or determined cautious reticence in speech **:** UNCOMMUNICATIVE ⟨*tight-lipped* friends keeping the matter secret⟩ **syn** see SILENT
tightlock \'⸗;⸗\ *adj* **:** of, relating to, or being a coupling device for cushioning the impact between railroad cars at starts or stops by taking up the slack
tight lock *n* **:** a disease of cotton caused by any of several fungi (esp. of the genus *Diplodia*) and characterized by failure of the affected locks to fluff and by discoloration and weakening of the fibers — **tight-locked** \'⸗;⸗\ *adj*
tight·ly *adv* **:** in a tight manner or state **:** so as to be tight
tight-mouthed \'⸗;⸗\ *adj* **:** CLOSEMOUTHED
tight·ness *n* -ES **:** the quality or state of being tight
¹tightrope \'⸗;⸗\ *n, often attrib* [¹*tight* + *rope*] **1 :** a rope or wire stretched taut on which acrobats perform — compare HIGH WIRE, SLACK ROPE **2 :** a hazardous situation
²tightrope \"\ *vt* **:** to walk on or along as if on a tightrope ⟨*tightroped* the foundation and jumped clear of the gooseberry bushes —Wallace Stegner⟩ ~ *vi* **1 :** to walk, dance, or perform acrobatics on a tightrope **2 :** to move or progress as if on a tightrope
tights \'tīts\ *n pl* [¹*tight* + *-s*] **1 :** close-fitting breeches usu. for men's formal wear (as in court dress) **2 :** skintight garments covering the body from the neck down or from the waist down and worn esp. for ease and display by dancers, acrobats, or gymnasts — compare LEOTARD
tight sap *n* **:** sapwood having close pores
tight scrummage *n* **:** a close formation of the forwards of each team in rugby
tight ship *n* **:** a ship with crew and officers working well together
tight side *n* **:** the concave face of a sheet of veneer — compare LOOSE SIDE
tight squeeze *n* **:** a passage or difficult situation that one barely manages to get through
tightwad \'⸗,⸗\ *n* **:** a person who spends, lends, or gives away money grudgingly or not at all **:** a close or miserly person
tightwire \'⸗,⸗\ *n* **:** a tightrope made of wire
tig·lal·de·hyde \ti'gladə,hīd\ *n* [ISV *tiglic* + *aldehyde*] **:** a liquid compound C_4H_7CHO that has the odor of bitter almonds and is obtained by distilling guaiacum resin; *α*-methyl-crotonaldehyde
tig·lic acid \'tiglik-\ *n* [ISV *tigl-* (fr. NL *tiglium*, specific epithet of *Croton tiglium*, fr. ML or NL, seed from a species of croton) + *-ic*] **:** a vesicant crystalline unsaturated acid $CH_3CH{=}C(CH_3)COOH$ that has a spicy odor, that is the stable stereoisomer of angelic acid and that occurs in the form of esters esp. in Roman chamomile oil and in croton oil; *trans-α*-methyl-crotonic acid
tiglic aldehyde *n* **:** TIGLALDEHYDE
ti·glon \'tīglən\ *n* -s [*tiger* + *lion*] **:** TIGON
ti·gnon \(')tē'yōⁿ\ *n* -s [LaF, fr. F, nape of the neck, chignon, fr. F dial. *tigne* moth, scalp disease, fr. L *tinea* moth, worm] **:** a madras handkerchief used esp. in Louisiana as a headdress
tig·num \'tignəm\ *n* -s [L, building material, beam — more at STAKE] **:** building material
ti·gog·e·nin \tə'gäjənən, tī'g-, -,nēn; ,tīgə'jenən, ,tig-\ *n* -s [blend of *tigonin* and *-gen*] **:** a crystalline steroid sapogenin $C_{27}H_{44}O_3$ obtained esp. by hydrolysis of tigonin
ti·gon \'tīgən\ *n* -s [*tiger* + *lion*] **:** a hybrid between a male tiger and a female lion — compare LIGER
ti·go·nin \tə'gōnən, tī'g-; 'tīgənən, 'tig-\ *n* -s [anagram of *gitonin*] **:** a steroid saponin obtained esp. from the leaves of either of two foxgloves (*Digitalis purpurea* and *D. lanata*)
ti·grai *or* **ti·gray** \tə'grī\ *n* -s *cap* **:** TIGRINYA
ti·gre \tə'grā\ *n* -s *cap* **:** a Semitic language of northern Ethiopia — see AFRO-ASIATIC LANGUAGES table
ti·gress \'tīgrəs\ *n* -ES [F *tigresse*, fr. *tigre* tiger + *-esse* -ess — more at TIGER] **:** a female tiger; *also* **:** a tigerish woman
ti·grid·ia \tī'gridēə\ *n, cap* [NL, fr. Gk *tigrid-, tigris* tiger + NL *-ia* — more at TIGER] **:** a small genus of Mexican and Central American plants (family Iridaceae) comprising the tigerflowers and having variegated evanescent flowers with spreading perianth segments and 2-parted style branches
ti·gri·gna \tə'grēnyə\ *n* -s *cap* **:** TIGRINYA

ti·grine \'tīgrən, -,grīn\ *adj* [L *tigrinus*, fr. *tigris* tiger + *-inus* -ine — more at TIGER] **:** of or relating to a tiger **:** resembling a tiger esp. in coloring

ti·gri·nya *also* **ti·gri·ña** \tə'grēnyə\ *n* -s *cap* **:** a Semitic language of northern Ethiopia — see AFRO-ASIATIC LANGUAGES table

ti·groid \'tī,grȯid\ *adj* [Gk *tigroeidēs*, fr. *tigris* tiger + *-oeidēs* -oid] **1 :** resembling a tiger esp. in being striped or spotted **2 :** being or consisting of Nissl substance

tigroid granules *n pl* **:** NISSL BODIES

tigroid substance *n* **:** NISSL SUBSTANCE

ti·grol·y·sis \tī'gräləsəs\ *n* [NL, fr. *tigro-* (fr. E *tigroid body*) + *-lysis*] **:** loss of Nissl bodies or substance accompanying degenerative changes in nervous tissue

tigs *pres 3d sing of* TIG, *pl of* TIG

tigua *usu cap, var of* TIWA

tig·u·rine \'tigyə,rīn\ *adj or n, usu cap* [L *Tigurinus* of or constituting a district in ancient Helvetia generally identified with Zürich, Switzerland] **:** ZWINGLIAN

TIH *abbr* Their Imperial Highnesses

tikal *var of* TICAL

tike *var of* TYKE

ti·ki \'tēkē\ *n* -s [Maori & Marquesan] **1** *usu cap* **:** an embodiment of the male principle in Polynesian mythology often depicted as the first man or the superhuman creator of mankind **2 a :** a Polynesian wood or stone image set up as a temporary abode or embodiment of a god or other supernatural power but not worshiped as an idol **b :** a Maori image representing an ancestor that is usu. either large and of wood or small, often in the form of a pendant, and of greenstone ⟨a greenstone ~ which has been in her family for many generations —*Auckland (New Zealand) Star*⟩ — compare HEI-TIKI

ti·ki·ti·ki \¦tēkē¦tēkē\ *n* -s [Tag & Bisayan] **:** RICE POLISHINGS; *also* **:** an alcoholic extract of rice polishings used in the treatment of beriberi

tik·ka \'tikə\ *n* -s [Hindi *ṭīkā* spot, mark] **:** a leaf spot disease of the peanut esp. in India that is caused by an imperfect fungus (*Cercospora personata*)

tik·ker *or* **ticker** \'tikə(r)\ *n* -s [*tikker* alter. of ¹*ticker*] **:** a form of interrupter used in the early days of radio as a detector of continuous waves consisting of a rapidly rotating wheel and a fine wire brush with the current made and broken by momentary contacts between the brush and a continuous strip of conducting material in the rim of the wheel

tik·kun \'tikůn\ *n* -s [NHeb *tiqqūn*, fr. MHeb, collection of excerpts from the Bible and Mishnah, fr. LHeb, arrangement, order] **:** a recital of prayers and excerpts from the Pentateuch, the Prophets, and rabbinic literature by observant Jews during the night on Shabuoth and Hoshana Rabbah

ti·kling \tə'kliŋ\ *n* -s [Tag *tikling*] *Philippines* **:** any of several rails; *esp* **:** a large slender rail (*Rallus philippensis*) that is olive brown with black spots above and has the underparts barred with black and white

tik·o·loshe *or* **tik·o·losh** \¦tikə¦läsh, -lȯsh\ *n, pl* **tikoloshes** [Xosa *utikoloshe*] **:** a mischievous spirit in southern African folklore taking the form of a short little man, living in the water, and being friendly to children

ti·ko·pia \tə'kōpēə\ *n, pl* **tikopia** *or* **tikopias** *usu cap* [fr. *Tikopia*, one of the Solomon islands] **1 a :** a Polynesian people on Tikopia, Solomon islands **b :** a member of such people **2 :** the language of the Tikopia people

tikor \'tikər, 'tēk-, -,kō(ə)r\ *n* -s [Hindi *tīkhur*] **1 :** a starch or arrowroot made from the tubers of an East Indian herb (*Curcuma angustifolia*) **2 :** a plant that yields tikor

ti·kug \tə'küg\ *n* -s [native name in the Philippines] **:** a tall coarse Philippine sedge (*Scirpus grossus*) the stems of which are used in weaving baskets and mats

¹**til** *var of* TILL

²**til** \'til, 'tē(ə)l\ *also* **teel** \'tē(ə)l\ *n* -s [Hindi *til*, fr. Skt *tila*] **:** SESAME

til·ak \'tilək\ *n* -s [Skt *tilaka*; perh. akin to Skt *tila* sesame] **:** an ornamental spot worn on the forehead chiefly by Hindus as a sectarian mark

ti·la·pia \tə'lāpēə\ *n* [NL] **1** *cap* **:** a genus of African freshwater food fishes (family Cichlidae) in many respects resembling the American sunfishes **2** -s **:** any fish of the genus *Tilapia*

til·as·ite \'tilə,sīt\ *n* -s [Sw *tilasit*, fr. Daniel *Tilas* †1772 Swedish mining engineer + Sw *-it* -ite] **:** a mineral $CaMg(AsO_4)F$ consisting of a magnesium calcium arsenate and fluoride and occurring in violet-gray granular masses (sp. gr. 3.3)

til·burg \'til,bərg\ *adj, usu cap* [fr. *Tilburg*, Netherlands] **:** of or from the city of Tilburg, Netherlands **:** of the kind or style prevalent in Tilburg

til·bury \'til,berē, -b(ə)rē\ *n* -ES [after *Tilbury*, 19th cent. London coach builder] **:** a light two-wheeled carriage with an elaborate spring suspension system and with or without a top

til·de \'tildə\ *n* -s [Sp, fr. L *titulus* superscription, sign, title — more at TITLE] **1 :** a mark ~ placed esp. over the letter *n* (as in Spanish *señor* sir) to denote the sound \nʸ\ or over vowels (as in Portuguese *não* no) to indicate nasality **2 :** the mark ~ used in logic and mathematics as a modified *n* generally read "not" and serving to indicate negation or denial or occas. used as the sign for the biconditional connective

¹**tile** \'tīl, *esp before pause or consonant* -īəl\ *n* -s *often attrib* [ME, fr. OE *tigel*, *tigele*; akin to OS *tiegla* tile, OHG *ziagala*, *ziagal*, ON *tigl*; all fr. a prehistoric WGmc-NGmc word borrowed fr. L *tegula* — more at THATCH] **1** *pl* **tiles** *or* **tile a :** a flat or curved piece of fired clay, stone, concrete, or other material used esp. for roofs, floors, or walls and often for such work of an ornamental nature — see ENCAUSTIC TILE, FACE TILE; compare BLOCK, BRICK **b :** a hollow or a semicircular and open earthenware or concrete drain (as a pipe or gutter) ⟨laying out underground ~ to drain fields —John Bird⟩; *also* **:** a piece used in constructing such a drain **c :** a hollow building unit made of burned clay or shale or of gypsum **2 :** TILING **3 :** a small flat piece of baked earth or earthenware used to cover vessels in which metals are fused **4 :** HAT; *esp* **:** a high silk hat **5 :** a thin piece of resilient material (as an asphalt composition, cork, linoleum, or rubber) used esp. for covering floors or walls **6 :** a flat usu. square ceramic plate used esp. as a coaster for hot dishes or as an ornament **7 :** a thin block used as a playing piece and usu. marked (as with letters or characters) for a particular game — **on the tiles** *or* **upon the tiles** *adv (or adj)* **:** on a debauch

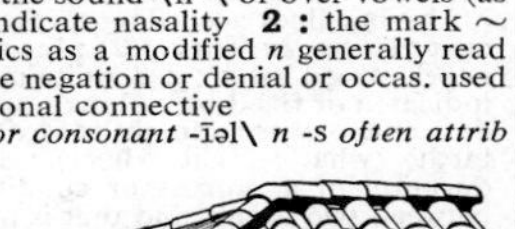
tiles 1a

²**tile** \"\ *vb* -ED/-ING/-S [ME *tilen*, fr. *tile*, n.] *vt* **1 :** to cover with or as if with tiles ⟨~ a house⟩ ⟨~ a floor⟩ **2** *also* **tyle** \"\ **a :** to protect (as a lodge meeting) from intrusion **:** GUARD ⟨~ the door⟩ **b :** to bind or swear (a member of a secret society) to secrecy **3 a :** to install drainage tile in **b :** to drain by use of tile ~ *vi* **:** to install drainage tile

tile blue *n* **:** a grayish blue that is redder, lighter, and stronger than electric, greener and stronger than copenhagen, redder, stronger, and slightly lighter than Gobelin, and greener, lighter, and stronger than average shadow blue

tileboard \'ₛ,ₛ\ *n* **1 :** a board used in interior finishing and made from a large sheet of any of various materials having a decorative coating simulating a tiled surface **2 :** a thin large square piece (as of wood) often with beveled edges that is fitted together with other like pieces to cover ceilings or walls

tile cell *n* **:** one of the apparently empty upright ray cells found interspersed with the procumbent cells in the wood of various trees (as basswood) usu. in horizontal series

tiled \'tī(ə)ld\ *adj* [ME *tyled*, fr. past part. of *tilen*, *tylen* to tile] **1 a :** covered or roofed with or as if with tiles **:** furnished with tiles **b :** drained by tiles ⟨~ fields⟩ **2 :** IMBRICATED **3 :** protected from intrusion **:** barred to intruders ⟨a lodge meeting within ~ doors⟩

tile drain *n* **:** a drain made of tiles

tile–drain \'ₛ,ₛ\ *vt* [*tile drain*] **:** to drain by or furnish with a tile drain

tilefish \'ₛ,ₛ\ *n* [*tile-* (modif. of NL *Lopholatilus*, genus of fishes including the tilefish) + *fish*] **:** a large deepwater violet blanquillo (*Lopholatilus chamaeleonticeps*) more or less thickly covered with large round yellow spots and having a fleshy appendage on the back of the head

tile hanging *n* **:** application of tiles to a vertical surface (as a wall) by hanging the tiles on battens

tile hat *n* **:** a high silk hat ⟨white-whiskered ancient in *tile hat* —Lucius Beebe⟩

tile ore *n* **:** an earthy cuprite often mixed with iron oxide

tile pipe *n* **:** pipe made of cement or pottery and used esp. for drains, chimney pots, and linings for chimney flues

til·er \'tīlə(r)\ *n* -s [ME *tyler*, fr. *tile*, *tyle* + *-er*] **1 :** one that lays tiles **2** *also* **tyl·er** \"\ **:** a doorkeeper in a lodge of a secret society (as of Freemasons)

tile red *n* **1 :** a strong brown that is redder, lighter, and stronger than average russet and redder and paler than rust **2 :** a moderate reddish orange that is yellower and duller than crab apple and yellower and darker than flamingo

til·ery \'tīlərē, -ri\ *n* -ES [¹*tile* + *-ery*] **1 :** a kiln or field where tiles are made or burned **2 :** the art of using tile for decorative effects in buildings

tileseed \'ₛ,ₛ\ *n* **:** an Australian tree of the genus *Geissois* (family Cunoniaceae) having imbricated seeds

til·ia \'tilēə\ *n, cap* [NL, fr. L, linden] **:** a genus (the type of the family Tiliaceae) of trees that are native in temperate regions and often planted as shade trees, that are distinguished by having cordate leaves, a winglike bract coalescent with the peduncle, indehiscent fruit with one or two seeds, and soft easily carved wood, and that have a strong hybridizing tendency — see BASSWOOD, LINDEN

til·i·a·ce·ae \,ₛₛ'āsē,ē\ *n pl, cap* [NL, fr. *Tilia*, type genus + *-aceae*] **:** a family of herbs, shrubs, or trees (order Malvales) distinguished chiefly by the free stamens and 2-celled anthers — **til·i·a·ceous** \¦ₛₛ¦āshəs\ *adj*

til·i·kum \'tiləkəm\ *var of* TILLICUM

til·ing \'tīliŋ, -lēŋ\ *n* -s [ME *tylynge*, fr. gerund of *tilen*, *tylen* to tile] **1 :** the act or work of one who tiles **2** [¹*tile* + *-ing*] **a :** TILES **b :** a surface of tiles

¹**till** *also* **til** \tᵊl (*often* d·ᵊl *after a vowel*), təl\ *prep* [ME, fr. OE *til*; akin to OFris & ON *til* to, till, OE *til* good, suitable — more at ³TILL] **1** *chiefly Scot* **a :** to a place of arrival **:** through to **:** as far as ⟨~ an end⟩ **b :** to or toward a limit or goal ⟨changed ~ a dragon⟩ **c :** TO — used to introduce an indirect object or complement of various adjectives and nouns ⟨gie it ~ him⟩ ⟨aye kind ~ his ain⟩ **d :** AT, BY, FOR, OF, CONCERNING **2 :** throughout the interval extending to **:** during the whole time from the starting point up to **:** up or down to a specified time **:** UNTIL — used with an implication of termination or change at the time mentioned ⟨~ his return⟩ ⟨~ after four o'clock⟩ ⟨~ next week⟩ ⟨to live ~ ninety⟩ **3 :** at any time before or before the arrival, appearance, or beginning of — used after a negative expression with an implication that the action or condition began or is to begin at the specified time ⟨a refund which I did not get ~ ten years later⟩ **4 —** used as a function word indicating position before the clock hour ⟨five minutes ~ three⟩

²**till** *also* **til** \"\ *conj* [ME, fr. *till*, *til*, prep.] **1 :** throughout the interval extending to the (specified) time thereafter **:** up to the time when **:** UNTIL ⟨wait ~ I come⟩ — formerly used with *that* ⟨~ that a capable and wide revenge swallow them up —Shak.⟩ ⟨~ that we see our cheeks ale-dyed —Robert Herrick †1674⟩ **2 a** *dial* **:** BEFORE ⟨felt like a frost ~ morning —Conrad Richter⟩ **b :** previous to the time when **:** at any time before **:** unless at some future time — used after a negative statement or an injunction ⟨you'll never succeed ~ you concentrate your efforts⟩ **c** *chiefly dial* **:** up to or at the time when **:** WHEN — used in negative constructions ⟨scarcely reached home ~ the rain started⟩ **3** *dial* **:** in extent of time intervening before ⟨it seemed long ~ dawn came⟩ **4 :** continuously up to the point at which **:** for so long that **:** so that finally ⟨ran and ran ~ he could run no more⟩ **5** *chiefly dial* **:** WHILE ⟨enjoy the roses ~ they flourish —Thomas Wright⟩ **6** *dial* **:** THAN ⟨more ~ one can play⟩ **7** *dial* **:** in order that **:** so that ⟨can't write my name ~ you can read it —J.H.Stuart⟩

³**till** \'til\ *vt* -ED/-ING/-S [ME *tilien*, *tilen*, *tillen* to strive for, obtain, work, cultivate, fr. OE *tilian*; akin to OE *til* good, suitable, OHG *zil* goal, *zilōn* to hurry, ON *aldrtili* death, Goth *gatils* suitable] **1 :** to turn or stir (as by plowing, harrowing, or hoeing) and prepare for seed **:** sow, dress, and raise crops from **:** CULTIVATE ⟨learned to ~ the soil —Eric Newton⟩ ⟨~*ed* the rocky land —E.W.Smith⟩ ⟨helping to ~ the fields —Will Irwin⟩ **2** *dial Eng* **:** PREPARE, SET ⟨~ a snare⟩ **3 a :** to improve by assiduous labor or study **:** foster the growth or development of **:** care for ⟨new ground, not adequately ~*ed* in any older book —Hugo Leichtentritt⟩ ⟨the president of a university in those days ~*ed* a very broad field —A.D.White⟩ ⟨whole broad field of liberty was being ~*ed* —W.H.Allison⟩ **b :** to make researches into **:** work upon ⟨~ a field of knowledge⟩

⁴**till** *vt* -ED/-ING/-S [ME *tullen*, *tillen*, fr. OE *-tyllan* (as in *fortyllan* to seduce, *betyllan* to allure); akin to OE *talu* talk, narrative, list — more at TALE] *obs* **:** ATTRACT, ENTICE, CHARM

⁵**till** \'til\ *n* -s [AF *tylle*] **1 a :** a box, drawer, or tray in a receptacle (as a cabinet or chest) used esp. for valuables **b :** a money drawer in or behind a counter or desk (as in a store or bank) **c :** a removable compartment fitting in the drawer of a cash register and used to hold or carry money ⟨gunmen . . . lifted $225 from the ~ —*Time*⟩ **d :** a place where money is kept for ready access ⟨bank . . . needs some cash in its ~ to meet day-to-day needs of customers for cash —*Federal Reserve System*⟩ **2 a :** the money contained in a till ⟨borrow from the ~⟩ **b :** a quantity or supply of ready money ⟨passion for a brimful ~ —E.O. Hauser⟩ ⟨amateur groups never forget the insistency of the ~ —Robertson Davies⟩ — compare TILL MONEY **3 :** one of the four spaces between projections above the platen of a hand press **4 :** TILL BASKET

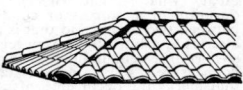

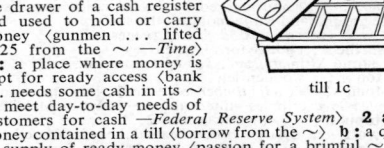

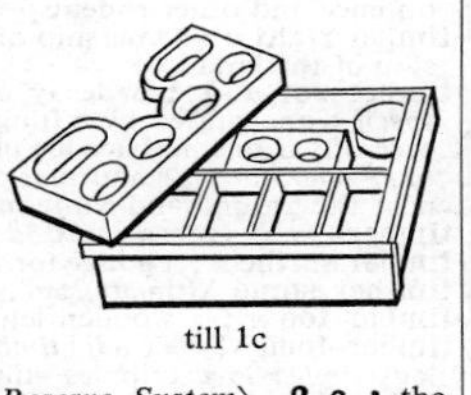
till 1c

⁶**till** \"\ *vt* -ED/-ING/-S **:** to put (as money) in a till

⁷**till** \"\ *n* -s [prob. fr. G *tülle* socket, mouth of a pitcher, fr. OHG *tulli* socket for an arrowhead; akin to OHG *tuolla* small valley — more at DOLE] **:** a horizontal piece fitted between the main uprights in an early handpress and supporting the sleeve with the spindle and screws

⁸**till** \"\ *n* -s [origin unknown] **1** *chiefly Scot* **:** a hard unproductive usu. clay subsoil often containing stones and gravel **2 :** unstratified drift deposited by a glacier and consisting of clay, sand, gravel and boulders intermingled in any proportions **:** BOULDER CLAY

till·able \'tiləbəl\ *adj* [³*till* + *-able*] **:** capable of being tilled **:** ARABLE ⟨an acre of irrigated land is equivalent to 4 acres of nonirrigated, ~ land —O.W.Israelsen⟩

till·age \-lij, -lēj\ *n* -s [ME, fr. *tilen*, *tillen* to till + *-age*] **1 :** the operation, practice, or art of tilling land **:** the improving of land for agricultural purposes **2 a :** a place tilled or cultivated **:** cultivated land ⟨forests have . . . given place to ~ and pasture —John Buchan⟩ **b :** crops growing on tilled ground — **in tillage :** under cultivation ⟨forty acres *in tillage*⟩

til·la·mook \'tilə,mu̇k\ *n, pl* **tillamook** *or* **tillamooks** *usu cap* [Chinook] **1 a :** a Salishan people of the Oregon coast **b :** a member of such people **2 :** a language of the Tillamook people **3** *or* **tillamook cheese** [fr. *Tillamook*, town and county in Oregon] **:** a cheddar cheese of crumbly texture and sharp flavor

til·lands·ia \tə'landzēə\ *n* [NL, fr. Elias *Tillands* †1693 Finnish botanist + NL *-ia*] **1** *cap* **:** a very large genus of chiefly epiphytic plants (family Bromeliaceae) confined to tropical and subtropical America and usu. bearing a rosette of narrow overlapping basal leaves that often hold a considerable quantity of water and spicate or paniculate flowers that have free perianth segments and are often subtended by colored bracts **2** -s **:** any plant of the genus *Tillandsia*

till basket *n* [⁵*till*] **:** a small rectangular basket for packing fruits or vegetables having its bottom and sides formed of two crossed pieces of veneer or of other material (as plastic or paperboard), usu. holding a pint or quart, and often fitting into a larger crate or other shipping container — compare BERRY BASKET, CLIMAX BASKET

¹**till·er** \'tilə(r)\ *n* -s [ME *tiliere*, *tilier*, *tiler*, fr. *tilien*, *tilen* *tillen* to till + *-ere*, *-er* -er] **1 :** one that tills **:** HUSBANDMAN, CULTIVATOR, PLOWMAN **2 :** an implement for tilling ground

²**til·ler** \"\ *n* -s [ME *tiler* stock of a crossbow, fr. MF *telier*, lit., beam of a loom, fr. ML *telarium*, fr. L *tela* web + *-arium* -ary — more at TOIL] **1 :** a notched stick used to hold a bow drawn during its shaping **2 a :** a lever of wood or metal that is fitted to the rudderhead and used for turning the rudder from side to side and that in small boats is usu. turned by hand but in ships is moved by mechanical appliances, is usu. in the form of a quadrant extending on each side of the rudderhead perpendicular to the keel, and has a rope or chain leading forward from each end to the wheel or other steering device **b :** a bar used for steering a vehicle (as an automobile) **3 :** a handle shaped like a boat's tiller: as **a :** the upper handle of a pit saw **b :** a two-handed bar for turning the rope in rope drilling **4** *or* **tiller wheel :** a steering wheel controlling the rear wheels or trailer section of a vehicle (as a ladder truck)

³**til·ler** \"\ *vb* -ED/-ING/-S *vi* **:** to use a tiller in archery ~ *vt* **:** to shape (a bow) to correct curvature

⁴**til·ler** \"\ *n* -s [fr. (assumed) ME, fr. OE *telgor*, *telgra* branch, twig, shoot; akin to OHG *zelga* twig, ON *tjalga* thin twig, *telgja* to shape by hewing, L *dolare* to hew — more at CONDOLE] **1 :** a young timber tree **:** SAPLING **2 :** SPROUT, STALK; *esp* **:** one from the base of a plant or from the axils of its lower leaves — compare STOOL 4

⁵**til·ler** \"\ *vi* -ED/-ING/-S **:** to put forth tillers ⟨some wheats and ryes ~ freely⟩

tiller chain *n* [²*tiller*] **:** a chain leading forward from either end of the tiller to the wheel or other steering device

til·ler·man \'ₛₛmən\ *n, pl* **tillermen** [²*tiller* + *man*] **:** one in charge of a tiller

tiller rope *n* [²*tiller*] **1 :** a rope leading forward from either end of the tiller to the wheel or other steering device **2 :** rope that consists of 6 strands of 42 wires each of ordinary lay about a hemp center and that is suitable where great flexibility is required (as for signal pulls and steering lines, and in the operation of tillers and of elevator controlling devices)

til·let \'tilət\ *n* -s [ME *tyllete*, fr. MF *tellette*, *teilete*, *toilete* — more at TOILET] **:** a glazed fabric used formerly for wrapping and protecting fabrics

til·le·tia \tə'lēsh(ē)ə\ *n, cap* [NL] **:** a genus (the type of the family Tilletiaceae) of smuts distinguished by single-celled chlamydospores that form a promycelium with a terminal tuft of sporidia — see ²BUNT; compare USTILAGO

til·le·ti·a·ce·ae \ₛ,ₛshē'āsē,ē\ *n pl, cap* [NL, fr. *Tilletia*, type genus + *-aceae*] **:** a family of smuts (order Ustilaginales) that is distinguished from the Ustilaginaceae by the simple promycelium bearing the spores in an apical cluster and that includes numerous genera some of which (as *Tilletia* and *Urocystis*) contain economically important parasites of cultivated plants — compare USTILAGO — **til·le·ti·a·ceous** \ₛ¦ₛₛ¦āshəs\ *adj*

til·leul \tə'yər(-ə)l, -'yəl,-'yəl\ *or* **tilleul green** *n* -s [F *tilleul* linden, fr. (assumed) VL *tiliolus*, fr. L *tilia*] **:** a pale greenish yellow that is very slightly paler than primrose green

tilleul buff *n* **:** ALABASTER 2

til·ley·ite \'tilē,īt\ *n* -s [fr. the name *Tilley* + E *-ite*] **:** a mineral $Ca_5(Si_2O_7)(CO_3)_2$ consisting of a carbonate and silicate of calcium

til·li·cum \'tiləkəm\ *n* -s [Chinook jargon, fr. Chinook *tlxam* people] **1** *Northwest* **:** PERSON, FRIEND **2** *Northwest* **:** PEOPLE; *esp* **:** the common people of an Indian tribe as distinguished from the chiefs

tilling *pres part of* TILL

till·ite \'ti,līt\ *n* -s [⁸*till* + *-ite*] **:** rock formed of consolidated or lithified till

till money *n* [⁵*till*] **:** money kept by a bank on its premises to meet day-to-day cash requirements

¹**til·lo·dont** \'tilə,dänt\ *adj* [NL *Tillodontia*] **:** of or relating to the Tillodontia

²**tillodont** \"\ *n* -s **:** a mammal or fossil of the order Tillodontia

til·lo·don·tia \ₛₛ'dänch(ē)ə\ *n pl, cap* [NL, fr. Gk *tillein* to pluck, tear + NL *-odontia*] **:** a small order of Eocene mammals of No. America and Europe probably derived from insectivores but having resemblances to rodents or carnivores

till plain *n* [⁸*till*] **:** a level or rolling land area covered by ground moraine

tills *pl of* TILL, *pres 3d sing of* TILL

till sheet *n* [⁸*till*] **:** GROUND MORAINE

¹**tilly** \'tilē -li\ *adj* -ER/-EST [⁸*till* + *-y*] **:** composed of or having the character of till ⟨~ land⟩ ⟨~ clay⟩

²**til·ly** \'tilē, -li\ *n* -ES [IrGael *tuilleadh*] *Irish* **:** something added for good measure

til·ma \'tilmə\ *n* -s [MexSp, fr. Nahuatl *tilmatl*] *chiefly Southwest* **:** a simple cloak of Indian origin

til oil *n* [²*til*] **:** SESAME OIL

ti·lop·te·ri·da·les \tə,läptərə'dā(,)lēz\ *n pl, cap* [NL, fr. *Tilopterid-*, *Tilopteris*, genus of algae (fr. Gk *tilos* something plucked — fr. *tillein* to pluck — + *pteris* fern) + *-ales* — more at PTERIS] **:** an order of brown algae (class Isogeneratae) resembling those of the genus *Ectocarpus* but with the cells of the prostrate lower portion of the thallus arranged in transverse tiers

til seed *n* [²*til*] **:** the seed of sesame

til·sit \'tilzət\ *or* **til·set cheese** \-zət-\ *n* -s *usu cap T* [fr. *Tilsit*, East Prussia (now Sovetsk, U.S.S.R.)] **:** a cheese consisting of whole or skim milk and having a plastic body and a mild to slightly sharp flavor

til·sit·er \'tilzəd·ə(r)\ *n* -s *usu cap* [G, fr. *Tilsiter* of Tilsit, one from Tilsit, fr. *Tilsit*] **:** TILSIT

¹**tilt** \'tilt\ *vb* -ED/-ING/-S [ME *tulten*, *tilten*; akin to OE *tealt* unstable, *tealtian*, *tealtrian* to totter, stumble, waver, MD *touteren* to tremble, Sw *tulta* to waddle, Norw dial. *tulta* to walk softly] *vt* **1 :** to cause to slope **:** INCLINE, SLANT, TIP ⟨~ a chair against a wall⟩ ⟨~*ed* sedimentary beds —*Jour. of Geol.*⟩ **2 :** to pour forth contents by tipping **:** empty or unload by inclining ⟨~ a cart⟩ **3 a :** to point or thrust in or as if in a tilt ⟨~ a lance⟩ **b :** to make a tilt or rush at **:** charge against ⟨~ an adversary⟩ **4 :** to hammer or forge with a tilt hammer ⟨~ a bar of iron⟩ **5 :** to rotate (a camera) about a horizontal axis that is at right angles to the lens axis so as to elevate or lower the viewing angle ~ *vi* **1 :** to move or shift so as to lean or incline **:** heel over **:** TIP, SLANT ⟨the board ~*ed* up when he stepped on it⟩ ⟨the tree ~*s* to the south⟩ **2 :** to move up and down **:** sway unsteadily **:** SEESAW, PITCH ⟨bird . . . ~*ing* among the leaves —Amy Lowell⟩ ⟨boats ~*ing* on the waves⟩ **3 a :** to engage in a combat with lances **:** ride or charge and thrust with a lance **:** JOUST **b :** to engage in an altercation or controversy **:** make an impetuous attack ⟨~ at wrongs⟩ **4 :** RUSH, BURST ⟨~ through the crowd⟩ ⟨~ into a room⟩ **5 :** to incline from a horizontal or vertical position ⟨roads that rise and dip and ~ past lively brooks —Frederick Nebel⟩ ⟨~*ing* strata⟩ **6 :** to tilt a camera — **tilt at windmills** [so called fr. the episode in *Don Quixote de la Mancha* in which Don Quixote battles with a windmill, thinking it a giant — more at DON QUIXOTE] **:** to fight imaginary enemies or illusory evils ⟨even though this rebellion may be a *tilting at windmills* —Rachel Frank⟩ ⟨viewed them as harmless literary eccentrics, *tilting at windmills* —Donald Davidson⟩

²**tilt** \"\ *n* -s **1 a** (1) **:** a military exercise on horseback in which two combatants (as knights in armor) charging with lances or similar weapons try to unhorse each other **:** JOUST (2) **:** a similar exercise in which an armed rider charges at a mark **b :** a tournament of tilts — compare QUINTAIN 2 **2 a :** an encounter in which opponents attack each other in a manner suggestive of that of tilting knights **:** ALTERCATION, DISPUTE ⟨had a sharp ~ with the manager⟩ ⟨fiery ~*s* against the evils of his day —Sarah G. Bowerman⟩ ⟨vocal ~*s* of legislators —T.C.Desmond⟩ **b :** SPEED — used esp. in the phrase *at full tilt* **3 a :** the act or fact of tilting **:** the state or position of being tilted **:** inclination from a vertical or horizontal position ⟨give a board a ~⟩ ⟨gave him a signal with a ~ of her gray head —Marcia Davenport⟩ **b :** a sloping surface ⟨warps, folds, or ~*s* that exist in rocks of the earth's crust —J.D.Forrester⟩ **4 :** BLACK-NECKED STILT **5 :** HELVE HAMMER **6 :** a contrivance used in fishing through the ice in which the tilting of a piece gives notice of the biting of a fish **7 :** any of various sports resembling or suggesting tilting with lances; *esp* **:** a water

sport in which the contestants stand on logs or in canoes or boats and thrust with poles **8 :** lack of parallelism between the plane of film in an aerial camera that is pointed downward and the plane of the ground — **at tilt :** ATILT ⟨lances *at tilt*⟩
[3]**tilt** \"\ *adj* [[2]*tilt*] **1 :** TILTED ⟨the ~ world returns from sun to ice —Philip Booth⟩ **2 :** that is emptied by tilting ⟨~ bucket⟩ ⟨~ pot⟩ ⟨~ wagon⟩
[4]**tilt** \"\ *n* -S [ME *teld, tild, telte* tent, canopy, fr. OE *teld;* akin to MLG & MD *telt* tent, OHG *zelt*, ON *tjald*, and perh. to L *dolare* to hew — more at CONDOLE] **1 :** a cloth covering or canopy (as of a cart, wagon, boat, or stall) ⟨bench under a little canvas ~ —J.G.Cozzens⟩ ⟨gaily colored ~*s* of the market stalls —*Courier (London)*⟩ **2** *Newfoundland & Labrador* **:** a log cabin or lean-to in which the logs are set upright
[5]**tilt** \"\ *vt* -ED/-ING/-S **:** to cover or provide with a tilt ⟨a ~*ed* jousting field⟩
tilt·able \'tiltəbəl\ *adj* **:** capable of being tilted
tiltboard \'=,=\ *or* **tilt table** *n* **:** an apparatus for testing perception of bodily position by rotating a blindfolded person from horizontal to vertical or oblique positions
tilt cart *n* **:** a cart having a body that can be tilted for emptying
tilted *adj* **:** taken with an aerial camera having the film plane out-of-parallel with the ground plane
[1]**tilt·er** \'tiltə(r)\ *n* -S [[1]*tilt* + *-er*] **1 :** one that tilts: as **a :** JOUSTER **b :** a workman who operates a helve hammer **c :** a workman who tilts out coal **d :** a contrivance for emptying something (as a barrel or carboy) by tilting **e :** a contrivance for varying the pitch of something (as the slats of a venetian blind) **f :** TILT 6 **2 a :** SPOTTED SANDPIPER **b :** SOLITARY SANDPIPER **c :** AVOCET
[2]**tilter** \"\ *vi* -ED/-ING/-S [freq. of [1]*tilt*] **:** to swing up and down **:** SEESAW, TEETER
tilth \'tilth *also* -ltth\ *n* -S [ME, fr. OE, fr. *tilian* to till + *-th* — more at TILL] **1 a :** the act, work, or occupation of tilling **:** cultivation of the soil **:** TILLAGE ⟨the ~ of the land⟩ **b :** mental or spiritual cultivation ⟨children without the ~ of kindness —Francis Hackett⟩ **2 :** cultivated land as distinguished from pasture, woodland, and waste land **:** PLOWLAND ⟨gradual extension of ~ drove the woods farther up the hills —Benjamin Farrington⟩ **3 :** the state of being tilled **:** condition when tilled ⟨land in good ~⟩ **4 a :** surface soil as prepared for sowing or planting **:** the depth of friable earth ⟨have never known the plow furrows break down so readily to a nice ~ —*Country Life*⟩ **b :** the state of aggregation of a soil ⟨a fine ~ is desirable —*New Zealand Jour. of Agric.*⟩
tilt hammer *n* **:** HELVE HAMMER
[1]**tilting** *n* -S [fr. gerund of [1]*tilt*] **:** the action or sport of one who tilts **:** JOUSTING ⟨was killed at a ~ —*Notes & Queries*⟩
[2]**tilting** *adj* [fr. pres. part. of [1]*tilt*] **1 :** that tilts, causes to tilt, or may be tilted **:** rising and falling **:** SLANTING, SWAYING **2 :** used for or in tilting ⟨~ field⟩ ⟨~ lance⟩ ⟨~ spear⟩
tilting board *n*, *NewEng* **:** SEESAW 2b
tilting fillet *n* **:** ARRIS FILLET
tilting helmet *or* **tilting helm** *n* **:** a helmet of great size and strength worn at tilts — called also *jousting helmet*
tilting table *n* **:** a mechanically controlled tabl⁄e used in casting a horse
tiltmeter \'=,==\ *n* **:** an instrument to measure tilting of the earth's surface
tilt mill *n* **:** a mill where metal (as steel) is tilted
tilt roof *n* **:** a roundheaded roof
tilts *pres 3d sing of* TILT, *pl of* TILT
tilt–top table \'=,=-\ *n* **:** TIP-TOP TABLE
tilt–up \'=¦=\ *adj* [fr. *tilt up*, v.] **:** of or relating to a method of constructing concrete walls in which the slabs are cast in horizontal position and then tilted up into place ⟨*tilt-up* building⟩
tiltup \'=,=\ *n* -S [fr. *tilt up*, v.] **:** TILT 6
tiltyard \'=,=\ *or* **tilting yard** *n* **:** a yard or place for tilting
til·yer \'tilyə(r)\ *n* -S [Hindi *tiliyar, tilyar* starling, small speckled bird, fr. *til* speck, sesame seed, fr. Skt *tila*] **:** ROSE=COLORED STARLING
tim \'tim\ *adj* [alter. of [1]*toom*] *Scot* **:** EMPTY
ti·ma·lia \tə'mālyə, -lēə\ *n, cap* [NL, prob. fr. native name in India] **:** the type genus of Timaliidae formerly including many Old World babblers but now usu. restricted to a single form of India and Java
tim·a·li·idae \,timə'līə,dē\ *n pl, cap* [NL, fr. *Timalia*, type genus + *-idae*] **:** a family of passerine birds comprising usu. a variety of forms not all of which may be closely related but having as typical representatives a group of babblers that are commonly isolated in a distinct subfamily and are characterized by short rounded wings with large outer primary, a bill like that of a thrush, and unspotted young
ti·ma·li·ine \tə'mālēən, -ē,īn\ *also* **tim·a·line** \'timə,līn\ *adj* [NL *Timalia* + E *-ine*] **:** of or relating to the genus *Timalia* or the family Timaliidae
ti·mar \tə'mär\ *n* -S [Turk *tımar* attendance, care, timar, fr. Per *tīmār* sorrow, care] **:** a Turkish fief formerly held under condition of military service
timarau *var of* TAMARAU
ti·mar·chy \'tī,märkē\ *n* -ES [Gk *timarchia*, fr. *timē* price, value, honor + *-archia* -archy — more at PAIN] **:** TIMOCRACY
ti·mar·i·ot \tə'märēət, -mar-\ *n* -S [F, fr. It *timariota*, fr. NGk *timariōtēs*, fr. *timarion* timar, fr. Turk *timar*] **:** one holding a timar
tim·bal *also* **tymbal** \'timbəl\ *n* -S [F *timbale*, fr. MF, alter. (influenced by *cymbale* cymbal) of *tamballe*, modif. (influenced by *tambour* drum) of OSp *atabal* — more at CYMBAL, TAMBOUR, ATABAL] **1 :** KETTLEDRUM 1 **2 :** the vibrating membrane in the shrilling organ of a cicada
tim·bale \'timbəl; tim'bäl, tam'-\ *n* -S [F, lit., kettledrum] **1 :** a creamy mixture (as of chicken, lobster, cheese, or fish) cooked in a drum-shaped mold or in individual molds or cups **2 :** a small pastry shell fried with a timbale iron and filled with a cooked timbale mixture or served with fruit sauce or dusted with powdered sugar — compare ROSETTE 9b
timbale iron *n* **:** an iron mold of varying design with a detachable handle used in making pastry shells for timbales

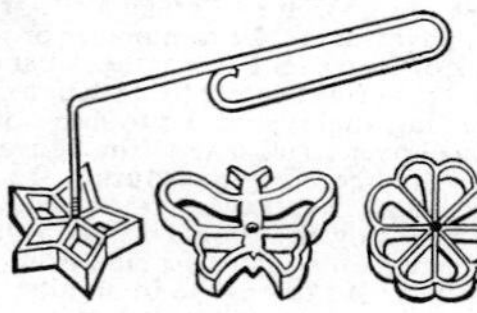
timbale irons

tim·be \'timbē\ *n* -S [MexSp *timbe, timbre*, name of various trees, esp. *Acacia angustissima*] **:** the bark or root of any of several Mexican trees and shrubs (esp. *Acacia angustissima* and *Calliandra anomala*) used in the manufacture of tepache
[1]**tim·ber** \'timbə(r)\ *n* -S [ME *timber, timmer*, fr. OE *timber* house, building, building material, wood, trees; akin to OHG *zimbar* house, room, wood, ON *timbr* timber, L *domus* house, Gk *domos* house, *demein* to build, Skt *dama* house] **1 a** (1) **:** growing trees or their wood ⟨standing ~⟩ (2) *Eng law* **:** trees (as oak, ash, elm over 20 years old) that are part of a freehold and may not be cut by a life tenant **b :** a wooded area **:** FOREST ⟨the early settlers had clung to rivers and ~*s* —Carl Sandburg⟩ ⟨hid out in the big ~ —Vance Randolph⟩ **c :** a standing tree or its trunk — often used interjectionally as a shout of warning to those near a falling tree **2 :** wood used for or suitable for building (as a house or boat) or for carpentry or joinery ⟨the turner, who concentrated on chair making, had beech for his favorite ~ —Andrew Phelan⟩ ⟨tropical wet evergreen forest producing valuable ~*s* —S.H. Howard⟩ **3 a :** MATERIAL, STUFF ⟨believe it's best-seller ~ —Richard Mallett⟩ **b :** something that helps to form a person **:** individual character or one of its constituents ⟨in this testing . . . inner ~*s* begin to part at once, the stuff of which he is made begins at once to deteriorate —F.R.Leavis⟩ **c :** human material suitable for a particular position or status ⟨presidential ~⟩ ⟨management ~⟩ ⟨officer ~⟩ **d :** bony structure in a dog **4 :** something that is made of wood or is likened to a wooden object: as **a :** a wooden gate, fence, post, or rail required to be jumped by a horse ⟨take a pull on your horse, considerably easing your pace as you near the ~ —C.C.W.Aldin⟩ **b** *slang* **:** LEG ⟨hobbled out on my gouty ~*s* for a walk —C.B.Fairbanks⟩ **5 a** (1) **:** a comparatively large squared or dressed piece of wood ready for use or forming part of a structure ⟨roof ~*s*⟩ ⟨bridge ~*s*⟩ ⟨floor ~*s*⟩; *esp* **:** one that in technical specifications usu. is not less than 5 inches in least dimension — compare PLANK; see ROOF illustration (2) *Brit* **:** a piece of sawed wood that in technical specifications usu. has a thickness of at least 4½ inches and a width of at least 6 inches **b** *Brit* **:** [2]LUMBER 2a **c :** a curving frame branching outward from the keel of a ship and bending upward in a vertical direction that is usu. composed of several pieces united **:** RIB 3b(1)
[2]**timber** \"\ *vb* **timbered; timbered; timbering** \-b(ə)riŋ\ **timbers** [ME *timbren*, fr. OE *timbran, timbrian;* akin to OHG *zimbarōn* to construct of wood, ON *timbra*, Goth *timrjan*, OE [1]*timber*] *vt* **1** *archaic* **:** to construct of wood **2 :** to frame, cover, or support with timbers ⟨the boards would suit admirably for ~*ing* cuts for drains —F.W.Crofts⟩ ~ *vi* **1 :** to cut timber ⟨a man ~*ing* in the wooded area —Don Browning⟩ **2 :** to provide timbers for support ⟨in all work in clay it was found advisable to ~ at once —*Military Engineer*⟩
[3]**timber** \"\ *adj* **1** *archaic* **:** formed of wood **:** WOODEN **2 :** of, relating to, or for timber **3** *Scot* **:** heavy as wood **:** DULL; *specif* **:** having no ear for music
[4]**timber** *var of* TIMBRE
timber and room *n* **:** ROOM AND SPACE
timber bar *n* **:** a crowbar having a working end that has a square section and ends in a right pyramid — called also *bridge bar*
timberbeast \'==,=\ *n, slang* **:** LOGGER
timber beetle *n* **:** any of various beetles (as the ambrosia beetles) whose larvae bore deeply in the wood of trees
timber borer *n* **:** any of numerous insects whose larvae develop as borers in living or dead trees or in timbers
timber connector *n* **:** CONNECTOR 2e
timber cruiser *n* **:** CRUISER 4a
tim·ber·doo·dle \¦==¦düdᵊl\ *n* [[1]*timber* + *doodle* (in *cock-a=doodle-doo*), euphemism for *cock* (associated with *cock* penis)] **:** the American woodcock ⟨the long-billed ~*s* were whistling all over the place as the flight came in —*N.Y.Times*⟩
tim·bered \'timbə(r)d\ *adj* [ME *timbred*, partly fr. [1]*timber* + *-ed;* partly fr. past part. of *timbren* to timber] **1 a :** furnished with, made of, or covered with timber ⟨one or two magnificently ~ old barns —Sinclair Lewis⟩ — often used in combination ⟨the waterlogged, rotten-*timbered*, barnacled old blubber hunter —H.A.Chippendale⟩ **b :** having walls framed by exposed timbers — compare HALF TIMBER **2 :** having a specified structure or constitution **:** BUILT, FORMED, MADE ⟨my arrows, too slightly ~ for so loud a wind —Shak.⟩ **3 :** covered with growing timber **:** WOODED ⟨sand hills whose thickly ~ ridges are clothed with loblolly pine, live oak, and holly —*Amer. Guide Series: N.C.*⟩ ⟨the hills, ~ up to their summits, formed an amphitheater —Anthony Trollope⟩
timber forest *n* **:** HIGH FOREST
timber grapple *n* **:** LUG HOOK
timber grouse *n* **:** a grouse (as the ruffed grouse) that inhabits woods — distinguished from *prairie chicken*
timberhead \'==,=\ *n* **1 :** the top end of a ship's timber used above the gunwale (as for belaying ropes) **2 :** a bollard bolted to the deck where the end of a timber would come
timber hitch *n* **1 :** a knot that is made by passing the end of a line around an object and twisting it back on itself, is used to secure a line (as to a log or spar), and is often supplemented by a half hitch to aid in towing and lifting **2 :** a knot resembling a timber hitch that is used to form the lower loop of an adjustable bowstring — called also *bowyer's knot*

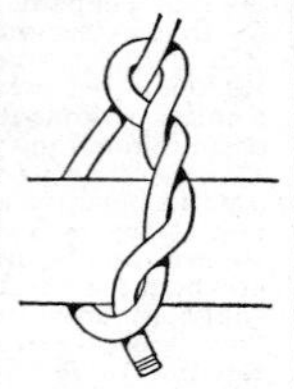
timber hitch 1

tim·ber·ing \'timb(ə)riŋ\ *n* -S [ME, fr. [1]*timber* + *-ing*] **:** a set of timbers **:** TIMBERWORK; *specif* **:** one used for support (as of a roof or wall)
timberjack \'==,=\ *n* **:** LOGGER
timber jumper *n* **:** a horse skilled in jumping over barriers (as fences or gates)
tim·ber·land \'==,land\ *n* **:** land covered with forest and esp. with marketable timber
tim·ber·less \-ˌləs\ *adj* **:** having no timber **:** not wooded
timberline \'==,=\ *n* **:** the upper limit of arboreal growth in mountains or in high latitudes ⟨all of the material included in the present study was obtained at ~ on the east slope . . . of the Rocky mountains —*Ecology*⟩
tim·ber·ling \-liŋ\ *n* -S [[1]*timber* + *-ling*] *Brit* **:** a small tree
tim·ber·man \-mən\ *n, pl* **timbermen** **1 :** LUMBERMAN **2 a :** a mine worker who frames and installs supporting timberwork **b :** a construction worker who cuts and puts together timbers and planking to form framing or supporting structures (as a retaining wall, trestle, or cofferdam) — called also *bracer*
timber mill *n* **:** a sawmill in which logs are cut into heavy timbers
timber mining *n* **:** ruthless cutting of timber with complete disregard for the future of the forests
timber rattlesnake *n* **:** a moderate-sized rattlesnake (*Crotalus horridus horridus*) that is widely distributed through the eastern half of the U. S., seeks rugged stony ground, and feeds largely on mice and other rodents — compare CANEBRAKE RATTLER
timber right *n* **:** ownership of standing timber without ownership of the land
timber rot *n* **1 :** a decay of lumber and building timbers; *specif* **:** one caused by a fungus (*Poria incrassata*) **2 :** a disease of various herbaceous plants caused by a fungus (*Sclerotinia sclerotiorum*) and marked by dry granular stem lesions near the ground and white mold on the surface
timbers *pl of* TIMBER, *pres 3d sing of* TIMBER
timber scribe *n* **:** a gouge for blazing trees
tim·ber·some \'timə(r)səm\ *var of* TIMORSOME
timber toe *n* **:** a wooden leg
timber–toed \¦==¦=\ *adj* [*timber toe* + *-ed*] **:** having a wooden leg ⟨*timber-toed* cripples stilted along —Herman Melville⟩
timber–topper \'==,==\ *n* **:** HURDLER 2
timber wolf *n* **:** a large broad-headed heavy-muzzled wolf (*Canis lupus lycaon*) of northern No. America that is extinct over much of the eastern and southern parts of its range and that has a dense heavy coat of clear or brownish gray or sometimes brownish white usu. with blackish shadowing along the back
timberwork \'==,=\ *n* **:** work made of timbers **:** a timber construction
timber worm *n* **:** a worm (as a timber borer) infesting timber
tim·bery \'timb(ə)rē, -ri\ *adj* [[1]*timber* + *-y*] **:** abounding in or characterized by timber ⟨the clean ~ look of her new house —P.H.Lowrey⟩
timbes *pl of* TIMBE
[1]**tim·bo** \tēm'bȯ, tim-, -bō\ *n* -S [Pg *timbó*, fr. Tupi] **1 :** an Amazonian woody vine (*Paullinia pinnata*) the bitter bark of which contains a fish poison **2 :** [3]CUBE 2
[2]**timbo** \"\ *n* -S [Sp *timbó*, fr. Guarani] **1 :** a timber tree (*Enterolobium timbouva*) of Argentina **2 :** the easily worked red wood of timbo used for furniture and interior woodwork
[1]**tim·bre** \'tambə(r), 'tim-,'taam-\ *n* -S [MF — more at [3]TIMBRE] **:** the crest on a coat of arms
[2]**timbre** \"\ *also* **tim·ber** \"\ *vt* -ED/-ING/-S **:** to surmount and adorn with a heraldic timbre
[3]**timbre** \"\ *also* **timber** \"\ *n* -S [F *timbre*, fr. MF, bell struck by a hammer, crest of a helmet, armorial crest, fr. OF, drum, fr. MGk *tymbanon* kettledrum, alter. of Gk *tympanon* — more at TYMPANUM] **1 :** a quality of sound that depends chiefly on the presence or absence and the relative intensity of various overtones: as **a :** the resonance quality of a voiced speech sound by which the ear recognizes and identifies it **b :** the quality of tone distinctive of a singing voice or an instrument **2 :** distinctive character, quality, or tone ⟨that consciousness is clearly very closely related to the author's own personal ~ —F.R.Leavis⟩ ⟨the dance did not prove to be one of dark ~ —*Dance Observer*⟩ ⟨would have shamed them forever, had they had the ~ of his world in their characters —*Yale Rev.*⟩
tim·brel \'timbrəl\ *n* -S [obs. E *timbre* tambourine (fr. ME, fr. OF, drum) + E *-el*] **:** a small hand drum or tambourine ⟨the shallow ~ . . . which itinerant jugglers carried—Curt Sachs⟩
tim·brelled \-ld\ *adj* [fr. past part. of obs. E *timbrel* to play upon or accompany with a timbrel, fr. E *timbrel*, n.] **:** played upon or accompanied with a timbrel ⟨there the ~ hymn rings to Osiris —W.L.Bowles⟩
[1]**time** \'tīm\ *n* -S [ME *time, tyme*, fr. OE *tīma, tȳma;* akin to ON *tīmi* time, OE *tīd* time — more at TIDE] **1 a :** a period during which something (as an action, process, or condition) exists or continues **:** an interval comprising a limited and continuous action, condition, or state of being **:** measured or measurable duration ⟨no one had spoken to him all the ~ we were at lunch —Ernest Hemingway⟩ ⟨could not sleep, and after a ~ he rose —Louis Bromfield⟩ ⟨gone a long ~⟩ ⟨written in three hours' ~⟩ **b :** a period set apart in some specified or implied way from others ⟨a ~ to weep, and a ~ to laugh; a ~ to mourn, and a ~ to dance —Eccles 3:4 (AV)⟩ ⟨Saturday evenings, traditional shopping ~ for millworkers and farmers —*Amer. Guide Series: N. H.*⟩ **c** (1) **:** a period sufficiently or conveniently long ⟨just ~ to reach shelter before the storm broke⟩ ⟨there is no ~ here to trace the means by which these errors of planning were corrected —*Amer. Guide Series: N. Y.*⟩ (2) **:** LEISURE ⟨there was ~ for athletic sports and private reading —Lucien Price⟩ ⟨as much good music as he has ~ to listen to —*Report: (Canadian) Royal Commission on Nat'l Development*⟩ (3) **:** the length of the period required for or consumed in performing an action or going over a course ⟨the winner's ~ was just under four minutes⟩ ⟨the ~ of the train trip was two hours⟩ (4) *slang* **:** progress in winning favor or sexual acceptance ⟨two guys tried to beat each other's ~ around the women —Russell Thacher⟩ ⟨the guy . . . trying to make ~ with his secretary — Bennett Cerf⟩ **d :** a period or segment of the radio or television broadcasting day ⟨one of the first to insist on the sale of radio ~ for both sides of a controversial issue —C.C.Barry⟩ **2 a :** a point or period when something occurs **:** the moment of an event, process, or condition **:** OCCASION ⟨we were not twenty yards from the rocks, at the ~ that the ship passed abreast of them —Frederick Marryat⟩ ⟨from that ~ she was his tennis instructor and patron —*Current Biog.*⟩ **b :** an opportune, convenient, or suitable moment or period **:** a favorable opportunity or occasion ⟨biding his ~⟩ ⟨the ~ has come to sift and synthesize the findings of these works —Julian Towster⟩ ⟨notice in him any sense of ~*s* and occasions and the demands of social etiquette —L.P.Smith⟩ **3 :** an appointed, fixed, or customary moment or hour for something to happen, begin, or end ⟨spring came ahead of ~ this year⟩ ⟨a half-hour before edition ~ —William DuBois⟩: as **a :** the normal or expected moment or period of death ⟨you'll die before your ~ —W.J. Reilly⟩ **b :** the normal end of the period of gestation **:** the expected moment of childbirth ⟨when her ~ has come, counted by the moons, she betakes herself to a special little hut built for the women —Corinne Feeney⟩ **c :** a scheduled moment of arrival or departure ⟨asked for the ~ of the next northbound train⟩ **d** *Brit* **:** the legally fixed closing hour of a public house **4 a :** a period associated with or characterized or dated by reference to a particular individual ⟨lived in the ~ of Elizabeth I⟩ ⟨one of the most popular writers of his ~⟩ **b** (1) **:** an historical period **:** AGE, ERA ⟨a fast moving ~ such as we are now in —T.K.Finletter⟩ ⟨geography could not fail to share in the mathematical advances of the ~ —Benjamin Farrington⟩ — often used in pl. ⟨ancient ~*s*⟩ ⟨modern ~*s*⟩ (2) **:** a division of geologic chronology **c :** conditions prevalent at present or in a specified or implied period of the past **:** state of things ⟨the ~ is out of joint —Shak.⟩ — usu. used in pl. ⟨refused to follow the trend of the ~*s* —Gerard MacGowan⟩ ⟨behind the ~*s*⟩ ⟨move with the ~*s*⟩ **d :** the present time — used with *the* ⟨many of the most important issues of the ~ —Brand Blanshard⟩ **5 :** a known, fixed, or anticipated period of existence or duration: as **a :** LIFETIME ⟨one man in his ~ plays many parts —Shak.⟩ **b :** a period of apprenticeship ⟨apprentices in the last year of their ~ —John Southward⟩ **c :** a term of military service ⟨had been enlisted for a short term only, and before the end of December . . . would have served their ~ —H.E.Scudder⟩ **d :** a prison sentence ⟨did ~ for lying about his bank accounts —P.F.Healy⟩ **6 a :** SEASON ⟨that ~ of year thou mayst in me behold —Shak.⟩ ⟨it's very hot for this ~ of year⟩ **b :** a point or portion of a day or year recurring periodically or established by routine — usu. used in combination ⟨dinner-*time*⟩ ⟨rest-*time*⟩ ⟨examination-*time*⟩ ⟨vacation=*time*⟩ **7 a :** a unit of duration as a basis for poetic meter; *esp* **:** MORA 2a **b :** rate of speed (as in marching, dancing, speaking) **:** TEMPO ⟨the woman dances regular ~ to the music —Chandler Brossard⟩ ⟨did this in slow ~, talking and laughing together —H.V.Morton⟩ **c** (1) **:** the grouping of the successive rhythmic beats or pulses as represented by a musical note taken as a time unit into measures or bars that are marked off by bar lines according to the position of the principal accent **:** METER, RHYTHM (2) **:** the rate or tempo at which a piece is performed **8 a :** a definite moment, hour, day, or year as indicated or fixed by a clock or calendar **:** a precise instant or date ⟨the ~ was midnight⟩ ⟨we do not know the exact ~ of his birth⟩ ⟨what ~ is it⟩ **b** (1) **:** a number that represents the duration of a process or condition or the interval elapsing between two events and that is obtained in effect by counting a series of arbitrarily chosen regularly recurrent events (as the swings of a pendulum) that take place during the interval to be measured (2) **:** a number (as on a clock dial or calendar) that marks the occurrence of a specified event as to hour or date and that is obtained by counting from a fiducial epoch (as that of a meridian passage of the sun or the birth of Christ) **c :** reckoning of time **:** a system of reckoning the lapse or progress of time — see SIDEREAL TIME, SOLAR TIME, STANDARD TIME **9 a :** one of a series of recurring instances or repeated acts or actions ⟨he took the stairs four at a ~ —*Phoenix Flame*⟩ ⟨a machine that can perform three operations at a ~⟩ ⟨you've been told that many ~*s*⟩ **b times** *pl* **:** multiplied instances ⟨five ~*s* greater⟩ ⟨many ~*s* stronger⟩ **c :** TURN ⟨got two hits out of three ~*s* at bat⟩ **10 a :** finite duration **:** the duration of one's life or of the material universe as contrasted with infinite duration ⟨~, that takes survey of all the world, must have a stop —Shak.⟩ **b :** FATHER TIME **11 a** *Platonism* **:** a reality that is an absolute flowing apart from the events filling it **b** *Aristotelianism* **:** the numerable aspect of motion **c** *Kantianism* **:** the a priori form of inner sensible intuitions that have no existence independently of the mind and are a subjective mode in which phenomena appear — see OBJECTIVE TIME, SUBJECTIVE TIME **12 a :** a person's experience during a specified period or on a particular occasion ⟨have the ~ of their lives putting on the yearly show —Louise Gerdts⟩ ⟨the student has a merry ~ of it trying to do three things at once —S.A. Constantino⟩ ⟨a good ~⟩ ⟨gave him a hard ~⟩ **b :** a highly enjoyable or disagreeable experience ⟨had himself a ~ drinking beer from a glass in one hand, milk from a glass in the other —*Time*⟩ ⟨had a ~ with them; couldn't figure any way to get them out —W.L.Gresham⟩ **c** *slang* **:** CAROUSAL, SPREE ⟨still thought he might be out on a ~ —Ernest Hemingway⟩ **13 a :** the hours or days given to or due to be given to one's work ⟨make up ~⟩ **b :** a rate of pay fixed in terms of a unit of time (as an hour) ⟨paid him straight ~ for his overtime work⟩ **c :** amount of pay due esp. according to an hourly rate; *specif* **:** a final payment of wages due ⟨any cowboy who hit a horse over the head or spurred one in the shoulders was asking for his ~ —Ross Santee⟩ ⟨asked for his ~, but it was just a misunderstanding and was straightened out —E.C. Abbott & Helena Smith⟩ **14 :** the shutter setting on a camera for making a time exposure **15 a :** official suspension of play during a game or contest ⟨the umpire called ~⟩ **b :** a temporary official stopping of the clock during a game or portion of a game (as basketball or football) scheduled to end after a specific number of minutes of play **syn** see OPPORTUNITY — **at the same time :** HOWEVER, NEVERTHELESS ⟨this frightened, insecure, querulous man . . . must *at the same time* possess the qualities of authority and command —Arthur Knight⟩ — **at times** *adv* **:** at intervals **:** now and then ⟨*at times* he sleeps, *at times* he tosses restlessly⟩ — **for the time being**

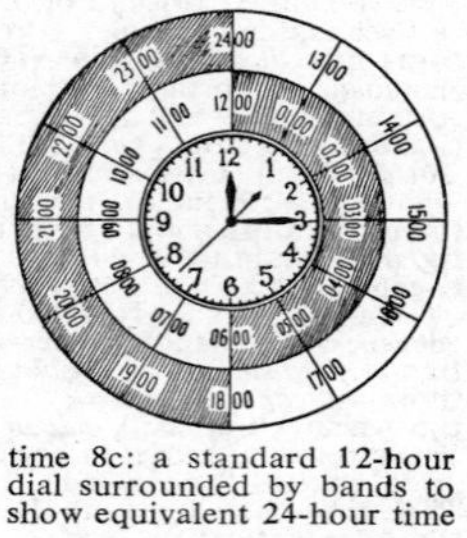

time 8c: a standard 12-hour dial surrounded by bands to show equivalent 24-hour time

: for the present : at the moment ⟨will take no action *for the time being*⟩ — **from time to time** : once in a while : OCCASIONALLY ⟨goes to the theater *from time to time*⟩ — **in good time** *adv* : in time — **in no time** *adv* : in the shortest possible time ⟨moved his fellows to a concerted attack, and *in no time* boulders were hurtling down the cliffs —*Amer. Guide Series: Minn.*⟩ — **in time** *adv* **1 a** : in due season : sufficiently early ⟨had they not been agreed upon *in time*, the states might have fallen asunder —Allan Nevins⟩ **2** : in the course of time : EVENTUALLY ⟨*in time* rose . . . to be general manager —*Current Biog.*⟩ **3** : in correct tempo ⟨has never learned to play *in time*⟩ **4** : on earth — used as an intensive ⟨why *in time* don't you come in the other room —Zona Gale⟩ — **on one's own time** : without being paid ⟨has done extra work *on his own time*⟩ — **on time** **1 a** : at the appointed time : PUNCTUALLY ⟨failed to arrive *on time* for his appointment⟩ **b** : on schedule ⟨the train is *on time*⟩ **2** : on the installment plan ⟨a portable typewriter he was buying *on time* —Hamilton Basso⟩ — **out of time** : not within the designated period : too late ⟨the appeal was filed *out of time*⟩ — **time and time again** : time and again

²**time** \"\ *vb* -ED/-ING/-S [ME *timen*, fr. ¹*time*] *vt* **1 a** : to arrange or set the time of : fix a time for : SCHEDULE ⟨*timed* his occasional calls to coincide with the hour of tea —Gertrude Atherton⟩ ⟨consciously *timed* that pause for dramatic effect —J.P.Marquand⟩ **b** : to regulate the speed or stops of (as a train) according to a timetable ⟨the train was *timed* to leave the station at 1:05 p.m.⟩ **c** : to adjust (as a watch) to keep correct time **2 a** : to set the tempo for ⟨the conductor *timed* the performance admirably⟩ **b** : to give a fixed or appropriate rhythm to ⟨gave a dragging tempo to the first movement, but *timed* the second movement effectively⟩ **c** : to regulate the moment, speed, or duration of for desired or maximum effect ⟨*timed* the exposure for two seconds⟩ ⟨*timed* his swing to hit the ball into right field⟩ **3** : to make coincident in time : cause to keep time with something ⟨*timed* his steps to the music⟩ **4 a** : to ascertain or record the time, duration, or rate of ⟨*timed* the horse in his last workout before the race⟩ **b** : to calculate or estimate the speed of ⟨*timed* the ball badly and missed it by a foot⟩ **5** : to dispose (as a mechanical part) so that an action occurs at a desired instant or in a desired way ⟨another factor which reduces distortion to a negligible value is the fact that the plate circuit is *timed* —L.E.Barton⟩ ~ *vi* : to keep or beat time : move in time ⟨beat, happy stars, *timing* with things below —Alfred Tennyson⟩

³**time** \"\ *adj* **1 a** : of or relating to time ⟨poetry, dance and music are ~ arts —J.M.Barzun⟩ ⟨a ~ salesman⟩ **b** : giving, recording, or marking time ⟨~ register⟩ **2** : timed to ignite or explode at a specific moment ⟨~ charge⟩ **3 a** : payable on a specified future day or a given length of time after presentation for acceptance **b** (1) : made with the understanding that extended terms will be given for settlement ⟨a ~ sale⟩ (2) : to be paid for in installments ⟨a ~ purchase⟩ : divided into installments ⟨a ~ payment⟩

time about *adv, chiefly Scot* : in turn : by turns : ALTERNATELY
time-advantage \⹀⹀,⹀⹀\ *n* : the accumulated time during which a wrestler is in a position of advantage over his opponent used as a limited basis of scoring in amateur bouts
time allowance *n* **1** : an allowance of time usu. in seconds per mile that is given a yacht in competition with one of a higher rating **2** : ALLOWED TIME 2
time and again *adv* : REPEATEDLY ⟨natural disasters recur *time and again* —O.N.Larsen⟩
time and a half *n* : payment of a worker (as for overtime or holiday work) at one and a half times his regular wage rate
time and motion study *or* **time-motion study** *n* : systematic observation, analysis, and measurement of the separate steps in the performance of a specific job for the purpose of establishing a standard time for each performance, improving procedures, and increasing productivity — called also *motion and time study, motion study, time study*
time and temperature method *n* : adjustment of the development time of a photographic negative in accordance with the developer solution temperature — called also *thermo development*
time at bat : AT BAT
time azimuth *n* : an observation by compass of the azimuth of a celestial body made at a specific time as a step in computing the compass error
time ball *n* : a large ball on a pole (as at an observatory) that is arranged to drop suddenly to mark a particular hour of day (as noon)
time base *n* : a part of an electronic circuit having a voltage varying accurately with time and used (as in radar) to provide range information or (as in television) to the scanning operation
time belt *n* : TIME ZONE
time bet *n* : a provisional bet on a race made with a bookmaker that is invalid if the purchase time noted on the betting slip is later than the official start of the race
time bill *n* **1** : a bill of exchange payable at a definite future time **2** *Brit* : TIMETABLE
time-binding \⹀,⹀⹀\ *n* : the characteristically human activity of transmitting experience from one generation to another esp. through the use of symbols
time bomb *n* **1** : a bomb so constructed as to explode at a predetermined time **2** : something (as a situation, conflict, personality trait) that has a delayed explosive action ⟨too many administrators sit unknowingly on *time bombs* —H.F. & Katharine Pringle⟩
time book *n* : a book in which hours spent on a job by workers are recorded
time buyer *n* : a person employed by an advertising agency to select and arrange radio and television coverage for clients
time capsule *n* : a container holding historical records or objects representative of current culture that is deposited (as in the earth or in a cornerstone) for preservation until discovery by some future age
time card *n* **1** *usu* **timecard** : TIMETABLE ⟨despite a greatly speeded-up *timecard*, it hit every stop on schedule —B.A. Long & W.J.Dennis⟩ **2** : a card on which is kept a daily record of the time worked by an employee or the time of his arrival and departure
time chart *n* **1** : a chart showing the standard times in various

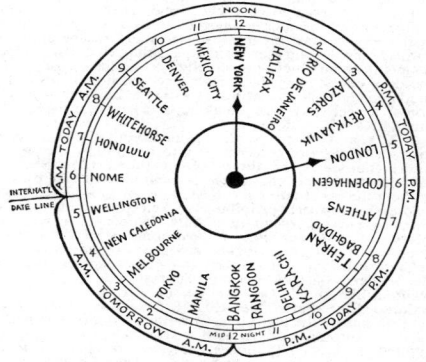

time chart

parts of the world with reference to a specified time at a specified place **2** : a table listing important events for successive years or groups of years within a particular historical period
time charter *n* : a contract for the cargo space of a manned ship for a specified period
time clerk *n* : TIMEKEEPER

time clock *n* : a clock with a device to record the times of arrival and departure of employees or the time at which a job is begun or completed — compare TELLTALE 3a
time constant *n* **1** : the time required for a current turned into a circuit under a steady electromotive force to reach to $\frac{e-1}{e}$ or 0.632 of its final strength (where *e* is the base of natural logarithms); *specif* : the ratio of the inductance of a circuit in henries to its resistance in ohms **2** : the relaxation time in the discharge of a capacitor that is equal to the product of the resistance in ohms of the discharging circuit and the capacity in farads of the condenser
time-consuming \⹀⹀,⹀⹀\ *adj* : using or taking up a great deal of time ⟨the development of young clone selections from such seedling material had proved to be rather *time-consuming* —*Farmer's Weekly (So. Africa)*⟩ **2** : wasteful of time ⟨efforts to block legislation may take the form of speech-making, roll-calls, and other *time-consuming* tactics —W.S.Sayre⟩
time copy *n* : newspaper or periodical copy usu. set in type beforehand that can be used at any time
timed *adj* [fr. past part. of ²*time*] : made to occur at or in a set time ⟨a ~ explosion⟩ ⟨a ~ examination⟩ **2** : done or taking place at a time of a specified sort ⟨a poorly ~ speech⟩ ⟨a propitiously ~ proposal⟩ ⟨ill-*timed*⟩
time deposit *n* : a bank deposit payable a specified number of days after deposit or after receipt by the bank of notice of withdrawal and considered by federal regulations as being any deposit payable after 30 days or after 30 days' notice
time depth *n* : a period of time during which a culture, language, or group of languages has been undergoing independent genetic development ⟨a language with a *time depth* of 5000 years⟩
timed fire *n* : target firing in which a given number of rounds are fired within a particular time limit
time draft *n* : a draft payable a specified number of days after date of the draft or presentation to the drawee
time error *n* : a systematic error in the comparison of magnitudes resulting from the fact that one magnitude follows the other in time
time-expired \⹀⹀\ *adj* : having completed a term of enlistment or military service ⟨fifteen hundred *time-expired* veterans had been discharged from the two regiments —Robert Graves⟩
time exposure *n* **1** : exposure of a photographic film for a definite time that is usu. more than one half second **2** : a photograph taken by time exposure
time fire *n* : artillery fire in which the projectile bursts or is intended to burst in air
time freight *n* : freight for movement on regularly scheduled trains providing expedited service and a guaranteed time of delivery; *also* : a train for handling such freight
time-ful \⹀⹀\ *adj* [ME, fr. ¹*time* + -*ful*] *archaic* : SEASONABLE, TIMELY — **time-ful-ly** \-fəlē\ *adv*
time fuze *n* : a fuze that detonates a bursting charge after a definite interval of time has elapsed
time hit *n* : a hit made by a time thrust
time-honored \⹀⹀\ *adj* **1** : honored or entitled to honor because of age or long usage ⟨a deep respect for *time-honored* institutions —*New Republic*⟩ **2** : long established ⟨begun to undermine the *time-honored* position of the traditional holders of authority —H.W.Glidden⟩ ⟨a *time-honored* phrase⟩
time immemorial *n* **1 a** : a time beyond legal memory formerly fixed by English law as the beginning of the reign of Richard I in 1189 but modified in common law by various prescription acts **2** : a time going back beyond the memory of any person living **2** : time so long past as to be indefinite in history or tradition ⟨field forces from *time immemorial* have dealt with such offenses on the spot —R.H.Jackson⟩
timekeeper \⹀⹀,⹀⹀\ *n* **1** : one that keeps, measures, regulates, or determines the time: as **a** : TIMEPIECE **b** : one who keeps records of the time worked by employees (as for use in making up a payroll) **c** : one appointed to mark and announce the time of participants or the elapsed time in a race, game, or contest
timekeeping \⹀⹀,⹀⹀\ *n* : the act, function, or process of keeping time
time killer *n* **1** : one who kills time : a person with time on his hands ⟨the reading room held many students, as well as a few *time killers*⟩ **2** : something that passes the time : DIVERSION ⟨made the experience full and memorable, made it an experience instead of a *time killer* —J.M.Barzun⟩
time killing *n* : the act or action of killing time
time lag *n* **1** : an interval of time between two related phenomena (as a cause and its effect) ⟨the *time lag* between the discovery of a scientific principle and its application —*Lamp*⟩ **2** : CULTURAL LAG ⟨have suffered a singular *time lag*, in bringing to the problems of today and tomorrow the elements of yesterday's thinking —Sidney Wallach⟩
time-lapse \⹀,⹀⹀\ *adj* [fr. the n. *time lapse*] : of, relating to, or constituting a motion picture taken at a speed slower than normal but usu. projected at a normal speed so that a slow action (as the opening of a flower bud) appears to be speeded up : STOP-MOTION
¹**time-less** \¹tīmləs\ *adj* [¹*time* + -*less*] *archaic* : PREMATURE, UNTIMELY ⟨a pack of sorrows which would press you down . . . to your ~ grave —Shak.⟩ **2 a** : having no beginning or end : ETERNAL, INTERMINABLE, UNENDING ⟨nothing on dry land can match the ghastly war for survival which continues ceaselessly in a ~ night and seasonless year —F.G.Kay⟩ **b** : not restricted to a particular time or date : DATELESS ⟨much of what seems contemporary in popular fiction is fairly ~ —W.H.Whyte⟩ ⟨criticize him from the perspective of some ~ realism —D.R.Meyer⟩ **3** : not affected by time : AGELESS, CHANGELESS ⟨one of those ~ people who sometimes looked younger as they grew older —J.P.Marquand⟩ — **time-less-ly** *adv* — **time-less-ness** *n* -ES
²**timeless** \"\ *adv, archaic* : TIMELESSLY
tim-e-li-idae \,timə'līə,dē\ *n* [NL, fr. *Timelia*, genus of babblers (prob. fr. native name in India) + -*idae*] *syn* of TIMALIIDAE
time limit *n* : a fixed period for doing or ending something; *specif* : a fixed amount of time allowed for a task with the object of measuring the amount of work an individual can accomplish in such time — contrasted with *amount limit*
time-li-ness \¹tīmlēnəs, -lin-\ *n* -ES : the quality or state of being timely
time loan *n* : a loan with a definite maturity date — compare CALL LOAN
time lock *n* : a lock controlled by clockwork to prevent its being unlocked before a set time
¹**time-ly** \¹tīmlē, -li\ *adv* [ME *timliche, timely*, fr. OE *tīmlice*, fr. *tīma* time + -*lice*, adv. suffix] **1** *archaic* : EARLY, SOON ⟨he did command me to call ~ on him —Shak.⟩ **2** : in time : OPPORTUNELY, SEASONABLY ⟨the present action was ~ brought within two years after his appointment —R.W.Starr⟩
²**timely** \"\ *adj* -ER/-EST [ME *timlich, timely*, fr. ¹*time* + -*lich*, -*ly* -ly, adj. suffix] **1 a** : done or occurring at a suitable time : OPPORTUNE ⟨if ~ treatment is available the patient has a good chance of recovery —*Nat'l Safety News*⟩ **b** : occurring at a normal or expected time ⟨in my habits, the ~ routine and oscillation of the hours —L.P.Smith⟩ **c** : falling within a time prescribed by law or contract ⟨the plaintiff filed a ~ claim for refund —T.M.Madden⟩ **d** : appropriate to the times or the occasion ⟨a ~ book⟩ ⟨a ~ remark⟩ ⟨a ~ hogshead of home-brewed beer . . . served effectively as fire extinguisher —*Amer. Guide Series: Vt.*⟩ **2** *archaic* : ADVANCE, EARLY ⟨I know that he will presently be summoned . . . I have ~ information —Charles Dickens⟩ *syn* see SEASONABLE
time money *n* : money loaned or ready to be loaned for a specified period of time
time-motion study *var of* TIME AND MOTION STUDY
ti-meno-guy \¹tī'menə,gi\ *n* -ES [prob. fr. F *timon* tiller, helm + E *guy* — more at TIMONEER] : a rope stretched taut from a projecting obstacle to prevent rigging from chafing or fouling
time note *n* : a note payable at a specified time — compare DEMAND NOTE
time of day **1 a** : the time as indicated by the clock ⟨asked him what *time of day* it was⟩ **b** : the present time ⟨it is unnecessary at this *time of day* to argue that the world is round⟩ **2 a** : the state of the case : the true situation ⟨he's been here long enough to know the *time of day*⟩ **b** : the latest fashion ⟨has long set the *time of day* in . . . champagnes —*New Yorker*⟩

time on target : a concentration of artillery fire on a target in which the time of firing by each unit participating is so regulated that all the projectiles reach the target simultaneously
time-ous \¹tīm(ē)əs, ¹timēəs\ *adj* [ME, fr. ¹*time* + -*ous*] : TIMELY ⟨has to give ~ notice to that effect —*Farmer's Weekly (So. Africa)*⟩ — **time-ous-ly** *adv*
time-out \⹀,⹀⹀\ *n* -S [fr. the phrase *to take time out*] **1** *usu* **time out** : a usu. brief suspension of activity or work : BREAK, INTERMISSION ⟨his eldest son died and he took *time out* to recover from the shock —*Newsweek*⟩ **2** : a brief period of suspension of play declared by an official in any of various organized sports (as for rest of players, treatment of an injured player, officials' conference)
time out of mind [ME] : TIME IMMEMORIAL
timepiece \⹀,⹀⹀\ *n* : an instrument (as a clock or watch) for measuring time; *esp* : one that has no striking or chiming mechanism
timepleaser *n, obs* : TIMESERVER
time policy *n* : a marine insurance policy covering property for a specified period of time
tim-er \¹tīmə(r)\ *n* -S [²*time* + -*er*] **1** : one that measures, records, or regulates time: as **a** : TIMEPIECE; *esp* : a stopwatch for timing races or contests **b** : TIMEKEEPER **c** : a device in the ignition system of an internal-combustion engine that causes the spark to be produced in the cylinder at the correct time either by the interruption or by the closing of the primary circuit — compare DISTRIBUTOR **d** : one who determines the exposure time to be used to obtain a satisfactory print of each scene of a motion-picture negative **e** : one who corrects the escapement of timepieces **f** (1) : a device (as a clock) that indicates by means of an audible signal the end of the interval of time for which it is set (2) : a device for automatically starting or stopping a machine or other device at a given time or for automatically controlling the operating interval **2** [¹*time* + -*er*] : one that does or serves in or for a specified time ⟨a first ~ in this office⟩ : one that has a specified relationship to time ⟨young-*timers* hep to the special needs of the holiday season —*advt*⟩
time rating *n* : the length of time a machine can carry a load without the specified conditions of load and temperature rise being exceeded
time recorder *n* : TIME CLOCK
¹**times** \(,)tīmz\ *prep* [ME, fr. pl. of ¹*time*] : multiplied by ⟨two ~ two is four⟩
²**times** \(¹)tīmz\ *adv* [fr. pl. of ¹*time*] *dial Eng* : many times : FREQUENTLY
time-saver \⹀,⹀⹀\ *n* : something that saves time
timesaving \⹀,⹀⹀\ *adj* : intended or serving to expedite something ⟨a ~ device⟩
time scale *n* : an arrangement of events used as a measure of the relative or absolute duration or antiquity of a period of history or geologic or cosmic time ⟨on the *time scale* of modern cosmology his brief and fevered existence seems a mere flash in the pan —*Times Lit. Supp.*⟩
time sense *n* : an ability to feel the lapse of time and to estimate and compare intervals esp. of short duration
time series *n* : a frequency distribution in which time is the independent variable
timeserver \⹀,⹀⹀\ *n* : one that shapes his behavior and ideas to fit the dominant pattern of his times or environment or to please his superiors : TEMPORIZER ⟨was in matters of principle inherently shifty, an opportunist and a ~ —S.H.Adams⟩
time service *n* : the determination and announcement of the precise time usu. conducted as a part of the work of an astronomical observatory, usu. based on transit observations of stars, and announced mainly by telegraphic and radio signals — compare TIME SIGNAL
¹**timeserving** \⹀,⹀⹀\ *n* : the behavior or practice of a timeserver ⟨discourages energy and initiative in public office, and encourages ~ —L.K.Caldwell⟩
²**timeserving** \"\ *adj* : marked by or revealing a lack of independence or integrity : TEMPORIZING ⟨a mean, ~ little man, grovelling odiously before the wealthy people in the district —Peter Forster⟩ ⟨we cannot afford a ~ tameness —*Times Lit. Supp.*⟩ — **time-serv-ing-ness** *n* -ES
time sheet *n* **1** : a sheet for recording the time of arrival and departure of workers and for recording the amount of time spent on each job **2** : a sheet for summarizing hours worked by each worker during a pay period
time-shift \⹀,⹀⹀\ *n* : a narrative method (as in a novel) that shifts back and forth in time from past to present instead of proceeding in strict chronological sequence
time sight *n* **1** : a set of observations for the determination of time that are usu. made with a transit instrument **2** : an observation by sextant of the altitude of a heavenly body to determine longitude by comparing the local time with Greenwich time
time signal *n* : a signal indicating an exact instant of time that is sent by telegraph or radio to regulate timepieces
time signature *n* **1** : a fraction that has a denominator indicating the kind of note (as a quarter note) taken as the time unit for the beat and a numerator indicating the number of these to the measure and that is placed at the beginning of a musical composition, movement, or section just after the key signature or at any point at which the meter changes to indicate the meter **2** : a symbol used to indicate the meter of a musical composition — compare ³C 1
time spirit *n* [trans. of G *zeitgeist*] : ZEITGEIST
time stamp *n* : a clock-actuated device for recording time; *specif* : one for recording the date and time of day that letters or papers are received or sent out
time-stratigraphic \⹀,⹀⹀,⹀⹀\ *adj* : of, relating to, or constituting rocks deposited during a specified time regardless of their composition, fossil content, or conditions of origin
time study *n* : TIME AND MOTION STUDY
time switch *n* : an electric switch that automatically operates at a set time
timetable \⹀,⹀⹀\ *n* **1** : a printed table showing times of departure and arrival (as of trains, buses, airplanes) from and at scheduled stopping points between two terminuses **2 a** : a schedule or plan listing or indicating the sequence in which things are to occur or be done and often the approximate or exact time of each ⟨a ~ that pinned the start and finish of each of this year's 133 events down to the minute —*Newsweek*⟩ ⟨determined resistance upset the ~ which had been set for the operation —H.L.Merillat⟩ **3** : a table showing the time value or relative duration of the various musical notes
time thrust *n* : a counterattack in fencing executed against and arriving in advance of the opponent's attack — compare STOP THRUST
time ticket *n* : TIME CARD 2
time train *n* : a train of wheels that drives the balance and escapement of a timepiece
time value *n* **1 a** : value measured by hours of labor **b** : value due to the date of receipt of goods or maturity of obligations **2** : the relative duration esp. of a musical note, tone, or rest
timework \⹀,⹀⹀\ *n* : work paid for at a standard rate for the hour or day — compare PIECEWORK
timeworker \⹀,⹀⹀\ *n* : a worker engaged on timework
timeworn \⹀,⹀⹀\ *adj* **1** : worn or impaired by time ⟨its graceful, ~ residences of the plantation type —*Amer. Guide Series: Texas*⟩ **2 a** : AGE-OLD, ANCIENT ⟨based on ~ procedures and the collocated experience of the ages —F.C.Neff⟩ **b** : HACKNEYED, STALE ⟨a ~ expression⟩
time zone *n* : one of 24 longitudinal zones into which the world has been divided for establishing a regular sequence of time changes, which are each 15 degrees wide, and which each keep standard time throughout its area the time of its central meridian except where variations to maintain national or local uniformity are necessary
tim-id \¹timəd\ *adj, usu* -ER/-EST [L *timidus*, fr. *timēre* to be afraid, fear] **1** : lacking in courage or self-confidence : easily frightened or overawed ⟨~, silent, crouching under oppression —J.R.Green⟩ ⟨a ~ person would rather remain miserable than do anything unusual —Bertrand Russell⟩ **2 a** : marked by or revealing a lack of boldness or determination ⟨a ~ policy⟩ ⟨a ~ look⟩ ⟨their ~ love of established ways —V.L. Parrington⟩ **b** : HESITANT, TENTATIVE ⟨this intellectual life was ~, cautious and derivative —Van Wyck Brooks ⟨the

darkness is broken by the ~ flare of a lamp or a candle —Lewis Mumford⟩
syn TIMOROUS: TIMID may stress lack of courage and venturesomeness and a tendency to cling to the safe, accustomed, undemonstrative, and unobtrusive ⟨meek, humble, *timid* persons, who accept things as they are, who tread in beaten paths, who are easily persuaded, who are cautious, prudent, and submissive —A.C.Benson⟩ ⟨in comparison with their fearlessness, their bold drawing, their dashing conception, their passion and action . . . how *timid* and conventional seemed his own friends —Edgar Johnson⟩ TIMOROUS may imply stronger influence of or domination by apprehension, fear, or terror causing one to shrink from independence or decision ⟨must have been a powerful, perhaps an insane, impulsion which drove the *timorous*, inconclusive Jesse, with his intuitive horror of guns, to send a bullet into his brain —S.H.Adams⟩ ⟨grew *timorous* and dejected, apprehending themselves to be haunted and possessed with vengeful spirits, on account of human blood that had been undeservedly spilt in this old town —William Bartram⟩

ti·mid·i·ty \tə'midəd·ē, -idətē, -i\ *n* -ES [L *timiditat-, timiditas*, fr. *timidus* timid + *-itat-, -itas* -ity] **:** the quality or state of being timid ⟨the animals have become so accustomed to motor traffic that they have quite lost their natural ~ —James Stevenson-Hamilton⟩ ⟨the ~ and conformity of the present day —C.V.Woodward⟩

tim·id·ly *adv* **:** in a timid manner

tim·id·ness *n* -ES [*timid* + *-ness*] **:** TIMIDITY

timing *n* -s [fr. gerund of ²*time*] **1 :** selection for maximum effect of the precise moment for beginning or doing something ⟨his bad luck or aim or ~ or whatever it was that caused him inevitably to be low man —Hamilton Basso⟩ ⟨the proper ~ of the operation in reference to the course of the disease —*Jour. Amer. Med. Assoc.*⟩: as **a :** the art or practice of regulating tempo (as in musical performance, utterance, dramatic action) so as to heighten the effectiveness of various moments by emphasis and of the whole by appropriate variations; *also* **:** the effect so produced ⟨often have to experiment with a comic scene, cutting it, changing its ~, before they can see how it works —*College English*⟩ **b :** the regulating of the speed of a motion, stroke, or blow so as to cause it to reach its maximum at the correct moment; *also* **:** the coordination of movements of body, arms, and hands to produce such effect **c :** coordination between a boxer's blows and the opportunities offered for attack **2 :** observation and recording of the elapsed time of an act, action, or process often by means of a stopwatch

timing gears *n pl* **:** the gear train with a two to one reduction through which the crankshaft drives the camshaft and thus controls valve timing in a four-stroke cycle internal-combustion engine

timing screw *n* **:** any of the adjustable screws in the rim of a watch balance that are used in timing the watch

timing valve *n* **:** an adjustable valve in a gas engine with hot tube ignition that automatically opens to permit a portion of the compressed explosive mixture to enter the ignition tube and so cause ignition at any desired point of the stroke — compare TIMER 1c

timing washer *n* **:** a small thin ring of metal (as gold or platinum) placed under the balance screws of a watch to slow the vibration period of the balance or to help poise it

ti·mis·ka·ming \tə'miskəmiŋ\ *adj, usu cap* [fr. *Timiskaming*, lake & district of southeast Ontario, Canada] **:** of or relating to a division of the Archeozoic — see GEOLOGIC TIME table

ti·mi·soa·ra \¦tēmə'shə¦wärə, ¦tim-, -¦shwä-\ *adj, usu cap* [fr. *Timişoara*, city of southwest Romania] **:** of or from the city of Timisoara, Romania **:** of the kind or style prevalent in Timisoara

tim·ist \'tīməst\ *n* -s [¹*time* + *-ist*] **:** one that keeps time or is concerned with time

tim·mer \'timər\ *chiefly Scot var of* TIMBER

timne *usu cap, var of* TEMNE

ti·moc·ra·cy \tī'mäkrəsē\ *n* -ES [MF *tymocracie*, fr. ML *timocratia*, fr. Gk *timokratia* polity based on honor or wealth, fr. *timē* price, value, honor + *-kratia* -cracy — more at PAIN] **1** *Aristotelianism* **:** a stage of political development in which political and civil honors are distributed according to wealth **2** [Gk *timokratia*] *Platonism* **:** a stage of political development in which love of honor or glory is the ruling principle

ti·mo·crat·ic \¦tīmə¦krad·ik\ *or* **ti·mo·crat·i·cal** \-d·əkəl\ *adj* [*timocratic* fr. Gk *timokratikos*, fr. *timokratia* timocracy + *-ikos* -ic; *timocratical* fr. Gk *timokratikos* + E *-al*] **:** of, relating to, or representative of timocracy

timo·neer \¦timə¦ni(ə)r, ¦tim-\ *n* -s [F *timonier*, fr. MF, fr. *timon* tiller, helm (fr. — assumed — VL *timon-, timo*, alter. of L *temon-, temo* shaft of a wagon, beam of a plow, pole) + *-ier* -ary] **:** HELMSMAN ⟨teach him the trade of a ~ —W.S.Gilbert⟩

ti·mon·ism \'tīmə,nizəm\ *n* -s *usu cap* [*Timon*, 5th cent. B.C. Athenian misanthrope + E *-ism*] **:** MISANTHROPY ⟨expressive of a period of *Timonism* and despair in the author's life —*Times Lit. Supp.*⟩

tim·o·rese \¦timə¦rēz, -ēs\ *n, pl* **timorese** *cap* [*Timor*, island in southern Malay archipelago + E *-ese*] **:** a native or inhabitant of the island of Timor

timo·ro·so \¦timə'rō(,)sō, ¦tēm-, -rō(,)zō\ *adj (or adv)* [It, fr. ML *timorosus*] **:** HESITATING, TIMID — used as a direction in music

tim·o·rous \'tim(ə)rəs\ *adj* [ME, fr. MF *temoros, timoureus*, fr. ML *timorosus*, fr. L *timor* fear (fr. *timēre* to be afraid, fear) + *-osus* -ous] **1 a :** experiencing or showing fear or apprehension **:** AFRAID ⟨the tunny is ~ when coming in to spawn —Alan Villiers⟩ — sometimes used with *of* ⟨one is ~ of change, another dissatisfied with the present —B.N.Cardozo⟩ ⟨is occasionally unduly ~ of these rule-givers —Thomas Pyles⟩ **b :** fearful by nature or character **:** TIMID ⟨a ~ incompetent who was lucky to have good men under him —W.A.Swanberg⟩ **2 :** marked by or expressing timidity ⟨spoke little, and generally in a ~ tone, as though silence had been enjoined —Arnold Bennett⟩ **syn** see TIMID

tim·o·rous·ly *adv* **:** in a timorous manner

tim·o·rous·ness *n* -ES **:** the quality or state of being timorous

tim·or·some \'timə(r)səm\ *adj* [fr. *timorous*, after such pairs as E *cumbrous: cumbersome*] *chiefly dial* **:** TIMOROUS

ti·mo·te \tə'mōd·ē\ *n, pl* **timote** *or* **timotes** *usu cap* **1 a :** an Indian people or peoples of western Venezuela **b :** a member of such people **2 :** the language of the Timote people

tim·o·thy \'timəthē, -thi\ *or* **timothy grass** *n* -ES [prob. after *Timothy* Hanson, 18th cent. Am. farmer said to have introduced it from New England to the southern States] **:** a European grass (*Phleum pratense*) with long cylindrical spikes that is grown in northern U. S. and in Europe for hay — called also *herd's-grass*

timpan *var of* TYMPAN

tim·pa·ni \'timpə(,)nē, -,ni\ *n pl but sometimes sing in constr* [It, pl. of *timpano* kettledrum, fr. L *tympanum* drum — more at TYMPANUM] **:** a set of usu. two or three kettledrums played by one performer in an orchestra or band

tim·pa·nist \'timpənəst\ *n* -s [*timpani* + *-ist*] **:** one who plays the kettledrums **:** TYMPANIST

tim·u·cua \¦timə'küə\ *n, pl* **timucua** *or* **timucuas** *usu cap* **1 a :** a possibly Muskogean people of central and northeastern Florida **b :** a member of such people **2 :** the language of the Timucua people

tim·u·cu·an \-üən\ *n, pl* **timucuan** *or* **timucuans** *usu cap* [*Timucua* + *-an*] **1 :** TIMUCUA 1 **2 :** a tentative language family comprising only the Timucua language and perhaps related to Muskogean

tim–whiskey \'tim,=\ *n* [*tim* (of unknown origin) + *whiskey*] **:** WHISKEY

¹**tin** \'tin\ *n* -s [ME, fr. OE; akin to OHG *zin* tin, ON *tin*] **1 :** a soft faintly bluish white lustrous low-melting metallic element that in this beta form exists as tetragonal crystals and is malleable and ductile at ordinary temperatures but changes gradually at low temperatures to a powdery gray cubic allotropic alpha form, that is bivalent and tetravalent in its compounds and is not oxidized by moist air, that occurs principally in the form of the dioxide cassiterite and various sulfides (as stannite), that is extracted by roasting and smelting with carbon, and that is used chiefly as a protective coating (as for steel and copper), in tinfoil, in collapsible tubes, and in soft solders, bronze, pewter, babbitt metals, type metals, and casting and other alloys — symbol *Sn;* see BLOCK TIN, FUSIBLE METAL, TERNE, TIN PEST, TINPLATE; ELEMENT table **2 :** a box, can, pan, or other vessel made of tinplate: **a :** any of various open tinplate sheets or pans used chiefly for baking ⟨drop the cookies on a greased ~⟩ ⟨pour the batter into a cake ~⟩ **b** *chiefly Brit* (1) **:** a vacuum-sealed can holding canned food ⟨a ~ of salmon⟩ ⟨open a ~ of tomatoes⟩ (2) **:** a tinplate container with cover or lid used for packaging biscuits, crackers, sweets, or tobacco **3 :** thin plates of iron or steel covered with tin **:** TINPLATE **4** *chiefly Brit* **:** CASH, MONEY ⟨pray them to advance the requisite ~ for ransom —H.C.Bunner⟩

²**tin** \"\ *adj* **1 :** of, relating to, or consisting of tin **2 :** of base or inferior material **:** SPURIOUS ⟨other narrow-minded little ~ gods —*N.Y. Times*⟩ ⟨the bright ~ divinity of the happy ending —Clifton Fadiman⟩

³**tin** \"\ *vt* **tinned; tinned; tinning; tins** [ME *tinnen*, fr. *tin*] **1 a :** to cover, coat, or plate (something) with tin **b :** to cover (as a soldering iron or the back of an electrotype shell) with solder or a tin alloy **2** *chiefly Brit* **:** to put up or pack in tins **:** CAN ⟨cannery workers ~ asparagus —*Nat'l Geographic*⟩ ⟨stopped to have lunch — tea and *tinned* food —Russell Hill⟩

⁴**tin** \"\ *n, pl* **tin** *or* **tins** *usu cap* **1 :** a people of the lower mountains of northeastern Thailand related to the Kha of Vietnam — called also *Khatin* **2 :** a member of the Tin people

ti·na·ja \tə'nä(,)hä\ *n* -s [Sp, aug. of *tina* jar, fr. L, wine jar] **1 :** a large porous water jar for cooling water by evaporation **2** *Southwest* **:** WATER POCKET, POTHOLE

ti·nam·i·dae \tə'namə,dē\ *n pl, cap* [NL, fr. *Tinamus*, type genus (fr. F *tinamou*) + *-idae*] **:** a family of large predominantly terrestrial birds (order Tinamiformes) comprising the tinamous

tin·a·mi·for·mes \,tinəmə'fȯr(,)mēz, tə,nam-\ *n pl, cap* [NL, fr. *Tinamus* + *-iformes*] **:** an order of birds (superorder Neognathae) coextensive with the family Tinamidae

tin·a·mine \'tinə,mīn, -,mən\ *adj* [*tinamou* + *-ine*] **:** of or relating to the tinamous

tin·a·mou \'tinə,mü\ *n* -s [F, fr. Galibi *tinamu*] **:** any of numerous birds that constitute the family Tinamidae, resemble gallinaceous birds in habits but are related to the ratite birds esp. in the structure of the palate though the sternum is deeply keeled, have a rudimentary tail without a pygostyle, and produce eggs with a peculiar enameled surface

ti·na process \¦tēnə-\ *n* [Sp *tina* jar, tub] **:** a process for amalgamation of silver ores in tubs

tin·cal \'tiŋkəl; 'tiŋ,kal, -käl, 'tin,k-\ *n* -s [Malay *tingkal*] **:** a mineral $Na_2B_4O_7.10H_2O$ consisting of a native borax formerly imported from Tibet and once the chief source of boric compounds

tin·cal·co·nite \tin'kalkə,nīt, tiŋ'k-\ *n* -s [*tincal* + Gk *konia* ashes, dust + E *-ite* — more at INCINERATE] **:** a mineral $Na_2B_4O_7.5H_2O$ consisting of sodium borate pentahydrate that is one of the principal ore minerals of borax and boron compounds — compare KERNITE

tin can *n* **1 :** a can or cup made of tin or similar metal **2** *slang* **:** DESTROYER 2

tin·chel \'tiŋkəl, 'tinkəl\ *n* -s [ScGael *timchioll* circuit, compass] *Scot* **:** a ring formed by hunters to drive or enclose deer

tin chloride *n* **:** a chloride of tin: as **a :** STANNIC CHLORIDE **b :** STANNOUS CHLORIDE

tinclad \'=,=\ *n* -s [²*tin* + *clad* (as in ²*ironclad*)] **:** a gunboat protected with light armor

tin cry *n* **:** the peculiar creaking noise made when a bar of tin is bent by twinning of the metal crystals

tin crystals *n pl but usu sing in constr* **:** stannous chloride dihydrate $SnCl_2.2H_2O$ used formerly as a mordant — called also *tin salt*

¹**tinct** \'tiŋ(k)t\ *adj* [L *tinctus*, past part. of *tingere* to tinge — more at TINGE] **:** TINGED, TINTED ⟨the blue in black, the green in gray is ~ —Edmund Spenser⟩

²**tinct** \"\ *n* -s [L *tinctus*, past part. of *tingere*] **:** TINCTURE, TINGE ⟨in the color or ~ lies the main difference between Irish and American glass —Dorothy Daniel⟩ ⟨new leaf and shadowy ~ —Wallace Stevens⟩

tinct *abbr* tincture

tinc·tion \'tiŋ(k)shən\ *n* -s [LL *tinction-, tinctio* act of dipping, fr. L *tinctus* (past part.) + *-ion-, -io* -ion] **:** the act or process of staining or dyeing; *also* **:** coloring matter

tinc·to·ri·al \(')tiŋk¦tōrēəl\ *adj* [L *tinctorius* of or relating to dipping (fr. *tinctus*, past part. + *-orius* -ory) + E *-al*] **:** of or relating to colors or to dyeing or staining **:** imparting a color ⟨has the greatest opacity and ~ strength of all white pigments —Andries Voet⟩ — **tinc·to·ri·al·ly** \-ēəlē\ *adv*

¹**tinc·ture** \'tiŋ(k)chə(r), -)sh-\ *n* -s [ME, fr. L *tinctura* act or instance of dyeing or tinging, fr. *tinctus* (past part. of *tingere* to tinge) + *-ura* -ure — more at TINGE] **1 a :** a substance that colors, dyes, or stains **:** PIGMENT, STAIN **b :** a color conveyed by or assumed from such a substance **:** HUE, TINT ⟨one dye of that ~ covered his clothes —Thomas Hardy⟩ ⟨all the ~s of the rainbow⟩ **2 a :** a characteristic or quality with which a person or thing is imbued or modified **:** TINGE, CAST ⟨both young men were Whigs of a radical ~ —*Current History*⟩ ⟨Protestantism has . . . a deep ~ of empiricism —A.N.Wilder⟩ **b :** a slight admixture or smattering of something **:** TOUCH, TRACE ⟨his followers were not altogether without a ~ of soldiership —T.B.Macaulay⟩ ⟨what he said had plausibility and perhaps a ~ of sincerity —Francis Hackett⟩ ⟨with a ~ of modern science added to . . . backwoods Calvinism —Carl Van Doren⟩ **3** *obs* **a :** an immaterial quintessential active alchemical principle capable of causing material and spiritual transmutations **b :** a chemical principle esp. when obtained by extraction; *also* **:** EXTRACT **4 :** a heraldic metal, color, or fur — usu. used in pl. ⟨the ~s of the armorial coat are carefully described⟩ **5 :** a solution of a medicinal substance (as a plant principle) in an alcoholic or hydroalcoholic menstruum or in a mixture of alcohol and ether

²**tincture** \"\ *vt* **tinctured; tinctured; tincturing** \-chəriŋ, -sh(ə)riŋ\ **tinctures 1 :** to tint or stain with a color **:** TINGE ⟨the islands were . . . so infused with the hues of the *tinctured* clouds —H.M.Tomlinson⟩ ⟨the blossom *tinctured* with deep green —*Parke-Bernet Galleries Cat.*⟩ **2 a :** to infuse or instill a physical property or entity in **:** IMPREGNATE ⟨the heavy traffic ~s the air with carbon monoxide⟩ ⟨the cytoplasm . . . is so *tinctured* by the products of the bacilli contained in it —*Amer. Jour. of Pathology*⟩ **b :** to imbue with a character or quality **:** AFFECT ⟨was not sure envy did not ~ his disdain —Waldo Frank⟩ ⟨*tinctured* political life with a similar monotony —Carleton Beals⟩ ⟨hardly ever spoke a sentence that was not *tinctured* . . . with his delightful and rare personality —Osbert Sitwell⟩

tincture press *n* **:** a cylindrical press used to express the menstruum adhering to the particles of a drug after extraction

tind \'tin(d), 'tīn\ *vb* -ED/-ING/-S [ME *tinden*, fr. (assumed) OE *tyndan;* akin to OE *tendan* to kindle — more at TINDER] *vt, dial Eng* **:** to set on fire **:** KINDLE, IGNITE ~ *vi, dial Eng* **:** to catch fire or become inflamed **:** BURN

tin·dal \'tindᵊl\ *n* -s [Hindi *ṭandail*] **:** a petty officer or supervisor of lascars or Indian workmen

tin·da·lo \'tində,lō\ *n* -s [Tag *tindalō*] **1 :** a timber tree (*Pahudia rhomboidea*) of the family Leguminosae of the Philippines having a hard valuable wood like that of the ipil **2 :** the wood of the tindalo

tin·der \'tində(r)\ *n* -s [ME, fr. OE *tynder, tyndre;* akin to OHG *zuntra* tinder, ON *tundr;* akin to OE *tendan* to kindle, OHG *zunten*, ON *tendra*, Goth *tandjan* to kindle, *tundnan* to burn] **1 :** an inflammable substance that readily takes spark or fire and is adaptable for use as kindling ⟨the woods are dry as ~⟩ — see ³PUNK **2 :** something that serves to incite, inflame, or spread abroad a movement, idea, or development ⟨men who are spiritually unfulfilled . . . are prey for the demagogue, ~ for the incendiary —C.T.Lanham⟩ ⟨the spark of your idea will . . . spread through the fresh ~ of new generations —L.J.Halle⟩ ⟨the human ~ that he writes about is best suited to kindle . . . wild mob rule —*Atlantic*⟩

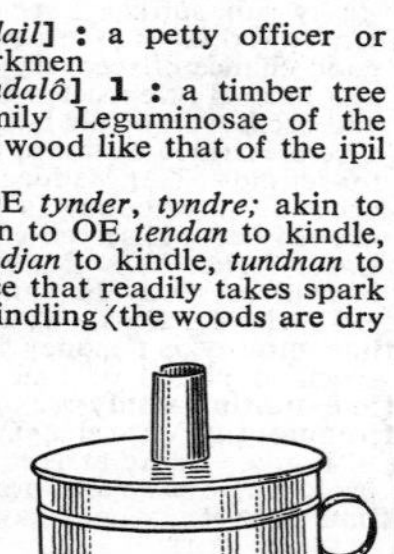

tinderbox 1

tinderbox \'==,=\ *n* **1 a :** a metal box for holding tinder and usu. a flint and steel for striking a spark **b :** an object (as a building) or place containing highly inflammable material ⟨the old tenements are ~*es* ready to go up in flame⟩ ⟨region 5 of the U. S. forest service is America's touchiest ~ —Frank Cameron⟩ **2 :** a person or thing containing inflammatory or explosive potentialities esp. for strife or conflict ⟨the whole Caribbean region was a ~; only a spark was needed to set it off —H.B.Murkland⟩ ⟨events that were potentially the ~ of World War III —*Saturday Rev.*⟩

tinder fungus *n* **:** a fungus that is a source of punk; *esp* **:** a destructive pore fungus (*Fomes fomentarius*) that attacks the beech, elm, and various fruit trees and is used in making tinder and a pliant feltlike material

tin·dery \'tind(ə)rē, -ri\ *adj* **:** resembling tinder **:** highly inflammable or inflammatory ⟨covered with dry, ~ sea moss —Herman Melville⟩ ⟨described the . . . drought with a ~ phrase capable of kindling this page —*Nat'l Geographic*⟩ ⟨ahead in the ~ future —*Time*⟩

tin dichloride *n* **:** STANNOUS CHLORIDE

tin dioxide *n* **:** STANNIC OXIDE

¹**tine** \'tīn, 'tin\ *vt* [ME *tinen*, fr. OE *tȳnan;* akin to OE *tūn* enclosure, fence, village, town — more at TOWN] *dial Eng* **:** CLOSE, SHUT, ENCLOSE

²**tine** \'tīn\ *n* -s [ME *tind*, fr. OE; akin to OHG *zint* point, spike, tine, ON *tindr* and prob. to OHG *zinna* pinnacle] **1 :** one of a set of slender pointed projecting parts of an implement or a weapon **2 :** a pointed branch of a deer's antlers ⟨prongs are not indicative of age . . . but the number of ~s on the antlers —*Wyo. Wild Life*⟩

³**tine** \'tīn\ *vb* **tined** \'tīnd\ *or* **tint** \'tint\ **tined** *or* **tint; tining; tines** [ME *tinen, tynen*, of Scand origin; akin to ON *týna* to lose, destroy; akin to ON *tjōn* injury — more at TEEN] *vt, dial Brit* **:** LOSE, WASTE ~ *vi, dial Brit* **:** to become lost **:** PERISH

⁴**tine** \"\ *n* -s [perh. fr. ³*tine;* fr. the trouble or damage it causes] *dial Eng* **:** any of various plants (as vetches) having twining or clasping tendrils

tin·ea \'tinēə\ *n* [ME, fr. ML, fr. L, worm, moth] **1** -s **:** any of several fungous diseases of the skin of man and domestic animals **:** RINGWORM **2** *cap* [NL, fr. L, worm, moth] **:** the type genus of the family Tineidae

ti·nea bar·bae \,tinēə'bär,bē\ *n* [NL, tinea of the beard] **:** BARBER'S ITCH

ti·nea ca·pi·tis \-'kapəd·əs\ *n* [LL, lit., worm of the head] **:** an infection of the scalp caused by fungi of the genera *Trichophyton* and *Microsporum* and characterized by scaly patches penetrated by a few dry brittle hairs

ti·nea cor·po·ris \-'kȯ(r)pərəs\ *n* [NL, tinea of the body] **:** a fungous infection involving parts of the body not covered with hair

ti·nea cru·ris \-'krürəs\ *n* [NL, crural tinea] **:** a fungous infection involving the groin, perineum, and the perianal region

tin·e·al \'tinēəl\ *adj* **:** of, relating to, or being tinea ⟨a ~ rash⟩

ti·nea pe·dis \,tinēə'pedəs\ *n* [NL, tinea of the foot] **:** ATHLETE'S FOOT

tin ear *n* **1 :** CAULIFLOWER EAR **2 :** a deafened or insensitive ear ⟨motorists . . . have developed a glass eye and a *tin ear* for traffic safety programs —*Springfield (Mass.) Union*⟩ ⟨only at his best does he transcend a *tin ear* and color blindness —George Mayberry⟩

ti·nea ton·su·rans \,tinēə,tän'sürənz, -,ranz\ *n* [NL, fr. ML *tinea* + NL *tonsurans* (specific epithet of the parasitic fungus *Trichophyton tonsurans*), pres. part. of *tonsurare* to shear, clip, fr. ML, fr. L *tonsura* act of shearing, tonsure — more at TONSURE] **:** tinea capitis involving any portion of the hairy parts of domestic animals

tined \'tīnd\ *adj* [²*tine* + *-ed*] **:** having or furnished with tines

¹**tin·e·id** \'tinēəd\ *adj* [NL *Tineidae*] **:** of or relating to the Tineidae

²**tineid** \"\ *n* -s **:** a moth of the family Tineidae

ti·ne·idae \tə'nēə,dē\ *n pl, cap* [NL, fr. *Tinea*, type genus + *-idae*] **:** a family of small usu. dully colored moths (superfamily Tineoidea) comprising the common clothes moths and related insects and in former classifications including all or most of the Microlepidoptera

tin·e·ina \,tinē'īnə, -ē'ēnə\ *n pl, cap* [NL, fr. *Tinea* + *-ina*] *in some esp former classifications* **:** a group of small moths variously ranked and nearly coextensive with the modern superfamily Tineoidea — **tin·e·ine** \'tinē,īn, -ē,ēn\ *adj*

tin·e·oid \'tinē,ȯid\ *adj* [NL *Tineoidea*] **:** of or relating to the Tineoidea

²**tineoid** \"\ *n* -s **:** a moth of the superfamily Tineoidea

tin·e·oi·dea \,tinē'ȯidēə\ *n pl, cap* [NL, fr. *Tinea* + *-oidea*] **:** a superfamily of small moths comprising the majority of the Microlepidoptera (as the clothes moths, carpet moths, leaf miners) and having narrow simply veined wings broadly fringed with hairs

ti·ne·o·la \tə'nēələ, ,tinē'ōlə\ *n* [NL, fr. LL, small worm, small moth, dim. of L *tinea*] **1** *cap* **:** a genus of clothes moths including the webbing clothes moth **2** -s **:** any moth of the genus *Tineola; esp* **:** WEBBING CLOTHES MOTH

tines *pl of* TINE, *pres 3d sing of* TINE

tin fish *n, slang* **:** TORPEDO

tinfoil \'=,=\ *sometimes* '='=\ *n* [ME, fr. ²*tin* + *foil*] **1 :** a thin metal sheeting now usu. made of aluminum or tin-lead alloy **2 a :** FOIL 4a **b :** SILVER PAPER 2

¹**ting** \'tiŋ\ *vb* -ED/-ING/-S [ME *tingen*, of imit. origin] *vt* **:** to cause (as a bell) to make a ting ~ *vi* **:** to sound with or make a ting

²**ting** \"\ *n* -s **:** a high-pitched sound (as made by a light stroke on a small bell) ⟨the ~ of the bell at . . . table —Nathaniel Burt⟩

³**ting** *var of* THING

⁴**ting** \'diŋ\ *n* -s [Chin (Pek) *ting*³] **:** an ancient Chinese ceremonial vessel consisting of a deep bowl with usu. two handles supported on three legs

ting–a–ling \¦tiŋə¦liŋ\ *n* -s [imit.] **:** the sound of a tinkling bell

¹**tinge** \'tinj\ *vb* **tinged; tinged; tingeing** *or* **tinging; tinges** [ME *tingen*, fr. L *tingere* to dip, moisten, tinge; akin to Gk *tengein* to wet, moisten, OHG *dunkōn, thunkōn* to dip] *vt* **1 a :** to color with a slight shade or stain **:** TINT ⟨kill plants that . . . will ~ the edge of the melting snow with early green —Alan Fraser⟩ ⟨the scarlet glare of the flames *tinged* her flesh with the color of rusty iron —Ellen Glasgow⟩ ⟨the sun . . . ~*ing* with colors of the rainbow the sandy beach —A.C. Whitehead⟩ **b :** to affect or modify with a slight odor or taste ⟨the roses ~ the air with their fragrance⟩ **2 :** to affect, modify, or influence in character, tone, or sensibility ⟨social relationships . . . peculiarly *tinged* by this postulate of intrinsic equality —Theodore Bienenstok⟩ ⟨a vague exasperation ~s his world view —Selig Harrison⟩ ⟨a darkling Renaissance look that might ~ mischief with cruelty —Claudia Cassidy⟩ ⟨the same deep respect *tinged* . . . with love and humor instead of hatred and fear —Nancy Mitford⟩ ~ *vi* **:** to undergo change in color or aspect ⟨day was breaking, the east was ~*ing* with strange fires —R.L.Stevenson⟩

²**tinge** \"\ *n* -s **1 :** a slight or modifying shade or color **:** TINT ⟨a faint ~ of color crept into her yellow face —J.C. Snaith⟩ ⟨houses . . . in the ~ of unpainted adobe —*Amer. Guide Series: Texas*⟩ ⟨the trees . . . beginning to take on here and there the ~s of autumn —R.H.Sampson⟩ **2 :** an affective or modifying property or influence taken from or imparted by something **:** CAST, TOUCH ⟨a slightly Celtic ~ in her diction —Mary Deasy⟩ ⟨eyes that . . . had some ~ of the oriental —Edmund Wilson⟩ ⟨half-baked eloquence without even a ~ of effective insight —H.J.Laski⟩ ⟨a ~ of exasperation in her tone —Ellen Glasgow⟩ ⟨his music assumed . . . a wild ~ —William Black⟩ ⟨almost every personal tragedy had a ~ of mild absurdity —Peter Quennell⟩ **3 :** a yellow discoloration of cotton lint by the plant juices resulting from field exposure of mature cotton after frost **syn** see COLOR

tin·gent \'tinjənt\ *adj* [L *tingent-, tingens*, pres. part. of *tingere* to tinge] *archaic* **:** having the power to tinge **:** COLORING

ting·gi·an *also* **tin·gui·an** \¦tiŋgē¦än\ *n, pl* **tinggian** *or* **tinggians** *also* **tinguian** *or* **tinguians** *usu cap* **1 a :** a predominantly pagan people inhabiting western Luzon, Philippines **b :** a member of such people **2 :** the Austronesian language of the Tinggian people

¹**tin·gid** \'tinjəd\ *adj* [NL *Tingidae*] **:** of or relating to the Tingidae

²**tingid** \"\ *n* -s **:** a bug of the family Tingidae **:** LACE BUG

tin·gi·dae \'tinjə,dē\ *n pl, cap* [NL, fr. *Tingis*, type genus (of unknown origin) + *-idae*] **:** a family of bugs (order Hemiptera) containing the lace bugs

tin·git·i·dae \tin'jid·ə,dē\ [NL, fr. *Tingit-, Tingis*, genus of lace bugs + *-idae*] *syn of* TINGIDAE

tin glaze *n* **:** an opaque glaze made of an oxide of tin or tin ashes and used on pottery

tin–glaze \'⸗,⸗\ *vt* **:** to coat (pottery) with a tin glaze

¹tin·gle \'tiŋgəl\ *n* -s [ME] **1 :** a small nail **:** TACK **2 :** a patch on a boat constructed to cover a hole or leak by overlapping

²tingle \"\ *vb* **tingled; tingled; tingling** \-g(ə)liŋ\ **tingles** [ME *tinglen*, alter. of *tinklen* to tinkle — more at TINKLE] *vi* **1 a :** to experience or feel a ringing, stinging, prickling, or thrilling sensation ⟨a great blast of his boat's whistle . . . made our ears ~ —R.P.Warren⟩ ⟨the blister on his right foot began to ~ —Fred Majdalany⟩ ⟨music that made . . . blood ~ —Sherwood Anderson⟩ ⟨like to weep, to laugh, to ~ with excitement, admiration, or fear —Rose Macaulay⟩ **b :** to cause such a sensation ⟨the trumpets ~ in his ears⟩ **2 :** to make a repeated light ringing or tinkling sound **:** TINKLE ⟨bells began to ~ above us —Ernest Beaglehole⟩ ⟨rain *tingled* steadily on the roof —Graham Greene⟩ ~ *vt* **1 :** to cause a thrilling, stinging, or pricking sensation in **:** STIR, STIMULATE ⟨an eagerness *tingled* him when he saw what he wanted —Alan Kapelner⟩ ⟨each is guaranteed . . . to ~ the brain —*advt*⟩ **2 :** to cause (a bell) to ring lightly **:** TINKLE

³tingle \"\ *n* -s **1 :** a tinkling sound **:** TINGLING **2 :** a tingling sensation or condition ⟨gave me a wincing ~ to see the deep marks of the murderously sharp talons —R.T.Bird⟩ ⟨feel the ~ of the hot blood of resentment mounting to our cheeks —B.N.Cardozo⟩ ⟨felt a ~ of excitement —Earle Birney⟩ ⟨was filled with a ~ of pleasure —Louis Auchincloss⟩

tingle–tingle \'tiŋgəl'tiŋgəl\ *n* [fr. native name in western Australia] **:** STRINGYBARK

tin·gling·ly *adv* **1 :** in a manner that causes one to tingle ⟨his book is . . . ~ provocative —Donald Harrington⟩ **2 :** with tingling ⟨~ conscious of it —Christine Weston⟩

tin·gly \'tiŋ(g)(ə)lē, -li\ *adj* **:** tingling or causing tingling

tings *pres 3d sing of* TING, *pl of* TING

ting·tang \'tiŋ,taŋ\ *n* [redupl. of ²*ting*] **:** the alternating sound of two differently toned bells esp. in a clock that sounds the quarter and half hours on only two bells

tin hat *n* **:** a metal hat or helmet worn (as by a soldier or industrial worker) for protection

tinhorn \'⸗,⸗\ *n* [²*tin* + *horn*] **:** a pretentious or boastful person or gambler having little money, power, or ability ⟨the gambling places were . . . swarming with ~s . . . dockhands, traveling men —H.L.Davis⟩ ⟨those ~s that spend all they got on dress suits and haven't got a decent suit of underwear to their name —Sinclair Lewis⟩

tinier *comparative of* TINY

tinies *pl of* TINY

tiniest *superlative of* TINY

tin·i·kling \,tinə'kliŋ\ *n* -s [Tag, fr. *tikling* tikling] **:** BAMBOO DANCE

ti·ni·ly \'tīn°lē, -nəl|, |ī\ *adv* **:** in the manner or condition of something tiny ⟨a miniature worm of train rolled ~ along the embankment —Bruce Marshall⟩

ti·ni·ness \'tīnēnəs, -īnin-\ *n* -ES **:** the quality or state of being tiny

tining *pres part of* TINE

¹tink \'tiŋk\ *vi* -ED/-ING/-S [ME *tinken*, of imit. origin] **:** to make a tinkling sound **:** TINKLE ⟨no roar came . . . and no bell ~*ed* —F.M.Ford⟩

²tink \"\ *n* -s **:** the sound of a light object striking against a resonant metal **:** PLINK ⟨the crackling of the fire, the ~ of sparks in the stovepipe —Dorothy Thomas⟩ ⟨the wind caught a ~ of harness rings and a jingle of spur rowels —Tom Lea⟩

¹tin·ker \'tiŋkə(r)\ *n* -s [ME *tinkere*, prob. fr. *tink* tinkle (of imit. origin) + *-ere* -er] **1 a :** a usu. itinerant repairman who mends kitchen or household utensils **b** *chiefly Irish* **:** GYPSY ⟨a story of wandering ~s and their struggle against the conventions of society —Paul Rotha⟩ **c :** an unskillful mender **:** BUNGLER **d :** TINNER 5 **2 :** TINKER MACKEREL **3 :** one that seeks to change, adjust, or improve often experimentally ⟨desire of every theatrical ~ and literary meddler —Richard Hanser⟩ ⟨social ~s —O.W.Holmes †1935⟩ ⟨all of us are . . . ~s of words —*Holiday*⟩

²tin·ker \"\ *vb* **tinkered; tinkered; tinkering** \-k(ə)riŋ\ **tinkers** *vi* **:** to work or act as or in the manner of a tinker; *esp* **:** to repair or adjust something in an unskilled or experimental manner ⟨the American likes to ~, and his passion for gadgets is notorious —H.S.Commager⟩ ⟨while he could read blueprints . . . he preferred to experiment and ~ —J.K. Galbraith⟩ ⟨even professionals have to ~ to make these sentences come out right —Milton Hall⟩ — often used with *with* or *at* ⟨spent . . . his spare time ~*ing* with machines —*Current Biog.*⟩ ⟨people ~ with their houses and keep adding to them —Mary H. Vorse⟩ ⟨the feeling they could also ~ with their social system and their psyches to reach a worldly paradise —J.D.Hart⟩ ⟨began to ~ at the wound in rather a clumsy way —Stephen Crane⟩ ⟨was always ~*ing* at verse —W.A. White⟩; sometimes used with *around* ⟨is not something that can be easily fixed merely by ~*ing* around with the curriculum —Norman Cousins⟩ ~ *vt* **:** to repair, adjust, or experiment with ⟨could expertly ~ pot, pan, or kettle —S.H.Adams⟩ ⟨they ~ everything, from decrepit hay rakes to railroad bridges —S.K.Farrington⟩ ⟨had ~*ed* their old car into shape —John Hermann⟩ — sometimes used with *up* ⟨~ up as many of the finished models as could be kept off the scrap heap —L.J.Carr⟩

tinkerbird \'⸗⸗,⸗\ *n* -s **:** any of various barbets with a harsh ringing note: as **a :** COPPERSMITH 2 **b :** any of several small African barbets of the genus *Pogoniulus*

tin·ker·er *n* -s **:** one that tinkers

tinker mackerel *n* **:** a small or young mackerel; *esp* **:** CHUB MACKEREL

tinker's curse *or* **tinker's cuss** *n* [prob. so called fr. the reputation of tinkers as being given to idle profanity] *Brit* **:** TINKER'S DAMN

tinker's damn *or* **tinker's dam** *n* [*tinker's damn* prob. so called fr. the tinkers' reputation for blasphemy; *tinker's dam* prob. by folk etymology fr. *tinker's damn;* prob. fr. the use by tinkers of a small dam of dough or mud to confine solder used in patching holes in pans] **:** something absolutely worthless ⟨people who didn't give a *tinker's damn* about poetry were . . . interested —James Blish⟩ ⟨pointed out a federal system isn't worth a *tinker's damn* —H.J.Laski⟩ ⟨is too involved . . . to make us care a *tinker's dam* what happens —R.B.Morris⟩

tin·ker's root \'tiŋkə(r)z-\ *or* **tinker's weed** *n* [*tinker* prob. fr. the name *Tinker*] **:** FEVERROOT

tin–kettling \(')tin'ket(°)liŋ\ *n* [fr. *tin kettle* + *-ing*] *Brit* **:** a mock serenade; *esp* **:** SHIVAREE

¹tin·kle \'tiŋkəl\ *vb* **tinkled; tinkled; tinkling** \-k(ə)liŋ\ **tinkles** [ME *tinklen*, freq. of *tinken* to make a tinkling sound] *vi* **1 :** TINGLE **2 a :** to make or emit a tinkle ⟨bells from distant sheep ~ through dreamy air —Lord Dunsany⟩ ⟨drums beating and marimbas *tinkling* —Dan Wickenden⟩ **b :** to make a sound suggestive of a tinkle esp. while flowing or moving ⟨the brook *tinkled* —George Meredith⟩ ⟨a footfall *tinkled* suddenly, incredibly tiny —Elinor Wylie⟩ ⟨the chaffinches *tinkled* excitedly —Gerald Durrell⟩ **c :** RHYME, JINGLE ⟨frames it in tripping rhythms and absurdly *tinkling* rhymes —Louis Untermeyer⟩ **3 a :** to produce a sound or sounds suggestive of a tinkle ⟨she *tinkled* on the piano but was not allowed to join an orchestra —Virginia Woolf⟩ ⟨can sit . . . and ~ away at waltzes —Claudia Cassidy⟩ **b :** to talk idly or foolishly or in a light gay manner **:** CHATTER, PRATE ⟨skipping and *tinkling* through all the social events of the town —Dorothy Parker⟩ **4 :** URINATE — not often in polite use ~ *vt* **1 :** to sound or make known (the time) by a tinkle ⟨through the tumult the bells . . . *tinkled* the hour —Hugh Walpole⟩ — sometimes used with *out* ⟨a small ornate clock . . . that *tinkled* out the hours —Mary Deasy⟩ **2 a :** to cause to make the sound of or as if of a tinkle ⟨likes to ~ the piano keys⟩ ⟨~s his guitar at every opportunity⟩ **b :** to produce (a sound or tune) by tinkling ⟨sitting idly *tinkling* a tune on his harpsichord⟩ — sometimes used with *out* ⟨found a Jew's harp . . . and began to ~ out an Irish jig tune —Henry Lapham⟩

²tinkle \"\ *n* -s **1 a :** a series of short high ringing or clinking sounds ⟨from the engine room the ~ of bells —R.H.Davis⟩ ⟨the ~ of glassware —H.A.Sinclair⟩ **b :** a sound suggestive of a tinkle ⟨the high ~ of the harp —Willa Cather⟩ ⟨the high ~ of their laughter —Irwin Shaw⟩ ⟨after the ~ of accompaniment . . . he made the old songs roar —Virginia D. Dawson & Betty D. Wilson⟩ **2 :** a jingling sound effect achieved in light repetitious verse or in wordy empty prose ⟨the ~ of words is all that strikes the ears —William Mason⟩

tin·kler \'tiŋk(ə)lə(r)\ *n* -s [ME *tinkeler*, prob. alter. (influenced by *-len* -le) of *tinkere* tinker — more at TINKER] *dial Brit* **:** TINKER

tinkling *n* -s [fr. gerund of ¹*tinkle*] **1 :** a tinkle or succession of tinkles ⟨drowsy ~s lull the distant folds —Thomas Gray⟩ **2** [so called fr. its note] **:** a grackle (*Quiscolus niger crassirostris*) that is native to Jamaica, often associates with domestic cattle, and rids them of insects

tin·kling·ly *adv* **:** in a tinkling manner **:** with a tinkling sound

tin·kly \'tiŋk(ə)lē, -li\ *adj* [²*tinkle* + *-y*] **:** TINKLING

tinks *pres 3d sing of* TINK, *pl of* TINK

tin liquor *n* **:** a solution of stannous chloride used formerly as a mordant in dyeing

tin liz·zie \(')⸗'lizē, -zi\ *n* [fr. *Tin Lizzie*, nickname for the Model T Ford automobile, fr. *tin* + *Lizzie*, nickname for *Elizabeth*] **:** a small and relatively inexpensive automobile ⟨they are in ancient *tin lizzies*, on motor scooters . . . in bicycle rickshas —Horace Sutton⟩

tin·man \'tinmən\ *n, pl* **tinmen 1 :** a maker of or worker in tinplate **:** TINSMITH **2 :** one who supervises the weighting of cloth or yarn with a tin solution — called also *tinner*

tinmouth \'⸗,⸗\ *n* [²*tin* + *mouth*] **:** BLACK CRAPPIE

tin·ne \'tinē\ *n, pl* **tinne** *or* **tinnes** *usu cap* [Athabascan, lit., people] **:** DÉNÉ

tinned *past of* TIN

tinnen *adj* [ME, fr. OE *tinen*, fr. *tin* + *-en*] *obs* **:** made or consisting of tin

tin·ner \'tinə(r)\ *n* -s **1 :** a tin miner **2 :** TINSMITH **3 :** one that tins metal articles **4 :** TINMAN 2 **5 :** one that makes or works with sheet metal

tin·nery \'tinərē\ *n* -ES [¹*tin* + *-ery*] **:** a tin mine **:** TINWORKS

tin·nevel·ly senna \tə'nevəlē-, |tinə|velē-\ *n, usu cap T* [fr. *Tinnevelly*, Madras, India] **:** senna from a cassia (*Cassia angustifolia*) — called also *Indian senna*

tin·ni·ent \'tinēənt\ *adj* [L *tinnient-, tinniens*, pres. part. of *tinnire* to ring, jingle, of imit. origin] **:** having a clear or ringing quality ⟨~ resonance of carillon music —P.D.Peery⟩ ⟨listened to the ting, ~ crackling of the coals —Mervyn Wall⟩

tin·ni·ly \'tin°lē, -nəl|, |i\ *adv* **:** in a tinny manner **:** with a tinny sound ⟨pots and pans . . . tinkling ~ as they jiggled and swung —Adria Langley⟩

tin·ni·ness \-nēnəs, -nin-\ *n* -ES **:** the quality or state of being tinny

tinning *n* -s [ME, fr. gerund of *tinnen* to tin — more at TIN] **1 :** the act or process of one who tins **2 :** a coating or lining of tin or tinfoil

tin·ni·tus \'tinətəs *also* tə'nīd·əs *or* -'nēd-\ *n* -ES [L, fr. *tinnitus*, past part. of *tinnire* to ring] **:** a ringing, roaring, hissing, or other sensation of noise in the ears that is purely subjective

tin·ny \'tinē, -ni\ *adj* -ER/-EST **1 :** of, abounding in, or yielding tin ⟨working a ~ lode⟩ **2 :** resembling or suggestive of tin: as **a :** having the appearance of tin **:** LIGHT, FRAGILE, SHINY ⟨the cheap ~ doorknob —Maritta Wolff⟩ ⟨wears a ~ dollar watch⟩ ⟨drives a small ~ car⟩ **b :** lacking resonance or depth of tone **:** THIN, METALLIC, HARSH ⟨could hear a ~ voice asking querulously —Hartley Howard⟩ ⟨the ~ alarm clock —Woody Klein⟩ ⟨the ceaseless ~ tumult of the jukebox —John McNulty⟩ ⟨the noble trumpet in F had to be given up in favor of a ~ little instrument in a higher key —Ralph Vaughan Williams⟩ ⟨a ~ paraphrase of the best-known . . . peroration —D.S. Berkeley⟩ **c :** tasting or smelling of tin **3 :** lacking matter, substance, or profundity of utterance **:** EMPTY, WORDY, INSIGNIFICANT ⟨the slick, well constructed, but ~ novels written by the literary engineers of today —Hiram Haydn⟩ ⟨power to drown out the ~ words of tiny men —*Reporter*⟩ ⟨the voice began to ring a ~ untruth —William Sansom⟩

tin ore *n* **:** CASSITERITE

tin oxide *n* **:** either of two oxides of tin; *esp* **:** STANNIC OXIDE — compare STANNOUS OXIDE

tin–pan \'⸗,⸗\ *or* **tin–panny** \'⸗|panē\ *adj* [E dial. *tin-pan*, v., to shivaree, fr. E *tin pan*] **:** NOISY, HARSH, TINNY

tin pan alley *n, usu cap T&P&A* **1 :** a district used or occupied chiefly by composers or publishers of popular music **2 :** the body or realm of composers or publishers of popular music ⟨the E major study which *Tin Pan Alley* has brought to the populace in the form of a song —A.H.Dent⟩

tin pants *n pl* **:** trousers of stout material soaked in paraffin for waterproofing and worn esp. by lumbermen

tin pest *also* **tin plague** *n* **:** the transformation of ordinary white metallic tin into powdery gray tin in extremely cold weather

tinplate \'⸗,⸗\ *n* [²*tin* + *plate*, n.] **:** thin sheet iron or steel coated with tin

tin–plate \"\ *vt* **:** to plate or coat (as a metal sheet) with tin

tin pot *n* **1 :** a pot made of tin or tinplate **2 :** the vessel holding the molten tin in the tin-plating process

tin–pot \'⸗,⸗\ *adj* [*tin pot*] **:** poor or paltry in quality **:** WRETCHED, INFERIOR ⟨this *tin-pot* town isn't the whole world —Hartley Howard⟩ ⟨when the *tin-pot* locomotive is unable to make the steepest grade, the passengers . . . pile out and push —E.A.Powell⟩ ⟨wasn't interested in his *tin-pot* politics —John Buchan⟩

tin putty *n* **:** PUTTY POWDER

tin pyrites *n* **:** STANNITE

tins *pl of* TIN, *pres 3d sing of* TIN

tin salt *n* **:** TIN CRYSTALS — sometimes used in pl.

¹tin·sel \'tin(t)səl *sometimes* -nzəl\ *adj* [earlier *tinselle*, fr. MF *etincellé, estencelé*, past part. of *etinceller, estenceler* to ornament with sparkling colors, to sparkle, fr. *etincelle, estencele* spark] **1 a :** interwoven with or overlaid with gold, silver, or metallic thread **b :** made of or covered with tinsel **2 :** cheaply glittering or gaudy **:** showily pretentious **:** SPECIOUS, TAWDRY ⟨wanders through its massive moldering architecture and ~ gaieties —Cecil Sprigge⟩ ⟨surrounded by the ~ splendor of his parties —J.W.Aldridge⟩ ⟨a world . . . with shoddy emotions and ~ values —Max Lerner⟩

²tinsel \"\ *n* -s [MF *etincelle, estincelle, estencele* spark, glitter, spangle — more at STENCIL] **1 a :** a silk or silk and wool fabric formerly interwoven or overlaid with glittering metallic threads or strips usu. of gold, silver, or copper **b :** LAMÉ **2 a :** a thread, strip, or sheet of metal, paper, or plastic used to produce a glittering and sparkling appearance in fabrics, yarns, Christmas decorations, or advertising materials **b :** a yarn of various fibers covered or combined with a thread of tinsel and used for knitting, weaving, or embroidering **3 :** something superficially showy, attractive, or glamorous that actually has little real worth ⟨those austere spirits who . . . had scorned the fumes and ~ of the loud world —L.P.Smith⟩ ⟨the ~ and power of high office did not appeal —J.C.Fitzpatrick⟩ ⟨a supergalamorous baggage of ~ — . . . a major movie star —Nolan Miller⟩ **4 :** DEEP STONE

³tinsel \"\ *vt* **tinseled** *or* **tinselled; tinseled** *or* **tinselled; tinseling** *or* **tinselling; tinsels 1 :** to interweave, overlay, or adorn with or as if with tinsel ⟨can produce ~*ed* or velvet surfaces by flocking —*Publishers' Weekly*⟩ ⟨dew ~*ed* the leaves —Truman Capote⟩ ⟨a gaudy ~*ed* dragonfly —Haldane Macfall⟩ **2 :** to impart to or cover with a meretricious brightness or appearance ⟨enraptured by all the ~*ed* glamour —Arthur Knight⟩ ⟨her ~*ed* picture of high life . . . thrilled the drab Victorian maiden —Robert Halsband⟩

⁴tinsel \"\ *n* -s [²*tinsel;* fr. the delicate filament or flimmer] **:** a flagellum (as on the zoospores of some phycomycetes) having a central axis from which extend short lateral hairs — compare FLIMMER, WHIPLASH

tin·sel·ly \'tin(t)s(ə)lē, -li *sometimes* -nzəl-\ *adj* **:** TINSELED ⟨a ~ star stuck high on a tree —Edwin Honig⟩ ⟨encompassing . . . all sides of life, the tawdry and ~ as well as the tautly tragic —E.J.West⟩ ⟨his playing . . . is elegant, sometimes ~ —Joseph Kerman⟩

tinsel of the feu *Scots law* **:** forfeiture of the feu right for failure to pay feu duty for two entire years

tin·sel·ry \'tin(t)səlrē, -ri *sometimes* -nzəl-\ *n* -s **:** tinseled material, ornamentation, or appearance **:** pretentious display ⟨the complacency of show and tangled ~ . . . had all been subdued into dust —Sean O'Casey⟩

tin·sey *also* **tin·sy** \'tin(t)sē, -nzē\ *n, pl* **tinseys** *also* **tinsies** [by alter.] **:** ²TINSEL

tinsmith \'⸗,⸗\ *n* [²*tin* + *smith*] **:** a worker who makes or repairs things of tin or other metal (as roofs, automobile equipment, kitchen utensils) — called also *tinman*

tin·smithy \'⸗,smithē, -ithē\ *n* **:** a tinsmith's workshop

tin soldier *n* **1 :** a toy soldier made of tin or other metal **2 :** one who plays at soldiering

tin spirit *n* **:** any of various solutions of tin salts used as mordants in dyeing — often used in pl.

tin spot *n* **:** a small hard white mass that is sometimes found in phosphor bronze, composed of an alloy of copper, tin, and phosphorus, frequently so hard as to be untouched by a file, and caused by excess of phosphorus

tinstone \'⸗,⸗\ *n* [²*tin* + *stone*] **:** CASSITERITE

tin stream *n* **:** an alluvial deposit of tin ore — usu. used in pl.

tin streaming *n* **:** the washing of tin from a tin stream

¹tint *past of* TINE

²tint \'tint\ *n* -s [alter. (prob. influenced by It or Sp *tinta* tint fr. LL *tincta* inked stroke, fr. fem. of L *tinctus*, past part. of *tingere* to tinge) of ³*tinct* — more at TINGE] **1 a :** a usu. slight or pale coloration **:** HUE ⟨colors as pure and delicate as the ~s of early morning —Willa Cather⟩ ⟨witch hazel and sumac add a variety of ~s —*Amer. Guide Series: Tenn.*⟩ ⟨dark it appeared, but the precise ~ was indeterminable —W.H.Hudson †1922⟩ ⟨made out the familiar pink and blue ~s of his anger —Louis Auchincloss⟩ **b :** any of various lighter or darker shades of a color **:** TINGE ⟨in the western sky a certain greenish phosphorescent ~ —J.C.Powys⟩ ⟨a ~ of yellow was creeping up the rushes —Richard Jefferies⟩ **2 :** a variation of a color produced by adding white to it and characterized by a low saturation with relatively high lightness — compare SHADE 9a **3 :** a usu. slight modifying quality or characteristic of something ⟨in it there was no ~ of fear for . . . the integrity of art —Sean O'Casey⟩ ⟨the purposeful political ~ of international loans —Herbert Feis⟩ ⟨showing a ~ of jealousy⟩ **4 :** a shaded effect in engraving produced by fine parallel lines close together **5 :** a panel of light, solid, or screened color often serving as background for matter in another color printed on top of it **6 :** dye for the hair **syn** see COLOR

³tint \"\ *vb* -ED/-ING/-S *vt* **1 :** to impart or apply a tint to **:** COLOR, TINGE ⟨spring ~*ing* her orchards with pastel hues —*advt*⟩ ⟨a small but gaudily ~*ed* society of women —G.N. Shuster⟩ ⟨having her hair ~*ed*⟩ — compare DYE **2 :** to modify or alter the aspect of by imparting an affective quality or characteristic ⟨the scent of roses just ~*ed* the clear . . . air —H.G.Wells⟩ ⟨the story's . . . ~*ed* with all the high colorings of adventure —Henry Cavendish⟩ ⟨his cheerfulness ~*ed* with some healthy cynicism —Henri Peyre⟩ ~ *vi* **:** to acquire a tint or color ⟨leaves ~ in the fall of the year⟩

⁴tint \"\ *n* -s [perh. alter. of ⁵*tent*] *dial Brit* **:** TASTE, FORETASTE, TRACE

tin tack *n, chiefly Brit* **:** a tin-plated tack

tin·ta·marre *also* **tin·ta·mar** \'tintə'mär\ *n* -s [F *tintamarre*, fr. MF, fr. *tinter* to ring (fr. L *tinnitare*, freq. of *tinnire* to ring) + *-amarre*, of unknown origin] **:** a great confused noise **:** UPROAR, DIN ⟨I did not know . . . though I did guess by such a ~ and cough and sneeze —Sir Walter Scott⟩

tint block *n* **:** a block or plate from which a tint is printed

tint·er \'tintə(r)\ *n* -s **:** one that tints; *specif* **:** one that mixes pigments to obtain paints of the desired color and shade

tin tetrachloride *n* **:** STANNIC CHLORIDE

tin·tic·ite \'tinti,kīt\ *n* -s [*Tintic* district, Utah, its locality + E *-ite*] **:** a mineral $Fe_3(PO_4)_2(OH)_3 \cdot 3H_2O$ consisting of a dense earthy to porcelaneous hydrous basic phosphate of iron

tinting *n* -s [fr. gerund of ³*tint*] **1 :** the act or process of one that tints: as **a :** the act or manner of producing an engraved tint **b :** the uniform dyeing of the gelatin layer of a transparency, lantern slide, or motion-picture film **2 :** the engraved or colored tint produced by the act of one that tints

tinting strength *n* **:** the ability of a pigment to change the hue of another pigment; *esp* **:** the depth of color produced by mixing a pigment or dye with white

tin·tin·nab·u·lar \'tintə'nabyələ(r)\ *adj* [L *tintinnabul*um bell + E *-ar*] **:** TINTINNABULARY

tin·tin·nab·u·lary \-,lerē\ *adj* [L *tintinnabul*um bell (fr. *tintinnare* to ring, jingle — fr. *tinnire*, of imit. origin — + *-bulum*, n. suffix) + E *-ary*] **:** of, relating to, or characterized by bells or their sounds ⟨has since enjoyed a . . . ~ fame as New York's Liberty Bell —*New Yorker*⟩

tin·tin·nab·u·la·tion \,⸗⸗,⸗⸗'lāshən\ *n* -s [L *tintinnabulum* + E *-ation*] **1 :** the ringing or sounding of bells ⟨all the church bells . . . tolled his knell in a quivering, melancholy ~ —Janet Flanner⟩ **2 :** a jingling or tinkling sound as of bells ⟨the splashing and ~ of a hundred country-scented showers —Osbert Sitwell⟩

tin·tin·nab·u·lous \|⸗⸗|⸗⸗ləs\ *adj* [L *tintinnabulum* + E *-ous*] **:** TINTINNABULARY ⟨bright ~ jewelry at ears and wrists —Audrey Barker⟩

tin·tin·nab·u·lum \,⸗⸗'⸗⸗ləm\ *n, pl* **tintinnabu·la** \-lə\ [L, bell] **:** a small tinkling bell

¹tin·tin·nid \tin'tinəd\ *adj* [NL *Tintinnidae*] **:** of or relating to the Tintinnidae

²tintinnid \"\ *n* -s **:** a ciliate of the family Tintinnidae

tin·tin·ni·dae \tin·'tinə,dē\ *n pl, cap* [NL, fr. *Tintinnus*, type genus (prob. fr. L *tintinnare* to ring) + *-idae*] **:** a large family that comprises loricate oligotrichous typically pelagic ciliates widely distributed in the seas and occas. found in fresh and brackish water and sometimes made coextensive with a suborder or other major division of Spirotricha

tintlaying \'⸗,⸗⸗\ *n* **:** the laying of a tint by the benday process

tint·less \'tintləs\ *adj* **:** having no tints **:** lacking color

tint tool *n* **:** a fine graver used for cutting the parallel lines that produce tints

tintype \'⸗,⸗\ *n* [²*tin* + *type*] **:** FERROTYPE 1

tinware \'⸗,⸗\ *n* [²*tin* + *ware*] **:** articles esp. utensils made of tinplate

tin whistle *n* **:** PENNY WHISTLE

tin–white \'⸗'⸗\ *adj* **:** bluish white

tinwork \'⸗,⸗\ *n* **1 :** work in tin; *also* **:** something made of tin **:** the part of a structure composed of tin **2 tinworks** *pl but sing or pl in constr* **:** an establishment where tin is smelted, rolled, or otherwise worked

¹ti·ny \'tīnē, -ni\ *adj* -ER/-EST [alter. (influenced by *-y*, adj. suffix) of ME *tine* tiny] **:** very small or diminutive **:** MINUTE ⟨a ~ baby⟩ ⟨a ~ mountain town —R.M.Coates⟩ ⟨a ~ hangar on a small flying field —*Amer. Guide Series: Conn.*⟩ ⟨a ~ army —C.S.Forester⟩ ⟨a ~ fraction of the money —H.G.Rickover⟩ ⟨the ~ clink of hammer and chisel —Tom Marvel⟩ **syn** see SMALL

²tiny \"\ *n* -ES *chiefly Brit* **:** a young child **:** INFANT ⟨rich food upsets the digestion of *tinies* —*Farmer's Weekly (So. Africa)*⟩

tiny tim \|⸗⸗'tim\ *n* -s *usu cap both Ts* [fr. *Tiny Tim*, crippled little boy in the story *A Christmas Carol* (1843) by Charles Dickens †1870 Eng. novelist] **:** a yellow-flowered prairie herb (*Thymophylla aurea*) of the family Compositae

tin·zen·ite \'tinzə,nīt, 'tin(t)sə,-\ *n* -s [*Tinzen*, Switzerland + E *-ite*] **:** a mineral $CaMnAl(SiO_4)_2$ consisting of a silicate of manganese, aluminum, and calcium and occurring in yellow monoclinic crystals at Tinzen, Grisons, Switzerland

ti·o·non·ta·ti \,tīə'nänt·ətē\ *n, pl* **tionontati** *or* **tionontatis** *usu cap* **1 :** an Iroquoian people of southern Ontario **2 :** a member of the Tionontati people

ti·ou *or* **ti·oux** \'tē(,)ü\ *n, pl* **tiou** *or* **tious** *or* **tioux** *usu cap* [F *Tioux*, fr. Tunica *Tiou*] **1 :** a Tunican people of northwestern Mississippi **2 :** a member of the Tiou people

¹tip \'tip\ *n* -s [ME *tip, tippe;* akin to MHG *zipf* tip, MD *tip*, MLG *timpe* — more at TAP] **1 a :** the pointed or rounded end or extremity of something ⟨the ~ of his finger⟩ ⟨~ of the spear⟩ ⟨tracks . . . led over the ~ of the hill —Robert Lund⟩ ⟨the very ~ of the nose of the fuselage —H.G.Armstrong⟩ ⟨at the southern ~ of the island —*Amer. Guide Series: Maine*⟩ ⟨the yellow ~ of the sun —V.G.Heiser⟩ ⟨the ~s of their wings⟩ **b** *obs* **:** the highest or utmost point or extremity **:** CROWN, SUMMIT **2 a :** a small piece or part (as of a belt,

shoe, cane, pen, or billiard cue) designed to serve as an end, cap, or point and made usu. of metal, leather, or other durable substance — see SHOE illustration **b :** the end of a feather or tail of fur used in trimming a hat; *specif* **:** a small ostrich plume **c** (1) **:** the piece or section of a jointed fishing rod farthest from the butt (2) **:** the terminal guide on the end of such a rod **d** (1) **:** FOOTHOLD 3 (2) **:** CAP 3a (3) **:** a short horseshoe made to reach only half round the hoof and worn to protect the crust **e** (1) **:** a thimble of leather used in archery for the protection of the drawing fingers (2) **:** PILE 4a **3 a :** a thin broad brush made of camel's or badger's hair and used in laying gold leaf (as in bookbinding) **b :** any insert pasted to the binding edge of a book or section **4 :** a triangular piece of beef cut from between the round and the sirloin and used for roasting or for steaks **5** *Austral* **:** the exposed weathered end of the fibers of wool on the sheep; *also* **:** an area or clump formed by the clotted ends of such fibers **6 tips** *pl* **:** a grade of tobacco comprising the top two or three leaves on a stalk

2tip \"\ *vt* **tipped; tipped** *also* **tipt; tipping; tips** [ME *tippen*, fr. *tip, tippe* tip] **1 a :** to attach a tip or point to or furnish a tip for ⟨the natives ~ their arrows with stone⟩ ⟨a summer settlement ~s the slender headland —*Amer. Guide Series: Maine*⟩ **b** (1) **:** to cover or adorn the tip of ⟨black wrought iron legs handsomely *tipped* with brass —*advt*⟩ ⟨*tipped* with gold-leaf trim —Frederick Way⟩ ⟨scales *tipped* with yellowish green above the back —P.M.Roedel⟩ (2) **:** to blend (furs) for improved appearance by brushing the tips of the hair with dye **2 :** to affix or paste (an insert) in a book at the binding margin — often used with *in* or sometimes with *into* or *on* ⟨one volume . . . with 105 full-color reproductions from photographs *tipped* in —*Yale Rev.*⟩ ⟨when plates are *tipped* on, they should be freed from the text —Edith Diehl⟩ **3 :** to remove the ends of (as living shoots) ⟨~ raspberries⟩ ⟨the cows' horns were *tipped* to prevent injury in shipping⟩

3tip \"\ *vb* **tipped; tipped** *also* **tipt; tipping; tips** [ME *tipen*] *vt* **1 a :** to cause to overturn or proceed downward **:** throw or cast down **:** UPSET — usu. used with *over* or *onto* ⟨the wind struck the car and nearly *tipped* it over —Ernest Hemingway⟩ ⟨the truck *tipped* its trailer onto the car⟩ **b :** to knock down (a bowling pin) otherwise than by direct impact of a bowl ⟨the bowled kingpin *tipped* three other pins⟩ **2 :** to turn (something) from a horizontal or vertical position to a slanting or inclined position **:** CANT, TILT ⟨*tipped* his head to one side —A.R.Wetjen⟩ ⟨neighborhood loafers *tipped* their chairs —S.T. Williamson⟩ ⟨were required to ~ their hats to the chemists —W.H.Whyte⟩ ⟨would eventually ~ the balance of power —*Time*⟩ **3** *chiefly dial* **:** to drink (liquor) esp. at one draft **4** *Brit* **:** to empty by tilting **:** DUMP ⟨a hole into which I had been *tipping* cinders —Francis King⟩ ⟨*tipped* it down gently off the spade onto the grass —*Punch*⟩ **~** *vi* **1 :** to become overturned or upset **:** TOPPLE — usu. used with *over* ⟨a canoe will sometimes ~ over quickly⟩ **2 :** to move from the vertical or horizontal **:** LEAN, SLANT ⟨the bench ~s on the uneven floor⟩ ⟨tall buildings ~ slightly in the wind⟩ — **tips the scales** *or* **tip the scale 1 :** to register weight on a scale or balance ⟨*tips the scales* at 210 pounds —*Current Biog.*⟩ **2 :** to shift the balance of fortune, influence, or power ⟨a blind world in which building and destroying successively *tip the scale* —W.L. Sperry⟩ ⟨Americans . . . *tipped the scales* decisively in two world wars —A.E.Stevenson b. 1900⟩ ⟨adding small gifts to *tip the scales* in my favor —Claudia Cassidy⟩

4tip \"\ *n* -s **1** *archaic* **:** the upsetting of a bowling pin by another that falls or rolls against it **2 :** the act or an instance of tipping **:** TILT ⟨the tower has a slight ~ to the south⟩ **3** *Brit* **a :** an elevated runway along which railroad cars or wagons can be run to have their contents tipped or dumped (as into a chute) at the end **b :** such a runway together with a crane that picks up a car or wagon and swings it bodily so that its contents can be tipped or dumped as desired — compare ⁴TIPPLE **4** *Brit* **:** a place for depositing something (as rubbish or garbage or material for embankments) by tipping or dumping **:** DUMP

5tip \"\ *n* -s [ME *tippe*; akin to LG *tippen* to tap] **:** the act or process of tipping **:** a light touch or blow **:** TAP ⟨giving him a ~ on the shoulder⟩

6tip \"\ *vb* **tipped; tipped** *also* **tipt; tipping; tips** *vt* **1 :** to strike lightly **:** TOUCH, TAP ⟨the sword *tipped* his shoulder —*Irish Digest*⟩ ⟨a baseball catcher sometimes ~s the batsman's bat illegally with his mitt⟩ **2 :** to hit (a baseball or cricket ball) a glancing blow with the edge or side of the bat ⟨the batter *tipped* the ball foul⟩ **3 :** to hit (as a basketball) lightly with the hand or fingers ⟨~s the ball to keep it rim high —*Scholastic Coach*⟩ — often used with in ⟨the forward *tipped* in another basket⟩ **~** *vi* **:** to move or proceed with mincing or light steps **:** TIPTOE ⟨*tipping* to the front windows, she closed them —J.B.Benefield⟩

7tip \"\ *vb* **tipped; tipped** *also* **tipt; tipping; tips** [perh. fr. ⁶*tip*] *vt* **1 :** GIVE, PRESENT ⟨be merry and ~ us a song⟩ ⟨*tipped* the head clerk a signal —Mark Twain⟩ **2 :** to give a tip or gratuity to ⟨the searchers, being *tipt* with half a crown, allowed us to proceed —Tobias Smollett⟩ ⟨*tipped* the servants liberally —W.F.DeMorgan⟩ ⟨~ them if they bring refreshments to your seat —Richard Joseph⟩ **~** *vi* **:** to bestow a tip or gratuity ⟨always ~s generously⟩ ⟨how much to ~ is a problem⟩ — **tip one the wink :** to give one a hint, suggestion, signal by or as if by a wink ⟨*tipped him the wink* as he passed, so he went over there —Richard Llewellyn⟩

8tip \"\ *n* -s **:** a gift or a usu. small sum of money tendered in payment or often in excess of prescribed or suitable payment for a service performed or anticipated ⟨cost 15 cents plus a 10-cent ~⟩ ⟨the redcaps had begun . . . to press for their interests in the question of ~s —*Current Biog.*⟩ ⟨at the entrance girl artists do portrait sketches for a ~ —*Amer. Guide Series: Fla.*⟩

9tip \"\ *n* -s [perh. fr. ⁷*tip*] **1 :** an item of expert or authoritative information imparted or sought for one's guidance ⟨take my ~ and do not venture in there without a guide —Fred Streeter⟩ ⟨wanted to pick up the ~s which experience had taught the pioneers —R.C.Snyder⟩ ⟨giving . . . useful ~s on all sorts of ways of spending the Christmas holidays —*N.Y.Times*⟩ **2 :** a piece of advance or confidential information given by or received from one thought to have access to special or inside sources **:** HINT, STEER: as **a :** a prediction concerning the expected change in the value or status of a stock, bond, or other security ⟨brokers . . . versed in the art of getting ~s and advance information of events likely to affect prices —Frederick Simpich †1950⟩ ⟨~s and rumors . . . send shares from quotations of a few cents up to thousands and down again —*Amer. Guide Series: Nev.*⟩ **b :** a forecast of the outcome or winner of a sporting event (as a horse or dog race) used chiefly for placing a bet ⟨through her I got that ~ on the horse race —Erle Stanley Gardner⟩ ⟨in one day you clean out half of what I had saved with your phoney ~s —*Ring*⟩ **c :** an advance notice or report concerning a newsworthy development of special interest to a reporter or a newspaper ⟨personnel frequently offer ~s or clues to news developments —*Banking*⟩ ⟨has been following obscure news ~s and developing stories of wide significance —*Current Biog.*⟩ ⟨even an hour's delay may mean the difference between ~ and fact —*Radio News*⟩

10tip \"\ *vt* **tipped; tipped; tipping; tips 1 a :** to impart a tip, a piece of information or advice, or a warning about often in a secret or confidential manner ⟨somebody was *tipping* their flights to the rebels —J.A.Phillips⟩ ⟨are you afraid I'll ~ the plot —Maurice Zolotow⟩ **b :** to make mention of as a prospective winner or a profitable investment ⟨has been *tipped* as council president⟩ ⟨practically nothing makes you look more foolish than *tipping* a loser —G.F.T.Ryall⟩ ⟨industrials are being *tipped* in the forecasts⟩ **2 :** to give a tip or private or confidential information to ⟨his wife . . . was *tipped* three days in advance and returned —*Newsweek*⟩ ⟨both had already been *tipped* to . . . keep top-secret documents face down on the desk —J.P.O'Donnell⟩ — often used with *off* ⟨a friend *tipped* him off that pianos were having a phenomenal sale —Green Peyton⟩ ⟨thousands . . . were *tipped* off in time to flee —T.H. Fielding⟩ — **tip one's hand :** to show one's hand ⟨the Justice department wouldn't *tip its hand* by saying what its next move . . . would be —*Newsweek*⟩

11tip \"\ *n* -s [perh. fr. ⁶*tip*] **:** a crowd gathered or attracted by a pitchman or barker ⟨the opening ~ consisted of all the roughnecks and loafers —G.A.Hamid⟩ ⟨for his horoscope pitch he often has his wife circulate among the ~ —W.L. Gresham⟩

ti palm *n* **:** ¹TI 1

tip and run *n, Brit* **:** a game similar to cricket in which a batsman is required to run each time he touches a bowled ball with his bat

tip-and-run \ˌ=ˌ=ˈ=\ *adj* [*tip and run*] *chiefly Brit* **:** characterized by bolting immediately upon striking ⟨a heavy bomb from a *tip-and-run* raider scored a direct hit —O.S.Nock⟩ ⟨sallied to make *tip-and-run* assaults —*Manchester Guardian Weekly*⟩

tip blight *n* **:** any of several diseases of plants characterized by death of terminal shoots: as **a :** a disease of balsam fir caused by a fungus (*Rehmielliopsis balsamae*) **b :** a virus disease of tomato

tipburn \ˈ=ˌ=\ *n* [¹*tip* + *burn*] **:** a disease of the potato, lettuce, and other cultivated plants characterized by burning or browning of the tips and margins of the leaflets and caused by loss of water due to excessive heat and sunshine — compare HOPPERBURN

tipcart \ˈ=ˌ=\ *n* [³*tip* + *cart*] **:** a cart whose body can be tipped on the frame to empty its contents

tipcat \ˈ=ˌ=\ *n* [⁶*tip* + *cat*] **:** a game in which one player using a bat strikes lightly a tapered wooden peg and as it flies up strikes it again to drive it as far as possible while fielders try to recover it; *also* **:** the peg used in this game

tip cheese *n* **:** a boy's game resembling tipcat

tip cutting *n* **:** TERMINAL CUTTING

tip-dye \ˈ=ˌ=\ *vt* **:** ²TIP 1b(2)

tip·ful \ˈtipˌfu̇l\ *adj* **:** BRIMFUL

tiph·ia \ˈtifēə\ *n* [NL, fr. Gk *tiphē* beetle + NL *-ia*] **1** *cap* **:** a genus (the type of the family Tiphiidae) of shining black wasps that includes a species (*T. vernalis*) of larval parasites of the Japanese beetle **2** -s **:** any wasp of the genus *Tiphia*

1tiph·i·id \ˈtifēəd\ *adj* [NL *Tiphiidae*] **:** of or relating to the Tiphiidae

2tiphiid \"\ *n* -s **:** a wasp of the family Typhiidae

ti·phi·idae \tə'fīəˌdē\ *n pl, cap* [NL, fr. *Tiphia*, type genus + *-idae*] **:** a family of rather small slender usu. black and often hairy wasps that as larvae parasitize the grubs of various scarabaeid beetles — see TIPHIA

tipi *var of* TEPEE

1tip-in \ˈ=ˌ=\ *n* -s [²*tip*] **:** ¹TIP 3b

2tip-in \"\ *n* -s [⁶*tip*] **:** a score made in basketball by deflecting the ball into the basket with the fingertips ⟨both guards trail the forward . . . for possible follow-up shots and *tip-ins* —G.K. Loveless⟩

tip-it *or* **tip·pit** \ˈtipət\ *n* -s [fr. the phrase *tip it;* fr. the command of the guesser when touching the other player's hand] **:** the game of up Jenkins sometimes played as a gambling game

tip·i·ti \ˈtipəd·ē, ˌtipə'tē\ *n* -s [Pg, fr. Tupi *tapeti*] **:** an elastic plaited cylinder of jacitara palm bark used in expressing the juice from the root in making cassava

tip layering *also* **tip layerage** *n* **:** the propagation of plants by bending a stem to the ground and covering the tip with soil so that roots and new shoots may develop

ti·ple \ˈtē(ˌ)plā\ *n* -s [Sp, lit., soprano, treble, prob. alter. of *triple*, fr. L *triplus* triple — more at TRIPLE] **:** a soprano guitar

tip·less \ˈtipləs\ *adj* **:** marked by the absence of tips or gratuities ⟨a ~ hotel⟩

tip·man \ˈtipmən\ *n, pl* **tipmen** [³*tip* + *man*] **:** DUMPER 1c

tip moth *n* **:** any of several moths esp. of the family Olethreutidae whose larvae bore in the tips of branches of trees

1tip-off \ˈ=ˌ=\ *n* -s [¹⁰*tip*] **:** an indication, hint, or warning of an otherwise unknown fact, development, or move **:** TIP, GIVEAWAY ⟨the only *tip-off* on his rank was the way the men addressed him —Dave Richardson⟩ ⟨the mysterious informer whose *tip-off* had brought them to witness the drug-running operation —Darrell Berrigan⟩ ⟨the production of certain . . . men's gloves or underwear might provide a *tip-off* on an impending military expedition —S.A.Rice & J.W.Kappel⟩ ⟨watch the blocking back for the *tip-off* as to where the play is going —A.J.Yunevich⟩

2tip-off \"\ *n* -s [⁶*tip*] **:** the act or an instance of putting the ball in play in basketball by a jump ball

tip-on \ˈ=ˌ=\ *n* -s [²*tip*] **:** ¹TIP 3b

ti·po·ni \ˈtēpənē\ *n* -s [Hopi *tiiponi* idol or amulet seen only by owner] **:** a sacred badge of authority of the Hopi Indians usu. consisting of an ear of corn decorated with feathers or a valued stone and worn or displayed by a chief, priest, or religious society

tip-over \ˈ=ˌ=\ *n* -s [fr. *tip over*, v.] **:** a disease of egg plant caused by a fungus (*Phomopsis vexans*) and characterized by girdling of the stem of seedlings just above the soil line

tip·pa·ble \ˈtipəbəl\ *adj* [⁷*tip* + *-able*] **:** able to be tipped or to receive tips

tipped *past of* TIP

tip·pee \(ˈ)ti'pē\ *n* -s [⁷*tip* + *-ee*] **:** one receiving or that receives a tip ⟨experienced ~s develop a pretty keen eye for what to expect —P.T.White⟩ ⟨standard ~s include hotel and railroad station porters . . . taxi drivers, doormen and delivery boys —*Wall Street Jour.*⟩

tip·per \ˈtipə(r)\ *n* -s **:** one that tips: as **a :** DUMPER 1c **b :** one whose work is making, fastening, or applying tips **c** *or* **tipper-in** \ˌ==ˈ=\ **:** a worker who tips pages into book or pamphlet signatures **d :** a worker who blocks felt hats **e :** a worker who picks and dresses poultry **f** *Brit* **:** a truck whose body tips for unloading **:** DUMP TRUCK

tip·pe·rary \ˌtipəˌre(ə)rē, ˌra(a)|, -ˌrāl, |ri\ *adj, usu cap* [fr. *Tipperary*, Ireland] **:** of or from County Tipperary, Ireland **:** of the kind or style prevalent in County Tipperary

tip·pet \ˈtipət, *usu* -əd·+V\ *n* -s [ME *tipet*, prob. fr. *tip, tippe* tip + *-et* — more at TIP (point)] **1 :** a long hanging end of cloth attached to a sleeve, cap, or hood and used esp. in the late medieval period — see LIRIPIPE **2 :** a shoulder cape of fur or cloth often with hanging ends worn esp. by women or by men as a garment of office **3 :** a scarf or band with long hanging ends worn over the robe or vestment esp. by Anglican or Episcopal clergymen **4** *Brit* **:** a hangman's rope **5 a :** a patagium of a lepidopteran **b :** a ruff of feathers on a bird **6 a :** a short length of fine gut, nylon, or horsehair used for securing a fly to the leader of a fishline **b :** a barb of a feather used as the tail of an artificial fly

tipping *pres part of* TIP

1tip·ple \ˈtipəl\ *vb* **tippled; tippled; tippling** \-p(ə)liŋ\ **tipples** [back-formation fr. obs. E *tippler* barkeeper, fr. ME *tipler, tipeler*] *vt* **1 :** to drink (intoxicating liquor) esp. continuously in small amounts ⟨farmers, artisans, and tradesmen *tippled* the stiffer drink —W.H.Lyon⟩ **2** *archaic* **:** to spend or lose by tippling **:** SQUANDER **~** *vi* **:** to drink intoxicating liquor esp. by habit or to excess ⟨had been *tippling* all that morning —Hamilton Basso⟩ ⟨the managers are afraid to drink . . . and the ex-boxers are usually too broke to ~ —A.J.Liebling⟩

2tipple \"\ *n* -s **:** an intoxicating beverage **:** DRINK ⟨trying to forget him and seeking oblivion in ~ —Norman Douglas⟩ ⟨an old gentleman . . . whose only ~ was straight vodka —A.J. Liebling⟩

3tipple \"\ *vb* -ED/-ING/-S [freq. of ³*tip*] *vi, dial Eng* **:** TUMBLE, OVERTURN **~** *vt, dial Eng* **:** to cause to fall, upset, or overturn

4tipple \"\ *n* -s **1 :** an apparatus by which loaded cars are emptied by tipping sometimes including an elevated runway or framework upon which the cars are run for tipping — compare ⁴TIP 3b **2 :** the place where tipping is done **:** TIP; *specif* **:** a coal-screening plant

tip·pler \ˈtip(ə)lə(r)\ *n* -s **:** one that tipples: as **a :** one that operates or works in a tipple **b :** ⁴TIPPLE 1 **c :** one of an English breed of pigeons similar to the tumblers but long-flying and commonly chocolate brown and white **d :** TUMBLER 3e

tippling house *n, archaic* **:** BARROOM

tip·ply \ˈtip(ə)lē, -li\ *adj* -ER/-EST [³*tipple* + *-y*] **:** ²TIPPY

1tip·py \ˈtipē, -pi\ *adj* [¹*tip* + *-y*] **1** *Brit* **:** TIPTOP, SMART, STYLISH **2** *Brit* **a :** full of tips **b** *of wool* **:** having an excessive or defective tip

2tippy \"\ *adj* -ER/-EST [⁴*tip* + *-y*] **:** given to tipping **:** liable to tip **:** UNSTEADY ⟨the ferry had a ~, untrustworthy feeling —Jean Stafford⟩ ⟨our canoe had . . . a certain ~ grace —*Outlook*⟩

tippy-toe \ˈtipēˌtō, -pi,-\ *n* [by alter.] **:** TIPTOE ⟨standing on my *tippy-toes*, I wedged it in the crotch of a limb —Helen Eustis⟩

tips *pl of* TIP, *pres 3d sing of* TIP

tip sheet *n* **:** a usu. folio publication containing special information or tips relating to a particular business or line of activity ⟨many mimeographed *tip sheets* are now on the market —Jo Ranson & R.M.Pack⟩; *esp* **:** a publication giving tips for gamblers (as on horse races or numbers games)

tip·si·fy \ˈtipsəˌfī\ *vt* -ED/-ING/-ES [*tipsy* + *-fy*] **:** to make tipsy **:** INTOXICATE

tip·si·ly \ˈtipsəlē, -li\ *adv* **:** in a tipsy manner **:** UNSTEADILY ⟨~ mutable, his mood changed . . . from hilarious to profoundly gloomy —Aldous Huxley⟩ ⟨the whole structure leaned ~ to the left —D.S.Mullen⟩

tip·si·ness \-sēnəs, -sin-\ *n* -ES **:** the quality or state of being tipsy

tip speed *n* **:** the velocity of the outer edge of a wheel or the tip of a propeller

tipstaff \ˈtipˌstaf\ *n, pl* **tipstaves** *or* **tipstaffs** [contr. of ME *tipped staf*, fr. *tipped* having a tip (fr. *tip, tippe* tip + *-ed*) + *staf* staff — more at TIP, STAFF] **1 :** a staff tipped with metal used as a badge of office **2 :** an officer who bears a tipstaff **:** a court attendant **:** CONSTABLE, BAILIFF ⟨the judges and *tipstaves* parted the combatants —T.B.Macaulay⟩

tip stall *n* **:** a stalling of the wing tip of an airplane before the remainder of the wing is stalled that frequently results in the loss of lateral control

tip·ster \ˈtipstə(r)\ *n* -s [⁹*tip* + *-ster*] **:** one who gives or sells tips or private information esp. for gambling, stock speculation, or news writing ⟨many touts and ~s prepared to sell inside information —Dennis Craig⟩ ⟨is best known as a stock market ~ —Martin Gardner⟩ ⟨was the first editor to employ secret ~s —W.A.Swanberg⟩ ⟨police are often informed of crimes by ~s⟩

tipstock \ˈ=ˌ=\ *n* [¹*tip* + *stock*] **:** the detachable or movable forepart of a gunstock that lies beneath the barrel and forms a hold for the left hand — compare BUTTSTOCK

tip·sy \ˈtipsē, -si\ *adj* -ER/-EST [³*tip* + *-sy* (as in *tricksy*)] **1 a :** mildly affected by an intoxicating drink **:** BEFUDDLED, UNSTEADY ⟨before offering to intoxicate others . . . getting well ~ himself —Herman Melville⟩ ⟨was not ~, but she fell in in the dark —Rachel Henning⟩ **b :** showing, marked by, or producing mild intoxication ⟨her manner seemed almost ~, as if she were drunk —Kay Boyle⟩ **2 a :** emotionally affected as if mildly intoxicated ⟨as ~ on self-pity as they were on blood and glory 15 years ago —Anthony West⟩ **b :** TIPPY, ASKEW ⟨stump-scarred fields bounded by ~ fences —*Amer. Guide Series: Pa.*⟩ ⟨a piece of ~ printing that incurred . . . disapproval —Rosamond Lehmann⟩ **syn** see DRUNK

tipsy cake *n* **:** a sponge layer cake soaked in wine or brandy with custard or preserves between the layers, frosted with whipped cream, and decorated with toasted almonds

tipsy pudding *n* **:** stale sponge cake soaked in wine and esp. sherry and served with boiled custard

tipt *past part of* TIP

tip table *n* **:** TIP-TOP TABLE

tiptail \ˈ=ˌ=\ *n* [³*tip* + *tail;* fr. the bobbing of its tail when walking] **:** SPOTTED SANDPIPER

1tip-tap \ˈ=ˌ=\ *n* -s [⁵*tip* + ⁵*tap*] **:** an alternating light knocking or tapping; *also* **:** the sound made by such tapping

2tip-tap \"\ *vi* **:** to make a tip-tap or its sound

tip-tilt \ˌ=ˈ=\ *vt* **:** to tilt or turn up at the tip — usu. used in past part. ⟨the scales *tip-tilted* with a slight excessive weight —J.G.Neihardt⟩ ⟨the mountain field *tip-tilted* by reason of its steepness —Willa Cather⟩ ⟨his nose was *tip-tilted* —Ethel Anderson⟩

1tiptoe \ˈtipˌtō\ *n* [ME *tiptoo*, fr. *tip, tippe* tip + *too* toe — more at TOE] **:** the tip or end of a toe; *collectively* **:** the ends of the toes — usu. used with reference to motion or posture on the balls of the toes ⟨he paced over . . . and on ~s whispered into his ear —L.M.Uris⟩ ⟨standing on ~ to see over the crowd⟩ ⟨craves ideals high enough to give him the thrill of standing on ~ to reach them —J.H.Baker⟩ — **on tiptoe :** AROUSED, ALERT, ATIPTOE ⟨she was very animated, very much *on tiptoe* —L.C. Douglas⟩ ⟨the contest of skill that puts one *on tiptoe* to win —*Deerfield (Wis.) Independent*⟩

2tiptoe \"\ *adv* **:** on or as if on tiptoe ⟨using one hand to support himself . . . because he was standing ~ —Margaret Shedd⟩ ⟨suddenly find yourself standing ~ and full of new breath —E.G.Anderson⟩ ⟨day stands ~ on the misty mountaintops —Shak.⟩

3tiptoe \"\ *adj* **1 :** standing or walking on or as if on tiptoe ⟨approaching with ~ step⟩ ⟨~ touches of sportful elves —E.J. Banfield⟩ **2 :** SILENT, CAUTIOUS, STEALTHY ⟨a stillness suggesting motion, what might be called a ~ effect —G.W. Knight⟩ ⟨offered to guard me and was amusing with his modest ~ air —George Meredith⟩

4tiptoe \"\ *vi* **1 :** to stand or raise oneself on tiptoe ⟨great difficulty of seeing anything . . . even by ~*ing* and craning —Arnold Bennett⟩ **2 :** to walk or proceed quietly or cautiously on or as if on tiptoe ⟨~*ing* extremely carefully past his door, they heard how restlessly he slept —Glenway Wescott⟩ ⟨a cat *tiptoed* from the shadow of a fence —Glenn Scott⟩ ⟨~*ing* progressively deeper into the uncharted channels of educational TV —Delbert Clark⟩

tip·ton weed \ˈtiptən-\ *n* [*tipton* prob. fr. the name *Tipton*] **:** SAINT-JOHN'S-WORT

1tip-top \ˈ=ˌ=\ *n* [¹*tip* + *top*] **1 :** the highest or utmost point **:** TOP, SUMMIT ⟨building a fire tower on the *tip-top* of the mountain⟩ **2 :** the highest degree or extent **:** CROWN, PINNACLE ⟨reaching the *tip-top* of happiness⟩ **3** *Eng* **:** the highest class or rank in society — usu. used in pl. ⟨hobnobbing with the *tip-tops*⟩ **4 :** ¹TIP 2c(2)

2tip-top \"\ *adj* **:** of or characteristic of the highest quality, rank, or class **:** EXCELLENT, FIRST-RATE ⟨a really *tip-top* man —H.J.Laski⟩ ⟨people from some *tip-top* West End house —Joseph Conrad⟩ ⟨kept the bridge in *tip-top* shape —Pearl Puckett⟩ ⟨horses . . . in *tip-top* shape, fit to run for the money —J.H.Winchester⟩

3tip-top \"\ *adv* **:** to the highest extent **:** very well **:** SURPASSINGLY ⟨colonel . . . uses me *tip-top* —Walt Whitman⟩ ⟨the mittens . . . fitted *tip-top* —J.C.Lincoln⟩

tip·top·per \ˈtip¦täpə(r)\ *n* **:** one of the first rank or class

tip-top table \ˈ=ˌ=-\ *n* **:** a table whose top is hinged to tip to a vertical position — called also *tilt-top table, tip table*

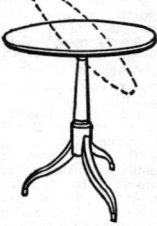

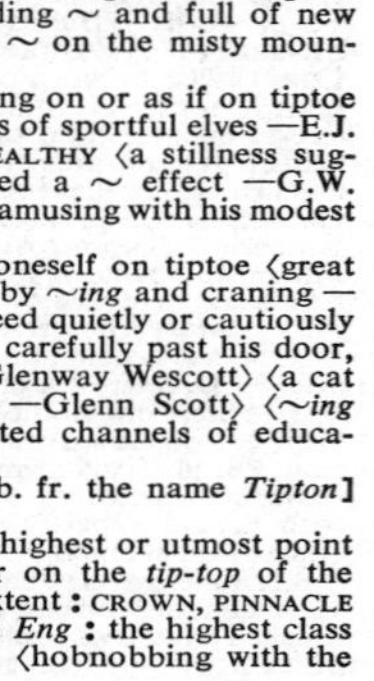
tip-top table

tip·u·la \ˈtipyələ\ *n* [NL, fr. L *tipula, tippula* water spider] **1** *cap* **:** the type genus of the family Tipulidae **2** -s **:** any fly of the genus *Tipula*

tip·u·lar·ia \ˌtipyə'la(a)rēə\ *n, cap* [NL, fr. *Tipula* + *-aria;* fr. the supposed resemblance of the flower to the crane fly] **:** a genus of delicate terrestrial orchids with solid bulbs that produce in late summer a racemose scape of greenish purple flowers and in autumn a single ovate purple leaf which persists through winter — see CRANE-FLY ORCHID

ti·pu·li·dae \tə'pyüləˌdē\ *n pl, cap* [NL, fr. *Tipula*, type genus + *-idae*] **:** a large family of long-legged usu. slender two-winged flies comprising the crane flies and often resembling enormous mosquitoes

tip·u·loi·dea \ˌtipyə'lȯidēə\ *n pl, cap* [NL, fr. *Tipula* + *-oidea*] **:** a superfamily of Nematocera including Tipulidae and various related families

1tip-up \ˈ=ˌ=\ *n* -s [fr. *tip up*, v.] **1** [prob. so called fr. the bobbing of its tail when walking] **:** SPOTTED SANDPIPER **2 :** TILT 6

2tip-up \"\ *adj* **:** constructed so as to tip up or out of the way ⟨sat neatly on the little *tip-up* seat of the taxi —Elizabeth Taylor⟩

tip·u·ra \ˈtipəˌrä, -ˌrə\ *n, pl* **tipura** *or* **tipuras** *usu cap* **1 a :** a people of the Tripura state, Bengal **b :** a member of such people **2 :** the Tibeto-Burman language of the Tipura people

tip worm *n* **:** a worm that is the larva of a gallfly (*Contarinia vaccinii*) that infests the tips of cranberry vines

ti·queur \(')tē¦kər(·)\ *n* -s [F, fr. *tiquer* to have a tic, to twitch (fr. *tic*) + *-eur* -or] **:** one subject to a tic

¹ti·rade *in sense 1* (')tī¦rād *sometimes* tə'räd *or* tə'rād *or* tə'räd, *in sense 2* tə'räd *or* tə'rȧd\ *n* -s [F, pull, shot, tirade, fr. MF, fr. OIt *tirata*, fr. fem. of *tirato*, past part. of *tirare* to draw, pull, shoot; akin to OSp & OPg *tirar* to draw, pull, shoot, OF *tirer*] **1 :** a protracted speech usu. marked by intemperate, vituperative, or harshly censorious language **:** a prolonged fire of invective **:** long-drawn-out harangue ⟨a tantrum of the utmost frenzy, screaming a ~ of protest and rage —Marcia Davenport⟩ **2 :** a baroque musical ornament consisting of a rapid run connecting two melody notes

²tirade \"\ *vi* -ED/-ING/-S **:** to make a tirade ⟨she might ~ at the moment —Rumer Godden⟩

ti·rak \tə'rak\ *n* -s [native name in India] **:** a physiological disease of Indian cotton prob. due to nutrient deficiency and characterized by premature yellowing and shedding of the leaves and cracking of the bolls before maturity

tir·a·lee \¦tirə¦lē\ *n* -s [imit.] **:** a succession of musical notes (as in a bugle call)

ti·ra·na \tə'ränə\ *adj, usu cap* [fr. *Tirana*, Albania] **:** of or from Tirana, the capital of Albania **:** of the kind or style prevalent in Tirana

ti·rasse \tə'ras, -räs\ *n* -s [F, drawnet, pedal coupler, fr. *tirasser* to catch with a drawnet, aug. of *tirer* to draw, pull, shoot — more at TIRADE] **:** a pedal coupler in an organ

¹tire \'tī(ə)r, -īə\ *vb* -ED/-ING/-S [ME *tyren, tyeren*, fr. OE *tȳrian, tēorian*] *vi* **1 :** to become weary **:** have one's strength decrease or fail ⟨*tired* long before the race was over⟩ ⟨the pitcher seems to be *tiring* although it is only the seventh inning⟩ **2 :** to have the patience, attention, interest, or liking reduced or exhausted ⟨never ~s of reading the Bible⟩ ⟨can describe it a thousand times before anyone ~s of it —Maxwell Mays⟩ ~ *vt* **1 :** to exhaust or considerably decrease the physical strength of **:** FATIGUE, WEARY ⟨the long hike *tired* the younger scouts⟩ **2 :** to wear out the patience of **:** satiate to the point of weariness or aversion **:** bore completely ⟨the endless chattering *tired* him and he left the room⟩ **3 :** to use up **:** wear out **:** OVERWORK ⟨*tiring* the land by overcultivation⟩

syn WEARY, FATIGUE, EXHAUST, JADE, FAG, TUCKER: TIRE is a general term indicating draining or bringing about loss of energy, strength, endurance, or resolution ⟨very *tired* after the long day's work⟩ WEARY suggests the cumulative effect of tiring until one is unable or unwilling to continue ⟨I am *wearied* out — it is too much — I am but flesh and blood, and I must sleep —Edna S. V. Millay⟩ ⟨I am *wearied* of keeping up deceits —Louis Bromfield⟩ FATIGUE suggests a tiring out by undue or excessive effort or strain that brings lassitude and enervation ⟨the passengers drooped on the wooden benches, too *fatigued* even to get the cool drinks —Dan Jacobson⟩ ⟨I rested for the remainder of the daylight in a shrubbery, being, in my enfeebled condition, too *fatigued* to push on —H.G. Wells⟩ EXHAUST is the strongest of these words in indicating utter draining or consuming of energy until one is without strength and energy ⟨his bonus system would have speeded up labor in a way to *exhaust* men in a few years —M.R.Cohen⟩ ⟨capacity for abstract thinking was *exhausted* by this effort —A.M.Young⟩ JADE applies to causing loss of freshness, spirit, animation, or interest and becoming dull, languid, or listless through overexertion or overindulging ⟨next morning I awoke *jaded* with the sense of having dreamed awful things all through the night —Max Beerbohm⟩ ⟨to minds *jaded* with debauches of over-emphasis it does contrive to give a thrill —C.E.Montague⟩ FAG suggests work or exertion to the point of sagging or drooping with weakness and weariness ⟨with a gasp for breath said, "Lord, what a run. I'm *fagged* to death" —John Masefield⟩ ⟨the long march up the river had *fagged* them brutally; overtired, the rest periods did them little good and laboring on the trail was torture —Norman Mailer⟩ TUCKER is a colloquial expression meaning to fatigue and leave without strength, breath, or resolution ⟨all *tuckered* out from the long climb⟩

²tire \"\ *n* -s **1 tires** *pl but sing in constr* **:** MILK SICKNESS 1, TREMBLE 3 **2 :** FATIGUE, WEARINESS

³tire \'tī(ə)r, -īə\ *n* -s [ME, short for *²attire*] **1** *obs* **:** wearing apparel **:** often sumptuous dress **:** ATTIRE **2 :** a woman's headband or hair ornamentation **3 :** PINAFORE

⁴tire \"\ *vt* -ED/-ING/-S [ME *tiren*, short for *attiren* to attire — more at ATTIRE] ATTIRE **:** to dress (the hair) with a tire ⟨painted her face, and *tired* her head —2 Kings 9:30 (AV)⟩

⁵tire \"\ *n* -s [ME, prob. fr. *³tire*] **1 :** the aggregate of strakes of a wheel **2 a :** the metal hoop forming the tread of a wheel; *specif* **:** the steel band shrunk on the fellies of a wagon wheel — see WHEEL illustration **b :** a continuous solid, partly solid, or pneumatic rubber cushion encircling and fitting into the rim of a wheel, and usu. consisting when pneumatic of an external rubber-and-fabric covering containing and protecting from injury an air-filled inner tube — see BICYCLE illustration **c :** the external rubber-and-fabric covering of a pneumatic tire

⁶tire \"\ *vt* -ED/-ING/-S **:** to put a tire on **:** provide with tires ⟨the blacksmith . . . and his young helper were *tiring* a wagon wheel —Jackson Burgess⟩

⁷tire *archaic var of* ¹TIER

⁸tire \'tī(ə)r, -īə\ *n* -s [F, prob. back-formation fr. *tirant* tie beam, tie rod, fr. pres. part. of *tirer* to pull, draw — more at TIRADE] **:** the member of a flying buttress that takes the thrust

tire bagger *n* **:** a worker who shapes flat uncured drum-built tires in a vacuum box and inserts air bags in the tires

tire chain *n* **:** a chain designed to be fastened over the tread of a tire in order to give a firmer grip on a road and esp. to prevent skidding or slipping — called also *chain, skid chain*

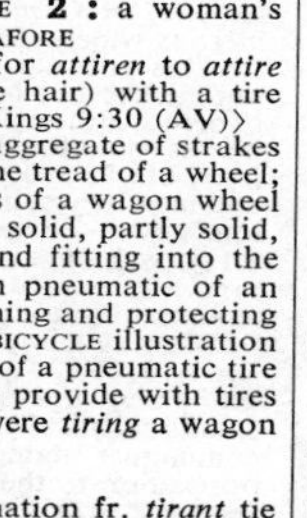

tire chain

¹tired \'tī(ə)rd, -īəd\ *adj, often* -ER/-EST [ME *tyred*, fr. past part. of *tyren, tyeren* to tire — more at TIRE] **1 :** drained of strength and energy **:** fatigued often to the point of exhaustion **:** WEARY ⟨when he was ~*est* he was least able to sleep —Robert Henderson⟩ **2 :** obviously worn by hard use **:** DILAPIDATED, RUN-DOWN ⟨decided to rejuvenate four ~ chairs —*McCall's Needlework*⟩ ⟨a neighborhood of ~ houses⟩ **3 :** completely out of patience **:** FED UP ⟨you make me ~ when you tell the same old story⟩ **4 :** devoid of freshness or originality **:** HACKNEYED ⟨no one could remember how often the ~ joke had been repeated —*Newsweek*⟩ ⟨can best be described by that ~ adjective *quaint* —Richard Joseph⟩

²tired \"\ *adj* [*⁵tire* + *-ed*] **:** equipped or fitted out with tires

tired·ly \'tī(ə)rdlē, -īəd-, -li\ *adv* **:** in a tired manner ⟨sank ~ into a big red chair —*Time*⟩

tired·ness \-dnəs\ *n* -ES **:** the quality or state of being tired ⟨a team of helpers who . . . look ready to drop with ~ —Mollie Panter-Downes⟩

tire gage *n* **:** a gage for measuring the air pressure in a tire

tire·less \'tī(ə)rləs, -īəl-\ *adj* **:** seemingly incapable of tiring **:** INDEFATIGABLE ⟨a man of distinguished presence and ~ industry —H.U.Faulkner⟩ — **tire·less·ly** *adv* — **tire·less·ness** *n* -ES

tire·man \", -,man, -,maa(ə)n\ *n, pl* **tiremen** [*⁵tire* + *man*] **1 :** a manufacturer of or dealer in tires **2 :** a worker who inspects and changes tires of buses

tire press *n* **:** a press for mounting or demounting solid tires

tires *pres 3d sing of* TIRE, *pl of* TIRE

tire·some \'tī(ə)rsəm, -īəs-\ *adj* **:** possessing a quality that tires, bores, or annoys **:** irritatingly tedious **:** WEARISOME ⟨the ~ chirping of a cricket —Mark Twain⟩ ⟨the endless flights of stone steps . . . were ~ —F. Tennyson Jesse⟩ ⟨there's some ~ engagement he wants to cut —John Buchan⟩ ⟨a nagging ~ woman —W.S.Maugham⟩ — **tire·some·ness** *n* -ES

tire·some·ly *adv* **:** in a tiresome manner ⟨tended to grow a little ~ facetious —A.C.Ward⟩

tiresomeweed \'==,=\ *n* **:** EELGRASS 1

tirewoman \'=,=\ *n, pl* **tirewomen** [*³tire* + *woman*] **1 :** a lady's maid; *esp* **:** a wardrobe woman in a theater **2 :** DRESSMAKER

tir·hu·tia \tir'hüd·ēə\ *n* -s *usu cap* **:** MAITHILI

tiring *pres part of* TIRE

tiring-house \'==,=\ *n* [*tiring* fr. gerund of *⁴tire*] **:** a section of a theater reserved for the actors and used esp. for dressing and preparing for stage entrances

tiring irons *n pl but sing in constr* [*tiring* fr. pres. part. of *¹tire*] **:** a puzzle game the object of which is to remove a series of rings from two or more metal loops which have but one opening and are intricately interlinked — called also *tarrying irons*

tiring-room \'==,=\ *n* [*tiring* fr. gerund of *⁴tire*] **:** a dressing room esp. in a theater

¹tirl \'tərl\ *vt* -ED/-ING/-S [prob. alter. (influenced by obs. E *tirve* to tirl, fr. ME *tirven*) of OE *tearflian* to turn, roll; akin to OHG *zerben* to turn over, OE *torfian* to throw, be tossed, ON *tyrfa* to cover with turf, *torf* turf — more at TURF] *chiefly Scot* **:** to strip the covering from **:** DIVEST, UNROOF

²tirl \"\ *vb* -ED/-ING/-S [alter. of *¹trill*] *vi* **1** *chiefly Scot* **:** to make a rattling sound with a door latch or pin **2** *chiefly Scot* **:** to whirl esp. in moving or falling ~ *vt* **1** *chiefly Scot* **:** to cause to revolve **:** turn rapidly **:** TWIRL **2** *chiefly Scot* **:** to rattle (as a pin) by moving rapidly up and down

³tirl \"\ *n* -s **1** *chiefly Scot* **:** a bout or turn usu. at drinking or dancing **2** *chiefly Scot* **:** something that revolves (as a turnstile or wheel)

tirlie-wirlie *or* **tirly-whirly** \¦tərli¦(h)wərli\ *n* [dim. of *³tirl* + *whirl*] *Scot* **:** an ornament consisting of a number of intervolved lines **:** an intricate contrivance

tir·ma \'tərmə\ *n* -s [native name in the Hebrides] *Scot* **:** OYSTER CATCHER

tiro *var of* TYRO

tir·o·dite \'tirə,dīt\ *n* -s [*Tirodi*, Central Provinces, India, its locality + E *-ite*] **:** a mineral (Mg, Mn)$_8$Si$_8$O$_{22}$(O, OH)$_2$ consisting of a basic silicate of magnesium and manganese of the amphibole group

tirolean *usu cap, var of* TYROLEAN

tirolese *usu cap, var of* TYROLESE

t iron *cap T, also* **tee iron** *n* **1 :** a rod with a short crosspiece at the end used as a hook **2 :** a T bar usu. of steel used in structures

ti·ro·ni·an \(')tī¦rōnēən\ *adj, usu cap* [L *tironianus*, fr. *tiron-* (fr. M. Tullius *Tiro fl* 1st cent. B.C. secretary of Cicero) + *-ianus* -ian] **:** of or relating to the learned freedman Tiro or the notae Tironianae

tirr \'tər\ *vb* -ED/-ING/-S [prob. short for obs. E *tirve* — more at TIRL (to strip)] *vt* **1** *chiefly Scot* **:** to tear off **:** STRIP, UNCOVER **2** *chiefly Scot* **:** to strip off the roof of **3** *chiefly Scot* **:** to remove the surface soil from esp. in quarrying ~ *vi, chiefly Scot* **:** to remove one's clothes **:** UNDRESS

tir·ra·lir·ra \,tirə'lirə\ *n* -s [imit.] **:** the note of a lark or robin or a sound resembling it

tir·ri·vee *also* **tir·ra·vee** *or* **tir·ri·vie** \'tərə,vē\ *n* -s [origin unknown] **1** *Scot* **:** an outburst of temper **2** *Scot* **:** a general uproar **:** COMMOTION

tir·than·ka·ra \tir'tənkərə\ *n* -s *often cap* [Skt *tīrthankara*, lit., ford-making, fr. *tīrtha* passage, ford + *karoti* he does, makes — more at KARMA] **:** one of the 24 founding jinas of Jain tradition venerated as breakers of the path across the stream of time to Nirvana who have shown the way to spiritual liberation in Jainism **:** a pioneer of faith

tir·u·chi·ra·pal·li \¦tirəchə¦räpəlē\ *adj, usu cap* [fr. *Tiruchirapalli* (Trichinopoly), India] **:** TRICHINOPOLY

tir·u·ray *also* **tir·u·rai** \¦tirə¦rī\ *n, pl* **tiruray** *or* **tirurays** *also* **tirurai** *or* **tirurais** *usu cap* **1 a :** a predominantly pagan people in the western part of Cotabato province, central Mindanao, Philippines **b :** a member of such people **2 :** the Austronesian language of the Tiruray people

tis *pl of* TI

ti·sane \tə'zan\ *n* -s [F, fr. L *ptisana* peeled barley, barley water — more at PTISAN] **:** an infusion orig. of barley but now usu. of dried leaves or flowers (as linden blossoms or camomile or cherry stems) that is used as a beverage or for mildly medicinal effects **:** PTISAN

ti·se·li·us apparatus *also* **tiselius cell** \tə¦sālēəs-, -¦zā\ *n, usu cap T* [after Arne *Tiselius* b1902 Swed. biochemist] **:** an apparatus characterized by a rectangular U-tube divided into two or three sections for carrying out electrophoresis esp. of proteins in a biological system (as blood plasma)

tish·ah b'ab *or* **tisha b'ab** *or* **tish·ah b'av** *or* **tisha b'av** \¦tishə¦bäv, -bȯv\ *n, usu cap T & Ab or Av* [Heb *tish'āh bĕ'ābh* ninth of Ab] **:** a Jewish fast day that is observed on the 9th day of Ab in commemoration of the destruction of the First and Second Temples at Jerusalem — called also *Ninth of Ab*

tish·chen·ko reaction \tə'shenkō-, təsh'ch\ *n, usu cap T* [after Vyacheslav E. *Tishchenko* †1941 Russian chemist] **:** the synthesis (as of ethyl acetate from acetaldehyde and aluminum ethoxide) of an ester from an aldehyde involving simultaneous oxidation and reduction of two molecules of the aldehyde in the presence of an aluminum alkoxide

tish·ri *or* **tiz·ri** \'tishrē\ *n* -s *usu cap* [Heb *tishri*, fr. Assyr-Bab *tashrītu* the seventh month] **:** the 1st month of the civil year or the 7th month of the ecclesiastical year in the Jewish calendar — see MONTH table

tis·su·al \'tish(y)əwəl, 'ti(,)shüəl, *chiefly Brit* 'tisyəwəl *or* 'ti(,)syüəl\ *adj* **:** of or relating to tissue

¹tis·sue \'ti(,)shü, 'tish(,)yü, 'ti(,)shü, 'tish(,)yü, *before a vowel often* -sh(y)əw; *chiefly South* -sh(y)ə *before a consonant or pause or before a vowel in a following word; chiefly Brit* 'ti(,)syü *or* 'ti(,)syü *or* 'tisyəw; *chiefly dial* 'tishē *or* -shi *in "tissue paper"*\ *n* -s [ME *tissu*, fr. OF, fr. past part. of *tistre* to weave, fr. L *texere* — more at TECHNICAL] **1 a (1)** *archaic* **:** a rich ornamented cloth usu. of silk interwoven with gold or silver threads **(2) :** a fine lightweight fabric often sheer or semitransparent; *esp* **:** a gauze of silk or wool **b :** something resembling a fabric of tissue **:** an intricate or interrelated number of things forming a web **:** a complicated mesh ⟨the testimony . . . is a ~ of lies —W.A.White⟩ ⟨most battlefield history of the past is a ~ of myths —S.L.A.Marshall⟩ **2 a :** TISSUE PAPER **b :** CARBON PAPER **2 c :** CLEANSING TISSUE **3 a :** an aggregate of cells usu. of a particular kind or kinds together with their intercellular substance that form one of the structural materials out of which the body of a plant or an animal is built up — see COLLENCHYMA, PARENCHYMA, PROSENCHYMA, SCLERENCHYMA; CONNECTIVE TISSUE, EPITHELIUM, MUSCLE, NERVE 2 **b :** something resembling the living tissue of a plant or animal ⟨give vitality and vigor to the ~s of our law —B.N. Cardozo⟩ ⟨collective bargaining . . . is part of the living ~ of society —*Current Biog.*⟩

²tissue \"\ *adj* [ME, fr. *tissu* tissue] **:** resembling a fabric of tissue in weight, texture, or appearance **:** characterized by unusual sheerness ⟨~ gingham⟩ ⟨~ faille⟩

³tissue \"\ *vt* -ED/-ING/-S [ME *tissuen*, fr. *tissu* tissue] **:** to weave into tissue **:** embroider by or as if by interweaving ⟨covered with cloth of gold *tissued* upon blue —Francis Bacon⟩

tissue culture *n* **:** the act, process, or technique of making body tissue grow in a culture medium outside of the organism; *also* **:** a culture of tissue (as fibrous tissue or epithelium)

tissued *adj* [fr. past part. of *³tissue*] **1 :** woven in the manner of tissue **:** having the splendor or delicacy of tissue **2 :** wrapped in tissue paper ⟨a pair of brown shoes and a pair of black all ~ up —Richard Llewellyn⟩

tissue fluid *n* **:** fluid permeating the spaces between individual cells, being in osmotic contact with the blood and lymph, and serving in interstitial transport of nutrients and waste

tissue paper *n* -s **:** a thin gauzy paper weighing not over 12 to 15 pounds for a ream of 480 sheets cut 24x36 inches

tissue space *n* **:** an intercellular space

tis·suey \'tish(y)əw|ē, 'ti(,)shü|, |i, *chiefly Brit* 'tisyəw| *or* 'ti(,)syü|\ *adj* **:** resembling tissue

tiss·wood \'ti,swüd\ *n* [*tiss* of unknown origin + *wood*] **1 a :** SNOWDROP TREE 1 **b :** RED BAY **2 :** the wood of a tisswood

tisty-tosty \¦tisti¦tästi\ *n* -ES [origin unknown] *dial Eng* **:** a ball made of flowers

tis·win *also* **tiz·win** \təz'wēn\ *n* -s [MexSp *tesguino, tejuino, tecuin*, fr. Nahuatl *tecuini* heartbeat] **:** a fermented beverage made by Indians of the southwestern U.S.

¹tit \'tit, *usu* -id·+V\ *n* -s [ME *titte*, fr. OE *titt, tit, tite* — more at TEAT] **1 a :** TEAT 1 **b :** BREAST 1a — usu. considered vulgar **2 :** something resembling or held to resemble a tit: **a :** a small metal part that ejects the finished nails from the bore in nail making **b :** TEAT 3

²tit \"\ *vb* **titted; titted; titting; tits** [ME *titten*] *chiefly Scot* **:** to pull forcibly **:** JERK, TUG, TWITCH

³tit \"\ *n* -s [ME *titte*, fr. *titten* to tit] *chiefly Scot* **:** a sharp or sudden pull **:** JERK, TUG, TWITCH

⁴tit \"\ *n* -s [*tit-* (as in *titmouse*)] **1 a :** a small horse **b :** an inferior or weedy horse **2** *archaic* **:** a girl or young woman: **a :** one of loose moral character **:** HUSSY **b :** one that is or is held to be admirable in some respect (as appearance)

⁵tit \"\ *n* -s [short for *titmouse*] **:** a small plump often long-tailed bird **:** TITMOUSE — often used with a qualifying term ⟨wren ~⟩ ⟨coal ~⟩

tit *abbr* **1** title **2** titular

¹ti·tan \'tīt^{ə}n\ *n* -s [Gk] **1** *usu cap* **:** one of a family or race of earth giants in ancient Greek mythology whose power was destroyed by the Olympian gods and who are usu. held to have been characterized by gigantic size, immense brute strength, and primitive force and appetite rather than intelligence or morality **2** *sometimes cap* **:** one gigantic in size or power **:** a titanic being **:** one that stands out among others of a group esp. for greatness of stature or achievement ⟨one of the ~s of American higher education —*Saturday Rev.*⟩ ⟨five mountain ~s higher than the highest of the . . . Alps —*Geog. School Bull.*⟩ ⟨grand old ~ of American law —Fred Rodell⟩ **3 :** TITAN CRANE

²titan \"\ *adj, usu cap* **:** TITANIC

titan- *or* **titano-** *comb form* [NL *titanium*] **:** titanium ⟨*titan*ate⟩ ⟨*titano*cyanide⟩ ⟨*titan*ofluoride⟩

ti·ta·nate \'tīt^{ə}n,āt, -^{ə}nət\ *n* -s [*titan-* + *-ate*] **1 :** any of various compounds (as barium titanate) that are multiple oxides or solid solutions of titanium dioxide with other metallic oxides **2 :** an ester of the general formula Ti(OR)$_4$ obtainable by reaction of titanium tetrachloride with an alcohol or phenol in the presence of a base

ti·ta·nat·ed \-ād·əd\ *adj* [*titanate* + *-ed*] **:** blended with titanium dioxide ⟨~ lithopone⟩

ti·tan-augite \¦tīt^{ə}n+\ *n* [G *titanaugit*, fr. *titan-* (fr. NL *titanium*) + *augit* augite (fr. L *augites*)] **:** a basaltic augite rich in titanium and usu. alkali

titan crane *n* **:** a massive crane with an overhanging counterbalanced arm carrying a traveler and lifting crab supported by a carriage mounted on track rails and used esp. for lifting and setting in place heavy masonry blocks for piers and breakwaters — compare GOLIATH CRANE

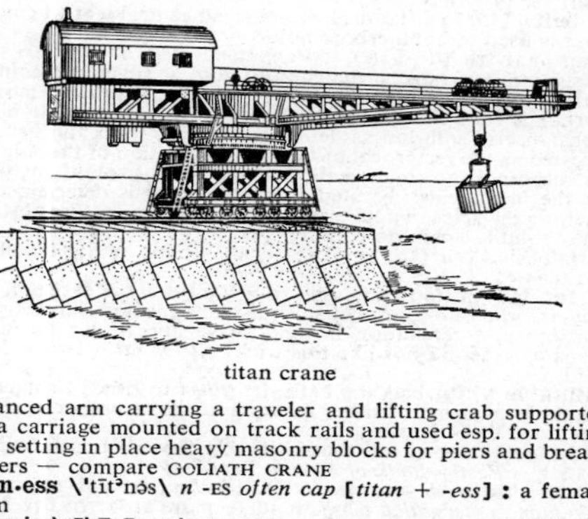

titan crane

ti·tan·ess \'tīt^{ə}nəs\ *n* -ES *often cap* [*titan* + *-ess*] **:** a female titan

ti·ta·nia \tī'tānēə, tə't- *sometimes* -'tan- *or* -nyə\ *n* -s [NL, fr. *titanium*] **1 :** TITANIUM DIOXIDE **2 :** RUTILE 2

¹ti·ta·ni·an \(')tī¦tānēən, -¦tan-, -nyən *sometimes* tə't-\ *adj, usu cap* [L *titanius* titanic (fr. Gk *titanios*, fr. *Titan* + *-ios* -y) + E *-an*] *archaic* **:** ¹TITANIC 1 ⟨begin with a *Titanian* revenge to shoot against heaven —John Florio⟩

²ti·ta·ni·an \(')tī¦tānēən, tə't-, -nyən, *sometimes* -¦tan-\ *adj* [NL *titanium* + E *-an*] **:** of, relating to, or containing titanium

¹ti·tan·ic \(')tī¦tanik, -nēk *sometimes* tə't-\ *adj* [Gk *titanikos*, fr. *Titan* + *-ikos* -ic] **1** *usu cap* **:** of, relating to, or held to have characteristics of the Titans of ancient Greek mythology **2** *sometimes cap* **:** resembling a titan (as in size or character): as **a :** marked by very great size **:** of enormous magnitude, power, scope, strength, or influence **:** COLOSSAL, GIGANTIC ⟨great factories hummed like one unanimous ~ loom —Donn Byrne⟩ ⟨a ~ archipelago —*Natural History*⟩ ⟨political change . . . on a ~ scale —H.J.Laski⟩ **b (1) :** manifesting superhuman power or force **:** exerting more than human strength **:** marked by tremendous brute force **(2) :** calling for the exertion of such strength or power ⟨the ~ labor of clearing away the debris after the air raid⟩ ⟨done a ~ job of streamlining and reorganizing the service —*Americas*⟩ **c :** EARTH-SHAKING ⟨a ~ civil war that all but destroyed the country —G.W.Johnson⟩ ⟨a ~ struggle⟩ **syn** see HUGE

²ti·tan·ic \(')tī¦tanik tə't-, -'tān-, -nēk\ *adj* [NL *titanium* + E *-ic*] **:** of, relating to, or containing titanium — used esp. of compounds in which this element is tetravalent; compare TITANOUS

titanic acid *n* [*²titanic*] **:** any of various amorphous weakly acid substances that are hydrates of titanium dioxide obtainable from solutions of titanium tetrachloride or basic titanium sulfate: as **a :** a gelatinous highly hydrated substance that is the ortho acid **b :** a less highly hydrated substance

ti·tan·i·cal·ly \(')tī¦tanək(ə)lē, -nēk-, -li *sometimes* tə't-\ *adv* [*¹titanic* + *-ally*] **:** in a titanic manner ⟨was ~ a failure at the job —Sinclair Lewis⟩ ⟨with ~ explosive results —*Atlantic*⟩

ti·tan·ich·thys \,tīt^{ə}n'ikthəs\ *n, cap* [NL, fr. Gk *Titan* + NL *-ichthys*] **:** a genus (the type of the family Titanichthyidae) of very large toothless arthrodiran fishes of the Upper Devonian of Ohio

titanic iron ore *or* **titaniferous iron ore** *n* [*²titanic*] **:** ILMENITE

titanic oxide *n* **:** TITANIUM DIOXIDE

ti·ta·nif·er·ous \¦tīt^{ə}n¦if(ə)rəs\ *adj* [*titan-* + *-iferous*] **:** containing or yielding titanium

ti·tan·ism \'tīt^{ə}n,izəm\ *n* -s *often cap* [*titan* + *-ism*] **:** the spirit characterizing or held to characterize a Titan: **a :** defiance of and headlong revolt against limits or restraints and esp. existing social or artistic conventions ⟨the *Titanism* of every kind that has marked our modern emancipation —Irving Babbitt⟩ **b :** a marked tendency to expansiveness in expression resulting in grandiosity and freedom from all restraint

ti·ta·nite \'tīt^{ə}n,īt\ *n* -s [G *titanit*, fr. NL *titanium* + G *-it* -ite] **:** SPHENE

ti·ta·ni·um \tī'tānēəm, tə't- *sometimes* -'tan- *or* -nyəm\ *n* -s [NL, fr. Gk *Titan* + NL *-ium*] **:** a lustrous silvery gray light strong high-melting metallic element that is usu. hard and brittle in the cold but malleable when heated and ductile when pure, that has good corrosion resistance at ordinary temperatures and is tetravalent in most of its compounds, that is found combined in ilmenite, rutile, and other minerals, is widely distributed in small amounts esp. in igneous rocks, soils, and clays, and is the ninth most abundant element in the earth's crust, that is usu. produced in the form of sponge from titanium tetrachloride by reduction with magnesium or sodium and consolidated by melting, and that is used chiefly in the form of ferrotitanium in making steel and in other alloys as a structural material (as in aircraft, jet engines, missiles, and chemical equipment) — symbol *Ti*; see ELEMENT table

titanium carbide *n* **:** a very hard gray metallic substance approximating the composition TiC, made by heating titanium dioxide and carbon in the electric furnace, and used chiefly with tungsten carbide in cemented carbide compositions for cutting steel

titanium dioxide *n* **:** the compound TiO$_2$ that occurs naturally in three different crystal forms as rutile, anatase, and brookite, that is produced commercially from rutile or ilmenite as a white amorphous powder or in the rutile or anatase crystal forms, and that is used chiefly as a pigment or opacifier (as in paint, vitreous enamel, linoleum, rubber and plastics, printing ink, paper) because of its high covering power, brilliance and reflectivity, and resistance to light and fumes, and also in ceramic components for electronic equipment and in the form of large synthetic rutile crystals as gems

titanium oxide *n* **:** any of several oxides of titanium; *esp* **:** TITANIUM DIOXIDE

titanium tetrachloride *n* **:** a volatile liquid compound $TiCl_4$ that is made by the action of chlorine at high temperature on either titanium or titanium dioxide and so serves as a means of separating the titanium content of crude ores by distillation and that is used otherwise chiefly in skywriting and smoke screens because it fumes in moist air

titanium white *n* **:** titanium dioxide used as a pigment; *also* **:** a composite pigment containing titanium dioxide and an extender (as calcium sulfate)

titano- — see TITAN-

ti·tano·magnetite \ˌtītᵊn(ˌ)ō, tīˈtanə, tə̇ˈt-, -ˈtānə+\ *n* [*titan-* + *magnetite*] **:** a titaniferous variety of magnetite

ti·tano·saur \tīˈtanəˌsȯ(ə)r, ˈtītᵊn-\ *n* -S [NL *Titanosaurus*] **:** a reptile or fossil of the genus *Titanosaurus*

ti·tano·sau·rus \tīˌtanəˈsȯrəs, ˌtītᵊn-\ *n, cap* [NL, fr. Gk *Titan* + NL *-o-* + *-saurus*] **:** a genus of large Cretaceous sauropod dinosaurs chiefly of the southern hemisphere

ti·tano·silicate \ˌtītᵊn(ˌ)ō, tīˈtanə, tə̇ˈt-, -ˈtānə+\ *n* [*titan-* + *silicate*] **:** SILICOTITANATE

ti·tano·there \tīˈtanəˌthi(ə)r, ˈtītᵊn-\ *n* -S [NL *Titanotherium*] **:** a mammal or fossil of the family Brontotheriidae **:** BRONTOTHERE

ti·tano·the·ri·idae \(ˌ)tīˌtanəthəˈrīəˌdē, ˌtītᵊn(ˌ)ōth-\ [NL *Titanotherium* + *-idae*] *syn of* BRONTOTHERIIDAE

ti·tano·the·ri·um \-nəˈthirēəm\ [NL, fr. Gk *Titan* + NL *-o-* + *-therium*] *syn of* MENODUS

ti·tanous \(ˈ)tīˈtanəs, tə̇ˈtan-, ˈtītᵊn-\ *adj* [ISV *titan-* + *-ous*] **:** of, relating to, or derived from titanium — used esp. of compounds in which this element is trivalent; compare TITANIC

ti·tanyl \ˈtītᵊnəl, -ᵊnˌēl; tīˈtanᵊl, tə̇ˈt-\ *n* -S [*titan-* + *-yl*] **:** the group TiO consisting of titanium and oxygen that is a bivalent radical

ti·tar \ˈtēd·ə(r)\ *n* -S [Hindi *tītar*, fr. Skt *tittira* — more at TURTLE (turtledove)] **:** a francolin (*Francolinus pondicerianus*) of southern Asia

tit babbler *n* [*⁵tit*] **:** any of several small East Indian and Asiatic timaliine birds of *Macronus* and related genera

titbit *var of* TIDBIT

tit drill *n* [*¹tit*] **:** a flat drill with a small central teat to guide it that is used to counterbore holes

ti·ter *or* **ti·tre** \ˈtīd·ə(r), ˈtēt·ə- *sometimes* ˈtē\ *n* -S [F *titre* title, designation of rank, proportion of gold or silver in a coin, fr. MF *title, tiltre* title, designation of rank, fr. OF *title* — more at TITLE] **1 :** the strength of a solution or the concentration of a substance in solution as determined by titration and usu. expressed as the reciprocal of the highest dilution of the solution or substance showing specific activity **2 :** the solidifying point of the fatty acids liberated from a fat that is determined by melting the acids in a tube and noting the temperature at which they solidify again on cooling

titfish \ˈ=,=\ *n* [*¹tit* + *fish*; fr. the shape of its tentacles] **:** TREPANG

tit for tat \ˌtitfə(r)ˈtat, *usu* -ad.+V\ [alter. of earlier *tip for tap*, fr. *⁵tip* + *for* + *tap*] **:** an equivalent given in return (as for an injury) **:** retaliation in kind ⟨gave him *tit for tat* in the debate⟩ ⟨she did not like this tricky *tit for tat* —Israel Zangwill⟩

¹tith·able \ˈtīthəbəl\ *adj* [ME, fr. *tithen* to tithe] **:** subject or liable to payment of tithes ⟨a tenth of his ~ property —F.M. Stenton⟩ ⟨a ~ person⟩

²tithable \"\ *n* -S **:** one that is tithable ⟨levied of each ~ in the parish —*Vestry Book of Bruton Parish (Va.)*⟩

¹tithe \ˈtīth\ *vb* -ED/-ING/-S [ME *tithen*, fr. OE *teogothian, tēothian*, fr. *teogotha, tēotha* tenth — more at ²TITHE] *vt* **1 :** to pay or give a tenth part of esp. for the support of the church **:** pay taxes in the form of tithes on ⟨~ an estate⟩ ⟨~ a crop⟩ ⟨~ one's income⟩ **2** *obs* **a :** to take a tenth part of or every tenth one from **:** divide into tenths ⟨divers of them were constrained to ~ themselves and eat the tenth man —Henry Spelman⟩ **b :** to reduce by one tenth of the original number (as by putting to death one man out of every ten) **:** DECIMATE **3 a :** to levy a tithe on **:** impose the payment of a tenth upon **:** tax to the amount of a tenth **:** exact tithe from **b :** to collect or exact one tenth from (as goods) as a tithe **:** take tithe of ⟨~ the product of the earth —Sydney Smith⟩ ~ *vi* **:** to pay tithe; *specif* **:** to give a tenth of one's income as a tithe esp. for the support of church or religious work ⟨church members are exhorted to ~⟩ ⟨a fundamentalist congregation . . . in which everyone ~*s* —Hugh Morrow⟩

²tithe \"\ *n* -S [ME *tigthe, tithe*, fr. OE *teogotha, tēotha* tenth; akin to OFris *tegotha* tenth, MLG *tegede*; all fr. a prehistoric WGmc alter. of the source of OHG *zehanto* tenth — more at TEIND] **1 :** a tenth part of something paid as a voluntary contribution or as a tax for religious purposes and esp. for the support of a priesthood or religious establishment: as **a :** a tenth part (as of a person's entire possessions or of the yearly increase thereof) paid in kind as a tax by the Hebrews and other ancient peoples **b :** an orig. voluntary but later legally required payment of one tenth of one's yearly income for the support usu. of the local parish church in medieval and later times **c :** a payment in kind or money consisting until the middle of the 19th century of one tenth of the yearly profits arising from land, stock, or personal industry and traditionally required of the inhabitants of a parish in the United Kingdom for the support of the parish church — see MIXED TITHE, PERSONAL TITHE, PRAEDIAL TITHE, TEIND **d :** a tenth of one's income given voluntarily for the support of church or religious work **2 :** the voluntary or required obligation represented by individual tithes — usu. used without article ⟨in the seventh century the payment of ~ was a religious duty —F.M.Stenton⟩ **3 a :** the tenth part of something **:** TENTH ⟨a hundred thousand a year . . . a cool ~ of a million a year to manipulate —G.A. Wagner⟩ **b :** a small part of something **:** an insignificant portion **:** one bit ⟨these are only a ~ of the treasures in the . . . museum —Elizabeth Montizambert⟩ ⟨passed over for men who have not a ~ of his ability —H.J.Laski⟩ ⟨no man . . . knows this country a ~ as well as the author —Louis Golding⟩ **4 a :** tax, levy, or tribute of usu. one tenth for a purpose other than a religious one ⟨forced to pay a fixed ~ that goes . . . into the private till of the Pasha —Joachim Joesten⟩

³tithe \"\ *adj* [ME, fr. *²tithe*] **1 a :** due as or given in payment of tithe — see TITHE PIG **b :** of or relating to tithes ⟨~ gatherer⟩ ⟨~ payer⟩ **2 :** TENTH ⟨a ~ part⟩

tithe barn *n* [*³tithe*] **:** a barn orig. built to hold ecclesiastical tithes paid in kind and common in many parts of England

tithe man *n* **:** TITHINGMAN 3

tithe pig *n* **:** a pig set apart or given in payment of tithe

tithe proctor *n* **:** a collector of tithes

¹tith·er \ˈtīthə(r)\ *n* -S [ME, fr. *tithen* to tithe + *-er*] **1 :** one that pays tithes ⟨practically every member of the church is a ~ —*Emporia (Kans.) Gazette*⟩ **2 :** one that collects or advocates the payment of tithes

²tith·er \ˈtithə(r)\ *var of* TOTHER

¹tithing *n* -S [ME *tething, tithing*, fr. OE *tēothung*, fr. *tēothian* to tithe, take one tenth + *-ung* -ing — more at TITHE, -ING] **:** a small administrative division locally preserved in many parts of England apparently orig. consisting of ten men with their families or of the tenth part of the hundred — compare FRANKPLEDGE

²tithing *n* -S [ME, fr. gerund of *tithen* to tithe] **1 :** the act of one that tithes **:** a paying, levying, or taking of tithes **2 :** something that is tithed **:** a tenth or set apart as tithe **:** TITHE

tith·ing·man \ˈtīthiŋmən\ *n, pl* **tithingmen** [ME, fr. OE *tēothingman*, fr. *tēothing* + *man*] **1 :** the chief man of an old English tithing **2 :** a British local peace officer **3** [*²tithing* + *man*] **:** a collector of tithes **4 a :** an elected local official having the functions of a peace officer in various American colonies (as Maryland and in New England) **b :** an annually elected official chosen in New England towns until well into the 19th century and charged primarily with preserving order in church during divine service and enforcing the observance of the Sabbath

tithing penny *n* [*¹tithing*] **:** a small customary duty traditionally paid under old English law: **a :** one paid by the tenants of a manor to the lord **b :** one paid by the lord of a manor at the hundred court **c :** one paid by each tithing to the sheriff to defray court expenses

tithing rod *n* [*tithing*man + *rod*] **:** a long rod used by tithingmen to keep order in church (as by tapping noisy or drowsy persons)

ti·tho·nia \tə̇ˈthōnēə, -nyə\ *n* [NL, prob. fr. L *Tithonis*, poetical name of Aurora, goddess of the dawn (fr. her marriage to *Tithonus*, son of Laomedon) + NL *-ia*] **1** *cap* **:** a genus of tall herbs (family Compositae) that are natives of Mexico and Central America but grown farther north as annual ornamentals and have alternate leaves and flower heads resembling sunflowers **2** -S **:** any plant of the genus *Tithonia* — called also *Mexican sunflower*

tithy·mal \ˈtithəməl, tə̇ˈthīm-\ *n* -S [L *tithymallus, tithymalus*, fr. Gk *tithymallos*] **:** SPURGE 1; *esp* **:** a spurge (*Tithymalus cyparissias*)

tith·y·ma·lop·sis \ˌtithəməˈläpsə̇s\ *n, cap* [NL, fr. *Tithymalus* + *-opsis*] *in some classifications* **:** a genus of chiefly perennial No. American spurges that is usu. included in *Euphorbia*

tith·y·ma·lus \ˌtithəˈmāləs, -mal-\ *n, cap* [NL, fr. L *tithymallus, tithymalus* tithymal] *in some classifications* **:** a genus of chiefly annual No. American spurges that is usu. included in *Euphorbia*

¹ti·ti \ˈtīˌtī, ˈtīd·ˌī\ *n* -S [prob. of Timucuan origin] **1 a :** a tree (*Cliftonia monophylla*) of the family Cyrillaceae that is found in the southern U.S. and has glossy leaves and racemes of fragrant white flowers succeeded by one-seeded drupes — called also *black titi, buckwheat tree* **b :** any of several trees of the genus *Cyrilla* — called also *white titi* **2 :** SOURWOOD **3** *Austral* **:** TI 1

²ti·ti \tə̇ˈtē\ *or* **tee·tee** \tēˈtē\ *n* -S [Sp *tití*, fr. Aymara *titi*, lit., little cat] **:** any of various small So. American monkeys of the genus *Callicebus* that resemble the squirrel monkeys of the genus *Saimiri* but have the head not so elongated posteriorly and the tail more thickly haired

³ti·ti \ˈtēˌtē\ *n* -S [Maori] **1** *NewZeal* **:** a blue-footed petrel (*Pterodroma cookii*) **2** *NewZeal* **:** SOOTY SHEARWATER

¹ti·tian \ˈtishən\ *n* -S *often cap* [after *Titian* (Tiziano Vecelli) †1576 Ital. painter] **1 :** a brownish orange that is less strong, slightly yellower and lighter than spice, slightly yellower and lighter than prairie brown or Windsor tan, and slightly redder and darker than amber brown or gold pheasant **2 :** one having titian hair ⟨blondes, brunets, and ~*s*⟩

²titian \"\ *adj, often cap* **:** of the color titian ⟨~ hair⟩

ti·tian·esque \ˌtishəˈnesk\ *adj, usu cap* [*Titian* †1576 Ital. painter + E *-esque*] **:** after the manner of or suggesting the style of the Venetian painter Titian noted for his breadth of treatment, realism, and rich but subdued coloring

ti·til·la \tīˈtilə, tə̇ˈt-\ *n, pl* **titil·lae** \tīˈti(ˌ)lē; tə̇ˈti(ˌ)lē, -ˌlī\ [NL, fr. L *titillare* to tickle] **:** any of various processes on the external genitalia of male invertebrate animals believed to play a role in sexual activities

ti·il·late \ˈtid·ᵊlˌāt, -itᵊl-, *usu* -ād.+V\ *vt* -ED/-ING/-S [L *titillatus*, past part. of *titillare* to tickle, titillate] **1 :** to stimulate by or as if by tickling ⟨they . . . ~ the nymphs with their antennae —J.D.Hood⟩ ⟨the static machine, used . . . to ~ the skin —L.R.Harrison⟩ **2 :** to excite pleasurably or agreeably **:** arouse by stimulation ⟨*titillated* the prurient with the frankness of its carnal detail —S.H.Adams⟩ ⟨~ rather than satiate the reader's interest —Raymond Walters b. 1912⟩ **syn** see PLEASE

titillating *adj* [fr. pres. part. of *titillate*] **:** being a source of, marked by, or inducing a state of titillation **:** pleasantly stimulating or exciting ⟨~ thoughts⟩ ⟨a ~ feeling⟩ ⟨~ reading⟩ — **tit·il·lat·ing·ly** *adv*

tit·il·la·tion \ˌtid·ᵊlˈāshən, -itᵊl-\ *n* -S [ME *titillacione*, fr. L *titillation-, titillatio*, fr. *titillatus* (past part. of *titillare* to titillate) + *-ion-, -io* -ion] **1 :** the action of titillating or the state of being titillated; *esp* **:** a pleasurable excitement or stimulation (as of the mind or senses) **2 :** a sensation of being titillated **:** a transient reaction from or as if from being tickled **:** a slight thrill esp. of pleasure

tit·il·la·tive \ˈ==ˌād·iv\ *adj* [*titillate* + *-ive*] **:** tending or serving to titillate ⟨a rowdy charmer with a ~ view of humanity —Charles Lee⟩

titius-bode law \ˌtētsēəsˈbōdə-\ *n, usu cap T&B* [after J.D. *Titius* †1796 Ger. mathematician, & Johann E. *Bode* †1826 Ger. astronomer] **:** BODE'S LAW

tit·i·vate *or* **tit·ti·vate** \ˈtid·əˌvāt, -itə-, *usu* -ād.+V\ *vb* -ED/-ING/-S [perh. fr. *¹tidy* + *-vate* (as in *renovate*)] **:** to dress up (as by making small additions or alterations in attire) **:** spruce up **:** smarten up

²titivate \"\ *vt* -ED/-ING/-S [by alter.] **:** TITILLATE ⟨few . . . fans felt *titivated* with pleasurable anticipations —E.F.Carter⟩

tit·i·va·tion \ˌ==ˈvāshən\ *n* -S [*titivate* + *-ion*] **:** the action of dressing up or making small additions or improvements in one's dress ⟨she must be a perfect beauty . . . to look so well without any ~ —Alix King⟩

tit·lark \ˈtitˌ=\ *n* [*tit-* (as in *titmouse*) + *lark*] **:** PIPIT

¹ti·tle \ˈtīd·ᵊl, -ītᵊl\ *n* -S [ME *titel, title*, fr. OF *titele, title*, fr. L *titulus* inscription, label, title] **1 a** *obs* **:** an inscription placed over, upon, or under something to describe, distinguish, explain, or entitle it **:** LEGEND **b :** an inscription placed on a cross usu. above a crucified person or on a crucifix ⟨Pilate wrote a ~, and put it on the cross —Jn 19:19 (AV)⟩ **c :** written material introduced into a motion picture or television program to give credits, explain an action, or represent dialogue — compare CREDIT, SUBTITLE **2 a :** the union of all the elements constituting legal ownership and being divided in common law into possession, right of possession, and right of property **b :** something that constitutes a legally just cause of exclusive possession **:** the body of facts or events that give rise to the ownership of real or personal property ⟨good ~ to an estate⟩ ⟨an imperfect ~⟩ **c :** the instrument (as a deed) that is evidence of a right **3 a :** something that justifies or substantiates a claim **:** sufficient proof or justification **:** a valid reason **:** a ground of right ⟨his services give him a ~ to our gratitude⟩ ⟨unable to establish his ~ of authorship⟩ **b :** an alleged or recognized right ⟨he has no ~ to anticipate our support⟩ **4 a :** a descriptive or general heading (as of a chapter in a book) **b :** the heading which names an act or statute, by which it is distinguished from others, and which at common law forms no part of the act but in case of ambiguity sometimes is referred to as an aid in interpretation **c :** the heading of a legal declaration setting forth the names of the parties and the court and the calendar or docket number of the case **5 a :** the distinguishing name of a written, printed, spoken, or filmed production (as a book, pamphlet, essay, or poem): as (1) **:** the principal name consisting of a word or phrase and sometimes appearing on the binding (as of a book) in the shortest form that will be distinctive — see HALF TITLE, SHORT TITLE, SUBTITLE (2) **:** all material on a title page preceding the author's name or its substitute and sometimes including a subtitle and various pieces of descriptive matter (3) **:** all the matter on a title page including punctuation marks esp. in an old or rare book **b :** a similar distinguishing name given to a picture, statue, musical composition, or other work **6 :** a sphere of work or a source of income or maintenance required by a bishop of a candidate for ordination **7 :** a descriptive name **:** a distinctive appellation or designation ⟨gallants, lads, boys, hearts of gold, all the ~*s* of good fellowship —Shak.⟩ ⟨earned for him the ~ of "father of the American psychological novel" —*Amer. Guide Series: N.J.*⟩ **8 :** a Roman Catholic parish church in or near Rome of which a cardinal is titular head **9 :** a division of an instrument or book; *esp* **:** one of a portion of a bill or act that usu. is larger than a section or article ⟨this act, divided into ~ and sections —*U.S.Code*⟩ **10** *obs* **:** an assertion of right **:** CLAIM ⟨an eagerness after employments in the state was looked upon . . . as the worst ~ a man could set up —Jonathan Swift⟩ **11 a :** an appellation of dignity, honor, distinction, or preeminence attached on a hereditary or acquired basis to a person or family by virtue of rank, office, precedent, privilege, or attainment, possession of or association with certain lands, or as a mark of respect ⟨no ~ of nobility shall be granted by the United States —*U.S.Constitution*⟩ — see COURTESY TITLE **b :** a person holding a title and esp. a title of nobility ⟨saw to it that their daughters married authentic foreign ~*s* —J.D.Hart⟩ **12 a :** TITLE PAGE **b :** the first book section containing the title page **c :** TITLE SPACE **d :** a gold-stamped leather label for a book backbone **e :** a specially printed title page for insertion in a deluxe book in place of or preceding a text title **13 :** a literary work or book as distinguished from a particular copy ⟨fifty ~*s* of fiction and ten copies of each in the library⟩ ⟨the press published 15 ~*s* last year —*Book Production*⟩ **14 :** CHAMPIONSHIP 1 ⟨won the boxing ~⟩ ⟨holder of the indoor tennis ~⟩

²title \"\ *vt* **titled; titled; titling** \-īd·ᵊliŋ, -īt(ᵊ)liŋ\ **titles** [ME *titelen*, fr. *titel* title] **1 a :** to provide a title for (as a book) **:** furnish with a title **:** give a title to **b :** to stamp or otherwise print the title of (a book) on the front cover or backbone **2 a :** to designate or call by a title (as of relationship, rank, or office) **:** TERM, STYLE ⟨their sovereign *titled* himself King of the Franks —James Bryce⟩ **b :** to dignify with an appellation or designation of rank **:** endow with a title

³title \"\ *adj* [*¹title*] **:** of or relating to a title: as **a :** used for or in the production of a printed title (as on the backbone of a book) ⟨~ leather⟩ **b :** having the same name as the title of a production ⟨act the ~ role in *Hamlet*⟩ **c :** having the same title as or providing the title for the collection or production of which it forms a part ⟨~ essay⟩ ⟨~ poem⟩ ⟨~ song⟩ ⟨~ story⟩ **d :** of, relating to, or involving a championship (as in sports) ⟨~ match⟩ ⟨~ contest⟩ **e :** of, used in, or involved in the production of written material introduced into a motion picture or television program ⟨~ artist⟩ ⟨~ background⟩ ⟨~ music⟩ ⟨~ card⟩

title by occupancy 1 : a legal right of property acquired by taking the first possession of a thing or possession of a thing which belonged to nobody and appropriating it **2 :** sovereignty acquired in international law by a political state over territory not under the dominion of another state by effective exercise of control (as by settlement or by air patrol) and by public proclamation of the extent of the territory involved

title catalog *n* **:** a library catalog in which books and other works are listed only under their titles usu. arranged alphabetically — compare AUTHOR CATALOG

ti·tled \ˈtīd·ᵊld, -ītᵊld\ *adj* [*¹title* + *-ed*] **:** having or bearing a title and esp. one of nobility **:** NOBLE ⟨a ~ family⟩

title deed *n* **:** the deed or one of the deeds constituting the muniments or evidences of a person's legal ownership

title entry *n* **:** a catalog entry of a writing under the title and usu. the first important or key word of the title — compare AUTHOR ENTRY

titleholder \ˈ==ˌ==\ *n* **:** one that holds a title; *specif* **:** CHAMPION

title insurance *n* **:** insurance against loss due to an unknown defect in a title or interest in real estate

title page *n* **:** a usu. recto page of a book on which is given its full title and usu. the names of the author and the publisher and the place and sometimes the date of publication — compare HALF TITLE 1, IMPRINT

title piece *n* **1 :** a label usu. of leather adhered to the front cover or backbone of a book and impressed with the title **2 :** a literary work (as a poem) having the same title as the collection of which it forms a part ⟨a volume . . . with this poem as *title piece* —H.S.Canby⟩

ti·tler \ˈtīd·ᵊlə(r), -īt(ᵊ)l-\ *n* -S [*¹title* + *-er*] **:** a device for holding a motion-picture camera and in front of it an easel or frame in which can be placed a card bearing a title

titles *pl of* TITLE, *pres 3d sing of* TITLE

title space *n* **:** a panel for the title between the bands of the backbone of a book

¹tit·ling \ˈtitlən, -liŋ\ *n* -S [ME, fr. *tit-* (as in *titmose* titmouse) + *-ling*] **1** *dial Brit* **:** PIPIT; *esp* **:** MEADOW PIPIT **2** *dial Brit* **:** HEDGE SPARROW

²ti·tling \ˈtīd·ᵊliŋ, -īt(ᵊ)liŋ\ *n* -S [ME *titeling*, fr. gerund of *titelen* to title] **1 :** the action or occupation of one that titles; *specif* **:** a marking (as by stamping in gold) with a title **2 :** the title marked on something ⟨the ~ on a book cover⟩

titling letter *n* [*²titling*] **:** a letter of any all-capital font formerly in common use in title pages

ti·tlist \ˈtīd·ᵊlə̇st, -īt(ᵊ)l-\ *n* -S [*¹title* + *-ist*] **:** TITLEHOLDER ⟨world auto-racing ~⟩

tit·man \ˈtitmən\ *n, pl* **titmen** [*tit-* (as in *titmouse*) + *man*] **1 :** the smallest in a litter of pigs **:** RUNT **2 :** a puny person **:** one stunted physically or mentally

tit·mouse \ˈtitˌmau̇s\ *n, pl* **tit·mice** \-ˌmīs\ [ME *titmose, titemose*, fr. (assumed) ME *tit, tite*, any small object or creature (perh. fr. OE *titt, tit* teat) + ME *mose* titmouse, fr. OE *māse*; akin to OHG *meisa* titmouse — more at TEAT] **:** any of numerous widely distributed small passerine birds of the family Paridae and esp. of the genus *Parus* that are related to the nuthatches but longer tailed, are arboreal and largely insectivorous although they do not creep up and down on tree trunks as do the nuthatches, have soft and fluffy plumage with gray, black, and white as the prevailing colors in most forms, and mostly nest in holes in trees although some build a pendulous nest — compare BLUE TIT, CHICKADEE, COAL TIT, CRESTED TITMOUSE, GREAT TIT, LONG-TAILED TIT, MARSH TIT, TUFTED TITMOUSE

titmouse blue *n* **:** MÉSANGE

ti·to·ism \ˈtēd·(ˌ)ōˌizəm, -ē(ˌ)tō-\ *n* -S *usu cap* [*Tito* (Josip Broz) *b*1890? Yugoslav premier + E *-ism*] **:** the political, economic, and social policies associated with Tito; *specif* **:** nationalistically oriented policies and practices followed by a communist state or group independently of and often in opposition to the U.S.S.R. — compare BOLSHEVISM, LENINISM, MARXISM, MARXISM-LENINISM, STALINISM, TROTSKYISM

¹ti·to·ist \-ōəst\ *n* -S *usu cap* [*Tito* + E *-ist*] **:** a follower of Tito **:** an adherent of Titoism

²titoist \"\ *adj, usu cap* **:** of, relating to, or having the characteristics of Titoism or Titoists

ti·to·ki \təˈtōkē\ *n* -S [Maori] **:** a New Zealand tree (*Alectryon excelsum*) with large panicles of reddish flowers

ti·tra·ble \ˈtī·trəbəl\ *adj* [*titer* + *-able*] **:** TITRATABLE

ti·trant \ˈtī·trənt\ *n* -S [*titer* + *-ant*] **:** the substance (as a standard solution) that is added in a titration

ti·trat·able \ˈtīˌtrād·əbəl\ *adj* [*titrate* + *-able*] **:** capable of being titrated ⟨~ acidity⟩

ti·trate \ˈtīˌtrāt\ *vb* -ED/-ING/-S [*titer* + *-ate*] *vt* **:** to subject to titration **:** standardize, analyze, or determine by titration ~ *vi* **:** to perform titration

ti·tra·tion \tīˈtrāshən\ *n* -S [*titer* + *-ation*] **1 :** a determination of the reactive capacity usu. of a solution; *esp* **:** the analytical process of successively adding from a burette measured amounts of a reagent (as a standard solution) to a known volume of a sample in solution or a known weight of a sample until a desired end point (as a color change or a large change in potential of the solution) is reached ⟨acid-base ~⟩ ⟨oxidation-reduction ~⟩ ⟨electrometric ~*s*⟩ — see INDICATOR 2a **2 :** a process of making mixtures of decreasing amounts of one substance usu. in solution with unvarying amounts of another, until a mixture which contains the smallest amount of the substance still produces the desired effect (as precipitation, agglutination, or neutralization) or contains the two reagents in optimum proportions as determined by adding an indicator (as a hemolytic system in the Wassermann reaction or agglutinable cells in some virus titrations), or by animal or tissue culture inoculation (as in titration of toxins and viruses), or by observing the times of reaction (as in optimum proportions titrations)

titre *var of* TITER

ti tree *n* **1** *Austral* **:** ¹TI 1 **2** *Austral* **:** TEA TREE 2a

Ti·trim·e·ter \tīˈtrimәd·ə(r)\ *trademark* — used for a titrimetric instrument

ti·tri·met·ric \ˌtī·trəˈme·trik\ *adj* [*titration* + *-i-* + *-metric*] **:** of, relating to, or carried out by titrimetry — **ti·tri·met·ri·cal·ly** \-e·trə̇k(ə)lē\ *adv*

ti·trim·e·try \tīˈtrimə·trē\ *n* -ES [*titration* + *-i-* + *-metry*] **:** measurement or analysis by titration

tits *pl of* TIT, *pres 3d sing of* TIT

tit-tat-toe *var of* TICKTACKTOE

titted *past of* TIT

¹tit·ter \ˈtid·ə(r), -itə-\ *vi* -ED/-ING/-S [imit.] **:** to give vent to laughter one is seeking to suppress **:** laugh lightly or in a subdued manner **:** laugh in a nervous, affected, or restrained manner esp. at a high pitch and with short catches of the voice

²titter \"\ *n* -S **:** an act or instance of tittering ⟨a ~ of feminine laughter —Willa Cather⟩

tit·ter·el \ˈtitərəl\ *n* -S [imit.] *dial Eng* **:** WHIMBREL

tittie *also* **titty** \ˈtitī\ *n, pl* **titties** [prob. baby talk alter. of *¹sister*] *chiefly Scot* **:** SISTER; *also* **:** a young girl or woman

titting *pres part of* TIT

tittivate *var of* TITIVATE

tit·tle \'tid·ªl, -it³l\ n -s [ME titel, fr. ML titulus title, label, diacritical mark, fr. L, title, label] **1 a :** a point or small sign used as a diacritical, punctuation, or similar mark in writing or printing: as **a** obs : CEDILLA **b :** TILDE **c :** the dot over i or j **d :** a vowel point or accent (as in Hebrew or Arabic) **2 a :** a very small or minute part **:** the smallest particle : an extremely small or the least possible amount (he meant not to lose one ~ of enjoyment —Winston Churchill) — often used in the phrase jot or tittle (burn books that depart one jot or ~ from the legends of the fathers —H.A.Overstreet) (better . . . that a million perish than that one jot or ~ of that unique value should be lost —Ruth Benedict)

tit·tle·bat \'tit²l.bat\ n -s [baby talk alter. of stickleback] dial Eng : STICKLEBACK

¹tittle-tattle \'tid·²l.tad·ªl, 'tit³l²tat²l\ n [redupl. of ²tattle] **:** idle trifling talk esp. about trivial matters : petty gossip **:** empty prattle

²tittle-tattle \"\ vi : to talk idly : CHATTER, GOSSIP, PRATE

³tittle-tattle \"\ adj : characterized by or addicted to tittle-tattle : given to gossip : GOSSIPY

¹tit·tup also **tit-up** \'tid·ªp\ n -s [imit. of the sound of a horse's hoofs] **:** the action of tittuping: as **a :** HAND GALLOP **b :** a lively movement (as a prance or caper)

²tittup also **titup** \"\ vi **tittupped** or **tittuped; tittupping** or **tittuping; tittups** or **tittups :** to move in a lively manner: as **a :** to walk with an up and down movement esp. in an affected manner designed to attract attention (pretty girls tittupped along the sidewalk) **b :** to gallop or canter easily although often with a false or exaggerated gait **c :** to hop here and there (the cuckoo . . . tittupped about the shrubs —Haldane Macfall)

tit·tup·py \-ope\ adj [²tittup + -y] : apt to tittup : RICKETY, SHAKY, UNSTEADY

tit·ty \'tid·ē, -it\, \i\ n -ES [¹tit + -y] **1 :** TEAT 1 **2** dial : milk from the breast

tit·u·bant \'tichəbənt, 'tid·əb-\ adj [L titubant-, titubans, pres. part. of titubare to titubate] **:** characterized by titubation **:** marked by wavering or vacillating : UNSTEADY

tit·u·bate \·.bāt\ vi -ED/-ING/-S [L titubatus, past part. of titubare to titubate] **:** to reel or stumble as if tipsy : STAGGER, TOTTER

tit·u·ba·tion \.⸱⸱'bāshən\ n -s [L titubation-, titubatio, fr. titubatus + -ion, -io -ion] **:** the action of titubating; specif **:** a staggering gait observed in some nervous disturbances

¹tit·u·lar \'tichələ(r)\ adj [L titulus title + E -ar] **1 :** existing in title or name only : NOMINAL (held ~ sovereignty) **b :** having the title and usu. the honors belonging to an office or dignity without exercising the associated duties, functions, or responsibilities (the ~ head of the executive power was the president of the republic —D.W.S.Lidderdale) **c :** having powers so limited and circumscribed or functions so few in number or restricted in scope as to resemble one having a title only (~ leader of the Democratic party) **2 a :** bearing a title **:** holding the title specified or involved (whether our ~ officers are running this nation —Samuel Crowther) **b :** bearing a title derived from a defunct ecclesiastical jurisdiction (as a monastery or an episcopal see) — see TITULAR ABBOT, TITULAR BISHOP **3 :** of, associated with, or arising from a title (~ rank) **4 :** of, relating to, of the nature of, or constituting a title (the ~ theme of the book —N.M.Lawrence) (sponsors two national ~ events —W.F.Brown b. 1903); esp : TITLE b (performed well in the ~ role) (~ hero) **5 :** referring a title or name; specif **:** constituting one of a group of Roman Catholic churches in or near Rome from which a cardinal derives his title

²titular \"\ n -s **1** or **titular of erection** or **titular of the teinds** or **titular of the tithes :** a layman having as a result of the Reformation title under Scots law to temporalities (as the title and revenues) but not the spiritualities of an ecclesiastical benefice — see LORD OF ERECTION **2 :** a person holding a title: as **a** (1) **:** one having the title and benefits of an office independently of the functions, duties, or other obligations attached to it (2) **:** a person entitled to enjoy an ecclesiastical benefice without performing its duties **b :** the incumbent (as a cardinal) of a Roman Catholic title in or near Rome **3 :** the sacred person or thing (as Blessed Sacrament) from which a church derives its title or name — compare PATRON, PATRON SAINT

titular abbot n : one who holds the title of abbot derived from a destroyed or suppressed abbey

titular bishop n : a Roman Catholic bishop with the title of but without jurisdiction in a defunct see (as in former Christian lands now under Muslim control) — called also bishop in partibus infidelium

tit·u·lar·i·ty \.⸱⸱²larəd·ē\ n -ES [¹titular + -ity] **:** the quality or state of being titular (the extreme ~ of titular party leadership —Blair Clark)

tit·u·lar·ly adv [¹titular + -ly] **:** in, by, or in respect of title (England is ~ a kingdom —W.S.Landor); esp **:** by title only **:** NOMINALLY (an adviser, he is actually the director)

¹tit·u·lary \'tichə.lerē\ adj [L titulus + E -ary] archaic : TITULAR

²titulary \"\ n -ES archaic : one holding a title; esp : TITULAR 2a(2)

titup var of TITTUP

tityre-tu \'tī.tᵊrē(t)(y)ü\ n -s usu cap 1st T [fr. L Tityre tu (patulae recubans sub tegmine fagi) Tityrus, thou reclining beneath the shelter of the spreading beech tree, opening line of the 1st Eclogue of Vergil; fr. their being regarded as wealthy and idle] **:** one of a gang of roistering brawling young blades in 17th century London similar to the Mohocks

tity·us \'tid·ēəs, 'tīd-\, n, cap [NL, fr. L or Gk; L Tityos, name of a mythical giant, fr. Gk] **:** a genus of scorpions (family Buthidae) containing several whose venom is highly toxic to man

tiv \'tiv\ n, pl **tiv** or **tivs** usu cap **1 a :** a prominent peasant people of central Nigeria noted for brass casting, wood carving, and music — called also Munchi **b :** a member of the Tiv people **2 :** the language of the Tiv people, belonging to the Central branch of the Niger-Congo language family

tiv·o·li \'tivəlē\ n -s [prob. fr. Tivoli, commune of central Italy, a pleasure resort near Rome] **:** a game resembling bagatelle and played on a special oblong board or table which has a curved upper end, a set of numbered compartments at the lower end, side alleys, and a surface studded with pins and sometimes furnished with numbered depressions or cups

ti·wa also **ti·gua** \'tēwə\ n, pl **tiwa** or **tiwas** also **tigua** or **tiguas** usu cap [Sp tigua, of AmerInd origin] **1 a :** any of several Tanoan peoples of north and south central New Mexico **b :** a member of any of such peoples **2 :** the language of the Tiwa peoples

ti·wi \'tē\, \wē\ n, pl **tiwi** or **tiwis** usu cap **1 :** an aboriginal people of Melville and Bathurst islands in northern Australia **2 :** a member of the Tiwi people

ti·zeur \()'tē²zər(r), 'tə³z-, 'tēzər\ n -s [modif. of F tiseur — more at TEASER] **:** ²TEASER

tizri usu cap, var of TISHRI

tizwin var of TISWIN

tiz·zick dial var of PHTHISIC

¹tiz·zy \'tizi\ n -ES [perh. alter. of ²tester] Brit : SIXPENCE

²tiz·zy \'tizē, -zi\ n -ES [origin unknown] **:** a highly excited and foolishly distracted or baffled state of mind esp. over a petty matter (the story threw the town into a ~)

tjae·le \'chāle, -lə\ n [Sw; akin to ON theli frozen ground, OE thel bone, plank, L tellus earth — more at THILL] **:** frozen ground; esp **:** permanently frozen (the depth to which ~ formerly existed in central Montana —Jour. of Geol.)

tjan·ting \'chäntiŋ\ n [Jav] **:** a Javanese instrument for applying hot wax in batik work usu. consisting of a small thin copper cup with one or more capillary spouts and a handle of reed or bamboo

---

t joint n, cap T **1 :** TEE 2a **2 :** TEE JOINT

tjurunga or **tjuringa** var of CHURINGA

tk abbr **1** tank **2** truck

TKO abbr or n -s technical knockout

tkof abbr take-off

tkr abbr tanker

tkt abbr ticket

tl abbr tael

TL abbr **1** thrust line **2** tie line **3** time loan **4** total loss **5** trade-last **6** truck load

Tl symbol thallium

tlach·tli \'tlächt(ə)lē\ n -s [Nahuatl] **:** a ball game played by Central American Indians (as the Aztecs and Mayas) in which the players endeavor by the use of only the leg, hip and elbow to send a solid rubber ball through two rings set vertically in the walls of an I-shaped court

tla·co \'tlä()kō\ also **tlac** \-äk\ n -s [Sp tlaco, fr. Nahuatl, half] **:** a small copper coin used in 19th century Mexico worth ⅛ of a real — called also claco

tla·co·pan \'tläkə.pän\ n, pl **tlacopan** or **tlacopans** usu cap **1 :** a Nahuatl people of the Valley of Mexico belonging to the Aztec confederacy **2 :** a member of the Tlacopan people

tla·pa·nec \'tläpə.nek, .·²²\ n, pl **tlapanec** or **tlapanecs** usu cap **1 a :** an Indian people of southeastern Guerrero, Mexico **b :** a member of such people **2 :** the Supanecan language of the Tlapanec people

tlas·ca·la \tlä'skälə\ also **tlas·ca·lan** \-lən\ n, pl **tlascala** or **tlascalas** also **tlascalan** or **tlascalans** usu cap **1 :** a Nahuatl people of the state of Tlaxcala, Mexico **2 :** a member of the Tlascala people

TLC abbr tender loving care

tld abbr tooled

tlingit \'tliŋ()ət\ also **tlin·kit** \-ŋkət\ n, pl **tlingit** or **tlingits** also **tlinkit** or **tlinkits** usu cap **1 a :** a group of Indian peoples of the islands and coast of southern Alaska including chiefly the Auk, Chilkat, Sitka, Stikine, Tongass, and Yakutat **b :** member of any of such peoples **2 :** the language of the Tlingit peoples **3 :** a language stock of the Na-dene phylum comprising only Tlingit — called also Koluschan

TLO abbr total loss only

tlr abbr **1** tailor **2** teller **3** trailer

TLZ abbr titanium-lead-zinc

TM abbr **1** technical manual; technical memorandum **2** tons per minute **3** trademark **4** traffic manager **5** training manual **6** trainmaster **7** trench mortar **8** true mean

Tm symbol thulium

t-man \'tē.man\ n, pl **t-men** usu cap T [Treasury man] **:** a special agent of the U. S. Treasury Department

t-maze \'⸱.⸱\ n, cap T **:** a maze for the study of learning usu. consisting of a wood or metal structure shaped like the letter T in which the experimental subject must at a given point make a choice between a left or right turn with one choice usu. involving a reward

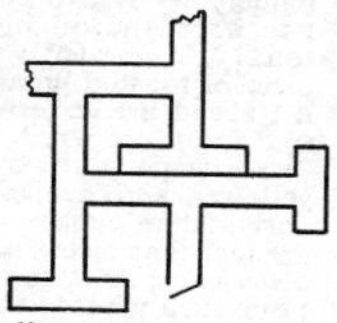

diagram of a partial T-maze

tmbr abbr timber

tme·sip·ter·is \.⸱⸱'mə'siptərəs\ n, cap [NL, fr. Gk tmēsis act of cutting + NL -pteris] **:** a genus of epiphytic Australasian fern allies related to Psilotum and characterized by conspicuous vertical leaves and boat-shaped 2-celled synangia

tme·sis \(t)ə'mēsəs\ n, pl **tme·ses** \-ē.sēz\ [LL, fr. Gk tmēsis act of cutting, fr. temnein to cut — more at TOME] **:** separation of parts of a compound word by the intervention of one or more words (as what place soever for whatsoever place)

TMG abbr track made good

TMH abbr tons per man hour

tmkpr abbr timekeeper

TML abbr three mile limit

TMO abbr telegraph money order

tmp abbr temperature

TMTD \'tē.em.tē'dē\ abbr or n -s [tetramethylthiuram disulfide] tetramethylthiuram disulfide

tn abbr **1** ton **2** town **3** train

TN abbr **1** tariff number **2** telephone number **3** thermonuclear **4** true north

tnaim var of TENAIM

TNB \'tē.en'bē\ abbr or n -s [trinitrobenzene] trinitrobenzene

tnd abbr tinned

t network n, cap T **:** a network consisting of three impedance branches connected in star

tng abbr training

tnge abbr tonnage

tnoyim var of TENAIM

tnpk abbr turnpike

TNT \'tē.en'tē\ abbr or n -s [trinitrotoluene] trinitrotoluene

t-number \'⸱.⸱⸱\ n, usu cap T [total light transmission + number] **:** a number that is similar to the f-number but takes into account the amount of light actually transmitted by a lens after loss by absorption and reflection and that equals the f-number divided by the square root of the transmittance

t nut n, cap T **1 :** a nut shaped like the head of a T bolt **2 :** a nut which may be driven into a board to receive a bolt inserted from the opposite side

¹to \.tə, before a vowel following without pause often or regularly təw, after a vowel usu d·ə(w), stressed consonant often də(w; ()tü, ()tü) prep [ME to, te, fr. OE tō (prep. & adv.) & te (prep.); akin to OFris to (adv.), to, te (prep.), OS tō (adv.), te (prep.), OHG zuo (adv.), za, zi, ze (prep.) to, L donicum, donec as long as, while, until, dum while, until, Gk -de toward, OLith do to, and prob. to Goth du to] **1** — used as a function word to indicate spatial relationships or relationships that suggest motion: as **a** — used as a function word to indicate movement or an action or condition suggestive of movement toward (1) a place, person, or thing that is reached or is thought of as being reached (drove ~ the city) (ran ~ his mother) (wore a new hat ~ the party) (a trip ~ the moon) (the boat is ~ the dock now) (went back ~ his original idea) (now ~ the matter at hand —A.J.Flynn) (on the telephone ~ central casting again —Lee Edson) or (2) a place, person, or thing that is not reached or that is not fully reached (turned his back ~ the door) (bowed ~ an acquaintance) (gazed philosophically ~ a burnished sea —R.W.Clark) (leaned ~ light verse and good humor —Phoenix Flame) (the great task . . . is now far along ~ completion —A.E.Stevenson b. 1900) (talks ~ the point) or (3) a physical force (bring the ship ~ the wind —C.S.Forester) **b** — used as an intensive with where (where will she go ~) **c** — used as a function word to indicate a place or a thing to which one goes for a temporary stay (has been ~ his uncle's house once) (went in and out ~ the sickroom —Seumas O'Kelly) (was ~ a show practically every night last week —Edward Newhouse) **d** — used as a function word to indicate direction (lived a few miles ~ the south) (a narrow paved road ~ the right just before the junction —Y.E.Soderberg) **e** — used as a function word to indicate a tendency ~ silliness) **f** — used as a function word to indicate contact or proximity: as (1) **:** close against **:** ON, UPON (his mother standing . . . with her hands ~ her eyes —Eve Langley) (applied polish ~ the table) (the houses had numbers painted ~ them —R.H.Newman) (2) **:** in a state of attention or ready availability to (stands ~ his post) (abundant slave labor was no longer ~ hand —Lancelot Hogben) (3) **:** before and straight ahead esp. in defiance (shall live and tell him ~ his teeth —Shak.) **i** archaic : AT **2** — used with verbs of seeing and smelling (a young girl's heart which he . . . smelled ~ like a rosebud —Nathaniel Hawthorne) **g** (1) chiefly substand : AT (that time we was making hay ~ her dad's place —Richard Bissell) (2) chiefly Brit : at the home of — usu. used with a personal name (went also ~ dinner ~ Birrell —H.J.Laski) **h** (1) — used as a function word to indicate the place or point that is the far limit (of a measured distance) (100 miles ~ the nearest town) (a short way ~ the store) (2) — used as a function word to indicate the limit of extent (as in space) (stripped ~ the waist) (hip deep ~ silliness) (saw through ~ the man's quality —Hallam Tennyson) **i** — used as a function word to indicate relative position (a beam perpendicular ~ the floor) (placed at right angles ~ the wall) (a line tangent

---

~ a circle) (stop the press if a sheet is not placed correctly ~ the guides —Theory & Practice of Pressmork) **2** — used as a function word to indicate purpose, intention, tendency, result, or end: as **a** (1) **:** for the purpose of : with a view to : aiming at : FOR (came ~ our aid) (trained ~ a religious life) (living ~ ends outside ourselves —O.W.Holmes †1935) (tailored ~ your particular needs) (liked to sit down ~ a game of bridge) (2) **:** in honor of : with all good wishes for (built temples ~ their gods) (drink ~ his health) (3) **:** for the making of : as a constituent part of (tons of ore go ~ a few ounces of gold) (4) **:** in support of (calls witnesses to speak ~ his character) (gives abundant testimony ~ the . . . committee's ignorance and inefficiency —R.L.Roy) (5) **:** for the cultivation of **:** WITH (when the land was drained he planted it ~ cabbages and onions —Sherwood Anderson) **b** (1) — used as a function word to indicate the result of an action or a process (broken all ~ pieces) (sharpened ~ a point) (warehouse converted ~ a church —Alice Griffin) (tulips going ~ seed) (a brushy wilderness growing up ~ scrub oak —Clifton Johnson) (2) **:** with the result of (seems to argue ~ the same effect —Herbert Read) (much ~ their surprise, the train left on time) **c** **:** in the capacity of : AS, FOR (a sincere desire to have her ~ wife —J.E.Tilford) **d** — used as a function word to indicate a determined condition or end (born ~ riches) (sentenced ~ death) **e** — used as a function word to indicate the object of a right or a claim (a title ~ the property) (the pretender ~ the throne) **3** — used as a function word to indicate a position or a relation in time: as **a** chiefly dial : AT 7 (all ~ once —Helen Eustis) (ready ~ three o'clock —F.T.Elworthy) **b** (1) **:** BEFORE (arrived at five minutes ~ five) (a quarter ~ six) (2) **:** TILL, UNTIL (stayed on ~ the last minute) (from eight ~ five o'clock) (his edition . . . had the fullest and best apparatus ~ that time —I.M.Price) (3) — used as a function word to indicate a limit in past time (a ceremony dating ~ the first century —Springfield (Mass.) Union) **c** — used as a function word usu. in combination with from to indicate recurrence or continued succession (a situation that changes from day ~ day) **d** — used as a function word to indicate the precise time of an occurrence (promised to pay ~ the day) **e** chiefly Brit — used as a function word to indicate occurrence at a set time (runs ~ schedule —advt) (a chance to get away ~ time —Noreen Routledge) **4** — used as a function word to indicate addition, attachment, connection, belonging, possession, accompaniment, or response: as **a** archaic : in addition to **:** BESIDES (foretell new storms ~ those already spent —Shak.) **b :** attached to (his fat pony that he drives ~ a basket phaeton —James Reynolds) (publishers would publish anything that had my name ~ it —G.B.Shaw) (a schooner riding ~ an anchor in the bay —Hall Caine) **c** — used as a function word to indicate belonging or possession (descendant of a great house with more than a dash of Italian blood ~ it —Eric Blom) (two rather obvious divisions ~ the investigation —McGill News) (there were green curtains ~ the bed —Virginia Woolf) (the key ~ the door) (had a severe sprain ~ her ankle —Lucien Price) (with a rasping bite ~ his voice —Current Biog.) **d** — used as a function word to indicate a special often close relationship of a person to another person, a group, or an organization (nephew ~ a powerful and wealthy man —Thomas Wolfe) (printer ~ the state —N.A.Crawford) **e** (1) **:** to the accompaniment of (sang ~ his guitar) (dancing ~ the radio —Louis Simpson) (rides ~ hounds) (nowadays you do it ~ cocktails —Arnold Bennett) (2) **:** in complement to **:** OPPOSITE (played Juliet ~ the Romeo of an unknown newcomer) **f** **:** in response or reaction to (comes ~ his call) (hardly knew what to say ~ it) (retaliate ~ mockery —Geoffrey Gorer) (flimsy houses that shake ~ the wind) **g** **:** with respect to (witnesses must speak only ~ facts of which they have direct knowledge —Edward Jenks) (liars they are ~ trade —J.M.Barrie) **5 a** — used as a function word to indicate (1) the extent or degree (as of completeness or accuracy) (assimilate penniless immigrants ~ a mankind is truly astonishing —Samuel Van Valkenburg & Ellsworth Huntington) (died two and a half centuries ago ~ a month —Times Lit. Supp.) (loyal ~ a man) (would lose his billet ~ a certainty —Henry Lapham) (liked to run his day's program ~ the fraction of a second —Osbert Sitwell) or (2) the extent and result (as of an action or a condition) (beaten ~ death) (worn ~ a frazzle) (case sense is thus feeble ~ extinction in English —Weston La Barre) (limited his criticism ~ a few pleasantries) (increased the amount ~ $1000) **b** (1) — used as a function word to indicate the last point or an intermediate point of a series (the climate over the period was moderate ~ cool —W.E.Swinton) (prices are firm ~ rising —U. S. News & World Report) (the quality ranges all the way from very poor ~ good ~ excellent) (a noncommittal word that might be used of anything from babies ~ furnaces —J.C.Swaim) (2) — INCLUDING (six spades ~ the ace queen) (3) **:** varying through the range between two similar colors or two slightly different magnitudes of a color characteristic (a dark grayish olive ~ olive green) (a pale ~ grayish blue) **6** — used as a function word to indicate a relation to one that serves as a standard: as **a** (1) — used as a function word to indicate similarity, correspondence, dissimilarity, or proportion (compared him ~ a god) (a hat identical ~ the one she had on) (forms different ~ those in which they familiarly present themselves —John Dewey) (seemed to be of another race ~ them —A. Conan Doyle) (knee-high ~ a grasshopper) (2) **:** in comparison with (the present annoyances are nothing ~ the real dangers that might develop) (inferior ~ the earlier works) **b** (1) — used as a function word to indicate agreement or conformity (add salt ~ taste) (found nothing ~ his purpose —N.J.G.Pounds) (composed three operas, all ~ his own librettos —J.T.Howard) (made ~ certain conventional patterns —C.P.Fitzgerald) (drawings give sufficient detail for a fairly skilled man to work ~ them —Brit. Bk. News) (2) **:** according to **:** within the range of (~ the best of my knowledge, this book is still the standard work) (~ all appearances is really ill) (arguing ~ supposed general principles —Times Lit. Supp.) **c** — used as a function word to indicate a proportion in terms of numbers or quantities: as (1) the proportion between two things in terms of a significant unit of measurement of one of the things; usu. used with the (two monsoon seasons ~ the year —D.G.Bridson) (750 persons ~ the square mile —John McNulty) or (2) the proportion between two things in terms of a common unit of measurement (is only 28 years old ~ his brother's 45) (hold 60 seats ~ their opponents' 40) (offered odds of nine ~ one) **7 a** (1) — used as a function word to indicate the application of an adjective (agreeable ~ everyone) (blind ~ art) (unknown ~ us) (necessary ~ progress) (adequate ~ our needs) (feels cold ~ your teeth) (observable ~ our senses —W.L.Sullivan) (unattainable ~ ambition —Hugh Wray) (2) — used as a function word to indicate the application of a noun (our attitudes ~ our friends) (enemies ~ cultivation —James Stevenson-Hamilton) (disaster ~ the army) (without charge ~ the parents —James Britton) (similarity ~ others) (a stranger ~ the country) (an interested observer ~ the changeover —Alaska Sportsman) (competitors ~ the printed word —Joseph Trenaman) (3) — used as a function word to indicate the relation of a verb to its complement or to a complementary element (refers ~ the traditions) (refers him ~ the traditions) (must look ~ our postural tensions —A.T.Weaver) (started ~ kindergarten —Newsweek) (admits ~ disappointments —R.W.Steel) (democracy succumbed ~ dictatorship —C.E.Black & E.C. Helmreich) (~ parentage . . . he owed the sturdy nature that served him well —Thomas Woody) **b** — used as a function word to indicate the object of address (spoke ~ his father about it) (hail ~ thee, blithe Spirit —P.B.Shelley) **c** (1) — used as a function word to indicate the receiver of an action or the one for which something is done or exists (gives a dollar ~ the man) (make alterations ~ the text —H.G.G.Herklots) (disputes certified ~ the board by the president —R.L. Putnam) (played the piano ~ royalty) (sat ~ a famous painter) (in the way of converts he died ~ something and had a moment of truth —W.J.Igoe) (~ their trained eyes and ears the fields are covered by red-hatted riders —W.B.Yeats); often used with a reflexive pronoun to indicate exclusiveness (as of possession or use) or separateness (the Dutch liner . . . which they had ~ themselves on the voyage —P.D.Whitney)

board used in tivoli

⟨medical school gets a chapter ~ itself —*Times Lit. Supp.*⟩ ⟨thought ~ himself⟩ ⟨kept himself ~ himself —F.W.Crofts⟩ (2) : in the opinion of : from the point of view of ⟨manifestly was somebody ~ them —Sidney Lovett⟩ ⟨~ him it seems unnecessary⟩ **d** (1) : at the hands of : through the agency of ⟨falls ~ the heavy blows of the enemy⟩ ⟨loses his closest friend ~ a violent death —Gene Baro⟩ ⟨captivities ~ thieving barons —R.B.Pearsall⟩ (2) : under the tutelage of ⟨went to school ~ the same teacher⟩ **8** — used as a function word to indicate that the following verb is an infinitive ⟨wants ~ go⟩ ⟨seems ~ evaporate⟩ ⟨something ~ do⟩ ⟨a happier place ~ be —Irving Kolodin⟩ ⟨overcame great opposition ~ launch modern sanitary legislation —David Spitz⟩ ⟨~ draw an analogy, we may be able —G.A.Miller⟩ ⟨sharpen their wits merely ~ survive —*Harper's*⟩ ⟨these people . . . whom it is our duty ~ properly represent —*Congressional Record*⟩; often used by itself at the end of a clause in place of an infinitive suggested by the preceding context ⟨knows more than he seems ~⟩ ⟨eats less than he ought ~⟩ ⟨maybe you'd like to go but I don't want ~⟩ ⟨I can't help it, I have ~⟩ ⟨Candy? I'd love ~⟩

²to \ˈtü\ *adv* [ME, fr. OE *tō* — more at ¹TO] **1 a** (1) — used as a function word to indicate direction toward ⟨birds with feathers wrong end ~⟩; used chiefly in the phrase *to and fro* ⟨children running ~ and fro⟩; used formerly in the phrase *to and again* ⟨work the boat ~ and again —Daniel Defoe⟩ (2) : close to the wind ⟨the gale having gone over, we came ~ —R.H.Dana⟩ **b** *obs* : in favor : PRO — used in the phrases *to and again* and *to and fro* ⟨all parties have been heard ~ and again —Thomas Burton⟩ **2 a** : into contact esp. with the frame of a door or a window ⟨the hall door snapped ~ —Nigel Dennis⟩ **b** (1) — used as a function word to indicate physical application or attachment ⟨set ~ his seal that it was true⟩ (2) : in or into harness ⟨put the horses ~⟩ **3** — used as a function word to indicate application or attention ⟨will stand ~ —Shak.⟩ **4 a** : to a state of consciousness or awareness ⟨brings her ~ with smelling salts⟩ **b** *archaic* : to a state of agreement or acquiescence ⟨forced to use a little fatherly authority to bring her ~ —Henry Fielding⟩ **5** *obs* : AGAIN — used in the phrase *to and again* **6** : at hand : BY ⟨get to see 'em close ~ —Richard Llewellyn⟩

TO \(ˈ)tēˈō\ *abbr or n* -S : a table of organization ⟨this company is 30 over its *TO* already —A.J.Guérard⟩ ⟨our *TO* quota of noncoms is all filled up —James Jones⟩

TO *abbr* **1** technical order **2** telegraph office **3** telephone office **4** tincture of opium **5** transport officer **6** turn over

toa \ˈtōə\ *n* -S [Samoan] **1** : a valiant Polynesian warrior **2** : a tree of the genus *Casuarina*; *esp* : a tall usu. spreading tree (*C. equisetifolia*) of northern Australia and the Pacific islands having very hard tough wood used locally for implements and war clubs and being often cultivated in southeastern Asia esp. for fuel and for its value in erosion control

¹toad \ˈtōd\ *n* -S *often attrib* [ME *tade, tadde, tode*, fr. OE *tāde, tādie, tādige*] **1 a** : any of numerous tailless leaping amphibians that comprise *Bufo* and various other genera esp. of the family Bufonidae, feed chiefly on insects and other small invertebrates, produce an acrid and irritating but not seriously harmful secretion from skin glands which is their only means of defense, and as compared with the related frogs are generally more terrestrial in habit though returning to water to lay their eggs, squatter and shorter in build and with weaker hind limbs, and rough, dry, and warty rather than smooth and moist of skin — see AGUA, NATTERJACK; compare HORNED TOAD **b** : TOADFISH **2** : a stupid contemptible person : a thing of no virtue or worth — sometimes used as a generalized term of abuse ⟨he's a perfect ~⟩ **3** *slang* : DERAIL

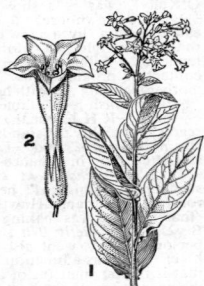

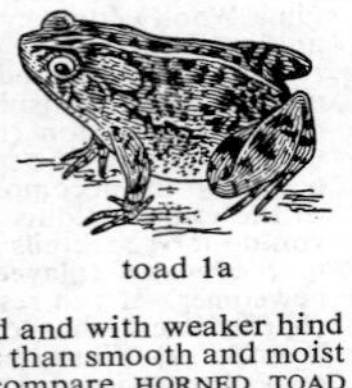
toad 1a

²toad \"\ *vb* -ED/-ING/-S : TOADY

toadback \ˈ=,=\ *adj* : having a section of 3-lobed shape with one of the lobes uppermost that gives a fancied resemblance to the back of a toad ⟨a ~ handrail⟩

toad bug *n* : any of several small predaceous bugs (family Gelastocoridae) having a broad flat body and projecting eyes

toad crab *n* : either of two relatively large rough spider crabs (*Hyas coarctatus* and *H. araneus*) living chiefly in deep water of arctic seas

toadeat \ˈ=,=\ *vb* [back formation fr. *toadeater*] : TOADY

toadeater \ˈ=,==\ *n* **1** *archaic* : a mountebank's assistant who eats or pretends to eat supposedly poisonous toads to permit his boss to show his skill in expelling the poison **2 a** : a fawning obsequious parasite : TOADY **b** : a servile dependent : a menial hanger-on

toadfish \ˈ=,=\ *n* **1** : any of various marine fishes having jugular pelvic fins, a large thick head, a wide mouth, and scaleless slimy skin, constituting the family Batrachoididae, and including some (as members of a widespread genus *Thalassophryne*) that have venomous spines; *esp* : a common fish (*Opsanus tau*) of the American Atlantic coast — compare MIDSHIPMAN 2 **2** : FROGFISH 1 **3** : GLOBEFISH

toadflax \ˈ=,=\ *n* **1** : a common European perennial herb (*Linaria vulgaris*) having showy yellow and orange flowers and being a naturalized weed in much of No. America; *broadly* : any of numerous plants of *Linaria* or the related genus *Kicksia* — see DEVIL'S FLAX **2** : any of various plants not closely related to but usu. somewhat resembling the common European toadflax — see BASTARD TOADFLAX

toad-frog \ˈ=,=\ *n* : a tailless amphibian : TOAD, FROG

toadhead \ˈ=,=\ *n, NewEng* : GOLDEN PLOVER

toadied *past of* TOADY

toad·i·er \ˈtōdē(r)\ *n* -S : one that toadies

toadies *pl of* TOADY, *pres 3d sing of* TOADY

toad-in-the-hole \ˈ===,=\ *n, pl* **toad-in-the-holes** : meat (as sausage) cooked in batter usu. by baking

toad·ish \ˈtōdish, -dēsh\ *adj* : suggestive of or suitable for toads ⟨a ~ hollow⟩ — **toad·ish·ness** *n* -ES

toad·less \ˈtōdləs\ *adj* : free from toads

toad·let \-lət\ *n* -S : a young or small toad

toad lily *n* **1** : a showy Japanese herb (*Tricyrtis hirta*) of the family Melanthaceae that is often cultivated for its delicately spotted white flowers **2** : a common white water lily (*Nymphaea odorata*) of No. America **3** : a cultivated bulbous herb (*Fritillaria pyrenaica*) of southern Europe with ill-smelling usu. solitary wine-purple flowers **4** : an Indian lettuce (*Montia chamissoi*) of moist areas at high elevations of western No. America with usu. decumbent stems and axillary or terminal racemes of small white or pink flowers

toad·ling \ˈtōdliŋ, -lēŋ\ *n* -S : TOADLET

toado \ˈtō(,)dō\ *n, pl* **toadoes** *or* **toados** [¹*toad* + -*o*] *Austral* : GLOBEFISH

toadpipe \ˈ=,=\ *n, dial chiefly Eng* : HORSETAIL 2 — often used in pl. but sing. in constr.

toadroot \ˈ=,=\ *n* : RED BANEBERRY

toad rush *n* : a low-growing nearly cosmopolitan annual rush (*Juncus bufonius*) of damp low-lying ground

toads *pl of* TOAD, *pres 3d sing of* TOAD

toad's-cheese \ˈ=,=\ *n, pl* **toad's-cheeses** *dial chiefly Eng* : a poisonous fungus

toad's-eye \ˈ=,=\ *or* **toad's-eye tin** *n, pl* **toad's-eyes** : a cassiterite with concentric structure and reddish color

toadshade \ˈ=,=\ *n* : a No. American trillium (*Trillium sessile*) with aromatic maroon sessile flowers

toad skin *n* : PHRYNODERMA

toad's-mouth \ˈ=,=\ *n, pl* **toad's-mouths** : a snapdragon (*Antirrhinum majus*)

toad snatcher *n, dial Brit* : REED BUNTING

toad sorrel *or* **toad's sorrel** *n* : SHEEP SORREL

toad spit *or* **toad spittle** *n* : CUCKOO SPIT 1a

toad spot *n* : one of the nonpigmented spots occurring on the genitals in dourine

toad-spotted \ˈ=,==\ *adj, obs* : foully blemished : most evil : INFAMOUS

toad-stabber \ˈ=,==\ *or* **toad-sticker** \ˈ=,==\ *n* **1** : JACKKNIFE, POCKETKNIFE **2** : SWORD

toadstone \ˈ=,=\ *n* **1** : a bufonite or other petrifaction, stone, or similar object held to have formed in the head or body of a toad and formerly often worn esp. as a charm or antidote to poison **2** : dark intrusive volcanic and usu. basaltic rock occurring in Carboniferous limestones of Derbyshire, England, often in broad sheets

toadstool \ˈ=,=\ *n* [ME *tadestool, todestool*, fr. *tade, tode* toad + *stool*] **1** : a fungus having an umbrella-shaped pileus **2** : a fleshy fungus that is poisonous or inedible as distinguished from an edible mushroom; *broadly* : a fleshy fungus with a conspicuous fruiting body usu. as distinguished from those (as bracket fungi or molds) with woody or inconspicuous fruiting structures

toadstool disease *n* : MUSHROOM ROOT ROT

¹toady \ˈtōdē, -di\ *adj* -ER/-EST [¹*toad* + -*y* (adj. suffix)] **1** : resembling a toad esp. in lack of beauty or grace : HIDEOUS **2** : full of toads ⟨a ~ path⟩

²toady \"\ *n* -ES [¹*toad* + -*y* (n. suffix)] : a truckler to the rich or powerful : SYCOPHANT, TOADEATER 2 **syn** see PARASITE

³toady \"\ *vb* -ED/-ING/-ES *vt* : to play the toady to : fawn upon with sycophancy ~ *vi* : to behave in the manner of a toady : engage in excessive deference and attention through motives of self-interest

toady·ish \-ish\ *adj* [²*toady* + -*ish*] : inclined to toady : marked by toadyism

toady·ism \-ē,izəm\ *n* -S : the behavior or attentions of a toady

to·a·la \təˈwälə\ *n, pl* **toala** *or* **toalas** *usu cap* **1** : a Veddoid people of the interior of southwestern Celebes **2** : a member of the Toala people

¹to-and-fro \ˈ=,=\ *n* -S [fr. the adv. phrase *to and fro*] **1 a** : FLUCTUATION, VACILLATION **b** : a bandying of words or questions : an argumentative discussion : SQUABBLE **2** : activity involving alternating movement in opposite directions ⟨the *to-and-fro* of the pendulum⟩ ⟨the noisy *to-and-fro* of a holiday crowd⟩

²to-and-fro \"\ *adj* [fr. the adv. phrase *to and fro*] : forward and backward : characterized by alternation (as in reciprocation or fluctuation) ⟨*to-and-fro* motion⟩ ⟨*to-and-fro* visiting between neighbors⟩

toa·ner *dial Eng var of* TONER

to-arrive \(,)==ˈ=\ *adj* : of, relating to, sold by, or being a contract providing that goods shipped will arrive at a specified point or be shipped from a point of origin within a prescribed time ⟨a *to-arrive* contract⟩ ⟨*to-arrive* prices⟩ ⟨trading in *to-arrive* cotton⟩

toas *pl of* TOA

¹toast \ˈtōst\ *vb* -ED/-ING/-S [ME *tosten*, fr. MF *toster*, fr. LL *tostare* to roast, fr. L *tostus*, past part. of *torrēre* to dry, parch — more at THIRST] *vt* **1** *obs* : to make thoroughly hot and dry by or as if by the action of fire or the sun **2 a** : to make (as bread) crisp, hot, and brown by the action of heat ⟨a ~*ed* cheese sandwich⟩ ⟨~ the bread very dark⟩ **b** : to warm thoroughly usu. before a fire ⟨~*ing* his toes on the fender⟩ ~ *vi* : to become toasted ⟨stale bread ~*s* best⟩; *usu* : to warm thoroughly ⟨sitting ~*ing* in the sun⟩

²toast \"\ *n* -S [ME *toste, toost*, fr. *tosten*, v.] **1 a** : a slice or piece of toasted bread — used in the phrase *as warm as a toast* **b** : sliced bread browned on both sides by a source of heat **c** : food prepared with toasted or other recooked bread — see FRENCH TOAST, MILK TOAST **d** : a light brown that is yellower and deeper than blush and stronger and slightly darker than cork — compare TOAST BROWN **2** [so called fr. the fact that pieces of spiced toast were used to flavor drinks] **a** *archaic* : a young woman in whose honor admirers drink : one such whose health is frequently proposed because of her beauty or charm **b** : a person whose health is drunk; *broadly* : something in honor of which persons drink : a sentiment that is drunk to **c** : a person who is the subject of public adulation ⟨as preacher at Notre Dame Cathedral, was the ~ of Paris —E.O.Hauser⟩ ⟨the unquestioned ~ of the season was the English soprano —*Information Please Almanac*⟩ **3** [³*toast*] : an act of proposing or of drinking in honor of a toast ⟨a dinner without ~*s*⟩

³toast \"\ *vb* -ED/-ING/-S [²*toast*] *vt* : to propose or drink to as a toast : drink to the health or in honor of ⟨~ the flag⟩ ⟨the two antagonists were ~*ing* each other's health —Mary K. Hammond⟩ ~ *vi* : to drink toasts : propose a toast

toast brown *n* : a moderate brown that is redder, lighter, and stronger than chestnut brown, coffee, auburn, or tobacco and lighter and slightly redder and stronger than bay — compare TOAST

toast·ee \(ˈ)tōˈstē\ *n* -S [³*toast* + -*ee*] : one whose health is drunk in a toast

toast·er \ˈtōstə(r)\ *n* -S [¹*toast* + -*er*] **1** : one that toasts bread or other food: as **a** : a device (as a toasting fork or a double hinged grill) for toasting bread on a stove or over a flame **b** : an electrical appliance with one or more grills for similar use **2** : a heated revolving inclined cylinder through which cut tobacco is passed to produce the effect of toasting

²toaster \"\ *n* -S [³*toast* + -*er*] : one that proposes toasts : TOASTMASTER

toasting fork *n* **1** : a long-handled fork used to toast bread, marshmallows, or other foods usu. over an open fire or live coals **2** : SWORD, RAPIER ⟨if I had given him time to get at his . . . pistol or his *toasting fork*, it was all up —Thomas Hughes⟩

¹toastmaster \ˈ=,==\ *n* [²*toast* + *master*] : one that presides (as at a banquet) and introduces the after-dinner speakers

²toastmaster \"\ *vt* : to serve as toastmaster at (a particular affair) ⟨~ a testimonial dinner⟩ ~ *vi* : to play the part or practice the art of a toastmaster

toastmaster's glass *n* : a drinking glass of apparently normal but actually minute capacity originally used by 18th century toastmasters

toastmistress \ˈ=,==\ *n* : a female toastmaster

toast rack *n* : a rack for holding several slices of toast on edge

toasts *pl of* TOAST, *pres 3d sing of* TOAST

toast tan *n* : a moderate brown that is lighter, stronger, and slightly yellower than chestnut brown, yellower, lighter, and slightly stronger than auburn, and yellower, lighter, and slightly less strong than bay

toasty \ˈtōstē, -ti\ *adj* -ER/-EST **1** : having the appearance or taste of toast **2** : pleasantly or comfortably warmed ⟨the room was snug and ~⟩

toa·toa \ˈtōəˌtōə\ *n* -S [Maori] : a New Zealand celery-topped pine (*Phyllocladus glaucus*) having striking whorled branches and often cultivated for ornament

to·at·tler \tōˈatlə(r)\ *n* -S [by alter.] *dial Eng* : TEETOTALER

tob *var of* TOBE

¹to·ba \ˈtōbə\ *n, pl* **toba** *or* **tobas** *usu cap* : a member of a Tatar people ruling northern China from the 4th to the 6th centuries

²toba \"\ *n, pl* **toba** *or* **tobas** *usu cap* [Sp, of AmerInd origin] **1 a** : a Guaicuru people of the Gran Chaco, Argentina **b** : a member of such people **2** : the language of the Toba people

³toba \"\ *n* -S *usu cap* : a dialect of Batak (sense 2)

to·bac \təˈbak\ *n* -S [short for *tobacco*] : TOBACCO BROWN

to·bac·co \təˈba(,)kō, -kə; -kəw, -ˌkō+V\ *n, pl* **tobaccos** *also* **tobaccoes** *often attrib* [Sp *tabaco*, prob. fr. Taino, roll of tobacco leaves smoked by the Indians of the Antilles at the time of Columbus] **1 a** : a plant of the genus *Nicotiana* esp. when cultivated for its leaves; *usu* : a tall erect annual So. American herb (*N. tabacum*) with large ovate to lanceolate leaves and terminal clusters of tubular white or pink flowers **b** : a crop of tobacco ⟨~ is hard on land⟩ ⟨just got his ~ into the barns⟩ **2 a** : the leaves of cultivated tobacco prepared and processed for use in smoking or chewing or as snuff ⟨a plug of chewing ~⟩ **b** : manufactured products of tobacco (as cigars or cigarettes) for personal use ⟨users of ~⟩ **c** : the use of tobacco : the habit of smoking or chewing ⟨swore off ~⟩ **3** : any of various plants felt to resemble or used like or as a substitute for tobacco — usu. used with a qualifying attributive — see INDIAN TOBACCO **4** : a moderate brown that is redder and deeper than chestnut brown or coffee, darker and slightly redder than auburn, duller and very slightly yellower than bay, and duller and slightly yellower than toast brown — compare TOBACCO BROWN

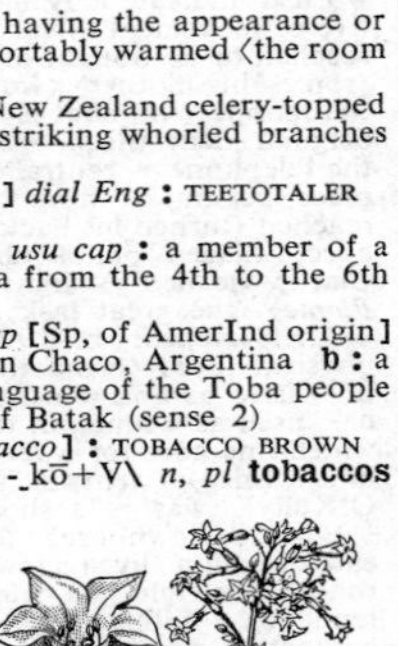
tobacco 1a: *1* flowering stem and leaves, *2* detached flower

tobacco barn *or* **tobacco shed** *n* : a building in which tobacco is cured with or without supplemental heat

tobacco beetle *n* : CIGARETTE BEETLE

tobacco box *n* **1** *or* **tobacco-box skate** : LITTLE SKATE **2** *Austral* : FRIARBIRD

tobacco brown *n* : a moderate to strong yellowish brown that is darker than clay and darker and slightly yellower than Aztec — called also *tobac* — compare TOBACCO

tobacco brush *n* : a snowbrush (*Ceanothus velutina*)

tobacco budworm *n* **1** : a small rusty often green-striped caterpillar that is the larva of a noctuid moth (*Heliothis virescens*) and that feeds on buds and young foliage esp. of various solanaceous plants **2** : CORN EARWORM

tobacco bug *n* : a small black mirid bug (*Dicyphus minimus*) that has green legs and underside and that sucks the sap of tobacco leaves — called also *suck fly*

tobacco cloth *n* : a loose-weave cotton fabric used esp. to shade growing tobacco plants

tobacco dove *n* : a West Indian ground dove (*Columbigallina passerina*)

tobacco etch *n* : a virus disease of tobacco characterized by mild leaf mottling, chlorosis, and linear traces of necrosis

tobaccoey *var of* TOBACCOY

tobacco flea beetle *n* : a tiny reddish brown flea beetle (*Epitrix hirtipennis*) that is esp. destructive to solanaceous plants

tobacco hatchet *or* **tobacco spud** *n* : a hatchet made with a broad thin blade with a sharp edge beveled on one side only and used for cutting the butt of tobacco plants in harvesting

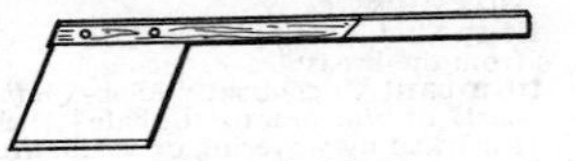
tobacco hatchet

tobacco hawkmoth *n* : the adult moth of a tobacco hornworm

tobacco heart *n* : a functional disorder of the heart characterized by irregularity of the heartbeat and caused by excessive use of tobacco

tobacco hornworm *n* : a large green obliquely white-striped caterpillar with a hornlike process near the posterior end that is the larva of a hawkmoth (*Manduca sexta*) and that feeds voraciously on tobacco and other solanaceous plants; *also* : the closely related and very similar tomato hornworm

tobacco indian *n, usu cap T&I* : a member of the Tionontati

tobacco juice *n* **1** : saliva colored brown by the use of chewing tobacco or snuff **2** : a dark brown oral discharge made by some grasshoppers when handled or disturbed

tobacco leaf miner *n* : POTATO TUBERWORM

tobacco mildew *n* : a disease of growing tobacco caused by a downy mildew (*Peronospora hyoscyami*); *also* : the fungus causing this disease

tobacco mosaic *n* : any of a complex of virus diseases of tobacco and other chiefly solanaceous plants that in their typical manifestation take the form of mosaics

tobacco moth *n* : a small brownish gray moth (*Ephestia elutella*) whose larva feeds in tobacco and other dried plant products — called also *cacao moth*

to·bac·co·nist \təˈbakənəst\ *n* -S [*tobacco* + connective -*n*- + -*ist*] **1** *obs* : a habitual user of tobacco **2** : a dealer in tobacco esp. at retail

tobacco road *n, often cap T&R* [fr. *Tobacco Road*, novel (1932) by Erskine Caldwell *b*1903 Amer. writer, and play (1933) adapted by Jack Kirkland †1969 Amer. playwright, about poor whites in a depressed rural area of Georgia traversed by a run-down thoroughfare ("tobacco road") made in earlier days by rolling hogsheads of tobacco to market] : a squalid poverty-stricken area or community in which the life of the inhabitants is characterized as wretched, disorganized, and hopeless

tobacco-roader \==ˈ==\ *n, often cap T&R* : one who dwells in or acts as if he dwelt in a tobacco road

tobacco-road·ish \-dish\ *adj, often cap T&R* : inclined to be like a tobacco road or its inhabitants

tobaccoroot \=ˈ=,=\ *n* **1** : BITTERROOT **2** : a tall erect perennial No. American valerian (*Valeriana edulis*) with small white or yellowish flowers in a long panicle and a large edible root

tobaccos *pl of* TOBACCO

tobacco-sick \=ˈ=(,)=ˈ=\ *adj, of land* : depleted in fertility and often heavily infested with parasites after repeated use for tobacco cultivation

tobacco splitworm *n* : POTATO TUBERWORM

tobacco stick *also* **tobacco lath** *n* : one of the laths on which tobacco leaves or stalks are hung for curing

tobacco stopper *n* : a device for pressing down tobacco in a pipe

tobacco thrips *n* **1** : a thrips (*Frankliniella fusca*) often injurious to growing tobacco and to peanuts in No. America **2** : ONION THRIPS

tobacco tongs *n pl but sing or pl in constr* : metal tongs for taking a live coal from a fire to light a tobacco pipe

tobacco water *also* **tobacco liquor** *n* : an extract of tobacco used (as in gardening) as an insecticide

tobaccoweed \=ˈ=(,)=,=\ *n* : DEVIL'S-GRANDMOTHER

tobacco wilt *n* : a wilt disease of tobacco caused by a bacterium (*Pseudomonas solanacearum*) : BROWN ROT — compare GRANVILLE WILT

tobaccowood \=ˈ=(,)=,=\ *n* : WITCH HAZEL 2a(1)

tobacco worm *n* : TOBACCO HORNWORM

to·bac·coy *or* **to·bac·co·ey** \-akəwē, -wi\ *adj* : full of tobacco fumes; *also* : like or like that of tobacco or tobacco smoking ⟨a warm ~ hue⟩ ⟨a gurgling ~ noise —Mary McCarthy⟩

tobacs *pl of* TOBAC

to·ba·go·nian \ˌtōbəˈgōnēən, -nyən\ *n* -S *cap* [*Tobago*, island in the West Indies + E -*onian* (as in *Patagonian*)] : a native or inhabitant of the island of Tobago in the British West Indies

tobas *pl of* TOBA

¹to-be \=ˈ=\ *adj* [fr. the infinitive phrase *to be*] : that is to be : FUTURE — usu. used postpositively and often in combination ⟨mothers-*to-be*⟩ ⟨his victim *to-be* —Stuart Atkins⟩ ⟨a charming bride-*to-be*⟩

²to-be \"\ *n* -S [fr. the infinitive phrase *to be*] : what is to be : FUTURE ⟨I work and write for the *to-be* —Marie Corelli⟩

tobe *also* **tob** \ˈtōb\ *n* -S [Ar *thawb* garment] : a long shapeless sometimes draped and usu. cotton garment made like a shirt and worn by peoples of northern and central Africa

to·ber \ˈtōbə(r)\ *n* -S [Brit. slang *tober* road, highway, fr. Shelta *tobar* — more at TOBY] *dial Brit* : a circus lot

to·bi·ad \təˈbīəd\ *n* -S *usu cap* [*Tobias*, father of Joseph *fl ab* 210 B.C. founder of the Tobiads + E -*ad* (member of a group)] : a member of a Jewish party of the Maccabean period favoring the Hellenization of the Jews

to·bi·as acid \təˈbīəs-\ *n, usu cap T* [after Georg *Tobias*, 19th cent. Ger. chemist] : a crystalline naphthylaminesulfonic acid $H_2NC_{10}H_6SO_3H$ used as a dye intermediate; 2-amino-1-naphthalenesulfonic acid

to·bi·khar \ˌtōbəˈkär\ *n* -S *usu cap* [Gabrielino] : GABRIELINO

to·bi·ra \təˈbīrə\ *n* -S [Jap, lit., door] : a commonly cultivated shrub (*Pittosporum tobira*) of China and Japan with ornamental glossy leaves and white fragrant flowers in terminal umbels

tobira family *n* : PITTOSPORACEAE

¹to·bog·gan \təˈbägən\ *n* -S [CanF *tobogan, tabagan, tabagane*, of Algonquian origin; akin to Micmac *tobâgun* drag made of skin, Abnaki *udâbâgân*, Cree *otâbânâsk*] **1** : a long flat-bottomed light sled made of thin boards curved up at one end with usu. low handrails at the

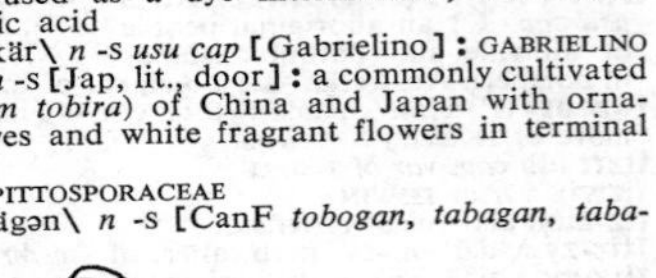
toboggan 1

sides and used for coasting, traveling, or transportation on snow or ice **2 a :** a slope or course of suitable steepness for use of a toboggan ⟨minutes are lost whenever we have to climb such a ~ —Michel Bouché⟩ **b :** a downward course (as of life or affairs) — used chiefly in the phrase *on the toboggan* ⟨on the ~ but still a long way from complete failure⟩ **c :** a sharp decline (as in value or price) ⟨prices hit the ~⟩ **3 :** a conveyor on which material moves down an incline under gravity **4** *or* **toboggan cap :** STOCKING CAP

²toboggan \"\ *vi* -ED/-ING/-S **1 :** to coast on a toboggan **:** slide rapidly on or as if on a toboggan **2 :** to decline suddenly and sharply (as in value) ⟨values ~*ed* on the market⟩ ⟨stocks may ~ in response to foreign tensions⟩

to·bog·gan·er \-gənə(r)\ *also* **to·bog·gan·ist** \-nəst\ *n* -S **:** one that toboggans

toboggan slide *or* **toboggan chute** *n* **:** a slide for coasting on toboggans usu. in the form of a steep wooden ice-covered chute

to·bo·sa grass \tə'bōsə-\ *n* [perh. after the *Toboso* Indians in northern Mexico, fr. Sp, of AmerInd origin] **:** a coarse range grass (*Hilaria mutica*) that is an important forage plant on semiarid plains and hills of the southwestern U. S. and adjacent Mexico

tobs *pl of* TOB

¹to·by \'tōbē, -bi\ *n* -ES [Shelta *tobar*, prob. modif. of IrGael *bōthar*] *Brit* **:** STREET, WAY, HIGHWAY; *also* **:** highway robbery — compare HIGHTOBY

²toby \"\ *n* -ES [fr. *Toby*, nickname for *Tobias*] **1** *or* **toby jug** *often cap T* **:** a small jug, pitcher, or mug that is generally used for ale and is shaped somewhat like a stout man with a cocked hat forming the brim; *also* **:** such a quantity (as of ale) as is served in a toby **2** *or* **to·bie** \"\ -S **:** a long slender cigar tapered at one end and made of strong inferior tobacco **3 :** *southern Africa* **:** GLOBEFISH

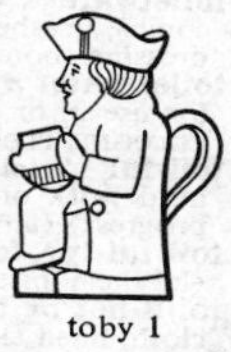

toby 1

toby fill·pot jug \-'fil,pät-\ *n, usu cap T&F* **:** TOBY 1

toby·man \'==,mən\ *n, pl* **tobymen** [¹*toby* + *man*] *archaic* **:** HIGHWAYMAN

to·ca·lo·te \,tōkə'lōd·ē\ *n* -S [modif. of Sp *chicalote* — more at CHICALOTE] **:** a weedy European annual herb (*Centaurea melitensis*) widely naturalized in the New World and esp. in California of some importance as a honey plant

toc·ca·ta \tə'kä|d·ə, -kȧ|, |tə\ *n* -S [It, fr. fem. of *toccato*, past part. of *toccare* to touch, play (a musical instrument) with the fingers, fr. (assumed) VL, to knock, strike a bell, touch — more at TOUCH] **:** a brilliant musical composition usu. for pipe organ or harpsichord, in free fantasia style, and usu. with many equal-timed notes in rapid movement

toc·ca·ti·na \,täkə'tēnə\ *n* -S [It, dim. of *toccata*] **:** a short toccata

to·cha·ri \tō'kärē\ *n pl, usu cap* [L, fr. Gk *Tocharoi*] **:** the Tocharian people

to·char·i·an *or* **to·khar·i·an** \tō'ka(a)rēən, -kär-\ *n* -S *cap* [L *Tochari* + E *-an*] **1 :** a member of a people of advanced culture and presumably European origin dwelling in central Asia during the first millennium of the Christian era until overrun by the Uighurs **2 a :** a language of central Asia known from documents from the seventh century A.D. and occurring in an eastern and a western dialect **b :** a branch of the Indo-European language family containing the Tocharian language — see INDO-EUROPEAN LANGUAGES table

tocharian A *n, cap T* **:** the eastern dialect of Tocharian

tocharian B *n, cap T* **:** the western dialect of Tocharian

to·cha·rish \tō'kärish\ *n, usu cap* [G *tocharisch*, fr. L *Tochari* + G *-isch* -ish] **:** TOCHARIAN 2

¹toch·er \'täkər\ *n* -S [IrGael *tochar*] *chiefly Scot* **:** marriage portion **:** DOT

²tocher \"\ *vt* -ED/-ING/-S *chiefly Scot* **:** to provide with a marriage portion **:** DOWER

tocher-good *n, Scot* **:** property given as a marriage portion

tock \'täk\ *n* -S [Pg *toco* toco, tock] **:** an African hornbill of the genus *Tockus*

¹to·co \'tō(,)kō\ *n* -S [Pg, fr. Tupi] **:** a large So. American toucan (*Ramphastos toco*) that is chiefly black with the rump and throat white, the latter tinged with yellow and bordered with red, and the under tail coverts crimson

²to·co *also* **to·ko** \"\ *n* -S [Hindi *toko*, imper. of *toknā* to blame] *Brit* **:** rigorous and usu. physical chastisement ⟨administer ~ to the wretched fags nearest at hand —Thomas Hughes⟩

toco- *or* **toko-** *comb form* [Gk *tokos*, fr. *tiktein* to bear, beget — more at THANE] **:** childbirth **:** offspring ⟨*toco*genetic⟩ ⟨*toco*logy⟩

toco·dynamometer *or* **toko·dynamometer** \¦tō(,)kō, ¦tä(+\ *n* [ISV *toco-* + *dynamometer*] **:** an instrument by means of which the force of uterine puerperal contractions can be measured

to·col·o·gy *also* **to·kol·o·gy** \tō'käləjē\ *n* -ES [Gk *tokos* + E *-logy*] **:** the science of obstetrics

to-come \tə'=\ *n* -S [fr. the infinitive phrase *to come*] **:** what is to come **:** FUTURE ⟨tides of the long past and the infinite *to-come* —Nathaniel Hawthorne⟩

to·coph·er·ol \tō'käfə,rōl, -rōl\ *n* -S [ISV *toco-* + *-pher* + *-ol*] **:** any of several pale yellow fat-soluble oily liquid phenolic compounds that are derived from chroman and differ in the number and locations of methyl groups in the benzene ring, that have antioxidant properties and vitamin E activity in varying degrees, that are found in the dextrorotatory form esp. in oils from seeds (as wheat-germ oil and cottonseed oil), in leaves, and in fish-liver oils, that are made synthetically in the racemic form, and that are used in a mixture chiefly as antioxidants (as for stabilizing vitamin A in fats and oils) and in nutrition and veterinary medicine: as **a :** the compound $C_{29}H_{50}O_2$ obtained usu. from germ oils or by synthesis (as from trimethylhydroquinone and phytyl bromide) and often used in the form of its acetate or other esters — called also *alpha-tocopherol, vitamin E* **b :** a compound $C_{28}H_{48}O_2$ occurring usu. with alpha-tocopherol and gamma-tocopherol — called also *beta-tocopherol* **c :** a compound $C_{28}H_{48}O_2$ isomeric with beta-tocopherol and occurring with it and alpha-tocopherol and predominating in corn oil and with delta-tocopherol in soybean oil — called also *gamma-tocopherol* **d :** a compound $C_{27}H_{46}O_2$ said to have the highest antioxidant activity of the tocopherols and found with the others but esp. in soybean oil — called also *delta-tocopherol*

to·co·ro·ro \,tōkə'rōr(,)ō\ *n* -S [AmerSp, of imit. origin] **:** a Cuban trogon (*Priotelus temnurus*) having the bill serrated and the tail feathers concave at the end

toco·stome \'täkə,stōm, 'tōk-\ *n* -S [*toco-* + *-stome*] **:** a genital pore

toc·sin \'täksən\ *n* -S [MF *toquassen, toquesin*, fr. OProv *tocasenh*, fr. *tocar* touch, ring a bell (fr. — assumed — VL *toccare* to ring a bell) + *senh* sign, bell, fr. ML & L *signum*; ML, bell, fr. LL, ringing of a bell, fr. L, mark, sign — more at TOUCH, SIGN] **1 :** an alarm bell or the ringing of a bell for the purpose of alarm **2 :** an urgent or warning thing or event ⟨these volumes . . . are both a ~ and an arsenal —S.K. Padover⟩ ⟨as so often thought of early summer as a time for ~*s* —*Economist*⟩ **3 :** something felt to resemble a warning bell (as in loudness, abruptness, or clarity) ⟨his ~ voice⟩

to·cus·so \tə'kü(,)sō\ *n* -S [Amharic *tokusso*] **:** a grass (*Eleusine tocussa*) cultivated in Ethiopia for its edible seeds which are used esp. in a dark heavy bread

¹tod \'täd\ *n* -S [ME] **1** *chiefly Scot* **:** FOX **2** *chiefly Scot* **:** a canny crafty person

²tod \"\ *n* -S [ME *todd, todde*; prob. akin to Fris *todde* rag, trash, D *tod, todde* rag, OHG *zotta* tuft of hair, ON *toddi* small piece, bit, and perh. to ON *tethja* to manure — more at TED] **1 :** any of various units of weight for wool; *esp* **:** a unit equal to 28 pounds **2** *chiefly dial* **:** a bundle, load, or mass (as of wool) often of a tod weight **3** *Brit* **:** a bushy clump or growth (as of ivy)

³tod \"\ *vi* **todded; todded; todding; tods** *archaic* **:** to produce or obtain a tod (as of wool)

⁴tod \"\ *n* -S [by shortening] **:** TODDY

to·da \'tōdə\ *n, pl* **todas** *also* **toda** *usu cap* **1 :** one of an aboriginal polyandrous people of light complexion and tall stature that reside in the Nilgiri hills of southern India and in Ceylon, that lead a peaceful pastoral life, and that practice a religion which is organized around the care and veneration of cattle and esp. the buffalo **2 :** the Dravidian language of the Todas

¹to·day \tə'dā\ *adv* [ME, fr. OE *tōdæge, tōdæg*, fr. *tō* to, at + *dæge*, dat. of *dæg* day — more at TO, DAY] **1 :** on or for this day **:** on the present day **2 :** at the present time **:** NOWADAYS

²today \"\ *n* -S **1 :** the day now present; *also* **:** any day construed as currently existing ⟨the tasks of ~⟩ **2 :** the present time, epoch, or age

to·day·ish \-ish, -ēsh\ *adj* **:** of or characteristic of today **:** CURRENT, UP-TO-DATE

tod·dick \'tädik, -dēk\ *n* -S [²*tod* + *-ick* (alter. of *-ock*)] **1** *South* **a :** a measure used by a custom miller to take out his toll from the grist **b :** a portion of flour or meal taken by a miller as his toll **2** *South* **:** a small amount

¹tod·dle \'täd°l\ *vi* **toddled; toddled; toddling** \-d(°)liŋ\ **toddles** [origin unknown] **1 :** to walk with short tottering steps in the manner of a young child **:** progress slowly and usu. irregularly **2 a :** to take a stroll **:** SAUNTER **b :** to take one's departure and go

²toddle \"\ *n* -S **:** an act of toddling **:** a toddling gait or progress

tod·dler \-d(°)lə(r)\ *n* -S **:** one that toddles; *esp* **:** a young child

tod·dy \'tädē, -di\ *n* -ES [Hindi *tāṛī* juice of the palmyra palm, fr. *tāṛ* palmyra palm, fr. Skt *tāla*, perh. of Dravidian origin; akin to Kannada *tar* palmyra palm, Telegu *tāḍu*] **1 :** the fresh or fermented sap of various chiefly East Indian palms **2 :** a hot drink consisting of an alcoholic liquor, water, sugar, and spices (as cinnamon, cloves, and nutmeg) and often garnished with fruit ⟨whiskey ~⟩ ⟨applejack ~⟩

toddy bird *n* **:** any of several Indian birds (as various weaverbirds and wood swallows) that feed on palm juice

toddy cat *n, India* **:** PALM CIVET

toddy palm *also* **toddy tree** *n* **:** any of several wine palms; *esp* **:** JAGGERY PALM

toddy stick *n* **:** a stick knobbed or flattened at the end and used in making toddy

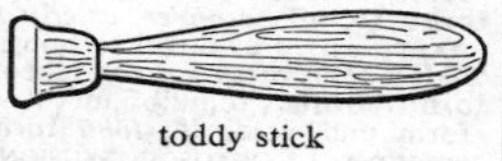

toddy stick

to·dea \'tōdēə, tə'dēə\ *n, cap* [NL, after H. J. *Tode* †1797 Ger. botanist] **:** a genus of delicate African and Australasian ferns (family Osmundaceae) distinguished from those of *Osmunda* by having the sporangia on the underside of the leaf — see CRAPE FERN

to·di·dae \'tōdə,dē\ *n pl, cap* [NL, fr. *Todus*, type genus + *-idae*] **:** a family of West Indian birds (order Coraciiformes) usu. comprising the single genus *Todus* — compare TODY

todlowrie \(')=¦==\ *n* -S [¹*tod* + *lowrie*] *Scot* **:** FOX, TOD

to-do \tə'dü\ *n* [fr. the infinitive phrase *to do*] **1 :** excited and usu. exaggerated stir **:** BUSTLE, COMMOTION ⟨the papers made a great *to-do* about his appointment⟩ ⟨a great flutter and *to-do* among the ladies of the church⟩ **2** *dial* **:** a formal or fancy party **:** a social affair of unusual style or show

tods *pl of* TOD, *pres 3d sing of* TOD

to·dus \'tōdəs\ *n, cap* [NL, fr. L, a small bird] **:** the type and usu. sole genus of the family Todidae — see TODY

to·dy \'tōdē, -di\ *n* -ES [modif. of F *todier*, fr. L *todus*, a small bird] **1 :** any of several tiny nonpasserine insectivorous West Indian birds constituting the genus *Todus*, being closely related to the kingfishers, having a long flattened bill with strong rictal bristles, and nesting in holes in banks — see GREEN TODY **2 :** any of various small brightly colored birds (as some American flycatchers) — compare ROYAL FLYCATCHER

¹toe \'tō\ *n* -S *often attrib* [ME *ta, to, too*, fr. OE *tā*; akin to OHG *zēha* toe, ON *tā* toe, L *digitus* finger, and prob. to Gk *deiknynai* to show — more at DICTION] **1 a (1) :** one of the terminal digits of a vertebrate's foot — distinguished from *finger* **(2) :** the fore end of a foot or hoof — opposed to *heel* **b (1) :** a terminal segment of a limb of an invertebrate **(2) :** either of the two processes in which the hinder part of the body of a rotifer usu. ends **c :** a part of something worn on or attached to a foot that covers or corresponds to its fore end ⟨the ~ of a boot⟩ ⟨the ~ of a horseshoe⟩ **2 :** a part that by its position, form or outline, or relation to other parts is felt to resemble a toe ⟨the ~ of Italy⟩: as **a (1) :** a prong or stub (as on a vinifera grape) from which vegetative growth arises **(2) :** one of the expanded extensions of a tree trunk where a root passes into the ground **(3) :** a single tuberous root of a dahlia **b (1) :** a journal or pivot supported in a step bearing **(2) :** a lateral projection at one end or between the ends of a piece (as a rod or bolt) by which it is moved; *often* **:** a projecting arm actuated by a cam on the valve-lifting rod in the beam type of steam engine **(3) :** a projection from the periphery of a revolving piece acting as a cam to lift another piece **c (1) :** the extreme bottom point of a seed trench prepared by a furrow opener (as of a grain drill) **(2) :** the lowest part of the slope of an earth embankment or a cliff **(3) :** the line of contact between the lower or downstream face and the base of a dam **(4) :** the bottom of a mine or quarry bench **(5) :** the lower edge of a mine dump **(6) :** the bottom of a drill hole for blasting **d :** a metal tip at the lower end of the foot of some wooden organ pipes; *also* **:** the lower end of a metal pipe foot or reed boot **e :** a board or other part of a structure occupying a low and forward position **f (1) :** the peen of a hammer **(2) :** the outer end of the hitting surface of a golf club or hockey stick — see GOLF illustration **g :** the corner of the butt of a gunstock that is lowermost when the gun is in firing position **h :** the front end of a railroad frog opposite the heel **3 :** TOE DANCE **4 :** a football player used solely or primarily for kicking — **on one's toes 1 :** full of life **:** ACTIVE, BUSY **2 :** alert and ready to seize any advantage or engage in any activity that comes one's way ⟨for a living working for real money you've got to be *on your toes* —W.L.Gresham⟩ — **toes up :** DEAD

²toe \"\ *vb* **toed; toed; toeing; toes** *vt* **1 :** to furnish with a toe; *esp* **:** to form the toe of (a knitted sock or stocking) by decreasing stitches — usu. used with *off* **2 :** to touch, reach, move, or crush with the forepart of the foot ⟨*toed* a chair into position⟩ ⟨~ your cigarette out⟩ ⟨simple homes *toeing* the sidewalk —P.J.Celliers⟩ ⟨~ a football⟩ **3 :** to drive (as a nail, spike, or rod) slantingly or aslant; *also* **:** to clinch or fasten by or with nails or rods so driven ⟨*toed* a brace between wall and floor⟩ ~ *vi* **:** to move the toes or move on the toes: as **a :** to move stealthily **:** TIPTOE ⟨~*ing* cautiously forward⟩ **b :** to stand, walk, or be placed so that the toes assume an indicated position or direction ⟨~ in⟩ ⟨~ along a straight line⟩ **c :** to tap with the toe in heel-and-toe dancing — **toe the line 1 :** to touch with the toes only in standing a line indicating a starting point (as in a race or match) **2 a** *or* **toe a line :** to act or conform rigorously to some rule or standard ⟨*toe a* party *line* without protest⟩ **b :** to accept one's responsibilities or stand to one's obligations — **toe the mark** *or* **toe a mark :** toe the line

¹toe-and-heel \¦=¦=\ *adj* **:** HEEL-AND-TOE

²toe-and-heel \"\ *vi* **:** DANCE; *usu* **:** to do tap-dancing, jigging, or other vigorous dancing — often used with *it*

toe-and-heel click *n* **:** the striking of the toe of one foot against the heel of the other in tap-dancing

toe-biter \'=,==\ *n* **1 :** TADPOLE 1 **2 :** any of several large aquatic insects that sometimes attack bathers: as **a :** a bug of the families Nepidae or Belostomatidae **b :** HELLGRAMMITE

toeboard \'=,=\ *n* **:** a support or reinforcement (as of board) for the toes or at the base of something ⟨the ~ of a swing⟩: as **a :** the sloping boards in the forward part of an automotive vehicle in front of the forward seat **b :** a curved piece of wood fastened to the ground at the front of the circle used for shot putting, throwing the weight, or similar contests to prevent overstepping **c :** a low border (as about a staging) esp. to prevent dropping of tools or other objects

toe box *n* **1 :** a piece of leather or other material placed between the toecap and lining of a shoe and treated with a substance (as a gum) that hardens after the shoe is lasted permanently **2 :** BOXING 5

toe calk *n* **:** a calk on the toe of the shoe of a horse or ox

toe cap *n* **:** a separate piece of leather or other material covering the toe of a shoe and reinforcing or decorating it

toe clip *n* **1 :** a device that fits the toe of a shoe and is attached to a cycle pedal to receive the foot and keep it from slipping **2 :** ²CLIP C

toe crack *n* **:** a sand crack in the front wall of a horse's hoof

toed \¦tōd\ *adj* [¹*toe* + *-ed*] **1 :** having a toe or such or so many toes — used esp. in combination ⟨long-*toed*⟩ ⟨five-*toed*⟩ **2** [fr. past part. of ²*toe*] **:** driven obliquely ⟨a carefully ~ nail⟩; *also* **:** secured by diagonal or oblique nailing

toe dance *n* **:** a dance executed on the tips of the toes

toe-dance \'=,=\ *vi* [*toe dance*] **:** to dance a toe dance — **toe dancer** *n*

toe dog *n* **:** a short usu. two to four inch long piece of bar steel made with one end flattened and the other cupped to receive the end of the setscrew of a screw plug and used esp. for clamping thin work to a table

toedrop \'=,=\ *n* **:** FOOT DROP

toe hardie *n* **:** a half-round hardie

toehold \'=,=\ *n* **1 :** a hold or place of support for the toes (as in climbing): as **a :** a means of progressing (as in gaining entry or surmounting barriers) ⟨hoped his uncle could give him a ~ in the import business⟩ **b :** a slight footing **:** very little power, influence, or territory ⟨at this time the Turks had only a ~ in Europe⟩ **2 :** a wrestling hold in which the aggressor bends or twists his opponent's foot

toe-in \'=,=\ *n* -S [fr. *toe in*, v.] **1 :** CAMBER 2 **2 :** inclination of the wheels of an automotive vehicle so that either pair is closer together at the front than at the back — compare TOE-OUT

toeing *pres part of* TOE

toe-iron \'=,=(=)\ *n* **:** one of two upright projections of metal plate fitted to a ski between which the toe of the boot is held firm

toe-kissing \'=,==\ *n* **:** an act of humble adoration **:** deeply obeisant conduct

toe·less \'tōləs\ *adj* **:** lacking a toe ⟨a ~ shoe⟩

¹toenail \'=,=\ *n* [¹*toe* + *nail*] **1 :** a nail of a toe **2 :** a nail that is toed (as in fitting a brace) **3 :** PARENTHESIS 3a

²toenail \"\ *vt* **:** to clinch or fasten by toed nails **:** TOE

toe-out \'=,=\ *n* -S [fr. *toe out*, v.] **:** inclination of the wheels of an automotive vehicle so that either pair is closer together at the back than at the front — compare TOE-IN

toepiece \'=,=\ *n* **:** a piece designed to form a toe (as of a shoe) or cover the toes of the foot

toe piling *n* **:** sharpened poles driven next to the upstream face of the mudsills of a dam to prevent water from getting under the foundations

toeplate \'=,=\ *n* **:** a metal tab attached to the toe of a shoe to prevent slipping or the wear due to heavy use

toep·ler pump \'tepl(r)-\ *n, usu cap T* [after August J. I. *Toepler* †1912 Ger. physicist, its inventor] **:** a gas pump that is used to produce vacuums or to transfer gases from one part of a system to another and that operates by the alternate lowering and raising of a column of mercury with the consequent alternate production of a vacuum in one tube and the exhausting of the gas through another

toe puff *n* **:** a piece of material (as fabric or metal) inserted as a stiffener in the toe of a shoe between the outside and the lining — compare BOXING 5, TOE BOX, TOE CAP

toe-punch \'=,=\ *also* **toe-mark** \'=,=\ *vt* **:** to mark (poultry) by punching holes through the membrane between the toes

toe ring *n* **1 :** a ring worn on the toe **2 :** a ferrule or a heavy ring on the end of a cant hook with a lipped lower surface that prevents slipping **3 :** a small paddock in which horses heated by exercise are walked to cool them off

toer·ne·bohm·ite *or* **tör·ne·bohm·ite** \'tərnə,bō,mīt, 'tōr-, ¦==¦==\ *n* -S [Alfred E. *Törnebohm* †1911 Swedish geologist + E *-ite*] **:** a mineral $Ce_3Si_2O_8OH$ that is a rare silicate of the cerium metals

toe rubber *n* **:** a rubber esp. for wear over a woman's high-heeled shoe that covers only the forepart of the shoe and is held in place by a strap extending around the back of the foot above the heel — compare FOOTHOLD 3, SANDAL 4

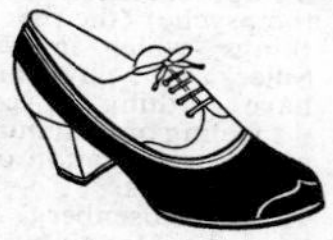

toe rubber

toes *pl of* TOE, *pres 3d sing of* TOE

toe shoe *also* **toe slipper** *n* **:** a ballet slipper with reinforced toe for toe dancing

toe strap *n* **:** any of various straps passing over or between the toes to give purchase (as on a deck) or hold something (as a ski) in position

toe-tap \'=,=\ *n* **:** tap-dancing done on the tips of the toes

toe·toe *also* **toi·toi** \¦tōē¦tōē, 'tōi,tōi\ *n* -S [Maori *toetoe*] **:** any of several coarse New Zealand sedges and grasses (as of the genera *Arundo* and *Cladium*); *specif* **:** a plant (*A. conspicua*) used by the Maoris for thatching

toe wall *n* **:** a low retaining wall; *esp* **:** an embankment wall in a railroad cut

toe weight *n* **:** a small metal weight attached to the toe of a horse's front hoof to regulate the gait

toey \'tōē\ *adj* [¹*toe* + *-y*, adj. suffix] *Austral* **:** NERVOUS, ANXIOUS, WORRIED

to-fall \'tü,fōl\ *n* [ME *tofall*, fr. *to*, adv. + *fall*, n.] **1** *chiefly Scot* **:** a building built against another **:** LEAN-TO **2** *Scot* **:** the fall of night **:** NIGHTFALL

toff \'täf, 'tȯf\ *n* -S [prob. alter. of *tuft* (student at Oxford)] *chiefly Brit* **:** a person of superior social status and often notably stylish or fashionable — often used disparagingly

tof·fee *also* **tof·fy** \'tȯfē, -'täf-, -fi\ *n, pl* **toffees** *also* **toffies** [alter. of *taffy*] **1 a :** candy of brittle but tender texture made by boiling sugar and butter together to approximately 310° F or the hard crack stage **b :** BUTTERSCOTCH ⟨~ pie⟩ ⟨~ cookies⟩ **2** *chiefly Brit* **:** a piece of toffee

toffee-nosed \¦=¦=\ *adj, Brit* **:** exhibiting undue airs of superiority **:** STUCK-UP

toff·ish \'täfish, 'tȯf-, -fēsh\ *adj, Brit* **:** resembling a toff esp. in smartness or style

to·fiel·dia \tə'fēldēə\ *n, cap* [NL, fr. Thomas *Tofield* †1779 Eng. botanist + NL *-ia*] **:** a genus of perennial herbs (family Liliaceae) growing in cool regions and having linear chiefly basal leaves and small spicate sessile flowers with 6 anthers and 3 styles — see FALSE ASPHODEL

tofore *adv* [ME *toforen, tofore*, fr. OE *tōforan*, fr. *tō* to + *foran* before, fr. *fore* — more at TO, FORE] *obs* **:** BEFORE ⟨would thou wert as thou ~ hast been —Shak.⟩

toft \'täft *also* 'tȯft\ *n* -S [ME, fr. OE, fr. ON *topt, tupt*] **1** *Brit* **a (1) :** a site for a dwelling and its outbuildings **:** HOMESTEAD **(2) :** a usu. enclosed garden plot attached to a homestead **b :** an entire holding comprising a homestead together with additional usu. arable land **2** *Brit* **:** an isolated hill or elevation **:** a knoll suitable for a building site

toft·man \'=mən\ *n, pl* **toftmen** *Brit* **:** a holder of a toft; *usu* **:** SMALLHOLDER

toft ware *n, usu cap T* [after Thomas *Toft*, 17th cent. Eng. potter] **:** slip-decorated ceramic ware of a style made orig. by Thomas Toft

to·fu \'tō(,)fü\ *n* -S [Jap *tōfu*] **:** BEAN CURD

¹tog \'täg *also* 'tȯg\ *n* -S [short for obs. E cant *togeman, togemans, togman* cloak, prob. fr. E *toge* + obs. E cant *-mans* (n. suffix of unknown origin)] **1** *slang* **:** an outer garment; *esp* **:** COAT **2 togs** *pl* **:** CLOTHING ⟨the old ~*s* he sat around in —Theodore Dreiser⟩; *esp* **:** an outfit of clothes and accessories for a specified use ⟨riding ~*s*⟩ ⟨beach ~*s*⟩ ⟨getting into play ~*s* for golf or boating —Vance Packard⟩ **3 togs** *pl, Austral* **:** BATHING SUIT

²tog \"\ *vt* **togged; togged; togging; togs :** to put togs on **:** dress up — usu. used with *out* or *up* ⟨went to school *togged* out in their Sunday best —Frank Sullivan⟩ ⟨*togged* up as an ordinary seaman of a century ago —Charles Hamblett⟩

tog *abbr* together

to·ga \'tōgə\ *n* -S [L; akin to L *tegere* to cover — more at THATCH] **1 a :** the outer garment worn in public by citizens of ancient Rome consisting of a semicircular or long elliptical usu. undyed woolen cloth sometimes ornamented along the borders and so draped as to cover the left arm and leave the right arm free **b :** a similar loose wrap ⟨the colorful ~ of an African chieftain⟩ **c :** a professional, official, or academic gown ⟨don the ~ of a judge⟩ **2 :** OFFICE; *esp* **:** SENATORSHIP ⟨will seek a ~ next November —*Newsweek*⟩

to·gaed \'tōgəd\ *adj* **:** clad in or as if in a toga **:** TOGATED ⟨a ~ Roman senator⟩ ⟨~ dancers⟩ ⟨parks, where ~ or equestrian Lincolns would look blandly down —*Nation*⟩

to·gat·ed \'tō,gād·əd\ *also* **to·gate** \-,āt\ *adj* [*togated* fr. L *togatus* togated + E *-ed*; *togate* fr. L *togatus*, fr. *toga* + *-atus*

-ate] **1 :** wearing a toga **:** TOGAED ⟨a ~ senator⟩ **2 :** DIGNIFIED, STATELY ⟨~ language⟩

to·ga vi·ri·lis \ˌtōgəwə'rēləs\ *n, pl* **to·gae viri·les** \ˌtō-ˌgiwə'rē(ˌ)lās\ [L, men's toga] **:** the white toga of manhood assumed by boys of ancient Rome at the end of their fourteenth year

toge *n* -s [ME, fr. MF *togue, toge,* fr. L *toga*] *obs* **:** TOGA, CLOAK

to·ged \'tōgəd\ *adj, obs* **:** TOGATED ⟨the ~ consuls can propose —Shak.⟩

to·geth·er \tə'gethə(r)\ *adv* [ME *togadere, togedere, togidere,* fr. OE *tōgadere, tōgædere, tōgædre,* fr. *tō* to + *gadere, gædere, gædre* together; akin to OFris *gader, gadur* together, MLG *tōgadere,* MHG *gater* together, *gatern* to unite — more at GATHER] **1 a :** in or into one place, mass, collection, or group (as body, company, or organization) ⟨sweep the rubbish ~⟩ ⟨call the members ~⟩ ⟨come ~ for discussion⟩ ⟨the girls got ~ by themselves⟩ ⟨gathered his scattered writings ~ for publication in one volume⟩ ⟨brought the two factions ~ in a new party⟩ **b :** in a body **:** as a group ⟨students and faculty ~ presented the petition⟩ ⟨~ our objective has been to hold tight to your attention —Richard Joseph⟩ **2 a :** in or into contact (as connection, collision, or union) ⟨fasten the parts ~⟩ ⟨mix these ingredients ~⟩ ⟨the opposing teams rushed ~⟩ ⟨held ~ by pins⟩ **b :** in or into a compacted or constricted mass or body ⟨folded and pressed the papers ~ into a small bundle⟩ ⟨sat all hunched ~⟩ **c :** in or into association or relationship (as of companionship, friendship, courtship, or cohabitation) ⟨colors that go well ~⟩ ⟨held ~ by ties of common interest⟩ ⟨circumstances threw them ~⟩ ⟨bringing industry and the liberal arts ~ —D.A.Shepard⟩ ⟨fought ~ in the war⟩ ⟨went ~ for years⟩ ⟨live ~ as man and wife⟩ **3 a :** at one time **:** SIMULTANEOUSLY, COINCIDENTALLY ⟨events that happened ~ —R.J.Goldwater⟩ ⟨what is learned through the most senses ~ will be most readily retained —I.A.Richards⟩ **b :** in succession **:** without intermission **:** on end **:** CONSECUTIVELY ⟨was moody for days ~ —Hugh Walpole⟩ ⟨sometimes lay hid for weeks ~ in cocklofts and cellars —T.B.Macaulay⟩ **4 a :** in or by combined action or effort **:** JOINTLY ⟨parents have ~ the responsibility for discipline⟩ ⟨~ we forced the door⟩ ⟨the family ~ earned one hundred dollars a week⟩ **b :** in or into agreement (as harmony, concert, or unison) **:** in unified action or interaction ⟨unable to get ~ on vacation plans⟩ ⟨the parts of the mechanism work ~ beautifully⟩ ⟨soloist and orchestra were not always quite ~⟩ **c :** in or into a unified or coherent structure or an integrated whole ⟨the play hangs ~⟩ ⟨the child who cannot put an easy sentence ~ —George Sampson⟩ ⟨have thrown ~ shacks of scrap lumber and tar paper —*Amer. Guide Series: Ark.*⟩ **5 a :** with each other **:** MUTUALLY, RECIPROCALLY ⟨were not on good terms ~⟩ ⟨consult ~ on possible . . . legislation —*New Republic*⟩ — used pleonastically and as an intensive after certain verbs ⟨join ~⟩ ⟨cooperate ~⟩ ⟨add a column of figures ~⟩ **b :** as a unit or sum **:** in the aggregate ⟨these arguments taken ~ make a convincing case⟩ ⟨the pair of meetings ~ seldom lasted more than three hours —J.K.Blake⟩ **c :** considered as a whole **:** counted or summed up ⟨richer than all his brothers ~⟩ ⟨all ~, there were 21 entries⟩ — compare ALTOGETHER 2 — **together with :** along with **:** in addition to **:** as well as ⟨the big island, *together with* its smaller neighbors⟩ ⟨these sums *together with* the previous balance⟩ ⟨arrested, *together with* a companion⟩

to·geth·er·ness *n* -ES **:** the quality or state of being or belonging together or of forming related parts of a unified whole: as **a :** ONENESS, UNITY ⟨a grasping of diverse entities into a value by reason of their real ~ in that pattern —A.N.Whitehead⟩ **b :** apprehension or sense of unity (as in the outer world or in the psyche) ⟨the psychology of ~⟩ **c :** ASSOCIATION ⟨the ~ of things, which impressed the artists of the North —G.C. Sillery⟩ **d :** physical closeness **:** PROPINQUITY ⟨the crowd . . . have nothing in common except ~ —Howard Griffin⟩ **e :** feeling of community **:** the emotional bond in a group (as a social organization or a family) **:** SOLIDARITY, COMMUNION ⟨a spontaneous . . . ~, as in invasions, floods, celebrations —Harold Rosenberg⟩ ⟨felt a deep flowing sense of ~ when we sang the Doxology —Lillian Smith⟩ ⟨that's what a home is made of — ~ —Edith Wharton⟩

tog·gen·burg \'tägənˌbərg\ *n* [fr. *Toggenburg,* district in northeastern Switzerland] **1** *usu cap* **:** a Swiss breed of brown hornless dairy goats with white stripes on the face **2** *often cap* -s **:** a goat of the Toggenburg breed

tog·gery \'täg(ə)rē, -ri\ *n* -ES *often attrib* [¹*tog* + *-ery*] **1 :** CLOTHING; *esp* **:** official or military dress ⟨the same ~ he first wore around the circuit —B.P.Thomas⟩ ⟨the campus ~ shop⟩ **2** *chiefly Brit* **:** a clothing shop ⟨opened a ~ on the town's main business street⟩

togging *pres part of* TOG

¹**tog·gle** \'tägəl\ *n* -s *often attrib* [origin unknown] **1 :** a piece or device for holding or securing: as **a :** a wood or metal pin inserted in a nautical knot to make it more secure or easier to slip **b** (1) **:** any crosspiece attached to the end of or to a loop in something (as a chain, rope, line, strap, belt) usu. to prevent slipping, to serve in twisting or tightening, or to hold something attached ⟨the ~ of a watch chain⟩ ⟨use a stick as a ~ in tightening a rope⟩ (2) **:** an object (as a chain or rope) with such a device **c :** a rod or screw with a T-head crosspiece or with a cone-shaped compressible nut that can pass through a hole in one direction but not in the opposite direction **d :** a button or frog capable of being engaged or disengaged for temporary purposes **e :** a short length of rope with a swivel and loop for tethering an animal **f :** a strap or cord fastened to the rear doorpost in an automobile as a handhold for passengers **g :** TOGGLE CHAIN **2 a :** TOGGLE JOINT **b :** a device having a toggle joint **c :** one of the bars of a toggle joint

²**toggle** \"\ *vt* **toggled; toggled; toggling** \-g(ə)liŋ\ **toggles** **1 :** to fasten with or as if with a toggle **:** hold fast with or as if with a toggle iron ⟨the sergeant would . . . ~ his holster —*Time*⟩ **2 a :** to furnish with a toggle **b :** to mend (as a harness) in makeshift or bungling fashion esp. with pieces of rope ⟨a *toggled* machine in danger of going to pieces at any moment —Hamlin Garland⟩ **c** *dial* **:** to add decoration to **:** make prettier **:** dress up ⟨put an ornament on a dress to ~ it up⟩ **3 :** to release (a bomb) from an airplane by a toggle switch instead of relying on the automatic release triggered by the bombsight ⟨all he had to do was ~ the bombs out —Bert Stiles⟩

toggle bolt *n* **:** a bolt that has a nut with pivoted flanged wings that close against a spring when passed through a constricted passage and open after emerging and that is used to fasten objects to thin or hollow walls

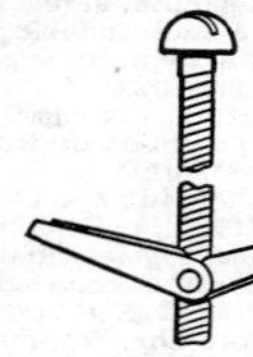

toggle bolt

toggle chain *n* **1 :** a device consisting of a short chain with a ring and toggle hook at one end and a ring at the other for regulating the effective length of a binding chain for a load of logs **2 :** a chain of any length with an end hook small enough to be inserted in a loose link that has been passed through a taut link

toggle clamp *n* **:** a clamp that locks by means of snap action across a dead center as in the toggle joint

toggle iron *or* **toggle harpoon** *n* **:** a harpoon with a pivoted crosspiece in a mortise near the point to prevent it from being drawn out when an animal is harpooned

toggle joint *n* **1 :** a device consisting of two bars jointed together end to end but not in line so that when a force is applied to the knee tending to straighten the arrangement the parts abutting or jointed to the ends of the bars will experience an endwise pressure which increases indefinitely as the bars approach a straight-line position ⟨*toggle joints* are used in stone crushers, in the double wagon brake, and in some kinds of presses⟩ **2 :** a joint consisting of a bar pivoted at its middle point to a supporting bar so that the former may be turned to any position and hence be used for lifting heavy objects (as tanks) by inserting the bar through a constricted opening and allowing it to assume a position normal to the supporting bar

toggle–joint press *or* **toggle press** *n* **:** a punch press operated by a toggle joint — called also *knuckle press*

toggle pin *n* **:** a pin with a shoulder and eye at one end and at the other a hinged locking device that prevents the pin from being withdrawn from a fitting until the locking device is in line with the pin

tog·gler \'täg(ə)lə(r)\ *n* -s **:** one that toggles

toggle riveter *n* **:** a riveter that upsets the stem and forms the rivet head by the action of a toggle mechanism

toggles *pl of* TOGGLE, *pres 3d sing of* TOGGLE

toggle switch *n* **:** an electric switch depending on a toggle-joint or knee-joint in conjunction with a spring to open or close the circuit quickly when the projecting lever is pushed through a small arc

to·ghuz·ghu \ˌtōˌgüzˌgü, -ˌgu̇z-\ *n, pl* **toghuzghus** \-üz\ *usu cap* **1 :** a Uighur people of central Asia held to be the only Turkish group professing the Manichaean religion **2 :** a member of the Toghuzghu people

to·go \'tō(ˌ)gō\ *adj, usu cap* [fr. *Togo,* country in western Africa] **:** of or relating to Togo **:** of the kind or style prevalent in Togo

to·go·land·er \'=(ˌ)=ˌlandə(r), -la(a)nd-\ *n* -s *cap* [*Togoland,* territory in western Africa + E *-er*] **:** a native or inhabitant of Togoland in western Africa

¹**to·go·lese** \ˌtō(ˌ)gō¦lēz, -lēs\ *adj, usu cap* [*Togo,* country in western Africa + E *-lese* (as in *Congolese*)] **1 :** of, relating to, or characteristic of the Republic of Togo in western Africa **2 :** of, relating to, or characteristic of the Togolese

²**togolese** \"\ *n, pl* **togolese** *cap* **:** a native or inhabitant of the Republic of Togo

togr *abbr* together

togs *pl of* TOG, *pres 3d sing of* TOG

togue \'tōg\ *n* -s [CanF] **:** LAKE TROUT

to·he·roa \ˌtōə'rōə\ *n, pl* **toheroa** *or* **toheroas** [Maori] **:** a large marine bivalve mollusk (*Amphidesma ventricosum*) of New Zealand used extensively for food

to·hi \'tōhē\ *n* -s [native name in eastern Africa] **:** a small tawny East African nagor (*Redunca redunca tohi*)

to·ho \tō'hō\ *v imper, chiefly Brit* [origin unknown] **:** STOP, HALT — used as a call to hunting dogs

TOHP *abbr, often not cap* takeoff horsepower

to·hu·bo·hu \ˌtōˌhüˌbōˌhü\ *n* -s [Heb *tōhū wā-bhōhū* without form and void, fr. *tōhū* formlessness, confusion + *bōhū* emptiness] **:** CHAOS, CONFUSION ⟨bringing order out of the ~ of human relations —Walter Lippmann⟩

to·hun·ga \ˌtōˌhu̇ŋgə\ *n* -s [Maori] *NewZeal* **:** a Maori priest or performer of sacred rites **:** SAGE, MEDICINE MAN

toi \'tȯi\ *n* -s [Maori] **:** ¹TI 1

¹**toil** \'tȯil, *esp before pause or consonant* 'tȯiəl\ *n* -s [ME *toile* argument, dispute, battle, fr. AF *toyl,* fr. OF *tooil, toeil* battle, trouble, confusion, fr. *tooillier, toeillier* to stir, mix, soil, sully, disturb, dispute — more at ²TOIL] **1** *archaic* **a :** a hard struggle **:** BATTLE, BROIL ⟨returning from their famous Trojan ~s —P.B.Shelley⟩ **b :** a laborious effort to achieve (as a task) despite the difficulties **:** LABOR ⟨some books are a ~ to read —J.E.Gloag⟩ **2 :** strenuous fatiguing labor marked usu. by long duration, lack of relief, and physical or mental strain **:** WORK, DRUDGERY ⟨for years he led a life of unremitting physical ~ —John Buchan⟩ ⟨fifty years of intellectual ~ . . . produced the greatest of all medieval storehouses of knowledge —H.O.Taylor⟩ ⟨nothing to offer but blood, ~, tears, and sweat —Sir Winston Churchill⟩ **syn** see WORK

²**toil** \"\ *vb* -ED/-ING/-S [ME *toilen* to argue, struggle, fr. AF *toiller,* fr. OF *tooillier, toeillier* to stir, mix, soil, sully, disturb, dispute, fr. L *tudiculare* to crush, grind, fr. *tudicula* machine for crushing olives, dim. of *tudes* hammer; akin to L *tundere* to beat — more at STINT] *vi* **1 :** to work hard and long at tiring labor **:** DRUDGE, SLAVE ⟨bathed in sweat as they ~*ed* at their . . . digging —W.F.Hambly⟩ ⟨inventors ~*ing* over drafting boards —R.A.Billington⟩ **2 :** to proceed with laborious exertion **:** advance with much effort or strain **:** PLOD — usu. used with *along, up, on,* or *over* ⟨father's bowed figure ~*ing* along the path —Ellen Glasgow⟩ ⟨~*ed* up the steepest part of the hill —Willa Cather⟩ ⟨feel obliged to ~ on through 559 more pages —O.W.Holmes †1935⟩ ~ *vt* **1** *archaic* **:** to weary or harass (as a person or animal) with labor or exertion **:** OVERWORK ⟨vex and ~ themselves to get what they have no need of —Izaak Walton⟩ **2 :** to work on (as the soil) **:** TILL ⟨~*ed* and tilled the rocky land —E.W.Smith⟩ **3** *archaic* **:** to accomplish (as a task) with great effort **:** get or effect after much labor **:** WORK ⟨at last the thing is ~*ed* and hammered into fit shape —S.T.Coleridge⟩

³**toil** \"\ *n* -s [MF *toile* cloth, net, fr. L *tela* web, fr. *texere* to weave, construct — more at TECHNICAL] **1 :** a net or a series of nets spread so as to enclose and entrap game already in the area or driven into it as quarry — usu. used in pl. ⟨the practice of enclosing the land with ~s and stirring it with dogs —H.A.J. Munro⟩ **2 :** something by which one is held fast, entangled, or involved in seemingly inextricable difficulties **:** SNARE, TRAP ⟨would catch another Anthony in her strong ~ of grace —Shak.⟩ — usu. used in pl. ⟨in the ~s of the law⟩ ⟨the immense genius . . . caught in the ~s of the moral and aesthetic conventions of his day —Herbert Read⟩

⁴**toil** \"\ *vt* -ED/-ING/-S **:** to entangle in or as if in toils **:** ENSNARE, ENTRAP ⟨a ~*ed* bird⟩

¹**toile** \'twäl\ *n* -s [F — more at ³TOIL] **1 :** cloth of various fibers; *specif* **:** TOILE DE JOUY **2 :** a muslin model of a garment

²**toi·lé** \(')twä¦lā\ *n* -s [F, fr. *toile* cloth, net + *-é* -ate (fr. L *-atus*)] **:** a closely worked solid pattern in lace making that is contrasted with a net ground

toile de jouy \ˌtwäldəzh¦wē\ *n, pl* **toiles de jouy** \"\ *usu cap J* [F, lit., cloth of Jouy, fr. *Jouy*-en-Josar, Seine-et-Oise dept., France] **:** an upholstery and drapery fabric usu. made of cotton or linen and printed with characteristic designs (as of landscapes or florals) in one color on a cream or white background — called also *Jouy print*

toil·er \'tȯilə(r)\ *n* -s [²*toil* + *-er*] **:** one that toils **:** WORKER; *specif* **:** one that works for wages or hire ⟨~s in the fields⟩ ⟨no captain of industry, just a ~ in the ranks⟩

¹**toi·let** \'tȯilət, *usu* -lәd·+V\ *n* -s *often attrib* [MF *toilette,* dim. of *toile* cloth — more at TOIL] **1 a** *obs* **:** a cloth or shawl put over the shoulders (as during shaving or hairdressing) **b** *archaic* **:** a cloth covering for a dressing table **:** TOILET CLOTH ⟨a ~ of blue velvet with a gold and silver fringe —*London Gazette*⟩ **2** *archaic* **a :** the equipment for a dressing room or dressing table **:** a toilet service or set **b :** DRESSING TABLE **3 a :** the act or process of dressing; *specif* **:** the process of washing, grooming, and arranging oneself for the day's activities or for a special occasion ⟨while making his ~ before dinner, he dropped his collar button⟩ ⟨hurried at her ~, which was soon made —Theodore Dreiser⟩ ⟨~ articles⟩ **b** *archaic* **:** the receiving of visitors by ladies while completing the final touches of their toilet **4** *archaic* **:** TOILETTE 3 **5 a :** TOILET ROOM, BATHROOM 1, LAVATORY 3a **b :** a fixture consisting typically of a water-flushed bowl with a toilet seat that is used for urination and defecation **:** WATER CLOSET **6 a :** local cleansing and application of aseptic dressings ⟨~ of an obstetrical patient⟩ ⟨~ of a surgical wound⟩ **b :** the removal of undesirable material (as mucus or dead tissue) from a passage or cavity ⟨tracheobronchial ~ after anesthesia⟩ ⟨~ of a tooth cavity before filling⟩

²**toilet** \"\ *vb* -ED/-ING/-S *vi* **1 :** to make one's toilet **:** DRESS **2 :** to go to the bathroom for washing or to the toilet for urinating or defecating — usu. used of a child ⟨learns all the accepted habits connected with eating, sleeping, and ~*ing* —J.D. Teicher⟩ ~ *vt* **1 :** GROOM **2 :** to see to the toileting of **:** set (as a child) on a toilet ⟨sly him up and ~ him —A.L. Gesell & Frances Ilg⟩

toilet cloth *or* **toilet cover** *n* **:** a covering of linen, silk, or tapestry spread over a dressing table

toilet glass *n* **:** a looking glass for a dressing table or dressing room

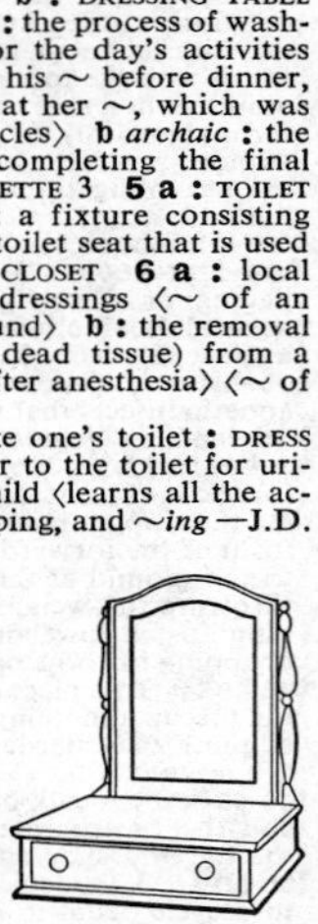

toilet glass

toilet paper *n* **:** a thin soft sanitary absorbent paper for use in toilet rooms

toilet powder *n* **:** a fine powder usu. with soothing or antiseptic ingredients for sprinkling or rubbing over the skin of the body (as after bathing) **:** DUSTING POWDER

toilet room *n* **1 :** a room for making the toilet **:** DRESSING ROOM **2 a :** a room or compartment equipped with one or more toilets **b :** a room (as in an office building or railroad station) equipped with one or more lavatories and toilets and if a men's room usu. with one or more urinals

toi·let·ry \'tȯilətrē, -ri\ *n* -ES *often attrib* [¹*toilet* + *-ry*] **:** an article or preparation used in making one's toilet (as a soap, lotion, cosmetic, toothpaste, shaving cream, cologne) ⟨~ manufacturers⟩ — usu. used in pl. ⟨a new line of *toiletries* for men⟩

toilet seat *n* **:** an oval or circular ring usu. of wood or plastic attached to the top of a toilet bowl at the back to support the buttocks and often covered with a hinged top

toilet set *n* **1 :** the vessels on a washstand (as a basin and ewer) **2 :** DRESSER SET

toilet soap *n* **:** a mild soap that is made from fatty materials of high quality usu. by milling and plodding to form cakes and that is often perfumed and colored and stabilized with preservatives

toilet table *n* **:** DRESSING TABLE

toi·lette \(')tȯi¦let, (')twä¦l-\ *n* -s [F — more at TOILET] **1** *archaic* **:** DRESSING TABLE **2 :** TOILET 3a **3 a :** formal or fashionable attire or style of dressing **b :** a particular costume or outfit ⟨noting each detail of her ~⟩ ⟨a ~ for each bridesmaid⟩

toilet training *n* **:** the process of training a child to control bladder and bowel movements and to use the toilet ⟨a great fuss about *toilet training* —Benjamin Spock⟩

toiletware \'==ˌ=\ *n* **:** merchandise comprising articles (as combs, brushes, mirrors, manicure sets) for the equipment of dressing room, dresser, vanity, or bathroom

toilet water *n* **:** a perfumed liquid largely alcoholic in content for use in or after a bath or as a skin freshener — compare COLOGNE, FLORIDA WATER

toil·ful \'=fəl\ *adj* [¹*toil* + *-ful*] **:** marked by or demanding hard work or industry **:** LABORIOUS, TOILSOME ⟨~ care⟩ ⟨~ progress⟩ ⟨a ~ servant⟩

toil·ful·ly \-fəlē, -li\ *adv* **:** in a toilful manner **:** INDUSTRIOUSLY ⟨let them loiter in pleasure or ~ spin —Park Benjamin⟩

toi·li·net *or* **toi·li·nette** \ˌtȯiləˌnet\ *n* -s [prob. fr. F *toile* cloth, linen cloth + E *-inet, -inette* (as in *satinet, satinette*) — more at TOIL] **:** a fabric with silk or cotton warp and wool weft in use in the 19th century for fancy waistcoats

toiling *pres part of* TOIL

toils *pl of* TOIL, *pres 3d sing of* TOIL

toil·some \'=səm\ *adj* [¹*toil* + *-some*] **:** marked by or full of toil or effort **:** ARDUOUS, LABORIOUS, WEARISOME ⟨a ~ life⟩ ⟨a ~ journey⟩ ⟨a slow and ~ process⟩

toil·some·ly *adv* **:** in a toilsome manner **:** LABORIOUSLY ⟨delivered the loaves, making his rounds slowly and ~ —D.C. Jenkins⟩

toil·some·ness *n* -ES **:** the quality or state of being toilsome **:** LABORIOUSNESS

toilworn \'=ˌ=\ *adj* **:** showing the effects of or worn out with toil ⟨a ~ traveler⟩ ⟨a ~ farmer⟩ ⟨~ eyes⟩

to·ing and fro·ing \ˌtüiŋən'frōiŋ\ *n, pl* **toings and froings** [fr. the phrase *to and fro*] **:** a passing back and forth **:** a going hither and thither ⟨the clatter and bustle, the . . . *toing and froing* of the soldiery —Sheridan Le Fanu⟩

toise \'tȯiz\ *n* -s [MF, fr. (assumed) VL *tensa, tesa,* fr. L *tensa,* fem. of *tensus,* past part. of *tendere* to stretch — more at THIN] **:** an old French unit of length equal to 6 French feet, 6.396 U.S. feet, or 1.949 meters

toitoi *var of* TOETOE

to·jo·la·bal \ˌtōhōlə¦bäl\ *n, pl* **tojolaba·les** \ˌ==='bä(ˌ)lās\ *usu cap* [Sp, of AmerInd origin] **1 a :** an Indian people of southeastern Chiapas in Mexico **b :** a member of such people **2 :** a Mayan language of the Tojolabal people

¹**to·kay** \(')tō¦kā\ *n* -s *usu cap* [fr. *Tokay* (Tokaj), Hungary] **1 :** a sweet unfortified dessert wine usu. dark gold in color that is made near the town of Tokaj on the Tisza river in northeastern Hungary **2 :** a sweet dessert wine made by blending Angelica, port, and sherry wines — called also *California Tokay*

²**tokay** \"\ *n* -s [Malay *toke,* of imit. origin] **:** a Malaysian house lizard (*Gekko gecko*)

toke \'tōk\ *n* -s [origin unknown] *Brit* **:** FOOD; *esp* **:** a portion of bread

to·ke·lau·an \ˌtōkə¦lau̇ən\ *n* -s *cap* [*Tokelau* islands, central Pacific ocean + E *-an*] **:** a native or inhabitant of the Tokelau islands of western Samoa

¹**to·ken** \'tōkən *sometimes* -kᵊŋ\ *n* -s [ME *taken, token,* fr. OE *tācen, tācn;* akin to OS *tēkan* sign, OHG *zeihhan,* ON *teikn,* Goth *taikn* sign, Gk *deiknynai* to show — more at DICTION] **1 :** an outward indication or expression (as a visible sign) **:** sensible evidence **:** PROOF ⟨~s of his profound grief⟩ ⟨saw the rainbow as . . . the ~ of a covenant between God and man —James Jeans⟩ ⟨from time to time said something . . . as a ~ of friendship —Douglas Stewart⟩ **2 :** a divine or miraculous sign **:** OMEN, PORTENT ⟨the most mighty gods by ~s send such dreadful heralds —Shak.⟩ ⟨the floor to the house where they stood up fell in and . . . folks said it was a bad ~ —Elizabeth M. Roberts⟩ **3 a :** something (as an act, gesture, or object) that serves as a sign or signification **:** MARK, EMBLEM ⟨a white flag is a ~ of surrender⟩ ⟨waved her handkerchief as a ~ of recognition⟩ ⟨gripped the clergyman's hand in ~ of his gratitude —Robert Grant †1940⟩ **b** (1) **:** a particular instance of an expression, symbol, or sentence ⟨if the word *man* is written twice and spoken once, there have arisen three ~s of the word *man*⟩ — contrasted with *type* (2) **:** the action of uttering, writing, or otherwise producing a token **4 :** a distinguishing mark **:** FEATURE, CHARACTERISTIC ⟨a boy of good make and mind, with the ~s on him of a refined nature —J.H.Newman⟩ **5** *archaic* **:** a usu. prearranged sign **:** SIGNAL ⟨he that betrayed him had given them a ~ —Mk 14:44 (AV)⟩ ⟨gave ~ that the host was closing for the night —E.A.Poe⟩ **6 a :** something given as a memento of regard or affection **:** SOUVENIR, KEEPSAKE ⟨an antique ~ my father gave my mother —Shak.⟩ ⟨give it to me as a going-away ~ —Lillian Hellman⟩ **b :** a vestige or reminder of something ⟨muse . . . over this ~ of bygone fashion —Virginia Woolf⟩ **c :** a small part or bit representing the whole **:** INDICATION ⟨only a ~ of what he hopes to accomplish⟩ ⟨this is the merest ~ of the subject —W.W.Howells⟩ **d :** something given or shown as a symbol or guarantee (as of authority, right, or identity) **:** PASSWORD ⟨say, by this ~, I desire his company —Shak.⟩ ⟨the book . . . was accompanied by no sign or ~ from him —William Black⟩ ⟨any member who reveals any ~ . . . is expelled —C.W.Ferguson⟩: as (1) **:** a small metal disk formerly given in the Church of Scotland as a warrant or voucher to members qualified to receive communion — called also *communion token* (2) *Brit* **:** a disk or strip of metal or leather having a peculiar mark designating a particular miner that is sent with each filled corf hewed or conveyed in a coal mine **7 :** a piece or disk (as of metal) certified as having a definite value for payment or exchange: as **a :** a piece (as of metal, cardboard, or hard rubber) fashioned in resemblance of a coin but not in imitation of any particular coin and issued for use as money by or on the authority of some person or body (as a bank or a business or commercial firm) other than a de jure government **b :** a piece resembling a coin issued on private or public authority for use by a particular group of people (as employees of a plantation or inmates of a prison) on specified terms **c :** a piece resembling a coin for use as a ticket on a public conveyance ⟨bus ~⟩ ⟨transportation ~⟩ ⟨a seven-and-a-half-cent ~⟩ **d :** TOKEN COIN **e :** a piece (as a coupon, certificate, label, or box top) redeemable for merchandise ⟨premium ~s⟩ ⟨a book ~⟩ **8 :** a piece resembling a medal issued as a souvenir or for advertising or political propaganda purposes **9 :** a game counter **10** *archaic* **a :** a quantity of paper sufficient for printing 250 impressions or for one hour's work for two men on a handpress **b :** a unit of presswork from one form varying from 250 to 500 impressions **syn** see PLEDGE, SIGN — **by the same token 1 :** for the same reason ⟨because his mind is flexible it responds quickly . . . to what is before it, and *by the same token* it can call up from within a host of appropriate ideas —J.M.Barzun⟩ **2 :** FURTHERMORE, ALSO — **more by token** *archaic* **:** the more so ⟨danger . . . from drug or pill; *more by token,* as there is a lot of apothecary's stuff aboard —Nathaniel Hawthorne⟩

²**token** \"\ *vb* **tokened; tokened; tokening** \-k(ə)niŋ\

tokens [ME *toknen, tokenen*, fr. OE *tācnian*, fr. *tācen, tācn*, n.] *vt* : to serve as a sign of : BETOKEN, SIGNIFY, SYMBOLIZE ⟨feeling remorse . . . ~s possible future pangs —F.B.Ebersole⟩ ~ *vi* : to occur as or provide with a token : INSTANCE

³**token** \"\ *adj* [¹*token*] : done or given as a token esp. in partial fulfillment of an obligation or engagement : having semblance or serving as a sign or sample of the real thing : SIMULATED, MINIMAL, PERFUNCTORY ⟨sent a ~ force to join in the unpopular war⟩ ⟨~ damages of six cents⟩ ⟨a ~ bequest⟩

token book *n* : a book listing parishioners receiving communion tokens

token coin *n* : a coin having an intrinsic value less than its face value — compare STANDARD COIN

token money *n* **1** : money (as paper currency or minor coins) of regular government issue having a greater face value than intrinsic value **2** : a conventional medium of exchange consisting of tokens privately issued (as by a trader or a company) and circulating by consent among private persons esp. during the 17th, 18th, and early 19th centuries usu. to alleviate a scarcity of small coins

token payment *n* : a very small payment made upon a debt and intended by the payer merely to acknowledge the existence of the obligation

tokens *pl of* TOKEN

token sheet *n, archaic* : the last sheet of each token printed that is turned down to help in counting

tokes *pl of* TOKE

tokharian *cap, var of* TOCHARIAN

toko *var of* TOCO

toko- — see TOCO-

to·ko·no·ma \ˌtōkə'nōmə\ *n* -s [Jap] : a niche or recess opening from the living room of a Japanese house in which a kakemono may be hung

-to·kous \d·əkəs, tək-\ *adj comb form* [Gk *-tokos*, fr. *tiktein* to bear — more at THANE] : producing (such or so many) offspring ⟨deutero*tokous*⟩

tok–tok·kie *also* **tok·tok·je** \'täk,täkē\ *n* -s [Afrik *toktokkie* (formerly spelled *toktokje*), of imit. origin] : any of several African beetles of the genus *Psammodes* (family Tenebrionidae)

to·kus \'tōkəs\ *n* -ES [Yiddish *tokhes*, fr. Heb *taḥath* under, below] *slang* : BUTTOCKS

to·ku·shi·ma \ˌtōkə'shēmə\ *adj, usu cap* [fr. *Tokushima*, Japan] : of or from the city of Tokushima, Japan : of the kind or style prevalent in Tokushima

-to·ky \d·əkē, tə-\ *n comb form* -ES [Gk *-tokia*, fr. *-tokos* + *-ia* -y] : parturition : delivery ⟨deutero*toky*⟩

to·kyo *also* **to·kio** \'tōkē,ō\ *adj, usu cap* [fr. *Tokyo* or *Tokio*, Japan] : of or from Tokyo, the capital of Japan : of the kind or style prevalent in Tokyo

tol- *or* **tolu-** *comb form* [ISV, fr. *tolu*] **1** : tolu ⟨*tol*uol⟩ **2** : toluene ⟨*tol*uic⟩ ⟨*tol*yl⟩ : toluic ⟨*tol*uate⟩

tol *abbr* tolerance

¹**to·la** \'tōlə\ *n* -s [Hindi *tolā*, fr. Skt *tulā* balance, scale, weight — more at TOLERATE] : a unit of weight of India equal to 180 grains troy or 0.4114 ounce

²**tola** \"\ *n* -s [AmerSp, fr. Aymara] : any of several So. American plants of the genera *Baccharis* and *Lepidophyllum*

³**tola** \"\ *n* -s [AmerSp] : a burial mound of Ecuador or Peru

to·la·ble \'tōləbəl\ *adj* [by alter.] *dial* : TOLERABLE

to·lan \'tō,lan\ *also* **to·lane** \-lān\ *n* -s [ISV *tol-* + *-an* or *-ane*] : a white crystalline unsaturated hydrocarbon $C_6H_5C{\equiv}CC_6H_5$ obtained synthetically from stilbene : diphenyl-acetylene

tolbooth *var of* TOLLBOOTH

tol·bu·ta·mide \täl'byüd·ə,mīd, -,məd\ *n* [*tol-* + *but-* + *amide*] : a crystalline sulfonamide $CH_3C_6H_4SO_2NHCONHC_4H_9$ that lowers the blood sugar level and is administered orally in the treatment of mild to moderate adult diabetes; 1-*n*-butyl-3-(*para*-tolyl-sulfonyl)-urea

told [ME *tolde* (past), *told* (past part.), fr. OE (northern and Midland dial.) *talde* (past), *getald* (past part.) — more at TELL] *past of* TELL

tol–de–rol \ˌtäldə'räl\ *n* -s [origin unknown] — used as a nonsense refrain in some old songs

tol·do \'tōl(,)dō, 'täl-\ *n* -s [AmerSp, fr. Sp, awning, canopy, cloth or canvas wagon covering, fr. OSp, fr. MF *taud* canopy on a ship, prob. of Gmc origin; akin to MLG & MD *telt* tent — more at TILT] : any of various Central or So. American shelters (as a covered dance platform or an Indian skin hut)

¹**tole** *var of* TOLL

²**tole** \'tōl\ *n* -s [F *tôle* sheet metal (esp. iron), fr. F dial. (Bordeaux area), table, slab, fr. L *tabula* board, tablet — more at TABLE] : a decorative japanned or painted tin or other metal finished in various colors (as black with gilt designs) and used esp. for trays, lamps, and boxes

¹**to·le·dan** \tə'lēdᵊn\ *adj, usu cap* [Sp *toledano*, fr. *Toledo*, Spain + Sp *-ano* -an] **1 a** : of, relating to, or characteristic of Toledo, Spain **b** : of, relating to, or characteristic of the people of Toledo **2** *also* **to·le·do·an** \-dəwən\ [*Toledo*, Ohio + E *-an*] **a** : of, relating to, or characteristic of Toledo, Ohio **b** : of, relating to, or characteristic of the people of Toledo

²**toledan** \"\ *n* -s *cap* **1** : a native or inhabitant of Toledo, Spain **2** *also* **toledoan** \"\ : a native or resident of Toledo, Ohio

¹**to·le·do** \tə'lē(,)dō\ *n* -s *usu cap* [fr. *Toledo*, Spain] : a finely tempered sword of a kind made in Toledo, Spain

²**toledo** \"\ *adj, usu cap* [fr. *Toledo*, Ohio] : of or from the city of Toledo, Ohio ⟨a *Toledo* factory⟩ : of the kind or style prevalent in Toledo

tol·er·a·bil·i·ty \ˌtäl(ə)rə'bilәd·ē, ˌtälər'b-, -lətē, -i\ *n* : the quality or state of being tolerable

¹**tol·er·a·ble** \'täl(ə)rəbəl, -älərb-, *dial* -äləb-\ *adj* [ME *tollerabill*, fr. L *tolerabilis*, fr. *tolerare* to endure, put up with + *-abilis* -able — more at TOLERATE] **1** : capable of being borne or endured : physically or morally supportable : BEARABLE ⟨a ~ compromise can be worked out —P.E.James⟩ ⟨the task . . . of making life secure and ~ for every class in the empire —John Buchan⟩ **2 a** : meeting some minimum standard of acceptability : fit to be countenanced or permitted : ALLOWABLE, SUFFERABLE ⟨socially ~ conduct⟩ ⟨there could be no ~ apology for injustice —Oscar Handlin⟩ ⟨a ~ paragraph must have gone through six or seven versions —J.M.Barzun⟩ **b** : of moderate worth, excellence, or magnitude : fairly good : merely passable : MEDIOCRE, MIDDLING ⟨the advantages of a ~ income —William Black⟩ ⟨bring lunar and solar times into ~, though not exact, harmony —J.G.Frazer⟩

²**tolerable** \"\ *adv, dial* : TOLERABLY

tol·er·a·ble·ness *n* -ES : the quality or state of being tolerable

tol·er·a·bly \-əblē, -li\ *adv* : in a tolerable manner : ALLOWABLY, BEARABLY

tol·er·ance \'täl(ə)rən(t)s\ *n* -s [ME *tolleraunce*, fr. MF *tolerance*, fr. L *tolerantia*, fr. *tolerant-, tolerans* (pres. part. of *tolerare* to endure, put up with) + *-ia* -y — more at TOLERATE] **1 a** : capacity to endure pain or hardship : ENDURANCE, FORTITUDE, STAMINA **b** (1) : the ability to endure the effects of a drug or food or of physiologic insults whether on single or repeated intake or experience without showing unfavorable effects ⟨the degree of work ~ of a diseased heart⟩ ⟨a diabetic's ~ for sugar before glycosuria is produced⟩ ⟨an addict's increasing ~ for a drug, requiring increasing doses to produce a desired effect⟩ ⟨a ~ dose of radiation⟩ (2) : relative capacity of an organism to grow or thrive in the presence of one or more unfavorable environmental conditions ⟨many forest understory plants exhibit a high degree of shade ~⟩ ⟨varying heat ~s of different strains of rye⟩ **c** : the maximum amount of a pesticide residue that may lawfully remain on or in food expressed in parts per million by weight **2 a** : a permissive or liberal attitude toward beliefs or practices differing from or conflicting with one's own : sympathy or indulgence for diversity in thought or conduct : breadth of spirit or of viewpoint ⟨the basis of ~ is the knowledge that there may be a measure of truth in theother camp —*Times Lit. Supp.*⟩ — compare BIGOTRY **b** : the act of allowing something : TOLERATION ⟨those years represented a low in our standards of ethics and the peak in our ~ for corruption —Estes Kefauver⟩ **3** : the allowable deviation from a standard: as **a** : the amount that coins either singly or in lots are legally allowed to vary above or below the standard of weight or fineness **b** : the range of variation permitted in maintaining a specified dimension in machining a piece : the difference between the upper and the lower limits between which a size must be held ⟨the blueprint called for a diameter of 0.255 inch plus or minus 0.0002, giving a manufacturing ~ of 0.0004 inch⟩ — compare ALLOWANCE **c** : a percentage difference allowed between a shipment's actual and its billed weight to compensate for variation between scales or between methods of weighing

tol·er·ant \-nt\ *adj* [F *tolérant*, fr. L *tolerant-, tolerans*, pres. part.] **1** : showing understanding or leniency for conduct or ideas differing from or conflicting with one's own : bearing contrariety mildly : ENDURING, FORBEARING, INDULGENT ⟨he was stoical under pain, serene under annoyance, and ~ of everything save injustice —Agnes Repplier⟩ **2 a** *of an organism* : exhibiting environmental tolerance; *esp, of a plant* : capable of growth in shade **b** : capable of enduring or resisting the effect of a drug or a physiologic shock **syn** see FORBEARING

tol·er·ant·ly *adv* : in a tolerant manner

tol·er·ate \'tälə,rāt, *usu* -ād·+V\ *vt* -ED/-ING/-S [L *toleratus*, past part. of *tolerare* to endure, put up with; akin to OE *tholian* to endure, put up with, OHG *dolēn*, ON *thola*, Goth *thulan* to endure, put up with, L *tollere* to lift up, take away, *latus* carried (suppletive past part. of *ferre* to bear), Gk *tlēnai* to bear, Skt *tulā* balance, scale, weight; basic meaning: to lift, bear] **1 a** : to endure or resist the action of (a drug, food, or physiologic factor) without grave or lasting injury ⟨a premature baby . . . does not ~ fats very well —H.R.Litchfield & L.H.Dembo⟩ ⟨the average pilot cannot ~ an average of over 85 hours in the air per month without eventually showing evidence of deterioration —H.G.Armstrong⟩ **b** : to thrive despite (something unfavorable in the environment) **2** : to permit the existence or practice of : allow without prohibition or hindrance : make no effort to prevent ⟨a legitimate government — that is, one that rests on consent — can ~ an opposition —Lindsay Rogers⟩ **3** : to endure with forbearance or restraint : put up with : BEAR ⟨recommends that we should learn to ~ one another —A.J.Franck⟩ ⟨public opinion . . . will ~ almost anything —Christopher Hollis⟩ ⟨~ the offstage egotism and eccentricities of artists —John Mason Brown⟩ **syn** see BEAR

tol·er·a·tion \ˌ≈≈'rāshən\ *n* -s [MF, fr. L *toleration-, toleratio*, fr. *toleratus* (past part. of *tolerare*) + *-ion-, -io* -ion] **1** *obs* : a legal permission or authorization : LICENSE **2 a** : the act or practice of tolerating something **b** : a government policy of permitting forms of religious belief and worship not officially favored, established, or approved **c** : TOLERANCE 2a **3** : TOLERANCE 1b(1)

tol·er·a·tion·ist \-shənəst\ *n* -s : one that practices or promotes toleration

tol·er·a·tor \'≈≈,rād·ə(r), -ātə-\ *n* -s : one that tolerates

tole·tan \tə'letᵊn, 'tälət·ᵊn\ *adj, usu cap* [L *Toletanus*, fr. *Toletum* (Toledo), Spain + L *-anus* -an] : of or relating to Toledo, Spain : TOLEDAN

toleware \'≈,≈\ *n* [²*tole* + *ware*] : ware made of tole ⟨a ~ tea caddy⟩

tol·gua·cha \tōl'wächə\ *or* **to·loa·che** \tōl'wächē\ *n* -s [MexSp *toloache, toloachi*, fr. Nahuatl *toloatzin*, fr. *toloa* to nod + *-tzin*, honorific particle; fr. the reverence borne such plants by the Indians] : any of several plants of the genus *Datura*; *esp* : a narcotic annual herb (*D. meteloides*) used ceremonially by some California Indians

tol·i·dine \'tälə,dēn, -dən\ *n* -s [ISV *tol-* + *-idine*] : any of several isomeric aromatic diamines $[-C_6H_3(CH_3)NH_2]_2$ that are homologues of benzidine and made from the nitrotoluenes by alkaline reduction: as **a** : a pearly crystalline compound made from *ortho*-nitrotoluene and used as a dye intermediate and in chemical analysis (as in testing for free chlorine after chlorination of water because of the intense blue color it gives with chlorine); 3,3′-dimethyl-benzidine — called also *ortho-tolidine* **b** : a crystalline compound made from *meta*-nitrotoluene and used as a dye intermediate; 2,2′-dimethyl-benzidine — called also *meta-tolidine*

tol·ite \'tä,līt\ *n* -s [ISV *tol-* + *-ite*] : TRINITROTOLUENE

¹**toll** \'tōl\ *n* -s *often attrib* [ME *toll, tol*, fr. OE *toll*; akin to OFris *tolen, tolene* toll, OS *tolna*, OHG *zol*, ON *tollr*; all fr. a prehistoric WGmc-NGmc word borrowed fr. (assumed) VL *tolonium*, alter. of LL *telonium* customhouse, fr. Gk *telōnion*, fr. *telōnēs* collector of tolls or taxes, fr. *telos* tax, tribute; akin to Gk *tlēnai* to bear — more at TOLERATE] **1 a** : a tax or fee paid for some liberty or privilege (as of passing over a highway or bridge or using a ferry, of keeping a booth or vending goods in a fair or market, or of importing or exporting goods) ⟨higher bridge and tunnel ~s —*Better Homes & Gardens*⟩ **2 a** : the right to take toll **b** : the former right of an English lord to levy a tallage or tax upon his villeins **3** : a compensation taken for services rendered: as **a** *dial* : a portion of grain taken by a miller as his fee **b** : a charge for transportation, conveyance, or use of facilities (as of a port) **c** : a charge for a long-distance telephone call **4** : the cost in loss or suffering at which something is achieved : damage done : EXACTION ⟨the flood took a heavy ~ —*Amer. Guide Series: Ind.*⟩ ⟨the large emotional ~ which expatriation usually exacts —Aline B. Saarinen⟩ ⟨defense takes an enormous ~ of money and manpower —Denis Healey⟩

²**toll** \"\ *vb* -ED/-ING/-S [ME *tollen*, fr. *tol, toll*, n.] *vi* **1** : to take or levy toll **2** *obs* : to enter a horse in the tollbook of a market as for sale — used with *for* ~ *vt* **1 a** : to exact part of as a toll or duty ⟨~*ed* his tenant's crops⟩ **b** : to take (something) as toll **2** : to exact a toll from (someone) : impose a levy on

³**toll** *or* **tole** \"\ *vb* -ED/-ING/-S [ME *tollen, tolen*; akin to ME *tullen, tillen* to attract, entice — more at TILL] *vt* **1** : to lure along : ATTRACT, ENTICE ⟨I'll shoot the man that ~s her off . . . a girl what's been learned to work and mind —Emmett Gowen⟩ ⟨wild mares on the ranges . . . had ~*ed* off 300 head of horses and mules from his 1500 guarded animals —J.F. Dobie⟩ ⟨the coal-oil lantern . . . would surely ~ any murdering redskins within miles —Mari Sandoz⟩ **2** : to lure (game) in any of various ways : DECOY ⟨they saw several loons and ~*ed* them by running towards them hallooing and waving a handkerchief, at which sight and cry the loon immediately swam towards them, until within 20 yards —J.J.Audubon⟩ **3** : to scatter (bait) for attracting fish : CHUM **4** : to lead or draw (domestic animals) in a desired direction (as by means of a bellwether or a lure) ⟨she had ~*ed* the young turkeys into the yard —Mary King⟩ ⟨~*ed* the sheep into the barn —E.B. White⟩ ~ *vi* : to respond to tolling : admit of being tolled ⟨these ducks ~ the most readily of all⟩

⁴**toll** \"\ *vb* -ED/-ING/-S [ME *tollen*, perh. fr. *tollen* to attract, entice] *vt* **1 a** : to give signal or announcement of : SOUND ⟨the clock ~s the hour⟩ ⟨the curfew ~s the knell of parting day —Thomas Gray⟩ **b** : to ring a toll for : announce by tolling ⟨~*ed* the president's death⟩ **c** : to call (someone) to or from a place or occasion ⟨forlorn! the very word is like a bell to ~ me back from thee to my sole self —John Keats⟩ **2** : to cause the sounding of (a bell) in a controlled and regular manner by pulling a rope, striking with a hammer, or manipulating the clapper usu. to announce a church service or other public occasion or a death or funeral or to give an alarm — compare PEAL ~ *vi* **1** : to sound with slow measured strokes ⟨never send to know for whom the bell ~s; it ~s for thee —John Donne⟩ **2** : to cause a bell to toll

⁵**toll** \"\ *n* -s [ME, fr. *tollen*, v.] **1 a** : an act or instance of tolling **b** : a single stroke on a bell **2** : the sound made by a toll

⁶**toll** \"\ *vt* -ED/-ING/-S [ME *tollen*, fr. AF *toller, touller*, fr. L *tollere* to lift up, take away — more at TOLERATE] : to take away : make null : REMOVE ⟨~ the statute of limitations⟩

toll·age \'tōlij, -lēj\ *n* -s [¹*toll* + *-age*] **1** : toll or payment or exaction of it **2** *obs* : TALLAGE

toll bait *n* [³*toll*] : chopped bait thrown out to attract fish

toll bar *n* [¹*toll*] : a bar or gate used to stop passengers at a tollhouse

toll board *n* [¹*toll*] : a telephone switchboard for making toll-call connections

tollbook *n* [¹*toll* + *book*] **1** *obs* : a register of goods for sale at an old English market or fair **2** *obs* : a tax register

toll·booth *or* **tol·booth** \'tōl,≈, *Scot* 'tō(l),≈ *or* 'täl,≈\ *n* [ME *tolbothe, tollbothe*, fr. *tol, toll* toll + *bothe* booth — more at BOOTH] **1** : a booth or other office where tolls are paid : CUSTOMHOUSE, TOLLHOUSE **2** *chiefly Scot* : a town or market hall **3** *Scot* : JAIL, PRISON

toll bridge *n* [¹*toll*] : a bridge at which a toll is charged for crossing

toll call *n* [¹*toll*] : a long-distance telephone call at charges above a local rate

toll collector *n* [¹*toll*] **1** : one who collects tolls or taxes of any kind **2** : an indicator showing the number of persons paying toll at a tollhouse **3** : a device automatically separating a miller's toll from his customer's grist

toll dish *n* [¹*toll*] : a measure for the miller's share of the grain he grinds for a customer

¹**toll·er** \'tōlə(r)\ *n* -s [ME, fr. OE *tollere*, fr. *toll* + *-ere* -er] : TOLL COLLECTOR 1, 3

²**toller** \"\ *n* -s [³*toll* + *-er*] : DECOY; *esp* : a dog trained to lure ducks

tollgate \'≈,≈\ *n* [¹*toll* + *gate*] : a point usu. at a tollhouse where vehicles pause to pay toll for using a turnpike, tunnel, or bridge

tollgatherer \'≈,≈≈≈\ *n* [ME *tol gaderer*, fr. *tol, toll* toll + *gaderer* gatherer — more at GATHERER] : a collector of tolls or taxes : PUBLICAN

tollhouse \'≈,≈\ *n* [ME *tolhowse*, fr. *tol, toll* + *hous, howse* house — more at HOUSE] : a house or booth where tolls are taken (as on a highway or bridge)

toll in *vi* [⁴*toll*] : to call people to a church service by tolling

tolling *pres part of* TOLL

toll·man \'≈-mən\ *n, pl* **tollmen** [¹*toll* + *man*] : a collector of tolls (as on a highway or bridge) : a tollhouse keeper

tol–lol \(')tä'läl\ *adj* [alter. of *tolerable*] : PASSABLE, TOLERABLE

tollon *var of* TOYON

toll road *n* [¹*toll*] : a road for the use of which a toll is collected

tolls *pl of* TOLL, *pres 3d sing of* TOLL

toll traverse *or* **toll travers** *n* : a toll paid in England for passage or traffic over the private property (as the ground, bridge, or ferry) of another

tollway \'≈,≈\ *n* [¹*toll* + *way*] : TOLL ROAD

tol·ly \'tälē, -li\ *n* -ES [alter. of *tallow*] : CANDLE

²**tolly** \"\ *n* -ES [native name in southern Africa] *southern Africa* : a young ox : STEER

tol·ly·gunge \'tälē,gənj\ *adj, usu cap* [fr. *Tollygunge*, India] : of or from the city of Tollygunge, India : of the kind or style prevalent in Tollygunge

toloache *var of* TOLGUACHA

tolonium chloride *n* [*tolonium*, NL, fr. *tol-* + *-onium*] : toluidine blue for medicinal use

to·lo·wa \'täləwə\ *n, pl* **tolowa** *or* **tolowas** *usu cap* **1 a** : an Athapaskan people of northwestern California **b** : a member of such people **2** : a language of the Tolowa people

toloxy- *comb form* [*tol-* + *oxy-*] : any of three univalent radicals $CH_3C_6H_4O-$ composed of a tolyl radical united with oxygen : tolyl-oxy ⟨*toloxy*-propane-diol⟩ — compare PHENOXY-

tol·ses·ter \'täl,sestə(r), ≈'≈≈\ *n* -s [ME, fr. OE, fr. *tol* toll + *sester*, a measure, fr. OE, fr. L *sextarius*, fr. *sextus* sixth + *-arius* -ary — more at TOLL, SEXT] : a toll paid to the feudal lord by a tenant for liberty to brew and sell ale

tol·sey *or* **tol·zey** \'tölzi\ *n* -s [ME *tolsell, tolsey*, fr. *tol, toll* toll + *-sell, -sey* (prob. fr. OE *sele* hall, house) — more at TOLL, SALOON] **1** *Brit* : TOWN HALL **2** *Brit* : a borough law court

¹**tol·stoy·an** *also* **tol·stoi·an** \'tōlz,tōiən, 'täl-,'tōl-, -l,st-, ≈'≈≈\ *adj, usu cap* [Count Lev (Leo) Nikolaevich *Tolstoy* (*Tolstoi*) †1910 Russ. novelist and religious philosopher + E *-an*] : of, relating to, or characteristic of Tolstoi or his writings

²**tolstoyan** *also* **tolstoian** \"\ *n* -s *usu cap* : a follower of Tolstoi, his philosophy of art, or his religious and moral doctrines

tol·stoy·ism \-ōi,izəm\ *n* -s *usu cap* [L. *Tolstoy* + E *-ism*] : the doctrines or practices of the Tolstoyans

tol·stoy·ist \-ōiəst\ *n* -s *usu cap* [L. *Tolstoy* + E *-ist*] : TOLSTOYAN

¹**tolt** \'tōlt\ *n* -s [AF *tolte*, fr. ML *tolta* act of taking away, fr. L *tollere* to take away — more at TOLERATE] : a writ by which a cause pending in a court baron is removed into a county court

²**tolt** \"\ *n* -s [origin unknown] : an isolated peak rising abruptly from a plain in Newfoundland

tol·tec \'tōl,tek, 'täl-\ *also* **tol·teca** \-'tekə, -'tākə\ *n, pl* **toltec** *or* **toltecs** *usu cap* [Sp *tolteca*, of AmerInd origin] **1** : a Nahuatlan people of central and southern Mexico **2** : a member of the Toltec people — **tol·tecan** \(')≈'tekən, -'tāk-\ *adj, usu cap*

to·lu \tə'lü, tō'-\ *or* **tolu balsam** *n* -s [Sp *tolú*, fr. Santiago de *Tolú*, Colombia] : BALSAM OF TOLU

tolu- — see TOL-

tolu·aldehyde \ˌtäl(,)yü+\ *n* [*tol-* + *aldehyde*] : any of four aldehydes C_7H_7CHO that give the corresponding toluic acids on oxidation — compare PHENYLACETALDEHYDE

tol·u·ate \'tälyə,wāt\ *n* -s [ISV *tol-* + *-ate*] : a salt or ester of a toluic acid

tol·u·ene \-ə,wēn\ *n* -s [ISV *tol-* + *-ene*] : a light mobile liquid aromatic hydrocarbon $C_6H_5CH_3$ that resembles benzene but is less volatile, less flammable, and less toxic, that was obtained orig. by distilling balsam of tolu, that is produced commercially from light oils from coke-oven gas and coal tar and esp. since World War II from petroleum (as by dehydrogenation of methyl-cyclohexane or by the reforming of dimethylcyclopentane), and that is used chiefly as a solvent, as a raw material for trinitrotoluene, dyes, pharmaceuticals, and other organic compounds, and as a blending agent for gasoline esp. for use in aviation because of its high antiknock property — called also *methylbenzene*

toluene diisocyanate *n* : TOLYLENE DIISOCYANATE

toluenesulfonic acid \'≈≈≈;≈≈≈-\ *n* [*toluene* + *sulfonic*] : any of three isomeric crystalline oily liquid strong acids $CH_3C_6H_4SO_3H$ of which the para and ortho isomers are obtained in a mixture by sulfonation of toluene and used in organic synthesis (as of dyes)

toluenesulfonyl \'≈≈≈;≈≈≈\ *n* [*toluene* + *sulfonyl*] : any of three radicals $CH_3C_6H_4SO_2-$ derived from the toluenesulfonic acids; *esp* : the radical of *para*-toluenesulfonic acid — compare TOSYL

toluenesulfonyl chloride *n* : any of three solid or liquid acid chlorides $CH_3C_6H_4SO_2Cl$ made from the corresponding toluenesulfonic acids or from toluene and chlorosulfonic acid; *esp* : the crystalline para isomer used in making chloramine-T and *para*-toluenesulfonyl derivatives (as of amines and sugars)

tolu·ic acid \tə'lüik, 'tälyəwik-\ *n* [ISV *tol-* + *-ic*] : any of four isomeric crystalline carboxylic acids C_7H_7COOH derived from toluene and obtainable in the case of the ortho, meta, and para isomers $CH_3C_6H_4COOH$ by oxidation of the three corresponding xylenes — see PHENYLACETIC ACID

to·lu·i·dide \tə'lüə,dīd\ *n* -s [*toluidine* + *-ide*] : an amide analogous to an anilide in which hydrogen of the amido group is replaced by tolyl : an *N*-acyl derivative of toluidine

to·lu·i·dine \-,dēn, -,dən\ *n* -s [ISV *tol-* + *-idine*] : any of three isomeric amino derivatives $CH_3C_6H_4NH_2$ of toluene that are the ortho, meta, and para methyl homologues of aniline, that are usu. obtained by reducing the corresponding nitrotoluenes, and that are used chiefly as dye intermediates

toluidine blue *also* **toluidine blue O** *n, often cap T&B* : a basic dye or its chloride of the thiazine class that is closely related chemically to methylene blue and is used chiefly as a biological stain and in medicine to treat hemorrhage (as in functional uterine bleeding) because of its ability to inhibit the anticoagulant effect of heparin

toluidine red toner *or* **toluidine red** *also* **toluidine toner** *n, sometimes cap both Ts&R* : any of a group of red organic pigments that are related to the para reds but are more permanent — see DYE table I (under *Pigment Red 3*)

tol·u·if·era \ˌtälyə'wifərə\ [NL, fr. Sp *tolú* + L *-ifera* (neut. pl. of *-ifer* -iferous)] *syn of* MYROXYLON

tol·u·ol \'tälyə,wōl, -,wōl\ *n* -s [ISV *tol-* + *-ol*] : TOLUENE — used esp. of commercial grades

tol·u·quinone \ˌtälyə+\ *n* [ISV *tol-* + *quinone*] : a methyl homologue $CH_3C_6H_3O_2$ of quinone; *esp* : a yellow crystalline compound made by oxidation of *ortho-* or *meta*-toluidine; 2-methyl-*para*-quinone

tolu tree *n* : a widely distributed usu. medium-sized tropical American tree (*Myroxylon balsamum*) that yields balsam of

Peru and balsam of Tolu and a fragrant durable rather hard showily figured yellowish to reddish or purplish wood which takes a fine polish and is used for high-grade furniture and cabinetwork
tol·u·yl·ene \'tälyəwə,lēn\ *n* -s [ISV *tol-* + *-yl* + *-ene*] **1** : STILBENE **2** : TOLYLENE
toluylene blue *n, often cap T&B* : an indamine dye derived from tolylenediamine (sense a) and used as an oxidation-reduction indicator and biological stain
toluylene orange G *n, usu cap T&O* : a direct dye — see DYE table I (under *Direct Orange 6*)
tol·yl \'tä,lil, -lēl\ *n* -s [ISV *tol-* + *-yl*] **1** : any of three univalent radicals $CH_3C_6H_4$— derived from toluene by removal of one hydrogen atom from a carbon atom in the benzene ring in a position ortho, meta, or para to the methyl group — called also *cresyl;* used in the system adopted by the International Union of Pure and Applied Chemistry **2** : BENZYL — used with an initial Greek alpha ⟨α-tolyl⟩
tol·yl·ene \'tälə,lēn\ *n* -s [*tolyl* + *-ene*] : any of six bivalent radicals $CH_3C_6H_3$< derived from toluene by removal of two hydrogen atoms from carbon atoms in the benzene ring : methyl-phenylene
tolylene·diamine \"+\ *n* [*tolylene* + *diamine*] : any of six isomeric crystalline bases $CH_3C_6H_3(NH_2)_2$ derived from toluene of which some are used as dye intermediates: as **a** : an isomer obtained by reduction of dinitrotoluene (sense a); toluene-2,4-diamine — called also *meta-tolylenediamine* **b** : an isomer obtained by reduction of aminoazo-toluene; toluene-2,5-diamine — called also *para-tolylenediamine;* see SAFRANINE b
tolylene diisocyanate *n* : any of six isomeric esters $CH_3C_6H_3$-$(NCO)_2$ of isocyanic acid or a mixture of them; *esp* : a liquid isomer made by reaction of tolylenediamine (sense a) and phosgene and used by itself or in a mixture with another meta isomer in making polyurethanes; 4-methyl-*meta*-phenylene diisocyanate
tol·y·peu·tes \,tälə'pyüd·(,)ēz\ *n, cap* [NL, fr. Gk *tolypeuein* to wind wool into a ball for spinning, fr. *tolypē* ball of wool; perh. akin to Gk *tylos* callus, knob — more at THOLE] : a genus of So. American armadillos containing the apar — **tol·y·peu·tine** \¦==¦pyü,tīn, -üd·ən\ *adj or n*
tol·y·po·sporium \,==,pō'spōrēəm\ *n, cap* [NL, fr. Gk *tolypē* + NL *-o-* + *-sporium*] : a genus of smut fungi that chiefly attack grasses — see LONG SMUT
tolzey *var of* TOLSEY
tom \'täm\ *n* -s [fr. *Tom,* nickname for *Thomas*] **1** *usu cap, obs* : TOM O'BEDLAM **2** : the male of various animals ⟨a ~ swan⟩: as **a** : a male cat : TOMCAT **b** : a male turkey : TURKEY-COCK **3** : a distance piece or small shore (as between frames in shipbuilding) **4** : a heavy lead weight by means of whose descent the bottom of a purse seine is puckered together **5** : LONG TOM 3
tom *abbr* tome
toma \'tōmə\ *n, pl* **toma** *or* **tomas** *usu cap* **1** : a people of adjacent parts of Liberia and Guinea **2** : a member of the Toma people
-to·ma \d·əmə, təmə\ *n comb form* -s [NL, fr. fem. of *-tomus* cutting, cut, segmented — more at -TOME] : animal having a (specified) type of segmentation — in generic names esp. of insects ⟨Tria*toma*⟩
¹tom·a·hawk \'tämə,hȯk *also* -mē,- *or* -mi,-\ *n* -s [fr. *tomahack* (in some Algonquian language of Virginia)] **1** : a light ax used both as a missile and as a hand weapon by the No. American Indians **2 a** : the stone hatchet of the Australian aborigines **b** : an ordinary hatchet

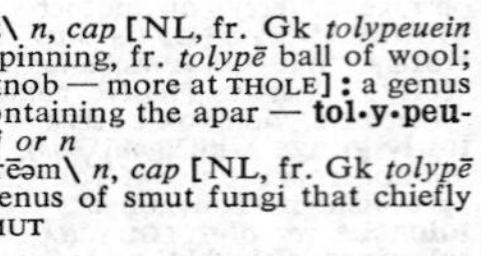

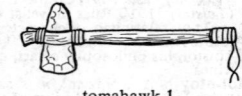

tomahawk 1

²tomahawk \"\ *vt* -ED/-ING/-s **1** : to cut, strike, or kill with a tomahawk **2** : to criticize or attack savagely : assail mercilessly ⟨battered, hacked, scalped, ~ed as I have been for three years —Hannah More⟩ **3** *Austral* : to cut (sheep) in unskillful shearing — **tom·a·hawk·er** \-kə(r)\ *n* -s
to·mal·ley \tə'mal·ē, 'täm,al·ē\ *n* -s [of Cariban origin; akin to Galibi *tumali* sauce of lobster or crab livers] : the liver of the lobster
¹to·man \tə'män\ *n* -s [Per *tōmān, tūmān,* of Mongol origin] **1** *also* **tu·man** \tə'm-\ **a** : an old Persian unit of monetary value equal at one time to 10,000 dinars **b** : a Persian gold coin issued up to 1927 **2** : a military division of 10,000 men among the Mongols and Tatars
²tom·an \'tämən\ *n* -s [ScGael, dim. of *tom* hill; akin to MIr *tomm* hill — more at TOMB] *Scot* : a mound or hillock
tom and jerry *n, pl* **tom and jerries** *usu cap T&J* [after Corinthian *Tom & Jerry* Hawthorne, chief characters of *Life in London* (1821) by Pierce Egan †1849 Eng. sportswriter] : a hot sweetened drink consisting of rum, water, and spices (as cinnamon and cloves) mixed with the yolk and white of an egg beaten separately and topped with nutmeg
to·mat·i·dine \tə'mad·ə,dēn\ *n* -s [*tomatine* + *-idine*] : a crystalline steroid amine $C_{27}H_{45}NO_2$ obtained by hydrolysis of tomatine and isolated from the roots of the tomato plant
to·ma·ti·llo \,tōmə'tē(,)(y)ō, -ēl(,)yō\ *n, pl* **tomatilloes** *or* **tomatillos** [Sp, dim. of *tomate* tomato] : any of several solanaceous plants with fruits resembling small tomatoes: as **a** : a ground cherry (*Physalis ixocarpa*) of Mexico and the southern U. S. with an edible purplish viscid fruit **b** : JERUSALEM CHERRY
tom·a·tine \'tämə,tēn\ *n* -s [ISV *tomato* + *-ine*] : a crystalline antibiotic glycosidic alkaloid $C_{50}H_{83}NO_{21}$ that is active against fungi and is obtained esp. from the juice of the stems and leaves of tomato plants resistant to wilt
to·ma·to \tə'mā|d·(,)ō, |(,)tō, |d·ə, |tə *also* -mä| *or* -mā| *sometimes* -ma|\ *n* -ES [alter. (prob. influenced by *potato*) of earlier *tomate,* fr. Sp, fr. Nahuatl *tomatl*] **1 a** : a plant of the genus *Lycopersicon; specif* : a So. American perennial herb (*L. esculentum*) widely cultivated usu. as an annual for its fruit and having interruptedly pinnate leaves and yellow flowers **b** : the large rounded or oblate pulpy berry of the tomato plant that is usu. red or yellow when ripe — see FRUIT illustration **2** *or* **tomato red** : a variable color averaging a deep reddish orange **3** *slang* **a** : WOMAN, GIRL **b** : PROSTITUTE
tomato black rot *n* : NAILHEAD SPOT
tomato blight *n* **1** : EARLY BLIGHT a **2** *or* **tomato yellows** : WESTERN TOMATO BLIGHT
tomato canker *n* : a bacterial canker of tomatoes caused by a spore-forming bacterium (*Corynebacterium michiganense*) and characterized by elongated brown cankers on the stems and sudden wilting of nearly mature plants and by spotting of the maturing fruits
tomato eggplant *n* : a tropical annual herb (*Solanum integrifolium*) sometimes grown for its white flowers and scarlet or yellow inedible fruit that resembles the fruit of the eggplant but is much smaller
tomato fruitworm *n* : CORN EARWORM — used esp. when the larva is infesting tomatoes
tomato gall *n* : a large irregular yellowish-green or reddish gall on the grapevine produced by a small two-winged fly (*Lasioptera vitis*)
tomato hornworm *n* : a caterpillar that is the larva of a hawkmoth (*Manduca quinquemaculata*), greatly resembles the tobacco hornworm, and feeds destructively on tomato, tobacco, and other solanaceous plants
tomato pinworm *n* : a pinworm that is the larva of a gelechiid moth (*Keiferia lycopersicella*) and that is an important pest of tomatoes esp. in parts of the western U. S.
tomato psyllid *n* : a psyllid bug (*Paratrioza cockerelli*) that is a pest on tomatoes and potatoes in parts of the western U. S.
tomato russet mite *or* **tomato mite** *n* : a widely distributed mite (*Vasates destructor*) that feeds on tomato leaves causing them to turn a russet color
tomato sphinx *n* : TOBACCO HAWKMOTH
tomato streak *n* : a virus disease of tomatoes, potatoes, peas, and a wide range of other plants believed to result from a mixed infection of potato mosaic and tomato mosaic and characterized by wilting and dark elongated streaks on stems and petioles and bronzing and necrosis of the leaves at first in spots but later in general — called also *spotted wilt*
tomato wilt *n* : either of two diseases of the tomato marked by wilting: **a** : a destructive disease caused by a fungus (*Fusarium lycopersici*) **b** : a disease caused by a bacterium (*Pseudomonas solanacearum*)
tomato worm *n* : TOBACCO HORNWORM — used esp. when the larva is feeding on tomato
¹tomb \'tüm\ *n* -s [ME *toumbe, tombe,* fr. AF *tumbe,* fr. LL *tumba* sepulchral mound, fr. Gk *tymbos;* akin to MIr *tomm* hill, L *tumēre* to be swollen — more at THUMB] **1 a** : a cavity in which a corpse is deposited : GRAVE **b** : any place of interment : the last resting place **2** : a house, chamber, or vault formed wholly or partly in the earth or entirely above ground for the reception of the dead ⟨was buried in a ~ in the institution he had founded —J.F.A.Jackson⟩ **3 a** : a monument (as in a church) erected to enclose the body and preserve the name and memory of the dead **b** : CENOTAPH **4** : a building or structure that resembles a tomb ⟨big, windowless stone buildings aptly known as ~s —*Christian Science Monitor*⟩
²tomb \"\ *vt* -ED/-ING/-s [ME *toumben,* fr. *toumbe* tomb] : to place or enclose in or as if in a tomb : BURY, ENTOMB
tom·bac *also* **tom·bak** \'täm,bak\ *or* **tam·bac** \'tam-\ *n* -s [*tombac* fr. F, fr. D *tombak; tombak* fr. D, fr. Malay *tĕmbaga* copper, prob. fr. Skt *tāmraka,* fr. *tāmra* dark red, copper; *tambac* fr. Siamese, fr. Malay *tĕmbaga*] : an alloy consisting essentially of copper and zinc and sometimes arsenic and used esp. for cheap jewelry and gilding
tomb·al \'tüməl\ *adj* [¹*tomb* + *-al*] : of, relating to, or serving as a tomb
tomb bat *n* : any of several Old World bats constituting the genus *Taphozous* of the family Emballonuridae and living in caves and tombs; *esp* : a common Egyptian bat (*T. perforatus*)
tom·bé \(')täm¦bā\ *adj* [F, fr. past part. of *tomber* to fall, fr. (assumed) VL *tumbare* to fall with a thump, of imit. origin] : fallen down — used of a ballet movement with accent on the descent
tomb·less \'tümləs\ *adj* : having no tomb
tom·bo·la \'tämbələ\ *n* -s [It, fr. *tombolare* to tumble, fr. *tombare* to fall, fr. (assumed) VL *tumbare* to tumble, fall with a thump, of imit. origin] *chiefly Brit* : HOUSE 15
tom·bo·lo \'tämbə,lō\ *n* -s [It, fr. L *tumulus* mound — more at TUMULUS] : a sand or gravel bar that connects an island with the mainland or with another island
tom·boy \'täm,bȯi\ *n* [*tom* + *boy*] **1** *obs* : STRUMPET, HARLOT **2** : a girl of boyish behavior : HOYDEN ⟨~ recalls the memory of a girl who could swim and fish, ride a bicycle, play tennis and baseball, shoot marbles, and win a snow fight as handily as any boy —Josephine Lawrence⟩
tom·boy·ful \-ȯifəl\ *adj* : TOMBOYISH
tom·boy·ish \-ȯi·ish\ *adj* : being or playing the tomboy : HOYDENISH ⟨even at her most ~, she had been dainty and fastidious —C.B.Kelland⟩ — **tom·boy·ish·ly** *adv* — **tom·boy·ish·ness** *n*
tombstone \'=,=\ *n* [*tomb* + *stone*] **1** : an inscribed stone placed horizontally over a grave : LEDGER **2** : GRAVESTONE, HEADSTONE
tombstone advertisement *n* [so called fr. its staid unexciting character] : a newspaper advertisement of the offering of a new issue of a security that does not give any specific information about it
¹tomcat \'=,=\ *n* [*tom* + *cat*] **1** : a male cat **2** *slang* : one who tomcats
²tomcat \"\ *vi, slang* : CAT 2 — often used with *around*
tomcat clover *n* : an annual clover (*Trifolium tridentatum*) of western No. America with usu. tridentate calyx lobes
tomcod \'=,=\ *n* [*tom* + *cod*] **1** : any of several small fishes of the genus *Microgadus* closely resembling the common codfish except in size: as **a** : a fish (*M. tomcod*) of the cold and temperate Atlantic coast that is olive to gray above and lighter below, has the ventral fins prolonged as filaments and a convex tail, and is sometimes taken by anglers **b** : a very similar fish (*M. proximus*) of the Pacific coast that is a minor sport fish and an excellent food fish though not fished commercially **2** : any of various croakers of the Pacific coast; *esp* : a kingfish (*Genyonemus lineatus*)
tom col·lins \-'kälənz\ *n, usu cap T&C* [fr. the name *Tom Collins*] : a collins with a base of gin
tom, dick, and harry *n, usu cap T&D&H* [fr. the names *Tom* (nickname for *Thomas*), *Dick* (nickname for *Richard*) & *Harry* (nickname for *Henry*)] : persons taken at random : the common run of humanity : EVERYBODY, EVERYONE — often used with *every* and disparagingly ⟨he hated the human race en masse, but truly loved *Tom, Dick, and Harry* —J.M. Barzun⟩ ⟨the government draws it all out and pays it to *Tom, Dick, and Harry* for relief —J.T.Flynn⟩ ⟨our columns thrown wide open for the views of every *Tom, Dick, and Harry* in the land —A.J.Russell⟩ ⟨an incessant helper of every *Tom, Dick, and Harry* who is in need —*Current Biog.*⟩
tome \'tōm\ *n* -s [MF or L; MF *tome,* fr. L *tomus,* fr. Gk *tomos* slice, section, roll of papyrus, tome, fr. *temnein* to cut; akin to Gk *tendein* to gnaw, L *tondēre* to shear, crop, MIr *tennaid* he splits] **1** : a volume forming part of a larger work ⟨a history in ten ~s⟩ **2** : BOOK ⟨over 259,000,000 copies of pocket-size ~s were printed —J.K.Hutchens⟩; *esp* : a large ponderous or a scholarly volume ⟨heavy books of reference or other large ~s that must stand much wear —Edith Diehl⟩ ⟨a huge twenty-seven-pound ~ as compared with the seven-and-a-half-pound volume —John Lawler⟩ ⟨adults often leave heavier ~s for cooler weather to dip into light summer fare —*N.Y. Times Bk. Rev.*⟩ ⟨two lines of poetry often tell us more, give us more, than the weightiest ~ of an erudite —Henry Miller⟩ ⟨waded conscientiously through many formidable ~s —W.S.Maugham⟩
-tome \,tōm\ *n comb form* -s [NL *-tomus,* fr. *-tomus* cutting, cut, segmented, fr. Gk *-tomos,* fr. *temnein* to cut] **1** : part : section ⟨angio*tome*⟩ ⟨gono*tome*⟩ **2** : cutting instrument ⟨micro*tome*⟩ ⟨pharyngo*tome*⟩
to·men·tel·la \,tōmən'telə\ *n, cap* [NL, fr. L *tomentum* cushion stuffing + *-ella* — more at TOMENTUM] : a genus of fungi (family Thelephoraceae) having basidia borne on a cobwebby layer of hyphae
to·men·tose \tə'men,tōs, 'tōmən-\ *adj* [NL *tomentosus,* fr. L *tomentum* cushion stuffing + *-osus* -ose] : covered with densely matted hairs ⟨a ~ leaf⟩ — compare PUBESCENT
to·men·tous \tə'mentəs\ *adj* [NL *tomentosus*] : TOMENTOSE
to·men·tu·lose \-nchə,lōs\ *adj* [NL *tomentulosus,* dim. of *tomentosus* tomentose] : minutely or slightly tomentose
to·men·tum \tə'mentəm\ *n, pl* **tomen·ta** \-tə\ [NL, fr. L, cushion stuffing consisting of matted wool, hair, feathers, fr. earlier (assumed) L *tovimentum,* fr. L *tovi-* (akin to L *tumēre* to be swollen) + *-mentum* -ment — more at THUMB] **1** : pubescence composed of densely matted woolly hairs **2** : a flocculent investment of the deep surface of the pia mater made up of minute blood vessels
tomes's fiber *or* **tomes's fibril** \'tōmzəz-\ *n, usu cap T* [after Sir John *Tomes* †1895 Eng. dental surgeon] : one of the fibers extending from the odontoblasts into the dental canals : a dentinal fiber
¹tom·fool \'täm'fül\ *n* [ME *Thome Fole,* name given to half-wits, fr. *Thome* (nickname for *Thomas*) + *fol, fole* fool] **1** *usu cap* : a buffoon in a play or pageant : a professional clown **2** : one lacking in sense or good judgment : a great fool : BLOCKHEAD ⟨if any ~ points a gun at you —L.S.Marceau⟩ **3 a** : RAINBIRD b **b** : a West Indian flycatcher (*Myiarchus stolidus*)
²tomfool \'=¦=\ *adj* : extremely foolish, stupid, or doltish; *also* : of, from, or characteristic of a tomfool ⟨don't know what ~ caper you're up to —C.B.Kelland⟩
³tomfool \'=¦=\ *vi* : to act the tomfool ⟨this ~*ing* is no sort of use —G.B.Shaw⟩
tom·fool·ery \(')täm¦fül(ə)rē, -ri\ *n* [¹*tomfool* + *-ery*] **1** : foolish or ridiculous trifling : nonsensical behavior or speech : NONSENSE ⟨indulge in ~⟩ **2** : an act, practice, speech, or thing that is nonsensical, foolish, or useless ⟨racehorses and football and *tomfooleries* of that sort —Sheila Kaye-Smith⟩ **3** : silly or trumpery trifles or ornaments ⟨among a lot of elegant ~ that makes it clear how the establishment got its name —*New Yorker*⟩
tom·fool·ish \-lish\ *adj* [¹*tomfool* + *-ish*] : given to tomfoolery : NONSENSICAL — **tom·fool·ish·ness** *n*
tom fool knot *or* **tom fool's knot** *n, often cap T&F* : a conjuror's knot consisting of two loops which disappear when the ends are pulled

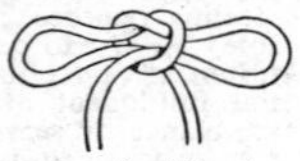

tom fool knot

to·mi·al \'tōmēəl\ *adj* [NL *tomium* + E *-al*] : relating to a tomium
-tomies *pl of* -TOMY
to·mis·to·ma \tə'mistəmə\ *n, cap* [NL, fr. Gk *tomos* cutting, sharp (fr. *temnein* to cut) + NL *-i-* + *-stoma;* more at TOME] : a genus of Malayan crocodilians resembling the gavials
to·mi·um \'tōmēəm\ *n, pl* **to·mia** \-ēə\ [NL, fr. Gk *tomos* cutting, sharp + NL *-ium*] : the cutting edge of the bill of a bird
tom·kin \'tämkən\ *n* -s : TAMPION
tom·my \'tämē, -mi\ *n* -ES [fr. *Tommy,* nickname for *Thomas*] **1** *dial Brit* **a** : a loaf or hunk of bread : a ration of bread; *also* : PROVISIONS **b** : the food carried by workmen as their daily allowance **2** : a short rod used as a key; *esp* : one for turning a capstan screw **3** *dial Eng* : SIMPLETON, FOOL **4** *usu cap* [*Tommy Atkins*] : a British soldier : TOMMY ATKINS **5 a** : TOMCOD 2 **b** : REQUIN
tommy at·kins \-'atkənz\ *n, pl* **tommy atkins** *usu cap T&A* [fr. *Thomas Atkins,* fictitious name used as model in official blank forms for private soldiers] : a white soldier of the British Army; *collectively* : such soldiers
tommy-ax \'==,=\ *n* [alter. (influenced by *ax*) of *tomahawk*] *Austral* : TOMAHAWK
tommy bar *n* : a bar used as a tommy to turn bolts and screws
tommycod \'==,=\ *n* [by alter.] : TOMCOD
tommy gun *n* [by shortening & alter.] : THOMPSON SUBMACHINE GUN; *broadly* : SUBMACHINE GUN
tommy-gun \'==,=\ *vt* [*tommy gun*] : to shoot with a tommy gun
tommy gunner *n* [*tommy gun* + *-er*] : an operator of a tommy gun
tom·my·hawk \'tämē,hȯk\ *vt* -ED/-ING/-s [alter. of ²*tomahawk*] *Austral* : TOMAHAWK 3
tommy hole *n* : a hole in a piece (as a collar) in which to insert the end of a tommy to turn it
tommy-knocker \'==,==\ *n, often cap T* [prob. fr. *Tommy* (nickname for *Thomas*) + *knocker;* fr. his being supposed to be responsible for the creaking of timbers in the mine] *West* : the ghost of a man killed in a mine
tommyrot \'=,=\ *n* [*tommy* + *rot*] : rank foolishness or nonsense ⟨such ~ has helped create a widespread and deep-rooted misunderstanding of science —John Pfeiffer⟩ ⟨how any sane and intelligent person can believe such ~ is inconceivable —A.H. & Ruth Verrill⟩
tommy rough *n, usu cap T* [*Tommy* (nickname for *Thomas*) + *rough;* fr. the roughness of the scales] : ROUGHY 1
tomnoddy \'=,==\ *n* [*Tom* (nickname for *Thomas*) + *noddy*] **1** *chiefly Scot* : ATLANTIC PUFFIN **2** : FOOL, DUNCE, NODDY
tom o'bed·lam \-ə'bedləm\ *n, pl* **tom o'bedlams** *usu cap T&B* [*Tom* (nickname for *Thomas*) + *o'* + *Bedlam,* popular name for the Hospital of St. Mary of Bethlehem, London, England, an insane asylum — more at BEDLAM] : a wandering mendicant either mad or feigning to be so : BEDLAMITE
to·mo·gram \'tōmə,gram\ *n* [ISV *tomo-* (fr. Gk *tomos* slice, section) + *-gram;* prob. orig. formed as G *tomogramm* — more at TOME] : a roentgenogram made by tomography
to·mo·graph \-raf, -räf\ *n* [ISV *tomo-* + *-graph*] : an X-ray machine used for tomography — **to·mo·graph·ic** \¦==¦grafik\ *adj*
to·mog·ra·phy \tə'mägrəfē\ *n* -ES [ISV *tomo-* (fr. Gk *tomos* slice, section) + *-graphy;* prob. orig. formed as G *tomographie*] : a technique of medical roentgenography by which details in one plane of body tissue appear clear and sharp while details of adjoining planes are blurred
¹to·mop·ter·id \tə'mäptərəd\ *adj* [NL *Tomopteridae,* family of polychaete worms, fr. *Tomopteris,* type genus + *-idae*] : of or relating to the genus *Tomopteris* or family Tomopteridae
²tomopterid \"\ *n* -s : a tomopterid worm
to·mop·ter·is \-rəs\ *n, cap* [NL, fr. Gk *tomos* slice, section + *pteris* fern; fr. its fernlike shape — more at TOME, PTERIS] : a genus (the type of the family Tomopteridae) of transparent free-swimming marine polychaete worms having long deeply divided or forked parapodia
to·morn \tə'mȯ(ə)rn\ *n or adv* [ME *to morne, to morn,* contr. of *to morgen, to morwen* — more at TOMORROW] *chiefly dial* : TOMORROW
¹to·mor·row \tə'mä|(,)rō, |rə *also* -'mȯ|; |rəw *or* |rō+V\ *adv* [ME *to morgen, to morwen,* fr. OE *tō morgenne, tō morgen,* fr. *tō* to + *morgenne,* dat. of *morgen* morning, morrow — more at MORN] : on or for the day after today : on or for the morrow
²tomorrow \"\ *n* -s [ME *to morwen,* fr. *to morwen* tomorrow (adv.)] **1** : the day after the present : MORROW ⟨the Senate took a recess until ~ —*Congressional Record*⟩ ⟨baffled as to how his ~s are to be spent —Florence Bullock⟩ **2** : FUTURE 1a
to·mor·row·er \|rəwə(r), |rōə(r)\ *n* -s [¹*tomorrow* + *-er*] : PROCRASTINATOR
to·mor·row·ness *n* -ES : the quality of being tomorrow
to·mo·sis \tə'mōsəs\ *n, pl* **tomoses** [NL, fr. Gk *tomos* slice, section + NL *-osis* — more at TOME] : a disease of cotton characterized by the fraying and perforation of the leaves
-to·mous \d·əməs, təməs\ *adj comb form* [NL *-tomus* — more at -TOME] **1** : cut : divided ⟨ortho*tomous*⟩ ⟨rhachi*tomous*⟩ **2** : cutting ⟨xylo*tomous*⟩
tompion *var of* TAMPION
toms *pl of* TOM
tom show *n, usu cap T* [after Uncle *Tom,* title character of *Uncle Tom's Cabin,* dramatization (1852) by George L. Aiken †1876 Am. actor & playwright of the novel *Uncle Tom's Cabin* (1852) by Harriet Beecher Stowe †1896 Am. author] : a traveling show performing *Uncle Tom's Cabin*
tomsk \'tämzk, 'tȯm-, -msk\ *adj, usu cap* [fr. *Tomsk,* city of western Siberia, U.S.S.R.] : of or from the city of Tomsk, U.S.S.R. : of the kind or style prevalent in Tomsk
tom·tate \'täm,tāt\ *n* -s [origin unknown] : a Florida and West Indian grunt (*Bathystoma rimator*); *also* : any of several related fishes
tom thumb *n, usu cap both Ts* [after *Tom Thumb,* legendary Eng. dwarf] : a dwarf type, race, or individual
tom tid·dler's ground \-'tidlə(r)z-\ *also* **tommy tiddler's ground** *n, usu cap both Ts* [fr. *Tom Tiddler, Tommy Tiddler,* name given to the player who is "it"] **1** : a game in which a player designated Tom Tiddler or Tommy Tiddler tries to catch the other players who invade the area designated as his property **2** : a place (as a no-man's-land) where pickings may be sought or had without effective interference ⟨this country was a *Tom Tiddler's ground* of raiding parties —T.E.Lawrence⟩ ⟨the border now became a sort of *Tom Tiddler's ground* filled with warring Kaffirs —Stuart Cloete⟩
tom·tit \(')täm'tit\ *n* [prob. short for *tomtitmouse*] : any of various small active birds: as **a** *dial Eng* : TITMOUSE; *esp* : BLUE TIT **b** *dial Eng* : WREN **c** *Irish* : TREE CREEPER **d** *South* : NUTHATCH **e** *Austral* : THORNBILL; *esp* : a common and widely distributed yellow-tailed thornbill (*Acanthiza chrysorrhoa*)
tomtitmouse \(')=¦=,=\ *n* [*Tom* (nickname for *Thomas*) + *titmouse*] *dial Eng* : BLUE TIT
¹tom-tom \'täm,täm\ *n* -s [Hindi *tamtam*] **1** : a small-headed drum of varying shape but typically long and narrow commonly beaten with the hands ⟨religious melodies chanted to the accompaniment of *tom-toms* —*Newsweek*⟩ **2** : TAM-TAM **3 a** : something used to make a noise suggestive of the tom-tom's beating **b** : an insistently monotonous beating, rhythm, or rhythmical sound ⟨the radiators beat an unending *tom-tom* like the Royal Watusi drums —S.J.Perelman⟩

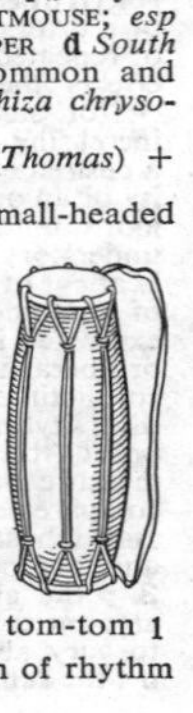

tom-tom 1

²tom-tom \"\ *vb* **tom-tomed** *or* **tom-tommed; tom-tomed** *or* **tom-tommed; tom-toming** *or* **tom-tomming; tom-toms** *vi* : to sound a tom-tom esp. as a signal : make tom-tom sounds ⟨waving genial greetings to thousands of *tom-toming,* grass-skirted Africans —*Newsweek*⟩ ⟨she observed her feet *tom-toming* out the pattern of rhythm

she was whistling —Jesse Lasky) ~ *vt* : to sound on the tom-tom : play or execute on or as if on a tom-tom

³**tom-tom** \"\ *adj* : of or relating to the tom-tom ⟨traditional *tom-tom* beaters —*Time*⟩ : characteristic or suggestive of the tom-tom ⟨*tom-tom* muffs, with cords around the middle —Lois Long⟩

tom tram \-ˈtram\ *n, usu cap both Ts* [fr. *Tom Tram*, name of a legendary Eng. buffoon] *obs* : a professional fool : JESTER

tom walker *n, sometimes cap T&W* [*Tom* (nickname for Thomas) + *walker*] **1 tom walkers** *pl, dial* : STILTS **2** *slang* : a man on stilts

-to·my \d·əmē, təm-, -mi\ *n comb form* -ES [NL *-tomia*, fr. Gk, fr. *-tomos* cutting + *-ia* -y — more at -TOME] : incision : section ⟨cranio*tomy*⟩ ⟨laparo*tomy*⟩ ⟨sclero*tomy*⟩

¹**ton** *obs var of* TUN

²**ton** \ˈtən\ *n, pl* **tons** *also* **ton** [ME *tonne, toun* tun, unit of ship capacity or of weight — more at TUN] **1** : any of various units of weight: **a** : a unit equal to 20 long hundredweight or 2240 pounds used chiefly in England — called also *long ton;* see MEASURE table **b** : a unit equal to 20 short hundredweight or 2000 pounds used chiefly in the U.S., Canada, and So. Africa — called also *short ton* **c** : METRIC TON **2 a** : a unit of internal capacity for ships equal to 100 cubic feet — called also *register ton;* see TONNAGE **b** : a unit approximately equal to the volume of a long ton weight of seawater used in reckoning the displacement of ships and equal to 35 cubic feet — called also *displacement ton* **c** : a unit of volume for cargo freight usu. reckoned at 40 cubic feet — called also *freight ton, measurement ton* **3** : a European unit of quantity for timber equal to 480 board feet **4** : a unit of cooling capacity equal to the cooling effect of a ton of ice melting in 24 hours **5** : a great quantity : a large supply : LOT, HEAP — used chiefly in pl. ⟨~*s* of propaganda flooding the country⟩ ⟨he's got ~*s* of money, so they say⟩

³**ton** \"\ *n* -S [F *thon* — more at TUNNY] : TUNNY

⁴**ton** \ˈtōⁿ\ *n* -S [F, lit., tone, fr. L *tonus* — more at TONE] **1 a** : the prevailing fashion or mode : VOGUE **b** : SMARTNESS, STYLE ⟨conversation as the evidence of ~, and the attribute of rank —E.G.Bulwer-Lytton⟩ **2** : the world of fashion : SMART SET ⟨the world of ~ which shook its head over a ruined friend —*Times Lit. Supp.*⟩

to·na·da \təˈnädə\ *n* -S [Sp, fr. *tono* tone (fr. L *tonus*) + *-ada* -ade, fr. LL *-ata*] : a Spanish folksong esp. of meditative character

to·na·di·lla \ˌtōnəˈdē(y)ə, -ēlyə\ *n* -S [Sp, dim. of *tonada*] : a short Spanish scenic intermezzo of the 18th century written for a few soloists for performance between the acts of a serious play and in the 19th century becoming a short comic opera with soloists, a chorus, and occas. instrumental movements

ton·al \ˈtōnᵊl\ *adj* [ML *tonalis*, fr. L *tonus* tone + *-alis* -al] **1** : of or relating to tone, tonality, or tonicity **2** : having tonality — compare ATONAL **3** : having the intervals of a melodic subject that is repeated at a new pitch so modified as to remain in the same key ⟨~ fugue⟩ ⟨~ sequence⟩ ⟨~ imitation⟩ — compare REAL — **ton·al·ly** \-ᵊlē, -ᵊli\ *adv*

to·na·la·ma·tl \təˈnäləˌmäd·ᵊl\ *n* -S [Nahuatl, lit., book of days, fr. *tonalli* day + *amatl* paper, book] **1** : an Aztec divinatory book based on the tonalpohualli **2** : TONALPOHUALLI

ton·al·ism \ˈtōnᵊlˌizəm\ *n* -S [*tonal* + *-ism*] : the practice of composing tonal music — opposed to *atonalism*

ton·al·ist \-ləst\ *n* -S [*tonal* + *-ist*] : one who adheres to tonality esp. in musical composition

to·nal·ite \ˈtōnᵊlˌīt\ *n* -S [G *tonalit*, fr. *Tonale* (*Pass*) in the Lombard Alps + G *-it* -ite] **1** : a granular igneous rock consisting of quartz, andesine, and small amounts of orthoclase **2** : QUARTZ-DIORITE

to·nal·i·tive \tōˈnaləd·iv\ *adj* [*tonality* + *-ive*] : tending to tonality

to·nal·i·ty \tōˈnaləd·ē, -ətē, -i *sometimes* təˈ-\ *n* -ES [*tonal* + *-ity*] **1** : tonal quality **2** : the principle of organizing all the tones and chords of a piece of music in relation to one tone : the quality of having a keynote or tonic : the recognition or acceptance of key and key relationships — opposed to *atonality* **3 a** : the arrangement or interrelation of the colors or color nuances of a picture : color scheme : tone system **b** : the effect or quality resulting from closely related tones esp. in the darker values

to·nal·po·hual·li \tōˈnälpōˌwälē\ *n* -S [Nahuatl] : an Aztec calendar period of 260 days like the tzolkin of the Maya calendar

tonal row *n* : TWELVE-TONE ROW

to-name \ˈ=,=\ *n* [ME, fr. OE *tōnama*, fr. *tō* to + *nama* name] **1** *obs* : SURNAME **2** *Scot* : NICKNAME

ton·a·wan·da pine \ˌtänəˈwändə-\ *n, usu cap T* [fr. *Tonawanda* Creek, northwestern N.Y.] : WHITE PINE 1a

tonca bean *var of* TONKA BEAN

ton·di·no \tänˈdē(ˌ)nō\ *n, pl* **tondi·ni** \-ēnē\ [It, dim. of *tondo* round] **1** : a circular molding **2** : a metal disk for striking a coin **3** : a small tondo

ton·do \ˈtän(ˌ)dō\ *n, pl* **ton·di** \-ndē\ [It, plate, circular plaque, fr. *tondo* round, short for *rotondo*, fr. L *rotundus* — more at ROUND] **1** : a circular painting **2** : a sculptured medallion

¹**tone** \ˈtōn\ *pron* [ME *ton*, alter. (resulting from incorrect division of *thet on* the one, fr. OE *thæt ān*) of *on* — more at THAT, ONE] *chiefly dial* : ONE ⟨and by my faith . . . the ~ of us shall die —*Childe Maurice*⟩

²**tone** \"\ *n* -S *often attrib* [ME *ton, tone*, fr. L *tonus* tension, pitch, tone, fr. Gk *tonos* act of stretching, tension, pitch, tone, cord; akin to Skt *tāna* fibre, tone, Gk *teinein* to stretch — more at THIN] **1** : vocal or musical sound; *esp* : sound quality of a specific character ⟨a voice with full, clear ~⟩ ⟨spoke in low ~*s*⟩ ⟨sweet ~ of a flute⟩ ⟨harsh ~⟩ **2 a** : a sound that has such regularity of vibration as to impress the ear with a definite pitch sensation and is further characterized musically by loudness and timbre : musical sound — compare NOISE **b** : WHOLE STEP **c** : TONE QUALITY **3** : an ecclesiastical mode or a traditional tune or plain chant of the church ⟨the Gregorian ~⟩ **4 a** : accent or inflection of the voice as adapted to the emotion or passion expressed : vocal expressiveness **b** : vocal inflection characteristic of the speech of an individual, region, or nation : ACCENT **c** : artificial modulation in speaking or reading : singsong or affected intonation ⟨I never liked a man who spoke in a ~ of voice —O.Henry⟩ **5 a** : the musical pitch or intonation of a sound, word, or sentence often used to express differences of meaning or function — see TONE LANGUAGE **b** : one of the four notes or keys in which Chinese Mandarin sounds are pitched and which are often indicated beside the character or its romanized spelling by the figures 1, 2, 3, 4 **6 a** : a particular pitch or change of pitch constituting an element in the intonation of a phrase or sentence ⟨high ~⟩ ⟨low ~⟩ ⟨mid ~⟩ ⟨low-rising ~⟩ ⟨falling ~⟩ **b** : WORD STRESS **7** : style or manner of approach in speaking or writing : method of address ⟨began in a defiant ~⟩ ⟨seemed wise to adopt a conciliatory ~⟩ **8 a** : color quality or value : a tint or shade of color : a modification of a chromatic or achromatic color with respect to lightness or saturation **b** : the color that appreciably modifies a hue or white or black ⟨a bright, dark, or light ~ of blue⟩ ⟨the gray walls took on a greenish ~⟩ ⟨the soft ~*s* of the old marble⟩ **9** : the general effect in painting of the harmonious combination of light and shade together with color **10 a** : the part of a print made from a photoengraving bearing the black or the color **b** : the relative darkness or color strength of different areas of a printed picture ⟨dark, middle, and light ~*s*⟩ **c** : the color of a photographic image ⟨sepia ~⟩ ⟨warm ~*s*⟩ **11 a** (1) : the state of a living body or of any of its organs or parts in which the functions are healthy and performed with due vigor (2) : overall vigor and well-balanced growth in a plant indicating satisfactory balance of environmental factors (as nutrients, moisture, light, heat) **b** : normal tension or responsiveness to stimuli : TONICITY; *specif* : TONUS **12 a** : healthy or normal elasticity : power to function or react under stress : RESILIENCY ⟨restore the ~ of the body politic⟩ ⟨fine ~ of a critical intelligence⟩ **b** : general or prevailing character, quality, or trend of moral or social behavior ⟨a city's low moral ~⟩ ⟨judge a school by its ~⟩ **c** : frame of mind : MOOD, TEMPER ⟨philosophical ~⟩ **d** : the character of a market as reflected in activity, supply and demand, and price trend ⟨the ~ of the stock market was steady⟩ **13** : FEELING TONE **syn** see COLOR

³**tone** \"\ *vb* -ED/-ING/-S [ME *tonen*, fr. ²*tone*] *vt* **1 a** *obs* : to sound with a musical quality **b** : to utter with a particular or affected tone : INTONE **2** : to give a particular intonation or inflection to ⟨fear *toned* his voice⟩ **3 a** : to impart tone to : improve or raise the quality of : STRENGTHEN ⟨exercise *toned* his muscles⟩ — used often with *up* ⟨prescribed a medicine to ~ up the system⟩ **b** : to reduce the emphatic or glaring quality of : make harmonious in color, appearance, or sound : SOFTEN, MELLOW — used usu. with *down* ⟨~ down clashing colors with brown tints⟩ ⟨advancing years had *toned* down his rash impulsiveness⟩ **c** : to change by treatment the tone or color of : modify in color; *specif* : to change the normal silver image of (a print, transparency, or lantern slide) into a colored image either by treatment with a solution containing some inorganic salt or by mordanting and dyeing ~ *vi* **1 a** : to assume a harmonious or pleasing color quality or tint ⟨the shingles will ~ with age and weathering⟩ — used often with *down* ⟨his clothes have *toned* down since his marriage⟩ **b** *of a photographic image* : to undergo a chemical reaction resulting in a change in color ⟨the average print will ~ in about 15 minutes —Jack Wright⟩ **2** : to blend with respect to tone or color quality : harmonize in color ⟨the rug ~*s* with the woodwork⟩

tone accent *n* : PITCH ACCENT 2

tone arm *n* : the movable part of a phonograph that carries the pickup and permits the needle to follow the record groove spiral

tone cluster *n* : a combination of musical tones sounded together each of which is a scale degree apart from one or two neighboring tones in the group ⟨C-D-E struck simultaneously are a *tone cluster*⟩

tone color *n* [trans. of G *klangfarbe*] **1** : TIMBRE 1b **2** : COLOR 10b

tone control *n* : a usu. manual control by which a listener can adjust the relative amplitude of the high, low, and intermediate frequencies in a radio set

toned \ˌtōnd\ *adj* [²*tone* + *-ed*] **1** : having or having been given tone or a specified tone : characterized or distinguished by a tone — often used in combination ⟨full-*toned*⟩ ⟨shrill-*toned*⟩ **2** : having or characterized by linguistic tones — see TONE LANGUAGE **3 a** *of paper* : having a slight tint : of an off-white color **b** *of a coin or medal* : having a mellow tint as a result of age

tone-deaf \ˈ=ˌ=\ *adj* : relatively insensitive to differences in the pitch of musical tones

tone language *n* : a language (as Chinese, Sudanic, or Bantu) in which variations in tone are regularly used to distinguish words of different meaning that otherwise would sound alike

tone·less \ˈtōnləs\ *adj* : lacking in tone, modulation, or expression ⟨speaks her first complete sentence in that ~ bird-shrill voice —Lee Rogow⟩ ⟨theatrically ~ — lacking in any real quality or spirit —H.E.Clurman⟩ — **tone·less·ly** *adv* — **tone·less·ness** *n* -ES

tone long *n* : a vowel that is not long in Semitic or pre-Hebrew but becomes long in Hebrew by virtue of its position in relation to the accent of the word or phrase and may be shortened when the position is changed

to·neme \ˈtōˌnēm\ *n* -S [²*tone* + *-eme*] : a phoneme consisting of a specific intonation in a tone language — **to·ne·mic** \tōˈnēmik\ *adj*

tone painting *n* : the use of varying timbres and sound symbolism in creating musical effects esp. in impressionistic composition or program music

tone picture *n* : a musical composition usu. for orchestra characterized by pictorial suggestion

tone poem *n* [²*tone* + *poem*] : an orchestral composition based on a literary subject or suggestive of poetic sentiments or images

tone poet *n* [trans. of G *tondichter*] : a composer of music; *esp* : a composer of program music

tone quality *n* **1** : TIMBRE 1 **2** : the character of musical tones with reference to their richness or perfection **3** : the character of the effect produced by a harmonic combination of musical tones

ton·er \ˈtōnə(r)\ *n* -S : one that tones: as **a** : an organic pigment that contains no inorganic pigment or inorganic carrier : a full-strength organic pigment — see DYE table I (under *Organic pigments*); compare ⁴LAKE 1b **b** : one that tests the quality and color of paints **c** : a chemical solution capable of converting a silver photographic image to a colored image

tone-row \ˈ=ˌ=\ *n* [trans. of G *tonreihe*] : TWELVE-TONE ROW

tones *pl of* TONE, *pres 3d sing of* TONE

tone syllable *n* : an accented syllable

to·net·ic \tōˈned·ik\ *adj* [²*tone* + *-etic*] : relating to linguistic tones or to tone languages : dealing with or expressing intonation ⟨~ notation⟩ — **to·net·i·cal·ly** \-d·ək(ə)lē\ *adv*

to·ne·ti·cian \ˌtōnəˈtishən *sometimes* ˌtän-\ *n* -S [*tonetic* + *-ian*] : a student of tonetics

to·net·ics \tōˈned·iks\ *n pl but sing in constr* [fr. *tonetic*, after E *phonetic*: *phonetics*] : the use or study of linguistic tones : the science of intonation

to·nette \(ˈ)tōˈnet\ *n* -S [²*tone* + *-ette*] : a small simple end-blown flute typically of plastic with a range somewhat exceeding an octave often used in elementary music education

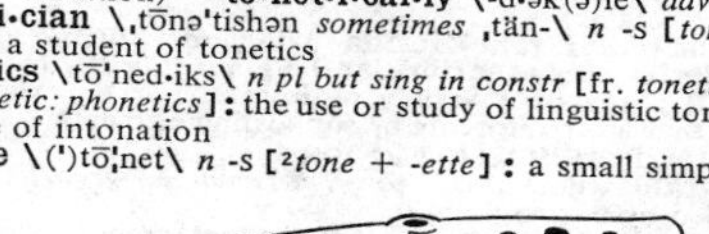

tonette

tone-up \ˈ=ˌ=\ *n* -S [fr. *tone up*, v.] : a toning-up exercise, treatment, or medicine

tone wheel *n* : a high-speed interrupter or commutator formerly used for producing a current of audio frequency in a radio receiver

toney *var of* TONY

ton-foot \ˈ=ˌ=\ *n* [²*ton* + *foot*] : FOOT-TON

¹**tong** \ˈtäŋ, ˈtȯŋ\ *n* -S [ME *tonge*, alter. of *tange* tang] **1** *dial* : TANG **2** *dial* : TINE

²**tong** \"\ *vb* -ED/-ING/-S [imit.] *vt, dial* : to cause (a bell) to give out a deep resonant tone ~ *vi, dial* : to give out a deep resonant tone

³**tong** \"\ *n* -S *dial* : a deep sound given out by a large bell

⁴**tong** \"\ *n* -S [fr. sing. of *tongs*] : TONGS

⁵**tong** \"\ *vb* -ED/-ING/-S [*tongs*] *vt* : to take, gather, hold, or handle with tongs ⟨~ oysters⟩ ⟨~ logs⟩ — often used with *up* ~ *vi* : to use tongs : take or gather something with tongs

⁶**tong** \"\ *n* -S [Chin (Cant) *t'ong* hall, meeting place] : a secret society or fraternal organization esp. among the Chinese in the U.S. formerly notorious for gang warfare and popularly associated with racketeering, gambling, and traffic in narcotics

⁷**tong** \"\ *n* -S [Afrik, tongue, flatfish, fr. MD *tonge, tong;* akin to OE *tunge* tongue — more at TONGUE] : a large commercially important southern African flatfish (*Austroglossus pectoralis*) much depleted by overfishing; *also* : a closely related fish (*A. microlepis*) distinguished by its minute scales

¹**ton·ga** \ˈtäŋgə\ *n* -S [Hindi *tāngā*] : a light 2-wheeled vehicle for two or four persons drawn by one horse and common in India

²**tonga** \ˈtäŋ(g)ə, ˈtȯŋ-\ *or* **ton·gan** \-)ən\ *n* -S [prob. fr. *Tonga* islands, southwest central Pacific ocean] **1** *also* **tongan creeper** : an epiphytic creeper (*Epipremnum mirabile*) of the family Araceae used in folk medicine in Malaysia **2** : a drug formerly used in pharmacy consisting of equal parts of tonga bark and the root of a verbenaceous tree (*Premna arborea*)

³**tonga** \"\ *n, pl* **tonga** *usu cap* **1 a** : any of several Bantu-speaking peoples found respectively in southern Portuguese East Africa, west of Lake Nyasa, and on the upper Zambezi river **b** : a member of one of these peoples **2** : any of the languages of the several Tonga peoples

⁴**ton·ga** \"\ *adj, usu cap* [fr. *Tonga* islands, southwest central Pacific ocean] : TONGAN

tonga bean *var of* TONKA BEAN

¹**ton·gan** \ˈtäŋ(g)ən, ˈtȯŋ-\ *n* -S *usu cap* [*Tonga* islands, southwest central Pacific ocean + E *-an*] **1** : a member of a Polynesian people native to the Tonga islands of the southwest Pacific **2** : the Polynesian language of the Tongans

²**tongan** \"\ *adj, usu cap* : of or relating to the Tonga islands or the Tongans or their language

ton·ga·re·van \ˌtäŋ(g)əˈrevən, ˌtȯŋ-, -ˈrāv-\ *adj, usu cap* [*Tongareva* island, central Pacific ocean + E *-an*] : of, relating to, or characteristic of the island, the people, or the language of Tongareva in the Manihiki islands in the central Pacific

ton·gass \ˈtäŋgəs\ *n, pl* **tongass** *or* **tongasses** *usu cap* **1** : a Tlingit people at the mouth of Portland canal, Alaska **2** : a member of the Tongass people

ton·ga·wal·la \ˌtäŋgəˈwälə\ *n* -S [Hindi *tāngāvālā*, fr. *tangā* tonga + *-vālā* man — more at WALLAH] : a driver of a tonga

tong·er \ˈtäŋə(r), ˈtȯŋ-\ *n* -S [⁵*tong* + *-er*] : one that tongs

tong·kang \ˈtäŋˈkaŋ\ *n* -S [Malay] : a large native boat or junk used in the East Indies in fishing and in local trading

tongkingese *usu cap, var of* TONKINESE

tong·man \ˈ=mən\ *n, pl* **tongmen** **1** [⁴*tong* + *man*] : one who handles tongs : TONGER **2** [⁶*tong* + *man*] : a member of a tong

tongs \ˈtäŋz, ˈtȯŋz\ *n pl but sometimes sing in constr* [ME *tanges, tonges*, pl. of *tange, tonge*, fr. OE *tang, tange;* akin to OHG *zanga* tongs, ON *tōng*, Gk *daknein* to bite, Skt *daśati* he bites, *daṁśa* bite] : any of numerous devices or instruments for taking hold of objects (as hot coals, hot metal, rails, logs, pipes), for ease and convenience in handling, or for lifting, dragging, or carrying and consisting commonly of two legs that are joined at one end by a pivot or spring or of two pieces hinged that are like scissors or pincers — often used with *pair* ⟨a pair of ~⟩

tongs·man \-zmən\ *n, pl* **tongsmen** [*tongs* + *man*] : TONGER

¹**tongue** \ˈtəŋ\ *n* -S *often attrib* [ME *tunge*, fr. OE; akin to OHG *zunga* tongue, ON *tunga*, Goth *tuggo*, OL *dingua*, L *lingua*] **1 a** : a process of the floor of the mouths of most vertebrates that is attached basally to the hyoid bone, that consists essentially of a mass of extrinsic muscle attaching its base to other parts, intrinsic muscle by which parts of the structure move in relation to each other, and an epithelial covering rich in sensory end organs and small glands, and that serves esp. for taking and swallowing food, as the principal seat of the sense of taste, as an instrument for cleansing and grooming, as a tactile organ (as in a snake), and in some forms (as the toad) as a prehensile organ for the seizing of prey **b** : an analogous part of various invertebrate animals (as the radula of a mollusk or the lingula or proboscis of some insects) **2** : the flesh of the tongue of an animal (as the ox or sheep) used as food **3** : the agent of articulated speech : the power of communication or expression through speech ⟨though I speak with the ~*s* of men and of angels —1 Cor 13:1 (AV)⟩ ⟨wonders that no ~ can tell⟩ ⟨done to death by slanderous ~*s* —Shak.⟩ ⟨you had better hold your ~⟩ ⟨used the strongest words he could lay ~ to⟩ ⟨gave him the rough side of my ~⟩ **4 a** : a spoken language; *esp* : a speech used by a particular people or class or in a particular region : DIALECT **b** : a language other than one's own : a foreign or strange language **c tongues** *pl, archaic* : the learned languages (as Hebrew, Greek, and Latin) — used with *the* **d** *archaic* : a people having a distinct language ⟨gather all nations and ~*s* —Isa. 66:18 (AV)⟩ **e** : manner or quality of utterance with respect to tone or sound ⟨a soft ~⟩ or the sense of what is expressed ⟨a flattering ~⟩ ⟨a foolish ~⟩ or the intention of the speaker ⟨a flattering ~⟩ **f** : ecstatic usu. unintelligible utterance called forth in a moment of religious excitation ⟨any believer might offer a hymn, or a revelation, or a ~ —C.T.Craig⟩ — see GIFT OF TONGUES **g** : the cry of or as if of a hound pursuing or in sight of game — used esp. in the phrase *to give tongue* **5** : TONGUEFISH **6 a** : a tapering cone of flame ⟨Pentecostal ~*s* of fire⟩ **b** : a tapering decorative element used in relief carvings esp. on moldings ⟨~ and dart molding⟩ — compare EGG AND DART **7 a** : a point or long narrow strip of land projecting from the mainland into a body of water **b** : a point of ice projecting nearly horizontally from the submerged part of an iceberg **c** : a current that runs rapidly between rocks **d** : the lower part of a valley glacier **e** : a minor subdivision or specifically developed part of a sedimentary formation that thins laterally to disappearance in one direction **f** : an offshoot from a body of intrusive igneous rock **g** : a narrow body of air projecting from a main air mass ⟨interlocking dry and moist ~*s* along a cold front⟩ **8** : something resembling an animal's tongue in being elongated and fastened at one end only: as **a** : a movable pin in a buckle that passes through a hole in the strap to be secured; *also* : the corresponding pin of a brooch or clasp **b** : the index of a balance or scale **c** : a metal ball freely suspended inside a bell so as to strike against the sides as the bell is swung **d** (1) : the free vibrating end of the reed in an organ pipe or wind instrument (2) : the vibrating part of a Jew's harp **e** : the pole of a 2-horse vehicle ⟨wagon ~⟩ **f** : the flap of leather or other material under the lacing or buckles of a shoe at the throat of the vamp **g** : a switch piece consisting of a movable point with a suitable enclosing or supporting body structure and designed for use on one side of a railroad track esp. of a street railway **h** : TANG 2a **i** : the swiveling part of a carpenter's bevel **j** : the endpiece of a mainspring serving as its attachment to the inside of the enclosing barrel **k** : a short block of wood or iron so placed in the jaws of a gaff as to facilitate its sliding up and down the mast **9 a** : the projecting rib on one edge of a board that fits into a corresponding groove in an edge of another board to make a flush joint **b** : FEATHER 6 **syn** see LANGUAGE — **on the tip of one's tongue 1** : about to be uttered or blurted out **2** : just eluding recall ⟨had his name *on the tip of my tongue* but it's gone now⟩

²**tongue** \"\ *vb* -ED/-ING/-S *vt* **1 a** *archaic* : UTTER, SPEAK **b** : SCOLD, ABUSE **2** : to touch or lick with or as if with the tongue ⟨cows *tonguing* the long grass⟩ ⟨~ a cigarette⟩ ⟨arms full of squirming, *tonguing* dog —Walter Karig⟩ **3 a** : to cut a tongue on ⟨~ a board⟩ **b** : to join (as boards) by means of a tongue and groove **4** : to articulate (notes) by tonguing ⟨in vain did he lip and ~ the notes as instructed —Israel Zangwill⟩ ⟨a lightning-*tongued* cornet solo⟩ ~ *vi* **1** : TALK, CHATTER — used often with *it* ⟨~ it all day long⟩ **2 a** : to project in a tongue : send out tongues ⟨forest belt of Siberia ~*s* southwards —C.D.Forde⟩ ⟨icebergs ~ out dangerously under the surface⟩ **b** : to thin to disappearance : taper off — used often with *out* ⟨the bed ~*s* out within 10 feet —*Jour. of Geol.*⟩ **3** : to give tongue ⟨hounds *tonguing* frantically on the scent⟩ **4** : to make a cut or slit in the stem of a plant before the operation of layering **5** : to articulate notes on a wind instrument

tongue and groove *n* : a joint made by a tongue on one edge of a board fitting into a corresponding groove on the edge of another board

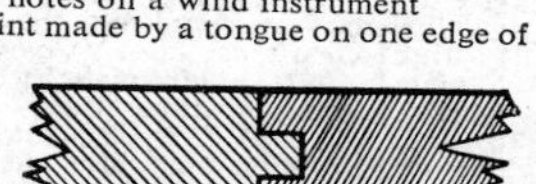

tongue and groove

tongue-and-lip joint \ˈ=ˌ=ˌ=-\ *n* : a tongue-and-groove joint for boards in which the board with the tongue has also a flush bead which serves to conceal the joint

tongue bit *n* : a horse's bit having a plate to keep the tongue under the mouthpiece

tongue-biter \ˈ=ˌ=ˌ=\ *n* : a large parasitic isopod (*Codonophilus imbricatus*) of Australian waters that attaches itself to the tongue of marine fishes

tongue bone *n* : HYOID BONE

tongued \ˌtəŋd\ *adj* [ME *tunged*, fr. *tunge* tongue + *-ed*] **1** : having a tongue or such a kind of tongue or so many tongues ⟨~ lightning⟩ — often used in combination ⟨double-*tongued*⟩ ⟨golden-*tongued*⟩ **2** : provided with a tongue ⟨a ~ shoe⟩ ⟨~ lid of a paper box⟩ ⟨~ board⟩

tongue depressor *or* **tongue blade** *n* : a thin wooden blade rounded at both ends that is used by physicians chiefly to depress the tongue to allow inspection of the throat

tongue fern *n* : any of several ferns (as *Cyclophorus lingua*) having fronds shaped like tongues

tonguefish \ˈ=ˌ=\ *n* : a small flatfish of the family Cynoglossidae

tongueflower \ˈ=ˌ=\ *n* [so called fr. its tongue-shaped lip] **1** : an Australian orchid of the genus *Glossodia* **2** : a plant or flower of the genus *Glossopetalon* (family Celastraceae)

tongue graft *n* : WHIP GRAFT 1

tongue grass *n* **1** : PEPPERGRASS 1 **2** : CHICKWEED

tongue in cheek *adv (or adj)* : with insincerity, irony, or whimsical exaggeration

tongue joint *n* : a joint usu. in metal with a tongue on one piece secured in a recess in the other

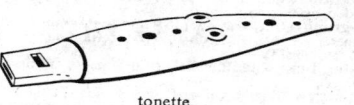

tongue-lash \ˈ=,=\ vb [back-formation fr. *tongue-lashing*] : CHIDE, REPROVE **syn** see SCOLD

tongue-lashing \ˈ=,==\ n [¹*tongue* + *lashing*] : a severe scolding

tongue·less \ˈtəŋləs\ adj [ME *tungles*, fr. *tunge* tongue + *-les* -less] **1** : having no tongue **2** : lacking power of speech : SPEECHLESS, MUTE ⟨best grief is ~ —Emily Dickinson⟩

tongue·let \-lət\ n -s [¹*tongue* + *-let*] : a small part, process, or object resembling a tongue

tonguelike \ˈ=,=\ adj [¹*tongue* + *like*] : resembling a tongue esp. in elongated form or in function

tongue of the trump [so called fr. the fact that the tongue is the essential part of a Jew's harp] *Scot* : the most important person

tongue-pad \ˈ=,=\ n, *dial chiefly Brit* : a great or glib talker

tongue pipe n : REED PIPE

tongu·er \ˈtəŋə(r)\ n -s [¹*tongue* + *-er*] **1** : one that makes or inserts tongues (as on shoes, buckles, or boards) **2** : a packing house worker who handles tongues

tongues *pl of* TONGUE, *pres 3d sing of* TONGUE

tongue-shaped \ˈ=,=\ adj : having the form of a tongue : LINGULATE

tongue shell n : a brachiopod of *Lingula* or a related genus

tongue sole n : TONGUEFISH

tongue·ster \ˈtəŋztə(r), -ŋ(k)st-\ n -s [¹*tongue* + *-ster*] : a glib or talkative person : a voluble speaker : BABBLER

tongue·tack·ed \ˈ=,takət\ adj, *Scot* : TONGUE-TIED

¹**tongue-tie** \ˈ=,=\ vt [back-formation fr. *tongue-tied*] : to deprive of speech or the power of distinct articulation by or as if by a tongue-tie or a gag : make speechless, silent, or unable to speak freely

²**tongue-tie** \ˈ"\ n [back-formation fr. *tongue-tied*] : limited mobility of the tongue due to shortness of the frenum or to its adhesion to the gums

tongue-tied \ˈ=,=\ adj [¹*tongue* + *tied*, past part. of *tie*] **1** : suffering from tongue-tie **2** : unable to speak freely from shyness or other cause ⟨he was *tongue-tied* by the sense that their minutes were numbered —Edith Wharton⟩

tongue tree n : the tongue of a vehicle

tongue twister n : a word, phrase, or sentence difficult to articulate readily because of a succession of similar chiefly consonantal sounds varied by small changes (as in "twin-screw steel cruiser", "shall he sell sea shells")

tongue-walk \ˈ=,=\ vt, *Brit* : SCOLD

tongue worm n : a parasitic arthropod of the group Linguatulida

tonguey *or* **tonguy** \ˈtəŋē, -ŋi\ adj [¹*tongue* + *-y*] **1** : ready or voluble in speaking : GARRULOUS **2** : of the nature of or affected by the tongue ⟨a ~ voice⟩

tongu·i·ness \-ŋēnəs\ n -ES : the quality of being tonguey

tonguing n -s [fr. gerund of ²*tongue*] **1** : the act of one who tongues; *also* : the product of the act of making tongues ⟨~ of matched boards⟩ **2 a** : the act of using or applying the tongue; *esp* : TONGUE-LASHING, SCOLDING **b** : the attack on or articulation of a note on a wind instrument by the use of the tongue ⟨~ rather than slurring is indicated for this passage⟩ — compare DOUBLE-TONGUE, SINGLE-TONGUE, TRIPLE-TONGUE

-to·nia \ˈtōnēə\ n *comb form* -s [NL, fr. *tonus* + *-ia* -y] : condition or degree of tonus ⟨hypo*tonia*⟩ ⟨somato*tonia*⟩

¹**ton·ic** \ˈtänik, -nēk\ adj [Gk *tonikos* of tension, of tone, fr. *tonos* tension, tone + *-ikos* -ic — more at TONE] **1 a** : relating to or characterized by tension **b** : producing or adapted to produce healthy muscular condition and reaction **c** *of muscular contraction* : maintained during prolonged periods : characterized by tonus — contrasted with *clonic* **d** *of bodily states* : marked or characterized by tonic muscular contraction ⟨~ convulsions⟩ **2 a** : increasing or restoring physical or mental tone : having the virtue or effect of a stimulant : INVIGORATING, REFRESHING, BRACING ⟨a ~ quality in her laughter —Agnes Repplier⟩ ⟨~ air of the upland morning put vigor into his blood —John Buchan⟩ ⟨~ therapy⟩ **b** : yielding a tonic substance **3** : relating to or based on the first tone of the scale ⟨~ harmony⟩ **4 a** : VOICED 2 — compare ATONIC **b** *of a syllable* : bearing a principal stress or accent — compare POSTTONIC, PRETONIC **5** : of or relating to speech tones or to languages using them : employing tones to distinguish words ⟨Chinese is a ~ language⟩

²**tonic** \ˈ"\ n -s **1 a** : a drug, medicine, or physical agent that increases body tone by stimulating tissue nutrition ⟨digitalis acts as a heart ~ by increasing cardiac tone⟩ ⟨sun baths are a ~ in some respiratory diseases⟩ **b** : something that invigorates, restores, refreshes, or stimulates ⟨his fear acted as a ~⟩ **c** : a liquid preparation for cleansing and toning the scalp **d** *NewEng* : a carbonated flavored beverage : SODA POP **2** : the first degree of a major or minor scale constituting the tonal center of a musical composition which has an established tonality — called also *keynote* **3** : a voiced sound

³**tonic** \ˈ"\ vt **tonicked; tonicked; tonicking; tonics** [²*tonic*] : to give a tonic to : strengthen by a tonic ⟨*tonicked* her children every winter with cod-liver oil⟩

tonic accent n **1** : relative phonetic prominence (as from greater stress or higher pitch) of a spoken syllable or word **2** : pitch stress as distinguished from dynamic stress

ton·i·cal \-nəkəl, -nēk-\ adj [Gk *tonikos* tonic + E *-al*] : TONIC 1,2

ton·i·cal·ly \-nək(ə)lē, -nēk-, -li\ adv [¹*tonic* + *-ally*] : in a tonic manner : BRACINGLY

to·nic·i·ty \tōˈnisəd·ē, -ətē, -i\ n -ES [¹*tonic* + *-ity*] **1** : the condition or property of possessing muscular, systemic, mental, or moral tone : VIGOR, HEALTH **2** : muscular tonus **3** : normal responsiveness of a plant to external stimuli

tonic sol-fa n : a system of solmization widely used in Great Britain and other countries to develop sightsinging that is based on tonality or key relationships and replaces the usual staff notation with the initial letters of the sol-fa syllables or the syllables themselves

tonier *comparative of* TONY

tonies *pl of* TONY

-tonies *pl of* -TONY

toniest *superlative of* TONY

ton·i·fy \ˈtänə,fī, ˈtōn-\ vt -ED/-ING/-ES [⁴*ton* + *-ify*] **1** : to give ton or style to **2** [¹*tone* + *-ify*] : to give tone to : tone up ⟨*tonifies* the system and rests the nerves⟩

¹**to·night** \təˈnīt, *usu* -īd·+V\ adv [ME *to night, to niht*, fr. OE *tō niht*, fr. *tō* to + *niht* night] : on this present night or the night following this present day

²**tonight** \ˈ"\ n [ME, fr. *to night*, adv.] : the present or the coming night : the night after the present day

tonikan *usu cap, var of* TUNICAN

toning [fr. gerund of ²*tone*] n -s *Brit* : a tint, shade, or tone (as of a fabric)

ton·ish *or* **ton·nish** \ˈtänish\ adj [⁴*ton* + *-ish*] : having ton : FASHIONABLE, STYLISH ⟨become a ~ poet and get into anthologies —Rose Macaulay⟩ — **ton·ish·ly** adv — **ton·ish·ness** n -ES

to·nite \ˈtō,nīt\ n -s [ISV *ton-* (fr. L *tonare* to thunder) + *-ite*] : a blasting explosive consisting of a mixture of guncotton with a nitrate and sometimes a nitro compound

ton·i·tro·cirrus \ˈtänə,(ˌ)trō+\ n [NL, fr. L *tonitrus* thunder + NL *-o-* + *cirrus*] : FALSE CIRRUS

to·nit·ru·ous \təˈni·trəwəs\ *also* **to·nit·ru·ant** \-wənt\ adj [*tonitruous* fr. L *tonitrum* thunder (fr. *tonitrus* thunder, fr. *tonare* to thunder) + E *-ous*; *tonitruant* fr. LL *tonitruant-, tonitruans*, fr. pres. part. of *tonitruare* to thunder, fr. L *tonitruum* thunder — more at THUNDER] : THUNDERING, FULMINATING

ton·jon \ˈtän,jän\ n -s [Hindi *tāmjhām, thāmjān*] : an open sedan chair used in India and Ceylon and carried by a single pole on men's shoulders

¹**tonk** \ˈtäŋk\ n -s [imit.] : a heavy unmusical clang ⟨~ of a cowbell⟩

²**tonk** *var of* TUNK

³**tonk** \ˈtäŋk\ n -s [by shortening] : HONKY-TONK

ton·ka bean *or* **ton·ca bean** *or* **ton·ga bean** \-ŋgə-\ *also* **ton·qua bean** \-ŋkə-\ n [prob. fr. Tupi *tonka*] **1** : the seed of any of several plants of the genus *Dipteryx* (esp. *D. odorata* and *D. oppositifolia*) that has a pleasant odor due to the presence of coumarin and is used in the manufacture of coumarin, in perfumes, as a flavor for tobacco, and in making artificial vanilla extracts; *also* : a plant whose seed is a tonka bean

ton·ka·wa \ˈtäŋkəwə\ n, *pl* **tonkawa** *or* **tonkawas** *usu cap* **1 a** : an Indian people of central Texas **b** : a member of such people **2** : the language of the Tonkawa people **3** : TONKAWAN

ton·ka·wan \-wən\ n -s *usu cap* [*tonkawa* + *-an*] : a language family perhaps related to Coahuiltecan and Karankawa of Texas that includes the Tonkawa language

ton-kilometer \ˈtən+\ n [²*ton* + *kilometer*] : a unit of freight carriage equal to the transportation of one metric ton of freight one kilometer

ton·kin \ˈtän'kin, -äŋ'-\ *also* **tonkin cane** n -s [fr. *Tonkin*, northern part of Vietnam] : a firm bamboo used for ski poles and fishing rods

¹**ton·kin·ese** \ˌtäŋkəˈnēz, -ēs\ *or* **tong·king·ese** \-kiŋˈēz, -ēs\ adj, *usu cap* [*Tonkin, Tongking*, northern part of Vietnam + E *-ese*] : of or belonging to Tonkin

²**tonkinese** \ˈ"\ *or* **tongkingese** \ˈ"\ n, *pl* **tonkinese** *or* **tongkingese** **1** *cap* : a native of Tonkin **2** *usu cap* : a dialect of Vietnamese spoken in Tonkin

ton·let \ˈtənlət\ n -s [F *tonnelet*, fr. MF, prob. fr. dim. of *tonnel, tonel* cask, barrel; fr. the resemblance of the bands to staves of a barrel — more at TUNNEL] : one of the horizontal overlapping bands forming a short skirt in late medieval armor

ton-mile \ˈ=,=\ n [²*ton* + *mile*] : a statistical unit of freight transportation equivalent to a ton of freight moved one mile — compare CAR-MILE

ton-mileage \ˈ=,==\ n [*ton-mile* + *-age*] **1** : the total ton-miles performed by a carrier in a period of time **2** : rate (as of fuel consumption) per ton-mile

ton·na \ˈtänə\ n, *cap* [NL, fr. ML *tunna, tonna* barrel, tun — more at TUNNEL] : a genus of large marine gastropods (family Tonnidae) lacking varix and operculum and having the body whorl greatly enlarged and the aperture very wide

ton·nage \ˈtənij, -nej\ n -s [in sense 1, fr. ME, fr. MF, fr. OF *tonne* barrel, tun + *-age*; in other senses, fr. ²*ton* + *-age*] **1** *also* **tun·nage** \ˈ"\ : a duty formerly levied on every tun of wine imported and exported **2 a** : a duty or impost on vessels based on cargo capacity **b** : a duty, toll, or rate on goods per ton transported on canals **3** : ships in terms of the total number of tons registered or carried or of the sum of their carrying capacity ⟨the ~ built in American shipyards is relatively small⟩ ⟨the ~ devoted to Oriental trade⟩ **4 a** : the cubical content of a merchant ship in units of 100 cubic feet — compare DEADWEIGHT CAPACITY, NET TONNAGE **b** : the displacement of a warship **5** : total weight in tons : aggregate of tons shipped, carried, or mined ⟨this mine's daily ~ is large⟩ ⟨a railroad with the year's record for ~⟩ **6** : the rating in tons of the pressure or thrust exerted by a machine or engine ⟨~ of a press⟩ ⟨~ of a rocket engine⟩

tonnage and poundage n [ME] : a duty on every tun of wine or pound of wool and other articles formerly granted as a subsidy to the crown on all goods exported or imported

tonnage coefficient n : the decimal by which the product of the length, breadth, and depth of a vessel must be multiplied to obtain the gross tonnage

tonnage deck n : the deck the space below which is included in estimating underdeck tonnage and which in vessels having more than one deck is the second from the keel

tonnage opening n : an opening left in a deck for bringing the space covered within the exemptions of a rule for calculating tonnage

tonnage train n : a freight train that is operated only when a definite tonnage of freight has accumulated

ton·neau \(ˌ)täˈnō\ n -s [F, barrel, tun, kind of carriage with rear entrance & seats parallel to the wheels, fr. OF *tonel, tonnel* barrel, tun — more at TUNNEL] **1** : the rear seating compartment of an automobile ⟨~ of a limousine⟩ ⟨sports car ~ with removable canvas cover⟩ **2** : a shape of watch case or dial resembling a barrel in profile

ton·neaued \-ōd\ adj [*tonneau* + *-ed*] : having a tonneau

tonneau lamp n : a lamp mounted on the back of the front seat of a vehicle

tonneau windshield n : a windshield that is directly in front of the tonneau and is usu. attached to the back of the front seat

ton·ner \ˈtənə(r)\ n -s [²*ton* + *-er*] : an object (as a ship) having tonnage — usu. used in combination ⟨a thousand-*tonner*⟩

ton·ni·dae \ˈtänə,dē\ n pl, *cap* [NL, fr. *Tonna*, type genus + *-idae*] : a family of gastropod mollusks (suborder Taenioglossa) comprising the tun shells — see TONNA

tonnish *var of* TONISH

tono- *comb form* [Gk *tonos* tension, pitch, tone — more at TONE] **1** : tone ⟨*tono*logy⟩ ⟨*tono*scope⟩ **2** : pressure ⟨*tono*meter⟩ ⟨*tono*taxis⟩

tono·fibril *also* **tono·fibrilla** \ˈtä(ˌ)nō, ˈtō(ˌ)nō+\ n, *pl* **tonofibrils** *also* **tonofibrillae** [NL *tonofibrilla*, fr. *tono-* + *fibrilla*] : any of a variety of intracellular or extracellular fibrils that are reinforcing or supporting elements

ton of refrigeration [²*ton*] : TON 4

ton·o·gram \ˈtänə,gram, ˈtōn-\ n -s [ISV *tono-* + *-gram*] : a curve recorded by a tonograph

ton·o·graph \-,raf, -,räf\ n [ISV *tono-* + *-graph*] : a recording tonometer — **ton·o·graph·ic** \ˌ==ˈgrafik\ adj — **to·nog·ra·phy** \tōˈnägrəfē\ n -ES

ton·o·log·i·cal \ˌtänᵊlˈäjəkəl, ˌtōn-\ adj : of or relating to tonology

to·nol·o·gy \tōˈnäləjē\ n -ES [*tono-* + *-logy*] : the comparative or historical science of tones or of speech intonation

to·nom·e·ter \tōˈnäməd·ə(r)\ n [*tono-* + *-meter*] **1** : an instrument or device for determining the exact pitch or the vibration rate of tones **2** : an instrument for measuring tension (as of the eyeball) or pressure (as of blood or a gas) **3 a** : a device for measuring vapor pressure

ton·o·met·ric \ˌtänəˈme·trik, ˌtōn-\ adj [ISV *tono-* + *-metric*] : of or relating to tonometry or to the use of a tonometer

to·nom·e·try \tōˈnämə·trē\ n -ES [ISV *tono-* + *-metry*] : the act or practice of measuring with a tonometer

ton·o·plast \ˈtänə,plast, ˈtōn-\ n -s [ISV *tono-* + *-plast*; orig. formed in G] : the semipermeable protoplasmic membrane surrounding a plant-cell vacuole orig. regarded as a self-perpetuating structural membrane that actively secreted the vacuolar content but usu. held to be comparable to the plasma membrane

ton·oscope \-,skōp\ n [*tono-* + *-scope*] : an acoustical instrument for enabling a singer or player to see instantly any deviation from proper pitch of the tone being produced

tono·taxis \ˈtä(ˌ)nō, ˈtō(ˌ)nō+\ n [NL, fr. *tono-* + *taxis*] : responsiveness to a difference of osmotic pressure of the surrounding medium

tonqua bean *var of* TONKA BEAN

tons *pl of* TON

ton·sil \ˈtän(t)səl\ n -s [L *tonsillae* (pl.) tonsils] **1 a** : either of a pair of prominent masses of lymphoid tissue that lie one on each side of the throat between the anterior and posterior pillars of the fauces and are composed of lymph follicles grouped around one or more deep crypts and except for the exposed surface which is covered only by epithelium are surrounded by diffuse lymphoid tissue in a fibrous capsule **b** : any of various similar masses of lymphoid tissue — see PHARYNGEAL TONSIL **2** : AMYGDALA 2

ton·sile \ˈtän(t)səl, -n,sīl\ adj [L *tonsilis*, fr. *tonsus* (past part. of *tondēre* to shear, clip, crop) + *-ilis* -ile — more at TOME] *archaic* : suitable for being shorn or clipped

tonsill- *or* **tonsillo-** *comb form* [L *tonsillae* tonsils] : tonsil ⟨*tonsill*ectomy⟩ ⟨*tonsillo*tomy⟩

ton·sil·lar \ˈtän(t)sələ(r)\ *or* **ton·sil·lary** \-sə,lerē\ adj [NL *tonsillaris*, fr. L *tonsillae* tonsils + *-aris* -ar] : of, relating to, or affecting the tonsils

ton·sil·lec·tome \ˌtän(t)səˈlek,tōm\ n -s [*tonsill-* + *-ectome*] : an instrument for removing tonsils

ton·sil·lec·to·my \-ktəmē, -mi\ n -ES [*tonsill-* + *-ectomy*] : the surgical removal of the tonsils

ton·sil·lit·ic \ˌ==ˈlid·ik\ adj [NL *tonsillitis* + E *-ic*] : of, relating to, or affected with tonsillitis

ton·sil·li·tis \ˌ==ˈlīd·əs, -ītəs\ n -ES [NL, fr. L *tonsillae* tonsils + NL *-itis*] : inflammation of the tonsils or a tonsil of varying degrees of severity and involving simple inflammation associated with acute pharyngitis, streptococcus infection (as in septic sore throat), or formation of an abscess (as in quinsy)

ton·sil·lo·tome \tänˈsilə,tōm\ n -s [ISV *tonsill-* + *-tome*] : a surgical instrument for cutting or removing tonsils

ton·sil·lot·o·my \ˌtän(t)səˈläd·əmē\ n -ES [*tonsill-* + *-tomy*] : incision of a tonsil

ton·sor \ˈtän(t)sə(r)\ n -s [L, fr. *tonsus* + *-or* — more at TONSURE] *archaic* : BARBER

ton·so·ri·al \(ˈ)tänˈsōrēəl, -ˈsȯr-\ adj [L *tonsorius* tonsorial (fr. *tonsus* + *-orius* -ory) + E *-al*] : of or relating to a barber or his work ⟨~ parlor⟩

¹**ton·sure** \ˈtänchə(r)\ n -s [ME, fr. ML *tonsura*, fr. L, act of shearing, clipping, fr. *tonsus* (past part. of *tondēre* to shear, clip, crop) + *-ura* -ure — more at TOME] **1** : the clipping or shaving of the head; *specif* : the shaving of a distinctive portion of the head as part of a rite accompanying admission to the clerical state **2** : the shaven crown or patch worn by monks and various clerics **3** : a bald spot that resembles a tonsure

²**tonsure** \ˈ"\ vt -ED/-ING/-S : to shave the head of : confer the tonsure upon

ton·sured \-(r)d\ adj [¹*tonsure* + *-ed*] **1** : shaven or shorn in the manner of one having a tonsure **2** : admitted by the rite of tonsure to the clerical state **3** : having a bald spot

¹**ton·tine** \ˈtän,tēn, =ˈ=\ n -s [F, fr. Lorenzo *Tonti* †1695 Ital. banker in Paris who invented the scheme + F *-ine*, fr. *-ine*, fem. of *-in* -ine, adj. suffix] : a financial arrangement (as an insurance policy) whereby a group of participants share various benefits or advantages on such terms that upon the death or default of any member a part or all of his advantages are distributed among all the remaining members until on the death of all but one the whole goes to him or on the expiration of an agreed period the whole goes to those then remaining in the group; *collectively* : the share or right of each individual

²**tontine** \ˈ"\ adj : relating to or involving the principle or system upon which the tontine is based ⟨~ fund⟩ ⟨~ loan⟩

tontine insurance n : participating life insurance providing for distribution of surplus according to the tontine principle — compare DEFERRED DIVIDEND

ton·tin·er \-ēnə(r)\ n -s [¹*tontine* + *-er*] : a sharer in a tontine

ton·to \ˈtän(ˌ)tō\ n, *pl* **tonto** *or* **tontos** *usu cap* [AmerSp, fr. Sp, fool, fr. *tonto* foolish] **1** : one of various subgroups of the Apache people **2** : an Indian of any one of several Apache subgroups

to·nus \ˈtōnəs\ n -ES [NL, fr. L, tension — more at TONE] : TONE 11a(1); *usu* : the state of partial contraction that is characteristic of normal muscle, is maintained at least in part by a continuous bombardment of motor impulses originating reflexly, and serves to maintain body posture and to hold the musculature in a state of readiness for specific demands — compare CLONUS

¹**tony** n -ES [fr. *Tony*, nickname for *Antony*] *obs* : FOOL, SIMPLETON

²**tony** *also* **toney** \ˈtōnē, -ni\ adj -ER/-EST [²*tone* + *-y*; influenced in meaning by ⁴*ton*] : HIGH-TONED, ARISTOCRATIC, STYLISH ⟨introduced me to all his ~ friends⟩ ⟨very expensive ~ restaurant⟩ : FASHIONABLE ⟨~ resort⟩ ⟨~ suburb⟩

³**tony** \ˈ"\ n, *pl* **tonys** *usu cap* [after *Tony*, nickname of *Antoinette* Perry †1946 Am. actress & producer] : any of several medallions awarded annually by a professional organization for notable performances in the theater

-to·ny \ˌtōnē, tᵊnē, -i\ n *comb form* -ES [NL *-tonia*] : -TONIA ⟨hyper*tony*⟩

too \(ˈ)tü\ adv [ME *to, too*, fr. OE *tō* to, too — more at TO] **1** : in addition : ALSO, BESIDES, MOREOVER ⟨must sell the house and the furniture ~⟩ ⟨in this group are, ~, the many species of frogfishes —R.E.Coker⟩ ⟨~, the reader will become aware of the ingenuity —J.D.Vehling⟩ ⟨naturally they become weaker . . . and ultimately must perish miserably from starvation, while many ~ are killed by their stronger companions —James Stevenson-Hamilton⟩ **2 a** : to an excessive degree : EXCESSIVELY ⟨the economic interpretation is ~ simple —M.R. Cohen⟩ ⟨~ often leans the other way —M.S.Watson⟩ ⟨a ~ easy formula —Max Lerner⟩ ⟨~ large a house for us⟩ ⟨~ old to walk —R.W.Hatch⟩ **b** : to such a degree as to be regrettable, painful, or reprehensible ⟨that's ~ bad⟩ ⟨all ~ true⟩ ⟨these suspicions were only ~ justified —*New Republic*⟩ ⟨has gone ~ far⟩ — often doubled for emphasis ⟨the peasants are just ~, ~ quaint — William Newberry⟩ **c** : to a high degree : EXTREMELY, EXTRAVAGANTLY, VERY ⟨standing and looking ~ languishing down by the door —Elizabeth Bowen⟩ ⟨how ~ terrible —Martha Gellhorn⟩ ⟨the first slope wasn't ~ bad although it was steep —L.A.Viereck⟩ ⟨an episodic work without ~ consistent a texture —Irving Kolodin⟩

toodle-oo \ˌtüdᵊlˈü\ interj [perh. imit. of an automobile horn] *chiefly Brit* : GOOD-BYE, SO LONG

took [ME (past), fr. OE *tōc* (past)] *past or dial past part of* TAKE

¹**tool** \ˈtül\ n -s *often attrib* [ME *tol, tool*, fr. OE *tōl*; akin to ON *tōl* tool, weapon, Goth *taujan* to do, make — more at TAW] **1 a** : an instrument (as a hammer or saw) used or worked by hand : an instrument used by a handicraftsman or laborer in his work : IMPLEMENT **b** (1) : the cutting or shaping part in a machine or machine tool (2) : a machine for shaping metal : MACHINE TOOL **c** : a particular kind of hand tool: as (1) : a bookbinder's instrument headed with a cut or engraved design with which impressions are made (as in finishing) (2) : a small brush used in painting window sashes **2 a** : an implement or object used in performing an operation or carrying on work of any kind : an instrument or apparatus necessary to a person in the practice of his vocation or profession ⟨a barber's chair, a photographer's camera, a scholar's books are all ~s⟩ **b** : something that serves as a means to an end : an instrument by which something is effected or accomplished ⟨words are the ~s with which men think —J.E.Gloag⟩ ⟨respected advertising as an indispensable ~ of business —*Newsweek*⟩ **c** *archaic* : SWORD, WEAPON **d** *slang* : PENIS **3** : one who is or allows himself to be used or manipulated by another : DUPE, PUPPET ⟨believes the whole business of witchcraft . . . and thinks that the old women who were burned were the ~s of a great conspiracy against religion and society —O.W.Holmes †1935⟩ ⟨an easy ~, deferential, glad to be of use —T.S.Eliot⟩ **syn** see IMPLEMENT

²**tool** \ˈ"\ vb -ED/-ING/-S vt **1 a** : to cause (a vehicle) to move along : DRIVE ⟨~*ed* the car expertly through dark alleys and back streets —John Faulkner⟩ **b** : to convey in a vehicle ⟨~*ed* him everywhere in a jeep —Hugh Fosburgh⟩ ⟨~*ing* him out to the starboard boat circle off the bow —K.M.Dodson⟩ **2** : to shape, form, or finish with a tool ⟨grotesque sandstone formations, ~*ed* by centuries of wind and weather into freak shapes —*Amer. Guide Series: Calif.*⟩ ⟨assumed that all aircraft parts are ~*ed* accurately —*Aero Digest*⟩: as **a** : to letter or ornament (a book cover) by means of heated hand tools **b** : to ornament the surface of (as a metal object) by means of hand tools **c** : to work on the surface of (a printing plate) with a hand tool (as to correct minor imperfections or engrave white lines) **3** : to equip (as a plant or industry) with the necessary tools, machines, and instruments for volume production ⟨the engine would be abandoned before the plant could be ~*ed* to make it —W.W.Stout⟩ — often used with *up* ⟨showed how easy it is to accumulate stockpiles, ~ up war industries —J.P. Baxter b. 1893⟩ ~ *vi* **1 a** : to drive or ride in a vehicle ⟨turned off the highway . . . and ~*ed* gently up the drive —R.P. Warren⟩ ⟨the usual crowd of space cadets ~*ing* along in a flying saucer —John McCarten⟩ **b** : to move along : PROCEED, TRAVEL ⟨my grandfather, in one race ~*ing* along at full gallop —Joyce Cary⟩ **2** : to use tools **3** : to equip a plant or industry for volume production by designing, building, and integrating the equipment (as machines, machine tools, precision instruments) required for making and assembling a product — often used with *up* ⟨the necessary time it takes to ~ up for new models —*Ethyl News*⟩

too·lach \ˈtü,lach\ n -s [native name in Australia] : a lightly built and heavily furred fawn gray wallaby (*Macropus greyi*) that is strikingly banded on face and rump and is nearly or wholly extinct due to excessive hunting

tool angle n **1** : the angle included between the top and front faces of a cutting tool **2** : an angle used to designate the form of the cutting edge of a tool — compare CLEARANCE 2e, CUTTING ANGLE, ⁶RAKE 3

tool apron n : APRON 3d(2)

toolbar \ˈ=,=\ n : a frame mounted at the rear of a tractor to which various implements may be attached

tool bit n : cutting material of square cross section a few inches

long that is shaped to perform a machining operation when clamped on a tool shank or holder
toolbox \'≈,≈\ *n* **1 :** a box or chest to hold tools — see BOX illustration **2 :** an adjustable mechanism containing the tool or cutter holder in a planing machine or other machine tool
tool crib *n* **:** CRIB 2g
tooled finish *n* **:** a finish on the face of a stone in which the corrugations made by the chisel or cutting tool extend in straight lines across the face of the stone
tooled joint *n* **:** a masonry joint in which the mortar is compressed and given a concave or V shape with a jointing tool while the mortar is still green — see JOINT illustration
tool engineer *n* **:** a specialist in tool engineering
tool engineering *n* **:** a division of industrial engineering whose function is to plan the processes of manufacture, develop the tools and machines, and integrate the facilities required for producing particular products with minimal expenditure of time, labor, and materials
tool·er \'tülə(r)\ *n* -s **:** one that tools ⟨a leather ~⟩
toolhead \'≈,≈\ *n* **:** a part of a machine (as of a lathe or planer) in which a tool or toolholder is clamped and which is provided with adjustments to bring the tool into the desired position
toolholder \'≈,≈≈\ *n* **:** a short steel bar having a shank at one end to fit into the toolhead of a machine and a clamp at the other end to hold small interchangeable cutting bits
toolhouse \'≈,≈\ *or* **toolshed** \'≈,≈\ *n* **:** a house or shed (as in a garden) for storing tools
tooling *n* -s [fr. gerund of ²*tool*] **1 :** a mechanical operation performed with or an effect produced by a tool: as **a :** stone dressing having a tooled finish **b :** a gilt or blind impression stamped in intaglio on ornamental leatherwork **c :** special ornamental handwork (as with a chisel or gouge) in any of various materials (as wood, metal, or ivory) **2 :** a set or group of tools; *specif* **:** an assembly of tools in a factory or workshop
tool·less \'tülləs\ *adj* **:** having no tools
toolmaker \'≈,≈≈\ *n* **:** one who makes and repairs tools; *specif* **:** a machinist who specializes in the construction, repair, maintenance, and calibration of the tools, jigs, fixtures, and instruments of a machine shop
toolmakers' button *n* **:** a small hardened steel jig for accurately locating holes to be drilled in a workpiece
toolmaking \'≈,≈≈\ *n* **:** the act, process, or art of making tools
tool·man \'≈mən\ *n, pl* **toolmen :** one who works with or makes tools; *specif* **:** a toolroom clerk
toolmark \'≈,≈\ *n* **:** a mark or impression made in tooling
toolmarking \'≈,≈≈\ *n* **:** the marking of a steel tool with figures, letters, or symbols
toolplate \'≈,≈\ *n* **:** TOOLBOX 2
tool post *n* **:** a slotted or channeled post or analogous part in a lathe or other machine tool in which the cutting tool is clamped
tool pusher *n, slang* **:** a foreman who supervises drilling operations at an oil well or group of oil wells
tool rest *n* **:** a support for a tool; *specif* **:** an adjustable horizontal bar for supporting a hand tool when turning
toolroom \'≈,≈\ *n* **:** a room where tools are kept; *esp* **:** a room in a machine shop in which tools are made, stored, or loaned out to the workmen
toolroom lathe *n* **:** an engine lathe designed for extremely accurate machining
tools *pl of* TOOL, *pres 3d sing of* TOOL
toolslide \'≈,≈\ *n* **:** a part that supports a cutting tool (as in a tool post) and that contains or is mounted upon sliding members which may be moved in ways provided for the purpose
toolsmith \'≈,≈\ *n* **:** a smith who forges, dresses, hardens, and tempers tools **:** TOOLMAKER
tool steel *n* **1 :** hard usu. electric steel capable of being tempered so as to be especially suitable as a material for tools **2 :** a high-carbon or alloy steel used to make a cutting tool for machining metals **3 :** steel used to make tools and dies for various purposes (as press tools, die-casting dies, forging dies, or extrusion tools)
tool subject *n* **:** a subject studied to achieve competence in a skill for use in other subjects ⟨graduate students in sociology are required to take statistics as a *tool subject*⟩ — compare CONTENT SUBJECT
¹toom \'tüm\ *adj* [ME *tom, toom* empty, fr. OE *tōm* — more at TEEM] *chiefly Scot* **:** being without content or substance **:** EMPTY
²toom \"\ *vt* -ED/-ING/-S *chiefly Scot* **:** EMPTY, POUR
³toom \"\ *n* -s [²*toom*] *Scot* **:** a dumping ground
too-much·ness \tü'mənchnəs\ *n* [fr. the phrase *too much* + *-ness*] **:** the quality or state of being excessive ⟨his prosodic devices, his lively games with adjectives and expletives, may weary us with a *too-muchness* today —*Times Lit. Supp.*⟩
¹toon \'tün\ *Scot var of* TOWN
²toon \"\ *n* -s [Hindi *tūn*, fr. Skt *tunna*] **1 :** an East Indian and Australian tree (*Cedrela toona*) with fragrant dark red wood and with flowers that yield a dye — called also *Moulmein cedar* **2 :** the wood of toon used esp. for furniture and general construction — called also *cedar, Indian mahogany, Moulmein cedar*
¹too·na \'tünə\ *n, cap* [NL, fr. E ²*toon*] **:** a small genus of Old World trees (family Meliaceae) closely related to *Cedrela* but having a short disk and completely winged seeds
²toona \"\ *n* -s [MexSp *tuna*] **:** a Mexican tree (*Castilloa elastica*) that is a minor source of rubber — compare CAUCHO
too·ner·ville \'tünə(r),vil, *esp south* -,vəl\ *adj, usu cap* [fr. the *Toonerville* (*trolley*), a rickety trolley car in the comic strip *Toonerville Trolley* by Fontaine Fox *b*1884 Am. cartoonist] **:** of, relating to, or constituting a rickety or inefficient railroad line ⟨even the *Toonerville* locals are terribly overcrowded, so make your reservations now —T.H.Fielding⟩
toor·ie \'türi\ *n* -s [*toor* (Sc, alter. of E *tower*) + *-ie*] **:** a tassel on a Scotch bonnet
¹toot \'tüt\ *vi* -ED/-ING/-S [ME *toten, tooten*, fr. OE *tōtian* — more at TOUT] **1** *chiefly dial* **:** to stand out **:** show above ground **:** SPROUT **2** *chiefly dial* **a :** GAZE, PEEP, SPY **b :** to look searchingly **:** PRY
²toot \'tüt, *usu* -üd·+V\ *n* -s [ME *tote*, fr. *toten, tooten*, v.] *chiefly dial* **:** an elevation used or capable of being used as a lookout; *specif* **:** a rocky promontory
³toot \"\ *vb* -ED/-ING/-S [prob. of imit. origin like MLG & MD *tūten* to toot] *vi* **1 a** *of a wind instrument* **:** to sound a short blast ⟨a horn ~*ed* in the distance⟩ **b :** to sound a note or call suggesting the short blast of a wind instrument ⟨the ~*ing* of the heath hen could be heard each spring —A.A. Allen⟩ **2 a :** to blow or sound a horn or other wind instrument esp. so as to produce short rapid blasts ⟨a trumpeter who has ~*ed* in many bands⟩ ⟨boarded a train a few miles out of town, and the entourage came puffing and ~*ing* up to the base of the platform —*Americas*⟩ **3 :** to drive, proceed, or move along esp. in a car ⟨agricultural-extension workers ~ around the . . . farmlands —Phil Gustafson⟩ **4** *slang* **:** to state the truth **:** assert something as a fact ⟨you're ~*ing*, you won't stop me —R.P.Warren⟩ ~ *vt* **1 :** to spread abroad **:** PROCLAIM, TRUMPET ⟨~*ed* his friend's praises wherever he went⟩ **2 a :** to sound (a note) on a horn or other wind instrument ⟨the bugle ~*ed* retreat⟩ **b :** to cause (a wind instrument) to produce a characteristic sound ⟨~ a horn⟩ ⟨~ a trumpet⟩ ⟨~ a whistle⟩ — **toot one's horn** *or* **toot one's own horn :** blow one's horn **:** BOAST ⟨goes around *tooting his horn* merely because he's charitable —Sinclair Lewis⟩
⁴toot \"\ *n* -s **:** a short blast sounded on a wind instrument (as a horn): *also* **:** a sound resembling or suggesting such a blast
⁵toot \'tüt\ *vb* -ED/-ING/-S [origin unknown] *vi, Scot* **:** to drink heavily ~ *vt, Scot* **:** to drink deeply of **:** QUAFF
⁶toot \'tüt, *usu* -üd·+V\ *n* -s **1** *Scot* **:** a drink of liquor **:** SNORT **2 a :** a drinking bout **:** SPREE ⟨used to go on a ~, and one night when he was drunk he told me —R.M.Dorson⟩ ⟨all hands went on a joyous ~ —James Dugan⟩ **b :** an act or period of unrestrained indulgence in some feeling or activity **:** BINGE, JAG ⟨any business taking off on an inflationary ~ —*Sacramento (Calif.) Bee*⟩ ⟨survived each of these emotional ~*s* —T.H.White b. 1915⟩
⁷toot \'tüt\ *interj* [prob. imit. of a tongue-clicking sound] *Scot* — used to express disapproval or disbelief
⁸toot \"\ *n* -s [origin unknown] *dial* **:** a worthless person **:** FOOL
⁹toot \'tu̇t\ *n* -s [PaG *dutt*, fr. MLG *tūte* horn, horn-shaped object; akin to Icel *tūta* sharp projection, Sw *tuta* fingerstall] *dial* **:** any of various conical containers: as **a :** a small paper bag **b :** a piece of paper twisted into the shape of a cone and used as a temporary container (as for mustard) **c :** ICE-CREAM CONE
toot·er \'tüd·ə(r), -ütə-\ *n* -s [³*toot* + *-er*] **:** one that toots
¹tooth \'tüth\ *n, pl* **teeth** \'tēth\ *often attrib* [ME *toth, tooth*, fr. OE *tōth*; akin to OHG *zand* tooth, ON *tönn*, Goth *tunthus*, L *dent-, dens*, Gk *odont-, odōn, odous*, Skt *danta* tooth, and prob. to OE *etan* to eat — more at EAT] **1 a :** one of the hard bony appendages that are borne on the jaws or in many of the lower vertebrates on other bones in the walls of the mouth or pharynx and serve esp. for the prehension and mastication of food and as weapons of offense and defense — see CANINE, FANG, INCISOR, MOLAR, PREMOLAR, TUSK; CROWN, ROOT; CEMENTUM, DENTIN, ENAMEL **b :** any of various usu. hard and sharp horny, chitinous, or calcareous processes about the mouth (as on the radula of a mollusk or the mastax of a rotifer) or about any part (as the forceps of an ear wig) of an invertebrate that functions like or resembles the vertebrate jaws **c :** a toothlike process on a bivalve shell — see HINGE TOOTH **2 a :** a fondness or taste for something specified **:** LIKING ⟨an insatiable ~ for candy⟩ **3 :** an angular or rounded projection resembling or suggesting the tooth of an animal in shape, arrangement, or action ⟨a saw ~⟩ ⟨the *teeth* of a comb⟩ ⟨the *teeth* of a rake⟩: as **a :** one of the regular projections on the circumference or sometimes on the face of a wheel (as in a machine) that engage with the corresponding projections on another wheel esp. to transmit force and motion **:** COG **b :** a small sharp-pointed marginal lobe (as of a leaf) **c :** a sharp jagged point or projection ⟨their slopes loaded with packed snow and fanged with the brittle *teeth* of icicles —Victor Canning⟩ ⟨to the westward . . . a line of jagged *teeth* proclaim . . . our ultimate objective —Wynford Vaughan-Thomas⟩ **d :** any of the bricks or stones left projecting from a wall to provide for a subsequent extension **e :** a projection of paper between perforation holes on a severed perforated edge (as of a stamp) — called also *perforation tooth* **4 a :** something that injures, tortures, devours, or destroys as if by a biting, piercing, or gnawing action ⟨only the classic can endure the ~ of time —Elinor Wylie⟩ ⟨the *teeth* of the wind⟩ **b teeth** *pl* **:** effective means of compulsion, enforcement, or punishment ⟨started turning out the arms which would put *teeth* into neutrality —E.O.Hauser⟩ ⟨reluctant to pass legislation with *teeth* regarding this issue —T.L.Reller⟩ **5 :** a roughness of surface produced by mechanical or artificial means on a surface or thing: as **a :** a roughness of surface on a material (as paper or canvas) that enables it readily to take ink, crayon, paints, or water colors **b :** the roughness given an undercoat of paint to anchor the next coat **c :** a mat surface on a negative film; *specif* **:** a fine varnish coating that permits pencil marks in retouching — **from the teeth forward** *or* **from the teeth outward** *archaic* **:** not from the heart **:** in outward appearance only **:** on the surface — **in the teeth of 1 :** in or into direct contact or collision with **:** so as directly to confront or be confronted with ⟨headed north *in the teeth of* the steadily rising gale —N.R.Raine⟩ ⟨*in the teeth of* conditions to drive a normal actor crazy —Kenneth Tynan⟩ **2 :** in direct opposition to **:** in defiance of ⟨to express such views was to fly *in the teeth of* the age —Roy Lewis & Angus Maude⟩ — **set one's teeth on edge** *also* **put one's teeth on edge 1 :** to cause a disagreeable sensation in the teeth ⟨the fathers have eaten sour grapes, and *the children's teeth are set on edge* —Jer 31:29(RSV)⟩ **2 :** EXASPERATE ⟨the constant chattering of the children *set his teeth on edge*⟩ — **to one's teeth** *archaic* **:** to one's face **:** OPENLY ⟨that I shall live and tell him *to his teeth* —Shak.⟩ — **to the teeth** *adv* **:** COMPLETELY, FULLY ⟨armed *to the teeth*⟩ ⟨a theory in which my father upheld her *to the teeth* —Della Lutes⟩

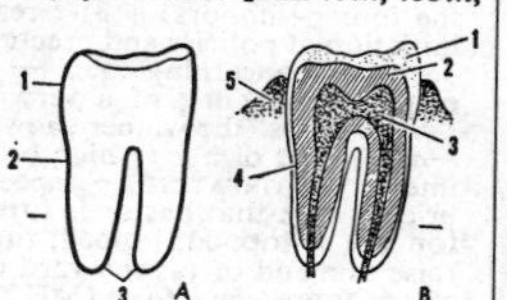

tooth 1a: *A*, outside of a molar: *1* crown, *2* neck, *3* roots; *B*, cross section of a molar: *1* enamel, *2* dentin, *3* pulp chamber, *4* cementum, *5* gum

²tooth \", 'tüth\ *vb* -ED/-ING/-S [ME *tothen, toothen*, fr. *toth, tooth*, n.] *vt* **1 :** to furnish with teeth; *specif* **:** INDENT, JAG ⟨~ a saw⟩ **2 :** to chew on **:** BITE **3 :** to lock into by means of teeth **4 :** to roughen the surface of (as with a toothing plane) ~ *vi* **:** to engage by means of teeth **:** GEAR, MESH
toothache \'≈,≈\ *n* [ME *tothache*, fr. *toth, tooth* tooth + *ache*] **:** pain in or about a tooth
toothache bark *n* **:** the bark of the prickly ash
toothache grass *n* **:** a tall grass (*Ctenium aromaticum*) of southern U. S. that has dense one-sided spikes and a very pungent taste
toothache tree *n* **:** PRICKLY ASH 1
toothachy \'≈,≈≈\ *adj* **:** suffering from or suggesting toothache
tooth and nail *adv* **:** with every available means of attack or defense **:** ALL OUT, FIERCELY ⟨swallowed their gallant words and fought the measure *tooth and nail* —C.G.Bowers⟩
toothbill \'≈,≈\ *n* **:** TOOTH-BILLED PIGEON
tooth-billed \'≈'≈\ *adj* **:** having a notched bill
tooth-billed pigeon *n* **:** a Samoan pigeon (*Didunculus strigirostris*) that has a bill superficially resembling that of the extinct dodo, a chiefly chestnut brown body with a greenish black head and neck, and a lower mandible with several notches near the end
toothbrush \'≈,≈\ *n* **:** a brush for cleaning the teeth
toothbrush mustache *n* **:** a small bristly mustache
toothbrush tree *n* **:** an Old World tree (*Salvadora persica*), whose twigs are sometimes bound in clusters and used as toothbrushes

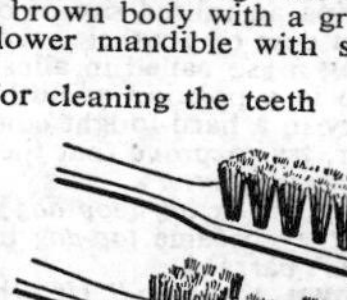
toothbrushes

tooth bud *or* **tooth germ** *n* **:** a mass of tissue having the potentiality of differentiating into a tooth
toothcomb \'≈,≈\ *n, Brit* **:** a comb with fine teeth
tooth coral *n* **:** CACTUS CORAL
toothcup \'≈,≈\ *n* **1 :** a low-growing No. American herb (*Rotala ramosior*) found on sandy shores and having solitary flowers and regularly splitting capsules **2 :** a low herb (*Ammania coccinea*) of the family Lythraceae chiefly found in southern U. S. and having narrow leaves and flowers in clusters of two, three, or several in the leaf axils
toothed \'tüths *sometimes* -üthd\ *adj* [ME *tothed, toothed*, fr. *toth, tooth* tooth + *-ed*] **1 a :** provided with teeth ⟨a ~ animal⟩ **:** BITING ⟨a gray world, with ice and ~ winds —*N.Y. Times*⟩ **b :** having such or so many teeth — usu. used in combination ⟨buck-*toothed*⟩ **c :** COGGED ⟨a ~ wheel⟩ **2 :** having marginal projecting points **:** DENTATE
toothed bur clover *n* **:** a bur clover (*Medicago hispida*)
toothed herring *n* **:** MOONEYE 2a
toothed spurge *n* **:** an annual weed (*Euphorbia dentata*) of northeastern No. America with dentate leaves
toothed whale *n* **:** any of various whales comprising the suborder Odontoceti and having numerous simple conical teeth — compare WHALEBONE WHALE
tooth·er \'tüthə(r), -üthə-\ *n* -s [²*tooth* + *-er*] **:** one that cuts out the teeth of saws
tooth·ful \'tüth,fu̇l\ *n* -s **:** a small bite or mouthful; *esp* **:** a small drink of liquor
tooth fungus *n* **:** a fungus of the family Hydnaceae
toothier *comparative of* TOOTHY
toothiest *superlative of* TOOTHY
tooth·i·ly \'tüthəlē, -li\ *adv* **:** in a toothy manner ⟨bowing low and grinning ~ —E.J.Kahn⟩
tooth·ing \'tüthiŋ, -üth-, -ēŋ\ *n* -s [in sense 1, fr. ¹*tooth* + *-ing*; in sense 2, fr. gerund of ²*tooth*] **1 a :** an arrangement, formation, or projection consisting of or containing teeth or parts resembling teeth **:** INDENTATION, SERRATION **b :** an arrangement of bricks alternately projecting at the end of a wall to permit bonding into a later continuation of the wall **2 :** the act or process of furnishing with teeth or a tooth
tooth·less \'tüthləs\ *adj* [ME *tothles, toothles*, fr. *toth, tooth* + *-les* -less] **1 a :** not yet supplied with teeth **:** not having cut one's teeth ⟨a ~ baby⟩ **b :** not provided with teeth ⟨a ~ animal⟩ ⟨a ~ saw⟩ **c :** having lost one's teeth ⟨a ~ old woman⟩ **2 a :** lacking in sharpness or bite ⟨spoke in ~ generalities —Arthur Hepner⟩ **b :** lacking in means of enforcement or coercion **:** FUTILE, INEFFECTUAL ⟨a ~ piece of legislation —*Nature Mag.*⟩ — **tooth·less·ly** *adv* — **tooth·less·ness** *n* -ES
tooth·let \-lət\ *n* -s **:** a small tooth (as on a shell)
toothlike \'≈,≈\ *adj* **:** resembling or suggesting a tooth or teeth **:** SERRATE
tooth ornament *n* **:** DOGTOOTH 2
toothpaste \'≈,≈\ *n* **:** a paste dentifrice
toothpick \'≈,≈\ *n* [ME (Sc) *tuthpik*, fr. *toth, tooth, tuth* tooth + *pik* pick — more at TOOTH, PICK] **1 a :** a slender pointed piece of wood used after eating to remove bits of food lodged between the teeth **b :** a similar instrument of metal, bone, or plastic used for picking the teeth and cleaned for reuse **2 :** a wooden toothpick or a small flat tapering piece of wood or plastic used for spearing and holding together small portions of prepared food or for conveying one mouthful to the mouth **3 toothpicks** *pl* **:** FRAGMENTS, SPLINTERS ⟨the ship was smashed into ~*s* by the storm⟩ **4 :** a long thin object or person ⟨wearing heels that are ~*s*⟩ ⟨a ~ of a man⟩: as **a** (1) **:** ARKANSAS TOOTHPICK (2) *usu cap* **:** ARKANSAN — used as a nickname **b :** a slender pointed boat
tooth·pick·er \-kə(r)\ *n* **:** a worker who places glass beads on toothpicks for further processing in the manufacture of synthetic pearls
tooth powder *n* **:** a dentifrice in powder form
tooth rail *n* **:** COGRAIL
tooth rash *n* **:** STROPHULUS
tooths *pres 3d sing of* TOOTH
tooth sac *n* **:** DENTAL SAC
tooth shell *n* **1 :** a mollusk of the class Scaphopoda **2 :** the shell of a tooth shell having the shape of an elephant's tusk and formerly used as money by the Indians along the northwest coast of No. America
tooth·some \'tüthsəm\ *adj* [¹*tooth* + *-some*] **1 :** pleasing to the taste **:** DELICIOUS ⟨grandmother's ~ battercakes —S.H. Adams⟩ **2 :** AGREEABLE, PLEASANT ⟨the taste of power is ~ —Helen Howe⟩ **3 :** sexually attractive **:** DELECTABLE, LUSCIOUS ⟨a ~ blond baggage . . . standing there in an unbelievably tight emerald gown —*New Yorker*⟩ **syn** see PALATABLE
tooth·some·ly *adv* **:** in a toothsome manner
tooth·some·ness *n* -ES **:** the quality or state of being toothsome
toothwort \'≈,≈\ *n* **1 :** a European plant (*Lathraea squamaria*) parasitic on the hazel and beech and having a rootstock covered with toothlike scales **2 :** any of various hardy perennial creeping herbs comprising the genus *Dentaria* and including several that are cultivated for their showy usu. white, rose, or purple flowers — called also *pepperroot*; compare CORALWORT, CRINKLEROOT

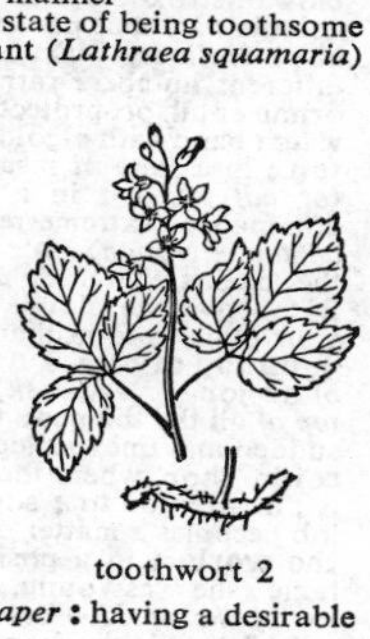
toothwort 2

toothy \'tüth|ē, -th|, |i\ *adj* -ER/-EST [¹*tooth* + *-y*] **1 :** having or showing prominent teeth ⟨he smiled broad ~ smiles —Walter Goodman⟩ **2 a** *archaic* **:** BITING, SHARP ⟨~ critics —Robert Burns⟩ **b :** equipped with teeth **:** EFFECTUAL ⟨the pact is not as ~ as once intended —*Time*⟩ **3 :** TOOTHSOME ⟨the ~ morsel within —*Manufacturing Confectioner*⟩ **4** *of paper* **:** having a desirable roughness of surface
tooting *pres part of* TOOT
¹too·tle \'tüd·ᵊl, -üt'l\ *vb* **tootled; tootled; tootling** \-d·ᵊliŋ, -t(ᵊ)liŋ\ **tootles** [freq. of ³*toot*] *vi* **1 a :** to make a repeated tooting noise ⟨the birds *tootling* in the trees⟩ **b :** to toot gently, repeatedly, or continuously on a wind instrument ⟨the final chorus with three high trumpets *tootling* for dear life —Virgil Thomson⟩ **2 :** to write or talk nonsense **3 :** to drive or move along **:** make one's way ⟨cheerfully *tootling* around England in their cars last weekend —Mollie Panter-Downes⟩ ⟨think I'll ~ off to bed —Dorothy Sayers⟩ ~ *vt* **1 :** to toot continuously on ⟨musical instruments which are scraped, *tootled*, and banged by millions —*Newsweek*⟩ **2 :** to produce by a continued or prolonged tooting ⟨birds began to ~ their songs of joy —P.G.Wodehouse⟩
²tootle \"\ *n* -s **1 :** the act, action, or sound of tootling ⟨can make it give off ~*s* of varying lengths —*New Yorker*⟩ **2 :** feeble or verbose writing or speech **:** TWADDLE
too·tler \'tüd·ᵊlə(r), -üt(ᵊ)l-\ *n* -s **:** one that tootles
toot net *n* [¹*toot*] *Scot* **:** a large anchored fishing net
¹too-too \'tü'tü\ *adv* [redupl. of *too*] **:** to an unpleasantly or affectedly excessive degree ⟨openly sneered . . . at those who prefer the *too-too* refined type of whodunit —*Time*⟩
²too-too \"\ *adj* **:** going beyond the bounds of convention, good taste, or common sense **:** EXCESSIVE, EXTREME; *esp* **:** affected in manner or behavior **:** LA-DI-DA ⟨isn't he just *too-too* —Chet Straight⟩
³too-too \(')tü'tü\ *vi* -ED/-ING/-S [imit.] **:** to produce or utter a flat monotonous tootling sound
¹toots *pres 3d sing of* TOOT, *pl of* TOOT
²toots \'tüts\ *Scot var of* ⁷TOOT
³toots \'tu̇ts\ *n* -ES [prob. short for *tootsie*] *slang* **:** WOMAN, GIRL ⟨hi, ~ . . . so you're out of jail again —H.T.Carter⟩
toot·sie \'tu̇tsē, -si\ *n* -s [origin unknown] **1** *slang* **:** DEAR, SWEETHEART **2** *slang* **:** PARTY GIRL ⟨a ~ he picked up in the lobby of a hotel —Alfred Hayes⟩
toot·sy *also* **toot·sie** \'tu̇tsē, -si\ *n, pl* **tootsies** [alter. of *footsie*] **:** FOOT ⟨cover baby's *tootsies* —Joy Warren⟩
tootsy-wootsy \'tu̇tsē'wu̇tsē\ *n* -ES [by redupl.] **:** TOOTSIE 1
¹top \'täp\ *n* -s [ME *top, toppe*, fr. OE *top*; akin to OHG *zopf* end, tip, tuft of hair, ON *toppr* tuft of hair, crest, top and perh. to OE *tæppa* tap — more at TAP] **1 a** (1) **:** the highest point, level, or part of something **:** the upper end, edge, or extremity **:** SUMMIT, CROWN ⟨looked over the ~*s* of his half-spectacles —Marcia Davenport⟩ ⟨slopes leading toward the mesa-*top* —*Amer. Antiquity*⟩ ⟨the ~ of the beach —Sally Carrighar⟩ ⟨the ~ of the pass⟩ (2) **:** the highest part of the body **:** the head or top of the head — used esp. in the phrase *top to toe* (3) **:** the head of a plant; *esp* **:** the part of a plant with edible roots that is above ground ⟨beet ~*s*⟩ (4) **:** the part of a cut gem above the girdle **:** CROWN, BEZEL (5) **:** the upper part of a garment; *esp* **:** the jacket of pajamas (6) **:** a garment worn on the upper body (7) **:** TOP MILK **b** (1) **:** the highest or uppermost region or parts ⟨dive bombers . . . dive off the ~ of the sky —Ira Wolfert⟩; *esp* **:** the uppermost story (as the attic) of a building ⟨at the ~ of the house lived a medical student —W.B.Yeats⟩ — compare TREETOP (2) **:** the surface normally or at present facing upward as opposed to the undersurface **:** the side that overlies the whole ⟨cumulus clouds . . . with flat bases and rounded ~*s* —O.W.Perrie⟩ ⟨marked at several places to indicate where the ~ of the concrete should be —*Building, Estimating & Contracting*⟩ (3) **:** the part of a thing placed uppermost in use ⟨the ~ of the page⟩ (4) **:** the surface of the land or ocean ⟨the submarine came to the ~⟩; *also* **:** the point at which an underground shaft, tunnel, or well reaches the surface **2 a** *dial* **:** a crowning tuft: (1) **:** the hair on the head (2) **:** CREST 1a **b** *dial* **:** a tuft of textile fiber; *specif* **:** a bunch of flax tow placed on a distaff **c** (1) **:** a continuous strand of the longer wool fibers after straightening and separating from the short fibers by combing (2) **:** a similar strand of rayon staple fiber **3 :** a fitted, integral, or attached part or unit serving as an upper piece, endpiece, lid, or covering ⟨an ornamented steamboat smokestack ~ —Frederick Way⟩ ⟨saving box ~*s* for premiums⟩ ⟨a jar with a threaded ~⟩: as **a :** a metal, plastic, or fabric roof over the passenger compartment of a vehicle that is permanent or capable of being folded back, lowered, or removed **b :** the turndown part or band on a top boot **c** *Brit* **:** a ceiling esp. in a mine **d :** the upper of a shoe; *esp* **:** the parts above the vamp **e :** a circus or carnival tent **4 a :** a platform surround-

ing the head of a lower mast that serves to spread the topmast rigging, strengthen the mast, and furnish a standing place for men aloft **b :** a comparable part of the superstructure; *esp* **:** such a part on a warship used as a fire-control station or antiaircraft gun platform **5 :** the part that is nearest in space or time to the source or beginning ⟨the ~ of the lake⟩ ⟨the ~ of the morning⟩; *specif* **:** the first half of an inning in the game of baseball **6 :** TOPSAIL **7 a** (1) **:** the highest degree conceivable, attainable, or attained **:** ACME, PINNACLE ⟨singing at the ~ of a form that is unmatched anywhere —*Theatre Arts*⟩ ⟨the high temperature reading . . . compared with an 87.2 ~ on Friday —*N.Y. Times*⟩ (2) **:** the loudest or highest range of a sound ⟨shouted at the ~ of his lungs⟩ ⟨a soprano with a weak ~⟩ (3) *Brit* **:** ³HIGH 2b (4) **:** the price of the most expensive seats for a performance ⟨a show having a six-dollar ~⟩ **b** *archaic* **:** the highest realization or embodiment **:** the most perfect actualization or instance **c :** the height at which something that has been advancing recedes **:** culminating point **:** MAXIMUM ⟨sail with the ~ of the tide —Rachel Henning⟩ ⟨the all-time ~ for fishermen's earnings —*Pacific Fisherman*⟩ ⟨stocks bought at the ~ of the market⟩ **8 a** (1) **:** the highest position in rank, achievement, honor, success, or fame ⟨the ~ of his profession⟩ ⟨~ of the bill⟩ ⟨the ~ of his class⟩; *esp* **:** the position of a person or group wielding supreme authority ⟨bribery has reached from the ~ right down to the lowest clerical level —*Atlantic*⟩ ⟨access to someone very near the ~ —Thomas Barman⟩ (2) **:** a person or thing at the top ⟨the news of the rising situation got through . . . to the Congress . . . ~s —*Spark*⟩ **b** (1) **:** a playing card higher than any held in the same suit by an opponent (2) **tops** *pl* **:** aces and kings in a hand or the three highest honors in a suit (3) *or* **top score :** the highest match-point score made at duplicate bridge on a particular board or the highest total of match points scored during a session by one contestant or team **9 a :** the choicest part **:** the best or finest of its lot or kind **:** CREAM, PICK **b tops** *pl* **:** the choicest animals in a flock or herd **c tops** *pl, Brit* **:** ARISTOCRATS **10 a :** the part of a thing that is conventionally highest or occupies the most important position ⟨the arctic, the frozen ~ of the world —Carey Longmire⟩ ⟨our pilots rolled to the ~ of the runway —P.J.C. Friedlander⟩ ⟨the ~ of the room⟩ ⟨set her down at the ~ of the street —Maurice Hewlett⟩ **b :** the end of a billiard table opposite to that marked with the balkline in English billiards ⟨a *top-of-the-table game*⟩ **11 :** TOP BOOT **12 :** a button finished (as by plating) only on the face **13 :** a forward spin given to a ball (as in golf, tennis, billiards, or cricket) by striking it on or near the top or above the center; *also* **:** the blow or stroke so given **14 :** FIRST SERGEANT 1 **15 :** the most volatile part that passes over first on distillation — often used in pl. ⟨refinery ~s⟩ **16 :** a die marked with usu. only three different numbers rather than the usual six **17 :** an outer ornamental or protective coating or layer ⟨a stainless steel watch band with a gold ~⟩ — compare BLACKTOP — **off one's top :** in a state of insanity or mental agitation — **on top** *adv* (*or adj*) **1 a :** in a state of accomplishment, success, or dominance ⟨extreme reactionary . . . elements have come out *on top* —*Nation*⟩ **b :** in the lead ⟨the horse went *on top* in the backstretch⟩ **2** *also* **on the top** *Brit* **:** in high gear **3 :** above the clouds or bad weather ⟨when flying *on top*, your plane is in brilliant sunshine —*What Goes On Up There*⟩ — **on top of** *prep* **1 a :** in control of ⟨acted like a man *on top of* his job —*Newsweek*⟩ **b :** informed about ⟨readers right *on top of* all the news that's fit to print —*N.Y. Times*⟩ **2 :** in sudden and unexpected proximity to ⟨I was right *on top of* the coffin shop when the door opened —Margery Allingham⟩ **3 :** in addition to **:** superadded to ⟨writing *on top of* a regular job becomes a matter of stamina —N.M.Loomis⟩ — **on top of the world :** in a position of eminent success, happiness, or fame ⟨she was young, and prettier than the sea, and I was *on top of the world* —Barnaby Conrad⟩ — **over the top** *adv* (*or adj*) **1 :** over the front of a trench in attacking **2 :** over the assigned goal or limit ⟨the drive had gone *over the top* and considerably more than 200 dollars was collected —*Irish Digest*⟩ — **the top of one's head** *or* **the top of one's mind :** mental elements not directly involved in a present task or only partially directed or controlled ⟨with *the top of his mind* he listened to them —William Faulkner⟩ ⟨countless conferences at which everyone talked off *the top of their heads* —Goodman Ace⟩

²**top** \"\ *n* -s [ME *top, toupe*, fr. OE *top* & OF *toupie, topoie*, of Gmc origin; akin to MD *dop* top, OHG *topf*] **1 :** a child's toy that is commonly cylindrical, pear-shaped, or conoidal and has a tapering usu. steel-shod point on which it is made to spin by means of the fingers, a string, or a spring, or by whipping — see PEG TOP, WHIPPING TOP **2 :** a conical block of wood with longitudinal grooves on its surface in which strands of rope slide in the process of twisting

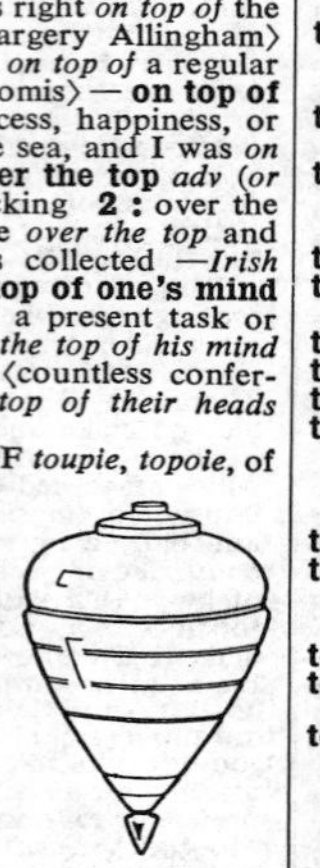
top 1

³**top** \"\ *vb* **topped; topped; topping; tops** [ME *topen, toppen*, fr. *top, toppe* top — more at TOP (head)] *vt* **1 :** to remove or cut the top of: as **a :** to prune the top or leaves of (a plant esp. of a root crop) ⟨~ carrots⟩ **b :** to execute by hanging **c :** to cut, break, or otherwise take off the top of (a steel ingot) to remove unsound metal **d :** to cut the top part from (a tree) in logging — compare CLIMBER 1a **e :** PINCH 1b (2) **f :** to remove the most volatile parts (as crude petroleum) from **:** STRIP 15a, SKIM **2 a :** to cover with a top or on the top **:** provide, form, or serve as a top for **:** complete by giving or serving as a covering, endpiece, crown, or cup for ⟨arches that ~ the windows —*Amer. Guide Series: N.H.*⟩ ⟨a black mop of curls *topping* a sleepy face —Winifred Bambrick⟩ ⟨the city's educational system is *topped* by four degree-granting colleges —*Amer. Guide Series: N.Y.*⟩ **b** (1) **:** to supply with a decorative or protective finish or a final touch — often used with *off* ⟨*topped* off the day with an hour's dancing—Bernard DeVoto⟩ (2) **:** to cover with another dye ⟨~ aniline black with methyl violet to prevent greening and crocking⟩ (3) **:** TIP 3 (4) **:** to resupply or esp. refuel (something partially exhausted) to capacity — usu. used with *off* ⟨log . . . showed she was *topped* off with fuel —Chesley Wilson⟩ (5) *West* **:** to finish breaking in (a horse) ⟨all these prospects had been *topped* and ridden several times —Jo Mora⟩ — usu. used with *off* or *out* ⟨the horse may still buck . . . but now the peeler can start *topping* it off —S.E.Fletcher⟩ **3 a** (1) **:** to be or become higher than **:** come to or over the top of **:** OVERTOP ⟨the water *topped* the boathouse⟩ ⟨*topped* by three other peaks in the state —*Amer. Guide Series: Vt.*⟩ (2) **:** to be in excess of ⟨ski crowds have *topped* 5000 in a single day —Jean Lunzer⟩ ⟨world wheat production has *topped* that of rice —Margaret K. Zieman⟩ ⟨the best year in its history . . . *topping* record 1953 —*Wall Street Jour.*⟩ **b** (1) **:** to be superior to **:** do better than **:** EXCEL, SURPASS, OUTDO ⟨intends to ~ herself in her next picture —Robert Trumbull⟩ ⟨~s everything of the kind in print —Alfred Frankenstein⟩ (2) **:** to perform (a part) eminently or better than before **c :** to gain ascendancy over **:** DOMINATE ⟨the base shall ~ the legitimate —Shak.⟩ **4 a** (1) **:** to rise to or reach the top of **:** ascend to the upper surface or esp. the summit of ⟨*topped* the backbone of the continent—A.B.Guthrie⟩ (2) **:** to go over the top of **:** CLEAR, SURMOUNT ⟨the horse *topped* the barrier⟩ (3) **:** to rise above the level of ⟨the plane was to ~ the storm —*Newsweek*⟩ **b** (1) **:** to be at the top of ⟨story that *topped* the nation's best-seller list —W.H.Whyte⟩ ⟨a great beech . . . *topped* a small knoll —Susan Ertz⟩ (2) **:** to be the highest card in (a suit) ⟨a suit *topped* by the ace⟩ (3) **:** to be in the most prominent or featured position of ⟨~ the bill⟩ **5 :** COVER 10a **6 :** to strike (a golf ball) above the center; *also* **:** to make (as a stroke) by hitting the ball in this way ~ *vi* **:** to make an end, finish, or conclusion — used with such prepositions as *off, out,* or *up* ⟨*topped* off with coffee⟩

⁴**top** \"\ *adj* [ME *top, toppe*, fr. *top, toppe*, n., top] **1 a :** of, relating to, or at the top **:** HIGHEST, TOPMOST, UPPERMOST ⟨~ floor⟩ ⟨in man the larynx sits at the ~ end of a windpipe —G. A.Miller⟩ **b :** serving as or constituting a top ⟨the ~ crust of a pie⟩ **2 a** (1) **:** foremost in order, rank, achievement, value, or precedence **:** CHIEF, HEAD, PREEMINENT ⟨the ~ painter of his time —Margaret Biddle⟩ ⟨two of the nation's ~ twenty-five banks —T.H.White b.1915⟩ ⟨ranked among the ~ six men of his class —*Current Biog.*⟩ ⟨~ priority⟩ **:** of prime importance or interest ⟨it should have been . . . the ~ thought and concern of theater men —Bosley Crowther⟩ ⟨~ essential for stained-glass making is lead —H.L.Morrow⟩ ⟨the ~ news . . . has dealt with cases of flagrant corruption —Sidney Warren⟩ (2) **:** being the highest or a high card of a suit ⟨a suit headed by the four ~ honors⟩ (3) **:** responsible for the planning and initiation of policies and practices and for making the principal decisions concerning them — distinguished from *middle* ⟨~ management⟩ **b :** of a very high quality **:** extremely good **:** FIRST-CLASS ⟨the winner showed ~ form⟩ ⟨~ sports coverage —*advt*⟩ **3 :** of a very high or the highest degree, amount, or intensity **:** GREATEST ⟨~ speed⟩ ⟨commodities selling at ~ prices⟩ **4 :** that has or is fitted with a top ⟨~ buggy⟩

⁵**top** \"\ *vt* **topped; topped; topping; tops** [perh. fr. ¹*top*] **:** to raise one end of (as the yard of a sail) higher than the other

top- *or* **topo-** *comb form* [ME, fr. LL, fr. Gk, fr. *topos* — more at TOPIC] **1 :** place **:** locality ⟨*topophobia*⟩ **2 :** local ⟨*topoalgia*⟩ ⟨*topectomy*⟩

top *abbr* topographic; topographical

TOP *abbr* temporarily out of print

top-and-butt \ˌ=ˈ=ˌ=\ *adj* **:** having the butt of one plank brought to the top of the other to make up a constant breadth in two layers ⟨*top-and-butt* planking⟩

toparch \ˈtōˌpärk, ˈtäˌp-\ *n* -s [LL *toparcha*, fr. Gk *toparchēs*, fr. *top-* + *-archēs* -arch] **:** a minor ruler or prince; *specif* **:** the governor of a toparchy

topar·chy \-kē\ *n* -ES [L *toparchia*, fr. Gk, fr. *toparchēs* toparch + *-ia* -y] **:** a small state or district consisting of a few cities or towns

top-armor \ˈ=ˌ==\ *n* **:** a railing of canvas or netting around a top on a ship

to·pa·to \təˈpād·(ˌ)ō\ *n* -ES [blend of *tomato* and *potato*] **:** POMATO

to·paz \ˈtōˌpaz\ *n* -ES [ME *topace*, fr. OF *topace, topaze*, fr. L *topazus, topazos*, fr. Gk *topazos, topazion*] **1 a :** a mineral $Al_2SiO_4(F,OH)$ consisting of a silicate of aluminum and usu. occurring in white orthorhombic translucent or transparent crystals or in white translucent masses **b :** a usu. yellow, reddish, or pink transparent mineral topaz used as a gem **c :** ORIENTAL TOPAZ **d :** a yellow quartz: as (1) **:** FALSE TOPAZ (2) **:** smoky quartz turned yellow by heating **2 :** either of two large brilliantly colored So. American hummingbirds (*Topaza pella* and *T. pyra*) that have a metallic yellowish green throat with a tint like topaz in the center, a bright crimson belly and red back, and in the male the two tail feathers next to the central ones much longer than the rest, curved, and crossed **3 :** a variable color averaging a dark orange yellow that is redder and duller than average amber (sense 3a)

to·paz·ine \ˈtōpəˌzēn, -əzən\ *adj* **:** resembling a topaz in color or luster

to·paz·o·lite \tōˈpazəˌlīt\ *n* -s [F, fr. *topaze* topaz + *-o-* + *-lite*] **:** a topaz-yellow or green garnet; *esp* **:** ANDRADITE

topaz quartz *n* **:** CITRINE

top banana *n* [so called fr. a burlesque routine involving three comedians in which the one that gets the punch line also gets a banana] **:** the leading comedian in a burlesque show

top billing *n* **1 :** the position at the top of a theatrical bill usu. featuring the star's name ⟨she got *top billing*⟩ **2 :** prominent emphasis, featuring, or advertising ⟨few of these incidents have received *top billing* in the U. S. press —Charles Abrams⟩

top block *n* **:** a block hung under the cap of a lower mast and used in lowering the topmast

top boot *n* **:** a high boot made often with light-colored leather bands around the upper part and worn esp. by riders (as in hunting or in livery)

top-bracket \ˈ=ˌ==\ *adj* **:** TOP-DRAWER ⟨the *top-bracket* group in capitalist society —D.J.Dallin⟩

top burton *n* **:** a burton having a fiddle block or double block and a single block used esp. for hoisting sails, yards, and rigging

topcap \ˈ=ˌ=\ *n* **:** the top part of a journal housing

top capping *n* **:** the application of a strip of camelback to the central area only of a worn tire tread — compare FULL CAPPING

top card *n* **:** TOP FLAT

topchrome \ˈ=ˌ=\ *vt or adj* [¹*top* + *chrome*] **:** AFTERCHROME

top cloth *n* **:** HAMMOCK CLOTH

topcoat \ˈ=ˌ=\ *n* [¹*top* + *coat*] **:** an outer coat: as **a :** a lightweight overcoat **b :** the long outer fur of an animal consisting of the part of the guard hairs that projects beyond the undercoat **c :** a final coating (as of paint) **:** OVERCOAT 2

top couple *n* **:** HEAD COUPLE

top cover *n* **:** combat airplanes flying at high altitude to protect from air attack a military force esp. of other airplanes flying at a lower altitude

top cow *n, dial* **:** BULL

top crop *n* **:** the harvest from the upper and younger portion of plants (as cotton)

topcross \ˈ=ˌ=\ *n* [¹*top* + *cross*] **1 :** a cross in which usu. male superior or purebred individuals are mated with inferior stock to improve the average quality of the progeny; *also* **:** the product of such a cross — compare GRADE 5 **2 :** a cross between an inbred line and a random-bred variety or strain of the same organism (as one between a strictly inbred line and a horticultural variety of maize); *also* **:** the first generation hybrid that is produced by such a cross — compare SINGLE CROSS

topcrossbred \ˈ=ˌ=ˌ=\ *n* **:** an individual produced by interbreeding an inbred sire of one breed or variety with a noninbred dam of another — compare TOPINCROSS

top dog *n* [so called in allusion to a dogfight] **:** a person or group in a position of authority or distinction esp. through victory in a hard-fought competition ⟨union leaders fight for power, try to prove that they should be *top dogs* —*Kiplinger Washington Letter*⟩

top-dog \ˈ=ˈ=\ *adj* [*top dog*] **:** of, relating to, or being a top dog ⟨they became *top-dog* in the government of the moment —T.R.Ybarra⟩

top-down \ˈ=ˈ=\ *adj* [fr. the phrase (*from the*) *top down*] **:** closely organized, controlled, and directed ⟨a *top-down* planned society —J.R.Chamberlain⟩

top drawer *n* **:** the highest level of society, authority, or excellence ⟨has a low social opinion of the . . . ruling class who do not come out of the *top drawer* —V.S.Pritchett⟩ ⟨the majority of critics currently place him in the *top drawer* —Granville Hicks⟩

top-drawer \ˈ=ˈ=(ə)\ *adj* [*top drawer*] **1 :** of the highest social level ⟨*top-drawer* socialites whom he has escorted —*Life*⟩ **2 :** of the highest level of rank, excellence, or importance ⟨the *top-drawer* officials of the railroad —S.K.Farrington⟩ ⟨one of the *top-drawer* secrets of the war —*N. Y. Times*⟩

topdress \ˈ=ˌ=\ *vt* [¹*top* + *dress*, v.] **:** to scatter manure or fertilizer over (a growing crop, meadow, or lawn)

topdresser \ˈ=ˌ==\ *n* **:** one that applies topdressing

topdressing \ˈ=ˌ==\ *n* [fr. gerund of *topdress*] **1 a :** the act of one who topdresses soil **b :** the material used to topdress soil **2 :** a surface layer of extraneous matter ⟨a sorry collection of old wheezes dressed out with a ~ of analytical jargon —Louis Untermeyer⟩

top-dye \ˈ=ˌ=\ *vt* **:** ³TOP 2b(2)

¹**tope** \ˈtōp\ *vb* -ED/-ING/-S [obs. *tope*, interj. used to wish good health before drinking, prob. fr. F, done! agreed!, fr. *tope*, 1st pers. sing. pres. indic. of *toper* to agree, consent, accept a bet, cover the opponent's stake, fr. Sp *topar* to take a bet, strike against, butt, bump, of imit. origin; prob. fr. the custom of drinking after a wager] *vt, archaic* **:** to drink (intoxicating liquor) frequently or to excess ~ *vi* **:** to drink intoxicating liquor to excess or in large drafts

²**tope** \"\ *n* -s [origin unknown] **:** any of several small sharks; *esp* **:** a cosmopolitan brownish or grayish bottom-dwelling shark (*Galeorhinus galeus*) having a liver extremely rich in vitamin A — called also *soupfin shark*

³**tope** \"\ *n* -s [Tamil *tōppu*] *India* **:** a grove, clump, or plantation of trees ⟨a mango ~⟩

⁴**tope** \"\ *n* -s [Hindi *top*, prob. fr. Skt *stūpa*] **:** a round cupola-topped building erected as a Buddhist shrine **:** STUPA

to·pec·to·my \təˈpektəmē, -mi\ *n* -ES [*top-* + *-ectomy*] **:** surgical removal of portions of the cortex of the frontal association area of the brain for the relief of mental disorders

to·pee *or* **to·pi** \tōˈpē, ˈ=ˌ=\ *n* -s [Hindi *topī*] **:** a lightweight helmetlike hat with a curved brim made orig. in India of sola pith that consists usu. of a cloth outer covering, an insulating layer of pith or cork, and a light inner framework to fit the head and is worn esp. for protection from the sun

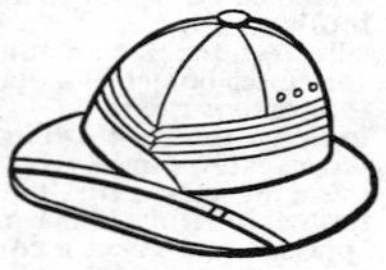
topee

to·pe·ka \təˈpēkə\ *adj, usu cap* [fr. *Topeka*, Kansas] **:** of or from Topeka, the capital of Kansas ⟨*Topeka* flour mills⟩ **:** of the kind or style prevalent in Topeka

to·peng \ˈtōˌpeŋ\ *n* -s [Jav *topèng*] **:** a Javanese dramatic performance in which the actors wear grotesque masks and act in pantomime

to·pepo \təˈpe(ˌ)pō\ *n* -s [blend of *tomato* and *pepper*] **:** a reputed hybrid between the tomato and the sweet pepper

¹**top·er** \ˈtōpə(r)\ *n* -s [¹*tope* + *-er*] **:** one that topes **:** a heavy drinker; *esp* **:** DRUNKARD

²**toper** \"\ *n* -s [²*tope* + *-er*] **:** TOPE

top facing *n* **:** a finishing piece of leather or fabric appearing at the top of a shoe lining and frequently bearing the maker's trademark

top fermentation *n* **:** a violent alcoholic fermentation at a temperature of 14 to 30° C during which the yeast cells are carried to the top of the fermenting liquid used in the production of such liquors as ale, porter, and wines of high alcohol content and in distilling — compare BOTTOM FERMENTATION

top flat *n* **:** one of a series of flat cards in a carding machine arranged in an endless chain and guided by rollers over the main cylinder

top flight *n* **:** the highest level or degree of achievement, excellence, or eminence **:** TOP DRAWER ⟨leading families intermarry; practically everyone in the *top flight* is thus related —*Reader's Digest*⟩

topflight \ˈ=ˈ=\ *adj* [*top flight*] **:** of topmost rank or eminence **:** TOP-DRAWER

top·flight·er \ˈ=ˈflīd·ə(r)\ *n* -s **:** one that is topflight **:** TOPNOTCHER ⟨a novice . . . not yet ready to challenge the ~*s* —Tom Siler⟩

top fruit *n, Brit* **:** TREE FRUIT

top·ful *or* **top·full** \ˈtäpˌfu̇l\ *adj* **:** full to the top **:** BRIMFUL

¹**top·gal·lant** \tăpˈgalənt, ˈ=ˌ==, *usu. naut* təˈg-\ *adj* [¹*top* + *gallant*] **1 a :** of, relating to, or being a part next above the topmast and below the royal mast ⟨~ sail⟩ ⟨~ mast⟩ — see SAIL illustration, SHIP illustration **b :** raised above the adjoining portions — used of a rail, bulwark, or deck **c :** such that topgallant sails may be used **:** fresh but light ⟨~ breezes⟩ **2 :** of the best or most excellent of its kind **:** very excellent **:** GRAND

²**topgallant** \"\ *n* -s **1 :** a topgallant mast or sail **2 a :** something loftier or more elevated than others of its kind or other parts of the same structure **b :** the topmost point **:** PINNACLE, SUMMIT

topgallant bulwarks *n pl* **:** QUARTER BOARDS

topgallant forecastle *n* **:** an extra deck above the forecastle in the bow of a ship

top gear *n, Brit* **:** ³HIGH 2b

top-graft \ˈ=ˌ=\ *vt* **:** TOPWORK

top grain *n* **:** leather made from the grain side of a hide with nothing taken off the surface except the hair and associated epidermis

top grass *n* **:** a tall grass suitable for hay

to·pha·ceous \təˈfāshəs\ *adj* [L *tophaceus, tofaceus*, fr. *tophus, tofus* tufa + *-aceus* -aceous] **1** *archaic* **:** of the nature of tufa **:** GRITTY, SANDY **2 :** having the characteristics of a tophus

top-hamper \ˈ=ˌ==\ *n* -s **1 :** matter or weight (as spars, rigging, superstructure, or cargo) in the upper part of a ship ⟨*top-hamper* of guns, three hundred and forty tons of landing craft together with six sets of heavy davits —K.M.Dodson⟩ **2 :** unnecessary cumbersome matter ⟨strip his long rambling paragraphs of their *top-hamper* of jargon —John Connell⟩

top hand *n* **:** a cowboy who is superior esp. as a rider or horsebreaker

top hat *n* **1 :** BEAVER 3a **2 :** SILK HAT **3 :** OPERA HAT

top-hat \ˈ=ˈ=\ *adj* [*top hat*] **:** of or relating to the upper social classes **:** TOP-DRAWER

top-heavily \ˈ=ˈ===\ *adv* **:** in a topheavy manner

top-heaviness \ˈ=ˈ===\ *n* **:** the quality or state of being top-heavy

top-heavy \ˈ=ˈ==\ *adj* **1 :** having the top part too heavy for the lower part **:** lacking in stability or in danger of toppling over because of too much weight at the top ⟨high *top-heavy* wagons —*Amer. Guide Series: Mich.*⟩ ⟨the lyrics are often *top-heavy* with ideas —*New Republic*⟩ **2 :** having a too high proportion of officers and esp. high-ranking officers ⟨a *top-heavy* bureaucracy⟩ **3 a** *of a financial structure* **:** OVERCAPITALIZED **b** *of a market* **:** technically weak with too many speculative holders likely to liquidate soon

to·phet \ˈtōfət\ *n -s usu cap* [ME *Tophet, Topheth*, shrine in the valley of Hinnom south of ancient Jerusalem where human sacrifices esp. those of children were performed to Moloch (Jer 7:31), Gehenna, hell, fr. Heb *tōpheth*] **:** GEHENNA, HELL ⟨what in *Tophet* is this —Cliff Farrell⟩

top-hole \ˈ=ˈ=\ *adj, chiefly Brit* **:** EXCELLENT, FIRST-CLASS

to·phus \ˈtōfəs\ *n, pl* **to·phi** \-ōˌfī\ [L *tophus, tofus* — more at TUFA] **1 :** TUFA **2 :** a deposit of urates in cartilage and other tissues characteristic of gout

¹**topi** *var of* TOPEE

²**to·pi** \ˈtōpē\ *n, pl* **topi** [of Mande origin; akin to Mende *ndopa, ndope* antelope] **:** an antelope (*Damaliscus corrigum jimela*) of eastern Central Africa having a glossy purplish brown coat with a watered-silk appearance; *also* **:** any of various related antelopes native to districts south of the Sahara

to·pi·ar·i·an \ˌtōpēˈa(a)rēən, -ˈer-\ *adj* [L *topiarius* + E *-an*] **:** TOPIARY

to·pi·a·rist \ˈtōpēərəst\ *n* -s **:** one skilled in topiary gardening

¹**to·pi·ary** \ˈ==ˌerē\ *adj* [L *topiarius*, fr. (*opera*) *topia* garden (work) (fr. Gk *topion* field, small place, dim. of *topos* place) + *-arius* -ary] **:** of, relating to, or being the practice or art of training, cutting, and trimming trees or shrubs into odd or ornamental shapes; *also* **:** characterized by such work

²**topiary** \"\ *n* -ES **1 :** topiary art or gardening; *also* **:** a topiary garden **2 a :** a plant (as a box or yew) shaped by topiary art **b :** topiary plants

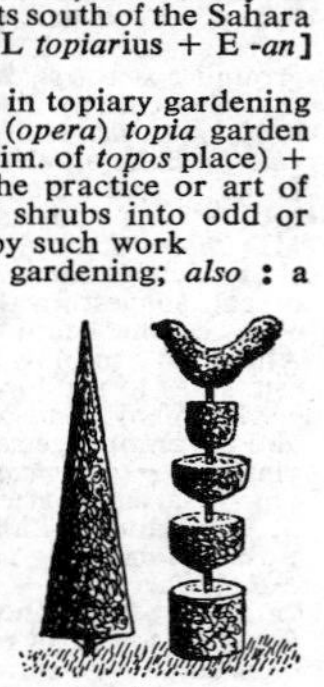
topiary 2b

topic \ˈtäpik, -pēk\ *n* -s [L *Topica* Topics, work by Aristotle in which the material is divided into topics, fr. Gk (*Ta*) *Topika*, fr. *topika*, neut. pl. of *topikos* of a place, of a commonplace, fr. *topos* place, commonplace + *-ikos* -ic; akin to Gk *topazein* to aim at, guess, Lith *tapti* to become, OE *thafian* to allow, agree, endure; basic meaning: to fall into place] **1 a** *obs* **:** a prepared form of argument applicable to a great variety of cases **:** a commonplace of argument or oratory **b** *obs* **:** one of the various general forms of argument employed in probable as distinguished from demonstrative reasoning **c :** ARGUMENT, REASON, CONSIDERATION **2 a :** a heading in an outlined argument or exposition **:** a phrase summarizing what is to be presented in a discourse or a section of it **b** (1) **:** the subject of a discourse or a section of it **:** THEME ⟨the ~ of his book⟩ (2) **:** a subject under discussion or consideration ⟨suggested inflation as the ~ for discussion⟩

¹**top·i·cal** \-pəkəl, -pēk-\ *adj* [Gk *topikos* of a place, of a commonplace + E *-al*] **1 :** of or relating to a place **:** local or designed for local application ⟨a ~ remedy⟩ ⟨a ~ anesthetic⟩ **2** *obs* **:** not demonstrative **:** merely probable **3 a :** of, relating to, or arranged by topics ⟨a detailed record, on both a chronological and a ~ basis —Jacob Viner⟩ **b :** referring to the topics of the day or place **:** of local or temporary interest ⟨the ~, the contingent and therefore ephemeral stuff which all novels contain —Edward Sackville-West⟩ ⟨a new, timely and useful study of civil liberty —J.B.Oakes⟩ — **top·i·cal·ly** \-k(ə)lē, -li\ *adv*

²topical \"\ *n* -s : a coin or postage stamp bearing a design relating to some general topic (as animals, flowers, or ships) that is often used as a theme for a collection

top·i·cal·i·ty \ˌ==ˈkaləd·ē, -lətē, -i\ *n* -ES **1** : the quality or state of being topical ⟨lectures and articles rather summarily thrown together . . . before they should lose ~ —*Times Lit. Supp.*⟩ **2** : an item of merely topical interest ⟨the thriller . . . did reasonably well with its international *topicalities* —J.S. Sandoe⟩

top ice *n* : shaved ice blown into loaded refrigerator cars to complete icing

topic sentence *also* **topical sentence** *n* : a sentence that states the main or central thought of a paragraph or of a larger unit of discourse and is usu. placed at or near the beginning

-topies *pl of* -TOPY

top·i·nam·bour \ˌtäpəˈnam,bu̇(ə)r, ˌ==ˌ=ˈ=\ *also* **top·i·nam·bou** \-bü\ *or* **tob·i·nam·bur** \ˌtäbəˈnam,bu̇(ə)r, ˌ==ˌ=ˈ=\ *n* -s [*topinambour* fr. F, fr. Pg *tupinambor*, alter. of *tupinamba*, short for *batata tupinamba*, fr. *batata* potato (fr. Taino) + *Tupinambá* Tupinamba; *topinambou* fr. obs. F, fr. Pg *tupinambo, tupinamba*; *tobinambur* modif. of AmerSp *topinámbur*, fr. Pg *tupinambor*] : JERUSALEM ARTICHOKE

topincross \ˈ=ˌ=\ *n* [¹*top* + *incross*] : an individual produced by interbreeding an inbred sire with a noninbred dam of the same breed or variety — compare TOPCROSSBRED

toping *pres part of* TOPE

top·i·nish \ˈtäpənish\ *n, pl* **topinish** *or* **topinishes** *usu cap* : a subdivision of the Yakima

topkick \ˈ=ˌ=\ *n* [¹*top* + *kick*, n.] : FIRST SERGEANT 1

topknot \ˈ=ˌ=\ *n* **1 a** : an ornament (as a knot of ribbons, a bunch of flowers or feathers, or a pompon) forming a headdress or worn on a cap or as part of a hairdress **b** (1) : a crest of feathers (as on a cock) (2) : a tuft of hair on the top or forward part of a head **c** : an arrangement of hair high on the head and usu. in a knot **2** : a small European flounder (*Zeugopterus punctatus*) having the anterior rays of the dorsal fin elongated; *also* : any closely related species

topknot pigeon *n* : a crested Australian wild pigeon (*Lopholaimus antarcticus*)

top·less \ˈtäpləs\ *adj* **1 a** : having no top ⟨~ bathing suit⟩ **b** *archaic* : so high as to reach up beyond sight **c** : nude above the waist ⟨~ waitress⟩ **d** : featuring topless waitresses or entertainers ⟨~ cabaret⟩ **2** *obs* : SUPREME

top-level \ˈ=ˈ==\ *adj* : very high or highest in level of authority, importance, or quality ⟨*top-level* management⟩ ⟨*top-level* news⟩ ⟨*top-level* scientists⟩

top lift *n* [¹*top*] : the bottom layer of a heel usu. made of leather, rubber, or composition — see SHOE illustration

top light *n* **1** : a light at one of the tops of a ship sometimes indicating a flagship **2** *or* **toplighting** \ˈ=ˌ==\ : light from above (as from a skylight)

topline \ˈ=ˌ=\ *n* : the outline of the top of an animal's body

top-line \ˈ=ˈ=\ *adj* **1** : named in or near the top line : most featured or prominently advertised : LEADING ⟨a *top-line* comedian⟩ ⟨*top-line* news⟩ **2** : TOP-LEVEL

top·lin·er \-nə(r)\ *n, chiefly Brit* : a top-line person or thing; *specif* : HEADLINER

top lining *n* : a cloth on the after side of the lower cloths of a topsail to prevent chafing

top load *n* : a load of logs more than one tier high

top loader *n* : a worker who places logs at the top of a deck or load

top·loft·ical \ˈtäˈplȯftəkəl\ *adj* [prob. fr. *top loft* + *-ical*] : TOPLOFTY ⟨a pedantic . . . ~ jargon —Marguerite Wilkinson⟩

top·loft·i·ly \-tələ̄, -li\ *adv* : in a toplofty manner ⟨looked down ~ on literary critics —Malcolm Cowley⟩

top·loft·i·ness \-tēnəs, -tin-\ *n* -ES : the quality or state of being toplofty

toplofty \ˈ=ˈ==\ *adj* [back-formation fr. *toplo[ftical]*] : very superior in air or in attitude : contemptuous of or elevated above the average or ordinary : DISDAINFUL, SUPERCILIOUS, HAUGHTY ⟨opinionated and ~ in its judgments —B.J.Stern⟩

topmaker \ˈ=ˌ==\ *n* : one who deals in wool tops

topmaking \ˈ=ˌ==\ *n* : the practice or trade of a topmaker

top·man \ˈ=mən\ *n, pl* **topmen** **1** : one whose work is done at or from the top: as **a** : TOP SAWYER 1 **b** : a miner who works at the surface **c** : a construction worker who works on the ground, shoveling dirt, loading, caring for equipment **d** : RACKMAN 2 **e** : a worker who attends to equipment and processing at the top of petroleum stills **2** : a sailor or marine stationed in a top **3** : a worker who assists in the operation of retort furnaces **4** : a supervisor of brick-chimney builders

top·mast \ˈtäpməst (*usu naut*), -p,mast, -,maa(ə)st, -,maist, -,mȧst\ *n* [ME *toppe maste*, fr. *toppe* top + *maste*, mast mast — more at TOP, MAST] : the mast next above the lower mast that is topmost in a fore-and-aft rig and below the topgallant mast in a square-rigged ship — see SHIP illustration

top milk *n* : the upper layer of milk in a container enriched by whatever cream has risen

topminnow \ˈ=ˌ=(ˌ)=\ *n* [¹*top* + *minnow*; fr. its swimming on the surface of the water] **1** : any of numerous small viviparous surface-feeding fishes that constitute the family Poeciliidae and include many brilliantly colored freshwater fishes some of which are much used in mosquito control and others extensively kept in the tropical aquarium — compare GAMBUSIA, HELLERI, PLATY, SWORDTAIL **2** : KILLIFISH 1

top·most \ˈtäp,mōst *also* -məst\ *adj* : that is at the very top : highest of all : UPPERMOST ⟨communication between the lowest classified worker and the ~ executive —H.F.Gracey⟩

top·most·ly *adv* : CHIEFLY

top-mounter \ˈ=ˈ==\ *n* : the member of a balance team whose position is atop the others

top necrosis *n* : a disease of potatoes caused by one or more of several viruses and characterized by death of the growing points and death of the plant progressively downward

topnotch \ˈ=ˌ=\ *n* : the highest point possible or attainable ⟨a boat in the ~ of perfection —H.A.Calahan⟩

top-notch \ˈ=ˈ=\ *adj* [*top notch*] : of the highest or best attainable : TIP-TOP, FIRST-RATE, UNSURPASSED

top·notch·er \-chə(r)\ *n* -s : one that is top-notch

to·po \ˈtō(,)pō\ *n* -s [It] : a flat-bottomed and half-decked Venetian fishing boat powered by sails or oars

topo- — see TOP-

topo *abbr* topographic; topographical

topo·chemical \ˌtäpə, ˌtōpə+\ *adj* [*top-* + *chemical*] **1** : of, relating to, or constituting a locally confined chemical reaction **2** : of, relating to, or constituting a combined tactile and chemical sense (as that of the antennae of insects) that is fundamentally equivalent to olfaction

topo·cli·nal \-ˈklīnᵊl\ *adj* : of or relating to a topocline — **topo·cli·nal·ly** \-nᵊlē\ *adv*

topo·cline \ˈ==,klīn\ *n* [*top-* + *cline*] : a cline along a geographical axis and usu. without apparent ecological explanation

topo·deme \-,dēm\ *n* [*top-* + *deme*] : a population occupying a specified geographical range

top off *vt* : FINISH 2d

topog *abbr* topographer; topographic; topographical; topography

to·pog·no·sia \ˌtä,päg'nōzh(ē)ə, ˌtō,p-\ *or* **to·pog·no·sis** \-ōsəs\ *n, pl* **topognosias** *or* **topognosises** [NL, fr. *top-* + *-gnosia* or *-gnosis*] : recognition of the location of a stimulus on the skin or elsewhere in the body

to·pog·ra·pher \təˈpägrəfə(r), tōˈ-\ *n* -s [Gk *topographos* (fr. *topographein* to describe a place) + E *-er* — more at TOPOGRAPHY] : one who is skilled in or practices topography : one who describes, maps, or surveys the topography of a region

topo·graph·ic \ˌtäpəˈgrafik, ˌtōp-, -fēk\ *adj* [MGk *topographikos*, fr. Gk *topographia* topography + *-ikos* -ic] : TOPOGRAPHICAL 1a

topographic adolescence *or* **topographic youth** *n* : the condition of a district soon after the beginning of erosion by streams when main branches have well-developed narrow valleys and the areas between the streams are little modified

topo·graph·i·cal \ˌ==ˈgrafək·əl, -fēk-\ *adj* [MGk *topographikos* + E *-al*] **1 a** (1) : of, relating to, or concerned with topography ⟨~ engineer⟩ (2) : discovering, measuring, or exhibiting the topography of a region ⟨a ~ description⟩ ⟨a ~ survey⟩ **b** : of, relating to, or concerned with the artistic representation of a particular locality ⟨a ~ poem⟩ ⟨~ painting⟩ **2** : of or relating to a mind made up of different strata and esp. of the conscious, preconscious, and unconscious **3** : of, relating to, or concerned with the delineation of the structure and relations of the parts of a group or subject — **topo·graph·i·cal·ly** \-k(ə)lē, -li\ *adv*

topographical anatomy *n* : REGIONAL ANATOMY

topographic infancy *n* : the condition of a district freshly exposed to the action of surface waters when the original hollows are still occupied by lakes and ponds and the plains are imperfectly dissected by narrow stream gorges

topographic map *n* : a map intermediate between a general map and a plan on a scale large enough to show roads, plans of towns, and contour lines

topographic maturity *n* : the condition of a district in which the land is reduced to slopes, the original upland has been completely dissected, a new plain of erosion has just begun to appear, and many of the individual river valleys are mature but some of the headwaters of the tributaries may still be in the youthful stage

topographic old age *n* : the condition of a district reduced by erosion nearly to base level

to·pog·ra·phize \təˈpägrə,fīz, tōˈ-\ *vt* -ED/-ING/-S [*topography* + *-ize*] : to describe topographically

topo·grapho·met·ric \ˌtäpəˌgrafəˈme·trik, ˌtōp-\ *adj* [*topography* + *-o-* + *-metric*] : concerned with or devised for the measurement of heights, angles, and distances

to·pog·ra·phy \təˈpägrəfē, tōˈ-, -fi\ *n* -ES [ME *topographie*, fr. LL *topographia*, fr. Gk, fr. *topographein* to describe a place (fr. *topos* place + *graphein* to write) + *-ia* -y — more at TOPIC, CARVE] **1 a** (1) *obs* : the description of a particular place (as a city, town, manor, parish, or tract of land) (2) : the art or practice of graphic delineation in detail usu. on maps or charts of selected natural and man-made features of a place or region esp. in a way to show their relative positions and elevations (3) : topographical surveying **b** (1) : the configuration of a surface including its relief and the position of its natural and man-made features ⟨a map showing the ~ of the county⟩ (2) : the physical or natural features of an object or entity and their structural relationships ⟨statistics which reveal the economic ~ of our time —R.D.Mack⟩ **2 a** : REGIONAL ANATOMY **b** : a chart or illustration showing the location of body parts (as of a bird or mammal)

topo·log·i·cal \ˌtäpəˈläjəkəl, ˌtōp-\ *also* **topo·log·ic** \-jik\ *adj* **1** : of or relating to topology **2** : concerned with relations between objects abstracted from exact quantitative measurement ⟨~ dating involves nothing more than the notion of *before* and *after* —C.F.Hockett⟩ ⟨the ~ statement that this angle is smaller than that⟩ — **topo·log·i·cal·ly** \-jək(ə)lē\ *adv*

topological equivalence *n* : the relationship of two geometric figures capable of being transformed one into the other by a one-to-one transformation continuous in both directions

topological psychology *n* : a system or theory that describes individual or group behavior in terms of topological relations within a life space

to·pol·o·gist \təˈpäləjəst, tōˈ-\ *n* -s : a student of or specialist in topology

to·pol·o·gy \-jē, -ji\ *n* -ES [ISV *top-* + *-logy*] **1** : topographical study of a particular place; *specif* : the history of a region as indicated by its topography **2** : REGIONAL ANATOMY **3** : a branch of mathematics that investigates the properties of a geometric configuration that are unaltered if the configuration is subjected to any one-to-one transformation continuous in both directions **4** : TOPOLOGICAL PSYCHOLOGY

top onion *n* **1** : one of the bulbils that often replace the flowers in the inflorescence of some onions and are used for propagation — called also *top set*; compare TREE ONION **2** : TREE ONION

top·onym \ˈtäpə,nim, ˈtōp-\ *n* -s [ISV, back-formation fr. *toponymy*] : PLACE-NAME

top·onym·ic \ˌ==ˈnimik, -mēk\ *or* **top·onym·i·cal** \-məkəl, -mēk-\ *adj* [*toponymy* + *-ic* or *-ical*] : of or relating to toponyms or toponymy

to·pon·y·my *also* **to·pon·o·my** \təˈpänəmē, tōˈ-, -mi\ *n* -ES [*toponymy* ISV *top-* + *-onymy*; *toponomy* fr. *top-* + Gk *onoma* name + E *-y* — more at NAME] **1** : the place-names of a region or language or the esp. etymological study of them **2** : the nomenclature of regional anatomy

topo·tax·is \ˌtäpəˈtaksəs, ˌtōp-\ *n* [NL, fr. *top-* + *-taxis*] : TROPISM

topo·type \ˈtäpə,tīp, ˈtōp-\ *n* [*top-* + *type*] : a specimen of a species collected at the locality at which the original type was obtained — **topo·typ·ic** \ˌ==ˈtipik\ *adj* — **topo·typ·i·cal** \-pəkəl\ *adj*

top out *vt* **1** : to separate (the best animals) from a group ⟨*top out* hogs⟩ **2** : to finish by putting on a cap or uppermost course ~ *vi* : to reach a summit or crest ⟨scraped through a willy-cherry thicket and *topped out* on the rock flat again —H.L. Davis⟩ ⟨investment boom . . . has *topped out* —*Newsweek*⟩

topped \ˈtäpt\ *adj* [ME, fr. ¹*top* + *-ed*] : having a top of a specified character — usu. used in combination ⟨flat-*topped*⟩

topped crude *n* [*topped* fr. past part. of ³*top*] : crude petroleum that has been treated (as by distillation) to remove some of its lighter components

top·per \ˈtäpə(r)\ *n* -s [¹*top* + *-er*] **1** : one that puts tops on (as on containers) or removes tops (as from vegetables); *specif* : CLIMBER 1a **2** : one that is at or on the top: as **a** : someone or something first-rate or surpassingly good **b** : a cover or a top layer or part **3 a** : SILK HAT **b** : OPERA HAT **4** : something (as a joke) that surpasses or climaxes everything preceding **5** : a woman's usu. short and boxy lightweight overcoat **6** : one that transfers hose from leggers to footers

toppiece \ˈ=ˌ=\ *n* : TOUPEE

¹top·ping \ˈtäpiŋ, -pēŋ\ *n* -s [ME, fr. gerund of *toppen* to top — more at TOP] **1** : something that forms a top (as of a tuft of hair or feathers on the head or a forelock): as **a** : something (as a sauce, nuts, or whipped cream) used to garnish food and esp. dessert **b** : a finishing layer of mortar about ½ to 1 inch in thickness placed on concrete (as on a floor or sidewalk) **2** : the action of one that tops: as **a** : the reduction of a tooth (as on a saw or gear) by filing **b** : the removal of volatile parts (as from crude oil) **3** : something removed by topping: as **a** : the cut tops of plants **b** : refuse separated from hemp in hackling **c** : the finest bran **4** : a feather from a golden pheasant's crest used in an artificial fly — see FLY illustration

²topping *adj* [fr. pres. part. of ³*top*] **1** : highest in rank, degree, or eminence **2** *NewEng* : PROUD, PRETENTIOUS, ARROGANT **3** *chiefly Brit* : very fine : EXCELLENT

topping lift *n* : a strong tackle or rope running from the masthead and used to support, raise, or top the outer end of a boom or a yard — see SHIP illustration

topping plant *n* : an extraction plant for removing the lighter components of oil

top plate *n* **1** : PLATE 5a(1) **2** : the plate at the top of a partition

top·ple \ˈtäpəl\ *vb* **toppled; toppled; toppling** \-p(ə)liŋ\ **topples** [freq. of ³*top*] *vi* **1** : to fall from or as if from top-heaviness : tumble down ⟨*toppled* backward to a sprawl on the pavement —Scott Fitzgerald⟩ **2** : to be or appear on the verge of toppling : be or seem unsteady : TOTTER ⟨upon his head ~s a fantastic structure of bull's horns and feathers —H.V. Morton⟩ ~ *vt* **1** : to cause to topple : push over : OVERTURN, UPSET ⟨the crowd outside *toppled* part of the churchyard wall in its crush —*Time*⟩ **2** : to eject from a position of authority, power, or eminence : OVERTHROW ⟨two world wars . . . *toppled* six colonial empires —*Newsweek*⟩

toppo *var of* TOPO

top rake *n* : the angle between the face of a cutting tool that receives the chip and the normal to the surface being cut

toprope \ˈ=ˌ=\ *n* : a rope for the hoisting or lowering of a topmast

top rot *n* **1** : a rotting of the upper part of a plant symptomatic of various diseases of sugarcane **2** : a rot starting in the upper part of the trunk (as in many trees)

top round *n* : the portion of a round steak situated on the inside of the round (sense 16a) — compare BOTTOM ROUND

tops \ˈtäps\ *adj* [fr. pl. of ¹*top*] : topmost in quality, ability, popularity, or eminence — used predicatively ⟨the opening essay . . . is ~ on the subject —*Commonweal*⟩ ⟨their personnel is ~ —Virgil Thomson⟩ — often used with *the* ⟨generally considered the ~ in the field —Fletcher Pratt⟩

top·sail \ˈtäpsəl (*usu naut*), -p,sāl\ *also* **tops'l** \ˈtäpsəl\ *n* -s [*topsail* fr. ME *topseil, topsail*, fr. ¹*top* + *seil, sail* sail; *tops'l* contr. of *topsail* — more at SAIL] **1** : the sail next above the lowermost sail on a mast in a square-rigged ship; *also* : one of two sails set one above the other next above the lowermost sail — see SAIL illustration, SHIP illustration **2** : the sail set above and sometimes on the gaff in a fore-and-aft rigged ship

topsail schooner *n* : a two-masted schooner having square-rigged topsails on the foremast and rarely on the mainmast

top sawyer *n* **1** : a worker at a sawpit who stands above the timber — compare BOTTOM SAWYER **2** *Brit* : a person in a position of advantage or eminence

top score *n* : TOP 8b(3)

top secret *adj* : demanding inviolate secrecy among top officials or a select few : classified as requiring the highest degree of concealment from a nation's enemies in a scale rating the value of information to a nation's security — compare CLASSIFICATION 1f

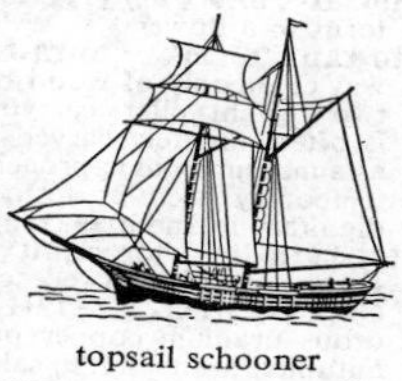

topsail schooner

top sergeant *n* : FIRST SERGEANT 1

top set *n* : TOP ONION

topset beds \ˈ=ˌ= -\ *n pl* : the nearly level layers of sediment deposited on the top of a delta

topset onion *n* : TREE ONION

top-shelf \ˈ=ˈ=\ *adj* : TOP-DRAWER

top shell *n* **1** : any of various marine snails constituting the family Trochidae and having a spiral and usu. regularly conical shell marked by a flat base and rhombic aperture and a multispiral operculum and sometimes used to make pearl buttons **2** : TURBAN SHELL

top sickness *n* : a boron deficiency disease of tobacco marked esp. by a pale green color appearing first in the leaves of the terminal bud and by bases that are paler than the tips

¹topside \ˈ=ˌ=\ *n, often attrib* [¹*top* + *side*] **1 a topsides** *pl* : the top portion of the outer surface of a ship on each side above the waterline **b** : the portion of a ship above the main deck and usu. below the top-hamper — distinguished from *side* **2** : high ranking personnel : the highest level of authority ⟨the ~ of the . . . armies and navies know about them —*Newsweek*⟩ ⟨got straight from ~ the picture of the war as it unfolded —*Coast Artillery Jour.*⟩ ⟨a former ~ government information man —R.E.Jones⟩ **3** : a place actually or figuratively above another (as the surface of the earth or sea) ⟨with a war surplus diving helmet, a painting machine air compressor and friends as a ~ crew, started diving —*N.Y.Times*⟩

²topside \ˈ=ˈ=\ *adv* **1** *also* **topsides** : on deck ⟨down in the engine room . . . quickly regretted ever having gone ~ —Joseph Whitehill⟩ **2** : in or into a high position ⟨to transport visitors ~, a businessman built the first cog railroad —B.M. Bowie⟩ : on top ⟨slept ~ in the bunk⟩ : to or on the surface ⟨miners coming ~⟩ **3** : in a position of authority : at a top level of rank ⟨charges of Communism ~ —*Newsweek*⟩

top side *n* : FELT SIDE

topside-turvy \ˌ==ˈtərvē\ *adv* [by alter.] : TOPSY-TURVY

top-size \ˈ=ˌ=\ *vt* : SURFACE-SIZE

top slicing *n* : a method of mining large ore bodies from the top downward by consecutively removing a series of horizontal slices under a caved capping

tops·man \ˈtäpsmən\ *n, pl* **topsmen** [*tops* (poss. of ¹*top*) + *man*] *Brit* : HANGMAN

top smelt *n* : a common silversides (*Atherinops affinis*) of the Pacific coast of No. America that attains a length of one foot and is of some importance as a food fish

¹topsoil \ˈ=ˌ=\ *n* : surface soil distinguished from subsoil and usu. including the average plow depth or the A-horizon — called also *loam*; distinguished from *solum*

²topsoil \"\ *vt* : to cover or dress with topsoil

top spin *n* [²*top*] : a rotary motion imparted to a ball which causes it to rotate forward in the direction of its flight

topstitch \ˈ=ˌ=\ *vt* : to make a line of stitching on the outside of (a garment) close to a seam

topstone \ˈ=ˌ=\ *n* : CAPSTONE

topswarm \ˈ=ˌ=\ *n, dial Brit* : the first swarm of bees from a hive

top·sy·turn \ˈtäpsē,tərn\ *vt* [¹*topsy*-turvy + *turn*] : to turn upside down

top·sy-tur·vi·ly \ˌtäpsēˈtərvəlē, -si,t-, -ˈtəv-, -ˈtəiv-, -li\ *adv* : in a topsy-turvy manner

top·sy·tur·vi·ness \-vēnəs, -vin-\ *n* -ES : the quality or state of being topsy-turvy

¹top·sy-tur·vy *also* **top·sy-tur·vey** \-vē,-vi\ *adv* [earlier *topsy-tirvy, topsy-tervy*, prob. fr. *tops* (pl. of ¹*top*) + *-y* (dim. suffix) + obs. E *tirve, terve* to turn, turn upside down (fr. ME *terven*, prob. fr. — assumed — OE *tierfan*) + E *-y* (dim. suffix); akin to OE *tearflian* to turn, roll — more at TIRL] **1** : in an inverted posture : with the top or head downward : upside down ⟨fall *topsy-turvy*⟩ **2** : in a state where proper or normal places, values, standards, objects, or facts are reversed ⟨the lives of two families are turned *topsy-turvy* —Evangeline Davis⟩

²topsy-turvy \"\ *adj, sometimes* -ER/-EST : turned topsy-turvy : totally disordered : REVERSED ⟨interprets the . . . licensing regulations to suit its own *topsy-turvy* hours of labor —Dorothy Sayers⟩

³topsy-turvy \"\ *vt* -ED/-ING/-ES : to turn or make topsy-turvy ⟨make in places the order of sedimentation a *topsy-turvied* sequence —W.E.Swinton⟩

⁴topsy-turvy \"\ *n* -ES : TOPSY-TURVINESS

top·sy-tur·vy·dom \-dəm\ *n* -s **1** : TOPSY-TURVINESS **2** : a state, existence, or world in which everything is turned topsy-turvy ⟨a quaint glimpse of *topsy-turvydom*; the laws of gravitation appear to be defied —F.A.A.Talbot⟩

top-timber \ˈ=ˌ==\ *n* : one of the highest timbers on the side of a ship above the futtocks

top water *n* : the water lying above oil or gas in productive formations — compare BOTTOM WATER

top-water minnow \ˈ=ˈ==-\ *n* : TOPMINNOW; *esp* : a common mosquito fish (*Gambusia affinis*)

top water plug *n* : an angling plug that floats on the surface of the water

topweight \ˈ=ˌ=\ *n* : the heaviest weight carried by a horse in a race; *also* : a horse carrying it

topwork \ˈ=ˌ=\ *vt* : to graft scions of another variety on the main branches of (as fruit trees) after removal of all smaller and some main and secondary branches usu. to obtain more desirable fruit — compare FRAMEWORK

-to·py \d·əpē, təp-, -pi\ *n comb form* -ES [NL *-topia*, fr. Gk, way, place, fr. *topos* place + *-ia* -y — more at TOPIC] : position : location ⟨hetero*topy*⟩

top yeast *n* : a yeast that produces carbon dioxide vigorously and has cells which tend to become clustered at the surface in brewing

toque \ˈtōk\ *n* -s [MF, fr. OSp *toca* woman's headdress, veil, toque] **1 a** : a soft hat with a very narrow brim and a full crown pleated into a snug headband, usu. ornamented with a plume, and worn esp. in the 16th century **b** : a woman's small brimless hat made in any of various soft close-fitting shapes **c** : TUQUE **2 a** : TOQUE MACAQUE **b** : BONNET MONKEY

toque macaque *or* **toque monkey** *n* [so called fr. the toquelike whorl of its scalp hair] : a small reddish or brown macaque (*Macaca sinica*) of southeastern Asia

to·qui·lla \tōˈkē(y)ə\ *n* -s [Sp, dim. of *toca* headdress, toque] **1** : JIPIJAPA **2** : a very flexible and durable fiber derived from the leaves of the jipijapa from which panama hats and other wares are plaited

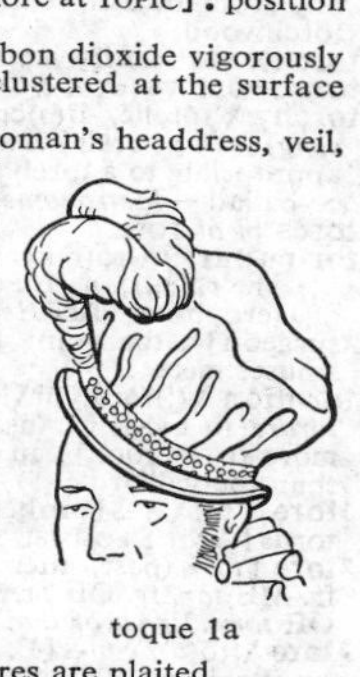

toque 1a

tor \ˈtȯ(ə)r\ *n* -s [ME *torre, tor*, fr. OE *torr*, prob. of Celt origin; akin to ScGael *torr* heap, mound, IrGael *torran* heap, hillock] : a high craggy hill : a rocky pinnacle or peak

tor *abbr* torpedo

to·ra \'tōrə\ *n* -s [Amharic *tōrā*] **:** a large reddish hartebeest (*Alcelaphus tora*) of eastern Africa

to·rad·ja *or* **to·ra·ja** \tə'räjə\ *n* -s *usu cap* [native name in central and south Celebes] **1 :** an Indonesian people of central Celebes **2 :** a member of the Toradja people

to·rah *or* **to·ra** \'tōrə, -ō(,)rä, tō'rä\ *n, pl* **to·roth** \tō'rōt(h), -rōs\ *or* **torahs** *or* **toras** *usu cap* [Heb *tōrāh*] **1 :** LAW, PRECEPT; *esp* **:** the body of divine knowledge and law found in the Jewish scriptures and tradition **2 a :** the first five books of the Old Testament **b :** SEPHER TORAH

to·ral \'tōrəl\ *adj* [NL *torus* + E *-al*] **:** of or relating to the torus of a flower

to·ran \'tōrən\ *or* **to·ra·na** \-nə\ *n* -s [Skt *toraṇa*] **1 :** a gateway commonly of wood but sometimes of stone consisting of two upright pillars carrying one to three transverse lintels that is often minutely carved with symbolic sculpture and serves as a monumental approach to a Buddhist temple in India **2 :** a temporary arch or festoon erected in honor of a visiting dignitary in India — compare PAI-LOU, TORII

tor·bern·ite \'tȯrbər,nīt\ *n* -s [G *torbernit*, fr. *Torbern* O. Bergman †1784 Swed. chemist + G *-it* -ite] **:** a mineral $Cu(UO_2)_2(PO_4)_2.8-12H_2O$ consisting of a tetragonal hydrous uranium copper phosphate that is isomorphous with autunite, uranocircite, saléeite, zeunerite, and uranospinite, is of micaceous structure, and occurs in green tabular crystals or in foliated form — called also *chalcolite*

torc *n* -s [by alter.] **:** [1]TORQUE

[1]**torch** \'tȯ(ə)rch, -ō(ə)ch\ *n* -ES *often attrib* [ME *torche*, fr. OF, bundle of twisted straw or tow, torch, fr. (assumed) VL *torca;* akin to L *torquēre* to twist — more at TORTURE] **1 :** a burning stick of resinous wood or twist of tow used to give light and usu. carried in the hand; *sometimes* **:** a chimneyless lamp mounted on a pole **:** FLAMBEAU **2 :** something (as wisdom or knowledge) likened to a torch as giving light or guidance ⟨the ~ of good reason was for the moment dimmed —Francis Hackett⟩ ⟨so that the ~ of his wisdom could be handed down the ages —H.J.Laski⟩ **3 :** any of various flowers that suggest a torch (as in being flame-colored, long-stemmed, and racemiform) or whose stalks are used for torches; *esp* **:** GREAT MULLEIN **4 :** any of various portable devices for emitting an unusually hot flame (as for vaporizing oil to start an oil engine, burning off old paint, or melting solder) ⟨an acetylene ~⟩ — compare BLOWTORCH **5** *chiefly Brit* **:** FLASHLIGHT **6 :** ARSONIST, INCENDIARY, PYROMANIAC ⟨the ~ . . . had touched off more fires than he could recollect —B.P.Battle & P.B.Weston⟩

[2]**torch** \"\ *vb* -ED/-ING/-ES *vt* **1 :** to set fire to, burn, sear, or illuminate with or as if with a torch **2 :** to catch (fish) with a jacklight ~ *vi* **:** to sing a torch song

[3]**torch** \"\ *vt* -ED/-ING/-ES [F *torcher* to daub or plaster with cob, to wipe, fr. OF, fr. *torche* bundle of twisted straw — more at [1]TORCH] **:** to point (slating) with a mixture of lime and hair or mortar

torch azalea *n* **:** FLAME AZALEA

torchbearer \'ˌ=ˌ=\ *n* **1 :** one that carries a torch (as in an ancient relay race) **2 a :** one that adds to or transmits light (as of knowledge, civilization, or truth) ⟨~*s* of culture and inspired creators —Susanne K. Langer⟩ **b :** someone in the forefront of a campaign, crusade, or movement **:** LEADER ⟨~*s* of a revolt against the introspective novel —Henri Peyre⟩ **3** *usu* **torch bearer** *usu cap T&B* **:** the highest of the four ranks attainable by a camp fire girl — compare FIRE MAKER, TRAIL SEEKER, WOOD GATHERER

torch cactus *or* **torch thistle** *n* **:** any of several columnar cacti of the genus *Cereus* whose stems were used by No. American Indians for torches

torch dance *n* **:** a festival serpentine dance in which lighted torches are carried

[1]**torch·er** \'tȯrchər, 'tō(ə)chə(r\ *n* -s [[1]*torch* + *-er*] **1 :** one that gives light with or as if with a torch **2 :** a fish jacker **3 :** TORCH SINGER

[2]**torcher** \"\ *n* -s [[3]*torch* + *-er*] **:** one that torches slate roofs

tor·chère \(')tȯr¦she(ə)r\ *n* -s [F, fr. *torche* torch] **1 :** a tall ornamental stand for a candlestick or candelabrum used in the 18th century and usu. set on a tripod base **2 :** an electric floor lamp giving indirect light

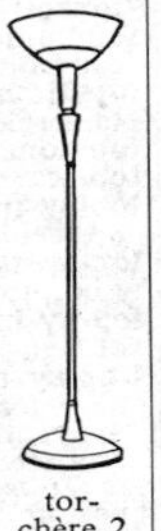

tor-chère 2

torch flower *n* **1 :** PRAIRIE SMOKE 1 **2 :** POKER PLANT

torch ginger *n* **:** an East Indian rhizomatous perennial herb (*Phaeomeria magnifica*) of the family Zingiberaceae that is cultivated in warm regions for its showy foliage and red or pink flower heads which resemble cones and are borne on tall stems arising directly from the rhizome

[1]**torchlight** \'ˌ=ˌ=\ *n* [ME *torche lyghte*, fr. *torche* torch + *lyghte*, *light* light] **1 :** light given by torches ⟨a flood of ~ surged and swirled about them —J.B.Cabell⟩ **2 :** TORCH ⟨some 15,000 ~*s* were carried there to be used in the great celebration upon the completion of the canal —F.J. Haskin⟩

[2]**torchlight** \"\ *adj* **:** composed of torchbearers ⟨a ~ parade⟩ **:** lighted by torches ⟨a ~ rally⟩

torch lily *n* **1 :** KNIPHOFIA 2 **2 :** SPEAR LILY

torchlit \'ˌ=ˌ=\ *adj* [[1]*torch* + *lit*] **:** lighted by torches

torch·man \'ˌ=mən\ *n, pl* **torchmen** **1 :** TORCHBEARER **2 :** one that uses a torch: as **a :** an acetylene welder **b :** a safecracker who uses a blowtorch

tor·chon \'tȯr,shän, ˌ=ˈ=\ *also* **torchon lace** *n* -s [F *torchon* dishcloth, duster, fr. OF, bundle of twisted straw, fr. *torche* — more at TORCH] **:** a coarse bobbin or machine-made lace made with fan-shaped designs forming a scalloped edge and used esp. for edgings and trimmings

torch pine *n* **1 :** LOBLOLLY PINE 1 **2 :** a pitch pine (*Pinus rigida*) of eastern No. America

torch singer *n* **:** a singer of torch songs

torch song *n* [fr. the phrase *carry a torch*] **:** a popular sentimental song of unrequited love

torch tree *n* **1 :** LOBLOLLY PINE 1 **2 :** an East Indian shrub (*Ixora parviflora*) with scarlet flowers **3 :** OCOTILLO 1

torch-tree family *n* **:** FOUQUIERIACEAE

torchweed \'ˌ=ˌ=\ *n* **:** MATCHWEED

torchwood \'ˌ=ˌ=\ *n* **1 :** a notably resinous or oily wood (as from the butt of some pines) suitable for burning as a torch **2 a :** any of several tropical American trees and shrubs constituting a genus (*Amyris*) that is usu. placed in the family Rutaceae and having fragrant resinous streaky yellowish brown wood that is very hard and heavy and is used locally for fuel and torches and to a limited extent in small cabinetwork; *esp* **:** either of two small trees (*A. elemifera* and *A. balsamifera*) chiefly of the West Indies and southern Florida with trifoliolate leaves, flowers in terminal panicles, and black oily aromatic drupes that ripen in the spring **b :** the wood of a torchwood

torchwood family *n* **:** BURSERACEAE

torchwort \'ˌ=ˌ=\ *n* **:** GREAT MULLEIN

torchy \'tȯrchē, -ō(ə)ch-, -chi\ *adj* -ER/-EST [*torch* (as in *torch song*) + *-y*] **:** of or relating to a torch song **:** characteristic of or appropriate to a torch song ⟨its leader's profound feeling for a ~ ballad —*Metronome*⟩ ⟨~ voice⟩

torcs *pl of* TORC

tor·cu·lar \'tȯ(r)kyələ(r)\ *also* **torcular he·ro·phi·li** \ˌ==hə'räfə,lī\ *n, usu cap H* [NL *torcular Herophili*, lit., press of Herophilus, after *Herophilus* fl 300 B.C. Greek anatomist and surgeon] **:** the point at which the four great cranial venous sinuses meet

tor·dion \(')tȯrd¦yōⁿ\ *n, pl* **tordions** \-ōⁿ(z)\ [F, fr. MF, fr. *tordre* to twist, fr. (assumed) VL *torquere*, fr. L *torquēre* — more at TORTURE] **:** an early French dance similar to but slower than the galliard

[1]**tore** \'tȯr\ *n* -s [prob. fr. L *torus* protuberance, bulge, cushion, torus] *Scot* **:** POMMEL

[2]**tore** [*tore* (past) alter. (influenced by *torn*) of archaic E *tare*, fr. ME *tar*, fr. OE *tær; tore* (past part.) fr. ME *tore, toren*, fr. OE *toren*] *past or dial past part of* TEAR

[3]**tore** \tō(ə)r\ *n* -s [F, fr. L *torus*] **1 :** the torus of an architectural column **2 :** TORUS 4

[4]**tore** \"\ *n* -s [origin unknown] *dial Eng* **:** long pasture grass

to·re·ador \'tȯrēə,dō(ə)r, 'tōr-, 'tär-, -dō(ə)\ *n* -s [Sp, fr. *toreado* (past part. of *torear* to fight bulls, fr. *toro* bull, fr. L *taurus*) + *-or* — more at STEER] **1 :** BULLFIGHTER, TORERO **2 :** DUTCH VERMILION

tored *dial past part of* TEAR

to·re·do \tə'rē(,)dō\ *n* -s [by alter.] **:** TEREDO

to·re·nia \tə'rēnēə, -nyə\ *n* [NL, fr. Olaf *Toren* †1753 Swedish ship's chaplain + NL *-ia*] **1** *cap* **:** a genus of chiefly tropical Asiatic and African herbs (family Scrophulariaceae) having simple opposite leaves and tubular 2-lipped showy flowers with four perfect stamens **2** -s **:** any plant of the genus *Torenia*

to·re·ro \tə're(,)rō\ *n* -s [Sp, fr. LL *taurarius*, fr. L *taurus* bull + *-arius* -ary] **:** a matador or a member of his cuadrilla **:** BULLFIGHTER — compare BANDERILLERO, PICADOR

to·reu·tic \tə'rüd·ik\ *adj* [Gk *toreutikos*, fr. *toreutos* worked in relief (fr. *toreuein* to bore through, chase, fr. *toreus* boring tool) + *-ikos* -ic; akin to Gk *tetrainein* to pierce, bore — more at THROW] **:** of or relating to work wrought in metal by embossing or chasing or less commonly to similar work in other materials esp. when comparatively minute and highly finished — not used of the sculpturing of statuary

to·reu·tics \-ks\ *n pl but sing in constr* [fr. *toreutic*, after such pairs as E *economic: economics*] **:** the art or process of making toreutic work

tor·goch \'tȯr,gōk̲\ *n* -s [W, fr. *tor* belly + *coch* red, fr. L *coccum* kermes berry, scarlet, fr. Gk *kokkos*] *Wales* **:** SAIBLING 1

tor·gos \'tȯrgəs, -,gäs\ *n, cap* [NL, fr. Gk, vulture; prob. akin to OE *storc* stork — more at STORK] **:** a genus of Old World vultures having fleshy lappets on the head — see PONDICHERRY VULTURE

tor·gut *also* **tor·god** *or* **tor·got** \'tȯrgət, -əd\ *n, pl* **torgut** *or* **torguts** *usu cap* **:** a member of a division of the Eastern Mongols who migrated to the Volga in the reign of Genghis Khan but later returned to the valley of the Ili

tori *pl of* TORUS

to·ric \'tȯrik, 'tōr-, 'tär-\ *adj* [ISV *tor-* (fr. NL *torus*) + *-ic*] **:** of, relating to, or shaped like a torus or segment of a torus

toric lens *n* **:** a simple lens having for one of its surfaces a segment of an equilateral zone of a torus and consequently having different refracting power in different meridians

tories *pl of* TORY

torify *usu cap, var of* TORYFY

to·rii \'tȯrē,ē, 'tōr-\ *n, pl* **torii** [Jap] **:** a Japanese gateway of light post-and-lintel construction designed usu. with delicately curved lines and commonly built at the approach to a Shinto shrine — compare PAI-LOU, TORAN

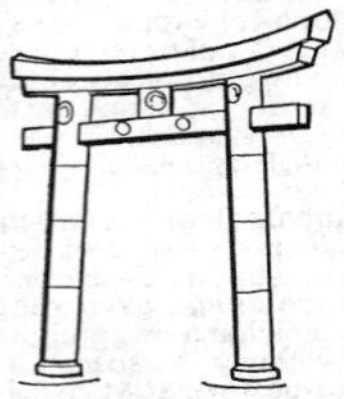

torii

to·ril \tə'rē(ə)l\ *n, pl* **to·ri·les** \-ē(,)lās\ *or* **torils** [Sp, fr. *toro* bull — more at TOREADOR] **:** a cell from which a bull enters the bullring

to·ri·lis \tə'rīləs, -rēl-\ *n, cap* [NL] **:** a genus of annual weedy herbs (family Umbelliferae) that are found in the northern hemisphere and have pinnately decompound leaves, compound umbels of white flowers, and fruits with five primary and four secondary ribs — see HEDGE PARSLEY

[1]**to·ri·nese** \¦tȯrə¦nēz, -ēs\ *adj, usu cap* [It, fr. *Torino* Turin, commercial and manufacturing commune of northwest Italy + It *-ese*] **1 :** of, relating to, or characteristic of Turin, Italy **2 :** of, relating to, or characteristic of the people of Turin

[2]**torinese** *n, pl* **torinese** \"\ *cap* **:** a native or inhabitant of Turin

to·rin·gin \tə'rinjən\ *n* -s [NL *toringo* (specific epithet of *Pyrus toringo*, syn. of *Malus sieboldii*) (fr. Jap, a crab apple tree) + E *-in*] **:** a crystalline flavone glucoside $C_{21}H_{20}O_9$ that occurs in the bark of a shrubby Japanese crab apple (*Malus sieboldii*) and in the buds of several poplars and that yields chrysin and glucose on hydrolysis

tor·ma \'tȯrmə\ *n, pl* **tor·mae** \-,mē, -,mī\ [NL, fr. Gk, socket, joint; akin to Gk *tormos* hole, socket, pivot — more at TERM] **:** either of a pair of small sclerites lying between the clypeus and labrum of a higher dipteran

[1]**tor·ment** \'tȯr,ment, -ō(ə),m- *sometimes chiefly Brit* -,mənt\ *n* -s [ME, fr. OF, fr. L *tormentum* torture, instrument of torture, engine for hurling missiles, fr. *torquēre* to twist, turn — more at TORTURE] **1 a :** the infliction of torture (as by rack or wheel) to punish or coerce someone **b :** the pain suffered by a victim of torture **2 :** extreme pain or anguish of body or mind **:** severe distress **:** AGONY ⟨showed the bodily ~ she was suffering —George Meredith⟩ ⟨five minutes of her were ~ to the ear —John Buchan⟩ ⟨the ~ of the betrayed husband —T.S.Eliot⟩ **3 :** a raging storm **:** TEMPEST **4 a :** a source or cause of physical or mental suffering or vexation **:** something that agitates, troubles, or pains ⟨the task of editing her . . . is both a tease and a ~ —Mark Van Doren⟩ **b :** someone that causes vexation or pain **:** TORMENTOR ⟨burst out into violent rages, and was a ~ to his friends —Rumer Godden⟩

[2]**tor·ment** \(')ˌ=¦ment\ *vt* -ED/-ING/-S [ME *tormenten*, fr. OF *tormenter*, fr. LL *tormentare*, fr. L *tormentum* torment] **1 a :** to cause (someone) severe suffering of body or mind **:** inflict pain or anguish on **:** AFFLICT, DISTRESS, RACK ⟨he was . . . ~*ed* with hunger and thirst —Nevil Shute⟩ ⟨she was . . . obviously ~*ed* by shyness —Compton Mackenzie⟩ ⟨problems that ~ men's hearts and warp men's lives —H.E.Fosdick⟩ **b :** to subject to extreme physical strain or agitation **:** stir up **:** DISTURB, TWIST ⟨the water is ~*ed* as if a hurricane had struck it —Alan Villiers⟩ ⟨lit another cigaret, or ~*ed* another pipe —Ellery Queen⟩ ⟨its atmosphere would be increasingly ~*ed* by aeroplanes —Eric Linklater⟩ **c :** to cause worry or vexation to **:** HARASS, PLAGUE, TROUBLE ⟨a last will and testament that was to ~ legal minds for a century to come —*Amer. Guide Series: Mass.*⟩ **2 :** to educe undue or unreal subtlety or complexity in **:** overrefine or complicate the interpretation of **:** read or explain deviously **:** DISTORT ⟨~*ed* the argument out of all honesty and directness⟩ ⟨~*s* the texts to yield readings more ingenious than probable⟩ **syn** see AFFLICT

tor·ment·ed·ly *adv* [*tormented* (past part. of [2]*torment*) + *-ly*] **:** in a tormented, distressed, or harassed manner **:** DISTRACTEDLY

tor·men·til \'tȯ(r)mən,til\ *n* -s [ME *turmentill*, fr. ML *tormentilla*, fr. L *tormentum* torment; fr. its use in allaying pain] **:** a yellow-flowered Eurasian herb (*Potentilla tormentilla*) with a root that contains an astringent and is used sometimes in tanning and dyeing; *broadly* **:** any of various plants of the genus *Potentilla*

[1]**tor·men·til·la** \ˌ==='tilə\ *n* -s [ML] **:** TORMENTIL

[2]**tormentilla** \"\ [NL, fr. ML, tormentil] *syn of* POTENTILLA

tor·ment·ing·ly *adv* [*tormenting* (pres. part. of [2]*torment*) + *-ly*] **:** in a tormenting, straining, or trying manner

tor·ment·ing·ness *n* -ES **:** the quality or state of being tormenting **:** the disposition to give pain

tor·men·tor *also* **tor·ment·er** \(')ˌ=¦mentə(r)\ *n* -s [ME *tormentor*, fr. OF *tormenteor*, fr. *tormenter* to torment + *-eor* -or — more at TORMENT, -OR] **1 :** an officer who inflicts penal or coercive torture ⟨delivered him to the ~*s*, till he should pay all that was due —Mt 18:34 (AV)⟩ **2 :** one that causes extreme pain, annoyance, or vexation **:** an agent of harassment **:** PEST, PLAGUE, PERSECUTOR **3 :** a long iron meat fork used by sea cooks **4 :** a fixed curtain or flat stage to the forward end of each side scene wall on a theater stage, running offstage parallel to the stage front, and serving to prevent the audience from seeing into the wings **5 :** a screen covered to prevent echo during the taking of motion picture scenes **6** *or* **tormentor pole :** a pole used to raise or brace an aerial fire ladder

tor·men·tress \-n·trəs\ *n* -ES [ME, fr. *tormentor* + *-ess*] **:** a female tormentor

tor·mo·gen cell \'tȯ(r)məjən-, -,jen-\ *n* [Gk *tormos* socket, hole + E *-gen* — more at TERM] **:** a specialized epidermal cell in insects that forms a socket at the base of some hairs

torn [ME *torn, toren*, fr. OE *toren*] *past part of* TEAR

tor·na·da \tō(r)'nädə\ *n* -s [OProv, fr. fem. of *tornat*, past part. of *tornar* to turn, return, fr. L *tornare* to turn in a lathe, round off — more at TURN] **1 :** the refrain of a Provençal poem **2** [alter. of *tornata*] **:** the envoy of an Italian canzone

tor·nad·ic \(')tō(r)¦nadik, -nad-, -dēk *sometimes* tə(r)'n-\ *adj* [*tornado* + *-ic*] **:** relating to, characteristic of, or constituting a tornado

tor·na·do \tō(r)'nā(,)dō *sometimes* tə(r)'n-\ *n, pl* **tornadoes** *or* **tornados** [modif. (influenced by Sp *tornado*, past part. of *tornar* to turn, return, fr. L *tornare* to turn in a lathe) of Sp *tronada* thunderstorm, fr. fem. of *tronado*, past part. of *tronar* to thunder, fr. L *tonare* — more at THUNDER] **1 a** *archaic* **:** a tropical thunderstorm **b** *obs* **:** the season of such storms **2 a :** a squall accompanying a thunderstorm in Africa **b :** a violent destructive whirling wind accompanied by a funnel-shaped cloud that progresses in a narrow path often for many miles over the land, occurs in many parts of the world but most frequently in the central Mississippi valley, and is associated with a fall in barometric pressure so rapid that wooden structures are often lifted and burst open by the air confined within them — compare CYCLONE, HURRICANE **3 :** a violent or destructive windstorm **:** WHIRLWIND **4 :** something likened to a storm: as **a :** a spectacular display of energy or power **:** DYNAMO ⟨he was a ~ when in action —Stanley Walker⟩ ⟨the maid was no respecter of persons when the ~ of work was in her —Adrian Bell⟩ **b :** a surge of destruction or devastation ⟨seemed torn by a ~ of grief and rage —Rumer Godden⟩ **c :** a torrential volume **:** FRESHET, SPATE, RUSH ⟨a ~ of words: too many at once to get into my ears —Hugh McCrae⟩ ⟨a ~ of protest⟩ **d :** a riotous showing (as of color or sound) ⟨a ~ of applause⟩ **syn** see WIND

tornado lantern *or* **tornado lamp** *n* **:** HURRICANE LAMP

tor·nal \'tȯrnᵊl\ *adj* [NL *tornus* + E *-al*] **:** of or relating to the tornus

tor·nar·ia \tō(r)'na(a)rēə\ *n* [NL, fr. L *tornus* lathe, chisel + NL *-aria* — more at TURN] **1** *pl* **tornarias** *or* **tornari·ae** \-ē,ē\ **:** a free-swimming larva that resembles a bipinnaria and is the immature form of an acorn worm or a closely related enteropneust **2** *cap* **:** any of various larval enteropneusts of which the adult is unknown — used as if a generic name ⟨*Tornaria alba*⟩ — **tor·nar·i·an** \(')ˌ=¦rēən\ *adj*

tor·na·ta \tō(r)'näd·ə\ *n* -s [It, fr. fem. of *tornato*, past part. of *tornare* to turn, return, fr. L *tornare*] **:** TORNADA 2

[1]**torn-down** \'ˌ=¦=\ *adj* [fr. past part. of *tear down*] *dial* **:** RIOTOUS, ROUGH, UNRULY, VIOLENT

[2]**torn-down** \'ˌ=,=\ *n, dial* **:** an unruly person

törnebohmite *var of* TOERNEBOHMITE

tor·nillo \tō(r)'nē(,)(y)ō, -ni(,)lō\ *or* **tor·nilla** \-nē(y)ə, -nilə\ *n* -s [Sp *tornillo*, lit., small lathe, clamp, screw, dim. of *torno* lathe, vise, fr. L *tornus* lathe — more at TURN] **:** SCREW BEAN 1

torniquet *var of* TOURNIQUET

tor·note \'tȯr,nōt\ *n* -s [Gk *tornōtos* rounded with a lathe, fr. *tornousthai* to round with a lathe, fr. *tornos* lathe — more at TURN] **:** a monaxon sponge spicule having both ends abruptly pointed

torn size *n* **:** the size of a piece of household linen (as a bed sheet) before hemming

tor·nus \'tȯrnəs\ *n, pl* **tor·ni** \-,nī, -,nē\ *or* **tornuses** [NL, fr. L, lathe — more at TURN] **:** the inner or anal angle of the wing of an insect (as a moth)

[1]**to·ro** \'tōr(,)ō, 'tō(,)rō\ *n* -s [Sp, fr. L *taurus* — more at STEER] **1** *chiefly Southwest* **:** BULL **2 a :** JACK CREVALLE **b :** a cowfish (*Lactophryes quadricornis*)

[2]**toro** \"\ *n* -s [Maori] **:** a New Zealand tree (*Myrsine salicina*) with reddish figured wood used for inlaying

toro bra·vo \ˌ=(,)=ˈbrä(,)vō\ *n* [Sp, lit., brave bull] **:** a fighting bull **:** a mettlesome animal in the bullring

to·roid \'tȯr,ȯid\ *n* -s [NL *torus* + E *-oid*] **1 :** a surface generated by the rotation of a plane closed curve about an axis lying in its plane and not intersecting it **2 :** a body whose surface has the form of a toroid

to·roi·dal \(')tȯ¦rȯidᵊl\ *adj* [NL *torus* + E *-oidal*] **:** of, relating to, or shaped like a torus or toroid **:** doughnut-shaped ⟨a ~ resistance coil⟩ ⟨the circulation in the atomic fireball develops a ~ form, with an updraft in the middle and a downdraft around the outside —W.W.Kellogg⟩ — **to·roi·dal·ly** \-ᵊlē\ *adv*

toroid coil *n* **:** a helical winding on a ring-shaped core

to·ron·to \tə'ränt·(,)ō, -n(,)tō, -ntə\ *adj, usu cap* [fr. *Toronto*, capital of Ontario, Canada] **:** of or from Toronto, the capital of Ontario **:** of the kind or style prevalent in Toronto

[1]**to·ron·to·nian** \¦tə¦rän·¦tōnēən, ¦tōrən-, ¦tärən-, ¦=rän-, -ōnyən\ *adj, usu cap* [*Toronto*, capital of Ontario + E *-onian* (as in *Bostonian*)] **1 :** of, relating to, or characteristic of Toronto, Ontario **2 :** of, relating to, or characteristic of the people of Toronto

[2]**torontonian** \"\ *n* -s *cap* **:** a native or inhabitant of Toronto

to·ro·sau·rus \¦tōrō¦sȯrəs\ *n, cap* [NL, prob. fr. L *torus* protuberance, bulge + NL *-saurus*] **:** a genus of dinosaurs (suborder Ceratopsia) of the Laramie formation

to·rose \'tōr,ōs, 'tō,rōs, ˌ='=\ *adj* [L *torosus*, fr. *torus* protuberance, bulge + *-osus* -ose] **1 :** having the surface covered with rounded prominences **:** KNOBBED **2 :** cylindrical (as a plant member) with alternate swellings and contractions

toroth *pl of* TORAH

to·ro·to·ro \¦tōrō¦tōr(,)ō\ *n* -s [origin unknown] **:** a kingfisher (*Halcyon torotoro*) of New Guinea having an orange beak

torp *abbr* torpedo; torpedoman

tor·pe·din·i·dae \,tȯrpə'dinə,dē\ *n pl, cap* [NL, fr. *Torpedin-*, *Torpedo*, type genus + *-idae*] **:** a family of elasmobranchs (order Batoidei) consisting of the electric rays

tor·pe·do \tō(r)'pē(,)dō\ *n* [L *torpedin-*, *torpedo* stiffness, numbness, crampfish, fr. *torpēre* to be stiff, numb — more at TORPID] **1** -ES **a** *or* **torpedo fish :** ELECTRIC RAY **b :** someone or something that paralyzes, benumbs, or stupefies **2** *cap* [NL *Torpedin-*, *Torpedo*, fr. L, crampfish] **:** the type genus of Torpedinidae **3** -ES **:** an engine or machine for destroying ships by blowing them up: as **a :** a metal case containing explosives that is anchored in a channel under water or at the surface or set adrift and so arranged that it will be exploded on contact by a vessel or electrically by an operator on shore — called also *submarine mine* **b :** a case containing high explosives carried on a long spar projecting from a war vessel or launch and exploded by contact or electrically — called also *spar torpedo* **c :** a dirigible self-propelling cigar-shaped submarine projectile filled with an explosive charge, projected from a ship often designed for that purpose against another at a distance, and controlled by compressed air and devices for keeping it on course and at a given depth **4** -ES **a :** a charge of explosive enclosed in a container or case and used for any of various military purposes — compare AERIAL TORPEDO **b :** an explosive cartridge or shell lowered or dropped into a bored oil well and there exploded to clear the well of obstructions or to open communication with a possible source of supply of oil **c :** a small firework that explodes when thrown against a hard object **d :** a detonating cartridge or shell placed on a rail to be exploded when crushed under the wheels of a railroad locomotive as a warning signal to the engineer **5** -ES **:** a professional gunman or assassin; *esp* **:** one employed by gangsters or racketeers

[2]**torpedo** \", *often* -ˌdə *in pres part*\ *vt* -ED/-ING/-ES **1 a :** to hit or sink (a ship) with a naval torpedo **:** strike (a military target) with a torpedo of any of various kinds **b :** to destroy or nullify altogether **:** EXPLODE, RUIN, SHATTER, WRECK ⟨this ~*es* the principal argument the union has relied on —A.H. Raskin⟩ ⟨the periodical which ~*ed* the great monthlies of the genteel age —H.S.Canby⟩ **2 :** to ignite or explode a charge in (an oil well or shaft) in order to clear away obstructions or increase output

torpedo boat *n* **:** a boat designed for firing torpedoes; *specif* **:** a small very fast thinly plated boat with one or more torpedo tubes carrying only light guns and relying on speed and inconspicuousness to get within torpedo range — compare MOTOR TORPEDO BOAT, SUBMARINE

torpedo-boat destroyer *n* [*torpedo boat*] **:** a large, swift, and powerful armed torpedo boat orig. intended principally for the destruction of torpedo boats but later used also as a formidable torpedo boat — compare DESTROYER

torpedo bomber *also* **torpedo plane** *n* **:** a military airplane designed to carry torpedoes

torpedo director *n* **:** a device for controlling the fire of torpedoes

torpedo grass *n* **:** a perennial grass (*Panicum repens*) that is native to the southeastern U.S., is used for pasture and forage, and has sharp-pointed rhizomes by which it spreads very aggressively

tor·pe·do·ist \tō(r)'pēdəwəst, -ēdō·ə-\ *n* -s **:** one that torpedoes; *esp* **:** TORPEDOMAN

torpedo juice *n* **:** a drink based on the fuel alcohol of naval torpedoes

¹torpedolike \'⸗⸗⸗,⸗\ *adj* [¹*torpedo* + *like*, adj.] **:** resembling a torpedo

²torpedolike \"\ *adv* [¹*torpedo* + *like*, adv.] **:** in the manner of a torpedo

tor·pe·do·man \-ēdō,man, -ēdə,m-, -mən\ *n, pl* **torpedomen** **:** a warrant officer (as in the U. S. Navy) whose specialty is supervision of underwater ordnance and related equipment

torpedo net *or* **torpedo netting** *n* **:** a netting made of steel links stretched by booms around a ship and extending beneath the surface of the water or extended across a harbor entrance as a protection against torpedoes

torpedo sand *n* **:** a coarse clean sand the particles of which all pass through a ⅜ inch mesh

torpedo tube *n* **:** a tube fixed near the waterline through which a torpedo is fired

tor·pex \'tȯr,peks\ *n* -ES *often cap* [*torpedo* + *explosive*] **:** a high explosive mixture consisting essentially of RDX, TNT, and aluminum and used for depth charges under water

¹tor·pid \'tȯrpəd, -ȯ(ə)p-\ *adj* [L *torpidus*, fr. *torpēre* to be stiff, numb, torpid; akin to Lith *tirpti* to become stiff, L *stirps* stem of a plant, trunk, stock, lineage, OE *starian* to stare — more at STARE] **1 a :** having lost motion or the power of exertion or feeling **:** DORMANT, NUMB **b :** sluggish in functioning or acting ⟨a ~ frog⟩ ⟨a ~ mind⟩ **2 :** lacking in energy or vigor **:** APATHETIC, DULL ⟨the bold and reckless young blood of ten years back was . . . turned into a ~, submissive, middle-aged, stout gentleman —W.M.Thackeray⟩ **syn** see LETHARGIC

²torpid \"\ *n* -S **:** a clinker-built eight-oared boat used for the Lent term races at Oxford university

tor·pid·i·ty \tȯ(r)'pidəd·ē, -idətē, -i\ *n* -ES [*torpid* + *-ity*] **:** the quality or state of being torpid **:** SLUGGISHNESS, TORPIDNESS

tor·pid·ly *adv* **:** in a torpid manner

tor·pid·ness *n* -ES [¹*torpid* + *-ness*] **:** TORPIDITY

tor·pi·fy *or* **tor·pe·fy** \'tȯ(r)pə,fī\ *vt* -ED/-ING/-ES [modif. (influenced by E *-ify*, *-fy*) of LL *torpefacere*, fr. *torpēre* to be torpid + *facere* to make — more at DO] **:** to make torpid **:** BENUMB, STUPEFY **syn** see DAZE

tor·pi·tude \-pə,tüd, -pə-,tyüd\ *n* -S [*torpid* + *-tude*] *archaic* **:** TORPIDITY

tor·por \'tȯrpər, 'tȯ(ə)pə(r *sometimes* -,pȯ(ə)r *or* -,pȯ(ə)\ *n* -S [L, fr. *torpēre* to be torpid] **1 :** a state of mental and motor inactivity with partial or total insensibility **:** suspended animation **:** sluggishness or stagnation of function **:** DORMANCY ⟨a deathlike ~ has succeeded to her former intellectual activity —W.H.Prescott⟩ **2 :** mental or spiritual sluggishness **:** APATHY, LETHARGY ⟨tradition may result merely in ~ —Walter Moberly⟩

tor·por·if·ic \,tȯ(r)pə¦rifik, -fēk\ *adj* [L *torpor* + E *-i-* + *-fic*] **:** producing torpor **:** DULLING, STUPEFYING

tor·quate \'tȯr,kwāt\ *adj* [L *torquatus*, lit., wearing a torque, fr. *torquis*, *torques* + *-atus* -ate] **:** having a ring esp. of color around the neck **:** COLLARED, RING-NECKED

¹torque \'tȯ(ə)rk, -ȯ(ə)k\ *n* -S [F *torque*, fr. L *torquis*, *torques*, fr. *torquēre* to twist — more at TORTURE] **:** a usu. metal collar or neck chain worn by the ancient Gauls, Germans, and Britons ⟨these hands won many a ~ of gold —W.B.Yeats⟩

²torque *n* -S [L *torquēre* to twist] **:** something which produces or tends to produce rotation or torsion and whose effectiveness is measured by the product of the force and the perpendicular distance from the line of action of the force to the axis of rotation **:** a moment of force ⟨a pound-foot of ~ is the ~ produced by a force of one pound acting one foot from the center of rotation —*Consumer Reports*⟩ ⟨if the handle of the wrench were 1 foot long and a 10-pound force is put on its end, 10 pound-feet of ~ would be applied on the nut —*Principles of Automotive Vehicles*⟩ ⟨in addition to transforming fuel into heat, the engine converts heat into reciprocal motion, and it changes reciprocal motion into ~ —George Hafferkamp & J.H.Zich⟩; *broadly* **:** a turning or twisting force **:** rotary effort

torque arm *n* [²*torque*] **:** an arm to take the torque of the rear axle of an automotive vehicle that is connected at the rear with the differential case either rigidly or by a joint and at the front is always jointed to a cross member of the frame

torque converter *n* **:** a device for converting the speed and torque at the driving shaft of an automobile to that required by the driven shaft

tor·que·ma·da \,tȯ(r)k(w)ə'mäldə, -mäl, ¦thə\ *n* -S *usu cap* [after Tomas de *Torquemada* †1498, Spanish Dominican monk and first inquisitor general for all Spanish possessions] **:** PERSECUTOR ⟨the youthful and ubiquitous *Torquemadas* who serve as the subcommittee's chief counsel and chief consultant —R.H.Rovere⟩

torque·me·ter \'tȯ(r)k,mēd·ə(r)\ *n* [²*torque* + *-meter*] **:** an instrument to measure or record torque

torque tube *n* [²*torque*] **:** a tube surrounding the propeller shaft of an automotive vehicle to take the torque and being usu. a unit with the rear-axle housing at the rear but with a universal joint at the front where it is supported by a cross-frame member or by the rear end of the transmission case

torque wrench *n* **:** a wrench that measures and indicates the

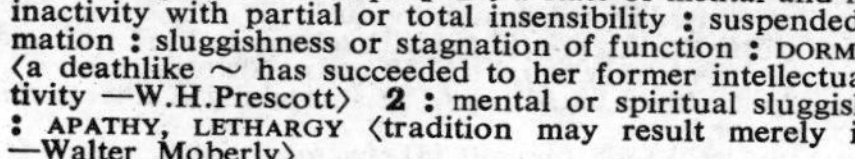

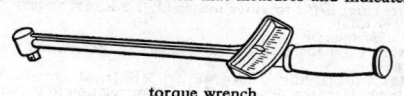

torque wrench

amount of turning and twisting force applied in tightening a nut or bolt

torr \'tȯ(ə)r\ *n, pl* **torr** [after Evangelista *Torricelli* †1647 Ital. mathematician and physicist and inventor of the barometer] **:** a unit of pressure equal to 1/760 of an atmosphere and very nearly equal to the pressure of a column of mercury 1 millimeter high at 0° C and standard gravity

tor·re·fac·tion \,tȯrə¦fakshən, ¦tär-\ *n* -S [L *torrefactus* (past part. of *torrefacere* to torrefy) + E *-ion*] **:** the act or process of torrefying or the state of being torrefied

tor·re·fy *also* **tor·ri·fy** \'⸗⸗,fī\ *vt* -ED/-ING/-ES [modif. (influenced by E *-fy*, *-ify*) of L *torrefacere*, fr. *torrēre* to dry, parch + *facere* to make — more at TORRENT, DO] **:** to dry or roast with fire **:** PARCH, SCORCH: as **a :** to subject (ores) to scorching heat so as to drive off volatile ingredients **:** ROAST **b :** to dry (drugs) on a hot metallic plate till they are friable or are reduced to the state desired

tor·rens system \'tȯ¦rənz-, 'tä¦\ *n, usu cap T* [after Sir Robert *Torrens* †1884, Brit. pioneer in Australia] **:** a system of land title registration first introduced in Australia and widely used in England, Canada, the U. S., and elsewhere according to which the government guarantees properly registered titles, simplifying transfers and making title insurance unnecessary

¹tor·rent \'tȯrənt, 'tär-\ *n* -S [F, fr. L *torrent-*, *torrens*, fr. *torrent-*, *torrens* burning, seething, rushing, fr. pres. part. of *torrēre* to dry, parch, burn; akin to OHG *derren* to dry, parch, ON *therra*, Skt *tarṣayati* he causes to thirst — more at THIRST] **1 :** a violent stream of a liquid (as water or lava); *esp* **:** a rushing stream of water (as a flooded river or one suddenly raised by a heavy rain or thaw and descending a steep incline) **2 a :** a mountain channel that is often dry though filled with rushing water at some times or seasons **b :** an intermittent branch **3 :** a raging flood **:** a tumultuous outpouring **:** FLUX, RUSH ⟨let loose a ~ of speculative buying —O.S.Nock⟩ ⟨engulfed in a ~ of enemy troops —H.L.Merillat⟩ ⟨philosophy . . . provided a foothold for man above the ~ of circumstance —John Buchan⟩

²torrent \"\ *adj* [L *torrent-*, *torrens*, adj.] **:** TORRENTIAL ⟨rich, grassy orchards and a ~ stream —M.C.A.Henniker⟩

torrent bow *n* [¹*torrent*] **:** a fragmentary rainbow formed in the spray of a torrent

torrent duck *n* **:** any of several ducks related to the mergansers and constituting the genus *Merganetta* that inhabit rushing streams of the Andes from Colombia to Chile

tor·ren·tial \tȯ'renchəl, tə'r-, tä'r-\ *adj* [¹*torrent* + *-ial*] **1 a :** relating to or having the character of a torrent ⟨~ rains⟩ **b :** caused by or resulting from action of rapid streams ⟨~ gravel⟩ **c :** of, relating to, or being inhabitants of swiftly flowing waters ⟨~ adaptations⟩ **2 :** resembling a torrent in violence or rapidity of flow **:** COPIOUS, RUSHING, VIGOROUS ⟨it has all the ~ facility and fecundity characteristic of his style —Winthrop Sargeant⟩ ⟨because of his splendid costumes and his ~ speeches —Malcolm Cowley⟩

tor·ren·tial·ly \-chəlē, -li\ *adv* **:** in a torrential manner

tor·ren·ti·cole \tə'rentə,kōl\ *n* -S [¹*torrent* + *-i-* + *-cole*] **:** an organism that lives in swiftly flowing water

¹tor·re·ón *or* **torreon** \¦tȯrē¦ōn, -ē,ōn, -ē¦än\ *adj, usu cap* [fr. *Torreón*, city of northeast Mexico] **:** of or from the city of Torreón, Mexico **:** of the kind or style prevalent in Torreón

²torreón \"\ *n, pl* **torreo·nes** \,⸗⸗'ōnēz, -'ō(,)nās\ [Sp, aug. of *torre* tower, fr. L *turris* — more at TOWER] **:** a prehistoric stone tower in the southwestern U.S.

tor·reya \'tȯrēə\ *n, cap* [NL, after John *Torrey* †1873 Am. botanist and chemist] **:** a genus of Asiatic and No. American trees (family Taxaceae) having two-ranked often ill-scented linear leaves and a large ovoid fruit resembling a drupe but being actually a large seed surrounded by a fleshy aril — see CALIFORNIA NUTMEG, STINKING CEDAR

tor·rey·ite \-ē,īt\ *n* -S [John *Torrey* †1873 + E *-ite*] **:** a mineral $(Mg,Mn,Zn)_7(SO_4)(OH)_{12}.4H_2O$ consisting of a basic hydrous sulfate of magnesium, manganese, and zinc

tor·rey pine \'tȯrē-\ *or* **torrey's pine** *n, usu cap T* [after John *Torrey* †1873] **:** a tall coniferous tree (*Pinus torreyana*) of California with dark green needles in fives and long cylindrical cones — called also *gray-leaf pine*, *Sabine pine*, *Soledad pine*

torrey tree *n, usu cap 1st T* [after John *Torrey* †1873] **:** STINKING CEDAR

tor·ri·cel·li·an \,tȯrə¦chelēən, ¦tär-, -rə¦sel-\ *adj, usu cap* [Evangelista *Torricelli* †1647 Ital. mathematician and physicist + E *-an*] **:** of or relating to the Italian physicist and mathematician Torricelli closely associated with Galileo and noted esp. for his researches in pneumatics

torricellian tube *n, usu cap 1st T* **:** a glass tube open at one end and hermetically sealed at the other and of such length that when filled with a liquid (as mercury) and immersed at the open end in a vessel of the same liquid allowing the enclosed liquid to descend till it is counterbalanced by the pressure of the atmosphere a vacuum will be produced at the upper end

torricellian vacuum *n, usu cap T* **:** the vacuum at the upper end of a Torricellian tube

tor·ri·cel·li's law *also* **torricelli's theorem** \-lēz-\ *n, usu cap Torricelli's* [after Evangelista *Torricelli* †1647] **:** a law in hydrodynamics: the speed of efflux of a liquid from an orifice is equal to that of a body falling freely through a distance equal to the total head of the liquid at the orifice

tor·rid \'tȯrəd, 'tär-\ *adj, usu* -ER/-EST [L *torridus*, fr. *torrēre* to dry, parch — more at TORRENT] **1 a :** parched with heat esp. of the sun **:** HOT, DRY, SCORCHED ⟨the ~ June boulevard —Bruce Marshall⟩ **b :** giving off intense heat **:** SCORCHING ⟨the ~ heat of the desert —C.A. & Mary Beard⟩ **2 :** emotionally aroused or arousing **:** ARDENT, PASSIONATE, SULTRY ⟨~ talk of dynamiting managers' homes⟩ ⟨the ~ love letters⟩ ⟨a ~ beauty⟩ ⟨hot trumpets and ~ rhythms —Green Peyton⟩

tor·rid·i·ty \tȯ'ridəd·ē, tä'r-, -idətē, -i\ *n* -ES [LL *torriditat-*, *torriditas*, fr. L *torridus* torrid + *-itat-*, *-itas* -ity] **:** TORRIDNESS

tor·rid·ly *adv* **:** in a torrid manner

tor·rid·ness *n* -ES **:** the quality or state of being torrid

tor·ri·do·ni·an \¦tȯrə¦dōnēən\ *adj, usu cap* [Loch *Torridon*, inlet on northwest coast of Scotland + E *-ian*] **:** of, relating to, or constituting a division of the Precambrian — see GEOLOGIC TIME table

torrid zone *n* **:** the belt of the earth between the tropics over which the sun is vertical at some period of the year — see ZONE illustration

torrify *var of* TORREFY

tor·ro·ne \tə'rōnē\ *n* -S [It, fr. Sp. *turrón*, fr. *turrar* to roast, toast, fr. L *torrēre* to dry, parch — more at TORRENT] **:** a candy made of honey and almonds

torrs *pl of* TORR

tor·ru·bia \tə'rübēə\ *n, cap* [NL, after José *Torrubia* †1768 Span. naturalist] **:** a genus of tropical American shrubs and trees (family Nyctaginaceae) with fleshy leaves, greenish dioecious panicled flowers, and fleshy fruit — see BLOLLY

tors *pl of* TOR

tor·sade \(')tȯr¦säd, -säd\ *n* -S [F, fr. obs. F *tors* twisted (fr. LL *torsus*) + F *-ade*] **:** a twisted cord or ribbon used esp. as a hat ornament ⟨the crown decked with ~s of pearls —*Harper's*⟩

tor·sa·lo \'tȯ(r)sə,lō\ *n* -S [AmSp *tórsalo*] **:** a botfly (*Dermatobia hominis*) that attacks man and other mammals in warm parts of the Americas

¹torse \'tȯ(ə)rs\ *n* -S [MF *torse*, *torce*, fr. fem. of *tors* twisted] **:** a twisted band or wreath by which a heraldic crest is joined to the helmet

²torse \"\ *n* -S [F, fr. It. *torso*] **:** TORSO

tor·sel \'tȯrsəl\ *or* **tas·sel** \'tasəl\ *n* -S [*torsel* alter. of *tassel*, fr. F *tassel*, *tasseau*, fr. OF *tassel* clasp — more at TASSEL] **:** a piece of stone, iron, or wood to support the end of a beam or joist and distribute the weight

torsi *pl of* TORSO

tor·si·bil·i·ty \,tȯ(r)sə'biləd·ē\ *n* -ES [LL *torsus* + E *-ibility*] **:** resistance to torsion; *also* **:** tendency (as of a twisted rope) to untwist

tor·si·gram \'tȯ(r)sə,gram\ *also* **tor·sio·gram** \-)shə,g-, -)sēə,g-\ *n* [*torsion* + *-gram*] **:** a torsion record made on a torsigraph

tor·si·graph *also* **tor·sio·graph** \-graf,-gräf\ *n* [ISV *torsion* + *-graph*] **:** a recording torsion meter

tor·sion \'tȯrshən, -ȯ(ə)sh-\ *n* -S [LL *torsus* (past part. of L *torquēre* to twist) + E *-ion* — more at TORTURE] **1 :** the act of turning or twisting **:** the state of being twisted **:** the twisting or wrenching of a body by the exertion of forces tending to turn one end or part about a longitudinal axis while the other is held fast or turned in the opposite direction **2 :** the limit of the ratio of the angle between the binormals at two points of a curve to the length of the arc joining the points as the length of the arc approaches zero — called also *second curvature* **3 :** the reactive torque that an elastic solid exerts by reason of being under torsion **4 :** the twisting of a body organ on its own axis ⟨the ~ of a loop of intestine around its own mesentery⟩ **syn** see STRESS

tor·sion·al *also* **tor·tion·al** \-shən°l,-shnəl\ *adj* **:** of, relating to, causing, or resulting from torsion — **tor·sion·al·ly** \-°l¦ē, -əl, ¦i\ *adv*

torsion balance *n* **1 :** an instrument used to measure minute forces (as electrostatic or magnetic attraction and repulsion) by the torsion of a wire or filament, the angle of torsion being proportional to the amount of force exerted **2 :** a spring balance in which the weight is balanced by the torsion of a wire — compare EÖTVÖS BALANCE

torsion bar *n* **:** a device to minimize sideway and road jolts in automobiles

torsion electrometer *n* **:** a torsion balance used for measuring electric attraction or repulsion

torsion head *n* **:** the part of a torsion balance from which the wire or filament is suspended and which is usu. graduated with an angular scale for measuring the counterrotation required to neutralize the deflection

tor·sion·ing \-sh(ə)niŋ\ *n* -S [*torsion* + *-ing*] **:** the producing of torsion esp. to close an opening (as by twisting the free end of a cut artery)

torsion meter *n* **:** an instrument for determining the torque on a shaft — compare TORSIGRAPH

torsion modulus *n* **:** SHEAR MODULUS

torsion pendulum *n* **:** PENDULUM 1b

torsion scale *n* **:** a weighing scale in which the fulcrums of the levers or beams are wires or strips acting by torsion

torsk \'tȯ(ə)rsk\ *n, pl* **torsk** *or* **torsks** [of Scand origin; akin to Norw & Sw & Dan *torsk* codfish, ON *thorskr*; akin to MLG *dorsch* codfish, and prob. to ON *therra* to dry — more at TORRENT] **:** CODFISH

¹tor·so \'tȯr(,)sō, -ȯ(ə)(,)sō\ *n, pl* **torsos** \-sōz\ *or* **tor·si** \-sē\ *also* **torsoes** [It, stalk, stem, torso, fr. L *thyrsus* thyrsus, stalk, stem — more at THYRSUS] **1 :** the trunk of a sculptured representation of a human body; *esp* **:** the trunk of a statue whose head and limbs are mutilated **2 :** something (as a work of art or letters) that is mutilated or left unfinished ⟨three volumes and only a ~ completed —*Infantry Jour.*⟩ **3 a :** the human trunk ⟨she lifted his ~ with great strength and infinite solicitude —F.M.Ford⟩ **b :** something likened to the human torso (as the trunk of a tree) ⟨cypress trees, tough twisted ~es lashed by long winds —Carl Sandburg⟩ **c :** the part of a garment that covers the torso ⟨a black-and-white checked cotton with a long, graceful ~ has a button-on collar —*New Yorker*⟩

²torso \"\ *n* -S [modif. (influenced by ¹*torso*) of F (*colonne*) *torse* twisted column, fr. *colonne* column (fr. MF *colomne*) + *torse*, fem. of obs. *tors* twisted — more at COLUMN, TORSADE] **:** a twisted or spiral shaft or column

tort \'tȯ(ə)r¦t, -ȯ(ə)l, *usu* ¦d·+V\ *n* -S [ME, fr. MF, fr. ML *tortum*, fr. L, neut. of *tortus*, twisted, distorted, fr. past part. of *torquēre* to twist — more at TORTURE] **1** *obs* **:** injury or wrong done someone **2 :** a wrongful act for which a civil action will lie except one involving a breach of contract **:** a civil wrong independent of a contract — compare CRIME, DELICT, INJURY, TRESPASS

tor·ta \'tȯrd·ə\ *n* -S [Sp, cake, fr. LL, round loaf of bread] **1 :** a flat heap of moist crushed silver ore prepared for the patio process **2 :** an open pie with a base of bread or biscuit dough and a sweet or savory filling — called also *tourte*

tor·te \'tȯrd·ə, ÷ -rt\ *n, pl* **tor·ten** \-rt°n\ *or* **tortes** [G, prob. fr. It *torta*, fr. LL, round loaf of bread] **:** a cake or pastry made of many eggs, sugar, and often grated nuts or dry bread crumbs in place of flour and baked in a large flat form, being sometimes filled with jam and usu. covered with a rich frosting (as chocolate, mocha, or strawberry meringue) — compare LINZER TORTE, SACHER

tor·teau *also* **tor·teaux** \(')tȯr¦tō\ *n, pl* **torteaux** \-ōz\ [MF *torteau*, fr. OF *tortel* wafer, small round loaf of bread, dim. of *torte*, *tourte* round loaf of bread, fr. LL *torta*] **:** a heraldic roundel gules

tor·tel·li·ni \,tȯ(r)d·°l'ēnē\ *n* -S [It (pl.), dim. of *tortelli* (pl.) a pasta, fr. LL *torta* round loaf of bread] **:** an alimentary paste of noodle dough cut in rounds, filled with savory fillings, and boiled

tort-feasor \'⸗¦fēzər, -,zȯ(ə)r\ *n* -S [F *tortfaiseur*, fr. MF, fr. *tort* wrong + *faiseur* doer, maker, fr. *fais-* (stem of *faire* to do, make, fr. L *facere*) + *-eur* -or — more at TORT, DO] **:** one that commits or is guilty of a tort

tor·ti·col·lis \,tȯrd·ə'käləs\ *n* -ES [NL, fr. L *tortus* twisted + *-i-* + *collum* neck — more at TORT, COLLAR] **:** an abnormal and more-or-less fixed twisting of the neck associated in man with muscular contracture esp. of a sternocleidomastoid and in domestic and other lower mammals occurring esp. in conjunction with severe intestinal parasitism or ear disorders — called also *wryneck*

tor·ti·cone \'tȯrd·ə,kōn\ *n* [L *tortus* + E *-i-* + *cone*] **:** a turreted spiral cephalopod shell as distinguished from one with coils in one plane

tor·tie *also* **tor·ty** \'tȯrd·ē\ *n, pl* **torties** [by shortening & alter.] **:** TORTOISESHELL CAT

tor·tile \'tȯrd·°l, -r,tīl, -r(,)til\ *adj* [L *tortilis*, fr. *tortus* (past part. of *torquēre* to twist) + *-ilis* -ile — more at TORTURE] **:** COILED, TWISTED, SINUOUS

tor·ti·lla \tȯ(r)'tē(y)ə\ *n* -S [AmSp, fr. dim. of Sp *torta* cake — more at TORTA] **:** a round thin cake of unleavened cornmeal bread usu. eaten hot with a topping or filling that may include ground meat, cheese, and any of various sauces — see ENCHILADA

tor·til·lé \¦tȯ(r)tē¦(y)ā\ *adj* [F, fr. past part. of *tortiller* to twist, wind, fr. (assumed) VL *tortiliare*, fr. L *tortilis* twisted — more at TORTILE] *heraldry* **:** wreathed with a spirally twisted band

tor·til·lon \¦tȯ(r)d·ē¦(y)än, -)ōn\ *n* -S [F, lit., twist, twisted object, fr. MF, fr. *tortiller* to twist] **:** a small rolled-paper stump used in charcoal drawing for rubbing or blending

tortional *var of* TORSIONAL

tor·tious \'tȯrshəs, -ȯ(ə)sh-\ *adj* [ME, fr. *tort* + *-ious*] **1** *obs* **a :** INJURIOUS, WRONGFUL **b :** IMPROPER, MISTAKEN **2 :** implying or involving tort for which the law gives damages ⟨~ conduct incurs liability⟩ — **tor·tious·ly** *adv*

tortious conveyance *n, old Eng law* **:** a wrongful conveyance of a greater estate than that of the conveyor

tor·tive \'tȯrd·iv\ *adv* [L *tortus* (past part. of *torquēre* to twist) + E *-ive* — more at TORTURE] **:** TWISTED, WREATHED

tor·tle \'tȯrd·°l\ *dial var of* TURTLE

tor·toise \'tȯr¦d·əs, -d(ə)s, ¦təs *sometimes* ¦,tȯiz *or* ¦,tȯis\ *n, pl* **tortoises** *also* **tortoise** [ME *tortuce*, *tortous*, *tortuse*, prob. alter. (the gen. being taken as the n. attrib.) of *tortu*, fr. MF *tortue* — more at TURTLE] **1 :** a reptile of the order Testudinata **:** TURTLE — used esp. of terrestrial forms; see GIANT TORTOISE **2 :** someone or something regarded as slow, tardy, or laggard ⟨complacent about the ~. Reaction, plodding up from the rear —H.L.Smith b. 1906⟩ **3 :** TORTOISESHELL **4 :** a strong brown that is yellower, less strong, and slightly lighter than average russet, yellower and less strong than rust, and yellower and slightly duller than gold brown **5 :** TESTUDO 2

tortoise beetle *n* **1 :** any of numerous small tortoise-shaped beetles of the family Chrysomelidae many of whom have a brilliant metallic luster and whose larvae feed upon the leaves of various plants **2 :** any of several Australian tenebrionid beetles of *Helaeus* and related genera having broad margins to the elytra and prothorax

tortoise-core \'⸗⸗(,)⸗¦⸗\ *n* **:** a stone core shaped like the carapace of a tortoise and constituting the nodule from which prehistoric man flaked off material for tools

tortoise plant *n* **:** ELEPHANT'S-FOOT 1b

tortoise scale *n* **:** any of various thick-bodied to hemispherical soft scales; *esp* **:** LECANIUM 2

¹tor·toise·shell \'tȯ(r)d·¦ə,shel, -)t¦, ¦əs(h),shel\ *n* **1 :** a substance that forms the horny plates covering the shell of some turtles and esp. the hawksbill turtle which provides almost all of the tortoiseshell of commerce and that is rich brown mottled with yellow, readily molded and welded when hot, and used in inlaying and in making ornamental articles **2** *or* **tortoiseshell butterfly :** any of several brilliantly colored butterflies of the genus *Nymphalis*; *esp* **:** either of two such butterflies (*N. milberti* and *N. j-album*) that in the larval state feed upon nettles

²tortoiseshell \"\ *adj* **:** made of tortoise shell or having a mottled coloration suggesting tortoise shell

tortoiseshell cat *or* **tortoiseshell** *n* **:** a usu. female domestic cat having a black, red, and cream or white blotched coat often with a white blaze on the face

tortoiseshell tiger *n* **:** CLOUDED LEOPARD

tortoiseshell turtle *n* **:** HAWKSBILL TURTLE

tor·to·ni \tȯ(r)'tōnē\ *n* -S [prob. after *Tortoni* 19th cent. Ital. restaurateur in Paris] **1 :** an ice cream made of heavy cream sometimes with minced almonds, chopped maraschino cherries, or other flavoring ingredients **2 :** BISCUIT TORTONI

¹tor·tri·cid \'tȯ(r)·trəsəd\ *adj* [NL *Tortricidae*] **:** of or relating to the Tortricidae

²tortricid \"\ *n* -S **:** a moth of the family Tortricidae

tor·tric·i·dae \tȯ(r)·'trisə,dē\ *n pl, cap* [NL *Tortric-*, *Tortrix*, type genus + *-idae*] **:** a family of small moths usu. having a stout body, oblong lightly fringed wings, threadlike antennae, and a tuft of scales at the end of the abdomen, many of the larvae being leaf rollers and others living in various fruits and galls

tor·trix \'tȯr·triks, -ȯ(ə)·t-\ *n* [NL *Tortric-*, *Tortrix*, lit., female twister, fr. L *tortus* (past part. of *torquēre* to twist) + *-ric-*, *-rix*, fem. of *-or*; fr. its habit of twisting or rolling leaves to make a nest — more at TORTURE] **1** *cap* **:** a genus of moths that is the type of the family Tortricidae **2** -ES **:** any moth of the genus *Tortrix* or family Tortricidae — see ORANGE TORTRIX, TEA TORTRIX

torts *pl of* TORT

tor·tu·la·ce·ae \,tȯ(r)chə'lāsē,ē\ [NL, fr. *Tortula*, genus of mosses (fr. L *tortus* twisted + *-ula*) + *-aceae*] *syn of* POTTIACEAE

tor·tu·os·i·ty \,tȯ(r)chə'wäsəd·ē, -sətē, -i\ *n* -ES [LL *tortuositat-*, *tortuositas*, fr. L *tortuosus* tortuous + *-itat-*, *-itas* -ity] **1 a :** the quality or state of being tortuous **b :** something winding or twisted **:** a crooked place or part **:** BEND, SINUOSITY ⟨she began to indicate the *tortuosities* of the tree with tentative and hesitant strokes —*New Yorker*⟩ **2 :** an instance or trait of deviousness or crookedness **:** INDIRECTNESS ⟨had begun to bog down in the subtleties and *tortuosities* of his own thought —J.R.Ullman⟩ ⟨*tortuosities* of behavior that pride, thwarted passion and almost ghoulish severities and prohibitions had effected —*N. Y. Herald Tribune Bk. Rev.*⟩

tor·tu·ous \'tȯ(r)chəwəs\ *adj* [ME, fr. MF *tortueux*, fr. L *tortuosus*, fr. *tortus* twist (fr. *tortus*, past part. of *torquēre* to twist) + *-osus* -ous] **1 :** marked by repeated twists, bends, or turns : WINDING ⟨the channel is ∼ and dangerous and constantly silting —L.F.Alexander⟩ ⟨we begin a ∼ climb into the highlands —Tom Marvel⟩ ⟨a ∼ length of water-cooled coils —D.W.Dresden⟩ ⟨products of a ∼ hereditary line —Faubion Bowers⟩ **2 a :** marked by or resorting to devious or indirect tactics or strategy : crooked, treacherous, or sharp in device or method : lacking in straightforwardness, candor, or simplicity : TRICKY ⟨pursued a ∼ policy in his testimony, disclosing this piece of evidence and withholding that —Rebecca West⟩ ⟨∼ haggling over the price of comradeship —*Time*⟩ **b :** wandering from a direct or consecutive course in thought or action : deviating into irrelevant complexity or intricacy : CIRCUITOUS, INVOLVED ⟨the ∼ workings of government by consent —*New Republic*⟩ ⟨the featureless hierophants of some ∼ ceremony —V.S.Pritchett⟩ ⟨∼ litigation⟩ **3 :** TORTIOUS 2 ⟨an agent who does a ∼ act is not relieved from liability by the fact that he acted at the command ... of his principal —J.D.Johnson⟩
tor·tu·ous·ly *adv* **:** in a tortuous manner
tor·tu·ous·ness *n* -ES **:** the quality or state of being tortuous
tor·tur·able \'tȯ(r)ch(ə)rəbəl\ *adj* [²torture + -able] **:** capable of being tortured
¹tor·ture \'tȯrchər, -ȯ(ə)chə(r\ *n* -s [F, fr. LL *tortura* act of twisting, torture, fr. L *tortus* (past part. of *torquēre* to twist, wind, torture) + *-ura* -ure; akin to OHG *drāhsil* turner, Gk *atraktos* spindle, Skt *tarku*] **1 a :** the infliction of intense pain (as from burning, crushing, wounding) to punish or coerce someone : torment or agony induced to penalize religious or political dissent or nonconformity, to extort a confession or a money contribution, or to give sadistic pleasure to the torturer ⟨no one shall be subjected to ∼ or to cruel, inhuman or degrading treatment or punishment —*U. N. Declaration of Human Rights*⟩ **b** *obs* **:** an implement of torture **2 a :** anguish of body or mind : excruciating agony : extremity of suffering ⟨long ∼ with Parkinson's disease —John Mason Brown⟩ ⟨she shrank in her convulsed, coiled ∼ from the thought of such a thing —D.H.Lawrence⟩ **b :** an extreme annoyance or severe irritation : an intense strain : something pernicious or baneful : PLAGUE ⟨plays ... would be torn line from line for the ∼ of high school boys and girls —J.D.Adams⟩ ⟨many of their sidehill and downhill lies would have been ∼ to a golfer with 20-20 vision —Tom Siler⟩ **3 :** distortion, overrefinement, or perversion of a meaning, an argument, or a line of thought or reasoning : STRAINING ⟨no ∼ in interpretation would be required —E.W.Knight⟩ **4 :** the subjecting of material or equipment to extreme strain or abuse as a test of strength, endurance, or quality ⟨cars are put through thousands of miles of ∼ —*Visit to the Proving Grounds*⟩
²torture \"\ *vb* **tortured; tortured; torturing** \-ch(ə)riŋ\ **tortures** *vt* **1 a :** to put to torture : punish or coerce by inflicting excruciating pain ⟨*tortured* my sister for three months ... disfigured her face and broke her hands and legs —Ben Hecht⟩ **b :** to extract or obtain by torture ⟨*tortured* a confession from the prisoner⟩ **2 :** to cause intense suffering to : inflict anguish on : subject to severe pain : TORMENT ⟨set himself to ∼ me as a schoolboy would devote a rapturous half hour to watching the agonies of an impaled beetle —Rudyard Kipling⟩ **3 :** to twist or wrench out of shape : DISTORT, WARP ⟨made it an easy matter to ∼ wooden boards into uncouth shapes —*Amer. Guide Series: Conn.*⟩ ⟨language ... strained and *tortured* —R.L.Cook⟩ ⟨unable to ∼ her religious experience into the Calvinistic system —C.A.Dinsmore⟩ ∼ *vi* **:** to cause excruciating pain or anguish **syn** see AFFLICT
tor·tured·ly \-chə(r)dlē\ *adv* [*tortured* (past part. of ²torture) + -ly] **:** in a tortured, strained, or anguished manner
tor·tur·er \-chərə(r)\ *n* -s **:** one that tortures
tor·ture·some \-chə(r)səm\ *adj* [¹torture + -some] **:** causing torture : intolerably painful ⟨slipped on their ∼ pumps —William Maxwell⟩
tor·tur·ing·ly \-chəriŋlē\ *adv* [*torturing* (pres. part. of ²torture) + -ly] **:** in a torturing manner : PAINFULLY
tor·tur·ous \'tȯrchərəs, -ȯ(ə)ch-\ *adj* [ME, fr. MF *tortureux*, fr. *torture* + *-eux* -ous] **1 :** causing, marked, or accompanied by torture : cruelly painful ⟨the ∼, far from finished battle —*Time*⟩ ⟨fell into ∼ sleep —C.O.Gorham⟩ **2** [alter. of *tortuous*] **:** DISTORTED, TORTUOUS, TWISTING ⟨the dark-stained after rafter, that seasoned crossarm of ∼ timber —Ralph Ellison⟩
tor·tu·rous·ly \-chə(r)dlē\ *adv* **:** in a torturous manner : PAINFULLY ⟨moved at a ∼ slow pace —Norman Mailer⟩
torty *var of* TORTIE
to·ru \'tȯr(ˌ)ü\ *n* -S [Maori] **:** a New Zealand tree (*Persoonia toru*) of the family Meliaceae with reddish wood that resembles toro
tor·u·la \'tȯr(y)ələ, 'tär-\ *n* [NL, fr. L *torus* protuberance, bulge, cushion + *-ula* —more at TORUS] **1** *pl* **tor·u·lae** \-ˌlē, -ˌlī\ *also* **torulas :** any of various yeasts or yeastlike fungi that lack sexual spores, do not produce alcoholic fermentations, and are typically acid formers **b :** CRYPTOCOCCOSIS **2** *cap* **a :** a form genus of usu. dark colored chiefly saprophytic imperfect fungi (family Dematiaceae) with hyphae that develop numerous crosswalls and are converted into chains of conidia — see BLACK YEAST **b** *in some classifications* **:** a genus of yeasts including pathogens usu. placed in the genus *Cryptococcus* and various others (as the food yeast *T. utilis*) that are sometimes segregated in the genus *Torulopsis*
tor·u·lop·sis \ˌtȯr(y)əˈläpsəs\ *n* [NL, fr. *torula* + *-opsis*] **1** *cap, in some classifications* **:** a genus of round, oval, or cylindrical yeasts that form no spores and no pellicle when growing in a liquid culture medium and that include forms which in other classifications are placed in *Torula* or *Cryptococcus* **2** *pl* **torulopsis :** TORULA 1a
tor·u·lose \'tȯr(y)əˌlōs, 'tär-\ *adj* [NL *torulosus*, dim. of L *torosus* torose] **:** somewhat torose
tor·u·lo·sis \ˌtȯrəˈlōsəs\ *n* -ES [NL, fr. *Torula* + *-osis*] **:** CRYPTOCOCCOSIS
tor·u·lous \ˈtȯrələs\ *adj* [NL *torulosus*] **:** TORULOSE
tor·u·lus \-ləs\ *n, pl* **tor·u·li** \-ˌlī, -ˌlē\ [NL, dim. of L *torus* cushion, couch] **:** the socket in which the antenna of an insect articulates
to·rus \'tȯrəs\ *n, pl* **to·ri** \-r(ˌ)ī, -r(ˌ)ē\ [NL, fr. L protuberance, bulge, cushion, couch, torus molding] **1 :** a smooth rounded protuberance on a body part; *esp* **:** any of several bony ridges that may be present on the skull ⟨a supraocular ∼⟩ **2 :** a large architectural molding of convex profile commonly occurring as the lowest molding in the base of a column or pilaster and next above the plinth — compare OVOLO; see BASE illustration, MOLDING illustration **3 a :** RECEPTACLE 3b **b :** the thickening of the membrane closing a bordered pit **4 :** a surface or solid shaped like a doughnut and formed by revolving a circle about a line in its plane without intersecting it : ANCHOR RING **5 :** a thickened vertical ridge bearing rows of uncini on the segments of many annelids **6 :** the driving member of a fluid coupling
¹to·ry \'tȯrē, 'tȯr-, -ri\ *n* -ES [IrGael *tōraidhe* pursued man, robber, fr. MIr *tōir* pursuit] **1** *often cap* **a :** a dispossessed Irishman of the 17th century subsisting primarily by highway robbery and agrarian outrages perpetrated esp. upon the English settlers and soldiers **b :** any armed Irish papist or royalist of later times **2** *obs* **:** one in another country resembling an Irish tory : BANDIT, MARAUDER, OUTLAW, ROBBER, TERRORIST ⟨among the *tories* in the Highlands —James Kirkton⟩ **3** *usu cap* **:** one opposing the exclusion in 1679–80 of the Duke of York from the line of succession to the British throne principally because of his Roman Catholicism : an opponent of the exclusioners **:** used as a term of obloquy or contempt — opposed to *Whig* **4** *usu cap* **:** a member or supporter of the Tory party in British politics **5** *usu cap* **:** an American upholding the cause of the British Crown against the supporters of colonial independence during the American Revolution : LOYALIST — opposed to *Whig* **6** *sometimes cap* **:** one held to resemble a British Tory in politics esp. in allegiance to the established order **7 :** one who emphasizes order, tradition, stability, or accepted canons of taste, opinion, or conduct in any area of human interest or concern esp. at the expense of innovation : one who by temperament or sentiment is inclined to conservative principles

²tory \"\ *adj* **:** of, relating to, or characterized by Toryism: as **a** *usu cap* **(1) :** of, relating to, or constituting one of the two major British political groups of the 18th and early 19th centuries arising from the Cavaliers and associated chiefly with support at first of the Stuarts but later of the monarchy itself and also of the established Anglican Church and with the preservation of the traditional political structure esp. as represented by the unreformed House of Commons — compare LIBERAL, RADICAL, WHIG **(2) :** CONSERVATIVE 2b(1) **(3) :** favoring, belonging to, or composed of members of such a political group or party ⟨openly *Tory* in his sympathies⟩ ⟨formation of a *Tory* Government⟩ ⟨the tradition of authority is naturally a *Tory* tradition —H.R.H.Cecil⟩ **b** *often cap* **:** characterized by Toryism esp. in social and economic relationships ⟨Roosevelt Republicanism which is ∼ in spirit but popular in its appeal —Walter Lippmann⟩ ⟨a slow-moving and ∼ society —C.W. de Kiewiet⟩ **c :** tending toward extreme political and economic conservatism ⟨∼ Democrats in the Senate —Henry Wallace⟩ **syn** see CONSERVATIVE
tory democracy *n, usu cap T&D* **:** a political philosophy advocating preservation of the established institutions and traditional principles characteristic of Toryism combined with political democracy and a social and economic program designed to benefit the common man ⟨the *Tory Democracy* of the British Conservative party⟩
tory democrat *n -s usu cap T&D* **:** an adherent or advocate of Tory Democracy
to·ry·fy *or* **to·ri·fy** \'tȯrəˌfī, -rē-ˌ\ *vt* -ED/-ING/-ES *usu cap* [²tory + -fy] **:** to make Tory **:** to influence by Tory principles or policies
to·ry·ish \'tȯrēish, -ri·ish\ *adj, usu cap* [²tory + -ish] **:** inclined toward Toryism
to·ry·ism \-rēˌizəm, -riˌiz-\ *n -s usu cap* [¹tory + -ism] **1 :** the principles, policies, and practices of or associated with Tories **2 :** the British Tory party or its members ⟨*Toryism* inflated its periphery to include ... working-class elements —L.G.Noonan⟩
tory-rory *adj* [origin unknown] *obs* **:** UPROARIOUS, ROISTERING ⟨*tory-rory* rakes —P.A.Motteux⟩
toryweed \ˈtȯrēˌwēd, -ri-\ *n* **:** HOUND'S-TONGUE 1
TOs *pl of* TO
to·sa·phist \ˈtȯsəfəst\ *n -s* [*tosaphoth* + *-ist*] **:** a writer of tosaphoth
to·sa·photh \-əˌfōt\ *n pl* [MHeb *tōsāphōth*, lit., additions] **:** critical and explanatory glosses on the Talmud usu. in the margin
tos·ca \'tȯskə\ *n -s* [AmerSp, fr. Sp, fem. of *tosco* rough, unpolished, uncouth, prob. fr. L *tuscus* Tuscan; fr. the disreputable character of the inhabitants of the *Vicus Tuscus* Tuscan Street in ancient Rome] **1 :** a calcium carbonate deposit occurring in the loess of the pampas — compare CALICHE **2 :** a soft coral limestone deposit used for various purposes in Puerto Rico (as for masonry, road surfacing, ballast, and as fertilizer)
¹tosh \'tȯsh\ *dial Brit var of* TUSH
²tosh \"\ *or* **toshy** \-shi\ *adj* [origin unknown] *Scot* **:** tidily trim or comfortable : NEAT, SNUG — **tosh·ly** *adv*
³tosh \"\ *vt* -ED/-ING/-ES *Scot* **:** to make neat : TIDY — usu. used with *up*
⁴tosh \"\ *n* -ES [origin unknown] **:** sheer nonsense : BOSH, TWADDLE ⟨nobody ... can possibly believe the sort of ∼ that is contained in these latest Kremlin outpourings —*N. Y. Times*⟩ — often used interjectionally to express disapproval or disbelief
to·side \ˈsˌt\ *n* [obs. to one (fr. ME, short for *ton*) + side — more at TONE, pron.] *archaic* **:** one side ⟨stepped a little *to-side* —John Bunyan⟩
tosk *also* **tosc** \'täsk\ *n -s usu cap* [Alb *tosk*] **1 :** one of the southern Albanians — compare GHEG **2** *also* **tosk·ish** \-kish\ **:** the dialect spoken by the Tosks of southern Albania
¹toss \'tȯs, 'täs\ *vb* **tossed** *or archaic* **tost** \-st\ **tossed** *or archaic* **tost; tossing; tosses** [prob. fr. Scand origin; akin to Sw dial. *tossa* to spread, scatter] *vt* **1 a :** to cause to rise and fall : throw around : HEAVE, TUMBLE ⟨storm-*tossed* sea⟩ ⟨waves from a passing steamer ∼ the small boats⟩ ⟨∼ed wildly on the rain came flocks of starlings —J.C.Powys⟩ **b :** to throw aloft : propel upward : CAST, FLIP ⟨∼ her up and caught her —Winifred Bambrick⟩ ⟨missed his footing and was ∼ed by the bull; *esp* **:** MATCH 5a ⟨I'll ∼ you for it⟩ **c :** to drive involuntarily : BUFFET, SHUNT ⟨∼ed to and fro and carried about with every wind of doctrine —Eph 4:14 (RSV)⟩ ⟨had begun life in poverty ... ∼ed about from one relative to another —Gamaliel Bradford⟩ **2 a :** to make uneasy : DISQUIET, DISTURB ⟨saintly aid to ... the sin-*tossed* soul —H.O. Taylor⟩ **b :** to discuss or canvass exhaustively : BANDY, DEBATE ⟨various figures ... were ∼ed around in conversation with tribal leaders —*New Republic*⟩ ⟨her brain was a steam wheel ... everything that could be thought of was ∼ed, nothing grasped —George Meredith⟩ **c :** to cause to shake up ⟨∼ it up herself —Clemence Dane⟩; *esp* **:** to mix lightly usu. with a fork and spoon until well coated with a dressing ⟨∼ a salad⟩ ⟨∼ carrots in butter⟩ **3 a :** to tilt suddenly or steeply so as to drain ⟨∼ed his glass to his lips, finished his drink —James Joyce⟩ **b :** to raise in a flourish or salute : BRANDISH, PEAK ⟨more fit ... to lift a pitchfork than to ∼ a pike —William Gouge⟩ — used chiefly in the phrase *toss oars* **c :** to elevate in a proud or spirited manner ⟨∼ed her head angrily⟩ ⟨∼ up your nose at obscure people —Christopher Smart⟩ **4 a :** to throw with force : FLING, HURL ⟨has been ∼ed into jail and convicted of libel —J.A.Morris b. 1904⟩ ⟨the challenge is ∼ed to the new president —Patrick McMahon⟩ ⟨Vesuvius ... ∼es out glowing bombs —Howel Williams⟩ **b (1) :** to throw gently often with an underhand motion : convey lightly ⟨∼ CHUCK, FLICK ⟨∼ a ball to and fro⟩ ⟨∼ peppermint sticks to ... children —*Amer. Guide Series: La.*⟩ **(2) :** to utter or include in an offhand manner : introduce casually : INTERJECT ⟨the book has its ... quota of gaily ∼ed metaphors —Rex Lardner⟩ ⟨for what it may be worth, I ∼ in ... a very minor statistic —Agnes Rogers⟩ ⟨∼ing off carefree farewells to shipboard friends —LaSelle Gilman⟩ ⟨criticism, ∼ed off ... in the most marginal way —F.R.Leavis⟩ **c :** to dispose of : CONSUME, SWALLOW ⟨∼es down a lemonade —J.A.Michener⟩ ⟨raised her glass to her mouth and ∼ed it off —*Encore*⟩ ⟨usually ∼ed off half a dozen papers with his morning coffee —Edith Wharton⟩ **d :** to get rid of : DISCARD, JETTISON ⟨∼ out the garbage⟩ ⟨the horse ∼ed his rider⟩ ⟨∼ed away $90,000 in film contracts to spend eighteen months on the road —J.K. Hutchens⟩ ⟨would you rather ∼ the evening and just go home now —Nicholas Monsarrat⟩ **e :** to put on carelessly or hurriedly ⟨∼ing on my bathrobe, I would run to the kitchen —Marjorie Houseplan⟩ **f :** to provide or turn out casually : execute in an apparently effortless manner ⟨∼es off science fiction as a by-product of his rocket research ⟨she can ∼ off roulades and staccati ... and other vocal acrobatics —Irving Kolodin⟩ ⟨his mind ∼ed up scheme after scheme —Lucien Price⟩ ⟨a monster cocktail party and buffet supper will be ∼ed in honor of former employees —Bennett Cerf⟩ ∼ *vi* **1 a :** to move restlessly : exhibit agitation or turbulence ⟨black water ... swirled and ∼ed over the ugly heads of jutting rocks —T.B.Costain⟩ ⟨his sentences pitched and ∼ed on a surging sea of righteous indignation —*Horizon*⟩; *esp* **:** to twist and turn repeatedly ⟨∼ed on their pillows worrying about their younger son —Josephine Pinckney⟩ **b :** to move jerkily or spasmodically : FLOUNCE, SWAY ⟨∼ed out of the room ... in one of her flighty humors —W.M.Thackeray⟩ ⟨the engine is ∼ing a little as she takes one reverse curve after another —O.S. Nock⟩ **c :** to mix together with a dressing ⟨tomato wedges ... and diced chicken go in a lettuce-lined salad bowl — ready to ∼ —*Better Homes & Gardens*⟩ **2 :** to decide an issue by lot esp. by the toss of a coin ⟨the skippers ∼ed and ours lost —Dal Stivens⟩ **3 :** to serve a handball **syn** see THROW
²toss \"\ *n* -ES **1** *archaic* **:** an act or instance of heaving or shaking : TOSSING ⟨the little boat ... pitches now with shorter ∼ upon the narrower swell —Robert Southey⟩ **b :** a state of agitation : TURMOIL ⟨Boston is in a great ∼ ... about Dr. Channing and the abolitionists —H.W.Longfellow⟩ **2 :** an act or instance of propelling through the air : PITCH, THROW ⟨after a few warm-up ∼es ... put the shot 63 feet 6 inches

—*Newsweek*⟩ ⟨put the Indians in front with a 5-yard run after catching a 10-yard ∼ —*N. Y. Times*⟩ **b :** an abrupt tilting or upward fling ⟨an almost disdainful ∼ of the head —T.G. Henderson⟩ ⟨with a ∼ of a hand ... issues half a dozen birthday pronouncements —Barbara B. Jamison⟩ **3 :** an act or instance of deciding by lot and esp. by flipping a coin ⟨choice of sides ... shall be decided by ∼ —*Official Lawn Tennis Guide*⟩ — called also *toss-up* **4 :** an act or instance of being thrown or jettisoned : DEFEAT, TUMBLE ⟨took a ∼ into a hole and ... broke his leg —John Buchan⟩ ⟨diplomat ... takes a professional ∼ —Eric Keown⟩
³toss \'tis\ *n* -ES *by alter.] Scot* **:** TOAST 1a
tos·sa \'tisə\ *or* **tossa jute** *n -s* [origin unknown] **:** a grayish or brown fiber obtained from a jute (*Corchorus olitorius*) — compare JUTE
toss bombing *n* ['toss + *bombing*, gerund of *bomb*] **:** bombing in which an airplane releases a bomb while pulling up in an Immelmann turn so that the bomb lobs forward as the plane flies away in an opposite direction
tossed salad [*tossed* (past part. of ¹toss) + *salad*] *n* **:** a salad made of greens often with added vegetables (as sliced tomato or cucumber) tossed in an oil dressing
toss·er \'tȯsə(r), 'täs-\ *n* -s **:** one that tosses
¹tossing [fr. gerund of ¹toss] *n* -S **1 :** an act or process of buffeting or shaking : AGITATION **2 :** an operation in tin refining in which the molten metal is lifted in a ladle and poured from a fine stream to oxidize impurities
²tossing *adj* [in sense 1, fr. pres. part. of ¹toss; in sense 2 fr. ¹tossing] **1 :** being in a state of tumultuous agitation : HEAVING, RESTLESS ⟨∼ skies⟩ ⟨a ∼ insomniac⟩ **2 :** of or relating to an act of flipping or jettisoning ⟨a ∼ pay⟩ ⟨process⟩ — **toss·ing·ly** *adv*
tosspot \ˌˌˌ\ *n* [¹toss + *pot*] **:** DRUNKARD, SOT ⟨assembled a group of ∼s —John McCarten⟩
toss-up \ˌˌˌ\ *n* [fr. the phrase *toss up*] **1 :** TOSS 3 **2 :** a matter of luck : an even bet or choice ⟨regard the election results as a ∼ —*N. Y. Times*⟩ ⟨it was a ∼ whether to go right or left —Fred Majdalany⟩
tost *archaic past of* TOSS
tos·ta·da \tōˈstädə\ *also* **tos·ta·do** \-ä(ˌ)dō\ *n -s* [MexSp *tostada*, fr. fem. of *tostado* fried, fr. Sp, toasted, roasted, browned, fr. past part. of *tostar* to toast, roast, fr. (assumed) VL *tostare* —more at TOAST] **:** a tortilla fried in deep fat
tos·ta·men·te \ˌtōstäˈmentē\ *adv* [It, fr. *tosto* quick, rapid] **:** RAPIDLY — used as a direction in music
tos·tão \tōs(h)ˈtauⁿ\ *n -s* [Pg, fr. It *testone* teston] **:** an old Portuguese silver coin equal to 100 reals : TESTON
tos·ti·cat·ed \'tästəˌkātəd\ *adj* [by shortening & alter.] *dial Brit* **:** INTOXICATED
tos·to \'tō(ˌ)stō\ *adv (or adj)* [It, fr. *tosto* quick, rapid, fr. (assumed) VL *tostus*, fr. L, past part. of *torrēre* to dry, parch, heat —more at TORRENT] **:** at a rapid tempo — used as a direction in music
tos·ton \tōˈstōn\ *n -s* [Sp *tostón*, fr. Pg or It; Pg *tostão*, fr. It *testone*] **:** a silver coin formerly in use in various Latin American countries and equal to ½ peso or 4 reals
tos·yl \'täsəl\ *n -s* [*toluenesulfonyl*] **:** the para isomer of toluenesulfonyl or tolyl-sulfonyl
tos·yl·ate \-sȯˌlāt\ *vt* -ED/-ING/-S [*tosyl* + *-ate*] **:** to introduce a tosyl group into (a compound) — **tos·yl·a·tion** \ˌˌˌˈ-\ *n*
¹tot \'tät, *usu* -äd-+V\ *vt* **totted; totted; totting; tots** [ME *totten*, fr. the L word *tot* (marked on the list)] *archaic* **:** to mark (an item on a list) with a tot
²tot \"\ *n* -S [L *tot* so much, so many; akin to Gk *tosos* so great, so many, Skt *tati* so many, L *istud*, neuter demonstrative pron. & adj. ∼ at THAT] **:** the word *tot* or letter *T* written against an item on a list to indicate receipt of a specified payment
³tot \"\ *n* -S [origin unknown] **1 :** a small child : TODDLER ⟨from tiny ∼s in kindergarten to the oldest pupil —F.T. Williams⟩ **2 a :** a small glass or mug; *esp* **:** a British soldier's drinking cup **b :** a small quantity or allowance esp. of an alcoholic beverage : DRINK, SHOT ⟨ladles out generous ∼s of ... whiskey punch —J.S.Bradford⟩ ⟨poured his cup, smuggling in a good ∼ of ... rum —Willa Cather⟩ ⟨not all jack-tars take grog; many prefer money instead of their ∼ —Luis Marden⟩
⁴tot \"\ *vb* **totted; totted; totting; tots** [*tot*, abbr.] *vt* **:** to add together : SUMMARIZE, TOTAL ⟨now your account is *totted* —John Masefield⟩ — usu. used with *up* ⟨the waiter ... *totted* up the bill —Virginia Woolf⟩ ⟨Clubs began *totting* up attendance records for the 12 months —*Rotarian*⟩ ⟨*totted* up exactly how far he had gone since he first entered ... journalism —*English Digest*⟩ ∼ *vi* **:** to come to a total : indicate a result : ADD ⟨hours spent on the project ∼ up to a staggering number⟩ ⟨intelligence reports all *totted* up one way —*Scribner's*⟩
⁵tot \"\ *n* -s *chiefly Brit* **:** an exercise in addition : column of figures : SUM ⟨an oriental clerk, faced by a simple long ∼ —Bryan Morgan⟩
⁶tot \'tät\ *Scot var of* ³TOTE
⁷tot \"\ *vi* **totted; totted; totting; tots** [prob. short for ¹totter] *dial Brit* **:** to move unsteadily : TODDLE, TOTTER
tot *abbr* total
TOT *abbr* time on target
tot·able \'tōdəbəl\ *adj* [¹tote + -able] **:** easily carried : PORTABLE
¹to·tal \'tōd.əl, 'tōt.əl\ *adj* [ME, fr. MF, fr. ML *totalis*, fr. L *totus* whole, entire + *-alis* -al] **1 :** of or relating to something in its entirety ⟨the ∼ effect of a room⟩ ⟨the writing is ... unified by a simple ∼ vision of the writer —William Barrett⟩ **2 a :** viewed as an entity : complete in all details : OVERALL, WHOLE ⟨culture ... is the ∼ spiritual product of any given time and place —*Modern Music*⟩ ⟨the ∼ university, with its galaxy of graduate and professional schools —N.M.Pusey⟩ ⟨after the introduction of gunpowder ... ∼ armor had gradually fallen into disuse —*New Yorker*⟩ **b :** constituting an entire number or amount : AGGREGATE ⟨∼ cost⟩ ⟨∼ value⟩ ⟨∼ extant manuscripts ... are of considerable number —I.M. Price⟩ ⟨∼ spending should be large enough to employ everyone who wants to work —George Soule⟩ **3 a :** unqualified in extent or degree : ABSOLUTE, UTTER ⟨∼ darkness⟩ ⟨a ∼ stranger⟩ ⟨the ∼ abolition of poverty ... is at the present moment technically possible —Bertrand Russell⟩ ⟨lines, characterized by ∼ simplicity, are by far the hardest to put into another language —Wallace Fowlie⟩ **b :** having dictatorial powers : OMNIPOTENT, TOTALITARIAN ⟨the liberal state acknowledged many limitations in its demands upon men; the ∼ state acknowledges none —A.M.Schlesinger b. 1917⟩ **c :** unlimited in character : concentrating all available personnel and resources on a single objective : ALL-OUT, THOROUGHGOING ⟨the nature of ∼ war has erased the distinction between combatants and civilians —J.N.Moody⟩ ⟨urges a bold effort at making a ∼ peace —*Atlantic*⟩ **syn** see WHOLE
²total \"\ *n* -s **1 a :** a result of addition : AGGREGATE, SUM ⟨column ∼⟩ ⟨cumulative ∼⟩ ⟨a ∼ of 319 students registered for summer school⟩ ⟨when the final ∼s were compiled they would show dollar volume close to ... the all-time high —S.C.Pace⟩ **b :** a summation of factors : final result ⟨deviations from a ∼ of zero cause the crane carriage to move forward or backward —T.W.Rodes⟩ **2 :** an entire quantity or configuration : AMOUNT, WHOLE ⟨a staggering ∼ of devastation and destruction —T.F.Mueller⟩ ⟨word-complexes that cannot be reconstructed by unit, but only as ∼s —John Ciardi⟩ **syn** see SUM — **in total** *adv* **:** as a whole ⟨little of the tie or shirt is visible, but the ∼ ... coat is seen in *total* —S.D.Barney⟩
³total \"\ *adv* **:** TOTALLY ⟨now is he ∼ gules, horridly tricked with blood —Shak.⟩
⁴total \"\ *vb* **totaled** *or* **totalled; totaling** *or* **totalling; totals** *vt* **1 :** to add up : COMPUTE ⟨these figures were arrived at by ∼ing all entries —H.J. Hanham⟩ ⟨the sensuous possibilities latent in silk, linen, wool, leather, and furs —Hunter Mead⟩ **2 :** to come to a total of : amount to : NUMBER ⟨in July of this year consumer credit ∼ed roughly $27 billion —*World*⟩ ⟨jute mills ... ∼ about a hundred —Walter Bally⟩ ⟨professing Christians ∼ed less than one percent of the population —K.S.Latourette⟩ ∼ *vi* **:** to compute a total : ADD ⟨this adding machine ∼s to 999,999.99⟩

total abstinence *n* **:** ABSTINENCE 1c

total adhesion locomotive *n* **:** a locomotive with all wheels coupled to act as driving wheels

total and permanent disability insurance *n* **:** insurance against loss due to inability to follow a gainful occupation because of mental or physical impairment classified as permanent under the terms of a life insurance policy usu. after such disability has continued for a stated period (as six months)

total–annular eclipse *n* **:** an eclipse of the sun in which totality is observed in the middle part of the path of the moon's shadow but an annular eclipse at the ends of the path near the sunrise and sunset points

total cleavage *n* **:** holoblastic cleavage of an egg

total depravity *n* **:** the theological doctrine asserting that man in his every part is infected with a sinfulness due to original sin inherited from Adam and that by his own unaided action man cannot make any efficacious effort toward his salvation but can only remain in a corrupt state until regenerated by the Spirit of God — see CALVINISM

total disability *n* **:** incapacity to perform the duties of any substantially gainful occupation either permanently or temporarily due to accident or illness — compare PARTIAL DISABILITY, TEMPORARY TOTAL DISABILITY

total eclipse *n* **:** an eclipse in which one celestial body is completely obscured by the shadow or body of another

total heat *n* **:** the thermal equivalent of the energy required to convert unit mass of a liquid at one temperature (as the melting point of the substance) into saturated vapor at any other given temperature

to·tal·ism \-ᵊlˌizəm\ *n* -s [¹*total* + *-ism*] **:** TOTALITARIANISM

to·tal·is·tic \ˌtōd·ᵊlˈistik, -ōtᵊl-, -tēk\ *adj* [¹*total* + *-istic*] **:** TOTALITARIAN

¹**to·tal·i·tar·i·an** \(ˌ)tōˌtaləˈterēən, -ˌta(a)r-, -ˌtär- *sometimes* ˌtōd·ᵊlə˞- *or* -ōtᵊl-\ *adj* [¹*total* + *-itarian* (as in *authoritarian*)] **1 a :** of or relating to centralized control by an autocratic leader or hierarchy **:** AUTHORITARIAN, DICTATORIAL ⟨~ theory and practice are solidly opposed to any institutional division of power —C.J.Friedrich⟩ ⟨fascism . . . is by ~ by necessity —Carlo Sforza⟩; *esp* **:** DESPOTIC ⟨Sparta's militarist ~ dictatorship —Peter Viereck⟩ **b :** of or relating to a political regime based on subordination of the individual to the state and strict control of all aspects of the life and productive capacity of the nation esp. by coercive measures (as censorship and terrorism) ⟨the limited state, the agent of man, has been converted to the ~ state, the master of man —C.P.Patterson⟩ ⟨will Europe in the future be ~ and collectivist, or will it be democratic and individualist —C.J.Friedrich⟩ **2 a :** advocating or characteristic of totalitarianism ⟨~ liberal⟩ ⟨the ~ concept that the end justifies the means —J.W.Fulbright⟩ ⟨cracks down on free speech and free press with ~ ease —*Time*⟩ ⟨seize power . . . by force and make Greece Communist, with the ~ liquidation of all opponents —Sir Winston Churchill⟩ **b :** completely regulated by the state esp. as an aid to national mobilization in an emergency ⟨it accomplishes a ~ control of atomic energy for the time being —A.H.Vandenberg †1951⟩ ⟨almost all governments adopt ~ measures in time of war —John Gunther⟩ **c :** exercising autocratic powers **:** tending toward monopoly ⟨by its very nature . . . religion is ~ —J.S.Roucek⟩ ⟨antitrust legislation . . . to reverse the trend toward the ~ collectivism of big business —*Jour. of Politics*⟩ **3 :** TOTAL 3c ⟨a ~ war, striking at civilians more than at armies —*N.Y. Times*⟩

²**totalitarian** \"\ *n* -s **:** an advocate or practitioner of totalitarianism

to·tal·i·tar·i·an·ism \-ēəˌnizəm\ *n* -s [¹*totalitarian* + *-ism*] **1 a :** centralized control by an autocratic ruler or hierarchy regarded as infallible ⟨in a democracy, forfeiture of sovereignty by the people means ~ —E.L.Klein⟩ ⟨ideally Christianity desires ~, too, but in the sense that men everywhere come to see the validity of its definition of man —*Times Lit. Supp.*⟩; *specif* **:** DESPOTISM ⟨the barbarism of the Turks and the ~ of the Spanish kings —*N. Y. Herald Tribune Bk. Rev.*⟩ **b :** the political concept of man as the servant of the state **:** COLLECTIVISM ⟨the essence of ~, in contrast with democracy, is that there is . . . no area where the citizen's initiative is supreme —Laurence Stapleton⟩ — compare INDIVIDUALISM **2 :** the quality or state of being totalitarian ⟨Pilgrim and Puritan women . . . functioned and reacted in the stern ~ of a male and theocratic civilization —*N. Y. Herald Tribune Bk. Rev.*⟩ ⟨~ is . . . not by accident the distinguishing characteristic of the Nazi state —H.J.Morgenthau⟩ **3 :** a totalitarian dogma, method, or regime ⟨championship of human values against all the insidious ~*s* —*New Yorker*⟩

to·tal·i·tar·i·an·ize \-ˌnīz\ *vt* -ED/-ING/-S **:** to make totalitarian

to·tal·i·ty \tōˈtaləd·ē, -ətē, -i\ *n* -ES [ML *totalitat-, totalitas,* fr. *totalis* total + L *-itat-, -itas* -ity] **1 :** an aggregate number or amount **:** SUM, WHOLE ⟨the ~ of universes —J.F.McComas⟩ ⟨a partial glimpse of the . . . ~ of truth —C.I.Glicksberg⟩ **2 a :** the quality or state of being complete or comprehensive **:** ENTIRETY, UNITY ⟨the port of New York, in its ~, includes all the navigable waterways within . . . twenty-five miles from the Statue of Liberty —*Amer. Guide Series: N. Y. City*⟩ ⟨your whole nature, in its physical and psychical ~ —J.C.Powys⟩ **b** (1) **:** the phase of an eclipse during which it is total **:** state of total eclipse (2) **:** the region from which the total phase of an eclipse may be observed **3 :** overall form or content **:** CONFIGURATION, ENTITY ⟨formal analysis . . . having to do with the ~ of a poem or a novel —C.W.Shumaker⟩ ⟨insists that the undivided ~ of the person must be the point of departure —Ruth Benedict⟩ **4 :** absolute or indiscriminate oppression ⟨weapons of ~ and terror —J.R.Oppenheimer⟩ ⟨the all-embracing ~ of the state —G.L.Dickinson⟩

to·tal·iza·tion \ˌtōd·ᵊləˈzāshən, -ōtᵊl-, -ᵊlˌīˈ-\ *n* -s [*totalize* + *-ation*] **:** an act or instance of totaling **:** SUMMATION

to·tal·i·za·tor *or* **to·tal·i·sa·tor** \ˈ==(ˌ)=ˌzād·ə(r), -ātə-\ *n* -s [*totalize* + *-ator*] **:** PARI-MUTUEL MACHINE

to·tal·ize \ˈtōd·ᵊlˌīz, -ōtᵊl-\ *vt* -ED/-ING/-S [¹*total* + *-ize*] **1 a :** to add up **:** TOTAL **b :** to express as a whole **:** SUMMARIZE **2 :** to make totalitarian

to·tal·iz·er \-zə(r)\ *n* -s **:** one that totalizes; *specif* **:** PARI-MUTUEL MACHINE

totalled *past of* TOTAL

totalling *pres part of* TOTAL

total loss *n* **:** loss that makes property valueless to an insured

total lunar eclipse *n* **:** an eclipse in which the moon is completely immersed in the umbra of the earth's shadow

to·tal·ly \ˈtōd·ᵊlē, -ōtᵊl-, -ᵊli *sometimes* -ōtlē *or* -li\ *adv* **1 :** in a total manner **:** COMPLETELY, WHOLLY **2 :** as a whole **:** IN TOTO

total–point scoring *n* **:** CUMULATIVE SCORING

total push *n* **:** a method of treating mental disorders by the employment of varied therapeutic techniques in a concerted and almost continuous series

total quantum number *n* **:** PRINCIPAL QUANTUM NUMBER

total recall *n* **:** the faculty of remembering with complete clarity and in complete detail

total reflection *n* **:** specular reflection in the more highly refractive of two media at their interface when the angle of incidence exceeds a certain critical value — compare CRITICAL ANGLE

totals *pl of* TOTAL, *pres 3d sing of* TOTAL

total score method *n* **:** a method of improving livestock by breeding animals selected for maximum excellence in as many desired traits as possible — compare TANDEM METHOD

total slip *n* **:** the part of a geologic fault displacement that is recorded by the maximum distance of separation of two originally contiguous points measured in the plane of the fault

total solar eclipse *n* **:** an eclipse of the sun in which the moon completely hides the solar surface or photosphere and thereby cuts off all direct rays of sunlight from the observer

total utility *n* **:** the degree of utility of an article, service, or other economic good considered as a whole — compare MARGINAL UTILITY

to·ta·nus \ˈtätᵊnəs\ *n, cap* [NL, fr. ML, moorhen] **:** a genus of shorebirds (family Scolopacidae) comprising various typical tattlers and being often included in the genus *Tringa*

to·ta·quine \ˈtōd·əˌk(w)ēn, -ˌk(w)ən\ *also* **to·ta·qui·na** \ˌ==-ˈkēnə\ *n* -s [NL *totaquina,* fr. ML *totalis* total + Sp *quina* cinchona bark; fr. its containing the total alkaloids of cinchona bark — more at QUININE] **:** an antimalarial drug that is obtained as a yellowish brown powder by extraction of American cinchona bark and that contains quinine and other alkaloids but is less effective than quinine

to·ta·ra \ˈtōd·əˌrä, tōˈtärə\ *n* -s [Maori] **:** a tall tree (*Podocarpus totara*) of New Zealand having hard reddish wood used for furniture and construction (as of bridges and wharves) and being the country's most valuable timber tree next to the kauri

¹**tote** \ˈtōt, *usu* -ōd·+V\ *vb* -ED/-ING/-S [origin unknown] *vt* **1 a :** to carry by hand **:** bear on the person **:** LUG, PACK ⟨longshoremen . . . ~ bananas on their shoulders —*Amer. Guide Series: La.*⟩ ⟨elegantly uniformed Army officers, *toting* briefcases —E.J.Kahn⟩ ⟨a-hollering for two of the little chaps to come and ~ the tub in for her —Frances Gaither⟩ **b :** to make a practice of carrying ⟨pistol-*toting* rangers patrol the sun-baked towns —H.H.Martin⟩ **2 :** to conduct or haul from one place to another **:** CONVEY, TRANSPORT ⟨*toted* her round to a few parties —B.C.L.Keelan⟩ ⟨horses . . . *toted* the ammunition —R.L.Neuberger⟩ ⟨carrier aircraft can ~ as many as 200 rockets —*Newsweek*⟩ ~ *vi* **1 a :** to carry a load ⟨you load and I'll ~⟩ **b** *South* **:** to take home leftover food ⟨Negro cooks will sometimes demand the right to ~ . . . as part of their wages —*Amer. Guide Series: Mo.*⟩ **2** *South* **:** GO, TRAVEL

²**tote** \"\ *n* -s *often attrib* **1 :** something that is carried **:** BURDEN, LOAD **2 :** an act of carrying or hauling

³**tote** \ˈtōt\ *n* -s [short for ²*total*] *dial Brit* **:** an entire number or amount **:** TOTAL

⁴**tote** \ˈtōt, *usu* -ōd·+V\ *vb* -ED/-ING/-S **:** TOT, TOTAL

⁵**tote** \"\ *n* -s [short for *totalizator*] **:** PARI-MUTUEL MACHINE

tote bag *n* [¹*tote*] **:** a woman's large handbag used esp. for carrying small packages

tote board *n* [⁵*tote*] **:** a usu. electrically operated board (as in the infield of a race track) on which betting odds are posted

tote–box \ˈ=ˌ=\ *n* [¹*tote*] **:** a box or tray for storing, handling, and transporting materials in industrial operations

tote double *n* [⁵*tote*] **:** DAILY DOUBLE

to·tem \ˈtōd·əm, ˈtōtəm\ *n* -s *often attrib* [Ojibwa *ototeman* his totem] **1 a :** an animal, plant, or other object serving as the emblem of a family or clan and often regarded as a reminder of its ancestry ⟨each clan has its ~ or ritualistic mascot —C.E. Wilson⟩ ⟨believes that . . . his own ancestors were birds like that which is now his ~ —Daisy Bates⟩ **b :** a usu. carved or painted emblem of a family or clan ⟨the aged and rotting raven ~ pictured at the right —*Alaska Sportsman*⟩ **c :** a family or clan identified by a common totemic object ⟨belonging to a ~ forbidden to marry either of the girls —Rex Ingamells⟩ **d :** a totemic object adopted by an individual ⟨the individual had his own ~, serving as familiar spirit in the case of shamans —C.S.Coon⟩ **2 :** something that serves as an emblem ⟨enamelled ~*s* of half the automobile clubs in Europe —*Times Lit. Supp.*⟩ esp. as a revered symbol ⟨his corpulent figure was the ~ of their belief —H.V.Gregory⟩ ⟨move uncritically among the ideological ~*s* of the modern world —W.F.Kerr⟩ **3 :** a dark reddish orange that is yellower, stronger, and slightly darker than average lacquer red, stronger and slightly lighter than ocher red, and redder and stronger than burnt sienna — called also *Mars red*

to·tem·ic \tōˈtemik, -mēk\ *adj* [*totem* + *-ic*] **1 a :** of, relating to, or characteristic of a totem or totemism ⟨~ animal⟩ ⟨~ ritual⟩ ⟨~ transfer of names and traits (especially brute strength, courage and cunning) from animals to men —B.A. Botkin⟩ **b :** resembling a totem ⟨ventilators in a roofscape become sculptured ~ figures —Howard Devree⟩ **2 :** based on or practicing totemism ⟨~ clan structure⟩ ⟨~ people⟩ — **to·tem·i·cal·ly** \-mək(ə)lē\ *adv*

to·tem·ism \ˈtōd·əˌmizəm, -ōtə-\ *n* -s [*totem* + *-ism*] **1 a :** belief in kinship with or a mystical relationship between a group or an individual and a totem ⟨~ . . . derives whole tribes or families from an animal or plant —*Internat'l Encyc.*⟩ ⟨with the idea of the powerful animal ~ is closely connected —J.E. Turner⟩ **b :** the rites and practices (as food and word taboos) associated with a totemic relationship ⟨~, one element of which is that the human group generally respects all members of the totem class and refrains from eating them —A.C. Andrews⟩ **2 :** a system of social organization based on totemic affiliations ⟨the primary object of ~ was to implement the incest taboo —*African Abstracts*⟩

to·tem·ist \-məst\ *n* -s [*totem* + *-ist*] **:** a practitioner of or specialist in totemism

to·tem·is·tic \ˌtōd·əˈmistik, -ōtə-, -tēk\ *adj* **:** of or relating to totemists or totemism **:** TOTEMIC

to·tem·ite \ˈ==ˌmīt\ *n* -s [*totem* + *-ite*] **:** TOTEMIST

totem pole *n* **1 a :** a pole or pillar carved and painted with a series of totemic symbols representing family lineage often interspersed with references to mythical or historical incidents and erected before the houses of Indian tribes of the northwest coast of No. America esp. of the Tlingit and Skittagetan language families ⟨the *totem pole* was . . . a symbol of family pride —L.H.Appleton⟩ **b :** something that resembles a totem pole ⟨made a big *totem pole* for the Scout jamboree⟩ **2 :** an order of rank **:** HIERARCHY ⟨entertain top men on the political *totem pole* —Mary Thayer⟩

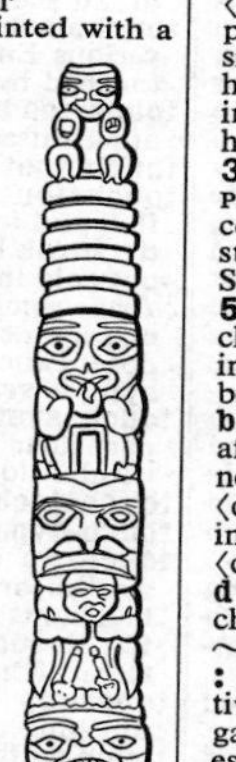

totem pole 1a

tot·er \ˈtōd·ə(r)\ *n* -s **:** one that totes

tote road *n* [¹*tote*] **:** a road for hauling supplies esp. into a lumber camp ⟨the *tote road* to our clearing where we lived —Robert Frost⟩ ⟨sent a gang of swampers . . . into the woods to break a *tote road* and make camp —*Mich. Log Marks*⟩

totes *pres 3d sing of* TOTE, *pl of* TOTE

¹**t'oth·er** *or* **t'oth·er** \ˈtəthə(r)\ *pron* [fr. earlier *the tother,* fr. ME, alter. (resulting from incorrect division) of *thet other,* fr. *thet* the (fr. OE *thæt*) + *other,* pron. — more at THAT, OTHER] *chiefly dial* **:** the other ⟨you cannot tell one from ~ —J.R. Lowell⟩

²**tother** *or* **t'other** \"\ *adj* [fr. earlier *the tother,* fr. ME, alter. (resulting from incorrect division) of *thet other,* fr. *thet* the (fr. OE *thæt*) + *other,* adj. — more at THAT, OTHER] *chiefly dial* **:** the other ⟨was obliged to go away . . . ~ night —W.M.Thackeray⟩

toti- *comb form* [L *totus* whole, entire] **:** whole **:** wholly ⟨*toti*palmate⟩

to·ti·es quo·ti·es \ˈtōd·ē,ēˈskwōd·ē,ās, ˈtōshē,ēz-ˈkwōshē,ēz\ *adv* [L, as many times as] **:** REPEATEDLY — used of an indulgence in the Roman Catholic Church that may be gained or granted as often as the required works are performed ⟨an indulgence granted *toties quoties*⟩

toting *n* -s [fr. gerund of ¹*tote*] *South* **:** the practice of taking food home from an employer's kitchen or the food so taken ⟨the Negro is . . . apt to regard a little ~ as a perquisite of the job —L.C.Stevens⟩ ⟨taking ~*s* from the icebox to her friends and family —David Riesman⟩

to·ti·pal·ma·tae \ˌtōd·əpalˈmād·ē\ [NL, fr. *toti-* + LL *palmatae,* fem. pl. of *palmatus* palmate] *syn of* PELECANIFORMES

to·ti·palmate \ˌtōd·ə+\ *adj* [*toti-* + *palmate*] **:** having all four toes united by a web ⟨birds of the order Pelecaniformes are ~⟩ — **to·ti·pal·ma·tion** \ˌtōd·əpalˈmāshən, -pä'-\ *n*

to·tip·o·ten·cy \tōˈtipədᵊnsē\ *n* -ES [*toti-* + *potency*] **:** ability to generate or regenerate a whole organism from a part ⟨~ of a begonia in producing a plant from a leaf cutting⟩

to·tip·o·tent \-nt\ *adj* [*toti-* + *potent*] **:** capable of development along any of the lines inherently possible to its kind ⟨a ~ homothallic fungus spore⟩ ⟨a mesenchyme cell is ~⟩ — **to·ti·potential** \ˌtōd·ə+\ *adj* — **to·ti·potentiality** \"+\ *n*

to·to \ˈtō,tō\ *n* -s [of Bantu origin; akin to Swahili *mtoto* child] **:** a young one **:** BABY, CHILD ⟨asked the chief if there was a small boy, a ~, who would like to enter my service —R.S.B. Baker⟩; *esp* **:** the young of an animal ⟨saw two more rhinos . . . a mother and a half-grown ~ —*Natural History*⟩

to·toa·ba *or* **to·tua·va** \tōˈtwävə\ *n* -s [MexSp *totuaba*] **:** a very large weakfish (*Cynoscion macdonaldi*) of the Gulf of California that reaches a weight of over 150 pounds and is highly prized as food

¹**to·to·nac** \ˌtōtəˈnäk\ *also* **to·to·na·co** \-ä(ˌ)kō\ *or* **to·to·na·ca** \-äkə\ *n, pl* **totonac** *or* **totonacs** *also* **totonaco** *or* **totonacos** *or* **totonaca** *or* **totonacas** *usu cap* **1 a :** an Indian people of Puebla and Veracruz, Mexico, constituting with the Tepehua the Totonacan language family **b :** a member of such people **2 :** the language of the Totonac people

²**totonac** \ˈ==ˌ=\ *adj, usu cap* **:** TAJIN

to·to·na·can \ˈ==ˌnäkən\ *n* -s *usu cap* [*totonac* + *-an*] **:** a language family comprising Totonac and Tepehua

to·to·ra \tōˈtōrə\ *n* -s [Quechua & Aymara *totora, tutura*] **:** a tall So. American cattail (*Typha domingensis*) having young shoots that are used as food in Peru and Bolivia and reedy stems that yield a fiber or are used in bunches (as for making fences or boats) ⟨canoe-shaped boats made of ~ with yellow matting sails⟩

totquot *n* -s [L *tot quot* as many as] *obs* **:** a dispensation permitting the holding of an unlimited number of benefices; *also* **:** a benefice held by such dispensation

tots *pres 3d sing of* TOT, *pl of* TOT

tot system *n* **:** a southern African system of paying colored agricultural workers part of their wages in tots of wine

totted *past of* TOT

tot·ten·ham \ˈtät(ᵊ)nəm\ *adj, usu cap* [fr. *Tottenham,* urban district of southeast England] **:** of or fr. the urban district of Tottenham, Middlesex, England **:** of the kind or style prevalent in Tottenham

tottenham pudding *n, usu cap T, Brit* **:** concentrated steam-sterilized swill for swine

¹**tot·ter** \ˈtäd·ə(r), -ätə-\ *vb* -ED/-ING/-S [ME *toteren, totren;* perh. akin to OE *tealtrian* to waver, totter — more at TILT] *vi* **1** *obs* **:** to be indecisive **:** WAVER ⟨many likelihoods . . . which hung so ~*ing* in the balance —Shak.⟩ **2 a :** to oscillate or lean dizzily **:** SHIMMY, SWAY ⟨~*ed* and fell forward upon her bicycle —Maurice Hewlett⟩ ⟨buildings were still ~*ing* and flames were raging —D.D.S.Pool⟩ **b :** to become unstable **:** threaten to collapse ⟨so many thrones had ~*ed* to their fall —Robert Grant †1940⟩ ⟨virtue could seem momentarily to ~ —Louis Kronenberger⟩ **3 :** to move unsteadily **:** STAGGER, WOBBLE ⟨weak with fever, he ~*ed* to the window —Jean Stafford⟩ ~ *vt* **:** to cause to totter ⟨~*ed* walls, gates and circuses —P.E. Deutschman⟩

²**totter** \"\ *n* -s **1** *NewEng* **:** SEESAW **2 :** an unsteady gait **:** WOBBLE

tot·ter·er \-ərə(r)\ *n* -s **:** one that totters

tottering *adj* [fr. pres. part. of ¹*totter*] **1 a :** being in an unstable condition **:** oscillating or threatening to collapse **:** SWAYING, WOBBLY ⟨buildings dilapidated and ~ —Wilkie Collins⟩ ⟨a ~ wineglass in her hand —George Meredith⟩ **b :** walking unsteadily **:** REELING, WAVERING ⟨a ~ child just learning to walk⟩ ⟨a black pony, a ~ skeleton covered with dirt —*Punch*⟩ **2 :** lacking firmness or stability **:** INSECURE, SHAKY ⟨try to bolster a ~ regime by force of arms⟩ ⟨made a clutch at his ~ reason and steadied it —F.V.W.Mason⟩ — **tot·ter·ing·ly** *adv*

tot·tery \-ərē, -ri\ *adj* [¹*totter* + *-y*] **:** of an infirm or precarious nature **:** SHAKY, TOTTERING ⟨a ~ old man⟩ ⟨the first floor of a ~ ruin —Ion Braby⟩ ⟨may . . . owe his ~ throne to the Soviet Union —*Time*⟩

totting *pres part of* TOT

tot·tle \ˈtäd·ᵊl\ *dial var of* TODDLE

tot·ty \ˈtäd·ē\ *adj* [ME *toty,* prob. fr. *toteren, totren* to totter + *-y*] *archaic* **:** DAZED, FUDDLED

totuava *var of* TOTOABA

to·tum \ˈtōd·əm\ *n* -s [L *totum* all, the whole — more at TEETOTUM] *archaic* **:** TEETOTUM 1

tot–up \ˈ=ˌ=\ [fr. the phrase *tot up,* fr. ⁴*tot* + *up*] *chiefly Brit var of* ⁵TOT

touareg *usu cap, var of* TUAREG

touart *var of* TUART

tou·can \ˈtüˌkan, -ˌkaa(ə)n, -ˌkän, (ˈ)tüˈkän *also* ˈtükən\ *n* -s [F, fr. Pg *tucano,* fr. Tupi] **1 :** any of numerous fruit-eating birds of tropical America of the family Ramphastidae that have a very large but light and thin-walled beak often nearly as long as the body and are usu. brilliantly colored in beak as well as plumage with red, yellow, white, and black in striking contrast — see BILL illustration **2 :** HORNBILL

tou·can·et \ˌtükəˈnet\ *n* -s [*toucan* + *-et*] **:** any of several small So. and Central American toucans constituting the genus *Aulacorhynchus* and having both sexes predominantly green in color

¹**touch** \ˈtəch, *dial* ˈtech *or* ˈtich\ *vb* -ED/-ING/-ES [ME *tochen, touchen,* fr. OF *tochier, tuchier,* fr. (assumed) VL *toccare* to knock, strike, strike a bell, touch, of imit. origin] *vt* **1 a :** to bring a bodily part briefly into contact with so as to feel ⟨~*ing* the delicate petals with gentle fingers⟩ **b :** to perceive or experience through the tactile sense ⟨afraid to ~ a hot iron⟩ ⟨~*ed* his face wonderingly with exploring fingertips⟩ **c :** to put one's fingers to (the hat or the forelock) as a salute or a sign of deference **2 :** to strike or push lightly **:** extend the hand or foot or an implement so as to reach, nudge, stir up, inspect, arouse ⟨if you ~ the snake he will strike⟩ ⟨turned as a hand ~*ed* his shoulder⟩ ⟨~*ed* the horse with the whip⟩ **3 a :** to examine by touching or feeling with the fingers **:** PALPATE **b :** to lay hands upon (one afflicted with scrofula) — compare KING'S EVIL **4 a** *archaic* **:** to play on (a stringed instrument) ⟨angels bending . . . to ~ their harps of gold —E.H. Sears⟩ **b** *archaic* **:** to perform (a melody) by playing or singing **5 a :** to take into the hands or mouth **:** make use of — used chiefly with expressed or implied negative ⟨never ~*es* alcohol in any form⟩ ⟨hardly ~*ed* his dinner⟩ ⟨had never ~*ed* a card before then⟩ ⟨hasn't ~*ed* the piano since his wife's death⟩ **b :** to put hands upon in any way or in any degree **:** disturb or affect by handling — used chiefly with expressed or implied negative ⟨your things haven't been ~*ed* while you were away⟩ ⟨don't ~ anything before the police come⟩ **c :** to have sexual intercourse with — used chiefly with real or implied negative ⟨doubt if he had ever ~*ed* a woman before his marriage⟩ **d :** to lay violent hands on **:** commit violence upon — used chiefly with expressed or implied negative ⟨swears he never ~*ed* the child⟩ **6 :** to have to do with **:** concern oneself with **:** meddle with — used chiefly with expressed or implied negative ⟨strictly his affair, I wouldn't ~ it for anything⟩ **7 a :** to gain the use of **:** get access to ⟨unable to ~ the capital of the estate⟩ **b** *slang* **:** pick up **:** STEAL **8 a** *obs* **:** to tamper with **:** BRIBE **b :** to rob by swindling **:** CHEAT **c :** pick the pocket of ⟨~*ed* him for his watch⟩ **d :** to induce to lend ⟨succeeded in ~*ing* him for ten dollars⟩ **9 a :** to cause to be briefly and lightly in contact or conjunction with something ⟨~*ed* his hand to his cap⟩ ⟨~*ed* his spurs to his horse⟩ ⟨solemnly raised and ~*ed* glasses⟩ ⟨~*ed* gloves with his opponent to start the last round⟩ **b :** to lay the scepter upon (an act of parliament) as a sign of royal assent **c :** to apply lightly to **:** spread thinly on ⟨~ a pimple with iodine⟩ **10 a :** to meet without overlapping or penetrating **:** be or become contiguous or adjacent to **:** impinge upon **:** ADJOIN ⟨where the edges of the figure ~ the border⟩ ⟨his farm ~*es* the river⟩ ⟨the speedometer needle ~*ed* 80⟩ **b :** to be tangent to **c :** to come up to in quality or value **:** compare with — used usu. with a negative ⟨nothing can ~ that cloth for durability⟩ ⟨not a fighter in his weight division to ~ him⟩ **d :** to sail as close to (the wind) as possible **11 a :** to deal with or treat of **:** HANDLE ⟨everything he ~*es* becomes clearer than before⟩ ⟨pamphlets ~*ing* nearly every aspect of rural life⟩ **b :** to make allusion or slight mention of **:** speak or tell of in passing ⟨~*ed* so many topics that only a confused impression remained at the end⟩ **12 :** to relate to **:** affect the interest of **:** CONCERN ⟨alert to anything that ~*ed* his personal honor⟩ ⟨their profession ~*es* our national defense very closely —Vannevar Bush⟩ **13 a :** to leave a mark or impression **:** make signs of wear, use, or slight damage on — used chiefly with a negative ⟨so hard no ordinary cutter will ~ it⟩ ⟨his war experiences seem not to have ~*ed* him at all⟩ **b** *obs* **:** MAGNETIZE **c :** to harm slightly by or as if by contagion, contamination, or blight **:** taint, blemish, sour, spoil in a slight degree ⟨fruit ~*ed* by frost⟩ ⟨this horse is ~*ed* in the wind⟩ **d :** to give a delicate tint, line, or expression to ⟨a smile ~*ed* her lips⟩ ⟨admiration faintly ~*ed* with envy⟩ **14 a :** to test the purity of (as gold) with a touchstone **:** ASSAY, TRY **b :** to stamp or mark (as gold, silver) after an official assay **15 a :** to draw or delineate with light strokes ⟨the lines though ~*ed* but faintly are drawn right —Alexander Pope⟩ **b :** to improve or modify by or as if by light strokes **:** touch up **16 :** to reach the heart or secret of **:** guess at correctly **:** FATHOM ⟨there you ~*ed* the life of our design —Shak.⟩ **17 a :** to hurt the feelings of **:** WOUND, STING ⟨the insult ~*ed* him to the quick⟩ **b :** to shame or discomfit by hitting the truth ⟨his face hardened, the last remark had ~*ed* him on a sore spot⟩ **c :** to move to sympathetic feeling (as pity, gratitude, remorse,

tenderness) ⟨~*ed* by the loyalty of his friends⟩ ~ *vi* **1 a :** to feel something with a body part (as the hand or foot) **b :** to lay hand or finger on a person to cure disease (as scrofula) ⟨he ~*ed* for the king's evil⟩ **2 a :** to be in such a position that no space exists between **:** be in contact ⟨two spheres can ~ only at points⟩ ⟨sat with their heads nearly ~*ing*⟩ **b :** to be next to another suit in rank of playing cards ⟨diamonds ~ hearts⟩ ⟨diamonds and clubs are ~*ing* suits⟩ **3 a :** to come close **:** APPROACH **:** VERGE ⟨his actions ~ on treason⟩ **b** *of a sail* **:** to turn so close to the wind that the weather leech shakes ⟨keep the royals ~*ing*⟩ **4 :** to have a bearing **:** RELATE, PERTAIN — used with *on* or *upon* **5 a :** to make a brief or incidental stop on shore during a trip by water — used usu. with *at* ⟨~*ed* at several ports on the return voyage⟩ **b :** to treat a topic in a brief or casual manner — used with *on* or *upon* ⟨~*ed* upon many points without enlarging upon any of them⟩ **6 :** to improve or modify something with slight strokes or alterations **:** RETOUCH ⟨endlessly ~*ing* and retouching before he was satisfied with the picture⟩ **syn** see AFFECT, MATCH — **touch and go 1** *obs* **:** to pass quickly from point to point (as in a discourse) **2 a :** to touch bottom or an obstacle without sticking fast or foundering **b :** to succeed by a very narrow margin — **touch bottom 1 :** to scrape or settle upon the sea bottom **2 :** to reach the lowest possible point ⟨prices seemed to have *touched bottom* and a rise is expected⟩ ⟨that day our hopes *touched bottom*⟩ — **touch elbows :** to be in close contact in work, play, viewpoint **:** have close association ⟨place where you *touch elbows* with all sorts of people⟩ — **touch wood :** to touch or rap on something made of wood as a charm to ward off bad luck esp. after boasting of good luck

[2]touch \"\ *n* -ES [partly fr. ME *touche*, fr. OF, fr. *tochier*, *tuchier* to touch; partly fr. [1]*touch*] **1 a :** a light stroke, tap, or push ⟨ready to fall at a ~⟩ **b :** a light stroke of wit or satire **:** KNOCK, DIG **c :** the contact of a fencer's point or blade against the opponent's target that scores a point **2 a :** the act or fact of touching, feeling, striking lightly, or coming in contact ⟨saluted with a ~ to his cap⟩ **b :** PALPATION **3 :** the sense by which pressure or traction exerted on the skin or mucous membrane is perceived **:** the tactile sense as distinguished from the pain, temperature, and kinesthetic senses **4 :** mental or moral sensitiveness, responsiveness, or tact ⟨she has a wonderful ~ in dealing with children⟩ ⟨our high task to use our power with a sure hand and a steady ~ —A.E.Stevenson b. 1900⟩ ⟨a skilled writer but lacking the popular ~⟩ **5 :** a specified sensation conveyed through the tactile receptors **:** FEEL ⟨the velvety ~ of a fabric⟩ **6 a :** the act of rubbing gold or silver on a touchstone to test its quality **b :** the quality or degree of fineness of metal so tested **c :** the official stamp upon a tested metal of standard quality **d :** TOUCHMARK **e** *archaic* **:** tested or proven quality or character ⟨friends of noble ~ —Shak.⟩ **7 a** *obs* **:** TOUCHSTONE 1 **b :** TEST, TRIAL — used chiefly in the phrase *put to the touch* **8 a :** a visible effect **:** STAMP, MARK ⟨~ of the tropical sun⟩ ⟨woman with what we used to call the ~ of good breeding upon her —Morris Markey⟩ **b :** WEAKNESS, DEFECT ⟨a ~ in his wits⟩ ⟨one ~ of nature makes the whole world kin —Shak.⟩ **c** *obs* **:** injury to reputation **:** REPROACH, BLAME **9 :** something slight of its kind: as **a :** a light attack ⟨~ of fever⟩ **b :** a small quantity **:** TRACE, DASH ⟨~ of spring in the air⟩ ⟨~ of garlic in the salad⟩ ⟨a ~ of unreality about the whole affair⟩ **c :** a transient emotion **:** a flash of feeling ⟨momentary ~ of compunction⟩ **d** *archaic* **:** a brief mention, hint, or reminder **e :** a near approach **:** a close call ⟨beaten in the . . . backstroke championships by a mere ~ —Kate Kerry⟩ **f :** BIT, LITTLE — used adverbially with *a* ⟨as though she had said something ridiculous and a ~ discreditable —R.V.Cassill⟩ ⟨aimed a ~ too low and missed⟩ **10** *archaic* **:** AGREEMENT, COVENANT — used in the phrase *to keep touch* **11 a** *archaic* **:** the playing of an instrument (as a lute or piano) with the fingers; *also* **:** musical notes or strains so produced ⟨with sweetest ~*es* pierce your mistress' ears —Shak.⟩ **b :** a manner or method of touching or striking esp. the keys of a keyboard instrument ⟨requiring a staccato ~⟩; *also* **:** one's characteristic style in striking keys ⟨have a firm ~⟩ **c :** particular or characteristic action of a keyboard instrument with reference to the resistance of its keys to pressure ⟨a piano with a stiff ~⟩ ⟨typewriter with a light ~⟩ **12 :** a set of changes in change ringing less than the total number possible or less than a peal **13 :** a light or delicate stroke in creating or improving an artistic composition **:** an effective or touching-up detail ⟨that was a vivid ~ in his last story⟩ ⟨the work is complete except for the finishing ~*es*⟩ ⟨hotel service with a personal ~⟩ **14 :** distinctive manner or method ⟨this room needs a woman's ~⟩ **:** characteristic skill of a workman or artist in the manipulation of his instruments or materials ⟨the billiard player had lost his ~⟩ ⟨the painting shows the ~ of a master⟩ **15 :** a characteristic or distinguishing trait or quality **16 a** *slang* **:** an act of borrowing, swindling, or stealing ⟨beggar making his ~⟩ **:** THEFT **b :** a victim of borrowing or swindling ⟨recognized him early as a soft ~ for a loan —John Lardner⟩ **17** *slang* **a :** a method of inducing someone to buy or to accept a deal **b :** something that will sell at a named price **c :** a sale effected by dubious means **18 :** the state or fact of being in contact or communication ⟨lost ~ with the other boats in the fog⟩ ⟨keeping in ~ with distant relations⟩ ⟨kept in close ~ with headquarters by phone⟩ ⟨out of ~ with modern methods⟩ **19 :** [3]TAG 1 **20 :** the broadest part of a plank worked top and butt **:** the angles of the stern timbers at the counters of a ship **21 :** the area outside of the sidelines in soccer or outside of and including the touchlines in rugby — used usu. with *in* or *into* ⟨kicked the ball into ~⟩ ⟨thrown in by a player standing in ~⟩

touch- *comb form* [obs. *touch-powder*, powder used for priming a gun, fr. ME *towchepoudre*, fr. MF *toucher* to touch, kindle (a fire) + ME *poudre* powder] **:** serving for quick ignition ⟨*touch*hole⟩ ⟨*touch*wood⟩

touch·able \'təchəbəl\ *adj* **1 :** capable of being touched **:** TANGIBLE **2 :** EATABLE — **touch·able·ness** *n* -ES

touch and go *n* [fr. the v. phrase *touch and go*] **1 :** rapid movement from point to point **:** continuous flitting ⟨its swift *touch and go* of actual talk —J.L.Lowes⟩ **2 :** a highly uncertain or precarious situation or condition **:** a state of affairs so critical that the slightest turn may bring disaster or failure ⟨*touch and go* of guerrilla warfare⟩

touch-and-go \¦=·=¦=\ *adj* [*touch and go*] **1 :** marked by restlessness or casualness of movement or execution ⟨*touch-and-go* dialogue⟩ **2 :** PRECARIOUS, HAIRBREADTH ⟨mule trains to haul your equipment the two *touch-and-go* miles —Horace Sutton⟩

touch-and-heal \'=·='=\ *n* -S [[1]*touch*] **:** an herb (*Hypericum perforatum*)

touchback \'=,=\ *n* -S **:** an act or instance in football of being in possession of the ball behind one's own goal line when the ball is declared dead, the impetus putting the ball over the goal line having been given by an opponent — compare SAFETY 6b(2)

touchball \'=,=\ *n* **:** TOUCH FOOTBALL

touch body *or* **touch corpuscle** *n* **:** TACTILE CORPUSCLE

touch·box \'təch,bäks\ *n* [*touch-* + *box*] **:** a box of lighted tinder formerly carried by soldiers for firing matchlocks

touch down *vt* **:** to place (the ball in rugby) by hand on the ground on or over an opponent's goal line in scoring a try or behind one's own goal line as a defensive measure ~ *vi* **:** to reach the ground **:** LAND ⟨the new bomber *touched down* just three hours later⟩

touchdown \'=,=\ *n* -S **1 a :** the act of touching a football down behind an opponent's goal; *specif* **:** the act of scoring six points by being lawfully in possession of the ball on, above, or behind an opponent's goal line when the ball is declared dead **b :** the act of a rugby player who first grounds the ball in his own in-goal **c :** the act of scoring two points in speedball by completion of a forward pass to a teammate in the opponent's end zone **2 :** the act or moment of making the landing gear of an airplane touch the surface with or without the intention of making a full landing

[1]tou·ché \tü'shā\ *interj* [F, past part. of *toucher* to touch] — used to acknowledge a hit in fencing or the success of an argument or the accuracy of an accusation

[2]touché \"\ *n* -S **1 :** a hit in fencing **:** TOUCH **2 :** a telling remark or home thrust in argument

touched *adj* [fr. past part. of [1]*touch*] **1 :** emotionally stirred ⟨she was both angry and in an odd way ~ —Sherwood Anderson⟩ **2 :** slightly unbalanced mentally **:** ECCENTRIC ⟨the ~ sea captain who remembers journeys to places that never were —Irving Howe⟩

touched bill *n* **:** a bill of health stating that a ship's company or a port is suspected of infectious disease

touch·eous \'təchəs, 'tech-\ *var of* TOUCHOUS

touch·er \'təchə(r)\ *n* -S [ME, fr. *touchen* to touch + *-er*] **1 :** one that touches **2 :** a bowl which has touched the jack during its original course on a bowling green

touches *pres 3d sing of* TOUCH, *pl of* TOUCH

touch football *n* **:** football played informally and chiefly characterized by the substitution of touching for tackling

touch·hole \'təch,hōl\ *n* [*touch-* + *hole*] **1 :** the vent in old-time cannons or firearms through which the charge was ignited **2 :** the hole in the cylinder of a gas engine with tube ignition in which the tube is inserted

touchier *comparative of* TOUCHY

touchiest *superlative of* TOUCHY

touch·i·ly \'təchəlē, -li\ *adv* **:** in a touchy manner ⟨~ refusing offers of help⟩

touch in *vt* **:** to insert (detail) by light strokes of pencil or brush

touch·i·ness \-chēnəs, -chin-\ *n* -ES **:** the quality or state of being touchy **:** IRRITABILITY

[1]touching *prep* [ME, fr. pres. part. of *touchen* to touch] **:** in reference to **:** as regards **:** CONCERNING ⟨good experimental verification of your hypothesis, ~ the cause of the abnormal phenomena —T.H.Huxley⟩ — often used with *as* ⟨now, as ~ things offered unto idols —1 Cor 8:1 (AV)⟩

[2]touching *adj* [fr. pres. part. of [1]*touch*] **:** capable of stirring emotions **:** AFFECTING, PATHETIC ⟨~ trust in her parents⟩ ⟨~ story⟩ **syn** see MOVING

touch·ing·ly *adv* [[2]*touching* + *-ly*] **:** in a touching manner **:** PATHETICALLY, MOVINGLY ⟨~ grateful⟩

touch·ing·ness *n* -ES **:** the quality or state of being touching ⟨~ of her devotion⟩

touch-in-goal \'=·='=\ *n* **:** any of the four areas of a rugby field back of the goal lines extended and outside of the touch-in-goal lines

touch-in-goal line *n* **:** a continuation of a touchline extending from a goal line to the nearest dead-ball line — see RUGBY illustration

touch judge *n* **:** either of two officials in rugby stationed one on each side of the field who assist the referee in determining when and where the ball goes into touch and when a goal has been kicked

touch·less \'təchləs\ *adj* [[2]*touch* + *-less*] **:** not touchable **:** INTANGIBLE

touchline \'=,=\ *n* **1 :** either of the lines between and at right angles to the goal lines that bound the sides of the field of play in rugby and soccer — see RUGBY illustration **2** *Brit* **:** SIDELINE 3b ⟨does not like people who boo from the ~ and refuse to help the game on —*Times Lit. Supp.*⟩

touchmark \'=,=\ *n* **:** an identifying maker's mark impressed on pewter

touch-me-not \'=·=,=\ *n* -S **1** [so called fr. the fact that the ripe pods burst open and scatter their seeds when touched] **a :** JEWELWEED **b :** SQUIRTING CUCUMBER **2** *obs* **:** LUPUS **3 :** a haughty, aloof, or prudish person; *esp* **:** a girl or woman inclined to be distant and cold

touch-me-not-ish \'təchmē,näd·ish\ *adj* **:** not readily approachable **:** STANDOFFISH, PRUDISH — **touch-me-not-ish·ness** *n* -ES

touch needle *n* **:** a small bar of gold either pure or alloyed with silver in a known proportion for trying the fineness of a gold or silver article by comparing the streaks made by the article and the bar on a touchstone

touch off *vt* **1 :** to describe or characterize to a nicety **:** hit off ⟨a fine job of *touching off* the shallowness and confusion of his interloper role —*Newsweek*⟩ **2** [*touch* (as in *touchhole*)] **a :** to cause to explode by or as if by touching with fire **b :** to release or initiate with the sudden violence of an explosion ⟨the charges *touched off* a storm of protest —R.A. Billington⟩ **3 :** to start (a relay runner) by touching his extended hand

touch-off \'=,=\ *n* -S [*touch off*] **:** something that is touched off; *specif* **:** a fire of incendiary origin

touch·ous \'təchəs, 'tech-\ *adj* [[2]*touch* + *-ous*] *dial* **:** TOUCHY

touch·pan \'təch,pan\ *n* [*touch-* + *pan*] **:** the pan of a flintlock

touch paper *n* [*touch-* + *paper*] **:** paper impregnated with potassium nitrate that burns steadily without flame and is used to aid the ignition of small fireworks

touchpiece \'=,=\ *n* **:** a coin (as an angel) or medal given by various English sovereigns as late as Queen Anne to persons touched by them for the cure of the king's evil

touch reader *n* **:** a blind person able to read braille or some other raised type with the fingers

touch spot *n* **:** PRESSURE SPOT

touchstone \'=,=\ *n* **1 :** a black siliceous stone related to flint and formerly used to test the purity of gold and silver by the streak left on the stone when rubbed by the metal ⟨holding out gold that's by the ~ tried —Shak.⟩ — called also *Basanite*, *Lydian stone* **2 :** a test or criterion for determining the quality or genuineness of a thing ⟨an original work is the ~ that exposes educated taste masquerading as sensibility —Clive Bell⟩ **syn** see STANDARD

touch system *n* **:** a method of typewriting that assigns a particular finger to each key and makes it possible to type without looking at the keyboard — compare HUNT AND PECK

touch-tackle \'='==\ *n* **:** TOUCH FOOTBALL

touch-type \'=¦=\ *vb* **:** to type by the touch system

touch up *vt* **1 :** to improve or perfect by small additional strokes or alterations ⟨*touch up* a picture by strengthening highlights and shadows⟩ ⟨the last act needs to be *touched up*⟩ **2 :** to stimulate by or as if by a flick of a whip ⟨*touch up* a team of horses⟩ ⟨his memory needs to be *touched up*⟩

touch-up \'=,=\ *n* -S [*touch up*] **1 :** an act or instance of touching up **:** RETOUCH **2 :** FLICK, HINT

touch watch *n* **:** a watch designed for reading in the dark or by the blind

touch·wood \'təch,wu̇d\ *n* [*touch-* + *wood*] **:** [3]PUNK 1, 2

touchy \'təchē, -chi, *dial* 'tech- *or* 'tich-\ *adj* -ER/-EST [[2]*touch* + *-y*] **1 :** marked by an oversensitive irritable temperament, by general readiness to take offense on slight provocation, or by delicate easily wounded sensitivity about specific matters ⟨a ~, uneasy friend . . . his intensest friendships generally came to grief —David Cecil⟩ ⟨a little ~ about my spoon-feeding at first —Stephen Haggard⟩ ⟨a man who had grown too ~ to make judicious decisions —*Time*⟩ **2 :** responding quickly to a touch **:** extremely reactive: as **a** *of a body part* **:** acutely sensitive or irritable **b** *of a chemical* **:** highly explosive or inflammable **3 :** calling for tact, care, and caution in treatment **:** likely to cause offense, chagrin, or hurt pride **:** uncertain in issue **:** fraught with danger **:** PRECARIOUS ⟨the job of governorship, when all men seemed set against change, was a brittle, ~ business —Julian Dana⟩ ⟨military training is a ~ subject in the aftermath of war —M.W.Childs⟩ **4 :** composed of dots or short strokes ⟨~ pencil drawing⟩ **syn** see IRASCIBLE

toucouleur *usu cap, var of* TUKULÖR

[1]tough \'təf\ *adj* -ER/-EST [ME *tow, togh, tough*, fr. OE *tōh*; akin to OHG *zāhi* tough, ON *tā* ground trodden to hardness, OE *tengan* to press forward, *tenge* pressing, resting on] **1 a :** having the quality of being strong or firm in texture but flexible and not brittle **:** yielding to force without breaking **:** capable of resisting great strain without coming apart ⟨the ligaments of animals are ~⟩ **b :** not easily chewed or masticated ⟨steak so ~ we could hardly cut it⟩ **2 :** having great viscosity **:** GLUTINOUS, STICKY, TENACIOUS ⟨~ phlegm⟩ ⟨~ tar⟩ **3 a :** characterized by severity **:** STIFF, FORCEFUL ⟨when the law gets too ~, the courts don't convict —Gregor Felsen⟩ ⟨one change will be a ~*er* boycott ban —S.K.Galpin⟩ **b** (1) **:** characterized by uncompromising determination **:** ADAMANT, MILITANT ⟨had something with which to back a ~ and inflexible foreign policy —*New Statesman & Nation*⟩ (2) **:** AGGRESSIVE, THREATENING ⟨the thing to do is get ~ with that country —Harry Schwartz⟩ **4 :** capable of enduring strain, hardship, or severe labor **:** having or manifesting great physical resistance **:** unusually sturdy **:** HARDY ⟨the rigorous climate . . . creates a ~ people —Douglas Carruthers⟩ ⟨the Scots . . . were almost without exception very ~ fighting men —G.W.Johnson⟩ **5 :** very hard to influence or move **:** STUBBORN, UNYIELDING ⟨they view him . . . as a ~ antagonist —*N.Y. Times*⟩ ⟨insight into certain deep and persistent . . . traits and into the ~ fidelities —Clifton Fadiman⟩ ⟨the ~*est* judge . . . single-minded and implacable —M.S.Mayer⟩ **6 :** making unduly heavy or arduous demands **:** extremely difficult to cope with or comprehend ⟨had been a ~ winter —Heywood Broun⟩ ⟨found himself in a ~ spot —Barnaby Conrad⟩ ⟨one of the ~*est* languages in the world —Albert Hubbell⟩ ⟨the work that men do is not the ~ part of their lives —G.W.Brace⟩ **7 :** stubbornly fought **:** stoutly maintained ⟨had lost a ~ contest that went into extra innings —R.O.Boyer⟩ **8 a :** pertinaciously unruly **:** ROWDYISH, RUFFIANLY **:** tending toward viciousness ⟨problem children who were too ~ for the other schools —Green Peyton⟩ **b :** frequented by rowdy or criminal elements ⟨a patrolman on . . . the ~*est* waterfront beat —*Current Biog.*⟩ ⟨had a reputation as one of the ~*est* places in the state —*Amer. Guide Series: Nev.*⟩ **9 :** marked by a steely quality **:** without softness or sentimentality **:** harshly even brutally realistic ⟨his book is . . . unbelievably ~ —W.H.Auden⟩ ⟨a writer . . . who is ~ and blunt and calls a spade a spade —M. D.Geismar⟩ ⟨strongly influenced by American writing of the ~ school —*Brit. Bk. News*⟩ **syn** see STRONG

[2]tough \"\ *vt* -ED/-ING/-S **:** to bear unflinchingly **:** ENDURE — often used with *out* ⟨a friend with whom he was ~*ing* the winter out —A.B.Guthrie⟩ ⟨been ~*ing* out a dry spell —W.D. Overholser⟩ ⟨the boy wanted to ~ it out and be a cowboy — Ross Santee⟩

[3]tough \"\ *n* -S **:** a tough person; esp **:** ROWDY

[4]tough \"\ *adv* **:** in a tough manner ⟨tried to tell why he and his buddies talked ~ —*Time*⟩ ⟨talks ~ and insensitively but sends money —A.E.Stevenson b. 1900⟩

tough check *n* **:** a very strong cardboard used for shipping tags and tickets and made on a cylinder machine

tough·en \'təfən\ *vb* **toughened; toughened; toughening** \-f(ə)niŋ\ **toughens** [[1]*tough* + *-en*] *vt* **:** to make tough ⟨~*ed* by a rough-and-tumble environment where each man's revolver . . . made the law —R.A.Billington⟩ ~ *vi* **:** to become tough ⟨the language has suddenly ~*ed* and acquired a new menacing cadence —Edmund Stevens⟩

toughened glass *n* [*toughened* (past part. of *toughen*) + *glass*] **:** glass tempered by a control process of sudden cooling

toughhead \'=,=\ *n* [[1]*tough* + *head*] *NewEng* **:** RUDDY DUCK

tough·ie *also* **toughy** \'təfē, -fi\ *n, pl* **toughies** [[1]*tough* + *-ie*] **:** one that is tough: as **a :** a loud rowdy person **:** tough character ⟨a square-jawed ~ who is not taking anything from anybody —Brand Blanshard⟩ **b :** a very intricate or difficult problem ⟨had worked on some real ~*s* . . . but this one topped them all —Franklin Sharpe⟩ **c :** a hard-boiled piece of writing ⟨the straight-out detective story as distinguished from . . . the ~ —Sergeant Cuff⟩

tough·ish \'təfish\ *adj* **:** rather tough

tough·ly *adv* [ME, fr. [1]*tough* + *-ly*] **:** in a tough manner ⟨~ vigorous and humanly sympathetic storytelling —Anthony Boucher⟩

tough-minded \'=¦==\ *adj* [[1]*tough* + *minded*] **:** tending toward or characterized by empiricism, materialism, or pessimism; *esp* **:** realistic or unsentimental in temper or habitual point of view **:** HARDHEADED, PRACTICAL — **tough-mind·ed·ly** *adv*

tough-mind·ed·ness *n* -ES **:** the quality or state of being tough-minded ⟨this educational process had the tendency to turn cynicism into *tough-mindedness* —C.G.Bolte⟩

tough·ness *n* -ES [ME *toughnes*, fr. [1]*tough* + *-nes* -ness] **1 :** the quality or state of being tough ⟨had a physical and moral ~ of fibre which enabled him . . . to endure misfortune —Sir Winston Churchill⟩ **2 :** the ability of a metal to absorb considerable energy before fracture **3 :** the quality of a paint or coating that causes it to resist chipping, abrasion, or cracking

tough pitch *n* **1 :** the exact state or quality of texture and consistency of refined and remelted copper containing about 0.02 to 0.05 percent oxygen **2** *also* **tough cake :** copper having the quality of tough pitch

tough-skinned \'=¦=\ *adj* **1 :** having a tough skin **2 :** lacking sensitivity **:** not easily offended

touk *var of* TUCK

tou·lon \(')tü¦län, tü'lōⁿ\ *adj, usu cap* [fr. *Toulon*, seaport of southeast France] **:** of or from the city of Toulon, France **:** of the kind or style prevalent in Toulon

[1]tou·louse \(')tü¦lüz\ *adj, usu cap* [fr. *Toulouse*, city of southern France] **:** of or from the city of Toulouse, France **:** of the kind or style prevalent in Toulouse

[2]toulouse \"\ *n, usu cap* **1 :** a French breed of large heavy geese having a large head, a short thick bill without a knob, and chiefly gray plumage **2** -S **:** a goose of this breed

tou·mey oak \'tümē-\ *n, usu cap T* [after James W. *Toumey* †1932 Am. forester] **:** an oak (*Quercus toumeyi*) of the southwestern U. S. having thin entire leaves and a thin shallow tomentose acorn cup

toun \'tün\ *Scot var of* TOWN

tou·pee \tü'pā\ *n* -S [alter. of *toupet*] **1 :** a curl or lock of hair made into a topknot on a periwig or natural hairdress and worn esp. in the 18th century by men and women; *also* **:** a periwig with such a topknot **2 :** a small wig or section of false hair worn to cover a bald spot

tou·pet \"\ *n* -S [F, tuft of hair, forelock, fr. OF, dim. of *top*, *toup*, of Gmc origin; akin to OHG *zopf* end, tip, tuft of hair — more at TOP] **:** TOUPEE

[1]tour \'tu̇(ə)r, 'tu̇ə, *in sense 1 sometimes* 'tau̇(ə)r *or* 'tau̇ə\ *n* -S [ME, fr. MF, fr. OF *tor, tour, torn, tourn* lathe, circuit, turn — more at TURN] **1 a :** one's turn in an orderly arrangement or schedule **:** a shift usu. in a factory **b :** a period during which an individual or unit is on a specific duty or at one place ⟨assigned to short ~*s* of duty at a number of United States Army stations —*Current Biog.*⟩ ⟨my ~ of duty in Kenya lasted fourteen months —John Muggeridge⟩ **c :** a single circuit of a postal carrier around his route **2** *obs* **:** a circuitous movement **:** a revolution esp. of a heavenly body **3 a** (1) **:** a journey in which one returns to the starting point **:** a circular trip usu. for business, pleasure, or education during which various places are visited and for which an itinerary is often planned ⟨an inexpensive ~ of Europe —T.R.Ybarra⟩ ⟨a motor ~ of New England⟩ (2) **:** something resembling such a tour ⟨making a ~ of all the problems confronting the West —*N.Y. Times*⟩ **b** (1) **:** a brief turn **:** ROUND ⟨the very walks of the garden are so moist that . . . no person can make a ~ of it —Tobias Smollett⟩ (2) **:** a short drive or outing often representing a social occasion **c :** a circuit of an island **d :** a visit (as to a museum, factory, or historic site) for enjoyment or instruction usu. under the auspices of a guide ⟨a brief opening ceremony followed by a ~ of the new school⟩ ⟨the group made a conducted ~ of the battleground⟩ **e :** a series of professional engagements involving travel from one place to another ⟨after a successful nationwide ~, the play was made into a motion picture —*Current Biog.*⟩ ⟨took his small theatrical company on ~ in the provinces⟩ **4 :** a headdress of the 17th and 18th centuries usu. built high by adding false hair, pads, or trimmings **5** *obs* **:** the compass or range of something **:** sum and substance **6 :** one of the distinct portions of a more or less continuous song of a canary

[2]tour \'tu̇(ə)r, 'tu̇ə\ *vb* -ED/-ING/-S *vi* **1 :** to direct one's steps **:** GO, PROCEED ⟨loves holding onto someone's hands and ~*ing* around the room —*Infant Care*⟩ **2 a :** to make a tour ⟨~*ed* through Central America and Mexico⟩ **b :** to go on tour esp. with or in a theatrical production ⟨the star headed an obedient company in the city or ~*ed* by himself —Margery Bailey⟩ ~ *vt* **1 a :** to make a tour of ⟨~*ed* the countryside instructing workers —*Americana Annual*⟩ **b :** to take on a tour ⟨the group was ~*ed* through the factory⟩ **2 :** to present (as a theatrical production) on a tour ⟨students . . . ~ a children's theater play for one week each spring —Alice Griffin⟩

tou·ra·co *or* **tu·ra·co** \¦tu̇rə¦kō\ *or* **tu·ra·cou** *or* **tu·ra·koo** \-kü\ *n* -S [native name in western Africa] **:** any of various African birds that constitute the family Musophagidae, are mostly from one to two feet long, have a long tail, an erectile crest, a short stout often colored bill, lax and fluffy plumage, and red wing feathers which yield turacin — called also *plantain eater*

tour·bil·lion *or* **tour·bil·lon** \tu̇r'bilyən, tu̇ə'-\ *n* -S [MF *tourbillon* whirl, vortex, whirlwind, fr. L *turbin-*, *turbo* — more

at TURBINE] **1 :** something that whirls around or moves spirally: as **a :** WHIRLWIND **b :** a vortex esp. of a whirlwind or whirlpool **c :** a firework making a spiral flight **2 :** a watch in which the escapement is mounted on an epicyclic train and assumes all the vertical positions in one minute thereby neutralizing the position errors **3 :** the whirl of the hair near the vertex of the human head

tour de force \ˌtu̇rdə¦fō(ə)rs, -¦fȯ(ə)rs; ¦tüədə¦fōəs, -¦fȯ(ə)s\ *n, pl* **tours de force** \"\ [F] **1 :** a feat of strength, skill, or artistic merit **2 :** a merely adroit or ingenious accomplishment or production

tou·relle \tü'rel\ *n* -s [F, fr. OF, dim. of *tor, tour* tower — more at TOWER] **1 :** a small tower (as one springing from corbeling or pier) : TURRET **2 :** something resembling a tourelle ⟨the pines' green ~s —Richard Llewellyn⟩

tour en l'air \ˌtu̇rän'ler\ *n, pl* **tours en l'air** \"\ [F] **:** a ballet turn in the air

tour·er \'tu̇rə(r)\ *n* -s [²*tour* + *-er*] : TOURING CAR

tou·rill \tü'ril\ *n* -s [G *tourill, tourille,* perh. modif. of F *tourie* carboy] **:** an absorption vessel in which a gas is passed over a liquid (as for removing moisture or a component of a gas mixture)

¹**touring** *n* -s [fr. gerund of ²*tour*] **1 :** the act of participating in a tour ⟨the ~ in quest of the picturesque —Anthony Trollope⟩ **2 :** TOURING CAR **3 :** cross-country skiing

²**touring** *adj* [in sense 1, fr. pres. part. of ²*tour;* in sense 2, fr. ¹*touring*] **1 :** traveling from place to place on a tour ⟨~ public⟩ **2 :** used in touring **:** suitable for use while touring **:** designed for the tourist trade

touring car *n* **:** an open automobile with two cross seats, usu. four doors, and a folding top — called also *phaeton, tourer*

tour·ism \'tu̇ˌrizəm\ *n* -s [¹*tour* + *-ism*] **1 :** the practice of touring **:** traveling for recreation **2 :** the guidance or management of tourists as a business or a governmental function **:** provision of itineraries, guidance, and accommodations for tourists **:** the economic activities associated with and dependent upon tourists

¹**tour·ist** \'tu̇rəst\ *n* -s [¹*tour* + *-ist*] **1 :** one that makes a tour **:** one that travels from place to place for pleasure or culture **:** one that stays overnight usu. at an inn or motel **2 :** TOURIST CLASS

²**tourist** \"\ *adj* **:** of, belonging to, suitable for, or serving tourists ⟨~ agency⟩ ⟨~ cottage⟩ ⟨~ rate⟩

³**tourist** \"\ *vb* -ED/-ING/-S *vi* **:** to make a tour ⟨would probably shudder at ~*ing* in his own country —Anne S. Mehdevi⟩ ~ *vt* **:** to visit while touring

tourist car *or* **tourist coach** *n* **:** a railway car equipped with less commodious and lower-priced sleeping accommodations than standard Pullman cars

tourist card *n* **:** a citizenship identity card issued to a tourist usu. for a stated period of time in lieu of a passport or a visa

tourist class *n* **:** a class of accommodations (as on a passenger ship) usu. less expensive and roomy than first or than second or cabin class

tourist court *n* **:** MOTEL

touristed *adj* [fr. past part. of ³*tourist*] **:** visited by throngs of tourists ⟨of the three islands, St. Thomas is the most ~ —Lawrence Martin⟩

tourist home *n* **:** a house in which rooms are available for rent to transients

tour·is·tic \(ˈ)tu̇¦ristik\ *also* **tour·is·ti·cal** \-təkəl\ *adj* [¹*tourist* + *-ic, -ical*] **:** of or relating to a tour or tourism **:** primarily catering or of interest to tourists ⟨traditional costumes are daily dress and not a holiday or ~ getup —Herbert Kubly⟩ ⟨one of two largest ~ hotels —Arnold Bennett⟩

tour·is·ti·cal·ly \-tək(ə)lē\ *adv* **:** in a touristic manner **:** with respect to tourists ⟨~ the country is probably twenty years behind —Horace Sutton⟩

tour·ist·ry \'tu̇rəstrē\ *n* -ES [¹*tourist* + *-ry*] **:** the fact or practice of touring; *also* **:** the whole body of tourists ⟨all the ruck and rabble of British ~ pour unhindered —R.L.Stevenson⟩

tour·isty \-tē\ *adj* [¹*tourist* + *-y*] **:** of, relating to, or characteristic of tourists **:** patronized by or popular with the tourist ⟨the shopfuls of ~ trinkets —*Mademoiselle*⟩ ⟨tourists descend . . . in busloads during summer, with the result the whole place is rather ~ —*N.Y.Times*⟩

tour je·té \ˌtu̇rzhə'tā\ *n, pl* **tour jetés** [F, lit., thrown turn] **:** a high turning leap in ballet starting with battement and finishing in arabesque — called also *jeté en tournant*

tou·lou·rou \ˌtu̇lü'rü\ *n* -s [F] **:** GREAT LAND CRAB

tour·ma·line *also* **tur·ma·line** \'tu̇rmələn, 'tüəm-, -məˌlēn\ *n* -s [Sinhalese *toramalli* carnelian] **1 :** a mineral $(Na,Ca)(Li,Mg,Fe,Al)(Al,Fe)_6B_3Si_6O_{27}(O,OH,F)_4$ that consists of a complex borosilicate, fluoride, and hydroxide of aluminum, iron, magnesium, calcium, lithium, and sodium, that occurs usu. in 3-, 6-, or 9-sided prisms vertically striated but sometimes in compact or columnar masses, that is strongly dichroic, piezoelectric, and pyroelectric, that shows double refraction but absorbs one of the rays, and that makes a gem of great beauty when transparent and cut (hardness 7–7.5, sp. gr. 2.98–3.2) — compare SCHORL **2 :** a very pale green that is bluer and darker than emerald tint or microcline green and bluer and deeper than celadon tint

tourmaline pink *n* **:** a grayish purplish red that is redder, lighter, and stronger than average rose plum, bluer, lighter, and stronger than Aztec maroon, and bluer and paler than daphne pink

tourmaline tongs *n pl but sometimes sing in constr* **:** a simple form of polariscope consisting of two transparent plates of tourmaline cut parallel to the optic axis and mounted on a tongs-shaped support so that the object to be examined can be held between them and used esp. by jewelers for distinguishing glass from crystal

tour·ma·lin·ic \ˌ≈≈¦linik\ *adj* **:** of the nature of or containing tourmaline

tour·ma·lin·iza·tion \ˌtu̇rmələnə'zāshən\ *n* -s [*tourmalinize* + *-ation*] **:** a process by which previously existing minerals are replaced wholly or in part by tourmaline

tour·ma·lin·ize \'tu̇rmələˌnīz\ *vt* -ED/-ING/-S [*tourmaline* + *-ize*] **:** to subject to tourmalinization

tourn \'tu̇(ə)rn\ *n* -s [AF, fr. OF *torn* circuit — more at TOUR] **1 :** the circuit or turn of an English sheriff to hold a court of record twice a year within a month after Easter and Michaelmas in every hundred in his county but abolished by the Sheriff's Act of 1887 **2 :** the court presided over by the sheriff

tour·na·ment \'tu̇rnəmənt, 'tər, 'tüən, 'tōn-, 'təin- *sometimes* 'tō(r)n-\ *n* -s [ME *tornement, turnement,* fr. OF *torneiement,* fr. *torneier* to engage in mounted combat + *-ment* — more at TOURNEY] **1 a** (1) **:** a knightly sport originating in the middle ages in which mounted armored combatants armed usu. with blunted lances or swords and divided into two parties engaged one another to exhibit their skill, prowess, and courage and to win a prize or favor bestowed by the lady of the tournament chosen for the occasion (2) **:** the whole series of knightly sports, jousts, and tilts occurring at a particular time and place (3) **:** a modern contest in which mounted men tilt with lances at suspended rings **b :** something resembling a medieval tournament ⟨it is the ~ of open minds that settles things —William Alfred⟩ **2** *obs* **:** shock of battle **:** BATTLE, ENCOUNTER ⟨with cruel ~ the squadrons join —John Milton⟩ **3 a :** an athletic meeting comprising contests in a large number of sports **b :** an event by the military in which contests esp. adapted to military training (as artillery driving, wall scaling, wrestling) are held **c :** a trial of skill in which many contestants compete for championship in a series of elimination contests **d :** a fishing contest in which many anglers participate

tour·na·sin \'tu̇rnəsən\ *n* -s [F, fr. *tournaser* to shape pottery on the wheel, fr. *tourner* to turn, fr. OF *torner*] **:** a tool for smoothing and finishing roughly thrown pottery while it revolves on a wheel

tour·ne·dos *n, pl* **tour·ne·dos** \¦tu̇rnə¦dō\ [F, fr. *tourner* to turn (fr. OF *torner*) + *dos* back, fr. L *dorsum*] **:** a small fillet of beef usu. cut from the tip of the tenderloin and encircled by a strip of suet, salt pork, or bacon for quick cooking

tour·nee \tu̇r'nā\ *n* -s [G *tourné, tournee,* fr. F *tourné,* past part. of *tourner* to turn] **:** a game of skat in which the player turns a card from the skat as trump and can exchange two cards for the skat cards

tour·ne·for·tia \ˌtu̇rnə'fȯrshēə, -rd·ēə\ *n, cap* [NL, fr. Joseph Pitton de *Tournefort* †1708 Fr. botanist + NL *-ia*] **:** a large genus of tropical trees and shrubs (family Boraginaceae) having alternate leaves and terminal cymes of small flowers and a fruit that is a fleshy or spongy 4-celled drupe

tour·nette \(ˈ)tu̇r¦net\ *n* -s [F, fr. MF, fr. *tourner* to turn + *-ette*] **:** a horizontal revolving tablet similar to a potter's wheel on which a piece of pottery is placed for painting

tour·neur *R* tu̇r'nər, +V -'nər-; -*R* tüə'nə, + *vowel in a word following without pause* -'nər- *or* -'nə *also* -'nər\ *n* -s [F, lit., turner, fr. OF *torneeur,* fr. LL *tornator,* fr. L *tornatus* (past part. of *tornare* to turn) + *-or* — more at TURN] **:** the employee of a casino who is in charge of a roulette game and whose duties include turning the wheel

¹**tour·ney** \'tu̇rnē, 'tər-, 'tüən-, 'tōn-, 'təin-, -ni\ *vi* **tourneyed; tourneyed; tourneying; tourneys** [ME *tourneyen,* fr. MF *torneier, tourneier,* fr. OF, fr. *torn* lathe, circular movement — more at TOUR] **:** to perform in a tournament

²**tourney** \"\ *n* -s [ME, fr. MF *tournei,* fr. OF *tornei,* fr. *torneier* to engage in a tournament] **:** TOURNAMENT

tour·ney·er \-ēə(r)\ *n* -s [¹*tourney* + *-er*] **:** one that enters a tourney

¹**tour·ni·quet** \'tu̇rnəkət, 'tər-, 'tüən-, 'tōn-, 'təin-, -nēk-\ *also* **tor·ni·quet** \'tō(r)n-\ *n* -s [F *tourniquet* instrument operated by turning, turnstile, tourniquet, fr. *tourner* to turn, fr. OF *torner* — more at TURN] **1 :** a device for arresting bleeding made of a bandage twisted tight usu. with a stick or of a piece of rubber tubing **2 :** TURNSTILE

²**tourniquet** \"\ *vt* -ED/-ING/-S **:** to apply a tourniquet or something resembling a tourniquet to

tour·nure \(ˈ)tu̇r¦nyü(ə)r\ *n* -s [F, manner in which a thing is fashioned, rounded form, bustle, fr. OF *torneüre* act of turning, rounded form, fr. ML *tornatura,* fr. L *tornatus* (past part. of *tornare* to turn) + *-ura* -ure — more at TURN] **:** BUSTLE; *sometimes* **:** the dress worn over this device

tours *pl of* TOUR, *pres 3d sing of* TOUR

tourte \'tu̇rt\ *n* -s [F, fr. OF *torte, tourte,* round loaf of bread, fr. LL *torta*] **:** TORTA 2

tourte bow \'tu̇rt-\ *n, usu cap T* [after François *Tourte* †1835 Fr. manufacturer of violin bows] **:** a violin bow made by François Tourte

¹**touse** *or* **towse** \'tau̇z\ *vb* -ED/-ING/-S [ME *-tusen, -tousen;* akin to Fris *tūsen* to pull, tear, OHG *zirzūsōn* to pull to pieces] *vt* **1 :** to pull or handle roughly **:** RACK, TEAR, WORRY **2 :** to tousle about **:** DISHEVEL ~ *vi* **:** to handle someone or something roughly **:** TUSSLE

²**touse** *or* **towse** \", 'tau̇s\ *n* -s **:** a noisy disturbance **:** ADO, FUSS

¹**tou·sle** *also* **tou·sel** *or* **tou·zle** *or* **tow·zle** *or* **tow·sle** \'tau̇zəl\ *vb* **tousled; tousled; tousling** \-z(ə)liŋ\ **tousles** [ME *touselen,* fr. *-tousen* to touse + *-len* -le] *vt* **1 :** to disorder by rough handling **:** DISHEVEL ⟨stood before the mirror arranging her hair which had been *tousled* by the wind —Thomas Wolfe⟩ **2 :** to indulge in tussling or horseplay with **:** pull or drag here and there ~ *vi* **:** to throw things into disorder **:** become disheveled ⟨full-cut hair ~*s* over his forehead and sideburns frame his . . . face —*Time*⟩

²**tousle** \", *in sense 1* 'tüzəl\ *n* -s **1** *Scot* **:** rough dalliance **:** TUSSLE **2 :** a tangled mass **:** disordered state ⟨~ of auburn curls —J.W.Vandercook⟩ ⟨the church . . . surrounded by a ~ of half-grown pines —Ruth Park⟩

tousled *adj* [fr. past part. of ¹*tousle*] **:** having a disheveled appearance **:** all tumbled together **:** extremely disordered ⟨his brown hair was ~, thick, and curly —Al Spiers⟩ ⟨a bed with the clothes ~ on it, a quilt . . . on the floor by the bed —Liam O'Flaherty⟩

tous-les-mois \ˌtülə'mwä\ *n* [F dial., by folk etymology (influence of F *tous les mois* all the months, every month) fr. F *tolomane,* fr. native name in West Indies] **:** starch from rootstocks of the edible canna often sold as arrowroot and used esp. in the preparation of foods for infants

tou·sly \'tau̇z(ə)lē\ *adj* -ER/-EST [¹*tousle* + *-y*] **:** TOUSLED

to usward *adv* [ME — more at USWARD] **:** USWARD ⟨the Lord . . . is long-suffering *to usward* —2 Pet 3:9 (ASV)⟩

tousy \'tüzi\ *adj* [¹*touse* + *-y*] **1** *chiefly Scot* **:** disheveled looking **:** TOUSLED **2** *chiefly Scot* **:** MAKESHIFT **:** ROUGH-AND-READY ⟨pretending you never took a ~ tea —Neil Munro⟩

¹**tout** \'tau̇t, *usu* -au̇d·+V\ *vb* -ED/-ING/-S [ME *tuten;* akin to OE *tōtian* to stick out, protrude, Norw *tyte* to stick out, ooze out, Fris *tūte* pipe, spout, snout] *vi* **1 :** to canvass for customers **:** solicit patronage **:** urge with annoying persistence ⟨peeled potatoes . . . and when otherwise unoccupied ~*ed* for custom from the passersby —E.M.Lustgarten⟩ **2 a** *chiefly Brit* **:** to spy out the movements of racehorses at their trials or to get by stealth or other improper means the secrets of the stable for betting purposes **b :** to give a tip on a racehorse ~ *vt* **1 :** to spy on **:** watch closely ⟨candidates are ~*ed* for possible political faux pas⟩ **2 a** *Brit* **:** to spy out information about (as a racing stable or horse) **b :** to give a tip on (a racehorse) to a bettor with the expectation of sharing in his winnings **3 :** to solicit importunately ⟨supplied the ideas and ~*ed* . . . businessmen for orders —Geoffrey Household⟩ **:** peddle in an annoyingly persistent manner ⟨the old woman of eighty who ~*ed Paris-Soir* . . . from café to café —Bruce Marshall⟩

²**tout** \"\ *n* -s **1 :** one that touts: as **a :** one who solicits custom ⟨tourists . . . besieged by ~*s* for tailoring and other establishments —H.R.Lieberman⟩ **b** *chiefly Brit* **:** one who secretly watches racehorses in training or gets racing information by improper means for betting purposes **c :** one who gives a tip on a racehorse for an expected compensation but esp. in hopes of a share in the winnings **2 :** the act of touting **:** LOOKOUT, WATCH ⟨a pickpocket on the ~ for a careless stroller⟩

³**tout** \'tau̇t, 'tüt\ *vt* -ED/-ING/-S [origin unknown] *Scot* **:** to tease in a vexing manner

⁴**tout** \'tau̇t\ *n* -s *chiefly Scot* **:** a slight illness

⁵**tout** \'tau̇t *also* 'tüt, *usu* -d·+V\ *vt* -ED/-ING/-S [alter. (perh. influenced by ¹*tout*) of ³*toot*] **:** to proclaim loudly **:** overly publicize **:** BALLYHOO ⟨~*ed* as the world's most elaborate suburban shopping development —*Wall Street Jour.*⟩ ⟨work is ~*ed* as the basic virtue —H.H.Mansfield⟩

tout·er \'tau̇d·ə(r)\ *n* -s [¹*tout* + *-er*] **:** ²TOUT

to·var·ia \tə'va(a)rēə\ *n, cap* [NL, fr. Simón *Tovario,* 18th cent. Span. physician + NL *-ia*] **:** a small genus (coextensive with the family Tovariaceae of the order Rhoeadales) of tropical American herbs having trifoliolate leaves and spicate flowers peculiar in having the sepals, petals, and stamens each eight while the gynoecium is composed of six carpels — **to·var·i·a·ceous** \tə¦va(a)rē¦āshəs\ *adj*

to·va·rich *or* **to·va·rish** \tə'värish, tō'-, -rēsh\ *n* -ES [Russ *tovarishch,* of Turkic origin] **1 :** COMRADE **2 :** an inhabitant of the Soviet Union

tove \'tōv\ *vi* -ED/-ING/-S [origin unknown] *Scot* **:** to smoke or emit a smoky smell

¹**tow** \'tō\ *vb* -ED/-ING/-S [ME *towen,* fr. OE *togian;* akin to OHG *zogōn* to tow, ON *toga;* akin to OE *tēon* to draw, pull, OHG *ziohan,* Goth *tiuhan* to draw, pull, L *ducere* to lead, draw, Gk *daidussesthai* to drag, Alb *nduk* to pull out, pluck] *vt* **1 :** to drag or pull along **:** HAUL, PROPEL ⟨tightening his hold on her wrist, he started through the . . . door, ~*ing* her along with him —Richard Burke⟩ ⟨men . . . ~*ed* and tugged by a perpetually retreating objective —Claud Cockburn⟩ **2 a :** to draw (as a ship or a disabled car) or pull along behind by a rope or chain ⟨~*ed* her into dry dock for repairs⟩ ⟨~*ed* the wrecked auto to the nearest garage⟩ ⟨a transport plane ~*ing* gliders⟩ ⟨more efficient for a tug to ~ the ship —*N. Y. Times*⟩ **b :** to push along (as a string of canal or river barges) — used of a powerboat behind a tow ~ *vi* **:** to move in tow ⟨piloting a ship that was ~*ing* into the river —Archie Binns⟩ ⟨riding out of town with a couple of pack ponies ~*ing* along behind him —H.L.Davis⟩ **syn** see PULL

²**tow** \"\ *n* -s *often attrib* **1 :** a rope or chain for towing ⟨coal barges . . . snapped their ~ in a storm —Joseph Mitchell⟩ **2 a :** the act or an instance of towing ⟨took a ~ for the last few miles —Alan Villiers⟩ **b :** the fact or state of being towed ⟨a damaged ship . . . in the ~ of a tug —E.L.Beach⟩ **3 :** something towed: as **a :** a boat or barge in tow or requiring towing **b :** a string of barges lashed together and pushed (as on the Mississippi river and tributaries) by a towboat ⟨watched the other ~ pass, the barges looming up in the night, and then the towboat —Richard Bissell⟩ ⟨puffing tugs with ~*s* of logs —*Amer. Guide Series: Wash.*⟩ ⟨flying the left glider in our ~ —J.W.Bellah⟩ **4 a :** something that tows (as a towboat or tugboat) ⟨two diesel-powered, screw-driven ~*s* —*Time*⟩ **b :** SKI TOW **5 :** the specimens taken in a towner ⟨sorting out the desired food from a plankton ~ —*Ecology*⟩ — **in tow** *adv* **1 :** in the state of being towed (as by a towline or towboat) ⟨passed a wrecker with a station wagon *in tow*⟩ **2 a :** under guidance or protection ⟨glad enough in such circumstances to be taken *in tow* by a friendly native⟩ **b :** in the character or position of a dependent, devoted, or subservient follower or admirer ⟨came round to see her with his latest protégé *in tow*⟩ ⟨kept him *in tow* . . . nearly six months —Dorothy Sayers⟩ ⟨a Navy officer passed with a good-looking girl *in tow* —Martin Dibner⟩

³**tow** \"\ *n* -s *often attrib* [ME, fr. OE *tow-* spinning; akin to ON *tō* tuft of wool for spinning, Goth *taui* work, doing, *taujan* to make, do — more at TAW] **1 :** short broken fiber removed from flax, hemp, or jute during scutching or hackling and used for yarn, twine, stuffing **2 :** HURDS **3 :** yarn or cloth made of tow — usu. used attributively ⟨~ trousers⟩ ⟨~ sack⟩ **4 :** a loose untwisted rope of textile filaments that is to be cut or broken into staple fiber ⟨rayon ~⟩

⁴**tow** \"\ *n* -s [ME (Sc), prob. fr. OE *toh-* (in *tohlīne* towline); akin to ON *tog, taug* rope, line, tow, OE *tēag* rope, cord, *togian* to tow — more at ¹TOW] **1** *archaic* **:** an attached iron chain or line for drawing a plow **2** *chiefly Scot & dial Eng* **:** ROPE: as **a :** a rope attached to a bell **b :** a ship's rope **c :** CABLE **d :** HANGMAN'S HALTER

towa \'tōə\ *n, pl* **towa** *or* **towas** *usu cap* **:** the language of the Jemez group of Pueblo Indians

tow·abil·i·ty \ˌtōə'biləd·ē\ *n* **:** the quality or state of being towable ⟨air transportability and ~ characteristics —*Aero Digest*⟩

tow·able \'tōəbəl\ *adj* **:** capable of being towed

tow·age \'tōij, -ōēj\ *n* -s *often attrib* [¹*tow* + *-age*] **1 :** the act or process of towing ⟨tugs available for deep-sea ~⟩ ⟨~ service⟩ ⟨~ fees⟩ **2 :** the price paid for towing

to·wai \'tōˌwī\ *n* -s [Maori] **:** KAMAHI

tow·an \'tau̇ən\ *n* -s [Corn] *dial Eng* **:** DUNE 1

¹**toward** \'t|ō(ə)rd, |ȯ(ə)rd, |ōəd, |ȯ(ə)d *also* 'tw| *or* tə'wȯ(ə)rd *or* tə'wō(ə)d\ *adj* [*toward* fr. ME, fr. OE *tōweard* facing, approaching, imminent, fr. *tō,* prep., to + *-weard* -ward; *towards* fr. ME *towardes,* alter. (influenced by *towardes,* prep., toward) of *toward* — more at TO] **1** *also* **towards a :** being about to take place **:** coming soon **:** being prepared ⟨could waddle fast enough if a meal was ~ —Kylie Tennant⟩ ⟨we have a trifling foolish banquet *towards* —Shak.⟩ **b** *obs* **:** threatening to happen **:** IMMINENT ⟨have you heard of no likely wars ~ —Shak.⟩ **c :** happening at the moment **:** AFOOT ⟨saw that there was a jest ~ and joined in —Charles Kingsley⟩ **d :** being planned or plotted — used predicatively ⟨the Governments . . . were privy to what was ~ —Hilaire Belloc⟩ **2 a** *obs* **:** quick to learn **:** APT, PROMISING ⟨spoken like a ~ prince —Shak.⟩ **b** *obs* **:** WELL-DISPOSED, AMIABLE, OBLIGING ⟨hath hitherto been very tractable and ~ —Richard Steele⟩ **c :** FAVORING, PROPITIOUS ⟨a ~ breeze⟩

²**toward** \"\ *or* **towards** \-dz\ *prep* [*toward* fr. ME, fr. OE *tōweard,* adv. & prep., fr. *tōweard,* adj.; *towards* fr. ME *towardes,* fr. OE *tōweardes,* alter. (influence of *-es* -s, gen. suffix) of *tōweard,* adj.] **1 a :** in the direction of **:** to a point approaching ⟨driving ~ town⟩ ⟨troops heading ~ the front⟩ ⟨comes ~ me —Willa Cather⟩ ⟨watch him lean over the dresser ~ the . . . mirror —R.P.Warren⟩ **b** *obs* **:** TO 1a(1) ⟨shall we ~ the Tower —Shak.⟩ **2 a :** along a course leading to **:** with a view to gaining **:** to the end or purpose of ⟨a long stride ~ disarmament⟩ ⟨a tendency ~ mischief⟩ ⟨the pressure ~ conformity⟩ ⟨looking ~ a mastery of the technique⟩ ⟨working ~ his doctorate⟩ ⟨beginnings ~ the formation of his own philosophy of life —H.F.West⟩ ⟨~ the goal of uniting all men of good will —*Harper's*⟩ **b :** in relation to **:** in the treatment or handling of ⟨an attitude ~ life⟩ ⟨measures taken ~ the colonies⟩ ⟨impartiality ~ the two —A.C.Sedgwick⟩ ⟨with malice ~ none —Abraham Lincoln⟩ ⟨the bias of many economists ~ government intervention —E.L.Dale⟩ ⟨an emotional block ~ mathematics —P.B.Sears⟩ **c** *usu* **towards :** in comparison with **:** with respect to ⟨how does it stand *towards* my past —Thomas Hardy⟩ **d :** in sympathy or affection for ⟨felt drawn ~ her without knowing why⟩ **e :** in tolerance for **:** in the presence of ⟨sensitized ~ tuberculin⟩ ⟨stable ~ . . . alkalies and solvents —H.J.Wolfe⟩ **3 a :** at a point in the direction of **:** NEAR ⟨took a cottage somewhere up ~ the Cape⟩ ⟨out ~ the blue-black ocean —William Beebe⟩ **b :** in such a position as to face **:** presented to **:** FACING ⟨pass the knife with the handle ~ the diner⟩ ⟨his back was ~ me⟩ ⟨lower left with face ~ camera —*N. Y. Times*⟩ ⟨with its northern outlook ~ the . . . Mountains —*Amer. Guide Series: N. H.*⟩ **4 :** at a time not long before **:** just prior to ⟨~ the end of the presidential campaign⟩ ⟨~ the dinner hour⟩ ⟨one afternoon ~ sundown —G.M. Smith⟩ **5 a :** in the way of help or assistance in **:** in furtherance of ⟨apply them ~ the solution of particular problems —W.L.Howard⟩ ⟨would do what he could ~ getting supper ready —W.D.Steele⟩ **b :** for the partial payment of **:** in defraying the costs of ⟨credited ~ the cost of your flight —Richard Joseph⟩ ⟨proceeds go ~ the provision of a scholarship⟩ **6** *obs* **:** in view or in store for ⟨something good was ~ me —Henry Fielding⟩ **7** *usu* **towards :** on the verge of **:** ABOUT, APPROXIMATELY ⟨there are *towards* six hundred persons —Edmund Burke⟩

toward·li·ness \-dlēnəs\ *n* -ES *archaic* **:** the quality or state of being toward or towardly: as **a :** APTNESS, PROMISE **b :** DOCILITY

¹**toward·ly** *adv* [ME, fr. ¹*toward* + *-ly* (adv. suffix)] *archaic* **:** in a towardly manner: as **a :** PROMISINGLY ⟨my scholars go ~ forward —Thomas Morley⟩ **b :** DOCILELY, OBLIGINGLY ⟨our friends will not behave ~ —William Penn⟩

²**towardly** *adj* [¹*toward* + *-ly,* adj. suffix] **1** *archaic* **:** likely to be favorable **:** ADVANTAGEOUS, PROPITIOUS ⟨choose a ~ hour —*Athenaeum*⟩ **2 :** developing favorably **:** PROMISING ⟨a child of ~ parts for her age —Jonathan Swift⟩ **3 a** *obs* **:** easily managed **:** DOCILE, OBLIGING **b :** favorably disposed **:** PLEASANT, AFFABLE ⟨she was very ~ and lenient in her behavior; she led him on to make pleasantries, and then applauded him —R.L.Stevenson⟩

towardness *n* -ES [ME *towardnesse,* fr. ¹*toward* + *-nesse* -ness] *obs* **:** the quality or state of being toward

towards \-dz\ *adv* [ME *towardes,* fr. *towardes,* adj., toward] *archaic* **:** FORWARD, ONWARD

towboat \'≈,≈\ *n* [¹*tow* + *boat*] **1 :** TUGBOAT **2 :** PUSH BOAT; *specif* **:** a compact usu. diesel-powered shallow-draft boat that is highly maneuverable by one-man controls and is equipped with squared bow and towing knees to enable it to push tows of barges on inland waterways

tow bug *n* [³*tow;* fr. its infestation of furniture upholstered in tow, flax, or straw] **:** CIGARETTE BEETLE

tow car *or* **tow truck** *n* **:** WRECKER 2b(3)

tow cloth *or* **tow linen** *n* **:** a coarse heavy linen in 18th century use for clothing — compare ³TOW 3

towed *past of* TOW

¹**towel** \'tau̇(ə)l\ *n* -s [ME *towele, towaille,* fr. OF *toaille,* of Gmc origin; akin to OS *thwahila, twahila* towel, MD *dwale, dwele,* OHG *dwahila, dwehila;* akin to OE *thwēal* washing, *thwēan* to wash, OHG *dwahan,* ON *thvā,* Goth *thwahan* to wash, OPruss *twaxtan* bath cloth] **1 :** a piece of absorbent cloth or paper often rectangular in shape for wiping or drying ⟨a bath ~⟩ ⟨a dish ~⟩ **2** *obs* **a :** NAPKIN 1 **b :** a piece of cloth used as a turban or sash **c :** VESPERAL 2 **d :** a cloth held by acolytes or spread over the rails before communicants during the celebration of the Eucharist

²**towel** \"\ *vb* **toweled** *also* **towelled; toweled** *also* **towelled; toweling** *also* **towelling** \-au̇(ə)liŋ\ **towels** *vt* **:** to rub or dry (as the body) with a towel ⟨~*ing* hard my hair, face, and the back of my neck —Joseph Conrad⟩ ⟨got out of the bath, ~*ed* herself dry —Aldous Huxley⟩ ~ *vi* **:** to use a towel

towel gourd *n* **:** DISHCLOTH GOURD

towel horse *n* **:** TOWEL RACK

toweling *also* **towelling** *n* -s **:** any of various absorbent fabrics used for making towels; *esp* **:** a fabric made of cotton or linen in any of various weaves and often woven in narrow widths with colored borders

towel rack *n* **:** a small rack with bars for hanging or drying towels (as in a kitchen or bathroom)

[1]**tow·er** \'tau̇(ə)r, 'tau̇ə, *esp in southern U.S.* 'tau̇wə(r\ *n* -s *often attrib* [ME *tour, tur, tor,* fr. OE *torr* & OF *tor, tur,* both fr. L *turris,* fr. Gk *tyrris, tyrsis*] **1 a :** a building or structure designed primarily for elevation that is higher than its diameter and high relative to its surroundings, that may stand apart (as a round tower, campanile, or pagoda), be attached (as a church belfry) to a larger structure, or project above or out from a wall, and that may be of skeleton framework (as an observation or transmission tower) **b :** such a structure used as a defense **:** CITADEL, FORTRESS **c :** a fortified prison **d :** a medieval engine of war for storming operations consisting of a tower on wheels having several platforms with the lowest sometimes occupied by a battering ram and the highest by soldiers (as archers and men with scaling ladders) **2 :** a structure or mass in the form of or resembling a tower: as **a :** a building for housing the mechanism (as levers) for operating the switches and signals of a railroad **:** SWITCH TOWER **b** (1) **:** FIRE TOWER 1 (2) **:** WATER TOWER 2 (3) **:** DRILL TOWER **c :** CONTROL TOWER **d :** a high office or apartment building **:** SKYSCRAPER ⟨the new owners of that uptown office ~ —*N. Y. Herald Tribune*⟩ **e :** a very high formation or pile (as of rock) **f :** a vertical structure of varying height through which gases or liquids are passed esp. to be purified, dried, fractionated, or absorbed — compare BUBBLE TOWER, COLUMN 3d, GLOVER TOWER, PLATE TOWER **g :** a structure on an elephant's back — compare HOWDAH **h :** a heraldic representation of a round tower closely resembling in form a modern rook in chess — compare CASTLE 6 **i :** [1]TOUR 4 **3 a :** one that provides support or protection **:** BULWARK, PILLAR ⟨thou hast been a shelter for me and a strong ~ from the enemy —Ps 61:3 (AV)⟩ — usu. used in the phrase *tower of strength* ⟨the king's name is a ~ of strength —Shak.⟩ ⟨has been a veritable ~ of strength in the affairs of this club —W.F.Brown b. 1903⟩ **b :** a place of refuge (as for contemplation or for avoidance of worldly problems) **:** RETREAT, SANCTUARY ⟨the only escape from this anguish of dissatisfaction was to ascend into those ~*s* of indifference —P.E. More⟩ ⟨content to stay within theology's safe academic ~ —*Newsweek*⟩ — compare IVORY TOWER **4 :** the high flight of a bird (as a hawk or eagle) **:** SOAR ⟨the peak of the ~⟩; *esp* **:** the steep flight upward of a wounded game bird

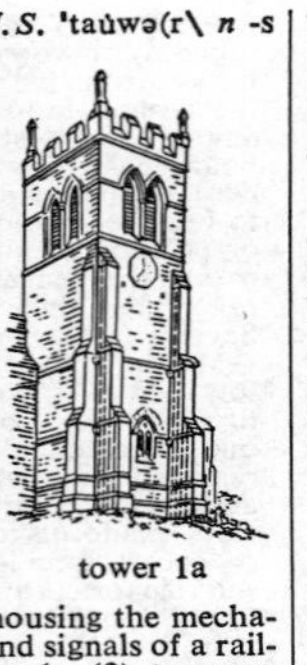
tower 1a

[2]**tower** \"\ *vb* -ED/-ING/-S [ME *towren, torren,* fr. *towr, tor* tower] *vi* **1 a :** to reach to a great height **:** RISE ⟨spires ~*ing* in the distance⟩ ⟨a great column of black smoke . . . ~*ing* up —Nevil Shute⟩ ⟨the powdered coiffures . . . ~*ed* as much as a yard high —Lois Long⟩ ⟨one moment he ~*ed* in imagination, the next he groveled in fear —G.D.Brown⟩ **b :** to rise above the surroundings **:** surpass others **:** OVERSHADOW — used with *above* or *over* ⟨the great forests ~*ed* above the toiling men and women —W.P.Webb⟩ ⟨~ above all the rest in vigor and height of intellect —Joshua Whatmough⟩ **2 a :** to fly high before swooping **:** SOAR ⟨the raven . . . ~*ed* steeply up from the rocks —Farley Mowat⟩ — used esp. of a hawk; compare STOOP **b :** to fly vertically upward before falling — used of a wounded game bird ⟨had another bird which ~*ed* —T.H.White b. 1906⟩ ~ *vt* **1** *archaic* **:** to raise aloft **:** lift up **:** ELEVATE ⟨gigantic trees . . . ~*ed* their lofty heads to the clouds —W.S.Mayo⟩ **2** *obs* **:** to soar into ⟨rising on stiff pennons ~ the mid aerial sky —John Milton⟩ **syn** see RISE

[3]**tow·er** \'tō(ə)r\ *n* -s [[3]*tow* + *-er*] **:** one that smooths ceramic ware with tow

tower bolt *n* **:** an esp. heavy sliding door bolt

tower clock *n* **1 :** a clock in a tower **2 :** TURRET CLOCK

tower cress *n* **:** a European cress (*Arabis turrita*) having stiff erect stems

towered *adj* [ME *toured,* fr. *tour* tower + *-ed* — more at TOWER] **:** having a tower **:** adorned or defended by towers ⟨a ~ church⟩ ⟨~ battlements⟩ ⟨~ cities please us then —John Milton⟩

tower house *n* **1 :** a medieval fortified castle (as in England and Scotland) **2 :** [1]TOWER 2a

[1]**towering** *adj* [fr. pres. part. of [2]*tower*] **1 a :** rising to a great height **:** IMPOSING ⟨the ~ pines⟩ ⟨the ~ structure of American prosperity —F.L.Allen⟩ **b :** impressively great **:** extremely high in relation to others **:** SURPASSING ⟨a figure of ~ prestige —R.H.Rovere⟩ **2 :** reaching a high point of intensity or violence **:** OVERWHELMING ⟨a ~ passion⟩ ⟨a ~ rage⟩ ⟨his superb and ~ contempt for his guilty stepfather —G.B.Shaw⟩ **3 :** going beyond proper bounds **:** EXCESSIVE, OVERWEENING ⟨~ ambitions⟩ ⟨a ~ poet's pride —William Cowper⟩

[2]**towering** *n* -s [fr. gerund of [2]*tower*] **:** a mirage in which objects some distance away appear to be stretched vertically to unnatural heights

tow·er·ing·ly *adv* **:** in a towering manner: as **a :** at a great height **:** LOFTILY ⟨elms standing ~ in the yard⟩ **b :** with great intensity **:** VIOLENTLY ⟨~ wrathful⟩

towerlike \'==,=\ *adj* **:** resembling a tower

tow·er·man \'=mən\ *n, pl* **towermen :** one who attends to or works in a tower: as **a :** one employed in a railroad switch tower to control and direct the movement of cars and trains **b :** one who erects and maintains electric-power transmission towers **c :** FIRE LOOKOUT **d :** one who fills towers with limestone to be used in preparing acid for cooking wood chips in pulp making and papermaking

tower mustard *n* **1 :** a widely distributed cress (*Arabis glabra*) **2 :** TOWER CRESS

tower of babel *often cap T&B* **:** BABEL

tower of ivory : IVORY TOWER

tower of silence : a circular stone wall having a height of 20 to 30 feet and an outside circumference of 200 to 270 feet on which the Parsis expose their dead to vultures — called also *dakhma*

tower owl *n, Brit* **:** BARN OWL

tower pound *n, often cap T* [so called fr. the standard pound kept in the Tower of London] **:** a pound of 5400 grains or 349.91 grams **:** the legal mint pound of England before 1527

towers *pl of* TOWER, *pres 3d sing of* TOWER

tower shell *n* **:** SCREW SHELL

tower shooting *n* **:** shooting at targets that are thrown from a trap mounted on an elevated place (as a high tower) to appear from overhead at a height of at least 40 feet

tower silo *n* **:** a tall cylindrical silo built above ground of masonry, wood, or enameled steel

tower skull *also* **tower head** *n* **:** OXYCEPHALY

tower telescope *n* **:** a long-focus telescope designed for observation of the sun that is set vertically and fed by a coelostat and mirror

tower wagon *n* **:** a wagon or motor truck with a high adjustable platform on which workmen can stand (as when repairing overhead wires or cleaning and replacing streetlights)

tow·ery \'tau̇(ə)rē\ *adj, sometimes* -ER/-EST **1 :** having towers **:** TOWERED ⟨~ city⟩ **2 :** LOFTY, TOWERING ⟨~ trees⟩

towhead \'=,=\ *n* [[3]*tow* + *head*] **1 a :** a head of hair resembling tow esp. in being flaxen or tousled **b :** a person having such a head of hair **2** *Midland & South* **:** a low alluvial island or shoal in a river **:** SANDBAR; *esp* **:** such a sandbar having clusters of cottonwoods on it ⟨paddled over to the ~ and hid in the cottonwoods —Mark Twain⟩ — **towheaded** \'=,==\ *adj*

tow·hee \tə'(h)wē, -'hē, 'tō,hē\ *also* **towhee bunting** *n* -s [*towhee* imit.] **:** any of numerous American finches (genera *Pipilo* and *Chlorura*); *esp* **:** a common finch (*P. erythrophthalmus*) of eastern No. America having the male black, white, and rufous and the female with brown instead of black — called also *chewink;* see CALIFORNIA TOWHEE, GREEN-TAILED TOWHEE

tow·ie \'tōē\ *n* -s [origin unknown] **:** contract bridge for three or more and usu. up to six players in which three play at one time and are replaced in turn after each hand by one of the inactive players if any and in which the players bid for the dummy hand after six cards of it have been exposed and play each for himself with no permanent partnerships

towing *n* -s [fr. gerund of [1]*tow*] **1 :** TOWAGE 1 **2 :** [2]TOW 5

towing basin *or* **towing tank** *also* **tow tank** *n* **:** a long open tank filled with water through which models of ship or seaplane hulls or floats are towed to test their hydrodynamic characteristics

towing bridle *n* **1 :** a bridle with a hook in the center to which a towline is fastened when two boats are towed abreast **2 :** a length of wire hawser for passing around part of a ship's structure (as an after turret) to the ends of which the towing hawser may be connected by a set of shackles

towing light *n* **:** one of the two or more white lights depending on the number of craft being towed that are carried in a vertical line by a steamer towing other ships

towing net *var of* TOWNET

towing path *var of* TOWPATH

towing post *or* **towing timber** *n* **:** a heavy timber on deck for attaching a towline **:** BITT 1

towing sleeve *n* **:** SLEEVE TARGET

towing spar *n* **:** FOG BUOY 2

tow iron *n* **:** a harpoon with a towline attached

to wit *adv* [ME *to witen,* lit., to know — more at WIT] **:** that is to say **:** NAMELY, SCILICET, VIDELICET — often used to enumerate and call attention to particular matters embraced in more general preceding language ⟨the prime cause of dissatisfaction at all times and in all countries, *to wit,* poverty —G.W. Johnson⟩

to within *prep* **1 —** used as a function word to indicate direction and movement to and somewhat past a point or to the outer limits of and some distance into a space ⟨jumped *to within* ½ inch of the record⟩ ⟨drove *to within* 50 yards of the green⟩ **2 —** used as a function word to indicate duration up to and somewhat past a point in time ⟨worked hard *to within* five minutes of closing time⟩

towline \'=,=\ *n* **:** a line (as a rope, cable, or hawser) used in towing (as a boat or automobile); *specif* **:** a line attached to an iron or harpoon by which a whaleboat is made fast to and often towed by a whale

tow linen *var of* TOW CLOTH

tow·man \'tōmən\ *n, pl* **towmen :** a garage worker who tows disabled vehicles

tow·mond \'tau̇mənd\ *or* **tow·mont** \-nt\ *n* -s [ME (Sc) *towlmonth,* fr. OE *twelf mōnath,* fr. *twelf* twelve + *mōnath* month — more at TWELVE, MONTH] *Scot* **:** TWELVEMONTH, YEAR

town \'tau̇n\ *n* -s *often attrib* [ME *town, toun,* fr. OE *tūn* enclosure, manor, village, town; akin to OHG *zūn* enclosure, fence, ON *tūn* hedge, enclosure, OIr *dūn* fortress] **1 a :** the chief dwelling usu. enclosed estate of a feudal lord including the chief dwelling (as a castle) and the community living in villenage around it **:** MANOR 2 **b** *Scot* **:** a farmhouse with its accompanying land and buildings **:** FARMSTEAD **2** *dial Eng* **:** a cluster or aggregation of houses recognized as a distinct place **:** a settlement with a place-name **:** VILLAGE, HAMLET **3 :** a place that is a population and business center and is so recognized geographically and politically: as **a :** a compactly settled area of any size as distinguished from surrounding rural territory **b :** a compactly settled area usu. larger than a village but smaller than a city in population and usu. incorporated and given definite boundaries and powers by law **:** a small municipality **c :** a large densely populated urban area; *specif* **:** CITY **d :** an English village without urban characteristics or the status of an episcopal see but having a periodic fair or market **:** MARKET TOWN **e :** an incorporated municipal unit in a Canadian province or an Australian state varying in population but usu. smaller than a city **4 a :** the particular town or city under consideration — usu. used without an article ⟨walked to the outskirts of ~⟩ ⟨new arrivals in ~⟩ ⟨was out of ~ all last week⟩ ⟨when the circus comes to ~⟩ ⟨left ~ in a hurry⟩ **b :** the capital city of a country (as London, England) ⟨aristocracy from every shire flocking to ~ for the coronation⟩ **c :** the neighboring large city **:** METROPOLIS ⟨commute daily to ~⟩ ⟨have an apartment in ~⟩ **d :** the business center of a city **:** DOWNTOWN ⟨parked on a residential street and walked the few blocks into ~⟩ ⟨a physician with an office at home and another in ~⟩ **e :** a section or district of a city characterized in some specified way (as by location, age, or inhabitants) ⟨the upper ~⟩ ⟨the old ~⟩ ⟨the French ~⟩ **5 :** the city as contrasted with the country **:** urban life — usu. used with *the* ⟨God made the country, and man made the ~ —William Cowper⟩ ⟨a poet not of nature but of the ~⟩ **6 a :** the citizens or inhabitants of a city or town **:** PUBLIC ⟨went to a number of plays that were drawing the ~ —W.S.Maugham⟩ **b :** the qualified voters of a town **:** ELECTORATE, CITIZENRY ⟨the ~ elects two representatives⟩ **c :** the governing officials of a town acting on behalf of the town as a corporation or of the whole body of inhabitants **d :** the townspeople of a college or university town that constitute a group distinct from and often antithetical to the academic community ⟨the usual battle between *Town* and Gown was developing, with clubs and quarterstaves as the weapons —T.B.Costain⟩ — compare GOWN 2b **e** *archaic* **:** the fashionable society of a city ⟨this vast universal Fool, the *Town* —John Dryden⟩ **7 :** a territorial area having the status of a unit of local government: as **a :** one of a number of territorial units into which the area of a New England state is divided usu. containing both rural and unincorporated urban areas under a single town government but sometimes containing or coterminous with an incorporated city or borough — called also *township* **b :** a territorial unit in a state (as New York) outside New England that usu. contains not only rural and unincorporated urban areas but also one or more incorporated villages or other municipal units **c :** TOWNSHIP 4b **8 :** a unit of local government found chiefly in the New England states constituting a municipal corporation or under broad grants from the state legislature exercising most of the powers of a municipal corporation and having a governmental structure in which the legislative power is exercised by the town meeting and administration is entrusted to a board of selectmen and other officials **9 :** something felt to resemble a town: as **a :** a collection of burrows of the prairie dog **b :** an aggregation of nests of penguins — **on the town** *adv (or adj)* **1** *also* **upon the town :** supported by poor relief provided by the town or parish **:** DESTITUTE ⟨a family *on the town* after the father's death⟩ **2 :** in carefree and often roving rollicking pursuit of the pleasures and diversions available (as in the night life of a big city) often in a spirit of welcome relief or abandon after a period of constraint or routine **:** out for a good time **:** footloose and fancy-free ⟨hired a baby-sitter and went out *on the town*⟩ ⟨a bunch of sailors *on the town* —Maxwell Griffith⟩ ⟨had decided to go out *on the town* . . . to all the dives —Dawn Powell⟩

town ball *n* [so called fr. the fact that it was played at the time of town meetings] **:** a ball game preceding and resembling baseball ⟨at recesses and at noon, we played . . . *town ball* and baseball —W.A.White⟩ — compare ROUNDER 3a

town car *n* **:** a 4-door automobile with a permanently enclosed passenger compartment in the rear separated from the driver's compartment by a sliding glass partition

town clerk *n* [ME *tounclerk,* fr. *toun* town + *clerk*] **1 :** a public officer charged with keeping the records (as marriage licenses and vital statistics) of a town and entering the official proceedings of its government **2 :** the secretary to the corporation, legal adviser, and chief administrative officer of a British local government (as of a town, borough, or city)

town crier *n* **:** a town officer who makes proclamations **:** CRIER b

town economy *n* **:** the stage or system in economic history in which the center of trade and commerce is a town (as a medieval walled town) with a distinct merchant class and considerable division of labor

town·ee \(')tau̇'nē\ *n* -s [*town* + *-ee*] **:** TOWNSMAN ⟨~*s* . . . who have had little more than an academic interest in agrarian questions —*Atlantic*⟩

town end *or* **town's end** *n* [ME] *dial* **:** one of the ends of a town or village street or road

town·er \'tau̇nə(r)\ *n* -s *slang* **:** a town or city dweller **:** TOWNSMAN ⟨the streets were crawling with people — ~*s* and visiting country cousins —Bill Ballantine⟩ — used esp. by circus troupes of the local citizenry ⟨the circus people, clannish and ever suspicious of ~*s* —Al Hine⟩

townet \'=,=\ *or* **towing net** *n* **:** a fine-meshed net usu. much tapered and more or less conical in shape and kept open by a ring or hoop that is towed through water (as for the taking of plankton)

town·gate \'tün,gāt, 'tau̇n-\ *n* [*town* + *gate* (way, street)] **:** the main street of a town

town hall *n* [ME] **1 a :** the chief public building of a town used for public offices and for meetings (as of the town council and the courts) **b :** a large hall for public assemblies **2 :** GUILDHALL

town house *n* **1 :** a house in town as distinguished from a house in the country ⟨there was a smart *town house* and a rococo summer estate —Harriot B. Barbour⟩; *specif* **:** the city residence of one having a countryseat or having a chief residence elsewhere ⟨stayed at their *town house* for a few weeks during the social season⟩ **2** *usu* **townhouse** \'=,=\ *chiefly Brit* **:** TOWN HALL 1

townier *comparative of* TOWNY

townies *pl of* TOWNY

towniest *superlative of* TOWNY

town·i·fy \'tau̇nə,fī\ *vt* -ED/-ING/-ES [*town* + *-ify*] **1 :** to cause to become urban ⟨a pleasant little village rapidly being *townified*⟩ **2 :** to stamp with the characteristics of the town or city or of urban life ⟨the long *townified* dress she'd put on —Christopher Isherwood⟩

town·i·ness \-nēnəs\ *n* -ES **:** the quality or state of being towny

town·ish \'tau̇nish\ *adj* [ME *townisch,* fr. *town* + *-isch* -ish] **1 :** of, relating to, or characteristic of a town or city or of the manners and style of urban life **:** appropriate for town or city **:** TOWNY ⟨the fabric . . . is definitely ~ —*N. Y. Times Mag.*⟩ **2 :** having the outlook or manners of a city-bred person ⟨always thought of myself as a ~ character⟩

town·ish·ly *adv* **:** in a townish manner

town·ish·ness *n* -ES **:** the quality or state of being townish

town·land \-nlənd\ *n, Irish* **:** a section of land constituted like a township as part of a parish ⟨looks after a ~ of 79 acres —J.M.Mogey⟩

town·let \-lət\ *n* -s **:** a small town ⟨this sleepy little ~ —Francis Ofner⟩

town library *n* **:** a public library serving a town and supported in whole or in part by public funds

town·ly *adj, archaic* **:** TOWNISH ⟨one of your ~ ladies —Henry Fielding⟩

town major *n* **:** an officer of a British garrison having the general supervision of good order (as in an occupied city during military operations)

town·man \-nmən\ *n, pl* **townmen** [ME *toun man,* fr. OE *tūnman* villager, fr. *tūn* town + *man* — more at TOWN] **:** TOWNSMAN 1

town manager *n* **:** an official appointed by the annual town meeting or by the selectmen to direct the administration of a town government

town mark *n* **:** a postmark showing the name of the town where mail has been stamped

town meeting *n* **:** a legal meeting of the inhabitants or taxpayers of a town entitled to vote on town matters for the transaction of public or governmental business

town order *n* **:** a nonnegotiable warrant approved by an auditor of a town (as in Maine) directing the treasurer to pay a specified sum of money to a designated person

town plan *n* **:** CITY PLAN

towns *pl of* TOWN

town·scape \'tau̇nz,kāp, -n,sk-\ *n* -s [*town* + *-scape*] **1 a :** a picture (as a painting) representing an urban scene ⟨spectacular ~*s* painted from rooftops —*Time*⟩ — compare CITYSCAPE **b :** the art of depicting such a scene (as by selection and composition of the man-made and natural elements that create a striking urban effect) **2 :** a portion of a town or city that the eye can comprehend in a single view ⟨viewed at twilight . . . a romantic ~, given a striking accent by the great arcs of viaduct —Lewis Mumford⟩ — compare LANDSCAPE 2b **3 :** the architectural art of achieving beauty in the design and spatial relationships created by the disposition and juxtaposition of structures (as civic buildings) in a town or city ⟨schools of architecture and planning . . . studying seriously the problems of ~ —H.M.Casson⟩

town·sen·dia \tau̇n'zendēə\ *n, cap* [NL, fr. David *Townsend* †1858 Am. botanist + NL *-ia*] **:** a genus of western American mostly low and tufted herbs (family Compositae) with large heads of purple-rayed or white-rayed flowers and achenes that are beset with bristly forked hairs — see EASTER DAISY

town·send's solitaire \'tau̇nzəndz-\ *n, usu cap T* [after John Kirk *Townsend* †1851 Am. ornithologist] **:** a solitaire (*Myadestes townsendi*) of western No. America

townsfolk \'=,=, 'tau̇nz,fōk\ *n pl* **:** TOWNSPEOPLE

town·ship \'tau̇n,ship\ *n* [ME *township,* fr. OE *tūnscipe,* fr. *tūn* town + *-scipe* -ship] **1 a :** the inhabitants of a vill, manor, or medieval town; *esp* **:** such a community constituting a corporate body **b :** VILL, MANOR **c :** an imaginary social or tribal unit among the Anglo-Saxons **2 :** an ancient unit of administration in England identical in area with or a division of a parish **:** the area of a parish or chapelry with reference only to the inhabitants **3 :** an administrative unit (as a self-governing town) in a foreign country **4 a :** TOWN 7a **b :** a territorial area having the status of a unit of local government in some 16 northeastern and north central states lying between New York on the east and the Dakotas and Kansas on the west and usu. having a chief administrative officer or board although having fewer functions and powers than a New England town **c :** an unorganized subdivision of the county in Maine, New Hampshire, and Vermont in the form of a tract of land laid off by the state authorities **d :** an administrative district of the county used esp. for electoral purposes in some parts of the southern U. S. (as in North and South Carolina and Arkansas) **5 :** a geographical rather than a political division: **a :** a piece of land that is bounded on the east and west by meridians six miles apart at its south border, has a north-south length of six miles, and forms one of the chief divisions of a U. S. public-land survey — compare SECTION 7, RANGE 13 **b :** a subdivision of some provinces in Canada having certain specified powers of local government **c** *Austral* (1) **:** TOWNSITE (2) **:** the temporary settlement on such a site **6** *Scot* **:** a farm held jointly **7** *Philippines* **:** MUNICIPAL DISTRICT

township line *n* **:** one of the imaginary lines running east and west at 6-mile intervals and marking the relative north and south locations of townships in a U. S. public-land survey — compare [1]RANGE 13, TOWNSHIP 5a

township road *n* **:** a highway maintained by a town or township

town·site \'=,=\ *n* **:** the site of a town ⟨each ~ must be selected with an eye to irrigation —R.A.Billington⟩; *specif* **:** a tract of land laid out with streets and subdivided into lots for the development of a town ⟨laid out a ~ on part of his extensive holdings —*Amer. Guide Series: La.*⟩

towns·man \'tau̇nzmən\ *n, pl* **townsmen** [ME *tounesman,* fr. OE *tūnesman,* fr. *tūnes* (gen. of *tūn* town) + *man* — more at TOWN] **1 a :** one born, residing, or holding citizenship in a town or city ⟨population . . . of whom one-third were *townsmen* and two-thirds countrymen —*Nineteenth Century & After*⟩ **b :** one marked by town or city ways ⟨designed for the . . . ~ spending a weekend in the country —*Brit. Bk. News*⟩ **2 :** a native, inhabitant, or citizen of a particular town ⟨a ~ . . . set up his blacksmith shop in front of his house —Allan Forbes & R.M.Eastman⟩ **3 :** one born, residing, or holding citizenship in the same town as another **:** fellow citizen ⟨earned the gratitude of his *townsmen*⟩ ⟨stopped to ask my fellow ~ —Dana Burnet⟩

townspeople \'=,==\ *n pl* [*towns* (gen. of *town*) + *people*] **1 :** the inhabitants of a town or city **:** TOWNSMEN ⟨the villagers seem . . . less envious of the ~ than they used to be —S.P.B. Mais⟩ **2 :** the citizens or inhabitants of a particular town ⟨reporters interviewed the ~ —J.C.Lincoln⟩

townswoman \'=,==\ *n, pl* **townswomen 1 :** a woman native, inhabitant, or citizen of a particular town ⟨the *townswomen* brought soups and custards for the invalid —Willa Cather⟩ **2 :** a woman born, residing, or holding citizenship in the same town as another ⟨the flag presented him . . . by his *townswomen* —Caroline Ticknor⟩

town talk *n* **1 :** the common talk of a place (as a city or town) **:** public gossip ⟨disregarded the rumor as mere *town talk*⟩ ⟨the only real evidence is the *town talk* —J.A.Froude⟩ **2 :** the matter (as the subject or object) of public gossip ⟨was *town talk* for at least three days —W.M.Thackeray⟩

town way *n* **:** a road maintained by a town

townwear \'=,=\ *n* **:** apparel (as of dark color or tailored style) that is suitable for wear in the city or to business

¹towny \ˈtau̇nē, -ni\ *n* -ES [*town* + *-y*, dim. suffix] : TOWNSMAN ⟨don't want the *townies* here to get any more ideas than they've got already —W.L.Gresham⟩ ⟨the people described by the exurbanites as the *townies* —A.C.Spectorsky⟩

²towny \"\ *adj* -ER/-EST [*town* + *-y*, adj. suffix] : of, relating to, or having the characteristics of a town or city or of town or city life ⟨the competitive, ~ culture —W.H.Hudson †1922⟩ ⟨a trifle showy and ~ . . . in her delicate high-heeled shoes —Miles Franklin⟩

towpath \ˈ=,=\ *or* **towing path** *n* : a path (as along a canal) traveled by men or animals towing boats

towplane \ˈ=,=\ *n* : an airplane that tows gliders

towrope \ˈ=,=\ *n* : a line (as a rope, cable, or chain) used in towing (as a boat, car, or skier) ⟨a tug's ~⟩ ⟨hauling the car on a short ~⟩ ⟨nylon ~*s* for gliders⟩

¹tow-row \ˈtau̇ˌrau̇\ *n* [redupl. & alter. of ⁶*row*] : a noisy outburst : RACKET, RUMPUS ⟨a great *tow-row* of thunder —R.L.Stevenson⟩ ⟨a furious *tow-row* at once began between him and Madame —Christina Stead⟩

²tow-row \"\ *vi* : to make a tow-row

tows *pres 3d sing of* TOW, *pl of* TOW

tow sack *n* [³*tow*] *Midland & South* : GUNNYSACK

towse *var of* TOUSE

tow·ser \ˈtau̇zə(r)\ *n* -S [¹*touse* + *-er*] **1** : a large dog ⟨great, lionhearted ~ that he is —*Springfield (Mass.) Union*⟩ **2** : a large rough person; *esp* : one full of energy — often used in the phrase *a towser for work*

towsle *var of* TOUSLE

towsy \ˈtau̇zē\ *var of* TOUSY

tow tank *var of* TOWING BASIN

tow target *n* : a practice target towed behind an airplane — compare SLEEVE TARGET

tow team *n* : an extra team of draft animals used to assist a regular team where the hauling is esp. difficult (as in towing logs up an incline)

tow truck *var of* TOW CAR

tow wheel *n* : a spinning wheel for making coarse tow yarn (as from flax fiber)

towz·ie \ˈtüzi\ *Scot var of* TOUSY

towzle *var of* TOUSLE

¹tox- *or* **toxi-** *or* **toxo-** *comb form* [LL, fr. L *toxicum* poison — more at TOXIC] **1** : toxic : poisonous ⟨*toxi*dermic⟩ ⟨*tox*in⟩ **2** : toxin : poison ⟨*tox*oid⟩

²tox- *or* **toxi-** *or* **toxo-** *comb form* [Gk, fr. *toxon* bow, arrow — more at TOXIC] **1** : bowed : arched ⟨*Toxo*donta⟩ **2** : arrow : shaped like an arrow ⟨*Toxo*glossa⟩ ⟨*Toxi*fera⟩ **3** : archery ⟨*toxo*phily⟩

tox *abbr* toxicology

toxa \ˈtäksə\ *n* -S [NL, fr. Gk *toxon* bow] : a sponge spicule curved like a bent bow

tox·al·bu·min \ˈtäksalˌbyümən\ *n* [ISV ¹*tox-* + *albumin*] : any of a class of toxic substances of protein nature : TOXIN

tox·a·phene \ˈtäksəˌfēn\ *n* -S [fr. *Toxaphene*, a trademark] : an insecticide obtained as a yellow waxy solid by chlorinating camphene

tox·as·ca·ris \täkˈsaskərəs\ *n, cap* [NL, fr. ²*tox-* + *Ascaris*] : a cosmopolitan genus of ascarid roundworms that infest the small intestine of the dog and cat and related wild animals

tox·ca·tl \ˈtōˌskäd·ᵊl\ *n* -S *usu cap* [Nahuatl *Toxcatl*, *Tozcatl*, lit., wet, slippery; fr. its occurring in the rainy season] : an Aztec new-year festival celebrated with a ceremonial including human sacrifice

tox·e·mia *also* **tox·ae·mia** \täkˈsēmēə\ *n* -S [NL, fr. ¹*tox-* + *-emia*] **1** : an abnormal condition associated with the presence of toxic substances in the blood: as **a** : a generalized intoxication due to absorption and systemic dissemination of bacterial toxins from a focus of infection **b** : intoxication due to dissemination of toxic substances (as some by-products of protein metabolism) that cause functional or organic disturbances (as in the kidneys) **2** : plant injury caused by insect or other toxin — **tox·e·mic** *also* **tox·ae·mic** \(ˈ)täkˈsēmik, -mek\ *adj*

toxemia of pregnancy : a disorder of unknown cause that is peculiar to pregnancy, is usu. of sudden onset, is marked by hypertension, albuminuria, edema, headache, and visual disturbances, and may or may not be accompanied by convulsions — compare ECLAMPSIA, PREECLAMPSIA

toxemic jaundice *n* : an enzootic hemolytic jaundice of Australian sheep that is associated with chronic copper poisoning and that results from feeding on pasture with a high copper and a low molybdenum content : YELLOWS

¹tox·ic \ˈtäksik, -sēk\ *adj* [LL *toxicus*, fr. L *toxicum* poison, fr. Gk *toxikon* (*pharmakon*) arrow (poison), fr. *toxikon*, neut. of *toxikos* of a bow, fr. *toxon* bow, arrow (prob. fr. the source of L *taxus* yew) + *-ikos* -ic] **1** : of, relating to, or caused by a poison or toxin ⟨~ drugs⟩ ⟨a ~ effect⟩ **2** : affected by a poison or toxin ⟨a ~ patient⟩ **3** : acting or likely to act as a poison : POISONOUS ⟨eggs are ~ to a hypersensitive or sensitized person⟩

²toxic \"\ *n* -S [F *toxique*, fr. L *toxicum* poison] : a toxic substance : something poisonous

toxic- *or* **toxico-** *comb form* [NL, fr. L *toxicum*] : poison ⟨*toxic*ology⟩ ⟨*toxico*phobia⟩ ⟨*toxic*emia⟩

tox·i·cal \-sə̇kəl, -sēk-\ *adj* [LL *toxicus* + E *-al*] : TOXIC — **tox·i·cal·ly** \-sə̇k(ə)lē, -sēk-, -li\ *adv*

¹tox·i·cant \ˈtäksə̇kənt, -sēk-\ *n* -S [¹*toxic* + *-ant*] : an agent or a substance that acts as a poison; *esp* : a preparation for insect control that kills rather than repels

²toxicant \"\ *adj* [ML *toxicant-*, *toxicans*, pres. part. of *toxicare* to poison, fr. L *toxicum* poison] : producing a toxic effect : POISONOUS

tox·ic·a·rol \täkˈsikəˌrōl, -rōl\ *n* -S [NL *toxicaria*, specific epithet of *Tephrosia toxicaria* (fr. *toxic-* + L *-aria* -ary) + E *-ol*] : a greenish yellow crystalline compound $C_{23}H_{22}O_7$ obtained from the roots of a tropical herb (*Tephrosia toxicaria*), derris, and cube : hydroxy deguelin

tox·ic·i·ty \täkˈsisəd·ē, -ətē, -i\ *n* -ES [ISV ¹*toxic* + *-ity*] : the quality, state, or relative degree of being toxic or poisonous ⟨the ~ of some antibiotics renders them clinically useless⟩

toxic jaundice *n* : hepatitis caused by toxic agents (as chemicals) and characterized by jaundice as a prominent symptom

tox·i·co·den·dron \-ndrən\ *n, cap* [NL, fr. *toxic-* + *-dendron*] *in some classifications* : a genus of trees, shrubs, or woody vines (family Anacardiaceae) comprising those members of the genus *Rhus* with fruits that are smooth and foliage that is poisonous to the touch

tox·i·co·der·ma \ˌtäksə̇kōˈdərmə\ *n* -S [NL, fr. *toxic-* + *-derma*] : a disease of the skin caused by a toxic agent

tox·i·co·dermatitis \ˌtäksə̇(ˌ)kō+\ *n* [NL, fr. *toxic-* + *dermatitis*] : an inflammation of the skin caused by a toxic substance

tox·i·co·gen·ic \ˌtäksə̇kōˌjenik\ *adj* [*toxic-* + *-genic*] : producing toxic products ⟨~ bacteria⟩

tox·i·cog·nath \ˈtäksə̇kəgˌnath\ *n* -S [*toxic-* + Gk *gnathos* jaw — more at -GNATHOUS] : either of a pair of poison fangs of a centipede that are structurally modified legs on the anterior segment of the body

tox·i·co·log·ic \ˌtäksə̇kəˈläjik, -sēk-, -jēk\ *also* **tox·i·co·log·i·cal** \-jə̇kəl, -jēk-\ *adj* : of or relating to toxicology or toxins

tox·i·col·o·gist \ˌtäksə̇ˈkäləjə̇st\ *n* -S : a specialist in toxicology

tox·i·col·o·gy \-jē, -ji\ *n* -ES [*toxic-* + *-logy*] : a science that deals with poisons and their effect on living organisms, with substances otherwise harmless that prove toxic under particular conditions, and with the clinical, industrial, legal, or other problems involved

tox·i·co·mania \ˌtäksə̇(ˌ)kō+\ *n* [NL, fr. *toxic-* + *mania*] : addiction to a drug (as opium or cocaine)

tox·i·co·sis \ˌtäksəˈkōsə̇s\ *n, pl* **toxicoses** [NL, fr. *toxic-* + *-osis*] : a pathological condition caused by the action of a poison or toxin : TOXEMIA

toxic paralysis *n* : botulism of sheep

tox·i·der·mi·tis \ˌtäksədə(r)ˈmīd·ə̇s\ *n* -ES [NL, fr. ¹*tox-* + *derm-* + *-itis*] : TOXICODERMATITIS

tox·if·era \täkˈsif(ə)rə\ [NL, fr. ²*tox-* + *-fera* (fr. L, neut. pl. of *-fer* -ferous)] *syn of* TOXOGLOSSA

tox·if·er·ine \täkˈsifəˌrēn, -rən\ *n* -S [NL *toxifera* (specific epithet of the woody vine *Strychnos toxifera* that yields calabash curare) (fr. ¹*tox-* + *-fera*, fr. L, fem. of *-fer* -ferous) + E *-ine*] : any of several alkaloids obtained from calabash curare; *esp* : one $C_{40}H_{46}N_4O_2$ obtained usu. as its crystalline dichloride

tox·if·er·ous \(ˈ)täkˈsif(ə)rəs\ *adj* [ISV ¹*tox-* + *-ferous*] : producing or conveying poison ⟨a ~ gland⟩

tox·i·fy \ˈtäksəˌfī\ *vb* -ED/-ING/-ES [¹*tox-* + *-fy*] : POISON

tox·i·gen·ic \ˌtäksəˈjenik\ *adj* [¹*tox-* + *-genic*] : producing toxin — used chiefly of bacteria — **tox·i·ge·nic·i·ty** \ˌtäksəjəˈnisəd·ē\ *n* -ES

tox·i·glos·sa \ˌtäksəˈgläsə\ [NL, fr. ²*tox-* + *-glossa*] *syn of* TOXOGLOSSA

tox·in \ˈtäksə̇n\ *n* -S [ISV ¹*tox-* + *-in*] : any of various poisonous substances that are specific products of the metabolic activities of living organisms, are colloidal substances related to proteins and usu. very unstable, are notably toxic when introduced into the tissues but are almost all destroyed by the digestive juices, and are typically capable of inducing antibody formation in suitable animals — see ANTITOXIN, ENDOTOXIN, EXOTOXIN; compare ABRIN, PTOMAINE, RICIN, VENOM **syn** see POISON

toxin-antitoxin \ˈ==ˈ===\ *n* : a mixture of toxin and antitoxin used esp. formerly in immunizing against the disease (as diphtheria) for which they are specific and characterized by engendering active immunity without the danger attendant upon use of a toxin alone

toxi·phobia \ˌtäksə+\ *n* [NL, fr. ¹*tox-* + *phobia*] : abnormal fear of poisons or of being poisoned

toxi·tabellae \"+\ *n pl* [NL, fr. ¹*tox-* + *tabellae* (pl. of *tabella*)] : tablets containing a poisonous ingredient (as mercuric chloride)

toxo- — see TOX-

tox·o·cara \ˌtäksəˈkarə\ *n, cap* [NL, fr. ²*tox-* + Gk *kara* head — more at CEREBRAL] : a genus of nematode worms (family Ascaridae) including the common ascarids of the dog and cat — compare TOXASCARIS

¹tox·o·dont \ˈtäksəˌdänt\ *or* **tox·o·don·tid** \ˌ==ˈdäntə̇d\ *adj* [*toxodont* fr. NL *Toxodontia*; *toxodontid* fr. NL *Toxodontia* + E *-id*] : of or relating to the Toxodontia

²toxodont \"\ *or* **toxodontid** \"\ *n* -S : a toxodont mammal or fossil

tox·o·don·ta \ˌ==ˈdäntə\ [NL, fr. ²*tox-* + *-odonta*] *syn of* TOXODONTIA

¹tox·o·don·tia \-nch(ē)ə\ *n pl, cap* [NL, fr. ²*tox-* + *-odontia*] : a suborder of Notoungulata comprising generalized ungulates of the Paleocene to Pleistocene of So. America mostly of huge size equaling a large rhinoceros and having mostly persistent teeth that consist of large incisors, small lower canines, and high-crowned curved molars

²toxodontia \"\ [NL, fr. ²*tox-* + *-odontia*] *syn of* NOTOUNGULATA

tox·o·glos·sa \ˌtäksəˈgläsə\ *n pl, cap* [NL, fr. ²*tox-* + *-glossa*; fr. the usu. strongly barbed and arrowlike radula] : a group of marine carnivorous gastropods (suborder Stenoglossa) including the families Conidae and Terebridae and having the teeth of the radula reduced in number, large, and often perforated to serve as poison fangs with which a large poison gland in the esophagus communicates by slender ducts — **tox·o·glos·sate** \ˌ==ˈgläˌsāt\ *adj or n*

tox·oid \ˈtäkˌsȯid\ *n* -S [ISV ¹*tox-* + *-oid*; orig. formed in G] : a toxin (as of diphtheria or tetanus) treated so as to destroy its toxicity but leave it capable of inducing the formation of antibodies on injection

¹tox·oph·i·lite \täkˈsäfəˌlīt\ *n* -S [²*tox-* + *-phil* + *-ite*] : one fond of or expert at archery

²toxophilite \"\ *also* **tox·oph·i·lit·ic** \=ˌ==ˈlid·ik\ *adj* : of or relating to archers or archery

tox·oph·i·ly \-lē\ *n* -ES [²*tox-* + *-phily*] : the study, practice, and love of archery : the sport or skill of archery

tox·oph·o·rous \(ˈ)täkˈsäf(ə)rəs\ *also* **tox·o·phor·ic** \ˌtäksəˈfȯrik, -ˈfär-\ *adj* [¹*tox-* + *-phorous* or *-phoric*] : having actively poisonous properties

tox·o·plasm \ˈtäksəˌplazəm\ *n* -S [NL *Toxoplasma*] : a microorganism of the genus *Toxoplasma*

tox·o·plas·ma \ˌ==ˈplazmə\ *n* [NL, fr. ¹*tox-* + *-plasma*] **1** *cap* : a genus of parasitic microorganisms of uncertain systematic position usu. held to be protozoans related to the sporozoans but possibly belonging among the Fungi, prob. comprising a single species of very low host specificity, and being typically serious pathogens of vertebrates that invade the tissues and induce widespread miliary granulomatous lesions and ulceration **2** *pl* **toxoplasmas** \-məz\ *or* **toxo·plasma·ta** \-məd·ə\ *also* **toxoplasma** : an organism of the genus *Toxoplasma* — see TOXOPLASMOSIS — **tox·o·plas·mic** \ˌ==ˈplazmik\ *adj*

tox·o·plas·mal \ˌ==ˈplazməl\ *adj* [NL *Toxoplasma* + E *-al*] : TOXOPLASMIC

tox·o·plas·mo·sis \ˌtäksəplazˈmōsə̇s\ *n, pl* **toxoplasmo·ses** \-ōˌsēz\ [NL, fr. *Toxoplasma* + *-osis*] : infection of man, dogs, or other mammals or of birds by toxoplasmas or disease caused by the presence of these organisms commonly involving extensive or fatal damage to the central nervous system and eyes esp. of infants, being apparently capable of transplacental transmission from mother to child, and in the adult being often subclinical in manifestation or resembling a mild influenza

tox·os·to·ma \täkˈsästəmə\ *n, cap* [NL, fr. ²*tox-* + *-stoma*] : a genus of American songbirds closely related to the mockingbirds and containing most of the thrashers

tox·o·tae \ˈtäksəˌtē\ *n pl* [NL, fr. Gk *toxotai*, pl. of *toxotēs* archer, fr. *toxon* bow, arrow — more at TOXIC] : public slaves of ancient Athens often of Scythian origin, armed with bows, and serving as police

tox·o·tes \ˈtäksəˌtēz\ *n, cap* [NL, fr. Gk *toxotēs* archer] : a genus (the type of the family Toxotidae) of percoid fishes including solely the archerfish

¹toy \ˈtȯi\ *n* -S [ME *toye* dalliance] **1** *obs* **a** : amorous dalliance : flirtatious or seductive behavior **b** : PASTIME, SPORT; *also* : a sportive or amusing act or acts : ANTIC **c** : a wild fancy : an odd conceit : WHIM, CAPRICE **d** : foolish dislike : AVERSION **2 a** : something (as a concern, preoccupation, interest) that is paltry or trifling : something without real or permanent value **b** : something uttered, written, or composed in jest or play or as a pure diversion : a light, gay, or diverting speech, play, or tune : a literary or musical trifle **c** : a small dainty, elegant, or showy article prized rather for its charm or interest than for utilitarian qualities : TRINKET, KNICKKNACK, BAUBLE **3 a** : something designed for amusement or diversion rather than practical use **b** : an article for the playtime use of a child either representational (as of persons, creatures, or implements) and intended esp. to stimulate imagination, mimetic activity, or manipulative skill or nonrepresentational (as balls, tops, jump ropes) and intended esp. to encourage manual and muscular dexterity and group integration **4 a** : something diminutive esp. in comparison with others of the same general class ⟨the tug was a ~ beside the ship that it guided⟩ **b** : a diminutive animal; *esp* : one of a breed or variety distinguished primarily by small size **5** : something that can be toyed with: as **a** : a small or insignificant person : WEAKLING; *also* : one that is an object of derision or contempt **b** : WOMAN; *esp* : MISTRESS **6** *Scot* : a headdress of linen or woolen hanging down over the shoulders and formerly worn by old women of the lower classes

²toy \"\ *vb* -ED/-ING/-S *vi* **1** : to dally amorously : indulge in a flirtation **2** : to act as though unconcerned, indifferent, or not serious : deal lightly or without vigor or purpose : TRIFLE ⟨~ with great issues⟩ ⟨~*s* with his dinner⟩ **3** : to while away the time in or as if in sport or play : amuse oneself as if with a plaything ~ *vt* : to spend or use up in toying; *also* : to bring (oneself) by toying into or out of a specified or implied condition

³toy \"\ *adj* **1** : designed or made for use as a toy ⟨a ~ stove⟩ ⟨a set of ~ soldiers⟩ **2** : resembling a toy esp. in diminutive size or delicate and fragile form ⟨a ~ house⟩

to·ya·ma \tōˈyämə\ *adj, usu cap* [fr. *Toyama*, Japan] : of or from the city of Toyama, Japan : of the kind or style prevalent in Toyama

toy dog *n* : a very small dog; *esp* : one of any of several breeds or varieties of tiny dogs kept purely as pets — compare ENGLISH TOY SPANIEL

to-year \təˈyi(ə)r\ *adv* [ME *to yeer*, fr. *to*, prep. + *yeer* year — more at YEAR] *dial Eng* : this year

toy·er \ˈtȯiə(r)\ *n* -S : one that toys

toy·ful \ˈtȯifəl\ *adj, archaic* : full of trifling play : SPORTIVE

toy·ish \ˈtȯi·ish\ *adj* **1** : lacking in solid worth or import : FRIVOLOUS, TRIVIAL **2** : resembling a toy esp. in diminutive or unsubstantial quality or in lack of real utility; *also* : fit for a plaything — **toy·ish·ly** *adv* — **toy·ish·ness** *n* -ES

toylike \ˈ=,=\ *adj* : resembling a toy esp. in small, dainty, or impractical quality ⟨~ masts⟩

toy·man \ˈtȯimən\ *n, pl* **toymen** : one who deals in toys: **a** *archaic* : a keeper of a trinket shop **b** : a maker of or dealer in children's toys

toy manchester *n* **1** *usu cap T&M* : an English breed of small long-legged black-and-tan terriers with erect ears **2** *or* **toy manchester terrier** *often cap both Ts & usu cap M* : a dog of the Toy Manchester breed

to·yo \ˈtō(ˌ)yō\ *n* -S [Jap] : a shiny smooth straw made chiefly in Japan from shellacked rice paper and used esp. for hats

to·yo·ha·shi \ˌtōyəˈhäshē\ *adj, usu cap* [fr. *Toyohashi*, Japan] : of or from the city of Toyohashi, Japan : of the kind or style prevalent in Toyohashi

toy·on *also* **to·llon** \ˈtōiˌän, ˈtōyən\ *n* -S [AmerSp *tollon*] : an ornamental evergreen shrub (*Photinia arbutifolia*) of the No. American Pacific coast having white flowers succeeded by persistent bright red berries — called also *California holly*, *Christmasberry*

toywort \ˈ=,=\ *n* [¹*toy* + *wort*] : SHEPHERD'S PURSE

toze \ˈtōz\ *vt* -ED/-ING/-S [ME *tosen*, prob. fr. (assumed) OE *tǣsan*; akin to OE *tǣsan* to pull, tear — more at TEASE] *archaic* : to pull about esp. in disentangling : TEASE, COMB

to·zee \ˈtōzē\ *n* -S [perh. fr. D *toezien* to look on, take care, be careful, fr. MD *toesien*, fr. *toe* to + *sien* to see; akin to OE *tō* to and to OHG *sehan* to see — more at TO, SEE] : a curling tee

tp *abbr* **1** telephone **2** township **3** troop

TP *abbr* **1** target practice **2** teaching practice **3** technical paper **4** teleprinter **5** [L *tempore Paschale*] at Easter time **6** title page **7** total points **8** transport pilot **9** treaty port

TPD *abbr* tons per day

TPH *abbr* tons per hour

TPI *abbr, often not cap* **1** teeth per inch **2** threads per inch **3** tons per inch **4** turns per inch

tpk *abbr* turnpike

t plate *n, cap T* : a T-shaped plate used as a splice and for stiffening a joint where the end of one beam abuts against the side of another

TPM *abbr, often not cap* title page mutilated

TPN \ˌtēˌpēˈen\ *abbr or n* -S triphosphopyridine nucleotide

TPO *abbr* traveling post office

tpr *abbr* **1** taper **2** *often cap T&P&R* teleprinter **3** trooper

TPR *abbr* temperature, pulse, respiration

tps *abbr* **1** townships **2** troops

tpt *abbr* **1** transport **2** trumpet

tptr *abbr* trumpeter

TPW *abbr, often not cap* title page wanting

TQM *abbr* transport quartermaster

tr *abbr* **1** tare **2** tincture **3** trace; traced **4** track **5** train **6** transaction **7** transferred **8** transit **9** transitive **10** translated; translation; translator **11** transom **12** transport; transportation **13** transpose **14** travel **15** tray **16** tread **17** treasurer **18** treble **19** trill **20** troop **21** truss **22** trustee

TR *abbr* **1** tariff reform **2** technical regulation; technical report; technical representative **3** [L *tempore regis*] in the time of the king **4** tons registered **5** training regulation **6** transmit-receive **7** trust receipt

tra·ba·co·lo \trəˈbäkəˌlō\ *also* **tra·bas·co·lo** \-ˈbäsk-\ *or* **trabaco·la** \-ələ\ *or* **trabaco·le** \-ə(ˌ)lā\ *n* -S [It *trabacolo*, *trabaccolo*] : a small coasting vessel of Italy

trabal \ˈtrābəl, -rab-\ *adj* [L *trabalis*, fr. *trabs*, *trabes* beam + *-alis* -al — more at THORP] **1** : of or relating to a beam : large or diverging like a beam **2** [NL *trabalis*, fr. *trabs* (*cerebri*) corpus callosum, lit., cerebral beam + L *-alis* -al] : of or relating to the corpus callosum : CALLOSAL

tra·bant \trəˈbänt\ *n* -S [G *trabant*, *drabant*, fr. Czech *drabant*, fr. Per *darwān* porter, doorkeeper — more at DURWAN] **1** : an armed attendant (as of a royal personage) **2** : SATELLITE 4a(1)

trab·el \ˈtrabəl\ *substand var of* TRAVEL

tra·bea \ˈtrābēə\ *n, pl* **trabe·ae** \-ēˌē, -ēˌī\ [L; akin to *trabs*, *trabes* beam] : a toga with a border of colored stripes worn ceremonially by various men of rank in ancient Rome

tra·be·at·ed \ˈ==ˌād·ə̇d\ *also* **tra·be·ate** \-ēˌāt, -ēə̇t\ *adj* [*trabeated* fr. *trabeation* + *-ed*; *trabeate* back-formation fr. *trabeated*] *archit* : designed or constructed of horizontal beams or lintels : not arcuate

tra·be·a·tion \ˌ==ˈāshən\ *n* -S [L *trabes* beam + E *-ation*] : beamed as distinguished from arched construction; *also* : ENTABLATURE

trab·e·cle \ˈtrabəkəl\ *n* -S [NL *trabecula*] : TRABECULA

tra·bec·u·la \trəˈbekyələ\ *n, pl* **trabecu·lae** \-əˌlē, -ˌlī\ *also* **trabeculas** [NL, fr. L, little beam, dim. of *trabs*, *trabes* beam, timber, roof — more at THORP] **1** : a small bar, rod, bundle of fibers, or septal membrane in the framework of a bodily organ or part (as the spleen) **2 a** : a row of cells bridging an intercellular space in a plant **b** : a fold, ridge, or bar projecting into or extending across a cell or into a sporangial cavity **c** : a row or plate of sterile cells extending in a moss across the cavity of a sporangium; *also* : one of the transverse thickenings on the peristome teeth of a moss **3** : one of a pair of longitudinally directed more or less curved cartilaginous rods in the developing skull of a vertebrate that develop under the anterior part of the brain on each side of the pituitary body and subsequently fuse with each other and with the parachordal cartilages to form the base of the cartilaginous cranium

tra·bec·u·lar \-lə(r)\ *also* **tra·bec·u·late** \-lə̇t\ *or* **tra·bec·u·lat·ed** \-ˌlād·ə̇d\ *adj* [*trabecular*, *trabeculate* fr. NL *trabecula* + E *-ar* or *-ate*; *trabeculated* fr. NL *trabecula* + E *-ate* + *-ed*] : of, relating to, or constituting a trabecula ⟨~ tissue⟩ : having or consisting of trabeculae ⟨a ~ partition⟩

tra·bec·u·la·tion \ˌ=ˌ==ˈlāshən\ *n* -S [NL *trabecula* + E *-ation*] **1** : the formation of trabeculae in the lumen or on the walls of an organ (as the bladder) **2** : trabecular condition ⟨the characteristic ~ of the spleen⟩

trab·e·cule \ˈtrabəˌkyül\ *n* -S [NL *trabecula*] : TRABECULA

tra·bes \ˈtrā(ˌ)bēz\ *n, pl* **trabes** [L] : BEAM

tra·bu·co \trəˈbü(ˌ)kō\ *n* -S [Sp, fr. Catal *trabuc* catapult, blunderbuss, fr. *tra-* across, through (fr. L *trans-*) + *buc* belly, bulk, hull, of Gmc origin; akin to OE *būc* belly — more at BUCKET] **1** : BLUNDERBUSS **2** : a strong Spanish cigar

trac \ˈtrak\ *abbr or n* -S tractor

tra·cau·lon \trəˈkȯˌlän, -lən\ *n, cap* [NL, prob. fr. *trachy-* + Gk *kaulos* stem, stalk — more at HOLE] *in some classifications* : a genus of herbaceous vines (family Polygonaceae) occurring in No. America and Asia, having prickly or bristly stems, prickly veined leaves mostly hastate or cordate at the base, racemose flowers, and angled fruits, and being commonly included in the genus *Polygonum*

¹trace \ˈtrās\ *n* -S [ME, fr. MF, fr. *tracer*, *tracier* to trace — more at ²TRACE] **1** *archaic* : a course or path that one follows : ROAD, ROUTE; *also* : a way of life or conduct **2 a traces** *pl* : the line of footprints left by an animal ⟨followed the ~*s* of the deer into the swamp⟩ **b** : the line or track left by something that has passed ⟨the ~ of a sleigh in the snow⟩ **c** : a path or trail beaten by or as if by the passage of feet ⟨a sheep ~ along the hill⟩; *also* : a marked or blazed trail through woods or over open lands **3 a** *obs* : FOOTPRINT **b** : a sign or evidence of something once present, influential, felt, or otherwise prominent : a mark left behind ⟨~*s* of an earlier civilization⟩ **c** : a neural or mental alteration produced by the learning process : ENGRAM **4** : something traced or drawn (as a traced or lightly marked line): as **a** : the marking made by a recording instrument (as a seismograph or kymograph) **b** : the ground plan of a fortified work, defensive position, minefield, or other military installation either in reproduction (as on a map or photograph) or on the ground **c** : an unbroken line of hair (as on the back of some dogs) darker than or otherwise distinguished from the remainder of the coat **5 a** : the intersection of a line or plane with a plane or other surface and esp. with a plane of projection **b** : the line of intersection of a plane (as a fault or bedding plane) with the surface of the ground — compare STRIKE **c** : the usu. bright line or spot that moves across the screen of a cathode ray tube

(as in a radar set or other electronic device); *also* : the path taken by such a line or spot **6 a** : a minute and often barely detectable amount or indication ⟨a mere ~ of a smile⟩ ⟨lost without a ~⟩ ⟨needs just a ~ more salt⟩ **b** : a very small quantity of a chemical constituent or component esp. when not quantitatively determined because of minuteness

²trace \"\ *vb* -ED/-ING/-s [ME *tracen*, fr. MF *tracer, tracier,* fr. (assumed) VL *tractiare* to drag, draw, fr. L *tractus,* past part. of *trahere* to draw, pull, drag — more at DRAW] *vt* **1** : to make or record by drawing : as **a** : DELINEATE, SKETCH, OUTLINE ⟨~ a design for a fresco⟩ **b** : to form (as characters in writing) with care : write (as letters or figures) carefully or with nicety **c** : to copy (as a drawing, engraving, or manuscript) by following the lines or letters as seen through a transparent sheet superimposed on the original **d** : to impress or imprint (as a design or pattern) with or as if with a tracer; *also* : to make an imprint of such an item for (as a fabric, metal) **e** : to record (as the movements of a muscle) in the form of a curved, wavy, or broken line : make a tracing of (the cardiograph ~s the heart action) **f** : to make marks or lines on : adorn with tracery, chasing, or other linear ornamentation ⟨traced windows in Gothic churches⟩ **2** *archaic* : to walk or travel over : to pass through : TRAVERSE ⟨~ this alley up and down —Shak.⟩ **3 a** : to follow the footprints of : pursue the trail of or course or route taken by : track down ⟨~ game to its lair⟩ **b** : to follow or study out in detail or step by step : outline or present the development, progress, or history of ⟨~ the history of a movement⟩ **c** : to discover or uncover by going backward over the evidence step by step : ascertain, establish, or attribute as a result of such retracing or reviewing ⟨~ the cause of an epidemic⟩ ⟨traced the failure of the project to indifference⟩ **d** : to discover traces or signs or evidence of : prove the existence or occurrence of ⟨could not ~ the hypothetical source of the Shakespearean play⟩ **e** : to make out by finding or examining traces or vestiges or remains : come to know, understand, or comprehend by such investigation ⟨~ the former course of a river⟩ ⟨~ him in his word, his works, his ways —William Cowper⟩ **f** : to find by following traces or the trail of; *esp* : to ascertain the whereabouts or disposition of (as something passing from hand to hand or place to place) ⟨unable to ~ a lost letter or one's relatives⟩ ⟨traced the missing man to Chicago⟩ **4** : to lay out the trace of (a military installation) ~ *vi* **1** : to make one's way : GO: as **a** : to follow a track, trail, or other indicated way **b** *dial Eng* : WALK, MARCH, TRUDGE; *also* : to ramble aimlessly **c** *archaic* : to perform dance steps : step a measure **d** *obs* : to tumble down : fall free **2** : to be traceable historically : go back in time — usu. used with *to* ⟨a family that ~s to the Norman conquest⟩ **3** : to record on the cataloguing card for a main entry the headings under which added entries have been made

³trace \"\ *n* -s [ME *trais,* pl., traces, fr. MF *trais, traiz,* pl. of *trait* pull, draft, strap for harnessing — more at TRAIT] **1** : either of two straps, chains, or ropes of a harness extending from the collar or breast collar to a whiffletree attached to a vehicle or thing to be drawn : TUG — see HARNESS illustration **2** : a short line usu. of wire or gut between a main fishing line and the hook or lure : LEADER **3** : the vascular supply of a leaf or branch consisting of one or more vascular bundles that are extensions of the central vascular cylinder; *also* : one of the individual bundles of such a supply — see BRANCH TRACE, LEAF TRACE; compare GAP 6 **4** : a connecting bar or rod pivoted at each end to the end of another piece and used for transmitting motion from one plane to another; *specif* : such a piece in an organ-stop action to transmit motion from the trundle to the lever actuating the stop slider

⁴trace \"\ *vt* -ED/-ING/-s *archaic* : to fasten (as a horse) by traces : hitch up

⁵trace \"\ *vt* -ED/-ING/-s [ME *trasen, trassen,* prob. alter. of MF *tresser* to tress, fr. OF *trecier*] : PLAIT, BRAID; *specif* : to fasten (as onion bulbs or ears of corn) in bunches by braiding together the dry herbage (as of tops or shucks)

⁶trace \"\ *n* -s : a traced string (as of onions or ears of corn)

trace·abil·i·ty \'trãsǝ'bilǝd·ē, -lǝtē, -i\ *n* : the quality or state of being traceable

trace·able \'trãsǝbǝl\ *adj* [²trace + -able] **1** : capable of being traced ⟨a ~ riverbed⟩ ⟨a barely ~ inscription⟩ **2** : suitable or of a kind to be attributed : DUE, ASCRIBABLE — used with *to* ⟨a failure ~ to lack of energy⟩ — **trace·able·ness** \-bǝlnǝs\ *n* -ES — **trace·ably** \-blē, -li\ *adv*

trace-bearer \"\ *n* [³trace] : LAZY STRAP

trace bud *n* : a plant bud having a vascular trace and developing in the elongating portion of a stem — compare ADVENTITIOUS BUD

trace chain *n* **1 a** : a harness trace of chain **b** : a short chain by which a leathern trace is linked with a whiffletree **2** : a long strong chain which is attached to a line and along which two or more pairs of draft animals are attached usu. by whiffletrees

trace element *n* [¹trace] : a chemical element (as zinc, boron, or iodine) found combined in minute quantities in plant or animal tissues and considered essential in the physiological processes of most plants and animals — called also *micro-element, micronutrient, minor element;* compare MACRONUTRIENT

trace horse *n* [³trace] : an extra horse hitched beside a team to assist in drawing a load through a difficult spot (as up an incline); *also* : an outside horse of a team in which more than two are driven abreast

trace·less \'trãslǝs\ *adj* [¹trace + -less] : having or leaving no trace — **trace·less·ly** *adv*

trace of precipitation *n* : a minute amount of precipitation (as of rain); *specif* : an amount measuring less than 0.01 inch

¹trac·er \'trãsǝ(r)\ *n* -s [²trace + -er] **1** : one that traces, tracks down, or searches out: as **a** : SEEKER **b** : a person professionally engaged in the tracing of missing persons or property and esp. of goods lost in transit ⟨a form or inquiry sent out to facilitate the tracing of an article or shipment lost in transit⟩ **2** : one that makes tracings or traceries: as **a** : a draftsman, gilder, stainer, or other worker that traces designs, patterns, or markings **b** : one that traces (as drawings) on semitransparent paper or cloth esp. for blueprint reproduction — compare TRACING CLOTH, TRACING PAPER **3** : a device (as a stylus) used in tracing a design or other matter: as **a** : TRACING WHEEL **b** : a tempered steel punch used in chasing or repoussé work on metal (as when cutting the outline of a design or when making and finishing corners or borders) **4 a** *or* **tracer ammunition** : ammunition containing a chemical composition to mark the flight of projectiles by a trail of smoke or fire **b** : a substance (as a fluorescent dye) used to trace the course of a process; *specif* : a labeled element or atom that can be traced throughout chemical, biological, or physical processes by its radioactivity or its unusual isotopic mass ⟨radioactive ~s administered to patients accumulate in tumors and other pathological tissue, where they can be detected⟩

²tracer \"\ *n* -s [³trace + -er] : TRACE HORSE

tracer bullet *n* : a bullet that contains a tracer and leaves a path of smoke or fire

trac·er·ied \'trãs(ǝ)rēd, -rid\ *adj* : decorated with or having tracery

trac·ery \-rē, -ri\ *n* -ES [²trace + -ery] **1** : architectural ornamental work with ramified lines: as **a** : decorative openwork in the head of a Gothic window: (1) : BAR TRACERY (2) : PLATE TRACERY **b** : ornamentation resembling window tracery on other decorative objects (as panels of wood or metal) **c** : a similar decoration in some styles of vaulting in which the ribs of the vault give off the minor bars of which the tracery is composed **2** : a decorative interlacing of lines suggestive of Gothic tracery : a pattern wrought by the interweaving or branching out of lines in ornamental or graceful figures ⟨the ~ of frost on a window pane⟩

tracery 1a(1)

traces *pl* of TRACE, *pres 3d sing* of TRACE

trache- *or* **tracheo-** *comb form* [NL, fr. ML *trachea*] **1** : trachea ⟨*tracheoscopy*⟩ **2** : tracheal and ⟨*tracheolaryngeal*⟩

tra·chea \'trãkēǝ, *chiefly Brit* trǝ'kēǝ\ *n, pl* **trache·ae** \-ē,ē, -ē,ī\ *also* **tracheas** [ME, fr. ML, windpipe, trachea, fr. LL *trachia,* fr. Gk *(artēria) tracheia* rough (artery), fr. fem. of *trachys* rough, harsh; akin to Gk *thrassein, thrattein* to trouble, disturb — more at DARK] **1** : the main trunk of the system of tubes by which air passes to and from the lungs in vertebrates that forms in man a tube about four inches long and somewhat less than an inch in diameter extending down the front of the neck from the larynx, bifurcating to form the bronchi, and having walls of fibrous and muscular tissue stiffened by incomplete cartilaginous rings which keep it from collapsing and lined with mucous membrane whose epithelium is composed of columnar ciliated mucus-secreting cells — compare SYRINX **2** [NL] : a xylem element or series of elements felt to resemble an animal trachea; *usu* : a xylem vessel — compare BOOK LUNG, SPIRACLE, STIGMA, TAENIDIUM **3** [NL] : one of the air-conveying tubules forming the respiratory system of most insects, millipedes, centipedes, many arachnids, and the onychophorans and in the insects constituting typically a system of ramifying and anastomosing tubules that are enlarged at various points into air sacs, penetrate to nearly all parts of the body, and have a cuticular lining which is stiffened by a spiral fiber or fibrous thickening — compare BOOK LUNG, SPIRACLE, STIGMA, TAENIDIUM

tra·che·al \-ēǝl\ *adj* [NL *trachealis,* fr. ML *trachea* + L *-alis*] **1** : of, relating to, or functioning in the manner of an animal trachea : resembling a trachea **2** : TRACHEARY

tracheal commissure *n* : one of the large transverse tubes that unite the tracheal systems of the opposite sides of the body in an insect

tracheal gill *n* : one of the external filaments or leaflike plates connected with the tracheae of the inside of the body that form part of the respiratory system of some aquatic insect larvae and nymphs but rarely persist in the adult

tra·che·alis \,trãkē'alǝs, -'ā-, -'ä-\ *n, pl* **trache·ales** \-(,)lēz\ [NL, lit., tracheal] : a muscle associated with the trachea and in man consisting of fibers that extend transversely between the ends of the cartilages and the intervals between them at the back of the trachea

tracheal sac *n* : an air sac of the tracheal system of an insect

tracheal tube *n* : a trachea of an insect or a branch of such a trachea

tracheal tug *or* **tracheal tugging** *n* : a downward pull of the trachea and larynx observed in aneurysm of the aorta

tracheal tympanum *n* : an enlarged and partially ossified segment of the trachea of some birds

tra·che·ar·ia \,trãkē'a(ǝ)rēǝ\ *n pl, cap* [NL, fr. trache- + -aria] *in former classifications* : a division of Arachnida comprising those that have no book lungs and including the mites, ticks, book scorpions, and harvestmen — **tra·che·ar·i·an** \-ēǝn\ *adj or n*

¹tra·che·ary \'trãkē,erē\ *adj* [trache- + -ary] **1** : breathing by means of tracheae **2** : of, relating to, made up of, or being plant tracheae ⟨~ tissue⟩ ⟨a ~ element⟩

²tracheary \"\ *n* -ES [NL *Tracheari*] : a member of the division Trachearia : an arachnid that lacks book lungs

¹tra·che·ata \,trãkē'äd·ǝ, -ād·ǝ\ *n pl, cap* [NL, fr. neut. pl. of *tracheatus* tracheate, fr. trache- + L *-atus* -ate] *in former classifications* : a class or other group of Arthropoda comprising all or most of the arthropods with tracheal respiration

²tracheata \"\ [NL] *syn of* TRACHEOPHYTA

¹tra·che·ate \'trãkē,āt, -kēǝt\ *n* -s [NL *Tracheata*] : a tracheate arthropod

²tracheate \"\ *adj* [NL *tracheatus*] : having tracheae as breathing organs

tra·che·a·tion \,trãkē'āshǝn\ *n* -s [trache- + -ation] : the distribution and arrangement of the tracheae in a tracheate arthropod and esp. in the developing wing of an insect previous to the formation of the veins

tra·cheid \'trãkēǝd, -ā,kēd\ *n, pl* **tracheids** *also* **tra·che·ides** \'trã'kē,dēz, trǝ'k-\ [ISV trache- + -id; prob. orig. formed in G] : a long tubular cell that is peculiar to xylem, functions in conduction and support, and is characterized by tapering closed ends which are not absorbed as in tracheae and by thickened strongly lignified walls which commonly have bordered pits — compare SIEVE CELL, TRACHEA 2, VESSEL; *also* : XYLEM — **tra·che·idal** \'trã'kēǝd³l, trǝ'k-, 'trãkē,id³l\ *adj*

tra·che·i·tis \,trãkē'ïd·ǝs\ *n* -ES [NL, fr. trache- + -itis] : inflammation of the trachea

trachel- *or* **trachelo-** *comb form* [NL, fr. Gk *trachēl-, trachēlo-,* fr. *trachēlos*] **1 a** : neck ⟨*tracheology*⟩ **b** : cervical and ⟨*tracheloscapular*⟩ **2** : necklike anatomical structure : cervix 2a ⟨*tracheloplasty*⟩

trache·late \'trãkǝ,lāt, 'trãk-\ *adj* [NL *trachelatus,* fr. trachel- + L *-atus* -ate] : having the look of a neck ⟨an insect with a narrowed ~ prothorax⟩

tra·che·li·um \trǝ'kēlēǝm\ *or* **tra·che·li·on** \-lē,än\ *n, pl* **trache·lia** \-lēǝ\ [NL, fr. Gk *trachēlos* neck + L *-ium* or Gk *-ion* (dim. suffixes)] : the part of the neck of a column above the gorgerin

trache·lo·mastoid \,trãkǝlō, 'trãkǝlō, 'trãkǝlō\ *adj* [ISV trachel- + mastoid] : relating to or joining the neck and mastoid

trachelo–occipital \"+\ *adj* [ISV trachel- + occipital] : relating to or joining the neck and occiput

trachelo·plasty \'trãkǝlō,plastē, 'trãkǝlō-, trǝ'kēlō-\ *n* -ES [trachel- + -plasty] : a plastic operation on the neck of the uterus

trache·lor·rha·phy \,trãkǝ'lórǝfē, 'trãk-\ *n* -ES [ISV trachel- + -rraphy] : the operation of sewing up a laceration of the uterine cervix

trachelo·spermum \,trãkǝlō'spǝrmǝm, ,trãkǝlō-, trǝ,kēlō-\ *n, cap* [NL, fr. trachel- + -spermum] : a genus of Asiatic woody vines (family Apocynaceae) with opposite leaves, showy flowers in loose cymes, and elongated terete follicles — see STAR JASMINE

tracheo- — see TRACHE-

tra·cheo·bronchial \,trãkē(,)ō, trǝ'kēō+\ *adj* [trache- + bronchial] : of, relating to, affecting, or produced in the trachea and bronchi ⟨~ secretion⟩ ⟨~ lesions⟩

tracheo·bronchitis \"+\ *n* [NL, fr. trache- + bronchitis] : inflammation of the trachea and bronchi

tra·che·o·lar \trǝ'kēǝlǝ(r)\ *adj* [tracheole + -ar] : of, relating to, or being a tracheole

tra·che·ole \'trãkē,ōl\ *n* -s [trache- + -ole] : one of the minute delicate endings of a branched trachea of an insect

tra·cheo·pho·nae \,trãkē'ō,fō,nē, trǝ,kē-\ *n pl, cap* [NL, fr. trache- + Gk *phōnē* sound, voice — more at BAN] *in former classifications* : a group comprising clamatorial birds with the syrinx thin-walled and tracheal, the syringeal muscles few, and the semirings few and thin and including the families Dendrocolaptidae, Formicariidae, and Conopophagidae — **tra·cheo·phone** \'trãkēǝ,fōn, trǝ'k-\ *n* -s

tra·cheo·pho·nine \,trãkē'ō,fō,nīn, trǝ,kē-, -,nôn\ *or* **tra·che·oph·o·nous** \,trãkē'äfǝnǝs\ *adj* [NL *Tracheophonae* + E *-ine* or *-ous*] : of or relating to the Tracheophonae

tra·che·oph·y·ta \,trãkē'äfǝd·ǝ\ *n pl, cap* [NL, fr. trache- + -phyta] : a division of plants comprising green plants with a vascular system that contains tracheids or tracheary elements (as vessel elements or fibers) and including the subdivisions Psilopsida, Sphenopsida, Lycopsida, and Pteropsida — **tra·cheo·phyte** \'trãkēǝ,fīt\ *n* -s

tra·che·os·to·my \,trãkē'ästǝmē\ *n* -ES [ISV trache- + -stomy; prob. orig. formed as F *trachéostomie*] : the surgical formation of an opening into the trachea through the skin

tra·che·ot·o·mize \,trãkē'äd·ǝ,mīz\ *vt* -ED/-ING/-s [ISV *tracheotomy* + -ize] : to perform tracheotomy on

tra·che·ot·o·my \-'äd·ǝmē\ *n* -ES [trache- + -tomy] : the surgical operation of cutting into the trachea esp. through the skin

trach·ich·thy·i·dae \,trã,kik'thīǝ,dē, ,trã,k-\ *n pl, cap* [NL, fr. *Trachichthys,* type genus (fr. Gk *trachys* rough + NL *-ichthys*) + *-idae*] : a family of reddish large-headed rough-bodied or spiny chiefly deep-sea fishes with numerous mucous channels about the head

trachin·i·dae \trǝ'kinǝ,dē\ *n pl, cap* [NL, fr. *Trachinus,* type genus (fr. ML *trachina,* a fish, fr. Gk *trachys* rough) + *-idae*] : a family of percoid fishes that is constituted by the weevers and sometimes with related elongated eellike fishes

placed in a separate suborder of Percomorphi or an independent order

¹trachi·noid \'trãkǝ,nóid, 'trãk-\ *adj* [NL *Trachinus* + E *-oid*] : resembling or related to the Trachinidae

²trachinoid \"\ *n* -s : a trachinoid fish

tra·chip·ter·us [NL] *syn of* TRACHYPTERUS

tra·chle \'trãkǝl, -rãk-\ *vb* -ED/-ING/-s [perh. fr. Flem *tragelen, trakelen* to walk with difficulty, drag; akin to MD *traechel* slow, heavy, sluggish, OHG *trägi* sluggish, slow, Lith *drižti* to become tired] *vt* **1** *Scot* : DISHEVEL, BEDRAGGLE, SOIL **2** *Scot* : to tire by overwork or overexertion; *also* : to put (as oneself) to inconvenience : BOTHER, TROUBLE ~ *vi, Scot* : to wear oneself out (as by work) : DRUDGE

²trachle \"\ *n* -s **1** *Scot* **a** : a source of fatigue (as a long and tiring walk or task) **b** : a cause of inconvenience, distress, or trouble **2** *Scot* : a listless sloven

trach·odon \'trãkǝ,dän, 'trãk-\ *n* [NL, fr. Gk *trachys* rough + NL *-odon*] **1** *cap* : a genus comprising large duck-billed dinosaurs of the Upper Cretaceous that resemble those of the *Iguanodon* but have a broad spatulate snout and commonly constituting a distinct family **2** : a dinosaur of the genus *Trachodon* — **trach·odont** \"\ *adj or n* — **trach·odon·tid** \"'düntǝd\ *adj*

tra·cho·ma \trǝ'kōmǝ\ *n* -s [NL, fr. Gk *trachōma,* fr. *trachys* rough, harsh + *-ōma* -oma] : a chronic contagious conjunctivitis characterized by the presence on the conjunctival surfaces of inflammatory granulations that are eventually replaced by scar tissue and caused by a rickettsia (*Chlamydia trachomatis*) — **tra·cho·ma·tous** \trǝ'kämǝd·ǝs, -kōm-\ *adj*

tracho·medusae \,trãkō, 'trãkō+\ *n pl, cap* [NL, alter. of *Trachymedusae*] : a suborder of Trachylina comprising medusae in which the tentacles arise from the edge of the umbrella and the gonads are developed in connection with the radial canals — **tracho·medusan** \"+\ *adj or n*

tra·chu·rus \trǝ'kyürǝs\ *n, cap* [NL, fr. Gk *trachouros* horse mackerel, fr. *trachys* rough + *oura* tail; akin to Gk *orrhos* buttocks — more at ASS] : a genus of marine carangid fishes including various important food fishes — compare COWAN-YOUNG, HORSE MACKEREL

trachy- *comb form* [in sense 1, fr. NL, fr. Gk, fr. *trachys* rough, harsh; in sense 2, fr. F, fr. *trachyte* — more at TRACHEA] **1** : rough : strong ⟨*trachyglossate*⟩ ⟨*trachychromatic*⟩ **2** : trachytic ⟨*trachydolerite*⟩ ⟨*trachyandesite*⟩

trachy·andesite \,trãkē, 'trãkē+\ *n* [F *trachyandésite,* fr. *trachy-* + *andésite* andesite] : a lava intermediate in composition between trachyte and andesite — compare LATITE

trachy·basalt \"+\ *n* [G, fr. *trachy-* + *basalt*] : a rock that is intermediate in composition between trachyte and basalt and that contains both orthoclase and basic plagioclase

trachy·car·pous \,trãkē'kärpǝs\ *adj* [ISV trachy- + -carpous] : rough-fruited

trachy·car·pus \,trãkē'kärpǝs\ *n, cap* [NL, fr. trachy- + -carpus] : a small genus of low East Asiatic fan palms having leaf sheaths with a dense fibrous network which is made into ropes and netting — see HEMP PALM

trachy·chromatic \"+\ *adj* [ISV trachy- + chromatic] : deeply staining (as some marrow cells)

trachy·li·na \,trãkē'līnǝ\ *n pl, cap* [NL, prob. fr. trachy- + L *linum* flax — more at LINEN] : an order of Hydrozoa comprising forms that lack a polyp stage and including the suborder Trachomedusae and Narcomedusae — **trachy·line** \',trãkǝ,līn, -lǝn\ *adj*

trachy·li·nae \,trãkē'lī,nē\ [NL] *syn of* TRACHYLINA

trachy·medusae \,trãkē+\ [NL, fr. trachy- + medusae] *syn of* TRACHOMEDUSAE

tra·chyp·ter·us \trǝ'kiptǝrǝs\ *n, cap* [NL, fr. trachy- + -pterus] : a genus of large oceanic fishes (order Allotriognathi) comprising the dealfishes and usu. constituting a distinct family

trachy·sper·mous \,trãkē'spǝrmǝs, 'trãk-\ *adj* [trachy- + -spermous] : rough-seeded

trachyte \'trã,kīt, 'trã,-, -ǝ\ *n* -s [F, fr. Gk *trachys* rough + F *-ite* — more at TRACHEA] : a usu. light-colored volcanic rock consisting of potash feldspar generally with more or less biotite, amphibole, or pyroxene, commonly exhibiting a subparallel texture, and being the effusive form of syenite

tra·chyt·ic \trǝ'kid,ik\ *adj* [F *trachytique,* fr. *trachyte* + -ique -ic] : of or relating to a texture of igneous rocks in which lath-shaped feldspar microlites are arranged in subparallel lines that flow around the larger phenocrysts

trachy·toid \'trãkǝ,tóid, 'trãk-\ *adj* [F *trachytoïde,* fr. *trachyte* + -oïde -oid] : resembling trachyte ⟨a ~ structure⟩

¹trac·ing \'trãsiŋ, -sēŋ\ *n* -s [ME, fr. gerund of *tracen* to trace — more at TRACE] **1** : the act of one that traces **2** : something that is traced or marked out: as **a** : a copy of a pattern or design made on a transparent sheet superimposed on an original or by use of transfer paper **b** : a record made by any of several instruments (as an ergogram or cardiogram) that register graphically some movement **c** : a mark left on the ice by a skate — called also *print* **3** : a record of additional entries in respect to a particular item placed on its main entry card in a catalog

²tracing \"\ *adj* [ME, fr. pres. part. of *tracen* to trace] : used in or for making tracings ⟨~ board⟩ ⟨a ~ machine⟩

tracing cloth *also* **tracing linen** *n* : a fine transparent linen or cotton cloth sized on one side and used (as by architects or designers) for making tracings esp. in ink

tracing paper *n* **1** : a tough semitransparent paper for tracing drawings **2** : lithographic transfer paper

tracing wheel *n* : a needle-pointed or saw-toothed wheel with an attached handle that is used (as by tailors or patternmakers) with or without carbon paper to mark construction lines on patterns or fabric

¹track \'trak\ *n* -s *often attrib* [ME *trak,* fr. MF *trac,* perh. of Gmc origin; akin to MD *tracken, trecken* to pull, haul, march, MLG *trecken* to pull — more at TREK] **1 a** : a detectable evidence that something has passed (as the wake of a ship, a line of footprints, or a wheel rut) **b** : a rough path or way formed by or as if by repeated chance footfalls : TRAIL **c** : a way or road constructed and maintained for a specific purpose: esp (1) : a path or course laid out esp. for racing or exercise ⟨a cinder ~⟩ ⟨a half-mile ~⟩; *esp* : a running track on which athletic races are contested — distinguished from *field* (2) : a metal way for wheeled vehicles; *specif* : one or more pairs of parallel lines of rails with the fastenings, ties, and sometimes ballast for a railroad, railway, or tramway **d** : a physical course by or on which something is recorded: as (1) : the portion of the dial of a timepiece on which minutes or seconds are marked off between concentric bands (2) : SOUND TRACK **2 a** : a footprint whether recent or fossil ⟨the huge ~ of an old bull elephant⟩ **b** *archaic* : a visible mark or sign : VESTIGE, TRACE **3 a** : the course along which something moves ⟨his ~ led him over mountains and through swamps⟩ ⟨the ~ of a bullet⟩ — used interjectionally by a skier to warn anyone ahead of him on a trail or run; see PACHISI illustration **b** : a way of life, conduct, or action : course ⟨one adopts or follows : METHOD, PROCEDURE ⟨afraid the new administration would choose a different ~ in foreign affairs⟩ **c** : one of two or more courses of study covering the same general field usu. at different levels of intensity and offered by a school to meet the diverse needs of particular groups of students **d** : the projection on the earth's surface of the path along which an aircraft has actually flown **4 a** : a sequence of events or train of ideas : the order in which things happen or ideas come ⟨my pen goes in the ~ of my thoughts —Edmund Burke⟩ ⟨the recurrent ~ of the years⟩ **b** : the condition or fact of being aware of or in touch with something or some aspect (as the progress, count, extent, or worth) of something specified ⟨lost ~ of his friend's address⟩ ⟨keeping careful ~ of the costs⟩ **5** : any of several things or paths that make or are associated with the making of a track: as **a** : the width of a wheeled vehicle as measured from wheel to wheel and usu. from the outside of the rims **b** : the tread of an automobile tire **c** : CATERPILLAR TREAD **6** : the lower face of the foot usu. of a bird **7** *Scot* : an odd spectacle : SIGHT **8** : track-and-field sports; *esp* : those (as running or hurdling events) that are performed on the running track — distinguished from *field event* — **across the tracks** *adv* : in a run-down or unfashionable neighborhood — **in one's tracks** : where one stands or is at the moment : on the spot : INSTANTLY ⟨shot the thief in his tracks⟩

[2]track \"\ vb -ED/-ING/-S vt **1 a** : to follow the tracks or traces of : pursue by following marks made by (the pursued) : TRAIL ⟨~ a deer⟩ **b** : to follow until caught up with — used with adverbs of direction (as *down*) ⟨~ down a criminal⟩ **2** : to mark out or beat down (a path or other course) **3 a** : to ascertain and follow up through vestiges : TRACE ⟨~ the course of an ancient wall⟩ **b** : to follow or plot the moving path of (a target) with an instrument (as a gun, telescope, or searchlight) for the purpose of determining point of aim, path of interception, or future position **4** : to pass over : TRAVEL, TRAVERSE ⟨~ a desert⟩ **5 a** : to make tracks upon ⟨new snow ~*ed* by rabbits⟩; *esp* : to carry mud or other soiling agent on the feet and deposit it upon — often used with *up* ⟨don't ~ up my clean floor⟩ **b** : to carry (as mud) on the feet and deposit in stepping ⟨~*ed* mud all over the house⟩ **6** : to furnish with tracks or rails — often used in compounds ⟨single-*track*⟩ ⟨double-*track*⟩ ~ *vi* **1** : to make one's way : WALK, GO, TRAVEL — often used with *around, about,* or *up* ⟨got up late and ~*ed* about for a while⟩ **2 a** : to follow a track in searching ⟨takes a woodsman to really ~⟩ **b** : to move a camera toward, beside, or away from a subject on a smooth moving trolley or tricycle **c** *of a phonograph needle* : to follow the groove undulations of a recording **3 a** *of a pair of wheels* (1) : to maintain a constant distance apart on the straightaway (2) : to fit a track or rails **b** *of a rear wheel of a vehicle* : to accurately follow its corresponding fore wheel on a straightaway **c** : to be in perfect alignment with a corresponding part — used esp. of a gear or cutter **4** : to leave tracks (as on a floor) ⟨~*ing* all over the house with his muddy boots⟩

[3]track \"\ n -S [by alter. of [3]*tract*] *chiefly dial* : EXTENT; *esp* : an extent of land

[4]track \"\ vb -ED/-ING/-S [prob. modif. (influenced by [2]*track*) of D *trekken* to pull, fr. MD *trecken* — more at TRACK (n.)] *vt* **1** : to draw along; *esp* : to tow (as a ship) from the shore **2** *chiefly Scot* : to prepare (tea) by infusing : DRAW ~ *vi* : to become towed : travel in a towed boat

[5]track \"\ n -S *chiefly Scot* : TEAPOT

track·able \'trakəbəl\ *adj* : capable of being tracked : suitable for tracking

[1]track·age \-kij, -kēj\ n -S [[4]*track* + *-age*] : an act of towing : TOWAGE

[2]trackage \"\ n -S [[1]*track* + *-age*] **1** : lines of railway track ⟨1000 miles of antiquated ~⟩ **2 a** *usu* **trackage right** : a right to use the tracks of another road **b** *usu* **trackage charge** : the charge for such right

track-and-field \¦==¦=\ *adj* : of, relating to, or being a sport performed on a running track or on the field usu. encircled by it — see TRACK 8; compare FIELD EVENT

track and slide n [[1]*track*] : a combination on a mast for hoisting and lowering a sail

trackbarrow \'=,=(,)=\ n [[1]*track* + *barrow*] : a wheelbarrow with a wheel grooved for use on railroad tracks

track boat n : a boat towed from the shore

track brake n : a brake (as on a streetcar) that presses the track instead of the wheels

track circuit n : an electrical circuit conducted partly through the rails of a track (as of a railway line)

tracked *past of* TRACK

[1]track·er \'trakə(r)\ n -S [[2]*track* + *-er*] **1** : one that tracks (as by tracing): as **a** : one that tracks down game or criminals **b** : an instrument used to track a gunnery target; *also* : the operator of such an instrument **2** : a maker of a track

[2]tracker \"\ n -S [[4]*track* + *-er*] : a tower of a boat or raft

tracker action n [[1]*tracker*] : a completely mechanical action in a pipe organ

track gage n : a tool by which the gage of a track (as of a railroad) is determined

track harness n : a light harness used in harness racing

trackhound \'=,=\ n : a hound that tracks by scent

track indicator n : a device used to indicate the condition of a railroad track section

tracking *pres part of* TRACK

tracking shot n [*tracking* fr. pres. part. of [2]*track*] : TRUCKING SHOT

track instrument n : a treadle device on a railroad track depressed by a passing train to operate an alarm (as near a crossing)

track jack n : a device for raising railway track during ballasting or other track operations

tracklayer \'=,=(=)\ n **1 a** : a workman engaged in work involved in putting railway tracks in place **b** : a machine used in track construction for advancing the rails and ties from supply cars in the rear to the point where they are to be placed in the track **2** : a Caterpillar tractor

[1]tracklaying \'=,==\ *adj* **1** : used in the laying of tracks **2** : of, relating to, or being a caterpillar tread vehicle

[2]tracklaying \"\ n [[1]*track* + *laying*, gerund of [1]*lay*] : the laying of track on a railway line

track·less \'trakləs\ *adj* **1** : having no track : UNTROD ⟨a ~ wilderness⟩ **2** : making or leaving no tracks ⟨~ footsteps⟩ **3** : not running on tracks or rails ⟨a ~ train⟩ — **track·less·ly** *adv* — **track·less·ness** n -ES

trackless trolley n : TROLLEYBUS

track·man \'trakmən\ n, pl **trackmen** : a worker engaged in the laying or maintenance of railway tracks or rails; *specif* : TRACKWALKER

track map n : a map showing existing physical plant including tracks, bridges, water service and mains, leases, station facilities, and all other physical property of a railway line

trackmaster \'=,==\ n : ROADMASTER 1

track-mile \'=¦=\ n : a mile of track (as of a railway line) ⟨costs per *track-mile*⟩

track oven n : a drying oven in which drying racks run on a track over a fire

track pan n : a very long shallow trough between the rails of a railroad track for holding water to be picked up by a moving steam locomotive

trackpot \'=,=\ n [[4]*track* + *pot*] *chiefly Scot* : TEAPOT

track road n [[4]*track*] : TOWPATH

tracks *pl of* TRACK, *pres 3d sing of* TRACK

track scale n : a scale fitted with tracks for the weighing of loaded or empty railway cars

trackshifter \'=,==\ n : an appliance used in shifting a railway track laterally

track shoe n **1** : the shoe of a track brake **2** : a heelless leather shoe having steel spikes on the sole to give traction to a runner

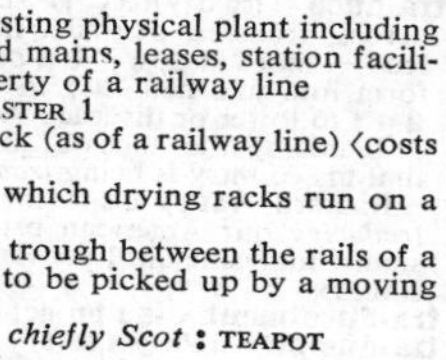
track shoe 2

[1]trackside \'=,=\ n [[1]*track* + *side*] : the space beside a track

[2]trackside \'=,=\ *adj* : of, relating to, or situated in the area immediately adjacent to a track and esp. a railway track

track spike n : an appliance driven or screwed into a tie to hold a rail and tie plate

track storage n : storage in railroad cars on other than private or industrial tracks beyond the free time allowed for loading or unloading for which a charge in addition to demurrage is usu. made; *also* : the charge for such storage

trackwalker \'=,==\ n : a worker employed to walk over and inspect a section of tracks

trackway \'=,=\ n [[1]*track* + *way*] **1** : a beaten or trodden path : ROADWAY **2 a** : one of two or more narrow paths of steel plates, smooth stone, or other suitable material laid in a public roadway otherwise formed of an inferior pavement (as of cobblestones) to provide an easy way for wheels **b** : a way (as a tramway or railway) with steel or other rails on which flange-wheeled vehicles travel **3** : a usu. grooved or curved guide in which a door, drawer, or other movable part runs often on ball bearings

tracs *pl of* TRAC

[1]tract \'trakt\ n -S *often cap* [ME *tracte*, fr. ML *tractus*, fr. L, action of drawing, extension, length; fr. its being sung without a break by one voice] : the verses of Scripture sung or recited in the Roman liturgy of the mass after the gradual or instead of the alleluia on penitential days from Septuagesima to Holy Saturday, on ember days, and at most vigils and requiems

[2]tract \"\ n -S [ME *tracte*, modif. of L *tractatus* action of handling, discussion, treatise — more at TRACTATE] **1** *archaic* : a literary work dealing with a particular topic : TREATISE **2** : a pamphlet, leaflet, or folder issued (as by a political or religious group) for propaganda; *esp* : one containing a religious exhortation, a doctrinal discussion, or a proselytizing appeal

[3]tract \'trakt\ n -S [L *tractus* action of drawing, trailing, extension, track, tract of land, space of time, fr. *tractus*, past part. of *trahere* to draw, pull, drag — more at DRAW] **1 a** *archaic* : extent or lapse of time : continued or protracted duration : COURSE **b** : a period in time : STRETCH ⟨hoping for a ~ of fair weather⟩ **c** *archaic* : a continuous course (as of action or events) : CONTINUITY **2** : an area either large or small: as **a** (1) : a region or stretch (as of land) that is usu. indefinitely described or without precise boundaries ⟨a few large ~s for settlement⟩ ⟨the wooded ~ between the two rivers⟩ ⟨a great ~ of unexplored sea⟩ (2) : a precisely defined or definable area of land ⟨an 80 acre ~⟩ ⟨an urban census ~⟩ **b** (1) : a system of body parts or organs acting in concert to perform some function or serve some special purpose ⟨the digestive ~⟩ ⟨upper respiratory ~⟩ (2) : a bundle of nerve fibers having a common origin, termination, and function; *esp* : such a bundle within the spinal cord or brain — called also *fiber tract*; compare FASCICULUS (3) : PTERYLA **c** : a particular and usu. identifiable part of something ⟨large ~s of the job about which I know nothing —Robertson Davies⟩ ⟨psychological ~s that ... lurk shapelessly outside the action of a novel —C.H. Rickword⟩ **3** *chiefly dial* : TRACK: as **a** : a footprint or other mark indicative of passage **b** : PATH, COURSE, WAY **c** : VESTIGE, TRACE

trac·ta·bil·i·ty \,traktə'bilədē, -lətē, -i\ n [L *tractabilitas*, fr. *tractabilis* tractable + *-itas* -ity] : the quality or state of being tractable ⟨was only too delighted at this ~ —Thomas Hardy⟩

trac·ta·ble \'traktəbəl\ *adj* [L *tractabilis*, fr. *tractare* to handle, treat + *-abilis* -able] **1 a** : capable of being easily led, taught, or controlled : DOCILE, GOVERNABLE, PLIANT ⟨~ children⟩ ⟨a ~ horse⟩ **b** : ready to listen, yield, conform, or agree — used with *to* ⟨thou shalt find me ~ to any honest reason —Shak.⟩ **2** : easily handled, managed, or wrought : MALLEABLE ⟨gold is ~⟩ **syn** see OBEDIENT

trac·ta·ble·ness n -ES : the quality or state of being tractable

trac·ta·bly \-blē, -li\ *adv* : in a tractable manner

[1]trac·tar·i·an \trak'terēən, -'ta(a)r-, -'tär-\ n -S [[2]*tract* + *-arian*] **1** : one who writes, prints, or distributes tracts **2** *usu cap* [so called fr. the *Tracts for the Times*, series of pamphlets expounding Tractarianism] **a** : one of the authors of the *Tracts for the Times* **b** : a promoter or supporter of Tractarianism

[2]tractarian \(')=¦==\ *adj* **1** : of or relating to tractarians **2** *usu cap* : of or relating to Tractarianism

trac·tar·i·an·ism \=¦===,nizəm\ n -S *usu cap* [[1]*tractarian* + *-ism*] : a system of principles set forth in a series of pamphlets issued at Oxford (1833–41) aimed at the Erastianism and liberalism of that day and urging a revival of the patristic sacramental piety and theology of the 17th century : the doctrines of the early leaders of the Oxford movement toward Catholicism in the Church of England — compare ANGLO-CATHOLICISM, LAUDIANISM

trac·tate \'trak,tāt, *usu* -ād.+V\ n -S [L *tractatus* action of handling, discussion, treatise, fr. *tractatus*, past part. of *tractare* to draw out, handle, discuss, treat — more at TREAT] : TREATISE, DISSERTATION, ESSAY ⟨an economic ~ of the first importance —*Manchester Guardian Weekly*⟩ **syn** see DISCOURSE

trac·ta·tor \-ād.ə(r), -ātə-\ n -S [LL, fr. L, handler, fr. *tractatus* (past part.) + *-or*] **1** *obs* : a writer of tracts or treatises **2** *usu cap* [so called fr. the *Tracts for the Times*, series of Tractarian pamphlets] : TRACTARIAN 2

trac·ta·tule \'traktə,tyül\ n -S [*tractate* + *-ule*] : a small or minor tractate

trac·tile \'traktəl, -k,tīl, -k(,)til\ *adj* [L *tractus* (past part. of *trahere* to draw, pull) + E *-ile*] : capable of being drawn and esp. of being drawn out in length : DUCTILE — **trac·til·i·ty** \trak'tilədē\ n -ES

tract index n [[3]*tract*] : a record kept by a register of deeds or other proper county official showing the location, size, and name of owner of each plot of land in a county

trac·tion \'trakshən\ n -S *often attrib* [ML *traction-, tractio*, fr. L *tractus* (past part. of *trahere* to draw, pull, drag) + *-ion-, -io* -ion — more at DRAW] **1 a** : the act of drawing or pulling : the state of being drawn; *also* : force exerted in drawing — opposed to *pulsion* **b** : the drawing of a body (as a vehicle) along a plane or gradient by motive power; *also* : the motive power employed in such drawing ⟨steam ~⟩ **2** : power or influence that attracts : ATTRACTION **3** : public utility transportation service (as electric railways and trolley lines) ⟨reviewing the interurban ~ charters⟩ ⟨sales of ~ bonds⟩ **4 a** : the adhesive friction of a body on a surface on which it moves (as of a wheel on a rail or a rope on a pulley) **b** (1) : the pulling of or tension established in one body part by another ⟨the gravitational ~ exerted by abdominal viscera on the diaphragm⟩ ⟨~ of skeletal muscle on the joints⟩ (2) : a pulling force exerted on a skeletal structure (as in fracture) by means of a special device or apparatus ⟨a ~ splint⟩; *also* : a state of tension created by such a pulling force ⟨a leg in ~⟩

trac·tion·al \-shənəl, -shnəl\ *adj* : of or relating to traction

traction engine n **1** : a locomotive for drawing vehicles on highways or in the fields — compare WALKING ENGINE **2** : a railway locomotive that moves by the friction of its driving wheels on rails — compare COG RAILWAY, RACK RAILWAY

traction fiber n : a spindle fiber that by its contraction is held to draw a mitotic chromosome to a pole of the spindle

traction sand n : sand carried by a locomotive or trolley car for spraying under the driving wheels to prevent slippage at starts or on grades — called also *engine sand*

traction sprayer n : an agricultural spray outfit on wheels that is operated by a power drive from the wheels and used esp. for spraying rows of truck crops

traction transport n : the rolling or sliding of particles along a stream bed by running water, over the ground surface by wind, or on a beach by waves and currents — compare SALTATION

traction wheel n **1** : a locomotive driving wheel that acts by frictional adhesion to a smooth track **2** : a smooth-rimmed friction wheel for giving motion (as to an endless link belt)

tract·ite \'trak,tīt\ n -S *usu cap* [[2]*tract* (in *Tract for the Times*, series of Tractarian pamphlets) + *-ite*] : TRACTARIAN

trac·tive \'traktiv, -tēv *also* -əv\ *adj* [L *tractus* (past part. of *trahere* to draw, pull) + E *-ive*] : that draws or is used or exerted in drawing or pulling; *also* : of or concerned with traction ⟨~ power⟩

tractive effort n : the force in pounds exerted by powered equipment (as a locomotive) as measured for statistical purposes at the rim of the driving wheels

trac·tor \'traktə(r)\ n -S *often attrib* [NL, fr. L *tractus* (past part. of *trahere* to draw, pull, drag) + *-or* — more at DRAW] **1 a** *archaic* : either of the pair of metal rods used in tractoration **b** : an instrument used to exert traction on a body part or tissue (as in surgical procedures) **2** : an apparatus or device for the draft or sometimes propulsion of another body: as **a** : TRACTION ENGINE 1 **b** (1) : a 4-wheeled or caterpillar-tread rider-controlled automotive vehicle used esp. for drawing agricultural or other implements or for bearing and propelling such implements (2) : a smaller 2-wheeled apparatus controlled through handlebars by a walking operator and used similarly with gardening and lawn implements **c** *also* **tractor truck** : a motive power unit in the form of a truck with short chassis and no body used in a combination highway freight vehicle — see FULL TRAILER, SEMITRAILER **d** : a small harbor tug (as one designed to draw barges) — called also *marine tractor* **3** *also* **tractor airplane** : an airplane having the propeller forward of the main supporting surfaces — compare PUSHER

trac·to·ra·tion \,=tə'rāshən\ n -S *archaic* : a technique of therapy first used about 1796 by Elisha Perkins of Norwich, Conn., consisting in the operation of drawing over an affected part the points of two small rods of different metals, and held to be helpful in local inflammation or pains (as of rheumatism)

trac·tor·ist \'==,rəst\ n -S : a tractor operator

trac·tor·iza·tion \,==rə'zāshən, -,rī'z-\ n -S [obs. E *tractorize* to use tractors (fr. E *tractor* + *-ize*) + E *-ation*] : adoption of tractors as a source of draft power — compare MOTORIZATION

tractor-mounted \¦==¦==\ *adj* : bolted or clamped to a tractor rather than drawn behind it ⟨*tractor-mounted* implements⟩

tractor propeller n : a propeller of an airplane that is placed at the forward end of its shaft and pulls on the thrust bearing instead of pushing — compare PUSHER

trac·tot·o·my \trak'tad.əmē\ n -ES [ISV [3]*tract* + *-o-* + *-tomy*] : CHORDOTOMY

trac·trix \'traktriks\ n, pl **tractri·ces** \trak'trī(,)sēz\ [NL, fr. L *tractus* (past part. of *trahere* to draw) + *-trix* — more at DRAW] : a curve in which the part of the tangent between the point of tangency and a given straight line is constant and which is an involute of a catenary

tracts *pl of* TRACT

tract society n : a society having as its aim the publication and distribution of religious tracts

trac·tus \'traktəs\ n, pl **tractus** [NL, fr. L, tract — more at TRACT] : TRACT 2b(2) — often used in combination ⟨~ solitarius⟩

trad *abbr* tradition; traditional

trad·able *also* **trade·able** \'trādəbəl\ *adj* : that can be traded

trad·al \'trādəl\ *adj* : COMMERCIAL

[1]trade \'trād\ n -S [ME, path, track, course of conduct, fr. MLG, path, track; akin to OS *trada* tread, track, OHG *trata* tread, track, course, OE *tredan* to tread — more at TREAD] **1 a** *obs* : a path traversed or for traverse : COURSE, WAY **b** *archaic* : a track or trail left by a man or animal : TREAD 1 ⟨some savage beast's ~ —Edmund Spenser⟩ **2 a** : a course of action or conduct : mode of procedure or life **b** : a customary course of action : HABIT, PRACTICE ⟨thy sin's not accidental, but a ~ —Shak.⟩ **3 a** : the business one practices or the work in which one engages regularly : one's calling : gainful employment : means of livelihood : OCCUPATION ⟨wherever a ... writer or any sort of artist is plying his ~ —C.E.Montague⟩ ⟨a doctor by ~ —*Times Lit. Supp.*⟩: as (1) : an occupation requiring manual or mechanical skill and training : a craft in which only skilled workers are employed ⟨the harness maker ... had learned his ~ after five years' service as an apprentice —Sherwood Anderson⟩ ⟨worked at the printer's ~ while preparing for the teaching profession⟩ ⟨a carpenter carrying the tools of his ~⟩ (2) : the occupation of a merchant (as a retail merchant) ⟨had demeaned herself a little, as the daughter of a doctor, by marrying into ~ ... when she married the matter-of-fact, industrious rising young cheese merchant —Florence Bullock⟩ ⟨English society ... preserved intact the distinction between ~ and gentility —G.H.Sabine⟩ **b** : a workman engaged in a trade ⟨mechanical ~s can move in as soon as ... sheets are placed —*Sweet's Catalog Service*⟩ **c** (1) : the group of persons engaged in a particular occupation, business, or industry ⟨as a member of the writing ~ —H.A. Smith⟩ ⟨the book and news ~ clearly oppose the adoption of a national censorship —*Publishers' Weekly*⟩ ⟨the word in the ~ is that May sales were not up to expectations —*Securities Outlook*⟩ (2) : a corporation, guild, union, or other organization of craftsmen in a Scottish burgh **4 a** (1) *archaic* : travel to and fro : coming and going (2) *obs* : dealings between persons or groups : INTERCOURSE ⟨have you any further ~ with us —Shak.⟩ (3) *dial* : FUSS, BOTHER **b** (1) : the business of buying and selling or bartering commodities : exchange of goods for convenience or profit : COMMERCE ⟨a materials shortage that affected first manufacturing, then ~⟩ : TRAFFIC ⟨a slump in the cotton ~⟩ ⟨laid off the new clerks when ~ was slack⟩ ⟨was doing a brisk ~ in umbrellas⟩ : MARKET ⟨souvenirs imported for the tourist ~⟩ ⟨children's books ... issued annually for the Christmas ~ —*Bookman's Glossary*⟩; *specif* : exchange of merchandise between different places on a large scale ⟨maritime nations for whom world ~ is an important source of income⟩ ⟨carried on ~ in tea and spices with the Orient⟩ ⟨a ship engaged in the coastwise ~⟩ (2) : commodities for barter ⟨salt ... which sold for 2 dollars cash per bushel, or 3 dollars in ~ —Andrew Ellicott⟩ (3) *archaic* : a trading expedition ⟨this new scheme of a ~ round the world —Daniel Defoe⟩ (4) : an act or instance of trading : TRANSACTION ⟨reported the ~ from the floor of the exchange⟩; *esp* : an exchange of property usu. without any use of money ⟨an even ~⟩ ⟨he's interested in making a ~ for another good pitcher —*N.Y.Times*⟩ ⟨repairing a car he had taken in ~⟩ (5) : a firm's customers : the clientele of a business ⟨a girl who waited on ~ in his father's shop —Sherwood Anderson⟩ ⟨sent notices to the ~ about the new location of the store⟩ ⟨a restaurant catering to the breakfast ~⟩ (6) : the group of firms or corporations engaged in a line of work : BUSINESS ⟨data reported for thirty-seven wholesale ~s —E.L.Smith⟩ : INDUSTRY ⟨in the rug and shawl ~s —C.M.Whittaker & C.C.Wilcock⟩ **5** *chiefly dial* **a** : STUFF; *specif* : FOODSTUFF ⟨all that ~ —Sir Walter Scott⟩ **b** : inferior matter or people : TRASH ⟨with beatings up ... by sailors and rough ~ —Gershon Legman⟩ **6** : TRADE WIND ⟨the steady drive of the ~ —Marjory S. Douglas⟩

[2]trade \"\ vb -ED/-ING/-S *vt* **1** *obs* : to make one's way along or through : TREAD, TRAVERSE, LEAD **2** *obs* **a** : to pursue constantly as a course, end, or occupation **b** : to use regularly or habitually ⟨the Greek language which then was the most *traded* ... through the whole universe —John Donne⟩ **c** : to bring to a state of practice, discipline, or familiarity : SCHOOL ⟨learned schoolmasters to ~ up the Christian youth in ... liberal arts —Thomas Becon⟩ **3** *archaic* : to resort to for trade : engage in trade with ⟨captain of a ship *trading* the Indies —Amy Lowell⟩ **4 a** (1) : to give in exchange for another commodity : BARTER ⟨the white men who penetrated to the ... wilds were always ready ... to ~ rifles and watches —J.F.Cooper⟩ ⟨stolen horses, which would only be sold or *traded* off ... hundreds of miles from home —J.F.Dobie⟩ (2) : to give in return : EXCHANGE ⟨reluctant to ~ the security and rewards of private life for the hazards ... and the low pay of government office —*Time*⟩ ⟨~ off the right to navigate the lower Mississippi for a slice of the Newfoundland fisheries —E.S.Corwin⟩ ⟨~ a proven pitcher to another team for four rookies⟩; *also* : to make an exchange of ⟨when parties ~ votes on certain bills on purely party grounds —G.H. Benton⟩ ⟨~ places with someone who likes to sit by open windows⟩ : exchange in give-and-take ⟨we *traded* shots and I got winged —Harvey Fergusson⟩ **b** : to buy and sell (as stock) regularly ⟨~ holdings at a good profit⟩ ~ *vi* **1 a** (1) *chiefly dial* : to make one's way : WALK, PASS, GO ⟨where be ye *trading* today —Thomas Hardy⟩ (2) : to pass to and fro : come and go — used esp. of birds ⟨a place ... over which the pigeons were *trading* between the stubbles and the wood —John Collier b. 1901⟩ **b** *obs* : to have dealings : NEGOTIATE ⟨would come and speak with him and ~ for a peace —Nicholas Lichefield⟩ **c** *archaic* : to occupy oneself : ENGAGE ⟨in private ... she *traded* more deeply in the occult sciences —Sir Walter Scott⟩ **2 a** : to go for purposes of trade ⟨all the vessels that ~ to or from the Red sea —Samuel Johnson⟩ **b** (1) : to engage in the exchange, purchase, or sale of goods or other property : carry on trade : do business for profit ⟨prohibits American firms from *trading* with the enemy⟩ ⟨a company is formed to ~ in building materials —Edward Jenks⟩ (2) : to buy and sell securities, real estate, or goods for quick profits rather than for long-term investment ⟨he likes the stock ... and he is accustomed to *trading* in and out of its shares —*A.B.C. of Puts & Calls*⟩ **c** : to deal in something not properly for sale : TRAFFIC — usu. used with *in* ⟨the chief justice ... *traded* largely in pardons —T.B.Macaulay⟩ **d** : to deal regularly or frequently as a customer ⟨~s only with merchants she knows⟩ : make one's purchases : SHOP ⟨~s at his store when she is in town⟩ **e** : to have a specified price in securities trading : SELL ⟨the common ~s around 15 —*Investor's Reader*⟩ **3** : to give one thing in return for another ⟨wanted to change his days off and got a friend to ~ with him⟩ : make an exchange ⟨wore each other's hat for a while and then *traded* back⟩ — **trade on** *also* **trade upon** : to take often unscrupulous advantage of : EXPLOIT ⟨*traded on* their influence ... in securing special favors for contractors —T.C.Pease⟩ ⟨individuals who attempt to *trade on* ... their social standing or their forebears —H.H.Arnold & I.C.Eaker⟩ ⟨the theater *trades on* a will to believe —Bernard DeVoto⟩ — **trade on the equity** : to use borrowed funds, bonds, or preferred stock in the operation of a company in order to augment profits for the common stockholder — compare LEVERAGE

[3]trade \"\ *adj* **1** : of or relating to trade ⟨~ channels⟩ ⟨~ statistics⟩ ⟨~ problems⟩ **2** : used in trade ⟨a ~ path⟩ ⟨a ~

ducat⟩ ⟨~ calendars⟩ ⟨~ catalogs of the mail-order houses⟩; *specif* **:** being merchandise for barter with primitive peoples usu. differing in material and form from the native product ⟨the relatively early displacement of native equipment by ~ goods —Eleanor Leacock⟩ ⟨~ tomahawks⟩ ⟨~ blankets⟩ **3 a :** intended for or limited to persons in business or industry rather than the general public ⟨a ~ fair⟩ ⟨a ~ show for film exhibitors⟩ ⟨a ~ price⟩ ⟨~ sales⟩ **b :** of, intended for, or used by people in a particular trade or occupation rather than the general public ⟨a ~ convention⟩ ⟨~ circles⟩ ⟨run ads in a ~ paper⟩ ⟨a ~ journal⟩ ⟨a ~ term not in most vocabularies⟩ **c :** that specializes in work for other craftsmen or concerns engaged in the same or a closely related business and that does not usu. deal directly with the ultimate user or consumer ⟨a ~ printing house⟩ ⟨a ~ compositor⟩ ⟨a ~ bindery⟩ **4 a** *also* **trades :** of, composed of, or representing the trades or trade unions ⟨a ~ club⟩ ⟨a ~ hall⟩ **b :** of, relating to, or training for a skilled manual or mechanical trade ⟨~ or professional work⟩ ⟨~ dictionaries⟩ ⟨~ students⟩ **5 :** of or associated with a trade wind ⟨the ~ belts⟩ ⟨~ clouds⟩

[4]**trade** \"\ *adv* [[1]*trade* (sense 2)] *archaic* **:** in a regular course **:** regularly and steadily in the same direction; *specif* **:** in the manner and direction of a trade wind ⟨the winds . . . seemed to be more steadily against us, blowing almost ~ —Daniel Defoe⟩

tradeable *var of* TRADABLE

trade acceptance *n* **:** a time draft or bill of exchange for the amount of a specific purchase drawn by the seller on the buyer, bearing the buyer's acceptance and often his specification of the place of payment (as a bank in which he has funds), and being negotiable when executed according to statute — compare BANK ACCEPTANCE

trade agreement *n* **1 :** an international agreement involving conditions of trade in goods and services **2 :** COLLECTIVE AGREEMENT

trade area *or* **trading area** *n* **:** a geographic area within which a business enterprise or center of retail or wholesale distribution draws most of its business ⟨the wholesale *trading area* for groceries of the city⟩ ⟨a department store's *trading area*⟩ ⟨the *trading area* of a shopping center⟩

trade association *n* **:** an association of tradesmen, businessmen, or manufacturers in a particular trade or industry for the protection and advancement of their common interests

trade balance *n* **:** BALANCE OF TRADE

trade bill *n* **:** a time draft or bill of exchange becoming a trade acceptance when signed by an acceptor

trade binding *n* **:** EDITION BINDING

trade board *n* **:** one of the former British official boards consisting of representatives from the employers and workers of an industry and neutral appointed members and charged with setting minimum wages for the industry

trade book *n* **1 :** a book intended for general readership ⟨a *trade book* . . . is not a juvenile, not a textbook, not a technical treatise, but the sort of thing that could (and the publisher hopes will) interest everybody —J.T.Winterich⟩ **2 :** TRADE EDITION

trade card *n, Brit* **:** BUSINESS CARD ⟨the *trade card* of an 18th century English instrument maker engraved with illustrations on a large sheet of paper⟩

trade coin *n* **:** a coin intended for use in foreign trade

trade commissioner *n* **:** a government official stationed in a foreign country and usu. subordinate in rank to a commercial attaché but with similar duties

trade council *also* **trades council** *n* **:** a central organization of local trade unions **:** a central labor union

trade cumulus *n* **:** a peculiar small detached cumulus cloud characteristic of trade-wind regions

trade cycle *n, Brit* **:** BUSINESS CYCLE

trade discount *n* **:** a percentage deduction from the list price of goods allowed by a manufacturer or wholesaler to customers engaged in trade

trade dollar *n* **:** a dollar issued as a trade coin; *esp* **:** the U. S. silver dollar weighing 420 grains .900 fine issued 1875–85 for use in oriental trade

trade down *vi* **:** to stock or purchase lower priced merchandise or property ⟨start the season with better goods and then *trade down* —*Women's Wear Daily*⟩

trade edition *n* **:** an edition of a book in a standard format intended for general distribution; *esp* **:** such an edition as contrasted with a deluxe or library-bound or paperback edition or sometimes with an edition published by a book club — compare TEXT EDITION, TRADE BOOK

trade fixture *n* **:** FIXTURE 2c(3)

trade·ful \ˈtrādfəl\ *adj* **:** full of trade **:** COMMERCIAL

trade gap *n* **:** the extent to which a country's imports during a period have exceeded its exports and have been obtained through gold shipments, the sale of foreign assets, or credit **:** an unfavorable balance of trade — compare DOLLAR GAP

trade guild *n* **1 :** a craft guild **2** *chiefly Brit* **:** TRADE UNION

trade in *vt* **:** to turn in as payment or part payment of a purchase or bill ⟨*trade* an old car *in* for a new one⟩

trade–in \ˈ=,=\ *n* -s [*trade in*] **:** an item of merchandise (as an automobile or refrigerator) taken as payment or part payment of a purchase

trade language *n* **:** a lingua franca (as a pidgin) used for trade

trade–last \ˈ=,=\ *n* -s **:** a complimentary remark by a third person that a hearer offers to repeat to the person complimented if the latter will first report a compliment made about the hearer — abbr. *T.L.*

trade·less \ˈtrādləs\ *adj* **:** having no trade

[1]**trademark** \ˈ=,=\ *n* **1 :** a word, letter, device, sound, or symbol or some combination of these that is used in connection with merchandise or service, distinctly points inherently or by association to the not necessarily known origin or ownership of that to which it is applied, and is legally reserved to the exclusive use of the owner according to statutory provisions **:** a name or symbol used by a maker or seller to identify distinctively his products ⟨sturdy display his ~ on his product for it to be legally valid⟩ ⟨a ~ can only be transferred in connection with the goodwill of the business —Edward Jenks⟩ — compare COPYRIGHT, SERVICE MARK **2 :** a distinctive feature, characteristic, or eccentricity that becomes so associated with a person or thing as to be a sign or designation of that person or thing **:** an identifying mark or feature ⟨the derringers . . . became almost a ~ of gamblers —Elmer Keith⟩

[2]**trademark** \"\ *vt* **1 :** to put or affix a trademark upon **:** label with a trademark **2 :** to secure trademark rights for **:** to register the trademark of

trademark infringement *n* **:** an appropriation or imitation that is likely to deceive ordinary or unwary buyers into accepting the goods of one trader as those of another — compare UNFAIR COMPETITION

[1]**trade name** *n* **1 a :** the name by which an article is called among traders ⟨blue vitriol, a common *trade name* for copper sulfate⟩ **b :** an invented or arbitrarily adopted name that is given by a manufacturer or merchant to an article or service to distinguish it as one produced or sold by him or is generally so used by purchasers and that may be used and protected as a trademark **2 :** the name or style under which a concern does business that will when it by association identifies a particular manufacturer or merchant be protected at common law against the use by others of a similar name which is calculated to deceive — compare UNFAIR COMPETITION

[2]**trade name** *vt* **:** to designate with a trade name

trade off *vi* **:** to exchange places with another or with each other at intervals **:** ALTERNATE ⟨*traded off* with each other several years for first place in the bowling tournament⟩ **~** *vt* **:** to use alternately ⟨*trade off* large and small brushes for rough and fine work⟩

trade practice *n* **:** a method of competition, operating policy (as the use of standards of size, shape, and quality of materials), or business procedure common to members of a line of business or industry that may be formally adopted sometimes as a rule under government auspices

trade publisher *n* **:** a publisher of trade books

trad·er \ˈtrādə(r)\ *n* -s **1 :** one that trades: **a :** a person whose business is buying and selling or barter **:** MERCHANT, DEALER ⟨a ~ to the East Indies⟩ **b :** a person who gets his livelihood by buying and selling for gain **c** (1) **:** one that buys and sells securities mainly for capital gains — often contrasted with *investor* (2) **:** an employee of a brokerage or investment house who actually executes orders either for customers or for the account of the house ⟨a government bond ~⟩ ⟨a bank stock ~⟩ **2** *obs* **:** PROSTITUTE **3 :** a ship engaged in the coasting or foreign trade

trade rat *n* [so called fr. its habit of replacing with some other article any article it takes away] **:** PACK RAT

trade route *n* **1 :** a route followed by traders (as in caravans) **2 :** one of the sea lanes ordinarily used by merchant ships

trad·er·ship \ˈtrādə(r),ship\ *n* **:** the position of a trader

trades *pl of* TRADE, *pres 3d sing of* TRADE

trad·es·can·tia \,tradə'skanch(ē)ə, -ntēə\ *n* [NL, fr. John *Tradescant* †1638 Eng. traveler and gardener + NL *-ia*] **1** *cap* **:** a genus of American herbs (family Commelinaceae) comprising the spiderworts and having mostly narrow elongated leaves and large white, pink, or violet ephemeral bracteate flowers **2** -s **:** any plant of the genus *Tradescantia* or of the related genus *Zebrina*

trade school *n* **:** a school usu. on the secondary level devoted esp. to teaching the practice and theory of skilled trades

trades council *var of* TRADE COUNCIL

trade secret *n* **:** a formula, pattern, process, or device that is used in one's business and that gives an advantage over competitors who do not know or use it

tradesfolk \ˈ=,=\ *n pl* **:** people in trade; *specif* **:** TRADESMEN

trades·man \ˈ=mən\ *n, pl* **tradesmen** [*trade's* (gen. of [1]*trade*) + *man*] **1 a :** one who trades **:** one who buys and sells things for a profit or means of living **:** SHOPKEEPER **b :** an employee of a shopkeeper **2 :** a workman in one of the skilled trades **:** ARTISAN, CRAFTSMAN

tradespeople \ˈ=,==\ *n pl* **:** TRADESMEN

trade test *n* **:** a test of proficiency in a given trade (as plumbing) standardized by obtaining norms for novices, apprentices, journeymen, and experts in the trade

trade union *also* **trades union** *n* **:** LABOR UNION; *specif* **:** one limited in membership to workmen engaged in the same trade rather than the same craft, company, or industry

trade–union \ˈ=ˈ==\ *adj* [*trade union*] **:** of or relating to trade unions or trade unionism

trade unionism *also* **trades unionism** *n* **:** the system or the principles and theory of trade unions or adherence to these principles **:** UNIONISM

trade unionist *n* **1 :** a member of a trade union **2 :** an advocate of trade unionism

trade up *vi* **:** to stock, promote the sale of, or purchase higher priced merchandise or property ⟨a big opportunity to *trade up* into higher price lines . . . is seen by Buffalo housedress buyers —*Women's Wear Daily*⟩ ⟨a certain percentage of the customers who come into a store . . . to buy the leader end by *trading up* and purchasing a higher-priced product —J.G.Lippincott⟩ ⟨a homeowner who wants to move or *trade up* —*Time*⟩ **~** *vt* **:** to persuade (a customer) to purchase a higher-priced item ⟨showing her the better garment . . . helps *trade* a good many of them *up* and out of the price bracket they had intended to stay within —*Dry Goods Jour.*⟩

tra·dev·man \trə'devmən\ *n, pl* **tradevmen** [*tra*ining *dev*ices *man*] **:** a petty officer in the U. S. Navy who installs, operates, maintains, and repairs training devices used esp. in gunnery, aviation, and electronics instruction

trade warranty *or* **trading warranty** *n* **:** a warranty in a marine insurance policy restricting the use of an insured ship to the type of cargo, the service (as the lake trade), and sometimes the season for which it was designed

trade waste *n, Brit* **:** an industrial waste

trade wind *n* [[4]*trade*] **:** a wind blowing almost constantly in one direction; *esp* **:** a wind that blows almost continually toward the equator from the northeast in the belt between the northern horse latitudes and the doldrums and from the southeast in the belt between the southern horse latitudes and the doldrums and is produced as a result of the rotation of the earth and movement of the air toward the equatorial regions during circulation between the warmer and colder portions of the earth — called also *trade;* compare ANTITRADES, MONSOON

trading *adj* **1 a :** engaged or used in trade ⟨Britons have been largely a ~ and industrial people —*Lamp*⟩ ⟨a ~ boat⟩ **b :** frequented by traders or purchasers ⟨a ~ center⟩ **2** *of an officeholder* **:** JOBBING, VENAL, CORRUPT

trading area *var of* TRADE AREA

trading bank *n, Austral* **:** COMMERCIAL BANK

trading card *n* **:** one of a collection of cards (as playing cards of different back designs) collected and traded esp. by children

trading company *n* **:** a company organized to carry on commerce with foreign nations or in overseas territories ⟨*trading companies* played an important part in the early settlement of America —O.M.Dickerson⟩: **a :** REGULATED COMPANY **b :** a joint stock company for trade and usu. colonization legally incorporated (as by the British Crown) under a charter granting the company rights to a specific territory within an area claimed by the authority granting the charter including legal title, a monopoly of trade, and governmental and military jurisdiction **c :** an unincorporated company with limited liability for its associates organized principally to settle and develop a land grant obtained from a legally incorporated company

trading estate *n, Brit* **:** INDUSTRIAL PARK

trading limit *n* **1 :** one of the prices above or below which trading on commodity exchanges is not allowed during any one day **2 :** a maximum number of contracts an individual is allowed to hold at one time in commodities covered by regulation

trading market *n* **:** a securities market without a definite price trend and with few traders other than professionals

trading post *n* **1 :** a station of a trader or trading company established in a sparsely settled region where trade in products of local origin is carried on with natives in exchange for goods they desire to purchase **2 :** [7]POST 4b

trading stamp *n* **:** a printed stamp of value given as a premium by a retail dealer to a customer and when accumulated in numbers redeemable in merchandise to be selected from a list of articles of various values — compare COUPON

tra·di·tion \trə'dishən\ *n* -s [ME *tradicion, tradicioun,* fr. MF & L; MF *tradition,* fr. L *tradition-, traditio* action of handing over, teaching, tradition — more at TREASON] **1 :** an act of delivering or surrendering something to another: as **a** *Roman, civil, & Scots law* **:** transfer or acquisition of property by mere delivery with intent of both parties to transfer the title in cases permitted by law (as in a sale or donation) **b :** the ecclesiastical offense committed by a traditor **2 :** the process of handing down information, opinions, beliefs, and customs by word of mouth or by example **:** transmission of knowledge and institutions through successive generations without written instruction ⟨a very different process from the ~ . . . which transmits culture from one generation of a society to another —A.L.Kroeber⟩ **3 :** an inherited or established way of thinking, feeling, or doing **:** a cultural feature (as an attitude, belief, custom, institution) preserved or evolved from the past ⟨a rebellious break with the ~s of their forebears⟩ **:** usage or custom rooted in the past (as of a family or nation) ⟨older universities rich in ~⟩: as **a** (1) **:** a doctrine or practice or a body of doctrine and practice preserved by oral transmission (2) **:** a belief or practice or the totality of beliefs and practices not derived directly from the Bible but arising and handed down within the Christian community orig. by oral transmission (3) *often cap* **:** a teaching of or the body of an unwritten code of Jewish law believed to have been given by God to Moses on Sinai and later reduced to writing in the Mishnah (4) *often cap, Islam* **:** HADITH **b :** a belief or story or a body of beliefs and stories relating to the past and commonly accepted as historical but not verifiable ⟨a ~ has grown up that it was put there by mistake —*Amer. Guide Series: Va.*⟩ ⟨portray beautiful old Japanese ~s, like the legend of the fisher . . . beloved by the Sea God's daughter —Lafcadio Hearn⟩ ⟨biographical details purporting to be based on family ~ —W.J. Ghent⟩ **c** (1) **:** an inherited principle, standard, or practice or body of principles, standards, and practices serving as the established guide of an individual or group ⟨held always to the religious and doctrinal ~s of his Puritan ancestry —T.D. Bacon⟩ ⟨the American ~ of democracy⟩ ⟨the company's ~ of safety⟩ ⟨the isolationist ~ still dominated American thought —H.H.Sprout⟩ **:** CONVENTION ⟨an old German theatrical ~ which allows you to start a quarter of an hour later than advertised —Barry Carman⟩ (2) **:** a literary or artistic rule or standard (as of theme, style, symbolism) or a body of such conventions normative for a period or group (as the followers of a great artist) ⟨followed the Arabic ~ of using no representations of living objects in their art —Edith Diehl⟩ ⟨the title poem . . . represents a complete break with nineteenth-century ~ —F.R.Leavis⟩ (3) **:** a technique or set of habits used in making the artifacts characteristic of a period or culture ⟨the flaked-flint ~⟩; *also* **:** the cultural continuity associated with such a tradition in a given region ⟨the Acheulean ~⟩ **d :** a practice or pattern of events of long standing **:** CUSTOM ⟨summer camps . . . are located by ~ on lakes —E.W.Smith⟩ ⟨the old ~ of the absence of the men from the village . . . is continued in modern times by soldiers and labor migrants —Mary Tew⟩ **e :** the manner characteristic of an individual group, or system **:** customary method or style — usu. used with *in* ⟨the movie . . . composed mainly in the British music-hall ~ —Roger Manvell⟩ ⟨the member companies . . . whoop it up for Douglas fir plywood in the best trade association ~ —*Monsanto Mag.*⟩ **4 :** a line of historical continuity or development marked by distinctive characteristics ⟨bred in the aristocratic ~⟩ ⟨psychiatry is an offshoot of the medical ~ —Edward Sapir⟩ ⟨the latter work . . . does not belong to the same manuscript ~ —Dorothy Robathan⟩ — often used with *in* ⟨in folk ~ singers almost invariably set new poems to tunes already in common use —S.P.Bayard⟩ **5 a :** cultural continuity embodied in a massive complex of evolving social attitudes, beliefs, conventions, and institutions rooted in the experience of the past and exerting an orienting and normative influence on the present ⟨a sense of ~⟩ **b :** the residual elements of past artistic styles or periods **6 :** the force exerted by the past upon the present **:** cultural inertia ⟨bound by family ~ in his choice of career⟩ ⟨resist political ~⟩ **7 :** something existing only in popular belief **:** inherited reputation or memory ⟨without social position save a ~ of gentility —Havelock Ellis⟩

tra·di·tion·al \-shən°l, -shnəl\ *adj* [ML *traditionalis,* fr. L *tradition-, traditis* tradition + *-alis* -al] **1 :** of or relating to tradition **:** consisting of or derived from tradition **:** handed down from age to age without writing ⟨~ history⟩ **2 :** following or conforming to tradition **:** based on an order, code, or practice accepted from the past **:** CONVENTIONAL ⟨~ morality⟩; *also* **:** observant of or holding to such traditions **:** TRADITIONALIST ⟨a ~ dramatist⟩ **3 :** designed with conscious adherence to architectural styles of the past — compare CONTEMPORARY, MODERN

tra·di·tion·al·ism \-shən°l,izəm, -shnə,li-\ *n* -s [F *traditionalisme,* fr. ML *traditionalis* traditional + F *-isme* -ism] **1 a :** the doctrines, principles, or practices of those who follow or accept tradition **b** *often cap* **:** the beliefs of those opposed to modernism, liberalism, radicalism **c :** FUNDAMENTALISM **2 :** orientation of a society toward old established values and institutions

tra·di·tion·al·ist \-shən°ləst, -shnəl-\ *n* -s [F *traditionaliste,* fr. *traditionalisme,* after such pairs as MF *athéisme* atheism: *athéiste* atheist] **:** one who adheres to or advocates adherence to tradition **:** a believer in or proponent of traditionalism — **tra·di·tion·al·is·tic** \trə¦dishən°l¦istik, -shnə¦li-, -tēk\ *adj*

tra·di·tion·al·i·ty \trə,dishə'naləd·ē\ *n* -es **:** TRADITIONALISM, CONVENTIONALITY

tra·di·tion·al·ize \trə'dishən°l,īz, -shnə,līz\ *vt* -ED/-ING/-S **:** to make traditional **:** imbue with traditions or traditionalism

traditional logic *n* **1 :** a system of formal logic mainly concerned with the syllogistic forms of deduction that is based on Aristotle and includes some of the changes and elaborations made by the Stoics and the Scholastics **:** ARISTOTELIAN LOGIC — compare IMMEDIATE INFERENCE, OPPOSITION, SUBJECT-PREDICATE, SYLLOGISM, SYMBOLIC LOGIC **2 :** inductive logic esp. as developed by Francis Bacon and J. S. Mill

tra·di·tion·al·ly \-n°lē, -nəlē, -i\ *adv* **1 :** in a traditional manner ⟨a modernistic interior contrasting with a ~ designed exterior⟩ **2 :** by tradition **:** CUSTOMARILY ⟨a district that ~ votes Republican⟩ **3 :** according to traditional belief ⟨~ claimed to be the poet's birthplace⟩

[1]**tra·di·tion·ary** \-shə,nerē, -ri\ *adj* **:** of the nature of a tradition **:** founded on or derived from tradition **:** full of traditions **:** TRADITIONAL ⟨a ~ dignity⟩ ⟨a ~ legend⟩

[2]**traditionary** \"\ *n* -ES **:** TRADITIONALIST

tra·di·tion·ate \-shə,nāt, *usu* -ād·+V\ *vt* -ED/-ING/-S **:** to indoctrinate with tradition

tra·di·tion·er \-sh(ə)nə(r)\ *n* -s **:** TRADITIONIST

tra·di·tion·ism \-shə,nizəm\ *n* -s **:** TRADITIONALISM

tra·di·tion·ist \-,nəst\ *n* -s **1 :** TRADITIONALIST **2 :** one versed in traditions **:** one who transmits a tradition

tradition·less \ˈ=ˈ==ləs\ *adj* **:** having no traditions

traditions *pl of* TRADITION

trad·i·tive \ˈtradəd·iv, -ətiv\ *adj* [prob. fr. obs. F, fem. of *traditif,* fr. L *traditus* (past part. of *tradere* to hand over) + F *-if* -ive — more at TRAITOR] **:** TRADITIONAL

trad·i·tor \ˈtradəd·ə(r)\ *n, pl* **tradito·res** \,tradə'tōr(,)ēz\ [ME *traditour* traitor, fr. L *traditor* — more at TRAITOR] **1** *obs* **:** TRAITOR **2 :** one of the Christians giving up to the officers of the law the Scriptures, the sacred vessels, or the names of their brethren during the Roman persecutions

tra·duce \trə'd(y)üs\ *vt* -ED/-ING/-S [L *traducere* to lead across, transfer, degrade, fr. *tra-, trans-* trans- + *ducere* to lead — more at TOW] **1 a** *obs* **:** to turn from one language or form into another **b :** to debase or pervert by translating **2 a :** to lower or disgrace the reputation of **:** expose to shame or blame by utterance of falsehood or misrepresentation ⟨feels that his country is being *traduced* and its war effort sneered at —Richard Watts⟩ **b :** to make mock of **:** VIOLATE, BETRAY ⟨is *traducing* our American principle of law that a man is presumed innocent until proven guilty —Agnes Meyer⟩ **syn** see MALIGN

tra·duce·ment *n* -s **:** an act of traducing

tra·duc·er \trə'd(y)üsə(r)\ *n* -s **:** one that traduces; *esp* **:** CALUMNIATOR

[1]**tra·du·cian** \-üshən\ *n* -s [ML *traducianus,* fr. *traduc-, tradux* heredity (fr. L, layer, layerage, fr. *traducere* to lead across) + L *-ianus* -ian] **:** a believer in traducianism

[2]**traducian** \"\ *adj* **:** of or relating to traducianism or traducians

tra·du·cian·ism \-ə,nizəm\ *n* -s [NL *traducianismus,* fr. ML *traducianus* + L *-ismus* -ism] **:** a theological doctrine that the human souls of new infants are generated from the souls of their parents at the moment of conception much in the same manner as the generation of human bodies — compare CREATIONISM, INFUSIONISM

tra·du·cian·ist \-ənəst\ *n* -s [NL *traducianista,* fr. ML *traducianus* traducian + L *-ista* -ist] **:** a believer in traducianism — **tra·du·cian·is·tic** \=¦=shə¦nistik\ *adj*

tra·duc·tion \trə'dəkshən\ *n* [LL *traduction-, tractio,* fr. L, act of transferring, fr. *traductus* (past part. of *traducere* to lead across, transfer) + *-ion-, -io* -ion] **1 :** the act or an instance of traducing; *specif* **:** an act of defaming **:** DEFAMATION, SLANDER **2 :** the repetition of a word or one of its derivatives or a term with a change in sense for rhetorical or argumentative effect **3** *obs* **:** something traduced; *esp* **:** TRADITION **4 :** logical inference in which premises and conclusion are of the same order of generality

tra·duc·tive \-ktiv\ *adj* [LL *traductivus,* fr. L *traductus* (past part.) + *-ivus* -ive] *archaic* **:** capable of being deduced **:** DERIVATIVE

traf *abbr* traffic

[1]**traf·fic** \ˈtrafik, -fēk\ *n* -s *often attrib* [MF *trafique,* fr. OIt *traffico,* fr. *trafficare*] **1 a :** commercial activity usu. involving import and export trade ⟨nurtured by land and water ~, it grew into a commercial center —*Amer. Guide Series: Ark.*⟩ **b :** the activity of exchanging commodities by bartering or buying and selling ⟨~ with the Indians, exchanging jewelry for horses⟩ ⟨perishable and livestock ~ . . . consigned to other than morning markets —*Farmer's Weekly (So. Africa)*⟩ ⟨middle classes . . . conducting the ~ by which they live —Agnes Repplier⟩ ⟨proud of his sung ~ in rich men's bonds, mortgages and deeds —Leo Marx⟩ **c :** illegal or disreputable usu. commercial activity ⟨a few such experiences sent him back to the narcotics ~ —Frank O'Leary⟩ ⟨~ in honors . . . and pardons was incessant —T.B.Macaulay⟩ ⟨evidence of Red ~

in contraband arms —*Wall Street Jour.*〉 〈prohibit transportation in interstate commerce for the white slave ~ —*Congressional Record*〉 **2 a :** communication or dealings between individuals or groups **:** INTERCOURSE, BUSINESS 〈held that there was no ~ between the human and the divine —John Buchan〉 〈realized for us in the three-hours ~ of the stage —J.I.M. Stewart〉 〈don't want any more ~ with his sort〉 〈for through our lively ~ all the day —W.H.Auden〉 **b :** reciprocal giving and receiving **:** EXCHANGE 〈facilitate a lively ~ in ideas —F.L. Allen〉 **3 a** *archaic* **:** GOODS 〈you'll see a draggled damsel . . . her fishy ~ bear —John Gay〉 **b traffics** *pl* **:** CARGO 〈move bulk ~*s* over long distances at reasonable speeds —P.E. Garbutt〉 **4 a** (1) **:** the circulation (as of vehicles or pedestrians) through an area **:** passage to and fro 〈flooring . . . suitable for light ~ —*Nat'l Fire Codes*〉 〈heavy lake ~ during the summer months〉 (2) **:** the flow of vehicles, pedestrians, ships, or planes (as along a street or sidewalk or air or sea lane) 〈will open a needed avenue . . . for passenger and freight ~ —M.M. Lilly & G.H.Kester〉 〈the full flood of the Christmas ~ —Compton Mackenzie〉 **b** (1) **:** the vehicles or pedestrians moving along a route 〈air and sea ~ will be notified —*Science*〉 〈construction of the building attracted the interest of sidewalk ~〉 (2) **:** the volume of vehicles or pedestrians moving along a route 〈engineers . . . who tabulate the ~ —A.W.Baum〉 **c** (1) **:** the information or signals transmitted or received over a communications system **:** MESSAGES 〈made arrangements for an interchange of ~ with other lines —H.W.Faulkner〉 (2) **:** the flow of messages or signals through a communications system 〈radio ~ has stepped up enormously —Pat Frank〉 **d :** the volume of customers visiting a business establishment 〈floor ~ in its showroom was up 60 percent —*Newsweek*〉 **5 a :** the number of passengers or amount of cargo carried by a transportation system 〈railroads handled more ~ than in the previous peak year —E.C.Helmreich〉 〈oceangoing passenger ~ —*Current Biog.*〉 **b :** the business of transporting passengers or freight 〈proposals . . . to get a proper share of international air ~ —C.H.Grattan〉 〈plans for a resurrected river ~ —*Amer. Guide Series: Minn.*〉 **6 :** TRAFFIC DEPARTMENT — **the traffic will bear :** existing conditions will allow or permit 〈their overhead is more than *the traffic will bear* —D.W.Brogan〉 〈getting all *the traffic will bear* —C.E.Wright〉 〈permitted to sell their surplus for whatever *the traffic will bear* —Joseph Wechsberg〉

²traffic \"\, *esp in pres part* -fək\ *also* **traf·fick** \"\ *vb* **trafficked; trafficked; trafficking; traffics** *also* **trafficks** [MF *trafiquer*, fr. OIt *trafficare*] *vi* **1 a :** to engage in commercial activity **:** buy and sell regularly **:** TRADE 〈got my living for a while by . . . *trafficking* in rabbit skins —Augusta Gregory〉 〈last of the impresarios . . . who *trafficked* in art in the grand manner —Bernard Simon〉 **b :** to engage in illegal or disreputable business or activity 〈began to ~ in army promotions —Geoffrey Bruun〉 **2 :** to carry on communication or negotiation **:** DEAL, BARGAIN 〈will not ~ with the breakers of the peace —H.S.Truman〉 〈convinced himself . . . the child was *trafficking* with bards, or druids, or witches —W.B.Yeats〉 **3 :** to concentrate one's effort or interest **:** SPECIALIZE 〈virtuoso soloists . . . continue to ~ in the well-worn favorites —Lawrence Morton〉 〈characteristic of a medium which ~*s* in comedy extremes —*Newsweek*〉 **4 :** to pass to and fro **:** WANDER 〈spilled out of their houses to laugh and ~ along its . . . streets —Lucy Embury〉 **~** *vt* **1 :** to journey over **:** TRAVEL 〈most heavily *trafficked* highway in the state —*Amer. Guide Series: Vt.*〉 〈venture to ~ them in the day, but few would risk such perilous thoroughfares by night —F.S.Merryweather〉 **2 :** to make an exchange of **:** TRADE, BARTER 〈pies and cakes being *trafficked* back and forth across the street —Arthur Miller〉

traf·fic·abil·i·ty \ˌtrafikəˈbiləd·ē\ *n* **1 :** the quality of a terrain to permit passage (as of vehicles and troops) 〈areas of low ~ and . . . beaches with steep gradients —J.F.Shaw〉 **2 :** the ability of a military force to move over a terrain 〈our failure to develop full cross-country ~ —*Combat Forces Jour.*〉

traf·fic·able \ˈtrafikəbəl\ *adj* [²*traffic* + *-able*] **1 :** suitable for trading **:** used in trade **:** MARKETABLE 〈required what may be called ~ material —Alexander Somerville〉 **2 :** open to traffic **:** PASSABLE 〈related . . . development to population and ~ roads —*Geog. Jour.*〉

traf·fi·ca·tor \ˈtrafəˌkād·ə(r\ *n* -s [blend of ¹*traffic* and *indicator*] *Brit* **:** a movable directional signal on a vehicle

traffic block *n, Brit* **:** TRAFFIC JAM

traffic circle *n* **:** ROTARY 2

traffic cone *n* **:** a conical marker used on a road or highway (as for indicating an area under repair)

traffic cop *n* **:** a policeman who regulates the movement of traffic 〈need a *traffic cop* at the intersection during rush hour〉

traffic court *n* **:** a minor court for disposition of petty prosecutions for violations of statutes, ordinances, and local regulations governing the use of highways and motor vehicles

traffic density *n* **:** DENSITY OF FREIGHT TRAFFIC

traffic department *n* **:** a department in a company or agency that supervises any of various operations (as sales, transportation, public relations, or the maintaining of production schedules)

traffic divider *n* **:** a barrier (as a guardrail, fence, or concrete wall) placed between the lanes of a highway to divide the traffic moving in opposite directions

traffic engineer *n* **:** an engineer whose training or occupation is traffic engineering

traffic engineering *n* **:** a branch of highway engineering dealing with the planning and design of streets and highways and the safe, economical, and convenient control of traffic

traffic island *n* **:** a paved or planted island in a roadway designed to guide the flow of traffic; *also* **:** MEDIAN STRIP

traffic jam *n* **:** a jamming up (as of vehicular traffic) into a disorganized standstill 〈the detour caused a *traffic jam* full of cursing honking drivers〉

traf·fick·er \ˈtrafikə(r), -fēk-\ *n* -s **:** one that traffics: **a :** NEGOTIATOR, SCHEMER 〈whole clan of . . . spies and ~*s* —R.L. Stevenson〉 **b :** MERCHANT, DEALER 〈groups of ~*s* who . . . made a market of their wares —Gilbert Parker〉 〈a ~ in ideas —Ellery Sedgwick〉

traffic lane *n* **:** LANE 3c

traffic management *n* **:** the management of the physical and cost-control phases of the receiving, handling, storing, and distributing of goods for industrial and commercial organizations

traffic manager *n* **1 :** an officer of the freight or passenger traffic department of a transport carrier who has charge of traffic solicitation, determination of rates and fares, and related traffic functions **2 :** a supervisor of the traffic functions of a commercial or industrial organization **3 :** the director of a large telegraph office

traffic pattern *n* **:** PATTERN 12

traffic sign *n* **:** a sign usu. on the side of a street or highway bearing symbols or words of warning or direction to motorists or pedestrians and often having a characteristic shape — compare STOP SIGN

traffic signal *or* **traffic light** *also* **traffic control signal** *n* **:** a usu. electrically operated signal (as a system of colored lights) for warning and controlling traffic 〈a car racing its motor, waiting for the *traffic signal* to turn green〉 — compare WIGWAG SIGNAL

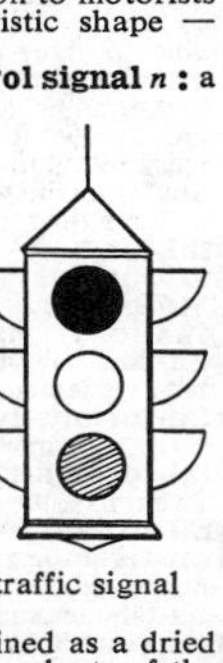

traffic signal

traffic unit *n* **:** a statistical unit combining ton-miles and passenger-miles and used by transportation agencies (as railroads, bus lines, airlines) in measuring the volume of passenger and freight traffic

trafficway \ˈ==ˌ=\ *n* **1 :** RIGHT OF WAY 2b **2 a :** a roadway open to traffic **b :** HIGHWAY

trag *abbr* tragedian; tragedy; tragic

trag·a·canth \ˈtrajəˌkan(t)th, -ˌkaa(ə)n- *also* -kən- *sometimes* -agə(ˌ)k- *or* -agə- *or* -gə(ˌ)s-\ *n* -s [MF *tragacanthe, tragacanth*, fr. L *tragacantha*, fr. Gk *tragakantha*, fr. *tragos* he-goat + *akantha* thorn — more at TRAGEDY, ACANTH-] **1 :** a gum that is obtained as a dried exudate from various Asiatic or East European plants of the genus *Astragalus* (esp. *A. gummifer*), that is constituted of bassorin and tragacanthin, that swells in water to a gel, and that is used chiefly as an emulsifying, suspending, and thickening agent and also as a demulcent and excipient for pills **2 :** a plant yielding tragacanth

trag·a·can·thin \ˌ==ˈk|an(t)thən, ˌ==ˈs|, |aan(-\ *n* -s **:** a substance obtained from tragacanth that is soluble in water forming a hydrosol — compare BASSORIN

tra·gal \ˈtrāgəl\ *adj* [NL *tragus* + E *-al*] **:** of or relating to the tragus

tra·ge·di·an \trəˈjēdēən\ *n* -s [ME *tragedien*, fr. MF, fr. *tragedie* + *-en* -an] **1 :** a writer of tragedies **2 :** an actor of tragedy; *esp* **:** one who specializes in tragic roles

tra·ge·di·enne \trəˌjēdēˈen\ *n* -s [F *tragédienne*, fr. MF *tragedienne*, fem. of *tragedien*] **:** an actress who specializes in tragic roles

trag·e·dize \ˈtrajəˌdīz\ *vt* -ED/-ING/-S [*tragedy* + *-ize*] *archaic* **:** to dramatize as a tragedy **:** make tragic

trag·e·dy \ˈtrajədē, -di\ *n* -ES [ME *tragedie*, fr. MF, fr. L *tragoedia*, fr. Gk *tragōidia*, fr. *tragos* he-goat + *-ōidia* (fr. *aeidein* to sing); prob. fr. the ancient Greek tragedy's having been influenced by the Peloponnesian satyr play, in which the satyrs were represented as goatlike rather than horselike creatures; akin to Gk *trōgein* to gnaw —more at ODE, TERSE] **1 a :** a medieval narrative poem or tale (as Chaucer's *Troilus and Criseyde*) typically describing the downfall of a great man **b** (1) **:** a drama in verse or prose and of serious and dignified character that typically describes the development of a conflict between the protagonist and a superior force (as destiny, circumstance, society) and reaches a sorrowful or disastrous conclusion that excites pity or terror 〈in the classical ~ the solution was death —Domenico Vittorini〉 — compare CATHARSIS, COMEDY (2) **:** a nondramatic work (as a novel) that resembles a tragic drama in character, development, and conclusion 〈forcing the rhetoric of his ~ . . . in the final pages most painfully —Vernon Young〉 **c :** an ancient Greek lyric poem sung by a chorus **d :** a literary genre consisting of tragic dramas 〈relies upon the Aristotelian account of ~ —Cleanth Brooks & R.B.Heilman〉 〈the study of ~ is the study of men at their best —G.K.Chalmers〉 **2 a** (1) **:** a disastrous often fatal event or series of events **:** CALAMITY 〈got back . . . to find myself in the midst of ~ —H.J.Laski〉 〈the scene of some of our most sickening road *tragedies* —Priscilla Hughes〉 〈revealed the evidence of a ~ of long ago —W.E.Swinton〉 (2) **:** an unfortunate, sad, or discouraging occurrence or situation **:** bad luck **:** unhappy fate **:** MISFORTUNE 〈the plight of these people is a human ~ which wrings the heart —H.G. Rickover〉 〈a ~ that this rich . . . corner of the state has been so sadly neglected —*Sydney* (*Australia*) *Bull.*〉 〈the ~ of plain women; to be valued, but not loved —Mary Austin〉 **b :** an unqualified failure **:** FLOP, DISASTER 〈the one architectural ~ on the university grounds —*Amer. Guide Series: Va.*〉 〈last night's party was a ~〉 **3** *obs* **:** LAMENTATION, JEREMIAD 〈I wail, and make my woes a ~ —Edmund Spenser〉 **4 :** the tragic quality or element 〈comprehension of the ~ of life as well as of its warmth and humor —*Current Biog.*〉

trag·e·laph \ˈtrajəˌlaf\ *n* -s [NL *Tragelaphus*] **:** an antelope of *Strepsiceros* or a related genus

tra·gel·a·phine \trəˈjeləˌfīn, -ˌfən\ *adj* [NL *Tragelaphus* + E *-ine*] **:** belonging or related to or typical of the genus *Strepsiceros* 〈~ antelopes〉 〈peculiarities of ~ anatomy〉

tra·gel·a·phus \-ˌfəs\ [NL, fr. L, a kind of antelope, fr. Gk *tragelaphos*, fr. *tragos* he-goat + *elaphos* deer — more at TRAGEDY, ELK] *syn of* STREPSICEROS

tragi *pl of* TRAGUS

¹trag·ic \ˈtrajik, -jēk\ *adj* [L *tragicus*, fr. Gk *tragikos* of a he-goat, of tragedy, fr. *tragos* he-goat + *-ikos* -ic] **1 :** of, marked by, or expressive of tragedy **:** DISASTROUS, FEARFUL 〈life will necessarily contain a ~ element —M.R.Cohen〉 〈witnessed many uneasy, wakeful . . . even ~ nights —Walter de la Mare〉 〈realize the ~ significance of the atomic bomb —H.S.Truman〉 **2 a :** dealing with or treated in narrative or dramatic tragedy 〈differentiates ~ fiction from the merely pathetic —Howard M. Jones〉 〈conceptions of the ~ hero —W.H.Auden〉 **b :** appropriate to or typical of dramatic tragedy 〈to be truly ~ . . . a plot must do more than bring . . . emotions to a head —B.A.G.Fuller〉 〈the ~ predicament of a mortal creature with immortal longings —Irwin Edman〉 **c :** composing or acting in tragedies 〈the Greek ~ poets〉 〈a notable ~ actress〉 **3 a :** saddeningly or regrettably serious or unpleasant **:** DEPLORABLE, LAMENTABLE 〈passionate and ~ sense of life —H.M.McLuhan〉 〈a . . . ~ symptom of our times that diplomats do punch nightclub girls —John Lardner〉 **b** (1) **:** marked by a sense of tragedy or pessimism 〈his account . . . is deeply ~ —Lionel Trilling〉 〈a ~ reading of history —F.L.Baumer〉 (2) **:** arousing feelings of melancholy **:** POIGNANT 〈the ~ peace of the long evening —Ellen Glasgow〉 〈a ~ little group of serious and gentle lads —W.E.Leonard〉

²tragic \"\ *n* -s **1** *archaic* **:** a writer of tragedy **2 :** a tragic quality or element 〈the ~ in life and art〉; *specif* **:** the aesthetic quality in tragic drama that excites emotions of pity and terror in the beholder — compare CATHARSIS 2a

trag·i·cal \-jəkəl, -jēk-\ *adj* [L *tragicus* + E *-al*] **:** TRAGIC 〈his subjects are frequently ~, sometimes shocking —Richard Garnett †1906〉 〈raised a hand in ~ dismissal —Rafael Sabatini〉 — **trag·i·cal·ness** *n* -ES

trag·i·cal·ly \-k(ə)lē, -li\ *adv* **1 :** in a tragic manner 〈ridiculously and ~ identifies his passion for her —Edmund Wilson〉 **2 :** to an unfortunate or disastrous degree **:** REGRETTABLY, WOEFULLY 〈died at a ~ early age —*Times Lit. Supp.*〉 〈was soon ~ evident that the cancer of totalitarianism was . . . spreading —Richard Hunt〉

tragic flaw *n* **:** a flaw in the character of the hero of a tragedy that brings about his downfall 〈the Oedipean *tragic flaw* is pride〉

tragi·comedy \ˌtrajə+\ *n* [MF *tragicomedie*, fr. OIt *tragicomedia*, fr. OSp, fr. L *tragicocomoedia, tragicomoedia*, fr. *tragicus* tragic + *comoedia* comedy — more at COMEDY] **1 a** (1) **:** a literary genre consisting of dramas that combine tragic and comic elements with the tragic predominating 〈Elizabethan ~ is . . . a subdivision of the larger classification, serious drama —P.W.Barber〉 (2) **:** a drama of this genre **b :** the tragicomic quality or element 〈some of the ~ remains and is the best thing in the film —*Time*〉 **2 :** an event or situation having both serious and comic aspects 〈the ~ of federal politics〉

tragi·comic \"+\ *adj* [¹*tragic* + *comic*] **1 a :** of, relating to, or having the characteristics of tragicomedy 〈a playwright specializing in ~ drama〉 **b :** manifesting both tragic and comic aspects 〈the ~ disparity . . . between man's aspirations and his accomplishments —B.R.Redman〉 **2 :** marked by both pathetic and ludicrous characteristics 〈a ~ character . . . an obscure and fatheaded young man —H.A.Smith〉

tragi·comical \"+\ *adj* [*tragic* + *comical*] **:** TRAGICOMIC 〈the girl's life . . . presented itself to me as a ~ adventure —Joseph Conrad〉 — **tragi·comically** \"+\ *adv*

trag·i·on \ˈtrajēˌän\ *n* -s [NL, fr. L *tragus* + Gk *-ion*, dim. suffix] **:** an anthropometric point in the notch of the tragus of the ear

trag·o·pan \ˈtragəˌpan\ *n* [NL, fr. L, a kind of vulture, fr. Gk *tragopan*, fr. *tragos* he-goat + *Pan*, ancient Greek god of woods and shepherds — more at TRAGEDY] **1** *cap* **:** a genus of brilliantly colored Asiatic pheasants having the back and breast covered usu. with white or buff ocelli and the head in the male ornamented with two bright-colored wattles and a pair of fleshy erectile horns — see CRIMSON TRAGOPAN **2** -s **:** any bird of the genus *Tragopan*

trago·po·gon \ˌtragəˈpōˌgän, -ōgən\ *n, cap* [NL, fr. L, salsify, fr. Gk *tragopōgōn*, fr. *tragos* he-goat + *pōgōn* beard; fr. the large pappus — more at -POGON] **:** a genus of Old World herbs (family Compositae) having entire linear leaves and long pedunculate heads of yellow or purple radiate flowers with a single series of involucral bracts — see SALSIFY, YELLOW GOATSBEARD

trag·ule \ˈtra(ˌ)gyül\ *n* -s [NL *Tragulus*] **:** CHEVROTAIN

¹trag·u·lid \ˈtragyələd\ *adj* [NL *Tragulidae*] **:** of or relating to the Tragulidae

²tragulid \"\ *n* -s **:** a mammal of the family Tragulidae **:** CHEVROTAIN

tra·gu·li·dae \trəˈgyüləˌdē\ *n pl, cap* [NL, fr. *Tragulus*, type genus + *-idae*] **:** a family of ruminant mammals (division Tragulina) comprising the chevrotains (as the kanchils, napus, and water chevrotain)

trag·u·li·na \ˌtragyəˈlīnə, -lēnə\ *n pl, cap* [NL, fr. *Tragulus* + *-ina*] **:** a division of Ruminantia comprising the chevrotains and extinct related forms — **trag·u·line** \ˈtragyəˌlīn, -ˌlēn, -lən\ *adj*

trag·u·loid \ˈtragyəˌlȯid\ *adj* [NL *Traguloidea*] **:** of or relating to the Traguloidea

¹trag·u·loi·dea \ˌtragyəˈlȯidēə\ [NL, fr. *Tragulus* + *-oidea*] *syn of* TRAGULINA

²traguloidea \"\ *n pl, cap* [NL, fr. *Tragulus* + *-oidea*] *in some classifications* **:** a division of Tragulina comprising the chevrotains and a few related forms

trag·u·lus \ˈtragyələs\ *n, cap* [NL, fr. Gk *tragos* he-goat + L *-ulus*, dim. suffix] **:** a genus (the type of the family Tragulidae) comprising the typical chevrotains

tra·gus \ˈtrāgəs\ *n, pl* **tragi** [NL, fr. Gk *tragos*, a part of the ear, lit., he-goat — more at TRAGEDY] **1 :** the prominence in front of the external opening of the ear **2 :** one of the hairs of the external auditory meatus

traik \ˈtrāk\ *vi* [origin unknown] *Scot* **:** to fall ill **:** break down

¹trail \ˈtrāl, *esp before pause or consonant* -āəl\ *vb* -ED/-ING/-S [ME *trailen*, fr. MF *trailler* to tow, fr. (assumed) VL *tragulare*, fr. L *tragula* dragnet, sledge; prob. akin to L *trahere* to pull, draw, drag — more at DRAW] *vi* **1 a :** to hang down so as to drag along a surface **:** sweep the ground 〈letting the flag ~ in the dust〉 〈my silken outer garment ~*ed* over withered leaves —Amy Lowell〉 〈his hand hit the wall and ~*ed* down it as he fell —Raymond Chandler〉 **b :** to hang so as to touch or pile up on a surface 〈the tablecloth ~*s* on the floor〉 **c :** to hang or extend over a surface loosely or stragglingly 〈no one looks right now with locks ~*ing* over one eye —*Country Life*〉 **d :** to hang or extend so as to float freely or loosely 〈would rather stroke faster with their arms and let their legs ~ —T.M. McDermott〉 〈allowing one of the propellers to ~, thereby reducing the drag on that side of the ship —*Manual of Seamanship*〉 **e :** to grow to such length as to droop over or rest upon the ground **:** spread and root extensively **:** CREEP 3c — used of a plant 〈knew where the first arbutus ~*ed* in the spring —Grace Metalious〉 **2 a :** to walk or proceed draggingly, heavily, or wearily **:** PLOD, TRUDGE 〈~*ed* along at a snail's pace〉 〈~*ed* dismally round his grounds praising the improvements —Virginia Woolf〉 **b :** to follow unthinkingly as if led or pulled along 〈his sister ~*ed* along after him —James Hensel〉 **c** (1) **:** to lag behind **:** do poorly in relation to others (as in a contest) **:** LOSE 〈bet on a horse that ~*ed* all the way and finished last〉 〈~*ing* in the election with only 30 percent of the vote〉 (2) *of a harness race driver* **:** to take a position behind the lead horse using him to set the pace and break the force of the wind **d** *archaic* **:** to fish by drawing the line along the water from a moving boat **:** TROLL **3 :** to move, flow, or extend slowly and esp. in thin or vaporous streams or spirals **:** DRIFT 〈blood ~*ing* over the floor〉 〈smoke ~*ing* from chimneys〉 〈a thin veil of mist ~*ed* below —John Connell〉 〈shadows o'er the landscape ~*ing* —H.W.Longfellow〉 **4 a :** to extend in an erratic or uneven course or line **:** STRAGGLE 〈stone walls ~ raggedly through the woods —*Amer. Guide Series: Vt.*〉 〈ropes ~ in loops and tangles across the slanting deck —*Phoenix Flame*〉 **b :** to wander (as from course, aim, or original character) so as to become weak, pointless, or ineffectual **:** DWINDLE — usu. used with *off* or *away* 〈the discussion ~*ed off* into futilities〉 〈voice ~*ing* off to a whisper —T.B.Costain〉 〈his book rather ~*s* away at the close —Allan Nevins〉 **5 :** to follow a trail **:** track game 〈spent long days ~*ing* over the desert〉 〈can . . . ~ like an Indian —W.P.Webb〉 **6 :** to play a card in casino without building or taking **7 :** to tour with a trailer carrying camping supplies or providing living accommodations 〈the art of ~*ing* lies in being away from the trailer as much as possible —*New Statesman & Nation*〉 **~** *vt* **1 a :** to draw or drag (as a garment) along a surface **:** allow to sweep the ground **:** DRAGGLE 〈when women ~*ed* long skirts through the dust —Justina Hill〉 **b :** to hold or carry so as to draw an end or part along a surface **:** DRAG 〈~ a log down a slope〉 〈~ a line in fishing〉 〈the winning crew ~*ed* their oars in salute〉 〈passing the marble table, she ~*ed* her aging fingertips across its mute surface —Harriet La Barre〉 **c :** to drag along by force **:** HALE 〈they shall not ~ me through their streets —John Milton〉 **d :** PULL, HAUL, TOW 〈~ the wagons of an overland train〉 **e :** to carry (as a firearm, pike, or lance) at the position of trail arms 〈~ arms at a military funeral〉 **2 a :** to drag heavily or wearily (as a limb or the body) 〈moved slowly, ~*ing* his wounded foot〉 **b :** to carry or bring along as an addition, burden, or encumbrance 〈always ~*s* along two or three uninvited friends〉 〈a dog ~*ing* a leash〉 〈stepped off the train still ~*ing* a little sand —Sybille Bedford〉 **c :** to draw along in one's wake 〈~*ing* clouds of glory do we come —William Wordsworth〉 〈~*ed* streamers of gray mist up the valley —Francis Ratcliffe〉 **d :** to draw or stretch out (as an utterance, discussion, or affair) **:** PROTRACT 〈no point in ~*ing* the business out any longer〉 **3 :** to adorn (as pottery) with a trailing pattern or ornament (as of tracery) **4 a :** to follow upon the scent or trace of **:** TRACK, HUNT 〈~*ed* the beast to its lair〉 〈had to ~ the suspect halfway across the country〉 **b :** to follow in the footsteps of **:** PURSUE, SHADOW 〈reporters ~*ing* him constantly〉 〈not daring to accost him . . . she had ~*ed* him to the railroad station —D.B.Chidsey〉 **c :** to follow along behind (as a person) 〈being careful always to ~ the queen at the prescribed distance〉 **d :** to play a bowl in lawn bowling so as to strike and carry (the jack) backward **e :** to lag behind (as others in a competition) 〈always ~*s* his classmates〉 〈~*ing* the league-leading team by two and a half games〉 〈~*ed* the other candidates on the ticket〉 **5 :** to urge (livestock) along (as from a summer to a winter range) 〈herders ~*ing* longhorns up from Texas —R.F.Adams〉 **syn** see FOLLOW — **trail a pike :** to serve as a soldier 〈*trailed a pike* in the Low Countries in the 1590s〉 — **trail one's coat** *or* **trail one's coattails :** to invite a quarrel by provoking argument or dissent

²trail \"\ *n* -s [ME, fr. *trailen*, v.] **1 a :** something that trails or is trailed: as (1) **:** a trailing plant 〈ivy had sent ~*s* down the steep banks —Flora Thompson〉 (2) **:** a running ornament representing leaves or tendrils (as in Gothic moldings) (3) **:** a trailing arrangement (as of flowers) **:** SPRAY 〈wore white roses on the shoulder — a ~, not a bunch —Clemence Dane〉 (4) **:** the rear part of a gun carriage that rests on the ground when the piece is unlimbered (5) **:** a flattened anterior prolongation of the shell of various brachiopods **b :** TRAIL ARMS — used in the phrases *at the trail* and *at trail* **2 a :** something that follows or moves along in or as if in a path or wake or as if being drawn along **:** TRAIN 〈the academic procession in a long ~〉 〈a ~ of clouds〉 〈a ~ of admirers〉 〈rocket ~*s*〉 〈smoke in thin blue ~*s* was coming from the brick chimneys —Calder Willingham〉 **b** (1) **:** the transitory luminous streak in the sky produced by the passage of a meteor (2) **:** a continuous line produced photographically by permitting the image of a celestial body (as a star) to move over the plate **c :** a chain of consequences **:** AFTERMATH 〈the . . . movement left a ~ of bitterness and prejudice behind it —Paul Blanshard〉 **3 a :** a trace or mark left by something that has passed or been drawn or dragged along **:** SCENT, SPOOR, TRACK 〈hounds picking up the ~〉 〈a ~ of blood from the house to the barn〉 〈got on the ~ of the killer〉 〈discovered a rattlesnake ~ in the sand —Jack Kerouac〉 **b :** SKIDDING TRAIL **c** (1) **:** a track made by passage (as through a wilderness or wild region) **:** a beaten path 〈an Indian ~〉 〈a deer ~〉 〈tortuous mountain ~*s*〉 〈wagon ~*s*〉 〈the era of the cattle ~*s*〉 〈stamping a ~ through the deep snow〉 (2) **:** a blazed or otherwise marked path through a forest or mountainous region 〈woodland ~*s*〉 〈the state provides a 300-mile ~ for those enjoying walking trips〉 (3) **:** a road or highway approximately following an historic trail or series of trails (as of Indians or pioneers) 〈the Mohawk *Trail*〉 **d :** SLOPE 1b **e :** a course followed or to be followed **:** ROUTE 〈a milestone on his educational ~〉 〈candidates hitting the campaign ~〉 **4 :** the horizontal distance from the point of impact of a bomb dropped from a moving airplane to a vertical line from the airplane at the instant of impact — **in trail** *adv* **:** in single file **:** one behind the other 〈planes flying *in trail*〉 〈the party had marched *in trail* —Thomas Hardy〉

³trail \"\ *n* -s [short for *entrail*] *archaic* **:** ENTRAIL 1; *esp* **:** the intestines of an animal (as a game bird or fish) served as food 〈the thrush is presented with the ~ —Tobias Smollett〉

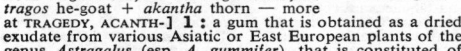

t rail *n, cap T* **:** a rail having a head, a web, and a flat flange base so that a section resembles the letter T — called also *Vignoles rail*

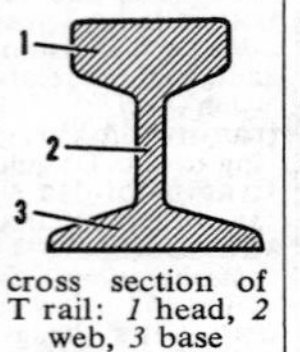

cross section of T rail: *1* head, *2* web, *3* base

trail angle *n* **:** the angle between the trail sight and a vertical line from an airplane drawn at the instant of impact of a bomb dropped from the airplane
trail arms *n pl but sing in constr* [fr. the imperative phrase *trail arms*] **:** a position in military drill in which a rifle butt is raised a few inches from the ground and the muzzle inclined forward so that the barrel makes an angle of about 30 degrees with the vertical — often used as a command
trailblazer \ˈ=,==\ *n* **1 :** one that blazes a trail to guide others through a wilderness or unknown country **:** PATHFINDER ⟨the . . . valley began to echo with the thud of the ∼'s ax —*Amer. Guide Series: Mich.*⟩ **2 :** one that discovers or tries out a new way (as of doing something) **:** PIONEER ⟨the ∼*s*, the setters of new patterns in business —Frieda Curtis⟩
trailblazing \ˈ=,==\ *adj* **:** making or pointing a new way **:** PATHBREAKING ⟨a ∼ experiment⟩ ⟨a unique and ∼ effort in coordinated . . . techniques —Paul Fejos⟩
trail board *n* **:** one of the curved and carved boards on the sides of the cutwater near the figurehead of a ship
trail boss *n, West* **:** one in charge of a trail herd ⟨the *trail boss* put three hands in front to hold the leaders back —S.E. Fletcher⟩
trailbreaker \ˈ=,==\ *n* **:** TRAILBLAZER
trail bridge *or* **trail ferry** *n* **:** a boat or raft attached to a pulley running on a rope stretched across a stream and moved from side to side by the action of the current
trail car *n* **:** TRAILER 4a
trail cutter *n* **:** a cowboy who breaks through a moving herd of cattle to search for strays
trailed *past of* TRAIL
¹trail·er \ˈtrālə(r)\ *n* -s [¹*trail* + *-er*] **1 :** one that trails or follows a trail: as **a :** one that tracks **:** HUNTER ⟨a master shot, a ∼ who was a match for any Apache —Stanley Walker⟩ **b :** one that travels over a trail ⟨the ∼*s* of yesterday . . . inscribed names and dates —A.B.Guthrie⟩ **2 :** something that trails or touches the ground in moving or hanging: as **a :** a trailing plant **:** CREEPER **3 b :** TRAILING WHEEL **c :** a sprag to prevent a vehicle from running backward **3 :** one that trails, follows, or lags behind: as **a :** a hunting dog that yields the initiative to its bracemate **b :** a player in various goal games (as hockey, basketball, or soccer) that follows closely a teammate who is dribbling the puck or ball **c** (1) **:** a short motion-picture film made up of snatches from a feature picture and displayed in advance for advertising purposes (2) **:** a short film shown for the purpose of making an announcement to the theater audience (3) **:** a short length of blank film attached to the finish end of a reel so that the film will continue to feed through the projector mechanism after the light and sound are turned off — compare LEADER 1m **d :** music played for the close or fade-out of a performance (as of a theatrical skit or a film) ⟨for my last ∼, I'll use *Only a Rose* —Gypsy Lee⟩ **4 :** a vehicle or one in a succession of vehicles hauled usu. by some other vehicle: as **a :** a car on a streetcar line pulled by another car **b :** a light 2-wheeled car pulled (as by a bicycle or motorcycle) **c :** a nonautomotive highway or industrial-plant vehicle designed to be hauled (as by a tractor, motor ruck, or passenger automobile) ⟨flatbed ∼⟩ ⟨truck ∼⟩ ⟨goods ∼⟩ **d :** one of several logging sleds that are hauled tandem by steam or gasoline power or by four to eight horses **e :** an automobile-drawn highway vehicle designed to serve wherever it is parked as a dwelling or as a place of business (as an office, laboratory, or field headquarters) **5 :** FROGGER 1 **6 :** PUSHER 1e
²trailer \"\ *vb* -ED/-ING/-S *vt* **:** to transport (a boat) by means of a trailer ⟨∼*ing* an outboard cruiser from one body of water to another⟩ ∼ *vi* **1 :** to live or travel in a trailer ⟨∼*ing* about the country⟩ **2 :** to be transportable by trailer ⟨a light boat that ∼*s* easily⟩
trailer camp *or* **trailer court** *or* **trailer park** *n* **:** an area where house trailers are congregated
trailer card *n* **:** a card that follows another card or group of cards in a computer and is provided to accommodate additional data or information
trailer coach *n* **:** HOUSE TRAILER
trail·er·ite \ˈtrālə,rīt\ *also* **trail·er·ist** \-,rəst\ *n* -s [¹*trailer* + *-ite* or *-ist*] **:** a person living or accustomed to live in a trailer ⟨a six-acre camp occupied by about 400 ∼*s* —Norma Browning⟩
trail·er·ship \-lə(r),ship\ *n* **:** a ship designed to carry trucks, trailers, and automobiles
trail·ery \ˈtrāl(ə)rē\ *n* -ES [²*trail* + *-ery*] **:** TRACERY, TRAIL 1a(2)
trail–eye \ˈ=,=\ *n* **:** LUNETTE 9
trail handspike *n* **:** a long stout handspike used in moving the trail of a gun carriage
trail herd *n, West* **:** a herd of cattle fit for trailing or being trailed esp. from the range to a railhead or market
¹trailing *n* -s [ME, fr. gerund of *trailen* to trail] **1 :** a trailing branch or shoot **:** RUNNER **2 :** the act or process of fusing bits of molten glass on glass articles to form decorative designs
²trailing *adj* [ME, fr. pres. part. of *trailen* to trail] **1 :** STRAGGLING, CREEPING ⟨a ∼ plant⟩ **2 :** of, relating to, or borne by the trailing wheels ⟨a ∼ truck⟩ ⟨∼ weight⟩ — **trail·ing·ly** *adv*
trailing arbutus *n* **:** ARBUTUS 3
trailing edge *n* **:** the rearmost edge of an airfoil — compare LEADING EDGE
trailing fuchsia *n* **:** a New Zealand fuchsia (*Fuchsia procumbens*) that is often used in hanging baskets and has procumbent slender stems and purplish flowers without petals followed by persistent red fruits
trailing lantana *n* **:** a common So. American trailing perennial (*Lantana sellowiana*) with rosy lilac flowers that is used as an ornamental
trailing line *n* **:** a line having one end fastened to a rowlock on a boat and the other to an oar to prevent loss of the oar
trailing myrtle *n* **:** ¹PERIWINKLE 1a
trailing pea *n* **:** GROUNDNUT 2a
trailing phlox *n* **:** a tufted spring-blooming perennial phlox (*Phlox nivalis*) that is similar to moss pink but has larger flowers with shorter stamens and styles
trailing–point switch *n* **:** a switch so set that the points are directed away from a passing train — distinguished from *facing-point switch*
trailing pole tip *also* **trailing horn** *n* **:** the edge of the pole piece of a dynamo or motor which the wires on the armature pass as they enter the gap
trailing raspberry *n* **:** any of several prostrate plants of the genus *Rubus* (esp. *R. parvifolius*)
trailing sumac *n* **:** a poison ivy (*Rhus toxicodendron*)
trailing truck *n* **:** the wheel unit of a locomotive that is located behind the driving wheels and that serves to help support the weight
trailing wheel *n* **:** a rear wheel of a locomotive to which the motive force is not directly applied — compare DRIVING WHEEL
trailing wild bean *n* **:** a sprawling leguminous vine (*Strophostyles helvola*) of eastern No. America with trifoliolate leaves, purple flowers, and linear nearly terete pods
trail knee *n* **:** a knee to stiffen the stem of a boat
trail's flycatcher \ˈtrā(ə)lz-\ *n, usu cap T* [after Thomas S. *Traill* †1862 Brit. encyclopedist] **:** ALDER FLYCATCHER
trail·man \ˈtrā(ə)lmən\ *n, pl* **trailmen 1 :** TRAILSMAN **2** *usu* **trail man :** one of a group of mounted cowboys driving a herd of cattle
trail net *n* **:** a net trailed or drawn behind a boat
trail plank *n* **:** a plank support for the trail of a gun carriage
trail plate *n* **:** the plate at the end of the trail of a gun carriage terminating in the lunette
trail rope *n* **:** DRAGROPE b
trails *pres 3d sing of* TRAIL, *pl of* TRAIL
trail seeker *n, usu cap T&S* **:** the first of four ranks attained by camp fire girls — compare FIRE MAKER, TORCH BEARER, WOOD GATHERER
trail sight *n* **:** the line of sight from a moving airplane to the point of impact of a bomb dropped by it taken at the instant of impact

trails·man \ˈtrā(ə)lzmən\ *n, pl* **trailsmen :** one that follows a trail
trail spade *n* **:** a metal spur, prong, or plate on the underside of the trail of a fieldpiece that is driven into the ground by the recoil and acts as a brake
trail teamster *n* **:** a logger that drives horses to tow logs over the flat part of a log chute
trail·way \ˈtrā(ə)l,wā\ *n* **:** a track or path esp. through a forest or mountainous region
¹train \ˈtrān\ *n* -s [ME *trayne, treyne,* fr. MF *traine*, fr. OF, fr. *traïr* to betray, fr. L *tradere* to betray, deliver — more at TRAITOR] **1** *obs* **a :** a scheme to deceive or betray **:** ARTIFICE, TRICK **b :** GUILE, TREACHERY, TRICKERY **2** *obs* **:** a trap for an animal **:** SNARE
²train \"\ *vt* -ED/-ING/-S [ME *traynen, treynen,* fr. *trayne, treyne,* n.] **1 :** to draw by artifice or stratagem **:** DECOY, ENTICE, LURE **2 :** ATTRACT, PERSUADE, WIN
³train \"\ *n* -s [ME *trayn, trayne,* fr. MF *train* action of drawing, trail, train of a dress, procession of animals or vehicles, fr. OF, fr. *trainer* to draw, drag — more at ⁴TRAIN] **1 a :** the extended part of a skirt, gown, or state robe that lies on the floor and trails behind the wearer **b :** an animal's tail; *esp* **:** the trailing tail feathers of a peacock **c :** the moving length of something (as a serpent or a stream) **d :** the luminous trail or tail of a meteor or comet sometimes persisting in the sky for several seconds or minutes after the meteor or comet itself has passed **2 a :** the retinue or suite of a person of rank or consequence **:** FOLLOWING ⟨he is bringing a staff of 80 in his ∼ —*Sydney (Australia) Bull.*⟩ **b :** a line or file of persons and often vehicles or animals proceeding together ⟨the little ∼ of silent people carried her out . . . to the family burying ground —Margaret Deland⟩ **:** CARAVAN ⟨a camel ∼⟩ **3 a :** an organization of military vehicles, men, and sometimes animals that furnishes supply, maintenance, and evacuation services to a combat unit — compare FIELD TRAIN **b :** the auxiliary ships assigned to supply and support a naval fleet or force **4 a :** proper arrangement or disposition **:** order designed or contrived to lead to some result ⟨was already in fair ∼ to develop party out of faction —Learned Hand⟩ ⟨the mathematics set in ∼ by these two pledges will force a reduction of the total armed forces —*New Statesman & Nation*⟩ **b :** a controlled or directed procedure **:** METHOD, PROCESS, WAY ⟨things proceeded in this ∼ for several days —T.L.Peacock⟩ **c :** a line, course, or sequence of thoughts, actions, or events **:** an orderly succession **:** a connected series ⟨the ∼ of years sped swiftly by —W.F.Brown b.1903⟩ ⟨his mind still upon his own ∼ of thought —Agnes S. Turnbull⟩ **d :** a set or progression of consequent or attendant events or conditions **:** a series of results or accompanying circumstances **:** AFTERMATH, SEQUEL ⟨in the ∼ of peace came industry and all the arts of life —T.B.Macaulay⟩ **5 a :** a line of black powder or other explosive laid to lead fire to a charge **:** FUSE **b :** a line of carrion pieces laid as a lure for game **6** *obs* **a :** the path followed by a horse **b :** the kind of travel experienced by a horse **c :** MANEGE, CONTROL **d :** a horse's gait **7 :** a series of moving machine parts (as gears, links, cams, chain drives, or belt drives) for transmitting and modifying motion ⟨the ∼ of a watch connects the barrel with the escapement⟩ ⟨gear ∼⟩ ⟨the valve ∼ of an automobile engine⟩ **8 a :** a connected line of railroad cars with or without a locomotive; *also* **:** an engine or motorcar with or without other engines or cars that displays markers **b :** an automotive tractor with one or more trailer units ⟨the number of truck-and-trailer ∼*s* has multiplied six or seven times in recent years —R.L.Neuberger⟩ **9 :** a long narrow geological deposit (as of gravel); *esp* **:** one composed of glaciofluvial sand and gravel extending down a valley far beyond the terminus of a glacier — called also *valley train* **10 :** a succession of physical oscillations or disturbances ⟨earthquake waves run in . . . ∼*s* —R.A. Daly⟩ ⟨the vibrations of a tuning fork cause a ∼ of sound waves to pass through the atmosphere⟩ **11 a :** a series of connected pieces of chemical apparatus **b :** a series of vats or large bowls for scouring wool **12 :** ROLL TRAIN **13 :** a series of bombs dropped from an airplane one after another in close succession — sometimes used in the phrase *in train*
⁴train \"\ *vb* -ED/-ING/-S [ME *traynen,* fr. MF *trainer*, fr. (assumed) VL *traginare;* akin to L *trahere* to pull, draw, drag — more at DRAW] *vt* **1 a :** to draw along **:** DRAG, TRAIL ⟨when a whale is harpooned . . . he ∼*s* with him the bold little creature who, greatly daring, has flung the fatal weapon —Francis Hackett⟩ **b :** to draw out **:** PROTRACT **2 :** to grow (a plant) in a manner designed to produce a desired form or effect usu. by bending, tying, and pruning; *esp* **:** to cause to grow symmetrically (as in an espalier or against a wall) by such means ⟨∼*ing* fruit trees as espaliers against a sheltering wall⟩ **3 a :** to instruct or drill in habits of thought or action **:** shape or develop the character of by discipline or precept ⟨∼ up a child in the way he should go, and when he is old he will not depart from it —Prov 22:6 (RSV)⟩ **b** (1) **:** to teach or exercise (someone) in an art, profession, trade, or occupation **:** direct in attaining a skill **:** give instruction to ⟨∼*ed* several generations of field and track athletes⟩ ⟨∼*ed* him in the law⟩ (2) **:** to cause (as judgment) to be disciplined **:** CULTIVATE ⟨perhaps we can ∼ our taste —Virginia Woolf⟩ **:** develop skill or habits in ⟨∼*ed* his hand to a patternmaker's delicate touch⟩ **c :** to teach (an animal) to obey commands **4 :** to aim or point at an object **:** bring to bear ⟨kept the shotgun ∼*ed* on him —F.B. Gipson⟩ ⟨had ∼*ed* his news camera on celebrities for 40 years⟩ ⟨∼*ed* his spotlight on the creative artist —W.F.Kerr⟩ **5 :** to adapt (a microorganism) to utilize a nutrient or to grow in an environment not normally suitable (as by continued exposure to such nutrient or environment) ∼ *vi* **1 :** DRAG, TRAIL ⟨her skirt ∼*ed* on the ground⟩ **2 a :** to undergo instruction, discipline, or drill ⟨recruits were ∼*ing* in army camps all over the nation⟩ ⟨∼*ed* in a nearby hospital for a nursing career⟩ **b :** to undertake an athlete's conditioning regimen of exercise, practice, and diet ⟨many baseball teams ∼ each spring in the South⟩ **3 :** to move in company **:** ASSOCIATE — used with *with* ⟨has always ∼*ed* with the moderates⟩ **4 :** to travel by rail **:** go by train ⟨had planed, ∼*ed*, and driven 1500 miles —Paul Gallico⟩ **syn** see TEACH
⁵train \"\ *n* -s [ME *trane,* fr. MD *traen, trane* fluid, drop, tear, train oil or MLG *trān;* akin to OS *trahni,* pl., tears, OHG *trahan* tear, *zahar* tear — more at TEAR] *archaic* **:** TRAIN OIL
train·able \ˈtrānəbəl\ *adj* [⁴*train* + *-able*] **:** capable of being trained ⟨labor supply is abundant, highly ∼, well educated —*advt*⟩
train·asi·um \trəˈnāzēəm, -zhəm\ *n* -s [⁴*train* + *-asium* (as in *gymnasium*)] **:** an intricate steel framework of bars, ladders, and other devices about 30 feet high designed to provide a climber with a succession of 22 gymnastic exercises
train·band \ˈtrān,=\ *n* [alter. of *trained band*] **:** a 17th or 18th century company of citizen soldiery in England or America **:** a militia company
trainbearer \ˈ=,==\ *n* **1 :** an attendant who holds up the train of a robe or gown (as at a wedding or on a ceremonial occasion) **2 :** a long-tailed So. American hummingbird (*Lesbia victoriae*)
trainboy \ˈ=,=\ *n* **:** a boy who sells newspapers, candy, or other small merchandise on railroad trains
train case *or* **train box** *n* **:** a small piece of luggage used esp. for toilet articles and other necessaries of overnight travel

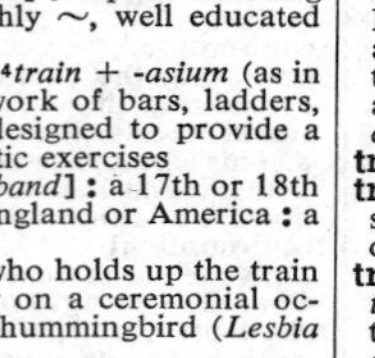
train case

train dispatcher *n* **:** a railroad employee who directs the movement of trains within a division and coordinates their movement from one division to another with other dispatchers — compare TOWERMAN
train down *vi* [⁴*train*] **:** to reduce one's weight by exercise and diet
trai·neau \(ˈ)trāˈnō\ *n, pl* **trai·neaux** \-ō(z)\ [F *traîneau*, fr. OF *trainel*, fr. *trainer* to draw, drag — more at TRAIN] **:** SLEDGE, SLEIGH
¹trained \ˈtrānd\ *adj* [fr. past part. of ⁴*train*] **1 :** having undergone a course of training ⟨we employ ∼ personnel⟩ ⟨a government-*trained* physician⟩ **2 :** formed, shaped, or disciplined by training **:** qualified or conditioned by training ⟨a ∼ mind⟩ ⟨a ∼ nose⟩ ⟨readers ∼ to be critical⟩
²trained \"\ *adj* [³*train* + *-ed*] **:** having a train ⟨a ∼ gown⟩

trained nurse *n* **:** GRADUATE NURSE
trained seal *n* **:** an author, celebrity, or expert hired by a newspaper to lend color or authority to its coverage of a conspicuous news story ⟨the veteran newsmen, big byliners and *trained seals* who covered the royal wedding —*Time*⟩
train·ee \(ˈ)trāˈnē\ *n* -s [⁴*train* + *-ee*] **:** someone being trained for a job **:** APPRENTICE, LEARNER ⟨industrial management ∼*s*⟩ ⟨job ∼*s*⟩; *esp* **:** an enlisted person receiving basic training
train·er \ˈtrānə(r)\ *n* -s [⁴*train* + *-er*] **1 :** someone or something that trains: as **a :** one that educates or teaches **b :** one that coaches athletes **c :** one that trains animals for performances, shows, or competitions **d :** one that trains a gun; *esp* **:** one that controls the horizontal aiming of a naval gun — compare POINTER **e :** a member of a trainband **:** MILITIAMAN **f** (1) **:** an airplane used in training airmen; *esp* **:** one with duplicate controls used in training pilots (2) **:** a mechanical device for training pilots that simulates flight conditions **g :** any of numerous machines and devices used in various forms of training **h :** a tree whose top is below the general forest canopy and whose shading and abrasive action prevents sucker formation and hastens natural pruning on the crop trees **2 :** someone being trained **:** TRAINEE ⟨∼*s* do practice teaching in connection with their teachers college courses⟩
train ferry *n* **:** a ferry equipped to carry railroad cars
train guard *n* **1 :** a force protecting a military train **2 :** a railroad guard
training *n* -s [fr. gerund of ⁴*train*] **1 a :** the teaching, drill, or discipline by which powers of mind or body are developed **:** EDUCATION ⟨many of us continue to believe in this ∼ of the mind by language —Charlton Laird⟩ ⟨the ∼ of statesmen is a large matter —Ernest Barker⟩ **b** (1) **:** the regimen of exercise, diet, and practice undergone by an athlete ⟨it was no light matter to break varsity football ∼⟩ (2) **:** a pitch of proficiency developed by an athlete's regimen ⟨he was in perfect ∼⟩ **c :** development of a particular skill or group of skills **:** instruction in an art, profession, or occupation **2 :** the control of plants, vines, or young trees so that they will grow in a desired shape or direction **3 :** the aiming or pointing of a gun, a camera, or a light
training aid *n* **:** a device (as a motion-picture film or a set of slides, charts, recordings, or models) to increase the effectiveness of training
training college *n, Brit* **:** TEACHERS COLLEGE
training day *n* **:** a day on which a volunteer military company is called out for drill or parade according to law
training school *n* **1 :** a school preparing students for a particular occupation or teaching a special skill **2 :** a correctional institution for the custody and reeducation of juvenile delinquents — compare INDUSTRIAL SCHOOL, REFORMATORY
training seat *n* **:** a small toilet seat fitted to a regular one and used for toilet training of children — compare POTTY-CHAIR

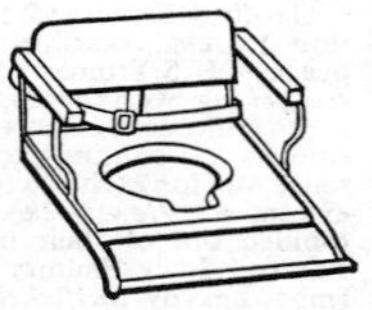
training seat

training ship *n* **1 :** a warship that carries naval-officer candidates on training cruises **2 :** a ship used to train men for the merchant marine
training table *n* **:** a table where men under an athletic training regimen eat meals planned to help in their conditioning ⟨a football *training table*⟩
training tackle *n* **:** TRAIN TACKLE
training wall *also* **training bank** *n* **:** a wall, bank, or jetty built to confine and direct the flow of a river or tide
train·less \ˈtrānləs\ *adj* **:** having no train
train line *n* **1 :** a continuous electric control circuit used on electric trains of two or more motor-driven cars for controlling the motors on the rear cars from the master controller in the cab of the first car **2** *or* **train pipe :** BRAKE PIPE
trainload \ˈ=,=\ *n* **:** the full freight or passenger cargo or capacity of a railroad train
train·man \ˈtrānmən, -,man\ *n, pl* **trainmen :** a member of a train crew supervised by a conductor
trainmaster \ˈ=,==\ *n* **1 :** an official in charge of the trains operating in a division or subdivision of a railroad **2 :** one in charge of the loading and unloading of a circus train
train–mile \ˈ=,=\ *n* **:** one mile traversed by one train used as a unit in railroad accounting
train off *vb* [⁴*train*] *vi* **1 :** to get out of training by relaxing a regimen or by going stale **2 :** SWERVE, VEER ∼ *vt* **:** to eliminate (excess body weight) by exercise and diet
train of rolls : ROLL TRAIN
train oil *n* [⁵*train*] **:** WHALE OIL; *also* **:** oil from various other marine animals
train order *n* **:** a written message to an engineer or conductor giving instructions about the operation of a railroad train
trains *pl of* TRAIN, *pres 3d sing of* TRAIN
train shed *n* **1 :** a part of a railroad station that covers the tracks **2 :** a building to protect trains from the weather
train sheet *n* **:** a sheet used by a dispatcher to record the movement of railroad trains
trainsick \ˈ=,=\ *adj* **:** affected with train sickness
train sickness *n* **:** motion sickness induced by riding on a train
train signal *n* **:** a signal conveyed from the cars of a railroad train to the locomotive by a mechanical device
train stop *n* **:** a device for automatically applying the brakes to stop a railroad train if a signal goes unheeded
train tackle *n* **:** a tackle formerly used for training and running out guns esp. on shipboard
¹traipse *also* **trapes** \ˈtrāps\ *vb* **traipsed** *also* **trapesed; traipsed** *also* **trapesed; traipsing** *also* **trapesing; traipses** *also* **trapeses** [origin unknown] *vi* **1 :** to walk or tramp about **:** GAD, WANDER **2 :** to trail or hang down in disorderly fashion ∼ *vt* **:** TRAMP, WALK
²traipse *also* **trapes** \"\ *n, pl* **traipses** *also* **trapeses 1 :** SLATTERN **2 :** a fatiguing walk
trait \ˈtrāt, *usu* -ād·+V; *Brit usu* ˈtrā\ *n* -s [MF, lit., pull, draft, fr. L *tractus* action of drawing, dragging, pulling, fr. *tractus*, past part. of *trahere* to draw, drag, pull — more at DRAW] **1 :** a stroke of or as of a pencil or brush **:** NOTE, TOUCH **2 :** a facial line or feature **:** LINEAMENT **3 :** a distinguishing quality (as of personal character) **:** FEATURE, MARK, PECULIARITY ⟨possessed what I think is the rarer ∼, great physical bravery —Gretchen Finletter⟩ ⟨familiar ∼*s* of church life —W.L.Sperry⟩ ⟨it is also a distinctly new medium with ∼*s* and features of its own —Milton Klonsky⟩ **4 :** a characteristic of behavior or a typical artifact that distinguishes a human culture — called also *culture trait*
trait–complex \ˈ=ˌ=,==\ *n* **:** ³COMPLEX 1a
trai·teur \(ˈ)trāˈtər(·)\ *n* -s [F, fr. *traiter* to treat, entertain, supply with food + *-eur* -or — more at TRATTORIA] **:** the keeper of a French or Italian eating house
trai·tor \ˈtrād·ə(r), -ātə-\ *n* -s [ME *traitre, traitour*, fr. OF *traitre, traitur*, fr. L *traditor*, fr. *traditus* (past part. of *tradere* to hand over, deliver, betray, fr. *trans-, tra-* trans- + *-dere* (fr. *dare* to give) + *-or* — more at DATE] **1 :** one that betrays another's trust or is false to an obligation or duty ⟨she sought to make me ∼ to myself —John Milton⟩ ⟨valley boys who play golf are ∼*s* to their class —M.S.Mayer⟩ **2 :** one that commits treason against his country (as by surrendering a fort or army unvanquished to an enemy) **:** one that violates his allegiance to his nation by levying war against it or by aiding its enemies
trai·tor·ism \-ə,rizəm\ *n* -s **:** BETRAYAL
trai·tor·ous \ˈtrād·ərəs, -ātər-, -ā·tr-\ *adj* [ME *traytrous*, fr. MF *traitreux*, fr. OF, fr. *traitre* traitor + *-eux* -ous — more at TRAITOR] **:** having the nature or quality of a traitor or of treason or betrayal **:** FALSE, PERFIDIOUS, TREACHEROUS, TREASONABLE **syn** see FAITHLESS
trai·tor·ous·ly *adv* [ME, fr. MF *traitreux* + ME *-ly*] **:** in a traitorous manner **:** FAITHLESSLY
trai·tor·ous·ness *n* -ES **:** the quality or state of being traitorous **:** PERFIDY
trai·tor·ship \-ād·ə(r),ship, -ātə-\ *n* **:** BETRAYAL, FALSITY
trai·tress *or* **trai·tor·ess** \ˈtrād·ərəs, -ātər-,-ā·tr-\ *n* -ES [ME *traitresse, traitouresse*, fr. traitre, traitour traitor + *-esse* -ess] **:** a female traitor
trai·vel \ˈtrāvəl\ *Scot var of* TRAVEL
¹traj·ect \ˈtra,jekt, -,jikt\ *n* -s [L *trajectus*, fr. *trajectus*, past part. of *trajicere, traicere* to throw across, cause to cross over,

cross over, fr. *trans-, tra-* trans- + *-jicere, -icere* (fr. *jacere* to throw) — more at JET] **1 :** a place for passing across **:** a crossing route **:** FERRY **2 :** an act of crossing or traversing **:** PASSAGE

²tra·ject \trəˈjekt\ *vt* -ED/-ING/-S [L *trajectus*, past part. of *trajicere, traicere*] **1 :** to cross over (as a river) **2 :** TRANSMIT ⟨~s sunlight through a prism⟩

tra·jec·tile \trəˈjektᵊl, -k,tīl\ *adj* [*trajection* + *-ile*] **:** of, capable of, or marked by trajection

tra·jec·tion \trəˈjekshən\ *n* -S [L *trajection-, trajectio*, fr. *trajectus* (past part. of *trajicere, traicere*) + *-ion-, -io* -ion] **1 :** transmission through space or some other medium **:** CROSSING **2 :** METATHESIS, TRANSPOSITION b(1)

¹tra·jec·to·ry \trəˈjekt(ə)rē, -ri\ *adj* [NL *trajectorius*, fr. L *trajectus* (past part. of *trajicere, traicere*) + *-orius* -ory] **:** of, relating to, or characteristic of a trajectory

²trajectory \"\ *n* -ES [NL *trajectoria*, fr. fem. of *trajectorius*] **1 a :** the curve that a body (as a planet or comet in its orbit, a projectile in passing from muzzle to first point of impact, or a rocket) describes in space **b :** a path, progression, or line of development likened to a physical trajectory ⟨the whole modern ~ from naturalism to symbolism —*New Republic*⟩ **2 :** a curve or surface that cuts all the curves or surfaces of a given system at the same angle

tra·jet \trȧzhā\ *n, pl* **trajets** \"\ [F, fr. L *trajectus* — more at TRAJECT] **:** TRAJECT, PASSAGE, COURSE, ROUTE, WAY

tra–la \trəˈlä, (ˈ)träˈlä\ *or* **tra–la–la** \ˌträləˈlä\ *also* **tra·li·ra** \ˌträləˈrä\ [origin unknown] — used to suggest gaiety, lightheartedness, or playful derision esp. in song

tral·a·ti·tious \ˌtraləˈtishəs\ *adj* [L *tralatitius, tralaticius* (fr. *tralatus, translatus*, suppletive past part. of *transferre* to transfer) + *-itius, -icius* -itious — more at TRANSLATE] **1 :** having a character, force, or significance transferred or derived from something extraneous **:** METAPHORICAL, FIGURATIVE ⟨the primary and ~ meanings of a word⟩ **2 :** passed along as from hand to hand, mouth to mouth, or from generation to generation **:** handed down **:** TRADITIONAL ⟨among Biblical critics a ~ interpretation is one received by expositor from expositor —William Withington⟩ — **tral·a·ti·tious·ly** *adv*

tral·les alcoholometer *or* **tralles hydrometer** \ˈträləs-\ *n, usu cap T* [after Johann G. *Tralles* †1822 Ger. physicist] **:** an alcoholometer graduated so that its degrees indicate percentages by volume at 15.6°C

tra·lu·cent \trəˈlüsᵊnt\ *adj* **:** TRANSLUCENT ⟨~ creatures as bright as rubies —Compton Mackenzie⟩

¹tram \ˈtram, -aa(ə)-\ *n* -S [F *trame* woof, weft, tram, fr. L *trama* woof, weft — more at TRAMA] **:** a loosely twisted silk yarn made by doubling and twisting two or more filaments together and usu. used for the weft of a fabric

²tram \"\ *n* -S [prob. fr. LG *traam* beam, handle of a barrow, fr. MLG *trāme;* akin to MD *traem, trame* beam, tooth of a rake, MLG *treme* crossbar] **1 a** *dial Brit* **:** a shaft of a vehicle (as a handbarrow or wheelbarrow) **b** *Scot* **:** LEG, LIMB **c** *dial Eng* **:** BENCH ⟨a ~ for dairy tubs⟩ **2 :** any of various vehicles: as **a :** a boxlike wagon often of steel running on a tramway or railway (as in a mine or logging camp) for conveying coal, ore, or logs **b** *chiefly Brit* **:** a passenger car of a street railway **:** STREETCAR ⟨that once characteristically British vehicle, the double-decked ~, is disappearing from one city after another —Paul Jennings⟩ **c :** a carrier that travels on an overhead cable or rails **3 a trams** *pl, chiefly Brit* **:** a streetcar line **b :** a tramway rail **c** (1) **:** TRAMWAY (2) **:** TRAMROAD

³tram \"\ *vb* **trammed; trammed; tramming; trams** *vi* **1** *Brit* **:** to travel in a tramcar **2** *Brit* **:** to operate a tram or a tramway system **~** *vt* **1 :** to haul (as coal) in a tram **2 :** to haul (lumber) over a tramway

⁴tram \"\ *n* -S [by shortening] **:** TRAMMEL 6c

⁵tram \"\ *n* -S [by shortening & alter.] *slang* **:** TROMBONE

tra·ma \ˈtrāmə\ *n* -S [NL, fr. L, woof, weft, fr. *trahere* to pull, draw, drag — more at DRAW] **:** the loosely woven hyphal tissue in basidiomycetous fungi forming the central substance of the lamellae or other projections of the hymenophore — **tra·mal** \-məl\ *adj*

tramcar \ˈ=,=\ *n* **1** *chiefly Brit* **:** ²TRAM 2b **2 :** ²TRAM 2a

tram crane *n* **:** a crane consisting of a short bridge without a trolley traveling on overhead rails

trame·tes \ˈtraməˌtēz, -rām-\ *n, cap* [NL, fr. *trama*] **:** a genus of pore fungi (family Polyporaceae) having leathery pileate sporophores with the meeting line between pores and context uneven

tram·less \ˈtramləs, -raam-\ *adj* **:** having no tram

tramline \ˈ=,=\ *n, Brit* **:** a tram line

¹tram·mel \ˈtraməl\ *n* -S [ME *tramayle, tramale*, fr. MF *tremail*, fr. LL *tremaculum*, fr. L *tres* three + *macula* mesh, spot — more at THREE] **1 :** a net for catching birds or fishes: as **a :** an anchored gill net **b :** TRAMMEL NET **2 :** a shackle used for regulating the motions of a horse and making him amble **3 :** something impeding activity, progress, or freedom as if by a net or shackle **:** RESTRAINT, CHECK — usu. used in pl. ⟨the poet's imagination must be free and has progressively thrown off the ~s of respectability, tradition, and more recently the established conventions of communication by language —N.E.Nelson⟩ ⟨bound by the ~s of human nature —Robert Graves⟩ ⟨the masses . . . sought to build an America free of the ~s of the Old World —H.J. Laski⟩ **4 :** an adjustable pothook for a fireplace crane **5 trammels** *pl, obs* **:** braids, plaitings, or tresses of a woman's hair **6 a** (1) **:** an instrument for drawing ellipses consisting of a cross with two grooves at right angles to each other and a beam carrying two pins which slide in those grooves and also a describing pencil (2) **:** any of various mechanical devices for drawing ellipses **:** ELLIPSOGRAPH **b** (1) **:** BEAM COMPASS — usu. used in pl. and often used with *pair* ⟨a pair of ~s⟩ (2) **:** either of the sliding parts on the beam of a beam compass **c :** any of various gages used for aligning or adjusting machine parts — called also *tram*

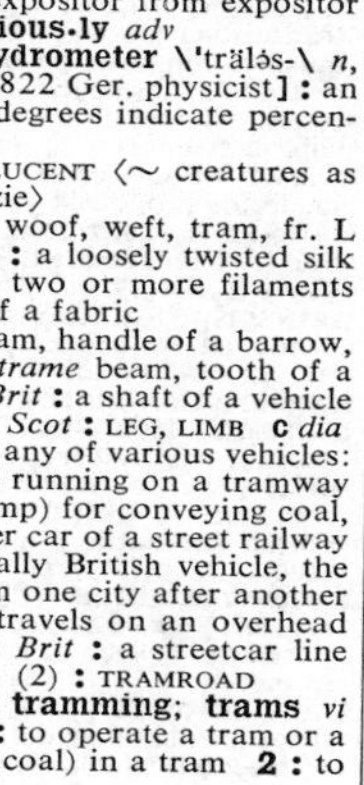

trammels 4

²trammel \"\ *vt* **trammeled** *or* **trammelled; trammeled** *or* **trammelled; trammeling** *or* **trammelling** \-m(ə)liŋ\ **trammels 1 a :** to catch (as fish) in a trammel **b** *obs* **:** to attach trammels to (a horse) **:** SHACKLE **2 :** to hold in or as if in a net **:** tie or fasten securely **:** ENMESH ⟨while suffering the almost irremediable homesickness of bereavement had now become ~ed in events —Ethel Wilson⟩ — sometimes used with *up* ⟨if the assassination could ~ up the consequence —Shak.⟩ **3 :** to impose restraints upon **:** prevent or impede the free play or exercise of **:** CONFINE ⟨writing about people whose speech and behavior were ~ed to a certain extent by the usages of polite society —Wolcott Gibbs⟩ ⟨their life was at once dangerously ~ed and dangerously free —John Buchan⟩ ⟨the classical models no longer ~, but assist him to be more effectively himself —H.O.Taylor⟩ ⟨these observations, by ~ing his every act, annihilate his freedom —J.G.Frazer⟩ **syn** see HAMPER

trammel net *n* **:** a rectangular net made of a middle layer that is slack and of fine mesh and two outer layers that are stretched and of coarse mesh so arranged that fish attempting to pass in either direction carry some of the fine net through the coarse and are thus pocketed

trammel point *n* **:** either of the metal points of a beam compass

tram·mer \ˈtramə(r), -raam-\ *n* -S [³*tram* + *-er*] **:** one that trams; *specif* **:** one that trams coal, ore, or waste rock **:** PUSHER

tra·mon·ta·na \ˌträ(ˌ)mōnˈtänə\ *n* -S [It, fr. fem. of *tramontano*] **:** the north wind; *esp* **:** a dry cold strong northerly wind off the west coast of Italy

¹tramon·tane \trəˈmänˌtān, ˈtramən-ˌ\ *adj* [It *tramontano*, fr. L *transmontanus*, fr. *trans-* + *montanus* of a mountain — more at MOUNTAIN] **1 a :** TRANSALPINE — compare CISMONTANE **b :** of or characteristic of the countries north of the Alps **c :** coming from the north beyond the Alps ⟨a ~ wind⟩ **2 :** lying or being beyond any mountains **:** coming from the other side of the mountains ⟨sectionalism in Virginia had reared its head in a contest between a cismontane and a ~ people —*Amer. Guide Series: Va.*⟩ **3 :** FOREIGN, OUTLANDISH, BARBAROUS

²tramontane \"\ *n* -S [It *tramontano*, fr. *tramontano*, adj.] **1 :** one dwelling in a tramontane region: as **a :** an inhabitant of a country north of the Alps **b :** FOREIGNER, STRANGER **c :** BOOR **2** [It *tramontana*] **:** TRAMONTANA

¹tramp \ˈtramp, -aa(ə)-, -ai-, *in senses vi 1 & vt 1 chiefly dial* ˈträmp *or* -rômp\ *vb* -ED/-ING/-S [ME *trampen;* akin to MLG *trampen* to stamp, tread, MD *tramperen* to stamp, Norw dial. *trumpa* to push, shove, Goth *anatrimpan* to crowd, MD *trappen* to stamp — more at TRAP] *vi* **1 a :** to walk or tread esp. with a heavy step ⟨a steady stream of visitors ~s every day through the magnificent exhibition —Mollie Panter-Downes⟩ ⟨man who was ~*ing* across the square in climbing boots —Willa Cather⟩ ⟨heard them ~ upstairs —Arnold Bennett⟩ ⟨~ on someone's toes⟩ **b :** to press one's foot ⟨~*ed* down on the gas pedal —Oakley Hall⟩ **2 a :** to travel about on foot **:** HIKE ⟨spent his holidays ~*ing* all over our native land —Joseph Conrad⟩ ⟨finds relaxation in . . . ~*ing* in the woods —*Current Biog.*⟩ ⟨~*ed* and climbed among the heights —H.N.Fowler⟩ **b :** to journey as a tramp **3 a :** to travel as a tramp ship ⟨three tiny steamers ~*ing* between Suez and Mukalla —Ladislas Farago⟩ **b :** to travel on a tramp ship **~** *vt* **1 :** to tread on forcibly and usu. repeatedly **:** trample so as to bruise or press down ⟨~ grapes for wine⟩ ⟨dig out the ground three feet deep, put in a foot of straw, leaves, or coarse litter, wet it thoroughly, and ~ it down one half —Emily Holt⟩ ⟨~*ing* the top of your silage 10 to 15 minutes a day for a week after filling will reduce top spoilage —*Deerfield (Wisc.) Independent*⟩ **2 a :** to travel or wander through on foot **:** hike or trudge through or along ⟨rode the subways and ~*ed* the streets —E.A.Weeks⟩ ⟨a naturalist ~*ing* the forests⟩ **b :** to make by trudging or hiking ⟨left home to ~ his way over the country —R.L.Taylor⟩

²tramp \ˈtramp, -aa(ə)-, -ai-, *in senses 3–5 chiefly dial* ˈträmp *or* -rômp\ *n* -S **1 a :** a foot traveler **:** TRAMPER ⟨youthful ~s in search of work —Siegfried Kracauer⟩ **b :** a begging or thieving vagrant; *esp* **:** a lazy good-for-nothing beggar or sponger who travels about but will not work ⟨the ~ reappeared time and again as the hero of screen adventures —Lewis Jacobs⟩ **c :** a woman of loose morals; *specif* **:** PROSTITUTE ⟨the rigid stateside demarcations between the nice girl and the ~ —*Christian Science Monitor*⟩ ⟨a girl who can't quite make up her mind whether she wants to be a wife or a kept woman or just a ~ off to try her luck in New York —Wolcott Gibbs⟩ **2 :** a journey on foot **:** a walking trip **:** HIKE ⟨forth for a long ~ —C.G.Bowers⟩ ⟨go for ~s on Saturday afternoons —Elizabeth Bowen⟩ **3 :** the act of tramping ⟨the dry ground was packed from the ~ of thousands of cattle and horses —J.F. Dobie⟩; *also* **:** a mark produced by this act **4 :** the succession of sounds made by the beating of feet of men or animals on a road, pavement, or floor ⟨the rhythmic ~ of marching armies —C.T.Lanham⟩ ⟨the ~s of so many horses —Walt Whitman⟩ **5 a :** a plate of iron worn to protect the sole of the foot or the shoe when digging with a spade; *also* **:** the part of the spade against which the foot is forced in digging **b :** a spiked piece of iron worn on the shoe in curling to prevent slipping **6** *or* **tramp ship** *or* **tramp steamer :** a ship not making regular trips between the same ports but taking a cargo when and where it offers and to any port **7 :** an unwanted up-and-down movement of an automobile on its front wheels ⟨tended to set up violent shimmy and ~ on the front end at high speeds —Roger Huntington⟩ **8 :** TRAMPOLINE **syn** see VAGABOND

³tramp \ˈtramp, -aa(ə)-, -ai-\ *adj* [²*tramp*] **1 :** having no fixed abode, connection, or destination ⟨a ~ dog⟩ ⟨a ~ printer⟩ ⟨a ~ and vagrant world, adrift in space —William James⟩ **2 :** UNWANTED, CONTAMINATING — used esp. of metallic particles ⟨whenever ~ iron threatens to contaminate a process or product, damage machinery, or give rise to sparking, magnets are the sentries that keep it out —*Steelways*⟩

tramp·dom \-dəm\ *n* -S **:** the realm of tramps; *also* **:** TRAMPS

tramp·er \-pə(r)\ *n* -S **1 :** one that tramps **:** VAGRANT: as **a :** a heavy walker **b :** one that takes long walks for pleasure or exercise **:** HIKER **2 :** an attachment for a cotton press for compacting the cotton during baling

tramp·ish \-pish\ *adj* **:** having the characteristics of a tramp esp. in appearance — **tramp·ish·ly** *adv* — **tramp·ish·ness** *n* -ES

¹tram·ple \ˈtrampəl, -raam-, -raim-\ *vb* **trampled; trampled; trampling** \-p(ə)liŋ\ **tramples** [ME *tramplen*, freq. of *trampen* to tramp — more at TRAMP] *vi* **:** TRAMP ⟨the little boys lay down in the dust, heedless of the feet *trampling* everywhere about them —Pearl Buck⟩ ⟨*trampling* up and down the front porch, nervous as a cat —R.P.Warren⟩ ⟨if in addition to the year's four seasons the fifth of famine ~s through the land —Frederic Morton⟩: as **a :** to tread heavily so as to bruise, crush, or injure — usu. used with *on, upon*, or *over* ⟨a runaway horse had *trampled* on him and broken his hipbone —Vicki Baum⟩ ⟨the boy who has a garden will not ~ on other people's flower beds —Bertrand Russell⟩ **b :** to inflict injury or destruction **:** have a contemptuous or ruthless attitude **:** TYRANNIZE — usu. used with *on, over*, or *upon* ⟨he liked to ~ on his foes —M.R.Cohen⟩ ⟨pride and sensitiveness were his chief foes, and he would ~ on them —George Meredith⟩ ⟨his grim, repressive mother, who *trampled* on every innocent pleasure —Van Wyck Brooks⟩ ⟨*trampled* on conventions —Henry Adams⟩ ⟨if the great powers show themselves irresponsibly ready to ~ over any weak nation that seemed to be in their way —Vera M. Dean⟩ **~** *vt* **1 :** to press down in walking **:** crush or injure by or as if by treading **:** STAMP ⟨man was standing on a large push truck and *trampling* down a great pile of old newspapers and other trash —Thomas Whiteside⟩ ⟨shoes ~ his camera underfoot —Ray Duncan⟩ ⟨used to ~ the lumps of hard clay into powder —*Amer. Guide Series: Tenn.*⟩ ⟨will rediscover the morality their oppressors *trampled* into the dust —*Times Lit. Supp.*⟩ ⟨the utility combine is pressuring Congress to ~ down the law and the will of the people —*N. Y. Times*⟩ **2 :** to extinguish by stamping with the feet — usu. used with *out* ⟨a forbidden book is like a fire one tries to ~ out —*Encore*⟩

²trample \"\ *n* -S **:** the act or sound of trampling **:** a heavy and repeated tread of or as if of many feet

tram·po·line *also* **tram·po·lin** \ˌtrampəˈlēn, -raam-, -raim-, *sometimes* ˈ==lən\ *n* -S [Sp *trampolín*, fr. It *trampolino*, fr. *trampoli* stilts, of Gmc origin; akin to MLG *trampen* to stamp, tread — more at TRAMP] **:** a resilient canvas sheet or web supported by springs in a metal frame used as a springboard in tumbling and exercising — **tram·po·lin·er** \ˌ==ˈlēnə(r)\ *or* **tram·po·lin·ist** \-nəst\ *n* -S

tramp's–trouble \ˈ=,=\ *n, pl* **tramp's–troubles :** CHINA BRIER

tram rail *n* **:** a rail for a tram: as **a :** a rail of plates as distinguished from the later edge rail **b :** an overhead rail on which a trolley runs to convey a load (as in a shop)

tramroad \ˈ=,=\ *n* **:** a roadway for trams consisting of parallel tracks made of usu. metal-faced wooden beams, stone blocks, metal plates, or rails; *specif* **:** a railway in a mine

trams *pl of* TRAM, *pres 3d sing of* TRAM

tramway \ˈ=,=\ *n* **:** a way for trams: as **a :** TRAMROAD **b** *Brit* **:** a streetcar line; *also* **:** STREETCAR **c :** TRAM RAIL b **d :** ROPEWAY **e :** a light or temporary logging railroad often with wooden rails and operated by horsepower

tram·way·man \ˈ"mən\ *n, pl* **tramwaymen** *Brit* **:** an employee of a streetcar line

tran *abbr* transit

¹trance \ˈtran(t)s, -raa(ə)n-, -rain-, -rȧn-\ *vb* -ED/-ING/-S [ME *transen* to die, swoon, be in fear, fr. MF *transir* — more at ²TRANCE] *vi, obs* **:** to be in great suspense or extreme fear **~** *vt* [²*trance*] **1 :** to hold (as a person) benumbed, immobile, or unnaturally still ⟨her heart was clutched by a grip of ice, and she went as one *tranced* —C.G.D.Roberts⟩ ⟨a dead hot silence *tranced* sea, land, and sky —R.H.Horne⟩ **2 :** ENTRANCE, ENRAPTURE ⟨a romance . . . held me rapt through many a *tranced* hour —R.M.Bell⟩ ⟨ever the fiery Pentecost . . . ~s the heart through chanting hours and through the priest the mind inspires —R.W.Emerson⟩

²trance \"\ *n* -S [ME *traunce, trance*, fr. MF *transe*, fr. *transir* to pass, pass away, die, swoon, be in fear, fr. L *transire* to pass, pass away — more at TRANSIENT] **1 :** a state of partly suspended animation or of inability to function **:** DAZE, STUPOR ⟨in a calm ~, like a dead person, she crossed the street —Mary McCarthy⟩ ⟨lay stone-still in a ~ of terror and mournfulness —George Meredith⟩ ⟨the neigh of some horse . . . loud and sudden, that had burst the shell of my ~, causing thought to start to life again —Owen Wister⟩ **2 :** a somnolent state such as that of deep hypnosis appearing also in hysteria and in some spiritualistic mediums and characterized by limited sensory and motor contact with the surroundings and subsequent lack of recall ⟨fell into . . . a light kind of ~ that, he explains, is the first stage of hypnosis —Vance Packard⟩ ⟨in ~ they divine auspicious times for various tasks —*African Abstracts*⟩ **3 :** a state of profound abstraction or absorption accompanied by exaltation ⟨went into a ~ closely resembling religious rapture —R.G.Hubler⟩ ⟨would work himself into a condition of ecstasy which resembled a ~ . . . would fall down, and foam would break out on his lips —Maurice Samuel⟩

³trance \ˈtrans\ *vi* -ED/-ING/-S [ME *trauncen*] *dial Brit* **:** to pass or travel over the ground **:** to move briskly **:** PRANCE

⁴trance \"\ *n* -S [perh. short for ¹*transit*] *chiefly Scot* **:** PASSAGE, PASSAGEWAY

tranced·ly \-nstlē, -nsədlē\ *adv* [*tranced* (past part. of ¹*trance*) + *-ly*] **:** in or as if in a trance

tranche \ˈträⁿsh\ *n* -S [F, fr. OF, fr. *trenchier, trancher* to cut — more at TRENCH] **:** SLICE, SECTION, PORTION; *specif* **:** a portion or series of a bond issue to be distributed in a foreign country

tran·chet \ˈträⁿˈshā\ *n* -S [F, cutting tool, fr. MF, fr. *trancher* to cut] **1 :** a chisel-shaped flint implement peculiar to Neolithic times **2 :** CHOPPER 2c

tra·neen \trəˈnēn\ *n* -S [IrGael *trāithnīn* blade of grass, herb bennet] *chiefly Irish* **:** something of little or no value **:** TRIFLE ⟨never cared a ~ for him —S.C.Hall⟩

tran·gam \ˈtraŋgəm\ *n* -S [origin unknown] *archaic* **:** an odd device or puzzle **:** TRINKET, GIMCRACK

trank \ˈtraŋk\ *n* -S [origin unknown] **1 :** a piece of leather large enough for one glove body **2 :** a cut glove body consisting of front and back without thumb, fourchettes, or gussets — see GLOVE illustration

tran·ky \ˈtraŋkē\ *n* -ES [Per dial. *trānki*] **:** an undecked bark used in the Persian gulf

tran·quil \ˈtraŋkwəl, -rank-, -raank-\ *adj, sometimes* **tranquiler** *or* **tranquiller;** *sometimes* **tranquilest** *or* **tranquillest** [L *tranquillus*] **1 a :** free from mental agitation **:** SERENE ⟨she became more ~, and was able to listen to his plans —Anthony Trollope⟩ ⟨the sort of heart that great men have, straightforward, undeviating, and ~ —Ruth Park⟩ **b :** free from disturbance or turmoil **:** QUIET, PEACEFUL ⟨~ as a rural church on a Sunday afternoon —Green Peyton⟩ ⟨a ~ twilight hour —Elinor Wylie⟩ ⟨has transformed a normally ~ agricultural region into one of factories —*Amer. Guide Series: Texas*⟩ ⟨celebrities . . . allowed to live and die in ~ privacy —E.M. Lustgarten⟩ ⟨peace can be made ~ and secure only by understanding and agreement —B.M.Baruch⟩ **2 :** unvarying in aspect **:** STEADY, STABLE ⟨when a few of the corpuscles have been fired across it, it becomes something very different from a ~ gas —K.K.Darrow⟩ ⟨her eyes and nostrils, usually so ~, were dilated —G.B.Shaw⟩ **syn** see CALM

tran·quil·iza·tion *or* **tran·quil·li·za·tion** \ˌtraŋkwələˈzāshən, -rank-, -raank-, -wəˌlīˈ-\ *n* -S **:** an act or process of tranquilizing

tran·quil·ize *or* **tran·quil·lize** \ˈtraŋkwəˌlīz, -rank-, -raank-\ *vb* -ED/-ING/-S [*tranquil* + *-ize*] *vt* **:** to cause to be or become tranquil **:** PACIFY ⟨the perfect balance she had held . . . stirred and yet *tranquilized* him —Edith Wharton⟩; *specif* **:** to reduce or bring to a quiet or unagitated state by means of a chemical reaction ⟨nicotinamide . . . also *tranquilized* animals —D.W. Woolley⟩ **~** *vi* **:** to become tranquil **syn** see CALM

tran·quil·iz·er *or* **tran·quil·liz·er** \-zə(r)\ *n* -S **1 :** one that tranquilizes **2 :** a drug used to reduce anxiety and tension states or mental disturbances in people and animals

tran·quil·li·ty *or* **tran·quil·i·ty** \tranˈkwilədē, traan-, traŋ'-, -ətē, -i\ *n* -ES [ME *tranquillite*, fr. MF *tranquillité*, fr. L *tranquillitat-, tranquillitas*, fr. *tranquillus* tranquil + *-itat-, -itas* -ity] **:** the quality or state of being tranquil ⟨emotion recollected in ~ —William Wordsworth⟩ ⟨the lasting peace which is the ~ of order —J.P.McGranery⟩ ⟨the ~ of the flowing stream is carefully measured⟩

tran·quil·lo \tränˈkwē(ˌ)lō\ *adv* (*or adj*) [It, fr. *tranquillo* tranquil, fr. L *tranquillus*] **:** in a quiet or calm manner — used as a direction in music

tran·quil·ly \ˈtraŋkwəlē, -rank-, -raank-, -li\ *adv* **:** in a tranquil manner

tran·quil·ness *n* -ES [*tranquil* + *-ness*] **:** TRANQUILLITY

trans \ˈtran(t)s, -nz\ *adj* [*trans-*] **:** having or characterized by certain atoms or groups on opposite sides of the molecule ⟨~ configuration around the double bonds⟩ — opposed to *cis*

trans- \(ˌ)tran(t)s, -raan-, -nz *sometimes chiefly Brit* -rȧn-\ *prefix* [L *trans-, tra-* across, beyond, to the other side, through, so as to change, fr. *trans* across, beyond, on or to the other side, through — more at THROUGH] **1 a :** across ⟨*trans*polar⟩ ⟨*trans*atlantic⟩ ⟨*trans*oceanic⟩ **b** (1) **:** beyond ⟨*trans*human⟩ ⟨*trans*mundane⟩ (2) **:** beyond (a specified chemical element) in the periodic table ⟨*trans*plutonium⟩ ⟨*trans*uranic⟩ **c :** through ⟨*trans*lucent⟩ ⟨*trans*cutaneous⟩ **d :** completeness of change ⟨*trans*shape⟩ **2 :** transverse ⟨*trans*frontal⟩ ⟨*trans*process⟩ **3 :** having certain atoms or groups on opposite sides of the molecule ⟨*trans*-dichloro-ethylene⟩ — opposed to *cis-* 3; compare ALL- 2b, ANTI- 7 **4 :** transfer **:** interchange — in names of chemical reactions and enzymes ⟨*trans*amination⟩

trans *abbr* **1** transaction **2** transfer; transferred **3** transformer **4** transit **5** transitional **6** transitive **7** translated; translation; translator **8** transmission **9** transmitter **10** transparent **11** transport; transportation **12** transpose **13** transverse

trans·abdominal \ˌtran(t)s, -raan-, -nz+\ *adj* [*trans-* + *abdomin-* + *-al*] **:** passing, occurring, or cutting across the abdomen or through the abdominal wall

trans·ac·ci·den·ta·tion \ˌtran(t)saksədenˈtāshən\ *n* -S [ML *transaccidentatio*, *transaccidentatio*, fr. L *accident-, accidens* accident, after L *substantia* substance: ML *transubstantiation-, transubstantiatio* transubstantiation] **:** an orig. medieval theological doctrine that the accidents of the eucharistic bread and wine are changed into the body and blood of Jesus Christ at the moment of their consecration — compare TRANSUBSTANTIATION

trans·acetylase \ˌtran(t)s, -raan-, -nz+\ *n* [*trans-* + *acetyl* + *-ase*] **:** any of several enzymes that catalyze the transfer of acetyl groups; *esp* **:** an enzyme that promotes the reversible conversion of acetyl coenzyme A to acetyl phosphate and is found in bacteria

¹trans·act \tran(t)ˈsakt, traan-, -nˈza-\ *vb* -ED/-ING/-S [L *transactus*, past part. of *transigere* to drive through, complete, transact, fr. *trans-* + *-igere* (fr. *agere* to drive, act, do) — more at AGENT] *vi* **1 :** to prosecute negotiations **:** carry on business **:** NEGOTIATE ⟨desires to ~ only with honest men⟩ **2 :** to compromise esp. by compliance or concession in a matter of principle **~** *vt* **1** *archaic* **:** to turn over (as for settlement) **:** TRANSMIT, TRANSFER **2 :** to carry out **:** EFFECT, PERFORM ⟨on his father's farm, he ~*ed* the imperative residuum of chores —Irving Stone⟩; *esp* **:** to carry on **:** DO, CONDUCT ⟨hold a meeting . . . choose a moderator, ~ their business —R.W. Hatch⟩ ⟨that such business, because of its technical nature, be ~*ed* solely by . . . experts —F.A.Ogg & Harold Zink⟩ **3** *archaic* **:** to trade in or with **:** HANDLE, EXCHANGE **4 :** to make a transaction of; *esp* **:** to compound or compromise (as a dispute) by mutual agreement

²trans·act \tranˈsakt\ *n* -S [LL *transactum*, fr. L, neut. of *transactus*] *dial Eng* **:** TRANSACTION

trans·ac·tion \tran(t)ˈsakshən, traan-, -nˈza-\ *n* -S [ME, fr. LL *transaction-, transactio*, fr. L *transactus* + *-ion-, -io* -ion] **1 :** an act, process, or instance of transacting: as **a** (1) **:** an adjustment or compromise in Roman and civil law of a disputed claim effected by mutual agreement and resembling the accord and satisfaction of the common law (2) **:** COMPACT, COVENANT ⟨the atonement is to him no mere ~ . . . but the consequence of God's own nature and will —*Times Lit. Supp.*⟩ **b :** a communicative action or activity involving two parties or two things reciprocally affecting or influencing each other ⟨to intensify the ~ between the lay listener and the esthetic object —Arthur Berger⟩ ⟨thought transference implies that there is some ~ . . . between the agent and the subject —A.G.N. Flew⟩ ⟨men . . . get perspectives upon events as the spur of

need drives them into interactions and ~s with events —H.L. Parsons⟩ **2 :** something that is transacted: as **a :** a business deal ⟨a profitable ~⟩ — often used in pl. ⟨service ~s were not sufficient to pay for necessary imports —W.M.W.Splawn⟩ **b transactions** *pl* **:** the often published record of action taken, matter discussed, or addresses read at the meeting of a society or association **:** PROCEEDINGS ⟨besides many contributions to ~s and periodicals he edited the American edition —F.R. Packard⟩

trans·ac·tion·al \-shən°l, -shnəl\ *adj* **:** of, relating to, or involving a transaction ⟨the ~ nature of the atonement⟩; *specif* **:** realized in actuality ⟨the general trend of science, however, is directed toward ~ conceptions —Ludwig Von Bertalanffy⟩ — **trans·ac·tion·al·ly** \-shən°l\|ē, -shnəl\|, \|i\ *adv*

transaction tax *n* **:** TURNOVER TAX

trans·ac·tor \-ktə(r)\ *n* -s [L, fr. *transactus* + *-or*] **:** one that transacts

trans·admittance \ˌtran(t)s, -raan-, -nz+\ *n* [*trans-* + *admittance*] **:** the ratio in an electron tube of the effective alternating-current component at one electrode to the corresponding effective voltage at another electrode with the potentials of the remaining elements being constant — compare TRANSCONDUCTANCE

¹**trans·alpine** \(ˈ)tran(t)s, -raan-, -nz+\ *adj* [L *transalpinus*, fr. *trans-* + *Alpes* the Alps, mountains of south central Europe + L *-inus* -ine] **1 :** of, relating to, or situated on the farther side of the Alps ⟨~ Gaul . . . was the country included between the Rhine, the ocean, the Pyrenees, the Mediterranean, and the Alps —J.A.Froude⟩ ⟨Cracow, one of the best of the ~ universities —G.C.Sellery⟩ — opposed to *cisalpine* **2 :** of, relating to, or characteristic of the region or peoples beyond the Alps

²**transalpine** \"\ *n* [L *Transalpini* (pl.), fr. pl. of *transalpinus*, adj.] **:** a native or inhabitant of a transalpine country

trans·am·i·nase \tran(t)ˈsaməˌnās, traan-, -nˈza-\ *n* [*transamination* + *-ase*] **:** any of a group of enzymes that promote transamination usu. if pyridoxal phosphate is present as coenzyme and that are found in almost all animal tissues, in higher plants, and in many bacteria

trans·am·i·na·tion \(ˌ)=,==ˈnāshən\ *n* [*trans-* + *amination*] **:** a reversible oxidation-reduction reaction in which an amino group is transferred typically from an alpha-amino acid to the carbonyl carbon atom of an alpha-keto acid and which is usu. promoted by a transaminase ⟨the ~ of glutamic acid in the presence of pyruvic acid yields alpha-ketoglutaric acid and alanine⟩

trans·an·i·ma·tion \(ˌ)tran(t)ˌsanəˈmāshən, -raan-, -nˌza-\ *n* [LL *transanimation-*, *transanimatio*, fr. L *trans-* + *anima* soul + *-ation-*, *-atio* -ation — more at ANIMATE] **:** METEMPSYCHOSIS

trans·an·nu·lar \(ˈ)tran(t)ˈsanyələ(r), -raan-, -nˈza-\ *adj* [*trans-* + L *annulus* ring + E *-ar* — more at ANNULUS] **:** relating to or being tautomerism characterized by migration (as of a hydrogen atom) across a ring

¹**trans·at·lan·tic** \ˌtran(t)sətˈlantik, -raan-, -nzə-, -ˈlaan-, -tēk\ *adj* [*trans-* + *Atlantic* (*ocean*)] **1 :** crossing or extending across the Atlantic ocean ⟨~ voyage⟩ ⟨~ cable⟩ **2 a :** lying or situated beyond the Atlantic ocean ⟨travels to a ~ country⟩ **b :** of, relating to, or characteristic of a people, country, or region beyond the Atlantic ocean ⟨the tacit conflict and mutual yearning of two cultures, the old European and the new ~ —*Times Lit. Supp.*⟩ — **trans·at·lan·ti·cal·ly** \-tək(ə)lē\ *adv*

²**transatlantic** \"\ *n* -s **1 :** one that is or lives across the Atlantic or in a transatlantic country **2 :** a transatlantic ship

trans·border \(ˈ)tran(t)s, -raan-, -nz+\ *adj* [*trans-* + *border*] **:** situated or living beyond the border or frontier — often used of Asian regions or peoples

trans·ca·lent \tranzˈkālənt, -n(t)ˈsk-\ *adj* [*trans-* + L *calent-*, *calens*, pres. part. of *calēre* to be warm — more at LEE] **:** pervious to or permitting the passage of heat

trans·callosal \ˌtranz, -raan-, -n(t)s+\ *adj* [*trans-* + NL (*corpus*) *callosum* + E *-al*] **:** passing through or by way of the corpus callosum ⟨a ~ section⟩ ⟨~ pathways⟩

¹**trans·caucasian** \ˌtranz, -raan-, -n(t)s+\ *adj, usu cap* [*Transcaucasia*, region south of the Caucasus mountains + E *-an*] **1 :** of, relating to, or characteristic of the region of Transcaucasia south of the Caucasus mountains **2 :** of, relating to, or characteristic of the people of Transcaucasia

²**transcaucasian** \"\ *n, cap* **:** a native or inhabitant of Transcaucasia

trans·ceiver \tranzˈsēvə(r), traan-, -n(t)(s)ˈ-\ *n* -s [*trans*mitter + *receiver*] **:** a radio transmitter-receiver that uses many of the same tubes for both transmission and reception

tran·scend \tranˈsend, traanˈ-\ *vb* -ED/-ING/-S [L *transcendere* to climb across, surmount, transcend, fr. *trans-* + *-scendere* (fr. *scandere* to climb) — more at SCAN] *vt* **1 a :** to rise above or go beyond the limits of **:** EXCEED ⟨servants whose loyalty and devotion ~ national and cultural boundaries —C.J. Friedrich⟩ ⟨instinctive courtesy which ~s mere good manners —Richard Joseph⟩ ⟨to possess by self-mastery the sources of love and hate is to ~ good and evil —Havelock Ellis⟩ **b :** to extend above or beyond (as the universe) ⟨~ material existence⟩ ⟨the Christian message ~s all temporal civilizations —Maria Sulzbach⟩ **2 :** to outstrip or outdo in some attribute, quality, or power **:** SURPASS ⟨some of the electrons . . . ~ this speed and take their leave —K.K.Darrow⟩ ⟨her compass ~ed that of her companions in the band —Thomas Hardy⟩ ⟨whose hatred, he says, ~s that of all other races —*Times Lit. Supp.*⟩ ⟨one who has infinitely ~ed him in reputation —Richard Garnett †1906⟩ **3** *obs* **:** to cross or climb over **:** MOUNT **4 :** to cause to rise or go upward **:** ELEVATE, RAISE ⟨man being ~ed toward the universal as worker and citizen —H.M. Parshley⟩ **~** *vi* **1** *obs* **:** to travel upward or onward **:** ASCEND **2 :** EXCEL, SURPASS ⟨it is the function of genius to ~⟩ **syn** see EXCEED

tran·scen·dence \-ndən(t)s\ *n* -s [LL *transcendentia*, fr. L *transcendent-*, *transcendens* + *-ia* -y] **:** the quality or state of being transcendent

tran·scen·den·cy \-nsē, -si\ *n* -ES [LL *transcendentia*] **:** TRANSCENDENCE

¹**tran·scen·dent** *also* **tran·scen·dant** \-nt\ *adj* [*transcendent* fr. L *transcendent-*, *transcendens*, pres. part. of *transcendere* to transcend; *transcendant* fr. F, fr. pres. part. of obs. *transcendre* to transcend, fr. L *transcendere*] **1 a :** going beyond or exceeding usual limits **:** EXCELLING, SURPASSING ⟨his own detestation of the rigors of winter made the children's courage appear ~ —Elinor Wylie⟩ ⟨the ~ importance of news . . . in a democracy —F.L.Mott⟩ ⟨the poet . . . fuses the elements of a profound perception into a single ~ vision —George Whalley⟩ **b :** proceeding beyond or lying outside of what is perceived or presented in experience ⟨philosophers . . . often explicitly reject the notion of any ~ reality beyond thought . . . and claim to be concerned only with thought itself and its immanent necessities —W.P.Alston⟩ **c** *Kantianism* **:** being beyond the limits of all possible experience and knowledge — contrasted with *transcendental* 1b **2 :** being beyond comprehension **:** VAGUE, OBSCURE ⟨too ~, too difficult, and too unrelated to the human heart to satisfy other men —H.O.Taylor⟩ **3 :** being above material existence or apart from the universe ⟨the ideal of a ~ and holy being —M.R.Cohen⟩ ⟨the idea of a source and end of life, too ~ to the . . . powers of human life to be either simply comprehended by the human mind or easily manipulated —Reinhold Niebuhr⟩ — contrasted with *immanent*

²**transcendent** *also* **transcendant** \"\ *n* -s **:** one that transcends: as **a :** a person or thing that escapes classification in any accepted category; *specif* **:** a predicate that cannot be classed among the Aristotelian predicaments **b** *Kantianism* **:** something beyond the limits of experience and knowledge ⟨spirit . . . is a ~ over against that which can be perceived by the senses —R.K.Bultmann⟩

¹**tran·scen·den·tal** \ˌtranˌsenˈdent°l, ˈtran(t)s°nˈ-, -raan-\ *adj* [ML *transcendentalis*, fr. L *transcendent-*, *transcendens* + *-alis* -al] **1 a** *Aristotelianism* **:** reaching or lying beyond the bounds of any category; *also* **:** METAPHYSICAL **b** *Kantianism* **:** of or relating to the a priori and necessary conditions of human experience as determined by the constitution of the mind itself (2) **:** transcending what is determined by the contingent particularity of experience though not transcending all human knowledge — contrasted with *transcendent* 1b **2 :** TRANSCENDENT 1a ⟨few men have had his ~ capacity to stir the heart —J.H.Plumb⟩ ⟨the trout fisherman . . . with that ~ patience —Richard Jefferies⟩ ⟨an event of ~ importance —Rodrigo Miró⟩ **3 :** incapable of being the root of an algebraic equation with rational integral coefficients ⟨π is a ~ number⟩ **4 a :** extending or being beyond the limits of ordinary experience ⟨extreme ~ idealism which viewed the world as the visionary creation of the fallen soul of man —E.S.Bates⟩ ⟨a ~ world of concepts has therefore been envisaged by the philosophers —C.K.Ogden & I.A.Richards⟩ **b :** of or relating to the supernatural ⟨the vital ~ soul, belonging to the spiritual realm —Lewis Mumford⟩ ⟨find ~ motives for sublunary action —Aldous Huxley⟩ **c :** ABSTRUSE, ABSTRACT ⟨that ~ phraseology which defies exact translation —Herbert Read⟩ ⟨insensitive plodders . . . regrettably unable to follow the ~ speculations —C.W.Shumaker⟩ **d :** of or relating to transcendentalism ⟨the ~ belief . . . that every part of nature is an emblem, symbol, or analogue of a spiritual or intellectual truth —R.L. Cook⟩

²**transcendental** \"\ *n* -s **:** something that is transcendental: as **a :** a transcendental idea or doctrine **b** *Scholasticism* **:** any one of the broadest conceptions of being (as being, thing, one, truth) ⟨he appears to assume, in many places but particularly in his demonstrations of God, both that being (or some equivalent ~) is a genus, and that God is in it —H.T.Schwartz⟩

transcendental aesthetic *n, Kantianism* **:** a doctrine of the a priori forms of perception esp. of time and space

transcendental curve *n* **:** a curve whose equations contain transcendental functions

transcendental equation *n* **:** an equation containing transcendental functions of the unknowns

transcendental function *n* **:** a function that is not algebraic

transcendental idealism *n, Kantianism* **:** a doctrine that the objects of perception are conditioned by the nature of the mind as to their form but not as to their content or particularity and that they have a kind of independence of the mind — called also *critical idealism*

tran·scen·den·tal·ism \-°lˌizəm\ *n* -s [¹*transcendental* + *-ism*] **1 a** (1) **:** a philosophic tendency or doctrine of Kantianism emphasizing a priori conditions of knowledge and experience or the unknowable character of ultimate reality (2) **:** a doctrine of post-Kantian idealism that emphasizes what transcends sense experience as being fundamental in reality **b :** a philosophy that asserts the primacy of the spiritual and the intuitive over the material and the empirical; *esp* **:** the 19th century New England movement stressing the presence of the divine within man as a source of truth and a guide to action **2 :** the quality or state of being transcendental; *esp* **:** visionary idealism of character or thought

¹**tran·scen·den·tal·ist** \-°ləst\ *n* -s [¹*transcendental* + *-ist*] **:** an advocate or adherent of transcendentalism

²**transcendentalist** \"\ *adj* **:** of or relating to transcendentalism

tran·scen·den·tal·is·tic \ˌ=(ˌ)=ˌdent°lˈistik\ *adj* [¹*transcendentalist* + *-ic*] **1 :** TRANSCENDENTALIST **2 :** held or believed by a transcendentalist

tran·scen·den·tal·i·ty \ˌ=(ˌ)=den·ˈtaləd·ē\ *n* -ES [¹*transcendental* + *-ity*] **:** the quality or state of being transcendental

tran·scen·den·tal·ize \ˌ=(ˌ)ˈdent°lˌīz\ *vt* -ED/-ING/-S [¹*transcendental* + *-ize*] **1 :** to make transcendent **:** cause to transcend ⟨other Christian critics . . . ~ the values out of all significant contact with action —E.E.Aubrey⟩ **2 :** to make transcendental **:** IDEALIZE ⟨was so easy for him to ~ this emotion —H.S.Canby⟩

tran·scen·den·tal·ly \ˌ=(ˌ)ˈdent°lē, -°li\ *adv* [¹*transcendental* + *-ly*] **:** in a transcendental manner **:** to a transcendent extent

transcendental number *n* **:** a number (as π or *e*) that is not the root of an algebraic equation with rational coefficients

transcendental object *n, Kantianism* **:** a thing in itself or the mere form of an object representing in knowledge our reference of the content of experience to an independent object

transcendental philosophy *n* **:** TRANSCENDENTALISM

transcendental truth *n* **:** METAPHYSICAL TRUTH

tran·scen·dent·ly *adv* **:** in a transcendent manner **:** to a transcendent extent

tran·scen·dent·ness *n* -ES [¹*transcendent* + *-ness*] **:** TRANSCENDENCE

transcending *pres part of* TRANSCEND

tran·scend·ing·ly *adv* [*transcending* (pres. part. of *transcend*) + *-ly*] **:** TRANSCENDENTLY

transcends *pres 3d sing of* TRANSCEND

tran·scen·sion \tranˈsenchən\ *n* -s [LL *transcension-*, *transcensio*, fr. L *transcensus* (past part. of *transcendere* to transcend) + *-ion-*, *-io* -ion] **:** an act, process, or instance of transcending

trans·conductance \ˌtranz, -raan-, -n(t)s+\ *n* [*trans-* + *conductance*] **:** the ratio of a change in the current through one electrode in an electron tube to the change of voltage responsible for it in another electrode with the potentials of the remaining elements being constant — compare MUTUAL CONDUCTANCE

trans·con·ti·nen·tal \ˌtranzˌkänt°nˈent°l, -raan-, -n(t)sk-, -tə¦ne-\ *adj* [*trans-* + *continent* + *-al*] **1 :** extending or going across a continent ⟨a ~ railroad⟩ ⟨a ~ journey⟩ ⟨a ~ traveler⟩ **2 :** of, relating to, or situated on the farther side of a continent ⟨a ~ city⟩ ⟨a ~ product⟩ — **trans·con·ti·nen·tal·ly** \-°lē\ *adv*

trans·cortical \(ˈ)tranz, -n(t)s+\ *adj* [*trans-* + NL *cortic-*, *cortex* cortex + E *-al*] **:** crossing the cortex of the brain; *esp* **:** passing from the cortex of one hemisphere to that of the other ⟨~ stimulation⟩

tran·scribe \tranzˈkrīb, traan-, -n(t)ˈsk-\ *vb* -ED/-ING/-S [L *transcribere*, fr. *trans-* + *scribere* to write — more at SCRIBE] *vt* **1 a :** to make a written copy of ⟨scrupulously *transcribed* from the surviving manuscripts of the war years —D.C.Mearns⟩ **b :** to make a copy of (dictated or recorded matter) in longhand or esp. on a typewriter ⟨taking dictation in the mornings, *transcribing* correspondence in the afternoons —Jean Holloway⟩ ⟨take letters down in shorthand or on the dictating machine and ~ them on the typewriter —E.M.Robinson⟩; *specif* **:** to read aloud (shorthand notes) ⟨lay aside this book and orally ~ your shorthand notes —*Law Stenographer*⟩ **c :** to reproduce in writing by more or less exact quotation **:** PARAPHRASE, SUMMARIZE ⟨I need not ~ any more of this part of the séance —Beverley Nichols⟩ ⟨what he expressed as a mere surmise was *transcribed* by others as a positive statement —Richard Semon⟩ **d :** to write down **:** RECORD ⟨a unique achievement in the amazing fidelity with which it ~s the life and mentality of an alien people —Amy Loveman⟩ ⟨if one looks the jungle straight in the face and ~s what is seen —William Beebe⟩ ⟨is endowed with . . . an unerring ear for *transcribing* speech —Angel Flores⟩ **2** *obs* **:** ASCRIBE, IMPUTE **3 a** (1) **:** TRANSLITERATE ⟨the larger part . . . would be unintelligible if *transcribed* in an alphabet or syllabary —K.S. Latourette⟩ ⟨*transcribed* into Cyrillic characters from the original Glagolitic —R.G.A.DeBray⟩ ⟨his hobby is *transcribing* books into braille —*N. Y. Herald Tribune*⟩ (2) **:** to represent (speech sounds) by means of phonetic symbols ⟨the letter *b* ~s Greek *beta*, which represented a phoneme with both stop and spirant allophones —W.G.Moulton⟩ (3) **:** to arrange (the letters of a cryptogram) by a prescribed route or system ⟨there are 39 routes by which the letters in the rectangle might have been *transcribed* to form the cryptogram —J.M.Wolfe⟩ **b :** TRANSLATE 2a ⟨*transcribed* English hymns into German —*Amer. Guide Series: Pa.*⟩ **c :** to transfer or convey (as information) from one recording form to another ⟨the account number could then be *transcribed* to the receiving ticket —H.D.McGuigan⟩ ⟨reproducers automatically ~ punching from one card to another —H.C.Zeisig & P.T.Martin⟩ **4** *obs* **:** COPY, IMITATE **5 :** to make a musical transcription of ⟨originally written for organ, the work was *transcribed* for symphony orchestra —*Current Biog.*⟩ **6 :** to broadcast (a radio or television program) by electrical transcription ⟨live shows are often replaced with *transcribed* programs⟩ **~** *vi* **1 a :** to make a copy of something in writing ⟨shall begin to ~ again and polish —T.B.Macaulay⟩ **b :** to reproduce in writing dictated or recorded matter ⟨ability to take dictation easily and ~ accurately on the typewriter —*Gregg Dictation Simplified*⟩ ⟨the belts are mailed to the . . . office for *transcribing* —*Dun's Rev.*⟩ **c :** to write down, set forth, or produce a factual or objective representation ⟨some ~ directly from nature —Thomas Munro⟩ ⟨no artist is content to ~ —*New Mexico Quarterly*⟩ **2 :** TRANSLATE 1a ⟨this question of whether they should . . . ~ into modern idiom —H.L.Savage⟩

tran·scrib·er \-bə(r)\ *n* -s **:** one that transcribes; *specif* **:** a person engaged in writing braille for the blind using either a slate and stylus or a braillewriter

transcribing machine *n* [*transcribing*, pres. part. of *transcribe*] **:** a business machine designed to play back electrically recorded dictation (as on a wax cylinder, plastic belt, disc, wire, or tape) for transcription

tran·script \ˈtranzˌkript, ˈtraan-, -n(t)ˌsk-\ *n* -s [ME, fr. ML *transcriptum*, fr. L, neut. of *transcriptus*, past part. of *transcribere* to transcribe] **1 a :** a written or printed copy ⟨a ~ of nine manuscript books —Gilbert Highet⟩ ⟨a volume . . . containing ~s from the papyrological collections —Jack Finegan⟩ **b :** a usu. typewritten copy of dictated or recorded matter ⟨the efficiency of shorthand instruction is to be judged entirely by . . . the ~s turned out by the pupils —C.G.Reigner⟩ **c :** an official or legal and often published copy or engrossment of a decree, testimony, or proceedings ⟨shall submit a ~ in duplicate of the ordinance⟩ ⟨courts have held that in a dispute as to what was said . . . the reporter's ~ must be accepted as final —*Law Stenographer*⟩ ⟨read the ~ of a round-table discussion appearing in the current issue —J.D.Adams⟩; *specif* **:** an official copy of a student's record at an educational institution **2 :** a copy, reproduction, or rendering (as of experience) set forth or expressed usu. in an art form ⟨inexperienced readers take literature more naïvely as ~ rather than interpretation of life —René Wellek & Austin Warren⟩ ⟨the book is a ~ from his own experience —*Brit. Bk. News*⟩ ⟨was an objective painter . . . returning always to his own type of studio-made ~s from life around him —Sheldon Cheney⟩ ⟨the formal content of the religion of the American Negro . . . is a ~, modified for his own uses, of the religion of his white masters in the days of slavery —W.L.Sperry⟩

tran·scrip·tion \tranzˈkripshən, traan-, -n(t)ˈsk-\ *n* -s [L *transcription-*, *transcriptio*, fr. *transcriptus* + *-ion-*, *-io* -ion] **1 :** an act, process, or instance of transcribing **2 :** something transcribed **:** COPY, TRANSCRIPT: as **a :** an arrangement of a musical composition often with some liberty in modification or embellishment for some instrument or voice other than that of the original composition **:** ARRANGEMENT ⟨his ripe scholarship is evidenced . . . in his ~s for organ of great symphonic works —E.C.Krohn⟩ **b :** a tape, disc, or other recording made for broadcast or rebroadcast of a radio or television program **:** ELECTRICAL TRANSCRIPTION ⟨continued on several hundred independent stations and . . . sent overseas by ~ —*Current Biog.*⟩

tran·scrip·tion·al \-shən°l, -shnəl\ *adj* **:** of, relating to, or produced by transcription — **tran·scrip·tion·al·ly** \-shən°lē, -shnəl-, -i\ *adv*

transcription machine *n* **:** PLAYBACK 2

tran·scrip·tive \-ptiv, -tēv *also* -təv\ *adj* [L *transcriptus* (past part. of *transcribere* to transcribe) + E *-ive*] **:** that transcribes or is given to transcription **:** IMITATIVE; *also* **:** produced by transcribing ⟨~ art resulting from the Renaissance scientific search for natural truth —Sheldon Cheney⟩ — **tran·scrip·tive·ly** \-təvlē\ *adv*

trans·crystalline \(ˈ)tranz, -raanz, -n(t)s+\ *adj* [*trans-* + *crystal* + *-ine*] **:** across or through individual crystals as opposed to between or around them — used of fractures or cracks in metals

trans·cultural \"+\ *adj* [*trans-* + *culture* + *-al*] **:** extending through all human cultures or types of human beings ⟨a ~ ideal of freedom which would embrace all the peoples of the world —David Bidney⟩ ⟨~ psychotherapy seems to involve . . . concepts applicable to all human beings —Paula Brown⟩

trans·cul·tu·ra·tion \ˌtranzˌkəlchəˈrāshən, -n(t)ˌsk-\ *n* -s [ISV *trans-* + *culture* + *-ation*; prob. orig. formed in Sp] **:** a process of cultural transformation marked by the influx of new culture elements and the loss or alteration of existing ones — compare ACCULTURATION

trans·cur·rent \(ˈ)tranz, -raanz, -n(t)s+\ *adj* [L *transcurrent-*, *transcurrens*, pres. part. of *transcurrere* to run across, fr. *trans-* + *currere* to run — more at CURRENT] **:** running or extending transversely

trans·cutaneous *also* **trans·cutaneal** \ˌtranz, -raanz, -n(t)s+\ *adj* [*trans-* + *cutaneous*, *cutaneal*] **:** passing or entering through the skin ⟨~ infection⟩ ⟨~ inoculation⟩

trans·dialect \(ˈ)tran(t)s, -raan-, -nz\ *vt* -ED/-ING/-S [*trans-* + *dialect*] **:** to translate from one dialect into another

trans·duc·er \tran(t)sˈd(y)üsə(r), traan-, -nzˈ-\ *n* -s [L *transducere* to lead across (fr. *trans-* + *ducere* to lead) + E *-er*] **:** a device actuated by power from one system and supplying power in the same or any other form to a second system (as a telephone receiver actuated by electric power and supplying acoustic power to the surrounding air or quartz crystals that produce electric power from mechanical power)

trans·duc·tion \-ˈdəkshən\ *n* -s [L *transductus* (past part. of *transducere*) + E *-ion*] **:** the act or process of leading or conveying over; *specif* **:** the carrying of hereditary material (as a gene) from one microorganism to another or from one strain of microorganism to another by a filterable agent (as a bacteriophage)

trans·duc·tor \-ktə(r)\ *n* -s [L *transductus* + E *-or*] **:** a device for controlling or regulating alternating current consisting of two or more coils with a common magnetic core with one of the coils carrying a direct current and the others carrying the alternating current

¹**tran·sect** \tranˈsekt, traan-\ *vt* -ED/-ING/-S [*trans-* + *-sect*] **:** to cut across or transversely ⟨dogs whose spinal cord had been ~ed —*Pharmacological Reviews*⟩ ⟨where a rock mass . . . is ~ed by natural cracks —W.J.Miller⟩ ⟨in ~ing these fields, the present study pursues . . . many patterns —*Books*⟩

²**transect** \ˈ=,=\ *n* -s **:** a sample area of vegetation usu. in the form of a narrow continuous strip that is used esp. for the tabulation of data (as of frequency, size, or yield of different kinds of plants) likely to vary within a stand or area

tran·sec·tion \tranˈsekshən, traan-\ *n* [*trans-* + *section*] **:** CROSS SECTION 1a

trans·el·e·ment \tran(t)ˈseləmənt, -nˈze-\ *also* **trans·el·e·ment·ate** \-mən,ˌtāt\ *vt* -ED/-ING/-S [*transelement* fr. ML *transelementare*, fr. L *trans-* + *elementum* element; *transelementate* fr. ML *transelementatus*, past part. of *transelementare*] **:** to change or transpose the elements of **:** TRANSFORM — **trans·el·e·men·ta·tion** \=,===ˈtāshən\ *n* -s

trans·empirical \ˌtran(t)s, -raan-, -nz +\ *adj* [*trans-* + *empirical*] **:** being beyond experience **:** TRANSCENDENT ⟨positivism had as its basic motivation the elimination of ~ metaphysics —E.C.Moore⟩

tran·sen·na \tranˈsenə\ *n, pl* **transen·nae** \-e,nē\ [L *trasenna*, *transenna* net, latticework, perh. of Etruscan origin] **:** a lattice or screen of stone or metal enclosing and protecting a shrine

tran·sept \ˈtranˌsept, ˈtraan-\ *n* -s [NL *transeptum*, fr. L *trans-* + *septum*, *saeptum* enclosure, wall — more at SEPTUM] **:** the transversal part of a cruciform church that crosses at right angles to the greatest length between the nave and the apse or choir — see BASILICA illustration

transept aisle *n* **:** the aisle of a transept corresponding to the side aisle of a nave

tran·sep·tal \(ˈ)tranˈsept°l, -raan-\ *adj* **:** of or relating to or like a transept ⟨~ style⟩ ⟨~ position⟩ ⟨~ towers⟩ — **tran·sep·tal·ly** \-°lē\ *adv*

transept chapel *n* **:** a chapel opening off a transept

trans·esterification \ˌtran(t)s, -raan-, -nz+\ *n* [*trans-* + *esterification*] **:** a reversible reaction in which one ester is converted into another (as by interchange of ester groups with an alcohol in the presence of a base)

trans·e·unt \ˈtran(t)sēənt\ *adj* [L *transeunt-*, *transiens*, pres. part. of *transire* to go across or beyond — more at TRANSIENT] **:** TRANSIENT 2

transeuntes *pl of* TRANSIENS

transf *abbr* **1** transfer; transferred **2** transformer

transfd *abbr* transferred

¹**trans·fer** *R* tranzˈfər, traan-, -n(t)sˈf-, ˈ=(ˌ)=, + *vowel* -fər-; *-R* -fə̄, + *suffixal vowel* -fər- *also* -fər, + *vowel in a following word* -fər- *or* -fə̄ *also* -fər\ *vb* **transferred; transferred; transferring; transfers** [ME *transferren*, fr. L *transferre*, fr. *trans-* + *ferre* to carry, bear — more at BEAR] *vt* **1 a :** to

carry or take from one person or place to another : TRANSPORT, REMOVE ⟨from underneath the litter he drew a packet . . . and *transferred* it deftly to the blue suit —D.M.Davin⟩ ⟨travelers were *transferred* to sloops to complete the journey —*Amer. Guide Series: N. J.*⟩ ⟨an effort was made to ~ a good share of the appointments from the president to congressmen —W.C. Ford⟩ **b :** to move or send to a different location esp. for business, vocational, or military purposes ⟨*transferred* her law practice to Greenville —*Current Biog.*⟩ ⟨the company plans to ~ him to its west coast plant⟩ ⟨was commandant at Fort Pitt . . . and in the latter year was *transferred* to the remote frontier —C.F.Cochran⟩ **c :** to cause to pass from one person or thing to another : TRANSMIT ⟨motion would be *transferred* from two cogged wheels to the big wheel through an endless chain —John Kobler⟩ ⟨no way in which he could ~ his own memories of European civilization into the Indian mind —Willa Cather⟩ **d :** to cause to transform : CHANGE — usu. used with *into* ⟨had *transferred* barren wastes . . . into fertile fields —Albert Hyma⟩ ⟨may upon occasion ~ himself into a tiger —Fay-Cooper Cole⟩ **2 :** to make over or negotiate the possession or control of (a right, title, or property) by a legal process usu. for a consideration : CONVEY ⟨to preserve the farm intact he ~*s* it to one heir⟩ ⟨*transferred* a part of their holdings . . . for $25,000 worth of stock —Marquis James⟩ **3 :** to print, impress, or otherwise copy (as a drawing or engraved design) from one surface to another ~ *vi* **1 :** to go or move to a different place or region to carry on a business or vocation ⟨*transferred* from the bookshop to the concert agency and was . . . placed in charge of that division —*Current Biog.*⟩ ⟨the company is *transferring* to an eastern location⟩ ⟨will ~ to the armored division as soon as his papers can be cleared⟩; *specif* **:** to withdraw from one educational institution to enroll at another ⟨students can ~ to other leading colleges . . . without loss of credits —Ruth Wilson⟩ **2 :** to change from one vehicle or transportation line to another ⟨took the streetcar and *transferred* to the bus —Robert Hazel⟩ **syn** see MOVE

²transfer \'=,=\ *n* -s *often attrib* **1 a :** the conveyance of right, title, or interest in either real or personal property from one person to another by sale, gift, or other process **b :** the removal or acquisition of property by mere delivery with intent of the parties involved to transfer the title **c :** an order transferring shares of stock or money; *specif* **:** a telegraphic order to pay to one party money deposited by another at a distant office **2 :** an act, process, or instance of transferring : TRANSFERENCE ⟨proposal for . . . a ~ of populations on a voluntary basis —*Current History*⟩ ⟨finds occasion for the ~ of his loyalty to a new cause⟩ **3 :** one that is transferred: as **a :** a picture produced by affixing to a support an image orig. developed on a separate temporary support — compare BROMOIL TRANSFER, CARBON TRANSFER **b :** a drawing or writing printed in reverse from one surface on another; *specif* **:** a reverse pattern (as for embroidery or a trademark) waxed or inked on tissue paper for printing on a textile material with the heat and pressure of an iron **c** (1) **:** a drawing in lithographic crayon made or printed on paper and then impressed on stone or other material from which it is to be printed by lithography (2) **:** a specially prepared sheet of lithographic paper containing a design to be transferred from the original stone to a stone or metal printing surface **d :** TRANSFER PICTURE **e :** an individual shifted from one military unit to another ⟨orders the sergeant to check in the new ~*s*⟩ **f :** a student that changes from one school to another ⟨a limited number of ~*s* can be accepted by the college⟩ **4 :** the distance a ship gains to the right or left from the time the helm is put over until it is on its new course — compare ADVANCE 8 **5 a :** a place where cars or trains are transferred to boats or ferries for water transportation; *also* **:** a boat or ferry used for this purpose **b :** TRANSFER HOUSE **c :** a point where a change is made from one form of power to another (as from electricity to steam) **d** (1) **:** a turnout connecting two tracks at a crossing with switches outside the end frogs of the crossing (2) **:** a track connecting roads that cross on separated grades **e** (1) **:** TRANSFER COMPANY (2) **:** a vehicle of such a company **f :** a ticket given with or without extra charge to a passenger on a public conveyance entitling him to continue his journey on another route or conveyance **6 a :** TRANSFERENCE 2 **b :** the carry-over or generalization of learned responses from one type of situation to another; *specif* **:** the application in one field of study or effort of knowledge, skill, power, or ability acquired in another ⟨there will be a certain degree of ~ from one skill to another if we direct our teaching to this end —Eliezer Rieger⟩ ⟨could not easily make the ~ from book to life —H.A.Overstreet⟩ **7 :** the moving of knitted stitches from one machine (as a ribber) to another

trans·fer·abil·i·ty \tranz,fərə'biləd·ē, ,tranz(,)f-, traan-, -n(t)(,)sf-, -lətē, -i\ *n* **:** the quality or state of being transferable ⟨sterling ~ affords a means of multilateral settlement for . . . trade between nondollar countries outside the sterling area —R.F.Mikesell⟩

trans·fer·able *also* **trans·fer·ra·ble** \tranz'fərəbəl, -n(t)'sf-, 'tranz(,)f-, -n(t)(,)sf-, -raan-\ *adj* **1 :** capable of being transferred or conveyed from one place or person to another ⟨good and bad are but names, very readily ~ to that or this —R.W. Emerson⟩ **2 :** capable of being made over from one party to another so as to vest in the transferee all the transferor's legal rights, title, or interest in the property being transferred : NEGOTIABLE ⟨~ stock⟩ ⟨a ~ account⟩ ⟨some tickets are not ~⟩

transferable vote *n* **:** a vote that in balloting by proportional representation may be transferred to a candidate other than the one marked as first choice — compare HARE SYSTEM

transfer agent *n* **:** the officer, bank, or trust company that keeps the ownership records and makes the transfer of title of corporate stock or other registered securities

trans·fer·al *also* **trans·fer·ral** \tranz'fərəl, traan-, -n(t)'sf-\ *n* -s [¹*transfer* + *-al*] **:** TRANSFERENCE, TRANSFER

trans·fer·ase \'tranzfə,rās, -n(t)sf-\ *n* -s [¹*transfer* + *-ase*] **:** any of various enzymes (as transaminases) that promote a transfer reaction

transfer book *n* **:** a register of transfers (as of shares of stock) from one party to another

transfer box *n* **:** a metal box in which one or more corresponding electric circuits are connected or branched

transfer caliper *n* **:** a caliper equipped with an adjustable or removable leg to permit use of the caliper in narrow or confined spaces — often used in pl.

transfer case *n* **1 :** a filing unit for storage of inactive correspondence or records **2 :** a housing containing gears used to distribute the driving power between the axles of vehicles equipped with more than one driving axle and usu. having a shifting lever for disengaging the front-wheel drive

transfer company *n* **:** a transportation company that transfers passengers or baggage usu. for a short distance between specified points or terminals

trans·fer·ee \¦tranzfə¦rē, -raan-, -n(t)sf-\ *n* -s [¹*transfer* + *-ee*] **1 :** a person to whom a transfer or conveyance is made — compare TRANSFERRER a **2 :** one who is transferred (as from one position or place to another) ⟨reserve officer ~*s* —*All Hands*⟩ ⟨the various population shifts of ~*s*, refugees, displaced persons —E.M.Kulischer⟩

trans·fer·ence \tranz'fərən(t)s, traan-, -n(t)'sf-; 'tranzfər(ə)n(t)s, 'traan-, -n(t)sf-, -frən-\ *n* -s [NL *transferentia*, fr. L *transferent-*, *transferens* (pres. part. of *transferre* to transfer) + *-ia* -y] **1 :** an act, process, or instance of transferring : CONVEYANCE, PASSAGE, TRANSFER **2 :** the redirection toward a new object (as a psychoanalyst) of feelings and desires esp. as unconsciously retained from childhood

transference neurosis *n* **:** a neurosis developed in the course of psychoanalytic treatment and manifested by the reliving of infantile experiences in the presence of the analyst

transference number *n* **:** the fraction of the total current carried either by the anion or the cation in electrolysis — called also *transport number*

trans·fer·en·tial \¦tranzfə¦renchəl, -raan-, -n(t)sf-\ *adj* [NL *transferentia* + E *-al*] **:** of or relating to transference

transfer house *n* **:** a station where freight is rehandled before proceeding to final destination

transfer ink *n* **:** ink used in transferring designs (as from paper to stone) that often contains wax, soap, lampblack, and shellac

transfer molding *n* **:** a process of molding plastics in which the molding material is softened by preheating and then forced into a closed heated mold

transfer of fire : the shifting of artillery fire from one target to another with the application of corrections determined from the adjustment on the first target to the initial firing data for the second

transfer of training : TRANSFER 6b

trans·fer·o·type *also* **trans·fer·ro·type** \tranz'fərə,tīp, -n(t)'sf-\ *n* [¹*transfer* + *-o-* + *type*] **:** a bromide print transferred from a paper backing to some other surface; *also* **:** the process by which this is done

transfer paper *n* **:** a paper coated with a special preparation for transferring a design or imprint to another surface by heat, pressure, or moisture — compare DECALCOMANIA

transfer payment *n* **1 :** any of various public expenditures (as veterans benefits or unemployment compensation) made for purposes other than procuring goods or current services — usu. used in pl. **2 :** money (as welfare payments or a pension) received by an individual or a family other than compensation (as wages or profits) for goods or services currently supplied or income (as interest or dividends) from investments

transfer picture *n* **:** a picture transferred or prepared for transference (as from specially prepared paper by means of the decalcomania process)

transfer printing *n* **1 :** DECALCOMANIA **2 :** a process of pottery decoration in which designs engraved on copper or drawn on stone are transferred to the ware by the use of tissue paper

transfer process *n* **:** any of several processes in which a pigmented or dyed image is transferred from one surface to another

transferrable *var of* TRANSFERABLE

transferral *var of* TRANSFERAL

transfer reaction *n* **:** a chemical reaction (as a transamination) in which a group is transferred from one molecule to another

transferred *past of* TRANSFER

transferred intent *n* **:** the intent to commit a specific wrong or crime that is imputed to a wrongdoer who in the execution of an intent to do some wrongful act commits an unintended wrong or crime

trans·fer·rer *also* **trans·fer·er** \tranz'fərə(r), traan-, -n(t)'sf-\ *or* **trans·fer·or** *or* **trans·fer·ror** \¦=(,)fər¦ȯ(ə)r, -ȯ(ə)\ *n* -s [¹*transfer* + *-er* or *-or*] **:** one that transfers: as **a** *usu* *transferor* **:** one that makes or executes a conveyance of a title, right, or property ⟨the validity of a transfer, as between the *transferor* and the transferee, is governed by the law —J.F. Spindler⟩ **b :** one that transfers images from photographic negatives to zinc plates for printing by the lithographic process **c :** one that transfers designs from engraved lithographic stones directly to zinc plates or to cellophane sheets that will be photographed on zinc plates in preparation for printing by the lithographic process **d :** a worker who prints numerals, minute and second tracks, and the company name on watch dials with an engraved plate in a transfer machine

transferrible *archaic var of* TRANSFERABLE

trans·fer·rin \tranz'ferən, -n(t)'sf-\ *n* -s [*trans-* + L *ferrum* iron + E *-in* — more at FARRIER] **:** a beta globulin in blood plasma that is capable of combining with ferric ions and of transporting iron to various parts of the body — called also *siderophilin;* compare FERRITIN

transferring *pres part of* TRANSFER

transferring machine *n* **:** a press for impressing an engraved and hardened steel die on a soft steel roller that is afterward hardened and used to impress a plate (as for printing bank notes or stock certificates)

transfers *pres 3d sing of* TRANSFER, *pl of* TRANSFER

transfer stamp *n* **:** a sales transfer tax stamp

transfer table *n* **:** a platform with one or more tracks moving laterally on wheels for shifting railroad locomotives or cars from one track to another one parallel to it

transfer tax *n* **1 :** INHERITANCE TAX 1 **2 :** an excise tax levied upon the transfer of real or esp. intangible property among the living and often signified by revenue stamps affixed to the instrument effecting the transfer

transfer track *n* **:** a railroad station track for loading or unloading freight

trans·fig·u·ra·tion \(,)=,==′rāshən\ *n* -s [ME, fr. MF, fr. L *transfiguration-*, *transfiguratio*, fr. *transfiguratus* (past part. of *transfigurare* to transfigure) + *-ion-*, *-io* -ion] **1 a :** an act, process, or instance of changing or being changed in form or appearance : METAMORPHOSIS ⟨the autumnal ~ had just begun —*New Yorker*⟩ ⟨astonished people by becoming a society man . . . a ~ —Norman Douglas⟩ **b :** an act, process, or instance of undergoing an exalting, glorifying, or spiritual change ⟨in poetry and art may be seen the ~ of nature⟩ ⟨a new elevation of the mind of man . . . in this ~ the arts have a noble and vital part to play —Sir Winston Churchill⟩ **2** *usu cap* **a :** a church feast observed in some branches of the Christian church on August 6 in commemoration of the Transfiguration of Jesus recorded in the New Testament **b :** an artistic representation of the Transfiguration

trans·fig·ure \tranz'figyə(r), traan-, -n(t)'sf-, ÷ -gə(r)\ *vt* [ME *transfiguren*, fr. L *transfigurare*, fr. *trans-* + *figurare* to shape, fashion, form, fr. *figura* figure] **1 :** to change the form or appearance of : TRANSFORM ⟨her face was *transfigured* by uncontrollable passion —Arnold Bennett⟩ ⟨his will has been *transfigured* by association with the wills of others —B.N. Cardozo⟩ — often used with *into* ⟨his . . . special gifts led him to ~ the wasteland into a circus —C.J.Rolo⟩ ⟨nationalism was *transfigured* into internationalism —C.B.Forcey⟩ **2 :** EXALT, GLORIFY, SPIRITUALIZE ⟨the great cliffs and domes were *transfigured* in the hazy golden air —John Muir †1914⟩ ⟨music . . . will ~ plain meanings and clothe the verbal substance with a kind of incandescence —A.T.Davison⟩ ⟨the same sacrifice *transfigured* the communicants who shared the mystery —Oscar Handlin⟩ — often used with *into* ⟨her beautiful face was *transfigured* into the ravishingly angelic —Arnold Bennett⟩ ⟨the moment when good verse . . . is *transfigured* into a thing that takes the breath away —C.D.Lewis⟩ **syn** see TRANSFORM

¹trans·finite \(')tranz, -raanz, -n(t)s+\ *adj* [G *transfinit*, fr. *trans-* (fr. L) + *finit* finite, fr. L *finitus*, past part. of *finire* to limit, finish, end — more at FINISH] **1 :** going beyond or surpassing any finite number, assemblage, or magnitude ⟨that world where pain and pleasure take on ~ values and all our arithmetic is dismayed —C.S.Lewis⟩ ⟨God . . . must be ~ beyond conception —C.O.Gorham⟩ **2 a :** being a power of a mathematical aggregate whose cardinal number is not finite ⟨aleph-null is the smallest ~ cardinal number⟩ **b :** being either an index of the ordered set of all natural numbers or generated from this index by purely algebraic means ⟨~ ordinal numbers⟩

²transfinite \"\ *n* -s **:** a transfinite number, assemblage, or magnitude

trans·fix \tranz'fiks, traan-, -n(t)'sf-\ *vt* [L *transfixus*, past part. of *transfigere* to transfix, fr. *trans-* + *figere* to fix, fasten, pierce — more at DIKE] **1 :** to pierce through with or as if with a pointed weapon or instrument : TRANSPIERCE, IMPALE ⟨he ~*es* the pig with his spear⟩ ⟨the knight must . . . ~ with his lance small rings suspended —*Amer. Guide Series: Md.*⟩ ⟨uses the hypodermic to puncture but not to ~ the vein⟩ ⟨he ~*ed* her with a piercing glance⟩ **2 :** to affix, fasten, or hold motionless by or as if by piercing esp. with an absorbing emotion or interest — often used with *to* or *into* ⟨plunged their stout spears into his belly and ~*ed* him to the earth —A.A. Grace⟩ ⟨was ~*ed* to the spot with eyes that pierced —Zane Grey⟩ ⟨had seen the pain ~ his friend's face and . . . it was white —Owen Wister⟩ ⟨an idea occurred to him and ~*ed* him into a statue —Alvin Johnson⟩ ⟨poetry . . . ~*es* its subject in a form which has a life of its own forever —R.P.Blackmur⟩

trans·fix·ion \-kshən\ *n* -s [LL *transfixion-*, *transfixio*, fr. L *transfixus* + *-ion-*, *-io* -ion] **1 :** an act, process, or instance of transfixing or of being transfixed ⟨there was only silence and ~ in the gray world above the forests —J.R.Ullman⟩ **2 :** a piercing of a part of the body (as by a suture, nail, or other device) in order to fix it in position

¹trans·form \tranz'fȯ(ə)rm, traan-, -n(t)'sf-, -ȯ(ə)m\ *vb* [ME *transformen*, fr. L *transformare*, fr. *trans-* + *formare* to form] *vt* **1 a :** to change completely or essentially in composition or structure : METAMORPHOSE — usu. used with *into* or *to* ⟨the sea king's daughter is ~*ed* into a river —Alfred Frankenstein⟩ ⟨life-giving water which ~*s* the dusty sagebrush lands into fertile fields —*Amer. Guide Series: Texas*⟩ ⟨the process which ~*ed* the lumber . . . into gunstocks —C.W.Mitman⟩ ⟨the processes by which policy is ~*ed* into law and administration —A.N.Holcombe⟩ **b :** to change the outward form or appearance of : ALTER ⟨for a moment the smile ~*ed* his face —J.C.Smith b.1924⟩ ⟨the drizzle that had so greatly ~*ed* the scene —Thomas Hardy⟩ ⟨science . . . has ~*ed* the world as the scene of the human drama —C.W.Eliot⟩ — often used with *into* or *to* ⟨an elaborate experiment in camouflage meant to ~ it into . . . farms and orange groves —J.G.Cozzens⟩ ⟨the setting sun suddenly ~*ed* the . . . peaks to furnace red —George Farwell⟩ **c :** to change in character or condition : CONVERT, TRANSFIGURE ⟨do not be conformed to this world but be ~*ed* by the renewal of your mind —Rom 12:2 (RSV)⟩ ⟨a change in the economic condition is not alone sufficient to ~ woman's situation —*Nation*⟩ — often used with *to* ⟨inventions and discoveries which quickly ~ the people . . . from barbarism to civilization —R.W.Murray⟩ **2 :** to subject to a usu. mathematical or logical transformation **3 a :** to change (one form of energy) into another ⟨the engine ~*s* potential energy into motion⟩ **b :** to change (a current) in potential (as from high voltage to low voltage) or in type (as from alternating to continuous) ~ *vi* **:** to become transformed : CHANGE ⟨the growing Crepidula first becomes a male and later . . . ~*s* into a female —W.C.Allee⟩ ⟨a proton . . . can ~ into a neutron —R. E.Marshak⟩ ⟨sofas that ~ for use as a bed⟩

syn METAMORPHOSE, TRANSMUTE, CONVERT, TRANSMOGRIFY, TRANSFIGURE: these all signify in common to change one thing into another or different thing. TRANSFORM can mean a change in outward shape or form or in character, nature, or function ⟨the old rock quarry . . . has been *transformed* into a large baseball and football field and is used as a skating rink in the winter —*Amer. Guide Series: Minn.*⟩ ⟨water, in the shape of rain, will always *transform* that gray soil into a sort of sticky black glue —C.E.W.Bean⟩ ⟨*transform* the hunger and misery of the people into hatred —Stanley Ross⟩ METAMORPHOSE may add the idea of a supernaturally or magically induced change; it may be confined to a change in structure or habits marking a stage in the development of some form of animal life or a change induced by chemicals or powerful natural agencies, in general, however, suggesting an abrupt, striking, or violent alteration ⟨a plain girl *metamorphosed* into a dazzling beauty⟩ ⟨a caterpillar *metamorphosed* into a butterfly⟩ ⟨rocks *metamorphosed* by heat into hard crystals⟩ TRANSMUTE suggests an elemental change esp. involving a metamorphosis of a lower element or thing into a higher ⟨the alchemists had believed that base metals could be *transmuted* into gold by such a process —S.F.Mason⟩ ⟨modern atomic science can actually *transmute* metals — plutonium is a *transmuted* metal —*Time*⟩ ⟨art not only adds something new, but seems to *transmute* and enrich the old —Clive Bell⟩ CONVERT usu. stresses a change in detail that fits a thing to a given or esp. a new use or function rather than an overall change ⟨the stupendous task of *converting* virgin wilderness into farms and homes —*Amer. Guide Series: Texas*⟩ ⟨the business of *converting* novels into musicals —Lewis Funke⟩ TRANSMOGRIFY suggests a metamorphosis that is often grotesque or bewildering and sometimes preposterous ⟨the classical heroes and heroines were *transmogrified* into medieval knights and ladies —J.L.Lowes⟩ ⟨the monarch *transmogrified* into a horse, a beast, but still royal —Jean S. Untermeyer⟩ TRANSFIGURE suggests an exaltation or glorification in outward appearance ⟨in Bonnard's paintings, the colors of nature are marvelously heightened, enriched, *transfigured* —David Sylvester⟩ ⟨all the tenderness that had *transfigured* his face the day before shone there, as he bent over her —Clive Arden⟩

²transform \'=,=\ *n* -s **:** TRANSFORMATION 6

trans·form·able \tranz'fȯ(r)məbəl, traan-, -n(t)'sf-\ *adj* **:** capable of being transformed

trans·form·ance \-ȯrmən(t)s\ *n* -s [¹*transform* + *-ance*] **:** TRANSFORMATION ⟨the ~ of any common event into a news story —Walter Rae⟩

trans·for·ma·tion \,tranzfə(r)'māshən, ,traan-, -n(t)sf-\ *n* -s [ME, fr. LL *transformation-*, *transformatio*, fr. L *transformatus* (past part. of *transformare* to transform) + *-ion-*, *-io* -ion] **1 :** an act, process, or instance of transforming or being transformed ⟨in the earliest time . . . ~*s* were common, and there was apparently no real line between animal and human —Frederica de Laguna⟩ ⟨~ of the farm lands into a magnificent estate —*Amer. Guide Series: Mich.*⟩ ⟨the ~ of policy into law —A.N.Holcombe⟩ ⟨the ~ of men's political thinking —Ellery Sedgwick⟩ ⟨the ~ of man's nature in Christ —Dietrich von Hildebrand⟩ **2 a** (1) **:** physiological change of one thing into another (as chemicals in assimilation and metabolism or larva into adult through metamorphosis) (2) **:** SPERMIOGENESIS (3) **:** EVOLUTION 5b **b :** TRANSMUTATION d **c :** a change in the atomic arrangement of a metal or metal alloy **3 :** TRANSFORMATION SCENE **4 :** false hair esp. as worn by a woman to replace or supplement natural hair — compare TOUPEE 2 **5 :** the changing of an expression, formula, or statement in logic into a different form without altering its substance or intent **6 a :** the substitution of one configuration (as by rotation or translation) for or the alteration of a mathematical expression (as by change of form or substitution of values) into another in accord with a mathematical rule **b :** a formula or rule governing such a substitution or alteration

trans·for·ma·tion·ist \-shənəst\ *n* -s [*transformation* + *-ist*] **:** TRANSFORMIST

transformation of coordinates : the introduction of a new set of mathematical coordinates that are stated distinct functions of the original coordinates

transformation range *n* **:** the range of temperature within which austenite forms or disappears when ferrous alloys are heated or cooled

transformation rule *n* **:** a principle in logic establishing the conditions under which one statement can be derived or validly deduced from one or more other statements esp. in a formalized language — called also *rule of deduction;* compare MODUS PONENS, MODUS TOLLENS

transformation scene *n* **:** a theatrical scene or setting that changes in sight of the audience; *specif* **:** a scene in the English pantomime in which the characters change to take part in the harlequinade proper

transformation temperature *n* **:** the temperature at which a change in phase occurs; *also* **:** the limiting temperature of a transformation range

trans·form·a·tive \tranz'fȯ(r)məd·iv, traan-, -n(t)'sf-, -ətiv\ *adj* [ML *transformativus*, fr. L *transformatus* (past part. of *transformare* to transform) + *-ivus* -ive] **:** having the power or a tendency to transform : TRANSFORMING ⟨the ~ experience that individuals undergo as . . . they focus their minds upon a significant piece of writing —H.A.Overstreet⟩

transformed *past of* TRANSFORM

trans·form·er \-ȯrmər, -ȯ(ə)mə(r\ *n* -s **:** one that transforms: as **a :** a device employing the principle of mutual induction to convert variations of current in a primary circuit into variations of voltage and current in a secondary circuit and typically consisting of two separate coils usu. with different numbers of turns wound on the same closed laminated iron core — see AUTOTRANSFORMER, CURRENT TRANSFORMER, PHASING TRANSFORMER **b :** a mythical figure (as a culture hero) in the legends of primitive cultures noted for bringing about the present order of the world by transforming its previous order

transformer oil *n* **:** an insulating oil (as a refined petroleum distillate) used esp. in transformers

transforming *pres part of* TRANSFORM

trans·form·ism \-ȯ(r),mizəm\ *n* -s [F *transformisme*, fr. *transformer* to transform (fr. L *transformare*) + *-isme* -ism] **:** EVOLUTION 5b ⟨regarded ~ as untenable . . . as no one had ever seen one species changing into another —R.H.Lowie⟩

trans·form·ist \-ȯrməst, -ȯ(ə)m-\ *n* -s [F *transformiste*, fr. *transformer* + *-iste* -ist] **:** an adherent of transformism

transforms *pres 3d sing of* TRANSFORM, *pl of* TRANSFORM

trans·fus·able *or* **trans·fus·ible** \tranz'fyüzəbəl, traan-, -n(t)'sf-\ *adj* **:** capable of being transfused ⟨~ blood⟩

trans·fuse \-üz\ *vt* -ED/-ING/-S [ME *transfusen*, fr. L *transfusus*, past part. of *transfundere* to transfuse, fr. *trans-* + *fundere* to pour — more at FOUND] **1 a** *archaic* **:** to transfer (a liquid) by or as if by pouring **b** (1) **:** to cause to flow or pass from one to another : TRANSMIT, INSTILL ⟨seeks to ~ his ideas throughout the land⟩ — often used with *into* or *to* ⟨~*s* his enthusiasm into others⟩ ⟨the animal spirits . . . are *transfused* from father to son —Laurence Sterne⟩ (2) **:** to flow or diffuse into or through

: PERMEATE ⟨the sunlight ~s the bay⟩ ⟨life is not merely an added property of matter but something that ~s and transforms it —H.J.Muller⟩ ⟨the wise men of the earth whose serenity ~s their style —H.S.Canby⟩ **2 a** : to transfer (as blood or saline) into a vein of a man or animal **b** : to subject (a patient) to transfusion ⟨the time to ~ patients is immediately after an injury occurs —*Commonweal*⟩

trans·fu·sion \-ˈfyüzhən\ *n* -s [L *transfusion-, transfusio*, fr. *transfusus* + *-ion-, -io ion*] : an act, process, or instance of transfusing; *esp* : the act or operation of transferring blood or other fluid into a vein or artery of a man or animal

transfusion cell *n* : PASSAGE CELL

trans·fu·sion·ist \-nəst\ *n* -s [*transfusion* + *-ist*] : one skilled in the transfusion of blood or other fluid

transfusion tissue *n* : tissue that is found characteristically around the vascular bundles of gymnosperm leaves and consists of both living and dead cells like those of parenchyma with walls that are not lignified and thin-walled but lignified tracheids with bordered pits

trans·ge·na·tion \ˌtran(t)sjəˈnāshən, ˌtraan-, ˌnzj-\ *n* -s [*trans-* + *gene* + *-ation*] : GENE MUTATION

trans·gran·u·lar \(ˈ)tran(t)s, ˌtraan-, -nz+\ *adj* [*trans-* + LL *granulum* little grain + E *-ar* — more at GRANULE] : TRANSCRYSTALLINE

¹**trans·gress** \tran(t)sˈgres, ˌtraan-, -nzˈ-\ *vb* -ED/-ING/-ES [F *transgresser*, fr. L *transgressus*, past part. of *transgredi* to step beyond or across, cross, fr. *trans-* + *-gredi* (fr. *gradi* to step, go) — more at GRADE] *vt* **1** : to go beyond limits set or prescribed by (law or command) : BREAK, VIOLATE ⟨had ~*ed* a solemn unwritten law and thereby fallen to the position of an enemy of society —Hamilton Basso⟩ ⟨~*ed* the divine law . . . is doomed to eternal punishment —A.C.McGiffert⟩ **2** : to pass beyond or go over (a limit or boundary) : CROSS ⟨the adjacent seas ~*ed* almost all the coast . . . at the close of the last glaciation —J.B.Bird⟩ ⟨can migrate . . . and ~ their natural climatic barriers —S.A.Cain⟩ ⟨the power . . . to ~ economic and political boundaries —C.D.Forde⟩ ~ *vi* **1** : to break or violate a command or law : TRESPASS, SIN ⟨we downrightly ~*ed* by . . . taking off our stockings to wade in the brook —Mary Austin⟩ **2** : to go beyond a boundary or limit ⟨an Arctic sea ~*ed* southward through western Canada —E.B.Branson & W.A.Tarr⟩

²**transgress** \ˈ⸗ˌ⸗\ *n* -ES : TRANSGRESSION b

trans·gres·sion \tran(t)sˈgreshən, ˌtraan-, -nzˈ-\ *n* -s [ME, fr. MF, fr. LL *transgression-, transgressio*, fr. L, act of crossing, passing over, fr. *transgressus* + *-ion-, -io ion*] : an act, process, or instance of transgressing: as **a** : the infringement or violation of a law, command, or duty : SIN, TRESPASS ⟨God, what are my ~*s* that they brought me here —Henry Baerlein⟩ ⟨summoned me for . . . some ~ of college rules —A.D.White⟩ ⟨simple ingratitude to a benefactor was a pardonable ~ —George Meredith⟩ **b** (1) : UNCONFORMITY 3a (2) : the spread of the sea over land areas and the consequent unconformable deposition of sediments on older rocks **syn** see BREACH

¹**trans·gres·sive** \-esiv, -sēv *also* -sov\ *adj* [L *transgressus* + E *-ive*] **1** *archaic* : disposed or tending to transgress, violate, or go beyond a limit **2** : progressively overlapping or passing over or beyond ⟨a suite of ~ sediments⟩ ⟨the deposits of ~ seas⟩ **3** : going beyond the limits set by the ancestral condition usu. because of segregation and recombination of polygenic factors in the progeny of a hybrid ⟨~ variation⟩ ⟨~ inheritance⟩ **b** *of a plant* : being at different stages of the life history a part of more than one section of the community of which it is a member — **trans·gres·sive·ly** \-sᵊvlē, -li\ *adv*

²**transgressive** \"\ *n* -s : a transgressive element of an ecological community

trans·gres·sor \-ə(r)\ *n* -s [ME, fr. LL, fr. L *transgressus* + *-or*] : one that transgresses; *esp* : one who breaks a law or violates any known rule or principle of rectitude : SINNER ⟨the way of ~*s* is hard —Prov 13:15(AV)⟩

transhape *var of* TRANSSHAPE

tranship *var of* TRANSSHIP

trans·hu·man \(ˈ)tranz, ˌtraan-, -nz+\ *adj* [*trans-* + *human*] : transcending human limits : SUPERHUMAN ⟨his profound intimation of ~ magnificence —the alien grandeur of nature —Robert Fitzgerald⟩

trans·hu·mance \tranzˈhyümən(t)s, ˌtraan-, -n(t)sˈ-\ *n* -s [F, fr. *transhumer* to practice transhumance (fr. Sp *trashumar*, fr. *tras-* trans- — fr. L *trans-* + L *humus* earth, ground) + *-ance* — more at HUMBLE] : seasonal movement of livestock and esp. sheep between mountain and lowland pastures either under the care of herders or (as among various pastoral peoples) accompanied by the whole population of owners — compare NOMADISM

¹**trans·hu·mant** \-mᵊnt\ *n* [F & Sp; F *transhumant* practicing transhumance, fr. Sp *trashumante*, fr. *trashumar* to practice transhumance] **1** *pl* **trans·hu·man·tes** \-ˌⸯhyüˈman-ˌtēz\ : a merino sheep of one of the great flocks kept in Spain by a system of transhumance esp. prior to the 19th century and esteemed for the quality and fineness of the wool **2** *pl* **transhumants** : a person who practices transhumance

²**transhumant** \"\ *adj* : of, relating to, or involving transhumance ⟨a ~ culture⟩ ⟨~ movements⟩

tran·sience \ˈtranchən(t)s, ˈtraan- *sometimes* -nzēən- *or* -n(t)sēən- *or* -nzhən- *or* -njən-\ *n* -s [fr. ¹*transient*, after such pairs as E *permanent: permanence*] **1** : the quality or state of being transient : PASSAGE, MOVEMENT ⟨the instability and ~ of all things in the stream of time —L.P.Smith⟩ ⟨the ~ of enthusiasms —O.S.J.Gogarty⟩ ⟨need for the canvass should be determined by the size of the city but by . . . a high rate of ~ —Katharine T. Kinkead⟩

tran·sien·cy \-ˌⸯⸯⸯⸯⸯⸯⸯⸯ, -si\ *n* -ES [¹*transient* + *-cy*] : TRANSIENCE ⟨a pervading sense of the ~ of all earthly things —Allan Nevins⟩ ⟨the lodging house . . . dates from the beginning of large-scale labor —Nels Anderson⟩

tran·si·ens \ˈtran(t)sēˌenz, -nzē-\ *n, pl* **tran·se·un·tes** \ˌtran(t)sēˈün-ˌtēz, -nzē-\ [NL *transeunt-, transiens*, fr. L, pres. part. of *transire*] : a phase in migratory locusts in which they exhibit characteristics in morphology and behavior intermediate between those typical of solitaria and gregaria

¹**tran·sient** \ˈtranchənt, ˈtraan- *sometimes* -nzēᵊnt *or* -n(t)sēᵊnt *or* -nzhᵊnt *or* -njᵊnt\ *adj* [L *transeunt-, transiens*, pres. part. of *transire* to go across or beyond, cross over, pass, pass away, fr. *trans-* + *ire* to go — more at ISSUE] **1 a** : passing away in time or ceasing to exist : IMPERMANENT, TRANSITORY, SHORT-LIVED ⟨not even spring beauty . . . was so ~ —like music fading away —Ruth Suckow⟩ ⟨features of their culture were ~; they do not exist —John Dewey⟩ ⟨the Leyden jar gave only ~ electrical current, but the voltaic cell . . . provided a continuous source of current —S.F.Mason⟩ ⟨if the patient is examined . . . when the circulatory impairment is ~ or rapidly compensated —Alfred Blalock⟩ **b** : passing through or by a place with only a brief stay or sojourn ⟨~ agricultural population with discouraged settlers constantly pulling up stakes and drifting on —*Amer. Guide Series: Ariz.*⟩ ⟨the hotel accommodates ~ guests⟩ ⟨the ~ butterfly —Edna S. V. Millay⟩ **c** *of a musical modulation* : introduced momentarily or in passing from one key to a third one **2** : passing beyond itself : outwardly effective or efficient : EMANANT ⟨the creation of the universe considered as a ~ act⟩ — contrasted with *immanent* **3** : passing from one person or thing to another ⟨dominant traits ~ through succeeding generations⟩

syn TRANSITORY, PASSING, EPHEMERAL, MOMENTARY, FLEETING, FUGITIVE, EVANESCENT, SHORT-LIVED: TRANSIENT often describes that which is short in its duration or stay and passes quickly ⟨after a *transient* seventh-century conquest by Assyria, Egypt experienced one more flourishing renascence (663–525) of its old patterns under native rulers —A.L.Kroeber⟩ ⟨guilt in Mrs. Clay's face as she listened . . . was *transient*: cleared away in an instant —Jane Austen⟩ ⟨the excitement of the examination may produce violent and rapid heart action, often associated with *transient* systolic murmur —H.G.Armstrong⟩ TRANSITORY and PASSING may suggest the notion of the inevitability of changing, ending, or dying out ⟨their eyes were lifted from the earth . . . not concerned with its *transitory* things, soon to be consumed —H.O.Taylor⟩ ⟨the pleasures of taste, at best, are *transitory* —Virgil Thomson⟩ ⟨have omitted no important event and no incident of more than *passing* interest —Bernard De Voto⟩ ⟨men are given to the trick of hav-

ing a *passing* fancy for somebody else in the midst of a permanent love, which reasserts itself afterwards just as before —Thomas Hardy⟩ EPHEMERAL may suggest the idea of living only for a day; it describes only that which endures for a similar brief period ⟨the life of the mayfly is *ephemeral*⟩ ⟨the very best of our experience is not as good as our dreams: our most exquisite moments are flawed and fragmentary . . . *ephemeral* —David Cecil⟩ MOMENTARY applies to that which endures only a moment or similar quite short period ⟨being a work of men's hands, it gave the child a *momentary* sense of comfort, of companionship in the dreadful wild —C.G.D.Roberts⟩ ⟨the *momentary* lulls between succeeding waves —C.B.Nordhoff & J.N.Hall⟩ FLEETING may suggest a flying transitoriness making it hard or impossible to arrest or apprehend the thing in question ⟨to take advantage of these *fleeting* opportunities, one must have a quick control over his own mind —S.M.Crothers⟩ ⟨how to seize the *fleeting* impressions of that dream —P.E.More⟩ FUGITIVE may suggest that whatever is described may be thought of as in flight and seeking to escape apprehension ⟨here is the last chance to feel young . . . but the days are *fugitive* and most of us are too busy —E.A.Weeks⟩ ⟨there were moments of *fugitive* sunshine, but of such brief duration that they but added to our misery —C.B.Nordhoff & J.N.Hall⟩ EVANESCENT describes that which is quite fleeting and likely to vanish away; it may apply to the delicate, fragile, unsubstantial, and airy ⟨the quality of her charm was *evanescent* . . . forever fleeing —Elinor Wylie⟩ ⟨of lusters with so *evanescent* a sheen their colours are felt, but never seen —Amy Lowell⟩ ⟨the scholar with perspective of his subject is aware . . . that part of his business is to distinguish the *evanescent* fad from permanent progress —A.L.Kroeber⟩ SHORT-LIVED stresses the fact of brevity of existence ⟨as *short-lived* as Wells' paper, lasting only from July 14 until October 15 —*Amer. Guide Series: Fla.*⟩

²**transient** \"\ *n* -s **1** : one that is transient: as **a** : a transient guest or boarder ⟨motels cater chiefly to ~*s*⟩ **b** : an often homeless person traveling about usu. in search of work or a living ⟨a city of permanent ~*s* who shift . . . from one section to another — wherever they can find food and coal —Norman Cousins⟩ ⟨the great bulk of ~*s* are law-abiding individuals . . . in pursuit of employment —H.A.Bloch⟩ **2 a** : a temporary or rapidly changing state or condition of an electrical system; *specif* : a temporary electrical oscillation that occurs in a circuit because of a sudden change of voltage or of load **b** : a transient current or voltage

transient cause *n*, *Spinozism* : a cause originating or having its effects outside an entity — contrasted with *immanent cause*

transient current *n* : an oscillatory or aperiodic current that flows in a circuit for a short time following an electromagnetic disturbance (as a nearby stroke of lightning)

tran·sient·ly *adv* : in a transient manner : for a short time : BRIEFLY

transient second class *n* : a class of mail in the U.S. and Canada comprising newspapers and periodicals sent as separate issues by the public or as samples by the publisher

transient vendor *or* **transient dealer** *or* **transient merchant** *n* : any person who either as principal or agent engages in a temporary or transient business either in one locality or in traveling from place to place buying or selling goods, wares, or merchandise

tran·sil·ience \tranˈsilēən(t)s, ˌtraan-, -lyən-\ *n* -s [fr. L *tran-silient*, after such pairs as E *resilient: resilience*] : an abrupt change or variation : TRANSITION; *specif* : such a change or variation in a geological formation

tran·sil·ient \-nt\ *adj* [L *transilient-, transiliens*, pres. part. of *transilire* to leap across, fr. *trans-* + *-silire* (fr. *salire* to leap) — more at SALLY] **1** : passing abruptly from one thing to another; *specif* : marked by breaches of continuity or abrupt transitions or variations in geological structure ⟨~ rocks⟩

trans·il·lu·mi·nate \(ˈ)tran(t)s, ˌtraan-, -nz+\ *vt* [*trans-* + *illuminate*] : to cause light to pass through; *specif* : to pass light through (a part of the body) to discover or examine a pathological condition

trans·il·lu·mi·na·tion \"+\ *n* : an act, process, or instance of transilluminating

trans·il·lu·mi·na·tor \"+\ *n* : an instrument for effecting transillumination

trans·in·di·vid·u·al \"+\ *adj* [*trans-* + *individual* (n.)] : going between individuals : passing from one to another ⟨the question whether environmental influences . . . have a ~ action —*Human Embryology*⟩ ⟨the ~ processes of interaction and societal circumstances —P.A.Sorokin⟩

trans·i·re \tranˈt)siˌrē\ *n* -s [L, to pass — more at TRANSIENT] *Eng* : a customs document describing the cargo, consignors, and consignees for clearance and entry of coasting vessels

trans·isth·mi·an \(ˈ)tran(t)s, ˌtraan-, -nz+\ *adj* [*trans-* + *isthmus* + *-ian*] : extending or going across an isthmus ⟨a ~ canal⟩ ⟨~ route⟩

tran·sis·tor \tranˈzistə(r), ˌtraan-, -n(t)sˈi-\ *n* -s [*transfer* + *resistor*; fr. its transferring an electrical signal across a resistor] : an electronic device similar in use to the electron tube consisting of a small block of a semiconductor (as germanium) on which are placed three electrodes of which the emitter and the collector make contact at points very close together on one side of the block while a metal plate makes contact on the opposite side with the operation of the device depending upon the peculiar conducting properties of semiconductors and the electrons moving in one direction are considered as leaving holes that serve as carriers of positive electricity in the opposite direction

tran·sis·tor·ize \-ˌrīz\ *vt* -ED/-ING/-s : to equip (a device) with transistors

¹**tran·sit** \ˈtran(t)sət, ˈtraan-, -nzət, *usu* -ᵊd-+V\ *n* -s [L *transitus*, fr. *transitus*, past part. of *transire* to go across, pass — more at TRANSIENT] **1 a** : an act, process, or instance of passing or journeying across, through, or over : JOURNEY, PASSAGE ⟨the ~ of so vast a body through Roman territory could not but be dangerous —J.A.Froude⟩ ⟨the ~ of radio signals from the earth to the moon and back —J.W.Townsend⟩ ⟨a fine case study of the ~ of ideas from Europe to America —R.E.Riegel⟩ ⟨our ~ across the little span of life —W.L.Sullivan⟩ **b** : passage across : CHANGE, TRANSITION ⟨to bolster morale . . . in the ~ from war to peace —Dixon Wecter⟩ ⟨the ~ from fall to winter, from this life to the next⟩ **c** (1) : the conveyance or carriage of persons or things from one place to another ⟨pigeons were used to provide the fastest ~ for written messages —W.G.East⟩ ⟨there were also commissions . . . on communications and ~ —C.E.Black & E.C.Helmreich⟩ ⟨uses all modes of ~ to ship his products⟩ (2) : the transportation esp. of people by means of bus, subway train, or other usu. local system of public conveyance ⟨the problems of urban ~ are complex⟩ — compare RAPID TRANSIT; *also* : the system, vehicles, or facilities engaged in such transportation ⟨within easy reach are . . . schools, shopping centers, and ~ —*advt*⟩ ⟨85 out of 100 shoppers . . . arrived there by ~, as against nine out of 100 by auto —Sam Stavisky⟩ **2** : the passing of a planet across or through any natural point or place on the zodiac **3 a** : the passage of a celestial body over the meridian of a place or through the field of a telescope — called also *culmination* **b** : the passage of a smaller body across the disk of a larger (as of Venus or Mercury across the sun's disk) **4** *or* **transit compass** : a variety of theodolite with the telescope mounted so that it can be transited — called also *transit theodolite* — **in transit** *adv* : in passage : in the process of transit ⟨billions of messages . . . are always in *transit* between individuals and group —Stuart Chase⟩ ⟨of those at sea half were in the combat zone and half in *transit* —J.P.Baxter b. 1893⟩ ⟨some are men who have never come to rest and are always in *transit* —Oscar Handlin⟩

²**transit** \"\ *vb* -ED/-ING/-s *vi* **1** : to go over or through : PASS ⟨ships use the canal to ~ to the west⟩ ⟨to steer to a destination through which the line ~*ed* —David Beaty⟩ **2** : to make a transit across a meridian, a celestial body, or the field of view of a telescope ⟨expects the planet to ~ shortly after midnight⟩ ~ *vt* **1 a** : to pass over or through : CROSS, TRAVERSE ⟨~*ed* La Perouse strait on the surface at night —E.L.Beach⟩ ⟨from San Juan to Guantánamo Bay you ~ the windward passage —Lee Rogow⟩ **b** : to cause to pass over or through : CONVEY ⟨the canal . . . can be operated around the clock to ~ a total of 36 ships daily —*Ships and the Sea*⟩ **2** : to pass across (a meridian,

a celestial body, or the field of view of a telescope) **3** : to turn (a telescope) over about its horizontal transverse axis in surveying

tran·sit·able \-ᵊd-əbəl\ *adj* [²*transit* + *-able*] : capable of being crossed or passed over

transit charge *n* [¹*transit*] : a charge provided in a carrier's transit tariff to cover costs incurred in serving a shipper with transit privileges

transit circle *n* : MERIDIAN CIRCLE

transit department *n* : the department of a bank that clears and collects checks or transit items drawn on out-of-town banks

transit duty *n* : a tax imposed on goods passing through a country

tran·sit·er \-ᵊd-ə(r)\ *n* -s [¹*transit* + *-er*] : a transit attachment consisting of a wire that can be made to traverse the field of a transit at a rate that will keep it continuously bisecting an object (as a star) passing across the field of view and of a device for registering such passage across definite points in the field

transit floater *n* : a blanket insurance policy covering all types of shipments without requiring the insured to report all the numerous items to the underwriter in advance

transit instrument *n* **1** : a telescope that is mounted at right angles to a horizontal east-west axis on which it revolves with its line of collimation in the plane of the meridian and that is used in connection with a clock and chronograph for observing the time of transit of a celestial body over the meridian of a place **2** : TRANSIT 4

tran·si·tion \tran(t)sˈishən, ˌtraan-, -nˈzi-\ *n* -s [L *transition-, transitio*, fr. *transitus* (past part. of *transire* to go across, pass) + *-ion-, -io ion* — more at TRANSIENT] **1 a** : a passage or movement from one state, condition, or place to another : CHANGE ⟨in what shadowy spot . . . does the ~ from the dead to the quick take place —*Treasury of Science*⟩ ⟨the ~ from childhood to adulthood⟩ ⟨the abrupt ~ of her features from assured pride to ludicrous astonishment and alarm —Arnold Bennett⟩ ⟨that evening at the time of ~ in the sky —Ethel Wilson⟩ ⟨here guided missiles can pass through a complete sea-land ~ —J.C.Waugh⟩ ⟨an age of ~ and flux⟩ **b** : a movement, development, or evolution from one stage, form, or style to another usu. of a later time or period ⟨the ~ to another usu. of a later time or period⟩ ⟨the ~ of American civilization from agricultural to urban —N.B.Fagin⟩ ⟨a ~ from native bronze to iron artifacts took place . . . under the influence of cultural borrowings —R.W.Murray⟩ ⟨the ~ of early English architecture ⟨a ~ . . . from the inorganic to the organic, from the inanimate to the living —W.R.Inge⟩ **2 a** : a passing from one subject to another esp. without abruptness ⟨having told all her griefs . . . was soon able to make a voluntary ~ to the oddities of her cousin —Jane Austen⟩; *specif* : a passage of discourse in which a shift of subject is gradually effected ⟨has a bleakly ungraceful habit of making his ~s in the form of a question as a topic sentence —B.H.Bronson⟩ **b** (1) : a musical modulation; *esp* : a transient modulation (2) : a sudden change of key (3) : a musical passage leading from one section of a piece to another usu. by a fade, moving from one dramatic scene to another usu. by a fade, sound effects, music, or narration ⟨uses an onstage narrator who streamlines the ~ between scenes —*Time*⟩ **3** : an abrupt change in the energy state or energy level of an atomic electron, a nucleus, or a molecule accompanied in general by the loss or gain of a single quantum of energy — compare QUANTUM THEORY

²**transition** \"\ *adj, usu cap* : of, relating to, or being a biogeographic zone having plants and animals of the zones on each side ⟨the *Transition* zone between the Boreal and Austral zones of No. America⟩

tran·si·tion·al \-shənᵊl, -shnᵊl\ *adj* **1** : of, relating to, or characterized by transition ⟨at this ~ point of its nightly roll into darkness —Thomas Hardy⟩ ⟨the Sudan is ~ between the hot desert . . . and the tropical rainy lands —D.D.Crary⟩ ⟨~ between gothic and roman —J.C.Tarr⟩ ⟨this ~ stage has become terminal in some races —Weston La Barre⟩ ⟨an effective ~ passage . . . which leads to the entry of the second subject —Dyneley Hussey⟩ **2** *usu cap* **a** : MESOLITHIC **b** : of or relating to Maya culture of the period A.D. 900–987 and overlapping and following the final stages of the Old Empire period — **tran·si·tion·al·ly** \-shᵊnᵊlē, -shnᵊl-, -li\ *adv*

transitional cell *also* **transitional** *or* **transitional leukocyte** *n* : MONOCYTE

transitional epithelium *n* : epithelium consisting of two or three layers of cells that are usu. more or less flattened or cuboidal

transition area *n* : GRADED AREA

tran·si·tion·ary \-shəˌnerē\ *adj* [*transition* + *-ary*] : TRANSITIONAL

transition curve *or* **transition spiral** *n* : EASEMENT CURVE

transition element *or* **transition metal** *n* : any of the series of metals (as scandium, titanium, vanadium, chromium, manganese, iron, cobalt, nickel) that fall in the center of the long form of the periodic table, that include as inner series the lanthanide series and the actinide series, that have valence electrons in two shells instead of only one, and that as characterized in most cases by variable oxidation states and magnetic properties

transition fit *n* : a mechanical fit in which a clearance or interference fit may be obtained within the specified tolerance

transition point *n* : a single point at which different phases of matter are capable of existing together in equilibrium — called also *inversion point*

transition region *n* : the region of a plant axis within which the vascular arrangement characteristic of the stem changes to that of the root

transition temperature *n* : a transition point on a temperature scale

¹**tran·si·tive** \ˈtran(t)sᵊd-iv, ˈtraan-, -nzə-, -ət\ *adj* [LL *transitivus*, fr. L *transitus* (past part. of *transire* to cross over, pass) + *-ivus* -ive — more at TRANSIENT] **1 a** *of a verb form* : expressing an action that carries over from an agent or subject to an object : taking a direct object **b** *of a grammatical construction* : containing a transitive verb form **2** : passing or leading successively on to members of a class or a series of developments : TRANSIENT 2 ⟨a moment connected with a wider complex of moments in a ~ chain that goes on indefinitely —Eliseo Vivas⟩ ⟨the main use of ~ parts is to lead us from one substantive conclusion to another —William James⟩; *specif* : of or relating to a logical relationship between *x*, *y*, and *z* such that if *x* has a specified relation to *y* and *y* to *z* then *x* has this relationship to *z* **3** : of, relating to, or involving transition : TRANSITIONAL **4** : passing or descending to another in law ⟨a ~ covenant binds not only its original maker but also his representatives⟩ — **tran·si·tive·ly** \-ᵊvlē, -li\ *adv* — **tran·si·tive·ness** \-ivnəs\ *n* -ES

²**transitive** \"\ *n* -s : a verb form or grammatical construction expressive of transitive force

tran·si·tiv·i·ty \ˌtran(t)siˈtivəd-ē, -nzə-\ *n* -ES [*transitive* + *-ity*] : the quality or state of being transitive

trans·i·tiv·ize \ˈtran(t)səd-əˌvīz, -nzə-\ *vt* -ED/-ING/-s [¹*transitive* + *-ize*] : to make (a verb form) transitive (as by adding a suffix)

tran·sit·man \ˈ⸗⸗mən\ *n, pl* **transitmen** [¹*transit* + *man*] : one who uses the surveyor's or engineer's transit

transit mix *n* : concrete or mortar moistened and mixed in a truck mixer en route to or at the work site — compare READY-MIX

transit number *n* : a number assigned to a bank by an official organization (as the American Bankers Association) and printed on its checks for identification

tran·si·to·ri·ly \ˈtranzəˌtōrəlē, ˌtraan-, -n(t)səˌ-, -tȯr-, -li\ *adv* : in a transitory manner : TRANSIENTLY, TEMPORARILY

tran·si·to·ri·ness \ˌ⸗⸗ˈtōrēnəs, -tȯr-, -rin-\ *n* -ES : the quality or state of being transitory ⟨the sense of the impermanence of things, the ~ of ~ the life —Laurence Binyon⟩

tran·si·to·ry \ˈ⸗⸗ˌtē, -ˌrij, -ˌtȯr\ *adj* [ME *transitorie, transitore*, fr. MF *transitoire*, fr. LL *transitorius*, fr. L, of or allowing passage, fr. *transitus* (past part. of *transire* to go across, pass, pass fr. *transire* — more at TRANSIENT] **1 a** : marked by the quality of passing away : EVANESCENT, TRANSIENT ⟨barter

the ~ pleasures of the world for the heavenly hope —Nathaniel Hawthorne⟩ ⟨thoughts are illusive, ~, fleeting, thin shadows of reality —William Zukerman⟩ ⟨objects of sense . . . are ~ and ephemeral —Frank Thilby⟩ **b :** of brief duration : existing momentarily : TEMPORARY ⟨the depression of occipital activity may be ~, lasting only for minutes or seconds —Oscar Sugar⟩ ⟨those who spend a ~ period in the public service —O.G.Stahl⟩ ⟨a ~ and impermanent occurrence like a shriek —Samuel Alexander⟩ ⟨the postage stamp renders only one ~ service, which is wholly exhausted within one financial period —S.W.Rowland & Brian Magee⟩ **2 :** TRANSITIONAL **syn** see TRANSIENT

transitory action *n* **:** an action (as for debt) that may be brought in any county or district where jurisdiction can be secured over the person of the defendant — compare LOCAL ACTION

transit privileges *n pl* [*transit*] **:** a carrier service available to a shipper by which a through rate instead of two local rates is applied to a shipment that is stopped en route for storage or processing — compare MILLING-IN-TRANSIT

transit rate *or* **transit charge** *n* **:** a rate applied to a shipment that is milled, stored, or treated in transit

tran·si·tron \ˈtran(t)sə,trän, -nzə-\ *n* -s [perh. fr. *transition* + *-tron*] **:** a pentode operating under conditions where the transconductance of the tube is negative and permits the tube to be used in oscillator, trigger, or similar circuits

transits *pl of* TRANSIT, *pres 3d sing of* TRANSIT

transit theodolite *n* [¹*transit*] **:** TRANSIT 4

transit time *n* **1 :** the observed or predicted time of the transit of a celestial body across the meridian **2 :** the time required for a particle (as an electron) to traverse the distance between two specified points (as from cathode to plate in a vacuum tube)

tran·si·tus \ˈtran(t)sədəs, ˈtraan-, -nzə-, -ətəs\ *n* -ES [L, passage, transit — more at TRANSIT] **:** transit of a person or property en route from one place to another — compare STOPPAGE IN TRANSITU

¹**trans-jordanian** \ˌtran(t)s, -raan-, -nz+\ *adj, usu cap* [fr. *Transjordania*, former name of Hashemite Kingdom of Jordan in northwest Arabia + E *-an*] **:** JORDANIAN

²**transjordanian** \"\ *n* -s *cap* **:** JORDANIAN

trans-jor·dan·ic \"+jȯ(r)ˈdanik\ *adj, usu cap J* [*trans-* + *Jordan*, river of eastern Palestine + *-ic*] **:** lying or situated beyond or across the Jordan river

transl *abbr* translated; translation

trans·lat·abil·i·ty \tran(t)ˌslādəˈbilədē, -nz,lā-\ *n* **:** the quality or state of being translatable ⟨such a literary work is beyond ~ —Murray Krieger⟩

trans·lat·able \tran(t)ˈslādəbəl, traan-, -nzˈl-, -ātəb-\ *adj* **:** capable of being translated ⟨sustenance readily ~ to the American home table —Lawton Mackall⟩ ⟨the social contacts . . . were all ~, sooner or later, into political manipulation —H.F.Graff⟩ ⟨languages . . . ~ into and from these symbolic characters —Caroline Yale⟩

trans·late \tran(t)ˈslāt, traan-, -nzˈ- *also* ˈ=,= , *usu* -ād.+V\ *vb* -ED/-ING/-S [L *translatus, tralatus* (suppletive past part. of *transferre* to transfer, translate), fr. *trans-* + *latus*, suppletive past part. of *ferre* to bear, carry — more at BEAR, TOLERATE] *vt* **1 a :** to bear, remove, or change from one place or condition to another : TRANSPORT, TRANSFER, CONVEY — usu. used with *to* ⟨I was *translated* from the country to the city —Kenneth Mackenzie⟩ ⟨he *translated* the fight . . . to the public arena —L.M.Hughes⟩ ⟨a fine play has been superlatively *translated* to the screen —*Current Biog.*⟩ ⟨the saint's relics were *translated* from the crypt to the . . . shrine —Dorothy G. Spicer⟩ ⟨*translated* him to the War Department —N.W.Stephenson & H.W.H.Knott⟩ **b :** to remove or convey to heaven or to a nontemporal condition without death ⟨by faith Enoch was *translated* that he should not see death —Heb 11:5 (AV)⟩ ⟨those Muslims who hold that the Mahdi was *translated* in an earlier century⟩ **c :** to transfer (a bishop) from one see to another ⟨if a bishop be *translated* he must be introduced as the holder of the see —T.E.May⟩ **2 a :** to turn into one's own or another language : RENDER ⟨is learning to ~ Latin⟩ — usu. used with *into* ⟨Chinese ideograms are *translated* into Japanese —David Diringer⟩ ⟨had to ~ the characters into spoken Korean —Cornelius Osgood⟩ **b :** to transfer or turn from any special system of representation, set of symbols, or calculus into another such system, set, or calculus : TRANSCRIBE — usu. used with *into* ⟨imperative that the reporter ~ his notes into longhand —B.M.Metzger⟩ ⟨~ books into braille⟩ ⟨a linguistic code . . . can be *translated* into a binary code —R.W.Brown b. 1925⟩ ⟨~ mathematical truths into logical truths⟩ **c :** DECODE, ENCODE ⟨this solution will permit the cryptanalyst to ~ additional messages —W.W.R.Ball⟩ ⟨when he ~s his message into a coded one —Aaron Bakst⟩ **d :** to express in different words : PARAPHRASE — usu. used with *into* ⟨what remains of the poetry after we have *translated* it into prose⟩ ⟨the terminology used by technicians . . . is *translated* into the language of the layman —Lucile Bagwell⟩ **e :** to express in explanatory or more comprehensible terms : EXPLAIN, INTERPRET ⟨the element which is so difficult to ~ in the idea of fair play —Margaret Mead⟩ ⟨it ~s my childish impressions accurately enough —A.T.Quiller-Couch⟩ ⟨all such novels have their special language which you must ~ . . . to learn the real intention of the artist —M.D.Geismar⟩ — often used with *into* ⟨has *translated* Moloc's words into contemporary human terms —Wayne Burns⟩ **3 a :** to change the substance, form, or appearance of : TRANSFORM, TRANSMUTE, CONVERT — usu. used with *into* ⟨~s the girl into a witch⟩ ⟨the projection kinescope . . . ~s the video signal into a pattern of light and shadows on the tube face —C.L.Dawes⟩ ⟨cars are *translated* into scrap —*New Yorker*⟩ ⟨the time required to ~ new ideas into practical military weapons —H.S.Truman⟩ ⟨the prime mover which ~s energy into power —Roger Burlingame⟩ ⟨designers ~ the . . . styling of an import into a modified and wearable version for the American woman —Dorothy O'Neill⟩ **b** *Brit* **:** to transform (old garments or shoes) by repairing, renovating, or remaking from old materials ⟨for two of these the costumes were *translated* from old sets —E.K.Chambers⟩ ⟨a number of men were fixing up — *translating* — old boots —Robert Sandall⟩ **4 :** TRANSPORT, ENRAPTURE, ENTRANCE **5 :** to change the position of (a body or figure) in space without rotation **6 :** to repeat or forward (a message) by telegraphic translation ~ *vi* **1 a :** to practice rendering from one language or representational system into another ⟨he ~s for the patent attorney⟩; *also* **:** to make such a rendering or translation ⟨no one but a language learner needs to be told . . . that a word-for-word transposition does not ~ —Jackson Mathews⟩ ⟨in class the teacher asks him to ~⟩ **b :** to admit of or be adaptable to translation ⟨words that ~ into every language —D.D.Eisenhower⟩ ⟨a Portuguese word that does not ~ easily —David Dodge⟩ **2 :** to repeat or forward a message by telegraphic translation

trans·lat·er \-ād·ə(r), -ātə-\ *n* -s [¹*translate* + *-er*] **:** TRANSLATOR

trans·la·tion \tran(t)ˈslāshən, traan-, -nzˈl-\ *n* -s [ME *translacioun*, fr. MF or L; MF *translation*, fr. L *translation-, translatio*, fr. *translatus* (suppletive past part. of *transferre* to transfer, translate) + *-ion-, -io* -ion] **:** an act, process, or instance of translating: as **a :** a rendering from one language or representational system into another ⟨~ is an art that involves the re-creation of a work in another language for readers with a different background —Malcolm Cowley⟩; *also* **:** the product of such a rendering ⟨collaborated on a Chippewa grammar and on ~s of the Bible —*Amer. Guide Series: Minn.*⟩ ⟨is in possession of a single cipher message with its ~ —W.W.R.Ball⟩ **b :** the removal, transfer, or conveyance from one place or condition to another ⟨the bishop's ~ to a different see⟩ ⟨promotion and ~ to a higher . . . sphere of activity —Harold Stein⟩ ⟨his ~ to an unaccustomed office life —Manfred Nathan⟩ **c :** a change or alteration to a different substance, form, or appearance : TRANSFORMATION, TRANSMUTATION, CONVERSION ⟨a mechanical ~ of sound into light and color —Leon Becker⟩ ⟨the ~ of the scientific knowledge into practical instruments —Lewis Mumford⟩ ⟨the ~ of the common will into action —Clement Attlee⟩ ⟨the ~ of habits of life and modes of thought into wood and stone —*Amer. Guide Series: Conn.*⟩ ⟨an almost immediate ~ from reality to art —Marya Mannes⟩ **d** *Roman & Scots law* **:** a transfer of property; *esp* **:** an assignment by an assignee of a debt by deed to another **e** (1) **:** a shift in position without rotation (2) **:** translational or translatory motion **f :** the automatic repeating or forwarding of a message (as by a telegraphic relay) **g :** a moving of rectangular axes parallel to themselves

trans·la·tion·al \-shənᵊl, -shnəl\ *adj* **:** of, relating to, or involving translation: as **a :** of, consisting in, or resulting from translation from one language or system to another ⟨~ differences in connotation⟩ **b :** of, relating to, or characterized by uniform motion in one line or direction — **trans·la·tion·al·ly** \-shənᵊlē, -shnəl-, -li\ *adv*

trans·la·tive \-ād.iv\ *adj* [L *translativus*, fr. *translatus* + *-ivus* -ive] **1 :** of, relating to, or involving removal or transference from one person or place to another: as **a :** of, involving, or marked by translational motion **b :** operating to transfer a right from one person to another **2 :** of, relating to, or serving to translate or render from one language or system into another **3 :** FACTIVE 2a

trans·la·tor \tran(t)ˈslād·ə(r), traan-, -nzˈl-, -ātə- *also* ˈ=,==\ *n* -s [ME *translatour, translatore*, fr. MF or L; MF *translatour*, fr. L *translator*, fr. *translatus* + *-or*] **:** one that translates: as **a :** one that translates or renders from one language or system to another **b** *Brit* **:** a repairer of clothing, umbrellas, or old shoes **c :** the relay apparatus used in translation : REPEATER **d :** a part of a dial telephone system that controls the routing of the connection

trans·la·tor·ese \tran(t)ˌslād·əˌrēz, -nzˌl-, -ēs\ *n* -s [*translator* + *-ese*] **:** the jargon of a translator : poorly translated matter

trans·la·to·ry \ˈtran(t)slə,tōrē, ˈtraan-, -nzl-, -tȯr-, -ri\ *adj* [L *translatus* + E *-ory*] **:** TRANSLATIONAL b

translatory motion *n* **:** motion in which all points of a moving body move uniformly in the same line or direction

trans·lit·er·ate \tran(t)ˈslid-ə,rāt, traan-, -nzˈl-, -itə,, *usu* -ād.+V\ *vt* -ED/-ING/-S [*trans-* + L *litera* letter + E *-ate* — more at LETTER] **1 :** to represent or spell (words, letters, or characters of one language) in the letters or characters of another language or alphabet ⟨~ Sanskrit words with roman letters⟩ ⟨the New Testament was *transliterated* into rabbinic characters —B.M.Metzger⟩ **2 :** TRANSLATE 2a ⟨the ability of a restaurant waiter to ~ orders into a language understood only by himself and the cook —*Coronet*⟩

trans·lit·er·a·tion \(ˌ)=,==ˈrāshən\ *n* -s [*transliterate* + *-ion*] **:** an act, process, or instance of transliterating ⟨a table of seven different systems of ~ of Russian —Gregory Razran⟩; *also* **:** the product of such transliterating ⟨Biblical Hebrew provides us with far stranger ~s from the cuneiform —S.L. Caiger⟩

trans·lit·er·a·tor \=ˈ==,rād·ə(r)\ *n* -s [*transliterate* + *-or*] **:** one that transliterates

trans·lo·cate \(ˈ)tran(t)ˈslō,kāt, traan-, -nzˈl-, *usu* -ād.+V\ *vt* [prob. back-formation fr. *translocation*] **:** to change the location or position of : DISLOCATE, DISPLACE; *esp* **:** to transfer (as food materials or products of metabolism) from one location to another in the plant body

trans·location \ˌtran(t)s, -raan-, -nz+\ *n* [*trans-* + *location*] **:** an act, process or instance of translocating ⟨water, wind, ice, and human agency are the chief factors in ~ and accumulation of dead shells in areas other than those in which they originate —H.J.Van Cleave⟩: as **a :** CONDUCTION 3; *esp* **:** the transfer of water from one part of a plant body to another **b :** the attachment of a broken-off segment of one chromosome to another; *esp* **:** the exchange of parts between nonhomologous chromosomes — compare CROSSING-OVER

trans·lu·cence \tran(t)ˈslüsᵊn(t)s, traan-, -nzˈl-\ *n* -s [fr. *translucent*, after such pairs as E *transparent: transparence*] **1 :** TRANSLUCENCY ⟨the soft ~ of the lighted globe⟩ **2 :** an act or instance of shining through or being outwardly apparent ⟨in his every act is the ~ of a noble character⟩

trans·lu·cen·cy \-nsē, -si\ *n* -ES [*translucent* + *-cy*] **:** the quality or state of being translucent : a partial transparency ⟨an X-ray picture . . . starting in the black, going up through the grays, and reaching a clear ~ —P.F.Titterington⟩ ⟨a ray of sunlight striking through the red or gold *translucencies* of wine in a glass —W.J.Locke⟩

trans·lu·cent \-nt\ *adj* [L *translucent-, translucens*, pres. part. of *translucēre* to shine through, fr. *trans-* + *lucēre* to shine — more at LIGHT] **1 :** shining or glowing through : PENETRATING, LUMINOUS ⟨the ~ rays of the sun⟩ **2 a :** TRANSPARENT ⟨materials used . . . for making windows or other ~ objects —*Notes & Queries on Anthropology*⟩ ⟨the water was ~, and I could readily watch from . . . the canoe what was going on —V.G. Heiser⟩ **b :** readily perceptible : CLEAR, LUCID ⟨his way of teaching, his ~ exposition —H.O.Taylor⟩ ⟨an interpretation . . . amazingly delicate and ~ —C.G.Poore⟩ ⟨the early piano is beautifully ~ throughout its compass —Robert Donington⟩ **3 :** admitting and diffusing light so that objects beyond cannot be clearly distinguished : partly transparent ⟨nothing could penetrate them except in the limited way that light penetrated ~ substances —Lewis Mumford⟩ ⟨the ~ skin showing the radiant rose beneath —W.H.Hudson †1922⟩ ⟨~ amber —Elinor Wylie⟩ **syn** see CLEAR

trans·lu·cent·ly *adv* **:** in a translucent manner

translucent reflector *n* **:** a partly transparent reflector used in semi-indirect lighting

trans·lu·cid \-üsəd\ *adj* [L *translucidus*, fr. *translucēre* to shine through] **:** TRANSLUCENT 3

trans·lu·nary \ˈtran(t)slü,nerē, -nzl-; (ˈ)tran(t)ˈslünərē, -nzˈl-\ *adj* [*trans-* + L *luna* moon + E *-ary* — more at LUNAR] **:** located beyond the moon : ETHEREAL, VISIONARY — compare SUBLUNARY ⟨who can imagine a ~ visitor in Times Square —O.S.J.Gogarty⟩ ⟨his high ~ dreams —John Buchan⟩

Trans-Lux \ˈtran(t)sləks, -nzˈl-\ *trademark* — used for a device for projecting on a translucent screen the ticker tape of a market or exchange

trans·make \(ˈ)tran(t)s, -raan-, -nz+\ *vt* [*trans-* + *make*; trans. of Gk *metapoiein*] **:** to make over : REFASHION

trans·marine \ˌtran(t)s, -raan-, -nz+\ *adj* [L *transmarinus*, fr. *trans-* + *mare* sea + *-inus* -ine — more at MARINE] **1 :** being or coming from beyond or across the sea ⟨a ~ people⟩ **2 :** passing over or extending across the sea : OVERSEAS ⟨the successive ~ thrusts of Britain, Japan, and the United States —*Foreign Policy Bull.*⟩

trans·median *also* **trans·medial** \(ˈ)tran(t)s, -raan-, -nz+\ *adj* [*trans-* + *median, medial*] **:** passing across or through the median plane

trans·methylation \ˌtran(t)s, -raan-, -nz+\ *n* [*trans-* + *methylation*] **:** a chemical reaction in which a methyl group is transferred from one compound to another

trans·mi·grant \tran(t)ˈsmīgrənt, traan-, -nzˈm-\ *n* [L *transmigrant-, transmigrans*, pres. part. of *transmigrare*] **:** one who transmigrates; *esp* **:** an emigrant passing through a country en route to the one in which he will be an immigrant

trans·mi·grate \-ī,grāt, *usu* -ād.+V\ *vb* [L *transmigratus*, past part. of *transmigrare* to migrate to another place, fr. *trans-* + *migrare* to migrate] *vi* **1** *of the soul* **:** to pass at death from one body or being to another ⟨some believe that the soul may ~ into an animal as well as a person⟩ **2 :** to go or move from one place or country to another : MIGRATE ⟨*transmigrated* from the rocky mountain slopes to the fertile plains⟩ ~ *vt* **:** to cause to pass from one place or state of existence to another : subject to transmigration : TRANSFER ⟨the new Lama has the soul of the old one that has been *transmigrated* into him⟩ — compare REINCARNATE

trans·mi·gra·tion \ˌ=,=ˈgrāshən\ *n* [LL *transmigration-, transmigratio*, fr. L *transmigratus* + *-ion-, -io* -ion] **:** an act, process, or instance of transmigrating: as **a** *also* **transmigration of souls :** the passing of the individual soul at death into a new body or new form of life usu. human or animal : METEMPSYCHOSIS — compare REINCARNATION **b :** the passage of cells through a membrane : DIAPEDESIS

trans·mi·gra·tor \tran(t)ˈsmī,grād·ə(r), traan-, -nzˈm-, -ātə-\ *n* [L *transmigratus* + E *-or*] **:** one that transmigrates — **trans·mi·gra·to·ry** \-īgrə,tōrē, -tȯr-, -ri\ *adj*

trans·mis·si·bil·i·ty \tran(t),smisəˈbilədē, traan-, -nz,m-, -lətē, -i\ *n* -ES **:** the quality or state of being transmissible

trans·mis·si·ble \tran(t)ˈsmisəbəl, traan-, -nzˈm-\ *adj* [L *transmissus* + E *-ible*] **:** capable of being transmitted ⟨~ disease⟩ ⟨~ tradition⟩ ⟨~ characteristics⟩

trans·mis·sion \-ishən\ *n* -s *often attrib* [L *transmission-, transmissio*, fr. *transmissus* (past part. of *transmittere* to transmit) + *-ion-, -io* -ion] **1 :** an act, process, or instance of transmitting: as **a :** the overall proportion of radiant energy homogeneous with respect to wavelength that is transmitted perpendicularly through a substance bounded by plane nondiffusing parallel surfaces (as a plate of glass or other homogeneous isotropic nondiffusing medium or series of such media in contact with one another) and that is the ratio of the amount of energy emerging from the last surface to the amount incident upon the first with the difference between the two amounts resulting from losses of radiant energy due to reflection at the surfaces and absorptance and scattering within the medium — called also *attenuation factor* — compare TRANSMITTANCE 2 **b :** the passage of radio waves in the space between transmitting and receiving stations; *also* **:** the act or process of transmitting by radio or television **2 :** the gear including the change gear and the propeller shaft or driving chain by which power is transmitted from the engine of an automobile to the live axle — called also *gearbox*; see SELECTIVE TRANSMISSION **3 :** the train of a watch **4 :** something that is transmitted : MESSAGE ⟨the machine records telegraphic ~s⟩

transmission bands *n pl* **:** the bands used in certain types of planetary transmission to clutch and stop the low and reverse speed drums

transmission case *n* **:** a jacket usu. of cast iron for the transmission of an automobile

transmission dynamometer *n* **:** a dynamometer in which power is measured without being absorbed or used up during transmission — compare ABSORPTION DYNAMOMETER

transmission efficiency *n* **:** the ratio of the power received over a transmission path to the power transmitted; *also* **:** the ratio of the output to the input power of a circuit or device

transmission grating *n* **:** a grating with opaque lines on a transparent background

transmission level *n* **1 :** the signaling-power amplitude at any point in a communication system **2 :** the radio field intensity at any point in a radio communication system

transmission line *n* **:** a metallic circuit of three or more conductors used to send energy usu. at high voltage over a considerable distance; *specif* **:** a usu. metallic line used for the transmission of signals or for the adjustment of circuit performance and often consisting of a pair of wires suitably separated, a coaxial cable, or a wave guide

transmission loss *n* **:** the loss of power or voltage of a transmitted wave or current in passing along a transmission line or path or through a circuit device — compare ABSORPTION 5, ATTENUATION 4

transmission rope *n* **:** a wire rope made of four or more strands of ordinary lay about a hemp center and used for the transmission of power on drive shafts and pulleys

transmission shaft *n* **:** a shaft in the transmission of an automotive vehicle that carries the sliding gears and makes the driving connection between the clutch and the propeller shaft

trans·mis·sive \tran(t)ˈsmisiv, traan-, -nzˈm-, -sēv *also* -səv\ *adj* [L *transmissus* (past part. of *transmittere* to transmit) + E *-ive*] **1 :** that transmits or serves to transmit ⟨the ~ function of the nerves⟩ ⟨the ~ powers of a legislature⟩ **2 :** that is or is capable of being transmitted or derived ⟨~ characteristics⟩

trans·mis·siv·i·ty \ˌtran(t)smə'sivəd·ē, -nzm-\ *n* -ES [*transmissive* + *-ity*] **:** the quality or state of being transmissive; *specif* **:** the transmittance of a unit thickness of absorbing nondiffusing matter

trans·mis·som·e·ter \-ˈsäməd·ə(r)\ *n* [*transmission* + *-o-* + *-meter*] **:** a photometer or other instrument used for measuring transmission; *specif* **:** an instrument that measures the visibility or the capability of the air to transmit light

trans·mit \tran(t)ˈsmit, traan-, -nzˈm-, ˈ=,=, *usu* -id.+V\ *vb* **transmitted; transmitted; transmitting; transmits** [ME *transmitten*, fr. L *transmittere*, fr. *trans-* + *mittere* to send — more at SMITE] *vt* **1 a :** to cause to go or be conveyed to another person or place : SEND ⟨he secured soldiers' pay and *transmitted* it to their families —A.V.D.Honeyman⟩ ⟨prophets who are . . . a vehicle through which to ~ a revelation to the people —W.W.Howells⟩ ⟨said it sounded to him like common sense, and he would ~ it to his father —Upton Sinclair⟩ ⟨lists they shall sign and certify and ~ sealed to the seat of government —W.S.Sayre⟩ **b** (1) **:** to pass on or spread about : DISSEMINATE, COMMUNICATE ⟨the knowledge that objects of different weights fall at different speeds was *transmitted* in western society —Ralph Linton⟩ ⟨visual aids . . . are no better than the amount of information they ~ —J.K.Blake⟩ ⟨some of the original power of the master is *transmitted* to the disciple —C.D.Lewis⟩ (2) **:** to pass on by inheritance or heredity : HAND DOWN ⟨through the legacy of their art the great ages have *transmitted* to us a dim image of their glorious vitality —J.W.Krutch⟩ ⟨drew the inference that acquired habits cannot be *transmitted* —G.B.Shaw⟩ ⟨selective breeding aims to eliminate bad characteristics and ~ the good⟩ **c :** to give or convey (a disease or infection) to another person or organism ⟨attempts to ~ colds artificially . . . are successful —C.H. Andrews⟩ ⟨human beings who are apparently well can ~ infectious disease —Morris Fishbein⟩ ⟨mosquitos ~ malaria⟩ **2 a** (1) **:** to cause (as light or force) to pass or be conveyed through space or a medium ⟨the telephone ~s sound⟩ ⟨the power which an engine develops is *transmitted* to the wheels . . . by certain essential parts —Joseph Heitner⟩ ⟨objects of higher temperature than the skin . . . ~ heat to it —F.A. Geldard⟩ ⟨arches . . . ~ their loads to the walls of the river gorge —*Amer. Guide Series: Minn.*⟩ (2) **:** to admit the passage of : CONDUCT ⟨glass ~s light⟩ ⟨metals ~ electricity⟩ **b :** to send out (a signal) either by radio waves or over a wire line ~ *vi* **1 :** to pass by transmission an obligation entailing either a right or a duty **2 :** to send out a signal either by radio waves or over a wire line **syn** see CARRY, SEND

trans·mit·ta·ble \tran(t)ˈsmid·əbəl, traan-, -nzˈm-, -itəb-\ *adj* **:** capable of being transmitted ⟨infections easily ~ to children —Morris Fishbein⟩ ⟨~ power⟩

trans·mit·tal \-id·ᵊl, -itᵊl\ *n* -s [*transmit* + *-al*] **:** TRANSMISSION ⟨report its findings and recommendations . . . for ~ to Congress —*New Republic*⟩ ⟨the ~ of evil from one generation to another —*Time*⟩ ⟨its values permeate the culture through the same process of ~ —J.K.Feibleman⟩

trans·mit·tance \-itᵊn(t)s\ *n* -s [*transmit* + *-ance*] **1 :** TRANSMISSION **2 :** the fraction of radiant energy that having entered a layer of absorbing matter reaches its further boundary — compare TRANSMISSION 1a

trans·mit·tan·cy \-ᵊnsē, -si\ *n* -ES [*transmit* + *-ancy*] **:** the capacity for transmission: **a :** the ratio of the transmittance of a solution of a material to that of an equal thickness of the solvent **b :** TRANSMITTANCE 2

trans·mit·ter \tran(t)ˈsmid·ə(r), traan-, -nzˈm-, -itə-\ *n* -s [*transmit* + *-er*] **:** one that transmits: as **a** (1) **:** a part on a telephone into which one speaks and which contains a mechanism for converting sound waves into equivalent electric waves (2) **:** the portion of a telegraph instrument by which the message is sent **b** (1) **:** a radio or television transmitting set (2) **:** TRANSMITTING STATION

transmitting set *n* [*transmitting* (gerund of *transmit*) + *set*] **:** an apparatus for transmitting radio waves; *specif* **:** the portion of a complete transmitting station that produces and modulates radio-frequency current and delivers it to the broadcasting antenna

transmitting station *n* **:** an assemblage of equipment to send out or transmit radio waves including an antenna transmitting set and telephone transmitter or key

trans·mog·ri·fi·ca·tion \tran(t)smägrəfəˈkāshən, traan-, -nz,m-\ *n* -s [fr. *transmogrify*, after such pairs as E *identify: identification*] **:** an act, process, or instance of transmogrifying ⟨~ into a porcupine —Florence B. Lennon⟩ ⟨in one of her more extensive ~s, imagined herself as a carpenter planing a board —R.S.Hillyer⟩

trans·mog·ri·fy \tran(t)ˈsmägrə,fī, traan-, -nzˈm-\ *vt* -ED/-ING/-ES [origin unknown] **:** to change or alter in form, appearance, or structure often with grotesque or humorous effect ⟨educational philosophy has been *transmogrified* since 1890 —*Amer. Council of Learned Soc. Newsletter*⟩ — usu. used with *into* ⟨wondering how the caricatured capitalism of his forbears can be *transmogrified* into a harmonious . . . way of life —*Current Biog.*⟩ ⟨plausibly *transmogrified* the sons of grocers . . . into haughty young bloods —H.M.McLuhan⟩ ⟨training which permits them to understand that an actress can be *transmogrified* into a rivet boy —C.J.Hitch⟩ **syn** see TRANSFORM

trans·mon·tane \tran(t)¦smän ¦tān, traan-, -nz¦m-\ *adj* [L *transmontanus* — more at TRAMONTANE] : TRAMONTANE ⟨~ country⟩ ⟨the ~ section of the state —J.H.Peeling⟩
trans·mun·dane \-mən¦dān\ *adj* [*trans-* + L *mundus* world + E *-ane* (as in *mundane*)] : extending or lying beyond the world ⟨whatever of ~ metaphysical insight . . . we may carry —William James⟩
trans·mu·ral \-myu̇rəl\ *adj* [*trans-* + L *murus* wall + E *-al* — more at MUNITION] : extending or lying across a wall; *esp* : involving the whole thickness of a wall ⟨~ myocardial infarction⟩
trans·mut·abil·i·ty \tran(t),smyüd·əˈbiləd·ē, -nz,m-\ *n* : the quality or state of being transmutable
trans·mut·able \tran(t)ˈsmyüd·əbəl, -nz'm-\ *adj* [ME, fr. ML *transmutabilis*, fr. L *transmutare* to transmute + *-abilis* -able] : capable of being transmuted
trans·mu·ta·tion \,tran(t)smyüˈtāshən, ,traan-, -nzm-\ *n* [ME *transmutacioun*, fr. MF or L; MF *transmutation*, fr. L *transmutation-, transmutatio*, fr. *transmutatus* (past part. of *transmutare* to transmute) + *-ion-, -io* -ion] : an act, process, or instance of transmuting or being transmuted: as **a** *or* **transmutation of metals** : the conversion of base metals into gold or silver **b** : TRANSFER 1 — used esp. in the phrase *transmutation of possession* **c** : the change of one species into another — compare LAMARCKISM **d** (1) : the conversion of one element into another by a nuclear reaction (2) : the conversion of one nuclide into another
trans·mu·ta·tion·ist \-sh(ə)nəst\ *n* -s [*transmutation* + *-ist*] : one who believes in or advocates a theory of transmutation esp. of species
trans·mut·ative \tran(t)ˈsmyüd·əd·iv, traan-, -nz'm-, -ütətiv\ *adj* [ML *transmutativus*, fr. L *transmutatus* + *-ivus* -ive] : of, relating to, or involving transmutation : serving or tending to transmute ⟨a ~ effect⟩ ⟨a ~ force⟩
trans·mute \-üt, *usu* -üd.+V\ *vb* -ED/-ING/-S [ME *transmuten*, fr. L *transmutare* to change, shift, fr. *trans-* + *mutare* to change — more at MISS] *vt* **1** : to change or alter in form, appearance, or nature : CONVERT ⟨a pronounced stabilization that will ~ the economic and social life of the African —Peter Scott⟩ ⟨the interaction of . . . forces ~*s* custom and produces a new tradition —B.N.Cardozo⟩ — often used with *into* ⟨how does the chlorophyll . . . ~ the dross of earth into living tissue —D.C.Peattie⟩ ⟨~ the abundant raw materials . . . into finished products —A.W.Long⟩ ⟨~ their national integrity into a decisive weapon of national defense —W.O.Douglas⟩ **2** : to change into another substance or element esp. gold or silver ⟨made it possible to smash atoms and ~ elements —*Current Biog.*⟩ — often used with *into* ⟨the alchemists . . . cared little for answers that did not lead them to the philosopher's stone, which would ~ base metals into gold —*Lamp*⟩ ~ *vi* : to undergo a change or transformation in form, nature, or substance ⟨the music gradually ~*s* and builds to a shattering climax —*Time*⟩ — often used with *into* ⟨energy converts into matter as naturally as matter ~*s* into energy —Gerard Piel⟩ **syn** see TRANSFORM
trans·national \(ˈ)tran(t)s, -raan-, -nz+\ *adj* [*trans-* + *national*] : extending or going beyond national boundaries ⟨an abatement of nationalism and the creation of ~ institutions which will render boundaries of minor importance —*New Republic*⟩ ⟨by the diffusion of culturally important words . . . ~ vocabularies have grown up —Edward Sapir⟩
transnatural \"+\ *adj* [*trans-* + *natural*] : being above or beyond nature : SUPERNATURAL ⟨credited many confusions in human knowledge to one's seeking natural causes . . . when the true reasons or causes were ~ —J.W.Yolton⟩
transnature \"+\ *vt* [*trans-* + *nature*] *archaic* : to change the nature of : TRANSELEMENT
trans–neptunian \¦tran(t)s, -raan-, -nz+\ *adj, usu cap N* [*trans-* + *Neptune*, formerly most distant known planet + E *-ian*] : lying beyond the orbit of the planet Neptune
trans·ocean \(ˈ)tran(t)s, -raan-, -nz+\ *adj* [*trans-* + *ocean*] : TRANSOCEANIC
trans·oceanic \¦(ˌ)tran(t)s, -raan-, -nz+\ *adj* [*trans-* + L *oceanus* ocean + E *-ic*] **1** : lying or dwelling beyond the ocean ⟨a ~ country⟩ **2** : crossing or extending across the ocean ⟨~ telephone⟩ ⟨the first to make a ~ crossing by air —H.G. Armstrong⟩
tran·som *also* **tran·some** \ˈtran(t)səm, ˈtraan-\ *n* -s *often attrib* [ME *traunsum, transom*, prob. fr. L *transtrum* crossbeam, transom, rowers' thwart, fr. *trans* across + *-trum*, suffix denoting an instrument — more at TRANS-, -TRON] **1** : a transverse piece in a structure : CROSSPIECE: as **a** : LINTEL **b** *or* **transom bar** : a horizontal crossbar in a window, over a door, or between a door and a window or fanlight above it — distinguished from *mullion* **c** : the horizontal bar or member of a cross or gallows **d** (1) : any of several transverse timbers or beams secured to the sternpost of a boat (2) *or* **transom frame** : the aftermost frame of the square body secured to the sternpost and supporting the overhanging stern **e** : a usu. broad and flat metal piece connecting the cheeks, the side-pieces of the trail, or similar parts of a gun carriage **f** : the vane of a cross-staff **g** : the board or planking forming the stern of a square-ended boat **h** : a transverse horizontal strut between parallel or nearly parallel members (as in a frame) **i** : a crossbeam joining the side frames of a truck of a railway car **2** *or* **transom window** : a window above a door or other window built on and commonly hinged to a transom **3** : a seat or couch built at the side of a cabin or stateroom of a boat usu. with lockers or drawers underneath
tran·somed \-md\ *adj* [*transom* + *-ed*] : having a transom — used of doors or windows
transom knee *n* : a knee bolted to a transom or after timber of a ship
transom stern *n* : a stern of a boat formed by or shaped from a transom frame
tran·son·ic \(ˈ)tran¦sänik, -raan-, -nēk\ *also* **trans-son·ic** \-nz¦s-, -n(t)s¦s-\ *adj* [*trans-* + *-sonic* (as in *supersonic*); fr. the fact that such speeds are transitional between subsonic and supersonic speeds] **1** : of, being, or relating to a speed approximating the speed of sound in air : relating to a speed in air of about 1087 feet per second or about 741 miles per hour at sea level — often used of aeronautical speeds between 600 and 900 miles per hour; compare SONIC, SUBSONIC, SUPERSONIC **2** : moving, capable of moving, or utilizing air currents moving at a transonic speed
trans·orbital \(ˈ)tran(t)s, -raan-, -nz+\ *adj* [*trans-* + *orbit* + *-al*] : passing through or occurring by way of the eye socket ⟨a ~ lobotomy⟩
trans·ovar·i·al \¦tran(t)sō¦va(a)rēəl, -nzō-\ *or* **trans·ovar·i·an** \-ēən\ *adj* [*trans-* + *ovary* + *-al* or *-an*] : passing through or occurring by way of the ovary ⟨~ passage⟩ ⟨wood ticks have been shown to be infectable . . . and capable of ~ transmission to their offspring —K.F.Maxcy⟩ — **trans·ovar·i·al·ly** \-lē\ *or* **trans·ovar·i·an·ly** *adv*
transp *abbr* **1** transparent **2** transportation
trans·pacific \¦tranz, -raan-, -n(t)s+\ *adj* [*trans-* + *Pacific* (*ocean*)] **1** : crossing or extending across the Pacific ocean ⟨~ flight⟩ ⟨steamships on the ~ run⟩ ⟨~ service⟩ **2** : lying, dwelling, or situated across or beyond the Pacific ⟨~ peoples⟩ ⟨~ regions⟩
trans·pa·dane \¦tranzpə¦dān, -n(t)sp-; (ˈ)tranz¦pā,dān, -n(t)¦sp-\ *adj* [L *transpadanus*, fr. *trans-* + *Padus* the Po, river in northern Italy + L *-anus* -an] : lying or situated on the farther or usu. north side of the river Po — opposed to *cispadane*
trans·palatine \(ˈ)tranz, -raan-, -n(t)s+\ *adj* [*trans-* + L *palatum* palate + E *-ine*] : of, relating to, or being the transverse bone of the skull of a reptile
trans·par·ence \tranzˈpa(a)rən(t)s, traan-, -n(t)ˈsp-, -per-\ *n* -s [ML *transparentia*] : TRANSPARENCY ⟨the ~ of water —George Copeland⟩ ⟨the sky above its domes . . . is of sheer ~ —E.O.Hauser⟩
trans·par·en·cy \-nsē, -si\ *n* -ES [ML *transparentia*, fr. *transparent-, transparens* transparent + L *-ia* -y] **1** : the quality or state of being transparent ⟨many marine invertebrates tend towards ~ —W.H.Dowdeswell⟩ ⟨the absolute ~ of the air on this gracious day —Walter Pater⟩ ⟨the marvelous fluidity, ~, and curiosity of his nature —V.S.Pritchett⟩ **2** : something that is transparent: as **a** : a picture or other matter for exhibition made upon glass, thin cloth, paper, or film and intended to be viewed by the aid of light shining through it or by projection — compare SLIDE 6b(1), LANTERN SLIDE **b** : a framework covered with thin cloth or paper bearing a device for public display and lighted from within
trans·par·ent \-nt\ *adj* [ME, fr. ML *transparent-, transparens*, pres. part. of *transparēre* to show through, fr. L *trans-* + *parēre* to be visible, appear, show — more at APPEAR] **1 a** : having the property of transmitting light without appreciable scattering so that bodies lying beyond are entirely visible : PELLUCID ⟨this plastic is more ~ than even high-quality plate glass —Harland Manchester⟩ ⟨the ~ or hazy air —Mary Webb⟩ — opposed to *opaque* and usu. distinguished from *translucent* **b** : so loose or open in texture as to admit the passage of light : SHEER, DIAPHANOUS ⟨~ velvet⟩ ⟨a ~ yoke⟩ **c** : TRANSLUCENT ⟨~ soap⟩ ⟨his ~ womanly hands —J.R.Green⟩ **2 a** : free from pretense or deceit : OPEN, FRANK, GUILELESS ⟨a man of such ~ sincerity that he is incapable of presenting a ghost-written speech —*N. Y. Times*⟩ ⟨the most important quality in a teacher . . . is genuine and ~ truthfulness —C.W.Eliot⟩ ⟨the child's ~ countenance⟩ **b** : easily detected or seen through : OBVIOUS ⟨embarked on an elaborate fraud ~ to the world —Otis Ferguson⟩ ⟨his writings . . . are so flat, so ~, so palpably taken from the nearest authorities —H.O.Taylor⟩ ⟨the man's ~ fear of discovery —Luke Short⟩ **c** : readily understood : PERSPICUOUS, CLEAR ⟨a style of ~ clarity that needs no artifices to make it vivid —C.H.Dreier⟩ ⟨that part of the chamber music which becomes ~ only after study or explication —Robert Evett⟩ ⟨the art . . . so ~ in all of its effects that the need is seldom felt to analyze —Philip Rahv⟩ **3** : pervious to any specified form of radiation (as X rays or ultraviolet light) **syn** see CLEAR
transparent chromium oxide *n* : a moderate to strong green that is bluer and darker than Hooker's green
trans·par·ent·ize \-n·,tīz\ *vt* -ED/-ING/-S : to make transparent ⟨a process developed to ~ tracing paper⟩
trans·par·ent·ly *adv* : in a transparent manner ⟨red brilliance of the wines shines ~ in the glasses —*Time*⟩ ⟨the concise and yet ~ lucid exposition —Ernest Nagel⟩ ⟨he was . . . ~ truthful —A.P.Davies⟩ ⟨sulked, faltered, and prevaricated ~ —Arthur Morrison⟩
trans·par·ent·ness *n* -ES [*transparent* + *-ness*] : TRANSPARENCY 1
trans·pep·ti·da·tion \(,)tranz,peptəˈdāshən, -n(t),spe-\ *n* -s [*trans-* + *peptide* + *-ation*] : a chemical reaction (as the reversible conversion of one peptide to another by a proteinase) in which an amino acid residue or a peptide residue is transferred from one amino compound to another
trans·personal \(ˈ)tranz, -raan-, -n(t)s+\ *adj* [*trans-* + *personal*] : extending or going beyond the personal or individual ⟨to transcend the immediacy of desire and to live for ends which are ~ —Walter Lippmann⟩ ⟨suggestions that he had enlisted ~ powers —Vernon Young⟩
trans·phenomenal \¦tranz, -raan-, -n(t)s+\ *adj* [*trans-* + *phenomenal*] : existing or lying beyond the phenomenal or apparent: **a** : of or relating to a reality that is beyond or above that which exists in itself and is the ground of what appears to our senses **b** : of or relating to what exists in itself and is the ground of what appears to our senses — compare THING-IN-ITSELF
trans·phosphorylase \(ˈ)tranz, -raanz, -n(t)s+\ *n* [*trans-* + *phosphorylase*] : any of a group of enzymes that promote transphosphorylation processes — compare KINASE 2, PHOSPHATASE, PHOSPHOGLUCOMUTASE, PHOSPHORYLASE
trans·phosphorylation \¦tranz, -raanz, -n(t)s+\ *n* [*trans-* + *phosphorylation*] : phosphorylation in which an organic phosphate group is transferred from one molecule to another and which is usu. promoted by a transphosphorylase
tran·spic·u·ous \tranzˈpikyəwəs, -n(t)ˈsp-\ *adj* [NL *transpicuus*, fr. L *transpicere* to look through, see through, fr. *trans-* + *-spicere* (fr. *specere* to look, see) — more at SPY] : clearly seen through or understood : TRANSPARENT
trans·pierce \tranzˈpi(ə)rs, -n(t)ˈsp-\ *vt* [MF *transpercer*, fr. OF, fr. *trans-* (fr. L) + *percer* to pierce — more at PIERCE] **1** : to penetrate sharply or painfully ⟨my spear . . . *transpierced* his back, and fixed him to the ground —Alexander Pope⟩ **2** : to pass or extend through ⟨a metal rod . . . ~*s* the box —*Athenaeum*⟩
tran·spir·able \tranzˈpīrəbəl, -n(t)ˈsp-\ *adj* [MF, fr. *transpirer* to transpire + *-able*] : capable of being transpired ⟨~ fluids⟩ : permitting transpiration ⟨a ~ membrane⟩
tran·spi·ra·tion \,tranzpəˈrāshən, ,traan-, -n(t)sp-\ *n* -s [MF fr. *transpirer* + *-ation*] : an act, process, or instance of transpiring: as **a** : the passage of fluid (as water) through skin or animal membrane in the form of a vapor; *also* : something that is transpired : PERSPIRATION **b** : the emission or exhalation of watery vapor from the surfaces of leaves or other parts of plants **c** : the passing of gases through fine tubes or porous substances because of differences of pressure or temperature — compare THERMAL TRANSPIRATION
transpiration ratio *n* : the amount of water used to produce one pound of dry matter in a plant
transpiration stream *or* **transpiration current** *n* : the current of water usu. containing many substances in solution that rises through the xylem of plants
tran·spire \tranzˈpī(ə)r, traan-, -n(t)ˈsp-, -īə\ *vb* -ED/-ING/-S [MF *transpirer*, fr. L *trans-* + *spirare* to breathe — more at SPIRIT] *vt* **1** : to cause (as a gas or liquid) to pass through a tissue or substance or its pores or interstices **2** : to excrete or give off (as moisture or vapor) through the skin, a membrane, or living cells : PERSPIRE, EXUDE, EXHALE ~ *vi* **1** : to emit moisture, vapor, or perfume; *specif* : to give off or exude watery vapor from the surfaces of leaves or other parts ⟨a plant ~*s* more freely on a hot dry day⟩ **2** : to pass out or escape in the form of a vapor from a living body ⟨moisture ~*s* through the skin⟩ **3 a** : to become known or apparent : DEVELOP ⟨it *transpired* that he had still been sitting . . . when the bomb struck —C.D.Lewis⟩ ⟨it soon *transpired* that there were two . . . conceptions of this problem —C.H.Malik⟩ ⟨only good faculties, it *transpired*, were inherited —Walter Lippmann⟩ **b** : to be revealed : leak out : come to light ⟨had to wait until 1934 for the secret to ~ —E.C.Wagenknecht⟩ ⟨it had just *transpired* that he had left gaming debts behind him —Jane Austen⟩ **4** : to come to pass : HAPPEN, OCCUR ⟨a course of events which ~ with unbelievable rapidity —H.G.Moseley⟩ ⟨I gave an honest account of what *transpired* —J.A.Michener⟩ ⟨more things ~ on a racetrack than are chronicled in the newspapers —Gerald Beaumont⟩ **syn** see HAPPEN
tran·spi·rom·e·ter \,tranzpəˈrämət·ə(r), -n(t)sp-\ *n* [*transpire* + *-o-* + *-meter*] : an instrument or apparatus for measuring plant transpiration
trans·place \tranzˈplās, -n(t)ˈsp-\ *vt* [*trans-* + *place*] **1** : to put in another place : TRANSPOSE **2** : to interchange the places of
trans·placental \¦tranz, -raan-, -n(t)s+\ *adj* [ISV *trans-* + NL *placenta* + ISV *-al*] : passing through or occurring by way of the placenta ⟨~ passage of nutrients⟩ ⟨~ immunization⟩
¹trans·plant \tranzˈplant, traan-, -n(t)ˈsp-, -laa(ə)nt, -laint, -lȧnt\ *vb* [ME *transplaunten*, fr. LL *transplantare*, fr. L *trans-* + *plantare* to plant] *vt* **1 a** : to remove and plant in another place; *specif* : to lift and reset in another soil or situation ⟨~*ed* mulberry trees from his . . . nursery —*Amer. Guide Series: Conn.*⟩ **b** : to remove from one location and introduce in another ⟨traps and ~*s* beaver to other sections of the state⟩ ⟨~ ladybirds⟩ **2** : to remove from a place or country and settle elsewhere : TRANSPORT — usu. used with *to* or *from* ⟨wished to ~ his family to America⟩ ⟨many institutions were ~*ed* from Europe⟩ ⟨his office staff is ~*ed* to his vacation spot —*U. S. News & World Report*⟩ **3** : to transfer (an organ or tissue) from one body or part of a body to another ⟨~*ed* one twin's kidney to the other⟩ ⟨reported that cancer tissues can be ~*ed* from man to other animals⟩ ~ *vi* **1** *obs* : to go elsewhere to settle : EMIGRATE **2** : to admit of being removed from one place or soil to another ⟨some plants do not ~ as well as others⟩
²transplant \ˈ=,=\ *n* **1** : the act or process of transplanting ⟨the operation called corneal grafting, or ~, can restore sight —Eleanor Early⟩ ⟨as long as six hours after death . . . successful ~*s* could be carried out —E.A.Graham⟩ **2** : a person or thing that is transplanted ⟨a tall Montanan, a Texas ~, pitched the grounds from his cup into the fire —Luke Short⟩ ⟨these tiny ~*s* . . . provide a kind of fishing that has no exact parallel —J.O.Cartier⟩ ⟨$2 a thousand for seedlings and $5 a thousand for ~*s* —*Amer. Guide Series: Pa.*⟩ ⟨never since doctors discovered how to replace fogged corneas . . . have there been eye ~*s* to go round —*Time*⟩
trans·plant·able *pronunc at* ¹TRANSPLANT + əbəl\ *adj* : capable of being transplanted
trans·plan·ta·tion \,tranz,planˈtāshən, ,traan-, -n(t),sp-, -laan-, -lȧn-\ *n* [¹*transplant* + *-ation*] : an act, process, or instance of transplanting or being transplanted: as **a** : a magical cure of a disease by causing it to pass from the afflicted person to another **b** : the removal of tissue from one part of the body or from one individual and its implantation or insertion in another esp. by surgery ⟨corneal ~⟩ ⟨the ~ of lung tissue⟩
trans·plant·er *pronunc at* ¹TRANSPLANT + ə(r)\ *n* : one that transplants; *esp* : a machine for transplanting plants by making furrows or holes and watering each transplant as it is dropped
trans·polar \(ˈ)tranz, -raan-, -n(t)s+\ *adj* [*trans-* + *polar*] : going or extending across either of the polar regions ⟨~ passage⟩ ⟨~ air route⟩ ⟨~ warfare⟩
tran·spon·der *also* **tran·spon·dor** \tranzˈpändə(r), traan-, -n(t)ˈsp-\ *n* -s [*transponder*, fr. *transmitter* + *responder*; *transpondor*, alter. (influenced by *responsor*) of *transponder*] : a radio or radar set that upon receiving a designated signal usu. in the form of a coded series of pulses emits a radio signal of its own that may also be coded — compare INTERROGATOR
trans·pon·tine \(ˈ)tranz¦pän-,tīn, -n(t)¦sp-\ *adj* [*trans-* + L *pont-, pons* bridge + E *-ine* — more at FIND] **1** : lying or situated on the other side of a bridge ⟨~ night life⟩ ⟨~ newspaper⟩ — opposed to *cispontine* **2** : resembling or characteristic of a class of melodramas once popular in theaters of the part of London south of the Thames
¹trans·port \tranzˈpō(ə)rt, traan-, -n(t)ˈsp-, -pȯ(ə)rt, -ōət, -ȯ(ə)t, ˈ=,=, *usu* -d.+V\ *vt* -ED/-ING/-S [ME *transporten*, fr. MF or L; MF *transporter*, fr. L *transportare*, fr. *trans-* + *portare* to carry — more at FARE] **1** : to transfer or convey from one person or place to another : CARRY, MOVE ⟨on this vessel he ~*ed* a heavy load of ammunition —L.H.Bolander⟩ ⟨in the early days copper ore was ~*ed* in wagons —*Amer. Guide Series: Tenn.*⟩ ⟨will ~ the industry to a better competitive level —T.D. Rice⟩ ⟨endeavor to ~ ourselves into the position of a contemporary spectator —Roger Fry⟩ **2** : to carry away with strong or intensely pleasurable emotion : INFLAME, ENRAPTURE ⟨his anger ~*s* him⟩ ⟨the test of greatness in a work of art is . . . that it ~*s* us —Herbert Read⟩ ⟨didn't realize that just a man and a red cloth and a bull could . . . ~ a person —Barnaby Conrad⟩ **3** : to convey or cause to be conveyed into banishment usu. to a penal colony ⟨was eventually ~*ed* for stealing a gentleman's gold watch —Osbert Sitwell⟩ **4** *Scot* **a** : to transfer (a minister) to another charge **b** : to remove (a parish church) to another part of the parish **syn** see BANISH, CARRY
²transport \ˈ=,=\ *n* -s *often attrib* [ME, fr. *transporten* to transport] **1** *obs* : the conveyance of property : TRANSFER **2 a** : TRANSPORTATION 1a ⟨the arduous ~ . . . of three and a half tons of stores —*Brit. Bk. News*⟩ ⟨then came the ~ of the huge disk to California —David England⟩ ⟨it is maintained that ~ in large tanks affects the wine quality —G.G.Weigend⟩ **b** : TRANSPORTATION 1b **3 a** : the state of being moved by strong or intensely pleasurable emotion : FRENZY, ECSTASY, RAPTURE ⟨in a ~ at possessing . . . a fortune —G.B.Shaw⟩ ⟨each expressed . . . an authentic ~ of personal joy —C.E. Montague⟩ **b** : an instance or fit of such transport ⟨~*s* of delight —T.B.Macaulay⟩ ⟨~*s* of rage —Jane Austen⟩ ⟨a bitter cynicism has succeeded to ~*s* of pugnacious hatred —G.B. Shaw⟩ **4 a** : a ship used for carrying soldiers or military equipment and stores ⟨a fleet of warships sailed with accompanying ~*s* filled with troops⟩ ⟨served as a seaman on ~*s* in the Pacific —*Current Biog.*⟩ — compare FREIGHTER **b** : a truck, plane, or other vehicle used to carry persons or goods from one place to another ⟨impatient drivers will . . . try to get around long, slow-moving trucks or ~*s* —T.S.Smith⟩ ⟨jet prototype that could be used as a bomber or a ~ —Horace Sutton⟩ **c** : TRANSPORTATION 4b ⟨the economics of ~ will . . . dictate the kind of vehicle to be used —John Kemp⟩ ⟨one must understand the whole picture of ~ —N.J.Curry⟩; *also* : a system or organized means of public conveyance or travel : TRANSIT ⟨they work in factories and offices, use ~, and live in residential suburbs —Sybille Bedford⟩ ⟨this shortage of efficient ~ —John Kobler⟩ **5** : a person who is transported or banished as a convict ⟨many early American settlers were ~*s*⟩ **6** : an exchange of molecules or other particles together with their kinetic energy and momentum across the boundary between adjacent layers of a fluid **syn** see ECSTASY
trans·port·abil·i·ty \tranz,pōr¦d·əˈbiləd·ē, traan-, -n(t),sp-, -pōə¦, -pȯ(r)¦, ¦tə- -lətē, -i\ *n* : the quality or state of being transportable
trans·port·able \tranzˈpōr¦d·əbəl, traan-, -n(t)ˈsp-, -pōə¦, -pȯ(r)¦, ¦təb-\ *adj* **1** : capable of being transported ⟨a tiny ~ organ —S.E.White⟩ **2** *chiefly Brit* : of, relating to, or incurring transportation or banishment ⟨committed a ~ crime⟩
trans·port·al \¦d·ᵊl\ *n* -s [¹*transport* + *-al*] : TRANSPORTATION
trans·por·ta·tion \,tranzpə(r)ˈtāshən, ,traan-, -n(t)sp-\ *n* -s [L *transportatus* (past part. of *transportare* to transport) + E *-ion*] **1 a** : an act, process, or instance of transporting or being transported ⟨arranging for the ~ of his luggage⟩ ⟨~ of the troops overseas is accomplished by ships and planes⟩ **b** : the conveyance or movement of sediment or rock materials either as solid particles or in solution from one place to another on or near the earth's surface by water, ice, air, or gravity **2** *obs* : TRANSPORT 3 **3** : banishment usu. to a penal colony — compare DEPORTATION ⟨was convicted and sentenced to ~ for life —Joseph Chiari⟩ **4 a** : means of conveyance or travel from one place to another ⟨his ~ is a battered coupé —*Phoenix Flame*⟩ ⟨cluttering up the road with ~ —G.S.Patton⟩; *also* : the cost of such means of conveyance or travel ⟨the state providing ~ for each child . . . to the extent of 70 cents per day —*Amer. Guide Series: Minn.*⟩ **b** : public conveyance of passengers, goods, or materials esp. as a commercial enterprise ⟨a single railroad . . . monopolizes all the railroad ~ through that valley —O.W.Holmes †1935⟩ ⟨nation whose very existence . . . depends on ~ —*Motor Transportation in the West*⟩
trans·por·ta·tion·al \¦==¦tāshənᵊl, -shnəl\ *adj* : of, relating to, or characteristic of transportation ⟨~ routes⟩ ⟨~ organization⟩ ⟨~ effect of eroding streams⟩
transportation insurance *n* : MARINE INSURANCE
trans·port·ed \(ˈ)tranz¦pōr¦d·əd, -raan-, -n(t)¦sp-, -pōr¦, -ōə¦, -ȯ(ə)¦, ¦təd\ *adj* [fr. past part. of ¹*transport*] **1** : carried or moved from one person or place to another: as **a** : condemned or sent into banishment usu. to a penal colony ⟨first seeing Australia as a ~ felon⟩ **b** : carried or moved along on or near the earth's surface by a natural force (as a river, ocean current, or glacier) ⟨~ clays⟩ ⟨~ soils⟩ **2** : impassioned or enraptured by strong and usu. pleasurable emotion ⟨instantly he felt ~ from the sphere of his work —R.L.Cook⟩ — **trans·port·ed·ly** *adv*
trans·port·ee \¦tranzpōrˈtē, -n(t)sp-, -pȯr-\ *n* -s [¹*transport* + *-ee*] : one who has been transported or banished as a convict
trans·port·er *pronunc at* ¹TRANSPORT + ə(r)\ *n* -s : one that transports or serves as a means of transportation; *specif* : any of various apparatus for moving loose material with dispatch esp. in loading or unloading ships
transporter bridge *n* : a bridge designed to span a navigable

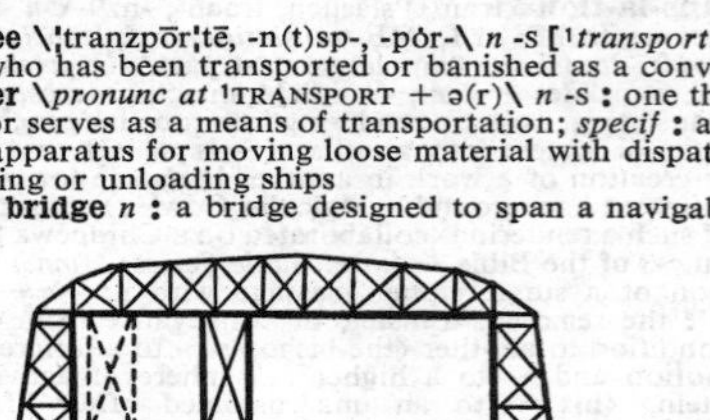

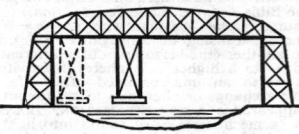

transporter bridge

waterway between low shores and made of a high framework from which is suspended a car for carrying traffic back and forth
transporting *pres part of* TRANSPORT

trans·port·ive *pronunc at* ¹TRANSPORT + iv\ *adj* [¹*transport* + *-ive*] : tending to transport or to cause transports ⟨~ and triumphant thought —Nathaniel Hawthorne⟩

transport number *n* : TRANSFERENCE NUMBER

transport pilot *n* : a pilot licensed by the federal government to operate a transport plane

transports *pres 3d sing of* TRANSPORT, *pl of* TRANSPORT

trans·pos·abil·i·ty \tranz,pōzə'biləd·ē, -n(t),sp-\ *n* : the quality or state of being transposable

trans·pos·able \tranz'pōzəbəl, traan-, -n(t)'sp-\ *adj* : capable of being transposed or interchanged

trans·pos·al \-ōzəl\ *n* -s [¹*transpose* + *-al*] : TRANSPOSITION

¹**trans·pose** \-ōz\ *vb* -ED/-ING/-S [ME *transposen*, fr. MF *transposer*, modif. (influenced by *poser* to put, place) of L *transponere* to change the position of, transfer (perfect stem *transpos-*), fr. *trans-* + *ponere* to put, place — more at POSITION, POSE] *vt* **1** : to change in form or nature : TRANSFORM, TRANSMUTE — usu. used with *into* or *to* ⟨Jesus the revealer is *transposed* into a figurine in a manger —I.G.Whitchurch⟩ ⟨~*s* himself completely from the role of systematic philosopher into that of biblical theologian —Joyce Hertzler⟩ ⟨what command has conceived . . . these groups now ~ to action —*Target Germany*⟩ **2** : to render into another language, style, or manner of expression : TRANSLATE — usu. used with *into* ⟨~*s* the Latin into English⟩ ⟨~*s* the verse into prose⟩ ⟨actual figures . . . are *transposed* into simple records which are kept by the client —*Jour. of Accountancy*⟩ **3** *obs* : to alter in use, significance, or intent : MISAPPLY, CORRUPT **4** : to transfer from one place or period to another : SHIFT, REMOVE — usu. used with *to* or *into* ⟨with the advance of astronomy, the domicile of the Deity had been *transposed* to the unknown center of the universe —S.F.Mason⟩ ⟨items which had no place . . . were not *transposed* into the new situation —D.J. Lehmer⟩ **5** : to change the relative place or normal order of : INTERCHANGE ⟨~*s* the letters to change the spelling⟩ ⟨had *transposed* economy and security in his table of priorities —*Atlantic*⟩ **6** : to write or perform (a musical composition) in a different key with consequent raising or lowering of pitch **7** : to bring (as a term of an algebraic equation) from one side to the other with the corresponding change of its sign **8** : to cause (the wires of a telegraph or telephone circuit) to cross at intervals to eliminate the effect of induction from neighboring wires or noise-making disturbances (as lightning) ~ *vi* : to transpose something, esp. a musical composition ⟨is learning to ~ with ease and skill⟩

²**transpose** \"\ *n* -s : TRANSPOSITION

transposing instrument *n* [*transposing* (pres. part. of ¹*transpose*) + *instrument*] **1** : a musical instrument that sounds pitches different from those indicated by the notation **2** : an instrument with a shifting keyboard for mechanically causing the music to sound in a different key

trans·po·si·tion \,tranzpə'zishən, ,traan-, -n(t)sp-\ *n* -s [ML *transposition-, transpositio*, fr. L *transpositus* (past part. of *transponere* to transpose) + *-ion-, -io* -ion] : an act, process, or instance of transposing or being transposed: as **a** : a transfer or removal from one place or time to another — usu. used with *into* or *to* ⟨the . . . ~ of the sentiments of the novel and its age into a different setting and a different period —Martin Turnell⟩ **b** (1) : a change or interchange in order or place esp. of letters or words : METATHESIS ⟨Latin admits the ~ of words more readily than English⟩ (2) : the rearrangement of the letters of a message in cryptography **c** (1) : a change of a musical composition or passage into another key (2) : a composition or passage so transposed **d** (1) : the transfer of any term of an equation from one side over to the other side with a corresponding change of the sign (2) : a mathematical permutation or interchange of two letters or symbols **e** : the displacement of a viscus to a side opposite from that which it normally occupies ⟨~ of the heart⟩ **f** : CONTRAPOSITION 2 **g** : the process of reversing the tonal or density values of a photographic image **h** : REARRANGEMENT 2

trans·po·si·tion·al \;==;zishən°l, -shnəl\ *adj* : of, relating to, or involving transposition

transposition cipher *n* : CIPHER 2a(2)

trans·prose \tranz, traanz, -n(t)s+\ *vt* [*trans-* + *prose*] *archaic* : to change from verse into prose

trans·rational \(')tran(t)s, -raan-, -nz+\ *adj* [*trans-* + *rational*] : going beyond or surpassing human reason or the rational ⟨an ultramundane and ~ Creator —J.A.Martin⟩

trans·rectification \;tran(t)s, -raan-, -nz+\ *n* [*trans-* + *rectification*] : the rectification taking place in the circuit of one electrode of a vacuum tube when an alternating voltage is applied to another electrode

trans·rhe·nane \;tran(t)s'rē,nān, -nzr-; tran(t)s'rē,nān, -nz'-, -re,-\ *adj* [L *transrhenanus*, fr. *trans-* + *Rhenus* the Rhine, river of western Europe + *-anus* -an] : situated or lying on the other side of the Rhine; *specif* : GERMAN — opposed to *cisrhenane*

trans·seg·men·tal \;tranzseg'ment°l, -n(t)sseg-, -nseg-\ *adj* [*trans-* + *segment* + *-al*] : extending across or beyond the limits of a body segment or segmental part

trans·shape \tranz, traanz, -n(t)s-, -nch+\ *also* **tran·shape** \tran, traan+\ *vt* [*trans-* + *shape*] : to change into another shape or form : TRANSFORM

trans·ship \"+\ *also* **tran·ship** \"+\ *vb* [*trans-* + *ship*] *vt* : to transfer for further transportation from one ship or conveyance to another ⟨sailed . . . in the *Speedwell* for Plymouth, England, where they *transshipped* to the larger *Mayflower* —Ralph Hammond-Innes⟩ ⟨the river steamer into which the . . . cargo had been *transshipped* —F.V.W.Mason⟩ ⟨about half this tonnage is *transshipped* by boat, truck, rail, and plane ~ *vi* : to change from one ship or conveyance to another ⟨men were *transshipping* from the . . . trucks to lorries and wagons —F.W.Crofts⟩

trans·ship·ment \"+mənt\ *also* **tran·ship·ment** \"+mənt\ *n* [*transship* + *-ment*] : the act or process of transshipping

trans·sonic *var of* TRANSONIC

trans·subjective \;tranz, -raanz, -n(t)s+\ *adj* [*trans-* + *subjective*] : of, relating to, or being in a state of existence independent of an individual mind or mode of thinking though not necessarily independent of the modes of thinking common to all men : objective in universal rather than individual experience ⟨concepts are necessarily ~, for they are of universal validity —Alfred Stern⟩

trans·temporal \(')tranz, -raanz, -n(t)s+\ *adj* [*trans-* + *temporal*] : crossing the temporal lobe of the cerebrum

trans·tracheal \"+\ *adj* [*trans-* + *trachea* + *-al*] : extending or effected through the trachea ⟨~ anesthesia⟩

tran·sub·stan·tial \;transəbz'tanchəl, -raan-, -b;st-, -taan-, -tain-\ *adj* [ML *transubstantiare* to transubstantiate + E *-al*] : changed or capable of being changed from one substance to another — **tran·sub·stan·tial·ly** \-chəlē\ *adv*

tran·sub·stan·ti·ate \;==='tanchē,āt, -b'st-, -taan-, -tain-, *usu* -ād·+V\ *vb* -ED/-ING/-S [ML *transubstantiatus*, past part. of *transubstantiare*, fr. L *trans-* + *substantia* substance] *vt* **1** : to change into another substance : TRANSFORM, TRANSMUTE — usu. used with *into* or *to* ⟨the ancient alchemists hoped to ~ base metals into gold⟩ ⟨the content of experience is not merely shuffled by the poet but is . . . *transubstantiated* —Eliseo Vivas⟩ **2** : to change (the eucharistic elements of bread and wine) into the body and blood of Christ according to the doctrine esp. of the Roman Catholic Church ⟨after the consecration . . . the bread is transmuted, *transubstantiated*, converted, and transformed into the true body itself of the Lord —R.M. French⟩ ~ *vi* : to undergo transubstantiation ⟨at what words and moment do the bread and wine ~ —Valentine Ughet & Eleanor Davis⟩

tran·sub·stan·ti·a·tion \,==,==,'āshən\ *also* **trans·sub·stan·ti·a·tion** \-nzsəb-, -n(t)ssəb-\ *n* [ME, fr. ML *transubstantiation-, transubstantiatio*; fr. *transubstantiatus* + L *-ion-, -io*, -ion] : an act, process, or instance of transubstantiating or being transubstantiated; *specif* : the change in the eucharistic elements at their consecration in the Roman Catholic mass from the substance of bread and wine to the substance of the body and blood of Christ with only the accidents (as taste, color, shape, and smell) of the bread and wine remaining — distinguished from *consubstantiation*; compare TRANSACCIDENTATION

tran·su·date \'tran(t)sə,dāt\ *n* -s [NL *transudatus*, past part. of *transudare* to transude] : a product of transudation

tran·su·da·tion \,==='dāshən\ *n* -s [NL *transudation-, transudatio*, fr. *transudatus* + L *-ion-, -io* -ion] **1** : the act or process of transuding or being transuded **2** : TRANSUDATE

tran·su·da·tive \tran'südəd·iv\ *adj* [NL *transudatus* + E *-ive*] : of, relating to, or constituting transudation or a transudate

tran·sude \tran'süd, traan-\ *vb* -ED/-ING/-S [NL *transudare*, fr. L *trans-* + *sudare* to sweat, perspire — more at SWEAT] *vi* : to pass through a membrane or permeable substance : EXUDE ⟨the serum of the blood has not *transuded* into the lung tissue proper —Robert Chawner⟩ ⟨a hand . . . squeezed and unsqueezed a blob of mud which *transuded* from the cracks of his fist —J.R.Guss⟩ ~ *vt* : to cause to pass through : permit passage of : EXUDE ⟨the capillary wall ~*s* fluids and dissolved matter into the tissue spaces⟩

tran·sumpt \-'səm(p)t\ *n* -s [ME, fr. ML *transumptum*, fr. neut. of *transumptus*, past part. of *transumere* to transcribe, fr. L, to take from one to another] *Scot* : a copy of a writing or legal document; *esp* : an exemplified copy

tran·sump·tion \-(p)shən\ *n* -s [ML *transumption-, transumptio* transcription, fr. L, transferal of terms, fr. *transumptus* (past part. of *transumere* to take from one to another, fr. *trans-* + *sumere* to take, fr. *sub-* up + *emere* to take) + *-ion-, -io* -ion — more at SUB-, REDEEM] : an act, process, or instance of making a copy ⟨only experts could read the original, a ~ in the ordinary hand —H.W.Smith⟩

tran·sump·tive \-(p)tiv\ *adj* [L *transumptivus*, fr. *transumptus* + *-ivus* -ive] : of, relating to, or characterized by the transfer or substitution of terms : METAPHORICAL ⟨the ~ power of poetry —R.P.Blackmur⟩

trans–uranian \;tran(t)s, -raan-, -nz+\ *adj*, *usu cap U* [*trans-* + *Uranus*, planet between Saturn and Neptune + E *-ian*] : extending or lying beyond the orbit of the planet Uranus

trans·u·ra·ni·um \;tran(t)syə;rānēəm, ;traan-, -nzy-\ *or* **trans·u·ran·ic** \-;ranik\ *also* **trans·u·ra·ni·an** \-;rānēən\ *adj* [*transuranium* fr. *trans-* + *uranium*; *transuranic*, ISV *trans-* + *uranium* + *-ic*; *transuranian*, ISV *trans-* + *uranium* + *-an*] : having an atomic number greater than that of uranium ⟨the known ~ elements belong to the actinide series⟩

trans·urethral \"+\ *adj* [ISV *trans-* + *urethra* + *-al*] : extending or effected through the urethra ⟨~ prostatectomy⟩ ⟨~ manipulation⟩

transv *abbr* transverse

trans·vaal daisy \(')tran(t)s;väl-, -raan-, -nz;-\ *n*, *usu cap T* [fr. *Transvaal*, province of northeast Union of So. Africa] : a widely cultivated southern African perennial herb (*Gerbera jamesoni*) having flower heads with orange to flame-colored strap-shaped rays — called also *Barberton daisy*

trans·val·u·ate \tran(t)s'valyə,wāt, traan-, -nz'-\ *vt* [back-formation fr. *transvaluation*] : TRANSVALUE

trans·val·u·a·tion \(,)=,==='wāshən\ *n* [*trans-* + *valuation*] : the act or process of transvaluing or altering the value or worth placed on something ⟨in his ~ of values, sought to do away with this Christian ethic and return to pagan standards —Grace Foster⟩ ⟨rebellion . . . involves a genuine ~ where the direct or vicarious experience of frustration leads to full denunciation of previously prized values —R.K.Merton⟩

trans·value \='val,yü\ *vt* [*trans-* + *value*] : to value on a different basis and esp. one that repudiates conventional or accepted standards : REEVALUATE ⟨war ~*s* all values —Curtis Bradford⟩ ⟨psychoanalysis . . . has not only permeated and *transvalued* the mental sciences, but indirectly also belles lettres —A.A.Brill⟩

trans·vase \tran(t)s'vās, -nz'-\ *vt* -ED/-ING/-S [F *transvaser*, fr. OF, fr. L *trans-* + *vas* vessel, vase] : to pour out of one vessel into another ⟨~*s* the water⟩

¹**trans·ver·sal** \(')tran(t)s;vərsəl, -raan-, -nz;-, -vōs-, -vəis-\ *adj* [ME, fr. ML *transversalis*, fr. L *transversus* transverse + *-alis* -al] : extending or lying across : TRANSVERSE ⟨a ~ line⟩ ⟨~ vibrations⟩ — **trans·ver·sal·ly** \-səlē, -li\ *adv*

²**transversal** \"\ *n* -s : a line that traverses or intersects a system of lines (as the sides of a triangle) or the sides produced

trans·ver·sale \,träⁿsver'säl\ *adj* [F, fem. of *transversal*, fr. ML *transversalis*] : placed so as to include three numbers in a row horizontally — used of a bet in roulette

trans·ver·sa·lis \,tran(t)svə(r)'salės, -raan-, -nzv-, -'säl-, -'säl-\ *n* -ES [NL, fr. ML, transversal] : any of several transverse bodily parts (as muscles or arteries) — usu. used with an orienting term ⟨~ abdominis⟩

trans·ver·sa·ry \tran(t)s'vərsərē, -nz'-\ *n* -ES [L *transversarium* crossbeam, fr. neut. of *transversarius* situated transversely, fr. *transversus* transverse + *-arius* -ary] : a crosspiece on a nautical cross-staff

¹**trans·verse** \tran(t)s'vərs, traan-, -nz'-, -'vōs, -'vəis\ *vt* -ED/-ING/-S [ME *transversen*, fr. MF *transverser*, fr. LL *transversare* to cross, fr. L *transversus* transverse] **1** : to lie or pass across : CROSS ⟨the artery ~*s* the bone⟩ **2** *archaic* : to go counter to : OPPOSE, TRAVERSE **3** : OVERTURN, REVERSE ⟨~ the saying⟩ **4** *obs* : ALTER, TRANSFORM

²**transverse** \(')=;=\ *adj* [L *transversus*, fr. past part. of *transvertere* to turn or direct across, fr. *trans-* + *vertere* to turn — more at WORTH] : extended or lying across or in a crosswise direction ⟨from the ~ hall, the stairway ascends gracefully —*Amer. Guide Series: Va.*⟩ ⟨uses ~ leaf springs set perpendicular to the axle⟩ ⟨the ~ strokes in the letter K⟩ — opposed to *longitudinal*

³**transverse** \"\ *n* -s : something (as a piece, muscle, or part) that is transverse or athwart; *specif* : TRANSEPT

⁴**transverse** \"\ *adv*, *archaic* : TRANSVERSELY

⁵**transverse** \=;=\ *vt* [*trans-* + *verse*] : to turn or render into verse : VERSIFY

transverse artery *n* [²*transverse*] : one of the small branches of the basilar artery supplying the pons and adjacent parts

transverse axis *n* : the axis through the foci of a conic and esp. of a hyperbola

transverse bone *n* : a bone connecting the pterygoid and maxilla in some reptiles and forming part of the apparatus for erecting the fangs in various snakes

transverse carpal ligament *n* : a dense transverse band of fibers passing over flexor tendons at the wrist

transverse colon *n* : the middle portion of the colon that extends across the abdominal cavity — see DIGESTION illustration

transverse crevasse *n* : a crevasse that commonly opens across a glacier where the slope of its floor abruptly steepens

transverse crural ligament *n* : a transverse band of fibers passing over the extensor tendons above the ankle

transverse dihedral *n* : DIHEDRAL 2

transverse facial artery *n* : a branch of the superficial temporal artery that supplies the parotid gland, masseter muscle, and adjacent parts

transverse facial vein *n* : a vein of the side of the face tributary to the temporal vein

transverse fault *n* : an extended dip fault

transverse fissure *n* **1** : the cleft below the hemispheres of the brain through which the pia mater extends to form the choroid plexuses **2** : a cleft of the liver **3** : a fracture that starts at a crystalline center inside a railhead and spreads outward

transverse flute *n* : the modern flute — compare RECORDER 3a

transverse framing *n* : a system of ship construction in which the frames are closely spaced to furnish most of the strength to the ship's structure — opposed to *Isherwood system*

transverse joint *n* : the metatarsal joint

transverse ligament *n* : any of various ligaments: as **a** : one that crosses between the greater and lesser tubercles of the humerus **b** : the transverse part of the cruciate ligament of the atlas **c** : one crossing the notch in the lower border of the acetabulum **d** : one connecting the digital ends of the metatarsal bones in the sole of the foot **e** : CORACOID LIGAMENT

trans·verse·ly *adv* [²*transverse* + *-ly*] : in a transverse direction or line : CROSSWISE, ATHWART

transverse mass *n* : the ratio of the accelerating force to the acceleration when the acceleration is perpendicular to the line of motion

trans·verse·ness *n* -ES : the quality or state of being transverse

transverse process *n* : a lateral process of a vertebra: **a** : DIAPOPHYSIS **b** : PARAPOPHYSIS

trans·vers·er \-sə(r)\ *n* -s [¹*transverse* + *-er*] **1** : one that transverses **2** : PLANE TABLE

transverse rib *n* [²*transverse*] : a rib in a vaulting that crosses a nave or aisle at right angles to the long axis of the building

transverse sinus *n* : either of two large venous sinuses of the cranium that begin at the internal occipital protuberance and terminate at the jugular foramen on either side to become the internal jugular vein — called also *lateral sinus*

transverse suture *n* : the suture between the frontal and facial bones

transverse table *n* : TRANSFER TABLE

transverse vein *n* : CROSSVEIN 2

transverse vibration *n* : a vibration in which the element moves to and fro in a direction perpendicular to the direction of the advance of the wave

transverse wave *n* : a wave in which the vibrating element (as the electric field in light waves or the particles of a vibrating medium) moves in a direction perpendicular to the direction in which the wave advances

trans·ver·sion \tran(t)s'vərzhən, -nz'-\ *n* -s [L *transversus* (past part. of *transvertere* to turn or direct across) + E *-ion* — more at TRANSVERSE] : an act, process, or instance of transversing

trans·ver·sum \tran(t)s'vərsəm, -nz'-\ *n* -s [NL, fr. L, neut. of *transversus* transverse] : the transverse bone of a reptile's skull

trans·ver·sus \-rsəs\ *n*, *pl* **transver·si** \-r,sī\ [NL, fr. L, transverse] : a transversalis muscle — often used in combination

transversus ab·dom·i·nis \-əb'dämənəs\ *n* [NL, lit., transversus of the abdomen] : a flat muscle with transverse fibers that forms the innermost layer of the anterolateral wall of the abdomen and ends in a broad aponeurosis which joins that of the opposite side at the linea alba with its upper three fourths passing behind the rectus abdominis muscle and the lower fourth in front of it

trans·vert·er \tran(t)s'vərd·ə(r), -nz'-\ *n* -s [L *transvertere* + E *-er*] : a machine that consists of a fixed transformer, commutator, and brushes which revolve at synchronous speed and by which a three-phase alternating current can be converted into a direct current at one end of the line and reconverted into a three-phrase alternating current at the terminal point

trans·ves·tic \tran(t)s'vestik, traan-, -nz'-, -tēk\ *adj* [*transvestism* + *-ic*] : of, relating to, or characterized by transvestism ⟨patients with ~ tendencies —*Jour. Amer. Med. Assoc.*⟩

trans·ves·tism \-e,stizəm\ *also* **trans·ves·ti·tism** \-estə,tizəm\ *n* -s [*transvestism* fr. G *transvestismus*, fr. L *trans-* + *vestire* to clothe + G *-ismus* -ism, fr. L; *transvestitism* fr. G *transvestitismus*, fr. *transvestit* transvestite + *-ismus* — more at VEST] : the practice of adopting the dress, the manner, and frequently the sexual role of the opposite sex

¹**trans·ves·tite** \-e,stīt, *usu* -īd·+V\ *n* -s [G *transvestit*, fr. L *trans-* + *vestitus*, past part. of *vestire* to clothe] : one who practices transvestism

²**transvestite** \"\ *adj* : addicted to wearing garments of the other sex

¹**tran·syl·va·nian** \;tran(t)səl;vānyən, -raan-, -nēən\ *adj*, *usu cap* [*Transylvania*, region of northwest & central Romania + E *-an*] **1** : of, relating to, or characteristic of Transylvania **2** : of, relating to, or characteristic of the people of Transylvania

²**transylvanian** \"\ *n* -s *cap* : a native or inhabitant of Transylvania

trant \'trant, 'tränt\ *vi* [back-formation fr. *tranter*] *dial Eng* : to work as a tranter

trant·er \-tə(r)\ *n* -s [alter. of earlier *trauenter*, *traunter*, fr. ML *travetarius*, perh. fr. L *transvectus* (past part. of *transvehere* to carry across, transport, fr. *trans-* + *vehere* to carry) + *-arius* -ary — more at WAY] *dial Eng* : one that does odd jobs of transporting or peddling usu. with a horse and cart

trant·lum \'trantləm\ *n* [origin unknown] *dial Brit* : TRIFLE, TRINKET — usu. used in pl.

tranz·sche·lia \tran(z)'shēlēə\ *n*, *cap* [NL, fr. *Tranzschel*, prob. a surname + NL *-ia*] : a genus of rusts (family Pucciniaceae) with 2-celled teliospores resembling those of the genus *Puccinia* but with two or more attached to a common stalk

¹**trap** \'trap\ *n* -s [ME *trap, trappe*, fr. OE *treppe, træppe* & OF *trape* (of Gmc origin); akin to MD *trappe* trap, step, stairs, MHG *trappe, treppe* step, stairs, MLG & MD *trappen* to stamp, OE *treppan* to tread, Lith *drebeti* to shake, quiver, Skt *dravati* he runs, melts; basic meaning: running, tripping] **1 a** : a device (as a pitfall, snare, or clamp that springs shut suddenly) for taking game or destructive animals : GIN ⟨sets his ~*s* along the river⟩ ⟨caught like a rat in a ~⟩ **b** (1) : FISH TRAP (2) : LOBSTER POT **c** : TRAP CROP **2** : something by which one is unsuspectingly or deceptively caught or stopped in an action or progress ⟨the Indians could be superb fighters . . . adepts at ~*s* and ambushes —Seth Agnew⟩ ⟨prepared defensive ~*s* for his opponent's attacks —G.A.Craig⟩ ⟨with ~*s* and obstacles . . . confronting us on every hand —B.N.Cardozo⟩ ⟨expensive ~*s* for ignorant tourists —Ann Leighton⟩ **3 a** (1) : a hinged or collapsible door or cover of an enclosed space or pit designed to give way when walked on (2) : DROP 3c **b** : any of various covered openings constructed in the floor of a stage for the passage of persons or scenery; *also* : a device or machinery used to effect such a passage **4 a** (1) : a wooden instrument used in playing trapball and consisting of a pivoted arm on one end of which is placed the ball to be thrown into the air by striking the other end (2) : a similar device used in knur and spell **b** : a device for hurling clay pigeons into the air **c** : SAND TRAP 2 **d** : the act or an instance of stopping or catching a ball close to or against the ground **e** : MOUSETRAP 2a **f** : ²TILT 6 **g** : a piece of leather webbing laced between the thumb and forefinger of a baseball glove to form a pocket for receiving the ball **5 a** *Brit* : DECEIT, TRICKERY ⟨a clever, ready-witted fellow, up to all sorts of ~ —Samuel Lover⟩ **b** *Brit* : POLICEMAN, DETECTIVE **c** *slang* : MOUTH ⟨shut your ~ and listen —Richard Llewellyn⟩ **6** : a light often sporty 2- or 4-wheeled horse-drawn carriage accommodating usu. 2 to 4 persons in various seating arrangements (as face-to-face or back-to-back) **7** : any of various devices for preventing the passage of something often while allowing other matter to proceed: as **a** : a device for drains or sewers consisting of a bend or partitioned chamber in which the liquid forms a seal to prevent the passage of sewer gas **b** : STEAM TRAP **c** : a device to separate sand and silt from flowing water **d** : a place in a water pipe or pump where something (as an air pocket) is held or retained **e** : a device to catch mercury or ammonia escaping from amalgamation plates **f** : a usu. sharply tuned circuit consisting of either conventional coils and condensers or transmission lines to eliminate an unwanted signal **g** : a site of imperfection in the crystal structure of a solid at which otherwise mobile electrons and holes can be confined or trapped often more or less temporarily **8** : SMASH 2b **9 a** : a percussion instrument — usu. used in pl. ⟨likes to play the ~*s*⟩ ⟨has a set of ~*s*⟩ **b traps** *pl* : the group of percussion instruments esp. in a dance or theater orchestra **10** : the degree to which printing ink will trap ⟨the sample definitely indicates poor ~ . . . due to improper tackiness of the inks, one printing over the other —*Graphic Arts Monthly*⟩

²**trap** \"\ *vb* **trapped** *or archaic* **trapt**; **trapped** *or archaic* **trapt**; **trapping**; **traps** [ME *trappen*, fr. *trap, trappe* trap] *vt* **1 a** : to catch or take in or as if in a trap or snare by skill, craft, or trickery : ENTRAP, ENSNARE ⟨~*s* muskrats in the fall of the year⟩ ⟨~ wasps in a jar containing beer and treacle —F.D. Smith & Barbara Wilcox⟩ ⟨*trapped* him . . . by forcing him to follow her into her home —Harrison Smith⟩ ⟨avoids the danger of being *trapped* upon cross-examination —Paul Wilson⟩ **b** : to place (as a person) in a restricted or difficult position : CONFINE, ENTANGLE ⟨the crash tools . . . useful in freeing persons *trapped* or imprisoned in a wrecked airplane —H.G.Armstrong⟩ ⟨those with food . . . share with the utterly *trapped* —Wallace Stegner⟩ ⟨*trapped* in a series of events over which he has no control —William Murray⟩ ⟨a story of people *trapped* in a criminal situation through their weakness rather than sin —David Dempsey⟩ — sometimes used with *into* ⟨his reliance on feeling . . . frequently *trapped* him into absurdities and muddleheadedness —F.B.Millett⟩ **c** : to induce (an opponent) usu. by passing to bid or bet unwisely in a card game **2** : to provide or set (a place) with traps: as **a** : to set (a place or area) with traps to catch an animal or a person ⟨had a permit from the mortgage company to ~ its lands —H.L.

Davis⟩ ⟨has the place *trapped* with all sorts of burglar alarms —Erle Stanley Gardner⟩ **b :** to install a trap in (as a drain) ⟨the law usually requires that drains be *trapped*⟩ **c :** to construct traps on (as a golf course) ⟨the greens are heavily *trapped* —*New Yorker*⟩ **3 :** to separate out : STOP, HOLD ⟨these mountains ~ rains and fogs generated over the ocean —*Amer. Guide Series: Calif.*⟩ ⟨a scheme which ~s sunlight and turns it into motive power —*English Digest*⟩ **4 a :** to stop or catch (as a soccer ball or baseball) when or immediately after it hits the ground **b :** to catch (as a baserunner) off base ⟨~s many runners with his quick pick-off throw⟩ **c :** MOUSETRAP ⟨one of the big problems we had on offense was *trapping* the guards —Bob Hicks⟩ **5 :** to accept (superimposed ink often of another color) during a subsequent printing **6 :** TRAPNEST ~ *vi* **1 :** to set traps for game; *also* **:** to make a business of trapping animals ⟨began to ~ for a living —R.L.Neuberger⟩ **2 :** to become trapped (as steam in a radiator) **3 :** to employ tactics in a card game designed to trap another player **syn** see CATCH

³trap \"\ *n* -s [ME *trappe*, modif. (prob. influenced by OSp *trapo* cloth, modif. of LL *drappus*) of MF *drap* cloth — more at DRAB] **1** *obs* **:** an ornamented cloth covering esp. for a horse **:** TRAPPING — usu. used in pl. **2 traps** *pl* **:** personal belongings **:** GOODS, LUGGAGE ⟨put our little household ~s into a freight car and went back —W.A.White⟩

⁴trap *vt* **trapped; trapped; trapping; traps** [ME *trappen*, fr. *trappe* cloth, trap] **:** to clothe or provide with or as if with traps or trappings **:** CAPARISON ⟨horse *trapped* for battle —P.H.Davis⟩ ⟨wrapped and *trapped* in their accouterments —Bruce Marshall⟩ ⟨feathers in which she has *trapped* out that idea —*Irish Digest*⟩

⁵trap \"\ *also* **traprock** \ˈ=,=\ *n* -s [*trap* fr. Sw *trapp*, fr. *trappa* stair, fr. MLG *trappe*; akin to MD *trappe* step, stair; *traprock* fr. ⁵*trap* + *rock*; fr. its occurring in sheetlike masses that rise above one another like steps — more at TRAP (snare)] **1 :** any of various dark-colored fine-grained igneous rocks (as basalt or amygdaloid) used esp. in road making **2 :** an arrangement of rock strata involving their structural relations or varied lithology and texture that favors the accumulation of oil and gas

⁶trap \"\ *n* -s [D, fr. MD *trappe*] *Scot* **:** a movable flight of steps **:** STEPLADDER

trapa \ˈtrāpə, -rapə\ *n*, *cap* [NL, prob. short for (assumed) ML *calcitrappa* caltrop — more at CALTROP] **:** a small Old World genus of aquatic herbaceous plants with finely dissected submerged leaves, rhombic floating leaves that have inflated spongy petioles, and solitary white flowers followed by horned or spiny fruits — see TRAPACEAE, WATER CHESTNUT

tra·pa·ce·ae \trəˈpāsē,ē\ *n pl*, *cap* [NL, fr. *Trapa*, type genus + *-aceae*] *in some classifications* **:** a family of dicotyledonous plants (order Myrtales) containing solely the genus *Trapa* and commonly treated as a subfamily or tribe of Onagraceae

trapball \ˈ=,=\ *n* **:** an old game of ball played with a trap; *also* **:** the ball used in the game

trap brilliant \ˈtrap-\ *n* [*trap* prob. fr. D, step, fr. MD — more at TRAP (snare)] **:** DOUBLE BRILLIANT

trap car *n* [¹*trap*] **:** a railroad car used for less-than-carload shipments usu. within terminal or city limits **:** FERRY CAR

trap crop *n* **:** a crop planted to attract noxious insects or other pests so that they may be destroyed to prevent damage to nearby or later crops

trap cut *n* [*trap* prob. fr. D, step] **:** STEP CUT

trapdoor \ˈ=,=\ *n* [ME *trappe dor*, fr. *trappe* trap + *dor* door — more at TRAP (snare), DOOR] **1 :** a lifting or sliding door covering an opening in a roof, ceiling, or floor **2 :** a ventilating door in a level of a mine — called also *weather door*

trap–door spider \ˈ=,=-\ *n* **:** any of various often large burrowing spiders esp. of the family Ctenizidae that construct a tubular subterranean silklined nest topped with a hinged lid

trap drum *n* **:** the bass drum in a set of traps to which are attached the various rhythm devices (as cymbal and block)

trap drummer *n* **:** a performer on traps

trapes *var of* TRAIPSE

¹tra·peze \(ˈ)traˈpēz *sometimes* trəˈp-\ *n* -s [F *trapèze*, fr. NL *trapezium*] **:** a gymnastic or acrobatic apparatus consisting of a short horizontal bar suspended by two parallel ropes

²trapeze \"\ *vi* -ED/-ING/-S **:** to perform or act on or as if on a trapeze ⟨hedges intertwined with crimson flowers, among which . . . birds were *trapezing* —Malcolm Lowry⟩ ⟨legal scholars *trapezing* around in cycles . . . without coming to rest on the floor of fact —F.S.Cohen⟩

trapeze artist *n* **:** a usu. professional performer on the trapeze

tra·pe·zi·al \traˈpēzēəl *sometimes* trəˈp-\ *adj* **:** of or relating to a trapezium or trapezius

tra·pe·zi·form \-zə,fȯrm\ *adj* [prob. fr. (assumed) NL *trapeziformis*, fr. *trapezium* + L *-iformis* -iform] **:** having the form of a trapezium

tra·pez·ist \-zəst\ *n* -s **:** TRAPEZE ARTIST

tra·pe·zi·um \-zēəm\ *n*, *pl* **trapeziums** \-ēəmz\ *or* **trape·zia** \-ēə\ [NL, fr. Gk *trapezion* small table, irregular four-sided figure, trapezium, dim. of *trapeza* table, fr. *tra-* four (akin to Gk *tettares* four) + *peza* foot; akin to *pod-*, *pous* foot — more at FOUR, FOOT] **1 :** a quadrilateral having no two sides parallel **2 a :** the greater multangulum of the carpus **b :** a bundle of transverse fibers in the dorsal part of the pons

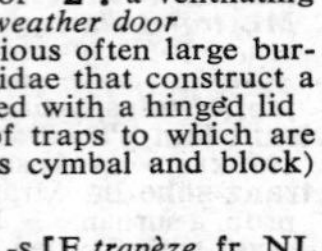

trapezium 1

tra·pe·zi·us \-zēəs\ *n* -ES [NL, fr. *trapezium*; fr. the pair on the back forming together the figure of a trapezium] **:** a large flat triangular superficial muscle of each side of the back that arises from the occipital bone, ligamentum nuchae, and the spinous processes of the last cervical and all the thoracic vertebrae, is inserted into the outer part of the clavicle, the acromion, and the spine of the scapula, and serves chiefly to rotate the scapula so as to present the glenoid cavity upward

trape·zo·he·dral \traˌpēzōˈhēdrəl, traˌpēz-, ˌtrapəz- *sometimes chiefly Brit* -hed-\ *adj* [NL *trapezohedron* + E *-al*] **:** of, relating to, or resembling a trapezohedron

tra·pe·zo·he·dron \-drən, -ˌdrän\ *n*, *pl* **trapezohedrons** \-nz\ *or* **trapezohe·dra** \-drə\ [NL, fr. *trapezium* + *-o-* + *-hedron*] **:** a crystalline form whose faces are trapeziums: **a :** a tetragonal trisoctahedron **b :** an 8-faced hemihedral form of the tetragonal system **c :** a 12-faced hemihedral form of the hexagonal system **d :** a 6-faced tetartohedral form of the hexagonal system — called also *trigonal trapezohedron*

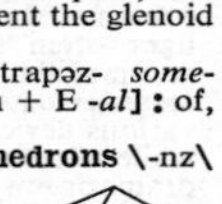

trapezohedron a

¹trap·e·zoid \ˈtrapə,zȯid\ *n* -s [NL *trapezoides*, fr. Gk *trapezoeidēs* trapezium-shaped, fr. *trapeza* table + *-oeidēs* -oid] **1** *archaic* **:** TRAPEZIUM 1 **2 :** a quadrilateral having only two sides parallel **3 :** the lesser multangulum of the carpus

²trapezoid \"\ *adj* **:** of, relating to, or having the form of a trapezoid; *sometimes* **:** TRAPEZIAL

trap·e·zoi·dal \ˌ=ˈzȯidᵊl\ *adj* [¹*trapezoid* + *-al*] **1 :** TRAPEZOID **2 :** TRAPEZOHEDRAL

trapezoidal projection *n* **:** a projection in which straight parallels and straight converging meridians divide the field into trapezoids

trapezoidal rule *n* **:** an approximate rule for determining the area under a curve

trapezoidal thread *n* **:** BUTTRESS THREAD

trapezoid body *n* **:** TRAPEZIUM 2b

trapfall \ˈ=,=\ *n* [¹*trap* + *fall*] **:** TRAP, PITFALL

trap gun *n* **:** a shotgun designed for trapshooting

trap house *n* **:** the enclosure from which clay targets are released in trapshooting and skeet shooting — see HIGH-HOUSE, LOW-HOUSE

tra·pi·che \trəˈpēchē\ *n* -s [Sp, fr. L *trapetes* oil mill, olive mill, fr. Gk *trapētēs* wine presser, fr. *trapein* to press grapes — more at TREPIDATION] **1 :** a sugar mill; *also* **:** a sugar plantation **2 :** a rude mill for grinding ores or minerals

traplight \ˈ=,=\ *n* **:** any of several devices using a light to trap or collect insects

trapline \ˈ=,=\ *n* **:** a line or series of traps; *also* **:** the route along which such a line of traps is set

trap load *n* **:** the charge of powder and shot best adapted for trapshooting; *also* **:** a shotshell loaded for trapshooting

¹trapnest \ˈ=,=\ *n* **:** a nest equipped with a hinged door designed to trap and confine a hen so that individual egg production may be determined

²trapnest \"\ *vt* **:** to determine the productivity of (individual domestic fowls) by means of a trapnest

trap net *n* **:** FISH TRAP, POUND NET

trapped *past of* TRAP

trapper \ˈtrapə(r)\ *n* -s [²*trap* + *-er*] **1 :** one that traps: as **a :** one whose business is trapping animals for furs or food or for sale alive **b :** one that traps fish **2 :** a boy who attends to the opening and closing of ventilation doors in a mine **3 :** one that manages a trap for trapshooting **4 :** a horse that draws a trap **5** *Brit* **:** a pointsman who points or switches trucks or cars into a siding

¹trap·ping \ˈtrapiŋ, -pēŋ\ *n* -s [ME, fr. gerund of *trappen* to trap — more at TRAP (to catch)] **:** the act of catching something or someone in a trap; *specif* **:** the occupation of a trapper

²trapping \"\ *n* -s [ME, fr. gerund of *trappen* to clothe — more at TRAP (to clothe)] **1 :** CAPARISON 1 — usu. used in pl. ⟨the heavy cart horses slipped and stamped . . . shaking their bells and ~s —Oscar Wilde⟩ **2 trappings** *pl* **:** outward decoration or dress **:** ornamental equipment **:** EMBELLISHMENT ⟨Christmas ~s such as lacy gilt butterflies, silver-paper harps . . . paper angels —*New Yorker*⟩ ⟨the usual ~s of rather shabby but gallant old age, which included . . . a cross gleaming gold on her breast —Virginia Woolf⟩ ⟨the visible ~s of success, the automobiles, the applause . . . the consciousness of opulence and distinction —F.A.Swinnerton⟩ ⟨little oligarchies masquerading in the ~s of democracy —F.A.Ogg & P.O.Ray⟩

³trapping \"\ *n* -s [*trap* (cut) + *-ing*] **1 :** the cutting of a gem in a step cut **2** [*trap* (*brilliant*) + *-ing*] **:** the cutting of a trap brilliant

¹trap·pist \ˈtrapəst\ *n* -s *usu cap* [F *trappiste*, fr. La *Trappe*, Normandy + *-iste* -ist] **:** a member of a reformed branch of the Roman Catholic Cistercian Order established in 1664 at the monastery of La Trappe in Normandy and united with the Cistercians since 1892

²trappist \"\ *adj*, *usu cap* **:** of or relating to the Trappist life, spirit, or system

trappist cheese *n*, *usu cap T* [so called fr. its having originated in the Trappist monastery of Mariastern in Bosnia] **:** a semisoft pale yellow cheese of mild flavor usu. made of fresh whole cow's milk — called also *Port du Salut*

trap·pist·ine \-pə,stēn, -tən\ *n* -s *usu cap* **:** a Roman Catholic nun of a group affiliated with the Cistercians of the Strict Observance

trap play *n* **:** MOUSETRAP 2a

trap·poid \ˈtra,pȯid\ *adj* [⁵*trap* + *-oid*] **:** of, relating to, or resembling trap or traprock

trap·py \ˈtrapē, -pi\ *adj* -ER/-EST **1 :** of, relating to, or containing traps or snares **:** TRICKY, DIFFICULT ⟨riding them through thickly timbered country over breakneck fences and ~ ground —W.A.Kerr⟩ ⟨the snow lies deep and soft over the ~ holes and crevices —F.G.Jackson⟩ **2 :** having a short quick rather high gait — used of a horse

traprock *var of* TRAP

traps *pl of* TRAP, *pres 3d sing of* TRAP

trapse *var of* TRAIPSE

trap seal *n* **:** the sealing value of a trap as measured vertically from the mean liquid surface level down to the dip of the trap

trap shoot *n* **:** a match at trapshooting

trapshooter \ˈ=,==\ *n* **:** one who engages in trapshooting

trapshooting \ˈ=,==\ *n* **:** shooting at clay pigeons sprung into the air from a trap

trap shot *n* **1 :** TRAPSHOOTER **2 :** a half volley (as in tennis) made by hitting the ball immediately after it hits the ground

trapstick \ˈ=,=\ *n* **:** a stick used in playing the game of trapball

trap strip *n* **:** a planted area in which the plants serve as a trap crop

trapt *archaic past of* TRAP

trap tree *n* **:** a tree deadened or felled for the purpose of luring insect pests where they can easily be destroyed

tra·pun·to \trəˈpün(,)tō\ *n* -s [It, fr. past part. of *trapungere* to embroider, fr. *tra-* across, through (fr. L *trans*) + *pungere* to prick, fr. L — more at TRANS-, PUNGENT] **:** a decorative quilted design in high relief worked through at least two layers of cloth by outlining the design in running stitch and then padding it from the underside by the insertion of yarn or cotton

trap weir *n* **:** a weir built in the form of a fish trap

¹trash \ˈtrash, -aa(ə)-,-ai-\ *n* -ES [of Scand origin; akin to Norw *trask* lumber, trash, *trase* rag; akin to OE *teran* to tear — more at TEAR] **1 :** something worth relatively little or nothing: as **a :** JUNK, RUBBISH ⟨trampling down a great pile of old newspapers and other ~ —Thomas Whiteside⟩ ⟨was sweeping the ~ in their backyard —Erskine Caldwell⟩ **b :** TRASH FISH ⟨none . . . attains any great size, and they are considered as ~ by fishermen —*Copeia*⟩ **c** (1) **:** empty talk or discourse **:** NONSENSE ⟨what ~ are you talkin' anyway —Owen Wister⟩ ⟨this book is utter ~ . . . pure quackery without scientific standing —Conway Zirkle⟩ (2) **:** inferior or worthless writing or artistic matter ⟨a corner of fiction in which sadistic and poorly written ~ is becoming the norm —Geoffrey Moore⟩ ⟨one of the most lugubrious bits of sentimental ~ . . . ever released —C.F.Wittke⟩ ⟨music that is only ~⟩ **d :** MONEY ⟨drudge, sweat . . . for every gain, for vile contaminating ~ —Edward Young⟩ **2 :** something in a crumbled or broken condition or mass: as **a :** woody or vegetable matter fallen or strewn on the ground ⟨a big drift of logs and ~ —F.B.Gipson⟩ **b :** CANE TRASH **3 :** a worthless person **:** NO-GOOD, POOR WHITE ⟨put a bullet past his ear, just to let the ~ know the sound of it —Winston Churchill⟩; *collectively* **:** such persons as a group or class **:** RIFF-RAFF ⟨the loudmouth ~ . . . from the slums of cities —T.H.Fielding⟩ ⟨I am a poor man . . . but I ain't ~ —R.P.Warren⟩ **4 :** the lower leaves of the burley tobacco plant **syn** see REFUSE

²trash \"\ *vt* -ED/-ING/-ES **:** to free from trash or refuse **:** LOP, CROP; *specif* **:** to strip outer leaves from (immature sugarcane)

³trash \"\ *vb* -ED/-ING/-ES [of Scand origin; akin to Sw *traska* to jog, trudge, tramp] *vi*, *dial Brit* **:** to plod about tiringly esp. in the wet **:** TRUDGE, TRAMP ~ *vt*, *dial Brit* **:** to wear out (as a person) with exertion **:** JADE, FATIGUE

⁴trash \"\ *vt* -ED/-ING/-ES [prob. fr. obs. F *trachier*, *tracier* to trace, track, fr. MF — more at TRACE] **1** *obs* **:** to hold back (as a hunting dog) by a trash **2** *archaic* **:** RESTRAIN, HINDER

⁵trash \"\ *n* -ES *dial Eng* **:** a long light cord used to slow or check a hunting dog in the field **:** LEASH

trash bug *n* **:** an aphis lion that is the larva of a lacewing of the family Chrysopidae and that piles debris on its back

trash can *n* **:** a metal receptacle for dry refuse

trash·ery \-shərē\ *n* -ES [¹*trash* + *-ery*] **:** TRASH, RUBBISH

trash farming *n* **:** a method of cultivation in which the soil is loosened by subsurface tillage or other methods that leave stubble and other vegetational residues on or near the surface to check erosion and serve as a mulch — called also *stubble-mulch farming*

trash fish *n* **1 :** ROUGH FISH **2 :** any of various sea fishes that have no market value as human food but are sometimes used for reduction (as to oil or meal for domestic animals)

trash fishery *n* **:** the business or practice of catching and marketing trash fish

trash ice *n* **:** broken or crumbled ice mixed with water

trash·i·ness \ˈtrashēnəs, -raash-,-raish-\ *n* -ES **:** the quality or state of being trashy

trashrack \ˈ=,=\ *n* **:** ³RACK 6

trash·trie \ˈtrashtri\ *n* -s [alter. of *trashery*] *Scot* **:** TRASH, RUBBISH

trashy \ˈtrashē, -raash-,-raish-, -shi\ *adj* -ER/-EST **1 :** resembling or containing trash **:** of inferior quality **:** WORTHLESS ⟨the cheap and ~ brandy . . . put into so many light wines —O.S.J.Gogarty⟩ ⟨crude in writing, ~ in feeling, implausible —Edmund Wilson⟩ ⟨its score contains some of the *trashiest* pages ever written —Winthrop Sargeant⟩ **2 :** covered or strewn with dried or withered vegetable matter usu. from a previous crop ⟨the seedbed was rough and ~ —Louis Bromfield⟩

trask·ite \ˈtra,skīt\ *n* -s *usu cap* [John *Trask* fl 1617 Eng. religious leader + E *-ite*] **:** SEVENTH-DAY BAPTIST

trass \ˈtras\ *also* **ter·race** *or* **tar·ras** \təˈras\ *n*, *pl* **trasses** *also* **terraces** *or* **tarrases** [D *trass*, *terras*, fr. F *terrasse* pile of earth, terrace, fr. MF — more at TERRACE] **:** a light-colored volcanic tuff resembling pozzolana in composition and occurring esp. on the lower Rhine where it is ground for use in a hydraulic cement

¹tras·tev·er·ine \(ˈ)traˈstevə,rēn, -ˌrən\ *adj*, *usu cap* [It *trasteverino*, fr. L *transtiberinus*, fr. *trans-* + *tiberinus* of the Tiber, fr. *Tiberis* Tiber river + *-inus* -ine] **1 :** of, relating to, or characteristic of the Trastevere region across the Tiber river from Rome **2 :** of, relating to, or characteristic of the people of the Trastevere

²trasteverine \"\ *n*, *pl* **trasteverines** \-nz\ *or* **trasteveri·ni** \ˌ=ˌ==ˈrē(,)nē\ *cap* [It *trasteverino*, fr. L *transtiberini*, pl., trasteverines] **:** a native or inhabitant of the Trastevere

¹trat·tle \ˈtratᵊl\ *vi* -ED/-ING/-S [ME (Sc) *tratlen*] *Scot* **:** PRATTLE, CHATTER, GOSSIP

²trattle \"\ *n* -s [earlier *tretle*, prob. alter. of obs. E dial. *treddle*, fr. ME *tredel*, *tyrdyl*, fr. OE *tyrdel*, dim. of *tord* turd — more at TURD] *dial Eng* **:** a pellet or dropping of any of various animals (as sheep or rabbits) — usu. used in pl.

trat·to·ria \ˌträd·əˈrēə\ *n* -s [It, fr. *trattore* innkeeper, restaurant owner (fr. F *traiteur*, fr. *traiter* to treat, settle, entertain — fr. OF *tretier*, *traitier* — + *-eur* -or) + *-ia* -y — more at TREAT] **:** an eating house **:** RESTAURANT

trau·chle \ˈträkəl\ *var of* TRACHLE

trau·lism \ˈtrȯ,lizəm, -raů,l-\ *n* -s [Gk *traulismos*, fr. *traulizein* to mispronounce, lisp, stammer, fr. *traulos*, adj., mispronouncing letters, lisping, stammering + *-izein* -ize] **:** STAMMERING, STUTTERING

trau·ma \ˈtraůmə *also* -rȯmə\ *n*, *pl* **trauma·ta** \məd·ə,-mətə\ *or* **traumas** [Gk, wound — more at THROE] **1 :** an injury or wound to a living body caused by the application of external force or violence ⟨injuries . . . such as sprains, bruises, fractures, dislocation, concussion — indeed *traumata* of all kinds —*Lancet*⟩ **2 a :** a psychological or emotional stress or blow that may produce disordered feelings or behavior ⟨separation from its mother was the greatest ~ to the young child —Carl Binger⟩ ⟨the moral energies of America were exhausted by the ~ of the Civil War —*New Republic*⟩ **b :** the state or condition of mental or emotional shock produced by such a stress or by a physical injury **:** TRAUMATISM ⟨effects of the ~ induced by the wound —J.W.Aldridge⟩ ⟨what was the nature of this ~, following as it did an acute anxiety state —Elizabeth Rosenberg⟩ ⟨the war left a lasting ~ —Edmund Wilson⟩ **syn** see WOUND

traumat- *or* **traumato-** *comb form* [LL, fr. Gk, fr. *traumat-*, *trauma*] **:** wound **:** trauma ⟨*traumatism*⟩

trau·mat·ic \(ˈ)trȯˈmad·ik, trəˈm-, -at|, |ēk *also* (ˈ)traůˈm-\ *adj* [LL *traumaticus*, fr. Gk *traumatikos*, fr. *traumat-*, *trauma* wound + *-ikos* -ic] **:** of, relating to, or resulting from a trauma ⟨cases of ~ rupture —*Jour. Amer. Med. Assoc.*⟩ ⟨bringing up the details of a ~ experience . . . so as to banish the effects of the experience and make it possible for them to live in the present —Malcolm Cowley⟩ — **trau·mat·i·cal·ly** \|ək(ə)lē, |ēk-, -li\ *adv*

traumatic acid *n* **:** a crystalline unsaturated dicarboxylic acid $HOOC(CH_2)_8CH{=}CHCOOH$ that is obtained esp. from the pods of green beans or by synthesis and that promotes healing of plant wounds; 2-dodec-ene-dioic acid — see WOUND HORMONE

trau·ma·tism \ˈtrȯmə,tizəm, ˈtraům-\ *n* -s [ISV *traumat-* + *-ism*] **:** the development of a state of mental or physical shock from a blow, injury, or stress ⟨fractures, sprains . . . burns, and similar ~s —*Jour. Amer. Med. Assoc.*⟩ ⟨the story of an adolescent ~ . . . of a wealthy child sheltered from reality —Edmond Taylor⟩ ⟨repressions and ~s which may have catastrophic results for whole nations —*Times Lit. Supp.*⟩; *also* **:** the condition produced by such a development **syn** see WOUND

trau·ma·ti·za·tion \ˌtrȯməd·əˈzāshən, ˌtraům-, |təˈz-, |d·,ī'z-, |,tī'z-\ *n* -s **:** the act or process of traumatizing

trau·ma·tize \ˈ=mə,tīz\ *vt* -ED/-ING/-S [*traumat-* + *-ize*] **:** to inflict a trauma upon (the body or mind) ⟨if the nerve is crushed so that the sheath is torn or *traumatized* —R.G. Grenell & H.S.Burr⟩ ⟨response to trauma is governed by . . . type of injury inflicted and region *traumatized* —*Yrbk. of Dentistry*⟩ ⟨case history of a young man who . . . was *traumatized* by an uncommonly hideous childhood, who took refuge in a violent fantasy —J.B.Martin⟩

trau·ma·to·pho·bia \ˌ=məd·əˈfōbēə\ *n* [NL, fr. *traumat-* + *-phobia*] **:** excessive or disabling fear of war or physical injury usu. resulting from experiences in combat

trau·ma·trop·ic \ˌ=mə¦träpik\ *adj* [*trauma* + *-tropic*] **:** of, relating to, or characterized by traumatropism

trau·mat·ro·pism \=ˈma·trə,pizəm\ *n* [*trauma* + *tropism*] **:** a modification of the orientation of an organ (as a plant root) as a result of wounding

trav *abbr* **1** travel **2** traveler **3** travels

¹travail \trəˈvā(ə)l, ˈtra,vāl *sometimes* traˈvā(ə)l *or* ˈtravəl\ *n* -s [ME, fr. OF, fr. *travailler*, *traveillier* to labor, travail] **1 a :** physical or mental work or exertion esp. of a painful or laborious nature **:** LABOR, TOIL, DRUDGERY ⟨tackles his outdoor ~ with the furious drive of a bulldozer —R.L.Taylor⟩ ⟨sat glum and thoughtful, his mind in unproductive ~ —Rafael Sabatini⟩ ⟨periods of high intellectual achievement and ~, of critical analysis and doubt —*Times Lit. Supp.*⟩ **b :** a physical or mental exertion or piece of work **:** TASK, EFFORT ⟨manfully undertakes his assigned ~⟩ ⟨my literary ~ —G.B.Shaw⟩ — often used in pl. ⟨reminisced on the ~s of campaigning —*N.Y. Times*⟩ **c :** pain or suffering resulting from physical struggle or mental conflict **:** AGONY, TORMENT ⟨chose . . . to share France's ~ as earlier he had shared her happier days —Paul Farmer⟩ ⟨rises joyously superior to the outward calamities . . . and celebrates the greatness of the human spirit whose ~ he describes —J.W.Krutch⟩ ⟨the ~ of an artist in a society of so many material conveniences —M.D.Geismar⟩ — sometimes used in pl. ⟨takes up some of the special ~s of the upper classes —Rex Lardner⟩ **2 :** LABOR, PARTURITION ⟨woman must marry because the race must perish without her ~ —G.B. Shaw⟩ ⟨suggested that the nation had been long in ~, and had at last produced a man —John Buchan⟩ **3** *obs* **:** TRAVEL 2 **syn** see WORK

²travail \"\ *vb* -ED/-ING/-S [ME *travailen*, *traveilen*, fr. OF *travaillier*, *traveillier* to labor, toil, trouble, torture, fr. (assumed) VL *tripaliare* to torture, fr. (assumed) VL *tripalium* instrument of torture, fr. L *tripalis* having three stakes, fr. *tri-* + *palus* stake — more at POLE] *vi* **1 :** to labor hard **:** DRUDGE, TOIL ⟨~s hard for his daily wage⟩ **2 :** LABOR 3 **3** *obs* **:** TRAVEL 2 ~ *vt* **1** *archaic* **:** TROUBLE, TORMENT, HARASS **2** *obs* **:** to put to laborious mental or physical work **:** DRIVE

³tra·vail \trəˈvī\ *n*, *pl* **travails** \-vīz\ *also* **tra·vaux** \-vō\ [F, fr. MF, fr. (assumed) VL *tripalium* instrument of torture] **:** TRAVOIS 1

tra·vat·ed \ˈtraˌvād·əd\ *adj* [It *travato* (fr. *trave* beam — fr. L *trabs*, *trabes* — + *-ato* -ate) + E *-ed*] *of a ceiling* **:** divided into traves

trave \ˈtrāv\ *n* -s [ME, fr. MF, beam, fr. L *trabs*, *trabes* — more at THORP] **1 :** a frame to confine an unruly horse or ox for shoeing **2 :** CROSSBEAM **3 :** a division or bay (as in a ceiling) made by or as if by crossbeams

¹travel \ˈtravəl\ *vb* **traveled** *or* **travelled; traveled** *or* **travelled; traveling** *or* **travelling** \-v(ə)liŋ\ **travels** [ME *travellen*, *travailen* — more at TRAVAIL] *vi* **1** *obs* **:** TRAVAIL **2 a :** to go or proceed on or as if on a trip or tour **:** JOURNEY ⟨the country through which we have been ~*ing* —Louis Bromfield⟩ ⟨many young birds ~ north during June —*Amer. Guide Series: La.*⟩ ⟨the surge . . . ~*ed* southwards along the coast —J.A.Steers⟩ ⟨even ideas and emotions ~*ed* slowly in those days —Clive Bell⟩ **b** (1) **:** to move or go as if by traveling **:** PASS ⟨my mind ~*ed* back to a hot sultry day in the little . . . town —Rex Keating⟩ ⟨her eyes ~*ed* about the room —Mary R. Rinehart⟩ ⟨US 190 ~s through a wide stretch . . . of virgin pine —*Amer. Guide Series: La.*⟩ ⟨most parts of the world are ~*ing* toward a tighter system —Bertrand Russell⟩ ⟨the path . . . for the inspired genius to ~ by —H.J.Laski⟩ (2) **:** to move or join in a company or group **:** ASSOCIATE ⟨~*ed* in left wing circles —Oden & Olivia Meeker⟩ — usu. used with *with* ⟨no harder a drinker than most of the crowd he ~*ed* with —Robert Sylvester⟩ ⟨the liberal intellectuals who . . . ~*ed* with the party —Margaret Marshall⟩ **c** *dial* **:** to go on foot **:** WALK ⟨did you ~ or come by boat —*Amer. Guide Series: N.C.*⟩ **d :** to go on a specified circuit or route ⟨in the frontier towns most ministers ~*ed*⟩ ⟨offering premiums for stallions to ~ —Robert Jarvis⟩ **e :** to go from place to place

as a salesman or business agent ⟨salesman . . . was *~ing* out of St. Louis —E.A.Duddy⟩ — often used with *in* ⟨man who *~ed* in ladies' undies, wholesale —O.S.J.Gogarty⟩ **3 a :** to move, advance, or undergo transmission from one place to another ⟨the bayonet entered the right rib cage . . . and *~ed* upward —Raymond Boyle⟩ ⟨the pain . . . *~ed* all the way into his head —Ira Wolfert⟩ ⟨the sound *~ed* onto the stage —Warwick Braithwaite⟩ **b :** to undergo transportation or dissemination ⟨loup, like weakfish, *~s* poorly and should be eaten within a few hours after being caught —A.J.Liebling⟩ ⟨cases . . . which ~ in freight cars must be securely packed —Edwin Sutermeister⟩ ⟨the whole concept of impressionism . . . didn't ~ well —R.M.Coates⟩ ⟨that typical regionalism which *~s* so poorly in literature —V.S.Pritchett⟩ **c :** to move in a given direction or path or through a given distance ⟨the needles . . . ~ down the face of the cam —W.E.Shinn⟩ ⟨the crankpin *~s* in a circular path⟩ ⟨the stylus *~s* in a groove⟩ **d :** to move briskly ⟨the souped-up car can really ~⟩ **4 :** to walk or run with the ball illegally (as in basketball) ~ *vt* **1** *obs* **:** TRAVAIL **2 a :** to journey through or over **:** TRAVERSE ⟨everyone should ~ at least part of its beautiful valley —Bernard DeVoto⟩ ⟨*~ed* the twenty feet of green carpet with his eyes fixed straight ahead —Scott Fitzgerald⟩ ⟨certain roads can be *~ed* only on horseback —W.E.Rudolph⟩ **b :** to follow (a course or path) as if by traveling **:** PURSUE ⟨no other social right has *~ed* so arduous a road —V.L.Parrington⟩ ⟨readers . . . often voyaged into the world celebrated by the romantic novelist, but few *~ed* the other way —J.D.Hart⟩ **c :** to pass over or along (a specified distance) ⟨individual cells often have to ~ great distances —*New Biology*⟩ ⟨the modern travel book has itself *~ed* a long way from the formal diary —*Geog. Jour.*⟩ **d :** to cover or visit (a place or region) as a commercial traveler ⟨*~ed* the Midwest for a soft drink firm —Tom Siler⟩ **3 :** to cause to travel **:** DRIVE, SHIP ⟨the beast . . . could scarcely be *~ed* upon a caravel —Galbraith Welch⟩ ⟨choose the best time of year to ~ cattle⟩ ⟨*~ing* the stallion to different farms —*Producing Farm Livestock*⟩ — **travel light :** to travel with a minimum of equipment or baggage ⟨the Australian *travels light:* a spear, a boomerang club, and perhaps a spear-thrower for a man —A.L.Kroeber⟩

²travel \"\ *n* -s [ME *travel, travail* — more at TRAVAIL] **1** *obs* **:** TRAVAIL **2 a :** the act of traveling, going, or journeying **:** PASSAGE ⟨dislikes the discomforts of ~ —Agnes Repplier⟩ ⟨outlined the probable steps leading to ~ in outer space —*Current Biog.*⟩ ⟨~ on the plateau is comparatively rapid —E.E.Shipton⟩ **b :** a journey esp. to a distant or unfamiliar place **:** TOUR, TRIP ⟨set out on another ~, this time to the Pacific —*Current Biog.*⟩ ⟨longest ~ for a cake to make without a bruise —*Postal Service News*⟩ ⟨to town and back is a long day's ~⟩ — often used in pl. ⟨extended our *~s* to parts of the rugged mountains totally unknown —C.B.Hitchcock⟩ **3 travels** *pl* **:** an account or narration of one's travels esp. in book form ⟨enjoys reading *~s*⟩ **4 :** power or speed of movement ⟨the most necessary qualifications of a dog are ~ . . . and nose —Eric Parker⟩ ⟨the new racing shell has tremendous ~⟩ **5 :** the number of persons or things traveling **:** TRAFFIC ⟨~ on the turnpike is heavy on holidays⟩ **6 a :** the movement or progression of something along a route or course ⟨the farther the film tray is from the workplace, the more reach or ~ is required —E.M.Harwell⟩ ⟨during combustion the ~ of the flame . . . should progress at a fairly uniform rate —Ernest Venk⟩ ⟨a device to time the ~ of satellites around the earth⟩ **b :** the motion of a piece of machinery esp. to and fro in a prescribed line or direction ⟨a timing device to make the high-voltage source perform at the set position of piston ~ —*Aircraft Power Plants*⟩

trav·el·able *or* **trav·el·la·ble** \ˈtrav(ə)ləbəl\ *adj* **:** capable of being traveled **:** PASSABLE ⟨highway crews soon had the roads ~ after the storm⟩

travel agency *or* **travel bureau** *n* **:** an office or enterprise engaged in selling, arranging, or furnishing information about personal transportation or travel

travel agent *n* **:** a person engaged in selling or arranging personal transportation, tours, or trips

traveled *or* **travelled** *adj* [fr. past part. of ¹*travel*] **1 :** that has traveled or is experienced in travel **2 :** ERRATIC 2 ⟨the ~ stones are of all dimensions —J.D.Dana⟩

trav·el·er *or* **trav·el·ler** \-v(ə)lə(r)\ *n* -s [ME *travellour, travaillour,* fr. *travellen, travailen* to travel + *-our* -or] **1 :** one that travels: as **a :** one that goes on a trip or journey ⟨the worst of ~s, detesting all modes of transportation —Agnes Repplier⟩; *specif* **:** one that travels to distant or unfamiliar places **b** *dial Brit* **:** TRAMP **c :** TRAVELING SALESMAN **2 :** something that travels fast or well (as a vehicle or draft animal) **3 a :** an iron ring (as on the inboard block of the sheet of a fore-and-aft sail) that travels on a line, bar, or spar of a ship and slides thereon **b** *or* **traveler iron :** a bar or rod running transversely on the deck on which a ring in one end of the sheet or the block of a sheet tackle of a fore-and-aft sail travels back and forth — called also *horse* **4 :** any of various devices (as a traveling crane) for carrying or suspending something being transported laterally; *esp* **:** a crab or winch moved on an elevated track and used in erecting steel bridges or other large work **5 :** a small metal clip that slides on the ring of a ring spinner and guides the yarn to the bobbin **6 :** a stage curtain that is drawn across the proscenium — contrasted with *drop curtain*

traveler's check *n* **:** a draft issued by a bank or express company payable on presentation by any correspondent of the issuer — called also *banker's check*

traveler's–delight \ˈ=(=)=ˌ=ˈ=\ *n, pl* **traveler's–delights :** GROUNDNUT 2a

traveler's–grass \ˈ=(=)=ˌ=\ *n, pl* **traveler's–grasses :** SETTLER'S TWINE

traveler's–joy \ˈ=(=)=ˌ=\ *n, pl* **traveler's–joys :** any of several climbing plants of the genus *Clematis; esp* **:** a vigorous woody climber (*C. vitalba*) of Europe and the Mediterranean region with fragrant greenish white flowers borne in axillary panicles in summer and autumn — compare OLD-MAN'S BEARD, VIRGIN'S BOWER

traveler's letter of credit : LETTER OF CREDIT 1

traveler's palm *n* **:** TRAVELER'S-TREE

traveler's–tree \ˈ=(=)=ˌ=\ *n, pl* **traveler's–trees :** a tree (*Ravenala madagascariensis*) of Madagascar having distichous leaves whose petioles contain large quantities of clear watery sap and yield a refreshing drink

traveling *or* **travelling** *adj* [ME *traveling,* fr. pres. part. of *travellen, travailen* to travel, travail — more at TRAVAIL] **1 :** that travels **2 :** that is carried, used by, or accompanies a traveler ⟨~ companion⟩

traveling apron *n* **:** APRON 3a(1)

traveling backstay *n* **:** a backstay attached to a mast by a traveler sliding up and down with the yard

traveling bag *n* **:** a bag carried by hand and designed to hold a traveler's clothing and other personal articles

traveling card *n* **:** a card issued by a local union that enables a worker to take a job outside the jurisdiction in which the card is issued

traveling carriage *n* **:** a carriage designed for long-distance travel

traveling case *n* **:** a usu. stiff and box-shaped traveling bag

traveling clock *n* **:** a small clock or large watch mounted in a folding case that serves as an easel when opened

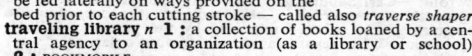

traveling clock

traveling crane *n* **:** CRANE 3a

traveling fellow *n* **:** the holder of a traveling fellowship

traveling fellowship *n* **:** a fellowship whose terms permit or direct the holder to travel or go abroad for study or research

traveling–head shaper *n* **:** a shaper whose reciprocating toolhead is mounted on a bed in such a way that the head may be fed laterally on ways provided on the bed prior to each cutting stroke — called also *traverse shaper*

traveling library *n* **1 :** a collection of books loaned by a central agency to an organization (as a library or school) **2 :** BOOKMOBILE

traveling microscope *n* **:** a microscope provided with cross hairs and mounted in such a way that it can be moved along a base with a screw for the purpose of making accurate measurements of distance

traveling nut *n* **:** a nut that travels on a revolving screw

traveling platform *or* **traveling sidewalk** *n* **:** a contrivance on the principle of the flat horizontal endless belt or conveyer designed for transporting objects or persons through a limited distance

traveling post office *n* **:** RAILWAY MAIL CAR

traveling rings *n pl* **:** swinging gymnastic rings arranged in a row — compare FLYING RINGS

traveling salesman *or* **traveling man** *n* **:** a traveling representative of a business concern who solicits orders usu. in an assigned territory by showing samples or catalogs or by demonstration of his company's products or services — called also *commercial traveler, drummer*

traveling staircase *or* **traveling stairs** *n* **:** MOVING STAIRCASE

traveling steady *n* **:** FOLLOW REST

traveling table *n* **:** a table or platform arranged to move on rollers or wheels

traveling wave *n* **:** a wave in which the particles of the medium move progressively in the direction of the wave propagation with such a gradation of speeds that the faster overtake the slower and are themselves in turn overtaken — compare STANDING WAVE

traveling–wave tube *n* **:** an electron tube used for the generation of microwave frequency radiation or for amplification at ultrahigh frequencies whose operation depends on the interaction of a beam of electrons with an electromagnetic wave

travellable *var of* TRAVELABLE

travelled *var of* TRAVELED

traveller *var of* TRAVELER

travel line *n, usu cap T* **:** LINE OF TRAVEL

travelling *var of* TRAVELING

travelling matt *or* **travelling matte** *n* **:** a film containing silhouettes of subjects or figures used to mask off selected areas during printing of motion-picture film

trav·el·ogue *also* **trav·el·og** \ˈtravəˌlȯg *also* -läg\ *n* -s [²*travel* + *-logue, -log*] **:** a talk, lecture, or discourse on travel usu. with illustrations (as slides or motion pictures) — **trav·el·ogu·er** \-gə(r)\ *n* -s

travel shot *n* **:** a motion-picture shot made with the camera on a dolly accompanying the actors as they move from one set or place to another

travel sickness *n* **:** sickness (as nausea or vertigo) due to the motion of travel in a vehicle

travel time *n* **:** a usu. specified period of time spent in traveling at work or from the entrance of a business establishment to the place where work is actually done (as in portal-to-portal travel or deadheading) for which compensation may be demanded or paid

tra·vers·able *pronunc at* ²TRAVERSE + əbəl\ *adj* **1 :** capable of being traversed or passed over **:** PASSABLE ⟨much of this . . . country is ~ only by four-wheel-drive vehicle or pack train —Joyce R. Muench⟩ **2 :** proper to be traversed in pleading **:** DENIABLE ⟨a ~ presentment⟩ ⟨a ~ issue⟩

tra·vers·al *pronunc at* ²TRAVERSE + əl\ *n* -s **:** the act or an instance of traversing

¹traverse \ˈ=(ˌ)= *or* =ˈ= — *see* ²TRAVERSE\ *n* -s [ME *travers;* partly fr. MF *traverse* crosspiece, fr. *traverser* to cross, traverse & L *transversa,* fem. of *transversus* lying across, past part. of *transvertere* to turn across; partly fr. MF *travers* way across, passage, fr. L *transversum,* fr. neut. of *transversus* — more at *transverse*] **1 :** something that crosses or lies or is laid across: as **a :** CROSSPIECE, TRANSOM **b :** BAR, BARRIER **c :** a screen, curtain, or sliding partition placed or drawn crosswise in a room, hall, or theater **d :** a collapsible fire screen with leaves usu. of pierced brass opening out like a fan from an upright standard **2 :** something that opposes or impedes **:** OBSTACLE, ADVERSITY ⟨~s, toils, and trouble⟩ **3 a :** a formal denial of some particular matter of fact alleged by the opposite party in a stage of legal pleadings ⟨matter was heard . . . on the petition, the returns, the ~s thereto —J.R.Martin⟩ **b** *obs* **:** DISPUTE, CONTROVERSY **4 a :** a compartment or recess formed by a partition, curtain, or screen **b :** a screened stall in a church or chapel **c :** a gallery or loft of communication extending from side to side in a church or other large building **5 :** a route or way across or over: as **a :** a zigzag course made by a sailing ship with contrary winds **b :** a zigzag road or course up a steep grade **c :** the course followed in a traverse (as on skis); *also* **:** a zigzag in such a course **6 a :** PASSAGE, TOLL TRAVERSE **b :** the act or an instance of traversing **:** CROSSING ⟨the only practicable route for human ~ —J.H.Bretz⟩ ⟨the ~ of a gorge might . . . take many weeks —E.E.Shipton⟩ ⟨their longest expeditions . . . have been mere ~s leaving great unexplored areas in between —Ralph Linton⟩ **c :** a horizontal or diagonal crossing of a mountainside or slope **d :** the crossing of a gap or pass from one side to the other **e :** a zigzag ascent or descent of a slope esp. on skis **f :** the act or position of traversing in fencing **7 :** a projecting wall or bank of earth in a trench constructed to protect the occupants from enfilading fire or to localize shell bursts **8 a :** a traversing or lateral movement (as of the saddle of a lathe carriage); *also* **:** a device for imparting such movement **b :** the lateral movement of a gun about a pivot or on a carriage to change the direction of fire; *also* **:** the total possible lateral movement of a gun on its carriage **9 :** a forward oblique movement of a horse with tail turned to one side and head to the other **10 a :** TRAVERSE SURVEY **b :** a line surveyed across a plot of ground **11** *New Eng* **:** BOBSLED 2 **12 :** the distance through which the yarn or roving laying device travels when winding the yarn

²tra·verse \trəˈvərs, -ˈvōs, -ˈvəis *sometimes* traˈv- *or* ˈtra,v- *or* ˈtra,və(r)s\ *vb* -ED/-ING/-S [ME *traversen,* fr. MF *traverser,* fr. LL *transversare* to cross, fr. L *transversus* lying across, transverse] *vt* **1 a :** to go against or act in opposition to **:** OPPOSE ⟨I accept nobody's precepts *traversing* my moral freedom —George Santayana⟩ ⟨since demands ~ each other we have to make a choice —H.J.Laski⟩ **b** (1) **:** to deny (an allegation of fact) formally at law (2) **:** to deny or take issue upon (an indictment) (3) **:** to deny or impeach the validity of (an inquest of office) **c** *obs* **:** DISCUSS, DEBATE **2 a :** to pass through (something) **:** PENETRATE ⟨gladness ~s his being⟩ **b** *archaic* **:** to cross or mark with a line, bar, or stripe **3 a :** to go or travel across or over ⟨walking through the streets they had *traversed* two nights before —Floyd Dell⟩ ⟨they drew close to the shore, having *traversed* a range of lofty hills —Elinor Wylie⟩ ⟨little water *~s* the steep rocky course of the river bed —N.R.Heiden⟩ ⟨the old community is *traversed* by heavy traffic —*Amer. Guide Series: Conn.*⟩ **b :** to move along or through (something) ⟨the current *traversing* the lamp is simply a migration of electrons —K.K.Darrow⟩ **c :** to advance or go through (as a time or an area of activity) ⟨the revolutionary period the world is *traversing* —André Mesnard⟩ ⟨the journeying of the individual scientist if he chooses to ~ the scientific circle —F.A.Geldard⟩ ⟨*traversing* new paths in the area of city planning —C.H.Sawyer⟩ **d :** to go over, consider, or make a study of **:** EXAMINE, SURVEY ⟨*~s* . . . the now century-old arguments against the well-known traditional dogmas —Irwin Edman⟩ ⟨a period . . . more thoroughly *traversed* by historians —R.B.Morris⟩ ⟨a wide area of investigation, only partially *traversed* in recent decades —René Wellek & Austin Warren⟩ **e :** to lie or extend across (something) **:** CROSS ⟨a small bridge which *~s* a rivulet —George Borrow⟩ ⟨a well-kept lawn *traversed* by concrete walks —*Amer. Guide Series: N.J.*⟩ ⟨the principal islands are *traversed* by large rivers —W.C. Forbes⟩ ⟨a career which . . . *~s* the whole scope of business opportunities —A.W.McCain⟩ **f :** to draw or construct (a geometrical figure) with one continuous stroke **4 :** to go or move to and fro over or along ⟨continued a long time *traversing* my bedchamber —Mary W. Shelley⟩; *specif* **:** to ascend, descend, or cross (a slope or gap) by means of a traverse ⟨the climber *traversing* the face of the cliff⟩ **5 :** to move or turn (something) laterally or crosswise; *specif* **:** to move (as a gun) to right or left on a pivot or mount ⟨so jammed . . . that it was impossible to ~ the gun turrets —E.J.Kohn⟩ **6 :** to plane (wood) across the grain esp. as a preliminary to trying up a board or floor **7 :** to make or carry out a traverse survey of ~ *vi* **1 a :** to move or go across or along ⟨deep in thought he *~s* to and fro⟩ ⟨watching cars *traversing* along the highway⟩ ⟨a glass tube which *~s* up and down the depth of the pot —H.R. Mauersberger⟩ **b** *archaic* **:** to move or shift from one topic or viewpoint to another **c :** to move or dodge from side to side ⟨the boxer *~s* cunningly⟩ **2 :** to move or turn laterally **:** SWIVEL, PIVOT ⟨the gun *~s* smoothly on its bearings⟩ **3 :** to execute a traverse on horseback **4 :** to slide one's blade in fencing toward the opponent's hilt while exerting prolonged pressure on his blade **5 :** to make a traverse in climbing or skiing ⟨one can zigzag or ~ up any length of slope with the least effort —Hans Georg⟩ **6 :** to make a traverse survey **syn** see DENY

³traverse \ˈ=ˌ= *or* ˈ=(ˌ)= — *see* ²TRAVERSE\ *adj* [ME *travers,* fr. MF, fr. L *transversus* — more at TRAVERSE, n.] **:** lying or being in a direction across something else **:** TRANSVERSE

⁴traverse *adv* [ME *travers,* fr. MF, fr. *travers,* adj.] *obs* **:** TRAVERSELY

traverse board *n* **:** a navigation device consisting of a small board marked with the four points of the compass with eight holes bored at each point to represent each half hour in a watch and used to peg the courses made by a ship in each half hour

traverse circle *n* **:** a circular track usu. of iron on which the wheels of a heavy gun carriage move when the gun is traversed

traverse drill *n* **1 :** a machine tool for drilling slots in which the work or tool has a lateral motion back and forth **2 :** a drilling machine in which the spindle holder can be adjusted laterally

traverse feed *n* **:** a feed on a machine operating in a lateral direction

traverse flute *n* **:** TRANSVERSE FLUTE

traverse jury *n* **:** a jury impaneled to try a civil or criminal case **:** TRIAL JURY — distinguished from *grand jury*

traverse·ly *pronunc at* ³TRAVERSE + lē *or* li\ *adv* **:** CROSSWISE, TRANSVERSELY

tra·vers·er *pronunc at* ²TRAVERSE + ə(r)\ *n* -s **:** one that traverses: **a :** a form of conveyor (as for moving fuel to furnaces) **b :** a turner who works with a traverse shaper **c :** one that traverses or denies at law **d :** TRANSFER TABLE

traverse rod *or* **traverse track** *n* **:** a metal rod or track with a pulley mechanism for drawing a curtain

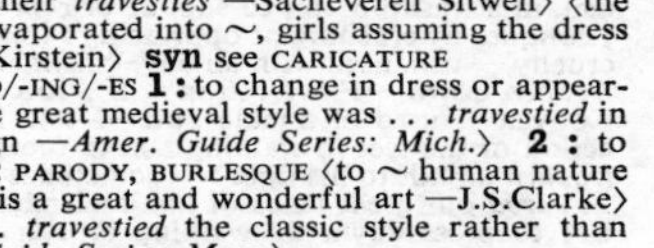

traverse rod

traverses *pl of* TRAVERSE, *pres 3d sing of* TRAVERSE

traverse sailing *n* **:** plane sailing in which a ship follows two or more courses in succession with the difference in latitude and departure being added algebraically to find a single resultant course and distance

traverse shaper *n* **:** TRAVELING-HEAD SHAPER

traverse survey *n* **:** a survey used esp. for long narrow strips of country in which a series of lines joined end to end are completely determined as to length and azimuth and are often used as a basis for triangulation

traverse table *n* **1 :** a navigation or surveying table giving the difference of latitude and departure corresponding to any given course and distance and containing the lengths of the two sides of a right-angled triangle usu. for every degree of angle and for all lengths of the hypotenuse from 1 to 100 **2 :** TRANSFER TABLE

traversing *pres part of* TRAVERSE

traversing bridge *n* **:** a movable bridge consisting of a structure like a girder that can be drawn backward

traversing circle *n* **:** TRAVERSE CIRCLE

traversing crane *n* **:** CRANE 3a

traversing gear *n* **:** the gear used in traversing a gun or other piece of machinery

traversing mandrel *n* **:** a mandrel that traverses or moves longitudinally; *specif* **:** a mandrel in a suitable support usu. driven by a separate belt for securing to a lathe carriage (as in order to carry a reamer)

traversing screw jack *or* **traversing jack** *n* **:** a screw jack that besides the raising and lowering device has a base piece with a slideway along which the jack proper can be traversed — called also *swing jack*

trav·er·tine *also* **trav·er·tin** \ˈtravə(r)ˌtēn, -tᵊn, -tən\ *n* -s [F, fr. It *travertino, tivertino,* fr. L (*lapis*) *tiburtinus* tiburtine (stone), fr. *lapis* stone + *tiburtinus* tiburtine — more at TIBURTINE] **:** a mineral consisting of a massive usu. layered calcium carbonate (as aragonite or calcite) formed by deposition from spring waters or esp. from hot springs — called also *calcareous sinter*

traves *pl of* TRAVE

¹travesty \ˈtravəstē, -sti\ *n* -ES [F *travesti,* past part. of *travestir* to disguise, fr. It *travestire,* fr. *tra-* across, through (fr. L *trans*) + *vestire* to dress, fr. L, fr. *vestis* garment — more at TRANS-, WEAR] **1 a :** a burlesque translation or literary or artistic imitation usu. grotesquely incongruous in style, treatment, or subject matter **:** PARODY ⟨achieves a ludicrous effect in his ~ of the epic as a melodramatic farce⟩ ⟨the image I saw there . . . but a ~, cunningly made of enameled clay or some other material, and put there by some malicious enemy to mock me —W.H.Hudson †1922⟩ **b :** a literary or artistic work that because of various inadequacies is only an inferior or grotesque imitation of its prototype ⟨some of them deliberately distort to achieve a primitive effect and the result is a ~—Esther Warner⟩ **c :** a debased or distorted imitation or representation **:** SHAM, MOCKERY ⟨such a ~ of a horse . . . that if it had been galloped it would have fallen down and broken its neck —David Masters⟩ ⟨dismembered so much and misinterpreted so much else as to leave . . . a ~ rather than a document —Irving Kolodin⟩ ⟨had been arrested and tried and four of them executed . . . a shocking ~ on justice —R.M.Lovett⟩ ⟨a ~ of democracy . . . votes were openly sold and openly quoted on the market —C.P.Fitzgerald⟩ **2 :** a change in dress or appearance usu. for dramatic purposes and often to represent the opposite sex **:** MAKEUP, DISGUISE ⟨the falling of the masks occasions a living change . . . when they continue dancing, unmasked, still in their *travesties* —Sacheverell Sitwell⟩ ⟨the male principle . . . evaporated into ~, girls assuming the dress of boys —Lincoln Kirstein⟩ **syn** see CARICATURE

²travesty \"\ *vt* -ED/-ING/-ES **1 :** to change in dress or appearance **:** DISGUISE ⟨the great medieval style was . . . *travestied* in materials and design —*Amer. Guide Series: Mich.*⟩ **2 :** to make a travesty of **:** PARODY, BURLESQUE ⟨to ~ human nature without . . . cruelty is a great and wonderful art —J.S.Clarke⟩ ⟨later examples . . . *travestied* the classic style rather than copied it —*Amer. Guide Series: Mass.*⟩

travis \ˈtrāvəs, -rav-\ *n* -ES [alter. of ¹*traverse*] *dial Brit* **:** a partition between stable stalls; *also* **:** STALL

travois \ˈtra,vȯi, trəˈvȯi, (ˈ)travˈwä\ *also* **travoise** \ˈtra,vȯiz, trəˈvȯiz\ *or* **travoy** \ˈtra,vȯi, trəˈvȯi\ *n, pl* **travois** \-ȯiz, -äz\ *also* **travoises** \-ȯizəz\ *or* **travoys** \-ȯiz\ [CanF *travois,* alter. of F *travail* — more at TRAVAIL] **1 :** a primitive vehicle used by the Plains Indians of No. America consisting of two trailing poles serving as shafts for dog or horse and bearing a platform or net for the load **2** *usu* **travoy :** ALLIGATOR 6b

travoy \ˈtra,vȯi, trəˈvȯi\ *vb* -ED/-ING/-S *vt* **:** to haul (a log) in or by a travois ~ *vi* **:** to transport a log or lumber by a travois

¹trawl \ˈtrȯl\ *vb* -ED/-ING/-S [prob. fr. obs. D *tragelen,* fr. MD, fr. *tragel* dragnet] *vi* **1 :** to fish or catch fish with a trawl **2 :** TROLL 2 ~ *vt* **:** to catch or gather (fish) with a trawl

²trawl \"\ *n* -s [prob. fr. obs. D *tragel* dragnet, fr. MD, prob. fr. L *tragula* — more at TRAIL] **1 :** a large conical net with a device for keeping its mouth open that is dragged along the sea bottom in gathering fish or other marine life **2 :** SETLINE

trawl·abil·i·ty \ˌtrȯləˈbiləd·ē\ *n* **:** suitability for trawling ⟨~ of the area —*Commercial Fisheries Rev.*⟩

trawl·able \ˈtrȯləbəl\ *adj* **:** capable of being trawled **:** suitable for trawling ⟨found the inshore waters . . . prolific in good ~ fish —W.J.Dakin⟩

trawl board *n* **:** OTTER BOARD

trawl·er \ˈtrȯlə(r)\ *n* -s **:** a person or craft that fishes by trawling

trawl·er·man \-mən\ *n, pl* **trawlermen :** a fisherman who uses a trawl or mans a trawler

trawl line *n* **:** SETLINE

trawlnet \ˈ=ˌ=\ *n* [¹*trawl* + *net*] **:** TRAWL

[1]**tray** \'trā\ *n* -s [ME *tray, trey*, fr. OE *trēg, trīg;* akin to OSw *trö* wooden grain measure, OE *trēow* tree, wood — more at TREE] **1 :** an open variously shaped receptacle of wood, metal, or other material with a flat bottom and a low rim for holding, carrying, or exhibiting articles ⟨a ~ of sandwiches⟩ ⟨a jeweler's ~⟩ ⟨a silver card ~⟩ **2** *dial Eng* **:** HURDLE 1a **3 :** a flat or curved piece of metal used to hold ammunition or any part of the mechanism of a gun; *specif* **:** a brass or steel part of the breech mechanism of a heavy cannon — called also *plugtray* **4 :** BOARD 5f(1) **5 :** an appliance consisting of a flanged body and a handle for use in holding plastic material against the gums or teeth in making negative impressions for dentures **6 :** PLATE 1a(3)

[2]**tray** \"\ *vt* -ED/-ING/-S **:** to arrange (as fruits for dehydration) on trays

[3]**tray** \"\ *n* -s [alter. of *trey*] **:** ROYAL ANTLER

tray agriculture *n* **:** HYDROPONICS

tray ceiling *n* **:** a ceiling under a gabled roof at a height part way up toward the ridge having the appearance of an inverted tray

tray·ful \'trā,fu̇l\ *n* -s **:** as much as a tray will hold

tray-top table *also* **tray table** *n* **1 :** a tea table with a raised edge, rim, or gallery (as on a tray) **2** *usu* *tray table* **:** a low table formed by a serving tray supported by a stand

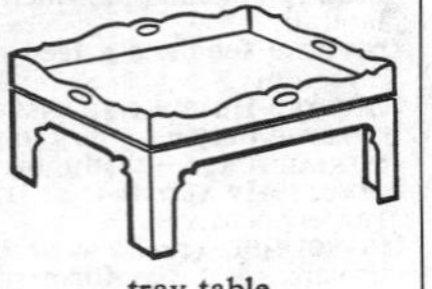

tray table

t-r box *n, often cap T&R* [transmit-receive *box*] **:** DUPLEXER

trc *abbr* tierce

treach·er·ous \'trech(ə)rəs\ *adj* [ME *trecherous, tricherous*, fr. MF *trecheros, tricheros*, fr. OF, fr. *trecherie, tricherie* + *-eus* -ous] **1 :** characterized by or manifesting treachery **:** marked by a ready disposition to betray confidence or faith pledged **:** violating or capable of violating allegiance **:** DISLOYAL, FALSE, PERFIDIOUS, TRAITOROUS ⟨the fiercest and most ~ of foes —H.O.Taylor⟩ ⟨his life, among these ~ demons, depended on a hair —R.L.Stevenson⟩ ⟨~ intrigues⟩ **2 a :** likely to betray confidence or trust **:** UNRELIABLE, UNTRUSTWORTHY ⟨a ~ memory⟩ **b :** providing insecure footing or support ⟨~ quicksands⟩ **c :** characterized by usu. hidden dangers, hazards, or perils ⟨found the inlets . . . too ~ and shallow to admit large vessels —*Amer. Guide Series: N.C.*⟩ ⟨the climbing was . . . exacting and ~ —D.L.Busk⟩ **syn** see FAITHLESS

treach·er·ous·ly *adv* [ME *tricherously*, fr. *trecherous, tricherous* + *-ly*] **:** in a treacherous manner **:** by or with treachery ⟨~ wounded by one of the enemy generals who had invited him to a parley —Robert Graves⟩ ⟨doomed . . . to a wife unworthy of him, just because of . . . a moon ~ sentimental —Donn Byrne⟩

treach·er·ous·ness *n* -ES **:** the quality or state of being treacherous ⟨his ~ was . . . concealed under an appearance of honest and awkward dullness —John Fiske⟩

treach·ery \-rē, -ri\ *n* -ES [ME *trecherie, tricherie*, fr. OF, fr. *trechier, trichier* to trick, cheat, deceive + *-erie* -ery] **1 a :** violation of allegiance or of faith and confidence **:** betrayal of trust **:** TREASON ⟨to oppose . . . the party organization would be regarded by most members as little short of ~ —R.M. Dawson⟩ **b :** an instance of treachery **:** an act of perfidy or treason ⟨blackmail the colonel into one of the greatest *treacheries* of history —Fletcher Pratt⟩ **2 :** something treacherous; *specif* **:** something that is or is likely to be unstable or unreliable

[1]**trea·cle** \'trēkəl\ *n* -s *often attrib* [ME *triacle, tryacle*, fr. MF *triacle, tiriacle*, fr. L *theriaca*, fr. Gk *thēriakē* antidote against a poisonous bite, fr. fem. of *thēriakos* of a wild animal, fr. *thērion* wild animal, poisonous animal, dim. of *thēr* wild animal — more at FIERCE] **1 a :** a medicinal compound formerly in wide use as a remedy against poison — compare THERIACA 1 **b** *archaic* **:** something resembling treacle in being a remedy **2** *chiefly Brit* **a :** MOLASSES **b :** a blend of molasses, invert sugar, and corn syrup used as a table syrup — called also *golden syrup* **3 :** something (as a tone of voice, manner, or compliment) resembling treacle in being heavily sweet and cloying ⟨collapsing at the close in a ~ of hideous sentimentality —*Dial*⟩

[2]**treacle** \"\ *vt* **treacled; treacled; treacling** \-k(ə)liŋ\ **treacles :** to smear, spread, or sweeten with treacle ⟨*treacled* the paper and attached it to the window —P.G.Wodehouse⟩

treacle mold *or* **treacle mould** *n* [prob. so called from its fancied resemblance to dripping treacle] **:** a rounded mold or nosing somewhat deeply undercut

treacle mustard *n* **1 :** a wallflower of the genus *Erysimum; esp* **:** WORMSEED MUSTARD **2 :** HARE'S-EAR 2

treaclewort \'==,=\ *n* -s **:** a pennycress (*Thlaspi arvense*)

trea·cly \-k(ə)lē, -li\ *adj* [*treacle* + *-y*] **:** resembling or held to resemble treacle (as in quality or appearance) **:** composed of treacle **:** as cloying or sticky as treacle ⟨saturated with black ~ oil —Audrey Barker⟩ ⟨purveyors of ~ Pollyannaish fiction —*Nashville Tennessean*⟩ ⟨~ sentimentalities⟩

[1]**tread** \'tred\ *vb* **trod** \'träd\ *also* **treaded; trodden** \'träd°n\ *or* **trod** *also* **tread; treading; treads** [ME *treden*, fr. OE *tredan;* akin to OHG *tretan* to step, tread, ON *trotha*, Goth *trudan* to tread, and perh. to Gk *dramein* to run, OE *treppan* to step — more at TRAP] *vt* **1 a :** to step or walk on **:** move about over esp. by walking ⟨went on to ~ the great smooth dome of the . . . summit —G.W.Murray⟩ ⟨the south pole, never before *trodden* by the foot of human beings —A.L.Kroeber⟩ **b :** to step or walk along **:** FOLLOW, PURSUE ⟨the avenue . . . she had *trodden* —Kathleen Freeman⟩ ⟨the safest road to ~ —H.J. Laski⟩ ⟨has *trod* the thin line between abstraction and strict realism —R.M.Coates⟩ **2 a** (1) **:** to step firmly or walk with pressure on (as a person) in an effort to crush, beat down, injure, or destroy — usu. used in phrases ⟨~ to dirt the rest of mankind —John Milton⟩ ⟨being *trod* to death like a frog —Jonathan Swift⟩ ⟨they were *trodden* under foot⟩ (2) **:** to thresh (as grain) usu. by trampling on a threshing floor — sometimes used with *out* (3) **:** to press out the juice of (grapes) by trampling usu. in a vat (4) **:** to wash (as clothes) by trampling usu. in a washtub **b :** to subdue or repress as if by trampling **:** conquer by crushing or oppressing **:** treat with contemptuous cruelty — usu. used with an adv. ⟨the masses were a good deal *trodden* down —F.E.Gretton⟩ **3 :** to copulate with (a hen) **:** COVER — used of a male bird **4 :** to form or make by the action of the feet in walking **:** BEAT ⟨countless footsteps have *trodden* a path to his door⟩ — sometimes used with *out* ⟨herds . . . *trod* out great lanes of habitual migration —C.D.Forde⟩ **5 :** to press down by walking or stamping upon ⟨~ soil⟩ **6 :** to execute by stepping or dancing ⟨~ a measure⟩ **7 :** to get, bring, or put into or out of some condition by walking or trampling — used with an adv. ⟨~ a grass fire out⟩ ⟨slippers *trodden* down at the heel⟩ **8 :** to step upon (as a treadle or pedal) in order to impart motion **:** press downward with the foot or feet (as in treadling or pedaling) ⟨this wheel . . . was *trodden* by a donkey —John Higgs⟩ **9 :** to brace (an archer's bow) by pressing the foot against the center **10 :** to apply the tread to (an automotive tire) ~ *vi* **1 a :** to move on foot **:** set down the feet in walking **:** PACE, STEP, WALK ⟨they *trod* cautiously, drawing closer and closer —O.E.Rölvaag⟩ ⟨where . . . the foot of a white man had rarely *trod* —Leslie Gardiner⟩ **b :** to proceed as if by walking ⟨in 18th century English history the author ~*s* with his accustomed ease and mastery —*Times Lit. Supp.*⟩ **2 :** to step or set foot on something ⟨fools rush in where angels fear to ~ —Alexander Pope⟩: as **a :** to set foot so as to press, crush, or injure **:** TRAMPLE — used with *on* or *upon* ⟨~ upon the grapes⟩ **b :** to put one's foot down upon something esp. in an accidental or unintentional manner **c :** to press firmly on something with a foot ⟨resolutely *trod* on the accelerator —James Lord⟩ **3 :** COPULATE — usu. used of a male bird **4** *chiefly dial* **:** to yield to treading or being trodden upon **:** become affected by tramping or trampling — used esp. of soil — **tread on one's toes :** to give offense (as by wounding in a tender spot or encroaching on one's rights, privileges, or feelings) — **tread the boards** *or* **tread the stage :** to act as a stage player **:** perform a part in a drama — **tread the steps of** *obs* **:** to walk in the steps of **:** follow the example of ⟨*tread the steps* of their parents merely by instinct —Thomas Brown⟩ — **tread water :** to keep the body nearly upright in the water and the head above water by a treading motion of the feet usu. aided by the hands ⟨trying to regain his breath while he *treaded water* —Nathaniel Benchley⟩ ⟨rose under the stern and *trod water* —Leslie Charteris⟩

[2]**tread** \"\ *n* -s *often attrib* [ME *trede, tred*, fr. *treden*, v.] **1 :** a mark (as a footprint, a rut of a wheel, or the imprint of a tire) made by or as if by treading **2 a** (1) **:** the action of treading ⟨that incessant ~ of feet wearing the rough stones smooth —Charles Dickens⟩ (2) **:** an act or an instance of treading **:** STEP **b :** manner of stepping **:** style of walking ⟨walked with a springy, catlike ~ —Tom Marvel⟩ ⟨the careful ~ of one conscious of his alcoholic load —Thomas Hardy⟩ **c :** the sound of treading ⟨I hear the ~ of hateful steps —John Milton⟩ ⟨the corner echoed . . . with the ~ of feet —Charles Dickens⟩ **3** *Scot* **a :** habitual course or manner of action **:** CUSTOM, PRACTICE **b :** customary occupation **:** regular business **:** EMPLOYMENT, LABOR, TRADE **4 a** *archaic* **:** the action of a male bird in copulation **b :** CHALAZA 1 **5 :** an injury of one foot by another foot of a horse (as in overreaching) **6 a** (1) **:** the part of the bottom surface of a shoe including or excluding the heel that touches level ground (2) **:** the part of a wheel that bears on a road or rail; *esp* **:** the thickened face of an automobile tire (3) **:** CATERPILLAR TREAD **b :** the design (as a raised or inset pattern of corrugations) on a tread ⟨a recognizable hobnail ~ —Frank Cameron⟩ **7 :** the distance in inches between the central points of contact with the ground of the two front wheels or the two rear wheels of a vehicle — compare WHEELBASE **8 a :** the upper horizontal part of a step (as in a stair) on which the foot is placed **b :** the width of such a part of a step **:** the horizontal distance between consecutive risers ⟨a stair with a 12-inch ~⟩ **c :** the flat or gently sloping surface of one of a series of steplike geologic landforms ⟨the ~ of a terrace⟩ **9 :** the length of the keel of a ship **10 :** the part of a rail on which the wheels of a railroad car bear

tread·er \-də(r)\ *n* -s [ME *treder*, fr. *treden* to tread + *-er* — more at TREAD] **:** one that treads ⟨automobile tire ~*s*⟩ ⟨the use of ~*s* in wine making⟩

[1]**trea·dle** \'tred°l\ *n* -s *often attrib* [ME *tredel* step of a stair, treadle, fr. OE, step of a stair, fr. *tredan* to step, tread + *-el*, suffix used to denote a means or an instrument] **1 a :** a swiveling or lever device pressed by the foot to drive a machine actuated by foot power and usu. operating a crank by means of a connecting rod **b :** one attached directly to the end of a crank (as in a bicycle) **:** PEDAL **c :** a device resembling such a treadle; *specif* **:** a lever actuated by a passing train to operate an alarm at a crossing or by a motor vehicle to operate a highway traffic control mechanism **2 :** CHALAZA 1

[2]**treadle** \"\ *vb* **treadled; treadled; treadling** \-d(°)liŋ\ **treadles** *vi* **:** to operate a treadle; *specif* **:** to proceed by pedaling a bicycle ~ *vt* **1 :** to operate (as a machine) by a treadle **2 :** to tread over (clay) ⟨a brickmaker, with boards or wooden shoes on his feet, ~*s* clay to pick out stones⟩

[1]**treadmill** \'=,=\ *n* [[1]*tread* + *mill*] **1 a :** a mill worked by persons treading on steps on the periphery of a wide wheel having a horizontal axis and used formerly in prison discipline **b :** a mill worked by an animal (as a horse or dog) treading an endless belt and used also on a stock farm or ranch to exercise a bull difficult to control as well as to utilize his power for belt operations **c :** a similar device used in studies of physiological functions **2 :** a wearisome routine resembling continued activity on a treadmill

[2]**treadmill** \"\ *vi* **:** to labor on or as if on a treadmill

tread plate *n* **:** a metal plate attached to a stair tread to prevent slipping

tread-softly \'=,==\ *n* -ES [fr. the imper. phrase *tread softly*] **:** SPURGE NETTLE

treadway bridge \'==,=\ *n* [*treadway* fr. [2]*tread* + *way*] **:** a floating bridge having two tracks as a roadway

treadwheel \'=,=\ *n* [[1]*tread* + *wheel*] **:** a wheel turned by a person or animal by treading, climbing, or pushing with the feet upon its periphery or face — compare TREADMILL 1

treas *abbr* treasurer; treasury

trea·son \'trēz°n\ *n* -s [ME *tresoun*, fr. OF *traison*, fr. ML *tradition-, traditio*, fr. L, action of handing over, teaching, tradition, fr. *traditus* (past part. of *tradere* to hand over, betray) + *-ion-, -io* -ion — more at TRAITOR] **1 :** the betrayal of a trust or confidence **:** breach of faith **:** PERFIDY, TREACHERY ⟨corruption in public office is ~ —A.E.Stevenson b.1900⟩ **2 a :** the offense of attempting by overt acts to overthrow the government of the state to which the offender owes allegiance or to kill or personally injure the sovereign or his family — see HIGH TREASON 1 **b** (1) **:** the betrayal in early English law of a lord by his vassal (2) **:** the violation in early feudal law by a vassal of his allegiance to his superior by one or more undefined acts of a serious nature (as betrayal to an enemy, adultery with the superior's wife, or forgery of his seal) — see PETIT TREASON **3** *obs* **:** an act or an instance of treason ⟨rebellions and ~*s* against their princes —Matthew Sutcliffe⟩

trea·son·able \-°nəbəl\ *adj* [ME *tresounable*, fr. *tresoun* treason + *-able*] **:** relating to, consisting of, or involving treason **:** having the characteristics of or partaking of the guilt of treason **:** PERFIDIOUS, TREACHEROUS ⟨a ~ betrayal of American interests —Elmer Davis⟩ ⟨participation in a ~ conspiracy —Henry Hallam⟩

trea·son·ably \-blē\ *adv* [ME *tresounably*, fr. *tresounable* + *-ly*] **:** in a treasonable manner

treason felony *n* **:** an offense under English law partaking of the nature of treason (as devising by overt act to depose or levy war against the sovereign to compel changes of policy or to intimidate or overawe Parliament) and usu. involving life imprisonment rather than the death penalty

trea·son·ous \-°nəs\ *adj* [ME *tresounous*, fr. *tresoun* + *-ous*] **:** full of, abounding in, or characterized by treason **:** TREASONABLE ⟨fired for ~ crimes —John Dryden⟩

treasr *abbr* treasurer

trea·sur·able \'trezh(ə)rəbəl, 'trāzh-\ *adj* [[2]*treasure* + *-able*] **:** worthy of being treasured **:** PRECIOUS ⟨~ additions to the record library —C.M.Smith⟩ ⟨the ~ stuff of English poetry —Robert Fitzgerald⟩

[1]**trea·sure** \-zhə(r)\ *n* -s *often attrib* [ME *tresor, tresour*, fr. OF *tresor*, fr L *thesaurus* hoard, treasure, fr. Gk *thēsauros*] **1 a** (1) **:** wealth (as money, plate, jewels, or precious metals) accumulated, stored, or hoarded up ⟨the pirate's ~⟩ ⟨digging for buried ~⟩ (2) **:** wealth of any kind or in any form **:** RICHES ⟨if the ~ of the men who run the railroad is elsewhere committed —*Value Line*⟩ ⟨a military victory won at unparalleled cost of blood and ~ —Henry Hazlitt⟩ **b :** a stock or store of money in reserve **2 a :** something of great worth or value **:** something valued and preserved as precious ⟨some of the richest ~*s* of sculpture and painting —Wilmot Harrison⟩ ⟨regions richest in these archeological ~*s* —*Amer. Guide Series: Ind.*⟩ **b :** a person esteemed as rare or precious **:** GEM 2b, JEWEL 2b(1) ⟨my maid is a ~⟩ **3 :** a valuable store, accumulation, or reserve supply **:** a collection of precious things ⟨this immense ~ of accumulated human thought and experience —Charlton Laird⟩ ⟨the illustrations are a ~ of charming Georgian houses —Anne Douglas⟩

[2]**treasure** \"\ *vt* **treasured; treasured; treasuring** \-zh(ə)riŋ\ **treasures** [ME *tresoren, tresouren*, fr. *tresor, tresour*, n.] **1 :** to collect and store up (something of value) for preservation, security, or future use **:** HOARD ⟨~ gold⟩ **2 :** to store away and preserve in or as if in the memory **:** retain and guard from being diminished, injured, forgotten, or lost ⟨not only did he ~ the lines of his favorite poets —Clark Wissler⟩ ⟨he ~*s* every least indication that she may be softer than her sister —E.K.Brown⟩ — sometimes used with *up* ⟨*treasured* up those pithy bits of local speech —Willa Cather⟩ **3 :** to hold or keep as precious **:** regard as dear and worthy of careful preservation **:** CHERISH, PRIZE ⟨those who *treasured* the New England tradition of local self-government —*Amer. Guide Series: N.H.*⟩ ⟨a book which will always be *treasured* —Herbert Read⟩ **syn** see APPRECIATE

treasure-house \'==,=\ *n* [ME *tresorhous, tresourhous*, fr. *tresor, tresour* treasure + *hous* house] **1 :** a building where treasure is kept **:** TREASURY **2 :** a place or source (as a collection) where many things of value can be found ⟨cities that are among Europe's finest *treasure-houses* of art and history —*Geog. Jour.*⟩ ⟨this book is a *treasure-house* of marvelous reading —Hal Lehrman⟩

treasure hunt *n* **1 :** an instance of searching for something that has real or imagined value **2 :** a game in which each player or team tries to be first to find whatever has been hidden

trea·sur·er \-zh(ə)rə(r)\ *n* -s [ME *tresorer, tresourer*, fr. OF *tresorier*, fr. *tresor* + *-ier*] **1 :** one having official charge of treasure; *esp* **:** a guardian of a collection of treasures (as in a cathedral church) **:** CURATOR **2 :** an officer entrusted with the receipt, care, and disbursal of funds: as **a :** one performing such functions for a king, noble, or other dignitary — see TREASURER OF THE HOUSEHOLD **b :** a governmental officer charged with receiving, keeping, and disbursing public revenues — compare CHANCELLOR OF THE EXCHEQUER, COMPTROLLER, FIRST LORD OF THE TREASURY, LORD HIGH TREASURER OF ENGLAND, TREASURER OF THE UNITED STATES **c :** the executive financial officer of a nongovernmental organization (as a club, society, or business corporation) **3 :** one having charge of keeping something valuable or precious ⟨the secrets of which thou seemest to be a too faithful ~ —Sir Walter Scott⟩ **4** *obs* **:** one that treasures something **:** a keeper, hoarder, or preserver of something precious

treasurer of the household *often cap T&H* **:** an officer of the English royal household who has only nominal duties and whose office is filled by a member of the House of Commons, usu. one of the principal Government whips

treasurer of the united states *often cap T & cap U&S* **:** an officer of the U.S. Treasury Department having charge of the receipt and keeping of all government moneys and their disbursal upon warrants properly drawn and countersigned

trea·sur·er·ship \-(r),ship\ *n* [ME *tresorership*, fr. *tresorer* + *-ship*] **:** the office of treasurer

treasure ship *n* **:** a ship with a cargo of gold, silver, jewels, or other valuables; *esp* **:** one returning from the New World to Spain in the 16th century

trea·sur·ess \-zhərəs\ *n* -ES [ME *tresouresse*, irreg. fr. *tresourer* + *-esse* -ess] **:** a female treasurer

treasure trove *n, pl* **treasure troves** [AF *tresor trové*, lit., found treasure, fr. OF *tresor* treasure + *trové*, past part. of *trover* to find, fr. (assumed) VL *tropare* — more at TREASURE, TROUVÈRE] **1 :** something in the nature of treasure that anyone finds; *specif* **:** gold or silver in the form of money, plate, or bullion which is found in the earth or otherwise hidden and the owner of which is not known **2 :** a discovery or something discovered that is full of treasures **:** a valuable and productive source ⟨natural gas and petroleum are veritable *treasure troves* of paraffin . . . and aromatic hydrocarbons —*Science*⟩ ⟨the diary . . . is a *treasure trove* to the abnormal psychologist —V.L.Parrington⟩

trea·sury \'trezh(ə)rē, 'trāzh-, -ri\ *n* -ES *often attrib* [ME *tresorie*, fr. OF *tresorie*, fr. *tresor* treasure + *-ie* -y — more at TREASURE] **1 a :** a place (as a room or building) in which stores of wealth or valuable objects are kept ⟨in the ~ of the cathedral . . . there is a fine, whole, uncut chasuble —Daniel Rock⟩ **b :** the place of deposit and disbursement of collected funds; *esp* **:** one where public revenues are deposited, kept, and disbursed **c :** the funds (as of a government, business corporation, or individual) kept or held to be kept in such a depository **2** *obs* **:** TREASURE ⟨thy sumptuous buildings . . . have cost a mass of public ~ —Shak.⟩ **3** *usu cap* **a :** a governmental department having charge of finances (as the collection, management, and expenditure of public revenues) **b :** the building in which the business of such a government department is transacted **4 :** TREASURE-HOUSE 2 ⟨the old house, a ~ of beams and paneling —Thomas Wood †1950⟩ ⟨edited another collection and called it *Treasury* of Science —G.I. Schwartz⟩ **5 :** the weekly payment of a theatrical company **6** *usu cap* **:** a government security (as a note or bill) issued by or under the authority of the Treasury ⟨a decline in *Treasuries* and . . . corporate bonds —*Mag. of Wall Street*⟩ **7** *often cap* **a :** an ancient Greek building for archives and treasures located near a sanctuary **b :** BEEHIVE TOMB

treasury bench *n, usu cap T&B* [so called fr. its being occupied by the First Lord of the Treasury] **:** the first row of seats on the right of the speaker in the British House of Commons and other Commonwealth parliamentary chambers that is occupied by cabinet ministers and other members of the Government — compare FRONT BENCH

treasury bill *n* **:** a short-term obligation issued by a government at a discount, bearing no interest, and payable at par at maturity

treasury bond *n* **:** a government bond issued by or under the authority of the Treasury

treasury certificate *n* **:** an interest-bearing obligation of the U.S. Treasury with a maturity up to one year

treasury currency *n* **:** currency (as coins, United States notes, or Federal Reserve notes) other than gold coin or gold certificates for which the U.S. Treasury is directly responsible

treasury note *n* **:** a currency note issued directly by a governmental treasury; *esp* **:** one issued by the U.S. Treasury in payment for silver bullion purchased under the Sherman Silver Purchase Act of 1890 — compare FEDERAL RESERVE NOTE, GREENBACK, SILVER CERTIFICATE

treasury of merits *or* **treasury of the church** *or* **treasury of the saints** *usu cap C* **:** the superabundant satisfaction of Christ for men's sins and the excess of merit of the Virgin Mary and the saints forming a store held in Roman Catholic theology to be effective to the salvation of others and to be available for dispensation through indulgences

treasury savings certificate *n* **:** a registered nontransferable certificate of the U.S. government issued between 1921 and 1924 in denominations of $25, $100, and $1000 maturity value five years from date of issue with the interest rate being about 4½ percent per annum compounded semiannually if held to maturity

trea·sury·ship \-rē,ship\ *n* **:** TREASURERSHIP ⟨took the ~ of the navy —George Bancroft⟩

treasury stock *n* **:** issued stock reacquired by a corporation and held as an asset — compare UNISSUED STOCK

treasury warrant *n* **:** a warrant for the payment of money into or from a public treasury

[1]**treat** \'trēt, *usu* -ēd·+V\ *vb* -ED/-ING/-S [ME *treten*, fr. OF *traitier* to treat, manage, fr. L *tractare* to pull violently, handle, manage, fr. *tractus*, past part. of *trahere* to draw, pull, drag — more at DRAW] *vi* **1 :** to carry on negotiations with another with the object of a settlement **:** discuss terms of accommodation or settlement **:** NEGOTIATE ⟨the commander-in-chief . . . was to ~ for an armistice —Bernard Pares⟩ ⟨willing to ~ with you but . . . afraid that your terms may be too high —W.M.Thackeray⟩ **2 :** to deal with a matter or subject esp. in writing or speaking **:** give an exposition **:** DISCOURSE — usu. used with *of* but sometimes with *with* ⟨the fifth essay ~*s* of the problems of map engraving —Jean Mitchell⟩ ⟨~*s* in detail of the origin of the council —R.A.Hall b.1911⟩ ⟨his article . . . ~*s* with an important conservation subject —*Nature Mag.*⟩ **3 :** to pay another's expenses (as for a meal or drink) usu. at a public place **:** bear the expense of another's entertainment **:** give or bear the expenses of a treat esp. as a compliment, an expression of regard or friendship, or as a bribe ~ *vt* **1 a :** to deal with (as a subject or theme) in speech or writing **:** ARGUE, DISCUSS, EXPOUND ⟨lectured enthusiastically about each of the poets . . . whom he ~*ed* —D.M.Allen⟩ ⟨literary history . . . has constantly to ~ problems of intellectual history —René Wellek & Austin Warren⟩ ⟨monthly programs ~ different aspects of astronomy —*Amer. Guide. Series: N.Y.City*⟩ **b :** to give artistic or literary treatment to **:** deal with in an artistic way **:** present or represent artistically esp. in a specified manner or style ⟨a romantically ~*ed* bronze group —*Amer. Guide Series: Minn.*⟩ ⟨the hall, ~*ed* in the Corinthian order —*Amer. Guide Series: Vt.*⟩ **c :** to handle, manage, or otherwise deal with ⟨food is plentiful and ~*ed* with imagination —Cecil Beaton⟩ **2** *obs* **:** to negotiate with a view to settling or arranging **:** discuss the terms of **:** ARRANGE **3 a :** to deal with or bear oneself toward in some specified way **:** behave or act towards **:** assume an attitude or form of behavior to **:** USE ⟨the worker's stay on the job depends on whether he is ~*ed* right or wrong —Carl Sandburg⟩ ⟨note with what scant respect the generals . . . were ~*ed* —C.H.Dewhurst⟩ ⟨the tones of nature require . . . to be ~*ed* relatively by the painter —C.W.H. Johnson⟩ **b :** to regard (as something or in a particular way) and act toward or deal with accordingly — usu. used with *as* ⟨asking me to ~ the news . . . as strictly confidential —O.S.

Nock⟩ ⟨adopted into the tribe and ~ed as an Indian squaw — *Amer. Guide Series: Md.*⟩ ⟨regional laws . . . ~ed defamation as a private delict —T.F.T.Plucknett⟩ **4 a :** to show hospitality to : ENTERTAIN, FEAST ⟨a host who ~s all the great persons in princely lodgings —John Evelyn⟩ **b** (1) : to provide (as another person) gratuitously with food, drink, entertainment, or some other source of enjoyment or gratification esp. as a compliment, gesture of kindness, or bribe — usu. used with *to* ⟨he ~ed her to a strawberry soda⟩ (2) : to provide (oneself) with a similar source of enjoyment or gratification — usu. used with *to* ⟨~ed herself to a new mink coat⟩ **c :** to provide with something that is or is held (as in irony or for amusement) to be a source of pleasure or gratification ⟨the Americans were ~ed to a remarkable display as the Tripolitan ship blew up —C.S.Forester⟩ ⟨when he punished he ~ed the culprit to ten minutes of biting irony first —Storm Jameson⟩ **5 a :** to care for (as a patient or part of the body) medically or surgically : deal with by medical or surgical means : give a medical treatment to ⟨during his hospital stay, he was ~ed with . . . transfusions of blood — *Jour. Amer. Med. Assoc.*⟩ ⟨120 persons were ~ed for miscellaneous . . . injuries — *Pasadena (Calif.) Independent*⟩ **b :** to seek cure or relief of (as a disease) ⟨~ a bruise with hot applications⟩ **6 a :** to subject to some action (as of a chemical reagent) : act upon with some agent ⟨~ a substance with sulfuric acid⟩ ⟨metals . . . ~ed to make maintenance a simple thing —Betty Pepis⟩ **b :** to subject (as a natural or manufactured article) to some process to improve the appearance, taste, usefulness, or some other quality : PROCESS ⟨~ rugs by washing⟩ ⟨port is a wine that is ~ed⟩
syn DEAL (*with*), HANDLE: TREAT in the sense of doing about, serving, or coping with is usu. accompanied by context indicating an attitude, temperament, point of view determining behavior or a manner of approach or execution ⟨*treat* all controversial questions impartially⟩ ⟨*treat* a subject realistically⟩ ⟨*treat* with care⟩ ⟨*treating* her guests cavalierly by *treating* with scorn nearly all the ancient virtues —A.W.Hummel⟩ ⟨before Massasoit died he made his sons promise to *treat* the Brown family kindly —J.R.Clift⟩ DEAL (*with*) may suggest managing, controlling, authoritative disposing ⟨she *dealt with* moral problems as a cleaver *deals with* meat —James Joyce⟩ ⟨the dean *dealt with* the matter promptly⟩ ⟨the only previous meeting . . . had *dealt* essentially *with* the immediate problems of military cooperation —F.W.D.Deakin⟩ and sometimes it suggests a relationship between persons or parties on a more or less even basis ⟨we're *dealing with* a ruthless foe that knows exactly what he wants —L.B.Salomon⟩ HANDLE is often interchangeable with TREAT and DEAL (*with*); it may suggest a placing, directing, disposing, or manipulating with or as if with the hand ⟨*handle* an ax skillfully⟩ ⟨*handle* the distribution of tickets⟩ ⟨*handling* the arrangement of flowers⟩ ⟨the federal government picked up a group of unfilled functions that the states could not *handle* —A.A.Berle⟩

²treat \"\ *n* -s **1** *obs* : ENTREATY **2 2 a** *archaic* : an entertainment of food and drink freely provided : FEAST ⟨when the tired glutton labors through a ~ —Alexander Pope⟩ **b :** an entertainment (as a picnic) given without expense to those invited : a pleasure party gratuitously arranged ⟨~s for young people are being organized —Frank Frost⟩ **3** *obs* **a :** the way in which one is treated : TREATMENT **b :** the treatment accorded to guests or visitors : RECEPTION, WELCOME **4 :** something that affords gratification or pleasure : a great satisfaction : a cause of joy, delight, or sometimes amusement : something highly enjoyable often by being unexpected ⟨there may be pineapple chunks . . . as a ~ for tea —A.D.Rees⟩ ⟨the London theatrical season is providing some distinguished ~s for Coronation visitors —Mollie Panter-Downes⟩ ⟨enjoy the ~ of hearing him talk —*Christian Science Monitor*⟩

³treat \ˈtrēt\ *n* -s [ME *trait, tret,* fr. AF *trait*] *dial Eng* : bran of medium coarseness — compare CHISEL

treat·able \ˈtrēd·əbəl, -ētəb-\ *adj* [ME *tretable,* fr. MF *traitable,* fr. L *tractabilis* — more at TRACTABLE] **1 a** *archaic* : easily managed, handled, or dealt with : open to appeal or argument : DOCILE, TRACTABLE ⟨those arts by which the people were rendered more ~ —A.A.Cooper⟩ **b** *obs* : gentle and moderate rather than violent in nature ⟨in France . . . changes of seasons are less ~ than they are with us —William Temple⟩ **2 :** capable of being treated : yielding or responsive to treatment ⟨~ aluminum alloys⟩ ⟨a ~ disease⟩

treat·er \ˈtrēd·ə(r), -ētə-\ *n* -s [ME *treyter,* fr. MF *traiteur,* fr. *traitier* to treat, negotiate + *-eur* -or — more at TREAT] **1 :** one that negotiates terms of a settlement : NEGOTIATOR **2** [¹*treat* + *-er*] : one that treats: as **a :** one that treats materials (as timber, oil, or beer) with chemicals **b :** an apparatus (as an agitator) for treating materials

treating *n* -s [ME *treting,* fr. gerund of *treten* to treat — more at TREAT] : the action of one that treats; *specif* : the gratuitous provision of food, drink, or entertainment to a person in order to influence one or more votes at an election ⟨~ is a statutory offense in the United Kingdom⟩

trea·tise \ˈtrēd·əs, *chiefly Brit* -əz\ *n* -s [ME *tretis,* fr. AF *tretiz,* prob. fr. OF *traitier* to treat — more at TREAT] **1 :** a writing (as a book or article) that treats a subject; *specif* : one that provides in a systematic manner and for an expository or argumentive purpose a methodical discussion of the facts and principles involved and conclusions reached ⟨the great source book and ~ on canon law —G.C.Sellery⟩ ⟨preparation of this ~ on the natural resources of Louisiana —J.B. Robson⟩ **2** *obs* : a spoken or written narrative : ACCOUNT, STORY, TALE ⟨my bell of hair would at a dismal ~ rouse and stir —Shak.⟩ **syn** see DISCOURSE

treat·ment \ˈtrētmənt\ *n* -s [¹*treat* + *-ment*] **1 :** the action or manner of treating: as **a :** conduct or behavior towards another party (as a person, thing, or group) ⟨regulations . . . for the ~ of all interned civilians —J.S.Pictet⟩ **b :** the action or manner of treating a patient medically or surgically ⟨diagnosis and ~ of tuberculosis⟩ ⟨required immediate medical ~⟩ **c :** subjection of something to the action of an agent or process ⟨the ~ of water supplies to make them safely potable —A.C. Morrison⟩ ⟨sewage ~⟩ **d :** the action or manner of dealing with something often in a specified way ⟨get capital gains ~ on income from a patent sale —J.T.Norman⟩ ⟨views . . . on the proper ~ of the conquered southern states —Carol L. Thompson⟩ ⟨a passage remarkable for its ~ of the age-old problem of freedom and authority —R.M.Weaver⟩ **e :** literary or artistic handling (as of a subject) esp. in terms of style ⟨two figures of sufficient importance to warrant ~ in separate chapters —R.A.Hall b.1911⟩ ⟨the architectural ~ is based . . . on the domestic style of northern Italy —*Amer. Guide Series: La.*⟩ **f :** preventive guidance and corrective training esp. of juvenile delinquents and youthful criminal offenders **2 :** an instance of treating ⟨the best ~s to date of several . . . bits of American history —John Bakeless⟩ ⟨a series of upper sidewall ~s in the architectural orders —*Amer. Guide Series: N.Y.*⟩ ⟨charges . . . $1 per ~ for occupational therapy —*Jour. Amer. Med. Assoc.*⟩ **3** *obs* : ENTERTAINMENT, FEAST ⟨accept such ~ as a swain affords —Alexander Pope⟩ **4 :** something (as a fertilizer or preserver) used in treating ⟨a seed disinfectant ~⟩ **5 :** an outline of the action of a proposed screenplay or television script that is considerably more detailed than a synopsis — compare SCENARIO, SCRIPT **6 :** the techniques or actions customarily applied in a specified situation: as **a :** a pattern of actions (as insults, annoyances, or physical punishment) designed to punish or persuade ⟨the new recruit got the ~ from a brutal sergeant⟩ **b :** a pattern of actions (as the bestowal of gifts and favors) designed to reward, encourage, or convince ⟨getting the standard ~ of cocktail parties, press interviews and deals with advertisers —*Time*⟩ **c :** the provision (as by a shop or restaurant) of the goods and services associated with a usu. specified fee or order ⟨the full ~ is $250 and up —Lois Long⟩

treats *pl of* TREAT, *pres 3d sing of* TREAT

trea·ty \ˈtrēd·ē, -ētē, |i\ *n* -ES *often attrib* [ME *tretee,* fr. MF *traité,* fr. ML & L; ML *tractatus* treaty, fr. L, handling, treatment, treatise, fr. *tractatus,* past part. of *tractare* to handle, manage, discuss, treat — more at TREAT] **1** *obs* : TREATISE ⟨in his excellent ~ of bodies—Sir Thomas Browne⟩ **2 :** the action of treating and esp. of negotiating : discussion aimed at an adjustment of differences or the reaching of an agreement — usu. used in the phrase *in treaty* ⟨unable to endure his loneliness, he was in ~ for a new wife —*Times Lit. Supp.*⟩ **3 a :** an agreement or arrangement made by negotiation: (1) : PRIVATE TREATY (2) : a contract in writing between two or more political authorities (as states or sovereigns) formally signed by representatives duly authorized and usu. ratified by the lawmaking authority of the state ⟨the president . . . shall have power, by and with the advice and consent of the Senate, to make *treaties* —*U.S. Constitution*⟩ — see PERSONAL TREATY, REAL TREATY; compare BILATERAL, CONVENTION, EXECUTIVE AGREEMENT, MULTILATERAL, PROTOCOL **b :** a document in which such a contract is set down **4 :** a formal meeting between representatives of the U. S. government and of one or more Indian tribes designed to produce a settlement (as of issues in dispute) ⟨Congress had promised them a ~, which was to have been holden about this time —Rufus Putnam⟩ **5 :** an agreement or contract (as between companies) providing for treaty reinsurance

treaty indian *n, usu cap I* : a No. American Indian belonging to a tribe that has signed a treaty with the U. S. or Canada

trea·ty·ite \ˈ|ē,īt\ *n* -s *usu cap* [*treaty* + *-ite*] : a supporter of the treaty of 1921 establishing the Irish Free State

treaty port *n* : one of a number of seaports, river ports, and inland cities in China, Japan, and Korea formerly open by treaty to commerce with other nations orig. as exceptions to a general policy of nonintercourse

treaty reinsurance *n* : reinsurance under a general agreement that automatically reinsures in accordance with its terms all risks of a given class to a predetermined extent as soon as they are insured by the direct underwriter

treb·bia·no \treˈbyä(,)nō\ *n* -s *usu cap* [It, perh. fr. L *Trebulanus* of Trebula, fr. *Trebula,* an ancient town in Campania, Italy + *-anus* -an] : UGNI BLANC

¹tre·ble \ˈtrebəl\ *n* -s [ME *treble, trible,* fr. MF *treble,* fr. *treble,* adj.] **1 a :** the highest of the four voice parts in vocal music : SOPRANO **b** (1) : a singer taking this part (2) *chiefly Brit* : a boy singer taking this part **c :** a musical instrument taking this part **d :** a high-pitched or shrill voice, tone, or sound ⟨a child's ~⟩ **e :** the highest bell of a ring in change ringing **f :** the upper half of the musical pitch range — contrasted with *bass* **g :** the higher portion of the audio frequency range in sound recording and broadcasting involving frequencies above 1000 cycles per second **2 :** something that is treble in construction, uses, amount, number, value, or other characteristic: **a :** a rack on which new sheets of handmade paper or sheets of newly printed paper are dried **b :** a win of three races by one horse

²treble \"\ *vb* **trebled; trebled; trebling** \-b(ə)liŋ\ **trebles** [ME *treblen,* fr. MF *trebler,* fr. *treble,* adj.] *vt* : to make three times as much or as many or as great : increase threefold : multiply by three ⟨the first daily penny paper . . . *trebled* its circulation —Alistair Cooke⟩ ⟨the commercial value of the looms was doubled or *trebled* overnight —*Irish Digest*⟩ ~ *vi* **1 :** to speak or sing in a treble tone **2 :** to become threefold : grow to three times the size, amount, or number ⟨its population has *trebled* since 1900 —*Amer. Guide Series: Pa.*⟩

³treble \"\ *adj* [ME *treble, trible,* fr. MF *treble,* fr. L *triplus* — more at TRIPLE] **1 a :** having three parts, elements, things, or uses : consisting of three members, sets, or layers : THREEFOLD ⟨a ~ row of bright red coral beads —R.M.Fox⟩ ⟨twenty-five strokes from the ~ whips —Lord Dunsany⟩ ⟨a lofty tower . . . with ~ walls —John Dryden⟩ **b :** having a threefold character : occurring in three kinds or existing in three ways ⟨every episode has its double and ~ meaning —Frederic Harrison⟩ **2 :** three times repeated : triple in number or amount : three times as much or as many ⟨~ salaries were paid —W.O.Douglas⟩ ⟨a newspaper with a circulation ~ that of its competitor⟩ ⟨sold for ~ the price⟩ ⟨a claim for ~ damages⟩ **3 a :** relating to or having the range of a musical treble ⟨~ violin⟩ ⟨~ voice⟩ **b :** high or sharp in tone : ACUTE, HIGH-PITCHED, SHRILL ⟨with her constant ~ cry —Ethel Wilson⟩ **c :** of, relating to, or having the range of treble in sound recording and broadcasting ⟨~ frequencies⟩ **4 :** of, relating to, or constituting a fishhook consisting of 3 single hooks fastened back to back usu. with an angle of 120 degrees between adjacent hooks — compare GANG HOOK

⁴treble *adv* [ME, fr. *treble,* adj.] *obs* : TREBLY

treble bob *n* : one of the chief methods of change ringing in which the treble has a uniform but zigzag course and all the bells dodge — see CHANGE RINGING illustration

treble clef *n* **1 :** G CLEF **2 :** TREBLE STAFF

treble staff *n* : the musical staff carrying the G clef

treblet *var of* TRIBLET

treble viol *n* : a 6-stringed viol made an octave higher than the bass viol and used chiefly in ensemble playing — called also *descant viol*

treble staff

tre·bly \-b(ə)lē\ *adv* [³*treble* + *-ly*] **1 :** in a threefold manner or degree : TRIPLY ⟨they have been ~ fortunate —Ernest Barker⟩ **2 :** in a treble tone ⟨listening to children ~ chant —*Brit. Books of the Month*⟩

treb·u·chet \ˈtrebyə,shet\ *n* -s [ME *trebochet,* fr. MF *trebuchet,* fr. OF, fr. *trebuchier* to stumble, trip, fall, fr. *tre-* (fr. L *trans-, tra-*) + *-bucher* (fr. *buc, bu* trunk of the body, of Gmc origin; akin to OHG *būh* belly — more at BUCKET] **1** *or* **tre·buck·et** \ˈtrē,bəkət\ : a medieval military engine designed to hurl stones and similar missiles with great force by means of a heavy weight fastened to the short arm of a lever which falls and raises the end of the long throwing arm with great velocity **2 :** a small delicately poised balance or scale made with a pan that tilts and used esp. in assaying and by chemists

tre·cen·tist \trāˈchentəst\ *n* -s *sometimes cap* [It *trecentista,* fr. *trecento* + *-ista* -ist] : a poet or artist of the trecento

tre·cen·to \-n·(,)tō\ *n* -s *sometimes cap* [It, lit., three hundred (abbr. of thirteen hundred), fr. *tre* three (fr. L *tres*) + *cento* hundred, fr. L *centum* — more at THREE, HUNDRED] : the 14th century; *specif* : the 14th century period in Italian literature and art

trech·mann·ite \ˈtrekmə,nīt\ *n* -s [Charles O. *Trechmann* †1917 Eng. mineralogist + E *-ite*] : a silver arsenic sulfide prob. $AgAsS_2$ occurring in small red rhombohedral crystals

tre cor·de \ˈtrāˈkȯrdā\ *adv (or adj)* [It, lit., three strings] : with soft pedal released — used as a direction in piano music at the close of a passage una corda

tre·cu·lia \trəˈkyülēə\ *n, cap* [NL, fr. Auguste A. L. *Trécul* †1896 Fr. botanist + NL *-ia*] : a small genus of African trees and shrubs (family Moraceae) having undivided coriaceous leaves, dioecious flowers, and large edible fruits — see BREADFRUIT

tre·dec·ile \trəˈdesəl\ *n* -s [L *tres* three + *decem* ten + E *-ile* — more at THREE, TEN] : the astrological aspect including 108 degrees

tre·decillion \ˌtrē+\ *n, often attrib* [L *tres* three + E *decillion*] — see NUMBER table

tre·drille \trəˈdril\ *or* **tre·dille** \-ˈdil\ *n* -s [alter. (influenced by L *tres* three) of *quadrille*] : a 3-handed card game similar to ombre popular in the 17th and 18th centuries

¹tree \ˈtrē\ *n* -s *often attrib* [ME *tree, tre,* fr. OE *trēow*; akin to OFris & ON *trē* tree, OS *trio, treo* tree, OHG *apholtra* apple tree, Goth *triu* tree, wood, Gk *drys* tree, *dory* spear, Skt *dāru* wood, *dru* tree, branch, wood] **1 a :** a woody perennial plant having a single main stem that may be short but is usu. considerably elongated, has generally few or no branches on its lower part, and is crowned with a head of branches and foliage or (as in palms) of foliage only — compare HERB, SHRUB **b :** a shrub or herb that grows naturally in or is trained into an arborescent form ⟨old rose ~s⟩ ⟨a sturdy banana ~⟩ ⟨some plants that are tall ~s under favorable conditions are mere shrubs at the extremes of their range⟩ **2 a** *archaic* : the substance of trees esp. as a source of structural material **b :** a piece of wood (as a stick, stave, post, or pole) either dressed or undressed and usu. adapted to a particular use: as (1) : a piece (as a bar, lever, brace, or support) forming a part of a structure or implement — usu. used in combination — see AXLETREE, CHESSTREE, CROSSTREE, DOUBLETREE, SINGLETREE, WHIFFLETREE (2) *obs* : the shaft of a spear or lance (3) *chiefly Scot* : STAFF, CUDGEL (4) *dial* : a wooden handle (as of a spade) **c :** a structure or fabrication of or typically or originally of wood: as (1) *obs* : SHIP (2) *archaic* : GALLOWS (3) *chiefly Scot* : a wooden container (as a cask for ale) (4) : SADDLETREE (5) : SHOE TREE **d** *sometimes cap* : CHRISTMAS TREE ⟨gifts clustered under the ~⟩ **3 :** something having the typical form of or felt to resemble a tree: as **a :** a design, diagram, or diagrammatic representation that depicts a branching from an original stem ⟨a genealogical ~⟩ **b :** an arborescent aggregation of crystals — see LEAD TREE **c :** a much-branched system of channels esp. in an animal body ⟨the vascular ~⟩; *also* : a cast of such a tree ⟨a bronchial ~ prepared by corrosion techniques⟩ — **as trees walking :** without clear definition or outlines : INDISTINCTLY, OBSCURELY — **up a tree** *adv (or adj)* : at a disadvantage or in an embarrassing position : CORNERED, TRAPPED

²tree \"\ *vb* **treed; treed; treeing; trees** *vt* **1 a :** to drive to or up a tree : cause to take refuge in a tree ⟨*treed* by a bull⟩ ⟨dogs ~*ing* small game⟩ **b :** to put into a position of extreme disadvantage : CORNER; *esp* : to bring (an evasive individual) to bay **2 a :** to furnish or construct with a tree ⟨~ an axle⟩ **b :** to plant or cover with trees **c** (1) : to fit (as a shoe) with a tree (2) : to shape and stretch (as a saddle) over a tree ~ *vi* **1 a :** to take refuge in a tree ⟨the coon soon *treed*⟩ **b :** to cause an animal to take refuge esp. in a tree ⟨the dogs *treed* early that night⟩ **2 :** to take the form of a tree ⟨crystals ~*ing* in a saturated solution⟩

tree agate *n* : moss agate when the dendritic markings resemble trees

tree aloe *n* : QUIVER TREE

tree ant *n* : any of several chiefly tropical ants (genus *Oecophylla*) that build their nests in trees of leaves sewn together by a secretion of the web-spinning larvae which the adults hold like shuttles

tree azalea *n* : a tall shrub (*Azalea arborescens*) of the southeastern U.S. often cultivated for its very fragrant white or pink flowers from which showy purple stamens protrude

tree bear *n* : RACCOON

tree belt *n* : a strip of ground lying between the sidewalk line and the curb line, usu. turfed, and commonly planted with shade trees — called also *tree lawn*

treebine \ˈ=,=\ *n* -s : any of various cultivated vines of the genus *Cissus*

tree boa *n* : an arboreal boa; *esp* : a member of either of two tropical American genera (*Boa* and *Epicrates*) of moderate-sized bird-eating boas

tree bracket *n* : a bracket-shaped fungus (as of the genus *Polyporus*)

tree burst *n* : the explosion of a projectile on contact with some part of a tree showering fragments down on the surrounding area

tree cactus *n* : any of several arborescent cacti; *esp* : SAGUARO

tree calf *n* : calfskin leather chemically treated so as to change its color and produce on it a treelike design ⟨a book bound in *tree calf*⟩

tree cat *n* : PALM CIVET

tree cat's-claw *n* : TEXAS CATCLAW

tree celandine *n* : PLUME POPPY

tree civet *n* : PALM CIVET b

tree class *n* : one of the size or age groups into which forest trees are commonly divided ⟨seedling, sapling, pole, standard are generally recognized *tree classes*⟩

tree clover *n* **1 :** WHITE SWEET CLOVER **2 :** an annual clover (*Trifolium ciliatum*) of the western U. S. having pink flowers with ciliate or bristle-margined calyx teeth

tree clubmoss *n* : a common and widely distributed clubmoss (*Lycopodium obscurum*) with underground creeping stems and erect aerial branches suggesting little trees

tree cobra *n* : MAMBA

tree cony *n* : TREE HYRAX

tree coral *n* : an arborescent coral; *usu* : a large branching ivory coral found esp. off the coast of Bermuda

tree cotton *n* **1 a :** an East Indian cotton plant (*Gossypium arboreum*) cultivated esp. for ornament **b :** the fiber obtained from tree cotton **c :** SEA ISLAND COTTON **2 a :** SILK COTTON TREE **b :** KAPOK

tree crab *n* **1 :** PURSE CRAB **2 :** MANGROVE CRAB

tree cranberry *n* : CRANBERRY BUSH

tree creeper *n* **1 :** a creeper of the family Certhiidae: as **a** (1) : a common European creeper (*Certhia familiaris*) that is brown streaked with buff above and silvery below and that has a slender curved bill (2) : the No. American brown creeper **b :** any of various Australian birds of the genus *Climacteris* **2 :** WOODHEWER 1

tree cricket *n* : any of several arboreal usu. pale or whitish American crickets (genus *Oecanthus*) noted for their loud stridulation — see SNOWY TREE CRICKET

tree cypress *n* : STANDING CYPRESS

treed *adj* [in sense 1, fr. ¹*tree* + *-ed*; in sense 2, fr. past part. of ²*tree*] **1 :** planted or grown with trees : WOODED **2 :** subjected to treeing: as **a :** driven up a tree ⟨a ~ animal⟩ **b :** fitted on a tree ⟨~ shoes⟩ ⟨no mark of stirrup iron across the instep of his freshly ~ boots —*Century Mag.*⟩

tree daisy *or* **tree aster** *n* : DAISYBUSH

tree digger *n* : a horse-drawn or tractor-drawn implement that consists essentially of a U-shaped blade which is passed under young trees in the nursery row to cut back roots and loosen the plant in the soil so that it may be lifted readily by hand (as for transplanting)

tree dog *n* : a dog (as a coonhound) used for treeing game

tree-dozer \ˈ=,==\ *n* : a device with heavy teeth mounted on the front of a track-laying tractor and used to clear land of brush, small trees, and roots

tree duck *n* : any of several long-legged and long-necked arboreal ducks (genus *Dendrocygna*) mostly of warm regions that are related to the sheldrakes and somewhat to the geese and have a complete bony orbit and the plumage usu. chestnut varied with black and white

tree farm *n* : an area of forest land managed in such a way as to ensure continuous commercial production under a systematic program of conservation and reforestation

tree farmer *n* : one engaged in tree farming

tree farming *n* : a systematic program of conservation and reforestation designed to ensure continuous commercial production of timber

tree fern *n* **1 :** any of various ferns exhibiting an arborescent habit with a caudex that is woody and elongated, belonging chiefly to the families Cyatheaceae and Marattiaceae but including some members of the Polypodiaceae, and being chiefly tropical and esp. abundant in Australia and New Zealand **2 :** any of several ferns that usu. grow on or about trees: as **a :** GRAY POLYPODY **b :** ROYAL FERN

treefish \ˈ=,=\ *n* : a California rockfish (*Sebastodes serriceps*) that is olive to blackish above, shades to yellow below, and is marked with transverse black bands

tree frog *n* : any of various Old World arboreal frogs (family Polypedatidae) related to those of the family Ranidae but distinguished by adhesive suckers on the toes; *broadly* : a tailless arboreal amphibian (as the New World spring peeper)

tree fruit *n* : a tree that produces table fruit; *also* : a fruit (as an apple, peach, or cherry) produced by such a tree — compare SMALL FRUIT

tree fuchsia *n* : KONINI

tree goose *n* [fr. the belief that the barnacle (shellfish) from which the goose was believed to stem is produced by trees] : BARNACLE GOOSE

tree guard *n* : any of various devices for protecting the trunk of a tree from animal and mechanical injury

tree heath *n* **1 :** a shrubby heath (*Erica arborea*) of the Mediterranean and Caucasian region cultivated for its nearly globular white flowers **2 :** a plant of the genus *Dracaena* **3 :** a New Zealand heathlike shrub or small tree (*Dracophyllum scoparium*) of the family Epacridaceae with tiny white flowers in dense racemes

tree hoopoe *n* : WOOD HOOPOE

treehopper \ˈ=,==\ *n* : any of numerous small leaping homopterous insects constituting the family Membracidae, living chiefly on branches and twigs, and injuring them by sucking sap — see BUFFALO TREEHOPPER

tree house *n* : a dwelling or playhouse built among the branches of a tree

tree huckleberry *n* : FARKLEBERRY

tree hyrax *or* **tree dassie** *n* : any of several largely arboreal African hyraxes that constitute the genus *Dendrohyrax* — called also *tree cony, tree dassie*

Representative Trees

Maximum Ht. 70 ft. **ARBORVITAE or WHITE CEDAR**

Maximum Ht. 130 ft. **ASH (White Ash)**

Ht. 50-60 ft. Maximum Ht. 100 ft. **BALSAM FIR**

Ht. Usually 60-70 ft. Sometimes 130 ft. **BASSWOOD or LINDEN**

Ht. Usually 70-80 ft. Maximum Ht. 130 ft. **BEECH**

Ht. Rarely over 60-80 ft. **PAPER BIRCH**

Ht. Usually 60-70 ft. Maximum Ht. 100 ft. **BUTTERNUT**

Ht. 40-50 ft. Maximum Ht. 100 ft. **RED CEDAR or JUNIPER**

Sometimes over 100 ft. **COTTONWOOD or POPLAR**

Ht. Usually not over 25-30 ft. **DOGWOOD (Blue Dogwood)**

Maximum Ht. 130 ft. **ELM**

(see also Tupelo) Maximum Ht. 140 ft. **GUM TREE or SWEET GUM**

Maximum Ht. 100 ft. **HEMLOCK**

Maximum Ht. 130 ft. **HICKORY (Shagbark)**

Maximum Ht. 100 ft. **HORSE CHESTNUT**

Ht. 70-80 ft. **LOCUST**

Maximum Ht. 130 ft. **MAPLE (Sugar Maple)**

Maximum Ht. 150 ft. **OAK (White Oak)**

Ht. Sometimes over 200 ft. **WHITE PINE**

Ht. Sometimes 80-90 ft. **SASSAFRAS**

Maximum Ht. 100 ft. **BLACK SPRUCE**

Maximum Ht. 180 ft. **SYCAMORE or BUTTONWOOD**

Maximum Ht. 200 ft. **TULIP TREE**

Occasionally over 100 ft. **TUPELO or SOUR GUM**

Ht. Sometimes 130 ft. **WALNUT (Black Walnut)**

treeing *pres part of* TREE
tree ipomoea *n* **:** any of various shrubby ipomoeas; *esp* **:** a plant (*Ipomoea crassicaulis*) native to tropical America and the southern U.S.
tree kangaroo *n* **:** TREE WALLABY
tree lark *n, Brit* **:** TREE PIPIT
tree lawn *n* **:** TREE BELT
tree·less \ˈtrēləs\ *adj* **:** lacking trees — **tree·less·ness** *n* -ES
tree·let \-lət\ *n* **:** a small or young tree (as a seedling or sapling)
treelike \ˈ=,=\ *adj* **:** resembling a tree esp. in form or size **:** ARBORESCENT
tree lilac *n* **:** a lilac of treelike form; *esp* **:** a broad-spreading white-flowered Japanese tree (*Syringa amurensis japonica* or *S. japonica*) that may exceed 35 feet in height
tree line *n* **:** TIMBERLINE
treelined \ˈ=,=\ *adj* **:** having a row of trees usu. on each side ⟨a ~ street⟩
treeling \ˈtrēliŋ\ *n* -S **:** a small or young tree **:** TREELET
tree lucerne *n, chiefly Austral* **:** TAGASASTE
tree lungwort *n* **1 :** a lichen (*Sticta pulmonacea*) growing on trees and rocks, having a lacunary thallus that suggests lung tissue, and used formerly in folk medicine in the treatment of pulmonary diseases **2 :** a bluebell (*Mertensia virginica*)
tree lupine *n* **:** an evergreen shrub (*Lupinus arboreus*) of the Pacific coast of the U.S. that has showy yellow or blue to violet flowers and is naturalized in New Zealand where it is used as a sand binder
tree mallow *n* **:** an arborescent mallow of the genus *Lavatera*
tree marten *n* **:** PINE MARTEN
tree martin *n* **:** TREE SWALLOW
tree medic *n* **:** a shrubby yellow-flowered medic (*Medicago arborea*) of southern Europe that is sometimes used as an ornamental
tree mildew *n* **:** a powdery mildew (*Phyllactinia corylea*) common on many trees and shrubs
tree milk *n* **1 :** the milky juice of an East Indian climbing plant (*Gymnema lactiferum*) of the family Asclepiadaceae that is used locally for food **2 :** the juice of a cow tree (*Brosimum galactodendron*)
tree molasses *n, chiefly dial* **:** MAPLE SYRUP
tree moss *n* **1 :** a moss or lichen growing on trees **2 :** a moss or club moss resembling a miniature tree; *esp* **:** a moss of the genus *Climacium*
tree mouse *n* **1 :** any of numerous small arboreal myomorph rodents: as **a :** any African long-clawed murid of *Dendromus* or related genera **b :** either of two cricetids of western No. America that are congeneric with the lemming mice **c :** any of a genus (*Vandeleuria*) of tropical eastern Asian climbing murids with very long tails and the great toe of the hind foot opposable and resembling a thumb **2 :** WHITE-BREASTED NUTHATCH
tree myrtle *n* **1 :** any of various shrubs of the genus *Ceanothus* (esp. *C. arboreus*) **2 :** any of various plants of the genus *Myrtus*
[1]**tre·en** \ˈtrēən\ *adj* [ME, fr. OE *trēowen*, fr. *trēow* tree, wood + *-en* — more at TREE] **1 :** made of wood **:** WOODEN **2** *obs* **:** of, relating to, or derived from trees
[2]**treen** \ˈtrēn\ *chiefly dial pl of* TREE
[3]**treen** \"\ *n, pl* **treen** [[1]*treen*] **1 :** small woodenware **2 :** an article (as a bowl or other utensil) made from wood — usu. used in pl.
[1]**tree·nail** *also* **tre·nail** *or* **trun·nel** \ˈtrē,nāl, ˈtrenᵊl, ˈtrənᵊl\ *n* -S [ME *trenayle*, fr. *tre, tree* tree, wood + *nayle, nail* nail — more at NAIL] **:** a wooden pin or peg made ordinarily of dry compressed timber so as to swell in its hole (as in a wooden ship) when moistened and used chiefly for fastening planking and ceiling to frames **2 :** GUTTA
[2]**treenail** \"\ *vt* **:** to fasten with treenails
treenware \ˈ=,=\ *n* [*treen* + *ware*] **:** TREEN
tree nymph *n* **:** a nymph (as a dryad or hamadryad) who is associated with a tree
tree of heaven *also* **tree of the gods :** an Asiatic tree (*Ailanthus altissima*) having foliage similar to that of the sumacs and ill-scented staminate flowers, being widely grown as a shade and ornamental tree esp. because of its resistance to smoke injury, and naturalized in many parts of the U.S.
tree of jesse *usu cap J* [after *Jesse*, father of David in the Bible] **:** JESSE TREE
tree of life 1 a [trans. of NL *arbor vitae*] **:** ARBORVITAE 1 **b :** BHUTAN CYPRESS **c :** [1]DATE 2 **2 :** a highly conventionalized and often ornate representation of a tree or vine used as a decorative motif and prob. of ultimately Assyrian origin
tree of porphyry *usu cap P* [after *Porphyry*, 3d cent. A.D. Greek philosopher] **:** a diagrammatic representation of the logical division of the highest genus, being, or substance into successive dichotomies

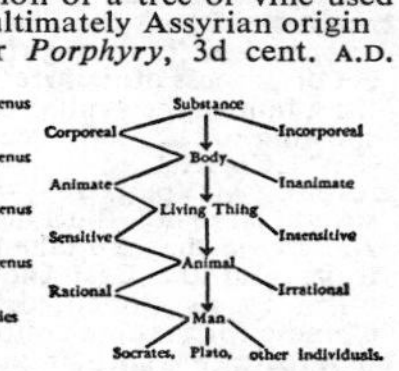

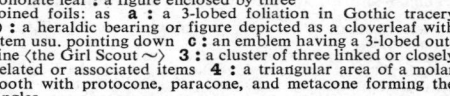

tree of Porphyry

tree onion *n* **:** any of several perennial garden onions that constitute a variety (*Allium cepa* var. *viviparum*) of the common onion, are grown chiefly as a curiosity or for early salad onions, and are propagated by bulbils that replace the flowers in the inflorescence — called also *Egyptian onion, top onion;* compare MULTIPLIER ONION
tree orchid *n* **:** an orchid of the genus *Epidendrum*
tree oyster *n* **:** MANGROVE OYSTER
tree partridge *n* **1 :** a Central American partridge of the genus *Dendrortyx* **2 :** HILL PARTRIDGE 1
tree peony *n* **:** a shrubby Chinese peony (*Paeonia suffruticosa*) having biternate leaves and large showy flowers and being the only woody cultivated peony and the source of many horticultural varieties
tree pie *n* **:** an Asiatic bird of the genus *Crypsirina* that is related to the common magpies and has a long graduated tail and plumage which is black or varied with orange-brown, buff, black, and white
tree pipit *n* **:** a European pipit (*Anthus trivialis*) of somewhat arboreal habits
tree planting *n* **:** the transplanting of a seedling or sapling tree to a permanent position; *also* **:** an exercise or ceremony attending such an act
tree poppy *n* **:** any of several shrubby to arborescent California plants of the family Papaveraceae: as **a :** MATILIJA POPPY **b :** BUSH POPPY
tree porcupine *n* **:** an American porcupine of the family Erethizontidae; *esp* **:** a So. or Central American prehensile-tailed porcupine of the genus *Coendou*
tree primrose *n* **:** an evening primrose (*Oenothera biennis*)
treer \ˈtrēə(r)\ *n* -S [[1]*tree* (boot tree) + *-er*] **:** a worker who cleans and dresses completed shoe uppers and irons out wrinkles
tree rat *n* **1** *Austral* **:** ROOF RAT **2 :** a member of an African murid genus (*Thallomys*) of arboreal rodents
tree ring *n* **:** ANNUAL RING
tree–ripe \ˈ=ˈ=\ *also* **tree–ripened** \ˈ=ˈ==\ *adj* **:** ripening or allowed to ripen on the tree to the stage of maximum palatability ⟨*tree-ripe* peaches⟩ — compare MARKET-RIPE
tree root rot *n* **:** MUSHROOM ROOT ROT
tree rose *n* **:** a rose that is budded at the apex of the stout trunk of the understock to produce a head of growth resembling the crown of a dwarf tree — called also *standard rose*
tree–run \ˈ=ˈ=\ *adj* **:** as taken from the tree without grading or sorting — used of fruits
tree runner *n* **:** NUTHATCH; *esp* **:** an Australian nuthatch of the genus *Neositta*
trees *pl of* TREE, *pres 3d sing of* TREE
tree·scape \ˈtrē,skāp\ *n* -S [[1]*tree* + *-scape*] **:** a landscape including many trees or groups of trees
tree shrew *n* **:** any of various small arboreal mammals (family Tupaiidae) of southeastern Asia that in appearance greatly resemble squirrels but may be distinguished by the very long pointed snout and sometimes by a distichous tail — compare PENTAIL
tree sparrow *n* **1 :** a European sparrow (*Passer montanus*) that is smaller than the house sparrow and has a black spot on the ear coverts **2 :** an American sparrow (*Spizella arborea*) that is larger than the chipping sparrow, breeds in northern No. America, and winters in the U.S.
tree·speel·er \ˈtrē,spēlə(r)\ *n* -S [[1]*tree* + [2]*speel* + *-er*] *Brit* **:** TREE CREEPER 1a(1)
tree spirit *n* **:** a supernatural being (as a deity or nymph) associated with a tree
tree squirrel *n* **:** an arboreal squirrel; *esp* **:** a typical squirrel of the genus *Sciurus* as distinguished from a ground squirrel or a flying squirrel
tree steppe *n* **:** land predominantly covered with grass but bearing scattered and usu. isolated trees ⟨much of the African veld is typical *tree steppe*⟩
tree stool *n* **:** the stump of a tree
tree sugar *n, chiefly dial* **:** MAPLE SUGAR
tree surgeon *n* **:** a specialist in tree surgery
tree surgery *n* **:** operative treatment of diseased trees esp. for the control of decay; *broadly* **:** practices (as pruning, spraying, fertilizing, repair of damage, protection from lightning injury, or moving) that form part of the professional care of specimen or shade trees
tree swallow *n* **1 :** WHITE-BELLIED SWALLOW **2 :** an Australian and Polynesian swallow (*Hirundo nigricans*) that nests in holes in trees — called also *tree martin*
tree swift *n* **:** any of several atypical swifts of the genus *Hemiprocne* of India and the East Indies which are often isolated in a distinct family, which have unusually soft plumage and are mostly crested, and in which the sexes are dissimilar and the young differ markedly from adults
tree toad *n* **:** any of numerous tailless amphibians of arboreal habits esp. of the family Hylidae **:** TREE FROG — see HYLA; compare SPRING PEEPER
tree tobacco *n* **:** an evergreen arborescent So. American tobacco (*Nicotiana glauca*) that has glaucous and glabrous foliage and yellow flowers, is naturalized in parts of the southwestern U.S. and in Australia and southern Africa, and is occas. responsible for poisoning of livestock **:** WILD TOBACCO
tree tomato *n* **1 :** a So. American arborescent shrub (*Cyphomandra betacea*) of the family Solanaceae **2 :** the egg-shaped reddish brown edible fruit of the tree tomato in flavor somewhat resembling a tomato
treetop \ˈ=,=\ *n* **1 :** the topmost branches or tuft of a tree **2 treetops** *pl* **:** the height or line marked by the tops of a row or clump of trees
tree trimmer *n* **:** OAK PRUNER
tree veld *n* **:** African tree steppe
tree viper *n* **:** any of several arboreal prehensile-tailed green and yellow vipers of equatorial Africa constituting a genus (*Atheris*) of the family Viperidae
tree wallaby *n* **:** any of several shapely arboreal wallabies (genus *Dendrolagus*) of tropical Australia and New Guinea having the tail long, slender, and furred, and the hind legs but slightly longer than the forelegs — called also *tree kangaroo*
tree warden *n* **:** a local officer charged in some jurisdictions with the care of trees — compare FIRE WARDEN
tree wax *n* **:** any of various fats, waxes, or waxy secretions produced by or found on trees or shrubs; *specif* **:** JAPAN WAX
treey \ˈtrē·ē\ *adj* [[1]*tree* + *-y*] **:** full of trees **:** WOODED
tree yucca *n* **:** JOSHUA TREE
[1]**tref** \ˈtrāv\ *n, pl* **tre·fi** \-vē\ [W, town, home, dwelling place, tref; akin to Corn *tref, tre* dwelling place, town, Bret *trev* division of a parish, OE *thorp* village — more at THORP] **:** a homestead or hamlet under old Cymric law; *usu* **:** a group or area acting as a single community as regards cattle and plowing, constituting a taxable unit, and consisting typically of nine houses, one plow, one oven, one churn, one cat, one cock, and one herdsman
[2]**tref** \ˈtrāf\ *or* **te·re·fah** *or* **te·re·fa** \təˈrāfə\ *or* **tre·fah** *or* **tre·fa** \ˈtrāfə\ *adj* [Yiddish & Heb; Yiddish *treyf, treyfe*, fr. Heb *ṭĕrēphāh* animal torn by wild beasts, torn flesh — more at TEREFAH] **:** ritually unclean or unfit according to Jewish law — opposed to *kosher*
trefah *or* **trefa** *var of* TEREFAH
tre·flée *also* **tre·flé** \trāˈflā\ *or* **tref·ly** \ˈtreflē\ *adj* [F *treflé* (fem. *treflée*), fr. *trefle* trefoil (fr. L *trifolium*) + *-é* -ate (fr. L *-atus*)] **1 :** BOTONÉE **2 :** ornamented with trefoils along the edge ⟨a bend ~⟩
[1]**tre·foil** \ˈtrē,fȯil, ˈtre,-\ *n* -S [ME, fr. MF *trefeuil, trefeul*, fr. L *trifolium*, fr. *tri-* + *folium* leaf — more at BLADE] **1 a** (1) **:** a clover of the genus *Trifolium* (2) **:** any of several similar trifoliolate leguminous herbs; *esp* **:** BLACK MEDIC — see BIRD'S-FOOT TREFOIL **b** *archaic* **:** WOOD SORREL **c :** a trifoliolate leaf (as of a clover) **2 a :** an ornament or symbol in the form of a stylized trifoliolate leaf **:** a figure enclosed by three joined foils: as **a :** a 3-lobed foliation in Gothic tracery **b :** a heraldic bearing or figure depicted as a cloverleaf with stem usu. pointing down **c :** an emblem having a 3-lobed outline ⟨the Girl Scout ~⟩ **3 :** a cluster of three linked or closely related or associated items **4 :** a triangular area of a molar tooth with protocone, paracone, and metacone forming the angles

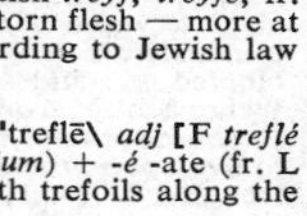
trefoils 2a

[2]**trefoil** \"\ *adj* **:** of, relating to, or having the shape of a trefoil: **a :** having three leaves or three lobes **b** *of an arch* **:** having an intrados with a 3-lobed outline — see ARCH illustration
tre·foiled \-ld\ *adj* **:** made like a trefoil or with trefoils
trefoth *or* **trefot** *pl of* TREFAH
trega– *or* **treg–** *comb form* [*trillion* + *-ega-, -eg-* (as in *mega-, meg-*)] **:** one million millions **:** trillion **:** 10^{12} ⟨*tregerg*⟩ ⟨*tregadyne*⟩
trega·dyne \ˈtregə,dīn\ *n* [*trega-* + *dyne*] **:** one trillion dynes
treg·erg \ˈtreg,ərg\ *n* [*trega-* + *erg*] **:** one trillion ergs
treg·et·our \ˈtrejəd·ə(r)\ *n* -S [ME, fr. OF *tresgeteor*, fr. *tresgeter* to throw across, juggle (fr. *tres-* across — fr. L *trans-* — + *geter, jeter* to throw, fr. L *jactare*) + *-eor* -or — more at JET] *archaic* **:** JUGGLER, MAGICIAN
tre·ha·la \trəˈhälə\ *n* -S [prob. fr. F *tréhala*, fr. Turk *tıgala*, fr. Per *tīghāl*] **:** a sweet edible substance constituting the pupal covering of an Asiatic beetle (prob. *Larinus maculatus*)
tre·ha·lase \ˈtrēhə,lās, trəˈhä,-\ *n* -S [ISV *trehala* + *-ase*] **:** an enzyme that accelerates the hydrolysis of trehalose and is found in yeasts and molds
tre·ha·lose \-,lōs\ *n* -S [ISV *trehala* + *-ose*] **:** a crystalline nonreducing disaccharide sugar $C_{12}H_{22}O_{11}$ that yields only glucose on hydrolysis and that is obtained from trehala, ergot of rye, and many fungi in which it is stored instead of starch; α-D-glucosyl α-D-glucoside
treil·lage \ˈtrālij\ *n* -S [F, fr. MF, fr. *treille* vine arbor (fr. L *trichila* arbor, summerhouse) + *-age*] **:** latticework for supporting vines or other growth **:** an espalier trellis; *also* **:** GRILL, LATTICE ⟨a room divided by ~⟩
treitz's muscle \ˈtrītsəz-\ *n, usu cap T* [after Wenzel *Treitz* †1872 Austrian physician] **1** *or* **treitz's ligament :** a band of smooth muscle extending from the junction of the duodenum and jejunum to the left crus of the diaphragm **2 :** RECTOCOCCYGEUS
[1]**trek** \ˈtrek\ *n* -S [Afrik, fr. MD *treck* pull, haul, fr. *trecken* to haul, migrate] **1** *chiefly southern Africa* **a :** a journey by ox wagon; *esp* **:** an organized expedition or migrational movement by a group of settlers to a new home **b :** a day's travel on such a journey or expedition **:** STAGE **2 :** a trip or movement esp. when involving difficulties or complex organization ⟨shortage of housing with the consequent ~ into apartments —*Yale Rev.*⟩ ⟨his ~ up from slavery —J.H.Johnson⟩ ⟨made a ~ to town⟩
[2]**trek** \"\ *vb* **trekked; trekked; trekking; treks** [Afrik, fr. MD *trecken* to pull, haul, march, migrate; akin to MLG *trecken* to pull, OHG *trechan*] *vi* **1** *chiefly southern Africa* **a :** to travel by ox wagon **b :** to migrate usu. by ox-wagon train to a new home **2 :** to make one's way slowly or arduously; *broadly* **:** to make a journey **:** GO — usu. used with *to* ~ *vt, chiefly southern Africa* **:** to provide draft for (as a vehicle) **:** PULL, DRAW
trekboer \ˈ=,=\ *n, pl* **trekboers** *or* **trekboere** [Afrik, fr. *trek* + *boer*] **:** a migratory grazier of southern Africa
trek·ker \ˈtrekə(r)\ *n* -S [Afrik, fr. *trek* to trek + *-er*] **:** one that treks
trek ox *n, southern Africa* **:** a draft ox
trek wagon *n* **:** a large 6-wheeled covered wagon used esp. in southern Africa in trekking and designed to provide lodging and storage space as well as seating for trekkers
trel·lage \ˈtrelij\ *n* -S [by alter.] **:** TREILLAGE
[1]**trel·lis** \ˈtreləs\ *n* -ES [ME *trelis*, fr. MF *treliz* fabric of coarse weave, trellis, fr. (assumed) VL *trilicius* woven with triple thread, fr. L *trilic-, trilix* — more at DRILLING] **1 a :** a structure or frame of latticework used as a screen or as a support for climbing plants **b :** a construction (as a bower or summerhouse) chiefly or wholly of latticework **c :** an arrangement that forms or gives the effect of a lattice ⟨a ~ of interlacing streams⟩ **2 :** a modification of the lattice in heraldic depiction in which the pieces are shown as nailed at the joints without interlacing
[2]**trellis** \"\ *vt* -ED/-ING/-ES [ME *trelesen*, fr. *trelis* trellis] **1 :** to provide with a trellis; *esp* **:** to train (as a vine) on a trellis **2 :** to cross or interlace on or through **:** INTERWEAVE ⟨an ornate design ~*ed* the wall⟩
[3]**trellis** \"\ *adj* [ME *trelis*, fr. *trelis*, n.] **:** having a latticed arrangement ⟨a ~ drainage pattern⟩

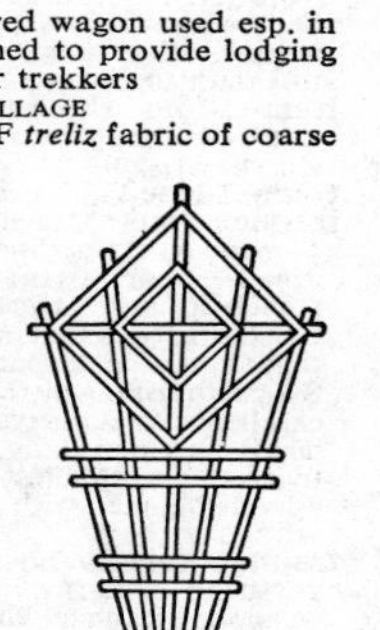
trellis 1a

trellis cipher *n* **:** a cipher that uses a grille to place the words of a hidden message in a cover text
trel·lised \-st\ *adj* [ME *trelest*, fr. past part. of *trelesen* to trellis] **:** having or furnished with a trellis or a latticed arrangement **:** trained upon a trellis ⟨~ roses⟩ ⟨a ~ cretonne⟩
trellised armor *n* **:** a medieval armor having bands crossing at right angles with a large rivethead or boss in each intervening square
trelliswork \ˈ==,=\ *n* **:** LATTICEWORK, MESHWORK
trem *abbr* tremolo
tre·ma \ˈtrēmə\ *n, cap* [NL *Tremat-, Trema*, fr. Gk *trēmat-, trēma* hole — more at THROW] **:** a genus of tropical shrubs and trees (family Ulmaceae) having alternate distichous leaves and cymose polygamous flowers succeeded by small drupes
-tre·ma \·ˈtrēmə\ *n comb form* [NL *-tremat-, -trema*, fr. Gk *trēmat-, trēma* hole — more at THROW] **1** *pl* **-tremas** \-məz\ *or* **-trema·ta** \-məd·ə, -mətə\ **:** hole **:** orifice **:** opening ⟨helico*trema*⟩ **2 :** creature having (such) an opening — in generic names ⟨Eury*trema*⟩
tre·mad·oc \trəˈmadək\ *adj, usu cap* [fr. *Tremadoc*, village of northwest Wales] **:** of or relating to a subdivision of the European Cambrian — see GEOLOGIC TIME table
trem·a·lith \ˈtremə,lith, ˈtrēm-\ *n* -S [Gk *trēma* hole + E *-lith* — more at THROW] **:** a minutely punctate coccolith — compare DISCOLITH
tre·man·do \traˈmän(,)dō\ *adj* [It, trembling, fr. verbal of *tremare* to tremble, modif. of L *tremere* — more at TREMBLE] **:** TREMOLANDO
tre·man·dra \trəˈmandrə\ *n, cap* [NL, fr. L *tremere* to tremble + NL *-andra*] **:** a small genus of Australian low shrubs that is the type of the family Tremandraceae
tre·man·dra·ce·ae \,trēmənˈdrāsē,ē\ *n pl, cap* [NL, fr. *Tremandra*, type genus + *-aceae*] **:** a family of exclusively Australian shrubs or undershrubs (order Geraniales) with solitary pink or purple regular flowers succeeded by 2-celled capsules — **tre·man·dra·ceous** \ˈ=;=ˈdrāshəs\ *adj*
-tre·ma·ta \·ˈtrēməd·ə, -mətə\ *n pl comb form* [NL, pl. of *-trema*] **:** creatures having (such) an opening — in names of orders and other higher taxa ⟨Dero*tremata*⟩
trem·a·to·da \,treməˈtōdə, ,trēm-\ *n pl, cap* [NL, fr. Gk *trēmatōdēs* pierced with holes, fr. *trēmat-, trēma* hole + *-ōdēs* -ode — more at THROW] **:** a class of Platyhelminthes including the flukes and related parasitic flatworms that usu. have no cellular epidermis or cilia but have a chitinous cuticle covering the body, suckers for adhesion, and a well-developed alimentary canal, and being commonly divided into three subclasses Monogenea, Aspidogastrea, and Digenea that differ significantly in reproductive behavior, in parasitic relations, and in structure — **trem·a·to·dan** \ˈ=;=ˈtōdᵊn\ *or* **trem·a·to·de·an** \-dēən\ *adj*
[1]**trem·a·tode** \ˈ===,tōd\ *adj* [NL *Trematoda*] **1 :** of or relating to the Trematoda **2 :** caused by a trematode worm
[2]**trematode** \"\ *n* -S **:** a flatworm (as a liver fluke) of the class Trematoda
trem·a·to·sau·rus \,treməd·əˈsȯrəs\ *n, cap* [NL, fr. Gk *trēmat-, trēma* hole + NL *-saurus*] **:** a genus of large labyrinthodont amphibians (order Stereospondyli) from the Triassic rocks of Germany having an elongated triangular roughly sculptured skull
[1]**trem·ble** \ˈtrembəl\ *vb* **trembled; trembled; trembling** \-b(ə)liŋ\ **trembles** [ME *tremblen*, fr. MF *trembler*, fr. ML *tremulare*, fr. L *tremulus* tremulous, fr. *tremere* to tremble; akin to Gk *tremein* to tremble, Lith *trimti*, Toch A *träm-*] *vi* **1 :** to shake involuntarily (as with fear, cold, excitement, fatigue) **:** SHIVER, SHUDDER, QUIVER **2 :** to move, sound, pass, or come to pass as if shaken or tremulous ⟨the building *trembled* but did not fall⟩ ⟨dusk was *trembling* on the verges of the hills —Nancy Hale⟩ **3 :** to become affected with tremulousness **:** fear greatly **:** become strongly affected ⟨I ~ for you⟩ ⟨*trembling* to think of what might have happened⟩ ~ *vt* **1** *obs* **:** to fear exceedingly **:** shudder at **2 :** to make tremble **:** cause to tremble **3 :** to speak or say tremulously ⟨*trembled* out a few words of appreciation⟩
[2]**tremble** \"\ *n* -S **1 :** an act of trembling **:** a fit or spell of involuntary shaking or quivering **:** a tremor or series of tremors **:** vibratory movement **2 :** AMERICAN ASPEN **3 trembles** *pl but sing in constr* **:** poisoning of livestock and esp. cattle caused by a toxic alcohol present in white snakeroot and rayless goldenrod which are common in parts of the western and central U.S., marked by muscular tremors, weakness, and constipation, and often progressing to coma and death — compare MILK SICKNESS, TREMETOL
trem·ble·ment \ˈtrembəlmənt\ *n* -S [F, fr. OF, fr. *trembler* to tremble + *-ment*] **1 :** a condition or instance of trembling or quivering **:** TREMOR **2 :** a terrifying thing **:** a cause of trembling **3 a :** TREMOLO **b :** a musical trill
[1]**trem·bler** \ˈtremb(ə)lə(r)\ *n* -S **1 :** one that trembles or causes or records trembling **2 :** any of various West Indian birds of the genera *Cinclocerthia* and *Rhamphocinclus* of the family Mimidae **3 :** the vibrating hammer or spring contact piece of an electrical hammer break (as of the electric ignition apparatus for an internal-combustion engine)
[2]**trembler** *or* **tremblor** *var of* TEMBLOR
trem·bleuse cup \trä^nˈbləz-\ *n* [F *trembleuse* trembleuse cup, fr. fem. of *trembleur* trembler, fr. *trembler* to tremble + *-eur* -er — more at -OR] **:** an old cup that fits into an elevated rim in the center of a saucer
[1]**trembling** *n* -S [ME, fr. gerund of *tremblen* to tremble] **:** the action or condition of one that trembles: as **a :** [2]TREMBLE 3 **b :** LOUPING ILL
[2]**trembling** *adj* [fr. pres. part. of [1]*tremble*] **:** that trembles **:** shaking with or as if with fear or other emotion **:** FEARFUL, VIBRATING, QUAKING — **trem·bling·ly** *adv* — **trem·bling·ness** *n* -ES
trembling hammer *n* [[2]*trembling*] **:** TREMBLER 3
trembling poplar *or* **trembling tree** *n* **1 :** EUROPEAN ASPEN **2** *or* **trembling aspen :** AMERICAN ASPEN
trembling prairie *n* **:** SHAKING PRAIRIE
trem·bly \ˈtremb(ə)lē, -li\ *adj* -ER/-EST [[1]*tremble* + *-y*] **:** marked by trembling **:** TREMULOUS; *also* **:** SHY, TIMID
tre·mel·la \trəˈmelə\ *n, cap* [NL, fr. L *tremere* to tremble + *-ella*] **:** a genus of fungi (family Tremellaceae) with yellowish and gelatinous sporophores having convolutions like those of the brain — **trem·el·line** \ˈtremə,līn, -,lən\ *adj*
trem·el·la·ce·ae \,treməˈlāsē,ē\ *n pl, cap* [NL, fr. *Tremella*, type genus + *-aceae*] **:** a family of basidiomycetous fungi (order Tremellales) having the basidium longitudinally or obliquely septate or divided
trem·el·la·les \-ā(,)lēz\ *n pl, cap* [NL, fr. *Tremella* + *-ales*] **:** an order of basidiomycetous fungi (subclass Heterobasidiomycetes) having the basidiocarp well developed and varying

from gelatinous to waxy or even horny in texture esp. when dry and being mostly saprophytes but including some parasites of mosses, other fungi, insects, or vascular plants — see AURICULARIACEAE, TREMELLACEAE

trem·el·loid \'tremə,loid\ *adj* [NL *Tremella* + E *-oid*] **1** : resembling or related to fungi of the genus *Tremella* **2** : GELATINOUS

trem·el·lose \-,lōs\ *adj* [NL *Tremella* + E *-ose*] : GELATINOUS

tre·men·dous \trə'mendəs, trē- *sometimes* -njəs\ *adj* [L *tremendus*, fr. gerundive of *tremere* to tremble, tremble at, dread — more at TREMBLE] **1** : such as may excite trembling : such as may arouse dread, awe, or terror : TERRIFYING, DREADFUL ⟨a ~ fact in human experience; that a whole civilization should be dependent on technology —Walter Lippmann⟩ **2 a** : astonishing by reason of extreme size, power, greatness, or excellence ⟨a countryside of ~ sweeping plains —Alan Moorehead⟩ **b** : unusually large or great : HUGE, VAST ⟨a ~ sensitivity to the slightest hint of criticism —Peggy Durdin⟩ ⟨an advertising man with ~ talents —M.E.Bennett⟩ **syn** see MONSTROUS

tre·men·dous·ly *adv* : to a tremendous degree or extent : EXTREMELY, GREATLY ⟨the ~ destructive powers of the new weapon —Raphael Demos⟩ ⟨the experience has been ~ educational —Sherwood Anderson⟩ ⟨~ preoccupied with his prestige and reputation —Margaret Mead⟩ ⟨~ bad films about the lives of celebrated musicians —London Times⟩

tre·men·dous·ness *n* -ES : the quality or state of being tremendous

trem·e·tol \'tremə,tól, -tōl\ *n* -S [irreg. fr. L *tremere* to tremble + *-ol* — more at TREMBLE] : an unsaturated alcohol obtained as an oil of aromatic odor from the white snakeroot and rayless goldenrod that causes trembles in animals

tre·mex \'trē,meks\ *n* [NL, prob. fr. Gk *trēma* hole + *-ex* (as in *Sirex*)] **1** *cap* : a genus of wood wasps (family Siricidae) with larvae that bore in weakened or dead wood of trees **2** -ES : any wood wasp of the genus *Tremex*

trem·ie \'tremē\ *n* -S [F *trémie* hopper, fr. L *trimodia* measure or vessel containing three modii, fr. *tri-* + *modius*] : an apparatus for depositing and consolidating concrete under water consisting essentially of a tube of wood or sheet metal with a top in the form of a hopper and being usu. handled by a crane

tre·mis·sis \trə'misəs\ *n, pl* **tremis·ses** \-'mi,sēz\ [LL *tremis, tremissis*, fr. L *tres* three + *-mis, -missis* (as in *semis, semissis*) — more at THREE, SEMIS] : a Byzantine triens or a similar gold coin of early western Europe

¹trem·o·lan·do *also* **trem·u·lan·do** \,tremō'lan(,)dō\ *adv (or adj)* [It, lit., trembling, fr. ML *tremulandum*, gerund of *tremulare* to tremble — more at TREMBLE] : TREMULOUS — used as a direction in music to play or perform in a tremolo

²tremolando *also* **tremulando** \"\ *n, pl* **tremolandos** \-,ōz\ *or* **tremolan·di** \-,ndē\ : a tremolo effect esp. by the strings of an orchestra

¹trem·o·lant \'tremələnt\ *also* **trem·u·lant** \-myəl-\ *n* -S [It *tremolante* tremolo stop, fr. *tremolante* tremulous, fr. ML *tremulant-, tremulans*, pres. part. of *tremulare* to tremble] **1** : an organ pipe having a tremulant note **2** : a device to impart a vibration causing a tremulant sound in a musical instrument

²tremolant \"\ *adj* : having a vibrant tremolo note

trem·o·lite \'tremə,līt\ *n* -S [F *trémolite*, fr. *Tremola* valley in the Alps, southern Switzerland + F *-ite*] : a mineral Ca₂Mg₅Si₈O₂₂(OH)₂ of the amphibole group that is a white or gray calcium magnesium silicate and occurs in long blade-shaped or short stout crystals and also in columnar, fibrous, or granular masses (sp.gr. 2.9–3.1) — **trem·o·lit·ic** \,=ə'lid·ik\ *adj*

trem·o·lo \'tremə,lō\ *n -S often attrib* [It, fr. *tremolo* tremulous, fr. L *tremulus*] **1 a** : the rapid reiteration of a musical tone or of alternating tones of a chord so as to produce a tremulous effect **b** : a perceptible rapid variation of pitch in the voice esp. in singing similar to the vibrato of a stringed instrument **2** *or* **tremolo stop** : a mechanical contrivance in an organ for periodically interrupting the flow of tone and causing a tremulous effect

trem·o·lo·so \,=ə'lō(,)sō\ *adv (or adj)* [It, fr. *tremolo* + *-oso* -ous (fr. L *-osus*)] : with tremolo — used as a direction in music

¹trem·or \'tremə(r) *sometimes* 'trēm-\ *n* -S [ME *tremour*, fr. MF, fr. L *tremor*, fr. *tremere* to tremble — more at TREMBLE] **1 a** (1) : a trembling or shaking of the body or one of its parts usu. associated with physical weakness or emotional stress ⟨the ~ of age⟩ (2) : a state of quivering excitement : tremulous agitation ⟨in a ~ of anticipatory delight⟩ (3) : an involuntary quivering of voluntary muscle involving an entire muscle, in muscle group, or some of the fibers of a muscle, varying in intensity and duration and occurring in conjunction with debilitated states or as a specific sign of organic disorders ⟨a coarse ~ of the hands⟩ ⟨the fine ~ associated with central nervous lesions⟩ **b** : a single shaking or quivering movement characteristic of a state of tremor ⟨cold ~s shook her from time to time⟩ **c** : a quaver in the voice esp. in speaking **2 a** : quivering or vibratory motion ⟨the ~ of a leaf in a breeze⟩ **3** : a feeling of uncertainty or insecurity ⟨not without ~s did we agree to the new plan⟩ ⟨all the ~s of arriving and departing ... forget its ~ —F.A.Swinnerton⟩

²tremor \"\ *vi* -ED/-ING/-S : to experience tremor

tremor disk *n* : the enlarged image of a star as registered on a photographic plate that results from the tremors of the atmosphere during the exposure

trem·or·less \-(r)ləs\ *adj* : free from tremor — **trem·or·less·ly** *adv*

trem·or·ous \-mərəs\ *adj* [*tremor* + *-ous*] : characterized by tremor : full of tremors ⟨a ~ state⟩ ⟨~ voices⟩

trem·our \'tremə(r)\ *archaic var of* TREMOR

¹trem·u·lant \'tremyələnt\ *adj* [ML *tremulant-, tremulans*, pres. part. of *tremulare* to tremble — more at TREMBLE] : TREMULOUS, TREMBLING

²tremulant \"\ *n* -S [G, fr. It *tremolante* — more at TREMOLANT] : TREMOLO 2b

trem·u·late \'tremyə,lāt\ *vi* -ED/-ING/-S [back-formation fr. *tremulation*] *archaic* : TREMBLE, QUIVER

trem·u·la·tion \,=ə'lāshən\ *n* -S [ML *tremulatus* (past part. of *tremulare* to tremble) + E *-ion*] : an act or the condition of trembling (as from fear or uncertainty)

trem·u·lous \'tremyələs\ *adj* [L *tremulus* — more at TREMBLE] **1** : characterized by or affected with trembling or tremors : QUIVERING, PALPITATING, SHAKING, VIBRATING ⟨~ hands⟩ ⟨leaves ~ in the breeze⟩ **2** : affected with fear or timidity : TIMOROUS, WAVERING ⟨a shy ~ girl⟩ **3** : such as is caused by a tremulous state or characteristic of a tremulous individual or thing ⟨a ~ handwriting⟩ ⟨a ~ reply⟩ ⟨night with no cloud to sully its ~ radiance —E.J.Banfield⟩ **4** : exceedingly sensitive : easily shaken or disordered ⟨a ~ and bitter joy —C.A.Lejeune⟩ — often used with to ⟨~ to criticism⟩ — **trem·u·lous·ly** *adv* — **trem·u·lous·ness** *n* -ES

trenail *var of* TREENAIL

¹trench \'trench\ *n* -ES *often attrib* [ME *trenche* track cut through a wood, fr. MF, fr. act of cutting, cut, fr. *trenchier* to cut] **1 a** : a long narrow cut in the ground : DITCH, FOSSE ⟨dig a ~ for sewer pipe⟩ **b** : a long narrow excavation used for military defense and often having the excavated dirt mounded up in front of it as an earthwork — compare APPROACH TRENCH, BUNKER, DUGOUT, FIRE TRENCH, PARALLEL 1c, SLIT TRENCH **c** *obs* : a protective earthwork ⟨resolved that the ditches ... should be deepened, and the ~es heightened —Fynes Moryson⟩ **2** : something that resembles a trench: as **a** archaic : FURROW, GROOVE ⟨these ~es made by grief and care —Shak.⟩ **b** : FIRING LINE 2 ⟨in the cultural struggle ... schools are the frontline ~es —Paul Blanshard⟩ **3 a** : a narrow steep-sided depression eroded by a stream : CANYON, GULLY **b** : a long straight comparatively narrow intermontane depression often occupied by parts of two or more drainage systems : TROUGH **c** : a long narrow steep-sided depression in an ocean floor : OCEAN DEEP — compare CANYON

²trench \"\ *vb* -ED/-ING/-S [in sense 1, fr. MF *trenchier* to cut, cut across, trench, prob. modif. of L *truncare* to cut off; in other senses, partly fr. ME *trenche*, n. and partly fr. MF *trenchier* — more at TRUNCATE] *vt* **1 a** : to make a cut in : CARVE, INCISE ⟨inscriptions ... ~ed in one of the stones

—John Webb⟩ ⟨surface ~*ing* at numerous points on the ... outcrop —W.H.A.Lawrence⟩ **b** *obs* : to make a gash in : SLASH ⟨the wide wound, that the boar had ~*ed* in his soft flank —Shak.⟩ **2 a** (1) : to dig a protective trench in ⟨~ a hill⟩ (2) : to protect with or as if with a trench ⟨~ an outpost⟩ **b** : to cut a drainage trench in : DITCH ⟨~ land to drain it⟩ **c** (1) : to turn over (soil) two or more times the depth of a spade (2) : to drain by trenches **d** : to bury in or confine by means of a trench ⟨~*ing* logs to prevent rolling —*Glossary of Terms Used in Forest Fire Control*⟩ ⟨stopping more than 3000 small fires and ~*ing* in nearly 100 big ones —W.B.Greeley⟩ **e** : ENTRENCH 2 ~ *vi* **1 a** *obs* : to approach a military objective by a series of trenches ⟨like powerful armies ~*ing* at a town —Edward Young⟩ **b** *archaic* : to extend out : STRETCH ⟨the land ~*ed* away best for fifteen hundred miles —Daniel Defoe⟩ **2 a** : ENTRENCH 2 ⟨~*ing* on other domains which were more vital —Sir Winston Churchill⟩ **b** : to come close : VERGE ⟨catches himself ... ~*ing* upon presumption —T.V.Smith⟩ **3** : INTRENCH ⟨~ around the spot right down to the clay —*Sydney (Australia) Bull.*⟩

tren·chan·cy \'trenchənsē, -si\ *n* -ES : the quality or state of being trenchant

tren·chant \-chənt\ *adj* [ME *trenchaunt*, fr. MF *trenchant*, pres. part. of *trenchier* to trench] **1 a** *archaic* : having a cutting edge : KEEN, SHARP ⟨a second less and the ~ blade had shorn through his heart —Bram Stoker⟩ **b** : adapted for cutting : SECTORIAL ⟨a ~ tooth⟩ **2** : vigorously effective : keenly articulate : BRISK ⟨a most ~ defender of civil rights —Zechariah Chafee⟩ ⟨discussed with a fearless and ~ pen the religious issues of the day —H.K.Rowe⟩; *specif* : CAUSTIC ⟨disillusioned satirist, ~ arrogant, and absolute master of a mordant pen —J.L.Lowes⟩ **3 a** : sharply perceptive : COGENT, PENETRATING ⟨a ~, plotless, constantly unfolding view of ... conditions brought by the war to our cities —Leslie Rees⟩ ⟨the author's ~ imagination —New Yorker⟩ **b** : well-defined : CLEAR-CUT, DISTINCT ⟨the ~ divisions between right and wrong, honest and dishonest —Edith Wharton⟩ **syn** see INCISIVE

tren·chant·ly *adv* : in a trenchant manner

trench artillery *n* : artillery emplaced in trenches for firing at high angles against targets at close range

trenchboard \'=,=\ *n* : duckboards running lengthwise of the bottom of a trench to keep the occupants out of accumulated mud and water

trench cart *n* : a low-wheeled narrow handcart for conveying ammunition through trenches

trench coat *n* **1** : a waterproof military overcoat with a removable woolen lining designed for wear in trenches **2** : a loose double-breasted raincoat or sport coat with a convertible collar, deep pockets, wide belt, tabs on the sleeves, and straps on the shoulders, usu. made of tan waterproofed gabardine or cotton twill

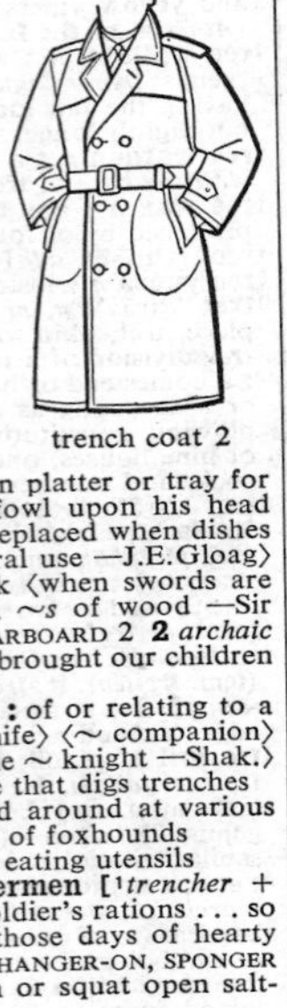

trench coat 2

trench digger *n* : a machine for excavating trenches

trenched *adj* [fr. past part. of ²*trench*] **1** : furrowed or drained by trenches : GROOVED, INCISED ⟨tributaries ran down north ... in deeply ~ valleys —W.G.East⟩ **2** [²*trench* + *-ed*] : provided with protective trenches ⟨stared at the ~ and fortified hill —Kenneth Roberts⟩

¹tren·cher \'trenchə(r)\ *n* -S [ME *trencher, trenchour* knife, wooden platter on which meat was cut up, trencher, fr. MF *trencheoir, trenchoir*, fr. *trenchier* to cut — more at TRENCH] **1 a** : a usu. wooden platter or tray for serving food ⟨balancing a ~ of roast fowl upon his head —Evelyn R. Sickels⟩ ⟨wooden ~s were replaced when dishes of pottery and porcelain came into general use —J.E.Gloag⟩ **b** *archaic* : a flat board or wooden disk ⟨when swords are blunted ... and spears are tipped with ~s of wood —Sir Walter Scott⟩ **c** *or* **trencher cap** : MORTARBOARD 2 **2** *archaic* : a source of nourishment : MEAL, TABLE ⟨brought our children to live upon others' ~s —Lewis Stucley⟩

²trencher \"\ *adj* [ME, fr. *trencher*, n.] **1** : of or relating to a trencher or to the eating of meals ⟨~ knife⟩ ⟨~ companion⟩ **2** *archaic* : PARASITIC, SYCOPHANTIC ⟨some ~ knight —Shak.⟩

trench·er \"\ *n* -S [²*trench* + *-er*] : one that digs trenches

trencher-fed \,=,=\ *adj, Brit* : boarded around at various places instead of in hunt kennels — used of foxhounds

trenchering *n* -S [*trencher* + *-ing*] *obs* : eating utensils

tren·cher·man \,=,=mən\ *n, pl* **trenchermen** [*trencher* + *man*] **1** : a hearty eater : GOURMAND ⟨soldier's rations ... so generous as to be improbable even in those days of hearty trenchermen —G.E.Fussell⟩ **2** *archaic* : HANGER-ON, SPONGER

trencher salt *n* : an individual salt dish or squat open saltcellar placed near a trencher

trencherwoman \,=,=,=\ *n, pl* **trencherwomen** : a female gourmand

trenches *pl of* TRENCH, *pres 3d sing of* TRENCH

trench fever *n* : an infectious disease characterized by fever and pain in muscles, bones, and joints, believed to be caused by a rickettsia transmitted by the body louse, and constituting a major medical problem during World War I

trench foot *n* [so called fr. its prevalence among soldiers serving in the trenches during World War I] : a painful condition of the feet resembling frostbite and marked by inflammation, swelling, mottled discoloration, burning pain, blisters, and in severe cases gangrene due to the combined effect of cold and wet upon the feet — compare IMMERSION FOOT

trenching *pres part of* TRENCH

trench knife *n* : a knife with a strong double-edged blade about eight inches long suited for use in hand-to-hand fighting

trench·more \'trench,mō(ə)r\ *n* -S [perh. fr. the name *Trenchmore*] : a boisterous English folk dance of the 16th and 17th centuries or its music in triple time and dotted rhythm

trench mouth *n* [so called fr. its prevalence among soldiers in the trenches] **1** : VINCENT'S ANGINA **2** : VINCENT'S INFECTION

trench-plow \'=,=\ *vb* [*trench* + *plow*, v.] *vi* : to bring lower soil to the surface by plowing a furrow a second time with a plow set much deeper ~ *vt* : to plow (a field) to double depth

trench plow *n* : a plow adapted for deep plowing

trench silo *n* : a trench often dug into a bank or slope, sometimes lined with concrete, and used mostly in regions of low rainfall for making and storing silage

trench warfare *n* : warfare in which the opposing forces attack and counterattack from a relatively permanent system of trenches protected by barbed-wire entanglements

¹trend \'trend\ *vb* -ED/-ING/-S [ME *trenden* to revolve, fr. OE *trendan*; akin to OFris *trind, trund* round, OE *trinda, trinde* round lump, ball, *trendel* circle, ring, MLG *trent* ring, boundary, MHG *trendel* disk, spinning top, *trinnen* to run forth, tear away from, *trennen* to break off, sever, OE *teran* to tear — more at TEAR] *vi* **1 a** : to extend in a general direction : follow a general course ⟨jagged ranges of mountains ... ~ north and south —G.R.Stewart⟩ ⟨the track led into caverns that ~*ed* upwards into the rock —John Masefield⟩ **b** : to take a turn : BEND, CURVE ⟨Penobscot Bay ... ~*s* deeply into Maine —Bernard De Voto⟩ **2 a** : to show an inherent tendency or general drift : INCLINE, MOVE ⟨selling costs have ~*ed* upward —Printers' Ink⟩ ⟨the direction Italian thought is ~*ing* —Fletcher Pratt⟩ ⟨people have a right to know how affairs of such great moment are ~*ing* —Arthur Krock⟩ **b** : to become deflected : SHIFT ⟨the flow of population may ~ his way —Alfred Marshall⟩ ~ *vt* : to cause to follow or conform ⟨laying the several courses ... and ~*ing* them to the abutments —*Civil Engineer & Architect's Jour.*⟩ ⟨~*ed* costs⟩

²trend \"\ *n* -S **1 a** : the line of direction or movement : ORIENTATION, FLOW ⟨the long northeastern ~ of the coast —Samuel Van Valkenburg & Ellsworth Huntington⟩ **b** : the directional line of a rock bed or petroleum deposit : STRIKE ⟨postulation of possible mineral ~s —*Economic Geology*⟩ ⟨~s of all the oil-bearing belts are known with considerable accuracy —John Pain⟩ **c** : the lower end of the shank of an anchor from about the middle of one of the arms to the throat **2 a** : a prevailing tendency or inclination : DRIFT, LEANING ⟨the ~ of opinion was distinctively conservative —C.L.Becker⟩ ⟨contemporary ~s in education⟩ ⟨the ~ toward government

participation in economic affairs —Louis Wasserman⟩ **b** : a general movement : SWING ⟨the ~ away from the land —Frank Hamilton⟩ ⟨the ~ toward shorter work periods —H.M.Diamond⟩ **c** : a current style or preference : VOGUE ⟨the ~ of yellow in longer waistline —Dun's Rev.⟩ **2** : a line of development : APPROACH ⟨important ~s in cancer have appeared in the clinical literature —D.A.Karnofsky⟩ **3 a** : the general movement in the course of time of some statistical progressive change ⟨a sufficiently long period of time of some statistical progressive change ~ of the stock market⟩ ⟨population ~⟩ ⟨upward ~ of the cost of living⟩ **b** : a straight line or other statistical curve showing the tendency of some function to grow or decline over a period of time ⟨a sensitive barometer of giving ~s through mass mailings —Jerome Ellison⟩ ⟨~s in parasitization —*Jour. of Economic Entomology*⟩ **syn** see TENDENCY

tren·del \'trend⁹l\ *n, pl* **trendels** *or* **trendel** [Yiddish *trendl*, fr. MHG *trendel* disk, spinning top] : DREIDEL

tren·de·len·burg position \'trend⁹lən,bərg-\ *n, usu cap* T [after Friedrich *Trendelenburg* †1924 Ger. surgeon] : a position of the body for medical examination or operation in which the patient is placed head down on a table inclined at about 45 degrees from the floor with the knees uppermost and the legs hanging over the end of the table

tren·dle \'trend⁹l\ *n* -S [ME, circle, ring, wheel, trendle, fr. OE *trendel* circle, ring; akin to MHG *trendel* disk — more at TREND] *dial Brit* : a large shallow round or oval usu. wooden tub or trough

trend line *n* : a line on a graph showing a statistical trend

tren·tal \'trent⁹l\ *n* -S [ME, fr. ML *trentale*, fr. (assumed) VL *trenta, trinta* thirty, fr. L *triginta* — more at TRICENARY] : a series of 30 Roman Catholic masses for the dead usu. celebrated 30 consecutive days

trente-et-qua·rante \,trä⁹tākə'ränt\ *or* **trente-qua·rante** \,trä⁹k-\ *n* [F *trente et quarante*, lit., thirty and forty; fr. the fact that the number dealt must never exceed 40 and the color nearest 31 wins] : ROUGE ET NOIR

tren·te·pohl·ia \,trentə'pōlēə\ *n, cap* [NL, fr. Johann F. *Trentepohl* †1806 Ger. botanist + NL *-ia*] : a genus of the type of the family Trentepohliaceae of terrestrial usu. reddish or orange-tinted green algae growing partly prostrate on rocks and tree trunks and found as the algal components of various lichens — see ROCK VIOLET

tren·te·pohl·i·a·ce·ae \,=,=,pōlē'āsē,ē\ *n pl, cap* [NL, fr. *Trentepohlia*, type genus + *-aceae*] : a family of aquatic or terrestrial green algae (order Ulotrichales) characterized by branching filaments without hairs and both prostrate and upright systems of growth and by isogamous sexual reproduction — see RED RUST 3a — **tren·te·pohl·i·a·ceous** \,=,=,=ēashəs\ *adj*

tren·tine \'tren-,tēn, -,tən\ *adj, usu cap* [Council of *Trent* (1545–63), nineteenth ecumenical council of the Roman Catholic Church held in the town of Trent, & *Trent*, town in northeastern Italy + E *-ine*] : TRIDENTINE

tren·ton \'trent⁹n\ *adj, usu cap* [*Trenton*, New Jersey] : of or from Trenton, the capital of New Jersey ⟨*Trenton* potteries⟩ : of the kind or style prevalent in Trenton

²trenton \"\ *n* -S *usu cap* [fr. *Trenton Falls*, New York] : a subdivision of the American Ordovician sometimes considered as the equivalent of the whole Middle Ordovician and sometimes restricted to a portion of this series

tren·to·ni·an \tren-'tōnēən\ *n* -S *cap* [*Trenton*, New Jersey + *-an*] : a native or resident of Trenton, New Jersey

tre·pak \trə'päk, 'trä-\ *n* -S [Russ, fr. *trepat'* to brake, beat, tap; akin to Lith *trepsti* to stamp with the feet, trample — more at TREPIDATION] : a fiery Ukrainian folk dance performed by men and featuring the leg-flinging prisiadka

¹tre·pan \trə'pan, trē-, -'paa(ə)n\ *n* -S [ME *trepane*, fr. ML *trepanum*, fr. Gk *trypanon* auger, trepan — more at TRYPAN-] **1** : TREPHINE **2 a** : a heavy tool consisting of vertical chisels fixed to a horizontal bar and used in boring mine shafts **b** : a machine tool for trepanning metals

²trepan \"\ *vt* **trepanned; trepanned; trepanning; trepans** [ME *trepanen*, fr. *trepane* trepan] **1** : to use a trephine on (the skull) **2 a** : to bore (as a mine shaft) with a trepan **b** (1) : to remove a disk or cylindrical core from (a metal plate, ingot, or forging) with a trepan (2) : to turn annular grooves or recesses in (as a metal block held in a lathe)

³trepan \"\ *n* -S [origin unknown] **1** *archaic* : DECOY, TRICKSTER **2** *archaic* : a deceptive device or maneuver : SNARE

⁴trepan \"\ *vt* **trepanned; trepanned; trepanning; trepans** **1** *archaic* : ENTRAP, LURE **2** *archaic* : SWINDLE

trep·a·na·tion \,trepə'nāshən\ *n* -S [ME *trepanacioun*, fr. MF *trepanation*, fr. *trepan* (fr. ML *trepanum*) + *-ation*] **1** : the act or process of perforating a skull with a surgical instrument **2** : a hole in the skull produced surgically ⟨hundreds of crania showing ~s ... have received close scrutiny from prehistorians —W.T.Corlett⟩

tre·pang \trə'paŋ, trē-, -'paaŋ\ *n* -S [Malay *tĕripang*] : any of several large holothurians mostly of the genera *Actinopyga* and *Holothuria* that are taken in vast quantities in northern Australia and the East Indies and to some extent along other warm coasts, boiled, dried, smoked, and used esp. by the Chinese for making soup — called also *bêche-de-mer*

trepanning *n* -S [ME, fr. gerund of *trepanen* to trepan] **1** : TREPANATION : the act or process of removing a disk or core of metal ⟨~ is a preliminary step in defusing an unexploded bomb⟩

treph·i·na·tion \,trefə'nāshən\ *n* -S [²*trephine* + *-ation*] : an act or instance of trephining; *esp* : TREPANATION

¹tre·phine \'trē,fīn; trē'fīn, -'fēn\ *n* -S [F *tréphine*, fr. obs. E *trefine, trafine*, fr. L *tres fines* three ends, fr. *tres* three + *fines*, pl. of *finis* end — more at THREE, FINAL] **1** : a surgical instrument for cutting out circular sections (as of bone or corneal tissue) **2** : TREPHINATION

²trephine \"\ *vb* -ED/-ING/-S *vi* : to perform a trephination ~ *vt* : to operate on with or extract by means of a trephine ⟨two young men whose skulls had been ~*d* because of head injury —R.S.Woodworth⟩ ⟨a graft ~*d* from a fresh cadaver eye —*Yrbk. of the Eye, Ear, Nose & Throat*⟩

treph·o·cyte \'trefə,sīt\ *n* -S [ISV *treph-* (fr. Gk *trephein* to nourish) + *-o-* + *-cyte* — more at ATROPHY] : a blood cell found in many invertebrates and concerned primarily with the transport of substances between the body cells

treph·one \'tre,fōn\ *n* -S [ISV, modif. of *treph-* (fr. Gk *trephein* to nourish)] : any of various substances in the blood serum and body fluids that promote the growth of cells

trep·id \'trepəd\ *adj* [L *trepidus*] : TIMOROUS, TREMBLING — **trep·id·ly** *adv*

trep·i·dant \'trepədənt\ *adj* [L *trepidant-, trepidans*, pres. part. of *trepidare* to trepidate] : TIMID, TREMBLING

trep·i·date \'trepə,dāt\ *vi* -ED/-ING/-S [L *trepidatus*, past part. of *trepidare* to trepidate] *archaic* : to feel trepidation ⟨causes our mind to ~ with quaking fear —Fraser's Mag.⟩

trep·i·da·tion \,trepə'dāshən\ *n* -S [L *trepidation-, trepidatio*, fr. *trepidatus* (past part. of *trepidare* to tremble, trepidate, fr. *trepidus* trembling, agitated) + *-ion-, -io -ion*; akin to OE *thrafian* to urge, push, press, OS *thrabon* to trot, high-step, MLG *draven, Sw trava* to trot, Gk *trapein* to press grapes, Lith *trepsti, trepseti* to stamp, trample, Skt *trpra* unsteady, hasty, anxious] **1 a** *archaic* : a tremulous motion : QUIVERING, TREMOR **b** : the quality or state of being trepid : nervous agitation : APPREHENSION ⟨the high quality ... should make readers turn with eagerness and without too much ~ to the 200-page anthology —*Times Lit. Supp.*⟩ ⟨shocked safe and sane businessmen into a state of indignant ~ —Thorstein Veblen⟩ **2 a** : a libration of one of the celestial spheres adduced under the Ptolemaic system to explain small changes in position of the ecliptic and the stars **b** : small fluctuation in the longitude of the sun or moon **syn** see FEAR

tre·pid·i·ty \trə'pidəd·ē\ *n* -ES [L *trepidus* trembling + E *-ity*] : TREPIDATION 1b

trep·o·ne·ma \,trepə'nēmə\ *n* [NL, fr. Gk *trepein* to turn + NL *-o-* + *-nema* — more at TROPE] **1** *cap* : the type genus of Treponemataceae comprising anaerobic spirochetes that are parasitic in warm-blooded animals and man, have an undulating or rigid body without a columella, and commonly terminate in tapering ends resembling flagella — see SYPHILIS, YAWS **2** *pl* **treponema·ta** \-məd·ə\ *or* **treponemas** : any spirochete of the genus *Treponema* — **trep·o·nem·a·tous** \,==,=nemad·əs, -,nēm-\ *adj*

trep·o·ne·mal \¦==¦nēməl\ *adj* [NL *Treponema* + E *-al*] **1 :** caused by treponemata **2 :** acting on or affecting treponemata

trep·o·ne·ma·ta·ce·ae \ˌtrepəˌnēmə'tāsēˌē\ *n pl, cap* [NL, fr. *Treponemat-, Treponema,* type genus + *-aceae*] **:** a family of Spirochaetales comprising small variable spirochetes without obvious structural differentiation and including a number of parasites of vertebrates, some of which are important pathogens — see BORRELIA, LEPTOSPIRA, TREPONEMA

trep·o·ne·ma·to·sis \-'tōsəs\ *n, pl* **treponemato·ses** \-ōˌsēz\ [NL, fr. *Treponemat-, Treponema* + *-osis*] **:** infection with or disease caused by spirochetes of the genus *Treponema* — compare BEJEL, PINTA, SYPHILIS, YAWS

trep·o·neme \'trepəˌnēm\ *n* -s [NL *Treponema*] **:** TREPONEMA 2

trep·o·ne·mi·ci·dal \¦==¦nēmə¦sīdᵊl\ *adj* **:** destroying treponemata

trep·o·ne·mi·cide \ˌ==='==ˌsīd\ *n* -s [ISV *treponem-* (fr. NL *Treponemata*) + *-i-* + *-cide*] **:** an agent that kills treponemata

trep·o·sto·ma·ta \ˌtrepə'stōmədə\ *n pl, cap* [NL, fr. Gk *trepein* to turn + NL *-o-* + *-stomata*] **:** an order of Bryozoa (class Gymnolaemata) comprising Paleozoic forms resembling corals and having conical or prismatic zooecial tubes with flat or curved partitions — **trep·o·stome** \'==ˌstōm\ *adj or n*

trep·pe \'trepə\ *n* -s [G, lit., step, stairs, fr. MHG *treppe, trappe* — more at TRAP] **:** the graduated series of increasingly vigorous contractions that results when a corresponding series of identical stimuli is applied to a rested muscle

tre·ron \'trēˌrän\ *n, cap* [NL, fr. Gk *trērōn* timid, shy, dove; akin to Gk *trein* to flee, be afraid — more at TERROR] **:** a genus comprising fruit-eating pigeons of southern Asia, the East Indies, and other warm parts of the Old World that have the plumage largely green shading into purple or maroon and being the type of a subfamily of Columbidae or sometimes of a distinct family

tres *abbr* trestle

tre·set·te \trā'set-ē, trə-\ *n* -s [It, lit., three-seven; fr. the fact that 3 or 7 points are scored at one time] **:** an Italian card game in which players may score by melding and by winning counting cards in tricks

-tre·sia \-'trēzh(ē)ə\ *n comb form* -s [NL, fr. Gk *trēsis* (akin to Gk *tetrainein* to pierce) + NL *-ia* — more at THROW] **:** perforation ⟨procto*tresia*⟩ ⟨spheno*tresia*⟩

¹tres·pass \'trespəs, -eˌspas, -eˌspaa(ə)s, -eˌspais, -eˌspȧs\ *n* -ES [ME *trespas,* fr. OF, passage, crossing, trespass, fr. *trespasser* to go across, pass through] **1 a :** a violation of moral or social ethics **:** OFFENSE, TRANSGRESSION ⟨forgive us our ~*es* —*Bk. of Com. Prayer*⟩; *esp* **:** SIN ⟨the fatal ~ done by Eve —John Milton⟩ **b :** an unwarranted infringement ⟨never worried about their . . . ~ on generosity —Audrey Barker⟩ **2 a** (1) **:** an unlawful invasion of the person, property, or rights of another that is committed with actual violence or violence implied by law **:** a tort involving actual or implied violence (2) **:** the action for injuries done by such an act **b :** TRESPASS QUARE CLAUSUM FREGIT **syn** see BREACH

²trespass \"\ *vb* -ED/-ING/-ES [ME *trespassen,* fr. MF *trespasser,* fr. OF, to go across, pass through, trespass, fr. *tres* across, through (fr. L *trans*) + *passer* to pass — more at TRANS-, PASS] *vi* **1 a :** to commit an offense **:** ERR, SIN ⟨his errors of taste, when he ~*es* . . . never consist in taking a subject too seriously or too lightly —T.S.Eliot⟩ ⟨scrupulous fairness even to those who ~ against him —S.L.A.Marshall⟩ **b :** to make an unwarranted or uninvited incursion **:** cross an established boundary line ⟨~ on an angler's casting area⟩ ⟨~ on a busy executive's time⟩ ⟨not their duty to train the infants . . . but merely to see that they do not ~ upon adult attention by outraging the rules of etiquette —Margaret Mead⟩ ⟨felt the ambassador had ~*ed* on domestic affairs —*Time*⟩ **2 :** to commit a trespass; *esp* **:** to enter unlawfully upon the land of another ~ *vt* **:** VIOLATE ⟨~ the bounds of good taste⟩ ⟨~*ed* a doctor's office —W.G.Eliasberg⟩

syn ENCROACH, ENTRENCH, INFRINGE, INVADE: TRESPASS applies to a usu. unwarranted, unlawful, or offensive intrusion ⟨farmers bothered by hunters *trespassing* on their fields⟩ ⟨have *trespassed* on your hospitality too long —Dorothy Sayers⟩ ENCROACH may apply to an invasion of another's territory or usurpation of his privileges, rights, or possessions, often accomplished gradually or stealthily ⟨leading his tribesmen in defense of their homes against *encroaching* white settlers —*Current Biog.*⟩ ⟨that the Argentine militarists would seek to *encroach* on the territories of neighboring states —Vera M. Dean⟩ ⟨their work is closely related but it is not synonymous; neither should ever *encroach* on the field of prerogatives of the other —H.H.Arnold & I.C.Eaker⟩ ENTRENCH may suggest an aggressive position and determination to maintain control ⟨the ultimate result was that the railroad *entrenched* itself so strongly in the state's political field —*Amer. Guide Series: N.J.*⟩ ⟨spokesmen for the coal industry have expressed concern that the unregulated producers may cut their prices sharply in strategic areas to *entrench* themselves at the expense of coal —Walter Goodman⟩ INFRINGE applies to any degree of encroachment that can be considered a clear breach of law, ethics, equity, or rights ⟨a well-regulated militia being necessary to the security of a free state, the right of the people to keep and bear arms shall not be *infringed* —*U.S.Constitution*⟩ ⟨was very critical whenever the military power seemed to *infringe* on civil rights —W.K.Boyd⟩ INVADE may indicate entrance into another's sphere or territory with hostile intent and injurious effect ⟨in the years after the Civil War, it was not only the carpetbaggers who had *invaded* the South —Oscar Handlin⟩ ⟨no good comes from attempts to *invade* authority and responsibility —Dean Acheson⟩ ⟨she'll probably insult you for *invading* what she calls their privacy —Hamilton Basso⟩

trespass board *or* **trespass notice** *or* **trespass sign** *n* **:** a notice on private property legally prohibiting trespass

tres·pass·er \-sə(r)\ *n* -s [ME *trespassour,* fr. MF *trespasseor,* fr. OF *trespasser* to trespass + *-or*] **:** one that trespasses; *specif* **:** one that commits a trespass against another or his property — compare INVITEE, LICENSEE

trespass offering *n* **:** GUILT OFFERING

trespass on the case : a form of action or a writ formerly employed to redress various wrongs or injuries to person or property which were not the immediate result of alleged violence and for which no adequate remedy was provided by the common-law action of trespass — called also *action on the case*

trespass quare clausum fregit : the tort of wrongful entry on real property

trespass to try title : an action of trespass quare clausum fregit or its equivalent under codes and practice acts brought as a means of determining the title to land

¹tress \'tres\ *n* -ES [ME *tresse,* fr. OF *trece*] **1 a** *archaic* **:** a plait of hair **:** BRAID ⟨her yellow golden hair was trimly woven and in ~*es* wrought —Edmund Spenser⟩ **b :** a long lock of hair; *esp* **:** the long unbound hair of a woman — usu. used in pl. ⟨a wealth of long and lustrous-dusky ~*es* tangled on the snow-white pillow —R.P.Warren⟩ **2 :** a flexible shoot or frond ⟨branches weaved like the ~*es* of marine weeds —William Sansom⟩

²tress \"\ *vt* -ED/-ING/-ES [ME *tressen,* fr. MF *tresser,* fr. OF *trecier*] **:** to form into tresses **:** BRAID, PLAIT ⟨~ hair⟩ ⟨beautiful liquid braids ~*ed* by the streamlet —Julian Green⟩

tressed \-st\ *adj* [ME, fr. past part. of *tressen* to tress] **1 :** BRAIDED, PLAITED ⟨beds of ~ gazelle hide —Ida Treat⟩ **2 :** having tresses — usu. used in combination ⟨a red-*tressed* ex-waitress —*Newsweek*⟩

tres·sure \'treshə(r)\ *n* -s [ME *tressour,* fr. MF *tressour, tressure* band for the hair, headdress, fr. MF *tresseor, tressure,* fr. *tresser* to tress + *-or, -ure*] **1 :** a narrow orle usu. enriched with fleurs-de-lis **2 :** an inner encircling ornamentation on a coin or medal bordering the device — **tres·sured** \-(r)d\ *adj*

tressy \'tresē\ *adj* -ER/-EST *archaic* **:** abounding in or resembling tresses

tres·tine \'treˌstīn\ *also* **trez·tine** \-ezˌt-\ *n* -s [prob. fr. L *tres* three + E *tine* (of an antler) — more at THREE] **:** ROYAL ANTLER

¹tres·tle *or* **tres·sel** \'tresəl\ *n* -s *often attrib* [ME *trestel,* fr. MF, modif. (influenced by OF *treste, trestre* trestle, var. of *traste, trastre,* fr. L *transtrum* crossbeam) of (assumed) VL *transtellum* trestle, fr. L *transtillum,* dim. of *transtrum* crossbeam, transom — more at TRANSOM] **1 a :** a movable support or scaffolding usu. having diagonally spreading legs **:** HORSE 2c ⟨put boards on a ~ to saw them⟩ ⟨painters at work on a ~⟩ **b** (1) **:** TRESTLE TABLE (2) **:** a divided foot on a piece of furniture (3) **:** a braced frame serving as a support (as for a table top or drawing board) **c :** a braced framework of timbers, piles, or steelwork usu. of considerable height for carrying a road or railroad over a depression — compare VIADUCT **2 a** *archaic* **:** a three-legged stool or support **:** TRIPOD **b :** a low usu. three-legged stool or bench used as a heraldic bearing

²trestle \"\ *vt* **trestled; trestled; trestling** \-s(ə)liŋ\ **trestles :** to set on or support by means of trestles

trestle bent *n* **:** a transverse frame supporting the ends of the stringers in adjacent spans of a trestle

trestle bridge *n* **:** a bridge supported by trestlework

tres·tle·man \'==mən\ *n, pl* **trestlemen :** a worker who unloads loose cargo (as sand or ore) from freight cars and puts it on conveyors or into boats

trestle table *n* **:** a table supported on trestles ⟨set up *trestle tables* for a church supper⟩ ⟨a large . . . *trestle table* rather like a drafting board —Carl Jonas⟩; *specif* **:** a table having two or three trestle supports connected by a longitudinal bar instead of legs

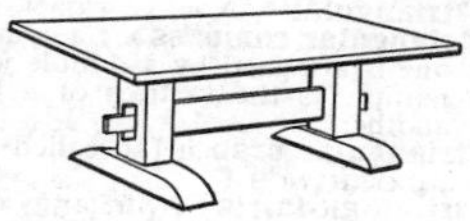

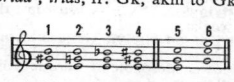

trestle table

trestletree \'==ˌ=\ *n* **:** one of a pair of timber crosspieces fixed fore and aft on the masthead to support the crosstrees, top, and fid of the mast — usu. used in pl.

trestlework \'==ˌ=\ *n* **1 :** a system of connected trestles supporting a structure (as a bridge, pier, or scaffold) **2 :** a structure composed of trestlework

trestling *n* -s **:** TRESTLEWORK 1

tret \'tret\ *n* -s [MF *trait* pull, draft, turn of the scale, pull of the scale — more at TRAIT] **:** an allowance of 4 pounds for every 104 pounds of suttle weight formerly added to various commodities (as spices) to offset deterioration in transit or chaff removed in cleaning

tre·ta yuga \'trād·ə-\ *n* [Skt *tretāyuga,* fr. *tretā* third throw of the dice, triad (fr. *traya* triple, threefold, fr. *tri* three) + *yuga* yoke, age of the world — more at THREE, YOKE] *Hinduism* **:** the second age of a world cycle

tre·val·ly \trə'valē\ *n* -ES [origin unknown] **1 :** an Australian carangid food fish (*Caranx georgianus*); *broadly* **:** any of several carangid fishes **2 :** BLACK TREVALLY; *broadly* **:** any of several related fishes chiefly of tropical and subtropical seas

tre·vis *or* **tre·viss** \'trāvəs, 'trev-\ *Scot var of* TRAVERSE

trev·or·ite \'trevəˌrīt\ *n* -s [T. G. *Trevor,* 20th cent. Brit. mine inspector + E *-ite*] **:** a black or brown-black mineral $NiFe_2O_4$ consisting of an oxide of nickel and iron and constituting a member of the magnetite series

trew \'trü\ *vi* -ED/-ING/-S [ME (Sc) *trewen,* fr. OE *trēowan, trēowian* — more at TROW] *Scot* **:** BELIEVE, TRUST

trews \'trüz\ *n pl* [ScGael *triubhas* — more at TROUSERS] **1 :** tight-fitting full-length trousers of tartan worn by some Scottish regiments **2 :** close-cut tartan short drawers sometimes worn under the kilt in Highland dress

trey \'trā\ *n* -s [ME *treye, treis,* fr. MF *treie* (fr. L *tria,* neut., three) & *treis,* fr. L *tres,* masc. & fem., three — more at THREE] **1 :** the side of a die or domino that has three spots **2 :** a card numbered three or having three main pips

trey–trip *n* -s [prob. fr. *trey* + *trip,* v.] *obs* **:** an old dicing game

trf *abbr* **1** tariff **2** transfer

TRF *abbr, often not cap* tuned radio frequency

trfd *abbr* transferred

trfr *abbr* transfer

TRH *abbr* Their Royal Highnesses

¹tri \'trī\ *adj* [by shortening] **:** TRICOLOR 1b ⟨a ~ dog⟩

²tri \"\ *n* -s **:** a tri dog

tri- *comb form* [ME, fr. L; akin to Gk *tri-,* L *tria* three — more at THREE] **1 :** three ⟨*tri*arch⟩ ⟨*tri*act⟩ **:** characterized by or having three or three parts ⟨*tri*crotic⟩ ⟨*tri*cycle⟩ ⟨*tri*pod⟩ **2 :** three times or in three ways ⟨*tri*farious⟩ ⟨*tri*sonant⟩; *also* **:** into three ⟨*tri*sect⟩ **3 :** thrice **:** every third ⟨*tri*weekly⟩ ⟨*tri*ennial⟩ **4 :** containing three atoms, radicals, or groups (of a specified kind) ⟨*tri*bromide⟩

tri·able \'trīəbəl\ *adj* [ME, fr. *trien* to try + *-able* — more at TRY] **1 :** liable or subject to undergo a judicial or quasi-judicial examination or trial ⟨a case ~ without a jury⟩ ⟨a case ~ by a national labor relations board examiner⟩ **2** *obs* **:** that may or can be tried **:** capable of being tested or put to a test

tri·a·can·thi·dae \ˌtrīə'kan(t)thəˌdē\ *n pl, cap* [NL, fr. *Triacantha,* type genus (fr. *tri-* + *acantha*) + *-idae*] **:** a family of marine fish (suborder Balistoidea) that have a protractile upper jaw, live chiefly on sandy bottoms where they feed on mollusks, and comprise the hornfishes

tri·acetate \(')trī+\ *n* [ISV *tri-* + *acetate*] **:** an acetate containing three acetate groups ⟨cellulose ~ fiber⟩

triacetin \"+\ *n* [ISV *tri-* + *acet-* + *-in*] **:** ACETIN

¹tri·acid \"+\ *adj* [ISV *tri-* + *acid,* adj.] **1 :** able to react with three molecules of a monobasic acid or one of a tribasic acid to form a salt or ester — used esp. of bases **2 :** containing three hydrogen atoms replaceable by basic atoms or radicals — used esp. of acid salts

²triacid \"\ *n* **:** an acid (as phosphoric acid or citric acid) having three acid hydrogen atoms

tri·a·con·tane \ˌtrīə'känˌtān, ˌtrēə-\ *n* -s [ISV *triacont-* (fr. Gk *triakonta* thirty) + *-ane* — more at TRICENARY] **:** a solid paraffin hydrocarbon $C_{30}H_{62}$; *esp* **:** the normal crystalline hydrocarbon $CH_3(CH_2)_{28}CH_3$ occurring in many mineral oils and in the wax coatings of apple skins and various flowers

tri·a·con·ta·no·ic acid \¦==¦käntə¦nōik-\ *n* [*triacontane* + *-oic*] **:** MELISSIC ACID

tri·a·con·ter \ˌ=='käntə(r)\ *n* -s [Gk *triakontērēs,* fr. *triakonta* thirty] **:** a Hellenic galley carrying 30 banks of oars

tri·act \'trīˌakt\ *n* -s [*tri-* + *-act*] **:** a triactinal sponge spicule

tri·actinal \(')trī¦aktənəl, ¦trīˌak¦tīnᵊl\ *also* **tri·ac·tine** \(')trī¦akˌtīn, -ˌtən\ *adj* [*tri-* + *-actinal* or *-actine*] **:** having three rays ⟨a ~ sponge spicule⟩

¹tri·ad \'trīˌad, -ïəd\ *n* -s [L *triad-, trias,* fr. Gk; akin to Gk *treis* three — more at THREE] **:** a union or group of three esp. of three closely related persons, beings, or things **:** TRINITY ⟨a ~ of deities⟩ ⟨a ~ of symptoms⟩: as **a :** a gnomic literature in medieval Wales and Ireland consisting of short aphorisms grouped in threes and in prose marked by rhythm and assonance and applying to various subjects (as history, laws, or morals) **b :** a trivalent element, atom, or radical **c :** a chord of three tones consisting of a root with its third and fifth and constituting the harmonic basis of tonal music — called also *common chord;* see MAJOR TRIAD, MINOR TRIAD; compare FIRST INVERSION, SECOND INVERSION **d :** a group of three individuals maintaining a sociologically significant relationship — compare DYAD **e :** a group of three strophes in a classical ode consisting of strophe, antistrophe, and epode

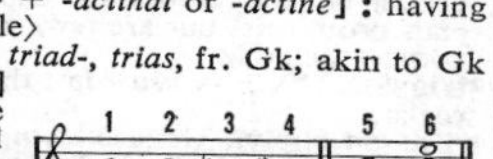

triads c: *1* major, *2* minor, *3* diminished, *4* augmented, *5* first inversion, *6* second inversion

²triad \"\ *adj* **:** having symmetry that results in repetition after every 120-degree rotation ⟨a ~ crystal axis⟩

tri·adel·phous \ˌtrīə¦delfəs\ *adj* [ISV *tri-* + *-adelphous*] **:** being or having stamens joined by filaments into three fascicles ⟨a ~ flower⟩

tri·a·denum \ˌtrīə'dēnəm\ *n, cap* [NL, fr. *tri-* + Gk *adēn* gland — more at ADEN-] *in some classifications* **:** a genus of No. American herbs (family Guttiferae) comprising two forms usu. included in the genus *Hypericum* but distinguished when separated chiefly by the pink or purple flowers and the three large glands alternating with three sets of stamens

tri·ad·ic \(')trī¦adik, -dēk\ *adj* **:** having the characteristics of or constituting a triad **:** consisting of or involving a triad ⟨a ~ poem⟩ ⟨the ~ nature of color vision —*Medical Physics*⟩ ⟨an erudite ~ biography of Lenin, Trotsky, and Stalin —R.A. Bauer⟩ ⟨suggested the use of ~ definitions in which the verbal symbol is made responsible both to an object or field of objects and to a detailed description of the objects —C.W. Shumaker⟩ ⟨thus language involves what logicians call a ~ relation. There is the speaker, the thing said, and the one spoken to —John Dewey⟩ — **tri·ad·i·cal·ly** \-dək(ə)lē, -dēk-, -li\ *adv*

tri·ad·ism \'trīəˌdizəm, -ī,a,d-\ *n* -s **1 :** state of being a triad **:** consisting of triads **:** threefold division or constitution ⟨the acceptance of ~ as the natural tonality —*ETC.*⟩ **2 :** a system based on a triad

tri·aene \'trīˌēn\ *n* -s [Gk *triaina* trident; akin to Gk *treis* three] **:** an elongated sponge spicule with three divergent rays at one end — **tri·ae·nose** \trī'ēˌnōs\ *adj*

¹tri·ae·noph·o·rid \¦trī,ē¦näf(ə)rəd\ *adj* [NL *Triaenophoridae,* family of tapeworms, fr. *Triaenophorus,* type genus + *-idae*] **:** of or relating to the genus *Triaenophorus* or the family Triaenophoridae

²triaenophorid \"\ *n* -s **:** a triaenophorid tapeworm

tri·ae·noph·o·rus \ˌ=='näf(ə)rəs\ *n, cap* [NL, fr. Gk *triaina* trident + NL *-phorus*] **:** a genus (the type of the family Triaenophoridae) of pseudophyllidean tapeworms that includes a form (*T. crassus*) parasitic as adults in pike and having larvae which form large cysts in the flesh of whitefish and make it unfit for human consumption

tri·age \trē'äzh, *in sense 1 also* 'trīij\ *n* -s [F, sorting, sifting, selecting, fr. *trier* to pick out, sift + *-age*] **1** *Brit* **a :** the process of grading marketable produce **b :** the lowest grade of coffee berries consisting of broken material **2 :** the sorting and first-aid treatment of battle casualties in collecting stations at the front before their evacuation to hospitals in the rear

¹tri·a·kid \'trīəkəd, trī'ak-\ *adj* [NL *Triakidae*] **:** of or relating to the Triakidae

²triakid \"\ *n* -s **:** SMOOTH DOGFISH

tri·ak·i·dae \trī'akəˌdē\ *n pl, cap* [NL, fr. *Triakis,* type genus (fr. Gk *triakis* three times) + *-idae;* fr. the three-pointed teeth] *in some classifications* **:** a family of elasmobranch fishes comprising the common smooth dogfishes

tri·a·kis·octahedron \¦trīəkəs, trī'ak-+\ *n* [ISV *triakis-* (fr. Gk *triakis* three times) + *octahedron;* akin to Gk *treis* three — more at THREE] **:** a trigonal trisoctahedron

tri·a·kis·tetrahedron \"+\ *n* [ISV *triakis-* + *tetrahedron*] **:** a trigonal tristetrahedron

¹tri·al \'trī(ə)l\ *n* -s [AF, fr. *trier* to try + E *-al* — more at TRY] **1 a :** the action or process of trying or putting to the proof **:** subjection of a person or thing to a test, examination, or participation in a contest or competition to determine something in question or to settle a controversy ⟨when several candidates are proposed for the chieftainship the choice is sometimes determined by a ~ of skill among the candidates —J.G.Frazer⟩ **b :** a trial match: as (1) **:** PRELIMINARY b (2) **:** HEAT 5a(2),5b **2 :** the formal examination of the matter in issue in a cause before a competent tribunal for the purpose of determining such issue **:** the mode of determining a question of fact in a court of law: as **a :** such an examination of an issue of law when it is before a judge alone or of fact when it is usu. before a judge and jury **b :** all proceedings from the time when the parties are called to try their cases in court or from the time when issue is joined to the time of its final determination **c :** such proceedings subsequent to swearing in a jury **3 a :** the state or fact of being tried by suffering; *esp* **:** a test (as of one's virtue, faith, patience, or stamina) by being subjected to affliction or temptation ⟨the 20th century . . . has been a time of recurring ~ —D.D.Eisenhower⟩ ⟨hotels are a ~ of both spirit and flesh —Nathaniel Peffer⟩ ⟨purified by ~⟩ ⟨the clock's greatest ~ occurred . . . when a bomb fell on the roof —Roy MacNab⟩ **b :** something that brings about such a trial ⟨despite all setbacks and hard ~*s* —*N.Y.Times*⟩ ⟨through the ~*s* of an epidemic —Martha T. Stephenson⟩ ⟨the ~*s* and tribulations of traveling over desert, across rocky divide, and floundering in the snowbanks —T.D.Clark⟩ ⟨the relinquishment of this work on account of illness was to her a great ~ —Elizabeth Hanscom⟩ ⟨I must have been a ~ to the secretary, for all my ideas were of the most precise and British order —Georgina Grahame⟩; *broadly* **:** a source of vexation or annoyance **4 :** a trying out as an experiment to test practicability, workability, or efficacy **:** a temporary and experimental use or application ⟨made his first ~ on the Delaware with a queer-looking boat having a row of paddles on each side —*Amer. Guide Series: N.J.*⟩ ⟨all sorts of sleeping bags have been developed and many have been given extensive ~*s* under various conditions —Morris Fishbein⟩ ⟨after many pauses and many ~*s* of other subjects —Jane Austen⟩ ⟨a conductor's duty to give all well-written works a ~ —Warwick Braithwaite⟩ ⟨a brief ~ of the plan would convince the people of its futility —F.A.Ogg & P.O.Ray⟩ **5** *obs* **:** direct personal knowledge **:** EXPERIENCE **6 :** an act of making an attempt **:** ENDEAVOR, EFFORT ⟨said he was willing to make the ~⟩ **7 a :** a sample or test piece used in proving the quality of a product or material or the progress and effectiveness of a mechanical operation **b** (1) **:** COLOR TRIAL (2) **:** an essay of a stamp **8 :** EXAMINATION: as **a :** the examination of a candidate for the Presbyterian ministry **b :** the final examination of the term in some English public schools

syn TRIBULATION, AFFLICTION, VISITATION, CROSS: TRIAL implies a test of one's patience, self-control, courage, or resistance to temptation ⟨the unfinished dresses . . . so saturated with smoke that he knew she found it a *trial* to work on them next morning —Willa Cather⟩ ⟨the child's disobedience in public was quite a *trial* to his mother⟩ TRIBULATION, when it is not completely interchangeable with TRIAL, stresses the suffering of a trial, sometimes connoting a suffering divinely imposed as a test of virtue ⟨the conquest of transatlantic trade by steam navigation softened the incredible *tribulations* of the old sailing ship voyage —Oscar Handlin⟩ ⟨a simple record of people trying to contend with the gigantic *tribulations* of poverty —*New Yorker*⟩ ⟨out of this time of trial and *tribulation* will be born a new freedom and glory for all mankind —Sir Winston Churchill⟩ AFFLICTION stresses the imposition of trouble or suffering ⟨the dark and senseless *afflictions* of a nightmare —Kenneth Roberts⟩ ⟨death and taxes . . . these twin *afflictions* —T.E.Ennis⟩ ⟨from early boyhood the sacrilegious and belligerent Simon had been a growing *affliction* to his parents —L.C. Douglas⟩ VISITATION heightens the idea of affliction, stressing the severity of suffering in suggesting an ordeal ⟨a maiming accident or some other *visitation* of blind fate —Joseph Conrad⟩ ⟨*visitations,* attacks, pestilences—Vicki Baum⟩ ⟨his inborn fatalism leads him to regard famines as inevitable *visitations* —Tom Marvel⟩ CROSS can suggest an undeserved suffering or a suffering borne for the sake of a larger unselfish or professedly unselfish good ⟨an ungrateful child was the *cross* she bore⟩ ⟨endure the *cross* of poverty and neglect⟩ — **on trial** *adv* (*or adj*) **:** in the state of being examined, tested, or tried out for a period ⟨became an itinerant preacher *on trial* —Marie A. Kasten⟩; *specif* **:** on approval for test or use for a specified period ⟨have goods sent out *on trial*⟩ ⟨coeducation was still *on trial* in the East —Hannah C. Hull⟩

²trial \"\ *adj* **1 :** of, relating to, or employed in a trial **2 :** made, done, or entered into by way of trial, experiment, or test **:** not intended to be permanent or final unless successful **3 :** used in trying, testing, fitting, or experimenting **4 :** serving as a sample, specimen, proof, or test piece ⟨a ~ subscription to a magazine⟩

³trial \"\ *adj* [ISV *tri-* + *-al*] **:** being or relating to forms of pronouns or nouns denoting three (as in the Polynesian and Melanesian languages) — compare DUAL, QUADRUAL

⁴trial \"\ *n* -s **:** the trial number, a form denoting it, or a word in that form

trial and error *n* **:** a finding out of the best way to reach a desired result or a correct solution by trying out one or more ways or means and by noting and eliminating errors or causes of failure; *also* **:** the trying of this and that until something succeeds

trial at bar 1 : a trial before three or more judges of the court in which the proceeding is brought used chiefly in causes célèbres or to consider novel points of law **2 :** trial before a judicial or quasi-judicial tribunal and esp. before a court of justice **:** trial by a court and by a jury

tri·alate \(')trī+\ *adj* [*tri-* + *alate*] **:** having three wings

trial at nisi prius 1 : a trial conducted as a result of the issuance of a writ of nisi prius **2 :** the original trial of the

facts in issue before a judge or jury as distinguished from the hearing of the case before an appellate court or on review
trial balance *n* **:** a list of the debit and credit balances of accounts in a double-entry ledger at a given date prepared primarily for the purpose of testing their equality or in the case of a subsidiary ledger of testing its accuracy against the control account
trial balloon *n* **1 :** a balloon sent up to test air currents and wind velocity **2 :** a project or scheme tentatively announced in order to test public opinion ⟨*trial balloons* . . . leaked to the press —Don Pryor⟩ — compare KITEFLYING
trial brief *n* **:** BRIEF 2d
trial by battle *or* **trial by combat :** a trial of a dispute formerly determined by the outcome of a personal battle or combat between the parties or in an issue joined upon a writ of right between their champions — called also *judicial combat, wager of battle*
trial by certificate : a trial of an issue formerly determined exclusively by the testimony of a person (as a military officer) certifying to what is peculiarly within his knowledge (as that a soldier is absent)
trial by inspection : a trial of a case formerly settled by the individual observation and decision of the judge upon the testimony of his own senses without the intervention of a jury
trial by jury : a trial in which the issue is determined by a judge and a jury usu. of 12 members whose province is to determine facts in issue
trial by ordeal : a trial formerly determined by the manner in which an accused sustains some form of ordeal
trial by record : a trial in which a matter of record is pleaded and in which the opposite party pleads that there is no such record and which involves inspection of the record itself and no other evidence — compare NUL TIEL RECORD
trial by the country : trial by a jury chosen from the country or vicinity
trial color proof *n* **:** COLOR TRIAL
trial court *n* **:** the court before which issues of fact and law are first determined as distinguished from an appellate court
trial docket *n* **:** DOCKET 2a(3)
trial examiner *n* **:** a person appointed to hold hearings on various matters and to investigate and report facts sometimes with recommendations to an administrative or quasi-judicial agency or tribunal
trial horse *n* **:** one set up as an opponent for a champion in trial competitions or workouts ⟨he offered his 12-meter yacht . . . and her crew to the syndicate as a *trial horse* —*Life*⟩
tri·al·ism \'trīə,lizəm\ *n* -s [*tri-* + *-alism* (as in *dualism*)] **1 :** TRIADISM **2** [G *trialismus*, fr. *tri-* + *-alismus* (as in *dualismus* dualism)] **:** a federation or union of three states
tri·al·ist \-ələ̇st\ *n* -s **1 :** an adherent or advocate of trialism **2 :** one that has an entry in or competes in a trial contest
trial judge *n* **:** a judge of a trial court
trial judge advocate *n* **:** a judge advocate detailed to act as a prosecutor of an accused before a court-martial
trial jury *n* **:** a jury impaneled to try a cause **:** PETIT JURY
tri·alkyl \(')trī+\ *adj* [*tri-* + *alkyl*] **:** containing three alkyl groups esp. in place of hydrogen
trial lawyer *n* **:** a lawyer who engages chiefly in the trial of cases before courts of original jurisdiction as distinguished from one whose functions are carried out mainly in his office or who is concerned with argument before appellate courts
trial marriage *n* **:** a proposed form of marriage in which a man and woman are married but for only a stated period — compare COMPANIONATE MARRIAGE
trial of the pyx : the annual assay of the coins in the British mint that have been placed in the pyx
tri·a·logue \'trīə,lȯg *also* -läg\ *n* -s [*tri-* + *-alogue* (as in *dialogue*)] **:** a scene, discourse, or colloquy in which three persons share
trial piece *n* **:** something made as a specimen: as **a :** a coin struck for testing a die often in a different metal and on a different size planchet from that used for the actual coin **b :** a carving done to test an artist's skill or conception found esp. in ancient art
trial run *n* **:** a testing exercise **:** EXPERIMENT, TEST ⟨a *trial run* of the seaworthiness of a new ship⟩ ⟨one great advantage of prose fiction is that it permits a kind of *trial run* for ideas under conditions approximating those of real life —H.O.Brogan⟩
trials *pl of* TRIAL
tri·amine \(;)trī+\ *n* [*tri-* + *amine*] **:** a compound containing three amino groups
tri·amino \"+\ *adj* [*triamino-*] **:** relating to or containing three amino or substituted amino groups
triamino- *comb form* [*tri-* + *amin-*] **:** containing three amino groups — in names of organic compounds ⟨1,2,4-*triamino*benzene⟩
tri·an·drous \(')trī¦andrəs\ *adj* [NL *triandrus*, fr. *tri-* + *-andrus* -androus] **:** having three stamens
tri·an·gle \'trī,aŋgəl, -aiŋ-\ *n* -s [ME, fr. L *triangulum*, fr. neut. of *triangulus* having three angles, triangular, fr. *tri-* three (akin to L *tria, tres* three) + *angulus* angle — more at THREE, ANGLE]

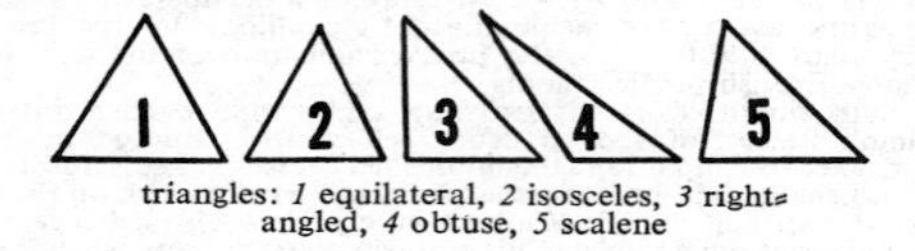

triangles: *1* equilateral, *2* isosceles, *3* right-angled, *4* obtuse, *5* scalene

1 : a usu. plane polygon having three sides — compare SPHERICAL TRIANGLE; see AREA table **2 :** a symbol (as of the Trinity in Christian art or as of life in primitive art), design, or decorative motif shaped like a triangle **3 :** a triangular object, marking, area, or arrangement **:** a triangle-shaped thing: as **a :** a hoisting or weighing device consisting of a tripod of poles or spars from the apex of which is suspended a pulley or balance **b :** a frame formed of three halberds or poles stuck in the ground and united at the top and used formerly to bind British soldiers undergoing corporal punishment — often used in pl. ⟨men were frequently sent to the ~s —*Time*⟩ **c :** a musical percussion instrument of indefinite pitch usu. made of a rod of steel bent into the form of a triangle open at one angle and sounded by striking with a small metal rod; *also* **:** a similar piece of metal used in the same way as an instrument of call ⟨a mess cook was beating the commissary ~ —K.M.Dodson⟩ **d :** a triangular area near the base of the wing in dragonflies **e :** a thin flat right-angled triangular instrument of wood or plastic usu. cut with acute angles of 45 degrees or of 30 degrees and 60 degrees and used in drafting **f :** a triangular postage stamp **4 a :** a group of three **:** TRIAD ⟨France's three-party coalition was described . . . as a type of ~ hard to break and impossible to maintain —P.S.Mowrer⟩ ⟨~ in an economic enterprise, composed of management, party leadership and labor-union organization —S.N.Harper & R.B.Thompson⟩ **b :** a situation involving three persons; *esp* **:** one involving the love of two men for one woman or of two women for one man and the resulting complications ⟨a comedy of the eternal ~, where the lover is a man . . . and the husband is a fat, lazy, hungry, cowardly, protesting cuckold —Leslie Rees⟩
triangle crab *n* **:** a small delicate triangular Australian crab (*Trigonoplax unguiformis longirostris*) living among weeds below the tide line
tri·an·gled \-gəld\ *adj* **:** having three angles **:** TRIANGULAR
triangle of forces : a vector diagram whose sides represent three forces in equilibrium — compare FORCE POLYGON
triangle of hes·sel·bach \-'hesəl,bäk\ *usu cap H* [after Franz K. *Hesselbach* †1816 Ger. surgeon] **:** an area of the abdominal wall bounded laterally by the deep epigastric artery, medially by the margin of the rectus muscle, and below by Poupart's ligament
triangle of mars \-'märz, 'mȧz\ *usu cap T&M* [after *Mars*, Roman god of war and agriculture] **:** GREAT TRIANGLE
triangle of scarpa *usu cap S* **:** SCARPA'S TRIANGLE
triangle spider *n* **:** a small American spider (*Hyptiotes cavatus*) that lives among the dead branches of evergreen trees, constructs a triangular web usu. composed of four radii crossed by a double elastic fiber, holds the thread at the apex of the web, and stretches it tight but lets go and springs the net when an insect comes in contact with it
¹tri·an·gu·lar \(')trī¦aŋgyələ(r), -aiŋ-\ *adj* [LL *triangularis*, fr. L *triangulum* triangle + *-aris* -ar] **1 a :** of, relating to, or consisting of a triangle **:** having three angles, corners, or sides **:** having the form of a triangle ⟨a ~ plot of land⟩ ⟨a ~ ruler⟩ ⟨he had a ~ face with high and broad forehead —J.M. Phalen⟩ **b :** having a principal surface of triangular shape ⟨a ~ chair⟩ ⟨a ~ table⟩ **2 a :** having a base that is a triangle ⟨a ~ prism⟩ ⟨a ~ pyramid⟩ **b :** shaped or edged like a triangular prism or pyramid **3 a** (1) **:** of, relating to, or involving three elements, factions, parts, persons, or states ⟨before the child enters the ~ mother-father-child relationship —Edmund Bergler⟩ ⟨a ~ trade between Peru, Europe, and the United States —H.T.Brundidge⟩ ⟨a ~ agreement⟩ (2) *of a military group* **:** based primarily on three units ⟨a ~ army division⟩ — compare SQUARE **b :** of or relating to a love triangle ⟨a ~ plot of a novel⟩ ⟨a ~ love affair⟩ — **tri·an·gu·lar·i·ty** \(')trī¦aŋgyə'larəd·ē, -aiŋ-, -lətē, -i *also* -ler-\ *n* -ES — **tri·an·gu·lar·ly** *adv*
²triangular \"\ *n* -s **:** TRIANGLE 3f
triangular compass *n* **:** a compass having three legs of which one is attached by a double joint used for transferring three points (as the vertices of a triangle) from one drawing to another
triangular crab *n* [so called fr. the shape of the carapace] **:** OXYRHYNCH 1
tri·an·gu·la·ris \(,)trī,aŋgyə'la(a)rə̇s\ *n, pl* **triangulares** [NL, fr. LL *triangularis*, adj., triangular] **:** a triangular body part (as a muscle); *specif* **:** a flat triangular muscle extending from the base of the mandible to the angle of the mouth and upper lip
triangular numbers *n pl* **:** the successive sums $\frac{n(n+1)}{2}$ of the first *n* natural numbers 1, 3, 6, 10, 15, . . . representable by dots arranged in triangles
triangular trade *n* **:** multilateral trade in which country A's purchases from country B are paid for by earnings from country B's sales to country C
¹tri·an·gu·late \(')trī¦aŋgyələt, -aiŋ-, -ə,lāt, *usu* -d·+V\ *adj* [ML *triangulatus*, past part. of *triangulare* to make triangles, fr. L *triangulum* triangle] **:** consisting of or marked with triangles **:** having triangular markings — **tri·an·gu·late·ly** *adv*
²tri·an·gu·late \-,lāt, *usu* -ād·+V\ *vb* -ED/-ING/-S [L *triangulum* triangle + E *-ate*] *vt* **1 :** to divide into triangles **:** give triangular form to **2** [back-formation fr. *triangulation*] **:** to survey, map, or determine by triangulation ⟨every culture is a moral geometry . . . a contingent means of *triangulating* one's course through reality —Weston La Barre⟩ ~ *vi* **:** to use triangulation **:** make a determination by triangulation
tri·an·gu·la·tion \(,)₌,₌₌'lāshən\ *n* -s [ML *triangulation-, triangulatio* action of making triangles, fr. *triangulatus* (past part. of *triangulare* to make triangles, fr. L *triangulum* triangle) + L *-ion-, -io* -ion — more at TRIANGLE] **1 :** the operation of measuring the elements necessary to determine the network of triangles into which any part of the earth's surface is divided in surveying and to fix the positions and distances apart of their vertices ⟨a surveyor who wants to measure the distance across a lake cannot use a tape measure or surveyor's chain so he must resort to a method called ~ —J.S.Allen⟩ ⟨as ~s cover only a small part of the continents and fail completely over the oceans, many geodetic systems exist —W.A. Heiskanen⟩; *broadly* **:** any similar trigonometric operation performed for finding a position or location by means of bearings from two fixed points a known distance apart ⟨~ on radio signals from the satellite will offer a supplemental means of location —*Science*⟩ **2 :** a calculation or prediction based on known facts ⟨a new isolationist formulation was bound to come — a new ~ by which the old emotions would try to make terms with the new realities —A.M.Schlesinger b.1917⟩
tri·an·gu·la·tor \₌'₌₌,lād·ə(r)\ *n* -s **:** one that triangulates
tri·annual \(')trī+\ *adj* [*tri-* + *annual*] **1** *obs* **:** TRIENNIAL **2 :** made, appearing, or occurring three times a year ⟨a ~ estimate of value⟩ ⟨a ~ advertisement⟩
tri·annulate \"+\ *adj* [*tri-* + *annulate*] **:** provided with or composed of three rings
tri·a·non \'trēə,nän\ *n* -s [fr. *Trianon*, one of two small villas in the royal park at Versailles, France] **:** a small elegant villa; *esp* **:** one in the grounds of a larger establishment
tri·ap·sal \(')trī¦apsəl\ *also* **tri·ap·si·dal** \-səd°l\ *adj* [*triapsal* fr. *tri-* + *apse* + *-al*; *triapsidal* fr. *tri-* + *apsidal*] **:** having three apses — used of a building ⟨the apses in a ~ church may be side by side at the east end or they may be projected from a central tower⟩
tri·arch \'trī,ärk, -ȧk\ *adj* [*tri-* + *-arch*] **:** having three xylem strands or groups ⟨a ~ root⟩
tri·ar·chy \-kē, -ki\ *n* -ES [Gk *triarchia*, fr. *tri-* three + *-archia* -archy — more at TRI-] **1 :** government by three persons **:** TRIUMVIRATE **2 :** a country under three rulers **3 :** one of three districts in a triarchy each under a ruler
tri·ar·thrus \trī'ärthrəs\ *n, cap* [NL, fr. *tri-* + Gk *arthron* joint — more at ARTHR-] **:** a genus of small Ordovician trilobites of which one form (*T. eatoni*) is often found with antennae and appendages in a good state of preservation
tri·articulate \¦trī+\ *adj* [*tri-* + *articulate*] **:** having three joints
tri·aryl \(')trī+\ *adj* [*tri-* + *aryl*] **:** containing three aryl groups in the molecule
triarylmethane dye \(')₌¦₌₌¦₌,₌-\ *n* [*triaryl* + *methane*] **:** any of a class of basic, acid, mordant acid, and direct dyes derived from triphenylmethane or diphenyl-naphthyl-methane usu. by introduction of one or more auxochromic groups (as amino, methylamino, dimethylamino, or hydroxyl groups) and characterized in general by brilliance but not by fastness — see TRIPHENYLMETHANE DYE
tri·as \'trīəs\ *adj or n, usu cap* [ISV, fr. L, triad] **:** TRIASSIC
¹tri·as·sic \(')trī¦asik\ *adj, usu cap* [ISV *triass-* (fr. L *trias* three, triad) + *-ic*; fr. the European Triassic being subdivided into the triad of Bunter, Muschelkalk, and Keuper] **:** of or relating to a division of the Mesozoic in which gymnosperms (as the cycads) are the most distinctive plants, the amphibians decline but the reptiles and ammonites develop rapidly, mammals prob. exist but are few, small, and primitive — see GEOLOGIC TIME table
²triassic \"\ *n* -s *usu cap* **:** the Triassic period or system of rocks
tri·as·so·chelys \trī¦asō+\ *n, cap* [NL, fr. *triasso-* (fr. ISV *triassic* + *-o-*) + *Chelys*] **:** a genus of extinct turtles of the lower Mesozoic of Europe believed to be the earliest true turtles
tri·as·ter \trī'astə(r)\ *n* -s [ISV *tri-* + *-aster*] **:** a mitotic figure resulting from tripolar usu. abnormal division of a nucleus
tri·at·ic stay \(')trī¦ad·ik-\ *n* [*triatic* prob. fr. *tri-* + *-ate* + *-ic*] **:** JUMPER STAY
tri·at·o·ma \trī'ad·əmə\ *n* [NL, fr. L *tria* three + NL *-toma* — more at TRI-] **1** *cap* **:** a genus of large blood-sucking bugs that are usu. placed in the family Reduviidae but sometimes assigned to a separate family and that feed on mammals and sometimes transmit Chagas' disease to their hosts — see CONENOSE **2** -s **:** any bug of the genus *Triatoma*
tri·a·tome \'trīə,tōm\ *n* -s [NL *Triatoma*] **:** TRIATOMID, CONENOSE
tri·atomic \¦trī+\ *adj* [ISV *tri-* + *atomic*] **1 :** consisting of three atoms **:** having three atoms in the molecule **2 :** having three replaceable atoms or radicals
tri·at·o·mid \(')trī¦ad·əmə̇d\ *also* **tri·atom·ic** \¦trīə¦tämik\ *adj* [NL *Triatoma* + E *-id* or *-ic*] **:** of or relating to *Triatoma* or various closely related genera
²triatomid \"\ *n* -s **:** a triatomid bug **:** CONENOSE
tri·axial \(')trī+\ *adj* [ISV *tri-* + *axial*] **:** having three axes **:** having three components ⟨~ ware composed of flint, clay, and feldspar⟩; *specif* **:** being a diagram with three axes for representing graphically three variables — **tri·axiality** \(;)trī+\ *n*
tri·ax·on \(')trī¦ak,sän\ *n* -s [NL, fr. *tri-* + Gk *axōn* axis — more at AXIS] **:** a sponge spicule having three axes crossing at right angles to form six rays
tri·ax·o·nia \,trī,ak'sōnēə\ *or* **tri·ax·on·i·da** \-'sänədə\ [NL, fr. *triaxon* + *-ia* or *-ida*] *syn of* HYALOSPONGIAE
tri·a·zine \'trīə,zēn, trī'a,z-, -,zə̇n\ *n* [ISV *tri-* + *azine*; orig. formed as Sw *triazin*] **1 :** any of three parent compounds $C_3H_3N_3$ containing a ring composed of three carbon and three nitrogen atoms that are distinguished by indication of the relative positions of the atoms in the ring or of only the nitrogen atoms; *esp* **:** the symmetrical or 1,3,5-isomer from which cyanuric compounds are derived — compare STRUCTURAL FORMULA **2 :** any of various derivatives of the three parent triazines

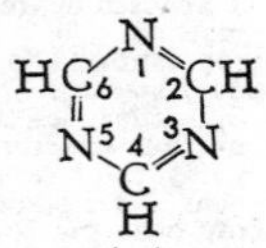

triazine

tri·az·i·nyl \trī'az°n,il\ *n* -s [*triazine* + *-yl*] **:** a univalent radical $C_3H_2N_3$ derived from one of the parent triazines
tri·azo \(')trī¦a(,)zō, -¦ā-\ *adj* [ISV *triazo-*] **1 :** AZIDO **2 :** TRISAZO — not used systematically
triazo- *comb form* [ISV *tri-* + *az-*] **:** AZIDO- — esp. in names of organic compounds
tri·a·zole \'trīə,zōl, trī'a,z-\ *n* [ISV *tri-* + *azole*] **1 :** any of four parent compounds $C_2H_3N_3$ containing a ring composed of two carbon atoms and three nitrogen atoms that are distinguished by indication of the relative positions of the atoms in the ring or of only the nitrogen atoms ⟨vicinal or 1,2,3-*triazole*⟩ **2 :** any of various derivatives of the four parent triazoles — see OSOTRIAZOLE — **tri·a·zol·ic** \¦trīə¦zälik\ *adj*
tri·az·o·lyl \trī'azə,lil\ *n* -s [ISV *triazole* + *-yl*] **:** a univalent radical $C_2H_2N_3$ derived from one of the parent triazoles
trib *abbr* **1** tribal **2** tribunal; tribune **3** tributary
tri·bade \'tribə̇d; trə̇'bäd, -'bad\ *n* -s [F, fr. L *tribad-, tribas*, fr. Gk, fr. *tribein* to rub; akin to L *terere* to rub — more at THROW] **:** a woman who practices tribadism — **tri·bad·ic** \trə̇'badik\ *adj*
trib·a·dism \'tribə,dizəm\ *n* -s [ISV *tribade* + *-ism*] **:** a homosexual practice among women which attempts to simulate heterosexual intercourse
trib·a·dy \-,dē\ *n* -ES [ISV *tribade* + *-y*] **:** TRIBADISM
trib·al \'trībəl\ *adj* **1 :** of, relating to, or characteristic of a tribe ⟨~ customs⟩ **2 :** resembling a tribe in possessing a sense of identification with and loyalty to the habits, traits, and values characteristic of a close-knit familistic, sociocultural, occupational, or political group or in ceremonial or ritualistic activity ⟨the ~ rites of rushing and initiation in a college fraternity⟩ — **trib·al·ly** \-bəlē, -li\ *adv*
trib·al·ism \-bə,lizəm\ *n* -s **1 a :** tribal life, organization, or society **b :** tribal feeling, peculiarities, or characteristics **2 :** strong ingroup loyalty and sentimental attachment to one's own group and its traits ⟨legislative ~⟩ ⟨a reversion to religious ~⟩
trib·al·ist \-ələ̇st\ *n* -s **:** an advocate of tribalism
trib·al·is·tic \¦₌₌¦listik\ *adj* **:** TRIBAL ⟨may leave the reader with the feeling that prejudices are ~ —E.R.Clinchy⟩
tri·basic \(')trī+\ *adj* [*tri-* + *basic*] **1 :** having three hydrogen atoms capable of replacement by basic atoms or radicals — used of acids (as phosphoric acid) **2 :** containing three atoms of a univalent metal or their equivalent ⟨~ sodium phosphate Na_3PO_4⟩ **3 :** having three basic hydroxyl groups **:** able to react with three molecules of a monobasic acid — used of bases and basic salts — **tri·basicity** \¦trī+\ *n*
tribe \'trīb\ *n* -s [ME *tribu, tribe*, fr. OF & L; OF *tribu*, fr. L *tribus* one third of the Roman people, division of the people, tribe; perh. akin to L *tria, tres* three — more at THREE] **1 a** (1) **:** a social group comprising numerous families, clans, or generations together with slaves, dependents, or adopted strangers ⟨the twelve ~s of Israel⟩ ⟨although the idea of consanguinity persists, the ~, as it expands, depends more and more on common social and political institutions, and less on actual kinship —A.H.Keane⟩ (2) **:** an endogamous social group held to be descended from a common ancestor and composed of numerous families, exogamous clans, bands, or villages that occupies a specific geographic territory, possesses cultural, religious, and linguistic homogeneity, and is commonly united politically under one head or chief — see CLAN; compare NATION (3) **:** a primitive group acting under a chief ⟨nomadic ~s⟩ **b** (1) **:** a large family group distinguished by close-knit ties, unusually well-marked family traits, or a number of eminent, talented, or successful members ⟨feeding and lodging . . . the whole ~ of near and distant cousins —Oliver La Farge⟩ (2) **:** a large family of offspring ⟨devotion . . . to children is graphically illustrated by the Christmas cards which . . . feature the smiling faces of the ~ —*Amer. Fabrics*⟩ **c** (1) **:** a political division of the Roman people orig. constituting one of the three voting units of the assembly of centuries and representing one of the three primitive tribes of ancient Rome and later being set up on a territorial basis, with the number of tribes increased — compare CURIA 1a (2) **:** PHYLE 1 **2 :** a group of persons having a common character, occupation, avocation, or interest ⟨of a ~ that accepts the failure of the large interests in life —Donn Byrne⟩ ⟨the whole ~ of American literary critics —C.I.Glicksberg⟩ ⟨as fishermen . . . we are beginners, and the humblest and greenest of the ~ —John Mason Brown⟩ **3 a :** a category of taxonomic classification to which various ranks have been assigned sometimes equivalent to or ranking just below a suborder but more commonly ranking below a subfamily; *also* **:** a natural group irrespective of taxonomic rank ⟨the cat ~⟩ ⟨rose ~⟩ **b :** a group of closely related animals or strains within a breed **4 :** a group of animals, birds, or sometimes inanimate objects having a common characteristic or being together in a flock or group ⟨this highly unbeloved feathered ~ —Morris Gilbert⟩ ⟨a ~ of sparrows⟩ ⟨a ~ of tray-shaped baskets —Elizabeth Bowen⟩
-tribe \,trīb\ *n comb form* -s [Gk *tribein* to rub — more at TRIBADE] **1 :** one that rubs against — used esp. of flowers during cross-fertilization ⟨pleuro*tribe*⟩ ⟨sterno*tribe*⟩ **2 :** instrument for crushing, compressing, or rubbing ⟨angio*tribe*⟩ ⟨osteo*tribe*⟩
tribe·less \'trīblə̇s\ *adj* **:** being without tribal affiliation
tribe·let \-lə̇t\ *n* -s **:** a small tribe
tribes·man \'trībzmən\ *n, pl* **tribes·men** \"\ **:** a member of a tribe
tribespeople \'₌,₌₌\ *n pl* **:** the people of a tribe
tribeswoman \'₌,₌₌\ *n, pl* **tribeswomen :** a female member of a tribe
tri·blas·tic \(')trī¦blastik\ *adj* [*tri-* + *-blastic*] **:** TRIPLOBLASTIC
tri·blet \'triblə̇t\ *or* **treb·let** \'treb-\ *n* -s [F *triboulet*, prob. fr. MF *tribouler, triboler* to press, oppress, trouble, afflict (fr. LL *tribulare* to oppress, afflict) + *-et* — more at TRIBULATION] **:** any of various mandrels used in making rings or nuts or in drawing tubes
tribo- *comb form* [F, fr. Gk *tribein* to rub — more at TRIBADE] **:** friction ⟨*tribo*fluorescence⟩ ⟨*tribo*phosphorescent⟩
tribo·electric \¦trībō, ¦tribō+\ *adj* [*tribo-* + *electric*] **:** of, relating to, or marked by triboelectricity
tribo·electricity \"+\ *n* -ES [*tribo-* + *electricity*] **:** a positive charge of electricity generated by friction (as by rubbing glass with silk) or a negative charge generated by friction (as by rubbing hard rubber with fur) — compare TRIBOELECTRIC SERIES
triboelectric series *n* **:** a sequence of substances so arranged that any one of them is positively electrified by rubbing it with any other substance farther on in the list — compare TRIBOELECTRICITY
tri·bo·li·um \trī'bōlēəm\ *n, cap* [NL, fr. Gk *tribolos*, any of various prickly plants + NL *-ium* — more at TRIBULUS] **:** a genus of small brown beetles (family Tenebrionidae) whose larvae feed on dry cereal products — see FLOUR BEETLE
tribo·luminescence \¦tribō, ¦tribō+\ *n* -ES [ISV *tribo-* + *luminescence*] **:** the emission of light from various substances usu. in flashes due to grinding, crushing, or tearing apart thought to be due to piezoelectric discharges — called also *piezoluminescence* — **tribo·luminescent** \"+\ *adj*
tri·bom·e·ter \trī'bämə̇d·ə(r)\ *n* [F *tribomètre*, fr. Gk *tribein* to rub + F *-mètre* -meter] **:** an instrument for measuring sliding friction
tribon \'tri,bōn, 'trī,bän\ *n* -s [LL, fr. Gk *tribōn*; akin to Gk *tribein* to rub — more at TRIBADE] **:** a garment made of coarse cloth worn the year round as the only garment by Spartan men — compare CHITON, CHLAMYS, HIMATION
tri·bo·ne·ma \,trībə'nēmə, ,trib-\ *n, cap* [NL, fr. Gk *tribos* action of rubbing (fr. *tribein* to rub) + NL *-nema*] **:** a genus

(the type of the family Tribonemaceae of the order Heterotrichales) of simple filamentous freshwater yellow-green algae having asexual spores formed within the cells and freed by the breaking of the filaments into H-shaped pieces — see CONFERVA

tribo·physics \ˌtrībō, ˌtribō+\ *n pl but usu sing in constr* [*tribo-* + *physics*] **:** the physics of friction

tri·borine triamine \(ˈ)trī+-\ *n* [*triborine* fr. *tri-* + *borine*] **:** BORAZOLE

¹tribrach \ˈtrīˌbrak, ˈtri-,\ *n* -s [L *tribrachys*, fr. Gk, having three short syllables, fr. *tri-* three (akin to Gk *treis* three) + *brachys* short — more at THREE, BRIEF] **:** a metrical foot of three short syllables of which two belong to the thesis and one to the arsis; *also* **:** a foot of three light syllables none of which carries a speech accent — **tri·brach·ic** \(ˈ)trīˈbrakik, trəˈb-\ *adj*

²tri·brach \ˈtrīˌbrak\ *n* -s [*tri-* + Gk *brachiōn* arm — more at BRACE] **:** a three-branched object, figure, or implement — **tri·brachi·al** \(ˈ)trīˈbrakēəl, -brāk-\ *adj*

tribrom- *or* **tribromo-** *comb form* [ISV *tri-* + *brom-*] **:** containing three atoms of bromine — in names of chemical compounds ⟨*tribromo*acetic acid⟩; compare BROM-

tri·bromide \(ˈ)trī+\ *n* [*tribrom-* + *-ide*] **:** a binary compound containing three atoms of bromine combined with an element or radical

tri·bro·mo·ethanol \(ˈ)trīˌbrōmō+\ *n* [*tribrom-* + *ethanol*] **:** a crystalline bromine derivative CBr_3CH_2OH of ethyl alcohol used as a basal anesthetic — called also *tribromoethyl alcohol*

tri·bro·mo·ethyl alcohol \"+-\ *n* [*tribromoethyl* fr. *tribrom-* + *ethyl*] **:** TRIBROMOETHANOL

trib·u·late \ˈtribyəˌlāt, *usu* -ād.+V\ *vt* -ED/-ING/-S [LL *tribulatus*, past part. of *tribulare* to oppress, afflict] **:** to cause to endure tribulation

trib·u·la·tion \ˌ==ˈlāshən\ *n* -s [ME *tribulacioun*, fr. OF *tribulacion*, fr. LL *tribulation-*, *tribulatio*, fr. *tribulatus* (past part. of *tribulare* to oppress, afflict, fr. L, to press, fr. *tribulum* threshing board) + L *-ion-*, *-io* -ion; akin to L *terere* to rub — more at THROW] **:** distress or suffering resulting from oppression, persecution, affliction, or sometimes contact with the physical environment ⟨found it nothing but a burden and a ~ —Jean Stafford⟩; *also* **:** an instance of such suffering **:** a trying experience ⟨explorers describing their hardships and ~*s* —*Report: Chapin Library*⟩ **syn** see TRIAL

trib·u·lus \ˈtribyələs\ *n*, *cap* [NL, fr. L, caltrop, fr. Gk *tribolos*, any of various prickly plants, threshing board studded with spikes; akin to L *tribulum* threshing board] **:** a genus of chiefly tropical or subtropical herbs (family Zygophyllaceae) introduced into No. America with pinnate leaves and yellow or white flowers succeeded by a spiny or prickly fruit of five indehiscent tuberculate carpels — see BURNUT, CALTROP 1b

tri·bu·na \trəˈb(y)ünə\ *n* -s [It — more at TRIBUNE] **:** ²TRIBUNE

tribu·nal \trīˈbyünᵊl, trəˈb- *sometimes* ˈtribyən-\ *n* -s [L, fr. *tribunus* Roman official, judge] **1 :** ²TRIBUNE: as **a :** the seat of a judge or one acting as a judge **:** the bench on which a judge and his associates sit for administering justice **b :** JUDGMENT SEAT ⟨appear before the august and holy ~ of God —J. N.Davies⟩ **2 :** a court or forum of justice **:** a person or body of persons having authority to hear and decide disputes so as to bind the disputants ⟨the Supreme Court is the highest ~ of the United States⟩ **3 :** something that decides or judges **:** something that determines or directs a judgment or course of action ⟨the ~ of events —George Santayana⟩ ⟨answerable to no ~ but that of their own judgment —Edith Wharton⟩

trib·u·nate \ˈtribyənət, -ˌnāt\ *n* -s [L *tribunatus*, fr. *tribunus* Roman official + *-atus* -ate] **:** TRIBUNESHIP

¹tribune \ˈtriˌbyün, trəˈb-\ *n* -s [ME, fr. L *tribunus* head of the tribe, chieftain, commander, tribune, fr. *tribus* tribe — more at TRIBE] **1 :** a Roman official under the monarchy and the republic: **a :** a commander of troops furnished the Roman army by the tribes **b :** a military commander chosen from the plebeians **c :** an officer elected from the plebeians with the specific function of protecting the individual citizen and esp. the plebeian from the arbitrary action of the patrician magistrates **2 a :** an officer or body in any country whose function is like that of a Roman tribune esp. in defending the common people ⟨Congress as the ~ of the people —Max Lerner⟩ **b :** a person other than a member of an official legislative, executive, or judicial body who defends the rights of the individual ⟨suggested that trade-union leaders serve as ~*s* in management with a veto power over management decisions —H.M. Magid⟩ ⟨the writer . . . is still the ~ of the person, the critic of institutions —Rex Warner⟩

²tribune \"\ *n* -s [F, fr. It *tribuna*, fr. ML, fr. L *tribunal*] **1 :** the raised platform in one end of a Roman basilica used esp. as the official station of the praetor and commonly placed in a semicircular apse **2 a :** the bishop's throne in a basilican church or the apsidal structure containing it **b :** an apsidal structure in a public building (as an Italian church) **3 :** a dais or platform from which an assembly is addressed

tribune·ship \-ˌship\ *n* **:** the office, function, or term of office of a tribune

trib·u·ni·cial *or* **trib·u·ni·tial** \ˌtribyəˈnishəl\ *adj* [LL *tribunicialis*, *tribunitialis*, fr. L *tribunicius*, *tribunitius* tribunician + *-alis* -al] **:** TRIBUNICIAN

trib·u·ni·cian *or* **trib·u·ni·tian** \-shən\ *adj* [L *tribunicius*, *tribunitius* (fr. *tribunus* Roman official + *-icius*, *-itius* -itious) + E *-an*] **:** of, relating to, characteristic of, or resembling a Roman tribune or his office

¹trib·u·tary \ˈtribyəˌterē, -ri\ *adj* [ME *tributarie*, fr. L *tributarius*, fr. *tributum* tribute + *-arius* -ary] **1 :** paying tribute to another to acknowledge submission, to obtain protection, or to purchase peace ⟨bringing one territory under the domination of the other, making it ~, or capturing its wealth —*Notes & Queries on Anthropology*⟩; *broadly* **:** SUBJECT, DEPENDENT, SUBORDINATE ⟨no conquering race ever lived . . . among a ~ one without begetting children on it —A.T.Quiller-Couch⟩ ⟨the freight rates and the tariffs which were to keep the South a ~ section —*Current Biog.*⟩ ⟨the elimination of poverty and the furtherance of social justice would in themselves cure all the ~ maladjustments —Oscar Handlin⟩ **2 :** paid or owed as tribute **:** of the nature of tribute **3 :** providing with or serving as a channel for supplies or additional matter ⟨receiving two ~ lanes from who should say what remote hamlets —Compton Mackenzie⟩ ⟨a ~ stream⟩ ⟨~ to the city are approximately 30,000,000,000 feet of pine timber —*Amer. Guide Series: Oregon*⟩

²tributary \"\ *n* -ES [ME *tributarie*, fr. LL *tributarius*, fr. L, adj., tributary] **1 :** a person (as a ruler) or state that pays tribute to a conquering power ⟨all the people that is found therein shall be *tributaries* unto thee —Deut 20:11 (AV)⟩ **2 :** one that is tributary to another: as **a :** a stream feeding a larger stream or a lake — compare BRANCH **b :** a vein that empties into a larger vein

¹trib·ute \ˈtri(ˌ)byü|t *also* -ˌbyə| *sometimes* -(ˌ)byü|; *usu* |d.+V\ *n* -s [ME *tribut*, fr. L *tributum*, fr. neut. of *tributus*, past part. of *tribuere* to bestow, grant, pay, allot, fr. *tribus* one third of the Roman people, tribe — more at TRIBE] **1 a :** an annual or stated sum of money or other valuable thing paid by one ruler or nation to another as an acknowledgment of submission, as the price of peace and protection, or by virtue of some treaty ⟨foreseen that foreigners would pay ~ to the country for the right to carry away a wealth of liquid gold —P.E.James⟩; *also* **:** the tax levied for such a payment **b** (1) **:** an esp. large or excessive tax, impost, duty, rental, or tariff imposed by a government, sovereign, lord, or landlord (2) **:** an exorbitant or extralegal impost levied by a person or group having the power of coercion ⟨the monopolistic combinations of war industries levied a ~ on the . . . consumer so wasteful that it led to proposals to draft capital —T.W.Arnold⟩ ⟨compelled to join unions and pay ~ against their wills —M.K.Hart⟩ **c :** the liability to pay tribute ⟨no English king had been more successful . . . in bringing British tribes under ~ —F.M.Stenton⟩ **2 a :** something given or contributed voluntarily as due or deserved **:** an offering, gift, a service rendered, or token manifesting respect, allegiance, gratitude, or affection ⟨floral ~*s* were placed at the community honor roll —*Springfield (Mass.) Union*⟩ ⟨a surprise cocktail party — a ~ they had paid to no other person —*Current Biog.*⟩ ⟨build a shrine and offer ~ —Agnes Repplier⟩ ⟨the work had been selected as a ~ in honor of the Coronation —*London Calling*⟩; *specif* **:** PRAISE, ENCOMIUM ⟨will receive so many ~*s* that it may seem unnecessary to add to the general paean —Harold Nicolson⟩ **b :** something usu. admirable or praiseworthy resulting from and attributable to something specified — usu. used in the phrase *a tribute to* ⟨this first semblance of law in the gold country is a ~ to the common sense of the majority —Julian Dana⟩ ⟨the sarcastic and bitter opposition must be taken as a ~ to the power of the art —Arnold Bennett⟩ **3 :** a proportion of the ore raised or of its value given to the miner or the owner of the land as his recompense in one system of payment

²tribute \"\ *vb* -ED/-ING/-S [ME *tributen*, fr. *tribut* tribute] *vt* **:** to pay as tribute ⟨deserve praise for the intention, and I ~ it the more willingly as it is the only praise I can give them —Bernhard Berenson⟩ ~ *vi* **:** to mine on the tribute system

tribute money *n* **:** money paid as tribute; *specif* **:** the annual tax of a didrachm or half shekel paid by each Jew for the support of the temple

trib·ut·er *or* **trib·u·tor** \|d-ə(r), |tə-\ *n* -s **:** one that mines on the tribute system

tri·butyl phosphate \(ˈ)trī+-\ *n* [*tributyl* fr. *tri-* + *butyl*] **:** a liquid inorganic ester $(C_4H_9)_3PO_4$ made from normal butyl alcohol and phosphorus oxychloride and used chiefly as a solvent and plasticizer (as for nitrocellulose lacquers and cellulose plastics)

tri·butyrin \"+\ *n* [ISV *tri-* + *butyrin*] **:** the bitter oily liquid triglyceride $C_3H_5(OOCC_3H_7)_3$ of butyric acid used as a plasticizer **:** glycerol tri-butyrate — called also *butyrin*

tri·calcium \(ˈ)trī+\ *also* **tri·calcic** \"+\ *adj* [*tricalcium* fr. NL, fr. *tri-* + *calcium*; *tricalcic* ISV *tri-* + *calcic*] **:** containing three atoms or equivalents of calcium in the molecule

tricalcium phosphate *n* **:** CALCIUM PHOSPHATE 1a(3)

tri·car \ˈtrīˌ=\ *n* [*tri-* + *car*] *Brit* **:** a 3-wheeled vehicle

tri·car·bal·lyl·ic acid \(ˌ)trīˌkärbəˈlilik-\ *n* [*tri-* + ISV *carballylic*, former name of tricarballylic acid, fr. *carb-* + *allyl* + *-ic*] **:** a crystalline tricarboxylic acid $C_3H_5(COOH)_3$ found in immature beets and obtainable from citric acid by dehydration followed by hydrogenation; 1,2,3,-propane-tricarboxylic acid

tri·carbocyanine \"+\ *or* **tricarbocyanine dye** *n* [*tri-* + *carbocyanine*] **:** any of a class of cyanine dyes in whose structure the two heterocyclic rings are joined by a seven-carbon chain (as =CH—CH=CH—CH=CH—CH=CH—); *esp* **:** any such dye containing two quinoline rings

tri·carboxylic \"+\ *adj* [*tri-* + *carboxylic*] **:** containing three carboxyl groups in the molecule

tricarboxylic acid cycle *n* **:** KREBS CYCLE

tri·carinate \(ˈ)trī+\ *adj* [*tri-* + *carinate*] **:** having three ridged keels

tri·carpellary \"+\ *also* **tri·carpellate** \"+\ *adj* [*tri-* + *carpellary* or *carpellate*] **:** having or made up of three usu. fused carpels

¹trice \ˈtrīs\ *vt* -ED/-ING/-S [ME *tricen*, *trisen*, fr. MD *trisen* to hoist by block and tackle, fr. *trise* windlass, capstan, pulley; akin to MLG *trītse* windlass, pulley] **1 :** to haul up or in and lash or secure with a small rope — usu. used with *up* ⟨prisoners are *triced* up by the wrists or hands —S.J.Barrows⟩ **2 :** to raise with or as if with a line — often used with *up* ⟨~ up a window shade⟩

²trice \"\ *n* -s [ME *trise*, fr. *trisen* to trice] **:** a brief space of time **:** INSTANT, MOMENT — used chiefly in the phrase *in a trice* ⟨in a ~ she was asleep —*Irish Digest*⟩

tri·ce·nar·i·um \ˌtrīsᵊnˈa(a)rēəm\ *n* -s [ML, fr. L, neut. of *tricenarius* of thirty] **:** TRENTAL

¹tri·ce·nary \ˈtrīsᵊnˌerē, ˈtris-; trīˈsenərē, -ˈsēn-\ *n* -ES [ML *tricenarium*] **:** TRENTAL

²tricenary \"\ *adj* [L *tricenarius* of thirty, fr. *triceni* tgirty each + *-arius* -ary; akin to L *triginta* thirty, Gk *triakonta*, Skt *trimśat* thirty, L *tres* three — more at THREE] **1 :** havinh or lasting 30 days ⟨a ~ month⟩ **2 :** based on the number 30 ⟨a ~ scale⟩

tri·cephalous \(ˈ)trī+\ *adj* [ISV *tri-* + *-cephalous*] **:** having or depicted with three heads

tri·ceps \ˈtrīˌseps\ *n*, *pl* **triceps·es** \-psəz\ *also* **triceps** [NL *tricipit-*, *triceps*, fr. L, three-headed, fr. *tri-* + *-cipit*, *-ceps* (fr. *capit-*, *caput* head) — more at HEAD] **:** a muscle that arises from three heads: **a :** the great extensor muscle situated along the back of the upper arm, arising by three heads, and inserted into the olecranon at the elbow **b :** the gastrocnemius and soleus muscles viewed as constituting together one muscle

tri·cer·a·tops \trīˈserəˌtäps\ *n* [NL, fr. *tri-* + *cerat-* + *-ops*] **1** *cap* **:** a genus of huge herbivorous ornithischian dinosaurs (suborder Ceratopsia) from the Cretaceous of Montana, Wyoming, and Colorado having a skull with two large horns above the eyes, a median horn on the nose, a horny beak, and a great bony hood or transverse crest over the neck, hoofed toes five in front and three behind, and a large strong tail **2** -ES **:** any animal or fossil of the genus *Triceratops*

tricerion *var of* TRIKERION

-trices *pl of* -TRIX

tricesimo-secundo *var of* TRIGESIMO-SECUNDO

trich- *or* **tricho-** *comb form* [NL, fr. Gk, *trich-*, *thrix* hair; akin to MIr *gairbdriuch* bristle, Lith *drīkti* to hang down in long threads, *driēkti* to stretch] **:** hair **:** filament ⟨*tricho*pathy⟩ ⟨*trich*atrophic⟩

-tri·cha \trəkə\ *n comb form*, *pl* **-tricha** [NL, fr. Gk *-trichos* -trichous] **:** one or ones having (such) ciliation — in names of taxa ⟨*Gastrotricha*⟩ ⟨*Oxytricha*⟩

tri·chal·cite \trīˈkalˌsīt\ *n* -s [G *trichalcit*, fr. *tri-* + *chalc-* + *-it* -ite] **:** a mineral $Cu_3(AsO_4)_2.5H_2O(?)$ that is a hydrous arsenate of copper

¹trich·ech·i·dae \trəˈkekəˌdē\ *n pl*, *cap* [NL, fr. *Trichechus*, type genus + *-idae*] **:** a family of aquatic mammals consisting of the manatees

²trichechidae \"\ [NL, fr. *Trichechus* + *-idae*] *syn of* ODOBENIDAE

¹trich·ech·odont \-kəˌdänt\ *adj* [NL *Trichechus* + E *-odont*] **:** having or being molar teeth with rows of tubercles confluent into transverse crests ⟨some sirenians, mastodons, and related animals have ~ molars⟩

²trichechodont \"\ *n* -s **:** a trichechodont mammal

trich·e·chus \ˈtrikəkəs, trəˈkekəs\ *n*, *cap* [NL, fr. *trich-* + Gk *echein* to have, hold — more at SCHEME] **:** a genus of mammals (family Trichechidae) comprising the manatees

-triches *pl of* -THRIX

trichi \ˈtrikē, -ki\ *n* -ES [by shortening] **:** TRICHINOPOLY

-tri·chi \trəˌkī\ *n pl comb form* [NL, fr. Gk *trich-*, *thrix* hair] **:** persons having (such) hair ⟨*leiotrichi*⟩

-trich·ia \ˈtrikēə\ *n comb form* -s [NL, fr. *trich-* + *-ia*] **1 :** condition of having (such) hair ⟨*oligotrichia*⟩ ⟨*hypotrichia*⟩ **2 :** hairiness ⟨*glossotrichia*⟩

tri·chi·a·sis \trəˈkīəsəs\ *n* -ES [LL, fr. Gk, fr. *trich-* + *-iasis*] **:** a turning inward of the eyelashes often causing irritation of the eyeball

-trichies *pl of* -TRICHY

tri·chil·ia \trīˈkilēə\ *n*, *cap* [NL, fr. Gk *tricheilos* three-lipped, fr. *tri-* three (akin to Gk *treis* three) + *cheilos* lip — more at THREE, GILL] **:** a genus of tropical African and American trees and shrubs (family Meliaceae) having odd-pinnate leaves and panicles of rather large flowers with four or five petals — see MAFURA

¹tri·chi·na \trəˈkīnə\ *n*, *pl* **trichi·nae** \-ˈī(ˌ)nē\ *also* **trichinas** [NL, fr. Gk *trichinos* of hair, fr. *trich-*, *thrix* hair + *-inos* -ine; akin to Lith *driēkti* to stretch — more at TRICH-] **1 :** a small slender nematode worm (*Trichinella spiralis*) that as an adult is a short-lived parasite of the intestines of a flesh-eating mammal (as man, rat, or hog) where it pairs and produces immense numbers of larvae which migrate to the muscles either directly or through the blood, establish themselves in or between the muscle fibers where they become encysted and may persist for years, and if consumed by a new host in raw or insufficiently cooked meat are liberated by the digestive processes and rapidly become adult to initiate a new parasitic cycle — see TRICHINOSIS **2 :** TRICHINOSIS — **tri·chi·nal** \-ˈnᵊl\ *adj*

²trichina \"\ [NL] *syn of* TRICHINELLA

trich·i·nat·ed \ˈtrikəˌnād.əd\ *adj* [NL *trichina* + E *-ate* + *-ed*] **:** parasitized by trichinae **:** TRICHINIZED

trich·i·nel·la \ˌtrikəˈnelə\ *n* [NL, fr. *trichina* + L *-ella*] **1** *cap* **:** a genus (coextensive with the family Trichinellidae of the order Enoplida) of nematode worms comprising the trichinae and being often isolated in a distinct superfamily **2** *pl* **trich·i·nel·lae** \-ˌe,lē, -lī\ **:** TRICHINA 1

trich·i·nel·li·a·sis \ˌtrikənəˈlīəsəs\ *n*, *pl* **trichinellia·ses** \-əˌsēz\ [NL, fr. *Trichinella* + *-iasis*] **:** TRICHINOSIS

trich·i·ni·a·sis \ˌ==ˈnīəsəs\ *n*, *pl* **trichinia·ses** \-əˌsēz\ [NL, fr. *trichina* + *-iasis*] **:** TRICHINOSIS

trich·i·niza·tion \ˌ==nəˈzāshən, -ˌnīˈz-\ *n* -s **:** the quality or state of being trichinized

trich·i·nize \ˈ==ˌnīz\ *vt* -ED/-ING/-S [NL *trichina* + E *-ize*] **:** to cause to become trichinous **:** affect with trichinae ⟨was estimated that at least 139 prisoners were *trichinized* —F.H. Hathaway⟩

¹trich·i·nop·o·ly \ˌ==ˈnäpəlē, -li\ *n* -ES [fr. *Trichinopoly*, city in southern India] **:** a cheroot made in India

²trichinopoly \"\ *adj*, *usu cap* [fr. *Trichinopoly*, India] **:** of or from the city of Trichinopoly, India **:** of the kind or style prevalent in Trichinopoly

tri·chi·no·scope \trəˈkīnəˌskōp\ *n* [ISV *trichina* + *-o-* + *-scope*] **:** a device for detecting larval trichinae in meat microscopically

trich·i·nosed \ˈtrikəˌnōst, -ōzd\ *adj* [NL *trichinosis* + E *-ed*] **:** TRICHINOUS

trich·i·no·sis \ˌ==ˈnōsəs\ *n*, *pl* **trichino·ses** \-ōˌsēz\ [NL, fr. *trichina* + *-osis*] **:** infestation with or disease caused by trichinae contracted by eating raw or undercooked infested food and esp. pork and marked initially by colicky pains, nausea, and diarrhea and later by muscular pain, dyspnea, fever, and edema

tri·chi·nous \ˈtrikənəs, trəˈkīn-\ *adj* ISV *trichin-* (fr. NL *trichina*) + *-ous*] **1 :** infested with trichinae ⟨~ meat⟩ **2 :** of, relating to, or involving trichinae or trichinosis ⟨~ infection⟩ ⟨~ manifestations⟩

trich·i·on \ˈtrikēˌän\ *n* -s [NL, fr. Gk, dim. of *trich-*, *thrix* hair — more at TRICH-] **:** the point where the normal hairline and middle line of the forehead intersect

trich·ite \ˈtriˌkīt\ *n* -s [in sense a, fr. G *trichit*, fr. *trich-* + *-it* -ite; in sense b, fr. NL *trichites*, fr. *trich-* + *-ites* -ite; in sense c, prob. fr. *trich-* + *-ite*] **:** a minute acicular body: as **a :** a hairlike crystallite occurring singly or in clusters **b :** a hairlike siliceous spicule occurring in some sponges in fascicles **c :** one of the slender rods supporting the cytopharynx of some ciliated protozoans

tri·chit·ic \trəˈkid.ik\ *adj* **:** containing, relating to, or having the characteristics of a trichite

trich·i·u·ri·dae \ˌtrikēˈyürəˌdē\ *n pl*, *cap* [NL, fr. *Trichiurus* type genus (fr. *trich-* + *-i-* + *-urus*) + *-idae*] **:** a family of deep-sea fishes including cutlass fishes and a few related forms and with the snake eels constituting a distinct suborder of Percomorphi

trichlor- *or* **trichloro-** *comb form* [ISV *tri-* + *chlor-*] **:** containing three atoms of chlorine — in names of chemical compounds ⟨*sym-trichloro*benzene⟩; compare CHLOR-

tri·chloride \(ˈ)trī+\ *n* [*trichlor-* + *-ide*] **:** a binary compound containing three atoms of chlorine combined with an element or radical

tri·chloroacetic acid \(ˌ)trī+-\ *also* **tri·chloracetic acid** \"+-\ *n* [ISV *trichlor-* + *acetic*] **:** a strong vesicant pungent deliquescent crystalline acid CCl_3COOH made usu. by chlorinating acetic acid or by oxidizing chloral and used in medicine as a caustic and astringent and esp. in the form of salts in weed control — abbr. *TCA*

tri·chlo·ro·ethane \(ˌ)trīˌklōr(ˌ)ō, -ō(ˌ)rō+\ *n* [*trichlor-* + *ethane*] **:** either of two nonflammable irritating liquid isomeric compounds $C_2H_3Cl_3$: **a :** the isomer CH_3CCl_3 that is made usu. by heating acetyl chloride with phosphorus pentachloride and is the parent compound of DDT and other insecticides — called also *1,1,1-trichloroethane* **b :** the isomer $CH_2ClCHCl_2$ that is made usu. by the action of chlorine on vinyl chloride or ethylene dichloride and is used chiefly as a solvent — called also *1,1,2-trichloroethane*

tri·chlo·ro·ethylene \"+\ *also* **tri·chlor·ethylene** \ˌtrīˌklōr+\ *n* [ISV *trichlor-* + *ethylene*] **:** a mobile nonflammable liquid $CHClCCl_2$ obtained usu. by heating symmetrical tetrachloroethane with hydrated lime and used chiefly as a solvent, a degreasing agent for metals, and in medicine as an inhalation analgesic and anesthetic

tri·chlo·ro·methane \(ˌ)trīˌklōr(ˌ)ō, -ō(ˌ)rō+\ *n* [ISV *trichlor-* + *methane*] **:** CHLOROFORM

tri·chlo·ro·nitrophenol \"+\ *n* [*trichlor-* + *nitrophenol*] **:** a pale yellow crystalline compound $O_2NC_6HCl_3OH$ derived from *ortho*-nitrophenol and used in streams for killing the sea lamprey — called also *3,4,6-trichloro-2-nitrophenol*

tri·chlo·ro·phenoxyacetic acid \"+-\ *n* [*trichlor-* + *phenoxy-* + *acetic*] **:** a crystalline irritating compound $Cl_3C_6H_2OCH_2COOH$ resembling dichlorophenoxyacetic acid, made from the corresponding trichloro-phenol and chloroacetic acid, and used chiefly in the form of esters as a weed killer esp. for woody plants — usu. used with initial numbers ⟨*2,4,5-trichlorophenoxyacetic acid*⟩; called also *2,4,5-T*

tri·chlo·ro·silane \"+\ *n* [*trichlor-* + *silane*] **:** a fuming flammable mobile liquid $SiHCl_3$ made usu. by heating silicon in hydrogen chloride and used in making organosilicon compounds — called also *silicochloroform*

tricho- — see TRICH-

trich·o·bacteria \ˌtrikō+\ *n pl* [NL, fr. *trich-* + *bacteria*] **1 :** filamentous bacteria **2 :** flagellated bacteria

tricho·bezoar \"+\ *n* [ISV *trich-* + *bezoar*] **:** HAIR BALL

tricho·bilharzia \"+\ *n*, *cap* [NL, fr. *trich-* + *Bilharzia*] **:** a genus of digenetic trematode worms (family Schistosomatidae) including forms that normally parasitize aquatic birds and are leading causers of swimmer's itch in man

trich·o·blast \ˈtrikəˌblast\ *n* [ISV *trich-* + *-blast*; orig. formed in G] **:** IDIOBLAST

trich·o·bothrium \ˌtrikə+\ *n*, *pl* **trichobothria** [NL, fr. *trich-* + *bothrium*] **:** a sensory hair on an arthropod or other invertebrate; *also* **:** a sensory organ consisting of one or more such hairs together with its supporting structures

trich·o·branchia \"+\ *n* [NL, fr. *trich-* + *-branchia*] **:** a gill of a decapod crustacean with filamentous branches arranged in series around an axis — **trich·o·branchiate** \"+\ *adj*

trich·o·ceph·a·li·a·sis \-ˌsefəˈlīəsəs\ *n*, *pl* **trichocephaliases** \-əˌsēz\ [NL, fr. *Trichocephalus* + *-iasis*] **:** TRICHURIASIS

trich·o·ceph·a·lus \ˈsefələs\ [NL, fr. *trich-* + *-cephalus*] *syn of* TRICHURIS

trich·o·ce·rat·i·dae \-ˌsəˈrad.əˌdē\ *n pl*, *cap* [NL, fr. *Trichocerat-*, *Trichoceras*, type genus (fr. *trich-* + *-cerat-*, *-ceras*) + *-idae*] **:** a small family of two-winged flies related to the Tipulidae and comprising the winter crane flies

trich·o·cer·cous \ˌ==ˈsərkəs\ *adj* [*trich-* + *cerc-* + *-ous*] *of a cercaria* **:** having a spiny tail

trich·o·cyst \ˈtrikəˌsist\ *n* [*trich-* + *-cyst*] **:** one of the minute projectile structures that release adhesive threads when discharged, are common in the ectoderm of protozoans, and are comparable to but less complex than nematocysts — **trich·o·cys·tic** \ˌ==ˈsistik\ *adj*

trichode \ˈtriˌkōd, -rīˌk-\ *n* -s [Gk *trichōdēs* like hair, fr. *trich-* + *-ōdēs* -ode] **:** TRICHOME

trich·o·dec·tes \ˌtrikəˈdekˌtēz\ *n*, *cap* [NL, fr. *trich-* + *-dectes*] **:** the type genus of Trichodectidae including various biting lice of domesticated mammals

trich·o·dec·ti·dae \-ktəˌdē\ *n pl*, *cap* [NL, fr. *Trichodectes*, type genus + *-idae*] **:** a widespread family of biting lice that have a single simple tarsal claw and include economically important parasites of mammals — see CAT LOUSE

trich·o·der·ma \ˌ==ˈdərmə\ *n*, *cap* [NL, fr. *trich-* + *-derma*] **:** a form genus of imperfect fungi (family Moniliaceae) having nonseptate conidia borne in heads on 2-branched or 3-branched conidiophores

trich·o·des·mi·um \-ˈdezmēəm\ *n*, *cap* [NL, fr. *trich-* + *desm-* + *-ium*] **:** a small genus of filamentous blue-green algae of the family Oscillatoriaceae — see SEA BLOOM

trich·odon·ti·dae \ˌ==ˈdäntəˌdē\ *n pl*, *cap* [NL, fr. *Trichodont-*, *Trichodon*, type genus (fr. *trich-* + *-odont-*, *-odon*) + *-idae*] **:** a family of elongate compressed scaleless large-eyed percoid fishes comprising the sandfishes

trich·o·gen \ˈtrikəjən\ *n* -s [ISV *trich-* + *-gen*; orig. formed in G] **:** a trichogenous cell

tri·chog·e·nous \trəˈkäjənəs\ *also* **trich·o·gen·ic** \ˌtrikəˈjenik\ *adj* [*trich-* + *-genous* or *-genic*] **:** producing hair; *esp* **:** being one of the hypodermal cells of insects and other arthropods that produce the chitinous hairs or spinules on the surface of the body and limbs

trich·o·gram·ma \ˌtrikəˈgramə\ *n, cap* [NL, fr. *trich-* + Gk *gramma* letter, small weight — more at GRAM] **:** a genus of minute hairy-winged chalcid flies that are parasitic as larvae in the eggs of other insects

trich·o·gyne \ˈtrikəˌjīn\ *n* -S [ISV *trich-* + *-gyne*] **:** a prolonged terminal receptive portion of a procarp or an archicarp — compare CARPOGONIUM — **trich·o·gyn·i·al** \ˌtrikəˈjinēəl\ *or* **trich·o·gyn·ic** \-nik\ *adj*

trich·oid \ˈtriˌkȯid\ *adj* [Gk *trichoeidēs*, fr. *trich-* + *-oeidēs* -oid] **:** HAIRLIKE, CAPILLARY

trich·o·lae·na \ˌtrikəˈlēnə\ *n, cap* [NL, fr. *trich-* + L *laena* cloak] **:** a genus of African grasses with one-flowered silky spikelets in small open panicles — see NATAL GRASS

tri·chol·o·gist \trəˈkäləjəst\ *n* -S **:** an expert in trichology

tri·chol·o·gy \-jē, -ji\ *n* -ES [ISV *trich-* + *-logy*] **:** scientific study of hair ⟨comparative ∼⟩

tri·cho·lo·ma \ˌtrikəˈlōmə\ *n, cap* [NL, fr. *trich-* + Gk *lōma* hem, fringe — more at LOMATINE] **:** a genus of white-spored agarics having a pileus with thin commonly sinuate lamellae and no volva or annulus and including both edible and inedible forms of various colors

tri·cho·ma \trəˈkōmə\ *n* -S [NL, fr. Gk *trichōma* growth of hair] **:** TRICHOME 1

tri·chom·a·nes \trəˈkäməˌnēz\ *n, cap* [NL, fr. L, a plant, fr. Gk, waterwort, fr. *trich-* + *-manes* (prob. fr. stem of *mainesthai* to rave, be mad about) — more at MIND] **:** a genus of chiefly tropical often epiphytic ferns (family Hymenophyllaceae) that have delicate usu. much-divided fronds with flattened sporangia within a transverse ring — see BRISTLE FERN

tri·cho·ma·to·sis \ˌtrəˌkōməˈtōsəs\ *n* -ES [NL, fr. *trichomat-*, *trichoma* + *-osis*] **:** PLICA 1

tri·chom·a·tous \trəˈkämədəs\ *adj* [ISV *trichomat-* (fr. NL *trichomat-*, *trichoma* trichome) + *-ous*] **:** bearing trichomes

tri·chome \ˈtriˌkōm, -rīˌk-\ *n* -S [G *trichom*, fr. Gk *trichōma* growth of hair, fr. *trichoun* to cover with hair, fr. *trich-*, *thrix* hair — more at TRICH-] **1 a :** an epidermal hair structure on a plant — compare EMERGENCE 3 **b :** a strand or chain of cells (as in a filamentous colony of bacteria or algae) **2 :** one of the tufts of brightly colored and often orange hairs on the bodies of myrmecophilous insects that releases an aromatic secretion attractive to ants; *also* **:** one of the constituent hairs — **tri·cho·mic** \trəˈkōmik\ *adj*

trich·o·mo·na·ci·dal \ˌtrikəˌmänəˈsīdᵊl, -ˌmōn-; trəˌkämənə-\ *adj* [*trichomonad* + *-cidal*] **:** tending or used to destroy trichomonads ⟨∼ action⟩ ⟨∼ agent⟩

trich·o·mo·nad \ˌtrikəˈmäˌnad, -ˈmōˌn-, -ˌnəd; trəˈkäməˌnad\ *n* -S [NL *Trichomonad-*, *Trichomonas*] **:** a flagellated protozoan of *Trichomonas* or a closely related genus

trich·o·mona·dal \ˌtrikəˈmänədᵊl, -ˈmōn-\ *or* **trich·o·mon·al** \ˌtrikəˈmänᵊl, -ˈmōn-; trəˈkämᵊnᵊl\ *adj* [*trichomonal* fr. *trichomonad* + *-al*] **:** of, relating to, or caused by trichomonads ⟨∼ vaginitis⟩

trich·o·mon·as \ˌtrikəˈmänəs, -ˈmōn-; trəˈkämənəs\ *n, cap* [NL, fr. *trich-* + *-monas*] **:** a genus (the type of the family Trichomonadidae) of polymastigote parasitic flagellated protozoans that have four anterior flagella and another at the margin of an undulating membrane or in some classifications also include forms with three or five anterior flagella and that are parasites of the alimentary or genitourinary systems of numerous vertebrate and invertebrate hosts including man — see TRICHOMONIASIS

trich·o·mo·ni·a·sis \ˌtrikəməˈnīəsəs, trəˌkäm-\ *n, pl* **trichomonia·ses** \-əˌsēz\ [NL, fr. *Trichomonas* + *-iasis*] **:** infection with or disease caused by trichomonads: as **a :** a human vaginitis characterized by a persistent discharge and caused by a trichomonad (*Trichomonas vaginalis*) that sometimes also invades the male urethra and bladder **b :** a venereal disease of domestic cattle marked by abortion, sterility, and pyometra and caused by a trichomonad (*T. foetus*) **c :** one or more diseases of various birds apparently caused by trichomonads (as *T. diversa* or *T. gallinorum*) and characterized by ulceration and necrosis of the upper digestive tract or by inflammatory changes of the ceca accompanied by severe diarrhea

trich·o·mycosis \ˌtrikə+\ *n* [NL, fr. *trich-* + *mycosis*] **:** a disease of the hair caused by fungi

trich·o·phyl·lous \-ˈfiləs\ *adj* [ISV *trich-* + *-phyllous*] **:** of, relating to, or having hairlike leaves or hairlike divisions of the leaf ⟨some xerophytes have the leaves reduced to ∼ processes⟩

trich·o·phyte \ˈtrikəˌfīt\ *n* -S [NL *Trichophyton*] **:** a fungus of the genus *Trichophyton*

tricho·phy·tia \ˌ══ˈfidēə\ *n* -S [NL, fr. *Trichophyton* + *-ia*] **:** TRICHOPHYTOSIS

trich·o·phy·tid \ˌtrikəˈfīdəd, trəˈkäfəd··\ *n* -S [ISV *trichophyte* + *-id*] **:** a skin eruption accompanying infection by trichophytes

trich·o·phy·ton \ˌtrikəˈfīˌtän, trəˈkäfəˌt-\ *n* [NL, fr. *trich-* + Gk *phyton* plant — more at PHYT-] **1** *cap* **:** a genus of ringworm fungi (family Moniliaceae) having hyaline single-celled spores and being parasitic in the skin and hair follicles of man and lower mammals — compare EPIDERMOPHYTON **2** *pl* **trichophy·ta** \-ədə\ *also* **trichophytons :** any fungus of the genus *Trichophyton*

trich·o·phyt·o·sis \ˌtrikəˌfīdˈōsəs, trəˌkäfəˈtō-\ *n* -ES [NL, fr. *Trichophyton* + *-osis*] **:** disease of the skin, nails, or hair caused by fungi of the genus *Trichophyton*

tricho·plax \ˈtrikəˌplaks\ *n, cap* [NL, fr. *trich-* + Gk *plax* flat surface — more at PLEASE] **:** a genus of minute marine animals that are sometimes classed among the Mesozoa but are prob. larval hydrozoans and that have a completely ciliated discoid body composed of three layers of cells but not otherwise differentiated

tricho·pore \-ˌpō(ə)r, -ō(ə)r, -ōə, -ō(ə)\ *n* [*trich-* + *-pore*] **:** a pore in the cuticle of an insect through which a sensory hair or bristle protrudes

tri·chop·ter \trəˈkäptə(r)\ *n* -S [NL *Trichoptera*] **:** CADDIS FLY

tri·chop·tera \-tərə\ *n pl, cap* [NL, fr. *trich-* + *-ptera*] **:** an order of insects consisting of the caddis flies and formerly treated as a suborder of Neuroptera — **tri·chop·ter·an** \-rən\ *adj or n* — **tri·chop·ter·ous** \-rəs\ *adj*

tri·chop·ter·on \-əˌrän\ *n, pl* **trichop·tera** \-ərə\ [NL, sing. of *Trichoptera*] **:** one of the Trichoptera

tri·chop·ter·yg·i·dae \═ˌ══ˈrijəˌdē\ *n pl, cap* [NL, fr. *Trichopteryg-*, *Trichopteryx*, type genus (fr. *trich-* + *-pteryx*) + *-idae*] **:** a family of clavicorn beetles having 3-jointed tarsi and the wings fringed with long hairs and including the smallest beetles known

tri·chord \(ˈ)trīˌkȯrd, -ō(ə)d\ *adj* [Gk *trichordos* three-stringed, fr. *tri-* three + *-chordos* stringed, fr. *chordē* string — more at TRI-, YARN] **:** of, relating to, or being a piano having three strings tuned in unison to each digital throughout most of its compass

trich·o·san·thes \ˌtrikəˈsanˌthēz\ *n, cap* [NL, irreg. fr. *trich-* + *-anthes*; fr. the fringed corolla lobes] **:** a large genus of Asiatic and Australian herbs (family Cucurbitaceae) having entire or lobed leaves and white flowers succeeded by fleshy fruits of various forms — see SNAKE GOURD

trich·o·sclereid \ˌ══+\ *n* [*trich-* + *sclereid*] **:** a long slender hairlike sclereid — compare BRACHYSCLEREID

tri·cho·sis \trəˈkōsəs\ *n, pl* **tricho·ses** \-ōˌsēz\ [NL, fr. Gk *trichōsis* growth of hair, fr. *trichoun* to cover with hair, fr. *trich-*, *thrix* hair — more at TRICH-] **:** a heavy growth of hair **:** HAIRINESS

trich·o·spo·ron \ˌtrikəˈspōrˌän, trəˈkäspəˌrän\ *n, cap* [NL, fr. *trich-* + *spora* seed, spore — more at SPORE] **:** a genus of parasitic imperfect fungi (order Moniliales) some of which are reputed skin or hair parasites of man

trich·o·spo·rum \ˌtrikəˈspōrəm, trəˈkäspərəm\ [NL, fr. *trich-* + *spora* seed] *syn of* AESCHYNANTHUS

tricho·stasis \ˌtrikəˈstāsəs, -ˈstas-; trəˈkästəsəs\ *n* -ES [NL, fr. *trich-* + *-stasis*] **:** persistence commonly with excessive development of the lanugo of a fetus

trich·o·ste·ma \ˌtrikəˈstēmə, trəˈkästəmə\ *n, cap* [NL, fr. *trich-* + Gk *stēma* stamen, fr. *stēmōn* thread — more at STAMEN] **:** a genus of No. American herbs or undershrubs (family Labiatae) having axillary whorls of small blue flowers with four exserted stamens and a deeply lobed ovary — see BLACK SAGE, BLUE CURLS

trich·o·stron·gyle \ˌtrikəˈstränˌjīl\ *n* -S [NL *Trichostrongylus*] **:** a worm of the genus *Trichostrongylus*

¹trich·o·stron·gy·lid \ˌ══ˈstränjələd\ *adj* [NL *Trichostrongylidae*] **:** of or relating to the Trichostrongylidae

²trichostrongylid \"\ *n* -S **:** a nematode worm of the family Trichostrongylidae

trich·o·stron·gyl·i·dae \ˌ══ˌstränˈjiləˌdē\ *n pl, cap* [NL, fr. *Trichostrongylus*, type genus + *-idae*] **:** a family of nematode worms (suborder Strongylina) that have a reduced buccal capsule with three or fewer basal teeth and parasitize the alimentary tract of vertebrates — see HYOSTRONGYLUS, TRICHOSTRONGYLUS

trich·o·stron·gy·lo·sis \ˌ══ˌ═jəˈlōsəs\ *n* -ES [NL *Trichostrongylus* + *-osis*] **:** infestation with or disease caused by roundworms of the genus *Trichostrongylus* chiefly in young sheep and cattle where it is commonly marked by diarrhea, inappetence, and loss of condition — compare BLACK SCOUR

trich·o·strongylus \ˌ══+\ *n, cap* [NL, fr. *trich-* + *Strongylus*] **:** a genus (the type of the family Trichostrongylidae) containing nematode worms that are parasites of birds and of mammals including man and comprising forms formerly placed in the genus *Strongylus* — see BLACK SCOUR WORM

trich·o·su·rus \ˌtrikəˈs(y)u̇rəs\ *n, cap* [NL, fr. Gk *trichōsis* growth of hair + NL *-urus* — more at TRICHOSIS] **:** a genus of marsupials comprising the common Australian opossums from which the opossum fur of commerce is obtained

trich·o·thal·lic \ˌ══ˈthalik\ *adj* [*trich-* + *thall-* + *-ic*] **:** having a filamentous thallus or one ending in hairs or hairlike branches — used esp. of an alga that grows by the action of an intercalary meristem

trich·o·the·ci·um \ˌ══ˈthēsh(ē)əm\ *n, cap* [NL, fr. *trich-* + *-thecium*] **:** a genus of imperfect fungi (family Moniliaceae) having erect unbranched septate conidiophores and 2-celled hyaline or bright-colored spores — see PINK ROT

trich·o·til·lo·ma·nia \ˌ══ˌtiləˈmānēə\ *n* [NL, fr. *trich-* + Gk *tillein* to pull, pluck + *mania*] **:** abnormal desire to pull out one's hair — **trich·o·til·lo·man·ic** \ˌ══ˌ══ˈmanik\ *adj*

trich·o·tom·ic \ˌ══ˈtämik\ *adj* [ISV *trichotomy* + *-ic*] **:** belonging to, characterized by, or based upon a trichotomy **:** TRICHOTOMOUS

tri·chot·o·mize \trīˈkädəˌmīz\ *vt* -ED/-ING/-S [*trichotomy* + *-ize*] **:** to make a trichotomy of

tri·chot·o·mous \-əməs\ *adj* [*trichotomy* + *-ous*] **:** divided or dividing into three parts or into threes **:** three-forked **:** THREEFOLD ⟨∼ branching⟩ — **tri·chot·o·mous·ly** *adv*

tri·chot·o·my \-ˌmē\ *n* -ES [prob. fr. (assumed) NL *trichotomia*, fr. Gk *trichotomein* to trisect (fr. *tricha* threefold — akin to Gk *treis* three — + *temnein* to cut) + L *-ia* -y — more at THREE, TOME] **1 :** a dividing into three parts, elements, or classes ⟨the ∼ of speech-sciences into phonetics, phonemics, and historical phonetics —R.S.Wells⟩ — compare POLYTOMY **2 :** a system divided or divisible into three constituents or elements ⟨to speak of man as a ∼, . . . having a division into three parts —Gottfried de Purucker⟩

-tri·chous \trəkəs\ *adj comb form* [Gk *-trichos*, fr. *trich-*, *thrix* hair — more at TRICH-] **:** having (such) hair **:** haired ⟨peri*trichous*⟩

tri·chro·ic \(ˈ)trīˌkrōik\ *adj* [Gk *trichroos* three-colored (fr. *tri-* three + *-chroos* -chroous) + E *-ic* — more at TRI-] **:** exhibiting trichroism

tri·chro·ism \ˈtrīˌkrōˌizəm\ *n* -S [ISV *trichro-* (fr. Gk *trichroos* three-colored) + *-ism*] **1 :** pleochroism in which the colors are unlike when a crystal is viewed in the direction of three different axes **2 :** polychromasia with three colors occurring in different individuals of a group or in different parts of one individual

tri·chro·mat \ˈtrīkrōˌmat\ *n* -S [back-formation fr. *trichromatic*] **:** one that requires that three primary colors be mixed in order to match the spectrum as he sees it **:** one having normal or nearly normal color vision — compare DICHROMAT, MONOCHROMAT; DEUTERANOMALY, PROTANOMALY

tri·chromatic \ˌtrī+\ *adj* [*tri-* + *chromatic*] **1 a :** of, relating to, consisting of, or employing three colors **b :** relating to, done by, or constituting three-color photography — compare PROCESS PRINTING **2 a :** relating to or exhibiting trichromatism **b :** characteristic of a trichromat

tri·chro·ma·tism \trīˈkrōməˌtizəm\ *n* [*trichromatic* + *-ism*] **1 :** the quality or state of being trichromatic **:** the use of three colors (as in photography) **2** *also* **tri·chro·ma·cy** \-əsē\ -ES **:** vision in which all of the fundamental colors are perceived though not necessarily with equal facility — compare DICHROMATISM, MONOCHROMATISM

tri·chrome \(ˈ)trīˌkrōm\ *adj* [ISV *tri-* + *-chrome*] **:** TRICHROMATIC: as **a :** of or relating to apparatus for printing three colors ⟨a ∼ typewriter⟩ **b :** coloring tissue elements differentially in three colors ⟨a ∼ biological stain⟩

tri·chromic \"+\ *adj* [*tri-* + *chromic*] **:** TRICHROMATIC

tri·chro·nous \ˈtrikrənəs\ *adj* [Gk *trichronos*, fr. *tri-* three + *-chronos* -chronous — more at TRI-] **:** TRISEMIC

trich·u·ra·ta \ˌtrikyəˈrādə, -rād-\ *n pl* [NL, fr. *Trichuris* + *-ata*] *syn of* DORYLAIMINA

trich·u·ri·a·sis \ˌ══ˈrīəsəs\ *n, pl* **trichuria·ses** \-əˌsēz\ [NL, fr. *Trichuris* + *-iasis*] **:** infestation with or disease caused by nematode worms of the genus *Trichuris*

¹trich·u·rid \trəˈkyu̇rəd\ *adj* [NL *Trichuridae*] **:** of or relating to the Trichuridae

²trichurid \"\ *n* -S **:** a nematode worm of the family Trichuridae

trich·u·ri·dae \trəˈkyu̇rəˌdē\ *n pl, cap* [NL, fr. *Trichurus* + *-idae*] **:** a family of nematode worms (order Enoplida) that are parasitic in the intestines of vertebrates and have a slender body sometimes with a thickened posterior end and a tubular capillary esophagus — see CAPILLARIA, TRICHURUS

trich·u·ris \-rəs\ *n, cap* [NL, fr. *trich-* + *-uris* (fr. Gk *oura* tail); fr. the lashlike anterior part that is often mistaken for a tail] **:** a genus (the type of the family Trichuridae) of nematode worms comprising the whipworms

trichy \ˈtrikē, -ki\ *n* -ES [alter. of *trichi*] **:** TRICHINOPOLY

-tri·chy \trəkē, -ki\ *n comb form* -ES [NL *-trichia*] **:** the condition of having (such) hair ⟨lisso*trichy*⟩

tricing *pres part of* TRICE

tri·cin·i·um \trīˈsinēəm\ *n* -S [LL, song by three voices, trio, fr. *tri-* + *-cinium* (fr. *canere* to sing) — more at CHANT] **:** a 16th century 3-part vocal composition

tri·cip·i·tal \(ˈ)trīˌsipədᵊl, -ətᵊl\ *adj* [NL *tricipit-*, *triceps* + E *-al* — more at TRICEPS] **1** *of a muscle* **:** having three heads **2 :** of, relating to, or being a triceps muscle ⟨the ∼ pull on the humerus⟩

tri-city \ˈ═ˌ══\ *n* **:** a group of three adjacent and usu. economically interacting cities; *also* **:** one of the cities of such a group

¹trick \ˈtrik\ *n* -S [ME *trik*, fr. ONF *trique*, fr. *trikier* to trick, cheat, deceive] **1 a :** a mean crafty procedure or practice **:** an artifice or stratagem designed to deceive, delude, or defraud ⟨scrupled at no ∼ however unfair that would get her her own way⟩ **b :** a mischievous or roguish act **:** a piece of tomfoolery (as a prank or practical joke) ⟨playing harmless ∼*s* on one another⟩ **c :** an unwise, indiscreet, or childish action **:** a stupid procedure ⟨it's a fool's ∼ to trust a stranger too far⟩ **d :** a deceptive, dexterous, or ingenious feat or procedure designed to puzzle or amuse ⟨a juggler's ∼*s*⟩ ⟨learned to do card ∼*s*⟩ ⟨taught his dog several ∼*s*⟩ **2 a** *archaic* **:** a small article (as a toy, trifle, or knickknack) **b tricks** *pl* **:** the small miscellaneous articles that supplement an arrangement ⟨the ∼*s* and bits that give a room personality⟩; *also* **:** PERSONAL EFFECTS, TRAPS ⟨left his ∼*s* at the camp⟩ **c** *dial* **:** an amulet or charm against misfortune **3 a :** an habitual peculiarity of behavior or manner **:** HABIT, CUSTOM ⟨a horse with the ∼ of shying at dead leaves⟩ ⟨a small stream that had the unfortunate ∼ of overflowing every spring⟩ ⟨had a ∼ of appearing to drowse while he listened⟩ **b :** a characteristic and identifying feature (as of fashion or expression) ⟨a ∼ of speech⟩ ⟨the ∼ of that voice, I do well remember —Shak.⟩ **c :** a delusive appearance esp. when caused by art or legerdemain **:** an optical illusion ⟨a mere ∼ of vision⟩; *also* **:** something causing such an effect ⟨some ∼ of lighting made her appear gaunt and haggard⟩ **4 :** a rough or preliminary outline sketch of a heraldic representation **5 :** KNACK: as **a :** a quick or effective way of getting a result or attaining an end ⟨knows the ∼ to make my lady laugh —Shak.⟩ **b** (1) **:** an artful or artificial expedient or contrivance **:** a technical device or formality (as of an art or craft) ⟨the ∼*s* of stage technique⟩ ⟨the ∼ of depicting perspective on a flat surface⟩ (2) **tricks** *pl* **:** the special skills and deft laborsaving methods that characterize an expert ⟨learning the ∼*s* of the trade⟩ **c** (1) **:** an act involving or requiring skillful dexterity or ingenuity ⟨the ∼ is to make everything appear natural⟩ (2) **:** a precise, skillful, and usu. rapid effecting of an aim or result often by the use of a substitute or an alternate means ⟨shaving a bit from the edge will do the ∼ and make the door fit⟩ **6 a :** the cards played in one round of a card game **b :** a scoring unit in a card game: as (1) **:** one consisting of the cards won in one round of play (2) **:** ODD TRICK (3) **:** HONOR TRICK **c :** a card as a potential score winner ⟨an ace of trumps is a sure ∼ in bridge⟩ **7 :** a continuous stretch of some activity: as **a :** a sailor's turn of duty at the helm usu. lasting for two hours **b :** SHIFT 2b(2) **c :** a trip taken as part of one's employment ⟨returned from a long ∼ in the rural areas⟩ **d** *slang* **:** a professional engagement of a prostitute **8 a :** a small creature (as a pony): as (1) **:** CHILD (2) **:** a neat trim pretty young woman ⟨the cutest ∼ you ever want to see⟩ **b** *slang* **:** the customer of a prostitute **9 :** a cut in a needlebar of a knitting machine to receive a needle

syn RUSE, STRATAGEM, MANEUVER, ARTIFICE, WILE, FEINT, DODGE: TRICK may indicate cheating or fraud, clever device or contrivance that pleases, deludes, or surprises, or a playful prank or practical joke ⟨such *tricks* as the substitution of goat's milk for cow's milk —Claire Sterling⟩ ⟨*tricks* and devices to conceal evasions and violations of ethical principles —H.A. Wagner⟩ ⟨a competent and resourceful musician who always knew what he was doing, was familiar with the *tricks* of the trade —P.H.Lang⟩ ⟨the *trick* is always to tag the other fellow as Red —T.H.White b. 1915⟩ ⟨ringing doorbells and extracting treats under threat of *tricks* has made Halloween a profitable grab bag for most kids —*Springfield (Mass.) Union*⟩ RUSE may imply an intention at false impression, as to divert attention from the truth or from what one intends ⟨used the old *ruse* of oxen dragging trees to create a dust that would give the English the impression of a large force moving —Stuart Cloete⟩ ⟨threw his cap and a large stone into the river and this *ruse* succeeded in convincing his pursuers that he was drowned —S.P.B.Mais⟩ STRATAGEM may apply to a single ruse that outwits or entraps; it is applicable to a more or less carefully laid plan involving deception ⟨driven to every possible trick and *stratagem* to entrap some man into marriage —G.B.Shaw⟩ ⟨a dazzling sea-fighter who by downright courage, *stratagem* and audacity succeeded in frightening the British people —C.B Palmer b. 1910⟩ MANEUVER may suggest an instance of tactics or manipulation, often adroit and astute ⟨the last of all the company to depart, and, by a *maneuver* of Mrs. Bennet, had to wait for their carriage a quarter of an hour —Jane Austen⟩ ⟨thanks to Italy's mysterious *maneuvers* by way of keeping valuable information well hidden —Claudia Cassidy⟩ ARTIFICE may suggest ingenious contrivance or invention, with or without deception ⟨the *artifices* by which friends endeavor to spare one another's feelings —G.B.Shaw⟩ ⟨the forthright story of a man's life told in a style of transparent clarity that needs no *artifices* to make it vivid —C.H.Driver⟩ WILE may imply an attempt to ensnare or beguile by deceptive allurement ⟨were I to lure him here with cunning *wile* —W.S.Gilbert & A.S. Sullivan⟩ FEINT indicates a diversion or distraction of attention away from one's genuine intent ⟨tricked the enemy commander by a *feint* off Tinian Town and sent Marines ashore at the opposite end of the island —*Current Biog.*⟩ DODGE refers to any artful expedient ⟨largely disfranchised by various police measures and legislative *dodges* which prevent his getting to the polls —W.L.Sperry⟩ ⟨a special *dodge* to get electric light for his father's house without paying for it —J.B.S.Haldane⟩

²trick \"\ *adj* **1 :** of or relating to or involving tricks or trickery ⟨∼ photography⟩ **:** skilled in or used for tricks ⟨∼ dice⟩ ⟨a ∼ horse⟩ **2 :** conspicuously smart, attractive, effective, or able; *esp* **:** trickily or intriguingly fashioned or devised **3 a :** somewhat defective and inclined to function abnormally on occasion ⟨a ∼ lock that doesn't always catch⟩ **b** *of a bodily joint* **:** inclined to lock or give way unexpectedly ⟨a ∼ knee resulting from a football injury⟩

³trick \"\ *vb* -ED/-ING/-S *vt* **1 :** to deceive by cunning or artifice **:** impose on, defraud, or cheat usu. by specious means **:** affect or induce by deceit or trickery ⟨∼ another in a sale⟩ ⟨∼ him into consent⟩ **2 :** to obtain or bring about by trickery ⟨advertising designed to ∼ your purse⟩ **3 a :** to dress or adorn esp. fancifully or ornately **:** ORNAMENT, DECORATE ⟨a request ∼*ed* with expressions of devotion⟩ — usu. used with *up*, *out*, *off* ⟨∼*ed* out in a gaudy lodge uniform⟩ ⟨planned to ∼ ourselves up for the party⟩ **b :** to put in order **:** ARRANGE, PREEN ⟨horses with manes and tails ∼*ed* and beribboned⟩ **4 :** to draw in outline (as with a pen); *specif* **:** to delineate (as a coat of arms) by outline sketches in which the tinctures are indicated by abbreviations and the repetition of a charge by numbers ∼ *vi* **1 :** to practice trickery or fraud **2 :** to practice or play tricks or pranks **:** TRIFLE — usu. used with *with* **syn** see DUPE

¹trick·er \-kə(r)\ *n* -S **:** one that tricks **:** TRICKSTER

²tricker \"\ *dial var of* TRIGGER

trick·ery \-k(ə)rē, -ri\ *n* -ES **1 :** deception by tricks and stratagems **:** the practice of crafty underhand ingenuity to deceive or cheat ⟨swindled by the sharper's ∼⟩ **2 :** tricks used or intended to deceive or harm **syn** see DECEPTION

trickier *comparative of* TRICKY

trickiest *superlative of* TRICKY

trick·i·ly \ˈtrikəlē, -li\ *adv* **:** in a tricky manner

trick·i·ness \-kēnəs, -kin-\ *n* -ES **:** the quality or state of being tricky

tricking *pres part of* TRICK

trick·ing·ly *adv* **:** in a tricking manner **:** so as to cheat or deceive **:** ARTFULLY

trick·ish \ˈtrikish\ *adj* **:** given to or characterized by tricks or trickery **:** somewhat tricky — **trick·ish·ly** \-kəshlē\ *adv* — **trick·ish·ness** \-kishnəs\ *n* -ES

¹trick·le \ˈtrikəl\ *vb* **trickled; trickled; trickling** \-k(ə)liŋ\ **trickles** [ME *triklen*] *vi* **1 a :** to run or fall in drops **:** flow in a thin gentle stream ⟨water *trickled* down the walls⟩ ⟨tears *trickling* from her eyes⟩ **b :** to drip with some liquid **:** emit a liquid in fine streams or drops ⟨onions made her eyes ∼⟩ **2 a :** to move (as in going or departing) one by one ⟨summer visitors are now *trickling* home⟩ ⟨his audience *trickled* out⟩ **b :** to dissipate slowly ⟨his enthusiasm *trickled* away⟩ ∼ *vt* **1 :** to pour forth or cause to flow in drops or in a thin stream **2 :** to let pass or go one by one

²trickle \"\ *n* -S **:** something that trickles or seems to trickle **:** a thin slow stream **:** DRIP ⟨a mere ∼ of water left in the river⟩

trickle charge *n* **:** a slow continuous charge for an electric storage battery

trickle charger *n* **:** a device for providing a storage battery with a trickle charge

trick·less \ˈ═ˌləs\ *adj* **:** free from tricks or trickery **:** having no trick

trick·let \-lət\ *n* -S [²*trickle* + *-et*] **:** a thin stream **:** RILL

trickling filter *n* **:** an artificial bed of broken rock or other coarse material through which sewage or industrial wastes trickle after being sprayed on intermittently so that organic matter present is oxidized and removed by biological growths formed on the surfaces of the rock

trick·ling·ly *adv* **:** in a trickling manner

trick·ly \ˈtrik(ə)lē\ *adj* -ER/-EST [¹*trickle* + *-y*] **:** marked by trickling

trick or treat *n* **:** a Halloween pastime in which children go from door to door asking for goodies supposedly with the idea of playing tricks on people who do not comply; *also* **:** the spoils so won

trick-or-treat \ˌ══ˈ═\ *vi* [*trick or treat*] **:** to engage in trick or treat — **trick-or-treater** \ˌ══ˈ══\ *n*

trick-o-the-loop \ˌ══ˈ═\ *n, Irish* **:** STRAP GAME

trick points *n pl* **:** TRICK SCORE 1

tricks *pl of* TRICK, *pres 3d sing of* TRICK

trick score *n* **1 :** a bridge score for odd tricks won or in contract bridge bid and won by the declarer's side **2 :** the section of a bridge score sheet reserved for recording the trick score

tricks·i·ness \ˈtriksēnəs, -sin-\ *n* -ES **:** the quality or state of being tricksy

trick·some \-səm\ *adj* **:** full of tricks **:** addicted to playing tricks **:** TRICKSY

trick·ster \-stə(r)\ *n* -S [¹*trick* + *-ster*] **:** one that tricks: as **a :** a dishonest person who defrauds others by trickery **:** a confidence man **b :** a person (as a stage magician) skilled in

the use of tricks and illusion **c :** a mischievous supernatural being found in the folklore of various primitive peoples, often functioning as a culture hero, and much given to capricious acts of sly deception

trick·ster·ing \-əriŋ, -rēŋ\ *n* -s **:** the acts or practices of a trickster

tricksy \'triksē, -si\ *adj* -ER/-EST [*tricks* (pl. of ¹*trick*) + -*y*] **1** *archaic* **:** tricked out **:** artfully embellished; *esp* **:** smartly attired ⟨the ~ pomp of fairy pride —J.R.Drake⟩ **2 :** full of tricks or pranks **:** given to roguish mischief **:** PRANKISH ⟨~ sprites of woods and fields⟩ **3 a** *archaic* **:** having or manifesting the cunning or craftiness of a trickster **:** UNCERTAIN, EVASIVE, DECEIVING, DECEPTIVE **b :** difficult to cope with or handle **:** TRYING ⟨a ~ job⟩

trick valve *n* **:** a slide valve (as of a steam engine) having a supplementary steam passage connecting the forward and back parts of its face and thus reducing the valve travel

trick work *n* **:** work involving a trick or knack or the use of tricks and esp. artificial devices; *specif* **:** literary or artistic work characterized solely by technical dexterity

tricky \'trikē, -ki\ *adj* -ER/-EST [¹*trick* + -*y*] **1 :** of or characteristic of a trickster **:** given to or manifesting trickery ⟨a ~ diplomat⟩ ⟨this ~ policy⟩ **2 a :** deceptively safe, easy, manageable, or orderly **:** TICKLISH ⟨a ~ situation⟩ ⟨a ~ passage in the final movement⟩ **b :** manifesting or requiring skill or aptitude in doing, making, or handling **:** INTRICATE ⟨a ~ set of controls⟩; *broadly* **:** INGENIOUS ⟨~ gadgets⟩ ⟨~ rhymes⟩ **3 :** TRICK 3 **syn** see SLY

¹**tri·clad** \'trī,klad\ *adj* [NL *Tricladida*] **:** of or relating to the Tricladida

²**triclad** \"\ *n* -s **:** a turbellarian worm of the order Tricladida **:** PLANARIAN

tri·clad·i·da \='kladədə\ *n pl, cap* [NL, fr. *tri-* + *clad-* + *-ida*] **:** an order of Turbellaria comprising chiefly free-living flatworms with the intestine composed of a median anterior division and two lateral posterior divisions with side branches and including marine, freshwater, and terrestrial forms — see PLANARIAN

tricli·nate \(')trī¦klīnət, 'triklə,nāt\ *adj* [*tri-* + L *clinatus*, past part. of *clinare* to bend — more at LEAN] **:** TRICLINIC

tri·clin·ic \(')trī¦klinik\ *adj* [ISV *tri-* + *-clinic*] **:** having or characterized by three unequal axes intersecting at oblique angles — used esp. of a crystal

triclinic system *n* **:** a crystal system characterized by three unequal axes intersecting at oblique angles — see CRYSTAL SYSTEM illustration

tri·clin·i·um \trī'klinēəm\ *n, pl* **triclin·ia** \-ēə\ [L, fr. Gk *triklinion*, fr. *tri-* three + *klinion*, dim. of *klinē* couch — more at TRI-, CLIN-] **1 :** a couch used by ancient Romans for reclining at meals, extending round three sides of a table, and usu. divided into three parts **2 :** a dining room furnished with a triclinium

tri·cli·no·he·dric \(')trī¦klīnō¦hēdrik, -hed-\ *adj* [ISV *tri-* + *clin-* + *hedr-* (fr. Gk *hedra* seat) + *-ic* — more at SIT] **:** TRICLINIC

tric·o·lette \¦trikə¦let, *usu* -ed·+V\ *n* -s [*tricot* + *-lette* (as in *flannelette*)] **:** a usu. silk or rayon knitted fabric used esp. for women's clothing

tri·colon \(')trī+\ *n* [Gk *trikōlon*, neut. of *trikōlos* 3-limbed, fr. *tri-* three + *kōlon* limb, part of a strophe — more at TRI-, CALK] **:** a period in classical prosody composed of three cola

¹**tri·col·or** \'trī,kələ(r)\ *sometimes* 'tre,k-, *chiefly Brit* 'tri,k-\ *n* [F *tricolore*, fr. *tricolore*, adj., three-colored, fr. LL *tricolor*, fr. L *tri-* + *color* — more at COLOR] **:** a flag of three colors ⟨the French ~⟩

²**tricolor** \"\ *adj* [F *tricolore* three-colored] **1 a** *or* **tri·col·ored** \'trī,kələ(r)d\ [*tricolored* fr. F *tricolore*, adj. + E *-ed*] **:** having three colors **:** marked with or employing three colors ⟨~ plumage⟩ ⟨a ~ process in photography⟩ **b** *of a dog* **:** having a coat of black, tan, and white **2 :** of, relating to, or characteristic of a tricolor or a nation whose flag is a tricolor; *often* **:** FRENCH ⟨the intricacies of ~ politics⟩

tri·conch \'trī,käŋk *also* -kȯŋk\ *adj* [Gk *trikonchos*, fr. *tri-* three + *konchē* conch, apse — more at TRI-, CONCH] **:** having apses on three sides of a square central mass ⟨many Syrian churches are built on a ~ plan⟩

tri·con·odon \trī'känə,dän\ *n* [NL, fr. *tri-* + *con-* + *-odon*] **1** *cap* **:** a genus of small generalized Jurassic mammals that have teeth with three simple cones and are associated with Marsupialia or Multituberculata or more usu. placed with a few related forms in the order Triconodonta **2** -s **:** any mammal or fossil of the genus *Triconodon* — **tri·con·odon·tine** \¦=;==¦dän·,tīn, -n·,tēn, -ntᵊn\ *n* -s

¹**tri·con·odont** \'trī'känə,dänt\ *adj* [NL *Triconodont-, Triconodon*] **1 :** having or being teeth with three simple cones — compare TRITUBERCULY **2** [NL *Triconodonta*] **:** of or relating to the Triconodonta

²**triconodont** \"\ *n* -s [NL *Triconodonta*] **:** a triconodont mammal

tri·con·odon·ta \(,)=,==¦däntə\ *n pl, cap* [NL *Triconodont-, Triconodon*] **:** an order of Jurassic primitive mammals that are of uncertain relationships and prob. not on the direct ancestral line of higher mammals — see TRICONODON

tri·consonantal \(')trī +\ *adj* [*tri-* + *consonantal*] **:** containing or consisting of three consonants

¹**tri·corn** \'trī,kȯrn\ *n* -s [L *tricornis* 3-horned, fr. *tri-* + *-cornis* -horned (fr. *cornu* horn) — more at HORN] **1 :** an imaginary 3-horned beast **2** *usu* **tri·corne** \"\ [*tricorne* fr. F, fr. *tricorne*, adj., having three corners] **:** COCKED HAT 1a **3 :** a lateral cerebral ventricle

²**tricorn** *also* **tricorne** \"\ *adj* [*tricorn* fr. L *tricornis*; *tricorne* fr. F, fr. L *tricornis*] **:** having three horns or corners

tri·cornered \(')trī+\ *adj* [*tri-* + *cornered*] **:** THREE-CORNERED, TRICORN

tri·cornute \(¦)=+\ *adj* [*tri-* + *cornute*] **:** having three horns or horn-shaped processes

tri·corporal \(')trī+\ *or* **tri·corporate** \"+\ *or* **tri·corpo·rated** \"+\ *adj* [L *tricorpor* (fr. *tri-* + *corpor-*, *corpus* body) + E *-al* or *-ate* or *-ate* + *-ed* — more at MIDRIFF] **:** having or represented with three bodies conjoined to one head

trico·sane \'trīkə,sān, 'trik-\ *n* -s [ISV *tri-* + *eicosane*] **:** a paraffin hydrocarbon $C_{23}H_{48}$; *esp* **:** the low-melting crystalline normal hydrocarbon $CH_3(CH_2)_{21}CH_3$

tri·costate \(')trī+\ *adj* [ISV *tri-* + *costate*] **:** having three costae

tri·cot \'trē(,)kō *also* 'trikət\ *n* -s [F, fr. *tricoter* to knit, fr. MF, to agitate, skip, hop, dance, fr. OF *estriquier* to move vivaciously, of Gmc origin; akin to OE *strīcan* to move, glide over — more at STRIKE] **1 :** a plain warp-knitted fabric in flat form that is more resistant to runs than jersey and is made of nylon, wool, rayon, silk, or cotton in sheer to opaque qualities esp. for use in clothing (as underwear) **2 :** a twilled clothing fabric of wool with fine warp ribs or of wool and cotton with fine weft ribs

tric·o·tine \¦trikə¦tēn\ *n* -s [F, fr. *tricot* + *-ine*] **:** CAVALRY TWILL

tri·cotyledonous \(¦)trī+\ *adj* [*tri-* + *cotyledon* + *-ous*] **:** having three cotyledons ⟨a ~ seedling⟩

tri·cou·ni \trī'kōnē\ *trademark* — used for a nail or iron fastened to the sole of a boot for mountain climbing

tri·cresol \(')trī+\ *n* [ISV *tri-* + *cresol*] **:** CRESOL 2

tri·cresyl \"+\ *n* [ISV *tri-* + *cresyl*] **:** TRITOLYL

tricresyl phosphate *n* **:** an oily flame-resistant mixture of isomeric inorganic esters $(CH_3C_6H_4)_3PO_4$ made from cresols or cresylic acid and usu. phosphorus oxychloride and used chiefly as a plasticizer and solvent, as a fire retardant, and as a lead scavenger in gasoline **:** tritolyl phosphate — called also *TCP*; not used systematically

tri·crot·ic \(')trī¦krädik\ *adj* [Gk *trikrotos* having a triple beat (fr. *tri-* three + *-krotos*, fr. *krotein* to beat, clap) + E *-ic* — more at TRI-, CROTAL] **:** of, relating to, or characterized by tricrotism

tricro·tism \'trīkrə,tizəm, 'trik-\ *n* -s [*tricrotic* + *-ism*] **:** a condition of the arterial pulse in which there is a triple beat

tric·trac *also* **trick·track** \'trik,trak\ *n* -s [F *trictrac*, of imit. origin; fr. the clicking sound made by the pegs] **:** a variety of backgammon formerly played with pegs; *broadly* **:** BACKGAMMON 1

¹**tri·cuspid** \(')trī+\ *adj* [NL *tricuspid-*, *tricuspis*, fr. L, having three points, fr. *tri-* + *cuspid-*, *cuspis* point] **1 :** having three cusps **2 :** of, relating to, or involving the tricuspid valve of the heart ⟨~ disease⟩

²**tricuspid** \"\ *n* **:** a tricuspid anatomical structure; *esp* **:** a tooth having three cusps

tri·cuspidate \"+\ *also* **tri·cuspidated** \"+\ *adj* [*tri-* + *cuspidate*, *cuspidated*] **:** cuspidate with three points **:** TRICUSPID ⟨a ~ leaf⟩

tricuspid valve *n* **:** a valve situated at the opening of the right auricle of the heart into the right ventricle and resembling in structure the mitral valve but consisting of three triangular membranous flaps

¹**tri·cy·cle** \'trī,sikəl, -,sȯk-, -,sēk- *sometimes* -,sīk-\ *n* [F, fr. *tri-* + Gk *kyklos* wheel — more at WHEEL] **:** a 3-wheeled vehicle propelled by pedals, hand levers, or a motor: as **a** (1) **:** a 3-wheeled velocipede used orig. by women or girls instead of a bicycle (2) **:** a child's vehicle with a pair of small rear wheels and a larger front wheel to which are attached the pedals and the handles for steering **b :** a 3-wheeled velocipede with two large wheels in the rear and one small wheel in front attached to a steering handle, propelled by pedals, and formerly used by girls **c :** a 3-wheeled velocipede equipped with a box or case for light haulage **d :** a 3-wheeled and often motorized invalid chair **e :** any of various power-driven 3-wheeled vehicles (as a motorcycle) — compare TRICAR

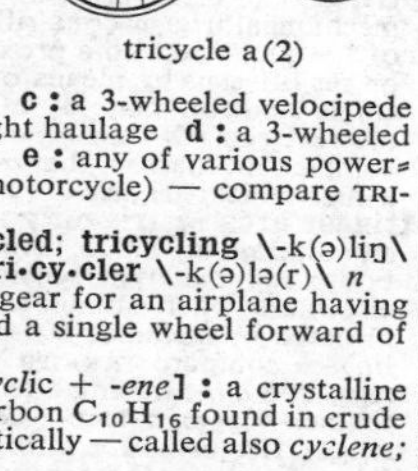

tricycle a(2)

²**tricycle** \"\ *vi* **tricycled; tricycled; tricycling** \-k(ə)liŋ\ **tricycles :** to ride a tricycle — **tri·cy·cler** \-k(ə)lə(r)\ *n*

tricycle landing gear *n* **:** landing gear for an airplane having two laterally-spaced wheels aft and a single wheel forward of the center of gravity

tri·cyclene \(')trī+\ *n* [ISV *tricyclic* + *-ene*] **:** a crystalline saturated tricyclic terpene hydrocarbon $C_{10}H_{16}$ found in crude alpha-pinene and also made synthetically — called also *cyclene*; not used systematically

tri·cyclic \(')trī+\ *adj* [*tri-* + *cyclic*] **:** containing three usu. fused rings in the molecular structure (as in anthracene)

tri·cy·clist \'trī,siklәst, -,sәk-, -,sēk-, -,sīk-\ *n* **:** one that rides a tricycle

tricyclo- *comb form* [ISV *tri-* + *cycl-*] **:** tricyclic ⟨*tricyclo*alkanes⟩

tri·dac·na \trə'daknə\ *n* [NL, fr. L, an oyster, fr. Gk *tridaknos* eaten at three bites, fr. *tri-* three + *-daknos* (fr. *daknein* to bite) — more at TONGS] **1** *cap* **:** a genus of marine bivalves (family Tridacnidae) having no anterior adductor muscle and an equivalve shell the valves of which are very thick and heavy and strongly plicated at the margin — see GIANT CLAM **2** -s **:** any mollusk of the genus *Tridacna* **:** GIANT CLAM

tri·dac·ni·dae \-nə,dē\ *n pl, cap* [NL, fr. *Tridacna*, type genus + *-idae*] **:** a small family of chiefly tropical thick-shelled marine bivalve mollusks (suborder Cardiacea) — see TRIDACNA

tri·dactyl \(')trī+\ *or* **tri·dactylous** \"+\ *also* **tri·dac·tyle** \-¦daktᵊl\ *adj* [*tridactyl*, *tridactylous* fr. Gk *tridaktylos*, fr. *tri-* three + *daktylos* finger; *tridactyle* fr. F, fr. Gk *tridaktylos* — more at TRI-] **:** having three fingers or toes ⟨the ~ foot of some reptiles⟩

tri·daily \(')trī+\ *adj* [*tri-* + *daily*] **:** occurring, appearing, or being made, done, or acted upon three times a day or every three days

trid·dler \'trid(ᵊ)lə(r)\ *n* -s [prob. alter. of obs. E *treadler* one who pedals, fr. E ²*treadle* + *-er*] *dial* **:** PECTORAL SANDPIPER

tri·decane \(')trī+\ *n* [ISV *tri-* + *decane*; fr. the number of carbon atoms] **:** a paraffin hydrocarbon $C_{13}H_{28}$; *esp* **:** the liquid normal hydrocarbon $CH_3(CH_2)_{11}CH_3$ obtained from petroleum

tri·decanoic acid \(')trī+-\ *n* [*tridecane* + *-oic*] **:** a crystalline fatty acid $C_{12}H_{25}COOH$ made synthetically

tri·dec·ene \trī'de,sēn\ *n* -s [*tridecane* + *-ene*] **:** any of six straight-chain isomeric olefin hydrocarbons $C_{13}H_{26}$

tri·dec·yl \trī'desәl\ *n* -s [ISV *tridecane* + *-yl*] **:** an alkyl radical $C_{13}H_{27}$ derived from a tridecane; *esp* **:** the normal radical $CH_3(CH_2)_{11}CH_2$—

tri·dec·yl·ene \-sə,lēn\ *n* -s [ISV *tridecyl* + *-ene*] **:** any of numerous isomeric olefin hydrocarbons $C_{13}H_{26}$ including the tridecenes

¹**tri·dent** \'trīdᵊnt\ *n* -s [L *trident-*, *tridens*, fr. *tri-* + *dent-*, *dens* tooth — more at TOOTH] **1 a** (1) **:** a 3-pronged scepter or spear serving in classical mythology as the attribute or symbol of a sea god (2) **:** a representation of such a trident serving as a symbol of naval power or supremacy and as such often borne by Britannia or appearing on coins **b :** a 3-pronged spear used by ancient Roman retiarii **c :** a 3-pronged fish spear **2 :** something felt to resemble a trident (as in shape, use, or emblematic significance)

²**trident** \"\ *adj* **:** having three teeth, processes, or points

tri·den·tal \(')trī¦dentᵊl\ *adj* **1 :** of or relating to a trident **:** having the form of a trident **2 :** divided into three points or prongs

tri·den·tate \-n·,tāt\ *adj* [NL *tridentatus*, fr. *tri-* + *-dentatus* -dentate] **:** having three teeth, processes, or points ⟨a ~ leaf⟩

trident bat *n* **:** any of numerous African and Asiatic leaf-nosed bats of *Asellia* and related genera distinguished by a tripartite frontal expansion of the nose leaf

¹**tri·den·tine** \(')trī¦dentᵊn, -en·,tēn, -en·,tīn\ *adj, usu cap* [NL *tridentinus*, fr. *Tridentum* Trent, town in northeastern Italy + L *-inus* -ine] **1 :** of or relating to Trent, Italy **2 :** of or relating to or based on the Council of Trent

²**tridentine** \"\ *n* -s *usu cap* **:** a Roman Catholic who conforms to the Tridentine profession of faith resulting from the Council of Trent and issued in 1564

tri·dermic \(')trī+\ *adj* [ISV *tri-* + *dermic*] **:** derived from all three germ layers

tri·digitate \"+\ *adj* [ISV *tri-* + *digitate*] **:** TRIDACTYL; *often* **:** having three slender elongated lobes, processes, or leaflets

tri·dimensional \¦trī+\ *adj* [ISV *tri-* + *dimensional*] **:** of, relating to, or concerned with three dimensions ⟨~ space⟩ ⟨a ~ motion-picture technique⟩ — **tri·dimensionality** \"+\ *n*

Tri·di·one \trī'dī,ōn\ *trademark* — used for trimethadione

tri·drachm \'trī,dram\ *n* [Gk *tridrachmon* three drachmas, fr. neut. of *tridrachmos* worth three drachmas, fr. *tri-* three + *-drachmos* (fr. *drachmē* drachma) — more at TRI-, DRAM] **:** an ancient Greek silver coin worth three drachmas

tri·duo \'tredə,wō\ *n* -s [It or Sp, fr. L *triduum*] **:** TRIDUUM

trid·u·um \'trijəwəm, -idyəw-\ *n* -s [L, space of three days, fr. *tri-* + *dies* day — more at DEITY] **:** a term of three days; *specif* **:** three days of prayer that in the Roman Catholic Church usu. precedes a feast or some religiously important occasion (as first communion)

trid·y·mite \'tridə,mīt\ *n* -s [G *tridymit*, fr. Gk *tridymos* threefold (irreg. fr. *tri-* three + *didymos* twin) + G *-it* -ite; fr. its common occurrence in trillings — more at TRI-, DIDYM-] **:** a mineral SiO_2 that is a silica, differs from quartz in its usu. minute thin tabular orthorhombic forms of crystallization, and is found in cavities in trachyte and similar rocks (hardness 7, sp. gr. 2.28–2.33)

triecious *var of* TRIOECIOUS

tried \'trīd\ *adj* [ME, fr. past part. of *trien* to try, test — more at TRY] **1 :** found good, faithful, or trustworthy through experience or testing ⟨a ~ friend⟩ ⟨a ~ recipe⟩ ⟨did not forget that which was old and ~ —Edison Marshall⟩ **2 :** subjected to trials or distress ⟨a kind but much-*tried* father⟩ **syn** see RELIABLE

tried and true *adj* **:** proved good, desirable, or feasible in actual practice **:** shown or known to be worthy ⟨a *tried and true* sales technique⟩ ⟨*tried and true* friends⟩

tri·ene \'trī,ēn, =¦=\ *n* -s [*-triene*] **:** a chemical compound containing three double bonds; *esp* **:** TRIOLEFIN

-tri·ene \¦trī,ēn, =¦=\ *n suffix* -s [*tri-* + *-ene*] **:** chemical compound containing three double bonds ⟨octa*triene*⟩

¹**tri·en·nial** \(')trī¦enēəl, -nyəl\ *adj* [L *triennium* period of three years (fr. *tri-* + *-ennium*, fr. *annus* year) + E *-al* — more at ANNUAL] **1 :** continuing or having a term of three years ⟨a ~ reign⟩ ⟨a ~ parliament⟩ **2 :** occurring, appearing, or being made, done, or acted upon every three years ⟨a ~ election⟩

²**triennial** \"\ *n* -s [L *triennium* + E *-al*, n. suffix] **:** a triennial event, appearance, or occasion: as **a :** a triennial episcopal visitation in the Church of England **b :** a third anniversary **c :** something (as a serial publication) that appears every three years

tri·en·nial·ly \-ēlē, -li\ *adv* **:** every three years

tri·en·ni·um \-ēəm\ *n, pl* **trienniums** \-ēəmz\ *or* **trien·nia** \-ēə\ [L] **:** a period of three years

tri·ens \'trī,enz, 'trē,än(t)s\ *n, pl* **trien·tes** \trī'en·,tēz, trē'en·,tās\ [L, third part, triens; akin to L *tres* three — more at THREE] **1 :** a bronze coin of ancient Rome equal to ⅓ as **2 :** an ancient Byzantine gold coin equal to ⅓ solidus; *also* **:** any of several similar ancient coins (as of Spain)

tri·en·ta·lis \,trī,en·'taləs, -āl-, -äl-\ *n, cap* [NL, prob. fr. L *triantalis* vessel, receptacle, fr. *trientalis* having a third of a foot, fr. *trient-*, *triens* third part + *-alis* -al] **:** a genus of delicate Eurasian and No. American herbs (family Primulaceae) having a whorl of entire leaves and several white stellate flowers on slender peduncles followed by 5-valved capsules — see STARFLOWER

tri·er \'trī(ə)r, -īə\ *n* -s [ME *triour*, fr. *trien* to try + *-our* -or] **1 :** a person who examines or studies a situation or problem and makes public a valid decision thereon: as **a :** one that tries judicially **:** JUDGE, JURY **b** *or* **tri·or** \"\ **:** a person appointed by an English court to try challenges of jurors **c :** a member of an English royal commission formerly allocating or referring petitions to the proper authority **d :** LORD TRIER **e** *usu cap* **:** one of a body of commissioners in the Church of England appointed in 1654 to examine those presented to benefices **f** *chiefly dial* **:** UMPIRE **2 :** one that tests or is used in testing something: as **a :** INVESTIGATOR, EXAMINER **b :** a worker that tests some product (as pipe or milk) **c :** an implement usu. in the form of a sharpened tapering tube or probe for sampling material (as flour, seeds, or processed meats) for inspection or testing **d :** something that constitutes a test of the individual and esp. of his character or mettle ⟨a ~ of men's spirit⟩ **3 :** one that tries: as **a :** one that separates a desired product from impurities **:** REFINER; *esp* **:** a renderer of fats **b :** one that makes an effort

trier 2c

tri·er·ar·chy \'trīə,rärkē, -,räk-, -ki\ *n* -ES [Gk *triērarchia*, fr. *triērarchos* one who furnishes a trireme, commander of a trireme (fr. *triērēs* trireme — akin to Gk *treis* three — + *-archos* -arch) + *-ia* -y — more at THREE] **:** the ancient Athenian plan whereby individual citizens furnished and maintained triremes or other naval equipment as part of their civic duty

tries *pres 3d sing of* TRY, *pl of* TRY

tri·este \(')trē¦est *sometimes* trē'estē *or* -,stā *or* -,stə\ *adj, usu cap* [fr. *Trieste*, Italy] **:** of or from the city of Trieste, Italy **:** of the kind or style prevalent in Trieste

tri·ester \(')trī+\ *n* [ISV *tri-* + *ester*] **:** a compound containing three ester groups

¹**tri·es·tine** \trē'estən, -,stēn, -,stīn\ *or* **tri·es·tene** \-,stēn\ *adj, usu cap* [*Trieste*, seaport in northeastern Italy + E *-ine*] **:** TRIESTE

²**triestine** \"\ *or* **triestene** \"\ *n* -s *cap* **:** TRIESTINO

tri·es·ti·no \-,tē(,)nō\ *n, pl* **triestinos** \-nōz\ *or* **triesti·ni** \-nē\ *cap* [It, fr. *Trieste*, Italy + It *-ino* (fr. L *-inus* -ine)] **:** a native or resident of Trieste, Italy

¹**tri·e·ter·ic** \¦trīə¦terik\ *n* -s [L *trieterica*, fr. fem. of *trietericus* occurring every third year] **:** a trieteric festival esp. in honor of Bacchus

²**trieteric** \"\ *adj* [L *trietericus*, fr. Gk *trietērikos*, fr. *trietēris* triennial festival (fr. *tri-* three + *etos* year) + *-ikos* -ic — more at TRI-, WETHER] **:** occurring in alternate years — used of an ancient Greek rite

tri·ethanolamine \(¦)trī+\ *n* [ISV *tri-* + *ethanolamine*] **:** a high-boiling viscous soluble hygroscopic basic amino alcohol $(HOCH_2CH_2)_3N$ that is usu. made from ammonia and ethylene oxide, often contains considerable amounts of diethanolamine and ethanolamine, and is used chiefly as a corrosion inhibitor in aqueous solution and in making fatty acid soaps; tris-(2-hydroxyethyl)-amine — not used systematically

tri·ethiodide \"+\ *n* [*tri-* + *ethiodide*] **:** a compound with three units of ethyl iodide

tri·ethyl \(')trī+\ *adj* [ISV *tri-* + *ethyl*] **:** containing three ethyl groups in the molecule

tri·ethylamine \(¦)trī+\ *n* [ISV *triethyl* + *amine*] **:** a water-soluble flammable liquid tertiary amine $(C_2H_5)_3N$ that has a strong ammoniacal odor, is usu. made by reaction of ethyl chloride with ammonia, and is used chiefly in synthesis (as of quaternary ammonium compounds)

tri·ethylene glycol \(')trī+ . . . -\ *n* [ISV *tri-* + *ethylene*] **:** a high-boiling hygroscopic liquid ether glycol $(-CH_2OCH_2CH_2OH)_2$ that resembles diethylene glycol, is made similarly, and is used chiefly as a solvent, as an air disinfectant, in the dehydration of gases, and in the form of esters as a plasticizer

triethylenemelamine \"+\ *n* [ISV *triethylene* + *melamine*] **:** a cytotoxic crystalline compound $C_3N_3(NC_2H_4)_3$ made from ethylenimine and cyanuric chloride and used chiefly as a textile finishing agent and in medicine like nitrogen mustard

tri·facial \(')trī+\ *adj or n* [ISV *tri-* + *facial*] **:** TRIGEMINAL

trifacial nerve *n* **:** TRIGEMINAL NERVE

tri·far·i·ous \(')trī¦fa(a)rēəs\ *adj* [L *trifarius* of three ways, fr. *trifariam* in three ways, fr. *tri-* + *-fariam* (akin to Skt *-dhā* in *dvidhā* in two ways) — more at BIFARIOUS] **:** facing three ways; *esp* **:** occurring in whorls of three ⟨~ leaves⟩

tri·fid \'trī,fid, -fəd\ *adj* [L *trifidus* split into three, fr. *tri-* + *-fidus* (fr. stem of *findere* to split) — more at BITE] **1 :** divided partway to the base into three lobes with narrow sinuses **:** TRIDENT **2** *of a cipher alphabet* **:** constructed by matching the letters of the alphabet with 3-unit equivalents of such a nature that exactly as many of them can be constructed as there are letters of the alphabet (as by using the twenty-seven 3-digit numbers made up of one or more of the numerals 1, 2, and 3 for a 27-letter alphabet) — compare FRACTIONAL SUBSTITUTION

tri·flagellate \(')trī+\ *adj* [*tri-* + *flagellate*] **:** having three flagella ⟨a ~ protozoan⟩

¹**tri·fle** \'trīfəl\ *n* -s [ME *trifle*, *trufle*, fr. OF *trufle*, *trufe* mockery, trickery] **1** *obs* **:** an idle, nonsensical, or fictitious tale **2 :** something of very little value or importance: as **a :** a paltry trinket or knickknack **:** BAUBLE **b :** a creative work of no great or enduring value and often of purely topical interest **c** *obs* **:** a person of no account **d :** an insignificant or relatively small amount (as of money) ⟨cost only a ~⟩ **3 a** *chiefly Brit* **:** a dessert of sponge cake spread with jam or jelly, sprinkled with crumbled macaroons, soaked in wine, and served with custard and whipped cream **b** *chiefly Brit* **:** a dessert (as of soft fruit) served with custard and whipped cream **4 a :** a pewter of moderate hardness (as of 83 parts tin and 17 antimony) used esp. for small utensils **b trifles** *pl* **:** utensils made of trifle — **a trifle** *adv* **:** to some small degree **:** SLIGHTLY ⟨*a trifle* annoyed at the delay⟩

²**trifle** \"\ *vb* **trifled; trifled; trifling** \-f(ə)liŋ\ **trifles** [ME *triflen*, *truflen*, fr. OF *trufler*, *trufer* to mock, trick] *vi* **1 a :** to talk jestingly or mockingly with intent to delude **:** indulge in beguiling or misleading talk ⟨I fear he did but ~ and meant to wreck thee —Shak.⟩ **b :** to act without seriousness of purpose or mood or due respect **:** speak, write, carry on an affair, or act with levity or flippancy **:** be heedless, indifferent, or frivolous where concern or respect are desirable **:** PLAY, FLIRT — often followed by *with* ⟨~ with your health⟩ ⟨*trifled* with the boy's affections⟩ **2 :** to waste time (as in idleness or foolish pastimes) **:** LOITER, DALLY ⟨*trifling* through the summer vacation⟩ **3 :** to handle something idly **:** TOY, FIDGET — usu. followed by *with* ⟨*trifling* with the silverware at his place⟩ ~ *vt* **1 :** to spend or waste in trifling or on trifles — usu. used with *away* ⟨~ away money⟩ **2** *obs* **:** to make or treat as trivial — **to be trifled with :** to be treated lightly or disrespectfully with impunity ⟨no man *to be trifled with*⟩ ⟨the text is not *to be trifled with*⟩ ⟨like a king not *to be trifled with* —Alfred Tennyson⟩

tri·fler \-f(ə)lə(r)\ *n* -s [ME, fr. *triflen* to trifle + *-er*] **:** one that trifles; *usu* **:** a shallow frivolous person **:** IDLER

¹tri·fling \-f(ə)liŋ, -lēŋ\ n -s [ME, fr. gerund of triflen to trifle] : trifling conduct: as **a** : light talk : BADINAGE **b** : a wasting or waste of time : effort or activity without value

²trifling \"\ adj [fr. pres. part. of ²trifle] : lacking in significance or solid worth: as **a** : FRIVOLOUS ⟨~ talk⟩ **b** : TRIVIAL ⟨a ~ gift⟩ ⟨these ~ quarrels⟩ **c** chiefly dial : LAZY, SHIFTLESS ⟨a ~ fellow who never amounted to much⟩ **syn** see PETTY

tri·fling·ly adv : in a trifling manner

tri·fling·ness n -ES : the quality or state of being trifling

trifluor- or **trifluoro-** comb form [ISV tri- + fluor-] : containing three atoms of fluorine ⟨trifluoroacetic⟩ — in names of chemical compounds; compare FLUOR-

tri·fluoride \(ˈ)trī+\ n [trifluor- + -ide] : a binary compound containing three atoms of fluorine combined with an element or radical

¹**tri·focal** \"+\ adj [tri- + focal] **1** : having three focal lengths **2** of an eyeglass lens : having one part that corrects for near vision, one for intermediate vision (as at arm's length), and one for distant vision

²**trifocal** \"\ n -s **1** : a trifocal glass or lens **2 trifocals** pl : eyeglasses with trifocal lenses — compare BIFOCAL 2

tri·fold \ˈtrīˌfōld\ adj [tri- + -fold] : THREEFOLD, TRIPLE

tri·fo·li·a·ta \(ˌ)trīˌfōlēˈādə, -ˈädə\ n -s [NL (specific epithet of Poncirus trifoliata), fr. tri- + L foliata, fem. of foliatus leaved — more at FOLIATE] : TRIFOLIATE ORANGE

tri·foliate \(ˈ)trī+\ adj [tri- + foliate] **1** or **tri·foliated** \"+\ [tri- + foliated] : having three leaves ⟨a ~ plant⟩ **2** : TRIFOLIOLATE — see TRIFOLIATE ORANGE

trifoliate orange n : a hardy deciduous Chinese orange (Poncirus trifoliata) that has trifoliolate leaves and small fragrant very acid fruits and is widely cultivated for ornament or hedging and esp. as a stock for budding various table oranges

tri·foliolate \(ˈ)trī+\ adj [ISV tri- + foliolate] : having three leaflets ⟨a ~ leaf⟩ — compare TRIFOLIATE; see LEAF illustration

tri·fo·li·o·sis \(ˌ)trīˌfōlēˈōsəs\ n, pl **trifolioses** [NL, fr. Trifolium + -osis] : CLOVER DISEASE

tri·fo·li·um \trīˈfōlēəm\ n [NL, fr. L, three-leaved grass, trefoil, fr. tri- + folium leaf — more at BLADE] **1** cap : a very large genus of herbs (family Leguminosae) comprising the common clovers, being widely distributed in temperate regions, and having digitately or pinnately trifoliolate leaves and red, purple, pink, or white chiefly globose heads of flowers with a persistent corolla followed by a membranous and indehiscent pod **2** -s : any plant of the genus Trifolium

tri·fo·ri·al \(ˈ)trīˈfōrēəl\ adj [ML triforium + E -al] : of or relating to a triforium

tri·fo·ri·um \trīˈfōrēəm\ n, pl **trifo·ria** \-ēə\ [ML, prob. fr. L tri- + fores door; fr. its often having three openings to each bay — more at DOOR] : a gallery or open space forming an upper story to the aisle of a church and typically constituting an arcaded story between the nave arches and clerestory

tri·form \(ˈ)trī+\ also **tri·formed** \"+\ adj [triform fr. L triformis, fr. tri- + forma form; triformed fr. L triformis + E -ed — more at FORM] : having a triple form, constitution, or character : having three manifestations

¹**tri·fur·cate** \ˈtrīfərˌkāt, -kət; (ˈ)trīˈfərkət\ also **tri·fur·cat·ed** \-ˌkādəd\ adj [L trifurcus (fr. tri- + furca fork) + E -ate or -ate + -ed — more at FORK] : having or divided into three branches or forks : TRICHOTOMOUS

²**tri·fur·cate** \ˈtrīfərˌkāt, (ˈ)trīˈfərˌkāt\ vi : to fork or divide into three branches — **tri·fur·ca·tion** \ˌtrī(ˌ)fərˈkāshən\ n

¹**trig** \ˈtrig\ adj, sometimes **trigger**; sometimes **triggest** [ME, of Scand origin; akin to ON tryggr faithful, trustworthy, Norw & Dan tryg easy, confident, safe — more at TRUE] **1** dial Brit : TRUSTY, FAITHFUL **2** chiefly Scot : ACTIVE, BRISK, LIVELY **3 a** chiefly Scot : pleasingly neat, trim, and orderly; sometimes : CONCISE ⟨a ~ summary⟩ **b** : pleasingly trim and stylish in dress : SPRUCE, SMART ⟨a ~ secretary in tailored black⟩; also : marked by trimness and style ⟨a ~ little hat⟩ **4** : extremely or excessively precise : STIFF, PRIM, FORMAL **5** dial chiefly Brit : marked by sound strong condition : FIRM, VIGOROUS **6** dial Brit : fully filled : STUFFED, CRAMMED **syn** see NEAT

²**trig** \"\ vt **trigged**; **trigged**; **trigging**; **trigs 1 a** dial chiefly Brit : to put in order : TIDY — usu. used with up **b** : to dress in a trig manner : make smart or noticeable in costume — usu. used with out or up ⟨trigged out in her best for the meeting⟩ **2** dial chiefly Brit : to fill completely : STUFF, CRAM

³**trig** \"\ vt **trigged**; **trigged**; **trigging**; **trigs** [perh. of Scand origin; akin to ON tryggja to make firm, make trusty, tryggr faithful, trustworthy] chiefly dial : to make secure or firm : restrain from moving or shifting: as **a** : to stop or slow the motion of (a wheel) usu. with a wedge or other block **b** : to support with props or wedges

⁴**trig** \"\ n -s **1 a** chiefly dial : something (as a stone or block) used as a support in trigging **b** : a brick bedded to the proper height to hold a mason's line level in the center of a course **2** : a manually operated eccentric cam mounted near the end of a scale beam by means of which the beam can be held stationary at the lower limit of its motion

⁵**trig** \"\ vi **trigged**; **trigged**; **trigging**; **trigs** [origin unknown] dial Eng : TROT, RUN

⁶**trig** \"\ n -s [perh. modif. (influenced by ¹trigger) of D trek pull, draft, tug, haul, fr. MD treck — more at TREK] **1** dial Eng : a line from which to start in a race or game **2** dial Brit : a small or shallow ditch or trench esp. when used to mark a boundary

⁷**trig** \"\ vt **trigged**; **trigged**; **trigging**; **trigs** dial Brit : to mark or bound with a trig ⟨trigged the ground with his heel⟩

⁸**trig** \"\ n -s [by shortening] : TRIGONOMETRY

trig abbr trigonometric; trigonometrical

tri·ga \ˈtrēgə, -rīgə\ n, pl **tri·gae** \-rēˌgī, -rīˌjē\ [LL, contr. of L trijuga, fem. of trijugus of a team of three, threefold, fr. tri- + jugum yoke, team — more at YOKE] **1** : an ancient Roman 3-horse chariot **2** : a 3-horse team (as for a triga)

trig·a·mist \ˈtrigəməst\ n -s : one who practices trigamy

trig·a·mous \-məs\ adj [Gk trigamos thrice married] **1** : being or relating to a trigamist or trigamy : living in trigamy **2** : having staminate, pistillate, and hermaphrodite flowers in the same head

trig·a·my \-mē\ n -ES [LL trigamia, fr. LGk, fr. Gk trigamos thrice married (fr. tri- three + gamos marriage) + -ia -y — more at BIGAMY] : the act of marrying or condition of being married three times; esp : the condition of having three spouses at one time

tri·gem·i·nal \(ˈ)trīˈjemənᵊl\ adj [NL trigeminus + E -al] **1** : of, relating to, or being the trigeminal nerve — see TRIGEMINAL NEURALGIA **2** [L trigeminus threefold, triple + E -al] : exhibiting or involving a pause after every third beat ⟨a ~ pulse⟩

trigeminal nerve also **tri·gem·i·nal** \"\ n -s : either of the fifth pair of cranial nerves that are mixed nerves and in man are the largest of the cranial nerves and that arise by a small motor and a larger sensory root which both emerge from the side of the pons with the sensory root bearing the Gasserian ganglion and dividing into ophthalmic, maxillary, and mandibular nerves and the motor root supplying fibers to the mandibular nerve and through this to the muscles of mastication

trigeminal neuralgia n : neuralgia involving one or more branches of the trigeminal nerve, being often extremely severe, and occurring in paroxysms

tri·gem·i·nus nerve \(ˈ)trīˈjemənəs-\ or **trigeminus** \⸗ˈ⸗⸗⸗\ n, pl **trigemini** [NL trigeminus, fr. L, threefold, triple, fr. tri- + geminus twofold, twin — more at GEMINATE] : TRIGEMINAL NERVE

tri·generic \¦trī+\ adj [tri- + generic] : of or relating to three types or kinds; esp : showing characteristics of or resulting from interbreeding members of three genera ⟨a ~ hybrid⟩

tri·ger process \trēˈzhā-\ n, usu cap T [after M. Triger, 19th cent. Fr. engineer] : a method of sinking through water-bearing ground in which a shaft is lined with tubbing and provided with an air lock so that work proceeds under air pressure

trigesimo-secundo \trīˈjesə(ˌ)mōsə¦kən(ˌ)dō\ or **tricesimo-secundo** \trīˈses-\ n -s [L trigesimo secundo, tricesimo secundo, abl. of trigesimus secundus, tricesimus secundus thirty-second, fr. trigesimus, tricesimus thirtieth (akin to L triginta thirty) + secundus second — more at TRICENARY, SECOND] : THIRTY-TWOMO — see BOOK tables

trigged past of TRIG

¹**trig·ger** \ˈtrigə(r)\ n -s [³trig + -er] **1** chiefly dial : a catch or block to hold the wheel of a carriage on a declivity **2** : a block used in shipbuilding to hold a boat on the ways — compare ²TRIGGER 1b

²**trigger** \"\ n -s [alter. (prob. influenced by ¹trigger) of earlier tricker, fr. D trekker, fr. MD trecker something that pulls, fr. trecken to pull, haul — more at TREK] **1** : a piece (as a lever) connected with a catch or detent as a means of releasing it: as **a** (1) : the part of the action of a firearm moved by the finger to release the hammer or firing pin in firing (2) : a device that fires an explosive ⟨using an A-bomb as ~ for an H-bomb⟩ **b** : a lever pivoted on the ground ways with the upper end forced against the sliding ways by a hydraulic ram against the lower end in such a manner that the releasing of the trigger allows a ship to be launched by sliding down the ground ways **2** : something that acts like or is felt to resemble a mechanical trigger esp. in being a sensitive means of initiating a process or reaction that produces a relatively large effect; esp : something (as an external stimulus) that initiates a physiological or pathological process ⟨the sight or odor of food may be a ~ for salivation⟩ **3** [by shortening] : TRIGGERFISH

³**trigger** \"\ adj **1** : of, relating to, or associated with a trigger ⟨~ covers⟩ **2** : functioning as or in a manner analogous to a trigger — see TRIGGER MECHANISM

⁴**trigger** \"\ vb -ED/-ING/-s vt **1** : to release by pulling a mechanical trigger ⟨~ a rifle⟩; broadly : to cause the explosion of ⟨~ a missile with a proximity fuse⟩ **2** : to initiate, actuate, or set off esp. by means of a comparatively weak impulse ⟨a single neutron may ~ an extensive chain reaction⟩ ⟨an indiscreet remark that ~ed off a long and costly strike⟩ ⟨the complex mechanism that ~s blood clotting⟩ ~ vi : to release a mechanical trigger

trigger area or **trigger zone** n : a sensitive area of the body stimulation of which gives rise to reaction elsewhere in the body; esp : a hypersensitive area that evokes referred pain elsewhere when stimulated ⟨an attack of trifacial neuralgia initiated by a chance brushing of the trigger area of the upper lip⟩ — compare TRIGGER MECHANISM

triggered adj : having a trigger — usu. used in combination ⟨a feather-triggered trap —Report: Smithsonian Institution⟩

trigger finger n **1** : a finger used in pressing the trigger of a firearm; also : the forefinger of the dominant hand **2** : a finger in which flexion or extension may be momentarily obstructed by spasm followed by a snapping into place

triggerfish \ˈ⸗⸗ˌ⸗\ n [²trigger + fish] : any of numerous deep-bodied fishes constituting Balistes and related genera of the family Balistidae, having an anterior dorsal fin with two or three stout erectile spines of which the second locks the larger first in position when both are erect, inhabiting chiefly warm seas, being often fantastically colored, and including edible forms and others that are distinctly poisonous — see QUEEN TRIGGERFISH

trigger guard n : a semicircular band of metal that encloses vertically the trigger of a firearm

trigger hair n : CNIDOCIL

trigger-happy \ˈ⸗⸗ˌ⸗⸗\ adj **1** : urgently desirous of shooting usu. to the point of overlooking or ignoring other factors involved : irresponsible in the use of firearms ⟨trigger-happy hunters determined to bag their limit⟩; esp : inclined to shoot before clearly identifying the target ⟨restraining trigger-happy sentries⟩ **2** : inclined to be irresponsible in matters that might lead to or precipitate war ⟨trigger-happy diplomats⟩ ⟨nations are not so trigger-happy as they once were —New Republic⟩; broadly : aggressively belligerent in attitude ⟨trigger-happy critics⟩

trig·ger·less \ˈtrigə(r)ləs\ adj : lacking a trigger

trig·ger·man \-mən, -ˌman, -ˌmaa(ə)n\ n, pl **triggermen 1** : a gunman who shoots the victim in a murder by a gang; also : a gangster's personal bodyguard **2** : a man who operates the trigger at the launching of a ship

trigger mechanism n : something (as a specific act or stimulus) that in interaction with the body constitutes a physiological trigger; esp : such a trigger by which an attack (as of disease or referred pain) is precipitated ⟨certain climatic and meteorological factors are required before the trigger mechanism setting off acute rheumatic fever can act —H.M.Margolis⟩ — compare TRIGGER AREA

trigger plant n : HAIR-TRIGGER FLOWER

trigger point n : a small trigger area

trigger pull n **1 a** or **trigger squeeze** : the pressure applied to a trigger to fire a firearm **b** : the weight in pounds that will cause complete movement of the trigger of a cocked firearm **2** : the mechanical linkage of trigger and other parts that directly fire the cartridge in a firearm; also : the movement of these parts

triggest superlative of TRIG

trigging pres part of TRIG

tri·gin·tal \trīˈjintᵊl\ n -s [ME trigental, fr. ML trigentale, trigintale, fr. L triginta thirty — more at TRICENARY] : TRENTAL

¹**trig·lid** \ˈtrigləd\ adj [NL Triglidae] : of or relating to the Triglidae

²**triglid** \"\ n -s : a fish of the family Triglidae : GURNARD

Trig·li·dae \-ləˌdē\ n pl, cap [NL, fr. Trigla, type genus (fr. LL, red mullet, fr. Gk trigla, triglē) + -idae; akin to Gk strix owl — more at STRIDENT] : a family of scorpaenid fishes comprising the gurnards

tri·glo·chin \trīˈglōkən\ n, cap [NL, fr. tri- + Gk glōchin-, glōchis projecting point; fr. the pronged look of the fruit — more at GLOSS] : a widely distributed genus of marsh herbs (family Juncaginaceae) having basal ligulate leaves, small spicate flowers, and tricarpellary fruits — see ARROW GRASS

trig loop n [⁴trig] : a steel loop in which the end of the weigh beam of a hand-operated grain scale moves up and down

¹**tri·glot** \ˈtrīˌglät, usu -äd·+V\ n -s [ISV tri- + Gk glōtta language — more at -GLOT] : a book or edition in three languages

²**triglot** \"\ adj [ISV tri- + -glot] : containing, printed in, or treating three languages

trig·ly adv [¹trig + -ly] : in a trig manner ⟨a ~ dressed woman⟩ ⟨~ kept homes⟩

tri·glyceride \(ˈ)trī+\ n [ISV tri- + glycer- + -ide] : a triester of glycerol with one, two, or three acids ⟨the ~s in natural fats —T.P.Hilditch⟩

tri·glyph \ˈtrīˌglif\ n [L triglyphus, fr. Gk triglyphos, fr. tri- three + glyphē carved work — more at TRI-, GLYPH] : an architectural ornament in the frieze of the Doric order consisting of a slightly projecting rectangular tablet, having two vertical channels of V section and two corresponding chamfers or half channels on the vertical sides, and being repeated alternately with the metopes — see GLYPH

tri·glyphed \-ft\ adj : provided or decorated with triglyphs

tri·glyph·ic \(ˈ)trī¦glifik\ adj : consisting of, relating to, or adorned with triglyphs

trig·ness n -ES [¹trig + -ness] : the quality or state of being trig ⟨the ~ of his quarters⟩

tri·gon \ˈtrīˌgän\ n -s [L trigonum, fr. Gk trigōnon, fr. neut. of trigōnos three-cornered, triangular, fr. tri- three + -gōnos -cornered, -angled (fr. gōnia corner, angle) — more at TRI-, -GON] **1** : TRIANGLE **2 a** : TRIPLICITY 1 **b** : TRINE 2 **3** : an ancient triangular harp of oriental and perhaps Assyrian origin having four strings and a shrill tone and often used for banquet music — called also sabbeka, sackbut, sambuca **4** : the cutting region of the crown of an upper molar that usu. comprises the anterior part and includes the protocone, paracone, and metacone

trigon- or **trigono-** comb form [L, fr. Gk trigōn-, trigōno-, fr. trigōnos] : triangular ⟨Trigonella⟩ ⟨trigonotype⟩

trigon abbr trigonometric; trigonometrical; trigonometry

¹**trigona** pl of TRIGONUM

²**tri·go·na** \trīˈgōnə\ n, cap [NL, prob. fr. fem. of L trigonus triangular, fr. Gk trigōnos] : a genus of stingless honeybees of the Old and New World tropics

trig·o·nal \ˈtrigənᵊl\ adj [L trigonalis, fr. trigonum triangle] **1** : of, relating to, or characteristic of triangles : having three angles : TRIANGULAR **2** : of or relating to a trigon or the trigone **3** : of, relating to, or being the division of the hexagonal crystal system or the forms belonging to it characterized by a vertical axis of threefold symmetry — see TRIGONAL SYSTEM — **trig·o·nal·ly** \-nəlē\ adv

trigonal system n : a crystal system that is characterized by three equal and equally inclined axes and that is commonly held to be a division of the hexagonal system

trigonal trapezohedron n : TRAPEZOHEDRON d

trigonal trisoctahedron n : a trisoctahedron whose faces are triangles

trigonal tristetrahedron n : a tristetrahedron whose faces are triangles

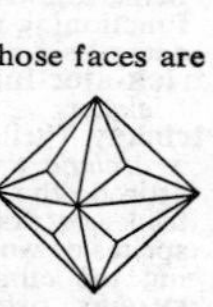
trigonal trisoctahedron

tri·gone \ˈtrīˌgōn\ n -s [F, fr. L trigonum] **1** also **tri·gon** \-ˌgän\ : a triangular body part; specif : a smooth triangular area on the inner surface of the bladder limited by the apertures of the ureters and urethra **2** : a thickening of plant cell walls that occurs when three or more cells adjoin

trig·o·nel·la \ˌtrigəˈnelə\ n, cap [NL, fr. L trigonum triangle + -ella — more at TRIGON] : a genus of widely distributed herbs (family Leguminosae) having pinnately trifoliolate leaves, capitate or racemose flowers, and linear pods — see FENUGREEK

trig·o·nel·line \-eˌlēn, -elən\ n -s [ISV trigonell- (fr. NL Trigonella) + -ine] : a crystalline alkaloid $CH_3N^+C_5H_4COO^-$ obtained esp. from the seeds of fenugreek, from coffee beans and other seeds, and from sea urchins and jellyfish and found in the urine (as after ingestion of nicotinic acid) : the N-methyl-betaine of nicotinic acid

tri·go·neu·tic \¦trīgō¦n(y)üd·ik\ adj [tri- + Gk goneuein to beget (akin to Gk gonos offspring) + E -tic (as in genetic) — more at GON-] : having three broods annually

tri·go·nia \trīˈgōnēə\ n, cap [NL, fr. L trigonus triangular (fr. Gk trigōnos) + NL -ia; fr. the shells suggesting the form of a triangle — more at TRIGON] **1** : a genus of pearly-shelled bivalve mollusks (suborder Arcacea) including many extinct forms which characterize the Mesozoic rocks and a few living forms which survive on the coast of Australia **2** [NL; fr. the often triangular shape of the fruit] : a genus (the type of the family Trigoniaceae) of chiefly climbing tropical American shrubs

tri·go·ni·a·ce·ae \⸗ˌ⸗⸗ˈāsēˌē\ n pl, cap [NL, fr. Trigonia, type genus + -aceae] : a family of tropical American shrubs or woody vines (order Geraniales) with irregular often spurred flowers and 2-celled capsular fruit — **tri·go·ni·a·ceous** \⸗¦⸗⸗¦āshəs\ adj

tri·go·nid \ˈtrīgəˌnid\ n -s [¹trigon + -id] : the part of a lower molar corresponding to the trigon of an upper molar

trigo·nite \ˈtrīgəˌnīt, ˈtrig-\ n -s [G trigonit, fr. trigon- + -it -ite] : a mineral $MnPb_3H(AsO_3)_3$ consisting of an acid lead manganese arsenite and occurring in yellow to brown triangular wedge-shaped crystals (hardness 2–3)

tri·go·ni·tis \ˌtrīgəˈnīdəs\ n -ES [NL, fr. trigonum trigone + -itis] : inflammation of the trigone of the bladder

trigono- — see TRIGON-

trigo·no·ceph·a·lous \¦trigənō¦sefələs, (ˌ)¦trī¦gōnə¦s-\ or **trigo·no·ce·phal·ic** \-səˈfalik\ adj [ISV trigon- + -cephalous or -cephalic] : having a somewhat triangular flat head — **trigo·no·ceph·a·ly** \ˌtrigənōˈsefəlē, (ˈ)trīˌgōnəˈs-\ n -ES

trig·o·noc·er·ous \ˌtrigəˈnäsərəs\ adj [trigon- + cer- (fr. Gk keras horn) + -ous — more at CEREBRAL] : having horns of triangular cross section ⟨some goats are ~⟩

trigono·dodecahedron \¦trigənō, (ˌ)¦trī¦gōnə+\ n [ISV trigon- + dodecahedron] : a trigonal tristetrahedron : the hemihedral form of the isometric trapezohedron

trig·o·nom·e·ter \ˌtrigəˈnämədə(r)\ n -s [prob. fr. (assumed) NL trigonometres, fr. NL trigonometria, after such pairs as L geometria geometry: geometres geometer] : one skilled in trigonometry or trigonometric surveying

trig·o·no·met·ric \¦trigənə¦me·trik, -rēk\ also **trig·o·no·met·ri·cal** \-trəkəl, -rēk-\ adj [trigonometric prob. fr. (assumed) NL trigonometricus, fr. NL trigonometria trigonometry + L -icus -ic; trigonometrical prob. fr. (assumed) NL trigonometricus + E -al] : of, relating to, or involving trigonometry : performed by the rules of trigonometry — **trig·o·no·met·ri·cal·ly** \-rək(ə)lē, -rēk-, -li\ adv

trigonometric curve n : a curve whose equation involves trigonometric functions

trigonometric equation n : an equation that involves trigonometric functions

trigonometric function also **trigonometric ratio** n : a function (as sine, cosine, tangent, cosecant, secant, cotangent) of an arc or angle usu. measured by the ratios of pairs of sides of a right-angled triangle

trigonometric identity n : an identity involving or based on trigonometric functions

trigonometric parallax n : the direct measurement of the parallax or distance of a celestial body from a base line of known length (as the earth's radius or the radius of its orbit) and the angles at the ends of the base line giving reliable results for stars up to distances of about 100 light-years

trigonometric series n : a mathematical series whose terms proceed by sines and cosines of integral multiples of a variable angle

trigonometric solution n : solution (as of a cubic equation) in terms of or by means of trigonometric functions

trig·o·nom·e·try \ˌtrigəˈnämətrē, -ri\ n -ES often attrib [NL trigonometria, fr. trigon- + -metria -metry] : a branch of mathematics dealing with the relations holding among the sides and angles of triangles and among closely related magnitudes and esp. with methods of deducing from given parts other required parts

tri·go·non \trīˈgōˌnän\ n -s [Gk trigōnon triangle — more at TRIGON] : TRIGON 3

trigo·no·type \ˈtrigənəˌtīp, trīˈgōnə-\ n [ISV trigon- + type] : TRAPEZOHEDRON d

trig·o·nous \ˈtrigənəs\ adj [L trigonus, fr. Gk trigōnos — more at TRIGON] : having three angles or corners : triangular in cross section

trigons pl of TRIGON

tri·go·num \trīˈgōnəm\ n, pl **trigonums** \-nəmz\ or **trigo·na** \-nə\ [NL, fr. L, triangle — more at TRIGON] : TRIGONE: as **a** or **trigonum men·ta·le** \-ˌmenˈta(ˌ)lē, -tā-, -ˈtä-\ [NL, trigone of the chin] : a somewhat triangular enlargement of the anteromedian part of the human mandible forming the bony support of the chin **b** or **trigonum ha·ben·u·lae** \-həˈbenyə(ˌ)lē, -ˌlī\ : a triangular area in the optic thalamus

tri·gram \ˈtrīˌgram, -aa(ə)m\ n [tri- + -gram] **1 a** : a three-letter inscription **b** : TRIGRAPH 2 **2 a** : a figure made by three lines or elements **b** : one of the eight possible combinations of three whole or broken lines used in Chinese and Japanese divination and symbolism

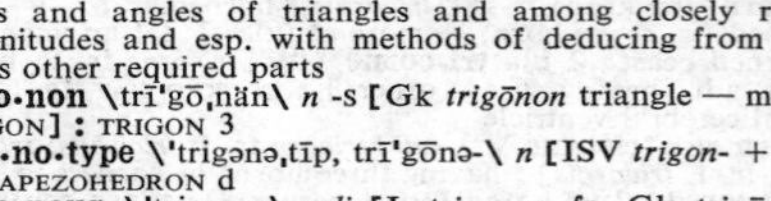
trigrams 2b

tri·gram·mat·ic \¦trīgrə¦mad·ik\ adj [Gk trigrammatos of three letters (fr. tri- three + grammat-, gramma letter) + E -ic — more at TRI-, GRAM] : of, relating to, or consisting of a trigram

tri·graph \ˈtrīˌgraf, -aa(ə)f, -aif, -āf\ n [tri- + -graph] **1** : three letters spelling a single consonant, vowel, or diphthong ⟨sch of schism, cch of bacchic, pph of sapphic, tth of Matthew, and eau of beau are ~s⟩ **2** : a cluster of three successive letters ⟨THE is a high frequency ~⟩

tri·graph·ic \(ˈ)trī¦grafik\ adj **1** : of, relating to, or consisting of a trigraph ⟨a ~ unit⟩ **2** : proceeding (as in encipherment) by groups of three letters at a time ⟨~ substitution⟩

trigs pres 3d sing of TRIG, pl of TRIG

tri·gyn·ia \trīˈjinēə, -ˈgi-\ n pl, cap [NL, fr. tri- + -gynia] in former classifications : an order of plants having flowers with three pistils — **tri·gyn·ian** \(ˌ)⸗¦⸗⸗ən\ adj

tri·halide \(ˈ)trī+\ n [tri- + halide] : a binary compound containing three atoms of halogen combined with an element or radical

tri·he·dral \(ˈ)trī¦hēdrəl\ adj [tri- + -hedral] : having three faces : of or relating to a trihedron

trihedral angle n : a polyhedral angle with three faces

tri·he·dron \trīˈhēdrən\ n, pl **trihedrons** \-drənz\ or **trihe·dra** \-drə\ [NL, fr. tri- + -hedron] : a figure formed by three planes meeting in a point

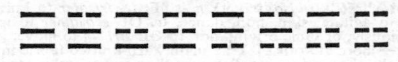

tri·hybrid \(')trī+\ n [tri- + hybrid] **1** : an individual or strain heterozygous for three factors and esp. for three recessive genes **2** : an individual or strain resulting from the interbreeding of three distinct kinds of individuals ⟨held the Australian aborigines to be ~s formed by admixture of Negrito and two distinct Australoid elements⟩ — **tri·hybrid·ism** \"+\ n

tri·hydrate \"+\ n [tri- + hydrate] : a chemical compound with three molecules of water

tri·hydrated \"+\ adj [tri- + hydrated] : combined with three molecules of water

tri·hy·dric \(')trī'hīdrik\ adj [ISV tri- + -hydric; prob. orig. formed as F trihydrique] **1** archaic : containing three atoms of acid hydrogen **2** : TRIHYDROXY — used esp. of alcohols and phenols

tri·hy·droxy \'trī,hī'dräksē\ adj [ISV trihydroxy-] : containing three hydroxyl groups in the molecule

trihydroxy- comb form [ISV tri- + hydroxy-] : containing three hydroxyl groups = in names of chemical compounds ⟨trihydroxybenzoic acid⟩

tri·iodide \(')trī+\ n [ISV tri- + iod- + -ide] : a binary compound containing three atoms of iodine combined with an element or radical

tri·iodothyronine \"+\ n [tri- + iod- + thyronine] : a crystalline iodine-containing phenolic amino acid $C_{15}H_{12}I_3NO_4$ that occurs in the levorotatory L-form in small amounts with thyroxine but is usu. made synthetically, is believed to be formed from thyroxine by loss of one iodine atom per molecule, has a more rapid and potent but briefer physiological action than thyroxine, and is used esp. in the form of its soluble sodium salt in the treatment of hypothyroidism and metabolic insufficiency

tri·ju·gate \'trīja,gāt; (')trī'jūgət, -,gāt\ adj [ISV trijug- (fr. L trijugus threefold) + -ate — more at TRIGA] : having three pairs of leaflets ⟨a ~ leaf⟩

tri·kaya \trə'kī(y)ə, -käyə\ n -s [Skt trikāya three bodies, fr. tri three + kāya body, mass (akin to Skt cinoti he heaps up) — more at THREE, POET] : a Mahayana Buddhist doctrine of the three bodies of the Buddha — see DHARMAKAYA, NIRMANAKAYA, SAMBHOGAKAYA

¹trike \'trīk\ n -s [by shortening & alter.] : TRICYCLE

²trike \"\ vi -ED/-ING/-S : TRICYCLE

tri·ke·rion \trī'kēryon\ or **tri·ce·ri·on** \trī'sirē,än\ n, pl **trike·ria** \-yə\ or **trice·ria** \-ēə\ [MGk trikērion, fr. Gk tri three + MGk kērion wax candle, fr. Gk, honeycomb, fr. kēros wax — more at TRI-, CEREUS] : a three-branched candlestick symbolizing the Trinity and used in the Eastern Orthodox Church by bishops (as in pronouncing a benediction)

triketo- comb form [ISV tri- + ket-] : containing three ketone groups = in names of chemical compounds ⟨triketocholanic acid⟩; compare KET-

tri·ketone \(')trī+\ n [tri- + ketone] : a chemical compound containing three ketonic carbonyl groups

tri·labiate \"+\ adj [tri- + labiate] : having three lips ⟨a ~ corolla on a flower⟩

tri·lacunar \'trī+\ also **tri·lacunate** \"+\ adj [tri- + laminar or laminate] : having three leaf gaps — compare MULTILACUNAR, UNILACUNAR

tri·laminar \'trī+\ also **tri·laminate** \"+\ adj [tri- + laminar or laminate] : having or built up of three layers

¹tri·lateral \'trī+\ adj [L trilaterus (fr. tri- + later-, latus side) + E -al — more at LATERAL] **1** : having three physical or material sides ⟨a ~ figure⟩ **2** : involving three interests often to the disadvantage of other interested parties ⟨a ~ agreement⟩ ⟨~ oligopoly in the market place —G.L.Bach⟩ — **tri·laterality** \(')trī+\ n — **tri·laterally** \(')trī+\ adv

²trilateral \"\ n : a figure having three sides : TRIANGLE

tri·lat·er·a·tion \(,)trī,lad·ə'rāshən\ n -s [trilateral + -ation] : the measurement of the lengths of the three sides of a series of touching or overlapping triangles on the earth's surface for the determination of the relative position of points by geometrical means (as in geodesy, map making, and surveying) — compare TRIANGULATION

tri·laurin \(')trī+\ n [ISV tri- + laurin] : the crystalline triglyceride $C_3H_5(OOCC_{11}H_{23})_3$ of lauric acid reported in laurel leaves and the fats of various seeds : glycerol tri-laurate

tril·by \'trilbē, -bi\ n -ES [fr. Trilby, heroine who is an artist's model whose feet are objects of admiration in the novel Trilby (1894) by George du Maurier †1896 Brit. artist and novelist] **1** : FOOT — usu. used in pl. **2** also **trilby hat** [so called fr. the fact that it was worn in the original London stage version (1895) of the novel Trilby] chiefly Brit : a soft felt hat with indented crown

tri·lem·ma \trī'lemə\ n -s [tri- + -lemma (as in dilemma)] **1** : an argument analogous to a dilemma but presenting three instead of two alternatives in the premises **2** : a state of things in which it is difficult to determine which one of three courses to pursue

tri·lete \'trī,lēt\ adj [NL Triletes, genus of spores with trigonous apertures, perh. irreg. fr. tri- + L latus side] : TRIGONOUS

tri·linear \'trī+\ adj [tri- + linear] : of, relating to, or included by three lines ⟨a ~ chart⟩

tri·lineate \"+\ also **tri·lineated** \"+\ adj [tri- + lineate, lineated] : marked with three usu. longitudinal streaks (as of color)

tri·lingual \"+\ adj [tri- + lingual] : consisting of, having, or expressed in three languages ⟨a ~ dictionary⟩; also : familiar with or able to use three languages ⟨~ students⟩ — **tri·lingual·ly** \-əlē, -li\ adv

trili·sa \'trīləsə, 'trīli-\ n, cap [NL, anagram of Liatris] : a genus of herbs (family Compositae) of the southern U.S. distinguished from Liatris by the corymbose panicles of flower heads and involucral bracts of two or three series only — see WILD VANILLA

¹tri·literal \(')trī+\ adj [tri- + literal] : consisting of three letters and esp. of three consonants ⟨~ roots in Semitic languages⟩ — **tri·literalism** \"+\ n — **tri·literally** \"+\ adv

²triliteral \"\ n : a root or word that is triliteral

tri·literality \(')trī+\ also **tri·literalness** \(')trī+\ n : the quality of being triliteral

tri·lithon \(')trī'lī,thän, 'trīlə,th-\ also **tri·lith** \'trī,lith\ n -s [NL trilithon, fr. Gk, neut. of trilithos of three stones, fr. tri- three + lithos stone — more at TRI-] : an ancient stone monument consisting of two upright megaliths carrying a third as a lintel

¹trill \'tril\ vb -ED/-ING/-S [ME trillen, prob. of Scand origin; akin to Sw & Norw trilla to roll, Dan trille; akin to MD trillen to tremble, vibrate, MLG trīseln to roll, reel, MHG trollen to run with short steps, OE treppan to tread — more at TRAP] vi **1** : TURN, TWIRL, ROLL, REVOLVE **2** : to flow in a small stream or in drops rapidly succeeding each other : TRICKLE ~ vt : to cause to flow in a small stream

²trill \"\ also **thrill** \'thril\ n -s [trill fr. It trillo; thrill alter. (influenced by ²thrill) of trill] **1 a** : the alternation of two musical tones a scale degree apart : SHAKE **b** : VIBRATO **c** : a rapid reiteration of the same tone esp. on a percussion instrument **2** : a sound felt to resemble a musical trill ⟨the liquid ~ of a thrush⟩ : the rapid vibration of one speech organ against another (as of the tip of the tongue against the teethridge, the uvula against the back of the tongue, or the lips against each other) **b** : a speech sound so made **c** : a letter or word pronounced with a trill

³trill \"\ vb -ED/-ING/-S [It trillare, prob. fr. D trillen to tremble, vibrate, fr. MD] vt : to impart the quality of a trill to : utter as or with a trill ⟨~ the r⟩; also : to vibrate, shake, or move to and fro so as to cause a trill ~ vi **1** : to utter a trill : play or sing with a trill : have a trembling sound : QUAVER **2** : to produce a vibration, shake, or quiver

tril·la·do \trə'yäd(,)ō, -ä(,)thō\ n [AmerSp, fr. Sp, past part. of trillar to thresh, prob. fr. trillo threshing machine, fr. L tribulum threshing board — more at TRIBULATION] : market coffee prepared by drying the beans in the sun

trill·er \'trilə(r)\ n -s [³trill + -er] : one that trills; esp : any of several cuckoo shrikes (genus Lalage) of Australia and the Pacific islands that are commonly largely black and white and are noted for their trilling calls — called also caterpillar-eater

tril·li·a·ceae \,trilē'āsē,ē\ n pl, cap [NL, fr. Trillium, type genus + -aceae] in some classifications : a small family of herbs (order Liliales) that have perennial rootstocks, entire leaves variously arranged, and often showy flowers of 3 petals and 3 sepals with 6 stamens followed by a globose or 3-lobed

berry, comprise the trilliums and closely related plants, and are usu. included in the family Liliaceae

tril·ling \'trilig, -lēg\ n -s [prob. fr. tri- + -ling] : a compound crystal consisting of three individuals — compare TWIN

tril·lion \'trilyən\ n -s often attrib [F, fr. tri- + -illion (as in million) — more at MILLION] **1** — see NUMBER table **2** : a very large number

¹tril·lionth \-n(t)th\ adj **1** : being number one trillion in a countable series — see NUMBER table **2** : being one of a trillion equal parts into which anything is divisible

²trillionth \"\ n, pl **trillionths** \-yən(t)s, -yən(t)ths\ **1** : number one trillion in a countable series **2** : the quotient of a number divided by one trillion : one of a trillion equal parts of anything **3** : a minute part

tril·li·um \'trilēəm\ n [NL, fr. tri- + -illium (as in cillium, verticillium)] **1** cap : a genus of chiefly No. American herbs (family Liliaceae) having short rootstocks and an erect stem bearing a whorl of three leaves and a large solitary flower at the summit with a corolla that is white, pink, purple, yellow, or greenish and is followed by a many-seeded berry — see WAKE-ROBIN **-s** : any plant of the genus Trillium **2 -s** : the dried rhizome of purple trillium formerly used as an astringent and tonic

trillium family n : LILIACEAE, TRILLIACEAE

trillium 1b

tril·lo \'tri(,)lō, 'trē(-\ n, pl **tril·li** \-lē\ or **tril·loes** [It] **1** : TRILL 1a **2** : TREMOLO

trills pl of TRILL, pres 3d sing of TRILL

tri·lobate \(,)trī+\ or **tri·lobated** \"+\ or **tri·lobed** \"+\ adj [tri- + lobate, lobated or lobed] : having or divided into three lobes ⟨a ~ leaf⟩

tri·lo·ba·tion \,trīlə'bāshən\ n : the condition of being trilobate

tri·lobe \'trī+\ n [tri- + lobe] : something having or distinguished by three lobes; esp : a trilobate gear wheel

tri·lo·bi·ta \,trīlə'bītə\ n pl, cap [NL, fr. Trilobites] : a division of Arthropoda that is treated as a subclass of Crustacea or made a separate class and comprises the trilobites

tri·lo·bite \'trīlə,bīt\ n -s [NL Trilobites division of Arthropoda comprising the trilobites, fr. Gk trilobos three-lobed (fr. tri- three + lobos lobe) + L -ites -ite — more at TRI-, SLEEP] : any of numerous extinct Paleozoic marine arthropods that constitute the group Trilobita, have delicate biramous appendages and the segments of the body divided by furrows on the dorsal surface into a median axis and two lateral pleura, are usu. of a flattened oval form, and besides the longitudinal lobes present the three transverse body regions of head, thorax, and pygidium of which the first is covered by a continuous shield, the second consists of a variable number of free segments, and the last of a number of coalescent segments — **tri·lo·bit·ic** \,-'bid·ik\ adj

trilobite larva n : a 3-lobed larva that is a developmental form of limulus and resembles a trilobite

tri·locular \(')trī+\ or **tri·loculate** \"+\ adj [ISV tri- + locular] : having three cells or cavities

tril·o·gy \'triləjē, -ji\ n -ES [Gk trilogia, fr. tri- + -logia -logy] **1** : a series of three dramas or sometimes three literary or musical compositions that although each is in one sense complete have a close mutual relation and form one theme or develop aspects of one basic concept **2** : a group of three connected classical Greek tragedies played serially (as at the festival of Dionysus) **3** : a group of three related things, topics, or sayings : TRIAD

tri·loph·odon \trī'läfə,dän\ n [NL, fr. tri- + loph- + -odon] syn of GOMPHOTHERIUM

tri·loph·odont \-nt\ adj [ISV tri- + loph- + -odont] : having or being teeth with three crests

¹trim \'trim\ vb trimmed; trimmed; trimming; trims [fr. (assumed) ME trimen, trymen, fr. OE trymian, trymman to strengthen, confirm, arrange, fr. trum strong, firm, secure; akin to Gk drymos forest, Skt druma tree, dāruna hard, dāru wood — more at TREE] vt **1 a** (1) archaic : to build or repair (a ship) and provide with fittings and supplies for sailing (2) obs : to furnish or prepare for use ⟨he had not so trimm'd and dressed his land as we this garden —Shak.⟩; also : to restore to a usable condition **b** : to prepare (as a lamp) for most efficient burning **2 a** : to embellish with or as if with ribbons, lace, or ornaments : DECORATE, ADORN ⟨these rich fabrics are often extravagantly trimmed with flowers —Women's Wear Daily⟩ ⟨a handsome edifice of . . . colonial sand-mold brick, trimmed with marble —Amer. Guide Series: Minn.⟩ **b** : to arrange a display of goods in (a shop window) **3 a** (1) : to administer a beating to : CHASTISE, THRASH (2) : to defeat esp. resoundingly ⟨trimmed him at chess⟩ **b** : DEFRAUD, CHEAT, SWINDLE **4 a** (1) : to make trim, neat, regular, or less bulky by or as if by cutting, shortening, or clipping ⟨has his hair trimmed before it needs cutting —H.W.Hayes⟩ ⟨~ a page of a book⟩ (2) : to prepare (an animal) for exhibition esp. by ordering and styling the coat **b** : to reduce by removing excess or extraneous matter : cut away matter to lessen the size of ⟨~s his 190 pounds down to a sinewy 170 by race time —Bill Wolf⟩ ⟨~ the hides of those parts which cannot be made into usable leather —advt⟩ ⟨trimmed of its branches, a ramrod-backed tree whisks out of the logging camp by rail —Monsanto Mag.⟩ ⟨~ the budget⟩ **c** : to take off or away by or as if by cutting, clipping, or lopping ⟨trimmed thousands from federal payrolls —Grit⟩ ⟨~ excess fat from meat —Better Homes & Gardens⟩ ⟨trimmed out description that intervenes between two consecutive actions —K.A.Spaulding⟩ **5 a** (1) : to cause (as a ship) to assume a desirable position in the water by the arrangement of ballast, cargo, or passengers ⟨the captain made us ~ the boat, and we got her to lie a little more evenly —R.L.Stevenson⟩ (2) : to adjust for horizontal movement or for motion toward or downward ⟨trimming the blimp satisfactorily⟩ ⟨trimmed to fly at a lift coefficient corresponding to a minimum glide angle —Aero Digest⟩ ⟨if the boat is properly trimmed, she submerges on a practically even keel —Kendall Banning⟩ **b** : to adjust (as a sail) to a desired position ⟨~ cargo⟩ ~ vi **1 a** : to maintain a middle position between opposing parties so as to appear to be neutral or to favor each equally **b** : to change one's views so as to correspond to the momentarily popular or winning opinion ⟨if . . . he begins to ~ or equivocate, then he won't be for us and we won't be for him —Amer. Mercury⟩ **2** : to assume or cause a boat or ship to assume a desired position in the water ⟨a boat that ~s badly ⟨the art of navigation lies in trimming to the storm —J.A.Froude⟩ syn see STABILIZE — **trim one's sails** : to adjust oneself or one's actions or expenditures to prevailing conditions ⟨trim his sails in accordance with the prevalent faith —C.H.Sykes⟩

²trim \"\ adj trimmer; trimmest **1** obs : EXCELLENT, FINE; also : PLEASANT, GAY **2** archaic : suitably adjusted, equipped, or prepared for service or use : in good order : well trimmed **3** : exhibiting neatness, good order, or compactness of line or structure : free from anything unkempt, disordered, or extraneous : having clean lines or proper proportion : being in good order or repair ⟨~, new bungalows —Amer. Guide Series: Ark.⟩ ⟨the gravel paths are squared and ~ —Emily Hahn⟩ ⟨not fat, like grass-fed cattle, but ~ and supple, like deer —John Burroughs⟩ syn see NEAT

³trim \"\ adv : TRIMLY : used chiefly in combination ⟨the trim-cut forest vistas —W.M.Thackeray⟩

⁴trim \"\ n -s **1 a** : the state of readiness to sail of a ship or its cargo, ballast, engines, or rigging **b** (1) : the condition or state of readiness for action or use of a person or thing : FITNESS ⟨weighing 160 pounds, the writer is in fine physical ~ —Current Biog.⟩; esp : a suitable or excellent condition for a particular task or for general action ⟨working himself into physical ~ to stand the strain —S.H.Adams⟩ ⟨get a strange system called democracy into working ~ —Elspeth Huxley⟩ ⟨cars in full road ~ —R.F.Baxter⟩ (2) : the condition of a person with respect to personal qualities : CHARACTER, DISPOSITION **2 a** : clothing, dress, or appearance esp. when rich or ornate

b : material used as adornment, ornament, or trimming or fully or partly ornamental fixtures ⟨sentences full of rich ~ . . . that a lesser man might forbear to use —Rex Lardner⟩: as (1) : TRIMMING 2 (2) : the lighter woodwork or metal in the finish of a building (as a molded architrave around an opening to protect the plastering); also : an ornamental or protective framing (as of wood, metal, or stone) around an opening or at a corner or eave ⟨a double-winged massive building of light brown brick with red stone ~ —Amer. Guide Series: Minn.⟩⟨serve as architectural ~ and have no structural value at all —G.E.Strehan⟩ (3) : the hardware of a building and esp. of its doors (4) : the interior furnishings of an automobile body including seat, floor, and sidewall coverings, hardware, lights, armrests, and other accessories; also : ornamental metalwork on the outside of an automotive vehicle ⟨chrome ~⟩ (5) : WINDOW DRESSING **3 a** : the position of a ship, boat, seaplane, or float in water esp. with reference to the horizontal ⟨could feel the altered ~ of the boat as her bows sank and her stern rose on the slope —C.S.Forester⟩ b : the measure of the difference between the draft of a ship forward and that aft ⟨designed . . . to float at a draft of 12 feet forward and 15 feet aft, giving a ~ of 3 feet by the stern —E.L.Aftwood⟩ **b** : the relation between the plane of a sail and the direction of motion of the ship **c** : the buoyancy status of a submarine ⟨using the ballast pumps to alter the ~ of the submarine —David Masters⟩ ⟨submarine custom for the diving officer to control the speed until he is satisfied with the submerged ~ —E.L.Beach⟩ **d** : the attitude of a lighter-than-air craft relative to a fore-and-aft horizontal plane ~ : the attitude with respect to several axes at which an airplane will continue in level flight with free controls **4** : something that is trimmed off or cut out ⟨a man making axle shafts . . . picked up a piece of discarded ~ —B.M.Bowie⟩ **5 a** : the portion of the outside edges of printed sheets or pages esp. of a book that is to be trimmed off **b** : the maximum width of finished paper with deckle edges removed that can be made on a paper machine **6** : a haircut that neatens up the lines of a previous haircut without changing the style **7** : the small strings at the top and throat of a racket which bind the main strings — **trim by the bow** of watercraft or aircraft : lower at the bow than at the stern — **trim by the stern** of watercraft or aircraft : lower at the stern than at the bow

tri·mas·ti·gote \(')trī'mastə,gōt\ adj [alter. of earlier tri-mastigate, fr. tri- + mastig- + -ate] : TRIFLAGELLATE

trime \'trīm\ n -s usu cap [prob. fr. tri- + -ime (as in dime)] : the U.S. silver three-cent piece issued 1851–1873

tri·mellitic acid \'trī+...\ n [ISV tri- + mellitic] : a crystalline tricarboxylic acid $C_6H_3(COOH)_3$ obtained indirectly from mellitic acid, by oxidation of coal, and in other ways; 1,2,4-benzene-tricarboxylic acid

tri·mer \'trīmə(r)\ n -s [ISV tri- + -mer] : a compound formed by the union of three molecules of a simpler compound or of a radical : a polymer formed from three molecules of a monomer — **tri·mer·ic** \(')trī'merik\ adj

trim·era \'trīmərə\ n [NL, fr. neut. pl. of trimerus trimerous] syn of PSEUDOTRIMERA

trim·ere·su·rus \,trīmərə'sürəs\ n, cap [NL, fr. Gk trimerēs of three parts + NL -urus] : a genus of usu. green prehensile-tailed arboreal Asiatic pit vipers closely related to the bushmaster — see HABU

tri·mer·ide \'trīmə,rīd, -,rəd\ n -s [trimer + -ide] : TRIMER

tri·mer·ite \'trīmə,rīt\ n -s [G trimerit, fr. Gk trimerēs of three parts + G -it -ite] : a mineral $Be(Mn,Ca)(SiO_4)$ consisting of a silicate of manganese, calcium, and beryllium and occurring in salmon-colored tabular crystals (hardness 6–7, sp. gr. 3.5)

tri·mer·iza·tion \,trīmərə'zāshən, -,rī'z-\ n -s [trimer + -ization] : polymerization resulting in a trimer

trim·ero·rhi·nus \,trīmərō'rīnəs\ n, cap [NL, fr. tri- + mer- + -rhinus] : a genus of African back-fanged snakes (family Boigidae) — see SCHAAPSTECKER

trim·er·ous \'trīmərəs\ adj [NL trimerus, fr. Gk trimerēs of three parts, fr. tri- three + meros part — more at TRI-, MERIT] **1** : having the parts in threes — used of a flower and often written 3-merous **2** of an insect : having three or apparently three segments in each tarsus **b** : belonging to the Pseudotrimera

tri·mes·ic acid \(')trī'mesik-\ n [ISV tri- + mes- (in mesity-lene) + -ic] : a crystalline tricarboxylic acid $C_6H_3(COOH)_3$ formed by the oxidation of mesitylene and in other ways; 1,3,5-benzene-tricarboxylic acid

tri·mes·ter \(')trī'mestə(r)\ n -s [F trimestre, fr. L trimestris of three months, fr. tri- + mensis month — more at MOON] **1** : a period of three or about three months **2** : one of three terms into which the academic year is divided at some educational institutions — **tri·mes·tral** \-strəl\ adj — **tri·mes·tri·al** \-rēəl\ adj

tri·metaphosphate \'trī+\ n [tri- + metaphosphate] : a cyclic trimeric metaphosphate — compare SODIUM PHOSPHATE

¹trim·e·ter \'triməd·ə(r)\ n [L trimetrus, fr. Gk trimetros, fr. tri- three + metron measure — more at TRI-, MEASURE] : a line of three measures consisting of three dipodies (as in classical iambic, trochaic, and anapestic verse) or three feet (as in modern English verse)

²trimeter \"\ adj : having three measures in a foot

tri·metha·di·one \'trī,methə'dī,ōn\ n [tri- trimethyl + connective -a- + -dione] : a crystalline anticonvulsant $C_6H_9NO_3$ used chiefly in the treatment of petit mal epilepsy; 3,5,5-trimethyl-2,4-oxazolidine-dione

tri·methine \'trī+\ n [tri- + methine] : CARBOCYANINE

trimethoxy- comb form [tri- + methoxy-] : containing three methoxy groups = in names of chemical compounds ⟨trimethoxycoumarin⟩

tri·methyl \'trī+\ adj [ISV tri- + methyl] : containing three methyl groups in the molecule

tri·meth·yl·amine \(,)trī'methəl+\ n [ISV trimethyl + amine] : an irritating gaseous or volatile liquid tertiary amine $(CH_3)_3N$ that has a fishy odor, that is only slightly more basic than ammonia, that is flammable and forms explosive mixtures with air, that is formed as a degradation product of many nitrogenous animal and plant substances (as in herring brine and the distillate of sugar-beet residues), that is made commercially by catalytic reaction of methanol and ammonia at high temperature, and that is used chiefly in making choline and other quaternary ammonium compounds

tri·meth·yl·benzene \(,)trī'methəl+\ n [ISV trimethyl + benzene] : any of three trimethyl derivatives of benzene: **a** : HEMIMELLITENE **b** : MESITYLENE **c** : PSEUDOCUMENE

tri·meth·yl·carbinol \"+\ n [ISV trimethyl + carbinol] : BUTYL ALCOHOL

tri·methylene \(')trī+\ n [ISV tri- + methylene] **1** : CYCLOPROPANE **2** : a bivalent radical —$CH_2CH_2CH_2$— containing three methylene groups and isomeric with propylene

tri·meth·yl·ene·tri·ni·tra·mine \(,)trī'methə,lēn,trī'nītrə,mēn, -,mēn\ n [trimethylene + trinitr- + amine] : CYCLONITE

tri·meth·yl·ethylene \(')trī+\ n [trimethyl + ethylene] : AMYLENE a

trimethyl·pyridine \(,)trī'methəl+\ n [trimethyl + pyridine] : COLLIDINE a

tri·metric \(')trī+\ adj [tri- + Gk metron measure + E -ic] : ORTHORHOMBIC

trimetric projection n : axonometric projection in which the three spatial axes are represented as unequally inclined to the drawing surface and whose distances along the axes are drawn unequal

tri·met·ro·gon \trī'me·trə,gän\ n -s [tri- + Gk metron measure + E -gon] : a system of aerial mapping involving the use of a single assembly containing three cameras with which one vertical and two oblique right and left aerial photographs are taken simultaneously at regular intervals over the area being mapped

trimline \'--,-\ n [⁴trim + line] : the boundary of an area from which a glacier has receded that is often indicated by changes in vegetation

trim·ly adv : in a trim manner : with trimness ⟨~ attired⟩

trimmed past of TRIM

trim·mer \'trimə(r)\ n -s [¹trim + -er] **1 a** : one that by hand or by machine trims articles in manufacturing or industrial processes: as (1) : one that puts the finishing touches or parts to a product (2) : one that cuts or smooths articles to the proper shape or size (3) : one that stows coal or

freight on a ship so as to distribute the weight properly **b** : an instrument or machine with which trimming is done: as (1) : any of various circular-saw machines for trimming lumber (2) : a machine for cutting stacks of books or paper (3) : an apparatus for trimming a pile of coal into a regular form (as a cone or prism) (4) : a flat board or metal surface having a movable cutting blade attached to one edge for trimming the edges of prints and films — called also *trimming board* (5) : a small adjustable circuit element and esp. a condenser used to tune a circuit to a desired frequency **2** : a beam that receives the end of a header in floor framing (as about a hole left for stairs or to avoid bringing joists near chimneys) **3** : one that does not adhere to one set of opinions esp. in politics : one that fluctuates or holds a middle position between parties so as to appear to favor each : one that for the sake of expediency will modify his policy, position or opinions ⟨a ~ who in the interests of his personal safety evaded the responsibility of joining the one or the other side —M.R.Cohen⟩ **4** : one that inflicts chastisement by words or blows **5** : a night line used in pike fishing **6** : one that arranges displays (as in a store) **7** : an engine in a hump classification yard assigned to retrieve misdirected cars

trimmer arch *n* : an arch built between trimmers in the thickness of an upper floor to support a hearth

trimmer condenser *n* : a small variable condenser used as a trimmer

trimmer joist *n* : TRIMMING JOIST

trimmer signal *n* : a signal near the summit in a hump yard to convey information about movements from the classification tracks toward the summit

trimmest *superlative of* TRIM

trimming *n -s* [fr. gerund of ¹*trim*] **1 a** : the act of one who trims **b** : the act or process of retrieving misdirected freight cars in a hump classification yard **2 a** : a decorative accessory or additional item which serves to finish, decorate, or complete ⟨~s for a hat⟩ **b** : an additional garnishing that is not essential but adds to the interest or attractiveness of a main item ⟨roast beef, Yorkshire pudding and all the ~s —Vera Caspary⟩ ⟨a factual report of what occurred, without adding the ~s of the public relations people —R.S.Low⟩ **c** : an extra figure, fill-in, or chorus in a square dance — usu. used in pl.

trimming board *n* : TRIMMER 1b(4)

trimming hatch *or* **trimming hole** *n* : a hatchway at a distance from a main hatch through which to load grain or similar cargo to bring it uniformly close up to the deck

trimming house *n* : the part of a railway shop in which the final stages of car rebuilding (as assembly, painting, and stenciling) are completed

trimming joist *n* : a joist into which timber trimmers are framed

trimming machine *n* : a woodworking machine consisting of a lever-operated knife and adjustable guides for shearing surfaces true to any required angle

trimming tab *n* : TAB 1h

trimming tank *n* : a tank either forward or aft and usu. in the extreme ends utilized for changing the trim of a ship by admitting or discharging water ballast

trim·ness *-es* : the quality or state of being trim

tri·modal \(')trī+\ *adj* [*tri-* + *modal*] : having three statistical modes — **tri·modality** \'trī+\ *n*

tri·mo·da ne·ces·si·tas \'trīˌmōdənə'sesəˌtas, ˌtrimə,dü-ˌneˈkesəˌtäs\ *n* [ML, lit., necessity of three kinds] : the threefold burden or charge on Anglo-Saxon landholders of army service, repair of strongholds, and repair of bridges

tri·molecular \'trī+\ *adj* [*tri-* + *molecular*] : relating to or formed from three molecules

tri·monthly \(')trī+\ *adj* [*tri-* + *monthly*] : occurring, appearing, or being made, done, or acted upon every three months

tri·morph \'trīˌmȯrf\ *n* [ISV, back-formation fr. *trimorphism*] : any of the three crystalline forms of a trimorphous substance ⟨rutile, brookite, and anatase are ~s of titanium dioxide⟩

tri·mor·phic \(')trīˈmȯrfik\ *adj* [*trimorphism* + *-ic*] : exhibiting trimorphism

tri·mor·phism \(')trīˈmȯr,fizəm\ *n -s* [ISV *trimorph-* (fr. Gk *trimorphos* having three forms) + *-ism*] **1** : polymorphism in which there are three distinct forms of a species or of a particular caste — compare DIMORPHISM a **2** : occurrence of three distinct forms of organs (as leaves or flowers) on individuals of the same species : HETEROGONY **3** : the property of crystallizing in three different forms

tri·mor·phous \-fəs\ *adj* [Gk *trimorphos*, fr. *tri-* three + *-morphos* -morphous — more at TRI-] : of, relating to, or characterized by trimorphism

tri·motor \'trī+\ *n* [*tri-* + *motor*] : an airplane powered with three motors

trims *pres 3d sing of* TRIM, *pl of* TRIM

trim size *n* : the actual size of something (as a magazine or book page) after excess material required in production has been cut off

trimstone \'ˌ¦-\ *n* : stone used to trim a wall of brick or stone masonry or for copings, cornices, and other ornament

trim tab *n* : TAB 1h

tri·myristin \'trī+\ *n* [ISV *tri-* + *myristin*] : the solid triglyceride $C_3H_5(OOCC_{13}H_{27})_3$ of myristic acid found esp. in nutmegs : glycerol tri-myristate

trin \'trin\ *n -s* [prob. fr. *trin* + *twin*] : TRIPLET 3

trin *abbr* trinity

tri·nacri·an \(')trīˈnakrēən, trə'n- *also* -nāk-\ *adj, usu cap* [*Trinacria*, ancient name of Sicily (fr. L, fr. Gk *Trinakria*) + E *-an*] : SICILIAN

¹tri·nal \'trīn³l\ *adj* [LL *trinalis* threefold, three, fr. L *trini* three each + *-alis* -al; akin to L *tres* three — more at THREE] **1** : THREEFOLD **2** : TRIAL

²trinal *n -s* : TRIAL

¹tri·na·ry \'trīnərē\ *adj* [LL *trinarius*, fr. L *trini* three each + *-arius* -ary] : TERNARY, THREEFOLD

²trinary *n -es* : a ternary group or set : TRIAD

tri·nate \'trīˌnāt\ *vi* -ED/-ING/-S [NL *trinatus*, past part. of *trinare*, prob. fr. L *trini* three each] : to celebrate three masses on the same day (as Christmas)

trin·co·ma·li wood *or* **trin·co·ma·lee wood** \'triŋkōˌmäˈlē-\ *n, often cap T* [fr. *Trincomali, Trincomalee*, seaport in Ceylon] **1** : a tropical Asiatic timber tree (*Berrya ammonilla*) of the family Tiliaceae with hard dark wood **2** : the wood of the trincomali wood tree

¹trin·dle \'trind³l, *dial* -n(d)³l\ *n -s* [ME *trindel, trendel* circle, ring — more at TRENDLE] **1** *dial Eng* : a round or circular object; *specif* : the wheel of a wheelbarrow **2** : either of a pair of metal plates that are inserted between the backbone and boards of a rounded and backed book to force the backbone temporarily into a flat shape while the fore edge is being trimmed

²trindle \-n(d)³l\ *vi* [ME *trindelen*, prob. fr. *trindel* trindle] *dial* : ROLL, TRUNDLE

¹trine \'trīn\ *vi* -ED/-ING/-S [ME *trinen*, of Scand origin; akin to Dan *trine*, to step, go, Sw *dial. trina* to go, march, OSw *trin* step, tread] **1** *archaic* : MARCH, GO **2** *archaic* : HANG

²trine \'ˌ\ *adj* [ME, fr. MF *trin, trine*, fr. L *trinus*, fr. *trini* three each — more at TRINAL] **1** : THREEFOLD, TRIPLE **2** : of, relating to, or being the favorable astrological aspect of two heavenly bodies 120 degrees apart

³trine \'ˌ\ *n -s* **1 a** : a group of three : TRIAD **b** *cap* : TRINITY **2** : the trine astrological aspect of two heavenly bodies **3** *trines pl* : TRIPLETS

⁴trine \'ˌ\ *vt* -ED/-ING/-S : to put in the aspect of a trine

trine immersion *n* : the practice of immersing a candidate for baptism three times in the names in turn of the Trinity

tri·neural fasciculus \(')trī+ - - -\ *n* [*trineural* fr. *tri-* + *neural*] : a bundle of fibers in the upper part of the spinal cord joined with the 9th, 10th, and 11th cranial nerves

t ring *n, cap T* : a ring such that T sections are formed by passing normal radial planes through the ring; *specif* : a piston ring having a T-shaped cross section

---

trin·ga \'triŋgə\ *n, cap* [NL, fr. Gk *tryngas*, a bird] : a genus of sandpipers including the solitary sandpipers and sometimes the tattlers

trin·gine \'triŋˌgīn, -rinˌjīn\ *or* **trin·goid** \-riŋˌgȯid\ *adj* [NL *Tringa* + E *-ine* or *-oid*] : of or relating to the genus *Tringa*

trin·gle \'triŋgəl\ *n -s* [F, rod, tringle, alter. of MF *tingle*, fr. MD *tingel, tengel* lath] : a narrow straight molding usu. of square section : FILLET

trin·i·dad \'trinəˌdad, -daa(ə)d, ˌ¦¦¦'¦\ *adj, usu cap* [fr. *Trinidad*, island in the West Indies] : of or from the West Indian island of Trinidad : of the kind or style prevalent in Trinidad : TRINIDADIAN

trinidad asphalt *also* **trinidad pitch** *n, usu cap T* : a natural asphalt found in a pitch lake in the island of Trinidad, widely used in the U. S. for sheet asphalt pavements, and containing when refined about 44 percent colloidal clay and 56 percent bitumen

¹trin·i·dadian \ˌ¦¦¦'dadēən, -dād-,-daad-\ *adj, usu cap* [*Trinidad* + E *-an*] **1** : of, relating to, or characteristic of the island of Trinidad **2** : of, relating to, or characteristic of the people of Trinidad

²trinidadian \"\ *n -s cap* [*Trinidad* + E *-an*, n. suffix] : a native or inhabitant of the island of Trinidad

tri·nil man \'trēˌnil-\ *n, usu cap T* [fr. *Trinil*, village in Java where parts of the Java man were found] : JAVA MAN

¹trin·i·tar·i·an \ˌtrinə'terēən, ˌ-nə'ta(ə)r-, -nə'tär-\ *adj* [LL *trinitarius* (fr. LL *trinitas* trinity + L *-arius* -ary) + E *-an* — more at TRINITY] **1** *usu cap* : of or relating to the order of Trinitarians **2** *usu cap* : of or relating to the Trinity, the doctrine of the Trinity, or adherents to that doctrine **3** : having three parts or aspects : THREEFOLD, TRIPLE

²trinitarian \"\ *n -s usu cap* [NL *trinitarius* + E *-an*, n. suffix] **1** : a member of the Roman Catholic Order of the Holy Trinity founded at Rome in 1198 for the ransoming of Christian captives from the Muslims but devoted today mainly to teaching and nursing — called also *Mathurin, Redemptionist* **2** : one who subscribes to the doctrine of the Trinity

trin·i·tar·i·an·ism \ˌ¦¦¦'¦¦əˌnizəm\ *n -s usu cap* **1** : the doctrine of the Trinity **2** : belief in or adherence to the doctrine of the Trinity

trinitr- *or* **trinitro-** *comb form* [ISV *tri-* + *nitr-*] : containing three nitro groups — in names of chemical compounds ⟨*trinitrocellulose*⟩

tri·nitramine \(')trī+\ *n* [*tri-* + *nitramine*] : a compound containing three nitramine groups in the molecule

tri·nitrate \"+\ *n* [*tri-* + *nitrate*] : a nitrate containing three nitrate groups in the molecule

tri·nitride \(')trīˈnī-,trīd, -nī-trōd\ *n* [ISV *trinitr-* + *-ide*] : a binary compound containing three atoms of nitrogen combined with an element or radical; *esp* : AZIDE

tri·ni·trin \(')trīˈnī-trən\ *n -s* [ISV *trinitr-* + *-in*] : NITROGLYCERIN

tri·ni·tro \(')trīˈnī-,(ˌ)trō\ *adj* [*trinitro-*] : containing three nitro groups in the molecule

tri·ni·tro·benzene \(')trīˈnī-trō+\ *n* [ISV *trinitr-* + *benzene*] : a light yellow crystalline compound $C_6H_3(NO_2)_3$ that is a more powerful yet more stable explosive than trinitrotoluene but is little used because of the difficulties of its preparation usu. indirectly from toluene — called also *TNB, 1,3,5-trinitrobenzene*

tri·ni·tro·cresol \"+\ *n* [ISV *trinitr-* + *cresol*] : any of several trinitro derivatives $(NO_2)_3C_6H(CH_3)OH$ of the three cresols; *esp* : a high explosive similar to picric acid made by nitrating *meta*-cresol — see CRESYLITE

tri·ni·tro·glycerin \"+\ *n* [*trinitr-* + *glycerin*] : NITROGLYCERIN

tri·ni·tro·phenol \"+\ *n* [ISV *trinitr-* + *phenol*] : any of six trinitro derivatives $(NO_2)_3C_6H_2OH$ of phenol; *esp* : PICRIC ACID

tri·ni·tro·phenylmethylnitramine \"+\ *pronunciations at* PHENYL, METHYL, & NITRAMINE\ *n* [*trinitr-* + *phenyl* + *methyl* + *nitramine*] : TETRYL

tri·ni·tro·toluene \(')trīˈnī-trō+\ *n* [ISV *trinitr-* + *toluene*] : the flammable toxic symmetrical trinitro derivative $CH_3C_6H_2(NO_2)_3$ of toluene that is obtained by nitrating toluene as the light yellow crystalline alpha form darkening to reddish brown on exposure to light, that is stable at temperatures up to 100° C and even higher and is insensitive to friction or ordinary shock but is a high explosive, and that is used either alone as bursting charge for shells, bombs, and grenades or as an ingredient of various explosives and is also used as an intermediate in chemical synthesis (as of phloroglucinol) — called also *TNT, 2,4,6-trinitrotoluene*

tri·ni·tro·toluol \"+\ *n* [ISV *trinitr-* + *toluol*] : TRINITROTOLUENE — not used systematically

tri·ni·tro·xylene \"+\ *n* [ISV *trinitr-* + *xylene*] : any of several trinitro derivatives $(CH_3)_2C_6H(NO_2)_3$ of the three xylenes or a mixture of such derivatives used as an explosive

¹trin·i·ty \'trinətē, -note, -əti-\ *n -s* [ME *Trinite, trinite*, fr. OF *trinité*, fr. LL *trinitat-, trinitas* (trans. of Gk *trias*), fr. L, triad, fr. *trini* three each (akin to L *tria*, three three) + *-itat-, -itas* -ity — more at THREE] **1 a** (1) *cap* : the union of three persons or hypostases (as the Father, the Son, and the Holy Spirit) in one godhead so that all the three are one God as to substance but three persons or hypostases as to individuality : the triune God (2) *usu cap* : the Christian doctrine of the Trinity **b** *often cap* : a union or group of three deities : TRIAD **2** *usu cap* : TRINITY SUNDAY **3** [ME *trinite*, fr. L *trinitas*] : the state of being threefold **4 a** : something having three parts or aspects **b** : a group of three (its ~ of churches standing in stately dignity —*Amer. Guide Series: Conn.*) **5 a** : HERB TRINITY **b** : a common No. American spiderwort (*Tradescantia virginiana*)

²trinity \"\ *adj, usu cap* **1** : of, dedicated to, or bearing a symbol of the Trinity **2** : associated with or occurring on or about Trinity Sunday ⟨*Trinity* Monday⟩ **3** [fr. *Trinity House*, established in 1514 in Deptford, England] : of or associated with a semigovernmental association of English mariners authorized by Parliament to erect and maintain English coastal lighthouses and other navigational aids and to license pilots ⟨*Trinity* pilots⟩ ⟨*Trinity* dues⟩ ⟨a *Trinity* buoy keeper⟩ **4** [fr. *Trinity* river, Texas] : of or relating to a subdivision of the Comanchean — see GEOLOGIC TIME table

trinity column *n* : a column of triangular plan for all or part of its height built as a religious memorial

trinity lily *n* : a large-flowered white trillium (*Trillium grandiflorum*)

trinity mixture *n* : a livestock concentrate that is made up of one quarter alfalfa meal, one quarter linseed oil meal, and one half tankage or meat scrap and is used esp. for feeding growing hogs

trinity sunday *n, usu cap T&S* [ME *trinite sonday*] : the Sunday next after Whitsunday observed as a feast in honor of the Holy Trinity

trinity term *n, usu cap 1st T* **1 a** : the term from May 22 to June 12 during which the superior courts of England were formerly open — compare EASTER TERM, HILARY TERM, MICHAELMAS TERM **b** *also* **trinity sitting** : the sitting of the High Court of Justice of England between June 9 and July 31 **2** : the third academic term in an English university from about mid April to about the end of June — compare HILARY TERM, MICHAELMAS TERM

trinitytide \ˌ¦¦¦¦'¦\ *n, usu cap* : the season of the church year between Trinity Sunday and Advent

¹trin·ket \'triŋkət, *usu* -ȱd-+\ *n -s* [perh. fr. ME *trenket, trynket* shoemaker's knife, small knife, fr. ONF *trenquet*, fr. *trenquer* to cut, prob. modif. of L *truncare* to cut off — more at TRUNCATE] **1** : a small article of equipment ⟨put up his ~s in his duffel bag⟩ **2 a** : a small ornament (as a jewel or ring) **b** : a vain ornament : GAUD **3** : a thing of little value

²trinket \"\ *vi* -ED/-ING/-S [perh. fr. ¹*trinket*] : to deal clandestinely ⟨*trinkets*... makes a big change in your costume — *Harper's Bazaar*⟩

trin·ket·ry \-strē, -ri\ *n -es* : small items of personal ornament (the finish ... makes a big change in your costume —*Harper's Bazaar*⟩

trin·kle \'triŋkəl\ *vi* -ED/-ING/-S [ME *trinkelen*, prob. alter. of *triklen* to trickle] *dial* : to flow down by drops : TRICKLE

---

trink·lied \'triŋˌklēt\ *n, pl* **trinklie·der** \-ˌēdə(r)\ [G, fr. *trinken* to drink (fr. OHG *trinkan*) + *lied* song, fr. OHG *liod* — more at DRINK, LAUD] : DRINKING SONG

trin·kums \'triŋkəmz\ *also* **trinkum·trankums** \ˌ¦-kəmˌtraŋkəmz\ *n pl* [*trinkums* alter. (influenced by L nouns ending in *-um*) of *trinkets*; *trinkum-trankums* redupl. of *trinkums*] : TRINKETS, FRIPPERY

tri·nodal \(')trī+\ *adj* [*tri-* + *nodal*] : having three nodes

tri·no·dine \(')trīˈnōd³n, trīˈnō,dīn, 'trīnə,dīn\ *adj* [L *trinodis* three-knotted (fr. *tri-* + *nodus* knot) + E *-al* or *-ine* — more at NODE] : having three nodes

tri·no·da necessitas \(')trī'nōdə-, (ˌ)trē'-\ *n* [NL, by alter. (influence of L *trinodis*)] : TRIMODA NECESSITAS

tri·no·men \(')trīˈnōmən\ *n* [*tri-* + L *nomen* name — more at NAME] : TRINOMIAL 2

¹tri·no·mi·al \(')trīˈnōmēəl\ *n -s* [*tri-* + *-nomial* (as in *binomial*, n.)] **1** : a polynomial of three terms **2 a** : a trinomial name (influence of *binomial*, adj.)] **1** : consisting of three mathematical terms **2** : being a name belonging to botanical or zoological nomenclature composed of a first term designating the species, a second term designating the subspecies or variety to which an organism belongs **3** : of or relating to trinomials ⟨~ nomenclature⟩

²trinomial \(')¦¦¦'¦¦¦\ *adj* [*tri-* + *-nomial* (as in *binomial*, adj.)] **1** : consisting of three mathematical terms **2** : being a name belonging to botanical or zoological nomenclature composed of a first term designating the species, a second term designating the subspecies or variety to which an organism belongs **3** : of or relating to trinomials ⟨~ nomenclature⟩

tri·no·mi·al·ism \ˌ¦¦¦'¦¦əˌlizəm\ *n -s* : a system of nomenclature (as in biological classification) involving the use of trinomial terms

tri·no·mi·al·ist \-ˈlȯst\ *n -s* : an adherent of trinomialism

tri·no·mi·al·ly \(')¦¦¦'¦¦ēˌlē, -li\ *adv* : in a trinomial manner

trins *pl of* TRIN

tri·nuclear \(')trī+\ *adj* [*tri-* + *nuclear*] : having three nuclei ⟨~ cyanine dyes⟩ — compare TRICYCLIC

tri·nucleate \"+\ *adj* [*tri-* + *nucleate*] : having three nuclei

tri·nucleotide \"+\ *n* [*tri-* + *nucleotide*] : a nucleotide consisting of three mononucleotides in combination

tri·nucleus \"+\ *n, cap* [NL, fr. *tri-* + *nucleus*] : a widely distributed genus (the type of the family Trinucleidae) of Ordovician trilobites in which the glabella and cheeks form three rounded elevations on the head

¹trio \'trē(ˌ)ō\ *n -s* [F, fr. It, modif. (influenced by *duo*) of L *tria* three — more at THREE] **1 a** : a musical composition for three voice parts or three instruments **b** : the secondary or episodic division of a minuet or scherzo (as in a sonata or symphony) or of a march or of various dance forms usu. contrasted in key and in a quieter style than the primary division **c** : a performance of such a composition **d** : a dance by three people **2** : a group or set of three: as **a** : the performers of a musical or dance trio **b** : three playing cards of the same rank **c** : male and two female domestic animals (as poultry) forming a breeding or exhibition group

²trio \"\ *n, pl* **trio** *or* **trios** *usu cap* **1 a** : a Cariban people of the boundary between Brazil and British and Dutch Guiana **b** : a member of such people **2** : the language of the Trio people

tri·obol \(')trī+\ *n* [L *triobolus*, fr. Gk *triōbolon*, fr. *tri-* three + *obolos* obol — more at TRI-, OBOL] : an ancient Greek coin worth 3 obols or ½ drachma

tri·octahedral \(')trī+\ *adj* [*tri-* + *octahedral*] : having all three of the available octahedrally coordinated positions occupied ⟨a ~ mica⟩

tri·ode \'trī,ōd\ *n -s* [*tri-* + *-ode*] : an electron tube with an anode, a cathode, and a control grid

tri·o·dia \trī'ōdēə\ *n* [NL, prob. fr. Gk, meeting of three roads, fr. *triodos* point where three roads meet (fr. *tri-* three + *hodos* way, road) + *-ia* -y — more at CEDE] **1** *cap* : a genus of Australian and in some classifications American perennial grasses having long narrow leaves and florets with prominently 3-nerved lemmas **2** *-s* : any grass of the genus *Triodia* : SPINIFEX 1

tri·odion \trē'ōthyōn\ *n, pl* **tri·odia** -yä\ [MGk *triōdion*, fr. Gk *tri-* three + *ōidē* ode — more at ODE] : a liturgical book of the Eastern church containing the offices from the fourth Sunday before Lent to Easter including canons having usu. only three odes instead of the regular nine

tri·odon \'trīə,dän\ *n, cap* [NL, fr. *tri-* + *-odon*] : a small genus (coextensive with the family Triodontidae) of Indo-Pacific puffers having the fused teeth of the lower jaw forming a single plate and those of the upper jaw two plates one on each side

¹tri·odon·toid \trī'ə,dän-,tȯid\ *adj* [NL *Triodont-, Triodon* + E *-oid*] : resembling or related to the genus *Triodon* or the family Triodontidae

²triodontoid \"\ *n -s* : a triodontoid fish

tri·odon·toph·o·rus \ˌtrīə,dän-'täfərəs\ *n, cap* [NL, fr. *tri-* + *odont-* + *-phorus*] : a genus of nematode worms (family Strongylidae) parasitic in the intestine of horses

tri·oe·cious *or* **tri·ecious** \(')trī'ēshəs\ *adj* [NL *Trioecia*, order of plants in former classifications (fr. *tri-* + *-oecia* + E *-ous*) : having staminate, pistillate, and hermaphrodite flowers on different plants ⟨a ~ species⟩ — **tri·oe·cious·ly** *adv*

tri·ol \'trī,ȯl, -ȯl\ *n -s* [*-triol*] : a chemical compound (as phloroglucinol) containing three hydroxyl groups

-tri·ol \ˌ¦\ *n suffix -s* [*tri-* + *-ol*] : chemical compound containing three hydroxyl groups ⟨1,2,4-benzene*triol*⟩

tri·ole \'trē,ōl, -ȯl\ *n -s* [prob. fr. *tri-* + *-ole*] : TRIPLET 4

tri·olein \(')trī+\ *n* [*tri-* + *olein*] : the oily liquid triglyceride $C_3H_5(OOCC_{17}H_{33})_3$ of oleic acid found in olive oil and other nondrying oils : glycerol tri-oleate

tri·o·let \ˌtrēə'lā\ *n -s* [F, prob. dim. of It *trio* — more at TRIO] **1** : a poem or stanza of eight lines in which the first is repeated as the fourth and seventh and the second as the eighth and the rhyme scheme is *ABaAabAB* **2 a** : TRIPLET 4 **b** : a short trio

tri·ol·o·gy \trī'äləjē\ *n -es* [by alter. (influence of *trio*)] : TRILOGY

Tri·o·nal \'trīə,nal\ *trademark* — used for sulfonethylmethane

-tri·one \'trī,ōn\ *n suffix -s* [*tri-* + *-one*] : chemical compound containing three carbonyl groups — in names of triketones or tri-oxo compounds that are not true triketones ⟨imidazole*trione*⟩

¹tri·on·y·chid \(')trī'änə,ˌ)kid, ˌtriə'nikəd\ *adj* [NL *Trionychidae*] : of or relating to the Trionychidae

²trionychid \"\ *n -s* : a turtle of the family Trionychidae

tri·onych·i·dae \ˌtrīə'nikəˌdē\ *n pl, cap* [NL *Trionych-, Trionyx*, type genus + *-idae*] : a family of soft-shelled freshwater turtles containing both fossil Tertiary and living forms in which the horny plates of carapace and plastron are replaced by leathery skin and constituting a distinct superfamily of Cryptodira

tri·on·y·choid \(')trīˈänəˌkȯid\ *or* **try·on·y·choi·de·an** \ˌtrīˌänə'kȯidēən\ *adj* [trionychoid fr. NL *Trionychoidea*, order of soft-shelled turtles, fr. *Trionych-, Trionyx* + *-oidea; trionychoidean* fr. NL *Trionychoidea* + E *-an*] : resembling or related to the Trionychidae

tri·onyx \'trīə,niks, -'ä(ə)n-\ *n, cap* [NL, fr. *tri-* + *-onyx*] : a genus (the type of the family Trionychidae) of soft-shelled turtles that usu. includes both Old World and New World forms and is sometimes restricted to Old World forms

tri·op·i·dae \trī'äpə,dē\ *n pl, cap* [NL *Triop-, Triops*, type genus + *-idae*] : a family of small active sessile-eyed aquatic crustaceans (order Notostraca) — see LEPIDURUS, TRIOPS

tri·ops \'trī,äps\ *n, cap* [NL, fr. *tri-* + *-ops*] : a genus of freshwater crustaceans (family Triopidae) having the head and thorax covered with an oval shield-shaped shell and a small third median eye

trior *var of* TRIER

trios *pl of* TRIO

tri·ose \'trī,ōs *also* -ōz\ *n -s* [ISV *tri-* + *-ose*] : either of two simple sugars $C_3H_6O_3$ containing three carbon atoms: **a** : GLYCERALDEHYDE **b** : a sweet crystalline compound $HOCH_2COCH_2OH$ that is formed usu. in an equilibrium mixture with glyceraldehyde by oxidation of glycerol and is the simplest ketose : dihydroxy-acetone

triose phosphate *n* : a phosphoric ester or acylal of a triose; *esp* : either of two monophosphates $C_3H_5O_2(OPO_3H_2)$ or an equilibrium mixture of them formed as intermediates in carbohydrate metabolism — compare ALDOLASE

---

trindles 2 (caption)

trio sonata *n* **:** a sonata of the Baroque period having two upper parts for like instruments (as violins or trumpets) and a figured bass part played by a bass instrument (as bass viol or cello) with the indicated harmony realized by a keyboard instrument

tri·os·te·um \trī'ästēəm\ *n, cap* [NL, short for *Triosteospermum*, fr. *tri-* + *oste-* + *-spermum*; fr. the usu. three bony nutlets of the fruit] **:** a genus of Asiatic and No. American herbs (family Caprifoliaceae) having connate or perfoliate entire leaves and purple or yellowish tubular flowers usu. sessile in the axils — see FEVERROOT

tri·ox·an \trī'äk,san, -sən\ *chiefly Brit var of* TRIOXANE

tri·ox·ane \-,sān\ *n* [ISV *tri-* + *oxa-* + cyclohex*ane*] **:** a crystalline combustible heterocyclic trimer $(CH_2O)_3$ of formaldehyde with an odor resembling chloroform that is depolymerized into formaldehyde by traces of mineral acids — called also *symmetrical trioxane;* compare PARAFORMALDEHYDE

tri·ox·ide \-,sīd, -,səd\ *n* [ISV *tri-* + *ox-* + *-ide*] **:** an oxide containing three atoms of oxygen

trioxy- *comb form* [ISV *tri-* + *oxy-*] **:** containing three oxy groups

tri·oxy·methylene \(ˌ)trī¦äksē+\ *n* [ISV *trioxy-* + *methylene*] **:** TRIOXANE — usu. used with initial Greek alpha ⟨*α-trioxymethylene*⟩

¹trip \'trip\ *n* -s [ME] *dial Eng* **:** a small flock (as of birds or mammals)

²trip \"\ *vb* **tripped** *also* **tript; tripped** *also* **tript; tripping; trips** [ME *trippen*, fr. MF *triper, treper* to dance, hop, trample, of Gmc origin; akin to LG *trippen, trippeln* to stamp, trample, MD *trepelen, trappelen* to stamp, trample, OE *treppan* to tread — more at TRAP] *vi* **1 a :** to dance, skip, or caper with light quick steps ⟨nymphs and shepherds . . . ~ no more in twilight ranks —John Milton⟩ **b :** to move with light quick steps **:** walk or move lightly **:** move the feet nimbly ⟨she . . . *tripped* lightly with him into the church —T.L.Peacock⟩ **2 :** to catch the foot against something so as to stagger, hop, or fall **:** stumble over something (as an obstacle in one's path) **:** make a false step ⟨the child . . . got up only to ~ on her skirt and tumble headlong again —O.E.Rölvaag⟩ ⟨*tripped* over his own feet⟩ **3 :** to fall into an error **:** make a mistake or false step **:** offend against morality, propriety, or accuracy **:** ERR, SLIP ⟨his careful reasoning which never ~*s* —H.O.Taylor⟩ ⟨nor do we ever find him *tripping* even in a matter of detail —Virginia Woolf⟩ **4 :** to stumble in articulation **:** falter in speaking ⟨drinking . . . till his tongue ~*s* —John Locke⟩ ⟨he shall stammer, cluck and ~ —Robert Graves⟩ **5 :** to make a journey or excursion ⟨*tripped* frequently to France to . . . visit troops —S.L.A.Marshall⟩ **6 :** to run past the pallet of the escapement without previously locking — used of a tooth of the escape wheel of a watch **7 :** to become strained or twisted out of the perpendicular — used of the floor of a ship between the keel and keelson **8 a :** to actuate a mechanism by the operation of some device **b :** to become operative or actuated as the result of the operation of some mechanical device ~ *vt* **1 a :** to cause to stumble or lose one's footing (as by suddenly checking the motion of a foot or leg) **:** cause to take a false step **:** throw off balance ⟨someone must have *tripped* him⟩ — often used with *up* **b :** to cause to fail or be checked by putting an obstacle in the way **:** HALT, OBSTRUCT **2 :** to detect in a misstep, error, or inconsistency **:** catch in a fault or blunder — usu. used with *up* ⟨any military man familiar with firearms could ~ you up —Kenneth Roberts⟩ ⟨wrongdoing inevitably ~*s* up itself —*Irish Digest*⟩ ⟨questions designed to ~ him up⟩ **3 a** *archaic* **:** to perform (as a dance) lightly or nimbly ⟨come and ~ it as you go, on the light fantastic toe —John Milton⟩ ⟨the young folks *tripped* it away on the grass —Harriet Martineau⟩ **b :** to dance upon (a surface) with a light and nimble step **4 :** to raise (an anchor) from the bottom by its cable or buoy rope so that it hangs free **5 a :** to pull (a yard) into a perpendicular position for lowering **b :** to hoist (a topmast) far enough to enable the fid to be withdrawn preparatory to housing or sending down **6 :** to release, let fall, set free, or otherwise operate (as a weight, compressed spring, switch, or other mechanism) esp. by removing a catch or detent **:** actuate (as a connecting, disconnecting, or controlling mechanism) by some device **7 :** to separate the petals of (a legume flower) in search of nectar causing vigorous springing apart of style and stamens and discharge of pollen that dusts over an insect (as a bee) and resulting in cross-pollination **8 :** WEDGE 5 **9 :** to raise (the bottom) even with the top of a scenery drop by an auxiliary set of lines in order to fold the drop in half and usu. out of audience view — **trip the light fantastic** [fr. the phrase *to trip on the light fantastic toe*] **:** DANCE

³trip \"\ *n* -s *often attrib* [ME, fr. *trippen* to trip] **1 :** a stroke, catch, or other movement by which one (as a wrestler) causes his antagonist to lose footing **:** the action of tripping someone **2 a :** a relatively short run of a vehicle usu. between two points or to a point and return ⟨extra ~*s* were scheduled by bus, railroad, and plane companies in anticipation of heavy holiday traffic⟩ **b :** VOYAGE, JOURNEY ⟨left China for a four-year . . . ~ abroad —Arthur Mathers⟩ ⟨my ~ around the world —Wendell Willkie⟩ ⟨a ~ to the moon⟩ ⟨missile on a ~ down the Atlantic range⟩; *esp* **:** one that is short or is undertaken for some usu. specified purpose ⟨a ~ to the dentist⟩ ⟨a day ~⟩ ⟨vacation ~*s*⟩ **c :** a single round of travel in the course of a business operation ⟨a delivery ~⟩ ⟨a postal carrier's two ~*s* a day⟩ **d :** the distance involved in a trip ⟨the only other village was one day's mule ~ farther into the interior —C.B.Hitchcock⟩ **e :** something held to resemble physical passage from one place to another ⟨their marriage and their ~ through life —J.P.Marquand⟩ ⟨the idea started on a long ~ around . . . conference tables —Laura Fermi⟩ **3 :** an error, failure, mistake, blunder, or similar misstep ⟨a ~ in one point would have spoiled all —John Berridge⟩ **4 :** a light lively movement of the feet **:** a quick light step ⟨the ~ of children's feet⟩ **5 :** a false step caused by stumbling over something or otherwise losing one's balance **:** STUMBLE **6 :** a single board in beating to windward **:** the distance covered by a sailing ship on a single tack **7 :** the action in coursing by a dog of throwing the hare off its feet or of seizing it but losing hold in an unsuccessful effort to kill **8 :** the catch of fish made or brought in on a single voyage to a fishing ground (as by a commercial fishing vessel) **9 a :** the action of tripping mechanically (as a valve held open against a spring) **b** (1) **:** a usu. automatic device for tripping a mechanism (as a catch or detent) (2) **:** TUP 2 **10 :** a number of cars coupled together and hauled as a train in mining operations

trip *abbr* triple; triplicate

tri·pack \'trī,-\ *n* [*tri-* + *pack*] **:** a combination of three superposed but separable films each sensitive to a different primary color for simultaneous exposure in one camera in color photography — compare BIPACK, INTEGRAL TRIPACK

tri·palmitin \(ˈ)trī+\ *n* [ISV *tri-* + *palmitin*] **:** the crystalline triglyceride $C_3H_5(OOCC_{15}H_{31})$ of palmitic acid found in small amounts in palm oils and various fats**:** glycerol tripalmitate

trip·a·ra \'tripərə\ *n* -s [NL, fr. *tri-* + *-para*] **:** a woman who has borne three children

tri·part \'trī+,-\ *adj* [*tri-* + *part*] **:** having or divided into three parts **:** THREEFOLD ⟨the conventional ~ balance of power system —Carleton Beals⟩

tri·par·tite \(ˈ)trī¦pär,tīt, -pȧ| *also* |d·,īt; *usu* -īd·+V\ *adj* [ME, fr. L *tripartitus*, fr. *tri-* + *partitus* — more at PARTITE] **1 a :** divided into or being in three parts **:** composed of three parts or kinds ⟨a ~ seismograph⟩ ⟨Plato's doctrine of the ~ soul —Helen North⟩ **b :** involving or of the nature of division into three parts ⟨a ~ division⟩ **2 :** having three corresponding parts or copies ⟨make indentures ~⟩ **3 a :** made between or involving three parties ⟨a ~ bloc⟩ ⟨a ~ treaty⟩ ⟨a ~ alliance⟩ ⟨~ discussions⟩ **b :** composed of or involving representatives of labor, management, and the public with each group having equal status with the other two ⟨a ~ pension board⟩ ⟨~ arbitration⟩ **4 a :** consisting of three parts or divisions ⟨these larvae had a . . . typically ~ gut —J.W.Jenkinson⟩ **b :** divided into three parts nearly to the base ⟨a ~ leaf⟩

²tripartite \"\ *n* -s [ME, fr. L *tripartitus*] **:** something (as a document, agreement, or work) divided into or made in three parts

tri·par·ti·tion \ˌtrī(ˌ)pär'tishən, ˌtripər-\ *n* [LL *tripartition-*, *tripartitio* threefold partition, fr. L *tripartitus* + *-ion-, -io* -ion] **:** the act of dividing or the state of being divided into three parts **:** partition into or among three ⟨~ of a uranium nucleus⟩

tri·par·tit·ism \ˌ≈'pär¦tīd·,izəm, -'pȧ|, -ī,tiz- *also* |d·,ī-\ *also* **tri·par·tism** \ˌ≈,pär,tizəm, -pȧ|, |d·,iz-\ *n* -s **:** the organization on a tripartite basis of a usu. governmental board concerned with labor relations ⟨~ . . . is designed to foster compromise —Clark Kerr⟩

tri·paschal \(ˈ)trī+\ *adj* [*tri-* + *paschal*] **:** including three passover feasts

trip coil *var of* TRIPPING COIL

tripe \'trīp\ *n* -s *often attrib* [ME, fr. OF] **1 a :** a wall of the stomach of a ruminant and esp. of the ox used as an article of food: (1) **:** the walls of the paunch or rumen — called also *plain tripe* (2) **:** the walls of the reticulum resembling honeycomb in form — called also *honeycomb tripe* **b :** an individual piece or portion of such a part of the stomach ⟨eaten . . . sheep ~*s* dipped in honey —Stephen Longstreet⟩ ⟨ox ~*s* are selected for good color and condition from ox stomachs —*New Zealand Jour. of Agric.*⟩ **2** *archaic* **:** BELLY 1a ⟨he hath his ~ full —James Howell⟩ **3 :** ENTRAIL 2 — usu. used in pl. ⟨shooting a man or cutting his ~*s* out —Joyce Cary⟩ ⟨felt a seasick rising of his ~*s* —Eric Linklater⟩ **4** *archaic* **:** a worthless or inferior and usu. disgusting person **5 :** something that is poor, worthless, and often offensive **:** inferior stuff **:** second-rate material **:** nonsensical rubbish **:** TRASH ⟨calling the report a mess of ~ —C.E.Montague⟩ ⟨the mass of popular-science ~ dished out to the American public —J.R.Newman⟩ ⟨get a little easy money by writing ~ —Bennett Cerf⟩

tripe-de-roche \ˌtrēpdə¦rōsh\ *n* [F] **:** ROCK TRIPE

tripehound \'≈,≈\ *n, Austral* **:** DOG

tri·pel·en·na·mine \ˌtrī,pe'lenə,mēn, -,mən\ *n* -s [*tri-* + *pyridine* + *ethylenediamine*] **:** an antihistamine drug $C_{16}H_{21}N_3$ derived from pyridine and ethylenediamine and used in the form of its crystalline citrate or hydrochloride

trip engine *n* **:** an engine with valves worked by a trip gear

tri·peptide \(ˈ)trī+\ *n* [ISV *tri-* + *peptide;* prob. orig. formed as G *tripeptid*] **:** a peptide that yields three molecules of amino acid on hydrolysis

tri·personal \"+\ *adj, sometimes cap* [*tri-* + *personal*] **:** consisting of or existing in three persons — used of the Godhead

tri·personality \(ˌ)trī+\ *n, often cap* [*tripersonal* + *-ity*] **:** the state of being tripersonal **:** existence as three persons in one Godhead **:** TRINITY ⟨the *Tripersonality* of the Deity is the very cornerstone of our religion —Clement Carlyon⟩

trip·ery \'trīp(ə)rē\ *n* -ES [F *triperie*, fr. OF, fr. *tripe* + *-erie* -ery] **:** a place where tripe is prepared or sold

tripe stone *n* **:** a variety of the mineral anhydrite composed of contorted plates suggesting pieces of tripe

tri·petaloid \(ˈ)trī+\ *adj* [*tri-* + *petaloid*] **:** having the appearance or form of three petals ⟨~ flowers⟩

tri·petalous \"+\ *adj* [*tri-* + *-petalous*] **:** having three petals

trip-free \'≈,≈\ *adj* **:** free to trip on the occurrence of any condition (as an overload) for which provision is made even if the normal operating lever or the control-switch closing contact is held in the closed position ⟨a *trip-free* circuit breaker⟩

trip gear *n* **:** a gear for tripping; *specif* **:** a rapid cutoff gear worked by a trip

¹trip-hammer \'≈,≈≈\ *n* **:** a massive power hammer having a head that is tripped and allowed to fall by cam or lever action

²trip-hammer \"\ *adj* **:** resembling or held to resemble the action of a trip-hammer esp. in being characterized by repeated pounding or involving great pressure ⟨*trip-hammer* motion⟩ ⟨under *trip-hammer* questioning⟩

tri·phane \'trī,fān\ *n* -s [F, fr. LGk *triphanēs* appearing threefold, fr. Gk *tri-* three + *-phanēs* appearing, shining (fr. *phainein* to show) — more at TRI-, FANCY] **:** SPODUMENE

tri·phase \'trī+,-\ *adj* [*tri-* + *phase*] **:** THREE-PHASE

tri·pha·sic \(ˌ)trī¦fāzik\ *adj* [ISV *triphase* + *-ic*] **1 :** having or occurring in three phases **2 :** THREE-PHASE

tri·phenol \(ˈ)trī+\ *n* [*tri-* + *phenol*] **:** a chemical compound containing three phenolic hydroxyl groups

tri·phenyl \"+\ *adj* [*triphenyl-*] **:** containing three phenyl groups in the molecule ⟨a ~ salt⟩

triphenyl- *comb form* [ISV *tri-* + *phenyl*] **:** three phenyl groups in the molecule

tri·phenyl·amine \(ˌ)trī¦fenᵊl, -fēn- +\ *n* [ISV *triphenyl-* + *amine*] **:** a crystalline tertiary amine $(C_6H_5)_3N$ that is practically neutral and that is made from diphenylamine, iodobenzene, and copper powder and in other ways

tri·phenyl·carbinol \"+\ *n* [ISV *triphenyl-* + *carbinol*] **:** a crystalline alcohol $(C_6H_5)_3COH$ made by reaction of methyl benzoate or benzophenone with phenyl-magnesium bromide and converted by acetyl chloride or hydrogen chloride into triphenylmethyl chloride — compare TRIPHENYLMETHYL

tri·phenyl·ene \trī'fenᵊl,ēn, -fēn-\ *n* [ISV *triphenyl-* + *-ene*] **:** a crystalline, tetracyclic aromatic hydrocarbon $C_{18}H_{12}$ present in coal tar and structurally constituted as though three *ortho*-phenylene radicals were joined to form a central hexagonal ring

tri·phenyl·formazan \(ˌ)trī¦fenᵊl, -fēn- +\ *n* [*triphenyl-* + *formazan*] **:** a red insoluble compound $C_6H_5N{=}NC(C_6H_5){=}NNHC_6H_5$ obtained by reaction of benzaldehyde phenylhydrazone with benzenediazonium chloride or by reduction of triphenyltetrazolium chloride

tri·phenyl·methane \"+\ *n* [ISV *triphenyl-* + *methane*] **:** a crystalline hydrocarbon $CH(C_6H_5)_3$ that is the parent compound of many dyes and that is made by the reaction of chloroform with benzene in the presence of aluminum chloride and in other ways

triphenylmethane dye *also* **triphenylmethane color** *n* **:** any of a group of triarylmethane dyes (as pararosaniline, crystal violet, or aurin) derived from triphenylmethane and used as mothproofing agents in the case of some colorless derivatives as well as dyes, organic pigments, and biological stains in the case of colored derivatives — compare LEUCO BASE, XANTHENE DYE

tri·phenyl·methyl \"+\ *n* [ISV *triphenyl-* + *methyl*] **:** the univalent radical $C(C_6H_5)_3$ derived from triphenylmethane by removal of the nonaromatic hydrogen atom and isolated as the first organic free radical in the form of very active yellow solutions by treating triphenylmethyl chloride $C(C_6H_5)_3Cl$ in solution usu. with finely divided silver or zinc — compare TRIPHENYLCARBINOL

triphenyl phosphate *n* **:** a crystalline nonflammable inorganic ester $(C_6H_5)_3PO_4$ used chiefly as a plasticizer and fire retardant (as for cellulose plastics)

tri·phenyl·tetrazolium chloride \(ˌ)trī¦fenᵊl, -fēn- +. . .-\ *n* [*triphenyl-* + *tetrazolium*] **:** a colorless crystalline salt $C(C_6H_5)_3N_4Cl$ that is obtained by oxidative ring closure of triphenylformazan and that gives back triphenylformazan on reduction (as by enzymes or reducing sugars) so that the red color formed can serve as a stain for tissues, as a test for viability (as of seeds), and as an analytical reagent — called also *tetrazolium chloride, 2,3,5-triphenyltetrazolium chloride, TTC*

¹tri·phib·i·an \(ˈ)trī¦fibēən\ *n* -s [*tri-* + *-phibian* (as in *amphibian*, n.)] **1 :** a person and esp. a military commander who is triphibian **2 :** a triphibian airplane

²triphibian \"\ *adj* [*tri-* + *-phibian* (as in *amphibian*, adj.)] **1 a :** adept at war alike on land, at sea, and in the air **b :** designed for or equipped to operate from land, water, snow, or ice as well as in the air ⟨a ~ airplane⟩ **2 :** TRIPHIBIOUS 1 ⟨a ~ military operation⟩

tri·phib·i·ous \(ˈ)trī¦fibēəs\ *adj* [*tri-* + *-phibious* (as in *amphibious*)] **1 :** employing, involving, or constituted by land, naval, and air forces and often including airborne troops in coordinated attack ⟨~ operations⟩ ⟨~ forces⟩ ⟨~ strategy⟩ ⟨~ warfare⟩ ⟨~ landing exercises⟩ **2 :** TRIPHIBIAN 1 ⟨~ marines⟩ ⟨~ airplanes⟩

trip hook *n* **:** SLIP HOOK

tripho·ra \'trifərə, -rīf-\ *n, cap* [NL, fr. *tri-* + *-phora;* fr. the fact that it usu. bears three flowers] **:** a genus of American terrestrial orchids having fleshy tubers, ovate usu. clasping leaves, axillary flowers that have an erect lip but are crestless and spurless, and fruit that is a drooping capsule — see NODDING CAP

tri·phosphate \(ˈ)trī+\ *n* [*tri-* + *phosphate*] **1 :** a salt or ester of triphosphoric acid — compare ADENOSINE TRIPHOSPHATE, SODIUM TRIPOLYPHOSPHATE **2 :** a salt containing three phosphate radicals

tri·phos·pho·pyridine nucleotide \(ˌ)trī¦fäsfō+. . .-\ *n* [*tri-* + *phosph-* + *pyridine*] **:** a coenzyme $C_{21}H_{28}N_7O_{17}P_3$ of numerous dehydrogenases (as that acting on glucose 6-phosphate) that occurs esp. in red blood cells and plays a role in intermediate metabolism similar to that of diphosphopyridine nucleotide but acting often on different metabolites — called also *codehydrogenase II, coenzyme II, TPN*

tri·phosphoric acid \¦trī+. . .-\ *n* [*tri-* + *phosphoric*] **:** a polyphosphoric acid $H_5P_3O_{10}$ that is a partial anhydride of three molecules of orthophosphoric acid, is capable of hydrolysis into orthophosphoric acid and pyrophosphoric acid, and is known chiefly in the form of salts and esters

triph·thong \'trif,thȯŋ, ÷ 'trip,- *also* -thäŋ\ *n* -s [*tri-* + *-phthong* (as in *diphthong*)] **1 :** a speech item consisting of three successive sounds (as in the first word following the consonant in *r*-droppers' pronunciation of *fire house* or *powerhouse* or of the word *wow* or for the letters preceding the *pe* of *yipe*) made with the tongue in vowel articulatory positions and serving or capable of serving metrically as a monosyllable — compare ²CENTERING, DIPHTHONG **2 :** TRIGRAPH

triph·thong·al \(ˈ)≈¦≈(g)əl\ *adj* **:** of, relating to, or having the character of a triphthong

triph·y·lite \'trifə,līt\ *also* **triph·y·line** \-lēn, -,lən\ *n* -s [*triphylite* alter. (influenced by *-ite*) of *triphyline*, fr. G *triphylin*, fr. *tri-* + *phyl-* + *-in* *-ine;* fr. its three bases] **:** a grayish green or bluish orthorhombic phosphate of lithium, iron, and manganese isomorphous with lithiophilite and commonly massive

tri·pinnate *also* **tri·pinnated** \(ˈ)trī+\ *adj* [*tri-* + *pinnate* or *pinnated*] **:** thrice pinnate **:** bipinnate with each division pinnate (as the leaves of an aralia or various ferns) — **tri·pin·nately** \"+\ *adv*

tri·pinnatifid \¦trī+\ *adj* [*tri-* + *pinnatifid*] **:** thrice pinnately cleft **:** bipinnatifid with segments again pinnatifid

tri·pinnatisect \"+\ *adj* [*tri-* + *pinnatisect*] **:** tripinnatifid with the divisions extending nearly to the base or midrib

tripl- *or* **triplo-** *comb form* [Gk *triploos*, fr. *tri-* three + *-ploos* (as in *diploos* double) — more at TRI-, DOUBLE] **:** triple ⟨*triplo*blastic⟩

tripl *abbr* triplicate

tri·plane \'trī+,-\ *n* [*tri-* + *plane*] **:** an airplane with three main supporting surfaces superposed

trip·lar·is \tri'pla(a)rə̇s\ *n, cap* [NL, fr. LL, threefold, fr. L *triplus* triple + *-aris* -ar] **:** a genus of tropical American shrubs and trees (family Polygonaceae) mostly with ant-infested hollow stems, dioecious flowers, and prominently winged fruit — see ANT TREE

¹tri·ple \'tripəl\ *vb* **tripled; tripled; tripling** \-p(ə)liŋ\ **triples** [ME *triplen*, fr. LL *triplare*, fr. L *triplus* triple] *vt* **1 :** to make three times as great or as much or as many **:** make threefold **:** multiply by three **:** TREBLE ⟨~ the possible 3 percent to 9 —Gabriel Kolko⟩ ⟨recreation facilities for children were *tripled* —*Current Biog.*⟩ **2 a :** to advance (a base runner in baseball) by a three-base hit **b :** to bring about the scoring of (a run in baseball) by a three-base hit ~ *vi* **1 :** to become three times as great **:** grow to three times the former number, size, or amount **:** increase threefold **:** TREBLE ⟨the population has almost *tripled* since 1930 —*Amer. Guide Series: Mich.*⟩ **2 :** to make a three-base hit in baseball

²triple \"\ *n* -s [ME, fr. L *triplus*] **1 a :** a triple sum, quantity, or number **:** a threefold amount **:** the product of a number multiplied by three ⟨add more than ~ to his income —H.C.W. Angelo⟩ ⟨increased to ~ its original size⟩ **b :** a combination of three usu. of related character and united **:** a group, set, or series of three **2 triples** *pl but sing or pl in constr* **:** a system for ringing changes on seven bells consisting of three pairs plus tenor **3 :** TRIPLET 2 **4 :** THREE-BASE HIT **5 :** TRIPLE VALVE **6 :** TURKEY 6

³triple \"\ *adj* [MF or L; MF, fr. L *triplus*, fr. *tri-* + *-plus* (as in *duplus* double) — more at DOUBLE] **1 :** being three times as much or as great or as many **:** multiplied by three **:** of three times the amount or quantity **:** THREEFOLD **2 :** consisting of three usu. combined members, things, or sets **:** having three parts joined together ⟨overcrowding produced ~ sessions in some schools⟩ **3 :** having a threefold relation or character **:** having three applications **:** combining three often dissimilar things or qualities **:** existing or occurring in three ways ⟨worked as a double or even ~ agent —*Time*⟩ **4 :** taken by threes or in groups of three **5 :** three times repeated **:** TREBLE **6 :** having three beats per measure ⟨~ time⟩ ⟨~ rhythm⟩ **7 a** *of meter* **:** having units of three components (as syllables) ⟨~ feet⟩ **b** *of rhyme* **:** involving correspondence of three syllables (as in *unfortunate-importunate*)

⁴triple \"\ *var of* TRIPPLE

triple-a \¦≈≈¦≈\ *adj, usu cap A* **:** A1 ⟨a *triple-A* priority⟩ ⟨*triple-A* rating⟩ ⟨*triple-A* investments⟩

triple-awned grass *or* **triple-awn grass** \¦≈≈¦≈-\ *n* **:** NEEDLEGRASS 2

tripleback \'≈≈,≈\ *adj* **:** constituting a sofa or settee (as in the Chippendale or Sheraton style) having a back in three parts like chair backs

triple block *n* **:** a pulley block with three sheaves

triple bond *n* **:** a chemical bond consisting of three covalent bonds between two atoms in a molecule and usu. represented in structural formulas by three lines, three dots, or six dots that denote three pairs of electrons (as in the formulas for acetylene HC≡CH, HC⋮CH, or HC:::CH) — compare DOUBLE BOND, UNSATURATED b

triple counterpoint *n* **:** three-part musical counterpoint so written that any part is transposable above or below any other

triple crown *n, usu cap T&C* **1 :** an unofficial title in horse racing representing the championship achieved by a horse that wins the three classic races for three year olds: **a :** one in English racing representing the winning of the Two Thousand Guineas, the Derby, and the St. Leger **b :** one in American racing representing the winning of the Kentucky Derby, the Belmont Stakes, and the Preakness Stakes **2 :** the unofficial title representing the championship attained by a baseball player who at the end of a single season leads his league in batting average, home runs, and runs batted in

triple-expansion engine *n* **:** a compound engine using three cylinders successively

triple first *n* **1 :** first-class honors in three different major courses of study esp. at Cambridge and Oxford universities **2 :** a student who takes a triple first

triple fugue *n* **:** a musical fugue with three subjects

triple fusion *n* **:** the fusion involving two polar nuclei and a sperm nucleus that occurs in double fertilization in a seed plant and results in the formation of the endosperm

tri·ple·gia \(ˈ)trī¦plēj(ē)ə\ *n* -s [NL, fr. *tri-* + *-plegia*] **:** hemiplegia plus paralysis of a limb on the opposite side

triple-header \¦≈'hedə(r)\ *n* **:** a sports program consisting of three consecutive contests ⟨a basketball *triple-header*⟩ — compare DOUBLEHEADER

triple-nerved \¦≈≈¦≈\ *adj* **:** having three nerves; *usu* **:** having a prominent vein on each side of the midrib above the base ⟨the *triple-nerved* leaf of a sunflower⟩

triple play *n* **:** a play or a continuous sequence of plays in baseball by which three outs are made during a single at bat

triple point *n* **1 :** a point of a plane curve such that every straight line through the point meets the curve in three coincident points there **2 :** a point on a phase diagram representing a set of conditions under which the gaseous, liquid, and solid phases of a substance (as water) can exist in equilibrium — compare ICE POINT

tri·pler \'trip(ə)lə(r)\ *n* -s **:** a circuit usu. associated with a vacuum tube in an electronic device that accepts a signal of one frequency and delivers a signal three times that at the input

triple-rivet \¦≈≈¦≈\ *vt* **:** to rivet (a joint) in such manner that all the rivets used are arranged in three rows

triple root *n* **:** a root x_0 of an algebraic equation $f(x)=0$ such that $(x-x_0)^3$ is a factor of $f(x)$ while $(x-x_0)^4$ is not

triples *pres 3d sing of* TRIPLE, *pl of* TRIPLE

triple salt *n* **1 :** a salt (as microcosmic salt) yielding on hydrolysis three different cations or anions **2 :** a salt regarded as a molecular combination of three distinct salts rather than as a coordination complex — compare DOUBLE SALT

triple scalar product *n* **:** the scalar product of a vector with the vector product of two other vectors

triple screw *n* **:** a screw with three parallel threads

Triple Sec *trademark* — used for a sweet colorless orange-flavored liqueur higher in alcoholic content than curaçao but distilled from spirit in which peel from the curaçao orange as well as neroli and orrisroot have been macerated

triple sheer *n* **:** a dress fabric of rayon or rayon and silk similar to sheer but made opaque instead of transparent

triple-space \¦==¦=\ *vt* **:** to type (copy) leaving two blank line spaces between lines of copy ~ *vi* **:** to type on every third line space

triple star *n* **:** a system of three stars apparently in close proximity

trip·let \'triplət, *usu* -əd.+V\ *n* -s [²*triple* + *-et*] **1 :** a unit of three lines of verse **2 :** a collection of three of a kind **:** a combination of three united **:** a set or group of three ⟨fraction ~s⟩ **3 a :** one of three children or offspring born at one birth **b triplets** *pl* **:** a group of three offspring born at one birth **4 :** a group of three musical notes or tones performed in the time of two of the same value **5 :** a combination of three lenses (as in a camera or microscope) **6 triplets** *pl* **:** three cards of a kind esp. in poker **7 :** a composite gemstone made by cementing together three parts of which the top and bottom are usu. genuine and the middle a colored substitute **8 a :** a spectrum line or an energy level of an atom, molecule, or nucleus having three components associated with the three possible orientations of one quantum unit of spin **b triplets** *pl* **:** three lines in a spectrum closely adjacent or in sets of three (as in the spectrum of iron)

tripletail \'==,=\ *n* **1 a :** a large edible marine percoid fish (*Lobotes surinamensis*) which occurs in the warm seas along the American Atlantic coast from Cape Cod to northern So. America and in which the long dorsal and anal fins extend backward and with the caudal fin appear like a three-lobed tail **b :** either of two fishes (*L. pacificus* and *L. erate*) of the Pacific and Indian oceans closely related to the Atlantic tripletail **2 :** a spadefish (*Chaetodipterus faber*)

triple thread *n* **:** one of three equal parallel threads on the same screw with each thread being 120 degrees ahead of the next succeeding — compare DOUBLE THREAD

triple threat *n* **:** a football player (as a back) adept at running, kicking, and forward passing

triple-threat \¦==¦=\ *adj* [*triple threat*] **:** adept in three different fields of activity or in three different phases of the same activity ⟨an international *triple-threat* man of the arts: he can draw, he can write, and he is an excellent photographer —*N.Y. Herald Tribune*⟩

triple-throw switch *n* **:** a switch that by a single throw makes a triple adjustment (as of circuits in an electrical connection, of organ stops on a console, or of tracks in a railroad switchyard)

triplet lily *n* **:** any plant of the genus *Brodiaea*

triple-tongue \¦==¦=\ *vi* **:** to articulate the notes of triplets in fast tempo on a wind instrument by using the tip and the back of the tongue alternately to interrupt the breath stream beginning each successive triplet with the tip — compare DOUBLE-TONGUE, SINGLE-TONGUE

triple tree *n, archaic* **:** GALLOWS

triple valve *n* **:** the automatic valve under a railroad car that controls the automatic air brake by regulating by three openings the intake, exhaust, and equalization of compressed air in the brake piston

¹**triplex** \'tri,pleks, -rī,p-\ *n* -ES [L, triple] **:** something (as a building or apartment) that is triplex

²**triplex** \"\ *adj* [L, fr. *tri-* + *-plex* -fold — more at SIMPLE] **1 :** having three parts or elements **:** THREEFOLD, TRIPLE ⟨~ windows⟩ ⟨~ cable⟩ **2 :** having three principal operative parts or motions **:** producing a threefold effect ⟨~ chain block⟩ ⟨~ pump⟩ — compare DUPLEX **3 a :** containing three apartments or dwelling units ⟨~ buildings⟩ **b :** having three floors or levels ⟨a ~ apartment⟩ **4 a :** consisting of a middle lined with paper on both sides ⟨~ paperboard⟩ **b :** consisting of three webs of paper laminated with an adhesive (as glue, wax, or asphalt) ⟨a ~ bag⟩ **5 :** having three doses of a given dominant gene — used of a tetraploid cell or individual

triplex process *n* **:** a process for making steel in which the material is partially treated in a Bessemer, transferred without interruption to an open-hearth furnace for the second stage of the treatment, and then finished in an electric furnace

¹**trip·li·cate** \'tripləkə̇t, -lēk- *sometimes* -lə,kāt; *usu* ¦d.+V\ *adj* [ME, fr. L *triplicatus*, past part. of *triplicare* to triple, fr. *triplic-*, *triplex* triple, threefold] **1 :** made in three identical copies **:** THREEFOLD ⟨a ~ agreement⟩ **2 :** THIRD — used of one of a set of copies ⟨the ~ copy shall be delivered directly to the collector of customs —*U.S.Code*⟩

²**trip·li·cate** \-lə,kāt, *usu* -ād.+V\ *vt* -ED/-ING/-S **1 :** to multiply by three **:** increase threefold **:** TRIPLE **2 :** to reproduce twice; *specif* **:** to make an original and two carbon copies of

³**triplicate** *like* ¹TRIPLICATE\ *n* -s **:** a third thing like two others of the same kind; *specif* **:** one of three identical copies of something (as a document or letter) ⟨the ~ . . . is forwarded to the administrative agency —*Jour. of Accountancy*⟩ — **in triplicate** *adv* **:** in an original and two identical copies ⟨prepared the manuscript *in triplicate* —W.A.White⟩

trip·li·ca·tion \,triplə'kāshən\ *n* -s [MF, fr. LL *triplication-*, *triplicatio* action of tripling, fr. L *triplicatus* + *-ion-*, *-io* -ion] **1 a :** a legal pleading showing why the last pleading of the opposing party should not be given legal effect **:** an equitable rebutter **b :** the plaintiff's reply to the defendant's rejoinder in Roman and civil law resembling the surrejoinder in common law **c :** the defendant's answer to the plaintiff's replication in early English law **2 :** the action of tripling or making threefold or adding three together **3 :** something that is triplicated or threefold

tri·plic·i·ty \tri'plisəd.ē, trī'p-\ *n* -ES [ME *triplicite*, fr. LL *triplicitas* threefold quality, fr. L *triplic-*, *triplex* triple + *-itas* -ity — more at TRIPLEX] **1 :** one of the groups of three signs each distant 120 degrees from the other into which the signs of the zodiac are divided — called also *trigon* **2 :** the quality or state of being triple or threefold ⟨~ of stars⟩ **3 :** a group or combination of three **:** TRINITY, TRIO **4 :** an extreme form of duplicity or double-dealing

trip line *n* **1 :** a line or light rope used to operate a trip (as to free a dog hook in logging) **2 :** HAULBACK 1

tripling *pres part of* TRIPLE

trip·lite \'tri,plīt\ *n* -s [G *triplit*, fr. *tripl-* + *-it* -ite; fr. its threefold cleavage] **:** a dark brown monoclinic basic phosphate of manganese, iron, magnesium, and calcium $(Mn,Fe,Mg,Ca)_2(PO_4)(F,OH)$ generally with a fibrous massive structure

triplo- — see TRIPL-

trip·lo·blas·tic \¦triplō¦blastik\ *adj* [*tripl-* + *-blastic*] **:** having three primary germ layers

trip·lo·blas·ti·ca \,==='stəkə\ *n pl, often cap* [NL, fr. *tripl-* + Gk *blastika*, pl. of *blastikos* budding, fr. *blast-* + *-ikos* -ic] **:** animals having three germ layers — used when these are held to form a natural group comprising the worms and all higher forms

trip·lo·caulescent \¦tri(,)plō+\ *adj* [*tripl-* + *caulescent*] **:** lacking the capacity of reproduction until an axis of the third order is attained — used of plants (as the common plantain) in which the primary axis produces foliage leaves, the secondary axis bracteal leaves, and the tertiary axis the flowers; compare DIPLOCAULESCENT, HAPLOCAULESCENT

trip·lo·chiton \,triplō+\ *n, cap* [NL, fr. *tripl-* + *chiton*] **:** a small genus comprising tall tropical African trees with palmately lobed alternate leaves like those of the maple and being included in Sterculiaceae or made the type of a separate family — see OBECHE

¹**trip·loid** \'tri,plȯid\ *adj* [ISV *tripl-* + *-oid*] **:** threefold in appearance or arrangement; *specif* **:** having or being a chromosome number that is three times the monoploid number ⟨a ~ cell⟩ — compare POLYPLOID

²**triploid** \"\ *n* -s **:** a triploid individual

trip·loid·ite \'tri,plȯi,dīt\ *n* -s [*triplite* + *-oid* + *-ite*] **:** a mineral $(Mn,Fe)_2(PO_4)(OH)$ consisting of a yellowish or reddish brown basic phosphate of manganese and iron isomorphous with wolfeite and probably with sarkinite

trip·loi·dy \'tri,plȯidē\ *n* -ES [*triploid* + *-y*] **:** the state of being triploid ⟨~ in higher animals is not common —H.P. Riley⟩

trip·lum \'tripləm\ *n* -s [ML, fr. neut. of L *triplus* triple — more at TRIPLE] **1 :** the third voice part in medieval polyphony counting upward from the tenor inclusive **2 :** a musical composition for three voice parts

tri·ply \'triplē, -li\ *adv* **:** to a triple degree **:** in three times the amount or sum **:** in a threefold manner ⟨mystery seems to be ~ and darkly compounded —B.R.Redman⟩ ⟨the ~ divine principle, Love —Mary B. Eddy⟩

¹**tri·pod** \'trī,päd\ *n* -s [L *tripod-*, *tripus*, fr. Gk *tripod-*, *tripous* three-footed, fr. *tri-* three + *pod-*, *pous* foot — more at TRI-, FOOT] **1 a :** a vessel (as a pot or caldron) resting on three legs or feet **b** (1) **:** the seat of the priestess of Apollo at Delphi in ancient Greece when delivering oracles ⟨a tone . . . less reminiscent of the priestess on the ~ —B.N.Cardozo⟩ (2) **:** an oracular seat held to resemble the one at ancient Delphi ⟨after the inauguration . . . the editor returned to his ~ —Arthur Krock⟩ **2 :** a structure or piece of apparatus (as a stool, table, or altar) supported on three legs **3 a :** a three-legged support; *esp* **:** a three-legged stand used to support a portable instrument (as a camera) and usu. consisting of a small table or head jointed to each of the three legs which are often telescopic **b :** a frame set in a field on which hay is piled for curing **4 a :** a tripodal bone **b :** a sponge spicule having three equal rays

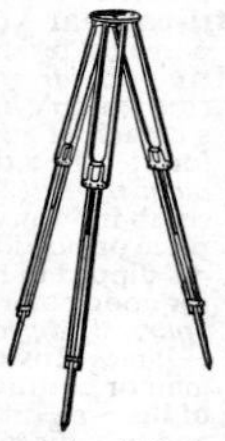

tripod 3a

²**tripod** \"\ *adj* **:** having or supported on three feet or legs ⟨a ~ vase⟩

trip·o·dal \'tripəd°l, 'trī,päd°l\ *adj* **1 :** having three feet or legs **:** forming a tripod **2 :** having three processes — used of a bone

tri·pod·ic walk \(')trī¦pädik-\ *n* **:** a mode of walking in which two feet on one side and one median foot on the other are used simultaneously (as in many insects)

tripod puller *n* **:** a stump puller that lifts the stump vertically out of the ground by means of chains passing over pulleys attached to a tripod

tripod table *n* **:** a table supported by a shaft from whose lower end radiate three curved or slanting legs

trip·o·dy \'tripədē\ *n* -ES [LL *tripodia*, fr. Gk, fr. *tripod-*, *tripous* three-footed + *-ia* -y] **:** a unit or group of three feet in prosody

tri·point·ed \'trī+,-\ *adj* [*tri-* + *pointed*] **:** having three points ⟨a ~ vase⟩

tri·polar \(')trī+\ *adj* [*tri-* + *polar*] **:** having three poles ⟨~ mitoses⟩

¹**trip·o·li** \'tripəlē, -li\ *n* -s [F, fr. *Tripoli*, region in northern Africa, its locality] **1 :** an earth consisting of very friable soft schistose deposits of silica regardless of their mode of origin and including diatomite and kieselguhr **2 :** an earth consisting of deposits of friable and dustlike silica not of diatomaceous material and possibly derived from the decomposition of siliceous limestone

²**tripoli** \"\ *adj, usu cap* [fr. *Tripoli*, Libya] **1 :** of or from Tripoli, a capital of Libya **:** of the kind or style prevalent in Tripoli **2** [fr. *Tripoli*, Lebanon] **:** of or from the city of Tripoli, Lebanon **:** of the kind or style prevalent in Tripoli

¹**tri·pol·i·tan** \trə'pälət°n\ *adj, usu cap* [*tripolitan* back-formation fr. *Tripolitania*; *tripolitanian* fr. *Tripolitania* + E *-an*] **1** *or* **tri·pol·i·ta·nian** \trə¦pälə¦tānyən, ¦tri,päl-, ¦tripəl-, -ānēən\ **:** of or belonging to Tripolitania, No. Africa **2** [*Tripoli*, former Barbary state in northern Africa + *-itan* (as in *metropolitan*)] **:** of or belonging to the Barbary state of Tripoli

²**tripolitan** \"\ *or* **tripolitanian** \"\ *n* -s *cap* [*tripolitan* back-formation fr. *Tripolitania*; *tripolitanian* fr. *Tripolitania* + E *-an*, n. suffix] **:** one of the people of Tripolitania, Libya, chiefly inhabited by Berbers and Arabs with some European, Turkish, and Negro elements

trip·o·lite \'tripə,līt\ *n* -s [*Tripoli*, northern Africa + E *-ite*] **:** TRIPOLI; *specif* **:** TRIPOLI 1

tri·polyphosphate \(¦)trī+\ *n* [*tri-* + *polyphosphate*] **:** TRIPHOSPHATE — not used systematically

tri·pos \'trī,päs\ *n* -ES [modif. (influenced by Gk nouns ending in *-os*) of L *tripus* tripod — more at TRIPOD] **1** *archaic* **:** TRIPOD **2** [so called fr. the three-legged stool on which he sat at the disputation] **a** (1) *usu cap* **:** a Bachelor of Arts (as at Cambridge University) formerly appointed to dispute humorously or satirically at commencement with candidates for degrees (2) *or* **tripos verses :** a set of humorous verses originally composed by this official but following the abolition of his office published independently at each commencement until 1894 (3) **:** the list of successful candidates for honors printed on the back of a paper containing tripos verses **b** (1) **:** the final examination instituted in the first half of the 18th century for honors in mathematical science (as at Cambridge university) — compare OPTIME, WRANGLER (2) **:** the final honors examination in classics to which formerly only those were admitted who had previously obtained honors in mathematics (3) **:** a final honors examination (as at Cambridge university) in a subject (as theology) other than mathematics and classics **c :** an honors course or school (as at Cambridge university)

trip·pant \'tripənt\ *adj* [²*trip* + *-ant*] **:** PASSANT 1 ⟨three goats ~ argent —Edward Almack⟩

tripped *past of* TRIP

trip·per \'tripə(r)\ *n* -s [ME *trippere*, fr. *trippen* to trip + *-ere* -er — more at TRIP] **1 :** a person that trips: as **a** *chiefly Brit* **:** one that takes a trip **:** EXCURSIONIST, TOURIST ⟨a kind of traveller's companion for the literary-minded ~ —*New Yorker*⟩ ⟨like a day ~ who has missed the last train home —Elizabeth Bowen⟩ **b :** one (as an extra employee on a street railway) employed by the trip **c :** DECKMAN 2c **2 :** a device or mechanism that trips: as **a :** a contrivance operated by a passing train to work a signal, switch, or alarm **b :** a projecting piece on a railroad track for operating a catch on a passing train to apply the brakes or sound a warning **c :** a mechanism for releasing the prop of a wicket in a movable dam **d :** a device for causing the load on a conveyor to be discharged into a hopper or other receptacle

trip·pery \'tripəri\ *adj* [*tripper* + *-y*] *chiefly Brit* **:** TOURISTY

¹**trip·pet** \'tripə̇t\ *n* -s [ME *tripet*, fr. *trippen* to trip + *-et*] **1** *dial* **:** the pointed piece of wood used in the game of tipcat **2 :** a cam, wiper, or projecting piece that strikes another piece at definite times

²**trippet** \"\ *dial Eng var of* TRIVET

tripping *adj* [fr. past part. of ²*trip*] **1 :** PASSANT 1 ⟨three hinds ~ proper —H.S.London⟩ **2 :** moving lightly and quickly **:** LIGHT-FOOTED, NIMBLE, QUICK ⟨bursts out into a ~ singing measure —H.S.Bennett⟩ ⟨~ lines⟩ **3** *archaic* **:** stumbling, erring, or sinning in moral behavior **4 :** used to trip a mechanism ⟨a ~ device⟩

tripping bracket *n* **:** a plate or bar attached to a ship's beam or structural member to prevent free flanges from bending

tripping coil *also* **trip coil** *n* **:** a coil forming part of an automatic circuit breaker

tripping line *n* **1 :** a small rope attached to a yard or upper mast and used to trip it and guide it to the deck **2 :** a line used in tripping or capsizing a sea anchor

trip·ping·ly *adv* **:** in a light, nimble, quick manner **:** with agility, dexterity, or smoothness of execution ⟨speak the speech . . . ~ on the tongue —Shak.⟩

tripping relay *n* **:** a trip-free relay

tripp·ke·ite \'tripkē,īt\ *n* -s [G *trippkeit*, fr. Paul *Trippke* †1880 Polish mineralogist + G *-it* -ite] **:** a tetragonal arsenite of copper of unknown formula characterized by short often bent prismatic crystals which can be broken into flexible fibers because of the excellent prismatic cleavages

¹**trip·ple** \'tripəl\ *n* -s [Afrik *trippel*, fr. *trippel* to tripple] *chiefly southern Africa* **:** a gait in which the horse moves both near and both off legs alternately and which somewhat resembles the amble

²**tripple** \"\ *or* **tri·ple** \"\ *vi* -ED/-ING/-S [Afrik *trippel*, fr. D *trippelen*, to trip along, amble; akin to LG *trippeln* to stamp, trample — more at TRIP] *chiefly southern Africa* **:** to go at a tripple

trips *pl of* TRIP, *pres 3d sing of* TRIP

trip·sa·coid \'tripsə,kȯid\ *adj, often cap* [NL *Tripsacum* + E *-oid*] **:** resembling or related to the genus *Tripsacum*

trip·sa·cum \'tripsəkəm\ *n, cap* [NL, fr. Gk *tripsis* rubbing, friction, resistance to rubbing; akin to Gk *tribein* to rub — more at THROW] **:** a genus of coarse perennial grasses of the southern U. S. and So. America having androgynous spikes with the 2-flowered staminate spikelets above and the pistillate below with the latter embedded in the joints of the rachis — see GAMA

trip scale *n* **:** an equal-arm balance having pans which are flat platforms or shallow trays elevated above the beam — compare PLATFORM SCALE

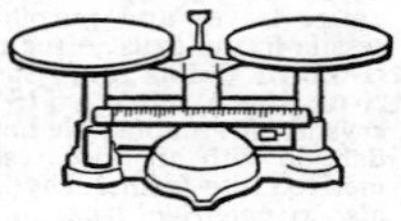

trip scale

tripsill \'=,=\ *n* [³*trip* + *sill*] **:** a timber placed across the bottom of the sluiceway in a splash dam against which rest the planks closing the dam

tript *past of* TRIP

trip·tane \'trip,tān\ *n* -s [*tri-* methyl + *p* (alter. of *b* in *butane*) + *butane*] **:** a liquid hydrocarbon $(CH_3)_3CCH(CH_3)_2$ that is one of the highest antiknock motor fuels known and hence is a valuable blending agent esp. for aviation gasolines to increase their power; 2,2,3-trimethyl-butane

trip·ter·al \'triptərəl\ *adj* [Gk *tripteros* having three wings (fr. *tri-* three + *-pteros* -pterous) + E *-al*] **:** having three rows of columns ⟨the later temple . . . ~ at the ends —D.S.Robertson⟩ — compare DIPTERAL

trip-toe \'=,=\ *n* **:** HOBBLEBUSH

trip·ton \'trip,tän, -ptən\ *n* -s [G, fr. Gk, neut. of *triptos* rubbed, ground, verbal of *tribein* to rub — more at THROW] **:** suspended nonliving debris (as bits of mineral matter or humus or organic remains) in a body of water — compare PLANKTON, SESTON

trip·tote \'trip,tōt\ *n* -s [LL *triptoton*, fr. LGk *triptōton*, neut. of *triptōtos* having only three cases, fr. Gk *tri-* three + *-ptōtos* (fr. *piptein* to fall, influenced in meaning by Gk *ptōsis* case, fall) — more at TRI-, PTOSIS, FEATHER] **:** a noun having three cases only — compare DIPTOTE

trip·tych *also* **trip·tich** \'trip(,)tik, -,tēk\ *n* -s [Gk *triptychos* threefold, fr. *tri-* three + *-ptychos* (fr. *ptychē* fold, layer)] **1 :** a writing tablet with three waxed leaves hinged for folding together and used by the ancient Romans for everyday writing **2 a :** a picture or carving in three compartments side by side; *esp* **:** a picture serving as an altarpiece and consisting of a central panel and two flanking panels of half its size that fold over it — compare DIPTYCH 3, POLYPTYCH **b :** something resembling or held to resemble such a 3-part picture; *esp* **:** a work (as in art, literature, or music) made up of three matching or contrasting parts

trip·tyque *also* **tryp·tyque** \(')trip¦tēk\ *n* -s [F *triptyque*, lit., triptych, fr. Gk *triptychos*] **:** a customs pass for the temporary importation of an automobile into a specified country

trip·u·hy·ite \,tripə'wē,īt\ *n* -s [*Tripuhy*, locality in eastern Brazil + E *-ite*] **:** a mineral $Fe_2Sb_2O_7$ (?) consisting of an oxide of antimony and iron in greenish yellow to dark brown fine-grained aggregates

trip wire *n* **1 :** a low-placed wire used to discourage trespassing on lawns or grass **2 :** a wire concealed close to the ground and used esp. in military operations to actuate a warning signal or set off an explosive device usu. when pulled or moved

tripy·laea \,tripə'lēə, ,trī,pī'l-\ *or* **tripy·lar·ia** \-la(a)rēə\ [NL *Tripylaea* fr. *tri-* + Gk *pylē* opening; NL *Tripylaria* fr. *tri-* + Gk *pylē* + NL *-aria*] *syn of* TRIPYLEA

tripy·lea \-lēə\ *n pl, cap* [NL, fr. *tri-* + Gk *pylē* opening, orifice — more at PYLON] **:** a suborder of Radiolaria comprising protozoans with or without spiculate skeletons and with the central capsule pierced by three openings

¹**tripy·le·an** *or* **tripy·lae·an** \¦=(,)=¦lēən\ *also* **tripy·lar·i·an** \-¦la(a)rēən\ *adj* **:** of or relating to the Tripylea

²**tripylean** *or* **tripylaean** \"\ *also* **tripylarian** \"\ *n* -s **:** a tripylean protozoan

tri·que \'trē(,)kā\ *n, pl* **trique** *or* **triques** *usu cap* **1 a :** an Indian people of the western part of the state of Oaxaca, Mexico **b :** a member of such people **2 :** the language of the Trique people

tri·que·an \(')trē¦kāən\ *n* -s *usu cap* **:** a language family comprising Trique

tri·quetra \trī'kwē·trə, -we·t-\ *n* -s [L, fem. of *triquetrus* three-cornered] **:** a triangle-shaped figure or decoration; *esp* **:** one formed of three interlaced arcs or loops

triquetra

tri·quet·ric \(')trī¦kwe·trik\ *adj* [L *triquetra* + E *-ic*] **:** of, relating to, or like triquetra

tri·quetrous \-wē·trəs, -we·t-\ *adj* [L *triquetrus*, fr. *tri-* + *-quetrus* -pointed, -cornered — more at WHET] **:** having three corners or salient angles or edges; *specif* **:** having three acute angles ⟨the ~ stems of many sedges⟩

tri·quetrum \=¦=·trəm\ *n, pl* **tri·quetra** \-rə\ [NL, fr. L, neut. of *triquetrus*] **1 a :** PYRAMIDAL BONE **b :** WORMIAN BONE **2 :** TRISKELION

tri·quinate \(')trī+\ *adj* [*tri-* + *quinate*] **:** ternate with the divisions quinate

tri·racial \"+\ *adj* [*tri-* + *racial*] **:** of, relating to, or descended from three divisions or stocks of mankind; *specif* **:** of Negro, white, and Indian ancestry ⟨the ~ group of Cajuns⟩

tri·radial \"+\ *adj* [*tri-* + *radial*] **:** TRIRADIATE — **tri·radially** \"+\ *adv*

¹**tri·radiate** \"+\ *adj* [*tri-* + *radiate*] **:** having three radiating branches ⟨~ sponge spicules⟩ — **tri·radiately** \"+\ *adv*

²**triradiate** \"\ *n* -s **:** something (as a sponge spicule) having three radiating branches

tri·radiated \(')trī+\ *adj* [*tri-* + *radiated*] **:** TRIRADIATE

tri·radius \"+\ *n* [*tri-* + *radius*] **:** a group of ridges forming a Y at the base of each finger on the palm of the hand

tri·rat·na \trē'rətnə\ *n* -s *usu cap* [Skt, three gems, fr. *tri* three + *ratna* gift, treasure, gem; akin to Skt *rāti* he gives, *rai* wealth, property — more at THREE, REAL] **1** *Buddhism* **:** the triad of the Buddha, the dharma, and the sangha **2** *Jainism* **:** the three conditions necessary for the attainment of nirvana: right knowledge, right faith, and right conduct

tri·rectangular \¦trī+\ *adj* [*tri-* + *rectangular*] *of a spherical triangle* **:** having three right angles

tri·reg·num \trī'regnəm\ *n* [NL, lit., triple reign, fr. L *tri-* + *regnum* reign — more at REIGN] **:** TIARA 1b

tri·reme \'trī,rēm\ *n* -s [L *triremis*, fr. *tri-* + *remus* oar — more at ROW] **:** an ancient galley having three banks of oars

tri·rhombohedral \(¦)trī+\ *adj* [*tri-* + *rhombohedral*] **:** of or relating to a group of the hexagonal system characterized by three different types of rhombohedrons

tris *pl of* TRI

tris- \(¦)tris\ *prefix* [Gk, fr. *tris*, fr. *treis* three — more at THREE] **:** thrice **:** tripled ⟨*tris*tetrahedron⟩ — esp. in complex chemical expressions ⟨*tris*-(2-chloroethyl)-amine⟩

tri·saccharide \(')trī+\ *n* [ISV *tri-* + *saccharide*] **:** any of a class of sugars (as raffinose) that yield on complete hydrolysis three monosaccharide molecules

tris·agion \trē'sȧyȯn\ *n, pl* **tris·agia** \-yȧ\ *usu cap* [MGk, fr. neut. of LGk *trisagios* thrice holy, fr. Gk *tris-* + *hagios* holy] **1 :** a hymn to or invocation of God as the thrice holy (the ~ of Isa 6:3) **2 :** a requiem service of the Eastern Church

trisail *var of* TRYSAIL

tris·azo \(')tris+\ *adj* [ISV *tris-* + *azo*] **:** containing three azo groups in the molecule ⟨~ dyes⟩

tri·sect \(')trī¦sekt\ *vt* -ED/-ING/-S [*tri-* + *-sect*] **:** to divide into three usu. equal parts

tri·sec·tion \(')trī¦sekshən\ *n* **:** the operation or result of trisecting

tri·sec·tor \-ktə(r)\ *n* -s **:** one that trisects

tri·sec·trix \-,triks\ *n, pl* **trisectri·ces** \,==='trī(,)sēz\ [*trisector* (fr. *trisector*) + *-trix*] **:** a curve that trisects an arbitrary angle

tri·seme \'trī,sēm\ *n* -s [Gk *trisēmos*] **:** a syllable or foot of three morae

tri·se·mic \(')trī¦sēmik\ *or* **tri·seme** \'trī,sēm\ *adj* [*trisemic* fr. Gk *trisēmos* of three time units (fr. *tri-* three + *-sēmos*, fr.

sēmeion unit of time, mark, sign, fr. *sēma* sign) + E *-ic*; *triseme* fr. Gk *trisēmos* — more at TRI-, SEMANTICS] : consisting of or equal in duration to three morae ⟨a ~ syllable⟩

tri·sep·tate \'(')trī+\ *adj* [*tri-* + *septate*] : having three septa

tri·se·tum \trī'sēd·əm\ *n, cap* [NL, fr. *tri-* + *sēta*] : a widely distributed genus of perennial tufted forage grasses having spikelets with several bisexual flowers and a lemma bearing a dorsal awn

tri·shaw *also* **tri·sha** \'trī,shò\ *n -s* [*tri-* + *rickshaw, ricksha*] : a light 3-wheeled vehicle propelled by pedaling and used in the Far East esp. for transporting passengers — compare PEDICAB

tri·sil·i·cate \'(')trī+\ *n* [ISV *tri-* + *silicate*] : a silicate containing three atoms of silicon in the molecule

tris·kai·deka·pho·bia \,trī,skī,dekə'fōbēə\ *n* [NL, fr. Gk *triskaideka* thirteen (fr. *treis* three + *kai* and + *deka* ten) + NL *phobia* — more at THREE, TEN] : fear of the number 13

tris·kele \'trī,skēl, 'trīs,-\ *or* **triske·lis** \'trīskələs\ *n, pl* **triskeles** \-kēlz, -lēz\ [Gk *triskelēs* three-legged, fr. *tri-* three + *-skelēs* (fr. *skelos* leg) — more at CYLINDER] : TRISKELION

tri·skel·i·on \trī'skelēən, trə'-, -ē,än\ *n, pl* **triskelions** \-nz\ *also* **triskel·ia** \-ēə\ [NL, fr. Gk *triskelēs*] : a figure composed of three usu. curved or bent branches radiating from a center — compare TETRASKELION

tris·mus \'trizməs\ *n -es* [NL, fr. Gk *trismos* grating, grinding; akin to Gk *trizein* to screech, creak — more at STRIDENT] : spasm of the muscles of mastication characterized by difficulty in opening the mouth and resulting from any of various abnormal conditions or diseases : LOCKJAW

triskelion

tris·octahedron \(')tris,tras+\ *n* [*tris-* + *octahedron*] : a solid (as a crystal) having 24 congruent faces meeting on the edges of a regular octahedron — compare TRAPEZOHEDRON

tri·sodium \'(')trī+\ *adj* [*tri-* + *sodium*] : containing three atoms of sodium in the molecule

trisodium phosphate *n* : SODIUM PHOSPHATE 1c

tri·some \'trī,sōm\ *n -s* [*tri-* + *-some*] : TRISOMIC

¹**tri·so·mic** \'(')trī,sōmik\ *adj* [*tri-* + *-somic*] : having one or a few chromosomes triploid in otherwise diploid nuclei usu. because of nondisjunction

²**trisomic** \"\ *n -s* : a trisomic individual

tri·so·my \'trī,sōmē\ *n -es* [¹*trisomic* + *-y*] : the condition of being trisomic

tri·splanch·nic \'(')trī+\ *adj* [ISV *tri-* + *splanchnic*] **1** : of or relating to the three splanchnic cavities of the head, chest, and abdomen **2** : of or relating to the sympathetic nervous system

tri·stach·y·ous \'(')trī'stākēəs, -'stak-\ *adj* [*tri-* + Gk *stachys* ear of grain + E *-ous* — more at STING] : having three spikes

tris·tania \trə'stānēə, -stan-\ *n* [NL, fr. Jules M. C. Tristan †1861 Fr. botanist + NL *-ia*] **1** *cap* : a genus of Australasian trees and shrubs (family Myrtaceae) having small yellow or white flowers with numerous stamens united in five columns — see RED BOX 2, WATER GUM **2** *-s* : any plant of the genus *Tristania*

tri·state \'trī·,-\ *adj* : of or relating to a region including three adjoining states or parts of three such states usu. centering around a point where the three states join ⟨the *tri-state* area of Arkansas, Mississippi, and Tennessee⟩ ⟨a *tri-state* commission⟩

triste \'trēst\ *adj* [ME *trist, triste*, fr. MF *triste*, fr. L *tristis*; perh. akin to OE *thrist, thriste* bold, brazen, shameless, OHG *dristi*] : SAD, DISMAL, DULL, DEPRESSING ⟨a ~ quartet could be heard —Donald Heiney⟩ ⟨the whole ~ thin landscape —May Sarton⟩

tri·stearate \'(')trī+\ *n* [*tri-* + *stearate*] : a stearate derived from three molecules of stearic acid

tri·stearin \"+\ *n* [ISV *tri-* + *stearin*] : the crystallizable triglyceride $C_3H_5(OOCC_{17}H_{35})_3$ of stearic acid reported esp. in hard fats, formed by the hydrogenation of various unsaturated fats or triglycerides (as triolein), and used chiefly in textile sizes, polishing materials, and leather stuffing : glyceryl tristearate

tris·tetrahedron \(')tris, tras+\ *n* [*tris-* + *tetrahedron*] : a solid (as a crystal) of the tetrahedral class of the isometric system having 12 triangular faces and related to the trapezohedron of the holohedral class — compare DELTOHEDRON

tris·te·za \trə'stäzə, -stēzə\ *n -s* [Pg, lit., sadness, sorrow, fr. L *tristitia*, fr. *tristis* sad] **1** : a highly infectious disease of grafted citrus trees with bitter orange rootstocks attributed to a virus and characterized by rotting of the rootlets and consequent wilting and death of the trees — compare QUICK DECLINE **2** : TEXAS FEVER

tristetrahedron

trist·ful \'tristfəl\ *adj* [ME *trist* sad + *-ful*] : SAD, MELANCHOLY — **trist·ful·ly** \-fəlē\ *adv* — **trist·ful·ness** *n -es*

tris·tich \'tris(,)tik, -,stēk\ *n -s* [*tri-* + *-stich*] : a strophic unit or stanza of three lines [TERCET, TRIPLET] — **tristich·ic** \(')tri'stikik, -,rī's-, -kēk\ *adj*

tris·ti·chous \'tristəkəs\ *adj* [LGk *tristichos* in three rows, fr. Gk *tri-* three + *stichos* row — more at DISTICH] : arranged in three esp. vertical rows ⟨a ~ leaf⟩

tri·stim·u·lus \'(')trī+\ *adj* [*tri-* + *stimulus*] : of or relating to values giving the amounts of three stimuli (as of the colors red, green, and blue) that when combined additively produce a match for the color being considered ⟨~ colorimetry⟩

tri·sty·lous \'(')trī'stīləs\ *adj* [*tri-* + *-stylous*] : having three styles ⟨~ flowers⟩ — **tri·sty·ly** \-,ē,lē\ *n -es*

tri·substituted \'(')trī+\ *adj* [*tri-* + *substituted*] : having three substituent atoms or groups in the molecule

tri·sul \trə'shül\ *or* **tri·su·la** \-lə\ *n -s* [Skt *triśūla*, lit., having three points, fr. *tri* three + *śūla* spit, spear, point — more at THREE, CULEX] : a trident or 3-pointed emblem or ornament associated esp. with the god Siva

tri·sulfide \'(')trī+\ *n* [*tri-* + *sulfide*] : a binary compound containing three atoms of sulfur combined with an element or radical

tri·sulfonic acid \'(')trī+...-\ *n* [*tri-* + *sulfonic*] : an acid containing three sulfonic acid groups

tri·syllabic \'(')trī+\ *adj* [prob. fr. (assumed) NL *trisyllabicus*, fr. L *trisyllabus* of three syllables, trisyllabic (fr. Gk *trisyllabos*, fr. *tri-* three + *syllabē* syllable) + *-icus -ic* — more at TRI-, SYLLABLE] : of or relating to a trisyllable : having three syllables ⟨a ~ word⟩ — **tri·syllabically** \"+\ *adv*

tri·syl·la·bism \trī'silə,bizəm, trī'-\ *n* [*trisyllabic* + *-ism*] : the state of being trisyllabic

tri·syllable \'(')trī, trī+\ *n* [modif. (influenced by *syllable*) of MF *trisyllabe*, fr. LL *trisyllaba* (pl.), fr. L, neut. pl. of *trisyllabus* trisyllabic] : a word of three syllables

trit- *or* **trito-** *comb form* [Gk, fr. *tritos*; akin to Gk *treis* three — more at THREE] : third : tertiary ⟨*tritonymph*⟩ ⟨*tritovum*⟩

trit *abbr* triturate

tri·tag·o·nist \trī'tagənəst, -,taig-\ *n -s* [Gk *tritagōnistēs*, fr. *trit-* + *agōnistēs* actor — more at PROTAGONIST] : the actor taking the part of third importance in a play (as in the ancient Greek theater) — compare DEUTERAGONIST, PROTAGONIST

trit·an·ope \'trīt'n,ōp, -rīt-\ *n -s* [ISV, fr. NL *tritanopia*] : one affected with tritanopia

trit·an·opia \,+'ōpēə\ *n -s* [NL, fr. *trit-* + *anopia* blindness, fr. *a-* + *-opia*; fr. the fact that only ⅓ of the colors of the spectrum can be perceived by a tritanope] : dichromatism in which the spectrum is seen in tones of red and green — called also *blue-yellow blindness*

trit·an·opic \,+'ōpik, -,āp-\ *adj* : characterized by or affected by tritanopia ⟨~ vision⟩ ⟨a ~ person⟩

tri·taph \'trī,taf\ *n -s* [Gk *taphos* tomb — more at EPITAPH] : a tomb containing three small chambers or cists

trite \'trīt\ *adj* TRITER/-EST [L *tritus*, past part. of *terere* to rub, wear out by use, make trite — more at THROW] **1 a** : used or occurring so often as to have lost interest, freshness, or force : STALE, VAPID ⟨~ diction⟩ and so commonplace observation —Earl of Chesterfield⟩ ⟨a subject which will seem ~ to some —J.M.Moore⟩ ⟨a ~ plot⟩ **b** : characterized by commonplace expression, treatment, or point of view : com-

---

posed of or employing clichés or platitudes ⟨a ~ speech⟩ ⟨poet . . . can be not only ~, he can be pompous, inflated —*Times Lit. Supp.*⟩ ⟨too many ~ objects in shiny yellow brass or dull black iron —*New Yorker*⟩ **2 a** : worn by much rubbing ⟨~ coins⟩ **b** : much-traveled : BEATEN ⟨~ a ~ path⟩ ⟨all these regions are ~ and familiar —Norman Douglas⟩

syn TRITE, HACKNEYED, STEREOTYPED, THREADBARE, and SHOPWORN all apply to something, esp. a once effective idea or expression in writing or art or a dramatic plot, lacking the power to evoke attention or interest because it lacks freshness. TRITE applies to something spoiled by too long familiarity with it, suggesting commonplaceness or total lack of power to impress ⟨the foregoing remarks doubtless sound *trite* and commonplace —M.R.Cohen⟩ ⟨it is as true as it is *trite* to liken the desert to a sea and the camel to a ship —C.S.Coon⟩ ⟨one could wish however that he had found a less *trite* and commonplace way of starting his chapters —*Geog. Jour.*⟩ HACKNEYED, often interchangeable with TRITE, stresses the idea of such constant use that all significance or force is dulled or destroyed ⟨the *hackneyed* pictures we have seen again and again —C.M. Smith⟩ ⟨used the *hackneyed* old theme of the vanity of earthly power for one of his best poems —Susanne K. Langer⟩ ⟨a *hackneyed* and cheap melodrama⟩ STEREOTYPED stresses an imitative quality, a usu. total lack of originality or creativity ⟨most advertising today is *stereotyped* — using the same words, the same ideas that we have had for more than 50 years —*Printers' Ink*⟩ ⟨a *stereotyped* novel about a young girl growing to womanhood⟩ THREADBARE applies to what has been used or exploited so much that its possibilities of interest have been totally exhausted ⟨when one writer hit upon a good phrase the others took it up and used it until it became *threadbare* —Stanley Walker⟩ ⟨this charge is becoming *threadbare* with repetition —J.H.Pollack⟩ ⟨our self-deceptive pretence of jollity at a *threadbare* joke —Nathaniel Hawthorne⟩ SHOPWORN suggests a loss, from constant use, of some or most of the qualities that appeal or arouse interest ⟨there hardly exists a more *shopworn* plot than the one about the show that during its preparation has to battle against all sorts of obstacles to emerge triumphant in the end a sensational success —Vicki Baum⟩ ⟨when a book as unusual as this appears the old adjectives seem too *shopworn* to do it justice —Graham Bates⟩ ⟨he has devoted his very considerable talents to a *shopworn* theme: the building of the first space platform —J.F.McComas⟩

tri·te·leia \,trīd·ə'līə, -ē(y)ə\ *n* [NL, fr. *tri-* + Gk *teleios* complete; so akin to Gk *telos* end, fr. the trimerous flowers — more at WHEEL] **1** *cap* : a genus of American bulbous herbs (family Liliaceae) that have grasslike leaves and umbels of white, blue, or violet flowers with the stamens borne on the tube of the perianth in two series and are sometimes included in *Brodiaea* **2** *-s* : any plant of the genus *Triteleia*

trite·ly *adv* : in a trite manner ⟨~ expressed sentiments⟩

trit·en·ceph·a·lon \,trīd·, ,trīd·, +\ *n* [NL *trit-* + *encephalon*] **1** : the third and hindmost of the primary brain vesicles **2** : TRITOCEREBRUM

trite·ness *n -es* : the quality of being trite ⟨there was a certain ~ in these reflections —Edith Wharton⟩ ⟨camera work of almost unbelievable ~ and stodginess —*Newsweek*⟩

triter *comparative of* TRITE

tri·ter·nate \'(')trī+\ *adj* [*tri-* + *ternate*] *of leaves* : thrice ternate : ternately decompound — **tri·ternately** \"+\ *adv*

tri·terpene \'(')trī+\ *n* [ISV *tri-* + *terpene*] : any of a class of terpenes $C_{30}H_{48}$ (as squalene) containing three times as many atoms in the molecule as monoterpenes; *also* : a derivative of such a terpene

tri·ter·pe·noid \'(')trī'tərpə,nòid\ *adj* [*triterpene* + *-oid*] : resembling a triterpene in molecular structure ⟨~ sapogenins⟩

²**triterpenoid** \"\ *n -s* : a triterpene or triterpene derivative (as lanosterol or oleanolic acid)

tri·the·ism \'trīthē,izəm, (')trī'th-\ *n, sometimes cap* [*tri-* + *-theism*] : a belief in three gods; *esp* : the doctrine that the Father, Son, and Holy Spirit of Christianity are three distinct Gods

tri·the·ist \'trīthēəst, (')trī'th-\ *n* [LGk *tritheos* believing in three gods + E *-ist*] : a believer in tritheism

tri·the·is·tic \'trīthē'istik\ *also* **tri·the·is·ti·cal** \-stəkəl\ *adj* : of, relating to, or adhering to tritheism

tri·the·ite \'trī(,)thē,īt, (')trī'th-\ *n -s* [LGk *tritheitēs*, fr. *tritheos* believing in three gods (fr. *treis* three + *theos* god) + Gk *-itēs* — more at TRI-, THE-] : TRITHEIST

trith·e·mim·er \,trithə'mimə(r)\ *n -s* [modif. (influenced by *trit-*) of NL *trihemimeris*, fr. *tri-* + *hemi-* + *-meris* (fr. Gk *meris* part) — more at MERIT] : a group of three half feet in classical prosody : a catalectic colon of a foot and a half

trith·e·mim·er·al caesura \,\•\\mimərəl-, \ *n* : a caesura in classical verse occurring after the third half foot

tri·thing \'trīthiŋ\ *n* [ME, fr. OE *thrithing* — more at RIDING] *archaic* : RIDING

trithio- *comb form* [ISV *tri-* + *thi-*] : containing three atoms of sulfur usu. in place of three oxygen atoms — in names of chemical compounds ⟨*trithiocarbonic*⟩

tri·thio·carbonate \"+\ *n* [*trithiocarbonic* + *-ate*] : a salt or ester of trithiocarbonic acid

tri·thio·carbonic acid \"+ . . .-\ *n* [*trithio-* + *carbonic*] : an unstable acid H_2CS_3 obtained by reaction of carbon disulfide with alkali sulfides in the form of its alkali salts from which it can be precipitated as a reddish ill-smelling oil

tri·thi·o·nate \trī'thīə,nāt, -,nāt\ *n* [ISV *trithionic* + *-ate*] : a salt of trithionic acid

tri·thi·on·ic acid \trī,thī'änik-\ *n* [ISV *tri-* + *thionic*] : the thionic acid $H_2S_3O_6$ containing three atoms of sulfur in the molecule

trithri·nax \trī'thrī,naks, 'trithrə,n-\ *n, cap* [NL, fr. *tri-* + Gk *thrinax* three-pronged fork, perh. fr. *thrin-* (akin to L *terni* three each) + *akmē* point, edge; fr. the form of the leaves — more at TERN, EDGE] : a genus of So. American fan palms having tough leaves with fibrous spiny sheaths, biconvex petiole, and prominent ligule

triti·at·ed \'trīd·ē,ād·əd *also* -ishē-\ *adj* [NL *tritium* + E *-ate* + *-ed*] : containing tritium esp. as a constituent of a chemical compound

triti·i·cal \'trīd·əkəl\ *adj* [*trite* + *-ical* (as in *critical*)] *archaic* : TRITE

triti·ca·le \,trīd·ə'kā(,)lē\ *n -s* [NL, blend of *Triticum* and *Secale*] : an amphidiploid hybrid between wheat and rye — sometimes used as if a generic name

tri·ti·ceous \trə'tishəs\ *adj* [NL *triticeus*, fr. L, of or resembling wheat, fr. *triticum* wheat + *-eus -eous*] : of, relating to, or being a small nodule of cartilage within the lateral thyrohyoid ligament

triti·ceum \trə'tish(ē)əm\ *n, pl* **triti·cei** \-shē,ī\ [NL, fr. neut. of *triticeus*] : a triticeous cartilage

triti·cum \'trīd·əkəm\ *n* [NL, fr. L, wheat; akin to L *terere* to rub, thresh — more at THROW] **1** *cap* : a genus of cereal grasses including the wheats and distinguished by the 2- to 5-flowered flattened spikelets in a terminal cylindrical spike with a flexuous rachis ⟨*Agropyron repens*⟩ **2** *-s* : the dried rhizome of a couch grass ⟨*Agropyron repens*⟩

trit·ide \'trīd·,īd\ *n -s* [NL *tritium* + E *-ide*] : a binary compound of tritium analogous to a hydride

triti·ish \'trīd·ish\ *adj* : somewhat trite ⟨~ expressions⟩

triti·um \'trīd·ēəm, -ish- *also* -ishē-\ *n -s* [NL, fr. *trit-* + *-ium*] : the radioactive isotope of hydrogen that has atoms of three times the mass of ordinary light hydrogen atoms, that has a half-life of about 12.5 years and emits beta rays to form helium of mass number 3, and that can be produced by bombardment of lithium with neutrons — symbol *t*

trito- — see TRIT-

tri·to·cerebral \'trīd·ō+\ *adj* [NL *tritocerebrum* + E *-al*] : of or relating to the tritocerebrum

tri·to·cerebrum \"+\ *n* [NL, fr. *trit-* + *cerebrum*] : the third lobe of the brain of an insect innervating the labrum — compare HINDBRAIN

trito·conid \,\•,-'kōnəd\ *n -s* [*tritocone* + *-id*] : the cusp of a lower molar corresponding to a metaconid of an upper molar of a true molar

tri·to·cone \'trīd·ə+,-\ *n* [*trit-* + *cone*] : the cusp of a mammalian premolar corresponding to the metacone of a true molar

tri·to·co·nid \,\•,-'kōnəd\ *n -s* [*tritocone* + *-id*] : the cusp of a lower molar corresponding to a metaconid

tri·tol·yl \'(')trī+\ *adj* [*tri-* + *tolyl*] : containing three tolyl radicals in the molecule

---

tritolyl phosphate *n* : TRICRESYL PHOSPHATE

¹**trit·o·ma** \'trīd·əmə\ *n* [NL, fr. Gk *tritomos* thrice cut, fr. *tri-* three + *-tomos* (fr. *temnein* to cut); fr. the trimerous flowers — more at TOME] *syn* of KNIPHOFIA

²**tritoma** \"\ *n -s* [Gk *tritomos*] : KNIPHOFIA 2

trit·o·mite \'trīd·ə,mīt\ *n -s* [G *tritomit*, fr. Gk *tritomos* thrice cut + G *-it -ite*; fr. the fact that the crystals leave trihedral cavities in the gangue] : a complex fluosilicate chiefly of calcium, thorium, cerium, yttrium, and containing boron

¹**tri·ton** \'trīt'n\ *n -s* [L *Triton*, Greco-Roman demigod of the sea, fr. Gk *Tritōn*] **1** *often cap* **a** : one of a class of minor sea divinities or partly human monsters usu. represented as having the upper body like that of a human being and the lower body like that of a fish — compare MERMAID **b** : a representation of a triton in art or heraldry **2** *or* **triton shell** \ fr. L *Triton*; fr. the sea god Triton being often represented holding a trumpet made of a conch shell⟩ **a** : any of various large marine gastropod mollusks esp. of the family Cymatiidae having a heavy elongated conical shell with the surface wrinkled and roughened or covered with a hairy periostracum and the lip usu. toothed or ridged **b** : a shell of one of these mollusks **3** : any of various aquatic salamanders : NEWT, EFT

²**triton** \"\ [NL] *syn* of TRITURUS

³**tri·ton** \'trī,tän\ *n -s* [*trinitrotoluene*] : TRINITROTOLUENE

⁴**tri·ton** \"\ *n -s* [Gk, neut. of *tritos* third — more at TRIT-] : the nucleus of the tritium atom consisting of one proton and two neutrons — symbol *t*; compare DEUTERON

tri·tone \'trī,tōn\ *n* [Gk *tritonos* of three tones, fr. *tri-* three + *tonos* tone — more at TRI-, TONE] **1** : a musical interval of three whole steps **2** : an augmented fourth — called also *mi contra fa*

tri·to·nia \trī'tōnēə\ *n* [NL, fr. L *Triton* + NL *-ia*] **1** *cap* : a genus of So. African bulbous plants (family Iridaceae) much cultivated for ornament and having ensiform leaves and yellow, red, or orange flowers with a tubular perianth that bears three stamens on the throat **2** *-s* : any plant of the genus *Tritonia* — see MONTBRETIA

tri·ton·ic \'(')trī'tänik\ *adj* **1** *usu cap* : of, relating to, or characteristic of the demigod Triton **2** *sometimes cap* : of, relating to, or characteristic of tritons

tri·ton·i·dae \trī'tänə,dē\ *n pl, cap* [NL, fr. ¹*triton* + *-idae*] *syn* of CYMATIIDAE

tri·ton·oid \'trīt'n,òid\ *adj* [¹*triton* + *-oid*] : resembling a triton mollusk

triton's horn *or* **triton's trumpet** *n, usu cap* Triton's : TRITON 2b

tri·to·nymph \'trīd·ō+,-\ *n* [*trit-* + *nymph*] : any of various acarids in their third developmental stage — compare DEUTONYMPH — **tri·to·nymphal** \,\•\ *adj*

tri·tor \'trīd·ə(r)\ *n -s* [L, grinder, fr. *tritus* (past part. of *terere* to rub, grind) + *-or* — more at THROW] : a grinding surface developed on a tooth — **tri·tor·al** \-ə,rəl\ *adj*

tri·tri·a·con·tane \'trī+\ *n* [ISV *tri-* + *triacontane*] : a paraffin hydrocarbon $C_{33}H_{68}$; *esp* : the normal hydrocarbon CH_3-$(CH_2)_{31}CH_3$

tri·trich·o·monas \"+\ *n, cap* [NL, fr. *tri-* + *Trichomonas*] : a genus of flagellates that is related to *Trichomonas* but distinguished by three anterior flagella and is often held to be distinguished from or a subgenus of *Trichomonas*

tri·tubercular *or* **tri·tuberculate** \'trī+\ *adj* [*tri-* + *tubercular, tuberculate*] **1** *of a tooth* : having three cusps : TRICUSPID **2** : of or relating to trituberculy

tri·tu·ber·cu·la·ta \,trītə,bərkyə'lād·ə, -läd·ə\ *n pl, cap* [NL, fr. neut. pl. of *trituberculatus* trituberculate, fr. *tri-* + *tuberculatus* tuberculate — more at TUBERCULATE] *syn* of PANTOTHERIA

tri·tu·ber·cu·lism \,trītə'bərkyə,lizəm\ *n -s* [*trituberculate* + *-ism*] : TRITUBERCULY

tri·tu·ber·cu·ly \-,lē\ *n -es* [*trituberculate* + *-y*] : the state of being tritubercular or showing evidence of having developed from a tritubercular ancestral type — used esp. in reference to a theory of the origin of mammalian molar teeth supposing them to have developed through tritubercular forms; compare MULTITUBERCULY

trit·u·ra·ble \'trichərəbəl\ *adj* [LL *triturare* to thresh + E *-able*] : capable of being triturated

trit·u·ral \'trichərəl\ *adj* [L *tritura* act of rubbing or threshing + E *-al*] : adapted for grinding ⟨the ~ border of a tooth⟩

¹**trit·u·rate** \'trichə,rāt\ *vt* -ED/-ING/-S [LL *trituratus*, past part. of *triturare* to thresh, fr. L *tritura* act of rubbing or threshing, fr. *tritus* (past part. of *terere* to rub, grind) + *-ura* — more at THROW] **1** : RUB, GRIND, BRUISE, MASTICATE ⟨~ one's food⟩ **2** : to rub or grind to a very fine or impalpable powder : pulverize and comminute thoroughly ⟨~ a drug with a diluent⟩

²**trit·u·rate** \,+-,rət\ *n -s* : a triturated substance : TRITURATION 2

trit·u·ra·tion \,trichə'rāshən\ *n -s* [LL *trituration-, trituratio* act or process of threshing, fr. *trituratus* (past part.) + L *-ion-, -io -ion*] **1** : the act or process of triturating or state of being triturated : COMMINUTION ⟨~ of food in the gizzard⟩ **2** : a triturated powder; *esp* : a powder made by triturating a substance with lactose as a diluent

trit·u·ra·tor \'trichə,rād·ə(r)\ *n -s* [LL, thresher, fr. *trituratus* (past part.) + L *-or*] : one that triturates; *specif* : an apparatus that triturates drugs

tri·tu·rus \'trīt·ūrəs, -ī,tyü-\ *n, cap* [NL, prob. fr. *Triton* the sea god + NL *-urus* — more at TRITON] : a genus of chiefly aquatic salamanders comprising the typical newts and having a small tongue free along the sides, four to five toes, and a compressed tail

tri·tyl \'trīd·'l\ *n -s* [ISV *triphenylmethyl*] : TRIPHENYLMETHYL

tri·tyl·odon \'trīd·ilə,dän\ *n, cap* [NL, fr. *tri-* + *tyl-* + *-odon*] : a genus of extinct vertebrates from the lower Mesozoic of Africa and Europe in many respects intermediate between reptiles and mammals and formerly classed as primitive mammals but now usu. placed among the reptiles forming with a few related forms the family Tritylodontidae

tri·tyl·odont \-,nt\ *adj* [NL *Tritylodon, Tritylodont-*] : of or relating to the genus *Tritylodon*

²**tritylodont** \"\ *n -s* : an animal or fossil of the genus *Tritylodon*

tri·tyl·odon·ti·dae \(,)trī,tilə'dänt·ə,dē\ *n pl, cap* [NL, fr. *Tritylodont-, Tritylodon, Tritylodon*typed + *-idae*] : a family of extinct vertebrates of the order Ictidosauria — see TRITYLODON

tri·um·fet·ta \,trīəm'fed·ə\ *n, cap* [NL, irreg. fr. Giovanni Battista *Trionfetti* †1708 Ital. botanist] : a large genus of tropical herbs and shrubs (family Tiliaceae) clothed with stellate hairs and bearing yellow flowers followed by bristly capsules — see BURBARK

¹**tri·umph** \'trīəm(p)f *also* -ī,əm-; before a consonant following without pause (as in "triumphs") often -m(p), before a pause or vowel sometimes -mp; *also* ÷ -m(p)th\ *n -s* [ME *triumphe*, fr. MF, fr. L *triumphus*, alter. of OL *triumpus*, fr. *triumpe!* shout repeated at the ceremonial departure of the Roman priests during the Arval fertility festival, prob. of non-IE origin; akin to the source of Gk *thriambos*, hymn sung in processions honoring the god of fruits Dionysus] **1 a** : an ancient Roman ceremonial in honor of a general after his decisive victory over a foreign enemy beginning with his entrance into the city preceded by the senate and magistrates, the spoils, and the captives in chains and followed by his army in marching order and ending with sacrificial offerings and a public feast **b** : a triumphal procession or stately esp. public show or pageant ⟨fishing and hunting expeditions had a sacred character. Their successes were celebrated with festivals and ~s —H.M.Parshley⟩ **2 a** : an occasion of victory esp. such as to elicit satisfaction, exultation, or acclaim : a decisive victory ⟨another great oratorical ~ —A.C.Cole⟩ ⟨wartime scientific and technical ~s —Gerard Piel⟩ ⟨the ~ of industrialism —C.I.Glicksberg⟩ **b** : satisfaction resulting from a victory : EXULTATION ⟨evil expression of ~ on the man's face —Georgina Grahame⟩ ⟨eyes were full of a wild hilarity and a wilder ~ —Elinor Wylie⟩ **c** : something resulting from or signifying a noteworthy victory or success ⟨conference room — ~ of fretwork and frenchified interior decoration —R.H.Rovere⟩ ⟨concedes in a ~ of understatement —M.W.Straight⟩ **3** : a state of joy or exultation for success ⟨great ~s and rejoicing was in heaven —John Milton⟩ **4 a** : a card game of medieval France or any of several games (as loo) derived from it **b** : a precursor of whist played

in England in the 16th century **c** *archaic* : TRUMP CARD **syn** see VICTORY

²triumph \"\, *sometimes in pres part* trī'əm-\ *vb* -ED/-ING/-S [L *triumphare*, fr. *triumphus* triumph] *vi* **1 a** : to receive the honor of a triumph **b** : to celebrate victory or success with exaltation : exult boastfully ⟨sorrow on thee and all the pack of you that ~ thus upon my misery —Shak.⟩ **2** : to obtain victory : be successful : PREVAIL ⟨~*ing* over death, and chance —John Milton⟩ ⟨proponents of the income tax ~*ed* eventually —W.B.Lockling⟩ ⟨originality constantly ~*ed* over convention —G.G.Coulton⟩ **3** : to be prosperous : FLOURISH ⟨where commerce ~*ed* on the favoring gales —John Trumbull⟩ ~ *vt* : CONQUER

tri·um·phal \(')trī¦əm(p)fəl *also* 'trī‚əm-\ *adj* [ME, fr. L *triumphalis*, fr. *triumphus* triumph + *-alis* -al] **1** : of, relating to, or used in a triumph : in honor of a triumph ⟨a ~ crown⟩ ⟨a ~ feast⟩ ⟨tricolored banners and ~ emblems —W.M. Thackeray⟩ ⟨paraded our prizes in a ~ procession through the streets —R.H.Davis⟩ **2** : TRIUMPHANT 4 ⟨~ success —Virgil Thomson⟩

triumphal arch *n* **1** : a monumental structure pierced by at least one lofty and typically arched passageway and usu. commemorating a notable victory, person, or event **2** : the great arch in an early esp. basilican church leading into the choir or sanctuary

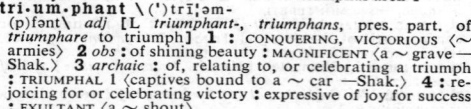

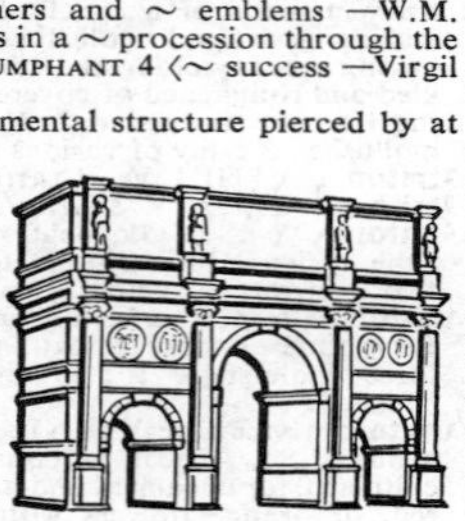
triumphal arch 1

triumphal arch motive *n* : a triple bay having an arch in the central and widest compartment

triumphal column *n* : a monumental column commemorating a victor or a victory

tri·um·phant \(')trī¦əm(p)fənt\ *adj* [L *triumphant-, triumphans*, pres. part. of *triumphare* to triumph] **1** : CONQUERING, VICTORIOUS ⟨~ armies⟩ **2** *obs* : of shining beauty : MAGNIFICENT ⟨a ~ grave —Shak.⟩ **3** *archaic* : of, relating to, or celebrating a triumph : TRIUMPHAL 1 ⟨captives bound to a ~ car —Shak.⟩ **4** : rejoicing for or celebrating victory : expressive of joy for success : EXULTANT ⟨a ~ shout⟩

tri·um·phant·ly *adv* : in a triumphant manner : VICTORIOUSLY

tri·um·pha·tor \'trīəm‚fād·ə(r)\ *n* -S [L, fr. *triumphatus* (past part. of *triumphare*) + *-or*] **1** : one granted a triumph in ancient Rome **2** : one to whom an ovation is given

triumphing *see* ²TRIUMPH\ *adj* : having or celebrating a triumph : TRIUMPHANT ⟨letting out a kind of ~ cry —Mary Deasy⟩ ⟨its abundance of telling detail and its dramatic solidity give it a crude and ~ power —Charles Lee⟩

tri·um·vir \trī'əmvə(r) *sometimes* 'trī‚əm-\ *n, pl* **triumvirs** \-z\ *also* **triumvi·ri** \-ˌvə‚rī, -və‚rē\ [L, back-formation fr. *triumviri*, pl., fr. *trium virum* of three men, fr. *trium* of three (gen. of *tres* three) + *viri*, pl. of *vir* man — more at THREE, VIRILE] : one of a commission or ruling body of three : a member of a triumvirate

tri·um·vir·al \(')trī¦əmvərəl\ *adj* [L *triumviralis*, fr. *triumvir* + *-alis* -al] : of or relating to triumvirs or a triumvirate

tri·um·vi·rate \trī'əmvərə̇t, -və‚rāt, *usu* \|d·+V\ *n* -S [L *triumviratus*, fr. *triumvir* + *-atus* -ate] **1** : the office or government of triumvirs **2** : a body of triumvirs **3** : a group, party, or association of three ⟨a world-famed ~ of painters —*Time*⟩ ⟨a ~ of little burros —William Beebe⟩ ⟨coalesce the ~ of foreign aid programs —*Foreign Policy Bull.*⟩

¹tri·une \'trī‚yün *also* -ī(‚)ün\ *n* -S [*tri-* + L *unus* one — more at ONE] : TRINITY

²triune \"\ *adj, sometimes cap* : being three in one — used esp. of unity of the Trinity in the Godhead ⟨professed faith in the ~ God —J.C.Brauer⟩

tri·un·gu·lin \trī'əŋgyələ̇n\ *n* -S [ISV *tri-* + *ungul-* (fr. L *ungula* claw, fr. *unguis* nail) + *-in* — more at NAIL] **1** : a larva that is the first larval stage of various hypermetamorphic beetles (as oil beetles and blister beetles), is active and of the campodeiform type but during later development becomes legless and parasitic, and in the best-known forms feeds on eggs of bees, wasps, or locusts **2** *or* **triungulid** : the active spiny campodeiform primary larva of a strepsipteral insect that seeks out and attacks the hymenopteran or sometimes homopteran host in which further development takes place

tri·uni·ty \(')trī¦yünəd·ē *also* -ī¦ü-\ *n* [*tri-* + *unity*] : the quality or state of being triune : TRINITY

tri·u·ret \‚trīyü'ret, '‚‚‚\ *n* -S [*tri-* + *-uret*] : a crystalline compound CO(NHCONH₂)₂ related to urea and biuret; 1,3-di-carbamoyl-urea

tri·u·rid \trī'yu̇rə̇d\ *n* -S [NL *Triurid-, Triuris*] : a plant of the family Triuridaceae

tri·u·ri·da·ce·ae \(‚)trī‚yu̇rə'dāsē‚ē\ *n pl, cap* [NL, fr. *Triurid-, Triuris*, type genus + *-aceae*] : a small family of saprophytic leafless herbs (order Triuridales) living in the tropics of both hemispheres and having star-shaped flowers with the perianth segments often fringed or tailed

tri·u·ri·da·les \-ā(‚)lēz\ *n pl, cap* [NL, fr. *Triurid-, Triuris* + *-ales*] : an order of monocotyledonous plants coextensive with the family Triuridaceae

tri·u·ris \trī'yu̇rə̇s\ *n, cap* [NL, fr. *tri-* + *-uris* (fr. Gk *oura* tail) — more at -UROUS] : a genus (the type of the family Triuridaceae) of saprophytic herbs

tri·valence *or* **tri·valency** \(')trī+\ *n, pl* **trivalences** *or* **trivalencies** [*trivalence* ISV, fr. *trivalent*, after such pairs as E *present: presence; trivalency* fr. *trivalent*, after such pairs as E *regent: regency*; trans. of G *dreiwertigkeit*] : the quality or state of being trivalent

¹tri·valent \"+\ *adj* [ISV *tri-* + *valent*; trans. of G *dreiwertig*] **1** : having a valence of three **2** : TRIPLE — used of homologous chromosomes when three are present and associate in synapsis

²trivalent \"\ *n* -S : a trivalent chromosome group

tri·valve \'trī+‚-\ *adj* [*tri-* + *valve*] : having three valves

tri·valvular \(')trī+\ *adj* [*tri-* + NL *valvula* valve + E *-ar*] : TRIVALVE

tri·van·drum \trə'vandrəm\ *adj, usu cap* [fr. *Trivandrum*, India] : of or from the city of Trivandrum, India : of the kind or style prevalent in Trivandrum

tri·variant \(')trī+\ *adj* [ISV *tri-* + *variant*] : capable of threefold variation : having three degrees of freedom — used of a physical-chemical system; compare PHASE RULE

tri·ver·bi·al \(')trī¦vərbēəl\ *adj* [*tri-* + L *verbum* word + E *-ial*; fr. the three words *do* (I grant), *dico* (I deliver), *addico* (I adjudge) used by praetors in court on the dies fasti — more at WORD] : of or relating to the dies fasti

¹triv·et \'trivə̇t, *usu* -ə̇d·+V\ *n* -S [ME *trevet*, fr. OE *trefet*, prob. modif. (influenced by OE *thrifēte* three-footed, fr. *thrīe*, *thrēo* three + *fēt* feet) of LL *tripes* tripod & L *triped-, tripes* three-footed, fr. *tri-* + *ped-, pes* foot — more at THREE, FOOT] **1** : a usu. three-legged stand (as to hold a kettle near a fire) : a tripod with short legs **2** : a usu. ornamental metal stand with short feet esp. for use under a hot dish at table and often electrified **3** : a metal rack for holding meat roasting in a pan

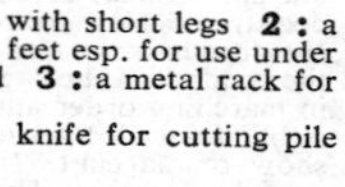
trivet 2

²trivet \"\ *n* -S [origin unknown] : a knife for cutting pile loops in fabrics or carpets

trivet table *n* : a three-legged table

triv·ia \'trivēə\ *n pl but sometimes sing in constr* [NL, fr. pl. of L *trivium* crossroads, influenced in meaning by L *trivialis* trivial] : unimportant matters : TRIFLES ⟨much of our research is wasted on ~ —P.G.Hoffman⟩ ⟨the undifferentiated ~ that impinge on consciousness —Robert Humphrey⟩ ⟨caught up in the ~ of everyday things —Honor Tracy⟩

triv·i·al \'trivēəl\ *adj* [in sense 1, fr. ME, fr. ML *trivialis*, fr. *trivium* + L *-alis* -al; in other senses, fr. L *trivialis* that may be found everywhere, common, ordinary, trivial, fr. *trivium* crossroads, place where three roads meet, fr. *tri-* + *via* way, road — more at VIA] **1** : of or belonging to the trivium **2** : COMMON, ORDINARY, COMMONPLACE ⟨the ~ round, the common task —John Keble⟩ ⟨~ pyrite —A.M.Bateman⟩ — see TRIVIAL NAME 2,3 **3 a** : of little worth or importance : INSIGNIFICANT, FLIMSY, MINOR, SLIGHT ⟨~ objections⟩ ⟨~ inconveniences⟩ ⟨where a painter discards many ~ points of exactness —C.E. Montague⟩ ⟨a ~ act of will —Allen Tate⟩ ⟨the capital as well as the ~ sins —Henry Miller⟩ ⟨wages from both jobs were ~, but he also got tips —Leonard Berry⟩ **b** : concerned with trivialities ⟨a ~ young woman —Sinclair Lewis⟩ ⟨dissertation need not be dull or ~ —J.M.England⟩ ⟨a ~ and badly ordered mind —John Dewey⟩ **4** : SPECIFIC ⟨the species of *Quercus* are notoriously variable in ~ characters —C.H.Muller⟩ — see TRIVIAL NAME 1 **syn** see PETTY

triv·i·al·i·ty \‚trivē'aləd·ē, -lətē, -i\ *n* -ES **1** : the quality or state of being trivial ⟨no one would wish to banish ~ from the theater —*New Republic*⟩ **2** : something trivial : TRIFLE ⟨tend to waste time on *trivialities* —Stewart Cockburn⟩ ⟨made such a fuss over a ~ —Elizabeth Taylor⟩ **3** : concern with or inclination to trivial matters ⟨forests . . . ground into pulp to minister to our ~ —Irving Babbitt⟩

triv·i·al·iza·tion \‚trivēələ'zāshən, -‚lī'z-\ *n* -S : the act, process, or result of trivializing ⟨take for granted the ~ of our lives —W.W.Phelps⟩ ⟨the ~ of education⟩

triv·i·al·ize \'‚‚‚‚līz\ *vt* -ED/-ING/-S : to make trivial : reduce to triviality ⟨a *trivialized* curriculum —Norman Foerster⟩

triv·i·al·ly \'trivēəlē, -li\ *adv* : in a trivial manner or by trivial means ⟨~ motivated demands —R.W.Firth⟩

trivial name *n* **1** : SPECIFIC EPITHET **2** : the vernacular name of an organism as distinguished from the scientific name **3** : the common name for a chemical substance (as camphor or quinoline) ⟨a *trivial name* . . . differs from a systematic name in that it tells little or nothing about structure —A.M.Patterson⟩

triv·i·al·ness *n* -ES : the quality or state of being trivial

triv·i·um \'trivēəm\ *n, pl* **triv·ia** \-ēə\ [ML, fr. L, place where three roads meet] **1** : the three liberal arts of grammar, rhetoric, and logic forming the elementary division of the seven liberal arts in medieval schools and required of all who would obtain bachelor's status — compare QUADRIVIUM **2** [NL, fr. L] : the three anterior rays in an echinoderm — opposed to *bivium*

tri·vol·tine \trī'vōl‚tēn, (')‚‚¦‚t°n\ *adj* [prob. fr. *tri-* + It *volta* turn (fr. — assumed — VL *volvita*, fr. *volvitare*, freq. of L *volvere* to roll) + E *-ine* — more at VOLT] : producing three broods a season — used esp. of silkworms

triv·vet \'trivə̇t\ *n* -S [prob. alter. of E dial. *trivant* truant, alter. of E *truant*] *dial* : a flighty frivolous person

¹tri·weekly \(')trī+\ *adj* [*tri-* + *weekly*] **1** : occurring, appearing, or being made, done, or acted upon three times a week ⟨a ~ publication⟩ ⟨~ train service⟩ **2** : occurring, appearing, or being made, done, or acted upon every three weeks

²triweekly \"\ *n* : a triweekly publication

³triweekly \"\ *adv* : three times a week ⟨a newspaper published ~⟩

-trix \(‚)(‚)triks, (‚)‚trēks\ *n suffix, pl* **-tri·ces** \(‚)‚trə‚sēz, (‚)'trī(‚)sēz\ *or* **-trixes** [ME, fr. L, fem. of *-tor*, ending of agent nouns, fr. *-tus*, past part. ending + *-or* — more at -ED] **1** : female that does or is associated with a (specified) thing ⟨aviatrix⟩ ⟨narratrix⟩ ⟨inheritrix⟩ — compare -TRESS **2** : straight line — in geometry ⟨trisectrix⟩ ⟨directrix⟩ ⟨tractrix⟩

tri·zo·ic \(')trī¦zōik\ *adj* [*tri-* + *-zoic*] : containing three sporozoites ⟨a ~ spore⟩

tri·zonal \(')trī+\ *adj, sometimes cap* [*tri-* + *zonal*] : of, relating to, or concerned with the combined affairs of three administrative areas

tri·zygotic \(')trī+\ *adj* [*tri-* + *zygotic*] : produced from three zygotes ⟨~ triplets⟩ — compare FRATERNAL 2

trk *abbr* **1** track **2** truck **3** trunk

trm *abbr* terminal

trml *abbr* terminal

trng *abbr* turning

tro·ad·ic \trō'adik\ *adj, usu cap* [*Troad*, territory surrounding the ancient city of Troy in northwestern Mysia in Asia Minor (fr. L *Troad-, Troas*, fr. Gk *Trōad-, Trōas*) + E *-ic*] : of or relating to ancient Troy ⟨a *Troadic* ornament⟩

troat \'trōt\ *vi* -ED/-ING/-S [obs. F *trout, trut*, interj., sound made to incite animals, fr. MF] : to cry in rutting time — used esp. of a buck

tro·bri·and·er \'trōbrēəndə(r), -ē‚an-\ *n* -S *cap* [*Trobriand* Islands, group of small islands in the Solomon Sea + E *-er*] : a native or inhabitant of the Trobriand Islands

tro·bri·and islander \'trōbrēənd-, -ē‚and-\ *n, cap T&I* [*Trobriand Islands* + E *-er*] : TROBRIANDER

tro·car *also* **tro·char** \'trō‚kär, -‚kȧ, 'trōkə(r)\ *n* -S [F *trocart*, fr. *trois* three (fr. L *tres*) + *carre* side of a sword blade, fr. *carrer* to square, make square, fr. L *quadrare*; fr. its triangular point — more at THREE, QUADRATE] : a sharp-pointed instrument fitted with a cannula and used to pierce a body cavity and be withdrawn leaving the hollow cannula in place to serve as a drainage outlet

tro·cas \'trōkəs\ *also* **tro·ca** \-kə\ *or* **trocas shell** *n, pl* **trocas** [NL *Trochus*] : a top shell that is fished commercially (as for making pearl buttons)

troch \'träk\ *chiefly Scot var of* TROUGH

troch *abbr* troche

troch- *or* **trocho-** *comb form* [NL, fr. Gk, fr. *trochos* wheel, fr. *trechein* to run — more at TROCHEE] : wheel : resembling a wheel : round ⟨*Troch*odendron⟩ ⟨*Troch*elminthes⟩ ⟨*trocho*phora⟩

-troch \‚träk\ *n comb form* -S [NL *-trocha*] : ciliated band ⟨meso*troch*⟩ ⟨proto*troch*⟩

tro·cha \'trōkə\ *or* **tro·chas** \-kəs\ *n, pl* **trochas** [NL *Trochus*] : TROCAS

-tro·cha \-trəkə\ *n comb form, pl* **-trochas** \-kəz\ *also* **-tro·chae** \-rə‚kē\ [NL, fr. fem. sing. of *-trochus* having (such) a ciliated band, fr. Gk *trochos* wheel] : creature or larva having (such) a ciliated band ⟨actino*trocha*⟩

¹tro·cha·ic \trō'kāik, -āek\ *adj* [MF *trochaïque*, fr. L *trochaicus*, fr. Gk *trochaikos*, fr. *trochaios (pous)* trochee + *-ikos* -ic — more at TROCHEE] : of, relating to, or consisting of trochees ⟨~ meter⟩ — **tro·cha·i·cal·ly** \-ā̇k(ə)lē\ *adv*

²trochaic \"\ *n* -S : a trochaic foot or verse

trochaic dactyl *n* **1** : a foot in classical prosody having the time value of a trochee but containing two short syllables instead of the usual one **2** : a cyclic dactyl

tro·cha·ize \'trōkā‚īz\ *or* **tro·che·ize** *or* **tro·chee·ize** \-kē‚-\ *vt* -ED/-ING/-S [*trochaize* fr. *trochaic* + *-ize*; *trocheize, trocheeize* fr. *trochee* + *-ize*] : to change into a trochee : make trochaic

tro·chal \'trōkəl\ *adj* [*troch-* + *-al*] : resembling a wheel

trochal disc *n* : the expanded flat to somewhat funnel-shaped disc at the anterior end of a rotifer's body that serves to draw in food or to propel the animal

tro·cha·lop·o·da \‚trōkə'läpədə, ‚träk-\ *n pl, cap* [NL, fr. Gk *trochalos* round (fr. *trochos* wheel) + NL *-poda*] *in some classifications* : a group of Hemiptera comprising terrestrial bugs with the coxae articulated by a ball-and-socket joint

tro·cha·lop·o·dous \¦‚‚¦läpədəs\ *adj* [NL *Trochalopoda* + E *-ous*] **1** : having the coxae articulated by a ball-and-socket joint — used of an insect **2** : of or relating to the Trochalopoda

tro·chan·ter \trō'kantə(r), -'kaan-\ *n* -S [NL, fr. Gk *trochantēr*, fr. *trechein* to run] **1** : a rough prominence or process at the upper part of the femur of many vertebrates serving for the attachment of muscles and in birds for articulation with the ilium, being usu. two on each femur in mammals though occasionally one or (as in horses and rhinoceroses) three, and in man constituting a larger prominence situated at the outer part of the upper end of the shaft at its junction with the neck and a smaller at the lower back part of the junction of the shaft and neck — called also respectively *great trochanter* or *greater trochanter, lesser trochanter* **2** : the second segment counting from the base of the leg of an insect that is usu. small and short and in some insects consists of two or rarely of several distinct parts — see TROCHANTIN 1

tro·chan·ter·al \-tərəl\ *adj* : of, relating to, or constituting a trochanter

tro·chan·ter·ic \¦trōkən·terik\ *adj* : of or relating to a trochanter

trochanteric fossa *n* : a depression at the base of the internal surface of the greater trochanter of the femur for the attachment of the tendon of the external obturator muscle

tro·chan·te·ri·on \‚‚‚'tirē‚än\ *n* -S [NL, dim. of *trochanter*] : TROCHANTER POINT

trochanter point *n* : the highest point upon the greater trochanter — called also *trochanterion*

tro·chan·tin *also* **tro·chan·tine** \trō'kantə̇n\ *n* -S [F *trochantin*, dim. of *trochanter*, fr. Gk *trochantēr*] **1** : the proximal of the two segments into which the trochanter of the leg of an insect may be divided and which is often united with the coxa **2** : the lesser trochanter of the femur — **tro·chan·ti·nal** \-tən°l\ *adj* — **tro·chan·tin·i·an** \¦trōkən¦tinēən\ *adj*

trochar *var of* TROCAR

tro·che \'trōkē, -ki\ *n* -S [short for *trochisk*, fr. ME *trocis*, fr. LL *trochiscus*, fr. Gk *trochiskos* small wheel, troche, dim. of *trochos* wheel — more at TROCH-] : a medicinal tablet or lozenge usu. of circular or oval form; *esp* : one used as a demulcent (as for soreness or irritation in the throat)

troch·e·am·e·ter \‚träkē'amədə(r)\ *n* [prob. fr. Gk *trochia* wheel track (fr. *trochos* wheel + *-ia* -y) + E *-meter*] : an instrument used to count the revolutions of a wheel

tro·chee \'trō(‚)kē\ *n* -S [F *trochée*, fr. L *trochaeus*, fr. Gk *trochaios (pous)* running (foot), trochee, fr. *trochaios* running, fr. *trochos* running race, racecourse, fr. *trechein* to run; akin to OIr *droch* wheel, Lith *drožti* to run quickly, Arm *durgn* potter's wheel] : a prosodic foot of two syllables of which the first is long and the second short (as in Latin *ante*) or the first stressed and the second unstressed (as in English *motion*) — symbol —⏑; compare IAMB

troch·el·minth \'träkəl‚min(t)th\ *n* -S [NL *Trochelminthes*] : an animal of the phylum Trochelminthes

troch·el·min·thes \‚‚‚'min(t)‚thēz\ *n pl, cap* [NL, fr. *troch-* + *helminthes*] *in some classifications* : a phylum of invertebrates including the Rotifera, the Gastrotricha, and a few obscure forms

trochi *pl of* TROCHUS

¹tro·chid \'trōkə̇d\ *adj* [NL *Trochidae*] : of or relating to the Trochidae

²trochid \"\ *n* -S : a mollusk of the family Trochidae

troch·i·dae \'träkə‚dē\ *n pl, cap* [NL, fr. *Trochus*, type genus + *-idae*] : a family of marine gastropod mollusks (suborder Rhipidoglossa) with a conical operculate shell flattened at the base and having an oblique aperture and a very lustrous nacreous lining — see TOP SHELL, TROCHUS

tro·chi·form \'trōkə‚fȯrm, 'träk-\ *adj* [NL *trochus* + E *-iform*] : shaped like a top or a top shell

troch·i·li \'träkə‚lī\ *n pl, cap* [NL, fr. pl. of *trochilus*] : a suborder of Apodiformes consisting of the hummingbirds

tro·chil·i·dae \trō'kilə‚dē\ *n pl, cap* [NL, fr. *trochilus* + *-idae*] : a family of small often brilliantly colored birds (order Apodiformes) consisting of the hummingbirds — **tro·chil·i·dine** \-‚dīn, -‚dən\ *adj*

troch·i·line \'träkə‚līn, -‚lən\ *adj* [NL *trochilus* + E *-ine*] : of or relating to the hummingbirds

troch·i·lus \-kələs\ *n* [NL, fr. L, a small bird, perh. the golden-crested kinglet, fr. Gk *trochilos* crocodile bird, wren; akin to Gk *trechein* to run — more at TROCHEE] **1** *pl* **troch·i·li** \-kə‚lī\ **a** : CROCODILE BIRD **b** : any of several Old World warblers (as the goldcrest or the willow warbler) **c** : HUMMINGBIRD **2** *cap* : a formerly extensive genus of hummingbirds that is usu. restricted to a long-tailed Jamaican hummingbird (*T. polytmus*) **3** *pl* **trochili** : SCOTIA

tro·ching \'trōkiŋ\ *n* -S [ME, fr. *troche* cluster of tines on an antler (fr. MF, cluster) + *-ing*] : a small point of a stag's antler

tro·chis·ca·tion \‚trōkə'skāshən\ *n* -S [ISV *trochisc-* (fr. LL *trochiscus*) + *-ation*] : the process of forming or forming into troches

tro·chis·cus \trō'kiskəs\ *n, pl* **trochis·ci** \-i‚s(k)ī\ [LL — more at TROCHE] : TROCHE

tro·chite \'trō‚kīt\ *n* -S [NL *trochites*, fr. Gk *trochos* wheel + L *-ites* -ite — more at TROCH-] : a joint of the stem of a fossil crinoid that suggests a wheel — **tro·chit·ic** \trō'kid·ik\ *adj*

troch·lea \'träklēə\ *n* -S [NL, fr. L, sheaf of pulleys, fr. Gk *trochileia, trochilea*; akin to Gk *trochos* wheel, *trechein* to run — more at TROCHEE] : an anatomical structure felt to resemble a pulley: as **a** : the articular surface on the medial condyle of the humerus that articulates with the ulna **b** : the fibrous ring in the inner upper part of the orbit through which the tendon of the trochlear muscle of the eye passes **c** : the smooth depression on the front of the femur between the condyles

troch·le·ar \-ēə(r)\ *adj* [NL *trochlearis*, fr. *trochlea* + L *-aris* -ar] **1 a** : of, relating to, or being a trochlea **b** : of, relating to, or being a trochlear nerve or trochlear muscle **2** : round and narrow in the middle like the wheel of a pulley ⟨a ~ plant embryo⟩

trochlear fossa *n* : a depression in the antero-medial aspect of each orbital plate of the frontal bone that forms a point of attachment for the corresponding superior oblique muscle

troch·le·ar·i·form \‚träklē¦a(a)rə‚fȯrm\ *adj* [NL *trochlearis* + E *-iform*] : TROCHLEAR 2

troch·le·ar·is \‚‚‚'a(a)rə̇s\ *n* -ES [NL] **1** : SUPERIOR OBLIQUE MUSCLE **2** : TROCHLEAR NERVE

trochlear muscle *n* : SUPERIOR OBLIQUE MUSCLE

trochlear nerve *n* *also* **trochlear** *n* -S : either of the 4th pair of cranial nerves arising from the dorsal aspect of the brainstem on either side of the anterior medullary velum and supplying the superior oblique muscle of the eye with motor fibers

trocho- — see TROCH-

troch·o·blast \'träkə‚blast\ *n* [*troch-* + *-blast*] : a ciliate cell on a trochophore

troch·o·ce·pha·lia \‚träkōsə'fālēə\ *n* -S [NL, fr. *troch-* + *-cephalia* -cephaly] : an abnormal roundness of the skull caused by premature union of the frontal and parietal bones — **troch·o·ce·phal·ic** \¦‚‚‚¦falik\ *adj*

troch·o·den·dra·ce·ae \‚träkō‚den'drāsē‚ē\ *n pl, cap* [NL, fr. *Trochodendron*, type genus + *-aceae*] : a family of eastern Asiatic trees (order Ranales) having apetalous flowers that are not aromatic — see EUPTELEA, TROCHODENDRON — **troch·o·den·dra·ceous** \¦‚‚‚¦drāshəs\ *adj*

troch·o·den·dron \‚träkō'dendrən\ *n, cap* [NL, fr. *troch-* + *-dendron*] : a genus (the type of the family Trochodendraceae) of evergreen trees growing in Japan and Korea and having bright green flowers in racemes and brown fruit

¹tro·choid \'trō‚kȯid\ *n* -S [Gk *trochoeidēs* round like a wheel, circular, fr. *troch-* + *-oeidēs* -oid] **1** : the curve generated by a point on the radius of a circle as the circle rolls on a fixed straight line — compare CYCLOID **2** *or* **trochoid joint** : PIVOT JOINT

²trochoid \"\ *adj* [in sense 1, fr. NL *Trochus* + E *-oid*; in sense 2, fr. ¹*trochoid*] **1 a** : TROCHIFORM **b** : of or relating to a top shell **2** : admitting of rotation on a longitudinal axis

tro·choi·dal \trō'kȯid°l\ *adj* [¹*trochoid* + *-al*] **1** : of, relating to, or having the properties of a trochoid **2** [obs. E *trochoid* mollusk of the family Trochidae, trochid (fr. NL *Trochus* + E *-oid*) + E *-al*] : TROCHOID — **tro·choi·dal·ly** \-°lē\ *adv*

tro·choi·des \trō'kȯi‚dēz\ *n, pl* **trochoides** [NL, fr. Gk *trochoeidēs* round like a wheel] : PIVOT JOINT

tro·chom·e·ter \trō'kämədə(r)\ *n* [*troch-* + *-meter*] : an odometer for vehicles

tro·choph·o·ra \trō'käf(ə)rə\ *n* -S [NL, fr. *troch-* + *-phora*] : TROCHOPHORE

troch·o·phore \'träkə‚fō(ə)r, -fȯ(ə)r\ *n* -S [NL *trochophora*] : a free-swimming larva characteristic of various aquatic invertebrates (as many worms, rotifers, mollusks) in typical cases having a bilaterally symmetrical ovoid or pyriform body with an equatorial preoral circlet of cilia, a mouth, an intestine, an anal opening, an apical sensory plate, and sometimes nephridial tubes and a second ciliated band behind the mouth — compare MÜLLER'S LARVA

troch·o·sphere \-‚sfi(ə)r\ *n* [*troch-* + *sphere*] : TROCHOPHORE

troch·o·tron \'träkə‚trän\ *n* -S [*troch-* + *-tron*] : a high-vacuum tube or a mass spectrograph in which the ion paths controlled by magnetic and electric fields are trochoids

troch·o·zoa \‚träkə'zōə\ *n pl, cap* [NL, fr. *troch-* + *-zoa*] *in some esp former classifications* : a group of Invertebrata including all those (as the annelids and mollusks) whose early larval stage is normally a trochophore — **troch·o·zo·ic** \¦‚‚¦zōik\ *adj*

troch·o·zo·on \‚‚'zō‚än\ *n, pl* **trocho·zoa** \-ōə\ [NL] **1** : an organism of the group Trochozoa **2** : a hypothetical ancestral organism having essentially the organization of a trochophore

-trochs *pl of* -TROCH

tro·chus \'trōkəs\ *n* [NL, fr. L, wheel, iron hoop, fr. Gk *trochos* wheel — more at TROCH-] **1 a** *cap* : a genus of chiefly Old World tropical marine gastropods (family Trochidae) with

beautifully nacreous bluntly conical shells including a large Indo-Pacific species (*T. niloticus*) extensively used in making buttons and ornamental objects **b** -ES : TOP SHELL **2** *pl*
tro·chi \-ō,kī\ *or* **trochuses** : the inner preoral band of cilia of a trochal disc; *broadly* : TROCHAL DISC
trock \'träk\ *chiefly Scot var of* TRUCK
tro·co \'trō(,)kō\ *n* -S [prob. modif. of It *trucco* trucks (game) — more at TRUCKS] : an old English game played on a lawn with wooden balls and cues with spoon-shaped iron tips and having as its object the sending of a ball through an iron ring on a pivot in the center of the field — called also *lawn billiards*
troc·to·lite \'träktə,līt\ *n* -S [G *troktolit*, fr. Gk *trōktēs*, a sea fish (in LL *trocta*, a trout) + G *-lit* -lite; fr. the resemblance to the speckled skin of a trout — more at TROUT] : gabbro that is chiefly labradorite and olivine with little or no pyroxene
1trod \'träd\ *n* -S [ME, fr. OE *trod* (neut.), *trodu* (fem.) track, trace; akin to ON *troth* act of treading, *trotha* to tread — more at TREAD] **1** *chiefly dial* : a footprint or other trace of passage **2** *chiefly dial* : FOOTPATH, TRAIL **3** *dial Eng* : a wheel's tread
2trod \"\ *vb, pres part* **trodding**; *pres 3d sing* **trods** [ME *trodden*, fr. *trod*, n.] *vt* **1** *chiefly Scot* : to follow the course of : TRACE, TRACK **2** : to follow as a chosen course or path ⟨the eccentric is forced . . . to ~ a lonely way —Martin Gardner⟩ ~ *vi, chiefly dial* : to progress by walking; *usu* : STROLL, RAMBLE
3trod [ME *troden* (past pl.), alter. of *treden* (past pl.), fr. OE *trǣdon* (past pl.)] *past of* TREAD
trodden [ME *troden* (past part.), alter. (prob. influenced by *trod*, n.) of *treden* (past part.), fr. OE *getreden*] *past part. of* TREAD
troe·ger·ite \'trōgə,rīt\ *n* -S [G *trögerit*, fr. R. *Tröger*, 19th cent. Ger. mining official + G *-it* -ite] : a mineral $(UO_2)_3(AsO_4)_2.12H_2O$ that is a hydrous arsenate of uranium and occurs in lemon-yellow crystals
trof·fer \'träfə(r), 'tröf-\ *n* -S [*troff* (alter. of *trough*) + *-er*] : an inverted trough serving as a support and reflector for a usu. fluorescent lighting unit
troft \'tröft, 'träft\ *n* -S [by alter.] *dial* : TROUGH
trog·gin \'trägən\ *n* -S [fr. obs. E dial. (Sc) *trog* to barter, bargain, prob. fr. F *troquer*] *Scot* : peddlers' wares
troglo- *comb form* [NL, fr. Gk *trōglo-*, fr. *trōglē* hole, cave] : cave-dwelling : troglodytic ⟨*troglo*biont⟩
trog·lo·bi·ont \,träglə'bī,änt, trä'glōbē,-\ *n* -S [*troglo-* + *-biont*] : an animal living in or restricted to caves; *esp* : one occurring in the lightless waters of caves
trog·lo·dyte \'träglə,dīt\ *n* -S [L *Troglodytae*, pl., a cave-dwelling people of Ethiopia, fr. Gk *trōglodytai* cave dwellers, fr. *trōglodytēs* one who enters caves, fr. *trōglē* hole, cave + *-dytēs* one who enters (fr. *dyein* to enter) — more at TERSE, ADYTUM] **1 a** : a member of a primitive people dwelling in caves or pits : CAVE DWELLER **b** : an animal (as an ant) that lives under the surface of the ground **2 a** : a person felt to resemble (as in appearance, ways of living, or degradation or brutality of nature) a troglodyte; *esp* : an unsocial seclusive person **b** : an anthropoid ape (as a chimpanzee or gorilla)
trog·lo·dy·tes \,träglə'dī,tēz, trä'glädə,-\ *n, cap* [NL, fr. Gk *trōglodytēs*] **1** : a genus of typical wrens including the common wren of the Old World, the American house wren, and related birds **2** *in former classifications* : a genus comprising the gorilla and chimpanzee and being an invalid homonym of the wren genus
trog·lo·dyt·ic \,träglə'did·ik\ *adj* [L *troglodyticus* of or relating to the cave dwellers of Ethiopia, fr. Gk *trōglodytikos* of or relating to cave dwellers, fr. *trōglodytēs* troglodyte + *-ikos* -ic] **1 a** : of or relating to cave dwellers or their ways **b** : dwelling in or involving residence in caves ⟨a ~ life⟩ **2** : coarse, brutal, or degraded in appearance, ways of living, or nature ⟨two ~ types . . . locked in unfraternal conflict —A.J.Liebling⟩ **3** : primitive or outmoded in character ⟨a ~ organization⟩ ⟨his ~ political ideas —G.W.Johnson⟩
trog·lo·dyt·i·dae \,==ˈdid·ə,dē\ *n pl, cap* [NL, fr. *Troglodytes*, type genus + *-idae*] : a family of passerine birds consisting of the wrens, formerly including also the thrashers, mockingbirds, and related forms and sometimes being made a subfamily of Timaliidae
trog·lo·dyt·ism \'===,dī,tizəm\ *n* -S : a condition or style of conduct typical of or suitable to a troglodyte
trog·lo·tre·ma \,träglə'trēmə\ *n, cap* [NL, fr. *troglo-* + *-trema*] : a genus (the type of the family Troglotrematidae) of small spiny egg-shaped digenetic trematodes including a worm (*T. salmincola*) responsible for salmon poisoning of dogs and other canines in the northwestern U.S.
trog·lo·tre·mat·i·dae \,träglətrə'mad·ə,dē\ *n pl, cap* [NL, fr. *Troglotrema*, type genus + *-idae*] : a small family of trematode worms that are parasitic for the most part in mammals — see PARAGONIMUS, TROGLOTREMA
tro·go·der·ma \,trōgə'dərmə\ *n, cap* [NL, fr. *trogo-* (fr. Gk *trōgein* to gnaw) + *-derma*] : a genus of dermestid beetles including several that are destructive to stored food — see KHAPRA BEETLE
tro·gon \'trō,gän\ *n* [NL, fr. Gk *trōgōn*, pres. part. of *trōgein* to gnaw — more at TERSE] **1** *cap* : the type genus of Trogonidae comprising tropical American birds with brilliant lustrous plumage **2** -S : any bird of the genus *Trogon*; *broadly* : a bird of the family Trogonidae — see QUETZAL
tro·gon·i·dae \trō'gänə,dē\ *n pl, cap* [NL, fr. *Trogon*, type genus + *-idae*] : a family (coextensive with the order Trogoniformes) of showy tropical nonpasserine forest birds that have a short stout dentate bill and heterodactylous feet — see TROGON
tro·gon·oid \'trōgə,nȯid\ *adj* [*trogon* + *-oid*] : resembling or related to the trogons
trogs *also* **troggs** \'trägz\ *n pl* [alter. of ME (Sc) *troughth* troth, fr. OE *trēowth* fidelity — more at TRUTH] *chiefly Scot* : TROTH
trogue \'trōg\ *n* -S [alter. of *trough*] *Brit* : a wooden trough forming a mine drain
tro·ic \'trōik\ *adj, usu cap* [L *troicus*, fr. Gk *trōikos*, fr. *Trōs*, *Trōos* Tros, legendary founder of Troy + *-ikos* -ic] : TROJAN
troi·ka \'trȯikə\ *n* -S [Russ *troĭka*, fr. *troe* three; akin to Lith *treji* three, Skt *tri* — more at THREE] : a Russian vehicle drawn by three horses abreast; *also* : a team for such a vehicle
tro·i·lite \'trōə,līt, 'trȯi,-\ *n* -S [G *troilit*, fr. Dominico *Troili*, 18th cent. Ital. scientist who described a meteorite in which it occurs + G *-it* -ite] : a mineral FeS that is a native ferrous sulfide, is a variety of pyrrhotite with almost no iron deficiency, and occurs in meteorites
troi·lus butterfly \'trȯiləs-, 'trōələs-\ *also* **troilus** *n* -ES [fr. *Troilus*, son of Priam, king of Troy, fr. L, fr. Gk *Trōilos*] : a large American swallowtail (*Papilio troilus*) that is black with yellow marginal spots on the front wings and blue on the rear
troilus verse *or* **troilus stanza** *n, usu cap T* [fr. *Troilus* and Criseyde, narrative poem in rhyme royal (*ab*1385) by Geoffrey Chaucer †1400 Eng. poet] : RHYME ROYAL
1tro·jan \'trōjən\ *n* -S [ME, fr. L *Trojani*, pl., Trojans, fr. *Troja, Troia* Troy] **1** *cap* : a native or inhabitant of Troy **2** *usu cap* : one who shows qualities (as pluck, endurance, determined energy) attributed to the defenders of ancient Troy — used chiefly in the phrase *like a Trojan* **3** *usu cap* : a gay and often somewhat irresponsible or disreputable companion
2trojan \"\ *adj, usu cap* [ME, fr. L *trojanus*, fr. *Troja, Troia* Troy, ancient city in Asia Minor that according to Greek legend was besieged, captured, and destroyed by the Greek armies during the ten-year Trojan War about 1200 B.C. (fr. *Tros*, legendary king of Phrygia and founder of Troy, fr. Gk *Trōs, Trōos*) + L *-anus* -an] **1** : of, relating to, or resembling that of ancient Troy or its inhabitants ⟨a *Trojan* spirit⟩ **2** : of, relating to, or constituting a Trojan horse ⟨a *Trojan* threat to our economy⟩
trojan asteroid *or* **trojan** *n* -S *usu cap T* [so called fr. its being one of the group whose members bear the names of Trojan heroes] : an asteroid whose average position is at one corner of an equilateral triangle formed with the sun and the planet Jupiter either eastward or westward of the planet
trojan group *n, usu cap T* : TROJAN ASTEROIDS
trojan horse *n, usu cap T* [so called fr. the gigantic and hollow wooden horse filled with soldiers by means of which the Greeks gained entrance into Troy during the Trojan War and insured the conquest of the city] **1** : a device of placing espionage and propaganda agents inside the country of an intended victim for purposes of sabotage and direction of native subversive groups — compare FIFTH COLUMN **2** : a person, organization, or factor that is intended or likely to undermine an established institution
1troke \'trōk\ *vb* -ED/-ING/-S [F *troquer*] *Scot* : BARTER, TRAFFIC, EXCHANGE, DEAL, NEGOTIATE — **trok·er** \-kər\ *n* -S *Scot*
2troke \"\ *n* -S *Scot* : 2TRUCK
tro·land \'trōlənd\ *n* -S [after Leonard T. *Troland* †1932 Am. psychologist and physicist] : PHOTON 2
1troll \'trōl\ *vb* -ED/-ING/-S [ME *trollen* to ramble, roll, prob. fr. MF *troller* to ramble, of Gmc origin; akin to MHG *trollen* to run with short steps — more at 3TROLL] *vt* **1** : to cause to move round and round : BOWL, ROLL ⟨~*ed* it . . . as a child does a hoop —R.S.B.Baker⟩ **2 a** : to sing the parts of (as a round or catch) in succession **b** : to sing loudly or freely **c** : to celebrate in song ⟨that all tongues shall ~ you —Francis Beaumont & John Fletcher⟩ **3** : to speak or recite in a rolling voice or very rapidly **4** *obs* : to move very rapidly : WAG ⟨to dress and ~ the tongue and roll the eye —John Milton⟩ **5 a** : to angle for with a hook and line drawn through the water from a moving boat **b** : to angle in ⟨~ the lakes —Jackson Rivers⟩ **c** : to pull through or as if through the water behind a boat ⟨two or three surface lures were ~*ed* continuously during daylight hours —*Commercial Fisheries Rev.*⟩ ~ *vi* **1** : to move around : CIRCULATE, ROLL **2** : to fish esp. by drawing a hook along or through the water with a line behind a moving boat ⟨~*ed* for bass —Walt Sibley⟩ **3 a** : to take part in a troll : sing or play in a jovial manner : sound with a rolling tone **b** : to be constantly in mind (as a melody) **4** : to speak rapidly : wag the tongue **5** *archaic* : to pass from hand to hand ⟨the wassail round in good brown bowls . . . blithely ~*s* —Sir Walter Scott⟩
2troll \"\ *n* -S **1** *Eng* : a hawker's cart : TROLLEY **2 a** : the process of trolling **b** (1) : the lure (as a spoon) used in trolling (2) : the line with its lure and hook used in trolling **3** : a song sung in parts successively : CATCH, ROUND **4** : a slovenly or loose woman : TROLLOP
3troll \"\ *n* -S [Norw *troll* & Dan *trold*, fr. ON *troll* giant, fiend, demon; akin to MHG *trolle* ghostly monster, boor, lout, *trollen* to run with short steps, ON *tramr* demon, monster, MHG *tremen* to totter, stagger, MLG *trampen* to stamp, tread, OE *treppan* to tread — more at TRAP] : a supernatural being in Germanic and Scandinavian folklore and mythology having sometimes the form of a dwarf and sometimes of a giant and inhabiting caves or hills
troll-drum \'=,=\ *n* [3*troll*] : a drum employed for shamanistic or magical purposes by the Lapps
troll·er \-lə(r)\ *n* -S : one that trolls: as **a** : one who fishes with a troll **b** : a singer of catches or rounds **c** : a boat used in trolling for fish
1trol·ley *or* **trol·ly** \'trälē, -li\ *n, pl* **trolleys** *or* **trollies** [prob. fr. 1*troll* + *-y* (dim. suffix)] **1 a** *dial Eng* : a low wheeled cart **b** *Brit* : a railroad dump car **c** *Brit* : a small truck used in mines **d** : a small wheeled car used usu. on a wooden track to move lumber from a portable sawmill to a yard **2 a** : a current collector operating in connection with a trolley wire — see BOW TROLLEY, PANTOGRAPH 2, WHEEL TROLLEY **b** : an electric car : TROLLEY CAR, STREETCAR **3** : a wheeled carriage running on an overhead rail or track (as of a parcel railway in a shop or store) : the wheeled truck of a traveling crane or of a ropeway from which a load is suspended **4** : a movable block used on a cable in skidding logs **5** *Brit* : a four-wheel stretcher used to transport patients in a hospital **6** *chiefly Brit* : a table or shelved stand on wheels usu. equipped with a handle and used for conveying something (as food or books) **7** *Brit* : a hand-propelled cart: as **a** : CADDIE CART **b** : PUSHCART — **off one's trolley** : mentally disorganized : unable for the time being to exhibit a reasonable and sensible course
2trolley *or* **trolly** \"\ *vb* **trolleyed** *or* **trollied**; **trolleyed** *or* **trollied**; **trolleying** *or* **trollying**; **trolleys** *or* **trollies** *vt* : to convey by a trolley ⟨was ~*ing* a packing case aboard a lift —Richard Church⟩ ~ *vi* : to ride on a trolley ⟨so ~ to your hotel for freshening up —James Cerruti⟩
3trolley *var of* TROLLY
trolleybus \'=,=\ *n* : a street-railway vehicle electrically propelled by power from two overhead wires and similar in appearance to a motor bus — called also *trolley coach*
trolley car *n* : a public conveyance for carrying passengers that runs on tracks with motive power derived through a trolley
trolley harp *n* : HARP 3a
trolley line *or* **trolley road** *n* : a system of transportation by means of trolley cars or trolleybuses
trolley locomotive *n* : an electrically operated locomotive that obtains power from an overhead wire
trol·ley·man *or* **trol·ly·man** \'==mən\ *n, pl* **trolleymen** *or* **trollymen** : a man who works on a trolley or electric car; *esp* : a motorman or conductor of an electric car
trolley pole *n* : the pole on various types of trolley cars and trolleybuses by which electrical contact is made with the power line
trolley retriever *n* : a trolley catcher with a supplementary movement to pull down the pole
trolley shoe *n* : a metal current-collecting device for an electrically propelled vehicle receiving power from overhead wires
trollflower \'=,=\ *n* [part trans. of G *trollblume*, prob. fr. *trollen* to trot, roll (fr. MHG, to run with short steps) + *blume* flower; prob. fr. the round shape — more at TROLL] : GLOBEFLOWER a
trolling *n* -S [fr. gerund of 1*troll*] : the act of one that trolls; *specif* : fishing with a troll
trol·li·us \'träləs\ *n, cap* [NL, fr. G *troll*blume trollflower] : a genus of herbs (family Ranunculaceae) that are native to the north temperate regions, have palmately lobed leaves and fruit consisting of a head of follicles, and are often cultivated as ornamentals for their large yellow or lilac flowers with sepals and petals colored alike — see GLOBEFLOWER a
troll-madam \'=,=\ *n* [modif. (influenced by 1*troll*) of MF *trou-madame*] : TROU MADAME
1trol·lop \'träləp\ *n* -S [prob. irreg. fr. G dial. *trolle* trollop, prostitute, fr. MHG *trulle* prostitute, mistress — more at TRULL] **1 a** : an unkempt slovenly woman : SLATTERN **b** : a woman of loose morals : WANTON **c** *Midland* : a dissatisfied restless woman **2** : something that dangles or drags untidily : a straggly mass ⟨a ~ of soldiery . . . out-of-step, blurred and miserable —Bruce Marshall⟩
2trollop \"\ *vi* -ED/-ING/-S **1** : to work, walk, or act in a sluggish or slovenly manner : slouch along : SLUMP **2** *chiefly Scot* : to dangle or hang soggily : become bedraggled **3** : to behave like a trollop : display a wanton manner
trol·lope \'träləp\ *interj, usu cap* [fr. Frances *Trollope* †1863 Eng. novelist known for her criticism of bad manners in her book *Domestic Manners of the Americans* (1832)] — used as a cry of protest against bad manners or boorish behavior esp. in a theater
1trol·lop·i·an *also* **trol·lop·e·an** \trə'läpēən, -'lōp-, ¦trälə¦pēən\ *adj, usu cap* [Anthony *Trollope* †1882 Eng. novelist + E *-an*, adj. suffix] : of, relating to, or characteristic of the works or the style of the English novelist Anthony Trollope
2trollopian \"\ *n* -S *usu cap* [Anthony *Trollope* †1882 + E *-an*, n. suffix] : an admirer of the writings of the English novelist Anthony Trollope
trol·lopy \'träləpē\ *adj* : resembling or characteristic of a trollop
troll plate *n* : a rotative disk with spiral ribs or grooves by which several pieces (as the jaws of a chuck) can be moved radially in or out
trolls *pres 3d sing of* TROLL, *pl of* TROLL
1trol·ly *or* **trol·ley** \'trälē, -li\ *n, pl* **trollies** *or* **trolleys** [prob. fr. Flem *tralie* trellis, lattice, mesh, network, lace, fr. MD *tralie*, *trallie* latticework, prob. fr. L *trichila, tricla* bower, arbor] : an English bobbin lace with a heavy thread outlining the designs on a net ground
2trolly *var of* TROLLEY
trom·ba \'trämbə, 'trōm-\ *n, pl* **trom·be** \-bā\ [It — more at TROMBONE] **1** : TRUMPET **2** : an organ stop imitating the tone quality of a trumpet
tromba da ti·rar·si \-datə'rärsē\ *n, pl* **trombe da tirarsi** [It] : a slide trumpet
trom·bic·u·la \träm'bikyələ\ *n, cap* [NL, fr. *Trombidium* + *-cula* -cle] : a genus of mites that is the type of the family Trombiculidae and that contains some mites that in the Orient transmit tsutsugamushi disease
1trom·bic·u·lid \-yələd\ *adj* [NL *Trombiculidae*] : of or relating to the Trombiculidae
2trombiculid \"\ *n* -S : a mite of the family Trombiculidae
trom·bi·cu·li·dae \,trämbə'kyülə,dē\ *n pl, cap* [NL, fr. *Trombicula*, type genus + *-idae*] : a large and widely distributed family of mites whose nymphs and adults feed on early stages of small arthropods but whose larvae are parasites on terrestrial vertebrates including man — compare TROMBIDIIDAE; see CHIGGER, TROMBICULA
trom·bi·di·a·sis \,trämbə'dīəsəs\ *also* **trom·bi·di·o·sis** \,==dī'ōsəs\ *n, pl* **trombidia·ses** \,==ˈdīə,sēz\ [NL, fr. *Trombidium* + *-iasis* or *-osis*] : infestation with chiggers
1trom·bid·i·id \träm'bidēəd\ *adj* [NL *Trombidiidae*] : of or relating to the Trombidiidae
2trombidiid \"\ *n* -S : a mite of the family Trombidiidae
trom·bi·di·idae \,trämbə'dīə,dē\ *n pl, cap* [NL, fr. *Trombidium* + *-idae*] : a large and widely distributed family of mites that feed in all stages on other arthropods — compare TROMBICULIDAE
trom·bid·i·um \träm'bidēəm\ *n, cap* [NL] : a genus of mites that is the type of the family Trombidiidae
trom·bi·doi·dea \,trämbə'dȯidēə\ *n pl, cap* [NL, fr. *Trombidium* + *-oidea*] *in some esp former classifications* : a superfamily of mites that includes the harvest mites, the red spiders, and others of minor importance
trom·bone \(')träm¦bōn, (,)trəm'bōn\ *n* -S [It, aug. of *tromba*

trombone

trumpet, of Gmc origin; akin to OHG *trumpa, trumba* trumpet — more at TRUMP (trumpet)] **1 a** (1) : a brass wind instrument that has a cupped mouthpiece, that consists of a long cylindrical metal tube bent twice upon itself and ending in a bell and that has its first crook as a movable slide thereby permitting the player to control the length of the vibrating column and produce any pitch within its compass of E to b♭′ — compare VALVE TROMBONE (2) : a player on this instrument **b** : a large-scale pipe-organ stop of a quality similar to that of the trombone **2** : an early blunderbuss having a large trumpet-shaped muzzle **3** : a U-shaped section that resembles the slide of a trombone and that adjusts tuning in a wave-guide or coaxial-line circuit
trombone-action *adj* : PUMP-ACTION
trombone coil *n* : a continuous steam or hot-water coil in which each intermediate section of pipe is connected at its ends by return bends to the parallel section on either side
trom·bon·ist \-nəst\ *n* -S : a player on the trombone
trom·mel \'träməl\ *n* -S [G, drum, fr. MHG *trummel*, fr. *trumme* — more at DRUM] : a screen usu. of cylindrical or conical shape that is mounted on a revolving and slightly inclined longitudinal shaft and is used esp. for screening or sizing rock, ore, or coal
tro·mom·e·ter \trō'mämәd·ə(r)\ *n* [Gk *tromos* trembling (akin to Gk *tremein* to tremble) + E *-meter* — more at TREMBLE] : an instrument for measuring or detecting minute earth tremors — **trom·o·met·ric** \¦trämə¦me·trik\ *or* **trom·o·met·ri·cal** \-rəkəl\ *adj* — **tro·mom·e·try** \trō'mämə·trē\ *n* -ES
trompe *also* **tromp** \'trämp\ *n* -S [F *trompe*, lit., trumpet, fr. OF — more at TRUMP] : an apparatus (as for a Catalan forge) in which air is sucked through sloping holes in the upper end of a large vertical wooden tube and led to a furnace by a stream of falling water that is discharged below
trompe l'oeil \trōⁿplər, -lə͞i\ *n, pl* **trompe l'oeils** \"\ [F] : deception of the eye esp. by a painting: as **a** : the intensification of the reality of component objects in an unnaturally arranged still life through the use of minute detail and the careful rendition of tactile and tonal values **b** : the use in mural and ceiling decoration of painted detail suggestive of architectural or other three-dimensional elements but often characterized by exaggerated perspective, abrupt contrast of light and shade, or general stylization which stresses artificiality
trom·pil \'trämpəl\ *n* -S [F *trompille*, fr. *trompe*] : an aperture in a trompe
trom·pil·lo \träm'pē(,)(y)ō\ *n* -S [Sp, prob. dim. of *trompa* horn, trumpet, nozzle, prob. of Gmc origin like It *tromba* trumpet — more at TROMBONE] : a weedy nightshade (*Solanum elaeagnifolium*) ranging from the central U.S. to So. America with silvery foliage, violet, blue, or white flowers, and a roundish berry widely used by the natives to curdle milk — called also *prairie berry, purple nightshade, silverleaf nightshade*
-tron \,trän\ *n suffix* -S [Gk, suffix denoting an instrument (as Gk *arotron* plow, fr. stem of *aroun* to plow); akin to OE *-thor*, suffix denoting an instrument, ON *-thr*, L *-trum*, MIr *-thar*, Skt *-tra*] **1** : vacuum tube ⟨magne*tron*⟩ **2** : device for the manipulation of subatomic particles ⟨cyclo*tron*⟩ ⟨iso*tron*⟩
tro·na \'trōnə\ *n* -S [Sw, prob. fr. Ar *natrūn* natron — more at NATRON] : a gray-white or yellowish white monoclinic mineral $Na_3H(CO_3)_2.2H_2O$ consisting of a hydrous acid sodium carbonate in crystals or fibrous or columnar masses as a deposit from various soda-brine springs and lakes (hardness 2.5–3, sp. gr. 2.11–2.14)
tro·na·dor \¦trōnə¦dȯ(ə)r\ *n* -S [AmerSp, lit., thunderer, fr. Sp, fr. *tronar* to thunder, modif. of L *tonare*; fr. its noisy dehiscence — more at THUNDER] **1** : a Central American, Mexican, and West Indian woody herb (*Abutilon trisulcatum*) **2** : the bast fiber of the tronador used esp. for ropes and nets
tron·age \'trōnij\ *n* -S [AF, fr. *trone* + OF *-age*] **1 a** : a medieval toll or duty for compulsory weighing of coarse goods (as wool) at the public trone **b** : the act of weighing such goods **2** : the right of demanding tronage
trone \'trōn\ *also* **tron** \'trän\ *n* -S [AF *trone*, fr. OF, fr. L *trutina* balance, scales, fr. Gk *trytanē*; akin to Gk *tryma* hole, *tetrainein* to pierce; fr. the opening in which the tongue of the scale moves — more at THROW] *chiefly Scot* : one of various weighing machines; *specif* : one for heavy wares having two horizontal bars crossing each other and beaked at the extremities
trone weight *n* : an old standard of weight used in Scotland before 1618 based on a pound containing 21 to 28 ounces avoirdupois
tro·nom·e·ter \trō'nämәd·ə(r)\ *n* [alter. of *tromometer*] : a device for measuring finger tremor used to diagnose nervous disturbances
tro·ö·don \'trōə,dän\ *n, cap* [NL, fr. *tro-* (prob. fr. Gk *trōgein* to gnaw) + *-odon* — more at TERSE] : a genus (the type of the family Troödontidae) of aberrant Upper Cretaceous No. American ornithopod dinosaurs with the skull expanded above into an enormous rugose bony dome ornamented with prongs and spikes
1tro·ö·dont \-nt\ *adj* [NL *Troödont-, Troödon*] : of or relating to the *Troödon*
2troödont \"\ *n* -S : a dinosaur of the genus *Troödon*
troo·lie \'trülē\ *n* -S [Galibi *turluri*] **1** : one of the immense leaves of the bussu used for thatching **2** *also* **troolie palm** : BUSSU
1troop \'trüp\ *n* -S [MF *troupe*, fr. *troupeau* herd, crowd, fr. OF, of Gmc origin; akin to OE *throp, thorp* group, village — more at THORP] **1 a** : a group of soldiers : a body of armed men ⟨the small ~ . . . that guarded the settlement was drawn up on parade —Leslie Thomas⟩ **b** (1) : a cavalry unit corresponding to an infantry company (2) : a company of horse artillery **c** : armed forces : SOLDIERS — usu. used in pl. ⟨victorious ~*s*⟩ **2 a** : a collection of people or things : COMPANY ⟨a mobile and dynamic ~ whose major aims are the improvement of the mind —E.O.Hauser⟩ **b** : a considerable number : a large quantity ⟨she had . . . ~*s* of friends —Havelock Ellis⟩ ⟨~*s* of servants and endless leisure —Letitia Fairfield⟩ **3** : a flock of animals or birds ⟨suddenly started a ~ of tall giraffes —H.R.Haggard⟩ ⟨a ~*s* of finches and linnets up here —Richard Jefferies⟩ **4 a** : a unit of at least five boy scouts of the Boy Scouts of America under the leadership of a scoutmaster **b** : a unit of the Girl Scouts comprising a group

of usu. 8 to 32 girls and 1 or 2 adult leaders who meet regularly to carry on Girl Scout activities

²troop \"\ *vb* -ED/-ING/-S *vi* **1 :** to gather in crowds **:** come together **:** ASSEMBLE ⟨armies at the call of trumpet . . . ~ to the standard —John Milton⟩ **2 :** to go one's way **:** WALK ⟨~*ed* off to market —Bessie Hackett⟩ ⟨~*ed* away to the ball game⟩ **3 :** to consort in company **:** ASSOCIATE — usu. used with *with* ⟨a snowy dove ~*ing* with crows —Shak.⟩ **4 :** to move in an orderly manner **:** march in or as if in file ⟨the fourth grade ~*ed* in —Frances G. Patton⟩ ⟨pushed back their chairs and ~*ed* into the kitchen —Kenneth Roberts⟩ **5 :** to move in large numbers **:** go as a big group **:** THRONG ⟨the miners ~ home . . . trailing slowly in gangs across the white field —D.H.Lawrence⟩ ⟨hordes of hysterical revelers ~*ing* through their rooms —Green Peyton⟩ ~ *vt, obs* **:** to unite with or form into a troop — **troop the colors** *Brit* **:** to perform a ceremony consisting essentially in carrying the colors slowly before elements of the Brigade of Guards (as on the sovereign's birthday)

troop carrier *n* **1 :** an armored cross-country vehicle designed esp. to carry infantry troops **2 :** a transport airplane used to carry troops and their supplies esp. in a tactical situation or area

troop committee *n* **:** a group of parents and other interested adults organized as a committee for advising and assisting a Girl Scout troop

troop duck *n* **:** GREATER SCAUP

troop·er \-pə(r)\ *n* -S **1 a** (1) **:** an enlisted cavalryman (2) **:** the horse of a cavalryman **b :** PARATROOPER **2 a :** a mounted policeman **b :** one of a body of state police usu. using motorized vehicles **3 :** TROOPSHIP

troopfowl \ˈ=,=\ *n* [¹*troop* + *fowl;* fr. its living in flocks] *dial* **:** SCAUP DUCK

troopial *var of* TROUPIAL

troop school *n* **:** a part of the system of military education in the U.S. armed forces in which both officers and enlisted men receive instruction within their own unit

troopship \ˈ=,=\ *n* **:** a ship built or fitted for the conveyance of troops **:** TRANSPORT

¹troost·ite \ˈtrü,stīt\ *n* -S [Gerard *Troost* †1850 Am. geologist + E *-ite*] **:** a variety of willemite occurring in large reddish crystals in which the zinc is partly replaced by manganese

²troostite \"\ *n* -S [F, fr. Louis J. *Troost* †1911 Fr. chemist + F *-ite*] **:** slightly tempered martensite that etches dark and cannot be resolved by the optical microscope — **troost·it·ic** \trüˈstid·ik\ *adj*

¹trop- *or* **tropo-** *comb form* [ISV, fr. Gk, fr. *tropos* — more at TROPE] **1 :** turn **:** turning **:** change ⟨*tropo*meter⟩ ⟨*tropo*sphere⟩ **2 :** affinity for **:** tendency to turn toward **:** tropism ⟨*trop*ic⟩ ⟨*tropo*taxis⟩

²trop- *also* **tropa-** *comb form* [ISV, fr. *tropine*] **1 :** tropine ⟨*trop*ate⟩ ⟨*tropa*cocaine⟩ **2 :** atropine ⟨*trop*oyl⟩

trop *abbr* tropic; tropical

tro·pa·cocaine \ˌtrōpə+\ *n* [ISV ²*trop-* + *cocaine*] **:** a crystalline alkaloid $C_{15}H_{19}NO_2$ that is obtained from coca leaves grown esp. in Java or is made synthetically and that acts like cocaine but is about one half as toxic **:** the ester of pseudotropine and benzoic acid

tro·pae·o·la·ce·ae \ˌtrōpēōˈlāsē,ē\ *n pl, cap* [NL, fr. *Tropaeolum*, type genus + *-aceae*] **:** a family of plants (order Geraniales) coextensive with the genus *Tropaeolum* — **tro·pae·o·la·ceous** \ˌ=====ˈlāshəs\ *adj*

tro·pae·o·lin *or* **tro·pe·o·lin** \trōˈpēəlēn\ *n* -S *often cap* [ISV *tropaeol-* (fr. NL *Tropaeolum*) + *-in*] **:** any of several orange or orange-yellow azo dyes some of which (as methyl orange) are used as acid-base indicators or as biological stains

tro·pae·o·lum \-ləm\ *n* [NL, dim. of L *tropaeum* trophy — more at TROPHY] **1** *cap* **:** a genus of tropical American diffuse or climbing pungent herbs constituting the family Tropaeolaceae and having lobed or dissected peltate leaves and showy variously colored spurred flowers succeeded by a fruit composed of three distinct rugose carpels — see CANARYBIRD FLOWER, NASTURTIUM 2 **2** -S **:** any plant or flower of the genus *Tropaeolum*

tro·pa·ion \trōˈpā,(y)än, -ˈpī,än\ *n* -S [Gk — more at TROPHY] **:** TROPHAEUM

tro·pane \ˈtrō,pān\ *n* -S [²*trop-* + *-ane*] **:** a bicyclic tertiary amine $C_8H_{15}N$ that is the parent compound of atropine, cocaine, and related alkaloids and that may be regarded as cycloheptane with a methyl-imino bridge **:** dihydro-tropidine

tro·pa·rion \trōˈpär(,)yōn\ *n, pl* **tropa·ria** \-yä\ [LGk, dim. of Gk *tropos* trope] **:** a short hymn in rhythmic prose sung or chanted liturgically in the Eastern Orthodox Church; *specif* **:** a stanza of an ode (sense 2)

tro·pate \ˈtrō,pāt\ *n* -S [ISV ²*trop-* + *-ate*] **:** a salt or ester of tropic acid

trope \ˈtrōp\ *n* -S [L *tropus*, fr. Gk *tropos* turn, way, manner, style; akin to Gk *trepein* to turn, L *trepit* he turns, and perh. to Skt *trapate* he is ashamed] **1 :** the use of a word or expression in a different sense from that which properly belongs to it for giving life or emphasis to an idea; *also* **:** an instance of such use **:** FIGURE OF SPEECH **2 a** (1) **:** any one of certain melodic decorations gradually developed in Gregorian music and employed at the close of psalms and responses (2) **:** a phrase or verse added as an embellishment or interpolation to the sung parts of the mass (as introit or kyrie) esp. during the medieval period **b :** any of the 44 groups or arrangements of the twelve-tone scales into two 6-note chords as developed by Josef Hauer and used by him as a basis of musical composition

¹-trope \ˌtrōp\ *n comb form* -S [F, fr. Gk *tropos* turn, direction, way] **1 :** turn **:** change **:** affinity for ⟨chromo*trope*⟩ ⟨neuro*trope*⟩ **2 :** body characterized by (such) an inversion ⟨hemi*trope*⟩ **3 :** instrument and esp. optical instrument that functions by rotating, reversing, or reflecting ⟨rheo*trope*⟩ ⟨thauma*trope*⟩

²-trope \"\ *adj comb form* [F, fr. Gk *-tropos*, fr. *trepein* to turn] **:** turning **:** being reverted ⟨aniso*trope*⟩ ⟨hemi*trope*⟩

tro·pe·ine \ˈtrōpē,ēn, -ˌən\ *n* -S [alter. of *tropine*] **:** any of a series of crystalline basic esters of tropine; *esp* **:** such an ester made synthetically

tro·per \ˈtrōpə(r)\ *n* -S [ME *tropere*, fr. OE, fr. ML *troparium, troperium*, fr. L *tropus* trope] **:** a medieval book containing tropes or sequences for farsing the sung parts of the mass

tro·pe·sis \trōˈpēsəs\ *n* -ES [NL, fr. Gk *tropē* action of turning (akin to Gk *tropos* turn) + NL *-sis*] *Haeckelism* **:** the rudimentary will or tendency to action possessed by all substance

troph- *or* **tropho-** *comb form* [F, fr. Gk, fr. *trephein* to nourish — more at ATROPHY] **:** nutrition ⟨*tropho*pathy⟩ ⟨*troph*allaxis⟩ ⟨*tropho*spore⟩

tro·phae·um \trōˈfēəm\ *n, pl* **tro·phaea** \-ēə\ [L — more at TROPHY] **:** an ancient Greek or Roman monument commemorating a military victory

tro·phal \ˈtrōfəl\ *adj* [NL *trophi* + E *-al*] **:** of, relating to, or constituting trophi

troph·al·lac·tic \ˌträfəˈlaktik\ *adj* [fr. NL *trophallaxis*, after such pairs as NL *prophylaxis:* E *prophylactic*] **:** of, relating to, constituting, or involving trophallaxis

troph·al·lax·is \ˌ==ˈlaksəs\ *n, pl* **trophallax·es** \-k,sēz\ [NL, fr. *troph-* + Gk *allaxis* barter, fr. *allassein* to change, fr. *allos* other — more at ELSE] **:** exchange of food (as from salivary or other glands) between organisms **:** the association of different organisms and esp. social insects on the basis of such a unilateral or mutual exchange

troph·amnion \ˈträf+\ *n* [NL, fr. *troph-* + *amnion*] **:** a nutritive sheath that sometimes invests the embryonic portion of the insect egg esp. in polyembryonic insects — see PARANUCLEUS

troph·ectoderm \"+\ *n* [*troph-* + *ectoderm*] **:** TROPHOBLAST

tro·phe·ma \trōˈfēmə\ *n* -S [NL, fr. *troph-* + Gk *haima* blood — more at HEM-] **:** the blood of the uterine mucous membrane that nourishes the embryo

tro·phi \ˈtrō,fī\ *n pl* [NL, pl. of *trophus* mouth, fr. Gk *trophos* feeder, fr. *trephein* to nourish] **1 :** the mouthparts of an arthropod (as an insect) including the labrum, labium, maxillae, mandibles, and hypopharynx with their appendages **2 :** the masticating organs of a rotifer including the incus and the two mallei; *broadly* **:** MASTAX

troph·ic \ˈträfik, -ˈfēk\ *adj* [F *trophique*, fr. Gk *trophikos*, fr. *trophē* food (fr. *trephein* to nourish) + *-ikos* -ic] **1 :** relating to or functioning in nutrition **:** NUTRITIONAL ⟨~ disorders⟩ ⟨~ hormones⟩ **2 :** ³TROPIC — **troph·i·cal·ly** \-fək(ə)lē, -fēk-, -li\ *adv*

-troph·ic \ˌ¦träfik, -rōf-, -fēk, *sometimes* -trə(,)fik\ *also* **-tro·phous** \ˌtrəfəs\ *adj comb form* [NL *-trophia* -trophy + E *-ic* or *-ous*] **1 a** *also* **-trophous :** of or relating to a (specified) type of nutrition ⟨hyper*trophic*⟩ ⟨hyper*trophous*⟩ **b :** having a (specified) nutritional requirement ⟨mono*trophic*⟩ **2 :** -TROPIC 1,2 ⟨glyco*trophic*⟩ ⟨lipo*trophic*⟩

tro·phied \ˈtrōfēd\ *adj* [*trophy* + *-ed*] **:** adorned with trophies ⟨the long ~ banquet hall⟩

trophies *pl of* TROPHY, *pres 3d sing of* TROPHY

-trophies *pl of* -TROPHY

tro·phis \ˈtrōfəs\ *n, cap* [NL, fr. Gk, well-fed, nursling, fr. *trephein* to nourish] **:** a small genus of tropical American trees (family Moraceae) having alternate leaves, small dioecious green flowers in usu. spicate or racemose clusters, and a nearly round thin-fleshed fruit with a single rather large seed

troph·ism \ˈträ,fizəm\ *n* -S [ISV *troph-* + *-ism*] **:** fundamental nutrition involving the actual metabolic exchanges of the tissues

troph·o·bi·ont \ˌ¦träfō¦bī,änt\ *n* -S [*troph-* + *-biont*] **:** a participant in trophobiosis

troph·o·bi·o·sis \ˌ==bīˈōsəs\ *n, pl* **trophobio·ses** \-ˈō,sēz\ [NL, fr. *troph-* + *-biosis*] **1 :** a relation in which an organism of one kind aids and protects an organism of another kind in return for some food product — compare CLEPTOBIOSIS **2 :** TROPHALLAXIS

troph·o·bi·ot·ic \ˌ==,=¦äd·ik\ *adj* [*troph-* + *-biotic*] **:** of, relating to, or engaging in trophobiosis ⟨~ insects⟩ ⟨the ~ relation between some ants and the aphids from which they obtain sweet secretions⟩

troph·o·blast \ˈträfə,blast\ *n* [ISV *troph-* + *-blast*] **:** a special layer of ectodermal tissue that forms the outer surface of the blastodermic vesicle of many mammals, destroys the tissues of the uterus with which it comes in contact, is held to supply nutrition to the embryo and to secure the attachment of the egg to the wall of the uterus, and becomes differentiated into an outer syncytial or plasmodial syntrophoblast and an inner cellular cytotrophoblast which enter into the formation of the placenta — **troph·o·blas·tic** \ˌ==¦blastik\ *adj*

tropho·chromatin \ˌträfō+\ *n* [ISV *troph-* + *chromatin;* orig. formed in G] **:** chromatin that is held to be concerned with vegetative functions only — compare IDIOCHROMATIN

troph·o·cyte \ˈträfə,sīt\ *n* -S [ISV *troph-* + *-cyte*] **1 :** a cell esp. of the insect fat body that has a trophic function **2 :** a nutritive cell of the insect ovary or testis

troph·o·derm \-,dərm\ *n* -S [*troph-* + *-derm*] **:** TROPHOBLAST

tropho·dynamic \ˌträfō+\ *adj* [*troph-* + *dynamic*] **:** of or relating to trophodynamics

tropho·dynamics \"+\ *n pl but sing or pl in constr* [*troph-* + *dynamics*] **:** the dynamics of nutrition

troph·o·gen·ic \ˌträfə¦jenik\ *adj* [*troph-* + *-genic*] **1 :** brought about by or resulting from differences in food or feeding rather than genetically determined ⟨the various castes of social insects are usu. held to be ~ in origin⟩ — compare BLASTOGENIC **2** *also* **tro·phog·e·nous** \trōˈfäjənəs\ [*troph-* + *-genous*] **:** of, relating to, or being the upper level in a lake in which inorganic matter is converted to organic through photosynthetic activity — compare TROPHOLYTIC

tro·phog·e·nist \ˈ=ˈ==nəst\ *n* -S [*trophogenic* + *-ist*] **:** an advocate of the trophogenic theory of caste determination in insects

tro·phol·o·gy \trōˈfäləjē\ *n* -ES [ISV *troph-* + *-logy*] **:** a branch of science dealing with nutrition

troph·o·lyt·ic \ˌträfə¦lid·ik\ *adj* [*troph-* + *-lytic*] **:** of, relating to, or being the deeper part of a lake in which dissimilation of organic matter tends to predominate — compare TROPHOGENIC

tro·phon \ˈtrō,fän\ *n* -S [NL, perh. fr. LGk *trophos* plaster, fr. *trophos* feeder — more at ATROPHY] **:** any of numerous small gastropod mollusks (family Muricidae) having the shell heavily sculptured and broadened by winglike varices

troph·o·ne·ma \ˌträfəˈnēmə\ *n, pl* **trophonema·ta** \-ˈnēməd·ə -ˈnem-\ [NL, fr. *troph-* + *-nema*] **:** one of the glandular filaments that develop from the inner uterine surface in viviparous elasmobranchs and secrete a nutritive fluid for the embryo

tropho·neurosis \ˌträfō+\ *n* [NL, fr. *troph-* + *neurosis*] **:** a functional disease of a part due to failure of nutrition from defective nerve action in the parts involved

tropho·neurotic \"+\ *adj* [ISV, fr. NL *trophoneurosis*, after such pairs as NL *narcosis:* ISV *narcotic*] **:** of, relating to, constituting, or affected by a trophoneurosis

tropho·nucleus \"+\ *n* [NL, fr. *troph-* + *nucleus*] **1 :** MACRONUCLEUS **2 :** the nucleus of a trypanosome or related flagellate as distinguished from the kinetoplast esp. when held to be a metabolic control center — compare KINETONUCLEUS

troph·o·phore \ˈträfə,fō(ə)r\ *n* -S [*troph-* + *-phore*] **:** one of the amoeboid cells that give rise to gemmules in a sponge — **tro·phoph·o·rous** \trōˈfäf(ə)rəs\ *adj*

troph·o·plasm \ˈträfə,plazəm\ *n* [ISV *troph-* + *-plasm*] **:** relatively unspecialized protoplasm held to be nutritive as distinguished from highly active differentiated protoplasm (as idioplasm, kinoplasm, archoplasm) — **troph·o·plas·mat·ic** \ˌ==plazˈmad·ik\ *adj* — **troph·o·plas·mic** \ˌ==¦plazmik\ *adj*

troph·o·plast \ˈträfə,plast\ *n* -S [ISV *troph-* + *-plast*, orig. formed in G] **:** a plant plastid

troph·o·some \-,sōm\ *n* -S [*troph-* + *-some*] **1 :** the nutritive zooids of a hydroid — compare GONOSOME **2 :** a storage organ in an adult mermithid worm consisting of the fat-filled syncytial remains of the intestine

troph·o·sphere \-,sfi(ə)r\ *n* [*troph-* + *sphere*] **:** the trophoblast of the hedgehog

troph·o·spon·gia \ˌ==ˈspənjēə, -pän-\ *n* -S [NL, fr. *troph-* + *-spongia*] **:** the vascular spongy mucous membrane between the wall of the uterus and the trophoblast — **troph·o·spon·gi·al** \ˌ==¦spənjēəl, -pän-\ *adj*

troph·o·spon·gium \ˌ==ˈspənjēəm, -pän-\ *n* -S [NL, fr. *troph-* + *-spongium*] **:** an intracellular canal system variously held to be the Golgi apparatus, ingrowths of surrounding cells, or an observational artifact

troph·o·tax·is \ˌ==ˈtaksəs\ *n, pl* **trophotax·es** \-k,sēz\ [NL, fr. *troph-* + *-taxis*] **:** a chemotaxis in which the stimulating agent may serve as food to the organism

troph·o·thy·lax \-ˈthī,laks\ *n* -ES [NL, fr. *troph-* + Gk *thylax* pouch, sack] **:** a depression or pocket on the underside of the body behind the mouth in various ant larvae in which food is placed by the attendant worker ants

troph·o·trop·ic \ˌ=ˈ==¦träpik\ *adj* [*trophotropism* + *-ic*] **:** of, relating to, or characterized by trophotropism

tro·phot·ro·pism \trōˈfä·trə,pizəm\ *n* [ISV *troph-* + *-tropism*] **:** a chemotropism in which food or a nutritive substance constitutes the orienting factor

-trophous — see -TROPHIC

troph·o·zo·ite \ˌträfəˈzō,īt\ *n* -S [*troph-* + *zo-* + *-ite*] **:** a vegetative protozoan as distinguished from a reproductive or resting form — used esp. of a parasite (as a sporozoan)

troph·o·zo·oid \-ō,ōid\ *n* [*troph-* + *zooid*] **1 :** an imperfect zooid or individual of the sexual generation of some free-swimming tunicates that never becomes sexually mature or detached from its parent **2 :** a nutritive zooid of a scyphozoan colony

¹tro·phy \ˈtrōfē, -fi\ *n* -ES *often attrib* [MF *trophee*, fr. L *trophaeum, tropaeum*, fr. Gk *tropaion*, fr. neut. of *tropaios* of turning, of defeat, fr. *tropē* action of turning, enemy's retreat; akin to Gk *trepein* to turn — more at TROPE] **1 a :** a memorial of an ancient Greek or Roman victory raised on the field of battle or in case of a naval victory on the nearest land or sometimes in the chief city either of the victorious or the conquered people and consisting originally of spoils (as armor or weapons) of the defeated enemy fixed to the trunk of a tree or to a post on an elevated site with an inscription and a dedication to a divinity **b :** a representation of such a memorial (as on a medal); *also* **:** an architectural ornament representing a group of arms and military weapons offensive and defensive **2 :** an evidence or memorial of victory or conquest: as **a :** something (as arms, flags, standards) taken from an enemy by force of arms and preserved as a memorial **b :** spoils of the hunting field esp. when suitable for mounting **c :** something (as a laurel wreath, a medal, or a piece of plate) given or received as an award for victory in a contest ⟨a mantel covered with tennis *trophies*⟩ **3 :** something kept or cherished usu. as a memento and gained by personal effort ⟨*trophies* of her social success⟩ ⟨gathered *trophies* of an earlier civilization⟩ ⟨less a wife than a ~⟩

²trophy \"\ *vt* -ED/-ING/-ES **:** to place trophies on or in **:** honor or adorn with a trophy

-tro·phy \ˌtrəfē, -fi\ *n comb form* -ES [NL *-trophia*, fr. Gk, fr. *troph-* + *-ia* -y] **:** nutrition **:** nourishment **:** nurture **:** growth ⟨eu*trophy*⟩ ⟨noso*trophy*⟩ ⟨pedo*trophy*⟩

trophy cress *n* **:** NASTURTIUM 2

tro·phy·less \ˈtrōfēləs\ *adj* **:** having or meriting no trophies

trophy money *or* **trophy tax** *n* **:** an annual English tax for militia equipment by housekeepers levied in the City of London

trophy room *n* **:** a room for the keeping and exhibition of trophies

trophywort \ˈ==,=\ *n* [*trophy* + *wort*] **:** NASTURTIUM 2

tro·pia \ˈtrōpēə\ *n* -S [NL, fr. Gk *tropē* action of turning + NL *-ia*] **:** deviation of an eye from the normal position with respect to the line of vision when the eyes are open **:** STRABISMUS

-tro·pia \-ˈtrōpēə\ *n comb form* -S [NL, fr. Gk, turn, deviation, fr. *-tropos* -trope + *-ia* -y] **:** condition of (such) a deviation in the line of vision ⟨eso*tropia*⟩ ⟨hyper*tropia*⟩

¹trop·ic \ˈträpik, -pēk\ *n* -S [ME *tropik*, fr. L *tropicus* of a turn, of a turning of the sun, fr. Gk *tropikos* of the solstice, fr. *tropē* action of turning (akin to Gk *trepein* to turn) + *-ikos* -ic — more at TROPE] **1** *obs* **:** either of the solstitial points; *also* **:** BOUNDARY, LIMIT **2 :** either of the two small circles of the celestial sphere on each side of and parallel to the equator at a distance of 23½ degrees which the sun reaches at its greatest declination north or south **3 a :** either of the two parallels of terrestrial latitude corresponding to the celestial tropics — see TROPIC OF CANCER, TROPIC OF CAPRICORN **b tropics** *pl, often cap* **:** the region lying between these parallels of latitude or near them on either side — usu. used with *the* ⟨life in the ~*s*⟩

²tropic \"\ *adj* **1 :** of, relating to, or occurring in the tropics **:** TROPICAL ⟨~ breezes⟩ ⟨~ fruits⟩ ⟨gorgeous ~ butterflies —William Beebe⟩ **2 :** associated with or occurring during the greatest north or south declination of the moon ⟨a ~ tide⟩

³tropic \"\ *adj* [¹*trop-* + *-ic*] **1 :** of, relating to, or characteristic of tropism or of a tropism **2** *of a hormone* **:** influencing the activity of a specified gland

-trop·ic \ˌ¦träpik, -pēk, *in some words* -rōp-\ *adj comb form* [F *-tropique*, fr. ¹*-trope* + *-ique* -ic] **1 :** turning, changing, or tending to turn or change esp. in a (specified) manner or in response to a (specified) stimulus ⟨bacterio*tropic*⟩ ⟨enantio*tropic*⟩ ⟨geo*tropic*⟩ ⟨helio*tropic*⟩ ⟨iso*tropic*⟩ ⟨chemo*tropic*⟩ **2 :** attracted specif. to (such) a tissue, organ, or system ⟨neuro*tropic*⟩ ⟨viscero*tropic*⟩ **3 :** -TROPHIC 1 ⟨ecto*tropic*⟩ ⟨endo*tropic*⟩

trop·ic acid \ˈträpik-\ *n* [*tropic* ISV, fr. *atropic* of or relating to atropine, fr. *atrop-* (in *atropine*) + *-ic*] **:** a crystalline acid $HOCH_2CH(C_6H_5)COOH$ known in dextrorotatory, levorotatory, and racemic forms of which the last is obtained by hydrolysis of atropine and various other alkaloids or by synthesis **:** α-phenyl-hydracrylic acid

¹trop·i·cal \ˈträpəkəl, -pēk-, *in sense 2* ˈtrōp-\ *adj* [¹*tropic* + *-al*] **1 a** (1) **:** of, relating to, characteristic of, or incident to the tropics ⟨~ fruits⟩ ⟨~ agriculture⟩ (2) **:** being within the tropics ⟨~ latitudes⟩ (3) **:** suitable for use in the tropics ⟨~ worsteds⟩ **b** *of a sign of the zodiac* **:** beginning at one of the tropics **c** *usu cap* **:** of, relating to, being, or native to an American biogeographic zone that lies next below the Austral, is bounded to the north by a line marking a minimum accumulation in growth season temperature above 43 degrees Fahrenheit of 26,000 degrees, is nearly or wholly frost-free, and includes most of the region between the tropics of Cancer and Capricorn **2** [L *tropicus* (fr. Gk *tropikos*, fr. *tropos* turn, style + *-ikos* -ic) + E *-al* — more at TROPE] **:** rhetorically changed from its exact original sense **:** having the nature of a trope **:** FIGURATIVE, METAPHORICAL

²trop·i·cal \ˈträpəkəl, -pēk-\ *n* -S **1 :** TROPICAL FISH **2 a :** a lightweight suiting of various fibers (as worsted) made in plain open weave with a clear finish and used esp. for hot-weather wear **b :** a garment (as a man's suit) of such a fabric

tropical air *n* **:** air of a mass originating in the tropics and characterized by high temperature and humidity

tropical almond *n* **:** MALABAR ALMOND

tropical apricot *n* **:** MAMMEE 1b

tropical aquarium *n* **:** an aquarium maintained at a uniform warmth by artificial heating and used for the keeping and breeding of tropical fish

tropical bleach *n* **:** a bleach for use under tropical conditions that is made by adding enough lime to a fairly dry bleaching powder to react with most of the water present

tropical cyclone *n* **:** a cyclone in the tropics characterized by winds rotating at the rate of 75 miles an hour or more — see HURRICANE, TYPHOON

tropical disease *n* **:** a disease that is indigenous to and may be endemic in a tropical area but may also occur in sporadic or epidemic form in a nontropical area

tropical duckweed *n* **:** WATER LETTUCE

tropical dysentery *n* **:** AMEBIASIS

tropical fish *n* **:** any of numerous exotic aquarium fishes requiring controlled water temperatures for satisfactory growth — compare BETTA, DANIO, MOLLIENISIA, PLATY, SWORDTAIL, TETRA

tropical fowl mite *n* **:** a poultry mite (*Bdellonyssus bursa*) that infests chickens and turkeys in warm regions of the New World including parts of southern U. S.

tropical hen flea *n* **:** STICKTIGHT FLEA

trop·i·ca·li·an \ˌträpəˈkālēən\ *adj, usu cap* [NL *Tropicalia*, marine realm including all tropical coral-reef seas (fr. L *tropicus* + Gk *hals* sea + NL *-ia*) + E *-an* — more at TROPIC, SALT] **:** of, relating to, being, or native to the marine biogeographic realm that includes all seas within the isocryme of 68° F and is characterized by the presence of reef-building corals

trop·i·cal·i·ty \ˌträpəˈkaləd·ē\ *n* -ES [¹*tropical* + *-ity*] **:** a thing or quality characteristic of the tropics

trop·i·cal·iza·tion \ˌträpəkələˈzāshən\ *n* -S **1 :** the quality or state of being tropicalized **2 :** an act of tropicalizing

trop·i·cal·ize \ˈträpəkə,līz\ *vt* -ED/-ING/-S *see -ize in Explan Notes* [¹*tropical* + *-ize*] **1 :** to make tropical (as in character, conditions, or appearance) **2 :** to fit or adapt for use in a tropical climate esp. by measures designed to combat the effects of fungi and moisture

tropical kudzu *n* **:** a tropical vine (*Pueraria phaseoloides*) grown esp. in the East Indies as a cover crop and for erosion control

tropical lake *n* **:** a lake with surface temperature constantly above 4°C

trop·i·cal·ly \-pək(ə)lē, -pēk-, -li\ *adv* **1 :** in a way typical of the tropics **2 :** by the use of tropes

tropical maritime air *n* **:** air of a mass originating over tropical oceans and characterized by high temperature and humidity

tropical medicine *n* **:** a branch of medicine dealing with tropical diseases and other special medical problems of tropical regions

tropical month *n* **:** a period that equals the mean time of the moon's revolution from any point of the ecliptic back to the same point and amounts to 27 days, 7 hours, 43 minutes, and 4.7 seconds of mean solar time

tropical rain forest *n* **:** RAIN FOREST 1

tropical rat mite *n* **:** a widely distributed mite (*Bdellomyssus bacoti* or a closely related species) that is primarily a parasite of rodents but sometimes bites humans causing painful itching and irritation and that has been implicated as a vector or potential vector of rodent and other diseases

tropical seal *n* **:** WEST INDIA SEAL

tropical storm *n* **:** a tropical cyclone with strong winds that are of less intensity than hurricane winds

tropical ulcer *n* **1 :** leishmaniasis of the skin — compare ORIENTAL SORE **2 :** a chronic sloughing sore of unknown cause occurring usu. on the legs and prevalent in wet tropical regions

tropical year *n* **:** the period occupied by the sun's center in passing from one equinox to the same again and having a

mean length of 365 days, 5 hours, 48 minutes, 45.5 seconds : SOLAR YEAR

tropic bird *n* : any of several totipalmate birds constituting the genus *Phaëthon* found chiefly in tropical seas often far from land, somewhat resembling terns but being more nearly related to the frigate bird and the gannets, and having plumage of a satiny texture and mostly white with a few black markings, a greatly elongated central pair of tail feathers, and a bright-colored bill

tropic of cancer *often cap T & usu cap C* [so called fr. the sign of the zodiac at which it touches the ecliptic] : the parallel of latitude that is 23½ degrees north of the equator and is the northernmost latitude reached by the overhead sun — see ZONE illustration

tropic of capricorn *often cap T & usu cap C* [so called fr. the sign of the zodiac at which it touches the ecliptic] : the parallel of latitude that is 23½ degrees south of the equator and is the southernmost latitude reached by the overhead sun — see ZONE illustration

trop·i·co·pol·i·tan \ˌträpəkō¦pälətᵊn\ *adj* [¹*tropic* + *-opolitan* (as in *cosmopolitan*)] : inhabiting all tropical countries : occurring throughout the tropics

trop·i·cor·bis \ˌträpə'kȯrbəs\ *n, cap* [NL, fr. *tropicus* tropical (fr. L, of a turning of the sun) + L *orbis* ring, circle — more at TROPIC, ORB] : a genus of New World freshwater snails (family Planorbidae) of medical importance as hosts of the schistosome (*Schistosoma mansoni*) in endemic focuses in No. and So. America

tropics *pl of* TROPIC

trop·i·dine \'träpəˌdēn, -dən\ *n* -s [ISV ²*trop-* + *-idine*] : an oily alkaloid $C_8H_{13}N$ obtained by the chemical dehydration of tropine

trop·i·do·lep·tus \ˌträpədō'leptəs\ *n, cap* [NL, fr. *tropido-* (fr. Gk *tropid-, tropis* ship's keel) + Gk *leptos* small; akin to Gk *tropos* turn — more at TROPE, LEPT-] : a genus of articulate brachiopods widely distributed in Devonian formations where they are important index fossils and characterized by a concavo-convex shell wide at the hinge and with broad rounded ribs

-tropies *pl of* -TROPY

tro·pine \'trōˌpēn, -ōpən\ *n* -s [ISV, fr. *atropine*] : a poisonous hygroscopic crystalline heterocyclic amino alcohol $C_8H_{15}NO$ derived from tropane and obtained by hydrolysis of atropine and other solanaceous alkaloids or by synthesis — see ECGONINE, TROPEINE

tro·pism \'trōˌpizəm\ *n* -s [ISV *-tropism*] **1 a** : involuntary orientation by an organism or one of its parts that involves turning or curving accomplished by active movement or more often by structural alteration (as through turgor changes or differential growth), that constitutes a positive or negative response to a source of stimulation (as a light or a temperature or chemical gradient), and that in motile organisms may be indistinguishable from a taxis — compare NASTIC MOVEMENT, REFLEX 4 **b** : a reflex reaction involving such movement **2** : an innate tendency to react in a definite manner to stimuli : a natural inborn inclination

-tro·pism \-trəˌpizəm, *in some words* ·ˌtrōˌpizəm\ *n comb form* -s [ISV, fr. ¹*-trope* + *-ism*] : tendency to turn toward : affinity for : tropism ⟨helio*tropism*⟩ ⟨neuro*tropism*⟩

tro·pis·mat·ic \ˌtrōpiz¦mad·ik\ *adj* [*tropism* + *-atic* (as in *automatic*)] : constituting a tropism esp. in being innate and essentially automatic

tro·pis·tic \trō'pistik, -tēk\ *adj* [fr. *tropism*, after such pairs as E *optimism: optimistic*] : of, relating to, or characteristic of tropism ⟨~ responses⟩

tropo- — see TROP-

trop·o·log·i·cal \¦träpə¦läjəkəl\ *also* **trop·o·log·ic** \-jik\ *adj* [*tropological* fr. LL *tropologicus* + E *-al; tropologic* fr. ME *tropologik*, fr. LL *tropologicus*, fr. LGk *tropologikos*, fr. *tropologia* tropology + Gk *-ikos* -ic] **1** : characterized or varied by tropes : TROPICAL, FIGURATIVE **2** : of, relating to, or involving tropology; *often* : MORAL — **trop·o·log·i·cal·ly** \-jək(ə)lē\ *adv*

tro·pol·o·gy \trō'päləjē\ *n* -ES [LL *tropologia*, fr. LGk, fr. *tropos* trope (fr. Gk, turn, manner, style) + Gk *-logia* -logy — more at TROPE] **1 a** : a figurative mode of speech or writing **b** : a mode of biblical interpretation stressing a moral meaning inhering in the metaphorical character of language **2** : a treatise on or compilation of tropes

trop·o·lone \'träpəˌlōn\ *n* -s [²*trop-* + *-ol* + *-one*] : a crystalline unsaturated enolic ketone $C_7H_6O_2$ containing the seven-membered ring of tropane and tropine — see STIPITATIC ACID, THUJAPLICIN

tro·pom·e·ter \trō'pämәd·ə(r)\ *n* [ISV ¹*trop-* + *meter*] : a device to measure rotation (as of the eyeball) or amount of torsion of a long bone

tropo·myosin \¦träpō+\ *n* [²*trop-* + *myosin*] : a crystallizable protein of relatively low molecular weight found in muscle and resembling myosin

tro·po·pause \'trōpəˌpȯz, 'träp-\ *n* [ISV ¹*trop-* + *pause*] : the region at the top of the troposphere

tro·poph·i·lous \trō'päfələs\ *also* **trop·o·phil** \'träpəˌfil\ *adj* [¹*trop-* + *-philous* or *-phil*] : physiologically adjusted to or thriving in an environment that undergoes marked periodic changes (as in temperature, soil moisture, or available light)

trop·o·phyte \'träpəˌfīt\ *n* -s [¹*trop-* + *-phyte*] : a tropophilous plant ⟨trees of the northern deciduous forests are typical ~s adapted to a mesophytic summer and a xerophytic winter⟩

tro·po·sphere \'trōpəˌsfi(ə)r, 'träp-, -iə\ *n* [ISV ¹*trop-* + *sphere*] : the portion of the atmosphere that is below the stratosphere, extends outward about 7 to 10 miles from the earth's surface, and is the portion in which temperature generally rapidly decreases with altitude, clouds form, and convection is active

tro·po·spher·ic \¦=='sfirik, -fer-\ *adj* : of, relating to, or occurring in the troposphere

tropo·stereoscope \¦träpō+\ *n* [¹*trop-* + *stereoscope*] : a stereoscope consisting essentially of two adjustable tubes side by side provided with caps to hold the images observed

trop·o·tac·tic \¦träpə¦taktik\ *adj* [¹*trop-* + *-tactic*] : of, relating to, or constituting a tropotaxis

trop·o·tax·is \ˌ=='taksəs\ *n* [NL, fr. ¹*trop-* + *-taxis*] : a taxis in which an organism orients itself through a process of simultaneous comparison of stimuli of different intensity acting on separate end organs

-tro·pous \-trəpəs\ *adj comb form* [Gk *-tropos* of a turn, fr. *trepein* to turn — more at TROPE] : turning or curving in (such) a way : exhibiting (such) a tropism ⟨ana*tropous*⟩

trop·o·yl \'träpəwəl\ *n* -s [²*trop-* + *-oyl* (as in *benzoyl*)] : the radical $HOCH_2CH(C_6H_5)CO$— of tropic acid

trop·po *also* **tropo** \'trä(ˌ)pō\ *n* -s [¹*tropic* + *-o*, n. suffix] *slang* : a condition of mental disorder or tension occurring in troops on tropical service

trop·tom·e·ter \träp'tämәd·ə(r)\ *n* [irreg. fr. ¹*trop-* + *-meter*] : an instrument for measuring the angular distortion of a bar or piece undergoing a torsion test

-tro·py \-trəpē, -pi\ *n comb form* -ES [F *-tropie*, fr. Gk *-tropia* turn, fr. *-tropos* -trope + *-ia* -y] **1** : a condition of turning or curving in (such) a way or of exhibiting (such) a tropism ⟨hemi*tropy*⟩ **2** : change in a (specified) way or in response to a (specified) stimulus

tro·pyl \'trōpəl\ *n* -s [²*trop-* + *-yl*] **1** : TROPOYL **2** : the univalent radical $C_8H_{14}N$ derived from tropine

¹trot \'trät, *usu* -äd·+V\ *n* -s [ME, fr. MF, fr. *troter* to trot] **1 a** (1) : a moderately fast gait of a horse or other quadruped in which the legs move in diagonal pairs — compare PACE 5b (2) : a gait of a man or other biped that falls between a walk and a run in speed and action : a jogging pace (as of one hurrying); *also* : brisk movement or activity ⟨tasks that kept him on the ~ all day⟩ (3) : an elastic running dance step in moderate tempo; *also* : a dance featuring such a step **b** : a journey or ride on horseback ⟨pleasant to go for a ~ on a fresh summer morning⟩ **c** : TROTTING RACE **d** : the sound of a trotting animal **2 a** : a small child **b** : an old woman ⟨one of the sourest ~s in the village⟩ **3** : a literal translation for student use — compare CRIB, PONY **4 trots** *pl but sing or pl in constr* : DIARRHEA — not often in polite use

²trot \"\ *vb* **trotted; trotted; trotting; trots** [ME *trotten*, fr. MF *troter*, fr. OF, of Gmc origin; akin to OHG *trottōn* to tread, MHG *trotten* to run, OE *tredan* to tread — more at TREAD] *vi* **1** : to ride, drive, or proceed at a trot ⟨the fox *trotted* over the knoll⟩ ⟨*trotting* behind a pair of matched bays⟩ **2** : to move or proceed briskly : JOG, HURRY ⟨keep him *trotting*⟩ ⟨the toddler *trotted* after his father⟩ ~ *vt* **1 a** : to ride, drive, or cause to go at a trot ⟨*trotting* the filly toward home⟩ **b** : to traverse at a trot ⟨loved to ~ the hills and valleys⟩ **2** : to draw (one) out so as to make sport of : subject to ridicule — **trot in double harness** : to get along smoothly; *esp* : to live contentedly in wedlock

³trot \"\ *n* -s [short for *trotline*] : TROTLINE; *also* : one of the short lines with hooks that are attached at intervals to the main line of a trotline

⁴trot \"\ *vi* : to use a trotline in fishing

trotcozy \'=,==\ *n* [²*trot* + *cozy*] *Scot* : a covering for the head and shoulders worn esp. when riding

¹troth \'trȯ|th, 'trō|, 'trä|\ *n, pl* **troths** \|ths, |t͟hz\ [ME *trouth*, fr. OE *trēowth* — more at TRUTH] **1** : loyal or pledged faithfulness : FIDELITY ⟨the evidence bespoke his perfect ~⟩ **2 a** : one's pledged word ⟨insisted on his ~ that such a thing could not be so⟩ **b** : one's faith as pledged in a solemn undertaking and esp. in an agreement to marry; *also* : the act of making such a pledge : BETROTHAL

²troth \", -o͟th\ *vt* -ED/-ING/-s [ME *trouthen*, fr. *trouth*, n., troth] : PLEDGE, BETROTH

troth·less *pronunc at* ¹TROTH +ləs\ *adj* : lacking in loyalty : FAITHLESS

¹trothplight \'=,=\ *n* [ME *trouth plight*, fr. *trouth* troth + *plight*] *archaic* : a solemn pledge usu. to enter into the married estate

²trothplight \"\ *vt* [ME *trouth plighten*, fr. *trouth* troth + *plighten* to pledge — more at PLIGHT] *archaic* : BETROTH

trotline \'=,=\ *n* [prob. fr. ²*trot* + *line*] : SETLINE 1; *esp* : a comparatively short setline used (as for catching catfish or crabs) near shore or along streams

trot out *vt* **1** : to lead out and show the paces of (as a horse) **2** : to bring forward and put on display ⟨always able to *trot out* some new excuse⟩

trot·sky·ism \'trätskēˌizəm\ *n* -s *usu cap* [Leon *Trotsky* †1940 Russ. Communist leader + E *-ism*] : the political, economic, and social principles advocated by Trotsky; *esp* : the theory and practice of communism developed by or associated with Trotsky and usu. including adherence to the concept of worldwide revolution as opposed to socialism in one country — compare STALINISM, TITOISM

¹trot·sky·ist \-ēəst\ *n* -s *usu cap* [Leon *Trotsky* + E *-ist*] : a follower of Trotsky : an adherent of Trotskyism

²trotskyist \"\ *adj, usu cap* : of, relating to, or having the characteristics of Trotskyism or Trotskyists

¹trot·sky·ite \-ēˌīt\ *n* -s *usu cap* [Leon *Trotsky* + E *-ite*] : TROTSKYIST

²trotskyite \"\ *adj, usu cap* : TROTSKYIST

¹trot·ter \'träd·ə(r), -ätə-\ *n* -s [ME *trotter*, fr. *trotten* to trot + *-er* — more at TROT] **1** : one that trots: as **a** : a horse that trots; *usu* : a standardbred trained for or used in harness racing **b** *Brit* : a person who runs errands : an errand boy : MESSENGER **2 a** : the foot of a quadruped esp. when prepared for use as food **b** : the human foot ⟨go in and wash your dirty little ~s⟩

²trotter \"\ *n* -s [⁴*trot* + *-er*] : a fisherman who uses a trotline

trotter oil *n* : NEAT'S-FOOT OIL

trot·teur *R* trä'tər, +V -'tər-; *-R* -'tō, + *vowel in a word following without pause* -'tər- *or* -'tō *also* -'tər\ *n* -s [F, fr. *trotter* to trot (fr. MF *troter*) + *-eur* -or — more at TROT] : a woman's tailored garment (as a suit, coat, dress, or hat) suitable for walking or outdoor wear

trotteur tan *n, often cap 1st T* : ²BAY 2

trot·tie \'träd·ē\ *n* -s [¹*trot* + *-ie*] : a small child : TODDLER

trotting *n* -s [fr. gerund of ²*trot*] : harness racing for trotters

trotting race *n* : a harness race for trotters

trot·toir \trä'twär\ *n* -s [F, fr. *trotter* to trot + *-oir* (fr. L *-orium* -ory)] : FOOTPATH, SIDEWALK

trot·ty \'träd·ē\ *adj* [¹*trot* + *-y*] : going at a trot; *broadly* : LIVELY, BRISK

tro·tyl \'trōd·ᵊl\ *n* -s [*trot-* (fr. *trinitrotoluene*) + *-yl*] : TRINITROTOLUENE

¹trou·ba·dour *also* **trou·ba·dor** \'trübəˌdō(ə)r, -dȯ(ə)r, -dü(ə)r, -ōə, -ō(ə), -üə\ *n* -s *often attrib* [F *troubadour*, fr. MF, fr. OProv *trobador*, fr. *trobar* to compose in verse, prob. fr. (assumed) VL *tropare* to compose, fr. L *tropus* trope — more at TROPE] **1** : one of a class of lyric poets and poet-musicians often of knightly rank flourishing from the 11th to the end of the 13th century chiefly in Provence, the south of France, and the north of Italy and cultivating a lyric poetry intricate in meter and rhyme and usu. of a romantic amatory strain — compare TROUVÈRE **2** : a strolling minstrel; *also* : anyone who in music, verse, or rhetorical prose promotes some cause

²troubadour \"\ *vi* -ED/-ING/-s : to act the part of a troubadour

trou·ba·dour·ish \-rish\ *adj* : suited to or like that of a troubadour

¹trou·ble \'trəbəl\ *vb* **troubled; troubled; troubling** \-b(ə)liŋ\ **troubles** [ME *troublen, troblen*, fr. OF *troubler, tourbler*, fr. (assumed) VL *turbulare*, fr. L *turbidare* to trouble, make turbid, fr. *turbidus* disordered, troubled, turbid — more at TURBID] *vt* **1 a** : to agitate mentally or spiritually : bring distress or uncertainty of mind to : WORRY, BOTHER ⟨sorrows that ~ the strongest spirit⟩ ⟨her failure to remember the address *troubled* her⟩ **b** (1) *archaic* : to do harm to : MISTREAT, OPPRESS (2) : to produce physical disorder in : cause physical distress or suffering to ⟨*troubled* with increasing deafness⟩ ⟨severe pain continued to ~ her⟩ **c** : to put to exertion or inconvenience usu. by asking some service ⟨did not want to ~ her sister with the care of the children⟩ ⟨~ you to pass the butter⟩ **2 a** : to put into confused motion : cause to become turbulent or turbid through moving ⟨a strong wind *troubled* and ruffled the sea⟩ **b** *archaic* : to interfere with or bring into disorder : CHECK, DISARRANGE ~ *vi* **1 a** : to become mentally agitated : WORRY, BOTHER ⟨a man who refuses to ~ over trifles⟩ **b** : to make an effort : be at pains ⟨the will to ~ infinitely with the problems of his position⟩ **2** *obs* : to become physically agitated (as of water) : become obscured or dark (as of the sky)

²trouble \":\ *n* -s [ME, fr. OF *trouble, tourble*, fr. *troubler, tourbler* to trouble] **1** : the quality or state of being troubled : UNEASINESS, ANNOYANCE; *also* : an instance of distress, annoyance, or perturbation **2** : a cause of disturbance, annoyance, or distress (as an annoying or injurious event or experience): as **a** : civil disorder : public unrest or demonstrations of dissatisfaction ⟨watched with concern the ~ in the neighboring state⟩ ⟨labor ~⟩ **b** : an effort made : EXERTION, PAINS ⟨took the ~ to call and inquire after his aunt⟩ **c** (1) : a condition of physical distress, debility, or ill health (2) : DISEASE, AILMENT (3) *dial Eng* : labor in childbirth **d** : pregnancy out of wedlock ⟨get a girl in ~⟩ **e** : a personal characteristic that is a handicap or a source of distress ⟨his greatest ~ was a too-trusting nature⟩ **3** : one (as a person) that is a source of distress, disturbance, and esp. inconvenience ⟨never meant to be such a ~ to her sister⟩ **syn** see EFFORT

troubled *adj* [ME, fr. past part. of *troublen* to trouble] : characterized by or indicative of trouble ⟨these ~ areas⟩ ⟨a ~ expression⟩

trou·bled·ly *adv* : in a troubled manner

trou·bled·ness *n* -ES : the quality or state of being troubled

troubled waters *n pl* : a situation or condition of disorder or confusion ⟨a mischievous rogue ready to make the most of *troubled waters*⟩

trouble light *n* : any of various lighting devices designed to provide emergency illumination or to provide light in places not normally illuminated

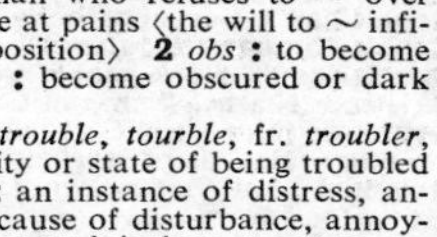

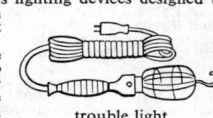

trouble light

troublemaker \'=,==\ *n* : one that is a source of trouble; *esp* : a person that consciously or unconsciously foments strife and disagreement often from ulterior motives

troublemaking \'=,==\ *n* : the behavior of a troublemaker

trouble man *n* : TROUBLESHOOTER 1

trou·ble·ment \'trəbəlmənt\ *n* -s [MF, fr. *trouble* + *-ment*] *chiefly dial* : a condition or source of trouble

troubleproof \'==,=\ *adj* : free from or not subject to trouble; *esp* : not readily put out of order

trou·bler \'trəb(ə)lə(r)\ *n* -s [ME *troublere*, fr. OF *troubleur*, fr. *troubler* to trouble + *-eur* -or — more at TROUBLE] : one that troubles

troubleshoot \'==,=\ *vb* [back-formation fr. *troubleshooter*] *vi* : to operate or serve as a troubleshooter ~ *vt* : to investigate or deal with in the role of troubleshooter

troubleshooter \'==,==\ *n* **1** : a skilled workman employed to locate causes of trouble in machinery and technical equipment and to make needed repairs — called also *trouble man* **2** : an expert at clearing or bridging an obstruction at a critical point or restoring flow past a bottleneck in political, military, or business affairs or industrial relations : a mediator of disputes come to an impasse

trou·ble·some \'trəbəlsəm\ *adj* **1** : giving trouble or anxiety : DISTURBING, VEXATIOUS ⟨a ~ infection⟩ ⟨these ~ activities of our enemies⟩ **2** *archaic* : characterized by disturbance : TURBULENT **3** *archaic* : AFFLICTED, DISTRESSED **4** : requiring or involving sustained or tiring effort, attention, study, or application : DIFFICULT, BURDENSOME, WEARISOME — **trou·ble·some·ly** *adv* — **trou·ble·some·ness** *n* -ES

trouble spot *n* : a spot at which trouble is esp. likely to occur or break out ⟨a *trouble spot* in a mechanism⟩ ⟨Asiatic *trouble spots*⟩

trou·bling·ly *adv* : in a troubling manner : so as to produce trouble

trou·blous \'trəbləs\ *adj* [ME *troubelous*, fr. OF *troubleus*, fr. *trouble* + *-eus* -ous] **1** : full of trouble : TROUBLED, AFFLICTED; *also* : AGITATED, STORMY **2** : causing trouble : TURBULENT, DISTURBING — **trou·blous·ly** *adv* — **trou·blous·ness** *n* -ES

trou–de–loup \ˌtrüdə'lü\ *n, pl* **trous–de–loup** \"\ [F, lit., wolf's hole] : a pit in the form of an inverted cone or pyramid having a pointed stake in the middle and forming one of a group constructed as an obstacle to the movements of an enemy — usu. used in pl.

¹trough \'trȯ|f *sometimes* 'trä|, *chiefly by bakers* 'trō, *chiefly by Brit bakers* 'trau̇, *dial* |th *or* |ft\ *n, pl* **troughs** \|fs, |vz, |ths, |t͟hz\ *n* -s *often attrib* [ME, fr. OE *trog, troh*; akin to OHG & ON *trog* trough, OE *trēow* tree, wood — more at TREE] **1 a** : a large long and usu. comparatively shallow open vessel that is often V-shaped in cross section and used esp. to hold water or feed for domestic animals **b** : any of various containers used for some domestic or industrial purpose: as (1) : a bowl, tank, or basin in which something is prepared or processed (as by kneading, washing, brewing, or tanning) (2) : the vessel under a grindstone that holds water for cooling in grinding; *also* : the place where a grindstone stands (3) : PNEUMATIC TROUGH (4) : a buddle or other vessel in which mining slimes are sorted in water (5) : the vessel used for the plating bath in the electroplating process **c** *chiefly dial* : TOMB, COFFIN **d** *chiefly dial* : any of various small boats (as a dugout) that somewhat resemble a trough for cattle **2 a** : a conduit for water: as (1) *chiefly dial* : a walled drain (2) *chiefly dial* : a wooden channel forming the headrace of a mill (3) : EAVES TROUGH **b** (1) : a long and narrow or shallow channel or depression (as between waves or hills) (2) : an elongated structural depression of the earth (as a graben, a geosyncline, a trench, or an ocean deep) **c** : a usu. recessed channel enclosing and concealing utilitarian structural elements (as piping or wiring) **3 a** : the part of a gravity wave or ripple on a liquid that is the lowest part of the oscillating surface at any given instant — contrasted with *crest* **b** : the minimum attained by a wave variable during the passage of a complete cycle: as (1) : an elongated area of low barometric pressure usu. with a minimum pressure at each end and between two anticyclones — opposed to *ridge* (2) : the low point in a business cycle (3) : a low part of a statistical curve that is between higher parts and is usu. concave upward

²trough \"\ *vt* -ED/-ING/-s : to make into or treat in a trough

trough conveyor *n* : a band conveyor with the sides of the band turned up to form a trough

trough gutter *n* : an eaves trough of rectangular or V-shaped section usu. hung below the eaves of a house

troughing *n* -s **1** : an arrangement or system of troughs : TROUGHS **2** : material for a trough

trough keel *n* : a keel in a yacht having the form of a trough into which molten lead is poured as ballast — compare BAR KEEL

trough roof *n* **1** : M ROOF **2** : a roof of hollowed-out split logs laid from ridge to eaves

trough shell *n* : a bivalve mollusk of the family Mactridae

trough·ton level \'trau̇tᵊn-\ *n, usu cap T* [after Edward *Troughton* †1835 Eng. instrument maker] : DUMPY LEVEL

troughway \'=,=\ *n* : the channel of a trough

troughy *pronunc at* ¹TROUGH +ē *or* i\ *adj* : having deep troughs

trou ma·dame \ˌtrümə'dam\ *n* [F *trou-madame*, lit., hole madam, fr. MF; fr. the exclamation of the women players when one of them fails to score] : a variety of bagatelle in which the arches are scored to the player and the holes against him

¹trounce \'trau̇n(t)s\ *vt* -ED/-ING/-s [origin unknown] : to thrash or punish severely: as **a** : FLOG, CUDGEL **b** : to defeat decisively **c** : to censure sternly : castigate verbally **d** *dial chiefly Eng* : INDICT, SUE

²trounce \'trau̇ns\ *vi* [prob. alter. of ³*trance*] *Scot & dial Eng* : to make a tiresome or rambling journey : TRAMP

³trounce \"\ *n* -s *dial Eng* : a long tiring ramble or journey

trounc·er \'trau̇n(t)sə(r)\ *n* -s [¹*trounce* + *-er*] : one that trounces: as **a** : WAISTER **b** *Brit* : a helper on a truck or delivery wagon

trou·pand \'trüˌpand\ *n* -s [Afrik, lit., wedding pledge, fr. *trou* to wed (fr. MD *trouwen*, fr. *trouw* faithful) + D *pand* pledge, pawn, fr. MF *pan*; akin to OE *trēowe* faithful — more at TRUE, PAWN] : a southern African bird that is a variety of the European roller (*Coracias garrulus*)

¹troupe \'trüp\ *n* -s [F, fr. MF — more at TROOP] : COMPANY, TROOP; *esp* : a group of performers on the stage

²troupe \"\ *vi* -ED/-ING/-s : to travel in a troupe; *also* : to perform as a member of a theatrical troupe

troup·er \-pə(r)\ *n* -s : a member of a troupe; *esp* : ACTOR

troup·i·al *also* **troop·i·al** \'trüpēəl\ *n* -s [F *troupiale*, fr. *troupe* flock, troop; fr. its living in flocks] : a bird of the family Icteridae; *esp* : one of the larger brilliant yellow-and-black or orange-and-black orioles of Central and So. America

trous–de–loup *pl of* TROU-DE-LOUP

trouse \'trüz, 'trau̇z\ *n* -s [ScGael *triubhas*] **1** *obs* : TREWS, DRAWERS **2** *archaic* : TROUSERS, BREECHES

trou·ser \'trau̇zə(r)\ *adj* [back-formation fr. *trousers*] : of, relating to, or designed for use with trousers ⟨~ pockets⟩ ⟨~ legs⟩ ⟨~ buttons⟩

trou·sered \-(r)d\ *adj* : wearing or accustomed to wear trousers

trou·ser·ing \-z(ə)riŋ\ *n* -s : a fabric used or suitable for trousers

trou·sers \-zə(r)z\ *n pl* [alter. (influenced by *-ers* as in *drawers*) of *trouse*, fr. ScGael *triubhas*, prob. fr. OF *trebus* breeches] **1** *archaic* : TREWS **2 a** *also* **trouser** : an outer garment extending from the waist to the ankle or sometimes only to or just below the knee, covering each leg separately, made close-fitting or loose-fitting in accord with the fashion of different periods, and worn typically by men and boys **b trouser** *n sing* : half or one leg of a pair of trousers ⟨snagged his left ~ on the wire⟩ **3** : baggy pantaloons worn by both sexes in the Near East **4** : PANTALETS **5** *also* **trouserings** : the hair on the hindquarters of a dog esp. when profuse and full

trous·seau \'trüsō\ *n, pl* **trous·seaux** \-ō(z)\ *or* **trousseaus** \-ōz\ [F, fr. OF, little bundle, dim. of *trousse* bundle — more at TRUSS] : the personal outfit of a bride usu. including clothes, accessories, and household linens

¹trout \'trau̇t, *usu* -au̇d·+V\ *n, pl* **trout** *also* **trouts** [ME *troute, trute*, fr. OE *trūht*, fr. LL *tructa, tructa*, a trout, a shark, fr. Gk *trōktēs* sea fish with sharp teeth, fr. *trōgein* to gnaw — more at TERSE] **1** : any of various fishes of the family Salmonidae that are on the average much smaller than the typical salmons, are mostly restricted to cool clear freshwaters though some are anadromous, and are highly regarded for their attractive colorations, rich well-flavored flesh, and gameness as an angling fish: **a** : any of various Old or New World

fishes of the genus *Salmo* — see BROWN TROUT, CUTTHROAT TROUT, RAINBOW TROUT, SEA TROUT 1, STEELHEAD 1 **b :** any of various No. American fishes of the genera *Salvelinus* or *Cristivomer* — see BROOK TROUT, CHAR, DOLLY VARDEN, LAKE TROUT **2 :** any of various fishes felt to resemble the salmonid trouts: as **a** *Austral* **:** a fish of the family Galaxiidae **b** *South* **:** LARGEMOUTH BLACK BASS **c :** a large cyprinid fish (*Gila elegans*) of the drainage of the Colorado and Gila rivers **d :** WEAKFISH

²trout \"\ *vi* -ED/-ING/-S **:** to fish for trout

troutbird \'ˌ=ˌ=\ *n* [so called fr. its speckled plumage] **:** GOLDEN PLOVER

trout–colored \'=ˌ==\ *adj* **:** white with spots of black, bay, or sorrel ⟨a *trout-colored* horse⟩

trout·er \'traủd·ə(r)\ *n* -S **:** one that fishes for trout

trout·less \'traủtləs\ *adj* **:** having or producing no trout ⟨~ waters⟩

trout·let \-lət\ *also* **trout·ling** \-liŋ\ *n* -S [¹*trout* + *-let* or *ling*] **:** a fingerling trout

trout lily *also* **trout flower** *n* [prob. so called fr. the speckled leaves] **:** DOGTOOTH VIOLET

trou·ton's rule \'traủtᵊnz-\ *n, usu cap T* [after Frederick T. *Trouton* †1922 Eng. physicist] **:** a statement in physical chemistry: the molar heats of vaporization of pure liquids are proportional to the absolute temperatures of their boiling points

trout–perch \'=ˌ=\ *n* **:** a small freshwater fish (*Percopsis omiscomaycus*) of the central and eastern U.S.

¹trouty \'traủd·ē\ *n* -ES [¹*trout* + *-y* (dim. suffix)] **:** a little trout

²trouty \"\ *adj* -ER/-EST [¹*trout* + *-y* (adj. suffix)] **:** containing or likely to contain abundant trout ⟨a ~ stream with deep pools and fast water⟩

trou·vaille \trü'vī\ *n* -S [F, fr. OF *trouver* to compose, find] **:** a lucky find **:** WINDFALL

trou·vère \trü'va(a)(ə)r\ *n* -S [F, fr. OF *troverre, troveor,* fr. *trover, trouver* to compose, find, fr. (assumed) VL *tropare* — more at TROUBADOUR] **:** one of a school of poets flourishing in northern France from the 11th to the 14th centuries and producing works that are typically the chansons de geste and are of a prevailingly narrative character — compare TROUBADOUR

trou·veur *R* trü'vər, + V -'vər· *or* -'vō, *-R* -'vō, + *vowel in a word following without pause* -'vər· *or* -'vō *also* -'vər\ *n* -S [MF, fr. OF *trouver* to compose] **:** TROUVÈRE

trove \'trōv\ *n* -S [short for *treasure trove*] **1 :** a thing found ⟨I was pleased by one of my ~*s* —Christopher Morley⟩ — compare TREASURE TROVE **2 :** a collection of objects ⟨a modest ~ of earrings —*New Yorker*⟩; *usu* **:** one deliberately concealed, previously lost sight of or not appreciated at its real value, or consciously assembled ⟨assembled a rich ~ of Chinese porcelain⟩ ⟨a ~ of new family letters . . . were made available to the biographer —*N.Y. Herald Tribune Bk. Rev.*⟩

tro·ver \'trōvə(r)\ *n* -S [MF, to compose, find (taken as a n.), fr. OF] **1 :** a coming into possession **2 :** an action to recover the value of personal chattels or goods wrongfully converted by another to his own use

¹trow \'trō\ *vb* -ED/-ING/-S [ME *trowen, trewen,* fr. OE *trēowan, trēowian;* akin to OS *triuwian* to believe, trust, ON *trūa* to believe, have faith in, Goth *trauan* to confide in, OE *trēowe* faithful — more at TRUE] **1** *obs* **a :** BELIEVE, TRUST **b :** HOPE, EXPECT **2** *archaic* **:** THINK, SUPPOSE **3** — formerly appended to questions to express contempt or indignant surprise ⟨what is the matter, ~ —Shak.⟩

²trow \"\ *n* -S [ME, fr. *trowen* to trow] **:** BELIEF, FAITH, COVENANT

³trow \"\ *Scot var of* TROLL

⁴trow \"\ *n* -S [ME, fr. OE *trog, troh* trough, canoe, boat — more at TROUGH] **:** any of several boats: as **a** *chiefly dial* **:** a catamaran or other double boat used in spearing salmon **b** *Brit* **:** a small fishing boat **c :** a bluff low flat-bottomed sailing barge used esp. in England for river and coastal haulage

⁵trow \"\ *dial chiefly Brit var of* TROUGH

¹trow·el \'traủ(ə)l\ *n* -S [ME *trowell, truel,* fr. MF *truelle,* fr. LL *truella, trulla* vessel for liquids, mason's trowel, fr. L *trulla* small ladle, dim. of *trua* ladle; akin to OE *thwiril* stick for stirring, OHG *dwiril,* Icel *thyrill,* Gk *torynē* stick for stirring, OHG *dweran* to stir — more at TURBID] **:** any of various hand tools or implements consisting of a flat or less commonly curved blade with a handle and used (as by bricklayers, plasterers, molders) to apply, spread, shape, and smooth loose or plastic material; *also* **:** a scoop-shaped or flat-bladed gardening implement used esp. for taking up and setting small plants

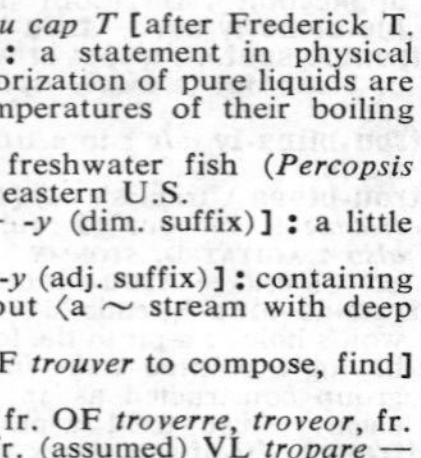

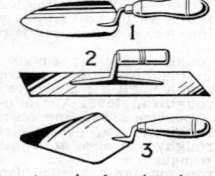

trowels: *1* gardener's, *2* plasterer's, *3* bricklayer's

²trowel \"\ *vt* **troweled** *or* **trowelled; troweled** *or* **trowelled; troweling** *or* **trowelling; trowels :** to smooth, dress, shape, mix, or apply with or as if with a trowel — **trow·el·er** \-lə(r)\ *n* -S

trow·el·man \-lmən\ *n, pl* **trowelmen :** a workman who uses a trowel

trow·ie \'trōī\ *adj* [³*trow* + *-ie*] *Scot* **:** belonging to or influenced by a troll

trow·ing \'trōiŋ\ *n* -S [ME, fr. gerund of *trowen* to believe, trust — more at TROW] **:** BELIEF, CREED, OPINION

trowl \'trōl\ *chiefly dial var of* TROLL

trowman \'=mən\ *n, pl* **trowmen** [ME, fr. ⁴*trow* + *man*] **:** an owner or operator of a fishing trow

trows·ers \'traủzə(r)z\ *n pl* [by alter.] **:** TROUSERS 2

trowth \'trōth\ *n* -S [ME(Sc) *trowth, trewth,* fr. OE *trēowth* — more at TRUTH] *chiefly Scot* **:** TROTH, TRUTH

trox \'trüks\ *n, cap* [NL, fr. Gk *trōx* gnawer, fr. Gk *trōgein* to gnaw — more at TERSE] **:** a genus of medium-sized brownish beetles with large vertical mandibles including several typical skin beetles and others that feed on carrion or dung

troy \'trȯi\ *adj* [ME *troye, troie,* fr. *Troyes,* city in France where it was prob. introduced] **:** expressed in troy weight — *abbr. t*

troy pound *n* [ME] **:** POUND 1a

troy weight *n* [ME] **:** a series of units of weight based on a pound of 12 ounces and the ounce of 20 pennyweights or 480 grains — see MEASURE table

trp *abbr* **1** troop **2** tropical

trs *abbr* **1** transfer **2** transpose **3** troops

trsd *abbr* **1** transferred **2** transposed

tru *abbr* trustee

tru·an·cy \'trüənsē, -si\ *n* -ES **:** an act or instance of playing truant **:** the state of being truant

¹tru·ant \'trüənt\ *n* -S [ME, fr. OF, vagrant, beggar, of Celt origin; akin to W *tru, truan* miserable, wretched, *truan* wretch, OIr *trōg* miserable, ScGael *truaghan* miserable person, *truagh* wretched] **1** *obs* **:** an idle vagrant **:** VAGABOND **2 :** one who stays away from business or shirks duty; *esp* **:** one who stays out of school without permission **syn** see VAGABOND

²truant \"\ *adj* **1 :** wandering from business or duty **:** shirking responsibility **:** IDLE; *esp* **:** absent from school without permission **2 :** resembling or characteristic of a truant ⟨try to govern this ~ pep —C.B.Fairbanks⟩ — **tru·ant·ly** *adv*

³truant *vb* -ED/-ING/-S [ME *truanten,* fr. *truant* vagrant] *vi* **:** to idle away time esp. while shirking some duty **:** willfully neglect a required task **:** absent oneself without permission ⟨have ~*ed* so much that . . . many can't do more than second-grade reading —Marjorie Rittwagen⟩ ~ *vt* **:** to waste or fritter away **:** play truant from

truant officer *n* **:** ATTENDANCE OFFICER

tru·ant·ry \-ntrē, -ntri\ *n* -ES **:** TRUANCY ⟨thought I had had enough of ~ —R.L.Stevenson⟩

¹trub \'trəb\ *n* -S [origin unknown] **:** TRUFFLE 1

²trub \'trüb, 'trəb\ *n* -S [G *trub, trüb;* akin to OHG *truobi* dim, murky, turbid, OE *drōf* dirty, muddy, turbid, ME *draf* dregs, draff — more at DRAFF] **:** a haze formed either during boiling or cooling of wort and removed as a step of the brewing process

tru·betz·koy·an \ˌtrübət¦skȯiən\ *adj, usu cap* [Nikolai *Trubetzkoi* †1938 Russ. linguist + E *-an*] **:** relating to or characteristic of the linguistic methods or terminology of Nikolai Trubetzkoi

¹truce \'trüs\ *n* -S [ME *trewes, triwes,* pl. of *trewe, triewe* agreement, treaty, truce, fr. OE *trēow* fidelity, allegiance, agreement, pledge; akin to OHG *triuwa* fidelity, ON *trū* trust, faith, Goth *triggwa* alliance, pact, OE *trēowe* faithful — more at TRUE] **1 :** a suspension of fighting esp. of considerable duration by agreement of the commanders of opposing forces **:** a temporary cessation of hostilities **:** ARMISTICE, CEASE-FIRE **2 :** a respite esp. from a disagreeable or painful state or action **:** an intermission of rest and quiet **:** a brief interruption ⟨the parts of his complex and tortured spirit come together in a ~ —Virginia Woolf⟩

²truce \"\ *vb* -ED/-ING/-S *vi* **:** to make a truce ⟨has *truced* with the party's younger strong man —*Springfield* (*Mass.*) *Union*⟩ ~ *vt* **:** to bring to an end with (a truce)

truce·less \-ləs\ *adj* **:** marked by unending hostilities **:** having no hope of a truce

truce of god *usu cap T & cap G* [trans. of ML *Treuga Dei*] **:** the cessation of hostilities between armies or individuals during part of the week (as from Wednesday evening to Monday morning) and during various holy seasons enjoined and imperfectly enforced in western Europe by the church from 1027 to as late as the 13th century — compare PEACE OF GOD 2

tru·cha \'trü(ˌ)chä\ *n* -S [Sp, fr. LL *tructa,* a trout — more at TROUT] *chiefly Southwest* **:** TROUT

tru·cial \'trüshəl, -üsēəl\ *adj, often cap* [¹*truce* + *-ial;* fr. the maritime truce made in 1835 between the British government and several Arab states of the Oman peninsula] **:** of, relating to, or involving several territorial areas in the vicinity of the Persian Gulf for which the government of Great Britain assumes responsibility nominally in an advisory capacity ⟨nearly 400 miles of coast belongs to the *Trucial* sheikhs —*Americana Annual*⟩

¹truck \'trək\ *vb* -ED/-ING/-S [ME *trukken, trukien,* fr. OF *troquer*] *vt* **1 :** to give in exchange **:** SWAP ⟨I would not ~ this brilliant day to rule —John Keats⟩ **2 a :** to exchange with an expectation of gain **:** BARTER ⟨maintain a trade with their neighbors and ~ their work with them for any necessaries —W.E.Roth⟩ **b :** to dispose of by bartering ⟨some of our kings have . . . ~*ed* away for foreign gold the interests and glory of their crown —Edmund Burke⟩ **3 :** to deal with or pay on the truck system ~ *vi* **1 :** to exchange commodities **:** BARTER ⟨the disposition peculiar to mankind to ~ —A.C. Pigou⟩ **2 a :** to negotiate or traffic esp. in an underhanded way **b :** to establish a familiar basis **:** have intercourse **3** *Scot* **:** to go about on insignificant affairs **:** PUTTER

²truck \"\ *n* -S **1 a :** the practice of trading by exchanging goods **:** BARTER **b :** a shrewd trade **:** DEAL **2 :** commodities appropriate for barter or for small trade ⟨accepted these simple gifts but ordered them all paid for out of the trading ~ —S.E. Morison⟩ **3 :** close association **:** CONTACT, DEALINGS ⟨with all such nonsense I have never had any ~ —Daniel George⟩ ⟨never at any time did he have the slightest ~ with . . . vulgarity —Clinton Rossiter⟩ ⟨wouldn't want you to have ~ with the family —Clemence Zane⟩ **4 :** payment of wages in goods instead of cash ⟨the worst conditions, long hours, irregular payment of wages, ~ . . . were to be found —J.H.Plumb⟩ — see TRUCK SYSTEM **5 :** vegetables that are grown for the market ⟨a good piece of land . . . by the springs to raise ~ on —J.F.Dobie⟩ **6 :** heterogeneous small articles often of little value **:** HODGE-PODGE; *also* **:** RUBBISH ⟨any such mess of ~ —Kenneth Roberts⟩ ⟨drawstring bags . . . hold almost enough ~ to be classified as luggage —*New Yorker*⟩

³truck \"\ *adj* **1 :** of or relating to the truck system **2 :** consisting of or dealing in garden stuff

⁴truck \"\ *n* -S [prob. fr. L *trochus* iron hoop, fr. Gk *trochos* wheel, fr. *trechein* to run — more at TROCHEE] **1 :** a small wheel; *specif* **:** a small strong wheel usu. of wood or iron for a gun carriage **2 :** a small wooden cap at the top of a flagstaff or a masthead usu. having holes in it for reeving flag or signal halyards — see SHIP illustration **3 :** a wheeled vehicle used for moving heavy articles: as **a :** a strong cart or wagon used for hauling ⟨the horses died of starvation and the men harnessed themselves to ~*s* —H.E. Scudder⟩ **b :** HAND TRUCK **c :** a small heavy rectangular frame supported on four wheels used instead of rollers for moving heavy objects **d :** a small flat-topped car sometimes with stakes or vertical ends to prevent the load from falling that is usu. pushed or pulled by hand **e :** a shelved stand mounted on casters **4 a** *Brit* **:** an open railroad freight car **b :** a swiveling carriage consisting of a frame with one or more pairs of wheels and the necessary boxes and springs esp. to carry and guide one end of a locomotive or a railroad car in turning sharp curves **5 a :** an automotive vehicle built for the transportation of goods on its own chassis **b :** a motorized vehicle equipped with a swivel for hauling a trailer

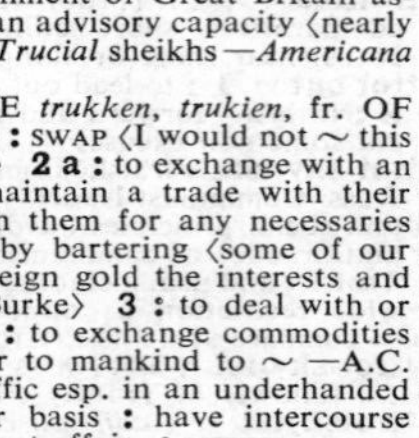

truck 3e

⁵truck \"\ *vb* -ED/-ING/-S *vt* **:** to load or transport on a truck ~ *vi* **1 :** to transport goods by truck **:** be employed in driving a truck **2 :** to execute a trucking step — usu. used with *down* ⟨singing at the top of his lungs . . . ~*ing* down the trail —Margaret Hastings⟩ **3 :** TRACK 2b

⁶truck \"\ *adj* **:** of, relating to, used by, or made for a truck ⟨a ~ tire⟩ ⟨~ route⟩

truck·age \'trəkij\ *n* -S [⁴*truck* + *-age*] **1 :** money paid for the conveyance of goods on a truck **:** FREIGHT **2 :** conveyance by trucks

truckaway \'=ˌ=ˌ=\ *n* -S [fr. *truck away,* v.] **:** the delivery of one or more vehicles or tractors mounted on special trailers usu. from an assembly plant to a dealer — compare DRIVEAWAY

truck box *n* **:** an open body on a motortruck

truck company *n* **:** LADDER COMPANY

truck crop *n* **:** a vegetable crop that is grown in truck farming ⟨lettuce is a *truck crop* in California⟩

truck·ee pine \'trəkē-\ *n, usu cap T* [*truckee* fr. Truckee river, western Nevada] **:** JEFFREY PINE

truckee trout *n, usu cap 1st T* [fr. *Truckee* river, Nevada] **:** TAHOE TROUT

¹truck·er \'trəkə(r)\ *n* -S [¹*truck* + *-er*] **1 a :** one that barters **b** *Scot* **:** an itinerant huckster **:** PEDDLER **2 :** TRUCK FARMER

²trucker \"\ *n* -S [⁵*truck* + *-er*] **1 a :** one whose business is transporting goods by truck **b :** a truck driver **2 :** a laborer who conveys materials from place to place within an industrial establishment usu. doing related jobs (as weighing, sorting, or loading)

truck farm *n* **:** a farm devoted to the production of vegetables for the market

truck farmer *n* **:** one that operates a truck farm

truck farming *n* **:** the production of crops of some vegetables on an extensive scale in regions esp. suited to their culture primarily for shipment to distant markets — compare MARKET GARDENING

truck garden *n* **:** a garden where vegetables are raised for market

truck gardener *n* **:** one that operates a truck garden

truck gardening *n* **:** the raising of vegetables for market

truckhead \'=ˌ=\ *n* [⁴*truck* + *head*] **:** a military installation where supplies that have been brought forward by truck are unloaded and distributed

truck horse *n* **:** DRAFT HORSE

truck house *n* **:** a storehouse for goods used for or received in barter esp. in the early trading with Indians

¹trucking *n* -S [fr. gerund of ¹*truck*] **1 :** BARTERING **2 :** TRUCK FARMING

²trucking *n* -S [fr. gerund of ⁵*truck*] **1 :** the process or business of transporting goods on trucks **2 :** a swaying shuffling jitterbug step in which the feet are moved forward alternately with the toes turned in and then turned out and which is performed with one upraised hand beating time

trucking shot *or* **truck shot** *n* **:** a scene photographed from a moving dolly — called also *tracking shot*

¹truck·le \'trəkəl\ *n* -S [ME *trookel, trocle,* fr. L *trochlea* sheaf of pulleys — more at TROCHLEA] **1 a :** a small wheel; *esp* **:** PULLEY **b :** a small roller used to move a heavy object **:** CASTER **2 :** TRUCKLE BED **3** *dial Eng* **:** a small barrel-shaped cheese

²truckle \"\ *vi* **truckled; truckled; truckling** \-k(ə)liŋ\ **truckles** [fr. *truckle* (in *truckle bed*)] **1** *obs* **:** to sleep in a truckle bed **2** [so called fr. the fact that the truckle bed was usu. pushed under the larger standard bed] **:** to act in a subservient manner **:** yield to the wishes or the will of another **:** bend obsequiously **:** SUBMIT ⟨he would ~ to no man —V.L. Parrington⟩ ⟨people who will always ~ to those who have money —Archibald Marshall⟩

truckle bed *n* [ME *trookel bed,* fr. *trookel* truckle + *bed*] **:** TRUNDLE BED

truck·ler \'trək(ə)lə(r)\ *n* -S **:** one that truckles

truck light *n* **:** a light at the truck of a mast

truckline \'=ˌ=\ *n* **:** a carrier using trucks and related freight vehicles to provide service to shippers

truckload \'=¦=\ *n* **1 :** a load that fills a truck **2 :** the minimum weight specified by the tariff for shipping at truckload rates

truckload rate *n* **:** a rate quoted for shipping a truckload

truck·man \'trəkmən\ *n, pl* **truckmen 1 :** one who conveys goods by truck **:** a truck driver **:** TRUCKER **2 :** a member of a ladder company

truckmaster \'=ˌ==\ *n* [²*truck* + *master*] **1** *archaic* **:** an officer in charge of trade with Indians esp. among the early settlers **2 :** a noncommissioned officer who supervises the operation and maintenance of military vehicles

truck mixer *n* **:** a concrete mixer mounted on the chassis of a truck used for mixing and delivering concrete

truck patch *n* **:** a small area devoted to the production of vegetables usu. for domestic use

¹trucks *pres 3d sing of* TRUCK, *pl of* TRUCK

²trucks \'trəks\ *n, pl* **trucks** [It *trucco* (fr. *truccare* to push, hit a ball, play at billiards, prob. fr. — assumed — VL *trudicare,* fr. L *trudere* to thrust, push) + E *-s,* pl. suffix — more at THREAT] **:** a table game resembling billiards played with little balls

truck system *n* **:** the system of paying wages in goods instead of cash

truck tractor *n* **:** TRACTOR 2c

truck trailer \'=¦==\ *n* **1 :** a nonautomotive freight vehicle to be drawn by a motortruck **2** *usu* **truck–trailer :** a combination of a truck trailer and its motortruck

truckway \'=ˌ=\ *n* **:** a roadway for trucks

truck wholesaler *n* **:** WAGON JOBBER

trucu·lence \'trəkyələn(t)s *sometimes* 'trük-\ *also* **trucu·len·cy** *n, pl* **truculences** *also* **truculencies** [*truculence* fr. *truculent; truculency* fr. L *truculentia* wildness, fierceness, fr. *truculentus* wild, cruel, fierce + *-ia -y*] **:** the quality or state of being truculent ⟨made up for his lack of stature by a great show of ~ —Carol Bache⟩ ⟨as sure a sign of ~ as the closed fist of a man —Edison Marshall⟩

trucu·lent \-nt\ *adj* [L *truculentus,* fr. *truc-, trux* wild, fierce; perh. akin to MIr *tru* given to death] **1 :** feeling or evincing savage ferocity **:** CRUEL, FIERCE ⟨the fangs of these powerful ~ brutes —W.H.Hudson †1922⟩ ⟨the swordfish . . . ~ and fearless —F.C.Lane⟩ **2 :** possessing an inherent capacity for destruction **:** DEADLY ⟨the sleek ~ ships steamed along blackly behind their guns —Ira Wolfert⟩ ⟨go out and inspect the ~ bomb —*Christian Science Monitor*⟩ **3 :** scathingly harsh **:** VITRIOLIC, VITUPERATIVE ⟨a ~ document devoted mostly to vilifying —*Time*⟩ ⟨when every English traveler . . . published a volume of ~ disparagement —V.L.Parrington⟩ **4 :** aggressively self-assertive **:** antagonistic to compromise **:** BELLIGERENT, PUGNACIOUS ⟨as ~ as a small boy who thinks his big brother can lick anybody —*Time*⟩ ⟨tribute is paid to . . . his rather ~ skill as a negotiator —Norman MacKenzie⟩

trucu·lent·ly *adv* **:** in a truculent manner ⟨he looked up ~ —L.C.Douglas⟩ ⟨strive for security by ~ asserting their vested interests —J.S.Schapiro⟩

tru·dell·ite \trü'deˌlīt\ *n* -S [Harry W. *Trudell* *b*1884 Am. mineralogist + E *-ite*] **:** a mineral $Al_{10}Cl_{12}(OH)_{12}(SO_4)_3 \cdot 3OH_2O$(?) consisting of a hydrous basic aluminum chloride and sulfate and occurring in amber-yellow masses

¹trudge \'trəj\ *vb* -ED/-ING/-S [origin unknown] *vi* **:** to walk or march on foot steadily and esp. toilsomely or wearily ⟨we *trudged* a hundred yards or so through deep, untrodden snow —John Connell⟩ ~ *vt* **:** to trudge along or over

²trudge \"\ *n* -S **:** a long tiring walk **:** TRAMP ⟨a strenuous ~ of twenty-three miles —R.L.Newberger⟩

trud·gen crawl \'trəjən-\ *n* [after John *Trudgen,* 19th cent. Eng. amateur swimmer] **:** a crawl stroke in which a scissors kick is combined with the flutter kick

trudgen stroke *or* **trudgen** *also* **trud·geon** \'trəjən\ *n* -S [after John *Trudgen*] **:** a swimming stroke in which a double overarm motion is used and the legs execute a scissors kick

trudg·er \'trejə(r)\ *n* -S **:** one that trudges

¹true \'trü\ *adj, usu* **truer** \-ü(ə)r; -ủ(ə)r, -ủə\ *usu* **truest** \-üəst\ [ME *trew, trewe,* fr. OE *trēowe* faithful, trustworthy; akin to OHG *gitriuwi* faithful, trustworthy, ON *tryggr,* Goth *triggws* faithful, trustworthy, OIr *dreb* certain, OPruss *druwis* faith, Lith *drūtas* strong, thick, Skt *dāruna* hard, *dāru* wood — more at TREE] **1 a :** steady, firm, and dependable in allegiance or devotion to a loved one, friend, leader, group, or cause **:** not false or perfidious ⟨his musical idiom was unique, and by remaining ~ to it, he expressed himself with the utmost clarity —J.D.Cook⟩ ⟨all ~ men were needed to save the country —Shelby Foote⟩; *specif* **:** steadfast in observing marriage or other vows ⟨a lover absolutely ~ in act and word and thought —H.O.Taylor⟩ **b :** HONEST, JUST, UPRIGHT ⟨he was absolutely ~, genuinely square in his relations to those about him —W.A.White⟩ **c** *archaic* **:** TRUTHFUL, VERACIOUS ⟨dare to be ~; nothing can need a lie —George Herbert⟩ **2 a** (1) **:** conformable to fact **:** in accordance with the actual state of affairs **:** not false or erroneous **:** not inaccurate ⟨mathematics, I thought, had a better chance of being ~ than anything else that passed as general knowledge —Bertrand Russell⟩ ⟨it is ~ that there is an underlying intention to keep patronage alive —Herbert Read⟩ (2) **:** conformable to nature, reality, or an original **:** accurate in delineating or expressing the essential elements ⟨fiction is *truer* than history, because it goes beyond the evidence —E.M.Forster⟩; *specif* **:** describing actual events that happened ⟨a ~ story⟩ **b** (1) **:** being on a level transcending phenomenal or everyday existence **:** IDEAL ⟨nobler ideas — *truer* because they are more in harmony with man's situation in the universe —Liston Pope⟩ ⟨the same event can be said to be ~ for faith but untrue for science —W.R.Inge⟩ ⟨appropriate to the inward search and responsive to ~ values —Pietro Belluschi⟩ (2) **:** being more genuinely characteristic of or operative in than manifest motives or appearances **:** ESSENTIAL ⟨the party's principles and policies, rather than its actual social composition, should be the criterion of its ~ nature —N.D.Palmer & S. C. Leng⟩ ⟨a better understanding of the ~ motives in human behavior —*Printers' Ink*⟩ **c :** being that which is the case rather than what is believed, assumed, or claimed ⟨the ~ dimension of the world refugee problem is clearly being ignored or sidestepped —Gertrude Samuels⟩ ⟨sent her back to bed without telling her the president's ~ condition —*Time*⟩ **d** (1) **:** consistent with expectation or previous performance ⟨remains ~ to its background of cattle barons —*Amer. Guide Series: Texas*⟩ (2) **:** confirmed by later experience or investigation ⟨the lawyer's premonition was ~ —Leo Marx⟩ **3 a :** properly so called: as (1) **:** void of deceit **:** SINCERE, UNFEIGNED ⟨~ love⟩ (2) **:** not sham, counterfeit, or adulterated **:** GENUINE ⟨returned to the ~ faith⟩ ⟨expect to make ~ and rapid progress in civil rights —D.D.Eisenhower⟩ (3) **:** being essentially what it is called ⟨the ~ coastline was . . . 140 kilometers from the apparent coastline —Valter Schytt⟩ ⟨the ~ stomach, the abomasum, forms only about one tenth of the total capacity of the ruminant stomach —S.J.Watson⟩ (4) **:** designed or functioning in a manner regarded as essential to meeting a standard ⟨none of these institutions could be regarded as a ~ university because none had a faculty capable of examining for the higher degrees —J.B.Conant⟩ ⟨a ~ textbook is one especially prepared for the use of pupil and teacher —*Textbooks in Education*⟩ **b** (1) **:** possessing all the fundamental characters of and belonging to the same natural group as ⟨a lizard is a ~ reptile⟩ ⟨a whale is a ~ but not a typical mammal⟩ (2) **:** TYPICAL ⟨the ~ cats may be distinguished

from fossil allies by characters of the dentition⟩ **4 a :** such as it should be **:** PROPER, FITTING ⟨facts presented in their ~ order and bearing⟩ **b** (1) **:** LEGITIMATE, RIGHTFUL ⟨the ~ and legal successors of the old régime —*Geog. Jour.*⟩ (2) **:** related by blood ⟨would a ~ child always take precedence of an adopted child —*Notes & Queries on Anthropology*⟩ **5 :** that can be relied on **:** TRUSTWORTHY ⟨heard by ~ telling that you have money and means —Augusta Gregory⟩ ⟨claim that his polls are a ~ representation of the opinions of the whole nation —*Current Biog.*⟩; *specif* **:** determined with respect to a statistical population rather than a sample ⟨prefer the narrow range with bias to a *truer* average with wider dispersed values —*Photogrammetric Engineering*⟩ **6 a :** placed, fitted, or formed accurately ⟨the blocks of granite were so ~ that practically no mortar was used —*Amer. Guide Series: Nev.*⟩ **b :** comformable to a standard, rule, or pattern **:** EXACT, ACCURATE, CORRECT ⟨supply the disposal agency with the originals or ~ copies of all documents —*U. S. Code*⟩ ⟨singing on ~ pitch⟩ **c :** molded by environment, family, or culture and marked by similar attitudes and characteristics ⟨a ~ product of his age, being neither more skeptical nor more credulous than any other —J.A.Rushing⟩ ⟨a ~ child of the rising West —H.E.Starr⟩ **d :** best fitting one's aptitudes or interests ⟨found his ~ vocation after many false starts⟩ **7 a :** reliable or accurate in function **:** EXACT ⟨the machine is *truer* than the hand —Edward Bellamy⟩ **b :** accurate, quick, or complete in measuring, grasping, or comprehending fact ⟨a ~ understanding of our heritage —W.R.Steckel⟩ ⟨whose turns and rhythms of speech have been caught by a ~ ear —B.R.Redman⟩ ⟨imagination is *truer* than reason is —O.S.J.Gogarty⟩ **8 :** related to a fixed point; *specif* **:** determined with reference to the earth's axis rather than the magnetic poles ⟨~ north⟩ ⟨~ west⟩ **9 :** logically necessary **:** universally valid **10 :** NARROW, RESTRICTED, STRICT ⟨a how-to-do-it booklet in the *truest* sense of the word —Mary S. Switzer⟩ **11 :** corrected for error — compare TRUE ALTITUDE **syn** see FAITHFUL, REAL

²true \"\ *n* -S **1 :** something that is true **:** ultimate truth **:** REALITY — usu. used with *the* **2 :** the quality or state of being accurate (as in alignment or adjustment) — used in the phrases *in true* and *out of true* ⟨the rail level may sag out of ~ —O.S.Nock⟩

³true \"\ *vt* **trued; trued; trueing** *also* **truing; trues :** to make level, square, balanced, or concentric **:** bring or restore to a desired mechanical accuracy or form ⟨*trued* an engine cylinder that had got out of round by boring it oversize⟩ ⟨*trued* an unbalanced grinding wheel with a dressing diamond⟩ ⟨repaired a worn housing by mounting it on centers in a lathe and taking a light *trueing* cut⟩ ⟨~s up a fixture with the machine spindle by using a dial indicator⟩

⁴true \"\ *adv, usu* -ER/-EST [ME *trewe*, fr. *trewe*, adj., true] **1 :** in accordance with fact or reality **:** TRUTHFULLY, HONESTLY ⟨your childish lips spoke *truer* than you suspected —Rosa Luxemburg⟩ **2 a :** without variation from path or position **:** in true **:** EXACTLY, ACCURATELY ⟨the bullet flew straight and ~⟩ ⟨the doors . . . still hang perfectly ~ —*Amer. Guide Series: Md.*⟩ — often used as an interjection for emphasis or as a signal of confirmation, admission, or endorsement of a fact ⟨~, there was a blot on the escutcheon of that lady —W.S. Gilbert⟩ **b :** without change ⟨a variety that comes ~ from seed⟩ **:** without variation from or of type ⟨genuine mutations usu. breed ~⟩

true airspeed *n* **:** the velocity of an airplane in its flight path relative to the air through which it is moving

true altitude *n* **:** the pressure altitude corrected for temperature

true balsam *n* **:** BALSAM 1b(2)

true bearing *n* **:** bearing relative to true north

true bill *n* **:** a bill of indictment returned by the grand jury endorsed as warranting prosecution of the accused under the indictment

true blue *n* **1 :** the blue color adopted from old association of blue with constancy and fidelity by the Covenanters; *also* **:** PRESBYTERIANISM **2 a :** thoroughgoing or uncompromising loyalty, fidelity, or orthodoxy **b :** a true-blue person ⟨a staunch Conservative himself, a *true blue*, and they knew his color when they went to vote —Flora Thompson⟩

true-blue \ˈ⸗ˌ⸗\ *adj* [*true blue*] **:** of unswerving loyalty esp. to a party or group using blue as its special color ⟨*true-blue* Presbyterians⟩ ⟨a *true-blue* Tory⟩

trueborn \ˈ⸗ˈ⸗\ *adj* **:** genuinely such by birthright ⟨though banish'd, yet a ~ Englishman —Shak.⟩

true branching *n* **:** a branched arrangement of filaments of bacteria or algae due to protoplasmic bifurcation or cell growth and fission along more than one axis — compare FALSE BRANCHING

truebred \ˈ⸗ˈ⸗\ *adj* **:** PUREBRED; *also* **:** THOROUGHGOING

true bug *n* **:** an insect of the order Hemiptera; *esp* **:** a typical winged insect of the suborder Heteroptera as distinguished from the highly varied members of the suborder Homoptera

true course *n* **:** the course of a ship or airplane measured with respect to true north

true discount *n* **:** ARITHMETICAL DISCOUNT

true dolphin *n* [so called to distinguish it from other cetaceans commonly called dolphins] **:** a dolphin of the genus *Delphinus*

true-false test \(ˈ)⸗ˈ⸗-\ *n* **:** an objective test consisting of a series of statements each of which is to be marked as either true or false

true fly *n* **:** ⁵FLY 2a

true fruit *n* **:** a fruit produced from only carpellary tissue — compare ACCESSORY FRUIT

true guest *n* **:** SYMPHILE

true heading *n* **:** the heading measured clockwise from true north

truehearted \ˈ⸗ˈ⸗⸗\ *adj* [ME, fr. ¹*true* + *hearted*] **:** FAITHFUL, STEADFAST, LOYAL — **true·heart·ed·ness** *n*

truehedge columnberry \ˈ⸗ˌ⸗ˈ⸗⸗- — *see* BERRY\ *n* [*true* + *hedge* + *column* + *berry*] **:** an upright barberry that is a variety (*Berberis thunbergii erecta*) of the Japanese barberry

true horizon *n* **:** HORIZON 1b(1); *also* **:** the horizon at sea

true leveller *n, usu cap T&L* **:** DIGGER 2

true-life \ˈ⸗ˈ⸗\ *adj* **:** true to life ⟨a *true-life* story⟩

truelove \ˈ⸗ˌ⸗\ *n* [ME *trewe love*, fr. OE *trēowe lufu* faithful love, fr. *trēowe* faithful + *lufu* love — more at TRUE, LOVE] **1 a :** faithful love **b :** one truly beloved or loving **:** SWEETHEART ⟨a lady young in beauty waiting until my ~ comes —J.C.Ransom⟩ **2 a :** HERB PARIS **b :** a trillium (*Trillium erectum*)

true lover's knot *also* **truelove knot** *n* [ME *trewe love knot*] **1 :** FISHERMAN'S KNOT **2 :** LOVE KNOT

true middle lamella *n* **:** the intercellular cementing layer of the middle lamella

true·ness *n* -ES [ME *trewenesse*, fr. OE *trēownes* object of trust, fr. *trēowe* faithful, trustworthy + *-nes* -ness] **:** the quality or state of being true: as **a :** correspondence with reality **b :** exactness of adjustment

true pelvis *n* **:** the lower more contracted part of the pelvic cavity

truepenny \ˈ⸗ˌ⸗\ *n* [¹*true* + *penny*] **:** an honest or trustworthy person

true plane *n* **:** a plane surface of metal made by repeated scrapping with a scraper and testing with a surface plate

¹truer *comparative of* TRUE

²tru·er \ˈtrüə(r); -ü(ə)r, -üə\ *n* -S [³*true* + *-er*] **:** one that trues: as **a :** a device for trueing abrasive wheels **b :** one that trues objects (as optical lenses, green clay blocks, or springs) to bring them into correct condition, size, or alignment

true rib *n* **:** one of the ribs whose costal cartilages connect directly with the sternum and that in man constitute the first seven pairs

trues *pl of* TRUE, *pres 3d sing of* TRUE

true seal *n* **:** a seal of the family Phocidae as distinguished from sea lions and eared seals of the family Otariidae

true skin *n* **:** DERMIS

true soil *n* **:** SOLUM 2

truest *superlative of* TRUE

true sun *n* **:** the sun that is observed in the sky — distinguished from *mean sun*

true time *n* **1 :** APPARENT TIME **2 :** MEAN SOLAR TIME

true-to-scale process *n* **:** a photomechanical process based on the insolubilizing action of iron salts on gelatin wherein a lithographic image is obtained by contact exposing a line original to blueprint paper that is squeegeed without development to the surface of a moist gelatin printing pad

true vocal cord *n* **:** either of the lower pair of vocal cords that enclose the lower part of the elastic membrane of the larynx, extend from the inner surface of the thyroid cartilage near the median line to a process of the corresponding thyroid cartilage, and when drawn taut, approximated, and subjected to the flow of breath produce voice

true wind *n* **:** the wind relative to a fixed point the observation of which is not affected by the motion of the observer — compare APPARENT WIND

truewood \ˈ⸗ˌ⸗\ *n* [¹*true* + *wood*] *Austral* **:** sound heartwood

truff \ˈtrəf\ *n* -S [origin unknown] **:** BULL TROUT 1

truf·fle \ˈtrəfəl, -rüf-, -rüf-\ *n* -S [modif. of MF *truffe*, fr. OProv *trufa*, fr. (assumed) VL *tufera*, *tufer*, alter. of L *tuber* hump, tumor, truffle — more at TUBER] **1 a :** the edible subterranean fruiting body of various European fungi of the genus *Tuber* usu. dark-colored, warty or rugose, resembling a rounded or ovoid tuber, and filled with ascospores; *broadly* **:** any similar fruiting body of a fungus of the family Tuberaceae **b :** a fungus that produces truffles **2 :** FALSE TRUFFLE **3 :** a candy made of chocolate, butter, and sugar shaped into balls and coated with cocoa, macaroon crumbs, or chopped nuts

truf·fled \-ld\ *adj* **:** cooked, stuffed, or garnished with truffles

trug \ˈtrəg, -rüg\ *n* -S [origin unknown] **1** *Brit* **:** an old unit of measure for wheat equal to 0.67 bushel **2** *Brit* **:** a coarse basket made of strips of wood and used esp. for carrying fruit, vegetables, or flowers

truing *pres part of* TRUE

tru·ism \ˈtrüˌizəm\ *n* -S [¹*true* + *-ism*] **:** an undoubted or self-evident truth; *esp* **:** one too obvious or unimportant for mention

tru·is·tic \(ˈ)trüˈistik\ *also* **tru·is·ti·cal** \-stəkəl\ *adj* [fr. *truism*, after such pairs as E *theism: theistic, theistical*] **:** of, relating to, or being a truism ⟨it is a ~ statement that a blind child can do everything but see —*Proceedings: Annual Education Congress*⟩

truk·ese \(ˈ)trüˈkēz, (ˈ)trüˈk-, ˈtrəˈk-\ *n, pl* **trukese** *cap* [*Truk* islands (fr. Trukese *Cuuk* Truk islands, fr. *cuuk* mountains, heights) + E *-ese*] **1 :** a Micronesian native or inhabitant of the Truk islands in the Caroline islands **2 :** the Austronesian language spoken in the Truk islands

trull \ˈtrəl\ *n* -S [obs. G *trulle* prostitute (now *trulle* lass, wench, hussy), fr. MHG, prostitute, mistress; akin to MHG *trolle* ghostly monster, boor, lout, blockhead, ON *troll* giant, fiend, demon — more at TROLL] **:** PROSTITUTE, STRUMPET

trul·lo \ˈtrü(ˌ)lō\ *n, pl* **trul·li** \-lē\ [It] **:** a round stone building made with conical roof and without mortar found in southern Italy and esp. in Apulia

¹tru·ly \ˈtrülē, -li\ *adv* [ME *trewely*, fr. OE *trēowlīce*, fr. *trēowe* faithful + *-līce* -ly — more at TRUE] **1 a** *archaic* **:** with constancy **:** FAITHFULLY **b :** SINCERELY — often used as a complimentary close after *yours* **2 a :** in agreement with fact **:** TRUTHFULLY ⟨a passion to see and to report ~ —Gladys Wrigley⟩ **b :** conformably with nature **:** REALISTICALLY ⟨the characters are all quietly funny; they are all ~ drawn —Coulton Waugh⟩ **3 :** with exactness of construction or operation **:** ACCURATELY ⟨the early engineers, who built so well, and so ~ —O.S.Nock⟩ **4 a :** INDEED — often used as an intensive ⟨~, she is fair⟩ or interjectionally to express astonishment or doubt **b :** without feigning, falsity, or inaccuracy in truth or fact **:** GENUINELY ⟨~ noble expressions of human feeling —M.R.Cohen⟩ ⟨whether you merely exist or ~ live —Dana Burnet⟩ **5 :** PROPERLY, RIGHTLY, RIGHTFULLY

²truly \"\ *n* -ES *Brit* **:** TRUTH, VERACITY, TRUSTWORTHINESS — used in such phrases as *by my truly*

tru·meau \(ˈ)trüˈmō\ *n, pl* **tru·meaux** \-ōz\ [F] **1 :** a central pillar supporting the tympanum of a large doorway esp in a medieval building **2 :** an overmantel treatment of 18th century France consisting of a pier glass surmounted by an oil painting or decorative often carved panel

¹trump \ˈtrəmp\ *n* -S [ME *trumpe*, *trompe*, fr. OF *trompe*, prob. of Gmc origin; akin to OHG *trumpa*, *trumba* trumpet, ON *trumba*; prob. of imit. origin like MHG *trumme* drum — more at DRUM] **1 a :** TRUMPET **b** *chiefly Scot* **:** JEW'S HARP **2 :** a sound of or as if of trumpeting ⟨would pick up this same shell . . . and wind a ~ that was heard in the far corner of the field —S.H.Holbrook⟩ ⟨roaring like the ~ of judgment —H.L. Davis⟩

²trump \"\ *n* -S [alter. of ¹*triumph*] **1 a :** any of various cards and usu. all the cards of a suit designated by chance or by an auction or declaration that if legally played will win over a card that is not a trump **b** *or* **trump suit :** the suit whose cards are all trumps — often used in pl. **c :** a card (as a heart or tarot) with a special function or value in a game (as hearts or tarok) **d :** TRUMP CARD **2 :** an old English card game that is a precursor of whist **3 a :** an influential factor or final resource kept in reserve ⟨kept a political ~ up his sleeve —*Economist*⟩ ⟨you put me to my ~s by asking me for additional matter . . . for I considered myself exhausted on that score long ago —*Harper's*⟩ **b :** a dependable and exemplary individual **:** CRACKERJACK, PEACH ⟨my father came out a ~ . . . he offered to pay for the furniture —H.J.Laski⟩

³trump \"\ *vb* -ED/-ING/-S *vt* **1 :** to take with a trump ⟨~ a trick⟩ **2 :** to get the better of **:** OUTDO, TOP ⟨giving the young men spades in years and effortlessly ~*ing* them with Old World charm —R.L.Shayon⟩ **~** *vi* **1 :** to play a trump **2 :** to take a trick with a trump

trump card *n* **1 a :** the last card that is dealt in a whist hand and is turned up to determine trump but if not played is restored to the dealer's hand after the first trick **b :** a card of a trump suit **2 :** a telling argument or decisive factor **:** CLINCHER ⟨justice . . . is the *trump card* of the western world —*Times Lit. Supp.*⟩ ⟨its real *trump card* . . . is its humane price —*New Yorker*⟩

trumped-up \ˈ⸗ˈ⸗\ *adj* [fr. past part. of *trump up*] **:** fraudulently concocted **:** MADE-UP, SPURIOUS ⟨*trumped-up* charges⟩ ⟨a *trumped-up* excuse⟩ ⟨an elaborately *trumped-up* trial —T.C. Chubb⟩

¹trum·pery \ˈtrəmp(ə)rē, -ri\ *n* -ES [ME *trompery*, fr. MF *tromperie*, fr. *tromper* to deceive + *-ie* -y] **1** *obs* **:** DECEIT, FRAUD — often used in pl. ⟨left none of his *trumperies* and double-dealings unrevealed —Robert Dallington⟩ **2 a :** trivial or useless articles of equipment **:** BRIC-A-BRAC, PARAPHERNALIA ⟨a wagon loaded with household ~ —Washington Irving⟩ ⟨farm families loaded down with balloons, dolls, and other ~ of the pitchman —*Amer. Guide Series: Pa.*⟩ **b :** worthless nonsense **:** MUMBO JUMBO, TWADDLE ⟨a piece of propaganda ~ —*Time*⟩ ⟨the *trumperies* of a forced symbolism —Robert Pick⟩ **c** *archaic* **:** tawdry finery ⟨the ~ in my house —Shak.⟩ **d** *dial Brit* **:** garden refuse **:** WEEDS

²trumpery \"\ *adj* **1 :** of small worth or poor quality **:** tastelessly superficial **:** CHEAP, TAWDRY ⟨charm primitive peoples with mirrors, glass beads, and other ~ baubles⟩ ⟨the demands mankind makes of fiction may be slight, ~, ridiculous, or meretricious —Bernard De Voto⟩ **2 a :** FRAUDULENT, TRUMPED-UP ⟨the ~ pathos of a tenth-rate novel —Hugh Walpole⟩ ⟨encourages the bringing of ~ actions . . . even though no damage has been suffered —*Manchester Guardian Weekly*⟩ **b :** worthy of contempt **:** DESPICABLE ⟨seemed in her own eyes both deluded and . . . ~ —Elizabeth Taylor⟩ ⟨encouraged two or three ~ fellows . . . to cut scurvy jokes at my expense —George Borrow⟩

¹trum·pet \ˈtrəmpət, *usu* -əd·+V\ *n* -S *often attrib* [ME *trumpette*, *trompette*, fr. MF *trompette*, fr. OF *trompe* trumpet + *-ette* — more at TRUMP (trumpet)] **1 a** (1) **:** a wind instrument consisting of a long cylindrical metal tube commonly once or twice curved and ending in a bell, producing its tones by the vibration of the player's lips against a cup-shaped mouthpiece, having valves that enable the use of all scale tones in its normal compass of written F sharp below middle C as indicated on the treble staff to the C two octaves above middle C, and usu. constructed in B flat thereby sounding a whole step lower than the notation indicates — compare BUGLE, CORNET (2) **:** a metal wind instrument (as the cornet) similar in shape and method of tone production to the trumpet **b :** a clarion call or one that utters it ⟨sounded forth the first tidings and ~ of Reformation —John Milton⟩ ⟨a powerful ~ who stirred the pulse of mankind —M.R.Cohen⟩ **2 a :** a trumpet player ⟨persuaded the ~s, who were satisfied with playing high notes, to play *good* notes —Cy Feuer⟩ **b** *obs* **:** MESSENGER, SPOKESMAN ⟨be thou the ~ of our wrath —Shak.⟩ **3 :** something that resembles a trumpet or its tonal quality: as **a :** an 8-foot pipe-organ reed stop with a penetrating tone **b :** TRITON 2 **c :** a funnel-shaped instrument (as a megaphone or a diaphragm horn) for collecting, directing, or intensifying sound — see EAR TRUMPET, SPEAKING TRUMPET **d** (1) **:** a trumpet-shaped flower esp. of a plant of the genera *Datura*, *Campsis*, *or Bignonia* (2) **trumpets** *South* **:** any of several pitcher plants having long trumpet-shaped leaves; *esp* **:** a swamp plant (*Sarracenia flava*) **e** (1) **:** a stentorian voice (2) **:** a penetrating cry (as of an elephant) (3) **:** a shrill hum (as of a mosquito) **f :** a funnel-shaped guide for material (as the fiber web leaving a carding machine)

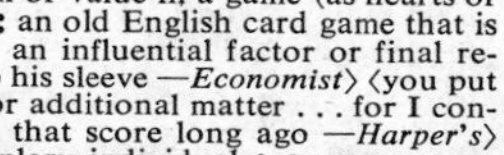

modern trumpet

²trumpet \"\ *vb* -ED/-ING/-S *vi* **1 :** to blow a trumpet ⟨practicing soldiers ~*ed* and bugled —Charles Dickens⟩ **2 a :** to make a shrill trumpetlike sound ⟨~ like . . . a wounded cow elephant —Charles Beadle⟩ **b :** to make a vociferous proclamation ⟨~s from his editorials on war and politics —H.S. Canby⟩ **~** *vt* **1 :** to give vociferous utterance to **:** proclaim loudly ⟨orders ~*ed* to us that morning —Kenneth Roberts⟩ ⟨was not going to ~ his criticisms while on foreign soil —Blair Clark⟩ **2 :** to herald by or as if by the sounding of trumpets ⟨a triumph which must be ~*ed* —Sophie Kerr⟩ ⟨Italy's most ~*ed* living writer —*Time*⟩; *also* **:** to summon or denounce by or as if by blowing a trumpet

trumpet animalcule *n* **:** a trumpet-shaped infusorian of *Stentor* or a related genus

trumpet arch *n* **:** a conical squinch

trumpetbush \ˈ⸗⸗ˌ⸗\ *n* [so called fr. the shape of the flowers] **:** YELLOW ELDER

trumpet call *n* **1 :** a call sounded on a trumpet; *specif* **:** FANFARE **2 :** an urgent or rousing summons ⟨*trumpet calls* to the European crusade against Bolshevism —*Manchester Guardian Weekly*⟩ ⟨a *trumpet call* to faith —H.E.Fey⟩

trumpet creeper *n* **:** a No. American woody vine (*Campsis radicans*) having pinnate leaves and large red trumpet-shaped flowers — called also *trumpet vine*

trumpet-creeper family *n* **:** BIGNONIACEAE

trum·pet·er \ˈtrəmpəd·ə(r), -ətə-\ *n* -S *except sense 3c(1)* [ME *trumpatour*, fr. *trumpete* trumpet + *-our* -or — more at TRUMPET] **1 a :** a trumpet player; *specif* **:** an agent (as a herald) who gives signals with a trumpet **b :** one that praises or advocates **:** EULOGIST, SPOKESMAN ⟨became his toady and ~ —Robertson Davies⟩ ⟨~ for democratic support of the League of Nations —*Saturday Rev.*⟩ **2** *or* **trumpeter muscle :** BUCCINATOR **3 a :** any of several large highly gregarious easily domesticated forest-dwelling So. American birds (genus *Psophia*) that are related to the cranes, have long legs, a long neck, a head and beak very similar to those of domestic fowl, soft plumage which is mostly blackish with yellowish green or purplish iridescence on neck and breast, and a loud clear prolonged cry, and are often kept in Brazil to protect poultry; *esp* **:** a bird (*P. crepitans*) of Guiana and Brazil **b :** TRUMPETER SWAN **c** (1) *usu cap* **:** an Asiatic breed of pigeons that have a shell crest, heavily feathered feet, and a prolonged melodious call and that are best known from a strain developed in Germany (2) **:** a bird of the Trumpeter breed **4 a :** any of several Australian and New Zealand marine spiny-finned fishes (family Latrididae); *esp* **:** a choice food fish (*Latris lineata*) that is silvery with olive longitudinal stripes and reaches a weight of 60 to 80 pounds **b :** any of several other fishes that make a trumpeting or grunting noise when caught: as (1) **:** an Australian striped perch (*Heliotes sexlineatus*) (2) *or* **trumpeter perch :** a related fish (*Pelates quadrilineatus*)

trumpeter bullfinch *n* **:** a thick-billed Afro-Asian terrestrial finch (*Erythrospiza githaginea*) that is predominantly pinkish tinged brown with a pale gray crown

trumpeter swan *n* **:** a No. American wild swan (*Olor buccinator*) that is found chiefly from the Mississippi valley westward but is becoming rare, is pure white with no yellow on the lores, and is noted for its sonorous voice

trumpet fish *n* **1 :** BELLOWS FISH 1 **2 :** CORNETFISH

trumpet flower *n* **1 :** a plant having trumpet-shaped flowers: as **a :** TRUMPET CREEPER **b :** TRUMPET HONEYSUCKLE **c :** CROSS VINE 1 **d :** DATURA 2 **e :** YELLOW ELDER **f :** YELLOW OLEANDER **2 :** a trumpet-shaped flower

trumpet fly *n* **:** BOTFLY

trumpet honeysuckle *n* **:** a No. American honeysuckle (*Lonicera sempervirens*) having coral-red or orange flowers with a slenderly trumpet-shaped corolla — called also *trumpet flower*, *trumpet vine*

trumpet hypha *n, pl* **trumpet hyphas :** one of the conducting cells in the tissues of the stems of brown algae of the family Laminariaceae that resemble sieve tubes and are long with swollen ends

trumpeting *n* -S [fr. gerund of ²*trumpet*] **1 :** the act or process of blowing a trumpet or producing a similarly penetrating sound ⟨startled awake by martial ~⟩ **2 :** an act or instance of heralding or proclaiming by or as if by the blowing of trumpets ⟨the ~ of Red peace banners —Han Suyin⟩

trumpet-leaf \ˈ⸗⸗ˌ⸗\ *n* **:** TRUMPET 3d(2)

trumpet leg *n* **:** a furniture leg turned in the shape of a horn with the flared end up and the small end joining the foot

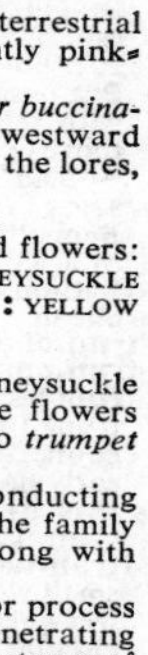

trumpet leg

trumpetlike \ˈ⸗⸗ˌ⸗\ *adj* **:** resembling a trumpet in shape or sound

trumpet lily *n* **1 a :** a lily (*Lilium longiflorum*) that is native to Formosa and the Ryukyu islands and is widely cultivated for its large fragrant pure white funnelform flowers which are borne singly or in pairs **b :** CALLA 2 **c :** DATURA 2 **2 :** the flower of a trumpet lily

trumpet marine *n* [prob. so called fr. its resemblance to large speaking trumpets used formerly on Italian and other European ships] **:** a triangular medieval bowed musical instrument about six feet long having one long catgut string that produces powerful and coarse-toned natural harmonics when played — called also *monochord*

trumpet milkweed *n* **:** WILD LETTUCE 1b(3)

trumpet narcissus *or* **trumpet daffodil** *n* **:** a plant of the genus *Narcissus* with the corona elongated into a trumpet **:** a typical daffodil

trum·pet·ry \ˈtrəmpətrē, -ri\ *n* -ES **:** the sound of trumpets ⟨amidst fanfare and ~ —J.C.Moloney⟩

trumpet-shaped \ˈ⸗⸗ˌ⸗\ *adj* **1 :** conical but flaring at the broad end **2** *bot* **:** tubular with the limb spreading

trumpet shell *n* **:** TRITON 2

trumpet tree *n* **:** TRUMPETWOOD

trumpet vine *n* **1 :** TRUMPET CREEPER **2 :** TRUMPET HONEYSUCKLE

trumpetweed \ˈ⸗⸗ˌ⸗\ *n* **:** any of several herbs: as **a :** TRUMPET MILKWEED **b** (1) **:** a boneset (*Eupatorium perfoliatum*) (2) **:** a joe-pye weed (*E. maculatum*)

trumpetwood \ˈ⸗⸗ˌ⸗\ *n* **:** a tropical American tree (*Cecropia peltata*) with large peltate leaves and hollow stems — called also *imbauba*

trumping *pres part of* TRUMP

trump-poor \ˈ⸗ˈ⸗\ *adj* [²*trump*] **:** lacking general strength but strong in trumps — used of a hand at cards

trumps *pl of* TRUMP, *pres 3d sing of* TRUMP

trump signal *n* **:** the high-low used in a card game as a request to a partner to lead a trump

trump suit *n* **:** TRUMP 1b

trump up *vt* [³*trump*] **1 :** to concoct esp. with intent to deceive **:** FABRICATE, INVENT ⟨*trump up* extra tasks to keep the children busy —Gertrude H. Hildreth⟩ ⟨*trump up* false charges of treason —R.A.Billington⟩ **2** *archaic* **:** to cite as support for an action or claim **:** ALLEGE ⟨necessity is *trumped up* for a plea —Samuel Palmer⟩ **3 :** to call forth by an act of will **:** EVOKE, SUMMON ⟨never able to *trump up* the courage to have a showdown —Mary B. Miller⟩

trun *dial past of* THROW

trun·cal \ˈtrəŋkəl\ *adj* [L *truncus* trunk + E *-al*] **:** of or relating to the trunk of the body

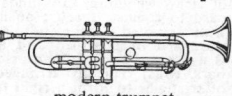

¹trun·cate \ˈtrəŋˌkāt, *usu* -ād.+V\ *vt* -ED/-ING/-S [L *truncatus*, past part. of *truncare* to cut off, mutilate, fr. *truncus* trunk, torso; prob. akin to W *trwch* broken, truncated, Lith *trenkti* to push violently, jolt and perh. to OE *thringan* to crowd, throng — more at THRONG] **1 :** to abbreviate by or as if by cutting off : LOP ⟨lower ends of the ridges . . . are *truncated* by glacial erosion —W.J.Miller⟩ ⟨~ the value of pi from eight decimal places to 3.14⟩ ⟨~ a news item to fit available space⟩ ⟨games . . . abruptly *truncated* by the arrival of the evening papers —H.G.Wells⟩ **2 :** to replace (as an edge or corner of a crystal) by a plane and esp. by a plane that is equally inclined to the adjoining faces

²truncate \ˈ"\ *adj* [L *truncatus*, past part. of *truncare*] **1 :** having the end square or even as if cut off ⟨a ~ leaf⟩ ⟨a ~ feather⟩ **2 :** lacking an apex — used of a spiral (as of a gastropod mollusk) shell in which the apex of the young shell breaks off naturally

trun·cat·ed \-ād·əd, -ātəd\ *adj* [ME, fr. L *truncatus* (past part. of *truncare* to cut off) + E *-ed*] **1 a :** having the apex replaced by a plane section and esp. by one parallel to the base ⟨volcanic mountains . . . bluntly ~, owing to the whole top of the original cone having been blown away —C.A.Cotton⟩ **b :** having the edges or corners cut off by a line or plane — compare BEVELED ⟨transformed into ~ spheres —D.W Van Krevelen & Johannes Schuyer⟩ **2 a :** abbreviated by or as if by lopping : cut short : CURTAILED ⟨~ headlands . . . are products of wave erosion —C.L.White & G.T.Renner⟩ ⟨the present disc . . . includes the whole of the usually ~ orchestral introduction —Edward Sackville-West & Desmond Shawe-Taylor⟩ ⟨words ~ by his impatience —Frances Winwar⟩ **b :** marred by mutilation : MAIMED, MANGLED ⟨a ~ body⟩ ⟨the ~ economy . . . must be made to grow new industrial limbs—*Time*⟩ ⟨such a ~ quotation does not do justice to the . . . argument —*Nation*⟩ **c :** lacking an expected or normal element (as a syllable) at beginning or end : ACEPHALOUS, CATALECTIC ⟨a ~ line of verse⟩ **3 :** squared off at the end; *specif* : TRUNCATE

truncated cone *or* **truncated pyramid** *n* **:** a cone section or pyramid lacking an apex and terminating in a plane usu. parallel to the base

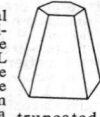

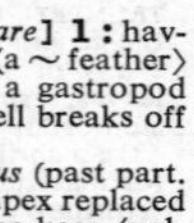
truncated pyramid

truncated cube *n* **:** a solid bounded by six equal regular octagons and eight equal regular triangles formed by cutting off the corners of a cube

trun·ca·tel·la \ˌtrəŋkəˈtelə\ *n, cap* [NL, fr. L *truncatus* (past part.) + *-ella*] **:** a genus (the type of the family Truncatellidae) of snails that are usu. terrestrial near the sea but occas. occur in either salt water or freshwater and that have a small somewhat cylindrical shell which is truncate in the adult and the ctenidium replaced by a pulmonary sac

trun·cate·ly *adv* **:** in a truncated form or manner

trun·ca·tion \ˌtrəŋˈkāshən\ *n* -S [LL *truncation-, truncatio*, fr. L *truncatus* (past part. of *truncare* to cut off) + *-ion-, -io* -ion] **1 a :** an act or instance of truncating ⟨loss of section . . . by ~ following uplift —*Jour. of Geol.*⟩ ⟨~ of street corners should be aimed at . . . to increase visibility —John Kemp⟩ **b :** omission at the beginning or end of an element (as an unstressed syllable) normally present or expected in a line or other unit of verse — compare CATALEXIS, BROKEN-BACKED LINE **c :** a truncated point or area ⟨the ~ on the edge of a crystal⟩ **2 :** the replacement of an edge or solid angle (as of a crystal) by a plane and esp. by one equally inclined to the adjoining faces **3 :** the quality or state of being truncated ⟨after revising his work . . . gave it an effect of ~ and bareness —Van Wyck Brooks⟩

trun·ca·ture \ˈtrəŋkəˌchu̇(ə)r\ *n* -S **:** TRUNCATION

¹trun·cheon \ˈtrənchən\ *n* -S [ME *tronchoun*, fr. MF *tronchon*, fr. (assumed) VL *truncion-, truncio*, fr. L *truncus* trunk, torso + *-ion-, -io* -ion — more at TRUNCATE] **1 :** a broken remnant esp. of a shattered spear or lance ⟨an arm embowed in armor . . . holding a ~ of a broken lance —*Burke's Peerage*⟩ **2 a** *obs* **:** a heavy club : BLUDGEON ⟨thy leg a stick compared with this ~ —Shak.⟩ **b :** a staff carried as a symbol of authority; *esp* : BATON ⟨a king at arms, whose hand the armorial ~ held —Sir Walter Scott⟩ **c :** a policeman's billy : NIGHTSTICK ⟨constables kept the crowd off with ~*s* —Arnold Bennett⟩ **3 :** a relatively thick stem cutting or long branch (as of a willow) used for propagating a plant

²truncheon \ˈ"\ *vt* -ED/-ING/-S *archaic* **:** to beat with a truncheon

trun·cheoned \-chənd\ *adj* **:** having a truncheon

trun·cus \ˈtrəŋkəs\ *n* -ES [L] **:** TRUNK 1a, 1b, 6a

truncus ar·te·ri·o·sus \ˈ==(ˌ)ärˌtirēˈōsəs\ *n* [NL, arterial trunk] **:** the part of the arterial system within the pericardium connecting the ventricle and ventral aorta in anamniotes and early developmental stages of amniotes; *specif* : the part of the truncus arteriosus between the bulbus arteriosus and the ventral aorta

¹trun·dle \ˈtrəndᵊl, ÷ -nᵊl\ *n* -S [alter. of *trendle*] **1 a :** a small wheel or roller ⟨the tip end of the nozzle rolls along on a freewheeling little ~ —*New Yorker*⟩ **b :** CIRCLET, HOOP ⟨the circular rampart being like a hoop or ~ —Jacquetta & Christopher Hawkes⟩ **c :** a small vertical pin in the action of an organ stop for transmitting motion from the stop knob to the trace **2 a :** LANTERN PINION **b :** any of the bars of such a trundle **3 :** a low-wheeled cart or truck

²trundle \ˈ"\ *vb* **trundled**; **trundled**; **trundling** \-n(d)(ᵊ)liŋ\ **trundles** *vt* **1 a :** to propel by causing to rotate : BOWL, ROLL ⟨*trundled* a new tire through the sand —Vicki Baum⟩ **b** *archaic* **:** to cause to revolve : SPIN ⟨attains the same result by *trundling* the glass during reheating —H.J.Powell⟩; *esp* : to remove water from (a mop) by twirling **2 a :** to transport in a wheeled vehicle : HAUL, WHEEL ⟨the local bus . . . *trundling* its load —Adrian Bell⟩ ⟨was put into a wheelchair and *trundled* down to the hospital library —Ben Benson⟩ ⟨*trundled* wheelbarrows of dirt —R.A.Billington⟩ **b :** to cause to move on trundles : CONVEY, PUSH ⟨machines . . . are *trundled* around on ball-bearing turntables —Bryan Morgan⟩ **~** *vi* **1 a :** to progress by revolving ⟨start a barrel *trundling* down a chute⟩ **b :** BOWL 4 **2 a :** to move on or as if on wheels : ROLL ⟨rickety old vehicles . . . ~ from city to city with loads of chickens —*N.Y.Times*⟩ ⟨the tram *trundled* away from them —Richard Blaker⟩ ⟨heaped-up cloud towers were *trundling* across the heavens —Eugene Walter⟩ **b :** to ride in a wheeled vehicle : TRAVEL ⟨called a taxi and *trundled* down to the offices —Dorothy Sayers⟩ ⟨*trundling* off aboard a suburban bus —Bennett Cerf⟩ **c :** to move ponderously : CHURN, LUMBER ⟨a battery had *trundled* into position . . . and was thoughtfully shelling the distance —Stephen Crane⟩ **3 :** to move or go at a constant rate esp. with a rolling gait ⟨a moving bundle of brush, he *trundled* away into the thicket —Margaret Peattie⟩

trundle bed *n* **1 :** a low bed usu. on casters that can be pushed under a higher bed — called also *truckle bed* **2 :** a two-bed unit designed to allow one bed to be slid under the other

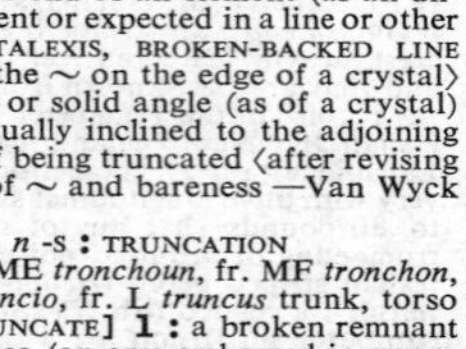
trundle bed

trundlehead \ˈ==ˌ=\ *n* **1 :** one of the disks forming the ends of a lantern pinion **2 :** the drumhead of a capstan

trun·dler \-n(d)(ᵊ)lə(r)\ *n* -S **:** one that trundles; *esp* : the bowler in cricket

trundle-tail \ˈ==ˌ=\ *n, archaic* **:** a curly-tailed dog : MONGREL ⟨bobtail tyke or *trundle-tail* —Shak.⟩

trung cha \ˈtru̇ŋˈchä\ *n, pl* **trung cha** *or* **trung chas** *usu cap T&C* **1 :** a mountain people of Tonkin in Vietnam **2 :** a member of the Trung Cha people

¹trunk \ˈtrəŋk\ *n* -S [ME *trunke, tronke* chest, box, trunk, fr. MF *tronc*, fr. L *truncus* trunk of a tree, torso, shaft of a column] **1 a :** the main stem of a tree apart from its limbs and roots **b** (1) **:** the human body apart from the head and appendages (2) *obs* : BODY **c** (1) **:** the thorax of an insect (2) **:** the body of a fish from the operculum to the anus **d :** the central part of anything; *specif* : the shaft of a column or pilaster **2 a** (1) **:** a box or tank for keeping fish alive after they are caught (2) *dial Brit* : HOOP NET **b** *obs* : an ornamental chest (as a jewel casket) or a box (as a packing case) used for storage **c** (1) **:** a piece of luggage that has a rigid frame, that is too large to be carried by hand, and that is used usu. for transporting a traveler's clothing and other personal effects (2) **:** the luggage compartment of an automobile **d** (1) **:** a superstructure over a ship's hatches usu. level with the poop deck, extending from one half to three quarters of the length of the ship, and having the main deck carried around it (2) **:** the roof and upper part of the sides of the cabin of a boat projecting above the deck (3) **:** the housing for a centerboard or rudder — see CENTERBOARD illustration **3 a :** PIPE, TUBE — compare TRUNK ENGINE **b :** PROBOSCIS; *esp* : the long muscular tubular extension of the nose of the elephant having the nostrils at its tip, serving as a prehensile organ either by coiling about an object to be seized or by the use of a small movable grasping process at its extremity, and used esp. to convey food or drink to the mouth and as a weapon **c** *or* **trunk glass** *obs* : TELESCOPE **4 trunks** *pl* **a** *obs* : TRUNK HOSE **b** *archaic* : BREECHES, KNICKERBOCKERS **c :** men's shorts worn chiefly for sports **5 a :** a passage or duct (as a wooden box conduit for carrying air to mine workings) **b :** LAUNDER **c :** WIND-TRUNK **d** (1) **:** a vertical shaft between decks (as a casing for access or ventilation) (2) **:** a chute for loading or coaling a ship **6 a :** the principal channel of a tributary system ⟨nerve ~⟩ ⟨~ of a river⟩ ⟨~ of an artery⟩ **b :** a circuit between two telephone exchanges or telephone switching devices for making connections between subscribers **c :** TRUNK LINE

²trunk \ˈ"\ *adj* **1 a :** of, relating to, or resembling a box or trunk ⟨~ lid⟩ ⟨~ load⟩ ⟨~ buoy⟩ **b :** used for storing luggage ⟨~ compartment⟩ **2 a :** of or relating to the torso ⟨determining ~ height . . . of these pygmies —*Amer. Anthropologist*⟩ **b :** of or relating to a tree trunk ⟨~ borer⟩ **3 :** having or consisting of a tube ⟨~ piston⟩ **4 :** having, using, or controlling the flow in a duct or chute ⟨~ machine⟩ **5 :** of, relating to, or constituting a primary segment or principal channel ⟨~ road⟩ ⟨~ stream⟩ ⟨~ pipeline⟩ ⟨~ wire of a teletype service⟩ ⟨~ airline⟩

³trunk \ˈ"\ *vt* -ED/-ING/-S **:** to enclose in a trunk or casing

trunkback \ˈ=ˌ=\ *n* **:** LEATHERBACK 1

trunk cabin *n* **:** a cabin on a boat (as a yacht) with the upper portion projecting above the deck

trunk call *n* **:** a long-distance telephone call

trunk deck *n* **:** the top of a ship's trunk usu. containing the hatchways, ventilators, and deck openings

trunk dial *n* **:** a spring-driven clock having an elongated case below the large dial to accommodate a pendulum

¹trunked *adj* [fr. past part. of obs. E *trunk* to cut off, truncate, fr. ME *trunken*, fr. L *truncare* — more at TRUNCATE] **:** having the head or top cut off : TRUNCATED

²trunked \ˈtrəŋkt\ *adj* [¹*trunk* + *-ed*] **1 :** having a trunk — often used in combination ⟨straight-*trunked*⟩ ⟨single-*trunked*⟩ ⟨gray-*trunked* beeches —E.W.Smith⟩ **2 :** having a proboscis ⟨~ mammal⟩

trunk engine *n* **1 :** a steam engine having a piston rod that is a pipe of sufficient diameter to enable one end of the connecting rod to be attached to the crank and the other end to pass within the pipe and be pivoted to the piston **2 :** an engine (as most internal-combustion engines) having a trunk piston

trunkfish \ˈ=ˌ=\ *n* **:** BOXFISH

trunk·ful \ˈtrəŋkˌfu̇l\ *n, pl* **trunk·fuls** *also* **trunks·ful** \-kˌfu̇lz, -kˌsfu̇l\ **1 :** as much or as many as a trunk will hold ⟨twenty ~*s* of memorabilia —R.L.Taylor⟩ ⟨*trunksful* of letters —*Time*⟩ ⟨elephants blowing ~*s* of the cooling water over parched . . . backs —Tom Marvel⟩ **2 :** a great many ⟨a ~ of ancient jokes —*Newsweek*⟩

trunk glacier *n* **:** a valley glacier formed by the flowing together of tributary glaciers

trunk hose *or* **trunk breeches** *n pl* [*trunk* prob. fr. obs. E *trunk* to cut off, truncate; fr. the fact that it was a truncated hose] **:** short full breeches reaching about halfway down the thigh and sometimes attached to the hose, usu. padded and slashed, and worn chiefly in the late 16th and early 17th centuries — see NETHERSTOCK illustration

trunking *n* -S [fr. gerund of ³*trunk*] **1 :** an act or instance of employing a trunk **2 a :** a casing to protect electrical conductors **b :** TRUNK 5d(1) **3 a :** the provision of adequate trunks and switching facilities in either a manual or automatic communications system **b :** the interconnections provided

trunk·less \ˈtrəŋkləs\ *adj* **:** lacking a body; *esp* : severed from the trunk ⟨~ head⟩ ⟨~ brushwood⟩

trunk line *n* **1 :** a system (as for transportation) handling long-distance through traffic : MAIN LINE ⟨like any highway system, the federal airways have their main *trunk lines* as well as feeder routes —*Monsanto Mag.*⟩; *specif* : one of the railway systems whose main lines run from Chicago to New York **2 a :** a main supply channel (as a natural-gas main) **b :** a direct link (as a telephone circuit between two switchboards)

trunkmaker \ˈ=ˌ==\ *n* [so called fr. the fact that in making trunks the pages were used as lining] *archaic* **:** a depository for unsalable books

trunknose \ˈ=ˌ=\ *n* **:** ELEPHANT SEAL

trunk piston *or* **trunk plunger** *n* **:** an elongated hollow piston in a single-acting engine or pump which is open at the end and in which the end of the connecting rod is pivoted

trunk room *n* **:** a storage room esp. for storing luggage

trunk scald *n* **:** winter sunscald affecting the trunk of a tree

trunk sleeve *n* [*trunk* prob. fr. obs. E *trunk* to cut off, truncate; fr. its being a truncated sleeve — more at TRUNKED] **:** a large usu. slashed and padded sleeve resembling trunk hose

trunk turtle *n* **:** LEATHERBACK 1

trunkway \ˈ=ˌ=\ *n* [²*trunk* + *way*] **:** TRUNK 5d(1)

trunk whale *n* **:** SPERM WHALE

trun·nel \ˈtrənᵊl\ *var of* TREENAIL

trun·nion \ˈtrənyən\ *n* -S [F *trognon* core, stalk, stump] **1 :** either of two opposite gudgeons on which a cannon is swiveled — see CANNON illustration **2 :** a pin or pivot usu. mounted on bearings for rotating or tilting something — **trun·nioned** \-yənd\ *adj*

¹truss \ˈtrəs\ *vt* -ED/-ING/-ES [ME *trussen*, fr. OF *trousser, tourser*, prob. fr. (assumed) VL *torciare*, fr. *torca* bundle, torch — more at TORCH] **1 a :** to secure closely or tightly : BIND, TIE ⟨attacked and ~*ed* a guard —*Springfield (Mass.) Union*⟩ — often used with *up* ⟨the victim, a middle-aged woman, had been expertly ~*ed up* —E.D.Radin⟩ **b :** to arrange for cooking by binding the wings or legs of (as fowl) close to the body **c :** to bind together the staves of (a barrel) with hoops to force into the desired shape and assure tightness of joints **2** *archaic* **:** to pack into a bundle **3 a :** to put clothes on (the body) so as to confine tightly ⟨gentlemen ~*ed* in broadcloth to the Adam's apple —*Amer. Guide Series: N. Y. City*⟩ **b** *archaic* **:** to fasten or arrange the clothing of; *specif* : to draw tight and tie firmly (as laces or strings) **c** *archaic* **:** to arrange (the hair) in a neat fashion : DRESS **4** *archaic* : HANG — often used with *up* **5 :** to take fast hold of; *esp* : to seize and bear off — used of a hawk or other bird of prey **6 :** to support by a truss : strengthen or stiffen (as a beam or girder) by a brace or braces esp. so as to constitute a truss

²truss \ˈ"\ *n* -ES [ME *trusse*, fr. OF *trousse, tourse*, fr. *trousser, tourser* to truss] **1 a :** something bound or packed together : BUNDLE, PACK ⟨bearing a ~ of trifles at his back —Edmund Spenser⟩ **b** *Brit* **:** any of various units of quantity for hay or straw: as (1) **:** a bundle of old hay weighing 56 pounds (2) **:** a bundle of new hay weighing 60 pounds (3) **:** a bundle of straw weighing 36 pounds **2 a :** a connection to secure a yard to a mast; *specif* : an iron band around a lower mast with a pivoted attachment to a lower yard at the center to keep the yard in position and allow it to be braced around **3 a :** BRACKET 1 **b :** an assemblage of members (as beams, bars, rods) typically arranged in a triangle or combination of triangles to form a rigid framework (as for supporting a load over a wide area) that cannot be deformed by the application of exterior force without deformation of one or more of its members **c :** a tripod of logs or timbers on which hay is piled for curing in the field **4 :** a device worn to hold a hernia in place **5 :** a compact flower cluster (as in the lilac) or fruit cluster (as in the tomato)

³truss \ˈ"\ *adj, archaic* **:** compactly framed

truss beam *n* **:** a beam reinforced by a truss rod or formed of straight or cambered pieces joined by trussing

truss bow *n* **:** a semicircular jointed portion of a truss holding the center of a lower yard to the mast

truss bridge *n* **:** a bridge supported mainly by trusses — see BRIDGE illustration

trus·sell \ˈtrəsəl\ *n* -S [ME, bundle, trussell, fr. MF *troussel, trousel*, dim. of OF *trousse* truss] **:** the upper die of an old English apparatus for striking coins by hand with a hammer — compare PILE 3a

truss·er \ˈtrəsə(r)\ *n* -S **:** one that trusses ⟨a ~ of hay⟩ ⟨a ~ of poultry⟩: as **a :** a machine for trussing barrels **b :** the operator of a trussing machine

truss hoop *n* **1 a :** the band of a truss encircling the mast **b :** one of the truss bands that encircle a yard **2 :** a hoop placed around the staves of a barrel (as by a trusser) to force them into shape and position

trussing *n* -S [fr. gerund of ¹*truss*] **1 :** the members forming a truss **2 :** the trusses and framework of a structure

truss leg *n* **:** a leg having the form of a prolonged corbel or console — see LEG illustration

truss rod *n* **1 :** a tensioned rod for trussing a wooden beam **2 :** a diagonal tie rod in a truss

trusswork \ˈ=ˌ=\ *n* **:** work consisting of trusses

¹trust \ˈtrəst\ *n* -S [ME *trust, trost*, prob. of Scand origin; akin to ON *traust* trust; akin to OHG *trōst* trust, Goth *trausti* agreement, pact, ON *trūa* trust, faith, OE *trūwian* to trust, inspire with trust, *trēowe* faithful, trustworthy — more at TRUE] **1 a :** assured reliance on some person or thing : a confident dependence on the character, ability, strength, or truth of someone or something : BELIEF ⟨nor should a physician do anything to diminish the ~ reposed by the patient in his own physician —W.T. & Barbara Fitts⟩ ⟨the ~ that farmer places in the fertilizer operator —*Monsanto Mag.*⟩ ⟨being ignorant of these matters, I take it all on ~ —H.J.Laski⟩ **b :** a person or thing in which confidence is placed : a basis of reliance, faith, or hope ⟨God, thou art my ~ from my youth —Ps 71:5 (AV)⟩ ⟨if I have made gold my ~ —Job 31:24 (RSV)⟩ **2 a :** dependence on something future or contingent : confident anticipation : HOPE ⟨hurried down to those who were waiting in joyful ~ —George Meredith⟩ **b :** reliance on future payment for merchandise or other property delivered : CREDIT ⟨sell on ~⟩ **3 a :** an equitable right or interest in property distinct from the legal ownership of it : a property interest held by one person for the benefit of another — see LIVING TRUST, MASSACHUSETTS TRUST, PASSIVE TRUST, SPENDTHRIFT TRUST, TESTAMENTARY TRUST **b** (1) **:** a combination of firms or corporations formed by an agreement legally establishing a trust whereby stockholders in the separate corporations exchange their shares for shares representing proportionate interest in the principal and income of the combination and surrender to the trustees the management and operation of the combined firms or corporations (2) **:** a combination or aggregation of business entities formed by any of various means; *esp* : one that reduces competition or is thought to present a threat of reducing competition **4** *archaic* : TRUSTWORTHINESS ⟨there's no ~, no faith, no honesty in men —Shak.⟩ **5 a** (1) **:** a charge or duty imposed in faith or confidence or as a condition of some relationship ⟨accept, as a sacred ~, the obligation to promote to the largest possible extent the welfare of such peoples —B.A.G.Cohen⟩ (2) **:** something committed or entrusted to one to be used or cared for in the interest of another ⟨no religious test shall ever be required as a qualification to any office or public ~ under the United States —*U. S. Constitution*⟩ **b :** the condition, obligation, or right of one to whom something is confided : responsible charge or office ⟨feel that my ~ as chairman of the board of this bank requires me to exert every effort —W.W.Aldrich⟩ ⟨sometimes people fail in their ~, but they live up to it far more often —*Boy Scout Handbk.*⟩ **c :** CARE, CUSTODY ⟨a child committed to his ~⟩

syn CONFIDENCE, RELIANCE, DEPENDENCE, FAITH: TRUST implies an assured attitude toward another which may rest on blended evidence of experience and more subjective grounds such as knowledge, affection, admiration, respect, or reverence ⟨to Miss Biddums he confided with equal *trust* his tattered garments and his more serious griefs —Rudyard Kipling⟩ ⟨his youthful optimism and his cheerful *trust* in men —Katherine McNamara⟩ CONFIDENCE may indicate a feeling of sureness about another that is based on experience and evidence without strong effect of the subjective ⟨both of whom had profound *confidence* in him —T.M.Spaulding⟩ ⟨he apparently has won the *confidence* of farm workers, merchants and others, who continue to elect him —Harold Callender⟩ RELIANCE may be used readily in contexts in which assuredness in another has formed the basis for some choice or decision ⟨his diffidence had prevented his depending on his own judgment in so anxious a case, but his *reliance* on mine made everything easy —Jane Austen⟩ ⟨had written out his Christmas sermon with a good deal of care and an excessive *reliance* on what other preachers had said before him —Compton Mackenzie⟩ DEPENDENCE is likely to suggest lack of independence and inability to act for one's self while relying on another ⟨the drastic effect on a girl's life of the mother's *dependence* on her —Leslie Rees⟩ ⟨a woman who did not regard the change from economic independence on an employer to economic *dependence* on a man, as an honorable promotion —Virginia Woolf⟩ FAITH may indicate a confidence that transcends, waives, or violates factual evidence ⟨although I already had great *faith* in the mental capacity of the Polynesians, even I was astounded at the facility with which the students forged ahead —V.G.Heiser⟩ ⟨a lasting *faith* that not everything in the dreams I dreamed as an undergraduate can possibly have been false —T.R.Ybarra⟩

— **in trust** *adv* **:** in the care or possession of a trustee ⟨the property of the State to be forever held *in trust* for the people —*Amer. Guide Series: Mich.*⟩

²trust \ˈ"\ *adj* **:** held in trust

³trust \ˈ"\ *vb* -ED/-ING/-S [ME *trusten, trosten*, prob. of Scand origin; akin to ON *treysta* to trust, *traust* trust] *vi* **1 a :** to place confidence : DEPEND — used with *in* or *to* ⟨hope for the best, and ~ in God —Sydney Smith⟩ ⟨flung together a jumble of material, and ~*ed* to its timeliness to sell —V.L.Parrington⟩ ⟨~ to luck⟩ **b :** to be confident : HOPE ⟨need not succumb to panic, however, if we will ~ and not be afraid —J.W.McKelvey⟩ ⟨will see you soon, I ~⟩ **2 :** to sell or deliver on credit **~** *vt* **1 a :** to commit or place with confidence : confer as a trust : ENTRUST ⟨~ my precious flowers to a mere man —Margaret Deland⟩ ⟨such trees must be cared for . . . almost no owner would, or does, ~ them to a tenant —B.H.Hibbard⟩ **b :** to permit to stay or go somewhere or to do something without fear or misgiving : venture confidently ⟨sealed my letter, and not ~*ing* it out of my own hands, delivered it myself —Charles Dickens⟩ **c :** to confer a trust on : give something into the care or possession of ⟨~*ed* his son with the family car⟩ ⟨~*ed* him with her story⟩ **2 a :** to rely on the truthfulness or accuracy of : BELIEVE, CREDIT ⟨if we may ~ him as a witness⟩ ⟨if rumor may be ~*ed*⟩ **b :** to place confidence in : have faith in : rely on ⟨~ the storekeeper from whom you buy your baseball mitt to sell you a good one —*Boy Scout Handbk.*⟩ ⟨was widely ~*ed* and loved by the community as a whole —K.S.Latourette⟩ ⟨~ him to know when to keep quiet⟩ **c :** to hope or expect confidently ⟨~*ed* the sight of that barren mountainside would compensate us for all the discomforts —W.H.Hudson †1922⟩ ⟨~*ed* to find oil on the land⟩ **3 :** to extend credit to ⟨do you suppose he'd mind ~*ing* me for the other dollar-ninety —MacKinlay Kantor⟩ **syn** see RELY

trust·abil·i·ty \ˌtrəstəˈbiləd·ē\ *n* **:** the quality or state of being trustable

trust·able \ˈtrəstəbəl\ *adj* **:** capable of being trusted

trust account *n* **:** an account opened with a trust company under which a living or testamentary trust is set up

trust agreement *n* **:** an agreement establishing and setting forth the material terms of a trust

trustbuster \ˈ=ˌ==\ *n* [¹*trust* + *buster*] **:** one who seeks to break up business trusts; *specif* : a federal official (as a district attorney) who prosecutes trusts under the antitrust laws

trust-busting \ˈ=ˌ==\ *n* **:** a legal action or political campaign to break up trusts

trust certificate *n* **:** a certificate issued and sold as one of a series by the trustee of designated trust property (as an investment trust, railroad equipment, or business trust) legally held evidencing a specified fractional equitable or beneficial interest

in the trust property existing in the holder or registered owner of the certificate, incorporating the particular trust agreement, setting forth the principal rights of the certificate owner to share in the income, profits, or gains realized from the trust property and in any current or future distributions of it, and prescribing the mode of transfer of the certificate

trust company *n* **:** a corporation organized to perform the fiduciary functions of trusts and agencies; *esp* **:** COMMERCIAL BANK

trust deed *n* **:** a deed conveying property in trust and often used as a mortgage to secure an obligation

¹**trust·ee** \ˌtrəˈstē\ *n* -S [³*trust* + *-ee*] **1 :** one to whom something is entrusted **:** one trusted to keep or administer something ⟨custodians of very glorious traditions, and the ~*s* of a spiritual wealth —W.R.Inge⟩: as **a :** a member of a board entrusted with administering the funds and directing the policy of an institution or organization (as a school, hospital, philanthropic foundation) **b :** a country charged with the supervision of a trust territory **2 a :** a person whether real or juristic to whom property is legally committed in trust **:** one holding legal title to property which he must administer for the benefit of a beneficiary or for a purpose recognized as legally charitable or as lawful by statute **b :** one in whose hands the effects of another are attached by the trustee process **c :** one held to a fiduciary duty similar in some respects to that of a trustee ⟨the directors of a bank may be ~*s* for the depositors⟩ ⟨directors of a corporation are ~*s* for the stockholders⟩ ⟨a guardian is ~ of his ward's property⟩

²**trustee** \"\ *vb* **trusteed; trusteed; trusteeing; trustees** *vt* **:** to commit to the care of a trustee ⟨required to either sell or ~ their holdings in one or the other end of the business —*Springfield (Mass.) Union*⟩ ⟨whose scheme of social organization is to be adopted in the *trusteed* areas of the world —Isaiah Bowman⟩ ~ *vi* **:** to serve as trustee

³**trustee** *var of* TRUSTY

trusteed plan *n* [*trusteed* fr. past part. of ²*trustee*] **:** a pension or retirement plan under which contributions are paid to a trustee who invests the funds and pays benefits to eligible employees — compare UNFUNDED PLAN

trustee ex ma·le·fi·cio \ˌekˌsmaləˈfikēˌō, -mäl-\ *or* **trustee ex de·lic·to** \-ˌeksdəˈlik(ˌ)tō\ *n* **:** a person treated as a trustee because guilty of wrongdoing and compelled to account as though he were a trustee for property to which he has legal title for the benefit of those injured and equitably entitled to it

trustee in bankruptcy : a person in whom the property of a bankrupt is vested by a court for the benefit of the creditors and who administers the property under the direction of the court for the purpose of distributing the net proceeds therefrom pro rata among his creditors according to the priority of their established claims

trustee in in·vi·tum \-ˌinənˈwēˌtüm, -ˈvīd·əm\ *n* **:** a person treated as a trustee of property because he has acted without authority or in excess of his authority in respect to that property

trustee process *n* **:** the process of attachment by garnishment or in the New England states by foreign attachment — compare EQUITABLE GARNISHMENT

trustee security *n* **:** a security in which a trustee may properly invest and which is often described in the trust instrument or in an approved list established in accordance with law

trust·ee·ship \ˌtrəˈstēˌship\ *n* **1 :** the office or function of a trustee **2 :** authorized supervisory control by one or more countries as trustee of the administration of a trust territory under the international system of the United Nations

trust·en \ˈtrəsᵊn\ *vi* -ED/-ING/-S [ME *trustnen*, fr. ¹*trust* + *-nen* -en] *dial Eng* **:** TRUST

trust·er \ˈtrəstə(r)\ *n* -S **1 :** one that relies, credits, or believes **2** *Scots law* **:** one that creates a trust

trust estate *n* **:** an estate subject to a trust or held in trust

trust·ful \-stfəl\ *adj* **:** full of trust **:** being without suspicion **:** CONFIDING ⟨great brown eyes, true and ~ —C.B.Nordhoff & J.N.Hall⟩ — **trust·ful·ly** \-fəlē, -li\ *adv* — **trust·ful·ness** *n* -ES

trust fund *n* **1 :** TRUST ESTATE; *esp* **:** money, securities, or similar property settled or held in trust **2 :** a property for which the holder or manager is held accountable as if he were a trustee

trustier *comparative of* TRUSTY

trusties *pl of* TRUSTY

trustiest *superlative of* TRUSTY

trust·ifi·ca·tion \ˌtrəstəfəˈkāshən\ *n* -S [fr. *trustify*, after such pairs as E *ramify: ramification*] **:** the process of forming a trust or of organizing into a system of trusts ⟨~ went on at a rapid pace; the size of American business expanded greatly —Isaac Lippincott⟩

trust·ify \ˈ==ˌfī\ *vb* -ED/-ING/-ES [¹*trust* + *-ify*] *vt* **:** to form into a trust ⟨a *trustified* industry⟩ ~ *vi* **:** to form a trust ⟨put a damper on the urge to ~ —J.R.Chamberlain⟩

trust·i·ly \ˈtrəstəlē\ *adv* [ME *trustily, trostily*, fr. *trusty, trosty* trusty + *-ly*] **:** in a trusty manner

trust indenture *n* **:** a document under which a trust (as a mutual investment fund) is conducted

trust·i·ness \ˈtrəstēnəs, -tin-\ *n* -ES **:** the quality or state of being trusty

trusting *pres part of* TRUST

trust·ing·ly *adv* **:** in a trusting manner

trust·ing·ness *n* -ES **:** the quality or state of being trusting

trust institution *n* **:** a corporation engaged in the business of administering estates and trusts; *also* **:** the trust department of a trust company or other banking institution

trust instrument *n* **:** the legal document (as a will, deed, agreement, or a declaration of trust) by which a trust is created

trus·tle \ˈtrəsəl\ *dial var of* TRESTLE

trust·less \ˈtrəstləs\ *adj* **1 :** not deserving of trust **:** FAITHLESS, FALSE, UNTRUSTWORTHY ⟨keep your heart for men like me and safe from ~ chaps —A.E.Housman⟩ **2 :** DISTRUSTFUL ⟨winning the trust of a ~ mind —Constance Woolson⟩ — **trust·less·ly** *adv* — **trust·less·ness** *n* -ES

trust·man \ˈtrəstˌman, -mən\ *n, pl* **trustmen :** one whose occupation is handling trusts either in the service of a trust institution or privately

trust mortgage *n* **1 :** a mortgage made to a trustee generally to secure an issue of bonds or a series of obligations wherein the rights of the parties are declared in a trust agreement set forth or referred to in the mortgage **2 :** a mortgage given by a debtor in distress to a trustee of all his business assets with authority to the trustee to operate the business until the debts are paid and then return the assets to the debtor or with authority to foreclose if the business cannot be operated profitably

trust officer *n* **:** an officer of a trust institution

trus·tor \ˈtrəstə(r), ˌtrəˈstȯ(ə)r\ *n* -S [³*trust* + *-or*] **:** the donor, settlor, grantor, or other person creating a trust by transferring his property to a trustee

trust property *n* **:** property held in or subject to a trust

trust receipt *n* **:** a trust agreement between a bank and its debtor by which the bank gives up possession of collateral security to the debtor without abandoning its title to the security and the debtor agrees to hold the security in trust for the bank and if the security is sold to hold the proceeds in trust for the bank and to pay them to the bank in settlement of the indebtedness

trusts *pl of* TRUST, *pres 3d sing of* TRUST

trust territory *n* **:** a non-self-governing territory placed under an administrative authority by the Trusteeship Council of the United Nations as being a former mandate under the League of Nations, a territory taken from a former enemy state as a result of World War II, or a territory voluntarily placed under the international system by the state responsible for its administration

trustwoman \ˈ=ˌ==\ *n, pl* **trustwomen :** a woman whose occupation is handling trusts either in the service of a trust institution or privately

trust·wor·thi·ly \ˈtrəsˌtwərthəlē, -wȯth-, -wəith-, -li\ *adv* **:** in a trustworthy manner

trust·wor·thi·ness \-thēnəs, -thin-\ *n* **:** the quality or state of being trustworthy

trust·wor·thy \-thē, -thi\ *adj* **:** worthy of confidence **:** DEPENDABLE ⟨an obedient and ~ officer —Stanley Pargellis⟩ ⟨no ~ story can be put together from the myth, tradition, and conscious fiction —H.O.Taylor⟩ **syn** see RELIABLE

¹**trusty** \ˈtrəstē, -sti\ *adj* -ER/-EST [ME *trusty, trosty*, fr. *trust, trost* trust + *-y* — more at TRUST] **1** *archaic* **:** having trust **:** CONFIDING, TRUSTFUL **2 :** fit to be trusted **:** deserving confidence **:** TRUSTWORTHY ⟨his ~, battered camera —Tom Marvel⟩ **3** *obs* **:** involving trust ⟨might at some great and ~ business in a main danger fail you —Shak.⟩ **syn** see RELIABLE

²**trusty** \"\ *also* **trust·ee** \ˌtrəˈstē *or like* TRUSTY\ *n, pl* **trusties** *also* **trustees** [*trustee* alter. (influenced by ¹*trustee*) of *trusty*] **:** a trusty or trusted person; *specif* **:** a convict considered trustworthy and allowed special privileges

truth \ˈtrüth\ *n, pl* **truths** \-üthz *also* -üths\ [ME *trewthe, treuthe*, fr. OE *trēowth, trīewth*; akin to OHG *getriuwida* fidelity, ON *tryggth* faith, trustiness; derivative fr. the root of E ¹*true*] **1 a** *archaic* **:** the quality or state of being faithful **:** FIDELITY, CONSTANCY ⟨whispering tongues can poison ~ —S.T.Coleridge⟩ **b :** sincerity in character, action, and speech **:** genuineness in expressing feeling or belief **:** TRUTHFULNESS, HONESTY ⟨gives a man a clear conscious view of his own opinions and judgments, a ~ in developing them —J.H. Newman⟩ ⟨the absolute ~ of his speech, and the rectitude of his behavior —R.W.Emerson⟩ **2 :** something that is true or held to be true: as **a** (1) **:** the real state of affairs **:** something that is the case **:** FACT ⟨the hard ~ was that few of America's allies believed that the . . . islands were worth fighting for —*Newsweek*⟩ ⟨the present definition of insanity has little relation to the ~*s* of mental life —B.N.Cardozo⟩ (2) **:** the body of things, events, and facts that make up the universe **:** actual existence **:** ACTUALITY ⟨the facets of reality . . . together comprising what the human spirit can call ~ —*General Education in a Free Society*⟩ (3) *often cap* **:** a fundamental or spiritual reality conceived of as being partly or wholly transcendent of perceived actuality and experience ⟨modern man . . . was capable of the relative and changing ~*s* of science, incapable and afraid of any supratemporal ~ reached by Reason's metaphysical effort or of the divine —Jacques Maritain⟩ ⟨got only the facts and not the ~ —W.A.White⟩ (4) **:** the world of a particular person or in a particular manner ⟨a psychotic's ~ is what "I" make it —Weston La Barre⟩ ⟨the ~ of speculative inquiry had been replaced by the ~ of empirical investigation —R.M.Weaver⟩ **b** (1) **:** a true relation or account ⟨to say ~, it can only be regarded as a kind of literary curiosity —Daniel George⟩ ⟨~ is stranger than fiction⟩ (2) **:** a judgment, proposition, statement, or idea that accords with fact or reality, is logically or intuitively necessary, or follows by sound reasoning from established or necessary truths ⟨two plus two equals four . . . that is a ~ anywhere —W.J.Reilly⟩ ⟨there are ~*s* which cannot be verified, yet we cannot help accepting them as true —Rubin Gotesky⟩; *specif* **:** a proposition or statement taken as an axiom, postulate, or principle in a field of study or inquiry ⟨questioned the basic ~*s* of thermodynamics⟩ (3) **:** TRUISM, PLATITUDE ⟨a ~ we are in danger of forgetting —Marie Hildegarde⟩ (4) **:** a notion having wide and uncritical acceptance among a group or in a field and liable to be proved false ⟨worshipped their flimsy hypotheses into ~*s* —Weston La Barre⟩ **c :** the body of true statements and propositions; *also* **:** the body of statements and propositions accepted, studied, or proved in a field ⟨seems to suggest that these are different and unrelated ~*s* — theological truth, psychotherapeutic truth, political truth —R.L.Howe⟩ ⟨every way of abstracting produces its own kind of ~ —S.I.Hayakawa⟩ **3 a :** relationship, conformity, or agreement with fact or reality or among true facts or propositions **:** the property in a conception, judgment, statement, proposition, belief, or opinion of being in accord with what is in fact or in necessity ⟨~ (or falsity) is a property of declarative sentences —Philip Hallie⟩ ⟨the test for ~ is objective and is not concerned with ministering to subjective feelings, needs, or desires —Jim Cork⟩ — see COHERENCE THEORY, CORRESPONDENCE THEORY, EMPIRICAL TRUTH, FORMAL TRUTH, METAPHYSICAL TRUTH, NORMATIVE TRUTH, PRAGMATISM, SEMANTIC CONCEPTION **b** *chiefly Brit* **:** TRUE 2 ⟨these squares must be tested for ~ —Laurence Town⟩ ⟨her propeller shaft was a trifle out of ~ —C.S. Forester⟩ **c** (1) **:** fidelity to an original or a possible original ⟨an ignorant, uneducated man may be a competent judge of the ~ of the representation of a sandal —Joshua Reynolds⟩ ⟨ability to build up the ~ of his characters through spare, pungent dialogue —Arthur Knight⟩ (2) **:** the conformity of a work of art to the essential significance of the subject, to the artist's conception or intent, or to some standard **:** the coherence of form and content in an apparently necessary whole ⟨what the imagination seizes as Beauty must be *Truth* — whether it existed before or not —John Keats⟩ ⟨a sturdy example of functional ~ in architecture —*Amer. Guide Series: Vt.*⟩ **4 a** *often cap* **:** abstract truth personified as a goddess **b** *cap, Christian Science* **:** GOD

syn VERACITY, VERITY, VERISIMILITUDE: TRUTH is a general term ranging in meaning from a transcendent idea to an indication of conformity with fact and of avoidance of error, misrepresentation, or falsehood ⟨the *truths* of religion are more like the *truths* of poetry than like the *truths* of science; that is, they are vision and insight, apprehended by the whole man, and not merely by the analysing mind —*Times Lit. Supp.*⟩ ⟨*truth* as the opposite of error and of falsehood —C.W.Eliot⟩ VERACITY commonly indicates rigid and unfailing adherence to, observance of, or respect for truth ⟨question an opponent's *veracity*⟩ ⟨his passion for *veracity* always kept him from taking any unfair rhetorical advantages of an opponent —Aldous Huxley⟩ ⟨I cannot, indeed, guarantee the absolute *veracity* of any of my apparently authentic law reports —J.R.Sutherland⟩ VERITY usu. designates the quality of a state or thing in being true or entirely in accordance with factual reality or with what should be so regarded; sometimes the word designates that which is marked by lasting, ultimate, transcendent value ⟨most primitive and national religions have also started out, naturally enough, with the assumption of their own *verity* and importance —A.L.Kroeber⟩ ⟨the old *verities* and truths of the heart, the old universal truths lacking which any story is ephemeral and doomed — love and honor and pity and pride and compassion and sacrifice —William Faulkner⟩ VERISIMILITUDE usu. indicates the quality of a representation that causes one to accept it as true ⟨to convey human nature in fiction requires the highest degree of *verisimilitude:* events that seem just like those of life as the reader's experience has led him to conceive of life must happen to people who seem just like human beings in a succession which seems just like the course of human affairs —E.K.Brown⟩

— **in truth :** in accordance with fact **:** ACTUALLY, REALLY

truth·ful \ˈtrüthfəl\ *adj* **:** telling or disposed to tell the truth **:** accurate and sincere in describing reality — **truth·ful·ly** \-fəlē, -li\ *adv* — **truth·ful·ness** *n* -ES

truth-function \ˈ=ˌ==\ *n* [trans. of G *wahrheitsfunktion*] **:** a sentential or propositional function whose truth-value depends only on the truth-values of its arguments — **truth-functional** \(ˈ)=ˌ=(=)=\ *adj* — **truth-functionally** \(ˈ)=ˌ=(=)==\ *adv*

truth·less \ˈtrüthləs\ *adj* **1 :** UNTRUTHFUL **2 :** UNTRUE — **truth·less·ness** *n* -ES

truth or consequences *n* **:** a game in which each participant in turn is asked a question by a leader and if he refuses to answer or answers falsely is punished by a penalty suggested by the leader or the group

truths *pl of* TRUTH

truth serum *also* **truth drug** *n* **:** any of several hypnotics or anesthetics said to be useful in inducing a subject under questioning to talk freely

truth table *n* [trans. of G *wahrheitstafel*] **:** a table that lists underneath one or more truth-functions the various truth-values of the truth-functions for given truth-values of their arguments (*see table at right*)

truth-value \ˈ=ˌ=(ˌ)=\ *n* [trans. of G *wahrheitswert*] **:** either the truth or the falsehood of a proposition or statement; *sometimes* **:** one of the interpreted or uninterpreted values attached to a formula in a many-valued logic

truthy \ˈtrüthē, -thē\ *adj* **:** TRUTHFUL

trut·ta \ˈtrəd·ə, -rüd·ə\ *n, cap* [NL, fr. ML *trutta, tructa* trout, fr. LL *tructa, troctа*, a trout, a shark — more at TROUT] *in some classifications* **:** a subgenus of *Salmo* or sometimes a separate genus comprising trouts that differ from the typical trouts in being marked with small black spots and in having smaller scales and fewer vertebrae and including the brown trout of Europe and the rainbow and cutthroat trouts of America

trut·ta·ceous \ˌtrəˈtāshəs\ *adj* [NL *truttaceus*, fr. ML *trutta* trout + L *-aceus* -aceous] **:** of, relating to, or resembling a trout

tru·xi·llic acid \(ˈ)trüˈhē(y)ik-, -hilik-; ˈtrəkˈsilik-\ *n* [ISV *truxilline* + *-ic*] **1 :** any of several crystalline stereoisomeric cyclic dicarboxylic acids $(C_6H_5)_2C_4H_4(COOH)_2$ that yield cinnamic acid on distillation; 2,4-diphenyl-cyclobutane-1,3-dicarboxylic acid: as **a :** an acid obtained from alpha-truxilline by hydrolysis or from cinnamic acid by irradiation — called also *alpha-truxillic acid* **b :** an acid obtained from alpha-truxillic acid by heating with acetic anhydride and sodium acetate and convertible again into the alpha isomer by stronger heating — called also *gamma-truxillic acid* **c :** an acid obtained from the potassium salt of alpha-truxillic acid by fusion with potassium hydroxide — called also *epsilon-truxillic acid* **2 :** TRUXINIC ACID

tru·xi·lline \trüˈhē(y)ən, -hilən; ˌtrəkˈsilən\ *n* -S [ISV *truxill-* (in *Truxillo coca*) + *-ine*] **:** either of two isomeric amorphous alkaloids $C_{38}H_{46}N_2O_8$ that are obtained from Truxillo coca and that yield on hydrolysis methanol, levorotatory ecgonine, and an acid: **a :** the isomer that yields alpha-truxillic acid — called also *alpha-truxilline* **b :** the isomer that yields beta-truxinic acid — called also *beta-truxilline*

tru·xi·llo coca \trüˈhē(ˌ)(y)ō-\ *n, usu cap T* [fr. *Truxillo* (Trujillo), city in northwestern Peru] **:** COCA 2b

trux·in·ic acid \ˌtrəkˈsinik-\ *n* [ISV *truxilline* + *-ic*] **:** any of several crystalline stereoisomeric cyclic dicarboxylic acids $(C_6H_5)_2C_4H_4(COOH)_2$ that are isomeric with the truxillic acids and also yield cinnamic acid on distillation; 3,4-diphenyl-cyclobutane-1,2-dicarboxylic acid: as **a :** an acid obtained from beta-truxilline by hydrolysis — called also *beta-truxillic acid, beta-truxinic acid* **b :** an acid obtained from the potassium salt of beta-truxinic acid by fusion with potassium hydroxide — called also *delta-truxillic acid, delta-truxinic acid*

trv *abbr* traverse

¹**try** \ˈtrī\ *vb* **tried; tried; trying; tries** [ME *trien*, fr. AF *trier*, fr. OF, to pick out, sift] *vt* **1 a :** to examine or investigate judicially **:** examine by witnesses or other judicial evidence and the principle of law ⟨no fact *tried* by a jury shall be otherwise reexamined in any court of the United States, than according to the rules of the common law —*U.S.Constitution*⟩ ⟨the paucity of women on the superior bench is a serious shortcoming in ~*ing* these cases —*Current Biog.*⟩ **b** (1) **:** to conduct the trial of ⟨they arrested him and he was *tried* before a Federal jury —*Amer. Guide Series: Md.*⟩ (2) **:** to participate as lawyer or counsel in the judicial examination of ⟨any lawyer who has ever *tried* a real case —A.T.Vanderbilt⟩ **2 a :** to put to test by experiment, investigation, or trial (as for determining strength, endurance, worth, accuracy, truth, or utility) ⟨taught school, practiced law, *tried* mining —*Amer. Guide Series: Oregon*⟩ ⟨put his shoulder to the door, then he *tried* the shutters —Elsie Singmaster⟩ ⟨some other apparently inaccessible peak on which to ~ their ardor and endurance —S.P.B.Mais⟩ ⟨~*ing* their luck casting plugs into the surf —R.M.Hodesh⟩ — often used with *out* ⟨*tried* out several occupations —Bernard Kalb⟩ ⟨*tried* out various hypotheses as to the nature of heat —S.F.Mason⟩ ⟨~ out a play on the road⟩ **b :** to test to the limit or breaking point **:** subject to extreme trial (as of severe or continuous strain or extreme or undue hardship, provocation, or affliction) ⟨don't work too hard, darling, or ~ your eyes —Elizabeth Taylor⟩ ⟨here is a tale that will ~ your credulity —O.S.J.Gogarty⟩ ⟨enough to ~ the patience of a saint —Alban Baer⟩ **c :** to demonstrate, discover, or settle by a test or trial ⟨hath still been *tried* a holy man —Shak.⟩ ⟨ready to ~ the question with his fists —George Meredith⟩ **3 a** *obs* **:** PURIFY, REFINE ⟨silver *tried* in a furnace of earth, purified seven times —Ps 12:6 (AV)⟩ **b :** to melt down (as oil, tallow, or lard) and procure in a pure state **:** RENDER — often used with *out* ⟨~ out whale oil from the blubber⟩ ⟨~ out chicken fat for cracklings⟩ **4** *obs* **:** to know by experience **:** EXPERIENCE **5 :** to fit or finish with accuracy — usu. used with *up* ⟨the steel square . . . is used . . . for laying out and ~*ing* up right angles —G.A.McGarvey & H.H.Sherman⟩ **6 :** to attempt through the exertion of effort, labor, or thought ⟨*tries* to stop short at irony —A.M.Mizener⟩ ⟨*tried* to demonstrate the existence of a real language of science —T.H.Savory⟩ ⟨~ to swim a mile⟩**:** make an effort for the purpose of ⟨*tried* walking without a crutch⟩ **7 :** TEASE 5 ~ *vi* **1** *of a ship* **:** to lie in a gale head to the wind under very little canvas **2 :** to make an attempt to achieve something or to carry out some action ⟨the girls will always be ~*ing* harder —*Management Behavior & Foreman Attitude*⟩ ⟨an adolescent urge to ~ for a good-night kiss —Lane Kauffmann⟩ — often used with *and* and a following verb ⟨a sad mistake to ~ and swim against the stream —George Santayana⟩ ⟨must therefore ~ and carry them with us on policy —Hugh Gaitskell⟩

syn ATTEMPT, ESSAY, ENDEAVOR, STRIVE, STRUGGLE: TRY is a simple word without much suggestive power; it may be used in reference to an attempt undertaken experimentally, tentatively, or uncertainly, or to an attempt ending in failure ⟨freedom in thought, the liberty to *try* and err —H.L.Mencken⟩ ⟨*tried* to have me assassinated three times —W.M. Thackeray⟩ ATTEMPT is almost always synonymous with TRY but may occas. be preferred in references to ventures of greater magnitude ⟨Father . . . do Thou finish above what I on earth have *attempted* —Thomas De Quincey⟩ ⟨here Shakespeare tackled a problem which proved too much for him. Why he *attempted* it at all is an insoluble puzzle —T.S.Eliot⟩ ESSAY, a rather formal term, may connote a preliminary canvassing or first beginning of a venture or its large and comprehensive nature ⟨the sculpture which attempted to unite repose and action . . . in a way which Phidias and Donatello were too prudent to *essay* —W.C.Brownell⟩ ⟨it is that continuity of evolution . . . that I have *essayed* to describe —J.L. Lowes⟩ ENDEAVOR may accentuate greater exertion, repeated effort, or continued search for expedients ⟨no art *endeavors* to express the emotions of the artist —Samuel Alexander⟩ ⟨the first step for every aspirant to culture is to *endeavor* to see things as they are —C.W.Eliot⟩ ⟨the wretch whom with such infinite pains and care I had *endeavored* to form —Mary W. Shelley⟩ STRIVE heightens notions of persistent, vigorous exertion to overcome opposition or hindrance ⟨her visitor, who held herself rigidly erect, and *strived* to mask her nervousness —G.B.Shaw⟩ ⟨was *striving* to come out of the filth, the flies, the poverty, the fishy smells —Sherwood Anderson⟩ ⟨loved his country deeply, and *strove* to serve her by lifting contemporary disputes into a larger air —John Buchan⟩ STRUGGLE implies continuing violent or strenuous exertion ⟨heroes fallen or *struggling* to advance —William Wordsworth⟩ **syn** see in addition AFFLICT, PROVE

— **try conclusions :** to test one's skill or strength against another person, an obstacle, or a challenging test — usu. used

TRUTH TABLE

a statement	a statement	p and q conjunction	p or q (inclusive) alternation	p if and only if q biconditional	if p then q conditional	not both p and q alternative denial	neither p nor q joint denial	p or q (exclusive) incompatibility	not p denial
p	q	$p \cdot q$	$p \vee q$	$p \equiv q$	$p \supset q$	$p \mid q$	$p \downarrow q$	$p + q$	$\sim p$
T	T	T	T	T	T	F	F	F	F
T	F	F	T	F	F	T	F	T	
F	T	F	T	F	T	T	F	T	T
F	F	F	F	T	T	T	T	F	

This table presents truth-values of the most important truth-functional connectives (conjunction ·, alternation ∨, biconditional ≡, conditional ⊃, alternative denial |, joint denial ↓, incompatibility +, and denial ~). Examples: A conjunction $p \cdot q$ is true only if both of its arguments are true; a biconditional $p \equiv q$ is true only if its arguments are either both true or both false.

with *with* ⟨the fascination of the mountains is only fully known to . . . hardy bush-walkers who . . . *try conclusions* with them —*Walkabout*⟩ — **try one's hand** : to attempt something for the first time as an experiment or out of curiosity — usu. used with *at* ⟨*trying his hand* at an adventurous romance for boys —J.D. Hart⟩

²**try** \"\ *n* -ES **1** *obs* : TRIAL, TEST **2** : an attempt esp. when undertaken with little hope of success, as one of a series, or when ending in failure ⟨an agreement . . . is not impossible, and they at least want to make a good ~ at it —Mark Gayn⟩ ⟨would go down in history as a nice ~ —R.M.Yoder⟩ ⟨hurled the cannonball farthest on the thirteenth through fifteenth *tries* —*Current Biog.*⟩ **3 a** : a play in rugby in which a player grounds the ball on or behind the opponent's goal line and which scores 3 points and entitles the scoring side to try for a placed goal **b** : TRY FOR POINT

try back *vi* : to return over or to repeat something already covered

try cock *n* **1** : one of two or more cocks arranged one above the other to ascertain the water level in a steam boiler : GAUGE COCK **2** : a cock for withdrawing a small quantity of liquid (as for testing)

try for point : an attempt made after scoring a touchdown in the game of football to kick a goal so as to score an additional point or to again carry the ball across the opponents' goal line or complete a forward pass in the opponents' end zone so as to score two additional points

try·gon \ˈtrī,gän\ *n* -S [L, fr. Gk *trygōn*, of imit. origin] : STINGRAY

try·gon·i·dae \trīˈgänə,dē\ [NL, fr. *Trygon*, genus of stingrays (fr. L *trygon* stingray) + *-idae*] *syn of* DASYATIDAE

try gun *n* : a gun having an adjustable stock to allow the user to determine the size and shape of stock best suited to him

trying *adj* [fr. pres. part. of ¹*try*] : causing severe hardship, annoyance, or irritation : severely straining the powers of endurance ⟨exposed their bodies to dangers greater than those of battle in long and ~ journeys —R.W.Southern⟩ ⟨no work on earth is more ~ than creative writing —Arnold Bennett⟩ ⟨his sorely tried and infuriatingly ~ wife —Charles Lee⟩ — **try·ing·ly** *adv* — **try·ing·ness** *n* -ES

try·ma \ˈtrīmə\ *n* -S [NL, fr. Gk, hole; fr. the inside of the drupe being hollow — more at TRONE] : a nutlike drupe (as the fruit of the walnut or hickory) in which the epicarp and mesocarp separate as a somewhat fleshy or leathery rind from the hard 2-valved endocarp

try on *vt* **1** : to put on (a garment) in order to ascertain how it fits **2** : to use or test experimentally esp. to determine convenience or simplicity of operation **3** *Brit* : to attempt to impose upon a person : try to outwit a person by means of ⟨if you'd *tried on* anything funny, he'd have said so —Robert Westerby⟩ ⟨I am not the right woman to *try* this *on* with —Elizabeth Bowen⟩

try-on \ˈ=,=\ *n* -S [*try on*] **1** : the action or an instance of trying on ⟨in a fitting room for a *try-on* —*Architect & Building News*⟩ **2** *Brit* : an attempt at deceit ⟨this letter's a *try-on*, doesn't mean what it says —Henry Green⟩

try out *vi* : to participate in competition for a position esp. on an athletic team or in a play ⟨*try out* for the basketball team⟩ ⟨*try out* for the male lead⟩

tryout \ˈ=,=\ *n* -S [*try out*] : an experimental performance or demonstration ⟨advisable to give actual classroom ~ to books under consideration before final adoption commitments —V.M.Rogers⟩ ⟨the first real ~ of collective security —T.J. Hamilton⟩: as **a** : a test of the performance of an athlete, actor, or other person to determine his ability to fill a part or position or meet the standards of a class ⟨scoring 590 points during ~s for U.S. shooting team —*Sports Illustrated*⟩ ⟨a card describing his radio ~ —*Current Biog.*⟩ **b** : a public performance or series of performances of a play prior to its official opening to determine public response and discover and make improvements ⟨the ~ period when he has to feed new lines to actors or to extract old lines from them fast enough for the changes to be incorporated by the next evening's performance —John Gassner⟩

try·pa \ˈtrīpə\ *n* -S [NL, fr. Gk *trypa*, *trypē* hole — more at TRYPAN-] : a pore in the front wall of the zooecium of a bryozoan — **tryp·i·ate** \ˈtrēpēət, -ē,āt\ *adj*

trypa·flavine \ˌtripə, ˈtripə+\ *n* [ISV *trypa* (fr. Gk, hole) + *flavine*; fr. its use in disinfecting wounds] : the hydrochloride of ACRIFLAVINE

trypan- *or* **trypano-** *comb form* [NL, fr. Gk, fr. *trypanon* auger, borer, trepan, fr. *trypan* to bore, pierce through, fr. *trypa* hole; akin to OSlav *truplŭ* hollow, Gk *tetrainein* to pierce — more at THROW] **1** : borer : auger ⟨*trypanosome*⟩ **2** : trypanosome ⟨*trypanocidal*⟩

trypan blue \ˈtripən-, ˈtri,pan-, trəˈpan-\ *n* [*trypan* ISV *trypan-*; fr. its being trypanocidal] : a disazo dye derived from tolidine and H acid that has limited use as an intravitam stain and esp. formerly in medicine

tryp·a·ne·id \ˌtripəˈnēəd\ *adj or n* [NL *Trypaneidae*] : TRYPETID

tryp·a·ne·idae \ˌtripəˈnēə,dē\ [NL, fr. *Trypanea*, genus of trypetids (fr. Gk *trypanon* borer) + *-idae*] *syn of* TRYPETIDAE

trypano·ci·dal \trəˌpanəˈsīdᵊl, ˌtripənōˈs-\ *adj* [*trypan-* + *-cidal*] : tending or used to destroy trypanosomes

trypano·cide \trəˈpanə,sīd, ˈtripənō,s-\ *n* -S [ISV *trypan-* + *-cide*] : a trypanocidal agent

trypano·rhyn·cha \trəˌpanəˈriŋkə, ˌtripənōˈr-\ *n pl, cap* [NL, fr. *trypan-* + Gk *rhynchos* snout — more at RHYNCH-] : an order of Cestoda comprising tapeworms parasitic in elasmobranch fishes and distinguished by a scolex with two or four bothridia and four spiny retractile tentacles for attachment to the host — **trypano·rhyn·chan** \=ˌ==ˈriŋkən, ˌ===-\ *adj or n*

trypano·so·ma \trəˌpanəˈsōmə, ˌtripənōˈs-\ *n* [NL, fr. *trypan-* (fr. Gk, fr. *trypanon* auger, borer) + *-soma*] **1** *cap* : a genus (the type of the family Trypanosomatidae) comprising flagellates that as adults are elongated and somewhat spindle-shaped, have a posteriorly arising flagellum which passes forward at the margin of an undulating membrane and emerges near the anterior end of the body as a short free flagellum, and are parasitic in the blood or rarely the tissues of vertebrates, that in the development phase which occurs in the digestive tract of a blood-sucking invertebrate and usu. an insect pass through a series of changes comparable to the typical forms of members of the genera *Leishmania*, *Leptomonas*, and *Crithidia*, multiply freely, and pass ultimately to the mouthparts or salivary structures whence they may be inoculated into a new vertebrate host bitten by the invertebrate host, and that are responsible for various serious diseases of man and domestic animals — compare CHAGAS' DISEASE, DOURINE, NAGANA, SLEEPING SICKNESS, SURRA **2** *pl* **trypanosomas** \-məz\ *or* **trypanosoma·ta** \-məd·ə\ : any flagellate of the genus *Trypanosoma*; *often* : any member of the family Trypanosomatidae that has the typical form of a mature blood trypanosome ⟨some leptomonads become typical ~s under culture in special media⟩

trypano·so·mat·i·dae \-ˌsōˈmad·ə,dē\ *n pl, cap* [NL, fr. *Trypanosomat-*, *Trypanosoma*, type genus + *-idae*] : a family of strictly parasitic more or less slender and elongated uniflagellate protozoans (order Protomonadina) having a single nucleus and a kinetoplast that includes serious pathogens of man and domestic animals usu. having complex host relations — see CRITHIDIA, HERPETOMONAS, LEISHMANIA, LEPTOMONAS, PHYTOMONAS, TRYPANOSOMA

trypano·some \trəˈpanə,sōm, ˈtripənō,s-\ *n* -S [NL *Trypanosoma*] : a protozoan of the genus *Trypanosoma*

trypano·so·mi·a·sis \=ˌ==ˌsōˈmīəsəs, ˌ===-\ *n, pl* **trypanosomia·ses** \-ə,sēz\ [NL, fr. *Trypanosoma* + *-iasis*] : infection with or disease caused by trypanosomes — compare CHAGAS' DISEASE, ENCEPHALITIS, SLEEPING SICKNESS, SURRA

trypan red \TRYPAN *as in* TRYPAN BLUE\ *n* [*trypan* ISV *trypan-*] : a disazo dye derived from benzidine and beta-naphthylamine and formerly used as a remedy in trypanosomiasis

tryp·ar·sa·mide \trəˈpärsə,mīd, -məd\ *n* [fr. *Tryparsamide*, a trademark] : a crystalline organic arsenical $H_2NCOCH_2NHC_6H_4AsO_3HNa.\frac{1}{2}H_2O$ used in the treatment of African sleeping sickness and syphilis of the central nervous system

¹**try·petid** \trəˈped·əd, -pēd-\ *adj* [NL *Trypetidae*] : of or relating to the Trypetidae

²**trypetid** \"\ *n* -S : a fly of the family Trypetidae

try·pet·i·dae \-ped·ə,dē\ *n pl, cap* [NL, fr. *Trypeta*, type genus (fr. Gk *trypētēs* borer, fr. *trypan* to bore) + *-idae* — more at TRYPAN-] : a family of acalyptrate muscoid flies having a piercing ovipositor and having the wings usu. banded or spotted that includes a number of important pests of various fruits (as the Mediterranean fruit fly)

tryp·o·graph \ˈtripə,graf, -ráf\ *n* [Gk *trypan* to bore, pierce through + E *-o-* + *-graph*] : a mimeograph using a stencil made by placing treated paper over a metal plate having sharp corrugations and writing with a stylus whose pressure causes the corrugations to pierce the paper and form the design — **tryp·o·graph·ic** \ˌ==ˈgrafik\ *adj*

try-pot \ˈ=,=\ *n* : a metallic pot used on a whaler or on shore to render blubber

tryp·sin \ˈtripsən\ *n* -S [ISV *tryp-* (fr. Gk *tryein* to wear out (i.e., digest) + *-psin* (as in *pepsin*) — more at THROE] **1** : a crystallizable proteinase that differs from pepsin in several ways (as in being most active in a slightly alkaline medium and in hydrolyzing esters as well as amides) and that is produced and secreted in the pancreatic juice in the form of inactive trypsinogen and activated in the intestine — compare CHYMOTRYPSIN **2** : a preparation from the pancreatic juice differing from pancreatin in containing principally proteolytic enzymes and used chiefly as a digestive and lytic agent

tryp·sin·ize \-sə,nīz\ *vt* -ED/-ING/-S : to subject to the action of trypsin

tryp·sin·o·gen \tripˈsinəjən, -,jen\ *n* -S [ISV *trypsin* + *-o-* + *-gen*] : the crystallizable precursor of trypsin present in the acinar cells of the pancreas and converted into trypsin by the action of trypsin itself, enterokinase, or other proteolytic enzyme

trypt·amine \ˈtriptə,mēn, tripˈta,m-, -mən\ *n* [*trypt-* (in *tryptophan*) + *amine*] : a crystalline amine $C_8H_6NCH_2CH_2NH_2$ formed by decomposition of tryptophan or made synthetically; 3-(2-amino-ethyl)-indole — compare SEROTONIN

tryp·tic \ˈtriptik\ *adj* [ISV *trypsin* + *-tic* (as in *peptic*)] **1** : of or relating to trypsin or to its action **2** : produced by trypsin ⟨~ digestion⟩

tryptique *also* **tryptyque** *var of* TRIPTYQUE

tryp·tone \ˈtrip,tōn\ *n* -S [ISV *trypsin* + *-tone* (as in *peptone*)] : a peptone produced by the action of trypsin

tryp·to·phan \ˈtriptə,fan\ *also* **tryp·to·phane** \-fān\ *n* -S [ISV *tryptic* + *-o-* + *-phane*] : a crystalline amino acid $(C_8H_6N)CH_2CH(NH_2)COOH$ that is obtained in the levorotatary L form from casein, fibrin, and other proteins (as by tryptic digestion) and in the racemic form by synthesis, that differs from most other naturally occurring amino acids in its instability toward mineral acids, and that is essential in the nutrition of animals and man; β-3-indolyl-alanine

tryp·topha·nase \ˈtriptəfə,nās, tripˈtäf-, -āz\ *n* -S [*tryptophan* + *-ase*] : an enzyme that catalyzes the decomposition of tryptophan into indole, pyruvic acid, and ammonia and that is present esp. in the colon bacillus

try·sail *also* **tri·sail** \ˈtrīsəl (*usual nautical pronunc*), -,sāl\ *n* [²*try* + *sail*] **1** : a fore-and-aft sail bent to a gaff, hoisted on a lower mast or a small mast close abaft and usu. connected to a lower mast, and used chiefly as a storm sail — see SHIP illustration **2** : a small and strongly made sail either triangular or with a very short gaff set in place of the mainsail of a yacht in heavy weather

try square *n* : an instrument consisting of two straightedges secured at right angles to each other and used for laying off right angles and testing whether work is square — called also *right-angle gauge*

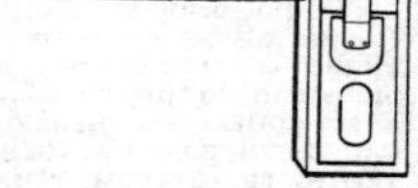
try square

¹**tryst** \ˈtrist, -rīst\ *n* -S [ME *tryst*, *trist*, *triste* agreement, tryst, appointed station in hunting, fr. OF *triste* appointed station in hunting, watch post, ambush, prob. of Scand origin; akin to ON *treysta* to make strong and safe, make firm, trust, *traust* trust — more at TRUST] **1** *Scot* : a mutual agreement **2 a** : an agreement often between lovers to meet at a specified time and place ⟨the merciless sea keeps ~ with the fury of the winds —Lilian S. Taylor⟩ **b** : an agreed upon meeting; *also* : a place specified for a tryst ⟨suburban ~s that offered real cover —Rebecca West⟩ **3** *Scot* : MARKET, FAIR; *esp* : a fixed annual cattle market **syn** see ENGAGEMENT

²**tryst** \"\ *vb* -ED/-ING/-S [ME *trysten*, *tristen*, fr. *tryst*, *trist* tryst] *vi* **1** *chiefly Scot* : to agree upon a meeting : make a tryst; *also* : to keep a tryst : MEET **2** *obs Scot* : to come to terms : NEGOTIATE **3** *obs* : to happen at the same time ~ *vt* **1** *Scot* : to agree to meet at a certain time or place : make tryst with **2** *Scot* : to affect with good or evil : VISIT

tryst·er \-stə(r)\ *n* -S : one that trysts

tryworks \ˈ=,=\ *n pl* [¹*try* + *works*] : a brick furnace in which trypots are placed; *also* : the furnace with the pots

ts *abbr* teaspoon; teaspoonful

TS *abbr* **1** *often not cap* tensile strength **2** test solution **3** tool steel **4** tough situation **5** transport and supply **6** transverse section **7** tub-sized **8** typescript

t's *or* **ts** *pl of* T

tsaddik *also* **tsadik** *var of* ZADDIK

tsa·de \ˈtsä·\ *n* -S [Heb *ṣādhē*] : SADHE

tsa·ko·ni·an \tsəˈkōnēən\ *n* -S *usu cap* [*Tsakon*, region in the eastern Peloponnesus, Greece + E *-an*] : a modern dialect of Greek spoken in a restricted area in the Peloponnesus and preserving some features of ancient non-Koine dialect

tsa·ma \ˈtsämə\ *n* -S [Afrik, fr. Hottentot (Nama dial.) *tsamas*] *Africa* : WATERMELON

tsam·ba \ˈtsämbə\ *also* **tsam·pa** \-mpə\ *n* -S [Tibetan *tsampa*] : flour made from parched ground barley or wheat that is the chief cereal food in and near Tibet

tsan·tsa \ˈtsäntsə\ *n* -S [Jivaro] : a shrunken head; *specif* : one prepared by a Jivaro Indian

tsao \ˈtsaü\ *n* -S [Chin (Pek) *tsao³*] : JUJUBE

tsar *var of* CZAR

tsat·lee \ˈtsatˌlē\ *n* -S [modif. of Chin (Pek) *Ch'i¹-li³*, lit., seven li] : rough irregular raw silk from China

t scale *n, usu cap T* [*t* (as in *t-test*)] : a scale for expressing the results of all tests in comparable form as standard scores orig. based upon the performance of a representative group of twelve-year-old children having a mean of 50 and a standard deviation of 10

tscheff·kin·ite \ˈchefkə,nīt\ *n* -S [G *tschewkinit* — more at CHEVKINITE] : CHEVKINITE

tscher·mig·ite \ˈchərmi,gīt, ˈcher-\ *n* -S [G *tschermigit*, fr. *Tschermig*, Bohemia, its locality + G *-it* -ite] : ALUM 1b

tsedakah *var of* TZEDAKAH

tsessebe *or* **tsesseby** *var of* SASSABY

tset·saut \ˈtset,saüt\ *n, pl* **tsetsaut** *or* **tsetsauts** *usu cap* **1 a** : an Athapaskan people of west central British Columbia **b** : a member of the Tsetsaut people **2** : the language of the Tsetsaut people

tset·se \ˈs|etsē, ˈt|, ˈts|, |ēt-, -tsi *sometimes* -tsə *or* ˈsēsē *or* ˈsēsi\ *or* **tsetse fly** *n, pl* **tsetse** *or* **tsetses** *or* **tsetse flies** [Afrik, fr. Tswana *tsêtsê*] : any of several muscoid flies of the genus *Glossina* that occur in Africa south of the Sahara desert — see NAGANA, SLEEPING SICKNESS

tsetse disease *or* **tsetse fly disease** *n* : NAGANA

TSH *abbr* **1** Their Serene Highnesses **2** thyroid stimulating hormone

t-shaped \ˈ=,=\ *adj, cap T* : having the shape of a capital T

tshi *usu cap, var of* TWI

tshi·lu·ba \chəˈlübə\ *n, usu cap* : one of the four major trade languages of Congo used most widely in the southern part of the country — called also *Luba*; compare KINGWANA, KONGO, LINGALA

t-shirt *cap T, also* **tee shirt** \ˈtē,=\ *n* [so called fr. its being T-shaped] **1** : a slipon collarless short-sleeved undershirt of cotton jersey for men **2** : a cotton or wool jersey outer shirt of similar design for men and women made with short or long sleeves and sometimes a collar

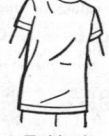

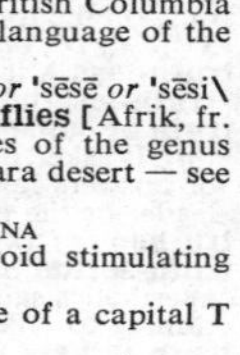
T-shirt 1

tshon \ˈchōn\ *usu cap, var of* CHON

tshwr *abbr* thundershower

tsim·shi·an \ˈchimshēən, ˈtsi-\ *or* **chimme·sy·an** \-mzēən, -msē-\ *n, pl* **tsimshian** *or* **tsimshians** *or* **chimmesyan** *or* **chimmesyans** *usu cap* **1 a** : an Indian people of the lower Skeena and Nass valleys and the adjacent coast of British Columbia **b** : a member of such people **2** : a language of the Tsimshian people **3** : a language family of the Penutian stock comprising only the Tsimshian language

tsi·nan \ˈjēˈnän, ˈtsē-\ *adj, usu cap* [fr. *Tsinan* (Chinan), China] : of or from the city of Tsinan, China : of the kind or style prevalent in Tsinan

tsine *n, pl* **tsine** \(t)sīn\ [Burmese *tsaiñ*] : BANTENG

tsing·tao \ˈchiŋˈdaü, ˈtsiŋˈtaü\ *adj, usu cap* [fr. *Tsingtao*, China] : of or from the city of Tsingtao, China : of the kind or style prevalent in Tsingtao

tsi·tsi·har \ˈtsētsē,här, ˈchēchē-\ *adj, usu cap* [fr. *Tsitsihar*, Manchuria] : of or from the city of Tsitsihar, Manchuria : of the kind or style prevalent in Tsitsihar

tsitsith *var of* ZIZITH

t slot *cap T, also* **tee slot** *n* : a T-shaped slot

t-slot cutter *n, cap T* : a small side-milling cutter with a necked-down shank for completing the bottoms of T slots

TSO *abbr* town suboffice

tsotsil *usu cap, var of* TZOTZIL

tsp *abbr* teaspoon; teaspoonful

TSP *abbr* trisodium phosphate

tspn *abbr* teaspoon; teaspoonful

tspt *abbr* transport

t square *cap T, also* **tee square** *n* [so called fr. its shape] : a

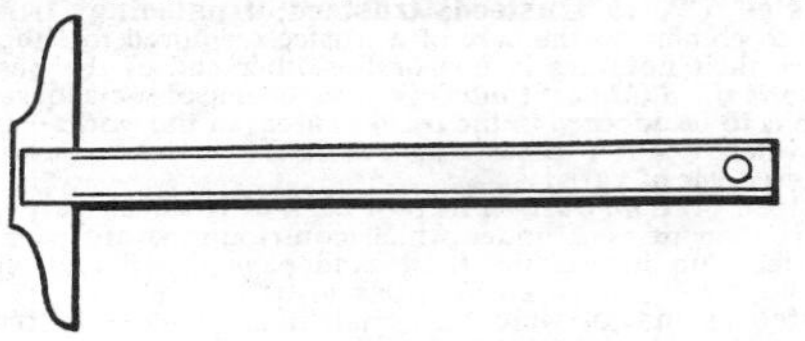
T square

ruler with a crosspiece or head at one end used in making parallel lines or as a support for triangles used in drawing lines at different angles to the ruler

TSR *abbr* traveling stock reserve

TSS *abbr* twin-screw steamer

tstm *abbr* thunderstorm

t-stop system *n, usu cap T* [*t* (symbol for *total light transmission*)] : a system for indicating camera apertures by means of T-numbers

t-strap \ˈ=,=\ *n, cap T* **1** : a T-shaped part of an open shoe formed by a strap rising from the throat over the instep and either fastening to an ankle strap or dividing at the top to form an ankle strap **2** : a shoe and esp. a sandal having a T-strap

TSU *abbr* this side up

tsu·bo \ˈ(t)sü(,)bō\ *n, pl* **tsubo** [Jap] : a Japanese unit of area equal to 35.58 square feet

tsu·ga \ˈ(t)sügə\ *n, cap* [NL, fr. Jap, larch] : a genus of Asiatic and No. American evergreen trees (family Pinaceae) comprising the hemlocks and being distinguished by drooping branches, linear leaves with persistent petiole bases, and reflexed cones

tsugaresinol \ˌ==ˈ==,=\ *n* [NL *Tsuga* + E *resinol*] : CONIDENDRIN

tsu·ku·pin \ˈ(t)sükəpən\ *n* -S [native name in the Yap islands] : a large sailing canoe of the Yap islands having a triangular sail and a single outrigger

tsu·meb·ite \ˈ(t)sümə,bīt\ *n* -S [*Tsumeb*, region in southwestern Africa + E *-ite*] : a mineral $Pb_2Cu(PO_4)(OH)_3.3H_2O$ consisting of a hydrous basic lead copper phosphate and occurring in small emerald-green monoclinic crystals (hardness 3.5, sp. gr. 6.1)

tsu·nami \(t)süˈnämē, -namē\ *n, pl* **tsunamis** *also* **tsunami** [Jap, fr. *tsu* port, harbor + *nami* wave, sea] : a seismic disturbance of the ocean : a great sea wave produced by submarine earth movement or volcanic eruption : TIDAL WAVE — **tsu·namic** \-mik\ *adj*

tsu·tsu·ga·mu·shi disease \ˌ(t)sütsəgəˈmüshē-\ *n* [*tsutsugamushi* fr. Jap, dangerous insect] : an acute febrile disease resembling louse-borne typhus orig. known from Japan but widely distributed in the western Pacific area and caused by a rickettsia (*Rickettsia tsutsugamushi* or *R. orientalis*) transmitted by larval mites (esp. *Trombicula akamushi*) that also occur on several voles which act as reservoir hosts of the infection — called also *scrub typhus*

tsutsugamushi mite *n* : any of several mites of the genus *Trombicula* that are vectors of the rickettsia causing tsutsugamushi disease

tswa \ˈ(t)swä, ˈchwä, chəˈwä\ *n, pl* **tswa** *or* **tswas** *usu cap* **1 a** : a southeastern African people chiefly of northern Transvaal and southern Mozambique **b** : a member of such people **2** : a Bantu language of the Tswa people

tswa·na *or* **chua·na** \ˈ(t)swänə, ˈchwä-, chəˈwä-\ *n, pl* **tswana** *or* **tswanas** *or* **chuana** *or* **chuanas** *usu cap* **1 a** : any of the various Bantu-speaking Negro peoples dwelling between the Orange and Zambezi rivers, particularly in Bechuanaland, southern Africa **b** : a member of any of such peoples **2** : a Bantu language of the Tswana people — compare SOTHO

tswett column \ˈswet-\ *n, usu cap T* [after Mikhail *Tswett* †1920 Russ. botanist] : a tubular glass device with a stopcock at the bottom used for the chromatographic separation of related compounds and esp. of plant pigments (as in chlorophyll) — compare CHROMATOGRAPHY

TT *abbr* **1** teetotaller **2** telegraphic transfer **3** teletype; teletypewriter **4** torpedo tube **5** Trinity term **6** tuberculin tested

Tt *symbol* trigesimo-secundo

TTC \ˌtēˌtēˈsē\ *abbr or n* -S triphenyltetrazolium chloride

t-test \ˈ=,=\ *n* [*t* (prob. abbr. of *true*)] : a statistical test involving means of normal populations with unknown standard deviations and using small samples based on a variable t equal to the difference between the mean of the sample and the mean of the population divided by a quotient formed by dividing the standard deviation of the sample by the square root of the number in the sample

TTL *abbr* to take leave

t-tube \ˈ=,=\ *n, cap 1st T* : a rubber tube in the form of a T used to drain the common bile duct

TU *abbr* **1** thermal unit **2** toxic unit **3** trade union **4** traffic unit **5** transmission unit

tu·a·mo·tu \ˌtüəˈmō(,)tü\ *n* -S *usu cap* [Tuamotu *tua* back + *motu* islet] : the Polynesian language of the Tuamotuan people

¹**tu·a·mo·tu·an** \ˌ==ˈmōtüən\ *adj, usu cap* [*Tuamotu* islands, So. Pacific Ocean + E *-an*, adj. suffix] : of or relating to the Tuamotu archipelago or its inhabitants

²**tuamotuan** \"\ *n* -S *usu cap* [*Tuamotu* islands + E *-an*, n. suffix] **1** : a native of the Tuamotu islands **2** : TUAMOTU

tuan \tüˈän\ *n* -S [Malay] : SIR, MASTER, LORD — used as a form of respectful address to a male by Malay-speaking persons

tuan be·sar \-bäˈsär\ *n* [Malay, great master] : a European boss in colonial Malaysia

tua·reg *also* **toua·reg** \ˈtwä,reg\ *n, pl* **tuareg** *or* **tuaregs** *also* **touareg** *or* **touaregs** *usu cap* [Ar *Tawāriq*] **1** : one of the dominant nomads of the central and western Sahara and along the Middle Niger from Timbuktu to Nigeria who are perhaps descendants of the ancient Gaetulians, have preserved their Hamitic speech in great purity and also their alphabet derived prob. from the Punic but have adopted the Muslim religion, are tall, of Mediterranean features, and occas. light-haired, and whose men wear a cloth about the face but whose women go unveiled — compare TIFINAGH **2** : TAMASHEK

tu·art *also* **tou·art** \ˈtüə(r)t\ *n* -S [native name in Western Australia] : an Australian white gum (*Eucalyptus gomphocephala*) yielding hard durable timber used esp. for ships

tu·a·ta·ra \ˌtüəˈtärə\ *also* **tu·a·te·ra** \-ˈtärə\ *n* -S [Maori *tuatāra*, fr. *tua* back + *tara* spine] : a large reptile (*Sphenodon punctatum*) formerly common in New Zealand but now confined to certain islets near the coast that is the only surviving rhynchocephalian, has a pineal body which shows distinct traces of having functioned as an eye in past ages, reaches a

length of two and a half feet, is dark olive-green with small white or yellowish specks on the sides, has yellow spines along the back except on the neck, and in general resembles an iguana

tu·ath \'tüə\ *n* -s [Ir, state, country, tribe, people, fr. OIr — more at DUTCH] **:** STATE 5a; *also* **:** the territory occupied by a tuath

¹tub \'təb\ *n* -s [ME *tubbe, tobbe,* fr. MD; akin to MLG *tubbe, tobbe* tub] **1 :** a wide low vessel usu. about the size of a half barrel and orig. formed with wooden staves, round bottom, and hoops but now often of metal or plastic ⟨a galvanized wash ~⟩ ⟨a ~ for lard⟩ **2** *Brit* **:** SAPPHIRINE GURNARD **3 :** something shaped like or felt to resemble a tub: as **a :** an old, inferior, or slow-moving boat **b :** an old-fashioned pulpit **c** (1) **:** a box or bucket in which coal or ore is sent up a shaft (2) **:** KEEVE (3) **:** a tram used underground (4) **:** a puddling tub **d :** an old-fashioned hand-drawn fire engine **e** *slang* **:** an excessively corpulent person **f :** a container in which a unit of commercial fishing gear is coiled down; *sometimes* **:** ¹SKATE 2b **g :** a mail hamper **4 :** a vessel to contain water for bathing **:** BATHTUB; *also* **:** a bath or the act of taking a bath ⟨nothing like a hot ~ to relax tired muscles⟩ **5 a :** the amount that a tub will hold **:** the contents of a tub ⟨a ~ of butter was consumed⟩ **b** *Brit* **:** a keg holding about four gallons and formerly used to smuggle spirits **6 a :** a pair-oared gig with a place for a coach in the stern used esp. in training oarsmen **b :** a rack for topsail halyards **c :** a lookout enclosure on a mast **7 :** a synchronized swimming stunt in which from a back layout position the knees are brought to the chest and the body is rotated at least once in a horizontal position

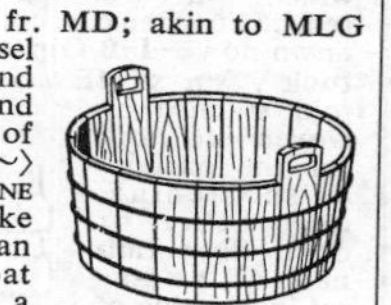
tub 1

²tub \"\ *adj* **1 :** of, relating to, or like a tub **:** using or kept in a tub ⟨~ butter⟩ **2 :** WASH ⟨~ silk⟩

³tub \"\ *vb* **tubbed; tubbed; tubbing; tubs** *vt* **1 :** to wash or bathe in a tub ⟨*tubbing* clothes bright and early on Monday⟩ **2 :** to line (as a mine shaft) with tubbing **:** keep back water with tubbing — sometimes used with *off* **3 a :** to put or store in a tub ⟨always *tubbed* his pork in sweetened brine⟩ **b :** to plant in a tub ⟨*tubbed* azaleas⟩ **4 :** to coach (a rower) in a tub ~ *vi* **1 :** to use a bathtub **:** take a bath **:** BATHE **2 :** to undergo washing ⟨synthetics that ~ well⟩ **3 :** to practice rowing in a tub

¹tu·ba \'tübə\ *n* -s [Ar *ṭūbā* blessed (found in Koran 13:28 and interpreted by various commentators as meaning a tree), fr. Aram. goodness] **:** a mythical tree believed to grow in the Muslim paradise

²tu·ba \'t(y)übə\ *n* -s *see sense 2* [It, fr. L, trumpet — more at TUBE] **1 :** a large low-pitched member of the bugle or saxhorn family of brass wind instruments having a conical bore and a cup-shaped mouthpiece and typically made to be held upright but in the largest sizes often made to encircle the player's body for easier carrying in marching bands — compare HELICON, SOUSAPHONE **2** *pl usu* **tu·bae** \-ü,bē\ **:** a straight bronze trumpet of the ancient Romans **3 :** a powerful organ reed stop of 8-foot pitch **4 :** a high-powered radar transmitter used to jam enemy radar

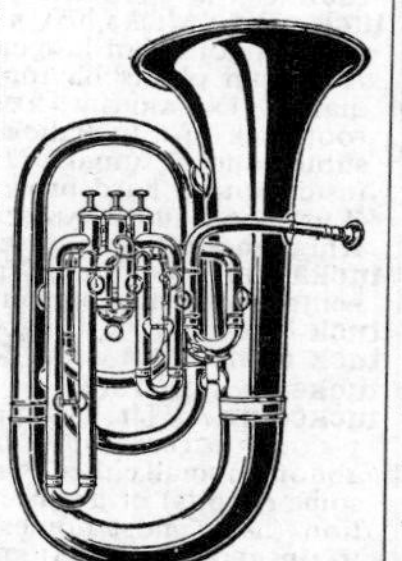
tuba 1

³tu·ba \'tübə\ *n* -s [Tag *tubâ*] **1 a :** any of various toxic substances derived from the sap, bark, or seeds of plants and used esp. in Malaysia and the Philippines as fish poisons: as (1) **:** PHYSIC NUT (2) **:** DERRIS **b :** a plant that yields a fish poison **2 a :** the usu. fermented sap of a palm (as a nipa or coconut palm) that is used esp. in the Philippines in the distillation of alcohol and is the source of beno **:** TODDY 1 **b :** BENO

⁴tuba \"\ *n, pl* **tuba** *or* **tubas** *usu cap* **:** one of the tatarized Samoyed

tuba clarion *n* **:** a 4-foot pipe-organ tuba

tub·age \'t(y)übij\ *n* -s [¹*tube* + *-age*] **1 :** TUBING **2 :** the act or process of inserting in a usu. smoothbore gun of large caliber a tube of wrought iron or steel that increases the strength but decreases the caliber of the gun

tu·ba·ic acid \tü'bāik-\ *n* [ISV ³*tuba* + *-ic*] **:** a crystalline phenolic acid $C_3H_5C_6H_5O(OH)COOH$ derived from coumaran and formed from rotenone by cleavage with strong alkali

tub·al \-bəl\ *adj* **:** of, relating to, or involving a tube and esp. a fallopian tube

tubal pregnancy *n* **:** ectopic pregnancy in a fallopian tube

tuba major *n* [NL, major tuba] **1 :** a 16-foot pipe-organ tuba **2 :** an 8-foot tuba mirabilis

tuba mi·rab·i·lis \-mə'rabələs\ *n* [NL, wonderful tuba] **:** a very loud high-pressure solo pipe-organ stop of the trumpet class

tu·bate \'t(y)ü,bāt\ *adj* [¹*tube* + *-ate*] **:** having or forming a tube **:** TUBIFORM, TUBULAR ⟨a ~ gland⟩

tü·ba·tu·la·bal \,tübətü'läbəl\ *n, pl* **tübatulabal** *or* **tübatulabals** *usu cap* [Shoshoni, pine-nut eaters] **1 a :** a Shoshonean people of the upper Kern river valley, south central California **b :** a member of such people **2 :** the language of the Tübatulabal

tub·ba·ble \'təbəbəl\ *adj* **:** suitable for tubbing **:** capable of being washed without damage

tub·bal \'təbəl\ *n* -s [prob. alter. of *twibil*] *dial Eng* **:** MATTOCK

tub basket *n* **:** a round basket having a wooden bottom and straight sides of veneer staves

tubbed *past of* TUB

¹tub·ber \'təbə(r)\ *n* -s [prob. alter. (influenced by *-er*) of *twibil*] **:** a Cornish mining pickax

²tubber \"\ *n* [¹*tub* + *-er*] **:** one that makes or works with tubs: as **a :** COOPER **b :** a worker who cleans jewelry in a tumbling machine **c :** a user of a tub (as a washer or bather)

tub·bie \'təbi\ *n* -s [¹*tub* + *-ie*] *dial Brit* **:** COOPER; *also* **:** a cooper's helper

tub·bi·ness \'təbēnəs\ *n* -ES **:** the quality or state of being tubby **:** CORPULENCE

tub·bing \'təbiŋ, -bēŋ\ *n* -s [¹*tub* + *-ing*] **1 :** the making of tubs; *also* **:** materials for making tubs **:** tub stock **2 :** a lining of timber or metal for a shaft (as in a mine); *esp* **:** a watertight shaft lining consisting of a series of cast-iron cylinders bolted together and used to sink through water-bearing strata

tub·bish \-bish\ *adj* **:** resembling a tub **:** rather tubby

tub·by \-bē, -bi\ *adj* -ER/-EST **:** resembling or suggesting a tub: as **a :** resembling a tub in round thick clumsy outline; *esp* **:** pudgily fat **b :** sounding dull and without proper resonance or freedom of sound ⟨a ~ violin⟩

tub–cart \'=,=\ *n* **:** GOVERNESS CART

tub chair *n* **:** a large rounded upholstered easy chair usu. with semicircular back and no separate arms — compare BARREL CHAIR

tub desk *n* **:** a desk with an open top having divisions for filing cards

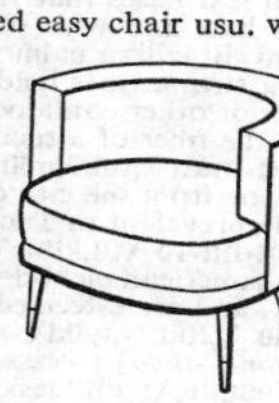
tub chair

¹tube \'t(y)üb\ *n* -s *often attrib* [F, fr. L *tubus;* akin to L *tuba* trumpet] **1 a :** a hollow elongated usu. cylindrical body that is used esp. to convey fluids and is mechanically nearly or precisely the same as a pipe but in use is arbitrarily associated with particular items and devices ⟨a melange of iron pipes and glass ~s⟩ ⟨pipes leading to a boiler and continuous through valves with the ~s of the boiler proper⟩ **b** (1) **:** a slender channel within a plant or animal body **:** DUCT — see BRONCHIAL TUBE, FALLOPIAN TUBE, POLLEN TUBE (2) **:** the narrow basal portion of a gamopetalous corolla or a gamosepalous calyx **:** the united part of a monadelphous androecium (3) **:** a more or less cylindrical sometimes crooked or spirally twisted case secreted or constructed by many annelids, a few larval insects, and some other animals for protection or concealment (4) **:** one of the siphons of a bivalve mollusk **2 a** *archaic* **:** something (as a telescope) with a tube or tubular part as its chief feature **b** *archaic* **:** a cannon or other firearm **c :** TUBULAR SKATE **3 :** any of various usu. cylindrical structures or devices felt to resemble or functioning in the manner of a tube: as **a :** the inner cylinder of a built-up gun usu. extending from the inner face of the breechblock to the muzzle, carrying the rifling on its inner surface, and surrounded by the jacket and hoops if any are used; *also* **:** the whole cylindrical piece of metal surrounding the bore **b** (1) **:** an often complex piece of laboratory or technical apparatus usu. of glass and commonly serving to isolate or convey a product of reaction ⟨a distillation ~⟩ — see FERMENTATION TUBE (2) **:** TEST TUBE **c :** a collapsible cylindrical metal container from which a paste is dispensed by squeezing ⟨a toothpaste ~⟩ **d** (1) **:** a tunnel for vehicular or rail traffic (2) **:** a tunnel housing an aqueduct or other underground duct **e :** a hollow cylindrical device (as a cannula) used for insertion into bodily passages or hollow organs for removal or injection of materials **f** (1) *archaic* **:** PIPE 6a (2) **:** the basically cylindrical part connecting the mouthpiece and bell of a wind instrument **g :** a cylindrical core without flange or head on which yarn or thread may be wound **h :** a woman's narrow fitted garment (as a skirt or dress) **4 :** INNER TUBE **5 :** ELECTRON TUBE **6 :** VACUUM TUBE

²tube \"\ *vb* -ED/-ING/-S *vt* **:** to furnish with, enclose in, or pass through a tube ⟨~ a well⟩ ⟨~ media in bacteriology⟩; *also* **:** to form into or wind on a tube ⟨~ yarn⟩ ~ *vi, chiefly Brit* **:** to go by subway

tube cell *n* **1 :** one of the two cells that is produced by division of the microspore nucleus in the development of the male gametophyte in higher plants and that functions in development of the pollen tube **2 :** any of the cells in a wheat grain having long axes parallel to those of the epicarp cells, appearing as rings in transection, and forming the inner epidermis of the grain

tube coral *n* **:** an organ-pipe coral or a related fossil coral

tu·bec·to·my \t(y)ü'bektəmē\ *n* -ES [¹*tube* + *-ectomy*] **:** surgical excision of a fallopian tube

tube culture *n* **:** a culture of microorganisms in a test tube

tube curare *n* **:** CURARE 3

tubed *adj, of a horse* **:** tracheotomized and fitted with a metal breathing tube (as for the relief of broken wind)

tube door *n* **:** a door in the smoke chamber of some boilers to permit access to the fire tubes

tube–feed \'=,=\ *vt* **:** to feed through or by means of a tube — compare GAVAGE

tubeflower \'=,==\ *n* **:** an East Indian shrub (*Clerodendron siphonanthus*) having white flowers with a long slender corolla tube

tube foot *n* **:** one of numerous small tentacular flexible tubular processes of starfishes, sea urchins, and most holothurians bearing at the end an adhesive sucker, being extensions of the water-vascular system, employed in crawling or in holding on to objects, and serving also in respiration and as tactile organs

tube generator *n* **:** a generator of alternating current in which electron tubes are used to convert the applied electric power into audio or radio-frequency power

tubehearted \'=,==\ *adj* **:** having pulsating sinuses functioning as a heart

tube·less \'t(y)übləs\ *adj* **:** lacking a tube; *specif* **:** being a pneumatic tire that does not depend on an inner tube for airtightness

tube·let \-lət\ *n* -s **:** a small tube **:** TUBULE

tubelike \'=,=\ *adj* **:** resembling or having the form of a tube

tubemaker \'=,==\ *n* **:** one that makes tubes; *esp* **:** an animal or larva that lives in a tubular case of its own fabrication

tube·man \'=mən\ *n, pl* **tubemen** *Brit* **:** an employee on a subway

tube mill *n* **:** a grinding mill that consists of a long revolving tube containing flint pebbles or steel balls or slugs and is used for pulverizing (as in cement manufacturing) — compare BALL MILL

tube–nosed \'=,=\ *adj* **:** having the nostrils prolonged in the form of horny tubes ⟨petrels are *tube-nosed* birds⟩

tube–nosed bat *n* **:** any of several fruit bats (genus *Nyctimene*) of Australia and the southwest Pacific distinguished by nostrils drawn out into diverging tubes

tube nucleus *n* **:** the one of the two nuclei formed by mitotic division of a microspore during the formation of a pollen grain that is held to control subsequent growth of the pollen tube and that does not divide again — compare GENERATIVE NUCLEUS

tube of bel·li·ni \-bə'lēnē\ *usu cap B* [after Lorenzo *Bellini* †1704 Ital. anatomist] **:** any of the large excretory ducts of the uriniferous tubules of the kidney that open on the free surface of the papillae

tube pan *n* **:** a deep round pan used for baking large cakes and having a hollow tube in the center that permits heat to reach the center of the batter

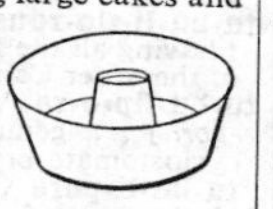
tube pan

tube plate *n* **:** a plate or sheet perforated with holes for the reception of tubes (as in a boiler)

¹tu·ber \'t(y)übə(r)\ *n* -s [L, hump, knob, tumor, truffle, tuber; akin to Gk *typhē* plant used as stuffing for beds, cattail, ON *thūfa* mound, OE *thūf* tuft, crest, L *tumēre* to swell — more at THUMB] **1 a :** a short thickened fleshy stem or terminal portion of a stem or rhizome that is usu. formed underground, bears minute scale leaves each with a bud capable under suitable conditions of developing into a new plant, and constitutes the resting stage of various plants (as the potato or the Jerusalem artichoke) — compare BULB, CORM, TUBEROUS ROOT **b :** a fleshy root, rhizome, or other plant structure resembling a tuber in appearance ⟨a dahlia ~⟩ — not used technically **c tubers** *pl* **:** a tuberous crop; *specif* **:** a crop of potatoes ⟨soon be time to harvest ~*s*⟩ **2** [NL, fr. L] **:** the type genus of Tuberaceae comprising fungi whose fruiting bodies are typical truffles **3 :** an anatomical prominence **:** TUBEROSITY, TUBERCLE, PROTUBERANCE

²tub·er \"\ *n* -s [¹*tube* + *-er*] **:** one that makes or works with tubes: as **a :** a worker who installs or fits tubes or tubing (as in a boiler assembly) **b :** an operator of a machine who forms material (as rubber or plastic) into a continuous strip or tube; *also* **:** such a machine ⟨a ~ that coats wire with insulation⟩ **c :** ⁴COPPER **d :** a textile worker who rewinds cloth from large rolls into smaller rolls to inspect it and cut out imperfections — called also *winder* **e :** a worker who makes round belting from strips of leather

tu·ber·a·ce·ae \,t(y)übə'rāsē,ē\ *n pl, cap* [NL, fr. *Tuber,* type genus + *-aceae*] **:** a family of ascomycetous fungi (order Tuberales) having ascocarps that resemble tubers and vary in size from that of an acorn to that of a large apple and bearing asci in a wholly enclosed hymenial layer — see TRUFFLE, TUBER 2 — **tu·ber·a·ceous** \;==;rāshəs\ *adj*

tube railway *n, chiefly Brit* **:** an underground railway **:** SUBWAY

tu·ber·a·les \,t(y)übə'rā(,)lēz\ *n pl, cap* [NL, fr. *Tuber* + *-ales*] **:** a small order of fungi (subclass Euascomycetes) with a closed hypogeal ascocarp — see TUBERACEAE

tuber ci·ne·re·um \sə'nirēəm\ *n* [NL, ashy hump] **:** an eminence of gray matter which lies on the lower surface of the brain between the optic tracts and in front of the mammillary bodies and of which the upper surface forms part of the floor of the third ventricle and the lower surface bears the infundibulum to which the pituitary body is attached

tu·ber·cle \'t(y)übə(r)kəl\ *n* -s [L *tuberculum,* dim. of *tuber*] **1 :** a small knobby prominence or excrescence: as **a** (1) **:** a prominence on the crown of a molar tooth (2) **:** a small rough prominence (as on the front of the head of the tibia for the patellar ligament or on the femur at the upper part of the junction of the neck and great trochanter or on the ulna at the base of the coronoid process) on a bone usu. being smaller than a tuberosity and serving for the attachment of one or more muscles or ligaments (3) **:** an eminence near the head of a rib that articulates with the transverse process of a vertebra **b :** any of several prominences in the central nervous system that mark the nuclei of various nerves ⟨the acoustic ~⟩ **c :** NODULE 2b(3) **d** (1) **:** a small tuber (2) **:** a tuberous root (as of a dahlia) that bears adventitious buds and functions like a true tuber **e :** TUBERCLE 2 **2 a :** a small discrete lump in the substance of an organ or in the skin: (1) **:** the specific lesion of tuberculosis consisting of a packed mass of epithelioid cells, giant cells, disintegration products of leukocytes and bacilli, and usu. a necrotic center (2) **:** a similar mass occurring as a local tissue reaction in diseases other than tuberculosis **b :** TUBERCULOSIS — not used technically

tubercle bacillus *n* **:** a bacterium (*Mycobacterium tuberculosis*) that is the cause of tuberculosis

tu·ber·cled \-ld\ *adj* **:** TUBERCULATE

tubercled orchid *also* **tubercled orchis** *n* **:** GREEN REIN ORCHIS

tubercle of darwin *usu cap D* **:** DARWIN'S TUBERCLE

tubercle of ro·lan·do \-rō'lan(,)dō\ *usu cap R* [after Luigi *Rolando* †1831 Ital. anatomist] **:** TUBERCULUM CINEREUM

tubercul- *or* **tuberculo-** *comb form* [NL, fr. L *tuberculum,* dim. of *tuber* — more at TUBER] **1 a :** tubercle ⟨*tubercular*⟩ **b :** tuberculous ⟨*tuberculid*⟩ **2 :** tubercle bacillus ⟨*tuberculin*⟩ **3 :** tuberculosis ⟨*tuberculo*therapy⟩

tubercula *pl of* TUBERCULUM

¹tu·ber·cu·lar \tə'bərkyələr, t(y)ü'-, -'bək-, -'bəik-, -lə(r)\ *adj* [NL *tubercularis,* fr. *tubercul-* + L *-aris* -ar] **1 :** of, relating to, resembling, or constituting a tubercle **:** TUBERCULATE ⟨a ~ process⟩ ⟨identification by ~ analysis⟩ **2 :** characterized by the presence of tubercular lesions ⟨~ leprosy⟩ — often distinguished from *tuberculous* **3 a :** of, relating to, or affected with tuberculosis **:** TUBERCULOUS ⟨a ~ child⟩ **b :** intended for tuberculars ⟨a ~ hospital⟩ **c :** caused by the tubercle bacillus ⟨~ meningitis⟩ **4 :** characterized by a weak or sickly state that requires cure or amendment ⟨~ finances⟩ — **tu·ber·cu·lar·ly** *adv*

²tubercular \"\ *n* -s **:** a person having tuberculosis

tu·ber·cu·lare \tə,bərkyə'la(a)rē\ *n* -s [NL, fr. neut. sing. of *tubercularis* tubercular] **:** DARWIN'S TUBERCLE

tu·ber·cu·lar·ia \-a(a)rēə\ *n, cap* [NL, fr. *tubercularis* + *-ia*] **:** a genus (the type of the family Tuberculariaceae) comprising fungi with often red or pink sporodochia and including some that cause diebacks of woody plants

tu·ber·cu·lar·i·a·ce·ae \=,==,la(a)rē'āsē,ē\ *n pl, cap* [NL, fr. *Tubercularia,* type genus + *-aceae*] **:** a large family of mainly saprophytic imperfect fungi (order Moniliales) having the conidia formed typically in sporodochia — see FUSARIUM, SPORODOCHIUM, TUBERCULARIA — **tu·ber·cu·lar·i·a·ceous** \=;==;==;āshəs\ *adj*

¹tu·ber·cu·late \tə'bərkyələt, t(y)ü'-, -'bək-, -'bəik-, -yə,lāt, *usu* -d·+V\ *or* **tu·ber·cu·lat·ed** \-yə,lād·əd, -ātəd\ *adj* [*tuberculate* fr. NL *tuberculatus,* fr. *tubercul-* + L *-atus* -ate; *tuberculated* fr. NL *tuberculatus* + E *-ed*] **1 :** having a tubercle **:** characterized by tubercles **2 :** TUBERCULAR — **tu·ber·cu·late·ly** *adv*

²tuberculate \"\ *n* -s [*tubercule* + *-ate*] **:** the aggregate of tubercules in an iron pipe

tu·ber·cu·la·tion \-=;==;lāshən\ *n* -s [*tubercule* + *-ation*] **1 a :** formation of or affection with tubercles **b :** a growth or arrangement of tubercles **2 :** the collection of tubercules in or on iron pipe **:** TUBERCULATE

tu·ber·cule \'t(y)übə(r),kyül\ *n* -s [F, fr. L *tuberculum*] **1 :** TUBERCLE **2 :** a small knob or button of rust formed on the inside of an iron pipe

tu·ber·culed \-ld\ *adj* **:** TUBERCULATE

tu·ber·cu·lid \tə'bərkyələd\ *or* **tu·ber·cu·lide** \-yə,līd\ *n* -s [ISV *tubercul-* + *-id, -ide*] **:** a tuberculous lesion of the skin; *esp* **:** one that is an id

tu·ber·cu·li·form \-yələ,fȯrm\ *adj* [NL *tuberculiformis,* fr. *tubercul-* + L *-iformis* -iform] **:** sufficiently short and blunt as to resemble a tubercle ⟨a ~ process on the head of an insect⟩

tu·ber·cu·lin \tə'bərkyələn, t(y)ü'-, -'bək-, -'bəik-\ *n* -s [ISV *tubercul-* + *-in*] **:** a sterile liquid containing the growth products of or specific substances extracted from the tubercle bacillus and used in the diagnosis of tuberculosis esp. in children and cattle — see OLD TUBERCULIN, TUBERCULIN TEST

tuberculin test *also* **tuberculin reaction** *n* **:** a test for hypersensitivity to tuberculin in which tuberculin is injected usu. into the skin of the individual tested and the appearance of inflammation at the site of injection is construed as indicating past or present tubercular infection — compare MANTOUX TEST

tuberculo- — see TUBERCUL-

tu·ber·cu·lo·cid·al \tə,bərkyəlō;sīd·ᵊl\ *adj* [*tubercul-* + *-cidal*] **:** destroying tubercle bacilli

tu·ber·cu·lo·derm \=';===,dərm\ *also* **tu·ber·cu·lo·der·ma** \=,===;'dərmə\ *n* -s [NL *tuberculoderma,* fr. *tubercul-* + *-derma*] **:** a tuberculous lesion of the skin **:** TUBERCULID

tu·ber·cu·loid \tə'bərkyə,lȯid\ *adj* [ISV *tubercul-* + *-oid*] **:** resembling tuberculosis esp. in being marked by the presence of tubercles **:** TUBERCULAR 2 ⟨~ leprosy⟩

tu·ber·cu·lo·ma \=,==;'lōmə\ *n, pl* **tuberculomas** \-məz\ *also* **tuberculoma·ta** \-məd·ə\ [NL, fr. *tubercul-* + *-oma*] **:** a large solitary caseous tubercle of tuberculous character occurring esp. in the brain

tu·ber·cu·lose \tə'bərkyə,lōs\ *adj* [NL *tuberculosus* tuberculous] **:** TUBERCULATE

tu·ber·cu·lo·sectorial \tə,bərkyə(,)lō+\ *adj* [*tubercul-* + *sectorial*] **:** of, relating to, or being a lower molar occurring in many carnivorous mammals (as the dog) and being laterally compressed with sharp anterior cusps and a heel composed of low blunt cusps

tu·ber·cu·lo·sis \tə,bərkyə'lōsəs, t(y)ü,-, -,bək-, -,bəik- *sometimes* ÷ -kə'- *or* ,t(y)übə(r)k-\ *n* -ES [NL, fr. *tubercul-* + *-osis*] **1 :** an acute or chronic highly variable communicable disease of man and some other vertebrates caused by the tubercle bacillus (*Mycobacterium tuberculosis*), found in any tissue in the body but esp. those of the respiratory tract whence it spreads from local lesions or by way of the lymph or blood vessels, and characterized by toxic symptoms (as fever, night sweats, or loss of weight) from absorption of toxic products of tissue destruction or by allergic manifestations that involve inflammatory infiltrations, formation of tubercles, caseation, and fibrosis — see MILIARY TUBERCULOSIS **2 :** any of several bacterial diseases of plants (as the olive or sugar beet) in which enlargements or pockets are formed

tu·ber·cu·lo·stat \tə'bərkyəlō,stat\ *n* -s [*tubercul-* + *-stat*] **:** an agent that inhibits the growth of the tubercle bacillus — **tu·ber·cu·lo·stat·ic** \=;==;==;stad·ik\ *adj*

tu·ber·cu·lo·stearic acid \tə;bərkyə(,)lō+...\ *n* [*tubercul-* + *stearic*] **:** a fatty acid $C_{18}H_{37}COOH$ obtained from the wax of tubercle bacilli and differing from most naturally occurring fatty acids in that it contains an odd number of carbon atoms and its structure is branched; 10-methyl-stearic acid

tu·ber·cu·lo·toxin \"+\ *n* [*tubercul-* + *toxin*] **:** a toxic substance from the tubercle bacillus

tu·ber·cu·lous \tə'bərkyələs, t(y)ü'-, -'bək-, -'bəik-\ *adj* [NL *tuberculosus,* fr. L *tuberculum* tubercle (dim. of *tuber*) + *-osus* -ose — more at TUBER] **1 :** of, relating to, or characterized by tubercles **:** TUBERCULAR, TUBERCULATE ⟨a ~ chitinized wing case⟩ **2 a :** constituting or affected with tuberculosis ⟨a ~ patient⟩ ⟨a ~ process⟩ **b :** caused by or resulting from the presence or products of the tubercle bacillus ⟨~ peritonitis⟩ ⟨~ meningitis⟩ — **tu·ber·cu·lous·ly** *adv*

tu·ber·cu·lum \-ləm\ *n, pl* **tubercu·la** \-lə\ [L] **:** TUBERCLE

tuberculum ci·ne·re·um \-sə'nirēəm\ *n* [NL, ashy tubercle] **:** an elevation on the lateral aspect of the medulla oblongata produced by the spinal trigeminal tract and its nucleus

tuber fern *n* **:** a common tropical fern (*Nephrolepis cordifolia*) with bright green leaves on shaggy stipes and small fleshy edible tubers along the prostrate stolons

tuber flea beetle *n* **:** a chrysomelid beetle (*Epitrix tuberis*) that is destructive to potatoes and some other plants in parts of western Canada and U.S.

tu·ber·in \'t(y)übərən\ *n* -s [*tuber* + *-in*] **:** a globulin constituting the principal protein of the potato tuber

tuber indexing *n* **:** EYE INDEXING

tu·ber·iza·tion \,t(y)übərə'zāshən\ *n* -s [*tuber* + *-ization*] **:** the process of forming tubers

tu·ber·less \'t(y)übə(r)ləs\ *adj* **:** lacking or deficient in tubers

tuber line *n* **:** a clonal population resulting from the continued propagation from one original tuber (as of the potato)

tuber moth *n* **:** POTATO MOTH

tu·ber·oid \'t(y)übə,rȯid\ *adj* [ISV *tuber* + *-oid*] **:** resembling a tuber ⟨a ~ root⟩

tube roll *n* **:** TABLE ROLL

tube·rose \'t(y)üb,rōz *sometimes* -übə,rōz *or* -ōs\ *n* -s [NL *tuberosa* (specific epithet of *Polianthes tuberosa*), fr. fem. of L *tuberosus* tuberous] **:** a Mexican bulbous herb (*Polianthes tuberosa*) commonly cultivated for its spike of fragrant white single or double flowers that resemble small lilies

tu·ber·os·i·ty \ˌt(y)übəˈräsəd·ē, -ətē, -i\ *n* -ES [MF *tuberosité*, fr. L *tuberosus* + MF *-ité* -ity] : an obtuse prominence: as **a** *archaic* : a swollen mass **b** : any of various large prominences on bones (as the lateral eminences of the head of the tibia, the rough eminence on the ischium on which the body rests when sitting, that on the inner front aspect of the radius for the attachment of the biceps tendon or on the cuboid and navicular bones of the foot) usu. serving for the attachment of muscles or ligaments **c** : TUBERCLE 1a(3)

tu·ber·ous \ˈt(y)übərəs\ *also* **tu·ber·ose** \-bəˌrōs\ *adj* [L *tuberosus*, fr. *tuber* + *-osus* -ose — more at TUBER] **1** *archaic* : covered with or divided into knobby prominences : KNOBBED **2 a** : consisting of, bearing, or resembling a tuber **b** : of, relating to, or being a tuber or tuberous root of a plant : having or reproducing by such structures — **tu·ber·ous·ly** *adv*

tuberous begonia *n* : any of various begonias that have tuberous roots and usu. large showy and often double flowers and that are complex hybrids commonly treated as a horticultural species (*Begonia tuberhybrida*) — compare FIBROUS-ROOTED BEGONIA, RHIZOMATOUS BEGONIA

tuberous root *n* : a thick fleshy root resembling a tuber but lacking buds or scale leaves, functioning esp. in storage in biennial or perennial plants in which new growth is from a crown, and being simple and solitary (as in the beet or turnip) or variously fascicled (as in the dahlia) — compare FIBROUS ROOT; see ROOT illustration — **tuberous–rooted** \ˈ;==ˈ;==\ *adj*

tuberous water lily *n* : a water lily (*Nymphaea tuberosa*) of the northeastern U. S. with large white or pale rose odorless flowers and tuberous creeping rhizomes

tuber root *n* : BUTTERFLY WEED 1

tubers *pl of* TUBER

tubes *pl of* TUBE, *pres 3d sing of* TUBE

tube saw *n* : TUBULAR SAW

tube set *n* : a radio receiving set containing electron tubes

tube shell *n* : BLIND SHELL 2

tube snout *n* : a slender marine fish (*Aulorhyndus flavidus*) having the head prolonged as a tubular snout with the small mouth at its end, related to the pipefishes, and sometimes occurring in dense schools off the Pacific coast of No. America

tube spinner *or* **tube weaver** *n* : any of various spiders (as of the genera *Tegenaria* and *Agelena*) that construct a flat web connected with a tubular nest in which the spider hides

tube transmitter *n* : a radio transmitting set using a tube generator

tube well *n* : a driven well

tube worm *n* : an annelid worm (as a serpulid) building and living in a tube

tube wrench *n* : PIPE WRENCH

tubfast \ˈ=,=\ *adj* [¹*tub* + *fast*] : able to resist ordinary domestic laundry procedures ⟨~ cottons⟩

tub file *n* : a file of cards or papers so housed that all or a large part of it may be consulted at one time

tubfish \ˈ=,=\ *Brit var of* TUB 2

tub front *n*, *chiefly Brit* : BLOCKFRONT

tubi- *comb form* [NL, fr. L *tubus* — more at TUBE] : tube ⟨*tubi*valve⟩ ⟨*Tubi*pora⟩

tu·bic·o·la \t(y)üˈbikələ\ *n pl*, *cap* [NL, fr. *tubi-* + *-cola* (fr. L *-cola* inhabitant) — more at -COLOUS] *in some esp former classifications* : an order of Annelida comprising the tube worms and being nearly equivalent to Sedentaria

tu·bic·o·lae \-kəˌlē\ *n pl*, *cap* [NL, fr. *tubi-* + *-colae* (pl. of *-cola*)] *in former classifications* : a group of animals distinguished by the tubes they construct: **a** : SEDENTARIA **b** : a group of spiders that build tubular nests

tu·bic·o·lous \-kələs\ *adj* [*tubi-* + *-colous*] **1** *also* **tu·bi·cole** \ˈt(y)übəˌkōl\ [*tubi-* + *-colous or -cole*] : living in a self-constructed tube ⟨a ~ annelid⟩ **2** [NL *Tubicolae* + E *-ous*] : spinning a tubular web ⟨~ spiders⟩ **3** *or* **tu·bic·o·lar** \t(y)üˈbikələ(r)\ [NL *Tubicola* + E *-ous or -ar*] : of or relating to the Tubicola or Tubicolae

tu·bi·fa·cient \ˌt(y)übəˈfāshənt\ *adj* [*tubi-* + *-facient*] : secreting or constructing a tube

tu·bi·fex \ˈt(y)übəˌfeks\ *n* [NL *Tubific-, Tubifex*, fr. *tubi-* + L *-fic-, -fex* (fr. *facere* to make, do) — more at DO] **1** *cap* : a genus (the type of the family Tubificidae) of slender red or brown oligochaete worms having four bundles of setae on each segment and living in tubes in fresh or brackish water and being widely used as food for aquarium fish **2** *pl* **tubifex** *or* **tubifexes** : any worm of the genus *Tubifex*

¹**tu·bif·i·cid** \t(y)üˈbifəsəd\ *adj* [NL *Tubificidae*] : of or relating to the Tubificidae

²**tubificid** \"\ *n* -S : a worm of the family Tubificidae

tu·bi·fic·i·dae \ˌt(y)übəˈfisəˌdē\ *n pl*, *cap* [NL *Tubific-, Tubifex*, type genus + *-idae*] : a nearly cosmopolitan family of aquatic oligochaete worms that do not reproduce asexually (as by budding or division) — see TUBIFEX

tu·bi·flo·rae \ˌt(y)übəˈflōrˌē\ [NL, fr. *tubi-* + *florae*] *syn of* POLEMONIALES

tu·bi·flo·ra·les \ˌt(y)übəflōrˈā(ˌ)lēz\ [NL, fr. *tubi-* + *flora* + *-ales*] *syn of* CAMPANULALES

tu·bi·flo·rous \ˈt(y)übəˈflōrəs\ *adj* [*tubi-* + *-florous*] : TUBULIFLOROUS

tu·bi·form \ˈt(y)übəˌfȯrm\ *adj* [*tubi-* + *-form*] : having the form of a tube : tubular in form

tu·bi·nar·es \ˌt(y)übəˈna(a)(ˌ)rēz\ [NL, fr. *tubi-* + L *nares*, pl. of *naris* nostril — more at NARIS] *syn of* PROCELLARIIFORMES

tu·bi·nar·i·al \ˌ;==ˈna(a)rēəl\ *also* **tu·bi·nar·ine** \-)rən, -)ˌrīn\ *adj* [NL *Tubinares* + E *-ial or -ine*] **1** : having the nostrils tubular **2** : of or relating to the Procellariiformes

tub·ing \ˈt(y)übiŋ, -bēŋ\ *n* -S [¹*tube* + *-ing*] **1 a** : material in the form of a tube : a length or piece of tube ⟨rubber ~⟩ ⟨a roll of copper ~⟩: as (1) : TUBULAR FABRIC (2) : a special grade of high-test pipe fitted with threads and couplings of special design **b** : a series of tubes : the tubes of a particular system or apparatus ⟨renewed the ~ of the boiler⟩ **2** [fr. gerund of ²*tube*] : the act or an instance of making or installing tubes

tu·bip·o·ra \t(y)üˈbipərə\ *n*, *cap* [NL, fr. *tubi-* + *-pora*] : a genus (the type of the family Tubiporidae of the order Alcyonacea) of corals comprising the organ-pipe corals — **tu·bi·pore** \ˈt(y)übəˌpō(ə)r\ *n*

tub·man \ˈtəbmən\ *n*, *pl* **tubmen** [¹*tub* + *man*] **1** [so called fr. the fact that his place in the Court was beside the tub used as a measure of capacity in excise cases] : a junior barrister in the former English Court of Exchequer having except in crown business precedence in motion over all juniors except the postman **2** : one whose work involves the use of tubs or vats: as **a** : a tender of the tubs in which hog carcasses are scalded preparatory to dehairing **b** : a worker who dyes hosiery or knit goods in a vat or dyeing machine

tu·bo·cu·ra·rine \ˌt(y)übōk(y)üˈräˌrēn, -ärən\ *n* [ISV *tubo-* (fr. L *tubus* tube) + *curare* + *-ine*; fr. its being shipped in sections of hollow bamboo] : a toxic alkaloid of the isoquinoline group or its crystalline quaternary ammonium chloride $C_{38}H_{44}Cl_2N_2O_6.5H_2O$ that is obtained chiefly from the bark and stems of the So. American pareira brava vine and in its dextrorotatory form constitutes the chief active constituent of curare (sense 3) and that is used similarly

tu·boid \ˈt(y)üˌbȯid\ *adj* [¹*tube* + *-oid*] : resembling a tube : approaching the tubular in form

tub orchard *n* : a group of fruit trees cultivated in tubs so that they may be brought indoors for storage (as for subsequent forcing into bloom in greenhouses or for culture beyond their normal limits of hardiness)

tub preacher *n* [¹*tub* (sense 3c)] : a ranting dissenting preacher

tubs *pl of* TUB, *pres 3d sing of* TUB

tub–size \ˈ=,=\ *vt* : to pass (paper) through a tub or vat containing a sizing solution (as of gelatin or starch) — compare BEATER-SIZE, SURFACE-SIZE

tub sugar *n* : soft maple sugar that is run into wooden or tin tubs for storage

tub–thumper \ˈ=,==\ *n* : one who engages in impassioned or ranting utterance ⟨at least one *tub-thumper* for every known variety of panacea —Earl Brown⟩

¹**tub–thumping** \ˈ=,==\ *n* : an act or instance of engaging in impassioned or ranting utterance ⟨a terrific job of *tub-thumping* for a novel —Bennett Cerf⟩

²**tub–thumping** \"\ *adj* : marked by tub-thumping ⟨a *tub-thumping* socialist —Anthony West⟩

tu·bu·lar \ˈt(y)übyələ(r)\ *adj* [L *tubus* tube + E *-ular* — more at TUBE] **1 a** : having the form of a tube ⟨a ~ process⟩ **b** : having or consisting of a tube ⟨a ~ calyx⟩ : made up of tubes : FISTULOUS ⟨a ~ hymenium⟩ **c** : provided with tubes ⟨a ~ boiler⟩ : involving the use of tubes or made of tubular stock ⟨a ~ chair⟩ ⟨a radiator of ~ construction⟩ **2** : relating to or sounding as if produced through tubes ⟨a ~ respiratory sound⟩

tubular bridge *n* **1** : a bridge supported chiefly by steel tubes **2** : a plate-girder bridge in the form of a rectangular tube

tubular chimes *or* **tubular bells** *n pl* : GLOCKENSPIEL 2

tubular fabric *n* : a woven, knitted, or braided fabric made in circular seamless form ⟨jersey is usually knit as a *tubular fabric*⟩ ⟨*tubular fabric* for pillowcases⟩

tubular floret *n* : DISK FLOWER

tubular girder *n* : a plate girder having two or more vertical webs with a space between them and solid members joining them top and bottom to form a tube of rectangular cross section with one or more cells

tu·bu·lar·ia \ˌt(y)übyəˈla(a)rēə\ *n* [NL, fr. L *tubulus* tubule, tube + NL *-aria*] **1** *cap* : a genus (the type of the family Tubulariidae) of anthomedusan hydroids having hydranths with two circles of tentacles at the summits of long, slender usu. simple stems and small adelocodonic gonophores that cluster at the bases of the outer tentacles **2** -S : any hydroid of the genus *Tubularia* or sometimes of the family Tubulariidae — **tu·bu·lar·i·an** \ˌ;==ˈla(a)rēən\ *adj or n*

tu·bu·lar·i·ae \ˌ==ˈla(a)rēˌē\ *or* **tu·bu·lar·i·da** \-ˈlarədə\ [NL *Tubulariae* fr. *Tubularia*; NL *Tubularida* fr. *Tubularia* + *-ida*] *syn of* ANTHOMEDUSAE

tu·bu·lar·i·ty \ˌt(y)übyəˈlarəd·ē, -ətē, -i *also* -ˈler-\ *n* -ES : the quality or state of being tubular

tubular lock *n* : a rim lock with the tumblers contained in a fixed tube that usu. projects through the door

tu·bu·lar·ly *adv* : in a tubular manner or form

tubular pile *n* : a pile consisting of a steel tube driven into the ground and filled with concrete after the enclosed earth has been removed

tubular–pneumatic action *n* : an action in a pipe organ in which the opening and closing of the mouth of the pipe is controlled by air pressure regulated by the depressing and releasing of the key

tubular rivet *n* : a rivet with a tubular shank

tubular saw *n* : a crown saw esp. when having considerable length compared to its diameter

tubular skate *n* : an ice skate having the frame composed of tubing

tu·bu·lary \ˈt(y)übyəˌlerē\ *adj* [L *tubulus* tubule, tube + E *-ary*] : being, made up of, or involving tubes ⟨~ ducts⟩

tu·bu·late \ˈt(y)übyələt, -yəˌlāt\ *also* **tu·bu·lat·ed** \-yəˌlād·əd\ *adj* [*tubulate* fr. L *tubulatus*, fr. L *tubulus* tubule, tube + *-atus* -ate; *tubulated* fr. L *tubulatus* + E *-ed*] **1** : provided with a tube **2** : having the form of a tube

tu·bu·la·tion \ˌ;==ˈlāshən\ *n* -S [L *tubulation-, tubulatio*, fr. *tubulus* + *-ation-, -atio* -ation] **1** : the act of shaping or making a tube or of providing with a tube **2 a** : arrangement or an array of tubes **b** : a tubular piece (as a juncture, connection, or orifice)

tu·bu·la·ture \ˈt(y)übyələˌchu̇(ə)r, -ˌchər\ *n* -S [*tubulate* + *-ure*] : TUBULATION 2

tu·bule \ˈt(y)üˌbyül\ *n* -S [L *tubulus* tubule, tube, dim. of *tubus* tube — more at TUBE] : a small tube; *esp* : a very slender elongated channel in an anatomical structure

tubuli- *comb form* [NL, fr. L *tubulus* tubule, tube] **1** : tubule : tubulus ⟨*tubuli*ferous⟩ **2** : tubular ⟨*tubuli*florous⟩

tu·bu·li·bran·chi·a·ta \ˌt(y)übyələˌbraŋkēˈäd·ə, -ˈād·ə\ *n pl* [NL, fr. *tubuli-* + *Branchiata*] *in former classifications* : an artificial group of gastropod mollusks including those (as of the genus *Vermetus*) having a tubular shell — **tu·bu·li·bran·chi·ate** \ˌ;===ˈbraŋkēət, -ēˌāt\ *adj or n*

tu·bu·li·den·ta·ta \ˌt(y)übyələdenˈtäd·ə, -ˈtād·ə\ *n pl*, *cap* [NL, fr. neut. pl. of *tubulidentatus* having tubelike teeth, fr. *tubuli-* + *-dentatus* -dentate] : an obscure order of Mammalia of protungulate or possibly creodont ancestry comprising the aardvark and extinct related forms that are distinguished by teeth composed of a cluster of upright parallel vasodentin columns with individual pulp canals — **tu·bu·li·den·tate** \ˌ;===ˈdenˌtāt\ *adj or n*

tu·bu·lif·era \ˌt(y)übyəˈlif(ə)rə\ *n pl*, *cap* [NL, fr. *tubulifer* tubuliferous] **1** *in some classifications* : a group of Hymenoptera comprising the families Serphidae and Chrysididae or the Chrysididae alone and being distinguished by a tubular ovipositor **2** : a suborder of Thysanoptera including those that have the last segment of the abdomen tubular — **tu·bu·lif·er·an** \-rən\ *n* -S

tu·bu·lif·er·ous \ˌ;==ˈlif(ə)rəs\ *adj* [NL *tubulifer*, fr. *tubuli-* + L *-fer* -ferous] : having or made up of tubules

tu·bu·li·floral \ˌ;t(y)übyələ+\ *adj* [ISV *tubuli-* + *floral*] : having tubular flowers

tu·bu·li·flo·rous \"+ˈflōrəs\ *adj* [ISV *tubuli-* + *-florous*] : having all the flowers with tubular corollas — used of plants of the order Campanulales and esp. of the family Compositae

tu·bu·lip·o·ra \ˌt(y)übyəˈlipərə\ *n*, *cap* [NL, fr. *tubuli-* + *-pora*] : a genus (the type of the family Tubuliporidae) of cyclostomate bryozoans having tubular calcareous calyculi — **tu·bu·li·pore** \ˈt(y)übyələˌpō(ə)r\ *n* -S

tubulo- *comb form* [L *tubulus* tubule, tube + E *-o-*] : tubular and ⟨*tubulo*racemose⟩

tu·bu·lo·saccular \ˌ;t(y)übyə(ˌ)lō+\ *adj* [*tubulo-* + *saccular*] : consisting of tubular and saccular elements

tu·bu·lous \ˈt(y)übyələs\ *also* **tu·bu·lose** \-yəˌlōs\ *adj* [NL *tubulosus*, fr. L *tubulus* + *-osus* -ose] **1** : resembling or having the form of a tube **2** : made up of or containing tubes or a tubular element (as florets) ⟨a ~ boiler⟩ — **tu·bu·lous·ly** *adv*

tu·bu·lure \ˈt(y)übyəˌlu̇(ə)r\ *n* -S [F, fr. *tubule* (fr. L *tubulus*) + *-ure*] : a short tubular opening (as at the top of a retort)

tu·bu·lus \ˈt(y)übyələs\ *n*, *pl* **tubu·li** \-yəˌlī\ [L — more at TUBULE] **1** : TUBULE **2** [NL, fr. L] : a slender tubular extensile ovipositor of some flies

tub wheel *n* : a drum used like a tumbling barrel esp. for washing skins

tu·can·de·ra *also* **tu·con·de·ra** \ˌtükənˈderə\ *n* -S [Pg *tocandera*, fr. Tupi *tocandira, tucanguira*, fr. *tucan* toucan + *guira* bird; fr. its size] : any of various large ponerine ants (esp. *Paraponera clavata*) of Central and So. America

tu·ca·no \tüˈkä(ˌ)nō\ *n*, *pl* **tucano** *or* **tucanos** *usu cap* **1 a** : a group of peoples of Colombia and northern Ecuador **b** : a member of any people of such group **2** : the language of the Tucano people

tu·ca·no·an \ˌ;tükaˌnōən\ *adj*, *usu cap* : of or relating to the Tucano or their language

tu·chun \ˈdüˈjün\ *n*, *pl* **tuchuns** *also* **tuchun** *often cap* [Chin (Pek) *tu¹-chün¹*, lit., overseer of troops] **1** : a Chinese military governor (as of a province) **2** : a Chinese warlord

tu–chung \ˈdüˈju̇ŋ\ *n* -S [Chin (Pek) *tu⁴ chung⁴*] : a very hardy Chinese tree (*Eucommia ulmoides*) that resembles an elm in appearance and is a potential source of rubber

¹**tuck** \ˈtək\ *vb* -ED/-ING/-S [ME *tuken, touken, tucken*, fr. OE *tūcian* to ill-treat, punish; akin to MD *tucken* to tug, OHG *zucken* to jerk, OE *togian* to pull — more at TOW] *vt* **1** *obs* : SCOLD, UPBRAID **2 a** : to pull up or gather into a fold — usu. used with *up* or *in* ⟨a geisha ~*s* her robe well up to her knees —Lafcadio Hearn⟩ **b** : to make a tuck in; *esp* : to shorten or ornament with a tuck ⟨the bodice was minutely ~*ed* —Kay Boyle⟩ **c** : to knit in tuck stitch **3** *archaic* : to draw up and gird the clothes of **4** : to put into a snug place ⟨~*ed* her notebook under her arm —Dorothy Sayers⟩; *specif* : to put into a snug place that affords concealment or isolation ⟨philosophically ~*ed* his handful of medals into an old cigar box —*Time*⟩ ⟨beaches lie ~*ed* in between its rocky cliffs —*Amer. Guide Series: Maine*⟩ — often used with *away* ⟨a modern colonial brick structure . . . has been ~*ed* away in a corner —*Amer. Guide Series: Conn.*⟩ ⟨many of his bitterest attacks were ~*ed* away in footnotes —J.S.Schapiro⟩ **5 a** : to push in the loose end or edge of so as to hold tightly ⟨~*ed* in the sheets⟩ ⟨forgot to ~ in your shirttail —John Steinbeck⟩ ⟨~*ed* a blanket around the child⟩ **b** : to cover (as a person) by tucking in the bedclothes ⟨is ~*ing* him in now⟩ ⟨~*ed* him up at last in his crib —Marcia Davenport⟩ **6** *archaic* : HANG 1b(1) — usu. used with *up* **7** : EAT — usu. used with *away* or *in* ⟨~*ed* away both steak and chicken —W.T.Musgrove⟩ ⟨~ in as much as they desire —*Strand Mag.*⟩ **8** : to take (fish) from a large seine with a tuck seine **9** : to put into a tuck position ⟨~ the legs to the chest —N.C.Loken⟩ ~ *vi* **1** : to draw together into tucks or folds **2** : to eat heartily — usu. used with *into* or *in* ⟨the careless abandon of a vegetarian ~*ing* into his beans —*Science*⟩ **3 a** : to fit in snugly ⟨the helicopter . . . ~*s* away into a hangar at the open end of the ship —Douglas Willis⟩ **b** : to fit in under something that binds ⟨tailored shirts which ~ in —*Women's Wear Daily*⟩ — **tuck one's tail** : to be reduced to shame or confusion ⟨hated to *tuck his tail* and back down now —F.B.Gipson⟩

²**tuck** \"\ *n* -S [ME *tucke*, fr. *tuken, tucken* to tuck] **1 a** (1) : a fold stitched or woven into cloth for the purpose of shortening, decorating, or controlling fullness (2) : a gusset in the side of a paper bag **b** : something that shortens or diminishes : CUT ⟨the opera lasts five hours if you take no ~*s* in score —Claudia Cassidy⟩ **2** : TUCK SEINE **3** : the part of a vessel where the ends of the lower planks meet under the stern **4** *Brit* **a** : a large meal : SPREAD **b** : FOOD; *esp* : sweet foods (as pastry, jam, and candy) **5 a** : an act or instance of pushing in a loose end or edge so as to secure ⟨gave the blankets a few more ~*s*⟩ **b** (1) : the act of tucking a strand of rope between or under other strands (2) : the joint so made **6 a** : a flap on a book cover that folds over and fits into a slot or a band on the opposite cover so as to keep the book closed — called also *tuck-in* **b** : the part of the end flap of a paperboard box that is inserted into the body to secure the end **7** : the end of a cigar that is to be lighted **8** : a body position used in diving, gymnastics, and dancing in which the knees are bent, the thighs drawn tightly to the chest, and the hands clasped around the shins — compare LAYOUT 5, ¹¹PIKE **9** : a fabric or leather covering for the steel shank of a shoe

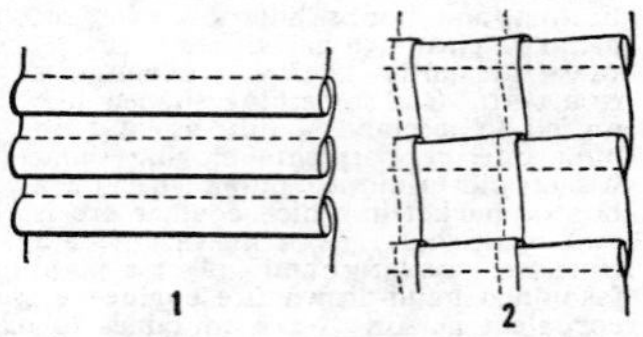

tuck 1a(1): *1* plain tucks, *2* cross tucks

³**tuck** \ˈtək\ *also* **touk** \ˈtük\ *n* -S [obs. E *tuk, touk* to beat the drum, sound the trumpet, fr. ME *tukken*, fr. ONF *toquer* to touch, strike, fr. (assumed) VL *toccare* — more at TOUCH] : a sound of or as if of a drumbeat ⟨danced silently to the ~ of drum —J.G.Frazer⟩

⁴**tuck** \ˈtək\ *n* -S [MF *estoc* thrusting sword, fr. OF, tree trunk, sword point — more at ESTOC] *archaic* : RAPIER

⁵**tuck** \"\ *n* -S [prob. fr. ²*tuck*] : VIGOR, ENERGY, TOUGHNESS ⟨seemed to kind of take the ~ all out of me —Mark Twain⟩

⁶**tuck** \"\ *n* -S [by shortening & alter.] : TUXEDO

tuck·a·hoe \ˈtəkəˌhō\ *n* -S [*tockawhoughe*, lit., it is round (in some Algonquian language of Virginia)] **1 a** : either of two American plants having rootstocks used as food by the Indians: (1) : ARROW ARUM (2) : GOLDEN CLUB **b** : the edible rootstock of a tuckahoe **2** : the large edible sclerotium of a subterranean fungus (*Poria cocos*) that is firm and white inside with a hard brown exterior — called also *Indian bread* **3** *usu cap* : VIRGINIAN; *esp* : a Virginian living east of the Blue Ridge mountains — used as a nickname

tuckaway \ˈ==,=\ *adj* [fr. the phrase *tuck away*] : capable of being folded and put out of the way ⟨~ table⟩

tuck box *n*, *Brit* : a box of delicacies from home

tuck comb *n* : a comb for holding the hair or a hat in place

tucked *past of* TUCK

tucked up *adj* [fr. past part. of *tuck up*, v.] **1** : drawn in or up : CONTRACTED; *esp* : having the flanks drawn in and the abdomen small either as a normal feature (as in greyhounds and some rabbits) or as an indication of ill health or poor condition (as in most domestic mammals) **2** *Brit* **a** : CRAMPED, HAMPERED **b** : EXHAUSTED

¹**tuck·er** \ˈtəkə(r)\ *n* -S [ME *touker*, fr. *tuken, touken* to tuck + *-er* — more at TUCK] **1** : one that tucks: as **a** (1) : an attachment on a sewing machine for making tucks (2) : an operator of a tucker attachment — called also *corder, pleater* **b** : the mechanism of a hay press or baler that folds in the hay to make the outside of the bales neat and square **2** : a piece of lace or cloth used to fill in the low neckline of a dress : CHEMISETTE — compare BIB AND TUCKER **3** *chiefly Austral* : FOOD **4** : SQUARE DANCE; *esp* : a square dance in which there is a dancer without a partner

²**tucker** \"\ *vt* -ED/-ING/-S [¹*tuck* + *-er* (freq. suffix as in *batter*)] : EXHAUST ⟨it ~*ed* me, that act —A.B.Guthrie⟩ — often used with *out* ⟨plain ~*ed* out —Laura Krey⟩ **syn** see TIRE

tucker-bag \ˈ==,=\ *n*, *chiefly Austral* : a bag used esp. by travelers in the bush to hold food

¹**tuck·et** \ˈtəkət\ *n* -S [prob. fr. ³*tuck* (influenced in meaning by obs. E *tuk* to beat the drum, sound the trumpet) + *-et*] : a fanfare on a trumpet

²**tucket** \"\ *n* -S [prob. of Algonquian origin; akin to *tockawhoughe* tuckahoe (in some Algonquian language of Virginia), Delaware *p'tuckqueu* it is round] : a green ear of corn

¹**tuck–in** \ˈ=,=\ *n* -S [fr. *tuck in*, v.] **1** *chiefly Brit* : a large meal : SPREAD **2** : ²TUCK 6a **3** : material (as cloth) that is to be tucked in

²**tuck–in** \"\ *adj* : designed to be held in place by being tucked in ⟨a *tuck-in* blouse⟩

tuck·ing \ˈtəkiŋ\ *n* -S [²*tuck* + *-ing*] : a fabric that has tucks woven or sewn into it

tucking–comb \ˈ==,=\ *n* : BACK COMB

tuck–out \ˈ=,=\ *n* -S [²*tuck*] *chiefly Brit* : a large meal : SPREAD

tuck plate *n* : OXTER PLATE

tuck–point \ˈ=,=\ *vt* [²*tuck*] : to finish (the mortar joints between bricks or stones) with a narrow ridge of putty or fine lime mortar — **tuck–pointer** \ˈ=,==\ *n*

tucks *pres 3d sing of* TUCK, *pl of* TUCK

tuck seine *also* **tuck net** *n* : a seine about 70 fathoms long and very deep in the middle that is used to take fish from a larger seine

tuck–shop \ˈ=,=\ *n*, *Brit* : a confectioner's shop : CONFECTIONERY

tuck stitch *n* : a pattern stitch for circular-knit garments that is made by taking on more than one loop in a stitch

tuck–up \ˈ=,=\ *n* -S [fr. *tuck up*, v.] : the sharp upward curve of the underline behind the ribs (as of a greyhound or other dog of racy build)

tucky \ˈtəkē\ *or* **tucky lily** *n* -ES [perh. fr. ²*tuck* + *-y*] : SPATTERDOCK

tucondera *var of* TUCANDERA

tu·co–tu·co \ˈtü(ˌ)kōˈtü(ˌ)kō\ *also* **tu·cu–tu·cu** \-kü . . . kü\ *n* -S [AmerSp *tucutuco*, imit. of its cry] : any of various So. American hystricomorph burrowing rodents comprising the genus *Ctenomys* and resembling the No. American pocket gophers but lacking cheek pouches

tu·cum \tüˈküm\ *also* **tu·cu·ma** \-mə\ *n* -S [Pg *tucumã*, fr. Tupi *tucumá*] **1** *also* **tucum palm a** : any of several chiefly Brazilian palms of the genus *Astrocaryum* (esp. *A. tucuma*) with leaf bases that yield a coarse fiber used esp. for cordage and hats and with seeds that yield an edible oil **b** : a low spiny Brazilian palm (*Bactris setosa*) with leaves that yield a long strong fiber held to resemble wool and used locally for bags or other containers, fishing nets, and shoemakers' twines **2** : the fiber of a tucum

tu·cu·mán \ˌ;tükuˈmän\ *adj*, *usu cap* [fr. *Tucumán*, Argentina] : of or from the city of Tucumán, Argentina : of the kind or style prevalent in Tucumán

tu·cu·na·ré \tüˌkünəˈrā\ *n* -S [Pg, fr. Tupi] : any of several So. American cichlid river fishes (genus *Cichla*) that resemble bass and are esteemed for sport and food

-tude \ˌtüd, ˌtyüd\ *n suffix* -S [MF or L; MF *-tude*, fr. L *-tudin-, -tudo*] : -NESS ⟨omni*tude*⟩ ⟨parvi*tude*⟩

tu·desque \t(y)üˈdesk\ *adj*, *usu cap* [F, fr. Sp *tudesco*, of Gmc origin; akin to OHG *thiutisc, diutisc* German — more at DUTCH] : GERMAN

tu·dor \ˈt(y)üdə(r)\ *adj*, *usu cap* [fr. *Tudor*, English royal house] **1** : of or relating to the English royal family reigning from 1485 to 1603 **2 a** : of or relating to the Tudor period or its culture ⟨*Tudor* drama⟩ **b** : marked by Tudor arches, shallow moldings, and an abundance of paneling on the walls ⟨a *Tudor* manor house⟩

tudor arch *n, usu cap T* **:** a low elliptical or pointed arch drawn from three, four, or five centers; *esp* **:** a pointed arch drawn from four centers — see ARCH illustration

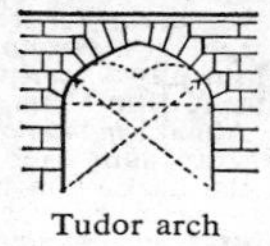
Tudor arch

tu·dor·esque \ˌt(y)üdəˈresk\ *adj, usu cap* [*Tudor,* royal house + E *-esque*] **:** of, relating to, or resembling the style of the Tudor period
tudor flower *n, usu cap T* **:** a trefoil flower used in the decorations of the late English Gothic art
tue iron \ˈtyü-\ *n* [alter. of earlier *tew iron,* by folk etymology fr. MF *tuyere* — more at TUYERE] **:** TUYERE
tues·day \ˈt(y)üzdē, -di *also* -z(ˌ)dā\ *n* -s *usu cap* [ME *tiwesday, tewisday,* fr. OE *tīwesdæg;* akin to OFris *tīesdei* Tuesday, OHG *ziostag,* ON *tȳsdagr, tȳrsdagr;* all fr. a prehistoric WGmc-NGmc compound formed from the components represented by OE *Tīw,* god of war, and *dæg* day; trans. of L *Martis dies,* lit., day of Mars (Roman god of war); trans. of Gk *hēmera Areios,* lit., day of Ares (Greek god of war) — more at DEITY, DAY] **:** the third day of the week **:** the day following Monday
tues·days \"+z\ *adv, usu cap* **:** on Tuesday repeatedly **:** on any Tuesday
tu·fa \ˈt(y)üfə\ *n* -s [It *tufo,* fr. OIt, fr. L *tophus, tofus,* prob. fr. Osco-Umbrian] **1 :** TUFF **2 :** a porous rock formed as a deposit from springs or streams — usu. used of calcareous deposits ⟨calcareous ~⟩
tu·fa·ceous \t(y)üˈfāshəs\ *adj* [It *tufaceo,* fr. L *tofaceus,* fr. *tofus* tufa + *-aceus* -aceous] **:** of, relating to, or resembling tufa
tu·fan \tüˈfän\ *n* -s [Ar *ṭūfān* deluge, fr. Gk *typhōn* typhoon — more at TYPHOON] *India* **:** a violent storm
tuff \ˈtəf\ *n* -s [MF *tuf,* fr. OIt *tufo* tufa] **:** a rock composed of the finer kinds of volcanic detritus usu. more or less stratified and in various states of consolidation — called also *tufa*
tuff·a·ceous \ˌtəˈfāshəs\ *adj* [*tuff* + *-aceous*] **:** of, relating to, or resembling tuff
tuf·fet \ˈtəfət\ *n* -s [alter. (influenced by *-et*) of ¹*tuft*] **1 :** TUFT 1b **2 :** a low seat (as a hassock or a stool)
tuf·foon \(ˌ)təˈfün\ *archaic var of* TYPHOON
¹**tuft** \ˈtəft\ *n* -s [ME, modif. of MF *tufe, tofe, toffe,* prob. of Gmc origin; akin to ON *toppr* tuft, OHG *zopf* — more at TOP] **1 :** a small cluster of elongated flexible outgrowths or parts attached or close together at the base and free at the opposite ends: as **a** (1) **:** a small bunch of hairs on the body (2) **:** a small beard on the chin **:** IMPERIAL **b :** a growing bunch of grass, leaves, flowers, or small plants **c :** a bunch of feathers; *specif* **:** the crest of a bird **d :** a bunch of soft fluffy threads cut off short and used to ornament cloth (as in a bedspread) **2 :** a small group (as of trees) **:** CLUMP, CLUSTER ⟨a ~ of pines —*U. S. Geographic Board*⟩ **3 :** MOUND ⟨the house . . . was set high on a ~ of land —*Yankee*⟩ **4 a :** a gold tassel formerly worn by titled undergraduates at Cambridge or Oxford Universities **b** *Brit* **:** a titled undergraduate at Cambridge or Oxford **5 a :** a cluster of loops or cut threads used as a finish for the tying threads of quilts, mattresses, or upholstery **b :** a covered button or leather disk for similar use **6 :** a coil of capillaries **7 :** one of the projections of extra warp or filling yarns drawn through a fabric or a carpet so as to produce a surface of raised loops or cut pile
²**tuft** \"\ *vb* -ED/-ING/-S *vt* **1 a :** to provide with a tuft **b :** to weave (a fabric) with tufts **2 a :** to beat (as a covert) for deer **b :** to rouse (game) by beating **3 :** to make (as a mattress or cushioned seat) firm by drawing stitches tightly through the padding at regular intervals and covering each depression on the surface with a tuft ~ *vi* **:** to form into tufts **:** grow into tufts
¹**tuf·taf·fe·ta** \ˌtəf+\ *n* -s [blend of ¹*tuft* + *taffeta*] **:** a taffeta having a pile that is arranged in tufts
²**tuftaffeta** \"\ *adj* **1 :** made of tuftaffeta **2** *obs* **:** clothed in tuftaffeta
tufted coquette *n* **:** a Central American hummingbird (*Lophornis ornatus*) having a large crest and cervical tufts; *broadly* **:** any of several related birds
tufted deer *n* **:** a deer of the genus *Elaphodus* related to the muntjacs but having minute antlers that are largely concealed by a frontal tuft of long coarse hair
tufted duck *or* **tufted pochard** *n* **1 :** an Old World duck (*Aythya fuligula*) having a tufted head but in most characteristics similar to the typical scaup ducks **2 :** RING-NECKED DUCK
tufted hair grass *n* **1 :** TUSSOCK GRASS a **2 :** a slender wiry grass (*Deschampsia caespitosa*) of the north temperate zone
tufted loosestrife *n* **:** a primulaceous bog or marsh herb (*Naumburgia thyrsiflora* of the north temperate zone that has small yellow flowers in heads on close racemes
tufted pansy *n* **:** a European violet (*Viola cornuta*) that has the spur of the corolla unusually prolonged — called also *horned violet*
tufted puffin *n* **:** a puffin (*Lunda cirrhata*) of the northern Pacific that is chiefly blackish brown above and below and has white cheeks and a large yellow plume over each eye
tufted titmouse *n* **:** an ashy gray titmouse (*Parus bicolor*) with a pointed crest that is found in the eastern U.S. chiefly south of New England and in the Midwest
tufted vetch *n* **:** a common perennial vetch (*Vicia cracca*) of temperate regions that has dense elongate clusters of flowers
tuft·er \ˈtəftə(r)\ *n* -s **:** one that tufts: as **a :** a hound used to drive deer out of cover **b :** a worker who tufts mattresses, cushions, quilts, or pads
tuft–hunted \ˈ=ˌ==\ *adj* **:** sought out by tuft-hunters
tuft–hunter \ˈ=ˌ==\ *n* [¹*tuft* (sense 4)] **:** one that seeks association with persons of title or high social status **:** SNOB
¹**tuft–hunting** \ˈ=ˌ==\ *n* **:** the practice of tuft-hunters
²**tuft–hunting** \"\ *adj* **:** of or relating to tuft-hunters **:** SNOBBISH
tuft·i·ly \ˈtəftəlē\ *adv* **:** in a tufty manner
tufting *n* -s [fr. gerund of ²*tuft*] **1 :** the act of one that tufts **:** a process of making tufts **2 :** TUFTS; *esp* **:** tufts used for decoration
tuft·let \ˈtəftlət\ *n* -s **:** a small tuft
tufts *pl of* TUFT, *pres 3d sing of* TUFT
tufty \-ftē\ *adj* -ER/-EST **1 :** growing in tufts **:** forming tufts ⟨little ~ plants —Katherine Mansfield⟩ **2 :** having many tufts ⟨a ~ stretch of marshland —Helen Eustis⟩
¹**tug** \ˈtəg\ *vb* **tugged; tugged; tugging; tugs** [ME *tuggen, toggen;* akin to OE *tēon* to pull, draw — more at TOW] *vi* **1 :** to pull hard ⟨*tugged* at the chains with the aid of two husky comrades —T.B.Costain⟩ ⟨jerked the shade and let it ~ halfway up —Barnaby Conrad⟩ ⟨insistent memories that *tugged* . . . from every cranny —Timothy Wharton⟩ **2 :** to struggle in opposition **:** CONTEND ⟨a person . . . *tugging* and wrestling with doubts and conflicts —*Omnibook*⟩ **3 :** to exert oneself laboriously **:** STRUGGLE, LABOR ⟨*tugged* all his life to make a living⟩ ~ *vt* **1 :** to pull at hard **:** strain at ⟨each oar was *tugged* by five or six slaves —T.B.Macaulay⟩ **2 a :** to move by pulling hard **:** pull with effort **:** DRAG, HAUL ⟨stuck fast until a team of cattle could . . . ~ them out of the slough —T.B.Macaulay⟩ ⟨the five year development plan now being *tugged* into shape —*Economist*⟩ **b :** to carry with difficulty **:** LUG ⟨~ about a mental burden of protest —J.G.Gilkey⟩ **3** *obs* **:** to handle roughly **:** MAUL **4 :** to tow with a tugboat **syn** see PULL
²**tug** \"\ *n* -s [ME *tugge,* fr. *tuggen* to tug] **1 :** something that is used as a connection for pulling: as **a :** a trace of a harness **b :** a short leather strap or loop **c :** a rope or chain used for pulling **d :** the iron hook of a hoisting tub to which a tackle is fastened to pull the tub up a mine shaft **2 a :** an act or instance of tugging **:** a hard pull ⟨making his own bed with a few careless ~*s* —Marcia Davenport⟩ **b :** a strong pulling force ⟨enables him to defy the awful ~ of gravity —G.E.Fox⟩ ⟨knows . . . why the ~ of the past has so much power —Norman Cousins⟩ **3 a :** a hard struggle **:** a big effort ⟨the stream was easy on the eastern side, but I saw that the ~ was to come, for the main torrent swept . . . near the western bank —A.W. Kinglake⟩ **b :** a struggle between two people or forces ⟨the ~ within him between conservative and liberal —John Mason Brown⟩ **4 a :** TUGBOAT **b :** an airplane used to pull a glider
³**tug** \"\ *n* -s [prob. alter. (influenced by ²*tug*) of ¹*tog & toge*] **1** *Brit* **a :** COLLEGER 1 **b :** KING'S SCHOLAR **2** *chiefly Brit* **:** an uncouth, dirty, or unscrupulous person

tugboat \ˈ=ˌ=\ *n* **:** a strongly built powerful boat used for towing and pushing esp. in harbors and on inland waterways — called also *towboat, tug*

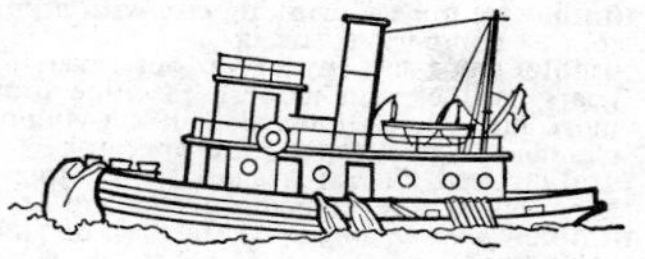
tugboat

tug chain *n* **1 :** a short chain at the end of a harness tug to attach it to the whiffletree **2 :** a harness tug made of chain
tug·ger \ˈtəgə(r)\ *n* -s **:** one that tugs: *specif* **:** a small portable hoist used in a mine and usu. mounted on a column and driven by air or electricity
tug·less \ˈtəgləs\ *adj* **:** not having a tug
tug·man \-gmən\ *n, pl* **tugmen :** one who works on a tugboat
tug–of–war \ˈ=ˌ=ˈ=\ *n, pl* **tugs–of–war 1 :** a struggle for supremacy ⟨a continual *tug-of-war* between the authorities and the masses —Alexander Dallin⟩ **2 :** an athletic contest in which two teams pull against each other at opposite ends of a rope
tu·grik *or* **tu·ghrik** \ˈtüˌgrēk\ *n* -s [Mongol *dughurik,* lit., round thing, wheel] **1 :** the basic unit of monetary value of the Mongolian People's Republic **2 :** a note or coin representing one tugrik
tugurium *var of* TEGURIUM
tui \ˈtüē\ *n* -s [Maori] **:** a predominantly glossy black New Zealand honey eater (*Prosthemadera novaeseelandiae*) with white markings on throat, neck, and wings that is a notable mimic and often kept as a cage bird — called also *parson bird*
tuille \ˈtwē(ə)l\ *n* -s [ME *toile,* fr. MF *tuille, teuille* tile, fr. L *tegula* — more at THATCH] **:** one of the hinged plates before the thigh in plate armor — see ARMOR illustration
tuil·lette \twēˈlet\ *n* -s [F *tuilette,* dim. of *tuile* tile, fr. MF *tuille, teuille*] **:** a small tuille for protecting the hip
tuil·yie *or* **tuil·zie** \ˈtülyi\ *n or vb* [ME (Sc) *tulȝe,* fr. MF *tooil, toeil* battle, trouble, fr. OF — more at TOIL] *chiefly Scot* **:** QUARREL, STRUGGLE
tu·in·ga \tüˈiŋgə\ *n* -s [Samoan] **:** a headdress of bleached human hair worn by Samoan men or women of very high rank in important ceremonies and dances
tu·ism \ˈt(y)üˌizəm\ *n* -s [L *tu* thou + E *-ism* — more at THOU] **:** the use of the second person (as in apostrophe or in rhetorical evasion of the first person); *also* **:** an instance of such use
tu·i·tion \t(y)üˈishən\ *n* -s [ME *tuicioun,* fr. OF *tuicion,* fr. L *tuition-, tuitio,* fr. *tuitus* (past part. of *tuērī* to look at, watch over, protect) + *-ion-, -io* -ion; perh. akin to OIr *tūath* left, northerly, lucky, favorable, Goth *thiuth* good, beneficial, ON *thȳdr* kind, meek] **1** *archaic* **:** protection, care, or custody esp. as exercised by a parent or guardian over a child or ward **:** GUARDIANSHIP ⟨powers which the father hath, in the right of ~ during minority —John Locke⟩ **2 :** the act of teaching **:** the services or guidance of a teacher **:** INSTRUCTION ⟨pursued his studies under private ~⟩ ⟨the high costs of ~⟩ ⟨received careful ~ from his mother⟩ **3 :** the price of or payment for instruction ⟨~ has risen sharply⟩
tu·i·tion·al \-shən³l\ *adj* **:** of or relating to tuition **:** designed to teach ⟨~ films⟩
t'u–jen \ˈtüˈrən\ *n, pl* **t'u–jen** *usu cap* [Chin(Pek) *t'u³-jen²*] **:** T'U-LAO
tuk·ra \ˈtu̇krə\ *n* -s [Hindi *ṭukṛā* piece, bit, scrap] **:** a disorder of the leaves and shoots of the mulberry tree in India caused by the feeding of a mealybug (*Phenacoccus hirsutus*) and characterized by curling of the leaves
tu·ku·lör \ˌtükü'lər\ *or* **tu·ku·ler** \-ˈle(ə)r\ *also* **tou·couleur** \-ˈlər\ *n* -s *usu cap* [F *Toucouleurs,* pl., Tukulörs, fr. Wolof *Tokoror,* fr. *Tekrur,* locality in Senegal] **:** any of a group of mixed negroid peoples of eastern Senegal who are tall and black and chiefly Muslim
tu·ku·tu·ku \ˈtü(ˌ)küˈtü(ˌ)kü\ *n* -s [Maori] **:** decorative Maori latticework usu. of flax or kiekie stems and in the form of panels that are used esp. between the carved posts of communal buildings (as a meetinghouse)
¹**tu·la** \ˈtülə\ *also* **tula metal** *n* -s [fr. *Tula,* city in central U.S.S.R.] **:** NIELLO 1
²**tula** \"\ *or* **tula istle** *n* -s [MexSp *tula*] **:** a coarse nearly white Mexican istle fiber that is sometimes used locally for cord or fabric and commercially esp. for brushes and that is obtained from an agave (*Agave lecheguilla*)
³**tula** \"\ *adj, usu cap* [fr. *Tula,* U.S.S.R.] **:** of or from the city of Tula, U.S.S.R. **:** of the kind or style prevalent in Tula
tu·la·di \ˈtülədē\ *n* -s [CanF *touladi,* fr. Montagnais] **:** LAKE TROUT b
tu·la·fa·le \ˌtüləˈfälā\ *n, pl* **tulafale** [Samoan *tūlāfale*] **:** a Samoan native chief functioning as an adviser and debater on matters of public policy and expected to be thoroughly informed on matters of traditional lore
t'u–lao \ˈtüˈlau̇\ *n, pl* **t'u–lao** *usu cap T* [Chin(Pek) *t'u³-lao³*] **:** any of various Tai groups of southern China
tu·la·pai \tüˈläˌpī\ *n* -s [Apache] **:** a fermented beverage made by Apache Indians of sprouted fermented corn often with various roots or herbs
tu·la·re \tüˈlärā\ *n* -s [AmerSp *tulares,* pl., tule fields, fr. Sp *tule*] **:** TULE LAND
tu·la·re·mia \ˌtüləˈrēmēə\ *n* -s [NL, fr. *Tulare* county, Calif. where it was first discovered + NL *-emia*] **:** an infectious disease of rodents, man, and some domestic animals caused by a bacterium (*Pasteurella tularensis*) that is transmitted by the bites of insects or is occas. acquired by man through handling infected animals and in man marked by headache, chills, fever, and other constitutional symptoms of toxemia — **tu·la·re·mic** \ˈ=ˌ=ˈrēmik\ *adj*
tu·la·si \ˈtüləsē\ *n* -s [Skt *tulasī* — more at TULSI] *India* **:** HOLY BASIL
¹**tul·bagh·ia** \ˌtəlˈbagēə\ [NL, fr. Ryk *Tulbagh* †1771 Dutch governor of Cape Colony + NL *-ia*] *syn of* AGAPANTHUS
²**tulbaghia** \"\ *n* -s [NL] **:** a plant of the genus *Agapanthus*
tul·chan \ˈtəlkən\ *also* **tul·chin** \-kən\ *n* -s [ScGael *tulchan*] **1 :** a stuffed calfskin used esp. formerly to induce a cow to let down her milk **2** *or* **tulchan bishop :** one of the bishops appointed in the Reformed Presbyterian Church of Scotland in 1572 who consented to hand over the larger part of the revenues of their dioceses to the lay patrons who had obtained their appointment
tu·le \ˈtülē, -li\ *n* -s [Sp, fr. Nahuatl *tollin, tullin*] **1 :** either of two large bulrushes (*Scirpus lacustris* and *S. acutus*) growing abundantly on overflowed land in the southwestern U.S. and adjacent Mexico and esp. in California at the junction of the Sacramento and San Joaquin rivers where large tracts are overgrown with these plants **2** *or* **tule land :** land on which tules are the dominant or characteristic native plant — usu. used in pl. and with *the* ⟨plans for draining and cultivating the ~*s*⟩ **3** *usu cap* **:** SAN BLAS
tule beetle *n* **:** a carabid beetle (*Agonum maculicolle*) of marshy areas of California that produces a strong nauseous odor
tule fog *n* **:** a dense low-flying mobile fog occurring esp. in the San Francisco area
tule goose *n* **:** a goose that winters in the Sacramento valley of California and prob. breeds in the arctic and that is a variety (*Anser albifrons gambelli*) of the white-fronted goose distinguished chiefly by its large size
tule mint *n, West* **:** CANADA MINT
tule potato *also* **tule root** *n, West* **:** WAPATOO
tule wren *n* **:** a long-billed marsh wren (*Telmatodytes palustris paludicola*) of the western U. S.
tu·li·ac \ˈt(y)üléˌak\ *n* -s [origin unknown] *dial Eng* **:** SKUA
tu·lip \ˈt(y)üləp\ *n* -s *often attrib* [NL *tulipa,* fr. Turk *tülbend* turban; fr. the flower's resemblance to a turban — more at TURBAN] **1 a (1) :** any of various plants constituting the genus *Tulipa* and including many that have been so long cultivated for their showy flowers as to make it impossible to identify them surely with existing tulip species though the dwarf early types commonly are assigned to a species (*T. suaveolens*) while later taller forms are assigned to a species (*T. gesneriana*) — see COTTAGE TULIP, DARWIN TULIP, LADY TULIP (2) **:** a flower or bulb of a tulip **b :** any of various southern African plants of the genus *Homeria* (family Iridaceae) having flowers that resemble tulips and including several forms that are poisonous to cattle **2 :** something felt to resemble a tulip: as **a :** a swelling of the metal of the muzzle of an old-fashioned gun **b** (1) **:** a wineglass that in silhouette suggests the flower of a tulip (2) **:** a style in women's dress in which a close waist and tight tapered skirt suggests an inverted tulip
tu·li·pa \ˈt(y)üləpə\ *n, cap* [NL] **:** a large genus of Eurasian bulbous herbs (family Liliaceae) having coated bulbs, linear or broadly lanceolate leaves, and commonly a single showy flower with six equal perianth segments and six hypogynous stamens — see TULIP
tulip ear *n* **:** an erect pointed ear (as of a dog) often with the tip drooping — **tulip–eared** \ˈ=ˌ=ˌ=\ *adj*
tulip fire *or* **tulip blight** *n* **:** a destructive disease of tulips caused by a mold (*Botrytis tulipae*) and marked by gray to brown lesions on leaves, petals, scapes, and bulb that often result in extensive necrosis
tulipflower \ˈ=ˌ=ˌ=\ *n* **:** WHEEL TREE 2
tulip lancewood *n, Austral* **:** TULIPWOOD 2a(2)
tulip mold *n* **:** TULIP FIRE; *also* **:** the fungus causing the disease
tulip mosaic *n* **:** a virus disease of tulips marked esp. by the striking color break in the flower which takes the form of irregular striping or marginal feathering
tulip oak *n* **:** an Australian tree of the genus *Tarrietia* (family Sterculiaceae) characterized by pink or reddish strong wood used for furniture and interior finish work
tu·lip·o·ma·nia \ˌt(y)üləpəˈmānēə\ *n* [*tulip* + *-o-* + *mania*] **:** an excessive fad or passion for acquiring or growing tulips; *specif* **:** such a mania prevailing in Holland about 1634 and accompanied by wild speculation in bulbs ultimately ended by governmental interference — **tu·lip·o·ma·ni·ac** \-ēˌak\ *n*
tulip orchid *n* **:** a Mexican epiphytic orchid (*Cattleya citrina*) much grown for its usu. solitary pendent very showy fragrant yellow flower with a white-bordered lip
tulip poppy *n* **1 :** a commonly cultivated glaucous annual poppy (*Papaver glaucum*) of Asia Minor with cup-shaped scarlet flowers on tall erect stems **2 :** a perennial Mexican herb (*Hunnemannia fumariaefolia*) of the family Papaveraceae that closely resembles the California poppy but has bright orange-colored stamens and two separate sepals
tulip root *n* **:** a disease of various grasses and esp. cereal grasses caused by a strain of the bulb eelworm and characterized esp. by bulbous swellings in the stem and distortions of leaves
tulip shell *n* **:** BAND SHELL; *esp* **:** a variable predominantly gray and brown mollusk (*Fasciolaria tulipa*) occurring on the coast of the southern U. S.
tulip tree *n* **1** *or* **tulip poplar :** a tall No. American timber tree (*Liriodendron tulipifera*) having truncate somewhat lobed leaves, large greenish yellow flowers that resemble tulips, and soft white wood that is much used esp. for cabinetwork and woodenware — see TREE illustration **2 :** any of various trees with tulip-shaped flowers: as **a :** MAJAGUA a **b :** PORTIA TREE **c :** BANANA SHRUB **d** *Austral* (1) **:** WARATAH (2) **:** an evergreen tree (*Lagunaria pattersonii*) of the family Malvaceae with large solitary axillary rosy pink flowers

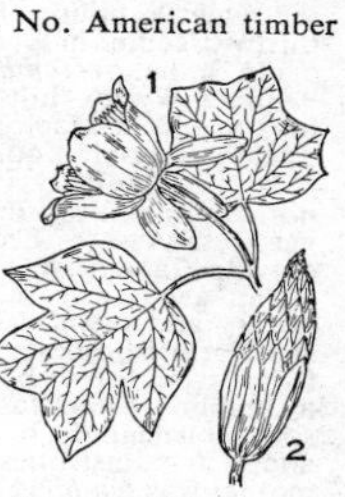
tulip tree; *1* flower and leaves, *2* fruit

tulip tree scale *n* **:** a scale (*Toumeyella liriodendri*) that occurs mainly in the eastern half of the U. S. on magnolia, poplar, and a few other trees
tulip valve *n* **:** an intake valve (as on an engine) with a cup-shaped to trumpet-shaped head
tulipwood \ˈ=ˌ=ˌ=\ *n* **1 :** wood of the No. American tulip tree **:** WHITEWOOD **2 a :** any of several showily striped or variegated woods: as (1) **:** the rose-colored wood of a Brazilian tree (*Physocalymma scabberimum* of the family Lythraceae) much used by cabinetmakers for inlaying (2) *Austral* **:** the wood of a tree (*Harpullia pendula*) — called also *Moreton Bay tulipwood* (3) *Austral* **:** the wood of the emu apple **b :** any tree that yields such a tulipwood **3 :** AUBURN
tu·li·san \ˌtüləˈsän\ *n, pl* **tulisa·nes** \-ä,nās\ [Tag *tulisán*] **:** a Philippine bandit **:** LADRONE
tulle \ˈtül *sometimes* ˈtəl *or* ˈtəl\ *n* -s [F, fr. *Tulle,* city in central France where it was orig. made] **:** a sheer and often stiffened machine-made net made with a usu. hexagonal mesh and of silk, rayon, or nylon and used chiefly for veils, evening dresses, or ballet costumes — compare ILLUSION
tulle gras *n* **:** fine-meshed gauze impregnated with a fatty substance (as vegetable oil or soft paraffin) and used in medicine as an application to raw surfaces
tul·li·bee \ˈtələˌbē\ *n* -s [CanF *toulibi,* prob. fr. Cree *otonabi,* lit., water-mouth] **:** any of several whitefishes of central and northern No. America; *esp* **:** a common cisco (*Leucichthys artedi*) that is a commercially important food fish
tul·ly's powder \ˈtəlēz-\ *n, usu cap T* [after William *Tully* †1859 Am. physician] **:** a powder composed of a mixture of morphine sulfate, camphor, powdered glycyrrhiza, and precipitated calcium carbonate and formerly used as an anodyne and antispasmodic
tul·nic \ˈtülnēk\ *n* -s [Romanian] **:** a very long wooden trumpet formerly used to convey warnings (as of invasion) between Romanian communities
tu·los·to·ma·ce·ae \ˌt(y)üˌlästəˈmāsēˌē\ *n pl, cap* [NL, fr. *Tulostoma,* type genus (prob. fr. *tyl-* + *stoma*) + *-aceae*] **:** a family of fungi (order Sclerodermatales) comprising the stalked puffballs and distinguished by having sporocarps similar to the Lycoperdaceae but with the unchambered gleba raised on a stalk
tul·sa \ˈtəlsə\ *adj, usu cap* [fr. *Tulsa,* Okla.] **:** of or from the city of Tulsa, Okla. ⟨a *Tulsa* oil company⟩ **:** of the kind or style prevalent in Tulsa
tul·san \-sən\ *n* -s *cap* [*Tulsa,* Okla. + E *-an*] **:** a native or resident of Tulsa, Okla.
tul·si \ˈtülsē\ *n* -s [Hindi *tulsī,* fr. Skt *tulasī,* prob. of Dravidian origin; akin to Tamil *tuḷāy,* Kanarese *toḷaci*] *India* **:** HOLY BASIL
tul–tul \ˈtülˈtül\ *n* -s [native name in New Guinea] **:** an assistant or deputy of a Polynesian native headman
tu·lu \ˈtü(ˌ)lü\ *n, pl* **tulu** *or* **tulus** *usu cap* **1 :** one of a Dravidian people in India on the coast near Mangalore **2 :** a Dravidian language of the west coast of Mysore in southern India
tul·war *also* **tul·waur** \ˈtəlˌwär\ *n* -s [Hindi *talwār, tarwār,* fr. Skt *taravārī*] **:** a curved saber or scimitar used in the Orient and esp. in northern India
¹**tum** \ˈtəm\ *vt* **tummed; tummed; tumming; tums** [origin unknown] **1 :** to card (wool) as a preliminary to finer carding **2 :** to open or tease out (wool) before carding
²**tum** \"\ *n* -s [imit.] **1 :** the sound of a plucked string (as of a banjo) **2 :** the sound of a drum
³**tum** \"\ *vi* **tummed; tummed; tumming; tums :** to make a tum or tum-tum
tuman *var of* TOMAN
tu·ma·ta·ku·ru *also* **tu·matu·ku·ru** \ˌtüˌmäd·əˌku̇(ˌ)rü, -mad·-\ *n* -s [Maori *tumatakuru*] **:** a New Zealand shrub or tree (*Discaria toumatou*) of the family Rhamnaceae having stout sharp spines used by the Maoris for tattooing — called also *Irishman, matagory, wild Irishman*
tum·bak \(ˌ)təmˈbäk, tüm-\ *or* **tum·ba·ki** \-bäkē\ *or* **tumbek** \-bek\ *or* **tumbeki** \-bekē\ *n* -s [Ar *tunbak* & Turk *tumbeki,* both fr. Per *tanbāku,* fr. Sp *tabaco* — more at TOBACCO] **:** a coarse Persian tobacco prob. derived from a tropical American plant (*Nicotiana tabacum*)
¹**tum·ble** \ˈtəmbəl\ *vb* **tumbled; tumbled; tumbling** \-b(ə)liŋ\ **tumbles** [ME *tumblen,* freq. of *tumben, tomben* to dance, jump, fr. OE *tumbian;* akin to MHG *tūmeln* to turn, reel, OHG *tūmōn* to turn, reel, ON *tumba* to tumble] *vi* **1 a :** to perform gymnastic feats of rolling and turning ⟨a man . . . paid for *tumbling* upon his hands —Samuel Johnson⟩ ⟨to keep in shape, the . . . general ~*s* —*Time*⟩ **b :** to turn end over end in falling or in flight ⟨rooks *tumbling* and cawing above the high elm tops —Flora Thompson⟩ ⟨a projectile ~*s* when the twist of the rifling is too slow for the bullet⟩ ⟨machine-gun

bullets, badly *tumbling*, fell in among the ridges —S.L.A. Marshall〉 **2 a :** to fall suddenly and helplessly **:** pitch headlong **:** fall to the ground 〈~ from a scaffold〉 〈tripped over a stone and *tumbled*〉 〈one . . . whose horse has *tumbled* —G.B. Shaw〉 **b :** to suffer a usu. sudden downfall, overthrow, or defeat 〈once again a government ~*s*〉 〈the small ~ with the great —Arnold Bennett〉 **c :** to decline suddenly and sharply (as in price or value) **:** DROP 〈the stock market *tumbled* —*N.Y. Times*〉 **d :** to fall into ruin or decay **:** break down **:** COLLAPSE 〈the wall finally *tumbled*〉 〈deserted buildings . . . *tumbling* into ruins —*Amer. Guide Series: Nev.*〉 — often used with *down* 〈old houses *tumbling* down〉 〈the structure of society does not ~ down when we probe its framework —Zechariah Chafee〉 **3 :** to roll over and over, back and forth, or around **:** thrash about **:** twist and turn **:** TOSS 〈*tumbled* in her sleep〉 〈his children *tumbled* like brown puppies about his threshold —Pearl Buck〉 〈laughed all day together *tumbling* in the hay —George Meredith〉 〈thoughts were *tumbling* about in her brain like cargo loose in a rolling ship —Arnold Bennett〉 **4 a :** to fall or issue forth hurriedly, confusedly, and all in a heap **:** pour out pell-mell 〈books *tumbling* from the presses〉 〈gold coins *tumbled* out on the counterpane —T.B.Costain〉 〈words *tumbling* eagerly from his lips〉 **b :** to move in a stumblingly hurried, confused, or disorderly way **:** rush helter-skelter 〈*tumbled* into his clothes〉 〈customers *tumbling* out of the tavern as the fire trucks arrived〉 **5 :** to come by chance or unexpectedly **:** STUMBLE, HAPPEN 〈treated his wife and children as the most delightful accidents against whom he had, most happily, *tumbled* —Hugh Walpole〉 — usu. used with *in, into,* or *upon* 〈the individuality you always *tumbled* upon in an English . . . village —H.J.Laski〉 **6 :** to have a receding upward slope — compare TUMBLE HOME **7 :** to come to understand the point or implication (as of something obscure or devious that is being said or done) **:** catch on **:** wise up 〈nobody ~*s* till we're dragging the damned aristocrats out of their cursed beds —W.G.Hardy〉 — usu. used with *to* 〈suspicious for some time . . . and all of a sudden I *tumbled* to it —W.S. Maugham〉 〈advertisers . . . had not *tumbled* to the extensive possibilities for fakery in photography —Andy Logan〉 **~** *vt* **1 a :** to cause to tumble or roll head over heels **:** make fall **:** throw down or over **:** PITCH, TOSS 〈*tumbled* him on the bed〉 **b :** to bring down (as in hunting) **:** DROP 〈~ a rabbit with a shotgun〉 **c :** to cause to fall from high place or power **:** TOPPLE 〈had reached a pinnacle . . . and now he was *tumbled* from it —Winifred Bambrick〉 **d :** to cause to fall to the ground **:** knock down **:** FELL 〈*tumbled* a policeman —Richard Free〉 〈*tumbled* the trees —V. W. Von Hagen〉 **2 :** to cause to fall into ruins **:** DEMOLISH 〈~*s* down steeples —Shak.〉 〈*tumbling* the majestic house of worship —Claudia Cassidy〉 **3 a :** to throw together in a confused and disorderly way **:** fling about or in a heap 〈*tumbled* them helter-skelter into the boxes —Elinor Wylie〉 〈hills lie *tumbled* about in a sort of mad confusion —Tom Marvel〉 **b :** to push or roll about **:** cause to pitch or stumble **:** BUNDLE, TOSS 〈*tumbled* about like a football —Tobias Smollett〉 〈*tumbling* him into the position at short notice〉 **c :** to put into a state of disorder or disarray **:** RUMPLE, DISHEVEL 〈~ bedclothes〉 〈one gets so *tumbled* in such a crowd —Jane Austen〉 **d** *archaic* **:** to turn over or throw about (as in a hasty search or examination) 〈walked through the library and *tumbled* books —Lord Byron〉 **e :** to turn (as a sheet printed on one side that is to be backed up by the same form) from top to bottom **4 :** to whirl (objects or material) in a tumbling barrel (as in polishing or coating metallic objects, softening leather, or drying clothes) — **tumble to** *Brit* **:** to adapt or adjust oneself to **:** fall in with **:** fit into 〈really his mother was *tumbling to* things wonderfully well —Sheila Kaye-Smith〉 — **tumble up 1 :** to go or come quickly on deck 〈men are still *tumbling up* from below, racing to their battle stations —E.L.Beach〉 **2** *dial* **:** to roll hay into bundles for pitching

²tumble \"\ *n* -s **1 a :** a random and disorderly collection **:** a mass of objects or material piled up or thrown together in confusion **:** HEAP 〈a ~ of books and papers on the floor〉 〈could look out . . . at the ~ of lesser hills and valleys, dotted here and there with towns and settlements —R.M.Coates〉 **b** *NewEng* **:** a small pile of hay in a field **c :** a confused, disorderly state or condition **:** DISARRAY, MESS 〈viewed the ~ of the bed〉 〈cut through the ~ of wordy, circular arguments〉 **2 :** an act of tumbling or falling: as **a :** a gymnastic or acrobatic feat of tumbling (as a somersault) 〈practice a ~〉 **b :** an accidental fall 〈take a ~〉 〈injured in a ~ from a horse〉 〈no ability to pick herself up after a ~ —F.A.Swinnerton〉 — compare ROUGH-AND-TUMBLE **c :** a usu. sudden descent from a higher level or position **:** DOWNFALL, DROP 〈the premier's ~ from office〉 〈a ~ in stock market prices〉 〈a ~ from high estate〉 **d :** a rolling, tossing, and falling movement (as of a watercourse) 〈the ~ of the waves〉 〈the . . . river does a series of ~*s* over rocky ledges —Y.E.Soderberg〉 **3 :** TUMBLING BARREL **4 :** a sign of recognition or interest; *esp* **:** an indication of responsive social or amatory interest 〈you wouldn't even give me a ~ —Dorothy Parker〉

tumblebug \ˈ==,=\ *n* [¹*tumble* + *bug*] **:** any of various scarabaeid beetles (as members of the genera *Scarabaeus, Canthon, Copris,* or *Phanaeus*) that form globular masses of dung which they roll and bury in holes excavated in the ground, in which they lay their eggs, and which serve as food for the larvae

tumble cart *also* **tumble car** *n* **:** a rough dumpcart having its wheels solid and made fast to the axle

tumbled *past of* TUMBLE

tumbledown \ˌ==ˈ=\ *adj* [fr. the phrase *tumble down*] **:** ready to fall **:** falling into decay **:** DILAPIDATED, RAMSHACKLE 〈a ~ shack〉 〈a ~ clapboard house, now serving as a junk shop —*Amer. Guide Series: N.Y. City*〉 〈~ temples —Glenway Wescott〉

tumbledung \ˈ==,=\ *n* [¹*tumble* + *dung*] **:** TUMBLEBUG

tumble grass *n* **:** WITCHGRASS 2

¹tumble home *vi* **:** to incline inward above the waterline or greatest breadth **:** FALL HOME — compare ³BATTER; used chiefly of the sides of a ship

²tumble home *n* **:** a receding upward slope (as of a ship's sides) **:** an inclination inward from the greatest breadth 〈as in all ships of the period, her sides have considerable *tumble home* —H.G. Smith〉 〈the *tumble home* of a building toward the top〉

tumble mustard *n* **:** a tall European biennial herb (*Sisymbrium altissimum*) that has pinnatifid leaves and long slender seed pods and is often a troublesome weed in No. America

tum·bler \ˈtəmb(ə)lə(r)\ *n* -s [ME, fr. *tumblen* to tumble + *-er* — more at TUMBLE] **1 :** one that tumbles: as **a :** one that performs gymnastic or acrobatic feats (as somersaults or handsprings) **:** ACROBAT **b :** a dog formerly bred for taking rabbits by suddenly seizing animals attracted or distracted by its circuitous tumbling progress **c** *or* **tumbler pigeon :** any of various domestic pigeons that tumble or somersault backward in flight or on the ground **d** (1) **:** the pupa of a mosquito (2) **:** TUMBLEBUG **e** *chiefly dial* **:** TUMBLE CART, TUMBREL **f :** ROLY-POLY 4b **2 :** a drinking glass made usu. without a foot or stem and orig. with a pointed or convex base so that it could not be set down until empty **3 a :** a movable obstruction in a lock (as a lever, latch, wheel, slide, pin) that must be adjusted to a particular position (as by a key) before the bolt can be thrown **b :** a piece that is attached to or forms part of the hammer of a gunlock, that is acted on by the mainspring, and that bears the notches for the sear point to enter **c** (1) **:** a projecting piece on a revolving shaft or rockshaft for actuating another piece; *specif* **:** the click that moves the rack in a striking mechanism one tooth for each blow struck (2) **:** the movable part of a tumbler gear **d :** a pin or one of a pair of pins engaging the ends of a ring stopper and shank painter **e :** one of the levers suspending the harness in a loom **f :** NEEDLE 8d **4 :** a device or mechanism for tumbling or revolving: as **a :** a clothes-drying device consisting of a revolving cage in which hot air is agitated by fan action **b :** TUMBLING BARREL **c :** a drum in which hides are treated (as washed and softened) in leather manufacturing **5 a :** a worker that operates a tumbling device (as a tumbling barrel) **b :** one that deburrs and cleans parts (as of watches or guns) by tumbling them with abrasives

tumbler bearing *n* **:** any of the intermediate swiveling or pivoted bearings for a square shaft (as in a gantry) that can be knocked aside (as by a traveling crab moving along the shaft and gearing with it)

tumbler cart *n* **:** a horse-drawn 2-wheeled farm cart with a tank for handling liquid or semiliquid materials

tumbler cup *n* **:** a drinking cup with a pointed or convex bottom — compare TUMBLER 2

tumbler gear *n* **:** any of various reversing or speed-changing gears used esp. in modern machine tools that have one or more idle wheels journaled in a swinging frame moved and clamped in position by the operator

tumbler switch *n* **:** a snap switch in which the blades are actuated by a lever being pushed up or pulled down

tumbles *pres 3d sing of* TUMBLE, *pl of* TUMBLE

tumbleweed \ˈ==,=\ *n* [¹*tumble* + *weed*] **:** any plant that habitually breaks away from its roots in the autumn and is driven by the wind as a light, rolling mass over the fields and prairies: as **a :** WINGED PIGWEED **b :** RUSSIAN THISTLE **c :** any of several amaranths (as *Amaranthus graecizans*)

¹tumbling *n* -s [ME, fr. gerund of *tumblen* to tumble — more at TUMBLE] **1 :** the act or process of tumbling **2 :** the skill, practice, or sport of executing gymnastic tumbles **3 :** a continuous violent pitching rotation of an aerodynamic body

²tumbling *adj* [ME, fr. pres. part. of *tumblen* to tumble] **:** tipped or slanted to the right or left of vertical position — used esp. of a cattle brand 〈the *Tumbling* T brand〉 — see BRAND illustration

tumbling barrel *n* **:** a revolving barrel, cask, or box in which objects or materials (as small metal parts, castings, plastics, leather, or clothing) undergo a process (as finishing, polishing, coating, softening, or drying) by being whirled about and so brought into vigorous frictional contact — called also *rattler, rumble, rumbler, scouring barrel*

tumbling bay *n* **:** an overfall in a canal **:** WEIR

tumbling box *n* **:** a tumbling barrel for small objects

tumbling mustard *n* **:** TUMBLE MUSTARD

tumbling pigweed *n* **:** PIGWEED a

tumbling rod *n* **:** a rod having a cam or lever rigidly attached to transmit an intermittent motion

tumbling shaft *n* **1 :** CAMSHAFT **2 :** COUNTERSHAFT 2

tumbling verse *n* **:** an early modern English verse form having four stresses but no prevailing type of foot and no regular number of syllables

tum·boa \ˌtəmˈbōə\ [NL, fr. native name in Mossamedes, southwestern Africa] *syn of* WELWITSCHIA

tum·brel *or* **tum·bril** \ˈtəmbrəl\ *n* -s [ME *tombrel, tumrel,* fr. ML & OF; ML *tumbrellum, tumberellum* cucking stool, fr. OF *tumberel, tomberel* dumpcart, tumble cart, fr. *tomber, tumer* to dance, leap, turn, tumble, of Gmc origin; akin to MLG *tummelen* to turn, leap, dance, OHG *tūmōn* to turn, reel — more at TUMBLE] **1** *obs* **:** an instrument of punishment **:** *specif* **:** CUCKING STOOL **2 a :** a farmer's dumpcart or wagon; *esp* **:** one for manure **b :** a vehicle carrying condemned persons (as political prisoners during the French Revolution) to a place of execution 〈gaping crowds . . . watch Shanghai's ~*s* rumble past —*Time*〉 **c** *archaic* **:** a two-wheeled cart accompanying troops to convey supplies (as tools or ammunition) **3** *dial Eng* **:** an osier or willow cage for fodder

tum·bu fly \ˈtu̇m,bü-\ *n* [*tumbu* of Bantu origin; akin to Kongo *timuka* fly, *mbu* mosquito, Swahili *imbu*] **:** an African fly (*Cordylobia anthropophaga*) of the family Muscidae whose larva lives as a subcutaneous parasite in various mammals and sometimes in man

tu·me·fa·cient \ˌt(y)üməˈfāshənt\ *adj* [L *tumefacient-, tumefaciens,* pres. part. of *tumefacere* to swell, cause to swell, fr. *tumēre* to swell + *facere* to make, do — more at THUMB, DO] **1 :** SWOLLEN **2 :** producing swelling

tu·me·fac·tion \ˌ==ˈfakshən\ *n* -s [MF, fr. L *tumefactus* (past part. of *tumefacere* to swell, cause to swell) + MF *-ion*] **1 :** the act or process of tumefying **:** state of being tumefied 〈incite previously normal tissue to ~ —*Amer. Jour. of Veterinary Research*〉 **2 :** SWELLING 〈~*s* on the chest wall or sinus tracts —J.B.Barnwell〉

tu·me·fac·tive \ˌ==ˌfaktiv, -tēv *also* -təv\ *adj* [L *tumefactus* (past part.) + E *-ive*] **:** TUMEFACIENT 2

tu·me·fy \ˈ==,fī\ *vb* -ED/-ING/-ES [MF *tumefier,* fr. L *tumēre* to swell + MF *-fier -fy*] *vi* **1 :** to rise in a tumor **:** SWELL **2 :** to become puffed up (as with pride) **~** *vt* **:** to cause to swell **:** produce a tumor in

tumeric *var of* TURMERIC

tu·mes·cence \t(y)üˈmesᵊn(t)s\ *n* -s [L *tumēre* to swell + E *-escence*] **1 :** the quality or state of being tumescent **:** DISTENTION, INFLATION: as **a :** swelling or teeming fullness 〈the lush ~ of equatorial vegetation〉 〈the ~ of the life force within him —Sidney Monas〉 〈lyrics . . . distinguished by a kind of ~ —Cyril Connolly〉 **b :** INFLATION 〈a current critical ~ —J.L. Lievsay〉 **c :** readiness for sexual activity marked by rising emotional excitement and physical tension with vascular congestion of the sex organs 〈~ . . . is the really essential part of the process —Havelock Ellis〉 **2 :** swollen part **:** SWELLING 〈prairie relieved only by . . . ~*s* —Clifton Fadiman〉

tu·mes·cent \-sᵊnt\ *adj* [L *tumescent-, tumescens,* pres. part. of *tumescere* to swell up, incho. of *tumēre* to swell] **1 :** somewhat tumid, swollen, or inflated 〈~ tissue〉 **2 :** BOMBASTIC, TUMID 3 **3 :** swelling with fullness of thought or emotion **:** TEEMING, PREGNANT 〈a ~ flow of thought —H.G.Wells〉

tum·fie \ˈtəm(f)fi\ *n* -s [origin unknown] *Scot* **:** a stupid or awkward person

tu·mid \ˈt(y)ümə̇d\ *adj* [L *tumidus,* fr. *tumēre* to swell — more at THUMB] **1 :** marked by swelling **:** SWOLLEN, DISTENDED 〈puffy, ~ flesh〉 〈a badly infected, ~ leg〉 **2 :** formed as if by swelling or inflation **:** BULGING, PNEUMATIC, PROTUBERANT 〈so high as heaved the ~ hills —John Milton〉 〈a ~ membrane〉 〈sails ~ in the spanking breeze〉 〈the ~ whorls of a shell〉 **3 :** overblown and pretentious (as in language or style) **:** BOMBASTIC, TURGID 〈the ~ . . . structure of our sentences —Thomas De Quincey〉 **syn** see INFLATED

tu·mid·i·ty \t(y)üˈmidəd·ē, -dətē, -i\ *n* -ES **:** the quality or state of being tumid **:** INFLATION; *specif* **:** inflation of language or style 〈speeches ridiculed for their ~ and bombast〉

tu·mid·ly *adv* **:** in a tumid manner

¹tu·mi·on \ˈt(y)ümē,än\ *n* [NL, prob. fr. Gk *thumion,* a yew] *syn of* TORREYA

²tumion \"\ *n* -s **:** STINKING CEDAR

tummed *past of* TUM

tum·mer \ˈtəmə(r)\ *n* -s [¹*tum* + *-er*] **:** a small drum similar to the doffer for transferring the cotton from the first to the second cylinder in the double carding process of cotton manufacture

tumming *pres part of* TUM

tum·mock \ˈtəmək\ *n* -s [ScGael *tom* hillock (akin to MIr *tomm* hill) + E *-ock* — more at TOMB] *chiefly Scot* **:** HILLOCK

tum·my \ˈtəmē, -mi\ *n* -ES [baby-talk for *stomach*] **:** ABDOMEN, BELLY, STOMACH 1c 〈makes that sweet . . . little baby cuddle down on his ~ —*Parents' Mag.*〉 〈sit square with their *tummies* in —*Irish Digest*〉 〈*tummies* are flattened by . . . foundations and girdles —*Corset & Underwear Rev.*〉

tu·mor \ˈt(y)ümə(r)\ *n* -s *see* -or *in Explan Notes* [L, fr. *tumēre* to swell — more at THUMB] **1** *obs* **:** TUMIDITY **2 a :** a swollen or distended part **:** SWELLING, PROTUBERANCE 〈houses that bulged with the ~*s* and warts of . . . ornamental architecture —W.A.White〉 **b :** a mass of abnormal tissue growing in or on the plant or animal body; *specif* **:** such a mass of noninflammatory and independent tissue arising without obvious cause from cells of preexistent tissue, possessing no physiologic function, and characteristically unrestrained in growth and structure — compare CANCER, NEOPLASM, SARCOMA **3** *archaic* **a :** swelling conceit **:** ARROGANCE 〈the ~ of insolence —Samuel Johnson〉 **b :** turgidity of style **:** BOMBAST 〈style . . . so far from ~ that it rather wanted a little elevation —Henry Wotton〉

tu·mor·al \-mərəl\ *adj* **:** of, relating to, or constituting a tumor 〈a ~ mass〉 〈a ~ syndrome〉

tumorlike \ˈ==,=\ *adj* **:** resembling a tumor

tu·mor·ous \ˈt(y)ümərəs\ *adj* [LL *tumorosus,* fr. L *tumor* + *-osus* -ose] **1** *obs* **a :** SWOLLEN **b :** ARROGANT, VAINGLORIOUS **c :** BOMBASTIC **2 :** of, relating to, or resembling a tumor 〈a ~ condition〉 〈~ porches and bays —Lewis Mumford〉

tumor virus *n* **:** a cell-free filtrate or an agent contained in such that is associated with or held to be a specific virus responsible for a neoplastic disease — compare MYXOMATOSIS 1, SHOPE PAPILLOMA

tump \ˈtəmp, ˈtu̇mp\ *n* -s [origin unknown] **1** *chiefly dial Eng* **:** a small rise of ground: as **a :** MOUND, HUMMOCK **b :** MOLEHILL **c :** ANTHILL **d :** ¹BARROW 2, TUMULUS **2 :** a clump of vegetation (as trees, shrubs, or grass); *esp* **:** one making a dry spot in a swamp

tum·phy \ˈtəm(p)fi\ *var of* TUMFIE

tump·line \ˈtəm,plīn\ *n* [*tump* of Algonquian origin (akin to Abnaki *mâdûmbi* pack strap) + *line*] **:** a sling formed by a strap slung over the forehead or chest for carrying a pack on the back or in hauling loads (as household goods or game) — see PACKSACK illustration

tums *pres 3d sing of* TUM, *pl of* TUM

¹tum–tum \ˈtəm,təm\ *also* **tum-ti-tum** \ˌtəm(p)tēˌtəm\ *n* -s [imit.] **:** a reiterated tum or strumming

²tum–tum \"\ *vi* **:** to make a tum-tum **:** STRUM

tum·tum \ˈtəm,təm\ *n* -s [perh. alter. of ¹*tandem*] *India* **:** DOGCART

tu·mu·lar \ˈt(y)ümyələ(r)\ *adj* [L *tumulus* mound, hillock + E *-ar* — more at TUMULUS] **:** of, relating to, or characterized by tumuli 〈a ~ cemetery〉 〈~ epoch〉

tu·mu·lary \-ə,lerē\ *adj* [L *tumulus* + E *-ary*] **1 :** of, relating to, or placed over a tomb **:** SEPULCHRAL 〈a ~ stone〉 〈a ~ style〉 **2 :** TUMULAR

tu·mu·lose \-ə,lōs\ *or* **tu·mu·lous** \-ələs\ *adj* [L *tumulosus,* fr. *tumulus* + *-osus* -ose] **:** full of small hills or mounds **:** TUMULAR 〈out there on those plains, in that ~ landscape —Malcolm Lowry〉

¹tu·mult \ˈt(y)ü,məlt *sometimes* -üˌməlt *or* ˈtəˌm-\ *n* -s [ME *tumulte,* fr. MF, fr. L *tumultus;* akin to Skt *tumula* noisy, L *tumēre* to swell — more at THUMB] **1 a :** disorderly and violent movement, agitation or milling about, of a crowd accompanied usu. with great uproar and confusion of voices **:** COMMOTION, TURMOIL 〈~ in the city〉 〈mob was in ~ over the death of its idol —Anthony Benis〉 **b :** a noisy and turbulent popular uprising **:** DISTURBANCE, RIOT 〈the ~*s* and disorders of the Great Rebellion —T.S.Eliot〉 〈during a hundred years . . . no ~ of sufficient importance to be called an insurrection —T.B. Macaulay〉 **2 a :** a confusion of loud noise and usu. turbulent or agitated movement **:** HUBBUB, DIN 〈the ~ of the elements〉 〈talking loudly enough to make himself heard above the ~ —John Bainbridge〉 〈the bells . . . made a jangling ~ —H.G. Wells〉 〈the sound of the lava, a ~ of rock in molten pressure under moving earth —Richard Llewellyn〉 **b :** a random or disorderly medley or profusion (as of objects or colors) **:** JUMBLE, RIOT 4 〈in the palace itself, what a ~ of statuary —*Horizon*〉 **3 a :** violent agitation of mind or feelings **:** highly disturbing mental or emotional excitement or stress **:** FERMENT, TURBULENCE 〈stood bewildered, her soul in a ~ —Hilaire Belloc〉 〈seek refuge in religion from the ~*s* of a strong emotional temperament —T.S.Eliot〉 **b :** a violent outburst of unrestrained emotion **:** PAROXYSM 〈a ~ of weeping —W.G. Hardy〉 〈a ~ of rejoicing in camp —H.E.Scudder〉 **syn** see COMMOTION

²tumult \"\ *vi* -ED/-ING/-S **:** to make a tumult **:** RIOT 〈a whole people . . . ~*ing* even to the fear of a revolt —John Milton〉

tu·mul·tu·ary \t(y)üˈməlchə,werē, təˈm-\ *adj* [L *tumultuarius,* fr. *tumultus* tumult + *-arius* -ary] **1 a :** composed of hastily levied and unorganized troops **:** UNDISCIPLINED, IRREGULAR 〈a ~ army〉 〈their ~ array is incapable of contending with the order and weapons of modern tactics —Edward Gibbon〉 **b :** carried on or brought about (as by a tumultuous mob) in a confused, wildly irregular, or sporadic manner 〈~ wars〉 〈~ violence〉 〈a ~ attack of the . . . peasantry —T.B.Macaulay〉 〈dread all rude and ~ innovation —V.L.Parrington〉 **2 :** marked by haste and confusion **:** done precipitately and without plan **:** huddled up **:** HAPHAZARD, AIMLESS 〈a ~ and giddy choice —Edmund Burke〉 〈rushed into a ~ discussion of chances and possibilities —Sir Walter Scott〉 **3 :** marked by or tending toward tumult **:** TUMULTUOUS 〈~ reception —J.G.Lockhart〉 〈the ~ . . . tide of life —R.L.Stevenson〉

tu·mul·tu·ate \-chə,wāt\ *vb* -ED/-ING/-S [L *tumultuatus,* past part. of *tumultuari* to make a tumult, fr. *tumultus*] *vi* **:** to raise a disturbance **:** TUMULT, RIOT 〈an oppressive action likely to make the people ~〉 **~** *vt* **:** to make tumultuous **:** cause to riot

tu·mul·tu·a·tion \=,==ˈwāshən\ *n* -s [ME *tumultuacion,* fr. L *tumultuation-, tumultuatio,* fr. *tumultuatus* (past part.) + *-ion-, -io* -ion] **:** the act or process of making a tumult **:** DISTURBANCE

tu·mul·tu·ous \t(y)üˈməlch(ə)wəs, təˈm-, -chəs\ *adj* [L *tumultuosus,* fr. *tumultus* tumult + *-osus* -ose] **1 :** marked by tumult **:** full of commotion and uproar **:** RIOTOUS, STORMY, BOISTEROUS 〈a ~ reception〉 〈~ applause〉 〈the ~ years of his administrations —F.L.Mott〉 〈a fierce, ~ battle —J.L.Motley〉 **2 :** tending or disposed to cause or incite a tumult 〈a ~ and irresponsible group〉 〈an unlawful and ~ design —Thomas Hobben〉 〈a factious and ~ person —*Amer. Guide Series: Md.*〉 **3 :** marked by violent or overwhelming turbulence or upheaval 〈~ passions〉 〈~ sensations〉 〈his blazing power . . . and his ~ creative imagination —Orville Prescott〉 〈a ~ river . . . overflowing its banks —W.S.Maugham〉

tu·mul·tu·ous·ly *adv* **:** in a tumultuous manner **:** STORMILY, BOISTEROUSLY, RIOTOUSLY 〈a crowd demonstrating ~〉

tu·mul·tu·ous·ness *n* -ES **:** the quality or state of being tumultuous **:** STORMINESS, BOISTEROUSNESS 〈the ~ of the sea〉

tu·mu·lus \ˈt(y)ümyələs\ *n, pl* **tumu·li** \-ə,lī\ [L; akin to L *tumēre* to swell — more at THUMB] **1 :** an artificial hillock or mound (as over a grave); *esp* **:** one over the grave of a person buried in ancient times **:** BARROW **2 :** a small domal mound of lava

¹tun \ˈtən\ *n* -s [ME *tonne, tunne, toun,* fr. OE *tunne* cask, barrel, tun, prob. of Celt origin; akin to MIr *tonn* skin, hide — more at TUNNEL] **1 a :** a large cask esp. for holding wine or beer **b :** a large receptacle (as a tub or chest) 〈sends you . . . this ~ of treasure —Shak.〉 〈the wash was made up freshly in a deep washing ~ —*Veterinary Record*〉 **c :** a brewer's fermenting vat **:** MASH TUN **2 :** any of various units of liquid capacity; *esp* **:** a unit equal to 252 wine gallons **3 a :** something that resembles a large barrel 〈that ~ of man —Leslie Hotson〉 **b** (1) *dial Eng* **:** CHIMNEY, CHIMNEY POT 〈the crooked smoke . . . from our cottage ~*s* —Llewelyn Powys〉 (2) **:** CHIMNEY STACK

²tun \"\ *vt* **tunned; tunned; tunning; tuns** [ME *tonnen, tunnen,* fr. *tonne, tunne* tun] **1** *archaic* **:** to put into or store in a tun **:** CASK **2** *archaic* **:** to cause to flow into or as if into a tun **:** POUR, SWILL 〈used to ~ down beer . . . during dinner —*Fraser's Mag.*〉

³tun \ˈtün\ *n* -s [Mayan] **:** a period of 360 days composed of 18 months of 20 days each and used as the basis of the Maya long count to which is added the uayeb to make the 365-day year of the Maya calendar — see UINAL; compare TZOLKIN

¹tu·na \ˈt(y)ünə\ *n* -s [Sp, fr. Taino] **1 :** any of various flat-jointed prickly pears of the genus *Opuntia*; *esp* **:** a tropical American plant (*O. tuna*) **2 :** the edible fruit of a tuna plant

²tuna \"\ *n, pl* **tuna** *or* **tunas** [AmerSp, alter. of Sp *atún* tunny, modif. of Ar *tūn,* fr. L *thunnus, thynnus* — more at TUNNY] **1 a :** any of numerous large vigorous scombroid fishes including forms highly esteemed for sport and as food — see ALBACORE, BLUEFIN 2, DOGTOOTH TUNA, YELLOWFIN TUNA **b :** any of various related but usu. smaller fishes — see BONITO, LITTLE TUNA **2** *or* **tuna fish :** the flesh of a tuna esp. when canned for use as food

³tu·na \ˈtünə\ *n* -s [Maori] **:** an eel (*Anguilla sucklandii*) of New Zealand waters

tun·able *also* **tune·able** \ˈt(y)ünəbəl\ *adj* **1** *archaic* **a :** full of melody **:** TUNEFUL **b :** sounding in harmony **:** ATTUNED **c :** free from discord **:** CONCORDANT **2 :** capable of being tuned or made harmonious 〈new receivers are ~ to an alternative station —E.B.Bishop〉 〈seemed to say that men were of ~ metal —Van Wyck Brooks〉 — **tun·ably** *also* **tune·ably** \-nəblē, -li\ *adv*

tun·able·ness *also* **tune·able·ness** *n* -ES *archaic* **:** the quality or state of being tunable

tuna clipper *n* **:** a diesel-powered boat used on the Pacific coast for tuna fishing and made with the deckhouse forward, bait tanks aft, and iron racks around the stern from which men fish with heavy bamboo poles

tunbellied \ˈ=ˌ==\ *adj* [¹*tun* + *bellied*] *archaic* **:** POTBELLIED

tunbelly \ˈ=,==\ *n* -ES [back-formation fr. *tunbellied*] *archaic* **:** POTBELLY 1, 2

tundish \ˈ=,=\ *n* [ME, fr. ¹*tun* + *dish*] **:** FUNNEL, POURING BASIN

tun·dra \ˈtəndrə, ˈtu̇n-\ *n* -s *often attrib* [Russ, of Finno-Ugric origin; akin to Finn *tunturi* arctic hill, Lapp *tundar* hill] **:** a level or undulating treeless plain that is characteristic of arctic

and subarctic regions, marks the limit of arborescent vegetation, consists of black mucky soil with a permanently frozen subsoil, and supports a dense growth of mosses and lichens (as the reindeer moss) and of dwarf caespitose herbs and shrubs often with showy flowers

tundra vole *n* : a vole (*Microtus operarius*) that constitutes an important part of the food supply of the smaller fur-bearing carnivores of far northern No. America

¹tune \'t(y)ün\ *n -s* [ME, alter. of *ton, tone* — more at TONE] **1 a** *archaic* : quality of sound : TONE ⟨thou hast a tongue: come, let us hear its —Horace Smith⟩ **b** : manner of utterance : INTONATION ⟨the straightforward ~ . . . of early English poetry —Louis Untermeyer⟩ *specif* : phonetic modulation ⟨differences . . . are probably more in language ~ than in actual pronunciation —A.J.Tresidder⟩ **c** : a general attitude or bearing : APPROACH ⟨when the tables are turned . . . changes his ~ —A.J.Toynbee⟩ ⟨so struck by facts he was . . . collecting that he altered his ~ —C.L.Boltz⟩ **d** *archaic* : a frame of mind ⟨being in . . . bad ~ for a fête —Thomas Moore⟩ **2 a** : a musical composition ⟨play a ~ on the piano⟩ : an easily remembered musical air, often being the uppermost part esp. of a short or simple construction (as of a ballad or psalm or of some operatic arias) : MELODY ⟨dance ~⟩ ⟨to the ~ of "America"⟩ **c** : a dominant course or theme ⟨stand the expense and not insist upon calling the ~ —I.I.Rabi⟩ ⟨the alluring ~ of the new Pied Piper —*Sydney (Australia) Bull.*⟩ **d** : a contrapuntal activity : ACCOMPANIMENT ⟨glowing speeches, delivered to the ~ of more cheers —*Phoenix Flame*⟩ **3 a** : correct musical pitch or consonance ⟨a competent musician knows with certainty when an instrument is out of ~ —Clive Bell⟩ **b** : a harmonious relationship : AGREEMENT, CONCORD ⟨drawings more in ~ with the text —*N.Y. Times Bk. Rev.*⟩ ⟨a portfolio of stocks . . . out of ~ with present market conditions —*Outlook*⟩ ⟨I was out of ~ with everything and everyone about me —Anne S. Mehdevi⟩ **b(2)** **4** : RESONANCE 1b(2) **4** : a scale of magnitude : AMOUNT, EXTENT ⟨technical difficulties . . . dehumanize us to such a ~ as to make us indifferent —J.C.Powys⟩ — usu. used in the phrase *to the tune of* ⟨subsidized Japan to the ~ of two billion dollars in five years —*Atlantic*⟩ ⟨custom-made to the ~ of $40 or $50 apiece —*Amer. Fabrics*⟩ ⟨turns out electricity from coal to the ~ of 150,000 kilowatts —*Newsweek*⟩

²tune \"\ *vb* -ED/-ING/-S *vi* **1** : to produce musical tones : SING, HUM ⟨a breeze *tuning* through the frigid silence —John Galsworthy⟩ ⟨my children could ~ before they could speak —A.B.Evans⟩ **2** : to become attuned or receptive ⟨develop new attitudes to their tasks as they sensitively ~ to the requirements of their responsibilities —C.C.Brown⟩ ⟨that other part of his mind *tuning* and clocking up the platitude —James Jones⟩ **3** : to adjust a receiver with respect to resonance ⟨~ in to a program⟩ ⟨~ about for good music —E. C.Aldrich⟩ ⟨by *tuning* in on just one station of known location, the direction from the direction finder to the station can be determined —*Introduction to Electronics*⟩ ~ *vt* **1 a** : to adjust in musical pitch or cause to be in tune ⟨~ a violin⟩ ⟨~ it up a minor or a major third —Deems Taylor⟩ **b** *archaic* **(1)** : to express in song ⟨little birds that ~ their morning's joy —Shak.⟩ **(2)** : to lead off (as a hymn) **c** : to give a musical intonation to ⟨he *tuned* a marvellous prose —Edmund Wilson⟩ **2** *archaic* : to influence in a desired direction ⟨the most effective way . . . of *tuning* public opinion —J.H.Blunt⟩ **3 a** : to bring into harmony : ATTUNE ⟨the actors . . . are not perfectly *tuned* to each other —Mildred J. O'Brien⟩ ⟨she was not *tuned* to a mood of self-reproach —Herman Wouk⟩ ⟨the stallion's sense is very keen . . . he knows instantly whether his man is *tuned* in to him —Henry Wyumalen⟩ **b** : to make responsive : ADAPT ⟨whether the touch is firm or light it can be *tuned* to the operator's rhythm —*Print*⟩ **c (1)** : to adjust for precise functioning : put in first-class working order ⟨has good plugs and points and has just recently been *tuned* —Phil Gresho⟩ — often used with *up* ⟨~ up a plane on the flight line⟩ **(2)** : to put in readiness : KEY ⟨we were tautly *tuned* for it —F.A.Perry⟩ — often used with *up* ⟨was pretty well *tuned* up for the challenge —Norman Cousins⟩ **4 a** : to adjust with respect to resonance ⟨a means of *tuning* the electrodes is . . . provided . . . to facilitate voltage adjustment —F.W.Curtis⟩ ⟨~ a television set to the local channel⟩ **b (1)** : to adjust for precise functioning ⟨~ in a program⟩ ⟨~ out static⟩ ⟨a hearing aid . . . that automatically ~s down loud and harsh noises —*Newsweek*⟩ **c** : to establish radio contact with ⟨~ in a directional beacon⟩

tuneable *var of* TUNABLE

tuned *adj* [fr. past part. of ²*tune*] **1 a** : put in tune : HARMONIZED, MELODIOUS ⟨a carillon of ~ bells⟩ **b** : furnished with a tune ⟨musical comedy well ~ —*New Yorker*⟩ **2** : adjusted for resonance ⟨~ amplifier⟩ ⟨~ circuit⟩

tuned-in \"⸗"\ *adj* : ALERT, RECEPTIVE ⟨grow attached to a teacher they think of as properly *tuned-in* —R.A.Arthur⟩

tune·ful \'t(y)ünfəl\ *adj* **1 a** : having a musical sound : MELODIOUS ⟨a ~ song⟩ ⟨a ~ bell⟩ **b** *archaic* : producing melody; *esp* : fond of singing ⟨free as the birds of the air, and like them . . . ~ —William Bartram⟩ **2** *archaic* : of or relating to music ⟨members of the ~ trade —John Dryden⟩ — **tune·ful·ly** \-fəlē, -li\ *adv*

tune·ful·ness \-nəs\ *n -ES* : the quality or state of being tuneful

tune·less \'t(y)ünləs\ *adj* **1** : lacking musical quality : UNMELODIOUS **2** : making no music : SOUNDLESS

tun·er \-nə(r)\ *n -s* : one that tunes or is used for tuning: as **a** : a specialist in tuning musical instruments ⟨piano ~⟩ **b** : a workman who adjusts a mechanism for peak performance ⟨power-loom ~⟩ ⟨typewriter ~⟩ ⟨a ~ of old cars⟩ **c (1)** : TUNING FORK **(2)** : PITCH PIPE **(3)** : a device for tuning an organ flue pipe consisting of an adjustable flap or opening near its top by which the vibrating length of the air chamber may be changed **(4)** : a device attached to the tailpiece of a bowed stringed musical instrument to facilitate the tuning of the upper strings ⟨~ ⟩ : an instrument (as a tuning capacitor) for tuning an electric circuit **(2)** : the part of a receiving set consisting of the circuit used to adjust resonance

tunes *pl of* TUNE, *pres 3d sing of* TUNE

tunesmith \'⸗"⸗"⸗\ *n* [¹*tune* + *smith*] : a composer esp. of popular songs

tune up *vi* **1** : to limber up the vocal chords : sing out ⟨the company *tuned* up and sang with goodwill —B.L.K.Henderson⟩ **2 a** : to bring the instruments of a musical ensemble to a common pitch ⟨the orchestra is *tuning up* and the concert is about to begin⟩ **b** : to make a tentative effort or a trial run ⟨a few soapbox orators are *tuning up* near the bandstand —Winston Brebner⟩

tune-up \'⸗"⸗"⸗\ *n -s* [*tune up*] **1** : a general adjustment to insure operation at peak efficiency ⟨periodic oil changes . . . and motor *tune-ups* in the spring and fall are essential —*Automobilist*⟩ **2** : a preliminary trial : WARM-UP ⟨takes a practice jump with her mount . . . in a *tune-up* for the rugged international kilowatt —*N.Y. Times*⟩

tung \'təŋ\ *var of* TUNG TREE

tun·ga \'təŋgə\ *n, cap* [NL, fr. Pg., fr. Tupi] : a genus of fleas having conspicuous mouthparts, the setae on the head very small or missing entirely, and no ctenidia on the head or pronotum — see CHIGOE

tun·gan \'tün-gán, (')tün-\ *also* **dun·gan** \('t)dü-\ *n, pl* **tungan** *or* **tungans** *also* **dungan** *or* **dungans** *usu cap* [G *Tunganen, Dunganen,* fr. Jagatai *Döngan,* prob. fr. *dönmek* to convert] **1 a** : a Mongoloid Turkish people of Turkestan found also in large numbers in Kansu Province and the Sining region of Chinghai Province in northwest China **b** : a member of such people **2** : the language of the Tungan people

tung-hu \'düŋ'hü\ *n pl, usu cap* : the eastern Tatars of ancient Chinese history

tun·go \'təŋgō\ *n -s* [native name in So. Australia] *Austral* : RAT KANGAROO

tung oil *n* [part trans. of Chin (Pek) *yu²-t'ung²* tung tree oil, fr. *yu²* oil + *t'ung²* tung tree] **1** : a pale yellow pungent drying oil obtained chiefly from the seeds of the tung tree and composed of glycerides esp. of eleostearic acid and other unsaturated acids, that polymerizes to a hard gel on long standing or on heating, and that is used chiefly in quick-drying varnishes and paints and as a waterproofing agent — called also *China wood oil, wood oil* **2** : JAPANESE TUNG OIL

tung oil tree *n* : TUNG TREE

tungst- *or* **tungsto-** *comb form* [ISV, fr. *tungsten*] **1** : tungsten ⟨*tungsto*boric⟩ **2** : tungstic acid ⟨*tungstate*⟩

tung·state \'təŋ₁stāt, -₁stät, usu ,stā-d.+V\ *n -s* [ISV *tungst-* + *-ate*] : a salt of tungstic acid; *esp* : a normal salt (as sodium tungstate Na_2WO_4) derived from the acid H_2WO_4 or its monohydrate — called also *wolframate*; compare METATUNGSTATE, PARATUNGSTATE

tung·sten \-₁stən\ *n -s* [Sw, fr. *tung* heavy + *sten* stone; akin to ON *thungr* heavy, OE *thīl, thixl* pole, shaft, OHG *dīhsala,* L *temo* pole, shaft, OSlav *tęgnoti* to drag, pull, Skt *tanoti* he stretches, and to ON *steinn* stone — more at THIN, STONE] **1** : a gray-white heavy high-melting ductile hard polyvalent metallic element that resembles chromium and molybdenum in many of its properties, that is found combined in scheelite, wolframite, and other minerals and is extracted by the successive formation of an alkali metal tungstate, tungstic acid, and tungsten trioxide, reduction of the trioxide with hydrogen to a gray-black metal powder, and compaction by powder metallurgy to massive metal, and that is used in the pure form chiefly for electrical purposes (as for filaments for incandescent lamps and contact points) and with other substances in hardening steel and other alloys and in making carbides — called also *wolfram;* symbol *W;* see ELEMENT table **2** *obs* **a** : SCHEELITE **b** : WOLFRAMITE

tungsten bronze *n* : any of a series of highly colored lustrous crystalline compounds of variable composition that are mixed oxides of tungsten and usu. sodium or other alkali metal, that are good conductors of electricity, and that can be made by reduction of a normal tungstate (as sodium tungstate Na_2WO_4 with tungsten) or of tungsten trioxide with sodium

tungsten carbide *n* : a compound of tungsten and carbon; *esp* : a fine very hard crystalline gray powder WC made by heating tungsten or tungsten trioxide with carbon at a high temperature and usu. bonded with cobalt or nickel in cemented carbide compositions esp. for cutting tools, abrasives, and dies

tung·sten·ite \-₁stə₁nīt\ *n -s* [*tungsten* + *-ite*] : a mineral WS_2 consisting of a tungsten sulfide and occurring in small lead-gray folia (hardness 2.5)

tungsten lamp *n* : an incandescent lamp with a filament of metallic tungsten — compare OSMIUM LAMP

tungsten trioxide *n* : a compound WO_3 found naturally as tungstite, obtained by chemical treatment as a heavy yellow crystalline powder (as in the extraction of tungsten), and used chiefly in the production of tungsten powder

tung·stic \-stik, -tēk\ *adj* [ISV *tungsten* + *-ic*] : of, relating to, or containing tungsten : WOLFRAMIC — used esp. of compounds in which this element is hexavalent

tungstic acid *n* **1** : TUNGSTEN TRIOXIDE **2** : any of various acids derived from tungsten trioxide; *esp* : the simplest acid H_2WO_4 analogous in composition to chromic acid and obtained as a yellow powder or as the white monohydrate $H_2WO_4.H_2O$ but known chiefly in the form of salts — compare HETEROPOLY ACID, METATUNGSTIC ACID, PHOSPHOTUNGSTIC ACID

tungstic ocher *n* : TUNGSTITE

tungstic oxide *n* : TUNGSTEN TRIOXIDE

tung·stite \'təŋ₁stīt, -ṇ(k)₁stīt\ *n -s* [*tungst-* + *-ite*] : a mineral $WO_3.H_2O(?)$ consisting of a hydrous tungsten trioxide and occurring in yellow or yellowish green pulverulent masses

tung·sto·boric acid \₁təŋ(₁)stō+-\ *n* [*tungst-* + *boric*] : BOROTUNGSTIC ACID

tung·sto·phosphate \"+-\ *n* [*tungst-* + *phosphate*] : PHOSPHOTUNGSTATE

tung·sto·phosphoric acid \"+-\ *n* [*tungst-* + *phosphoric*] : PHOSPHOTUNGSTIC ACID

tung·sto·silicate \"+-\ *n* [ISV *tungst-* + *silicate*] : SILICOTUNGSTATE

tung·sto·silicic acid \"+-\ *n* [ISV *tungst-* + *silicic*] : SILICOTUNGSTIC ACID

tung tree \'təŋ-\ *also* **tung** *n -s* [Chin (Pek) *t'ung²*] : any of several plants of the genus *Aleurites*; *esp* : a Chinese tree (*A. fordii*) grown for its seeds which yield tung oil

tun·gus *also* **tun·guz** \(')tu̇ŋ¦gu̇z\ *n, pl* **tungus** *or* **tunguses** *also* **tunguz** *or* **tunguzes** *usu cap* [Russ, one of the Tungus, prob. fr. Turko-Tatar *tonguz* hog; fr. the fact that they are often hog breeders] **1 a** : a Mongoloid people related to the Manchu that are widely spread over Eastern Siberia and include many still nomadic groups — called also *Evenk;* see GOLDI, LAMUT; compare OLCHA **b** : a member of such people **2** *also* **tun·guse** \-z-\ : the Tungusic languages of the Tungus peoples

¹tun·gu·sic \-zik\ *n -s usu cap* : a subfamily of Altaic languages spoken in Manchuria and northward and including Tungus, Lamut, Manchu, and Goldi

²tungusic \"\ *adj, usu cap* **1** *also* **tun·guse** \-z\ *or* **tun·gu·sian** \-zēən, -zhən\ : of or relating to the Tungus people or their language **2** : of or relating to Tungusic

tu·nic \'t(y)ünik, -nēk\ *n -s* [L *tunica* tunic, integument, membrane, of Sem origin; akin to Heb *kuttōneth* coat — more at CHITON] **1 a** : a simple slip-on garment made with or without sleeves and usu. knee-length or longer, belted at the waist, and worn as an under or outer garment by men and women of ancient Greece and Rome **b** : SURCOAT **2 a (1)** : MANTLE 2b(2) **(2)** : TUNICA **b** : a natural integument ⟨the ~ of a seed⟩ **3 a** : a long usu. plain close-fitting jacket made with a high collar and worn (as by a soldier or policeman) esp. as part of a uniform **b** : an undress coat worn by British soldiers **4** : TUNICLE 1b, 1c **5 a** : a short overskirt usu. cut in one piece with the bodice and either belted or fitted at the waist **b** : a usu. belted overblouse or jacket that is hip length or longer **c** : a short loose garment resembling a Grecian tunic worn by women for active sports (as for dance practice)

¹tu·ni·ca \'t(y)ünəkə\ *n, pl* **tuni·cae** \-nə,kē, -,kī, -,sē\ [L] **1** : an enveloping or covering membrane or layer of body tissue **2** [NL, fr. L] : the outer of the two growth regions into which the apical meristem is held to be divisible in the tunica-corpus theory

²tunica \"\ *n -s* [NL (genus name of the coat flower *Tunica saxifraga*), fr. L *tunic*] : COAT FLOWER

³tu·ni·ca \'t(y)ünəkə, -'nēkə\ *n, pl* **tunica** *or* **tunicas** *usu cap* [Tunica, the people] **1 a** : an Indian people of the lower Yazoo river valley in Mississippi **b** : a member of such people **2** : the language of the Tunica people

tunica al·bu·gin·ea \-₁albyə'jinēə, -bə'gi-\ *n, pl* **tunicae albugine·ae** \-'jinē,ē, -'ginē,ī\ [NL, white-spotted coat] : a white fibrous capsule esp. of the testis, ovary, eye, or spleen

tunica-corpus theory \"⸗'⸗⸗-\ *n* : a theory in plant morphology: each apical meristem consists of an outer tunica and an inner corpus

¹tu·ni·can \'t(y)ünəkən, ⸗'nēkən\ *also* **to·ni·kan** \'tōnəkən, tə'nēk-\ *adj, usu cap* **1** : of or relating to the Tunica or their language **2** : of or relating to Tunican

²tunican \"\ *n -s usu cap* **1** : a language family of the Gulf phylum comprising the Tunica language **2** *in former classifications* : a language stock comprising Tunican, Atakapan, and Chitimachan

¹tu·ni·cary \'t(y)ünə,kerē\ *n -ES* [L *tunica* + E *-ary,* n. suffix] : TUNICATE

²tunicary \"\ *adj* [L *tunica* + E *-ary,* adj. suffix] : of or relating to a covering membrane

tu·ni·ca·ta \₁t(y)ünə'kād·ə, -'käd-ə\ *n pl, cap* [NL, fr. neut. pl. of L *tunicatus* tunicate] *syn of* UROCHORDA

¹tu·ni·cate \'t(y)ünə,kāt, -nēk-, *sometimes* -nə,kāt; *usu* ¦d-+V\ *also* **tu·ni·cat·ed** \-nə,kād·əd, -ātəd\ *adj* [*tunicate* fr. L *tunicatus,* past part. of *tunicare* to clothe with a tunic, fr. *tunica* tunic; *tunicated* fr. L *tunicatus* + E *-ed* — more at TUNIC] **1 a** : covered with a tunic **b** : coated with layers (as an onion) **2 a (1)** : having a tunic or mantle **(2)** : of or relating to the Urochorda **b** : having each joint buried in the preceding funnel-shaped one ⟨the ~ antennae of an insect⟩

²tunicate \"\ *n -s* [NL *Tunicata*] : an animal of the subphylum Urochorda

tunica va·gi·na·lis \-₁vajə'nalēs, -nā-\ *n, pl* **tunicae vaginales** \-a(₁)lēz, -ā,(₁)lēz\ [NL, vaginal coat] : a pouch of serous membrane covering the testis and derived from the peritoneum

tunic flower *n* : COAT FLOWER

tu·ni·cin \'t(y)ünəsən\ *n -s* [²*tunicate* + *-in*] : a substance in the cell walls of many tunicates that resembles the cellulose of plants

tu·nicked *also* **tu·niced** \'t(y)ünikt, -nēkt\ *adj* : having or

wearing a tunic ⟨wearing ~ bathing suits —Elizabeth Enright⟩

tu·ni·cle \'t(y)ünik'l, -nēk-\ *n -s* [ME, fr. L *tunicula* little tunic, little membrane, dim. of *tunica* tunic, membrane] **1 a** *obs* : a small tunic **b** : a short dalmatic worn by a subdeacon over the alb during mass **2** : a short close-fitting vestment worn by a bishop under the dalmatic at pontifical ceremonies **2** : a covering membrane or integument : MANTLE 2b(2), ²TUNICA

tunics *pl of* TUNIC

tuning *n -s* [fr. gerund of ²*tune*] **1 a (1)** : the act or process of putting in tune ⟨final assembly, regulating, ~ and voicing of . . . pianos —*Baldwin Piano Co. Catalog*⟩ **(2)** : the quality or state of being tuned ⟨a small violoncello of standard ~ —Robert Donington⟩ **b** : an adaptive influence or state of adaptation ⟨gave him the right ~ for feeling like a piece of God's creation —Eric Manners⟩ **2** *obs* : the production of musical sounds ⟨sentimental and rapturous ~s —Henry Brooke⟩ **3** : an act or process of adjusting with respect to resonance; *specif* : adjustment of the frequency response of receiving equipment (as of a radio) so as to be resonant with the received signal — compare FLAT TUNING, SHARP TUNING

tuning bar *n* : a tuning instrument used esp. by bands and orchestras and made of a steel bar set on a resonance box that gives the pitch when struck

tuning capacitor *or* **tuning condenser** *n* : a variable capacitor used to vary the resonant frequency of an oscillatory circuit (as in tuning a radio receiver)

tuning coil *n* : a tuner consisting of a coil of variable inductance

tuning cone *n* : a hollow metal cone used in tuning open organ pipes

tuning eye *n* : a cathode ray tube designed to aid in precise tuning of a radio circuit

tuning fork *n* : a two-pronged metal implement not affected by moderate differences of temperature that gives a persistent fixed tone nearly free from harmonics when struck and is useful for tuning musical instruments and ascertaining standard pitch

tuning fork

tuning hammer *or* **tuning wrench** *n* : a hammer-shaped wrench used in tuning pianos and made with heads hollowed to fit over the tuning pegs

tuning peg *or* **tuning pin** *n* : an adjustable pin to which the strings (as of a piano or a violin) are fastened and by means of which the pitch may be varied ⟨the creak of *tuning pegs* in their sockets —Mark Harris⟩

tuning pipe *n* : PITCH PIPE; *specif* : one of a set of pitch pipes used esp. for tuning stringed musical instruments

tuning slide *n* : an adjustable crook or slide in a metal wind musical instrument used for tuning to another instrument

tu·nis \'t(y)ünəs\ *n* [fr. *Tunis* (Tunisia), country in No. Africa where the breed originated] **1** *usu cap* : an old Asiatic breed of hornless medium-wooled fat-tailed sheep valued esp. for their ability to breed and develop rapidly a good quality meat lamb **2** [*Tunis* (often *cap* : a sheep of the Tunis breed

²tunis \"\ *adj, usu cap* [fr. *Tunis,* Tunisia] : of or from Tunis, the capital of Tunisia : of the kind or style prevalent in Tunis : TUNISIAN

tunis grass *n, usu cap T* [fr. *Tunis* (Tunisia), No. Africa] : a No. African grass (*Sorghum virgatum*) used for forage

tu·ni·sia \t(y)ü'nēzh(ē)ə, -nizh-\ *adj, usu cap* [fr. *Tunisia,* country in No. Africa] : of or from Tunisia : of the kind or style prevalent in Tunisia : TUNISIAN

¹tu·ni·sian \-zh(ē)ən\ *n -s cap* [*Tunisia,* No. Africa + E *-an,* n. suffix] : a native or inhabitant of Tunis or Tunisia

²tunisian \"\ *adj* [*Tunisia* + E *-an,* adj. suffix] : TUNISIA

¹tunk \'təŋk\ *also* **tonk** \'tȯŋk, 'tȯŋk\ *n -s* [imit.] **1** : TAP, RAP, THUMP ⟨got a bad ~ on her head, and a few scratches —Marguerite Tate⟩

²tunk \"\ *also* **tonk** \"\ *vb* -ED/-ING/-S *vt* : to strike lightly or sharply : RAP, TAP ⟨~ed their heads together⟩; *esp* : to tap (as car wheels) with a hammer to test for flaws ~ *vi* : to give a tunk : TAP ⟨~ing on a drum⟩

³tunk \"\ *or* **tonk** \"\ *n -s* [prob. fr. ¹*tunk*] : a game of rummy for two to five players with deuces wild

tunker *usu cap, var of* DUNKER

tun·ket \'təŋkət, *usu* -ₔd-+V\ *n -s* [prob. euphemism for *tophet*] : HELL — used interjectionally to express curiosity, puzzlement, or exasperation ⟨what in ~ did he mean, upside-down eyes⟩ ⟨why in ~ didn't you tell me so —Della Lutes⟩

tunnage *var of* TONNAGE

tunned *past of* TUN

¹tun·nel \'tən²l\ *n -s often attrib* [ME *tonel,* fr. MF *tonel, tonnel* cask, tun, fr. OF, fr. *tonne* tun, fr. ML *tunna,* prob. fr. barrel, tun, of Celt origin; akin to MIr *tonn* skin, hide, W *tonn;* akin to L *tondēre* to shear, crop — more at TOME] **1** : TUNNEL NET 1 **2 a** *archaic* : a chimney flue **b** *dial* : FUNNEL 2 : a hollow conduit or recess : TUBE, WELL ⟨drive shaft ~ ⟨drying ~⟩; *specif* : SHAFT TUNNEL **b** : a bodily channel ⟨a more or less circular ~, the neural canal —W.E.Swinton⟩ **c** : WIND TUNNEL **3 a** : a covered passageway ⟨~ of a long nave —George Santayana⟩; *specif* : a nearly horizontal passageway through or under an obstruction ⟨railroad ~ through a mountain⟩ ⟨take the midtown ~ from Long Island to New York⟩ **b (1)** : a subterranean gallery (as in a cave or mine) ⟨2⟩ : ADIT **c (1)** : a narrow enclosed pressurized corridor connecting two pressurized personnel compartments of an airplane **d** : the burrow of an insect or other animal ⟨mole's ~⟩ ⟨termite ~s in beams⟩ **e** : something that resembles a corridor ⟨a ~ of trees⟩ ⟨headlights created their own ~ of light —Paul Scott⟩ ⟨trapped in the ~ of their own logic —Douglas Stewart⟩; *specif* : an arch formed by partners' joined hands in a square dance

²tunnel \"\ *vb* **tunneled** *or* **tunnelled; tunneled** *or* **tunnelled; tunneling** *or* **tunnelling** \-n(ə)liŋ\ **tunnels** *vt* **1** *archaic* : to catch in a tunnel net **2 a** : to pass through a covered channel : advance by or as if by excavating a tunnel ⟨belt ~ed through wide black patent girdle —*Women's Wear Daily*⟩ ⟨larvae . . . ~ing their way through the cappings —*Gleanings in Bee Culture*⟩ **b** : to penetrate with or as if with a tunnel ⟨make a passage through or under ⟨the acid water . . . ~ed it, so that it is honeycombed —Marjory S. Douglas⟩ ⟨lights ~ the darkness⟩ ~ *vi* **1** : to make or use a tunnel ⟨with a view to keeping the gradient down . . . proposed to ~ under the ridge —O.S.Nock⟩ ⟨a creaking train . . . ~ed through the hill —J.A. Michener⟩ **b** : UNDERMINE ⟨appeared to be ~ing under all the established values —Sherwood Anderson⟩ **2** *physics* : to pass through a potential barrier ⟨electrons . . . ~ back to the vacant sites —Frederick Seitz⟩

tunnel effect *n* : the quantum mechanical phenomenon sometimes exhibited by moving particles that succeed in passing from one side of a potential barrier to the other although of insufficient energy to pass over the top

tun·nel·er *or* **tun·nel·ler** \-n(ə)lə(r)\ *n -s* : one that tunnels: as **a** : a workman employed in excavating a tunnel **b** : a machine used in tunneling (as in mining) to cut a drift)

tunneling *or* **tunnelling** \"⸗⸗⸗\ *n -s* [fr. gerund of ²*tunnel*] **1** : a tunnel or series of tunnels **2** : the act or process of making a tunnel

tunnel kiln *n* : CONTINUOUS KILN

tunnellike \'⸗⸗,⸗\ *adj* : resembling a tunnel

tunnel net *n* **1** : a long conical net for game or fish : FYKE **2** : the narrow part of a pound net connecting the heart with the pot

tunnel of cor·ti \-'kȯrd·ē, -,r,tē\ *usu cap C* [after Alfonso Corti †1876 Ital. anatomist] : a spiral passage in the organ of Corti

tunnel of love *n* : a dark tunnel in an amusement park through which passengers are conveyed usu. by boat

tunnel right *n* : the mineral right to all previously undiscovered veins and lodes within 3,000 feet of the portal of an exploratory tunnel and 300 feet on each side of its center line and to a claim 1500 feet in length on any vein that crosses it at right angles

tunnel vault *n* : BARREL VAULT

tunnel vision *n* : a field of vision of 70 percent or less from the straight-ahead position resulting in elimination of the peripheral field

tunnel weaver *n* : TUBE SPINNER

tun·ner \ˈtənə(r)\ *n* -s *Brit* **:** a brewer's workman in charge of a tun
tunning *pres part of* TUN
tun·ny \ˈtənē, -ni\ *also* **tunnyfish** \ˈ≈,≈\ *n, pl* **tunnies** *also* **tunny** [earlier *tonny, tony,* modif. (prob. influenced by *-y,* dim. suffix) of MF *thon* or OIt *tonno,* both fr. OProv *ton,* fr. L *thunnus, thynnus,* fr. Gk *thynnos,* of non-IE origin; akin to the source of Heb *tannīn* serpent, sea monster] **:** TUNA; *esp* **:** BLUEFIN 2
tu·no \ˈtü(,)nō\ *or* **tu·nu** \-nü\ *n* -s [AmerSp, prob. fr. Miskito *túno*] **1 :** a Central American tree (*Castilloa fallax*) closely related to the Central American rubber tree but producing a nonelastic rubber **2** *also* **tuno gum :** the resinous gum of the tuno tree
tun of gold [¹*tun*] *obs* **:** 100,000 gold coins (as guilders or florins)
tuns *pl of* TUN, *pres 3d sing of* TUN
tun shell *n* [¹*tun*] **1 :** a gastropod mollusk of the family Tonnidae **2 :** a shell of one of the Tonnidae
¹**tup** \ˈtəp\ *n* -s [ME *tupe, tuppe*] **1 a :** *chiefly Brit* **:** RAM 1a **b** *archaic* **:** one who is likened to a ram; *specif* **:** CUCKOLD **2 :** a heavy metal body (as the hammer head of a steam hammer or the weight of a pendulum)
²**tup** \ˈ"\ *vb* **tupped; tupped; tupping; tups** *vi, chiefly Brit* **:** to come in heat **:** be ready to accept a ram ~ *vt, chiefly Brit* **:** to copulate with (a ewe) **:** COVER
tu·paia \t(y)üˈpīə\ *n* [NL, fr. Malay *tupai* squirrel] **1** *cap* **:** a genus (the type of the family Tupaiidae) that is the chief genus of tree shrews **2** *also* **tu·paya** \ˈ"\ -s **:** TREE SHREW
¹**tu·pai·id** \-īəd\ *adj* [NL *Tupaiidae*] **:** of or relating to the Tupaiidae
²**tupaiid** \ˈ"\ *n* -s **:** a member of the Tupaiidae **:** TREE SHREW
tu·pai·idae \t(y)üˈpīə,dē\ *n pl, cap* [NL, fr. *Tupaia,* type genus + *-idae*] **:** a family of small arboreal mammals of southeastern Asia and the Pacific islands that comprise the tree shrews and are held to be insectivores or treated as primates of lowly organization and then placed with the lemurs and tarsiers in the suborder Prosimii
tu·pe·lo \ˈt(y)üpə,lō\ *n* -s [Creek *ito opilwa,* lit., swamp tree] **1 :** a tree of the genus *Nyssa:* as **a :** BLACK GUM 1a — see TREE illustration **b :** TUPELO GUM **2 :** the wood of a tupelo
tupelo gum *n* **:** a swamp tree (*Nyssa aquatica*) occurring esp. in the southeastern U. S. and having brilliant glossy foliage and softer wood than the related black gums
tu·pi \ˈtü,pē, ≈ˈ≈\ *n, pl* **tupi** *or* **tupis** *usu cap* **1 a :** a group of Tupi-Guaranian peoples of Brazil esp. living in the valleys of the Amazon, Tapajoz, Araguaia, and Xingu **b :** a member of any of such peoples **2 :** the language of the Tupi people serving as a lingua franca in the valley of the Amazon
tu·pi·an \-ēən\ *adj, usu cap* **:** of, relating to, or designating the Tupi or other Tupi-Guaranian peoples or their languages
tupi–guarani \¦≈¦≈¦≈\ *n, usu cap T&G* **1 a :** a So. American people spread over an area from far eastern Brazil to the Peruvian Andes and from the Guianas to Uruguay **b :** a member of such people **2 a :** TUPI-GUARANIAN **b :** GUARANI 2
¹**tupi–guaranian** \¦≈¦≈¦≈\ *adj, usu cap T&G* **:** of or relating to Tupi-Guarani
²**tupi–guaranian** \ˈ"\ *n, usu cap T&G* **:** a language stock widely distributed in tropical So. America including Tupi, Guarani, and many other languages
tu·pik *also* **tu·pek** \ˈtüpik\ *n* -s [Esk] **:** an Eskimo summer dwelling; *specif* **:** a sealskin tent
tu·pi·nam·ba \,tüpəˈnambə, -ˌnamˈbä\ *n, pl* **tupinamba** *or* **tupinambas** *usu cap* **1 a :** a group of extinct Tupian peoples of the Brazilian coast from the mouth of the Amazon to the southern part of the State of São Paulo **b :** a member of any of such peoples **2 :** the language of the Tupinamba people
tuppence *var of* TWOPENCE
tuppenny *var of* TWOPENNY
tupping *n* -s [fr. gerund of ²*tup*] *chiefly Brit* **:** BREEDING — used of sheep
tups *pl of* TUP, *pres 3d sing of* TUP
tuque \ˈt(y)ük\ *n* -s [CanF, fr. F *toque,* fr. MF — more at TOQUE] **:** a warm knitted stocking cap; *esp* **:** a close-fitting pointed cap of double thickness made by folding one of the closed ends of a tapered tubular knitted piece up into the other
tu quo·que \ˈt(y)üˈkwōkwē\ *n, pl* **tu quoques** [L, you also] **:** a retort charging an adversary with being or doing what he criticizes in others ⟨has always the same childlike defence, a *tu quoque* —*Times Lit. Supp.*⟩
¹**tur** \ˈtü(ə)r\ *n* -s [Russ, urus, Caucasian goat; akin to L *taurus* bull — more at STEER] **:** any of several Caucasian wild goats (as *Capra cylindricornis* of the eastern, *C. severtzowi* of the western, and *C. caucasica* of the central Caucasus)
²**tur** \ˈ"\ *n* -s [Hindi *tuar,* fr. Skt *tubarī,* of Dravidian origin; akin to Tamil *tuvarai* tur, Kanarese *togari*] *India* **:** PIGEON PEA
tu·ra·cin \ˈt(y)ürəsən\ *n* -s [NL *Turacus* + E *-in*] **:** an amorphous red porphyrin pigment containing copper obtained from feathers of the touraco — compare UROPORPHYRIN
turaco *or* **turacou** *or* **turakoo** *var of* TOURACO
tu·ra·cus \ˈt(y)ürəkəs\ *n, cap* [NL, fr. F *touraco*] **:** a genus of birds (family Musophagidae) comprising various typical touracos
¹**tu·ra·ni·an** \t(y)əˈrānēən, t(y)üˈ-, t(y)ůˈ-\ *n* -s *usu cap* [Per *Tūrān* Turkistan, the region north of the Oxus + E *-ian*] **1 a** (1) **:** a member of any of the peoples of Ural-Altaic stock (2) **:** a member of any division of a nomadic people held to have preceded the Aryans in Europe and Asia **b :** a member of any tribe or nationality of Turkic or Tataric stock **2 :** the total body of Turanian languages
²**turanian** \ˈ"\ *adj, usu cap* **1 :** of, relating to, or constituting various language families of Asia (as Altaic and Uralic) **2 a :** of, relating to, or constituting peoples speaking the Turanian languages **b :** of, relating to, or constituted by Turanians
tu·ran·ite \ˈt(y)ůrə,nīt, t(y)ůˈra,-\ *n* -s [Russ *turanit',* fr. Per *Tūrān* Turkistan + Russ *-it'* -ite (fr. L *-ita, -ites*)] **:** a basic vanadate of copper prob. $Cu_5(VO_4)_2(OH)_4$
tu·ran·ose \-,nōs\ *n* -s [G *turanos,* fr. Per *Tūrān* Turkistan + G *-os* -ose; fr. its being obtained from a manna found in Turkistan] **:** a crystalline reducing disaccharide sugar $C_{12}H_{22}O_{11}$ obtained by the partial hydrolysis of melezitose; 3-α-glucosyl-fructose
turb \ˈtərb\ *n* -s [ME *turbe,* fr. MF, fr. L *turba* crowd — more at TURBID] *archaic* **:** a number of individuals or units gathered together (as a crowd, swarm, heap, troop, or clump)
¹**tur·ban** \ˈtərbən, ˈtə̄b-, ˈtəib-\ *n* -s *often attrib* [MF *turbant,* fr. It *turbante,* modif. of Turk *dülbend, tülbend,* fr. Per *dulband*] **1 :** a headdress worn chiefly in countries of the eastern Mediterranean and southern Asia esp. by Muslims and made of a cap around which is wound a long cloth **2** *archaic* **:** MUSLIM **3 :** an emblematic representation of a turban (as on a Muslim funeral monument or in a heraldic device) **4 :** a symbolic representation of Islam in the form of a turban ⟨I was better fitted for the ~ than the cowl —Linda Villari⟩ **5 :** a headdress resembling a Muslim turban: as **a :** a fashionable headdress for women esp. in the 19th century **b :** a cloth, bandanna, or towel wrapped or tied about the head ⟨their black skins and snow-white linen being set off by colored ~s —C.R.Darwin⟩ **c :** a woman's brimless close-fitting hat usu. of draped fabric **6 :** TURBAN SHELL **7 :** a dish (as a fillet of fish) formed in the shape of a turban to permit the center to be filled with a suitable accompanying mixture ⟨~ of filet of sole with quenelles of shrimp and lobster-and-caviar sauce —*Newsweek*⟩

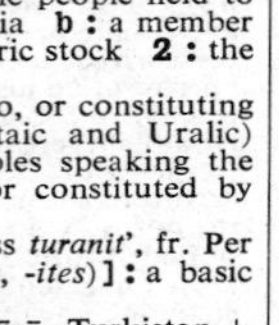
turban 5c

²**turban** \ˈ"\ *vt* -ED/-ING/-S **:** to envelop with or as if with a turban ⟨the wreaths, like mist, that ~ thy dusk brow —H.H. Milman⟩ ⟨~*ed* in a wet huck towel —Peter De Vries⟩
turban buttercup *n* **:** any of several commonly cultivated double-flowered buttercups derived from a Eurasian tuberous-rooted buttercup (*Ranunculus asiaticus*) and characterized by bright yellow flowers often nearly two inches across
tur·baned *or* **tur·banned** \-nd\ *adj* [¹*turban* + *-ed*] **:** wearing a turban ⟨~ police —*Nat'l Geographic*⟩ ⟨~, long-robed Moslems —Jill Donisthorpe⟩ ⟨~ Indian generals —*Newsweek*⟩
turban lily *n* **:** a European lily (*Lilium pomponium*) cultivated for its deep-red spotted flowers shaped like turbans
turban shell *n* [modif. (influenced by ¹*turban*) of NL *turbin-, turbo*] **1 :** any of numerous marine snails (family Turbinidae) with a thick spiral nacreous operculate shell — see CAT'S-EYE, GREEN SNAIL, STARSHELL **2 :** the shell of a turban shell
turban squash *n* **:** any of various winter squashes constituting a distinct variety (*Cucurbita maxima turbaniformis*) and having hard-shelled fruit shaped somewhat like a turban and usu. with an evident rounded central portion protruding from the end farthest from the stem
¹**tur·ba·ry** \ˈtərbərē\ *n* -ES [ME, fr. ML *turbaria,* fr. *turba* turf, peat (of Gmc origin; akin to OE *turf*) + L *-aria* -ary — more at TURF] **1 :** the ground where turf or peat may be dug esp. for fuel **:** PEAT BOG **2 :** an easement under English law to dig turf or peat on a common or on another's land
²**turbary** \ˈ"\ *adj* [¹*turbary;* fr. the fact that the remains of such sheep are found in turbaries of the period] **:** of, relating to, or constituting hogs or sheep domesticated in prehistoric times
tur·ba·trix \,tərˈbā·triks\ *n, cap* [NL *Turbatric-, Turbatrix,* fr. L, female disturber, fem. of *turbator* one that disturbs, fr. *turbatus* (past part. of *turbare* to disturb) + *-or* — more at TURBID, -TRIX] **:** a genus of small slender nematode worms (family Cephalobidae) including the vinegar eel
tur·beh *or* **tur·be** \ˈtər,be\ *n* -s [Turk *türbe,* fr. Ar *turbah*] **:** a Muslim tomb or mausoleum
tur·bel·lar·ia \,tərbəˈla(a)rēə\ *n pl, cap* [NL, fr. L *turbellae* (pl.) bustle, stir (dim. of *turba* crowd, confusion, tumult) + NL *-aria;* fr. the tiny eddies created in water by their cilia — more at TURBID] **:** a class of Platyhelminthes comprising mostly free-living comparatively small soft-bodied more-or-less leaf-shaped externally ciliated flatworms widely distributed in salt or fresh water but occas. living on land or as parasites — see ACOELA, ALLOIOCOELA, POLYCLADIDA, RHABDOCOELA, TRICLADIDA
¹**tur·bel·lar·i·an** \¦≈≈¦la(a)rēən\ *adj* [NL *Turbellaria* + E *-an*] **:** of or relating to the Turbellaria
²**turbellarian** \ˈ"\ *n* -s **:** a turbellarian worm
tur·bid \ˈtərbəd, ˈtə̄b-, ˈtəib-\ *adj* [L *turbidus* confused, disordered, turbid, fr. *turba* confusion, tumult, crowd; akin to L *turbare* to throw into disorder, disturb, make turbid, Gk *tyrbē* confusion, tumult, ON *thorp* crowd, *thyrpask* to crowd, OHG *dweran* to stir, Skt *tvarati* he hurries] **1 a :** having the lees or sediment disturbed **:** thick or opaque with matter in suspension **:** cloudy or muddy in physical appearance ⟨near the banks the waters become ~ —Mark Van Doren⟩ ⟨grossly ~ urine need not necessarily mean pyuria —*Jour. Amer. Med. Assoc.*⟩ ⟨many of the feldspars . . . are ~ owing either to minute inclusions or to partial kaolinization —*Jour. of Geol.*⟩ **b :** heavy with smoke or mist **:** DARK, DENSE, THICK ⟨the air without had the ~ yellow light of sandstorms —Willa Cather⟩ **2 a :** having an appearance held to resemble physical turbidity **:** characterized by being cloudy, muddy, dull, impure, or polluted **:** lacking in clarity or translucence ⟨whirled onward . . . in that ~ stream of wrong-belief and lust —L.P.Smith⟩ ⟨~ depths of degradation and misery —C.I.Glicksberg⟩ **b :** confused in thought or feeling **:** characterized by or producing obscurity (as of thought or feeling) **:** mentally confused, muddled, perplexed, disturbed, or troubled **:** lacking in lucidity ⟨making the imagination ~ with monstrous fancies and misshapen dreams —Oscar Wilde⟩ ⟨~ longings and passionate regrets —Curtis Dahl⟩
syn MUDDY, ROILY: TURBID modifies whatever is literally or figuratively stirred up and disturbed by or as if by sediment so that it is made opaque, obscured, or confused ⟨similar treatments, generally applied to *turbid* water and frequently to clear water suspected of pollution —A.C.Morrison⟩ ⟨*turbid* feelings, arising from ideas not fully mastered, had to clarify and adjust themselves —H.O.Taylor⟩ ⟨the *turbid* ebb and flow of human misery —Matthew Arnold⟩ MUDDY suggests turbidness resulting from mixture with or suspension of mud, dross, or impurity that muddles and makes unclear or impure ⟨the pond was *muddy* after the storm⟩ ⟨the *muddy* and slow-moving plot has something to do with spying and counterspying —Anthony Boucher⟩ ROILY describes what is turbid and agitated and swirling ⟨where the *roily* Monongahela meets the clear Allegheny —J.M.Weed⟩
tur·bi·dim·e·ter \,tərbəˈdimədˑər\ *n* [ISV *turbidity* + *-meter*] **1 :** an instrument for measuring and comparing the turbidity of liquids by viewing light through them and determining how much light is cut off by them **2 :** NEPHELOMETER
tur·bi·di·met·ric \¦tərbədə¦me·trik\ *adj* [*turbidimetry* + *-ic*] **:** of, relating to, or using turbidimetry or a turbidimeter ⟨~ methods⟩ ⟨~ control tests⟩
tur·bi·di·met·ri·cal·ly \-rək(ə)lē\ *adv* [*turbidimetric* + *-ally*] **:** by the use of turbidimetry or a turbidimeter ⟨the rate of coagulation is followed ~ —*Eastman Kodak Monthly Abstract Bull.*⟩
tur·bi·dim·e·try \,tərbəˈdimə·trē\ *n* -ES [ISV *turbidity* + *-metry*] **:** the determination and measurement of the concentration of suspended matter in a liquid by use of a turbidimeter
tur·bid·i·ty \,tərˈbidəd·ē\ *n* -ES [ML *turbiditat-, turbiditas,* fr. L *turbidus* turbid + *-itat-, -itas* -ity] **:** the quality or state of being turbid **:** CONFUSION, MUDDINESS, OBSCURITY
tur·bid·ly *adv* **:** in a turbid manner **:** with muddiness, confusion, or obscurity
tur·bid·ness *n* -ES [*turbid* + *-ness*] **:** TURBIDITY ⟨lime water produces a ~ when added to the fresh water —William Saunders⟩
tur·bi·na·do \¦tərbə¦nä(,)dō\ *also* **turbinado sugar** *n* -s [AmerSp, prob. fr. Sp *turbina* turbine (fr. F *turbine*) + *-ado* -ate; fr. its being sprayed with water while spinning in a centrifuge — more at TURBINE] **:** partially refined cane sugar that has been washed and dried, is off-white, yellowish, or grayish in color, and is used in industry and food processing
¹**tur·bi·nal** \ˈtərbənᵊl, ˈtə̄b-, ˈtəib-\ *adj* [L *turbin-, turbo* top, whirlwind, whirl + E *-al* — more at TURBINE] **1 :** TURBINATE 1, 2 **2 :** of, relating to, or being one of the usu. several thin plicated bony or cartilaginous plates covered with olfactory and mucous membrane and borne on the walls of the nasal chambers
²**turbinal** \ˈ"\ *n* -s **:** a turbinal bone or cartilage
¹**tur·bi·nate** \-bənət, bə,nāt, *usu* -d·+V\ *adj* [L *turbinatus* shaped like a top, fr. *turbin-, turbo* top, whirlwind, whirl + *-atus* -ate — more at TURBINE] **1 :** spiral with whorls decreasing rapidly from base to apex — used of a gastropod shell **2 :** shaped like a top or an inverted cone **:** narrow at the base and broad at or near the apex ⟨a ~ seed capsule⟩ **3 :** TURBINAL
²**turbinate** \ˈ"\ *n* -s **1 :** a turbinate shell **2 :** TURBINATE BONE
turbinate bone *n* **:** a turbinal bone or process; *esp* **:** one of three such bones or processes which in man are borne on the lateral wall of the nasal fossa on each side and of which the middle and superior are processes of the ethmoid and the inferior and largest is a separate curved bony plate horizontally placed and separating the inferior and middle meatuses in the nose — called also *nasal concha*
tur·bi·nat·ed \-bə,nād·əd\ *adj* [L *turbinatus* turbinate + E *-ed*] **:** TURBINATE
turbinato- *comb form* [L *turbinatus* turbinate] **:** conically ⟨*turbinato*concave⟩ ⟨*turbinato*cylindrical⟩ ⟨*turbinato*globose⟩
tur·bine \ˈtər|bən, ˈtə̄|, ˈtəi|, |,bīn\ *n* -s *often attrib* [F, fr. L *turbin-, turbo* spinning object, whirlwind, top, whirl; akin to L *turbare* to throw into disorder, disturb, make turbid — more at TURBID] **:** a rotary engine actuated by the reaction or impulse or both of a current of fluid (as water, steam, gas, or mercury vapor) subject to pressure and usu. made with a series of curved vanes on a central spindle arranged to rotate with the whole being enclosed by a casing provided with redirecting vanes and passageways which permit the inlet and outlet of the fluid in a desired manner — compare AXIAL-FLOW, RADIAL-FLOW
tur·bi·nec·to·my \,tərbəˈnektəmē\ *n* -ES [ISV *turbinal* + *-ectomy*] **:** surgical removal of one or more turbinate bones
turbine–electric locomotive *n* **:** an electric locomotive having generators powered by turbine engines for the production of its own electric power
turbine generator *n* **:** an electric generator driven by a steam, gas, or hydraulic turbine
tur·bi·nel·la \¦tərbə¦nelə\ [NL, fr. L *turbin-, turbo-* top, whirl + *-ella* — more at TURBINE] *syn of* XANCUS
turbinella oak *n* [NL *turbinella* (specific epithet of *Quercus dumosa turbinella*), fr. L *turbin-, turbo* + *-ella*] **:** a scrub oak (*Quercus dumosa turbinella*) of No. America having acorn cups shaped like tops
turbine locomotive *n* **:** a locomotive powered by a steam or gas turbine engine that transmits motion directly to the driving wheels through gearing or that drives generators for producing electricity for the electric motors that move the driving wheels
turbine–propeller engine *n* **:** an airplane propulsion system in which a turbine drives a compressor and a propeller with thrust being derived from the propeller and also from the exhaust jet of the turbine
tur·bin·er \ˈtərbənər, -r,bīn-\ *n* -s [*turbine* + *-er*] **:** a turbine-propelled ship
tur·bin·i·dae \,tərˈbinə,dē\ *n pl, cap* [NL, fr. *Turbin-, Turbo,* type genus + *-idae*] **:** a family of gastropod mollusks (suborder Rhipidoglossa) of which *Turbo* is the type genus
tur·bit \ˈtərbət\ *n* [origin unknown] **1** *usu cap* **:** a breed of fancy pigeons having a short head and beak, a frilled breast, a peak or a shell crest, variously colored wings except the quills, and a white body **2** -s *often cap* **:** a bird of the Turbit breed
¹**tur·bo** \ˈtər(,)bō\ *n* [NL *Turbin-, Turbo,* fr. L, top, whirl — more at TURBINE] **1** *cap* **:** a genus (the type of the family Turbinidae) of marine snails that usu. have a heavy turbinate shell with a pearly lining, a rounded aperture, and a calcareous operculum **2** *pl* **tur·bi·nes** \-rbə,nēz\ *or* **turbos :** TURBAN SHELL
²**turbo** \ˈ"\ *n* -s [*turbo-*] **1 :** TURBINE **2** [by shortening] **:** TURBOSUPERCHARGER
turbo- *comb form* [*turbine*] **1 :** coupled directly to a driving turbine ⟨*turbo*alternator⟩ ⟨*turbo*blower⟩ ⟨*turbo*compressor⟩ ⟨*turbo*dynamo⟩ ⟨*turbo*exciter⟩ ⟨*turbo*fan⟩ ⟨*turbo*generator⟩ ⟨*turbo*pump⟩ **2 :** consisting of or incorporating a turbine ⟨*turbo*machine⟩ ⟨*turbo*motor⟩ ⟨*turbo*ventilator⟩
tur·bo·car \ˈtərbō+,-\ *n* [*turbo-* + *car*] **:** an automotive vehicle propelled by a gas turbine
tur·bo·charge \ˈ"+,-\ *vt* [*turbo-* + *charge*] **:** to supercharge (an engine) by means of a turbine-driven compressor
tur·bo·charger \ˈ"+,-\ *n* [*turbo-* + *charger*] **:** a centrifugal blower driven by exhaust gas turbines and used to supercharge an engine
tur·bo·compound engine \ˈ"+. . .-\ *n* [*turbo-* + *compound*] **:** an engine compounded by using the exhaust jet of the principal component to drive smaller auxiliary turbines
tur·bo·jet \ˈtərbō,jet, ˈtə̄b-, ˈtəib-, *usu* -ed·+V\ *n* [*turbojet engine*] **1 :** TURBOJET ENGINE **2 :** an airplane powered by turbojet engines
turbojet engine *n* [*turbo-* + *jet* + *engine*] **:** an airplane propulsion system in which the power developed by a turbine is used to drive a compressor that supplies air to a burner and hot gases from the burner pass through the turbine and thence to a rearward-directed thrust-producing exhaust nozzle
tur·bo·prop \-,präp\ *n* [by shortening] **1 :** TURBO-PROPELLER ENGINE **2 :** an airplane powered by turbo-propeller engines
tur·bo–propeller engine \¦tər(,)bō+. . .-\ *n* [*turbo-* + *propeller* + *engine*] **:** a jet engine having a turbine-driven propeller and designed to produce thrust principally by means of a propeller although additional thrust is usu. obtained from the hot exhaust gases which issue in a jet
turboprop engine *n* [*turbo-propeller engine*] **:** TURBO-PROPELLER ENGINE
turboprop–jet engine *n* [*turbo-propeller (engine)* + *jet engine*] **:** TURBO-PROPELLER ENGINE
tur·bo·ram·jet engine \ˈtərbōˈram,jet-\ *n* [*turbo-* + *ramjet engine*] **:** a jet engine consisting essentially of a turbojet engine with provisions for burning additional fuel in the tail pipe or the portion of the engine to the rear of the turbine and thus making it possible to obtain higher gas temperatures in the exhaust jet than can be tolerated by the turbine blades
tur·bo·supercharged \¦tər(,)bō+\ *adj* [*turbosupercharger* + *-ed*] **:** equipped with a turbosupercharger
tur·bo·supercharger \ˈ"+\ *n* [*turbo-* + *supercharger*] **:** a turbine compressor driven by hot exhaust gases of an airplane engine for feeding rarefied air at high altitudes into the carburetor of the engine at sea-level pressure so as to increase engine efficiency and the plane's rate of climb
tur·bot \ˈtərbət\ *n, pl* **turbot** *also* **turbots** [ME, fr. OF *turbut, tourbot*] **1 a :** a large European flatfish (*Psetta maxima*) that is highly esteemed as a food fish, may reach a weight of 30 to 40 pounds, and has a brownish upper surface marked with scattered tubercles and a white undersurface **b :** any of various other flatfishes (as of the families Pleuronectidae and Bothidae) that are felt to resemble the European turbot: as (1) **:** HALIBUT (2) **:** DIAMOND FLOUNDER (3) **:** a New Zealand flatfish (*Ammotretis guntheri*) **2 :** any of several triggerfishes or filefishes esp. of the Caribbean area
turbt *abbr* turbulent
tur·bu·la·tion \,tərbyəˈlāshən\ *n* -s [*turbulent* + *-ation*] **:** the enforced movement of photographic bath to overcome stagnation at the surface of film or paper during processing
tur·bu·la·tor \ˈ≈≈,lād·ə(r)\ *n* -s [*turbulent* + *-ator*] **:** a device to cause turbulence of fluids (as for mixing or scrubbing)
tur·bu·lence \ˈtərbyələn(t)s, ˈtə̄b-, ˈtəib-, ÷ -bəl-\ *n* -s [LL *turbulentia,* fr. L *turbulentus* turbulent + *-ia* -y] **1 :** the quality or state of being turbulent: as **a :** wild unruly disorderly commotion **:** disposition to stormy unruliness **:** violent agitation or disturbance **:** great perturbation **:** disorderly or tumultuous conduct ⟨the landmark of order in the midst of ~ and crime —S.H.Holbrook⟩ ⟨the ~ of the Scottish border in the early seventeenth century —Henry Cavendish⟩ ⟨the political changes accomplished this day do not imply ~, upheaval, or disorder —D.D.Eisenhower⟩ **b :** highly irregular atmospheric motion characterized by rapid changes in wind speed and direction and the presence of up and down currents **c :** departure in a fluid from a smooth or streamline flow with accompanying sinuosity and eddies due to an obstruction or to exceeding a critical speed **2 :** an instance or case of turbulence ⟨gigantic ~s set up in this vast poisonous atmosphere by the planet's . . . rapid rotation —*Springfield (Mass.) Daily News*⟩
syn see COMMOTION
tur·bu·len·cy \-nsē\ *n* -ES [LL *turbulentia*] *archaic* **:** TURBULENCE ⟨what a tale of terror . . . its ~ tells —E.A.Poe⟩ ⟨like *turbulencies* in the affairs of men —John Milton⟩
tur·bu·lent \-nt\ *adj* [L *turbulentus* tumultuous, stormy, turbulent, fr. *turba* confusion, tumult, crowd + *-ulentus* -ulent] **1 :** disposed or given to insubordination and disorder **:** causing great unrest **:** inciting violence or disturbance ⟨their physical courage and prowess . . . were the talk of the less ~ settlers —*Amer. Guide Series: Minn.*⟩ ⟨the hot and ~ feelings which boiled and surged in her —Virginia Woolf⟩ **2 :** being in a state of violent commotion **:** characterized by great agitation or tumult **:** violently disturbed or agitated **:** STORMY, TEMPESTUOUS ⟨a ~ childhood filled with frustration and fears —*Diseases of the Nervous System*⟩ ⟨the ~ waters of party politics —Victor Lewis⟩ ⟨the ~ years of the revolutionary period⟩ **3** *obs* **:** causing or tending to cause turbulence **:** having a disturbing or exciting effect ⟨whose heads that ~ liquor fills with fumes —John Milton⟩ **4 :** characterized by random fluctuations of velocity — see TURBULENT FLOW; compare CRITICAL VELOCITY
turbulent flow *n* **:** a fluid flow in which the velocity at a given point varies erratically in magnitude and direction with time and is thus essentially variable in pattern — contrasted with LAMINAR FLOW; compare STREAMLINE FLOW
tur·bu·lent·ly *adv* **:** in a turbulent manner ⟨the river rolls ~ boiling —W.C.Baldwin⟩
turcism *n* -s *usu cap* [ML *turcus* Turk + E *-ism*] *obs* **:** TURKISM
türck's column \ˈtürks-\ *n, usu cap T* [after Ludwig *Türck* †1868 Austrian neurologist] **:** DIRECT PYRAMIDAL TRACT
tur·co \ˈtür(,)kō\ *n* -s [AmerSp, fr. Araucanian *thurcu*] **:** a tapacolo (*Pteroptochos megapodius*) of Chile
turco- *or* **turko-** *comb form, usu cap* [*turco-* fr. ML *Turcus* Turk; *turko-* fr. ¹*turk*] **1 :** Turkic ⟨*Turko*-Tatar⟩ **2 :** Turkish ⟨*Turko*man⟩ **3 :** Turkish and ⟨*Turco*-Greek⟩
tur·col·o·gist \,tərˈkäləjəst\ *n, usu cap* [*turco-* + *-logist* (as in *geologist*)] **:** a specialist in Turkic languages and literature
turcoman *usu cap, var of* TURKOMAN
tur·co·phil \ˈtərkə,fil\ *n* -s *usu cap* [*turco-* + *-phil*] **:** one who admires or is partial to Turkey or Turkish ways
tur·co·pole \ˈtərkə,pōl\ *n* -s [ML *turcopulus, turcopolus,* fr. MGk *tourkopoulos,* lit., son of a Turk, fr. LGk *Tourkoi* (pl.) Turks (fr. Turk *Türk* Turk) + MGk *-poulos* child of, alter.

(prob. influenced by L *pullus* young of an animal) of Gk *pōlos* young animal, young man or woman — more at FOAL] **:** a light-armed soldier of the Order of St. John of Jerusalem

tur·co·po·lier \ˈ==pō,li(ə)r\ *n* -s [alter. (influenced by F *turcopolier*, fr. ML *turcopolarius*) of ME *turkepler*, fr. ML *turcopolarius*, fr. *turcopolus* turcopole + L *-arius* -ary] **:** a high official of the Order of St. John of Jerusalem who is ex officio the commander of the turcopoles

turd \ˈtərd\ *n* -s [ME *tord, turd*, fr. OE *tord;* akin to MD *tort* dung, ON *tordyfill* dung beetle, OE *teran* to tear — more at TEAR (divide)] **1 a :** a piece of dung — sometimes considered vulgar **b** *archaic* **:** EXCREMENT, FILTH **2 :** one that is esp. vile and contemptible — usu. considered vulgar

tur·di·dae \ˈtərdə,dē\ *n pl, cap* [NL, fr. *Turdus* + *-idae*] **:** a widely distributed family of singing birds (suborder Passeres) containing the true thrushes and a greater or lesser number of related birds (as often the bluebirds, wheatears, stonechats, Old World warblers, Old World redstarts, solitaires, and water ouzels, and the mockingbirds and thrashers)

tur·di·form \-,fȯrm\ *adj* [L *turdus* thrush + E *-iform*] **:** having the form or structure of a thrush

tur·doid \ˈtər,dȯid\ *adj* [L *turdus* + E *-oid*] **:** THRUSHLIKE

tur·dus \ˈtərdəs\ *n, cap* [NL, fr. L, thrush — more at THRUSH] **:** a genus of thrushes that is the type of the family Turdidae and includes the European blackbird, the mistle thrush, fieldfare, ring ouzel, and the American robin

tu·reen \t(y)əˈrēn, t(y)ùˈ-, t(y)ü'-\ *n* -s [alter. of earlier *terrene, terene*, fr. F *terrine*, fr. MF, fr. fem. of *terrin* of earth, fr. (assumed) VL *terrinus*, fr. L *terra* earth + *-inus* -ine — more at TERRACE] **1 :** a deep footed vessel with a cover from which cooked foods (as soup, sauce, or eggs) are served at table **2 :** CASSEROLE 2

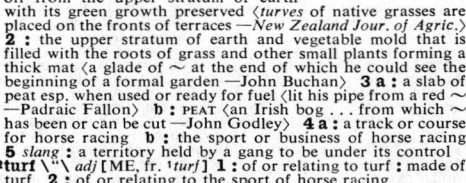

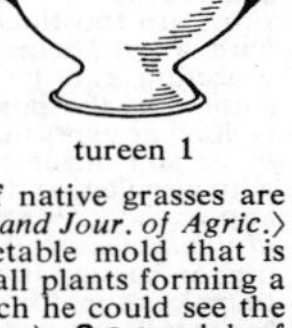
tureen 1

¹turf \ˈtər\|f, ˈtə̄\|, ˈtəi\|\ *n, pl* **turfs** \|fs\ *or* **turves** \|vz\ [ME, fr. OE; akin to OHG *zurba* turf, ON *torf*, Skt *darbha* tuft of grass] **1 :** a piece cut or pared off from the upper stratum of earth with its green growth preserved ⟨*turves* of native grasses are placed on the fronts of terraces —*New Zealand Jour. of Agric.*⟩ **2 :** the upper stratum of earth and vegetable mold that is filled with the roots of grass and other small plants forming a thick mat ⟨a glade of ~ at the end of which he could see the beginning of a formal garden —John Buchan⟩ **3 a :** a slab of peat esp. when used or ready for fuel ⟨lit his pipe from a red ~ —Padraic Fallon⟩ **b :** PEAT ⟨an Irish bog . . . from which ~ has been or can be cut —John Godley⟩ **4 a :** a track or course for horse racing **b :** the sport or business of horse racing **5** *slang* **:** a territory held by a gang to be under its control

²turf \"\ *adj* [ME, fr. ¹*turf*] **1 :** of or relating to turf **:** made of turf **2 :** of or relating to the sport of horse racing

³turf \"\ *vb* -ED/-ING/-S [ME *turven*, fr. ¹*turf*] *vt* **1 a :** to cover with turf **b :** to lay under the turf **:** BURY **2 :** to dig for turf **3 :** take turf from **3** *chiefly Brit* **:** to eject forcefully **:** KICK, THROW — usu. used with *out* ⟨going to ~ out those corny souvenirs of yours —Earle Birney⟩ ⟨his body must be ~*ed* out of the chair —Joanna Cannan⟩ ~ *vi* **:** to gather turfs

turf accountant *n, Brit* **:** BOOKMAKER 2

turf ant *n* **:** PAVEMENT ANT

turf·dom \|fdəm\ *n* -s [¹*turf* + *-dom*] **:** the horse-racing world

turf·en \|fən\ *adj* [¹*turf* + *-en*] **:** made of turf **:** covered with turf

turfing daisy *n* [fr. gerund of ³*turf*] **:** a low densely tufted perennial herb (*Matricaria tchihatchewii*) of Asia Minor that has small white flower heads and is used as a ground cover in dry places

turf·ite \|,fīt\ *n* -s [¹*turf* + *-ite*] **:** TURFMAN

turf·man \|fmən\ *n, pl* **turfmen** [²*turf* + *man*] **1 :** a devotee of horse racing **:** one who owns and races horses **2 :** one who specializes in the study of fine grasses, their care, and uses

turf tan *n* **:** a light brown that is yellower and deeper than blush and redder and deeper than cork

turf webworm *n* **:** GRASS WEBWORM

turfy \|fē, |fi\ *adj, sometimes* -ER/-EST [¹*turf* + *-y*] **1 :** abounding with turf **:** made of or covered with turf ⟨green ~ knolls —William Bartram⟩ **2 :** having the nature or appearance of peat **3 :** of, relating to, or smacking of horse racing

tur·gen·cy \ˈtərjənsē, ˈtə̄j-, ˈtəij-, -si\ *n* -ES [*turgent* + *-cy*] *archaic* **:** the quality or state of being swollen

tur·gent \-nt\ *adj* [ME, fr. L *turgent-, turgens*, pres. part. of *turgēre* to be swollen — more at TURGID] *obs* **:** noticeably swelling **:** SWOLLEN

tur·ges·cence \,tərˈjesᵊn(t)s, ,tə̄ˈ-, ,təiˈ-\ *n* -s [L *turgescere* to swell, begin to swell (inchoative of *turgēre* to be swollen) + E *-ence* — more at TURGID] **1 :** the act of swelling **:** the quality or state of being turgescent **2 :** the quality or state of being pompous **:** BOMBAST ⟨something out of the . . . romantic mode to give this book a ~ it does not need —N.L.Rothman⟩ **3 :** a tumid or turgid state **:** TURGOR

tur·ges·cen·cy \-nsē, -si\ *n* -ES [L *turgescere* + E *-ency*] *archaic* **:** TURGESCENCE

tur·ges·cent \-nt\ *adj* [L *turgescent-, turgescens*, pres. part. of *turgescere* to swell, become swollen] **:** becoming turgid, distended, or inflated **:** SWELLING

tur·gid \ˈtərjəd, ˈtə̄j-, ˈtəij-\ *adj* [L *turgidus*, fr. *turgēre* to be swollen; perh. akin to L *tumēre* to swell, be swollen — more at THUMB] **1 :** distended by or as if by some internal agent or expansive force **:** being in a normal or abnormal state of distention **:** SWOLLEN, TUMID ⟨~ limbs⟩ ⟨healthy living cells are ~⟩ **2 :** excessively embellished esp. in style or language **:** vainly ostentatious **:** BOMBASTIC, POMPOUS ⟨an effete classical tradition long ago . . . given over to ~ rhetorical display —Roger Fry⟩ **syn** see INFLATED

tur·gid·i·ty \,tərˈjid·əd·ē, ,tə̄ˈ-, ,təiˈ-, -ətē, -i\ *n* -ES [L *turgidus* + E *-ity*] **:** the quality or state of being turgid **:** condition of being swollen ⟨plants . . . placed in a moist chamber to determine if they would regain ~ —*Jour. of Forestry*⟩ ⟨an unrelieved ~ settles over the movie —Hollis Alpert⟩

tur·gid·ly *adv* **:** in a turgid manner ⟨incidents, unpleasant fragments of . . . life churned ~ in his brain —Norman Mailer⟩

tur·gid·ness *n* -ES [*turgid* + *-ness*] **:** TURGIDITY

tur·gor \ˈtərgər; ˈtə̄gə(r, ˈtəig-\ *n* -s [LL, turgidity, swelling, fr. L *turgēre* to be swollen] **:** the normal state of turgidity and tension in living cells; *esp* **:** the distention of the protoplasmic layer and wall of a plant cell by the fluid contents that is an essential feature of growth and movements in many parts of plants — compare TURGOR PRESSURE, WILT

turgor deficit *n* **:** DIFFUSION PRESSURE DEFICIT

turgor movement *n* **:** a reversible change in position of a plant part due to a change in turgor pressure of various cells (as in sleep movements) — compare NYCTITROPISM

turgor pressure *n* **:** the actual pressure developed by the fluid in a turgid plant cell as a result of endosmosis as contrasted with the potential maximum pressure that fluid of the same concentration could theoretically develop

tu·ri \ˈtürē\ *n, pl* **turi** *or* **turis** *usu cap* **1 :** a Pathan people inhabiting northern West Pakistan **2 :** a member of the Turi

tu·ri·ca·ta \,türəˈkäd·ə\ *n* -s [MexSp] **:** an argasid tick (*Ornithodoros turicata*) of Mexico and the southwestern U. S. that is a pest on hogs and cattle and sometimes transmits relapsing fever to man

tu·rin \ˈt(y)ürən, t(y)ùˈrin\ *adj, usu cap* [fr. *Turin*, commercial & manufacturing commune of northwest Italy] **:** of or from the city of Turin, Italy **:** of the kind or style prevalent in Turin

tu·ri·on \ˈt(y)ürē,än\ *n* -s [NL *turion-, turio*, fr. L, sprout, tendril, young branch; prob. akin to L *tumēre* to swell, be swollen — more at THUMB] **:** a scaly shoot (as of asparagus and some duckweeds) developed from a bud on a subterranean or submerged rootstock — **tu·ri·on·if·er·ous** \,t(y)ürēə,ˈnif(ə)rəs\ *adj*

¹turk \ˈtərk, ˈtə̄k, ˈtəik\ *n* -s [ME, fr. MF or Turk; MF *Turc*, fr. ML or Turk; ML *Turcus* fr. Turk *Türk*] **1** *usu cap* **a :** a member of any of numerous Asiatic peoples speaking Turkic languages who live in the region ranging from the Adriatic to the Okhotsk and who are racially mixed but are held to have risen in the Altai mountains and western Siberia **b :** a member of the dominant race of the Ottoman Empire **2** *cap* **:** a native or inhabitant of Turkey **3** *usu cap, archaic* **:** one who is cruel, hardhearted, or tyrannical ⟨a terrible *Turk* at keeping his wife up to her social duties —W.W.Hunter⟩ **4** *usu cap* **:** MUSLIM; *specif* **:** a Muslim subject of the Turkish sultan **5** *usu cap* **:** a Turkish horse; *specif* **:** a Turkish strain of Arab and crossbred horses **6** *usu cap* **:** one of a group of people of mixed white, Indian, and Negro ancestry esp. in So. Carolina — often used disparagingly

²turk \"\ *n* -s [F *turc;* prob. fr. *Turc* Turk] **:** PLUM CURCULIO; *also* **:** the larva of various destructive beetles

tur·ka·na \tùrˈkänə\ *n, pl* **turkana** *or* **turkanas** *usu cap* **1 :** a people resembling the Masai and living between Lake Rudolf and the Nile in East Africa **2 :** a member of the Turkana people

türk cell \ˈtirk-\ *or* **türk's cell** *n, usu cap T* [after Wilhelm *Türk* †1916 Austrian physician] **:** a large cell resembling a lymphocyte, having densely basophilic cytoplasm and eccentric nucleus with peripheral chromatin and central clear area, and being rare in normal blood but commonly present in diseases of lymphoid tissues

turk·dom \ˈtərkdəm\ *n* -s *usu cap* [¹*turk* + *-dom*] **:** the realm controlled by the Turks

tur·ken \ˈtərkən\ *also* **turk·hen** \-k,hen\ *n* -s [*turken* blend of *turkey* and *chicken; turkhen* fr. *turkey* + *hen*] **:** a type of chicken sometimes held to constitute a separate breed and distinguished by a rough red unfeathered neck; *also* **:** one of these birds often erroneously reported to be a hybrid between turkey and chicken

¹turkey *n* -s *usu cap* [ME, fr. *Turkey*, country of southeast Europe and southwest Asia] *obs* **:** TURQUOISE 1

²tur·key \ˈtərkē, ˈtə̄k-, ˈtəik-, -ki\ *adj, usu cap* [fr. *Turkey*, country of southeast Europe and southwest Asia] **1 :** of or from Turkey **:** of the kind or style prevalent in Turkey **:** TURKISH **2 :** believed to be of Turkish origin

³turkey \"\ *n* -s *often attrib* [short for *turkey-cock*] **1 :** a bird of the family Meleagrididae: as **a** (1) **:** a large American bird (*Meleagris gallopavo*) orig. distributed from southern Mexico throughout much of the eastern and central U. S. and northward into Canada but extinct over much of the northern and western part of its range though reintroduced as a game bird in some regions and successfully reestablished as far north as Pennsylvania, occurring in several subspecies in various parts of its range, and having typically a bronzy lustrous plumage, a naked carunculate head, and a tail that in the male is spread fanlike in display (2) **:** any of various domesticated birds derived primarily from a Mexican variety of the wild turkey and raised chiefly for their flesh — see BELTSVILLE SMALL WHITE, BOURBON RED, BRONZE, NARRAGANSETT **b :** OCELLATED TURKEY **2** *Austral* **a :** a bustard (*Choriotis australis*) **b :** BRUSH TURKEY **3 :** a lumberman's kit or itinerant worker's pack ⟨carrying a long-handled double-bitted ax and a ~ of clothes across his shoulder —J.H.Stuart⟩ **4 a :** a theatrical production that is a failure **:** FLOP ⟨a ~ about a rich actor who financed a play to star himself —Stanley Frank⟩ **b :** something that has a conspicuous lack of success ⟨the idea was a complete ~ —Mac Davis⟩ **5 :** practical action without delay or evasion **:** straight facts leading to a realistic solution **:** BUSINESS — usu. used in the phrase *talk turkey* ⟨will be willing to talk ~ . . . and to end the war —*Kiplinger Washington Letter*⟩ **6 :** three successive strikes in bowling — called also *triple*

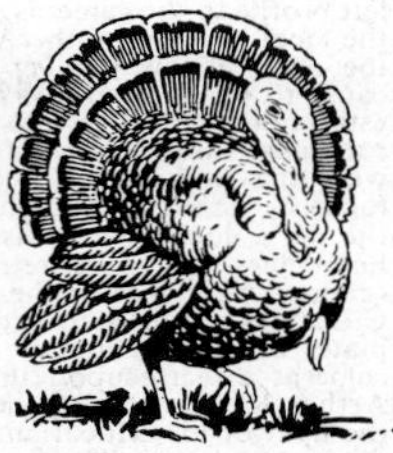
domestic turkey-cock

⁴turkey \"\ *n* -s *usu cap* **:** TURKEY LEATHER

turkeyback \ˈ==,=\ *n* [³*turkey*] *NewEng* **:** GREATER YELLOWLEGS; *esp* **:** one of large size

turkey beard *n* **:** an American plant of the genus *Xerophyllum* (esp. *X. asphodeloides*)

tur·key·berry \ˈ==- — *see* BERRY\ *n* **1 a :** either of two nightshades (*Solanum mammosum* and *S. torvum*) of the West Indies **b :** the fruit of either of these plants **2 a** *also* **turkeyberry tree :** a West Indian tree (*Cordia collococca*) **b :** the berry of the turkeyberry **3 :** CORALBERRY 1 **4 :** PARTRIDGEBERRY 1

turkey berry *n, usu cap T* [²*turkey*] **:** PERSIAN BERRY

turkey bird *n* [³*turkey*] *dial Eng* **:** WRYNECK

turkey blue *n, often cap T* [²*turkey*] **:** TURKISH BLUE

turkeybush \ˈ==,=\ *n* [³*turkey*] **:** a tropical African spiny shrub (*Caesalpinia oligophylla*) introduced into Australia where it forms dense weedy scrub

turkey buzzard *n* **1 :** an American vulture (*Cathartes aura*) that is common in So. and Central America and in the southern U. S. but rare north of Pennsylvania, that is blackish brown with the nearly naked wrinkled skin of the head and foreneck red, that is about five feet in spread of wings and very graceful in flight, and that feeds on carrion only — called also *turkey vulture* **2** *Africa* **:** BROMVOEL

turkey call *n* **1 :** the gobbling sound made by a turkey-cock **2 :** an instrument imitating a gobbling sound and used as a decoy by hunters of wild turkey

turkey carpet *n, usu cap T* [²*turkey*] **1 :** TURKISH CARPET **2 :** ORIENTAL RUG

turkey–cock \ˈ==,=\ *n* [²*turkey* + *cock;* fr. confusion with the guinea fowl, supposed to be imported from Turkish territory] **1 :** a male turkey **2 :** a strutting pompous person

turkey corn *n* [³*turkey*] **:** SQUIRREL CORN

turkey cup sponge *or* **turkey cup** *n, usu cap T* [²*turkey*] **:** a Turkey sponge (*Spongia officinalis mollissima*) with fine elastic durable fibers

turkey dance *n* [³*turkey*] **:** a mimetic social dance of American Indians with a jigging step, erratic course, and often realistic head jerking

turkey fig *n, usu cap T* [²*turkey*] **1 :** a common cultivated fig (*Ficus carica*) **2** *Austral* **:** INDIAN FIG 2a(2)

turkey fish *n* [³*turkey*] **:** LION-FISH 1

turkeyfoot \ˈ==,=\ *n, pl* **turkeyfoots** [³*turkey* + *foot;* fr. the shape of the spike] **:** any of several No. American grasses of the genus *Andropogon*

turkey gnat *n* **:** a small black fly (*Simulium meridionale*) that injures poultry esp. in the southern and western U. S. and has been reported as a vector of leucocytozoan diseases of turkeys; *broadly* **:** any of various simuliid flies

turkey–gobbler \ˈ==,==\ *n* **:** TURKEY-COCK 1

turkey grape *n* **:** POST-OAK GRAPE

turkey grass *n, dial Eng* **:** CLEAVERS

turkey gum *n, usu cap T* [²*turkey*] **:** GUM ARABIC

turkey leather *n, usu cap T, Brit* **:** an oil-tawed leather used esp. for bookbindings

turkey louse *n* [³*turkey*] **:** a biting louse (*Lipeurus gallipavonis*) that infests turkeys and eats their feathers

turkey morocco *n, usu cap T* [²*turkey*] **:** morocco made in Turkey or as if in Turkey

turkey mullein *n* [³*turkey*] **:** a prostrate soft-leaved annual weed (*Eremocarpus setigerus*) of the family Euphorbiaceae of the Pacific coast of the U. S. whose small black seeds are said to be eaten by turkeys and whose herbage is used by Indians to stupefy fish — called also *doveweed*

¹turkey oak *n, usu cap T* [²*turkey*] **:** a brittle-branched oak (*Quercus cerris*) that is a native of the Balkans but widely planted — called also *Adriatic oak, cerris*

²turkey oak *n* [³*turkey*] **:** any of several oaks of the southern U. S.: as **a :** RED OAK 1b **b :** an oak (*Quercus laevis*) of dry sandy barrens having shining leaves with bristle-tipped lobes suggesting a turkey's toes **c :** an oak (*Quercus incana*) of the southeastern U. S. with heavily tomentose young branchlets

turkey pea *n* [³*turkey*] **1 a :** SQUIRREL CORN **b :** HOARY PEA **c :** HARBINGER-OF-SPRING **2 :** DEVIL'S SHOESTRINGS

turkey pod *n* **:** MOUSE-EAR CRESS

turkey red *n* [²*turkey*] **1** *usu cap T* **a :** a brilliant durable red produced upon cotton by means of alizarin or formerly madder in connection with an aluminum mordant and oil or other fatty matter — called also *alizarine red* **b :** cotton cloth dyed with this red **2** *often cap T* **:** a moderate red that is yellower and very slightly darker than cerise, yellower and darker than claret (sense 3a), yellower and very slightly lighter than Harvard crimson (sense 1), and yellower, slightly darker, and very slightly less strong than average strawberry (sense 2a) — called also *Adrianople red, Levant red, Turkish red* **3** *usu cap T* **:** an iron oxide pigment similar to Indian red

turkey–red oil *n* **1 :** an inferior grade of olive oil used in producing Turkey red **2 :** a sulfonated oil used in dyeing (as with alizarin dyes) and as a wetting and emulsifying agent; *esp* **:** sulfated castor oil or its sodium salt

turkey rhubarb *n, usu cap T* **:** Chinese rhubarb formerly imported through Turkey

turkeys *pl of* TURKEY

turkey shoot *n* [³*turkey*] **1 a :** a contest of marksmanship with a gun using live turkeys as targets **b :** a similar contest for prizes usu. using moving targets **2 :** something resembling a turkey shoot

turkey sponge *n, usu cap T* [²*turkey*] **:** any of various superior commercial sponges of the Adriatic and Mediterranean seas

turkey stone *also* **turkey slate** *n, usu cap T* [²*turkey*] **1 :** TURQUOISE **2** *or* **turkey oilstone a :** a whetstone or oilstone from Turkey **b :** NOVACULITE

turkey toilet sponge *also* **turkey toilet** *n, usu cap 1st T* **:** a Turkey sponge (*Spongia officinalis adriatica*) of fine quality but less valuable than the Turkey cup sponge

turkey trot *n* [³*turkey*] **:** a ragtime dance of the period of World War I danced with the feet well apart and with a characteristic rise on the ball of the foot followed by a drop upon the heel

turkey–trot \ˈ==,=\ *vi* [*turkey trot*] **:** to dance the turkey trot

turkey umber *n* [²*turkey*] **1** *usu cap T* **:** raw umber from the island of Cyprus **2** *often cap T* **:** RAW UMBER 2

turkey vulture *n* [³*turkey*] **:** TURKEY BUZZARD

turkey wheat *n, usu cap T* [²*turkey*] **1 :** INDIAN CORN **2 :** CRIMEAN WHEAT

turkey wing *n* [³*turkey*] **:** an ark shell (*Arca occidentalis*)

turkey work *n, often cap T* [²*turkey*] **:** needlework imitating the designs and texture of Oriental rugs made by knotting worsted yarn on canvas or coarse cloth and used formerly for upholstery and carpets

turkhen *var of* TURKEN

¹tur·ki \ˈtərkē, ˈtürkē, ˈtə̄k-, ˈtəik-, ˈtù(ə)k-, -ki\ *adj, usu cap* [Per *turkī*, fr. *Turk* Turk, fr. Turk *Türk*] **1 :** of or relating to the peoples of Turkic speech **2 :** of or relating to any central Asian Turkic language particularly of the eastern group

²turki \"\ *n* -s *usu cap* **1 :** one of the Turki peoples **2 :** any central Asian Turkic language particularly of the eastern group

¹turk·ic \ˈtərkik, ˈtə̄k-, ˈtəik-, -kēk\ *adj, usu cap* [¹*turk* + *-ic*] **1 a :** of or relating to a subfamily of Altaic languages **b :** of or relating to the peoples speaking these languages **2 :** TURKISH

²turkic \"\ *n* -s *usu cap* **:** a subfamily of Altaic languages including Azerbaijani, Kazak, Kirghiz, Turkish, Turkoman, Uighur, Uzbek, and Yakut

turk·i·cize \-kə,sīz\ *vt* -ED/-ING/-S *often cap* [¹*turkic* + *-ize*] **:** TURKIZE

¹tur·kis \ˈtərkəs\ *n pl but sometimes sing in constr* [ME *turkas*, fr. MF *turquoises, turquaises* (pl.), prob. fr. fem. pl. of *turquoys, turqueis* Turkish — more at TURQUOISE] *Scot* **:** a pair of pincers

²turkis \"\ *n* -ES [ME *turkeis* — more at TURQUOISE] **:** TURQUOISE ⟨that all the turf was rich in plots that looked each like a garnet or a ~ in it —Alfred Tennyson⟩

¹turk·ish \ˈtərkish, ˈtə̄k-, ˈtəik-, -kēsh\ *adj, usu cap* [¹*turk* + *-ish*] **1 a :** of, relating to, or characteristic of Turkey **b :** of, relating to, or characteristic of the Turkish people **2 :** of, relating to, or characteristic of the Turkic subfamily of Ural-Altaic languages; *specif* **:** of, relating to, or characteristic of the Turkish language

²turkish \"\ *n* -ES *usu cap* **1 :** the Turkic language of the Republic of Turkey **2 :** TURKIC

turkish bath *n, usu cap T* **:** a bath in which the bather passes through a succession of steam rooms of increasing temperature followed by a rubdown, massage, and cold shower

turkish bean *n, usu cap T* **:** SCARLET RUNNER

turkish blue *n, often cap T* **:** a grayish purplish blue that is redder than average delft and redder, lighter, and stronger than average navy blue — called also *Turkey blue*

turkish boxwood *n, usu cap T* **:** the wood of a box (*Buxus sempervirens*)

turkish carpet *n, usu cap T* **1 :** a handmade one-piece carpet made in Turkey having a deep generally woolen pile with a weft of different material **2 :** an English carpet woven in the Turkish manner

turkish checkers *n pl but usu sing in constr, usu cap T* **:** checkers in which each player has 16 men and all 64 squares of the checkerboard are used, single men move forward, sideward, or diagonally forward, and kings move any distance in any direction

turkish coffee *n, usu cap T* **:** a decoction of pulverized coffee in thin sugar syrup

turkish crescent *n, usu cap T* **:** PAVILLON CHINOIS

turkish–crescent red *n, often cap T* **:** CHRYSANTHEMUM 4

turkish delight *or* **turkish paste** *n, usu cap T* **:** a confection of jellylike or gummy consistency usu. cut in cubes and dusted with sugar

turkish geranium oil *n, usu cap T* **:** PALMAROSA OIL

turkish knot *n, usu cap T* **:** GHIORDES KNOT

turk·ish·ly *adv, usu cap* **:** in a characteristically Turkish manner ⟨his defense was *Turkishly* impregnable —T.E.Lawrence⟩

turkish music *n, usu cap T* **:** JANISSARY MUSIC 1b

turk·ish·ness *n* -ES *usu cap T* **:** the quality or state of being Turkish

turkish oak *n, usu cap T* **:** VALONIA OAK

turkish pepper *n, usu cap T* **:** PIMIENTO; *also* **:** a paprika made from it

turkish red *n, often cap T* **:** TURKEY RED

turkish saddle *n, usu cap T* [trans. of NL *sella turcica*] **:** SELLA TURCICA

turkish tobacco *n, usu cap 1st T* **:** a very aromatic tobacco of small leaf size grown chiefly in Turkey and Greece and adjoining territories and used esp. in blended cigarettes

turkish towel *n, usu cap 1st T* **:** a towel made of Turkish toweling

turkish toweling *n, usu cap 1st T* **:** a cotton terry cloth used esp. for towels

turkish walnut *n, usu cap T* **:** ENGLISH WALNUT

turk·ism \ˈtər,kizəm\ *n* -s *usu cap* [¹*turk* + *-ism*] **:** the customs, beliefs, institutions, and principles of the Turks

turk·ize \-,kīz\ *vt* -ED/-ING/-S *often cap* [¹*turk* + *-ize*] **:** to make Turkish

tur·kle \ˈtərkəl\ *n* -s [by alter.] *dial* **:** TURTLE

turk·man \ˈtərkmən, ˈtə̄k-, ˈtəik-\ *n, pl* **turkmen** *usu cap* [alter. (influenced by ¹*turk* & *man*) of *turkoman*] **:** TURKOMAN 1

¹turk·men \-kmən, -k,men\ *adj, usu cap* [Per *Turkmēn* Turkoman] **:** TURKMENIAN

²turkmen \"\ *n* -s *usu cap* **:** TURKOMAN 2

turk·me·ni·an \,tərkˈmēnēən\ *adj, usu cap* [Per *Turkmēn* Turkoman + E *-ian*] **:** of or relating to the Turkomans or the Republic of Turkmen, U. S. S. R.

turko- — see TURCO-

tur·ko·man *or* **tur·co·man** \ˈtərkəmən, ˈtə̄k-, ˈtəik-\ *n, pl* **turkomans** *or* **turcomans** *usu cap* [ML *Turcomannus*, fr. Per *Turkmān, Turkmēn*, fr. *turkmān, turkmēn* resembling a Turk, fr. *Turk* Turk — more at TURKI] **1 :** a member of a group of peoples of East Turkic stock living chiefly in the Turkmen, Uzbek, Kazak, and Karakalpak republics of the U. S. S. R. **2 :** the Turkic language of the Turkoman people

turkoman carpet *or* **turkoman rug** *n, usu cap T* **:** any of a number of oriental rugs made by various Turkoman peoples

tur·ko–tatar \ˌtər(,)kō+\ *n, cap both Ts* [*turco-* + *tatar*] **:** TURKIC

turks *pl of* TURK

turk's–cap lily \ˈ=,=-\ *also* **turk's cap** *n, usu cap T* **:** either of two lilies having nodding flowers with strongly revolute perianth segments: **a :** a widely cultivated lily (*Lilium martagon*) with rather small dull purple flowers **b :** an American native lily (*Lilium superbum*) with flowers resembling those of the tiger lily

turk's–cap moss *n, usu cap T* **:** an urn moss (*Physcomitrium turbinatum*)

türk's cell *usu cap T, var of* TÜRK CELL

turk's head *n, usu cap T* **1** *or* **turk's-head cactus** \'=,=-\ *or* **turk's cap** *or* **turk's-cap cactus** \'=,=-\ : a globular West Indian cactus (*Cactus intortus*) deeply furrowed and spiny with a cap of whitish hairs resembling a fez from which the red flowers and fruit arise **2 :** a knot that is ornamental as well as practical and is considered to resemble a small turban

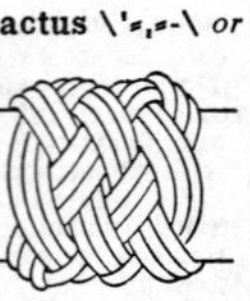
Turk's head 2

turk's-turban \'=¦==\ *n, pl* **turk's-turbans** *usu cap 1st T* : TUBEFLOWER

tur·ku \'tu̇r(,)kü\ *adj, usu cap* [fr. *Turku*, seaport city of southwest Finland] : of or from the city of Turku, Finland : of the kind or style prevalent in Turku

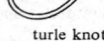

turle knot \'tərl-\ *n* [after Major W. G. *Turle*, 19th cent. Eng. fisherman] : a knot made with a variety of slip noose and used in angling to tie a gut or nylon leader to a hook or fly — called also *turtle knot*

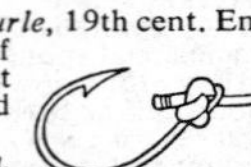
turle knot

tur·lough \'tər,läk\ *n* -s [IrGael *turloch*, fr. *tur* dry + *loch* lake, fr. OIr — more at LAKE] *Irish* : a winter lake that is dry or marshy in summer

turmaline *var of* TOURMALINE

[1]**tur·mer·ic** \'tərmərik, 'tə̄m-, 'təim-, -rēk\ *or* **tu·mer·ic** \'t(y)üm-\ *n* -s [modif. of MF *terre merite* saffron, fr. ML *terra merita*, lit., deserving or deserved earth] **1 a** (1) : an East Indian perennial herb (*Curcuma longa*) with a large aromatic deep yellow rhizome (2) : the cleaned, boiled, sun-dried, and usu. pulverized rhizome of the turmeric plant used as a coloring agent, a condiment (as in pickling and in curry powder), or a stimulant (3) : a yellow to reddish brown dyestuff obtained from turmeric **b :** any of several closely related plants yielding a similar product **2 :** any of several plants (as the bloodroot or goldenseal) yielding colored juices or otherwise felt to resemble the East Indian turmeric **3 :** MIMOSA 3

[2]**turmeric** \"\ *adj* : of, relating to, or obtained from turmeric

turmeric paper *n* : paper impregnated with an extract of turmeric and used as a test for alkaline substances which turn it from yellow to reddish brown and for boric acid which turns it red brown

turmeric root *n* **1 :** BLOODROOT **2 :** GOLDENSEAL 2

turmeric yellow *n* : CURCUMIN

tur·mit \'tərmət\ *or* **tur·mut** \-mət\ *dial Brit var of* TURNIP

[1]**tur·moil** \'tər,mȯil, 'tə̄,-, 'təi,-\ *n* -s [origin unknown] : an utterly confused, extremely agitated, or tumultuous state or condition: as **a :** the inner confusion of a disturbed or distressed mind or spirit ⟨the child's inner life is often a ~ of terrors and anxieties —W.R.Inge⟩ ⟨an odd ~ of shame and triumph in her heart —Louis Bromfield⟩ **b :** disruptive commotion : disordered activity ⟨the mad ~ of governmental investigation —W.S.Lynch⟩ ⟨keep executives in a constant ~ making decisions —R.E.Cross⟩ **c :** active strife ⟨rose to his greatest heights in the excitement and ~ of battle —Robert Bruce⟩ **syn** see COMMOTION

[2]**turmoil** \"\ *vb* -ED/-ING/-S *vt* **1 :** to produce a state of harassment in : DISQUIET, WORRY **2 :** TOSS, UPSET ~ *vi* : LABOR, TOIL

tur·moil·er \-lə(r)\ *n* -s [[2]*turmoil* + *-er*] : one that makes or causes turmoil

[1]**turn** \'tərn, 'tə̄n, 'təin\ *vb* -ED/-ING/-S [ME *turnen;* partly fr. OE *tyrnan & turnian* to turn, fr. ML *tornare*, fr L, to turn on a lathe, round off, fr. *tornus* lathe, chisel, fr. Gk *tornos* dividers, lathe; partly fr. OF *torner, tourner*, fr. ML *tornare;* akin to L *terere* to rub — more at THROW] *vt* **1 a :** to cause to move in a curved esp. circular path around or as if around an axis or a center : make rotate or revolve ⟨~ a wheel⟩ ⟨~ a crank⟩ ⟨great wheel ~*s* its axle when it can —Theodore Roethke⟩ ⟨shaft . . . can be ~*ed* . . . at higher than 50,000 revolutions per minute —*Ford Times*⟩ ⟨how that little scrapper could hold and ~ a miner's drill —N.C.Wilson⟩ **b** (1) : to cause to move around in such a path far enough or enough times to effect a desired end (as of locking, opening, or shutting) ⟨~ a key in a lock⟩ ⟨~*ed* the knob till the door opened⟩ ⟨~ a screw tight⟩ ⟨shut the door and ~*ed* the bolt —Paul Horgan⟩ ⟨~ the cap to release it⟩ ⟨~*ed* the handle to the shut position⟩ (2) : to affect or alter the functioning of (as a mechanical device) by or as if by operation of a control moving in this way ⟨~*ed* the lamp as low as it would go⟩ ⟨~*ed* the heating pad too high⟩ ⟨~*ed* the steam iron to *rayon*⟩ **c :** to execute or perform by rotating or revolving like a rolling wheel ⟨~ a double somersault⟩ ⟨~ handsprings⟩ or like a spinning top ⟨~*s* a clumsy pirouette —G.C.Menotti⟩ **d :** to twist to one side or out of line or shape : WRENCH ⟨so easy . . . to plant a swift blow, to ~ a fragile wrist —H.A.Overstreet⟩ ⟨stumbled along, ~*ing* his ankle at frequent intervals —Peggy Bennett⟩ **2 a** (1) : to cause to change position, posture, or part exposed by moving through an arc of a circle ⟨nurse could easily ~ a patient twice her size⟩ ⟨leaned out, and ~*ed* his heavy shoulders . . . around to gaze up into the dark night —Glenway Wescott⟩ ⟨kept ~*ing* his hat in his hands⟩ ⟨~*ed* his chair to the fire⟩ (2) : to cause to move around a center so as to see or to show another side or angle ⟨~*ing* the pages of the book⟩; *specif* : to turn the leaves of (a book) : read or search through (3) : to cause (as the beam or platform of a scale) to move up or down : cause to register weight ⟨~*ed* the scale at 160 pounds⟩ (4) : to cause to move or stir in any way ⟨a fate she did not ~ a finger to escape —V.L.Parrington⟩ **b :** to revolve mentally : consider and reconsider in various aspects or from several points of view : think over : PONDER ⟨~*ed* the question every which way but could find no answer⟩ ⟨was still ~*ing* the idea about when he fell asleep⟩ — usu. used with *over* ⟨~*ing* the scenes and characters over in his mind —Ernest Newman⟩ ⟨appeared to be ~*ing* something over in his mind —Douglas Stewart⟩ ⟨disturbing thought . . . persisted. He ~*ed* it over continuously as he rode —T.B.Costain⟩ **3 a :** to reverse the position of (as by making the uppermost side or part the undermost, or the outermost side or part the innermost, or the front the back) : reverse the sides or surfaces of : INVERT ⟨~ an hourglass⟩ ⟨~ pancakes⟩ ⟨~ a phonograph record⟩ ⟨coat can be ~*ed* and worn either side out⟩ ⟨~ 4 thin veal fillets in 1 oz. seasoned flour —*Modern Woman*⟩ ⟨~*ed* the rug frequently to equalize wear⟩: (1) : to dig or plow so as to invert the turf or bring the lower soil to the surface ⟨soil should be ~*ed* after the harvest⟩ ⟨was eager to get home and begin ~*ing* his ground —G.S.Perry⟩ ⟨sod . . . almost had to be ~*ed* by main strength, piece by piece —O.E. Rölvaag⟩ (2) : to make (as a garment) over by unpicking the stitching, reversing the material, and resewing ⟨~ a dress⟩ ⟨~ a collar⟩ (3) : to invert feet up and face down (as a character, rule, or slug) in setting type (as in place of a letter or matter temporarily unavailable or to draw attention to a change to be made) **b :** to reverse or upset the order or disposition of : change drastically the arrangement of things in ⟨found everything ~*ed* topsy-turvy⟩ ⟨robbers had ~*ed* the room upside down⟩ ⟨in adapting the novel . . . have ~*ed* the story on its head —Arthur Knight⟩ **c** (1) : to disturb or upset the mental balance of : DERANGE, UNSETTLE ⟨thwarted affections had ~*ed* her brain —Kathleen Freeman⟩ ⟨a mind ~*ed* by grief⟩ (2) : to affect the power of judgment of (as by causing to become infatuated or to harbor extravagant notions of pride or conceit) — used chiefly in the phrase *turn one's head* ⟨success had not ~*ed* his head⟩ ⟨silly girl's head had been ~*ed* by a handful of compliments⟩ **d :** to cause (the stomach) to revolt (as at something swallowed) : UPSET ⟨very thought of food ~*ed* his stomach⟩ **e :** to set in another esp. contrary direction ⟨~*ed* his horse and rode away⟩ ⟨hard car to ~ in a narrow street⟩ **4 a :** to cause to have or take another path or direction : bend or change the course of ⟨~ the channel of a stream⟩ ⟨saddle stock spooked and I had to run them two miles to ~ them —Bruce Siberts & W.D.Wyman⟩ ⟨~ a car into a stream of traffic⟩: as (1) : to reverse the course or direction of : make go back ⟨captured cart was ~*ed* and rumbled past —F.V.W.Mason⟩ ⟨series of revolts which was definitely to ~ the tide against reaction —C.L.Jones⟩ (2) : to cause to retreat ⟨police used fire hoses and tear gas to ~ the mob⟩ (3) : to check the course of (as by interposing an obstacle) : make go back or go aside : keep out or off ⟨wires are close enough together . . . to ~ hogs and sheep —*Fence*⟩ ⟨struck like a club in the dark . . . not to be ~*ed* by any plea —R.O.Bowen⟩ (4) : to cause (a ball) to break — used of a cricket bowler ⟨flights the ball well, ~*s* it markedly any way —*Sunday Express (Johannesburg) So. Africa*⟩ **b** (1) : to alter the drift, tendency, or natural or expected result of (as a course of thought, action, or progress) ⟨alliance . . . led directly to war, and ~*ed* the course of history —L.L.Snyder⟩ ⟨is not facts . . . but what people think about the facts that ~*s* elections —*Times Lit. Supp.*⟩ ⟨~*ed* the talk to baseball⟩ (2) : to divert esp. from a course of action, an intention, an attitude ⟨would not be ~*ed* from his life of senseless pleasure⟩ ⟨a plea that would have ~*ed* a heart of stone⟩ **c** (1) : to change direction by bending a course around or about : take a usu. circular or elliptical path around : ROUND ⟨~*ed* the corner at full speed⟩ ⟨watched the leading boat ~ the first marker⟩ (2) : to get around in this way : get to the other side of ⟨ship had ~*ed* the cape and was now homeward bound⟩ ⟨a play designed to ~ the end of the defensive line⟩ ⟨was so intent on surprising the enemy . . . that his right flank was ~*ed*, and he suffered . . . a crushing defeat —R.L.Conolly⟩ **d :** to pass or go beyond (as an amount) ⟨was waiting for the clock to ~ ten⟩ ⟨~*ed* seventeen the day he graduated⟩ ⟨this robust man, just ~*ed* fifty, died of cerebral hemorrhage —Padraic Colum⟩ ⟨~*ed* of seventy years, he had withdrawn from active business —F.L. Paxson⟩ **5 a** (1) : to direct or point (as a glance) in a specified way ⟨had ~*ed* his face from the curious onlookers⟩ ⟨~*ed* a pair of stricken eyes on his mother —T.B.Costain⟩ ⟨~*ing* more and more hostile looks in her direction —Charles Lee⟩ ⟨will find anxious eyes all over the town ~*ed* toward the dropping mercury —Judson Philips⟩ (2) : to present by or as if by a change in direction or position ⟨~ the cheek even to the smiter's hand —P.B.Shelley⟩ ⟨apologized for ~*ing* his back to his guests⟩ ⟨face she ~*ed* to the world was always serene⟩ ⟨cattle had ~*ed* tail to the storm —F.B.Gipson⟩ ⟨the novel, a powerful modern agency for civilization . . . must ~ to the light many ugly realities —Carl Van Doren⟩ ⟨always ~*ed* his left profile to the cameras⟩ (3) : to change the direction of (as the face) : direct another way or various ways ⟨stood alone in the open doorway ~*ing* his eyes speculatively⟩; *often* : to cause to be directed away or aside ⟨~*ed* her face and wept⟩ ⟨staring match to see who would first ~ his eyes⟩ (4) *archaic* : to cause (as oneself) to face or go another way or a specified way **b :** to bring to bear by moving, aiming, pointing, or focusing esp. from a point of rest : TRAIN ⟨~*ed* his light into the dark doorway⟩ — usu. used with *on* or *upon* ⟨~*ed* the binoculars on those retreating backs —Maurice Duggan⟩ ⟨cannon were ~*ed* on the city and street fighting broke out —C.L.Jones⟩ ⟨had been vaguely ~*ing* his torch on the number plates of a short line of cars —Elizabeth Bowen⟩ ⟨~*ed* his cameras directly upon the violence and brutality of life —Arthur Knight⟩ ⟨bring them into his study and ~ upon them the light of his critical analysis —V.L.Parrington⟩ **c** (1) : to direct (as the mind) toward or away from something ⟨~ his thoughts to home⟩ ⟨recording companies must ~ their attention . . . to other kinds of music —P.H.Lang⟩ ⟨was free to ~ his whole mind and will to work —Carl Van Doren⟩ ⟨urging him to ~ his thoughts towards religion —R.A.Hall b. 1911⟩ ⟨sought to ~ man's curious mind from this world to the next —Marjory S. Douglas⟩ ⟨~ public attention to the fascinating underworld of the unconscious —C.I.Glicksberg⟩ ⟨cool evenings and heavy dews that ~ the mind toward sweaters —Virgil Thomson⟩ (2) *archaic* : to direct (oneself) toward or away from a concern with someone or something **d** (1) *obs* : to lead or bring (a person) to or into some state or situation by influencing or causing to become involved ⟨all the trouble thou hast ~*ed* me to —Shak.⟩ (2) : to induce or influence (a person) to change his way of life (as from ungodly to godly or from one religious faith to another) ⟨a popish place like that! They'll ~ her . . . sure as death and taxes —Angus Mowat⟩ (3) *archaic* : to direct the course of (as a series of events) ⟨Apollo ~ all to the best —Shak.⟩ **e** (1) : to direct the employment of (as to some use or purpose) : make use of : APPLY, DEVOTE — used with *to* ⟨~ anthropological knowledge to practical uses —Ralph Linton⟩ ⟨studying how they could best ~ to their own benefit the doctrines they found —F.L. Paxson⟩ ⟨~*ed* misfortune to good account —Sir Winston Churchill⟩ ⟨~*s* her compassion to finding ways in which she and her staff can help —*Lamp*⟩ ⟨sawmill and gristmill were erected . . . and a soda spring nearby ~*ed* to the use of the Saints —R.A.Billington⟩ (2) : to make use of (as a person) for or in the accomplishment of a purpose ⟨~*ed* every available workman on the unexpected order⟩ ⟨~*ed* all hands onto the job of cleaning up⟩ **f** (1) : to direct or bring to bear in opposition esp. by reversing the use or application of something : cause to rebound or recoil ⟨tests the Communists' underlying contention . . . and ~*s* their argument against them —Arthur Knight⟩ ⟨secured or collected Japanese swords, then ~*ed* them upon their former owners —R.W.Thorp⟩ (2) : to lead or cause to dislike : make antagonistic : PREJUDICE — used with *against* ⟨~ a child against its mother⟩ ⟨campaign to ~ the people against their leaders⟩ ⟨had an arrogant manner that ~*ed* many against him⟩ **g** (1) : to cause to go or move in a particular direction ⟨~*ed* his steps homeward⟩ (2) : to make go or move elsewhere : DRIVE, SEND ⟨~ cows to pasture⟩ ⟨farmers round about ~ into these woods their young cattle —John Burroughs⟩ ⟨~*ed* the cat into the cellar for the night⟩; *esp* : to send or order away ⟨officers were ~*ed* adrift by the mutineers⟩ — usu. used with *away, from, off, out of* ⟨kind of man who would ~ a homeless child from his door⟩ ⟨~*ed* his wayward son out of his house⟩ ⟨no deserving person is ever ~*ed* away from that mission⟩ ⟨kept busy ~*ing* hunters off his land⟩ (3) : to convey or direct into or out of a receptacle by turning (as by inverting a container or operating a cock or faucet) ⟨don't need a recipe — just ~ the meat into a pot, heat, and serve⟩ ⟨mixture was ~*ed* into a baking tin and popped into a preheated oven⟩ ⟨asked by the police to ~ the contents of her handbag out onto the table⟩ **6 a** (1) *archaic* : to change the nature or appearance of : METAMORPHOSE, TRANSMUTE (2) : to make acid or sour : CURDLE, FERMENT ⟨hot weather may ~ milk⟩ (3) : to change the color of (as foliage) **b** (1) : to cause to become something specified : CONVERT, TRANSFORM — used with *into* or *to* ⟨giant elms that ~ those streets into great cathedrals in summer —Maxwell Mays⟩ ⟨~*ed* an almost impossible challenge into a remarkable personal triumph —C.H. Driver⟩ ⟨had ~*ed* disappointment into contentment and failure into success —Ellen Glasgow⟩ ⟨would ~ their ancient town into just another dormitory-suburb —Sam Pollock⟩ ⟨device that ~*s* the sun's light directly into electricity —E.C.Bullard⟩ ⟨tries to ~ every contact into a vote —R.L.Duffus⟩ ⟨gadget that was going to ~ us all into a nation of gawking illiterates —R.M. Yoder⟩ ⟨claim the desert can be ~*ed* to farmland —*Newsweek*⟩ ⟨cannot leave his comedy ~*ed* to sadness by the sentencing of the youths —K.F.Thompson⟩ (2) : to render in another language or another form of expression : TRANSLATE, PARAPHRASE — usu. used with *into* ⟨beautifully sculptured French has been ~*ed* into equally impressive English —*Times Lit. Supp.*⟩ ⟨selected a group of translators . . . to ~ into Latin a considerable number of important Greek books —G.C. Sellery⟩ ⟨struggled to ~ Indian legends and colonial tales into verse —Howard M. Jones⟩; *also* : to phrase differently : give a different cast or form to **c :** to cause to become of a specified nature or appearance — used with *into* or *to* ⟨~*s* the marble pillars above into a dusky silver⟩ ⟨salt air of the Cape is said to ~ the shingles on roofs and walls to a distinctive gray —Jackson Rivers⟩ ⟨wondered if the contortionist would be able to ~ himself into his right shape again⟩ **d :** to exchange for something else : dispose of by exchanging for an equivalent ⟨~*ed* his stocks and bonds into cash⟩ ⟨~ a pocketful of coins into paper money⟩ **e :** to change (as a person) so as to make different in a specified way : affect so as to cause a specified reaction ⟨starvation, thirst, heat and chills ~ them mad or sullen —Charles Lee⟩ ⟨~*s* your tongue black if you drink too much of it —R.H.Newman⟩ ⟨last year's drought ~*ed* things worse —*Christian Science Monitor*⟩ ⟨improvements ~*ed* them obsolete —Roger Burlingame⟩ ⟨if the resulting bungles . . . do not ~ the cold war hot —*Times Lit. Supp.*⟩ **f :** to cause to be regarded in a particular way : make the subject (as of ridicule) — used esp. in the phrase *turn to ridicule* ⟨humiliates him by patronizing him and ~*s* to ridicule his abilities and ambitions —Edmund Wilson⟩ **7 a :** to shape or fashion esp. in a rounded form by applying a cutting tool while revolving in a lathe : form in a lathe ⟨~ a set of table legs⟩ ⟨craftsmen ~*ing* small ivory figurines⟩ ⟨most effective cutting rate in relation to the material being ~*ed* —*Industrial Improvement*⟩ **b :** to give a rounded form to by any means (as carving or molding) ⟨showed him how to ~ the volute of a capital —Van Wyck Brooks⟩: as (1) *archaic* : to cause (as an arch) to be built : CONSTRUCT (2) : to cut off the rind or skin of (as an orange) in a narrow spiral strip : remove the stone from (as an olive) by paring off the flesh in such a strip (3) : to make a curved section in (a piece of needlework); *specif* : to perform the operations necessary to make the curved form of (a heel of a stocking) ⟨looking down at her as she sat ~*ing* a heel —J.M.Barrie⟩ **c** (1) : to shape or mold artistically, gracefully, or neatly esp. in curved or rounded form as if on a lathe ⟨girl with magnificently ~*ed* ankles —*New Yorker*⟩ ⟨a long nyloned leg, a trifle thin but well ~*ed* —Earle Birney⟩ (2) : to fashion skillfully (as a piece of literary work) ⟨really knows how to ~ a sentence⟩ ⟨has a knack for ~*ing* a phrase —W.O.Douglas⟩ ⟨man's obviously literate, can ~ neat and precise phrases —Rex Ingamells⟩ ⟨slick, quick, well ~*ed* plays —H.A.L.Craig⟩ ⟨speaks rather elegant and carefully ~*ed* English —Winthrop Sargent⟩ ⟨a gentle squib of beautifully ~*ed* parody —*Britain Today*⟩; *sometimes* : to execute skillfully ⟨performances are . . . well ~*ed* —Edward Sackville-West & Desmond Shawe-Taylor⟩ **d** *obs* : to equip specially by nature : ADAPT, FIT ⟨by nature ~*ed* to play the rake —Jonathan Swift⟩ **8 :** to make a fold, crook, bend, or curve in by or as if by pressure: as **a** *obs* : FOLD **b** *obs* : PLAIT **c :** to bend or twist so as to encircle ⟨creepers ~*ed* their tendrils about a picket fence⟩ ⟨had a snake ~*ed* round his arm⟩ **d :** to form by bending ⟨~ a lead pipe⟩ ⟨tubing had been ~*ed* in a U-shaped curve⟩ **e** (1) : to cause (the edge of a blade) to bend back or over : cause to give by meeting resistance (as from a hard surface) ⟨even ordinary slicing tends to ~ a fine edge —L.D.Bement⟩ : BLUNT, DULL ⟨if skins are too thick, they are reduced . . . with a moon knife with a ~*ed* edge —H.R.Procter⟩ ⟨thinks the edge of this objection can be ~*ed* —R.J.Spilsbury⟩ (2) : to dull or soften (as the power to cut or penetrate) in something that is done or expressed — used chiefly in the phrase *turn the edge of* or sometimes *turn the point of* ⟨spoke slowly and softly with a smile that did little to ~ the edge of his attack⟩ ⟨this . . . approach . . . ~*s* the edge of certain hostile criticisms —*Jour. of Philosophy*⟩ **9 a :** to keep (as money) moving, circulating, or passing in trade; *specif* : to dispose of (a stock) so as to make room for another ⟨pushcart vendor of oranges may ~ his stock every day —J.W.Wingate⟩ **b :** to make or gain chiefly by buying or selling or performing work or services) ⟨were not able to ~ a penny in the present market⟩ ⟨scheme to sell tea cheaply to the colonies and ~ a quick penny at the same time —James Street⟩ ⟨known to be ~*ing* a profit this year —Doyle Smee⟩ ⟨doing odd jobs to ~ an honest penny —John Dos Passos⟩ ⟨tricks . . . by which a more or less dishonest dollar can be ~*ed* —V.O.Key⟩ ~ *vi* **1 a :** to move around on an axis or about a center : move in circles or through an arc of a circle : revolve or rotate as a wheel does : wheel or whirl around ⟨wheel ~*ed* rapidly⟩ ⟨gate creaked as it ~*ed* on its hinges⟩ ⟨heavens . . . ~ in silence round the pole —A.E. Housman⟩ ⟨key would not ~ in the lock⟩ ⟨meat was ~*ing* on the spit⟩ **b :** *of the head or brain* : to have a sensation of whirling : become giddy or dizzy : REEL ⟨I'll look no more lest my brain ~ —Shak.⟩ ⟨hated heights; they always made his head ~⟩ **c** (1) : to have as a decisive factor : HINGE — usu. used with *on* or *upon* ⟨problems will rarely ~ on simple questions of right or wrong —H.G.Rickover⟩ ⟨the second act . . . the one upon which the whole work ~*s* —Virgil Thomson⟩ ⟨the trouble ~*ed* substantially on the failure . . . to consult and inform our allies —*New Republic*⟩ ⟨guilt or innocence . . . ~*s* on the identification of the weapon —*Irish Digest*⟩ ⟨argument ~*s* upon a point not of ethics but logic —Gail Kennedy⟩ (2) : to have a center (as of interest) in something specified : concentrate attention : relate principally — used with *around* or *about* ⟨social activity ~*ed* largely around official and church activities —C.L.Jones⟩ ⟨story ~*s* about a tormented passion felt by a dying young girl —Charles Lee⟩ or with *on* or *upon* ⟨discussion ~*ed* solely upon the feasibility of the scheme⟩ ⟨differences of opinion have ~*ed* mainly upon . . . how the success in Vienna can be turned to advantage here —J.E. Williams⟩ **2 a :** to shift one's position as if by moving on an axis or through the arc of a circle ⟨suffer with cramps in the muscles . . . when they ~ or stretch —Morris Fishbein⟩ ⟨had lain twisting and ~*ing* as he bemoaned their fate —O.E. Rölvaag⟩ ⟨~*ed* on his side⟩ ⟨tossed and ~*ed*, sighing and groaning —Kenneth Roberts⟩ ⟨enough to make a person ~ in his grave⟩ **b :** to move in a circular course or as if on an axis so as to face in various directions or in the opposite direction ⟨cabin was so small that a dog could hardly ~ in it —Tobias Smollett⟩ ⟨can ~ on a dime for repeated depth-charge attacks —J.C.Furnas⟩ ⟨~*ed* on his heel and walked away⟩ ⟨boat could ~ in its own length⟩ **c :** to incline from a horizontal position (as up or down from a point of rest) — used of a scale or balance **d :** to come by turning the leaves of a book ⟨~ ahead to the third chapter⟩ ⟨one can only leaf through the pictures or ~ to a list at the end of the book —Jane G. Mahler⟩ **3 a :** to direct one's course ⟨was completely lost, hadn't the faintest idea which way to ~⟩ ⟨was content to go whichever way his feet ~*ed*⟩ ⟨they ~*ed* into a street in which there was considerable activity —Irwin Shaw⟩ **b** (1) : to reverse a course or direction : go backward or in the opposite direction : become reversed ⟨market ~*ed* sharply in the afternoon⟩ ⟨nervous footpad ~*ed* and fled⟩ ⟨luck ~*ed* and he went broke⟩; *specif* : to change from ebb to flow or flow to ebb ⟨you should start half an hour to an hour before the tide ~*s* —Peter Heaton⟩ (2) : to have a reactive usu. adverse effect : RECOIL ⟨the . . . advantage — the buoyancy and liveliness of their lightly loaded craft — abruptly ~*ed* against them —Walter O'Meara⟩ **c :** to change one's course : take a different course or direction ⟨~*ed* toward home⟩ ⟨~ to the left at the foot of the hill⟩ ⟨~*ed* from the road into a tree-shaded lane⟩ ⟨rabbit ran out and ~*ed* along the hedge —Adrian Bell⟩ ⟨surge which had traveled southwards along our east coast later ~*ed* and moved northwards —J.A.Steers⟩ ⟨economy has begun to ~ downward —L.H.Keyserling⟩ ⟨corporate profits are ~*ing* upward —*Newsweek*⟩: as (1) : to execute or perform any of various maneuvers or procedures for changing course or direction (as of a ship or a fleet, a body of troops, a swimmer, skater, skier, or dancer); *specif* : to change direction by tacking (2) : to walk here and there : take a turn — used with *about* ⟨was at home in the country . . . ~*ing* about his grounds, sauntering by a brookside —Van Wyck Brooks⟩ (3) *of the wind* : to blow from a different quarter : SHIFT ⟨in the afternoon the wind ~*ed* into the east —Kenneth Roberts⟩ ⟨the wind ~*ed* and the sky cleared⟩ (4) : BREAK 5b(1) **d :** to change direction at, along, or by means of a bend or curve ⟨main road ~*s* sharp right at the fork⟩ ⟨highway ~*s* gradually away from the river⟩ ⟨river did indeed finally ~ to the left —Tom Marvel⟩ ⟨long hall runs the length of the building without ~*ing*⟩ **4 a :** to change position so as to face or be directed another way ⟨everywhere the eye ~*s* . . . it encounters propaganda —*N. Y. Times Mag.*⟩; *often* : to move one's head or body so as to face in another direction or to see something behind or to one side : face about ⟨heard his name called but did not ~⟩ ⟨astonished dignitaries were ~*ing* to stare at him —Al Hine & J.P.O'Neill⟩ **b :** to change position so as to face toward or away from someone or something ⟨however one ~*s*, one cannot evade the truth —R.M.Weaver⟩ ⟨~ from a gruesome sight⟩ ⟨~*ed* expectantly toward the door⟩ ⟨had taken fright at our behavior and ~*ed* to the captain pitifully —Joseph Conrad⟩ **c :** to change one's position or attitude or reverse one's course of action to one of opposition or hostility: (1) : to change from submission or friendliness to resistance or opposition ⟨even a worm will ~⟩ — usu. used with *against* ⟨felt that the whole world had suddenly ~*ed* against him⟩ ⟨even the younger men had ~*ed* against me —W.B.Yeats⟩ (2) : to vent anger or resentment — used with *on* or *upon* ⟨~*ed* upon them with a ferocity which made a savage of him on the spot —Virginia Woolf⟩ ⟨must come up with solutions or his party will be quick to ~ on him —*New Republic*⟩ (3) : make a sudden violent assault ⟨bulls often ~*ed* on the wounded, and the hunter could thus induce a fight —C.D.Forde⟩ ⟨dog had suddenly and for no apparent reason ~*ed* on his master⟩ **5 a :** to direct one's attention or thoughts to or away from someone or something ⟨men have

~ed from the discussion of universals —H.O.Taylor⟩ ⟨~s away in this book from his previous shock-treatment style of writing —Henry Cavendish⟩ ⟨played for society dances before ~ing to the blues —Hubert Creekmore⟩ ⟨former has ~ed to religion while the latter is still trying to live with uncertainty —Granville Hicks⟩; *also* **:** to find itself directed in this way ⟨riding to Canterbury, his mind naturally ~ed to church history —S.M.Crothers⟩ ⟨the thoughts of pioneers ~ed to self-government —R.A.Billington⟩ ⟨English prose ~ed to the sea in the early eighteenth century —W.P.Webb⟩ **b** (1) **:** to change one's way of life or thought by being converted to religion or a godly life ⟨~ to God⟩ ⟨disciples must ~, i.e. change their dispositions and habits —*Interpreter's Bible*⟩; *specif* **:** to change one's religion esp. as between Roman Catholic or Protestant ⟨he's a Catholic and I'm going to ~ —Victoria Lincoln⟩ ⟨feeling . . . that you've been praying for me to ~ —Ruth Park⟩ (2) **:** to go over to another side or party esp. by deserting or revolting **:** DEFECT **c :** to address oneself or direct one's attention to another subject **:** concern oneself with something different ⟨let us ~ now from mechanics to medicine —Benjamin Farrington⟩ ⟨now let us ~ to the United States and its theater —Marc Connelly⟩ ⟨kept wishing the speaker would ~ to something less gloomy⟩; *also* **:** to come in its course **:** move on ⟨talk, by some odd chance, had ~ed to the value of reticence in art —Thomas Wood †1950⟩ ⟨one evening over a cocktail the conversation ~ed to trout —Alexander MacDonald⟩ **d :** to betake oneself (as for information, help, or support) **:** have recourse — used with *to* ⟨for the historical presentation of contemporary literature one must ~ to . . . foreign critics —F.B.Millett⟩ **:** REFER ⟨the book to which one ~s inevitably for information on whaling —Hal Nielson⟩ ⟨book . . . that can be ~ed to again and again —Arthur Knight⟩ **:** RESORT ⟨government is not likely to ~ to private sources for dollars at higher rates of interest —J.C.Harsch⟩ ⟨for relaxation he ~s to tennis —*Current Biog.*⟩ ⟨painful illness led him to ~ to drugs⟩ ⟨employers ~ed to the regions where cheap labor was to be found —Oscar Handlin⟩ ⟨few experts . . . to whom it could ~ for knowledge and counsel —C.W.de Kiewiet⟩ ⟨a man to ~ to in time of need⟩ **e :** to direct one's efforts or interests **:** devote or apply oneself ⟨fewer studying medicine and more ~ing to agriculture and dairy science —*Irish Digest*⟩ ⟨came out of the army with nothing in mind to ~ to⟩ ⟨~ed to the study of the law with enthusiasm⟩ **6 a :** to become changed, altered, or transformed (as in nature, character, or appearance): as (1) *archaic* **:** to become different (2) **:** to change color — used esp. of leaves ⟨by the first of October most of the leaves have ~ed —W.H.Upson⟩ ⟨hickories were ~ing slowly and here and there the boughs were brushed with wine-color —Ellen Glasgow⟩ (3) **:** to become sour, rancid, or tainted ⟨found that the milk had ~ed⟩ (4) **:** to be variable or inconstant (5) **:** to become mentally unbalanced **:** become deranged **b** (1) **:** to become transformed or converted into something else (as by receiving a new character or new properties) **:** pass from one state to another **:** CHANGE — used with *into* or *to* ⟨water had ~ed to ice⟩ ⟨passive neglect ~ed into active antagonism —G.G.Coulton⟩ ⟨went away a fledgling and he has ~ed into a man —Louis Bromfield⟩ ⟨friendship . . . ~s into conflict, and in the end a formal duel is held —R.A.Hall b. 1911⟩ ⟨puzzled look . . . ~ed quickly to one of understanding —T.B.Costain⟩ ⟨no clear dividing line between fluids and jellies . . . one may ~ readily into the other —*New Biology*⟩ (2) **:** to become changed so as to be of a specified nature **:** change to **:** GROW ⟨hair had ~ed gray⟩ ⟨face ~ed white⟩ ⟨milk ~ed sour⟩ ⟨animal ~ed nasty⟩ ⟨weather ~ed bad⟩ ⟨voice ~ed shrill⟩ ⟨cautious ones ~ed moderately optimistic —*Biddle Survey*⟩ ⟨country ~ed thin and poor, with great patches of naked ground —H.L.Davis⟩ (3) **:** to become someone or something specified by change from another state **:** come to be ⟨~ state's evidence⟩ ⟨both poets in the end ~ed men of action —Osbert Sitwell⟩ ⟨dancing-school teacher who ~s call girl —Anthony Boucher⟩ ⟨in Latin America physicians frequently ~ author and statesman —*Americas*⟩ ⟨wartime diary of a journalist ~ed lieutenant commander —A.A. Ageton⟩ ⟨walls rise sheer around the courtyard ~ed theater —Claudia Cassidy⟩ ⟨picture themselves ~ing explorer and going home down the Amazon —*Geog. Jour.*⟩ **7 :** to become curved or bent (as from pressure); *esp* **:** to become blunted by bending ⟨the knife's edge had ~ed⟩ **8 :** to become upset **:** become nauseated — used of the stomach **9 a :** to operate a lathe **b :** to admit of fashioning on a lathe ⟨beech is largely used . . . since it ~s easily in the lathe —F.D.Smith & Barbara Wilcox⟩ ⟨ivory ~s well⟩ **10** *of merchandise* **:** to become stocked and disposed of **:** turn over **:** change hands **11** *of a goat* **:** to come in heat again after service by a buck

syn REVOLVE, ROTATE, GYRATE, CIRCLE, SPIN, TWIRL, WHIRL, WHEEL, EDDY, SWIRL, PIROUETTE: TURN is a general rather colorless word interchangeable with most of the others in their less specific uses. REVOLVE may suggest regular circular motion on an orbit around something exterior to the item in question; it may refer to the dependence of the less important, the secondary, on something cardinal or pivotal which resolves or determines ⟨though local questions, such as the State Bank and state aid to railroads, gave rise to sharp contests, politics usually *revolved* around national questions —A.B.Moore⟩ ⟨everything in that house *revolved* upon Aunt Mary —Margaret Deland⟩ ROTATE is likely to suggest a circular motion on an interior axis within the thing under consideration which may be not moving otherwise ⟨the earth *rotates* on its axis while it revolves on its orbit⟩ GYRATE may suggest the regularity of REVOLVE but it is likely to be used to indicate a fluctuating or swinging back and forth which describes circular or spiral patterns ⟨stocks *gyrated* dizzily on uncertainty over the foreign situation —*Wall Street Jour.*⟩ ⟨a low cloud of dust raised by the dog *gyrating* madly about —Joseph Conrad⟩ CIRCLE may simply indicate a movement around in a more or less circular pattern, or it may indicate any lack of straight directness in a winding course ⟨a flock of black ibises *circled* high overhead wheeling endlessly on the ascending air currents —Dillon Ripley⟩ ⟨the essayist's licence to *circle* and meander —Virginia Woolf⟩ SPIN indicates rapid sustained rotation on an inner axis or fast circling around an exterior point ⟨he who but ventures into the outer circle of the whirlpool is *spinning*, ere he has time for thought in its dizzy vortex —Bayard Taylor⟩ TWIRL adds to the ideas of SPIN those of dexterity, lightness, or easy grace ⟨this . . . book . . . I toss i' the air, and catch again, and *twirl* about —Robert Browning⟩ WHIRL stresses force, power, speed, and impetus of rotary or circular motion ⟨and collections of opaque particles *whirled* to shore by the eddies —William Bartram⟩ ⟨the withered leaves had gathered violence in pursuit, and were *whirling* after her like a bevy of witches —Ellen Glasgow⟩ WHEEL may suggest either going in a circular or twisted course or turning on an arc or curve to a new course ⟨a familiar sight is the turkey vulture *wheeling* against the skies to the north —*Amer. Guide Series: Ariz.*⟩ ⟨she had crossed the threshold to the porch, when, *wheeling* abruptly, she went back into the hall —Ellen Glasgow⟩ EDDY suggests the circular movement, sometimes fast, sometimes slow, of an eddy; it may be used in situations involving indirection, futility, or isolation from main currents ⟨as the smoke slowly *eddied* away —Stephen Crane⟩ ⟨the dead leaves which *eddied* slowly down through the windless calm —Rebecca West⟩ ⟨waves of friends and reporters *eddied* through the apartment —*Time*⟩ SWIRL suggests more rapidity, flow, or graceful attractiveness than EDDY ⟨further than ever comet flared or vagrant star-dust *swirled* —Rudyard Kipling⟩ ⟨the black water was running like a millrace and raising a turbulent coil as it *swirled* and tossed over the ugly heads of jutting rocks —T.B.Costain⟩ ⟨her dark hair *swirled* about her face —Helen Howe⟩ PIROUETTE suggests the light graceful turning of a ballet dancer ⟨ashes *pirouetted* down, coquetting with young beeches —Alfred Tennyson⟩ **syn** see in addition DEPEND

syn DIVERT, DEFLECT, AVERT, SHEER: TURN is comprehensive in its scope and devoid of specific connotation; it could be used in any of the citations in the following, although with some loss of force and distinctness. DIVERT stresses the idea of turning a thing or a person from a natural, expected course, way, or pattern into another ⟨vast quantities of water can be *diverted* from one to the other watershed with very little engineering work —B.K.Sandwell⟩ ⟨the machinery of our economic life has been *diverted* from peace to war —Clement Attlee⟩ DEFLECT is more likely to be used in reference to bouncing, refraction, or ricochet from a straight course or fixed direction ⟨when they were fired at a thin film of metal, the majority passed through without being substantially *deflected* from their courses —James Jeans⟩ In more figurative uses, it implies a turning, refracting, or deviating from a clearly evident course, direction, or pattern ⟨he underwent all those things — but none of them *deflected* his purpose —Hilaire Belloc⟩ ⟨after all, she had perhaps purposely *deflected* the conversation from her own affairs —Edith Wharton⟩ ⟨the spirit . . . of the Romance tongues *deflecting* it from classical constructions —H.O. Taylor⟩ AVERT implies no particular previously set course or pattern but usu. indicates either a turning away of one's eyes, attention, or the like from the unpleasant or a turning of the course of exterior developments to avoid the dangerous or unpleasant ⟨tried unsuccessfully to *avert* her horrified eyes from the sight⟩ ⟨Athenian statesmen *averted* a social revolution by successfully carrying through an economic and political revolution —A.J.Toynbee⟩ SHEER, orig. nautical, is likely to involve a sharp turning or veering, as of a ship, or, in more figurative use, a sharply sudden divergence from a path or course previously followed ⟨a griffon, wheeling here and there about, kept reconnoitring us . . . till he *sheered* off —John Keats⟩

— **turn a blind eye :** to refuse to see **:** be oblivious ⟨might *turn a blind eye* to the use of violence —Arthur Krock⟩ — **turn a cold shoulder to :** to treat with neglect or indifference **:** SNUB — **turn a deaf ear :** to refuse to listen — **turn a flange :** to form a flange on (as around a metal sheet or boiler plate) by stretching, bending, and hammering or rolling the metal — **turn a hair :** to give a sign of discomposure or disturbance — used in negative constructions ⟨came through the ordeal without *turning a hair*⟩ ⟨never *turned a hair*⟩ — **turn around one's finger** *or* **turn around one's little finger :** to do what one likes with **:** manage easily — **turn color 1 :** to become of a different color ⟨leaves are *turning color*⟩ ⟨dyes are fast and cloth will not *turn color*⟩ **2 a :** BLUSH, FLUSH **b :** to grow pale — **turn edge** *archaic, of a blade* **:** to have the edge turned over **:** become blunt — **turn flukes** *of a whale* **:** to raise the tail and dive — **turn loose 1 a :** to set free (as a tied horse) so as to have the run of a pasture **b :** to free from all restraints **:** permit to go one's own way ⟨is going to *turn* the savages *loose* on us —Dorothy C. Fisher⟩ ⟨poetry is not a *turning loose* of emotion —T.S.Eliot⟩ **2 :** to fire off (as a gun or a bullet) **:** DISCHARGE **3 :** to open fire ⟨everything aboard *turned loose* on him —Bill Alcine⟩ **4 :** to speak esp. at length and without restraint ⟨after the director spoke the workers *turned loose* on him —A.R.Williams⟩ — **turn one's back on** *or* **turn one's back upon 1 :** to put behind one **:** depart from ⟨with this month of March we *turn our backs on* winter —Faith Baldwin⟩ ⟨Eskimo *turn their backs* abruptly *on* the sea . . . up a valley from the shore —C.D.Forde⟩ **2 :** REJECT, DENY ⟨my conscience will not let me *turn my back upon* a call to service —F.D.Roosevelt⟩ ⟨would be *turning one's back on* history —Pius Walsh⟩; *often* **:** to reject unceremoniously or treat with contempt **3 :** ABANDON, FORSAKE, DESERT ⟨*turning our backs upon* the rest of mankind and refusing to enter the cooperative scheme —Stephen Duggan⟩ ⟨*turned his back on* his own people⟩ — **turn one's coat :** to change one's uniform or colors **:** go over to the opposite party — **turn one's hand 1** *archaic* **:** to lay one's hand esp. to kill — used with *upon* **2** *or* **turn a hand a :** to engage in manual work ⟨plans must be drawn before *a hand* can be *turned* to building⟩ **b :** set to work **:** be employed **:** apply oneself — used with *to* ⟨had begun *turning his hand* to occasional literary journalism —Cecil Sprigge⟩ ⟨could *turn their hand* to almost anything in the line of pantomime —Winthrop Palmer⟩ — **turn one's stomach :** to disgust completely **:** NAUSEATE, SICKEN ⟨wanted to change the public mind . . . succeeded mainly in *turning its stomach* —J. D.Hart⟩ — **turn over a new leaf :** to make a radical change esp. for the better in one's way of living or doing ⟨*turned over a new leaf* at forty and became a pillar of the church⟩; *also* **:** to promise or attempt such a change ⟨forever involved in scandals . . . and forever *turning over a new leaf* —Jean Stafford⟩ — **turn tail 1 :** to run away (as from danger or opposition) ⟨might have to carry him out on a stretcher, but he wouldn't *turn tail* again —Hamilton Basso⟩ **:** retreat from a position ⟨administration *turned tail* and ran —Elmer Davis⟩ **2 :** to turn one's back **:** ABANDON, FORSAKE, REJECT — used with *on* or *upon* ⟨fellows who *turned* their *tails* on the land —John Galsworthy⟩ — **turn the other cheek :** to respond to injury or unkindness with patience **:** forgo retaliation — **turn the scale** *also* **turn the balance 1 :** to register weight — used with *at* ⟨hand baggage *turned the scale* at 60 pounds⟩ **2 :** to decide or determine something doubtful **:** prove decisive ⟨sharper claw or oilier feather might *turn the balance* —W.C.Allee⟩ ⟨air support can make much difference, but can it . . . *turn the scales* —B.H.Liddell Hart⟩ — **turn the tables** [fr. *turn the tables* to reverse the relative positions as in a board game] **1 :** to bring about a reversal of the relative conditions or fortunes of two contending persons or parties **2 :** to show that an argument advanced for or against a thesis actually favors the other side — **turn the trick :** to bring about the desired result or effect — **turn thumbs down :** to express disapproval, condemnation, or rejection ⟨at least one legislative body has *turned thumbs down* on a proposal to investigate the schools —*Nation*⟩ — **turn to windward :** to beat to windward — **turn turtle 1 :** to capsize bottom upward — used of a boat **2 :** OVERTURN ⟨automobile *turned turtle*⟩

[2]**turn** \"\ *n* -s [ME; partly fr. OF *tor, tour, torn, tourn* lathe, circuit, turn (partly fr. L *tornus* lathe; partly fr. OF *torner, tourner* to turn); partly fr. ME *turnen*, v.] **1 a :** the action or an act of turning or moving about or as if about a center or axis **:** REVOLUTION, ROTATION ⟨~ is the motion employed to turn the hand either empty or loaded by movement that rotates the hand, wrist, and forearm about the long axis of the forearm —*Methods-Time Measurement*⟩ ⟨knowledge and entertainment are brought with the ~ of a dial —*Girl Scout Handbk.*⟩ ⟨almost any ~ of the kaleidoscope of nature may set up in the artist this . . . vision —Roger Fry⟩ **b :** a single revolution or turning motion ⟨twists and ~s of the head⟩ ⟨each ~ of the wheels brought them nearer home⟩ ⟨only three ~s of the moon —Virginia Woolf⟩ ⟨grand old leaps and ~s of the imperial ballet discipline —*Time*⟩: as (1) **:** any of various rotating or pivoting movements in dancing whether executed singly or in couples — see CIRCLE TURN, OPEN TURN, REVERSE TURN, ROCK TURN (2) **:** a revolution by a gymnast of less than a circle around a bar **2 a :** the action or an act of giving or taking a direction or a different direction **:** change of course or posture ⟨forgot to make the usual ~ at the corner⟩ ⟨illegal left ~⟩ ⟨gentle ~s may be performed by rudder alone —R.P.Holland⟩ ⟨controls had jammed in a ~ —Phil Gustafson⟩: as (1) **:** a drill maneuver in which troops in mass formation change direction without preserving alignment and which is executed by the pivot file facing in the new direction and marching at the half step until the others move up and place themselves in succession on the new line — compare WHEEL (2) **:** a change of course by a ship in formation or a simultaneous change of course by the ships of a unit (3) **:** any of various shifts of direction in skiing — see CHRISTIANIA, JUMP TURN, KICK TURN, SNOWPLOW TURN, STEM CHRISTIANIA, STEM TURN, STEP TURN, TELEMARK (4) **:** an interruption of a curve in figure skating **b :** the action or an act of turning aside (as from a straight course, a normal development, or a manifest trend) **:** DEFLECTION, DEVIATION ⟨gave the story so many twists and ~s the reader becomes lost⟩: as (1) **:** a sudden change of not less than a right angle in direction made by the quarry in coursing when hotly pursued ⟨hound gave the hare a ~⟩ (2) **:** BREAK 4c(6) (3) **:** a forward stroke in cricket made with the face of the bat at an angle that sends the ball to the on side ⟨would open his account with a ~ to the on side, generally forward of square leg —*Calling All Cricketers*⟩ **c :** the action or an act of turning so as to face or move in the opposite direction **:** reversal of posture or course ⟨an about ~⟩ ⟨wait for the ~ of the tide⟩ ⟨sales have never been higher at this season — and there are few signs of a ~ —*Nation's Business*⟩: as (1) **:** a complete reversal of direction in a swimming race (2) **:** a complete reversal of a skate in figure skating **d :** a change effected by turning over to another side or face about ⟨lost a fortune on one ~ of the cards⟩ **e :** a place at which something turns, turns off, or turns back **:** point or part at or along which a change of course or direction takes place **:** ANGLE, BEND, CURVE ⟨stopped at a ~ in the road⟩ ⟨river has many ~s⟩ ⟨couldn't get the piano around the ~ in the hallway⟩ ⟨swept around a ~ of the trees, down the nearest avenue toward us —B.T.Cleeve⟩: as (1) *dial Eng* **:** a pit sunk in some part of a drift in lead mining (2) **:** a curved part of a running track or racetrack ⟨took the lead on the run to the clubhouse ~ —*N.Y.Times*⟩ ⟨too big to move easily around the ~s —Albion Hughes⟩ (3) **:** the point on a golf course at which the return journey is begun **:** end of the first nine holes or start of the last nine holes ⟨was three up at the ~⟩ ⟨made the ~ in 35 —*N.Y.Times*⟩ (4) **:** a point of junction between two curves in figure skating **3 a** (1) *obs* **:** JOURNEY, TOUR, TRIP (2) **:** TOURN **b** (1) **:** the action or an act of walking esp. briefly around or out and back ⟨usually took a ~ around the block before going to bed⟩ ⟨going to have a ~ under the stars before I follow you —Agnes S. Turnbull⟩ ⟨took a short ~ through the garden — to the row of tamarisk trees and back —Willa Cather⟩ ⟨so incurably soft as not to be able to face a gentle ~ round an ordinary suburban garden —Osbert Lancaster⟩ (2) **:** a short trip (as a walk, ride, drive) out and back or round about ⟨had enough gas for a half hour's ~ in the park⟩ ⟨studied navigation — why, if I had taken one ~ down the harbor I should have known more about it —H.D.Thoreau⟩ **c** *chiefly dial* **:** a single trip and return (as by a team in hauling logs) **4 a :** a movement by a wrestler intended to throw his opponent **b** *archaic* **:** ARTIFICE, STRATAGEM, TRICK, WILE ⟨beheld in either field a farmer at work and proposed to play the two a ~ —Joseph Campbell⟩ **5 a :** an act or deed affecting another esp. when performed out of the usual course **:** a usu. incidental or unexpected act of service or disservice ⟨one good ~ deserves another⟩ ⟨when you turned me out you did me the best ~ you ever did me —W.S.Maugham⟩ ⟨actually the worms do the cattle farmers a good ~ —B.C.Cronwright⟩ ⟨you've had a rotten deal . . . The man . . . has done you a bad ~—Dorothy Sayers⟩ **b** *chiefly Scot* **:** a stroke of work **:** piece of work **:** JOB, TASK — compare HAND'S TURN **6 :** something that comes in its own due order or at often regular intervals: as **a :** a period of action or activity **:** GO, SPELL ⟨went on deck and took a ~ at the wheel⟩ ⟨a ~ at the lathe in his cellar workshop —Otis Fellows⟩ ⟨catch their breath between ~s on the ice —H.W. Wind⟩ ⟨enjoys spectator sports, bridge, and a ~ on the dance floor —*Current Biog.*⟩; *specif* **:** a bout of wrestling **b :** a place, time, or opportunity accorded an individual or unit of a series in simple succession or in or as if in a scheduled order ⟨rooms were thoroughly cleaned each in its ~⟩ ⟨was waiting his ~ in a doctor's office⟩ ⟨is pointed out to him that his ~ will come —Richard Joseph⟩ ⟨took our ~ and did our bit —G.B.Shaw⟩ ⟨class took ~s expressing opinions —Eleanor S. Lowman⟩ ⟨~ of the surrealists for market appreciation is probably next —J.T.Soby⟩; *often* **:** a recurring chance or opportunity coming to each in alternation or succession (as in a game) **c :** a period during which one of a number of persons or groups successively employed is on duty **:** SHIFT, TOUR ⟨increases . . . to 6 cents from 4 cents on the afternoon ~ —*Wall Street Jour.*⟩ ⟨will add a second ~ employing another 1000 —*Wall Street Jour.*⟩ **d :** a short act or piece of any kind esp. in or for a variety show ⟨announced each act and said a few words between ~s —Pete Martin⟩ ⟨can recall virtually every routine and ~ he ever learned —R.B.Gehman⟩ ⟨a song-and-dance ~⟩ ⟨cabaret ~s⟩ ⟨chief ~ consisted of four performing elephants —Osbert Sitwell⟩; *also* **:** the performer of such an act ⟨commended only one of the ~s, a young man . . . who sang *Danny Boy* —Patrick Campbell⟩ **e** (1) **:** an event in any gambling game after which bets are settled — called also *coup* (2) **:** the order of the last three cards in faro — used in the phrase *call the turn* **7 :** something that revolves or that turns or moves around or as if around a center: as **a** (1) LATHE; *esp* **:** a watchmaker's lathe (2) *chiefly dial* **:** SPINNING WHEEL (3) **:** a catch or latch for a cupboard or cabinet door that is operated by turning a knob or handle **b** (1) **:** a musical ornament consisting of a group of four or more notes that wind about the principal or written note by including the notes next above and next below beginning either on the upper note or (as often in 19th century music) on the principal note ⟨executes the ~s with beautiful ease —Irving Kolodin⟩ (2) **:** a sign indicating this musical ornament **8 :** a special purpose, need, or requirement **:** CONVENIENCE, EXIGENCY — used chiefly in the phrase *serve one's turn* ⟨the philosophy that serves one's ~ best —J.C.Powys⟩ ⟨hoping . . . to exploit and then disown him after he had served their ~ —*Times Lit. Supp.*⟩ **9** *obs* **:** an event or course or series of events **10 a :** the action or an act of changing **:** ALTERATION, MODIFICATION ⟨a nasty ~ in the weather⟩ ⟨tea too weak and not hot enough, and the milk verging to the ~ —E.O.Schlunke⟩ **b :** a change in tendency, trend, or drift or in conditions, circumstances, or affairs ⟨hoped for a ~ in his luck⟩ ⟨credit situation probably won't cause an adverse ~ in the economy —M.S.Rukeyser⟩ ⟨~ of fortune which made him a prisoner of war —G.F.Hudson⟩ ⟨fairly sharp ~s characterize British history —*Current History*⟩ ⟨a ~ for the better in the bitter labor-management feud —Mary K. Hammond⟩ ⟨market for used cars took a definite ~ for the worse —Leo Wolman⟩ ⟨laughing up their sleeves at the ~ of affairs —Edward Bok⟩ **c :** the time when something changes its direction or its course (as of development) or when a change in trend or circumstances takes place ⟨the ~ of the seasons — the low point between the end of the winter season and the pickup of the spring-summer boom —*N.Y.Times*⟩ ⟨decided to wait until the ~ of the year⟩ ⟨our literary taste at the ~ of the century —M.D.Geismar⟩ ⟨born just after the ~ of the century⟩ ⟨years at the ~ of the twentieth century were vintage years —W.A.White⟩ **d** *Brit* **:** the middle price between a stock jobber's buying and selling prices **:** change in price **11 a :** distinctive quality or character ⟨peculiar ~ of the Greek genius —H.J.J.Winter⟩ ⟨the ~ and genius of our language —Thomas Gray⟩ **b** (1) **:** a turning or fashioning of language esp. skillfully or for a special effect **:** arrangement of words ⟨saw in the ~ of her phrase an opportunity to exhibit a small verbal neatness —Dorothy C. Fisher⟩ ⟨stylist . . . will appreciate the ~ of the phrase —Gilbert Seldes⟩ ⟨never at a loss for a ~ of a phrase to illustrate a point —Harvey Graham⟩ ⟨shocks us . . . by its Machiavellian ~ of phrase —Béla Menczer⟩ (2) **:** a particular form of expression or detail of style of discourse; *esp* **:** a peculiarity of phrasing ⟨some of the most felicitous ~s of thought and phrase in poetry —J.L.Lowes⟩ ⟨Scandinavian strain . . . is shown more clearly by ~s of expression than by the forms of individual words —F.M. Steuton⟩ ⟨altered his dress, his mannerisms, and his ~s of speech —Geoffrey Gorer⟩ ⟨studded with his special capering marks and ~s of style —Richard Eberhart⟩ ⟨uses many dialect ~s —H.H.Reichard⟩ ⟨even an advanced student misses idiomatic ~s —Geoffrey Bullough⟩ **c :** the shape or mold in which something is fashioned ⟨gown showed off the ~ of her neck and shoulder⟩ **:** CAST ⟨an unbelievably evil ~ of countenance⟩ **12 a :** the state or manner of being coiled or twisted ⟨spinning yarns . . . in various grades, sizes, and degrees of twist or ~ —*Whitlock Cordage*⟩; *specif* **:** the distance along the axis of a rope in which a strand makes one spiral **b :** a single round (as of rope passed about an object or laid in a coil or of wire wound on the core of an induction coil), twist (as of the strands of a rope), or whorl (as of a convoluted form) ⟨snail shell with seven ~s⟩ ⟨stove was cracked and held together with many ~s of heavy wire —Brian Harwin⟩ ⟨~s around the drum of the windlass began to slip —H.A.Chippendale⟩ ⟨one ~ of wire when carrying one ampere of current is known as one ampere turn —Irving Frazee⟩ ⟨give a yarn ten ~s of twist per inch of length —Werner Von Bergen & H.R.Mauersberger⟩ ⟨the axial length of one complete ~ or helix of a wire in a cable —L.F.Hickernell & A.A.Jones⟩ **c :** a coiling, twisting, or winding of one thing (as a cord, rope, or wire) about another ⟨a ~ is taken round the most convenient article

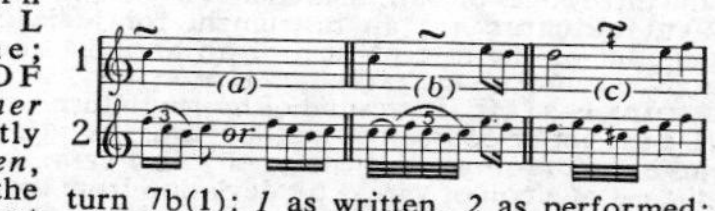

turn 7b(1): *1* as written, *2* as performed: *a* with sign over the note, *b* with sign following, *c* with chromatic

that will take the strain —*Fire Service Drill Bk.*⟩ **13 :** any of several measures of quantity (as for some commodities): as **a :** a varying measure for selling fish **b :** a load of wood; *esp* **:** a number of logs hauled on one trip **c :** a bundle of 60 skins in the fur trade **d** *chiefly dial* **:** a quantity of corn (as a sackful) taken to a mill at one time for grinding **14 a :** natural or special ability or aptitude **:** BENT, INCLINATION ⟨renown . . . rests not on his geometry or his ~ for affairs —Benjamin Farrington⟩ ⟨a fellow with a real practical ~—O.W.Holmes †1894⟩ ⟨a ~ for logical presentation —Jane Addams⟩ ⟨a pretty ~ for anecdote —W.S.Gilbert⟩ ⟨must possess . . . artistic sensibility and a ~ for clear thinking —Clive Bell⟩ — used esp. in the phrase *turn of mind* ⟨am of an optimistic ~ of mind —G.P.Brockway⟩ ⟨had a philosophic ~ of mind —John Mason Brown⟩ ⟨help to stimulate an inquiring ~ of mind —Warwick Braithwaite⟩ ⟨men of a speculative ~ of mind —M.R.Cohen⟩ **b** (1) *obs* **:** a particular characteristic (as of a person) or a characteristic act (2) *dial* **:** DISPOSITION, PERSONALITY **15 a :** direction of movement **:** DRIFT, TENDENCY, TREND ⟨the individuals who took a decisive part in them — who gave a ~ to the events —Herbert Read⟩ ⟨the oriental ~ of seeking nirvana —Warren Weaver⟩ ⟨provide a clue as to the ~ of events a few seconds before they happen —Princess Indira⟩ **b :** a special twist, construction, or interpretation ⟨gave the hoary old yarn a new ~⟩ ⟨gave a native ~ to the designs which they imitated —O. Elfrida Saunders⟩ **16 a :** a disordering spell or attack (as of illness, faintness, dizziness) ⟨some ~ of disease had begun to parade erotic images before his eyes —W.B.Yeats⟩ ⟨a delicate man, who had survived, mother alone knows how many bad ~s —Blanche E. Baughan⟩ ⟨isn't a real snake on the carpet, it is only one of my ~s —Margaret Macdonald⟩ **b :** a nervous start or shock (as from alarm, fright, or surprise) ⟨gives one quite a ~ to discover that one's husband is a murderer —Denis Johnston⟩ ⟨had given me a ~ . . . she was so close to the edge —Joseph Conrad⟩ ⟨gave him a nasty ~, but he put on a bold front —W.S.Maugham⟩ **c : turns** *pl* **:** MENSES **17 a :** a complete transaction involving a purchase and sale of securities or vice versa; *also* **:** a profit from such a transaction **b :** TURNOVER 8c ⟨wash goods department may find that three ~s a year are feasible —J.W. Wingate⟩ **18 :** something turned or to be turned: as **a** (1) **:** a character or slug inverted in setting type (2) **:** a piece of type placed bottom up or a character temporarily keyed (as by a Monotype operator) in place of another of the same width to be inserted later by hand; *also* **:** the replacement of a turn by the proper character ⟨~s have been made in most of the galleys⟩ **b :** TURN SHOE — **at every turn** *adv* **:** on every occasion **:** in every instance **:** CONSTANTLY, CONTINUALLY ⟨commission would find itself hampered *at every turn* —T.W. Arnold⟩ ⟨fights public housing *at every turn* —*New Republic*⟩ — **by turns** *adv* **:** one after another in regular succession **:** ALTERNATELY, SUCCESSIVELY ⟨was praised and blamed *by turns*⟩ ⟨washed the dishes *by turns*⟩ ⟨stores that are *by turns* curious, tragic, ennobling, disturbing, and heartening —C.R. Hewitt & Jenifer Wayne⟩ — **in turn** *adv* **:** in due order of succession **:** SUCCESSIVELY ⟨new waves of hope arise to shatter themselves *in turn* against the sands of despair —M.R.Cohen⟩ ⟨revision of estimated sales . . . and this, *in turn*, will mean revision in production schedules —J.K.Blake⟩ **:** ALTERNATELY ⟨*in turn* caustic and idyllic —Mark Gayn⟩ ⟨each *in turn* comes into the ascendant at the other's expense —A.J.Toynbee⟩ — **on the turn** *adv (or adj)* **:** in the act or course of turning **:** at the point of turning ⟨tide is *on the turn*⟩ — **out of turn** *adv* **1 :** not in turn **:** not in due order of succession ⟨play *out of turn*⟩ **2 :** imprudently, unadvisedly, or at a wrong time or place ⟨throwing their weight around . . . and talking *out of turn* —Joseph Mitchell⟩ ⟨might be condemned for heresy if he spoke *out of turn* —Peter Wiles⟩ — **to a turn** *adv* **:** to perfection **:** precisely right **:** EXACTLY, PERFECTLY ⟨food was superb, the roast done *to a turn*⟩ ⟨sung and danced *to a turn* by the comedy team —*Theatre Arts*⟩

[3]**turn** \'tərn, 'tu̇rn\ *vi* -ED/-ING/-S [G *turnen*, fr. OHG *turnēn* to turn (in general), fr. ML *tornare* — more at [1]TURN] **:** to practice or perform gymnastic exercises

turn·able \'tərnəbəl\ *adj* [ME *turneabylle*, fr. *turnen* to turn + *-able*] **:** capable of being turned

[1]**turn about** *vb* [[1]*turn* + *about*, adv.] *vi* **:** to face about **:** reverse one's position, direction, course, or policy ~ *vt* **:** to cause to face in the opposite direction ⟨*turn* a car *about*⟩

[2]**turn about** *or* **turn and turn about** *adv* [[2]*turn* + *about*, adv.] **:** by turns

turnabout \'≈,≈\ *n* -S [[1]*turn about*] **1 a :** an act or instance of turning about **:** a change or reversal of direction ⟨boat capable of a quick ~⟩ or trend ⟨sharp ~ in farm prices⟩ or policy or of relative position or role ⟨~ humor of husbands who bake cookies and send them to wives —Walter Karig⟩ **b :** a changing from one side or allegiance to another ⟨~ witness⟩ **c :** TURNCOAT, RENEGADE **2 a** *obs* **:** TURNSTILE **b :** MERRY-GO-ROUND **3 :** a reversible garment

turn and bank indicator *n* **:** an instrument combining the functions of a turn indicator and a lateral inclinometer

turn around *or* **turn round** *vb* **:** to turn about

turnaround \'≈≈,≈\ *n* -S [*turn around*] **1 :** a space (as a widened section of a driveway) designed to permit the turning around of a vehicle **2 :** a reversal of one's course, attitude, position, or policy **:** TURNABOUT **3 :** the time required for a round trip (as of a ship, airplane, or other vehicle) including loading and unloading at both points and necessary maintenance; *also* **:** the overhauling of a vehicle

turn away *vt* **1 :** DEFLECT, AVERT ⟨proper clothing and genteel speech would *turn away* the adverse criticisms —Oscar Handlin⟩ ⟨a soft answer *turneth away* wrath —Prov 15:1 (AV)⟩ **2 a :** to send away **:** REJECT, DISMISS **b :** REPEL **c :** to refuse admittance or acceptance to ⟨hundreds were *turned away* from the theater⟩ ~ *vi* **:** to start to go away **:** LEAVE, DEPART, ABANDON ⟨when the audience *turns away* there is something wrong with the writer's communication line —Stuart Chase⟩

turnaway \'≈≈,≈\ *n* -S [*turn away*] **1 :** a turning away **:** DESERTION **2 :** the act of refusing admittance

turn back *vi* **1 a :** to stop going forward **:** refuse to go ahead **b :** to go in the reverse direction **:** RETURN ⟨it was getting late, time to *turn back*⟩ **2 :** to refer to an earlier time or place ⟨*turn back* to the first page⟩ ~ *vt* **1 :** to drive back or away **:** cause to return or to reverse direction ⟨refugees were *turned back* at the frontier⟩ **2 :** to stop the advance of **:** CHECK **3 :** to fold back

[1]**turnback** \'≈,≈\ *n* -S [*turn back*] **1 :** COWARD, QUITTER **2 :** a part (as of a garment) that is turned back ⟨~ of a hat brim⟩

[2]**turnback** \"\ *or* **turned-back** \'≈,≈\ *adj* [*turn back* or *turned back*, past part. of *turn back*] **:** folded back on itself ⟨~ sleeve⟩

turn bench *n* **:** a watchmaker's lathe

turn bolt *n* **:** a latch bolt that operates by turning a knob or handle

turn bridge *n* **:** PIVOT BRIDGE

turnbuckle \'≈,≈≈\ *n* **1 :** a link with a screw thread at one end and a swivel at the other or a right-and-left screw link used for tightening a rod or stay **2 :** a gravitating catch for fastening a shutter, the end of a chain, or a hasp

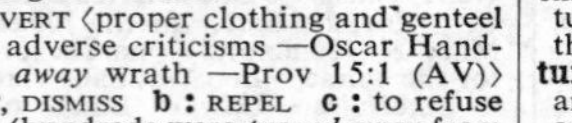

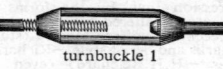

turnbuckle 1

turn·bull's blue \'tərn,bu̇lz-\ *n, usu cap T* [prob. fr. the name *Turnbull*] **:** an iron blue pigment having a coppery luster formed as a precipitate when an alkali metal ferricyanide and a ferrous salt are brought together in solution and formerly regarded as ferrous ferricyanide — compare PRUSSIAN BLUE

turn button *n* **:** BUTTON 5a

turncap \'≈,≈\ *n* **:** a chimney cap that turns with the wind so as to present its opening to leeward

turncoat \'≈,≈\ *n* [[1]*turn* + *coat*, n.] **:** one who forsakes his party or his principles **:** RENEGADE, APOSTATE

turncock \'≈,≈\ *n* **1 :** a stopcock with a plug that is turned in opening or closing **2 :** a person employed to turn on or off water supplied intermittently (as to dwellings or street flushing operations)

turn down *vi* **1 :** to take a downward course or direction ⟨corners of his mouth began to *turn down*⟩ **2 :** to be capable of being folded or doubled down ⟨collar *turns down*⟩ ~ *vt* **1 :** to fold or double down ⟨corner of the page has been *turned down*⟩ **2 :** to turn upside down **:** INVERT ⟨*turn down* the first card dealt⟩ **3 :** to reduce in height or intensity by turning a valve or stopcock or control ⟨*turn down* the lights⟩ ⟨*turn down* the thermostat for the night⟩ ⟨*turn* the radio *down*⟩ **4 :** to refuse to accept **:** DECLINE, REJECT ⟨reasons . . . for *turning down* two such eligible suitors —Leon Edel⟩ **5** *chiefly Brit* **:** to liberate or release for stocking purposes ⟨*turn down* foxes⟩

[1]**turndown** \'≈,≈\ *adj* [*turn down*] **:** capable of being turned down; *esp* **:** made to wear with the upper part turned down ⟨blouse with a ~ collar⟩

[2]**turndown** \"\ *n* -S [*turn down*] **1 :** the act of turning down **:** REJECTION **2 :** something turned down ⟨the ~ of the sheet covered the frayed edge of the blanket⟩ **3 :** DOWNTURN

turn·dun \'tərn,dən\ *n* -S [native name in Australia] **:** BULL-ROARER

turned \'tərnd, 'tə̄nd, 'təind\ *adj* [ME, fr. past part. of *turnen* to turn — more at TURN] **1 :** shaped in or as if in a lathe ⟨chair made entirely of ~ members⟩ ⟨well-*turned* phrases⟩ — see LEG illustration **2 :** REVERSED, INVERTED ⟨~ letters⟩

turned shoe *var of* TURN SHOE

turned trump *n* **:** TRUMP CARD 1a

tur·nel \'tərnᵊl\ *n* -S [origin unknown] *dial Eng* **:** TUB

[1]**turn·er** \'tərnər, 'tə̄nə(r, 'təinə(r\ *n* -S [ME, fr. *turnen* to turn + *-er*] **1 :** one that turns or is used for turning ⟨cake ~⟩ ⟨log ~ in a sawmill⟩; *specif* **:** a tool used for shaping material in a lathe **2 :** one whose work is turning: as **a :** one that shapes pottery, stone, or wooden articles on a lathe **b :** an operator of a machine for cutting out jewelry stock or watch parts **c :** a garment worker who turns finished parts or articles of clothing to the right side

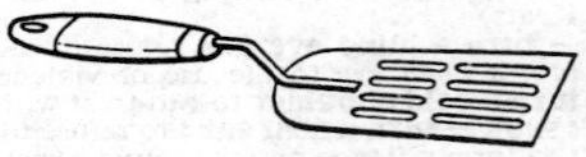

food turner

[2]**tur·ner** \"\ *n* -S [prob. alter. of *tournois*] **:** a 17th century copper coin of Scotland worth two Scots pennies

[3]**turn·er** \'tərnər, 'tu̇rn-\ *n* -S [G, fr. *turnen* to perform gymnastic exercises + *-er* — more at TURN] **:** a member of a turnverein **:** GYMNAST

tur·nera \'tərnərə\ *n, cap* [NL, after William *Turner* †1568 Eng. physician and botanist] **:** a large genus (the type of the family Turneraceae) of tropical American dicotyledonous plants having alternate leaves and solitary axillary yellow flowers often with the peduncle and petiole coherent — see DAMIANA, YELLOW ALDER

tur·ner·a·ce·ae \,tərnə'rāsē,ē\ *n pl, cap* [NL, fr. *Turnera*, type genus + *-aceae*] **:** a family of mostly tropical American herbs or shrubs (order Parietales) having flowers with five stamens, three styles, and a free ovary — **tur·ner·a·ceous** \;≈≈;rāshəs\ *adj*

tur·ner·esque \,tərnə;resk\ *adj, usu cap* [Joseph M. W. *Turner* †1851 Eng. landscape painter + E *-esque*] **:** resembling or suggesting the work of the painter Turner **:** having brilliant color effects in the manner of Turner's paintings of landscapes and seascapes ⟨*Turneresque* sunset⟩

turner harp *n* [[1]*turner*; fr. its being between the immature and mature stages of development] **:** a harp seal three years old

turner hood *n* [[1]*turner*] **:** a hooded seal three years old

turner's yellow *n* [after J. M. W. *Turner*] **1** *often cap T* **:** ORPIMENT **2** *usu cap T* **:** CASSEL YELLOW 1

tur·nery \'tərnərē, 'tə̄n-, 'təin-, -nəri\ *n* -ES [[1]*turner* + *-y*] **1 :** the process of fashioning material into cylindrical or other forms by means of a lathe **2 :** things or forms made by a turner or in the lathe; *esp* **:** turned ornamentation ⟨chairs of wood, the seats triangular, the backs, arms, and legs loaded with ~ —Horace Walpole⟩ **3 :** MACHINE SHOP

turn–furrow \'≈,(,)≈\ *n* [[1]*turn* + *furrow*] **:** MOLDBOARD 1a

turngate \'≈,≈\ *n* **:** TURNSTILE

turn·halle \'tu̇rn,hälə\ *also* **turn·hall** \'tərn,hȯl\ *n* -S [G *turnhalle*, fr. *turnen* to perform gymnastic exercises + *halle* hall, fr. OHG *halla* — more at TURN, HALL] **:** a building used as a school of gymnastics

tur·ni·ces \'tərnə,sēz\ *n pl, cap* [NL, pl. of *Turnic-*, *Turnix*] **:** a small suborder of Gruiformes comprising the button quails and the plain wanderer

tur·nic·i·dae \,tər'nisə,dē\ *n pl, cap* [NL, fr. *Turnic-*, *Turnix*, type genus + *-idae*] **:** a usu. monotypic family of Old World chiefly terrestrial birds (suborder Turnices) comprising the button quails — see TURNIX — **tur·ni·cine** \'tərnə,sīn, -sən\ *adj*

tur·ni·co·mor·phae \,tərnəkō'mȯr,fē\ *n pl, cap* [NL, fr. *Turnic-*, *Turnix* + *-o-* + *-morphae*] *in former classifications* **:** superfamily equivalent to Turnices

turn in *vt* **1 a :** to deliver up **:** hand over ⟨*turn in* an expense account⟩ ⟨*turned in* his badge and quit⟩ **b :** to inform on **:** BETRAY ⟨*turn in* a wanted man to police⟩ **c :** to give an account of oneself respecting **:** acquit oneself of ⟨*turns in* a fine performance as the hero's father⟩ ⟨*turned in* a piece of good reporting —Ellen Smith⟩ **2 :** to turn under ⟨*turn in* a fodder crop as green manure⟩ ~ *vi* **1 :** to turn from a road or path so as to enter ⟨their neighbors were *turning in* at their own gate —Dorothy C. Fisher⟩ **2 :** to go to bed ⟨must have known how late he had *turned in* —Edward Newhouse⟩ — **turn in upon oneself :** to be or become absorbed in one's own thoughts and feelings **:** INTROVERT ⟨are Americans *turning in upon themselves* . . . allowing an almost neurotic concern with internal subversion to do duty for a genuine policy —Barbara Ward⟩

turn–in \'≈,≈\ *n* -S [*turn in*] **:** something that turns in or is turned in; *specif* **:** the portion of a book covering that overlaps the three edges of both boards and is secured smoothly to them

turn indicator *n* **:** an instrument for indicating either the amount or the rate of turn of an airplane about its vertical axis — compare RELATIVE INCLINOMETER

turning *n* -S [ME, fr. gerund of *turnen* to turn — more at TURN] **1 :** the act or course of one that turns: as **a :** rotation about an axis ⟨the slow ~ of the earth⟩ **b :** BEND, FLEXURE ⟨count the ~s of a coil of wire⟩ **c :** deviation from the way or proper course ⟨straighten out the ~s of the old road⟩ ⟨a kind act that was to lead, after many ~s, to his own undoing —*Time*⟩ **d :** the act of reversing direction **:** ABOUT-FACE **2 :** the place or point of a change in direction ⟨when we come to the ~ I shall run right past it —Margaret Kennedy⟩ ⟨let only the few wrong ~s be retraced —Oscar Handlin⟩ ⟨one of the major ~s in the cultural history of the West —Irving Horne⟩ **3 a :** the art or process of forming by use of the lathe **:** TURNERY **b :** the shape of a turned member ⟨staircase with balusters of three different ~s on each tread —*Amer. Guide Series: Conn.*⟩ ⟨a trumpet-shaped ~⟩ **c turnings** *pl* **:** the chips or curls detached in the process of turnery from the material turned ⟨cleaning pads made from metal ~s⟩ **4 :** the amount of cloth (as the width of a seam) folded under along a raw edge for a seam or narrow hem

turning bar *n* **:** HORIZONTAL BAR

turning basin *n* **:** an enlarged space at the end of a canal or narrow channel to permit boats to turn around

turning bridge *n* **:** PIVOT BRIDGE

turning chisel *n* **:** a chisel used for shaping or finishing work in a lathe — see CHISEL illustration

turning engine *n* **1 :** LATHE 1 **2 :** a small engine for turning over a larger engine or turbine (as for inspection or adjustment)

turning gouge *n* **:** a tool used in woodworking for roughing down surfaces in a lathe

turning movement *n* **:** an attack in which a command is separated into two parts operating out of mutual supporting distance one of which is to hold the enemy while the other is to make a wide detour and strike at a vital point deep in the enemy's rear — compare ENVELOPMENT

turning plow *n* **:** MOLDBOARD PLOW

turning point *n* **1 :** a point at which a course of events or a situation undergoes a significant change of direction or character **:** CLIMAX, CRISIS ⟨1858 marked the *turning point* in the resistance of science to the new ideas concerning man's antiquity —R.W.Murray⟩ ⟨*turning point* in a disease⟩ ⟨*turning point* in a tragedy⟩ **2 :** a high or low point on a graph or plotted curve **3 :** a point the height of which is determined before a differential leveling instrument is moved and which is used to determine the height of the instrument after the resetting

turning rest *n* **:** a rest (as a T-shaped rest) serving as a fulcrum for a turning tool

turning saw *n* **:** COMPASS SAW

turning sickness *n* **:** an African cattle disease marked by circling movements, incoordination of the hind legs, loss of orientation, and frequently death and believed to be related to East Coast fever

turning spur *n* **:** a spur track with a curved branch returning to the main line for reversing the direction of a locomotive or train

turning square *n* **:** a square piece of lumber suitable for turning into a roller

tur·nip \'tərnəp, 'tə̄n-, 'təin-\ *n* -S *often attrib* [alter. of earlier *turnepe*, prob. fr. [1]*turn* + *neep*; fr. the well-rounded root] **1 :** either of two biennial herbs having thick edible roots eaten as a vegetable or used for feeding stock: **a :** a plant (*Brassica rapa*) having hairy leaves and typically flattened roots much broader than long **b :** RUTABAGA **2 :** a large or thick pocket watch ⟨after consulting a large ~ watch of florid gold and enamel —Ann Bridge⟩ **3 a :** a stupid person **:** BLOCKHEAD **b :** a dull or unexciting work

turnip aphid *or* **turnip louse** *n* **1 :** CABBAGE APHID **2 :** a greenish plant louse (*Rhopalosiphum pseudobrassicae*) destructive to turnips and other brassicas

turnip bean *n* **:** YAM BEAN

turnip beetle *n* **:** a chrysomelid beetle (*Entomoscelis americana*) that injures turnip plants in parts of Canada

turnip cabbage *n* **1 :** KOHLRABI **2 :** RUTABAGA

turnip flea *or* **turnip flea beetle** *or* **turnip jack** *n* **:** STRIPED FLEA BEETLE

turnip fly *n* **1** TURNIP FLEA **2 :** the adult of the cabbage maggot **3 :** TURNIP SAWFLY

turnip foot *n* **:** a ball foot with a long curved neck

turnip ghost *n, Brit* **:** a jack-o'-lantern made from a turnip rind; *broadly* **:** BUGABOO

turnip grass *n* **:** a grass (*Panicum bulbosum*) of the southwestern U. S. and adjacent Mexico used for hay

turnip leaf miner *n* **:** the maggot of a small fly (*Scaptomyza flaveola*) related to the drosophilas and introduced into America from Europe that is destructive to turnips and related vegetables

turnip maggot *n* **:** the larva of the turnip fly

turnip radish *or* **turnip–rooted radish** *n* **:** any of various radishes with somewhat spherical roots

turnip–rooted \'≈≈;≈≈\ *adj* **:** having a round flattened root

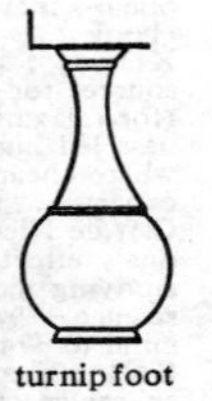

turnip foot

turnip–rooted celery \'≈,≈≈-\ *also* **turnip celery** *n* **:** CELERIAC

turnip–rooted chervil *n* **:** the edible spindle-shaped tuber of a European biennial (*Chaerophyllum bulbosum*); *also* **:** the plant itself

turnip–rooted parsley *n* **:** HAMBURG PARSLEY

turnip sawfly *n* **:** a European sawfly (*Athalia spinarum*) that cuts slits on the margins of turnip leaves in which to lay its eggs

turnip shell *n* **:** any of several large thick shelled marine gastropod mollusks of *Rapa* and related genera of the group Rachiglossa; *also* **:** the shell of such a mollusk

turnip tops *or* **turnip greens** *n pl* **:** the fresh young leaves of the turnip used as a green vegetable

turnipweed \'≈≈,≈\ *n* **:** JOE-PYE WEED

turnipwood \'≈≈,≈\ *n* **1 :** BASTARD ROSEWOOD **2 :** an Australian rosewood (*Dysoxylum fraserianum*) with bark that when fresh smells like a rutabaga

tur·nipy \'tərnəpē\ *adj* **1 :** resembling a turnip in shape or taste **2 :** lacking vitality **:** BLOODLESS, SOULLESS

tur·nix \'tərniks\ *n* [NL, short for L *coturnix* quail] **1** *cap* **:** a genus comprising small 3-toed birds that live on grassy plains of southern Europe, Asia, and northern Africa and are related to the plovers and sand grouse and constituting with the genus *Pedionomus* the family Turnicidae **2** -ES **:** any bird of the genus *Turnix* **:** BUTTON QUAIL

turnkey \'≈,≈\ *n* -S [[1]*turn* + *key*] **:** one who has charge of the keys of a prison **:** JAILER, WARDER

turn–key job \'≈,≈-\ *n* **:** a job or contract in which the contractor agrees to complete the work of building and installation to the point of readiness for operation or occupancy

turn meter *n* **:** an instrument that measures the angular velocity of an airplane about a predetermined axis

turn of a hair : the narrowest possible chance or closest approach without contact ⟨missed the approaching car by a *turn of a hair*⟩

turn off *vt* **1 a :** DISMISS, DISCHARGE ⟨at Jamaica he *turned off* the troublesome crew —W.P.Webb⟩ **b :** to dispose of **:** get rid of **:** SELL; *esp* **:** to consign (fat stock) to market **2 :** to turn aside **:** DEFLECT, EVADE ⟨*turn off* an importunate question with a laugh —H.G.Dwight⟩ **3 :** to turn out **:** PRODUCE, ACCOMPLISH, EXECUTE ⟨so versatile an artist . . . who can . . . *turn off* half a dozen Viennese songs —Irving Kolodin⟩ **4 :** to shut off or stop the flow of by or as if by turning a valve or stopcock or switch ⟨*turn off* the water⟩ ⟨*turn off* the ignition of a motor⟩ ⟨*turn off* a gas burner⟩ **5 a :** HANG 1b(1) ⟨when he was caught at last and *turned off* —Richard Hallet⟩ **b** *Brit* **:** to join in marriage **6 a :** to remove (material) by the process of turning **b :** to shape or produce by turning ~ *vi* **1 :** to deviate from a straight course or from a main road or route ⟨*turn off* into a side road⟩ ⟨*turned off* when he ought to have gone straight on⟩ **2 a** *Brit* **:** to go off **:** turn bad **:** SPOIL **b :** to change to a specified state **:** BECOME ⟨the evening had *turned off* cool —Hamilton Basso⟩

turnoff \'≈,≈\ *n* -S [*turn off*] **1 a :** a turning off **b :** a place where one turns off ⟨a wrong ~⟩ **c :** a side road **:** BRANCH **d :** a ramp leading from an express highway or turnpike **2 a :** completed product (as from a loom) **b :** number or weight of marketed livestock ⟨average annual ~ of fat bullocks —R.M.Bowman⟩

turn of speed : ability to go fast **:** capacity for speed ⟨develop great hardiness, courage, and a *turn of speed* —Richard Pollock⟩ ⟨showed a remarkable *turn of speed* —John Buchan⟩

turn of the bilge : the part of the hull between the keel and vertical sides

turn of the market *Brit* **:** [2]TURN 10d

turn of the scale : the slight excess in weight that turns a scalepan downward and that usu. constitutes an advantage to a buyer

turn on *vt* **1 :** to cause to flow by or as if by opening a valve or tap ⟨*turn* the water *on* full⟩ ⟨her charm could be *turned on* and off at will⟩ **2 :** to cause to operate ⟨*turn* the radio *on*⟩

turn out *vt* **1 a :** to drive out **:** EXPEL, EVICT ⟨voters have never *turned* a party *out* of power during a period of prosperity —*Newsweek*⟩ ⟨if you can't behave decently I'll have you *turned out* —Margaret Kennedy⟩ **b :** to put (as a horse) to pasture **2 a :** to turn inside out ⟨*turning out* his pockets to show they were empty⟩ **b :** to empty the contents of esp. for cleaning or rearranging; *also* **:** CLEAN ⟨three maids who were *turning out* the drawing room —Ethel Anderson⟩ **3 :** to cause to point outward ⟨*turns* his toes *out* like a dancer⟩ **4 :** to produce by or as if by machine **:** make with rapidity or regularity ⟨*turned out* literally thousands of airplanes and trained pilots —W.L.Davidson⟩ ⟨*turns out* books faster than most men write letters —Arthur Knight⟩ **5 :** to equip, dress, or finish in a careful or elaborate way ⟨*turned out* in a cutaway, striped trousers, a careful collar-and-tie effect, white carnation —C. W.Morton⟩ ⟨many of them are married, with wives who insist on *turning* them *out* well groomed —S.P.B.Mais⟩ **6 :** to put out (a light) by turning a valve or a switch **7 :** to call (as a company) out from rest or from shelter and into formation ~ *vi* **1 a :** to come or go out from home in answer to a summons or invitation ⟨students and faculty *turn out* to aid in shoveling the streets clear —Corey Ford⟩ ⟨*turn out* for football practice⟩ **b :** to get out of bed ⟨*turned out* about two in the morning to make our final preparations for landing —H. L.Merillat⟩ **2 :** to prove to be in the result or end ⟨if what he envisages *turned out* to be really a frontier —W.P.Webb⟩ **:** END ⟨stories that *turn out* happily⟩ ⟨waiting to see how the game *turned out*⟩ **:** become in maturity or eventually ⟨the oldest boy . . . *turned out* ornery as a bobcat —Jean Stafford⟩

turnout \'≈,≈\ *n* -S [*turn out*] **1 :** an act of turning out ⟨fireman ready for a sudden ~⟩ ⟨drank beer . . . for the few minutes until ~ time —Nigel Balchin⟩ ⟨party work did stimulate ~ —R.M.Goldman⟩ **2** *chiefly Brit* **a :** STRIKE 7a **b :** STRIKER 8 **3 :** a gathering of people for a special purpose ⟨largest ~ ever

to appear at a board meeting —David Clinton⟩ ⟨the opening game brought only a small ~⟩ **4 a :** a place where something turns out or branches off ⟨on the highway just beyond the ~ to the white church⟩ **b :** a widened space in a highway for vehicles to pass each other or for parking **c :** a track arrangement enabling locomotives and cars to pass from one track to another and consisting of a switch and frog with all connecting and operating parts **d :** a device or structure (as a joint of pipe) through which material (as water from an irrigation canal) is released **5 a :** a clearing or emptying out **b :** an act of cleaning and setting in order ⟨gave all the rooms a good ~ twice a year⟩ **6 a :** a coach or carriage together with the horses, harness, and attendants **:** EQUIPAGE ⟨smart ~ with two men on the box and a crest on the door —Frances P. Keyes⟩ **b :** manner of furnishing or outfitting **:** EQUIPMENT, RIG **c :** manner of dress **:** clothes or costume esp. for a particular occasion **:** GETUP ⟨belief that smart ~ on parade was the be-all and end-all of the military life —Al Newman⟩ **7 :** net quantity of produce yielded **:** OUTPUT, PRODUCT **8 turnouts** *or* **turnout clothes** *pl* **:** BUNKER SUIT **9 :** a position of the feet in ballet with the heels back to back

turn over *vt* **1 a :** to turn or roll from one side to the other **:** INVERT ⟨*turn* a stone *over*⟩ **b :** to turn from an upright position **:** OVERTURN, UPSET ⟨a big wave *turned* the boat *over*⟩ **2 :** to reverse the layers of (as soil) **3 :** to search (as papers) by lifting or moving one by one ⟨*turn over* clothes⟩ ⟨*turning over* old letters⟩ **4 :** to think over **:** meditate on ⟨*turning* the advice *over* in his mind⟩ **5 :** to read or examine (as a book) while turning the pages ⟨idly *turning over* a magazine⟩ **6 :** to hand over **:** DELIVER, TRANSFER ⟨funds thus collected are *turned over* to union officials —H.M.Diamond⟩ ⟨*turn over* a regiment to a new commander⟩ **7 a :** to receive and dispose of (a stock of merchandise) ⟨*turn over* its inventory 18 times a year —*Time*⟩ **b :** to handle in business **:** do business to the amount of ⟨wrote home . . . that he was *turning over* a hundred pounds a week —H.V.Morton⟩ **8 :** to transfer (as a word) from the end of one line to the beginning of the next line or from the foot of one column or page to the head of the next ~ *vi* **1 :** to tip or roll over **:** UPSET, CAPSIZE, OVERTURN **2 :** ROTATE ⟨engine *turning over* at 6000 revolutions per minute⟩ **3 a** *of one's stomach* **:** to heave with nausea **b** *of one's heart* **:** to seem to leap or lurch convulsively

[1]**turnover** \ˈ=,==\ *n* -s [*turn over*] **1 :** an act or result of turning over ⟨~ on a horizontal bar⟩ **:** UPSET ⟨collision and ~ of a bus⟩ **2 :** a turning from one side, place, or direction to its opposite **:** SHIFT, REVERSAL; *esp* **:** a marked shift of votes from one party to another **3 :** a reorganization with a view to a shift in personnel **:** SHAKE-UP **4 :** something that is turned over **:** a part (as the leaf of a book, the flap of an envelope, or a welt in a shoe) turned or folded over **5 :** a triangular or semicircular pocket of filled pastry made by turning half of a square or circle of pastry over the other and enclosing a filling ⟨apple ~⟩ ⟨chicken ~⟩ **6** *or* **turnover apprentice** *archaic* **:** one whose indentures are transferred from one master (as a master printer) to another to enable him to complete his apprenticeship **7 a :** the amount of business done **:** degree of business activity ⟨gilt-edged securities were firm but the ~ small⟩ **b :** the amount of material on which some process has been performed ⟨the ~ of a mine⟩ or the rate at which material is processed ⟨~ of a machine⟩ **8 a :** movement (as of goods, animals, or people) into, through, and out of a place considered all as a single process ⟨a rapid ~ of patients in a well-organized hospital⟩ ⟨daily ~ of hogs in the stockyards⟩ **b :** the receipt, placing on sale, and disposal of a stock of merchandise; *also* **:** the rate at which goods are sold **c :** a cycle of purchase, sale, and replacement of a stock of goods, ⟨a ~ four times a year⟩; *also* **:** the ratio of sales for a stated period to average inventory **d :** the number of persons hired within a period to replace those leaving or dropped from a working force; *also* **:** the ratio of this number to the number in the average force maintained **9** *Brit* **:** a light essay on a matter of current interest beginning in the last column of page one of a newspaper and continuing onto page two **10 :** TURNOVER FREQUENCY

[2]**turnover** \"\ *adj* [*turn over*] **:** capable of being turned over **:** made with a part folded over ⟨~ collar⟩

turnover frequency *n* **:** the frequency (as 500 cycles per second) at which the transition is made from constant velocity recording to constant amplitude recording in making phonograph records

turnover hinge *n* **:** a hinge designed so that the door to which it is attached can be swung open flat against the wall

turnover tax *n, Brit* **:** a tax on total transactions or gross sales usu. applicable to all sales of commodities by manufacturers, wholesalers, and retailers

[1]**turnpike** \ˈ=,=\ *n* [ME *turnepike*, fr. *turnen* to turn + *pike* (point)] **1** *obs* **:** a revolving frame bearing spikes and used as a barrier in medieval warfare **2 :** TOLL BAR, TOLLGATE **3** *or* **turnpike road a :** a toll road; *esp* **:** a toll expressway **b :** a free road orig. maintained as a toll road **c :** a main road **:** a paved highway having a crowned surface **4** *Scot* **:** a winding spiral stairway

[2]**turnpike** \"\ *vt* -ED/-ING/-S **1 :** to make into or like a turnpike road **2 :** CROWN 5c

turnpike geranium *n* **:** JERUSALEM OAK 1

turnpike man *n* **:** a man who collects tolls at a turnpike

turn·pik·er \-kə(r)\ *n* [[1]*turnpike* + *-er*] **:** one that travels on a turnpike

turnpin \ˈ=,=\ *n* **:** a tapered hardwood pin used to enlarge the ends of lead pipe

turnplate \ˈ=,=\ *n* **1 :** TURNTABLE **2 :** TURNSHEET

turnplow \ˈ=,=\ *n* **:** MOLDBOARD PLOW

turn ratio *or* **turns ratio** *n* **:** the ratio of the number of turns in one of two inductively coupled circuits to the number in the other

turn round *var of* TURN AROUND

turn-round \ˈ=,=\ *n* -s [*turn round*] **1 :** a place for turning around **2 :** TURNABOUT 3

turnrow \ˈ=,=\ *n* **:** a strip of usu. uncropped land at the side or end of a field upon which a plow may be turned at the end of the furrow

turns \ˈtərnz\ *n pl* [fr. pl. of [2]*turn*] **:** a watchmaker's lathe — often used with *pair*

turnscrew \ˈ=,=\ *n* [[1]*turn* + *screw*] **:** a device for turning screws **:** SCREWDRIVER, WRENCH

turnsheet \ˈ=,=\ *n* **:** a heavy, flat, iron or steel plate used in place of rails at track intersections for turning cars from one line to another — called also *turnplate*

turn shoe *also* **turned shoe** *n* **:** a light flexible single-soled shoe or slipper usu. worn by women and made by sewing upper and sole together both wrong side out, removing the last, turning right side out, attaching the heel, and finishing

turn-sick \ˈ=,=\ *n* [obs. E *turn-sick* vertigo, fr. ME *turnseke*, fr. *turnseke*, adj., dizzy, fr. *turn* + *seke* sick] **:** GID

turn·sole \ˈtərn,sōl\ *n* -s [ME *turnesole*, fr. MF *tournesol*, fr. OIt *tornasole*, fr. *tornare* to turn (fr. ML) + *sole* sun, fr. L *sol* (acc. *solem*) — more at TURN, SOLAR] **1 :** any of several plants whose flowers or stems are supposed to follow the movement of the sun: **a :** HELIOTROPE 1b **b :** SUNFLOWER **c :** SUN SPURGE **d :** a double-flowered tulip (*Tulipa suaveolens*) of southern Russia **2 :** a European annual herb (*Chrozophora tinctoria*) of the family Euphorbiaceae the juice of which is turned blue by ammonia **3 a :** a purple dye obtained from the turnsole (sense 2) **b :** LITMUS

turnspit \ˈ=,=\ *n* [[1]*turn* + *spit*] **1 a :** one who turns a spit **b :** a small dog with long body and short crooked legs formerly used in a treadmill to turn a spit **c :** ROASTING JACK **2 :** a spit that may be rotated

turnstile \ˈ=,=\ *n* **1 a :** a post with four arms pivoted on the top set in a gateway or passageway so that persons can pass through but cattle cannot **b :** a similar device set in an entrance for controlling or counting the persons entering ⟨~s at the ball park were clicking busily⟩ **2 :** a device resembling in appearance a turnstile and turned by hand to traverse the turret slide of a lathe **3** *or* **turnstile antenna :** a television transmitting antenna consisting of two horizontal dipoles at right angles to each other usu. used in the VHF-UHF frequency range and when it is desired to have signals transmitted in all directions equally well

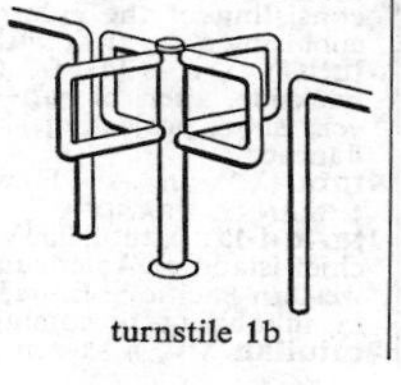

turnstile 1b

turnstone \ˈ=,=\ *n* [[1]*turn* + *stone*; fr. its habit of turning over stones to find food] **:** any of various widely distributed migratory shorebirds (genus *Arenaria*) of the family Charadriidae that typically resemble the related plovers and sandpipers in form and habits; *esp* **:** a widely distributed New and Old World bird (*A. interpres*) having the upperparts variegated with black and chestnut, the breast black, and the abdomen white — see BLACK TURNSTONE, RUDDY TURNSTONE

turntable \ˈ=,==\ *n* **1 :** a revolvable platform: as **a :** a pivoted structure that supports a platform or track and revolves in a horizontal plane for turning wheeled vehicles ⟨locomotive ~⟩ **b :** LAZY SUSAN **c :** a support with horizontal bearings for holding a reel for winding or unwinding rope **d :** a rotating platform that carries a phonograph record **2 :** a machine that reproduces speech or music from records and transcriptions for radiobroadcasting **3 :** a stunt performed on the trampoline consisting of a front drop followed by a horizontal rotation of the body in the air into a second front drop

turntable ladder *n* **:** AERIAL LADDER

turntail \ˈ=,=\ *n* [fr. the phrase *turn tail*] **:** one who turns tail and runs away **:** DESERTER, COWARD

turn the trencher *n* **:** SPIN THE PLATE

turn to *vi* **:** to apply oneself to work **:** act vigorously ⟨all hands *turn to* and help the cook with the dishwashing —H.A. Calahan⟩ ⟨must sometimes *turn to* and earn a living like other persons —Jacob Epstein⟩

turn-to \ˈ=,=\ *n* -s [*turn to*] **1 :** FIGHT, BOUT **2 :** a turning of one's attention and efforts to the business at hand **:** a setting to work

turn-tree \ˈ=,=\ *n, Brit* **:** the drum of a windlass

turn under *vt* **1 :** to bend or fold downward or underneath ⟨pull the end of the sheet down and *turn* it *under*⟩ **2 :** to put (as soil) underneath from the surface by plowing or digging ~ *vi* **:** to bend or curve toward the underside

turn-under \ˈ=,==\ *n* -s [*turn under*] **1 :** the act of turning under **2 :** a curving at or toward the underside or the amount of such curvature

turn up *vt* **1 a :** to turn or fold so as to bring the bottom side on top or on the outside ⟨*turn up* a coat collar⟩ ⟨*turned up* his shirt cuffs⟩ **b :** to shorten (as a skirt) esp. by making a hem or increasing the width of a hem **c :** to make (a cuff) by folding over the bottom of a sleeve or pant leg **2 a :** to bring from underneath to the surface (as by digging or plowing) **b :** FIND, DISCOVER ⟨readily have *turned up* additional examples of the term —C.J.Lovell⟩ ⟨the papers soon *turned up* evidence of skullduggery —*Newsweek*⟩ **3 :** to raise or increase by turning a valve or stopcock ⟨*turn up* the flame of a burner⟩ ⟨*turn* the lights *up*⟩ **4** *Brit* **a :** to look up (as a word) in a book ⟨assuming again that the interested reader will *turn up* the poem —F. R.Leavis⟩ **b :** to refer to (a book) **:** CONSULT **5 a :** to bring to a supine position **b :** KILL **6 :** to call (a crew) on deck **7 :** to turn (a card) face upward **8** *Brit* **a :** to give up **:** RELINQUISH **b :** to turn loose **:** set free **9 :** to reach a rotational speed of **:** develop power to the extent of ⟨engine *turns up* 101 horsepower⟩ ~ *vi* **1 :** to appear or come to light unexpectedly or after being lost ⟨number of new species will *turn up* —C.H. Curran⟩ **2 a :** to turn out to be ⟨*turned up* missing at roll call⟩ **:** become visible or evident ⟨name is always *turning up* in the newspapers⟩ **b :** to arrive or show up at an appointed or expected time or place ⟨*turned up* half an hour late for work⟩ **3 :** to happen or occur unexpectedly ⟨something always *turned up* to prevent their meeting⟩ **4** *of a ship* **:** TACK — **turn up one's nose :** to show scorn or disdain — **turn up one's toes** *slang* **:** DIE

[1]**turnup** \ˈ=,=\ *n* -s [*turn up*] **1** *chiefly Brit* **:** DISTURBANCE, FUSS, ROW; *esp* **:** FISTFIGHT, SET-TO **2 a :** the turned-up part of an article of clothing **b** *chiefly Brit* **:** a cuff on a trouser leg ⟨the black mud closed over his shoes and the ~s of his trousers —Graham Greene⟩ **3 a :** a card turned faceup to fix or propose the trump **b :** UPCARD 1a

[2]**turnup** \"\ *adj* [*turn up*] **1 :** turned up ⟨~ nose⟩ **2 :** made or fitted to be turned up ⟨~ collar⟩

turn·ver·ein \ˈtərnvə,rīn, ˈtu̇rn-, -nfə,-\ *n* [G, fr. *turnen* to perform gymnastic exercises + *verein* society, club — more at TURN, VEREIN] **:** an association of gymnasts and athletes **:** an athletic club

[1]**turn·wrest** \ˈ=,rest\ *or* **turn·wrist** \-rist\ *adj* [[1]*turn* + *wrest* or *wrist* (dial. var. of *wrest*)] *Brit* **:** having a reversible moldboard ⟨~ plow⟩

[2]**turnwrest** \"\ *or* **turnwrist** \"\ *n, Brit* **:** SWIVEL PLOW

tu·ro·ni·an \t(y)u̇ˈrōnēən\ *adj, usu cap* [F *turonien* of Tours, fr. LL *Turoni* Tours, France (fr. L *Turones, Turoni*, a people of ancient Gaul) + F *-en* -an] **:** of, relating to, or constituting a subdivision of the European Cretaceous — see GEOLOGIC TIME table

tu·ro·phile \ˈt(y)u̇rə,fīl\ *n* -s [irreg. fr. Gk *tyros* cheese + E *-phile* — more at TYR-] **:** a gourmet of cheese **:** a cheese fancier

turp \ˈtərp\ *vb* -ED/-ING/-S [by shortening] **:** TURPENTINE

[1]**tur·pen·tine** \ˈtərpən,tīn, ˈtə̄p-, ˈtəip-, -pᵊm,-\ *n* -s [ME *terebentyne, terbentyne, turpentyne*, fr. MF & ML; MF *terebentine, terbentine, tourbentine*, fr. ML *terbentina* (fr. L *terebinthina*) & L *terebinthina*, fem. of *terebinthinus* of terebinth, fr. *terebinthus* terebinth (fr. Gk *terebinthos*) + *-inus* -ine] **1 a :** a yellow to brown semifluid oleoresin that exudes from the terebinth tree — called also *Chian turpentine* **b :** any of various oleoresins that are derived from coniferous trees and are obtained in crude form as yellowish viscous exudates of characteristic odor and taste from incisions in the tree trunks and that usu. thicken and solidify in the air: as (1) **:** CANADA BALSAM (2) **:** VENICE TURPENTINE (3) **:** STRASBOURG TURPENTINE (4) **:** GALIPOT (5) **:** RUSSIAN TURPENTINE **2** *or* **turpentine oil a :** the colorless or slightly yellowish mobile flammable pungent biting essential oil that is obtained by distillation from turpentine oleoresins esp. from longleaf, slash, and other pines, that is a mixture of terpenes with alpha-pinene usu. as the principal component, that oxidizes in air to a solid, and that is used chiefly as a solvent and thinner (as in paints and varnishes), as a raw material for synthetic camphor and other chemicals, and in medicine — called also *gum spirits, gum turpentine, spirits of turpentine* **b :** a similar oil obtained by steam distillation of chipped pine stumpwood and butt logs or of extracts of the chips — called also *steam-distilled wood turpentine, wood turpentine;* compare PINE OIL a **c :** a similar oil obtained by the carbonization of pinewood — called also *destructively distilled wood turpentine* **d :** a similar oil obtained as a by-product of the sulfate process — called also *sulfate turpentine* **3 a :** TURPENTINE TREE c **b :** TURPENTINE WEED

[2]**turpentine** \"\ *vb* -ED/-ING/-S *vt* **1 :** to saturate or rub with turpentine **:** apply turpentine to **2 :** to extract turpentine from (pine trees) by scarifying or wounding the surface to make resin exude ~ *vi* **:** to collect or make turpentine

turpentine beetle *n* **:** any of several bark beetles of the genus *Dendroctonus* (esp. *D. valens*) whose larvae live under the bark of pine stumps or trees

turpentine borer *n* **:** a borer that is the larva of a buprestid beetle (*Buprestis apricans*) and that bores in pines in the southeastern U.S.

turpentine moth *n* **:** any of several small moths (family Tortricidae) whose larvae eat the tender shoots of pine and fir trees causing an exudation of pitch or resin

turpentine orchard *n* **:** a stand of pine bled for turpentine

turpentine pine *n* **:** LONGLEAF PINE

tur·pen·tin·er \-īnə(r)\ *n* -s **:** a worker who gathers turpentine

turpentine substitute *n* **:** a petroleum distillate intermediate between gasoline and kerosine

turpentine tree *n* **:** a tree that yields a turpentine or turpentinic product: as **a :** TEREBINTH **b :** a pine or other turpentine-producing conifer — compare VENICE TURPENTINE **c :** any of several Australian trees (as various eucalypts) that yield a resinous fluid; *esp* **:** a tree (*Syncarpia laurifolia*) of the family Myrtaceae that is often grown for shelterbelts and hedging

turpentine weed *n* **:** any of several No. American herbs with an odor resembling that of turpentine: as **a** (1) **:** PRAIRIE DOCK 1 (2) **:** COMPASS PLANT a **b :** a California blue curls (*Trichostema laxum*) with purple or deep blue flowers

tur·pen·tin·ic \;tərpən;tinik\ *also* **tur·pen·tin·ous** \ˈ==,tīnəs\ *or* **tur·pen·tiny** \-nē\ *adj* **1 :** of or relating to turpentine **2 :** resembling turpentine

tur·peth \ˈtərpəth\ *n* -s [alter. (influenced by NL *turpethum* turpeth, fr. Ar *turbid*) of earlier *turbith*, fr. ME *turbit*, fr. MF *turbit*, fr. Ar *turbid*] **1 :** the root of a tropical Asiatic and Australian vine (*Operculina turpethum*) formerly used in medicine as a purgative; *also* **:** the plant itself — called also *Indian jalap, vegetable turpeth* **2** *also* **turpeth mineral :** CALOMEL

tur·pis cau·sa \ˈtərpə̇sˈkōzə\ *n* [L, base cause] **:** a cause or consideration that is base or immoral and therefore not sufficient to support a contractual obligation

turpis con·trac·tus \-kənˈtraktəs\ *n* [L, base contract] **:** an immoral and therefore unenforceable contract

tur·pi·tude \ˈtərpə,tüd, ˈtə̄p-, ˈtəip-, -ə,tyüd\ *n* -s [MF, fr. L *turpitudo*, fr. *turpis* vile, foul, base + *-tudo* -tude; prob. akin to L *trepit* he turns — more at TROPE] **:** inherent baseness or vileness of principle, words, or actions **:** DEPRAVITY ⟨moral ~⟩; *also* **:** a base act or action ⟨the various ~s of modern society⟩

turps \ˈtərps\ *n pl but usu sing in constr* [by shortening & alter.] **:** TURPENTINE

[1]**tur·quoise** *also* **tur·quois** \ˈtər,k(w)ȯiz, ˈtə̄,-, ˈtəi,-\ *n, pl* **turquoises** [ME *turkeis, torcas, turcas*, fr. MF *turquoyse, turquaise*, fr. fem. of *turquoys, turqueis* Turkish, fr. OF, fr. *Turc* Turk] **1 :** a mineral $CuAl_6(PO_4)_4(OH)_8.5H_2O$ consisting of a blue, bluish green, or greenish gray hydrous basic copper aluminum phosphate isomorphous with chalcosiderite, occurring usu. in reniform masses with a botryoidal surface, taking a high polish, and changing sometimes to a green tint but when sky blue valued as a gem and mined in Persia and Arizona and New Mexico **2 a :** a variable color averaging a light greenish blue that is deeper and slightly greener than average turquoise blue and greener and deeper than average aqua or average robin's-egg blue (sense 1) **b :** a light bluish green that is bluer and paler than average turquoise green, slightly deeper and very slightly bluer than average aqua green (sense 1), and bluer, lighter, and stronger than robin's-egg blue (sense 2)

[2]**turquoise** *also* **turquois** \"\ *adj* **1 a :** consisting of turquoise ⟨a ~ carving⟩ **b :** set or set off with turquoise or turquoises ⟨a ~ brooch⟩ **2 :** of either of the colors turquoise or turquoise blue

tur·quoise·berry \ˈ=,=- — *see* BERRY\ *n* **1 :** a Tasmanian herb (*Drymophila cyanocarpa*) of the family Liliaceae with white flowers and blue fruits **2 :** ASIATIC SWEETLEAF

turquoise blue *n* **:** a variable color averaging a light greenish blue that is paler and slightly bluer than average turquoise (sense 2a), deeper and very slightly greener than average aqua, and greener and deeper than average robin's-egg blue (sense 1)

turquoise green *n* **:** a variable color averaging a light bluish green that is greener and deeper than turquoise (sense 2b) or average aqua green (sense 1) and bluer and deeper than robin's-egg blue (sense 2)

tur·ret \ˈtər·ət, ˈtə·rət, ˈtu̇rət *usu* -əd·+V\ *n* -s *often attrib* [ME *turet, touret*, fr. MF *torete, turete, tourete*, fr. OF, dim. of *tor, tur* tower — more at TOWER] **1 :** a little tower; *specif* **:** an ornamental structure at one of the angles of a larger structure **2** *heraldry* **:** a small tower on top of a larger tower **3 :** a holder for several tools or devices: as **a :** a pivoted toolholder in a machine tool by which each of various tools can be rapidly moved to the work — called also *turrethead* **b :** a device for supplying steam from the boiler of a locomotive to auxiliary devices (as a whistle or injector) **c** (1) **:** a manifold on a fire apparatus supplying heavy streams of water directly from pumps (2) *also* **turret nozzle** *or* **turret pipe :** a monitor mounted on the bed of a fire truck or on the deck of a fireboat **d :** a television device holding usu. four lenses and used in association with the camera tube **:** LENS TURRET **4 a :** a military siege device consisting of a building often square in form, sometimes having as many as 20 stories, usu. moved on wheels, and carrying soldiers, rams, ladders, and bridges for breaching or scaling a wall **b :** an enclosed, cylindrical, or dome-shaped armored structure usu. revolving, containing one or more guns, and forming part of a military vehicle, airplane, or ship: as (1) **:** a gunner's fixed or movable enclosure in an airplane usu. capable of being rotated on one or more axes and often of being raised or lowered so as to protrude a maximal distance only when manned for action (2) **:** a revolving structure on a warship protecting the breech portion of the one or more guns mounted within it — compare BARBETTE (3) **:** the upper structure of a tank rotatable for swinging the gun mounted within it

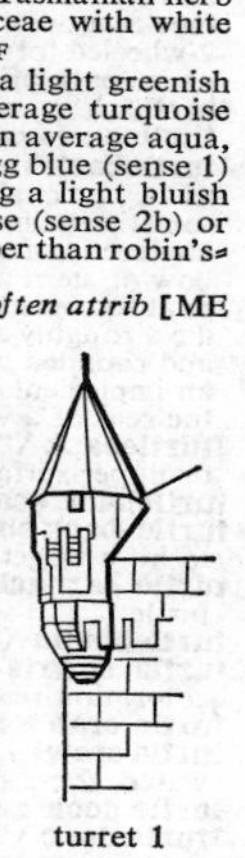

turret 1

turret angle-rack tool *n* **:** a tool for turning short tapers in a turret lathe

turret captain *n* **:** a petty officer (as in the U.S. Navy) appointed to the command of a turret crew and ranking next to the officer while in a turret

turret clock *n* **:** a clock for a turret or tower having one or more dials separate from the movement

turret cutter *n* **:** a coal cutter adjustable to various heights of coal cutting and mounted on a pivoted frame — called also *overcutter*

turret deck *n* **:** a narrow superstructure running from stem to stern on the upper deck of a steam cargo ship having a rounded gunwale and sides curved inward convexly

turret drier *n* **:** a wooden building of usu. five stories with ventilating and heating devices used for drying leather

turret drill *n* **:** a single-spindle or gang drill in which the spindle supports a head carrying a number of tools and so designed that each tool may in turn be brought to a position suitable for performing its function

tur·ret·ed \-əd·əd\ *adj* [*turret* + *-ed*] **1 :** furnished with or as if with turrets ⟨a ~ fortress⟩ ⟨a ~ cloud⟩ **2** *of a seashell* **:** having whorls forming a high conical spiral

turrethead \ˈ==,=\ *n* **:** TURRET 3a

turret lathe *n* **:** a lathe having a turret for holding various different cutting tools

turret slide tool *n* **:** a vertically or horizontally adjustable slide that supports one or more cutting tools for use with a turret lathe

turret spider *n* **:** a Californian spider (*Atypoides riversi*) that forms burrows with external turrets

turret steamer *n* **:** a whaleback steamer with hatch coamings extending almost continuously fore and aft

turret taper tool *n* **:** a tool held in the turret of a turret lathe and used for turning tapers

turret tuner *n* **:** a radio tuner having a number of complete circuits mounted in a drum by whose rotation switching to different stations is done

tur·ri·cal \ˈtərəkəl\ *adj* [L *turris* tower + E *-ical* — more at TOWER] **:** of, relating to, or resembling a turret or tower

tur·ric·u·la \(,)təˈrikyələ\ *n, pl* **turricu·lae** \-yə,lē\ [NL, fr. L, small tower, dim. of *turris* tower] **:** a utensil or ornament (as a candlestick) shaped like a tower

tur·ric·u·lar \-lə(r)\ *adj* [L *turricula* small tower + E *-ar*] **:** shaped like or resembling a tower

tur·ric·u·late \-yələt, -yə,lāt\ *or* **tur·ric·u·lat·ed** \-ād·əd\ *adj* [L *turricula* + E *-ate* or *-ated* (fr. *-ate* + *-ed*)] **:** having a small turret **:** formed like a small turret **:** TURRETED

tur·ri·dae \ˈtərə,dē\ [NL, fr. *Turris*, type genus + *-idae*] *syn of* TURRITIDAE

tur·rif·er·ous \(,)təˈrif(ə)rəs\ *adj* [L *turrifer* turriferous (fr. *turris* tower + *-fer* -ferous) + E *-ous*] **:** bearing towers

tur·ri·lite \ˈtərə,līt\ *n* -s [NL *Turrilites*] **:** an ammonoid or fossil of the genus *Turrilites*

tur·ri·li·tes \,==ˈlīd·(,)ēz\ *n, cap* [NL, fr. L *turris* tower + Gk *lithos* stone] **:** a genus of Cretaceous ammonoid cephalopods having a spiral sinistral turreted shell with the later whorls more or less separate

tur·ri·lit·i·cone \,tərəˈlid·ə,kōn\ *n* -s [*turrilite* + *-i-* + *cone*] **:** an ammonite asymmetrically coiled like a gastropod with a high spire

tur·ris \ˈtərə̇s\ *n, cap* [NL, fr. L, tower — more at TOWER] **:** a genus of small marine snails having a graceful shell shaped like a spindle and being the type of the family Turritidae

tur·ri·tel·la \,tərəˈtelə\ *n* [NL, irreg. fr. L *turris* + NL *-ella*] **1** *cap* **:** a genus (the type of the family Turritellidae) of marine gastropod mollusks having an elongated turreted shell com-

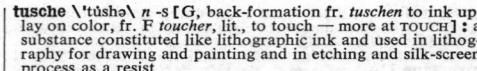

posed of many whorls with a rounded aperture and a horny multispiral operculum **2** *also* **tur·ri·tel·lid** \-ləd\ -s : any mollusk or shell of the genus *Turritella* or family Turritellidae — see SCREW SHELL

¹tur·ri·tid \'tərəd\ *also* **tur·rid** \'tor'id\ *adj* [NL *Turridae* & *Turritidae*] : of or relating to the Turritidae

²turrid \"\ *n* -s : a mollusk of the family Turritidae

tur·rit·i·dae \(,)tə'rid.ə,dē\ *n pl, cap* [NL, irreg. fr. *Turris*, type genus + *-idae*] : a large and widely distributed family of marine gastropod mollusks (suborder Stenoglossa) — see TURRIS

tur·rum \'tərəm\ *n* -s [native name in Australia] : a large Australian trevally prob. of the genus *Caranx*

turs *pl of* TUR

turse \'tərs\ *n* -s [ME(Sc) *turs* bundle, truss, fr. MF *tourse*] — more at TRUSS *chiefly Scot* : BUNDLE, LOAD

tur·si·ops \'tərsē,äps\ *n, cap* [NL, fr. *Tursio*, genus of dolphins (fr. L, a kind of dolphin, fr. Gk *thyrsiōn*, fr. *thyrsos* thyrsus) + *-ops*] : a genus of rather large heavy-bodied dolphins having a truncate beak and a dorsal fin shaped like a sickle

¹tur·tle \'tərtəl, 't(ə)l, 'tə(r)l, 'tə(r)l\ *n* -ES [ME *turtle*, *turtle*, fr. OE *turtla*, fr. L *turtur*, of imit. origin like Gk *tetraōn* heath cock, *tetrix*, a bird (perh. the pipit), Skt *tittira* francolin] *archaic* : TURTLEDOVE ⟨the voice of the ∼ is heard in our land —Song of Sol 2:12 (AV)⟩

²turtle \"\ *n, pl* **turtles** *also* **turtle** *often attrib* [prob. by folk etymology (influence of ¹*turtle*) fr. F *tortue*, prob. fr. (assumed) VL *tartaruca*, fr. LL *tartarucha*, fem. of *tartaruchus* of Tartarus, fr. Gk *tartarouchos*, fr. *Tartaros* Tartarus, the infernal regions; fr. the turtle's having been regarded in ancient times as an infernal creature] **1** : a reptile of the order Testudinata — used esp. of the more aquatic and esp. marine members of the order; compare TERRAPIN, TORTOISE; see GREEN TURTLE **2** : SIENNA BROWN **3 a** : the curved section of the plate cylinder of a type-revolving press to which the type matter is locked **b** : a 2-wheeled form truck for making up and transporting a newspaper page prior to stereotyping **4** : TURTLENECK

turtle 1a

³turtle \"\ *vi* **turtled; turtling; turtling** \|d·liŋ, |t(ə)l-\ **turtles** : to catch turtles esp. as an occupation

¹turtleback \'∠∠,∠\ *n* [¹*turtle* + *back*] : a raised convex surface: as **a** : an oval boss esp. on furniture **b** : a raised obstruction sometimes illuminated and placed in the pavement at a street intersection for the guidance of traffic **c** : a convex deck at the bow or stern and sometimes extending from bow to stern of a boat so made to shed the seas quickly — called also *turtle deck* **d** : a roughly shaped artifact of stone chipped flat on one side and rounded on the other and prob. a blank form from which an implement might be chipped **e** : a rounded projection on the rear of a vehicle

²turtleback \"\ *or* **turtle-backed** \'∠∠,∠\ *adj* : having a back or upper surface shaped like the back of a turtle

turtleback scale *n* : a soft scale (*Lecanium hesperidium*)

turtle-back shooting *n* : archery shooting with high trajectory to hit a target laid flat on the ground

turtle barnacle *n* : a barnacle living on the shell of a marine turtle

turtlebloom \'∠∠,∠\ *n* : TURTLEHEAD

turtle cowrie *n* : a large cowrie (*Cypraea testudinaria*) in coloration resembling the shell of a tortoise

turtle crab *n* : GULF-WEED CRAB

turtle crawl *n* : the trail of a tortoise between its nest and the water **2** : a pen in which turtles are kept

turtle deck *n* : TURTLEBACK c

¹turtledove \'∠∠,∠\ *n* [ME *turtildove*, fr. *turtil*, *turtle* turtledove + *dove* — more at TURTLE] **1 a** : an Old World wild dove of *Streptopelia* or related genera; *esp* : a common European bird (*S. turtur*) noted for its plaintive cooing and being mostly cinnamon brown with a white-bordered black patch on each side of the neck and white-tipped outer tail feathers **b** : MOURNING DOVE **c** : a small Australian dove (*Stictopeleia cuneata*) of terrestrial habits **2** : BELOVED, SWEETHEART **3** : a dark gray to reddish gray

²turtledove \"\ *vi* -ED/-ING/-s : to be affectionately demonstrative

turtle grass *n* **1** : EELGRASS 1 **2** : a submerged marine plant (*Thalassia testudinum*) of the family Hydrocharitaceae of the coasts of Florida and the West Indies with elongated linear leaves and dioecious flowers

turtle green *n* : a moderate yellow green that is greener and paler than average moss green and yellower and paler than average pea green or apple green (sense 1)

turtlehead \'∠∠,∠\ *n* [²*turtle* + *head*; so called fr. the shape of the flower] : CHELONE; *esp* : a showy perennial herb (*Chelone glabra*) of marshy lands of eastern and central No. America with waxy lanceolate to ovate leaves and flowers with the lower parts creamy white and the upper parts pale pink to deep purple

turtle knot *n* : TURLE KNOT

turtleneck \'∠∠,∠\ *n* **1 a** : a high close-fitting turnover collar used esp. for sweaters; *also* : a sweater with a turtleneck

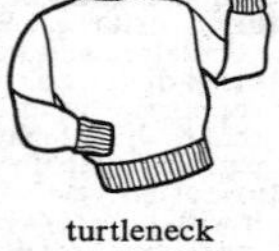

turtle peg *n* : a detachable sharp steel spearhead attached to a cord for use in harpooning sea turtles

tur·tler \|d·lə(r), |t(ə)l-\ *n* -s [²*turtle* + *-er*] : one that hunts turtles or their eggs **2** : one that deals in turtles

turtles *pl of* TURTLE, *pres 3d sing of* TURTLE

turtle twist *n* **1** : TORTOISE SHELL **2** : TURTLE COWRIE

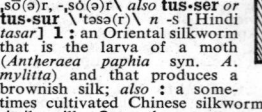

turtleneck

turtle stone *n* : a calcareous concretion divided in the interior by cracks partly or wholly filled by crystallized minerals : SEPTARIUM

turt·let \-lət\ *n* -s [²*turtle* + *-et*] : a young or small-sized turtle

turtling *pres part of* TURTLE

tur·to·sa \,tər'tōsə\ *n* -s [origin unknown] : AFRICAN OAK

turves *pl of* TURF

¹tus·can \'təskən\ *n* -s [ME, fr. L *tuscanus*, adj., Etruscan, fr. *Tusci* Etruscans + *-anus* -an] **1** *cap* **a** *archaic* : ETRUSCAN **b** : a native or inhabitant of Tuscany in Italy **2** *cap* **a** : the Italian language spoken in Tuscany **b** : the standard literary dialect of Italian **3** *usu cap* : a fine wheat straw of Italian origin used for hats

²tuscan \"\ *adj, usu cap* [L *tuscanus*] **1 a** *archaic* : ETRUSCAN **b** : relating to, situated in, inhabiting, or coming from Tuscany in Italy **2 a** : of or relating to one of the classical orders of architecture that is of Roman origin and is rudely plain in style **b** : of or relating to the art of Tuscany principally from the 14th through the 16th centuries and comprising the Florentine and Sienese schools

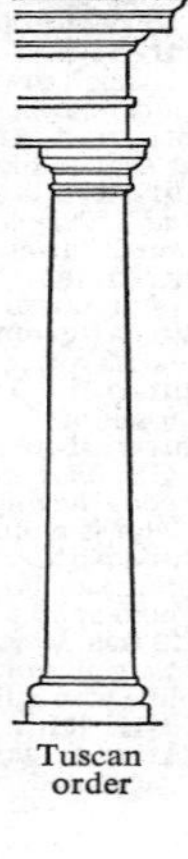

tuscan brown *n, often cap T* : a moderate brown to reddish brown that is darker than pencilwood — called also *Etruscan, Mecca, Mohawk*

tuscan red *n, often cap T* **1** : a moderate reddish brown that is yellower and deeper than roan, redder, slightly darker, and much stronger than mahogany, and redder, stronger, and slightly darker than oxblood — called also *madder Indian red, mascara* **2** : a purplish red pigment that is an iron red made by treating ferric oxide with a lake (as an alizarin lake)

tuscan tan *n, often cap 1st T* : SAUTERNE 2

tus·ca·ny \-nē, -ni\ *n* -ES *often cap* [fr. *Tuscany*, region in west-central Italy] : COLCOTHAR 2

tus·ca·ro·ra *or* **tuscaroras** *usu cap* [Tuscarora *Skǎ-rū-rē²*] **1 a** : an Iroquoian people of No. Carolina and later of New York and Ontario **b** : a member of such people **2** : the language of the Tuscarora people

tusch \'tủsh\ *n* -ES [G] : a flourish or fanfare of brass wind musical instruments and drums

tusche \'tủshə\ *n* -s [G, back-formation fr. *tuschen* to ink up, lay on color, fr. F *toucher*, lit., to touch — more at TOUCH] : a substance constituted like lithographic ink and used in lithography for drawing and painting and in etching and silk-screen process as a resist

tusch·er \-shə(r)\ *n* -s [*tusche* + *-er*] : one that prepares drawings on lithographic stones or plates using tusche and a steel pen

tus·cu·lan \'təskyələn\ *adj, usu cap* [L *Tusculanus*, fr. *Tusculum*, ancient town of Latium + L *-anus* -an] : of or relating to ancient Tusculum

¹tush \'tỏsh\ *n* -ES [ME *tusch*, fr. OE *tūsc*; akin to OFris *tusk* tooth, Goth *tunthus* — more at TOOTH] : a long pointed tooth : TUSK: as **a** : a horse's canine **b** : a small or dwarfed tusk in an Indian elephant

²tush \"\ *interj* [ME *tussch*] — used to express disdain, contempt or reproach ⟨∼; these are trifles, and mere old wives' tales —Christopher Marlowe⟩

³tush \'tỏsh\ *or* **tush·in** \-shən\ *n, pl* **tush** *or* **tushes** *or* **tushin** *or* **tushins** *usu cap* : a member of a Georgian people north of Tiflis

tushed \'tỏsht\ *adj* : having tushes : TUSKED

tush·ery \'tỏshərē\ *n* -ES [²*tush* + *-ery*] : writing of poor quality distinguished esp. by the presence of affectedly archaic diction

tu·si *also* **tus·si** \'tūsē, -si\ *or* **tut·si** \'tūts-\ *n, pl* **tusi** *or* **tusis** *also* **tussi** *or* **tussis** *or* **tutsi** *or* **tutsis** *usu cap* : the ruling and cattle-owning class of the Rundi in Urundi in East Africa who presumably are cognate with the Hima people northward and whose extreme average height suggests an affinity with the Nilotes — called also *Watusi*

¹tusk \'təsk\ *n* -s [ME, alter. of *tux*, fr. OE *tūx*; akin to OE *tūsc* tush — more at TUSH] **1 a** : an elongated greatly enlarged tooth that projects when the mouth is closed, serves to dig up food or as a weapon, and is usu. a canine tooth but on an elephant an incisor **b** : a long protruding tooth **c** : one of the small projections on a tusk tenon

²tusk \"\ *vb* -ED/-ING/-s *vt* **1** : to dig or turn up with a tusk; *also* **2** : to gash or gore with a tusk in the manner of an elephant **2** : to equip or adorn with or as if with tusks ∼ *vi* **1** : to thrust or dig up the ground with a tusk **2** : to bare or gnash the teeth

³tusk \"\ *n* -s [Shetland Norse; akin to Norw, Dan, & Sw *torsk* codfish — more at TORSK] : CUSK 1

tusked \-kt\ *adj* [*tusk* + *-ed*] **1** : furnished with or having tusks **2** *heraldry* : having teeth or tusks

tus·ke·gee \,təs'kēgē\ *n, pl* **tuskegee** *or* **tuskegees** *usu cap* **1** : a Muskogean people of east central Alabama **2** : a member of the Tuskegee people — compare CRUK

tusk·er \'təskə(r)\ *n* -s [*tusk* + *-er*] : an animal having tusks; *specif* : a male elephant with two normally developed tusks — compare HINE

tusk·less \'∠∠\ *adj* : devoid of a tusk

tusklike \'∠∠,∠\ *adj* : resembling a tusk esp. in exceptional size or in form ⟨a ∼ canine tooth⟩

tusk shell *n* : TOOTH SHELL

tusk tenon *n* : a tenon strengthened by one or more smaller tenons underneath forming a steplike outline

tusky \'təskē\ *adj* -ER/-EST : having tusks

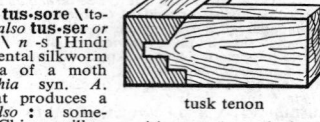

tusk tenon

tus·sah \'təsə\ *or* **tus·sore** \'tə,sō(ə)r, -,sȯ(ə)r\ *also* **tus·ser** *or* **tus·sur** \'təsə(r)\ *n* -s [Hindi *tasar*] : an Oriental silkworm that is the larva of a moth (*Antheraea paphia* syn. *A. mylitta*) and that produces a brownish silk; *also* : a sometimes cultivated Chinese silkworm (*A. pernyi*) producing a similar silk **2 a** : the uneven tan filament produced by the wild silkworms of China and India that is coarser, stronger, and shorter than cultivated silk **b** : any of various fabrics (as pongee and shantung) made of this silk and used in its natural tan color or dyed

tus·sal \'təsəl\ *adj* [L *tussis* cough + E *-al*; perh. akin to L *tundere* to strike — more at STUTTER] : relating to or manifested by a cough

tus·sic \'təsik\ *adj* [LL *tussicus*, fr. L *tussis* + *-icus* -ic] : relating to or manifested by cough

tussie-mussie *var of* TUZZY-MUZZY

tus·si·la·go \,təsə'lā(,)gō\ *n, cap* [NL, fr. L, coltsfoot, irreg. fr. *tussis* cough; prob. fr. the use of the coltsfoot in folk medicine as a cough remedy] : a monotypic genus of low creeping yellow-flowered perennial composite herbs comprising the coltsfoots

tus·sis \'təsəs\ *n* -ES [L] : COUGH

tus·sive \'təsiv, -sēv *also* -səv\ *adj* [L *tussis* + E *-ive*] : relating to, of the nature of, or caused by a cough

¹tus·sle \'təsəl\ *vb* **tussled; tussled; tussling** \-s(ə)liŋ\ **tussles** [ME *tussillen*, freq. of *-tusen*, *-tousen* to touse — more at TOUSE] *vi* : to struggle esp. roughly or violently : SCUFFLE — usu. used with *with* ⟨likes to ∼ with a large tuna⟩ ⟨will ∼ with the university's postwar development budget —*Newsweek*⟩ ⟨a strong man who could ∼ with evil and conquer —Vera Caspary⟩ ∼ *vt, archaic* : to struggle or scuffle with **syn** see WRESTLE

²tussle \"\ *n* -s **1** : a physical contest or struggle : SCUFFLE ⟨a ∼ to get through the door first⟩ ⟨a hard ∼ with the nasty sea —*Appalachia*⟩ **2** : a rough argument, controversy, or struggle against difficult odds for success ⟨a constant ∼ with insomnia —Lucien Price⟩ ⟨a sharp ∼ with temptation —Samuel Butler †1902⟩ ⟨a constant ∼ to find the money to pay our bills —Eileen McCarthy⟩ ⟨his lifelong ∼ . . . with the intricacies of the language —B.D.Wolfe⟩

tus·sock \'təsək, -sēk\ *n* -s [origin unknown] **1 a** : a dense tuft (as of grass or hair) **b** : a small hummock of more solid ground in marsh or bog usu. covered with and bound together by the roots of low vegetation (as grasses or sedges) ⟨raised ∼s of blueberries⟩ ⟨crossed the marsh by jumping from ∼ to ∼⟩ **c** *also* **tussock land** *chiefly NewZeal* : land covered with tussock grasses : TUSSOCK SEDGE **2** : TUSSOCK MOTH

tussock bellflower *n* : a perennial bellflower (*Campanula carpatica*) that grows in clumps with stems decumbent and spreading and has solitary flowers with an open bell-shaped corolla

tussock caterpillar *n* : a caterpillar that is the larva of a tussock moth, is covered with long tufts or bushes of hair, and includes several which eat the leaves of various shade and fruit trees and often become destructive pests

tus·socked \-kt\ *adj* : having or characterized by the presence of tussocks; *also* : covered with tussock grass

tus·sock·er \-kə(r)\ *n* -s *NewZeal* : TRAMP

tussock grass *n* : any of various grasses or sedges that typically grow in tussocks: as **a** : a tall stout cespitose grass (*Poa flabellata*) valuable for fodder introduced into Scotland from the Falkland islands **b** : an Australian grass (*Poa caespitosa*) **c** : SMUT GRASS **d** : GREAT BULRUSH **e** : a sedge that forms dense tufts in wet meadows or boglands; *esp* : TUSSOCK SEDGE

tussock moth *n* : any of numerous dull-colored moths esp. of the family Lymantiidae which in most of the common forms have wingless females

tussock sedge *n* : a common No. American sedge (*Carex stricta*) growing in dense tufted clumps and having wiry stems and leaves that are much used in making matting

tus·socky \-kē\ *adj* : having the form of tussocks : full of or covered with tussocks or tufts ⟨a cliff covered with ∼ bents —H.S.Tegner⟩

tussore *var of* TUSSAH

²tus·sore \'tə,sō(ə)r, -,sȯ(ə)r\ *n* -s : SEASHELL PINK

tussur *var of* TUSSAH

tut \'tủt, 'tət\ *n* -s [origin unknown] : a game of ball (as rounders); *also* : a base in rounders

²tut *the actual sound represented by the spelling "tut" is made by placing the tip of the tongue against the alveolar ridge and suddenly sucking in air; often read as* 'tǝt, *usu read* ∨\ **tut-tut** *interj* [ME] — used to express disapproval or disbelief ⟨∼, ∼, you shouldn't listen in on such conversations —Erle Stanley Gardner⟩

³tut \'tət\ *n* -s [origin unknown] *dial Eng* : PIECE — used esp.

in the phrases *by tut, by the tut,* and *upon tut*; compare TUTWORK

tu·ta·nia \t(y)ü'tānēə\ *n* -s [William *Tutin*, 18th cent. Eng. manufacturer + *Britannia* (metal)] : a silver-white alloy of tin with other metals (as antimony and copper) that is used for tableware

tutball \'∠,∠\ *n* [¹*tut* + *ball*] *dial Eng* : STOOLBALL, ROUNDERS

tu·tcho·ne \tü'chōnē\ *n, pl* **tutchone** *or* **tutchones** *usu cap* **1** : an Athapaskan people of southwestern Yukon, Alaska **2** : a member of the Tutchone people

tu·tee \t(y)ü'tē\ *n* -s [²*tutor* + *-ee*] : one who is being tutored : PUPIL ⟨each advisee or ∼ was working . . . in a different corner of a very wide field —Mary McCarthy⟩

tu·te·la \t(y)ü'tēlə\ *n, pl* **tute·lae** \-,lē\ [L, protection, guardianship, guardian] **1** *Roman, civil, & Scots law* : the right or power of a tutor over his ward : the relation of a tutor to his ward or pupil **2** *Roman law* : a guardianship over a woman regardless of age who is not under marital or paternal power exercised by certain of her relatives by law

tu·te·lar \-lə(r)\ *n* -s : one that is tutelary

²tutelar \"\ *adj* : TUTELARY ⟨a ∼ deity⟩

tu·te·lage \t(y)üd·l·lij, -ūtʹl-, -ᵊlij\ *n* -s [L *tutela* protection, guardianship, guardian (fr. *tutus*, past part. of *tuērī* to watch, protect, guard) + E *-age* — more at TUITION] **1** : an act or action of guarding or protecting : GUARDIANSHIP, PROTECTION **2** : the state of being under a guardian or tutor; *also* : the right or power of a tutor over his pupil : DEPENDENCE **3 a** : INSTRUCTION; *esp* : individual instruction accompanied by close personal attention and a conscious attempt at guidance ⟨were held together by the firm social ∼ of the publisher's widow —Willa Cather⟩ ⟨under his ∼ she trained for a contest —*Current Biog.*⟩ **b** : a determining influence exerted over an individual by a person, school, or movement ⟨began his intellectual career under the ∼ of the neo-Kantians —J.G.Gray⟩

¹tu·te·lar \-lə(r)\ *adj* [LL *tutelaris*, fr. L *tutela* + *-aris* -ar] : TUTELARY ⟨a ∼ deity⟩

²tutelar \"\ *n* -s : one that is tutelary

tu·te·lary \t(y)üd·ᵊl,erē, -ütʹl-, -ri\ *adj* [L *tutelarius*, n., guardian, fr. *tutela* + *-arius* -ary] **1** : having the guardianship or charge of protecting a person or a thing : GUARDIAN, PROTECTING ⟨∼ goddesses⟩ **2** : of or relating to a guardian or to the protection afforded by a guardian ⟨∼ authority⟩ **3** : of a tutelary power (as a deity)

tu·te·lo \tü'tā,lō\ *n, pl* **tutelo** *or* **tutelos** *usu cap* **1 a** : a Siouan people of Virginia and No. Carolina **b** : a member of such people **2** : the language of the Tutelo people

tu·tin \'tūtən\ *n* -s [*tutu* + *-in*] : a poisonous crystalline glucoside $C_{15}H_{18}O_6$ obtained from the tutu and other plants of the genus *Coriaria*

tu·ti·or·ism \t(y)üshēə,rizəm, -üd·ē-\ *n* -s [L *tutior* safer (comp. of *tutus* safe, fr. past part. of *tuērī* to watch, protect, guard) + E *-ism* — more at TUITION] : a viewpoint in the probabilistic controversy that the argument favoring liberty as distinguished from law must be either certain or the most probable of all possible opinions to furnish a basis for action — compare PROBABILISM 2

tu·ti·or·ist \-răst\ *n* -s [L *tutior* + E *-ist*] : an adherent or advocate of tutiorism

tut money *n, dial Eng* : pay for tutwork

¹tu·tor \t(y)üd·ə(r), -ütə-\ *n* -s [ME *tutour, tutor,* fr. MF & L; MF *tuteur,* fr. L *tutor,* fr. *tutus* (past part. of *tuērī* to look at, protect, guard) + *-or* — more at TUITION] **1** : a person charged with the instruction and guidance of another: as **a** : a private teacher or instructor : MENTOR **b** : a college teacher esp. in a British university who guides the individual studies of undergraduates working in his special field **c** : a college teacher ranking below an instructor **d** : a college officer having administrative or counseling functions **2** : a person in Roman and civil law who has the charge of the person and estate of a pupil or child under the age of puberty — see TUTOR DATIVE; compare CURATOR 1, GUARDIAN 3

²tutor \"\ *vb* -ED/-ING/-s *vt* **1** : to have the guardianship, tutelage, or care of **2** : to teach, guide, or instruct usu. on an individual basis and in a special subject or for a particular occasion or purpose : COACH ⟨∼ed in Latin⟩ ⟨has never been ∼ed in patience⟩ **3** : to inform or instruct secretly or underhandedly ⟨∼ a witness⟩ ⟨∼ed in the art of deceit⟩ ∼ *vi* **1** : to do the work of a tutor; *specif* : to give private instruction **2** : to receive instruction esp. privately ⟨had to ∼ in Latin in order to pass⟩ **syn** see TEACH

tu·tor·age \-ərij\ *n* -s [¹*tutor* + *-age*] : the office, function, or work of a tutor : TUTORSHIP, TUITION

tutor dative *n* [part trans. of L *tutor dativus*] : a guardian appointed by a Roman magistrate in the absence of a testamentary guardian or a statutory guardian from among the close relatives who is entitled to act without confirmation by any magistrate in accordance with a certain order of preference; *sometimes* : a testamentary guardian

tu·tor·ess \-ərəs\ *n* -s : a female tutor

tu·tor·hood \-ə(r),hủd\ *n* -s [¹*tutor* + *-hood*] **1** : TUTORSHIP, TUTORAGE **2** : TUTORS

¹tu·to·ri·al \t(y)ü'tōrēəl, -'tȯr-\ *adj* [L *tutorius* of a tutor (fr. *tutor*) + E *-al*] : of, relating to, or involving a tutor ⟨a ∼ position⟩ ⟨the ∼ staff⟩ ⟨a ∼ manner⟩ ⟨the ∼ method⟩

²tutorial \"\ *n* -s : a class or seminar that is conducted by a tutor for a single student or for a small number of students and that consists mainly of discussion and individual instruction

tu·tor·less \'t(y)üd·ə(r)ləs\ *adj* : being without a tutor

tu·tor·ly *adj* : of, relating to, or befitting a tutor

tu·tor·ship \-(r),ship\ *n* -s [¹*tutor* + *-ship*] **1** : the office, function, or practice of a tutor ⟨the ∼ may be held for a year⟩ **2** : TUTELAGE 3 ⟨under the ∼ of her parents⟩

tu·toy·er \,tütwȯ'yā\ *vt* -ED/-ING/-s [F, to address with the pronoun *tu* ("thou"), fr. MF, fr. *tu* thou, fr. L — more at THOU] : to address familiarly

tu·trix \'t(y)ü·triks, -ēks\ *n, pl* **tu·tri·ces** \t(y)ü'trī(,)sēz, 't(y)ütrə-, -,sēz\ *or* **tutrixes** [LL, fem. of L *tutor*] : TUTORESS

tuts *pl of* TUT

tut·san \'tətsən\ *n* -s [ME *totsane, toutsayne,* fr. (assumed) MF *toute-saine* (whence F), fr. *toute* (fem. of *tout* all, fr. — assumed — VL *tottus,* alter. of L *totus*) + *saine,* fem. of *sain* healthy, fr. L *sanus* healthy, sane] : a Eurasian St.-John's-wort (*Hypericum androsaemum*) from which a healing salve is made in Spain

tutsi *usu cap, var of* TUSI

tut·te le cor·de \'tüd-ālā'kȯrdə\ *adv (or adj)* [It, lit., all the strings] : TRE CORDE

¹tut·ti \'tü|d·ē, 'tül, |tl, |i\ *adj (or adv)* [It, masc. pl. of *tutto* all, fr. (assumed) VL *tottus,* alter. of L *totus*] : ALL — used as a direction in music for voices or instruments to sing or play together; compare SOLO

²tutti \"\ *n* -s **1** : a passage performed by all the players or singers **2** : the total tonal effect produced by an orchestra or chorus performing together

tut·ti-frut·ti \'tüd·ē'früd·ē, 'tỏt|...ütʹ, |i...ʹi\ *n* -s [It *tutti frutti,* lit., all fruits] : a confection or ice cream containing chopped usu. candied fruits

tut-tut *var of* TUT

¹tut·ty \'tət·ē\ *n* -ES [ME *tutie,* fr. MF, fr. Ar *tūtiyā,* fr. Per, fr. Skt *tuttha, tūtaka*] : a yellow or brown amorphous substance that is obtained as a sublimation product in the flues of furnaces smelting zinc and that consists of a crude zinc oxide

²tut·ty \'tȯti\ *n* -ES [origin unknown] *dial Eng* : FLOWER, NOSEGAY

¹tu·tu \'tü,tü\ *n* -s [Maori] : any of several New Zealand shrubs or small trees of the genus *Coriaria; esp* : a shrubby tree (*C. ruscifolia*) with a juicy black edible receptacle consisting of the enlarged fleshy petals and enclosing a dry fruit with a poisonous seed

²tutu \"\ *n* -s [F, fr. (baby talk) *cucu, tutu* backside, alter. of *cul* — more at CULET] : a very short projecting skirt worn by a ballet dancer

³tutu \"\ *n* -s [Hawaiian *tūtū*] *Hawaii* : GRANNY, GRANDPA

¹tu·tu·i·lan \tüt(ü)'ēlən\ *adj, usu cap* [*Tutuila,* chief island of American Samoa in the southwestern Pacific + E *-an*] : relating to, situated in, inhabiting, or coming from Tutuila

²tutuilan \"\ *n* -s *cap* : a native or inhabitant of Tutuila

tutu

tutu ta·glio·ni \-täl'yōnē\ *n, usu cap 2d T* [after Maria *Taglioni* †1884 Ital. ballet dancer] **:** an ankle-length tutu

tu·tut·ni \tü'tütnē\ *n, pl* **tututni** *or* **tututnis** *usu cap* **1 :** an Athapaskan people or group of peoples of the lower Rogue river valley and adjacent Pacific coast in Oregon **2 :** a member of the Tututni people or group of peoples

tutwork \'ˌ=ˌ=\ *n* [*³tut* + *work*] *dial Eng* **:** PIECEWORK; *specif* **:** excavation in Cornwall paid for by measure or by weight

tu·vin·i·an \tü'vinēən\ *n* -s *cap* [*Tuva,* autonomous region in U. S. S. R. + E *-inian* (as in *Abyssinian*)] **:** TANNU-TUVAN

tu-whit tu-whoo \tü'(h)wit·tü'(h)wü\ *n* [imit.] **:** the cry of an owl

tux \'təks\ *n* -ES [by shortening] **:** TUXEDO

tux·e·do \ˌtək'sē(ˌ)dō, -ēdə\ *n* -ES [fr. *Tuxedo* Park, resort near *Tuxedo* Lake, N. Y.] **1 a** *also* **tuxedo jacket :** a single-breasted or double-breasted jacket usu. black or midnight blue made with notched silk lapels **b :** semiformal evening dress for men — compare EVENING DRESS b(2) **2** *also* **tuxedo coat :** a woman's unbelted straight-hanging coat characterized by a single band forming the collar and the wide full-length lapels

tuxedo sofa *n* **:** an upholstered sofa with slightly curved arms that are the same height as the back

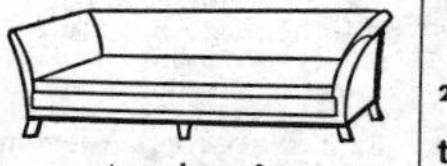

tuxedo sofa

tu·yere \tü'ye(ə)r, twē'-, 'twi(ə)r\ *n* -s [F *tuyère,* fr. MF *tuyere,* fr. *tuyau* pipe, fr. OF *tuel, tuyau* — more at TEWEL] **:** a nozzle through which an air blast is delivered to a forge or blast furnace; *also* **:** a port or vent between tiered grate sections of a boiler furnace

tuyere box *n* **:** an air belt or air chamber from which air is supplied to the tuyeres in a Bessemer converter

tuyere notch *also* **tuyere arch** *n* **:** an opening in the wall of a furnace hearth or crucible for a tuyere

tuz·la \'tüzlə\ *n* -s *usu cap* [Turk, fr. Lake *Tuz,* Turkey] **:** a central Anatolian rug very similar to a Konia

tuz·zy-muz·zy \'təzē'məzē\ *also* **tus·sie-mus·sie** \'təsē'məsē\ *n, pl* **tuzzy-muzzies** *also* **tussie-mussies** [ME *tusmose, tussemose*] *archaic* **:** a garland of flowers **:** NOSEGAY

TV \(')tē'vē *sometimes* 'tē,vē *or* -vi\ *abbr or n* -s television

TV *abbr* terminal velocity

TVI *abbr* television interference

tw *abbr* **1** *cap* Twaddell (hydrometer) **2** twisted

¹twa \'twä, 'twȯ\ *or* **twae** \'twē\ *Scot var of* TWO

²twa \'twä\ *n, pl* **twa** *or* **twas** *usu cap* **1 :** any of several diverse peoples of central and southern Africa **2 :** a member of one of the Twa peoples

twad·dell \(')twä¦del *also* (')twȯ¦del *or* '=ˌdᵊl\ *adj, usu cap* [*Twaddell (hydrometer)*] **:** according to the reading of a Twaddell hydrometer ⟨degrees ~⟩

twaddell hydrometer *n, usu cap T* [after William *Twaddell* †1840? Scot. inventor] **:** a hydrometer for liquids heavier than water graduated with an arbitrary scale to give specific gravity when a reading is multiplied by 0.005 and added to 1

¹twad·dle \'twädᵊl *also* -wȯd-\ *n* -s [prob. alter. of *²twattle*] **1 :** empty silly talk **:** idle chatter **:** GABBLE ⟨~ about the poet's amorous intrigues —*Times Lit. Supp.*⟩ ⟨that reasoning was unadulterated ~ —F.D.Roosevelt⟩ **2 :** TWADDLER

²twaddle \"\ *vb* **twaddled; twaddled; twaddling** \-d(ᵊ)liŋ\ **twaddles** [prob. alter. of *¹twattle*] **:** PRATE, BABBLE

twad·dler \-d(ᵊ)lə(r)\ *n* -s **:** one that writes or talks twaddle

twaddling *adj* **1 :** EMPTY, TRIVIAL **2 :** given to talking twaddle ⟨boot out that ~ doctor —Marcia Davenport⟩

twad·dly \-d(ᵊ)lē, -li\ *adj* **:** talking twaddle **:** composed of twaddle

¹twain \'twān\ *adj* [ME *tweyen, twein, twain,* adj. & pron., fr. OE *twēgen,* nom. & accus. masc. — more at TWO] *archaic* **:** TWO ⟨Nature's ~ circumscriptions of man's station —H.B.Alexander⟩

²twain \"\ *pron* [ME *tweyen, twein, twain*] **:** TWO ⟨mark ~⟩

³twain \"\ *n* -s [ME *tweyen, twein, twain,* fr. *tweyen, twein, twain,* adj. & pron.] **1 :** TWO **2 :** COUPLE, PAIR ⟨the doings of this talented ~ —Osbert Sitwell⟩ — **in twain** *adv* **:** in halves **:** into two parts **:** APART, ASUNDER ⟨one mountain at the base of which we passed was literally split *in twain* —Francis Kingdon-Ward⟩

⁴twain \"\ *vb* -ED/-ING/-S [ME *twaynen,* fr. *tweyen, twein, twain,* adj.] **:** DIVIDE, PART, SUNDER

twain cloud *n* **:** CUMULOSTRATUS

twaite \'twāt\ *or* **twaite shad** *also* **thwaite** *or* **thwaite shad** \'t(h)wāt-\ *n* -s [origin unknown] **:** a European shad (*Alosa finta*)

twal *or* **twall** \'twal\ *Scot var of* TWELVE

twa·na \'twänə\ *n, pl* **twana** *or* **twanas** *usu cap* **1 a :** a Salishan people of the Hood canal region in Washington **b :** a member of such people **2 :** a language of the Twana people

¹twang \'twaŋ, -aiŋ\ *n* -s [imit.] **1 :** a harsh quick ringing sound like that of a plucked bowstring ⟨could hear the ~ and slam of a screen door —Laurence Critchell⟩ **2 a :** nasal speech or resonance — called also *nasal twang* ⟨the ~ of the backwoods journalist —Ben Crisler⟩ **b :** the characteristic speech of a region, locality, or group of people ⟨a cockney ~⟩ ⟨the ~ of native speech —Hersteinn Palsson⟩ ⟨a good clean American ~ —D.C.Peattie⟩ **3 a :** an act of plucking or twitching **:** a sharp picking or pulling **b :** PANG, TWINGE ⟨feel ~*s* of conscience —R.L.Neuberger⟩

²twang \"\ *vb* -ED/-ING/-S *vi* **1 a :** to give forth the quick harsh ringing sound of or as if of the plucked string of a bow or a musical instrument ⟨the bow ~*ed* and the arrow shot across —T.B.Costain⟩ ⟨the fence gate ~*ed* —Elizabeth Bowen⟩ **b :** to produce a twanging sound by or as if by plucking a stringed musical instrument ⟨~*ed* away at his guitar⟩ **2 :** to speak or sound with a nasal intonation ⟨the voices of the card players came ~*ing* up the stairwell —Jean Stafford⟩ **3 :** to vibrate, throb, or twitch with or as if with pain or tension ⟨a blistered heel, a ~*ing* tendon —D.R.Brower⟩ ⟨their eyeballs danced and their muscles ~*ed* —*English Digest*⟩ ~ *vt* **1 a :** to cause to sound with a twang **:** pluck the strings of ⟨encouraged them to ~ lutes, scrape fiddles and burst into humorous song —John Blofeld⟩ **b :** to play (music) by plucking a stringed instrument **:** pick or beat out (a tune) ⟨banjo players ~*ed* music for a breakdown —*Amer. Guide Series: Fla.*⟩ **2 :** to utter or pronounce with a nasal twang ⟨the high timbre with which he ~*ed* out his cynicisms —Josephine Pinckney⟩ **3 a :** to pluck the string of (a bow) ⟨~*ed* his bow⟩ **b :** to discharge (an arrow) from a bow ⟨~*ed* off an arrow that missed the deer⟩

³twang \"\ *n* -s [alter. (influenced by *¹twang*) of *tang*] **1 :** a persisting flavor, taste, or odor **:** TAINT, TANG ⟨butter left uncovered in a refrigerator readily takes on a ~ from other foods⟩ **2 :** NOTE, SUGGESTION, TRACE ⟨likes a sporty ~ about his apparel —*advt*⟩

twang·i·ness \'twaŋēnəs, -aiŋ-, -ŋinəs\ *n* -ES **:** the quality or state of being twangy **:** the resonance of a plucked string or of nasal intonation

¹twan·gle \'twaŋgəl, -aiŋ-\ *vb* **twangled; twangled; twangling** \-g(ə)liŋ\ **twangles** [freq. of *²twang*] **:** TWANG ⟨held the strands on either side so that the snapped ends could not ~ as they broke loose —John Brophy⟩

²twangle \"\ *n* -s **:** a twanging sound ⟨the spinet player . . . was playing ~*s* on his keyboard —Christopher Morley⟩

twangy \-gē, -gi\ *adj* -ER/-EST **1 :** having the resonance of a plucked string ⟨heard the parlor clock strike twelve with its old ~ chime —Helen Eustis⟩ **2 :** having the resonance of nasal intonation ⟨his voice was a high, ~, unmusical New England drawl —Irving Stone⟩

twank \'twaŋk, -aiŋk\ *vb* -ED/-ING/-S [imit.] *vi, dial chiefly Eng* **:** to sound with an abrupt twang ~ *vt, dial chiefly Eng* **:** to cause to sound with an abrupt twang

twan·kay tea *or* **twan·key tea** \'twaŋˌkā-, -(ˌ)kē-\ *n, usu cap 1st T* [fr. Chin (Pek) *T'un²-ch'i¹* (Tunki), town in Anhwei prov., China] **:** a green tea of inferior quality and of open leaves

twa·some \'twäsəm, -wȯs-\ *Scot var of* TWOSOME

twat \'twä¦t *also* 'twȯ¦; *usu* ¦d·+V\ *n* -s [origin unknown] **1 :** VULVA — usu. considered vulgar **2** *slang* **:** BUTTOCKS **3** *slang* **:** WOMAN

twatch·el \'twachəl\ *n* -s [ME angel*twacche* earthworm + *-el* — more at ANGLETWITCH] **:** an earthworm used as bait by a fisherman

¹twat·tle \'twätᵊl\ *vi* -ED/-ING/-S [perh. alter. of *¹tattle*] *dial Eng* **:** to talk idly **:** CHATTER, PRATE, TWADDLE

²twattle \"\ *n* -s *dial* **:** the act of prating **:** idle talk **:** TWADDLE

t wave \'tē,wāv\ *n, usu cap T* **:** the deflection of the electrocardiogram produced during the retreat of the excitation wave from the ventricle — compare P WAVE, QRS COMPLEX

tway \'twā\ *dial Brit var of* TWO

tway·blade \'twā,blād\ *n* **:** any of several orchids having a pair of leaves; *esp* **:** a plant of either of two genera (*Listera* and *Liparis*)

tweag \'twēg\ *dial var of* TWEAK

¹tweak \'twēk\ *vb* -ED/-ING/-S [alter. of earlier *twick,* fr. ME *twikken,* fr. OE *twiccian* to pluck, catch hold of — more at TWITCH] *vt* **1 :** to pinch and pull with a sudden jerk and twist **:** JERK, JOG, SNATCH, TWITCH ⟨elevated the gun barrel . . . and ~*ed* the lanyard —Arthur Mayse⟩ ⟨~*ed* his memory —Olive H. Prouty⟩ ⟨figures long standard . . . are ~*ed* across a minuscule stage —H.M.Robinson⟩ ⟨~*ed* the bulbous end of his nose —Francis King⟩ **2 :** to pull the nose of **:** pull by the nose ⟨political techniques of ~*ing* babies and shaking hands —*Springfield (Mass.) Union*⟩ ~ *vi* **:** TWITCH ⟨he sat . . . ~*ing* feebly and blinking his eyes —Richard Church⟩ ⟨has been ~*ing* at my conscience ever since —K.I.Brown⟩

²tweak \"\ *n* -s **1 :** an act of tweaking **:** a sharp pinch or jerk **:** TWIST, TWITCH ⟨a ~ of the nose⟩ **2 :** AGITATION, DISTRESS

tweaky \'twēkē, -ki\ *adj* -ER/-EST **1 :** THIN, NERVOUS, TWITCHY **2 :** ACID, BITING, SHARP

twee \'twē\ *n* -s [imit.] **:** a thin or shrill piping note (as of a horn or small bird)

tweed \'twēd\ *n* -s [alter. (influenced by *Tweed* river, Scotland) of *¹tweel*] **1 a :** a woolen coating and suiting fabric of Scottish origin having a rough appearance and made usu. in twill weaves **b :** an imitation of this fabric **2 tweeds** *pl* **:** tweed clothing **:** a tweed suit ⟨the man in the gray ~*s* —P.B.Kyne⟩

tweed·dale \'twēd,dāl\ *adj, usu cap* [fr. *Tweeddale* (Peeblesshire) County, Scotland] **:** PEEBLESSHIRE

tweed·ed \'twēdəd\ *adj* **:** wearing tweeds **:** clothed in tweeds ⟨a sprucely ~ man in his fifties —*New Yorker*⟩

tweed·i·ness \'twēdēnəs, -din-\ *n* -ES **:** the quality or state of being tweedy **:** a homely, informal, or outdoor look or character seen in one wearing tweeds

¹twee·dle \'twēdᵊl\ *vb* **tweedled; tweedled; tweedling** \-d(ᵊ)liŋ\ **tweedles** [prob. of imit. origin] *vi* **1 :** to sing or whistle in modulation **:** PIPE, CHIRP **2 :** to play negligently on a musical instrument ~ *vt* **:** to cajole or entice by music

²tweedle \"\ *n* -s **:** a sound of tweedling ⟨the squeal and the blare and the ~ of bagpipes —W.C.Williams⟩

³tweedle \"\ *dial var of* TWIDDLE

twee·dle·dum and twee·dle·dee \ˌtwēdᵊl'dəmən,twēdᵊl'dē\ *n, usu cap both Ts* [*¹tweedle* + *dum* (imit. of a low musical note) & *dee* (imit. of a high musical note)] **:** two objects, persons, or groups differing superficially or insignificantly **:** a practically indistinguishable pair

tweedy \'twēdē, -di\ *adj, usu* -ER/-EST **1 :** of tweed **:** resembling or suggesting tweed in texture, color, or appearance ⟨~ attire⟩ **2 a :** given to or fond of wearing tweeds **:** dressed in tweeds **b :** homely, informal, or outdoorsy in taste, inclination, or habits

tweeg \'twēg\ *n* -s [Delaware *twi'kw*] **:** HELLBENDER 1a

¹tweel \'twēl, *esp before pause or consonant* -ēəl\ *Scot var of* TWILL

²tweel \"\ *n* -s [F *tuile,* lit., tile, alter. of OF *teule, tiule,* fr. L *tegula* — more at THATCH] **:** the closure of a glass furnace: **a :** a clay covering for the furnace mouth **b :** a counterweighted furnace door

tween \'twēn\ *prep* [ME *twene,* short for *betwene* — more at BETWEEN] **:** BETWEEN

tween-brain \'=ˌ=\ *n* **:** DIENCEPHALON

tween-deck \'=¦=\ *adj* **:** located or carried between decks

tween deck *n* **:** any deck of a ship but the upper or the lowest

tweeny *or* **tween·ie** \'twēnē, -ni\ *n, pl* **tweenies** [*tween* + *-y, -ie*] **:** BETWEENMAID

tweer *var of* TWIRE

¹tweet \'twēt, *usu* -ēd·+V\ *n* -s [imit.] **1 :** a chirping note ⟨the sharp ~*s* of the referee's whistle —Nathaniel Benchley⟩ **2 :** a high note emitted by sound-reproducing equipment — contrasted with *woof*

²tweet \"\ *vb* -ED/-ING/-S **:** CHIRP ⟨songbirds are ~*ing* —Richard Bissell⟩

tweet·er \'twēd·ə(r), -ētə-\ *n* -s **:** a small loudspeaker responsive only to the higher acoustic frequencies and reproducing sounds of high pitch — compare WOOFER

twee·tle \'twēdᵊl, -ētᵊl\ *vb* **tweetled; tweetled; tweetling** \-d·ᵊliŋ, -t(ᵊ)liŋ\ **tweetles** [by alter.] **:** TWEEDLE ⟨the flutes *tweetling* high —Mary Deasy⟩

¹tweeze *or* **tweese** \'twēz\ *n* -s [short for *etweese,* fr. pl. of *etwee,* fr. F *étui,* fr. OF *estui* container, fr. *estuier* to keep, preserve, retain, perh. fr. (assumed) VL *studiare* to take care of, fr. L *studium* zeal, application, study — more at STUDY] *obs* **:** a case of small instruments (as of a surgeon or barber) **:** ETUI

²tweeze \'twēz\ *vt* -ED/-ING/-S [back-formation fr. *tweezers*] **:** to extract, pluck, or remove with tweezers ⟨~*s* the hairs out of his ears —*Newsweek*⟩ ⟨*tweezed* out the little triangular stitches of black thread —Robert Hazel⟩

¹tweez·er \-zə(r)\ *n* -s [*¹tweeze* + *-er*] **1** *obs* **:** TWEEZE **2 :** TWEEZERS

²tweezer \"\ *vb* -ED/-ING/-S [back-formation fr. *tweezers*] *vt* **:** to draw, place, or hold with or as if with tweezers ⟨coaxing smoke from a cigarette stub which . . . he had ~*ed* between two pieces of wire —A.M.Robinson⟩ ~ *vi* **:** to use tweezers

³tweezer \"\ *n* -s [origin unknown] *dial* **:** AMERICAN MERGANSER

tweez·ers \-ə(r)z\ *n pl but sometimes sing in constr* [*¹tweeze* + *-er* + *-s*] **1 :** any of various small pincer-shaped tools used for plucking, holding, or manipulating (as for removing superfluous hair or handling watch parts) **2** *obs* **:** ETUI, TWEEZE

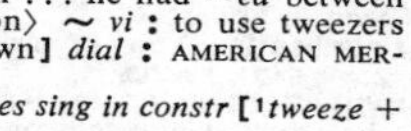

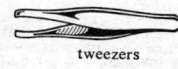

tweezers

¹twelfth \'twel¦f(t)th, ¦ft, -eü¦, *rapid or substand* ¦th; *the sound transcribed* f *may be bilabial instead of labiodental — the voiceless cognate of* b\ *adj* [ME *twelfte, twelfthe,* adj. & n., fr. OE, fr. OE *twelfta* (akin to OHG *zwelifto* twelfth, ON *tolfti*), fr. *twelf* twelve + *-ta* (fr. *-otha, -tha* -th) — more at TWELVE] **1 :** being number 12 in a countable series ⟨the ~ day⟩ — see NUMBER table **2 :** being one of 12 equal parts into which something is divisible ⟨a ~ share of the money⟩

²twelfth \"\ *n, pl* **twelfths** \¦f(t)ths, ¦f(t)s\ [ME *twelfte, twelfthe*] **1 :** number 12 in a countable series ⟨the ~ of the month⟩ **2 :** the quotient of a unit divided by 12 **:** one of 12 equal parts of something ⟨one ~ of the total⟩ **3** *usu cap* **a** [ME *twelthe,* short for *twelfte day, twelthe day*] **:** EPIPHANY **b** [by shortening] **:** TWELFTHTIDE **4 a :** a musical interval comprising an octave and a fifth **b :** a note or tone at this interval **c :** an organ stop that produces tones at this interval above the pitch indicated by the notation

twelfth-cake \'=ˌ=\ *also* **twelfth-night cake** \'=¦=ˌ=\ *n, sometimes cap T* **:** a cake made for a Twelfth Night celebration that contains a bean or a coin for determining the ruler of the feast

twelfth cranial nerve *or* **twelfth nerve** *n* **:** HYPOGLOSSAL NERVE

twelfth day *n, usu cap T* [ME *twelfte day*] **:** EPIPHANY

twelfth night *n, usu cap T&N* [ME *twelfte niht,* fr. OE *twelfte niht*] **1 :** the eve preceding Epiphany marking the end of medieval Christmas festivities **2 :** the evening of Epiphany

twelfthtide *n, usu cap, obs* **:** the 12-day season after Christmas ending with Epiphany

twell \twel, (ˌ)twel\ *dial var of* ¹TILL

¹twelve \'twelv, -eüv, *chiefly South* -e(ə)v\ *adj* [ME *twelf, twelve,* adj. & pron., fr. OE *twelf;* akin to OHG *zwelif* twelve, ON *tolf,* Goth *twalif;* all fr. a prehistoric Gmc compound whose first constituent is represented by OE *twēgen, twā, tū* two, and whose second constituent is prob. akin to Lith *-lika* (as in *dvylika* twelve, *vënúlika* eleven) — more at TWO, ELEVEN] **:** being one more than 11 in number ⟨~ years⟩ — see NUMBER table

²twelve \"\ *pron, pl in constr* [ME *twelf, twelve*] **:** 12 countable persons or things not specified but under consideration and being enumerated ⟨~ are here⟩ ⟨~ were found⟩

³twelve \"\ *n* -s [ME *twelf, twelve,* fr. *twelf, twelve,* adj. & pron.] **1 :** 10 and two **:** twice six **:** six times two **:** three times four **2 a :** 12 units or objects ⟨a total of ~⟩ **b :** a group or set of 12 ⟨arranged by ~*s*⟩ **3 :** the numerable quantity symbolized by the arabic numerals 12 **4 :** 12 o'clock — compare BELL table, TIME illustration **5 :** the 12th in a set or series; *esp* **:** an article of clothing of the 12th size ⟨wears ~*s*⟩ **6 twelves** *pl* **:** TWELVEMO

¹twelve·fold \'=¦fōld\ *adj* [*¹twelve* + *-fold*] **1 :** having 12 parts or aspects **2 :** being 12 times as large, as great, or as many as some understood size, degree, or amount ⟨a ~ increase⟩

²twelvefold \"\ *adv* **:** to 12 times as much or as many **:** by 12 times ⟨increased ~⟩

twelve hours *n pl* **1** *Scot* **a :** NOON **b** MIDNIGHT **2** *Scot* **:** a noon lunch

twelve-men's morris \'=ˌ=-\ *n* **:** morris played with 12 counters

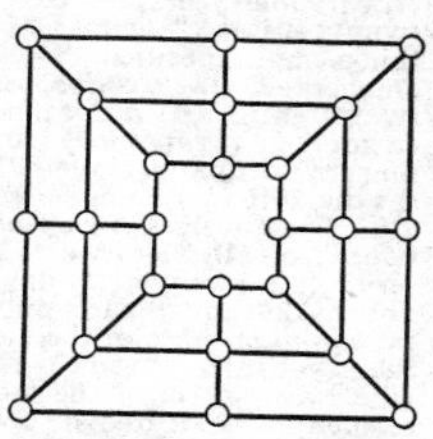

twelve-men's morris board

twelve-mile limit \'=ˌ=-\ *n* **:** a limit of the marginal sea of 12 miles included in the territorial waters of a state

twelve·mo \'=ˌmō\ *n* -s [*¹twelve* + *-mo* (as in *duodecimo*)] **:** the size of a piece of paper cut 12 from a sheet; *also* **:** paper or a page of this size — called also *duodecimo;* abbr. *12 mo;* symbol *12°;* see BOOK tables

twelvemonth \'=ˌ=\ *n* [ME *twelfmoneth,* fr. *twelf* twelve + *moneth* month] **:** YEAR ⟨kept out of the police courts for a whole ~ —*Punch*⟩

twelve-note \'=¦=\ *adj* **:** TWELVE-TONE

twelve·pen·ny \'=pəni *or* -nē *or* -ˌpen- *Brit* '=pəni\ *adj* **:** sold for, worth, or costing a shilling

twelv·er \-və(r)\ *n* -s *usu cap* **:** a member of a major Shi'ite sect which acknowledges 12 imams and holds that the 12th will reappear as the Mahdi before the Last Day and of which the tenets and organization have been the state religion of Persia since the 16th century — called also *imami;* compare SEVENER

twelve-spotted asparagus beetle \'=¦=-\ *n* **:** a European asparagus beetle (*Crioceris duodecimpunctata*) that is naturalized in eastern No. America

twelve-tone \'=¦=\ *adj* **:** of or relating to music based on the 12 chromatic tones of the octave used in any chosen order without regard for the major-minor system ⟨*twelve-tone* technique of composition⟩

twelve-tone row *n* **:** the 12 chromatic tones of the octave placed in a chosen fixed order and constituting with some permitted permutations and derivations the melodic and harmonic material of a movement or work — called also *tone row*

twelve-wired bird of paradise \'=¦=-\ **:** a bird of paradise (*Seleucides ignotus*)

¹twen·ti·eth \'twentēəth, -ntiəth, *in rapid speech sometimes* -wənē- *or* -ni-\ *adj* [ME *twentithe,* fr. OE *twentigotha,* fr. *twentig* twenty + *-otha* -th] **1 :** being number 20 in a countable series ⟨the ~ day⟩ — see NUMBER table **2 :** being one of 20 equal parts into which something is divisible ⟨a ~ share of the money⟩

²twentieth \"\ *n* -s **1 :** number 20 in a countable series ⟨the ~ of the month⟩ **2 :** the quotient of a unit divided by 20 **:** one of 20 equal parts of something ⟨one ~ of the total⟩

twentieth-century cut \¦=ˌ==ˌ==-\ *n* **:** a gem cut with 80 or 88 facets with the table replaced by a low pyramidal range of facets carried to a central point — compare BRILLIANT

¹twen·ty \'twentē, -nti, *in rapid speech sometimes* -wənē *or* -ni\ *adj* [ME, fr. OE *twēntig, twentig,* n., group of 20, fr. *twēn-, twen-* (akin to OE *twēgen, twā, tū* two) + *-tig* group of 10 — more at TWO, EIGHTY] **:** being one more than 19 in number ⟨~ years⟩ — see NUMBER table

²twenty \"\ *pron, pl in constr* [ME, fr. *twenty,* adj.] **:** 20 countable persons or things not specified but under consideration and being enumerated ⟨~ are here⟩ ⟨~ were found⟩

³twenty \"\ *n* -ES [ME, fr. *twenty,* pron.] **1 :** two tens **:** twice 10 **:** 10 times two **:** four times five **2 a :** 20 units or objects ⟨a total of ~⟩ **b :** a group or set of 20 ⟨arranged by *twenties*⟩ **3 :** the numerable quantity symbolized by the arabic numerals 20 **4 twenties** *pl* **a :** the numbers 20 to 29 inclusive ⟨a score in the *twenties*⟩ ⟨low grades in the *twenties*⟩ **b :** the members of a series or set of successive numbers that end in 20 to 29 inclusive ⟨the *twenties* of the preceding century⟩ ⟨lives in the *twenties* in the next block⟩ **c :** the portion of a continuum lying between 20 and 30 on a scale of measurement or segmentation ⟨temperatures in the *twenties* tomorrow⟩ ⟨a man in his *twenties*⟩ ⟨dresses selling in the *twenties*⟩ ⟨in the latitude of the *twenties*⟩ **5 :** the 20th in a set or series; *esp* **:** an article of clothing of the 20th size ⟨wears a ~⟩ **6 a :** a twenty-pound note **b :** a twenty-dollar bill

¹twenty-eight \¦=¦=¦=\ *adj* **:** being one more than 27 in number ⟨*twenty-eight* years⟩ — see NUMBER table

²twenty-eight \"\ *pron, pl in constr* **:** 28 countable persons or things not specified but under consideration and being enumerated ⟨*twenty-eight* are here⟩ ⟨*twenty-eight* were found⟩

³twenty-eight \"\ *n* **1 :** eight and 20 **:** four times seven **2 a :** 28 units or objects ⟨a total of *twenty-eight*⟩ **b :** a group or set of 28 **3 :** the numerable quantity symbolized by the arabic numerals 28 **4 :** the 28th in a set or series; *esp* **:** an article of clothing of the 28th size ⟨wears a *twenty-eight*⟩

⁴twenty-eight \"\ *n* **:** a West Australian yellow-collared parakeet (*Platycercus zonarius semitorquatus*)

¹twenty-eighth \¦=¦=¦=\ *adj* **1 :** being number 28 in a countable series ⟨the *twenty-eighth* day⟩ — see NUMBER table **2 :** being one of 28 equal parts into which something is divisible ⟨a *twenty-eighth* share of the money⟩

²twenty-eighth \"\ *n* **1 :** number 28 in a countable series ⟨the *twenty-eighth* of the month⟩ **2 :** the quotient of a unit divided by 28 **:** one of 28 equal parts of something ⟨one *twenty-eighth* of the total⟩

¹twenty-fifth \¦=¦=¦=\ *adj* **1 :** being number 25 in a countable series ⟨the *twenty-fifth* day⟩ — see NUMBER table **2 :** being one of 25 equal parts into which something is divisible ⟨a *twenty-fifth* share of the money⟩

²twenty-fifth \"\ *n* **1 :** number 25 in a countable series ⟨the *twenty-fifth* day of the month⟩ **2 :** the quotient of a unit divided by 25 **:** one of 25 equal parts of something ⟨one *twenty-fifth* of the total⟩

¹twenty-first \¦=¦=\ *adj* **1 :** being number 21 in a countable series ⟨the *twenty-first* day⟩ — see NUMBER table **2 :** being one of 21 equal parts into which something is divisible ⟨a *twenty-first* share of the money⟩

²twenty-first \"\ *n* **1 :** number 21 in a countable series ⟨the *twenty-first* of the month⟩ **2 :** the quotient of a unit divided by 21 **:** one of 21 equal parts of something ⟨one *twenty-first* of the total⟩

twenty-first·er \ˌ==¦=ə(r)\ *n* -s [*twenty-first* + *-er*] **:** the celebration of a 21st birthday

¹twenty-five \¦=¦=¦=\ *adj* **:** being one more than 24 in number ⟨*twenty-five* years⟩ — see NUMBER table

²twenty-five \"\ *pron, pl in constr* **:** 25 countable persons or things not specified but under consideration and being enumerated ⟨*twenty-five* are here⟩ ⟨*twenty-five* were found⟩

³twenty-five \"\ *n* **1 :** five and 20 **:** five fives **:** the square of five **2 a :** 25 units or objects ⟨a total of *twenty-five*⟩ **b :** a group or set of 25 ⟨arranged by *twenty-fives*⟩ **3 :** the numerable quantity symbolized by the arabic numerals 25 **4 :** the 25th in a set or series; *esp* **:** an article of clothing of the 25th size ⟨wears a *twenty-five*⟩ **5 :** a 25-caliber pistol — usu. written .25

¹twenty-four \¦=¦=¦=\ *adj* **:** being one more than 23 in number ⟨*twenty-four* years⟩ — see NUMBER table

²twenty-four \"\ *pron, pl in constr* **:** 24 countable persons or things not specified but under consideration and being enumerated ⟨*twenty-four* are here⟩ ⟨*twenty-four* were found⟩

³twenty-four \"\ *n* **1** : four and 20 : twice 12 : 12 times two : three times eight : four times six : two dozen **2 a** : 24 units or objects ⟨a total of *twenty-four*⟩ **b** : a group or set of 24 **3** : the numerable quantity symbolized by the arabic numerals 24 **4** : the 24th in a set or series; *esp* : an article of clothing of the 24th size ⟨wears a *twenty-four*⟩ **5 twenty-fours** *pl, archaic* : TWENTY-FOURMO

twenty-four·mo \¦==¦=,mō\ *n* -s [*twenty-four* + *-mo*] : the size of a piece of paper cut 24 from a sheet; *also* : paper or a page of this size — abbr. *24mo*; symbol *24°*; see BOOK tables

¹**twenty-fourth** \¦==¦=\ *adj* **1** : being number 24 in a countable series ⟨the *twenty-fourth* day⟩ — see NUMBER table **2** : being one of 24 equal parts into which something is divisible ⟨a *twenty-fourth* share of the money⟩

²**twenty-fourth** \"\ *n* **1** : number 24 in a countable series ⟨the *twenty-fourth* of the month⟩ **2** : the quotient of a unit divided by 24 : one of 24 equal parts of something ⟨one *twenty-fourth* of the total⟩

¹**twenty-nine** \¦==¦=\ *adj* : being one more than 28 in number ⟨*twenty-nine* years⟩ — see NUMBER table

²**twenty-nine** \"\ *pron, pl in constr* : 29 countable persons or things not specified but under consideration and being enumerated ⟨*twenty-nine* are here⟩ ⟨*twenty-nine* were found⟩

³**twenty-nine** \"\ *n* **1** : nine and 20 **2 a** : 29 units or objects ⟨a total of *twenty-nine*⟩ **b** : a group or set of 29 **3** : the numerable quantity symbolized by the arabic numerals 29 **4** : the 29th in a set or series; *esp* : an article of clothing of the 29th size ⟨wears a *twenty-nine*⟩

¹**twenty-ninth** \¦==¦=\ *adj* **1** : being number 29 in a countable series ⟨the *twenty-ninth* day⟩ — see NUMBER table **2** : being one of 29 equal parts into which something is divisible ⟨a *twenty-ninth* share of the money⟩

²**twenty-ninth** \"\ *n* **1** : number 29 in a countable series ⟨the *twenty-ninth* of the month⟩ **2** : the quotient of a unit divided by 29 : one of 29 equal parts of something ⟨one *twenty-ninth* of the total⟩

¹**twenty-one** \¦==¦=\ *adj* : being one more than 20 in number ⟨*twenty-one* years⟩ — see NUMBER table

²**twenty-one** \"\ *pron, pl in constr* : 21 countable persons or things not specified but under consideration and being enumerated ⟨*twenty-one* are here⟩ ⟨*twenty-one* were found⟩

³**twenty-one** \"\ *n* **1** : one and 20 : three times seven **2 a** : 21 units or objects ⟨a total of *twenty-one*⟩ **b** : a group or set of 21 **3** : the numerable quantity symbolized by the arabic numerals 21 **4** : the 21st in a set or series; *esp* : an article of clothing of the 21st size ⟨wear a *twenty-one*⟩ **5** *or* **21** [trans. of F *vingt-et-un*] : a card game the object of which is to be dealt cards having a higher count than those of the dealer up to but not exceeding 21 — called also *blackjack, vingt-et-un*

twenty-penny nail \¦==¦==-\ *n* : a 4-inch nail

twenty questions *n pl but sing in constr, often cap T&Q* : a game in which one player or team tries to determine from yes and no answers to not more than 20 questions what word or object the others have chosen to be guessed

¹**twenty-second** \¦==¦==\ *adj* **1** : being number 22 in a countable series ⟨the *twenty-second* day⟩ — see NUMBER table **2** : being one of 22 equal parts into which something is divisible ⟨a *twenty-second* share of the money⟩

²**twenty-second** \"\ *n* **1** : number 22 in a countable series ⟨the *twenty-second* of the month⟩ **2** : the quotient of a unit divided by 22 : one of 22 equal parts of something ⟨one *twenty-second* of the total⟩ **3** : a pipe-organ stop of 1-foot pitch

¹**twenty-seven** \¦==¦==\ *adj* : being one more than 26 in number ⟨*twenty-seven* years⟩ — see NUMBER table

²**twenty-seven** \"\ *pron, pl in constr* : 27 countable persons or things not specified but under consideration and being enumerated ⟨*twenty-seven* are here⟩ ⟨*twenty-seven* were found⟩

³**twenty-seven** \"\ *n* **1** : seven and 20 : three times nine : the cube of three **2 a** : 27 units or objects ⟨a total of *twenty-seven*⟩ **b** : a group or set of 27 **3** : the numerable quantity symbolized by the arabic numerals 27 **4** : the 27th in a set or series; *esp* : an article of clothing of the 27th size ⟨wears a *twenty-seven*⟩

¹**twenty-seventh** \¦==¦==\ *adj* **1** : being number 27 in a countable series ⟨the *twenty-seventh* day⟩ — see NUMBER table **2** : being one of 27 equal parts into which something is divisible ⟨a *twenty-seventh* share of the money⟩

²**twenty-seventh** \"\ *n* **1** : number 27 in a countable series ⟨the *twenty-seventh* day of the month⟩ **2** : the quotient of a unit divided by 27 : one of 27 equal parts of something ⟨one *twenty-seventh* of the total⟩

¹**twenty-six** \¦==¦=\ *adj* : being one more than 25 in number ⟨*twenty-six* years⟩ — see NUMBER table

²**twenty-six** \"\ *pron, pl in constr* : 26 countable persons or things not specified but under consideration and being enumerated ⟨*twenty-six* are here⟩ ⟨*twenty-six* were found⟩

³**twenty-six** \"\ *n* **1** : six and 20 : two times 13 **2 a** : 26 units or objects ⟨a total of *twenty-six*⟩ **b** : a group or set of 26 **3** : the numerable quantity symbolized by the arabic numerals 26 **4** : the 26th in a set or series; *esp* : an article of clothing of the 26th size ⟨wears a *twenty-six*⟩

⁴**twenty-six** \"\ *n* : a gambling game in which one wins if he rolls his chosen number 26 or more times in 13 rolls of 10 dice

¹**twenty-sixth** \¦==¦=\ *adj* **1** : being number 26 in a countable series ⟨the *twenty-sixth* day⟩ — see NUMBER table **2** : being one of 26 equal parts into which something is divisible ⟨a *twenty-sixth* share of the money⟩

²**twenty-sixth** \"\ *n* **1** : number 26 in a countable series ⟨the *twenty-sixth* of the month⟩ **2** : the quotient of a unit divided by 26 : one of 26 equal parts of something ⟨one *twenty-sixth* of the total⟩

¹**twenty-third** \¦==¦=\ *adj* **1** : being number 23 in a countable series ⟨the *twenty-third* day⟩ — see NUMBER table **2** : being one of 23 equal parts into which something is divisible ⟨a *twenty-third* share of the money⟩

²**twenty-third** \"\ *n* **1** : number 23 in a countable series ⟨the *twenty-third* of the month⟩ **2** : the quotient of a unit divided by 23 : one of 23 equal parts of something ⟨one *twenty-third* of the total⟩

¹**twenty-three** \¦==¦=\ *adj* : being one more than 22 in number ⟨*twenty-three* years⟩ — see NUMBER table

²**twenty-three** \"\ *pron, pl in constr* : 23 countable persons or things not specified but under consideration and being enumerated ⟨*twenty-three* are here⟩ ⟨*twenty-three* were found⟩

³**twenty-three** \"\ *n* **1** : three and 20 **2 a** : 23 units or objects ⟨a total of *twenty-three*⟩ **b** : a group or set of 23 **3** : the numerable quantity symbolized by the arabic numerals 23 **4** : the 23d in a set or series; *esp* : an article of clothing of the 23d size ⟨wears a *twenty-three*⟩ **5** : a railway telegraph signal for a message of greatest urgency **6** : the end : that's all — compare TWENTY-THREE SKIDDOO

twenty-three skiddoo *vi imper* : SCRAM ⟨*twenty-three skiddoo* to anyone who says different —H.A.Smith⟩

twenty-twenty \¦==¦==\ *or* **20/20** \"\ *adj* : having the normal visual acuity of the human eye that according to one common scale can distinguish at a distance of 20 feet characters one-third inch in diameter

¹**twenty-two** \¦==¦=\ *adj* : being one more than 21 in number ⟨*twenty-two* years⟩ — see NUMBER table

²**twenty-two** \"\ *pron, pl in constr* : 22 countable persons or things not specified but under consideration and being enumerated ⟨*twenty-two* are here⟩ ⟨*twenty-two* were found⟩

³**twenty-two** \"\ *n* **1** : two and 20 : twice 11 : 11 times two **2 a** : 22 units or objects ⟨a total of *twenty-two*⟩ **b** : a group or set of 22 **3** : the numerable quantity symbolized by the arabic numerals 22 **4** : the 22d in a set or series; *esp* : an article of clothing of the 22d size ⟨wears a *twenty-two*⟩ **5** : a 22-caliber rifle or pistol — usu. written .22

twerp *also* **twirp** \'twərp, -wəp\ *n* -s [origin unknown] : an insignificant or contemptible fellow ⟨can't mind the silly ~ —Earle Birney⟩

twi *or* **tshi** *also* **tchi** \'chwē, 'twē, 'chē\ *n* -s *usu cap* **1** : a dialect of Akan spoken by the Akwapim people **2** : a literary language based on the Twi dialect and used by the Akim, Akwapim, Ashanti, and other Akan-speaking peoples

twi- *prefix* [ME, fr. OE; akin to OFris & OS *twi-*, OHG *zwi-*, ON *tvi-*, *tvē-*, L *bi-* (fr. OL *dui-*), Gk *di-*, Lith *dvi-* twi-, OE *twēgen, twā, tū* two — more at TWO] : two : double : doubly : twice ⟨*twi*-circle⟩ ⟨*twi*-faced⟩

twi *abbr* twilight

twi·bil *or* **twi·bill** \'twī,bil, -,bəl\ *n* -s [ME, a kind of two-bladed ax, mattock, fr. OE *twibill*, fr. *twi-* + *bill* two-edged sword — more at BILL] **1** : a double-headed battle-ax **2** *dial Eng* : a reaping hook esp. for cutting beans

¹**twice** \'twīs\ *adv* [ME *twies, twys*, fr. OE *twiges*, fr. *twiga, twiwa* twice + *-es* -s; akin to OE *twi-* — *more at* TWI-] **1** : for a first and second time : on two occasions ⟨~ absent without leave⟩ **2** : two times : as multiplied by two : in doubled quantity, amount, or degree ⟨~ two is four⟩ ⟨would be guaranteed ~ over —*Newsweek*⟩ — **at twice** *adv* **1** : at two different times or operations ⟨pay a debt *at twice*⟩ **2** : at the second time or operation ⟨succeeded *at twice*⟩

²**twice** \"\ *adj, archaic* : TWOFOLD

twice-accented octave \¦==¦==-\ *n* : TWO-LINE OCTAVE

twice-born \'=¦=\ *adj* [ME *twys borne*] **1** : born a second time : REINCARNATED **2** : having undergone a definite experience of fundamental moral and spiritual renewal : having experienced a religious conversion : REGENERATE ⟨the Anabaptist view that the church should consist exclusively of *twice-born* individuals⟩ **3** : of or being one of the three upper Hindu varnas of ancient Aryan origin in which boys undergo an initiation ceremony symbolizing spiritual birth and are invested with the sacred thread

twice-laid \'=¦=\ *adj* : made from the ends of rope and strands of used rope ⟨*twice-laid* rope⟩

twic·er \'twīsə(r)\ *n* -s [¹*twice* + *-er*] **1** : one that does something twice or does two things: as **a** : one that attends two Sunday church services **b** *Brit* : a printer who works as both compositor and pressman — usu. used disparagingly **2** *chiefly Brit* **a** : CHEAT, CROOK **b** : a two-time loser ⟨he's already a ~. Any time he's picked up carrying a gun he's liable to get life —Hartley Howard⟩

twice-stabbed ladybird \'=¦=-\ *n* : a small black predatory beetle (*Chilocoris stigma*) of the family Coccinellidae marked with a bright orange dot on each wing cover and important as a predator on citrus scale insects in Florida

twicet \'twīst\ *substand var of* TWICE

twice-told \'=¦=\ *adj* [ME *twies told*] **1** *obs* : counted twice : reckoned or added up two times **2 a** : narrated twice **b** : HACKNEYED, OLD, TRITE — used chiefly in the phrase *a twice-told tale*

twi·child \'twichəl(d)\ *n* [*twi-* + *child*] **1** : one who is in his dotage **2** : DOTAGE

twick·en·ham \'twik(ə)nəm\ *adj, usu cap* [fr. *Twickenham*, England] : of or from the municipal borough of Twickenham, England : of the kind or style prevalent in Twickenham

¹**twid·dle** \'twid°l\ *vb* **twiddled; twiddled; twiddling** \-d(°)liŋ\ **twiddles** [origin unknown] *vi* **1** : to be busy with trifles : act or play negligently with something : FIDDLE ⟨*twiddled* with his moustaches⟩ **2** : to turn or jounce lightly : JIGGLE, QUIVER, TWIRL ⟨the log . . . ~s round and round in the water —J.B.S.Haldane⟩ ~ *vt* : to rotate (something) lightly or idly : play with : TURN, TWIRL ⟨vaguely *twiddled* his cigar —James Lord⟩ ⟨I closed the safe door and *twiddled* the knob —C.B.Kelland⟩ — **twiddle one's thumbs** : to spend time vacantly : do nothing ⟨kept the manager busy and left me *twiddling my thumbs*⟩

²**twiddle** \"\ *n* -s : an act of twiddling or twirling something : TURN, TWIST ⟨gave the wheel a ~ to avoid a casual dog —P.G.Wodehouse⟩

³**twiddle** \"\ *vi* **twiddled; twiddled; twiddling** \-d(°)liŋ\ **twiddles** [imit.] **1** : to chatter or gabble idly **2** : to play negligently on a musical instrument

twiddle-twaddle \¦==¦==\ *n* [redupl. of *twaddle*] : empty chatter : TWADDLE

twiddling line *n* **1** *obs* : a line fastened to a ship's steering wheel to steady or secure it **2** : a line holding the rudder of an open boat in a desired position

twid·dly \'twid(°)lē, -li\ *adj* -ER/-EST : TWIDDLING, TWISTING, TRIVIAL ⟨they would walk through the ~ lanes —Aldous Huxley⟩ ⟨~ food⟩

twifallow *vt* [*twi-* + *fallow*] *obs* : to plow for the second time

twi·fold \'twī,fōld\ *adj* [ME, fr. OE *twifeald*, fr. *twi-* + *-feald* -fold] : TWOFOLD

twi-formed \'=¦=\ *also* **twi-form** \'=¦=\ *adj* [*twi-* + *formed* or *-form*] : having two shapes or bodies : combining incongruous constituents

¹**twig** \'twig\ *n* -s [ME *twigge*, fr. OE; akin to OE *twig*, MLG *twich*, OHG *zwīg* twig, OE *twēgen, twā, tū* two — more at TWO] **1** : a small shoot or branch usu. without its leaves : a portion of stem of no definite length or size **2** : a minute branch of a nerve or artery ⟨auricular ~s of the coronary arteries —C.H.Best & N.B.Taylor⟩ **3** : a divining rod ⟨with the twirl of a hazel ~ has found water on dozens of small holdings —*Irish Digest*⟩

²**twig** \"\ *vt* **twigged; twigged; twigging; twigs** : to beat with or as if with a twig : SWITCH

³**twig** \"\ *vt* **twigged; twigged; twigging; twigs** [prob. alter. of E dial. *twick* to twist, twitch, tweak, fr. ME *twikken* — more at TWEAK] : PULL, TWITCH

⁴**twig** \"\ *n* -s : PULL, TUG

⁵**twig** \"\ *vb* **twigged; twigged; twigging; twigs** [perh. fr. ScGael *tuig* I understand, perceive] *vt* **1** : NOTICE, OBSERVE, PERCEIVE, WATCH ⟨reflected that the paratrooper might not have *twigged* him —Earle Birney⟩ **2** : to understand the meaning of : COMPREHEND ⟨by their use of words you can ~ what is wrong with them —Christopher Morley⟩ ~ *vi* : NOTICE, UNDERSTAND ⟨she probably *twigged* instinctively about things being a bit rough for him —H.E.Bates⟩

⁶**twig** \"\ *n* -s [origin unknown] *Brit* : FASHION, MODE, STYLE ⟨a plan she formed for going to the ball in proper ~ —Samuel Lover⟩

twig beetle *n* : any of various small beetles that bore in twigs; *esp* : BARK BEETLE

twig blight *n* : a dying back (as in fire blight or brown rot) of the terminal branches or twigs of woody plants — compare DIEBACK, WITHERTIP

twig borer *n* : any of various small beetles or their larvae or the larvae of small moths that bore in twigs of trees or shrubs — compare APPLE TWIG BORER, PEACH TWIG BORER

twig budding *n* : a modified shield budding (as in budding dormant English walnuts in California) in which the scion consists of a prong, spur, or twig

twig caterpillar *n* : any of several slender loopers (family Geometridae) that assume a resting and protective position on the side of a twig to which they attach by the anal prolegs

twig drop *n* : the shedding of twigs or small branches because of nutritional disturbances

twig gall *n* : any of numerous galls that develop on the twigs of trees or shrubs

twigged \'twigd\ *adj* [¹*twig* + *-ed*] : having twigs esp. of a specified kind or color

twig·gen \'twigən\ *adj* [¹*twig* + *-en*] *archaic* : made of twigs : covered with wickerwork

twig·gery \'twigərē, -ri\ *n* -ES [¹*twig* + *-ery*] : all the twigs of a shrub or tree ⟨this ailing tree was the only survivor . . . and so its ~ had to accommodate the sparrows —C.D.Stewart⟩

twig girdler *n* : GIRDLER 2

twig·gy \'twigē, -gi\ *adj* -ER/-EST [¹*twig* + *-y*] : of, relating to, or suggesting twigs: as **a** : DELICATE, SLIGHT, THIN ⟨the sandpipers staggered on ~ legs —Christopher Morley⟩ **b** : abounding in twigs ⟨~ trees —John Evelyn⟩

twig insect *n* : STICK INSECT

twig·let \'twiglət\ *n* -s : a small twig

twiglike \'=,=\ *adj* : resembling a twig

twig pruner *n* : any of numerous small beetles whose larvae bore in twigs of trees and cut them off as if pruned; *esp* : a longicorn beetle (*Elaphidion villosum*) infesting various hardwood trees in America

twig rush *n* : any of the rushlike sedges of the genus *Cladium* (esp. *C. mariscoides*) most of which have harsh-edged leaves

twigwithy \'=¦==\ *n* [¹*twig* + *withy*] : OSIER 1a

twi·light \'twī,līt, *usu* -īd·+V\ *n, often attrib* [ME, fr. *twi-* + *light*] **1** : the light from the sky between full night and sunrise or between sunset and full night produced by diffusion of sunlight through the atmosphere and its dust — compare ASTRONOMICAL TWILIGHT, CIVIL TWILIGHT, NAUTICAL TWILIGHT **2 a** : state of imperfect clarity, of dubiety, indefiniteness, or indistinctness, or of deepening obscurity, darkness, or gloom ⟨approaching the inglorious ~ of his career —Oscar Handlin⟩ ⟨the cynical, truculent democratic ~ to which they are expected to be loyal —R.S.Lynd⟩ ⟨he created a ~ which dimmed the brightness of Mother's success —Dorothy C. Fisher⟩ **3** *or* **twilight blue a** : a variable color averaging a pale purplish blue to pale violet that is lighter than dusk blue **b** : a grayish blue that is redder and paler than electric, greener and paler than copenhagen, and redder, lighter, and stronger than Gobelin

twilight arch *n* : the shadow of the earth on the atmosphere seen rising in the eastern sky during evening twilight and setting in the western sky during morning twilight as an arched pinkish band with a dark bluish area beneath

twilight band *n* : a narrow zone in which a pilot flying at the edge of the on-course radio beam can detect both the on-course and off-course signals

twi·light·ed \-,līd·əd, -līt·əd\ *adj* [*twilight* + *-ed*] : TWILIT

twilight effect *n* : a serious error in radio bearings that may arise from upheavals in the Heaviside layer which occur about sunset

twilight sleep *n* : a state in which awareness of pain is dulled and memory of pain is dimmed or effaced and which is produced by hypodermic injection of morphine and scopolamine and used chiefly in childbirth

twilight state *n* : a dreamy state lacking touch with present reality, occurring in epilepsy, hysteria, and schizophrenia, and sometimes induced with narcotics

twilight vision *n* : rod vision by the dark-adapted eye in dim light : SCOTOPIA — compare DUPLICITY THEORY, PURKINJE PHENOMENON

twi·lighty \'twī,līd·ē, -līt·ē, -i\ *adj* : having the color or brightness of twilight

twilight zone *n* **1** : the lowest part of the photic region of the ocean **2** : a zone lying on the border between two distinguishable fields, situations, subjects, or groups and exhibiting a blend of the characteristics of both without the distinctness of either ⟨a kind of *twilight zone* between East and West, an area which declines to be dominated by either —J.C.Harsch⟩ ⟨this *twilight zone* of what is implied but not actually stated —*Jour. of the Patent Office Society*⟩ ⟨increasing the area and the obscurity of the *twilight zone* which lies between state and federal functions —*New Republic*⟩ **3** : TWILIGHT BAND

twi·lit \'twī,lit\ *adj* [*twi-* + *lit*] : lighted by or as if by twilight : DIM ⟨a boat on a ~ river —Anthony West⟩

¹**twill** \'twil\ *n* -s [ME *twyll, twylle*, fr. OE *twilic* having a double thread, modif. (influenced by *twi-*) of L *bilic-, bilix*, fr. *bi-* + *-lic-, -lix* (akin to L *licium* thread)] **1** : a fabric with a twill weave (gabardine and serge are ~*s*) **2** *or* **twill weave** : a basic textile weave producing an allover surface pattern of fine diagonal lines or ribs usu. all running to the left or right and made by floating weft or warp threads over groups of two or more threads and staggering these floats regularly or irregularly to form a slanting line ⟨herringbone is a reversed or pointed ~⟩ ⟨gabardine has a steep ~⟩ **3** : a basketry pattern made by passing one or more wefts over two or more warps

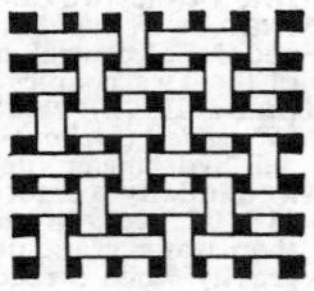

twill 2

²**twill** \"\ *vt* -ED/-ING/-S : to make (cloth) with a twill weave

³**twill** \"\ *n* -s [by alter.] *dial Eng* : QUILL

twilled \'twild\ *adj* : made with a twill weave

twill·ing \'twiliŋ, -lēŋ\ *n* -s : a twilled weave or part or the act or process by which it is produced

twil·ly \'twilē, -li\ *n* -ES [by alter.] : WILLOW 3a

twilt \'twilt\ *dial var of* QUILT

TWIMC *abbr* to whom it may concern

¹**twin** \'twin\ *adj* [ME, fr. OE *twinn* twofold, double, two by two; akin to OHG *zwinal* born a twin, *zwiniling* twin, ON *tvinnr, tvennr* two by two, in pairs, OE *twēgen, twā, tū* two — more at TWO] **1 a** : born with one other at the same birth ⟨a ~ brother⟩ ⟨a ~ lamb⟩ **b** : born as a pair at one birth ⟨~ girls⟩ **2 a** : made up of two similar, related, or connected members or parts : DOUBLE ⟨meet this ~ (not alternative) responsibility —H.M.Wriston⟩ ⟨this is the first half of the Crisis Question, this time a ~ question —Hazel Sullivan⟩ **b** : paired in a close or necessary relationship : MATCHING ⟨the ~ threats of war and inflation —*New Republic*⟩ **c** : having or consisting of two identical units **d** (1) : constituting two similar, closely associated, or otherwise paired persons, topics, or objects ⟨~ waiting rooms —*Amer. Guide Series: N.Y. City*⟩ ⟨two girls in ~ yellow dresses —Scott Fitzgerald⟩ ⟨the ~ realms of tactics and strategy —S.L.A.Marshall⟩ (2) : being one of a pair of similar or associated persons or things ⟨across the bay lies its ~ city⟩ **3** : formed by twinning of crystals

²**twin** \"\ *n* -s [ME, fr. OE *getwinn*; akin to OE *twinn* twofold — more at ¹TWIN] **1 a** : either of two offspring produced at a birth esp. in a species that ordinarily brings forth but one at a birth — see IDENTICAL TWIN **b twins** *pl, usu cap* : GEMINI 1 **2** : one of two persons or things closely related to or resembling each other ⟨a powder compact that was the ~ of the one the old guy had found —Hartley Howard⟩ **3** : a pair of offspring that are twins ⟨he was one of a ~⟩ **4** *or* **twin crystal** : a compound crystal composed of two or more crystals or parts of crystals of the same kind that are grown together in a specific rational manner so that there is at least one plane and the direction perpendicular thereto that are related in the same way to the crystallographic axes of both parts of the twin **5** : a well drilled on the same location as an existing oil well or gas well to tap a different producing formation ⟨an oil well may have four or five ~*s*⟩

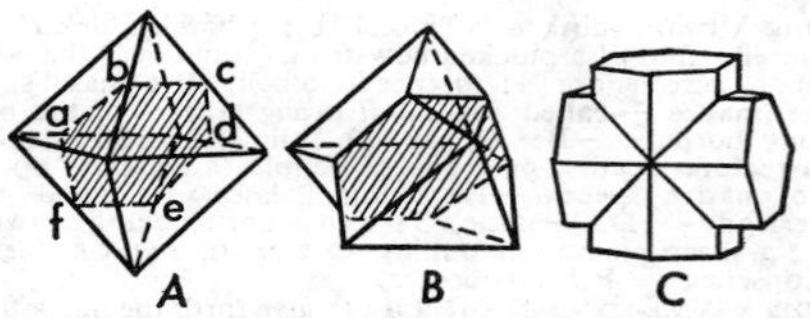

twin 4: *A* octahedron showing twinning plane *a b c d e f*; *B* contact twin; *C* penetration twin

³**twin** \"\ *vb* **twinned; twinned; twinning; twins** [ME *twinnen*, fr. *twin*, adj. & n.] *vt* **1** *Scot* : to put asunder : cause to be separated : PART, DIVIDE, SUNDER **2** : to bear as twins **3 a** : to bring together in close association : LINK, COUPLE, JOIN ⟨whose name will always remain *twinned* with that of the . . . institute —B.R.Redman⟩ **b** : DUPLICATE, MATCH, PARALLEL ⟨sat at a spacious desk whose highly polished surface *twinned* his upper half in reverse —V.V.Nabokov⟩ ~ *vi* **1** *Scot* : to go apart : SEPARATE **2** : to bring forth twins **3** *archaic* : to be born at the same birth with another **4** *obs* : to become coupled or combined : JOIN **5** : to grow as a twin crystal

twin-axis \(')=¦==\ *n* : the axis common to both individuals of a twin crystal

twin band mill *n* : a sawmill with both a right-hand and a left-hand saw that are adjustable and may be mounted on separate frames

twin bed *n* : one of a pair of matching single beds

twin·berry \'=- — *see* BERRY\ *n* **1** : a shrubby No. American honeysuckle (*Lonicera involucrata*) with purple involucrate flowers **2** : PARTRIDGEBERRY

twin bill *n* : DOUBLEHEADER

twinborn \'=¦=\ *adj* : born at the same birth

twin city *adj, usu cap T&C* [fr. the *Twin Cities*, nickname for Minneapolis and St. Paul, Minn.] : of or relating to the adjoining cities of Minneapolis and St. Paul, Minn. ⟨*Twin City* newspapers⟩

t winding *n, cap T* : an electrical T connection

twin disease *var of* TWIN-LAMB DISEASE

twin·dle \'twin°l\ *n* -s [²*twin* + *-le*] *dial* : TWIN

¹**twine** \'twīn\ *n* -s [ME *twin, twyne*, fr. OE *twīn*; akin to MD

twijn & twern twine, MHG *zwirn*, ON *tvinni* twine, OE *twēgen, twā, tū* two — more at TWO] **1 :** a strong string composed of two or more plies or strands twisted together and used for various purposes (as binding small parcels and making nets) **2 :** a twined or interlaced part or object: as **a :** the stem of a plant or vine **b :** a coil, twist, or convolution formed or seeming to be formed by winding **c :** something snarled or knotted **:** TANGLE **3 :** an act of twining, interlacing, or embracing **4** *dial Brit* **:** a peculiar ocean ripple preceding a southeast gale on the coast of Great Britain **5 :** a light grayish olive color that is greener and paler than hemp, darker than Quaker gray, and redder and darker than average citron gray — called also *anamite, dune*

²twine \"\ *vb* -ED/-ING/-S [ME *twinen*, fr. *twin, twyne*, n.] *vt* **1 :** to twist together **:** form by twisting or winding of threads **:** BRAID, WEAVE ⟨~ a wreath of flowers⟩ **2 a :** INTERLACE ⟨remembered . . . the way she had *twined* and untwined her fingers —John Buchan⟩ **b :** to cause to encircle or enfold another **:** clasp (something) about another **:** WRAP ⟨*twined* her arms around him⟩ **c :** to cause to be encircled with something else ⟨*twined* the porch pillars with wreathed flowers⟩ **3** *dial* **:** TWIST, WRENCH, WREST **~** *vi* **1 :** to coil about something **:** twist in spirals ⟨a vine that ~s about the tree trunk⟩ **:** WIND **2 :** to stretch or move in a winding or sinuous manner **:** MEANDER, UNDULATE ⟨a snake *twined* over the ground⟩ ⟨a river ~s through the valley⟩ **3** *dial Brit* **:** SQUIRM **syn** see WIND

twin–engine \'=,=\ *or* **twin–engined** \'=¦=\ *adj* **1 :** having two cylinders or two rows of cylinders **2 :** having two engines — used of an airplane

twin·er \'twīnə(r)\ *n* -S **:** one that twines: as **a :** a plant (as a morning glory) that climbs by twining about a support **b :** TWINE REELER

twine reeler *n* **:** a machine similar to the spinning mule for twisting twine and ply yarns

twinflower \'=,=\ *n* **:** LINNAEA 2: **a :** a low prostrate subshrub (*Linnaea borealis*) of northern parts of Europe and Asia with opposite leaves and fragrant usu. pink flowers borne in pairs **b :** a similar plant (*L. borealis americana* or *L. americana*) of northern No. America

¹twinge \'twinj\ *vb* -ED/-ING/-S [ME *twengen*, fr. OE *twengan*; prob. akin to OHG *dwengen* to compel, apply force to, *dwingan* to oppress, overcome, compel — more at THONG] *vt* **1** *dial* **:** PLUCK, TWEAK, TWITCH **2 :** to cause (one) a sharp or smarting pain **:** PRICK **~** *vi* **:** to feel a sudden sharp local pain **:** suffer a stabbing or smarting sensation

²twinge \"\ *n* -S **1** *obs* **:** TWEAK, TWITCH **2 a :** a sudden sharp stab of pain ⟨would have shrugged off ~s and creakings like mine as something quite to be expected in their early fifties —Edith M. Stern⟩ **b :** a moral or emotional pang **:** PRICKING ⟨a ~ of fear⟩ ⟨a ~ of conscience⟩ ⟨a ~ of envy⟩ **syn** see PAIN

twin·gle \'twiŋ(g)əl\ *vb* -ED/-ING/-S [origin unknown] *dial Brit* **:** TWIST, WRIGGLE

twingle–twangle \¦=¦=¦=\ *also* **twing–twang** \'twiŋ¦=\ *n* [*twingle-twangle* redupl. of ²*twangle; twing-twang* redupl. of *twang*] **:** the twang of a musical instrument

twinier *comparative of* TWINY

twiniest *superlative of* TWINY

twi–night \'twī,=\ *adj* [*twilight* + *night*] **:** of or relating to a baseball doubleheader in which the first game is played in the late afternoon and the second continues into the evening under lights

¹twink \'twiŋk\ *vi* -ED/-ING/-S [ME *twinken* — more at TWINKLE] **:** WINK, TWINKLE

²twink \"\ *n* -S [ME, fr. *twinken*, v.] **:** WINK, TWINKLING — used esp. in the phrase *in a twink*

³twink \"\ *vt* -ED/-ING/-S [origin unknown] *dial Eng* **:** PUNISH, THRASH

⁴twink \"\ *n* -S [imit.] *dial Brit* **:** CHAFFINCH

¹twin·kle \'twiŋkəl\ *vb* **twinkled; twinkled; twinkling** \-k(ə)liŋ\ **twinkles** [ME *twinklen*, fr. OE *twinclian*; akin to ME *twinken* to wink, twinkle, MD *twinc* wink of an eye, MHG *zwinken* to blink] *vi* **1 :** to shine with a flickering, sparkling, or intermittent light **:** give off a fluctuating radiance **:** SCINTILLATE ⟨stars *twinkled* in the night sky⟩ ⟨street lamps *twinkled* dully —Wilson Collison⟩ ⟨tiny wavelets *twinkling* among the black boulders —William Beebe⟩ **2 a :** to flutter the eyelids **:** blink the eyes open and shut **b :** to emit gleams of joy, merriment, or other vivid usu. happy feeling **:** FLASH, GLITTER, SPARKLE ⟨his eyes *twinkled* in a friendly way —T.B.Costain⟩ **c :** to beam with gay or lively feeling ⟨~s happily through gold-rimmed spectacles —*Irish Digest*⟩ **3 :** to move in flashing or evanescent manner **:** flutter or flit rapidly ⟨the buggy *twinkled* away in the sunlight —Katherine Mansfield⟩ ⟨her little feet *twinkled* on the pavement —A.R.Foff⟩ **~** *vt* **1 :** to cause to shine with fluctuating or intermittent light **:** give off radiance from ⟨*twinkled* her blue eyes⟩ ⟨in the dark coverts the . . . beetle ~s its tiny lamp —Haldane MacFall⟩ **2 :** to transmit or communicate by a gleam of the eyes ⟨stopped *twinkling* mischief at him —Richard Blaker⟩ ⟨not one bright star to ~ hope and light to him —Meg Dyan⟩ **3 :** to flicker or flirt rapidly **:** twitch with flashing motions ⟨deer feeding, *twinkling* their scuts as they moved —Maurice Hewlett⟩

²twinkle \"\ *n* -S **1 :** a winking or blinking of the eyes **:** a flutter or quiver of the eyelids **2 :** the instant's duration of a flicker of the eyelids **:** TWINKLING, WINK — used esp. in the phrase *in a twinkle* ⟨and in a ~ it is gone —D.G.Campbell⟩ **3 :** an intermittent radiance **:** FLICKER, GLEAM, SPARKLE ⟨a laughing ~ in his bright eye —Charles Dickens⟩ **4 :** a rapid flashing motion **:** FLIRT ⟨a ~ of long, black-stockinged legs —Flora Thompson⟩ **5 :** a ballroom dance step in which one foot is brought forward, then to the side of the other, and finally to the rear or these movements executed in reverse order

twin·kler \-k(ə)lə(r)\ *n* -S **:** one that twinkles ⟨some very new, very young stars who proved to be rather ineffectual ~s —A.H.Dent⟩

twin·kling \-k(ə)liŋ, -liŋ\ *n* -S [ME, fr. gerund of *twinklen* to twinkle — more at TWINKLE] **1 a :** a winking of the eye **b :** the time required for a wink **:** INSTANT ⟨the kettle will boil in a ~ —*Punch*⟩ ⟨his patient would be carried off by meningitis in the ~ of an eye —Jean Stafford⟩ **2 a :** a momentary repetitive variation in brightness of a star due to the varying density of the air which produces constantly changing refractive and interference effects **:** SCINTILLATION **b :** a radiance likened to the twinkling of a star (as the gleam of an eye or the glimmering of city lights) **3 :** a rapid flashing motion ⟨the ~ of their wings was as in sweet rhythm to the ~ of their hues —Jack McLaren⟩

twin·kly \-k(ə)lē, -li\ *adj* [²*twinkle* + *-y*] **:** TWINKLING, BEAMING, SMILING ⟨a tall, ~ Scotsman —Philip Hamburger⟩

twin–lamb disease \'=¦=-\ *or* **twin disease** *n* **:** PREGNANCY DISEASE

twinleaf \'=,=\ *n* **:** an American perennial herb (*Jeffersonia diphylla*) with leaves of two leaflets and simple naked one-flowered scapes

twin–lens camera \'=¦=-\ *n* **:** a camera fitted with two lenses optically corrected to make them identical in their application

twin·ly *adj* [²*twin* + *-ly*] **:** of, relating to, or appropriate to a twin

twinned \¦twind\ *adj* [²*twin* + *-ed*] **1 :** born two at one birth **2 :** closely linked or associated **:** COUPLED **3 :** formed by twinning ⟨~ crystal⟩

twin·ner \'twinə(r)\ *n* -S **:** one that bears twins

twinning *n* -S [fr. gerund of ³*twin*] **1 :** the bearing of twins **:** production of a pair instead of one **2 :** the coupling, association, or comparison of two persons or things ⟨the usual ~ of Homer and Vergil —George Saintsbury⟩ **3 :** the assemblage of two or more crystals or parts of crystals in nonparallel but rational position with reference to each other — compare TWIN 4, SECONDARY TWINNING

twins *pl of* TWIN, *pres 3d sing of* TWIN

twin–screw \'=¦=\ *adj* **:** having a right-handed screw propeller and a left-handed screw propeller parallel to each other one on each side of the plane of the keel — compare SINGLE-SCREW

twin–screw pump *n* **:** a displacement pump consisting of a casing containing two parallel screws with intermeshing threads fitted to prevent backward movement of fluid

twin·ship \'twin,ship\ *n* [¹*twin* + *-ship*] **:** the quality or state of being twin **:** close similarity or association ⟨regimes . . . that hide their ~ to communism —*N. Y. Times Mag.*⟩

twin sister *n* **1 :** a girl born as one of twins **2 :** TWINFLOWER

twinspur \'=,=\ *n* **:** an erect annual herb (*Diascia barberae*) with flowers colored rosy pink with a yellow spot in the throat and growing in terminal racemes

¹twin·ter \'twintə(r)\ *n* -S [ME, fr. OE *twiwintre* two years old, fr. *twi-* + *winter*] *dial Brit* **:** a sheep, ox, or horse that has lived through two winters

²twinter \"\ *adj* [fr. (assumed) ME, fr. OE *twiwintre*] *dial Brit* **:** two years old — used esp. of sheep and cattle ⟨a ~ ewe⟩

twin valve *n* **:** a valve with one supply and two discharge openings

twiny \'twīnē, -ni\ *adj* -ER/-EST [in sense 1, fr. ¹*twine* + *-y*; in sense 2, fr. ²*twine* + *-y*] **1 :** of, relating to, or resembling twine **2 :** TWINING, INTERLACING

twire \'twī(ə)r\ *or* **tweer** \'twi(ə)r\ *vi* -ED/-ING/-S [perh. akin to MHG *zwieren* to wink] **1** *archaic* **:** to peep out **:** PEER **2** *obs* **:** TWINKLE

¹twirl *R* 'twərl, *esp before pause or consonant* 'twər·əl; *–R* 'twəl *or* 'twəil\ *vb* -ED/-ING/-S [perh. of Scand origin; akin to Norw dial. *tvirla, tvilla* to spin, twirl; akin to Fris *dwerlje, dwirlje* to whirl, MD *dwerelen* to whirl, OHG *dweran* to stir — more at TURBID] *vi* **1 :** to revolve rapidly **:** become whirled round **:** SPIN ⟨~*ing* about the floor⟩ **2 :** to writhe like a snake **:** move with sinuous twisting motion **:** UNDULATE **3 :** to pitch in a baseball game **~** *vt* **1 a :** to rotate rapidly **:** cause to take a circular, curving, or spiral course **:** SPIN, TWIST, WHIRL ⟨~*ed* his moustaches⟩ ⟨she ~*ed* the beater furiously —Christopher Bloom⟩ ⟨~*ed* an auburn curl about her finger⟩ ⟨spied two policemen ~*ing* their billies —W.A.Swanberg⟩ **b :** to flourish (a drum major's baton) in more or less elaborate whirling figures **2 :** PITCH 3b(2) **syn** see TURN

²twirl \"\ *n* -S **1 :** an act of rotating or spinning something or of revolving **:** a rapid circling or turning **:** WHIRL ⟨stood watching a skater's ~s and figure eights⟩ ⟨the flash and ~ of batons to strident martial music⟩ **2 :** something that turns or is turned or has a round or spiral form **:** COIL, CONVOLUTION, TWIST, WHORL ⟨distinctive loops and ~s of individual handwriting⟩ ⟨the spiral ~ of a seashell⟩

twirl·er \'twərlər; 'twələ(r, 'twəil-\ *n* -S **:** someone or something that twirls: as **a :** a baseball pitcher **b :** BATON TWIRLER **c :** any of various whirling toys

twirl·i·gig \-lē,gig, -lə,g-\ *n* -S [alter. of *whirligig*] **:** WHIRLIGIG BEETLE

twirling *n* -S **:** the act or practice of one that twirls; *esp* **:** the act or technique of a baseball pitcher or a baton twirler

twirly \'twərlē, -wəl-, -wəil-, -li\ *adj* -ER/-EST **:** CURLED, CURVED, TWISTED, SPIRAL ⟨exercise books with a ~ wire binder —Christopher Morley⟩

twirp *var of* TWERP

twis *pl of* TWI

¹twist \'twist\ *vb* -ED/-ING/-S [ME *twisten*, fr. OE *-twist* (in compounds) rope; akin to OFris & MLG *twist* quarrel, MD, quarrel, twine, OE *twēgen, twā, tū* two — more at TWO] *vt* **1 a :** to unite by winding a thread, strand, or wire around another **:** join by or as if by winding threads or strands together ⟨not less than two yarns are . . . ~*ed* together to form a strand —*Manual of Firemanship (Gt. Brit.)*⟩ **b :** PLAIT, WREATHE **c :** ENTWINE, INTERLACE **2 :** to coil around something **:** TWINE ⟨~*ed* her hair in ringlets around her finger⟩ **3 :** to associate intimately (as by a Luddite initiation) **4 a :** to wring, wrench, or wrest so as to dislocate or distort; *esp* **:** SPRAIN ⟨~*ed* my ankle⟩ **b :** to wrest the meaning or sense of **:** PERVERT, TORTURE ⟨one of those political phrases which can be ~*ed* to mean whatever the user wants it to mean —Arthur Krock⟩ ⟨tends to exaggerate and ~ many facts out of proportion —H.E.Salisbury⟩ **c :** to tighten up (facial muscles) **:** CONTORT ⟨~*ed* his face into a grin⟩ **d :** to pull off, turn, or break by means of a turning strain **:** force by torsion ⟨kept on tightening the nut until he ~*ed* it right off the bolt⟩ **e :** to cause to move with any of various turning motions (as by pivoting, revolving, or spiraling) ⟨~*ed* her rocking chair toward the table —Arnold Bennett⟩ **f :** to form into a spiral shape ⟨a pig's tail ~*ed* into a corkscrew⟩ **g :** to cause to take on moral, mental, or emotional deformity **:** WARP ⟨their lives and minds have been warped, ~*ed* and soured by the boom-boom, big-hit policy that now governs the game —John Lardner⟩ **h :** to wrest into an alien or unnatural form **:** force into a desired shape **:** DEFLECT, DISTORT, DIVERT ⟨~*ed* as many things as I could into laughing matters —J.B.Benefield⟩ ⟨~*ed* the authority of the church to the side of wealthy pewholders —V.L.Parrington⟩ **i :** to take (a winding, indirect, or devious course) to a destination or objective ⟨excitement one gets from watching a good broken-field runner ~*ing* his way to a long touchdown —Jerome Stone⟩ **5 :** to turn (a sheet of paper) for printing on the reverse by the work-and-twist method **6 :** to use misrepresentation or trickery to induce someone to drop (a life insurance policy) and buy (another) usu. in a different company **:** switch (life insurance) unscrupulously for someone **~** *vi* **1 :** to coil or wind with sinuous or tortuous motion **:** follow a winding course ⟨a narrow stream that ~s through green valleys —*Amer. Guide Series: N. C.*⟩ **2 a :** to turn or change shape under torsion ⟨the blade ~*ed* in the vise⟩ **b :** to bend into or assume a spiral shape **c :** SQUIRM, WRITHE ⟨he ~*ed* uneasily in his chair —T.B.Costain⟩ **3** *of a ball* **:** to rotate while taking a curving path or direction **4 :** to turn around **:** face about ⟨~*ed* around to see the approaching procession⟩ **5 :** to move forward while turning on an axis **:** advance while spinning ⟨if you travel fast . . . you might easily ~ over the edge into one of the steep ravines —Rose Macaulay⟩ ⟨the ball ~*ed* slowly from the pitcher's hand⟩ **syn** see CURVE, WIND — **twist one's arm :** to subject to overmastering pressure **:** COMPEL ⟨*twisted my arm* until I consented to drink —Hyman Goldberg⟩ — **twist around one's finger :** to influence (another) at will **:** dominate wholly (as by wiles or cajolery) — **twist the lion's tail** *often cap L* **:** to vex or anger Britain

²twist \"\ *n* -S [ME, fr. *twisten*, v.] **1 :** something formed by twisting or winding: as **a :** a thread, yarn, cord, or rope formed by twisting two or more strands together **b :** a strong tightly twisted sewing silk used esp. for buttonholes **c :** a complete turn of a fiber, yarn, roving, or cord about its axis: (1) **:** the hardness of a cord expressed as the number of such turns per inch (2) **:** the state of being so twisted **d :** a baked piece of twisted dough ⟨a bread ~⟩ ⟨cinnamon ~s⟩ **e :** tobacco leaves twisted into a thick compact roll **f :** a strip of citrus peel twisted above a drink in order to flavor it with the expressed oils and sometimes dropped into the drink itself **2 a :** the fleshing between an animal's hind legs; *esp* **:** the juncture of the thighs of cattle or sheep **b :** the curved tail of an animal (as a pug) **3** *obs* **:** the continuing thread of life **4 a :** the act of turning something or the state of being turned on or as if on its axis ⟨rounded a sharp corner with deft ~s of a file⟩ **b :** the spin given the ball in any of various games (as baseball) — compare CURVE, ENGLISH **c :** a spiral turn or curve (as that of an animal's horn) **d :** the spiral rifling of a gun barrel; *esp* **:** the distance in which rifling makes one complete turn of the barrel ⟨a 12-inch ~⟩ **e** (1) **:** torque or torsional stress applied to a body (as a rod or shaft) (2) **:** torsional strain (3) **:** the angle through which a thing is twisted **f :** a warp in lumber that bends one or more of the four corners of a board out of the plane of the others **5** *Brit* **:** a vigorous appetite **6 a :** a turning aside **:** BEND, DEFLECTION, DEVIATION ⟨the road wound through the hills with many a ~ and turn⟩ **b :** a local or individual peculiarity of pronunciation or inflection ⟨his outlandish ~ of tongue —Harriot B. Barbour⟩ **c :** a strong individual tendency or bent **:** a marked inclination or bias **:** ECCENTRICITY, IDIOSYNCRASY ⟨all sorts of strange characters, of every race and mind, poets, philosophers, cranks of every ~, were in our class —John Reed⟩ **d :** a wresting or distortion of meaning or sense **:** PERVERSION ⟨gave the facts an imperceptible ~ here and there to make the prisoner seem guilty⟩ **e :** a kinked or tangled confusion **:** an involved or intricate mess **7** *Brit* **:** a screw of paper used as a container **:** CORNET ⟨eats his sour olives out of a ~ of paper —Elizabeth Monroe⟩ **8 a :** an unexpected turn or development **:** a movement of action, plot, or policy in an unpredictable or astonishing direction ⟨~s of history which give piquancy to the past —G.P. Musselman⟩ ⟨provides a fictional account with an unusual ~ —T.C.Chubb⟩ **b :** DEVICE, TRICK ⟨all the old ~s of oratory were tried, but where there had been cheers before, there were now embarrassed silences —*Atlantic*⟩ ⟨acquainted with all the ~s that make for efficient cooking —Jane Nickerson⟩ **c :** a novel approach, procedure, or method **:** GIMMICK ⟨a teacher uses a new ~ for an assignment —W.D.Baker⟩ ⟨a new ~ in spending and saving habits —Sylvia F. Porter⟩ ⟨a ~ on the chain-letter idea —Saul Carson⟩ **9** *also* **twist disease :** a disease of wheat and rye that is caused by a fungus (*Dilophospora alopecuri*) often in association with an eelworm (*Anguina tritici*) and that causes earcockle of wheat **10 :** a front or back dive in which the diver beginning usu. at the highest point of the dive executes in corkscrew fashion but without bending the body a half turn or a complete turn by twisting the shoulders sideways so that the body follows the movement — compare FULL TWIST, HALF TWIST **11** *slang* **:** GIRL, WOMAN; *esp* **:** FLOOZY ⟨the blonde . . . looked like a two-bit ~ —Mickey Spillane⟩ **12** *Brit* **:** a warp thread **13 :** a spiral often colored line in the stem of a glass — compare AIR TWIST

twist bit *n* **:** a boring bit resembling a twist drill — compare SPUR BIT

twist disease *n* **1 :** a destructive disease of young salmonoid fishes due to injury of cartilage and perichondrium resulting from invasion of these tissues by a myxosporidian protozoan (*Myxosoma cerebralis*) **2 :** TWIST 9

twist dive *n* **:** a competitive diving category including those dives in which the body from a standing or running approach rotates around both a transverse and a longitudinal axis — compare *back dive, front dive, inward dive, reverse dive*

twist drill *n* **:** a drill having one or usu. two deep helical grooves extending from the point to the smooth portion of the shank

twisted *past of* TWIST

twisted cubic *n* **:** a cubic space curve cut by an arbitrary plane in three points

twisted curve *n* **:** SPACE CURVE

twisted flower *n* **:** a plant of the genus *Strophanthus*

twisted gear wheel *n* **:** SCREW WHEEL; *esp* **:** one having its axis parallel to that of another wheel that meshes with it

twisted heath *n* **:** a low evergreen shrub (*Erica cinerea*) of southern Europe naturalized at Nantucket in the U. S. with small bell-shaped rosy purple flowers — called also *Scotch heath*

twist·ed·ly *adv* **:** in a twisted manner

twisted pair *n* **:** an electric cable consisting of two insulated conductors twisted together for minimized induction and having no common wrap

twisted pine *n* **:** LODGEPOLE PINE a

twisted shovel *n* **:** a shovel cultivator with curved and twisted blades for throwing soil toward the roots of cultivated crops

twisted–stalk \'==,=\ *n* **:** a plant of the genus *Streptopus* of the family Liliaceae with slightly twisted stem, nodding usu. greenish or purplish flowers, and red berries — called also *liverberry*; *see* ROSE MANDARIN

twisted stomach worm *or* **twisted wireworm** *n* **:** a stomach worm (*Haemonchus contortus*)

twist·er \'twistə(r)\ *n* -S [¹*twist* + *-er*, n. suffix] **1 :** one that twists: as **a :** TWISTER-IN **b :** THROWSTER **c :** one that twists (as dough or yarn) or shapes (as pretzels or tobacco) into twists **d :** a ball with a combined onward and spinning motion ⟨a curve in baseball, a break ball in cricket, and a ball with English in billiards are all called ~s⟩ **e :** a textile machine or device for twisting single yarns into plied yarns or for adding twist to yarns without plying **f :** SPANISH WINDLASS **g :** SWIVEL PLOW **h :** a device for twisting small stumps out of the ground **i :** a device by which an arm or hand may be painfully twisted (as to subdue a prisoner) **2 :** a tornado, waterspout, sand column, or dust whirl in which the rotatory ascending movement of a column of air is esp. apparent ⟨a ~ may change from a tornado to a waterspout and back again many times as it crosses bays and rivers —S.D.Flora⟩ **3 :** a somersault in which an acrobat performs a difficult twist of his body in air **4 :** a twisted roll, doughnut, or cruller **5 a :** a shifty, tricky, or unprincipled person **:** someone evasive, devious, or unreliable ⟨he's a ~, but I'll be able to make him see that it'll pay him to be straight with me —Dorothy Sayers⟩ **b :** an insurance agent who unscrupulously induces someone to drop one policy and buy another usu. in a different company **6 a :** something difficult, overwhelming, confusing, or dumbfounding **:** POSER ⟨I might believe it tomorrow, but it's a bit of a ~ now, this minute —A.E.Coppard⟩ **b :** TONGUE TWISTER **7** *dial* **:** MALLARD **syn** see WIND

twister–in \'=¦=\ *n, pl* **twisters–in** [*twist in*, v. + *-er*] **:** a textile worker who twists or ties new warp threads onto ends left in the harness

twisthand \'=,=\ *n* [¹*twist* + *hand*] **:** a lace maker

twist·i·cal \'twistəkəl\ *adj* [²*twist* + *-ical*] **:** CROOKED, DEVIOUS, TORTUOUS

twist·i·fi·ca·tion \,twistəfə'kāshən\ *n* -S [¹*twist* + *-i-* + *-fication*] **1 :** an act of twisting **:** something twisting or twisted **:** TORTUOSITY ⟨his reporting articles are nearly totally free from ~ of fact into doctrine —W.R.Cross⟩ **2** *South & Midland* **:** a dancing game in which each couple in turn weaves in and out among others who stand in two lines

twist·i·fy \'==,fī\ *vt* -ED/-ING/-ES [back-formation fr. *twistification*] **:** to make twisting

twist·i·ness \-tēnəs, -tin-\ *n* -ES **:** the quality or state of being twisty **:** SINUOSITY, TORTUOSITY

twisting *n* -S [fr. gerund of ¹*twist*] **:** the use of misrepresentation or trickery to get someone to lapse a life insurance policy and buy another usu. in another company

twisting–in \¦=¦=\ *n, pl* **twistings–in** [fr. gerund of *twist in*, v.] **:** the attaching of the ends of a new warp to those of the old by twisting them together — compare TYING-IN

twisting paper *n* **:** a paper with high tensile strength in the machine direction that is cut into narrow strips and twisted into yarn or in lighter weights used for wrapping small pieces of candy

twis·tle \'twisəl\ *n* -S [²*twist* + *-le* (alter. of *-el*)] *Scot* **:** TWIST, WRENCH

twists *pres 3d sing of* TWIST, *pl of* TWIST

twist serve *n* **:** an overhand tennis serve that imparts spin to the ball and causes it to bounce high and to the left of the receiver

twist–set \'=¦=\ *vt* **:** to fix the twist in (yarns) by a steam treatment in order to prevent kinking or snarling during weaving or knitting

twisty \'twistē, -ti\ *adj* -ER/-EST [²*twist* + *-y*] **1 :** full of twists, bends, or sinuosities **:** WINDING ⟨~ roads are a pleasure to drive on —J. Eason Gibson⟩ **2 :** DEVIOUS, EVASIVE, TRICKY ⟨she begged him for love of her to beware of all that ~ sex —James Stephens⟩

¹twit \'twit, *usu* -id·+V\ *vt* **twitted; twitted; twitting; twits** [alter. of earlier *twite*, short for *atwite*, fr. ME *atwiten*, fr. OE *ætwītan* fr. *æt* at + *wītan* to guard, look after, reproach, blame; akin to OHG *wīzan* to punish, reproach, ON *vīta* to punish, blame, Goth *fraweitan* to avenge, *witan* to observe — more at AT, WIT] **1 :** to subject to ridicule or reproach **:** TAUNT ⟨nearly every day finds him . . . *twitting* reporters on their personal and professional weaknesses —*New Republic*⟩ ⟨some seamen were *twitting* him about dressing so formally —Joseph Whitehill⟩ **2 :** to impute or make game of as a fault ⟨*twitted* his laziness⟩ **syn** see RIDICULE

²twit \"\ *n* -S **1 :** an act of twitting **:** TAUNT **2** *Brit* **:** a silly peevish person **:** FOOL ⟨making a silly ~ of yourself —Noel Coward⟩ **3 :** a nervous or jumpy state **:** JITTERS ⟨what a ~ she had been in —Martha Gellhorn⟩ ⟨giving everybody the ~s —Richard Llewellyn⟩

³twit \"\ *n* -S [imit.] **:** TWITTER, CHIRP

⁴twit \"\ *n* -S [origin unknown] **:** a defect in yarn or roving; *usu* **:** a thin and weak place caused by too much twist

¹twitch \'twich\ *vb* -ED/-ING/-ES [ME *twicchen*; akin to OE *twiccian* to pluck, catch hold of, LG *twicken* to pinch, tweak, OHG *gizwickan*] *vt* **1 :** to pull with a sudden motion **:** JERK, PLUCK ⟨be sure he does not ~ his handwheel back and forth —*Coast Artillery Jour.*⟩ ⟨~*ed* him by the sleeve⟩ **2 :** to nip or pinch with or as if with pincers **:** inflict a pinching sting or smart on ⟨misgivings ~*ed* him at the prospect⟩ **3 :** to move (a body part) with a sudden jerky motion ⟨cows ~*ed* their flanks to drive off flies⟩ **4 :** to snatch as a thief or pickpocket ⟨~*ed* a purse from his pocket⟩ **5** *dial Brit* **a :** to draw tight with a cord **b :** draw (a cord) tight **6 :** to close on (a mineral lode) **:** NARROW — used of the surrounding rock **7** *NewEng* **:** SKID

— used of logs ~ *vi* **1 :** PULL, PLUCK ⟨~*ed* at my sleeve⟩ ⟨~*ed* at her skirt⟩ **2 a :** to move jerkily **:** JUMP, QUIVER ⟨her lips began to ~ —Marcia Davenport⟩ ⟨chestnuts ~*ed* on hot tin drums —Horace Sutton⟩ **b :** to ache with a sudden stabbing pain or twinge ⟨his corn ~*ed* like a bad tooth⟩ ⟨her conscience ~*ed* at the memory⟩ **3 :** PINCH 4 **syn** see JERK

²twitch \"\ *n* -ES **1 :** an act of twitching **:** a short sudden pull or jerk ⟨by a dexterous ~ got possession of the cuttings —John Buchan⟩ **2 :** a sudden sharp pain **:** PANG, TWINGE ⟨felt again the ~ of an old wound⟩ ⟨ignored a passing feeble ~ of conscience⟩ **3 :** a loop of rope or strap that is tightened over a horse's upper lip as a restraining device by twisting an attached stick **4 :** PINCH 4 **5 a :** a short spastic contraction of the muscle fibers **:** a simple muscular contraction **:** an involuntary muscular jerk ⟨the nerve was electrically stimulated and the muscle ~ was recorded —C.H.Thienes⟩ **b :** a slight jerk or motion of a body part ⟨saw by an icy ~ of her eyebrows that this would be presuming —Marcia Davenport⟩

³twitch \"\ *or* **twitch grass** *n* -ES [alter. of *quitch (grass)*] **1 :** COUCH GRASS 1a **2 :** SLENDER FOXTAIL

⁴twitch \"\ *vi* -ED/-ING/-ES **:** to clear land of twitch grass **:** gather and burn twitch grass

¹twitch·el \'twichəl\ *n* -S [ME *twychel*, alter. of *twychen*, fr. OE *twicen* fork in a road; akin to OE *twi-* — more at TWI-] *dial Eng* **:** a path between hedges

²twitchel \"\ *n* -S [¹*twitch* + *-el* (suffix used to denote an instrument)] *dial Eng* **:** NOOSE, TWITCH

³twitchel \"\ *vt* **twitchelled; twitchelled; twitchelling; twitchels** *dial Eng* **:** to tie up with a twitchel

twitch·ell process \'twichəl-\ *n, usu cap T* [after Ernst *Twitchell* †1929 Am. chemist] **:** a process for the acid hydrolysis of fats into fatty acids and glycerol that employs live steam and a Twitchell reagent as catalyst

twitchell reagent *n, usu cap T* [after E. *Twitchell*] **:** any of various sulfonated products used as catalysts in the Twitchell process: as **a :** a sulfonic acid made by condensing oleic acid with naphthalene in the presence of sulfuric acid **b :** a sulfonated petroleum product

twitch·er \-chə(r)\ *n* -S [¹*twitch* + *-er*] **:** one that twitches

twitchfire \'=,=\ *n* [³*twitch* + *fire*] **:** a fire for burning twitch grass from land ⟨like the drift of ~*s* blown in June —John Drinkwater⟩

twitch road *n* **:** a logging road

twitchy \'twichē, -chi\ *adj* -ER/-EST [¹*twitch* + *-y*] **:** FIDGETY, IRRITABLE

twite \'twīt\ *or* **twite finch** *n* -S [*twite* of imit. origin] **:** a linnet (*Carduelis flavirostris*) of northern Europe and Great Britain

twitlark \'=,=\ *n* [³*twit* + *lark*] *dial Eng* **:** MEADOW PIPIT

twits *pres 3d sing of* TWIT, *pl of* TWIT

twitted *past of* TWIT

twit·ten \'twitᵊn\ *n* -S [perh. alter. of ME *twichen* — more at TWITCHEL] *dial Eng* **:** a narrow lane

¹twit·ter \'twid·ə(r), -itə-\ *vb* **twittered; twittered; twittering** \-id·əriŋ, -itər-, -i·tr-\ **twitters** [ME *twiteren*; akin to OHG *zwizzirōn* to twitter, chirp; both of imit. origin] *vi* **1 :** to utter the successive chirping notes of a bird **:** make a bird's continuing small noises ⟨birds ~*ed* in the trees⟩ **2 a :** to chatter in light inconsequential fashion **:** talk busily of small or negligible things ⟨a home filled with ~*ing* gentlewomen —*Times Lit. Supp.*⟩ **b :** to laugh a light or silly laugh **:** GIGGLE, TITTER **3 :** to tremble with agitation **:** FLUTTER, QUIVER ⟨held up the amulet in a hand that ~*ed* —*Strand Mag.*⟩ ~ *vt* **1 :** to chirp out (as a bird's small noises) **2 :** to shake rapidly back and forth **:** FLUTTER ⟨raised his right hand above his head and ~*ed* his fingers —*Literary Review*⟩

²twitter \"\ *n* -S **1 :** a trembling agitation **:** a pitch of wild excitement **:** QUIVER ⟨your father's being so bent on it sets me all in a ~ —W.D.Howells⟩ **2 :** the chirping sounds of birds **3 :** a light chattering **:** GABBLE ⟨the ~ of the sportscasters and sports reporters —*Harper's*⟩

³twitter \"\ *n* -S [prob. fr. E dial. *twitter* pus, quittor, alter. of ¹*quitter* & *quittor*] **1 :** the refuse of the case of a sperm whale after the oil is pressed out **2 :** the thick tough tissue lining the case of a sperm whale

twit·ter·a·tion \,twid·ə'rāshən\ *n* -S [¹*twitter* + *-ation*] **:** FLUTTER, TWITTER, TIZZY

twitterboned \'=:=,=\ *adj* [E dial. *twitter* pus, quittor + *boned*] *dial Brit, of a horse* **:** having an excrescence on the hoof

twit·ter·er \'twid·ərə(r), -itə-\ *n* -S **:** one that twitters

twit·tery \-ərē, -ri\ *adj* [¹*twitter* + *-y*] **:** nervously agitated or infirm ⟨women for our mates who have great constitutional strength and are not ~ —James Thurber⟩

twitting *pres part of* TWIT

twit-twat \'twi·,twät, -it·,w-\ *n* -S [imit.] **:** HOUSE SPARROW

¹twit·ty \'twid·ē, -itē, -i\ *adj* -ER/-EST [²*twit* + *-y*] **1** *dial Brit* **:** ILL-TEMPERED, PEEVISH **2 :** CHIRPING, TWITTERING ⟨a little ~ bird —Kenneth Roberts⟩

²twitty \"\ *adj* -ER/-EST [⁴*twit* + *-y*] *of yarn* **:** varying in diameter **:** full of twits **:** UNEVEN

twixt \'twikst\ *prep* [ME *twix*, short for *betwix* — more at BETWIXT] **:** BETWEEN ⟨~ the charge and the conviction there is frequently great difference —Philip Wittenberg⟩

twiz·zle \'twizəl\ *vb* -ED/-ING/-S [prob. alter. of ²*twistle*] *Brit* **:** SPIN, TWIRL

twizzle-twig \'=,=,=\ *n, dial Eng* **:** a common rush (*Juncus articulatus*) of the north temperate zone

¹two \'tü\ *adj* [ME *twa, two*, adj. & pron., fr. OE *twā* (fem. & neut.); akin to OE *twēgen* two (masc.), *tū* (neut.), OHG *zwēne* (masc.), *zwā, zwō* (fem.), *zwei* (neut.), ON *tveir* (masc.) *tvær* (fem.), *tvau* (neut.), Goth *twai* (masc.), *twos* (fem.), *twa* (neut.), L *duo*, Gk *dyo*, Skt *dva*] **:** being one more than one in number ⟨~ years⟩ — see NUMBER table

²two \"\ *pron, pl in constr* [ME *twa, two*] **1 :** two countable persons or things not specified but under consideration and being enumerated ⟨~ are here⟩ ⟨~ were found⟩ **2 :** a small approximate number of indicated things **:** SO — used with a unitary noun and *or* ⟨fire a shot or ~⟩ ⟨come in a minute or ~⟩

³two \"\ *n* -S **1 :** twice one **2 a :** two units or objects ⟨a total of ~⟩ **b :** a group or set of two ⟨arranged by ~*s*⟩ **3 a :** the numerable quantity symbolized by the arabic numeral 2 **b :** the figure 2 **4 :** two o'clock — compare BELL table, TIME illustration **5 :** the second in a set or series: as **a :** a playing card marked to show that it is second in a suit **b :** a domino with two spots on one of its halves **c :** a die with two spots on the side uppermost **d :** an article of clothing of the second size ⟨wears a ~⟩ **6 :** a two-dollar bill **7 :** something having as an essential feature two units or members; *specif* **:** an opening bid in contract bridge of two in a suit when treated as a forcing bid and essential to a system of bidding — used chiefly in the phrases *forcing two* and *two demand* ⟨*two*-demand system⟩ — **in two** *adv* **:** into two more or less equal parts ⟨cut it *in two*⟩ — **in two twos** *adv, Brit* **:** in a very short time ⟨if she isn't here *in two twos* —James Stephens⟩

¹two-a-day \'=='=\ *adj* **1 :** used or presented twice a day ⟨a *two-a-day* theatrical attraction⟩ **2 :** presenting an entire vaudeville bill twice daily ⟨a *two-a-day* house⟩

²two-a-day \"\ *n* [¹*two-a-day*] **:** something used or presented twice daily; *esp* **:** a vaudeville show with two performances daily

two-along \'==,=\ *or* **two-on** \'=,=\ *adv* **:** with hand-sewn threads fastened on alternate ends of the sections ⟨a book sewed *two-along*⟩

two-and-one-half striper \'==(,)=,=-\ *n* **:** LIEUTENANT COMMANDER

two-arched \'=,=\ *adj* **:** having two temporal openings separated by a bony bar consisting of the fused prolongations of the postorbital and squamosal bones — used of a diapsid reptile

two-base hit \'=,=-\ *or* **two-bagger** \'=,==\ *n* **:** a base hit that enables a batter to reach second base safely **:** DOUBLE

two-beat \'=,=\ *adj* **1** *of jazz* **:** characterized by the accentuation of alternate beats in four-four time **2 :** playing or devoted to two-beat jazz (as Dixieland) ⟨a *two-beat* jazzman⟩ ⟨*two-beat* fans⟩

two-bid \'=,=\ *n* **:** an opening bid in contract bridge of two in a suit; *esp* **:** one treated as a forcing bid

two-bit \'=,=\ *adj* [*two bits*] **1 :** of the value of two bits ⟨a *two-bit* cigar⟩ **2 :** of small worth or importance **:** TRIFLING, PETTY, SMALL-TIME ⟨the attitude of a lot of the big cattlemen was that the *two-bit* ranchers were a nuisance —Bruce Siberts & W.D.Wyman⟩

two bits *n pl but sing or pl in constr* **1 :** the value of a quarter of a dollar ⟨shot craps for *two bits* a throw —C.G.Norris⟩ **2 :** something of small worth or importance ⟨an era that would make the achievements of the past look like *two bits* —W.S. Maugham⟩

two-block \'=,=\ *vt* [fr. the n. phrase *two blocks*] **1 :** to haul upon (tackle) so that the two blocks are chockablock ⟨*two-blocked* the tackle and snapped the cable⟩ **2 :** to hoist (as a signal flag or anchor) to the full extent

two-blocks \'=,=\ *adv* [fr. the n. phrase *two blocks*] **:** CHOCKABLOCK

two-body problem \'=,==-\ *n* **:** the problem of determining the previous or subsequent motion and the data for computing the places at any time of two bodies when given the Newtonian law of gravitation and the masses of two bodies with their positions and motions at any moment

two-bottom plow \'=,==-\ *n* **:** a plow having two moldboards or disks for plowing two furrows at a time

¹two-by-four \'=bə'=\ *adj* **1 :** measuring two units (as inches) by four **2 :** SMALL ⟨from *two-by-four* enterprises set up in barns and kitchens . . . to the big industrial plants —*N.Y. Herald Tribune Bk. Rev.*⟩ **:** PETTY, CRAMPED ⟨narrow, tight, *two-by-four* lives —Manuel Komroff⟩

²two-by-four \"\ *n* [¹*two-by-four*] **:** a piece of lumber having finished dimensions of 1⅝ by 3⅝ inches

two-by-twice \'=-bə'=\ *adj* **:** limited in size **:** SMALL, CRAMPED ⟨a *two-by-twice* sandwich shop⟩

two-card poker \'=,=-\ *n* **:** poker in which each player's hand contains only two cards, a pair is the highest-ranking hand, and unpaired hands are ranked by the rank of their cards with no counting of straights or flushes

two-centered arch \'==-\ *n* **:** an arch whose intrados curve is described from two centers

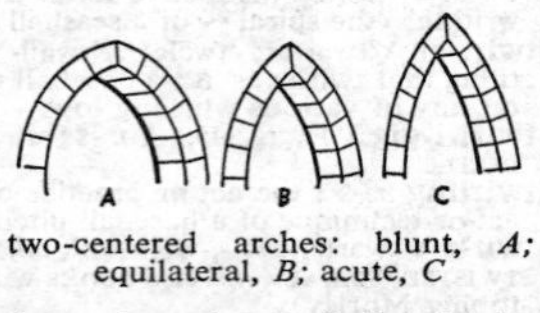

two-centered arches: blunt, *A*; equilateral, *B*; acute, *C*

two cents *n pl* **1 :** a sum or object of very small value **:** practically nothing ⟨said angrily that for *two cents* he'd punch your nose⟩ ⟨realized it was my mistake and felt like *two cents*⟩ **2** *or* **two cents worth :** an opinion offered on a topic under discussion ⟨giving each speaker the feeling that he is getting in his *two cents worth* —Dwight MacDonald⟩

two-charge rate \'=,=-\ *n* **:** a rate based upon the amount (as of electricity) used by a customer and upon his maximum demand

two-club system \'=,=-\ *n* **:** a system of bidding in contract bridge in which an opening bid of two clubs is artificial and forcing to game and the bidder's partner responds two diamonds to show a hand with less strength than one ace and one king

two-color \'=,==\ *adj* **1 :** having two colors **2** *of a photomechanical process* **:** printing in two colors

two-control airplane \'==,=-\ *n* **:** an airplane with no rudder in which control is achieved by means of ailerons and elevators only

two-course \'=,=\ *adj* **:** TWO-FIELD

two-cycle \'=,==\ *adj, of an internal combustion engine* **:** having a two-stroke cycle

2-D \'=,=\ *adj* **:** TWO-DIMENSIONAL 3

¹two-decker \'=,==\ *n* -S **1 a :** a ship with two decks **b :** an old-time warship with guns on two decks **2 :** something (as a bus) having two levels or layers

²two-decker \"\ *adj* **:** having two decks, levels, layers, or classifications ⟨a *two-decker* bus⟩ ⟨a *two-decker* tariff⟩ **:** DOUBLE-DECK

two-demand bid \'=,=-\ *n* **:** DEMAND BID

two-demand system *n* **:** CULBERTSON SYSTEM

two-dimensional \'==(=)=\ *adj* **1 :** having two dimensions; *specif* **:** having the coordinates of its points depending on two independent variables **2 a :** designed or effective primarily as a flat or surface composition ⟨*two-dimensional* painting or sculpture in the round⟩ **b :** lacking depth of literary characterization **:** MECHANICAL, WOODEN **3 :** not specially designed to give an illusion of depth or varying distances — used esp. of a motion picture; compare THREE-DIMENSIONAL — **two-dimensionally** \'==(=)=\ *adv*

two-dimensionality \'===,==\ *n* [*two-dimensional* + *-ity*] **:** the aspect or quality of being two-dimensional

two-dimensional motion *n* **:** UNIPLANAR MOTION

two-dimensional ramjet engine *n* **:** an airplane propulsion system of the ramjet type in which the flow passage of rectangular cross section has two sides parallel

two-dollar broker \'=,==-\ *n* **:** a broker who executes orders for other exchange members on the floor for a commission formerly of two dollars per 100 shares

two-double \'=,==\ *adj* **:** DOUBLE; *specif* **:** bent over in posture ⟨ran back to their bench *two-double* with laughter —Mary Webb⟩

two-edged \'=,=\ *adj* **:** DOUBLE-EDGED

two-egg \'=,=\ *adj* **:** DIZYGOTIC

two-em dash \'=,=-\ *n* **:** a printing dash that is two ems wide

two-eye berry \'=,=-\ *n* **1** *also* **two-eyes** \'=,=\ *pl but sing or pl in constr* **:** PARTRIDGEBERRY 1 **2 :** TWINFLOWER

two-faced \'=|fāst\ *adj* **1 :** having two faces **2 :** DOUBLE-DEALING **:** FALSE **3 :** AMBIGUOUS — **two-fac·ed·ly** \'=|fāsədlē, -āstlē, -li\ *adv* — **two-fac·ed·ness** \-sədnəs, -stnəs\ *n*

two-family house \'=(=)=-\ *n* **:** a house divided either vertically and designed for two families living side by side but separated by a party wall or horizontally and designed for two families occupying separate apartments one above the other — called also *duplex house*

two·fer \'tüfə(r)\ *n* -S [alter. of *two for* (as in such phrases as *two for a nickel*)] **1 :** a cheap item of merchandise; *specif* **:** a cigar selling at two for a nickel **2 :** a free coupon entitling the bearer to purchase two tickets to a specified theatrical production for the price of one at the box office

two-field \'=,=\ *adj* **:** of, using, or being a system of crop rotation in which the land is divided into two parts alternately left fallow

two-fisted \'=,==\ *adj* **:** VIRILE, VIGOROUS ⟨a red-blooded, go-getting, *two-fisted* American he-man —Weston La Barre⟩ ⟨a real *two-fisted* battle training —Carl Mann⟩

¹twofold \'=,=\ *adj* [ME *twafald, twofold*, fr. *twa, two* two + *-fald, -fold* -fold] **1 :** having two parts or aspects ⟨the office of a clergyman is ~: public preaching and private influence —R.W.Emerson⟩ **:** DOUBLE, DUAL, BINARY **2 :** being twice as large, as great, or as many as some understood size, degree, or amount ⟨a ~ increase⟩ **3 :** DIAD ⟨~ symmetry⟩

²twofold \"\ *adv* [ME *twafald, twofold*, fr. *twafald, twofold*, adj.] **1 :** to twice as much or as many **:** by two times ⟨increased ~⟩ **2** *Scot* **:** so as to be doubled up or bent over (as with age)

two-fold \"\ *n* [¹*two* + *fold*] **:** two stage flats hinged together so that they fold face to face

two·fold·ness *n* -ES **:** the quality or state of being twofold

twofold purchase *or* **twofold tackle** *n* **:** a tackle of two double blocks with the standing part of the rope fast to the block from which the hauling part comes ⟨the *twofold purchase* . . . is commonly used for hoisting boats —*Manual of Seamanship*⟩

twofold truth *n* **:** a theory that truth is not necessarily unitary but may have a theological side and a philosophic side each governing in its own realm even though it may contradict the other

two-foot octave \'=,=-\ *n* **:** ONE-LINE OCTAVE

two-foot pitch *n* **:** the pitch of a two-foot stop on a pipe organ

two-foot stop *n* **:** a pipe-organ stop sounding pitches two octaves higher than the notes indicate — compare EIGHT-FOOT STOP

two-forked \'=,=\ *adj* **:** divided into two parts somewhat after the manner of a fork **:** DICHOTOMOUS, BIFURCATE

two-forty \'=,==\ *n* [so called fr. its having once been a trotting record] **1 :** a speed of a mile in two minutes and forty seconds ⟨ran like *two-forty*⟩ **2 :** high speed

two-four \'=,=\ *or* **two-four time** *n* **:** the time of a musical composition having two quarter notes or tones or their equivalent to a measure and indicated by the time signature 2/4 ⟨a quick dance in *two-four*⟩

2, 4-D \'=,=,=\ *abbr or n* -S dichlorophenoxyacetic acid

2, 4, 5-T \'=,=,=\ *abbr or n* -S trichlorophenoxyacetic acid

two-gun \'=,=\ *adj* **:** carrying two guns **:** adept at the use of two guns ⟨a fighting *two-gun* marshal —*Popular Western*⟩

two-handed \'=,==\ *adj* [ME *too-honded*, fr. *too, two* two + *honded, handed* handed] **1** *or* **two-hand** \'=,=\ **:** designed for or requiring the use of both hands ⟨a *two-hand* manual alphabet⟩ **2 :** requiring two persons for operation ⟨a *two-handed* saw⟩ **3 :** STOUT, STRONG **4 :** having or efficient with two hands — **two-hand·ed·ly** *adv* — **two-hand·ed·ness** *n*

two-headed snake \'=,==-\ *n* **1 :** a snake (as some small boas and the cylinder snakes) with a blunt tail that resembles a head **2 :** a limbless lizard of the family Amphisbaenidae

two-high \'=,=\ *adj* **:** of or being a rolling mill with two rolls one over the other — compare THREE-HIGH

two-hole \'=,=\ *n* **:** the favored position at the rail behind the lead horse in harness racing

two-holer \'=,==\ *n* **:** a privy with two openings

two kettle *n, pl* **two kettle** *or* **two kettles** *usu cap T&K* **:** a Dakota people constituting a division of the Tetons

two-leaved solomon's-seal \'=,=-\ *n, usu cap 1st S* **:** FALSE LILY OF THE VALLEY

two leg *n* **:** MIDDLE AND LEG

two-line \'=,=\ *adj* **:** of twice the depth or point size of the type or letter named or understood ⟨a *two-line* initial⟩ ⟨a *two-line* letter⟩ — distinguished from *double*

two-lined chestnut borer \'=,=-\ *n* **:** a chestnut borer (*Agrilus bilineatus*)

two-line octave \'=,=-\ *n* [so called fr. the two accent marks of the symbol C″ representing the first C above middle C] **:** the musical octave that begins on the first C above middle C — see PITCH illustration

two·ling \'tüliŋ, -lēŋ\ *n* -S [¹*two* + *-ling*] **:** a twin crystal

two-man \'=,=\ *adj* **:** of or relating to two individuals: as **a :** consisting of two individuals ⟨a *two-man* committee⟩ **b** (1) **:** done, presented, or produced by two individuals ⟨a *two-man* comedy act⟩ (2) **:** that features the work of two artists ⟨a *two-man* exhibition⟩ **c** (1) **:** designed for or limited to two individuals ⟨a *two-man* bobsled⟩ or requiring two individuals to operate or handle ⟨a *two-man* saw⟩ (2) **:** managed or controlled by only two individuals ⟨a *two-man* shop⟩

two-mast·er \'=,=ə(r)\ *n* -S [¹*two* + *mast* + *-er*] **:** a ship having two masts

two-minded \'=,==\ *adj* **:** having two inconsistent attitudes toward something

two-name paper \'=,=-\ *n* **:** negotiable paper on which two signatures appear with both parties liable for payment

two-nerved \'=,=\ *adj* **:** having two nerves; *specif* **:** having two main veins ⟨a *two-nerved* leaf⟩

two·ness \'tünəs\ *n* -ES **:** the quality or state of being two **:** DUALITY

two old cat \'tüə'kat, ¦tü,ōl¦k-\ *also* **two o' cat** \¦tüə¦k-\ *n* **:** one old cat played with two batters

two-on *var of* TWO-ALONG

two pair *n* **1** *Brit* **:** a lodging situated on the third floor **2** *or* **two pairs :** a pair of one denomination and another of different denomination held in the same hand in poker and ranking between one pair and triplets — see POKER illustration

two-pair \'=,=\ *adj* [*two pair*] **1** *Brit* **:** situated on the third story above two flights of stairs ⟨a *two-pair* front room⟩ **2 :** containing two pairs ⟨a *two-pair* poker hand⟩

two-part \'=,=\ *n, Scot* **:** two thirds

two-part code *n* **:** a code book having an encoding part listing the plaintext segments in alphabetical and logical order each with its code group or groups assigned at random and a decoding part listing in alphabetical or numerical order the code groups with their plaintext equivalents — compare ONE-PART CODE

two-part form *n* **:** a song form composed of two repeated parts or sections of which the first often modulates to a related key and the second returns to the original key

two-part time *or* **two-part measure** *n* **:** DUPLE TIME

two-party \'=,==\ *adj* **:** consisting of two major political parties having almost equal voting strength with little or no opposition from other parties ⟨the *two-party* system in U.S. politics⟩

two-pence *Brit* 'təpən(t)s *or* -p°m(-, *US* " *or* 'tü,pen-\ *also* **tup·pence** \'təpən(t)s, -p°m(-\ *n, pl* **twopence** *or* **twopences** [ME *two pens*] **1 :** the sum of two usu. British pennies **2 :** a coin worth two pennies now in Britain issued only for maundy money

¹two·pen·ny *Brit* 'təp(ə)ni, *US* " *or* -nē *or* 'tü,pen-\ *adj* [¹*two* + *penny*] **1 :** of the value of or costing twopence **2 :** CHEAP, MEAN

²twopenny \"\ *also* **tup·pen·ny** \'təp(ə)n-\ *n* **1 :** weak ale orig. sold at twopence for a quart or more **2 :** TWOPENCE 2 **3 :** BIT, WHIT — usu. used in the phrase *don't care a tuppenny*

twopenny grass *n* **:** MONEYWORT

twopenny-halfpenny \¦təp(ə)ni¦hāp(ə)ni\ *adj* **1 :** of the value of or costing twopence halfpenny **2 :** PETTY

two-phase \'=,=\ *adj* **:** supplying or supplied with two alternating currents in separate circuits differing in phase usu. by a quarter cycle ⟨a *two-phase* generator⟩ ⟨a *two-phase* motor⟩

¹two-piece \'=,=\ *adj* [¹*two* + *piece*] **:** consisting of two separate pieces; *esp* **:** forming a clothing ensemble with matching but separate top and bottom parts (as jacket and skirt, halter and shorts) ⟨a *two-piece* dress⟩ ⟨a *two-piece* playsuit⟩

²two-piece \"\ *or* **two-piec·er** \'=¦pēsə(r)\ *n* **:** a garment or ensemble consisting of a matching but separate top and bottom

two pipe *adj* **:** of or being a steam or water heating system in which there are separate supply and return pipes so that each radiator receives a direct supply of the hot water or steam

two-platoon system \'==,=-\ *n* **:** a practice in football of training and playing separate offensive and defensive units

¹two-ply \'=,=\ *adj* [¹*two* + *ply*] **1 :** woven as a double cloth ⟨*two-ply* carpet⟩ **2 :** consisting of two strands ⟨*two-ply* yarn⟩

²two-ply \"\ *n* **:** a board consisting of two layers of wood

two-point \'=,=\ *adj* **1 :** having or concerned with two points ⟨a *two-point* equidistant map projection⟩ **2 :** being in contact or supported at two points

two-point landing *n* **:** a landing of an airplane in which the initial contact with the landing surface is made with the two main wheels

two-point perspective *n* **:** linear perspective in which parallel lines along the width and depth of an object are represented as meeting at two separate points on the horizon that are 90 degrees apart as measured from the common intersection of the lines of projection

two-point problem *n* **:** a problem in plane-tabling in which two points are mapped on the paper and a third is occupied on the ground to do which a fourth point is occupied temporarily

two-point threshold *or* **two-point limen** *n* **:** the smallest separation at which two points applied simultaneously to the skin can be distinguished from one

two-price \'=,=\ *adj* **:** of or being a system of government regulation of farm commodity prices providing fixed supports for domestic sales and none for export sales

two-revolution press \(¦)=,==,==-\ *n* **:** a cylinder press in which the cylinder revolves continuously during the forward and return strokes of the bed — compare STOP-CYLINDER PRESS

two-rowed barley \'=,=-\ *n* **:** a barley having only the central spikelet of each cluster fertile so that the spike appears to have two rows — compare FOUR-ROWED BARLEY

twos \'tüz\ *vi* -ED/-ING/-ES [fr. pl. of ³*two*] **:** to go around in the company of a member of the opposite sex ⟨you don't have to be always *twosing* with a person if you feel that way about them —S.V.Benét⟩

twoscore \'=,=\ *adj* **:** being 40 in number

two-seat·er \'=¦sēd·ə(r)\ *n* [¹*two* + *seat* + *-er*] **1 :** something seating two persons: as **a :** an automobile with one seat accommodating a driver and one passenger **b :** an airplane with two open cockpits in tandem **2 :** something having two seats; *specif* **:** an automobile having front and back seats

two-seed-in-the-spirit predestinarian baptist *n, usu cap 1st T & both Ss & P & B* **:** a member of a strongly Calvinistic Baptist sect resembling the Primitive Baptists but believing that mankind is divided into the offspring of God who will be saved and the offspring of the Devil who will be lost

two-shear \ˈ=,=\ *adj, Brit, of a sheep* **:** that has been shorn twice ⟨a *two-shear* ram⟩
two-shot \ˈ=,=\ *n* **:** a camera shot of two persons
two-sided \ˈ=¦==\ *adj* **1 a :** having two sides **:** BILATERAL **b** *of a sheet of paper* **:** having opposite surfaces that are different in color or texture **2 :** DOUBLE-FACED, HYPOCRITICAL — **two-sid·ed·ness** *n*
two·some \ˈtüsəm\ *n* -s [ME (Sc) *twasum*, fr. *twa* two + *-sum* -some] **1 :** a group of two persons or things **:** COUPLE, DUO ⟨the dancer and her husband have been a popular ~ —*Springfield (Mass.) Daily News*⟩ **2 :** a golf single
two-speed \ˈ=¦=\ *adj* **:** adapted for producing or for receiving either of two speeds ⟨a *two-speed* motor⟩ ⟨a *two-speed* axle⟩
two-spined stickleback \ˈ=¦=-\ *n* **:** a stickleback that is a variety of the three-spined stickleback and is distinguished from the typical form by the presence of two rather than three dorsal spines
two-spot \ˈ=,=\ *n* **1 :** an unimportant person or thing; *esp* **:** a two of any card suit **2 :** a two-dollar bill
two-spotted ladybird \ˈ=¦=-\ *n* **:** a European predaceous ladybird (*Adalia bipunctata*) that is now common in the northern U.S., feeds on aphids on hardwoods, and often hibernates in houses
two-spotted spider mite *also* **two-spotted mite** *n* **:** a widely distributed plant-feeding mite (*Tetranychus bimaculatus*) that feeds on various usu. herbaceous plants but is sometimes a serious pest in orchards
two-star \ˈ=¦=\ *adj* **1 :** of a moderate degree of excellence ⟨a *two-star* restaurant⟩ **2 :** being or having the military rank of major general or rear admiral ⟨a *two-star* general⟩
¹two-step \ˈ=,=\ *n* [¹*two* + *step*] **1 :** a ballroom dance executed with a sliding step-close-step in march or polka time **2 :** a piece of music for the two-step **3 :** a walking step used in skiing in which a forward swing of both poles and a walking step with one ski is followed by a strong push of the poles and a gliding step with the other ski
²two-step \"\ *vi* **:** to dance the two-step
two-story \ˈ=¦==\ *or* **two-storied** \ˈ=¦==\ *adj* **:** having two floors or levels ⟨a *two-story* house⟩
two-striped grasshopper \ˈ=¦=-\ *n* **:** a short-horned grasshopper (*Melanoplus bivittatus*) with two yellow stripes along its back that is sometimes a destructive pest of field crops (as alfalfa) in many parts of the U.S.
two-strip·er \ˈ=¦strīpə(r)\ *n* **:** LIEUTENANT 2b
two-stroke cycle \ˈ=¦=-\ *n* **:** a working cycle of a piston in an internal combustion engine consisting of two strokes in which the piston during the first stroke compresses the fuel mixture on one side while receiving the expansive thrust of previously compressed gases on the other side and during the second draws in a fresh charge on one side while expelling burnt gases on the other — compare FOUR-STROKE CYCLE
two-suit·er \ˈ=ˈsüd·ə(r)\ *n* -s **1** *or* **two-suit hand** \ˈ=,=-\ **:** a bridge hand containing two suits each of five or more cards **2 :** a man's wardrobe case designed to hold two suits and accessories
two-third·er \ˈ=¦=ə(r)\ *n* -s [*two thirds* + *-er*] **:** an apprentice printer who has served most of his apprenticeship
two-thirds rule \ˈ=¦=-\ *n* **:** a political principle requiring that two thirds rather than a simple majority of the members of a politically organized group must concur in order to exercise the power to make decisions binding upon the whole group — compare MAJORITY RULE
two-thirds vote *n* **:** a vote requiring the concurrence of two-thirds of the members of a politically organized group
two-three \ˈtü¦, ˈtü¦=\ *adj* **:** ²FEW 2, SEVERAL
two-throw \ˈ=¦=\ *adj* **1 :** capable of being thrown or cranked in two directions usu. opposite to one another ⟨a *two-throw* crank⟩ ⟨a *two-throw* switch⟩ **2 :** having two cranks set near together and opposite to one another ⟨a *two-throw* crankshaft⟩
¹two-time \ˈ=¦=\ *vt* **1 :** to betray (a spouse or lover) by secret lovemaking with another **2 :** DOUBLE-CROSS — **two-tim·er** \ˈ=,tīmə(r)\ *n*
²two-time \ˈ=¦=\ *adj* **:** that has done, suffered, or received something twice ⟨a *two-time* medal winner⟩
two-toed \ˈ=¦=\ *adj* **:** having two toes on each foot
two-toed anteater *n* **:** SILKY ANTEATER
two-toed sloth *n* **:** a sloth of the genus *Choloepus* having two functional claws on each front foot and three on each back foot; *specif* **:** a Central American sloth (*C. hoffmanni*)

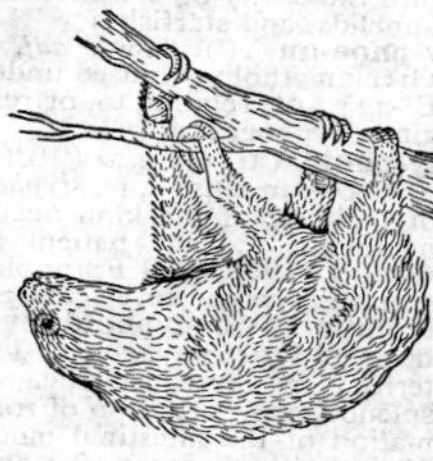
two-toed sloth of Central America

two-tone \ˈ=¦=\ *or* **two-toned** \ˈ=¦=\ *adj* **:** having some parts of one color and others of another color or of a different shade of the same color
two-to-one \ˈtüd·ə¦wən\ *adj* **:** of or being a gear for reducing or increasing a velocity ratio two to one
two-tooth \ˈ=,=\ *n, pl* **two-tooths** *Brit* **:** a sheep having two permanent teeth erupted and being usu. between one and two years old ⟨buy more *two-tooths* to build up the ewe flock⟩
two-toothed longhorn \ˈ=¦=-\ *n* **:** a cerambycid beetle (*Ambeodontus tristis*) the larva of which is a destructive wood borer in New Zealand
¹two-track \ˈ=¦=\ *vi* [¹*two* + *track*] *of a horse* **:** to move forward and to one side simultaneously without turning the neck or body
²two-track \ˈ=,=\ *n* **:** an act of two-tracking **:** a two-tracking movement
two-twenty \ˈ=¦==\ *n* **:** a 220-yard race common in running, skating, and swimming
two-up \ˈ=¦=\ *n* **:** a gambling game in which players bet that two coins tossed from a small wooden kip will fall both heads or both tails
two-valued \ˈ=¦==\ *adj* **:** possessing only the truth-values of truth and falsehood ⟨*two-valued* logic⟩ — compare MANY-VALUED
two-way \ˈ=¦=\ *adj* **1 :** being a cock or valve that will connect a pipe or channel with either of two others at will **2 a :** moving or allowing movement in opposite directions at the same time ⟨*two-way* traffic⟩ ⟨a *two-way* street⟩ **b :** moving or allowing movement in either of two directions ⟨*two-way* adjustment⟩ **3 a :** involving or allowing an exchange between two individuals or groups ⟨*two-way* communication by radiotelephone⟩ ⟨a *two-way* scholarship program for U.S. and foreign universities⟩ ⟨*two-way* trade⟩; *specif* **:** of or being equipment designed for both sending and receiving messages by wire or radio ⟨a mobile *two-way* radio for his taxi⟩ **b :** involving mutual responsibility or reciprocal relationships **:** affecting, entered into by, or binding on both parties ⟨a *two-way* guarantee⟩ ⟨political alliance is a *two-way* thing —T.H.White b. 1915⟩ **4 :** involving two participants **:** TWO-SIDED ⟨lost to his opponent in the *two-way* race for the governorship⟩ **5 a :** that may be used in either of two manners ⟨a shirt with a *two-way* collar⟩ ⟨*two-way* cattle fat enough to sell to either slaughterers or feeders⟩ **b** *of a bid in contract bridge* **:** made sometimes on a strong and sometimes on a weak hand for the purpose of withholding information from the opponents ⟨a *two-way* three-bid⟩ ⟨a *two-way* no-trump bid⟩
two-way plow *n* **:** SWIVEL PLOW
two-way plug *n* **:** CURRENT TAP
two-way stretch *n* **1 :** a characteristic of some materials of being stretchable in two directions **2 :** a woman's girdle of two-way stretch material
two-way switch *n* **:** one of two electrical switches (as at the top and bottom of a stair) controlling a single outlet
two-wheel·er \ˈ=ˈ(h)wēlə(r)\ *n* **:** a 2-wheeled vehicle: as **a :** a 2-wheeled cab or hansom **b :** BICYCLE ⟨a child learning to ride his new *two-wheeler*⟩
two-winged \ˈ=¦=\ *adj* **:** having one pair of wings **:** DIPTEROUS
two-winged fly *n* **:** an imaginal insect of the order Diptera having typically a single pair of wings and halteres instead of a second pair

two-worlds theory \ˈ=¦=-\ *n* **:** philosophic dualism; *specif* **:** interactionist dualism
twp *abbr* township
twr *abbr* tower
t wrench *n, cap T* **:** a T-shaped wrench that consists of a handle or lever with a fixed or removable socket to fit over a nut or bolt head
twy·er \ˈtwīə(r), -īə\ *n* -s [by alter.] **:** TUYERE
tx *abbr* tax
txn *abbr* taxation
-ty \d·ē, t|, |i\ *n suffix* -ES [ME *-te, -tee, -tie*, fr. OF *-té*, fr. L *-tat-, -tas;* akin to Gk *-tēt-, -tēs* -ty, Skt *-tāt, -tāti*] **:** quality **:** condition **:** degree ⟨aprior*ity*⟩
ty *abbr* **1** territory **2** truly **3** type
ty·chism \ˈtī,kizəm\ *n* -s [Gk *tychē* chance, fortune + E *-ism;* akin to Gk *tynchanein* to happen, happen on, attain, *teuchein* to make, build — more at DOUGHTY] **1 :** a theory that chance is an objective reality; *esp* **:** a theory in evolution that variation may be purely fortuitous — contrasted with *uniformitarianism* **2 :** a proposition that absolute chance is operative in the cosmos
tychite \ˈtī,kīt, ˈti,k-\ *n* -s [Gk *tychē* + E *-ite;* fr. its chance discovery among other crystals] **:** a rare mineral $Na_6Mg_2(SO_4)(CO_3)_4$ that is an octahedral sulfate and carbonate of sodium and magnesium (hardness 3.5–4, sp. gr. 2.59)
tychi·us \ˈtikēəs, ˈtik-\ *n, cap* [NL, fr. Gk *Tychios*, name of a maker of shields in Homer's *Iliad*] **:** a genus of weevils containing some that feed destructively esp. on clovers
ty·chon·ic \(ˈ)tīˈkänik, (ˈ)tē¦-\ *or* **ty·cho·ni·an** \-kōnēən\ *adj, usu cap* [NL *Tychon-, Tycho* (Latinized form of *Tycho* Brahe †1601 Dan. astronomer) + E *-ic* or *-ian*] **:** of or relating to Tycho Brahe or his system of astronomy
ty·cho·parthenogenesis \¦tīkō+\ *n* [NL, fr. Gk *tychē* chance + NL *-o-* + *parthenogenesis* — more at TYCHISM] **:** parthenogenesis occurring in a species in which it is not the usual method of reproduction
ty·cho·potamic \¦tī(,)kō+\ *adj* [ISV *tych-* (fr. Gk *tychē*) + *-o-* + *potamic*] *of an aquatic organism* **:** thriving chiefly in still waters (as of ponds) and occurring only incidentally in flowing waters — compare AUTOPOTAMIC, EUPOTAMIC
ty·coon \(ˈ)tīˈkün\ *n* -s [Jap *taikun*, fr. Chin (Pek) *ta*⁴ great + *chün*¹ ruler] **1 :** SHOGUN **2 a :** a businessman of exceptional wealth, power, and influence **b :** a masterful and potent leader (as in politics)
tyd·den *or* **tyd·dyn** \ˈtithən, ˈtəth-\ *n* -s [W *tyddyn*, fr. MW, fr. *tŷ* house + *dyn* hill; akin to L *tegere* to cover and to OIr *dūn* fortress — more at THATCH, TOWN] *Wales* **:** a small farm **:** HOMESTEAD
tyd·ie \ˈtidē\ *n* -s [prob. fr. ME *tydife*] **:** a small bird variously identified as a wren or the blue titmouse — compare TIDLEY
¹tye \ˈtī\ *n* -s [ME, casket, fr. OE *tēag*, of unknown origin] **1** *obs* **:** a small box (as for the storage of valuables) **2** *Brit* **:** a launder for washing ores
²tye \"\ *vt* -ED/-ING/-S *Brit* **:** to wash (ores) in a tye
³tye \"\ *n* -s [ME, fr. OE *tēag*, of unknown origin] **1** *obs* **:** a piece of enclosed land **2** *dial Eng* **:** a large pasture or common
⁴tye \"\ *n* -s [ME, tie — more at TIE] **:** a chain or rope one end of which passes through the mast or through a block and is made fast to the center of a yard, the other end being attached to a tackle by means of which a yard is hoisted or lowered — see SAIL illustration
ty·ee \ˈtī,ē\ *n* -s [Chinook jargon, fr. Nootka *ta·yi·* elder brother, senior] **1 :** CHIEF, BOSS, LEADER **2** *also* **tyee salmon :** a king or chinook salmon esp. when of large size
tyer *var of* TIER
Ty·fon \ˈtī,fän\ *trademark* — used for a diaphragm horn used esp. in signaling during a fog at sea
tyg \ˈtig\ *n* -s [origin unknown] **:** a large usu. slip-decorated ceramic drinking cup with two or more handles
tyigh \ˈtī\ *n, pl* **tyigh** *or* **tyighs** *usu cap* **1 :** a Shahaptian people of west central Oregon **2 :** a member of the Tyigh people
tying *adj* [fr. *tying*, pres. part. of ²*tie*] **:** relating to, constituting, or putting into effect a tying agreement ⟨~ contract⟩ ⟨~ clause⟩ ⟨~ arrangement⟩
tying agreement \¦==-\ *n* **:** an often illegal agreement by one party to sell a product or service only on condition that the buyer will also purchase another and different product or service or will not purchase the product or service from any other supplier or will adhere to some other restriction; *esp* **:** one that compels a buyer to purchase an undesired product or service in order to purchase a desired product or service
tying-in \¦==ˈ=\ *n* -s **:** the attaching of the ends of a new warp to those of the old by tying them together — compare TWISTING-IN
tyke *also* **tike** \ˈtīk\ *n* -s [ME *tyke*, fr. ON *tīk* bitch; akin to MLG *tīke* bitch] **1 :** DOG; *esp* **:** an inferior or mongrel dog **2 a :** an unpleasing and usu. clumsy, churlish, or eccentric person **b :** a small child esp. when an object of pity or commiseration ⟨poor little ~⟩ **c :** YORKSHIREMAN
tyl- *or* **tylo-** *comb form* [Gk, fr. *tylos, tylē* knob, lump, callus, pad — more at THOLE] **:** knob **:** knobbed ⟨*tyl*aster⟩ ⟨*Tylo*saurus⟩ **:** pad ⟨*Tylo*poda⟩
tyl·a·rus \ˈtilərəs, təˈla(a)rəs\ *n, pl* **tyla·ri** \ˈ==,rī, -,rē; =ˈ=,rī, -,rē\ [NL, modif. of Gk *tylēros* callous, fr. *tylos, tylē* callus] **:** a pad on the undersurface of a bird's toe
tyl·as·ter \ˈtī,lastə(r), ˈti,l-\ *n* [NL, fr. *tyl-* + *-aster*] **:** a small sponge spicule with the ends of the rays knobbed
tyle *var of* TILE
ty·lench \ˈtī,leŋk, təˈl-\ *n* -s [NL *Tylenchus*] **:** ²TYLENCHID
¹ty·len·chid \tīˈleŋkəd, təˈl-\ *adj* [NL *Tylenchidae*] **:** of or relating to the Tylenchidae
²tylenchid \"\ *n* -s **:** a worm of the family Tylenchidae
ty·len·chi·dae \-kə,dē\ *n pl, cap* [NL, fr. *Tylenchus*, type genus + *-idae*] **:** a family of soil-dwelling or plant-parasitic phasmid nematode worms (superfamily Tylenchoidea) related to the Heteroderidae but usu. having a bursa in the male — see TYLENCHULUS, TYLENCHUS; compare HETERODERA
ty·len·choid \-ŋ,kȯid\ *adj* [NL *Tylenchoidea*] **:** of or relating to the Tylenchoidea
tylen·choi·dea \,tī,leŋˈkȯidēə, ,ti,l-, -enˈk-\ *n pl, cap* [NL, fr. *Tylenchus* + *-oidea*] **:** a superfamily of soil-dwelling or plant-parasitic nematodes (order Rhabditida) with a dorsal esophageal gland opening near the base of the buccal spear — see HETERODERA, TYLENCHIDAE
ty·len·chu·lus \tīˈleŋkyələs, təˈl-\ *n, cap* [NL, fr. *Tylenchus* + *-ulus*] **:** a genus of nematode worms (family Tylenchidae) that includes the destructive citrus nematode
ty·len·chus \-kəs\ *n, cap* [NL, fr. *tyl-* + Gk *enchos* spear] **:** a genus of nematode worms (family Tylenchidae) usu. restricted to soil-dwelling forms that are saprophagous or feed on roots but formerly including numerous serious plant parasites (as the bulb eelworm) that are mostly placed in the genus *Anguina*
tyler *var of* TILER
tyl·i·on \ˈtilē,än\ *n, pl* **tyl·ia** \-ēə\ [NL, fr. *tyl-* + *-ion* (as in *rhinion*)] **:** a craniometric point on the anterior edge of the optic groove at the median line of the skull
tylo- — see TYL-
ty·lo·pod \ˈtīlə,päd\ *n* -s [NL *Tylopoda*] **:** a mammal or fossil of the suborder Tylopoda — **ty·lop·o·dous** \(ˈ)tīˈläpədəs\ *adj*
ty·lop·o·da \tīˈläpədə\ *n pl, cap* [NL, fr. *tyl-* + *-poda*] **:** a suborder of Artiodactyla or in some classifications a division of Ruminantia comprising the camels and extinct related forms
ty·lo·ri·an \(ˈ)tīˈlōrēən\ *adj, usu cap* [Sir Edward B. *Tylor* †1917 Eng. anthropologist + E *-an*] **:** of, relating to, or constituting the anthropological writings or theories of Sir Edward Burnett Tylor
ty·lo·sau·rus \,tīləˈsȯrəs\ *n, cap* [NL, fr. *tyl-* + *-saurus*] **:** a genus of large pythonomorph reptiles from the Upper Cretaceous of Kansas, New Mexico, and Texas having a short body, long tail, and pentadactyl limbs functioning as paddles
ty·lose \ˈtī,lōs, təˈl-\ *n* -s [F, fr. Gk *tylōsis*] **:** TYLOSIS
ty·lo·sis \tīˈlōsəs\ *n, pl* **tylo·ses** \-ō,sēz\ [NL, fr. Gk *tylōsis* act of making or becoming callous, fr. *tyloun* to make callous, make knobby, fr. *tylos* callus, knob — more at THOLE] **1 :** one of the protrusions from plant parenchyma cells into adjacent tracheary elements usu. through a pit-pair and often numerous enough to completely fill the lumen **2 :** a thickening and hardening of an organ or body part **:** CALLOSITY
ty·lo·soid \tīˈlō,sȯid\ *n* -s [NL *tylosis* + E *-oid*] **:** a protrusion into a resin canal of a conifer resembling a tylosis but produced by proliferation of epithelial cells
ty·lo·style \ˈtīlə,stīl\ *n* [*tyl-* + *style*] **:** a uniradiate pointed sponge spicule with a knob at the blunt end
ty·lo·stylus \¦tīlō+\ *n, pl* **tylostyli** [NL, fr. *tyl-* + *stylus*] **:** TYLOSTYLE
ty·los·u·rus \,tīləˈsůrəs\ *n, cap* [NL, irreg. fr. Gk *tylos* callus, pad, knob + NL *-urus;* fr. the structure of the caudal keel — more at THOLE] **:** a genus of needlefishes (family Belonidae) including commercially important food fishes
ty·lo·tate \ˈtīlə,tāt\ *adj* [NL *tylotus* tylote + E *-ate*] **:** knobbed at both ends ⟨a ~ sponge spicule⟩
ty·lote \ˈtī,lōt\ *n* -s [NL *tylotus*, fr. Gk *tylōtos* knobbed, fr. *tyloun* to make knobby — more at TYLOSIS] **:** a slender elongate sponge spicule with a knob at both ends
ty·lot·ic \(ˈ)tīˈläd·ik\ *adj* [fr. NL *tylosis*, after such pairs as NL *narcosis*: E *narcotic*] **:** of, relating to, or marked by tylosis
ty·lot·ox·ea \,tīləˈtäksēə, -,täkˈsēə\ *n, pl* **tylotox·e·ae** \-ē,ē\ [NL, fr. *tylotus* tylote + *oxea*] **:** a rodlike sponge spicule tapering toward the ends one of which is sharp and one knobbed — **ty·lot·ox·e·ate** \sēət\ *adj*
ty·lus \ˈtīləs\ *n, pl* **tyli** [NL, fr. Gk *tylos* knob — more at THOLE] **:** a central prominence on the upper front side of the head of some hemipterons
ty·lwyth teg \,tə,lüithˈteg\ *n* [W *tylwyth* family (fr. *tŷ* house + *llwyth* tribe) + *teg* fair, beautiful; akin to L *tegere* to cover and to OHG *loh* enclosure — more at THATCH, LOCK, THIG] **:** the fairies of Welsh folklore
tymbal *var of* TIMBAL
tym·ba·lon \ˈtimbə,län\ *n* -s [by alter.] **:** TIMBAL
tymp \ˈtimp\ *n* -s [short for *tympan*] **:** the stone or the water-cooled iron casting protecting the top of the opening through which molten slag and iron continually pass into the forehearth in an old type open-front iron blast furnace
tym·pan *also* **tim·pan** \ˈtimpən\ *n* -s [in sense 1a, fr. ME *tympan, timpan*, fr. OE *timpana*, fr. L *tympanum;* in sense 1b, fr. IrGael *tiompan*, fr. L *tympanum* drum; in other senses fr. ML *tympanum* eardrum & L *tympanum* drum, architectural panel — more at TYMPANUM] **1 a :** DRUM **b :** a Celtic bowed stringed musical instrument **2 a** *obs* **:** TYMPANUM 1a(1) **b :** any of various membranous plates functioning basically like the membranous tympanum of the ear **3 a** *or* **tympan sheet :** a sheet of material (as paper or cloth) in a printing press that is placed between the impression surface (as the platen or impression cylinder) and the paper to be printed **:** DRAWSHEET **b** *or* **tympan frame :** either of two frames that hold the tympan sheet of a handpress: (1) **:** an inner frame over which the tympan sheet is drawn (2) **:** an outer frame that holds the tympan sheet in place **4 :** an architectural panel **:** TYMPANUM
tympan- *or* **tympano-** *comb form* [NL *tympanum*] **1 :** tympanum **:** tympanic membrane ⟨*tympan*itis⟩ ⟨*tympano*tomy⟩ **2 :** tympanic and ⟨*tympano*eustachian⟩
tym·pa·nal \ˈtimpənᵊl\ *adj or n* [NL *tympanum* + E *-al*] **:** TYMPANIC
tym·pa·ni *n pl but sometimes sing in constr* [modif. (influenced by *tympanum*) of It *timpani*] **:** TIMPANI
¹tym·pan·ic \(ˈ)timˈpanik, -nēk\ *adj* [L & NL *tympanum* + E *-ic*] **1 :** of, relating to, associated with, or constituting an anatomical tympanum and esp. the eardrum — see TYMPANIC ANTRUM, TYMPANIC BONE, TYMPANIC CANAL, TYMPANIC MEMBRANE, TYMPANIC NERVE **2 :** of or relating to an architectural tympanum **3 :** resembling or resembling that of a drum ⟨a ~ roll of steady artillery —P.S.Wolff⟩
²tympanic \"\ *n* -s **:** a tympanic body part (as a bone or nerve)
tympanic antrum *n* **:** a large air-containing cavity in the mastoid process communicating with the tympanum and often being the seat of dangerous inflammation
tympanic bone *n* **:** a bone of the skull of a mammal that encloses a part of the middle ear, supports the tympanic membrane, and is often fused with the temporal bone
tympanic canal *n* **:** a minute canal leading into the middle ear and transmitting the tympanic nerve (sense 1)
tympanic cavity *n* **:** the cavity of the middle ear
tympanic membrane *n* **:** a thin membrane closing externally the cavity of the middle ear like the head of a drum and in mammals being deeply located at the bottom of the external auditory meatus, in birds and reptiles more superficially, and in frogs and toads on the surface — see EAR illustration
tympanic nerve *n* **1 :** a branch of the glossopharyngeal nerve arising from the petrosal ganglion and distributed to the walls of the tympanum of the ear where it takes part in forming a plexus — called also *Jacobson's nerve* **2 :** a branch of the facial nerve to the stapedius muscle
tympanic notch *n* **:** a notch in the tympanic plate filled by Shrapnell's membrane
tympanic plate *n* **:** the tympanic bone of man having in the adult the form of a plate fused with the petrous part of the temporal bone
tym·pani·form \ˈtimpənə,fȯrm, (ˈ)timˈpan-\ *adj* [*tympan-* + *-iform*] **:** resembling a tympanum
tym·pan·ing \ˈtimpəniŋ\ *n* -s [*tympan* + *-ing*] **:** material used in making a tympan for a printing press
tym·pa·nism \ˈtimpə,nizəm\ *n* -s [ISV *tympany* + *-ism*] **:** TYMPANITES
tym·pa·nist \ˈtimpənəst\ *n* -s [L *tympanista*, fr. Gk *tympanistēs*, fr. *tympanizein* to beat a drum, fr. *tympanon* drum + *-izein* -ize — more at TYMPANUM] **:** one that beats a drum; *specif* **:** a member of an orchestra who plays the kettledrums
tym·pa·ni·tes \,timpəˈnīd·(,)ēz\ *also* **tym·pa·ni·tis** \-d·əs\ *n* -ES [ME *tympanites*, fr. LL, fr. Gk *tympanitēs*, fr. *tympanon*] **:** a distension of the abdomen caused by accumulation of air or gas in the intestinal tract or peritoneal cavity — compare BLOAT
tym·pa·nit·ic \¦==ˈnid·ik\ *adj* [LL *tympaniticus*, fr. *tympanites* + L *-icus* -ic] **1 :** of, relating to, or affected with tympanites **2 :** resonant on percussion **:** hollow-sounding
tym·pa·ni·tis \,timpəˈnīd·əs\ *n* -ES [NL, fr. *tympan-* + *-itis*] **:** OTITIS MEDIA
tym·pa·no·hy·al \¦timpənō¦hīəl\ *n* -s [*tympan-* + *hy-* + *-al*] **:** the proximal segment in the hyoid arch becoming a part of the styloid process of the temporal bone in adult man
tym·pa·non \ˈtimpə,nän\ *n, pl* **tympa·na** \-pənə\ *also* **tympanons** [Gk — more at TYMPANUM] **:** TYMPAN 1a
tympan paper *n* **:** a hard paper treated with oil or glycerin and used as a tympan on printing presses
tym·pa·nu·chus \,timpəˈn(y)ükəs\ *n, cap* [NL, fr. Gk *tympanon* drum + *-ochos* (fr. *echein* to have, hold) — more at SCHEME] **:** a genus of American grouse consisting of the prairie chickens
tym·pa·num \ˈtimpənəm\ *n, pl* **tympa·na** \-nə\ *also* **tympanums** [ML & L; ML *tympanum* eardrum, fr. L, drum, architectural panel, fr. Gk *tympanon* drum, kettledrum; akin to Gk *typtein* to strike, beat — more at TYPE] **1 a** (1) **:** the tense double membrane separating the outer and middle ear **:** TYMPANIC MEMBRANE — called also *eardrum* (2) **:** MIDDLE EAR **b :** a thin tense membrane covering an organ of hearing (as in the leg) of an insect — see INSECT illustration **c** (1) **:** a membrane in a sound-producing organ that acts as a resonator (2) **:** TRACHEAL TYMPANUM **d :** one of the naked areas on the neck of the prairie chicken and other grouse that are expanded when the esophagus is inflated in display **2 a :** the recessed face of a pediment situated within the frame made by the upper and lower cornices and usu. shaped like a triangle or panel **b :** the space within an arch and above a lintel or a subordinate arch spanning the opening below the arch **3 :** TYMPAN 1a **4 :** a water-raising wheel resembling a Persian wheel **5 :** EPIPHRAGM 2a **6 :** the diaphragm of a telephone
tym·pa·ny \ˈtimpənē\ *n* -ES [ML *tympanias*, fr. Gk, fr. *tympanon* drum] **1 a :** TYMPANITES **b :** resonance on percussion **2** *archaic* **a :** a condition of being swollen out or inflated (as with pride, arrogance, or self-satisfaction) **b :** bombastic or turgid style (as of expression) **3 :** TYMPAN
tymps *pl of* TYMP
tymp stick \ˈtimp,=\ *n* [*tymp*, short for *tympani*] **:** a timpani drumstick
tyn·dall beam *or* **tyndall cone** \ˈtindᵊl-\ *n, usu cap T* [after John *Tyndall* †1893 Brit. physicist] **:** the luminous path formed in the Tyndall effect by the breaking up of the entering light by the suspended particles

tyndall blue *n, usu cap T* **:** bluish plane-polarized light (as in the sky) scattered in the Tyndall effect

tyndall effect *also* **tyndall phenomenon** *n, usu cap T* [after John *Tyndall* †1893] **:** the scattering of a beam of light when passed through a medium containing small suspended particles (as smoky or mist-laden air or colloidal solutions) — compare RAYLEIGH SCATTERING

tyn·dall·om·e·ter \ˌtindᵊlˈäməd·ə(r)\ *n* [*tyndall* (*beam*) + *-o-* + *-meter*] **:** an apparatus for measuring the brightness of the Tyndall beam — called also *Tyndall meter;* compare NEPHELOMETER

tyne *var of* TINE

typ- *or* **typo-** *comb form* [Gk, fr. *typos* — more at TYPE] **:** type **:** image **:** model ⟨*typ*onym⟩ ⟨*typ*ology⟩

typ *abbr* **1** typewriter; typewritten **2** typical **3** typographer; typographic; typographical

typ·able *or* **type·able** \ˈtīpəbəl\ *adj* **:** that may be typed

typ·age \ˈtīpij\ *n* -s [²*type* + *-age*] **:** TYPECASTING

typ·al \ˈtīpəl\ *adj* [¹*type* + *-al*] **1 :** of or relating to a type **2 :** serving as a type **:** TYPICAL

¹**type** \ˈtīp\ *n* -s *often attrib* [LL *typus*, fr. L & Gk; L *typus* image, fr. Gk *typos* blow, impression, image, model, type, fr. *typtein* to strike, beat; akin to L *stuprum* defilement, dishonor, Skt *tupati*, *tumpati* he hurts] **1 a :** something that serves as a symbolic representation usu. of a thing yet to come into being **:** PREFIGURATION, TOKEN ⟨concludes that the whole of the Old Testament is one great prophecy, one great ~ of what was to come —A.J.Maas⟩ ⟨a ~ of the one who was to come —Rom 5:14 (RSV)⟩ ⟨a Christian ~ differs from an allegory in that the historical reference is not lost sight of —*Oxford Dict. of the Christian Church*⟩ **b :** one (as an object, a person, or a kind of entity) that possesses or exemplifies qualities of a higher category **:** MODEL, EXEMPLAR: as (1) **:** a lower taxonomic category selected as a standard of reference for a higher category and usu. chosen as the subgroup most perfectly exemplifying the higher category; *also* **:** the specimen or series of specimens on which a taxonomic species or subspecies is actually based — see TYPE SPECIMEN (2) **:** a simple chemical compound used as a model or pattern to which other compounds are conveniently regarded as being related and from which they may be actually or theoretically derived **2 a** *obs* **:** a figurative representation **:** IMAGE **b :** a distinctive mark or sign ⟨the banked foundations that are such a ~ of old-time rural winter life⟩ **c :** the central figure on either side of a coin, medal, or piece of paper money **d** (1) **:** a postage stamp design esp. when differing from another only in small details ⟨~ one has thin, ~ two thick letters and numerals⟩ or when appearing on stamps of more than one denomination or on stamps differing in other details (as paper, perforation, or watermark) ⟨the 1 cent and 3 cent stamps were of the same ~⟩ (2) **:** the arrangement of a particular overprint or surcharge on a stamp **3 a :** a usu. metal, wood, or plastic rectangular block having on its face a relief character of which an inked impression will produce a printed character ⟨a piece of ~⟩ **b :** a collection of such blocks ⟨a case of ~⟩ ⟨a font of ~⟩; *also* **:** a composed assembly of such single blocks from which something is to be printed or of comparable units cast in the form of a solid slug ⟨a ~ page⟩ ⟨a galley of ~⟩ **c :** characters forming the faces of typebars (as in a typewriter) **d :** characters functioning as type in photocomposition **e :** TYPEFACE ⟨a very condensed ~⟩ **f :** a printed impression from type **:** printed matter ⟨very small ~ can be hard to read⟩ **4 a :** qualities common to a number of individuals that serve to distinguish them as an identifiable class or kind: as (1) **:** a set of determinable and usu. physically measurable qualities that on the average is held in common by the members of a relatively homogeneous human group (as a family, a tribe, or a race) (2) **:** the combination of characters that fits an individual or kind of individual to a particular use or function ⟨meat ~ poultry⟩ ⟨a strong horse of draft ~⟩ (3) **:** the morphological, physiological, or ecological characters by which relationship between organisms may be recognized (4) **:** qualities (as of bodily contour and carriage) that are felt to indicate excellence in members of a group ⟨won the show with a beagle of superior ~⟩ (5) **:** a form of structure or symmetry common to a group of crystals (6) **:** the general form of a word as contrasted with its particular instances in speech or writing — called also *type-word;* contrasted with *token* ⟨if a man twice says "it's raining," he utters two tokens of one ~ —D.C.Williams⟩ **b :** an individual exhibiting distinguishable qualities of its kind **:** a typical and often superior specimen ⟨a dog that is a ~ beagle⟩ **c :** a group or category exhibiting such type **:** a particular kind, class, or group ⟨infections of the most deadly ~⟩ ⟨oranges of a seedless ~⟩ ⟨a physique of the pyknic ~⟩: as (1) **:** a large taxonomic category characterized by basic rather than detailed similarities among its members and being essentially equivalent to division or phylum of other taxonomic systems (2) **:** any of various closely related minor categories usu. distinguishable on physiologic or serological bases — compare BLOOD GROUP, PHYSIOLOGIC RACE, SEROTYPE (3) **:** a group of soils developed from like parent material and having similar horizons, texture, and profile arrangement (4) **:** a class of objects or a style peculiar to a particular archaeological site or period (5) **:** one of a hierarchy of mutually exclusive classifications of arguments in a logical calculus suggested as a means of resolving the logical paradoxes ⟨individuals, classes of individuals, and classes of classes of individuals are entities of progressively higher ~s⟩ ⟨a class cannot be of the same ~ as its members⟩ — compare RUSSELL'S PARADOX **d :** something felt to be distinguishable as a variety or kind **:** SORT ⟨a new ~ submarine⟩ ⟨won't stand for that ~ of behavior⟩ **5** [origin unknown] **:** a canopy sounding board for a pulpit

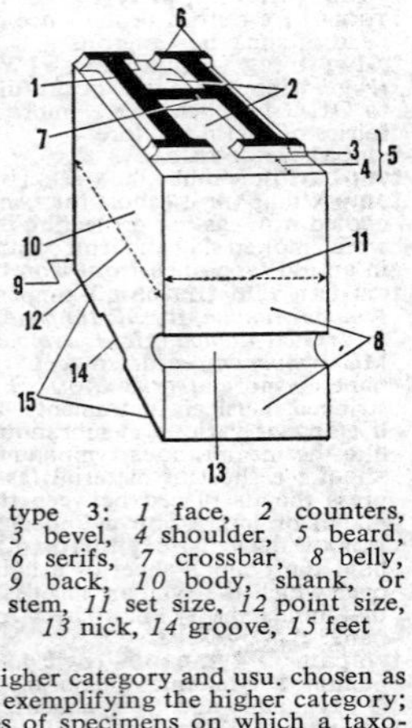

type 3: *1* face, *2* counters, *3* bevel, *4* shoulder, *5* beard, *6* serifs, *7* crossbar, *8* belly, *9* back, *10* body, shank, or stem, *11* set size, *12* point size, *13* nick, *14* groove, *15* feet

syn KIND, SORT, STRIPE, KIDNEY, ILK, DESCRIPTION, NATURE, CHARACTER: TYPE may suggest strong and clearly marked similarities throughout the items included, so that each is typical of the group ⟨the land forms are related to these rock *types* —A.E.Trueman⟩ ⟨that most dangerous *type* of critic: the critic with a mind which is naturally of the creative order —T.S.Eliot⟩ KIND in most uses is likely to be very indefinite and involve any criterion of classification whatever ⟨each *kind* of mental or bodily activity —Herbert Spencer⟩ ⟨their soil yields treasures of every *kind* —H.T.Buckle⟩ ⟨the *kind* of fear here treated of is purely spiritual —Charles Lamb⟩ It may suggest criteria of grouping dependent on natural, intrinsic characteristics ⟨Sinic philosophers conceived yin and yang as two different *kinds* of matter . . . yin symbolized water and yang fire —A.J.Toynbee⟩ SORT is often a close synonym of KIND ⟨the *sort* of culture I am trying to define —J.C.Powys⟩ and may be used in situations having a suggestion of disparagement ⟨the *sort* of journals put out by the learned societies —*New Republic*⟩ ⟨Victorianism of a meaner and baser *sort* —F.B.Millett⟩ ⟨what *sort* of idiots have you got around here —A.W.Long⟩ TYPE, KIND, and SORT are usu. interchangeable and are used most of the time without attention to special connotations. STRIPE and KIDNEY are used mostly of people rather than things; the first may suggest political attitude or affiliation, the second persuasion, disposition, or social level ⟨all Fascists are not of one mind, one *stripe* —Lillian Hellman⟩ ⟨economic dogmatists of whatever *stripe* —*Atlantic*⟩ ⟨the crown representative and comptroller were political appointees, and like many men of that *kidney* had never done a fair share of the work —S.E.Morison⟩ ILK, orig. indicating clan or family, may suggest grouping on the basis of status, attitude, or temperament ⟨no matter if . . . your ancestors spoke only to Cabots and their *ilk* —Stanley Walker⟩ ⟨one great composer is worth twenty of your *ilk* —Bella & Samuel Spewack⟩ DESCRIPTION, NATURE, and CHARACTER are close synonyms of TYPE and KIND mostly in phases beginning with *of*. DESCRIPTION may suggest a grouping in which all salient details of description or definition are involved; NATURE may suggest inherent, essential characteristics rather than superficial, ostensible, or tentative ones; and CHARACTER may stress distinctive or individualizing criteria ⟨all embargoes are not of this *description*. They are sometimes resorted to . . . with a single view to commerce —John Marshall⟩ ⟨the few hitherto known phenomena of a similar *nature* —*Amer. Jour. of Science*⟩ ⟨until the invention of printing advertising was necessarily of this primitive *character* —Charles Presbrey⟩ **syn** see in addition SYMBOL

²**type** \"\ *vb* -ED/-ING/-S *vt* **1 :** to represent beforehand as a type **:** PREFIGURE **2 :** to produce a copy of; *also* **:** REPRESENT, TYPIFY **3** [by shortening] **:** TYPEWRITE **4 :** to subsume under, classify as a member of, or identify as belonging to a type: as **a :** to determine the natural type of (as a sample of blood or a culture of bacteria) **b :** TYPECAST **c :** to cast (an actor) repeatedly in the same sort of role ⟨~ an actor as a butler or a gangster⟩ **~** *vi* [by shortening] **:** TYPEWRITE

typeable *var of* TYPABLE

typebar \ˈ=,=\ *n* **1 :** one of the bars on a typewriter that bears type for printing **2 :** ³SLUG 2c

typecase \ˈ=,=\ *n* **:** CASE 1d(1)

typecast \ˈ=,=\ *vt* [in sense 1, prob. back-formation fr. *typecasting;* in sense 2, fr. ¹*type* + *cast*] **1 :** to produce by typecasting ⟨~ ornament⟩ ⟨~ sorts⟩ **2 :** to cast (a theatrical performer) in a part calling for the same type of physique, personal quality, and temperament as that characterizing the actor in real life

typecasting *n* [¹*type* + *casting*] **:** the casting of printing type (as letters, rules, slugs, or borders) by pouring or forcing material (as type metal) in a molten or plastic state into a mold or matrix

type culture *n* **:** a viable culture of an organism that is directly descended from the strain or isolation on which the original description of the organism is based

type cutter *n* **:** an engraver of punches for making type

typeface \ˈ=,=\ *n* **1 :** the face of printing type; *also* **:** its printed impression **2 :** all type of a single design regardless of size ⟨our wide latin ~ comes in ten sizes, from 6 to 48 point⟩ — called also *face*

type family *n* **:** FAMILY 4c

typeform \ˈ=,=\ *n* **:** FORM 8a

typefounder \ˈ=,==\ *n* [¹*type* + *founder*] **:** one that is engaged in the design and production of metal printing type for hand composition

typefounding \ˈ=,==\ *n* [¹*type* + *founding*] **:** the business or occupation of a typefounder **:** the manufacture of metal printing type

typefoundry \ˈ=,==\ *n* [¹*type* + *foundry*] **:** the manufacturing establishment of a typefounder

type gauge *n* **:** LINE GAUGE

type genus *n* **:** the genus of a taxonomic family or subfamily from which the name of the family or subfamily is formed and which in practice is more often selected because it is the largest, best-known, or earliest-described genus or the one first used as the basis of a family or subfamily name than because its structure is most representative of the larger group as a whole

type height *n* **:** HEIGHT TO PAPER

type–high \ˈ=ˈ=\ *adj* (*or adv*) **:** having the same foot-to-face height as printing type and being 0.9186 inch in English-speaking countries ⟨plates must be mounted *type-high*⟩

type–high gage *n* **:** a fixed gage for measuring height to paper

typeholder \ˈ=,==\ *n* **:** a bookbinder's tool consisting of a head for holding set type and a handle and used for hand-stamping lettering (as on a book cover) — called also *pallet*

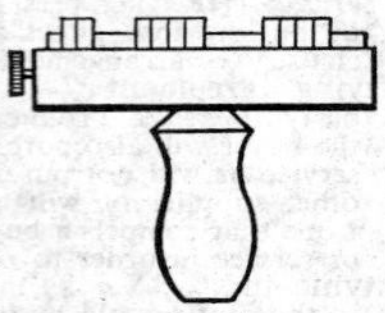

typeholder

type lice *n pl* **1 :** imaginary lice that the victim of a printer's joke is invited to observe by close scrutiny of set type previously soaked with water and squeezed together by the jokester at the moment of the victim's inspection thereby squirting dirty water in his face **2 :** the joke involving the scrutiny for type lice

type locality *n* **1 :** the source of an original type specimen **2 a :** the place whence a geological item (as a formation or series) derives its name and where it is typically displayed **b :** the first or original source of a geologic feature (as a fossil or particular kind of igneous rock)

type material *n* **:** a group of equivalent specimens collected at the type locality at one time and used wholly or partially in the identification and description of a new taxonomic entity

type·embryo \(ˈ)tī¦p+,\ *n* [*typ-* + *embryo*] **:** an embryo at the stage of development in which it first exhibits specific characteristics of the major natural group to which it belongs

type metal *n* **:** an alloy used in making type or stereotype or other plates and in backing up electrotype plates and consisting essentially of lead, antimony, and tin often with a little copper

type method *n* **:** the practice of basing the name of a taxon upon a type and accepting as validly published only those names so based

type o *n, usu cap O* **:** a blood group characterized by a serum that does not agglutinate the cells of any other member of the ABO system — called also *universal donor*

type object *n* **:** an object on which the original scientific description of a given class of objects is based

type page *n* **:** the printed area of a page (as of a book)

typ·er \ˈtīpə(r)\ *n* -s [²*type* + *-er*] **:** TYPIST

type–revolving press \ˈ=,==-\ *n* **:** an early rotary press printing from special tapered type fastened around the circumference of a cylinder

type rule *or* **type scale** *n* **:** LINE GAUGE

types *pl of* TYPE, *pres 3d sing of* TYPE

typescript \ˈtīp,skript\ *n* [²*type* + manu*script*] **:** typewritten matter esp. when used as printer's copy

type section *n* **:** the original sequence of strata as described for a given locality

type series *n* **1 :** a group of representatives of a taxon (as a subspecies or species) selected to demonstrate the extent of variation of that unit ⟨a syntypic *type series*⟩ **2 :** SERIES 10

typeset \ˈ=,=\ *vt* **:** to set in type **:** COMPOSE ⟨~ a magazine article⟩ ⟨surcharges and overprints are usually ~ and printed in black —*Scott's Standard Postage Stamp Catalogue*⟩

typesetter \ˈ=,==\ *n* **:** one that sets type: **a :** COMPOSITOR, KEYBOARDER **b :** TYPESETTING MACHINE

typesetting machine *n* [fr. gerund of *typeset*] **:** any of various keyboard machines for automatically composing printing type either by assembling and sometimes distributing ordinary foundry type or a modification of it or more often by producing keyboarded matter through forcing hot metal into matrices

type species *n* **:** the species of a genus with which the generic name is permanently associated and upon which the original generic description is largely or wholly based **:** the type of a genus **:** GENOTYPE

type specimen *n* **:** a specimen or individual designated as type of a species or lesser group and serving as the final criterion of the characteristics of that group — compare HOLOTYPE, ISOTYPE, PARATYPE, TOPOTYPE

type station *or* **type site** *n* **:** the place of discovery of prehistoric remains that have been agreed upon as the standard for a specified culture

type theory *n* **:** the theory that chemical compounds are derived by substitution from a limited number of type compounds (as hydrogen, water, ammonia, and methane) and that developed into the modern unitary theory

type wash *n* **:** an ink solvent for cleaning type or printing plates

type wheel *n* **:** a wheel made with raised characters on its periphery and used in some typewriters, printing telegraphs, and other printing devices

type–word \ˈ=,=\ *n* **:** TYPE 4a(6) ⟨twenty tokens of the *type-word* "the" may occur on a single page⟩

type·write \ˈtī,prīt, *usu* -īd·+V\ *vb* [back-formation fr. *typewriter*] *vt* **:** to write (as a letter) with a typewriter **~** *vi* **:** to use a typewriter

type·writ·er \-īd·ə(r), -ītə-\ *n* [¹*type* + *writer*] **1 :** any of various instruments or machines for writing in characters similar to those produced by printers' types; *esp* **:** one in which the characters are produced by steel types striking the paper through an inked ribbon with the types being actuated by corresponding keys on a keyboard and the paper being held by a platen that is automatically moved along with a carriage when a key is struck **2** [*typewrite* + *-er*] **:** TYPIST **3 :** a printing typeface that is designed to imitate typewriting and that usu. has all characters of the same set

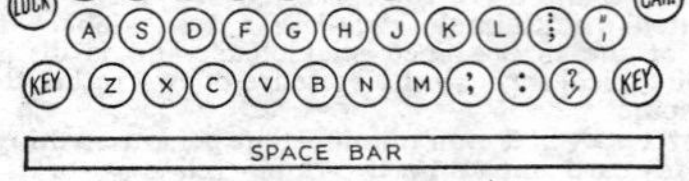

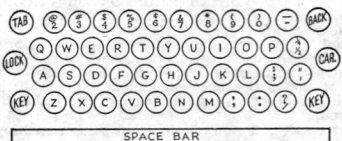

typewriter keyboard

typewriting *n* [fr. gerund of *typewrite*] **1 :** the act, study, or art of using a typewriter **2 :** the printing done with a typewriter **3 :** a typewritten paper

typewriting telegraph *n* **:** a telegraph system using apparatus similar to a typewriter as transmitter or receiver or both

typey *var of* TYPY

typh- *or* **typho-** *comb form* [NL *typhus*] **:** typhus **:** typhoid ⟨*typho*sepsis⟩

ty·pha \ˈtīfə\ *n, cap* [NL, fr. Gk *typhē* cattail — more at TUBER] **:** a genus of tall erect herbs (family Typhaceae) that occur in fresh and salt marshes and have sword-shaped leaves and monoecious flowers in dense spikes with the staminate uppermost — see CATTAIL

ty·pha·ce·ae \tīˈfāsē,ē\ *n pl, cap* [NL, fr. *Typha*, type genus + *-aceae*] **:** a family of perennial marsh plants (order Pandanales) with creeping rootstocks, long linear leaves, and cylindrical spikes of flowers — **ty·pha·ceous** \(ˈ)tī¦fāshəs\ *adj*

ty·phic \ˈtīfik\ *adj* [ISV *typh-* + *-ic*] **1 :** of or relating to typhus **2 :** TYPHOID

typhl- *or* **typhlo-** *comb form* [in sense 1, fr. Gk, blind, fr. *typhlos;* in sense 2, fr. Gk *typhlon*, fr. neut. of *typhlos* blind — more at DEAF] **1 :** blind ⟨*typhlo*sole⟩ **:** blindness ⟨*typhlo*logy⟩ **2 :** cecum ⟨*typhl*itis⟩ ⟨*typhlo*tomy⟩

typh·li·tis \tiˈflīd·əs\ *n* -ES [NL, fr. *typhl-* + *-itis*] **:** inflammation of the cecum

typh·lo·cy·ba \ˌtiflōˈsībə\ *n, cap* [NL, prob. fr. *typhl-* + Gk *kybistan* to turn somersaults, tumble] **:** a widely distributed genus of leafhoppers that includes several destructive pests of various cultivated trees and crop plants

typh·lol·o·gy \tiˈflälәjē\ *n* -ES [*typhl-* + *-logy*] **:** the scientific study of blindness, its causes, effects, and control **:** a branch of science that deals with blindness

typh·lo·molge \¦tiflō+\ *n, cap* [NL, fr. *typhl-* + *Molge*] **:** a genus of neotenic salamanders (family Plethodontidae) of underground waters that are known from a single species (*T. rathburni*) of Texas and that lack functional eyes

typh·lop·i·dae \tiˈfläpə,dē\ *n pl, cap* [NL, fr. *Typhlops*, *Typhlops*, type genus (fr. Gk *typhlōp-*, *typhlōps* blind-eyed, fr. *typhl-* + *-ōp-*, *ōps* eye) + *-idae* — more at EYE] **:** a widely distributed family of small burrowing snakes having the whole body covered with uniform cycloid scales, the mouth not distensible, and the teeth restricted to the upper jaw — see BLIND SNAKE

typh·lo·so·lar \¦tiflə¦sōlə(r)\ *adj* **:** of, relating to, or constituting a typhlosole

typh·lo·sole \ˈ==,sōl\ *n* -s [*typhl-* + Gk *sōlēn* channel, pipe — more at SYRINGE] **:** a longitudinal fold of the wall projecting into the cavity of the intestine esp. in bivalve mollusks, some annelids, and starfishes

ty·phoe·an \(ˈ)tī¦fēən\ *adj, usu cap* [L *Typhoe*us, giant of Greek mythology buried under Mt. Etna (fr. Gk *Typhōeus*) + E *-an*] **:** of, relating to, or resembling the mythical monstrous giant Typhoeus

¹**ty·phoid** \ˈtī,fȯid *also* (ˈ)tīˈf-\ *adj* [in sense 1, fr. NL *typh*us + E *-oid;* in sense 2, fr. ²*typhoid*] **1 :** of, relating to, or typical of typhus **:** of the kind occurring in typhus ⟨in tuberculous meningitis . . . the patient sinks into the ~ state —R.M. Goepp †1950 & H.F.Flippin⟩ **2 :** of, relating to, or constituting typhoid fever ⟨the ~ bacillus⟩

²**typhoid** \"\ *or* **typhoid fever** *n* -s [*typhoid* fr. *typhoid fever*, trans. of F *fièvre typhoïde*] **1 :** a communicable disease characterized by fever, diarrhea, prostration, apathy, headache, splenomegaly, eruption of rose spots, leukopenia, and inflammation of the intestinal mucosa and caused by a bacterium (*Salmonella typhosa*) **2 :** any of several diseases of domestic animals in some respects felt to resemble human typhus or typhoid: as **a :** FOWL TYPHOID **b :** HOG CHOLERA **c :** INFECTIOUS ANEMIA **d :** shipping fever of horses

ty·phoi·dal \(ˈ)tī¦fȯidᵊl\ *adj* [²*typhoid* + *-al*] **:** of, relating to, or resembling typhoid fever

typhoid fly *n* **:** HOUSEFLY

typhoid mary *n, usu cap T&M* [after *Typhoid Mary*, name given to Mary Mallon †1938 Irish cook in U.S. who was found to be a typhoid carrier] **:** one that is by force of circumstances a center or focus from which something undesirable spreads ⟨authoritarianism . . . is carried by *Typhoid Marys*, unwitting sources of infection —S.P.Hayes b. 1910⟩

ty·pho·ni·an \(ˈ)tī¦fōnēən\ *also* **ty·phon·ic** \-fänik\ *adj, often cap* [L *Typhon*, monster of Greek mythology identified with the Egyptian god Set (fr. Gk *Typhōn*) + E *-ian*, *-ic*] **:** of, relating to, or resembling the monster Typhon of ancient mythology or the Egyptian god Set ⟨the gazelle is a ~ symbol in Egyptian art⟩

typhonic \"\ *adj* [Gk *typhōnikos*, fr. *typhōn* whirlwind + *-ikos* -ic] **:** of, relating to, resembling, or suggestive of a typhoon

ty·phoon \(ˈ)tī¦fün\ *n* -s [alter. (influenced by Gk *typhōn* whirlwind and Chin — Cant — *taai fung* typhoon, fr. *taai* great + *fung* wind) of earlier *touffon*, *tufan*, fr. Ar *ṭūfān* hurricane, deluge, fr. Gk *typhōn* whirlwind; akin to Gk *typhein* to smoke — more at DEAF] **:** a tropical cyclone occurring in the region of the Philippines or the China sea **syn** see WIND

ty·phous \ˈtīfəs\ *adj* [NL *typh*us + E *-ous*] **:** of or relating to typhus **:** resembling or characteristic of typhus

typh·u·la \ˈtifyələ\ *n, cap* [NL, fr. Gk *typhē* cattail + NL *-ula* — more at TUBER] **:** a genus of club fungi (family Clavariaceae) with simple or slightly branched filamentous sporophores

ty·phus \ˈtīfəs\ *also* **typhus fever** *n* -ES [NL *typhus*, fr. Gk *typhos* fever, delusion, pride; akin to Gk *typhein* to smoke — more at DEAF] **1 :** any of three human rickettsial diseases: **a :** a severe febrile disease characterized by high fever, stupor alternating with delirium, intense headache, and a dark red rash and caused by a rickettsia (*Rickettsia prowazekii*) that is transmitted esp. by body lice **b :** MURINE TYPHUS **c :** TSUTSUGAMUSHI DISEASE **2 :** CANICOLA FEVER

typ·ic \ˈtipik, -pēk\ *adj* [F *typique*, fr. LL *typicus*, fr. Gk *typikos*, fr. *typos* type + *-ikos* -ic] **:** TYPICAL; *esp* **:** conforming to type

typ·i·cal \ˈtipəkəl, -pēk-\ *adj* [LL *typicalis*, fr. *typicus* typical + L *-alis* -al] **1 :** constituting or having the nature of a type **:** representing something by a form, model, or resemblance **:** EMBLEMATIC, PREFIGURATIVE **2 a :** combining or exhibiting the essential characteristics of a group sharing the nature of a type ⟨a ~ Victorian Sunday dinner⟩ ⟨the ~ modern girl⟩ **b :** conforming to a type ⟨a ~ species⟩ **syn** see REGULAR

typical bathyal zone *n* **:** the upper half of the bathyal zone

typ·i·cal·i·ty \ˌtipəˈkaləd·ē, -lətē, -i\ *n* -ES [*typical* + *-ity*] **:** TYPICALNESS

typ·i·cal·ly \ˈtipək(ə)lē, -pēk-, -li\ *adv* **:** in a typical manner

typ·i·cal·ness \-kəlnəs\ *n* -ES **:** the quality or state of being typical

ty·pi·con or **ty·pi·kon** \ˈtēpēˌkón\ n, pl **typi·ca** \-kä\ or **typicons** \-kónz\ or **typi·ka** \-kä\ [MGk typikon, fr. neut. of typikos prescribed, regular, fr. Gk, typical] : a book containing rules and rubrics for the religious services of the church year in the Eastern Church

typier comparative of TYPY

-typies pl of -TYPY

typiest superlative of TYPY

typ·i·fi·ca·tion \ˌtipəfəˈkāshən\ n -s [fr. typify, after such pairs as E purify: purification] 1 : the act of typifying 2 : something that constitutes a type

typ·i·fy \-ˌī\ vt -ED/-ING/-ES [LL typus type + E -ify — more at TYPE] 1 : to represent by an image, form, model, or resemblance : PREFIGURE 2 : to embody the essential or salient characteristics of : be the type of ⟨the genus Rosa typifies the family Rosaceae⟩

typ·i·ness \ˈtipēnəs\ n -ES : the quality or state of being typy ⟨a difficult class to judge because all the animals showed marked ~ and finish⟩

typing n -s [fr. gerund of ²type] : TYPEWRITING

typ·ist \ˈtipəst\ n -s [²type + -ist] : one who typewrites; specif : one employed to type letters, records, memoranda, and other business papers and often to do office clerical work

typ·iste \ˈtipəst\ chiefly Austral var of TYPIST

ty·po \ˈtī(ˌ)pō\ n -s 1 [short for typographer] : PRINTER; esp : COMPOSITOR 2 [short for typographical (error)] : a typographical error

typo- — see TYP-

¹ty·po·graph \ˈtipəˌgraf, -ˌráf sometimes 'tip-\ n [typ- + -graph] 1 : a keyboard-operated slugcasting machine that uses circulating matrices and functions on principles basically similar to those of the linotype 2 : LUDLOW

²typograph \"\ vt -ED/-ING/-S [back-formation fr. typography] : to produce (stamps) by letterpress ⟨the stamp will be ~ed instead of engraved —Edwin Mueller⟩ ⟨made excellent lithographed forgeries of two of the ~ed German stamps for the use of agents —John Easton⟩

ty·pog·ra·pher \tīˈpägrəfə(r) sometimes təˈp-\ n -s [ML typographus printer (fr. Gk typos impression, cast + -graphos writer) + E -er — more at TYPE, -GRAPHER] 1 : COMPOSITOR, TYPESETTER ⟨newspaper ~s⟩ 2 : PRINTER ⟨printed in foreign countries by foreign ~s —André Morize⟩ 3 : a printing designer who specializes in the choice and arrangement of type matter

ty·po·graph·ic \ˌtipəˈgrafik, -fēk sometimes 'tip-\ or **ty·po·graph·i·cal** \-fəkəl, -fēk-\ adj [typographic fr. NL typographicus, fr. ML typographia typography + L -icus -ic; typographical fr. NL typographicus + E -al] 1 a : of, relating to, or occurring or used in typography ⟨the ~ art⟩ ⟨a ~ error⟩ b : of or relating to letterpress or relief printing as distinct from other forms of printing (as lithography, intaglio, or stencil) 2 : of or relating to representation by types or symbols : EMBLEMATIC, FIGURATIVE — **ty·po·graph·i·cal·ly** \-fək(ə)lē, -fēk-, -li\ adv

typographical printing n : LETTERPRESS 1a

ty·pog·ra·phy \tīˈpägrəfē sometimes təˈp-\ n -ES [ML typographia, fr. Gk typos impression, cast + -graphia -graphy — more at TYPE] 1 : LETTERPRESS ⟨in ~ the ink is deposited only on the raised parts of the plate —Andries Voet⟩ 2 : the art of letterpress printing esp. with regard to design or execution ⟨books of fine format and ~ —Amer. Guide Series: Oregon⟩ 3 a : the style, arrangement, or appearance of matter printed by letterpress ⟨this advertisement has good ~, is easily seen and read —W.M.Krieger⟩ ⟨the ~ seems curiously fitted to the personality of the poems —Commonweal⟩ b : matter and esp. lettering that resembles letterpress but is produced by some other means ⟨photocomposed ~⟩ ⟨an offset printing job with excellent ~⟩

ty·po·lithography \ˌtī(ˌ)pō+\ n [ISV typ- + lithography] : a branch of lithography in which impressions from printers' types are transferred to stone for reproduction

ty·po·log·i·cal \ˌtipəˈläjəkəl sometimes 'tip-\ also **ty·po·log·ic** \-jik\ adj [typology + -ical or -ic] 1 : of or relating to typology 2 : of or relating to types — **ty·po·log·i·cal·ly** \-jək(ə)lē\ adv

ty·pol·o·gist \tīˈpäləjəst sometimes təˈp-\ n -s [typology + -ist] : a student of or expert in typology; broadly : one that is preoccupied with types

ty·pol·o·gize \-ˌjīz\ vt -ED/-ING/-S [typology + -ize] : to deal with in a typological manner : interpret through use of types or make a type of

ty·pol·o·gy \-jē\ n -ES [typ- + -logy] 1 : a doctrine or theory of types; specif : a doctrine that things in the Christian dispensation are symbolized or prefigured by things in the Old Testament (as the sacrifice of Christ and the Eucharist by the sacrifice of the Paschal Lamb) 2 : study of or study based on types ⟨the ~ of the idealistic morphology —Franz Schwanitz⟩: as a : classification (as of archeological remains or bacterial strains) based on comparative study of types b : comparative study of languages or aspects of languages as to their structures rather than their historical relations c : the distinction in the study of prose rhythm of types of internal structure of rhythmic systems or series in terms of combination of word-units, juncture, and pause d : study and esp. analysis or division of humanity in terms of social types ⟨the ~ of union-management relations⟩ ⟨the ~ of religious groups⟩

ty·po·mor·phic \ˌtipəˈmórfik sometimes 'tip-\ adj [typ- + -morphic] : characteristically occurring under particular conditions (as of temperature and pressure) or in particular processes of formation ⟨~ texture due to formation from a gel⟩ ⟨a ~ mineral⟩

ty·po·nym \ˈtipəˌnim sometimes 'tip-\ n -s [typ- + -onym] 1 : a taxonomic name based on an indication of a type specimen or type species rather than on a description or diagnosis 2 : a rejected isogenotypic name — **ty·po·ny·mal** \(ˈ)tīˈpänəməl sometimes təˈp-\ or **ty·po·nym·ic** \ˌtipəˈnimik sometimes 'tip-\ or **ty·po·ny·mous** \(ˈ)tīˈpänəməs sometimes təˈp-\ adj

ty·po·phile \ˈtipəˌfīl sometimes 'tip-\ n -s [typ- + -phil] : a lover of printed matter or typography — **ty·po·phil·ic** \ˌtipəˈfilik\ adj

typos pl of TYPO

ty·po·script \ˈtipəˌskript\ n [typ- + manuscript] : typewritten matter : TYPESCRIPT

ty·po·telegraph \ˌtī(ˌ)pō+\ n [typ- + telegraph] : a printing telegraph — **ty·po·telegraphy** \"+\ n

ty·po·there \ˈtipəˌthi(ə)r sometimes 'tip-\ n -s [NL Typotheria] : a mammal or fossil of the suborder Typotheria

ty·po·the·ria \ˌ=ˈthirēə\ n pl, cap [NL, fr. pl. of Typotherium, genus of herbivorous mammals, fr. typ- (prob. influenced in meaning by F slang type peculiar individual, fr. F type type, fr. Gk typos) + -ˈherium] : a suborder of Notoungulata sometimes a separate order comprising small So. American Tertiary and Pleistocene mammals somewhat similar to the rodents and having clavicles, usu. five toes, and single persistently growing teeth

ty·poth·e·tae \tīˈpäthəˌtē sometimes təˈp-\ n pl but sing in constr [NL, lit., typesetters, fr. typ- + Gk -thetai, pl. of -thetēs (fr. tithenai to place, set) — more at DO] : an association of master printers (as in the U.S. and Canada)

typp \ˈtip\ n -s [thousand yards per pound] : a unit of yarn size representing the number of thousands of yards of a yarn that weigh one pound

typw abbr typewriter

typy or **typ·ey** \ˈtipē\ adj typier; typiest [¹type + -y] : characterized by strict conformance to type : exhibiting superior bodily conformation ⟨a sound ~ heifer⟩ ⟨one of the typiest litters we have seen⟩

-ty·py \ˌtipē, ˌd·əpē, -pi\ n comb form -ES [¹type + -y] : condition, process, or art related to or involving the use of (such) a type ⟨heliotypy⟩

tyr- or **tyro-** comb form [Gk, fr. tyros cheese — more at BUTTER] : cheese ⟨tyramine⟩ ⟨tyrotoxin⟩

ty·ra·mine \ˈtīrəˌmēn, 'tir-; tīˈramən, təˈr-\ n [ISV tyrosine +

amine] : a crystalline phenolic amine $HOC_6H_4CH_2CH_2NH_2$ obtained from tyrosine by strong heating or by bacterial action and found also in the secretions of cephalopods and in various plants (as mistletoe and ergot)

ty·ran·ni \təˈraˌnī, -a(ˌ)nē; tīraˌnī\ n pl, cap [NL, fr. L, pl. of tyrannus tyrant] : a suborder of Passeriformes that comprises birds possessing little power of song and having the tendon of the hind toe separate and the intrinsic muscles of the syrinx reduced to usu. one pair the ends of which are inserted on the sides instead of the tips of its cartilaginous semirings and that includes the So. American antbirds, oven birds, and woodhewers together with the tyrant flycatchers and related birds of both hemispheres

ty·ran·ni·cal \təˈranəkəl, -nēk- also (ˈ)tī-r-\ also **ty·ran·nic** \-nik,-nēk\ adj [tyrannic fr. L tyrannicus, fr. Gk tyrannikos, fr. tyrannos tyrant + -ikos -ic; tyrannical fr. L tyrannicus + E -al] 1 a archaic : of, relating to, or associated with an absolute rule or ruler b : behaving as if an absolute ruler esp. in unjust severity in government : DESPOTIC ⟨a ~ administration⟩ c : given to oppressive, harsh, unjust, or arbitrary behavior or exercise of power ⟨a ~ parent⟩ ⟨some men become ~ when raised to a position of authority⟩ 2 a : typical of a tyrannical individual : of the kind associated with tyranny ⟨~ abuse⟩ ⟨a ~ suppression of liberty⟩ b : tending to dominate in a stultifying or repressive manner usu. by reason of inexorability or omnipresence ⟨~ tasks⟩ ⟨tradition ... more powerful, continuous, and even ~ —Laurence Binyon⟩ syn see ABSOLUTE

ty·ran·ni·cal·ly \-nək(ə)lē, -nēk-, -li\ adv : in a tyrannical manner

ty·ran·ni·ci·dal \təˈranəˈsīd²l, (ˌ)tīr-\ adj : of, relating to, or dealing with tyrannicide ⟨~ schemes⟩

ty·ran·ni·cide \təˈranəˌsīd\ n -s [in sense 1, fr. F, fr. L tyrannicidium, fr. tyrannus tyrant + -cidium -cide (killing); in sense 2, fr. F, fr. L tyrannicida, fr. tyrannus + -i- + -cida -cide (killer)] 1 : the act of killing a tyrant 2 : the killer of a tyrant

tyran·nid \ˈtirəˌnid, ˈtirən-\ n -s [NL Tyrannidae] : a bird of the family Tyrannidae

ty·ran·ni·dae \təˈranəˌdē, tīˈr-\ n pl, cap [NL, fr. Tyrannus, type genus + -idae] : a large exclusively American family of birds that are most numerous in So. and Central America but well represented in the U.S. and Canada, comprise the tyrant flycatchers, are mostly strictly insectivorous and take their prey on the wing, have a flattened bill often hooked at the tip and usu. bristly at the gape, and with the pittas, cotingas, and related birds constitute a superfamily of the suborder Tyranni

tyran·nis \ˈtiranəs, 'tirən-\ n -es [L, fr. Gk, fr. tyrannos tyrant] : absolute rule (as by a local dictator in ancient Greece or medieval Italy)

tyr·an·nize \ˈtirəˌnīz\ vb -ED/-ING/-S see -ize in Explan Notes [MF tyranniser, fr. LL tyrannizare, fr. tyrannus tyrant + -izare -ize] vi : to act the tyrant : exercise arbitrary power : rule or act with unjust and oppressive severity — often used with over ⟨no habit could ~ over him⟩ ~ vt : to treat tyrannically : OPPRESS

tyr·an·niz·er \-zə(r)\ n -s : one that tyrannizes

ty·ran·no·saur \təˈranəˌsò(ə)r, tīˈr-\ n -s [NL Tyrannosaurus] : a very large bipedal carnivorous dinosaur (Tyrannosaurus rex) of the Upper Cretaceous of No. America

ty·ran·no·sau·rus \təˈranəˌsòrəs, (ˌ)tīˌr-\ n [NL, fr. Gk tyrannos tyrant + NL -saurus] 2 cap : a genus of theropod dinosaurs from the Upper Cretaceous of Montana and Wyoming closely related to Ceratosaurus and including a single species (T. rex) — see TYRANNOSAUR 2 -ES : TYRANNOSAUR

tyr·an·nous \ˈtirənəs\ adj [ME, fr. L tyrannus + ME -ous] : marked by tyranny and esp. by unjust severity : OPPRESSIVE ⟨~ disregard of human rights⟩ ⟨a proper protest against all ~ demands ... that insist upon everybody's using a word in a particular sense —R.G.F.Robinson⟩ ⟨escaping the ~ heat of the sun by the custom of siesta⟩ syn see ABSOLUTE

tyr·an·nous·ly adv : in a tyrannous manner : so as to be tyrannous

tyr·an·nous·ness n -ES : the quality or state of being tyrannous

ty·ran·nus \təˈranəs, tīˈr-\ n, cap [NL, fr. L, tyrant] : the type genus of Tyrannidae comprising the kingbird and closely related birds or in former classifications the greater part of the family

tyr·an·ny \ˈtirənē, -ni\ n -ES [ME tyrannie, fr. MF, fr. ML tyrannia, fr. L tyrannus tyrant + -ia -y] 1 a : absolute government (as of an ancient Greek city state) in which power is vested in a single ruler — compare AUTOCRACY b : the power, authority, office, and administration of such a ruler c : a city or other administrative unit under such government 2 : rigorous, cruel, oppressive, and unjustly severe government whether by a single absolute ruler or other controlling power 3 a : oppressive, severe, and unjust domination ⟨the ~ of a harsh overseer⟩ ⟨subject to the ~ of fanaticism⟩ b : a severe and rigorous condition or effect ⟨the ~ of the open night's too rough for Nature to endure —Shak.⟩ c : an oppressive effect that derives from the inexorable, relentless, or omnipresent quality of something in question ⟨the useful ~ of the normal —Edward Sapir⟩ ⟨two travelers escaped from the ~ of ham and eggs —John Buchan⟩ 4 a : a tyrannical act : an instance of tyranny ⟨all the petty tyrannies of domestic life⟩ b obs : lawless and violent activity

¹ty·rant \ˈtirənt\ n -s [ME tyran, tirant, tirand, fr. OF tyran, tyrant, fr. L tyrannus, fr. Gk tyrannos] 1 a : an absolute ruler unrestrained by law or constitution; often : a usurper of sovereignty b obs : a ruling personage (as a prince or governor) c : a ruler who exercises absolute power oppressively or brutally : DESPOT 2 a : a person in a position of control who exercises unlawful or improper authority or lawful or proper authority in an arbitrary or oppressive manner : one who by unfair or unreasonable demands or rigorous exploitation imposes burdens and hardships on those under his control ⟨our Latin teacher was a bitter ~⟩ b : something that imposes burdens and hardships like a human tyrant ⟨that ~, time⟩ 3 : TYRANT FLYCATCHER

²tyrant \"\ vi -ED/-ING/-S : to act the tyrant : TYRANNIZE

tyrant flycatcher also **tyrant bird** n : a flycatcher of the family Tyrannidae

tyrant wren n : a small yellow-crested So. American tyrant flycatcher (Tyrannulus elatus)

tyre chiefly Brit var of TIRE

¹tyr·i·an \ˈtirēən\ adj [L tyrius Tyrian (fr. Gk tyrios, fr. Tyros Tyre, famous maritime city of ancient Phoenicia) + E -an] 1 usu cap : of or relating to ancient Tyre or its people 2 often cap : of the color Tyrian purple

²tyrian \"\ n -s cap : a native or inhabitant of ancient Tyre

tyrian alphabet n, usu cap T : a Moabite alphabet prevailing in Phoenicia during the ascendancy of Tyre

tyrian blue n, often cap T : a grayish blue to grayish purplish blue

tyrian pink n, often cap T : a strong to vivid purplish red that is bluer and slightly darker than spring beauty

tyrian purple n, often cap T [so called fr. its chief source in ancient times, the city of Tyre] 1 : a crimson or purple dye $C_{16}H_8Br_2N_2O_2$ of the indigo class used by the ancient Greeks and Romans and prepared from the adrectal glands of gastropod mollusks (as of the genus Thais) or made synthetically; 6,6'-dibromo-indigo — see DYE table I (under Vat Blue); compare MUREX 1b 2 : a strong to vivid purplish red that is redder and darker than Tyrian pink

tyrian rose n, often cap T : a vivid purplish red that is redder and less strong than Indiana, redder and lighter than rubellite, and redder and darker than Persian rose

tyro- — see TYR-

ty·ro also **ti·ro** \ˈtī(ˌ)rō\ n -s [ML tyron-, tyro, tiron-, tiro, fr. L tiron-, tiro young soldier, new recruit, tyro] : a beginner in any field : one familiar with the rudiments of a subject but lacking in practical experience : NOVICE ⟨advice from the expert to the ~⟩

ty·ro·ci·dine \ˌtirəˈsīd²n, -ˌdēn\ or **ty·ro·ci·din** \-ˌīd²n\ n -s [tyrosine + -cide + -ine] : a crystalline antibiotic of a basic

polypeptide nature produced by a soil bacillus (Bacillus brevis) and constituting the major component of tyrothricin

ty·rode solution \ˈtiˌrōd-\ or **tyrode's solution** n, usu cap T [after Maurice V. Tyrode †1930 Am. pharmacologist] : physiological saline containing sodium chloride 0.8, potassium chloride 0.02, calcium chloride 0.02, magnesium chloride 0.01, sodium bicarbonate 0.1, and sodium dihydrogen phosphate 0.005 percent

¹ty·rog·ly·phid \tīˈrägləfəd, 'tirəˌglifəd\ adj [NL Tyroglyphidae] : ACARID 2

²tyroglyphid \"\ also **ty·ro·glyph** \ˈtirəˌglif\ n -s [tyroglyphid fr. ¹tyroglyphid; tyroglyph fr. NL Tyroglyphus] : ACARID 2

ty·ro·glyph·i·dae \ˌtirəˈglifəˌdē\ n [NL, fr. Tyroglyphus + -idae] syn of ACARIDAE

ty·rog·ly·phus \tīˈrägləfəs, ˌtirəˈglif-\ n, pl. Gk tyr- -glyphos (fr. glyphein to carve) — more at CLEAVE] syn see ACARUS

¹tyro·le·an also **tiro·le·an** \təˈrōlēən also (ˈ)tī,rōl- or 'tirō,l-\ adj, usu cap [Tyrol, Tirol, province in western Austria + E -ean] : of, relating to, or characteristic of the Tirol or its inhabitants : of the kind or style used or made in the Tirol

²tyrolean also **tirolean** \"\ n -s cap : a native or inhabitant of the Tirol

tyro·lese also **tiro·lese** \ˌtirəˈlēz, -ēs also ˈtīr-\ adj or n, usu cap [Tyrol, Tirol, Austria + E -ese] : TYROLEAN

tyrolese green n, often cap T : MALACHITE GREEN 3

tyrol green n, often cap T [fr. Tyrol (Tirol), Austria] : TERRE VERTE 2

ty·ro·li·an \təˈrōlēən\ adj or n, usu cap [Tyrol (Tirol), Austria + E -ian] : TYROLEAN

ty·ro·li·enne \təˌrōlēˈen\ n -s sometimes cap [F, fr. fem. of tyrolien Tyrolean, fr. Tyrol + F -ien -ian, fr. L -ianus] : a Tyrolean peasants' song or melody characterized by the yodel

tyr·o·lite \ˈtirəˌlīt\ n -s [G tirolit, fr. Tirol, Austria + G -it -ite] : a mineral $Cu_5Ca(AsO_4)_2(CO_3)(OH)_4.6H_2O$(?) that is a hydrous hydroxide, arsenate, and carbonate of copper and calcium

tyrolite green n, often cap T : APHRODITE 3

ty·rone \təˈrōn, by outsiders (ˈ)tīˌr-\ adj, usu cap [fr. Tyrone, county of west central Northern Ireland] : of or from County Tyrone, Northern Ireland : of the kind or style prevalent in County Tyrone

ty·ron·ic \(ˈ)tīˈränik\ adj [L tiron-, tiro tyro + E -ic] : of, relating to, or characteristic of a tyro : AMATEURISH

tyro·sin·ase \ˈtirəsəˌnās, 'tir-, -āz\ n -s [ISV tyrosine + -ase] : a copper-containing enzyme that promotes the reaction of oxygen and tyrosine or other phenols (as para-cresol) giving rise to a series of oxidation products including an ortho diphenol, an orthoquinone, and a melanin and that is widely distributed in plants and animals — compare POLYPHENOL OXIDASE

tyro·sine \-ˌsēn, -sən\ n -s [irreg. fr. Gk tyros cheese + ISV -ine — more at BUTTER] 1 : a crystalline phenolic alpha-amino acid $HOC_6H_4CH_2CH(NH_2)COOH$ obtained in the levorotatory L form by the hydrolysis of proteins (as casein or fibroin) and also made synthetically in the racemic form; para-hydroxyphenylalanine 2 : either of two crystalline acids that are ortho and meta isomers of tyrosine — compare DIIODOTYROSINE, DOPA, THYRONINE

tyro·sin·osis \ˌtirəsəˈnōsəs\ n -es [NL, fr. ISV tyrosine + -osis] : a condition of faulty metabolism of tyrosine marked by the excretion of unusual amounts of tyrosine in the urine

tyro·sin·uria \-səˈn(y)ùrēə\ n -s [NL, fr. ISV tyrosine + NL -uria] : the excretion of unusual amounts of tyrosine in the urine

tyro·syl \-ˌsil\ n -s [ISV tyrosine + -yl] : the acyl radical $HOC_6H_4CH(NH_2)CO$- of tyrosine

ty·ro·thricin \ˌtirəˈthrisᵊn, -risᵊn\ n -s [NL Tyrothric-, Tyrothrix, generic name formerly applied to various spore-forming bacteria (fr. tyr- + -thrix) + E -in] : an antibiotic mixture consisting chiefly of tyrocidine and gramicidin usu. extracted from a soil bacillus (Bacillus brevis) as a gray to brown powder and used for local applications esp. for infections caused by gram-positive bacteria

tyr·rhe·ni \ˈtirēˌnī\ n pl, usu cap [L, fr. pl. of tyrrhenus Etruscan] : the Etruscan people; also : the supposed immigrant ancestors of the historic Etruscans

tyr·rhe·ni·an \təˈrēnēən\ also **tyr·rhene** \ˈti,rēn, təˈr-\ adj, usu cap [tyrrhene fr. L tyrrhenus, fr. Gk tyrrhēnos; tyrrhenian fr. L tyrrhenus + E -ian] : of or relating to the Tyrrheni

tyr·tae·an \(ˈ)tərˈtēən\ adj, usu cap [Tyrtaeus 7th cent. B.C. Greek elegiac poet + E -an] : of, relating to, or styled in the manner of the Spartan poet Tyrtaeus noted as a writer of spirited martial and patriotic songs in the 7th century B.C.

ty·son·ite \ˈtisᵊnˌīt\ n -s [S. T. Tyson 19th cent. Am. naturalist + E -ite] : FLUOCERITE

ty·son's gland \ˈtisᵊnz-\ n, usu cap T [after Edward Tyson †1708 Eng. anatomist] : GLAND OF TYSON

tys·tie \ˈtisti, 'tēs-\ n -s [of Scand origin; akin to ON theist, theisti black guillemot] Brit : BLACK GUILLEMOT

tythe chiefly Brit var of TITHE

ty·to \ˈti(ˌ)tō\ n, cap [NL Tyton-, Tyto, fr. Gk tytō owl, of imit. origin] : a cosmopolitan genus of owls coextensive with the family Tytonidae

ty·ton·i·dae \tīˈtänəˌdē\ n pl, cap [NL, fr. Tyton-, Tyto, type genus + -idae] : a monotypic family of owls comprising the barn owls and being distinguished by an unnotched sternum and large clavicles fused with it — compare BUBONIDAE, STRIGIDAE

tyu·ya·mu·nite \ˌtyü(y)ə²mü,nīt, ˌchü-\ n -s [Tyuya Muyun, name of a hill in Fergana, Turkistan, U.S.S.R. + E -ite] : a mineral $Ca(UO_2)_2(VO_4)_2.nH_2O$ that is a hydrous vanadate of copper and uranium and important as an ore of uranium

tzaddik also **tzadik** var of ZADDIK

tzar var of CZAR

tze·da·kah or **tse·da·kah** or **ze·da·kah** \tsəˈdò(ˌ)kó\ n, pl **tzeda·koth** or **tzeda·kot** or **tseda·koth** or **tseda·kot** \tsəˈdòkəs, -ˌkä'dòt(h)\ [Heb ṣĕdāqāh, lit., righteousness] : voluntary aid : CHARITY ⟨circulate a ~ box for the support of orphan asylums⟩

tzel·tal \(ˌ)tselˈtäl\ or **tzen·tal** \-enˈtäl\ n, pl **tzeltal** or **tzelta·les** \-ˈtä(ˌ)läs\ or **tzental** or **tzenta·les** usu cap 1 a : an Indian people of the central part of the state of Chiapas, Mexico b : a member of such people 2 a : a Mayan language of the Tzeltal people

¹tzi·gane \(ˌ)tsēˈgän\ n -s sometimes cap [F tzigane, tsigane, fr. Hung cigány, czigány] : GYPSY

²tzigane \"\ adj, sometimes cap : of or relating to gypsies : of the kind or style used or made by gypsies ⟨~ music⟩

tzim·mes also **tzim·es** \ˈtsiməs\ n, pl **tzimmes** also **tzimes** [Yiddish tsimes] : a sweetened combination of vegetables (as carrots and potatoes) or of meat and carrots often with dried fruits (as prunes) that is stewed or baked in a casserole

tzitzith var of ZIZITH

tzol·kin \(ˈ)tsólˌkēn\ n [Mayan tzol to set in order + kin day] : a period of 260 days constituting a complete cycle of all the permutations of 20 day names with the numbers 1 to 13 that constitutes the Maya sacred year — compare TUN

tzo·tzil also **tso·tsil** \(ˈ)tsóˈtsē(ə)l, -)sót-\ or **zo·tzil** \(ˈ)só-, 'zó-\ n, pl **tzotzil** or **tzotziles** usu cap 1 a : an Indian people of central Chiapas, Mexico b : a member of the Tzotzil people 2 a : a Mayan language of the Tzotzil people

tz'u-chou \(ˈ)t)sü²jōⁿ\ n -s usu cap T [fr. Tz'u-chou, district in southern Hopeh province, northeast China] : a Chinese pottery made in Honan province during the Sung period and having usu. a cream-colored glaze over a buff body as the base, an incised or slip-painted decoration, and a transparent overglaze

tzut \(ˈ)t)süt\ or **tzu·te** \-ü(ˌ)tä\ n -s [of AmerInd origin] : a brightly patterned square of cotton used by Guatemalans esp. as a head cover

tzu·tu·hil also **zu·tu·hil** or **zu·tu·gil** \(ˈ)tsüd-əˌwē(ə)l, -d·ò)hē-\ n, pl **tzutuhil** or **tzu·tuhi·les** \ˌ=ˈwē(ˌ)läs, -ˌhē-\ usu cap 1 a : an Indian people of the south shore of Lake Atitlan, Guatemala b : a member of such people 2 a : a Mayan language of the Tzutuhil people

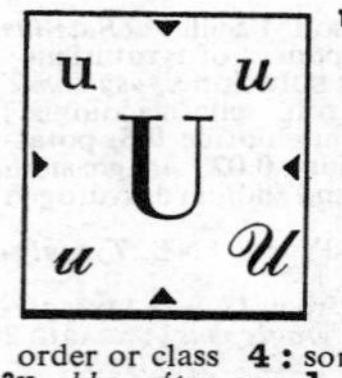

¹u \ˈyü\ *n, pl* **u's** *or* **us** \ˈyüz\ *often cap, often attrib* **1 a :** the 21st letter of the English alphabet **b :** an instance of this letter printed, written, or otherwise represented **c :** a speech counterpart of orthographic *u* (as long *u* in *mute,* short *u* in *cut,* or *u* in *rule*) **2 :** a printer's type, a stamp, or some other instrument for reproducing the letter *u* **3 :** someone or something arbitrarily or conveniently designated *u* esp. as the 20th or when j is used for the 10th the 21st in order or class **4 :** something having the shape of the letter U

²u *abbr, often cap* **1** uncirculated **2** uncle **3** [G *und*] and **4** under **5** unified **6** uniform **7** union; unionist **8** unit; united **9** universal **10** university **11** unpleasant **12** upper

³u *symbol, cap* **1** *ital* intrinsic energy **2** uranium

UA *abbr* **1** ultra-audible **2** underwriting account

uakari *var of* OUAKARI

U and O *abbr* use and occupancy

uang \ˈwäŋ\ *n* -s [Atjehnese *uĕng*] **:** a rhinoceros beetle (*Oryctes rhinoceros*)

ua·yeb \ˈwī,eb\ *n* -s *sometimes cap* [Mayan] **:** a period consisting of five nameless days added to a tun to make the 365-day year of the Maya calendar

ubaid \üˈbād, -bīd\ *or* **al 'ubaid** \,alə¦b-\ *adj, usu cap U* [fr. *al 'Ubaid* (Tell el-Obeid), locality in southern Iraq] **:** of or relating to an early Bronze Age culture in Mesopotamia prior to 3000 B.C.

uban·gi \yüˈbaŋ(g)ē, -aaŋ-, -aiŋ- *sometimes* üˈbäŋ-\ *n* -s *usu cap* [fr. *Ubangi-Shari,* territory in French Equatorial Africa] **:** a Sara woman of the district of Kyabé village in Africa with lips pierced and distended to unusual dimensions with wooden disks

ube \ˈübē, ˈü,bā\ *adj, usu cap* [fr. *Ube,* seaport city of southwest Honshu, Japan] **:** of or from the city of Ube, Japan **:** of the kind or style prevalent in Ube

uber·ri·ma fi·des \yüˈberəməˈfī(,)dēz\ *n* [L, lit., most abundant faith] **:** GOOD FAITH ⟨the rights of the parties . . . should be interpreted in a spirit of *uberrima fides* —H.B.Brown⟩

ubi·e·ty \yüˈbīəd·ē\ *n* -ES [L *ubi* where + E *-ety* (as in *society*) — more at UBIQUITY] *archaic* **:** the quality or state of being in a place **:** as **a :** the state of being placed in a definite local relation **:** POSITION, LOCATION **b :** the abstract quality of being in position **:** WHERENESS ⟨no woozy timelessness or lack of ~ in the drama —R.B.Heilman⟩

ubi·quar·i·an \,yübəˈkwa(a)rēən\ *n* -s *usu cap* [L *ubique* everywhere + E *-arian*] **:** UBIQUITARIAN

ubi·quist \ˈyübəkwəst\ *n* -s [L *ubique* everywhere + E *-ist*] **1** *usu cap* **:** UBIQUITARIAN **2 :** an organism that is distributed more or less uniformly through a region

¹**ubiq·ui·tar·i·an** \(,)yü¦bikwə¦ta(a)rēən\ *adj, often cap* [*ubiquity* + *-arian*] **:** of or relating to the doctrine of the Ubiquitarians

²**ubiquitarian** \"\ *n* -s *usu cap* **:** one of a school of Lutheran clergymen holding that as Christ is omnipresent his body is everywhere (as in the Eucharist)

ubiq·ui·tism \yüˈbikwə,tizəm\ *n* -s *usu cap* [*ubiquity* + *-ism*] **:** the doctrine that Christ's body is omnipresent

ubiq·ui·tous \-wəd·əs, -wətəs\ *adj* [*ubiquity* + *-ous*] **:** existing or being everywhere at the same time **:** occurring or capable of appearing everywhere or in many places throughout a particular area, sphere, or production **:** OMNIPRESENT ⟨the ~ little wolf of the high country —*Amer. Guide Series: Oregon*⟩ ⟨bricks . . . made from a ~ gray mud —Christopher Rand⟩ ⟨the ~ functionalism of modern society —Hannah Arendt⟩ ⟨nothing . . . escapes the ~ eyes of our Treasury Department —Harvey Breit⟩ ⟨the ~ paperback⟩ ⟨a ~, active salesman —J.S.Redding⟩ — **ubiq·ui·tous·ly** *adv* — **ubiq·ui·tous·ness** *n* -ES

ubiq·ui·ty \-wəd·ē, -wətē, -i\ *n* -ES [L *ubique* everywhere (fr. *ubi* where + *-que,* enclitic generalizing particle) + E *-ity;* akin to Oscan *puf* where, L *quis* who and to L *-que* and — more at WHO, SESQUI-] **1 :** the theological doctrine formulated by Luther that Christ's glorified body is omnipresent **2 :** presence everywhere or in many places esp. simultaneously **:** OMNIPRESENCE ⟨the ~ of the printed word —Reinhold Niebuhr⟩ ⟨the ~ of unreliable editions —Abram Chasins⟩ ⟨achieved a certain ~ by shuttling back and forth in hot and dusty trains —Agnes & W.E.Hocking⟩

ubi sunt \ˈübē¦sünt, ˈüb-\ *adj* [L, where are] **:** of or relating to a type of esp. medieval verse in which the poem or its stanzas begin with the Latin words *ubi sunt* or their equivalent in another language and which has as a principal theme the transitory nature of all things

ubi su·pra \,==ˈsüprə\ *adv* [L, where above] **:** where above mentioned

u-boat \ˈ=,=\ *n, usu cap U* [trans. of G *u-boot,* short for *unterseeboot,* lit., undersea boat] **:** a German or an Austrian submarine

u-bolt \ˈ=,=\ *n, cap U* **:** a U-shaped bolt having both arms threaded to receive nuts and used as a fastening device

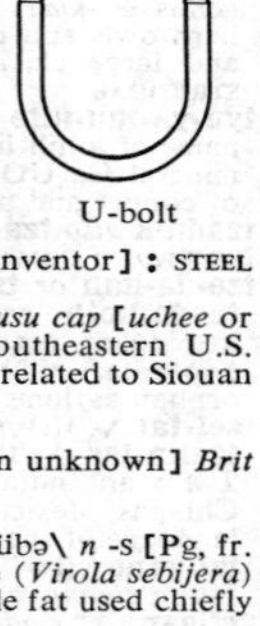
U-bolt

ubus·su \,übəˈsü\ *or* **ubussu palm** *n* [Pg *ubussú, bussú, ubuçu, buçu* — more at BUSSU] **:** BUSSU

UC *abbr* **1** undercarriage **2** under charge **3** under construction **4** *often not cap* uppercase **5** utility cargo

uca \ˈyükə\ *n, cap* [NL, fr. Tupi *uça, usa*] **:** a genus consisting of the typical fiddler crabs

ucha·ti·us bronze *or* **uchatius metal** \üˈkätsēəs-\ *n, usu cap U* [after Franz, Baron *Uchatius* †1881 Austrian general & inventor] **:** STEEL BRONZE

uche·an *also* **yu·chi·an** \ˈyüchēən, =ˈ==\ *n, usu cap* [*uchee* or *yuchi* + *-an*] **:** a language family of the southeastern U.S. comprising the Yuchi language and possibly related to Siouan and Muskogean

uchee *usu cap, var of* YUCHI

uck·ers \ˈekəz\ *n pl but sing in constr* [origin unknown] *Brit* **:** LUDO

ucs *abbr* unconscious

ucu·uba \,ükəˈ(w)übə\ *also* **ucu·hu·ba** \-ˈhübə\ *n* -s [Pg, fr. Tupi *ucu-uva*] **:** BANAK; *esp* **:** a Brazilian tree (*Virola sebifera*) having seeds that yield a hard yellowish edible fat used chiefly in candles and soap

ucuuba butter *or* **ucuuba tallow** *or* **ucuuba oil** *n* **:** a yellowish white fat obtained from the seeds of banaks (esp. *Virola sebifera*) and used in soap and candles

UD *abbr* **1** upper deck **2** urban district **3** [L *ut dictum*] as directed

¹**udal** \ˈyüdᵊl\ *adj* [ON *ōthal* inherited property — more at ODAL] **:** of, relating to, or constituting udal

²**udal** \"\ *n* -s **:** an alodial system of land tenure extant only in Shetland and Orkney — compare ODAL

UDC *abbr* urban district council

ud·der \ˈədə(r)\ *n* -s [ME, fr. OE *ūder;* akin to OHG *ūtar* udder, ON *jūgr,* L *uber,* Gk *outhar,* Skt *ūdhar*] **1 :** a large pendulous organ consisting of two or more mammary glands enclosed in a common envelope and each provided with a single nipple ⟨a cow's ~⟩ **2 :** MAMMARY GLAND, BREAST ⟨the ~s of a sow⟩ ⟨a lioness, with ~s all drawn dry —Shak.⟩

ud·der·less \ˈ==ləs\ *adj* **:** destitute or deprived of an udder

udi \ˈüdē\ *also* **udic** \-dik\ *or* **udin** \-dᵊn\ *n* -s *usu cap* **:** a north Caucasic language

udish \ˈüdish\ *n* -ES *usu cap* **:** UDI

ud·murt \(ˈ)üd¦mü(ə)rt\ *n* -s *usu cap* [Votyak, Votyak man] **:** VOTYAK

udo \ˈü(,)dō\ *n* -s [Jap] **:** a stout Japanese herb (*Aralia cordata*) the blanched young shoots of which are used esp. as a vegetable and in salads

udom·e·ter \yüˈdäməd·ə(r)\ *n* [L *uvidus, udus* damp, moist, wet + E *-o-* + *-meter* — more at HUMOR] **:** RAIN GAGE — **udo·met·ric** \¦yüdə¦me·trik\ *adj*

udom·o·graph \yüˈdämə,graf\ *n* [*udometer* + *-o-* + *-graph*] **:** a self-registering rain gage

UDT *abbr* **1** underdeck tonnage **2** underwater demolition team

UE *abbr* university extension

ufa \(ˈ)ü¦fä\ *adj, usu cap* [fr. *Ufa,* capital of Bashkir Republic, U.S.S.R.] **:** of or from the city of Ufa, U.S.S.R. **:** of the kind or style prevalent in Ufa

ufer \ˈyüfə(r)\ *n* -s [D *juffer* miss, lady, pole, beam, euphroe — more at EUPHROE] **:** a fir pole from 4 to 7 inches in diameter and from 20 to 40 feet in length

UFO \,yü,ef¦ō\ *abbr or n* -s **:** an unidentified flying object — compare FLYING SAUCER

ufra disease \ˈüfrə-\ *n* [prob. fr. Ar *'ufrah* dust color] **:** a disease of rice (as in India) caused by an eelworm (*Ditylenchus angustus*) and characterized by first whitish and then brownish leaf tips, stem distortion above the last node, and arrested development of the ear and in heavily attacked plants by decay

ugan·da \(y)üˈgandə, üˈgän-\ *adj, usu cap* [fr. *Uganda,* British protectorate in eastern Africa] **:** of, relating to, or characteristic of Uganda **:** UGANDAN

¹**ugan·dan** \-dən\ *adj, usu cap* [*Uganda,* British protectorate in eastern Africa + E *-an*] **:** of, relating to, or characteristic of Uganda

²**ugandan** \"\ *n* -s *cap* **:** a native or inhabitant of Uganda

uga·ra·ño \,ügəˈrän(,)yō\ *n* -s *usu cap* [Sp, of AmerInd origin] **:** a dialect of the Zamuco people

uga·ri·tian \,ügəˈrishən, -rēsh-\ *n* -s *usu cap* [*Ugarit,* ancient city + E *-ic*] **:** UGARITIC

¹**uga·rit·ic** \,==¦rid·ik\ *adj, usu cap* [*Ugarit,* ancient city in northwest Syria + E *-ic*] **1 :** of, relating to, or characteristic of the ancient city of Ugarit or its inhabitants **2 :** of, relating to, or characteristic of the Ugaritic language

²**ugaritic** \"\ *n* -s *usu cap* **:** the Semitic language of ancient Ugarit closely related to Phoenician and Hebrew

ug·gle·some \ˈəgəlsəm\ *adj* [obs. E *uggle* horrible (fr. ME *uggen* to inspire horror or disgust, to fear, fr. ON *ugga* to fear) + E *-some;* akin to ON *uggr* fear — more at UGLY] *archaic* **:** HORRIBLE

ugh *often read as* ˈəg *or* ˈə\ *interj* — used to indicate the sound of a cough or grunt or to express disgust or horror

ug·li \ˈəgli\ *n, pl* **uglis** *or* **uglies** [prob. alter. of ³*ugly;* fr. the unattractive appearance of its wrinkled skin] *Brit* **:** TANGELO

uglies *pl of* UGLY

ug·li·fi·ca·tion \,əgləfəˈkāshən\ *n* -s [fr. *uglify,* after such pairs as E *purify: purification*] **:** the action of making ugly

ug·li·fi·er \ˈəglə,fī(ə)r, -īə\ *n* -s [*uglify* + *-er*] **:** one that uglifies ⟨~s of the landscape⟩

ug·li·fy \-,fī\ *vt* -ED/-ING/-ES [¹*ugly* + *-fy*] **:** to make ugly ⟨beautifying our environment instead of ~*ing* it —Matthew Lipman⟩

ug·li·ly \-lə̇lē, -li\ *adv* [ME, fr. ¹*ugly* + *-ly*] **:** in an ugly manner

ug·li·ness \-lēnə̇s, -lin-\ *n* -ES [ME *uglines,* fr. ¹*ugly* + *-nes* -ness] **1 :** the quality or state of being ugly ⟨observe the ~ of poverty —John Reed⟩ ⟨moral ~ trespasses into the aesthetic —E.M.Forster⟩ **2 :** an ugly thing or characteristic

¹**ug·ly** \ˈəglē, -li\ *adj* -ER/-EST [ME *uglike, ugly* frightful, unpleasing in appearance, fr. ON *uggligr* frightful, fr. *uggr* fear + *-ligr* -ly — more at -LY] **1 :** FRIGHTFUL, TERRIBLE, HORRIBLE, DIRE ⟨inflicting a very ~ though not necessarily fatal wound —D.D.Martin⟩ **2 a** (1) **:** offensive to the sight **:** of unpleasing, disagreeable, or loathsome appearance **:** not beautiful **:** UNSIGHTLY, HIDEOUS ⟨~ people⟩ ⟨an ~ color⟩ ⟨houses were cheaply constructed and ~ —Sherwood Anderson⟩ (2) **:** INAESTHETIC ⟨an ~ line⟩ **b :** offensive or unpleasing to any sense ⟨~ sounds⟩ ⟨~ smells⟩ **3 :** morally offensive or objectionable **:** REPULSIVE, VILE, BASE ⟨~ crimes⟩ ⟨~ habits⟩ **4 a :** causing or likely to cause inconvenience, embarrassment, or discomfort **:** TROUBLESOME ⟨an ~ situation⟩ ⟨told him the ~ truth about himself —Eden Phillpotts⟩ **b** (1) **:** THREATENING ⟨~ weather⟩ ⟨an ~ cloud⟩ (2) **:** HEAVY, VIOLENT ⟨an ~ sea⟩ **c :** ILL-NATURED, SURLY, QUARRELSOME ⟨an ~ temper⟩

syn HIDEOUS, ILL-FAVORED, UNSIGHTLY: UGLY may apply to whatever is strongly displeasing to view or contemplate or to whatever calls forth repulsion, repugnance, loathing, or dread ⟨an *ugly* sight he was, thin, stooping, bald, stiff-jointed, with an ulcered face patched with plasters —Robert Graves⟩ ⟨acres of *ugly* wooden tenement houses line the drab streets —*Amer. Guide Series: Mass.*⟩ ⟨an *ugly* story of low passion, delusion, and waking from delusion —George Eliot⟩ HIDEOUS applies to what is extremely ugly and revolting, horrible, or odious ⟨false eyebrows and false moustaches were stuck upon them, and their *hideous* countenances were all bloody and sweaty —Charles Dickens⟩ ⟨a yell of agony so appalling and *hideous* —Sheridan Le Fanu⟩ ⟨a *hideous* business, in which nearly all the humane alleviations of brutal violence, introduced and practiced in the days when professional armies fought for a dynasty or for a point of honor, were disregarded —W.R. Inge⟩ ILL-FAVORED describes one with unpleasing, disagreeable, or unpleasant features but not in general have more dire connotation ⟨*ill-favored* and lean-fleshed —Gen 41:3 (AV)⟩ UNSIGHTLY, close to UGLY, may apply to something unattractive that blemishes what might have been pleasing ⟨*unsightly* hovels⟩ ⟨*unsightly* areas of houses quickly built and poorly kept —*Amer. Guide Series: Va.*⟩ ⟨an *unsightly* scar⟩

²**ugly** \"\ *adv* [ME, fr. ¹*ugly*] *chiefly dial* **:** UGLILY

³**ugly** \"\ *n* -ES [¹*ugly*] **:** one that is ugly

ugly duckling *n* [fr. *The Ugly Duckling* (1835?), story by Hans Christian Andersen †1875 Dan. author] **:** an immature or dependent person or thing that is despised or neglected because of unprepossessing appearance or unpromising qualities but that develops or is capable of developing into a person or thing worthy of attention or respect ⟨from the beginning Alaska was treated pretty much as our *ugly duckling* —W.O.Douglas⟩ ⟨bacteriology is still too often taught as the *ugly duckling* of botany —Justina Hill⟩

ugly-nest caterpillar *n* **:** a gregarious caterpillar that is the larva of a tortricid moth (*Archips cerasivorana*) and that feeds chiefly on black cherry and chokecherry in northern U.S. and Canada and webs the leaves together into an irregular nest

ugni blanc \ˈügnē¦bläⁿ, ˈünyē-\ *n* [F, fr. *Ugni,* name of a type of grape + *blanc* white, fr. MF — more at BLANK] **:** a white table wine of Chablis type made in California — called also *Trebbiano*

¹**ugri·an** \ˈ(y)ügrēən\ *adj, usu cap* [Old Russian *Ugre* (pl.) Hungarians + E *-ian*] **1 :** of, relating to, or characteristic of the Ugrians **2 :** UGRIC

²**ugrian** \"\ *n* -s *usu cap* **:** a member of the eastern division of the Finno-Ugrian peoples including the Magyars, Voguls, and Ostyaks — compare FINNO-UGRIAN

ugric \-grik\ *adj, usu cap* [*ugrian* + *-ic*] **:** of, relating to, or characteristic of the languages of the Ugrians — see URALIC LANGUAGES table

ugro- *comb form, usu cap* [*ugrian*] **:** Ugrian and ⟨*Ugro*-Aryan⟩ ⟨*Ugro*-Finnic⟩

ug·rug \ˈə,grəg\ *n* -s [Esk] *Alaska* **:** BEARDED SEAL

ug·some \ˈəgsəm\ *adj* [ME, fr. *uggen* to fear, inspire dread or loathing + *-some* — more at UGGLESOME] *archaic* **:** FRIGHTFUL, HORRID, LOATHSOME ⟨the depth of the wood beyond was so ~ —John Masefield⟩

ugt *abbr* urgent

UH *abbr* upper half

UHF *abbr, often not cap* ultrahigh frequency

uh-huh *a disyllabic sound with* m-*sounds at beginning & end, an h-like interval of voicelessness between, & heavier stress on the first member; in the registering of gratification the voiced members are more prolonged, about equal in stress, & the sound is higher in pitch*\ *interj* — used to indicate affirmation, agreement, or gratification

uh·lan \(ˈ)ü¦län, ˈ(y)ülən\ *n* -s [G *ulan, uhlan,* fr. Pol *ulan,* fr. Turk *oğlan* boy, servant] **:** a lancer of a class of Tatarian origin introduced into European armies in Poland and esp. prominent in the Prussian armies (as in the Franco-Prussian war of 1870) who were armed with lances, pistols, sabers, and later with carbines and were employed chiefly as skirmishers and scouts

ui *abbr* [L *ut infra*] as below

UI *abbr* unemployment insurance

ui·ghur *or* **ui·gur** \ˈwē,gü(ə)r, -,gər\ *n, pl* **uighur** *or* **uighurs** *or* **uigur** *or* **uigurs** *usu cap* [Uighur *Uighur*] **1 :** a member of a Turkic people who developed a powerful kingdom and a considerable culture in Mongolia and eastern Turkestan between the 8th and 12th centuries A.D. and who now form a majority of the population of Chinese Turkestan and are found chiefly in the oasis towns of the Tarim basin — compare YARKANDI **2 a :** the Turkic language of the Uighur people **b :** an alphabet based on Sogdian and employed for Turkic languages from the 6th to the 12th centuries — called also *neo-Sogdian*

²**uighur** *or* **uigur** \"\ *adj, usu cap* **1 :** of, relating to, or characteristic of the Uighurs **2 a :** of, relating to, or characteristic of the Uighur language **b :** of, relating to, or characteristic of the Uighur alphabet

ui·ghu·ri·an *or* **ui·gu·ri·an** \(ˈ)wē¦gürēən\ *adj or n, usu cap* [¹*uighur* + *-ian*] **:** UIGHUR

ui·ghu·ric *or* **ui·gu·ric** \-rik\ *adj, usu cap* [¹*uighur* + *-ic*] **:** UIGHUR

ui·nal \wēˈnäl\ *n* -s [Mayan] **:** one of the eighteen 20-day periods into which a tun is divided in the Maya calendar **:** a Maya month

uin·ta *also* **uin·tah** \yüˈ(w)intə, yəˈwi-\ *n, pl* **uinta** *or* **uintas** *or* **uintah** *or* **uintahs** *usu cap* **1 :** a division of the Ute in northeastern Utah **2 :** a member of the Uinta division of the Ute

uin·ta·ite *also* **uin·tah·ite** \-tə,īt\ *n* -s [*Uinta* or *Uintah* mountains of northeast Utah + E *-ite*] **:** a black lustrous asphalt occurring esp. in Utah that is useful in the arts (as in the manufacture of paints, varnishes, and inks) and for waterproofing

uin·ta·there \-ə,thi(ə)r\ *n* -s [NL *uintatherium*] **:** UINTATHERIUM 2

uin·ta·the·ri·um \=,==ˈthirēəm\ *n* [NL, fr. *Uinta* co., southwest Wyo. + NL *-therium*] **1** *cap* **:** a genus (the type of the family Uintatheriidae) of large herbivorous ungulate mammals of the order Dinocerata from the Eocene of Wyoming resembling elephants in size and in the conformation of their limbs and having three pairs of bony protuberances respectively on the parietal, maxillary, and nasal bones of the skull, a pair of canine tusks guarded by downwardly directed processes of the lower jaw but no upper incisors, and a proportionately very small brain **2** *pl* **uin·ta·the·ria** \-rēə\ **:** a mammal of the genus *Uintatherium*

uin·tjie \ˈānchē\ *n* -s [Afrik *euntjie, uintjie,* a species of *Moraea,* dim. of MD *enioen, eyuun* onion, fr. L *union-, unio* — more at ONION] *southern Africa* **:** the edible corm of various plants esp. of the family Iridaceae that when boiled tastes like a chestnut

uit·land·er \ˈāt,landə(r)\ *n* -s *often cap* [Afrik, fr. MD *utelander,* fr. *utelant* foreign territory (fr. *ute* out + *land, lant* land) + *-er,* fr. L *-arius;* akin to OE *ūt* out & to OE *land* — more at OUT, LAND, -ER] **:** FOREIGNER, OUTLANDER; *esp* **:** a British resident in the former So. African republics of the Transvaal and Orange Free State

uitotoan *usu cap, var of* WITOTOAN

uitoto *usu cap, var of* WITOTO

uit·span \(ˈ)āt¦span\ *vb* [Afrik, fr. MD *utespannen,* fr. *ute* out (akin to OE *ūt* out) + *spannen* to bind, hitch up — more at OUT, SPAN] *southern Africa* **:** OUTSPAN

uji \ˈü(,)jē\ *n* -s [Jap, maggot] **:** a silkworm disease in Japan caused by the parasitic larva of the uji fly

uji fly *n* **:** a tachinid fly (*Sturmia sericaria*) of Japan

ukase \yüˈkās *sometimes* yüˈkāz *or* (y)üˈkäz *or* (y)üˈkäs; ˈ=,=\ *n* -s [F & Russ; F *ukase,* fr. Russ *ukaz,* fr. *ukazat'* to show, direct, order; akin to OSlav *u-* away, thoroughly, L *au-* away, Skt *ava-* away, and to OSlav *kazati* to show; prob. akin to Gk *tekmōr* tekmar sign, token, Skt *kāśate* he appears, shines] **1** *also* **ukaz** \üˈkäz, -kaz\ -ES **:** a proclamation or order by a Russian emperor or government having the force of law **2 :** EDICT, DECREE ⟨the ~ of a board of trustees, a legislature, a political party —A.M.Schlesinger b. 1917⟩ ⟨government by ~⟩

uke \ˈyük\ *n* -s [by shortening & alter.] **:** UKULELE

uki·yoe \üˈkēyō,yā\ *also* **uki·yo** \-ē(,)yō\ *or* **uki·yo·ye** \-ēyō,yā\ *n* -s [Jap *ukiyoe* genre picture, fr. *ukiyo* world, life + *e* picture] **:** a Japanese artistic movement from the 17th through the 19th centuries specializing in simple paintings and color prints of everyday life

¹**ukrain·ian** \(ˈ)yü¦krānēən, -ānyən *sometimes* (ˈ)(y)ü¦krīn-\ *adj, usu cap* [fr. *Ukraine,* constituent republic of the U.S.S.R. in east central Europe + E *-ian*] **1 a :** of, relating to, or characteristic of the Ukraine **b :** of, relating to, or characteristic of the people of the Ukraine **2 :** of, relating to, or characteristic of the Ukrainian language

²**ukrainian** \"\ *n* -s *cap* **1 :** a native or inhabitant of the Ukraine **2 :** the Slavic language of the Ukrainian people **3 :** RUTHENIAN 2

uku \ˈü,kü\ *n* -s [Hawaiian] **:** a grayish blue-tinged snapper (*Aprion virescens*) of Hawaiian seas that is common in the markets and highly esteemed as food

uku·le·le *also* **uke·le·le** \,yükəˈlālē, -āli, *sometimes* ,ük-\ *n* -s [Hawaiian *'ukulele,* fr. *'uku* small person, flea + *lele* jumping; prob. fr. the Hawaiian nickname of Edward Purvis 19th cent. Brit. army officer who was small and quick and who popularized the instrument] **:** a small guitar of Portuguese origin popularized in Hawaii in the 1880s, strung typically with four strings that are plucked or strummed with the fingers, and used esp. in accompanying songs or dances

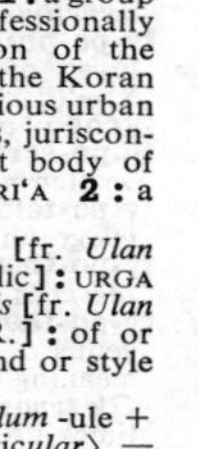
ukulele

UL *abbr* upper left

ula \ˈyülə\ *n pl* [NL, fr. Gk *oula,* pl. of *oulon;* prob. akin to Gk *eilein* to roll, *eilyein* to roll, wrap — more at VOLUBLE] **:** GUMS

¹**-u·la** \(y)ələ\ *n suffix, pl* **-ulas** \-ləz\ *or* **-ulae** \-,lē, -,lī\ [L — more at -ULE] **:** small one ⟨Cang*ula*⟩ ⟨siphon*ula*⟩ ⟨plac*ula*⟩

²**-ula** *pl of* -ULUM

ulae \(ˈ)ü¦lī\ *n* -s [Hawaiian *'ulae*] *Hawaii* **:** LIZARD FISH

ula·ma *or* **ule·ma** \ˈülə¦mä\ *n, pl* **ulama** *or* **ulamas** *or* **ulema** *or* **ulemas** [Ar, Turk & Per; Turk & Per *'ulemā,* fr. Ar *'ulamā,* fr. pl. of *'ālim* knowing, learned, fr. *'alama* to know] **1 :** a group of Muslim theologians and scholars who are professionally occupied with the elaboration and interpretation of the Muslim legal system from a study of its sources in the Koran and hadith, are usu. found gathered in groups at various urban centers where they function individually as teachers, jurisconsults, and theologians, and constitute the highest body of religious authorities in Islam — compare ALIM, SHARI'A **2 :** a member of an ulama

ulan ba·tor \ˈü,län¦bä,tò(ə)r\ *adj, usu cap U&B* [fr. *Ulan Bator* (Urga), capital of Mongolian People's Republic] **:** URGA

ulan ude \ˈü¦län¦ü(,)dā, -nü¦dā\ *adj, usu cap both Us* [fr. *Ulan Ude,* capital of Buryat-Mongol Republic, U.S.S.R.] **:** of or from the city of Ulan Ude, U.S.S.R. **:** of the kind or style prevalent in Ulan Ude

-u·lar \yələ(r)\ *adj suffix* [L *-ularis,* fr. *-ulus, -ula, -ulum* -ule + *-aris* -ar] **:** of, relating to, or resembling ⟨crevic*ular*⟩ — chiefly in words where the base word is derived from a Latin word having a diminutive in *-ulus, -ula,* or *-ulum* ⟨tub*ular*⟩ ⟨valv*ular*⟩

ula·ula \ˈülə¦ülə\ *n* -s [Hawaiian *'ula'ula*] *Hawaii* **:** any of several brightly colored snappers commonly used as food

ULC *abbr* upper left center

¹**ul·cer** \ˈəlsə(r)\ *n* -s [ME, fr. L *ulcer-, ulcus* sore, ulcer; akin to Gk *helkos* wound, ulcer, Skt *arśas* hemorrhoids] **1 :** a break in skin or mucous membrane that is characterized by loss of surface tissue on an inflammatory base and by disintegration and necrosis of epithelial tissue and that is associated with slow healing and if infected with pus ⟨a stomach ~⟩ ⟨a varicose ~⟩ — compare ABSCESS **2 :** something that festers and corrupts like an ulcer

²**ulcer** \"\ *vb* -ED/-ING/-S **:** ULCERATE

ul·cer·ate \-ə,rāt, *usu* -ād·+V\ *vb* -ED/-ING/-S [ME *ulceraten,* fr. L *ulceratus,* past part. of *ulcerare* to ulcerate, fr. *ulcer-, ulcus* ulcer] *vt* **:** to affect with or as if with an ulcer ⟨an *ulcerated* stomach⟩ ~ *vi* **:** to undergo ulceration

ul·cer·a·tion \,==ˈrāshən\ *n* -s [L *ulceration-, ulceratio,* fr. *ulceratus* + *-ion-, -io* -ion] **1 :** the process of forming an ulcer or of becoming ulcerated **2 :** the state of being ulcerated **3 :** ULCER

ul·cer·a·tive \ˈəlsə,rād·|iv, -s(ə)rəl, |t|, |ēv *also* |əv\ *adj* [L *ulceratus* + E *-ive*] **:** of, relating to, or characterized by an ulcer or by ulceration

ulcerative colitis *n* **:** a nonspecific inflammatory disease of

the colon of unknown cause characterized by diarrhea with discharge of mucus and blood, cramping abdominal pain, and inflammation and edema of the mucous membrane with patches of ulceration

ulcerative lymphangitis *n* **:** pseudoglanders or a related condition in cattle

ulcer disease *n* **:** a common and destructive bacterial disease of young trout esp. in hatcheries that is characterized by extensive skin lesions and sloughing ulcerations and is distinguished with difficulty from furunculosis

ul·cered \ˈəlsə(r)d\ *adj* [¹*ulcer* + *-ed*] **:** ULCEROUS, ULCERATED

ulcero- *comb form* [L *ulcer-, ulcus*] **1 :** ulcer ⟨*ulcero*genic⟩ **2 :** ulcerous and ⟨*ulcero*glandular⟩

ul·cero·membranous \ˌəlsərō+\ *adj* [ISV *ulcero-* + *membranous*] **:** characterized by ulceration and the formation of a membrane or esp. a false membrane

ul·cer·ous \ˈəls(ə)rəs\ *adj* [L *ulcerosus* affected with sores or ulcers, fr. *ulcer-, ulcus* ulcer + *-osus* -ous] **1 :** having the nature or character of an ulcer ⟨~ lesions⟩ **2 :** affected with an ulcer **:** ULCERATED ⟨an ~ person⟩

ul·cus \ˈəlkəs\ *n, pl* **ul·cera** \-lsərə\ [L *ulcer-, ulcus*] **:** ULCER

ule *or* **hu·le** \ˈü(ˌ)lā\ *n* -s [AmerSp *ule, hule,* fr. Nahuatl *ulli*] **1** *also* **ule tree :** a tree of the genus *Castilloa* that yields caucho **2 :** CAUCHO

-ule \ˌyül\ *n suffix* -s [F&L; F *-ule,* fr. L *-ulus,* masc. dim. suffix, *-ula,* fem. dim. suffix, *-ulum* neut. dim. suffix] **:** small one ⟨*cym*ule⟩ ⟨*vein*ule⟩

ulema *var of* ULAMA

-u·lent \(y)ələnt\ *adj suffix* [L *-ulentus, -olentus;* prob. akin to L *olēre* to smell — more at ODOR] **:** that abounds in (a specified thing) **:** that has (a specified thing) in marked amount or degree ⟨*nidor*ulent⟩

ulet·ic \yüˈled·ik\ *adj* [NL *ula* + E *-etic*] **:** of or relating to the gums

ulex \ˈyüˌleks\ *n* [NL *Ulic-, Ulex,* fr. L, a shrub resembling rosemary] **1** *cap* **:** a genus of Eurasian spiny shrubs (family Leguminosae) including the common furze that are usu. destitute of true leaves and have solitary or racemose yellow flowers with a 2-lipped colored calyx **2** -ES **:** any plant of the genus *Ulex*

ulex·ine \yüˈlekˌsēn, -ksən\ *n* -s [NL *Ulex* + E *-ine*] **:** cytisine from the seeds of a furze (*Ulex europaeus*)

ulex·ite \ˈ(y)üˌlekˌsīt\ *n* -s [George L. *Ulex* †1883 Ger. chemist + E *-ite*] **:** a mineral $NaCaB_5O_9.8H_2O$ consisting of a hydrous sodium calcium borate and occurring in white rounded crystalline masses rather common in borate deposits (hardness 1, sp. gr. 1.65)

-uli *pl of* -ULUS

ulig·i·nous \yüˈlijənəs\ *adj* [L *uliginosus,* fr. *uligin-, uligo* moisture, marshiness, fr. *udus, uvidus* damp, moist — more at HUMOR] **:** growing in wet or swampy ground

ul·lage \ˈəlij, -lēj\ *n* -s [ME *ulage, oylage,* fr. MF *eullage, oillage* act of filling a cask, filling to replace leakage, fr. *eullier, ouiller* to fill a cask (fr. OF *ouil* eye, bunghole, fr. L *oculus* eye) + *-age* — more at EYE] **:** the amount that a container (as a cask or tank) lacks of being full **:** OUTAGE

ul·laged \-jd\ *adj* [*ullage* + *-ed*] **:** short of the full measure of its contents ⟨an ~ cask⟩

ul·la·gone \ˌələˈgōn\ *also* **ul·li·can** \ˌələˈkän\ *n* -s [IrGael *olagān, olagān,* of imit. origin] *Irish* **:** a cry of sorrow **:** DIRGE

ul·la grass \ˈülə-\ *n* [Bengali *ulu*] **:** a coarse East Indian and Australian grass (*Themeda gigantea*) that is used as a source of paper pulp — called also *kangaroo grass, oat grass*

ull·mann·ite \ˈəlməˌnīt\ *n* -s [G *ullmannit,* fr. Johann C. *Ullmann* †1821 Ger. mineralogist + G *-it* -ite] **:** a mineral NiSbS consisting of nickel antimonide and sulfide, usu. containing a little arsenic, and occurring massive with steel-gray color and metallic luster

ul·lo·a's ring *or* **ulloa's bow** *or* **ulloa's circle** \ü(l)ˈyōəz-\ *n, usu cap U* [after Antonio de Ulloa †1795 Span. naval officer and scientist] **:** FOGBOW

ullu·cu \üˈyü(ˌ)kü\ *or* **ollu·co** \ōˈyü(ˌ)kō\ *n* -s [AmerSp & Quechua; AmerSp *ulluco, alluco, olluca,* fr. Quechua *ullucu*] **:** an Andean plant (*Ullucus tuberosus*) of the family Basellaceae having a creeping stem that roots wherever it touches the ground and tuberous roots which are used in place of potatoes

ul·ma·ce·ae \ˌəlˈmāsēˌē\ *n pl, cap* [NL, fr. *Ulmus,* type genus + *-aceae*] **:** a family of trees and shrubs (order Urticales) distinguished by the alternate stipulate pinnately veined simple leaves and small apetalous perfect or unisexual flowers — see CELTIS, PLANERA, TREMA, ULMUS

ul·ma·ceous \-shəs\ *adj* [NL *Ulmaceae* + E *-ous*] **:** of or relating to the Ulmaceae

ul·mar·ia \ˌəlˈma(a)rēə\ *n* [NL, fr. L *ulmus* elm + NL *-aria;* fr. the resemblance of its leaves to those of the elm — more at ELM] *syn of* FILIPENDULA

ul·mic \ˈəlmik\ *or* **ul·mous** \-məs\ *adj* [*ulmin* + *-ic* or *-ous*] **:** of or relating to ulmin

ul·min \-mən\ *n* -s [L *ulmus* elm + E *-in*] **:** any of a group of brown to black organic substances found esp. in soil, peat, or coal and obtained artificially by the action of various reagents on sugars

ul·min·ic \ˌəlˈminik\ *adj* [*ulmin* + *-ic*] **:** ULMIC

ul·mo \ˈül(ˌ)mō\ *n* -s [Sp, fr. Araucanian] **:** MUERMO

ul·mus \ˈəlməs\ *n, cap* [NL, fr. L, elm — more at ELM] **:** a genus of trees (the type of the family Ulmaceae) comprising the elms that are widely distributed in temperate regions and have simple serrate oblique leaves, often drooping branches, and fascicled perfect flowers unfolding before the leaves and succeeded by orbicular samaras

ul·na \ˈəlnə\ *n, pl* **ul·nae** \-ˌnē, -ˌnī\ *or* **ulnas** [NL, fr. L, elbow, arm, ell — more at ELL] **1 :** the postaxial or inner one of the two bones of the forearm or corresponding part of the forelimb of vertebrates above fishes that in man forms with the humerus the elbow joint and serves as a pivot in rotation of the hand and that in many animals is fused with the radius and then often much reduced in size — see CORONOID PROCESS, OLECRANON, SEMILUNAR NOTCH, SIGMOID CAVITY **2 :** the hypercoracoid bone of a fish

ul·nad \ˈəlˌnad\ *adv* [NL *ulna* + E *-ad*] **:** toward the ulna

ul·nar \ˈəlnə(r)\ *adj* [NL *ulnaris,* fr. *ulna* + L *-aris* -ar] **1 :** of or relating to the ulna **2 :** located on the same side of the forearm as the ulna

ulnar artery *n* **:** an artery that is the larger of the two terminal branches of the brachial artery, runs along the ulnar side of the forearm, and gives off near its origin the anterior and posterior ulnar recurrent arteries

ul·nare \ˌəlˈna(a)rē, -ˈnārē\ *or* **ul·nar** \ˈəlnə(r)\ *n, pl* **ulnar·ia** \-a(a)rēə, -ārēə\ *or* **ulnars** [NL *ulnare,* fr. neut. of *ulnaris* ulnar] **1 :** the third carpal bone or element of the proximal row counting from the radial side; *specif* **:** CUNEIFORM 1b **2** *or* **ulnar carpal :** a bone of a bird prob. representing the ulnare and centrale and sometimes also the fifth metacarpal

ulnar nerve *n* **:** a large nerve arising from the medial part of the brachial plexus, passing down the inner side of the arm and forearm, and resting upon the medial epicondyle of the humerus at the elbow

ulnar recurrent artery *n* **:** either of the two small terminal branches of the ulnar artery that innervate the upper forearm and elbow region

ulnar vein *n* **:** any of several veins of the forearm; *esp* **:** either of the two veins running up the anterior and posterior aspects of the inner side of the forearm and opening into the median basilic vein either separately or uniting to form a short single trunk and constituting with it the basilic vein

ulno- *comb form* [NL *ulna*] **:** ulnar and ⟨*ulno*carpal⟩ ⟨*ulno*radial⟩

ul·no·condylar \ˌəlnə+\ *adj* [*ulno-* + *condylar*] **:** of, relating to, or constituting the medial epicondyle of the humerus

ulo *var of* ULU

ulo- *comb form* [NL *ula*] **:** connection with or relation to the gums ⟨*ulo*rrhagia⟩

¹ulob·o·rid \yüˈläbərəd\ *adj* [NL *Uloboridae*] **:** of or relating to the Uloboridae

²uloborid \ˈ"\ *n* -s **:** a spider of the family Uloboridae

ulo·bor·i·dae \ˌyüləˈbōrəˌdē\ *n pl, cap* [NL *Uloborus,* type genus + *-idae*] **:** a family of spiders having a cribellum and calamistrum and spinning an orb web

ulob·o·rus \yüˈläbərəs\ *n, cap* [NL, fr. Gk *ouloboros* having a deadly bite, fr. *oulos* deadly, destructive (akin to Gk *ollynai* to destroy) + *-boros* (fr. *bibrōskein* to eat, devour) — more at VORACIOUS] **:** a genus (the type of the family Uloboridae) of orb-spinning spiders

-u·lose \(y)əˌlōs *also* -ōz\ *n suffix* -s [lev*ulose*] **:** ketose sugar — esp. in names of 2-keto sugars ⟨hept*ulose*⟩ ⟨xyl*ulose*⟩

ulo·thrix \ˈyüləˌthriks\ *n, cap* [NL *Ulotrich-, Ulothrix,* fr. Gk *oulotrich-, oulothrix* having curly hair — more at ULOTRICHOUS] **:** a genus (the type of the family Ulotrichaceae) of green algae that are common in ponds and consist of simple filaments with band-shaped green chloroplasts

ulot·ri·cha·ce·ae \yüˌlätrəˈkāsēˌē\ *n pl, cap* [NL, fr. *Ulotrich-, Ulothrix,* type genus + *-aceae*] **:** a family of green algae (order Ulotrichales) — see ULOTHRIX — **ulot·ri·cha·ceous** \ˌ⁼ˌ⁼⁼ˈkāshəs\ *adj*

ulot·ri·cha·les \ˌ⁼ˌ⁼⁼ˈkā(ˌ)lēz\ *n pl* [NL *Ulotrich-, Ulothrix* + *-ales*] **:** an order of green algae that includes the family Ulotrichaceae and in some classifications also Ulvaceae and that comprises freshwater or marine forms having a multicellular thallus with usu. simple or branched filaments sometimes aggregated to form pseudoparenchymatous masses or sheets, asexual reproduction effected by zoospores, and sexual reproduction by fusion of isogametes or of differentiated egg and sperm cells

ulot·ri·chan \⁼ˈlätrəkən\ *adj* [NL *Ulotrichi* + E *-an*] **:** ULOTRICHOUS

ulot·ri·choid \-rəˌkȯid\ *adj* [NL *Ulotrichales* + E *-oid*] **:** resembling or related to the order Ulotrichales

ulot·ri·chous \-rəkəs\ *adj* [NL *Ulotrichi* (pl.) division of mankind having crisp or woolly hair (fr. Gk *oulotrich-, oulothrix* having curly or woolly hair, fr. *oulos* curly, woolly + *trich-, thrix* hair) + E *-ous;* akin to Gk *eilein* to roll, *eilyein* to roll, wrap — more at TRICH-, VOLUBLE] **:** exhibiting ulotrichy **:** having woolly or crisp hair

ulot·ri·chy \-kē\ *n* -ES [NL *Ulotrichi* + E *-y*] **:** the condition of having woolly or crisp hair

-u·lous \yələs\ *adj suffix* [L *-ulus,* dim. suffix] **:** being slightly or minutely ⟨*hirsut*ulous⟩ ⟨*viscid*ulous⟩

ul·pan \ˈülˌpän\ *n, pl* **ulpa·nim** \ˌülpäˈnēm\ [NHeb *ūlpān,* fr. Mishnaic Aram (*bēth*) *ūlpānā* (house) of study, fr. Aram *alaph* to teach, train] **:** an Israeli study center for newcomers in which intensive training in Hebrew and cultural subjects is given

¹ul·ster \ˈəlstə(r), -lst-\ *adj, usu cap* [fr. *Ulster,* former province of northern Ireland (now partly in the Republic of Ireland)] **1 :** of or from the former province or the present region of Ulster, Ireland **:** of the kind or style prevalent in Ulster **2 :** NORTHERN IRELAND **3 :** of or from the province of Ulster, Republic of Ireland **:** of the kind or style prevalent in Ulster province

²ulster \ˈ"\ *n* -s **:** a long loose overcoat of Irish origin made of frieze or other heavy overcoating

ul·ster·ette \ˌ⁼təˈret\ *n* -s [²*ulster* + *-ette*] **:** a light ulster

ul·ste·ri·an \ˌəlzˈtirēən, ˌəlˈst-\ *adj, usu cap* [*Ulster,* former province of northern Ireland + E *-ian*] **:** of or relating to a subdivision of the American Devonian — see GEOLOGIC TIME table

ul·ster·ite \ˈəlztəˌrīt, -lst-\ *n* -s *cap* [*Ulster,* former province of northern Ireland + E *-ite*] **:** ULSTERMAN

ulster king of arms *also* **ulster** *usu cap U&K&A* **:** the chief officer of arms for Ireland from 1552 to 1943 — compare IRELAND KING OF ARMS, NORROY AND ULSTER KING OF ARMS

ul·ster·man \ˈ⁼⁼mən\ *n, pl* **ulstermen** *cap* **:** a native or inhabitant of Ulster or of Northern Ireland

ulster office *n, usu cap U&O* **:** the office of arms of which Ulster King of Arms was head **:** OFFICE OF ARMS 2

ulsterwoman \ˈ⁼⁼ˌ⁼⁼\ *n, pl* **ulsterwomen** *cap* **:** a woman born in Ulster or of Ulster descent

ult *abbr* **1** ultimate; ultimately **2** ultimo

ul·te·ri·or \ˌəlˈtirēə(r), -tēr-\ *adj* [L, situated beyond, farther, further, compar. of (assumed) *ulter* situated beyond (whence *ultra* beyond, adv. & prep.), fr. *uls* beyond (prep.) — more at ALL] **1 a :** occurring at a subsequent time **:** FURTHER, FUTURE ⟨~ actions⟩ ⟨without ~ argument⟩ **b :** more distant **:** REMOTER ⟨without . . . any purpose, immediate or ~ —G.B. Shaw⟩ ⟨~ reasons⟩ **c :** situated on the further side **:** THITHER ⟨~ regions⟩ **2 :** going beyond what is avowed, manifest, or proper **:** not apparent **:** HIDDEN, LATENT ⟨eyes . . . with no ~ thought behind —Gilbert Parker⟩ ⟨look too closely for an ~ purpose in all knowledge —Bertrand Russell⟩ ⟨not a line in the book without an ~ motive —A.J.A.Waldock⟩ — **ul·te·ri·or·ly** *adv*

ul·ti·ma \ˈəltəmə\ *n* -s [L, fem. of *ultimus* last] **:** the last syllable of a word ⟨antepenult, penult, and ~⟩ ⟨"Mama," she said, accenting the ~ —Jean Stafford⟩

ul·ti·ma·cy \-məsē, -si\ *n* -ES [*ultimate* + *-cy*] **1 :** the quality or state of being ultimate ⟨denied the ~ of these social values —F.I.Carpenter⟩ **2 :** ULTIMATE, FUNDAMENTAL ⟨not to pry into the *ultimacies* of metaphysics —C.H.Whiteley⟩

ul·ti·ma ra·tio \ˌültəməˈräd·ēˌō; ˌəltəməˈrāshēˌō, -āˌshō\ *n* [NL] **:** the last or final argument **:** the last resort (as force) ⟨impaired by methods in which violence is the *ultima ratio* —*New Republic*⟩ ⟨the strike is the *ultima ratio* of Trade Unionism —Hewlett Johnson⟩

¹ul·ti·mate \ˈəltəmət, *usu* -əd·+V\ *adj* [ML *ultimatus* completed, last, final, fr. LL, past part. of *ultimare* to come to an end, be last, fr. L *ultimus* farthest, furthest, last, final, superl. of (assumed) *ulter* situated beyond — more at ULTERIOR] **1 a :** most remote in space or time **:** FARTHEST, EARLIEST ⟨man's ~ destiny⟩ ⟨~ origins⟩ ⟨faded farther and farther away into ~ distance —Hugh Walpole⟩ **b :** last in a progression **:** FINAL ⟨swallowing the ~ crumb of gingerbread —Elinor Wylie⟩ ⟨this ~ book of my autobiography —Osbert Sitwell⟩ **c :** EVENTUAL ⟨saw no hope of any ~ escape —R.L. Stevenson⟩ ⟨endurance based on a serene faith in ~ rescue —W.J.Ghent⟩ **d :** EXTREME, UTMOST ⟨at the ~ rakish angle, she wore a black . . . beret —Raymond Chandler⟩ ⟨certainty of an ~ act — murder —Frederic Morton⟩ ⟨not averse to immense sacrifice — even to the ~ sacrifice — if it will win the war —*Jour. Amer. Med. Assoc.*⟩ **2 a :** tended toward by all that precedes **:** arrived at as the last result ⟨~ truths⟩ ⟨consideration of the ~ questions of religion —*McCormick Theological Seminary Cat.*⟩ ⟨the fugue was considered the ~ vehicle for profound musical expression —A.E.Wier⟩ **b :** finally reckoned ⟨the ~ damage of that hurricane was not known for weeks —Marjory S. Douglas⟩ **c :** using an economic good in a way that diminishes or destroys its utility ⟨~ buyer⟩ ⟨~ consumer⟩ ⟨~ purchaser⟩ **3 a :** BASIC, FUNDAMENTAL, ORIGINAL, PRIMITIVE ⟨the English alphabet . . . owes its ~ origin to the Phoenician —Norbert Wiener⟩ ⟨~ title to the soil —D.E.Clark⟩ ⟨the ~ control of education —*General Education in a Free Society*⟩ ⟨the ~ nature of things —A.N. Whitehead⟩ **b :** incapable of further analysis, division, or separation ⟨the ~ ingredients of matter —James Jeans⟩ **c :** ELEMENTAL 2a(2) ⟨~ analysis⟩ ⟨~ composition⟩ **4 :** MAXIMUM ⟨~ speeds which may be attained by airplanes in the future —H.G.Armstrong⟩ — used esp. of strain, strength, or stress at the instant of breaking or rupture ⟨the ~ strength of any concrete structure —*Building, Estimating & Contracting*⟩ **syn** see LAST

²ultimate \ˈ"\ *n* -s **1 :** something that is ultimate **:** something final or fundamental ⟨search for ~s and grand generalizations ends in a universality devoid of all content —E.H.Eby⟩ ⟨an absurdity . . . carried to its ~ —W.H.Camp⟩ **2 :** ACME, PEAK, LAST WORD ⟨an automobile that is the ~ in luxurious transportation⟩

³ul·ti·mate \-ˌmāt, *usu* -ād·+V\ *vb* -ED/-ING/-S *vi* **:** to come to an end or issue **:** EVENTUATE, END ~ *vt* **:** to bring to an end or issue

ultimate analysis *n* **:** the determination of the percentage of constituent elements of a chemical substance

ultimate destination *n* **:** the final destination in the territory of an enemy or under its control making goods contraband under the doctrine of continuous voyage

ultimate fact *n* **:** a basic fact essential to maintain a cause of action or to establish a defense thereto as distinguished from the subsidiary individual facts that are offered in evidence as tending to prove a basic fact

ultimate line *n* **:** RAIE ULTIME

ul·ti·mate·ly *adv* [¹*ultimate* + *-ly*] **:** in the ultimate stage **:** in the end **:** at last **:** FINALLY, BASICALLY, FUNDAMENTALLY ⟨doubted not that I should ~ succeed —Mary W. Shelley⟩ ⟨~ the towns were able to establish themselves as centers of freedom —R.A.Hall b. 1911⟩ ⟨were estranged; but ~ they became friends again —E.E.Hume⟩

ultimate mortality table *n* **:** a mortality table based on experience from which the effect of medical selection has been eliminated by the passage of a stated period (as five years)

ul·ti·mate·ness *n* -ES **:** the state or degree of being ultimate

ultimate reality *n, often cap U&R* **:** something that is the supreme, final, and fundamental power in all reality ⟨*ultimate reality* in Judaism, Christianity, and Islam is God⟩

ultimate tensile strength *n* **:** TENSILE STRENGTH

ul·ti·ma thu·le \ˌəltəmə-\ *n, usu cap U&T* [L, farthest Thule] **:** THULE

ul·ti·ma·tion \ˌəltəˈmāshən\ *n* -s [LL *ultimatus* (past part. of *ultimare* to come to an end) + E *-ion* — more at ULTIMATE] **:** the act or result of ultimating **:** the state of being ultimate

ul·ti·ma·tum \ˌəltəˈmā|d·əm, |təm *also* -mä| *or* -mā|\ *n, pl* **ultimatums** \-mz\ *or* **ultima·ta** \|d·ə, |tə\ [NL, fr. ML, neut. of *ultimatus* final — more at ULTIMATE] **1 :** a final proposition, condition, or demand; *esp* **:** one whose rejection will end negotiations and cause a resort to force or other direct action **2 :** the farthest point or stage to be reached **:** a final objective or end **:** ULTIMATE

ul·ti·mo \ˈəltəˌmō\ *adj* [L *ultimo* (*mense*) in the last month, fr. abl. sing. masc. of *ultimus* last — more at ULTIMATE] **:** of or occurring in the month preceding the present — abbr. *ult.* ⟨your letter received on the 25th *ult.*⟩; compare INSTANT, PROXIMO

ul·ti·mo·branchial \ˌəltəmō+\ *adj* [L *ultimus* last + E *-o-* + *branchia* + *-al*] **:** relating to or derived from the last gill pouch

ultimobranchial body *n* **:** a hollow vesicle of the embryo believed to be derived from the fifth pharyngeal pouch

ul·ti·mo·gen·i·tary \-ˌjenədˌerē\ *adj* [fr. *ultimogeniture,* after E *primogeniture: primogenitary*] **:** of or relating to ultimogeniture

ul·ti·mo·geniture \ˌ⁼⁼⁼+\ *n* -s [L *ultimus* last + E *-o-* + *-geniture* (as in *primogeniture*)] **:** a system of inheritance by which the youngest son or sometimes daughter or collateral heir succeeds to the estate — called also *postremogeniture;* opposed to *primogeniture;* compare BOROUGH-ENGLISH

ul·ti·mus he·res \ˌültəməsˈhāˌrās\ *or* **ultimus hae·res** \-ˈhīˌ-\ *n* [ML] **:** the last heir — in feudal law often applied to the sovereign as taking property when other capable heirs fail

¹ul·to·ni·an \ˌəlˈtōnēən\ *adj, usu cap* [ML *Ultonia* Ulster, former province of northern Ireland + E *-an*] **1 :** of, relating to, or characteristic of Ulster **2 :** of, relating to, or characteristic of the people of Ulster

²ultonian \ˈ"\ *n* -s *cap* **:** ULSTERMAN

¹ul·tra \ˈəltrə\ *adj* [*ultra-*] **:** going beyond others or beyond due limit **:** EXTREME, FANATICAL, UNCOMPROMISING, SUPERLATIVE ⟨~ political individualism taught by liberal political leaders —*Metropolitan Mag.*⟩ ⟨treat yourself to . . . ~ dinners —Michael Frome⟩

²ultra \ˈ"\ *n* -s [*ultra-*] **1 :** ULTRAIST, EXTREMIST, RADICAL **2** *usu cap* [F, short for *ultraroyaliste,* fr. *ultra-* (fr. L) + *royaliste* royalist, fr. *royal* + *-iste* -ist] **:** a member of a political group active in 19th century France following the Bourbon restoration composed largely of returned emigrés and associated principally with a desire to restore the political and social order prevailing before the Revolution of 1789

ultra- *prefix* [L, fr. *ultra* beyond (adv. & prep.), fr. abl. sing. fem. of (assumed) *ulter* situated beyond — more at ULTERIOR] **1 :** beyond in space **:** on the other side **:** TRANS- ⟨*ultra*tropical⟩ ⟨*ultra*median⟩ **2 :** beyond the range or limits of **:** transcending **:** SUPER- ⟨*ultra*microscopic⟩ ⟨*ultra*sonic⟩ **3 :** beyond what is common, ordinary, natural, right, proper, or moderate **:** excessively **:** exceedingly **:** HYPER- ⟨*ultra*complex⟩ ⟨*ultra*critical⟩ ⟨*ultra*formal⟩ ⟨*ultra*modern⟩

ul·tra-atomic \ˌəltrə+\ *adj* [*ultra-* + *atomic*] **:** of, relating to, or constituting particles smaller than atoms

ul·tra·basic \"+\ *adj* [ISV *ultra-* + *basic*] **:** extremely basic **:** very low in silica and rich in ferromagnesian minerals ⟨~ igneous rocks⟩ ⟨peridotite is ~⟩

ul·tra·centrifugal \"+\ *adj* [¹*ultracentrifuge* + *-al*] **:** of, relating to, or obtained by means of an ultracentrifuge — **ul·tra·centrifugally** \"+\ *adv*

ul·tra·centrifugation \"+\ *n* [²*ultracentrifuge* + *-ation*] **:** processing in an ultracentrifuge ⟨purified by repeated ~s —*Jour. of General Microbiology*⟩

¹ul·tra·centrifuge \"+\ *n* [*ultra-* + *centrifuge*] **:** a very high-speed centrifuge that effects the sedimentation of colloidal and other small particles and is useful esp. in determining mean size and size distribution of such particles and molecular weights of proteins and other high polymers

²ultracentrifuge \"\ *vt* **:** to subject to the action of an ultracentrifuge

ul·tra·condenser \"+\ *n* [ISV *ultra-* + *condenser*] **:** the condenser of an ultramicroscope

ul·tra·conservatism \"+\ *n* [*ultra-* + *conservatism*] **:** extreme conservatism ⟨~ is the chief characteristic of their cult —H.H.Shenk⟩

ul·tra·conservative \"+\ *adj* [*ultra-* + *conservative*] **:** extremely conservative ⟨a few ~ newspapers —E.A.Peers⟩ ⟨there exists a large ~ religious group —R.W.Murray⟩

ul·tra·dolichocephalic \"+\ *adj* [*ultra-* + *dolichocephalic*] **:** having a very long or narrow head or both and a cephalic index of 64 or less

ul·tra·dolichocephaly \"+\ *n* [*ultra-* + *dolichocephaly*] **:** the quality or state of being ultradolichocephalic

ul·tra·dolichocranial \"+\ *adj* [*ultra-* + *dolichocranial*] **:** having a very long or narrow skull or both and a cranial index of 60 to 65

ul·tra·dolichocrany \"+\ *n* [*ultra-* + *dolichocrany*] **:** the quality or state of being ultradolichocranial

ul·tra·fashionable \"+\ *adj* [*ultra-* + *fashionable*] **:** extremely fashionable

Ul·tra·fax \ˈəltrəˌfaks\ *trademark* — used for a very high-speed facsimile transmission that uses television techniques for scanning, transmission, and reproduction

¹ul·tra·filter \ˌəltrə+\ *n* [ISV *ultra-* + *filter*] **:** a dense filter used for the filtration of a colloidal solution that holds back the dispersed particles but not the liquid

²ultrafilter \"\ *vt* **:** to cause to pass through an ultrafilter

ul·tra·filtrate \"+\ *n* [²*ultrafilter* + *-ate*] **:** the liquid that has passed through an ultrafilter

ul·tra·filtration \"+\ *n* [ISV *ultra-* + *filtration*] **:** the process of passing through an ultrafilter

ul·tra·gaseous \"+\ *adj* [*ultra-* + *gaseous*] **:** having the properties exhibited by gases under pressures of one millionth of an atmosphere or less

ul·tra·high frequency \"+-\ *n* [*ultra-* + *high*] **:** a radio frequency in the second from the highest range of the radio spectrum — see RADIO FREQUENCY table

ultrahigh-frequency *adj* [*ultrahigh frequency*] **:** of or relating to ultrahigh frequency or a radio wave having such a frequency

ul·tra·ism \ˈəltrəˌizəm\ *n* -s [¹*ultra* + *-ism*] **1 :** the principles of those who advocate extreme measures (as radicalism) **2 :** an instance or example of radicalism ⟨he pleaded for freedom of speech and of the press, denounced sectionalism and ~ on either side —W.E.Smith⟩

¹ul·tra·ist \-əəst\ *n* -s [¹*ultra* + *-ist*] **:** an adherent of ultraism **:** EXTREMIST, RADICAL ⟨the organ of the Argentine ~s . . . roundly rejected Madrid's claim to chieftainship —*Times Lit. Supp.*⟩

²ultraist \"\ *or* **ul·tra·is·tic** \ˌ⁼⁼ˈistik\ *adj* **:** of, relating to, or characteristic of ultraism

ul·tra·mafic \ˌəltrə+\ *adj* [*ultra-* + *mafic*] **:** ULTRABASIC

¹ul·tra·marine \"+\ *or* **ultramarine blue** *n* [ML *ultramarinus* coming from beyond the sea; fr. the fact that lapis lazuli came originally from Asia] **1 a :** a costly pure blue pigment formerly prepared by powdering lapis lazuli **b :** a brilliant blue pigment of similar composition but having commonly a reddish or greenish cast that is usu. prepared by powdering the product from calcining essentially a mixture of kaolin, soda ash, sulfur, and charcoal or other reducing agent and that is used chiefly in paints, printing inks, paper, and laundry bluing — called also *French blue, new blue* **c :** any of various pigments that are usu. produced by modifications of the

above process or by replacing the sodium or the sulfur in ordinary ultramarine by other elements ⟨silver ~⟩ **2 :** a vivid blue that is redder, lighter, and stronger than Ch'ing and redder than Cleopatra — called also *Armenian blue*

[2]ultramarine \"\ *adj* [ML *ultramarinus*, fr. L *ultra-* + *mare* sea + *-inus* -ine — more at MARINE] **:** situated beyond the sea ⟨~ provinces⟩ **:** coming from beyond the sea

ultramarine ash *n* [¹*ultramarine*] **1 :** a delicate bluish gray pigment obtained as a residuum from lapis lazuli after the extraction of ultramarine and used by the old masters as a middle or neutral tint for flesh, skies, and draperies **2 :** a variable color averaging from blue ultramarine ash to gray ultramarine ash

ultramarine green *n* **1 :** an ultramarine pigment of strong green cast **2 :** a blackish green that is bluer and paler than cannon

ultramarine yellow *n* **1 :** YELLOW ULTRAMARINE **2 :** LIGHT CHROME YELLOW

ul·tra·metamorphic \ˌəltrə+\ *adj* [*ultrametamorphism* + *-ic*] **:** of or relating to ultrametamorphism

ul·tra·metamorphism \"+\ *n* [*ultra-* + *metamorphism*] **:** metamorphism at temperatures and pressures just below the fusion temperature of rock

ul·tra·micro \"+\ *adj* [ultramicro-] **:** smaller in size than micro **:** being on a scale smaller than micro

ultramicro- *comb form* [*ultra-* + *micr-*] **:** of, involving, or being for quantities of material smaller than micro quantities **:** on a scale smaller than micro

ul·tra·microanalysis \"+\ *n* [*ultramicro-* + *analysis*] **:** chemical analysis (as of quantities of the order of a few micrograms) on a scale smaller than microanalysis

ul·tra·microbe \"+\ *n* [ISV *ultra-* + *microbe*] **:** ULTRAVIRUS

ul·tra·microchemical \"+\ *adj* [fr. *ultramicrochemistry*, after E *chemistry: chemical*] **:** of, relating to, or using the methods of ultramicrochemistry

ul·tra·microchemistry \"+\ *n* [*ultramicro-* + *chemistry*] **:** chemistry dealing with very minute quantities of substances (as a microgram or less) — compare MICROCHEMISTRY

ul·tra·micrometer \"+\ *n* [*ultra-* + *micrometer*] **:** an extremely sensitive micrometer (as one capable of measuring to one millionth of an inch or less) frequently utilizing a variable capacitance that controls the frequency of an oscillator

ul·tra·micron \"+\ *n* [*ultra-* + *micron*] **:** SUBMICRON

ul·tra·microorganism \"+\ *n* [*ultra-* + *microorganism*] **:** ULTRAVIRUS

ul·tra·microscope \"+\ *n* [back-formation fr. *ultramicroscopic*] **:** an apparatus for making ultramicroscopic particles visible consisting of a compound microscope with a condenser that projects intense light from one side so that what is actually seen against an otherwise dark field is the light scattered by the particles rather than the particles themselves — called also *dark-field microscope* — **ul·tra·microscopy** \"+\ *n*

ul·tra·microscopic \"+\ *adj* [ISV *ultra-* + *microscopic*] **1 :** too small to be seen with an ordinary microscope **:** SUBMICROSCOPIC **2** [*ultramicroscope* + *-ic*] **:** of or relating to an ultramicroscope or to ultramicroscopy

[1]ul·tra·modern \"+\ *adj* [*ultra-* + *modern*] **:** being beyond the norm of the modern **:** extreme in typically modern ideas or tendencies ⟨~ ideas⟩ ⟨~ equipment⟩ ⟨~ artists⟩

[2]ul·tra·modern \"+\ *n* **:** one that is ultramodern

ul·tra·modernist \"+\ *n* **:** ULTRAMODERN

[1]ul·tra·montane \"+\ *n* -s [in sense 1, fr. ML *ultramontanus*, fr. *ultramontanus* situated beyond the mountains; in other senses fr. ²*ultramontane*] **1** *usu cap* **:** a Roman Catholic ecclesiastic in a country north of the Alps **2 :** one who lives beyond the mountains: as **a** *archaic* **:** one who lives north of the Alps — compare TRAMONTANE **b :** one who lives south of the Alps **3** *sometimes cap* **:** a supporter of ultramontanism

[2]ultramontane \"\ *adj* [ML *ultramontanus*, fr. L *ultra-* + *mont-, mons* mountain + *-anus* -an — more at MOUNT] **1 :** situated beyond the mountains **:** of or relating to countries or peoples beyond the mountains: as **a :** of or relating to countries or peoples to the north of the Alps **b :** of or relating to Italy **2** *sometimes cap* [fr. the fact that the papal seat was located the other side of the Alps from the French] **:** of, relating to, or supporting ultramontanism ⟨~ party⟩ **3 :** claiming an absolute supremacy or a privileged superiority

ul·tra·montanism \"+\ *n* -s *sometimes cap* [F *ultramontanisme*, fr. *ultramontain* ultramontane (fr. ML *ultramontanus*) + *-isme* -ism] **:** the policy of advocating the greatest possible enhancement of papal power and authority — compare GALLICANISM

ul·tra·montanist \"+\ *n* [²*ultramontane* + *-ist*] **:** a supporter of ultramontanism

ul·tra·mundane \"+\ *adj* [L *ultramundanus*, fr. *ultra* beyond + *mundus* world + *-anus* -an — more at ULTERIOR] **:** situated beyond the world or beyond the limits of the solar system

ul·tra·nationalism \"+\ *n* [*ultra-* + *nationalism*] **:** great or excessive devotion to or advocacy of national interests and rights esp. as opposed to international considerations

[1]ul·tra·nationalist \"+\ *or* **ul·tra·nationalistic** \"+\ *adj* [*ultra-* + *nationalist* or *nationalistic*] **:** of, relating to, or characterized by ultranationalism

[2]ul·tra·nationalist \"+\ *n* **:** a supporter of ultranationalism

ul·tra·profound \"+\ *adj* [*ultra-* + *profound*] **:** extremely profound

ul·tra·rapid picture \"+-\ *n* [*ultra-* + *rapid*] **:** a slow-motion picture

ul·tra·red \"+\ *adj* [*ultra-* + *red*] **:** INFRARED

ul·tra·short \"+\ *adj* [*ultra-* + *short*] **:** having a wavelength below 10 meters and frequencies above 30 megacycles per second ⟨~ radiations⟩

[1]ul·tra·sonic \"+\ *adj* [*ultra-* + *sonic*] **:** SUPERSONIC — **ul·tra·sonically** \"+\ *adv*

[2]ultrasonic \"\ *n* **:** an ultrasonic wave or frequency

ul·tra·son·ics \ˌəltrəˈsäniks, -nēks\ *n pl but usu sing in constr* [fr. ¹*ultrasonic*, after such pairs as E *economic: economics*] **:** the science of ultrasonic phenomena **:** SUPERSONICS

ul·tra·sound \ˈəltrə+\ *n* [*ultra-* + *sound*] **:** a wave phenomenon of the same physical nature as sound but with frequencies above the range of human hearing — called also *supersound*

ul·tra·structure \"+\ *n* [*ultra-* + *structure*] **:** the invisible ultimate physicochemical organization of protoplasm

[1]ul·tra·violet \"+\ *adj* [*ultra-* + *violet*] **1** *of radiation* **:** beyond the visible spectrum at its violet end **:** having a wavelength shorter than those of visible light and longer than those of X rays — compare INFRARED **2 :** relating to, producing, or employing ultraviolet radiation ⟨~ lamp⟩ ⟨~ filter⟩

[2]ultraviolet \"\ *n* **:** ultraviolet radiation

ultraviolet light *n* **:** ultraviolet radiation

ultraviolet microscope *n* **:** FLUORESCENCE MICROSCOPE

ultraviolet spectrum *n* **:** a spectrum of ultraviolet radiation characterized by short wavelengths and high quantum energies as compared to visible light

ul·tra vi·res \ˌəltrəˈvī(ˌ)rēz\ *adv (or adj)* [NL] **:** beyond the scope or in excess of legal power or authority (as vested in a corporation, an official, or a legislative body) ⟨an *ultra vires* contract⟩ ⟨the official acted *ultra vires*⟩

ul·tra·virus \ˌəltrə+\ *n* [ISV *ultra-* + *virus*; prob. formed in F] **:** an ultramicroscopic or filterable virus

ul·tro·ne·ous \ˌəlˈtrōnēəs\ *adj* [L *ultroneus* voluntary, spontaneous, fr. *ultro* beyond, beyond expectation, spontaneously, fr. abl. sing. masc. or neut. of (assumed) *ulter* situated beyond — more at ULTERIOR] *Scots law* **:** that voluntarily offers testimony without being cited ⟨an ~ witness⟩

[1]ulu \ˈüˌlü\ *also* **ulo** \-ˌlō\ *n* -s [Inupik] **:** an Eskimo woman's knife resembling a food chopper with a crescent-shaped blade

[2]ulu \ˈüˌlü\ *n* -s [prob. fr. Bengali, ulla grass] **:** an Indian grass (*Imperata arundinacea*) used for forage and pasture

ulua \üˈlüwə\ *n* -s [Hawaiian] **:** any of several large cavallas (genus *Caranx*) of Hawaiian waters highly prized as food and sport fishes

ulu-juz \ˈüləˈjüz\ *n, pl* **ulu-juz** *or* **ulu-juzes** *usu cap U* **1 :** one of the major divisions of the Kazak **2 :** a member of the Ulu-juz people

ulu·lant \ˈəlyələnt, ˈyül-\ *adj* [L *ululant-, ululans*, pres. part. of *ululare*] **:** HOWLING, WAILING ⟨a dark wasteland . . . ~ with bitter wind —Rudi Blesh⟩ ⟨yell . . . had a keening, ~ quality —C.B.Goolrick⟩

ulu·late \-əˌlāt, *usu* -ād.+V\ *vi* -ED/-ING/-S [L *ululatus*, past part. of *ululare* to howl, wail, of imit. origin] **:** to utter a loud mournful usu. protracted and rhythmical sound **:** cry out **:** HOWL, WAIL ⟨the *ululating* air raid danger signal —J.D. Mabbott⟩ ⟨*ululating* wolves⟩ ⟨crowds on the stands *ululated* with joy —Robert Lynd⟩ **syn** see ROAR

ulu·la·tion \ˌ==ˈlāshən\ *n* -s [L *ululation-, ululatio*, fr. *ululatus* + *-ion-, -io* -ion] **1 :** a loud mournful usu. protracted and rhythmical sound **:** HOWL **2 :** the action of ululating **:** HOWLING ⟨the ~ of the ambulance —Christopher Morley⟩ ⟨the ~ of our despair —Sidney Alexander⟩

-u·lum \yələm\ *n suffix, pl* **-ulums** \-ləmz\ *or* **-u·la** \-lə\ [L — more at -ULE] **:** small one ⟨*septulum*⟩ ⟨*frenulum*⟩

-u·lus \yələs\ *n suffix, pl* **-u·lus·es** \-ləsəz\ *or* **-u·li** \-ˌlī\ [L — more at -ULE] **:** a small one ⟨phoeniculus⟩

[1]ul·va \ˈəlvə\ *n, cap* [NL, fr. L, sedge] **:** a genus of green seaweeds (the type of the family Ulvaceae) having a thin flat edible thallus that resembles a lettuce leaf and is two cells thick — see SEA LETTUCE

[2]ul·va \ˈülvə, ˈül(ˌ)və\ *or* **ul·ua** \ˈülwə\ *n, pl* **ulva** *or* **ulvas** *or* **ulua** *or* **uluas** *usu cap* **1 a :** a people of Nicaragua and Honduras **b :** a member of such people **2 :** a language of the Ulva people

ul·va·ce·ae \ˌəlˈvāsēˌē\ *n pl, cap* [NL, fr. ¹*Ulva*, type genus + *-aceae*] **:** a widely distributed family of thin green algae having either a flat or a hollow tubular thallus, reproducing by the conjugation of planogametes or of zoospores, and being classed among the Ulotrichales or now more commonly placed in the order Ulvales — **ul·va·ceous** \ˌ=ˈvāshəs\ *adj*

ul·va·les \ˌ=ˈvā(ˌ)lēz\ *n pl, cap* [NL, fr. ¹*Ulva* + *-ales*] **:** an order of green algae (class Chlorophyceae) that is coextensive with the family Ulvaceae

ul·ya·novsk \ülˈyänəfsk, -əvsk\ *adj, usu cap* [fr. *Ulyanovsk*, city of eastern Soviet Russia] **:** of or from the city of Ulyanovsk, U.S.S.R. **:** of the kind or style prevalent in Ulyanovsk

ulys·se·an \yüˈlisēən\ *adj, usu cap* [*Ulysses*, hero of Homer's *Odyssey* + E *-an*] **:** of, relating to, or resembling Ulysses

um *a prolonged* m *sound*\ *interj* [imit.] — used to express hesitation or doubt or to indicate inarticulateness

um *abbr* unmarried

'um *like* 'EM\ *pron* [alter. of *'em*] *chiefly dial* **:** THEM

uma \ˈ(y)ümə\ *n* [NL, perh. fr. Aymara, head, helmet] **1** *cap* **:** a genus of American lizards (family Iguanidae) comprising the fringefoots **2** -s **:** FRINGEFOOT

uman·gite \(y)üˈmaŋˌgīt\ *n* -s [G *umangit*, fr. Sierra de *Umango*, province in northwestern Argentina + G *-it* -ite] **:** a mineral Cu_3Se_2 consisting of a copper selenide and occurring in dark red masses (hardness 3, sp. gr. 5.62)

uma·til·la \ˌyüməˈtilə\ *n, pl* **umatilla** *or* **umatillas** *usu cap* **1 :** a Shahaptian people of northeastern Oregon **2 :** a member of the Umatilla people

umay·yad \üˈmī(y)əd, əˈm-\ *or* **omay·yad** \ōˈmī(y)əd, əˈm-\ *also* **om·mi·ad** \ōˈmīəd, əˈm-\ *n* -s *usu cap* [*Umayyah* (*Ommiah*), ancestor of Muawiyah I †A.D.680 founder of the dynasty + E *-ad*] **1 :** a member of a dynasty of caliphs ruling the Muslim empire from A.D. 661 to 750 **2 :** a member of a dynasty of caliphs established in Spain from A.D. 756 to 1031

umb *abbr* umbilicus

um·bel \ˈəmbəl\ *n* -s [L *umbella* parasol, umbrella — more at UMBRELLA] **1 :** a racemose inflorescence that is characteristic esp. of the family Umbelliferae and has the flower stalks in a cluster arising from a common point at the apex of the main stalk and reaching approximately the same height and sometimes branching again to form similar secondary clusters — see INFLORESCENCE illustration **2 :** an arrangement of parts resembling an umbel

um·beled *or* **um·belled** \-ld\ *adj* **:** bearing or producing umbels **:** UMBELLATE

umbell- *or* **umbelli-** *comb form* [NL, fr. L *umbella* parasol, umbrella] **:** umbel **:** umbellate ⟨*umbell*oid⟩ ⟨*umbelli*form⟩

um·bel·la \ˌəmˈbelə\ *n, pl* **umbel·lae** \-eˌlē, -ˌlī\ *or* **umbellas** [NL, fr. L, parasol, umbrella] **:** UMBEL

um·bel·la·les \ˌəmbəˈlā(ˌ)lēz\ *n pl, cap* [NL, fr. *umbell-* + *-ales*] **:** a large order of chiefly herbaceous dicotyledonous plants that have umbels or corymbs of small uniovulate flowers with epigynous stamens and 1 to 5 carpels followed by fruits which are drupes or cremocarps and that include several economically important plants (as the carrot and parsnip) — see CORNACEAE, UMBELLIFERAE

um·bel·lar \ˈəmbələ(r), ˌəmˈbel-\ *adj* [*umbell-* + *-ar*] **:** of or relating to an umbel **:** UMBELLATE

um·bel·late \ˈəmbəˌlāt, ˌəmˈbelət\ *also* **um·bel·lat·ed** \ˈəmbəˌlād·əd\ *adj* [*umbellate* fr. NL *umbellatus*, fr. *umbell-* + L *-atus* -ate; *umbellated* fr. NL *umbellatus* + E *-ed*] **1 :** bearing, consisting of, or arranged in umbels **2 :** resembling an umbel in form — **um·bel·late·ly** *adv*

um·bel·let \ˈəmbələt\ *n* -s [*umbell-* + *-et*] **:** UMBELLULE

umbellic acid *n* [*umbellic* fr. *umbell-* (in *umbelliferone*) + *-ic*] **:** an acid $C_6H_3(OH)_2CH{=}CHCO_2H$ formed as a yellow powder by hydrolysis of umbelliferone; 2,4-dihydroxy-cinnamic acid

um·bel·li·fer \ˌəmˈbeləfə(r)\ *n* -s [NL *Umbelliferae*] **:** a plant of the family Umbelliferae

um·bel·lif·er·ae \ˌəmbəˈlifəˌrē\ *n pl, cap* [NL, fr. fem. pl. of *umbellifer* umbelliferous] **:** a large and economically important family of often fragrant or aromatic plants (order Umbellales) with alternate mostly compound leaves, small flowers in simple or compound involucrate umbels, and dry 2-carpellary ribbed fruits that split at maturity and are borne from the apex of a common axis — compare ANISE, CARAWAY, CARROT, CELERY, DILL, PARSLEY

um·bel·lif·er·one \-əˌrōn\ *n* -s [ISV *umbellifer* + *-one*, orig. formed as G *umbelliferon*] **:** a crystalline phenolic lactone $C_9H_6O_3$ found in many plants, obtained by the distillation of resins (as galbanum or asafetida) from various umbellifers, and also made synthetically; 7-hydroxy-coumarin — compare HERNIARIN

um·bel·lif·er·ous \ˌ==ˈlif(ə)rəs\ *adj* [NL *umbellifer* umbelliferous (fr. *umbella* umbel — fr. L, parasol, umbrella — + L *-ifer* -iferous) + E *-ous* — more at UMBRELLA] **1 :** producing umbels **2** [NL *Umbelliferae* + E *-ous*] **:** of or relating to the Umbelliferae

um·bel·li·florae \ˌəmˈbelē+\ [NL, fr. *umbell-* + *florae*] *syn of* UMBELLALES

um·bel·lu·la \ˌəmˈbelyələ\ *n, cap* [NL, dim. of *umbella* umbel] **:** a genus (the type of the family Umbellulidae) of deep-sea alcyonarians consisting of a cluster of large flowerlike polyps at the summit of a long slender stem that stands upright in the mud and is supported by a bulbous base

um·bel·lu·late \-əˌlāt\ *adj* [NL *umbellula* umbellule + E *-ate*] **:** arranged in umbellules

um·bel·lule \ˈəmbəˌlül, -əlˌyül, ˌəmˈbel(ˌ)yül\ *n* -s [NL *umbellula*, dim. of *umbella*] **:** a secondary umbel in a compound umbel

um·bel·lu·lif·er·ous \ˌəmˌbelyəˈlif(ə)rəs\ *adj* [*umbellule* + *-iferous*] **:** bearing umbellules

um·bel·lu·lone \ˌəmˈbelyəˌlōn\ *n* -s [ISV *umbellul-* (fr. NL *Umbellularia*, genus of dicotyledonous trees, fr. *umbellula* — dim. of *umbella* umbel — + *-aria*) + *-one*] **:** an unsaturated oily compound $C_{10}H_{14}O$ that is derived from the leaves of California laurel and is a ketonic derivative of thujene

[1]um·ber \ˈəmbə(r)\ *n* -s [ME *umbre*, fr. MF, fr. L *umbra* shade, shadow, grayling] **1 :** a grayling (*Thymallus thymallus*) **2** *also* **umber bird :** HAMMERKOP

[2]umber \"\ *n* -s [prob. fr. obs. E, shade, shadow, color, fr. ME *umber, umbre* shade, shadow, fr. MF *umbre*, fr. L *umbra* — more at UMBRAGE] **1 :** a brown earth that is darker in color than ocher and sienna because of its content of manganese oxides as well as iron oxides, that is highly valued by artists as a permanent pigment, and that is used either in the greenish brown raw state or dark brown burnt state — see BURNT UMBER **2 a :** RAW UMBER 2 **b :** BURNT UMBER 2

[3]umber \"\ *adj* **:** of, relating to, or having the characteristics of umber; *specif* **:** of the color of raw umber or burnt umber

[4]umber \"\ *vt* **umbered; umbered; umbering** \-b(ə)riŋ\ **umbers :** to stain umber **:** DARKEN ⟨each battle sees the other's *~ed* face —Shak.⟩

[5]umber \"\ *vt* [L *umbrare*, fr. *umbra* shade, shadow] *chiefly dial* **:** ²SHADE 1

umbilic *n* -s [L *umbilicus* navel, middle, center] *obs* **:** a middle point **:** CENTER

um·bil·i·cal \ˌəmˈbiləkəl, -ˈbilēk- *sometimes* ˌəmbəˈlīk-\ *adj* [NL *umbilicalis*, fr. L *umbilicus* navel, center + *-alis* -al — more at NAVEL] **1 a :** of, relating to, or used at the navel ⟨~ infection⟩ ⟨~ discharge⟩ ⟨~ surgery⟩ ⟨~ tape⟩ **b :** of or relating to the central region of the abdomen — see ABDOMINAL REGION illustration **2** *archaic* **:** relating to or occupying the center **:** CENTRAL ⟨supported, as to its arched roof, by one ~ pillar —Daniel Defoe⟩ **3 :** attached by or as if by an umbilical cord **:** intimately related ⟨the connection between the hard-core . . . supporters and the know-nothings . . . seems at times almost ~ —R.H.Rovere⟩

umbilical artery *n* **:** either of a pair of arteries that arise from the hypogastric arteries of the mammalian fetus and pass through the umbilical cord to the placenta to which they carry the impure blood from the fetus

umbilical cord *n* **1 a :** a cord arising from the navel that connects the fetus with the placenta and contains the two umbilical arteries and the umbilical vein **b :** YOLK STALK **2 :** a cable conveying power to a rocket or spacecraft before takeoff; *also* **:** a tethering or supply line (as for an astronaut outside a spacecraft or an aquanaut underwater)

umbilical fissure *n* **:** the anterior part of the longitudinal fissure on the undersurface of the liver that lodges the umbilical vein in the fetus

umbilical hernia *n* **:** a hernia of abdominal viscera at the umbilicus

um·bil·i·cal·ly \-k(ə)lē, -li\ *adv* **:** by means of or as if by means of an umbilical cord **:** INTIMATELY ⟨embryos nourished ~⟩ ⟨~ tied to . . . complex, tentative liberalism —H.J.Bresler⟩

umbilical vein *n* **:** a vein that passes through the umbilical cord to the fetus and returns the purified and nutrient blood from the placenta to the fetus

umbilical vesicle *n* **:** the yolk sac of a mammalian embryo usu. having the form of a fluid-filled pouch, corresponding to the yolk sac of an oviparous vertebrate, and having a transitory connection with the alimentary canal by way of the vitelline duct

um·bil·i·car·ia \ˌəmˌbiləˈka(a)rēə\ *n, cap* [NL, fr. LL *umbilicaris* umbilical (fr. L *umbilicus* navel + *-aris* -ar) + NL *-ia*] **:** a small genus related to *Lecanora* and composed of foliose umbilicate lichens that are used esp. in folk medicine as a purgative — see ROCK TRIPE

um·bil·i·cate \ˌəmˈbiləkət, -ləˌkāt, *usu* -d.+V\ *or* **um·bil·i·cat·ed** \-ləˌkād·əd\ *adj* [*umbilicate* fr. L *umbilicatus*, fr. *umbilicus* navel + *-atus* -ate; *umbilicated* fr. L *umbilicatus* + E *-ed*] **1 :** resembling a navel; *specif* **:** depressed like a navel **2** *of a mollusk shell* **:** PERFORATE

um·bil·i·ca·tion \ˌəmˌbiləˈkāshən\ *n* -s [L *umbilicus* + E *-ation*] **1 :** a depression resembling a navel ⟨an ~ in the center of a nodule⟩ **2 :** the condition of having umbilications ⟨vesicles . . . with a greater tendency to ~ —Joseph Stokes⟩

um·bil·i·cus \ˌəmˈbiləkəs, -ˈbilēk- *also* ˌəmbəˈlīkəs\ *n, pl* **umbili·ci** \ˌ=ˈ==ˌkī, -ˌsī, -ˌkē; ˌ==ˈ=ˌkī, -ˌsī\ *or* **umbilicuses** [L — more at NAVEL] **1 a :** a small depression in the middle of the abdomen where the umbilical cord is attached in the embryo **b :** the place where the extraembryonic structures are continuous with those of the body proper of the embryo **2 :** a cavity in the center of the base of a spiral shell that is surrounded by the whorls **3 a :** HILUM **b :** a rootlike attachment of the thallus in a lichen **4 :** a central point **:** CORE, HEART ⟨the key to control, the ~ of this . . . sea —J.P.O'Donnell⟩

um·bil·root \ˈəmbəl,=\ *n* [prob. fr. ME *umble* humble, low-growing + *root* — more at HUMBLE] **:** SHOWY LADY'S-SLIPPER

um·ble pie \ˈəmbəl-\ *n* [*umbles*] *archaic* **:** HUMBLE PIE 1

um·bles \ˈəmbəlz\ *n pl* [ME, alter. (prob. influenced by *umble* humble) of *noumbles, nombles* numbles — more at NUMBLES] **:** the entrails of an animal (as a deer, hog, or sheep) used as food **:** NUMBLES, HUMBLES ⟨sat beside the hearth with the menials and ate ~ —Robert Graves⟩

um·bo \ˈəm(ˌ)bō\ *n, pl* **umbo·nes** \ˌəmˈbō(ˌ)nēz\ *or* **umbos** [L — more at NAVEL] **1 :** the boss of a shield sometimes having a sharp spike **2 :** a rounded elevation often accompanied by a corresponding depression on the opposite surface: as **a :** an elevation in the tympanic membrane of the ear **b :** an elevation in a cone scale of a pine tree **3 :** one of the lateral prominences just above the hinge of a bivalve shell **:** BEAK 1d(1)

um·bo·lateral \ˌəmbō+\ *adj* [*umbo* + *lateral*] **:** of, relating to, or located at the sides of the umbo of a bivalve shell

um·bo·nal \ˈəmbənᵊl, ˌəmˈbōn-\ *adj* [L *umbon-, umbo* + E *-al*] **:** of, relating to, or having the characteristics of an umbo ⟨long ~ projections frequently contain hollow spaces between . . . calcareous layers —K.H.Barnard⟩

um·bo·nate \-ˌnət, -ˌnāt\ *or* **um·bo·nat·ed** \ˌ==ˈnād·əd\ *adj* [*umbonate* fr. L *umbon-, umbo* + E *-ate*, *umbonated* fr. L *umbon-, umbo* + E *-ate* + *-ed*] **:** having or forming an umbo

um·bone \ˈəmˌbōn\ *n* -s [L *umbon-, umbo* boss of a shield, projection, knob] **1** *obs* **:** PISTIL, STYLE **2 :** UMBO 3

um·bon·ic \ˌəmˈbänik\ *also* **um·bo·ni·al** \-bōnēəl\ *adj* [L *umbon-, umbo* + E *-ic* or *-ial*] **:** UMBONAL

um·bon·u·late \ˌəmˈbänyələt, -ˌlāt\ *adj* [dim. of *umbonate*] **:** slightly umbonate

um·bra \ˈəmbrə\ *n, pl* **umbras** \-brəz\ *or* **um·brae** \-ˌbrē, -ˌrī\ *except sense 5* [L] **1 a :** GHOST, PHANTOM ⟨a spectral ~ pointing heavenward —Walter Besant & James Rice⟩ **b :** one that tags along with another **:** SHADOW 10a ⟨the dependable ~ of the guest of honor⟩ **2 :** a shaded area **:** DARKNESS ⟨sealed off in the ~ beyond the flame tips —Robert Hazel⟩ **3 a :** a shadow excluding all light from a given source; *specif* **:** the part of the shadow of a celestial body having all the light from the primary source geometrically excluded and having a conical shape in bodies of the solar system — compare PENUMBRA 1 **b** (1) **:** PENUMBRA 2 (2) **:** the central dark part of a sunspot **4 :** any of several food fishes of the genus *Umbrina; esp* **:** a Mediterranean food fish (*U. cirrhosa*) that is much esteemed as a market fish **5** *cap* [NL, fr. L, shade, shadow, grayling, umbra] **:** a genus (the type of the family Umbridae) of small bottom-dwelling freshwater fishes containing the mudminnows of northern No. America and southern Europe

um·brac·u·la \ˌəmˈbrakyələ\ *n, cap* [NL, fr. L *umbraculum* parasol, umbrella, fr. *umbrare* to shade] **:** a genus (the type of the family Umbraculidae) of gastropod mollusks comprising the typical umbrella shells

um·bra·cu·li·dae \ˌəmbrəˈkyüləˌdē\ *n pl, cap* [NL, fr. *Umbracula*, type genus + *-idae*] **:** a family of gastropod mollusks (suborder Tectibranchia) that includes the umbrella shells

[1]um·brage \ˈəmbrij, -rēj\ *n* -s [ME, fr. MF, fr. L *umbraticum*, neut. of *umbraticus* of the shade, fr. *umbratus* (past part. of *umbrare* to shade, fr. *umbra* shade, shadow) + *-icus* -ic; akin to Lith *unksna* shadow] **1 a :** an area of comparative darkness **:** SHADE ⟨lying . . . at the foot of some tree of friendly ~ —Charlotte Brontë⟩ **b :** an overshadowing influence or power **:** SHADOW ⟨compete in the ~ of big city printing wages and other costs —J.R.Malone⟩ **2 :** the thick shady branches of a tree or bush **:** FOLIAGE ⟨the thrush sings in that ~ —L.P. Smith⟩ ⟨chimney pots veiled under blossomy ~ —Thomas Carlyle⟩ **3** *archaic* **:** something providing protection **:** SHELTER, REFUGE **4 a :** an indistinct indication **:** vague suggestion **:** SUSPICION, HINT ⟨the least ~ of a reflection upon this accident —Roger North⟩ **b :** a reason for doubt **:** SUSPICION ⟨the man toward whom our . . . State Department has never felt ~, let alone taken exception —H.L.Ickes⟩ **5 :** DISPLEASURE, RESENTMENT, ANNOYANCE ⟨persons who feel most ~ from the overshadowing aristocracy —Sir Walter Scott⟩ — usu. used in the phrases *give umbrage* or *take umbrage* ⟨would give ~ to them by not sending an invitation⟩ ⟨never take ~ unless you can lick the guy —Jackie Gleason⟩ **6** *obs* **:** an alleged purpose or motive **:** PRETEXT, PRETENSE ⟨veiling the murder with the ~ of devotion and justice —Edmund Hickeringill⟩ **7** *obs* **:** the state of being in disfavor **:** DISESTEEM **syn** see OFFENSE

[2]umbrage \"\ *vt* -ED/-ING/-S **1 :** to cast into shadow **:** SHADE **2 :** to cause to become insulted or angry ⟨*umbraged* . . . by finding no crumbs —Sylvia T. Warner⟩

um·bra·geous \ˌəmˈbrājəs\ *adj* **1 a :** providing protection from heat and light **:** SHADY ⟨~ willow trees⟩ ⟨his winged cloak and ~ fedora —*Times Lit. Supp.*⟩ **b :** protected by shade **:** filled with shade or shadows **:** SHADOWY ⟨making a glowworm halo in the ~ alleys —R.L.Stevenson⟩ ⟨cool ~ woodlands⟩ **2 :** inclined to take offense easily **:** BELLIGERENT, RESENTFUL ⟨have not been as ~ . . . in demanding their terri-

tory back —John Gunther⟩ ⟨~ students⟩ — **um·bra·geous·ly** *adv* — **um·bra·geous·ness** *n* -ES

um·bral \'əmbrəl\ *adj* [*umbra* + *-al*] **:** of or relating to an umbra **:** SHADED, DARKENED ⟨the moon's ~ cone⟩ ⟨whispering somewhere in the ~ reaches of the room —*Omnibook*⟩

umbral symbol *n* **:** a symbol indicating substitution in turn of each of *n* given values followed by addition of the results obtained ⟨the *umbral symbol a* in the expression $x^a y_a$ which stands for $x^1y_1+x^2y_2+\ldots+x^ny_n$⟩

um·brat·ed \ˌəmˈbrād·əd\ *adj* [L *umbratus* (past part. of *umbrare* to shade) + E *-ed*] **:** drawn indistinctly or in outline on a heraldic field ⟨many an ~ charge is . . . displayed upon a parti-colored field —M.R.Holmes⟩

um·brat·ic \ˌəmˈbrad·ik\ *or* **um·brat·i·cal** \-d·əkəl\ *adj* [*umbratic* fr. L *umbraticus* of the shade, secluded, fr. *umbratus* (past part. of *umbrare*) + *-icus* -ic; *umbratical* fr. L *umbraticus* + E *-al*] **1** *archaic* **:** SECLUDED, RETIRING **2** *obs* **:** SHADOWY, INDISTINCT

um·bra·tile \'əmbrəˌtīl\ *adj* [L *umbratilis*, fr. *umbratus* (past part. of *umbrare*) + *-ilis* -ile] **1 :** carried on in seclusion **:** RECONDITE **2** *archaic* **:** of an insubstantial nature **:** SHADOWY

umbra tree *n* [*umbra* modif. (influenced by L *umbra* shade) of Tupi *umbu*] **:** a So. American tree (*Phytolacca dioica*) that has large dark leaves and is cultivated in southern Europe

um·bre \'əmbə(r)\ *n* -S [prob. fr. NL *umbra*, fr. L, shade] **:** HAMMERKOP

¹um·brel·la \ˌəmˈbrelə *also* ˈ=ˌ==\ *n* -S [It *ombrella*, modif. (influenced by *ombra* shade, shadow, fr. L *umbra*) of L *umbella* parasol, umbrella, dim. of *umbra* — more at UMBRAGE] **1 a :** a small portable usu. cloth canopy that is fastened to a frame with hinged ribs radiating from a center pole, has a circular convex shape when open, can be opened or closed by means of a sliding catch, and provides protection against the weather — see PARASOL **b :** a large canopy of similar design whose center pole may be placed firmly in the ground or attached esp. to a table ⟨garden furniture with colored ~s —Christopher Morley⟩ — see BEACH UMBRELLA **2 :** something resembling an umbrella in shape or function: as **a :** a metal cover secured over a ship's smokestack to keep out precipitation **b :** a bell-shaped structure composed chiefly of jellylike mesoglea that forms the main part of the body of a jellyfish, has muscular ectodermal cells lining the lower concave surface, and serves as a swimming organ by means of contractions **c** (1) **:** the arched overhanging foliage of a tree ⟨the creamy ~s of the hemlock —C.G.Glover⟩ (2) **:** the canopy formed by leaves and branches in a wooded area ⟨see the pine wood spread its broad ~ —Cyril Connolly⟩ **d :** the open canopy of a parachute **e :** a formation of planes maintained over surface operations or a landmass for defense against attack ⟨throwing up an air ~ over Europe —*Springfield (Mass.) Union*⟩ **f :** a heavy barrage of shell fire ⟨the main battery guns were laying an ~ over the carrier —F.J.Bell⟩ **3 :** a unifying, conditioning, stabilizing, or controlling factor, agency, category, or authoritative influence ⟨both parties are ~s for diverse groups —J.E.McLean⟩ ⟨organization cost, an ~ which covers the publisher's expenses —H.M.Silver⟩ ⟨maintain a price ~ over the industry —A.D.H.Kaplan⟩ ⟨combined under the ~ of Fascism —T.E.M.McKitterick⟩

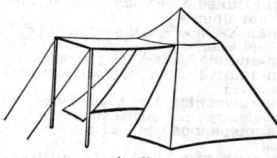

umbrella 1a

²umbrella \"\ *adj* **1 :** of, relating to, or having the characteristics of an umbrella **2 :** taking in many individuals or groups **:** ALL-EMBRACING ⟨an ~ organization sheltering a host of subdivided activities —O.O.Trullinger⟩ **3 :** having a roof supported on a single post ⟨a series of ~ sheds on a train platform⟩

³umbrella \"\ *vt* -ED/-ING/-S **1 :** to protect or cover with or as if with an umbrella ⟨each man ~*ed* from the downpour —*Manchester Guardian Weekly*⟩ **2 :** to provide with or as if with an umbrella ⟨the new job . . . : to ~ the invasion —*Time*⟩

umbrella ant *n* [so called fr. the fact that it sometimes carries bits of leaves on its back] **:** LEAF-CUTTING ANT

umbrella bird *n* **:** any of several So. and Central American birds of the genus *Cephalopterus* (as *C. ornatus*) that are about the size of a jackdaw and in the male are entirely black with a radiating crest curving forward over the head and a long feathered lappet depending from the breast

umbrella bush *n* **:** a small Australian acacia (*Acacia oswaldi*) used in hedges

umbrella catalpa *n* **:** a horticultural catalpa that is obtained by grafting a scion or scions of a dwarf variety (*C. bignonioides* var. *nana*) on a tall straight bole of the common catalpa (*C. bignonioides*) and that is characterized by a dense umbrella-shaped head formed of numerous leaf-bearing branches

umbrella fern *n* **:** an Australasian fern of the genus *Gleichenia*

umbrella grass *n* **:** any of several plants having outspread inflorescence: as **a :** AUSTRALIAN MILLET **b :** an Australian grass (*Aristida ramosa*) **c :** a sedge of the genus *Fuirena*

umbrella leaf *n* **:** a No. American herb (*Diphylleia cymosa*) with two large peltate stem leaves or a solitary lobed basal one

umbrellalike \ˌ=ˈ==ˌ=, ˈ=ˌ==ˌ=\ *adj* **:** resembling an umbrella ⟨an ~ dome fourteen feet in diameter —S.M.Spencer⟩

umbrella palm *n* **1 :** a widely cultivated pinnate-leaved palm (*Hedyscepe canterburyana*) native to Lord Howe Island and having a crown of recurved leaves **2 :** UMBRELLA PLANT 1

umbrella patent *n* **:** a patent in which claims are made all-embracing in order to give some color of right for litigating against those alleged to infringe it

umbrella pine *n* **1 :** a tall Japanese evergreen tree (*Sciadopitys verticillata*) of the family Pinaceae that has a symmetrical crown and needle-shaped leaves borne in umbrellalike whorls at the ends of the twigs **2 a :** STONE PINE 2 **b :** TANYOSHO PINE

umbrella plant *n* **1** *or* **umbrella sedge :** an African sedge (*Cyperus alternifolius*) that bears large terminal whorls of slender leaves and is often cultivated as an ornamental aquatic **2 :** any of several plants of the genus *Eriogonum* of the western U.S. **3 :** MAYAPPLE 1

umbrella pulley *n* **:** a pulley having a semispherical projecting skeleton boss

umbrella shell *n* **:** a marine gastropod of *Umbracula* or a related genus having a large thick foot, small head, and small external shell resembling that of a limpet and only partly covering the body

umbrella tent *n* **:** a tent resembling an umbrella and having a center pole with a framework of metal ribs

umbrella thorn *n* **:** an acacia (*Acacia heteracantha* or *A. litakunensis*) of the African bushveld having a flat-topped crown, straight thorns, and curved prickles — called also *haak-en-steek*

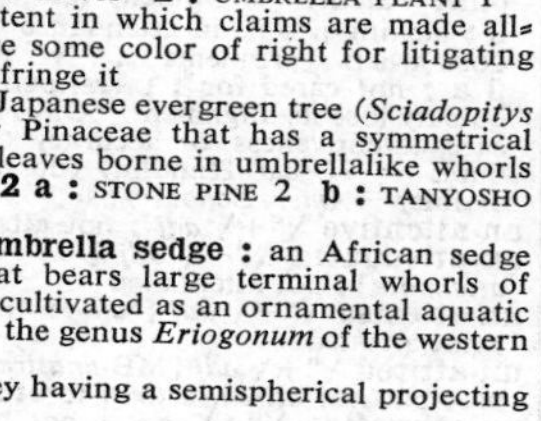
umbrella tent

umbrella tree *n* **1** *or* **umbrella magnolia :** an American magnolia (*Magnolia tripetala*) having large leaves clustered at the ends of the branches **2 a :** an Australian tree (*Brassaia actinophylla*) of the family Araliaceae having digitate leaves arranged like the ribs of an umbrella **b :** UMBRELLA BUSH **3 :** any of various other trees or shrubs resembling an umbrella esp. in the arrangement of leaves or the shape of the crown of foliage: as **a :** BLUE DOGWOOD **b :** PORTIA TREE **c :** MALABAR ALMOND 1 **d :** a cultivated tree of the southern U.S. that forms a variety (*Melia azedarach umbraculiformis*) of the chinaberry and is characterized by branches arising at a common level and radiating from the trunk like the ribs of an umbrella

umbrellawort \ˌ=ˈ==ˌ=, ˈ=ˌ==ˌ=\ *n* [¹*umbrella* + *wort*] **:** a plant of the genus *Mirabilis*

um·brette \ˌəmˈbret\ *or* **om·brette** \(')ăm-\ *n* -S [NL *umbretta*, fr. F *ombrette*, fr. *ombre* shade, shadow (fr. L *umbra*) + *-ette* — more at UMBRAGE] **:** HAMMERKOP

Um·bri·an \'əmbrēən\ *adj, usu cap* [L *Umbria*, province in central Italy + E *-an* (adj. suffix)] **1 a :** of, relating to, or characteristic of the Italian province of Umbria **b :** of, relating to, or characteristic of the people inhabiting Umbria **2 :** of, relating to, or characteristic of the Italic language of ancient Umbria

²umbrian \"\ *n* -S *cap* [L *Umbria* + E *-an* (n. suffix)] **1 a :** a member of a people of ancient Italy occupying Umbria **b :** a native or inhabitant of the Italian province of Umbria **2 :** the Italic language of ancient Umbria

um·bri·dae \'əmbrəˌdē\ *n pl, cap* [NL, fr. *Umbra*, type genus + *-idae*] **:** a family of small bottom-dwelling freshwater fishes (order Haplomi) including the genus *Umbra*

um·brif·er·ous \ˌəmˈbrif(ə)rəs\ *adj* [L *umbrifer*, fr. *umbra* shade, shadow + *-ifer* -iferous] *archaic* **:** UMBRAGEOUS 1a

um·bri·na \ˌəmˈbrīnə\ *n, cap* [NL, fr. L *umbra* + NL *-ina*] **:** a common widely distributed genus of croakers (family Sciaenidae) including a European umbra (*U. cirrhosa*) and the yellowfin croaker of the Pacific coast of No. America

um·brine \'əmˌbrīn, -brən\ *n* -S [NL *Umbrina*] **:** UMBRA 4

um·brous \'əmbrəs\ *adj* [L *umbrosus*, fr. *umbra* shade, shadow + *-osus* -ose — more at UMBRAGE] **:** SHADY, SHADOWED

um·bun·du \əmˈbünˌdü\ *n* -S *usu cap* **:** a Bantu language of central Angola — called also *Mbundu*

umbu-rana \ˌümbəˈrānə\ *n* -S [Tupi, fr. *umbu* umbra tree + *rana* false] **:** a So. American timber tree (*Torresia cearensis*) of the family Leguminosae that yields a yellow wood used for furniture — called also *roble*

ume \ə'mā, m'mā\ *n* -S [Jap] **:** JAPANESE APRICOT

um·faan \'əmˌfän\ *n* -S [Afrik, fr. Zulu *umfana* boy, dim. of *umfo* man, person] **:** a boy employed in southern Africa to care for small children or perform general work

um-hum *a sound made with the organs of speech in position for* m, *a voiced beginning which usu. has the heaviest stress, and a voiced ending separated by an* h-*like period of voicelessness*\ *interj* [origin unknown] — used to express affirmation, agreement, comprehension, or interest

umi·ak *also* **oo·mi·ak** *or* **oo·mi·ack** \'ümēˌak\ *n* -S [Esk] **:** an open Eskimo boat that consists of a wooden frame covered with hide and is usu. propelled with broad paddles — compare KAYAK

umiak

umi·ri *or* **umi·ry** \ˌüməˈrē\ *n, pl* **umiris** *or* **umiries** [Pg *umiri*, fr. Tupi *umiri*] **1 :** a fragrant balsam derived from So. American trees of the genus *Humiria* (esp. *H. floribunda* and *H. balsamifera*) **2 :** a tree of the genus *Humiria*

um·land \'ümˌland\ *n* -S [G, fr. *um-* around + *land*, fr. OHG *lant* — more at LAND] **:** the environs of a city, town, or village that is part of the main community through common economic and cultural activities — compare HINTERLAND 2

¹um·laut \'ümˌlau̇t\ *n* -S [G, fr. *um-* around, about (fr. MHG *um-, umb-*, fr. *umbe*, prep., around, about, fr. OHG *umbi*) + *laut* sound, fr. MHG *lūt*, akin to OE *hlūd* loud — more at EMBER DAY, LOUD] **1 a :** the change of a vowel caused by partial assimilation to a succeeding sound; *esp* **:** the fronting or raising of a back or low vowel (as *a, o,* or *u*) caused by an *i* or *j* orig. standing in the following syllable but now usu. lost or altered ⟨~ is a striking characteristic of the Germanic languages⟩ **b :** a vowel resulting from such partial assimilation **2 :** a diacritical mark ¨ placed esp. over a German vowel to indicate umlaut

²umlaut \"\ *vt* -ED/-ING/-S **1 :** to produce by umlaut **2 :** to write or print an umlaut over

umlaut vowel *n* **:** a reflex of a vowel produced by umlaut; *broadly* **:** a front-rounded vowel

umo·ho·ite \'yüməˌhōˌīt\ *n* -S [*U* (symbol for *uranium*) + *Mo* (symbol for *molybdenum*) + *H* (symbol for *hydrogen*) + *O* (symbol for *oxygen*) + *-ite*] **:** a mineral $(UO_2)MoO_4.4H_2O$ consisting of hydrous uranium molybdate

ump \'əmp\ *n* -S [by shortening] **:** UMPIRE 1b ⟨calling the ~s . . . dirty names in close decisions —L.M.Uris⟩

¹umph *like* ¹HUMPH\ *interj* [origin unknown] — usu. used to express skepticism or disgust

²umph \'üm(p)f, 'əm-\ *n* -S [by alter.] **:** OOMPH ⟨needs that ~, even if he is just 30 —*Springfield (Mass.) Daily News*⟩

um·pir·age \'əmˌpīrij, -rēj\ *n* -S [¹*umpire* + *-age*] **1 :** the office or authority of an umpire ⟨hoped the ~ of the war would fall into their hands —Gilbert Burnet⟩ **2 a :** an act or instance of umpiring ⟨cemented by the mild ~ of the federal union —Edward Everett⟩ **b :** a decision of an umpire **:** ARBITRAMENT ⟨the time for making the ~ was further extended —E.H.East⟩

¹um·pire \'əmˌpī(ə)r, -pīə\ *n* -S [ME *umpere, oumpere*, alter. (resulting from incorrect division of *a noumpere*) of *noumpere*, fr. MF *nomper, nonper* not equal, not paired (i.e., a third person), fr. *non-* + *per* equal, even, fr. L *par* — more at PAIR] **1 :** one having authority to arbitrate and make a final decision: as **a** (1) **:** an attorney at law appointed to judge a legal matter disputed by arbitrators (2) **:** an impartial third party chosen by labor and management to arbitrate disputes arising under the terms of a labor agreement **b :** an official in a sport (as baseball or cricket) who rules on the plays **2 :** a military officer who observes and evaluates training maneuvers ⟨~s rushed about to decide how this battle of blank ammunition was going —O.N.Bradley⟩

²umpire \"\ *vb* -ED/-ING/-S *vt* **:** to supervise and decide in the capacity of umpire ⟨differences have to be . . . *umpired* by the president —Anthony Leviero⟩ ⟨can see . . . policemen *umpiring* the roughest games —Margaret Mead⟩ ~ *vi* **:** to act in the capacity of umpire **:** ARBITRATE ⟨appointed to ~ in the labor disputes⟩ ⟨*umpired* for the California league —Darrell Berrigan⟩

umpire assay *n* **:** an assay to decide the value of a shipment (as of ore, concentrate, bullion) when previous assays made by the buyer and seller are not in agreement

umpire-in-chief \ˈ=ˌ=ˌ=ˈ=\ *n, pl* **umpires-in-chief :** an umpire stationed behind the catcher in baseball or softball who calls balls and strikes

umpire·ship \ˈ=ˌ=ˌship\ *n* **:** UMPIRAGE

ump·qua \'əm(p)kwə\ *n, pl* **umpqua** *or* **umpquas** *usu cap* [Umpqua *ăkwa*] **1 a :** an Athapaskan people of western Oregon **b :** a member of such people **2 :** a language of the Umpqua people

ump·teen *also* **um·teen** \ˌəm(p)ˈtēn\ *adj* [blend of *umpty* and *-teen* (as in *thirteen*)] **:** very many **:** indefinitely numerous ⟨tonight, like ~ other nights —W.H.Auden⟩ ⟨an . . . audience estimated in the ~ millions —R.B.Considine⟩

ump·teenth *also* **um·teenth** \-ēn(t)th\ *adj* **:** being the latest or last in an indefinitely numerous series ⟨postponed for the ~ time —*Time*⟩ ⟨made the ~ mistake that day⟩

ump·ti·eth \'əm(p)tēəth\ *adj* **:** UMPTEENTH

ump·ty \'əm(p)tē, -ti\ *adj* [prob. alter. of *-enty* (as in *twenty, seventy*)] **:** such and such ⟨~ percent of all new houses —*Kansas City Star, Mo.*⟩ — often used in combination ⟨the *umpty*-fifth regiment —Bill Mauldin⟩

um·quhile *also* **um·while** \'əmˌ(h)wīl\ *adj* [ME, fr. OE *ymbhwīle*, adv., at times, sometimes, fr. *ymb, ymbe* around, about, at + *hwīle* while — more at EMBER DAY, WHILE] *chiefly Scot* **:** of old **:** FORMER, LATE, DECEASED

UMS *abbr* universal military service

um suff \ümˈsüf\ *n* -S [Ar *umm ṣūf* sudd, lit., mother (i.e., source) of wool, fr. *ṣūf-al-baḥr*, a maritime plant, lit., wool of the sea] **:** a wiry grass (*Vossia procera*) that is found in the Nile and often makes up a considerable part of the river's sudd

UMT *abbr* universal military training

¹un \ən, ³n\ *pron* [alter. of ¹*hin*] *dial* **:** HIM

²un \"\ *pron* [by alter.] *dial* **:** ONE ⟨that ~ got away clean —Frank Yerby⟩ ⟨some of them were bad ~s —A.L.Burt⟩ — often used in combination ⟨we will but you-*uns* won't —J.M. Allen⟩

¹un- *prefix* [ME, fr. OE: akin to OHG *un-* un-, ON *ō, ū-*, Goth *un-*, L *in-*, Gk *a-, an-*, Skt *a-, an-* un-, OE *ne* not — more at NO] **1 :** not **:** IN-, NON- — in adjectives formed from adjectives ⟨*un*capacious⟩ ⟨*un*gratifiable⟩ ⟨*un*neighborlike⟩ ⟨*un*strenuous⟩ including adjectivally used past and present participles ⟨*un*camouflaged⟩ ⟨*un*chosen⟩ ⟨*un*dressed⟩ ⟨*un*soothing⟩ and adjectives formed by adding *-ed* to nouns ⟨*un*bearded⟩, in nouns formed from nouns ⟨*un*ostentation⟩, and rarely in verbs formed from verbs ⟨*un*be⟩; sometimes in words that have a meaning that merely negates that of the base word and are thereby distinguished from words that prefix *in-* or a variant of it (as *im-*) to the same base word and have a meaning positively opposite to that of the base word ⟨*un*artistic⟩ ⟨*un*moral⟩ **2 :** opposite of **:** contrary to — in adjectives formed from adjectives ⟨*un*constitutional⟩ ⟨*un*graceful⟩ ⟨*un*palatable⟩ ⟨*un*warlike⟩ including adjectivally used past and present participles ⟨*un*affected⟩ ⟨*un*stinting⟩ and adjectives formed by adding *-ed* to nouns ⟨*un*principled⟩, and in nouns formed from nouns ⟨*un*rest⟩

²un- *prefix* [ME, fr. OE *un-, on-*, alter. of *and-* against — more at ANTE-] **1 a :** do the opposite of **:** reverse (a specified action) **:** DE- 1a, ¹DIS- 1a — in verbs formed from verbs ⟨*un*bend⟩ ⟨*un*dress⟩ ⟨*un*fold⟩ **b :** cause to cease to — in verbs formed from verbs ⟨*un*be⟩ **2 a :** deprive of **:** remove (a specified thing) from **:** remove — in verbs formed from nouns ⟨*un*flesh⟩ ⟨*un*frock⟩ ⟨*un*sex⟩; compare DE-, ¹DIS- **b :** release from **:** free from — in verbs formed from nouns ⟨*un*hand⟩ **c :** remove from **:** extract from **:** bring out of — in verbs formed from nouns ⟨*un*bosom⟩ ⟨*un*heaven⟩; compare DE-, ¹DIS- **d :** cause to cease to be — in verbs formed from nouns ⟨*un*king⟩; compare ¹DIS- **3 :** completely ⟨*un*loose⟩ — compare ¹DIS-

un *abbr* **1** unified; unifying **2** union **3** unit **4** united **5** university

un·abashed \ˌənəˈbasht, -aa(ə)sh, -aish-\ *adj* [¹*un-* + *abashed*, past part. of *abash*] **:** not abashed ⟨a tinseled charm and ~ sentimentality —Jerome Stone⟩ — **un·abashed·ly** \-shədlē, -shtl-, -li\ *adv*

un·abated \ˌən+\ *adj* [¹*un-* + *abated*, past part. of ¹*abate*] **:** not abated **:** at full strength or force ⟨the popularity of his books among young people has continued almost ~ —Sarah G. Bowerman⟩ — **un·abat·ed·ly** *adv*

un·abbreviated \"+\ *adj* **:** not abbreviated

unability *n* [ME *unabilite*, fr. ¹*un-* + *abilite* ability] *obs* **:** INABILITY

¹un·able \ˌən+\ *adj* [ME, fr. ¹*un-* + *able*, adj.] **1 :** not able **:** INCAPABLE ⟨the sun is ~ to melt the snow down to this underlying part —*Amer. Guide Series: N.H.*⟩ **2 a :** UNQUALIFIED, INCOMPETENT, INEFFICIENT **b :** IMPOTENT, HELPLESS ⟨like an ~ phoenix in hot ashes —*Time*⟩

²un·a·ble \ˌəˈnābəl\ *vt* [ME *unablen*, prob. fr. ²*un-* + *ablen* to enable — more at ABLE] **:** DISABLE, INCAPACITATE ⟨so *unabled* by the gout that she cannot dress herself —Samuel Johnson⟩

una boat \'yünə-\ *n, usu cap U* [fr. *Una*, the first boat of this kind taken to England (1853)] *Brit* **:** CATBOAT

¹un·abridged \ˌən+\ *adj* [¹*un-* + *abridged*, past part. of *abridge*] **1 :** not abridged **:** COMPLETE ⟨presented an ~ version of the play⟩ ⟨an ~ reprint of a novel⟩ **2 :** being the most complete of its class ⟨an ~ dictionary⟩

²unabridged \"\ *n* -S **:** an unabridged dictionary

un·absolved \"+\ *adj* [¹*un-* + *absolved*, past part. of *absolve*] **:** not absolved

un·absorbable \"+\ *adj* **:** not capable of being absorbed

un·absorbed \"+\ *adj* [¹*un-* + *absorbed*, past part. of *absorb*] **:** not absorbed

un·abused \"+\ *adj* [¹*un-* + *abused*, past part. of *abuse*] **:** not abused **:** used or treated properly

un·academic *also* **un·academical** \"+\ *adj* **:** not academic or scholarly **:** not formal or conventional **:** belonging to or arising from the realities of common life rather than the rules or theories of the schoolroom

un·accented *also* **un·accentuated** \"+\ *adj* [¹*un-* + *accented* (past part. of *accent*) *or accentuated* (past part. of *accentuate*)] **:** not accented **:** UNSTRESSED

un·acceptable \"+\ *adj* [ME *unacceptabylle*, fr. ¹*un-* + *acceptabylle, acceptable* acceptable] **:** not acceptable **:** not pleasing or welcome ⟨a slang word ~ in polite society —Scott Seegers⟩ — **un·ac·cept·able·ness** *n* -ES

un·acceptance \"+\ *n* **:** lack of acceptance

un·accepted \ˌən+\ *adj* [¹*un-* + *accepted*, past part. of *accept*] **:** not accepted; *specif* **:** not having had responsibility for its maintenance accepted by a government ⟨a street ~ by the city⟩

un·accessible \"+\ *adj* **:** INACCESSIBLE

un·acclimated *or* **un·acclimatized** \"+\ *adj* [¹*un-* + *acclimated* (past part. of *acclimate*) *or acclimatized* (past part. of *acclimatize*)] **:** not acclimatized

un·accommodated \"+\ *adj* [¹*un-* + *accommodated*, past part. of *accommodate*] **:** not accommodated **:** UNPROVIDED

un·accommodating \"+\ *adj* **:** not accommodating — **un·ac·com·mo·dat·ing·ly** *adv*

un·accompanied \"+\ *adj* [¹*un-* + *accompanied*, past part. of *accompany*] **:** not accompanied ⟨dramatic energy was ~ by a sufficiently developed sense of dramatic form —Leslie Rees⟩; *specif* **:** being without instrumental accompaniment ⟨the soloist sang ~⟩

un·accomplishable \"+\ *adj* [¹*un-* + *accomplish* + *-able*] **:** not capable of being accomplished

un·accomplished \"+\ *adj* [¹*un-* + *accomplished*, past part. of *accomplish*] **1 :** not accomplished **:** INCOMPLETE, UNFINISHED **2 :** lacking talent, poise, grace, or achievement

un·accountability \"+\ *n* **:** the quality or state of being unaccountable

¹un·accountable \"+\ *adj* **1 :** not to be accounted for **:** INEXPLICABLE ⟨perceptible only as ~ influences that distort and hinder progress —C.H.Rickword⟩ ⟨gave her an ~ thrill of pleasure —G.B.Shaw⟩; *esp* **:** not consonant with reason or rule **:** STRANGE, MYSTERIOUS **2 :** not accountable or responsible **:** free from control ⟨the power of management has been aggrandized and left largely exempt and ~ —G.B.Hurff⟩ — **un·ac·count·able·ness** *n* -ES — **un·accountably** \"+\ *adv*

²unaccountable \"+\ *n* **:** a person or thing that is unaccountable

un·accounted \"+\ *adj* [¹*un-* + *accounted*, past part. of *account*] **:** not accounted — often used with *for* ⟨the balance remained ~ for⟩

un·accredited \"+\ *adj* **:** not accredited

un·accusable \ˌən+\ *adj* [¹*un-* + *accuse* + *-able*] **:** not accusable — **un·accusably** \"+\ *adv*

un·accused \"+\ *adj* [¹*un-* + *accused*, past part. of *accuse*] **:** not accused

un·accustomed \"+\ *adj* **1 :** not customary **:** UNUSUAL, UNCOMMON, STRANGE, NEW ⟨in contact with many varieties of ~ foods —*Current Biog.*⟩ **2 :** not habituated **:** UNFAMILIAR — usu. used with *to* ⟨toxic substances to which it is ~ in its native habitat —W.H.Dowdeswell⟩

un·achievable \"+\ *adj* **:** not capable of being achieved

un·achieved \"+\ *adj* [¹*un-* + *achieved*, past part. of *achieve*] **:** not achieved

un·aching \"+\ *adj* **:** not aching

un·acknowledged \"+\ *adj* [¹*un-* + *acknowledged*, past part. of *acknowledge*] **:** not acknowledged

unacknowledging *adj* [¹*un-* + *acknowledging*, pres. part. of *acknowledge*] **:** not acknowledging

una cor·da \ˌünəˈkȯrdə\ *adv (or adj)* [It, lit., one string; fr. the fact that the soft pedal shifts the hammers so that they do not strike all the strings available for each note] **:** with soft pedal depressed — used as a direction in piano music; compare TRE CORDE

una corda pedal *n* **:** SOFT PEDAL

un·acquaintance \"+\ *n* **:** the quality or state of being unacquainted **:** lack of acquaintance **:** IGNORANCE ⟨displays a brilliant ~ with the thought, manners, and beliefs of the period —R.E.Roberts⟩

un·acquainted \"+\ *adj* **1 :** not having experience or knowledge **:** IGNORANT **2 :** not acquainted — **un·ac·quaint·ed·ness** *n* -ES

un·acquired \"+\ *adj* **:** not acquired; *esp* **:** INNATE

un·actable \"+\ *adj* **:** not actable ⟨an ~ play⟩

un·acted \"+\ *adj* [¹*un-* + *acted*, past part. of *act*] **:** not performed ⟨the fault unknown, is as a thought ~ —Shak.⟩ ⟨an ~ play⟩ ⟨is not fermentable and so is ~ on by yeast —William Jago⟩

un·active \"+\ *adj* **:** INACTIVE

un·actuated \"+\ *adj* [¹*un-* + *actuated*, past part. of *actuate*] **:** not actuated

un·adaptable \"+\ *adj* **:** not adaptable

un·adapted \"+\ *adj* **:** not adapted

un·addicted \"+\ *adj* **:** not addicted

un·addressed \"+\ *adj* [¹*un-* + *addressed*, past part. of *address*] **:** not addressed ⟨an ~ envelope⟩

uña de ga·to \ˈünyədəˈgä(ˌ)tō\ *n* [AmerSp, lit., cat's claw] **:** any of various shrubs or trees of the southwestern U.S. and Spanish America having sharp recurved prickles or thorns; *esp* **:** CAT'S-CLAW
un·adept \ˌən+\ *n* **:** one who is not an adept **:** LAYMAN
un·adjusted \ˌən+\ *adj* **:** not adjusted ⟨~ children⟩
un·administered \"+\ *adj* [¹*un-* + *administered*, past part. of *administer*] **:** not administered
un·admirable \"+\ *adj* **:** not worthy of admiration
un·admiring \"+\ *adj* **:** not admiring
un·admonished \"+\ *adj* [¹*un-* + *admonished*, past part. of *admonish*] **:** not admonished
un·adopted \"+\ *adj* [¹*un-* + *adopted*, past part. of adopt] **:** not adopted ⟨an heroic manner of a kind hitherto ~ in symphonic works —H.J.Foss⟩
un·adored \"+\ *adj* [¹*un-* + *adored*, past part. of *adore*] *archaic* **:** not adored **:** UNWORSHIPED
un·adorned \ˌənəˈdȯ(ə)rnd, -ō(ə)nd\ *adj* [¹*un-* + *adorned*, past part. of *adorn*] **:** not adorned **:** lacking adornment, embellishment, or decoration ⟨a simple ~ account of the coronation —Elinor Wylie⟩ — **un·adorn·ed·ness** \-nədnəs\ *n* -ES
un·adulterated *also* **un·adulterate** \ˌən+\ *adj* [¹*un-* + *adulterated* (past part. of *adulterate*) or *adulterate*, adj.] **:** not adulterated **:** PURE, UNMIXED, UNCORRUPTED ⟨here is genius ~, superb, enormous —Amy Loveman⟩ — **un·adul·ter·at·ed·ly** *adv*
un·advanced \"+\ *adj* [alter. (influenced by ¹*advance*) of ME *unavanced*, fr. ¹*un-* + *avanced*, *avaunced*, past part. of *avancen*, *avauncen* to advance] **:** not advanced ⟨the relatively ~ state of descriptive theory —*Psycholinguistics*⟩
un·advantageous \"+\ *adj* **:** not advantageous — **un·ad·van·ta·geous·ly** *adv*
un·adventurous \"+\ *adj* **:** not adventurous **:** lacking in boldness ⟨our clothes were for the most part ~ like our conversation —W.B.Yeats⟩ — **un·ad·ven·tur·ous·ly** *adv* — **un·ad·ven·tur·ous·ness** *n*
un·advertised \"+\ *adj* [¹*un-* + *advertised*, past part. of *advertise*] **:** not advertised **:** UNANNOUNCED
un·advisable \"+\ *adj* **1 :** not capable of being advised **2 :** INADVISABLE — **un·ad·vis·able·ness** *n* — **un·advisably** \"+\ *adv*
un·ad·vised \ˌənədˈvīzd\ *adj* [alter. (influenced by *advised*) of ME *unavised*, fr. ¹*un-* + *avised* advised] **1 :** done without due consideration **:** RASH, INCONSIDERATE **2 :** not prudent **:** INDISCREET — **un·ad·vis·ed·ly** \-zədlē, -li\ *adv* —**un·ad·vis·ed·ness** \-dnəs\ *n* -ES
un·aerated \ˌən+\ *adj* [¹*un-* + *aerated*, past part. of *aerate*] **:** not aerated
un·aesthetic \"+\ *adj* **:** INAESTHETIC
un·affable \"+\ *adj* **:** not affable
un·affected \"+\ *adj* [¹*un-* + *affected*, past part. of *affect* (to act upon)] **1 a :** not influenced mentally or emotionally **:** UNMOVED ⟨remained almost entirely ~ by each other's writings —Richard Garnett †1906⟩ **b :** undergoing no change when acted upon ⟨fibers remain apparently ~ when subjected to quite severe hydrolytic treatments —H.R.Mauersberger⟩ **2** [¹*un-* + *affected*, adj.] **a :** GENUINE, SINCERE ⟨stared at me in ~ astonishment —Allen Upward⟩ **b :** free from affectation **:** PLAIN, SIMPLE, NATURAL ⟨consciously elaborate fashion which began to supplant the ~ early American style —*Amer. Guide Series: N.C.*⟩ ⟨spoke with the confidence of the —Marguerite Steen⟩ **syn** see NATURAL
un·af·fect·ed·ly *adv* **:** in an unaffected manner
un·af·fect·ed·ness *n* **:** the quality or state of being unaffected
un·affecting \"+\ *adj* **1** *archaic* **:** being without affectation **2 :** not affecting **:** creating no effect on the feelings **:** UNMOVING
un·affectionate \"+\ *adj* **:** lacking affection **:** not affectionate — **un·af·fec·tion·ate·ly** *adv*
un·affianced \"+\ *adj* [¹*un-* + *affianced*, past part. of *affiance*] **:** not affianced
un·affiliated \ˌən+\ *adj* [¹*un-* + *affiliated*, past part. of *affiliate*] **:** not affiliated
un·afflicted \"+\ *adj* **:** not afflicted
un·affrighted \"+\ *adj* **:** UNAFRAID — **un·af·fright·ed·ly** *adv*
un·affronted \"+\ *adj* [¹*un-* + *affronted*, past part. of *affront*] **1 :** not insulted **2 :** not met face to face **:** not confronted
unaflow *var of* UNIFLOW
un·afraid \ˌən+\ *adj* [ME *unaffraid*, fr. ¹*un-* + *affraid*, *affraied* afraid] **:** not afraid or frightened **:** not fearful **:** oblivious of dangers or perils or calmly resolute in braving them **syn** see BRAVE
un·aggravated \"+\ *adj* [¹*un-* + *aggravated*, past part. of *aggravate*] **:** not aggravated
un·aggressive \"+\ *adj* **:** not aggressive **:** not given to fighting or assertiveness — **un·ag·gres·sive·ly** *adv* — **un·ag·gres·sive·ness** *n*
un·agitated \"+\ *adj* **:** not mentally or physically disturbed — **un·ag·i·tat·ed·ly** *adv*
un·aided \"+\ *adj* [¹*un-* + *aided*, past part. of *aid*] **:** not aided **:** being without help — **un·aid·ed·ly** *adv*
un·aimed \"+\ *adj* [¹*un-* + *aimed*, past part. of *aim*] **:** being without a fixed target **:** not aimed **:** RANDOM
un·aired \"+\ *adj* [¹*un-* + *aired*, past part. of *air*] **:** not ventilated
un·akin \"+\ *adj* **:** not akin **:** UNRELATED
una·lach·ti·go \ˌünəˈlächtəˌgō\ *n*, *pl* **unalachtigo** *or* **unalachtigos** *usu cap* [Delaware, lit., tidewater people] **1 :** a Delaware Indian people of northern Delaware, southeastern Pennsylvania, and southern New Jersey **2 :** a member of the Unalachtigo people
un·alarmed \ˌən+\ *adj* [¹*un-* + *alarmed*, past part. of *alarm*] **:** not alarmed
un·alarming \"+\ *adj* [¹*un-* + *alarming*, pres. part. of *alarm*] **:** not alarming
un·alert \"+\ *adj* **:** not alert
un·alienable \"+\ *adj* **:** INALIENABLE — **un·alienably** \"+\ *adv*
un·alienated \"+\ *adj* [¹*un-* + *alienated*, past part. of *alienate*] **:** not alienated ⟨good and accessible land . . . left ~ from the Crown —B.K.Sandwell⟩
un·alike \"+\ *adj* **:** not alike **:** DISSIMILAR ⟨as ~ as any two people could be —Edita Morris⟩
unal·ist \ˈyünᵊləst\ *n* -S [L *unus* one + E *-alist* (as in *pluralist*) — more at ONE] **:** a holder of one benefice
un·alive \ˌən+\ *adj* **:** slow of perception or feeling **:** not alive **:** UNALERT ⟨~ to the beauties of the music⟩
un·allayed \"+\ *adj* [¹*un-* + *allayed*, past part. of *allay* (to alloy)] **:** UNALLOYED
un·alleviated \"+\ *adj* [¹*un-* + *alleviated*, past part. of *alleviate*] **:** not alleviated **:** acting at full strength ⟨~ pain⟩
un·allied \"+\ *adj* **:** not allied **:** having no connection or relation ⟨~ species⟩
un·allowable \"+\ *adj* **:** not allowable **:** IMPERMISSIBLE
un·allowed \"+\ *adj* [¹*un-* + *allowed*, past part. of *allow*] **:** not allowed **:** UNPERMITTED
un·alloyed \"+\ *adj* [¹*un-* + *alloyed*, past part. of *alloy*] **:** not alloyed **:** UNMIXED, UNQUALIFIED, PURE ⟨~ metals⟩ ⟨~ happiness⟩
un·alluring \"+\ *adj* **:** not alluring **:** UNATTRACTIVE, PLAIN
un·alterability \"+\ *n* **:** INALTERABILITY
un·alterable \"+\ *adj* **:** not capable of being altered **:** INALTERABLE, UNCHANGEABLE ⟨an ~ ground rule to be followed —C.F.Robinson⟩ — **un·al·ter·able·ness** *n* -ES — **un·alterably** \"+\ *adv*
un·altered \ˌən+\ *adj* [¹*un-* + *altered*, past part. of *alter*] **:** not altered **:** remaining in an original state **:** UNCHANGED ⟨persisting ~ through time —Arthur Pap⟩
un·amalgamated \"+\ *adj* [¹*un-* + *amalgamated*, past part. of *amalgamate*] **:** not amalgamated
un·amazed \"+\ *adj* **:** not amazed **:** being without astonishment or surprise
un·ambiguity \"+\ *n* **:** lack of ambiguity **:** possession of one clear meaning
un·ambiguous \"+\ *adj* **:** not ambiguous **:** having or being a single clearly defined or stated meaning **:** CLEAR, PRECISE ⟨~ evidence⟩ — **un·am·big·u·ous·ly** *adv*
un·ambition \"+\ *n* **:** lack of ambition

un·ambitious \"+\ *adj* **:** not ambitious **:** lacking ambition ⟨happy ~ irresponsibility —*Partisan Rev.*⟩ — **un·am·bi·tious·ly** *adv* — **un·am·bi·tious·ness** *n* -ES
un·amenable \"+\ *adj* **:** not amenable ⟨~ to persuasion⟩ — **un·amenably** \"+\ *adv*
un·amendable \"+\ *adj* [ME, fr. ¹*un-* + *amenden* to amend + *-able*] **:** not amendable
un·amended \"+\ *adj* [ME, fr. ¹*un-* + *amended*, past part. of *amenden* to amend] **:** not amended
un·american \"+\ *adj*, *usu cap A* **:** not American **:** not characteristic of or consistent with American customs, principles, or traditions
un·americanism \"+\ *n*, *usu cap A* **:** the quality or state of being un-American **:** lack of or contrariety to Americanism
una·mi \üˈnämē\ *n*, *pl* **unami** *or* **unamis** *usu cap* **1 :** a Delaware Indian people chiefly of central New Jersey and southeastern Pennsylvania **2 :** a member of the Unami people
un·amiability \ˌən+\ *n* **:** lack of amiability
un·amiable \"+\ *adj* [ME, fr. ¹*un-* + *amiable*] **:** not amiable — **un·ami·a·ble·ness** *n* — **un·amiably** \"+\ *adv*
una·mo \üˈnä(ˌ)mō\ *n* -S [AmerSp] **:** a So. American palm (*Jessenia polycarpa*) the seeds of which yield an oil
un·amortized \ˌən+\ *adj* [¹*un-* + *amortized*, past part. of *amortize*] **:** not amortized
un·amused \"+\ *adj* **:** not amused
un·amusing \"+\ *adj* **:** not amusing — **un·amus·ing·ly** *adv*
unan *abbr* unanimous
un·analogous \ˌən+\ *adj* **:** not analogous
un·analyzable \"+\ *adj* **:** not analyzable ⟨this weight of evidence is something mystical and ~ —M.R.Cohen⟩
un·analyzed \"+\ *adj* [¹*un-* + *analyzed*, past part. of *analyze*] **:** not analyzed ⟨an ~ compound⟩
un·anchor \"+\ *vt* [²*un-* + *anchor*, v.] **:** to loosen from or as if from an anchor ⟨any marked disturbance of the society . . . ~s him —Paul Radin⟩
un·aneled \"+\ *adj* [¹*un-* + *aneled*, past part. of *anele*] *archaic* **:** not having received extreme unction
un·angelic \"+\ *adj* **:** not angelic **:** HUMAN, DEMONIC
un·animated \"+\ *adj* [¹*un-* + *animated*, past part. of *animate*] **1 :** INANIMATE **2 :** not enlivened **:** DULL
unan·i·mism \yüˈnanəˌmizəm\ *n* -S [F *unanimisme*, fr. *unanime* unanimous (fr. L *unanimus*) + *-isme* -ism] **:** a doctrine that the unifying principles in human groups are more significant (as for representation in literature) than personal individualities
una·nim·i·ty \ˌyünəˈnimədˌē, -mətē, -i\ *n* -ES [ME *unanimite*, fr. MF *unanimité*, fr. L *unanimitat-*, *unanimitas*, fr. *unanimus* unanimous + *-itat-*, *-itas* -ity] **:** the quality or state of being unanimous
unan·i·mous \yüˈnanəməs\ *adj* [L *unanimus*, fr. *unus* one + *animus* soul, mind — more at ONE, ANIMATE] **1 :** being of one mind **:** agreeing in opinion, design, or determination **:** CONSENTIENT ⟨the assembly was ~⟩ ⟨the members of the council were ~ in their approval of the report⟩ **2 :** formed with or indicating unanimity **:** having the agreement and consent of all without dissent ⟨a ~ vote⟩ — **unan·i·mous·ly** *adv*
unanimous consent *n* **:** the silent consent of an assembly to a routine or minor matter proposed by the chairman
un·annealed \ˌən+\ *adj* [¹*un-* + *annealed*, past part. of *anneal*] **:** not annealed
un·annotated \"+\ *adj* [¹*un-* + *annotated*, past part. of *annotate*] **:** not annotated
un·announced \"+\ *adj* [¹*un-* + *announced*, past part. of *announce*] **:** not announced **:** being without announcement
un·anointed \"+\ *adj* [¹*un-* + *anointed*, past part. of *anoint*] **:** not anointed
un·answerable \"+\ *adj* **:** not answerable ⟨an ~ question⟩; *specif* **:** IRREFUTABLE, CONCLUSIVE, DECISIVE ⟨an ~ argument⟩ — **un·an·swer·able·ness** *n* -ES — **un·answerably** \"+\ *adv*
un·answered \"+\ *adj* [ME, fr. ¹*un-* + *answered*, past part. of *answeren* to answer] **1 :** not replied to ⟨an ~ letter⟩ **2 :** not refuted ⟨an ~ argument⟩ **3 :** not responded to in kind **:** UNREQUITED ⟨~ love⟩
un·anticipated \"+\ *adj* [¹*un-* + *anticipated*, past part. of *anticipate*] **:** not anticipated **:** UNEXPECTED, UNFORESEEN ⟨~ and disconcerting lines of development —H.W.Glidden⟩
un·anxious \"+\ *adj* **:** not anxious **:** being without worries, fears, or doubts — **un·anx·ious·ly** *adv*
un·apologetic \"+\ *adj* **:** not apologetic **:** offering or being put forward with no apology ⟨an ~ believer⟩
un·apostolic \"+\ *adj* **:** not in accordance with apostolic belief, doctrine, or practice — **un·apostolically** \"+\ *adv*
un·appalled \ˌən+\ *adj* [¹*un-* + *appalled*, past part. of *appall*] **:** not appalled **:** UNFRIGHTENED
un·apparent \"+\ *adj* **:** not apparent ⟨the answer was at first ~⟩
un·appealable \"+\ *adj* **:** not appealable **:** not subject to appeal — **un·appealably** \"+\ *adv*
un·appealing \"+\ *adj* **:** not appealing **:** UNATTRACTIVE
un·appeasable \"+\ *adj* **:** not appeasable **:** IMPLACABLE — **un·appeasably** \"+\ *adv*
un·appeased \"+\ *adj* [¹*un-* + *appeased*, past part. of *appease*] **:** not appeased
un·appetizing \"+\ *adj* **:** not appetizing **:** INSIPID, UNINTERESTING, UNATTRACTIVE ⟨durably bound and ~ volumes on zoological and chemical subjects —Edmund Wilson⟩ — **un·ap·pe·tiz·ing·ly** *adv*
un·applauded \"+\ *adj* [¹*un-* + *applauded*, past part. of *applaud*] **:** not applauded **:** UNPRAISED
un·applicable \ˌən+\ *adj* **:** INAPPLICABLE
un·applied \"+\ *adj* [¹*un-* + *applied*, past part. of *apply*] **:** not applied
un·appreciable \"+\ *adj* **:** INAPPRECIABLE
un·appreciated \"+\ *adj* [¹*un-* + *appreciated*, past part. of *appreciate*] **:** not appreciated **:** without recognition or thanks
un·appreciative \"+\ *adj* **:** not appreciative
un·apprehensive \"+\ *adj* **1 :** slow to comprehend **:** DULL, UNINTELLIGENT **2 :** slow to recognize danger; *also* **:** not recognizing danger **:** UNAFRAID — **un·ap·pre·hen·sive·ness** *n*
un·apprised \"+\ *adj* [¹*un-* + *apprised*, past part. of *apprise*] **:** not apprised **:** UNINFORMED
un·approachable \"+\ *adj* **1 :** not approachable **:** physically inaccessible ⟨the scholastic notion of a material substance ~ by us —William James⟩ **2 :** discouraging intimacies **:** RESERVED — **un·ap·proach·able·ness** *n* -ES — **un·approachably** \"+\ *adv*
un·approached \"+\ *adj* [¹*un-* + *approached*, past part. of *approach*] **:** not approached; *specif* **:** of a standard unattained by any other in its class ⟨as a description of manners . . . the book is ~ by any others —Carl Van Doren⟩
un·appropriated \"+\ *adj* [¹*un-* + *appropriated*, past part. of *appropriate*] **1 :** not granted to any one to the exclusion of others ⟨~ public domain⟩ **2 :** not granted for or applied to a specific purpose ⟨~ taxes⟩
un·approved \"+\ *adj* [¹*un-* + *approved*, past part. of *approve* (to sanction)] **:** not approved **:** UNSANCTIONED
un·apt \"+\ *adj* [ME, fr. ¹*un-* + *apt*] **1** *obs* **:** UNADAPTED, UNFIT **2 :** UNSUITABLE, INAPPROPRIATE ⟨an ~ citation⟩ **3 :** not accustomed and not likely **:** not disposed ⟨I am a soldier and ~ to weep —Shak.⟩ **4 :** INAPT, SLOW, DULL, BACKWARD — **un·apt·ly** *adv* — **un·apt·ness** *n*
un·architectural \"+\ *adj* **:** not consonant with architectural principles
un·arguable \"+\ *adj* **:** INARGUABLE — **un·arguably** \"+\ *adv*
un·argued \"+\ *adj* [¹*un-* + *argued*, past part. of *argue*] **1 :** being without debate **2 :** not argued against **:** UNDISPUTED
un·argumentative \"+\ *adj* **:** not argumentative — **un·ar·gu·men·ta·tive·ly** *adv*
un·arm \"+\ *vt* [ME *unarmen*, fr. ²*un-* + *armen* to arm] **:** DISARM
un·armed \"+\ *adj* [ME, fr. ¹*un-* + *armed*] **1 :** not armed or armored **:** having or bearing no weapons **2 :** having no hard and sharp projections (as spines, prickles, spurs, or claws)
un·armored \"+\ *adj* **:** not armored; *also* **:** lightly armored
unarmored scale *n* **:** any of various scales (as a soft scale) belonging to families other than Diaspididae and usu. lacking a substantial waxy covering; *esp* **:** COCCID
un·arrested \"+\ *adj* [ME *unarested*, fr. ¹*un-* + *arested*, past part. of *aresten* to arrest] **:** not arrested

un·artful \"+\ *adj* **1 :** lacking craft **:** ARTLESS **2 :** lacking skill — **un·artfully** \"+\ *adv*
un·articulate \"+\ *adj* **:** INARTICULATE
un·articulated \"+\ *adj* [¹*un-* + *articulated*, past part. of *articulate*] **:** not articulated
un·artificial \"+\ *adj* **:** INARTIFICIAL — **un·artificially** \"+\ *adv*
un·artistic \"+\ *adj* **:** not artistic
una·ry \ˈyünərē\ *adj* [L *unus* one + E *-ary*, adj. suffix — more at ONE] **1 :** occurring as molecules of only one kind **2 :** containing only one component — used of a physical-chemical system
un·ascertainable \ˌən+\ *adj* **:** not ascertainable
un·ascertained \"+\ *adj* [¹*un-* + *ascertained*, past part. of *ascertain*] **:** not ascertained
unasgd *abbr* unassigned
un·ashamed \ˌən+\ *adj* **:** not ashamed **:** being without guilt, self-consciousness, or doubt **:** PROUD, UNABASHED ⟨~ individualism⟩ — **un·ashamedly** \"+\ *adv* — **un·ashamedness** \"+\ *n*
un·asked \"+\ *adj* [ME, fr. ¹*un-* + *asked*, past part. of *asken* to ask] **1 :** not being asked **:** UNINVITED **2 :** not requested ⟨~ advice⟩
un·asking \"+\ *adj* [¹*un-* + *asking*, pres. part. of *ask*] **:** not asking **:** not expressing a desire
un·aspirated \"+\ *adj* [¹*un-* + *aspirated*, past part. of *aspirate*] **:** not aspirated
un·aspiring \"+\ *adj* [¹*un-* + *aspiring*, pres. part. of *aspire*] **:** not aspiring **:** satisfied with one's possessions or position — **un·as·pir·ing·ness** *n* -ES
un·assailable \"+\ *adj* **:** not assailable **:** not liable to doubt, attack, or question ⟨an ~ argument⟩ ⟨an ~ alibi⟩ — **un·as·sail·able·ness** *n* -ES — **un·assailably** \"+\ *adv*
un·assailed \"+\ *adj* [¹*un-* + *assailed*, past part. of *assail*] **:** not assailed **:** free from attack
un·assayed \ˌən+\ *adj* [ME, fr. ¹*un-* + *assayed*, past part. of *assayen* to assay] **:** not assayed **:** UNATTEMPTED
un·assented \"+\ *adj* **:** not assented — used of a stock or bond the holder of which refuses to deposit it by way of assent to an agreement altering its status (as in a readjustment)
un·assertive \"+\ *adj* **:** not assertive **:** MODEST, SHY, RETIRING
un·assignable \"+\ *adj* **:** not assignable
un·assigned \"+\ *adj* [ME, fr. ¹*un-* + *assigned*, past part. of *assignen* to assign] **:** not assigned ⟨~ personnel⟩
un·assimilable \"+\ *adj* **:** not assimilable ⟨eccentrics who are ~ in a civilized society —Bernard Frechtman⟩
un·assimilated \"+\ *adj* [¹*un-* + *assimilated*, past part. of *assimilate*] **:** not assimilated ⟨a disturbing ~ element in the whole society —Oscar Handlin⟩
un·assisted \"+\ *adj* [¹*un-* + *assisted*, past part. of *assist*] **:** not assisted **:** lacking help
un·associated \"+\ *adj* [¹*un-* + *associated*, past part. of *associate*] **:** not associated
un·assorted \"+\ *adj* **:** UNSORTED, MIXED
un·as·suage·able \ˌənəˈswājəbəl\ *adj* [¹*un-* + *assuage* + *-able*] **:** not capable of being assuaged
un·assuaged \ˌən+\ *adj* [¹*un-* + *assuaged*, past part. of *assuage*] **:** not assuaged ⟨an ~ desire⟩
un·assuming \"+\ *adj* **:** not assuming **:** not bold or forward **:** not arrogant or presuming **:** MODEST, RETIRING ⟨~ to a fault, skeptical about the value of his work —*Man*⟩ — **un·as·sum·ing·ness** *n* -ES
un·assured \"+\ *adj* [ME, fr. ¹*un-* + *assured* safe, assured] **1 :** UNSAFE **2 :** not assured **:** lacking boldness or confidence
un·astonished \"+\ *adj* [¹*un-* + *astonished*, past part. of *astonish*] **:** not astonished
un·aton·able \ˌənəˈtōnəbəl\ *adj* [¹*un-* + *atone* + *-able*] **:** IRRECONCILABLE
un·atoned \ˌən+\ *adj* [¹*un-* + *atoned*, past part. of *atone*] **:** not atoned **:** UNEXPIATED
un·attached \"+\ *adj* [¹*un-* + *attached*, past part. of *attach*] **1 a :** not assigned or committed to a particular task, organization, or person; *specif* **:** not committed by engagement, marriage, date, or other promise to a particular person of the opposite sex ⟨an unhappily married man whose passion for his acres is interrupted by his meeting an ~ girl —James Stern⟩ **b :** not seized, taken, or arrested as security for any legal judgment or decree that may later be obtained **2 :** not joined or united ⟨~ polyps⟩
un·attack·able \ˌənəˈtakəbəl\ *adj* **:** not attackable — **un·at·tack·ably** \-blē\ *adv*
un·attacked \ˌən+\ *adj* [¹*un-* + *attacked*, past part. of *attack*] **:** not attacked **:** free from attack
un·at·tain·able \ˌənəˈtānəbəl\ *adj* **:** not attainable ⟨an ~ ideal⟩ — **un·at·tain·able·ness** *n* — **un·at·tain·ably** \-blē\ *adv*
un·attained \ˌən+\ *adj* [¹*un-* + *attained*, past part. of *attain*] **:** not attained **:** UNREACHED
un·attainted \"+\ *adj* [¹*un-* + *attainted*, past part. of *attaint*] **1** *obs* **:** IMPARTIAL ⟨with ~ eye, compare her face with some that I shall show —Shak.⟩ **2** *archaic* **:** UNINFECTED, UNTAINTED **3 :** not attainted
un·attempted \"+\ *adj* [¹*un-* + *attempted*, past part. of *attempt*] **1 :** not attempted **:** UNTRIED **2** *obs* **:** UNATTACKED
un·attended \"+\ *adj* [¹*un-* + *attended*, past part. of *attend*] **1 :** not attended: **a :** lacking a guard, escort, caretaker, or other watcher ⟨~ women⟩ ⟨an ~ lighthouse⟩ ⟨a fire left ~⟩ **b :** lacking people in attendance ⟨an ~ meeting⟩ **2 :** UNACCOMPANIED ⟨problems . . . ~ with dangers —G.F.Eliot⟩ **3 a :** not cared for **:** UNTENDED ⟨if left ~ the road would quickly lose its alignment —O.S.Nock⟩ **b :** not watched with care, attentiveness, or accuracy ⟨sudden August storms that burst ~ —Oscar Handlin⟩ ⟨do not live out our lives ~ by divinity —*Amer. Scholar*⟩
un·attentive \"+\ *adj* **:** not attentive
un·attenuated \"+\ *adj* [¹*un-* + *attenuated*, past part. of *attenuate*] **:** not attenuated
un·attested \"+\ *adj* [¹*un-* + *attested*, past part. of *attest*] **:** not attested
un·attired \"+\ *adj* [ME *unatired*, fr. ¹*un-* + *atired*, *attired*, past part. of *atiren*, *attiren* to attire] **:** UNCLOTHED
un·attractive \"+\ *adj* **:** not attractive **:** lacking beauty, interest, or charm **:** PLAIN, DULL, DREARY ⟨the ~ appearance and slovenly habits of his third wife —Alan Hynd⟩ ⟨~, as are most mining regions —Samuel Van Valkenburg & Ellsworth Huntington⟩ — **un·attractively** \"+\ *adv* — **un·attractiveness** \"+\ *n*
un·attuned \"+\ *adj* [¹*un-* + *attuned*, past part. of *attune*] **:** not attuned
unau \yüˈnō, ˈ=,=, üˈnau̇\ *n* -S [F, of Tupian origin; akin to Tupi *unáu*] **:** a two-toed sloth (*Choloepus didactylus*)
un·audible \ˌən+\ *adj* **:** INAUDIBLE
un·audited \"+\ *adj* [¹*un-* + *audited*, past part. of *audit*] **:** not audited
un·augmented \"+\ *adj* [¹*un-* + *augmented*, past part. of *augment*] **:** not augmented
un·auspicious \"+\ *adj* **:** INAUSPICIOUS — **un·aus·pi·cious·ly** *adv*
un·authentic \"+\ *adj* **:** INAUTHENTIC — **un·authenticity** \"+\ *n*
un·authenticated \"+\ *adj* [¹*un-* + *authenticated*, past part. of *authenticate*] **:** not authenticated
un·authoritative \"+\ *adj* **:** not authoritative — **un·au·thoritatively** \"+\ *adv*
un·au·tho·rized \ˌənˈȯthəˌrīzd\ *adj* **:** not authorized ⟨an ~ use of government airplanes⟩ ⟨~ speeches⟩ — **un·au·tho·riz·ed·ly** \-zədlē\ *adv*
un·availability \ˌən+\ *n* **:** lack of availability ⟨the ~ of medical supplies endangered the wounded⟩
un·avail·able \ˌənəˈvāləbəl\ *adj* **1 :** UNAVAILING **2 :** not available — **un·avail·able·ness** *n* — **un·avail·ably** \-blē\ *adv*
unavailable energy *n* **:** energy that is incapable of doing work under existing conditions — compare AVAILABLE ENERGY, DEGRADATION OF ENERGY, ENTROPY
un·availing \ˌən+\ *adj* [¹*un-* + *availing*, pres. part. of *avail*] **:** not availing **:** FUTILE, USELESS — **un·avail·ing·ly** *adv*
un·avenged \"+\ *adj* [¹*un-* + *avenged*, past part. of *avenge*] **:** not avenged
un·averted \"+\ *adj* [¹*un-* + *averted*, past part. of *avert*] **:** not turned aside

una vo·ce \'ünə'vōkā, 'yünə'vōsē\ *adv* [L, with one voice] : with one voice : UNANIMOUSLY

un·avoid·abil·i·ty \,ənə,vȯidə'biləd·ē\ *n* : the quality or state of being unavoidable

un·avoidable \,ən+\ *adj* [1*un-* + *avoid* + *-able*] : not avoidable : incapable of being shunned or prevented : INEVITABLE ⟨~ mistakes⟩ ⟨natural and ~ material of verse —H.O.Taylor⟩ — **un·avoid·able·ness** *n* -ES — **un·avoidably** \"+\ *adv*

unavoidable casualty *or* **unavoidable accident** *n* : an unintended occurrence that cannot be avoided by the degree of care required of a person under all the circumstances : a casualty or accident happening without fault of any person involved — compare ACT OF GOD

un·avowed \"+\ *adj* : not avowed : not affirmed, mentioned, or declared — **un·avowedly** \"+\ *adv*

un·awakened \"+\ *adj* [1*un-* + *awakened*, past part. of *awaken*] : not awakened; *specif* : not enlivened or activated ⟨~ taste buds⟩ ⟨~ emotions⟩

1un·aware \,ənə,wa(ə)(ə)r, -weⅼ, ǀə\ *adv* [back-formation fr. *unawares*] : UNAWARES ⟨may involve himself ~ —W.G.Perry & C.P.Whitlock⟩

2unaware \"\ *adj* [1*un-* + *aware*] : not aware : lacking knowledge or acquaintance : UNCONSCIOUS ⟨~ of the seriousness of the situation —H.W.Van Loon⟩ — **un·aware·ly** *adv* — **un·aware·ness** *n*

un·awar·ed·ly \-wa(ə)rədlē, -wer-\ *adv* [obs. E *unawared*, adj., not forewarned (fr. E 1*un-* + assumed obs. E *awared*, past part. of assumed obs. E *aware*, v., to alert, fr. E *aware*, adj.) + E *-ly*] : without warning : UNEXPECTEDLY ⟨his voice became ~ loud —H.D.Skidmore⟩

un·awares \-wa(ə)(ə)rz, -weⅼ, ǀəz\ *adv* [1*un-* + *aware* + *-s*, adv. suffix (fr. ME *-s*, *-es*, gen. sing. ending of nouns) — more at -'s] **1** : without design, attention, preparation, or premeditation ⟨as to my pronunciation, it improved rapidly and ~ —George Santayana⟩ **2** : without warning : SUDDENLY, UNEXPECTEDLY ⟨a malicious gust of wind caught them ~ —Aldous Huxley⟩ — **at unawares** *or* **at unaware** *adv*, *archaic* : UNAWARES ⟨let destruction come upon him *at unawares* —Ps 35:8 (AV)⟩

un·awed \,ən+\ *adj* : not awed

unb *abbr* unbound

un·backed \,ən+\ *adj* [1*un-* + *backed*, past part. of *back*] **1** : never mounted by a rider : UNBROKEN **2** : not supported or encouraged : UNAIDED **3** : having no back ⟨an ~ stool⟩

un·baffled \"+\ *adj* [1*un-* + *baffled*, past part. of *baffle*] : not baffled: as **a** : UNPERPLEXED **b** : UNHINDERED **c** : having no baffles ⟨an ~ boiler⟩

un·bag \"+\ *vt* [2*un-* + *bag*] : to pour, take, or let go out of a bag

un·bailable \"+\ *adj* : not bailable ⟨an ~ offense⟩

un·baked \"+\ *adj* [1*un-* + *baked*, past part. of *bake*] **1** : not baked ⟨~ tile⟩ **2** *obs* : IMMATURE

1un·balance \"+\ *vt* [2*un-* + *balance*, v.] : to put out of balance ⟨raise taxes and ~ the budget —Reinhold Niebuhr⟩ ⟨everybody's face has a feature or features that ~ it —Wally Westmore⟩; *specif* : to derange mentally ⟨ardor in the cause . . . threatened to ~ his mind —J.F.Fulton⟩

2unbalance \"\ *n* [1*un-* + *balance*, n.] : lack of balance : IMBALANCE; *specif* : mental derangement ⟨the ~ of even the full-fledged paranoiac is sometimes hard to detect —H.A.Overstreet⟩

un·balanced \"+\ *adj* **1 a** : not in equipoise : having no counterpoise or having insufficient counterpoise **b** : being or being thrown out of equilibrium **c** : mentally disordered or deranged **2** : not brought to an equality of debit and credit ⟨an ~ account⟩ **3** : of, relating to, or being an offensive line or backfield formation in football with more players on one side of the center **4** : containing a singleton or void with reciprocally greater length in another suit or suits — used of a hand in bridge or its distribution

un·ballast \,ən+\ *vt* [2*un-* + *ballast*] : to remove ballast from

un·ballasted \"+\ *adj* [1*un-* + *ballasted*, past part. of *ballast*] **1** : not furnished with or steadied by ballast : UNSTEADY **2** : lightly provided with reason or sense

un·bandage \"+\ *vt* [2*un-* + *bandage*] : to remove a bandage from

un·banded \"+\ *adj* **1** : not provided with a band ⟨an ~ bird⟩ **2** *obs* : UNFASTENED

un·banked \"+\ *adj* [1*un-* + *banked*, past part. of *bank* (to deposit in a bank)] : not deposited in a bank

un·baptize \"+\ *vt* [2*un-* + *baptize*] : to remove the effect of baptism from

un·baptized \"+\ *adj* [ME, fr. 1*un-* + *baptized*, past part. of *baptizen* to baptize] : not baptized; *also* : HEATHENISH, PROFANE

un·bar \"+\ *vt* [ME *unbarren*, fr. 2*un-* + *barren* to bar] : to remove a bar from : UNBOLT, OPEN

un·barbarize \"+\ *vt* [2*un-* + *barbarize*] : to make less barbarous : CIVILIZE

un·barbed \,ən+\ *adj* [1*un-* + *barbed*, past part. of *barb*] : not provided with a barb ⟨an ~ fishhook⟩

un·barbered \"+\ *adj* [1*un-* + *barbered*, past part. of *barber*] : not barbered : UNCUT, UNSHAVEN

un·bare \"+\ *vt* [2*un-* + *bare*] : STRIP, UNCOVER, BARE

un·barred \"+\ *adj* [1*un-* + *barred*, past part. of *bar*] **1** : not secured by a bar : UNLOCKED **2** [1*un-* + *barred*] : not marked with bars ⟨~ plumage⟩

un·bashful \"+\ *adj* : not bashful — **un·bashfully** \"+\ *adv*

un·bated \"+\ *adj* [1*un-* + *bated*, past part. of *bate* (to moderate)] **1** : UNABATED **2** *archaic* : not blunted

un·bathed \"+\ *adj* [1*un-* + *bathed*, past part. of *bathe*] : not bathed

un·battered \"+\ *adj* [1*un-* + *battered*, past part. of *batter* (to beat)] : not battered : free from blows

unbd *abbr* unbound

1un·be \,ən'bē\ *vi* [ME *unbeen*, fr. 1*un-* + *been* to be] *archaic* : to lack or cease to have being

2unbe *vt* [2*un-* + *be*] *obs* : to cause to cease to be

un·bearable \,ən+\ *adj* [ME *unberable*, fr. 1*un-* + *beren* to bear + *-able*] : not bearable : UNENDURABLE — **un·bear·able·ness** *n* -ES — **un·bearably** \"+\ *adv*

un·bearded \"+\ *adj* : having no beard

un·bearing \"+\ *adj* : BARREN, INFERTILE

un·beat·able \,ən'bēd·əbəl, -ētəb-\ *adj* [1*un-* + *beat* + *-able*] : not capable of being defeated : possessing unsurpassable qualities

un·beaten \,ən+\ *adj* **1** : not ground into small bits by beating **2** : UNTROD **3** : UNDEFEATED

un·beauteous \"+\ *adj* : not beauteous : PLAIN, UNATTRACTIVE — **un·beau·te·ous·ness** *n*

un·beautified \"+\ *adj* [1*un-* + *beautified*, past part. of *beautify*] : not beautified : not provided with beautiful features

un·beautiful \"+\ *adj* : not beautiful : UNATTRACTIVE; *esp* : UGLY — **un·beautifully** \"+\ *adv*

un·beautify \"+\ *vt* [2*un-* + *beautify*] : to deprive of beauty

un·beclouded \"+\ *adj* [1*un-* + *beclouded*, past part. of *becloud*] : UNCLOUDED

un·become \"+\ *vt* [1*un-* + *become*] : not to become : MISBECOME

un·becoming \"+\ *adj* : not becoming : UNSUITABLE, INDECOROUS, IMPROPER ⟨charged with conduct ~ to a soldier —James Jones⟩ — **un·be·com·ing·ly** *adv* — **un·be·com·ing·ness** *n*

un·bed \"+\ *vt* [2*un-* + *bed*] : to stir or remove from a bed

un·befitting \"+\ *adj* : not befitting : UNSUITABLE — **un·be·fit·ting·ly** *adv* — **un·be·fit·ting·ness** *n*

un·befriended \"+\ *adj* [1*un-* + *befriended*, past part. of *befriend*] : having no friend

un·beginning \"+\ *adj* [1*un-* + *beginning*, pres. part. of *begin*] : having no beginning

un·begot \"+\ *adj* [1*un-* + *begot*, past part. of *beget*] *archaic* : UNBEGOTTEN

un·begotten \"+\ *adj* [1*un-* + *begotten*, past part. of *beget*] **1** : not begotten **2** : having never been generated : SELF-EXISTENT, ETERNAL

un·be·gun \,ənbə'gən, -bē'-\ *adj* [ME *unbegunnen*, fr. OE, fr. 1*un-* + *begunnen*, past part. of *beginnan* to begin] **1** : existing from all eternity without beginning **2** : not yet begun

un·beheld \,ən+\ *adj* [1*un-* + *beheld*, past part. of *behold*] : UNSEEN

un·beholden \"+\ *adj* [1*un-* + *beholden*, adj.] **1** : not beholden **2** [1*un-* + *beholden*, archaic past part. of *behold*] : UNBEHELD

un·be·known \,ənbə'nōn, -bē'-\ *or* **un·be·knownst** \-ōnzt, -ōn(t)st\ *adj* [*unbeknown* fr. 1*un-* + obs. E *beknown* known, familiar, fr. ME *beknowen*, past part. of *beknowen* to become acquainted with, fr. OE *becnāwan*, fr. *be-* + *cnāwan* to know; *unbeknownst* irreg. fr. *unbeknown* — more at KNOW] : happening without one's knowledge : UNKNOWN — usu. used with *to* ⟨two elderly women ~ to anybody —J.H.Holmes⟩

un·belief \,ən+\ *n* [ME *unbeleve*, fr. 1*un-* + *beleve* belief] : withholding of belief : incredulity or skepticism esp. in matters of religious faith ⟨a reaction . . . against rationalism and ~ —A.C.McGiffert⟩

un·believable \"+\ *adj* [1*un-* + *believable*] : not believable : INCREDIBLE — **un·believably** \"+\ *adv*

1un·believe \"+\ *vb* [1*un-* + *believe*] : DISBELIEVE

2unbelieve \"\ *vt* [2*un-* + *believe*] : to reject from belief

un·believer \"+\ *n* [1*un-* + *believer*] **1** : one that does not believe : an incredulous person : DOUBTER, SKEPTIC **2** : DISBELIEVER, INFIDEL

un·believing \"+\ *adj* [ME *unbylefynge*, fr. 1*un-* + *bylefynge*, *bilevinge*, pres. part. of *bileven* to believe] **1** : not believing : INCREDULOUS, DOUBTING, DISTRUSTING, SKEPTICAL **2** : disbelieving esp. a particular divine revelation — **un·be·liev·ing·ly** *adv* — **un·be·liev·ing·ness** *n* -ES

un·belonging \"+\ *adj* [1*un-* + *belonging*, pres. part. of *belong*] : not belonging ⟨never taking a thing ~ to them —James Still⟩

un·be·loved \,ənbə'ləvd\ *adj* : UNLOVED

un·belt \,ən+\ *vt* [ME *unbelten* to ungird, fr. 2*un-* + *belten* to belt] : to remove one's belt; *also* : to remove (as a sword) by removing a belt

un·belted \"+\ *adj* : not furnished with a belt

un·bend \"+\ *vb* [ME *unbenden*, fr. 2*un-* + *benden* to bend] *vt* **1** : to free from flexure : make or allow to become straight ⟨~ a bow⟩ **2** : to remit from strain or exertion : set at ease for a time : cause to relax ⟨~ the mind from study⟩ **3** *obs* : SLACKEN **4 a** : to unfasten (as a sail) from a spar or stay **b** : to cast loose or untie (as a rope) ~ *vi* **1 a** : to relax one's severity, stiffness, or austerity ⟨she *unbent* a little, losing something of her marble acquiescence —A.J.Cronin⟩ **b** : to give oneself wholeheartedly to affability, mirth, or amusement ⟨an office party where everyone ~*s* and regrets it —Frederick Laws⟩ **2** : to cease to be bent : become straight or relaxed

un·bendable \"+\ *adj* : not bendable; *esp* : not capable of being turned from a goal : of set purpose : SINGLE-MINDED, FIRM ⟨a man of ~ perseverance —*Times Lit. Supp.*⟩

1un·bending \"+\ *adj* [1*un-* + *bending*, pres. part. of *bend*] **1** : not bending : UNYIELDING ⟨the ~, wind-swept ruggedness of that tree —H.A.Overstreet⟩ **2 a** : not given to altering a purpose or opinion : RESOLUTE, INFLEXIBLE ⟨a man of violent temper, stern and ~ in the performance of what he considers to be his duty —C.B.Nordhoff & J.N.Hall⟩ **b** : that does not unbend : cool, aloof, or unsocial in manner or mien : RESERVED — **un·bend·ing·ly** *adv* — **un·bend·ing·ness** *n* -ES

2unbending *adj* [fr. pres. part. of *unbend*] : that unbends : given to relaxation

un·beneficed \,ən+\ *adj* [1*un-* + *beneficed*, past part. of *benefice*] : not beneficed

un·beneficial \"+\ *adj* : not beneficial : HARMFUL

un·benefited \"+\ *adj* [1*un-* + *benefited*, past part. of *benefit*] : not benefited : UNHELPED

un·benevolent \"+\ *adj* : not benevolent : desiring or causing harm

un·benight \"+\ *vt* [2*un-* + *benight*] *archaic* : to free from night or darkness

un·benign \"+\ *adj*, *archaic* : UNBENIGNANT

un·benignant \"+\ *adj* : not benignant : MALIGNANT — **un·be·nig·nant·ly** *adv*

un·bent \"+\ *adj* [ME, fr. 1*un-* + *bent*] **1** : not bent : UNBOWED **2** *obs* : UNWRINKLED **3** : UNSUBDUED

un·bequeathed \"+\ *adj* [1*un-* + *bequeathed*, past part. of *bequeath*] : not bequeathed

un·bereft \"+\ *adj* [1*un-* + *bereft*, past part. of *bereave*] *archaic* : not bereft

un·beseem \"+\ *vt* [1*un-* + *beseem*] : to be unbecoming or unbefitting to

un·besought \"+\ *adj* [1*un-* + *besought*, past part. of *beseech*] : not requested : not asked for

un·bespoken \"+\ *adj* [1*un-* + *bespoken*, past part. of *bespeak*] : not bespoken

un·be·think \,ənbi'thiŋk\ *vt* [ME *unbethinken*, *umbethinken*, *umbethenken* to bethink, consider, fr. OE *ymbthencan*, *ymbethencan* to consider, fr. *ymb*, *ymbe* around + *thencan* to think — more at EMBER DAY, THINK] *dial Brit* : BETHINK

un·beveled \"+\ *adj* [1*un-* + *beveled*, past part. of *bevel*] : not beveled

un·bewailed \"+\ *adj* [1*un-* + *bewailed*, past part. of *bewail*] *archaic* : UNMOURNED

unbewitch *vt* [2*un-* + *bewitch*] *obs* : DISENCHANT

un·biased \,ən+\ *adj* **1** : free from bias **2** : characterized by complete absence of prejudice, favoritism, undue or unwarranted preference, or personal interest : resolute in evenness and equality ⟨~ by self-profit —Alfred Tennyson⟩ ⟨a daughter's story of her father, startlingly honest and ~ —*English Jour.*⟩ **3** *of a statistic* : having an expected value equal to a population parameter being estimated **syn** see FAIR

un·bi·ased·ly *adv* : in an unbiased manner

un·bib·li·cal \,ən'bibləkəl\ *adj* : contrary to, or not conforming with, or unsanctioned by the Bible : UNSCRIPTURAL — **un·bib·li·cal·ly** \-lək(ə)lē\ *adv*

un·bid \,ən'bid\ *adj* [ME *unbedde*, fr. 1*un-* + *bedde*, *biden*, past part. of *bidden* to entreat, invite — more at BID] : UNBIDDEN

un·bid·da·ble \-dəbəl\ *adj*, *Brit* : INTRACTABLE

un·bid·den \,ən'bid°n\ *adj* [ME *unbiden*, *unbeden*, fr. OE *unbeden*, fr. 1*un-* + *beden*, past part. of *biddan* to entreat — more at BID] : not bidden : UNASKED, UNINVITED

un·bigoted \,ən+\ *adj* : not bigoted : UNBIASED

un·bind \,ən'bīnd\ *vt* [ME *unbinden*, fr. OE *unbindan*, *onbindan*, fr. *un-*, *on-* un- + *bindan* to bind] **1 a** : to remove a band from : free from shackles or fastenings : UNTIE, UNFASTEN, LOOSE **b** : to set free : give or restore liberty to : RELEASE **2 a** : to free (as a cord) by or as if by untying a knot or releasing a catch; *also* : to untangle or loose (a knot) by separating the parts **b** : to make less binding, controlling, or restrictive ⟨~*s* the strictures which restrain the full joy in marriage —J.A.Pike⟩

un·binding \,ən+\ *adj* : not binding; *esp* : not imposing a duty or obligation : without restrictive force ⟨the contract was ~⟩

un·bitt \,ən+\ *vt* [2*un-* + *bitt*] : to remove the turns of (a rope or cable) from a bitt

un·bitted \"+\ *adj* [1*un-* + *bitted*, past part. of *bit*] : UNBRIDLED, UNCONTROLLED

un·bitter \"+\ *adj* : not bitter : having or exhibiting no feelings of malice, resentment, or revenge ⟨remarkably ~ toward . . . her captors —J.K.Hutchens⟩

un·blacked \"+\ *adj* [1*un-* + *blacked*, past part. of *black*] : not blacked ⟨~ shoes⟩

un·blackened \"+\ *adj* [1*un-* + *blackened*, past part. of *blacken*] : not blackened

un·blamable \"+\ *adj* : BLAMELESS — **un·blamably** \"+\ *adv*

un·blamed \"+\ *adj* [ME, fr. 1*un-* + *blamed*, past part. of *blamen* to blame] : not blamed

un·blanched \"+\ *adj* [ME, fr. 1*un-* + *blanched*, *blaunched*, past part. of *blanchen*, *blaunchen* to blanch] : not whitened : UNBLEACHED

un·blasted \"+\ *adj* : UNBLIGHTED

un·bleached \"+\ *adj* [1*un-* + *bleached*, past part. of *bleach*] : not bleached

un·blemished \,ən+\ *adj* [ME *unblemisshed*, fr. 1*un-* + *blemisshed*, past part. of *blemisshen* to blemish] : not blemished : free from physical or moral spots or stains : PURE

un·blenched \"+\ *adj* [1*un-* + *blenched*, past part. of *blench* (to flinch)] : not disconcerted : UNDAUNTED

un·blenching \"+\ *adj* [1*un-* + *blenching*, pres. part. of *blench* (to flinch)] : UNBLENCHED, UNFLINCHING — **un·blench·ing·ly** *adv*

un·blended \"+\ *adj* [ME, fr. 1*un-* + *blended*, past part. of *blenden* to blend, mix] : not blended : UNMIXED

un·blent \"+\ *adj* [1*un-* + *blent*, past part. of *blend*] : UNBLENDED

un·blessed *also* **un·blest** \,ən'blest\ *adj* [ME, fr. 1*un-* + *blessed*, *blest*] **1 a** : UNCONSECRATED **b** : UNHOLY, EVIL, ACCURSED **c** : excluded from or not having received blessing and esp. religious blessing **2** : not provided with a good : UNFORTUNATE, LACKING ⟨his hut which was ~ with electricity —L.K.Liang⟩ — **un·bless·ed·ness** \-sədnəs\ *n*

un·blighted \,ən+\ *adj* : not blighted : FRESH, PURE — **un·blight·ed·ly** *adv*

un·blind \"+\ *vt* [2*un-* + *blind*] : to free from blindness or illusion

un·blinded \"+\ *adj* : not blinded; *also* : being without illusion : UNDECEIVED

un·blinking \"+\ *adj* [1*un-* + *blinking*, pres. part. of *blink*] **1** : not blinking **2** : not exhibiting signs of emotion, doubt, or confusion ⟨stood ~ in District Court and accepted a sentence of a year —*Springfield (Mass.) Daily News*⟩ **3** : honest, accurate, and fearless in examination ⟨~ sincerity is the first requisite in writing amateur plays —*Harper's*⟩ — **un·blink·ing·ly** *adv*

un·block \"+\ *vt* [2*un* + *block*] : to free from being blocked ⟨~ an alien's assets⟩; *specif* : to play the cards of (a suit) so that the last trick on which a hand can follow suit will be taken by a higher card in the hand of the partner who has the remaining cards of a combined holding

un·blocked \"+\ *adj* [1*un-* + *blocked*, past part. of *block*] : not shaped by a block ⟨an ~ hat⟩

un·blooded \"+\ *adj* [1*un-* + *blooded*, past part. of *blood*] **1** : UNBLOODIED **2** [1*un-* + *blooded*, adj.] : not purebred

un·bloodied \"+\ *adj* [1*un-* + *bloodied*, past part. of *bloody*] : not bloodied

unbloodily *adv* : in an unbloody manner

un·bloody \,ən+\ *adj* : not bloody ⟨pagan emperors who fought easy and ~ wars —Albert Solomon⟩; *specif* : BLOODLESS

unbloody sacrifice *n* : EUCHARIST

un·blotted \,ən+\ *adj* [1*un-* + *blotted*, past part. of *blot*] : not blotted; *esp* : PURE, UNDEFILED

1un·blown \"+\ *adj* [1*un-* + *blown* (open, having bloomed)] : not blown; *esp* : not yet in blossom

2unblown \"\ *adj* [1*un-* + *blown* (moved or acted upon by moving air)] : not blown by the wind

un·blunted \"+\ *adj* [1*un-* + *blunted*, past part. of *blunt*] : not blunted : SHARP, KEEN

un·blurred \"+\ *adj* : not blurred : sharply delineated : CLEAR

un·blushing \"+\ *adj* **1** : not blushing **2** : SHAMELESS, UNABASHED ⟨the most ~ of self-portrayals —P.R.Levin⟩ — **un·blush·ing·ly** *adv* — **un·blush·ing·ness** *n* -ES

un·boastful \"+\ *adj* : not boastful : MODEST — **un·boast·fully** \"+\ *adv*

un·bodied \"+\ *adj* [partly fr. 1*un-* + *bodied* (having a body); partly fr. past part. of *unbody*] **1** : having no body : INCORPOREAL; *also* : DISEMBODIED **2** : FORMLESS

un·bodily \"+\ *adj* [ME, fr. 1*un-* + *bodily*] : INCORPOREAL

un·body \"+\ *vt* [2*un-* + *body*] : DISEMBODY

un·boiled \,ən+\ *adj* : not boiled

un·bolt \"+\ *vt* [2*un-* + *bolt* (to fasten)] : to open, loosen, or unfasten by or as if by withdrawing a bolt

1un·bolted \"+\ *adj* [1*un-* + *bolted*, past part. of *bolt* (to sift)] : not bolted : UNSIFTED ⟨~ flour⟩; *also* : COARSE, GROSS

2unbolted \"\ *adj* [1*un-* + *bolted*, past part. of *bolt* (to fasten)] : not fastened by bolts

un·bonnet \"+\ *vb* [2*un-* + *bonnet*, n.] *vi* : to remove one's bonnet esp. as a mark of respect ~ *vt* : to take a bonnet from

un·bon·net·ed \,ən'banəd·əd\ *adj* [1*un-* + *bonnet*, n. + *-ed*] : having no bonnet or other headgear on : UNCOVERED, BAREHEADED

un·bookish \,ən+\ *adj* : not bookish : not given to reading; *also* : UNLEARNED

un·bored \"+\ *adj* [1*un-* + *bored*, past part. of *bore* (to pierce)] : not bored : UNPIERCED; *also* : not provided with a bore

un·born \"+\ *adj* [ME, fr. OE *unboren*, fr. 1*un-* + *boren* born] : not born : not brought into life ⟨his male descendant, as yet ~ —Joseph Hitrec⟩; *broadly* : still to appear : FUTURE ⟨projected figures are ~ statistics, statistics of the future —*New Yorker*⟩ **2** : existing without birth

un·borrowed \"+\ *adj* [1*un-* + *borrowed*, past part. of *borrow*] : not borrowed; *esp* : NATURAL, NATIVE, INHERENT

un·bosom \"+\ *vt* [2*un-* + *bosom*, n.] **1 a** : to give expression to : DISCLOSE, REVEAL ⟨freely ~*ing* his perplexities and his anguish —J.S.C.Abbott⟩ **b** : to express the thoughts or feelings of (oneself) ⟨~*s* herself in conversations, in letters, in intimate diaries —H.M.Parshley⟩ **2** *archaic* : to spread out : DISPLAY ~ *vi* : to unbosom oneself

un·bottomed \"+\ *adj* [1*un-* + *bottomed*, past part. of *bottom*] : BOTTOMLESS

un·bought \"+\ *adj* [ME, fr. OE *unboht*, fr. 1*un-* + *boht* bought, past part. of *bycgan* to buy — more at BUY] : not bought

1un·bound \"+\ *adj* [ME *unbounden*, fr. OE *unbunden*, fr. 1*un-* + *bunden* bound, past part. of *bindan* to bind — more at BIND] : not bound: as **a** (1) : UNFASTENED (2) : UNCONFINED **b** : not having the leaves fastened or sewn together ⟨an ~ book⟩ **c** : not held in chemical or physical combination

2unbound *adj* [prob. fr. 1*un-* + (assumed) obs. E *bound*, past part. of E *bound* (to set limits to)] *obs* : UNBOUNDED

un·bounded \,ən+\ *adj* [1*un-* + *bounded*, past part. of *bound* (to set limits to)] **1** : having no bound : unlimited in extent, degree, or quantity ⟨wealth poured in . . . and luxury grew more ~ —J.S.Froude⟩ ⟨~ space⟩ ⟨the work was received with ~ enthusiasm —*Amer. Guide Series: Ind.*⟩ **2** : UNCHECKED, UNCONTROLLED, UNRESTRAINED ⟨the ~ freedom of pure mathematics —Samuel Alexander⟩ — **un·bound·ed·ly** *adv* — **un·bound·ed·ness** *n*

un·bowdlerized \"+\ *adj* [1*un-* + *bowdlerized*, past part. of *bowdlerize*] : not bowdlerized : UNEXPURGATED

un·bowed \"+\ *adj* [ME, fr. 1*un-* + *bowed* (bent down)] **1** : not bowed down **2** : UNSUBDUED

un·box \,ən+\ *vt* [2*un-* + *box*] : to remove from a box

un·boyish \"+\ *adj* : not boyish : uncharacteristic of a boy

un·brace \,ən'brās\ *vt* [ME *unbracen* to carve, remove clothing or armor from, fr. 2*un-* + *bracen* to fasten tightly — more at BRACE] **1** *archaic* : CARVE, DISJOINT **2 a** : to remove the holding power of by or as if by untying a bond **b** : to free or detach by or as if by untying a brace; *specif* : to untie the string from (a bow) **3** : ENFEEBLE, WEAKEN

un·braced \,ən+\ *adj* [partly fr. 1*un-* + *braced*, past part. of *brace*; partly fr. past part. of obs. E *unbrace* to unfasten, remove clothing or armor from, fr. ME *unbracen*] **1 a** *obs* : not tied by braces ⟨his doublet all ~ —Shak.⟩ **b** : wearing unfastened or loosened clothing **2 a** *obs*, *of a drum* : not taut : free from tension **b** : UNFLEXED, RELAXED

un·bracketed \"+\ *adj* [1*un-* + *bracketed*, past part. of *bracket*] : not bracketed : not enclosed in brackets

un·braid \"+\ *vt* [2*un-* + *braid*] : to separate the strands of (as a braid) : UNRAVEL

un·braided \"+\ *adj* [1*un-* + obs. E *braided* tarnished, fr. E *braided*, adj.] **1** *obs* : UNTARNISHED **2** [1*un-* + *braided*, adj.] : not braided

un·branched \"+\ *adj* [1*un-* + *branched*, past part. of *branch*] **1** : having no branch ⟨an ~ trunk⟩ **2** : not branched ⟨a leaf with ~ veins⟩ **3** : having a straight chain of atoms in the molecule : NORMAL 10e

un·branching \"+\ *adj* [1*un-* + *branching*, pres. part. of *branch*] : not branching

un·branded \"+\ *adj* [1*un-* + *branded*, past part. of *brand*] : not branded; *specif* : not marked with the owner's name or mark ⟨~ cattle⟩

un·breakable \"+\ *adj* [ME *unbrekable*, fr. 1*un-* + *breken* to break + *-able*] : not breakable; *also* : not breakable under ordinary usage

un·breakfasted \"+\ *adj* [1*un-* + *breakfasted*, past part. of *breakfast*] **1** : not having eaten breakfast **2** : not supplied with breakfast

un·breaking \"+\ *adj* [1*un-* + *breaking*, pres. part. of *break*] : not breaking

un·breathable \ˌən+\ *adj* : not breathable ⟨sufficient carbon dioxide gas to render the atmosphere absolutely ~ —Valentine Williams⟩

un·breathed \"+\ *adj* [¹*un-* + *breathed*, past part. of *breathe*] : not breathed

un·breathing \"+\ *adj* [¹*un-* + *breathing*, pres. part. of *breathe*] **1** : not breathing; *esp* : holding one's breath **2** *archaic* : not stirred by a breeze or wind : CALM, STILL

un·bred \"+\ *adj* [¹*un-* + *bred*, past part. of *breed*] **1** *obs* : UNBORN **2** *obs* : not well-bred : ILL-BRED **3** : UNTAUGHT, UNTRAINED **4** : not now bred and usu. never having been bred ⟨an ~ heifer⟩

un·breech \"+\ *vt* [²*un-* + *breech*] : to remove the breeches of

un·breeched \"+\ *adj* [¹*un-* + *breeched*] : not wearing breeches

un·bribable \"+\ *adj* [¹*un-* + *bribe*, v. + *-able*] : not bribable : INCORRUPTIBLE

un·bribed \"+\ *adj* [¹*un-* + *bribed*, past part. of *bribe*] **1** : uncorrupted by bribery **2** : not obtained by bribery

un·bridgeable \"+\ *adj* [¹*un-* + *bridge*, v. + *-able*] : not bridgeable ⟨an ~ stream⟩ ⟨the ~ gap between the experiences and attitudes of frontline soldiers and of the civilians back home —R.G.Davis⟩

un·bridged \"+\ *adj* [¹*un-* + *bridged*, past part. of *bridge*] : not crossed by a bridge

un·bridle \"+\ *vt* [ME *unbridlen*, fr. ²*un-* + *bridlen* to bridle] : to free or loose from a bridle; *broadly* : to set loose : FREE ⟨his annoyance had *unbridled* his tongue —J.H.Wheelwright⟩

un·bridled \"+\ *adj* [ME, fr. ¹*un-* + *bridled*, past part. of *bridlen* to bridle] **1** : not confined by a bridle **2** : completely at liberty : UNRESTRAINED, UNGOVERNED, UNCHECKED ⟨extolled the benevolence of ~ competition in human affairs —Joseph Schiffman⟩ ⟨fantastic charges and ~ insults —William Ridsdale⟩ ⟨~ enthusiasm⟩

un·british \"+\ *adj, usu cap B* : not characteristic of or consistent with British customs, habits, or traditions

un·broached \"+\ *adj* [¹*un-* + *broached*, past part. of *broach* (to tap)] : not broached

un·broke \"+\ *adj* [ME, fr. ¹*un-* + *broke*] **1** : UNBROKEN **2** : not broke ⟨a few raw ~ horses —Bruce Siberts & W.D. Wyman⟩

un·broken \"+\ *adj* [ME, fr. ¹*un-* + *broken*] : not broken: as **a** : UNVIOLATED **b** : WHOLE, INTACT, COMPLETE ⟨~ control of the economic, social and political life —G.M.McBride⟩ **c** : UNSUBDUED, UNTAMED ⟨half-educated and totally ~ to society —*Punch*⟩; *esp* : not trained for service or use ⟨~ range horses⟩ **d** : not interrupted ⟨magnificent gleaming cars in an ~ procession —Winifred Bambrick⟩ ⟨an ~ series of evolving organisms —Waldemar Kaempffert⟩ ⟨100 miles of ~ forest —*Amer. Guide Series: Maine*⟩ **e** : UNPLOWED **f** : not disorganized — **un·bro·ken·ly** *adv* — **un·bro·ken·ness** *n*

un·brook·able \ˌən¦brůkəbəl\ *adj* [¹*un-* + *brook*, v. + *-able*] : UNENDURABLE

un·brother \ˌən+\ *vt* [²*un-* + *brother*] : to deprive of the status of brother

un·broth·er·ly *adj* : not characteristic of or befitting a brother

un·bruised \ˌən+\ *adj* [ME *unbrused*, fr. ¹*un-* + *brused*, past part. of *brusen* to bruise, crush] : not bruised : UNINJURED, SOUND

un·brushed \"+\ *adj* [¹*un-* + *brushed*, past part. of *brush* (to use a brush on)] : not brushed

un·buckle \"+\ *vb* [ME *unboclen*, fr. ²*un-* + *boclen* to buckle] *vt* : to loose the buckle of : UNFASTEN ⟨~ a shoe⟩ ~ *vi* : to loosen a buckle

un·budded \"+\ *adj* [¹*un-* + *budded*, past part. of *bud*] : not budded

un·budge·abil·i·ty \ˌən,bəjə¦biləd·ē\ *n* : the quality or state of being unbudgeable

un·budge·able \ˌən¦bəjəbəl\ *adj* [¹*un-* + *budge*, v. + *-able*] : that cannot be budged ⟨smile blandly with ~ composure —G.N.Kates⟩ — **un·budge·ably** \-blē\ *adv*

un·budging \ˌən+\ *adj* [¹*un-* + *budging*, pres. part. of *budge*] : not budging : resisting movement or change — **un·budg·ing·ly** *adv*

un·build \"+\ *vb* [²*un-* + *build*] : DEMOLISH, RAZE

un·built \"+\ *adj* [ME *unbylyt*, fr. ¹*un-* + *bylyt*, *bilt*, past part. of *bilden* to build — more at BUILD] **1** : not built : not yet constructed **2** : not occupied with a building ⟨an ~ plot⟩ — often used with *on* ⟨ground as yet ~ on⟩

un·bulky \"+\ *adj* : not bulky

un·bung \"+\ *vt* [²*un-* + *bung*] : to remove the bung from

un·burden \"+\ *vt* [²*un-* + *burden*] **1** : to free or relieve from a burden and esp. from something oppressing or depressing the mind or spirit ⟨~s himself . . . of all the accumulated resentment and dislike of years —S.M.Fitzgerald⟩ **2** : to relieve oneself from esp. by expression ⟨~ the worries he can't confess in the office —W.H.Whyte⟩ **syn** see RID

un·burdened \"+\ *adj* [¹*un-* + *burdened*, past part. of *burden*] : not burdened : having no weight or load ⟨~ by an overarching theory —Alex Inkeles⟩

un·buried \"+\ *adj* [ME, fr. OE *unbyrged*, fr. ¹*un-* + *byrged*, past part. of *byrgan* to bury] : not buried

un·burned \"+\ *adj* [ME *unbirned*, fr. ¹*un-* + *birned*, past part. of *birnen* to burn] : not burned ⟨built of ~ bricks⟩

un·burnished \"+\ *adj* : not burnished : UNPOLISHED, DULL

un·burnt \ˌən+\ *adj* [¹*un-* + *burnt*, past part. of *burn*] : UNBURNED

un·burst \"+\ *adj* : not burst

un·bury \"+\ *vt* [ME *unberien*, fr. ²*un-* + *berien* to bury] : DISINTER, EXHUME

un·busy \"+\ *adj* : not busy : UNOCCUPIED

un·buttered \"+\ *adj* [¹*un-* + *buttered*, past part. of *butter*] : not buttered : lacking butter ⟨water and ~ bread⟩

un·button \"+\ *vb* [ME *unbotonen*, fr. ²*un-* + *botonen* to button] *vt* **1** : to loose the buttons of : unfasten by loosing buttons ⟨~*ed* his coat⟩; *also* : to remove (a button) from a buttonhole **2** : to open as if by unbuttoning ⟨~*ed* my heart to him —*Omnibook*⟩ ⟨a team of experts in the code room has ~*ed* it —E.O.Hauser⟩; *specif* : to open the hatches or apertures of (an armored vehicle) ~ *vi* : to undo a button

un·buttoned \"+\ *adj* [¹*un-* + *buttoned*, adj.] **1 a** : not buttoned **b** : not provided with buttons **2** : not under constraint : free and unrestricted in action or expression ⟨this ~ and disrespectful age —Curtis Bok⟩ ⟨outburst of ~ rhetoric —F.L. Allen⟩ **3** : deprived of strength or stability ⟨her moral fiber had suddenly become ~ —Ellen Glasgow⟩

un·buttressed \"+\ *adj* [¹*un-* + *buttressed*, past part. of *buttress*] : not buttressed : UNSUPPORTED ⟨one of the few really ~ statements in the book —Priscilla Robertson⟩

unc *abbr* **1** uncertain **2** uncirculated **3** uncut

un·cage \ˌən+\ *vt* [²*un-* + *cage*] : to release from or as if from a cage

un·cal \ˈəŋkəl\ *adj* [*uncus* + *-al*] : of or relating to an uncus

un·calcified \ˌən+\ *adj* [¹*un-* + *calcified*, past part. of *calcify*] : not calcified

un·calculated \"+\ *adj* : not planned or thought out beforehand : IMPROVISED ⟨a rough and ~ style —Winthrop Sargeant⟩

un·calculating \"+\ *adj* : not based on or marked by calculation : not self-interested ⟨flung his defiance at the entrenched enemy with the courage of ~ youth —V.L.Parrington⟩ — **un·cal·cu·lat·ing·ly** *adv*

un·called \"+\ *adj* [ME, fr. ¹*un-* + *called*, past part. of *callen* to call] : not asked for or invited; *specif* : not called up for payment ⟨protected by paid-up and ~ capital —*Economist*⟩

un·called-for \ˌən¦kȯld,fȯ(ə)r, -ȯ(ə)\ *adj* [¹*un-* + *called for*, past part. form of the phrase *call for*] **1** : not called for or needed : UNNECESSARY ⟨in those areas rationing has on the surface seemed *uncalled-for* —*Harper's*⟩ **2 a** : not warranted : being without cause or occasion : GRATUITOUS ⟨much of his bitterness is *uncalled-for* —Thomas Halton⟩ **b** : RUDE, IMPERTINENT ⟨an *uncalled-for* comment⟩ ⟨his display of temper was *uncalled-for*⟩

¹**un·cal·low** \ˌən'kalō\ *vb* -ED/-ING/-S [²*un-* + *callow*, n.] *vt, dial Eng* : to remove the layer of soil above the subsoil from ~ *vi, dial Eng* : to clear off the layer of soil above the subsoil

²**uncallow** \"\ *n, dial Eng* : the layer of soil above the subsoil

un·candid \ˌən+\ *adj* : not frank or aboveboard : DISINGENUOUS ⟨was sometimes ~, to put no harsher name to his conduct —Broadus Mitchell⟩ — **un·can·did·ly** *adv* — **un·can·did·ness** *n*

un·candor \"+\ *n* : lack of candor

un·cannily \"+\ *adv* : in an uncanny manner : to an uncanny degree ⟨the present crop of ~ human robots —H.W.Baldwin⟩

un·canniness \"+\ *n* : the quality or state of being uncanny ⟨a curlew added to the ~ of the quiet solitude as its wail swept across the night —Myrtle R. White⟩

un·canny \"+\ *adj* **1 a** : arousing feelings of dread or of inexplicable strangeness : seeming to have a supernatural character, cause, or origin : EERIE, MYSTERIOUS, WEIRD ⟨it was that saddest, most ~ thing — a deserted house —Clara Morris⟩ ⟨~ as the shadows of unfamiliar furniture on the walls of an inn —A.T.Quiller-Couch⟩ **b** : extending to a degree beyond what is normal or expected : suggesting superhuman or supernatural powers or qualities ⟨showed an ~ ability to gauge the public's taste —A.E.Peterson⟩ ⟨his ~ skill with firearms —S.H.Holbrook⟩ **2** *chiefly Scot* : PUNISHING, SEVERE **3** *chiefly Scot* : DANGEROUS **syn** see WEIRD

un·canonical \"+\ *adj* **1** : not being in accord with church canons ⟨an ~ marriage⟩ **2** : not belonging to the canon of biblical books ⟨an ~ work⟩ **3** : UNSANCTIONED, UNORTHODOX ⟨his ~ religious ideas⟩ — **un·canonically** \"+\ *adv*

un·canonize \"+\ *vt* [²*un-* + *canonize*] : to deprive of canonical authority or status

un·cap \"+\ *vt* [²*un-* + *cap*] : to remove a cap or covering from; *specif* : to remove the caps from (a honeycomb) preparatory to extracting honey

un·capable \"+\ *adj* : INCAPABLE

un·capitalized \"+\ *adj* [¹*un-* + *capitalized*, past part. of *capitalize*] : not capitalized

un·cared-for \ˌən¦ka(a)r|d,fȯ(ə)r, -ke|, |əd,fȯ(ə)\ *adj* [¹*un-* + *cared for*, past part. form of the phrase *care for*] **1** : not cared for : UNHEEDED ⟨the *uncared-for* and undisciplined life of the medieval student —G.M.Trevelyan⟩ **2** : RUN-DOWN ⟨an *uncared-for* look has begun to pervade the residential areas —Faubion Bowers⟩

un·careful \ˌən+\ *adj* **1** : not taking care : CARELESS **2** : having no care : CAREFREE

un·car·ia \ˌəŋ'ka(a)rēə\ *n, cap* [NL, fr. L *uncus* hook + NL *-aria* — more at ANGLE] : a large genus of chiefly tropical Asiatic woody vines (family Rubiaceae) having axillary heads of yellow flowers with valvate corollas succeeded by large septicidal many-seeded capsules — see GAMBIER

un·caring \ˌən+\ *adj* [¹*un-* + *caring*, pres. part. of *care*] : HEEDLESS, OBLIVIOUS ⟨sat around as bored and ~ as castaways on a Pacific atoll —Truman Capote⟩

un·carpeted \"+\ *adj* [¹*un-* + *carpeted*, past part. of *carpet*] : not covered or provided with a carpet

un·cart \"+\ *vt* [²*un-* + *cart*, n.] : to take or discharge from a cart

un·case \"+\ *vb* [²*un-* + *case*] *vt* **1** *archaic* : to take off the clothes of ⟨at once ~ thee —Shak.⟩ **2** : to take out of or free from a case or covering : DISCLOSE, UNCOVER; *specif* : to spread to view : DISPLAY ⟨~ the colors⟩ ~ *vi, archaic* : STRIP, UNDRESS ⟨I proceeded to ~, entrenching myself behind a chair —*Spirit of the Times*⟩

un·castrated \"+\ *adj* [¹*un-* + *castrated*, past part. of *castrate*] **1** : not castrated : ENTIRE, INTACT **2** : not expurgated ⟨has printed the ~ text for the first time⟩

un·cataloged \"+\ *adj* [¹*un-* + *cataloged*, past part. of *catalog*] : not cataloged

un·catch·able \ˌən¦kachəbəl, -kech-\ *adj* : not able to be caught ⟨the ~ quality of a shooting star —*View*⟩

un·catholic \ˌən+\ *adj* : not catholic; *specif* : not adhering to, favoring, accepted by, or suitable to a universal Christian church

un·catholicize \"+\ *vt* [²*un-* + *catholicize*] : to make uncatholic

un·caught \"+\ *adj* [ME, fr. ¹*un-* + *caught*, past part. of *cacchen* to catch — more at CATCH] : being at large : FREE ⟨was a bonny girl and could not in the nature of things be long ~ —Israel Zangwill⟩

un·caused \"+\ *adj* [¹*un-* + *caused*, past part. of *cause*] : having no antecedent cause : SELF-EXISTENT ⟨argues backward to a first great cause, which is itself ~ —G.W.Knox⟩

un·ceasing \"+\ *adj* [ME *uncesinge*, fr. ¹*un-* + *cesinge*, pres. part. of *cesen* to cease] : not ceasing : CONTINUOUS, INCESSANT ⟨high hills whose owners wage ~ warfare with drought and isolation —*Amer. Guide Series: Texas*⟩ — **un·ceas·ing·ly** *adv* — **un·ceas·ing·ness** *n* -ES

un·celebrated \"+\ *adj* [¹*un-* + *celebrated*, past part. of *celebrate*] **1** : not formally honored or commemorated ⟨baseball is . . . new to song and story and ~ in the fine arts —M.R. Cohen⟩ **2** : not famous : OBSCURE ⟨untried or ~ author —*Manchester Guardian Weekly*⟩

un·celestial \"+\ *adj* : EARTHY, WORLDLY ⟨a gift from heaven, designed to serve his own rather ~ purpose —R.D.Altick⟩

un·cemented \"+\ *adj* [¹*un-* + *cemented*, past part. of *cement*] : not held together by cement or other substance

un·censored \"+\ *adj* **1** : not subjected to censorship ⟨~ news reports⟩ **2** : not inhibited or restrained in expression ⟨the presentation of ~ observations by the characters of each other —Robert Humphrey⟩

un·censured \"+\ *adj* [¹*un-* + *censured*, past part. of *censure*] : not subjected to blame or criticism

un·center \"+\ *vt* [²*un-* + *center*] : to remove from a center

un·ceremonious \ˌən+\ *adj* **1** : not ceremonious : INFORMAL **2** : ABRUPT, RUDE ⟨his ~ dismissal from office⟩ — **un·cer·e·mo·ni·ous·ly** *adv* — **un·cer·e·mo·ni·ous·ness** *n*

¹**un·certain** \"+\ *adj* [ME, fr. ¹*un-* + *certain*] **1 a** : not fixed in time : being of indefinite date ⟨the exact moment of departure is ~⟩ **b** : indeterminate in number, amount, or extent ⟨engagements being irregular, the income is ~ —*Official Register of Harvard Univ.*⟩ ⟨a tract of ~ acreage —*Amer. Guide Series: Md.*⟩ **2** : not certain to occur : PROBLEMATICAL ⟨her success in new parts was very ~ —G.B.Shaw⟩ **3 a** : not known, demonstrated, or apparent beyond doubt : open to doubt : QUESTIONABLE ⟨unless further evidence is found, his story must remain ~⟩ **b** : AMBIGUOUS ⟨told him, in no ~ terms, what he thought of his behavior⟩ **c** : not clearly identified, defined, or located ⟨a fire of ~ origin destroyed the capitol —*Amer. Guide Series: Pa.*⟩ ⟨a play of ~ authorship⟩ ⟨the two bartenders, sallow women of ~ age —William Sansom⟩ **4 a** : not fixed in place, direction, or course : WANDERING ⟨the silver thread of water tracing its ~ course along the valley floor —E.A.McCourt⟩ **b** : not assured, consistent, or dependable in action, behavior, or effect : ERRATIC, UNRELIABLE ⟨ramshackle buildings lean over the water on their ~ stilts —*Amer. Guide Series: N.Y.City*⟩ ⟨a gun with a rather ~ trigger —D.M.MacKay⟩ **c** : not settled or fixed in character, quality, or state : subject to accident, chance, or change : UNPREDICTABLE ⟨everything is ~ about the army —Walt Whitman⟩ ⟨leading a somewhat ~ existence —*Fortnight*⟩ ⟨~ health⟩ **5 a** : not having certain knowledge or conviction : not assured : DOUBTFUL ⟨tolerant but never ~ of his convictions —W.A. White⟩ **b** : not definitely directed : UNDECIDED ⟨of great ambition, but ~ aim⟩ **c** : HESITANT, TENTATIVE ⟨touching the flowers, the ornaments, the books with ~ fingers —Edith Sitwell⟩ ⟨an ~ gentleness in his tone —Marguerite Steen⟩ **6** : CHANGEABLE, FICKLE, VARIABLE ⟨an ~ breeze⟩ ⟨an ~ friend⟩ ⟨a beautiful and ~ time, cold and wet and dry and warm —Josephine Johnson⟩ — **un·cer·tain·ly** *adv* — **un·cer·tain·ness** *n*

²**uncertain** \"\ *adv* : UNCERTAINLY

un·cer·tain·ty \"+tē *or* tï\ *n* [ME *uncertainte*, fr. ¹*uncertain* + *-te* -ty] **1** : the quality or state of being uncertain : lack of certainty **2** : something that is uncertain : something doubtful or unknown

syn UNCERTAINTY, DOUBT, DUBIETY, DUBIOSITY, SKEPTICISM, SUSPICION, and MISTRUST can all indicate a lack of sureness about something or someone. UNCERTAINTY stresses a lack of certitude ranging from a small falling short of definite knowledge to an almost complete lack of it or even any conviction, esp. about an outcome or result ⟨drove without any *uncertainty* or hesitation as to her route —Margaret Deland⟩ ⟨renewed *uncertainty* about the business outlook —Leo Wolman⟩ ⟨convince others without having experienced either *uncertainty* or conviction himself —C.D.Lewis⟩ ⟨the long *uncertainty* and bloody confusion that attended the breakdown of the Roman Empire —Lewis Mumford⟩ DOUBT can imply uncertainty about the truth or reality of something or an inability to make a decision in respect to it or arrive at conviction even after study, esp. about religious belief ⟨no man likes to have his intelligence or good faith questioned, especially if he has *doubts* about it himself —Henry Adams⟩ ⟨after a very few days more of *doubt* and indecision, the great question of whither he should go was settled —Jane Austen⟩ ⟨a *doubt* about the existence of evil⟩ ⟨the strong religious *doubt* of the nineteenth century⟩ DUBIETY is close to UNCERTAINTY in stressing a questionableness, a lack of sureness, commonly implying also a wavering between conclusions ⟨it threw a kind of *dubiety* upon Susan's moral conduct —Charles Lamb⟩ ⟨no matter how small the technical probable error of the measurements might be, the *dubiety* of the result cannot be less than 3 in 105 —N.E.Dorsey & Churchill Eisenhart⟩ ⟨with presumable Scotch *dubiety* he would be inclined to distrust such items on the table as potatoes and ice cream and coffee—completely unknown in his day in Scotland —Alan Gregg⟩ DUBIOSITY is interchangeable with DUBIETY but may be distinguished from it in often suggesting vagueness, indistinctness, or mental confusion ⟨she pronounced distinctly and without a shadow of *dubiosity* —George Meredith⟩ SKEPTICISM suggests an unwillingness to believe without definitive demonstration, often applying to an habitual or temperamental frame of mind that tends to oppose belief not based on rational or scientific demonstration ⟨*skepticism* about all facile answers to basic questions of conduct⟩ ⟨created *skepticism* about the wisdom of foreign aid —Henry Wallace⟩ ⟨has found that *skepticism* rather than dogmatism is the key to human freedom —*New Republic*⟩ ⟨a religious *skepticism*⟩ SUSPICION stresses a conjectural belief that something is not true, real, or right, generally carrying also the idea of an accompanying uncertainty, doubt, or skepticism ⟨a strong *suspicion* that the new instrument with which Einstein has presented the mathematicians is being put to uses for which it was never intended —W.R.Inge⟩ ⟨public *suspicion* of the colleges —J.B.Conant⟩ ⟨the basic and healthy *suspicion* of power that is not strictly circumscribed by the rule of the law —Max Lerner⟩ MISTRUST, in this context, implies a doubt based on suspicion or an anticipation of wrong, falsehood, or evil, in action or result, and precluding faith, confidence, or trust ⟨most physicists have a traditional *mistrust* of philosophy —W.V.Houston⟩ ⟨intracommunity bickering, conflict and *mistrust* obscure the steady vision of extracommunity danger —A.E.Stevenson b. 1900⟩ ⟨his general *mistrust* of the human race —L.P.Stryker⟩

uncertainty principle *n* : a principle in quantum mechanics: it is impossible to assert in terms of the ordinary conventions of geometrical position and of motion that a particle (as an electron) is at the same time at a specified point and moving with a specified velocity for the more accurately either factor can be measured the less accurately the other can be ascertained

un·certitude \ˌən+\ *n* : INCERTITUDE

un·ces·sant \ˌən¦ses³nt\ *adj* [ME, alter. (influenced by ¹*un-*) of *incessaunt, incessant* incessant] *archaic* : INCESSANT

un·chain \ˌən+\ *vt* [²*un-* + *chain*] : to free by or as if by removing a chain : set loose : RELEASE ⟨reflexes ~*ed* by localized mechanical stimuli —Piero Leonardi⟩

un·chal·lenge·able \ˌən¦chalənjəbəl, -alēn-\ *adj* : not able to be challenged or disputed ⟨a position of ~ supremacy —*Harper's*⟩ — **un·chal·lenge·ably** \-blē\ *adv*

un·challenged \ˌən+\ *adj* [¹*un-* + *challenged*, past part. of *challenge*] : not challenged : UNDISPUTED ⟨emerged the ~ political head —A.L.Funk⟩

un·chambered \"+\ *adj* [¹*un-* + *chambered*, past part. of *chamber*] : not having a chamber

un·chancy \"+\ *adj* **1** *chiefly Scot* : ILL-FATED, ILL-OMENED, UNLUCKY **2** *chiefly Scot* : unsafe to meddle with : DANGEROUS

un·changeability \"+\ *n* [ME *unchangeabilite*, fr. *unchangeable, unchangeabil* unchangeable + *-ite* -ity] : the quality or state of being unchangeable

un·changeable \"+\ *adj* [ME, fr. ¹*un-* + *changeable*] : not changeable : IMMUTABLE ⟨a fixed and ~ part of the germ plasm —M.F.A.Montagu⟩ — **un·change·able·ness** *n* — **un·change·ably** \"+\ *adv*

un·changed \ˌən¦chānjd\ *adj* [ME *unchaunged*, fr. ¹*un-* + *chaunged, changed*, past part. of *chaungen, changen* to change] : not changed : UNALTERED ⟨the causes which produced them have remained ~ —*World's Work*⟩ — **un·chang·ed·ness** \-jədnə̇s\ *n* -ES

un·changing \ˌən+\ *adj* [ME *unchaunginge*, fr. ¹*un-* + *chaunginge, changinge*, pres. part. of *chaungen, changen* to change] : CHANGELESS, CONSTANT ⟨a country of immovable and ~ traditions —Laurence Binyon⟩ — **un·chang·ing·ly** *adv* — **un·chang·ing·ness** *n* -ES

un·chaperoned \"+\ *adj* [¹*un-* + *chaperoned*, past part. of *chaperon*] : not accompanied by a chaperon

un·characteristic \"+\ *adj* : not characteristic : not typical or distinctive ⟨a book ~ of its author⟩ — **un·characteristic·ally** \"+\ *adv*

uncharge *vt* [ME *unchargen* to remove a load or burden from, fr. ²*un-* + *chargen* to load, put a load on — more at CHARGE] *obs* : ACQUIT ⟨even his mother shall ~ the practice and call it accident —Shak.⟩

un·charged \ˌən+\ *adj* [ME, not burdened, fr. ¹*un-* + *charged*, past part. of *chargen*] : not charged; *specif* : having no electric charge

un·charitable \"+\ *adj* [ME, fr. ¹*un-* + *charitable*] : not charitable : HARSH, SEVERE ⟨a thing all pious words and ~ deeds —Charles Reade⟩ ⟨criticism . . . which he now feels to have been unjust and ~ —Richard Garnett †1906⟩ — **un·char·i·ta·ble·ness** *n* — **un·charitably** \"+\ *adv*

un·charity \ˌən+\ *n* : lack of charity ⟨a double sin, that of ~ and that of pride —Ruth Park⟩

un·charm \"+\ *vt* [²*un-* + *charm*] **1** : to divest of power to charm **2** : to free from or as if from a charm

un·charming \"+\ *adj* [¹*un-* + *charming*, adj.] : lacking charm ⟨writes an ugly ~ style —O.W.Holmes †1935⟩

un·charnel \"+\ *vt* -ED/-ING/-S [²*un-* + *charnel*, n.] : to remove from a charnel house or the grave : EXHUME

un·charred \"+\ *adj* [¹*un-* + *charred*, past part. of *char* (to burn)] : not charred

un·charted \"+\ *adj* [¹*un-* + *charted*, past part. of *chart*] : not charted : not recorded or plotted on a map, chart, or plan : UNKNOWN ⟨headed westward into the ~ wilderness —*Amer. Guide Series: Texas*⟩ ⟨assigned to explore previously ~ areas of space —*Springfield (Mass.) Republican*⟩ ⟨the great ~ region in the realm of letters —J.L.Lowes⟩

un·chartered \"+\ *adj* [¹*un-* + *chartered*, past part. of *charter*] : not chartered : IRREGULAR

un·chary \"+\ *adj* : not chary : not cautious or reserved ⟨have said too much unto a heart of stone and laid mine honor too ~ out —Shak.⟩

un·chaste \ˌən+\ *adj* [ME, fr. ¹*un-* + *chaste*] : not chaste : lacking in chastity ⟨an ~ woman⟩ ⟨~ conduct⟩ — **un·chaste·ly** *adv* — **un·chaste·ness** *n*

un·chastened \"+\ *adj* [¹*un-* + *chastened*, past part. of *chasten*] : not chastened

un·chastity \"+\ *n* [ME *unchastite*, fr. ¹*un-* + *chastite, chastete* chastity] : the quality or state of being unchaste : lack of chastity

un·check \"+\ *vt* [¹*un-* + *check*] : to impose no check on

un·checked \"+\ *adj* [ME *unchekked*, fr. ¹*un-* + *chekked, cheked*, past part. of *chekken, cheken* to check] **1** : not checked : not curbed or hindered : UNRESTRAINED ⟨a harmonious development that continued ~ for more than fifty years —*Amer. Guide Series: Maine*⟩ ⟨~ extravagance⟩ **2** *obs* : not contradicted ⟨it lives there ~ that Antonio hath a ship of rich lading wrecked —Shak.⟩

un·cheerful \"+\ *adj* [ME *uncherefull*, fr. ¹*un-* + *chereful, cherefull* cheerful] : not cheerful or cheering : GLOOMY ⟨a moody and ~ person⟩ ⟨an ~ place⟩ — **un·cheerfully** \"+\ *adv* — **un·cheer·ful·ness** *n*

un·child \"+\ *vt* [²*un-* + *child*, n.] **1** *archaic* : to bereave of children **2** : to divest of childhood or childlike characteristics

un·chivalrous \"+\ *adj* : not chivalrous : lacking in chivalry ⟨~ scorners of its old maids —G.D.Brown⟩ — **un·chiv·al·rous·ly** *adv*

un·choke \"+\ *vt* [²*un-* + *choke*] : to clear of obstruction ⟨~ the clogged channels of international trade —E.S.Griffith⟩

un·christen \"+\ *vt* [²*un-* + *christen*] : to annul the christening or baptism of

un·christened \"+\ *adj* [ME *uncristned,* fr. ¹*un-* + *cristned,* past part. of *cristnen* to christianize, christen] : not made Christian : not christened : UNNAMED

un·christian \"+\ *adj* **1** : not of the Christian faith ⟨love for the ~ neighbor —John Dillenberger & Claude Welch⟩ **2 a** : contrary to Christianity or the Christian spirit or character : not becoming to or like a Christian ⟨ashamed to have to recognize how fundamentally ~ his actual assumptions, motives, and attitudes are —F.R.Leavis⟩ **b** : BARBAROUS, UNCIVILIZED ⟨sitting up to ~ hours —Arnold Bennett⟩

un·christianize \"+\ *vt* [²*un-* + *christianize*] : to make unchristian : turn from Christianity

un·chris·tian·ly *adv* : in an unchristian manner

un·church \ˌən+\ *vt* [²*un-* + *church,* n.] **1** : to expel from or cause to be separated from a church : EXCOMMUNICATE **2** : to deprive of a church or of status as a church

un·churched \"+t\ *adj* [¹*un-* + *church,* n. + *-ed*] : not belonging to or connected with a church ⟨the vast masses of ~ peoples —J.C.Brauer⟩

unci *pl of* UNCUS

un·cia \ˈənchēə\ *n, pl* **unci·ae** \-ēˌē\ [L — more at OUNCE] : a twelfth part: as **a** : INCH **b** : a bronze coin of the ancient Roman republic worth 1/12 as **c** : a bronze coin of ancient Sicily worth 1/12 litra

¹**un·cial** \ˈənchəl\ *adj* [L *uncialis,* fr. *uncia* twelfth part, ounce, inch + *-alis* -al] **1** : of or relating to an inch or ounce **2** [LL *uncialis,* fr. L] : written or in the style or size of uncials ⟨~ script⟩ — **un·cial·ly** \-chəlē\ *adv*

²**uncial** \"\ *n* -s **1** : a book hand used esp. in Greek and Latin manuscripts of the 4th to the 8th centuries A.D. and consisting of somewhat rounded separated majuscules but having cursive forms for some letters **2** : an uncial letter **3** : a manuscript written in uncial

uncials 1

un·cif·er·ous \ˌənˈsif(ə)rəs\ *adj* [*uncus* + *-iferous*] : bearing a hook or hooklike structure

¹**un·ci·form** \ˈən(t)səˌfȯrm\ *adj* [NL *unciformis,* fr. LL *unci-* (fr. L *uncus* hook) + L *-formis* -form — more at ANGLE] : UNCINATE, HOOKLIKE

²**unciform** \"\ *n* -s [NL *unciforme,* fr. neut. of *unciformis*] : HAMATUM

unciform process *n* **1** : the hamulus of the hamatum **2** : the uncinate process of the ethmoid bone

un·ciliated \ˌən+\ *adj* : not ciliate

un·ci·nal \ˈən(t)sənᵊl\ *adj* [L *uncinus* hook (fr. *uncus* hook) + E *-al*] : UNCINATE

un·ci·nar·ia \ˌən(t)səˈna(a)rēə\ *n* [NL, fr. L *uncinus* hook + NL *-aria*] **1** *cap* : a genus of hookworms (family Ancylostomatidae) usu. restricted to a few parasites of carnivorous mammals but formerly often including most of the common hookworms **2** -s : HOOKWORM

un·ci·na·ri·a·sis \ˌən(t)sənəˈrīəsəs\ *n, pl* **uncinaria·ses** \-īəˌsēz\ [NL, fr. *Uncinaria* + *-iasis*] : ANCYLOSTOMIASIS

un·ci·nate \ˈən(t)sənət, -səˌnāt\ *adj* [L *uncinatus,* fr. *uncinus* hook + *-atus* -ate] **1** : bent at the tip like a hook : HOOKED **2 a** : of, relating to, or constituting an uncus **b** : affecting or involving the uncinate gyrus; *also* : marked by hallucinatory sensations of taste and smell ⟨an ~ fit⟩

un·ci·nat·ed \-səˌnād·əd\ *adj* [L *uncinatus* + E *-ed*] : UNCINATE

uncinate gyrus *or* **uncinate convolution** *n* : a subdivision of the hippocampal convolution containing olfactory association centers and marked by a thick layer of myelinated fibers upon its surface

uncinate process *n* **1** : a backwardly directed and often somewhat curved process on many ribs of birds that is in such a position that it crosses or overlaps one or more other ribs and serves to stiffen the walls of the thorax **2** : an irregular downwardly and backwardly directed process of each lateral mass of the ethmoid bone that articulates with the inferior turbinate bones

un·ci·na·tum \ˌən(t)səˈnād·əm\ *n, pl* **uncina·ta** \-d·ə\ *or* **uncinatums** [NL, fr. L, neut. of *uncinatus*] : HAMATUM

un·cin·u·la \ˌənˈsinyələ\ *n, cap* [NL, fr. L *uncinus* hook + *-ula*] : a genus of powdery mildews (family Erysiphaceae) having perithecia with several asci and simple or rarely forked appendages hooked or coiled at the apex

un·ci·nus \ˌənˈsīnəs\ *n, pl* **unci·ni** \-īˌnī\ [NL, fr. L, hook] : a small hooklike structure or process: as **a** : one of the minute chitinous hooks found in large numbers in the tori of some tubicolous annelids **b** : one of the hooklike lateral teeth of the radula of a gastropod **c** : a hooked cilium of various infusorians

un·circulated \ˌən+\ *adj* [¹*un-* + *circulated,* past part. of *circulate*] *of a coin* : issued for use as money but kept out of circulation (as for preservation in a collection) — compare PROOF

un·circumcised \"+\ *adj* [ME, fr. ¹*un-* + *circumcised,* past part. of *circumcisen* to circumcise] **1** : not circumcised ⟨this ~ Philistine —1 Sam 17:26 (RSV)⟩ **2** : spiritually impure : HEATHEN ⟨it fell into . . . ~ hands —F.H.Ellis⟩

un·circumcision \"+\ *n* **1 a** : the state or condition of being uncircumcised ⟨neither circumcision counts for anything nor ~, but keeping the commandments of God —1 Cor 7:19 (RSV)⟩ **b** : repudiation of one's circumcision **2** : those not circumcised : GENTILES

un·circumscribed \"+\ *adj* [¹*un-* + *circumscribed,* past part. of *circumscribe*] : not circumscribed : UNBOUNDED

un·circumstantial \"+\ *adj* : not circumstantial : not entering into minute particulars

un·civil \"+\ *adj* **1** : not civilized : BARBAROUS, SAVAGE ⟨keep them from ~ outrages —Shak.⟩ **2** : lacking in courtesy : ILL-MANNERED, IMPOLITE ⟨want nothing from you but to get away from your ~ tongue —Willa Cather⟩ **3** : not conducive to civic harmony and welfare ⟨civilization is ~ because human beings are divided into . . . sects, races, nations, classes and cliques —John Dewey⟩ **syn** see RUDE

un·civilized \"+\ *adj* **1** : not civilized : BARBAROUS, RUDE, SAVAGE ⟨fighting is crude and ~, especially if the weapons are efficient —Margaret Mead⟩ ⟨shuddered at the responsibility for getting them up at that ~ hour —Jean & Franc Shor⟩ **2** : remote from civilization : WILD ⟨a hidden river, entirely ~ with no roads or trails touching it —Patricia Spring⟩

un·civilly \"+\ *adv* : in an uncivil manner

un·claimed \"+\ *adj* [¹*un-* + *claimed,* past part. of *claim*] : not claimed; *specif* : not called for by an owner or consignee ⟨~ goods⟩

un·clamp \"+\ *vt* [²*un-* + *clamp*] : to loosen the clamp of : free from a clamp

un·clarity \"+\ *n* : lack of clarity : AMBIGUITY, OBSCURITY ⟨the *unclarities* in the theory of instincts —Abram Kardiner⟩

un·clasp \"+\ *vb* [²*un-* + *clasp*] *vt* **1 a** : to open the clasp of ⟨~*ed* his briefcase and took out his notes⟩ **b** : to open or cause to be opened (as a clenched hand) **2** *obs* : to open up : REVEAL ⟨in her bosom I'll ~ my heart —Shak.⟩ ~ *vi* : to loosen a hold or grip

un·classifiable \"+\ *adj* : not capable of being classified ⟨this ~ zoological freak —R.K.Buehrle⟩

un·classified \"+\ *adj* **1** : not placed in or belonging in a class ⟨an ~ specimen⟩ ⟨an ~ student⟩ **2** : not subject to a security classification ⟨~ documents⟩

¹**un·cle** \ˈəŋkəl\ *n* -s [ME, fr. OF *uncle, oncle,* fr. L *avunculus* mother's brother; akin to OE *ēam* uncle, mother's brother, OHG *ōheim* mother's brother, ON *afi* grandfather, Goth *awo* grandmother, L *avus* grandfather, OIr *aue* grandson, Lith *avynas* mother's brother] **1 a** : the brother of one's father or mother **b** : the husband of one's aunt — often used as a term of affectionate respect for an older man (as a close friend of the family) **2** : one who helps, advises, or encourages ⟨he played ~ to so many movements —H.G.Wells⟩ **3** *slang* : PAWNBROKER ⟨~ gave little for them but you got the money readily —Albert Szent-Györgyi⟩ **4** — used as a cry of surrender ⟨you want me to holler ~, you want me to crawl for you —Maritta Wolff⟩

²**uncle** \"\ *vt* -ED/-ING/-S : to refer to as uncle : address as uncle ⟨grace me no grace nor ~ me no uncle —Shak.⟩

³**uncle** \"\ *usu cap* — a communications code word for the letter *u*

un·clean \ˌənˈklēn\ *adj* [ME *unclene,* fr. OE *unclǣne,* fr. ¹*un-* + *clǣne* clean] **1 a** : morally impure ⟨something sneaking and ~ about secret code messages —Fletcher Pratt⟩ ⟨feels ~ when he discovers he has been used for an experiment —A.P. Davis⟩ **b** : WICKED ⟨commands even the ~ spirits, and they obey him —Mk 1:27 (RSV)⟩ **2 a** : ritually prohibited as food ⟨an ~ animal⟩ ⟨~ meat⟩ **b** : ceremonially unfit or defiled ⟨people who were ~ in the eyes of the law —C.T.Craig⟩ **3 a** : DIRTY, FILTHY ⟨an ~ shirt⟩ ⟨an ~ glass⟩ **b** : not desirable or wholesome as food — used of fish that have just spawned **4** : lacking in clarity and precision of conception or execution : IMPURE, MUDDLED ⟨a compromised and ~ design —N.W. Sharpe⟩ ⟨had some trouble with her intonation, and much of her double-stopping was ~ —*Musical Digest*⟩ — **un·clean·ness** \-ēnnəs\ *n*

unclean hands *n pl* : the condition of being guilty of unfair, inequitable, fraudulent, oppressive, or other unconscionable or illegal misconduct constituting grounds for refusing an application for relief in a court of equity

un·clean·li·ness \ˌənˈklenlēnəs, -enlin-\ *n* [¹*uncleanly* + *-ness*] : the quality or state of being uncleanly

¹**un·clean·ly** \-enlē, -li\ *adj* [ME *unclenly,* fr. OE *unclǣnlic,* fr. ¹*un-* + *clǣnlic* pure — more at CLEANLY] **1** : morally unclean : IMPURE ⟨~ thoughts⟩ **2** : physically unclean : FILTHY ⟨his ~ habits of spitting —Hamlin Garland⟩

²**un·clean·ly** \ˌənˈklēnlē\ *adv* [*unclean* + *-ly*] : in an unclean manner

un·clear \ˌən+\ *adj* [ME *unclere,* fr. ¹*un-* + *clere* clear] **1** : difficult to grasp or understand : INDISTINCT, OBSCURE ⟨their descriptions of human behavior become vague, dull, and ~ —P.A.Sorokin⟩ **2** : confused or uncertain in statement or understanding ⟨are very ~ in their religious thinking —Vilhjalmur Stefansson⟩ ⟨the law itself was ~ as to the distinction —*World's Work*⟩ — **un·clear·ly** *adv* — **un·clear·ness** *n*

un·cleared \"+\ *adj* [¹*un-* + *cleared,* past part. of *clear*] : not cleared; *specif* : not cleared of trees or brush ⟨~ land⟩

un·cleave \"+\ *vi* [²*un-* + *cleave* (to adhere)] : to become detached

un·cleft \"+\ *adj* : not cleft

un·cle·hood \ˈəŋkəlˌhu̇d\ *n* : the state of being an uncle

uncle–in–law \ˈ===,=\ *n, pl* **uncles–in–law** **1** : the husband of one's aunt **2** : the uncle of one's spouse

un·clench \ˌən+\ *vb* [²*un-* + *clench*] *vt* **1** : to open or force open from a clenched position : RELAX ⟨~*ed* his hands⟩ ⟨with a determined effort he ~*ed* her grasp⟩ **2** : to release from a grip ~ *vi* : to become unclasped or relaxed ⟨his hands continued to clench and ~⟩

uncle sam *n, usu cap U&S* [fr. *U. S.,* abbr. of *United States;* prob. fr. an originally jocular interpretation of the letters U. S. stamped on casks of meat supplied to the U.S. Army during the War of 1812 as standing for *Uncle Sam,* nickname of Samuel Wilson †1854 Am. meat packer] **1** : the U.S. government personified ⟨doesn't like people who work for *Uncle Sam* —Merle Miller⟩ **2** : the American nation or people ⟨a distorted picture of *Uncle Sam*⟩

un·cle·ship \ˈəŋkəlˌship\ *n* : the quality or state of being an uncle

uncle tom *n, usu cap U&T* [after *Uncle Tom,* hero of the novel *Uncle Tom's Cabin* (1851–52) by Harriet Beecher Stowe †1896 Am. author] : a Negro having a humble and submissive attitude or philosophy

un·clinch \"+\ *vt* [²*un-* + *clinch*] : UNCLENCH

un·clipped *or* **un·clipt** \"+\ *adj* [ME *unclipped,* fr. ¹*un-* + *clipped,* past part. of *clippen* to clip, cut] : not clipped ⟨~ hair⟩ ⟨~ wings⟩ ⟨an ~ coin⟩

un·cloak \"+\ *vb* [²*un-* + *cloak*] *vt* **1** : to remove a cloak or cover from **2** : REVEAL, UNMASK ~ *vi* : to take off a cloak

un·clog \"+\ *vt* [²*un-* + *clog*] : to free from a difficulty or obstruction

un·cloister \"+\ *vt* [²*un-* + *cloister*] : to release from a cloister or confinement : set free

un·close \"+\ *vb* [ME *unclosen,* fr. ²*un-* + *closen* to close] *vt* **1** : OPEN ⟨~ the window⟩ **2** : DISCLOSE, REVEAL ~ *vi* : to become opened ⟨her eyes *unclosed*⟩

un·closed \"+\ *adj* [ME, fr. ¹*un-* + *closed*] : not closed or settled : not concluded

un·clothe \"+\ *vt* [ME *unclothen,* fr. ²*un-* + *clothen* to clothe] **1 a** : to strip of clothes : UNDRESS **b** : to take cloths from ⟨~ the sails of a windmill⟩ **2 a** : DIVEST ⟨*unclothed* his heart of bitterness⟩ **b** : UNCOVER ⟨*unclothed* his secret thoughts⟩

un·clothed \"+\ *adj* [ME, fr. ¹*un-* + *clothed,* past part. of *clothen* to clothe] : not clothed : NAKED

un·cloud \ˌən+\ *vb* [²*un-* + *cloud*] *vt* : to free from or as if from clouds : clear from obscurity or gloom ~ *vi* : to become free from clouds

un·clouded \"+\ *adj* [¹*un-* + *clouded,* past part. of *cloud*] : not covered by clouds : not darkened : CLEAR ⟨ideas given to the ~ mind by intuition —S.F.Mason⟩ — **un·cloud·ed·ly** *adv* — **un·cloud·ed·ness** *n* -ES

un·clubbable *also* **un·clubable** \"+\ *adj* : not clubbable : UNSOCIABLE ⟨an ~ man⟩

un·clutch \"+\ *vt* [²*un-* + *clutch*] : UNCLENCH

un·clutter \"+\ *vt* [²*un-* + *clutter*] : to make neat and orderly : straighten out ⟨instead of trying to clean out or ~ the old one, he would simply build a new shack —G.S.Perry⟩

un·cluttered \"+\ *adj* [¹*un-* + *cluttered,* past part. of *clutter*] : not cluttered : having nothing extraneous or unnecessary : NEAT ⟨his prose is ~, pungent, witty —Nona B. Brown⟩

¹**un·co** \ˈəŋ(ˌ)kō\ *adj* [ME (Sc) *unkow,* alter. of ME *uncouth* strange, unaccustomed — more at UNCOUTH] **1** *chiefly Scot* **a** : STRANGE, UNKNOWN **b** : UNCANNY, WEIRD **2** *chiefly Scot* : out of the ordinary : REMARKABLE

²**unco** \"\ *adv* : EXTREMELY, REMARKABLY ⟨the ~ refined and the queasy had best give it a wide berth —Orville Prescott⟩

³**unco** \"\ *n* -s **1 uncos** *pl, chiefly Scot* : NEWS, TIDINGS **2** *chiefly Scot* : STRANGER

un·coach \ˌən+\ *vt* [²*un-* + *coach*] : to remove from a coach or car

un·coagulable \"+\ *adj* : INCOAGULABLE

un·coagulated \"+\ *adj* : not coagulated; *specif, of blood* : kept from coagulating esp. by additives (as oxalate ion)

un·coated \"+\ *adj* : not having a coating ⟨~ paper⟩

un·cock \"+\ *vt* [²*un-* + *cock*] **1** : to remove the hammer of (a firearm) from a cocked position ⟨~ my gun and went sneaking back on my tiptoes —Mark Twain⟩ **2** : to let down the brim of (a cocked hat) ⟨his three-cornered hat with one side ~*ed* so that it flapped —Kenneth Roberts⟩

un·codified \"+\ *adj* [¹*un-* + *codified,* past part. of *codify*] : not codified ⟨their ~ theology —D.S.Taylor⟩

un·coffin \"+\ *vt* [²*un-* + *coffin*] : to remove from or as if from a coffin ⟨~ warfare from the winding sheets of the past —Tom Wintringham⟩

un·coffined \"+\ *adj* [¹*un-* + *coffined,* past part. of *coffin*] : not coffined : not placed in a coffin

unco guid *n, pl in constr* : those who profess a strict morality — used with *the* ⟨the *unco guid* magnified the scandal . . . in order piously to deplore it —R.D.Altick⟩

un·coil \ˌən+\ *vb* [²*un-* + *coil*] *vt* : to release or pay out from a coiled state or position : UNWIND ⟨~*ing* the scarf from his throat —Eve Langley⟩ ⟨we all ~*ed* ourselves — it had been a tight fit —Thomas Wood †1950⟩ ~ *vi* : to become released from a coiled state or position ⟨~*ed* to his full height and glared down on the bewildered bartender —Edna Ferber⟩

un·coiled \"+\ *adj* [¹*un-* + *coiled,* past part. of *coil* (to wind)] : not coiled

un·coined \"+\ *adj* [ME *unkoyned,* fr. ¹*un-* + *koyned, coyned,* past part. of *koynen, coynen* to coin] **1** : not minted ⟨~ metal⟩ **2** : not fabricated : not artificial or counterfeit : NATURAL ⟨a fellow of plain and ~ constancy —Shak.⟩

uncolike \ˈ==,=\ *adj, Scot* : STRANGE

un·collected \ˌən+\ *adj* **1** : not self-composed : DISCONCERTED ⟨was in a very ~ and nervous state⟩ **2** : not gathered into one place or body ⟨his poems are as yet ~ —W.B.Cairns⟩ **3** : not yet paid ⟨an ~ debt⟩

¹**un·collectible** \"+\ *adj* : not capable of being collected ⟨an ~ debt⟩

²**uncollectible** \"\ *n* -s : an uncollectible account : a bad debt

un·colored \"+\ *adj* **1** : having no color ⟨~ cloth⟩ ⟨~ paper⟩ **2** : not distorted by an irrelevant, prejudiced, or deceptive quality or addition ⟨gave a plain ~ account of the accident⟩ **syn** see FAIR

un·colt \"+\ *vt* [²*un-* + *colt,* n.] : UNHORSE

un·combed \"+\ *adj* [¹*un-* + *combed,* past part. of *comb*] : not combed : UNKEMPT ⟨unwashed, ~, with his clothes half buttoned —Hall Caine⟩

un·com·bine \ˌənkəmˈbīn\ *vt* [²*un-* + *combine*] : to break apart : SEPARATE

un·com·bined \-nd\ *adj* [¹*un-* + *combined,* adj.] : not combined : FREE

un·come–at–able \ˌən+\ *adj* [¹*un-* + *come-at-able*] : INACCESSIBLE, UNATTAINABLE

un·comeliness \"+\ *n* : the quality or state of being uncomely

¹**un·comely** \"+\ *adj* [ME *uncomly,* fr. ¹*un-* + *comly* comely] **1** : not fitting : IMPROPER ⟨clumsy, ~ methods of management and care —Brooks Atkinson⟩ **2** : not pleasing to the sight : UNATTRACTIVE ⟨she had always been ~ in his eyes —Agnes Repplier⟩

²**uncomely** *adv* [ME *uncomly,* fr. *uncomly,* adj.] *obs* : in an uncomely manner : IMPROPERLY ⟨behaveth himself ~ toward his virgin —1 Cor 7:36 (AV)⟩

un·comfortable \ˌən+\ *adj* **1 a** : causing annoyance, embarrassment, or uneasiness : DISCONCERTING ⟨has an ~ way of surprising me just when I feel surest —J.O.Hannay⟩ ⟨was at once a valuable and an ~ contributor —M.A.D.Howe⟩ **b** : causing physical discomfort ⟨an ~ chair⟩ ⟨an ~ day⟩ **2** : feeling discomfort : physically or mentally ill at ease : UNEASY ⟨even when the heat is not extreme, a sudden rise may make us ~ —Ellsworth Huntington⟩ ⟨grew ~ beneath his sideward, estimating eye —G.D.Brown⟩ — **un·com·fort·a·ble·ness** *n* — **un·comfortably** \"+\ *adv*

un·comforted \"+\ *adj* [¹*un-* + *comforted,* past part. of *comfort*] : not comforted

un·comforting \"+\ *adj* **1** : not giving comfort ⟨a foreign country in wartime . . . is an ~ place to be —Max Beerbohm⟩ **2** : causing discomfort ⟨vital and sometimes ~ truths —William Plomer⟩

un·comfy \"+\ *adj* : UNCOMFORTABLE

un·commercial \"+\ *adj* **1** : not engaged in or related to commerce **2** : not based on commercial principles : not conducive to financial success ⟨might prove arty and hence ~ —H.E.Clurman⟩

un·commissioned \"+\ *adj* [¹*un-* + *commissioned,* past part. of *commission*] : not commissioned

un·committed \"+\ *adj* [¹*un-* + *committed,* past part. of *commit*] : not committed; *specif* : not obligated or pledged to a particular belief, allegiance, or program ⟨have stayed ~ in the great controversy that divides the world —Patrick O'Donovan⟩

¹**un·common** \ˌən+\ *adj* **1** : not ordinarily encountered : INFREQUENT, RARE ⟨during the worst of the blitz, it was no ~ experience for him to hear a nearby building collapse —*Current Biog.*⟩ **2** : more than ordinary : unusually large or great ⟨has been doing an ~ amount of business —*N. Y. Times*⟩ **3** : remarkable in character, quality, or kind : EXCEPTIONAL, OUTSTANDING ⟨it was to the ~ character and ability of his mother that . . . he owed the greatest debt —C.A.Dinsmore⟩ — **un·com·mon·ly** *adv* — **un·com·mon·ness** *n*

²**uncommon** \"\ *adv, chiefly dial* : UNCOMMONLY ⟨the route back . . . was ~ hard —Bernard DeVoto⟩

un·communicable \"+\ *adj* : INCOMMUNICABLE

un·communicated \"+\ *adj* [¹*un-* + *communicated,* past part. of *communicate*] **1** : not communicated : not told or imparted **2** : not having partaken of Communion

un·communicative \"+\ *adj* **1** : unwilling to talk or impart information ⟨when he works . . . is quiet, withdrawn, ~ —Barbara B. Jamison⟩ ⟨~ regarding plans —*Current Biog.*⟩ **2** : not disposed to associate with others : RESERVED **syn** see SILENT

un·com·mu·ni·ca·tive·ly *adv* : in an uncommunicative manner

un·com·mu·ni·ca·tive·ness *n* : the quality or state of being uncommunicative

un·compacted \ˌən+\ *adj* [¹*un-* + *compacted,* past part. of *compact* (to compress)] : not packed together; *specif* : not compressed ⟨~ soil⟩

un·com·pah·gre \ˌənkəmˈpägrē\ *n, pl* **uncompahgre** *or* **uncompahgres** *usu cap* [*Uncompahgre* valley, southwestern Colorado, site of the reservation to which this people was assigned] **1** : a Ute people of southwestern Colorado **2** : a member of the Uncompahgre people

un·companied \ˌən+\ *adj* [¹*un-* + *companied,* past part. of *company*] : UNACCOMPANIED

un·companionable \"+\ *adj* : UNSOCIABLE ⟨thought her morose and ~ —Elmer Davis⟩

un·companioned \"+\ *adj* [¹*un-* + *companioned,* past part. of *companion*] **1** : having no companion ⟨the ~ boy beyond them working away in almost total darkness —Daniel Corkery⟩ **2** : marked by a lack of companionship : LONELY, SOLITARY ⟨one of those contemplative ~ walks which it was his habit to take —G.W.Cable⟩

un·compassionate \"+\ *adj* : HARDHEARTED, UNFEELING ⟨nor silver-shedding tears could penetrate her ~ sire —Shak.⟩

un·compelled \"+\ *adj* [ME, fr. ¹*un-* + *compelled,* past part. of *compellen* to compel] : not compelled

un·compensated \"+\ *adj* [¹*un-* + *compensated,* past part. of *compensate*] : not compensated or compensated for ⟨this last ~ federal post —*Current Biog.*⟩ ⟨~ differences in polarization at glass surfaces —D.L.Drabkin⟩

un·complaining \"+\ *adj* [¹*un-* + *complaining,* pres. part. of *complain*] : not complaining : PATIENT ⟨~ courage⟩ — **un·com·plain·ing·ly** *adv* — **un·com·plain·ing·ness** *n*

un·complete \"+\ *adj* [ME *uncomplet,* fr. ¹*un-* + *complet* complete] : INCOMPLETE

un·completed \"+\ *adj* [¹*un-* + *completed,* past part. of *complete*] : not completed : UNFINISHED ⟨an ~ building⟩ ⟨an ~ play⟩

un·complex \"+\ *adj* : not complex ⟨an ~, uniform culture —Margaret Mead⟩

un·compliant \ˌən+\ *adj* : not compliant : INFLEXIBLE

un·complicated \"+\ *adj* [¹*un-* + *complicated,* past part. of *complicate*] **1** : not complicated by something outside itself ⟨~ adrenal insufficiency —*Jour. Amer. Med. Assoc.*⟩ ⟨men whose understanding is obviously ~ by any personal acquaintance with the classics —Albert Lynd⟩ **2** [¹*un-* + *complicated,* adj.] : not complex : easy to understand or manage : SIMPLE ⟨a big, bouncy, ~ girl —Frances G. Patton⟩ ⟨small and ~ cars for those who are really interested in motoring —*Country Life*⟩

un·complimentary \"+\ *adj* : not complimentary : DEROGATORY ⟨an ~ remark⟩

un·complying \"+\ *adj* [¹*un-* + *complying,* pres. part. of *comply* (to accord)] : not complying : RIGID, STIFF ⟨an ~ attitude⟩

un·composed \"+\ *adj* : not composed : not properly organized : SHAPELESS, UNFORMED ⟨the fitness of publishing so ~ a thing —John Howe⟩

un·compounded \"+\ *adj* [¹*un-* + *compounded,* past part. of *compound*] **1** : not constituting a compound : UNMIXED ⟨an ~ substance⟩ **2** : not involved : SIMPLE, UNCOMPLICATED ⟨a simple and ~ idea —Virginia Woolf⟩

un·comprehended \"+\ *adj* [¹*un-* + *comprehended,* past part. of *comprehend*] : not understood ⟨an ~ mystery⟩

un·comprehending \"+\ *adj* [¹*un-* + *comprehending,* pres. part. of *comprehend*] : not comprehending : lacking understanding ⟨her able and ~ father —Harry Levin⟩ ⟨a kind woman and magnificently ~ —Sinclair Lewis⟩ — **un·com·pre·hend·ing·ly** *adv*

un·comprehensible \"+\ *adj* [ME, alter. (influenced by ¹*un-*) of *incomprehensible*] : INCOMPREHENSIBLE

un·comprehensive \"+\ *adj* **1** *obs* : INCOMPREHENSIBLE **2** : not comprehensive

un·compressed \"+\ *adj* : not compressed

un·compromising \ˌən+\ *adj* [¹*un-* + *compromising,* pres. part. of *compromise*] **1** : not making or accepting a compromise : making no concessions : INFLEXIBLE, UNYIELDING ⟨was as conciliatory in the moment of triumph as he had been ~ while the conflict lasted —A.L.Kennedy⟩ **2** : marked by an

absence or avoidance of compromise or concession : being without reservation : WHOLEHEARTED ⟨the same deep sense of duty and ~ honesty which characterized his whole life —J.T. Sellin⟩ — **un·com·pro·mis·ing·ly** *adv* — **un·com·pro·mis·ing·ness** *n* -ES

un·concealed \"+\ *adj* : not concealed : OPEN ⟨regarded him with ~ hatred⟩

un·conceivable \"+\ *adj* [¹*un-* + *conceive* + *-able*] : INCONCEIVABLE — **un·con·ceiv·able·ness** *n* — **un·conceivably** \"+\ *adv*

un·concern \"+\ *n* **1** : lack of care or interest : INDIFFERENCE ⟨~ for the great problems of our day —H.G.Rickover⟩ ⟨a tone of casual ~ —E.T.Thurston⟩ **2** : lack of anxiety ⟨flinging itself with confidence and ~ over wide spaces in the trees —Weston LaBarre⟩

un·concerned \"+\ *adj* [¹*un-* + *concerned*] **1** : lacking care, interest, or feeling ⟨convincing the ~, the apathetic, and the downright hostile —Benjamin Fine⟩ ⟨~ if his girl deserts him —K.E.Read⟩ **2** : not occupied or engaged ⟨readers ~ with style and philosophical illumination —R.A.Cordell⟩ **3** : not anxious or solicitous : easy in mind : not worried ⟨the prisoner seems entirely ~ as to the outcome of the examination —D.D. Martin⟩ **syn** see INDIFFERENT

un·concernedly \"+\ *adv* : in an unconcerned manner

un·concernedness \"+\ *n* : the quality or state of being unconcerned

un·concernment \"+\ *n* [¹*un-* + *concernment*] : UNCONCERN

un·conditional \"+\ *adj* : not limited in any way : not bound or restricted by conditions or qualifications : ABSOLUTE, UNRESERVED ⟨~ surrender⟩ ⟨an ~ offer⟩ ⟨an ~ admirer⟩ — **un·conditionally** \"+\ *adv* — **un·con·di·tion·al·ness** *n* -ES

un·conditionality \"+\ *n* [*unconditional* + *-ity*] : the quality or state of being unconditional

un·conditioned \¦ən+\ *adj* **1 a** : not subject to limitations or conditions : ABSOLUTE, INFINITE ⟨it is a consciousness of the ~ and universal that makes people religious —Clive Bell⟩ **b** : INCONCEIVABLE, UNKNOWABLE **c** : not dependent on conditioning or learning : NATURAL ⟨an ~ response⟩ — **un·con·di·tioned·ness** *n* -ES

unconditioned reflex *n* : a reflex that is inborn or dependent on physiological maturation rather than on learning

un·condoned \¦ən+\ *adj* [¹*un-* + *condoned*, past part. of *condone*] : not condoned

un·confessed \"+\ *adj* [¹*un-* + *confessed*, past part. of *confess*] : not confessed

un·confident \"+\ *adj* : lacking in confidence : UNSURE — **un·con·fi·dent·ly** *adv*

un·confiding \"+\ *adj* : not confiding : UNCOMMUNICATIVE ⟨had been singularly glum and ~ during the last week of preparation —Gerald Beaumont⟩

un·confine \"+\ *vt* [back-formation fr. *unconfined*] : to release from confinement or restraint

un·confined \"+\ *adj* [¹*un-* + *confined*] **1** : not kept within limits : UNBOUNDED, UNCONTROLLED ⟨on with the dance! let joy be ~ —Lord Byron⟩ **2** : not secured or kept confined ⟨her ~ hair fell to her shoulders⟩

un·confirmed \"+\ *adj* **1** *obs* : not instructed : IGNORANT **2** : not finally established or authorized : not settled : TENTATIVE ⟨an ~ letter of credit⟩ **3** : not corroborated or supported by evidence ⟨~ rumors⟩

un·conformability \"+\ *n* : the quality or state of being unconformable

un·conformable \"+\ *adj* **1** : not correspondent ⟨a description ~ to previous accounts⟩ **2** : not conforming; *specif* : not conforming to the practices and teachings of the Church of England esp. as prescribed by the Acts of Uniformity **3** : exhibiting geological unconformity — **un·conformably** \"+\ *adv*

un·conformist \"+\ *n* : NONCONFORMIST

un·conformity \¦ən+\ *n* **1** *archaic* : lack of conformity **2 a** : lack of continuity in deposition between rock strata in contact corresponding to a period of nondeposition, weathering, or erosion either subaerial or subaqueous prior to the deposition of the younger beds and consequently to a gap in the stratigraphic record **b** : the surface of contact between unconformable strata — compare DISCONFORMITY, NONCONFORMITY

un·congeal \"+\ *vi* [²*un-* + *congeal*] : THAW

un·congenial \"+\ *adj* **1 a** : not sympathetic ⟨the ~ roommates were always fighting⟩ **b** : not compatible — used of a plant stock or scions **2 a** : not fitted : UNSUITABLE ⟨their work had been ~ to the social structure and traditions of the land —G.M.Trevelyan⟩ ⟨an ~ soil⟩ **b** : not to one's taste : DISAGREEABLE ⟨the task was ~ to one sensitive to rebuffs —H.K. Rowe⟩ ⟨found the pursuit ~ and resolved to abandon it —U.B.Phillips⟩ — **un·congenially** \"+\ *adv*

un·congeniality \"+\ *n* : the quality or state of being uncongenial

un·connected \"+\ *adj* **1 a** : not joined or grouped together : SEPARATE ⟨the supreme agent by which disparate and hitherto ~ things are brought together in poetry —I.A.Richards⟩ **b** : not coherent : DISJOINTED ⟨spoke in ~ phrases⟩ ⟨an ~ argument⟩ **2** : having no family or other personal ties ⟨a lonely ~ person⟩ — **un·con·nect·ed·ly** *adv* — **un·con·nect·ed·ness** *n*

un·con·quer·able \¦ən¦käŋkərəbəl *sometimes* -¦kȯŋ-\ *adj* [¹*un-* + *conquer* + *-able*] **1** : incapable of being conquered : INDOMITABLE ⟨a tribute to his courage, his sagacity, and his ~ will —R.E.Danielson⟩ **2** : incapable of being surmounted : INSUPERABLE ⟨seems to create ~ difficulties in man's life —H.E.Salisbury⟩ — **un·con·quer·able·ness** *n* -ES — **un·con·quer·ably** \-blē\ *adv*

un·conquered \¦ən+\ *adj* [¹*un-* + *conquered*, past part. of *conquer*] : not conquered ⟨this stark, ~ land —Guy Priest⟩

un·conscient \"+\ *adj* : lacking consciousness

un·conscientious \"+\ *adj* : not conscientious — **un·con·sci·en·tious·ly** *adv* — **un·con·sci·en·tious·ness** *n*

¹**un·con·scio·na·ble** \¦ən¦känch(ə)nəbəl\ *adj* **1** : not guided or controlled by conscience : UNSCRUPULOUS ⟨an ~ villain⟩ **2 a** : EXCESSIVE, EXORBITANT ⟨advertising and promotion costs an ~ amount —G.P.Brockway⟩ ⟨was staying up there an ~ time —Joseph Conrad⟩ **b** : lying outside the limits of what is reasonable or acceptable : shockingly unfair, harsh, or unjust : OUTRAGEOUS ⟨the grinding poverty, the ~ death rate, and the appalling illiteracy —*Commonweal*⟩

²**unconscionable** \"\ *adv* : UNCONSCIONABLY

un·con·scio·na·bly \-blē, -li\ *adv* : in an unconscionable manner or to an unconscionable extent

¹**un·conscious** \¦ən+\ *adj* **1 a** : not knowing or perceiving : not aware ⟨seemed quite ~ of her scrutiny —A.T.Quiller-Couch⟩ ⟨happily ~ of the new calamity at home —Charles Dickens⟩ **b** : free from self-awareness ⟨would never again be quite the same ~ creature —John Galsworthy⟩ **2 a** : not possessing mind or consciousness : NONCONSCIOUS ⟨~ matter⟩ **b** (1) : not marked by conscious thought, sensation, or feeling ⟨~ processes behind conscious mental states⟩ (2) : of or relating to the unconscious **c** : having no consciousness for the time being ⟨he lay inert, breathing heavily and ~ —Dorothy Sayers⟩ **3** : not consciously held, exercised, or displayed : not realized ⟨found in the countryside the profound, ~ content that animals find —Rose Macaulay⟩ ⟨~ bias⟩ **4** : not deliberately planned, organized, or carried out : not consciously directed ⟨is language an ~ collective growth, with a life of its own, beyond individual control —A.L.Guérard⟩ ⟨the ~ choice of words —W.F.Mackey⟩ — **un·con·scious·ly** *adv* — **un·con·scious·ness** *n* -ES

²**unconscious** \"\ *n* **1** : the absolute principle of the universe according to the doctrine of panpneumatism **2** : the greater part of the psychic apparatus accumulated through life experience that is not ordinarily integrated or available to consciousness yet is manifested as a powerful motive force in overt behavior esp. in neurosis and is often revealed (as through dreams, slips of the tongue, or dissociated acts) **3** : COLLECTIVE UNCONSCIOUS — compare SUBCONSCIOUS

un·consecrated \"+\ *adj* [¹*un-* + *consecrated*, past part. of *consecrate*] : not consecrated

un·consequential \"+\ *adj* : INCONSEQUENTIAL

un·considered \"+\ *adj* [¹*un-* + *considered*, past part. of *consider*] **1** : not considered or worth consideration : INCONSIDERABLE ⟨a snapper-up of ~ trifles —Shak.⟩ ⟨too humble and ~, himself, to view with alarm the discomfiture of his superiors —Katharine F. Gerould⟩ **2** : not resulting from consideration ⟨what he should avoid is prejudice — the holding of ~ opinions —R.B.West⟩

un·consolable \"+\ *adj* [by alter.] : INCONSOLABLE — **un·consolably** \"+\ *adv*

un·consolidated \"+\ *adj* : loosely arranged : not stratified ⟨~ soil⟩

un·consonant \"+\ *adj* : INCONSONANT

un·conspicuous \"+\ *adj* : INCONSPICUOUS

unconstancy *n* [*unconstant* + *-cy*] *obs* : INCONSTANCY

un·constant \¦ən+\ *adj* [ME, fr. ¹*un-* + *constant*] *archaic* : INCONSTANT

un·constellated \"+\ *adj* [¹*un-* + *constellated*, past part. of *constellate*] : not forming part of a constellation ⟨a star in exile, ~ at the south —Hugh McCrae⟩

un·constitutional \"+\ *adj* : not according to or consistent with the constitution of a state or society; *specif* : contrary to the U. S. Constitution — **un·constitutionality** \"+\ *n* — **un·constitutionally** \"+\ *adv*

un·constrained \"+\ *adj* [ME *unconstreynd*, fr. ¹*un-* + *constreynd*, past part. of *constreynen, constrainen* to constrain] : not constrained : not acting or done under constraint — **un·constrainedly** \"+\ *adv*

un·constraint \"+\ *n* : freedom from constraint : EASE ⟨there was a perfect ~, and they all seemed to feel like one enormous family —Bernard Pares⟩

un·consumed \"+\ *adj* [¹*un-* + *consumed*, past part. of *consume*] : not consumed

un·con·tain·able \¦ənkən¦tānəbəl\ *adj* [¹*un-* + *contain* + *-able*] : not containable : IRREPRESSIBLE ⟨felt ~ indignation —N.M.Pusey⟩

un·contaminated \¦ən+\ *adj* [¹*un-* + *contaminated*, past part. of *contaminate*] : not contaminated ⟨~ primitive societies still going their own way —A.L.Kroeber⟩

un·content \"+\ *adj* [¹*un-* + *content*, adj.] : UNCONTENTED

un·contented \"+\ *adj* : not contented : DISCONTENTED

un·contestable \"+\ *adj* [by alter.] : INCONTESTABLE — **un·contestably** \"+\ *adv*

un·contested \"+\ *adj* [¹*un-* + *contested*, past part. of *contest*] : not contested : UNCHALLENGED ⟨~ superiority⟩

un·continuous \"+\ *adj* : DISCONTINUOUS

un·contradicted \"+\ *adj* [¹*un-* + *contradicted*, past part. of *contradict*] : not contradicted

un·control \"+\ *n* : lack of control ⟨the keen, grey eyes, with their dash of wildness and ~ —H.W.Nevinson⟩

un·controllability \"+\ *n* : the quality or state of being uncontrollable ⟨the ~ of a forest fire whipped by a dry south wind —A.R.Mead⟩

un·controllable \"+\ *adj* [¹*un-* + *controllable*] **1** *obs* : INDISPUTABLE **2** *archaic* : free from the control of a superior power : ABSOLUTE **3** : incapable of being controlled : UNMANAGEABLE ⟨rumor, irresponsible and ~, is dangerous to public morale —F.L.Mott⟩ — **un·con·trol·la·ble·ness** *n* -ES — **un·controllably** \"+\ *adv*

un·con·trolled \¦ənkən¦trōld\ *adj* : not being under control : UNRESTRAINED ⟨the greatest ~ public health problem —G.T. Harrell⟩ — **un·con·trolled·ly** \-l(ə)dlē\ *adv*

un·controvertible \¦ən+\ *adj* : INCONTROVERTIBLE — **un·controvertibly** \"+\ *adv*

un·conventional \"+\ *adj* : not conventional : not bound by or in accordance with convention : being out of the ordinary ⟨~ behavior⟩ ⟨~ weapons⟩ — **un·conventionally** \"+\ *adv*

un·conventionalism \"+\ *n* : UNCONVENTIONALITY

un·conventionality \"+\ *n* : the quality or state of being unconventional

un·conversable \"+\ *adj, archaic* : not inclined or suited to conversation or sociability

un·convert \"+\ *vt* [²*un-* + *convert*] : to reverse the conversion of : restore to a state before conversion

un·converted \"+\ *adj* [¹*un-* + *converted*, past part. of *convert*] **1** : not changed in opinion or action; *specif* : not induced to accept a religious faith : UNREGENERATE ⟨the minds of men as yet ~ —H.O.Taylor⟩ **2** : not changed in form or function ⟨~ wood⟩ ⟨a plant that has stood idle, ~ to war use —*Christian Science Monitor*⟩

un·convertibility \"+\ *n* [*unconvertible* + *-ity*] : INCONVERTIBILITY

un·convertible \"+\ *adj* : INCONVERTIBLE — **un·convertibly** \"+\ *adv*

un·convince \¦ən+\ *vt* [²*un-* + *convince*] : to cause to abandon a conviction ⟨a man thus steeled to his beliefs . . . is not easily *unconvinced* —John Dollard⟩

un·convinced \"+\ *adj* [¹*un-* + *convinced*, past part. of *convince*] : not convinced : DUBIOUS ⟨admitted the force of the argument but remained ~⟩

un·convincing \"+\ *adj* : not convincing : IMPLAUSIBLE ⟨as ~ as a forced smile —Jan Struther⟩ — **un·con·vinc·ing·ly** *adv* — **un·con·vinc·ing·ness** *n* -ES

un·convoluted \"+\ *adj* : not convoluted

un·cooked \"+\ *adj* [¹*un-* + *cooked*, past part. of *cook*] : not cooked : RAW ⟨an ~ dish⟩ ⟨an ~ and slapdash theory of human nature —W.L.Sullivan⟩

un·cooled \"+\ *adj* [¹*un-* + *cooled*, past part. of *cool*] : not cooled

un·cooperative \"+\ *adj* : not cooperative : REFRACTORY ⟨an ~ attitude⟩ ⟨an ~ witness⟩

un·coordinated \"+\ *adj* : not coordinated : lacking proper or effective coordination ⟨~ scheduling often resulted in conflicting games in the same neighborhood —*Current Biog.*⟩ ⟨~, scattered agencies —*Scientific American*⟩

un·coquettish \"+\ *adj* : not coquettish : not trifling or insincere ⟨~ behavior⟩ — **un·co·quet·tish·ly** *adv*

uncor *abbr* uncorrected

un·cord \¦ən+\ *vt* [ME *uncorden*, fr. ²*un-* + *cord*, n.] : to release from cords : loosen the cords of

un·cordial \"+\ *adj* : not cordial : lacking in friendly warmth ⟨looked ~ and standoffish as they drove past —H.L.Davis⟩ — **un·cordially** \"+\ *adv*

un·core prist \ˈən,kō(ə)rˈprist\ *n* [AF, still ready] : an old plea at law that payment of a debt was and still is tendered

un·cork \¦ən+\ *vt* [²*un-* + *cork*] **1** : to draw a cork from ⟨~*ed* the bottle of wine⟩ **2 a** : to release from a sealed or pent-up state ⟨~*ed* another surprise last week —*Springfield (Mass.) Union*⟩ **b** : to let go or propel with sudden force ⟨~*ed* a wild pitch that got past the catcher⟩

un·corporal \"+\ *adj, archaic* : INCORPOREAL ⟨~ as the light —S.V.Benét⟩

un·corrected \"+\ *adj* [ME, fr. ¹*un-* + *corrected*, past part. of *correcten* to correct] **1** : not made correct : left faulty or wrong ⟨an ~ error⟩ **2** : not subjected to correction or improvement by discipline or guidance ⟨let her children grow up ~⟩ **3 a** : not neutralized ⟨~ astigmatism⟩ **b** : not adjusted ⟨an ~ score⟩

un·corrupt \"+\ *adj* [ME, fr. ¹*un-* + *corrupt*] : INCORRUPT

un·corrupted \"+\ *adj* [ME, fr. ¹*un-* + *corrupted*, past part. of *corrupten* to corrupt] **1** : not subjected to corruption : not decomposed **2** : free from moral corruption : not debased or made corrupt ⟨though his associates were dishonest, he remained ~⟩ ⟨~ values⟩ — **un·cor·rupt·ed·ly** *adv* — **un·cor·rupt·ed·ness** *n*

un·corruptible \"+\ *adj* [ME, fr. ¹*un-* + *corruptible*] *archaic* : INCORRUPTIBLE ⟨the glory of the ~ God —Rom 1:23 (AV)⟩

un·cor·rupt·ness *n* [*uncorrupt* + *-ness*] *archaic* : the quality or state of being incorrupt

un·corseted \¦ən+\ *adj* [¹*un-* + *corset* + *-ed*] **1** : not wearing a corset **2** : not controlled, inhibited, or restricted ⟨their language is as ~ and robust as English —Harrison Smith⟩

uncos *pl of* UNCO

un·costly \"+\ *adj* : INEXPENSIVE

¹**un·countable** \"+\ *adj* **1 a** : INNUMERABLE ⟨~ shingles devastated by white ants —William Beebe⟩ **b** : impossible to count ⟨uncounted and ~ sums paid out by various individuals for electioneering activities of their own —*Nation*⟩ **2** : INESTIMABLE ⟨a source of ~ joy⟩

²**uncountable** \"\ *n* : MASS NOUN

un·counted \"+\ *adj* [ME *uncountit*, fr. ¹*un-* + *countit*, past part. of *counten* to count] **1** : not counted ⟨a stack of ~ bills⟩ **2** : INNUMERABLE ⟨~ millions of people —W.J.Reilly⟩

un·couple \"+\ *vb* [ME *uncouplen*, fr. ²*un-* + *couplen* to couple] *vt* **1** : to loose (dogs) from a couple : RELEASE ⟨*uncoupled* the hounds⟩ **2** : DETACH, DISCONNECT ⟨~*s* the 20-foot lengths of aluminum pipe —W.C.Fournier⟩ ⟨~ railroad cars⟩ ⟨~ their minds from all their usual interests —Susanne K. Langer⟩ **3** : to throw off or release a coupler of (a pipe organ) ~ *vi* **1** : to unleash hounds for the chase ⟨~ in the western valley; let them go —Shak.⟩ **2** : to detach a connection ⟨don't ~ until she drains —Wirt Williams⟩

un·coursed \"+\ *adj* [¹*un-* + *course*, n. + *-ed*] : not laid or placed in courses — used of masonry

un·courteous \"+\ *adj* [ME *uncurteis*, fr. ¹*un-* + *curteis* courteous] : lacking in courtesy ⟨the idea of being ~ to any man in my own house is particularly grievous to me —Anthony Trollope⟩ — **un·cour·te·ous·ly** *adv* — **un·cour·te·ous·ness** *n*

un·courtly \"+\ *adj* **1** : not suitable for a court : lacking in courtliness ⟨a little squat, ~ figure —Laurence Sterne⟩ **2** : not favoring a court ⟨an ~ faction⟩

un·couth \¦ən¦küth\ *adj* [ME, fr. OE *uncūth*, fr. ¹*un-* + *cūth* known, familiar — more at COUTH] **1 a** *archaic* : not known or familiar to one : UNACCUSTOMED ⟨toiled out my ~ passage —John Milton⟩ **b** *archaic* : seldom experienced : WONDERFUL, UNCOMMON, RARE **c** *obs* : MYSTERIOUS, UNCANNY ⟨surprised with an ~ fear —Shak.⟩ **d** : not usually or normally encountered or used : ODD, UNFAMILIAR ⟨the air was full of the sounds of ~ instruments —Arnold Bennett⟩ ⟨whipped the crutch out of his armpit, and sent that ~ missile hurtling through the air —R.L.Stevenson⟩ **2 a** : seldom visited or frequented : DESOLATE, SOLITARY ⟨if this ~ forest yield anything savage —Shak.⟩ **b** : UNCOMFORTABLE, UNPLEASANT ⟨found conditions rough and ~ —E.M.Coulter⟩ **3 a** : strange or clumsy in shape or appearance : OUTLANDISH ⟨crouching down behind the bulwarks, ~ in his equipment —Nevil Shute⟩ ⟨made his own glass, thick and ~ but homemade —O.S.J. Gogarty⟩ **b** : lacking in polish and grace : RUGGED ⟨a composer with a bold, ~ quality —Aaron Copland⟩ ⟨the essential jargon is necessarily ~ —*Times Lit. Supp.*⟩ **c** : awkward and uncultivated in appearance, manner, or behavior : RUDE ⟨the inherent courtesy and tenderness of the untutored and ~ human being —Harrison Smith⟩ **d** : marked by or revealing a lack of cultivation and refinement : BOORISH ⟨their laughter was often ~, often boastful —Bergen Evans⟩ ⟨~ to converse while at meals —Nora Waln⟩ ⟨embarrassed by the ~ stare —Liam O'Flaherty⟩ — **un·couth·ly** *adv* — **un·couth·ness** *n* -ES

un·covenanted \¦ən+\ *adj* [¹*un-* + *covenanted*, past part. of *covenant*] **1 a** : not granted or entered into under a covenant; *specif* : not assured by divine promises or conditions ⟨the ~ mercies of God⟩ **b** : not having entered into relationship with God through the appointed means **2 a** : not having joined in a league or assented to a covenant or agreement; *specif* : not having signed or adhered to the Scottish National Covenant of 1638 or the Solemn League and Covenant of 1643 **b** : not employed under a covenant ⟨served for many years as an ~ official of the Indian Civil Service⟩ — compare COVENANTED 1a

un·cover \"+\ *vb* [ME *uncoveren*, fr. ²*un-* + *coveren* to cover] *vt* **1** : to make known : bring to light : DISCLOSE, REVEAL ⟨~*ing* political scandals —*Phoenix Flame*⟩ ⟨acquaintance with her ~*s* the reason for this success —S.J.Beck⟩ **2 a** : to expose to view by removing some covering object or material ⟨fragments ~*ed* by excavating parties —*Amer. Guide Series: Pa.*⟩ ⟨~*ed* seventy villages in the valley —*Current Biog.*⟩ **b** : to lay bare by removing clothes from ⟨opened his shirt to ~ his chest⟩ **c** : to drive (as a fox) from cover **3 a** : to take the cover from : divest of covering ⟨~ the box⟩ **b** : to take off the hat from ⟨~*ed* his head⟩ **4 a** : to expose (a line of soldiers) by the moving of forward units to right or left **b** : to deprive of protection : leave open to enemy fire or attack ~ *vi* **1** : to remove a cover or covering ⟨~, dogs, and lap —Shak.⟩ **2** : to take off the hat as a token of respect : bare one's head ⟨the crowd stood and the men ~*ed* —Tom Lea⟩

un·covered \"+\ *adj* [ME *uncovert*, fr. ¹*un-* + *covert, covered*, past part. of *coveren* to cover] **1** : not supplied with a cover or covering ⟨an ~ pit⟩: as **a** : having no roof ⟨an ~ shed⟩ **b** : BARE ⟨~ legs⟩ **c** : BAREHEADED ⟨was caught ~ by the downpour⟩ **2** : not protected: as **a** : not covered by insurance or included in a social insurance or welfare program **b** : not covered by collateral ⟨an ~ note⟩ **3** : not taken care of; *specif* : not provided with a teacher ⟨an ~ class⟩

un·cowl \"+\ *vt* [²*un-* + *cowl*] : to remove a cowl or similar covering from ⟨think us friends — ~ your face —S.T.Coleridge⟩

un·creased \"+\ *adj* [¹*un-* + *creased*, past part. of *crease*] : lacking a crease ⟨~ trousers⟩

¹**un·create** \"+\ *adj* [¹*un-* + *create*, adj.] : UNCREATED

²**un·create** \"+\ *vt* [²*un-* + *create*, v.] : to deprive of existence : ANNIHILATE

un·created \"+\ *adj* [¹*un-* + *created*, past part. of *create*] **1** : not existing by creation : ETERNAL, SELF-EXISTENT **2** : not yet created ⟨misery ~ till the crime of thy rebellion —John Milton⟩ — **un·cre·at·ed·ness** *n*

un·creation \"+\ *n* [²*uncreate* + *-ion*] : the act of uncreating

un·creative \"+\ *adj* : not creative : STERILE ⟨an ~ imagination⟩ — **un·cre·a·tive·ness** *n*

un·creditable \¦ən+\ *adj* : DISCREDITABLE

un·credited \"+\ *adj* [¹*un-* + *credited*, past part. of *credit*] : not credited : not believed or trusted ⟨what the light of your mind . . . pronounces incredible . . . leave ~ —Thomas Carlyle⟩

un·crippled \"+\ *adj* [¹*un-* + *crippled*, past part. of *cripple*] : not crippled or deformed ⟨grow up emotionally ~ —Alfred Werner⟩

un·critical \"+\ *adj* **1** : not critical : lacking in discrimination : not evaluating or judging ⟨she was absolutely ~, she believed everything —Audrey Barker⟩ ⟨a devoted, almost ~ admirer —D.W.Brogan⟩ **2** : marked by a disregard for or improper use of critical standards or procedures ⟨news sources reflected ~ estimates of the number of juvenile addicts —D.W. Maurer & V.H.Vogel⟩ — **un·critically** \"+\ *adv*

un·criticized \"+\ *adj* [¹*un-* + *criticized*, past part. of *criticize*] : not subjected to criticism ⟨many of the most ~ concepts of science and philosophy are . . . human constructions —J.W. Krutch⟩

un·cropped \"+\ *adj* [¹*un-* + *cropped*, past part. of *crop*] **1** : not cut or picked : not browsed ⟨~ flowers⟩ **2** : not subjected to cutting or trimming ⟨~ hair⟩ ⟨an ~ dog⟩ ⟨the dog's ~ ears⟩ **3** : not used for a crop : not cultivated ⟨~ soil⟩ ⟨~ land⟩

un·cross \"+\ *vt* [²*un-* + *cross*] : to change the position of so as no longer to be crossed ⟨~*ed* her legs and smoothed her skirt —J.P.Marquand⟩

un·crowded \"+\ *adj* : not crowded : having or allowing sufficient room ⟨an ~ train⟩ ⟨an ~ view⟩

un·crown \"+\ *vt* [ME *uncrounen*, fr. ²*un-* + *crounen* to crown] **1** : to deprive of a crown : DEPOSE, DETHRONE **2** : to reveal as if by taking off a crown : DISPLAY

un·crowned \"+\ *adj* [¹*un-* + *crowned*] **1** : not having or wearing a crown ⟨the coin shows an ~ head⟩ **2** : having royal power or status without formal royal rank or title ⟨an almost mythical figure, one of the ~ rulers of Europe and Asia —*Manchester Guardian Weekly*⟩

un·crumple \"+\ *vb* [²*un-* + *crumple*] *vt* : to smooth the creases and wrinkles from ⟨*uncrumpled* the letter . . . laid it on his knee, and ironed it with the palm of his hand —J.F. Powers⟩ ~ *vi* : to become free from creases or wrinkles

un·crystallized \"+\ *adj* : not crystallized; *specif* : not finally or definitely formed ⟨~ ideas⟩

unct *abbr* uncut

unc·tion \ˈəŋ(k)shən\ *n* -S [ME *unctioun, unccioun*, fr. L *unction-, unctio* act of anointing, fr. *unctus* (past part. of *unguere* to anoint, smear) + *-ion-, -io* -ion — more at OINTMENT] **1 a** : the act of anointing that is a symbol of consecration ⟨this act of ~, not the act of crowning, which is the essential feature of a coronation —H.V.Morton⟩ **b** (1) : the anointing of the sick with oil that is a religious rite of healing (2) *often cap* : the seventh and last sacrament of the Eastern Orthodox Church — compare EXTREME UNCTION, HOLY UNCTION **2** : a benign spiritual influence ⟨all human systems based on material premises are minus the ~ of divine Science —Mary B. Eddy⟩ **3 a** : the application of a soothing or lubricating oil

or ointment **b :** something that is used for anointing : OINTMENT, UNGUENT ⟨bought an ~ of a mountebank —Shak.⟩ **c :** something that soothes or eases ⟨lay not that flattering ~ to your soul —Shak.⟩ **4 a :** religious or spiritual fervor or the expression (as in language or manner) of such fervor ⟨was always a powerful preacher; but oh, the ~ of the discourse this morning —George Borrow⟩ **b :** exaggerated, assumed, or superficial earnestness of language or manner : UNCTUOUSNESS ⟨students like polemics, but they detest preachment and they loathe ~ —H.N.Fairchild⟩ **c :** an earnest and sympathetic absorption in something one is acting, doing, or speaking ⟨an intelligent, not very original man — but doing his work with pleasant ~ —O.W.Holmes †1935⟩

unc·tion·al \-shənᵊl, -shnəl\ *adj* [*unction* + *-al*] : full of or characterized by spiritual or devotional fervor

unc·tion·less \-shənləs\ *adj* : lacking in unction

unc·tious \ˈəŋ(k)shəs\ *adj* [ME *unctius*, alter. (influenced by *unctioun* unction) of *unctuous*] : UNCTUOUS — **unc·tious·ness** *n* -ES

unc·tu·os·i·ty \ˌəŋ(k)chəˈwäsəd·ē, -sətē, -i\ *n* -ES [ME *unctuosite*, fr. MF or ML; MF *unctuosité*, fr. ML *unctuositat-*, *unctuositas*, fr. *unctuosus* unctuous + L *-itat-*, *-itas* -ity] : the quality or state of being unctuous

unc·tu·ous \ˈəŋ(k)chəwəs, -)chəs, -)sh-\ *adj* [ME, fr. MF or ML; MF *unctueux*, fr. ML *unctuosus*, irreg. fr. L *unctum* ointment (fr. neut. of *unctus*, past part. of *unguere* to anoint) + *-osus* -ous — more at OINTMENT] **1 a :** having the nature or qualities of an unguent or ointment : FATTY, GREASY, OILY ⟨rubbed on an ~ preparation⟩ **b :** rich in oil or fat : containing a great deal of grease ⟨it took floods of drink to wash down these ~ and heavily flavored courses —Silas Spitzer⟩ **c :** having some of the nature or qualities of grease ⟨an ~ vapor⟩ **d :** smooth and greasy in texture or appearance ⟨~ with kitchen smoke —Nathaniel Hawthorne⟩ : suggestive of fat or grease ⟨~ feel⟩ **2 a :** rich in organic matter and easily workable ⟨~ soil⟩ **b :** PLASTIC ⟨a layer of fine ~ clay —C.O.Dunbar⟩ **3 :** full of unction; *esp* : revealing or marked by a smug, ingratiating, and false earnestness or spirituality : OILY ⟨the devastating portrait of the ~ literary opportunist —R.A Cordell⟩ ⟨his ~ morality, which sickens later ages —Roy Lewis & Angus Maude⟩ — **unc·tu·ous·ly** *adv* — **unc·tu·ous·ness** *n* -ES

un·culled \ˌən+\ *adj* [¹*un-* + *culled*, past part. of *cull*] : not subjected to culling

un·cultivable \"+\ *adj* : not able to be cultivated ⟨thickets of indigenous trees are preserved on ~ land —C.B.Palmer⟩

un·cultivatable \"+\ *adj* : UNCULTIVABLE

un·cultivated \"+\ *adj* **1 a :** lacking in education or refinement : UNCULTURED ⟨the people are ignorant and ~ —Edmund Wilson⟩ **b :** BARBAROUS, UNCIVILIZED ⟨an ~ age⟩ **2 a :** not put under cultivation : not tilled ⟨~ land⟩ **b :** growing or developing without care ⟨an ~ plant⟩ **3 :** not developed by training or education ⟨an ~ genius⟩

un·cultivation \"+\ *n* : lack of cultivation

un·culture \"+\ *n* : lack of culture ⟨ignorance, ~ or, at the best, mediocrity has triumphed —Malcolm Cowley⟩

un·cultured \"+\ *adj* [¹*un-* + *cultured*, past part. of *culture*] **1 :** not subjected to cultivation ⟨a wild ~ scene —T.L.Peacock⟩ **2 :** not improved or refined by education : BACKWARD ⟨its dreary, unjust, and ~ society —Edward Shils⟩

un·cumbered \"+\ *adj* [¹*un-* + *cumbered*, past part. of *cumber*] : UNENCUMBERED

un·curable \"+\ *adj* [by alter.] : INCURABLE

uncurbable *adj* [¹*un-* + *curb* + *-able*] *obs* : not capable of being curbed

un·curbed \ˌən+\ *adj* [¹*un-* + *curbed*, past part. of *curb*] : not curbed : not restrained or held back ⟨sat erect in his saddle with the innate confidence of the ~ —Francis Hackett⟩

un·cured \"+\ *adj* [¹*un-* + *cured*, past part. of *cure*] **1 :** not made healthy ⟨an ~ wound⟩ ⟨an ~ patient⟩ **2 :** not subjected to a preservative process ⟨~ hides⟩ ⟨~ meat⟩

un·curious \"+\ *adj* : INCURIOUS

un·curl \"+\ *vb* [²*un-* + *curl*] *vi* : to become straightened out from a curled or coiled position ~ *vt* : to straighten the curls of : UNROLL

un·curled \"+\ *adj* [¹*un-* + *curled*, past part. of *curl*] : not having curls ⟨~ hair⟩ : not having a curled shape or position ⟨lay ~ on the bed⟩

un·current \"+\ *adj* : not current; *specif* : not passing in common payment : not receivable at par or full value ⟨~ coins⟩

un·curse \"+\ *vt* [²*un-* + *curse*] : to free from a curse ⟨somebody discovered that it was a moral book, and so a good many people *uncursed* him —*Manchester Guardian Weekly*⟩

un·cursed \"+\ *adj* [¹*un-* + *cursed*, adj.] : not cursed or afflicted ⟨his dialogue is ~ with flabbiness —John Mason Brown⟩

un·curtain \"+\ *vt* [²*un-* + *curtain*] : to remove a curtain from : REVEAL, UNVEIL

un·curtained \"+\ *adj* [¹*un-* + *curtained*, past part. of *curtain*] : not having a curtain ⟨the ~ windows⟩

un·cus \ˈəŋkəs\ *n, pl* **un·ci** \ˈənˌsī\ [NL, fr. L, hook, barb — more at ANGLE] : HOOK, CLAW: as **a :** the anterior curved end of the hippocampal convolution **b :** the head of the malleus of the mastax in a rotifer that is often hooked or bears one or more teeth **c** (1) : a median beaked plate or process dorsal to the copulatory apparatus of a male insect (2) : an appendix of the copulatory bulb in a male spider

un·customary \"+\ *adj* : not customary : RARE, UNCOMMON ⟨an ~ access of rage shook my body —L.A.Fiedler⟩

un·customed \"+\ *adj* [in sense 1, fr. ME, fr. ¹*un-* + *custom*, *customs* + *-ed*; in other senses, fr. ¹*un-* + *customed*, past part. of *custom*] **1 :** not having passed through the customs ⟨was charged with being in possession of ~ goods —*Auckland (New Zealand) Weekly News*⟩ **2** *archaic* : UNACCUSTOMED **3** *archaic* : UNUSUAL

un·cut \"+\ *adj* [ME *unkitt*, fr. ¹*un-* + *kitt* cut] **1 a :** not subjected to a cut or incision (as with a knife) ⟨glad to get out of the house with my throat ~ —Tobias Smollett⟩ **b :** not subjected to cutting ⟨~ grass⟩ ⟨~ trees⟩ **2 :** not reduced or shaped by cutting ⟨an ~ diamond⟩ **3** *of a book or periodical* : having leaves whose edges have not been trimmed subsequent to the printing of the sheets; *broadly* : not having the folds of the leaves slit — compare UNOPENED **4 :** not abridged or curtailed ⟨an ~ text⟩ ⟨an ~ performance of the opera⟩

uncut velvet *n* : a velvet with a looped pile

un·dam \ˌən+\ *vt* [²*un-* + *dam*] : to release from or as if from a dam

un·damaged \"+\ *adj* [¹*un-* + *damaged*, past part. of *damage*] : not damaged or injured : UNHURT, SOUND

un·da ma·ris \ˌəndəˈma(a)rəs\ *n* [NL, lit., wave of the sea] : an 8-foot pipe organ stop producing undulations from two ranks of pipes tuned slightly apart or from one rank tuned slightly flat and used in connection with other stops — compare VOIX CELESTE

un·damped \ˌən+\ *adj* [¹*un-* + *damped*, past part. of *damp*] **1 :** not stifled or checked : not depressed ⟨proceed with ~ ardor⟩ **2 :** not checked or retarded by a damper ⟨~ vibrations⟩ ⟨~ musical strings⟩ **3 :** not dampened by moisture **4** *of an electrical or mechanical oscillation* : not damped : maintained with undiminished amplitude

undamped waves *n pl* : CONTINUOUS WAVES

un·dangerous \"+\ *adj* : not dangerous

un·daring \"+\ *adj* : not daring : afraid or unwilling to venture or take risks : TIMID

un·darkened \"+\ *adj* [¹*un-* + *darkened*, past part. of *darken*] : not darkened : CLEAR

un·dashed \"+\ *adj* [¹*un-* + *dashed*, past part. of *dash*] **1 :** not dashed : not qualified or diluted ⟨belief ~ with doubt⟩ : UNDAUNTED **2 :** provided with no dash

un·datable \"+\ *adj* : not capable of being given a date

un·dated \"+\ *adj* [¹*un-* + *dated*, past part. of *date*] **1 :** not dated : bearing no date ⟨an ~ letter⟩ **2 :** having no specified date of termination : having no limit or no end ⟨~ securities⟩

un·daughterliness \"+\ *n* : attitude or behavior unbecoming a daughter

un·daughterly \"+\ *adj* [¹*un-* + *daughterly*] : unbecoming a daughter

un·daunt·able \ˌənˈdȯntəbəl, -dän-, -dan-\ *adj* [¹*un-* + *daunt*, v. + *-able*] : incapable of being daunted : INTREPID, FEARLESS, INDOMITABLE

un·daunted \ˌən+\ *adj* [¹*un-* + *daunted*, past part. of *daunt*] : not daunted : courageous with an undiminished resolution or boldness : UNDISMAYED, UNDASHED ⟨~ by repeated failure⟩ ⟨~ in the face of death⟩ **syn** see BRAVE

un·daunt·ed·ly *adv* : in an undaunted manner : with undiminished spirit or courage

un·daunt·ed·ness *n* -ES : unshaken courage or resolution

un·dazzled \ˌən+\ *adj* [¹*un-* + *dazzled*, past part. of *dazzle*] : not dazzled

un·dé *or* **un·dée** \ˈəndā\ *or* **on·dé** \ōⁿˈdā\ *or* **on·dy** \ˈändē\ *or* **un·dy** \ˈəndē\ *adj* [AF *undé* & *undee* (fem. of *undé*), fr. OF *unde*, *onde* wave (fr. L *unda*) + *-é* (fr. L *-atus* -ate) — more at WATER] : WAVING, WAVY — used of division lines

un·dead \ˌən+\ *n, pl* **undead** : VAMPIRE 1 — used with *the*

un·dealt \"+\ *adj* [¹*un-* + *dealt*, past part. of *deal*] : not dealt ⟨~ cards⟩ ⟨problems still ~ with⟩

un·dear \"+\ *adj* : not dear : DISESTEEMED, CHEAP

un·debatable \"+\ *adj* : not subject to debate : INDISPUTABLE ⟨~ facts⟩

un·debauched \"+\ *adj* : INNOCENT, UNCORRUPTED

undec- *comb form* [L *undecim*, prob. fr. *unus* one + *decem* ten — more at ONE, TEN] : eleven ⟨*undec*ane⟩ ⟨*undec*ennial⟩ ⟨*undec*illion⟩

un·dec·a·gon \ˌənˈdekəˌgän\ *n* -S [*undec-* + *-agon* (as in *decagon*)] : a plane figure having eleven angles and eleven sides

un·de·cane \ˈəndəˌkān, ˌənˈde,-\ *n* -S [*undec-* + *-ane*] : any of several liquid isomeric paraffin hydrocarbons $C_{11}H_{24}$; *esp* : the normal hydrocarbon $CH_3(CH_2)_9CH_3$ — called also *hendecane*

un·dec·a·no·ic acid \ˌənˌdekəˈnōik-\ *n* [*undecane* + *-oic*] : a crystalline acid $CH_3(CH_2)_9COOH$ usu. made by hydrogenation of undecylenic acid — called also *undecylic acid*

un·deceivable \ˌən+\ *adj* **1** *obs* : not deceiving : not deceitful **2 :** not capable of being deceived ⟨~ common sense⟩

un·deceive \"+\ *vt* [²*un-* + *deceive*] : to free from deception, fraud, fallacy, or mistaken ideas : set straight : DISABUSE — **un·deceiver** \"+\ *n*

un·dec·e·no·ic acid \ˌənˌdesəˈnōik-\ *n* [*undec-* + *-ene* + *-oic*] : any of several isomeric straight-chain unsaturated acids $C_{10}H_{19}COOH$ (as undecylenic acid)

un·decent \ˌən+\ *adj, archaic* : INDECENT

un·de·cep·tion \ˌəndəˈsepshən\ *n* : the act of undeceiving : a being undeceived

un·decidable \ˌən+\ *adj* : not capable of being decided

un·decided \"+\ *adj* [¹*un-* + *decided*, past part. of *decide*] **1 :** not yet determined : UNSETTLED **2 :** WAVERING, INCONSTANT, IRRESOLUTE ⟨fitful, ~ rain on the face of the land —Rudyard Kipling⟩ — **un·de·cid·ed·ly** *adv* — **un·de·cid·ed·ness** *n*

un·de·cil·lion \ˌəndəˈsilyən\ *n, often attrib* [*undec-* + *-illion* (as in *million*)] — see NUMBER table

un·decimal \ˌənˈdesəməl\ *adj* [*undec-* + *-imal* (as in *decimal*)] : numbered or proceeding by elevens : based on the number 11

un·de·ci·pher·abil·i·ty \ˌəndəˌsīfərəˈbiləd·ē\ *n* : the quality or state of being undecipherable

un·decipherable \ˌən+\ *adj* : not capable of being deciphered ⟨scratched with marks which were long ~ —Charlton Laird⟩ ⟨looked at him with a face which was quite ~ —G.K.Chesterton⟩ — **un·decipherably** \"+\ *adv*

un·deciphered \"+\ *adj* [¹*un-* + *deciphered*, past part. of *decipher*] : not deciphered

un·decisive \"+\ *adj* : INDECISIVE — **un·decisively** \"+\ *adv* — **un·decisiveness** \"+\ *n*

un·deck \"+\ *vt* [²*un-* + *deck*] : to divest of ornament

un·decked \"+\ *adj* [in sense 1, fr. ¹*un-* + *decked*, past part. of *deck*, v.; in sense 2, fr. ¹*un-* + *deck*, n. + *-ed*] **1 :** not decked : UNADORNED **2 :** not having a deck ⟨a ~ rowboat⟩

un·declared \"+\ *adj* [¹*un-* + *declared*, past part. of *declare*] : not declared : not announced or openly acknowledged ⟨~ war⟩ ⟨~ emergency⟩

un·declinable \"+\ *adj* [¹*un-* + *decline*, v. + *-able*] **1 :** INDECLINABLE **2 :** that cannot be refused or rejected ⟨~ offer⟩ **3** *obs* : UNAVOIDABLE — **un·de·clin·able·ness** *n* -ES — **un·de·clin·ably** \-blē\ *adv*

un·declined \ˌən+\ *adj* [¹*un-* + *declined*, past part. of *decline*] : having no inflected forms ⟨~ noun⟩

un·de·co·ic acid \ˌəndəˈkōik-\ *n* [*undecane* + *-oic*] : any of the monocarboxylic acids $C_{10}H_{21}COOH$ derived from the undecanes

un·decomposable \ˌən+\ *adj* : not subject to decomposing or division ⟨a soul postulated as ~ and immortal activity —M.T. Keeton⟩ ⟨a feeling is a simple and ~ mental state —G.S. Brett⟩

un·decomposed \"+\ *adj* : not decomposed

un·decorated \"+\ *adj* : not decorated : left without ornament or embellishment : PLAIN ⟨~ arch⟩ ⟨~ facts⟩

un·decorative \"+\ *adj* [¹*un-* + *decorate* + *-ive*] : not decorative ⟨~ use of adjectives —Josephine Miles⟩; *sometimes* : UNSIGHTLY, UGLY

un·decorous \"+\ *adj* : INDECOROUS

un·decorticated \"+\ *adj* [¹*un-* + *decorticated*, past part. of *decorticate*] : not decorticated : WHOLE ⟨~ cottonseed⟩

un·decyl \ˌənˈdesəl, -dēs-\ *n* [ISV *undec-* + *-yl*] : an alkyl radical $C_{11}H_{23}$ derived from an undecane; *esp* : the normal radical $CH_3(CH_2)_9CH_2$ — called also *hendecyl*

un·dec·y·len·ate \ˌən,desəˈle,nāt, -ˈlē,-\ *n* -S [*undecylenic* + *-ate*] : a salt or ester of undecylenic acid

un·dec·y·len·ic acid \ˌ≈;≈ˈlenik-, -lēnik-\ *n* [*undecylene* $C_{11}H_{22}$ (fr. *undecyl* + *-ene*) + *-ic*] : a liquid or crystalline acid $CH_2{=}CH(CH_2)_8COOH$ that is a component of perspiration, that is formed from ricinoleic acid in the vacuum distillation of castor oil, and that is used sometimes in the form of a salt in the treatment of fungous infections esp. of the skin; 10-undecenoic acid

un·de·cyl·ic acid \ˌəndəˈsilik-\ *n* [*undecyl* + *-ic*] : UNDECOIC ACID; *esp* : UNDECANOIC ACID

un·dedicated \ˌən+\ *adj* : not dedicated

undée *var of* UNDÉ

undeeded *adj* [¹*un-* + *deed*, n. + *-ed*] *obs* : not exploited in deeds ⟨my sword . . . I sheathe again ~ —Shak.⟩

un·defaced \ˌən+\ *adj* [ME, fr. ¹*un-* + *defaced*, past part. of *defacen* to deface — more at DEFACE] : not defaced or obliterated

un·de·feat·able \ˌəndəˈfēd·əbəl\ *adj* [¹*un-* + *defeat*, v. + *-able*] : incapable of being defeated or of accepting defeat : UNCONQUERABLE, INVINCIBLE

un·defeated \ˌən+\ *adj* [¹*un-* + *defeated*, past part. of *defeat*] : not defeated : not having suffered a defeat ⟨the team was ~ and untied all season⟩

un·defendable \"+\ *adj* : not capable of being defended esp. by military action ⟨~ islands⟩ — **un·de·fend·able·ness** *n* -ES

un·defended \"+\ *adj* [¹*un-* + *defended*, past part. of *defend*] **1 :** not guarded or protected ⟨left the goal ~⟩ ⟨~ frontier⟩ **2 :** not provided with legal assistance

un·defiled \"+\ *adj* [ME, fr. ¹*un-* + *defiled*, past part. of *defilen* to defile — more at DEFILE] : UNTAINTED, UNCORRUPTED, PURE ⟨learn to speak pure English ~ —Van Wyck Brooks⟩

un·definable \"+\ *adj* : INDEFINABLE — **un·de·fin·able·ness** *n* -ES — **un·definably** \"+\ *adv*

un·defined \"+\ *adj* [¹*un-* + *defined*, past part. of *define*] **1 :** not defined : not precisely limited, determined, or distinguished : VAGUE ⟨some ~ sense of excitement —W.H. Wright⟩ **2 :** not capable of being described or limited in words : PRIMITIVE ⟨~ term⟩ ⟨~ concept⟩ — **un·de·fined·ly** \-nədlē, -nd-\ *adv* — **un·de·fined·ness** \-nədnəs, -n(d)nəs\ *n* -ES

un·deflected \ˌən+\ *adj* [¹*un-* + *deflected*, past part. of *deflect*] : not deflected ⟨~ ray⟩

un·deflowered \"+\ *adj* [¹*un-* + *deflowered*, past part. of *deflower*] : VIRGIN, INNOCENT, UNTOUCHED

un·deformed \"+\ *adj* : not deformed : free of deformity or deformation

un·degenerate \"+\ *adj* : not degenerate : showing no loss of vigor

un·deify \"+\ *vt* [²*un-* + *deify*] : to degrade from the state of deity

un·delayed \"+\ *adj* [ME, fr. ¹*un-* + *delayed*, past part. of *delayen* to delay — more at DELAY] : not delayed : IMMEDIATE

un·deliberate \ˌən+\ *adj* : not intended : not calculated — **un·de·lib·er·ate·ness** *n*

un·delight \ˌən+\ *n* : want of delight : UNHAPPINESS

un·delightful \"+\ *adj* : not delightful : UNPLEASANT — **un·delightfully** \"+\ *adv*

un·deliverable \"+\ *adj* : not capable of being delivered to an addressee ⟨~ mail⟩ ⟨~ parcel⟩

un·delivered \"+\ *adj* [ME, fr. ¹*un-* + *delivered*, past part. of *deliveren* to deliver — more at DELIVER] : not delivered

un·delude \"+\ *vt* [²*un-* + *delude*] : UNDECEIVE

un·demanding \"+\ *adj* : not demanding : not exacting ⟨simple, ~ affection⟩

un·democratic \"+\ *adj* : not democratic : not agreeing with democratic doctrine or practice or ideals ⟨objected to volunteering on the ground that it was ~ —*World's Work*⟩ — **un·democratically** \"+\ *adv*

un·democratize \"+\ *vt* [²*un-* + *democratize*] : to cause to cease to be democratic

un·demonstrable \"+\ *adj* : INDEMONSTRABLE — **un·demonstrably** \"+\ *adv*

un·demonstrated \"+\ *adj* [¹*un-* + *demonstrated*, past part. of *demonstrate*] : not supported by proof or logical demonstration ⟨~ faith⟩

un·demonstrative \ˌən+\ *adj* : restrained or reserved in expression of feeling : not effusive — **un·demonstratively** \"+\ *adv* — **un·demonstrativeness** \"+\ *n*

un·deniable \"+\ *adj* [¹*un-* + *deny* + *-able*] **1 :** plainly true : readily conceded : INCONTESTABLE, INDISPUTABLE ⟨~ evidence of a witness⟩ ⟨~ guilt⟩ **2 :** unquestionably excellent or genuine ⟨~ literary classic⟩ ⟨applicant would have to produce ~ references —*Country Life*⟩ — **un·de·ni·able·ness** *n* -ES — **un·de·ni·ably** \-blē, -li\ *adv*

un·denied \ˌən+\ *adj* [¹*un-* + *denied*, past part. of *deny*] : not denied : not contested or disputed

un·denominational \ˌən+\ *adj* : not restricted or belonging to a denomination : UNSECTARIAN ⟨~ religious instruction⟩ — **un·denominationally** \"+\ *adv*

un·dependable \"+\ *adj* : not dependable : UNRELIABLE — **un·de·pend·able·ness** *n* — **un·dependably** \"+\ *adv*

un·depressed \ˌən+\ *adj* **1 :** not dejected **2 :** not pressed down or sunken

un·deprivable \"+\ *adj* **1 :** that cannot be deprived : not deposable **2 :** that one cannot be deprived of ⟨~ possession of property⟩

¹un·der \ˈəndə(r)\ *adv* [ME, adv. & prep., fr. OE; akin to OHG *untar*, adv. & prep., under, ON *undir*, adv. & prep., Goth *undar*, prep., under, L *infra* below, underneath, *inferus* low, situated beneath, Skt *adha* below] **1 :** further down or along in a writing ⟨see ~ for further discussion⟩ **2 a :** in or into a position below or beneath something ⟨wears a girdle ~⟩ : down below ⟨get ~ quick⟩ **b :** below the surface of the water ⟨a gust put the lee deck ~ —Nelson Hayes⟩ **c :** below the horizon ⟨sun went ~ an hour ago⟩ **3 :** below some quantity or limit ⟨ten dollars or ~⟩ — often used in combination ⟨*under*bid⟩ ⟨*under*ripe⟩ ⟨*under*staffed⟩ **4 :** in or into a condition of subjection, regulation, or subordination ⟨kept his disappointment ~⟩ ⟨I keep my body ~ —1 Cor 9:27 (AV)⟩ **5 a :** down to defeat, ruin, or death ⟨weaker competitors will be forced ~⟩ **b :** into unconsciousness ⟨enough ether to put him ~⟩ **c :** so as to be overwhelmed : out of sight ⟨buried ~ by the avalanche⟩ ⟨snowed ~ in the election⟩ **6 :** through a range downward ⟨children of eight and ~⟩

²under \"\ *prep* [ME — more at ¹UNDER] **1 a :** during the ascendancy of ⟨born ~ a lucky star⟩ **b :** lower than and overhung by : having directly overhead ⟨every place ~ the sun⟩ ⟨~ tropical skies⟩ **2 :** in the shelter of ⟨living ~ the same roof⟩ ⟨huddled ~ the tree⟩ ⟨at anchor close ~ the island⟩ ⟨crawled out from ~ the bed⟩ ⟨~ the lee of the bank⟩ **3 :** using for concealment ⟨fled ~ cover of darkness⟩ ⟨entered the house ~ the pretext of asking for directions⟩ **4 :** at the foot of ⟨cottage nestling ~ the hill⟩ ⟨encamped ~ the town walls⟩ ⟨in this little combe ~ the Downs —T.W.Sharp⟩ **5 a :** below or beneath so as to be covered or enveloped or concealed ⟨sleeping ~ blankets⟩ ⟨wore a sweater ~ his jacket⟩ ⟨a kind heart ~ a gruff manner⟩ ⟨mailed ~ separate cover⟩ **b :** below the surface of ⟨diving ~ water⟩ ⟨burrowing ~ the earth⟩ **6 a :** below so as to support or carry ⟨with a good horse ~ him⟩ ⟨put runners ~ a sleigh⟩ ⟨put jacks ~ a beam⟩ **b :** topped or crowned with ⟨~ a huge periwig⟩ : surmounted by ⟨sailing ~ full canvas⟩ ⟨marching ~ a foreign flag⟩ **7 :** at a point below and close to ⟨hit him just ~ the ear⟩ ⟨drew a line ~ the last word⟩ ⟨put one number ~ the other and add them⟩ **8 a :** required by : in accordance with : bound by ⟨~ contract to deliver⟩ ⟨statement ~ oath⟩ ⟨~ the necessity of selling⟩ ⟨rights ~ the law⟩ **b :** suffering restriction, restraint, or control by ⟨sent home ~ guard⟩ ⟨ship placed ~ quarantine⟩ ⟨living ~ strict disciplinary rules⟩ ⟨~ a system of collective security —A.O.Walfers⟩ **c :** in conditions or circumstances of ⟨shocks and strains any language undergoes ~ rapid diffusion —I.A.Richards⟩ **9 a :** weighed upon or oppressed by ⟨travel ~ a heavy load⟩ ⟨laid ~ heavy obligation⟩ ⟨prohibited ~ severe penalties⟩ ⟨laboring ~ a misapprehension⟩ ⟨collapsed ~ the intolerable strain of waiting⟩ ⟨lawmakers are ~ conflicting pressures —*Wall Street Jour.*⟩ **b :** receiving or undergoing the action or application of : exposed to the effect of ⟨land ~ irrigation⟩ ⟨go ~ the surgeon's knife⟩ ⟨~ the influence of a strong emotion⟩ ⟨bravery ~ fire⟩ ⟨came ~ suspicion of theft⟩ ⟨stand up ~ punishment⟩ ⟨in London ~ the bombing —A.N.Whitehead⟩ **c :** in process of ⟨~ repair⟩ ⟨~ discussion⟩ ⟨~ construction⟩ **d :** devoted to the cultivation of : planted to ⟨most of the acreage ~ corn⟩ **e :** contained or enclosed by ⟨thousands of acres ~ fence —*Amer. Guide Series: Texas*⟩ **10 a :** subject to the bidding or authority of : led by ⟨served ~ three colonels⟩ **b :** during the reign or administration of ⟨extended the empire ~ the next king⟩ **c :** subject to the guidance and instruction of ⟨studied piano ~ a famous virtuoso⟩ **11 a :** within the grouping or designation of ⟨matters that come ~ this head⟩ ⟨classified ~ Diptera⟩ **b :** having as name or title ⟨traveling ~ an assumed name⟩ : in the section designated as ⟨looked for it ~ Minerals⟩ ⟨listed ~ Occupations⟩ **c :** attested or warranted by ⟨issued ~ the royal seal⟩ **d :** bearing as signature or indication of authorship ⟨published several works ~ a pen name⟩ **12 a :** inferior to : falling short of : exceeded by : *of, for*, or *in* less than ⟨exempting incomes ~ four thousand⟩ ⟨boys ~ fifteen⟩ ⟨sold ~ the list price⟩ ⟨a mile ~ four minutes⟩ **b :** lower in rank or quality than ⟨hardly speak to anyone ~ a colonel⟩ **c :** lower than or less than the standard or required degree of ⟨while his children are still ~ age⟩ ⟨company was so fearfully ~ strength —F.V.W.Mason⟩ — often used in combination ⟨this whiskey is considerably *under*proof⟩ **d :** one thirty-second less than ⟨~ ½ means 1⁵⁄₃₂⟩ — used on the London stock exchange **13 :** next after in a card game ⟨betting ~ the opener⟩ — **under ditch :** below the water level of a ditch or canal and therefore capable of irrigation — **under night** *Scot* : during the night : concealed by the darkness — **under one** *obs* : at the same time : TOGETHER — **under one's hat 1 :** in one's head **2 :** to oneself : SECRET ⟨keep the news *under your hat*⟩

³under \"\ *adj* [ME, fr. ¹*under*] **1 a :** lying below or beneath ⟨gnawed his ~ lip⟩ — often used in combination ⟨sea's *under*current⟩ ⟨*under*surfaces of furniture⟩ **b :** placed on the ventral side of an animal's body — often used in combination ⟨*under*parts of fish⟩ **c :** facing or protruding downward — often used in combination ⟨*under*surface of a leaf⟩ **2 :** enclosed beneath a covering — often used in combination ⟨*under*layer of a bud⟩ **3 :** lower in rank or authority : SUBORDINATE ⟨~ bookkeepers⟩ — often used in combination ⟨*under*servants of a household⟩ **4 :** lower than usual, proper, or desired in amount, quality, or degree ⟨~ dose of medicine⟩ ⟨ready to fill in if the program proves to be ~⟩ **5 :** SUBDUED ⟨keep the musical accompaniment ~ during the scene⟩

⁴under \"\ *n* -S [¹*under*] : something that falls short in amount, quality, length, or duration; *specif* : a broadcast program lasting less than the time allotted for it

underact \ˌ≈≈ˈ≈\ *vb* [¹*under* + *act*] *vt* **1 :** to perform (a dramatic part) with less than the requisite skill or vigor **2 :** to perform with restraint for greater dramatic impact or personal force ~ *vi* : to perform feebly or with restraint ⟨the rest of the cast knew how to ~ for the greatest small-screen effectiveness —Saul Carson⟩

underaction \ˈ≈≈ˌ≈≈\ *n* [³*under* + *action*] **1 :** subordinate action : a minor action incidental or subsidiary to the main story : EPISODE **2 :** subnormal or insufficient action ⟨~ of focusing muscles of the eye⟩

underactivity \ˌ≈≈ˌ≈ˈ≈≈≈\ *n* [³*under* + *activity*] : an abnormally low degree of activity ⟨~ of thyroid gland⟩

underactor \ˈ==,==\ *n* [³*under* + *actor*] **:** a subordinate actor
¹**un·der·age** \ˌ==ˈ=\ *adj* [²*under* + *age*, n.] **:** of less than mature or legal age
²**un·der·age** \ˈəndərij\ *n* -s [¹*under* + -*age*] **:** SHORTAGE, DEFICIT
underair \ˈ==,=\ *n* [³*under* + *air*] **:** the lowest strata of the atmosphere
¹**underarm** \ˈ==,=\ *adj* [in sense 1, fr. ²*under* + *arm*, n.; in sense 2, fr. ³*under* + *arm*, n.] **1 :** placed under or on the underside of the arm ⟨~ seams⟩ ⟨~ handbag⟩ **2 :** UNDERHAND ⟨~ bowling⟩ ⟨~ pitching delivery⟩ ⟨~ pass in basketball⟩
²**underarm** \ˌ==ˈ=\ *adv* [³*under* + *arm*] **:** UNDERHAND ⟨learning to throw ~⟩
underback \ˈ==,=\ *n* [²*under* + *back*] **:** a vessel used in brewing that receives the wort as it flows from the mash tun
underbake \ˌ==ˈ=\ *vt* [¹*under* + *bake*] **:** to bake less than fully
underbarring \ˈ==,==\ *n* [³*under* + *barring*] **:** barring on the part of the feathers not visible on the surface
underbear \ˌ==ˈ=\ *vt* [ME *underberen*, fr. OE *underberan*, fr. *under*, adv. + *beran* to bear — more at BEAR] **1** *archaic* **:** SUPPORT, ENDURE **2** *obs* **:** to line or trim at the bottom
underbearer \ˈ==,==\ *n* [³*under* + *bearer*] **:** one who assists in bearing the coffin at a funeral — compare PALLBEARER
underbed \ˈ==,=\ *n* [³*under* + *bed*] **:** a mass or layer underlying or supporting something laid over it; *specif* **:** a mattress laid under a feather bed
underbelly \ˈ==,==\ *n* [³*under* + *belly*] **:** the lower surface of a body or mass ⟨see a vast ruddy brilliance flash on the *underbellies* of clouds —Marjory S. Douglas⟩ ⟨~ of a bomber⟩; *esp* **:** a vulnerable area ⟨Sicilian and Italian campaigns . . . could now be launched across the sea against the ~ of Hitler's Europe —Sir Winston Churchill⟩
under bevel *n* **:** a bevel whose angle is acute
¹**underbid** \ˌ==ˈ=\ *vb* [¹*under* + *bid*] *vt* **1** *obs* **:** UNDERVALUE **2 :** to bid less than (a competing bidder) **3 :** to bid (a hand of cards) at less than the strength of the hand warrants ~ *vi* **:** to offer too little in bidding; *specif* **:** to bid less than should be bid or than can reasonably be made on a hand of cards — **underbidder** \ˌ==ˈ==\ *n*
²**underbid** \"\ *n* **1 :** an act of underbidding **2 :** a contract in bridge that is lower than can be made
underbill \ˌ==ˈ=\ *vt* [¹*under* + *bill*] **:** to bill (goods) at less than the real amount
underbit \ˈ==,=\ *n* [³*under* + *bit*] **:** an earmark for cattle corresponding to the overbit but on the lower side of the ear — see EARMARK illustration
underbite \ˌ==ˈ=\ *vt* [¹*under* + *bite*] **:** to etch insufficiently
underblow \ˌ==ˈ=\ *vt* [¹*under* + *blow*] **:** to blow (as a pipe or other wind instrument) with insufficient energy to sound the fundamental tone so that only a set of feeble high overtones is heard — compare OVERBLOW
underbodice \ˈ==,==\ *n* [³*under* + *bodice*] **:** a bodice worn under an open blouse or jacket
underbody \ˈ==,==\ *n* [³*under* + *body*] **1 a** *obs* **:** the lower part of a woman's dress **b** *dial* **:** a garment (as a petticoat, corset cover, slip) worn under an outer garment **2 a :** the lower part of an animal's body **:** UNDERPARTS **b :** the underwater part of a ship's hull **c :** the lower parts of the body of a vehicle or airplane; *esp* **:** the undersurfaces of an automotive vehicle
underbowed \ˌ==ˈ=\ *adj* [¹*under* + *bowed* (furnished with a bow)] **:** using a bow that is too weak or beneath one's strength
underbraced \ˌ==ˈ=\ *adj* [¹*under* + *braced*, past part. of *brace*] **1 :** strengthened underneath by stretchers ⟨~ table legs⟩ **2 :** not sufficiently braced; *specif* **:** depending upon some of its joints for its rigidity ⟨~ truss⟩
underbranch \ˈ==,=\ *n* [³*under* + *branch*] **:** a lower branch
underbreath \ˈ==,=\ *n* [³*under* + *breath*] **:** WHISPER, UNDERTONE ⟨spoke in an ~ —George Meredith⟩
¹**underbred** \ˌ==ˈ=\ *adj* [¹*under* + *bred*] **1 :** marked by lack of good manners or social poise **:** not well-bred **:** ILL-BRED **2 :** of inferior or mixed breed ⟨~ dog⟩
²**underbred** \ˈ==,=\ *n* -s **:** an underbred animal
underbreeding \ˌ==ˈ==\ *n* [³*under* + *breeding*] **:** the condition or quality of being underbred
underbright \ˈ==,=\ *n* -s [³*under* + *bright* (brightness)] **:** a streak of very bright light occasionally seen below clouds near the horizon
underbrim \ˈ==,=\ *n* [³*under* + *brim*] **:** a facing on the underside of a hat brim
¹**underbrush** \ˈ==,=\ *n* [³*under* + *brush*] **1 :** shrubs, bushes, or small trees growing beneath large trees in a wood or forest **:** BRUSH **2 :** a tangled, obstructing, or impeding mass ⟨heavy ~ of footnotes to impede the general reader —Owen Lattimore⟩
²**underbrush** \"\ *vt* **:** to clear of underbrush ~ *vi* **:** to cut or clear away underbrush
underbuild \ˌ==ˈ=\ *vt* [¹*under* + *build*] **1 :** to build a supporting structure underneath **:** build beneath **2 :** to build below the standard of (one's position) **3 :** to fall short of standards of construction in the building of
underburn \ˌ==ˈ=\ *vt* [¹*under* + *burn*] **:** to burn (as clay) at a less than normal temperature
underbush \ˈ==,=\ *n* [³*under* + *bush*] **:** UNDERBRUSH
underbutler \ˈ==,==\ *n* [³*under* + *butler*] **:** a butler's assistant
underbuy \ˌ==ˈ=\ *vi* [¹*under* + *buy*] **:** to buy insufficient quantities
undercanopy \ˈ==,===\ *n* [³*under* + *canopy*] **:** UNDERSTORY
un·der·capitalize \ˌəndə(r)+\ *vt* [¹*under* + *capitalize*] **1 :** to supply with insufficient capital for efficient operation **2 :** to issue a relatively small amount of securities in relation to the earnings and assets of (a business)
undercard \ˈ==,=\ *n* [³*under* + *card*] **:** a program (as of boxing matches) supporting the featured match
undercarriage \ˈ==,==\ *n* [³*under* + *carriage*] **1 :** a supporting framework ⟨~ of a field gun⟩ ⟨~ of a wagon⟩ ⟨~ of an automobile⟩ **2 :** the landing gear of an airplane
undercart \ˈ==,=\ *n* [³*under* + *cart*] *Brit* **:** LANDING GEAR
undercast \ˈ==,=\ *n* [³*under* + *cast*] **1 :** a passage for air carried under a road or floor of a mine **2 :** a cloud layer beneath a flying aircraft
¹**undercharge** \ˌ==ˈ=\ *vt* [¹*under* + *charge*] **1 :** to charge less than is usual or suitable for; *also* **:** to charge (a person) too little for something ⟨~ an oil company for shipments⟩ **2 a :** to load (a gun) with too small an explosive charge **b :** to give (a storage battery) an insufficient charging
²**undercharge** \ˈ==,=\ *n* **:** a charge that is less than is usual or suitable; *specif* **:** a rate assessed a shipper or consignee that is less than the rate prescribed by the tariff
underchurched \ˌ==ˈchərcht\ *adj* [¹*under* + -*churched* (fr. *church*, n. + -*ed*)] **:** not having sufficient churches to meet existing needs ⟨an ~ suburb⟩
underclass \ˌ==ˈ=\ *adj* [back-formation fr. *underclassman*] **:** being or belonging to an underclassman
underclassman \ˌ==ˈ=mən\ *n, pl* **underclassmen** [³*under* + *class*, n. + *man*] **:** a member of the freshman or sophomore class in a college or secondary school
underclay \ˈ==,=\ *n* [³*under* + *clay*] **:** a layer of clay beneath a coal bed often containing fossil roots of coal plants and constituting fireclay
undercliff \ˈ==,=\ *n* [³*under* + *cliff*] **:** a terrace or subordinate cliff on a shore consisting of material fallen from the cliff above
un·der·clothe \ˈ==,klōth\ *vt* [back-formation fr. *underclothing*] **:** to supply with underclothes
underclothed \ˌ==ˈ=\ *adj* [¹*under* + *clothed*, past part. of *clothe*] **:** inadequately clothed
underclothes \ˈ==,=\ *n pl* [³*under* + *clothes*] **:** clothes worn under others; *esp* **:** UNDERWEAR
underclothing \ˈ==,==\ *n* [³*under* + *clothing*] **:** UNDERWEAR
underclub \ˌ==ˈ=\ *vi* [¹*under* + *club*, n.] **:** to use a golf club not designed to yield the distance needed to be covered ⟨failed to reach the green through *underclubbing*⟩
¹**undercoat** \ˈ==,=\ *n* [³*under* + *coat*] **1 :** a coat or jacket formerly worn under another **2 :** a growth of short hair or fur partly concealed by a longer growth ⟨a dog's ~⟩ **3 a :** a coat of paint under another **b :** a paint prepared for use under a finishing coat ⟨red lead ~⟩ **c :** GROUND COAT 2b **4** *Brit* **:** the course of crushed stone that is immediately under the wearing surface of a bituminous pavement **5** *dial* **:** PETTICOAT
²**undercoat** \"\ *vt* **1 :** to apply an undercoat to ⟨~ steelwork with a primer⟩ **2 :** to apply a special waterproof coating to the undersurfaces of a vehicle
undercoater \ˈ==,==\ *n* **:** UNDERCOAT 3b
undercoating \ˈ==,==\ *n* [fr. gerund of ²*undercoat*] **:** UNDERCOAT 3
under–color \ˈ==,==\ *n* [³*under* + *color*] **:** the color of the undercoat of an animal
undercolored \ˌ==ˈ==\ *adj* [¹*under* + *colored*] **1 :** having less color than needed or proper **2 :** having or relating to undercolor
un·der·compounded \ˌəndə(r)+\ *adj* [¹*under* + *compounded*] *of a dynamo or motor* **:** having the shunt and series field coils so related that voltage decreases with increasing load
underconsciousness \ˌ===ˈ===\ *n* [³*under* + *consciousness*] **:** SUBCONSCIOUS
underconsumption \ˌ===ˈ==\ *n* [³*under* + *consumption*] **:** consumption of less than is produced that is caused by insufficient purchasing power and is a cause of business depression
undercook \ˌ==ˈ=\ *vt* [¹*under* + *cook*] **:** to cook insufficiently or less than thoroughly
undercool \ˌ==ˈ=\ *vt* [¹*under* + *cool*] **1 :** to cool less than required for some specified or understood purpose **2 :** SUPERCOOL ⟨glass is an ~*ed* liquid which does not form crystals upon solidification —*Electrical Manufacturing*⟩
undercourse \ˈ==,=\ *n* [³*under* + *course*] **:** a layer (as of flooring) immediately under a course of tiles **:** a course (as of shingles) laid beneath a covering course
undercover \ˌ==ˈ==\ *adj* [²*under* + *cover*] **:** acting or executed in secret **:** SURREPTITIOUS ⟨~ scheme⟩; *specif* **:** employed or engaged in spying or secret investigation ⟨~ agent⟩
undercover man *n* **:** one who undertakes to secure evidence of criminal or illegal actions by working with or among those who are under suspicion; *also* **:** one who secures a position (as in a business or factory) for the purpose of illicitly obtaining confidential information
undercovert \ˈ==,==\ *n* [³*under* + *covert*] **1 :** a covert of underbrush **2 :** one of the small basal feathers of the underside of a bird's wing or tail
undercroft \ˈ==,=\ *n* [ME *under croft*, fr. ³*under* + *croft*, *crofte* vault, crypt — more at CROFT] **:** a subterranean room; *esp* **:** a vaulted chamber under a church **:** CRYPT
undercrossing \ˈ==,==\ *n* [³*under* + *crossing*] **:** UNDERPASS
undercrowded \ˌ==ˈ==\ *adj* [¹*under* + *crowded*] **:** having fewer than the usual or desirable number of members ⟨~ insect population⟩ ⟨~ profession⟩
undercrowding \ˌ==ˈ==\ *n* [³*under* + *crowding*, gerund of *crowd*] **:** the condition or fact of being undercrowded
¹**undercurrent** \ˈ==,==\ *n* [³*under* + *current*] **1 :** a current below the upper currents or surface of a fluid body (as water or air) **2 :** a tendency of opinion or feeling not openly displayed and often contrary to the one publicly shown ⟨an ~ in favor of the accused had set in⟩ **3 undercurrents** *pl* **:** broad branch sluices in placer mining set at small inclination into which water carrying fine gold is diverted from the main sluice to lessen the velocity of flow in order to promote the settling **4 :** an electric current whose intensity is lower than a specified amount
²**undercurrent** \"\ *adj* **:** running under the surface **:** passing in secret **:** HIDDEN ⟨~ protest⟩
¹**undercut** \ˌ==ˈ=\ *vb* [¹*under* + *cut*, v.] *vt* **1 :** to cut away the underpart of ⟨~ a vein of ore⟩ **2 :** to cut away material from the underside of (an object) so as to leave an overhanging portion in relief ⟨~ the leaves of a wood carving⟩ **:** cut free from beneath ⟨~ the skin of the cheek in plastic surgery⟩ **3 a :** to offer to sell at lower prices than or to work for lower wages or serve for lower fees than (a competitor) **b :** to accept or offer to accept a lower scale of (prices or wages) than is standard or general **c :** to have in gin rummy a count as low as or lower than the count of (the knocker) **4 a :** to cut (a book cover) in stamping with an improperly prepared die **b :** to hollow out or trim off a part of (a stamping die) to reduce impression pressure **5 :** to eat under laterally so as to leave without proper support — used of the action of etching acid on the lines of a printing surface **6 :** to cut obliquely into (a tree) below the main cut and on the side toward which the tree will fall **7 :** to strike (the ball) in golf, tennis, or hockey obliquely downward so as to give a backspin or elevation to the shot **8 :** to cut from (a forest) less timber than the growth warrants or less than the estimated annual cut ~ *vi* **1 :** to perform the action of cutting away beneath **2 :** to cut one foot into the place occupied by the other in dancing
²**undercut** \ˈ==,=\ *n* [partly fr. ¹*undercut*; partly fr. ³*under* + *cut*, n.] **1 :** the action or result of cutting away from the underside of anything ⟨~ of a vehicle⟩ ⟨~ of a tooth cavity for anchoring a filling⟩ **2** *Brit* **:** TENDERLOIN 1 **3 a :** a notch cut before felling in the base of a tree to determine the direction of falling and to prevent splitting **b :** KERF 2 **c :** part of a founding mold cut away so as to require special measures in removing the pattern from the mold **4 a :** a cut (as in tennis) made with an underhand stroke **b :** BACKSPIN **5 :** a replacement of one foot by the other in dancing **:** COUPÉ

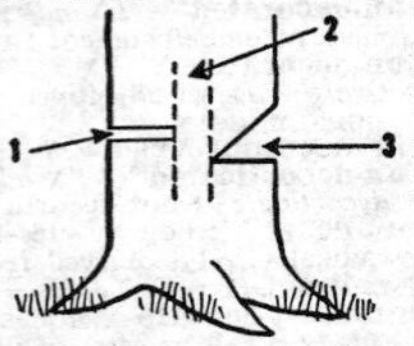

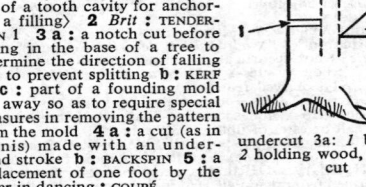

undercut 3a: *1* back cut, *2* holding wood, *3* undercut

³**undercut** \ˌ==ˈ=\ *adj* [fr. past part. of ¹*undercut*] **:** cut away below or on the underside **:** having under material cut or carved away so as to be left standing out in relief ⟨~ rims and figures on pottery⟩
undercutter \ˌ==ˈ==\ *n* **:** one that undercuts or makes undercuts: as **a :** a logger who chops the undercut in a tree that is to be felled **b :** a mine worker who operates a machine for cutting the bottom or side of the working face of coal so that it will not shatter when blasted
¹**underdeck** \ˈ==,=\ *n* [³*under* + *deck*] **:** a lower deck of a ship
²**underdeck** \"\ *adj* [²*under* + *deck*, n.] **:** belonging to or carried in a space below the main deck or the tonnage deck
underdeck tonnage *n* **:** the gross cubical capacity of a ship less the spaces above the tonnage deck
underdeveloped \ˌ===ˈ==\ *adj* [¹*under* + *developed*, past part. of *develop*] **1 :** not normally or adequately developed ⟨~ muscles⟩ ⟨~ sense of responsibility⟩ ⟨~ chin⟩ **2 :** insufficiently developed to give a satisfactory photographic image ⟨~ negative⟩ **3 :** failing to realize a potential economic level of industrial production and standard of living because of lack of capital for exploitation of natural resources, shortage of technically trained personnel, low medical standards, or because of culture traits resistant to change ⟨a program of technical assistance for ~ areas⟩
underdevelopment \ˌ===ˈ===\ *n* **:** lack of adequate development ⟨~ of film⟩ ⟨~ of industrial resources⟩
underditch \ˌ==ˈ=\ *vt* [¹*under* + *ditch*] **:** to dig an underground ditch in (a field or farm) so as to drain the surface
underdo \ˌ==ˈ=\ *vb* [¹*under* + *do*] *vi* **:** to do less than one can or than is requisite or proper ~ *vt* **1 :** to do less thoroughly than one can or should; *esp* **:** to cook (as meat) rare **2** *obs* **:** UNDERACT
underdog \ˈ==,=\ *also* \ˈ==ˈ=\ *n* [³*under* + *dog*] **1 :** a loser in a struggle **2 :** a victim of social injustice or of ruthless persecution **3 :** the predicted loser of a game or match **:** one not favored in the odds
underdone \ˌ==ˈ=\ *adj* [¹*under* + *done*] **:** not thoroughly done; *esp* **:** cooked for a comparatively short or an insufficient time **:** RARE ⟨~ steak⟩ ⟨~ cabbage⟩
¹**underdrag** \ˌ==ˈ=\ *vb* [¹*under* + *drag*] *vt* **:** to exert pull on the underside of (an overlying mass of rock) ~ *vi* **:** to undergo a pull from the underside
²**underdrag** \ˈ==,=\ *n* **:** the combined tensile stresses exerted by an overthrust rock mass upon rocks which overlie it but are not themselves under compressive thrusting stresses and therefore tend to be stretched and broken by normal faulting
¹**underdrain** \ˈ==,=\ *n* [³*under* + *drain*] **:** a concealed drain with openings through which the water enters when the water table reaches the level of the drain ⟨an ~ below a filter bed⟩
²**underdrain** \ˌ==ˈ=\ *vt* **:** to drain by forming an underdrain ⟨~ a meadow⟩
underdrainage \ˈ==,==\ *n* **:** the drainage of soil by means of drains placed beneath the surface
underdraw \ˌ==ˈ=\ *vt* [¹*under* + *draw*] **1 :** to draw a line under **:** UNDERSCORE **2 :** to draw or depict inadequately **3 :** to overlay or line (a roof or ceiling) with thin boards or lath and plaster **4 :** to draw from (an account) less than the amount credited
underdrawers \ˈ==,==\ *n pl* [³*under* + *drawers*] **:** an article of underwear covering the lower body and the legs ⟨calf-length ~⟩
¹**underdress** \ˈ==,=\ *n* [³*under* + *dress*, n.] **:** clothing worn under outer clothing; *esp* **:** a decorative petticoat showing where the overskirt is draped back
²**underdress** \ˌ==ˈ=\ *vi* [¹*under* + *dress*, v.] **:** to dress more simply or less formally than is customary ⟨after three winters of wartime ~*ing* —*Time*⟩
underdrift \ˈ==,=\ *n* [³*under* + *drift*] **:** UNDERCURRENT
underdrive \ˈ==,=\ *n* [³*under* + *drive*] **:** a transmission gear which transmits to the driven shaft a speed less than engine speed or less than the speed provided by the normal gear set
underdriven \ˌ==ˈ==\ *adj* [¹*under* + *driven*, past part. of *drive*] **:** driven from below ⟨~ millstone⟩
¹**underearth** \ˌ==ˈ=\ *adj* [²*under* + *earth*, n.] **:** SUBTERRANEAN
²**underearth** \"\ *n* [³*under* + *earth*] **1 :** the soil beneath the earth's surface **:** an underlying layer (as of clay) **2 :** the depths of the earth
undereaten \ˌ==ˈ==\ *adj* [¹*under* + *eaten*, past part. of *eat*] **:** eaten or worn away from beneath ⟨~ cliffs⟩
underemployed \ˌ===ˈ=\ *adj* [¹*under* + *employed*, past part. of *employ*] **:** having less than full-time employment
underemployment \ˌ===ˈ==\ *n* [³*under* + *employment*] **1 :** a state of less than full employment of the labor force in an economy **:** the existence of numbers of workers without jobs **2 :** the partial employment of a worker **3 :** the utilization of workers at more menial or less skilled tasks than their training or abilities permit
¹**underestimate** \ˌ==ˈ==(,)=\ *vt* [¹*under* + *estimate*, v.] **1 :** to estimate as being less than the actual size, quantity, or number ⟨~ the cost of new building⟩ **2 :** to place too low a value on **:** take too lightly ⟨~ an opponent⟩ ⟨~ the seriousness of a threat of suicide⟩
²**underestimate** \"\ *or* **underestimation** \ˌ==,==ˈ==\ *n* [³*under* + *estimate*, n., or *estimation*] **1 :** the act of underestimating **2 :** an estimate that falls below the truth or actuality
underexcited \ˌ===ˈ==\ *adj* [¹*under* + *excited*] **:** operated with field excitation below normal ⟨~ dynamo⟩
¹**underexercise** \ˌ==ˈ===\ *vi* [¹*under* + *exercise*, v.] **:** to exercise too little ⟨overeating and *underexercising*⟩
²**underexercise** \"\ *n* [³*under* + *exercise*, n.] **:** inadequate amount or frequency of exercise
underexpose \ˌ===ˈ=\ *vt* [¹*under* + *expose*] **:** to expose (a photographic plate or film) for less time than is needed ⟨an *underexposed* negative is lacking in density and in shadow detail —C.B.Neblette⟩
underexposure \ˌ===ˈ==\ *n* **:** the act or result of underexposing
underfall \ˈ==,=\ *n* [³*under* + *fall*] **:** a lower mountain slope — usu. used in pl.
¹**underfeed** \ˌ==ˈ=\ *vt* [¹*under* + *feed*] **1 :** to feed with too little food **2 :** to feed with fuel from the underside
²**underfeed** \ˈ==,=\ *adj* **:** being fed or feeding from beneath ⟨~ stoking of a furnace⟩ — opposed to *overfeed*
underfill \ˈ==,=\ *n* -s [³*under* + *fill*] **1 :** a rolled or forged member (as of steel) that is imperfect because of insufficient material **2 :** an incompletely filled can or container
underfire \ˌ==ˈ=\ *vt* [¹*under* + *fire*] **1 :** to fire (as brick) insufficiently **2 :** to fire from beneath ⟨~ a coke oven⟩
underfit \ˌ==ˈ=\ *adj* [¹*under* + *fit*, past part. of *fit*] **:** greatly reduced in volume and therefore in ability to erode or transport as a consequence of stream piracy ⟨an ~ stream⟩
underflow \ˈ==,=\ *n* [³*under* + *flow*] **:** a flowing under **:** movement of water through subsurface material
¹**underfold** \ˌ==ˈ=\ *vt* [¹*under* + *fold*, v.] **:** to fold within so as to hide
²**underfold** \ˈ==,=\ *n* [³*under* + *fold*, n.] **:** a fold lying under or beneath a surface or beneath another fold
¹**underfoot** \ˌ==ˈ=\ *adv* [ME *underfot*, *underfoot*, fr. ²*under* + *fot*, *foot* foot] **1 a :** under the foot esp. against the ground ⟨hated emblem torn down and trampled ~⟩ **b :** on the bottom of the foot **:** between the foot and the ground ⟨soles with no inside seams or nails ~⟩ ⟨felt the soft turf ~⟩ **2 a :** below, at, or before one's feet ⟨violets growing ~⟩ **b :** UNDERGROUND ⟨felt a tremor ~⟩ **3 a :** under the bottom (as of a ship) ⟨a strong current ~⟩ **b** *of an anchor* **:** under the forefoot **4 :** in the way ⟨the children are always getting ~⟩
²**underfoot** \"\ *adj* **1 :** being under or obstructing the foot ⟨clear a factory floor of ~ hazards⟩ **2 :** ABJECT, DOWNTRODDEN, DESPISED ⟨the city's most famous ~ characters, the cats of New York —*Park East*⟩
³**underfoot** \"\ *vt* -ED/-ING/-S [¹*under* + *foot*, n.] **1 :** to support beneath **:** PROP, UNDERPIN **2 :** to replace the footings beneath
underfooting \ˈ==,==\ *n* [¹*underfoot* + -*ing*] **:** FOOTING 1 ⟨treacherous ~ resulted in scores of injuries —*N. Y. Times*⟩
underframe \ˈ==,=\ *n* [³*under* + *frame*] **:** the lower or lowermost of two or more superimposed frames **:** a frame supporting a superstructure (as of a railroad car) **:** CHASSIS
underframing \ˈ==,==\ *n* [³*under* + *framing*] **:** the material or structural members of an underframe
underfrequency relay \ˈ==,===-\ *n* [³*under* + *frequency*] **:** a relay actuated by a fall in electrical frequency
underfur \ˈ==,=\ *n* [³*under* + *fur*] **:** the thick soft sometimes curly and barbed fur lying beneath the longer and coarser hair of a mammal — compare UNDERCOAT 2
undergage \ˈ==,=\ *n* [³*under* + *gage*] **:** a no-go gage of the limit-gage type used for metal sheets or plates
undergarment \ˈ==,==\ *n* [³*under* + *garment*] **:** a garment to be worn under another
undergear \ˈ==,=\ *n* [³*under* + *gear*] **:** gear placed below or under something else **:** running gear and chassis of a vehicle
undergird \ˌ==ˈ=\ *vt* [¹*under* + *gird*] **1 :** to gird below **:** make secure underneath ⟨took measures to ~ the ship —Acts 27:17 (RSV)⟩ **2 :** to brace up **:** STRENGTHEN, SUPPORT ⟨faith ~*s* moral principles —I.G.Whitchurch⟩
undergirth \ˈ==,=\ *n* [³*under* + *girth*] **:** a band or rope used in undergirding
underglaze \ˈ==,=\ *adj* [²*under* + *glaze*] **1 :** applied before the glaze is put on ⟨~ painting on porcelain⟩ **2 :** suitable for applying under the glaze ⟨~ color⟩ ⟨~ pigment⟩ — compare OVERGLAZE
undergo \ˌ==ˈ=\ *vb* [ME *undergon*, *undergoon*, fr. ¹*under* + *gon*, *goon* to go — more at GO] *vt* **1** *obs* **:** to move or pass under or underneath **2** *obs* **:** UNDERTAKE **3** *obs* **:** to partake of **4 :** to submit to **:** ENDURE, SUFFER, SUSTAIN ⟨tragic hero rises above . . . the world man ~*es* —W.E.Allen⟩ **5 :** to go through **:** be the subject of (as a process) **:** receive the effect of ⟨~ martyrdom⟩ ⟨~ surgery⟩ ⟨~ examination⟩ ⟨~ a moral conversion⟩ ⟨words which had *undergone* certain derivational processes —Stanley Newman⟩ ⟨~ complete metamorphosis⟩ ~ *vi* **:** ENDURE ⟨the self acts as well as ~*es* —John Dewey⟩ ⟨the inarticulate merely ~ —S.V.Benét⟩ **syn** see EXPERIENCE
undergoer \ˌ==ˈ==\ *n* **:** one that undergoes
undergown \ˈ==,=\ *n* [³*under* + *gown*] **:** a gown worn under another gown or other garment usu. so that the neckline, sleeves, or skirt shows for contrast
undergrad \ˌ==ˈ=\ *n* -s [by shortening] *slang* **:** UNDERGRADUATE
undergrade \ˌ==ˈ=\ *adj* [²*under* + *grade*, n.] **1 :** below or inferior to standard grade **:** not of first grade ⟨~ fruit⟩ ⟨~ lumber⟩ **2 :** below the grade of the track or roadway ⟨~ crossing⟩
¹**un·der·graduate** \ˌəndə(r)+\ *n* [²*under* + *graduate*] **1 :** a student at a college or university who has not taken a first degree **:** a candidate for a bachelor's degree or a first degree in a school or profession (as medicine) **:** a member of one of the four traditional collegiate classes **2 :** one whose training is not yet perfect **:** NOVICE
²**undergraduate** \"\ *adj* **1 :** of, relating to, or engaged in college or university studies prior to the first degree ⟨~ course⟩ ⟨~ student⟩ ⟨~ medical studies⟩ **2 :** of, relating to, or charac-

teristic of undergraduates ⟨retain the ~ fervor —H.M. McLuhan⟩
undergraduate·ship \"+ˌship\ *n* **:** the condition or status of an undergraduate
un·der·grad·u·ette \ˌəndə(r)ˌgrajəˈwet\ *n* [blend of 1*undergraduate* and *-ette*] *Brit* **:** CO-ED
undergreen \ˈ≈ˌ≈\ *adj* [1*under* + *green*] **:** green on the underside ⟨~ willow⟩
undergroom \ˈ≈ˌ≈\ *n* [3*under* + *groom*] **:** a groom's helper **:** STABLEBOY
1**underground** \ˈ≈ˌ≈\ *adv* [2*under* + *ground*, n.] **1 :** beneath the surface of the earth ⟨water flowing ~⟩ ⟨burrowing ~⟩ **2 :** in or into hiding or secret operation ⟨an ideology driven ~ develops into a more virulent form —W.O.Douglas⟩ ⟨the association soon became subversive and went ~ —Harold Ingrams⟩
2**underground** \ˈ≈ˌ≈\ *adj* **1 :** being, growing, or situated below the surface of the ground ⟨~ cave⟩ ⟨~ cellar⟩ ⟨~ stream⟩ ⟨~ rhizomes⟩ **2 :** dwelling in an underworld ⟨mythical ~ people⟩ **3 :** used or adapted for use or wear underground **:** employed or performing duties underground ⟨~ foreman⟩ ⟨~ shovel⟩ **4 :** done or occurring underground esp. away from public knowledge **:** conducted or conveyed by secret or stealthy means ⟨~ revolutionary activity⟩ ⟨the ~ life of civilized societies —Edward Sapir⟩
3**underground** \"\ *n* [2*underground*] **1 :** the place or space beneath the surface of the ground **:** a subterranean space or channel **2 :** ground or soil lying beneath the surface or beneath something else **3 :** an underground city railway system ⟨the London *Underground*⟩ **4 a :** a movement or group organized in strict secrecy among citizens in an occupied or totalitarian country for maintaining communications, popular solidarity, and concerted resistive action pending liberation ⟨the ~ in Occupied France⟩ **b :** a clandestine conspiratorial cell or organization set up for revolutionary or other disruptive purposes esp. against a civil order — used with *the* ⟨the Communist ~ in wartime Germany⟩
underground·er \"+ə(r)\ *n* -s [3*underground* + *-er*] **1 a :** one that works underground **b :** one that rides on an underground railway **2 :** a member of the underground
underground railroad *n* **1 :** UNDERGROUND RAILWAY **2** *usu cap U&R* **:** a system of cooperation among active antislavery people in the U.S. before 1863 by which fugitive slaves were secretly helped to reach the North or Canada
underground railway *n* **:** a railway running in a subway usu. beneath the street level of a city
undergrove \ˈ≈ˌ≈\ *n* [3*under* + *grove*] **:** a grove of shrubs or low trees under taller ones
undergrow \ˌ≈ˈ≈\ *vi* [1*under* + *grow*] **:** to grow beneath something or up from beneath
undergrown \ˌ≈ˈ≈\ *adj* [1*under* + *grown*] **1 :** of small stature **:** not grown to full height or size **2 :** grown over with an undergrowth
undergrowth \ˈ≈ˌ≈\ *n* [3*under* + *growth*] **1 :** low growth more or less completely covering the floor of a forest and including seedlings and saplings and shrubs and herbs **2 :** a condition of incomplete or imperfect growth
underhair \ˈ≈ˌ≈\ *n* [3*under* + *hair*] **:** a growth of fine hair underneath the coarser outer hair of some mammals
1**underhand** \ˈ≈ˌ≈\ *adv* [1*under* + *hand*] **1 a :** by secret means **:** in a clandestine manner **:** not openly **:** not fairly ⟨mean revenge, committed ~ —John Dryden⟩ **b** *archaic* **:** QUIETLY, UNOBTRUSIVELY **2 :** with the target seen below the bow hand **3** [1*under* + *hand*] **:** with an underhand motion ⟨toss a ball ~⟩
2**underhand** \ˈ≈ˌ≈\ *adj* **1 :** aimed so that the target is seen below the bow hand ⟨~ shooting at long range⟩ **2 :** marked by or treated with secrecy, chicanery, and deception or by hidden craft and deceit **:** not honest, open, and aboveboard **:** SLY ⟨a coward with an ~ streak of cruelty —G.J.Becker⟩ ⟨stooping to ~ methods to gain his end⟩ **3 :** done so as to evade notice **:** marked by quiet unobtrusiveness or subtlety ⟨from his intellectual superiority he is deemed to exert an ~ influence against the officers —Herman Melville⟩ **4 :** performed with the hand kept below the level of the shoulder ⟨flip an ~ pass in football⟩ ⟨~ shot for the basket⟩; *also* **:** using such a manner of throwing ⟨~ bowler⟩ ⟨~ pitcher⟩ **5 :** working from above downward ⟨~ surface mining⟩ **syn** see SECRET
3**underhand** \"\ *n* [2*underhand*] **:** a ball delivered underhand **:** an underhand delivery
4**underhand** \ˌ≈ˈ≈\ *vt* [1*underhand*] **:** to throw, pass, or pitch (a ball) in an underhand manner
1**underhanded** \ˌ≈ˈ≈≈\ *adj* [1*underhand* + *-ed*] **1 :** UNDERHAND ⟨did not look quite like a professional gambler, but something ... in his countenance suggested an ~ mode of life —Willa Cather⟩ **2 :** insufficiently provided with hands or workers **:** SHORTHANDED, UNDERMANNED **syn** see SECRET
2**underhanded** \"\ *adv* **:** UNDERHAND ⟨the ball must be delivered ~, not thrown or jerked —*Quarterly Rev.*⟩
un·der·hand·ed·ly *adv* **:** in a secret or deceitful manner ⟨old line aristocratic diplomats ~ undermined the attempt ... to align Germany with the Western democracies —C.G.Bowers⟩
un·der·hand·ed·ness *n* -ES **:** DECEITFULNESS, TRICKERY
underhanging \ˌ≈ˈ≈≈\ *adj* [1*under* + *hanging*, pres. part. of *hang*] **:** UNDERHUNG 1 ⟨~ jaw⟩
underharvest \ˌ≈ˈ≈≈\ *vt* [1*under* + *harvest*] **:** to take less of the crop of (as fishes) than is desirable to maintain a satisfactory balance of nature
underhew \ˌ≈ˈ≈\ *vt* [1*under* + *hew*] **:** to hew (timber) to scant dimensions
underhive \ˌ≈ˈ≈\ *vt* [1*under* + *hive*] **:** to hive (bees) in insufficient space
underhold \ˈ≈ˌ≈\ *n* [3*under* + *hold*] **1 :** an encircling grip secured advantageously by a wrestler under his opponent's arms **2 :** a handhold with which a climber maintains balance by pulling against the pressure of his feet — see LAYBACK
underhole \ˌ≈ˈ≈\ *vt* [1*under* + *hole*] **:** to cut away the lower portion of or to cut under (a coal seam)
underhook \ˌ≈ˈ≈\ *vt* [1*under* + *hook*] **:** to pass an arm under so as to hook in wrestling
un·der·housed \ˌəndə(r)ˈhau̇zd\ *adj* [1*under* + *-housed* (fr. *house*, n. + *-ed*)] **1 :** having too few houses **2 :** inadequately housed
underhousemaid \ˈ≈≈ˌ≈≈\ *n* [3*under* + *housemaid*] **:** an assistant housemaid
underhung \ˌ≈ˈ≈\ *adj* [1*under* + *hung*, past part. of *hang*] **1** *of a lower jaw* **:** projecting beyond the upper jaw **:** UNDERSHOT **2 :** having an underhung jaw ⟨this poor creature, heavy-bodied, bowlegged and ~ —J.A.Thomson⟩ **3 :** suspended so that the point of support is beneath the load; *specif* **:** resting on a track at the bottom instead of being suspended from above ⟨~ sliding door⟩
underinsurance \ˌ≈≈ˈ≈≈\ *n* [3*under* + *insurance*] **:** insurance in an amount insufficient to cover the possible loss or to satisfy the requirements of a coinsurance clause
un·derivative \ˌən+\ *adj* **:** not derivative or imitative **:** ORIGINAL ⟨a natural and ~ poet —Florence B. Lennon⟩
un·derived \"+\ *adj* **:** not derived or secondary **:** PRIMARY, SIMPLE
underjaw \ˈ≈ˌ≈\ *n* [3*under* + *jaw*] **:** lower jaw
underjawed \ˌ≈ˈ≈\ *adj* **:** having the underjaw prominent
underkeeper \ˈ≈ˌ≈≈\ *n* [3*under* + *keeper*] **:** a subordinate keeper ⟨~ of a game forest⟩
underlaid \ˌ≈ˈ≈\ *adj* [fr. past part. of *underlay*] **1 :** laid or placed underneath **2 :** having something laid or lying underneath often by way of support or strengthening ⟨bed of sand ~ with shale⟩ ⟨the theology of India is ~ with pantheism —J.W. Draper⟩
underlain *past part of* UNDERLIE
1**underlap** \ˌ≈ˈ≈\ *vt* [1*under* + *lap*] **:** to project under the edge or end of ⟨the forward end of each plank ~s the overlapping rear end of the next⟩
2**underlap** \ˈ≈ˌ≈\ *n* **:** a section of a garment extending beneath another; *esp* **:** the front edge of a coat or dress that is closed by placing one side of the front under the other
1**underlay** *past of* UNDERLIE
2**underlay** \ˌ≈ˈ≈\ *vt* [ME *underleyen, underleggen*, fr. OE *underlecgan*, fr. 1*under* + *lecgan* to lay — more at LAY] **1 :** to cover, line, or traverse the bottom of ⟨~ the Atlantic with a cable⟩ **:** give support to on the underside or below **:** place a line or layer beneath or inside of — used with *with* ⟨slates *underlaid* with roofing paper⟩ ⟨~ the pavement with traprock⟩ **2 a :** to raise or support by something laid under ⟨~ a cut to bring it up to the right height for printing⟩ **b** *obs* **:** to put a tap on (a shoe)
3**underlay** \ˈ≈ˌ≈\ *n* **1 :** something that is laid under: as **a :** a piece of leather or other material placed between the outside and the lining of a shoe upper beneath a cutout or perforation **b :** a thickness of paper placed under type or a cut to bring it up to the proper height for printing — compare OVERLAY **c :** a contrasting facing or lining used esp. with sheer fabrics **d :** material placed under flooring or carpeting for insulation or reducing noise and wear **2 :** a basic trend not evident upon the surface **:** UNDERCURRENT ⟨beneath all the wild rumors there was an ~ of fact⟩
underlayer \ˈ≈ˌ≈≈\ *n* [3*under* + *layer*] **:** a layer that underlies another **:** SUBSTRATUM
un·der·lay·ment \ˌəndə(r)ˈlāmənt\ *n* -s **:** UNDERLAY 1d ⟨plywood ~ for flooring tile⟩
underleaf \ˈ≈ˌ≈\ *n* [3*under* + *leaf*] **1 :** the underside of a leaf **2 :** AMPHIGASTRIUM
1**underlease** \ˈ≈ˌ≈\ *n* [3*under* + *lease*] **:** SUBLEASE
2**underlease** \ˌ≈ˈ≈\ *vb* **:** SUBLET
un·der·les·see \ˌəndə(r)ˌleˈsē\ *n* [3*under* + *lessee*] **:** one to whom an underlease is granted **:** SUBTENANT
1**underlet** \ˌ≈ˈ≈\ *vt* [1*under* + *let*, v.] **1 :** to let below the real value **2 :** SUBLET
2**underlet** \"\ *adj* [1*under* + *let*, past part. of *let*] **:** let in or introduced from below or from the bottom
3**underlet** \ˈ≈ˌ≈\ *n* -s **:** the water introduced into the mash tun from beneath the false bottom in brewing
1**underlie** \ˌ≈ˈ≈\ *vt* [ME *underliggen, underligen, underlien*, fr. OE *underlicgan*, fr. 1*under* + *licgan* to lie — more at LIE] **1 a** *obs* **:** to submit to the will or direction of **b** *obs* **:** to undergo the infliction of (a penalty or judgment) **c** *Scot* **:** to surrender oneself to (law) **d** *obs* **:** to assume the expense of or responsibility for **2 :** to lie or be situated under ⟨shale ~s the coal⟩ ⟨delta *underlain* by a clay bed⟩ ⟨granite on the outside *underlain* with basalt —*Science*⟩ **3 :** to be at the basis of **:** form the foundation of **:** SUPPORT ⟨political ideas *underlying* the revolution⟩ ⟨law of gravitation and his equations of motion apply to and ~ immense realms of physical experience —Julian Huxley⟩ **4 :** to lie concealed beneath the obvious exterior of ⟨the human and personal actualities that ~ the impersonality of justice —F.R.Leavis⟩ ⟨probe the mysterious causality that may ~ chance —H.C.Webster⟩ **5 :** to exist as a claim or security superior and prior to (another) ⟨a first mortgage ~s a second⟩ **~ vi 1** *obs* **:** to lie in the grave **2** *Brit* **:** to incline from the vertical **:** HADE
2**underlie** \ˈ≈ˌ≈\ *n* **1** *Brit* **:** SLOPE, HADE **2 :** the angle made by the center line of a stull with a line normal to the hanging wall at their point of incidence — called also *underset*
un·der·li·er *pronunc at* 1UNDERLIE + ə(r)\ *n* **:** something that lies under; *specif* **:** UNDERLYING COMPANY
underlife \ˈ≈ˌ≈\ *n* [3*under* + *life*] **:** life beneath the surface or concealed from common knowledge
1**underline** \ˌ≈ˈ≈\ *vt* [1*under* + *line* (to cover inner surface of)] **:** to provide with an underlining ⟨collar *underlined* with black —*advt*⟩
2**underline** \"\ *vt* [1*under* + *line* (to mark with a line)] **1 a :** to mark (a word) with a line underneath **:** UNDERSCORE **b :** to put emphasis upon **:** stress in or as if in utterance ⟨~s the unity of knowledge and the consequent unity which should be aimed at in education —R.M.Hutchins⟩ **2 :** to make evident the significant character or importance of ⟨British weakness was *underlined* when the French fleet escaped from Toulon —J.H.Plumb⟩ ⟨hydrogen bomb explosions *underlined* in a horrifying fashion the likely consequences of atomic attack —Barbara Ward⟩ **3 :** to announce in advance by or as if by an underline ⟨his book is *underlined* for publication next month⟩
3**underline** \ˈ≈ˌ≈\ *n* **1 a :** a horizontal line placed underneath something ⟨words with a single ~ are to be set in italics⟩ **b underlines** *pl* **:** a set of guiding lines placed underneath a sheet to be written on **2 a :** explanatory or descriptive wording underneath an illustration **:** LEGEND **b :** a line placed below the notice of a current performance announcing a performance shortly to follow **3 :** the outline of the lower part of an animal's body between the front and rear legs ⟨~ well tucked up⟩; *also* **:** the ventral surface of a quadruped's body ⟨brown above, with the ~ lighter⟩
underlineation \ˌ≈≈ˌ≈≈ˈ≈≈\ *n* [3*under* + *lineation*] **:** the action of underlining or the markings so made
underlinen \ˈ≈ˌ≈≈\ *n* [3*under* + *linen*] **:** underwear usu. of lightweight material
1**un·der·ling** \ˈəndə(r)liŋ, -lēŋ\ *n* -s [ME, fr. 1*under* + *-ling*] **1 a :** one who is under the orders of another **:** SUBORDINATE, INFERIOR ⟨the fault ... is ... in ourselves, that we are ~s —Shak.⟩ **b :** a person of small importance ⟨scientists need to be used not as lackeys or ~s —Vannevar Bush⟩ **2** *dial* **:** an underdeveloped, imperfect, or weakly offshoot or offspring
2**underling** \"\ *adj* [ME, fr. *underling*, n.] **1 :** subordinate or inferior in authority or prestige to another **:** serving under another ⟨fearful of ~ aggression —V.L.Parrington⟩ **2** *dial* **:** underdeveloped, imperfect, or weakly in growth
1**underlining** \ˈ≈ˌ≈≈\ *n* [3*under* + *lining*] **:** lining placed on the under or the inner side of something
2**underlining** \"\ *n* [fr. gerund of 2*underline*] **:** the action of drawing lines underneath in writing or printing or lines so drawn **:** UNDERSCORING ⟨letters ... with their ~s and broken sentences and postscripts —G.H.Genzmer⟩
underlip \ˌ≈ˈ≈\ *n* [3*under* + *lip*] **1 :** the lower lip **2 :** the lower edge of the mouth in an organ flue pipe
underlit \ˌ≈ˈ≈\ *adj* [1*under* + *lit*, past part. of *light*] **:** insufficiently lighted ⟨working in dingy ~ rooms⟩
underload \ˈ≈ˌ≈\ *n* [3*under* + *load*] **:** a load markedly below full capacity **:** an inadequate or insufficient load
underload starter *n* **:** a motor starter provided with an underload switch
underload switch *n* **:** a switch that opens a circuit when the current falls below a predetermined value and that is used to protect a motor from racing upon decrease of load
1**underlook** \ˌ≈ˈ≈\ *vt* [1*under* + *look*, v.] **1 :** to look or glance at from underneath or from lowered eyes **:** look covertly at **2 :** to miss or omit because one has looked too low
2**underlook** \ˈ≈ˌ≈\ *n* [3*under* + *look*, n.] **:** a covert glance
underlooker \ˈ≈ˌ≈≈\ *n* [3*under* + *looker*] **:** an assistant to a manager (as of a mine) usu. engaged in superintendence and overseeing
un·der·ly \ˈəndə(r)lē\ *adj* [1*under* + *-ly*] **:** below average **:** not in health
underlying \ˌ≈ˈ≈≈\ *adj* [fr. pres. part. of *underlie*] **1 :** lying under or beneath **:** IMPLICIT, FUNDAMENTAL ⟨~ principles⟩ **2 :** innate or organic but evident only on close inspection ⟨~ identity about the motley immigrants⟩ **3 :** anterior and prior in claim ⟨~ mortgage⟩
underlying bond *n* **:** a bond secured by a mortgage on corporate property prior to other claims
underlying company *n* **:** a company that is part of a larger consolidated organization and is kept in existence only because of nontransferable rights or franchises that it possesses
underman \ˈ≈ˌ≈\ *n, pl* **undermen** [3*under* + *man*] **1 :** a man who is subordinate to, inferior to, or in some way disadvantageously placed with respect to others ⟨unreasoning revolt of the ~ —A.E.Wiggam⟩ **2 :** a member of an acrobatic team who supports the others in his act
undermanned \ˌ≈ˈ≈\ *adj* [1*under* + *manned*, past part. of *man*] **:** furnished with an inadequate force of men **:** SHORTHANDED, UNDERSTAFFED ⟨attract labor to ~ industries —*Economist*⟩
undermatched \ˌ≈ˈ≈\ *adj* [1*under* + *matched*, past part. of *match*] **:** married to a social inferior
undermeaning \ˈ≈ˌ≈≈\ *n* [3*under* + *meaning*] **:** a meaning implied or discoverable but not directly expressed ⟨saw in the Old Testament stories an allegorical ~ which explained ... the relation of matter and spirit —*New Statesman*⟩
undermentioned \ˌ≈ˈ≈≈\ *adj* [1*under* + *mentioned*, past part. of *mention*] *Brit* **:** mentioned below **:** included in the list that follows **:** FOLLOWING
undermill \ˌ≈ˈ≈\ *vt* [1*under* + *mill*] **:** to mill (grain) without loss of all the bran and other particles eliminated by full milling
undermine \ˌ≈ˈ≈\ *vt* [ME *underminen*, fr. 1*under* + *minen* to mine — more at MINE] **1 :** to excavate the earth beneath esp. for the purpose of causing to fall **:** form a mine under **:** SAP ⟨~ a wall⟩ **2 a :** to wash away supporting material from under ⟨flood water *undermined* the building's foundation⟩ ⟨stream ~s the glacier⟩ **b :** to make a passage under ⟨fence *undermined* by dogs⟩ **c :** to erode underneath or the underlayer of ⟨an ulcer may ~ the adjacent mucous membrane⟩ **3 :** to remove the foundation or support of subtly or by underhand means **:** subvert or weaken insidiously or secretly ⟨the way a writer handles the social situation either supports or ~s it —Peter Crowcroft⟩ ⟨selling below cost ... to ~ competition —*Time*⟩ ⟨~ public confidence in its judicial system⟩ **4 :** to weaken or ruin by degrees ⟨prolonged overwork had *undermined* his health⟩ **syn** see WEAKEN
underminer \ˌ≈ˈ≈≈\ *n* -s **:** one that undermines
un·der·min·ing·ly *adv* **:** so as to undermine
1**undermost** \ˈ≈ˌ≈\ *adj* [3*under* + *-most*] **:** lowest in relative position ⟨~ layer⟩
2**undermost** \"\ *adv* **:** in the lowest or lower position **:** on the underside ⟨with the dark layer ~⟩ ⟨put the rubber sheet ~⟩
un·dern \ˈəndə(r)n, ˈun-\ *n* -s [ME, third hour of the morning (9:00 a.m.), noon, fr. OE; akin to OHG *untarn, untorn* noon, ON *undorn* midafternoon, midmorning, Goth *undaurni*mats noon meal, and prob. to OHG *untar* between, among — more at INTER-] **1** *dial* **:** the time from noon to sundown **:** AFTERNOON **2** *dial* **:** a light meal in the forenoon or in the afternoon
1**un·der·neath** \ˌəndə(r)ˈnēth\ *prep* [ME *undernethe, undernethen*, prep. & adv., fr. OE *underneothan*, fr. 2*under* + *neothan* below — more at BENEATH] **1 :** directly beneath ⟨put the date ~ the address⟩ **:** close under esp. so as to be covered or hidden ⟨beetles found ~ stones and logs⟩ ⟨stowed away ~ the flooring⟩ **2 :** below an upper layer of or inside an outer surface or covering of ⟨wore his swim suit ~ his slacks⟩ ⟨blood vessels just ~ the skin⟩ **3 :** under subjection or submission to ⟨living ~ a crushing tyranny⟩ **4 :** under the outward appearance or obvious aspect of ⟨~ the discursive chat of his letters is the firm fabric of economic fact —V.L.Parrington⟩ ⟨treachery lying ~ a mask of friendliness⟩
2**underneath** \"\ *adv* [ME *undernethe, undernethen*] **1 :** under or below an object or a surface often with the implication of being covered or concealed ⟨scrape off the paint to show the grain of the wood ~⟩ ⟨soaked through his jacket to the shirt ~⟩ **2 :** beneath by way of support ⟨house with a solid foundation ~⟩ **3 :** farther or lower down on the page ⟨column of figures with the totals given ~⟩ **4 :** on the lower or downward side ⟨pot blackened ~⟩
3**underneath** \ˌ≈ˈ≈\ *adj* **1** *dial* **:** SECRET, SURREPTITIOUS **2 :** not evident on the surface ⟨~ meanings⟩ **3 :** lying or working underneath ⟨~ wrestler⟩ ⟨~ man of an acrobatic team⟩
4**underneath** \ˌ≈ˈ≈\ *n* -s **:** UNDERSIDE **:** the bottom surface ⟨wipe the ~ of the glass⟩ ⟨looking at the ~s of the china for makers' names⟩
undernote \ˈ≈ˌ≈\ *n* [3*under* + *note*] **:** a subdued note **:** UNDERTONE ⟨spoke abruptly, low and cold, but with that same ~ of excitement —J.H.Wheelwright⟩
undernoted \ˌ≈ˈ≈≈\ *adj* [1*under* + *noted*, past part. of *note*] *chiefly Brit* **:** mentioned or listed below or in what follows ⟨applications are invited for the ~ posts —*advt*⟩
undernourished \ˌ≈≈ˈ≈≈\ *adj* [1*under* + *nourished*, past part. of *nourish*] **:** supplied with insufficient nourishment or less than the minumum quantity of foods essential for sound health and growth
undernourishment \ˌ≈≈ˈ≈≈≈\ *n* **:** lack of sufficient nourishment
undernutrition \ˌ≈≈ˌ≈ˈ≈≈\ *n* [3*under* + *nutrition*] **:** a condition of deficient body nutrition from an inadequate intake of food or from failure to assimilate or utilize food elements
underpaid \ˌ≈ˈ≈\ *adj* [3*under* + *paid*, past part. of *pay*] **:** receiving less than adequate pay
underpaint \ˌ≈ˈ≈\ *vt* [1*under* + *paint*] **:** to apply preliminary layers of paint to
underpainting \ˈ≈ˌ≈≈\ *n* **:** preliminary painting; *specif* **:** such painting done on a canvas or panel and covered completely or partially by the final layers of paint
underpan \ˈ≈ˌ≈\ *n* [3*under* + *pan*] **:** a protective metal covering fitting under the engine, clutch, and transmission case of an automobile
underpants \ˈ≈ˌ≈\ *n pl* [3*under* + *pants*] **:** short or long pants worn under an outer garment **:** DRAWERS
underpart \ˈ≈ˌ≈\ *n* [3*under* + *part*] **1 :** a part lying on the lower side or underneath; *specif* **:** one of the parts on the ventral side of a bird or animal's body ⟨a rodent with ~s approaching pure white⟩ **2 :** a subordinate or auxiliary part or role
1**underpass** \ˈ≈ˌ≈\ *n* [3*under* + *pass*] **:** a passage beneath: **a :** a grade separation where clearance to traffic on the upper level is obtained by depressing partially or completely (as with a tunnel) the grade of the lower level — compare OVERPASS **b :** the lower level of a grade separation — called also *undercrossing*
2**underpass** \"\ *vt* **:** to provide (a crossing) with an underpass
underpay \ˌ≈ˈ≈\ *vt* [1*under* + *pay*] **:** to pay inadequately
underpayment \ˌ≈ˈ≈≈\ *n* [3*under* + *payment*] **1 :** insufficient payment ⟨~ of a tax obligation⟩ **2 :** payment of inadequate salary or wages
underpeopled \ˌ≈ˈ≈≈\ *adj* [1*under* + *peopled*] **:** sparsely populated
1**underpick** \ˈ≈ˌ≈\ *adj* [3*under* + *pick*, n. (throw of the shuttle)] *of a loom* **:** having the picking arm or shuttle-driving device under the shuttle boxes — compare OVERPICK
2**underpick** \"\ *n* **:** an underpick loom
underpin \ˌ≈ˈ≈\ *vt* [1*under* + *pin*] **1 :** to replace or strengthen the foundation of ⟨~ a sagging building⟩ **2 :** to form part of the foundation of ⟨*underpinning* wall⟩ ⟨principles which should ~ a free society —Barbara Ward⟩ **3 :** SUPPORT, SUBSTANTIATE ⟨~ his thesis that American democracy is not an exportable commodity —V.O.Key⟩ ⟨*underpinned* with thick footnotes —*Newsweek*⟩ ⟨is this section of the play the acting is strongly *underpinned* by a script —E.R.Bentley⟩
underpinner \ˈ≈ˌ≈≈\ *n* **:** a supporting brace **:** PROP
underpinning \ˈ≈ˌ≈≈\ *n* [3*under* + *pinning*] **1 a :** the material and construction used for support and introduced beneath a wall already constructed **b :** the foundation of a frame house **2 :** a method of lining a mine shaft by supporting the upper section of brickwork on a curb by shores or props, excavating below, and building up to this curb from another curb inserted lower down **3 :** SUPPORT, PROP ⟨military security depends upon a strong economic ~ —H.S.Truman⟩ **4 :** UNDERWEAR — used usu. in pl. **5 :** a person's legs — used usu. in pl. ⟨still unsteady on his ~s when he came out for the seventh —*Ring*⟩
underpitch \ˈ≈ˌ≈\ *adj* [1*under* + *pitch*, v.] **:** formed by the incomplete intersection of unequal usu. cylindrical vaults springing from the same level ⟨~ groining⟩
underplant \ˌ≈ˈ≈\ *vt* [1*under* + *plant*] **1 :** to plant or sow among or under other taller growing plants or trees **2 :** to plant a crop or trees under (an existing stand or plantation)
1**underplay** \ˌ≈ˈ≈\ *vb* [1*under* + *play*] *vt* **1 :** to play a card lower than (a held high card) ⟨~*ed* his ace⟩ **2 :** to act or present (as a role or a scene) with restraint or subdued force **:** refrain from emphasizing or exaggerating **:** play down ⟨the comic elements of an opera⟩ ⟨continued briskly ~*ing* the drama of his news —Louis Auchincloss⟩ **~ vi :** to play a role or scene with restraint or subdued force
2**underplay** \ˈ≈ˌ≈\ *n* **1 :** an act or instance of underplaying **2 :** hidden or underlying action ⟨a subtle ~ of antagonism beneath the polite conversation⟩
underplot \ˈ≈ˌ≈\ *n* [3*under* + *plot*] **1 :** a dramatic plot that is subordinate to the main action **2 :** a hidden scheme or trick
underpole \ˌ≈ˈ≈\ *vt* [1*under* + *pole*] **:** to pole (as copper) insufficiently
underpopulated \ˌ≈ˈ≈≈ˌ≈≈\ *adj* [1*under* + *populated*, past part. of *populate*] **:** having a lower density of population than is normal or desirable
underpowered \ˌ≈ˈ≈≈\ *adj* [1*under* + *powered*] **:** driven by an engine of insufficient power ⟨~ truck⟩
underpower relay \ˌ≈≈≈-\ *n* **:** a relay actuated by a fall in wattage below a set level

underpraise \¦==¦=\ *vt* [¹*under* + *praise*] **:** to withhold due praise from
underpresence \'==,==\ *n* [³*under* + *presence*] **:** a force or personality felt as present in inanimate nature
underprice \¦==¦=\ *vt* [¹*under* + *price*] **1 :** to set a price on that is below the current price or below the real value **2 :** to undercut (a competitor) in prices
¹**underprint** \¦==¦=\ *vt* [¹*under* + *print*] **1 :** to print or impress on the under side of **2 :** to print with less density or firmness of outline than is needed
²**underprint** \'==,=\ *n* **1 :** a light-colored overall pattern printed on a stamp underneath the design **2 :** printing on the back of a stamp
underprivilege \¦==¦=(=)=\ *n* [³*under* + *privilege*] **:** condition of being deprived of or barred from enjoyment of an average or accepted standard of living **:** relative poverty ⟨right of labor to speak their protests against economic ~ —R. M. La Follette †1953⟩
underprivileged \¦==¦=(=)=\ *adj* [¹*under* + *privileged*] **:** deprived through social or economic oppression of some of the fundamental rights theoretically belonging to all members of a civilized society ⟨children from ~ homes⟩ **:** socially and economically deprived **:** POOR ⟨epidemics in ~ areas of the city⟩
underprize \¦==¦=\ *vt* [¹*under* + *prize*] **:** UNDERVALUE
underproduction \¦==¦==\ *n* [³*under* + *production*] **:** the production of less than is demanded or of less than the usual supply
underproductive \¦===¦=\ *adj* [¹*under* + *productive*] **:** not capable of adequate production ⟨~ agricultural system⟩
underpromotion \¦===¦=\ *n* [³*under* + *promotion*] **:** the promotion of a pawn to bishop, knight, or rook in chess
underproof \¦==¦=\ *adj* [²*under* + *proof*, n.] **:** containing less alcohol than proof spirit
¹**underprop** \¦==¦=\ *vt* [¹*under* + *prop*] **1 :** to prop up from below **:** UNDERPIN **2 :** UPHOLD, SUPPORT ⟨~ a reputation⟩ **3 :** to serve as a prop or support underneath
²**underprop** \'==,=\ *n* **:** a prop placed underneath or supporting something
underpropping \'==,==\ *n* -s **:** FOUNDATION, SUPPORT
underquote \¦==¦=\ *vt* [¹*under* + *quote*] **:** to quote a lower price than ⟨~ competitors⟩
underrate \¦==¦=\ *vt* [¹*under* + *rate*] **:** to rate too low **:** set too low an estimate upon **:** UNDERVALUE ⟨human nature is consistently *underrated* in business —John Galsworthy⟩ ⟨overpraised by some critics, who have thus naturally provoked others to ~ it —A.T.Quiller-Couch⟩
¹**underreach** \¦==¦=\ *vt* [¹*under* + *reach*] **:** to reach under or below **:** clear under (as a log) so as to pass a chain
²**underreach** \'==,=\ *n* **:** a pole used to lever up a bogged log
underread \¦==¦=\ *vt* [¹*under* + *read*] **1 :** to take a reading below the correct reading of (a test) **:** to read (as a temperature, measurement, or weight) as lower than that actually registered **2 :** to read with less than full or due understanding, appreciation, or alertness ⟨~ the poets whose reputations they wish to demolish —F.A.Pottle⟩
underreader \'==,==\ *n* [³*under* + *reader*] **:** an assistant reader
underream \¦==¦=\ *vt* [¹*under* + *ream*] **:** to enlarge (an oil-well hole) below the casing
underreamer \'==,==\ *n* **:** a reamer for operating below the casing of a borehole to enlarge the hole for the reception of the pipe
underreport \¦===¦=\ *vt* [¹*under* + *report*] **:** to report an amount for (as income) less than the actual one
underrepresented \¦==¦==¦==\ *adj* [¹*under* + *represented*, past part. of *represent*] **:** inadequately represented ⟨in pollen statistics . . . species producing small quantities will tend to be ~ —S.A.Cain⟩ ⟨farm laborers . . . are also ~ in unemployment figures —*Harper's*⟩
underripe \¦==¦=\ *adj* [¹*under* + *ripe*] **:** not fully ripe ⟨~ berries⟩
underround \¦==¦=\ *vt* [¹*under* + *round*] **:** to round (the lips or a vowel) less than usual in relation to the height of the tongue
¹**underruff** \¦==¦=\ *vi* [¹*under* + *ruff*] **:** to ruff with a trump smaller than one already played so as to avoid discarding from another suit
²**underruff** \'==,=\ *n* **:** the act of underruffing
¹**underrun** \¦==¦=\ *vb* [¹*under* + *run*] *vt* **1 :** to pass or extend under ⟨~ and uplifted by advancing masses of colder air⟩ **2 a :** to pass along under in order to examine (a cable) **b :** to separate and put in order the parts of (a tackle) **c :** to take in (a net or trawl line) for emptying and resetting **d :** to lift and empty out (a hose) by walking along and shifting the hold successively along the length ~ *vi* **:** to flow or persist in a suppressed or underlying stream
²**underrun** \'==,=\ *n* **1 :** UNDERCURRENT **2 :** a run (as of goods or printed copies) short of the quantity ordered by a customer **3 :** the amount by which the actual cut of merchantable lumber falls below a log scale estimate **4 :** the lower contact surface of a third rail or trolley wire
unders *pl of* UNDER
undersailed \¦==¦=\ *adj* [¹*under* + *-sailed* (fr. *sail*, n. + *-ed*)] **:** equipped with too small or too few sails
undersanded \¦==¦==\ *adj* [¹*under-* + *-sanded* (fr. *sand*, n. + *-ed*)] *of concrete* **:** not containing enough sand for normal use and working conditions
undersaturated \¦==¦=,==\ *adj* [¹*under* + *saturated*] **:** UNSATURATED ⟨~ rocks⟩
undersaturation \¦==,==¦==\ *n* **:** the quality or state of being undersaturated
¹**underscore** \¦==¦=\ *vt* [¹*under* + *score*] **1 :** to draw a line under **:** UNDERLINE ⟨twenty lines of it were heavily *underscored* in red ink —L.C.Douglas⟩ **2 :** EMPHASIZE ⟨the conference also *underscored* the very great importance of isotopes to industry, biology, and medicine —R.J.Bunche⟩ **3 :** to provide (action on film) with accompanying music
²**underscore** \'==,=\ *n* **1 :** a line drawn under a word or line esp. for indicating emphasis or italic letters **:** UNDERSCORING **2 :** music accompanying the action and dialogue of a film
underscrub \'==,=\ *n* [³*under* + *scrub*] **:** scrubby growth under trees **:** UNDERBRUSH
¹**undersea** \¦==¦=\ *adj* [²*under* + *sea*, n.] **1 :** being or carried on under the sea or under the surface of the sea ⟨~ oil deposits⟩ ⟨~ fighting⟩ **2 :** designed for use under the surface of the sea ⟨~ fleet⟩ ⟨~ cable⟩
²**undersea** \"\ *or* **underseas** \¦==¦=\ *adv* [²*under* + *sea*, n. or *seas*, pl. of *sea*, n.] **:** under the sea **:** beneath the surface of the sea ⟨photographs taken ~⟩
undersecretariat \¦==¦==(,)=\ *n* [³*under* + *secretariat*] **:** the office and staff of an undersecretary **:** a subdivision of a ministry
un·der·secretary \¦əndə(r)+\ *n* [³*under* + *secretary*] **:** a subordinate or assistant secretary; *specif* **:** a secretary immediately subordinate to a principal secretary ⟨~ of the Treasury⟩ ⟨the British ~ for India⟩
undersecretary·ship \"+,ship\ *n* **:** the position of undersecretary
undersell \¦==¦=\ *vt* [¹*under* + *sell*] **1 :** to sell articles at a lower price than **:** to sell cheaper than (the same article offered elsewhere) **:** UNDERCUT **2 :** to appeal to or persuade inadequately or with restraint ⟨discovered that ~*ing* actually boosted its business —*Time*⟩
undersense \'==,=\ *n* [³*under* + *sense*] **1 :** an inner awareness **:** SUBCONSCIOUSNESS **2 :** an underlying sense or meaning ⟨the mind has to make no effort to get the ~ of what is happening —J.C.Powys⟩
underservant \'==,==\ *n* [³*under* + *servant*] **:** a subordinate servant
¹**underset** \¦==¦=\ *vt* [ME *undersetten*, fr. ¹*under* + *setten* to set — more at SET] **1 :** UNDERPIN **2 :** to place underneath something else
²**underset** \'==,=\ *n* **1 :** UNDERCURRENT **2 a :** an underlying vein of ore **b :** UNDERLIE
³**underset** \"\ *adj* [fr. past part. of ¹*underset*] **:** insufficiently filled (as with printed matter) so as to be partly blank ⟨~ page⟩ ⟨~ column⟩
undersetting \'==,==\ *n* [ME, fr. ³*under* + *setting*, gerund of *setten* to set] **:** something set or built under as a support **:** UNDERPINNING
un·der·set·tle \'əndə(r),sed·ᵊl\ *n* [ME *undersetle*, fr. ³*under* + *-setle* dweller, fr. OE *-setla*; akin to OE *sitan* to sit — more at SIT] **:** one of a class of subtenants formerly under the peasant proprietors in England
undersexed \¦==¦=\ *adj* [¹*under* + *sexed*] **:** characterized by a subnormal or inadequate degree of sexual desire or interest ⟨the American woman has become cold and ~ —William Faulkner⟩
undersheriff \'==,==\ *n* [³*under* + *sheriff*] **:** a sheriff's deputy; *specif* **:** one on whom the sheriff's powers devolve by the sheriff's direction or in case of his incapacity or a vacancy in the office
undershirt \'==,=\ *n* [³*under* + *shirt*] **:** a collarless undergarment with or without sleeves and usu. of cotton jersey
¹**undershoot** \¦==¦=\ *vt* [¹*under* + *shoot*, v.] **1 :** to shoot short of or below (a target) **2 :** to fall short of (a runway) in landing an airplane ~ *vi* **:** to shoot so as to strike below or short of the mark
²**undershoot** \'==,=\ *n* **:** an act or an instance of undershooting
³**undershoot** \"\ *n* [³*under* + *shoot*, n. (branch)] **:** a shoot (as of a plant) that springs out below a higher or more important shoot
undershore \¦==¦=\ *vt* [ME *undershoren*, fr. ¹*under* + *shoren* to shore — more at SHORE (to support)] **1 :** to shore up **2 :** to furnish support or justification for **:** UPHOLD ⟨~ an argument⟩
undershorts \'==,=\ *n pl* [³*under* + *shorts*] **:** short loose-fitting underpants
undershot \'==,=\ *adj* [¹*under* + *shot*, past part. of *shoot*] **1 :** having the lower incisor teeth or lower jaw projecting beyond the upper when the mouth is closed ⟨~ bulldog⟩ **2 :** moved by water passing beneath
undershot wheel *n* **:** a vertical waterwheel into the circumference of which are set blades that are pushed by water passing underneath

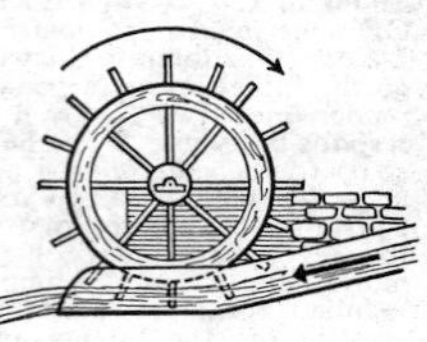
undershot wheel

undershrub \'==,=\ *n* [³*under* + *shrub*] **1 :** SUBSHRUB 1 **2 :** a small low-growing shrub; *esp* **:** a woody chamaephyte
undershrubby \'==,==\ *adj* **:** tending to be a low shrub or subshrub
underside \'==,=, ,=='=\ *n* [³*under* + *side*] **1 :** the side or surface lying underneath ⟨~ of a leaf⟩ **2 :** the side usu. hidden from sight **:** the worse side ⟨with the ~ of civilization revealing itself in slum and brothel —R.M.Kain⟩
undersign \¦==¦=\ *vt* [¹*under* + *sign*] **:** to write one's name at the foot or end of (as a letter or legal instrument)
undersigned \¦==¦=\ *n, pl* **undersigned** [fr. past part. of *undersign*] **:** one who signs his name at the end of a document — used with *the* ⟨the ~ testifies⟩ ⟨the ~ all agree⟩
undersigner \¦==¦=\ *n* **:** one that undersigns **:** UNDERSIGNED, SUBSCRIBER
undersize \'==,=\ *n* [³*under* + *size*] **1 :** size below the normal or average **2 :** the portion of ground material (as ore or coal) that passes through a specific size of screen
¹**undersized** *also* **undersize** \¦==¦=\ *adj* [*undersized* fr. ¹*under* + *sized*; *undersize* fr. ²*under* + *size*, n.] **:** of a size less than is common, proper, normal, or average ⟨~ trout⟩
²**undersized** *adj* [¹*under* + *sized*, past part. of *size* (to treat with size)] **:** not sufficiently sized ⟨~ paper⟩
underskirt \'==,=\ *n* [³*under* + *skirt*] **:** a skirt worn under an outer skirt; *esp* **:** PETTICOAT
underslip \'==,=\ *n* [³*under* + *slip*] **:** SLIP 6a
underslope \'==,=\ *n* [³*under* + *slope*] **:** an earmark for cattle corresponding to the overslope but on the lower side of the ear — see EARMARK illustration
undersluice \'==,=\ *n* [³*under* + *sluice*] **:** a sluice covered from view or lying beneath another structure; *specif* **:** a wasteway for sluicing out canals in which the waste escapes beneath other structures
underslung \'==,=\ *adj* [¹*under* + *slung*, past part. of *sling*] **1 a** (1) **:** having the point of support above rather than underneath ⟨~ desk drawer⟩ **:** having the principal bulk below the point of support ⟨~ bowl of a pipe⟩ (2) *of a vehicle frame* **:** suspended so as to extend below the axles **b :** having a low center of gravity **:** built low to the ground **:** having short legs **:** SQUAT **2 :** UNDERSHOT 1 ⟨bullet head and ~ jaw⟩
undersold *past of* UNDERSELL
undersong \'==,=\ *n* [³*under* + *song*] **1 a :** a subordinate melody or part; *esp* **:** a droning accompaniment **b :** UNDERTONE **2** *archaic* **:** REFRAIN
undersow \¦==¦=\ *vt* [¹*under* + *sow*] **:** to sow (a crop) with or after a main crop to grow on after the main crop has been harvested ⟨barley was *undersown* with lespedeza⟩
underspend \¦==¦=\ *vb* [¹*under* + *spend*] *vt* **:** to spend less than or less than the whole of ~ *vi* **:** to spend at less than the normal rate
underspin \'==,=\ *n* [³*under* + *spin*] **:** BACKSPIN
undersquare \'==,=\ *n* [³*under* + *square*] **:** an earmark for cattle made on the lower side of the ear **:** UNDERCROP — see EARMARK illustration
understaffed \¦==¦=\ *adj* [¹*under* + *staffed*, past part. of *staff*] **:** having an inadequate staff ⟨overcrowded and ~ hospitals⟩
un·der·stand \,əndə(r)'stand, -aa(ə)nd\ *vb* **un·der·stood** \-tůd\ **understood** *or archaic* **understanded**; **understanding**; **understands** [ME *understanden*, *understonden*, fr. OE *understandan*, *understondan*, fr. ¹*under* + *standan*, *stondan* to stand — more at STAND] *vt* **1 :** to grasp the meaning of **:** COMPREHEND: as **a :** to apprehend the meaning or idea of by knowing what is conveyed by the words or signs used ⟨~ Russian⟩ ⟨~ a message in code⟩ ⟨~ a wink⟩ ⟨a tongue not ~*ed* of the people —*Bk. of Com. Prayer*⟩ **b :** to grasp the reasonable or logical character of **:** interpret or explain successfully to oneself ⟨I can ~ why he was disappointed⟩ ⟨his behavior is hard to ~⟩ ⟨must be made to ~ the importance of this step⟩ **c :** to make out clearly the speech of ⟨spoke in such a thick accent no one could ~ him⟩ **d :** to have thorough or technical acquaintance with or expertness in the practice of ⟨being well informed about science is not the same thing as ~*ing* science —J.B.Conant⟩ ⟨~ finance⟩ ⟨master builders had to ~ both carpentry and stonework —G.B.Saul⟩ **e :** to be thoroughly familiar with the character or essential nature and propensities of ⟨need someone who ~*s* children⟩ ⟨liked him better when he came to ~ him better⟩ **2 a :** to know, consider, or accept as a fact, truth, or principle without further mention or explanation or without utter certainty ⟨*understood* that customary procedures obtained⟩ **b :** to consider as a possible fact **:** infer or come to regard as plausible or probable without certain knowledge or proof **:** know through rumor or hearsay ⟨we ~ that he is returning from abroad next week⟩ ⟨was *understood* to be in favor of the plan⟩ **c :** to accept as established or laid down as a condition whether or not explicitly stated ⟨am I to ~ that your refusal is final⟩ **3 :** to regard in a particular way or with a particular meaning in mind **:** interpret in a single one of a number of possible ways ⟨by the money price of goods . . . I ~ always the quantity of pure gold or silver for which they are sold —Adam Smith⟩ ⟨by poetical colors the neoclassicist ~*s* words, elegant phrases, figures of speech —Irving Babbitt⟩ **4 :** to supply in thought as if present **:** take as meant though not expressed ⟨the phrase "to be married" is commonly *understood* after the word *engaged*⟩ ⟨~ the subject of an imperative⟩ **5** *archaic* **:** to be familiar with **:** recognize from previous knowledge ⟨abundance of kinds of creatures that we did not ~ —Daniel Defoe⟩ **6** *obs* **:** to know how to conduct (oneself) properly **7** *obs* **:** to prop up **:** SUPPORT ~ *vi* **1 :** to have the use of the intellectual faculties **:** have the power of comprehension **2 :** to achieve a mental grasp of the nature, significance, or causal explanation of something ⟨the more he was educated, the less he *understood* —Henry Adams⟩ ⟨doubt if they really can ~ about politics —Christopher Hollis⟩ **3 :** to show a sympathetic or tolerant or indulgent attitude toward something ⟨she relied on him to ~ and sympathize —John Galsworthy⟩
syn COMPREHEND, APPRECIATE: UNDERSTAND and COMPREHEND are very often interchangeable. For very wide and general concepts UNDERSTAND is more likely to be used than COMPREHEND ⟨*understand* Shakespeare's preeminence⟩ ⟨*comprehend* the dramatic action of Macbeth⟩ ⟨to *understand* the present institutions, we must therefore *comprehend* something of their history —J.B.Conant⟩ UNDERSTAND is wider in its use, ranging from the mere physical act of sensory perception or very casual consideration to a full and profound realization of inner nature, rationale, or significance ⟨the racket prevented my *understanding* the telephone operator⟩ ⟨when you throw an apple upward and let it fall . . . the mechanics of the thing . . . seem natural; you *understand* them without even using your intellect —Wolfgang Langewiesche⟩ ⟨those enlightened ones who in the clear beam of their purified vision beheld and *understood* the sorrows, the struggles, the vain angers and hatreds of imperfect mortality —Laurence Binyon⟩ COMPREHEND may focus attention on thought processes rather than their conclusions ⟨with what terrible earnestness Woodrow Wilson was trying to *comprehend* the problem —W.A.White⟩ COMPREHEND may stand between *sense* or *feel* and *understand* in suggesting less reflection and analysis than the latter ⟨dissimilar as her parents had appeared to be, there was a bond between them which Dorinda felt without *comprehending* —Ellen Glasgow⟩ APPRECIATE stresses full and just perception, esp. of value, arrived at with insight and discrimination ⟨I could not *appreciate* its excellence, having no background of previous displays to use for purposes of comparison —Robert Graves⟩ ⟨fully to *appreciate* the American experience . . . would require a rehearsal of the whole of American history —H.S.Commager⟩
— **give one to understand 1 :** to intimate or convey to one without direct or positive assertion ⟨it is reported that the Democrats have been quietly *given to understand* that the White House approves of their action —*New Republic*⟩ **2 :** to make one understand **:** tell plainly and forcibly — **understand each other :** to be in agreement esp. without having exchanged explicit declarations or assurances; *often* **:** to be in collusion
un·der·stand·abil·i·ty \,əndə(r),standə'biləd·ē, -aan-, -lətē, -i\ *n* **:** the quality or state of being understandable
un·der·stand·able \¦əndə(r)¦standəbəl, -aan-\ *adj* [ME, fr. *understanden* + *-able*] **1 :** capable of being readily understood **:** INTELLIGIBLE **2** *obs* **:** able to understand or comprehend — **un·der·stand·able·ness** *n* -ES — **un·der·stand·ably** \-blē, -li\ *adv*
understanded *archaic past part of* UNDERSTAND
un·der·stand·er \,əndə(r)'standə(r), -aan-\ *n* -s [ME *understander*, *understonder*, fr. *understanden*, *understonden* + *-er*] **1 :** one that understands **2 :** one that stands under or supports; *specif* **:** UNDERMAN 2 **3** *obs* **a :** FOOT **b :** BOOT **4** *obs* **:** a spectator in the pit of a theater
¹**understanding** *n* -s [ME, fr. OE, fr. *understandan* to understand + *-ing*] **1 :** the act of grasping mentally **:** COMPREHENSION, DISCERNMENT, INTERPRETATION ⟨a clear ~ of the reasons for his failure⟩ **2 a :** the ability to understand **:** the power of comprehending, analyzing, distinguishing, and judging ⟨an argument aimed at the ~ rather than the emotions⟩ **b :** the condition of having attained to full comprehension ⟨the book deals with matters beyond a child's ~⟩ **3 a :** the faculty or ability of subsuming the particular under the general or of apprehending general relations of particulars; *also* **:** JUDGMENT 10b **b :** the power to make experience intelligible by bringing perceived particulars under appropriate concepts **c :** the capacity to formulate and apply to experience concepts and categories, to judge, and to draw logical inferences — distinguished from *reason*; compare DIANOIA, RATIO 1b, TECHNE **4 a :** friendly or harmonious relationship ⟨working for better ~ between nations⟩ ⟨had never been much ~ between the brothers⟩ **b :** an agreement of opinion or feeling **:** adjustment of differences ⟨reached an ~ with the children about television programs⟩ **c :** a mutual agreement not formally entered into but in some degree binding on each side ⟨a monetary ~ between two countries⟩; *esp* **:** an informal engagement to marry **d :** an understood or acknowledged condition, limitation, or provision ⟨allowed to plow up the footpaths during the war on the ~ that they restored them afterward —S.P.B.Mais⟩ **5 :** SIGNIFICATION, MEANING ⟨according to the usual ~ of the word⟩ **syn** see REASON
²**understanding** *adj* [ME, fr. pres. part. of *understanden* to understand] **1** *archaic* **:** KNOWING, INTELLIGENT, SKILLFUL **2 :** endowed with or displaying understanding ⟨~ heart⟩ **3 :** possessed of a tolerant, kindly, humane, or sympathetic attitude ⟨~ parents⟩ — **un·der·stand·ing·ly** *adv* — **un·der·stand·ing·ness** *n* -ES
understands *pres 3d sing of* UNDERSTAND
understate \¦==¦=\ *vt* [¹*under* + *state*] **1 :** to represent as being less than the true number, size, intensity **:** state inadequately or less strongly than may be done truthfully ⟨~ taxable income⟩ ⟨~ the logical difficulties of a proposed scheme⟩ **2 :** to state or describe with deliberate restraint esp. so as to achieve an effective contrast **:** withhold obvious emphasis from ⟨story is told with . . . *understated* force —*Time*⟩
understated \¦==¦=\ *adj* [fr. past part. of *understate*] **:** simply effective **:** avoiding obvious emphasis or embellishment ⟨handsome, ~ suit with simple details —Dorothy Hawkins⟩
understatement \¦==¦==\ *n* [³*under* + *statement*] **1 :** the act of understating **:** a statement below the truth ⟨~ of population growth⟩ **2 :** restrained statement in ironic contrast to what might be said **:** studied avoidance of emphasis or exaggeration ⟨we have been taught to value terseness and ~ —Irving Howe⟩
understeer \'==,=\ *n* **:** the tendency of an automobile to go straight ahead and turn less sharply than the driver intends — **understeer** \,=='=\ *vi*
¹**understock** \¦==¦=\ *vt* [¹*under* + *stock*] **:** to stock (as a farm or store) with less than the usual or desirable number or quantity
²**understock** \'==,=\ *n* **1 :** an inadequate supply **2 :** STOCK 5b(1)
understocking \'==,==\ *n* [³*under* + *stocking*] **1** *archaic* **:** a stocking for the lower leg **2 :** a stocking worn for support or warmth under another stocking
un·der·stood \¦əndə(r)¦stůd\ *adj* [fr. past part. of *understand*] **1 :** fully apprehended as to meaning or causal relations or essential nature **2 :** settled or settled upon by common often tacit agreement **:** IMPLICIT ⟨our breakfasts together had become habitual, the invitation ~ —R.C.Peace⟩
understory \'==,==\ *n* [³*under* + *story*] **1 :** a foliage layer lying beneath and shaded by the main canopy of a forest **2 a :** the plants (as seedlings, shrubs, and herbs) that form the foliage understory of a forest — sometimes distinguished from *ground cover* **b :** a layer of low vegetation underlying a layer of taller (as of grama grass beneath wheatgrass)
understrapper \'==,==\ *n* [³*under* + *strapper*] **:** an inferior agent or official **:** a petty subordinate **:** UNDERLING ⟨country being run into the ground by a bunch of big-headed ~*s* who went around lording it over the taxpayers —H.L.Davis⟩
understratum \'==,==\ *n* [³*under* + *stratum*] **:** SUBSTRATUM
understrength \¦==¦=\ *adj* [²*under* + *strength*, n.] **:** deficient in strength ⟨~ solution of disinfectant⟩; *specif* **:** having fewer personnel than prescribed by a table of organization
understress \¦==¦=\ *vt* [¹*under* + *stress*] **:** to stress insufficiently **:** fail to give due emphasis to
understring \¦==¦=\ *vt* [¹*under* + *string*] **:** to string (a bow) with too long a cord
¹**understroke** \¦==¦=\ *vb* [¹*under* + *stroke*] *vt* **:** UNDERLINE, UNDERSCORE ~ *vi* **:** to execute an understroke
²**understroke** \'==,=\ *n* **:** a stroke executed underneath or with a downward sweep
understructure \'==,==\ *n* [³*under* + *structure*] **:** a structure for supporting something above **:** FOUNDATION, BASIS
understrung \¦==¦=\ *adj* [¹*under* + *strung*, past part. of *string*] **:** LOW-STRUNG
¹**understudy** \'==,==\ *vb* [¹*under* + *study*] *vi* **:** to study another actor's part in order to be his substitute in an emergency ~ *vt* **1 :** to study (a part or character) as understudy **:** prepare as understudy to (an actor) **2 :** to learn (as a job or procedure) thoroughly by observation or apprenticeship ⟨~ a banking operation⟩
²**understudy** \"\ *n* **:** one who stands prepared to act another's part or take over the work or duties of another
undersupply \¦==¦=\ *n* [³*under* + *supply*] **:** an inadequate supply or amount
¹**undersurface** \'==,==\ *n* [³*under* + *surface*] **:** the surface that lies underneath **:** UNDERSIDE

²undersurface \"\ *adj* [²*under* + *surface*, n.] **:** existing or moving below the surface ⟨~ craft⟩

undertail \ˈ==,=\ *adj* [²*under* + *tail*, n.] **:** lying or extending under the tail ⟨~ wing coverts⟩

undertake \ˌ==ˈ=\ *vb* [ME *undertaken*, fr. ¹*under* + *taken* to take — more at TAKE] *vt* **1 :** to take in hand **:** enter upon **:** set about **:** ATTEMPT ⟨~ a task⟩ ⟨~ a journey⟩ ⟨~ to campaign for office⟩ ⟨when armed uprisings have been *undertaken* by single oppressed classes —M.R.Cohen⟩ **2 :** to take upon oneself solemnly or expressly **:** put oneself under obligation to perform **:** CONTRACT, COVENANT ⟨a player ~*s* to win nine tricks provided he may declare his own trumps —J.B.Pick⟩ **3 :** GUARANTEE, PROMISE ⟨the magician who ~*s* to make or stop rain —J.G.Frazer⟩ **4 :** to accept as a charge **:** engage to look after or attend to **:** accept the responsibility for the care of ⟨~ a patient⟩ ⟨lawyer may refuse to ~ a case which appears to him unsound —H.S.Drinker⟩ **5** *archaic* **a :** to engage with in combat **b :** to engage with in argument or competition **:** take on **6** *obs* **:** REPROVE, CHIDE **7** *obs* **:** to take in or receive by hearing or interpreting ~ *vi* **1** *archaic* **:** to enter into an engagement or contract **:** PLEDGE — used with *for* **2** *archaic* **:** to give surety or assume responsibility — used with *for* **3** *obs* **:** to engage in a venture or enterprise

un·der·tak·er \ˈəndə(r)ˌtākə(r), *in sense 4* ˌ==ˈ==\ *n* [ME, fr. *undertaken* + *-er*] **1 :** one that undertakes **:** one that launches an enterprise **:** one that engages in any project or business **:** one that takes the risk and management of business **:** ENTREPRENEUR **2** *obs* **a :** one engaged in scholarly and scientific exploration of a subject **b :** one engaged upon the compiling or composition of a work for publication **c :** a book publisher **d :** an organizer of a stage production **3 :** one that stipulates or covenants to perform work for another **:** CONTRACTOR, SUBCONTRACTOR **4 :** one whose business is to prepare the dead for burial and to arrange and manage funerals **5 a :** an Englishman taking over ownership of forfeited lands in Ireland in the 16th and 17th centuries **b :** a political leader undertaking to influence members of Parliament esp. in securing supplies for the sovereign in 17th century England

un·der·tak·er·ly *adj* **:** having the manner or tone of an undertaker ⟨sees my grief, and assumes an ~ air —George Meredith⟩

¹undertaking *n* [ME, fr. gerund of *undertaken* to undertake] **1 :** the act of one who undertakes or engages in a project or business; *specif* **:** the business of an undertaker **2 :** something undertaken **:** a business, work, or project which one engages in or attempts **:** ENTERPRISE ⟨large-scale ~*s* involving large expenditures of money —E.L.Bernays⟩ **3 :** PLEDGE, PROMISE, GUARANTEE; *specif* **:** a promise or security required by law

²undertaking *adj* [ME, fr. pres. part. of *undertaken* to undertake] *archaic* **:** willing to undertake an enterprise assuming the risks as organizer or manager; *esp* **:** ready to engage in literary production or act as publisher

undertenancy \ˈ==,===\ *n* [³*under* + *tenancy*] **:** a tenancy held from a tenant

undertenant \ˈ==,==\ *n* [³*under* + *tenant*] **:** the tenant of a tenant **:** one who holds lands or tenements by an underlease

under-the-counter \ˌ===ˈ==\ *adj, of a sale* **:** made from concealed stocks of scarce or rare goods or goods priced below the legal fixed price; *broadly* **:** UNLAWFUL, ILLICIT

under-the-table \ˌ===ˈ==\ *adj* [fr. the phrase *under the table*] **:** carried out in a secret or confidential manner **:** SUB-ROSA ⟨has the *under-the-table* backing of the remnants of the discredited political faction —*New Orleans (La.) Times-Picayune*⟩

underthings \ˈ==,=\ *n pl* [³*under* + *things*, pl. of *thing*] **:** women's underwear

underthought \ˈ==,=\ *n* [³*under* + *thought*] **:** a suppressed or concealed thought

¹underthrust \ˌ==ˈ=\ *vt* [¹*under* + *thrust*] **1 :** to thrust underneath or out from underneath ⟨sulky ~ lower lip⟩ **2 :** to insert or move (a rock mass) into position by underthrust faulting

²underthrust \ˈ==,=\ *n* **1 :** the insertion by compressive stresses and faulting of one mass of rock under another — compare THRUST FAULT **2 :** the stress that produces an underthrust

undertide \ˈ==,=\ *n* [³*under* + *tide*] **:** UNDERCURRENT

¹undertime \ˈ==,=\ *n* [³*under* + *time*, n.] **1 :** a time less than the time allotted for the performance of some task or the completion of a program or speech **2 :** working time that is less than full time or a required minimum

²undertime \ˌ==ˈ=\ *vt* [¹*under* + *time*, v.] **:** to allow too short a time for ⟨~ a photographic exposure⟩

undertint \ˈ==,=\ *n* [³*under* + *tint*] **:** a subdued tint

¹undertone \ˈ==,=\ *n* [³*under* + *tone*] **1 a :** a low or subdued utterance ⟨gossiping in a corner in ~*s*⟩ **b :** an underlying or accompanying sound ⟨~ of droning insects⟩ **c :** COMBINATION TONE **2 a :** a subdued or implicit emotional quality underlying the surface of an utterance or action ⟨sneering and malicious ~ on nearly every page —John Morris⟩ ⟨uneasiness in Paris had deeper ~*s* of fear —*Atlantic*⟩ **b :** the underlying tendency of a market as distinguished from its behavior at any one time ⟨despite a weak start, utilities displayed a strong ~ in today's session⟩ **3 :** a subdued color: as **a :** the color of a pigment thinly laid on a white or light-colored ground **b :** a color seen through and modifying another or other colors **c :** the color of the light transmitted (as by a paint or varnish film) — compare OVERTONE 2

²undertone \"\ *vt* **:** to express in an undertone

undertook *past of* UNDERTAKE

undertow \ˈ==,=\ *n* [³*under* + *tow*] **:** the current beneath the surface that sets seaward or along the beach when waves are breaking upon the shore — compare OFFSET, ⁵RIP 2, SEA PUSS

undertread \ˌ==ˈ=\ *vt* [¹*under* + *tread*] *archaic* **:** to tread beneath the feet **:** SUBJUGATE, OPPRESS

undertrick \ˈ==,=\ *n* [³*under* + *trick*] **:** a trick by which a declarer in bridge falls short of making his contract

undertrimmer \ˈ==,==\ *n* [³*under* + *trimmer*] **:** one that fits and sews linings to shoe uppers

undertrump \ˌ==ˈ=\ *vb* [¹*under* + *trump*] **:** UNDERRUFF

underturner \ˈ==,==\ *n* [³*under* + *turner* (after *turn under*, v.)] **:** a worker that removes burrs from clock pinions

underutilization \ˌ==ˌ=(ˌ)=ˈ==\ *n* [³*under* + *utilization*] **:** insufficient utilization **:** wasteful failure to utilize fully

undervaluation \ˌ==ˌ==ˈ==\ *n* [³*under* + *valuation*] **1 :** the act of undervaluing **2 :** a rate or value not equal to the real worth

¹undervalue \ˌ==ˈ=(ˌ)=\ *vt* [¹*under* + *value*, v.] **1 :** to value, rate, or estimate below the real worth **:** set too low a value upon ⟨*undervalued* the things he did not know —Agnes Repplier⟩ **2 :** to esteem lightly **:** treat as of little worth **3 :** to cause to decrease in value or estimation **:** DEPRECIATE ⟨the dollar was *undervalued* in terms of foreign currencies —E.W.Kemmerer⟩

²undervalue \"\ *n* [³*under* + *value*] **:** a rate or price less than the real worth

undervest \ˈ==,=\ *n* [³*under* + *vest*] **:** UNDERSHIRT

undervitalized \ˌ==ˈ==,=\ *adj* [¹*under* + *vitalized*, past part. of *vitalize*] **:** lacking normal vitality or energy ⟨pallid, ~, shy, sensitive creatures —O.W.Holmes †1894⟩

undervoltage \ˈ==,==\ *adj* [²*under* + *voltage*] **:** devised so as to become operative when the voltage in a line drops below a definite value ⟨~ relay⟩

undervoltage protection *n* **:** the protection of a circuit by an automatic device against operation on reduced voltage

undervoltage release *n* **:** the automatic release of connections to the main circuit during an interval of reduced or no voltage

underwaist \ˈ==,=\ *n* [³*under* + *waist*] **:** a waist for wear under another garment; *specif* **:** WAIST 4a(3)

¹underwater \ˌ==ˈ==\ *adj* [²*under* + *water*, n.] **1 :** lying, growing, performed, worn, or operating below the surface of the water ⟨~ caverns⟩ ⟨~ operation of a submarine⟩ ⟨~ signaling⟩ **2 :** being below the waterline of a ship ⟨~ body⟩ ⟨~ valve⟩ **3** *of a security* **:** not backed by assets **:** having no equity if all liabilities were paid

²underwater \"\ *adv* [²*under* + *water*, n.] **:** under the water **:** under the surface of the water ⟨once stayed ~ for twenty-four hours —*New Yorker*⟩ ⟨could move more quickly ~ —Sir Winston Churchill⟩

³underwater \ˈ==,==\ *n* [³*under* + *water*] **:** the water under the surface (as of the ocean) ⟨fired from ~⟩ ⟨the ~*s* were infested by submarines —*Irish Statesman*⟩ ⟨knows the ~ of the bay . . . like the back of her hand —George Bradshaw⟩

under way *adv* [prob. fr. D *onderweg*, *onderwege*, fr. MD *onderwegen*, *onderwege*, fr. *onder* between, among + *wegen*, *wege*, dat. & acc. pl. of *wech* way; akin to OHG *untar* between, among and to OHG *wec* way — more at INTER-, WAY] **1 :** in motion **:** not at rest **:** not moored **:** not at anchor **2 :** into motion from a standstill ⟨an electric train gets *under way* rapidly⟩ **3 :** in process of development **:** in progress toward completion **:** AFOOT ⟨preparations for a big celebration were *under way*⟩ ⟨before the discussion was well *under way*⟩

underway \ˌ==ˈ=\ *adj* [*under way*] **:** occurring, performed, or used while traveling or in motion ⟨~ training unit⟩ ⟨~ refueling⟩ ⟨~ clothing⟩

underwear \ˈ==,=\ *n* [³*under* + *wear*] **:** a garment worn next to the skin and under other clothing ⟨stripped down to his ~⟩ ⟨filmy silk ~⟩ ⟨heavy woollen ~⟩

under weigh *adv* [by folk etymology] **:** under way

¹underweight \ˌ==ˈ=\ *n* [³*under* + *weight*] **1 :** weight below normal, average, or requisite weight **:** want of weight **:** the amount of the deficiency; *specif* **:** the amount by which the actual shipping weight of lumber differs from the standard weight upon which freight charges are computed **2 :** the condition of weighing less than the weight normal for an age or height **3 :** a person or article whose weight is less than normal or standard

²underweight \"\ *adj* [²*under* + *weight*, n.] **:** weighing less than the normal amount; *esp* **:** below the normal weight for the age

underwent *past of* UNDERGO

¹underwing \ˈ==,=\ *n* [³*under* + *wing*] **1 :** one of the posterior wings of an insect ⟨~ of a moth⟩ **2 :** any of numerous noctuid moths belonging to *Catocala* and related genera and having the hind wings banded with red and black or other contrasting colors **3 :** the surfaces underneath a bird's wing

²underwing \"\ *adj* [²*under* + *wing*, n.] **:** placed or growing underneath the wing ⟨~ coverts⟩

underwit \ˈ==,=\ *n* [³*under* + *wit*] **:** an underwitted person **:** HALF-WIT

underwitted \ˌ==ˈ==\ *adj* [¹*under* + *witted*] **:** weak in intellect **:** HALF-WITTED

underwood \ˈ==,=\ *n* [ME *underwode*, fr. ³*under* + *wode* wood — more at WOOD] **1 :** UNDERGROWTH, UNDERBRUSH **2 :** the sprout growth in a cutover forest which is reproducing itself

underwooded \ˈ==,==\ *adj* **:** covered with undergrowth

underwool \ˈ==,=\ *n* [³*under* + *wool*] **:** short woolly underfur or underhair (as of a rabbit)

¹underwork \ˌ==ˈ=\ *vb* [¹*under* + *work*, v.] *vi* **1 :** to do less work than is proper or suitable **2 :** to do work for less than current rates ~ *vt* **1** *obs* **:** to work against secretly **:** UNDERMINE **2 a :** to expend too little work upon ⟨~ a painting⟩ **b :** to exact too little work from ⟨~ a horse⟩ ⟨~*ed* committee⟩ **3 :** to do like work at a less price than

²underwork \ˈ==,=\ *n* [³*under* + *work*, n.] **:** a supporting structure built underneath

underworker \ˈ==,==\ *n* [³*under* + *worker*] **1 :** one that underworks **2 :** an assistant workman

underworld \ˈ==,=\ *n* [³*under* + *world*] **1** *archaic* **:** the world lying below the heavens **:** EARTH **2 :** the place of departed souls **:** HADES **3 a :** a region underground or in the ocean depths **b :** the side of the earth opposite to one **4 a :** the world of activity among the lower forms of life **b :** a social sphere or level of society regarded as lying below the level of ordinary life and experience; *esp* **:** the world of organized crime

underwrite \ˌ==ˈ=\ *vb* [ME *underwriten*, fr. ¹*under* + *writen* to write — more at WRITE] *vt* **1 :** to write under or at the end of something else **2 :** to write one's name under or set one's name to (an insurance policy) for the purpose of thereby becoming answerable for a designated loss or damage on consideration of receiving a premium percent **:** insure on life or property; *also* **:** to assume (a sum or risk) by way of insurance **3 :** to subscribe to **:** agree to **:** CONFIRM ⟨U.S. might tolerate, accept, permit a compromise in Indochina without fully *underwriting* it —Frank Gorrell⟩ **4 a :** to agree to purchase (a security issue) on a fixed date at a fixed price with a view to public distribution **b :** to contract for the purchase of (securities) under an agreement to buy any portion of issues offered to a corporation's existing shareholders that remain unsold ⟨~ a stock issue on a standby basis⟩ **c :** to put up funds for or guarantee financial support of ⟨corporations have undertaken to ~ a sizable proportion of the orchestras' deficits —Howard Taubman⟩ **5 a :** to write in a manner inadequate to represent the real worth or importance of ⟨~ his parts, lightly sketching the characters and counting on the actors to fill them in —W.S.Maugham⟩ **b :** to drop below (as a person or a standard) in quality of writing ~ *vi* **1** *obs* **:** to give a guarantee or become surety **2 :** to carry on the business of an underwriter

underwriter \ˈ==,==\ *n* **1 :** one that underwrites **:** GUARANTOR, SUPPORTER ⟨the citizen taxpayer has succeeded . . . as the principal ~ of the costs of science —*Scientific American Reader*⟩ **2 :** one that underwrites a policy of insurance **:** an individual or company that insures **:** INSURER **3 :** one that underwrites or shares in underwriting a security issue **4 :** one who selects risks to be solicited ⟨life ~⟩ or classifies and rates the acceptability of risks solicited ⟨fire ~⟩ ⟨home-office ~⟩

underwriting \ˈ==,==\ *n* [³*under* + *writing*] **:** the earlier writing in a palimpsest

un·descended \ˌən+\ *adj* [¹*un-* + *descended*, past part. of *descend*] **:** not having descended; *specif* **:** retained in the inguinal canal instead of descending normally into the scrotum ⟨~ testicle⟩

un·describable \"+\ *adj* [¹*un-* + *describe* + *-able*] **:** INDESCRIBABLE

un·described \"+\ *adj* [¹*un-* + *described*, past part. of *describe*] **:** not described

un·descried \"+\ *adj* [¹*un-* + *descried*, past part. of *descry*] **:** not descried **:** UNSEEN

un·descriptive \"+\ *adj* **:** not effective in describing

un·deserve \"+\ *vt* [back-formation fr. *undeserved*] **:** to fail to deserve

un·deserved \"+\ *adj* [ME, fr. ¹*un-* + *deserved*, past part. of *deserven* to deserve — more at DESERVE] **:** not deserved **:** not merited **:** not justified ⟨~ reputation as a coward⟩ ⟨~ praise⟩ — **un·deservedly** \"+\ *adv* — **un·deservedness** \"+\ *n*

un·deserving \"+\ *adj* [¹*un-* + *deserving*, pres. part. of *deserve*] **:** not deserving ⟨~ of forgiveness⟩

un·de·serv·ing·ly *adv* **1 :** UNWORTHILY ⟨~ honored⟩ **2 :** UNJUSTLY ⟨~ punished⟩

un·designated \"+\ *adj* [¹*un-* + *designated*, past part. of *designate*] **:** not designated

un·designed \"+\ *adj* [¹*un-* + *designed*, past part. of *design*] **:** not designed **:** UNINTENTIONAL — **un·designedly** \"+\ *adv*

un·designing \"+\ *adj* **:** having no artful, ulterior, or fraudulent purpose **:** SINCERE, ARTLESS — **un·de·sign·ing·ly** *adv* — **un·de·sign·ing·ness** *n* -ES

un·desirability \"+\ *n* **:** the quality or state of being undesirable ⟨~ of concentrating all authority in a single individual —N.R.Collins⟩

¹un·desirable \"+\ *adj* [¹*un-* + *desirable*] **:** not desirable **:** UNWANTED, OBJECTIONABLE ⟨~ impurities in steel⟩ ⟨led astray by ~ companions⟩ ⟨legislation excluding ~ aliens⟩ — **un·de·sir·able·ness** *n* — **un·desirably** \"+\ *adv*

²undesirable \"\ *n* **:** one that is undesirable ⟨rounding up vagrants, drunks, ~*s*⟩

undesirable discharge *n* **:** a formal release from military service under conditions other than honorable

un·desire \ˌən+\ *n* **:** absence of desire

un·desired \"+\ *adj* [ME, fr. ¹*un-* + *desired*, past part. of *desiren* to desire — more at DESIRE] **:** not desired **:** UNSOUGHT, UNWANTED ⟨~ result⟩ ⟨~ unemployment⟩ — **un·de·sired·ly** \-ī(ə)rdlē, -īəd-, -īrəd-, -li\ *adv*

un·desiring \"+\ *adj* [¹*un-* + *desiring*, pres. part. of *desire*] **:** not desiring **:** UNDESIROUS

un·desirous \"+\ *adj* **:** lacking desire **:** feeling no desire

un·despairing \"+\ *adj* [¹*un-* + *despairing*, pres. part. of *despair*] **:** not despairing **:** UNDAUNTED

un·despoiled \"+\ *adj* [¹*un-* + *despoiled*, pres. part. of *despoil*] **:** not despoiled ⟨~ wilderness⟩

un·destroyable \"+\ *adj* [ME *undistriable*, fr. ¹*un-* + *destroyen*, *distrien* to destroy + *-able* — more at DESTROY] **:** INDESTRUCTIBLE

un·detachable \"+\ *adj* **:** not detachable ⟨~ part of a property⟩

un·detached \"+\ *adj* **:** not detached **:** INTEGRAL 1

undetd *abbr* undetermined

un·detectable \ˌən+\ *adj* **:** not detectable **:** escaping observation ⟨~ traces of poison⟩

un·detected \"+\ *adj* [¹*un-* + *detected*, past part. of *detect*] **:** not detected **:** UNOBSERVED

un·determinable \"+\ *adj* **:** INDETERMINABLE

un·determinate \"+\ *adj* **:** INDETERMINATE

un·determined \"+\ *adj* [ME, fr. ¹*un-* + *determined*, past part. of *determinen* to determine — more at DETERMINE] **1 :** not yet definitely or authoritatively decided, settled, or fixed ⟨~ boundary⟩ **:** not yet positively identified or ascertained ⟨~ species⟩ **2 :** not bounded by definite limits or restrictions **:** not fixed or precise in signification or use **:** VAGUE **3 :** not determinate in form or character **4 :** undecided in purpose — **un·determinedness** \"+\ *n*

un·deterred \"+\ *adj* [¹*un-* + *deterred*, past part. of *deter*] **:** not deterred ⟨pursued his own path . . . ~ by lack of popular appreciation and understanding —Osbert Sitwell⟩

un·developable \"+\ *adj* **:** not capable of being developed ⟨~ surface⟩

un·developed \"+\ *adj* [¹*un-* + *developed*, past part. of *develop*] **:** not developed ⟨~ natural resources⟩ **:** lacking in development **:** IMMATURE ⟨~ social awareness⟩

un·deviable \"+\ *adj* **:** UNDEVIATING

un·deviating \"+\ *adj* [¹*un-* + *deviating*, pres. part. of *deviate*] **:** keeping a true course **:** UNSWERVING ⟨evolution as an ~ upward march from the level of very simple organisms to much more complex ones —L.C.Eiseley⟩ ⟨~ loyalty⟩ — **un·de·vi·at·ing·ly** *adv*

un·devil \"+\ *vt* [²*un-* + *devil*, n.] **1** *archaic* **:** to free from diabolical possession **2** *archaic* **:** to divest of the character of a devil

un·devised \ˌən+\ *adj* [¹*un-* + *devised*, past part. of *devise*] **1 :** not devised by will ⟨~ portion of an estate⟩ **2 :** not intended **:** UNPLANNED

un·devout \"+\ *adj* [ME, fr. ¹*un-* + *devout*] **:** lacking in devoutness — **un·de·vout·ly** *adv*

un·diagnosable \"+\ *adj* [¹*un-* + *diagnose* + *-able*] **:** not capable of being diagnosed ⟨~ complaint⟩

un·diagnosed \"+\ *adj* [¹*un-* + *diagnosed*, past part. of *diagnose*] **:** not diagnosed **:** eluding diagnosis ⟨~ disease⟩

undid *past of* UNDO

un·didactic \ˌən+\ *adj* **:** not didactic **:** simply informative or descriptive

un·dies \ˈəndēz, -diz\ *n pl* [by shortening & alter. fr. *underwear*] **:** UNDERWEAR; *esp* **:** women's underwear

un·differenced \ˌən+\ *adj* [¹*un-* + *differenced*, past part. of *difference*] **:** UNDIFFERENTIATED

un·differentiated \"+\ *adj* [¹*un-* + *differentiated*, past part. of *differentiate*] **:** not differentiated **:** UNIFORM

un·digested \"+\ *adj* [¹*un-* + *digested*, past part. of *digest*] **1 :** not digested **:** UNASSIMILATED ⟨~ food⟩ ⟨~ mass of facts gathered at random⟩ **2** *of securities* **:** not absorbed by the market **:** not sold to permanent investors

un·dignified \"+\ *adj* **:** not dignified **:** lacking in dignity or injurious to dignity ⟨felt it to be ~ to accept a tip⟩ ⟨scrambling on all fours in an ~ manner⟩ — **un·dignifiedly** \"+\ *adv*

un·dignify \"+\ *vt* [²*un-* + *dignify*] **:** to take dignity from

un·diluted \"+\ *adj* **:** not diluted **:** PURE, UNQUALIFIED, UNMITIGATED ⟨~ racial strain⟩ ⟨~ pleasure⟩ ⟨~ nonsense⟩

un·diminishable \"+\ *adj* [¹*un-* + *diminish* + *-able*] **:** not capable of being diminished ⟨~ greatness⟩

un·diminished \"+\ *adj* [¹*un-* + *diminished*, past part. of *diminish*] **:** not lessened or weakened ⟨zeal ~ through the years⟩

un·dimmed \"+\ *adj* [¹*un-* + *dimmed*, past part. of *dim*] **:** not dimmed **:** CLEAR, BRIGHT

¹un·dine \ˌənˈdēn\ *n* -S [NL *undina*, fr. L *unda* wave + *-ina*, fr. fem. of *-inus* -ine (adj. suffix) — more at WATER] **:** a water nymph **:** an elemental spirit of the water **:** NIX — compare GNOME, SALAMANDER, SYLPH

²un·dine \", ˈən,dīn\ *or* **undine dropper** *n* -S [*undine*, ISV, fr. *und-* (fr. L *undare* to wave, overflow, inundate, fr. *unda* wave) + *-ine*] **:** a glass vessel used by physicians for irrigating the eye or a nasal passage

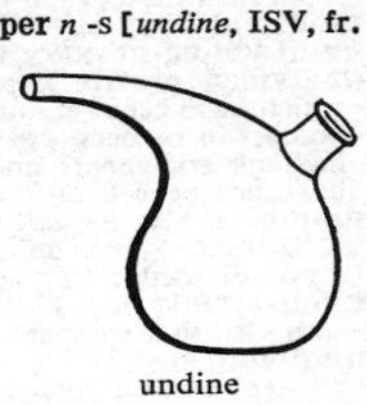

undine

un·diocesed \ˌən+\ *adj* [¹*un-* + *diocese* + *-ed*] **:** unprovided with a diocese **:** having no diocese

un·diplomatic \"+\ *adj* **:** TACTLESS, IMPOLITIC

un·dipped \"+\ *adj* [¹*un-* + *dipped*, past part. of *dip*] **1 :** not dipped **2 :** UNBAPTIZED

un·directed \"+\ *adj* [¹*un-* + *directed*, past part. of *direct*] **1 :** not directed **:** not guided **:** left without direction ⟨earnest but ~ efforts⟩ **2 :** not addressed **:** not superscribed ⟨~ letter⟩

un·disbanded \"+\ *adj* [¹*un-* + *disbanded*, past part. of *disband*] **:** not disbanded

un·discerned \"+\ *adj* [¹*un-* + *discerned*, past part. of *discern*] **:** not discerned **:** UNSEEN

un·discernible \"+\ *adj* **:** INDISCERNIBLE — **un·dis·cern·ible·ness** *n* — **un·discernibly** \"+\ *adv*

un·discerning \"+\ *adj* [¹*un-* + *discerning*, pres. part. of *discern*] **:** lacking discernment — **un·dis·cern·ing·ly** *adv*

un·discharged \"+\ *adj* [¹*un-* + *discharged*, past part. of *discharge*] **:** not discharged ⟨~ ammunition⟩ ⟨~ debts⟩

un·disciplinable \"+\ *adj* **:** resisting discipline **:** UNRULY

un·discipline \ˌən+\ *n* **:** want of discipline

un·disciplined \"+\ *adj* [ME, fr. ¹*un-* + *disciplined*] **1 :** lacking in discipline **:** UNRULY, WILD ⟨~ behavior⟩ **2 :** not subjected to discipline **:** UNTRAINED ⟨~ talent⟩ — **un·dis·ci·plined·ness** *n* -ES

un·disclosed \"+\ *adj* [¹*un-* + *disclosed*, past part. of *disclose*] **:** not made known ⟨sold for an ~ sum⟩ **:** not named or identified ⟨acting on information from an ~ source⟩ ⟨acting in behalf of an ~ principal⟩

un·dis·cour·age·able \ˌəndəˈskər-ijəbəl, -kə-ri-\ *adj* [¹*un-* + *discourage* + *-able*] **:** not capable of being discouraged

un·discouraged \ˌən+\ *adj* [¹*un-* + *discouraged*, past part. of *discourage*] **:** not discouraged

un·discoverable \"+\ *adj* **:** not discoverable **:** resisting or escaping discovery — **un·dis·cov·er·ably** \-blē\ *adv*

un·discovered \"+\ *adj* [¹*un-* + *discovered*, past part. of *discover*] **:** not discovered **:** HIDDEN, UNEXPLORED

un·discriminated \"+\ *adj* [¹*un-* + *discriminated*, past part. of *discriminate*] **:** not discriminated **:** INDISCRIMINATE

un·discriminating \"+\ *adj* **:** not discriminating **:** failing to make or to recognize distinctions ⟨~ condemnation of a class⟩ ⟨sweeping, ~ generalization⟩ — **un·dis·crim·i·nat·ing·ly** *adv*

un·discussed \"+\ *adj* [ME, fr. ¹*un-* + *discussed*, past part. of *discussen* to discuss — more at DISCUSS] **:** not discussed ⟨leaving the main question still ~⟩

un·disgraced \"+\ *adj* [¹*un-* + *disgraced*, past part. of *disgrace*] **:** not disgraced

un·disguisable \"+\ *adj* [¹*un-* + *disguise*, v. + *-able*] **:** not disguisable ⟨~ voice⟩

un·disguise \"+\ *n* [¹*un-* + *disguise*, n.] **:** absence of disguise or pretense

un·disguised \"+\ *adj* [ME, fr. ¹*un-* + *disguised*, *disgised* disguised — more at DISGUISED] **:** not disguised or concealed **:** PLAIN, FRANK, OPEN ⟨~ admiration⟩ ⟨~ hatred⟩ — **un·disguisedly** \"+\ *adv*

un·dismayed \ˌən+\ *adj* [¹*un-* + *dismayed*, past part. of *dismay*] **:** not dismayed **:** not discouraged **:** unshaken in purpose ⟨wholly ~ by the commercial failure of the three movies he had made —R.L.Taylor⟩

un·dispensed \"+\ *adj* [¹*un-* + *dispensed*, past part. of *dispense*] **:** not freed by dispensation

un·display \"+\ *n* **:** advertising run usu. in the classified columns of a newspaper and set solid without illustration or surrounding white space

un·disposed \"+\ *adj* [ME, fr. ¹*un-* + *disposed*] **:** not disposed: as **a :** INDISPOSED, DISINCLINED **b :** not distributed **:** not placed **:** not sold **:** not assigned to a use

un·disputable \"+\ *adj* : INDISPUTABLE — **un·dis·put·able·ness** *n* — **un·disputably** \"+\ *adv*

un·disputed \"+\ *adj* [¹*un-* + *disputed*, past part. of *dispute*] : not disputed : UNCHALLENGED, UNQUESTIONED ⟨~ leader of his party⟩ ⟨~ claims to excellence⟩ ⟨man of ~ competence⟩ ⟨~ possession of a region⟩ — **un·dis·put·ed·ly** *adv*

un·dissected \"+\ *adj* : not dissected ⟨~ coastal plain⟩

un·dissembled \"+\ *adj* [¹*un-* + *dissembled*, past part. of *dissemble*] **1** : not pretended : GENUINE ⟨~ cordiality⟩ **2** : UNDISGUISED ⟨expression of ~ hatred⟩

un·dissembling \"+\ *adj* [¹*un-* + *dissembling*, pres. part. of *dissemble*] : lacking guile or pretense : FRANK, OPEN ⟨~ friendliness⟩

un·dissociated \"+\ *adj* : not electrolytically dissociated ⟨~ molecules of a salt solution⟩

un·dissolved \ˌən+\ *adj* [¹*un-* + *dissolved*, past part. of *dissolve*] : not dissolved

un·distinct \"+\ *adj* [ME, fr. ¹*un-* + *distinct*] : INDISTINCT — **un·dis·tinct·ly** *adv* — **un·dis·tinct·ness** *n*

un·distinctive \"+\ *adj* **1** : not distinctive **2** : making no distinctions : not discriminating : IMPARTIAL

un·distinguishable \"+\ *adj* [¹*un-* + *distinguish* + *-able*] : INDISTINGUISHABLE — **un·dis·tin·guish·able·ness** *n* — **un·distinguishably** \"+\ *adv*

un·distinguished \"+\ *adj* [¹*un-* + *distinguished*, past part. of *distinguish*] : not distinguished: as **a** : not to be distinguished or set off as separate from others or each other : not recognized as distinct **b** : confusedly mingled with something else ⟨an ~ shriek in the general uproar⟩ **c** : indistinctly heard or seen **d** : incapable of resolution into constituent parts or forms by the perceptive powers **e** : unmarked by any distinction or elevation above the rest : receiving no special respect : having no special fame, honor, or notoriety ⟨~ record of service⟩

un·distinguishing \"+\ *adj* [¹*un-* + *distinguishing*, pres. part. of *distinguish*] : INDISCRIMINATE — **un·dis·tin·guish·ing·ly** *adv*

un·distorted \"+\ *adj* **1** : not distorted : FAITHFUL ⟨~ image⟩ ⟨~ reproduction of sound⟩ **2** : not extreme : NORMAL ⟨~ point of view⟩

un·distracted \"+\ *adj* : not distracted : not drawn aside ⟨~ pursuit of a goal⟩

un·distributed \"+\ *adj* [¹*un-* + *distributed*, past part. of *distribute*] : not distributed

undistributed middle *n* : a syllogistic fallacy in which neither premise conveys information about all members of the class designated by the middle term ⟨the argument "All men are sinners, and all weaklings are sinners, therefore all men are weaklings" says nothing about all sinners and has an *undistributed middle*⟩

un·disturbed \ˌən+\ *adj* [¹*un-* + *disturbed*, past part. of *disturb*] : not disturbed

un·disturbedly \"+\ *adv* : in an undisturbed manner

un·dis·turbed·ness *n* : the quality or state of being undisturbed

un·disturbing \ˌən+\ *adj* [¹*un-* + *disturbing*, pres. part. of *disturb*] : not disturbing

un·diversified \"+\ *adj* : not diversified

un·diverted \"+\ *adj* [¹*un-* + *diverted*, past part. of *divert*] **1** : not diverted : UNDEFLECTED **2** : not amused

un·diverting \"+\ *adj* : not diverting

un·dividable \"+\ *adj* [¹*un-* + *divide*, v. + *-able*] : INDIVISIBLE

un·divided \"+\ *adj* [ME, fr. ¹*un-* + *divided*, past part. of *dividen* to divide — more at DIVIDE] **1** : not divided: as **a** : not parted by conflict of opinion ⟨presented an ~ front⟩ **b** : not separated out into parts or shares ⟨an ~ interest in a hardware store⟩ **c** : not directed or given to more than one object ⟨~ attention⟩ ⟨~ affection⟩ **d** : not shared by or among others ⟨~ responsibility⟩ **2** : not lobed or cleft : not branched : ENTIRE **3** : held under the same common title by joint tenants or tenants in common whose shares may be equal or unequal in value or quantity and who often are entitled to share joint possession before partition and assignment of a separate title to each owner in severalty

un·di·vid·ed·ly *adv* : in an undivided manner

un·di·vid·ed·ness *n* : the quality or state of being undivided

undivided profits *n pl* : earnings of a business enterprise which have been retained instead of being distributed to stockholders or owners; *esp* : a net worth account often appearing in bank statements and showing accumulated profits which have not been transferred to surplus

un·divine \ˌən+\ *adj* : not divine

un·divined \"+\ *adj* [¹*un-* + *divined*, past part. of *divine*] : not divined : UNFORESEEN, UNIMAGINED, UNPERCEIVED

un·di·vine·ly *adv* **1** *obs* : in a manner unworthy of a clergyman **2** : in a manner unlike God

un·divulged \ˌən+\ *adj* [¹*un-* + *divulged*, past part. of *divulge*] : not divulged

un·do \ˌən'dü\ *vb* [ME *undon*, fr. OE *undōn*, fr. ²*un-* + *dōn* to do — more at DO] *vt* **1 a** : to open or loose by releasing a lock or other fastening ⟨*undid* the door⟩ ⟨*undid* the package⟩ **b** : to fix (any of various closures) in an open or free position ⟨*undid* the bolt⟩ ⟨*undid* a button⟩ **c (1)** : to loosen or remove the clothing of : UNDRESS **(2)** : to unbutton or untie the fastenings of (as a garment) : OPEN **2** : to make of no effect or as if not done : make null : bring to naught : CANCEL ⟨lead to a hostility to science, to a wish that its work could be *undone* —D.W.Brogan⟩ ⟨*undid* the spell by an incantation —Ben Riker⟩ **3 a** : to destroy the worldly means or standing of : ruin the reputation or hopes of ⟨held to an intransigence that *undid* him⟩ ⟨technological advances had taken away his market and *undone* him⟩ **b** : to upset the composure of : UNMAN ⟨mention of the boy would still ~ her sometimes⟩ **c** : to entice or betray into unchastity : SEDUCE ⟨*undid* a neighbor's young daughter⟩ **4** : to unravel the secret of : EXPLAIN, INTERPRET ~ *vi* : to come open ⟨the newspaper . . . *undid* with the suddenness of a pocket map —Elizabeth Bowen⟩ **syn** see DESTROY

un·do·able \-üəbəl\ *adj* : impossible to do : not feasible ⟨seems to me to have done the almost ~ —*Saturday Rev.*⟩

un·dock \ˌən+\ *vb* [²*un-* + *dock* (to take a ship to a dock)] *vt* **1** : to take (a ship) away from a dock or wharf **2** : to take (a ship) out of dry dock ~ *vi* : to move away from a dock (as at sailing time) ⟨some luggage in new trunks came on board in the afternoon. We ~*ed* at midnight —Joseph Conrad⟩

un·docked \"+\ *adj* [¹*un-* + *docked*, past part. of *dock* (to cut off)] : not docked : UNABRIDGED

un·doctored \"+\ *adj* [¹*un-* + *doctored*, past part. of *doctor*] : not doctored

un·doctrinaire \"+\ *adj* : not doctrinaire : not rigidly theoretical or devoted to preconceived notions : not committed to a party program : not dogmatic ⟨knowledgeable, clearheaded, ~, civilized . . .; his independent intelligence kept free of all labels and fashions —*Manchester Guardian Weekly*⟩

un·documented \"+\ *adj* [¹*un-* + *documented*, past part. of *document*] **1** : lacking documents : unsupported by the evidence of documents or the conclusions of scholarship **2** : not registered or enrolled : not licensed — used of a boat

un·doer \"+\ *n* [ME, fr. *undon* to undo + *-er* — more at UNDO] : one that undoes : DESTROYER; *esp* : one that ruins a woman : SEDUCER

un·dog \"+\ *vt* [²*un-* + *dog* (to fasten with a dog)] : to loose from a fastening dog or catch ⟨the quartermaster . . . *undogged* the ports —Gordon Webber⟩

un·dogmatic *also* **un·dogmatical** \"+\ *adj* : not dogmatic : not committed to dogma ⟨spoke of my ~ state, no longer influenced by or dependent on any formal religious observance —*Atlantic*⟩

undoing *n* [ME, fr. gerund of *undon* to undo — more at UNDO] **1** : LOOSING, UNFASTENING **2 a** : a bringing to naught : DESTRUCTION, RUIN ⟨cocaine . . . leads to his complete ~ by destroying his mental equipment —A.C.Morrison⟩ **b** : a cause of ruin ⟨a redhead who was to prove my ~ —C.C.Wertenbaker⟩ **3** : the reversal, cancellation, or annulment of something done : reinstatement of a condition existing previous to some act or accomplishment ⟨would settle for nothing less than the complete ~ of his country's calamitous defeat and humiliation⟩

un·domestic \ˌən+\ *adj* : not domestic: as **a** : unrelated to home **b** : not home-loving **c** : not homelike

un·domesticate \"+\ *vt* [²*un-* + *domesticate*] : to make undomestic : undo the taming of

un·domesticated \"+\ *adj* [¹*un-* + *domesticated*, past part. of *domesticate*] : not domesticated ⟨a few ~ horses left⟩

¹un·done \ˌən'dən\ *adj* [ME *undon*, *undoon*, fr. ¹*un-* + *don*, *doon* done — more at DONE] : not done ⟨a task ~⟩

²undone \"\ *adj* [ME *undon*, *undoon*, fr. past part. of *undon*, *undoon* to undo — more at UNDO] **1** : DESTROYED, RUINED ⟨a mind ~⟩ **2** : UNFASTENED ⟨his package came ~ while passing through the New York post office —Jane Shellhase⟩

un·double \ˌən+\ *vb* [²*un-* + *double*] : UNFOLD

un·doubled \"+\ *adj* [¹*un-* + *doubled*, past part. of *double*] : not doubled

un·doubtable \"+\ *adj* [ME *undoutable*, fr. ¹*un-* + *doutable* doubtable — more at DOUBTABLE] : not open to doubt or challenge : SURE, UNQUESTIONABLE

un·doubted \"+\ *adj* [ME *undouted*, fr. ¹*un-* + *douted*, past part. of *douten* to doubt — more at DOUBT] : not doubted : ASSURED, CERTAIN, GENUINE, UNDISPUTED ⟨produced several ~ masterpieces —K.S.Davis⟩

un·doubt·ed·ly *adv* [ME *undoutedly*, fr. *undouted* + *-ly*] : in an undoubted manner : ASSUREDLY ⟨mounds that ~ contain human bones —*Amer. Guide Series: Minn.*⟩

un·doubtful \ˌən+\ *adj* [ME *undouteful*, fr. ¹*un-* + *douteful* doubtful — more at DOUBTFUL] **1** : not open to doubt : firmly established ⟨an ~ pedigree⟩ **2** : feeling no doubt : CONFIDENT ⟨a child ~ of the stork —W.J.Locke⟩

un·doubting \"+\ *adj* [¹*un-* + *doubting*, pres. part. of *doubt*] : not doubting : CONFIDENT

un·doubt·ing·ly *adv* : in an undoubting manner : without hesitation : CONFIDENTLY

un·dowered \ˌən+\ *adj* [¹*un-* + *dowered*, past part. of *dower*] : given no dowry

un·drain·able \ˌən'drānəbəl\ *adj* **1** : INEXHAUSTIBLE **2** : incapable of being drained ⟨an ~ swamp⟩

un·drained \ˌən+\ *adj* : not drained

un·dramatic \"+\ *adj* : lacking dramatic force or quality : UNSPECTACULAR ⟨moved with quiet assurance and ~ bearing⟩

un·dramatically \"+\ *adv* : in an undramatic or unshowy manner : QUIETLY

un·drape \"+\ *vt* [²*un-* + *drape*] : to strip of drapery : UNCOVER, UNVEIL

un·draw \"+\ *vb* [²*un-* + *draw*] *vt* : to draw aside (as a curtain) : OPEN ~ *vi* : to become drawn back or aside

un·drawn \"+\ *adj* [¹*un-* + *drawn*, past part. of *draw*] : not drawn: as **a** : not milked or tapped : not eviscerated **b** : not extended or dragged : not pulled or stretched **c** : not represented in a drawing

un·dreaded \"+\ *adj* [¹*un-* + *dreaded*, past part. of *dread*] : not dreaded

un·dreading \"+\ *adj* [¹*un-* + *dreading*, pres. part. of *dread*] : not dreading

un·dreamed *also* **un·dreamt** \"+\ *adj* [¹*un-* + *dreamed*, *dreamt*, past part. of *dream*] : not thought of : UNIMAGINED — usu. used with *of* ⟨*undreamed-of* capacity for cooperation with their fellows —J.H.Robinson †1936⟩ ⟨impersonal forces have been set in motion on a scale ~ of in the early days of the republic —John Dewey⟩ ⟨the printing press was probably ~ of a half century before its invention⟩

un·dreaming \"+\ *adj* [¹*un-* + *dreaming*, pres. part. of *dream*] : not dreaming

¹un·dress \ˌən+\ *vb* [²*un-* + *dress*, v.] *vt* **1** : to remove the clothes or covering of : DIVEST, STRIP ⟨~*ed* himself and went to bed⟩ **2** *obs* : to undo the dressing of (the hair) : take down : UNBIND **3** : to free or deprive of concealment or privacy : EXPOSE ⟨asked to ~ his past —Eugene Gressman⟩ ~ *vi* : to take off one's clothes : DISROBE

²undress \"\ *n* [¹*un-* + *dress*, n.] **1** : informal dress: as **a** : a loose robe or dressing gown for lounging or informal wear **b** : ordinary dress — distinguished from *full dress* **c** : UNDRESS UNIFORM **2** : NAKEDNESS, NUDITY ⟨the usual models in differing degrees of ~ —*New Orleans States*⟩

³undress \"\ *adj* **1** : of, relating to, or worn as informal attire ⟨made the engine-room staff change from dungarees to ~ blues before going to chow —Fletcher Pratt⟩ **2** : marked by relaxed informality or unpretentiousness ⟨the ~ style which a man keeps for his intimates —John Buchan⟩ ⟨look at the ~ side of things —*New Yorker*⟩

un·dressed \"+\ *adj* [ME, fr. ¹*un-* + *dressed*, past part. of *dressen* to dress — more at DRESS] **1** : not dressed: as **a** : DISARRANGED, UNGROOMED ⟨with hair ~ and clothing in disarray she bore down like an avenging fury⟩ **b** : ROUGH, UNFINISHED ⟨~ granite⟩ ⟨~ hides⟩ **c** : left without medication, bandage, or dressing ⟨an ~ wound⟩ **d** : UNTENDED, UNTRIMMED ⟨~ grounds⟩ ⟨an ~ vine⟩ **e** : left without sauce, garnish, or condiment — used of foods **f** : prepared so as not to deteriorate but not fully processed or ready for use — used of game fish, game animals, or hides **2 a** : not clothed or not fully clothed : nearly or altogether naked **b** : not ordered or prepared for public presentation or appearance : not arranged to be seemly, persuasive, or attractive ⟨man's ~ thoughts —C.T. Ryan⟩ **3 a** : wearing informal or ordinary dress **b** : not properly dressed

undressed kid *n* : kid leather finished with a nap surface usu. on the flesh side of the skin

undress uniform *n* : a military or naval uniform for use on other than formal occasions

un·dried \ˌən+\ *adj* [ME, fr. ¹*un-* + *dried*, past part. of *drien* to dry — more at DRY] : not dried

un·drinkable \"+\ *adj* : not drinkable

un·driven \"+\ *adj* [¹*un-* + *driven*, past part. of *drive*] **1** : not driven **2** : DRIVEN — used of snow ⟨pure as ~ snow —*Times Lit. Supp.*⟩

un·drooping \"+\ *adj* : not drooping

un·drowned \"+\ *adj* [¹*un-* + *drowned*, past part. of *drown*] : not drowned

un·drugged \"+\ *adj* [¹*un-* + *drugged*, past part. of *drug*] **1** : not drugged **2** : freed of the effects of a drug

un·drunk \"+\ *adj* [¹*un-* + *drunk*, past part. of *drink*] **1** : UNSWALLOWED **2** [¹*un-* + *drunk* (intoxicated)] : not intoxicated

undsgd *abbr* undersigned

undtkr *abbr* undertaker

un·dubbed \ˌən+\ *adj* [¹*un-* + *dubbed*, past part. of *dub*] : not dubbed

un·dubitable \"+\ *adj* : INDUBITABLE ⟨~ piety —*Nation*⟩ — **un·du·bi·ta·bly** \-blē\ *adv*

un·due \"+\ *adj* [ME *undewe*, *undue*, fr. ¹*un-* + *dewe*, *due* due — more at DUE] **1** : not due : not yet payable ⟨an ~ debt⟩ ⟨an ~ bond⟩ **2 a** : unsuited to the time, place, or occasion : IMPROPER, INAPPROPRIATE, INOPPORTUNE ⟨~ behavior⟩ **b** : exceeding or violating propriety or fitness : EXCESSIVE, IMMODERATE, UNWARRANTED ⟨desire for ~ private profit —T.W.Arnold⟩ ⟨his sartorial equipment stops just short of ~ elegance —Philip Hamburger⟩ **3** *archaic* : contrary to justice, right, or law : UNLAWFUL

undue influence *n* : such influence over another often presumed from the existence of very close relationships as destroys his free agency in the eye of the law : such influence as prevents a person from exercising his own will and substitutes in its place the will of another (as by constraint, machination, or urgency of persuasion)

un·dug \ˌən+\ *adj* [¹*un-* + *dug*, past part. of *dig*] : not dug

un·duke \"+\ *vt* [²*un-* + *duke*] : to deprive of dukedom

un·du·lance \'ənjələn(t)s, 'ənd(y)əl-\ *n* -s [fr. undulant, after such pairs as E *abundant*: *abundance*] : the quality or state of being undulant ⟨his prose has some of the ~ of the sea —*New Yorker*⟩

un·du·lant \-lənt\ *adj* [²*undulate* + *-ant*] **1** : moving with the rise and fall of waves : FLUCTUATING, HEAVING, RIPPLING ⟨~ waters away —Amy Lowell⟩ ⟨a ripe and ~ figure, which she covered no more than sufficiently to meet the police requirements —R.L.Taylor⟩ **2** : having a form or outline like that of waves : ROLLING ⟨well-kept farms and ~ meadows —*Amer. Guide Series: Vt.*⟩

undulant fever *n* : BRUCELLOSIS a

un·du·lar \-lə(r)\ *adj* [LL *undula* + E *-ar*] : having the form or movement of waves

¹un·du·late \'ənjələt, 'ənd(y)əl-, -ˌlāt, *usu* -d·+V\ *adj* [L *undulatus*, fr. (assumed) *undula* small wave (dim. of *unda* wave) + *-atus* -ate — more at WATER] **1** : bending in gradual curves ⟨the ~ margin of a leaf⟩ : WAVY — compare REPAND, SINUATE **2** : UNDULATING ⟨slumber in ~ rhythms —Amy Lowell⟩

²un·du·late \-ˌlāt, *usu* -ād·+V\ *vb* -ED/-ING/-S [LL *undula* small wave (fr. — assumed — L) + E *-ate*, v. suffix] *vi* **1** : to form or move in waves : rise and fall with the movement or appearance of the ocean surface : FLUCTUATE, SURGE ⟨the water seemed bound down with a dark, oily skin that stirred and *undulated* —Victor Canning⟩ ⟨veiled women *undulating* to the sound of gongs —Anthony Carson⟩ ⟨the orange candle flame . . . made the jades ~ like green pools —Amy Lowell⟩ **2** : to rise and fall in volume, pitch, or cadence ⟨the rooftop siren's wail *undulated* for minutes⟩ ⟨his prose flows and ~*s* in beguiling patterns of rhythm⟩ **3** : to exhibit a form or outline like that of waves : present a wavy appearance ⟨a sandy waste ~*s* southward —Rex Keating⟩ ~ *vt* **1** : to move or cause to move in wavy, sinuous, or flowing manner ⟨danced . . . with their entire bodies, moving slowly, *undulating* their abdomens —Richard Wright⟩ **2** : to give (something) a wavy form **syn** see SWING

un·du·lat·ed \-ād·əd, -ātəd\ *adj* [L *undulatus* + E *-ed*] **1** : having wavy markings or a wavy form or outline **2** : UNDULATE 1

undulating *adj* [fr. pres. part. of *undulate*] **1** : rising and falling in waves : FLUCTUATING ⟨I often gaze on that waste of ~ water —L.P.Smith⟩ **2** : resembling waves in form : having a wavy outline : ROLLING, SCALLOPED ⟨broad, ~ prairie land —*Amer. Guide Series: Minn.*⟩ ⟨her small white straw hat had an ~ brim —*Sydney (Australia) Bull.*⟩ **3** : rising and falling in volume, pitch, or metrical stress or quantity ⟨~ string arpeggios —Julian Herbage⟩

undulating cadence *n* : a metrical cadence in which the foot is an amphibrach or an amphimacer — called also *rocking rhythm*; compare FALLING RHYTHM, RISING RHYTHM

undulating membrane *n* : a vibratile cytoplasmic membrane: **a** : a lateral expansion of the periplast in some flagellates that is usu. bordered by a flagellum **b** : a row of laterally fused long cilia associated in many ciliates with the oral structures

un·du·la·tion \ˌ==ˈlāshən\ *n* -s [fr. (assumed) NL *undulation-*, *undulatio*, fr. LL *undula* small wave + L *-ation-*, *-atio* -ation] **1 a** : a rising and falling in waves : HEAVING, POLLING, SURGING, SWELLING ⟨the bay broke up into long oily ~*s* —Edith Wharton⟩ **b** : a wavelike motion to and fro, up and down, or from side to side in a fluid or elastic medium propagated continuously among its particles but with little or no permanent translation of the particles in the direction of the propagation : VIBRATION **2 a** : TREMOLO 1a **b** : the pulsation caused by the vibrating together of two tones not quite in unison **c** : VIBRATO **3** : a wavy appearance, outline, or form : a wavelike curve or series of curves : a rippling, rolling, or corrugated surface : WAVINESS ⟨the country spread all about us . . . rolling in gentle swells and ~*s* like a summer sea —Blanche E. Baughan⟩ ⟨the ~*s* of his dark, old-fashioned locks of hair —Kay Boyle⟩

un·du·la·tor \'==ˌlād·ə(r), -ātə-\ *n* -s : one that undulates ⟨a lovely blonde lady ~ —*Wall Street Jour.*⟩

un·du·la·to·ry \'ənjələˌtōrē, 'ənd(y)əl-, -tòr-, -ri\ *adj* : of or relating to undulation : moving in or resembling waves : UNDULATING

undulatory theory *n* : a theory in physics: light is transmitted from luminous bodies to the eye and other objects by an undulatory movement — called also *wave theory*

un·dulled \ˌən+\ *adj* [¹*un-* + *dulled*, past part. of *dull*] : not dulled ⟨~ by time, he was worn smoother by it —Stuart Cloete⟩

un·du·lous \'ənjələs, 'ənd(y)əl-\ *adj* [*undul*ate + *-ous*] : UNDULATING, UNDULATORY

un·du·ly \ˌən'd(y)ülē, -li\ *adv* [ME *undewely*, *unduely*, fr. *undewe*, *undue* undue + *-ly* — more at UNDUE] : in an undue manner; *esp* : EXCESSIVELY ⟨~ pessimistic about the chance for the reward of merit —J.M.England⟩

un·dunged \ˌən+\ *adj* [¹*un-* + *dunged*, past part. of *dung*] : not dunged : not manured ⟨~ and untilled land —Fred Bradbury⟩

un·duplicated \"+\ *adj* [¹*un-* + *duplicated*, past part. of *duplicate*] : not duplicated

un·durable \"+\ *adj* : not durable

un·duteous \"+\ *adj* : UNDUTIFUL

un·dutiful \"+\ *adj* : not dutiful

un·dutifully \"+\ *adv* : in an undutiful manner

un·du·ti·ful·ness *n* : the quality or state of being undutiful

undutiful will *or* **unduteous will** *n* : a will that does not make the minimum provision required by law for some heir of the testator who may then claim his legitimate share unless the testator had a lawful reason for disinheriting him : an inofficious will subject to being declared entirely void

undy *var of* UNDÉ

un·dyed \ˌən+\ *adj* [¹*un-* + *dyed*, past part. of *dye*] : not dyed

un·dying \"+\ *adj* [ME, fr. ¹*un-* + *dying*] : not dying : IMMORTAL, PERPETUAL ⟨~ fame⟩ — **un·dy·ing·ly** *adv* — **un·dy·ing·ness** *n* -ES

un·dynamic \"+\ *adj* : not dynamic : STATIC ⟨a static village community and a completely ~ type of agriculture —Barbara Ward⟩

un·eager \ˌən+\ *adj* **1** : lacking spirit or animation : IMPASSIVE, UNEXPRESSIVE ⟨decrepit, colorless, ~ things —Arthur Symons⟩ **2** : showing no eagerness : RELUCTANT ⟨foreigners stubbornly ~ to accept our way of life —Joseph Barnes⟩ ⟨fresh from college and ~ for the moment to marry the boy back home —P.E.Deutschman⟩ — **un·eagerly** \"+\ *adv* — **un·eagerness** \"+\ *n*

un·earned \"+\ *adj* [¹*un-* + *earned*, past part. of *earn*] : not earned: **a** : not due to worth or merit : UNMERITED ⟨felt he was enjoying an ~ importance⟩ ⟨~ luck —Shak.⟩ **b** : not gained by labor or service ⟨~ revenue⟩ ⟨accepted the ~ rewards that came his way⟩ **c** : received in advance of delivery (as of goods) or of service performed ⟨~ collections amounting to several thousand dollars⟩ **d** : scored as a result of an error by the opposing team — used of a run in baseball

unearned income *n* **1** : income (as dividends) that is not derived from personal labor or service but usu. merely from ownership of personal property and that is sometimes taxed at a higher rate than earned income **2** : income resulting from transfer payments

unearned increment *n* : an increase in the value of property (as land) that is due to no labor or expenditure on the part of the owner but to natural causes (as the increase of population or the general progress of society) creating an increased demand for it and that is sometimes specially taxed

unearned premium *n* : the share of a total insurance premium applicable to the unexpired portion of a policy term

unearned premium reserve *n* : a reserve established at the end of any accounting period in insurance to represent premiums paid in advance for which protection is to be given in the future

un·earth \ˌən+\ *vt* [ME *unerthen*, fr. ²*un-* + *erthen* to earth] **1 a** : to dig up out of the earth : bring up, uncover, or recover from underground : EXHUME, DISINTER ⟨~ a hidden treasure⟩ ⟨~*ed* a cache of . . . whiskey —Georg Meyers⟩ ⟨archaeologists . . . have ~*ed* many valuable Indian relics —*Amer. Guide Series: Conn.*⟩ **b** : to drive out of the ground (as from a hole or burrow) ⟨~ a badger⟩ **2** : to bring from concealment, obscurity, or oblivion : bring to light : UNCOVER, DISCOVER ⟨~ carefully hidden evidence⟩ ⟨~ a plot⟩ ⟨the facts ~*ed* by patient research⟩ ⟨~*ed* proof that the accused was innocent —Robert Brennan⟩ ⟨~*ed* a sheaf of yellowing catalogs —David Anderson⟩ **syn** see DISCOVER

un·earthed \"+\ *adj* [¹*un-* + *earthed*, past part. of *earth*] *chiefly Brit* : not grounded electrically ⟨the death of a man at an ~ pasteurizing plant —*Farmers Weekly (London)*⟩

un·earthliness \"+\ *n* : the quality or state of being unearthly: as **a** : SPIRITUALITY, UNWORLDLINESS ⟨the impressive ~ of the preacher's expression⟩ **b** : EERINESS, PRETERNATURALNESS ⟨amid its amazing thrill, a strange ~ —Gilbert Murray⟩

un·earthly \"+\ *adj* : not earthly: as **a** : not belonging to or characteristic of this earth : not terrestrial ⟨the ~ beauty of the fish and plant life . . . were probably comparable to a trip to the moon —John Tassos⟩ ⟨the most ~ region within reach of man —Walter Sullivan⟩ **b** : passing beyond natural limits : PRETERNATURAL, SUPERNATURAL, CELESTIAL ⟨beings of ~ splendor —W.M.Thackeray⟩ ⟨an ~ melody⟩ ⟨an ~ light⟩

c : WEIRD, EERIE ⟨a moonlit . . . landscape ~ with expectancy —Ann F. Wolfe⟩ ⟨an ~ soaring wail —D.C.Peattie⟩ **d** : not worldly or mundane : SPIRITUAL, IDEAL ⟨~ love⟩ ⟨revelation granted to us of what is ~ —Algernon Blackwood⟩ **e** : not conforming to the usual experience, observation, or custom of everyday life : FANTASTIC, PREPOSTEROUS ⟨his picture of the ~ leisureliness of English journalism —*New Yorker*⟩ ⟨have to get up at ~ hours —George Meredith⟩

un·ease \¦ən+\ *n* [ME *unese*, fr. ¹*un-* + *ese* ease] **1** : mental or spiritual discomfort: **a** : vague dissatisfaction : MISGIVING ⟨my ~ over the lack of stylistic assurance —R.D.Darrell⟩ **b** : anxiety and foreboding : DISQUIET ⟨worry and ~ harried her for the next weeks —Adria Langley⟩ **c** : emotional strain : TENSION ⟨a sense of menace, of ~ runs through their conversation —T.H.White b. 1915⟩ **d** : lack of ease (as in social relations) : EMBARRASSMENT ⟨in the presence of . . . the great man —H.S.Canby⟩ **2** *obs* : physical discomfort ⟨such ~ as in a coach . . . in passing over a furrow —Thomas Hobbes⟩ **3** : AWKWARDNESS, UNCOMFORTABLENESS ⟨the ~ of their garments —William Faulkner⟩ ⟨the ~ of this divorce of tradition from environment —*Times Lit. Supp.*⟩

un·easily \"+\ *adv* [ME *unesily*, fr. *unesy* uneasy + *-ly*] : in an uneasy manner: **a** *obs* : not easily : with difficulty **b** : with troubled feelings (as of discomfort, worry, or foreboding) : APPREHENSIVELY, DISTURBEDLY ⟨strange fish . . . sought ~ for an outlet to the ocean —William Beebe⟩ ⟨astronomers ~ ignoring irregularities in the movements of the heavenly bodies —Benjamin Farrington⟩ **c** : with embarrassment : UNCOMFORTABLY ⟨coloring ~ under his gaze —Israel Zangwill⟩ **d** : RESTLESSLY, FIDGETINGLY ⟨kept shifting his position ~⟩ **e** : AWKWARDLY ⟨his body . . . is punily, ~ built —Osbert Sitwell⟩ ⟨a little self-consciously and ~ aggressive —M.P. O'Connor⟩ **f** : not firmly : PRECARIOUSLY ⟨held the chairmanship ~ against mounting opposition⟩

un·easiness \"+\ *n* **1** : the quality or state of being uneasy: **a** : mental or spiritual discomfort : DISTRESS, PERTURBATION ⟨the ~ that our most generous . . . ideals have their roots in childhood guilts —Irwin Edman⟩ **b** : a feeling of worry, apprehension, or foreboding : ANXIETY, DISQUIET ⟨reluctant to be awake . . . her ~ amounted almost to alarm —Jean Stafford⟩ **c** : RESTLESSNESS, INSTABILITY ⟨the misery and ~ of the incompletely assimilated —Edward Shils⟩ **d** : physical discomfort : MALAISE, QUEASINESS ⟨conscious of a certain ~ in the organs —Arnold Bennett⟩ **e** : AWKWARDNESS ⟨~ of diction —R.W.Southern⟩ **f** : EMBARRASSMENT, DISCOMPOSURE ⟨conscious of her ~ among these sophisticated women⟩ **2** *archaic* : HARDSHIP, VICISSITUDE ⟨without these ~*es* to mingle with these benefits, I might be too much puffed up —Samuel Richardson⟩

¹**un·easy** \"+\ *adj* [ME *unesy*, fr. ¹*un-* + *esy* easy] **1 a** *archaic* : causing physical discomfort : UNCOMFORTABLE ⟨why rather, sleep, liest thou . . . upon ~ pallets —Shak.⟩ **b** *archaic* : causing mental discomfort : DISTRESSING ⟨a great and ~ disappointment —Samuel Johnson⟩ **c** *obs* : disagreeable in behavior : ANNOYING ⟨a sour . . . nature makes him ~ to those who approach him —Joseph Addison⟩ **2** *archaic* **a** : not easy : DIFFICULT ⟨the road will be ~ to find —Sir Walter Scott⟩ ⟨I think it not ~ to get the cause —Shak.⟩ **b** : hard to traverse — used esp. of a road or watercourse ⟨the flood . . . roars horrible along the ~ race —John Dryden⟩ **3** : marked by lack of ease : AWKWARD, EMBARRASSED ⟨gave an ~ laugh⟩ ⟨an ~ . . . silence fell on the group —John Steinbeck⟩ **4** : mentally upset : WORRIED, APPREHENSIVE ⟨~ about his health⟩ ⟨~ at the threat of expulsion —*Amer. Guide Series: Calif.*⟩ **5 a** : RESTLESS, UNQUIET ⟨the first ~ stir of the sleeper —Lewis Mumford⟩ ⟨the ~ atmosphere of the city —Winifred Bambrick⟩ **b** : CHOPPY, TROUBLED ⟨~ waters⟩ **6** : PRECARIOUS, UNSTABLE ⟨an ~ coalition government⟩ ⟨an ~ peace⟩

²**un·easy** \"\ *adv* : UNEASILY ⟨~ lies the head that wears a crown —Shak.⟩

un·eatable \¦ən+\ *adj* : not fit to be eaten : INEDIBLE ⟨so undercooked as to be ~ —Sylvia T. Warner⟩ ⟨food atrocious and ~ —*Harper's*⟩

un·eaten \"+\ *adj* [ME *unete, uneten*, fr. ¹*un-* + *ete, eten*, past part. of *eten* to eat] : not eaten : UNCONSUMED ⟨gave the dog the ~ remnants of the roast⟩

¹**un·eath** \"+\ *adj* [ME *uneathe*, fr. OE *unēathe*, fr. ¹*un-* + *ēathe* easy — more at EATH] *archaic* : not easy : DIFFICULT, HARD ⟨who he was, ~ was to descry —Edmund Spenser⟩

²**uneath** \"\ *adv* [ME *uneathe*, fr. OE *unēathe*, fr. *unēathe* uneasy] *archaic* : not easily : with difficulty : SCARCELY ⟨I ~ the fancy might control —S.T.Coleridge⟩

un·economic *also* **un·economical** \¦ən+\ *adj* : not economic : COSTLY, WASTEFUL ⟨~ ebb and flow of manpower —Welles Hangen⟩ — **un·economically** \"+\ *adv* — **un·economicalness** \"+\ *n* -ES

un·edified \"+\ *adj* [¹*un-* + *edified*, past part. of *edify*] : not edified : UNINSTRUCTED, UNENLIGHTENED ⟨the ~ heathen —Charles Lamb⟩

un·edifying \"+\ *adj* [¹*un-* + *edifying*, pres. part. of *edify*] : not edifying: as **a** : not instructive : UNENLIGHTENING, UNILLUMINATING ⟨that rare and useful but ~ variation —G.B. Shaw⟩ **b** : not inspiring or uplifting : IMMORAL, UNSAVORY ⟨~ conduct⟩ ⟨an ~ story⟩ ⟨~ episodes . . . enliven the histories of travellers —T.H.Savory⟩

un·edited \"+\ *adj* [¹*un-* + *edited*, past part. of *edit*] : not edited: as **a** : left unrevised ⟨this first novel . . . bravely ~ —E.B.Garside⟩ **b** : UNCENSORED, UNCUT ⟨an ~ record⟩ ⟨~ film not yet reviewed by the censors⟩ **c** : not yet edited : still unpublished ⟨found an ~ manuscript of a famous medieval mystic⟩

un·educable \¦ən+\ *adj* : INEDUCABLE

un·educated \"+\ *adj* [¹*un-* + *educated*, past part. of *educate*] : not educated: as **a** : lacking in education : UNTAUGHT **b** : ILLITERATE **syn** see IGNORANT

un·effectual \"+\ *adj* : INEFFECTUAL

un·elaborate \"+\ *adj* : INELABORATE

un·elastic \"+\ *adj* : INELASTIC

un·elected \"+\ *adj* : not counted among the elect ⟨died ~⟩ ⟨the ~ multitude⟩

un·elegant \¦ən+\ *adj* : INELEGANT

un·elevated \"+\ *adj* : not elevated : EARTHBOUND

un·eligible \"+\ *adj* : INELIGIBLE

un·eloquent \"+\ *adj* : lacking in eloquence : INELOQUENT ⟨an earnest but ~ speaker⟩ — **un·eloquently** \"+\ *adv*

un·emancipated \"+\ *adj* : not emancipated : not freed: **a** : held in the power of another; *specif* : held in slavery or bondage ⟨~ serfs⟩ **b** : subject to the paternal power ⟨an ~ minor child —E.B.Denny⟩ **c** : bound by or adhering to accepted social mores implying or entailing subservience or restraints ⟨the ~ woman⟩

un·embarrassed \"+\ *adj* [¹*un-* + *embarrassed*, past part. of *embarrass*] **1** : free from embarrassment : UNASHAMED, UNABASHED ⟨an ~ greeting as if nothing untoward had happened⟩ **2** : not constrained : NATURAL ⟨their ~ good breeding —Earl of Chesterfield⟩ **3** : free of encumbrance : UNENCUMBERED ⟨dream of punctual tenants and ~ properties —Anthony Trollope⟩ — **un·embarrassedly** \"+\ *adv*

un·embellished \¦ən+\ *adj* [¹*un-* + *embellished*, past part. of *embellish*] : lacking embellishment : UNADORNED, PLAIN ⟨~ walls⟩ ⟨a forthright, ~ style⟩

un·embittered \"+\ *adj* [¹*un-* + *embittered*, past part. of *embitter*] : not embittered : UNRESENTFUL ⟨take their stings with gay ~ lips —Sara Teasdale⟩

un·embodied \"+\ *adj* [¹*un-* + *embodied*, past part. of *embody*] **1** : DISEMBODIED, INCORPOREAL ⟨~ spirits⟩ **2** : not collected into a body : not yet organized ⟨~ militia⟩

un·embroidered \"+\ *adj* [¹*un-* + *embroidered*, past part. of *embroider*] : lacking adornment or elaboration : PLAIN, SIMPLE ⟨the author's ~ . . . approach will appeal to readers looking for a concise account —*Jour. of Accountancy*⟩

un·emendable \"+\ *adj* : not emendable

un·emotional \"+\ *adj* : not emotional: as **a** : not easily aroused or excited : IMPASSIVE, COLD, STOLID ⟨in the little church he had seemed most ~, and had been most moved —John Galsworthy⟩ **b** : little influenced by emotion or sentiment : UNFEELING, HARD-BOILED ⟨could be cruel in a completely ~ way⟩ **c** : marked by less than usual emotion : UNIMPASSIONED ⟨made an ~ appeal to the audience⟩ **d** : involving a minimum of emotion : INTELLECTUAL ⟨put disagreements on an intelligent and ~ basis —K.D.Miller⟩ — **un·emotionally** \"+\ *adv*

un·emotionality \"+\ *n* : the quality or state of being unemotional : IMPASSIVITY, OBJECTIVITY ⟨handled the delicate matter with complete ~⟩ ⟨the scientific virtue of ~⟩

un·emphatic \"+\ *adj* : not emphatic: **a** : lacking emphasis or force of expression ⟨~ student writing⟩ **b** : commanding little attention : INCONSPICUOUS ⟨cruel at first only in an ~ and spasmodic way —E.K.Brown⟩ **c** : marked by a lack of stress or insistence ⟨was ~ in his refusal⟩ ⟨an ~ affirmation⟩ **d** : not sharply delineated : not salient ⟨an ~ detail in a painting⟩ **e** : carrying no stress in pronunciation ⟨an ~ syllable⟩ — **un·emphatically** \"+\ *adv*

un·employability \"+\ *n* : the quality or state of being unemployable

¹**un·employable** \"+\ *adj* : not acceptable for employment as a worker

²**unemployable** \"\ *n* -S : an unemployable person

un·employed \¦ən+\ *adj* [¹*un-* + *employed*, past part. of *employ*] : not employed: **a** : not being used ⟨~ time⟩ ⟨~ tools⟩ ⟨a method as yet ~⟩ **b** : not engaged in a gainful occupation : out of work ⟨~ workers⟩ **c** : not invested ⟨~ capital⟩ **d** : FREE 5g

un·employment \"+\ *n* : lack of employment : IDLENESS; *specif* : involuntary idleness of a worker seeking work at prevailing wages

unemployment benefit *n* : payment (as by a union or an employer or according to the provisions of a governmental social security program) to an unemployed worker of a sum of money per week — compare DOLE

unemployment compensation *n* : the system of unemployment benefits provided in the U. S. by state laws adopted pursuant to the Federal Social Security Act

unemployment insurance *n* : insurance (as provided by state laws adopted pursuant to the Federal Social Security Act) against loss of earnings by payments for a limited period during which a worker is involuntarily unemployed

un·encapsulated \¦ən+\ *adj* : not encapsulated ⟨an ~ tumor⟩

un·enciphered \"+\ *adj* [¹*un-* + *enciphered*, past part. of *encipher*] : not converted to cipher ⟨~ messages⟩

un·enclosed \"+\ *adj* [¹*un-* + *enclosed*, past part. of *enclose*] : not enclosed: **a** : not fenced in : COMMON ⟨~ land⟩ **b** : not kept within convent walls ⟨~ nuns⟩

un·encrypted \"+\ *adj* [¹*un-* + *encrypted*, past part. of *encrypt*] : not encoded : not cryptic : CLEAR ⟨~ language⟩

un·encumbered \"+\ *adj* [¹*un-* + *encumbered*, past part. of *encumber*] **1** : free of encumbrance : UNBURDENED, UNHAMPERED ⟨a lucid, ~ book, sparing of footnotes⟩ ⟨planning to live an ~ life⟩; *specif* : free from a temporary estate or interest (as a mortgage, lien, or dower right) ⟨pass it on to their heirs . . . intact and ~ —H.P.Becker⟩ **2** : having no dependents (as spouse or children) ⟨reliable, ~ woman . . . would like position as housekeeper —*Vancouver (Canada) Sun*⟩

un·encysted \"+\ *adj* [¹*un-* + *encysted*, past part. of *encyst*] : not encysted

un·ended \"+\ *adj* [ME, fr. ¹*un-* + *ended*, past part. of *enden* to end] : not ended : UNFINISHED ⟨that contest was still ~ —C.L.Jones⟩

un·ending \"+\ *adj* [¹*un-* + *ending*, pres. part. of *end*] : never ending : ENDLESS: **a** : not coming to an end : continuing indefinitely into the future : CONTINUOUS, EVERLASTING ⟨the . . . dream of ~ progress —W.R.Inge⟩ **b** : going on from time immemorial : TIMELESS, AGELONG ⟨the reef's ~ creation —P.A. Zahl⟩ **c** : UNDYING, ETERNAL ⟨~ love⟩ **d** : going on continually : INCESSANT, PERPETUAL ⟨an ~ struggle carried on at every club meeting⟩ **e** : extending with no apparent end : INTERMINABLE ⟨the ~ levee, covered with scraggly grass —*Amer. Guide Series: La.*⟩ **f** : passing all limits : EXTRAVAGANT, EGREGIOUS ⟨the most ~ ass in Christendom —Thomas Carlyle⟩

un·end·ing·ly \¦ən¦endiŋlē, -dēŋ-, -li\ *adv* : in an unending manner : EVERLASTINGLY ⟨a good housekeeper who is ~ mopping out dark corners —Dwight MacDonald⟩

un·end·ing·ness \-ŋnəs\ *n* -ES : the quality or state of being unending

un·endorsed \¦ən+\ *adj* [¹*un-* + *endorsed*, past part. of *endorse*] **1** : bearing no endorsement ⟨an ~ check⟩ **2** : not approved ⟨a proposal as yet ~ by the governor⟩

un·endowed \"+\ *adj* [¹*un-* + *endowed*, past part. of *endow*] **1** *archaic* : having no dowry : DOWERLESS **2** : not equipped or provided ⟨~ with . . . genius —J.L.Lowes⟩ ⟨~ with the finer graces⟩

un·endued \"+\ *adj* [¹*un-* + *endued*, past part. of *endue*] : not supplied : UNENDOWED ⟨~ with foresight⟩

un·endurable \"+\ *adj* : not endurable : UNBEARABLE ⟨~ agony⟩ ⟨he is under ~ domestic . . . pressure —Nicolas Monjo⟩

un·endurably \"+\ *adv* : in an unendurable manner : INTOLERABLY

un·enduring \"+\ *adj* : not lasting : SHORT-LIVED

un·energetic \¦ən+\ *adj* : lacking energy or enterprise : SLOW-GOING ⟨~ incompetents —S.P.Sherman⟩

un·enforceable \"+\ *adj* : not enforceable ⟨an ~ law⟩ : not capable of being brought about by compulsion ⟨~ reforms⟩

un·enforced \"+\ *adj* : not enforced : UNFORCED, UNCOMPELLED; *specif* : not enforced by legal or police action : DORMANT ⟨an ~ speed limit⟩

un·enfranchised \"+\ *adj* : not free; *specif* : not granted or not allowed to exercise political rights (as suffrage) ⟨he and his still ~ fellow citizens are restless —*Manchester Guardian Weekly*⟩

un·engaged \"+\ *adj* : not engaged: **a** : not pledged or promised; *specif* : not promised in marriage ⟨agreed to continue seeing him but on an ~ basis⟩ **b** : not occupied or employed : not busy : FREE ⟨left her ~ a good part of the afternoon⟩

un·engaging \"+\ *adj* : not engaging : lacking in charm : UNATTRACTIVE ⟨an ~ manner⟩

un–english \¦ən+\ *adj, usu cap E* **1** : not characteristically English ⟨what could be more *un-English* than a languid female in a turban —George Santayana⟩ **2** : not agreeing with standard or generally accepted usage of the English language ⟨*un-English* pronunciation⟩ ⟨an *un-English* sentence⟩

un–englished \"+\ *adj, usu cap E* [¹*un-* + *englished*, past part. of *english*] : not translated into English ⟨left certain passages of the Latin *un-Englished*⟩

un·enjoyable \"+\ *adj* : not capable of being enjoyed : producing no pleasure : JOYLESS ⟨had a thoroughly ~ time⟩

un·enjoyed \"+\ *adj* [¹*un-* + *enjoyed*, past part. of *enjoy*] : not enjoyed: as **a** : not partaken of : UNUSED ⟨pleasures passed by ~⟩ **b** : giving no joy : DREARY, JOYLESS ⟨a disconsolate and ~ matrimony —John Milton⟩

un·enjoying \"+\ *adj* [¹*un-* + *enjoying*, pres. part. of *enjoy*] : not able to experience or express enjoyment : SAD, MELANCHOLY ⟨an ~ miser⟩

un·enlarged \¦ən+\ *adj* **1** : not enlarged upon : kept brief ⟨leave the notice ~ —Elizabeth B. Browning⟩ **2** : NARROW, ILLIBERAL ⟨a man of ~ views⟩ **3** : not enlarged : not larger or greater than formerly, normally, or usu. present ⟨the ~ first pair of legs of a lobster⟩

un·enlightened \"+\ *adj* **1** *archaic* : not lighted : not illuminated ⟨a place ~ by the cheery rays of the sun⟩ **2 a** : not enlightened : IGNORANT, UNINSTRUCTED, UNINFORMED ⟨lamentably ~ as to the laws —Helen Martin⟩ **b** : BACKWARD, BENIGHTED ⟨the devices by which ~ men . . . preserved the unjust social order —C.C.Walcutt⟩

un·enlightening \"+\ *adj* : not enlightening : not tending to inform or clarify ⟨an ~ comment⟩

un·enlivened \"+\ *adj* [¹*un-* + *enlivened*, past part. of *enliven*] : not enlivened : not brightened or made lively — often used postpositively ⟨a life ~ by romance⟩

un·ennobled \"+\ *adj* : not ennobled : LOWLY, SIMPLE ⟨the ~ soldier in the ranks⟩

un·enquiring \"+\ *adj* [¹*un-* + *enquiring*, pres. part. of *enquire*] : marked by unquestioning, uncritical, or unconsidered acceptance or action : ACQUIESCENT, UNTHINKING ⟨deplored a too trustful, ~ repetition of the teacher's opinion⟩

un·enriched \"+\ *adj* [¹*un-* + *enriched*, past part. of *enrich*] **1** : not made wealthy — often used postpositively ⟨a politician ~ by graft⟩ **2** : not improved by addition of new content; *specif* : not improved in nutritive value by addition of vitamins and minerals in processing ⟨~ bread⟩

un·enrolled \"+\ *adj* [¹*un-* + *enrolled*, past part. of *enroll*] : not enrolled : not holding membership in a group or organization

un·enslaved \"+\ *adj* [¹*un-* + *enslaved*, past part. of *enslave*] **1** : not enslaved : EMANCIPATED, FREE ⟨happy ~ citizenry⟩ **2** : not disposed to be servile ⟨an ~ spirit⟩

un·entailed \"+\ *adj* [¹*un-* + *entailed*, past part. of *entail*] : not restricted as to course of descent upon the owner's death ⟨an ~ estate⟩

un·entangle \"+\ *vt* [²*un-* + *entangle*] : DISENTANGLE

un·entangled \"+\ *adj* [¹*un-* + *entangled*] : not entangled: **a** : not trapped or caught **b** : not complicated : UNINVOLVED ⟨dream-consciousness, blessedly ~ with all one's own problems —*Publ's Mod. Lang. Assoc. of Amer.*⟩

un·entered \¦ən+\ *adj* [ME, fr. ¹*un-* + *entered*, past part. of *enteren, entren* to enter] : not entered: **a** : not recorded or registered **b** : not penetrated ⟨an ~ cave⟩

un·enterprising \"+\ *adj* : lacking in enterprise : not bold or venturesome : LETHARGIC, CONSERVATIVE ⟨has become ~ and sluggish because . . . so prosperous and comfortable —H.G.Wells⟩

un·entertained \"+\ *adj* [¹*un-* + *entertained*, past part. of *entertain*] : not entertained : not amused ⟨a play that left the audience completely ~⟩

un·entertaining \"+\ *adj* : not entertaining : UNAMUSING ⟨a quite ~ letter⟩

un·entertainingly \"+\ *adv* : in an unentertaining manner

un·enthralled \"+\ *adj* [¹*un-* + *enthralled*, past part. of *enthrall*] : not enslaved : free of the domination of others ⟨judgment ~ —John Milton⟩

un·enthusiasm \"+\ *n* : lack of enthusiasm : PERFUNCTORINESS ⟨said . . . with polite ~ —Edna Ferber⟩

un·enthusiastic \"+\ *adj* **1** : lacking ardor or excitement : SPIRITLESS ⟨an ~ performance by an orchestra⟩ **2** : marked by a lack of sympathy or disinclination to praise : LUKEWARM ⟨an ~ review⟩ ⟨was . . . ~ about most of her relatives —Margaret Mead⟩ **3** : not buoyant : not optimistic ⟨~ about the prospects of success⟩

un·enthusiastically \"+\ *adv* [*unenthusiastic* + *-ally*] : in an unenthusiastic manner : with no great warmth or interest ⟨agreeing to the proposal ~⟩

un·entitled \¦ən+\ *adj* [¹*un-* + *entitled*, past part. of *entitle*] : not entitled : having no title or right : UNWORTHY ⟨a distinction to which he was ~⟩

un·entombed \"+\ *adj* [¹*un-* + *entombed*, past part. of *entomb*] : not entombed : UNBURIED

un·entreated \"+\ *adj* [¹*un-* + *entreated*, past part. of *entreat*] : not entreated : not asked or requested

un·enviable \"+\ *adj* **1** : not so desirable as to attract envy ⟨a very low, altogether ~ standard of living⟩ ⟨what an ~ problem has the writer of a classic in his next work —Leslie Rees⟩ **2** : so undesirable as to be incapable of arousing envy ⟨~ notoriety⟩ ⟨an ~ reputation for bad dealing⟩ **3** : AWKWARD, EMBARRASSING ⟨placed in the ~ position of resorting to an act which he planned to make a major campaign issue —Mary K. Hammond⟩

un·envied \"+\ *adj* [¹*un-* + *envied*, past part. of *envy*] **1** : not envied : inspiring no envious feelings ⟨lived in an unostentatious and so ~ way⟩ **2** : not coveted ⟨the submerged fifth of the present population . . . forgotten because it lives upon ~ land —*Harper's*⟩

un·envious \"+\ *adj* : marked by an absence of envy : not malicious : UNGRUDGING ⟨an amiable, ~ person⟩ ⟨in friendly and thoroughly ~ correspondence with them all —J.G. Lockhart⟩ ⟨~ irony —R.P.Warren⟩

un·enviously \"+\ *adv* : in an unenvious manner ⟨had gone his own way ~ —Meredith Nicholson⟩

un·envying \"+\ *adj* [¹*un-* + *envying*, pres. part. of *envy*] : free of envy ⟨strains . . . which charm to silence the ~ nightingales —P.B.Shelley⟩

un·episcopal \¦ən+\ *adj* **1** : having no bishops **2** : not episcopalian **3** : not befitting a bishop — **un·episcopally** \"+\ *adv*

un·epitaphed \"+\ *adj* [¹*un-* + *epitaphed*, past part. of *epitaph*] : not provided or honored with an epitaph ⟨lived a niggardly patron and died ~⟩

un·equable \"+\ *adj* **1** : not equable or temperate ⟨an ~ climate⟩ **2** : IRREGULAR, UNSTABLE ⟨~ movement⟩

un·equably \"+\ *adv* : in an unequable manner : IRREGULARLY

¹**un·equal** \"+\ *adj* **1 a** : not of the same measurement, quantity, amount, or number as another : UNLIKE ⟨cutting planks of ~ length⟩ ⟨~ amounts of butter⟩ ⟨classes of ~ size⟩ ⟨~ costs⟩ **b** : not like or not the same as another in degree, worth, quality, ability, or status ⟨two machines operating at ~ speeds⟩ ⟨several pieces of ~ workmanship⟩ ⟨men of ~ capacity⟩ ⟨statistics . . . ~ in value —*Geog. Jour.*⟩ ⟨poems . . . of widely ~ merit —*College English*⟩ **c** *archaic* : ODD — used of numbers **2 a** : not like or not the same for each member of a group or class ⟨~ chances for success⟩ **b** : not uniform in quantity or quality, measure or degree : VARIABLE, IRREGULAR, UNEVEN ⟨~ pulsations⟩ ⟨an ~ and different movements of the heavenly bodies —Benjamin Farrington⟩ ⟨a most ~ writer —*Times Lit. Supp.*⟩ **c** : showing variation in appearance, structure, or proportion ⟨the tips of the ~ towers —Janet Flanner⟩ **d** : not level : RUGGED ⟨an ~ surface⟩ **3 a** : badly balanced or matched : UNEVEN ⟨~ odds⟩ ⟨an ~ fight⟩ ⟨farmers were ready to abandon their ~ struggle with a stubborn soil —*Amer. Guide Series: Mass.*⟩ **b** : contracted between unequals ⟨~ marriages⟩ ⟨~ treaties⟩ ⟨an ~ match⟩ **c** *archaic* : not equable : INTEMPERATE ⟨her spirits . . . were more disturbed, more ~, than she had often seen them —Jane Austen⟩ **4 a** *archaic* : not equitable : UNJUST, UNFAIR ⟨to punish me for what you made me do seems much ~ —Shak.⟩ **b** *obs* : acting unfairly : PARTIAL ⟨an ~ parent —Matthew Prior⟩ **5** : incapable of meeting the requirements of a situation or task : INADEQUATE, INSUFFICIENT — usu. used with *to* ⟨~ to the pace⟩ ⟨a mere politician will prove ~ to the position⟩ ⟨timber ~ to the strain⟩ ⟨felt ~ to the coming interview⟩ ⟨they were ~ to the wild country —Emil Lengyel⟩

²**unequal** \"\ *n* **1** : one that is not equal to or not on a basis of equality with another — usu. used in pl. ⟨a comparison of ~*s*⟩ ⟨a society of ~*s* —Walter Moberly⟩ **2** : a mathematical quantity that is either less or greater than another ⟨if ~*s* are added to ~*s* in the same order, the sums are unequal in the same order⟩

³**unequal** \"\ *adv, archaic* : UNEQUALLY ⟨~ match'd —Shak.⟩

un·equal·able \¦ən¦ēkwələbəl\ *adj* [¹*un-* + *equal*, v. + *-able*] : incapable of being equaled : UNSURPASSABLE, INCOMPARABLE ⟨two ~ men —Robert Lonthey⟩

unequal counterpoint *n* : counterpoint in which the musical parts move in unequal notes

un·equaled \¦ən+\ *adj* [¹*un-* + *equaled*, past part. of *equal*] : not equaled : UNPARALLELED ⟨~ cruelty⟩ ⟨~ success⟩ ⟨an ~ job of shirking —S.E.Hyman⟩ ⟨an ~ degree of resistance —*Steinway Cat.*⟩ : UNRIVALED, MATCHLESS ⟨flowers ~ for size and beauty⟩ ⟨craftsmen whose skill is ~ —*Quarterly Rev.*⟩ : UNPRECEDENTED ⟨for killing two . . . bulls he would receive the ~ sum of thirty thousand dollars —Barnaby Conrad⟩

unequal hour *n* : HOUR 5

un·equality \¦ən+\ *n* [by alter.] : INEQUALITY

un·equal·ize \¦ən¦ēkwə,līz\ *vt* [¹*unequal* + *-ize*] : to cause to be unequal ⟨the more you ~ opportunity, the more you ~ men —A.E.Wiggam⟩

un·equally \¦ən+\ *adv* : in an unequal manner: **a** : in unequal amounts or shares ⟨profits divided ~⟩ **b** : with unequal treatment for each : with partiality : UNJUSTLY ⟨angry that they had been dealt with so ~⟩ **c** : not uniformly : UNEVENLY, IRREGULARLY ⟨snow scattered ~ over the mountainside⟩

un·equalness \"+\ *n* [¹*un-* + *equalness*] *archaic* : INEQUALITY

unequal temperament *n* : a temperament that keeps pure or nearly pure intonation in some keys and accumulates the dissonances in the little-used keys

unequal voices *n pl* : mixed voices in singing

un·equipped \¦ən+\ *adj* [¹*un-* + *equipped*, past part. of *equip*] : not provided with what is needed : UNPREPARED ⟨~ with the necessary outfit for the sport⟩ ⟨his gentle background left him ~ to face today's realities —Gordon Merrick⟩

un·equitable \"+\ *adj* : INEQUITABLE

un·equivocal \"+\ *adj* **:** not equivocal **:** leaving no doubt: **a :** expressing only one meaning **:** leading to only one conclusion **:** CLEAR, UNAMBIGUOUS ⟨~ evidence⟩ ⟨take an ~ position on an issue⟩ **b :** expressed in full and definite terms **:** EXPLICIT, CERTAIN ⟨the plain and ~ language of the laws —R.B.Taney⟩ **c :** expressing finality **:** carrying no implication of later change or revision **:** CONCLUSIVE, ABSOLUTE ⟨her dangerous inability to make an ~ refusal⟩ ⟨an ~ promise⟩ ⟨an ~ guarantee to respect the nation's sovereignty in the future⟩ ⟨the ~ diagnosis . . . is at present difficult —*Jour. Amer. Med. Assoc.*⟩ **d :** not open to challenge **:** UNQUESTIONABLE, UNMISTAKABLE ⟨had an ~ success in the role⟩ ⟨an ~ loss of prestige⟩ ⟨these people enjoy . . . an ~ social position —W.H.Auden⟩

un·equivocally \"+\ *adv* **:** in an unequivocal manner: **a :** CLEARLY, UNAMBIGUOUSLY ⟨come out ~ with their own position —K.S.Latourette⟩ **b :** EXPLICITLY ⟨little . . . can be said ~ about the theoretical work —G.E.K.Branch & Melvin Calvin⟩ **c :** CONCLUSIVELY, ABSOLUTELY ⟨clinical experience ~ demonstrates —*Therapeutic Notes*⟩ **d :** UNMISTAKABLY ⟨speaks . . . ~ with the voice of his literary age —T.S.Eliot⟩

un·equivocalness \"+\ *n* **:** the quality or state of being unequivocal

un·eradicable \"+\ *adj* [¹*un-* + *eradicate* + *-able*] **:** INERADICABLE

un·erasable \"+\ *adj* [¹*un-* + *erase* + *-able*] **:** incapable of being erased

un·erect \"+\ *adj* **:** not erect **:** bowing down **:** SUBMISSIVE ⟨no merit but a love, slavish and ~ —R.L.Stevenson⟩

un·erected \"+\ *adj* [¹*un-* + *erected*, past part. of *erect*] **:** not erected **:** not uplifted or inspired ⟨an ~ spirit⟩

un·erring \"+\ *adj* **1 :** committing no error **:** FAULTLESS ⟨people of ~ taste in clothes and furniture —Albert Dasnoy⟩ **2 :** matching a standard with the greatest exactness or accuracy ⟨perform with ~ exactness⟩ ⟨aped his mannerisms in ~ fashion⟩ ⟨the youngsters noted his weakness with . . . ~ precision —G.D.Brown⟩ **3 :** not wandering from the intended course or purpose **:** going right to the mark **:** UNDEVIATING, SURE ⟨~ marksmanship⟩ ⟨~ as a shaft of light —J.L.Lowes⟩ ⟨the ~ and merciless power of retribution in Nature —E.T. Thurston⟩ **syn** see INFALLIBLE

un·erringly \"+\ *adv* **:** in an unerring manner: **a :** INFALLIBLY ⟨believed capable of interpreting the Bible ~⟩ **b :** with precision **:** ACCURATELY, NEATLY ⟨a play ~ performed⟩ ⟨caught the traits of his rustic characters ~⟩

un·err·ing·ness \,=ˈ==nə̇s\ *n* -ES **:** the quality or state of being unerring **:** INFALLIBILITY

un·erupted \ˌən+\ *adj* [¹*un-* + *erupted*, past part. of *erupt*] *of a tooth* **:** not yet emerged through the gum

un·escapable \"+\ *adj* [¹*un-* + *escape*, v. + *-able*] **1 :** incapable of being escaped or ignored **:** INESCAPABLE, UNAVOIDABLE ⟨every Tube station . . . is papered with ~ assertions —C.E.Montague⟩ **2 :** necessarily to be considered and dealt with ⟨an ~ crisis⟩ ⟨the ~ expansion of the nation's foreign policy —D.S.Freeman⟩ **3 :** following logically or from the evidence **:** INEVITABLE ⟨an ~ conclusion⟩

un·escapably \"+\ *adv* **:** in an unescapable manner **:** UNAVOIDABLY, INEVITABLY ⟨no other writer . . . is more ~ national in his every gesture and trick of mind —H.L.Mencken⟩

un·escaped \"+\ *adj* [¹*un-* + *escaped*, past part. of *escape*] **:** not escaped **:** RETAINED ⟨~ vapors⟩

un·escorted \ˌən+\ *adj* [¹*un-* + *escorted*, past part. of *escort*] **:** not escorted **:** lacking an escort **:** UNATTENDED, UNACCOMPANIED ⟨~ ladies not admitted⟩

un·espied \"+\ *adj* [ME, fr. ¹*un-* + *espied*, past part. of *espien* to espy] **:** passing unseen **:** escaping notice or detection ⟨got into the forbidden area ~⟩

un·essayed \"+\ *adj* [¹*un-* + *essayed*, past part. of *essay*] **:** not essayed **:** UNATTEMPTED ⟨leaves no tyrannical evasion ~ —John Milton⟩

¹**un·essential** \"+\ *adj* **1 :** not essential **:** DISPENSABLE, UNIMPORTANT ⟨~ illustrations⟩ ⟨other freedoms . . . seem vague and ~ —E.H.Erikson⟩ **2** *archaic* **:** void of essence **:** having no real being **:** INSUBSTANTIAL ⟨the void profound of ~ night —John Milton⟩

²**unessential** \"\ *n* **:** something that is unessential or that can be dispensed with as unimportant or unneeded ⟨not . . . waste time in attacking ~*s* —F. Tennyson Jesse⟩

un·established \"+\ *adj* [¹*un-* + *established*, past part. of *establish*] **:** not firmly based ⟨a reputation as yet ~⟩: **a :** having little or no previous success; *specif* **:** not yet published ⟨short stories by ~ writers —*Atlantic*⟩ **b** *of a church* **:** not made a national or state institution **c** *Brit* **:** outside the permanent or regular staff of a business or institution ⟨an ~ post⟩ ⟨an ~ appointment⟩

un·esteemed \"+\ *adj* [¹*un-* + *esteemed*, past part. of *esteem*] **:** not esteemed **:** UNHONORED, UNRESPECTED ⟨~ worth⟩

un·esthetic \"+\ *adj* **:** not esthetic ⟨something ~ about the word —Edward Sapir⟩

un·estimable \"+\ *adj* [by alter.] **:** INESTIMABLE

un·ethical \"+\ *adj* **:** not conforming to approved standards of behavior, a socially accepted code, or professionally endorsed principles and practices ⟨~ practices in the handling of public funds⟩ ⟨considered such advertising by physicians ~⟩ — **un·ethically** \"+\ *adv*

un·etymological *also* **un·etymologic** \"+\ *adj* **:** not based on or in accordance with etymology ⟨the *unetymologic* doubling of consonants —R.C.Clark⟩

un·evadable \"+\ *adj* [¹*un-* + *evade* + *-able*] **:** not evadable ⟨the . . . downright ~ pressures of realities —Thomas De Quincey⟩

un·evad·ably \¦==¦==blē\ *adv* **:** in an unevadable manner **:** INESCAPABLY ⟨the images are . . . ~ concrete —F.R.Leavis⟩

un·evaluated \ˌən+\ *adj* [¹*un-* + *evaluated*, past part. of *evaluate*] **:** not examined and appraised as to worth or significance ⟨~ data⟩

un·evangelical \"+\ *adj* **:** not conforming to or agreeing with the Christian gospels **:** not according with the doctrines or practices of Protestant Christianity ⟨~ rites⟩

un·evaporated \"+\ *also* **un·evap·o·rate** \¦==¦==ˌrə̇t\ *adj* [*unevaporated* fr. ¹*un-* + *evaporated* past part. of *evaporate; unevaporate* fr. ¹*un-* + obs. *evaporate* evaporated, fr. L *evaporatus*, past part. of *evaporare* to evaporate] **1 :** not dissipated **:** EXTANT ⟨an ~ remnant⟩ **2 :** not passed off in the form of vapor ⟨the ~ residue⟩

un·even \ˌən+\ *adj* [ME, fr. OE *unefen*, fr. ¹*un-* + *efen* even] **1 a** *archaic* **:** not equal in size, number, or quantity **:** UNEQUAL 1a ⟨two pipes of glass very ~ in length —Robert Boyle⟩ **b :** not divisible by two without a remainder **:** ODD 3 **2 a :** not even **:** not level or flat **:** RUGGED ⟨proceeding slowly over the ~ ground⟩ ⟨miles of ~ country —*Amer. Guide Series: Pa.*⟩ **:** having irregularities of surface (as breaks, indentations, or roughnesses) **:** RAGGED ⟨large, ~ teeth⟩ ⟨~ ranks⟩ ⟨~ handwriting⟩ **b :** varying from the straight or parallel ⟨a building with ~ vertical lines⟩ **c :** varying or inconsistent **:** not uniform **:** SPOTTY, IRREGULAR ⟨~ earnings⟩ ⟨~ combustion⟩ ⟨~ subway traffic —*N.Y.Times*⟩ ⟨a stove at one end . . . gave very ~ heat —*Amer. Guide Series: Calif.*⟩ ⟨germination may be ~ or poor —*Farmer's Weekly (So. Africa)*⟩ **d :** varying markedly in quality ⟨an ~ performance⟩ ⟨an ~ achievement . . . its writing ranges from the human and impassioned to the dully academic —David Hall⟩ **3** *obs* **:** UNJUST, INEQUITABLE ⟨complains of the bishops' ~ hand over these pamphlets —John Milton⟩ **4 :** UNEQUAL 3a ⟨vaudeville troupes . . . waged an ~ battle against the church —*Amer. Guide Series: N.J.*⟩ **syn** see ROUGH

uneven-aged \¦=¦=¦=\ *adj* [*uneven* + *aged*] *of a forest* **:** consisting of trees of three or more age classes

un·evenly \ˌən+\ *adv* [ME, fr. *uneven* + *-ly*] **:** in an uneven manner or degree: **a :** in unequal parts ⟨time ~ divided between play and study⟩ **b :** not uniformly or consistently **:** IRREGULARLY ⟨mowed the lawn very ~⟩ ⟨~ fitted boards —*Amer. Guide Series: Oregon*⟩ ⟨when biographical facts are scanty, they are also apt to be ~ distributed —*Times Lit. Supp.*⟩ **c :** without proper balance **:** on unequal terms **:** UNFAIRLY ⟨teams ~ matched⟩

un·evenness \"+\ *n* [ME *unevennesse*, fr. *uneven* + *-nesse* -ness] **1 :** the quality or state of being uneven: **a :** INEQUALITY ⟨~ of height⟩ **b :** ROUGHNESS ⟨the ~ of land surfaces⟩ ⟨the ~ of the path⟩ **c :** lack of uniform quality **:** IRREGULARITY, INCONSISTENCY ⟨the ~ of the essays detracts from the book's overall effect —F.R.Dulles⟩ **d :** temperamental instability ⟨the ~ of his moods and behavior⟩ **2 :** an uneven place ⟨file down the ~*es*⟩

un·eventful \"+\ *adj* **1 :** marked by no noteworthy incidents **:** PLACID, COMMONPLACE ⟨an ~ life⟩ ⟨the voyage . . . was throughout pleasant and ~ —Havelock Ellis⟩ **2 :** passing without untoward incident **:** NORMAL ⟨made an ~ landing⟩ ⟨recovery was ~ —*Lancet*⟩ **3 :** unworthy of particular notice **:** ORDINARY

un·eventfully \"+\ *adv* **:** in an uneventful manner

un·eventfulness \"+\ *n* **:** the quality or state of being uneventful

un·evoked \ˌən+\ *adj* [¹*un-* + *evoked*, past part. of *evoke*] **:** not evoked **:** DORMANT ⟨a law that has gone ~ since its passage⟩

un·evolved \"+\ *adj* [¹*un-* + *evolved*, past part. of *evolve*] **:** not evolved **:** not unfolded **:** UNDEVELOPED, PRIMITIVE

un·exact \"+\ *adj* **:** INEXACT

un·exacting \ˌən+\ *adj* **:** not demanding **:** UNCRITICAL

un·exaggerated \"+\ *adj* [¹*un-* + *exaggerated*, past part. of *exaggerate*] **:** not magnified or colored **:** UNVARNISHED ⟨an ~ report of the event⟩ ⟨the ~ truth of the matter⟩

un·exalted \"+\ *adj* **:** UNELEVATED, UNINSPIRED ⟨not ~ by religious faith —William Wordsworth⟩

un·examinable \"+\ *adj* **1 :** not susceptible to inquiry **:** INSCRUTABLE ⟨~ intention —John Milton⟩ **2 :** not determinable by examination ⟨what a student most needs to get from literature is intangible and . . . ~ —*Quarterly Jour. of Speech*⟩

un·examined \"+\ *adj* [ME, fr. ¹*un-* + *examined*, past part. of *examinen* to examine] **:** not subjected to examination (as critical scrutiny, analysis, or comparison) **:** not carefully weighed **:** not collated ⟨an ~ premise⟩ ⟨several ~ copies of the manuscript are being made available for study⟩

un·examining \"+\ *adj* [¹*un-* + *examining*, pres. part. of *examine*] **:** not weighing or considering **:** UNCRITICAL, UNTHINKING ⟨an ~ and undiscriminating public⟩

un·ex·am·pled \¦==¦pəld\ *adj* [¹*un-* + *example* + *-ed*] **:** having no example, precedent, or parallel **:** UNIQUE ⟨a time of ~ prosperity⟩ — often used postpositively ⟨its system of public parks ~ to my knowledge —A.B.Guthrie⟩

un·excelled \ˌən+\ *adj* [¹*un-* + *excelled*, past part. of *excel*] **:** not capable of being bettered or improved upon **:** UNSURPASSED, SUPERB ⟨an ~ view of the mountains⟩ ⟨an ~ academic record⟩

un·excepted \"+\ *adj* [¹*un-* + *excepted*, past part. of *except*] **1** *obs* **:** not objected to **:** UNQUESTIONED, UNCRITICIZED **2 :** having no exception **:** UNALTERABLE ⟨nature's ~ law —P.J.Bailey⟩

un·ex·cep·tion·abil·i·ty \ˌənik,sepsh(ə)nəˈbiləd-ē\ *n* [*unexceptionable* + *-ity*] **:** UNEXCEPTIONABLENESS

un·ex·cep·tion·able \¦==¦sepsh(ə)nəbəl\ *adj* [¹*un-* + obs. *exception* to take exception (fr. *exception*, n.) + *-able*] **:** not open or liable to objection, criticism, or reproach **:** ACCEPTABLE, UNIMPEACHABLE ⟨starts from an ~ premise⟩ ⟨two ~ witnesses —G.G.Coulton⟩ ⟨had always maintained an ~ character —Sheridan Le Fanu⟩ ⟨his work was ~ —S.F. Mason⟩ ⟨this part of the . . . plan is perhaps ~ —*New Republic*⟩

un·ex·cep·tion·able·ness \,==ˈ=(=)==nə̇s\ *n* -ES **:** the quality or state of being unexceptionable **:** ACCEPTABILITY, IRREPROACHABILITY

un·ex·cep·tion·ably \¦==¦sepsh(ə)nəblē, -li\ *adv* **1 :** in an unexceptionable manner **:** UNIMPEACHABLY, IRREPROACHABLY ⟨behaving ~⟩ **2** *archaic* **:** without exception **:** UNEXCEPTIONALLY, UNIVERSALLY

un·ex·cep·tion·al \-shənᵊl,-shnəl\ *adj* [¹*un-* + *exception* + *-al*] **1 :** open to no objection **:** UNEXCEPTIONABLE ⟨only the ~ work of the aircraft and engine manufacturers . . . enabled the expedition to take place —*World Today*⟩ **2 :** allowing no exception **:** UNALTERABLE ⟨an ideal language, with ~ rules —E.W.Hall⟩ **3 :** constituting no exception to the general rule **:** ORDINARY, COMMONPLACE ⟨as ~ an incident as this must be in a doctor's career —*New Republic*⟩

un·ex·cep·tion·al·ly \-ᵊlē, -əl|, |i\ *adv* [*unexceptional* + *-ly*] **:** without exception **:** in every case **:** UNIVERSALLY ⟨have ~ taken for granted the one thing which they were attempting to prove —M.F.A.Montagu⟩

un·exchangeable \ˌən+\ *adj* **:** not capable of being substituted one for another **:** INCOMMUTABLE

un·excitable \"+\ *adj* **:** incapable of being stirred or energized **:** not responsive to stimuli ⟨an ~ temperament⟩

un·excited \"+\ *adj* [¹*un-* + *excited*, past part. of *excite*] **1 :** marked by a lack of excitement **:** CALM ⟨make an ~ appraisal of the situation⟩ **2 :** not affected by outward stimuli

un·exciting \"+\ *adj* **:** not exciting **:** PROSAIC, COMMONPLACE ⟨an ~ life⟩ ⟨an ~ novel⟩

un·excluding \"+\ *adj* [¹*un-* + *excluding*, pres. part. of *exclude*] **:** not excluding **:** COMPREHENSIVE ⟨a taste so catholic, so ~ —Charles Lamb⟩

un·exclusive \"+\ *adj* **:** not exclusive **:** INCLUSIVE, COMPREHENSIVE

un·exclusively \"+\ *adv* **:** in an unexclusive manner **:** COMPREHENSIVELY, UNIVERSALLY

un·excogitable \ˌə,nekˈskijəd-əbəl\ *adj* [modif. of LL *inexcogitabilis*, fr. L *in-* ¹in- + *excogitare* to excogitate + *-abilis* -able] **:** not capable of being thought out or contrived

un·excusable \ˌən +\ *adj* [¹*un-* + *excusable*] **:** INEXCUSABLE

un·excused \ˌən+\ *adj* [¹*un-* + *excused*, past part. of *excuse*] **:** not excused; *specif* **:** not officially excused or permitted ⟨~ absences⟩

un·executed \"+\ *adj* [¹*un-* + *executed*, past part. of *execute*] **:** not carried out **:** UNPERFORMED ⟨an ~ plan⟩; *specif* **:** not carried out legally according to its terms ⟨an ~ agreement⟩

un·exemplary \"+\ *adj* [¹*un-* + L *exemplum* example + E *-ary*] **1** *obs* **:** having no precedent **:** UNEXAMPLED **2 :** not exemplary **:** not fit to be taken as a model ⟨an ~ husband⟩

un·exemplified \"+\ *adj* [¹*un-* + *exemplified*, past part. of *exemplify*] **1** *obs* **:** UNEXAMPLED **2 :** not provided with an illustrative example **:** not exemplified ⟨titles of odd form and ~ significance —E.A.Robinson⟩

un·exercised \"+\ *adj* [ME, fr. ¹*un-* + *exercised*, past part. of *exercisen* to exercise] **:** not exercised: **a :** not put to use or trial **:** UNTRIED, UNPRACTICED ⟨a faculty left ~⟩ ⟨I cannot praise a fugitive and cloistered virtue, ~ and unbreathed —John Milton⟩ **b :** not made effective in action **:** not exerted **:** UNCLAIMED ⟨an ~ right⟩ ⟨a privilege ~ for years⟩ **c :** not accustomed to physical exercise **:** SEDENTARY, INACTIVE ⟨skiing . . . within the reach of the most ~ —*Times Lit. Supp.*⟩ **d** *archaic* **:** not fitted or prepared by exercise **:** UNTRAINED

un·exhausted \ˌən+\ *adj* [¹*un-* + *exhausted*, past part. of *exhaust*] **1 :** not emptied or drawn off completely ⟨an ~ well⟩ **2 :** not completely expended **:** not used up ⟨an ~ fund⟩

un·exhaustible \"+\ *adj* [by alter.] **:** INEXHAUSTIBLE

un·existence \"+\ *n* **:** absence of existence **:** NONEXISTENCE

un·existing \ˌən+\ *adj* [¹*un-* + *existing*, pres. part. of *exist*] **:** NONEXISTENT

un·ex·or·cis·able \¦=¦=(,)=¦sīzəbəl\ *adj* [¹*un-* + *exorcise* + *-able*] **:** incapable of being exorcised

un·ex·or·cis·ably \-blē\ *adv* **:** in an unexorcisable manner ⟨image ~ haunting him —Aldous Huxley⟩

un·exorcised \ˌən+\ *adj* [¹*un-* + *exorcised*, past part. of *exorcise*] **:** not exorcised **:** not driven off or expelled ⟨an ~ specter⟩

un·expanded \"+\ *adj* [¹*un-* + *expanded*, past part. of *expand*] **1 :** not enlarged upon **:** not expounded or developed fully ⟨an ~ comparison⟩ ⟨left the idea ~⟩ **2 :** not unfolded **:** not spread open ⟨~ leaves⟩

un·expansive \"+\ *adj* **:** not expansive: **a :** showing no tendency or inclination to expand ⟨~ bodies⟩ **b :** not given to high spirits or effusiveness **:** RESTRAINED ⟨an ~ man⟩

un·expectable \"+\ *adj* [¹*un-* + *expect* + *-able*] **:** incapable of being expected **:** UNPREDICTABLE ⟨kept bringing out one unexpected and wholly ~ thing after another —Nathaniel Hawthorne⟩ ⟨who could have been more ~ —Christopher Morley⟩

un·expected \"+\ *adj* [¹*un-* + *expected*, past part. of *expect*] **:** not expected **:** UNLOOKED-FOR, UNFORESEEN, SURPRISING ⟨~ news⟩ ⟨an ~ guest⟩ ⟨the ~ always happens⟩

un·ex·pect·ed·ly \"lē, -li\ *adv* **:** in an unexpected manner **:** SURPRISINGLY ⟨arrived ~ early⟩ ⟨was ~ successful⟩

un·ex·pect·ed·ness \,==ˈ==nə̇s\ *n* -ES **:** the quality or state of being unexpected ⟨the ~ of the warm welcome⟩

un·expedient \ˌən+\ *adj* [ME, fr. ¹*un-* + *expedient*] *archaic* **:** INEXPEDIENT

un·expended \"+\ *adj* [¹*un-* + *expended*, past part. of *expend*] **:** not expended **:** not consumed **:** not used up ⟨~ provisions⟩ **:** not spent ⟨an ~ portion of a fund⟩ ⟨an ~ balance⟩

un·expensive \"+\ *adj* **:** INEXPENSIVE — **un·expensively** \"+\ *adv* — **un·expensiveness** \"+\ *n*

un·experienced \"+\ *adj* [partly fr. ¹*un-* + *experience*, n. + *-ed*; partly fr. ¹*un-* + *experienced*, past part. of *experience*] **:** not experienced: **a :** having no experience **:** INEXPERIENCED ⟨an ~ practitioner⟩ **b :** UNTRIED ⟨quite unknown and ~ by most —R.C.McCall⟩

unexpert *adj* [ME, fr. ¹*un-* + *expert*] *obs* **:** lacking practical knowledge or experience **:** UNEXPERIENCED ⟨a pure celibate and altogether ~ of women —Aphra Behn⟩

un·expiated \"+\ *adj* [¹*un-* + *expiated*, past part. of *expiate*] **:** not expiated **:** not atoned for ⟨~ crimes⟩

un·expired \ˌən+\ *adj* [¹*un-* + *expired*, past part. of *expire*] **:** not yet run out **:** not terminated ⟨elected to fill the senator's ~ term⟩ ⟨an ~ lease⟩

un·explainable \"+\ *adj* **:** not capable of being explained **:** UNACCOUNTABLE, INEXPLICABLE ⟨an ~ fear⟩ ⟨an ~ custom of changing the ship's name —*N. Y. Herald Tribune*⟩

un·ex·plain·ably \¦==¦==blē, -bli\ *adv* **:** in an unexplainable manner **:** INEXPLICABLY

un·explained \ˌən+\ *adj* [¹*un-* + *explained*, past part. of *explain*] **:** not explained or accounted for ⟨an ~ error⟩

un·explicit \"+\ *adj* **:** not explicit **:** lacking full and clear expression **:** VAGUE, AMBIGUOUS ⟨the more basic the premise the more likely it is to remain ~ —L.A.White⟩

un·explicitly \"+\ *adv* **:** in an unexplicit manner **:** UNCLEARLY, VAGUELY

un·exploded \"+\ *adj* [¹*un-* + *exploded*, past part. of *explode*] **:** not exploded **:** charged with explosive **:** UNDISCHARGED, LIVE 3c ⟨~ ammunition⟩ ⟨an ~ shell⟩

un·exploited \"+\ *adj* [¹*un-* + *exploited*, past part. of *exploit*] **:** not exploited **:** not taken advantage of **:** UNUSED ⟨left a blunder of the opposition completely ~⟩; *specif* **:** not turned to economic account **:** UNDEVELOPED ⟨vast ~ natural resources —*Amer. Guide Series: Oregon*⟩

un·explored \"+\ *adj* [¹*un-* + *explored*, past part. of *explore*] **:** not explored **:** not looked into or investigated ⟨minor writings still ~ by scholars⟩ ⟨~ areas of the subconscious mind⟩; *specif* **:** not penetrated or ranged over for purposes of geographical discovery ⟨~ wilderness⟩

un·exposed \"+\ *adj* **:** not exposed: **a :** not laid open to view **:** not brought to light ⟨many ~ cases of official corruption⟩ **b :** not made subject to an action or influence; *specif* **:** not subjected (as sensitive photographic film) to the action of radiant energy

un·expressed \"+\ *adj* [¹*un-* + *expressed*, past part. of *express*] **:** not expressed: **a :** not uttered in words **:** UNSPOKEN ⟨~ emotion⟩ ⟨vague ~ ideas⟩ **b :** not conveyed **:** TACIT ⟨the ~ terms of the agreement⟩

un·expressible *also* **un·expressable** \"+\ *adj* [¹*un-* + *express* + *-ible, -able*] **:** INEXPRESSIBLE

un·expressive \"+\ *adj* [¹*un-* + *express* + *-ive*] **1** *obs* **:** incapable of being expressed in words **:** transcending expression or description **:** INEFFABLE, INEXPRESSIBLE ⟨the fair, the chaste, and ~ she —Shak.⟩ **2 :** not expressive **:** lacking expression **:** failing to convey the meaning or feeling intended ⟨an ~ face⟩ ⟨~ voices chanting the correct service —L.P.Smith⟩

un·expugnable \"+\ *adj* [ME, modif. of L *inexpugnabilis* inexpugnable] **:** INEXPUGNABLE 1

un·expurgated \"+\ *adj* [¹*un-* + *expurgated*, past part. of *expurgate*] **:** not expurgated **:** UNCENSORED ⟨volumes of the best plays, ~ —Havelock Ellis⟩

un·extended \"+\ *adj* **1 :** not extended **:** not stretched out ⟨an ~ arm⟩ **2 :** not having the property of extension ⟨an ~ substance⟩

un·extenuated \ˌən+\ *adj* [¹*un-* + *extenuated*, past part. of *extenuate*] **:** having no extenuation **:** UNMITIGATED

un·extinct \"+\ *adj* **1 :** still burning **:** UNEXTINGUISHED ⟨one spark of fire . . . ~ —John Fletcher⟩ **2 :** still in use **:** not superseded **:** ACTIVE, EXTANT

un·extinguishable \"+\ *adj* **1 :** incapable of being stopped from burning **:** UNQUENCHABLE **2 :** incapable of being ended or suppressed ⟨~ laughter⟩

un·extinguished \"+\ *adj* [¹*un-* + *extinguished*, past part. of *extinguish*] **:** not extinguished: **a :** not put out **:** UNQUENCHED ⟨an ~ fire⟩ **b :** not ended **:** still living ⟨observed . . . tokens of ~ or returning passion —T.L.Peacock⟩

un·extirpated \"+\ *adj* [¹*un-* + *extirpated*, past. part. of *extirpate*] **:** not rooted out **:** not wholly destroyed ⟨vicious habits still ~⟩

un·extorted \"+\ *adj* [¹*un-* + *extorted*, past part. of *extort*] **:** not extorted **:** freely given ⟨~ affection⟩

un·extricable \"+\ *adj* **:** INEXTRICABLE

un·eyed \"+\ *adj* [¹*un-* + *eyed*, past part. of *eye*] **:** UNOBSERVED, UNSEEN

un·fabled \"+\ *adj* **:** not fictitious **:** REAL, ACTUAL

un·fabricated \"+\ *adj* [¹*un-* + *fabricated*, past part. of *fabricate*] **:** not worked, shaped, or processed into final form **:** not manufactured ⟨~ material⟩

un·face·able \ˌənˈfāsəbəl\ *adj* [¹*un-* + *face*, v. + *-able*] **:** not capable of being faced **:** REVOLTING ⟨an unknown and ~ horror —John Strachey⟩

un·faced \ˌən+\ *adj* **:** not provided with a facing ⟨~ surface⟩ ⟨~ brick⟩

un·fact \"+\ *n* **:** a deliberate falsehood made to pass as fact (as for partisan or propagandistic purpose)

un·fad·able \ˌənˈfādəbəl\ *adj* [¹*un-* + *fade* + *-able*] **1 :** not subject to fading **:** FAST, EVERLASTING ⟨a fabric of ~ color⟩ **2 :** incapable of being forgotten **:** MEMORABLE, DEATHLESS ⟨an ~ act of political courage —*Manchester Guardian Weekly*⟩

un·faded \ˌən+\ *adj* [¹*un-* + *faded*, past part. of *fade*] **:** not faded **:** FRESH ⟨moments that live again in remembrance ~ —W.W.Gibson⟩

un·fading \"+\ *adj* [¹*un-* + *fading*, pres. part. of *fade*] **1 :** not losing color or freshness ⟨~ flowers⟩ **2 :** not losing value, importance, effectiveness, or appeal ⟨an ~ honor⟩

un·fail·ing \ˌənˈfāliŋ, -lēŋ\ *adj* [ME, fr. ¹*un-* + *failing*, pres. part. of *failen* to fail] **:** not failing or liable to fail: **a :** not desisting **:** CONSTANT, UNFLAGGING ⟨~ good spirits⟩ ⟨~ courtesy⟩ **b :** EVERLASTING, INEXHAUSTIBLE ⟨a subject of ~ interest⟩ ⟨~ pleasure⟩ **c :** INFALLIBLE, SURE ⟨an ~ test⟩ ⟨the ~ mark of an amateur⟩

un·fail·ing·ly *adv* [ME, fr. *unfailing* + *-ly*] **:** in an unfailing manner **:** without fail **:** INVARIABLY, UNFLAGGINGLY ⟨prolific and ~ bad writers —Whitney Balliett⟩ ⟨no other living conductor so ~ attentive . . . to the music —Virgil Thomson⟩

un·fail·ing·ness *n* -ES **:** the quality or state of being unfailing

un·fainting \"+\ *adj* [¹*un-* + *fainting*, pres. part. of *faint*] **:** not losing courage or vigor **:** PERSISTING ⟨~ diligence⟩

un·fair \"+\ *adj* **:** not fair: **a :** marked by injustice, partiality, or deception **:** UNJUST, DISHONEST ⟨~ methods⟩ ⟨an ~ trial⟩ ⟨an ~ critic⟩ ⟨an ~ judgment⟩ ⟨taking an ~ advantage of another person⟩ **b :** providing an insufficient or inequitable basis for judgment or evaluation **:** not representative ⟨an ~ instance to cite⟩ **c :** not according with merit or importance **:** DISPROPORTIONATE, EXCESSIVE ⟨an ~ share⟩ **d** *of the wind* **:** UNFAVORABLE 2a **e** (1) **:** not straight or smoothly curving ⟨~ lines⟩ (2) **:** not properly aligned or fitted together ⟨drilled ~ holes⟩ **f :** not equitable in business dealings (as in competition, wage scales, or attitude toward a labor union) ⟨~ to organized labor⟩

unfair competition *n* **1 a :** business competition effected by an act that is deceptive and in effect a fraud on the public or that otherwise violates the legal or equitable rights of a competitor or the public **b :** an improper or inequitable obtaining by one competitor of the benefits belonging to another ⟨passing off on the public the goods of one person as those of another is a form of *unfair competition*⟩ **2 :** a competitive practice contrary to the ethical standards of business or in violation of existing law as interpreted by a federal trade commission or a state agency

unfair labor practice *n* **:** a practice on the part of an employer or of an employee declared unfair under a national or state

labor relations act that provides civil remedies to employer or employee administered by a labor relations board
unfair list *n* : a list of employers declared by the union compiling and publishing it to be unfair to organized labor
un·fairly \“+\ *adv* : in an unfair manner: **a** : UNJUSTLY, INEQUITABLY ⟨raised his prices ~⟩ **b** : with partiality ⟨decided the case ~⟩ **c** : UNREASONABLY ⟨it might, therefore, not ~ be assumed —T.H.Huxley⟩ **d** : not in accordance with the rules governing a competition ⟨played so ~ no one enjoyed playing with him⟩
unfair method of competition : UNFAIR TRADE PRACTICE
un·fairness \“+\ *n* : the quality or state of being unfair: **a** : INJUSTICE ⟨recognized the ~ of the decision⟩ **b** : improper alignment or fit ⟨noticed the ~ of the rivet holes⟩
unfair practice *n* **1** : a trade practice with respect to the public or a competitor that is forbidden by statute and that is therefore subject to control by a federal trade commission **2** : UNFAIR COMPETITION
unfair trade practice *n* : a trade practice declared by a federal trade commission to be an unfair method of competition pursuant to power given it by a legislative act designed to curb dishonesty, misrepresentation, and unethical and monopolistic business practices contrary to public policy and good morals in the business community
un·faith \¦ən+\ *n* [ME *unfeith*, fr. [1]*un-* + *feith* faith] **1** : absence of faith : DISBELIEF ⟨a silent manifesto of ~ in the future of our body politic —Max Beerbohm⟩ **2** : a nonreligious faith; *esp* : a faith actively opposed to religion
un·faithful \“+\ *adj* [ME *unfeithful*, fr. [1]*un-* + *feithful* faithful] : not faithful: **a** : having no religious faith : INFIDEL **b** (1) : not observing or adhering to vows, allegiance, or duty : DISLOYAL ⟨an ~ servant⟩ (2) : failing to perform a function or duty ⟨defects . . . make him ~ to his work —Samuel Alexander⟩ **c** : not faithful to marriage vows ⟨his ~ wife had eloped with her latest lover —Harrison Smith⟩ **d** *archaic* : wanting in good faith : DISHONEST ⟨this ~ dealing with your brother —Thomas Otway⟩ **e** : INACCURATE, UNTRUSTWORTHY ⟨an ~ copy of a document⟩
un·faithfully \“+\ *adv* [ME *unfeithfully*, fr. *unfeithful* + *-ly*] : in an unfaithful manner
un·faithfulness \“+\ *n* [ME *unfeithfulnesse*, fr. *unfeithful* + *-nesse* -ness] : the quality or state of being unfaithful
un·fallen \“+\ *adj* [[1]*un-* + *fallen*, past part. of *fall*] : not morally fallen : marked by a state of prelapsarian innocence ⟨~ man⟩ ⟨an atmosphere as ~ as the original Garden —L.A. Fiedler⟩
un·fallible \“+\ *adj* : INFALLIBLE
un·faltering \“+\ *adj* [[1]*un-* + *faltering*, pres. part. of *falter*] : not wavering or weakening : UNHESITATING, STEADY, FIRM ⟨a leader who demanded ~ belief from his followers⟩
un·falteringly \“+\ *adv* : in an unfaltering manner : UNHESITATINGLY, FIRMLY ⟨has ~ held to the old idea of liberal democracy —M.R.Cohen⟩
un·famed \¦ən+\ *adj* : unknown to fame : not famous ⟨passed his life ~⟩
un·familiar \“+\ *adj* : not familiar: **a** : not well known : STRANGE, UNACCUSTOMED ⟨new and ~ tasks⟩ ⟨an ~ place⟩ ⟨an industrial aspect ~ in this section of the state —*Amer. Guide Series: Ark.*⟩ **b** : UNKNOWN ⟨an artist ~ to all of us⟩ **c** : not well acquainted ⟨technical students . . . ~ with the study of the humanities —G.W.Chapman⟩
un·familiarity \“+\ *n* [*unfamiliar* + *-ity*] : the quality or state of being unfamiliar : STRANGENESS, NOVELTY ⟨his ~ with this quarter of the city⟩ ⟨an ~ with the new rules slowed down his play⟩ ⟨the ~ of the scene⟩
un·familiarized \“+\ *adj* [[1]*un-* + *familiarized*, past part. of *familiarize*] : not made familiar or accustomed ⟨the plan itself would . . . startle an ~ conscience —S.T.Coleridge⟩
un·fancied \“+\ *adj* : UNIMAGINED ⟨some growth ~ yet —Robert Browning⟩
un·fanned \“+\ *adj* [[1]*un-* + *fanned*, past part. of *fan*] : not fanned : not excited : not aroused ⟨~ by any enthusiasm⟩
un·fantastic \“+\ *adj* : not fantastic : EVERYDAY, REALISTIC ⟨a completely rational, ~ plan⟩
un·fashionable \¦ən+\ *adj* [[1]*un-* + *fashion*, n. + *-able*] **1** *obs* : poorly fashioned : UNSHAPELY, DISTORTED **2** : not in accord with or not following current fashion : not favored socially : OUT-OF-DATE, OUTMODED ⟨~ clothes⟩ ⟨melodrama of the now ~ kind —Daniel George⟩ ⟨it is ~ and indiscreet to profess admiration —Saul Maloff⟩
un·fashionableness \“+\ *n* : the quality or state of being unfashionable
un·fashionably \“+\ *adv* : in an unfashionable manner
un·fashioned \“+\ *adj* [[1]*un-* + *fashioned*, past part. of *fashion*] : not fashioned: **a** : not shaped : UNWROUGHT ⟨an ~ jewel⟩ **b** *archaic* : not polished : UNREFINED, INELEGANT ⟨a precise ~ fellow —Richard Steele⟩
un·fasten \“+\ *vt* [ME *unfastnen*, fr. [2]*un-* + *fastnen* to fasten] : to make loose: **a** *obs* : make less firm : WEAKEN ⟨~ his resolutions —Thomas Carte⟩ **b** : UNPIN, UNBUCKLE ⟨~ the bolt of a door⟩ ⟨~ a belt⟩ **c** : UNDO ⟨~ the buttons of a dress⟩ **d** : DETACH ⟨~ a boat from its moorings⟩ **e** : UNTIE ⟨~*ed* the string and opened the package⟩
un·fastened \“+\ *adj* [[1]*un-* + *fastened*, past part. of *fasten*] : not fastened: **a** : UNBOUND, LOOSE ⟨~ hair⟩ **b** : UNLOCKED ⟨an ~ door⟩
un·fastidious \¦ən+\ *adj* : not fastidious: **a** : UNTIDY, CARELESS ⟨~ in her dress⟩ **b** : lacking in refinement : COARSE
un·fathered \“+\ *adj* [[1]*un-* + *father*, n. + *-ed*] **1** : having no father : FATHERLESS, ILLEGITIMATE, BASTARD ⟨~ offspring⟩ **2** : having no known origin ⟨~ slanders⟩
un·fatherly \“+\ *adj* : not befitting a father ⟨an ~ attitude⟩
un·fathomable \“+\ *adj* [[1]*un-* + *fathom* + *-able*] : not capable of being fathomed ⟨~ depths⟩: **a** : INCOMPREHENSIBLE, INSCRUTABLE ⟨the ~ mentality of a child⟩ ⟨all that is cryptic and ~ in humanity —J.L.Lowes⟩ **b** : IMMEASURABLE, IMPENETRABLE ⟨the ~ darkness of empty space —H.G.Wells⟩ — **un·fath·om·able·ness** *n* -ES
un·fath·om·ably \¦=¦===blē, -bli\ *adv* : to an unfathomable degree: **a** : IMMEASURABLY ⟨~ deep⟩ **b** : INCOMPREHENSIBLY ⟨continued ~ to eat —A.J.Cronin⟩
un·fathomed \¦ən+\ *adj* [[1]*un-* + *fathomed*, past part. of *fathom*] **1** : not fathomed : UNSOUNDED ⟨the dark ~ caves of ocean —Thomas Gray⟩ **2** : UNDETERMINED, IMMENSE ⟨the thought of the ~ might of man —J.J.Chapman⟩
un·fatigued \“+\ *adj* [[1]*un-* + *fatigued*, past part. of *fatigue*] : not fatigued : UNWEARIED
un·fatiguing \“+\ *adj* [[1]*un-* + *fatiguing*, pres. part. of *fatigue*] : not fatiguing : UNTIRING ⟨~ work⟩
un·faulty \“+\ *adj*, *archaic* : free of fault : BLAMELESS, INNOCENT ⟨the poor ~ baby —Samuel Richardson⟩
un·favorable \“+\ *adj* [ME, fr. [1]*un-* + *favorable*] **1 a** : not disposed to favor : OPPOSED, CONTRARY ⟨~ comment⟩ ⟨reasons for being ~ to the proposal⟩ **b** : expressing disapproval : NEGATIVE ⟨an ~ response⟩ **2 a** : tending to retard, discourage, or make more difficult : DISADVANTAGEOUS ⟨an atmosphere ~ to calm discussion⟩ ⟨an ~ business climate⟩ ⟨an ~ wind⟩ **b** : indicative of an unsuccessful outcome : boding ill ⟨~ weather for a camping trip⟩ ⟨conditions ~ for a new enterprise⟩ **3 a** : not pleasing : DISAGREEABLE, UNDESIRABLE ⟨an ~ feature of the plan⟩ **b** : having the value of imports exceed that of exports ⟨an ~ balance of trade⟩ **4** *archaic* : repulsive in looks : ILL-FAVORED, UGLY
un·favorableness \“+\ *n* : the quality or state of being unfavorable
un·favorably \“+\ *adv* [ME, fr. *unfavorable* + *-ly*] : in an unfavorable manner
un·feared \¦ən+\ *adj* [in sense 1, fr. ME *unferd*, fr. [1]*un-* + *fered*, *ferd*, past part. of *feren* to frighten; in sense 2, fr. [1]*un-* + *feared*, past part. of *fear* — more at FEAR] **1** *obs* : not frightened : UNAFRAID ⟨stand upright and ~ —Ben Jonson⟩ **2** : not feared ⟨an ~ adversary⟩
un·fearful \“+\ *adj* : free of fear : FEARLESS
un·fearing \“+\ *adj* [[1]*un-* + *fearing*, pres. part. of *fear*] : having no fear : DAUNTLESS ⟨~ minds —Sir Walter Scott⟩
un·feasibility \“+\ *n* : the quality or state of being unfeasible : IMPRACTICABILITY
un·feasible \“+\ *adj* : not feasible : IMPRACTICABLE ⟨a suggested reform that was ~ in the prevailing circumstances⟩
un·feather \“+\ *vt* [ME *unfetheren*, fr. [2]*un-* + *fetheren* to feather] : to deprive (as a bird) of feathers : PLUCK, DEPLUME, STRIP
un·feathered \“+\ *adj* [[1]*un-* + *feathered*, past part. of *feather*] **1 a** : having no plumage ⟨~ legs of the Orpington⟩ : UNFLEDGED ⟨the ~ brood⟩ **b** : PLUCKED ⟨an ~ goose⟩ **2** : not fully developed : CALLOW ⟨that ~, two-legg'd thing, a son —John Dryden⟩ **3** : not equipped with feathers ⟨~ arrows⟩
un·featured \“+\ *adj* **1** *obs* : having ill-formed features : DEFORMED **2** : lacking features : UNVARIED ⟨an ~ wilderness⟩ ⟨my highway is ~ air —W.E.Channing⟩ **3** : not displayed or advertised as a feature attraction ⟨an ~ performer⟩
un·fed \¦ən+\ *adj* [ME *unfedd*, fr. [1]*un-* + *fedd*, past part. of *feden* to feed] **1** : not provided with food ⟨worrying over her ~ pets⟩ **2** : not given support or sustenance ⟨a grudge that remained ~⟩
un·feed \“+\ *adj* [[1]*un-* + *feed*, past part. of *fee*] : not rewarded with a fee or gratuity : UNPAID, UNTIPPED ⟨the breath of an ~ lawyer —Shak.⟩ ⟨cork crumbs in wine opened by an ~ waiter —O.Henry⟩
un·feeling \“+\ *adj* [ME *unfeling*, fr. [1]*un-* + *feling* feeling] **1 a** : devoid of feeling or sensation : INSENSATE ⟨an ~ tree⟩ ⟨an ~ corpse⟩ **b** *archaic* : INSENSITIVE, COLD ⟨should to fame your hearts ~ be —James Thomson †1748⟩ **2** : devoid of kindness or sympathy : HARDHEARTED, CRUEL ⟨an ~ wretch⟩ ⟨~ enough to laugh at her predicament⟩ ⟨the ~ governor sought to terrify her into compliance with his demands —Herman Melville⟩ — **un·feel·ing·ly** *adv* — **un·feel·ing·ness** *n*
un·feigned \“+\ *adj* [ME *unfeined*, fr. [1]*un-* + *feined* feigned] : not feigned or pretended ⟨an ~ interest in people —Geoffrey Bruun⟩ ⟨with ~ curiosity —Louis Auchincloss⟩ **syn** see SINCERE
un·feignedly \“+\ *adv* : in an unfeigned manner : SINCERELY ⟨~ glad to see his old teacher⟩
un·felicitous \“+\ *adj* : INFELICITOUS
un·fel·lowed \¦ən¦fe(ˌ)lōd, -ˌləd\ *adj* [in sense 1, fr. [1]*un-* + *fellowed*, past part. of *fellow*, in sense 2, fr. [1]*un-* + *fellow*, n. + *-ed*] **1** *obs* : having no equal : PEERLESS, MATCHLESS **2** : having no companion : UNMATED, ALONE
un·felted \“+\ *adj* : not felted ⟨~ material⟩
un·feminine \“+\ *adj* : not suitable to or appropriate for a woman : not characteristic of a woman : unexpected in a woman ⟨an ~ depth of voice⟩ ⟨a quite ~ insight into the mystique of fly-fishing —Stuart Keate⟩
un·fenced \“+\ *adj* [[1]*un-* + *fenced*, past part. of *fence*] **1** : not protected : UNGUARDED ⟨the ~ shore⟩ **2** : not enclosed; *esp* : not closed in with a fence ⟨an ~ pasture⟩
un·fermentable \“+\ *adj* : incapable of undergoing fermentation ⟨~ sugar⟩
un·fermented \“+\ *adj* [[1]*un-* + *fermented*, past part. of *ferment*] : not fermented ⟨~ grape juice⟩
un·fertile \“+\ *adj* : not fertile : INFERTILE
un·fertilized \“+\ *adj* [[1]*un-* + *fertilized*, past part. of *fertilize*] : not fertilized ⟨an ~ egg⟩
un·festive \“+\ *adj* : not festive : lacking holiday atmosphere or spirit ⟨~ streets⟩ ⟨unpopular domestic measures . . . hinted at in his ~ Christmas broadcast —Mollie Panter-Downes⟩
un·fetter \“+\ *vt* [ME *unfeteren*, fr. [2]*un-* + *feteren* to fetter] **1** : to free from fetters : UNSHACKLE ⟨~ a prisoner⟩ **2** : to loose from restraint : EMANCIPATE, LIBERATE ⟨~ the mind from prejudice⟩
un·fettered \“+\ *adj* [[1]*un-* + *fettered*, past part. of *fetter*] : not fettered or bound : not restrained or limited : UNTRAMMELED, FREE ⟨~ competition⟩ ⟨believe in freedom of opinion and the ~ pursuit of knowledge —*advt*⟩
un·feued \¦ən+\ *adj* [[1]*un-* + *feued*, past part. of *feu*] *Scots law* : not in feu : free or freed from feu-duties
un·figured \“+\ *adj* **1** : not marked by figurative language ⟨an ~ style⟩ **2 a** : containing no artistic patterns or figures ⟨an ~ pattern⟩ **b** : not including human figures ⟨~ paintings⟩
un·filed \“+\ *adj* [in sense 1, fr. [1]*un-* + *filed*, past part. of *file* (to rub); in sense 2, fr. [1]*un-* + *filed*, past part. of *file* (to arrange)] **1** *archaic* : not smoothed : UNPOLISHED ⟨my rude ~ apology —George Wither⟩ **2** : not placed on file or in a file ⟨several ~ documents⟩
un·filial \“+\ *adj* : not observing the obligations of a child to a parent : not befitting a son or daughter : UNDUTIFUL ⟨an ~ child⟩ ⟨~ behavior⟩ ⟨gave his father an ~ answer⟩
un·fillable \“+\ *adj* [ME, fr. [1]*un-* + *fillable* capable of being filled, fr. *fillen* to fill + *-able*] : incapable of being filled : INSATIABLE ⟨an ~ hole⟩ ⟨an ~ maw⟩
un·filled \“+\ *adj* [[1]*un-* + *filled*, past part. of *fill*] **1** : not filled : EMPTY, BLANK ⟨an ~ bottle⟩ ⟨~ spaces⟩ **2** : not containing a filler
un·filtered \“+\ *adj* [[1]*un-* + *filtered*, past part. of *filter*] : not filtered
un·financial \“+\ *adj* : not current in payment of dues : not in good financial standing — used esp. of a member of a fraternal organization
un·findable \“+\ *adj* [[1]*un-* + *find* + *-able*] : not capable of being found — used esp. of a person sought by law enforcement authorities ⟨he was ~, and finally . . . we all gave up looking for him —Edmond Taylor⟩
un·fine \“+\ *adj* [ME, fr. [1]*un-* + *fine*] **1** *obs*, *of a wine* : poor in flavor : ROUGH **2** *of the weather* : INCLEMENT, STORMY
un·finish \“+\ *n* : lack of finish : unfinished state ⟨canvases in various stages of ~ —*Time*⟩
un·finishable \“+\ *adj* [[1]*un-* + *finish*, v. + *-able*] : incapable of being finished ⟨an ~ tale⟩
un·finished \“+\ *adj* [[1]*un-* + *finished*, past part. of *finish*] : not finished: **a** : not brought to an end or to completion ⟨an ~ poem⟩ ⟨an ~ house⟩ ⟨~ work⟩ **b** : left in the rough state : UNPOLISHED, CRUDE ⟨~ wood⟩ ⟨~ steel⟩ **c** (1) : subjected to no other processes (as bleaching or dyeing) after coming from the loom : UNBLEACHED, UNDYED — used of a wool fabric ⟨~ cloth⟩ (2) *of a worsted fabric* : finished with a slight nap in contrast to the usual hard napless finish **d** (1) *of a market animal* : inadequately fattened (2) *of a feeder* : not yet fattened
unfinished business *n* : matters postponed from a previous meeting : matters pending at adjournment
un·fin·ished·ness \ˌ=¦==nə̇s\ *n* -ES : the quality or state of being unfinished : CRUDENESS
un·fired \¦ən+\ *adj* [[1]*un-* + *fired*, past part. of *fire*] **1** : not set on fire : not ignited ⟨~ coals⟩ **2** : not subjected to or treated by fire; *esp* : not yet baked in a kiln : GREEN 7a(8) ⟨the ~ clay⟩ **3** : not exploded : UNDISCHARGED ⟨an ~ shell⟩ **4** : not animated : not aroused : UNINSPIRED ⟨so grave and ~ a countenance —*McClure's*⟩
un·firm \“+\ *adj* : not firm: **a** : not compact : LOOSE ⟨~ earth⟩ **b** : not firmly set : UNSTEADY, INSECURE ⟨an ~ stance⟩ — **un·firmly** \“+\ *adv* — **un·firmness** \“+\ *n*
un·fir·ma·ment·ed *adj* \¦ən¦fərməˌmentə̇d *sometimes* -ˌmən-\ [[1]*un-* + *firmament* + *-ed*] : having no bounding firmament : UNBOUNDED ⟨~ space⟩
un·fishable \¦ən+\ *adj* : unsuitable for fishing ⟨an ~ stream⟩ ⟨turbulent, ~ water —Edward Grey⟩
un·fished \“+\ *adj* [[1]*un-* + *fished*, past part. of *fish*] : not used for fishing ⟨~ waters⟩
[1]**unfit** \“+\ *adj* : not fit: **a** : not adapted to an end, object, or design : UNSUITABLE, INAPPROPRIATE ⟨land ~ for farming⟩ ⟨food ~ for human consumption⟩ **b** : not fitted : not qualified : INCAPABLE, INCOMPETENT ⟨clearly ~ by temperament to assume such a responsibility⟩ ⟨eliminated ~ candidates by examination⟩ **c** (1) : physically or mentally unsound ⟨certified as ~ for army service⟩ (2) : not qualified by reason of poor physical condition ⟨reported drunk and ~ for duty⟩
[2]**unfit** \“\ *n* : one that is unfit ⟨many are moral failures . . . or physical ~*s* —D.D.Lescohier⟩
[3]**unfit** \“\ *vt* [[2]*un-* + *fit*] : to make unfit : DISABLE, DISQUALIFY ⟨has a record that ~*s* him for the presidency⟩ ⟨an education that *unfitted* him for the life of a farmer⟩ ⟨doing one's duty . . . apparently *unfitted* one for doing anything else —Edith Wharton⟩
un·fit·ly *adv* : in an unfit manner : UNSUITABLY, INAPPROPRIATELY
un·fit·ness *n* : the quality or state of being unfit: **a** : UNSUITABILITY, INAPPROPRIATENESS ⟨the ~ of the gesture⟩ **b** : poor physical condition ⟨the ~ of many factory workers⟩ **c** : INCOMPETENCE ⟨could not conceal his ~ for the work⟩
un·fitted \¦ən+\ *adj* [[1]*un-* + *fitted*, past part. of *fit*] : not adapted : not qualified ⟨felt himself temperamentally ~ for the ministry⟩
un·fitting \“+\ *adj* : not fitting : UNSUITABLE, IMPROPER ⟨an ~ atmosphere⟩
un·fit·ting·ly *adv* : in an unfitting manner : UNSUITABLY
un·fix \¦ən+\ *vt* [[2]*un-* + *fix*] **1** : to loosen from a fastening : detach from something that holds ⟨~ the flagpole⟩ : DISENGAGE ⟨~ bayonets⟩ **2** : to make unstable : UNSETTLE, UNHINGE ⟨~ the mind⟩ ⟨a new discovery that ~*ed* all established notions⟩ **3** : to make (a chemical compound) soluble : DISSOLVE
un·fixable \“+\ *adj* **1** : incapable of being held in a fixed state : UNSTABLE, INDETERMINATE **2** : incapable of breeding true : manifest only in the heterozygous state -- used of a genetic character
un·fixed \“+\ *adj* **1** : not set in a definite place : DETACHED, FREE **2** : not settled upon definitely : UNDETERMINED ⟨a date as yet ~⟩ **3** : UNSTABLE, VAGUE ⟨~ as were her general notions of what men ought to be —Jane Austen⟩
un·fixedness \“+\ *n* : the quality or state of being unfixed : INSTABILITY
un·flagging \“+\ *adj* : not flagging : continuing with vigor : SUSTAINED, TIRELESS ⟨~ energy⟩ ⟨~ enthusiasm⟩ ⟨~ courtesy⟩
un·flaggingly \“+\ *adv* : in an unflagging manner : STEADILY, PERSEVERINGLY ⟨waved and smiled ~ —R.H.Rovere⟩
un·flattering \“+\ *adj* : not flattering : revealing or displaying truly or in a starkly realistic way : CANDID, ACCURATE ⟨an ~ mirror⟩ ⟨an ~ portait⟩; *esp* : tending to show or represent unfavorably ⟨an ~ remark⟩ ⟨the full ~ light of morning —Walter de la Mare⟩ ⟨an ~ illustration of the tone of our civilization —*Popular Science Jour.*⟩
un·flatteringly \“+\ *adv* : in an unflattering manner
un·flavored \“+\ *adj* : not flavored
un·flawed \“+\ *adj* : free of flaws : FLAWLESS, PERFECT ⟨an ~ gem⟩ ⟨flowers and shrubs glowing under a blazing sun and an ~ sky —Sean O'Faolain⟩
un·flecked \“+\ *adj* [[1]*un-* + *flecked*, past part. of *fleck*] : not flecked : stainlessly pure : SPOTLESS ⟨the pure heart, by thoughts of ill ~ —Gilbert Murray⟩
un·fledged \“+\ *adj* [[1]*un-* + *fledged*, past part. of *fledge*] **1 a** : not fledged : not feathered : not ready for flight ⟨found a small, ~ English sparrow on the doorstep —*advt*⟩ **b** *of an arrow* : not equipped with vanes ⟨shot an ~ arrow⟩ **2 a** : not fully developed : IMMATURE, CALLOW ⟨an ~ writer⟩ ⟨~ judgment⟩ **b** : of, relating to, or characteristic of youth and inexperience ⟨in those ~ days was my wife a girl —Shak.⟩
un·flesh \“+\ *vt* [[2]*un-* + *flesh*, n.] : to deprive of flesh
[1]**un·fleshed** \“+\ *adj* [[1]*un-* + *fleshed*, past part. of *flesh*] : not fleshed: **a** : not incited to the hunt by the taste of flesh ⟨an ~ hound⟩ **b** : not initiated : INEXPERIENCED ⟨an ~ novice⟩
[2]**unfleshed** \“\ *adj* [[2]*un-* + *flesh*, n. + *-ed*] : deprived of flesh ⟨an ~ skull⟩
un·fleshliness \¦ən+\ *n* : the quality or state of being unfleshly : SPIRITUALITY
un·fleshly \“+\ *adj* : not carnal : SPIRITUAL
un·flexed \¦ən+\ *adj* [[1]*un-* + *flexed*, past part. of *flex*] : not flexed : UNBENT ⟨performing the movement with an ~ position of the knees⟩
un·flexible \“+\ *adj* : INFLEXIBLE
un·flickering \“+\ *adj* : not flickering : STEADY ⟨an ~ light⟩ — **un·flick·er·ing·ly** *adv*
un·flinching \“+\ *adj* [[1]*un-* + *flinching*, pres. part. of *flinch*] : not flinching or shrinking : UNWAVERING, STEADFAST ⟨remain ~ when a gun roars out —*Amer. Guide Series: Maine*⟩ ⟨lived a life of ~ probity —R.G.Swing⟩ ⟨an ~ determination to take the whole evidence into account —A.N.Whitehead⟩
un·flinch·ing·ly *adv* : in an unflinching manner : without shrinking or wincing : STEADFASTLY, RESOLUTELY ⟨bear pain ~ and . . . without complaint —D.C.Buchanan⟩ ⟨took ~ the severe blow of the defeat —W.H.Chamberlin⟩
un·flower \¦ən+\ *vt* [[2]*un-* + *flower*, n.] : to strip (as a plant) or empty (as a basket) of flowers
un·fluctuating \“+\ *adj* [[1]*un-* + *fluctuating*, pres. part. of *fluctuate*] : not fluctuating : UNWAVERING ⟨an ~ guide⟩ : UNVARYING, STEADY ⟨~ in his principles⟩ : CONSTANT ⟨~ health⟩ ⟨an ~ amount⟩ : STABLE ⟨an ~ currency⟩
un·flurried \“+\ *adj* : not flurried : free of agitation or nervous tension : CALM ⟨~ service⟩ ⟨~ and good-natured as they pass your baggage through —E.A.Weeks⟩
un·flustered \“+\ *adj* [[1]*un-* + *flustered*, past part. of *fluster*] : not flustered : SERENE
un·focused *also* **un·focussed** \“+\ *adj* [[1]*un-* + *focused*, past part. of *focus*] **1** : not adjusted to a focus ⟨her eyes . . . stared blankly, ~ —Raymond Chandler⟩ **2** : not concentrated at one point or upon one objective ⟨an uncertain, ~ young man⟩ ⟨diversity . . . in our huge ~ country —Owen Wister⟩
un·fold \“+\ *vb* [ME *unfolden*, fr. OE *unfealdan*, fr. [2]*un-* + *fealdan* to fold — more at FOLD] *vt* **1 a** : to open the folds of : spread or straighten out : EXPAND ⟨~ a tablecloth⟩ ⟨~*ed* the map⟩ ⟨~ the arms⟩ **b** : to open wide (as a gate) ⟨hell shall ~ . . . her widest gates —John Milton⟩ **c** : to remove (as a package) from the folds : UNWRAP ⟨began ~*ing* a brown paper parcel —W.B.Yeats⟩ **2** : to open to the view or understanding : make known : REVEAL ⟨stand and ~ yourself —Shak.⟩; *esp* : to make clear by gradual disclosure and often by recital or explanation ⟨~*ed* his story through dialogue —W.K.Ferguson⟩ ⟨~*ed* to me his desires for the university —A.C.Benson⟩ ~ *vi* **1 a** : to open from a folded state : open out : EXPAND ⟨plane . . . wheels began to ~ —Howard Hunt⟩ **b** : BLOSSOM ⟨buds beginning to ~⟩ **c** : to move toward full development ⟨if the . . . child were permitted to ~ amid rich and stimulating surroundings —Margaret Mead⟩ **2** : to open out gradually to the view : become visible or known ⟨a panorama of carefully tilled farm lands . . . ~*s* before the visitor's eyes —*Amer. Guide Series: Mich.*⟩ ⟨suppressed his comment and let the narrative ~ simply and objectively —R.A.Cordell⟩ **3** : to develop a parasitic vowel by anaptyxis

syn UNFOLD, EVOLVE, DEVELOP, ELABORATE, and PERFECT can mean in common to cause something to emerge from a state in which its potentialities are not apparent, are unrealized, or are incompletely realized, into a state where they are apparent or partly or fully realized. UNFOLD usu. suggests a natural process by which the true or complete character of something is unveiled or disclosed ⟨a bud *unfolds* itself into a flower⟩ ⟨hitherto chemistry has not succeeded in *unfolding* the principles by which metals are formed —*Encyc. Americana*⟩ ⟨the creative spirit gains sustenance and vigor for its own *unfolding* —Edward Sapir⟩ ⟨the episodes of this life began to *unfold* themselves in his mind —Fred Majdalany⟩ EVOLVE implies an unfolding gradually and in an orderly way, often suggesting a slowness and complexity of process, sometimes carrying strongly the idea of natural development by an inner process ⟨slowly, through ages and centuries, we have *evolved* a picture of the world we live in —*Fortune*⟩ ⟨the program we have *evolved* as a result of a year of deliberation is now complete in general outline —J.B.Conant⟩ ⟨the new order which seemed to be *evolving* —E.M.Forster⟩ ⟨the germinal situation out of which this book *evolves* —N.L.Rothman⟩ DEVELOP, in this connection, implies a passing through several stages, stressing the unfolding, usu. slow, of latent possibilities ⟨the scientific writer must also have a broad point of view, *developed* by experience, reading, and reflection —C.E.Kellogg⟩ ⟨the viscose process was *developed* from the inventions of three Englishmen —*Amer. Guide Series: Va.*⟩ ⟨the quarrel grew hot, and finally *developed* into a lawsuit —Gilbert Highet⟩ ELABORATE implies labor or effort to develop or realize the clear possibilities of something that is only in the germ or only partly formulated ⟨only a system with order and progress in the heart of it could *elaborate* itself so perfectly and so intricately —J.A.Thomson⟩ ⟨escapes death from surgical infection because a Frenchman, Pasteur, and a German, Koch, *elaborated* a new technique —R.B.Fosdick⟩ ⟨did the tubercle bacillus *elaborate* some strange substance which tended to stimulate the mind —Harry Sylvester⟩ PERFECT implies an unfolding or developing of something so that it stands as a complete or finished product ⟨a series of complementary inventions, the phonograph, the moving picture, the gasoline engine, the steam turbine, the airplane, were all sketched in, if not *perfected*, by 1900 —Lewis Mumford⟩ ⟨conditions required of both Japanese and Americans a relent-

less *perfecting* of such cooperative efforts —T.C.Mendenhall b. 1910⟩ **syn** see in addition SOLVE

¹un·fold·ed \ˌən¦fōldəd\ *adj* [¹*un-* + *folded*, past part. of *fold* (to pen)] : not confined in a sheepfold

²unfolded \"\ *adj* [in sense 1, fr. past part. of *unfold;* in sense 2, fr. ¹*un-* + *folded*, past part. of *fold* (to double over)] **1** : opened out : DISCLOSED, DISPLAYED ⟨~ flowers⟩ ⟨littering with ~ silks the polished counter —William Cowper⟩ **2** : not folded

un·fold·ing \-ldiŋ, -ldēŋ\ *n* -s [fr. gerund of *unfold*] : the act or process of unfolding: **a** : expansion or opening out from or as if from folds ⟨the ~ of a bud⟩ **b** : DEVELOPMENT, EVOLUTION ⟨profoundly influenced the ~ of her childish mind —Norman Douglas⟩ **c** : EXPLICATION, EXPOSITION ⟨a lengthy and patient ~ only possible in a book —H.N.Southern⟩

un·fold·ment \-l(d)mənt\ *n* -s [*unfold* + *-ment*] **1** : the act or process of unfolding : DEVELOPMENT, EVOLUTION ⟨during the story's ~ the character grows —*Sat. Eve. Post*⟩ ⟨help those who are seeking spiritual ~ —*Amer. Mercury*⟩ **2** : full manifestation or realization ⟨the journey of the soul to its final ~ —M.L.Bach⟩

un·foliaged \¦ən+\ *adj* : lacking foliage ⟨trees still ~⟩

un·followed \"+\ *adj* [¹*un-* + *followed*, past part. of *follow*] : having no followers or retainers ⟨come back . . . alone, ~ —Sir Walter Scott⟩

unfooled \"+\ *adj* [²*un-* + *fooled*, past part. of *fool*] : not fooled : not taken in ⟨remaining ~ high-flown idealism —Max Lerner⟩

un·footed \¦ən+\ *adj* [¹*un-* + *footed*, past part. of *foot*] : UNTROD ⟨the ~ woods —Owen Wister⟩

un·forced \"+\ *adj* : not forced: **a** : not compelled : VOLUNTARY, WILLING ⟨gained the ~ attention of the group⟩ **b** : achieved without strain : marked by ease and naturalness ⟨a voice with a pleasingly ~ quality⟩ : apparently effortless ⟨one of the most ~ humorous sagas of our time —G.F. Whicher⟩ ⟨so sure and ~ is its pathos —*Manchester Guardian Weekly*⟩

un·fordable \"+\ *adj* : incapable of being forded : IMPASSABLE ⟨an ~ river⟩

un·foreknowable \"+\ *adj* : not capable of being foreknown ⟨the ~ future⟩

un·forensic \"+\ *adj* : not forensic : unsuitable for courts or in public debate ⟨~ rhetoric⟩

un·foreseeable \"+\ *adj* [¹*un-* + *foresee* + *-able*] : incapable of being foreseen, foretold, or anticipated : UNPREDICTABLE ⟨the ~ future⟩ ⟨~ events⟩ ⟨an ~ effect⟩ ⟨~ consequences⟩ ⟨if no ~ disabilities or restraints are put upon us —*Economist*⟩

un·foreseen \"+\ *adj* [¹*un-* + *foreseen*, past part. of *foresee*] : not foreseen : UNEXPECTED ⟨~ circumstances⟩ ⟨~ developments⟩ ⟨an ~ contingency⟩

un·forest \"+\ *vt* [²*un-* + *forest*, n.] : deprive of woods : DEFOREST

un·forested \"+\ *adj* [¹*un-* + *forested*] : not wooded ⟨~ land⟩

un·forethoughtful \¦ən+\ *adj* : not forethoughtful : IMPROVIDENT, CAREFREE

un·forewarned \"+\ *adj* [¹*un-* + *forewarned*, past part. of *forewarn*] : not forewarned : taken by surprise

un·forfeitable \"+\ *adj* : not subject to forfeiture : INALIENABLE ⟨an ~ right⟩

un·forgettable \"+\ *adj* [¹*un-* + *forget* + *-able*] : incapable of being forgotten : MEMORABLE ⟨an ~ occasion⟩ ⟨an ~ face⟩ ⟨that exciting and ~ night —Arnold Bennett⟩ ⟨a poignant and ~ expression of one of the deepest truths of human life —J.L. Lowes⟩

un·for·get·ta·bly \¦=;=¦==blē, -bli\ *adv* : in an unforgettable manner : to an unforgettable degree ⟨the thought takes hold and clings ~ —J.A.Macy⟩

un·forgivable \"+\ *adj* [¹*un-* + *forgive* + *-able*] : incapable of being forgiven : UNPARDONABLE ⟨the ~ sin⟩ ⟨an ~ crime⟩

un·forgivably \"+\ *adv* : in an unforgivable manner : to an unforgivable extent : UNPARDONABLY, INTOLERABLY ⟨careful not to offend ~⟩ ⟨was ~ impartial in his arrests —Morley Callaghan⟩

un·forgiveness \"+\ *n* : UNFORGIVINGNESS

un·forgiving \"+\ *adj* : marked by an inability or unwillingness to forgive : RELENTLESS

un·forgivingness \"+\ *n* [*unforgiving* + *-ness*] : the quality or state of being unforgiving : IMPLACABILITY, VINDICTIVENESS ⟨the ~ of passionate hearts —John Galsworthy⟩

un·fork \"+\ *vt* [²*un-* + *fork*] : to dismount from (a horse) ⟨~*ed* his horse and walked along with him —A.B.Guthrie⟩

un·forked \"+\ *adj* [¹*un-* + *forked*] : not forked ⟨the ~ tail of a bird⟩

un·form \¦ən+\ *vt* [²*un-* + *form*] : to undo the form of : make formless

un·formal \"+\ *adj* : INFORMAL

un·formalized \"+\ *adj* [¹*un-* + *formalized*, past part. of *formalize*] **1** *archaic* : not made rigid or unbending : FLEXIBLE **2** : not put into definite shape or arrangement

un·formed \"+\ *adj* [ME *unfourmed*, fr. ¹*un-* + *fourmed*, past part. of *fourmen* to form] : not formed ⟨an as yet ~ government⟩ : not arranged in regular shape, order, or relations: **a** : UNDEVELOPED, IMMATURE ⟨an ~ character⟩ ⟨~ still in body and mind —Kathleen Freeman⟩ **b** : marked by crudity or lack of finish : UNPOLISHED **c** : INCHOATE, AMORPHOUS ⟨this ~ government is the "legitimate" one —Frank Gorrell⟩

un·formidable \"+\ *adj* : not formidable : UNIMPOSING

un·formulable \"+\ *adj* : not reducible to formula : incapable of being formulated ⟨~ presuppositions —*New Republic*⟩

un·formulated \"+\ *adj* [¹*un-* + *formulated*, past part. of *formulate*] : not formulated : not expressed by formula or in systematic form ⟨~ desires⟩ ⟨~ plans⟩

un·fortified \"+\ *adj* [¹*un-* + *fortified*, past part. of *fortify*] : not fortified: **a** : not protected by fortification ⟨an ~ frontier⟩ **b** : lacking moral strength or stamina : UNSTABLE, WEAK ⟨shows . . . a heart ~, a mind impatient —Shak.⟩ **c** : not strengthened : UNSUPPORTED ⟨~ premises⟩; *esp* : not strengthened or enriched (as a food or drink) ⟨~ wine⟩ ⟨~ margarine⟩

¹un·fortunate \"+\ *adj* : not fortunate: **a** : not favored by fortune : UNSUCCESSFUL, UNLUCKY ⟨sending the ~ naval commander into exile —A.J.Toynbee⟩ **b** : marked or accompanied by or resulting in misfortune ⟨an ~ decision⟩ ⟨~ investments⟩ ⟨an ~ night for all concerned⟩ ⟨had an ~ experience with a neighborhood cleaner —Richard Joseph⟩ **c** : UNTOWARD, UNPROMISING ⟨an ~ location for the business⟩ ⟨~ social consequences —Willy Richardson⟩ **d** : UNSUITABLE, INEPT ⟨rather an ~ choice in the circumstances —Denis Johnston⟩ ⟨his ~ personality —P.I.Wellman⟩ **e** : lacking felicity of expression : INFELICITOUS ⟨an ~ term⟩ ⟨his phrasing was rather ~ —*Nation*⟩ **f** : DEPLORABLE, REGRETTABLE ⟨an ~ lapse of taste —Saul Maloff⟩ **g** *of a sign of the zodiac* : having an unfortunate influence : UNPROPITIOUS **syn** see UNLUCKY

²unfortunate \"\ *n* : an unfortunate person ⟨leave off tormenting that ~ —Ellen Glasgow⟩ ⟨one of those ~*s* without influence or money —Kenneth Roberts⟩ : a social outcast (as a prisoner or prostitute) ⟨one more ~ . . . gone to her death —Thomas Hood †1845⟩

un·fortunately \¦ən+\ *adv* : in an unfortunate manner : UNLUCKILY

un·fortunateness \"+\ *n* : the quality or state of being unfortunate

un·fossiliferous \"+\ *adj* : not fossiliferous ⟨~ sandstone⟩

un·fought \"+\ *adj* [¹*un-* + *fought*, past part. of *fight*] : not fought : UNCONTESTED ⟨an ~ field⟩

un·foul \"+\ *vt* [²*un-* + *foul*] : to cause to become disentangled ⟨dived into the river, ~*ed* the lines, and made them fast —*N.Y.Times*⟩

un·found \"+\ *adj* [¹*un-* + *found*, past part. of *find*] : not found : remaining unknown : UNDISCOVERED ⟨a path that links our shores with a shore ~ —S.R.Lysaght⟩

un·founded \"+\ *adj* [¹*un-* + *founded*, past part. of *found*] **1** *obs* : BOTTOMLESS, UNSTABLE ⟨the ~ deep —John Milton⟩ **2** : lacking a sound basis in reason or fact : BASELESS, GROUNDLESS, ILLUSIVE ⟨an ~ accusation⟩ ⟨~ suspicions⟩ ⟨his . . . rash and most ~ assertion —J.M.Kemble⟩ ⟨that hope proved to be ~ —Edith Sitwell⟩

un·found·ed·ly \¦=¦==lē\ *adv* [*unfounded* + *-ly*] : without foundation or reasonable cause : UNWARRANTABLY

un·frame \"+\ *vt* [²*un-* + *frame*] **1** : to take apart : break down : DESTROY ⟨the women's exuberance will . . . the houses ~ —Robinson Jeffers⟩ **2** *obs* : to throw into confusion : DISRUPT

un·framed \"+\ *adj* [¹*un-* + *framed*, past part. of *frame*] : not provided with a frame ⟨an ~ picture⟩

un·frank \"+\ *adj* : not candid : DISINGENUOUS, SLY ⟨men with . . . that glistening ~ expression that wives know —Sinclair Lewis⟩

un·fraternal \"+\ *adj* : not fraternal : UNBROTHERLY

un·fraught \"+\ *adj* : not fraught : not burdened ⟨minds empty and ~ with matter —Francis Bacon⟩

un·free \ˌən+\ *adj* [ME, fr. ¹*un-* + *free*] : not free : lacking freedom: **a** : bound to the land ⟨a primarily agrarian society of . . . landlords and their ~ tenants —R.H.Hilton⟩ **b** *obs* : not holding the status or privileges of membership (as in a civic body or guild) **c** : marked by a lack of political freedom ⟨colonies do not have to remain ~ —Wendell Willkie⟩ **d** : marked by a lack of personal liberty ⟨we are all to some degree oppressed, ~ —William James⟩ **e** : brought about by coercion ⟨a unity which is artificial because it is ~ —*Atlantic*⟩

un·freedom \"+\ *n* : lack of freedom ⟨these newcomers — black and white — toiled under some degree of ~ . . . were bound servants for greater or lesser terms —Oscar Handlin⟩ ⟨gains his sense of security by this very ~ of conforming —H.A.Overstreet⟩

un·freeman \"+\ *n* [ME *unfreman*, fr. *unfree* + *man*] *archaic* : one that is not a freeman

un·freeze \"+\ *vb* [²*un-* + *freeze*] *vt* **1** : to cause to thaw ⟨unseasonably warm temperatures *unfroze* the ground early⟩ **2** : to free (as prices or raw materials) from regulation or control ⟨the liberals wanted land rents *unfrozen* immediately —Arnaldo Cortesi⟩ **3** : to release (as funds) for expenditure, withdrawal, or exchange ⟨the Fund must ~ the vast resources it now has cached away in various central banks —*New Republic*⟩ ~ *vi* : THAW

un·french \"+\ *adj, usu cap F* : not characteristically French ⟨the work of these Odéon actors seemed strangely *un-French* —*New Republic*⟩

un·frequency \"+\ *n* [*unfrequent* + *-cy*] *archaic* : INFREQUENCY

un·frequent \"+\ *adj* : INFREQUENT

un·frequented \"+\ *adj* [¹*un-* + *frequented*, past part. of *frequent*] : not often visited or traveled over ⟨trails . . . lead to ~ lakes —*Amer. Guide Series: Mich.*⟩ ⟨the car . . . soon turned into an ~ street —Alexander Forbes⟩

un·frequently \¦ən+\ *adv* : not frequently : INFREQUENTLY, RARELY, SELDOM ⟨in these conflicts, the animals were by no means ~ the conquerors —C.W.Webber⟩

un·friend \"+\ *n* [ME *unfrend*, fr. ¹*un-* + *frend* friend] *chiefly Scot* : one that is not a friend : ENEMY ⟨I am no ~ to plainness —R.L.Stevenson⟩

un·friended \"+\ *adj* [¹*un-* + *friended*, past part. of *friend*] : having no friends : not befriended : FRIENDLESS ⟨leave me to go through the remainder of my life ~ —W.S.Gilbert⟩

un·friendliness \"+\ *n* : the quality or state of being unfriendly : ill feeling : HOSTILITY, ANTAGONISM ⟨greeted each other with obvious ~⟩ ⟨a miserable business to have any ~ on the raft —Mark Twain⟩

un·friendly \"+\ *adj* [ME *unfrendly*, fr. ¹*un-* + *frendly* friendly] : not friendly: **a** : not showing or marked by the disposition or attitude of one that is or wishes to be a friend ⟨an ~ action for him to take after years of close association⟩ **b** : not well disposed : UNSYMPATHETIC, HOSTILE ⟨an ~ reviewer⟩ ⟨an ~ nation⟩ **c** : marked by lack of warmth : COLD ⟨received an ~ reception⟩ **d** : INHOSPITABLE, UNFAVORABLE ⟨a place ~ to meditation⟩ ⟨the ~ and lonesome environment at high altitude —H.G.Armstrong⟩ **e** *of a fire* : spreading beyond intended limits : out of control

un·friendship \"+\ *n* [ME *unfrendship*, fr. *unfrend* unfriend + *-ship*] *chiefly Scot* : ill will : ENMITY

un·frightened \"+\ *adj* : not frightened : FEARLESS

un·frock \"+\ *vt* [²*un-* + *frock*, n.] **1** : to deprive or divest of a frock; *specif* : to deprive of priestly function or privilege : DEGRADE 1b, DEPOSE ⟨trained for the . . . ministry but was ~*ed* 27 years ago on charges of modernism and heresy —*Time*⟩ **2** : to remove from a position of honor or privilege : DISCHARGE ⟨a physician ~*ed* by the medical association⟩

un·frozen \"+\ *adj* [¹*un-* + *frozen*] : not frozen: **a** : not congealed ⟨~ ground⟩ **b** : not chilled ⟨an ~ dessert⟩

un·fructify \"+\ *vt* [²*un-* + *fructify*] : to make unfruitful

un·frugal \"+\ *adj* : EXTRAVAGANT, LAVISH

un·fruitful \"+\ *adj* [ME, fr. ¹*un-* + *fruitful*] : not fruitful: **a** : not producing offspring : INFERTILE, STERILE ⟨an ~ marriage⟩ **b** : yielding no valuable result : FRUITLESS, UNPROFITABLE ⟨an ~ effort⟩ ⟨this unsavory and ~ piece of research —Douglass Cater⟩ **c** (1) : not bearing fruit ⟨an ~ tree⟩ (2) : not producing crops : BARREN ⟨~ soil⟩ **syn** see STERILE

un·fruitfully \"+\ *adv* [ME, fr. *unfruitful* + *-ly*] : in an unfruitful manner : UNPRODUCTIVELY, UNPROFITABLY ⟨negotiations proceeded ~⟩

un·fruitfulness \"+\ *n* : the quality or state of being unfruitful : UNPRODUCTIVENESS, STERILITY

un·fueled \¦ən+\ *adj* [¹*un-* + *fueled*, past part. of *fuel*] : not provided with fuel : UNFED, SELF-SUSTAINED

un·fulfill \"+\ *vt* [back-formation fr. *unfulfilled*] : to fail to fulfill (as an obligation) : NEGLECT

un·fulfillable \"+\ *adj* [¹*un-* + *fulfill* + *-able*] : incapable of being fulfilled : UNREALIZABLE ⟨an ~ offer⟩ ⟨~ wishes⟩

un·fulfilled \"+\ *adj* [ME, fr. ¹*un-* + *fulfilled*, past part. of *fulfillen* to fulfill] : not fulfilled : **a** : not filled : UNSUPPLIED, UNSATISFIED ⟨vital ~ needs of the nation —H.S.Truman⟩ **b** : not carried out : not accomplished ⟨a great mission ~ —*Quarterly Rev.*⟩ **c** : not converted into reality : not completely achieved ⟨a still ~ desire⟩ ⟨the inheritors of ~ renown —P.B.Shelley⟩ **d** : marked by failure to realize or attain to full potentialities of experience or development ⟨~ and uneasy men —Sinclair Lewis⟩ ⟨~ as a woman —H.M.Parshley⟩

un·fulfillment \"+\ *n* **1** : failure to fulfill : lack of execution ⟨~ of an obligation⟩ **2** : failure to achieve fulfillment : lack of consummation : DISSATISFACTION ⟨had arrived at this . . . final ~ —Fred Majdalany⟩ ⟨consume themselves in ~ —*Yale Rev.*⟩

un·fumed \"+\ *adj* [¹*un-* + *fumed*, past part. of *fume*] **1** *obs* : not distilled **2** : not exposed to fumes : not fumigated

un·functional \"+\ *adj* : not functional: **a** : not related directly to or fitted for everyday needs or activities : IMPRACTICAL, INEFFICIENT **b** : not conforming to functionalist theory

un·funded \"+\ *adj* [¹*un-* + *funded*, past part. of *fund*] : not funded : FLOATING ⟨an ~ debt⟩

unfunded life insurance trust *n* : a life insurance trust under which the insured agrees to pay the premiums on the subject policies during his lifetime

unfunded plan *n* : a pension or retirement plan under which the employer is free to finance payments to retired workers on a pay-as-you-go basis — compare INSURED PLAN, TRUSTEED PLAN

un·funny \¦ən+\ *adj* : not funny : failing to achieve the humor intended : UNAMUSING ⟨an ~ joke⟩ ⟨a feverish and ~ comedy —Robert Hatch⟩

un·furl \"+\ *vb* [²*un-* + *furl*] *vt* **1** : to release or open out (as a sail or flag) from a furled state : cast loose ⟨~ the sails and get under way⟩ : spread out for display ⟨the flag which the legation ~*ed* on state occasions —Jenny G. Walker⟩ **2** : to open out (as a scene) to the view : UNFOLD, UNROLL ⟨with nature's wonders all ~*ed* to our delighted vision —W.S. Gilbert⟩ ~ *vi* : to open wide : UNFOLD ⟨strange plants ~*ed* —D.D.Randall⟩

un·furnish \"+\ *vt* [²*un-* + *furnish*] **1** *archaic* : to strip (as a place or a man) of means of defense **2** *obs* : DIVEST ⟨that which may ~ me of reason —Shak.⟩ **3** : to clear (as a house or apartment) of furniture : DISMANTLE

un·furnished \"+\ *adj* [¹*un-* + *furnished*, past part. of *furnish*] : not furnished: **a** : not provided or equipped : UNPREPARED ⟨~ with money or skill⟩ ⟨valleys . . . ~ with tracks —E.E.Shipton⟩ **b** : not provided with furniture; *specif* : not so provided by the landlord ⟨an ~ apartment⟩

un·furrowed \"+\ *adj* [¹*un-* + *furrowed*, past part. of *furrow*] : having no furrows : **a** : UNPLOWED, UNTRENCHED ⟨an ~ field⟩ **b** : UNWRINKLED ⟨an ~ throat⟩ ⟨~ fruit⟩

un·fused \"+\ *adj* : not fused: **a** : not blended by or as if by melting ⟨~ material in a blast furnace⟩ **b** : not joined ⟨~ lower leg bones⟩

un·fussing \"+\ *adj* [¹*un-* + *fussing*, pres. part. of *fuss*] : UNFUSSY

un·fussy \"+\ *adj* : not fussy: **a** : not easily flustered : EASYGOING ⟨managed the motel in an efficient, ~ way⟩ **b** : not greatly concerned with ways and means : not particular ⟨was quite ~ about the choice of a restaurant⟩ **c** : not cluttered with pretentious or nonessential matters : SIMPLE, UNCOMPLICATED ⟨keep the affair as ~ as possible⟩ ⟨the color pictures are just right, plain and realistic and ~ —Harvey Breit⟩

ung *abbr* [L *unguentum*] ointment

un·gag \¦ən+\ *vt* [²*un-* + *gag*] : to remove a gag from; *esp* : to release from censorship

un·gain \ˌən¦gān\ *adj* [ME *ungeyn*, fr. ¹*un-* + *geyn* gain — more at GAIN (direct)] **1** *dial Brit* **a** : hard to reach or do : INACCESSIBLE, INCONVENIENT **b** : INTRACTABLE **2** *dial* : UNGAINLY

un·gained \¦ən+\ *adj* [¹*un-* + *gained*] : not gained ⟨men prize the thing ~ more than it is —Shak.⟩

un·gainful \"+\ *adj* : not gainful

un·gain·li·ness \ˌən¦gānlēnəs, -lin-\ *n* -ES : the quality or state of being ungainly

¹un·gain·ly \ˌən¦gānlē, -li\ *adj, sometimes* -ER/-EST **1 a** : lacking in smoothness or dexterity : CLUMSY ⟨a very tall ~ gentleman . . . made her one of the clumsiest bows that was ever performed —W.M.Thackeray⟩ ⟨~ and eloquent, monstrous and exquisite . . . by turns —Virginia Woolf⟩ **b** : hard to handle : UNWIELDY ⟨the cello, some thought . . . was rather an ~ instrument for a girl —Osbert Lancaster⟩ **2** : lacking in grace or refinement : COARSE, UGLY ⟨an ~ grey homespun coat —Robert Lynd⟩ ⟨~ frame houses with scrollwork —*Amer. Guide Series: Calif.*⟩ **syn** see AWKWARD

²ungainly \"\ *adv, archaic* : in an ungainly manner ⟨waddles ~ by —*Westminster Gazette*⟩

un·gain·say·able \ˌən¦gān¦sāəbəl\ *adj* [¹*un-* + *gainsay* + *-able*] : incapable of being contradicted — **un·gain·say·ably** \-blē\ *adv*

un·gallant \¦ən+\ *adj* : not gallant; *esp* : DISCOURTEOUS — **un·gallantly** \"+\ *adv*

un·garbled \"+\ *adj* [ME *ungarbeled*, fr. ¹*un-* + *garbeled*, past part. of *garbelen* to garbie] **1** *archaic* : not sorted or sifted **2** : not distorted : CLEAR

un·garmented \"+\ *adj* [¹*un-* + *garmented*, past part. of *garment*] : not garmented

un·garnish \"+\ *vt* [²*un-* + *garnish*] *archaic* : to divest of decoration or equipment

un·garnished \"+\ *adj* [ME, fr. ¹*un-* + *garnished*] : free of embellishment : PLAIN, SIMPLE ⟨the village church's ~, stone facade —Kay Boyle⟩

un·gartered \"+\ *adj, archaic* : not gartered ⟨chid . . . for going ~ —Shak.⟩

un·gathered \"+\ *adj* [ME *ungadered*, fr. ¹*un-* + *gadered*, past part. of *gaderen* to gather] **1** : not collected or drawn together; *esp* : not assembled in book sequence ⟨~ signatures⟩ **2** : not harvested ⟨~ crops⟩

un·gear \"+\ *vt* [²*un-* + *gear*] **1** *archaic* : to remove the harness from (a draft animal) : UNHITCH ⟨~*ed* the mules, and crawled under the wagon for shade —J.H.Beadle⟩ **2** : to disconnect by or as if by throwing out of gear ⟨~ the pinion of a machine⟩ ⟨jangle your nerves . . . ~ you for the life you might have selected —Isa Glenn⟩

un·ge·mach·ite \'əŋgəˌmäˌkīt\ *n* -s [Henri-Léon *Ungemach* †1936 Belgian crystallographer + E *-ite*] : a mineral $K_3Na_9Fe(SO_4)_6(OH)_3.9H_2O$ consisting of a hydrous basic sulfate of potassium, sodium, and iron

un·generosity \¦ən+\ *n* [*ungenerous* + *-ity*] : lack of magnanimity : MEANNESS, SPITE ⟨the ill-tempered *ungenerosities* of a nerve-wracked woman —W.J.Locke⟩

un·generous \"+\ *adj* **1** : lacking in courtesy or magnanimity : PETTY, SMALL ⟨it seems ~ to end this review of a splendid work of scholarship on a critical note —*Times Lit. Supp.*⟩ **2** : lacking in largess : NIGGARDLY, PARSIMONIOUS ⟨~ response to an appeal for funds⟩ — **un·generously** \"+\ *adv*

un·genial \"+\ *adj* : DISAGREEABLE; *esp* : not arousing a sympathetic response ⟨considered the most ~ theory with scrupulous faith —Elinor Wylie⟩

un·genteel \¦ən+\ *adj* : lacking in courtesy or refinement : IMPOLITE, INELEGANT — **un·genteelly** \"+\ *adv*

un·gentle \"+\ *adj* [ME *ungentil*, fr. ¹*un-* + *gentil* gentle] **1 a** : not of the nobility : LOWBORN **b** *archaic* : UNGENTEEL **2** : lacking in softness or congeniality : HARSH, ROUGH — **un·gently** \"+\ *adv*

ungentleman *vt* [²*un-* + *gentleman*, n.] *obs* : to disqualify as a gentleman

un·gentlemanlike \¦ən+\ *adj* [¹*un-* + *gentlemanlike*] *archaic* : UNGENTLEMANLY

un·gentlemanliness \"+\ *n* [*ungentlemanly* + *-ness*] : the quality or state of being ungentlemanly

un·gentlemanly \"+\ *adj* : unworthy of a gentleman : ILL-BRED, IGNOBLE

un·gentleness \"+\ *n* [ME *ungentilnesse*, fr. *ungentil* ungentle + *-nesse* -ness] **1** *obs* : lack of civility : DISCOURTESY, RUDENESS **2** : lack of kindness or consideration : INHUMANITY

un·genuine \"+\ *adj* : not genuine — **un·genuinely** \"+\ *adv*

un·getatable \"+\ *adj* [¹*un-* + *getatable*] : hard to reach : INACCESSIBLE

un·ghosted \¦ən+\ *adj* [¹*un-* + *ghosted*, past part. of *ghost*] : not ghostwritten : FIRSTHAND ⟨asked the maestro himself to write an ~ introduction —Lionel Trilling⟩

un·ghostly \"+\ *adj, archaic* : not spiritual

un·gifted \"+\ *adj* **1** : lacking talent **2** *archaic* : EMPTY-HANDED

un·gild \"+\ *vt* [²*un-* + *gild*] : to remove gilding from

un·gilded *or* **un·gilt** \"+\ *adj* [*ungilded* fr. ¹*un-* + *gilded*; *ungilt* fr. ME, fr. ¹*un-* + *gilt*] *archaic* : not overlaid with gilding ⟨frames gilded and ~ —*London Gazette*⟩

un·ginned \"+\ *adj* [¹*un-* + *ginned*, past part. of *gin*] : not ginned ⟨~ cotton⟩

un·gird \"+\ *vt* [ME *ungyrden*, fr. OE *ongyrdan*, fr. *on-* ²un- + *gyrdan* to gird] **1** : to divest of a restraining band or girdle : free from constriction ⟨~*ed* his camels —Gen 24:32 (RSV)⟩ **2** *archaic* : to loosen or lay aside by or as if by undoing a belt ⟨*ungirt* and cast off that cloak —John Jackson⟩ ⟨~ thy strangeness, and tell me —Shak.⟩

un·girdled \"+\ *adj* [¹*un-* + *girdled*, past part. of *girdle*] : not girdled

un·girt \"+\ *adj* [ME *ungyrt*; partly fr. past part. of *ungyrden* to ungird; partly fr. ¹*un-* + *gyrt*, past part. of *gyrden*, *girden* to gird] **1** : wearing no belt or girdle or wearing one that is not snugly fastened ⟨wandering through the woods . . . ~, unsandaled —P.B.Shelley⟩ **2** : lacking in discipline or compactness : LOOSE, SLACK ⟨did not run on in ~ dithyrambs . . . but worked quietly with her finely chosen materials —Carl Van Doren⟩

un·girth \"+\ *vt* [²*un-* + *girth*] *archaic* : to release by undoing a girth ⟨~*ing* his saddle —Henry Brooke⟩

un·give \"+\ *vi* [²*un-* + *give*] *dial Brit* : to lose rigidity : become pliable : MELT

un·given \"+\ *adj* : not given ⟨a person not ~ to words —John Mason Brown⟩

un·giving \"+\ *adj* [¹*un-* + *giving*, pres. part. of *give*] **1** : exhibiting parsimony : FRUGAL, STINGY ⟨stingy, ~ people —Vance Packard⟩ **2** : characterized by rigidity : ADAMANT, INFLEXIBLE ⟨if the mother is a cold, ~, stern and disciplinary one —Carl Binger⟩

un·glaciated \¦ən+\ *adj* [¹*un-* + *glaciated*, past part. of *glaciate*] : not glaciated

un·glad \"+\ *adj* [ME, fr. OE *unglæd*, fr. ¹*un-* + *glæd* glad] : not glad

un·glamorous \"+\ *adj* : lacking romantic appeal : COMMONPLACE, HUMDRUM ⟨~ jobs . . . greasing engines, operating turntables, wielding a shovel —*advt*⟩ ⟨a relatively small and ~ settlement —R.L.Beals⟩ — **un·glamorously** \"+\ *adv*

un·glazed \"+\ *adj* : not glazed: as **a** : lacking a vitreous finish ⟨~ pottery⟩ **b** *of paper* : having a smooth machine finish : not calendered **c** : not furnished with glass ⟨~ openings . . . to admit as much light and air as possible —*Materials Handling in the Wool Industry*⟩

un·glorified \"+\ *adj* [ME, fr. ¹*un-* + *glorified*, past part. of *glorifien* to glorify] : not glorified

un·glorious \"+\ adj [ME, fr. ¹un- + glorious] archaic : INGLORIOUS

un·glossed \"+\ adj [¹un- + glossed, past part. of gloss] : not glossed

un·glove \,ən+\ vt [ME ungloven, fr. ²un- + glove, n.] : to uncover by or as if by removing a glove ⟨her hand . . . when ungloved, glitters with heavy rings —Israel Zangwill⟩ ⟨Soviet Russia ungloved its winged fist —Time⟩

un·glue \"+\ vt [²un- + glue] : to disjoin by or as if by dissolving an adhesive ⟨~ a stamp from an envelope by steaming⟩ ⟨~ children from a TV set⟩

un·gna·dia \,ən'nādēə, ,əŋgə'nā-\ n, cap [NL, fr. Baron David von Ungnad 16th cent. Austrian diplomat + NL -ia] : a monotypic genus of shrubs or small trees (family Sapindaceae) comprising the buckeyes of southwestern No. America and distinguished by shining dark green leaves, rose-colored flowers, and poisonous black seeds

un·god \,ən+\ vt [²un- + god] archaic : to strip of divinity ⟨men cannot come to pull God out of his throne, and ~ him —William Gurnall⟩

un·goddess \"+\ vt [²un- + goddess, n.] archaic : to deprive of the status of a goddess

un·godlike \"+\ adj : not godlike

un·godlily \"+\ adv [ungodly + -ly] : in an ungodly manner

un·godliness \"+\ n [ungodly + -ness] : the quality or state of being ungodly : WICKEDNESS

¹un·godly \"+\ adj 1 a : denying God or disobedient to him : IMPIOUS, IRRELIGIOUS b : contrary to moral law or Christian precepts : SINFUL, WICKED 2 a : offensive to civilized taste : INDECENT b : OUTRAGEOUS ⟨do you expect me to get up at that ~ hour —Zane Grey⟩ ⟨stir up an ~ scandal —W.H. Wright⟩

²ungodly \"\ adv, dial : EXTREMELY ⟨I was ~ proud —Saul Bellow⟩

ungored adj [¹un- + gored, past part. of gore] obs : unwounded by or as if by stabbing ⟨keep my name ungor'd —Shak.⟩

un·gotten or **un·got** \,ən+\ adj [ME, fr. ¹un- + gotten or got, past part. of getten to get] 1 obs : not begotten 2 : not gathered or obtained

un·governable \"+\ adj : not capable of being governed, ruled, or restrained : UNBRIDLED ⟨make France nearly ~ —D.W.Brogan⟩ ⟨a harsh and ~ temper⟩ **syn** see UNRULY

un·governableness \,ən+\ n : the quality or state of being ungovernable ⟨the ~ of youth⟩

un·gov·er·na·bly \¦=;===blē, -bli\ adv : in an ungovernable manner ⟨made him ~ ferocious —T.B.Macaulay⟩

un·governed \"+\ adj [¹un- + governed, past part. of govern] : not subjected to regulation or control : UNRESTRAINED, WILD ⟨~ trade⟩ ⟨~ youth⟩ ⟨~ rage⟩

un·gowned \"+\ adj [¹un- + gowned, past part. of gown] : not gowned

un·grace \"+\ n [ME, fr. ¹un- + grace] : lack of grace

un·graced \"+\ adj [¹un- + grace, n. + -ed] : lacking in beauty or distinction : GRACELESS ⟨thatched cottages overrun by ~ building —Manchester Guardian Weekly⟩

un·graceful \,ən+\ adj : lacking in charm or felicity : AWKWARD, INELEGANT ⟨his stature low . . . his bearing ~ —Sir Walter Scott⟩ ⟨his concessions were ~ —S.E.Morison & H.S. Commager⟩ — **un·gracefully** \"+\ adv

un·gracefulness \"+\ n : the quality or state of being ungraceful

un·gracious \"+\ adj [ME, fr. ¹un- + gracious] 1 archaic : lacking in spiritual grace : PROFANE, WICKED ⟨take heed of . . . converse with lewd, profane and ~ company —Joseph Mede⟩ 2 a obs : exhibiting bad breeding : BOORISH, CRUDE ⟨~ wretch, fit for the mountains . . . where manners ne'er were preached —Shak.⟩ b : showing bad taste or lack of courtesy : SURLY ⟨it seems ~ to insist upon the futility of so much earnest . . . effort, prompted by motives which are so splendid —Norman Angell⟩ ⟨this curt summary is not meant to be ~ —B.R. Redman⟩ 3 a : lacking in attraction : UNCONGENIAL ⟨urban life tends to put an ~ stamp upon the human face —Irwin Shaw⟩ b : DISAGREEABLE, THANKLESS ⟨it would be an ~ task to catalog them —M.R.Cohen⟩ **syn** see RUDE

un·graciously \"+\ adv [ME, fr. ungracious + -ly] : in an ungracious manner

un·graciousness \"+\ n : the quality or state of being ungracious

un·graded \"+\ adj [¹un- + graded, past part. of grade] 1 : not leveled or reduced to a gradual slope or gradient ⟨~ road⟩ 2 a : not classified according to grades ⟨~ material⟩ ⟨~ jobs⟩ b : not assigned to a specific grade ⟨~ teacher⟩

ungraded school n : a usu. rural one-room elementary school with one teacher in which pupils are not classified by grades

un·graduated \,ən+\ adj : not graduated

un·grafted \"+\ adj [¹un- + grafted, past part. of graft] : not grafted

un·grammatical also **un·grammatic** \"+\ adj 1 : not following rules of grammar ⟨the colloquial and ~ Latin he spoke —Gilbert Highet⟩ 2 a : INCORRECT 5 b : SUBSTANDARD b 3 : varying from established practice ⟨~ oppositions of tonality —W.H.Mellers⟩ — **un·grammatically** \"+\ adv

un·granted \"\ adj [¹un- + granted, past part. of grant] : not granted

ungranted land n : PUBLIC LAND

un·graspable \"+\ adj [¹un- + grasp, v. + -able] : incapable of being seized or comprehended ⟨of all the eluding and ~ objects that ever I tried to get mind or hands on —Mark Twain⟩

un·grasped \"+\ adj [¹un- + grasped, past part. of grasp] : not fully apprehended ⟨the ~ infinite ground of all being —Philip Wheelwright⟩

un·grateful \,ən+\ adj [¹un- + grateful] 1 a : showing no gratitude : THANKLESS ⟨an ~ child refusing help to his aging parents⟩ b : appearing to lack appreciation ⟨few composers being professional conductors, the unfortunate guest is likely to give a pretty ~ . . . performance —Deems Taylor⟩ c archaic : failing to respond to cultivation : LISTLESS ⟨where vegetation is found at all, it is more ~ than . . . blankness —Herman Melville⟩ 2 a : of a disagreeable nature : DISTASTEFUL ⟨the work of security boards is an ~ task at best —Sidney Hook⟩ b : offensive to the senses : HARSH, REPELLENT ⟨unidiomatic instrumental writing and ~ chord dispositions —Virgil Thomson⟩ ⟨the reeds . . . sent forth an ~ stench —Jonas Hanway⟩ — **un·gratefully** \"+\ adv

un·gratefulness \"+\ n : the quality or state of being ungrateful

un·gratified \"+\ adj [¹un- + gratified, past part. of gratify] : not satisfied : DISCONTENTED, RESTLESS

un·grave \"+\ vt [²un- + grave, n.] : to dig up : DISINTER

un·graven \,ən+\ adj [ME, fr. ¹un- + graven, past part. of graven to grave, engrave] archaic : not engraved

un·greased \"+\ adj [ME ungrecyd, fr. ¹un- + grecyd, past part. of grecen, gresen to grease] : not greased

un·greeted \"+\ adj [¹un- + greeted, past part. of greet] : not greeted

un·gregarious \"+\ adj : not gregarious

un·groomed \"+\ adj [¹un- + groomed, past part. of groom] : not groomed

un·ground \"\ adj [ME ungrond, fr. ¹un- + grond, past part. of grinden to grind] : not ground

un·grounded \"+\ adj [ME, fr. ¹un- + grounded, past part. of grounden to ground] 1 a : lacking a solid foundation : BASELESS b : lacking basic information : UNINSTRUCTED 2 : not connected electrically with the ground

un·grown \"+\ adj : not grown

un·grudged \"+\ adj [¹un- + grudged, past part. of grudge] : not grudged

un·grudging \"+\ adj : being without envy or reluctance : GENEROUS, WHOLEHEARTED ⟨~ admiration⟩ ⟨~ hospitality⟩ — **un·grudgingly** \"+\ adv

¹un·gual \'əŋgwəl, 'əŋ-\ also **un·gui·nal** \-wənᵊl\ adj [ungual fr. L unguis nail, claw, hoof + E -al; unguinal, irreg. (influenced by L unguin-, unguen ointment, fr. unguere to anoint) fr. L unguis + E -al — more at NAIL, OINTMENT] : of, relating to, or resembling a nail, claw, or hoof

²ungual \"\ n -s : NAIL, HOOF, CLAW

un·guaranteed \,ən+\ adj [¹un- + guaranteed, past part. of guarantee] : not guaranteed

un·guard \"+\ vt [back-formation fr. unguarded] : to expose to attack : leave unprotected

un·guarded \"+\ adj [¹un- + guarded] 1 a : unprotected by a guard : vulnerable to attack ⟨an ~ gate⟩; specif : not protected by another piece or card ⟨an ~ queen⟩ b : not having a protective shield or barrier ⟨an ~ precipice⟩ 2 a : free from guile or wariness : DIRECT, INCAUTIOUS ⟨their ~, childish gaze —New Yorker⟩ b : marked by lack of caution : having the guard down ⟨in an ~ moment spilled the beans⟩ c : not disguised : OPEN, REVEALING ⟨every indiscreet and ~ expression of yours —Earl of Chesterfield⟩ — **un·guardedly** \"+\ adv

un·guent \'əŋgwənt, 'əngwə-, ÷'ənjə- sometimes ÷'əŋgənt or ÷'əngə-\ n -s [ME, fr. L unguentum — more at OINTMENT] : a lubricant or salve (as for sores or burns) : CERATE, OINTMENT

un·guen·tar·i·um \,əŋgwən'ta(a)rēəm, ,əngwə-, ÷,ənjə- sometimes ÷,əŋgə- or ÷,əngə-\ n, pl **unguentaria** [L unguentarium (vas), fr. neut. of unguentarius of or relating to ointment, fr. unguentum ointment + -arius -ary] : an ancient Greek or Roman glass jar to hold unguents

un·guerdoned \¦ən+\ adj [ME unguerdonned, fr. ¹un- + guerdonned, past part. of guerdonnen, gerdonen to guerdon] : not guerdoned

un·guessable \"+\ adj [¹un- + guess, v. + -able] : incapable of being guessed ⟨the angler forever bets . . . against unknowable odds for ~ returns —Philip Wylie⟩

un·guessed \"+\ adj [ME ungessid, fr. ¹un- + gessid, past part. of gessen to guess] 1 : lying beyond conjecture : MYSTERIOUS, UNIMAGINABLE 2 : not taken into consideration : UNFORESEEN, UNSUSPECTED

ungui- comb form [L unguis nail, claw, hoof — more at NAIL] : nail : claw

un·guic·u·la·ta \,əŋ,gwikyə'lād·ə, ,ən,g-, -lād·ə\ n pl, cap [NL, fr. neut. pl. of unguiculatus unguiculate] in former classifications : a major division of Mammalia comprising mammals with nails or claws as distinguished from hoofed mammals and cetaceans — compare UNGULATA

¹un·guic·u·late \¦=¦=kyəlᵊt, -,lāt\ also **un·guic·u·lat·ed** \-,lād·əd\ adj [unguiculate fr. NL unguiculatus, fr. L unguiculus fingernail (fr. L unguis + -culus -cle) + -atus -ate; unguiculated fr. NL unguiculatus + E -ed] 1 a : having nails or claws b : of or relating to the Unguiculata 2 : tapering below into a claw or a stalklike base ⟨an ~ petal⟩

²unguiculate \"\ n -s [NL Unguiculata] : a mammal of the division Unguiculata

un·guided \,ən+\ adj : not guided: as a : lacking one to show the way ⟨~ tour⟩ b : lacking leadership or control ⟨~ days and rotten times —Shak.⟩ c : not subject to guidance after launching ⟨~ missile⟩

un·guif·er·ate \,əŋ¦gwifərᵊt, ,ən¦g-\ adj [ungui- + -fer + -ate] : having nails, claws, or hooklike processes

un·guiltily \,ən+\ adv [unguilty + -ly] : INNOCENTLY

un·guilty \"+\ adj [ME ungilty, fr. OE ungyltig, fr. ¹un- + gyltig guilty — more at GUILTY] : not guilty : INNOCENT

un·gui·rostral \,əŋgwə, 'əŋ-+\ adj [ungui- + rostral] : having a horny nail at the end of the bill ⟨~ duck⟩

un·guis \'əŋgwəs, 'əŋ-\ n, pl **ungues** [L — more at NAIL] 1 a : a nail, claw, or hoof on a digit of a vertebrate b : one of the tarsal claws or terminal chitinous hooks on the foot of an insect c : the hard chitinous hook through which the poison gland opens on the chelicera of a spider 2 : a narrow pointed base of a petal

un·gui·trac·tor \-wə,traktə(r)\ n -s [ungui- + retractor] : a sclerite of the insect pretarsus that is partially invaginated within the tarsus

un·gu·la \'əŋgyələ\ n, pl **ungu·lae** \-,lē\ [L, dim. of unguis] : UNGUAL — **un·gu·lar** \-lə(r)\ adj

un·gu·la·ta \,==lād·ə, -'lād·ə\ n pl, cap [NL, fr. neut. pl. of LL ungulatus ungulate] in former classifications : a major division of Mammalia comprising hoofed mammals as distinguished from cetaceans and those with nails or claws — compare UNGUICULATA

¹un·gu·late \'əŋgyəlᵊt, -,lāt\ also **un·gu·lat·ed** \-,lād·əd\ adj [ungulate fr. LL ungulatus, fr. L ungula + -atus -ate; ungulated fr. LL ungulatus + E -ed] 1 : having hoofs 2 : of or relating to the Ungulata

²ungulate \"\ n -s [NL Ungulata] : a mammal of the division Ungulata

un·guled \'əŋ,g(y)üld, -g(y)əld\ adj [L ungula + E -ed] : having hoofs or claws of a heraldic tincture different from that of the body

un·gu·li·grade \'əŋgyələ,grād, 'əŋ-\ adj [L ungula + E -i- + -grade] : walking on hoofs

un·gum \,ən'gəm\ vt [²un- + gum] 1 : UNGLUE 2 : DEGUM

un·gummed \-md\ adj [¹un- + gummed, past part. of gum] : devoid of adhesive

un·gutted \,ən+\ adj [¹un- + gutted, past part. of gut] : not gutted

un·gyved \"+\ adj [¹un- + gyved, past part. of gyve] : not gyved : UNFETTERED

un·habitable \"+\ adj [ME, fr. ¹un- + habitable] : not habitable

un·habitual \,ən(h)ə-\ adj : not habitual

un·habituated \,ən(h)ə-\ adj [¹un- + habituated, past part. of habituate] : UNACCUSTOMED

un·hackneyed \,ən+\ adj [¹un- + hackneyed] 1 archaic : lacking knowledge or proficiency : GREEN, INEXPERIENCED ⟨a man ~ and unpracticed in the world —Laurence Sterne⟩ 2 : being out of the ordinary : FRESH, ORIGINAL ⟨children have such an ~ way of looking at their world —Alice Dalgliesh⟩

un·hailed \"+\ adj [¹un- + hailed, past part. of hail] : not hailed

un·hair \"+\ vb [ME unheeren, fr. ²un- + heer hair] vt 1 archaic : to deprive of hair : make bald ⟨I'll ~ thy head —Shak.⟩ 2 : DEHAIR; specif : to remove (guard hairs) from pelts used for garments by hand or machine to improve appearance of the fur ~ vi : to become dehaired

un·hair·er \,ən'ha(a)rə(r), -he|\ n -s [unhair + -er] : a workman who unhairs hides or skins

un·hair·ing \|riŋ, |rēŋ\ n -s [fr. gerund of unhair] : an act or process of removing hair; esp : depilation of skins or hides

unhairing machine n : a machine for removing hair from hides and skins preparatory to tanning

un·hallow \,ən+\ vt [²un- + hallow] archaic : to make profane ⟨nothing more ~s a man . . . than a habit of wrath —John Milton⟩

un·hallowed \"+\ adj [ME unhalewed, fr. OE unhālgod, fr. ¹un- + halgod, past part. of hālgian to hallow — more at HALLOW] 1 : not blessed : UNCONSECRATED ⟨buried in ~ ground⟩ 2 a : unsanctioned by or showing lack of reverence for religion : IMPIOUS, PROFANE ⟨bow before the idol, and taste the ~ ecstasy —L.P.Smith⟩ b : suited for or inhabited by devils : FIENDISH 3 a : contrary to law or accepted social standards : ILLEGITIMATE ⟨~ relations between men and women —Anne D. Sedgwick⟩ b : used for immoral purposes ⟨wrecked health and ~ hotel rooms —Chad Walsh⟩

un·halted \"+\ adj [¹un- + halted, past part. of halt] : not halted

un·halved \"+\ adj [¹un- + halved, past part. of halve] : not played in the same number of strokes as one's opponent at golf ⟨~ holes⟩

un·hammered \"+\ adj : not hammered

un·hampered \"+\ adj [¹un- + hampered, past part. of hamper] 1 a : not held in check : LIBERATED, LOOSED ⟨outlet for healthy and ~ action —B.N.Cardozo⟩ b : not impeded by external influences ⟨~ by tradition⟩ ⟨the priest was ~ by scruple —V.L.Parrington⟩ ⟨bridle paths, ~ by thoroughfares —Amer. Guide Series: Texas⟩ 2 : not subjected to control and esp. to government control : FREE, UNRESTRICTED ⟨~ dissemination of any news a reporter can smell out —Alistair Cooke⟩ 3 : not obstructed : CLEAR ⟨had an ~ view over the whole town —A.V.Borosini⟩

un·hand \,ən+\ vt [²un- + hand, n.] : to remove the hand from : let go

un·handily \"+\ adv : in an unhandy manner

un·handiness \"+\ n : the quality or state of being unhandy

un·handled \"+\ adj [¹un- + handled, past part. of handle] : not tamed or disciplined : WILD ⟨youthful and ~ colts —Shak.⟩

un·handsome \"+\ adj 1 a : lacking in external beauty or refinement : HOMELY, INELEGANT ⟨her portrait . . . is very pretty or at least not ~ —Robert Lynd⟩ b obs : AWKWARD, CLUMSY 2 : not gratifying : DISAGREEABLE, UNPLEASANT ⟨the ~ business of losing money —U.S.Investor⟩ 3 : deficient in courtesy or taste : IMPOLITE, RUDE ⟨~ language or behavior⟩ — **un·handsomely** \"+\ adv

un·handsomeness \"+\ n : the quality or state of being unhandsome

un·handy \,ən+\ adj 1 : hard to handle : UNWIELDY ⟨an ~, sprit-rigged, shallow-draft sloop —Vincent McHugh⟩ 2 : lacking in skill or dexterity : AWKWARD, INCOMPETENT ⟨a clumsy dissector . . . and ~ at most of the practical work —H.G. Wells⟩ ⟨have not shown themselves ~ in foreseeing trouble, and checking it —Contemporary Rev.⟩

un·hang \"+\ vt [ME unhangen, fr. ²un- + hangen to hang] : to detach from a hanging support ⟨~ a mirror from the wall⟩

un·hanged \"+\ adj [ME, fr. ¹un- + hanged, past part. of hangen to hang] : not executed by hanging ⟨there lives not three good men ~ in England —Shak.⟩

un·happily \"+\ adv [ME, fr. unhappy + -ly] : in an unhappy manner : LAMENTABLY, UNFORTUNATELY

un·happiness \"+\ n [ME unhappynes, fr. unhappy + -nes -ness] : the quality or state of being unhappy : MISERY, SADNESS

un·happy \"+\ adj [ME, fr. unhap misfortune, trouble (fr. ¹un- + hap) + -y] 1 archaic : OBSTREPEROUS, TROUBLESOME ⟨these ~ Highland clans are again breaking into general commotion —Sir Walter Scott⟩ 2 a : being out of luck : MISERABLE, UNFORTUNATE ⟨~ caravans, straggling afoot through swamps and canebrakes —Amer. Guide Series: Ark.⟩ b : causing or subject to disaster : INAUSPICIOUS, ILL-STARRED ⟨a particularly ~ moment for a scandal to blow up —Green Peyton⟩ ⟨in a few ~ regions the people swim to work in . . . record precipitation —T.H.Fielding⟩ c : full of misery : WRETCHED ⟨people may play with impunity at any game in this ~ world except . . . Life, Love, and Death —Lafcadio Hearn⟩ 3 : lacking in skill or felicity : AWKWARD, INEPT ⟨~ references to "unsystematic systems" —S.E.Martin⟩ ⟨two fine singers a little ~ in the French language —Edward Sackville-West & Desmond Shawe-Taylor⟩ 4 a : dejected in spirit : MELANCHOLY, SAD ⟨was ~ when alone, always craved a public —M.R.Cohen⟩ b : mentally disquieted : DISTURBED, DISSATISFIED ⟨~ . . . with the outcome of our China policy —W.W.Kaufmann⟩ ⟨if you're ~ without statistics —Richard Joseph⟩ c : causing dejection or discontent : DISCOURAGING ⟨the ~ history of eleven months of truce talks shows that every difficulty solved begets a difficulty to be solved —Time⟩ 5 a : of an unpleasant nature : DISAGREEABLE, DISTRESSING ⟨nagging has been defined as the constant reiteration of the ~ truth —English Digest⟩ ⟨the whole ~ problem of school integration —Newsweek⟩ b : of a depressing character : CHEERLESS, DREARY ⟨an ~ view of twisted antennae and grimy rooftops⟩

un·harbor \,ən+\ vt [²un- + harbor] Brit : to drive (an animal) from cover

un·harden \"+\ vt [²un- + harden] : to make soft : DISARM, MELT ⟨sang in a manner . . . to ~ the most critical heart —Musical Digest⟩

un·hardened \"+\ adj [¹un- + hardened] : not hardened

un·hardy \"+\ adj [ME, fr. ¹un- + hardy] : not hardy

un·harmed \"+\ adj [ME, fr. ¹un- + harmed, past part. of harmen to harm] : not harmed : SAFE, UNSCATHED

un·harmful \"+\ adj : not harmful — **un·harmfully** \"+\ adv

un·harming \"+\ adj [¹un- + harming, pres. part. of harm] : doing no injury

un·harmonious \"+\ adj : INHARMONIOUS — **un·harmoniously** \"+\ adv

un·harness \,ən+\ vt [ME onharnesen, fr. on- ²un- + harnesen, harneisen to harness] : to divest of harness ⟨~ a horse⟩

un·harnessed \"+\ adj : not harnessed; esp : not utilized ⟨seething with ~ energy —Henry Miller⟩

un·harried \"+\ adj : not harried

un·harrowed \"+\ adj [¹un- + harrowed, past part. of harrow] : not harrowed

un·harvested \"+\ adj [¹un- + harvested, past part. of harvest] : not harvested

un·hasp \"+\ vt [ME unhaspen, fr. ²un- + haspen to hasp] archaic : to unfasten the hasp of : OPEN ⟨endeavored to ~ the casement —Emily Brontë⟩

un·hasting \"+\ adj [¹un- + hasting, pres. part. of haste] : DELIBERATE, UNHURRIED

un·hasty \"+\ adj : LEISURELY, SLOW

un·hat \"+\ vi [²un- + hat, n.] archaic : to doff the hat as a mark of respect

un·hatched \"+\ adj [¹un- + hatched, past part. of hatch] 1 : not hatched from or as if from the egg ⟨an ~ chick⟩ ⟨an ~ plot⟩ 2 : not fully incubated ⟨an ~ egg⟩

un·hatted \"+\ adj : not wearing a hat

un·haunted \,ən+\ adj [¹un- + haunted, past part. of haunt] 1 : not inhabited : UNFREQUENTED ⟨a region . . . ~ by birds —Alfred Sutro⟩ 2 : not disturbed : UNTROUBLED ⟨~ by any pang —W.D.Howells⟩

un·hazarded \"+\ adj [¹un- + hazarded, past part. of hazard] archaic : not hazarded : UNTRIED

un·hazardous \"+\ adj : not dangerous

un·head \"+\ vt [ME unhevden, fr. ²un- + heved head, n. — more at HEAD] archaic : to separate the head or top from

un·healable \,ən+\ adj [ME unheleable, fr. ¹un- + helen to heal + -able] : incapable of being healed

un·healed \"+\ adj [ME unheled fr. ¹un- + heled, past part. of helen to heal] : not healed

un·health \"+\ n [ME unhelthe, fr. OE unhǣlth, fr. ¹un- + hǣlth health] : lack of health or vigor : ILLNESS, INFIRMITY

un·healthful \"+\ adj [¹un- + healthful] 1 obs : UNHEALTHY 2 : detrimental to good health : UNWHOLESOME

un·healthfulness \"+\ n : the quality or state of being unhealthful

un·healthily \"+\ adv : in an unhealthy manner

un·healthiness \"+\ n : the quality or state of being unhealthy

un·healthy \"+\ adj [¹un- + healthy] 1 : UNHEALTHFUL 2 ⟨an ~ climate⟩ 2 a : not in good health : SICKLY, WEAK b : evincing abnormality : DISEASED, MORBID ⟨~ wounds and ulcers —Robert Chawner⟩ ⟨register . . . unhappiness, the boy with nightmares, the girl with ~ greed —Caroline H. Tunstall⟩ 3 a : of a dangerous nature : RISKY, UNSOUND ⟨dropping depth charges at six knots is ~ for the boat that does it —Alexander Forbes⟩ ⟨it would be ~ . . . to criticize the regime —Atlantic⟩ ⟨on the lookout for ~ speculative developments —C.E.Egan⟩ b : of a harmful nature : BAD, INJURIOUS ⟨had an ~ habit . . . of borrowing money —R.W.Thorp⟩ ⟨produce inflation, or other ~ results —Internat'l Bank for Reconstruction & Development Report⟩ c : morally contaminated : CORRUPT, DEPRAVED ⟨an ~ alliance between thugs and politicians⟩

un·heard \,ən+\ adj [ME unherd, fr. ¹un- + herd, past part. of heren to hear] 1 a : not perceived by the ear b : not given a hearing 2 archaic : UNHEARD-OF

un·heard-of \,=¹=,=\ adj [¹un- + heard of, past part. form of the phrase hear of, fr. ¹hear + of] : previously unknown : NEW, UNPRECEDENTED ⟨a first novel by an unheard-of writer⟩ ⟨amphibious operations . . . would soon be necessary on an unheard-of scale —J.P.Baxter b. 1893⟩

un·hearing \,ən+\ adj [¹un- + hearing, pres. part. of hear] : not hearing

un·heartsome \"+\ adj, chiefly Scot : CHEERLESS, SAD

un·heated \"+\ adj : not heated

un·heaven \"+\ vt [²un- + heaven, n.] archaic : to separate from heaven

un·heavenly \"+\ adj : not heavenly : GROSS, SINFUL

un·hedged \"+\ adj [¹un- + hedged, past part. of hedge] : not hedged : UNPROTECTED, UNQUALIFIED

un·heeded \"+\ adj [¹un- + heeded, past part. of heed] : not heeded : DISREGARDED, IGNORED — **un·heed·ed·ly** adv

un·heedful \"+\ adj, archaic : not attentive : CARELESS, NEGLIGENT

un·heeding \,ən+\ adv (or adj) [¹un- + heeding, pres. part. of heed] : in an inattentive manner : ABSENTLY, UNOBSERVANTLY ⟨so sunk was he in . . . abstraction that he walked ~ by a large circle of people —Herman Wouk⟩ — **un·heed·ing·ly** adv

unheedy adj [¹un- + obs. E heedy attentive, careful, fr. E heed + -y] obs : HEEDLESS

un·hele \ˌən'hē(ə)l\ *vt* [ME *unhelen*, fr. OE *unhelian*, fr. ²*un-* + *helan*, *helian* to conceal — more at HELL] **1** *obs* : UNCOVER, REVEAL **2** *dial* : to strip of thatch
un·helm \ˌən+\ *vt* [ME *unhelmen*, fr. ²*un-* + *helmen* to helm] *archaic* : to divest of a helmet ⟨~*ed* themselves to quench their thirst —G.A.Lawrence⟩
un·helped \"+\ *adj* [ME, fr. ¹*un-* + *helped*, past part. of *helpen* to help] : not helped : UNAIDED
un·helpful \"+\ *adj* : not helpful : offering no assistance : USELESS, UNCOOPERATIVE ⟨a curiously ~ manual —Robertson Davies⟩ ⟨icily neutral, disagreeably ~ —H.H.Johnston⟩ — **un·helpfully** \"+\ *adv*
un·helping \"+\ *adj*, *archaic* : UNHELPFUL
un·hemmed \"+\ *adj* [ME, fr. ¹*un-* + *hemmed*, past part. of *hemmen* to hem] : not hemmed
un·heralded \ˌən+\ *adj* [¹*un-* + *heralded*, past part. of *herald*] **1** : not publicly acclaimed : ANONYMOUS, UNRECOGNIZED ⟨~ in his large charities —D.S.Muzzey⟩ ⟨a new and ~ talent —Eric Newton⟩ **2** : UNEXPECTED, UNFORESEEN ⟨a totally ~ telegram that his daughter . . . died last night —M.A.D.Howe⟩
un·heroic *also* **un·heroical** \"+\ *adj* : not heroic : TIMID, UNIMPRESSIVE ⟨~ policy of nonintervention —H.S.Commager⟩ ⟨the gasoline drums were heavy, ~, yet dangerous to handle —K.M.Dodson⟩ — **un·heroically** \"+\ *adv*
un·hesitant \"+\ *adj* : not hesitant : IMMEDIATE, FORTHRIGHT
un·hesitating \"+\ *adj* [¹*un-* + *hesitating*, pres. part. of *hesitate*] : not curbed or qualified : FREE, WHOLEHEARTED — **un·hesitatingly** \"+\ *adv*
un·hewn \ˌən+\ *adj* : not given a finished form by or as if by hewing : ROUGH, UNPOLISHED ⟨houses . . . of ~ gray stone roughly cemented together —Martha Kean⟩ ⟨a rough, ~ soldier —Susanna Centlivre⟩
un·hidden \"+\ *adj* : not hidden
un·highlighted \"+\ *adj* [¹*un-* + *highlighted*, past part. of *highlight*] : not highlighted
un·hindered \"+\ *adj* [¹*un-* + *hindered*, past part. of *hinder*] : not hindered or restrained
un·hinge \"+\ *vt* [²*un-* + *hinge*] **1 a** : to remove (as a door) from the hinges **b** : to swing open or as if on hinges ⟨will not . . . ~ my jaws to speak again —A.J.Munby⟩ **2 a** : to interrupt the normal functioning of : DISRUPT, DISORDER ⟨dislocates a shoulder, ~s a joint —Lafcadio Hearn⟩; *specif* : DERANGE ⟨a shock so great as almost to ~ the mind —Bernard DeVoto⟩ **b** : to stir up or throw into turmoil : DISCOMPOSE, UPSET ⟨the obvious sarcasm *unhinged* his temper⟩ ⟨sudden excitement *unhinged* all precision —R.L.Shayon⟩ **c** : to make precarious or cause to waver : SWAY, UNSETTLE ⟨neither oratory, anticlericalism, nor last-minute attempts to capitalize on the threat of "Fascism" . . . could ~ the Italian voter —*Newsweek*⟩ ⟨supplies are coming in very irregularly and ~ the trade —*London Daily News*⟩ **3** : to split or break apart : CRACK, DISMEMBER ⟨smashed . . . where they threatened to ~ the entire Allied line —Milton Lehman⟩
un·hinged \ˌən'hinjd\ *adj* [in sense 1, fr. past part. of *unhinge*; in sense 2, fr. ¹*un-* + *hinged*, past part. of *hinge*] **1 a** : no longer joined by or as if by a hinge **b** : DERANGED, DISORGANIZED ⟨a belief . . . that the United Nations could keep the world from becoming *unhinged* in another war —Norman Cousins⟩ **2** *of a stamp* : never mounted or hinged
un·hinge·ment \ˌ=ˈ=mənt\ *n* -S [*unhinge* + *-ment*] : an act or instance of unhinging or state of being unhinged
un·hired \ˌən+\ *adj* [¹*un-* + *hired*, past part. of *hire*] : not hired
un·historical *also* **un·historic** \"+\ *adj* : not historical — **un·historically** \"+\ *adv*
un·hit \"+\ *adj* [¹*un-* + *hit*, past part. of *hit*] : not hit ⟨the bear lumbered off, ~, up the canyon to safety —*Time*⟩
un·hitch \"+\ *vt* [²*un-* + *hitch*] : to free from or as if from being hitched : UNFASTEN
un·hive \"+\ *vt* [²*un-* + *hive*] : to drive from or as if from a hive
un·holily \ˌən+\ *adv* : in an unholy manner
un·holiness \"+\ *n* : the quality or state of being unholy
un·hollowed \"+\ *adj* [¹*un-* + *hollowed*, past part. of *hollow*] : not hollowed
un·holpen \"+\ *adj* [ME, fr. ¹*un-* + *holpen*] *archaic* : UNHELPED
¹un·holy \"+\ *adj* [ME, fr. OE *unhālig*, fr. ¹*un-* + *hālig* holy — more at HOLY] **1** : irreligious or showing disregard for what is holy : PROFANE, WICKED ⟨souls ~ and unclean —John Wesley⟩ ⟨may excommunicate the heretical as well as the ~ —A.C. McGiffert⟩ **2 a** : violating accepted civil or social standards : CORRUPT, IMMORAL ⟨an ~ reputation for branding everything they could, regardless of ownership —*Amer. Guide Series: Ariz.*⟩ **b** : deserving of censure : DAMNING, REPREHENSIBLE ⟨add condescension to bad manners in a singularly ~ combination —*Geog. Jour.*⟩ ⟨an ~ alliance between public utility companies⟩ **3 a** : of a sinister character : FIENDISH, MALICIOUS ⟨delirium of grandeur is more dangerous still if the man is ready to live and to die . . . for his ~ dream —A.L.Guérard⟩ ⟨takes ~ joy . . . in telling off brutally his family of three —Parker Tyler⟩ **b** : shockingly big or barbarous : GOD-AWFUL, RAUCOUS ⟨rarely . . . has society been in such an ~ mess —*Nation*⟩ ⟨an ~ clatter as of ash and refuse cans being dragged across sidewalks —Charles Breasted⟩ ⟨every morning, at an ~ hour, I heard . . . an air-raid siren —*Sydney (Australia) Bull.*⟩
²unholy \"\ *n* : an impious or disreputable person
un·home \ˌən+\ *vt* [²*un-* + *home*] : to make homeless
un·homelike \"+\ *adj* : not homelike
un·homeliness \"+\ *n* [*unhomely* + *-ness*] : lack of intimacy or warmth : ALOOFNESS, FORMALITY
un·homely \"+\ *adj* : UNINVITING
un·homogeneity \"+\ *n* [*unhomogeneous* + *-ity*] : the quality or state of being inhomogeneous
un·homogeneous \"+\ *adj* : INHOMOGENEOUS
un·honest \"+\ *adj* [ME, fr. ¹*un-* + *honest*] : DISHONEST — **un·honestly** \"+\ *adv*
un·honesty \"+\ *n* [ME *unhoneste*, fr. ¹*un-* + *honeste* honesty] *archaic* : DISHONESTY
un·honored \"+\ *adj* : not honored
un·hood \"+\ *vt* [²*un-* + *hood*] : to remove a hood or covering from : EXPOSE
un·hooded \"+\ *adj* [in sense 1, fr. past part. of *unhood*; in sense 2, fr. ¹*un-* + *hooded*] **1** : divested of a hood **2** : not having a hood
un·hoodwinked \ˌən+\ *adj* [¹*un-* + *hoodwinked*, past part. of *hoodwink*] : not deceived
un·hook \"+\ *vt* [²*un-* + *hook*] **1** : to remove from a hook ⟨~*ing* a mug from the rack —Richard Llewellyn⟩ **2** : to unfasten by disengaging a hook ⟨~*ed* the collar of his uniform —*Irish Digest*⟩
un·hooked \"+\ *adj* [in sense 1, fr. ¹*un-* + *hooked*; in sense 2, fr. past part. of *unhook*] **1** : not hooked **2** : having the hooks unfastened
un·hoped \ˌən+\ *adj* [ME, fr. ¹*un-* + *hoped*, past part. of *hopen* to hope] *archaic* : UNHOPED-FOR
un·hoped-for \ˌ=ˈ=,=\ *adj* [¹*un-* + *hoped-for*, past part. form of the phrase *hope for*, fr. ¹*hope* + *for*] : not anticipated : UNEXPECTED ⟨an *unhoped-for* piece of luck⟩
un·hopeful \ˌən+\ *adj* [ME, fr. ¹*un-* + *hope*, n. + *-ful*] : not hopeful — **un·hopefully** \"+\ *adv*
un·hoping \"+\ *adj* [¹*un-* + *hoping*, pres. part. of *hope*] : DESPAIRING, HOPELESS
un·hopped \"+\ *adj* : made without hops ⟨~ beer worts⟩
un·horned \"+\ *adj* : not horned
un·horse \"+\ *vt* [ME *unhorsen*, fr. ²*un-* + *horsen* to horse] **1** : to dislodge from or as if from a horse : put out of action : OVERTHROW, UNSEAT ⟨~ a rider⟩ ⟨Republicans are in a scramble . . . to try to ~ the state's Democratic senator —*N.Y. Times*⟩ ⟨reports of the maltreatment of the sick and wounded nearly *unhorsed* the . . . general staff —James Dugan⟩
unhorsing *n* -S [fr. gerund of *unhorse*] : an act or instance of overthrowing ⟨the definitive ~ of the militarists —*Commonweal*⟩
un·hospitable \ˌən+\ *adj* : INHOSPITABLE — **un·hospitably** \"+\ *adv*
un·hostile \"+\ *adj* : not hostile : AMICABLE, BENIGN
un·house \ˌən'hau̇z\ *vt* [ME *unhousen*, fr. ²*un-* + *housen* to house] : to eject from or deprive of a protective shelter ⟨thousands of refugees are still *unhoused*⟩ ⟨*unhoused* his bleating flock —Phineas Fletcher⟩
un·housed \-zd\ *adj* [¹*un-* + *housed*, past part. of *house*] : not housed
un·houseled \ˌən+\ *adj* [¹*un-* + *houseled*, past part. of *housel*] *archaic* : not having received the sacrament ⟨cut off even in the blossoms of my sin, ~, disappointed —Shak.⟩
un·hulled \"+\ *adj* [in sense 1, fr. ¹*un-* + *hull*, n. + *-ed*; in sense 2, fr. ¹*un-* + *hulled*, past part. of *hull*] **1** : not having a hull **2** : not having been hulled
un·human \"+\ *adj* : INHUMAN — **un·humanly** \"+\ *adv*
un·humanize \"+\ *vt* [²*un-* + *humanize*] : DEHUMANIZE
un·humble \"+\ *adj* : not humble
un·humbled \"+\ *adj* [¹*un-* + *humbled*, past part. of *humble*] : not humbled
un·humorous \"+\ *adj* : not funny or jocular : SERIOUS, SOBER — **un·humorously** \"+\ *adv*
un·hung \"+\ *adj* [¹*un-* + *hung*, past part. of *hang*] : not hung; *esp* : not executed by hanging
un·hunted \"+\ *adj* : not hunted
un·hurried \"+\ *adj* : not hurried : LEISURELY — **un·hurriedly** \"+\ *adv*
un·hurriedness \"+\ *n* : the quality or state of being unhurried : CALMNESS, PLACIDITY
un·hurt \"+\ *adj* [ME, fr. ¹*un-* + *hurt*] : not hurt or damaged : INTACT, UNINJURED
un·hurtful \"+\ *adj* [¹*un-* + *hurtful*] *archaic* : HARMLESS
un·hurting \"\ *adj* [¹*un-* + *hurting*] : not causing hurt : BENIGN, GENTLE ⟨smiled . . . in her ~ way —N.H.Matson⟩
un·hus·band·ed \ˌən'həzbəndəd\ *adj* [in sense 1, fr. ¹*un-* + *husbanded*, past part. of *husband*; in sense 2, fr. ¹*un-* + *husband*, n. + *-ed*] **1** : not tilled : UNCULTIVATED ⟨~ land⟩ **2** : not having a husband ⟨the ~ young lady . . . lives with her married sister —John Gould⟩
un·husk \ˌən+\ *vt* [²*un-* + *husk*] : to strip of or as if of a husk : EXPOSE, SHUCK
un·husked \ˌən'həskt\ *adj* [in sense 1, fr. past part. of *unhusk*; in sense 2, fr. ¹*un-* + *husked*] **1** *obs* : stripped of the husk **2** : still in the husk : not shucked
un·hygienic \ˌən+\ *adj* : not healthful or sanitary — **un·hygienically** \"+\ *adv*
un·hymned \"+\ *adj* [¹*un-* + *hymned*, past part. of *hymn*] : not hymned : UNSUNG
un·hyphenated \"+\ *adj* : not hyphenated
un·hysterical \"+\ *adj* : not hysterical — **un·hysterically** \"+\ *adv*
uni- *prefix* [ME, fr. MF, fr. L, fr. *unus* — more at ONE] : one : single ⟨*uni*axial⟩ ⟨*uni*cellular⟩ ⟨*uni*lateral⟩
uni·algal \ˌyünē+\ *adj* [*uni-* + *algal*] : of, relating to, or derived from a single algal individual or cell ⟨a ~ culture⟩
uni·ate \'yünēˌat, -ēət *also* -ēˌät\ *or* **uni·at** \-ēˌat, -ēət\ *n* -S *usu cap* [Russ *uniyat*, fr. Pol *uniat*, fr. *unja* union (of the Greek and Roman Catholic churches), fr. LL *unio* — more at UNION] : a Christian of an Eastern rite not belonging to the Latin patriarchate but in union with and submitting to the authority of the Roman papacy : one who belongs to an ecclesiastical body that accepts Roman Catholic doctrines in matters of faith but utilizes different forms of liturgy and discipline and is directly governed by a patriarch of its own
uni·at·ism \-əˌtizəm\ *n* -S *often cap* : the system of faith, practice, and ecclesiastical government of the Uniates or Uniate bodies
uni·axial \ˌyünē+\ *adj* [*uni-* + *axial*] **1** : having but one axis: as **a** : having but one optic axis or line of no double refraction ⟨~ crystals of calcite or quartz⟩ **b** : MONAXIAL **2** : of, relating to, or affecting but one axis ⟨~ stress⟩ — **uni·axially** \"+\ *adv*
uni·bi·va·lent \ˌyünə+, ˌyünəˌbivələnt\ *adj* [*uni-* + *bivalent*] : of, relating to, or being an electrolyte (as sodium carbonate Na_2CO_3) that dissociates into two univalent ions and one bivalent ion
unica *pl of* UNICUM
uni·cameral \ˌyünə+\ *adj* [*uni-* + *camera* + *-al*] : having a single chamber: as **a** : consisting of a single legislative chamber ⟨a ~ government⟩ **b** : UNILOCULAR ⟨a ~ fruiting body of a fungus⟩ — **uni·camerally** \"+\ *adv*
uni·cameralism \"+\ *n* : use or advocacy of a unicameral system in government
uni·capsula \ˌyünə+\ *n*, *cap* [NL, fr. *uni-* + *capsula*] : a genus of myxosporidian parasites — see WORMY HALIBUT
un·iced \ˌən+\ *adj* : not containing or chilled with ice : not specially cooled
uni·cell \'yünəˌsel\ *n* [*uni-* + *cell*] : a unicellular organism
¹uni·cellular \ˌyünə+\ *adj* [*uni-* + *cellular*] : having or consisting of a single cell — **uni·cellularity** \"+\ *n*
²unicellular \"\ *n* -S : a unicellular organism
unicellular animal *n* : PROTOZOAN
uni·cen·tric \ˌyünəˌsen·trik, -rēk\ *adj* [*uni-* + *-centric*] : having a single center (as of origin or dispersal) ⟨a ~ genus of plants⟩
uni·cist \'yünəsəst\ *n* -S [*unicity* + *-ist*] : an advocate or adherent of a theory of unicity
unic·i·ty \yü'nisədē, -sətē, -i\ *n* -ES [L *unicus* sole, single, unique + E *-ity* — more at UNIQUE] : the quality or state of being unique of its kind : ONENESS ⟨the question of the ~ of the distemper virus⟩ ⟨the ~ of each angelic form within its species —W.N.Clarke⟩
uni·color \ˌyünə+\ *or* **uni·colored** \"+\ *adj* [*uni-* + *color* or *colored*] : of a uniform color
uni·col·or·ous \ˌ=ˈ=kələrəs\ *adj* [*uni-* + *color* + *-ous*] : of one color throughout ⟨a ~ insect⟩
uni·consonantal \ˌyünə+\ *also* **uni·consonantic** \"+\ *adj* [*uni-* + *consonantal* or *consonantic*] : of or containing one consonant
uni·constant \"+\ *adj* [*uni-* + *constant*] : having, characterized by, or based on one constant ⟨a ~ theory of isotropy⟩
¹uni·corn \'yünəˌkȯrn\ *n* -S [ME *unicorne*, fr. OF, fr. LL *unicornis* (trans. of Gk *monokeros*), fr. L, adj., having one horn, fr. *uni-* + *cornu* horn — more at HORN] **1 a** (1) : a fabulous animal possibly based on faulty old descriptions of the rhinoceros and generally depicted (as in heraldry) with the body and head of a horse, the hind legs of a stag, the tail of a lion, and in the middle of the forehead a single long straight horn held to be a sovereign remedy against poisoning (2) : a representation of a unicorn **b** (1) *obs* : the one-horned rhinoceros (2) *or* **unicorn whale** : NARWHAL (3) : a normally bicorn mammal (as an ox) having the horn buds surgically altered to produce a single median horn **2** : a Scottish gold coin of the 15th and 16th centuries weighing 59 grains and having the figure of a unicorn on the obverse **3** *or* **unicorn horn** : material reputed to be the horn of the fabulous unicorn and formerly used for ornament, as an antidote, or as a talisman **4** : a team of three horses harnessed with one as leader to a pair; *also* : an equipage with such a team **5** *obs* : HOWITZER **6** : any of several plants (as a colicroot or blazing star) felt to resemble unicorn horn (as in form of root or reputed medical worth)

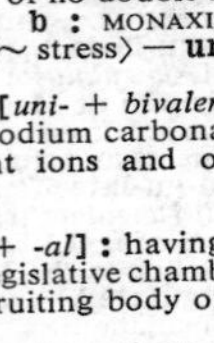
unicorn 1a(1)

²unicorn \"\ *adj* [L *unicornis*] : having a single horn or hornlike process ⟨a ~ uterus⟩
unicorn antelope *n* : TAKIN
unicorn beetle *n* : any of various large beetles (as some scarabaeids) having a hornlike prominence on the head or prothorax
unicorn bird *n* : HORNED SCREAMER
unicorn caterpillar *n* : a caterpillar that is the larva of a unicorn moth
unicorn fish *n* **1** : NARWHAL **2 a** : any of several surgeonfishes (genus *Teuthis*) of the Pacific ocean having a long bony hornlike projection extending forward from the skull above the eye **b** : any of various filefishes having a long dorsal spine
unicorn moth *n* : a moth (*Schizura unicornis*) of the family Notodontidae whose caterpillar has a horn on its back
unicorn plant *n* : a No. American annual herb (*Martynia louisianica*) having large whitish or yellowish flowers mottled with purple or yellow within and a capsule with a long curving beak
unicorn-plant family *n* : MARTYNIACEAE
unicorn root *n* **1** : COLICROOT 1 **2** : GRUBROOT **3** : SWAMP PINK 3
unicorn shell *n* : any of several marine snails of the division Rachiglossa (as members of the genus *Latirus*) having a prominent spine on the lip of the shell
unicorn's horn *n* **1** : UNICORN 3 **2** : UNICORN ROOT
uni·cum \'yünəkəm, -nēk-\ *n*, *pl* **uni·ca** \-kə\ [L, neut. of *unicus* sole, single, unique — more at UNIQUE] : a thing unique in its kind; *esp* : a sole existing exemplar (as of a writing)
uni·cur·sal \ˌyünəˈkərsəl\ *adj* [*uni-* + L *cursus* course + E *-al* — more at COURSE] *of an irreducible curve* : having coordinates expressible rationally through a single parameter — opposed to *bicursal*
uni·cuspid \ˌyünə+\ *also* **uni·cuspidate** \"+\ *adj* [*uni-* + *cuspid* or *cuspidate*] : having a single cusp ⟨canines and other ~ teeth⟩
uni·cy·cle \'yünəˌsīkəl\ *n* [*uni-* + *-cycle* (as in *tricycle*)] : any of various vehicles that have a single wheel, are used for personal transport, exercise, or haulage, and are propelled usu. by pedals or applied draft — **uni·cy·clist** \-klәst\ *n*

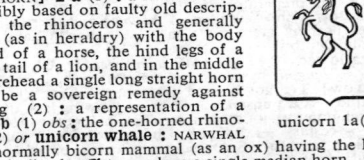

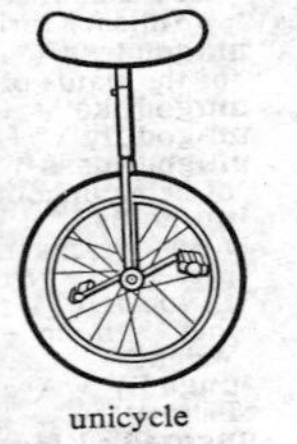
unicycle

un·ideaed \ˌən+\ *adj* [¹*un-* + *idea* + *-ed*] : lacking in originality of thought : deficient in ideas
un·ideal \"+\ *adj* : lacking ideals or ideal qualities : deficient in idealism
un·identifiable \"+\ *adj* : impossible to identify : so defective, damaged, or altered as to defy recognition
un·identified \"+\ *adj* [¹*un-* + *identified*, past part. of *identify*] : not identified though not necessarily unidentifiable
uni·dextral \ˌyünə+\ *adj* [*uni-* + *dextral*] : using one hand preferentially : exhibiting handedness either right or left — **uni·dextrality** \"+\ *n*
uni·dimensional \"+\ *adj* [*uni-* + *dimensional*] **1** : having a single dimension that is usu. construed as length **2** : having or dealing with a single aspect ⟨a prose statement of fact is ~, its value being measured wholly in terms of its truth —Mary Sheehan⟩ — **uni·dimensionality** \"+\ *n*
un·idiomatic \ˌən+\ *adj* : not conforming to established or accepted idiom — **un·idiomatically** \"+\ *adv*
uni·direct \ˌyünə+\ *vt* [back-formation fr. *unidirectional*] : to cause to go in a single direction : RECTIFY
uni·directional \"+\ *adj* [*uni-* + *directional*] : having, involving, moving, or responsive (as to sound) in a single direction : not subject to change or reversal of direction ⟨a ~ antenna⟩ ⟨a ~ approach to a problem⟩
unidirectional current *n* : DIRECT CURRENT
uni·directivity \"+\ *n* [*uni-* + *directivity*] : a property (as of a microphone, loudspeaker, or antenna) of operating more effectively in one direction than another
uni·face \"+\ *also* **uni·faced** \"+\ *adj* [*uni-* + *face*, n. or *faced*] : having a design on only one side ⟨~ coin⟩ ⟨~ medal⟩ ⟨~ bank note⟩
uni·facial \ˌyünə+\ *adj* [*uni-* + *facial*] : having but one principal or in some way specialized surface ⟨~ corals in which all the polyps are on one surface⟩ ⟨a primitive ~ flint tool flaked only on one face⟩ — **uni·facially** \"+\ *adv*
uni·factorial \"+\ *adj* [*uni-* + *factorial*] : relating to or controlled by a single gene
uni·fi·able \'yünəˌfīəbəl\ *adj* [*unify* + *-able*] : capable of being unified
unif·ic \yü'nifik\ *adj* [*uni-* + *-fic*] : tending to produce unity
uni·fi·ca·tion \ˌyünəfəˈkāshən\ *n* -S [fr. *unify*, after such pairs as E *identify*: *identification*] **1** : the act, process, or result of unifying : state of being unified **2** : the use of the same set of pipes for securing on the same organ manual two or more stops at different pitches
uni·fi·ca·tion·ist \-sh(ə)nəst\ *n* -S : an advocate or adherent of a scheme of unification and esp. one of political unification (as of separate or divided states)
unified *past of* UNIFY
unified command *n* : an armed force (as a task force containing army, navy, and air force units) of two or more services operating under a single commander
unified field theory *n* : a mathematical theory of fields developed by Einstein and involving Maxwell's electromagnetic theory and Einstein's mathematical theory of gravitation as special cases
uni·fi·er \'yünəˌfī(ə)r, -fīə\ *n* -S : one that unifies
unifies *pres 3d sing of* UNIFY
uni·filar \ˌyünə+\ *adj* [*uni-* + *filar*] : having or involving use of only one thread, wire, or fiber
uni·flagellate \"+\ *adj* [*uni-* + *flagellate*] : having a single flagellum
uni·flo·rous \ˌyünəˈflōrəs\ *also* **uni·floral** \"+\ *adj* [*uni-* + *-florous* or *floral*] : bearing a solitary flower
uni·flow *also* **una·flow** \ˌyünə+\ *adj* [*uni-* or *una-* (alter. of *uni-*) + *flow*, n.] : flowing in one direction without reversal ⟨~ traffic⟩
uniflow engine *n* : an engine in which the steam or gas enters through admission valves at the ends of the cylinder and escapes through exhaust ports uncovered by the piston as it nears the end of its stroke
uni·foliate \ˌyünə+\ *also* **uni·foliar** \"+\ *adj* [*uni-* + *foliate* or *foliar*] **1** : having only one leaf **2** : UNIFOLIOLATE
uni·i·foliolate \"+\ *adj* [*uni-* + *foliolate*] *of a leaf* : compound but having only a single leaflet and distinguishable from a simple leaf by the basal joint
¹uni·form \'yünəˌfȯrm\ *adj*, *sometimes* -ER/-EST [MF *uniforme*, fr. L *uniformis*, fr. *uni-* + *-formis* -form] **1** : marked by lack of variation, diversity, change in form, manner, worth, or degree : showing a single form, degree, or character in all occurrences or manifestations ⟨the Shasta dam . . . will keep the flow of the Sacramento relatively ~ throughout the year —*Amer. Guide Series: Calif.*⟩ ⟨Great Russian itself has dialects, though generally speaking for so widespread a language it is remarkably ~ —W.J.Entwistle & W.A.Morison⟩ **2** : marked by complete conformity to a rule or pattern or by similarity in salient detail or practice : CONSONANT, ALIKE ⟨how far churches are bound to be ~ in their ceremonies —Richard Hooker⟩ **3** : marked by unvaried and changeless appearance (as of surface, color, or pattern) ⟨so many ~ red hills —Willa Cather⟩ **4** : consistent in conduct, character, or effect : lacking in variation, deviation, or unequal or dissimilar operation ⟨the constitution has conferred on Congress the right to establish a ~ rule of naturalization —R.B.Taney⟩ **syn** see LIKE, STEADY
²uniform \"\ *vt* -ED/-ING/-S **1** : to bring into uniformity **2** : to clothe with a uniform ⟨~ soldiers in khaki⟩
³uniform \"\ *n* -S [F *uniforme*, fr. *uniforme*, adj.] **1** : dress of a distinctive design or fashion adopted by or prescribed for members of a particular group (as an armed service, an order, or a social or work group) and serving as a means of identification ⟨the blue ~ of the navy⟩ ⟨a school ~⟩ ⟨the gang's ~ of blue jeans and red caps⟩ **2** : a garment or outfit of a widely copied style or prescribed design ⟨her usual ~ of white gloves with a tailored suit⟩ — **out of uniform** : wearing a military uniform that is not according to regulations
⁴uniform \"\ *usu cap* — a communications code word for the letter *u*
uni·for·mal \ˌ=ˈ=ˈfȯrməl, -fō(ə)m-\ *adj* [L *uniformis* + E *-al*] *archaic* : UNIFORM
uniform flow *n* : flow of a fluid in which each particle moves along its line of flow with constant speed and in which the cross section of each stream tube remains unchanged — compare STEADY FLOW
uni·form·ist \'=ˌ=ˌfȯrməst\ *n* -S : an advocate of uniformity
¹uni·form·i·tar·i·an \ˌyünəˌfȯrməˈterēən, -ta(ə)r-, -tār-\ *n* -S [*uniformity* + *-arian*] : a believer in uniformitarianism : an advocate of uniformity
²uniformitarian \"\ *adj* : of, relating to, or adhering to a doctrine of uniformitarianism
uni·form·i·tar·i·an·ism \-əˌnizəm\ *n* -S **1** : a geological doctrine that existing processes acting in the same manner and with essentially the same intensity as at present are sufficient to account for all geological changes — compare CATASTROPHISM **2** : a philosophical doctrine that the world is subject to law — contrasted with *tychism*

uni·form·i·ty \ˌ==ˈfȯ(r)məd·ē, -ətē, -i\ *n* -ES [ME *uniformite*, fr. MF *uniformité*, fr. LL *uniformitat-, uniformitas*, fr. L *uniformis* uniform + *-itat-, -itas* -ity — more at UNIFORM] **1** : the quality or state or an instance of being uniform (as by conformance to one pattern or adherence to one standard) ⟨the insistence on ~ in religion⟩ ⟨a rule of ~ that all duties, imposts, and excises shall be uniform throughout the U.S.⟩ **2** : the condition of having the constituent elements lacking in individuality or variability or so arranged as to give a uniform effect to the whole to which they belong; *often* : SAMENESS, MONOTONY

uniformity of nature : a doctrine or principle of the invariability or regularity of nature; *specif* : one that holds identical antecedent states or causes to be uniformly followed by identical effects — called also *principle of the uniformity of nature*

uni·form·ize \ˈ==,fȯr,mīz\ *vt* -ED/-ING/-S [F *uniformiser*, fr. *uniforme* uniform + *-iser* -ize] : to make uniform

uni·form·less \-mləs\ *adj* : having no uniform : not wearing a uniform

uni·form·ly \ˈ==ˌ=lē\ *adv* : in a uniform manner : so as to be uniform

uni·form·ness *n* -ES : the quality or state of being uniform

uniform system *n* : a system of photographic diaphragm or stop marking in which the numbers are proportional to the intensities of the light permitted to pass and hence to the times required for exposure

uni·fy \ˈyünə,fī\ *vb* -ED/-ING/-ES [LL *unificare*, fr. L *uni-* + *-ficare* -fy] *vt* **1 a** : to cause to be one : make into a coherent group or whole : give unity to : HARMONIZE ⟨war *unifies* a people torn by rivalries⟩ ⟨a *unified* design⟩ ⟨would also be technically possible to ~ the world and abolish war —Bertrand Russell⟩ **b** : to issue (as bonds) in order to combine several issues into one ⟨a *unified* bond⟩ **2** : to secure (a stop in a pipe organ) by unification ~ *vi* : to become one : CONSOLIDATE

syn INTEGRATE, CONSOLIDATE, COMPACT, CONCENTRATE agree with UNIFY in meaning to gather or combine parts or elements so as to form a close mass or coherent structure. UNIFY, the most general term, emphasizes unity in action or harmony in effect; the elements involved may be similar or diverse; they may be physically close or far apart; things may be *unified* deliberately or as a result of evolution, but rarely by imposition from without ⟨making only slow progress in *unifying* the economy of the world —W.S.Thompson⟩ ⟨frequently a minority group is *unified* by persecution⟩ ⟨the room, despite its clutter of furniture, was *unified* by the use of blue in the drapes and the rug⟩ INTEGRATE implies a close and harmonious relation both between individual parts and between each part and the whole and has favorable connotation; more than any of the other terms here discussed, it implies a beneficial effect for the components as well as for the whole ⟨an *integrated* personality⟩ ⟨a well-adjusted child is one that is *integrated* into his group⟩ ⟨narrative and background are *integrated* in their proper proportions —John Barkham⟩ ⟨its culture is more stable and better *integrated* —A.L.Kroeber⟩ CONSOLIDATE, usu. used of things that are alike or homogeneous, orig. points to a drawing together or thickening; likewise, in its transferred uses, it implies strengthening through solidarity ⟨organize state leagues for political action in order to *consolidate* the labor vote —G.S.Watkins⟩ ⟨two marriages with the Dutch Vandergraves had *consolidated* these qualities of thrift and handsome living —Edith Wharton⟩; when used of organizations, corporations, or the like, *consolidate* suggests close union not only in purpose or effect, but in administration ⟨several agencies were *consolidated* in one department⟩ ⟨the two companies were *consolidated* under one management⟩ COMPACT, when used of physical objects, means to stick or cake together, reducing the size of the whole by reducing the space between parts ⟨rain *compacts* the soil⟩ ⟨dry, powdered snow is better for skiing than wet snow which is soon *compacted*⟩ COMPACT in its transferred uses means to shape (a whole) from various parts, joined closely enough to hold together, without any implication as to the balance or harmony of the whole ⟨the loosely *compacted* hosts of thegns and peasants —F.M.Stenton⟩ COMPACT may, however, imply density, leaving no room for any but the parts mentioned ⟨it is based on solid facts, nay, is *compacted* of solid facts from the first sentence to the last —*Times Lit. Supp.*⟩ CONCENTRATE usu. carries the implication of bringing together things or parts that were scattered or diffused and of massing them around a point or center; the emphasis is not so much on unity or integrity of a whole as on accumulation of like elements ⟨people of Scandinavian and German origin are *concentrated* in the Middle West⟩ ⟨the control of the major part of the country's wealth is *concentrated* in a few hands⟩; figuratively, CONCENTRATE means to fix one's mental powers on one thing, so that all distracting thoughts or objects are eliminated ⟨the ability to *concentrate* on the task at hand is essential to all achievement⟩; a similar implication of eliminating that which weakens, dilutes, or adulterates is found in scientific and technical use ⟨evaporated milk is more *concentrated* than fresh milk⟩ ⟨a miner *concentrates* ores by separating the base from the precious materials⟩

uni·grav·i·da \ˌyünəˈgravədə\ *n* [NL, fr. *uni-* + L *gravida*] : a woman in her first pregnancy

uni·ju·gate \yüˈnijə̇,gāt, ˌyünəˈjü|, |gə̇t\ *adj* [*uni-* + *jugate*] : having one pair of leaflets — used of a pinnate leaf

uni·lacunar \ˌyünə+\ *adj* [*uni-* + *lacunar*] : having a single leaf gap — compare MULTILACUNAR, TRILACUNAR

uni·lateral \"+\ *adj* [*uni-* + *lateral*] **1 a** : of, relating to, or involving one side : done, made, undertaken, or shared by one of two or more persons or parties : dealing with or affecting one side of a subject : ONE-SIDED ⟨~ denunciation of such treaties is justified —I-Kua Chou⟩ **b** : constituting or relating to a contract or engagement by which an express obligation to do or forbear is imposed on but one party (as in a deed poll) ⟨in a ~ simple contract, a promise is exchanged for an act or forbearance⟩ **2 a** : produced or arranged on or directed toward one side : having dependent parts so oriented ⟨a ~ raceme⟩ ⟨~ flowers⟩ **b** : affecting or occurring in but one side of the body or a body part or organ **c** : pronounced with the oral passage open on one side of the tongue only — compare LATERAL 4 **3** : tracing descent through either the maternal or paternal line only ⟨a ~ clan⟩ — contrasted with *bilateral* **4** : having only one side; *specif* : being a surface on which a continuous path may be drawn from any point to any other point even to the exactly opposite point through the surface without piercing the surface or crossing its border — compare MÖBIUS BAND **5** *of a machined part* : having for a nominal diameter the smallest or largest size that the specified tolerances permit — **uni·laterally** \"+\ *adv*

unilateral compound pitting *n* : pitting in plant cell walls in which one large pit occurs opposite two or more small pits in an adjacent cell

uni·lateralism \ˌyünə+\ *n* -S : the state of being unilateral

uni·lateralist \"+\ *adj* : UNILATERAL

uni·laterality \"+\ *n* : UNILATERALISM

unilateral system *n* : a system of tolerances and allowances as applied to cylindrical mating surfaces having for its basis unilateral holes and involving measurement of the high and low limits of tolerance in one direction from the basic size

uni·lineal \ˌyünə+\ *adj* [*uni-* + *lineal*] : UNILATERAL 3

uni·linear \"+\ *adj* [*uni-* + *linear*] : progressing or unfolding in a linear manner : developing in or involving a series of stages usu. from the primitive to the more advanced ⟨~ social evolution⟩; *also* : involving such a trend ⟨a ~ cultural sequence⟩

unilinear evolution *n* : EVOLUTION 6a

uni·lingual \ˌyünə+\ *adj* [*uni-* + *lingual*] : composed in or using one language only

uni·literal \"+\ *adj* [*uni-* + *literal*] : consisting of or involving one letter only

un·illuminated \ˌən+\ *adj* [ˡ*un-* + *illuminated*, past part. of *illuminate*] **1** : deficient in mental or spiritual enlightenment **2** : not lighted : LIGHTLESS, DARK ⟨the ~ side of Mars —R.S. Richardson⟩

un·illuminating \"+\ *adj* : not providing light; *esp* : failing to enlighten or clarify ⟨an ~ report⟩ — **un·illuminatingly** \"+\ *adv*

un·illusioned \"+\ *adj* : free from illusion — compare DISILLUSION

uni·locular \ˌyünə+\ *adj* [*uni-* + *locular*] : containing a single cavity

un·imaginable \ˌən+\ *adj* : not imaginable or comprehensible usu. because of the extreme degree at which some cogent factor exists ⟨~ privations⟩ ⟨intergalactic distances that are ~ to the lay mind⟩ — **un·imaginableness** \"+\ *n* — **un·imaginably** \"+\ *adv*

un·imaginative \"+\ *adj* : not imaginative: as **a** : deficient in creative or imaginative quality : PROSAIC ⟨an ~ work of art⟩ ⟨~ development of a musical theme⟩ **b** : dealing or adapted to deal only with concrete facts : PRACTICAL ⟨the ~ calculating machine⟩ — **un·imaginatively** \"+\ *adv* — **un·imaginativeness** \"+\ *n*

un·imagined \"+\ *adj* [ˡ*un-* + *imagined*, past part. of *imagine*] : not imagined : not yet thought of : UNIMAGINABLE

uni·manual \ˌyünə+\ *adj* [*uni-* + *manual*] : of or relating to one hand : executed with one hand

un·imitable \ˌən+\ *adj* [alter. (influenced by ˡ*un-*) of *inimitable*] *archaic* : INIMITABLE

uni·modal \ˌyünə+\ *adj* [*uni-* + *modal*] : having a single mode ⟨a ~ statistical distribution⟩ — **uni·modality** \"+\ *n*

uni·molecular \"+\ *adj* [*uni-* + *molecular*] : relating to or involving a single molecule or single molecular species : MONOMOLECULAR ⟨~ reactions⟩

un·impaired \ˌən+\ *adj* [ˡ*un-* + *impaired*, past part. of *impair*] : not damaged or made less ⟨an argument ~ by logic⟩ ⟨his speech remained ~⟩ ⟨emerged from the trial with ~ prestige⟩

un·impassioned \"+\ *adj* : not impassioned; *esp* : marked by calm reasonableness and free from purely emotional appeal ⟨an ~ discussion of the problem⟩ **syn** see SOBER

un·impassionedly \"+\ *adv* : in an unimpassioned manner

un·im·peach·abil·i·ty \ˌənə̇m,pēchəˈbiləd·ē\ *n* : the quality or state of being unimpeachable

un·impeachable \ˌən+\ *adj* : not impeachable : not to be called in question : exempt from liability to accusation : IRREPROACHABLE, BLAMELESS ⟨an ~ reputation⟩ ⟨information from an ~ source⟩ ⟨an easy and ~ literary style⟩ — **un·im·peach·able·ness** \-əbəlnəs\ *n* -ES — **un·im·peach·ably** \-əblē\ *adv*

un·impeached \"+\ *adj* [ˡ*un-* + *impeached*, past part. of *impeach*] : not impeached; *also* : UNIMPEACHABLE

un·impeded \"+\ *adj* [ˡ*un-* + *impeded*, past part. of *impede*] : free from anything that impedes or hampers ⟨an ~ sweep of meadows and hills formed a peaceful setting⟩ ⟨~ demands⟩ — **un·im·ped·ed·ly** *adv*

un·implemented \"+\ *adj* [ˡ*un-* + *implemented*, past part. of *implement*] : not yet brought into effect ⟨an ~ trade agreement⟩

un·importance \"+\ *n* : the quality or state of being unimportant

un·important \"+\ *adj* : lacking in importance : TRIVIAL, MINOR, UNIMPRESSIVE — **un·importantly** \"+\ *adv*

un·imposing \"+\ *adj* : not imposing ⟨~ kindness⟩; *esp* : lacking in impressiveness

un·impregnated \ˌən+\ *adj* : not impregnated; *esp* : not inseminated

un·impressed \"+\ *adj* : not impressed: as **a** : bearing no impress **b** : not moved to serious regard

un·impressible \"+\ *adj* : not impressible; *esp* : lacking in mental sensibility or responsiveness

un·impressionable \"+\ *adj* : not sensitive or susceptible to impression : UNFEELING, UNYIELDING ⟨an ~ mind⟩ ⟨the ~ stones⟩

un·impressive \"+\ *adj* : not impressive — **un·impressively** \"+\ *adv* — **un·impressiveness** \"+\ *n*

un·improvable \"+\ *adj* : not improvable

ˡ**unimproved** *adj* [ˡ*un-* + *improved*, past part. of *improve* (to reprove)] *obs* : not subjected to censure : UNREPROVED

²**un·improved** \ˌən+\ *adj* [ˡ*un-* + *improved*, past part. of *improve* (to better)] : not improved: as **a** *of land* : not tilled, built upon, or otherwise improved for use : retained in the wild or natural state ⟨a farm with 50 acres of improved and 68 acres of ~ land⟩ ⟨~ woodlands⟩ **b** : not used or employed advantageously or for a valuable purpose ⟨opportunity ~ may become a source of repining⟩ **c** : not selectively bred for better quality or productiveness : of the kind occurring in nature or as a result of chance interbreeding; *often* : being a scrub ⟨~ native cattle yielding little meat and less milk⟩ **d** *of a road* : lacking a hardened surface and usu. unsuitable for all year travel

un·incisive \"+\ *adj* : deficient in incisiveness

un·incorporate \"+\ *adj* **1** : UNEMBODIED **2** : UNINCORPORATED

un·incorporated \"+\ *adj* : not incorporated : lacking corporate status ⟨an ~ village⟩

un·indifferent \"+\ *adj* : not indifferent; *esp* : lacking in impartiality : PREJUDICED — **un·indifferently** \"+\ *adv*

un·indorsed \"+\ *adj* [ˡ*un-* + *indorsed*, past part. of *indorse*, var. of *endorse*] : not indorsed; *esp* : lacking a formal written endorsement ⟨an ~ check⟩

un·industrialized \ˌən+\ *adj* [ˡ*un-* + *industrialized*, past part. of *industrialize*] : not industrialized

un·industrious \"+\ *adj* : not industrious : LAZY — **un·industriously** \"+\ *adv*

un·infected \"+\ *adj* : free from infection

un·infectious \"+\ *adj* : incapable of causing infection

un·inflammable \ˌən+\ *adj* : not flammable : incapable of combustion — not used technically

un·inflected \"+\ *adj* : not inflected ⟨an ~ voice⟩ ⟨~ words⟩

un·influenced \"+\ *adj* [ˡ*un-* + *influenced*, past part. of *influence*] : not influenced

un·informed \"+\ *adj* : not informed; *esp* : lacking in knowledge, awareness, or information : IGNORANT ⟨the ~ public⟩

un·inhabitable \"+\ *adj* [ME, fr. ˡ*un-* + *inhabitable*] : not inhabitable : unfit for habitation

un·inhabited \"+\ *adj* [ˡ*un-* + *inhabited*, past part. of *inhabit*] : not inhabited : UNOCCUPIED, VOID ⟨a barren nearly ~ country⟩; *esp* : not used as a regular dwelling place by human beings ⟨gaping doors of ~ houses⟩

un·in·hab·it·ed·ness *n* -ES : the quality or state of being uninhabited

un·inhibited \ˌən+\ *adj* : free from inhibition; *often* : boisterously informal ⟨a thoroughly ~ party⟩ — **un·in·hib·it·ed·ly** *adv*

ˡ**un·initiate** \"+\ *adj* [ˡ*un-* + *initiate*, adj.] : UNINITIATED

²**uninitiate** \"\ *n* : one that is not initiated or that lacks relevant knowledge and experience : TYRO

un·initiated \ˌən+\ *adj* [ˡ*un-* + *initiated*, past part. of *initiate*] : not initiated : deficient in relevant experience : INEXPERIENCED, GREEN

un·injured \"+\ *adj* [ˡ*un-* + *injured*, past part. of *injure*] : not injured

un·injurious \"+\ *adj* : doing no harm : incapable of causing injury (as to health) ⟨toys with ~ paints⟩

un·inked \"+\ *adj* [ˡ*un-* + *inked*, past part. of *ink*] : not inked : free from ink

uni·nodal \ˌyünə+\ *adj* [*uni-* + *nodal*] : having a single node

uni·nominal \"+\ *adj* [F, fr. *uni-* + *nominal*, fr. ML *nominalis* — more at NOMINAL] **1** : based on the principle of having only one member (as of a legislature) selected from each electoral district ⟨a ~ electoral system⟩ ⟨a ~ ballot⟩ — compare LIST SYSTEM, PROPORTIONAL REPRESENTATION, SINGLE-MEMBER DISTRICT **2 a** : having, relating to, or consisting of a single name or identifying term **b** : of, relating to, or constituting a system of nomenclature in which items have single names

un·inquiring \ˌən+\ *adj* : not inquiring; *esp* : deficient in curiosity

un·inspected \"+\ *adj* [ˡ*un-* + *inspected*, past part. of *inspect*] : not inspected

un·inspired \"+\ *adj* : not inspired; *esp* : deficient in originality of thought and development ⟨~ writing⟩ ⟨a perfunctory and ~ treatment⟩

un·inspiring \"+\ *adj* : not inspiring; *often* : unattractive and depressing to the spirit

un·instructed \"+\ *adj* : not instructed: as **a** : deficient in knowledge or enlightenment : IGNORANT ⟨the ~ masses⟩ **b** : not provided with instructions; *esp* : not directed how to vote ⟨an ~ delegation⟩

un·insurable \"+\ *adj* : not insurable; *esp* : too risky to be coverable by insurance

un·insured \"+\ *adj* [ˡ*un-* + *insured*, past part. of *insure*] : not insured

uninsured plan *n* : a usu. funded pension or retirement plan not providing for the guarantee of benefits by an insurance company — compare INSURED PLAN

un·integrated \"+\ *adj* : not integrated; *esp* : deficient in personality integration

un·integration \"+\ *n* : the quality or state of being unintegrated

un·intelligence \"+\ *n* : the quality or state of being unintelligent

un·intelligent \"+\ *adj* : lacking intelligence : UNWISE, IGNORANT — **un·intelligently** \"+\ *adv*

un·intelligibility \"+\ *n* **1** : the quality or state of being unintelligible **2** : something that is unintelligible ⟨depending too much on jargon and other *unintelligibilities* for effect⟩

un·intelligible \"+\ *adj* [ˡ*un-* + *intelligible*] : not intelligible : difficult to comprehend : OBSCURE — **un·intelligibleness** \"+\ *n* — **un·intelligibly** \"+\ *adv*

un·intended \ˌən+\ *adj* : not intended; *esp* : not deliberate

un·intentional \"+\ *adj* : not intentional — **un·intentionally** \"+\ *adv*

un·interest \"+\ *n* : a condition of lacking means to stir interest ⟨the drab ~ of the town —T.H.Jones⟩

un·interested \"+\ *adj* [ˡ*un-* + *interested*, past part. of *interest*] : not interested: as **a** : having no interest and esp. no property interest in : not personally concerned **b** : not having the mind or feelings engaged : INATTENTIVE, APATHETIC **syn** see INDIFFERENT

un·interestedly \"+\ *adv* : in an uninterested manner

un·interestedness \"+\ *n* : the quality or state of being uninterested

un·interesting \"+\ *adj* : not attracting interest or attention : DULL, BORING ⟨a very ~ account of her trip⟩ — **un·interestingly** \"+\ *adv* — **un·interestingness** \"+\ *n*

un·intermitted \"+\ *adj* [ˡ*un-* + *intermitted*, past part. of *intermit*] : not intermitted : CONTINUOUS — **un·in·ter·mit·ted·ly** *adv*

un·intermittent \"+\ *adj* : not intermittent

un·interpreted \"+\ *adj* [ˡ*un-* + *interpreted*, past part. of *interpret*] : not interpreted

un·interrupted \"+\ *adj* : not interrupted : CONTINUOUS — **un·interruptedly** \"+\ *adv* — **un·interruptedness** \"+\ *n*

un·intimate \"+\ *adj* : not intimate; *often* : distant or shy in social relationships

uni·nucleate \ˌyünə+\ *also* **uni·nuclear** \"+\ *adj* [*uni-* + *nucleate* or *nuclear*] : having a single nucleus

un·inventive \ˌən+\ *adj* : not inventive : lacking powers of invention — **un·inventively** \"+\ *adv* — **un·inventiveness** \"+\ *n*

un·invested \"+\ *adj* : not invested ⟨~ funds⟩

un·invited \"+\ *adj* [ˡ*un-* + *invited*, past part. of *invite*] : not invited

un·inviting \"+\ *adj* : not inviting; *esp* : not appealing to the senses

un·involved \"+\ *adj* : not involved

unio \ˈyünē,ō\ *n* [NL, fr. L, a large pearl — more at ³UNION] **1** *cap* : the type genus of the family Unionidae comprising freshwater mussels that have an oblong shell pearly within and covered without by a greenish or blackish epidermis **2** *pl* **unios** \-ōz\ *or* **uni·on·i·des** \ˌ==ˈänə,dēz\ : any mussel of *Unio* or a related genus — **uni·oid** \ˈ==,ȯid\ *adj*

uni·ocular \ˌyünē+\ *adj* [*uni-* + *ocular*] : MONOCULAR

uni·o·la \yüˈnīələ, ˌyünēˈōlə\ *n, cap* [NL, fr. LL, a kind of plant, prob. fr. *unio* oneness, unity, union] : a small genus of showy No. American perennial grasses having ample panicles of 2-edged spikelets of which the lowermost glumes are empty and that are valued as sand stabilizers — see SEA OAT

ˡ**un·ion** \ˈyünyən\ *n* -S [ME, fr. MF, fr. LL *union-, unio* oneness, unity, union, fr. L *unus* one + *-ion-, -io* -ion — more at ONE] **1 a** : an act or instance of uniting or joining two or more things into one : a bringing into intimate and usu. fixed association: as (1) : an associating of nonmaterial or abstract items ⟨a ~ of Latin and Nordic elements⟩ ⟨a gracious ~ of elegance and strength⟩ (2) : a uniting (as of groups, factions, people) into a coherent and usu. harmonious whole ⟨bring about the ~ of the troubled household⟩ ⟨arranged a ~ of the opposing factions in the church⟩; *esp* : the formation of a single political unit from two or more separate and independent units usu. through a surrender to the whole of the principal governmental powers of the parts or by the incorporation of separate entities into an already existing unit ⟨the ~ of Scotland and England took place on May 1, 1707⟩ (3) : a consolidation of benefices or churches (4) : a uniting in marriage; *also* : sexual intercourse : COPULATION (5) : the growing together of severed parts ⟨the slow ~ of a fractured bone⟩ (6) : the concious identification of one's will with that of divinity which constitutes the third and highest stage in mystical striving and in which the soul is held to have experimental knowledge of God — called also *unitive way* **b** : the state or result of being subjected to union : a unified condition : COMBINATION, JUNCTION ⟨exhibiting an excellent ~ of beef and milk qualities⟩ **2** *obs* : ONENESS **3** : something that is made one : something formed by a combining or coalition of parts or members : a consolidated body or group: as **a** : a confederation or league of independent individuals (as nations or persons) for some common end or purpose — see CUSTOMS UNION, LABOR UNION, POSTAL UNION **b** : a political unit constituting an organic whole formed usu. from previously independent units which have surrendered their principal powers to the government of the whole that may be the government of one of the units (as in the case of England and Scotland in 1707) or a newly created government (as of the U. S. in 1789) ⟨we, the people of the United States, in order to form a more perfect ~ —*U. S. Constitution*⟩ — compare CONFEDERATION, FEDERATION, LEAGUE **c** : a 19th century British governmental unit primarily for the administration of poor relief formed by uniting two or more parishes under a board of guardians — called also *poor-law union*; compare RURAL DISTRICT **d** *usu cap* : an organization on a college or university campus providing facilities for recreational, social, and cultural activities and sometimes dining facilities; *also* : the building in which such an organization is housed **e** : a union cloth **f** : a chemical combination : BOND 3e **g** : a plant society esp. when consisting of plants linked by common habit ⟨an herbaceous perennial ~ within the greasewood-shad-scale association⟩ **h** : the point of joining or state of being joined of stock and scion in a plant graft ⟨weak ~s may need to be bridged by mutually compatible intermediates⟩ **4 a** : a device emblematic of the union of two or more sovereignties borne on a national flag typically in the upper inner corner or constituting the whole design of the flag **b** : the upper inner corner of a flag : CANTON **5** : any of various devices for connecting machine or other parts: as **a** : the elastic pipe connecting a tender with the locomotive feed pipe **b** : a coupling for pipes or pipes and fittings designed to facilitate connection or disconnection — compare FLANGE UNION

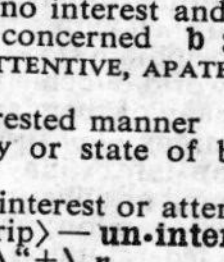

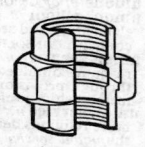

pipe union, partly cut away

²**union** \"\ *adj* **1 a** : of, relating to, dealing with, or constituting a union (as a labor union) ⟨~ affairs⟩ ⟨a ~ contract⟩ **b** (1) *of yarn* : spun from a mixture of two or more fibers (2) *of cloth* : having warp and weft threads of different fibers **c** *of a literary language* : artificially created by a selection of vocabulary and usages from related dialects or languages with the intent of serving all equally **2** : formed by union usu. of diverse elements ⟨a ~ ticket in politics⟩

³**union** \"\ *n* -S [L *union-, unio*, fr. *unus* one — more at ONE] *archaic* : a large pearl of exceptional quality and worth

⁴**union** \"\ *usu cap* — a communications code word for the letter *u*

un·ion·alls \ˈyünyə,nȯlz\ *n pl* [ˡ*union* + *-alls* (as in *overalls*)] : COVERALL

union calendar *n, usu cap U* : a legislative calendar of the U.S. House of Representatives listing all public bills for raising

revenue or involving a governmental expenditure or government property — compare PRIVATE CALENDAR
union card *n* **1 :** a card certifying personal membership in good standing in a labor union **2 :** something felt to resemble a union card esp. in being a prerequisite to employment or in providing evidence of ingroup status ⟨the Ph.D. . . . a *union card* for the teaching profession —Douglas Bush⟩
union catalog *n* **:** a library catalog combining in one series and usu. alphabetically by authors a number of catalogs or the contents of more than one library
union day *n, usu cap U&D* **:** the anniversary of the founding of the Union of South Africa on May 31, 1910 observed in the Union as a legal holiday
union depot *n* **:** UNION STATION
union district *n* **:** a school district made by uniting two or more elementary or secondary school districts
union down *adv* **:** with the flag reversed so that its union is downward ⟨a flag flown *union down* is a signal of distress at sea⟩
un·ion·eer \ˌyünyəˈni(ə)r, -iə\ *n* -S **:** a member or advocate of a union; *esp* **:** a labor union executive
union elbow *n* **:** an elbow pipe union
¹uni·o·nid \ˈyünēəˌnid\ *adj* [NL *Unionidae*] **:** of or relating to the Unionidae
²unionid \"\ *n* -S **:** a mollusk of the family Unionidae
uni·on·i·dae \ˌ==ˈänəˌdē\ *n pl, cap* [NL, fr. *Union-, Unio,* type genus + *-idae*] **:** a very large family of freshwater mussels (suborder Submytilacea) having a pearly often roughly sculptured shell with a thick epidermis and larvae that pass through a glochidium stage and being represented in nearly all parts of the world but chiefly in No. America where the nacreous shells of many of them are used for button making
unionides *pl of* UNIO
un·ion·ism \ˈyünyəˌnizəm\ *n* -S **:** the principle or policy of forming or adhering to a union **:** an advocacy or movement in favor of union: as **a** *usu cap* **:** adherence to the policy of a firm federal union between the states of the United States esp. during the Civil War period **b :** the principles, theory, or system of combination of workers in the same occupation, trade, or industry ⟨horizontal ~⟩; *also* **:** the labor union movement ⟨the advance of ~⟩ **c :** advocacy of the principles of the British Unionists
un·ion·ist \-nəst\ *n* -S **:** an advocate or promoter of union and esp. of some form of unionism: as **a** *usu cap* **:** one loyal to the federal union of the U. S. during the Civil War **b** *usu cap* **:** a member of a former British political party advocating legislative union between Great Britain and Ireland **c :** an adherent or supporter of the labor union movement; *esp* **:** an active member of a labor union **d :** an advocate of religious union and esp. of the amalgamation of related Protestant sects
un·ion·is·tic \ˌ==ˈnistik, -tēk\ *adj* **:** of, relating to, characteristic of, or favoring union or unionists
un·ion·ization \ˌyünyənəˈzāshən, -əˌnīz-\ *n* -S **1 :** the quality or state of being unionized **2 :** the act of unionizing
un·ion·ize \ˈ==ˌnīz\ *vt* -ED/-ING/-S *see -ize in Explan Notes* [¹*union* + *-ize*] **:** to cause to become a member of or subject to the rules of a labor union ⟨planned to ~ the shop⟩ **:** form into a labor union ⟨*unionizing* previously unorganized groups⟩
union jack *n, often cap U&J* **:** a jack consisting of the union of a national ensign
union jet burner *n* **:** a gas burner in which two jets unite to produce a single flat flame
union joint *n* **:** a joint (as between pipes) formed by means of a union
union label *n* **:** an identifying mark attached to goods indicating that they have been produced by union labor or that particular goods or services have been sold or done by that labor
union list *n* **:** a usu. alphabetical catalog of periodicals or other serials that provides bibliographical information and locates files in libraries
union-made \ˈ==ˈ=\ *adj* **:** made by union labor
unions *pl of* UNION
union school *n* **:** an elementary, secondary, or combined elementary and secondary school that serves a union district — compare CONSOLIDATED SCHOOL
union security *n* **:** guaranteed preservation of union status or revenues obtained through clauses in a labor contract and esp. through provisions for closed or union shop, maintenance of membership, preferential hiring, or the checkoff
union service *n* **:** a worship service sponsored jointly by two or more religious denominations or communions ⟨urged to attend the *union service* in the Congregational or Baptist Churches⟩
union shona *n, usu cap U&S* **:** SHONA 3
union shop *n* **:** an establishment in which the employer by agreement is free to hire nonmembers as well as members of the union but retains nonmembers on the payroll only on condition of their becoming members of the union within a specified time ⟨a *union shop* clause in a collective agreement⟩ — compare CLOSED SHOP
union station *n* **:** a station used jointly by two or more railroad or other transport companies (as bus or truck lines)
union suit *n* **:** an undergarment with shirt and drawers in one piece
union tannage *n* **:** tannage by means of a mixture of vegetable tanning materials
union tee *n* **:** a T pipe fitting with a male or female union on one end of the main run
unios *pl of* UNIO
uni·oval \ˌyünē+\ *or* **uni·ovular** \"+\ *adj* [*uni-* + *oval* or *ovular*] **:** MONOVULAR
uni·ovulate \"+\ *adj* [*uni-* + *ovulate*] **:** having a single ovule or ovum
unip·a·ra \yüˈnipərə\ *n* -S [NL, fr. *uni-* + *-para*] **:** a woman who has borne one child
uni·parental \ˌyünə+\ *adj* [*uni-* + *parental*] **:** having or involving a single parent; *esp* **:** PARTHENOGENETIC — **uni·parentally** \"+\ *adv*
unip·a·rous \yüˈnipərəs\ *adj* [*uni-* + *-parous*] **1 a :** producing but one egg or offspring at a time **b :** having produced but one offspring **:** once heretofore pregnant **2 :** producing but one axis at each branching ⟨a ~ cyme⟩
uni·partite \ˌyünə+\ *adj* [*uni-* + *partite*] **:** not divided or divisible into parts

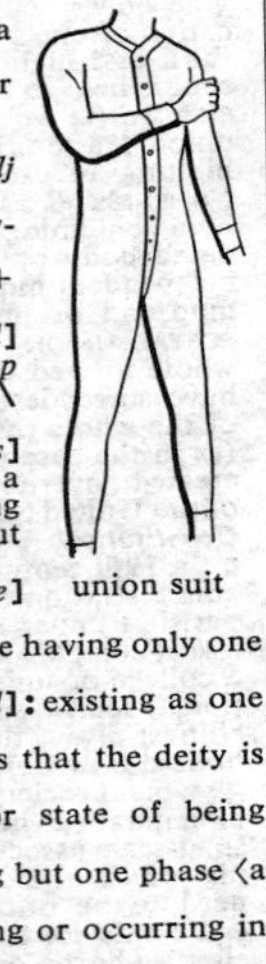
union suit

uni·ped \ˈyünəˌped\ *n* -S [*uni-* + *-ped*] **:** one having only one foot or leg
uni·personal \ˌyünə+\ *adj* [*uni-* + *personal*] **:** existing as one person
uni·personalist \"+\ *n* **:** one who believes that the deity is unipersonal
uni·personality \"+\ *n* **:** the quality or state of being unipersonal
uni·phase \"+\ *adj* [*uni-* + *phase*] **:** having but one phase ⟨a ~ conflict⟩; *esp* **:** SINGLE-PHASE
uni·planar \"+\ *adj* [*uni-* + *planar*] **:** lying or occurring in one plane **:** PLANAR 1
uniplanar motion *n* **:** motion of a rigid body or fluid such that each point or particle moves in a plane parallel to a given plane — called also *two-dimensional motion*
uni·pod \ˈyünəˌpäd\ *n* -S [*uni-* + *-pod* (as in *tripod*)] **:** a one-legged support (as for a camera)
uni·polar \ˌyünə+\ *adj* [*uni-* + *polar*] **:** having or oriented in respect to a single pole: as **a :** having, produced by, or acting by a single magnetic or electrical pole **b** *of a nerve cell* **:** having but one process ⟨~ ganglion cells⟩ **c :** based on or controlled by a single compelling factor ⟨a ~ coalition in politics⟩ — **uni·polarity** \"+\ *n*
unipolar induction *n* **:** induction (as in a conducting circuit) by only one pole of a magnet
unip·o·rous \yüˈnipərəs\ *adj* [*uni-* + *porous*] **:** having one pore; *specif* **:** having wood cells with a single row of bordered pores or disk-shaped markings
unip·o·tent \yüˈnipədˌənt\ *adj* [*uni-* + *potent*] **:** having power in one way only; *esp* **:** capable of developing only in one direction or to one end product ⟨~ cells⟩
uni·potential \ˌyünə+\ *adj* [*uni-* + *potential*] **1 :** UNIPOTENT **2 :** having the same electrical potential as something else ⟨a ~ lens⟩
uni·pulse \ˈ==ˌ=\ *n* [*uni-* + *pulse*] **:** a single wave **:** PULSE
uni·quantic \ˌyünə+\ *adj* [*uni-* + *quantic*] **:** of, relating to, or giving rise to a single quantum of energy
¹unique \yüˈnēk, ˈ=ˌ=\ *adj, sometimes* -ER/-EST [F, fr. L *unicus* sole, single, unique, fr. *unus* one + *-icus* -ic — more at ONE] **1 a :** being the only one **:** SOLE ⟨earning money whose ~ object could be nothing but Cyril's welfare —Arnold Bennett⟩ ⟨has thus preserved the original and often ~ records —G.B. Parks⟩ ⟨you are a miracle, a wonder, a mystery . . . one single ~ and inimitable living thing —J.C.Powys⟩ **b** *of a book* **:** known to exist in no other copy **2 :** being without a like or equal **:** single in kind or excellence **:** UNEQUALED ⟨they stand alone, ~, objects of supreme interest —A.B.Osborne⟩ ⟨as historian he knows that events, like persons, are ~ —J.M. Barzun⟩ ⟨remains singularly himself, a ~ lyrist of the first water —L.L.Salomon⟩ ⟨an almost ~ experience —Havelock Ellis⟩ ⟨tendencies present in our contemporary world which make our own times somewhat ~ —M.B.Smith⟩ ⟨story of his life is considerably more ~ than most autobiographies —Dorothy C. Fisher⟩ ⟨the more we study him, the less ~ he seems —Harry Levin⟩ — sometimes used with *to* ⟨the problem of what to do with surplus women is by no means ~ to our own society — Ralph Linton⟩ or *with* ⟨by no means ~ with the song sparrow —*Nature Mag.*⟩ **3 :** UNUSUAL, NOTABLE ⟨possessed ~ ability in the raising of funds —C.F.Thwing⟩ ⟨the wife of a career diplomat has a ~ opportunity to observe the world political scene —Ray Pierre⟩ ⟨a frankness ~ in literature —David Daiches⟩ ⟨~ peace and privacy —R.W.Hatch⟩ ⟨cheap, nourishing, and a ~ dining experience —T.H.Fielding⟩ ⟨the most ~ characteristic of that environment —R.A.Billington⟩ ⟨she's the most ~ person I ever met —Arthur Miller⟩ ⟨the most ~ theater in town —*advt*⟩ **4 :** capable of being performed in only one way ⟨the factorization of a number into its prime factors is ~⟩ **syn** see SINGLE, STRANGE
²unique \"\ *n* -S **:** something (as a specimen, thing, circumstance, or person) that is unique **:** the only one of its kind ⟨mistaking the ~ for the typical —W.J.Reilly⟩ ⟨the zest of the collector for possession of a ~ —Roy Bedichek⟩ ⟨a display of glass, including undercoated ~*s* —*Danish Foreign Office Jour.*⟩ ⟨the phoenix, the ~ of birds —Thomas De Quincey⟩
unique·ly *adv* **:** in a unique manner **:** so as to be unique
unique·ness *n* -ES **:** the quality or state of being unique
uniqueness theorem *n* **:** a theorem in mathematics: a given problem has at most one solution
uniq·ui·ty \yüˈnikwədˌē, -wətē, -i\ *n* -ES [*unique* + *-ity*] **1 :** UNIQUENESS **2 :** a unique item
uni·radiate \ˌyünə+\ *adj* [*uni-* + *radiate*] **:** having a single ray or radius; *esp* **:** MONAXON
uni·ramous \"+\ *or* **uni·ramose** \"+\ *adj* [*uni-* + *ramous* or *ramose*] **:** consisting of a single process **:** UNBRANCHED ⟨the appendages of crustaceans may be ~ or biramose⟩
uni·reme \ˈyünəˌrēm\ *n* -S [*uni-* + *-reme* (as in *trireme*)] **:** a galley having but one tier of oars
un·ironed \ˌən+\ *adj* [¹*un-* + *ironed,* past part. of *iron*] **1 :** not restrained or confined with fetters **2 :** not pressed with a flatiron
unis *abbr* unison
uni·serial \ˌyünə+\ *or* **uni·seriate** \"+\ *adj* [*uni-* + *serial* or *seriate*] **:** forming or arranged in a single series **:** having parts in a single row or on one side only of an axis
uni·sexual \"+\ *adj* [*uni-* + *sexual*] **:** of, relating to, or restricted to one sex: **a :** male or female but not hermaphroditic **b :** DICLINOUS ⟨a ~ flower⟩ — **uni·sexuality** \"+\ *n* — **uni·sexually** \"+\ *adv*
¹uni·son \ˈyünəsən, -əzən\ *n* -S [MF, fr. ML *unisonus,* adj., having the same sound, fr. L *uni-* + *sonus* sound — more at SOUND] **1** *archaic* **:** a tone identical in pitch with another; *also* **:** a tone from which intervals are reckoned **2 a :** identity in musical pitch; *specif* **:** the interval of a perfect prime represented by the vibration ratio of 1:1 **b :** the state of being so tuned or sounded **c :** the writing, playing, or singing of parts in a musical passage at the same pitch or in octaves — compare HARMONY 2b **3 a :** a harmonious agreement or union **:** CONCORD **b :** an instance or means of such agreement **:** a sympathetic response **:** ASSENT ⟨~*s* of overmastering thoughts⟩ — **in unison** *adv* **:** in precise and perfect agreement **:** so as to harmonize exactly ⟨speaking *in unison*⟩
²unison \"\ *adj* **1** *archaic* **:** CONCORDANT, CONSONANT **b :** EQUIVALENT **2 a :** identical in musical pitch **:** UNISONOUS ⟨~ singing⟩ ⟨a ~ passage⟩ **b :** tuned to the same pitch — used of a string and esp. of any one of two or three piano strings ⟨~ strings⟩ **c :** having a pitch that are struck by one hammer that corresponds with the notation (as of a pipe-organ stop)
unis·o·nal \yüˈnisˀnəl\ *adj* [¹*unison* + *-al*] **:** UNISONOUS 1
unis·o·nance \-nən(t)s\ *n* -S [²*unison* + *-ance*] **:** a blending of sound into unison ⟨the first two sounds reach the ear as a ~ —*Newsweek*⟩
unis·o·nant \-nt\ *adj* [¹*unison* + *-ant*] **:** UNISONOUS 1
uni·so·no \ˌünēˈsō(ˌ)nō\ *adv (or adj)* [It, fr. ML *unisonus*] **:** in unison — used as a direction esp. in ensemble instrumental music
unis·o·nous \yüˈnisˀnəs\ *adj* [ML *unisonus*] **1 :** being in unison **:** having the same degree of gravity or acuteness **:** sounded alike in pitch **2 :** alike in nature **:** CONCORDANT
un·issued stock \ˌən+ -\ *n* [¹*un-* + *issued,* past part. of *issue*] **:** stock authorized (as under the charter of a corporation) but not yet issued — compare TREASURY STOCK
¹unit \ˈyünət, *usu* -əd·+V\ *n* -S [back-formation fr. *unity*] **1 a** (1) **:** the first natural number **:** a number that is the least whole number and is expressed by the numeral 1 (2) **:** a single thing (as a magnitude or number) that constitutes an undivided whole **b :** a number that divides every element of a set of numbers **c :** a determinate quantity (as of length, time, heat, value, or housing) adopted as a standard of measurement for other quantities of the same kind: as (1) **:** a fractional part of the width of a printing character (as ⅛ of ordinary roman capital M) used in measuring the set of a piece of type and being of the same width for all type of the same point size and proportionally wider or narrower for larger or smaller point sizes (2) **:** an amount of work (as 120 hours of classroom work in a completed course of a secondary school) used in education in calculating student credits (as for graduation or college entrance) (3) **:** an amount of a biologically active agent (as a drug, serum, vitamin, or antigen) required to produce a specific result under strictly controlled conditions — compare BIOASSAY, RAT UNIT (4) **:** one percent per ton of a fertilizing ingredient ⟨a fertilizer containing 5 percent of nitrogen, 10 percent of phosphoric acid, and 10 percent of potash includes 25 fertilizer ~*s*⟩ **2 a :** a single thing or person or group that is a constituent and isolable member of some more inclusive whole **:** a member of an aggregate that is the least part to have clearly definable separate existence and that normally forms a basic element of organization within the aggregate ⟨the township in the usual ~ of government⟩ ⟨the family as a basic ~ of society⟩ **b :** one of the commonly more or less repetitive sections combined in assembling a manufactured article (as a bookcase or kitchen cabinet) **c :** a part of a military establishment that has a prescribed organization (as of personnel and materiel) ⟨in the army ~*s* vary in size and complexity from the squad to the army⟩ **d :** a piece or complex of apparatus serving to perform one particular function ⟨a train drawn by two diesel ~*s*⟩ ⟨a power station with one ~ out of order⟩ **e :** a combination of two or more securities offered at a single price ⟨a ~ of one share of preferred stock and two shares of common offered at $110⟩ **f :** a course or part of a course in an elementary or secondary school focusing on a central theme and making use of resources from numerous subject areas and the pupils' own experience **g :** BARGAINING UNIT **h :** a fraction of an annual pension or a retirement income benefit earned as a result of each year's service prior to retirement **i :** a subdivision of a Girl Scout camp comprised of girls and counselors who live together and plan their own activities in a manner comparable to a Girl Scout troop **j :** a molecule or portion of a molecule esp. as combined in a larger molecule **:** RESIDUE ⟨repeating ~*s* in a polymer⟩
²unit \"\ *adj* **1 a :** of, relating to, forming, or involving some unit ⟨~ sales⟩ ⟨studies of ~ distribution⟩ **b :** existing or occurring per unit ⟨the ~ weight of cement⟩ ⟨a ~ increment⟩ ⟨calculating the ~ rise or vertical change per running foot⟩ **2 :** having independent existence **:** INDIVIDUAL
unit·able *also* **unite·able** \yüˈnīd·əbəl, -ītə-\ *adj* [*unite* + *-able*] **:** capable of union by growth or otherwise **:** that can be joined together
unit·age \ˈyünəd·ij\ *n* -S [¹*unit* + *-age*] **1 :** specification of the amount constituting a unit (as of a vitamin) **2 :** amount in units ⟨a ~ of 50,000 per capsule⟩
unit·al \-nəd·ᵊl\ *adj* [¹*unit* + *-al*] **:** UNITARY
¹uni·tar·i·an \ˌyünəˈterēən, -ta(a)r-, -tār-\ *n* -S [NL *unitarius* unitarian (fr. L *unitus* — past part. of *unire* to unite — + *-arius* -ary) + E *-an*] **1** *usu cap* **a :** a Christian who believes that the deity exists only in one person **:** a unipersonalist who denies the doctrine of the Trinity **:** a member of a Christian denomination who in general affirms the principles of individual freedom of belief, the free use of reason in religion, commitment to advancing truth, religious tolerance, universal brotherhood of man, a creedless church, a united world community, and support of a vigorous program of liberal social action **b :** an advocate of a non-Christian monotheist (as a Muhammadan) **2 a :** an advocate of a theory or doctrine founded upon unity; *specif* **:** MONIST **b :** an advocate of unity or a unitary system; *specif* **:** one who advocates centralization in government **c :** an observer of the dramatic unities
²unitarian \"\ *adj* **1** *usu cap* **:** of, relating to, or involving Unitarians or their doctrines **2 :** UNITARY 1: as **a :** MONISTIC **b :** of, relating to, or advocating centralization in government or administration
unitarian hypothesis *also* **unitarian view** *n* **:** a theory in immunology: a single pure antigen will produce only one variety of antibody which when brought into contact with the antigen in appropriate form can react in various ways (as by agglutinating, precipitating, fixing complement, or opsonizing)
uni·tar·i·an·ism \-əˌnizəm\ *n* -S **1** *cap* **:** the principles and practices of Unitarians **2** *sometimes cap* **:** a unitarian or unitary system (as of government)
uni·tar·i·ness \ˈyünəˌterēnəs, -rin-\ *n* -ES **:** the quality or state of being unitary
uni·tary \-ˌterē, -ri\ *adj* [¹*unit* & *unity* + *-ary*] **1 :** of, relating to, based upon, or characterized by unity ⟨a ~ movement in politics⟩ **:** MONISTIC **2 a :** having the character of a unit **:** not divided or discontinuous ⟨a ~ process⟩ **b :** functioning as a unit esp. in regard to measurement ⟨established a ~ distance on which to base subsequent calculations⟩ ⟨a ~ university⟩ **c :** of, relating to, or constituting a system of government in which power is held by a central authority and may be delegated to but is not derived from constituent subdivisions — distinguished from *federal* **3 a :** of, relating to, or involving the use of units ⟨a ~ approach to a problem⟩ ⟨the ~ method in arithmetic⟩ **b :** made up of discrete units ⟨a ~ loudspeaker with four speaker units associated in a single assembly⟩
unitary color *n* **:** PSYCHOLOGICAL PRIMARY
unitary theory *n* **:** a theory in chemistry: molecules are units whose parts are bound together in definite structure with mutual and reciprocal influence on each other — compare DUALISM 4
unit banking *n* **:** banking carried on by individual banks without branches or corporate relationships with other banks
unit card *n* **:** a library catalog card containing full information about a book or other printed item and reproduced in quantity so that it may be not only used for a main entry but adapted for all secondary entries
unit cell *n* **:** the simplest polyhedron that by indefinite repetition makes up the lattice of a crystal and embodies all the characteristics of its structure
unit character *n* **1 :** a natural character that is inherited on an all or none basis **2 :** a natural character dependent on the presence or absence of a single gene **:** a typical Mendelian or qualitative character
unit class *n* **:** a class with a single member
unit construction *n* **:** a system of building in which large sections (as of a ship) can be fabricated independently and subsequently assembled
unit cost *n* **:** the cost allocated to a selected unit and commonly calculated as the cost over a period of time divided by the number of items produced
¹unite \yüˈnīt, *usu* -īd·+V\ *vb* -ED/-ING/-S [ME *uniten,* fr. LL *unitus,* past part. of *unire,* fr. L *unus* one — more at ONE] *vt* **1 a :** to put together to form a single unit ⟨~ the fighting forces of the friendly nations⟩ **b :** to cause to adhere ⟨~ bricks with mortar⟩ **c :** CONNECT ⟨a dirt road ~*s* the farm road with the main highway⟩ **d :** to relate integrally ⟨often the ideas are yoked, but not *united* —T.S.Eliot⟩; *esp* **:** to link by a legal or moral bond ⟨a purpose that *united* all factions⟩ ⟨a treaty to ~ all the independent nations⟩ **2 :** to possess (as qualities) in combination ⟨the bride *united* beauty and intelligence⟩ ~ *vi* **1 a :** to become one or as if one ⟨particles which can ~ to form a new compound —T.S.Eliot⟩ ⟨mutterings of the crowd *united* in a thunderous cheer —Darrell Berrigan⟩ **b :** to become combined by or as if by adhesion or mixture ⟨the broken bones of a child ~ easily⟩ ⟨clouds of devastating smoke that ~ with the river fog . . . to form smog —*Amer. Guide Series: Pa.*⟩ **2 :** to act in concert ⟨all parties *united* in signing the petition⟩ **3 :** to enter into association for or as if for a common purpose ⟨the group *united* to improve the city's schools⟩
syn COMBINE, CONJOIN, CONCUR, COOPERATE: UNITE often indicates joining, merging, coalescing, adhering together to form a new unit, permanent or temporary ⟨the North West Company *united* with the Hudson's Bay Company —*Amer. Guide Series: Wash.*⟩ ⟨in France the whole people saw at once what was upon them; the single word *patrie* was enough to *unite* them in a common enthusiasm and stern determination — W.R.Inge⟩ COMBINE may apply to a temporary uniting or joining or to one which leaves the components distinct ⟨a gift for *combining,* for fusing into a single phrase, two or more diverse impressions —T.S.Eliot⟩ ⟨wealth and sophistication *combine* with breezy western characteristics in this town —*Amer. Guide Series: Texas*⟩ ⟨innumerable factors *combine* in the inextricable complexity of our general story —Hilaire Belloc⟩ CONJOIN is likely to stress the notion of jointure, often of more or less equal things or forces, at a specific point ⟨nature had lavished gifts and aspirations upon him, but they were so mixed and contradictory that only by a fortunate miracle did some of them *conjoin* to produce the rich poetry by which he is remembered —R.D.Altick⟩ CONCUR is likely to be used of things that happen to merge, work together, or coincide when another course of action is probable or plausible ⟨two opposite forces *concurred* in bringing about the Council of Nicaea — A.P.Stanley⟩ COOPERATE indicates a joining of strength or force in some specific situation with no fusion or loss of identity ⟨sent a joint expedition, under British command, to *cooperate* with the White Russians at Murmansk and Archangel against the Bolshevist forces —J.M.Hanson⟩ **syn** see in addition JOIN
²unite \ˈyüˌnīt, =ˈ=\ *n* -S [fr. obs. *unite* joint, united, fr. ME *unit,* fr. LL *unitus*] **:** an old British gold 20-shilling piece issued first by James I in 1604 for England and Scotland and bearing in the design and inscription reference to the uniting of the two crowns — called also *jacobus*
uniteable *var of* UNITABLE
united *adj* [fr. past part. of ¹*unite*] **1 :** made one **:** COMBINED, JOINED **2 :** relating to or produced by joint action **:** CONJOINT ⟨their ~ consent⟩ **3 :** formed by or resulting from union **4 :** being or living in agreement **:** HARMONIOUS ⟨a ~ family⟩ — **unit·ed·ly** *adv* — **unit·ed·ness** *n* -ES
united baptist *n, usu cap U&B* **:** a member of a Baptist sect formed in the late 18th century by a union of some Separate Baptist and Regular Baptist churches of the South
united brethren *n pl, usu cap U&B* **1 :** MORAVIANS **2 :** Christians of several denominations descending from the United Brethren in Christ originating among Germans in the U.S. during the religious awakening of the late 18th century, formally organized in 1800, and resembling Methodism in doctrine and polity
united front *n* **1 :** a state or appearance of unity, common purpose, or general agreement usu. presented by a heterogeneous group in the face of opposition or danger from an outside source ⟨that Western Europe will continue to present a *united front* against the threat of Communist aggression — *Springfield (Mass.) Union*⟩ **2 :** POPULAR FRONT ⟨the appearance of a *united front* in each country controlled by the Russians after World War II⟩

united kingdom *adj, usu cap U&K* [fr. the *United Kingdom* (Great Britain and Northern Ireland)] **:** of or from the United Kingdom **:** of the kind or style prevalent in the United Kingdom

united nations *adj, usu cap U&N* **1 :** of or relating to the United Nations organization or community **2 :** of or relating to the United Nations territory which is an enclave of New York, N.Y.

united presbyterian *n, usu cap U&P* **:** a Presbyterian of the United Presbyterian Church of North America formed by merger in 1858 or of the United Presbyterian Church in the U.S.A. formed by a merger including the former in 1958

1united states *n pl but usu sing in constr* [fr. the *United States* of America] **1** *usu cap* **:** a federation of states esp. when forming a nation in a usu. specified territory ⟨advocating a *United States* of Europe⟩ **2 :** United States English **:** written or spoken English exhibiting peculiarities typical of the United States of No. America

2united states *adj, usu cap U&S* [fr. the *United States* of America] **:** of or from the United States of No. America ⟨a *United States* ship⟩ **:** of the kind or style prevalent in the United States

united states court of appeals *usu cap U&S* **:** a court in each of the 11 federal judicial districts of the U. S. that functions as a court of record, exercises appellate jurisdiction, is presided over by three or sometimes two judges, and may be overruled only by the Supreme Court of the U. S.

united statesian \¦==¦stātsēən\ *n* -s *cap U&S* [*United States* of America + *-ian*] **:** a native or resident of the United States of No. America

united-statesian \"\ *adj, usu cap U&S* **:** UNITED STATES

united states note *n, usu cap U&S* **:** a piece of United States paper money

united states standard thread *n, usu cap U&S* **:** an American screw thread that has a thread angle of 60 degrees and varies from 3½ to 64 threads per inch

united states value *n, usu cap U&S* **:** a value of imported merchandise that is obtained by deducting from its value in U. S. wholesale markets specified enumerated expenses of importation and that is used esp. as a basis for assessing customs duties

unit·er \yü'nīd·ə(r), -ītə-\ *n* -s **:** one that unites

uni·terminal \¦yünə+\ *adj* [*uni-* + *terminal*] **:** POLAR 2b

unites *pres 3d sing of* UNITE, *pl of* UNITE

unit factor *n* **:** a gene that controls the inheritance of a unit character — compare POLYGENE

unit fraction *n* **:** a fraction whose numerator is unity and whose denominator is an integer

unit heater *n* **:** a heater consisting essentially of a fan or blower and an indirect radiator enclosed in a common casing and designed to circulate and warm the air of a continuous enclosed space (as a room)

unities *pl of* UNITY

uniting *pres part of* UNITE

uni·tion \yü'nishən\ *n* -s [LL *unition-, unitio,* fr. *unitus* (past part. of *unire* to unite) + L *-ion-, -io* -ion — more at UNITE] **:** an act of uniting or the state of being united **:** JUNCTION

unit·ism \'yünə,tizəm\ *n* -s [¹*unit* + *-ism*] **:** MONISM

uni·tive \'yünəd·iv, -ətiv\ *adj* [LL *unitivus,* fr. *unitus* (past part. of *unire* to unite) + L *-ivus* -ive] **:** characterized by or tending to produce union — **uni·tive·ly** *adv* — **uni·tive·ness** *n* -ES

unitive way *n* **:** UNION 1a(6)

unit·ization \,yünəd·ə'zāshən, -nətə'z-, -nə,tī'z-\ *n* -s **1 :** the quality or state of being unitized **2 :** the act of unitizing: as **a :** the uniting of diverse properties into a single operational unit **b :** the assembling and securing of goods or packages into a unit of use or sale

unit·ize \'yünə,tīz\ *vt* -ED/-ING/-S *see -ize in Explan Notes* [¹*unit* + *-ize*] **:** to convert into a unit: as **a :** to aggregate discrete elements into (a functional whole) ⟨~ an oil field⟩ ⟨a car with a *unitized* body⟩ **b :** to divide and package or otherwise finish (an aggregate of material) into units designed for the ultimate buyer or user ⟨~ bulk merchandise⟩

unit·iz·er \-zə(r)\ *n* -s **:** an auto factory stock clerk who packs parts or accessories in matched sets

unit line *n* **:** a field line (as in a magnetic field) representing one unit of flux

unit lock *n* **:** a lock set whose parts are permanently combined and which can be applied to a door as a single unit

unit magnetic pole *n* **:** a unit of magnetic pole strength equal to the strength of a magnetic pole that repels an identical pole at a distance of one centimeter with a force of one dyne

unit marker *n* **:** a device (as a guidon) that serves to identify a unit (as of a military force)

unit modifier *n* **:** a compound adherent adjective or a phrase or sentence used as an adherent modifier

unit of account : a monetary unit or measure of value (as a coin) in terms of which accounts are kept and values stated

unit of fire : a prescribed quantity of ammunition for a given organization or weapon based on the number of rounds that on the average are expected to be used in one day

unit of value 1 : the amount of some one thing taken as a standard by comparison with which to reckon the value of other things **2** *or* **unit of assessment :** the unit of length, surface, capacity, or weight that an assessor uses in calculations of or values for the assessment of taxes

unit operation *n* **:** a physical change to which material is subjected esp. in coordination with a unit process (as filtration, distillation, or extraction)

unit organ *n* **:** an organ with comparatively few sets of pipes that by the use of duplexing and unification are made available by means of different stop names on all manuals and at various pitches

unit price *n* **:** a price quoted in terms of so much per agreed or standard unit of product or service ⟨agreed to take the gravel at a *unit price* of 50 cents a yard⟩; *often* **:** an inclusive price quoted to cover all incidentals (as transportation or installation) as well as the basic unit of product or service ⟨purchasing on a *unit price* relieves the buyer of inconvenience but may be more expensive⟩ ⟨quoted a *unit price* for the funeral⟩

unit process *n* **:** a chemical change (as nitration, diazotization, or esterification) to which material is subjected as a step in manufacture

unit pulse *n* **:** the shortest telegraphic signaling pulse **:** BAND

uni·trivalent \¦yünə+\ *adj* [*uni-* + *trivalent*] **:** of, relating to, or designating an electrolyte that dissociates into three univalent ions and one trivalent ion

unit rule *n* **:** a rule that may be adopted optionally by a delegation to a Democratic national convention under which the entire vote of the delegation shall be cast as a unit as determined by a majority vote

units *pl of* UNIT

unit-set \¦==¦=\ *adj, of printing type* **:** cast with a set expressible in units — compare POINT-SET

unit solid angle *n* **:** STERADIAN

unit switch *n* **:** a switch designed to establish or interrupt an electric-power circuit repeatedly under normal operating conditions

unit value *n* **:** the set of a printing character measured in units

unit vector *n* **:** a vector of unit magnitude used to specify a particular spatial direction

unit vote *n* **:** a vote cast by a political subdivision as a single unit regardless of the number of persons voting or eligible to vote

unit watermark *n* **:** a watermark on a stamp that is a single entire design — called also *simple watermark*

uni·ty \'yünəd·ē, -ətē, -i\ *n* -ES [ME *unite,* fr. OF *unité,* fr. L *unitat-, unitas,* fr. *unus* one + *-itat-, -itas* -ity — more at ONE] **1 a :** the quality or state of being or consisting of one **:** ONENESS, SINGLENESS **b** (1) **:** a definite quantity or aggregate of quantities or magnitudes taken as one or for which 1 is made to stand in calculation ⟨in a table of natural sines the radius of the circle is regarded as ~⟩ (2) **:** the singular multiplier in any system multiplication by which leaves the multiplicand unchanged and which is distinguished from a unit in not entering into addition ⟨in any system there may be many units (as 1 and *i* in complex numbers) yet only one if any ~⟩ (3) *archaic* **:** UNIT 1a(1) **2 a :** a condition of concordant harmony **:** the state of those that are in full agreement **:** ACCORD ⟨attaining ~ of purpose through thorough discussion⟩ ⟨living in contented ~⟩ **b :** continuity without deviation or change (as in purpose or action) **:** absence of diversity **3 a :** the quality or state of being made one **:** a uniting into one **:** UNIFICATION ⟨the strength that lies in ~⟩ ⟨seeking ~ with the several groups in order that they might become a more effective competitor in world markets⟩ **b :** a combination or ordering of parts in a literary or artistic production such as to constitute a whole or promote an undivided total effect **:** the reference of the elements of a composition to a single main idea or point of view; *also* **:** conformity to this principle or the singleness of effect or symmetry and consistency of style and character secured **4 a :** the quality or state of constituting a whole and esp. one organized from distinguishable parts or elements **b :** a totality of related parts **:** an entity that is a complex or systematic whole — compare ORGANIC 5b **5 :** any of four peculiar characteristics of an estate held by several in joint tenancy according to which joint tenants have one and the same interest accruing by one and the same conveyance, commencing at the same time, and held by one and the same undivided possession **6 :** any of three principles governing the structure of drama, derived by writers of the French classical school from the Aristotelian canon, and as rigidly formulated requiring the action of a play to be represented as occurring in one place, within one day, and with nothing irrelevant to the plot — called also respectively *unity of place, unity of time, unity of action* **7** *usu cap* **:** a 20th century American religious movement that utilizes for the most part a conservative Protestant Christian theology in its teachings but adds the two distinctive doctrines of reincarnation and the regeneration of the body, and emphasizes health, successful living, and prosperity

unity in variety : a principle that aesthetic value or beauty in art depends on the fusion of various elements into an organic whole which produces a single impression

unity of science movement : SCIENTIFIC EMPIRICISM 1

unity stress *n* **:** accent (as of *up* and *on* in *upon*) that unites the meanings of words

uni·univalent \¦yünə, -nē+\ *adj* [*uni-* + *univalent*] **:** of, relating to, or designating an electrolyte that dissociates into two univalent ions

univ *abbr* universal; universally; universe; university

1uni·va·lent \¦yünə¦vālənt, yü'nivələnt\ *adj* [ISV *uni-* + *valent*] **:** having a valence of one: as **a :** capable usu. of combining with only one atom of another element ⟨the hydrogen atom . . . is taken to be ~ —N.N.Greenwood⟩ **b** *of a chromosome* **:** lacking a synaptic mate **:** SINGLE **c** *of an antibody* **:** capable of agglutinating or precipitating but not both **:** having only one combining group

2univalent \"\ *n* **:** a univalent chromosome

1uni·valve \¦yünə+\ *also* **uni·valved** \"+\ *adj* [*uni-* + *valve* or *valved*] **:** having or consisting of one valve only ⟨a ~ shell⟩ ⟨a ~ diatom⟩

2univalve \"\ *n* **1 :** a mollusk with a univalve shell; *esp* **:** GASTROPOD — compare BIVALVE **2 :** a mollusk shell consisting of one piece

uni·variant \¦yünə+\ *adj* [ISV *uni-* + *variant*] **:** having one degree of freedom — used of a physical-chemical system; compare BIVARIANT, PHASE RULE

uni·variate \"+\ *adj* [*uni-* + *variate*] **:** having or involving one variate only

1uni·ver·sal \¦yünə¦vərsəl, -vəs-, -vəis-\ *adj* [ME *universel, universal,* fr. MF, fr. L *universalis,* fr. *universus* entire, whole + *-alis* -al — more at UNIVERSE] **1 :** including or covering all or a whole collectively or distributively without limit or notable exception or variation ⟨~ human weakness —T.S.Eliot⟩ ⟨most of the twigs, pearled with water, were patterned very naked against ~ gray —John Galsworthy⟩ **2 a :** present or occurring as indicated throughout the whole world **:** encountered everywhere ⟨~ as the air —Samuel Rogers⟩ **b :** existent or operative as indicated everywhere or under all conditions ⟨far from being infrequent, the crystalline state is almost ~ among solids —K.K.Darrow⟩ **c :** having effectiveness, power, or action through a salient part of the world ⟨a ~ state, in the shape of the Roman Empire —A.J.Toynbee⟩ **3 :** pertinent to or inclusive of all or much of mankind: **a :** practiced, observed, or occurring throughout all peoples or groups or a great many of them **:** commonly or unanimously followed, approved, or subscribed to by a people or group ⟨petty gambling is nearly ~ —W.C.Brownell⟩ ⟨feudalism was not so ~ there . . . as in the north —H.O.Taylor⟩ ⟨~ cultural patterns⟩ **b :** marked by width and inclusiveness **:** embracing a very wide range of interests or pursuits **:** comprehensively broad and versatile ⟨a ~ genius. He wrote . . . logic, rhetoric, poetics, physics, botany, zoology . . . —Frank Thilly⟩ **c :** designed for general or worldwide use or applicability ⟨interested in ideas of ~ citizenship, in Esperanto and Ido and ~ languages —H.G. Wells⟩ **4 :** relatively unrestricted in application **:** of general relevance: as **a** *of a logical proposition* **:** affirming or denying something of all members of a class **b :** constituting a general term capable of denoting every member of a class **c :** common to all members of a class ⟨food is a ~ need of living beings⟩ ⟨color is a ~ attribute of visible objects⟩ **5 :** of, relating to, or involving the totality of a person's legal rights and liabilities ⟨a ~ partnership⟩ — compare UNIVERSAL SUCCESSION **6 :** adapted or adjustable to meet varied requirements (as of use, shape, or size) ⟨a ~ gear cutter⟩ — compare UNIVERSAL JOINT, UNIVERSAL MOTOR, UNIVERSAL VISE **7 :** of, relating to, or constituting a universal

syn COSMIC, ECUMENICAL, CATHOLIC, COSMOPOLITAN: UNIVERSAL is likely to suggest that which is worldwide rather than pertinent to or characteristic of the whole universe; it is often further narrowed to refer to the world of men and human affairs or to important or significant parts of this world. It is likely to indicate a unanimity or conformity of practice or belief or a broad comprehensiveness ⟨no other theory which has won *universal* acceptance —Laurence Binyon⟩ ⟨the *universal* favor with which the New Testament is outwardly received —H.D.Thoreau⟩ ⟨replaced a philosophy which was crude and raw and provincial by one which was, in comparison, catholic, civilized and *universal* —T.S.Eliot⟩ COSMIC is used to suggest matters pertinent to the whole universe as opposed to the earth, esp. in suggestions of infinite vastness, distance, or force ⟨sardonic phantoms, whose vision is *cosmic,* not terrestrial —J.L.Lowes⟩ ⟨the great *cosmic* rhythm of the spirit which sets the currents of life in motion —Laurence Binyon⟩ ECUMENICAL applies to situations involving people throughout the whole world or all people in groups or divisions as indicated, often in religious contexts ⟨the incorporation of all the broken fragments of the former Iranic and Arabic societies into the wholly different structure of a Western World which has grown into an *ecumenical* "Great Society" —A.J.Toynbee⟩ CATHOLIC may stress an attitude involved, as well as a fact, in including, comprehending, or appreciating of all or many peoples, places, or periods ⟨he was a *catholic* nature lover. The tropics, the desert, the tundra, the glaciers and the prairies all found a place in his heart —D.C.Peattie⟩ COSMOPOLITAN may imply an understanding and appreciation of other lands, sections, nations, or cities coming about through personal experience in traveling or living elsewhere; it often contrasts with *provincial* ⟨one of the most entertaining and most *cosmopolitan* of novelists. Born in Tuscany, he was educated in New England, England, Germany, and Italy, became interested in Sanskrit, edited a newspaper in India —Carl Van Doren⟩

syn GENERIC, GENERAL, COMMON: UNIVERSAL implies applicability to each one of a whole and usu. precludes significant exception ⟨a prehistoric and *universal* principle that the burden of defense should rest upon all able-bodied males —G.G.Coulton⟩ ⟨habits both *universal* among mankind and peculiar to individuals —F.H.Allport⟩ GENERIC applies to that which characterizes every individual in a category or group and may suggest further that what is designated may be thought of as a clear and certain classificatory criterion ⟨erect pointed ears are *generic* among foxes⟩ ⟨natural that the preaching of men of all religious categories — except ranters — should have a *generic* likeness —Douglas Bush⟩ GENERAL is used to refer to all, nearly all, or the great majority of a class, type, group, or number; it is less inclusive than *universal* and less precise in suggestion than *generic* ⟨ethylene has come into *general* but not yet universal favor with surgeons —A.C. Morrison⟩ ⟨nightfall brings about a *general* upward movement of the animal species, each striving to attain its optimum illumination —W.H.Dowdeswell⟩ COMMON indicates frequency, applicability to a majority, usu. without being an identifying or classifying attribute; it may suggest a certain participation, sharing, mutual relationship, tendency to group together ⟨the *common,* the perpetually repeated mistake of judging the savage by the standard of European civilization —J.G.Frazer⟩ ⟨crowds . . . swept along by a *common* animating impulse —Laurence Binyon⟩

2universal \"\ *n* -s **1 :** the whole of something specified **:** a thing in its entirety — used with *the* **2 :** one that is universal (as in power, currency, interest, scope, or applicability): as **a** (1) **:** a universal proposition in logic — called also *abstract universal;* compare CONCRETE UNIVERSAL (2) **:** a predicable of traditional logic (3) **:** a general concept or something in reality to which it corresponds **:** an abstract and general term or something denoted by such a term **:** the essence of a particular logical genus **:** ABSTRACTION **b** *obs* **:** a remedy affecting or altering the entire bodily mechanism **c** *obs* **:** UNIVERSE **d** (1) **:** a pattern or mode of behavior existing in all cultures ⟨the institution of the family is a ~ in human culture⟩ (2) **:** a culture trait characteristic of all normal adult members of a particular society **3 :** a metaphysical being (as the ego or self) that preserves or evinces an identity of nature through a series of changes or as embodying different relations ⟨self-consciousness, wherein the ~, or self, is the organic total of the facts of consciousness —Josiah Royce⟩ — compare CONCRETE UNIVERSAL

3universal \"\ *adv* **:** UNIVERSALLY

universal affirmation *n* **:** a universal proposition that affirms something of all members of a class

universal agent *n* **:** one to whom has been delegated powers to act for the principal in all business and in all matters rather than in a particular business **:** GENERAL AGENT

universal calling *n* **:** the divine summons to all men to repent and accept the gospel

universal cause *n* **:** the ultimate or all-comprehensive cause **:** FIRST CAUSE; *often* **:** GOD

universal chuck *n* **:** a chuck in which the jaws are moved simultaneously to center the workpiece

universal class *n* **:** a class comprising all members of a universe of discourse

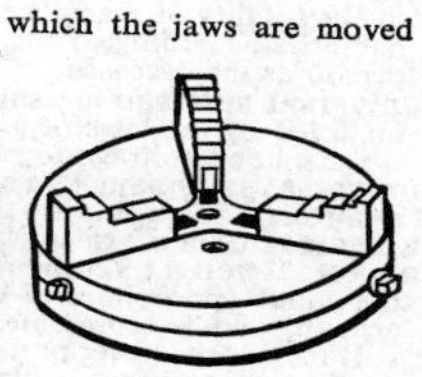

universal chuck

universal compass *n* **:** a large compass with hollow adjustable legs each containing a complete bow compass that may be used as a part of the large compass or independently

universal constant *n* **:** a physical constant of wide application and frequent occurrence in physical formulas ⟨the speed of light, *c,* the electronic charge, *e,* and the Planck constant, *h,* are *universal constants*⟩

universal conversion *n* **:** conversion of a proposition in logic into a universal proposition

universal decimal classification *n* **:** an expanded decimal classification widely used in Europe — called also *Brussels classification*

universal dial *n* **:** a sundial with an adjustable gnomon by which the hour may be found in any part of the world or under any elevation of the pole

universal donor *n* **1 :** TYPE O **2 a :** a person with type O blood **b :** the blood of such a person

universal grammar *n* **:** GENERAL GRAMMAR

uni·ver·sa·lian \¦yünə(,)vər¦salyən, -lēən\ *adj, usu cap* [¹*universal* + *-ian*] **:** UNIVERSALIST

uni·ver·sal·ism \,==¦vərsə,lizəm, -vəs-, -vəis-\ *n* -s **1** *often cap* **a :** a theological doctrine that all men will eventually be saved or restored to holiness and happiness **b :** the principles and practices of Universalists including centrally the belief that all men will ultimately be saved **2 :** a thing universal in scope; *also* **:** addiction to universal knowledge or pursuits **3 :** the state of being universal **:** UNIVERSALITY **4 a :** a theory according to which the whole is logically or valuationally prior to its parts **b :** an ethical theory that the good of all men should take precedence over that of an individual — contrasted with *individualism* **c :** a social relationship in which behavior is determined by an impersonal code or standard — contrasted with *particularism*

1uni·ver·sal·ist \-ləst\ *n* -s [¹*universal* + *-ist*] **1 a :** one who believes in universalism **b** *usu cap* **:** a member of a Christian denomination founded in America in the 18th century and holding the view that all men will be ultimately saved, employing a modified congregational polity, having at its head a general convention, and using no strictly creedal basis but having members who for the most part acknowledge their common purpose to be the performance of the will of God as revealed by Jesus Christ and the establishment of the kingdom for which he lived and died and who acknowledge belief in God, in the leadership of Jesus Christ, in the supreme worth of every human personality, in the authority of truth now known or to be known, in the power of men of goodwill to overcome evil, and in their power to establish progressively God's kingdom on earth **2 a :** one who affects or is credited with universal knowledge, interests, or aptitudes **b :** one who regards or acts with regard to the whole

2universalist \"\ *adj* **1** *usu cap* **:** of or relating to Universalists or their principles and practices **2 :** UNIVERSALISTIC

uni·ver·sal·is·tic \¦==,==¦listik, -tēk\ *adj* **1 :** of or relating to the whole **:** universal in scope or nature **2 :** of or relating to universalism or the universal **:** resembling or tending toward universalism **3** *usu cap* **:** UNIVERSALIST 1

universalistic hedonism *n* **:** an ethical theory that the supreme good and the determining consideration of moral conduct is the greatest happiness of the greatest number **:** UTILITARIANISM 1 — contrasted with *egoistic hedonism;* compare PSYCHOLOGICAL HEDONISM

uni·ver·sal·i·ty \,==(,)vər'saləd·ē, -lətē, -i\ *n* -ES [ME *universalite,* fr. LL *universalitas,* fr. L *universalis* universal + *-itas* -ity — more at UNIVERSAL] **1 :** the quality or state of being universal (as in extent, occurrence, or application) **2 :** universal comprehensiveness in range (as of subjects, pursuits, or acquaintances) **:** unrestricted versatility or power of adaptation or comprehension ⟨the ~ of Shakespeare's insight⟩ **3 :** the entire body of a specified group; *sometimes* **:** the mass of the people as distinguished from those deserving (as by reason of class or special notability) to be particularized **4** *obs* **:** GENERALITY

uni·ver·sal·ization \,==vərsələ'zāshən, -ə,lī'z-\ *n* -s **:** the quality or state of being universalized

uni·ver·sal·ize \,==¦vərsə,līz\ *vt* -ED/-ING/-S *see -ize in Explan Notes* [¹*universal* + *-ize*] **:** to make universal (as in character, application, or distribution) **:** GENERALIZE ⟨to observe what is best in the schools and to strive to ~ these qualities —*Amer. Child*⟩ — **uni·ver·sal·iz·er** \-zə(r)\ *n* -s

universal joint *or* **universal coupling** *n* **:** a shaft coupling capable of transmitting rotation from one shaft to another not collinear with it and typically consisting of a cross-shaped piece having pivots on its arms so arranged that each pair of pivots engage with the eyes of a yoke on the end of one shaft

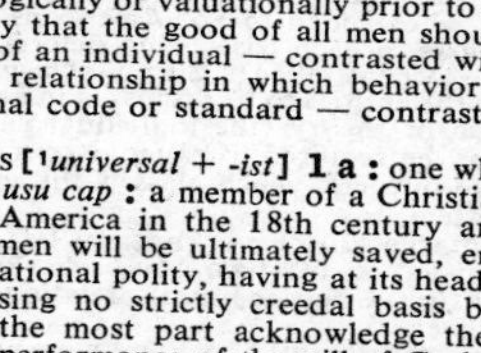

universal joint

universal language *n* **:** an international auxiliary language

universal legacy *n* **:** a legacy under Roman or civil law resembling the residuary legacy of Anglo-American law by which a testator gives to one or more persons all his estate subject to the duty of paying particular legacies and debts and carrying out fideicommissary bequests

uni·ver·sal·ly \-s(ə)lē, -li\ *adv* [ME, fr. *universal* + *-ly*] **:** in a universal manner **:** so as to be universal (as in influence or effect) ⟨a ~ applicable rule⟩

universal military service *n* **:** a system under which all male citizens with some specified exceptions are required to serve a prescribed length of time in an active unit of the armed forces
universal military training *n* **:** a system under which all male citizens with some specified exceptions are required to train for a short period in a special organization and a longer period in a reserve unit
universal mill *n* **:** a rolling mill in which metal is acted upon by two sets of rollers commonly horizontal and vertical at each pass and which is used esp. in rolling girder and channel-bar sections
universal milling machine *n* **:** a milling machine having a table fitted with all motions and a dividing head with change gears so that it can perform any type of milling operation
universal motor *n* **:** an electric motor (as for small household and workshop appliances) that can be used on either an alternating or a direct current supply
universal negative *n* **:** a universal proposition that denies something of all members of a class
uni·ver·sal·ness *n* -ES **:** the quality or state of being universal
universal partnership *n* **:** a partnership that includes all the present and future property of the partners and all burdens or losses which without fraud are incurred by either partner and that is exemplified by the community of property between husband and wife under Roman Dutch law or the civil law
universal postulate *n* **:** a criterion of truth: something whose negative is inconceivable must be true
universal quantifier *n* **:** a logical quantifier that asserts all values of a given variable in a formula
universal rule *n* **:** a rule of measurement for the racing of yachts including as factors the waterline length, sail area, and displacement with modifying limitations
universals *pl of* UNIVERSAL
universal scale *n* **:** an architect's or engineer's scale
universal shunt *n* **:** AYRTON SHUNT
universal solvent *n* **:** ALKAHEST
universal stage *n* **:** a small theodolite made in dimensions suitable for a petrographic microscope and used to obtain detailed optical and petrofabric data
universal succession *n* **:** succession under Roman or civil law to the totality of a man's estate including both his rights and liabilities according to the principle that the heir is the same person as the deceased
universal suffrage *n* **:** suffrage of all adults not legally disqualified by the laws of a country: **a :** MANHOOD SUFFRAGE **b :** manhood suffrage together with woman suffrage
universal syllogism *n* **:** a syllogism the conclusion of which is a universal proposition
universal time *n* **:** GREENWICH TIME
universal veil *n* **:** a membrane that initially completely invests the young sporophore of various mushrooms, is ruptured by growth, and is represented in the mature sporophore by a volva about the lower part of the stem and sometimes by scales on the upper surface of the cap — compare PARTIAL VEIL
universal vise *n* **:** a vise (as on some milling machines) that can be swung either horizontally or vertically — compare SWIVEL VISE
uni·verse \ˈyünəˌvərs, -vəs, -vəis *sometimes* ˈyünēˌ-\ *n* -S [L *universum* (trans. of Gk *to holon*), fr. neut. of *universus* entire, whole, fr. *uni-* + *versus*, past part. of *vertere* to turn — more at WORTH] **1 :** the whole body of things and phenomena **:** the totality of material entities **:** COSMOS: as **a :** a systematic whole held to arise by and persist through the direct intervention of divine power **b :** the world of human experience **:** this earth that is the seat of mankind; *also* **:** the inhabitants of earth **:** human beings **c** (1) **:** the entire celestial cosmos **:** the totality of the observed or postulated physical whole — compare EXPANDING UNIVERSE (2) **:** MILKY WAY GALAXY (3) **:** an aggregate of stars comparable to the Milky Way galaxy — see ISLAND UNIVERSE **2 :** a distinct field or province of thought or reality that forms a closed system or self-inclusive and independent organization; *often* **:** UNIVERSE OF DISCOURSE **3 :** POPULATION 4
universe of discourse 1 : a collection of facts, ideas or entities that is tacitly implied or understood in a given statement, context, or discussion ⟨a proposition concerning "Americans" may be intended to apply only to American aborigines, or to citizens of the U. S., it may include all No. Americans, or be extended to So. Americans as well, the *universe of discourse* in each case being determined by the sense in which the word is taken⟩ **2 :** an inclusive class explicitly containing all the entities to be discussed in a given discourse or investigation or theory ⟨the individual variables of an axiom system may be required to range over members of the class of positive integers, which class is the *universe of discourse* for that system⟩
universe vine *n* **:** BEARBERRY 1
¹**uni·ver·si·tar·i·an** \ˌ==ˌ=səˈterēən, -ta(a)r-, -tār-\ *adj* [*university* + *-arian*] **:** of, relating to, or characteristic of a university
²**universitarian** \"\ *n* -S **:** a member of a university
uni·ver·si·tas \ˌ==ˈ=səˌtas\ *n, pl* **universita·tes** \ˌ==ˌ==ˈtāˌtēz\ [L, lit., totality] **:** something whether in fact composed of one or more than one unit that is treated as an indivisible whole by the law
universitas ju·ris \-ˈju̇rəs\ *n* [L, totality of right] **:** the totality of the rights and liabilities of a person
universitas per·so·na·rum \-ˌpərsᵊnˈa(a)rəm, -ˈer-, -ˈār-\ *n* [L, totality of persons] **:** a number of persons (as a college, corporation, or state) functioning together as an independent entity
universitas re·rum \-ˈrērəm, -rār-\ *n* [L, totality of things] **:** a totality of objects treated in one or more respects as a whole in law
uni·ver·si·ty \ˌyünəˈvərsəd·ē, -vəs-, -vəis-, -s(ə)tē, -i\ *n* -ES *often attrib* [ME *universite*, fr. OF *université*, fr. ML, LL, & L; ML *universitat-, universitas* university (sense 1), fr. LL, company, corporation, guild, fr. L, totality, universe, fr. *universus* entire, whole + *-itat-, -itas* -ity — more at UNIVERSE] **1 a** *archaic* **:** a body of persons gathered at a particular place for the disseminating and assimilating of knowledge in advanced fields of study **b :** an institution of higher learning providing facilities for teaching and research and authorized to grant academic degrees: as (1) **:** an institution in the British Commonwealth authorized to hold examinations and confer degrees and usu. consisting of several affiliated or associated colleges (2) **:** a continental European institution concentrating on or exclusively concerned with advanced or professional study (3) **:** an institution made up of an undergraduate division which confers bachelor's degrees and a graduate division which comprises a graduate school and professional schools each of which may confer master's degrees and doctorates **c :** the physical plant of a university **2** *obs* **a :** UNIVERSE **b :** a body of persons **c :** the mass of the people **3 :** a corporation, guild, association, or other body (as of persons) that is treated as a unit at law **:** UNIVERSITAS
university college *n* **1 :** a college attached to or affiliated with a university **2** *Brit* **:** a college lacking the right to confer its own degrees and for this purpose attached to but physically separate from a university
university extension *n* **:** EXTENSION 6
university press *n* **:** a press connected with a university and esp. concerned with the publication of scholarly works
uni·ver·sol·o·gy \ˌ==(ˌ)vərˈsäləjē\ *n* -ES [*universe* + *-o-* + *-logy*] **:** science of the universe
¹**univ·o·cal** \yüˈnivəkəl\ *adj* [LL *univocus* having only one meaning (fr. L *uni-* + *-vocus*, fr. *voc-, vox* voice) + E *-al* — more at VOICE] **1 :** unmistakable in meaning: as **a** *archaic* **:** symptomatic of but one thing **b :** having one meaning only **:** subject to a single interpretation **c :** UNAMBIGUOUS — contrasted with *equivocal* **2** *obs* **a :** UNANIMOUS **b :** UNIFORM **3** *archaic* **:** characteristic of or restricted to things of the same nature — **univ·o·cal·ly** \-vək(ə)lē, -li\ *adv*
²**univocal** \"\ *n* **:** a word or term having but one meaning
uni·vocalic \ˌyünə+\ *adj* [*uni-* + *vocalic*] **:** having one vowel — compare PLURIVOCALIC
uni·vocality \"+\ *n* **:** the quality or state of being univocal
uni·vo·ci·ty \ˌyünəˈväsəd·ē\ *n* -ES [*univocal* + *-ity*] **:** the character or quality of being univocal
uni·vol·tine \ˌyünəˈvōlˌtēn, -ltᵊn\ *adj* [F *univoltin*, fr. *uni-* + It *volta* time, instance + F *-in* -ine — more at BIVOLTINE] **:** producing one brood in a season and esp. a single brood of eggs capable of hibernating — used of insects; compare BIVOLTINE
un·jaded \ˌən+\ *adj* **:** not jaded **:** FRESH, KEEN ⟨the most lively and ~ fancy may . . . need direction —*Atlantic*⟩
un·jaundiced \"+\ *adj* **:** free from jaundice; *esp* **:** free from hurtful prejudice ⟨good citizens, with well-balanced, ~ minds —Louis Bromfield⟩
un·jelled \"+\ *adj* [¹*un-* + *jelled*, past part. of *jell*] **:** not stabilized in final or definitive form ⟨an ~ agreement⟩
un·join \"+\ *vt* [ME *unjoinen*, fr. ²*un-* + *joinen* to join — more at JOIN] **:** to separate from a state of union **:** DIVORCE
un·joined \"+\ *adj* **:** not joined
un·joint \"+\ *vt* [²*un-* + *joint*, n.] **:** to sever or dislocate at a joint (as in carving) **:** DISJOINT
un·jointed \"+\ *adj* **:** not jointed
un·joyous \"+\ *adj* **:** deficient in joy **:** lacking the capacity to convey joyous emotion
un·judicial \"+\ *adj* **:** unbecoming or unsuitable to a judge — **un·judicially** \"+\ *adv*
un·judicious \"+\ *adj* **:** INJUDICIOUS
un·just \"+\ *adj* [ME, fr. ¹*un-* + *just*] **1 :** characterized by injustice **:** deficient in justice and fairness **:** WRONGFUL ⟨an ~ judge⟩ ⟨an ~ sentence⟩ ⟨such a proposal was ~ to the consumers⟩ **2** *archaic* **:** DISHONEST, FAITHLESS — **un·justly** \"+\ *adv* — **un·justness** \"+\ *n*
unjust enrichment *n* **:** acquisition of property under such circumstances that one is legally or equitably bound to make restitution of it
un·justice \ˌən+\ *n, chiefly Scot* **:** INJUSTICE
un·justifiable \"+\ *adj* **:** not justifiable **:** lacking in propriety or justice ⟨~ noise⟩ ⟨an ~ decision⟩ — **un·justifiableness** \"+\ *n* — **un·justifiably** \"+\ *adv*
un·justification \"+\ *n* **:** the quality or state of being unjustified
un·justified \"+\ *adj* [¹*un-* + *justified*, past part. of *justify*] **:** not justified: as **a :** not demonstrably correct or judicious **:** unwarranted in the light of surrounding circumstances ⟨~ abuse⟩ **b** *of a line of type* **:** not adjusted to properly fill the measure
unk *abbr* unknown
un·kar \ˈəŋˌkär\ *adj, usu cap* [fr. the *Unkar* valley, Arizona] **:** of, relating to, or constituting the lower division of the Algonkian rocks in the Grand Canyon region, Arizona, consisting mainly of sandstone with some limestone and conglomerate and forming a layer nearly 7000 feet in thickness
un·ked *also* **un·kid** \ˈəŋkəd, ˈu̇ŋ-\ *or* **un·ket** \-kət\ *adj* [ME *unkid*, fr. ¹*un-* + *kid*, past part. of *kithen* to make known — more at KITHE] **1** *dial Brit* **:** UNKNOWN, STRANGE, ODD **2** *archaic* **:** UNCOUTH, AWKWARD **3** *dial Brit* **:** DESOLATE, LONELY **4** *dial Brit* **:** UNCANNY, WEIRD, GHASTLY
un·keeled \ˌən+\ *adj* [¹*un-* + *keel*, n. + *-ed*] **:** having no keel — opposed to *carinate*
un·kempt \"+\ *adj* [¹*un-* + *kempt*, past part. of *kemb*] **1 a** *of hair* **:** not combed **b :** deficient in order or neatness of person **:** DISHEVELED **2 :** not trimly finished or ordered **:** lacking in formal neatness and order **:** ROUGH ⟨native vistas and ~ rambling paths⟩ **syn** see SLIPSHOD
un·kempt·ly *adv* **:** in an unkempt manner **:** so as to be unkempt
un·kempt·ness *n* -ES **:** the quality or state of being unkempt
un·kenned \ˌən+\ *adj* [ME, fr. ¹*un-* + *kenned*, past part. of *kennen* to ken — more at KEN] *chiefly dial* **:** UNKNOWN, STRANGE
un·kennel \"+\ *vt* **1 a :** to drive (as a fox) from a hiding place or den **b :** to free (dogs) from a kennel **2 :** to cause to come to light **:** bring out into the open **:** DISCOVER, DISCLOSE ⟨seeking to ~ traitors⟩
un·kenning \"+\ *adj* [¹*un-* + *kenning*, pres. part. of *ken*] *Scot* **:** not knowing **:** IGNORANT
un·kent \"+\ *adj* [¹*un-* + *kent*, past part. of *ken*] *chiefly Scot* **:** not known or recognized
un·kept \"+\ *adj* [ME, fr. ¹*un-* + *kept*, past part. of *kepen* to keep — more at KEEP] **:** not kept: as **a :** NEGLECTED **b :** DISREGARDED **c :** UNDEFENDED
un·key \"+\ *vt* [²*un-* + *key* (insert a keystone)] **:** to remove the key from (as an arch)
un·kind \"+\ *adj* [ME, fr. ¹*un-* + *kind*] **1 a** *of weather or climate* **:** marked by harshness and rigor **:** deficient in pleasant mildness **b** *chiefly dial* **:** exhibiting unfavorable or undesirable qualities **:** inherently bad or unsuitable — used esp. of soil **c** *chiefly dial* **:** not thriving **2** *obs* **a :** deficient in appreciation of or gratitude for benefits **:** UNGRATEFUL **b :** unduly or unnaturally ungenerous or severe **3 :** deficient in humane and kindly feeling, expression, or outlook **:** lacking in sympathy and kindness **:** HARSH, RIGOROUS, CRUEL — **un·kindness** \"+\ *n*
un·kindliness \"+\ *n* [ME *unkindlinesse*, fr. *unkindly* + *-nesse* -ness] **:** the quality or state of being unkindly
¹**un·kindly** \"+\ *adj* [ME, fr. ¹*un-* + *kindly*] **:** UNKIND
²**unkindly** \"\ *also* **un·kind·li·ly** \-lᵊlē\ *adv* [*unkindly* fr. ME, fr. *unkindly*, adj.; *unkindlily* fr. ¹*unkindly* + *-ly*] **:** in an unkind manner **:** so as to be unkind
un·king \ˌən+\ *vt* [²*un-* + *king*, n.] **1 :** to cause to cease to be a king **2 :** to deprive (a monarchy) of having a king
un·kink \ˌən+\ *vt* [²*un-* + *kink*] **:** to free from kinks **:** STRAIGHTEN, UNTWIST
unkn *abbr* unknown
un·knit \ˌən+\ *vb* [ME *unknitten*, fr. OE *uncnyttan*, fr. ²*un-* + *cnyttan* to tie, bind, fasten — more at KNIT] *vt* **1 :** to cause to become undone or unraveled ⟨~ that threatening unkind brow —Shak.⟩ **2 :** to cause to become disunited **:** DISPERSE, DISSOLVE, RELAX ~ *vi* **:** to become unknitted
un·knot \"+\ *vt* [²*un-* + *knot*] **:** to undo a knot in; *also* **:** UNTIE, LOOSE
¹**un·know** \"+\ *vt* [ME *unknowen*, fr. ¹*un-* + *knowen* to know — more at KNOW] **:** to be ignorant of
²**unknow** \"\ *vt* [²*un-* + *know*] **:** to cease to know **:** FORGET
un·knowability \ˌən+\ *n* **:** the quality or state of being unknowable
¹**un·knowable** \"+\ *adj* [ME, fr. ¹*un-* + *knowen* to know + *-able*] **:** not knowable **:** of a kind that cannot be comprehended; *esp* **:** lying beyond the limits of human experience or of human powers of apprehension or understanding — **un·knowableness** \"+\ *n* — **un·know·ably** \-əblē, -li\ *adv*
²**unknowable** \"\ *n* **:** something that is unknowable: as **a :** absolute reality lying beyond human experience or human understanding **b :** the reality of things as they are in themselves which is outside space and time and underlies phenomena as they appear to human minds **c :** the ultimate reality that we experience but that we can understand only in terms of images and symbols inadequate to its true nature — usu. used with *the*
un·know·en \ˌə(n)ˈnōən\ *chiefly dial var of* UNKNOWN
¹**un·knowing** \ˌən+\ *adj* [ME, fr. ¹*un-* + *knowing*, pres. part. of *knowen* to know — more at KNOW] **1 :** not knowing; *esp* **:** IGNORANT **2 :** UNKNOWN — usu. used with *to* ⟨people who ~ to him had come —James Lerner⟩ — **un·knowingly** \"+\ *adv* — **un·know·ing·ness** \"+\ *n*
²**unknowing** \"\ *n* [ME, fr. ¹*un-* + *knowing*, n.] **:** IGNORANCE
³**unknowing** \"\ *adv* [ME, fr. *unknowing*, adj.] **:** without knowing
un·knowledgeable \ˌən+\ *adj* **1 :** deficient in or not based on knowledge ⟨an ~ assistant⟩ ⟨such ~ comments⟩ **2 :** UNKNOWABLE ⟨~ splendours —Mary Austin⟩
¹**un·known** \"+\ *adj* [ME *unknowen, unknawen*, fr. ¹*un-* + *knowen, knawen* known — more at KNOWN] **1 :** not known: as **a :** STRANGE, UNFAMILIAR **b :** not apprehended **:** not ascertained **c :** INCALCULABLE, INEXPRESSIBLE **d :** lacking an established or normal status **:** having no formal recognition ⟨~ to the court⟩ **2** *obs* **:** not knowing **:** IGNORANT — **un·known·ness** *n* -ES
²**unknown** \"\ *n* **1 :** one that is unknown: as **a :** an unknown or unidentified person — usu. used with *the* ⟨the fair ~⟩ **b :** a thing, state, or region that is unknown or imperfectly known or defined ⟨left to seek his fortune in the western ~⟩ ⟨this ~ may alter our plans⟩ **2 :** something requiring to be discovered, identified, or made clear; *esp* **:** a letter or other symbol in a mathematical equation representing a number that is to be found and often consisting of one of the last letters of the alphabet — see UNKNOWN QUANTITY
unknown quantity *n* **1 :** a quantity for which a mathematical value is sought and which is usu. denoted symbolically by a mathematical unknown **2 :** something that constitutes a factor (as in a particular situation) of which the bearing and importance is not apparent
unknown soldier *n, usu cap U&S* **:** an unidentified soldier whose body is selected as a representative of all of the same nation who died in a war and esp. in one of the world wars to receive national honors
un·knownst \ˌə(n)ˈnōn(t)st\ *adj* [by alter.] *chiefly dial* **:** UNKNOWN
unl *abbr* unlimited
un·labeled \ˌən+\ *adj* [¹*un-* + *labeled*, past part. of *label*] **:** not labeled
un·labored \ˌən+\ *adj* [ME *unlaboured*, fr. ¹*un-* + *laboured*, past part. of *labouren* to labor — more at LABOR] **1 :** not cultivated **:** UNTILLED **2 :** produced without labor or toil **3 :** accomplished or attained seemingly without effort **:** NATURAL, SPONTANEOUS ⟨a cheerful, friendly, and ~ book —Harrison Smith⟩
un·laboring \"+\ *adj* [¹*un-* + *laboring*, pres. part. of *labor*] **:** having no necessity to labor or make an effort
un·laborious \"+\ *adj* **:** not requiring work or striving **:** EFFORTLESS
un·lace \"+\ *vt* [ME *unlacen*, fr. ²*un-* + *lacen* to lace — more at LACE] **1 a :** to loose by undoing a lacing **:** untie the laces of ⟨*unlaced* her skates⟩ **b** (1) **:** to free by or as if by undoing the laces **:** unloose the dress of (2) *obs* **:** to expose to disgrace ⟨what's the matter that you ~ your reputation thus —Shak.⟩ **2 :** to loose and take off (a bonnet from a sail) **:** cast off (lacing in the rigging) **:** UNTIE
un·laced \"+\ *adj* [ME, fr. past part. of *unlacen*] **:** loosed from laces **:** UNRESTRAINED ⟨~ behavior in a neighborhood pub —Robert Hatch⟩
un·lade \"+\ *vb* [ME *unladen*, fr. ²*un-* + *laden* to load — more at LADE] *vt* **1 :** to take the load from **:** take out the cargo of ⟨didn't ~ the ponies —C.A.Spring-Rice⟩ **2 :** to have removed (as a load or burden) **:** DISCHARGE, UNLOAD ⟨here freighters . . . lade and ~ cargo with cranes —*Amer. Guide Series: Fla.*⟩ ~ *vi* **:** to discharge cargo ⟨the wharf where the fishing boats ~⟩
un·laden \"+\ *adj* [fr. past part. of *unlade*] **:** UNLOADED
un·ladylike \"+\ *adj* **:** lacking the behavior, manner, or style considered proper for a lady
un·laid \"+\ *adj* [ME *unleyd*, fr. ¹*un-* + *leyd, leyed*, past part. of *leyen* to lay — more at LAY] **1 :** not laid or placed **:** not fixed ⟨his supper still ~ —Israel Zangwill⟩ **2 :** not allayed **:** not pacified **:** not laid finally to rest ⟨stubborn, ~ ghost —John Milton⟩ **3 :** not laid out — used esp. of a corpse **4** *of a rope* **:** not twisted
un·lamented \"+\ *adj* [¹*un-* + *lamented*, past part. of *lament*] **:** not grieved for **:** causing no mourning ⟨interred in an ~ grave —E.J.Mann⟩
un·landed \"+\ *adj* [ME, fr. ¹*un-* + *landed*] **:** possessing no land ⟨uphold the rights of ~ tenants⟩
un·lan·guaged \ˌənˈlaŋgwijd\ *adj* [¹*un-* + *language* + *-ed*] **:** lacking articulateness **:** not expressed in clear articulate speech ⟨the ~ prattling of infants —J.R.Lowell⟩
un·lap \ˌən+\ *vt* [ME *unlappen*, fr. ²*un-* + *lappen* to lap — more at LAP (to fold over)] **:** to uncover by or as if by the removal of an outer wrapper
un·lash \"+\ *vt* [²*un-* + *lash*] **1 :** to detach in order to make use of (something lashed or tied down) **:** untie the lashing of ⟨quickly ~*ed* a sledge he was carrying on the pontoon of his helicopter —Glen Jacobsen⟩ **2 :** LOOSE, UNDO
un·latch \"+\ *vb* [²*un-* + *latch*] *vt* **:** to open or loose by lifting the latch ~ *vi* **:** to become loosed or opened
un·latched \"+\ *adj* [¹*un-* + *latched*] **:** not fastened with a latch or a similar device ⟨went through the ~ gate into the street⟩
un·lat·ined \ˌənˈlatᵊnd\ *adj* [¹*un-* + *Latin* + *-ed*] **:** uninstructed in Latin ⟨the ~ English reader —M.H.Fisch⟩
un·launched \ˌən+\ *adj* [¹*un-* + *launched*, past part. of *launch*] **:** not launched; *esp* **:** not set afloat ⟨left ~ and dry —John Keats⟩
un·laureled \"+\ *adj* [¹*un-* + *laureled*, past part. of *laurel*] **:** not crowned with laurel **:** having no acclaim or reward ⟨the ~ heroism of endurance —Francis Parkman⟩
¹**un·law** \ˈ=,lȯ\ *n* [ME *unlawe*, fr. OE *unlagu*, of Scand origin; akin to ON *ōlǫg, ūlǫg* illegality, lawlessness, fr. *ō-, ū-* un- + *lǫg* law — more at LAW] **1 :** a violation of law **:** disregard of the restraints of law **:** ILLEGALITY, LAWLESSNESS ⟨times of ~ alternate with times of law —Frederick Pollock & F.W.Maitland⟩ **2** *Scots law* **:** a fine or amercement for a violation of law
²**unlaw** \"\ *vt* [ME (Sc) *unlawen*, fr. *unlawe*, n.] **1** *Scots law* **:** to impose a fine upon **2** [²*un-* + *law*, n.] *obs* **:** to deprive of the character of a law **:** ANNUL
un·lawed \"+\ *adj* [¹*un-* + *lawed*, past part. of *law* (to expeditate)] **:** not expeditated — used esp. of a dog
un·lawful \"+\ *adj* [ME *unlaweful*, fr. ¹*un-* + *laweful* lawful — more at LAWFUL] **1 :** not lawful **:** contrary to or prohibited by law **:** not authorized or justified by law **:** not permitted or warranted by law ⟨~ measures⟩ ⟨~ money⟩ **2 :** acting contrary to or in defiance of the law **:** disobeying or disregarding the law ⟨~ buyer⟩ ⟨~ hunter⟩ **3 :** contrary to normal or acceptable procedure **:** IRREGULAR; *esp* **:** not morally right or conventional ⟨~ love⟩ ⟨~ pleasures⟩ **4 :** born out of wedlock **:** ILLEGITIMATE
unlawful assembly *n* **:** a meeting of three or more persons in pursuance of a common plan and in such a way as to cause a reasonable apprehension that they will disturb the peace tumultuously
un·lawfully \"+\ *adv* [ME *unlawefully*, fr. *unlaweful* + *-ly*] **:** in an unlawful manner ⟨accused of having ~ and willfully entered the waters . . . in search of loot —Frank Yerby⟩
un·law·ful·ness *n* **:** the quality or state of being unlawful
un·lax \ˌənˈlaks\ *vb* -ED/-ING/-ES [²*un-* + *-lax* (as in *relax*)] *vi* **:** RELAX ⟨lie in the hot sun, feeling yourself gradually ~ —Bennett Cerf⟩ ~ *vt* **:** to gradually relieve the tension in ⟨took only a few minutes of the caressing air of Rome . . . to ~ cramped muscles —Kay Halle⟩
un·lay \ˌən+\ *vb* [²*un-* + *lay*] *vt* **:** to untwist the strands of (as a rope) ~ *vi* **:** UNTWIST
un·leached \"+\ *adj* [¹*un-* + *leached*, past part. of *leach*] **:** not leached — used esp. of wood ashes
un·lead \"+\ *vt* [²*un-* + *lead* (to place leads)] **:** to remove lead from (as between lines of type)
un·leaded \"+\ *adj* [in sense 1, fr. past part. of *unlead*; in sense 2, fr. ¹*un-* + *leaded*, past part. of *lead*] **1 :** stripped of lead **2 :** not having leads between the lines in printing
un·leaf \"+\ *vt* [²*un-* + *leaf*, n.] **:** to strip of leaves
un·learn \"+\ *vb* [ME *unlernen*, fr. ²*un-* + *lernen* to learn — more at LEARN] *vt* **1 :** to put out of one's knowledge or memory **:** discard the habit of **:** discover the falsity of ⟨it took him a long time to ~ the puritanism of his childhood —Aldous Huxley⟩ **2 :** UNTEACH ~ *vi* **:** to discard previously acquired habits or knowledge ⟨they do not learn because they cannot or will not ~ —R.G.Vansittart⟩
un·learned *in senses 1, 2 & 4* ˌənˈlərnəd, -ˈlən-, -ˈləin- *sometimes* -nd, *in senses 3 & 5* -nd *or* -nt, *dial* ˈlärn- *or* ˈlán-\ *adj* [ME *unlerned*, fr. ¹*un-* + *lerned* learned — more at LEARNED] **1 :** possessing little or no learning or education **:** UNSCHOOLED, UNTAUGHT ⟨recounts the experiences of an ~ man in the search for truth and understanding —*Brit. Bk. News*⟩ **2 :** characterized by or revealing ignorance **:** not exhibiting learning ⟨~ speech⟩ **3 :** not gained by study ⟨things better ~⟩ **4 :** lacking in skill or knowledge **:** UNVERSED — usu. used with *in* ⟨~ in the arts of war⟩ ⟨he was not ~ in philosophy⟩ **5 :** independent of experience, training, or the process of learning **:** NATURAL ⟨breathing is an example of man's ~ behavior⟩ **syn** see IGNORANT
un·learned·ly *adv* **:** in an unlearned manner
un·leased \ˌən+\ *adj* [¹*un-* + *leased*, past part. of *lease*] **:** not leased **:** being without a lease ⟨the house had been ~ for a year⟩
un·leash \"+\ *vt* [²*un-* + *leash*] **:** to free from a leash or as if from a leash **:** let loose from control or restraint ⟨a bold and imaginative approach that will ~ the energies of free men —*Nation's Business*⟩ ⟨corruptions of power could ~ great evil in the world —A.M.Schlesinger b. 1917⟩
un·leavened \"+\ *adj* [¹*un-* + *leavened*, past part. of *leaven*] **:** not leavened **:** containing no leaven ⟨~ bread is usu. flour mixed with water⟩ ⟨these works are tedious, ~ by imaginative power, and cramped in diction —L.N.Richardson⟩

un·led \"+\ *adj* [1*un-* + *led*, past part. of *lead*] : not led : lacking leadership or guidance ⟨the ~ or misled welter of a commercial century —John Masefield⟩

un·legal \"+\ *adj* : NONLEGAL

un·leisured \"+\ *adj* [1*un-* + *leisure* + *-ed*] : having no leisure ⟨the feverish ~ scrambling lives we live in the big cities —J.C. Powys⟩

1un·less \(ˌ)ən'les *sometimes* ᵊn-\ *conj* [ME *unlesse* (*than*), *unlesse* (*that*), alter. (influenced by 1*un-*) of *onlesse* (*than*), *onlesse* (*that*), fr. *on* + *lesse* less — more at ON, LESS] **1** : under any other circumstance than that : except on the condition that : if . . . not ⟨would have been destroyed ~ a regiment . . . had been sent —J.J.Chapman⟩ ⟨modern man is obsolete . . . ~ he can stop world wars —Stuart Chase⟩ ⟨no person shall be convicted of treason ~ on the testimony of two witnesses —*U. S. Constitution*⟩ **2** : without the accompanying circumstance or condition that : but that : BUT ⟨never a day goes by ~ at least one collision occurs —Priscilla Hughes⟩

2unless \"\ *prep* [ME *unlesse* (*than*), alter. of *onlesse* (*than*), fr. *on* + *lesse*] : except possibly : EXCEPT ⟨no one (~ the psychotherapists who have to deal with the casualties) seems seriously to have considered the dangers —*New Republic*⟩

un·lessened \ˌən+\ *adj* [1*un-* + *lessened*, past part. of *lessen*] : marked by constancy : not diminished ⟨in spite of the treatment he received his loyalty was ~⟩

un·lessoned \"+\ *adj* [1*un-* + *lesson*, n. + *-ed*] : lacking lessons or instruction ⟨an ~ girl . . . happy in this, she is not so old but she may learn —Shak.⟩

un·let \"+\ *adj* [1*un-* + *let*, past part. of *let*] : not rented ⟨examined the room . . . which was still ~ —F.W.Crofts⟩

un·lettable \"+\ *adj* : not able to be rented

un·lettered \"+\ *adj* [ME, fr. 1*un-* + *lettered*] **1 a** : not lettered : lacking scholarship ⟨regarded as an ~ rhymester —Van Wyck Brooks⟩ **b** : ILLITERATE ⟨many country priests were stupid and ~ —G.B.Sansom⟩ **2** : not marked with letters ⟨an ~ tombstone⟩ ⟨an ~ police car —*Springfield (Mass.) Daily News*⟩ **syn** see IGNORANT

1un·level \"+\ *adj* [1*un-* + *level*, adj.] : not level : UNEVEN ⟨tennis lawns grown lank and ~ —Adrian Bell⟩

2unlevel \"\ *vt* [2*un-* + *level*, v.] : to destroy the level character of : make uneven ⟨moles ~*ed* the lawn⟩

un·lev·el·ness *n* : the quality or state of being unlevel

un·liable \ˌən+\ *adj* : not liable ⟨pictured . . . as being somehow ~ to human frailties —Arnold Bennett⟩

un·licensed \ˌən+\ *adj* **1 a** : unauthorized by license to engage in a specified activity ⟨an ~ airplane pilot⟩ ⟨~ moneylender⟩ **b** *archaic* : not granted permission or authority **2 a** : printed without a license — used of a publication **b** : lacking sanction or authorization ⟨imprisoned for ~ preaching —*Dial*⟩ **3** : lacking restraint : LAWLESS ⟨the ~ passions of a guilty people —W.E.Channing⟩

un·licked \"+\ *adj* [1*un-* + *licked*, past part. of *lick*] **1** : not licked dry : lacking proper form or shape ⟨an ~ bear whelp —Shak.⟩ **2** : revealing youthful naïveté or crudeness of manner : lacking finish or polish ⟨was just an ~ kid when I knew him⟩ ⟨a kind of ~ attempt at civility —Mary Deasy⟩

un·lid \"+\ *vt* [2*un-* + *lid*, n.] : to take the lid off : UNCOVER ⟨she *unlidded* the second box —T.W.Duncan⟩

un·lidded \"+\ *adj* [1*un-* + *lid*, n. + *-ed*] : not having or equipped with a lid

un·lifelike \"+\ *adj* : not lifelike : lacking realism

un·light \ˌən'līt\ *vi* [2*un-* + *light*] *dial Eng* : to get down (as from a vehicle or horse) : ALIGHT

un·lighted \ˌən+\ *adj* [1*un-* + *lighted*, past part. of *light*] : not lighted : UNLIT

un·lightened \"+\ *adj* [1*un-* + *lightened*, past part. of *lighten*] : not lighted up : lacking brightness

un·likable *also* **un·likeable** \ˌən+\ *adj* : not likable

1un·like \"+\ *prep* [ME *unlik*, fr. 1*un-* + *lik*, prep., like — more at LIKE] : not like: as **a** (1) : different from : dissimilar to ⟨felt strangely ~ a successful lover —Floyd Dell⟩ (2) : not characteristic of ⟨it was ~ him to be late⟩ **b** (1) : in a different manner from : differently from ⟨become, ~ all other human beings, altogether free from personal or class bias —M.R. Cohen⟩ (2) : in a manner that is not characteristic of ⟨so many fine men were outside the charmed circle that, ~ most colleges, there was no disgrace in not being a club man —John Reed⟩

2unlike \"\ *adj* [ME *unlik*, fr. *un-* + *lik*, adj., like — more at LIKE] **1** : not like: as **a** : marked by dissimilarity : DISSIMILAR, DIFFERENT ⟨men are profoundly ~ —E.W.Sinnott⟩ **b** : marked by inequality : UNEQUAL ⟨contributed ~ amounts⟩ **2** *archaic* : UNLIKELY ⟨it's ~ to dry off the grass before midnight —MacKinlay Kantor⟩

3unlike \"\ *n* : a person or thing marked by difference

4unlike \"\ *conj* : in a manner that is different than : not as ⟨~ in the gasoline engine, fuel does not enter the cylinder with air on the intake stroke —Irving Frazee⟩

un·likelihood \ˌən+\ *n* **1** : IMPROBABILITY ⟨his present financial status adds to the ~ of his attending college⟩ **2** : something improbable

un·likeliness \"+\ *n* **1** *obs* : a rank discrepancy **2** : UNLIKELIHOOD

1un·likely \"+\ *adj*, *sometimes* -ER/-EST [ME *unlikli*, fr. 1*un-* + *likli*, adj., likely — more at LIKELY] **1** : not likely : IMPROBABLE, UNBELIEVABLE ⟨laughed at the . . . description of the ~ animal —C.A.Nicholson⟩ ⟨his nomination seemed an ~ event⟩ **2** : not such as to inspire liking : DISAGREEABLE, OBJECTIONABLE, UNATTRACTIVE ⟨fractured himself with . . . too little work and too many ~ companions —*Time*⟩ **3** : seemingly lacking in any prospect of success : likely to fail : UNPROMISING ⟨a place full of good things, but it looked so ~ at first glance —Maristan Chapman⟩ ⟨discovers poetry in the most ~ places —C.D.Lewis⟩

2unlikely \"\ *adv* [ME *unlikli*, fr. 1*un-* + *likli*, adv., likely — more at LIKELY] : in an unlikely manner

un·like·ness *n* [ME *unliknesse*, fr. *unlik*, adj., unlike + *-nesse* -ness] : the quality or state of being unlike : an instance of dissimilarity **syn** see DISSIMILARITY

un·limber \ˌən+\ *vb* [2*un-* + *limber*, n.] *vt* **1** : to detach the limber from and so make ready ⟨~ a gun for action⟩ **2** : to prepare for action : arrange for use ⟨~*ed* his cameras . . . and began to work —R.L.Taylor⟩ ~ *vi* : to perform the task of preparing something for action

un·lime \"+\ *vt* [2*un-* + *lime*, n.] : DELIME

un·limited \ˌən+\ *adj* [ME, fr. 1*un-* + *limited*, past part. of *limiten* to limit — more at LIMIT] **1** : lacking any controls : UNRESTRICTED, UNCONFINED ⟨to start with a theory of ~ freedom is to end up with ~ despotism —Philip Rahv⟩ ⟨not in favor of ~ experiment; he was in favor of rigid control from above —H.L.Mencken⟩ **2** : having no bounds : wanting limits : BOUNDLESS, INFINITE ⟨ceiling ~⟩ ⟨an ~ expanse of ocean⟩ **3** : not bounded by exceptions : UNDEFINED ⟨the ~ and unconditional surrender of the enemy —Sir Winston Churchill⟩

unlimited company *n* : a company in which liability of members is not limited

un·lim·it·ed·ly *adv* : in an unlimited manner : without limitations

un·lim·it·ed·ness *n* : the quality or state of being unlimited

unlimited policy *n* : an insurance policy covering substantially all hazards or types of loss contemplated under the particular kind of insurance or setting no maximum limitation on the company's liability

1un·lined \ˌən+\ *adj* [1*un-* + *lined* (having a lining)] : made or constructed without a lining ⟨his jacket was ~⟩

2unlined \"\ *adj* [1*un-* + *lined* (marked with lines)] : not traced with lines ⟨his cheeks were ~, his speech was soft —J.S. Reeves⟩

un·link \"+\ *vb* [2*un-* + *link*] *vt* **1** : to unfasten the links of **2** : to separate by or as if by undoing the links of a chain ~ *vi* : to become detached

un·liquid \"+\ *adj* : not readily converted into cash

un·liquidated \"+\ *adj* [1*un-* + *liquidated*, past part. of *liquidate*] : not liquidated

un·listed \"+\ *adj* **1** : not appearing upon a list ⟨telephone number was ~⟩ **2** : of or relating to a stock or bond not listed on an organized securities exchange

un·listened \"+\ *adj* [1*un-* + *listened*, past part. of *listen*] not listened to : not heard

un·listening \"+\ *adj* : not listening : lacking sensitivity ⟨his speech fell upon ~ ears⟩

un·lit \"+\ *adj* : not lighted: as **a** : not kindled ⟨the table was bare, the fire ~⟩ **b** : not illuminated with or as if with light ⟨through the dark ~ streets —Erskine Caldwell⟩

un·literal \"+\ *adj* : not literal : lacking complete accuracy

un·literary \ˌən+\ *adj* : not literary : marked by lack of affectation or pedantry ⟨her talk was very ~ —W.D.Howells⟩

un·literate \"+\ *adj* : not literate

un·livable \"+\ *adj* **1** : unfit to live in or with ⟨~ substandard housing⟩ ⟨~ conditions⟩ **2** : not conducive to comfortable or easy living ⟨the room was very beautiful, but . . . ~ because there was no place in it where you could settle down —Frances Crane⟩

un·live \"+\ *vt* [2*un-* + *live*] : to live down : ANNUL, REVERSE ⟨history cannot be *unlived* —*New Republic*⟩

un·lively \"+\ *adj* : not lively : lacking animation : DULL ⟨a particularly ~ session of the Senate⟩

un·livery \"+\ *n* [1*un-* + *livery*] : the unloading or discharge of cargo

un·living \"+\ *adj* : LIFELESS ⟨entreat all living and ~ things to weep —Matthew Arnold⟩

1un·load \"+\ *vb* [2*un-* + *load*] *vt* **1 a** (1) : to take off : DELIVER, DISCHARGE, REMOVE ⟨call for your car at the port where it is to be ~*ed* —Richard Joseph⟩ (2) : to take the cargo from ⟨the whole crew may drop their tools to help ~ an arriving . . . sloop —Stuart Chase⟩ **b** : to give outlet to : pour forth ⟨head buried in his mother's lap, he ~*ed* his small problems⟩ **2 a** : to relieve of something burdensome : take a load from ⟨~*ed* the pack animals and began making camp⟩ **b** : to relieve from something oppressive or difficult ⟨~*ed* his heart in passionate utterance⟩ **3** : to draw the charge from ⟨~*ed* the gun⟩ **4** : to sell esp. in large quantities : get rid of : DUMP ⟨investors who keep their eyes on fundamental business trends made no move to ~ their holdings —*Newsweek*⟩ ⟨might be able to ~ more of its grain . . . abroad —*Wall Street Jour.*⟩ **5 a** : to discard (worthless or dangerous cards) from one's hand **b** : to meld or discard (high cards) in playing rummy to reduce the count of one's hand ~ *vi* **1** : to perform the act of unloading ⟨there were certain types of shipping which could ~ in a matter of hours —E.C.R.Lasher⟩ **2** : to sell large quantities of stock esp. in expectation of a market decline or for an inordinate price **3** : to meld or discard cards that would be costly if they remained in one's hand at the end of play

2unload \"\ *n* : a commodity, consignment, or cargo after it has been unloaded — compare SHIPMENT

un·loader \"+\ *n* **1 a** : one that unloads by hand or by machine **b** : a machine used for unloading **2** : a valve in an ammonia compressor system that shunts the head pressure so the compressor has less to work against

un·lobed \ˌən+\ *adj* : having no lobes

un·localized \"+\ *adj* [1*un-* + *localized*, past part. of *localize*] : lacking a specific location

un·located \"+\ *adj* [1*un-* + *located*, past part. of *locate*] **1** : not located or placed **2** : not surveyed or designated by marks, limits, or boundaries as appropriated ⟨~ lands⟩

un·lock \"+\ *vb* [ME *unlokken*, fr. 2*un-* + *lokken* to lock — more at LOCK] *vt* **1** : to unfasten the lock of ⟨~*ed* the trunk of his car⟩ **2 a** : to lay open by or as if by undoing a lock ⟨struggle to ~ the lands held by a handful of squatters —*Times Lit. Supp.*⟩ **b** : to gain or grant admission to ⟨how to ~ one of the greatest of all mysteries — photosynthesis —Bruce Bliven b. 1889⟩ ⟨reference books are the keys that quickly ~ the doors to . . . stored knowledge and golden wisdom —G.B. Shaw⟩ **3** : to cause to open : free from restraints or restrictions ⟨the reaction to the shock ~*ed* a flood of emotions⟩ **4 a** : to open by a physical action : spread apart ⟨they ~*ed* their cramped fingers from the paddles —Bill Wolf⟩ **b** : to release from immovability ⟨sheer anger finally ~*ed* his tongue and he shouted at the mob⟩ **5** : to furnish a key to ⟨the three cipher men ~*ed* the whole letter —Fletcher Pratt⟩ ~ *vi* : to become unfastened or freed from restraints

un·locked \"+\ *adj* [fr. past part. of *unlock*] : not locked ⟨the ~ door⟩

un·lodge \"+\ *vt* [2*un-* + *lodge*] : to deprive of lodgment : DISLODGE

un·logical \"+\ *adj* : ILLOGICAL

un·looked at \ˌənˌlu̇kˌtat\ *adj* [1*un-* + *looked at*, past part. form of the phrase *look at*] : lacking attention : UNHEEDED ⟨the magazines lay *unlooked at*⟩

un·looked-for \ˌənˌlu̇ktˌfȯ(ə)r, -ȯ(ə)\ *adj* [1*un-* + *looked for*, past part. form of the phrase *look for*] : not observed or foreseen : UNEXPECTED ⟨a virtue perhaps *unlooked-for* in a people so full of energy —E.A.Peers⟩

un·looped \ˌən+\ *adj* : not looped

un·loose \"+\ *vb* [ME *unloosen*, *unlosen*, fr. 2*un-* + *loosen*, *losen* to loose — more at LOOSE] *vt* **1** : to moderate or relax the strain of ⟨he *unloosed* his grip —I.L.Idriess⟩ **2** : to release from or as if from restraints : set free ⟨a flood of dark memories and fears had been *unloosed* —John Buchan⟩ **3** : to loosen the ties of ⟨in *unloosing* the traditional social bonds Puritanism awakened aspirations —V.L.Parrington⟩ ~ *vi*, *obs* : to become loose

un·loosen \"+\ *vt* [ME *unlosnen*, fr. 2*un-* + *losnen*, *loosnen* to loosen — more at LOOSEN] : UNLOOSE

un·lopped \"+\ *adj* [1*un-* + *lopped*, past part. of *lop*] : not lopped : UNCUT

un·lord \"+\ *vt* [2*un-* + *lord*] : to deprive of the rank or position of a lord

un·lordly \"+\ *adj* [1*un-* + *lordly*] : not lordly : not arbitrary

un·lost \"+\ *adj* : not lost : SECURE

un·lovable \"+\ *adj* : incapable of inspiring love or admiration ⟨she was in some mysterious way . . . ~ —Joseph Conrad⟩

1un·love \"+\ *vb* [ME *unloven*, fr. 2*un-* + *loven* to love — more at LOVE] *vt* : to cease to love ⟨he must not ~ her but he must certainly leave her —*Delineator*⟩ ~ *vi* : to stop loving something ⟨he can . . . ~ so easily —Robert Hichens⟩

2un·love \'ənˌləv\ *n* [1*un-* + *love*, n.] : absence of love : HATE ⟨after months of gnawing ~ —Martha Gellhorn⟩

un·loved \ˌən+\ *adj* [ME, fr. 1*un-* + *loved*, past part. of *loven* to love] : not loved ⟨a poet ~ by most critics —C.R.Woodring⟩

un·loveliness \"+\ *n* : the quality or state of being unlovely

un·lovely \"+\ *adj*, *sometimes* -ER/-EST [ME, fr. 1*un-* + *lovely*] **1** : lacking the ability to evoke affection : possessing qualities that inspire dislike : DISAGREEABLE, UNPLEASANT **2** : not attractive to the senses : displeasing in appearance : UNSIGHTLY ⟨planked a most ~ boot firmly —Ngaio Marsh⟩

un·loving \"+\ *adj* : not loving : not giving or reciprocating affection — **un·lov·ing·ly** *adv* — **un·lov·ing·ness** *n*

un·luck \"+\ *n* [1*un-* + *luck*] *chiefly South* : bad luck : MISFORTUNE

un·luckily \"+\ *adv* : in an unlucky manner : UNFORTUNATELY ⟨~ I have lost my memorandum —B.N.Cardozo⟩

un·luckiness \"+\ *n* : the quality or state of being unlucky

un·lucky \"+\ *adj* [1*un-* + *lucky*] **1** : characterized by adversity or failure ⟨this has been an ~ year for us⟩ **2** : seemingly presaging misfortune : ILL-OMENED ⟨born under an ~ star⟩ **3** : having or meeting with bad luck ⟨the ~ prisoner was again put in irons —W.H.Prescott⟩ **4** *dial chiefly Eng* : causing trouble or mischief **5** : producing dissatisfaction : REGRETTABLE ⟨the ~ fact is that . . . it is not a formal biography —*Times Lit. Supp.*⟩

syn DISASTROUS, ILL-STARRED, ILL-FATED, UNFORTUNATE, LUCKLESS, HAPLESS: UNLUCKY implies that in spite of effort or merit one has bad luck, often chronically, or, as applied to an occasion or action, that it proves to be unfavorable, esp. in outcome or consequences ⟨if you're *unlucky* enough to lose or break your glasses —Richard Joseph⟩ ⟨the loss of over $200,000 in an *unlucky* coffee speculation —H.G.Pearson⟩ ⟨the child who is born on an *unlucky* day —Abram Kardiner⟩ ⟨an *unlucky* throw of the dice⟩ DISASTROUS, applying to anything that is or brings calamity, applies often to anything that has a calamitous fate ⟨a *disastrous* flood⟩ ⟨in so *disastrous* a plight that he died on the following day —W.H.Prescott⟩ ⟨a *disastrous* armaments race —*Current Biog.*⟩ ⟨a *disastrous* expedition against a superior force⟩ ILL-STARRED is interchangeable with DISASTROUS both in the sense of bringing calamity ⟨the *ill-starred* depression year of 1929 —*Springfield (Mass.) Union*⟩ and in the sense of having or doomed to have a calamitous fate ⟨the return trip was *ill-starred*: they narrowly escaped a serious accident —Willa Cather⟩ ⟨the *ill-starred* fellow is pummeled on deck —Herman Melville⟩ ⟨the *ill-starred* lady who perished —Allen Upward⟩ ILL-FATED is ILL-STARRED in the second of the two senses suggested immediately above ⟨an *ill-fated* expedition that perished at sea⟩ UNFORTUNATE, though often interchangeable with UNLUCKY, is weaker in implying mere bad luck ⟨an *unfortunate* day at the races⟩ and stronger in suggesting misfortune, misery, or desolation ⟨expecting some *unfortunate* woman to instruct simultaneously a crowd of fifty urchins of all degrees of ignorance and stupidity —C.H.Grandgent⟩ ⟨assist an *unfortunate* people suffering the calamities of war⟩ though it can often mean only regrettable ⟨the building was completed with *unfortunate* stylistic admixtures —*Amer. Guide Series: N.Y.*⟩ LUCKLESS and HAPLESS usu. apply to a person or thing notably or chronically unfortunate ⟨the *luckless* small investors were ruined —O.S.Nock⟩ ⟨all his speculations had of late gone wrong with the *luckless* old gentleman —W.M.Thackeray⟩ ⟨as the sea dried up, the *hapless* ship sank beneath shifting dunes —*Amer. Guide Series: Calif.*⟩ ⟨these *hapless* creatures now wander as displaced persons —R.H.Jackson⟩

un·lucrative \"+\ *adj* : not gainful : lacking in profit ⟨made life exciting, but altogether ~ —*Time*⟩

un·luminous \"+\ *adj* : lacking illumination : not luminous

un·lustrous \"+\ *adj* : lacking luster : having no brilliance or shine

un·lute \"+\ *vt* [2*un-* + *lute* (to seal)] : to take apart (as things cemented) : take the clay from

un·luxurious \"+\ *adj* : lacking luxury : PLAIN, SPARTAN

unm *abbr* unmarried

un·made \ˌən+\ *adj* [ME *unmad*, fr. 1*un-* + *mad*, past part. of *maken* to make — more at MAKE] : not made

unmade-up *adj* [1*un-* + *made up*, past part. of *make up*] : not made or worked up into final form : not ready : not manufactured

un·magical \ˌən+\ *adj* : not magical ⟨life that can be comprehended in ~ terms —*Dial*⟩

un·magnetic \"+\ *adj* : not magnetic

un·magnetized \"+\ *adj* [1*un-* + *magnetized*, past part. of *magnetize*] : not magnetized

un·magnified \"+\ *adj* [1*un-* + *magnified*, past part. of *magnify*] : not magnified

un·maidenly \ˌən+\ *adj* [1*un-* + *maidenly*] : not maidenly ⟨high-minded, flat-bosomed young women who embrace world problems with ~ ardor —M.G.Bishop⟩

un·mailable \"+\ *adj* : not mailable ⟨found the novel ~ under post office decency clauses —*Newsweek*⟩ — **un·mail·able·ness** *n* -ES

un·maimed \"+\ *adj*, *archaic* : not maimed

un·maintainable \"+\ *adj* : not maintainable

un·maintained \"+\ *adj* [1*un-* + *maintained*, past part. of *maintain*] : not maintained

un·make \"+\ *vt* [ME *unmaken*, fr. 2*un-* + *maken* to make — more at MAKE] **1** : to undo the creation of : cause to disappear : DESTROY ⟨couldn't ~ the public image his press agents had so carefully built⟩ **2** : to deprive of rank or office : DEPOSE ⟨people have elected me . . . and they can ~ me —John Steinbeck⟩ **3** : to deprive of essential characteristics : change the nature of ⟨enough to ~ any man —Katherine Mansfield⟩ **4** : to change an attitude of (one's mind) ⟨ladies are allowed to ~ their minds —R.D.Blackmore⟩

un·maker \"+\ *n* [ME *unmakere*, fr. *unmaken* + *-ere* -er] : one that unmakes

un·malicious \"+\ *adj* : not malicious

un·malleable \"+\ *adj* : not malleable

un·malted \"+\ *adj* [1*un-* + *malted*, past part. of *malt*] : not malted ⟨~ barley⟩

un·man \ˌən+\ *vt* [2*un-* + *man*, n.] **1 a** *archaic* : to deprive of the characteristics of man ⟨I may put forth angel's plumage, once *unmanned*, but not before —Robert Browning⟩ **b** : to deprive of courage, strength, or vigor : cause to become weak or unmanly ⟨the tenderness that threatened to ~ him —Frances G. Patton⟩ ⟨fell prostrate . . . exhausted and *unmanned* —W.H. Hudson †1922⟩ **c** *obs* : to place below the level of man : DEGRADE ⟨habits of vice ~ men's minds —William Wotton⟩ **2** : to deprive of sexual or procreative potency : CASTRATE, EMASCULATE ⟨*unmanned* themselves during . . . wild transports, which resemble those of dancing dervishes —R.H.Pfeiffer⟩ **syn** see UNNERVE

un·manacle \"+\ *vt* [2*un-* + *manacle*] : to free from manacles

un·manageable \"+\ *adj* : not manageable : UNCONTROLLABLE, INTRACTABLE ⟨became so ~ . . . she was committed to an asylum —H.A.Overstreet⟩ — **un·man·age·able·ness** *n* — **un·manageably** \"+\ *adv*

un·managed \"+\ *adj* [1*un-* + *managed*, past part. of *manage*] : not controlled : UNREGULATED ⟨natural ~ populations in excess of a bird per acre —A.S.Leopold⟩

un·manful \"+\ *adj* : not manful — **un·manfully** \"+\ *adv*

un·manifest \"+\ *adj* : not manifest

un·manifested \"+\ *adj* [1*un-* + *manifested*, past part. of *manifest*] : not manifested

un·manlike \"+\ *adj* : not manlike

un·manliness \"+\ *n* : the quality or state of being unmanly

1un·manly \"+\ *adv* [ME, fr. 1*un-* + *manly*, adv.] *archaic* : in an unmanly manner ⟨a dominion so ~ cruel —John Cleveland⟩

2unmanly \"\ *adj* [ME, fr. 1*un-* + *manly*, adj.] : not manly: as **a** : of weak character : PUSILLANIMOUS, COWARDLY ⟨~ despair which bids men eat and drink for tomorrow they die —J.R.Green⟩ **b** : EFFEMINATE, SISSY ⟨looked upon the arts as ~ forms of escape —Lewis Mumford⟩

un·manned \ˌən+\ *adj* [1*un-* + *manned*, past part. of *man*] **1** : having no men aboard : not guided by men on board ⟨an ~, globe-girdling artificial satellite —J.K.Hutchens⟩ ⟨forbade the operation of remotely controlled ~ airplanes —A.R.Weyl⟩ **2** *obs*, *of a hawk* : not trained

un·mannered \"+\ *adj* **1** : marked by a lack of good manners : RUDE, COARSE ⟨a beautiful but ~ people, primitively callous —Rose Macaulay⟩ ⟨resentment flared at such an ~ intrusion —Joseph Hergesheimer⟩ **2** : characterized by an absence of artificiality or insincerity : UNAFFECTED, STRAIGHTFORWARD ⟨the doctor's quiet, ~ entry —Viola Meynell⟩ — **un·man·nered·ly** *adv*

un·mannerliness \"+\ *n* : the quality or state of being unmannerly

1un·mannerly \"+\ *adv* [ME *unmanerly*, fr. 1*un-* + *manerly*, adv., mannerly] : in an unmannerly fashion : RUDELY ⟨reformers . . . did not ~ reject those offices of the church —J.J. Blunt⟩

2unmannerly \"\ *adj* [ME *unmanerly*, fr. 1*un-* + *manerly*, adj., mannerly] : not mannerly : IMPOLITE, DISCOURTEOUS ⟨disliked for his ~ behavior⟩

un·mantle \"+\ *vt* [2*un-* + *mantle*] : to remove a mantle or cover from : UNCOVER

un·manufactured \"+\ *adj* [1*un-* + *manufactured*, past part. of *manufacture*] : not manufactured

un·manumitted \"+\ *adj* [1*un-* + *manumitted*, past part. of *manumit*] : not manumitted ⟨we strive with proud, ~ soul —J.W.Watson⟩

un·manured \"+\ *adj* [1*un-* + *manured*, past part. of *manure*] **1** *obs* : UNCULTIVATED, UNTILLED ⟨the soil is wonderfully fruitful, but ~ —John Dryden⟩ **2** : not fertilized with manure ⟨~ lawns⟩

un·mapped \"+\ *adj* [1*un-* + *mapped*, past part. of *map*] : not mapped : UNCHARTED ⟨wild and ~ areas of the physical world —H.G.Rickover⟩

un·marked \ˌən+\ *adj* [ME *unmarked*, fr. 1*un-* + *marked*, past part. of *merken*, *marken* to mark — more at MARK] **1 a** : lacking a mark ⟨handed him an ~ card⟩ **b** *of a road* : not having a marker giving a street name or route number ⟨an ~, graveled road running parallel with the levee —*Amer. Guide Series: La.*⟩ **2** : not noticed : UNOBSERVED ⟨his retirement . . . was not allowed to go ~ —*Wesfarmers News*⟩ **3** : not characterized ⟨wrote political articles ~ by a regard for truth⟩

un·marketable \"+\ *adj* : not marketable

un·marred \"+\ *adj* [ME *unmerred*, *unmarred*, fr. 1*un-* + *merred*, *marred*, past part. of *merren*, *marren* to mar — more at MAR] : not marred

un·married \"+\ *adj* [ME *unmaried*, fr. ¹*un-* + *maried* married — more at MARRIED] **:** not married: **a :** not now or previously married **b :** DIVORCED **c :** WIDOWED
un·marry \"+\ *vb* [²*un-* + *marry*] *vt* **:** to release from marriage **:** cancel the marriage of **:** DIVORCE ~ *vi* **:** to release oneself from marriage
un·martial \"+\ *adj* **:** not martial
un·martyr \"+\ *vt* [²*un-* + *martyr*] **:** to deprive of martyrdom
un·masculine \"+\ *adj* **:** not masculine
un·mask \"+\ *vb* [²*un-* + *mask*] *vt* **1 :** to remove a mask from ⟨a law to ~ the Ku Klux Klan —*Time*⟩ **2 :** to reveal the true nature of **:** remove a false or misleading appearance from **:** EXPOSE ⟨dramatically ~*s* herself on her deathbed when she confesses all —*Irish Digest*⟩ ⟨~ the process of deception —R.W.Southern⟩ ~ *vi* **:** to remove one's mask ⟨at midnight the dancers ~*ed*⟩
un·masker \"+\ *n* **:** one that unmasks
un·mastered \ˌən+\ *adj* [¹*un-* + *mastered*, past part. of *master*] **:** not mastered
un·matchable \"+\ *adj* [¹*un-* + *match*, v. + *-able*] **:** not matchable: **a :** INCOMPARABLE, UNEQUALED ⟨state the issue with ~ clarity —R.M.Goldman⟩ **b :** not capable of being paired or duplicated ⟨furniture . . . interspersed with modern and ~ makeshifts —Bret Harte⟩ — **un·match·ably** \-blē\ *adv*
un·matched \"+\ *adj* [¹*un-* + *matched*, past part. of *match*] **1 :** UNMATCHABLE **a** ⟨infamy . . . ~ in the Western world —H.E.Rieseberg⟩ **2 :** not matching ⟨~ pieces of dinnerware⟩
un·mated \"+\ *adj* [¹*un-* + *mated*, past part. of *mate* (to join)] **:** not mated
un·material \"+\ *adj* [ME *unmateriall*, fr. ¹*un-* + *materiel*, *material*, *materiall* material] **:** IMMATERIAL, INSUBSTANTIAL ⟨their . . . almost ~ structure —Simon Newcomb⟩
un·maternal \"+\ *adj* **:** not maternal
un·mathematical \"+\ *adj* **:** not mathematical
un·matted \"+\ *adj* **:** not matted ⟨an ~ watercolor⟩
un·meaning \"+\ *adj* **1 :** lacking intelligence **:** VAPID ⟨an ~ facial expression⟩ **2 :** having no meaning **:** SENSELESS ⟨his response . . . is picayune and ~ —R.B.Pearsall⟩ — **un·mean·ing·ly** *adv* — **un·mean·ing·ness** *n*
un·meant \"+\ *adj* [¹*un-* + *meant*, past part. of *mean*] **:** not meant **:** UNINTENTIONAL ⟨an ~ harshness in her reply⟩
un·measurable \"+\ *adj* [ME *unmesurable*, fr. ¹*un-* + *mesurable* measurable — more at MEASURABLE] **1 :** not measurable **:** of a degree, extent, or amount incapable of being measured **:** INDETERMINABLE ⟨~ reaches of outer space⟩ ⟨satellite is slowing down at an almost ~ rate —J.P.Hagen⟩ **2 :** of an excessive degree or amount **:** IMMODERATE, BOUNDLESS ⟨an ~ desire for fame⟩ ⟨~ enthusiasm⟩ — **un·mea·sur·able·ness** *n* — **un·measurably** \"+\ *adv*
un·measured \ˌən+\ *adj* [ME *unmesured*, fr. ¹*un-* + *mesured*, past part. of *mesuren* to measure — more at MEASURE] **:** not measured **:** LIMITLESS, UNRESTRAINED ⟨~ vastness of our . . . solar system —L.P.Smith⟩ ⟨his hypocrisy and duplicity were ~, almost magnificent —Francis Hackett⟩ ⟨~ scorn⟩; *specif* **:** not metrical ⟨~ verse⟩ — **un·mea·sured·ly** *adv* — **un·mea·sured·ness** *n*
un·mechanical \"+\ *adj* **:** not mechanical; *esp* **:** ignorant of or not interested in mechanics ⟨the difficulty of talking mechanics with an ~ person —C.S.Forester⟩ — **un·mechan·ically** \"+\ *adv*
un·mechanized \"+\ *adj, see -ize in Explan Notes* [¹*un-* + *mechanized*, past part. of *mechanize*] **:** not mechanized ⟨production of furniture remained largely ~ —Gordon Russell⟩
un·meddled \"+\ *adj* [¹*un-* + *meddled*, past part. of *meddle*] **:** not meddled — usu. used with *with* ⟨have the enjoyment of his goods . . . ~ with by others —C.S.C.Bowen⟩
un·meddling \"+\ *adj* [¹*un-* + *meddling*, pres. part. of *meddle*] **:** not meddling
un·mediated \"+\ *adj* [¹*un-* + *mediated*, past part. of *mediate*] **:** not mediated ⟨~ relation between God and the soul of man —*Contemporary Rev.*⟩
un·medical \"+\ *adj* **:** not medical
un·meditated \"+\ *adj* [¹*un-* + *meditated*, past part. of *meditate*] **:** not meditated **:** SPONTANEOUS, UNPREMEDITATED
un·medullated \"+\ *adj* **:** having no medullary sheath ⟨~ nerve fiber⟩
un·meek \"+\ *adj* [ME *unmeoc*, *unmek*, *unmeek*, fr. ¹*un-* + *meoc*, *mek*, *meek* meek — more at MEEK] **:** not meek
un·meet \ˌən+\ *adj* **:** not meet **:** UNSUITABLE, IMPROPER ⟨would be ~ . . . to pursue that story to its close —A.E.Coppard⟩ — **un·meet·ly** *adv* — **un·meet·ness** *n*
un·mellowed \"+\ *adj* [¹*un-* + *mellowed*, past part. of *mellow*] **:** not mellowed
un·melodious \"+\ *adj* **:** not melodious — **un·me·lo·di·ous·ly** *adv*
un·melted \"+\ *adj* [¹*un-* + *melted*, past part. of *melt*] **:** not melted
un·melting \"+\ *adj* [¹*un-* + *melting*, pres. part. of *melt*] **:** not melting
un·memorable \"+\ *adj* **:** not memorable **:** not worth remembering ⟨an ~ dramatic production⟩
un·mend·able \ˌən¦mendəbəl\ *adj* [¹*un-* + *mendable* capable of being mended, fr. *mend* + *-able*] **:** not capable of being mended
¹**un·mentionable** \ˌən+\ *adj* [¹*un-* + *mentionable*] **:** not mentionable **:** UNSPEAKABLE, HUSH-HUSH ⟨suffered ~ cruelties —M.R.Cohen⟩ ⟨discussion of formerly ~ topics⟩
²**unmentionable** \"\ *n* -s **:** one that is not to be mentioned or discussed ⟨a long list of advertising ~*s* —*Time*⟩: as **a unmentionables** *pl* **:** TROUSERS ⟨chaste young men in checked ~*s* —Cyril Pearl⟩ **b unmentionables** *pl* **:** UNDERWEAR ⟨having trouble with public laundries shrinking my ~*s* —*Reader's Digest*⟩
un·mentioned \"+\ *adj* [¹*un-* + *mentioned*, past part. of *mention*] **:** not mentioned **:** left out **:** OMITTED ⟨the director was ~ in the program credits⟩
un·mercantile \"+\ *adj* **:** not mercantile
un·mercenary \"+\ *adj* **:** not mercenary
un·merchantable \"+\ *adj* **:** not merchantable **:** not fit for market **:** UNSALABLE
un·merciful \"+\ *adj* **1 :** not merciful **:** MERCILESS ⟨an ~ tyrant⟩ **2 :** EXCESSIVE, EXTREME ⟨sat beside a bore who talked for an ~ period⟩ — **un·mercifully** \"+\ *adv* — **un·mer·ci·ful·ness** *n*
un·merge \"+\ *vt* [²*un-* + *merge*] **:** to dissolve a merger ⟨should be brought under the antitrust laws and *unmerged* —Edward Wimmer⟩
un·meritable \"+\ *adj* **:** not worthy of merit
un·merited \"+\ *adj* **:** not merited **:** UNDESERVED ⟨these defeats, which he believed wholly ~ —J.D.Hicks⟩ ⟨received an ~ honorary degree⟩ — **un·mer·it·ed·ly** *adv*
un·meriting \"+\ *adj* [¹*un-* + *meriting*, pres. part. of *merit*] **:** UNDESERVING
un·mesh \ˌən+\ *vt* [²*un-* + *mesh*] **1 :** to free from a mesh **:** DISENTANGLE **2 :** to release (as gear teeth) from meshing
un·met \"+\ *adj* [¹*un-* + *met*, past part. of *meet*] **1 :** not met **2 :** not yet considered or solved **:** UNANSWERED ⟨find out . . . where ~ needs exist —*New South*⟩
un·metalled \"+\ *adj* [¹*un-* + *metalled*, past part. of *metal*] *chiefly Brit* **:** not provided with road metal ⟨saw an ~, sandy track leading toward some beech woods —M.C.A.Henniker⟩
un·metallic \"+\ *adj* **:** NONMETALLIC
un·metamorphosed \"+\ *adj* [¹*un-* + *metamorphosed*, past part. of *metamorphose*] **:** not metamorphosed ⟨the arrangement of mineral grains in ~ sediments —*Jour. of Geol.*⟩
un·metaphysical \"+\ *adj* **:** not metaphysical
un·methodical \"+\ *adj* **:** not methodical **:** DESULTORY ⟨the project failed through ~ planning⟩ — **un·methodically** \"+\ *adv*
un·methodized \"+\ *adj* [¹*un-* + *methodized*, past part. of *methodize*] **:** not handled methodically
un·metrical \"+\ *adj* **:** not metrical ⟨~ lines of poetry⟩
un·military \"+\ *adj* **:** not military: as **a :** not conforming to military standards or practice ⟨~ posture⟩ ⟨an ~ approach to handling people⟩ **b :** not belonging to or associated with the military ⟨~ circles of government⟩
un·milked \"+\ *adj* [¹*un-* + *milked*, past part. of *milk*] **:** not milked ⟨~ cows⟩
un·milled \"+\ *adj* [¹*un-* + *milled*, past part. of *mill*] **:** not milled
un·minded \"+\ *adj* [¹*un-* + *minded*, past part. of *mind*] *archaic* **:** not attended to **:** UNHEEDED, IGNORED
un·mindful \"+\ *adj* [ME *unmyndeful*, fr. ¹*un-* + *myndeful* mindful — more at MINDFUL] **:** not mindful **:** CARELESS, UNAWARE ⟨while thus ~ of his steps, he stumbled —G.B.Shaw⟩ ⟨not ~ of the heavy responsibility —Ernest Bevin⟩ **syn** see FORGETFUL
un·mined \"+\ *adj* [¹*un-* + *mined*, past part. of *mine*] **:** not mined ⟨deposits of ~ uranium⟩
un·mingled \"+\ *adj* [¹*un-* + *mingled*, past part. of *mingle*] **:** not mingled **:** UNADULTERATED
un·minished \"+\ *adj* [¹*un-* + *minished*, past part. of *minish*] **:** UNDIMINISHED ⟨one everlasting, ~, unchanging joy —E.B. Pusey⟩
un·ministerial \"+\ *adj* **:** not ministerial
un·minted \"+\ *adj* [¹*un-* + *minted*, past part. of *mint*] **:** not minted
un·miraculous \"+\ *adj* **:** not miraculous
un·mirthful \ˌən+\ *adj* **:** not mirthful **:** SERIOUS, HUMORLESS ⟨glanced around a tableful of sober, ~ faces —Caroline Ticknor⟩
un·misgiving \"+\ *adj* [¹*un-* + *misgiving*, pres. part. of *misgive*] **:** not having misgivings **:** CERTAIN, CONFIDENT ⟨a small and unambitious, yet ~ and happy production —Leigh Hunt⟩ — **un·mis·giv·ing·ly** *adv*
un·miss·able \ˌən¦misəbəl\ *adj* [¹*un-* + *miss*, v. + *-able*] **:** that cannot or should not be missed ⟨a large ~ target⟩ ⟨~ tourist attractions⟩
un·missed \ˌən+\ *adj* [ME *unmist*, fr. ¹*un-* + *mist*, past part. of *missen* to miss — more at MISS] **:** not missed ⟨could sneak out and be ~ all night⟩
un·mistakable \"+\ *adj* **:** not capable of being mistaken or misunderstood **:** CLEAR, PLAIN, OBVIOUS, MANIFEST ⟨the ~ odor of alcohol is on his breath —Wayne Hughes⟩ ⟨his opposition to slavery was ~ —Broadus Mitchell⟩ — **un·mis·tak·able·ness** *n* -ES — **un·mistakably** \"+\ *adv*
un·mistrusting \"+\ *adj* [¹*un-* + *mistrusting*, pres. part. of *mistrust*] **:** not mistrusting **:** INGENUOUS
un·miter \"+\ *vt* [²*un-* + *miter*] **:** to deprive of a miter
un·mitigable \"+\ *adj* [¹*un-* + *mitigate* + *-able*] **:** not mitigable ⟨stern and ~ accusations —Sir Walter Scott⟩
un·mitigated \"+\ *adj* [¹*un-* + *mitigated*, past part. of *mitigate*] **1 :** not made less severe or intense **:** UNRELIEVED ⟨the heat is ~ —D.M.Poole⟩ ⟨sounds . . . like an ~ horror of profanity —Agnes Repplier⟩ ⟨had the most ~ contempt —Gertrude Atherton⟩ **2 :** not qualified **:** ARRANT, DOWNRIGHT, OUT-AND-OUT ⟨must think that the . . . public is just a bunch of ~ suckers —R.W.Robey⟩ ⟨an absolutely ~ triumph of wit and writing skill —Brendan Gill⟩ — **un·mit·i·gat·ed·ly** *adv*
un·mix \"+\ *vi* [²*un-* + *mix*] **:** to undergo the separation of a second solid phase from a homogeneous phase ⟨homogeneous synthetic feldspars . . . ~ when held at lower temperatures —*Jour. of Geol.*⟩
un·mixable \"+\ *adj* [¹*un-* + *mix*, v. + *-able*] **:** not mixable **:** INCOMPATIBLE ⟨has brought together in conference . . . apparently ~ groups —Walter Moberly⟩
un·mixed \"+\ *adj* [¹*un-* + *mixed*, past part. of *mix*] **:** not mixed **:** UNADULTERATED, PURE ⟨the course of action . . . is direct and ~ with dissenting viewpoints —F.L.Ryan⟩ ⟨none of them is an ~ blessing —*Modern Industry*⟩ — **un·mixedly** \"+\ *adv*
un·modern \"+\ *adj* **:** not modern **:** OLD-FASHIONED ⟨come from a family too ~ —R.M.Nixon⟩
un·modest \ˌən+\ *adj* **:** IMMODEST
un·modifiable \"+\ *adj* **:** not modifiable **:** UNALTERABLE, INFLEXIBLE ⟨these variations from custom are illogical, incomprehensible, and ~ —*Science News Letter*⟩
un·modified \"+\ *adj* [¹*un-* + *modified*, past part. of *modify*] **:** not modified ⟨the germ cells . . . are ~ by these activities —W.E.Castle⟩ ⟨~ verbs⟩
un·modish \"+\ *adj* **:** UNFASHIONABLE ⟨~ hats⟩ — **un·mo·dish·ly** *adv*
un·modulated \"+\ *adj* [¹*un-* + *modulated*, past part. of *modulate*] **:** not modulated ⟨lectured in an ~ voice edged with hysteria⟩
un·moist \"+\ *adj* **:** not moist
un·moistened \"+\ *adj* [¹*un-* + *moistened*, past part. of *moisten*] **:** not moistened
un·mold \"+\ *vt* [in sense 1, fr. ²*un-* + *mold*, v. (to form); in sense 2, fr. ²*un-* + *mold*, n. (form)] **1 :** to destroy the mold of ⟨'til his very soul ~s its essence —S.T.Coleridge⟩ **2 :** to remove from a mold ⟨~ the gelatin on a plate of lettuce or endive⟩
un·molded \"+\ *adj* [¹*un-* + *molded*, past part. of *mold*, (to form)] **:** not molded ⟨envisioned the sculpture latent in the ~ marble⟩
un·molested \"+\ *adj* [¹*un-* + *molested*, past part. of *molest*] **:** not molested **:** not interfered with **:** UNTOUCHED ⟨communities in the Latin-American countries were ~ —Shlomo Katz⟩ ⟨small game . . . roam ~ —*Amer. Guide Series: Maine*⟩ — **un·mo·lest·ed·ly** *adv*
un·monarch \ˌən+\ *vt* [²*un-* + *monarch*, n.] **:** to depose from the position of monarch
un·moneyed \"+\ *adj* **:** not having money **:** PENNILESS ⟨the ~ young man who has married the heiress —Henry James †1916⟩
un·moor \"+\ *vb* [ME *unmooren*, fr. ²*un-* + *mooren*, *moren* to moor — more at MOOR] *vt* **1 :** to loose from or as if from moorings ⟨~*ed* the punt, leaving the moorings marked with an old tin can —G.G.Carter⟩ ⟨expected to . . . turn the pillows or to ~ the counterpane —Jean Stafford⟩ **2 :** to heave up (an anchor) leaving a second anchor down ~ *vi* **:** to cast off moorings ⟨the ship ~*ed* and swung slowly about⟩
un·moral \"+\ *adj* **1 :** having no moral perception or quality **:** lacking a sense of morality **:** AMORAL ⟨the characters are depicted as being like savages, innocently ~ —Haldeen Braddy⟩ ⟨a triumphant glorification of rascality, the most ~ narrative ever told —Agnes Repplier⟩ **2 :** not influenced or guided by moral considerations or ethical customs ⟨the great ~ power of the modern industrial revolution —F.L.Wright⟩ **3 :** lying outside the bounds of morals or ethics **:** NONMORAL ⟨imagination is, of its very nature, ~ —*Times Lit. Supp.*⟩ — compare IMMORAL
un·morality \"+\ *n* -ES **:** the quality or state of being unmoral ⟨there was something about him, a recklessness, an ~ —Louis Bromfield⟩
un·moralized \"+\ *adj* [¹*un-* + *moralized*, past part. of *moralize*] **:** not influenced or guided by a moral sense ⟨even in his ~ condition he is a social being —James Ford⟩
un·mordanted \"+\ *adj* [¹*un-* + *mordanted*, past part. of *mordant*] **:** not mordanted ⟨~ wool⟩
un·mortared \"+\ *adj* [¹*un-* + *mortared*, past part. of *mortar*] **:** not mortared ⟨roofed with turf and built of ~ stones —R.L. Stevenson⟩
un·mortgaged \"+\ *adj* [¹*un-* + *mortgaged*, past part. of *mortgage*] **:** not mortgaged ⟨an ~ estate⟩
un·mortified \"+\ *adj* [ME, fr. ¹*un-* + *mortified*, past part. of *mortifien* to mortify — more at MORTIFY] **:** not spiritually mortified ⟨an undisciplined and ~ spirit —Jeremy Taylor⟩
un·mothered \"+\ *adj* [¹*un-* + *mother*, n. + *-ed*] **:** deprived of a mother **:** MOTHERLESS ⟨adolescent gosling that, ~, attached itself to him —Della Lutes⟩
un·motherly \"+\ *adj* **:** not motherly
un·motivated \"+\ *adj* [¹*un-* + *motivated*, past part. of *motivate*] **:** lacking an appropriate or understandable motive ⟨began to indulge in odd, ~ behavior⟩
un·motived \"+\ *adj* [¹*un-* + *motive*, n. + *-ed*] **:** UNMOTIVATED
un·mounted \ˌən+\ *adj* **:** not mounted ⟨~ . . . fifteen-inch speakers with integral tweeters —R.S.Lanier⟩ ⟨~ photographs⟩ ⟨~ artillery⟩; *esp* **:** not mounted on or provided with a horse ⟨~ troops⟩
un·mourned \"+\ *adj* [¹*un-* + *mourned*, past part. of *mourn*] **:** not mourned
un·movable \"+\ *adj* [ME *unmevable*, *unmovable*, fr. ¹*un-* + *mevable*, *movable* movable — more at MOVABLE] **:** IMMOVABLE — **un·mov·able·ness** \"+\ *n* — **un·movably** \"+\ *adv*
un·moved \ˌən¦müvd\ *adj* [ME *unmeved*, *unmoved*, fr. ¹*un-* + *meved*, *moved*, past part. of *meven*, *moven* to move — more at MOVE] **1 :** not emotionally affected **:** CALM, INDIFFERENT, UNDISTURBED ⟨had always appeared completely ~ and imperturbable —Elinor Wylie⟩ **2 :** remaining in the same place or position **:** FIRM ⟨after 10 years of redevelopment, some houses were still ~⟩ ⟨could be endured . . . with an ~ countenance —W.H. Hudson †1922⟩ — **un·moved·ly** \-vədlē, -vd-\ *adv*
unmoved mover *n* **:** PRIME MOVER 1
un·moving \ˌən+\ *adj* **:** not moving ⟨bade the sun to stay a while ~ —Frederick O'Brien⟩; *esp* **:** not emotionally stirring ⟨only those with an adamant prejudice . . . can find it meaningless or ~ —W.P.Clancy⟩
un·mown \"+\ *adj* [¹*un-* + *mown*, past part. of *mow*] **:** not mown ⟨~ hay⟩
un·muffle \"+\ *vt* [²*un-* + *muffle*] **:** to free from something that muffles ⟨~ a face⟩ ⟨the sunlight seemed . . . to ~ the incessant noise —Osbert Sitwell⟩
un·murmuring \"+\ *adj* [¹*un-* + *murmuring*, pres. part. of *murmur*] **:** not murmuring discontentedly **:** UNCOMPLAINING — **un·mur·mur·ing·ly** *adv*
un·musical \"+\ *adj* **:** not musical: as **a :** not musical in nature **:** HARSH, DISCORDANT ⟨~ call of the bluejay⟩ **b :** not gifted in or appreciative of music ⟨an entirely ~ crooner —Douglas Watt⟩ ⟨too ~ to care for concerts⟩ — **un·musi·cally** \"+\ *adv*
un·mutation \"+\ *n* [trans. of G *rückumlaut*] **:** RÜCKUMLAUT
un·muted \"+\ *adj* **:** not muted ⟨~ trumpets⟩
un·mutilated \"+\ *adj* [¹*un-* + *mutilated*, past part. of *mutilate*] **:** not mutilated ⟨fragile tracery that must be preserved ~ and distinct —B.N.Cardozo⟩
un·muzzle \"+\ *vt* [²*un-* + *muzzle*] **:** to remove a muzzle from ⟨~ the dog after the mailman has left⟩
un·myelinated \"+\ *adj* **:** lacking a myelin sheath ⟨the ~ fiber found in the mammalian central nervous system —H.J.Curtis & K.S.Cole⟩
un·mysterious \"+\ *adj* **:** not mysterious
un·nail \ˌən+\ *vt* [²*un-* + *nail*] **:** to unfasten by removing nails
un·nailed \"+\ *adj* [¹*un-* + *nailed*, past part. of *nail*] **:** not nailed
un·nameable \"+\ *adj* [¹*un-* + *name*, v. + *-able*] **:** not capable of being named or described **:** NAMELESS, UNSPEAKABLE, INEFFABLE ⟨a mongrel, ~ as to breed —*Harper's*⟩ ⟨experienced ~ horrors⟩ ⟨contemplation of ~ transcendence —Evelyn Underhill⟩
un·named \"+\ *adj* **:** not named **:** UNIDENTIFIED, UNSPECIFIED ⟨a gray slate stone marks the grave of two ~ British soldiers —Phyllis Duganne⟩ ⟨petroleum gas converted by an ~ process —J.H.Kuney⟩
un·na's boot \ˈünəz-\ *n, usu cap U* [after Paul G. *Unna* †1929 Ger. dermatologist] **:** GELATIN BOOT
un·national \ˌən+\ *adj* **:** not belonging to or characteristic of an individual nation ⟨~, as well as deliberately un-English in style —Osbert Sitwell⟩ — compare SUPRANATIONAL
un·natural \"+\ *adj* [ME, fr. ¹*un-* + *natural*] **1 a :** not innately characteristic of the nature of man ⟨scientific inventions . . . to stimulate depraved appetites, to invent ~ wants —T.L. Peacock⟩ ⟨this secrecy . . . is against my disposition, ~ —Joseph Hergesheimer⟩ **b :** not being in accordance with nature **:** not determined by or consistent with a normal course of events ⟨if idleness is ~ a five-hour work week would be disastrous —Stuart Chase⟩ ⟨nothing impossible or ~ in being in love with two women at the same time —Aldous Huxley⟩ ⟨his abhorrence of men who advocated ~ change —A.S.Link⟩ ⟨shaping her economy along grotesquely ~ lines —O.P. Echols⟩ **2 a :** not being in accordance with normal feelings or behavior **:** PERVERSE, ABNORMAL ⟨she had been vicious and ~ . . . had thrived on hatred —W.H.Wright⟩ ⟨something ~ between him and his now-dead closest friend —*Time*⟩ **b :** not marked by naturalness or genuineness **:** ARTIFICIAL, CONTRIVED ⟨when one . . . is ~ with all who are not intimate friends —W.B. Yeats⟩ ⟨an ~ and not very intelligent simplification of a very complex issue —H.J.Laski⟩ **c :** inconsistent with what is natural or expected **:** STRANGE, IRREGULAR ⟨exaltations in which piety and sensuality kept ~ company —F.J.Mather⟩ ⟨his ~ alliance with the nationalists —Michael Clark⟩ **d :** going beyond what is normal **:** SUPERNATURAL, UNCANNY ⟨an almost ~ gift for winning musical prizes —*Amer. Guide Series: N.J.*⟩ **3 :** not having a natural claim **:** ILLEGITIMATE ⟨the ~ children of my brain that I should wish . . . to disinherit —Ellen Glasgow⟩ — **un·naturally** \"+\ *adv* — **un·nat·u·ral·ness** *n*
unnatural act *n* **:** CRIME AGAINST NATURE
un·naturalize \"+\ *vt* [²*un-* + *naturalize*] **1** *archaic* **:** to deprive of natural characteristics **:** make unnatural **2 :** to deprive of the rights of citizenship
un·naturalized \"+\ *adj* [¹*un-* + *naturalized*, past part. of *naturalize*] **:** not having citizenship
un·navigable \"+\ *adj* **:** not navigable ⟨up rapid-broken, ~ streams —*World's Work*⟩
un·neat \"+\ *adj* **:** not neat ⟨all the edges are ~ —*Nation*⟩
un·necessaries \ˌən+\ *n pl* **:** expendable material **:** needless or unimportant things ⟨nowhere are the ~ of life . . . sold at such extravagant prices —*Quarterly Rev.*⟩
un·necessarily \"+\ *adv* **:** not by necessity **:** to an unnecessary degree ⟨gave an ~ detailed description⟩ ⟨prolonging his journey ~ —Sir Walter Scott⟩
un·necessariness \"+\ *n* **:** the quality or state of being unnecessary
un·necessary \"+\ *adj* [¹*un-* + *necessary*] **:** not necessary **:** USELESS, NEEDLESS ⟨a striker's tent camp . . . was burned with ~ loss of life —F.L.Paxson⟩ ⟨ordered to cut out ~ words —F.P.Donovan⟩
un·necessitated \"+\ *adj* [¹*un-* + *necessitated*, past part. of *necessitate*] **:** not necessitated
un·needed \"+\ *adj* [¹*un-* + *needed*, past part. of *need*] **:** not needed **:** UNNECESSARY ⟨~ public works —*N. Y. Herald Tribune*⟩
un·needful \"+\ *adj* [ME *unnedefull*, fr. ¹*un-* + *nedefull* needful — more at NEEDFUL] **:** not needful **:** UNNECESSARY, NEEDLESS
un·neighbored \"+\ *adj* [¹*un-* + *neighbored*, past part. of *neighbor*] **:** having no neighbors ⟨an ~ isle, and far from all resort of busy man —William Cowper⟩
un·neighborly \"+\ *adj* **:** not neighborly ⟨found the new people on the street an ~ bunch who kept to themselves⟩
un·nerve \"+\ *vt* [²*un-* + *nerve*, n.] **1 :** to deprive of courage and physical strength **:** cause to become weak and ineffective esp. from fear ⟨a steeplejack . . . was exhausted and *unnerved* and could not hold on to his dangerous perch much longer —*Boy Scout Handbk.*⟩ ⟨the sudden revulsion of feeling *unnerved* him —F.W.Crofts⟩ **2 :** to cause to become nervous or discomposed **:** UPSET ⟨a lady . . . so emotional in her acting that she ~*s* me —John McCarten⟩ ⟨waiting for something to happen was starting to ~ everybody⟩ **3 :** DENERVATE ⟨~ a chronically lame leg of a horse⟩
syn UNNERVE, ENERVATE, UNMAN, and EMASCULATE can mean in common to deprive of strength, vigor, or the capacity to advance, to overcome difficulties, or often to stand up under even the normal physical or moral strains of existence. UNNERVE implies marked loss of courage, self-control, or power to act ⟨utterly *unnerved* by her surprise, Fara leaned limply against him —L.C.Douglas⟩ ⟨the magnitude of problems in other fields (education, health, housing, social welfare) is equally *unnerving* —Hal Lehrman⟩ ⟨so *unnerved* . . . that he threw away his pistol —Peter Forster⟩ ENERVATE implies a gradual physical or moral weakening, often as a result of luxury or indolence, until one is too feeble to exert effort ⟨work had not made him strong, but *enervated* him. He was pale and thin, with no chest, no buttocks, not even a stomach —Donald Windham⟩ ⟨such a power does not destroy, but . . . *enervates*, extinguishes, and stupefies a people, till each nation is reduced to nothing better than a flock of timid and industrious animals —Alexis de Tocqueville⟩ ⟨a love of luxury has *enervated* the virile race that swarmed in cabins —Russell Lord⟩ UNMAN implies loss of manly vigor, control, or spirit ⟨debilitated and *unmanned* by factory-produced comforts —*Time*⟩ ⟨every tiny animal he roused in its burrow startled him, *unmanned* him with the noise of its movement —Norman Mailer⟩ ⟨*unmanned* by a woman's tears⟩ EMASCULATE implies a loss of force, esp. by the removal of something essential ⟨a plan *emasculated* by lack of funds⟩ ⟨supporters voted against the treaty . . . rather than have it passed in *emasculated* form —H.S.Quigley⟩ ⟨how to . . . *emasculate* homemade bombs —J.A.Maxwell⟩
un·nest \ˌən+\ *vt* [²*un-* + *nest*, n.] **:** to put out of or as if out of a nest

un·neurotic \"+\ *adj* **:** not neurotic **:** well-adjusted ⟨successful mothers — mothers with many ~ children —E.G.Boring⟩
un·neutral \"+\ *adj* [[1]*un-* + *neutral*] **:** not neutral **:** PARTISAN ⟨regarded the . . . policy as ~ and likely to lead . . . into war —F.M.Russell⟩
un·neutrality \"+\ *n* **:** the quality or state of being unneutral ⟨his policy of ~ and of assistance to the allies —Dexter Perkins⟩
un·noble \"+\ *adj* [ME, fr. [1]*un-* + *noble*] **:** not noble **:** COMMON
un·notched \"+\ *adj* **:** not notched ⟨~ surface⟩
un·noted \"+\ *adj* [[1]*un-* + *noted*, past part. of *note*] **:** not noted **:** UNOBSERVED, DISREGARDED ⟨would have lived and died, ~ —S.H.Adams⟩
un·noteworthy \"+\ *adj* **:** not noteworthy **:** UNREMARKABLE, COMMONPLACE ⟨the theater season opened with an ~ comedy⟩
un·noticeable \"+\ *adj* [[1]*un-* + *notice*, v. + *-able*] **:** not noticeable **:** not drawing attention **:** UNDISTINGUISHED, INSIGNIFICANT ⟨her clothes were simple and ~ —J.G.Cozzens⟩ ⟨an ~ cigarette burn on the rug⟩ — **un·noticeably** \"+\ *adv*
un·noticed \"+\ *adj* [[1]*un-* + *noticed*, past part. of *notice*] **:** not noticed **:** UNOBSERVED, UNRECOGNIZED ⟨the guests begin to slip away, one by one, ~ —Lafcadio Hearn⟩ ⟨managed to get through the reception line ~⟩
un·noticing \¦ən+\ *adj* [[1]*un-* + *noticing*, pres. part. of *notice*] **:** not noticing
un·nourishing \"+\ *adj* **:** not nourishing or beneficial ⟨an ~ diet⟩ ⟨the irreligion and the cult of success that were so fatally ~ to . . . the Edwardians —V.S.Pritchett⟩
un·numberable \"+\ *adj* [ME, alter. (influenced by [1]*un-*) of *innumerable*] **:** INNUMERABLE ⟨with starry globes ~ —P.J. Bailey⟩
un·numbered \"+\ *adj* [ME *unnumbred, unnombred*, fr. [1]*un-* + *noumbred, nombred*, past part. of *noumbren, nombren* to number — more at NUMBER] **:** not numbered: as **a :** more than are countable **:** INNUMERABLE ⟨through my heart's palace thoughts ~ throng —Rupert Brooke⟩ **b :** not having an identifying number ⟨~ page⟩ ⟨you turn west up an ~ dirt road —Bernard DeVoto⟩
un·nurtured \"+\ *adj* [[1]*un-* + *nurtured*, past part. of *nurture*] **:** not nurtured
un·obedient \¦ən+\ *adj* [ME, fr. [1]*un-* + *obedient*] **:** DISOBEDIENT
un·obeyed \"+\ *adj* [[1]*un-* + *obeyed*, past part. of *obey*] **:** not obeyed **:** DISOBEYED
un·objected \"+\ *adj* [[1]*un-* + *objected*, past part. of *object*] **:** not objected to
un·objectionable \"+\ *adj* **:** not objectionable **:** ACCEPTABLE — **un·objectionableness** \"+\ *n* — **un·objectionably** \"+\ *adv*
un·objective \"+\ *adj* **:** not possessing or representing objective reality **:** SUBJECTIVE
un·obligated \"+\ *adj* [[1]*un-* + *obligated*, past part. of *obligate*] *of funds* **:** appropriated but remaining uncommitted by contract at the end of a fiscal period
un·obliging \"+\ *adj* **:** not obliging **:** DISOBLIGING
un·obliterated \"+\ *adj* [[1]*un-* + *obliterated*, past part. of *obliterate*] **:** not obliterated ⟨an ~ stain⟩
un·obnoxious \"+\ *adj* [[1]*un-* + *obnoxious*] **1 :** UNLIABLE **2 :** not obnoxious **:** INOFFENSIVE
un·obscured \"+\ *adj* [[1]*un-* + *obscured*, past part. of *obscure*] **:** not obscured **:** UNHIDDEN, CLEAR
[1]**un·observable** \"+\ *adj* **:** not observable **:** INDISCERNIBLE, IMPERCEPTIBLE
[2]**unobservable** \"\ *n* **:** something unobservable esp. even in principle ⟨multiply ~*s* and subsistent entities at pleasure —A. E.Duncan-Jones⟩
un·observance \¦ən+\ *n* **:** want or neglect of observance **:** NONOBSERVANCE
un·observant \"+\ *adj* **:** not observant **:** not noticing — **un·observantly** \"+\ *adv*
un·observed \"+\ *adj* [[1]*un-* + *observed*, past part. of *observe*] **:** not observed **:** UNPERCEIVED ⟨looking quickly around to be sure she was ~ —Sherwood Anderson⟩ — **un·observedly** \"+\ *adv*
un·observing \"+\ *adj* **:** not observing **:** UNNOTICING, INCURIOUS, INATTENTIVE
un·obstinate \"+\ *adj* **:** not obstinate **:** ACCOMMODATING, AGREEABLE
un·obstructed \"+\ *adj* [[1]*un-* + *obstructed*, past part. of *obstruct*] **:** not obstructed **:** CLEAR, UNHINDERED ⟨an ~ view⟩ ⟨~ progress⟩ — **un·ob·struct·ed·ly** *adv* — **un·ob·struct·ed·ness** *n* -ES
un·obtainable \¦ən+\ *adj* **:** not obtainable
un·obtrusive \"+\ *adj* **:** not obtrusive **:** not blatant, immodest, or overly aggressive in manner, action, or appearance ⟨a quiet, ~ life of self-denial —Samuel Butler †1902⟩ — **un·obtrusively** \"+\ *adv* — **un·obtrusiveness** \"+\ *n*
un·obvious \"+\ *adj* **:** not obvious **:** not immediately apparent ⟨in mathematical science connections are exhibited which . . . are extremely ~ —A.N.Whitehead⟩
un·occupancy \"+\ *n* **:** the state of being unoccupied
un·occupied \"+\ *adj* [ME *unoccupyed*, fr. [1]*un-* + *occupyed* occupied] **1 :** not busy **:** UNEMPLOYED **2 a :** not occupied by inhabitants ⟨~ ground⟩ **b :** of, relating to, or being premises on which no one is living although the furniture and fixtures have not been removed — compare VACANT 6 **c :** not occupied by enemy or conquering troops
un·offended \"+\ *adj* [ME, fr. [1]*un-* + *offended*, past part. of *offenden* to offend] **:** not offended **:** not given offense — **un·of·fend·ed·ly** *adv*
un·offending \"+\ *adj* [[1]*un-* + *offending*, pres. part. of *offend*] **:** not offending or offensive; *esp* **:** not harming **:** HARMLESS, INNOCUOUS
un·offensive \"+\ *adj* **:** INOFFENSIVE
un·offered \"+\ *adj* [[1]*un-* + *offered*, past part. of *offer*] **:** not offered
un·officered \¦ən+\ *adj* [[1]*un-* + *officer* + *-ed*] **:** not provided with or led by officers
[1]**un·official** \"+\ *adj* **1 a :** not belonging to, emanating from, or sanctioned or acknowledged by a government or governing body ⟨a sort of ~ mayor of the village —Siegfried Sassoon⟩ ⟨the ~ capital⟩ ⟨an ~ estimate⟩ **b** *of a drug* **:** not recognized by the legal standards or government of a country **c :** nominated or elected from among the native inhabitants of a British dependency and holding no appointment from the Colonial Office in the public service ⟨a governor's council with an ~ minority⟩ ⟨there is no legislative council in the Dependent Empire without ~ members —Martin Wight⟩ — compare OFFICIAL **2 :** not sanctioned, authorized, or acknowledged by a group, class, or society ⟨proud of their ~ power as mothers —E.H.Erikson⟩ ⟨the custom of awarding prizes . . . substitutes one certified good play for half a dozen ~ good plays —Russell Maloney⟩ — **un·officially** \"+\ *adv*
[2]**unofficial** \"\ *n* **:** an unofficial member of a legislature in a British dependency
un·officinal \¦ən+\ *adj* **:** not commonly kept in stock by pharmacists ⟨~ drugs⟩
un·often \"+\ *adv* **:** not often **:** SELDOM
un·oiled \"+\ *adj* **:** not oiled
uno·na \yəˈnōnə\ *n, cap* [NL, alter. of *Anona*] **:** a genus of tropical Asiatic and African trees, shrubs, or woody vines (family Annonaceae) having flowers with flat spreading petals succeeded by an aggregate of stalked berries
unop *abbr* **1** unopened **2** unopposed
un·open \¦ən+\ *adj* **:** not open **:** CLOSED, SHUT, SEALED
un·opened \"+\ *adj* [[1]*un-* + *opened*, past part. of *open*] **:** not opened; *specif* **:** having adjacent leaves still joined together at the fore edge — used of a book or periodical
un·operated \"+\ *adj* [[1]*un-* + *operated*, past part. of *operate*] **:** not operated upon
un·operative \"+\ *adj* **:** INOPERATIVE
un·opposable \"+\ *adj* **:** not opposable
un·opposed \"+\ *adj* **:** not opposed ⟨~ to earning an honest dollar —R.L.Taylor⟩; *esp* **:** having no opponent ⟨the incumbent was ~ for the nomination⟩
un·oppressed \"+\ *adj* [[1]*un-* + *oppressed*, past part. of *oppress*] **:** not oppressed esp. emotionally
un·oppressive \"+\ *adj* **:** not oppressive **:** MILD, BENEFICENT
un·ordained \"+\ *adj* [[1]*un-* + *ordained*, past part. of *ordain*] **:** not ordained in the ministry or priesthood ⟨an ~ preacher⟩
un·ordered \"+\ *adj* [ME *unordred*, fr. [1]*un-* + *ordred*, past part. of *ordren* to order] **1 :** not arranged in order **:** DISORDERED **2 :** not decreed or commanded
un·orderly \"+\ *adj* [ME, fr. [1]*un-* + *order* + *-ly*] **:** DISORDERLY, DISORDERED
un·ordinary \"+\ *adj* **:** not ordinary; *esp* **:** being out of the ordinary **:** UNUSUAL, EXTRAORDINARY
un·organizable \"+\ *adj* **:** not organizable
un·organized \"+\ *adj* **1 a :** not brought into a coherent or well-ordered whole **b :** not having a formally organized government ⟨~ territories⟩ **c :** not belonging to a labor union **2 :** not having the characteristics of a living organism
un·oriented \"+\ *adj* **:** not oriented: as **a :** not having a position, direction, and bearing definitely ascertained **b :** of, relating to, or being a texture in igneous rock in which the individual crystals lie crisscross in orientation **c :** lacking a set goal, purpose, or direction ⟨engaged in ~ study⟩
un·original \"+\ *adj* **:** not original: as **a :** not exerting, capable of exerting, or arising from the use of originality ⟨his life had been ~, conforming completely to the given pattern —Gwethalyn Graham⟩ **b :** not present at the origin ⟨containing ~ emendations⟩ — **un·originality** \"+\ *n*
un·orig·i·nate \ˌənəˈrijənət, -əˌnāt\ *adj* [back-formation fr. *unoriginated*] **:** UNORIGINATED
un·originated \¦ən+\ *adj* [[1]*un-* + *originated*, past part. of *originate*] **1 :** not originated **:** existing from all eternity **:** UNCREATED **2 :** not yet caused to be or to be made
un·originative \¦ən+\ *adj* **:** having no talent for originating **:** UNORIGINAL
un·ornamental \"+\ *adj* **:** not used as or decorated by ornament — **un·ornamentally** \"+\ *adv*
un·ornamented \"+\ *adj* [[1]*un-* + *ornamented*, past part. of *ornament*] **:** not ornamented **:** UNADORNED, BARE ⟨stark, ~ functional clusters of concrete —*Amer. Guide Series: Minn.*⟩
un·orthodox \"+\ *adj* **:** not orthodox **:** not in accord with approved, standardized, or conventional doctrine, method thought, custom, or opinion ⟨~ religious views⟩ ⟨the ~ field of parapsychology —A.G.N.Flew⟩ ⟨an ~ news-gathering tactic —*Newsweek*⟩ — **un·orthodoxly** \"+\ *adv*
un·orthodoxy \"+\ *n* **1 :** an unorthodox opinion, doctrine, or method **2 :** a group or the body of people holding unorthodox doctrines
un·ossified \"+\ *adj* **:** not ossified
un·ostentatious \"+\ *adj* **:** not ostentatious **:** not showy, forward, flamboyant **:** quiet and restrained esp. in taste ⟨~ elegance⟩ — **un·ostentatiously** \"+\ *adv* — **un·ostentatiousness** \"+\ *n*
un·owned \¦ən+\ *adj* [[1]*un-* + *owned*, past part. of *own*] **1 :** having no owner **:** OWNERLESS **2 :** UNACKNOWLEDGED
un·oxygenated \"+\ *adj* [[1]*un-* + *oxygenated*, past part. of *oxygenate*] **:** not oxygenated
unp *abbr* unpaged
un·pacific \¦ən+\ *adj* **:** not pacific **:** VIOLENT, WARLIKE
un·pack \"+\ *vb* [ME *unpakken*, fr. [2]*un-* + *pakken* to pack] *vt* **1 a :** to remove the contents of ⟨~ a trunk⟩ **b :** to reveal the feelings of **:** UNBURDEN ⟨must . . . ~ my heart with words —Shak.⟩ **2 a :** to remove or undo from packing or a container ⟨packed and ~*ed* all the gear in traveling —Weston La Barre⟩ **b :** to reveal or decipher (as thought or meaning) by interpretation ⟨the meaning of such statements can be ~*ed* in a series of hypothetical propositions —R.J.Spilsbury⟩ ~ *vi* **:** to engage in unpacking a container
un·packed \"+\ *adj* [ME *unpakked*, fr. [1]*un-* + *pakked*, past part. of *pakken* to pack] **:** not packed
un·padded \"+\ *adj* **:** not padded
un·paged \"+\ *adj* [[1]*un-* + *paged*, past part. of *page*] **:** having no page numbers ⟨an ~ pamphlet⟩ ⟨~ inserts⟩
un·paid \"+\ *adj* [ME *unpayd*, fr. [1]*un-* + *payd*, past part. of *payen* to pay] **1 :** not paid **:** serving without pay ⟨~ officials⟩ **2 a :** not presented as payment ⟨~ wages⟩ **b :** not cleared by payment ⟨an ~ bill⟩ **c :** not purchased or as yet unpurchased by payment — usu. used with *for* ⟨a car partially ~ for⟩ **3 :** not paying a salary ⟨an ~ position⟩
unpaid-letter stamp *n* **:** POSTAGE-DUE STAMP
un·pained \¦ən+\ *adj* [ME *unpeyned*, fr. [1]*un-* + *peyned*, past part. of *peynen* to pain] **:** having no pain **:** feeling no pain
un·painful \"+\ *adj* **:** not painful
un·paintable \"+\ *adj* **:** not paintable; *esp* **:** not suitable for artistic representation on canvas — **un·paintableness** \"+\ *n*
un·painted \"+\ *adj* **:** not painted **:** not having a coat of paint; *also* **:** badly in need of a fresh coat of paint
un·paired \"+\ *adj* [[1]*un-* + *paired*, past part. of *pair*] **1 :** not paired; *esp* **:** not matched or mated ⟨an ~ shoe⟩ ⟨an ~ electron⟩ **2 a :** situated in the median plane of the body ⟨an ~ fin⟩ **b :** having no mate on the opposite side
un·palatability \"+\ *n* **:** the quality or state of being unpalatable
un·palatable \"+\ *adj* **1 :** not palatable **:** DISTASTEFUL **2 :** UNPLEASANT, DISAGREEABLE ⟨harshly ~ but honest statements —Linton Wells⟩ — **un·palatableness** \"+\ *n* — **un·palatably** \"+\ *adv*
un·palliated \"+\ *adj* [[1]*un-* + *palliated*, past part. of *palliate*] **:** not palliated **:** SEVERE
un·palpable \"+\ *adj* **:** IMPALPABLE
un·palped \"+\ *adj* **:** having no palp
un·paper \"+\ *vt* [[2]*un-* + *paper*] **:** to strip paper from
un·papered \"+\ *adj* [[1]*un-* + *papered*, past part. of *paper*] **:** having no paper; *esp* **:** not covered with wallpaper
un·paradise \"+\ *vt* -ED/-ING/-S [[2]*un-* + *paradise*, n.] **1 a :** to expel from paradise **b :** to make unhappy **2 :** to remove the character of paradise from
un·paragoned \"+\ *adj* [[1]*un-* + *paragoned*, past part. of *paragon*] **:** having no paragon **:** UNEQUALED, MATCHLESS, PEERLESS
un·parallel \"+\ *adj* **:** not parallel ⟨~ lines intersect⟩
un·par·al·lel·able \-ləbəl\ *adj* [[1]*un-* + *parallel* + *-able*] **:** not capable of being paralleled; *esp* **:** that cannot be equalled or matched **:** INCOMPARABLE
un·paralleled \¦ən+\ *adj* [[1]*un-* + *paralleled*, past part. of *parallel*] **:** having no parallel; *esp* **:** having no equal or match **:** UNSURPASSED, UNEQUALED ⟨rains of ~ intensity —W.E. Swinton⟩ ⟨an ~ gift for invective —C.I.Glicksberg⟩
un·paralyzed \"+\ *adj* [[1]*un-* + *paralyzed*, past part. of *paralyze*] **:** not paralyzed
un·pardonable \"+\ *adj* **:** not admitting of pardon **:** UNFORGIVABLE, INEXCUSABLE ⟨falsification of results in any way, even by implication is the ~ sin —Jessie Bernard⟩ — **un·pardonableness** \"+\ *n* — **un·pardonably** \"+\ *adv*
un·pardoned \"+\ *adj* [[1]*un-* + *pardoned*, past part. of *pardon*] **:** not pardoned **:** UNFORGIVEN
un·pardoning \"+\ *adj* [[1]*un-* + *pardoning*, pres. part. of *pardon*] **:** not pardoning **:** withholding forgiveness
un·par·ent·ed \¦ənˈpa(a)rəntəd, -per-\ *adj* [[1]*un-* + *parent* + *-ed*] **:** having no parent or acknowledged parent **:** ORPHAN
un·park \¦ən+\ *vt* [[2]*un-* + *park*] **:** to remove from a parking place ⟨could ~ the trucks and cars and wagons and mules —William Faulkner⟩
un·parliamentary \"+\ *adj* **:** not parliamentary **:** contrary to the practice of parliamentary bodies
un·parted \"+\ *adj* **:** not parted **:** UNSEPARATED; *specif* **:** not subjected to the operation of separating gold from silver — used of gold bullion containing silver or silver bullion containing gold
un·participated \"+\ *adj* [[1]*un-* + *participated*, past part. of *participate*] **:** not participated in **:** UNEQUALED, UNIQUE
un·partisan \"+\ *adj* **:** NONPARTISAN — **un·partisanship** \"+\ *n*
un·partitioned \"+\ *adj* [[1]*un-* + *partitioned*, past part. of *partition*] **:** not partitioned **:** having no partitions
un·passable \"+\ *adj* **1 :** IMPASSABLE **2** *obs* **:** not usable as currency
un·passed \"+\ *adj* [[1]*un-* + *passed*, past part. of *pass*] **:** not passed **:** still to be crossed
un·passioned \¦ən+\ *adj* **:** DISPASSIONATE
un·pastoral \"+\ *adj* **:** not pastoral; *also* **:** not characteristic of or consonant with the tradition of pastoral verse
un·patentable \"+\ *adj* **:** not patentable
un·patented \"+\ *adj* [[1]*un-* + *patented*, past part. of *patent*] **:** not patented ⟨~ inventions⟩
un·pathed \ˌənˈpa\|tht, -ˈpaa(ə)\|, -ˈpai\|, -ˈpȧ\|, \|t͟hd\ *adj* [[1]*un-* + *path* + *-ed*] **:** not having a path **:** PATHLESS
un·patient \¦ən+\ *adj* [ME *unpacient*, fr. [1]*un-* + *pacient* patient] **:** IMPATIENT
un·patriotic \"+\ *adj* **:** not patriotic **:** not giving or expressing due regard to one's country or its interests; *esp* **:** SUBVERSIVE ⟨~ obstruction by any corporation in defense work —F.D. Roosevelt⟩ — **un·patriotically** \"+\ *adv*
un·patrolled \"+\ *adj* [[1]*un-* + *patrolled*, past part. of *patrol*] **:** not patrolled esp. by sentinels or police ⟨an ~ section of the highway⟩
un·patronized \"+\ *adj* [[1]*un-* + *patronized*, past part. of *patronize*] **:** not patronized **:** having little or no patronage ⟨a restaurant ~ by the elite⟩
un·pausing \"+\ *adj* [[1]*un-* + *pausing*, pres. part. of *pause*] **:** continuing without cease — **un·pausingly** \"+\ *adv*
un·pave \"+\ *vt* [[2]*un-* + *pave*] **:** to remove the paving from
un·paved \"+\ *adj* **:** not paved **:** not furnished with a pavement
un·pawned \"+\ *adj* [[1]*un-* + *pawned*, past part. of *pawn*] **:** not pawned
un·payable \"+\ *adj* **1 :** not capable of being paid **2 :** not capable of being profitably worked ⟨~ ore deposits⟩
un·paying \"+\ *adj* [[1]*un-* + *paying*, pres. part. of *pay*] **:** not paying ⟨~ customers⟩
un·peace \"+\ *n* **:** lack of peace **:** STRIFE, DISUNITY, DISSENSION
un·peaceable \"+\ *adj* [[1]*un-* + *peaceable*] **1 :** given to disturbing the peace **:** DISSENTIENT **2 :** lacking peace **:** DISTURBED, UNPEACEFUL
un·peaceful \"+\ *adj* **:** not peaceful **:** INHARMONIOUS, AGITATED, TURBULENT — **un·peacefully** \"+\ *adv*
un·pedantic \"+\ *adj* **:** not pedantic **:** not characterized by the dryness and dead mechanical manner of a pedant **:** LIVELY — **un·pedantically** \"+\ *adv*
un·pedestal \¦ən+\ *vt* [[2]*un-* + *pedestal*, n.] **:** to oust from a position of superiority
un·pedigreed \"+\ *adj* [[1]*un-* + *pedigreed*, past part. of *pedigree*] **1 :** not distinguished by a pedigree **2** *of a domestic animal* **:** lacking a recorded pedigree **:** not of the pure blood of a recognized breed — used esp. of a high grade
un·peel \"+\ *vt* [[2]*un-* + *peel*] **:** to remove an outer covering (as bark, a rind, or a peel) from ⟨~ a banana⟩
un·peeled ginger \"+-\ *n* **:** BLACK GINGER
un·peg \"+\ *vt* [[2]*un-* + *peg*] **1 a :** to remove a peg from **b :** to unfasten by or as if by removing a peg **2 :** to cease pegging transactions in (a security or a currency)
un·pen \"+\ *vt* [[2]*un-* + *pen*] **:** to release from a pen or from confinement
un·penetrable \"+\ *adj* **:** IMPENETRABLE
un·penetrated \"+\ *adj* [[1]*un-* + *penetrated*, past part. of *penetrate*] **:** not penetrated
un·penned \"+\ *adj* [[1]*un-* + *penned*, past part. of *pen* to enclose & *pen* to write] **1 :** not confined by a pen **2 :** UNWRITTEN
un·pensioned \"+\ *adj* [[1]*un-* + *pensioned*, past part. of *pension*] **:** not pensioned **:** having no pension
un·pent \"+\ *adj* **:** not pent **:** UNCONFINED, RELEASED
un·people \"+\ *vt* [[2]*un-* + *people*] **:** to deprive of inhabitants **:** DEPOPULATE ⟨the failure of the harvest again produced famine — *unpeopling* farms and hamlets —G.M.Trevelyan⟩
un·peopled \"+\ *adj* [[1]*un-* + *peopled*, adj.] **:** UNPOPULATED, UNINHABITED
un·perceivable \"+\ *adj* [ME, fr. [1]*un-* + *perceivable*] **:** IMPERCEPTIBLE; *esp* **:** logically or by nature imperceptible
un·perceived \"+\ *adj* [ME, fr. [1]*un-* + *perceived*, past part. of *perceiven* to perceive] **:** not perceived, noticed, or remarked
un·perceiving \"+\ *adj* **:** not perceiving or prone to perceive **:** UNOBSERVANT
un·perceptive \"+\ *adj* **:** lacking perception **:** UNPERCEIVING ⟨as ~ as a boulder —Edmund Wilson⟩
un·perch \¦ən+\ *vt* [[2]*un-* + *perch*] **:** to remove from a perch
un·percipient \"+\ *adj* **:** UNPERCEIVING
un·perfect \"+\ *adj* [alter. (influenced by L *perfectus* perfect) of ME *unperfit*, fr. [1]*un-* + *perfit* perfect] **1 :** IMPERFECT **2** *obs* **:** poorly trained **:** UNSKILLED — **un·perfectness** \"+\ *n*
un·perfected \"+\ *adj* **1 :** not brought to completion **:** UNFINISHED **2 :** poorly trained **:** INEXPERT
un·perforate \"+\ *adj* **:** IMPERFORATE
un·perforated \"+\ *adj* **:** having no perforations **:** IMPERFORATE
un·performable \"+\ *adj* **:** not performable; *also* **:** difficult to perform
un·performed \"+\ *adj* [ME, fr. [1]*un-* + *performed*, past part. of *performen* to perform] **:** not performed ⟨the author of an ~ play⟩
un·performing \"+\ *adj* **:** not performing
un·perilous \¦ən+\ *adj* **:** not perilous **:** free from danger
un·perishable \"+\ *adj* **:** IMPERISHABLE
un·perished \"+\ *adj* [ME *unperist*, fr. [1]*un-* + *perist, perisshed*, past part. of *perissen, perisshen* to perish] **:** not dead **:** ALIVE
un·perishing \"+\ *adj* **:** IMMORTAL
un·perjured \"+\ *adj* **:** not perjured
un·permanent \"+\ *adj* **:** IMPERMANENT
un·permissive \"+\ *adj* **:** not permissive **:** STRICT
un·permitted \"+\ *adj* **:** not permitted **:** DISALLOWED, BANNED
un·perplex \¦ən+\ *vt* [[2]*un-* + *perplex*] **:** to free from perplexity
un·perplexed \"+\ *adj* [[1]*un-* + *perplexed*, adj.] **1 :** not perplexed **:** UNBAFFLED **2 :** SIMPLE, STRAIGHTFORWARD, CLEAR
un·persuadable \"+\ *adj* **:** not persuadable **:** ADAMANT — **un·persuadableness** \"+\ *n*
un·persuaded \"+\ *adj* [[1]*un-* + *persuaded*, past part. of *persuade*] **:** not persuaded
un·persuasive \"+\ *adj* **:** not persuasive — **un·persuasively** \"+\ *adv* — **un·persuasiveness** \"+\ *n*
un·perturbed \"+\ *adj* [ME, fr. [1]*un-* + *perturbed*, past part. of *perturben* to perturb] **:** not perturbed **:** unaffected by worry, interruption, disturbance, or disarrangement ⟨a fox who was completely ~ by my appearance —S.P.B.Mais⟩ — **un·perturbedly** \"+\ *adv* — **un·per·turbed·ness** \-b(ə)dnəs\ *n* -ES
un·perverted \¦ən+\ *adj* **:** not perverted
un·petticoated \"+\ *adj* **:** not wearing a petticoat
un·philosophic \"+\ *or* **un·philosophical** \"+\ *adj* **1 :** not in accordance with philosophic knowledge or methods ⟨an ~ judgment⟩ **2 :** lacking philosophic breadth, insight, or temperament ⟨the ~ specialist may be a fool in every field not his own —A.L.Guérard⟩ — **un·philosophically** \"+\ *adv*
un·phonetic \"+\ *adj* **:** characterized by or showing lack of regular correspondence of spelling to sound — **un·pho·net·ic·ness** \-knəs\ *n* -ES
un·physical \¦ən+\ *adj* **1 :** not physical **:** MENTAL, SPIRITUAL **2 :** not according with the doctrines or methods of physics
un·physiologic \"+\ *also* **un·physiological** \"+\ *adj* **:** not such as would ordinarily conduce to an organism's normal healthy functioning ⟨an ~ regime⟩ ⟨~ dosage of vitamin D⟩
un·pick \"+\ *vt* [[2]*un-* + *pick*] **:** to undo (as sewing, embroidery, or knitting) by taking out stitches
un·pickable \"+\ *adj* **1 :** not pickable or easily pickable ⟨an ~ lock⟩
unpicked \"+\ *adj* **1 :** UNSORTED **2 :** not picked
un·pictorial \"+\ *adj* **:** not susceptible to pictorial representation — **un·pictorially** \"+\ *adv* — **un·pictorialness** \"+\ *n*
un·picturesque \"+\ *adj* **:** not picturesque — **un·picturesquely** \"+\ *adv* — **un·picturesqueness** \"+\ *n*
un·pierceable \"+\ *adj* **:** not pierceable
un·pierced \"+\ *adj* **:** not pierced
un·pigmented \"+\ *adj* [[1]*un-* + *pigmented*, past part. of *pigment*] **:** having no pigment
un·pile \"+\ *vb* [[2]*un-* + *pile*] *vt* **:** to take or disentangle from a pile ⟨waiters *unpiling* the wicker chairs —Cyril Connolly⟩ ~ *vi* **:** to become separated or disentangled from a pile ⟨at the referee's whistle the players *unpiled*⟩
un·pillared \"+\ *adj* **:** having no pillar
un·pillowed \"+\ *adj* [[1]*un-* + *pillowed*, past part. of *pillow*] **:** not resting on a pillow
un·piloted \"+\ *adj* [[1]*un-* + *piloted*, past part. of *pilot*] **:** not piloted **:** being without a pilot ⟨~ missiles⟩

un·pin \"+\ *vt* [ME *unpinnen*, fr. ²*un-* + *pinnen* to pin] **1 :** to remove a pin from **2 :** to loosen, free, or unfasten by or as if by removing a pin ⟨~ a dress⟩ ⟨~ a frame⟩
unpinion *vt* [²*un-* + *pinion*] *obs* : to loose from or as if from pinions : free from restraint
un·pinioned \ˌən+\ *adj* [¹*un-* + *pinioned*] **1 :** having no pinions **2 :** not bound by or as if by pinions ⟨perfectly free and ~ —Edward Grey⟩
un·pitiable \ˌən+\ *adj* : not pitiable — **un·pitiably** \"+\ *adv*
un·pitied \"+\ *adj* [¹*un-* + *pitied*, past part. of *pity*] **1 :** not pitied **2** [¹*un-* + *pity*, n. + *-ed*] *obs* : PITILESS, MERCILESS
un·pitiful \"+\ *adj* [ME *unpiteful*, fr. ¹*un-* + *piteful*, *petefull* pitiful] : PITILESS — **un·pitifully** \"+\ *adv*
un·pitying \"+\ *adj* : not pitying : UNMERCIFUL — **un·pityingly** \"+\ *adv*
un·placed \"+\ *adj* [¹*un-* + *placed*, past part. of *place*] **1 :** not placed : not having a definite or assigned place, position, station, or office **2 :** not winning one of the first three places in a horse race
un·plagued \"+\ *adj* : not plagued ⟨a town rich in traditions . . . and ~ by ambition —*Amer. Guide Series: Md.*⟩
un·plait \"+\ *vt* [²*un-* + *plait*] : to undo the plaits of
un·plaited \"+\ *adj* [¹*un-* + *plaited*] : not plaited
un·planed \"+\ *adj* [¹*un-* + *planed*, past part. of *plane* to level] : not planed ⟨~ planks⟩
un·plank \"+\ *vt* [²*un-* + *plank*] : to remove the planks from
un·planked \ˌən+\ *adj* [¹*un-* + *planked*, past part. of *plank*] : not planked; *specif* : not covered with planks
un·planned \"+\ *adj* **1 :** not planned ⟨an ~ economy⟩ **2 :** UNEXPECTED ⟨accepts an ~ order —J.S.Berliner⟩
un·plant \"+\ *vt* [²*un-* + *plant*] : to remove from the soil : UPROOT
un·plantable \"+\ *adj* : not plantable : INFERTILE ⟨land hitherto regarded as ~ —*Ulster Yr. Bk.*⟩
un·planted \"+\ *adj* [¹*un-* + *planted*, past part. of *plant*] **1** *of a plant* : growing spontaneously and freely in nature without human intervention : UNCULTIVATED **2 :** not colonized : UNSETTLED **3 :** not placed in position : not set out
un·plastered \"+\ *adj* [¹*un-* + *plastered*, past part. of *plaster*] : not plastered : having no plaster ⟨~ walls⟩
un·plastic \"+\ *adj* : not plastic; *specif* : not amenable to plastic representation
un·plausible \"+\ *adj* : IMPLAUSIBLE — **un·plausibly** \"+\ *adv*
un·playable \ˌən+\ *adj* : not playable: as **a :** not capable of being played on a musical instrument **b :** being in a position where a stroke or shot is impossible ⟨an ~ lie in golf⟩
un·pleasant \"+\ *adj* : not pleasant : not amiable or agreeable : DISPLEASING, OFFENSIVE ⟨~ odors⟩ ⟨~ repercussions⟩ ⟨an ~ personality⟩ — **un·pleasantly** \"+\ *adv*
un·pleasantness \"+\ *n* **1 a :** the quality or state of being unpleasant : DISAGREEABLENESS **b :** an unpleasant situation, experience, or event ⟨murders, bankruptcies, and other ~*es* —Charles Spielberger⟩ **2 :** the elementary feeling ordinarily awakened by painful or disagreeable stimuli
un·pleasantry \"+\ *n* **1 :** an unpleasant incident **2 :** an unpleasant remark or speech : INSULT ⟨the candidates exchanged *unpleasantries*⟩
un·pleased \"+\ *adj* [ME *unplesed*, fr. ¹*un-* + *plesed* pleased] : not pleased : DISPLEASED, UNSATISFIED
un·pleasing \"+\ *adj* : not pleasing : DISAGREEABLE ⟨full of ~ blots and sightless stains —Shak.⟩ — **un·pleasingly** \"+\ *adv*
un·pleasurable \"+\ *adj* : not pleasurable : not giving pleasure or satisfaction — **un·pleasurably** \"+\ *adv*
un·pleasure \"+\ *n* **1 :** lack of pleasure **2 :** UNPLEASANTNESS 2
un·pleated \"+\ *adj* : not pleated : having no pleats ⟨an ~ skirt⟩
un·pledged \"+\ *adj* [¹*un-* + *pledged*, past part. of *pledge*] : not bound by a pledge or vow; *specif* : not pledged to vote for a specified candidate ⟨the state sent an ~ delegation to the convention⟩
un·pliable \"+\ *adj* **1 :** not liable to persuasion : OBSTINATE ⟨the most ~ mind I ever met —H.J.Laski⟩ **2 :** not pliable ⟨~ substances⟩ — **un·pliableness** \"+\ *n*
un·pliancy \"+\ *n* : lack of pliancy
un·pliant \"+\ *adj* **1 :** not pliant **2 :** UNPLIABLE, OBSTINATE **3 :** resistant to use : not easily managed
un·plowed \"+\ *adj* [¹*un-* + *plowed*, past part. of *plow*] : not plowed
un·plucked \"+\ *adj* [¹*un-* + *plucked*, past part. of *pluck*] : not plucked
un·plug \"+\ *vt* [²*un-* + *plug*] **1 a :** to take a plug out of ⟨~ a sink⟩ **b :** to remove an obstruction from ⟨~ the channel⟩ **2 a :** to remove (as an electric plug) from a socket or receptacle **b :** to disconnect from an electric circuit by removing a plug ⟨~ a refrigerator⟩
un·plumbed \"+\ *adj* [¹*un-* + *plumbed*, past part. of *plumb*] **1 :** not tested with a plumb line **2 a :** not measured with a plumb **b :** not explored in depth, intensity, meaning, or significance ⟨a fascinating variety of ~ possibilities —I.I. Rabi⟩
un·plume \"+\ *vt* [²*un-* + *plume*] **1 :** to strip of plumes or feathers **2** *obs* : HUMILIATE
un·plumed \"+\ *adj* [¹*un-* + *plumed*, adj.] : not furnished or decorated with plumes
un·plundered \"+\ *adj* [¹*un-* + *plundered*, past part. of *plunder*] : not plundered
un·pocket \"+\ *vt* [²*un-* + *pocket*] : to remove from a pocket
un·poetic \"+\ *or* **un·poetical** \"+\ *adj* : not poetic : not having the characteristics of poetry — **un·poetically** \"+\ *adv*
un·pointed \ˌən+\ *adj* **1 :** not pointed : having no point **2 :** unprovided with vowel points ⟨an ~ Hebrew text⟩
un·poise \"+\ *vt* [²*un-* + *poise*] : to upset the equilibrium of
un·poised \"+\ *adj* [¹*un-* + *poised*, adj.] : not poised : UNBALANCED
un·poisoned \"+\ *adj* [¹*un-* + *poisoned*, past part. of *poison*] : not poisoned
un·polarized \"+\ *adj* [¹*un-* + *polarized*, past part. of *polarize*] : not polarized ⟨~ light⟩
unpolicied *adj* [¹*un-* + *policy* + *-ed*] *obs* : IMPOLITIC, IMPRUDENT
un·polish \ˌən+\ *vt* [²*un-* + *polish*] : to deprive of polish
un·polishable \"+\ *adj* : not polishable
un·polished \"+\ *adj* [ME *unpolisshed*, fr. ¹*un-* + *polisshed* polished] **1 a :** not smoothed by polishing ⟨an ~ gem⟩ **b :** not coated with polish ⟨~ shoes⟩ **2 a :** not marked by careful reworking and finishing : CRUDE ⟨an ~ literary style⟩ **b :** not marked by refinement : relatively untouched by urbane or civilizing influences : BOORISH, UNCULTURED
unpolished rice *n* : rice from which the hulls, germs, and outer bran layers but not the inner bran layers have been removed
un·polite \ˌən+\ *adj* : IMPOLITE — **unpolitely** *adv* — **un·politeness** \"+\ *n*
un·politic \"+\ *adj* : IMPOLITIC
un·political \"+\ *adj* **1 :** not according with sound political doctrine **2 :** APOLITICAL **3 :** NONPOLITICAL
un·polled \"+\ *adj* [¹*un-* + *polled*, past part. of *poll*] **1 :** not registered as a voter **2 :** not included or interviewed in a poll
un·polluted \"+\ *adj* : not polluted : CLEAN, PURE ⟨an ~ water supply⟩
un·polymerized \"+\ *adj* [¹*un-* + *polymerized*, past part. of *polymerize*] : not polymerized
un·pope \"+\ *vt* [²*un-* + *pope*, n.] *archaic* : to divest of the character, office, or authority of a pope
un·popular \"+\ *adj* : not popular : viewed or received unfavorably by the public ⟨suspected of ~ ideas —Herbert Agar⟩ — **un·popularity** \"+\ *n*
un·populated \"+\ *adj* [¹*un-* + *populated*, past part. of *populate*] : not populated : not occupied or settled : not inhabited
un·portable \"+\ *adj* [ME, unbearable, fr. ¹*un-* + *portable*] : not portable : too bulky or heavy or too complexly or firmly fixed to be easily moved
un·posed \"+\ *adj* [¹*un-* + *posed*, past part. of *pose*] : not posed : CANDID ⟨impromptu, ~ portraits —H.L.Mencken⟩
un·possessed \"+\ *adj* **1 :** having no possessor : UNOWNED, UNOCCUPIED **2 :** not having a possession — **un·possessedness** \"+\ *n*

unpossessing *adj* [¹*un-* + *possessing*, pres. part. of *possess*] *obs* : not possessing : lacking a possession
un·possibility \ˌən+\ *n* : IMPOSSIBILITY
un·possible \"+\ *adj* [ME, fr. ¹*un-* + *possible*] : IMPOSSIBLE
un·powdered \"+\ *adj* : not powdered
un·powered \"+\ *adj* : not powered; *specif* : not self-powered ⟨an ~ glider⟩ ⟨~ artificial satellites⟩
un·practicable \"+\ *adj* : IMPRACTICABLE — **un·practicableness** \"+\ *n*
un·practical \"+\ *adj* : IMPRACTICAL — **un·practically** \"+\ *adv* — **un·practicalness** \"+\ *n*
un·practicality \"+\ *n* : IMPRACTICALITY
un·practiced \"+\ *adj* **1 :** not put to use or test : UNTRIED **2 :** not practiced : UNSKILLED, INEXPERT
un·praised \"+\ *adj* [¹*un-* + *praised*, past part. of *praise*] : not praised : not extolled in praise
un·prayed \"+\ *adj* [ME *unpreyed*, fr. ¹*un-* + *preyed*, past part. of *preyen* to pray] **1 :** not addressed in prayer **2 :** not sought : UNSOLICITED, UNINVITED — often used with *for*
un·preach \"+\ *vt* [²*un-* + *preach*] *archaic* : to undo or retract by preaching
un·preaching \"+\ *adj* [¹*un-* + *preaching*, pres. part. of *preach*] : not preaching : failing to preach
un·precarious \"+\ *adj* : not precarious : SAFE
un·precedented \"+\ *adj* [¹*un-* + *precedent* + *-ed*] : having no precedent : NOVEL, NEW, UNEXAMPLED ⟨inaugurated an ~ expansion in population and industry —*Amer. Guide Series: N.Y.*⟩ — **un·prec·e·dent·ed·ly** *adv* — **un·prec·e·dent·ed·ness** *n* -ES
un·precipitated \ˌən+\ *adj* [¹*un-* + *precipitated*, past part. of *precipitate*] : not precipitated
un·precise \"+\ *adj* : IMPRECISE — **un·precisely** \"+\ *adv*
un·predictability \"+\ *n* : the quality or state of being unpredictable ⟨the characteristic of the kaleidoscope is ~ —Margery Sharp⟩
¹**un·predictable** \"+\ *adj* : not predictable : not to be foretold ⟨the uncertainty and hazards of bad weather and other ~ factors —H.G.Armstrong⟩ ⟨the very essence of harlequinade to be spontaneous, ~ —*Amer. Guide Series: Calif.*⟩ — **un·pre·dict·able·ness** \-bəlnəs\ *n* -ES — **un·predictably** \ˌən+\ *adv*
²**unpredictable** \"\ *n* -S : an unpredictable person, thing, or event ⟨the vocation of her husband, his success, and location are ~*s* —L.W.Norris⟩
un·predicted \ˌən+\ *adj* [¹*un-* + *predicted*, past part. of *predict*] : not predicted : UNFORESEEN
unpreferred *adj* [ME, fr. ¹*un-* + *preferred*, past part. of *prefer*] *obs* : not advanced or promoted
unpregnant *adj*, *obs* : INAPT
un·prejudiced \ˌən+\ *adj* : not prejudiced : free from undue bias, warp, or prepossession : IMPARTIAL ⟨an ~ judge⟩ ⟨an ~ appraisal of the pros and cons —J.L.Lowes⟩ — **un·prejudicedly** \"+\ *adv* — **un·prej·u·diced·ness** *n* -ES
un·prelatical \ˌən+\ *adj* : not prelatic
un·premeditated \ˌən+\ *adj* : not premeditated — **un·premeditatedly** \"+\ *adv* — **un·premeditatedness** \"+\ *n*
un·premeditation \"+\ *n* : lack of premeditation
un·preoccupied \"+\ *adj* : not preoccupied
un·prepare \"+\ *vt* [²*un-* + *prepare*] : to cause to be unprepared : make unfit or unready ⟨the purpose . . . is precisely to ~ the reader —W.M.Frohock⟩
un·prepared \"+\ *adj* [¹*un-* + *prepared*, adj.] **1 a :** not prepared : not on the alert or in a state of readiness : having made no preparation ⟨our treaty makers approached their immensely difficult problems ~, unsure, inexperienced —R.E.Danielson⟩ **b :** not put into a state of preparedness : UNREADY ⟨the machinery was ~ for the extra load⟩ **2 :** happening without preparation : arriving or taking place unexpectedly or without warning ⟨the shock was ~⟩ — **un·preparedly** \"+\ *adv* — **un·preparedness** \"+\ *n*
un·prepossessed \"+\ *adj* [¹*un-* + *prepossessed*, past part. of *prepossess*] : having no prior bias or opinion : UNPREJUDICED ⟨a mind . . . entirely ~ with any theory or system —John Foster⟩
un·prepossessing \"+\ *adj* : not prepossessing : creating an unfavorable or neutral first impression ⟨a very ~ lot . . . being fat, skinny, old, young, gawky, commonplace —Rex Ingamells⟩
un·prescient \"+\ *adj* : not prescient : lacking foresight
un·prescribed \"+\ *adj* [¹*un-* + *prescribed*, past part. of *prescribe*] : not prescribed : FREE, VOLUNTARY
un·presentable \"+\ *adj* : not presentable; *esp* : having a disreputable or unprepossessing character, background, or appearance ⟨~ friends . . . sometimes fleeing from the police —Upton Sinclair⟩ — **un·pre·sent·able·ness** *n* -ES
un·presented \ˌən+\ *adj* [¹*un-* + *presented*, past part. of *present*] : not presented ⟨the meeting adjourned with several proposals ~⟩
un·pressed \"+\ *adj* : not pressed
un·presuming \"+\ *adj* : not presumptuous : keeping to an inherited or appropriate social status : MODEST — **un·pre·sum·ing·ness** *n* -ES
un·presumptuous \ˌən+\ *adj* : UNPRESUMING — **un·presumptuously** \"+\ *adv*
un·pretended \"+\ *adj* : not pretended : REAL, GENUINE
un·pretending \"+\ *adj* [¹*un-* + *pretending*, pres. part. of *pretend*] : not pretending; *esp* : UNPRETENTIOUS, UNPRESUMING ⟨our mode of living . . . is plain and ~ —Jane Austen⟩ — **un·pre·tend·ing·ly** *adv* — **un·pre·tend·ing·ness** *n*
un·pretentious \ˌən+\ *adj* : not pretentious : free from ostentation, pomp, elegance, or affectation : MODEST ⟨comfortable but ~ homes —*Amer. Guide Series: La.*⟩ ⟨a quiet, frank, and ~ disposition —F.C.Baker⟩ **syn** see PLAIN
un·pretentiously \"+\ *adv* : in an unpretentious manner
un·pretentiousness \"+\ *n* : the quality or state of being unpretentious
un·prettiness \"+\ *n* : lack of prettiness : PLAINNESS, UGLINESS
un·pretty \"+\ *adj* **1 :** not pretty : lacking in beauty ⟨so ~ she ought to be funny —Eudora Welty⟩ **2 :** not deserving moral approval; *esp* : REPREHENSIBLE ⟨as conquerors they make an ~ lot —*Time*⟩
un·prevailing \"+\ *adj* : not culminating or not capable of culminating in success : INEFFECTIVE
un·preventable \"+\ *adj* : not preventable : UNAVOIDABLE ⟨~ hysteria⟩ — **un·pre·vent·able·ness** \-bəlnəs\ *n* — **un·pre·vent·ably** \-blē, -li\ *adv*
un·prevented \ˌən+\ *adj* [¹*un-* + *prevented*, past part. of *prevent*] : not prevented
un·pricked \"+\ *adj* : not pricked : not punctured or wounded by a prick
un·priest \"+\ *vt* [²*un-* + *priest*] : to deprive of priesthood : UNFROCK
un·priestly \"+\ *adj* [¹*un-* + *priestly*, adj.] : not priestly : unbefitting a priest
un·prime \"+\ *adj*, *of a fur* : not prime ⟨an ~ fur taken when the animal was molting and growing a new coat⟩
un·primed \"+\ *adj* [¹*un-* + *primed*, past part. of *prime*] : not primed
un·primitive \"+\ *adj* : not primitive : DEVELOPED ⟨a highly advanced ~ state —*Times Lit. Supp.*⟩
un·princely \"+\ *adj* : not princely : exhibiting or being characteristics unbefitting a prince
un·principled \"+\ *adj* : lacking or exhibiting a lack of moral principles ⟨brash, ~, and conscienceless —J.R.Cominsky⟩ ⟨freedom from coarse, ~ calumny —A.E.Stevenson b. 1900⟩ — **un·prin·ci·pled·ness** *n* -ES
un·printable \ˌən+\ *adj* : that cannot be printed specif. because considered offensive to morals or good taste ⟨an ~ epithet⟩ ⟨an ~ picture⟩ — **un·print·able·ness** \-bəlnəs\ *n* — **un·print·ably** \-blē, -li\ *adv*
un·printed \ˌən+\ *adj* [¹*un-* + *printed*, past part. of *print*] **1 :** not printed upon ⟨would cover . . . the ~ newspaper with charcoal sketches —H.A.Overstreet⟩ **2 :** not transferred to or expressed in print ⟨an ~ manuscript⟩
un·prison \"+\ *vt* [ME, fr. ²*un-* + *prison*] : to free from prison
un·privileged \"+\ *adj* : not privileged; not enjoying special rights or benefits ⟨the ~, the disaffected are probably the most amenable recruits —W.E.Moore⟩

un·prized \ˌən+\ *adj* [¹*un-* + *prized*, past part. of *prize*] *archaic* : not valued or properly valued
un·probable \"+\ *adj* : IMPROBABLE
un·probed \"+\ *adj* [¹*un-* + *probed*, past part. of *probe*] : not probed : not thoroughly investigated or explored
un·problematic \"+\ *adj* : not problematic : not presenting puzzles or raising questions or doubts
un·processed \"+\ *adj* [¹*un-* + *processed*, past part. of *process*] : not processed; *esp* : not altered from an original or natural state
un·proclaimed \"+\ *adj* [¹*un-* + *proclaimed*, past part. of *proclaim*] : not proclaimed : UNANNOUNCED
un·produced \"+\ *adj* [¹*un-* + *produced*, past part. of *produce*] **1 :** not formed, made, or created **2 :** not extended or abnormally extended — **un·pro·duc·ed·ness** \-sədnəs, -stnəs\ *n* -ES
¹**un·productive** \ˌən+\ *adj* : not productive ⟨elimination of ~ or high-cost industries —Harold Callender⟩ ⟨efforts of early missionaries to proselyte Minnesota Indians were largely ~ —*Amer. Guide Series: Minn.*⟩ — **un·productively** \"+\ *adv* — **un·productiveness** \"+\ *n*
²**unproductive** \"\ *n* -S : an unproductive point in a field trial
unproductive consumption *n* : consumption of food, fuel, or materials without creation of corresponding values in some other form
un·profane \ˌən+\ *adj* : not profane : HOLY, SAINTLY
un·profaned \"+\ *adj* [¹*un-* + *profaned*, past part. of *profane*] : not profaned : PURE, INVIOLATE
un·professed \"+\ *adj* : not professed ⟨an ~ sister⟩
un·professional \"+\ *adj* **1 :** not belonging to or gainfully employed at a particular profession ⟨drawings of the ~ architect, which have commanded the admiration of the critics —C.G.Bowers⟩ **2 :** not characteristic of or befitting a member of a profession ⟨in such ~ language that the high school student could understand it as easily as the lawyer —M.L. Ernst⟩ — **un·professionally** \"+\ *adv*
un·profitability \"+\ *n* : the quality or state of being unprofitable ⟨the chaos and ~ of cutthroat price competition —*Economist*⟩
un·profitable \"+\ *adj* [ME, fr. ¹*un-* + *profitable*] : not profitable : producing no profit, gain, good, or result : PROFITLESS, USELESS, VAIN, IDLE ⟨in all this straining after symmetry there is an ~ overcomplication —Robert Humphrey⟩ ⟨miners . . . turned to the deposits that the companies had abandoned as ~ —*Amer. Guide Series: Pa.*⟩ — **un·profitableness** \"+\ *n* — **un·profitably** \"+\ *adv*
un·profited \"+\ *adj* [¹*un-* + *profited*, past part. of *profit*] : PROFITLESS
un·progressive \"+\ *adj* : not progressive; *esp* : not devoted to or showing economic, social, or political progress : BACKWARD ⟨the supposedly volatile but really conservative and, on the whole, industrious but ~ character of the main mass —Samuel Van Valkenburg & Ellsworth Huntington⟩ — **un·progressively** \"+\ *adv* — **un·progressiveness** \"+\ *n*
un·prohibited \"+\ *adj* [¹*un-* + *prohibited*, past part. of *prohibit*] : not prohibited : PERMITTED, ALLOWED
un·projected \"+\ *adj* : UNPLANNED, UNEXPECTED
un·prolific \"+\ *adj* : not prolific : INFERTILE
un·promising \"+\ *adj* : appearing unlikely to be enjoyable or result favorably ⟨hesitation before an ~ task —M.R. Cohen⟩ ⟨devising beautiful and interesting music for ~ combinations of instruments —Edward Sackville-West & Desmond Shawe-Taylor⟩ — **un·promisingly** \"+\ *adv*
un·prompted \"+\ *adj* [¹*un-* + *prompted*, past part. of *prompt*] : not prompted : SPONTANEOUS
un·promulgated \"+\ *adj* [¹*un-* + *promulgated*, past part. of *promulgate*] : not promulgated
un·pronounceable \"+\ *adj* **1 :** not pronounceable **2 :** presenting difficulty in correct pronunciation
un·pronounced \"+\ *adj* [¹*un-* + *pronounced*, past part. of *pronounce*] : not pronounced : MUTE
un·prop \"+\ *vt* [²*un-* + *prop*] : to remove a prop from : deprive of support
unproper *adj* [ME *unpropre*, fr. ¹*un-* + *propre* proper] *obs* : IMPROPER
un·propertied \ˌən+\ *adj* : PROPERTYLESS
un·prophetic \"+\ *adj* : not prophetic : not foreseeing correctly — **un·prophetically** \"+\ *adv*
un·propitious \"+\ *adj* : not propitious ⟨made a by-election necessary at a time highly ~ for the Government —Stewart Cockburn⟩ **syn** see OMINOUS
un·propitiously \"+\ *adv* : in an unpropitious manner
un·propitiousness \"+\ *n* : the quality or state of being unpropitious
un·proportionable \"+\ *adj* : DISPROPORTIONATE — **un·proportionably** \"+\ *adv*
un·proportionate \"+\ *adj* : DISPROPORTIONATE — **un·proportionately** \"+\ *adv*
un·proportioned \"+\ *adj* : DISPROPORTIONATE
un·propped \"+\ *adj* [¹*un-* + *propped*, past part. of *prop*] : having no prop : UNSUPPORTED
un·prosecuted \"+\ *adj* [¹*un-* + *prosecuted*, past part. of *prosecute*] : not prosecuted
un·prospected \"+\ *adj* [¹*un-* + *prospected*, past part. of *prospect*] : not prospected : not investigated esp. for minerals
un·prosperous \ˌən+\ *adj* **1 :** not indicative of or resulting in a favorable issue ⟨suggested that some irregular love affair was ~ —Walter Bagehot⟩ **2 :** not prospering with respect to money, health, or general welfare — **un·prosperously** \"+\ *adv* — **un·prosperousness** \"+\ *n*
un·prostituted \"+\ *adj* [¹*un-* + *prostituted*, past part. of *prostitute*] : not prostituted
un·protected \"+\ *adj* : lacking protection or defense — **un·pro·tect·ed·ly** *adv* — **un·pro·tect·ed·ness** *n* -ES
un·protestantize \ˌən+\ *vt* [²*un-* + *protestantize*] : to make other than Protestant : cause to change from Protestantism to another form of religion; *also* : to deprive of a Protestant characteristic ⟨the attempt to ~ the Church of England —J.A.Froude⟩
un·protested \"+\ *adj* : not protested : accepted without challenge
un·proud \"+\ *adj* : not proud : MODEST, MEEK
un·provable \"+\ *adj* [ME, fr. ¹*un-* + *provable*] : not provable — **un·provableness** \"+\ *n*
un·proved \"+\ *or* **un·proven** \"+\ *adj* [¹*un-* + *proved* or *proven*, past part. of *prove*] : not proved ⟨~ allegations⟩ ⟨~ assumptions⟩
un·provide \"+\ *vt* [²*un-* + *provide*] : to deprive of necessary provision
un·provided \"+\ *adj* [¹*un-* + *provided*, adj.] **1 :** not provided : lacking supplies, equipment, or funds ⟨left his family ~ for⟩ **2 :** not warned or made ready : UNPREPARED **3 :** not provided for : UNEXPECTED — **un·pro·vid·ed·ness** *n* -ES
un·provocative \"+\ *adj* : not provocative
unprovoke *vt* [²*un-* + *provoke*] *obs* : to rid of a motive, desire, or capability
un·provoked \ˌən+\ *adj* [¹*un-* + *provoked*, past part. of *provoke*] : lacking provocation ⟨~ and dastardly attack —F.D.Roosevelt⟩ — **un·pro·vok·ed·ly** \-kədlē, -ktlē, -i\ *adv* — **un·pro·vok·ed·ness** \-nəs\ *n* -ES
un·provoking \ˌən+\ *adj* : not provoking : not given to provocation
un·pruned \"+\ *adj* [¹*un-* + *pruned*, past part. of *prune*] : not pruned : allowed to grow naturally ⟨~ trees⟩ ⟨an ~ vine⟩
un·publicized \"+\ *adj* [¹*un-* + *publicized*, past part. of *publicize*] : not publicized
un·publishable \"+\ *adj* : not publishable
un·published \"+\ *adj* [¹*un-* + *published*, past part. of *publish*] : not published ⟨~ memoirs⟩
un·pulled \"+\ *adj* [ME, fr. ¹*un-* + *pulled*, past part. of *pullen* to pull] : not pulled
un·pulverized \"+\ *adj* [¹*un-* + *pulverized*, past part. of *pulverize*] : not pulverized
un·pumpable \"+\ *adj* : not capable of being pumped esp. for information
un·pumped \"+\ *adj* [¹*un-* + *pumped*, past part. of *pump*] : not pumped
un·punctual \"+\ *adj* : not punctual : late or habitually late — **un·punctuality** \"+\ *n*

un·punctuated \"+\ *adj* [1*un-* + *punctuated*, past part. of *punctuate*] : not punctuated : lacking punctuation

un·punishable \"+\ *adj* : not punishable ⟨a sin ~ by law⟩ — **un·punishably** \"+\ *adv*

un·punished \"+\ *adj* [ME *unpunished*, fr. 1*un-* + *punissed*, past part. of *punissen* to punish] : not punished ⟨the impious . . . ought not to go ~ —Benjamin Jowett⟩

un·purchasable \"+\ *adj* **1** : not purchasable : too rare or expensive to be or not of a type that can be bought ⟨the ~ beauties of the countryside⟩ **2** : not bribable ⟨it is only the man ~ by society that can create the sound society —O.L. Reiser & Blodwen Davies⟩

un·purchased \"+\ *adj* [1*un-* + *purchased*, past part. of *purchase*] : not purchased

un·pure \"+\ *adj* [ME, fr. 1*un-* + *pure*] : IMPURE

un·purged \"+\ *adj* [1*un-* + *purged*, past part. of *purge*] : not purged

un·purified \"+\ *adj* [1*un-* + *purified*, past part. of *purify*] : not purified

un·purposed \"+\ *adj* [1*un-* + *purposed*, past part. of *purpose*] **1** : not done from purpose : UNINTENDED **2** : having no purpose : PURPOSELESS

un·pursued \"+\ *adj* [1*un-* + *pursued*, past part. of *pursue*] : not pursued

un·put \"+\ *adj* [ME, fr. 1*un-* + *put*, past part. of *putten* to put] : not put ⟨~ questions⟩ ⟨as yet ~ on the shelf⟩

un·putrefied \"+\ *adj* [1*un-* + *putrefied*, past part. of *putrefy*] : not putrefied

un·quailing \¦ən+\ *adj* [1*un-* + *quailing*, pres. part. of *quail*] : not quailing : DAUNTLESS, FEARLESS — **un·quail·ing·ly** *adv*

un·qualifiable \¦ən+\ *adj* [1*un-* + *qualify* + *-able*] : not capable of qualifying

un·qualified \"+\ *adj* [1*un-* + *qualified*, adj.] **1** : not fit : not having requisite qualifications **2 a** : not limited by sensible or other qualities or by sensible experience **b** : not modified or restricted by reservations ⟨an ~ denial⟩ — **un·qualifiedly** \"+\ *adv*

un·qualify \"+\ *vt* [2*un-* + *qualify*] : DISQUALIFY

unqualitied *adj, obs* : deprived of the usual faculties

un·quantified \¦ən+\ *adj* [1*un-* + *quantified*, past part. of *quantify*] : not quantified: **a** : not qualified by a quantifier ⟨an ~ term⟩ **b** : containing no quantifier ⟨an ~ expression⟩

un·quarried \"+\ *adj* : not quarried ⟨~ rock⟩ ⟨~ from the hidden depths of the human mind —*Times Lit. Supp.*⟩

un·queen \"+\ *vt* [2*un-* + *queen*] : to divest of the rank or authority of queen

un·quelled \"+\ *adj* [1*un-* + *quelled*, past part. of *quell*] : not quelled ⟨~ pockets of resistance left behind the advance⟩

un·quenchable \"+\ *adj* [ME, fr. 1*un-* + *quenchen* to quench + *-able*] **1** : not quenchable : INEXTINGUISHABLE ⟨an ~ underground fire⟩ **2** : not capable of being satisfied, quelled, or discouraged : INSATIABLE ⟨the author's ~ enthusiasm for his theories —Ralph Linton⟩ — **un·quench·ably** \-əblē, -li\ *adv*

un·quenched \¦ən+\ *adj* [ME *uncwenced*, fr. 1*un-* + *cwenced*, past part. of *cwencen* to quench, fr. (assumed) OE *cwencan* — more at QUENCH] : not quenched : UNEXTINGUISHED, UNQUELLED, UNSATIATED ⟨~ appetites⟩ ⟨~ curiosity⟩

un·questionable \"+\ *adj* **1** *obs* : averse to questions or conversation **2** : acknowledged as beyond question or doubt ⟨regarded as an ~ legal authority —M.R.Cohen⟩ ⟨~ status as a statesman⟩ **3** : not questionable : INDISPUTABLE, INDUBITABLE ⟨~ evidence⟩ — **un·questionableness** \"+\ *n* — **un·questionably** \"+\ *adv*

un·questioned \"+\ *adj* [1*un-* + *questioned*, past part. of *question*] **1** : not interrogated : not examined or examined into **2** : not called in question : UNDOUBTED ⟨the claims of literature are no longer supported by an ~ tradition —R.K. Welsh⟩ **3** : not open to question : UNQUESTIONABLE ⟨holds an ~ control over individual members —N.D.Palmer & S.C. Leng⟩ ⟨the ~ masterpieces of our epoch —Herbert Read⟩

un·questioning \"+\ *adj* : not questioning : accepting without examination or hesitation ⟨simple ~ trust in God's loving-kindness toward his children —C.B.Nordhoff & J.N.Hall⟩ ⟨~ obedience to authority⟩ — **un·questioningly** \"+\ *adv* — **un·ques·tion·ing·ness** *n* -ES

un·quickened \¦ən+\ *adj* [1*un-* + *quickened*, past part. of *quicken*] : not quickened : not infused with life, energy, or spirit

1un·quiet \"+\ *vt* [ME, fr. 2*un-* + *quiet*, n.] : DISQUIET

2unquiet \"+\ *adj* [1*un-* + *quiet*, adj.] **1** : not quiet : AGITATED, DISTURBED, TURBULENT ⟨the ~ days of the riots⟩ ⟨was windy and spitting rain and ~ —G.B.Shaw⟩ **2** : physically, emotionally, or mentally restless or perturbed : UNEASY ⟨the human understanding is ~; it cannot stop or rest —Francis Bacon⟩ — **un·quietly** \"+\ *adv* — **un·quietness** \"+\ *n*

3unquiet \"+\ *n* [1*un-* + *quiet*, n.] : a state of uneasiness or disturbance : DISQUIET

un·quivering \¦ən+\ *adj* [1*un-* + *quivering*, pres. part. of *quiver*] : not quivering

un·quote \"+\ *vi* [2*un-* + *quote*] : to end a quotation by or as if by the insertion of closing quotes ⟨the candidate said quote I will not run for office ~⟩

un·quoted \"+\ *adj* [1*un-* + *quoted*, past part. of *quote*] : not quoted

un·railed \"+\ *adj* [1*un-* + *railed*, past part. of *rail*] : not equipped with a railing

un·raised \"+\ *adj* : not raised

un·rake \"+\ *vt* [ME *unraken*, fr. 2*un-* + *raken* to rake] : to rake off the top or cover of : expose with raking

un·raked \"+\ *adj* [1*un-* + *raked*, past part. of *rake*] : not raked

un·rallied \"+\ *adj* [1*un-* + *rallied*, past part. of *rally*] : not rallied : UNCOLLECTED

un·ransacked \"+\ *adj* [1*un-* + *ransacked*, past part. of *ransack*] : not ransacked

un·ransomed \"+\ *adj* [1*un-* + *ransomed*, past part. of *ransom*] : not ransomed

un·raptured \"+\ *adj* [1*un-* + *raptured*, past part. of *rapture*] : untouched by ecstasy, passion, or transport

un·ratable \"+\ *adj* : not ratable

un·rated \"+\ *adj* [1*un-* + *rated*, past part. of *rate*] : not rated

un·ratified \"+\ *adj* [1*un-* + *ratified*, past part. of *ratify*] : not ratified

un·ravaged \"+\ *adj* [1*un-* + *ravaged*, past part. of *ravage*] : not ravaged or pillaged

un·ravel \"+\ *vb* [2*un-* + *ravel*] *vt* **1** : to disengage or separate the threads of : DISENTANGLE ⟨~*ed* the cord into its separate strands⟩ ⟨~*ed* the woven fabric⟩ **2** : REVERSE, UNDO ⟨many of them have had to ~ their training in this direction —John McDonald⟩ **3** : to resolve the intricacy, complexity, or obscurity of : trace the origin or the elements of : clear up ⟨many attempts have been made to ~ the origin of language —Edward Sapir⟩ ⟨there is always the pleasure of ~*ing* a difficulty —O.W.Holmes †1935⟩ ⟨poking far into the atom to ~ the heart of matter —Norman Cousins⟩ ~ *vi* : to become unraveled : RAVEL ⟨an old rope had frayed and ~*ed*⟩ ⟨a tangled skein of hardly won evidence which gradually ~*s* into strands of horse-doping, blackmail, and fear —Vernon Knowles⟩ **syn** see SOLVE

un·raveler \"+\ *n* : one that unravels

un·ravelment \"+\ *n* : the act of unraveling or the state of being unraveled : DENOUEMENT, DISENTANGLEMENT ⟨he is a shrewd critic of historical ideas and an apt dialectician in the ~ of their intention —Irwin Edman⟩

un·ravished \¦ən+\ *adj* [1*un-* + *ravished*, past part. of *ravish*] : not ravished

un·razed \"+\ *adj* [1*un-* + *razed*, past part. of *raze*] : not razed

un·ra·zored \¦ən¦rāzə(r)d\ *adj* [1*un-* + *razor* + *-ed*] : untouched by a razor : UNSHAVEN

un·reachable \¦ən+\ *adj* : incapable of being reached

un·reached \"+\ *adj* [1*un-* + *reached*, past part. of *reach*] : not reached

un·reacted \"+\ *adj* [1*un-* + *reacted*, past part. of *react*] : not having reacted

un·reactive \"+\ *adj* : not reactive; *specif* : INERT 2

un·read \"+\ *adj* [ME *unred*, fr. 1*un-* + *red*, past part. of *reden* to read] **1** : not read : left unexamined ⟨through sheer mischance the letter remained ~⟩ **2** [1*un-* + *read*] : lacking the experience or the benefits of reading : having no familiarity with a (specified) field ⟨he seems to have been wholly ~ in political theory —V.L.Parrington⟩

un·readability \"+\ *n* : UNREADABLENESS

un·readable \"+\ *adj* **1** : lacking attraction or interest as reading : alien or dull in vein or spirit ⟨to us, the writings of most of the original 14th and 15th century humanists seem wholly ~ —Aldous Huxley⟩ **2 a** : not clear or plain enough to be read or understood : ILLEGIBLE, UNDECIPHERABLE ⟨penned a page of ~ scribbles⟩ **b** : not open to confident interpretation : INCOMPREHENSIBLE, INDISTINCT, UNINTELLIGIBLE, CONFUSED, OPAQUE ⟨tire tracks in the roadside sand were confused and ~ —E.S.Sullivan⟩ ⟨she raised her eyes, glistening softly in the light with a sort of ~ appeal —Joseph Conrad⟩

un·readableness \"+\ *n* : the quality or state of being unreadable

un·readably \"+\ *adv* : in an unreadable manner

un·readily \"+\ *adv* : not readily or easily : HARDLY

un·readiness \"+\ *n* : the quality or state of being unready

un·reading \"+\ *adj* : little given to reading ⟨the idle and ~ world —Frederic Harrison⟩

un·ready \"+\ *adj* [ME *unredy*, fr. 1*un-* + *redy* ready] **1** : not ready : UNPREPARED **2** *dial* : being in a state of undress or deshabille **3** : lacking in ready wit, presence, or prompt address ⟨thrice over she cursed her ~ tongue —Josephine Pinckney⟩

un·real \"+\ *adj* **1** : lacking in reality, substance, or genuineness : ARTIFICIAL ⟨considering it in ~ separation from all the other elements with which it actually fuses —E.K.Brown⟩ **2** : lacking in truth : failing to correspond to acknowledged facts, standards, or criteria : FALSE ⟨seems fantastically ~ and utterly remote from the slightest vestige of truth —John Russell b. 1872⟩ **3** : related only to fantasy or fiction : ILLUSORY, IMAGINARY ⟨the idealistic, ~ world of advertising art —Coulton Waugh⟩ ⟨~ as a cinemascope slightly out of focus —E.B.Garside⟩

un·realism \"+\ *n* : lack of realism : failure of verisimilitude : ineptitude in dealing with reality

un·realist \"+\ *n* : one who exhibits unrealism in words or action ⟨neither of them believes anything which has the slightest actual bearing on the course of economic events. They are ~*s*, illusionists, players with ideas —*Nation*⟩

un·realistic \"+\ *adj* : not realistic : inappropriate to reality or fact : DELUSIVE ⟨the school's ~ program —M.H.Fouracre⟩ ⟨prices for both commodities have reached ~ high levels —*Wall Street Jour.*⟩ — **un·realistically** \"+\ *adv*

un·reality \"+\ *n* **1 a** : the quality or state of being unreal : lack of substance or validity : NONEXISTENCE ⟨there is an air of ~ about life among diplomats anywhere —G.S.Gale⟩ **b** : something unreal, insubstantial, or visionary : a figment of imagination ⟨born of silly parents, and trained to *unrealities* —Samuel Butler †1902⟩ **2** : ineptitude or incapacity in recognizing or dealing with reality ⟨the ~ of the ivory-tower attitude of mind —Leslie Rees⟩

un·realizable \"+\ *adj* **1** : incapable of being understood or sensed : INCOMPREHENSIBLE, UNINTELLIGIBLE, UNTHINKABLE **2** : incapable of being brought to reality or given substance or tangible accomplishment ⟨an immense and ~ series of electoral pledges —John Gunther⟩

un·realize \"+\ *vt* : to make unreal : deprive of substance or validity : make fanciful ⟨his fancy . . . ~*s* everything at a touch —J.R.Lowell⟩

un·realized \"+\ *adj* [1*un-* + *realized*, past part. of *realize*] **1 a** : not reduced to real or actual form : not brought to fruition or accomplishment ⟨an ~ ambition⟩ **b** : not turned into cash by sale : PAPER ⟨an ~ profit⟩ ⟨~ appreciation in the value of property —*U. S. Code*⟩ **2** : not recognized or known : not understood : not brought to conscious awareness ⟨found he had ~ strength and endurance⟩

un·really \"+\ *adv* : in an unreal manner : not genuinely : IMPROBABLY ⟨~ dark shadows —Gilbert Highet⟩

un·reaped \"+\ *adj* [1*un-* + *reaped*, past part. of *reap*] : not reaped

1un·reason \"+\ *n* [ME *unresoun*, fr. 1*un-* + *resoun* reason] **1** : an act devoid of rational excuse or justification : conduct based on unconsidered impulse rather than on prudence, calculation, or morality ⟨sought to moderate the new church; to prevent the monstrous riot and ~ which followed —A.D. White⟩ **2 a** : the absence of reason or sanity : disorder of mind : want of rational faculty or competence : IRRATIONALITY, MADNESS ⟨her thoughts went quickly down this ladder of ~ —Jean Stafford⟩ ⟨this hysterical state of ~ —Dorothy C. Fisher⟩ **b** : lack of systematic or intelligible order : absence of arrangement, control, or guidance according to reasoned plan : CHAOS, CONFUSION ⟨waste, ~, moral conflict everywhere abound —J.A.Hobson⟩

2unreason \"\ *vt* [2*un-* + *reason*, n.] **1** : to unhinge the reason or sanity of **2** *obs* : DISPROVE

un·reasonable \¦ən+\ *adj* [ME *unresonable*, fr. 1*un-* + *resonable* reasonable] **1** : lacking equipment of mind on the full human scale : not endowed with reason ⟨the ~ beasts⟩ **2 a** : not governed by or acting according to reason : evincing indifference to reality or appropriate conduct : ill regulated in behavior **b** : not conformable to reason : ABSURD, INAPPROPRIATE, INCONGRUOUS ⟨the ~ nimbus of romance with which she had encircled that man —Thomas Hardy⟩ **3** : exceeding the bounds of reason or moderation : INORDINATE, UNCONSCIONABLE ⟨the right of the people to be secure in their persons, houses, papers, and effects, against ~ searches and seizures —*U. S. Constitution*⟩ ⟨the general level of their rates was found unjust and ~ —J.C.Nelson⟩ — **un·reasonableness** \"+\ *n* — **un·reasonably** \"+\ *adv*

un·reasoned \"+\ *adj* : not founded on reason or reasoning : UNREASONABLE ⟨~ pity is a passion of weakness —M.R. Cohen⟩

un·reasoning \"+\ *adj* [1*un-* + *reasoning*, pres. part. of *reason*] **1** : not reasoning; *esp* : swayed by emotion that is uncontrolled by prudence or intelligence ⟨instinctive, ~ as he was, entirely at the mercy of the emotion or impression which, for the moment, had seized upon him —Arthur Symons⟩ **2** : not moderated by reason : not controlled or kept in proportion by intelligence : EXTRAVAGANT ⟨~ terror⟩ ⟨~ prejudice⟩ — **un·rea·son·ing·ly** *adv*

un·reave \¦ən+\ *vt* [2*un-* + *reave*] : UNRAVEL ⟨the web is plaiting which nothing ~*s* —Amy Lowell⟩

un·rebated \"+\ *adj* [1*un-* + *rebated*, past part. of *rebate*] **1** *obs* : UNDIMINISHED, UNREDUCED **2** : not subject to rebate

un·rebukable \"+\ *adj* : not deserving rebuke or censure : BLAMELESS

un·rebuked \"+\ *adj* [ME, fr. 1*un-* + *rebuked*, past part. of *rebuken* to rebuke] : not rebuked : UNREPROVED

un·recalled \"+\ *adj* [1*un-* + *recalled*, past part. of *recall*] : not recalled

un·receivable \"+\ *adj* : not receivable : UNACCEPTABLE

un·received \"+\ *adj* [1*un-* + *received*, past part. of *receive*] : not received : not acknowledged or accepted

un·receptive \"+\ *adj* : not receptive or responsive : not open : UNSYMPATHETIC

un·recited \"+\ *adj* [1*un-* + *recited*, past part. of *recite*] : not recited

un·recking \"+\ *adj* [1*un-* + *recking*, pres. part. of *reck*] : not recking : HEEDLESS

un·reckonable \"+\ *adj* : not reckonable : INCALCULABLE ⟨the prospective candidate himself was the ~ factor —S.H. Adams⟩

un·reckoned \"+\ *adj* [ME *unrekened*, fr. 1*un-* + *rekened*, past part. of *rekenen* to reckon] : not reckoned, counted, or calculated ⟨whilst time was yet ~, the koala flourished —Bill Beatty⟩

un·reclaimable \"+\ *adj, archaic* : IRRECLAIMABLE

un·reclaimed \"+\ *adj* [1*un-* + *reclaimed*, past part. of *reclaim*] **1** : UNREFORMED, UNREGENERATE **2** *obs* : UNTAMED **3** : not brought from wildness or desolation into fitness for cultivation or use ⟨water-splotched pastures and ~ prairie lands —*Amer. Guide Series: La.*⟩

un·recognition \"+\ *n* : want of recognition

un·recognizable \"+\ *adj* : not recognizable — **un·rec·og·niz·able·ness** \¦ən+\ *n* — **un·recognizably** \¦ən+\ *adv*

un·recognized \¦ən+\ *adj* [1*un-* + *recognized*, past part. of *recognize*] : not recognized

un·recognizing \"+\ *adj* [1*un-* + *recognizing*, pres. part. of *recognize*] : not recognizing

un·recognizingly \"+\ *adv* : in an unrecognizing manner

un·recollected \"+\ *adj* : not recollected

un·recompensed \"+\ *adj* [ME, fr. 1*un-* + *recompensed*, past part. of *recompensen* to recompense] : not recompensed

un·reconcilable \"+\ *adj* : IRRECONCILABLE — **un·reconcilableness** \"+\ *n* — **un·reconcilably** \"+\ *adv*

un·reconciled \"+\ *adj* [ME, fr. 1*un-* + *reconciled*, past part. of *reconcilen* to reconcile] : not reconciled

un·reconciliable \"+\ *adj* [1*un-* + L *reconciliare* to reconcile + E *-able* — more at RECONCILE] *obs* : IRRECONCILABLE

un·reconstructed \¦ən+\ *adj* [1*un-* + *reconstructed*, past part. of *reconstruct*] : not reconstructed; *esp* : adhering to an attitude, position, or standard widely held to be outmoded ⟨the peasants are still ~ small capitalists at heart —W.C.Huntington⟩

un·recorded \"+\ *adj* [1*un-* + *recorded*, past part. of *record*] **1** : not recorded **2** : not made a matter of official record : UNREGISTERED ⟨an ~ deed to property⟩

un·recoverable \"+\ *adj* [ME, fr. 1*un-* + *recoverable*] **1** : incapable of being recovered, recaptured, or regained : hopelessly lost : IRRECOVERABLE **2** : INCURABLE, IRREMEDIABLE

un·recovered \¦ən+\ *adj* : not recovered

un·recruited \"+\ *adj* [1*un-* + *recruited*, past part. of *recruit*] : not recruited

un·rectified \"+\ *adj* [1*un-* + *rectified*, past part. of *rectify*] : not rectified

un·redeemable \"+\ *adj* : IRREDEEMABLE

un·redeemed \"+\ *adj* [1*un-* + *redeemed*, past part. of *redeem*] : not redeemed — **un·re·deem·ed·ly** \-mədlē, -li\ *adv*

un·redressed \¦ən+\ *adj* [1*un-* + *redressed*, past part. of *redress*] : not redressed

un·reduced \"+\ *adj* : not reduced

un·reducible \"+\ *adj* : IRREDUCIBLE

un·reel \"+\ *vb* [2*un-* + *reel*] *vt* : to unwind from or as if from a reel ⟨~*ed* a spectacular 66-yard pass play —*N.Y.Times*⟩ ~ *vi* : to become unwound ⟨one more postwar colonial tragedy has begun to ~ —Denis Healey⟩

un·reelable \"+\ *adj* [1*un-* + *reel* + *-able*] : incapable of being wound on a reel

un·reeler \"+\ *n* : a textile worker who reels cloth during processing

un·reeve \"+\ *vt* [2*un-* + *reeve*] : to withdraw (a rope) from a ship's block, thimble, or other opening

un·refined \"+\ *adj* : not refined: as **a** : lacking moral or social cultivation or the graces of manners or speech : COARSE, UNCOUTH **b** : not separated from dross, impurity, or unwanted matter ⟨~ ore⟩

un·reflected \"+\ *adj* **1** : not reflected on : UNCONSIDERED **2** : not turned back by physical reflection

un·reflecting \"+\ *adj* : not reflecting : UNTHINKING ⟨the ~ mirth of a sailor when on shore —Sir Walter Scott⟩

un·reflectingly \"+\ *adv* : in an unreflecting manner : THOUGHTLESSLY

un·reflective \"+\ *adj* : not reflective : UNTHINKING, HEEDLESS ⟨the most ~ forms of historical optimism —Reinhold Niebuhr⟩

un·reflectively \"+\ *adv* : in an unreflective manner : THOUGHTLESSLY

un·reformable \"+\ *adj* **1** : INCORRIGIBLE **2** : UNCHANGEABLE

un·reformed \"+\ *adj* **1** : not reformed : UNCORRECTED **2** : not originating with or shaped by the Protestant Reformation ⟨~ churches⟩

un·re·form·ed·ness \-m(ə)dnəs\ *n* : the quality or state of being unreformed

un·refracted \¦ən+\ *adj* [1*un-* + *refracted*, past part. of *refract*] : not refracted

un·refreshed \"+\ *adj* [1*un-* + *refreshed*, past part. of *refresh*] : not refreshed

un·refreshing \"+\ *adj* : not refreshing — **un·refreshingly** \"+\ *adv*

un·refusable \"+\ *adj* : not refusable

un·refutable \"+\ *adj* : IRREFUTABLE

un·refuted \"+\ *adj* [1*un-* + *refuted*, past part. of *refute*] : not refuted

un·regal \"+\ *adj* : not regal

un·regarded \"+\ *adj* [1*un-* + *regarded*, past. part. of *regard*] : not regarded : IGNORED

un·regardful \"+\ *adj* : not regardful

un·regeneracy \"+\ *n* : the quality or state of being unregenerate

1un·regenerate \"+\ *also* **un·regenerated** \"+\ *adj* [*unregenerate* fr. 1*un-* + *regenerate*, adj.; *unregenerated* fr. 1*un-* + L *regeneratus* (past part. of *regenerare* to regenerate) + E *-ed* — more at REGENERATE] **1** : not regenerated : not renewed in heart : remaining or being at enmity with God : UNREPENTANT ⟨sounded a warning of what science could do if it became the mere servant of ~ human nature —Roy Lewis & Angus Maude⟩ **2 a** : unpersuaded by or unconverted to a particular doctrinaire viewpoint, cult, or cause : UNRECONSTRUCTED **b** : persisting in a reactionary stand : OBSTINATE, STUBBORN ⟨in ~ conservatism and unreasoning fear, we supported a regime that had no support among its own people —*New Republic*⟩ — **un·regenerately** \"+\ *adv*

2unregenerate \"\ *n* [1*un-* + *regenerate*, n.] : an unregenerate person

un·regimented \"+\ *adj* [1*un-* + *regimented*, past part. of *regiment*] **1** : not organized or disciplined in military regiments ⟨~ soldiers roved the countryside⟩ **2** : not dominated by a tightly organized social or economic system : INDEPENDENT, INDIVIDUALISTIC

un·registered \"+\ *adj* [1*un-* + *registered*, past part. of *register*] : not registered: as **a** : not having entered one's name on a voting list ⟨an ~ citizen⟩ **b** : unrecorded or not filed in the place provided by law ⟨an ~ mortgage⟩ ⟨an ~ trademark⟩ **c** : not recorded with or certified by an appropriate breeders' association ⟨~ dairy cattle⟩

un·regretful \"+\ *adj* : not regretful

un·regretfully \"+\ *adv* : not regretfully

un·regretted \"+\ *adj* [1*un-* + *regretted*, past part. of *regret*] : not regretted : UNLAMENTED

un·regular \"+\ *adj* : IRREGULAR

un·regulated \"+\ *adj* [1*un-* + *regulated*, past part. of *regulate*] : not regulated: as **a** : DISORDERLY, CHAOTIC ⟨an ~ mind⟩ **b** : UNCONTROLLED, UNDISCIPLINED, UNGOVERNED ⟨~ traffic⟩

un·rehearsed \"+\ *adj* [ME *unrehersed*, fr. 1*un-* + *rehersed*, past part. of *rehersen* to rehearse] **1** : not narrated : UNTOLD **2** : not practiced or prepared : SPONTANEOUS ⟨an ~ speech⟩

un·rein \"+\ *vt* [2*un-* + *rein*] : to loosen the reins of : remove restraint from

un·rejoicing \¦ən+\ *adj* [1*un-* + *rejoicing*, pres. part. of *rejoice*] : not rejoicing

un·related \"+\ *adj* **1** : not connected by birth or family **2** : DISCRETE, DISJOINED, SEPARATE ⟨hard to imagine a rule more completely ~ to the realities of life —B.N.Cardozo⟩ **3** : not told ⟨an ~ tale⟩

un·relatedness \"+\ *n* : the quality or state of being unrelated

un·relative \"+\ *adj* : UNRELATED, DISPROPORTIONATE

un·relaxed \"+\ *adj* [1*un-* + *relaxed*, past part. of *relax*] : not relaxed ⟨his life was drawing to a close in baffled zeal and ~ strain —U.B.Phillips⟩

un·relaxing \"+\ *adj* [1*un-* + *relaxing*, pres. part. of *relax*] : not relaxing

un·released \"+\ *adj* [ME *unrelesed*, fr. 1*un-* + *relesed*, past part. of *relesen* to release] : not released

un·relenting \"+\ *adj* [1*un-* + *relenting*, pres. part. of *relent*] **1** : not softening, yielding, or swerving in resolution or determination : HARD, STERN ⟨a fierce and ~ partisan leader —*Amer. Guide Series: Tenn.*⟩ **2** : maintaining undiminished speed, vigor, or pace : not letting up or weakening ⟨an intense and ~ struggle is being waged —Sir Winston Churchill⟩

un·relentingly \"+\ *adv* : in an unrelenting manner

un·re·lent·ing·ness *n* -ES : the quality or state of being unrelenting

un·reliability \ˌən+\ *n* **:** the quality or state of being unreliable
un·reliable \"+\ *adj* **:** not reliable **:** UNDEPENDABLE, UNTRUSTWORTHY — **un·reliableness** \"+\ *n* — **un·reliably** \"+\ *adv*
un·relievable \"+\ *adj* [¹*un-* + *relieve* + *-able*] **:** not relievable
un·relieved \"+\ *adj* [¹*un-* + *relieved,* past part. of *relieve*] **1 :** not given relief **:** furnished no assistance, remedy, or mitigation ⟨drudgery was ~ by labor-saving devices —*Amer. Guide Series: Ind.*⟩ **2 :** having or likened to a flat unbroken surface without heights or depths or without lights or shadows **:** lacking diversity, alternation, or chiaroscuro **:** MONOTONOUS, UNVARYING ⟨gowns . . . of ~ black —Victoria Sackville-West⟩ ⟨an ~ slum —Gus Tyler⟩ ⟨simple pity that such a career should end in ~ banality —L.B.Gowing⟩ — **un·relievedly** \"+\ *adv*
un·religious \"+\ *adj* [ME, fr. ¹*un-* + *religious*] **1 :** IRRELIGIOUS **2 :** having no connection with or relation to religion **:** involving no religious import or idea **:** NONRELIGIOUS ⟨~ education⟩ — **un·religiously** \"+\ *adv*
un·relinquished \"+\ *adj* [¹*un-* + *relinquished,* past part. of *relinquish*] **:** not relinquished
un·reluctant \"+\ *adj* **:** not reluctant
un·reluctantly \"+\ *adv* **:** not reluctantly
un·remarkable \"+\ *adj* **:** calling for no notice **:** lacking interest or distinction **:** JEJUNE, ORDINARY
un·remarked \"+\ *adj* [¹*un-* + *remarked,* past part. of *remark*] **:** not remarked **:** UNNOTICED ⟨the streets were crowded, and we found ourselves wholly ~ —Kenneth Roberts⟩
un·remedied \"+\ *adj* [¹*un-* + *remedied,* past part. of *remedy*] **:** not remedied
un·rememberable \"+\ *adj* **:** not worth remembering or likely to be remembered
un·remembered \"+\ *adj* [ME *unremembred,* fr. ¹*un-* + *remembred,* past part. of *remembren* to remember] **:** not remembered **:** FORGOTTEN
un·remembering \"+\ *adj* [¹*un-* + *remembering,* pres. part. of *remember*] **:** not remembering **:** FORGETFUL, OBLIVIOUS
un·remitted \"+\ *adj* [¹*un-* + *remitted,* past part. of *remit*] **1 :** not remitted **:** UNPARDONED ⟨~ sin⟩ ⟨an ~ debt⟩ **2 :** continuously or assiduously maintained **:** UNBROKEN, UNINTERRUPTED ⟨~ attention⟩
un·re·mit·ted·ly *adv* **:** in an unremitted manner **:** without interruption **:** STEADILY
un·remittent \ˌən+\ *adj* [¹*un-* + L *remittent-, remittens,* pres. part. of *remittere* to remit — more at REMIT] **:** UNREMITTING
un·remitting \"+\ *adj* [¹*un-* + *remitting,* pres. part. of *remit*] **:** not remitting **:** CONSTANT, INCESSANT, STEADY, UNINTERRUPTED ⟨exhausted her strength with ~ work —Harrison Smith⟩ ⟨the blatting of automobile horns off yonder, not too loud but variegated and ~ —R.P.Warren⟩ ⟨few other American statesmen have been such careful and ~ students of political thought —Dumas Malone⟩ **syn** see CONTINUAL
un·re·mit·ting·ly *adv* **:** in an unremitting manner **:** STEADILY, UNINTERRUPTEDLY
un·remorseful \ˌən+\ *adj* **:** not remorseful: **a :** REMORSELESS **b :** bringing no remorse **:** INNOCENT
un·removable \"+\ *adj* **1** *obs* **:** IMMOVABLE **2** *archaic* **:** IRREMOVABLE
un·removed \ˌən+\ *adj* [ME, fr. ¹*un-* + *removed,* past part. of *removen* to remove] **:** not removed: **a :** not eliminated **b :** not moved from one place to another **c :** firmly placed or grounded **:** IRREMOVABLE, FIXED, STEADFAST
un·remunerated \"+\ *adj* [¹*un-* + *remunerated,* past part. of *remunerate*] **:** not remunerated **:** UNPAID
un·remunerative \"+\ *adj* **:** not remunerative **:** returning no gain or profit or an inadequate one **:** UNREWARDING ⟨an ~ occupation⟩ ⟨its first reading is arduous and apparently ~ —T.S.Eliot⟩
un·renderable \"+\ *adj* **:** not renderable **:** UNTRANSLATABLE
un·renewed \"+\ *adj* [¹*un-* + *renewed,* past part. of *renew*] **:** not renewed; *esp* **:** UNREGENERATE
un·renowned \"+\ *adj* **:** not renowned **:** little known **:** OBSCURE
un·rent \"+\ *adj* [¹*un-* + *rent,* past part. of *rend*] **:** not rent **:** UNTORN
un·rentable \"+\ *adj* **:** incapable of being rented
un·repaid \"+\ *adj* [¹*un-* + *repaid,* past part. of *repay*] **:** not repaid
un·repair \"+\ *n* **:** want of repair **:** DISREPAIR
un·repaired \"+\ *adj* [¹*un-* + *repaired,* past part. of *repair*] **:** not repaired
un·re·pass·able \ˌən(ˌ)rēˈpasəbəl, -paas-, -pais-, -pas-\ *adj* [¹*un-* + *repass* + *-able*] *archaic* **:** incapable of being passed again **:** not to be traversed in returning
unrepealable *adj* **:** not repealable **:** IRREVOCABLE
un·repealed \ˌən+\ *adj* [ME *unrepeled,* fr. ¹*un-* + *repeled,* past part. of *repelen* to repeal] **:** not repealed **:** remaining in force or effect **:** UNREVOKED
un·repeatable \"+\ *adj* **1 :** not fit to be repeated **:** offensively coarse **:** INDECENT **2 :** not repeatable **:** incapable of being duplicated **:** UNIQUE ⟨dogs, mice, and flies are as individual and ~ as men are —Theodosius Dobzhansky⟩
un·repeated \"+\ *adj* **:** not repeated
un·repelled \"+\ *adj* [¹*un-* + *repelled,* past part. of *repel*] **:** not repelled
un·repentance \"+\ *n* [ME *unrepentaunce,* fr. ¹*un-* + *repentaunce* repentance] **:** IMPENITENCE
un·repentant \"+\ *adj* [ME *unrepentaunt,* fr. ¹*un-* + *repentaunt* repentant] **1 :** not repentant **:** IMPENITENT ⟨~ sinners⟩ **2 :** holding to a prior conviction or attitude **:** OBSTINATE, STUBBORN ⟨an avowed and ~ protectionist —David Thomson⟩
un·repented \"+\ *adj* [¹*un-* + *repented,* past part. of *repent*] **:** not repented **:** not regretted and renounced ⟨~ sin⟩
un·repenting \"+\ *adj* [¹*un-* + *repenting,* pres. part. of *repent*] **:** not repenting
un·repining \"+\ *adj* [¹*un-* + *repining,* pres. part. of *repine*] **:** not repining **:** UNCOMPLAINING
un·repiningly \"+\ *adv* **:** in an unrepining manner **:** UNCOMPLAININGLY
un·replaceable \"+\ *adj* **:** IRREPLACEABLE
un·replenished \"+\ *adj* [¹*un-* + *replenished,* past part. of *replenish*] **:** not replenished
un·replying \ˌən+\ *adj* [¹*un-* + *replying,* pres. part. of *reply*] **:** not replying
un·reportable \"+\ *adj* **1** *obs* **:** too extreme or monstrous to report **:** UNSPEAKABLE **2 :** too coarse or indecent to report **:** UNREPEATABLE
un·reported \"+\ *adj* [¹*un-* + *reported,* past part. of *report*] **:** not reported
un·representative \"+\ *adj* **1 :** not representing an electorate ⟨a parliament which was ~ and corrupt —J.H.Plumb⟩ **2 :** not exemplifying a class **:** ATYPICAL ⟨behavior quite ~ of the profession⟩
un·represented \"+\ *adj* **1 :** not represented **:** having no member or advocate in a legislature ⟨an ~ minority⟩ ⟨an ~ viewpoint⟩ **2 :** not exemplified **:** shown by no instance
un·repressed \"+\ *adj* **:** not repressed
un·reprieved \"+\ *adj* [¹*un-* + *reprieved,* past part. of *reprieve*] **:** not reprieved
un·reproachable \"+\ *adj, archaic* **:** IRREPROACHABLE
un·reproached \"+\ *adj* [¹*un-* + *reproached,* past part. of *reproach*] **:** not reproached
un·reproachful \"+\ *adj* **:** not reproachful
un·reproaching \"+\ *adj* [¹*un-* + *reproaching,* pres. part. of *reproach*] **:** not reproaching
un·reproducible \"+\ *adj* **:** not reproducible
un·re·prov·able \ˌənrəˈprüvəbəl, -rē;-\ *adj* [*unreprovable* fr. ME, fr. ¹*un-* + *reprovable* open to reproof, fr. *reproven* to reprove + *-able*] **:** not open to reproof **:** not meriting censure **:** BLAMELESS
un·reproved \ˌən+\ *adj* [ME, fr. ¹*un-* + *reproved,* past part. of *reproven* to reprove] **:** not reproved
un·repugnant \"+\ *adj* **:** not repugnant **:** causing or offering no opposition
un·requested \ˌən+\ *adj* [¹*un-* + *requested,* past part. of *request*] **:** not requested **:** UNASKED
un·required \"+\ *adj* [ME *unrequered,* fr. ¹*un-* + *requered,* past part. of *requeren* to require] **:** not required
un·requisite \"+\ *adj* **:** not requisite
un·re·quit·able \ˌənrəˈkwīd·əbəl, -rē;-\ *adj* [¹*un-* + *requite* + *-able*] **:** incapable of being requited **:** not returnable in kind
un·requited \ˌən+\ *adj* [¹*un-* + *requited,* past part. of *requite*] **:** not requited **:** not reciprocated **:** not returned in kind ⟨~ love⟩
un·resembling \"+\ *adj* [¹*un-* + *resembling,* pres. part. of *resemble*] *archaic* **:** not resembling **:** DISSIMILAR
un·resented \"+\ *adj* [¹*un-* + *resented,* past part. of *resent*] **:** not resented
un·resentful \"+\ *adj* **:** not resentful
un·resenting \"+\ *adj* [¹*un-* + *resenting,* pres. part. of *resent*] **:** not resenting
un·reserve \"+\ *n* **:** absence of reserve **:** FRANKNESS, OPENNESS
un·reserved \"+\ *adj* **1 :** not limited or partial **:** ENTIRE, FULL, UNQUALIFIED ⟨a book to which one awards an ~ enthusiasm —Carl Van Vechten⟩ **2 :** not cautious or reticent **:** FRANK, OPEN
un·reservedly \"+\ *adv* **:** in an unreserved manner
un·reservedness \"+\ *n* **:** the quality or state of being unreserved
un·resistant \"+\ *adj* **:** not resistant
un·resisted \ˌən+\ *adj* [¹*un-* + *resisted,* past part. of *resist*] **:** not resisted **:** not withstood **:** UNOPPOSED — **un·re·sist·ed·ly** *adv*
un·resistible \"+\ *adj* **:** IRRESISTIBLE
un·resisting \ˌən+\ *adj* **:** not resisting **:** YIELDING — **un·resistingly** \"+\ *adv*
un·resolvable \"+\ *adj* **:** not resolvable
un·resolve \"+\ *vb* [²*un-* + *resolve*] **:** to revoke a resolution
un·resolved \"+\ *adj* [¹*un-* + *resolved,* past part. of *resolve*] **1 :** UNDECIDED, UNSOLVED ⟨depends upon answers to the many ~ questions —J.A.R.Pimlott⟩ ⟨an ~ conflict⟩ **2 a :** IRRESOLUTE, WAVERING ⟨restless and ~, seeking purpose of some sort from his love —*Times Lit. Supp.*⟩ **b :** unsettled or uncertain in opinion **3 :** remaining discordant or dissonant **:** not modulated to a consonance ⟨~ discords⟩
un·resolvedness \"+\ *n* **:** IRRESOLUTION
un·resolving \"+\ *adj* [¹*un-* + *resolving,* pres. part. of *resolve*] **:** not resolving
un·resounding \"+\ *adj* **:** not resounding
un·respectable \"+\ *adj* **:** not respectable **:** unworthy of respect **:** DISREPUTABLE ⟨says nothing so ~ has happened in years —Louis Bromfield⟩
un·respected \"+\ *adj* [¹*un-* + *respected,* past part. of *respect*] **:** accorded no respect
un·respectful \"+\ *adj* **:** not respectful **:** DISRESPECTFUL
un·respective \"+\ *adj* **1** *archaic* **:** NEGLIGENT, INATTENTIVE **2 :** UNDISCRIMINATING
un·respirable \ˌən+\ *adj* **:** unfit to breathe ⟨~ air⟩
un·responsible \ˌən+\ *adj* **:** IRRESPONSIBLE
un·responsive \"+\ *adj* **:** not responsive — **un·responsively** \"+\ *adv* — **un·responsiveness** \"+\ *n*
un·rest \"+\ *n* [ME, fr. ¹*un-* + *rest*] **:** want of rest **:** a disturbed or uneasy state **:** DISQUIET, TURMOIL ⟨revolt is brewing, there is hatred and ~, and explosion in the atmosphere —Stanley Ross⟩ ⟨social ~⟩ ⟨labor ~⟩
un·rested \"+\ *adj* [¹*un-* + *rested,* past part. of *rest*] **:** not rested
un·restful \"+\ *adj* [ME, fr. ¹*un-* + *restful*] **:** not restful: as **a :** not feeling or not conducing to repose **b :** lacking calmness or confidence **:** DISTURBED, FIDGETY, NERVOUS ⟨one's conducting is apt to become angular and ~ —Warwick Braithwaite⟩
un·resting \"+\ *adj* **:** not resting **:** taking no repose **:** continuing without pause or interruption
un·restored \"+\ *adj* [ME, fr. ¹*un-* + *restored,* past part. of *restoren* to restore] **:** not restored
un·restrainable \"+\ *adj* [ME *unrestraynable,* fr. ¹*un-* + *restraynen* to restrain + *-able*] **:** not restrainable **:** UNCONTROLLABLE — **un·restrainably** \"+\ *adv*
un·restrained \"+\ *adj* **1 :** not restrained **:** IMMODERATE, INTEMPERATE, UNCONTROLLED ⟨~ praise⟩ ⟨~ development resulted in more than 30 subdivisions within the limits of the city —*Amer. Guide Series: Mich.*⟩ **2 :** free of constraint, inhibition, or timidity **:** SPONTANEOUS, UNEMBARRASSED ⟨never before in all her life had she so desired to be spontaneous and ~ —H.G.Wells⟩
un·restrainedly \"+\ *adv* **:** in an unrestrained manner
un·restrainedness \"+\ *n* **:** the quality or state of being unrestrained
un·restraint \"+\ *n* **:** freedom from restraint
un·restricted \ˌən+\ *adj* **:** not restricted
un·restrictedly \"+\ *adv* **:** in an unrestricted manner
un·restrictive \"+\ *adj* **:** not restrictive
un·retaliated \"+\ *adj* [¹*un-* + *retaliated,* past part. of *retaliate*] **:** not retaliated
un·retarded \"+\ *adj* **:** not retarded **:** UNDELAYED
un·retentive \"+\ *adj* **:** not retentive
un·reticent \"+\ *adj* **:** not reticent
un·retouched \"+\ *adj* [¹*un-* + *retouched,* past part. of *retouch*] **:** not retouched
un·retracted \"+\ *adj* **:** not retracted
un·returnable \"+\ *adj* **:** not returnable
un·returned \"+\ *adj* [¹*un-* + *returned,* past part. of *return*] **:** not returned
un·returning \"+\ *adj* **:** not returning
un·revealed \"+\ *adj* [¹*un-* + *revealed,* past part. of *reveal*] **:** not revealed
un·revealing \"+\ *adj* **:** not revealing
un·revenged \"+\ *adj* [¹*un-* + *revenged,* past part. of *revenge*] **:** not revenged
un·revengeful \"+\ *adj* **:** not revengeful
un·reverenced \ˌən+\ *adj* [ME, fr. ¹*un-* + *reverenced,* past part. of *reverencen* to reverence] **:** not reverenced
un·reverend \"+\ *adj* **1 :** IRREVERENT **2 :** not reverend **:** not meriting reverence
un·reverent \"+\ *adj* [ME, fr. ¹*un-* + *reverent*] **:** IRREVERENT
un·reversed \"+\ *adj* **:** not reversed
un·reviewable \"+\ *adj* **:** not subject to review (as by superior authority) ⟨discretion may, as a rule, be ~ —*Yale Law Jour.*⟩
un·revised \"+\ *adj* [¹*un-* + *revised,* past part. of *revise*] **:** not revised
un·revived \"+\ *adj* [¹*un-* + *revived,* past part. of *revive*] **:** not revived
un·revoked \"+\ *adj* [ME, fr. ¹*un-* + *revoked,* past part. of *revoken* to revoke] **:** not revoked
un·rewarded \"+\ *adj* [ME, fr. ¹*un-* + *rewarded,* past part. of *rewarden* to reward] **:** not rewarded
un·rewarding \"+\ *adj* **:** not rewarding **:** not repaying effort or attention **:** UNPROFITABLE ⟨reading him proved to be an ~ labor⟩
un·rhetorical \ˌən+\ *adj* **:** not rhetorical **:** LITERAL, PLAIN
un·rhymed \"+\ *adj* [¹*un-* + *rhymed,* past part. of *rhyme*] **:** not rhymed
un·rhythmic \"+\ *or* **un·rhythmical** \"+\ *adj* **:** not rhythmic **:** lacking rhythm **:** irregular in beat, pulse, or accent
un·ribbed \"+\ *adj* **:** having no ribs
un·rid \"+\ *adj* [¹*un-* + *rid,* past part. of *rid* (to clear)] *dial Brit* **:** DISORDERED
un·ridden \"+\ *adj* **:** not ridden
un·riddle \"+\ *vt* [²*un-* + *riddle,* n.] **:** to read the riddle of **:** find the explanation of **:** SOLVE ⟨patiently *unriddled* a situation of extreme complexity —John Buchan⟩
un·riddler \"+\ *n* **:** one that unriddles ⟨the poet can no longer be the seer, the ~ of the universe —Peter Viereck⟩
¹un·rifled \"+\ *adj* [¹*un-* + *rifled,* past part. of *rifle* (to rob)] **:** not rifled **:** UNDESPOILED, UNROBBED
²unrifled \"\ *adj* [¹*un-* + *rifled,* past part. of *rifle* (to cut grooves)] *of a gun barrel* **:** not having internal spiral grooves
un·rig \ˌən+\ *vt* [²*un-* + *rig*] **1 :** to strip of rigging ⟨~ a ship⟩ **2 :** UNCLOTHE, UNDRESS
¹un·right \"+\ *adj* [ME *unriht, unright,* fr. OE *unriht,* fr. ¹*un-* + *riht,* adj., right] **:** WRONG, UNJUST
²unright \"\ *n* [ME *unriht, unright,* fr. OE *unriht,* fr. ¹*un-* + *riht,* n., right] **:** WRONG, INJUSTICE
un·righteous \"+\ *adj* [alter. (influenced by *-eous*) of earlier *unrightwise, unrightuous,* fr. ME *unrightwise, unrihtwise,* fr. OE *unrihtwīs,* fr. ¹*un-* + *rihtwīs* righteous] **1 :** not righteous **:** EVIL, SINFUL, WICKED ⟨an ~ man⟩ ⟨an ~ act⟩ **2 :** UNJUST, INEQUITABLE, UNMERITED ⟨an ~ sentence⟩ — **un·righteously** \"+\ *adv* — **un·righteousness** \"+\ *n*
un·rightful \"+\ *adj* [ME, fr. ¹*un-* + *rightful*] **:** not rightful **:** WRONG, UNJUST
un·ringed \"+\ *adj* **:** not having or wearing a ring
un·rinsed \"+\ *adj* [¹*un-* + *rinsed,* past part. of *rinse*] **:** not rinsed
un·rip \"+\ *vt* [²*un-* + *rip*] **1 :** to rip or slit up **:** cut or tear open ⟨*unripped* a seam⟩ **2 :** DISCLOSE, REVEAL ⟨~ your plan, captain —J.M.Barrie⟩
un·ripe \"+\ *adj* [ME, fr. OE *unrīpe,* fr. ¹*un-* + *rīpe* ripe] **1 :** not ripe **:** less than fully developed **:** IMMATURE ⟨~ fruit⟩ ⟨an ~ lover⟩ ⟨lived to the not ~ age of 77 —Harvey Graham⟩ **2 :** UNREADY, UNPREPARED, UNSEASONABLE ⟨~ for any call to national self-extinction —*Current History*⟩ ⟨the time is ~⟩
un·ripely \"+\ *adv* **:** in an unripe manner
un·ripened \"+\ *adj* [¹*un-* + *ripened,* past part. of *ripen*] **1 :** not ripened **:** not having attained maturity **:** UNDEVELOPED **2** *of cheese* **:** ready for use without curing
un·ripeness \"+\ *n* [ME *unripnes,* fr. *unripe* + *-nes* -ness] **:** the quality or state of being unripe
un·rippled \"+\ *adj* [¹*un-* + *rippled,* past part. of *ripple*] **:** not rippled **:** glassy smooth ⟨~ water⟩
un·risen \"+\ *adj* **:** not risen
un·rivaled *or* **un·rivalled** \"+\ *adj* [¹*un-* + *rivaled, rivalled,* past part. of *rival*] **:** having no rival **:** INCOMPARABLE, SUPREME, UNEQUALED, UNPARALLELED ⟨the island offered ~ opportunities for spying —C.S.Forester⟩ ⟨the ~ literary colossus of the age —W.R.Thayer⟩
un·riven \"+\ *adj* [¹*un-* + *riven,* past part. of *rive*] **:** not riven **:** UNTORN, UNBROKEN
un·rivet \"+\ *vt* [²*un-* + *rivet*] **1 :** to unfasten or separate by removing the rivets of **2 :** DETACH, UNDO, UNLOOSE ⟨the diversion ~*ed* his gaze⟩
un·roasted \"+\ *adj* [¹*un-* + *roasted,* past part. of *roast*] **:** not roasted
un·robbed \"+\ *adj* [ME, fr. ¹*un-* + *robbed,* past part. of *robben* to rob] **:** not robbed
un·robe \"+\ *vb* [²*un-* + *robe*] **:** DISROBE, UNDRESS
un·roll \"+\ *vb* [ME *unrollen,* fr. ²*un-* + *rollen* to roll] *vt* **1 :** to unwind a roll of **:** open out **:** UNCOIL, EXTEND ⟨the limitless exuberance with which America ~*s* the carpet for the imported prodigy —E.O.Hauser⟩ **2 :** to spread out like a scroll for reading or inspection ⟨the novel itself ~*s* their previous histories to the reader —Frederic Morton⟩ ~ *vi* **:** to be unrolled **:** UNWIND ⟨the landscape ~*s* under the speeding plane⟩
un·rolled \"+\ *adj* **:** not rolled
un·romantic \"+\ *also* **un·romantical** \"+\ *adj* **:** not romantic — **un·romantically** \"+\ *adv*
un·roof \"+\ *vt* [²*un-* + *roof*] **:** to strip off the roof or covering of ⟨would wreck the castle and ~ every house —C.S. Forester⟩
un·roost \"+\ *vb* [²*un-* + *roost,* n.] *vt* **:** to drive from the roost **:** DISLODGE ~ *vi* **:** to leave a roost
un·root \"+\ *vb* [ME *unrooten,* fr. ²*un-* + *rooten* to root] *vt* **:** to tear up by the roots **:** ERADICATE, UPROOT ~ *vi* **:** to become uprooted
un·rooted \"+\ *adj* [¹*un-* + *rooted,* past part. of *root*] **1 :** not torn up by the roots — used with *out* **2 :** having no roots **:** ROOTLESS ⟨an ~ and vagrant life —A.L.Kroeber⟩
un·rope \"+\ *vb* [²*un-* + *rope*] *vt* **:** to remove a rope from **:** free from a rope ~ *vi* **:** to detach a rope **:** loose oneself from a rope ⟨once on gentler slopes we *unroped* and swiftly descended —*Appalachia*⟩
un·rotten \"+\ *adj* **:** not rotten
un·rouged \"+\ *adj* [¹*un-* + *rouged,* past part. of *rouge*] **:** not rouged
un·rough \"+\ *adj* **:** not rough; *esp* **:** BEARDLESS
un·round \"+\ *vt* [²*un-* + *round*] **1 :** to spread (the lips) laterally ⟨necessary to ~ the lips in pronouncing \ē\⟩ **2 :** to pronounce (a sound) without lip rounding or with decreased lip rounding
un·rounded \"+\ *adj, of a sound* **:** produced with lips spread laterally
un·roused \"+\ *adj* [¹*un-* + *roused,* past part. of *rouse*] **:** not roused **:** UNAWAKENED, DORMANT
un·routed \"+\ *adj* [¹*un-* + *routed,* past part. of *rout*] **:** not routed
un·royal \ˌən+\ *adj* **:** not royal
un·rude \"+\ *adj* [ME, alter. (prob. influenced by *rude*) of *unride* rough, violent, fr. OE *ungerȳde,* fr. ¹*un-* + *gerȳde* prepared, easy, fr. *ge-* (perfective prefix) + *-rȳde,* of unknown origin] *dial* **:** ROUGH, RUDE
un·ruffle \"+\ *vb* [²*un-* + *ruffle*] *vi* **:** to become calm **:** quiet down ~ *vt* **:** CALM, QUIET
un·ruffled \"+\ *adj* [¹*un-* + *ruffled,* past part. of *ruffle*] **1 :** emotionally undisturbed **:** CALM, STEADY, UNFLUSTERED ⟨an efficient organizer, smooth and ~ —Flora Lewis⟩ **2 :** not ruffled **:** SMOOTH ⟨~ water⟩ **syn** see COOL
un·ruffledness \"+\ *n* -ES **:** the quality or state of being unruffled
un·ruinable \"+\ *adj* [¹*un-* + *ruin* + *-able*] **:** IMPERISHABLE
un·ruined \"+\ *adj* [¹*un-* + *ruined,* past part. of *ruin*] **:** not ruined
un·rulable \"+\ *adj* **:** not rulable **:** UNGOVERNABLE
un·ruled \"+\ *adj* [ME, fr. ¹*un-* + *ruled,* past part. of *rulen* to rule] **1 :** not ruled **:** UNGOVERNED **2 :** lacking ruled lines ⟨~ writing paper⟩
un·rul·i·ness \ˌənˈrülēnəs, -lin-\ *n* -ES **:** the quality or state of being unruly
un·ruly \-lē, -li\ *adj, often* -ER/-EST [ME *unreuly,* fr. ¹*un-* + *reuly, ruly* amenable to rule, disciplined, fr. *reule* rule + *-y* (adj. suffix) — more at RULE] **1 :** not readily ruled, disciplined, or managed **:** TURBULENT, UNCONTROLLABLE ⟨began his greatest editorial effort, his battle royal with that stubborn and ~ writer —Harrison Smith⟩ ⟨could imagine no such ~ urgence in man's perfect estate —J.H.Robinson †1936⟩ **2 :** STORMY, TEMPESTUOUS, WILD ⟨cleared the land, dug ditches and dammed ~ streams —*Amer. Guide Series: Ariz.*⟩

syn UNGOVERNABLE, INTRACTABLE, REFRACTORY, RECALCITRANT, WILLFUL, HEADSTRONG: UNRULY calls attention to lack of being disciplined; it may suggest incapacity for discipline, turbulence, disorder, or waywardness ⟨*unruly* children⟩ ⟨a wrought-iron collar with three bells attached, used to subdue an *unruly* or runaway slave —*Amer. Guide Series: La.*⟩ ⟨with judicious officers the most *unruly* seamen can at sea be kept in some sort of subjection —Herman Melville⟩ UNGOVERNABLE centers attention on the fact of not being governed, subdued, restrained, or checked; it may apply to whatever has never been subdued or to whatever has thrown off control ⟨in the case of a consistently obstreperous and *ungovernable* slave, he should be sold rather than lashed —C.G.Bowers⟩ INTRACTABLE may suggest a stubborn disposition to resist guidance or restraint ⟨inclined to display a savage, domineering and *intractable* temper —Robert Graves⟩ ⟨to submit to authority — human nature even then remaining so *intractable* that the only assurance of safety against its marauding instincts is subjection to sovereignty —John Dewey⟩ REFRACTORY may connote manifest resistance and rebelliousness, disobedience, and protest ⟨lawlessness is a term applied to the behavior of a social group which is considered to be consistently *refractory* and to be habitually breaking important legal rules —Jerome Frank⟩ ⟨some of them again became most *refractory,* breathing nothing but downright mutiny —Herman Melville⟩ RECALCITRANT may suggest determined resistance, temperamental defiance to authority, or obstinate rebellion ⟨some trouble about a *recalcitrant* miner who wanted to quit work. He shouted something about being a free man. When I ordered him to work, he rushed at me with his pick —John Steinbeck⟩ ⟨the establishment and maintenance of any orderly state generally involves the extermination of some of the *recalcitrant* opposition —M.R.Cohen⟩ WILLFUL implies determination to have one's own will, sometimes capricious, and to flout authority or wise guidance in achieving it ⟨*willful* men whom even the common frontier perils cannot reconcile or make tolerant —V.L.Parrington⟩ ⟨peevish because he called her and she did not come, and he threw his bowl of tea on the ground like a *willful* child —Pearl Buck⟩ HEADSTRONG may suggest

obdurate and mulish self-will impatient of restraint, advice, or suggestion ⟨testy and *headstrong* through an excess of will and bias —R.W.Emerson⟩ ⟨*headstrong* enough to make it a very difficult task for him to manage her —Anthony Trollope⟩
un·rumpled \ˌən+\ *adj* [¹*un-* + *rumpled*, past part. of *rumple*] **:** not rumpled **:** SMOOTH
un·rung \"+\ *adj* **:** UNRINGED
un·rusted \"+\ *adj* [¹*un-* + *rusted*, past part. of *rust*] **:** not rusted
un·ruth \"+\ *n* **:** lack of mercy or compassion **:** PITILESSNESS
uns *abbr* unsymmetrical
uns- *or* **unsym-** *comb form, usu ital* [fr. *unsymmetrical*] **:** unsymmetrical — in names of organic compounds ⟨*uns*-dichloro-ethane⟩
un·sabbatical \ˌən +\ *adj* [¹*un-* + *sabbatical*] **:** not suited to the sabbath
un·sack \ˌən+\ *vt* [²*un-* + *sack*, n.] **1 :** to remove the sack from **2 :** to remove from a sack
un·sacred \"+\ *adj* **:** not sacred **:** PROFANE
un·sadden \"+\ *vt* [²*un-* + *sadden*] **:** to free from sadness
un·saddle \"+\ *vb* [ME *unsadlen*, fr. ²*un-* + *sadlen* to saddle] *vt* **1 :** to strip of a saddle **:** take the saddle from (as a horse) **2 :** to throw from the saddle **:** UNHORSE ~ *vi* **:** to remove the saddle from a horse
un·saddled \"+\ *adj* [¹*un-* + *saddled*, past part. of *saddle*] **:** not saddled
un·safe \"+\ *adj* **:** not safe **:** exposed or exposing to danger **:** UNRELIABLE ⟨an ~ bridge⟩ ⟨an ~ method⟩ — **un·safely** \"+\ *adv* — **un·safeness** \"+\ *n*
un·safetied \"+\ *adj* [¹*un-* + *safetied*, past part. of *safety*] **:** not made safe
un·safety \"+\ *n* **:** want of safety **:** INSECURITY
un·said \"+\ *adj* [ME, fr. OE *unsægd*, fr. ¹*un-* + *sægd*, past part. of *secgan* to say — more at SAY] **:** not said; *esp* **:** thought but not spoken or expressed in words
un·sailed \"+\ *adj* [¹*un-* + *sailed*, past part. of *sail*] **:** not sailed
un·saint \ˌən+\ *vt* [²*un-* + *saint*] **:** to deprive of status as a saint
un·sainted \"+\ *adj* [¹*un-* + *sainted*, adj.] **:** not sanctified **:** not canonized
un·saintly \"+\ *adj* **:** unbecoming to a saint
un·salability \"+\ *n* **:** the quality or state of being unsalable
un·salable \"+\ *adj* **:** not salable **:** UNMERCHANTABLE ⟨goods which are ~ lose their dollar value —T.W.Arnold⟩ ⟨drama, economics and philosophy were ~ —G.B.Shaw⟩ — **un·sal·ableness** \"+\ *n*
un·salaried \"+\ *adj* **:** not paid a salary ⟨an ~ officer⟩
un·salted \"+\ *adj* [ME, fr. ¹*un-* + *salted*, past part. of *salten* to salt] **:** not salted
un·salutary \"+\ *adj* **:** not salutary **:** HARMFUL, UNHEALTHY
un·saluted \"+\ *adj* [¹*un-* + *saluted*, past part. of *salute*] **:** not saluted
un·salvable \"+\ *adj* **:** not salvable
un·sanctification \"+\ *n* **:** absence or lack of sanctification
un·sanctified \"+\ *adj* [¹*un-* + *sanctified*, adj.] **:** not holy or sanctified **:** not made sacred or holy **:** not reserved for religious use ⟨the daring half-hope is expressed that the lovers' ~ union may be blessed with issue —*New Republic*⟩ — **un·sanc·ti·fi·ed·ly** \-ˌfī(ə)dlē, -li\ *adv*
un·sanctify \ˌən+\ *vt* [²*un-* + *sanctify*] **:** to remove the sanctification from **:** make unsanctified
un·sanctimonious \"+\ *adj* **1 :** not making a show of or giving the appearance of sanctity **2 :** IRRELIGIOUS, UNHOLY — **un·sanctimoniously** \"+\ *adv* — **un·sanctimoniousness** \"+\ *n*
un·sanctioned \"+\ *adj* [¹*un-* + *sanctioned*, past part. of *sanction*] **:** not sanctioned **:** not morally acceptable
un·sandaled \"+\ *adj* **:** not sandaled
un·sane \"+\ *adj* **:** lacking in sanity ⟨people are ~ when their mental maps of reality are slightly out of correspondence with the real world —Martin Gardner⟩ ⟨the noble but somewhat ~ faith that by some principle of truth men can be conditioned to perfectly rational behavior —H.J.Muller⟩
un·sanguinary \"+\ *adj* **:** not sanguinary **:** UNBLOODY ⟨sports-car . . . meet has had a relatively ~ history —J.M. Flagler⟩
un·sanguine \"+\ *adj* **:** not sanguine **:** not optimistic ⟨this ~ appraisal⟩ — **un·sanguineness** \"+\ *n*
un·sanitary \"+\ *adj* **:** not sanitary **:** INSANITARY ⟨~ methods of disposing of sewage —Ellsworth Huntington⟩ ⟨frequently ~ and generally grim conditions —E.G.Harrison⟩ ⟨~ places are placed off limits —*Science News Letter*⟩
un·saponifiable \"+\ *adj* **:** incapable of being saponified — used esp. of the portion of oils and fats other than the glycerides ⟨~ fractions such as steroids or vitamin A⟩
un·saponified \"+\ *adj* [¹*un-* + *saponified*, past part. of *saponify*] **:** not saponified
un·sated \ˌən+\ *adj* **:** not satiated **:** not satisfied **:** INSATIABLE ⟨youth, with its ~ and unbounded desires —Laurence Binyon⟩ ⟨curiosity was still ~ —R.A.Billington⟩
un·satiable \"+\ *adj* [ME *unsaciable*, fr. ¹*un-* + L *satiare* to satiate + E *-able* — more at SATIATE] **:** INSATIABLE — **un·sa·tia·ble·ness** \-bəlnəs\ *n* -ES — **un·sa·tia·bly** \-blē, -li\ *adv*
un·satiate \ˌən+\ *adj* **:** INSATIATE
un·satiated \"+\ *adj* **:** not satiated
un·satisfaction \"+\ *n* **:** absence of satisfaction
un·satisfactorily \"+\ *adv* **:** in an unsatisfactory manner
un·satisfactoriness \"+\ *n* **:** the quality or state of being unsatisfactory
un·satisfactory \"+\ *adj* **:** not satisfactory: as **a :** not yielding content **b :** not meeting the issue or problem **:** not answering the question **c :** failing to make amends or to give satisfaction
un·satisfiable \"+\ *adj* **:** not capable of being satisfied
un·satisfied \"+\ *adj* [ME, fr. ¹*un-* + *satisfied*, past part. of *satisfien* to satisfy] **:** not satisfied ⟨the curiosity was ~ —Sherwood Anderson⟩ ⟨has any claim been left ~ —B.H. Hibbard⟩ ⟨unfilled orders and an ~ demand for passenger cars —*Report: General Motors Corp.*⟩ — **un·sat·is·fied·ly** *adv* — **un·sat·is·fied·ness** *n* -ES
unsatisfied judgment fund *n* **:** a state-administered fund for the payment of damages incurred in automobile accidents provided the parties responsible are unable to pay
un·satisfying \ˌən+\ *adj* **:** failing to satisfy ⟨an ~ meal⟩
un·saturate \"+\ *n* -S **:** an unsaturated chemical compound (as an olefinic or acetylenic hydrocarbon)
un·saturated \"+\ *adj* **:** not saturated: as **a :** capable of absorbing or dissolving to a greater degree ⟨an ~ salt solution⟩ **b** *of a chemical compound or mixture* **:** able to form addition products — used esp. of organic compounds containing double or triple bonds between carbon atoms ⟨ethylene, acetylene, and oleic acid are ~ compounds⟩ ⟨hydrogenation of ~ vegetable and marine oils —O.B.J.Fraser⟩ **c :** relating to minerals (as nepheline and leucite) that generally do not form in the same rock with quartz
un·saturation \"+\ *n* **:** the quality or state of being unsaturated
un·savable \"+\ *adj* **:** not savable
un·saved \"+\ *adj* **:** not saved; *esp* **:** not rescued from eternal punishment
un·savorily \"+\ *adv* **:** in an unsavory manner
un·savoriness \"+\ *n* **:** the quality of being unsavory
un·savory \"+\ *adj* [ME, fr. ¹*un-* + *savory*] **1 :** not savory **:** INSIPID, TASTELESS **2 :** unpleasant to taste or smell **:** DISAGREEABLE, DISTASTEFUL ⟨dropped the ~ morsel —John Burroughs⟩ ⟨punishing students . . . by assigning them more work, has made education ~ and unappealing to the average student —H.C.McKown⟩ **3 :** morally offensive ⟨an ~ character . . . could be as harmful to youngsters as a man who beat them or starved them —Ross Annett⟩ ⟨an ~ reputation for providing a friendly haven for pirates —*Amer. Guide Series: R.I.*⟩ ⟨make an example of men around him caught in ~ acts —*New Republic*⟩
un·say \"+\ *vt* [ME *unsayen*, fr. ²*un-* + *sayen* to say] **:** to make as if not said **:** RECANT, RECALL, RETRACT ⟨he would not deny it; he would just ~ it —Nathaniel Peffer⟩ ⟨ten million graves record what youth has said, and cannot now ~ —Alfred Noyes⟩
un·sayable \"+\ *adj* **:** incapable of being said

un·scabbard \ˌən+\ *vt* [²*un-* + *scabbard*] **:** to remove from a scabbard ⟨~ a sword⟩
un·scalable \"+\ *adj* **:** not scalable ⟨an ~ fence⟩ ⟨an ~ barrier⟩
un·scale \"+\ *vt* [²*un-* + *scale*, n.] **:** to divest of scales **:** remove scales from
un·scaled \"+\ *adj* [¹*un-* + *scaled*, past part. of *scale*] **:** not scaled ⟨an ~ mountain⟩
un·scannable \"+\ *adj* **:** not scannable ⟨denouncing his verse as ~ —F.R.Leavis⟩
un·scanned \"+\ *adj* [¹*un-* + *scanned*, past part. of *scan*] **:** not scanned
un·scared \"+\ *adj* **:** not scared
un·scarred \"+\ *adj* [¹*un-* + *scarred*, past part. of *scar*] **:** not scarred ⟨a foot trail leads through heavy, ~ woods —*Amer. Guide Series: Mich.*⟩ ⟨~ by his thirty years as a teacher —H.F. & Katharine Pringle⟩
un·scathed \"+\ *adj* [ME, fr. ¹*un-* + *scathed*, past part. of *scathen* to scathe] **:** wholly unharmed **:** not injured ⟨believed that . . . his devotees pass ~ over this burning charcoal although they actually stamp their feet on it —J.G.Frazer⟩ ⟨emergence from the war physically ~ —A.E.Stevenson †1965⟩
un·scented \"+\ *adj* **:** deprived of scent **:** having no scent ⟨an ~ soap⟩
un·sceptered \ˌən+\ *adj* **:** deprived of a scepter **:** having no scepter
un·scheduled \"+\ *adj* [¹*un-* + *scheduled*, past part. of *schedule*] **:** not scheduled ⟨an ~ airplane flight⟩
un·scholarly \"+\ *adj* **:** not scholarly
un·school \"+\ *vt* [²*un-* + *school*] **:** to make (one) disregard schooling or training
un·schooled \"+\ *adj* [¹*un-* + *schooled*, past part. of *school*] **1 :** not schooled **:** UNTAUGHT, UNTRAINED ⟨comfort and leisure came to people ~ to use them —A.N.Whitehead⟩ **2 :** not artificial **:** NATURAL ⟨employed his ~ talents on vigorous . . . paintings of colonial families —*Amer. Guide Series: N.Y.*⟩
un·scientific \"+\ *adj* **:** not scientific: as **a :** not used in scientific work **b :** not according with the principles and methods of science ⟨essential national resource . . . dwindling from day to day because of ~ management —F.D.Roosevelt⟩ **c :** not showing scientific knowledge or familiarity with scientific methods — **un·scientifically** \"+\ *adv*
un·scorched \"+\ *adj* [¹*un-* + *scorched*, past part. of *scorch*] **:** not scorched
un·scored \"+\ *adj* [¹*un-* + *scored*, past part. of *score*] **:** not scored
un·scorned \"+\ *adj* [¹*un-* + *scorned*, past part. of *scorn*] **:** not scorned
un-scottish \"+\ *adj, usu cap S* **:** not Scottish **:** not characteristic of or consistent with Scottish customs or principles
un·scoured \"+\ *adj* [ME, fr. ¹*un-* + *scoured*, past part. of *scouren* to scour] **:** not scoured
un·scramble \"+\ *vt* [²*un-* + *scramble*] **1 :** to separate (as a conglomeration, mass, or tangle) into original components **:** RESOLVE, CLARIFY ⟨airfreight carriers, are trying to ~ a merger omelet —*Wall Street Jour.*⟩ ⟨the various possible meanings of *di-* and *de-* are so confused that only an expert can ~ them —Charlton Laird⟩ ⟨the *unscrambling* of a composite race into its original pure-race constituents —A.L.Kroeber⟩ ⟨had to ~ the financial operations which had taken place —*Brit. Bk. News*⟩ ⟨no adult can ever successfully ~ his complex mental life —Kathryn Maxwell⟩ ⟨jars or cans dumped on table are instantly *unscrambled* and regimented into a single file —*advt*⟩ **2 :** to restore (a scrambled telephonic, radio, or television transmission) to intelligible form ⟨each process by different methods would enable the home television viewer to ~ special telecast programs —Alvin Shuster⟩
un·scraped \"+\ *adj* [¹*un-* + *scraped*, past part. of *scrape*] **:** not scraped
unscraped ginger *n* **:** BLACK GINGER
un·screen \ˌən+\ *vt* [²*un-* + *screen*] **:** to remove the screen from **:** UNVEIL, REVEAL
un·screened \"+\ *adj* [¹*un-* + *screened*, past part. of *screen*] **1 :** not shut off or protected by a screen ⟨his eyes ~ from the glare⟩ ⟨the now met the college world, ~ —Edmund Wilson⟩ **2 :** not passed through a screening device or procedure ⟨~ sand⟩ ⟨this material was . . . wholly ~ —*Newsweek*⟩
un·screw \"+\ *vb* [²*un-* + *screw*] *vt* **1 :** to draw the screws from **:** loose from screws ⟨~*s* the metal plate⟩ **2 a :** to loosen or withdraw (as a screw or a cover) by turning **b :** to loosen or remove the cover of (as a jar) by turning ~ *vi* **:** to become unscrewed **:** to admit of being unscrewed ⟨vibration often causes the bolts to ~⟩ ⟨the attachment ~*s* easily for removal⟩
un·scripted \"+\ *adj* [¹*un-* + *scripted*, past part. of *script*] **:** not furnished with or using a script ⟨spot interviews, unrehearsed and ~, are the feature of the first part —Roger Manvell⟩ ⟨brought to the microphone . . . for ~ discussion on topics of the moment —Angus Mackay⟩
un·scriptural \"+\ *adj* **:** not in accordance with or in contradiction to the Scriptures ⟨the conservative members were opposed to missionary societies and instrumental music . . . as ~ —Brooke P. Church⟩ ⟨rejected infant baptism as ~ —F.S. Mead⟩ — **un·scripturally** \"+\ *adv* — **un·scripturalness** \"+\ *n*
un·scrupulosity \"+\ *n* **:** UNSCRUPULOUSNESS ⟨at times had a look of cynical ~ —O.W.Holmes †1935⟩
un·scrupulous \"+\ *adj* **1 :** not scrupulous **:** UNPRINCIPLED ⟨~ enough to betray his comrades . . . again and again —Desmond Ryan⟩ ⟨ambitious, ~, and cruel, a master of intrigue —Victor Seroff⟩ ⟨~ politicos who would be happy to sell . . . their country in order to gain power —Green Peyton⟩ **2 :** marked or characterized by unscrupulousness ⟨a witty woman of ~ tongue —Walter Bagehot⟩ ⟨the ~ procession of thieves is led by proud states and lofty statesmen —W.L. Sullivan⟩
un·scrupulously \"+\ *adv* **:** in an unscrupulous manner **:** without scruple ⟨~ uses her personal fascination to make men give her whatever she wants —G.B.Shaw⟩
un·scrupulousness \"+\ *n* **:** the quality or state of being unscrupulous
un·seal \"+\ *vt* [ME *unselen*, fr. ²*un-* + *selen* to seal] **1 :** to break or remove the seal of **:** OPEN ⟨~ the tomb⟩ ⟨~ the letter⟩ **2 a :** to free from constraint or restriction ⟨drink can ~ the shiest tongue⟩ **b :** to release from the necessity of being closed ⟨this event did not ~ her lips —Francis Hackett⟩
un·sealed \"+\ *adj* [ME *unseled*, fr. ¹*un-* + *seled*, past part. of *selen* to seal] **:** not sealed: as **a :** not marked or stamped with a seal ⟨~ goods⟩ **b :** not closed or fastened shut with or as if with a seal ⟨the letter came ~⟩ ⟨passengers should not be flown . . . above 18,000 feet in ~ cabins —H.G.Armstrong⟩ ⟨his lips remain ~⟩ **c :** not verified or confirmed ⟨his doom is as yet ~⟩
un·seam \"+\ *vt* [²*un-* + *seam*] **:** to open the seam of **:** rip open ⟨~ the garment⟩
un·seamanlike \"+\ *adj* **:** not seamanlike ⟨the boats appeared unseaworthy and the men ~ —J.H. & Edward Quick⟩
un·seamed \"+\ *adj* **:** not having any seams **:** SEAMLESS ⟨the dominant expression of his ~ face —B.F.Shambaugh⟩ ⟨an ~ garment made of a plastic⟩
un·searchable \"+\ *adj* [ME *unserchable*, fr. ¹*un-* + *serchen* to search + *-able*] **:** not capable of being explored **:** INSCRUTABLE, HIDDEN, MYSTERIOUS ⟨the ~ ways of Providence⟩ — **un·search·able·ness** \-bəlnəs\ *n* -ES — **un·search·ably** \-blē, -li\ *adv*
un·searched \ˌən+\ *adj* [¹*un-* + *searched*, past part. of *search*] **:** not searched, examined, or investigated ⟨leaving no piece of baggage ~⟩
un·seasonable \"+\ *adj* [ME *unsesounable*, fr. ¹*un-* + *sesounable* seasonable] **1 :** not seasonable **:** being, done, or occurring out of the proper season **:** UNTIMELY, INAPPROPRIATE ⟨you think my intrusion ~ —T.L.Peacock⟩ ⟨their aim . . . to guard the free income of the lesser vested interests against the ~ rapacity of the greater ones —Thorstein Veblen⟩ ⟨lovers will drop in at most ~ hours —Anthony Trollope⟩ **2 :** not being in season ⟨after spawning when the fish . . . are thin, weak, and ~ —C.R.A.Martin⟩ ⟨this partridge was evidently a diseased bird, and the ~ egg was probably due to some abnormal condition —*Country Life*⟩ **3 a :** not usual or normal and usu. undesirable for the season of the year ⟨to forestall losses from sudden ~ northers —*Amer. Guide Series: Texas*⟩ ⟨an ~ April blizzard⟩ **b :** characterized by unseasonable weather ⟨boarding houses . . . had suffered from the ~ summer —Mollie Panter-Downes⟩
un·seasonableness \"+\ *n* **:** the quality or state of being unseasonable
un·seasonably \"+\ *adv* **:** in an unseasonable manner **:** at an unseasonable time **:** not in season ⟨he ~ and precipitously made his decision⟩ ⟨tributes to German generosity fall ~ at this moment on French ears —Sir Winston Churchill⟩ ⟨the night had been ~ hot —Elinor Wylie⟩
un·seasonal \"+\ *adj* **:** not suitable or appropriate for the season **:** UNSEASONABLE ⟨to store . . . the few ~ clothes —Max Steele⟩ ⟨if rains are ~ they may scarcely bloom —*Amer. Guide Series: Texas*⟩ — **un·seasonally** \"+\ *adv*
un·seasoned \"+\ *adj* **:** not seasoned: as **a** *obs* **:** UNSEASONABLE 1 **b :** not matured or developed by growth or passage of time **:** IMMATURE ⟨~ timber⟩ ⟨the stone was often used ~ and without regard for the lie of the strata in the quarry —*Time*⟩ **c :** lacking age or seasoning **:** INEXPERIENCED ⟨~ men who are not used to responsibility because they have never exercised it —Walter Lippmann⟩ ⟨~ artillery volunteers who ought never to have been placed in such a position —H.G.Wells⟩ ⟨~ by any saving knowledge of human nature —V.L.Parrington⟩
un·seat \"+\ *vt* [²*un-* + *seat*] **1 :** to dislodge from one's seat esp. on horseback ⟨gave up horseback riding when a low-hanging limb ~*ed* him⟩ **2 a :** to displace in a political rank or office usu. by an elective process ⟨defeated an attempt . . . to ~ him in the primary —*Current Biog.*⟩ ⟨party caucus that ~*ed* the Old Guard regime —*N. Y. Times*⟩ **b :** to remove or depose from rank or office by legal action or force ⟨by a close vote . . . declined to ~ him —C.A.Berdahl⟩ ⟨had been ~*ed* for bribery —J.A.Froude⟩ ⟨in his second army coup . . . ~*ed* the president of the island republic —*Current Biog.*⟩
un·seated \"+\ *adj* [¹*un-* + *seated*, adj.] **:** not seated: **a :** having been dislodged from one's seat esp. as a rider **:** UNHORSED **b :** having been removed or deposed from political rank or position **c** *of land or territory* **:** not settled or occupied ⟨if all the states rush to claim the ~ lands within the limits of their overlapping —H.R.Warfel⟩
un·seaworthiness \"+\ *n* **:** the quality or state of being unseaworthy
un·seaworthy \"+\ *adj* **:** not seaworthy
un·seconded \"+\ *adj* [¹*un-* + *seconded*, past part. of *second*] **:** not seconded; *esp* **:** not supported or assisted ⟨the motion is ~⟩ ⟨the attempt was ~⟩
¹un·secret \"+\ *adj* [¹*un-* + *secret*, adj.] **:** not secret ⟨ringing his footfalls deliberate and ~ in the hollow silence —William Faulkner⟩
²unsecret *vt* [²*un-* + *secret*] *obs* **:** DISCLOSE, REVEAL
un·sectarian \ˌən+\ *adj* **:** not sectarian **:** not bound to or devoted to the promotion of the interests of a sect ⟨had a wide and ~ interest in religion —Bertrand Russell⟩ — **un·sectarianism** \"+\ *n*
un·secular \"+\ *adj* **:** not secular; *esp* **:** of or relating to religion or the church
un·secularize \"+\ *vt* [²*un-* + *secularize*] **:** to cause to become unsecular ⟨a movement to ~ public education⟩
un·secured \ˌən+\ *adj* [¹*un-* + *secured*, past part. of *secure*] **:** not secured; *esp* **:** not having specific security pledged ⟨~ bond⟩ ⟨~ note⟩
un·seduced \"+\ *adj* [¹*un-* + *seduced*, past part. of *seduce*] **:** not seduced ⟨remains ~ by temptations of personal gain⟩
un·see \"+\ *vt* [¹*un-* + *see*] **:** to fail to see **:** avoid seeing ⟨to prove scientifically the error or unreality of disease, you must mentally ~ the disease —Mary B. Eddy⟩
un·seeable \"+\ *adj* [ME *unseable*, fr. ¹*un-* + *seable* seeable] **:** not seeable **:** INVISIBLE
un·seeded \"+\ *adj* **:** not seeded; *esp* **:** not selectively placed in the draw for a tournament
un·seeing \"+\ *adj* **:** not seeing; *esp* **:** not consciously observing ⟨looking through him with blank ~ eyes⟩ — **un·seeingly** \"+\ *adv* — **un·see·ing·ness** *n* -ES
unseel *vt* [²*un-* + *seel*] *obs* **:** to cause (as the eyes of a hawk) to become uncovered
un·seemliness \ˌən+\ *n* [ME *unsemelines*, fr. *unsemely* unseemly + *-nes* -ness] **:** the quality or state of being unseemly
¹un·seemly \"+\ *adj* [ME *unsemely*, fr. ¹*un-* + *semely* seemly] **:** not seemly: as **a :** not according with established standards of good form or taste **:** UNBECOMING, INDECENT ⟨very ~ to talk in this loose fashion before young men —Willa Cather⟩ ⟨an ~ outbreak of temper —Nathaniel Hawthorne⟩ ⟨one of the *unseemliest* squabbles . . . grew out of the bitterness sowed between a strong administrator and his teaching staff —V.L. Parrington⟩ ⟨rescuing its historic monuments from a century and a half of ~ neglect —Lewis Mumford⟩ **b :** not comely, handsome, or attractive in appearance ⟨a man of ~ aspect⟩ ⟨country farmhouses . . . resembling dingy boxes surrounded by ~ household litter —S.E.Morison & H.S.Commager⟩ **c :** not suitable for time or place **:** INAPPROPRIATE, UNSEASONABLE ⟨at the most ~ hours — eleven at night, four in the morning — alarm clocks shrieked, taps gushed —Jean Stafford⟩ ⟨we demand to know the reason for this ~ intrusion —T.B. Costain⟩ ⟨useless and ~ sorrow for the irrevocable past —W.M.Thackeray⟩
²unseemly \"\ *adv* [ME *unsemely*, fr. ¹*un-* + *semely*, adv., seemly] **:** in unseemly fashion or manner
¹un·seen \ˌən+\ *adj* [ME *unseyn, unsene*, fr. ¹*un-* + *seyn, sene*, past part. of *seen, sen* to see] **1 a** *obs* **:** not hitherto seen or known **:** UNFAMILIAR **b :** SIGHT 1 ⟨an ~ translation⟩ **2 :** not seen or perceived **:** INVISIBLE ⟨~ natural resources⟩ ⟨the visible incarnation of that ~ ideal —Oscar Wilde⟩
²unseen \"\ *n* -S **1 :** something not seen **2** *Brit* **:** a sight translation ⟨was doing an ~ —*Oxford Mag.*⟩
unseen companion star *n* **:** a member of a binary or multiple star system that is known to exist only by its gravitational effect on the visible components whose apparent motions it usu. alters in a cyclic manner
un·segmented \ˌən+\ *adj* [¹*un-* + *segmented*, past part. of *segment*] **:** not divided into or made up of segments
un·segregated \"+\ *adj* **:** free from segregation ⟨Negro students would be admitted . . . on an ~ basis —*New Republic*⟩ ⟨an ~ audience⟩
un·seiz·able \ˌən¦sēzəbəl\ *adj* [¹*un-* + *seize* + *-able*] **:** incapable of being seized ⟨an unshorn lamb . . . now ran round, bleating, terror-stricken, and ~ —Israel Zangwill⟩ ⟨noticed an ~ resemblance between these second cousins —John Galsworthy⟩ ⟨remains as ~ to their wits as a high flight of metaphysics —R.L.Stevenson⟩ — **un·seiz·able·ness** *n* -ES
un·seized \ˌən+\ *adj* [¹*un-* + *seized*, past part. of *seize*] **:** not seized ⟨the ~ opportunity may not return⟩
un·seldom \"+\ *adv* **:** FREQUENTLY — often used with *not* ⟨often becomes tired and not ~ exhausted⟩
un·selected \"+\ *adj* **:** not selected **:** chosen at random
un·selective \"+\ *adj* **:** not selective
un·self \"+\ *vt* [²*un-* + *self*, n.] **:** to do away with selfhood or selfishness in (oneself) ⟨man has the idealism to ~ himself⟩
un·selfconscious \"+\ *adj* **1 :** not self-conscious ⟨the beautifully ~ straight-faced way he plays the scene —Manny Farber⟩ ⟨grew up with him in ~ friendship —G.L.Keynes⟩ **2 :** marked or characterized by unselfconsciousness ⟨the experience of unadorned, ~ goodness —*Times Lit. Supp.*⟩ ⟨she laughed . . . the gayest, most ~ sound in the world —Vincent Sheean⟩
un·selfconsciously \"+\ *adv* **:** in an unselfconscious manner ⟨no choice but ~ to play his role —*School & Society*⟩
un·selfconsciousness \"+\ *n* **:** the quality or state of being unselfconscious ⟨he has the ~ of a child⟩
un·selfish \"+\ *adj* **:** not selfish **:** GENEROUS ⟨his deep devotion and ~ service —W.C.Ford⟩
un·selfishly \"+\ *adv* **:** in an unselfish manner **:** with unselfishness ⟨~ give of their time . . . and money to improve the lot of all farmers —*Farmer's Weekly (So. Africa)*⟩
un·selfishness \"+\ *n* **:** the quality or state of being unselfish
un·sell \"+\ *vt* [²*un-* + *sell*] **1 :** to dissuade from a belief in the truth, value, or desirability of something ⟨has undertaken to ~ the American people on several debatable ideas . . . foisted on them —R.E.Lauterbach⟩ ⟨others won't be able to ~ him on the things he's sold on —*Time*⟩ **2 :** to dissuade one from a belief in the truth, value, or desirability of ⟨comes to

~ the idea that his country wants war⟩ ⟨rushed back before the press release to try to ~ the proposal⟩

unseminared *adj* [1*un-* + *seminary* + *-ed*] *obs* **:** deprived of seminal energy

un·sensational \ˌən+\ *adj* **:** not sensational; *esp* **:** not of such character as to arouse intense interest, curiosity, or emotional reaction ⟨in a detached ~ fashion he describes the hell of the camps —W.H.Auden⟩ ⟨the text of these two ~ documents discloses no reason why the negotiations should have attracted the world's attention —*Living Age*⟩ — **un·sensationally** \"+\ *adv*

un·sense \"+\ *vt* [2*un-* + *sense*, n.] **:** to make insensible

un·sensed \"+\ *adj* [1*un-* + *sensed*, past part. of *sense*] **:** lacking a distinct meaning **:** having no certain sense

un·sensible \"+\ *adj* [ME, fr. 1*un-* + *sensible*] *dial chiefly Brit* **:** INSENSIBLE

un·sensitive \"+\ *adj* **:** INSENSITIVE

un·sensualize \"+\ *vt* [2*un-* + *sensualize*] **:** to elevate from the domain of the senses **:** PURIFY, SUBLIMATE ⟨~ love and raise it above passion⟩

un·sent \"+\ *adj* [1*un-* + *sent*, past part. of *send*] **:** not sent or dispatched ⟨the missive remains unwritten and ~⟩

un·sentenced \"+\ *adj* [1*un-* + *sentenced*, past part. of *sentence*] **:** not sentenced; *esp* **:** not condemned to penalty or punishment

un·sentimental \"+\ *adj* **:** not sentimental; *esp* **:** not characterized or dominated by excessive or unwarranted sentiment ⟨a fine, original novel, written with affectionate but ~ understanding of the Norwegians —R.A.Cordell⟩ ⟨much quite ~ appeal to the emotions —M.R.Ridley⟩ ⟨a hard core of ~ intelligence beneath their romantic paganism —Richard Watts⟩ — **un·sentimentality** \"+\ *n* — **un·sentimentally** \"+\ *adv*

un·separable \"+\ *adj* [ME *unseperable*, fr. 1*un-* + *seperable* separable] **:** INSEPARABLE

un·separated \ˌən+\ *adj* [1*un-* + *separated*, past part. of *separate*] **:** not separated ⟨inevitable that a great deal of bad painting should remain ~ from the good —Walter Pach⟩

un·septate \"+\ *adj* **:** not septate or partitioned

un·sepulchered \"+\ *adj* [1*un-* + *sepulchered*, past part. of *sepulcher*] **:** not buried or entombed

un·serious \"+\ *adj* **:** not serious ⟨the ~ intermezzi, originally presented between the acts of serious pieces, were . . . put together to form the first light or comic operas —Sheldon Cheney⟩ ⟨flight into an ~ career as an actress —*New Republic*⟩

un·serried \"+\ *adj* **:** not in close order or array

un·served \"+\ *adj* [ME, fr. 1*un-* + *served*, past part. of *serven* to serve] **:** not served: as **a :** not attended to **:** not furnished with something ⟨many customers waiting ~⟩ ⟨concentrated in the cities, the broadcasting stations leave large rural areas ~⟩ **b** *of a church or parish* **:** not having a clergyman in attendance **c** *of a legal writ or summons* **:** not served on a person

un·serviceable \"+\ *adj* **1 :** not capable of being used usu. by reason of wear, impairment, or obsolescence ⟨an ~ car was defined as one which had been driven 40,000 miles —*Newsweek*⟩ ⟨~ equipment may be discarded and replaced⟩ **2 :** not able to give service or aid **:** USELESS, INEPT ⟨~ and grossly insolent civil servants —G.B.Shaw⟩ ⟨despite our best efforts, we proved to be quite ~ for his purposes⟩ **3** *chiefly Brit* **:** incapable of doing military service ⟨ragged, ill-fed, and ~ troops⟩ — **un·serviceableness** \"+\ *n* — **un·serviceably** \"+\ *adv*

1un·set \"+\ *adj* [ME *unsett*, fr. 1*un-* + *sett* set] **:** not set: as **a** *archaic* **:** not allotted or assigned **b :** not fixed in a setting **:** UNMOUNTED ⟨auctioning off a collection of ~ stones⟩ ⟨an ~ sawtooth⟩ **c :** not firmed or solidified ⟨~ concrete⟩

2unset \"\ *vt* [2*un-* + *set*] **:** DISPLACE, UNSETTLE

1un·setting \ˌən+\ *adj* [1*un-* + *setting*, pres. part. of *set*] **:** not setting ⟨where suns ~ light the sky and flowers and fruit abound —J.H.Newman⟩

2unsetting \"\ *n* [1*un-* + *setting*, n.] **:** a supporting of the opposite masonry walls of a cut through loose strata by means of buttresses resting on inverted arches

un·settle \ˌən+\ *vb* [2*un-* + *settle*] *vt* **1 :** to unfix or loosen from a settled state **:** DISPLACE ⟨a lusty shock . . . *unsettled* another rock up the mountain —Burtt Evans⟩ **2 :** to force or move from a quiet or settled condition **:** DISTURB ⟨the heavy diet ~*s* his stomach⟩ ⟨this theory, though intended to strengthen the foundations of government, altogether ~*s* them —T.B. Macaulay⟩ ⟨major strikes could ~ 1959 economy —*News Front*⟩ **3 a :** to cause to be doubtful or uncertain **:** UPSET ⟨new trends ~ old beliefs and opinions⟩ ⟨to ~ the traditional notion —F.R.Leavis⟩ ⟨the cold war has *unsettled* the minds of men —M.B.Travis⟩ **b :** to perturb or agitate mentally or emotionally **:** DISCOMPOSE ⟨a clumsy driver had *unsettled* the horses —C.S.Forester⟩ ⟨his narratives ~ us, force us to make comparisons in our own terms —E.R.May⟩ ⟨the impact of the momentary glamorous life could ~ a woman —Herbert Mitgary⟩ ~ *vi* **:** to become unsettled or unfixed ⟨the congregation *unsettled*, produced handkerchiefs, and knelt upon them —James Joyce⟩ **syn** see DISORDER

un·settled \"+\ *adj* [partly fr. 1*un-* + *settled*; partly fr. past part. of *unsettle*] **:** not settled: as **a** (1) **:** not calm or tranquil **:** DISTURBED, UNQUIET ⟨an ~ air — an echo of turbulence and war — now hangs over every campus —F.E.Robin⟩ ⟨this utterly ~ and uncertain condition —C.S.Peirce⟩ (2) **:** INCONSTANT, VARIABLE ⟨homebound . . . meeting ~ weather all the way, rain, snow, hail, and sunshine —*Crowsnest*⟩ (3) **:** remaining in a state of motion or change **:** not settled down ⟨clouds of ~ dust⟩ ⟨the murky ~ water⟩ **b** (1) **:** not decided or determined **:** DOUBTFUL ⟨in an ~ state of mind⟩ (2) **:** not resolved or worked out **:** UNDECIDED ⟨~ constitutional questions . . . came up for solution —H.W.H.Knott⟩ ⟨specifications were still ~ —*Fortune*⟩ **c** (1) **:** not firm or steadfast in disposition or outlook **:** ERRATIC, UNSTABLE ⟨~ young people without any roots in the past⟩ (2) **:** characterized by uncertainty, irregularity, or instability ⟨living an ~ life after leaving his family⟩ ⟨the old tribal customs now ~ by modern civilization⟩ **d** (1) **:** not living or staying in one place ⟨the ~ nomads of the desert⟩ (2) **:** not inhabited or populated ⟨land within the territory . . . that was then ~ or uncultivated has been peopled or reclaimed —B.N.Cardozo⟩ **e :** mentally unbalanced ⟨minds ~ by excessive ascetic observances —W.G. Sumner⟩ ⟨at one time he was insane or at least ~ —A.B. Guthrie⟩ **f** (1) **:** not disposed of according to law ⟨the estate remains ~⟩ (2) **:** not paid or discharged ⟨borrowing money to pay off all ~ debts⟩ — **un·settledness** \"+\ *n*

un·settlement \"+\ *n* **1 :** an act, process, or instance of unsettling ⟨in the teaching of foreign languages there has been at least some ~ in consequence of army courses —*Language*⟩ ⟨did not relish the theological ~ that came with the advance of scientific inquiry —V.L.Parrington⟩ **2 :** the quality or state of being unsettled ⟨the disturbance and ~ that now marks . . . man's life —John Dewey⟩

un·settling \"+\ *adj* [fr. pres. part. of *unsettle*] **:** having the effect of upsetting, disturbing, or discomposing ⟨his ornate and exuberant grandiosity that is a bit ~ —R.M.Coates⟩ ⟨the swift pace of scientific discovery . . . has had a profoundly ~ effect upon our modern world view —Melvin Rader⟩ ⟨found even the simplest political questions ~ —R.H.Rovere⟩

un·severed \"+\ *adj* [ME, fr. 1*un-* + *severed*, past part. of *severen* to sever] **:** not severed ⟨our ties remain ~⟩

un·sew \"+\ *vt* [ME *unsewen*, fr. 2*un-* + *sewen* to sew] **:** to take the stitches out of; *also* **:** to rip apart or separate by removing the sewing

un·sewered \"+\ *adj* [1*un-* + *sewer* + *-ed*] **:** not provided with a sewer or drain ⟨~ slums⟩

un·sex \"+\ *vt* [2*un-* + *sex*, n.] **1 :** to deprive of sex or sexual power **2 :** to remove the qualities typical of one's sex ⟨come you spirits, that tend on mortal thoughts, ~ me here —Shak.⟩ ⟨if she earned money in the one profession that was open to her, the oldest profession of all, she ~*ed* herself —Virginia Woolf⟩

un·sexual \"+\ *adj* **:** not sexual **:** lacking sex

unsgd *abbr* unsigned

un·shackle \ˌən+\ *vt* [2*un-* + *shackle*] **1 a :** to loose from a shackle or bond ⟨giving orders to ~ the prisoner and bring him on deck⟩ **b :** to set free from restraint ⟨conversation was *unshackled* —B.M.Bowie⟩ ⟨when the mind has been *unshackled* from ignorance —H.G.Rickover⟩ **2 :** to remove a shackle from (as an anchor) ⟨*unshackled* the port anchor and lowered it —H.A.Chippendale⟩

un·shaded \"+\ *adj* **:** not shaded: as **a :** not darkened or bedimmed by shade **:** EXPOSED ⟨an ~ meadow⟩ ⟨a bright and ~ lane through the trees⟩ **b :** not having shades in coloring or tone ⟨sharp ~ colors⟩ ⟨a clear ~ voice⟩ **c :** not provided with a shade ⟨an ~ lamp⟩ ⟨~ windows⟩

un·shadow \"+\ *vt* [2*un-* + *shadow*] *archaic* **:** to rid of shadow

un·shadowed \"+\ *adj* [1*un-* + *shadowed*, past part. of *shadow*] **:** not darkened or obscured by shadow ⟨on the rough sea ice you may on an ~ day . . . fall over a chunk of ice that is knee-high —Vilhjalmur Stefansson⟩ ⟨in times of ~ prosperity —Claire Sterling⟩

un·shakable \"+\ *adj* **:** not shakable **:** firmly grounded ⟨a sense of deep conviction and ~ faith —*Manchester Guardian Weekly*⟩

un·shak·able·ness *or* **un·shake·able·ness** \-bəlnəs\ *n* -ES **:** the quality or state of being unshakable **:** FIRMNESS, SOLIDITY

un·shak·ably *or* **un·shake·ably** \-blē, -li\ *adv* **:** in an unshakable manner **:** FIRMLY

un·shaked \ˌən+\ *adj* [1*un-* + *shaked*, dial. past part. of *shake*] *obs* **:** UNSHAKEN

un·shaken \"+\ *adj* [ME, fr. 1*un-* + *shaken*, past part. of *shaken* to shake] **:** not shaken **:** FIRM, STEADY ⟨although physically only the wreck of a man, his nerve was ~ and his remarkable mental faculties unimpaired —Sir Winston Churchill⟩ — **un·shak·en·ly** *adv* — **un·shak·en·ness** *n* -ES

un·shamed \ˌən+\ *adj* [ME, fr. 1*un-* + *shamed*, past part. of *shamen* to shame] **1 :** not shamed **2 :** UNASHAMED

un·shaped \"+\ *adj* **:** not shaped: as **a :** not dressed or finished to final form ⟨an ~ timber⟩ **b :** imperfect in form or formulation ⟨~ ideas⟩

un·shapeliness \"+\ *n* **:** the quality or state of being unshapely

un·shapely \"+\ *adj* [ME *unshaply*, *unshaplich*, fr. 1*un-* + *shap* shape + *-ly*, *-lich* -ly] **:** not shapely **:** wanting the beauty of fully realized or developed form ⟨she was a stout, ~ woman —Ellen Glasgow⟩

un·shapen \"+\ *adj* [ME, fr. 1*un-* + *shapen*] **:** UNSHAPED

un·shared \"+\ *adj* [1*un-* + *shared*, past part. of *share*] **:** not shared

un·sharp \"+\ *adj* **:** not sharp

unsharp mask *n* **:** a copy of a photographic image that is intentionally blurred for use over the original image in making final copies which are thereby modified in contrast and edge sharpness

un·sharpness \ˌən+\ *n* **:** the quality or state of being unsharp; *esp* **:** a low degree of photographic sharpness

un·shattered \"+\ *adj* [1*un-* + *shattered*, past part. of *shatter*] **:** not shattered

un·shaved \"+\ *adj* **:** not shaved

un·shaven \"+\ *adj* [ME, fr. 1*un-* + *shaven*] **:** not shaved **:** having a beard or the stubble of a beard

un·shawl \"+\ *vi* [2*un-* + *shawl*] **:** to remove one's shawl

un·sheared \"+\ *adj* **:** not sheared

un·sheathe \"+\ *vt* [2*un-* + *sheathe*] **:** to draw from or as if from a sheath or scabbard ⟨*unsheathed* his sword⟩ **:** BARE, UNCOVER

un·shed \"+\ *adj* **:** not shed

un·shell \"+\ *vt* [2*un-* + *shell*, n.] **:** to remove from the shell

un·sheltered \"+\ *adj* [1*un-* + *sheltered*, past part. of *shelter*] **:** not sheltered **:** having or offering no shelter

un·sheltering \"+\ *adj* [1*un-* + *sheltering*, pres. part. of *shelter*] **:** not sheltering

un·shent \ˌən+\ *adj* [ME, fr. 1*un-* + *shent*, past part. of *shenden* to shend] **:** UNHARMED, UNSPOILED

un·shepherded \"+\ *adj* [1*un-* + *shepherded*, past part. of *shepherd*] **:** not shepherded

un·shielded \"+\ *adj* [1*un-* + *shielded*, past part. of *shield*] **:** not shielded **:** UNPROTECTED

un·shiftable \"+\ *adj* [1*un-* + *shift* + *-able*] **:** IMMOVABLE

un·shifted \"+\ *adj* [1*un-* + *shifted*, past part. of *shift*] **:** unchanged for a fresh article of clothing ⟨a shirt ~⟩

un·ship \"+\ *vb* [ME *unschippen*, fr. 2*un-* + *schippen* to ship] *vt* **1 :** to take out of a ship **:** DISCHARGE, UNLOAD ⟨*unshipped* a cargo⟩ **2 :** to remove (as an oar) from position ~ *vi* **1 :** to become detached or removed **2 :** to become unloaded

un·shipped \"+\ *adj* [1*un-* + *shipped*, past part. of *ship*] **1 :** not shipped ⟨the ~ goods⟩ **2 :** having no ship **3 :** detached from position in a ship or boat

un·shirted \"+\ *adj* [1*un-* + *shirted*, past part. of *shirt*] **:** NAKED, UNDISGUISED, PLAIN — usu. used in the phrase *unshirted hell* ⟨given . . . ~ hell for a speech —Sherman Adams⟩ ⟨old guerrillas were raising ~ hell —*N. Y. Herald Tribune Bk. Rev.*⟩

un·shocked \"+\ *adj* [1*un-* + *shocked*, past part. of *shock*] **:** not shocked **:** not subject to shocks

un·shod \"+\ *adj* [ME, fr. OE *unscōd*, past part. of *unscōgan* to unshoe, fr. 2*un-* + *scōgan* to shoe — more at SHOE] **1 :** wearing no shoes **:** BAREFOOT **2** *of a horse* **:** not shod **:** having cast a shoe **3 :** having no tire or rim ⟨an ~ wagon wheel⟩ **:** lacking a sharp iron point ⟨an ~ pole⟩

un·shoe \"+\ *vt* [2*un-* + *shoe*] **:** to remove a shoe from

un·shorn \ˌən+\ *adj* [ME, fr. 1*un-* + *shorn*, past part. of *sheren* to shear] **1 :** not cut ⟨his grizzly ~ beard —Anthony Trollope⟩ **2 :** not harvested ⟨the ~ fields, boundless and beautiful —W.C.Bryant⟩ **3 :** not diminished ⟨hues with all their beams ~ —Lord Byron⟩

un·shortened \"+\ *adj* [1*un-* + *shortened*, past part. of *shorten*] **:** not shortened **:** UNDIMINISHED

un·shot \"+\ *adj* **1 :** not shot ⟨an ~ gun⟩ ⟨an ~ arrow⟩ **2 :** not hit by a shot **3 :** not mingled or variegated **:** not interwoven ⟨methods of beef preparation . . . not ~ with cunning and imagination —C.H.Baker⟩

un·shoulder \"+\ *vt* [2*un-* + *shoulder*] **:** to remove from the shoulder ⟨~*ed* their knapsacks⟩

un·shown \"+\ *adj* [1*un-* + *shown*, past part. of *show*] **:** not shown

un·showy \"+\ *adj* **:** not showy

un·shrine \"+\ *vt* [2*un-* + *shrine*] **:** to remove from a shrine

un·shrinkable \"+\ *adj* [1*un-* + *shrink* + *-able*] **:** incapable of being shrunken, diminished, or reduced

un·shrinking \"+\ *adj* [1*un-* + *shrinking*, pres. part. of *shrink*] **:** not shrinking

un·shrinkingly \"+\ *adv* **:** without shrinking

un·shrived \"+\ *adj* [1*un-* + *shrived*, past part. of *shrive*] **:** UNSHRIVEN

un·shriven \"+\ *adj* [1*un-* + *shriven*, past part. of *shrive*] **:** not shriven

un·shroud \"+\ *vt* [2*un-* + *shroud*] **:** to remove a shroud from **:** EXPOSE, UNCOVER

un·shun·na·ble \ˌən¦shənəbəl\ *adj* [1*un-* + *shun* + *-able*] **:** not to be shunned or evaded **:** INESCAPABLE

1un·shut \ˌən+\ *vb* [ME *unshutten*, fr. 2*un-* + *shutten* to shut] **:** OPEN

2unshut \"\ *adj* [ME, fr. past part. of *unshutten* to unshut] **:** not shut **:** OPEN

un·shutter \ˌən+\ *vt* [2*un-* + *shutter*] **:** to open or remove the shutters of

un·shy \"+\ *adj* **:** not shy ⟨they were naked, ~, beautiful, and full of grace —John Cheever⟩

un·shyly \"+\ *adv* **:** not shyly

un·shyness \"+\ *n* **:** absence of shyness or timidity

un·sicker \"+\ *adj* [ME *unsiker*, fr. 1*un-* + *siker* safe, sicker] *Scot* **:** UNSURE, UNSAFE

un·sifted \"+\ *adj* [1*un-* + *sifted*, past part. of *sift*] **1 :** not passed through a sieve or strainer **2 :** not inspected or scrutinized

1un·sight \"+\ *vt* [2*un-* + *sight*] **:** to prevent from seeing ⟨a gust of wind blew his . . . hat over his face and ~*ed* him so that he dropped the catch —*N.Y. Times*⟩

2unsight \"\ *adj* [1*un-* + *sight*, n.] **:** not sighted or examined ⟨buying the horse ~, unseen⟩

un·sightliness \ˌən+\ *n* **:** the quality or state of being unsightly

un·sightly \"+\ *adj* **:** not sightly **:** not comely ⟨an ~ swamp and dump grounds —*Amer. Guide Series: Minn.*⟩ ⟨a distortion of the back . . . ~ to behold —Herman Melville⟩ **syn** see UGLY

un·signed \"+\ *adj* [1*un-* + *signed*, past part. of *sign*] **:** not signed **:** lacking a signature

un·significant \"+\ *adj* **:** lacking meaning or significance **:** INSIGNIFICANT

un·similar \"+\ *adj* **:** DISSIMILAR — usu. used with *not* ⟨implements . . . not ~ to those still in occasional use —*Economic Geology*⟩ ⟨for reasons not ~ to those cherished —*Current History*⟩

un·sin \"+\ *vt* [2*un-* + *sin*] **:** to annul (a sin) by subsequent action

un·sinew \"+\ *vt* [2*un-* + *sinew*, n.] **:** to deprive of sinews or of strength **:** ENERVATE, ENFEEBLE ⟨seeking every way to ~ the enemy⟩

un·singable \"+\ *adj* **:** not fitted for singing

un·sinkable \"+\ *adj* **:** incapable of being sunk ⟨~ ships⟩

un·sizable \"+\ *adj* **:** of insufficient size or maturity ⟨throwing back all ~ fish he finds in the net⟩

1un·sized \"+\ *adj* **:** not fashioned to a size or to regular sizes ⟨~ pieces of slate⟩

2unsized \"\ *adj* [1*un-* + *sized*, past part. of *size* to treat with size] **:** not treated with size ⟨~ paper⟩

un·skill \ˌən+\ *n* **:** lack of skill or proficiency ⟨his failure could only be a matter of technical ~ —Samuel Alexander⟩

un·skilled \"+\ *adj* **1 :** not skilled or proficient ⟨~ copyists cannot be relied on in matters of punctuation —R.P.Blackmur⟩ ⟨is ~ in parliamentary debate⟩; *specif* **:** not skilled in a specified branch of work **:** lacking technical training ⟨all workers — skilled, semiskilled, and ~ —G.S.Watkins⟩ **2 :** not requiring or involving skill ⟨the book lists all skilled and ~ occupations⟩ **3 :** displaying lack of skill or proficiency ⟨a rude and comparatively ~ poem —Gilbert Highet⟩

unskilled labor *n* **:** labor that requires relatively little or no training or experience for its satisfactory performance; *also* **:** workers or personnel engaged in such labor ⟨an accident attributed to the use of *unskilled labor* —*Current Biog.*⟩

un·skillful \ˌən+\ *adj* [ME *unskilful*, fr. 1*un-* + *skilful*] **1 :** not skillful **:** lacking in skill or proficiency ⟨although a keen mountaineer, I am a pretty ~ one —Wynford Vaughan-Thomas⟩ **2 :** displaying lack of skill or proficiency ⟨an ~ attempt⟩ ⟨~ manner⟩ — **un·skillfully** \"+\ *adv* — **un·skillfulness** \"+\ *n*

un·skimmed \"+\ *adj* [1*un-* + *skimmed*, past part. of *skim*] **1 :** not skimmed ⟨~ milk⟩ **2 :** not covered with a skim coat ⟨~ plaster⟩

un·slacked \"+\ *adj* [1*un-* + *slacked*, past part. of *slack*] **1 :** not slackened or relaxed **2 :** UNSLAKED 1

un·slaked \"+\ *adj* [1*un-* + *slaked*, past part. of *slake*] **1** *of lime* **:** not slaked **2 :** not lessened or brought to an end ⟨~ thirst⟩ ⟨demonstrators went home with their wrath ~ —*Newsweek*⟩ ⟨would leave human longing ~ —F.R.Leavis⟩

un·slate \"+\ *vt* [2*un-* + *slate*] **:** to remove the slate from ⟨the wind can ~ the roof⟩

un·sleeping \"+\ *adj* [1*un-* + *sleeping*, pres. part. of *sleep*] **:** not sleeping or resting **:** WAKEFUL, WATCHFUL, ACTIVE ⟨~ waters of the ocean⟩ ⟨face and eyes of ~ passion —S.H. Adams⟩ ⟨that ~ interest in everything about him —B.J. Hendrick⟩

un·slept \"+\ *adj* [1*un-* + *slept*, past part. of *sleep*] **1 :** not having slept ⟨arose early ~⟩ **2 :** not used for sleeping — usu. used with *in* ⟨his bed is ~ in⟩

un·sling \"+\ *vt* [2*un-* + *sling*] **:** to remove from being slung **:** DETACH, UNHITCH ⟨would ~ the yellow tape from his shoulders and measure . . . the man's waist —Michael McLaverty⟩ ⟨having dismounted he *unslung* his binoculars —J.T. McNish⟩; *specif* **:** to take off the slings of or remove from a sling esp. aboard ship ⟨climbing the rigging to ~ the sail⟩ ⟨lowered the cask into the hold and *unslung* it⟩ ⟨was ordered to ~ his hammock⟩

un·slip \"+\ *vt* [2*un-* + *slip*] **:** to set loose **:** FREE ⟨~*s* the yelping pack of hounds⟩

un·slotted \ˌən+\ *adj* **:** not slotted

un·sluice \"+\ *vt* [2*un-* + *sluice*] *archaic* **:** to open the sluice of **:** let flow **:** SLUICE

un·smart \"+\ *adj* **:** not smart ⟨is a young accountant — hard up, shy, ~ —R.P.Fleming⟩

un·smeared \"+\ *adj* [1*un-* + *smeared*, past part. of *smear*] **:** not smeared

un·smiling \"+\ *adj* [1*un-* + *smiling*, pres. part. of *smile*] **:** not smiling — **un·smilingly** \"+\ *adv*

un·smirched \"+\ *adj* [1*un-* + *smirched*, past part. of *smirch*] **:** not smirched

un·smoked \"+\ *adj* [1*un-* + *smoked*, past part. of *smoke*] **1 :** not smoked or exposed to smoke ⟨there is no industry here and that's . . . why it's so calm, so ~ and unsoiled —Richard Joseph⟩ ⟨~ bacon⟩ **2 :** not used up by smoking ⟨leaving his cigar ~ in the ashtray⟩

1un·smooth \"+\ *adj* [1*un-* + *smooth*, adj.] **:** not smooth **:** ROUGH, HARSH ⟨strokes his ~ face⟩ ⟨awkward and ~ writing⟩ — **un·smoothly** \"+\ *adv*

2unsmooth \"\ *vt* [2*un-* + *smooth*] **:** to make unsmooth or uneven **:** ROUGHEN ⟨the passing ship ~*s* the water⟩

un·smoothed \ˌən+\ *adj* [1*un-* + *smoothed*, past part. of *smooth*] **:** not smoothed

un·snap \"+\ *vt* [2*un-* + *snap*] **:** to loosen or free by or as if by undoing a snap **:** UNDO, RELEASE ⟨the groom ~*s* the halter⟩ ⟨the great beast ~*s* its jaws⟩

un·snarl \"+\ *vt* [2*un-* + *snarl*] **:** to disentangle a snarl in ⟨helping ~ the yarn⟩ ⟨worked hard to ~ the company's affairs⟩

un·snuffed \"+\ *adj* [1*un-* + *snuffed*, past part. of *snuff*] **:** not snuffed

un·sober \"+\ *adj* [ME *unsober*, *unsobre*, fr. 1*un-* + *sober*, *sobre* sober] **:** not sober: as **a** *obs* **:** marked by extremes **:** IMMODERATE, EXCESSIVE **b :** not serious or sober-minded **:** undisciplined in conduct or thought ⟨an ~, temperamental person⟩ **c :** given to drinking **:** INTOXICATED ⟨comes often ~ from the taproom⟩ — **un·soberly** \"+\ *adv*

un·sociability \"+\ *n* **:** the quality or state of being unsociable

un·sociable \"+\ *adj* **1 a :** not inclined to society or conversation **:** SOLITARY, RESERVED, WITHDRAWN ⟨is generally ~ except with intimate friends⟩ ⟨my ~ nature . . . shy, awkward, reserved —Havelock Ellis⟩ **b :** marked by or resulting from unsociability ⟨~ behavior⟩ ⟨~ demeanor⟩ **2** *archaic* **:** not mutually accordant **:** INCOMPATIBLE, DISCORDANT **3 :** lacking or preventing social intercourse ⟨living an ~ distance apart⟩ — **un·sociableness** \"+\ *n* — **un·sociably** \"+\ *adv*

un·social \"+\ *adj* **1 a :** not social **:** not seeking or given to association ⟨as Christians, they are ~, since they find themselves unable to go along with any . . . organized groups —Katharine F. Gerould⟩ **b :** marked by or resulting from an unsocial quality or state ⟨the ~ disposition to neglect one's neighbor's appreciations —W.C.Brownell⟩ ⟨his desire to escape notoriety . . . did not denote an ~ nature —Caroline Ticknor⟩ **2 :** ANTISOCIAL 1b ⟨hoarding of money, lending it on interest, cornering of foodstuffs — all these ~ tendencies are sternly prohibited —P.G.Waris⟩ ⟨a margin . . . such as would make for ~ profits and induce to a larger capital formation than might be proper —S.E.Harris⟩ — **un·socially** \"+\ *adv*

un·socialized \"+\ *adj* [1*un-* + *socialized*, past part. of *socialize*] **:** not socialized; *specif* **:** not sufficiently socialized to adjust to societal norms ⟨~ and aggressive delinquents⟩

un·socket \"+\ *vt* [2*un-* + *socket*] **:** to loose or take from a socket ⟨a severe twist can ~ the bone⟩

un·sodden \ˌən+\ *adj* **:** not sodden; *esp* **:** not wet or soaked **:** not weighed down by moisture ⟨the wet leaves are rendered ~ by the drying wind⟩

un·soil \"+\ *vb* [2*un-* + *soil*, n.] *vt* **:** to strip the top layer of soil or mold from ~ *vi* **:** to remove the soil (as in opening a deposit of clay for brickmaking)

un·soiled \"+\ *adj* [1*un-* + *soiled*, past part. of *soil*] **:** not soiled or dirtied ⟨an ~ towel⟩ **:** not sullied ⟨his ~ name⟩

un·sold \"+\ *adj* [ME, fr. 1*un-* + *sold*, past part. of *sellen* to sell] **:** not sold; *esp* **:** not disposed of by purchase

un·solder \"+\ *vt* [2*un-* + *solder*] **:** to separate or disunite (something that has been soldered) **:** DIVIDE, SUNDER ⟨~ all electrical connections⟩ ⟨nothing would ~ fraternal bonds⟩

un·soldierly \"+\ *adj* **:** not characteristic of or befitting a soldier ⟨~ maneuver⟩ ⟨~ appearance and conduct⟩

un·solemn \"+\ *adj* **1 :** not solemn **:** not solemnized by formalities **2** *of a will* **:** lacking the name of an executor
un·solicited \"+\ *adj* [1*un-* + *solicited*, past part. of *solicit*] **:** not solicited: as **a :** not subjected to solicitation ⟨the old pastor sent for him and ~ granted him the request —Willa Cather⟩ ⟨half the block is as yet ~ for contributions⟩ **b :** not asked for **:** granted or given without request ⟨his early adherence to the principles . . . brought him an ~ nomination and election to Congress —J.D.Hicks⟩ ⟨some information . . . was obtained ~ from anonymous sources —W.E.Welmers⟩
un·solicitous \"+\ *adj* **:** not solicitous; *esp* **:** not manifesting anxiety or concern ⟨is ~ about the welfare of others⟩
un·solid \"+\ *adj* **1 :** not solid ⟨~ materials crumble⟩ **2 :** lacking a sound or substantial basis ⟨an ~ argument⟩ ⟨~ thinking⟩
un·solidified \ˌən+\ *adj* [1*un-* + *solidified*, past part. of *solidify*] **:** not solidified
un·soluble \"+\ *adj* **:** INSOLUBLE
un·solvable \"+\ *adj* **:** not solvable **:** INSOLUBLE ⟨public finance . . . had long presented problems ~ or at least unsolved —C.L.Jones⟩
un·solved \"+\ *adj* [1*un-* + *solved*, past part. of *solve*] **:** not solved ⟨many crimes remain ~⟩ ⟨an ~ *x* in all equations —Ralph Linton⟩ ⟨~ problems⟩
un·son \"+\ *vt* **unsonned; unsonned; unsonning; unsons** [2*un-* + *son*] **:** to dispossess of the station or character of a son ⟨denied his heritage and took steps to ~ himself⟩
un·sonsy \"+\ *adj* **1** *dial Brit* **:** boding or causing misfortune **:** UNLUCKY, FATAL **2** *dial Brit* **:** UNPLEASANT, DISAGREEABLE
un·sophisticate \"+\ *adj* **:** UNSOPHISTICATED ⟨a simple, genuine ~ nature⟩
un·sophisticated \"+\ *adj* **:** not sophisticated: as **a** (1) **:** not altered in substance **:** UNADULTERATED (2) **:** not changed or corrupted **:** GENUINE ⟨pure loyalty ~ by hypocrisy⟩ **b** (1) **:** not worldly-wise **:** lacking sophistication **:** NAÏVE, ARTLESS, INGENUOUS ⟨~ Indians who would barter bales of furs for a handful of trinkets —R.A.Billington⟩ ⟨has scaled the Hollywood heights but remains essentially ~, untouched by it all —Donald Foley⟩ ⟨were either too ~ or too honest to promise . . . more than they thought they could reasonably deliver —*Newsweek*⟩ (2) **:** lacking adornment or complexity of structure **:** PLAIN, SIMPLE ⟨the earliest buildings in Philadelphia and its vicinity were . . . ~ with gable or sometimes gambrel roofs —*Amer. Guide Series: Pa.*⟩ ⟨his rhythms are basic, regular, and generally ~ —Harold Rogers⟩ ⟨is dealing with a relatively ~ problem⟩ **syn** see NATURAL
un·sophistication \"+\ *n* **:** a lack of or freedom from sophistication
un·sordid \"+\ *adj* **:** not sordid
un·sorted \"+\ *adj* [1*un-* + *sorted*, past part. of *sort*] **1 :** not sorted or classified ⟨a lot of ~ goods⟩ **2** *obs* **:** not well selected or chosen
un·sought \ˌən+\ *adj* [ME *unsouht, unsought*, fr. 1*un-* + *souht, sought*, past part. of *seken* to seek] **:** not sought: as **a :** not searched for or sought out ⟨kindness receives ~ compliments⟩ **b :** not acquired by effort or search ⟨help ~ may sometimes come when all seeking has failed⟩ **c :** not requested **:** UNSOLICITED ⟨reads the mind's desires and grants favors ~⟩ **d** *obs* **:** not explored or examined
un·soul \"+\ *vt* [2*un-* + *soul*] **:** to deprive of soul or spirit
un·sound \"+\ *adj* [ME, fr. 1*un-* + *sound*] **:** not sound: as **a** (1) **:** not physically healthy or whole **:** UNHEALTHY, DISEASED ⟨an ~ limb⟩ ⟨the teeth were ~⟩; *esp* **:** having a disease, abnormality, or defect of such a nature or to such a degree as to impair usefulness — used esp. of a horse (2) **:** not in good or edible condition **:** STALE, ROTTEN ⟨poultry in a state of decomposition must be regarded as ~ —C.R.A.Martin⟩ ⟨all ~ produce is refused at the market⟩ (3) **:** not mentally sound or normal **:** not wholly or consistently sane ⟨is said to be of ~ mind⟩ **b :** not morally sound **:** CORRUPT, EVIL ⟨a strong nation cannot be built of an ~ people⟩ **c :** not firmly made, placed, or fixed ⟨if pure copper . . . was cast thinly, the ingots proved ~ —John Craig⟩ ⟨in detail design it was fundamentally ~ —O.S.Nock⟩ **d** (1) **:** not based on logical reasoning or established fact **:** FALSE, INVALID, SPECIOUS ⟨it is doubtless ~ to argue that what can be done by the government in time of war can also be effected in time of peace —M.R.Cohen⟩ ⟨contained exaggerated statements and ~ prophecies —W.O.Lynch⟩ (2) **:** not based on proven practice, established procedure, or practical knowledge ⟨the economic collapse . . . brought on by ~ banking and wild speculation in public utilities —*Amer. Guide Series: Nev.*⟩ ⟨the present arrangement is obviously a precarious and ~ one, dangerous to the long-term stability of the . . . area —G.F.Kennan⟩ — **un·soundly** \"+\ *adv*
un·soundable \"+\ *adj* [1*un-* + *sound* + *-able*] **:** not capable of being sounded or fathomed ⟨a silence ~ —Thomas Carlyle⟩ ⟨~ depths⟩
1un·sounded \"+\ *adj* [1*un-* + *sounded*, past part. of *sound*] **:** not pronounced or spoken **:** not made to sound ⟨the words stopped at her lips ~⟩ ⟨in French certain letters are often ~⟩
2unsounded \"\ *adj* [1*un-* + *sounded*, past part. of *sound* to fathom] **:** not fathomed or probed ⟨remote and ~ caverns —S.A.Coblentz⟩ ⟨the ~ depths of human misery⟩
un·soundness \ˌən+\ *n* **1 :** the quality or state of being unsound ⟨recognize the substantial ~ of certain conclusions —M.R.Cohen⟩ ⟨the ~ of the island's economy⟩ **2 :** something (as a disease) that causes one to be unsound ⟨heaves is an ~ in the horse⟩
un·soured \"+\ *adj* [1*un-* + *soured*, past part. of *sour*] **:** not soured ⟨giving him the taste of opulence ~ by satiety —Norman Lewis⟩
un·sown \"+\ *adj* [1*un-* + *sown*, past part. of *sow*] **1 :** not sown in the ground ⟨it is so cold this year that the seed is still ~⟩ **2 :** not planted with seed ⟨farmland . . . still ~ —Benjamin Waife⟩
un·spaced \"+\ *adj* **:** not spaced
un·spar \"+\ *vt* [ME *unsperren*, fr. 2*un-* + *sperren* to bolt, spar] *archaic* **:** to take the spars, stakes, or bars from **:** OPEN
un·sparing \"+\ *adj* [1*un-* + *sparing*, pres. part. of *spare*] **1 :** not merciful or forbearing **:** HARD, RUTHLESS ⟨portrait, at once ~ and compassionate —Coleman Rosenberger⟩ ⟨both artists have been ~ with their social comments —*Amer. Guide Series: Minn.*⟩ ⟨become an ~ critic of himself and of others —Walter Silz⟩ **2 :** not frugal **:** LIBERAL, PROFUSE ⟨worked and expected others to work with the same ~ energy —Roger Cary⟩ ⟨has periods of niggardliness followed by impulses of ~ generosity⟩
un·sparingly \"+\ *adv* **:** in an unsparing manner ⟨drove himself ~ and often beyond his strength —J.C.Fitzpatrick⟩ ⟨~ portrayed the money-grabbing society of the Gilded Age —*Amer. Guide Series: N.Y.*⟩ ⟨his book . . . is ~ comprehensive —F.P.Rous⟩
unspeak *vt* [2*un-* + *speak*] *obs* **:** UNSAY
un·speakable \ˌən+\ *adj* [ME *unspekeable*, fr. 1*un-* + *speken* to speak + *-able*] **1 a :** not capable of being verbally expressed **:** UNUTTERABLE, INDESCRIBABLE ⟨watching the ~ beauties of that wondrous bay —Martha Kean⟩ ⟨with ~ delight . . . took and divided the gifts —Francis Parkman⟩ ⟨all creative work starts as a feeling . . . or some other ~ affective state —A.H.S.Korzybski⟩ **b :** indescribably objectionable or hateful ⟨that ~ odor came sweeping into the room, wave upon wave of the breath of all corruption —Arthur Grimble⟩ ⟨so likable as a man, so ~ as a politician —Francis Biddle⟩ ⟨those poor painted females . . . plied their ~ trade —D.B.Chidsey⟩ **2 :** that may not or cannot be uttered or spoken ⟨oddest of all are the bawdy thoughts that come into one's head — the ~ words —L.P.Smith⟩ ⟨our job to see that a speaker does not have to contend with ~ collections of consonants —Rosemary Jellis⟩
un·speakableness \"+\ *n* **:** the quality or state of being unspeakable
un·speakably \"+\ *adv* **:** UNUTTERABLY, INEXPRESSIBLY ⟨~ glad⟩ ⟨~ obnoxious⟩
un·specialized \"+\ *adj* **:** not specialized; *esp* **:** not adapted or modified in form or structure for a particular purpose or function **:** GENERALIZED
un·specific \"+\ *adj* **:** not specific ⟨the statement of his hero's disillusionment is ~ —H.E.Clurman⟩ ⟨is deterred . . . by an ~ dread which is not placed in any time sequence of rewards and punishments —Margaret Mead⟩

un·specificness \"+\ *n* **:** the quality or state of being unspecific
un·specified \"+\ *adj* [1*un-* + *specified*, past part. of *specify*] **:** not specified
un·spectacular \"+\ *adj* **:** not spectacular ⟨studious and ~ . . . one of labor's ablest parliamentarians —*Current Biog.*⟩ ⟨does well an ~ but necessary task⟩ — **un·spectacularly** \"+\ *adv*
un·speculative \"+\ *adj* **:** not speculative: as **a :** not pondering or given to thought ⟨exhibits a facile and ~ mind⟩ **b :** not risky **:** of a conservative nature **:** SOUND ⟨containing a large number of bonds and blue-chip stocks, his investment portfolio is clearly ~⟩
un·sped \"+\ *adj* [ME, fr. 1*un-* + *sped*, past part. of *speden* to succeed — more at SPEED] **:** not performed or accomplished ⟨returns with his mission ~⟩
un·spell \ˌən+\ *vt* [2*un-* + *spell*, n.] **:** to break the power of or release from a spell
un·spent \"+\ *adj* [ME, fr. 1*un-* + *spent*] **1 :** not spent or used **:** UNEXPENDED ⟨a corresponding amount of income will be left ~ —W.M.Dacey⟩ **2 :** not consumed or used up ⟨continuing on with ~ momentum⟩
un·sphere \"+\ *vt* [2*un-* + *sphere*] **:** to remove (as a planet) from its sphere **:** DISPLACE
un·spike \"+\ *vt* [2*un-* + *spike*, n.] **:** to remove a spike from (as the vent of a cannon)
un·spin \"+\ *vt* [2*un-* + *spin*] **:** UNTWIST
unspirited *adj* [1*un-* + *spirited*, adj.] *obs* **:** lacking in spirit **:** SPIRITLESS
un·spiritual \ˌən+\ *adj* **:** not spiritual ⟨the ~ man does not welcome the teachings of the Spirit of God —W.F.Howard⟩ — **un·spiritually** \"+\ *adv* — **un·spiritualness** \"+\ *n*
un·spiritualize \"+\ *vt* [2*un-* + *spiritualize*] **:** to remove spiritual qualities from ⟨materialism can ~ man⟩
un·spit \"+\ *vt* [2*un-* + *spit*] *archaic* **:** to take or release from a spit
un·split \"+\ *adj* **:** not split or divided
un·spoiled \"+\ *adj* [1*un-* + *spoiled*, past part. of *spoil*] **1 a :** not pillaged or plundered ⟨the land is ~ by war⟩ **b :** not spoiled or decayed **2 a :** not worn or damaged ⟨stamps . . . in perfect condition with the gum ~ —Barbara Hooper⟩ **b :** not marred or altered from a natural or original state esp. by industry, commerce, or tourism ⟨a paradise of color and silence which has somehow remained ~ and uncommercialized —Guy Priest⟩ ⟨primitive, ~, breathtaking in the ruggedness of its mountains and the simplicity of its people —T.H.Fielding⟩ ⟨magnificent coast . . . is ~ by industry —L.D.Stamp⟩ **c :** not deteriorated or impaired in character or disposition by excessive pampering or indulgence or contaminating influences ⟨thanks to the sturdy simplicity of their parents, quite ~ —Nevil Shute⟩ ⟨liked each other at once, both being good-humored . . . and ~ by fame —*Irish Digest*⟩
un·spoken \"+\ *adj* [ME, fr. 1*un-* + *spoken*, past part. of *speken* to speak] **1 :** not spoken or uttered **:** TACIT, UNEXPRESSED ⟨the ~ conclusion is obvious —M.W.Straight⟩ ⟨by some sort of ~ agreement, they patronize a less pretentious shop in the opposite direction —Cabell Phillips⟩ **2 :** not spoken to or addressed — often used with *to* ⟨sitting for hours ~ to⟩ **3 :** not speaking **:** SILENT
un·sporting \"+\ *adj* **:** not sportsmanlike ⟨had beaten . . . at tennis with a nasty, ~ serve —Sinclair Lewis⟩
un·sportsmanlike \"+\ *adj* [1*un-* + *sportsman* + *like*] **:** not sportsmanlike **:** not characteristic of or exhibiting good sportsmanship ⟨to shoot down a bear . . . when he is off his guard is too ~ —A.W.Long⟩
un·spotted \"+\ *adj* [ME, fr. 1*un-* + *spotted*] **:** not spotted **:** free from spot or stain; *esp* **:** free from moral stain ⟨~ by such alleged vices as drinking, smoking, card playing —F.L.Allen⟩ — **un·spottedness** \"+\ *n*
un·spring \"+\ *vt* [2*un-* + *spring*, n.] **:** to loosen or release by or as if by pressing a spring
un·sprung \"+\ *adj* [1*un-* + *sprung*, past part. of *spring*] **:** not sprung; *esp* **:** not equipped with springs ⟨~ parts and units . . . depend entirely upon the resiliency of the tires for protection from road shock —Joseph Heitner⟩
unsprung weight *n* **:** weight (as of a vehicle) not supported by springs
un·spun \ˌən+\ *adj* [1*un-* + *spun*, past part. of *spin*] **:** not spun
un·stability \"+\ *n* [ME *unstabilite*, fr. 1*un-* + *stabilite* stability] **:** INSTABILITY
un·stable \"+\ *adj* [ME, fr. 1*un-* + *stable*] **:** not stable: as **a** (1) **:** not firm or fixed in one place **:** apt to move **:** MOVABLE ⟨snow as ~ as aspic trembled on the steep slope —R.L.Neuberger⟩ ⟨the ~ shifting sands of the desert⟩ (2) **:** lacking steadiness **:** apt to sway or fall ⟨the tower proved to be ~ in a high wind⟩ ⟨the bird flutters on its ~ perch⟩ (3) **:** not steady in movement **:** IRREGULAR ⟨felt the ~ tripping beat of her heart⟩ (4) **:** not firm or substantial **:** WEAK, INSECURE ⟨the young earth was yet ~, the molten forces within were constantly looking for escape —W.E.Swinton⟩ ⟨the road may become so ~ as to compel the imposition of a speed limit —O.S.Nock⟩ ⟨built on an ~ foundation⟩ **b** (1) **:** wavering in purpose or intent **:** VACILLATING ⟨an ~ and uneasy class of yeomen —S.E.Morison & H.S.Commager⟩ ⟨his rather ~ religious convictions —H.E.Starr⟩ ⟨woman's love . . . is volatile, insoluble, ~ —Marcia Anderson⟩ (2) **:** exhibiting or characterized by emotional instability ⟨an ~ temperament —Rex Ingamells⟩ ⟨the ~ prisoners . . . placed in the vague but convenient category of psychopaths —A.H.MacCormick⟩ ⟨had brought an inherently ~ nature to the point of mental and emotional collapse —E.J.Simmons⟩ **c** (1) **:** variable in character or condition **:** liable to change or alteration **:** CHANGEABLE ⟨an ~ world economy . . . subjected to periods of wars, inflation, and depression —*Farmer's Weekly (So. Africa)*⟩ ⟨the wind might change; for it is an ~ world —Charles Kingsley⟩ ⟨~ climate⟩ ⟨~ relationship⟩ (2) **:** readily decomposing or changing otherwise in chemical composition or biological activity — compare LABILE 3, SENSITIVE 4e (3) **:** readily changing in physical state or properties ⟨~ emulsions tend to separate into layers⟩ (4) **:** spontaneously radioactive **syn** see INCONSTANT
unstable equilibrium *n* **:** a state of equilibrium of a body (as a pendulum standing directly upward from its point of support) such that when the body is slightly displaced it departs further from the original position — compare STABLE EQUILIBRIUM
un·stableness \ˌən+\ *n* [ME *unstablenesse*, fr. *unstable* + *-nesse* -ness] **:** the quality or state of being unstable
unstable oscillation *n* **:** an oscillation (as of an airplane) whose amplitude increases continuously until an altitude is reached from which there is no tendency to return toward the original altitude, the motion becoming a steady divergence — compare STABLE OSCILLATION
un·stably \ˌən+\ *adv* [ME, partly fr. 1*un-* + *stably* & partly fr. *unstable* + *-ly*] **:** in an unstable manner **:** without steadiness
un·stack \"+\ *vt* [2*un-* + *stack*] **:** to remove from a stack or pile
un·staid \"+\ *adj* **1** *obs* **:** not demure, reserved, or well ordered in behavior **2 :** UNCONTROLLED, UNRESTRAINED ⟨~ thoughts⟩ ⟨~ delights⟩ **3** *obs* **:** CHANGEABLE, VACILLATING, UNSTABLE
un·stained \"+\ *adj* **1 :** not stained or discolored **:** not spotted ⟨keeps his clothing ~⟩ **2 :** not morally blemished or stained **:** UNSULLIED ⟨his thoughts were ~ with selfishness and lust —John Steinbeck⟩ ⟨felt a wild longing for the ~ purity of his boyhood —Oscar Wilde⟩
un·stalked \"+\ *adj* **:** lacking a stalk or stem
un·stamped \"+\ *adj* [1*un-* + *stamped*, past part. of *stamp*] **:** not stamped with an official device or impression; *also* **:** not affixed with an official stamp or adhesive label to certify payment of a tax or duty
un·starred \"+\ *adj* **:** not starred; *esp* **:** not marked or decorated with a star or asterisk
un·state \"+\ *vt* [2*un-* + *state*] **:** to deprive of state dignity or rank ⟨Caesar will ~ his happiness —Shak.⟩
un·stated \"+\ *adj* [1*un-* + *stated*, adj.] **:** not stated or set forth ⟨his action is clear but his reason remains ~⟩
un·statesmanlike \"+\ *adj* [1*un-* + *statesman* + *like*] **:** not statesmanlike ⟨~ procedure⟩
un·statutable \"+\ *adj* [1*un-* + *statute* + *-able*] **:** contrary to or not according with a statute ⟨an ~ procedure⟩

1un·stayed \"+\ *adj* [1*un-* + *stayed*, past part. of *stay* to hinder] **:** not hindered or checked **:** UNIMPEDED ⟨goes his way ~ by any minor obstacles⟩
2unstayed \"\ *adj* [1*un-* + *stayed*, past part. of *stay* to support] **:** not steadfast **:** not firmly supported ⟨~ in his weakness except by faith⟩
3unstayed \"\ *adj* [1*un-* + *stay*, n. + *-ed*] **:** not fastened or secured with stays ⟨the bowsprit was a makeshift sort of spar, crooked and ~ —Alan Moore⟩
unstdy *abbr* unsteady
un·steadfast \ˌən+\ *adj* [ME *unstedefast*, fr. 1*un-* + *stedefast* steadfast] **1 :** not steadfast in thought or action **:** VACILLATING ⟨an ~ backslider⟩ ⟨a man of ~ heart⟩ **2 :** UNSTABLE a(1) ⟨the ~ waters of the ocean⟩ — **un·steadfastness** \"+\ *n*
un·steadily \"+\ *adv* [1*un-* + *steadily*] **:** in an unsteady or unstable manner
un·steadiness \"+\ *n* **:** the quality or state of being unsteady
1un·steady \"+\ *vt* [2*un-* + *steady*] **:** to make unsteady ⟨joy *unsteadies* his voice⟩ ⟨the drop in ammunition *unsteadied* the artillery action⟩ ⟨he was *unsteadied* by the sudden turn of events⟩
2unsteady \"\ *adj* [1*un-* + *steady*, adj.] **:** not steady: as **a :** not firm or solid **:** not fixed in position ⟨the man's hand was ~ as he poured the wine —George Meredith⟩ ⟨climbing carefully up the ~ ladder⟩ **b :** UNSTABLE b(1) ⟨we were excited and ~ and . . . required time to collect themselves —J.A. Froude⟩ ⟨his mind becomes ~ in a crisis⟩ **c :** marked by change or fluctuation **:** CHANGEABLE ⟨a new and yet ~ world of discovery, hope, failure, glory —H.A.L.Craig⟩ ⟨~ business conditions⟩ ⟨this ~ time⟩ **d :** not uniform or even **:** IRREGULAR ⟨the gas jet . . . threw an ~ light on her features —Ellen Glasgow⟩ ⟨the lady feels her pulse's beat ~ —Elinor Wylie⟩ ⟨a decade . . . of somewhat ~ growth —F.A.Ogg & Harold Zink⟩
un·steel \ˌən+\ *vt* [2*un-* + *steel*] **:** to make soft or penetrable **:** DISARM ⟨the gentle appeal ~*ed* his heart⟩
un·stemmed \"+\ *adj* **:** not having the stem removed
un·step \"+\ *vt* [2*un-* + *step*] **:** to remove (a mast) from its step ⟨the canvas came down with a rush, and the mast was *unstepped* —Luis Marden⟩
un·sterilized \"+\ *adj* [1*un-* + *sterilized*, past part. of *sterilize*] **:** not sterilized ⟨~ milk⟩
un·stick \"+\ *vt* [2*un-* + *stick*] **:** to cause to draw apart **:** RELEASE, UNFASTEN
un·stiffen \"+\ *vt* [2*un-* + *stiffen*] **:** to remove the stiffness from **:** make limp or flexible ⟨the penetrating heat ~*s* his joints⟩ ⟨pragmatism ~*s* all our theories, limbers them up and sets each one at work —William James⟩
un·stimulating \"+\ *adj* [1*un-* + *stimulating*, pres. part. of *stimulate*] **:** not stimulating
un·sting \"+\ *vt* [2*un-* + *sting*] **:** to remove the sting of
un·stinted \"+\ *adj* [ME, fr. 1*un-* + *stinted*, past part. of *stinten* to stint] **:** not restrained or restricted **:** generously or freely given ⟨his bravery and resourcefulness won him . . . ~ praise —E.M.Coulter⟩ ⟨the deep civic convictions, the integrity, and the ~ devotion —C.T.Lanham⟩ — **un·stintedly** \"+\ *adv*
un·stinting \"+\ *adj* [1*un-* + *stinting*, pres. part. of *stint*] **:** not restricting or holding back **:** giving or contributing freely or generously ⟨teachers who sent in reports on his model lessons were ~ in their praise —Robertson Davies⟩ ⟨called for ~ support of the United Nations —I.G.Blake⟩ ⟨gave his unqualified backing to . . . ~ aid to Britain —Roscoe Drummond⟩ — **un·stintingly** \"+\ *adv*
un·stirred \ˌən+\ *adj* [ME *unstired*, fr. 1*un-* + *stired*, past part. of *stiren* to stir] **:** not stirred
un·stitch \"+\ *vt* [2*un-* + *stitch*] **:** to take out the stitches of; *also* **:** to undo or separate by removing the stitches
un·stock \"+\ *vt* [2*un-* + *stock*] **:** to remove the stock from (as a gun)
un·stocked \"+\ *adj* [ME *unstokked*, fr. 1*un-* + *stokked*, past part. of *stokken* to stock] **:** not stocked: as **a :** not equipped or provided with a stock ⟨~ rifle⟩ **b :** not furnished with animals, fish, or livestock ⟨~ woods⟩ ⟨~ pond⟩
un·stop \"+\ *vt* [ME *unstoppen*, fr. 2*un-* + *stoppen* to stop] **1 :** to free from any obstruction **:** OPEN **2 :** to remove the stopper or plug from (as a bottle, cask, or vent) ⟨~ this flask —William Alfred⟩
un·stoppable \"+\ *adj* [1*un-* + *stop* + *-able*] **:** not stoppable ⟨as ~ as the wind —Han Suyin⟩ ⟨at his present pace, he may just be ~ —*Newsweek*⟩ — **un·stop·pa·bly** \-blē, -li\ *adv*
un·stopped \ˌən+\ *adj* [ME, fr. 1*un-* + *stopped*] **:** not stopped: as **a :** not stoppered or plugged **:** not closed ⟨an ~ rabbit hole⟩ **b :** not prevented or hindered ⟨is coming on ~⟩ **c** *of a consonant* **:** OPEN, CONTINUANT **d :** RUN-ON ⟨~ lines often occur in his verse⟩
un·stopper \"+\ *vt* [2*un-* + *stopper*] **:** to remove the stopper from **:** UNSTOP ⟨~*ed* the decanter —William Faulkner⟩ ⟨will ~ the economy so that the forces for full employment . . . are freed —*Time*⟩
un·storied \"+\ *adj* **:** not having a history **:** not told or celebrated in story ⟨the land . . . still ~ —Robert Frost⟩
un·stow \"+\ *vt* [2*un-* + *stow*] **:** to empty of cargo or contents **:** UNLOAD ⟨~ the ship⟩ ⟨~ the goods in the hold⟩ ⟨began to ~ the panniers —Henry Green⟩
un·strain \"+\ *vt* [2*un-* + *strain*] **:** to relieve from strain
un·strained \"+\ *adj* [ME *unstreined*, fr. 1*un-* + *streined*, past part. of *streinen* to strain] **:** not strained: as **a :** not placed under a strain **:** not stretched ⟨the campaign would not leave party loyalties ~⟩ ⟨~ iron⟩ **b :** not forced or resulting from undue effort ⟨his playing is facile and ~⟩ **c :** not put through a strainer ⟨~ juice⟩ **:** not cleared or purified by straining ⟨~ oil⟩
un·strap \"+\ *vt* [2*un-* + *strap*] **:** to unfasten, remove, or loose a strap from ⟨~*s* the trunk⟩ ⟨the hikers ~ their packs⟩ ⟨the cowboy ~*s* his gun belt⟩
un·stratified \"+\ *adj* [1*un-* + *stratified*, past part. of *stratify*] **:** not stratified; *specif* **:** not deposited in layers ⟨glacial till is ~⟩
un·strengthen \"+\ *vt* [2*un-* + *strengthen*] **:** to make weak **:** WEAKEN
un·stress \"+\ *n* **:** a syllable having relatively weak stress or lacking in phonetic prominence
un·stressed \"+\ *adj* [1*un-* + *stressed*, past part. of *stress*] **:** not stressed or emphasized; *specif* **:** not bearing a stress or accent
un·stretch \ˌən+\ *vb* [2*un-* + *stretch*] *vt* **:** to release the tension of **:** RELAX ~ *vi* **:** SLACKEN
un·string \"+\ *vt* [2*un-* + *string*] **1 a :** to loosen or remove the string from (a bow or musical instrument) **b :** to untie the strings of (a purse) **2 :** to remove from a string ⟨~*s* the beads⟩ **3 :** to make weak, disordered, or unstable ⟨the news *unstrung* his nerves⟩ ⟨getting married ~*s* some men —Owen Wister⟩
un·striped \"+\ *adj* **:** not striped or striated ⟨~ muscle⟩
un·stripped \"+\ *adj* [1*un-* + *stripped*, past part. of *strip*] **:** not stripped **:** not detached by stripping
un·structured \"+\ *adj* **:** lacking structure or organization: as **a** (1) **:** not having an integrated system or hierarchy of the roles, functions, or statuses of an organized society ⟨the situation was ~, for there were no persons vested with authority by virtue of station or public office —*Amer. Anthropologist*⟩ ⟨were experiencing a permissive and relatively ~ situation that included strong demands for individual participation —G.E. Swanson⟩ ⟨in a neighborhood gang . . . with a relatively ~ system —*Jour. of Social Issues*⟩ (2) **:** not forming a part of such an integrated system or hierarchy ⟨the position of the poet is ~ . . . in our society —*Report: Harvard Laboratory of Social Relations*⟩ ⟨the defeated candidate has an extremely ~ status —R.M.Goldman⟩ **b :** not formally organized into a set or conventional pattern **:** AMBIGUOUS ⟨questions on the effect of price and flavor were ~ . . . purposely vague to encourage respondents to give an answer —*Australian Jour. of Dairy Tech.*⟩ ⟨in an ~ or new situation the person feels insecure because the psychological directions are not defined —Kurt Lewin⟩ ⟨an ~ situation . . . with no frame of reference except such as may be created by the subject himself —W.S.Ray⟩
un·strung \"+\ *adj* [1*un-* + *strung*, past part. of *string*] **1 :** having the strings loosened or detached **2 :** nervously relaxed or weakened **:** UNNERVED, DISCOMPOSED ⟨the nerves of the men were much ~ —H.A.Chippendale⟩ ⟨felt weak, ~, incapable of rational effort —Ellen Glasgow⟩

un·stuck \"+\ *adj* [*1un-* + *stuck*, past part. of *stick*] **1 :** released from being glued, fastened, or bound ⟨glancing through the photographs one day . . . she had found that one beginning to come ~ —Elizabeth Taylor⟩ ⟨the gears locked in second and would not come ~ —Herbert Passin⟩ **2 :** brought to a state of disorder, disorganization, or incoherence ⟨the government's stabilization program . . . has recently shown signs of coming ~ —*N.Y. Times*⟩ ⟨price programs became ~ because little grain was available —*Newsweek*⟩ ⟨projects were always coming ~ at the last minute —Bruce Catton⟩

un·studied \"+\ *adj* [ME, fr. *1un-* + *studied*, past part. of *studien* to study] **1** *obs* **:** not studied or contemplated **:** NEGLECTED **2 :** lacking knowledge gained by study often in a specified field **:** UNLEARNED ⟨is ~ in Latin as he is in many other matters⟩ **3 :** not forced or unnecessarily elaborated by study or artifice: as **a :** UNAFFECTED, NATURAL ⟨the clusters of houses set beside these winding lanes have a simple ~ charm —*Amer. Guide Series: Mich.*⟩ ⟨was possessed of a nervous temperament and his gestures were rapid and ~ —Marie B. Owen⟩ **b :** CASUAL, OFFHAND, IMPROMPTU ⟨an air of ~ spontaneous utterance is apt to be as painstakingly achieved as any other quality in the poetic fiction —Susanne K. Langer⟩

un·studious \"+\ *adj* **:** not studious

un·stuff \"+\ *vt* [*2un-* + *stuff*] **:** to take the stuffing from or out of

un·stylish \"+\ *adj* **:** not stylish ⟨wearing ~ clothes⟩ — **un·stylishly** \"+\ *adv* — **un·stylishness** \"+\ *n*

un·subdued \ˌən+\ *adj* **:** not subdued — **un·subduedness** \"+\ *n*

un·suberized \"+\ *adj* [*1un-* + *suberized*, past part. of *suberize*] **:** not corky **:** not converted into phellem

un·subsidized \"+\ *adj* [*1un-* + *subsidized*, past part. of *subsidize*] **:** not subsidized ⟨the shipping industry . . . is not only privately owned and managed but ~ —E.K.Lindley⟩

un·substantial \"+\ *adj* [ME, fr. *1un-* + *substantial*] **:** not substantial: as **a :** lacking a basis in fact ⟨an ~ argument⟩ ⟨an ~ hope⟩ ⟨~ speculation⟩ **b :** not having matter or substance **:** VISIONARY, UNREAL ⟨an ~ phantom . . . luring men away from the safety and ease —Bertrand Russell⟩ ⟨remote and ~ as the most distant nebulae —G.W.Russell⟩ ⟨pale and ~ in the moonlight, the shadowy figure of a man was moving —C.B.Nordhoff & J.N.Hall⟩ **c :** lacking firmness or strength in construction **:** WEAK, UNSTABLE ⟨a chipping sparrow . . . collecting stray hairs from the farm horses' tails for lining her very ~ nest —W.P.Smith⟩ ⟨a child of wax, delicate and charming and ~ —H.G.Wells⟩ ⟨birds and butterflies and such ~ things —W.H. Hudson †1922⟩ — **un·substantially** \"+\ *adv*

un·substantiality \"+\ *n* **:** the quality or state of being unsubstantial **:** INSUBSTANTIALITY

un·substantiate \"+\ *vt* [*2un-* + *substantiate*] **:** to divest of substantiality **:** make unsubstantial

un·substantiated \"+\ *adj* [*1un-* + *substantiated*, past part. of *substantiate*] **:** not substantiated; *esp* **:** not supported or borne out by fact ⟨another example of making an ~ assertion and then treating it as an established fact —Ruth P. Randall⟩

un·substituted \ˌən+\ *adj* [*1un-* + *substituted*, past part. of *substitute*] **:** not substituted

un·subtle \"+\ *adj* **:** not subtle ⟨thinks these characteristics are rather barbarian and ~ —Owen & Eleanor Lattimore⟩ ⟨the ~ statement that love and years are the only tragedy —Malcolm Cowley⟩ ⟨weaves a light romance with all the direct charm of a strong and ~ plot —*Times Lit. Supp.*⟩

un·subtly \"+\ *adv* **:** in an unsubtle manner

un·success \"+\ *n* **:** lack of success **:** FAILURE ⟨effort which has been waged . . . for over 15 years usually with disheartening ~ —H.L.Varney⟩ ⟨~*es* and futilities —D.C.Peattie⟩

un·successful \"+\ *adj* **:** not successful **:** not meeting with or producing success ⟨his early efforts to raise capital were ~ —Frank Monaghan⟩ ⟨attempted some short stories and novels which were ~ —Witmer Stone⟩ ⟨was the son of an illiterate and ~ . . . immigrant —F.L.Paxson⟩ ⟨was an ~ . . . candidate for congress —H.K.Beale⟩

un·successfully \"+\ *adv* **:** in an unsuccessful manner **:** without success

un·successfulness \"+\ *n* **:** the quality or state of being unsuccessful

un·successive \"+\ *adj* **:** not successive **:** not following in order or in series

un·sufferable \"+\ *adj* [ME, fr. *1un-* + *sufferable*] **1 :** not to be suffered or borne with patience or composure **:** INTOLERABLE, INSUFFERABLE ⟨an ~ wrong⟩ ⟨~ pride⟩ ⟨an ~ snob⟩ **2 :** so painful or severe as to be physically unbearable ⟨~ cold⟩ ⟨~ torment⟩ ⟨~ pain⟩ — **un·sufferably** \"+\ *adv*

un·sufficient \"+\ *adj* [ME, fr. *1un-* + *sufficient*] **1** *obs* **:** INSUFFICIENT **a 2 :** lacking in the required strength, quality, or amount **:** INADEQUATE ⟨the present aid is quite ~ to meet the requirements —*Dawn*⟩ — **un·sufficiently** \"+\ *adv*

un·suggestive \"+\ *adj* **:** not suggestive **:** UNSTIMULATING ⟨his walk was curiously uninspiring and ~ —Willa Cather⟩

un·suit \ˌən+\ *vt* [*2un-* + *suit*] **:** to make unfit ⟨long periods of staff duty tend to disqualify and ~ the once promising commander —H.H.Arnold & I.C.Eaker⟩

un·suitability \"+\ *n* **:** UNSUITABLENESS

un·suitable \"+\ *adj* **:** not suitable or fitting **:** UNBECOMING, INAPPROPRIATE ⟨a new element in life renders . . . the operation of the old instincts ~ —A.N.Whitehead⟩ ⟨in certain conditions alcohol is ~ as an antifreeze⟩ — often used with *to* or *for* ⟨compositions most ~ to this medium —Osbert Sitwell⟩ ⟨an ~ article for export —Vernon Bartlett⟩

un·suitableness \"+\ *n* **:** the quality or state of being unsuitable

un·suitably \"+\ *adv* **:** in an unsuitable manner **:** without suitability

un·suited \"+\ *adj* [*1un-* + *suited*, past part. of *suit*] **:** not suited or fit **:** not adapted **:** UNFIT ⟨a mental and physical fatigue . . . will break down the less rugged and the temperamentally ~ —H.H.Arnold & I.C.Eaker⟩ ⟨a material utterly ~ for such use —Lafcadio Hearn⟩ ⟨thinks your hobby ~ to your position in life —Dorothy Sayers⟩

un·sullied \"+\ *adj* [*1un-* + *sullied*, past part. of *sully*] **:** not sullied or stained **:** spotlessly clean **:** IMMACULATE ⟨the ~ snow of mountains —L.P.Smith⟩ ⟨the ~ splendor of eternal youth —Oscar Wilde⟩ ⟨~ name⟩ ⟨~ reputation⟩

un·sulliedness \"+\ *n* -ES **:** the quality or state of being unsullied

un·summed \"+\ *adj* [ME *unsumed*, fr. *1un-* + *sumed*, past part. of *sumen* to sum] **:** UNCOUNTED

un·sung \"+\ *adj* [*1un-* + *sung*, past part. of *sing*] **1 :** not sung **:** not rendered in song **2 :** not celebrated in song or verse or otherwise praised ⟨our writers, artists, and musicians . . . go ~ —Cornelia O. Skinner⟩ ⟨the creator of infiltration is the ~ prophet of the new age in warfare —S.L.A.Marshall⟩ ⟨massed infantry to do the bloody ~ job of mopping up the enemy —*Time*⟩

un·sunned \"+\ *adj* [*1un-* + *sunned*, past part. of *sun*] **1 a :** not exposed to sunlight ⟨the ~ northerly face of the cliff⟩ **b :** not affected or changed by the sun's light or heat ⟨a creeping chilliness . . . probably caused by the ~ morning air —Thomas Hardy⟩ **c :** not burned or tanned by the sun ⟨the pale ~ features of the city dweller⟩ **d :** unlighted by the sun ⟨the ~ landscape⟩ **2 :** not conveyed or open to the public ⟨the ~ art treasures kept locked up in a private gallery⟩

un·supervised \"+\ *adj* [*1un-* + *supervised*, past part. of *supervise*] **:** not supervised **:** not under constant observation ⟨the school maintains ~ study halls during free periods⟩ ⟨reliable workers are generally ~⟩

un·supplied \"+\ *adj* [*1un-* + *supplied*, past part. of *supply*] **:** not supplied: as **a** *archaic* **:** not furnished or provided with **b :** not satisfied **:** UNFILLED ⟨a tremendous ~ book demand —Edward Bok⟩ ⟨the ~ needs of the poor⟩

un·supportable \"+\ *adj* **:** not supportable: as **a** *archaic* **:** OFFENSIVE, VEXATIOUS **b :** hardly to be suffered or borne **:** INTOLERABLE, INSUPPORTABLE ⟨war would be ~ to the human conscience —H.C.Dillard⟩

un·supported \"+\ *adj* [*1un-* + *supported*, past part. of *support*] **1 a :** not supported or verified **:** UNSUBSTANTIATED ⟨his assumption . . . is an ~ hypothesis —W.G.Byron⟩ **b :** not backed up or assisted ⟨the artillery rolled off leaving the infantry ~⟩ **2 :** not held up or sustained ⟨removal of the center post will leave the roof ~⟩ ⟨~ portions of the body, due to their inertia, may tend to lag behind —H.G.Armstrong⟩ — **un·sup·port·ed·ly** *adv* — **un·sup·port·ed·ness** *n* -ES

un·suppressed \"+\ *adj* [*1un-* + *suppressed*, past part. of *suppress*] **:** not suppressed ⟨~ feelings⟩ ⟨~ rage⟩

un·sure \"+\ *adj* [ME, fr. *1un-* + *sure*] **1** *obs* **a :** not safe from danger or mishap **:** INSECURE **b :** lacking in security or safety **:** DANGEROUS, UNSAFE **2 a :** lacking confidence or assurance **:** UNCERTAIN ⟨approached their . . . problems unprepared, ~, inexperienced —R.E.Danielson⟩ ⟨a young man . . . ~ of himself and of his future —L.A.G.Strong⟩ **b :** not having certain knowledge ⟨was still ~ whether they were human or not —J.D. Beresford⟩ — often used with *of* ⟨~ of public support —Paul Rosenfeld⟩ ⟨is ~ of the results of his calculations⟩ **c :** marked by lack of confidence, assurance, or certainty ⟨his memory was curiously ~ —H.G.Wells⟩ ⟨moving with ~ steps⟩ ⟨the place of either manifestation in a cultural sequence remains ~ —A.L. Kroeber⟩ **3 a :** not steadfast or stable **:** CONTINGENT, PRECARIOUS ⟨the ~ state of our existence⟩ **b** *archaic* **:** of doubtful or uncertain prospect **4 :** not reliable **:** UNTRUSTWORTHY ⟨an ~ deceitful man⟩

un·sureness \"+\ *n* [ME *unsurenesse*, fr. *unsure* + *-nesse* -ness] **:** the quality or state of being unsure ⟨his ~ of himself —Osbert Sitwell⟩

un·surety \"+\ *n* [ME *unsuirte*, fr. *1un-* + *suirte*, *surete* surety] **:** lack of surety **:** UNCERTAINTY, INSECURITY ⟨the forced jocularity which is really ~ masquerading —H.M.Reynolds⟩

un·surmountable \"+\ *adj* **:** INSURMOUNTABLE ⟨an ~ barrier⟩ ⟨an ~ obstacle⟩ — **un·sur·mount·able·ness** *n* -ES

un·sur·pass·able \ˌənsərˈpasəbəl, -paas-, -pais-, -pàs-\ *adj* [*1un-* + *surpass* + *-able*] **:** incapable of being surpassed **:** not to be exceeded ⟨was hailed with ~ enthusiasm —Fred Whishaw⟩ ⟨~ standards of workmanship⟩ ⟨~ skill⟩ — **un·sur·pass·ably** \-blē, -li\ *adv*

un·surpassed \ˌən+\ *adj* [*1un-* + *surpassed*, past part. of *surpass*] **:** not surpassed or exceeded usu. in excellence ⟨as a teacher of practical chemistry he was ~ by his contemporaries —L.C.Newell⟩ ⟨the swamp is an ~ laboratory for biologists —*Amer. Guide Series: La.*⟩ ⟨the ~ beauty of the scenes —Matthew Arnold⟩

un·surprised \"+\ *adj* [*1un-* + *surprised*, past part. of *surprise*] **:** not surprised **:** not expressing surprise ⟨~ . . . at such gaps in his vocabulary —Jack London⟩ ⟨that ~ obstinate look of his —Edith Sitwell⟩

un·surprising \"+\ *adj* [*1un-* + *surprising*, pres. part. of *surprise*] **:** not surprising or unexpected ⟨the ~ findings of the report⟩ ⟨his violent reaction was ~⟩ — **un·surprisingly** \"+\ *adv*

un·susceptibility \"+\ *n* **:** the quality or state of being unsusceptible

un·susceptible \"+\ *adj* **:** not susceptible **:** not able to be moved, affected, or impressed ⟨is generally ~ to disease⟩ ⟨such a missile . . . must also be ~ to electronic countermeasures —*Scientific Monthly*⟩

un·suspected \ˌən+\ *adj* [*1un-* + *suspected*, past part. of *suspect*] **1 :** not being suspected ⟨observing ~ all their secret plottings⟩ **2 :** not regarded or considered suspiciously ⟨remaining ~ as the head of the spy ring⟩ **3 :** not known to exist **:** UNEXPECTED, UNKNOWN ⟨saw myriads of minute living creatures, the existence of which had hitherto been ~ —R.W. Miner⟩ ⟨things obscurely felt surged up from ~ depths in her —Edith Wharton⟩ ⟨~ turnings in roadways —Ludwig Lewisohn⟩

un·suspectedly \"+\ *adv* **:** in an unsuspected manner **:** without being suspected

un·suspectedness \"+\ *n* **:** the quality or state of being unsuspected ⟨the ~ of the evidence is as bad a shock as the immediate effects⟩

un·suspecting \"+\ *adj* [*1un-* + *suspecting*, pres. part. of *suspect*] **:** not suspecting **:** not being suspicious ⟨took refuge . . . in the doorway of Mount Vernon church, all ~ of the fact that I would one day be its minister —Sidney Lovett⟩ ⟨deceiving the ~ public —A.E.Wiggam⟩

un·sus·pect·ing·ly *adv* **:** without suspicion ⟨you couldn't all at once ~ have been caught —Mary Austin⟩

un·suspicion \ˌən+\ *n* **:** lack of suspicion ⟨sometimes a man's ~ is wiser —Booth Tarkington⟩

un·suspicious \"+\ *adj* **:** not suspicious **:** UNSUSPECTING ⟨as long as one remains inside the car, the animals are ~ —Jan Juta⟩ ⟨a carefree ~ fellow —C.B.Nordhoff & J.N.Hall⟩ — **un·suspiciously** \"+\ *adv* — **un·suspiciousness** \"+\ *n*

un·sustainable \"+\ *adj* [*1un-* + *sustain* + *-able*] **:** not capable of being sustained

un·sustained \"+\ *adj* [*1un-* + *sustained*, past part. of *sustain*] **:** not sustained: as **a** *obs* **:** not physically sustained or supported **b :** not kept up or supported by some aid ⟨leaving the station feeling empty and ~ —S.H.Adams⟩ ⟨~ any longer by loans, the business failed⟩ **c :** not kept or continued at a consistently high level ⟨a convolution of plots makes for ~ interest —*Current Biog.*⟩

un·swaddle \"+\ *vt* [*2un-* + *swaddle*] **:** to free or take from a swaddle **:** UNSWATHE

un·swallowable \"+\ *adj* [*1un-* + *swallow* + *-able*] **:** not able to be swallowed

un·swallowed \"+\ *adj* [*1un-* + *swallowed*, past part. of *swallow*] **:** not swallowed

un·swathe \"+\ *vt* [ME *unswathen*, fr. *2un-* + *swathen* to swathe] **:** to take a swathe from **:** relieve from a bandage ⟨~ the child⟩

un·swayed \"+\ *adj* [*1un-* + *swayed*, past part. of *sway*] **:** not moved or affected **:** not influenced ⟨~ by personal considerations⟩

un·swear \"+\ *vb* [*2un-* + *swear*] *vi* **:** to unsay or retract something sworn or firmly stated ⟨the false swear and ~ easily⟩ ~ *vt* **:** to recant or recall (as an oath) esp. by a second oath ⟨he swore his oath only to ~ it next day⟩

un·sweet \"+\ *adj* [ME *unswete*, fr. OE *unswēte*, fr. *1un-* + *swēte* sweet] **:** not sweet: as **a :** not pleasant or agreeable **:** DISTASTEFUL ⟨he sometimes finds life ~⟩ **b** (1) **:** not sweet or pleasing to the taste ⟨~ fruit⟩ (2) **:** DRY 16a, 16b **c :** not pleasant to hear ⟨has a fine voice . . . not ~ in its lower ranges —*Theatre Arts*⟩ **d :** having an unpleasant smell **:** FOUL ⟨the ~ sewers of the city⟩

un·sweetened \"+\ *adj* [*1un-* + *sweetened*, past part. of *sweeten*] **:** not sweet **:** not made sweet

un·swell \"+\ *vb* [ME *unswellen*, fr. *2un-* + *swellen* to swell] *vi*, *archaic* **:** to reduce from swelling **:** SUBSIDE ~ *vt*, *archaic* **:** to reduce the swelling of

un·swelled \"+\ *adj* [*1un-* + *swelled*, past part. of *swell*] **:** not swelled or swollen

un·swept \"+\ *adj* [*1un-* + *swept*, past part. of *sweep*] **:** not swept

un·swerving \"+\ *adj* [*1un-* + *swerving*, pres. part. of *swerve*] **1 :** not swerving or turning aside ⟨a straight narrow clay road . . . tree-lined and ~ across the far-reaching lowlands —*Amer. Guide Series: Vt.*⟩ **2 :** STEADY, UNREMITTING ⟨~ loyalty⟩ ⟨~ integrity⟩ ⟨holds an ~ belief in the democratic form of government —Victor Lewis⟩

un·swerv·ing·ly *adv* **1 :** without swerving or turning aside ⟨the ship drives ~ through the night⟩ ⟨the businessman who goes ~ to business —J.W.Aldridge⟩ **2 :** STEADILY, UNREMITTINGLY ⟨an ~ loyal man —*Current Biog.*⟩ ⟨~ supported . . . foreign policy —R.J.Kerner⟩ ⟨these compulsions do not operate ~ —Max Lerner & Edwin Mims⟩

un·swerv·ing·ness *n* -ES **:** the quality or state of being unswerving

un·swoll·en \ˌən+\ *adj* **:** not swollen

un·sworn \"+\ *adj* **1 :** not sworn in or bound by oath ⟨the witness stands ~⟩ **2 :** not verified or stated on oath ⟨~ testimony⟩

un·syllabic \"+\ *adj* **:** NONSYLLABIC

un·syllabled \"+\ *adj* [*1un-* + *syllabled*, past part. of *syllable*] **:** not articulated in syllables

unsym- — see UNS-

un·symbolic \"+\ *adj* **:** not symbolic — **un·symbolically** \"+\ *adv*

un·symmetrical \"+\ *also* **un·symmetric** \"+\ *adj* **1 :** not symmetrical **:** lacking symmetry **:** ASYMMETRIC **2** *of an equation or logical proposition* **:** of such a structure that its terms may not be interchanged without altering its value, character, or truth — **un·symmetrically** \"+\ *adv*

un·sympathetic \ˌən+\ *adj* **:** not sympathetic **:** UNRESPONSIVE ⟨his dignity made of him an aloof and ~ figure —Stringfellow Barr⟩ ⟨could tackle a theme that was temperamentally ~ to him —Eric Newton⟩ ⟨the revolt was directed against an unrepresentative and ~ officialdom —G.M.Trevelyan⟩ — **un·sympathetically** \"+\ *adv*

un·sympathizing \"+\ *adj* [*1un-* + *sympathizing*, pres. part. of *sympathize*] ⟨an uncharitable and ~ attitude⟩ — **un·sympathizingly** \"+\ *adv*

un·systematic \"+\ *also* **un·systematical** \"+\ *adj* **:** not systematic **:** lacking systematic arrangement, method, or organization ⟨the ~ and fragmentary records that have come down to us —J.G.Edwards⟩ ⟨does his work in an ~ manner⟩ — **un·systematically** \"+\ *adv*

un·systematized \"+\ *adj* [*1un-* + *systematized*, past part. of *systematize*] **:** not systematized **:** not planned, ordered, or done according to a system ⟨an ~ procedure⟩ ⟨in an ~ fashion⟩

unt \ˈənt\ *n* -S [origin unknown] *dial Eng* **:** a European mole (*Talpa europaeus*)

un·tackle \ˌən·+\ *vt* [*2un-* + *tackle*] **:** to take the tackle from **:** rid of tackling or harness

un·tactful \"+\ *adj* **:** lacking in tact ⟨an intelligent but overzealous and ~ officer —*Nation*⟩ — **un·tactfully** \"+\ *adv* — **un·tact·ful·ness** *n*

un·tainted \"+\ *adj* [*1un-* + *tainted*, past part. of *taint*] **1 :** not corrupted or infected **:** not spoiled **:** free from taint **:** UNBLEMISHED ⟨a young dreamer with ~ senses —W.J.Fisher⟩ ⟨is gratifyingly ~ by . . . stuffy critical phraseology —Henri Peyse⟩ **2** *obs* **:** not attainted ⟨~, unexamined, free, at liberty —Shak.⟩ — **un·taint·ed·ly** *adv* — **un·taint·ed·ness** *n* -ES

un·takable \"+\ *adj* **:** not capable of being taken ⟨an ~ fortress⟩

un·taken \"+\ *adj* [ME, fr. *1un-* + *taken*, past part. of *taken* to take] **:** not taken ⟨an ~ city⟩ ⟨left no opportunity ~⟩

un·talented \"+\ *adj* **:** not talented **:** not endowed with superior talent ⟨the talented child of ~ parents⟩

un·talked-of \ˌən·ˈtȯk,təv, -,täv\ *adj* [*1un-* + *talked of*, past part. form of the phrase *talk of*] **:** not talked about **:** not mentioned

un·tamable \ˌən·+\ *adj* **:** not capable of being tamed ⟨an ~ animal⟩ ⟨sweeps along the ~ flood —J.C.Mangan⟩ — **un·tam·able·ness** *n* — **un·tam·ably** \-blē\ *adv*

un·tamed \"+\ *adj* [*1un-* + *tamed*, past part. of *tame*] **:** not tamed **:** UNSUBDUED, WILD ⟨the ~ background of forest and prairie —Dorothy Dondore⟩ ⟨a haughty, almost fierce, uneasy look — an ~ look —John Galsworthy⟩ — **un·tamed·ly** *adv* — **un·tamed·ness** *n* -ES

un·tangible \"+\ *adj* **:** INTANGIBLE

un·tangle \"+\ *vt* [*2un-* + *tangle*] **:** to loose from tangles **:** straighten out **:** DISENTANGLE ⟨drank, set down his glass, and *untangled* his legs —Hamilton Basso⟩ ⟨aided in the reorganization of municipal administration, *untangled* financial difficulties —T.H.Jack⟩ **syn** see EXTRICATE

un·tanned \"+\ *adj* **:** not put through a tanning process ⟨~ leather⟩

un·tapped \"+\ *adj* [*1un-* + *tapped*, past part. of *tap*] **1 :** not subjected to tapping ⟨an ~ sugar maple⟩ ⟨an ~ keg⟩ **2 :** not drawn upon or utilized ⟨the ~ stockrooms of our minds —G.R.Harrison⟩ ⟨~ natural resources⟩

un·tarnished \"+\ *adj* [*1un-* + *tarnished*, past part. of *tarnish*] **:** not tarnished **:** free from stain or blemish ⟨an ~ reputation⟩

un·tarred \"+\ *adj* [*1un-* + *tarred*, past part. of *tar*] **:** not tarred

un·tasted \"+\ *adj* [*1un-* + *tasted*, past part. of *taste*] **:** not tasted ⟨~ food⟩ **:** not sampled or tried out ⟨all his virtues . . . are like to rot ~ —Shak.⟩

un·taught \"+\ *adj* [ME *untaght*, fr. *1un-* + *taght*, past part. of *techen* to teach] **1 :** not instructed or trained **:** IGNORANT, UNTUTORED ⟨unusually interesting . . . not only for the ~ music lover, but also for many who think they know a thing or two —Richard Aldrich⟩ **2 :** NAÏVE, NATURAL, SPONTANEOUS ⟨~ kindness⟩ **syn** see IGNORANT

un·taught·ness *n* **:** the quality or state of being untaught

un·tax \ˌən·+\ *vt* [*2un-* + *tax*] **:** to take a tax from **:** remove from taxation

un·taxed \"+\ *adj* [*1un-* + *taxed*, past part. of *tax*] **:** not subjected to taxation ⟨an ~ expense account⟩

un·teach \"+\ *vt* [*2un-* + *teach*] **1 :** to cause to unlearn something ⟨an employee who has learned outmoded procedures on previous jobs must first be *untaught*⟩ **2 :** to demonstrate the falsity of **:** teach the contrary of something previously believed or accepted ⟨will take a generation to ~ this monstrous lie —Upton Sinclair⟩

un·teachable \"+\ *adj* [ME, fr. *1un-* + *techen* to teach + *-able*] **1 :** not teachable **:** resisting guidance or instruction **:** STUBBORN ⟨is opinionated and rather ~ —Stephen Haggard⟩ **2 :** not capable of being conveyed or developed by teaching ⟨an ~ skill⟩ — **un·teach·able·ness** *n*

un·team \"+\ *vt* [*2un-* + *team*] *archaic* **:** to unyoke a team from

un·technical \"+\ *adj* **1 :** lacking technical training or skill ⟨may seem wearisome to an ~ reader —*Amer. Mercury*⟩ **2 :** not technical in meaning or style ⟨in clear, ~, effective style —*School & Society*⟩ — **un·technically** \"+\ *adv*

untell *vt* [*2un-* + *tell*] *obs* **:** to make as if not counted **:** nullify the passage of ⟨that time could turn up his swift sandy glass, to ~ the days —Thomas Heywood⟩

un·tell·able \ˌən·ˈteləbəl\ *adj* [ME, fr. *1un-* + *tellen* to tell + *-able*] **:** INEXPRESSIBLE ⟨a thing of ~ splendor —Lucius Beebe⟩ ⟨the ecstasy of this experience is ~ —A.J.Russell⟩ — **un·tell·ably** \-blē\ *adv*

un·tempered \ˌən·+\ *adj* [ME, fr. *1un-* + *tempered*] **1 a :** lacking in moderation **:** INTEMPERATE, UNCONTROLLED ⟨the inhumanity of his ~ principles —M.S.Dworkin⟩ **b :** not made less extreme **:** UNMODIFIED ⟨individualism ~ by social responsibilities and loyalties —F.M. & Marie Keesing⟩ **2 :** not brought to a proper consistency ⟨~ mortar⟩ **:** not hardened ⟨~ steel⟩ **3** *of a musical scale* **:** PURE 1b(2)

un·tempting \"+\ *adj* **:** UNATTRACTIVE, UNINVITING ⟨~ food⟩ ⟨find the night dark and windy and ~ —F.A.Swinnerton⟩ — **un·tempt·ing·ly** *adv*

un·tenability \"+\ *n* **:** the quality or state of being untenable

un·tenable \"+\ *adj* **1 :** not able to be defended or maintained **:** INDEFENSIBLE ⟨an ~ position⟩ ⟨their arguments were found so ~ that they themselves renounced them —Samuel Butler †1902⟩ **2 :** not able to be occupied ⟨found the place ~ —Edith Wharton⟩ — **un·ten·able·ness** *n*

un·tenant \"+\ *vt* [*2un-* + *tenant*] **1 :** to remove a tenant from **2 :** LEAVE, QUIT

un·ten·ant·able \"+əbəl\ *adj* **:** incapable of being occupied or lived in ⟨an ~ house⟩ ⟨an ~ island⟩

un·tenanted \ˌən·+\ *adj* [*1un-* + *tenanted*, past part. of *tenant*] **:** not tenanted **:** not leased to or occupied by a tenant ⟨very little unclaimed and ~ land —*Amer. Guide Series: Mich.*⟩ ⟨look up at the ~ air —Sidney Alexander⟩

un·tended \"+\ *adj* [*1un-* + *tended*, past part. of *tend*] **:** not tended or cared for **:** NEGLECTED ⟨the candles may gutter out at their own greasy will — unsnuffed, ~ —Israel Zangwill⟩

un·tender \"+\ *adj* **1 :** not tender in manner or approach **:** not gentle or sympathetic ⟨an amusing companion . . . but fundamentally an unloving, ~ woman —C.D.Lewis⟩ ⟨so young and so ~ —Shak.⟩ **2** *archaic* **:** not guided or influenced by religious feelings **3 :** not soft or fragile **:** not easily hurt **:** TOUGH ⟨my throat was stiff and my jaw was not ~ —Raymond Chandler⟩ — **un·ten·der·ly** *adv* — **un·ten·der·ness** *n*

un·tent \"+\ *vt* [*2un-* + *tent*, n.] **:** to bring out of a tent

1un·tented \"+\ *adj* [*1un-* + *tented*, past part. of *tent* to probe] **:** not probed or attended to ⟨the ~ woundings of a father's curse —Shak.⟩

2untented \"+\ *adj* [*1un-* + *tented*, past part. of *tent* to attend to] *archaic* **:** UNHEEDED

un·tenty \"+\ *adj*, *Scot* **:** INATTENTIVE, INCAUTIOUS

un·terrified \"+\ *adj* **:** UNDAUNTED ⟨the committee's most ~ man on any political question —W.S.White⟩

un·terrifying \"+\ *adj* **:** not arousing terror

un·tested \"+\ *adj* **:** not put to a test **:** not proved by trial or experience ⟨an ~ theory⟩

un·thanked \ˌən·+\ *adj* [*1un-* + *thanked*, past part. of *thank*] **:** not thanked **:** UNAPPRECIATED ⟨performs its dreary and ~ job —T.O.Heggen⟩

un·thankful \"+\ *adj* [ME, fr. ¹*un-* + *thankful*] **1 :** not such as to call for thanks : DISAGREEABLE, THANKLESS, UNPLEASANT ⟨an ~ assignment⟩ **2 :** not giving thanks : UNAPPRECIATIVE ⟨an ~ child⟩ — **un·thankfully** \"+\ *adv* — **un·thank·ful·ness** *n*

un·thatch \"+\ *vt* [²*un-* + *thatch*] : to remove the thatch of ⟨a haystack which had been ~*ed*, ready for removal —Flora Thompson⟩

un·thatched \"+\ *adj* [¹*un-* + *thatched*, past part. of *thatch*] : not thatched ⟨an ~ cottage⟩

un·thaw \"+\ *vb* [²*un-* + *thaw*] : THAW

un·thawed \"+\ *adj* [¹*un-* + *thawed*, past part. of *thaw*] : not thawed : FROZEN

un·theatrical \"+\ *adj* **1 :** not suited to the stage ⟨a beautifully written but ~ play⟩ **2 :** not of a nature or quality characteristic of the stage ⟨an ~ personality⟩

un·think \"+\ *vb* [²*un-* + *think*] *vi* : to terminate or reverse a thought process ⟨learned how to think and how to ~ —Peggy Bennett⟩ ~ *vt* : to put out of mind ⟨~ your speaking and . . . say so no more —Shak.⟩

un·think·abil·i·ty \ˌən,thiŋkəˈbiləd·ē\ *n* : the quality or state of being unthinkable

¹**un·thinkable** \ˌən+\ *adj* [ME, fr. ¹*un-* + *thinken* to think + *-able*] **1 :** EXTRAORDINARY, UNIMAGINABLE ⟨~ joy⟩ **2 a :** incapable of being thought : not conceivable by the mind ⟨either alternative is ~⟩ **b :** contrary to what is reasonable or probable : INCREDIBLE ⟨it seemed ~ that this quiet and apparently worthy citizen should be connected with crimes —F.W.Crofts⟩ **3 :** not to be considered : being out of the question ⟨the average tenor was ~ in these youthful parts —James Joll⟩ — **un·think·able·ness** *n* — **un·thinkably** \"+\ *adv*

²**unthinkable** \"\ *n* : something unthinkable ⟨the realm of the disharmonic ~*s* —A.E.Wiggam⟩

un·thinking \"+\ *adj* **1 :** not taking thought : HEEDLESS, INATTENTIVE, UNMINDFUL ⟨an exploit performed thousands of times a day by ~ New Yorkers —Bennett Cerf⟩ **2 :** not indicating thought or reflection : VACANT ⟨with earnest eyes, and round ~ face —Alexander Pope⟩ **3 :** not having the power of thought ⟨vicious ~ animal —Richard Sale⟩ — **un·think·ing·ly** *adv* — **un·think·ing·ness** *n*

un·thorough \"+\ *adj* : not thorough : SLIPSHOD ⟨incapable of an ~ or conscienceless job —Olin Downes⟩

¹**un·thought** \"+\ *adj* [¹*un-* + *thought*, past part. of *think*] **1 :** not anticipated : UNEXPECTED ⟨shooting off at ~ angles —William Sansom⟩ — often used with *of* or *on* **2 :** not thought : UNPREMEDITATED

²**unthought** \"\ *n* [¹*un-* + *thought*, n.] : lack of thought

un·thoughted \"+\ *adj* **1 :** not thought of **2** *dial* : ill-considered : THOUGHTLESS

un·thoughtful \"+\ *adj* **1 :** not thoughtful : lacking in thought ⟨a mechanical, ~ process —W.H.Hale⟩ **2 :** THOUGHTLESS ⟨careless, ~ behavior⟩ — **un·thoughtfully** \"+\ *adv* — **un·thought·ful·ness** *n*

un·thread \ˌən+\ *vt* [²*un-* + *thread*] **1 :** to draw or take out a thread from ⟨~ a needle⟩ **2 :** to loosen the threads or connections of ⟨he with his bare wand can ~ thy joints —John Milton⟩ **3 :** to make one's way through ⟨~*ed* the maze⟩

un·threaded \"+\ *adj* [¹*un-* + *threaded*, adj.] : lacking a thread ⟨~ pipe⟩

un·threshed \"+\ *adj* [¹*un-* + *threshed*, past part. of *thresh*] : not threshed

¹**un·thrift** \"+\ *n* [ME, fr. ¹*un-* + *thrift*] **1 :** lack of thrift : EXTRAVAGANCE, WASTEFULNESS ⟨the repression of ~ and dissipation —James Ford⟩ **2 :** an extravagant person : SPENDTHRIFT, WASTREL ⟨like ~*s*, having spent your stock, and needy grown —John Drinkwater⟩

²**unthrift** \"\ *adj* : EXTRAVAGANT, LAVISH, UNTHRIFTY ⟨in an ~ generosity, has given it with a much more valuable present —J.G.Lockhart⟩

un·thriftily \"+\ *adv* [ME, fr. *unthrifty* + *-ly*] : in an unthrifty manner

un·thriftiness \"+\ *n* [ME *unthriftinesse*, fr. *unthrifty* + *-nesse* -ness] : the quality or state of being unthrifty

un·thrifty \"+\ *adj* [ME, fr. ¹*un-* + *thrifty*] **1 :** marked by lack of thrift : of little value or effect in proportion to the effort or expenditure involved : UNPROFITABLE, WASTEFUL ⟨nothing is cooked, and nobody is warmed — a most ~ fire —Edna S. V. Millay⟩ **2** *obs* : DISSOLUTE, PROFLIGATE ⟨can no man tell me of my ~ son —Shak.⟩ **3 a :** not thriving or prospering ⟨an ~ tree⟩ **b** *of livestock* : lacking in vigor or bloom : constitutionally unsound ⟨the intelligent buyer of choice feeders rejects all lambs that appear in the least ~ —W.C.Coffey⟩ **4 :** not given to thrift or saving : EXTRAVAGANT, IMPROVIDENT, PRODIGAL

un·thriven \"+\ *adj* [¹*un-* + *thriven*, past part. of *thrive*] *Scot* : UNTHRIVING

un·thriving \"+\ *adj* : not thriving

un·throne \"+\ *vt* [²*un-* + *throne*] : to remove from or as if from a throne : DETHRONE ⟨the dahlias that flaunted for so many royal weeks to be *unthroned* in a single night —C.G. Glover⟩

un·tidily \ˌən+\ *adv* : in an untidy manner

un·tidiness \"+\ *n* : the quality or state of being untidy

¹**un·tidy** \"+\ *adj* [ME, fr. ¹*un-* + *tidy*, adj.] **1 :** UNFIT, UNSUITABLE ⟨is an ~ walk on a glaring afternoon in July —Michael Arlen⟩ **2 a :** not neat in appearance : CARELESS, SLOVENLY ⟨~ tufts of grizzled hair —Walter de la Mare⟩ **b :** not neat in habits or procedure : not orderly ⟨was ~ and casual about money —Frank O'Connor⟩ **3 a :** not neatly organized or carried out : having loose ends ⟨convert an ~ manuscript into a great book —S.E.Harris⟩ ⟨instinct for illogical and ~ but highly effective compromise —G.B. Baldwin⟩ **b :** marked by or conducive to a lack of neatness ⟨~ tasks like bathing the baby —*New Yorker*⟩

²**untidy** \"\ *vt* [²*un-* + *tidy*] : DISARRANGE, DISORDER

un·tie \"+\ *vb* [ME *untyen*, fr. OE *untīegan*, fr. ²*un-* + *tīegan* to tie — more at TIE] *vt* **1 :** to detach from something by loosing a connecting rope or other tie ⟨*untied* the horse from the fence⟩ **2 :** to free from something that fastens or restrains : let loose : UNBIND ⟨*untied* him from his promise⟩; *specif* : to set free from a rope or other confining bond ⟨*untied* his hands⟩ ⟨*untied* the package⟩ **3 a :** to disengage the knotted parts of ⟨*untied* his tie, took it off, and opened his collar⟩ ⟨found it hard to ~ the knot⟩ **b :** DISENTANGLE, RESOLVE ⟨the worst traffic tangle . . . when 75,000 cars choked all roads leading out of the city, was *untied* —*Sydney (Australia) Bull.*⟩ **c :** DISSOLVE, UNDO ⟨~ the spell —Shak.⟩ ~ *vi* **1 :** to become loosened or unbound ⟨all cords easily *untied* but the one binding me to what I loved —Anais Nin⟩ **2 :** to unfasten a knot or loosen a bond ⟨those who tangled must ~ —Robert Browning⟩

un·tied \"+\ *adj* [ME *untyed*, fr. *un-* + *tyed*, past part. of *tyen* to tie] : not tied; *specif* : not limited or restricted ⟨an ~ loan⟩

un·tight \"+\ *adj* [¹*un-* + *tight*, adj.] : not tight : LOOSE, LEAKY

un·tighten \"+\ *vt* [²*un-* + *tighten*] : to make less tight : LOOSEN ⟨an expulsion of breath ~*s* the chest —William Faulkner⟩

¹**un·til** \(ˌ)ənˈ|til, -t°l, *often* °n| *after* t, d, s, z, *often* °m *after* p, b, *often* °ŋ *after* k, g; *sometimes* ˈən·t°l *or* ˌən·til *or* |ˈtel\ *prep* [ME, fr. *un-* unto, until (akin to OE *ōth*, prep. & conj., to, up to, until, OHG *unt*, prep., unto, until, ON & Goth *und*, prep., unto, until, OE *end* end) + *til* till — more at END, TILL] **1** *chiefly Scot* **a** — used as a function word to indicate movement to and arrival at a destination **b** — used as a function word to indicate something reaching as far as a limit or stopping point **c :** AGAINST **2** *chiefly Scot* : TO, TOWARD **3** — used as a function word to indicate continuance (as of an action, condition, or state) up to a particular time ⟨a tedious task which took ~ almost ten o'clock that night —M.M.Musselman⟩ ⟨the accident remained undiscovered ~ morning⟩ **4 a** — used as a function word after a negative expression to indicate performance or occurrence at a specified time ⟨the final ordering cannot be achieved ~ page proof —*Amer. Institute of Physics*⟩ **b :** BEFORE ⟨had barely heard of the mayor ~ this evening —Nigel Dennis⟩

²**until** \"\ *conj* [ME, fr. *until*, prep.] **1 :** up to the time that : till such time as ⟨the game continued ~ it got dark⟩ **2 :** before the time that ⟨often years pass by ~ the new ruler is found —Heinrich Harrer⟩ — often used after a negative or qualified statement ⟨had never been able to relax ~ he took up fishing⟩ **3 :** to the point or degree that : so long or so far that ⟨would clamber up the stairs ~ he was breathless —Martha Gellhorn⟩

un·tile \ˌən·+\ *vt* [ME *untilen*, fr. ²*un-* + *tilen* to tile] : to take the tiles from ⟨the storm *untiled* part of the roof⟩

un·tiled \"+\ *adj* [¹*un-* + *tiled*, adj.] : not supplied with tiles

un·tillable \"+\ *adj* : not tillable : BARREN, UNPRODUCTIVE

un·tilled \"+\ *adj* [ME *untiled*, fr. ¹*un-* + *tiled*, past part. of *tilen* to till] : not tilled : not cultivated ⟨~ land⟩

until that *conj* [ME] *archaic* : UNTIL

un·timbered \ˌən·+\ *adj* **1 :** lacking timbers ⟨an ~ boat⟩ **2 :** TREELESS, UNWOODED ⟨an ~ area⟩

un·timeliness \"+\ *n* : the quality or state of being untimely

¹**un·timely** \"+\ *adv* [ME *untimliche*, *untimely*, fr. ¹*un-* + *timliche*, *timely*, adv., timely] **1 :** at an inopportune time : UNSEASONABLY ⟨thought I was mad, or most ~ merry —T.E. Lawrence⟩ **2 :** PREMATURELY ⟨died ~ a few months ago at the age of thirty-nine —Gerald Bullett⟩

²**untimely** \"\ *adj* [¹*un-* + *timely*, adj.] **1 :** occurring or done before the due, natural, or proper time : too early : PREMATURE ⟨come to an ~ end through passion —Cyril Connolly⟩ **2 :** INOPPORTUNE, UNSEASONABLE ⟨an ~ joke⟩ ⟨the only passenger who came on board at that ~ hour —Charles Dickens⟩ ⟨an ~ frost⟩ **3 :** not observing fitness of time or occasion ⟨during the performance of music when ~ people come in or go out —Owen Wister⟩

un·timeous \"+\ *adj*, *chiefly Scot* : UNTIMELY — **un·time·ous·ly** *adv*, *chiefly Scot*

un·tinged \"+\ *adj* [¹*un-* + *tinged*, past part. of *tinge*] : not tinged : not colored or affected ⟨based on a two-year study, ~ by politics —*N.Y. Times*⟩ ⟨their cheeks ~ by shame —William Blacker⟩

un·tir·abil·i·ty \ˌən·ˌtīrəˈbiləd·ē\ *n* : the quality or state of being untirable

un·tir·able \ˌən·ˈtīrəbəl\ *adj* [¹*un-* + *tire* + *-able*] : incapable of being tired ⟨seemed invigorated and ~ —H.H.Johnston⟩

un·tire \ˌən·+\ *vt* [²*un-* + *tire*] : to give rest to : REFRESH ⟨a bench or two on which the drinkers ~ themselves —Richard Ford⟩

un·tired \"+\ *adj* [¹*un-* + *tired*, adj.] : not tired or worn out ⟨his head was hot, but he was singularly ~ —Stephen McKenna⟩ — **un·tired·ly** *adv*

un·tiring \"+\ *adj* [¹*un-* + *tiring*, pres. part. of *tire*] : incapable of tiring : INDEFATIGABLE, UNWEARYING ⟨to the end of his life he was an ~ worker —A.C.McGiffert⟩ — **un·tir·ing·ly** *adv*

un·titled \"+\ *adj* **1 :** having no title or right ⟨O nation miserable, with an ~ tyrant —Shak.⟩ **2 :** not named ⟨still ~ autobiography —*Publishers' Weekly*⟩ **3 :** not called by a title ⟨a dignity and prestige which can never be maintained among ~ civilians —Eugene Field⟩

un·to \ˌəntə, -n·tu̇, -n·(ˌ)tü, +V *often* -ntəw\ *prep* [ME, fr. *un-* unto, until + *to* — more at UNTIL, TO] **1 a** — used as a function word to indicate direction and completion of movement toward a place, destination, or object ⟨come ~ these yellow sands —Shak.⟩ ⟨they had gone ~ the wars —E.A.Poe⟩ **b** — used as a function word to indicate movement, inclination, or tendency toward an unreached object ⟨we stretch our hands ~ the Egyptians —John Donne⟩ ⟨my inwardness and love is very much ~ the prince —Shak.⟩ **c** *archaic* : AT **2 a** — used as a function word to indicate a limit of reach or extension ⟨my nails can reach ~ thine eyes —Shak.⟩ **b** — used as a function word to indicate a limit of contact, juxtaposition, or union ⟨pressed his dead child ~ his heart —Robert Browning⟩ **c** — used as a function word to indicate a limit in amount, extent, or degree ⟨lay sick almost ~ death —H.J.Johnson⟩ ⟨assume the configuration of a balancer, even ~ the finer details —V.C.Twitty⟩ **d** *obs* : next to : in front of ⟨flout me thus ~ my face —Shak.⟩ **3** — used as a function word to indicate the end of an interval of time or continuance ⟨her sentence that subsists ~ this day —Robert Browning⟩ **4 a** — used as a function word to indicate aim, purpose, or destiny ⟨went ~ his doom⟩ **b** — used as a function word to indicate a result, condition, or situation achieved or imposed ⟨our wars will turn ~ a peaceful comic sport —Shak.⟩ ⟨dust thou art, and ~ dust shalt thou return —Gen 3:19 (AV)⟩ **5 a** — used as a function word to indicate a person spoken to ⟨the serpent said ~ the woman, ye shall not surely die —Gen 3:4 (AV)⟩ **b** (1) — used as a function word to indicate the recipient of an action, benefit, or feeling or the person affected by an event ⟨and ~ thy seed, I will give all these countries —Gen 26:3 (AV)⟩ ⟨~ you is born this day . . . a Savior —Lk 2:11 (AV)⟩ (2) — used as a function word to indicate reference, concern, or interest ⟨is a law ~ himself —Raymond Daniell⟩ ⟨each town lived ~ itself —*Amer. Guide Series: Conn.*⟩ **c** — used as a function word to indicate the recipient of care, regard, faith, or reverence ⟨attended ~ his friend⟩ ⟨hearkened ~ his words⟩ ⟨trusted ~ his good fortune⟩ **6** — used as a function word to indicate comparison, agreement, or relationship ⟨are dangerously like ~ cancerous cells in the social organism —B.M.Beck⟩: as **a :** with respect to ⟨as strange ~ your town as to your talk —Shak.⟩ ⟨the effort of the individual reader to live ~ God —L.A.Weigle⟩ **b :** in agreement with ⟨and ~ this he frames his song —William Wordsworth⟩ **c :** in comparison with ⟨as water ~ wine —Alfred Tennyson⟩ **7** — used as a function word to indicate possession, belonging, or relationship ⟨documents pertaining ~ the case⟩ ⟨servant ~ the king⟩ ⟨cousin ~ his wife⟩ **8 a** — used as a function word to limit or direct the application of a quality or attribute to a specific individual or group ⟨forgiving ~ his enemies⟩ ⟨liberties which are designed to be available even ~ the most iconoclastic —*New Republic*⟩ **b** — used as a function word to indicate range of perception or knowledge ⟨a secret known ~ few⟩ ⟨a name known ~ many⟩ **9** — used as a function word to indicate something arousing a response or responsive action ⟨yielded ~ their prayers⟩ ⟨bowed ~ their demands⟩ **10 :** BESIDES ⟨should have given him tears ~ entreaties —Shak.⟩

un·toggle \ˌən·+\ *vt* [²*un-* + *toggle*] : to unfasten by removing a toggle from its loop

un·told \"+\ *adj* [ME, fr. OE *unteald*, fr. ¹*un-* + *teald*, past part. of *tellan* to tell] **1 a** *obs* : not numbered or counted ⟨in the number let me pass ~ —Shak.⟩ **b :** too great or numerous to count : VAST ⟨~ wealth⟩ ⟨destroy ~ quantities of fish —Tom Marvel⟩ ⟨the boulder, product of ~ ages —*Amer. Guide Series: Mich.*⟩ **c :** being without limit : IMMEASURABLE ⟨~ happiness⟩ ⟨~ suffering⟩ ⟨~ damage⟩ **2 a :** not related **b :** kept secret : UNREVEALED ⟨the effect of mystery, of ~ implications —C.D.Lewis⟩

un·tomb \"+\ *vt* [²*un-* + *tomb*] : to take from a tomb : DISENTOMB, DISINTER

un·tombed \"+\ *adj* [¹*un-* + *tombed*, past part. of *tomb*] : not supplied with a tomb : UNBURIED

un·tone \"+\ *vt* [²*un-* + *tone*] : to put out of tone

un·tooth \"+\ *vt* [²*un-* + *tooth*] : to take out the teeth of

un·torn \"+\ *adj* [¹*un-* + *torn*, past part. of *tear*] : not torn : unmarred by tears : WHOLE

un·touch·abil·i·ty \ˌən·ˌtəchəˈbiləd·ē\ *n* : the quality or state of being untouchable; *specif* : the state of being an untouchable

¹**un·touchable** \ˌən·+\ *adj* [¹*un-* + *touch* + *-able*] **1 a :** forbidden to the touch : not to be handled ⟨in most museums such articles are ~⟩ **b :** exempt from criticism or control ⟨for the first time criticism was directed at a hitherto ~ target —*Newsweek*⟩ **2 :** lying beyond the reach : being out of reach ⟨~ resources buried deep within the earth⟩ **3 :** disagreeable or defiling to the touch — **un·touch·ably** \-blē\ *adv*

²**untouchable** \"\ *n* -s : one that is untouchable; *specif* : a member of a large hereditary group in India having in traditional Hindu belief and practice the quality of defiling by contact the person, food, or drink of a member of a higher caste and formerly being strictly segregated and restricted to menial work

un·touched \"+\ *adj* [ME, fr. ¹*un-* + *touched*, past part. of *touchen* to touch] **1 a :** not subjected to touching : not handled ⟨the new piano stood ~ for weeks⟩ **b :** not traveled or explored ⟨free to pursue their explorations in almost ~ territory —*Times Lit. Supp.*⟩ **c :** not reached ⟨an enormous and hitherto ~ audience —Harrison Smith⟩ **2 :** not described or dealt with ⟨in the second volume he left few areas of our life ~ —J.D.Adams⟩ **3 a :** left in an intact state or condition : not damaged or injured ⟨it refreshed him to see something ~, unscarred, unhardened by suffering —Joseph Conrad⟩ **b :** UNTASTED ⟨stood at the edge of the group with an ~ cocktail in her hand —Louis Auchincloss⟩ **c** (1) : being in the first state or condition : not altered, treated, or worked on ⟨this small cherrywood chest-on-chest . . . is in its original ~ condition —*Antiques*⟩ ⟨published the full and ~ text of his father's diary —W.C.Ford⟩ (2) : ABORIGINAL, PRIMEVAL ⟨its brooding magic of an ~ world —Anita Leslie⟩ ⟨a very early human being, standing upon an ~ earth —Emma Hawkridge⟩ **4 a :** not influenced : UNAFFECTED ⟨stewed in its petty provincialism ~ by the brisk debates that stirred the old world —V.L.Parrington⟩ **b :** not disturbed or swayed by emotion : CALM, UNMOVED ⟨the difficulty is to keep oneself ~ in a crowd —Lewis Vogler⟩ **5 :** UNEQUALED ⟨a perfection of form . . . ~ in English letters —H.J.Laski⟩ — **un·touched·ness** *n* -ES

un·toward \ˌən·ˈt|ō(ə)rd, |ȯ(ə)rd, |ōəd, |ȯ(ə)d *also* -tw| *or* -ntəˈwȯ(ə)rd *or* -ntəˈwȯ(ə)d\ *adj* [¹*un-* + *toward*, adj.] **1 a :** difficult to guide, manage, or influence : UNRULY ⟨an ~ wife⟩ **b :** resistant to manipulation, treatment, or use ⟨~ land⟩ ⟨~ material⟩ **c** *archaic* : AWKWARD, UNGRACEFUL **2 a :** marked by or causing trouble or unhappiness : UNFORTUNATE, UNLUCKY ⟨the oppressive realities of an ~ life —*Times Lit. Supp.*⟩ ⟨an ~ accident⟩ ⟨~ circumstances plunged it into bankruptcy —*Amer. Guide Series: Oregon*⟩ **b :** not favoring or assisting : ADVERSE, UNPROPITIOUS ⟨have managed to make a place for themselves under the most ~ conditions —M.F.A.Montagu⟩ **c :** not usual or expected : OUT-OF-THE-WAY ⟨~ scrap losses —Harold Koontz & Cyril O'Donnell⟩ ⟨some ~ and amusing incident —*Spectator*⟩ **3 :** not in accordance with propriety : IMPROPER, INDECOROUS ⟨moving to curb the ~ enthusiasm of the standees —Irving Kolodin⟩ — **un·toward·ness** *n*

¹**un·toward·ly** *adj* [¹*un-* + *towardly*, adj.] **1** *archaic* : OBSTINATE, PERVERSE **2** *archaic* : UNFAVORABLE

²**un·toward·ly** *adv* [*untoward* + *-ly*] : in an untoward manner

un·trace \ˌən+\ *vt* [²*un-* + *trace*, n.] : to loose from a trace

un·traceable \"+\ *adj* [¹*un-* + *trace* + *-able*] : not traceable — **un·trace·able·ness** *n* — **un·traceably** \"+\ *adv*

un·track \"+\ *vt* [²*un-* + *track*] : to cause to move out of one's tracks : cause to get going ⟨the eventual victors were unable to ~ themselves right away —*N.Y. Times*⟩

un·tracked \"+\ *adj* [¹*un-* + *tracked*, past part. of *track*] **1 :** not provided with a track : TRACKLESS ⟨the ~ wilderness⟩ **2 :** not traced ⟨the getaway car is still ~⟩

untraded *adj* [¹*un-* + *traded*, past part. of *trade*] *obs* : not common or hackneyed : UNUSUAL ⟨mock not that I affect the ~ oath —Shak.⟩

un·train \ˌən+\ *vt* [²*un-* + *train*] : to undo the training of ⟨~ a badly trained painter⟩

un·trained \ˌən·ˈtrānd\ *adj* [¹*un-* + *trained*, adj.] **1 :** not trained : not made adept or expert by instruction or experience ⟨the afflicted person is ~ in the habit of concentration —H.A. Overstreet⟩ ⟨an ~ listener⟩ ⟨~ troops⟩ ⟨an ~ voice⟩ **2 :** not based on training or knowledge : INEXPERT ⟨an ~ diagnosis —Leon Gellert⟩ — **un·trained·ly** \-nədlē, -nd-\ *adv* — **un·trained·ness** \-nədnəs, -n(d)n-\ *n* -ES

un·trammeled \ˌən+\ *adj* [¹*un-* + *trammeled*, past part. of *trammel*] **1 :** not confined or limited : not hindered ⟨melted with the same ~ rush that the snows had shown in the first spring sun —Farley Mowat⟩ ⟨the gift of a fresh eye and an ~ curiosity —Russell Lord⟩ ⟨command ~ by orders from committees of weak and treacherous noblemen —J.A.Froude⟩ **2 :** being free and easy ⟨the old ~ days —D.W.Brogan⟩ — **un·tram·meled·ness** *n* -ES

un·tranquil \"+\ *adj* : DISTURBED, RESTLESS ⟨despite my ~ night —A.J.Liebling⟩

un·tranquilize \"+\ *vt* [²*un-* + *tranquilize*] : to make untranquil : disturb the quiet of

un·transcended \"+\ *adj* [¹*un-* + *transcended*, past part. of *transcend*] : not transcended : not surpassed : not risen above or gone beyond

un·transferable \"+\ *adj* : not subject to transfer : incapable of being transferred

un·transformed \"+\ *adj* [¹*un-* + *transformed*, past part. of *transform*] : not transformed : not changed in form

un·translatability \"+\ *n* : the quality or state of being untranslatable

un·translatable \"+\ *adj* [¹*un-* + *translate* + *-able*] : not translatable : not capable of being put into another form, style, or language ⟨an ~ idiom⟩ ⟨an ~ art⟩ — **un·trans·lat·able·ness** *n* -ES — **un·trans·lat·ably** \-blē\ *adv*

un·translated \"+\ *adj* [¹*un-* + *translated*, past part. of *translate*] **1 :** not put into another language **2 :** not removed to another place or condition

un·transparent \"+\ *adj* : OPAQUE

un·traveled \ˌən·+\ *adj* **1 :** not having traveled : lacking direct knowledge of other countries or regions ⟨an intelligent but ~ inland girl —Carl Van Doren⟩ **2 :** not passed over or through by travelers : UNTRAVERSED ⟨an ~ desert⟩

un·traversed \"+\ *adj* [¹*un-* + *traversed*, past part. of *traverse*] : not traversed; *esp* : not journeyed : not traveled over or through ⟨an ~ region⟩

un·tread \"+\ *vt* [²*un-* + *tread*] : to tread back : RETRACE ⟨treads the path that she ~*s* again —Shak.⟩

un·treasure \"+\ *vt* [²*un-* + *treasure*] **1 :** to rob or deprive of a treasure ⟨found the bed *untreasured* of their mistress —Shak.⟩ **2 :** to bring forth (something precious) : EXHIBIT ⟨*untreasured* . . . the stores of his memory —John Mitford⟩

un·treatable \"+\ *adj* [ME *untretable*, fr. ¹*un-* + *tretable*] : incapable of being treated; *specif* : not susceptible of medical treatment ⟨its striking effectiveness against types of the disease previously ~ —*Newsweek*⟩

un·treated \"+\ *adj* [¹*un-* + *treated*, past part. of *treat*] : not subjected to treatment ⟨an ~ disease⟩ ⟨an ~ fabric⟩

un·tremulous \"+\ *adj* : not tremulous : STEADY

un·trenched \"+\ *adj* : not trenched

un·tressed \"+\ *adj* [ME, fr. ¹*un-* + *tressed*] : not tied up in tresses ⟨~ hair⟩

un·tried \"+\ *adj* [¹*un-* + *tried*, past part. of *try*] **1 :** not tested or proved by experience or trial ⟨an illustrator ~ in monumental painting —F.J.Mather⟩ **2** *obs* : not noted or examined : not commented on ⟨slide o'er sixteen years and leave the growth ~ —Shak.⟩ **3 :** not tried in court ⟨had accompanied us as an ~ prisoner —R.H.Davis⟩

untried horse *n* : a horse whose get are maidens in racing

un·trim \ˌən·+\ *vt* [²*un-* + *trim*] : to strip of trimming : put in disorder

un·trimmed \"+\ *adj* [¹*un-* + *trimmed*, past part. of *trim*] : not made or kept neat : DISORDERED ⟨by chance, or nature's changing course, ~ —Shak.⟩; *specif* : not cut for trimness ⟨style is often ~ to the point of tediousness —Duncan Aikman⟩ ⟨the black hair was tangled and unkempt and the beard ~ —Israel Zangwill⟩ — **un·trimmed·ness** *n* -ES

un·tripe \"+\ *vt* -ED/-ING/-S [²*un-* + *tripe*] : DISEMBOWEL

un·trod *or* **un·trodden** \"+\ *adj* [¹*un-* + *trod* or *trodden*, past part. of *tread*] : not trod : UNTRAVERSED ⟨~ snow⟩ ⟨~ wilderness⟩

un·troubled \"+\ *adj* [ME, fr. ¹*un-* + *troubled*] **1 :** not given trouble : not made uneasy ⟨could pursue my hobby ~ by the dislike of needless waste —Francis Birtles⟩ **2 :** CALM, TRANQUIL ⟨the pictorial value of the large ~ rectangular spaces —Roger Fry⟩ ⟨a huge stretch of ~ harbor, sheltered from the winds —Julian Dana⟩ — **un·trou·bled·ness** *n*

un·troublesome \"+\ *adj* : not troublesome : EASY ⟨an ~ guest⟩ ⟨an ~ procedure⟩ — **un·trou·ble·some·ness** *n*

un·true \"+\ *adj* [ME *untrewe*, fr. OE *untrēowe*, fr. ¹*un-* + *trēowe* true] **1 :** not true to an obligation, love, or trust : DISLOYAL, UNFAITHFUL ⟨is ~ to his highest opportunity and duty —Bruno Lasker⟩ ⟨finally locates her lover, finds that he has been ~ and shoots him —W.E.Roberts⟩ **2 :** not according with a standard of correctness : not level or exact ⟨unsightly cracks, off-level floors, and ~ doors and windows —*Building, Estimating & Contracting*⟩ **3 :** not according with the facts : FALSE ⟨the claim presented to the government contained an ~ statement —R.L.Taylor b. 1889⟩ **4 :** not honest or fair : WRONG ⟨~ methods⟩ — **un·true·ness** *n*

2untrue *adv* [ME *untrewe*, fr. *untrewe*, adj.] *obs* : UNTRULY
un·truism \ˌən+\ *n* : something obviously not true ⟨revel in platitudes, truisms, and ~ —Anthony Trollope⟩
un·truly \"+\ *adv* [ME *untrewely*, fr. OE *untrēowlīce*, fr. 1*un-* + *trēowlīce* truly] : in an untrue manner
un·truss \"+\ *vb* [ME *untrussen*, fr. 2*un-* + *trussen* to truss] *vt* **1** *archaic* : to loose from a fastening : set free **2** *archaic* **a** : UNTIE, UNFASTEN, UNDO — used in the phrase *untruss one's points*; compare 1POINT 10a **b** : UNDRESS ~ *vi*, *archaic* : to unfasten or take off one's clothes and esp. one's breeches ⟨is condemned for ~*ing* —Shak.⟩
un·trust \"+\ *n* [ME, fr. 1*un-* + *trust*] *archaic* : DISTRUST
un·trustworthiness \"+\ *n* : the quality or state of being untrustworthy
un·trustworthy \"+\ *adj* : not trustworthy : UNRELIABLE ⟨an ~ person with whom, when I discovered his true character, I had no wish to associate —Eric Linklater⟩
un·trusty \"+\ *adj* [ME, fr. 1*un-* + *trusty*] : UNTRUSTWORTHY
un·truth \"+\ *n* [ME *untreuth*, fr. OE *untrēowth*, fr. 1*un-* + *trēowth* truth] **1** *archaic* : DISLOYALTY, UNFAITHFULNESS **2** : lack of truthfulness : FALSITY ⟨literary art may be associated with ~ —Aldous Huxley⟩ **3** : something that is untrue : FALSEHOOD, MISSTATEMENT ⟨motivated to cling to these childish ~*s* —Weston La Barre⟩ ⟨told you ~*s* yesterday morning merely to cheer you up —Arnold Bennett⟩
un·truth·ful \"+\ *adj* : not truthful : FALSE, INACCURATE ⟨an ~ report⟩ **syn** see DISHONEST
un·truthfully \"+\ *adv* : in an untruthful manner
un·truth·ful·ness *n* : the quality or state of being untruthful
unts *pl of* UNT
un·tuck \ˌən+\ *vt* [2*un-* + *tuck*] : to release from a tuck or from being tucked up ⟨stooping to ~ the rug —Clive Arden⟩ ⟨~*ed* her legs, and stuck her feet into her shoes —Frances G. Patton⟩
un·tufted \"+\ *adj* [1*un-* + *tufted*, past part. of *tuft*] : not tufted : not having tufts ⟨~ ears⟩
un·tunable \"+\ *adj* : not melodious : DISCORDANT, HARSH — **un·tun·able·ness** *n* — **un·tun·ably** \-blē\ *adv*
un·tune \"+\ *vt* [2*un-* + *tune*] **1** : to put out of tune : make incapable of harmony or harmonious action ⟨~ that string, and hark, what discord follows —Shak.⟩ **2** : DISARRANGE, DISCOMPOSE ⟨his troubles had *untuned* his mind⟩
un·tuned \"+\ *adj* [1*un-* + *tuned*, adj.] **1** : made untuneful or discordant ⟨with ~ tongue she hoarsely calls her maid —Shak.⟩ **2** : not tuned : being out of tune ⟨an ~ violin⟩
un·tuneful \"+\ *adj* : not pleasing in sound : HARSH — **un·tunefully** \"+\ *adv* — **un·tune·ful·ness** *n*
un·turn \"+\ *vt* [2*un-* + *turn*] : to turn in a reverse way
un·turned \"+\ *adj* [1*un-* + *turned*, past part. of *turn*] : not turned ⟨would leave no stone ~ to secure its success —W.B. Shaw⟩
un·tutored \"+\ *adj* [1*un-* + *tutored*, past part. of *tutor*] **1 a** : having no formal learning or training : UNEDUCATED ⟨~ in local history and Moslem architecture —Douglas Carruthers⟩ ⟨to the ~ ear they are meaningless — these queer noises —Waldemar Kaempffert⟩ **b** : NAÏVE, SIMPLE, UNSOPHISTICATED ⟨a growing and powerful, if politically ~, body of industrial workers —T.H.White b. 1915⟩ **2** : owing nothing to education : not produced or developed by instruction ⟨the ~ ethical judgment of the individual —Alfred Cobban⟩ **syn** see IGNORANT
un·twine \"+\ *vb* [ME *untwinen*, fr. 2*un-* + *twinen* to twine] *vt* **1 a** : to break up : DISSOLVE ⟨~ the ties of custom which bind a people to the established and the old —William Hamilton †1856⟩ **b** : to unwind the twisted or tangled parts of ⟨~*s* the ball of thread⟩ **c** : DISENTANGLE, UNCLASP **2** : to remove by unwinding ~ *vi* : to become disentangled or unwound
un·twist \"+\ *vb* [2*un-* + *twist*] *vt* **1 a** : to separate the twisted parts of : UNTWINE ⟨~ a knot⟩ **b** *archaic* : DISENTANGLE **2** : to bring to nothing : FRUSTRATE ⟨able to overcome prejudices and vested interests, to ~ wrong purposes and unmask false ideals —G.A.L.Sarton⟩ **3** *archaic* : to let loose : FREE ~ *vi* : to become separated : become untwined
un·twisted \"+\ *adj* [1*un-* + *twisted*, past part. of *twist*] : not twisted
untwisting *n* [fr. gerund of *untwist*] : the act or action of untwisting
un·typical \ˌən+\ *adj* : not typical : not representative ⟨too small and ~ to serve as a cross section of national opinion —E.K.Lindley⟩ — **un·typically** \"+\ *adv*
un·understandable \ˌən+\ *adj* : not understandable : PUZZLING, UNINTELLIGIBLE
un·understanding \"+\ *adj* : lacking in understanding : UNCOMPREHENDING
un·understood \"+\ *adj* : not understood ⟨should not tamely submit to the unpredictable and ~ cycles of wars —*Psychiatry*⟩
un·uniform \"+\ *adj* : not uniform — **un·uni·form·ly** *adv*
un·uniformed \"+\ *adj* : not dressed in uniform
un·united \"+\ *adj* : DISUNITED
un·upbraided \"+\ *adj* [1*un-* + *upbraided*, past part. of *upbraid*] *archaic* : not accused : UNREPROACHED
un·upbraiding \"+\ *adj* [1*un-* + *upbraiding*, pres. part. of *upbraid*] *archaic* : not reproachful
un·upholstered \"+\ *adj* : not upholstered
un·urbane \"+\ *adj* : not urbane : CHURLISH, VULGAR
un·urged \ˌən+\ *adj* [1*un-* + *urged*, past part. of *urge*] : without being urged : VOLUNTARILY ⟨goes ~ for the mail because it's his birthday⟩
un·usable \"+\ *adj* : not serviceable : USELESS — **un·usably** \"+\ *adv*
un·use \"+\ *n* [1*un-* + *use*] : lack of usage
un·used \"+\ *adj* [ME, fr. 1*un-* + *used*, past part. of *usen* to use] **1** : not habituated : UNACCUSTOMED ⟨a country boy ~ to city ways⟩ **2** : not used: as **a** : recently made or acquired : FRESH, NEW ⟨set an ~ canvas on the easel and got out a fresh brush⟩ **b** : not being in use : IDLE, VACANT ⟨stay in a friend's ~ apartment⟩ **c** : waiting to be used : ACCRUED, ACCUMULATED ⟨~ annual leave⟩ **d** *of a postage stamp* : not canceled **3** *archaic* : not familiar : STRANGE ⟨strange dainty things they ate, of ~ savor —William Morris⟩
un·useful \"+\ *adj* : of no practical value : UNHELPFUL, USELESS ⟨nameless and ~ plants such as flourish under barrels —Thomas Wolfe⟩ — **un·usefully** \"+\ *adv*
un·use·ful·ness *n* : the quality or state of being impractical or worthless
un·usual \ˌən+\ *adj* **1 a** : being out of the ordinary : EXCEPTIONAL, REMARKABLE ⟨a scholar of ~ ability⟩ ⟨a scene of ~ beauty⟩ **b** : deviating from the normal : PECULIAR, STRANGE ⟨devoted to all that was strange, ~ and exotic in humanity —B.K.Malinowski⟩ ⟨excessive bail shall not be required . . . nor cruel and ~ punishments inflicted —*U.S.Constitution*⟩ **2** : being unlike others : DIFFERENT, UNIQUE ⟨~ and highly entertaining variations of the . . . trick-ending story —William Peden⟩ ⟨discovered an ~ meteorite —Walter Granger⟩ — **un·usually** \"+\ *adv*
un·u·su·al·i·ty \ˌənˌyüzhəˈwaləd·ē\ *n* -ES **1** : UNUSUALNESS **2** : something unusual
un·usu·al·ness *n* : the quality or state of being unusual
un·utilized \ˌən+\ *adj* [1*un-* + *utilized*, past part. of *utilize*] : not utilized
un·utterable \"+\ *adj* : being beyond the powers of description : INEXPRESSIBLE, UNSPEAKABLE ⟨longed with ~ longing . . . for those nights in the wagon on the prairie —Edna Ferber⟩ ⟨the ~ miseries and wretchedness of mankind —M.R.Cohen⟩ — **un·ut·ter·ably** \-blē, -li\ *adv*
un·utterables \"+\ *n pl*, *archaic* : UNMENTIONABLES
un·uttered \"+\ *adj* [1*un-* + *uttered*, past part. of *utter*] : not expressed in words : UNSPOKEN ⟨meeting glances tell the ~ tale of love —Amelia Welby⟩
un·vaccinated \"+\ *adj* [1*un-* + *vaccinated*, past part. of *vaccinate*] : not vaccinated
un·valuable \"+\ *adj* **1** *obs* : INVALUABLE **2 a** : not valuable **b** : having negative value
un·value \"+\ *n* : a negative value; *esp* : ethical or aesthetic badness ⟨truth, goodness, and beauty . . . contrast with their ~*s* of error, evil, and ugliness —Samuel Alexander⟩
un·valued \"+\ *adj* [1*un-* + *valued*, past part. of *value*] **1** *obs* : of inestimable worth : INVALUABLE **2 a** : not important or prized : DISREGARDED, INSIGNIFICANT ⟨the inestimable, tho' ~ benefit of health —Edward Hyde⟩ ⟨he may not, as ~ persons do, carve for himself —Shak.⟩ **b** : not appraised ⟨an ~ estate⟩
unvalued policy *n* : an insurance policy in which absence of prior agreement leaves losses to be settled on the basis of indemnity
un·van·quish·able \ˌənˈvaŋkwishəbəl, -ank-\ *adj* [ME *unvenkusable*, fr. 1*un-* + *venkussen*, *venquissen* to vanquish + *-able*] : incapable of being subdued : UNCONQUERABLE
un·vanquished \ˌən+\ *adj* [ME *unvenquissed*, fr. 1*un-* + *venquissed*, past part. of *venquissen* to vanquish] : not vanquished : UNDEFEATED
un·vaporized \"+\ *adj* [1*un-* + *vaporized*, past part. of *vaporize*] : not vaporized
un·variable \"+\ *adj* [ME, fr. 1*un-* + *variable*] : INVARIABLE
un·varied \"+\ *adj* : not varied : MONOTONOUS, UNDIVERSIFIED
un·variegated \"+\ *adj* : not variegated : PLAIN, UNIFORM
un·varnished \"+\ *adj* [1*un-* + *varnished*, past part. of *varnish*] **1 a** : free from ambiguity or subterfuge : PLAIN, STRAIGHTFORWARD ⟨straight talk to the Turks, who appreciate ~ discourse —Welles Hangen⟩ ⟨more concerned with making himself look good . . . than he was with telling the ~ truth —K.S.Davis⟩ **b** : free from affectation : ARTLESS, FRANK ⟨the thought of that other woman, so ~, so undefended —Ida A. R. Wylie⟩ ⟨the ~ candor of old people and children —Janet Flanner⟩ **2** : not coated with or as if with varnish : CRUDE, UNFINISHED ⟨an ~ floor⟩ ⟨legal methods shall be substituted for ~ use of force —P.C.Nash⟩
un·varying \"+\ *adj* [1*un-* + *varying*, pres. part. of *vary*] : not varying : CONSTANT, UNCHANGING ⟨principles of ~ validity —B.N.Cardozo⟩ ⟨Latin as an artificial, ~ language —R.A.Hall b. 1911⟩ — **un·vary·ing·ly** *adv*
un·vaulted \"+\ *adj* [1*un-* + *vaulted*, past part. of *vault*] : not vaulted
un·veil \"+\ *vb* [2*un-* + *veil*] *vt* **1 a** : to divest of or as if of a veil ⟨ended child marriage, ~*ed* the women —*Time*⟩ ⟨~*ed* Olympus before my enraptured vision —W.J.Locke⟩ **b** : to expose by or as if by removing a veil : UNMASK ⟨~*s* a hidden alter ego by playing the piccolo for his astonished guests⟩ ⟨the physicist, wishing to ~ the . . . architecture of the atom —G.W. Gray b. 1886⟩ **c** (1) : to display publicly for the first time by drawing aside a curtain or covering ⟨~ a statue⟩ (2) : to make public for the first time : INTRODUCE ⟨brought from London by the Theater Guild and ~*ed* here last Thursday —John Lardner⟩ **2 a** : to disclose to the public : DIVULGE, REVEAL ⟨these addresses ~ as do no other writings of the great preacher his own personal experiences —C.A.Dinsmore⟩ ⟨~*ed* a vision of society in the twentieth century —R.M.Lovett⟩ **b** : to present to the eye : EXHIBIT, SHOW ⟨in its wide windows and slender piers . . . unconventional verticality is frankly ~*ed* —*Amer. Guide Series: N.Y.*⟩ ~ *vi* : to remove a veil : discard a protective cloak ⟨~*ed* before each other concerning it —Richard Blaker⟩
un·veiled \"+\ *adj* [1*un-* + *veiled*, past part. of *veil*] : not veiled : OPEN, REVEALED
unveiling *n* [fr. gerund of *unveil*] : an act or instance of revealing or putting on display esp. for the first time : EXPOSURE, PRESENTATION ⟨the ~ of some of nature's most precious secrets —Johnny Antillon⟩ ⟨~ of his latest film —A.H.Weiler⟩ ⟨~*s* of the new models⟩
un·vendible \"+\ *adj* : not salable
un·venerable \"+\ *adj* : unworthy of veneration ⟨forever ~ be thy hands, if thou tak'st up the princess —Shak.⟩
un·vented \"+\ *adj* [1*un-* + *vented*, past part. of *vent*] : not vented
un·ventilated \"+\ *adj* [1*un-* + *ventilated*, past part. of *ventilate*] : not ventilated
un·ventured \"+\ *adj* [1*un-* + *ventured*, past part. of *venture*] : not ventured
un·veracious \"+\ *adj* : not veracious : FALSE
un·veracity \"+\ *n* : lack of truthfulness : FALSEHOOD, MENDACITY
un·verbalized \"+\ *adj* [1*un-* + *verbalized*, past part. of *verbalize*] : not put into words or given conscious expression ⟨the ~ resentment the patient might have —M.M.Gill & Margaret Brenman⟩ ⟨deep ~ levels of the mind —Lillian Smith⟩
un·verifiability \ˌən+\ *n* : the quality or state of being unverifiable
un·verifiable \"+\ *adj* : incapable of being verified ⟨~ reports of flying saucers⟩ — **un·ver·i·fi·a·bly** \-blē\ *adv*
un·verified \"+\ *adj* [1*un-* + *verified*, past part. of *verify*] : not verified : lacking substantiation
un·vernalized \"+\ *adj* [1*un-* + *vernalized*, past part. of *vernalize*] : not subjected to vernalization
un·versed \"+\ *adj* : displaying lack of knowledge or proficiency : IGNORANT, INEXPERIENCED ⟨~ in the jargon of the social scientist —*Dun's Rev.*⟩
un·vest \"+\ *vi* [2*un-* + *vest*] : to take off ecclesiastical vestments
un·vexed \"+\ *adj* [ME *unvext*, fr. 1*un-* + *vext*, past part. of *vex*] : free from disturbance : CALM, SERENE
un·viable \"+\ *adj* : incapable of growth or development
un·vicious \"+\ *adj* : not vicious : GENTLE, TRACTABLE
un·victorious \"+\ *adj* : not victorious : DEFEATED
un·viewed \ˌən+\ *adj* [1*un-* + *viewed*, past part. of *view*] : not viewed : UNSEEN
un·vigilant \"+\ *adj* : not vigilant : INATTENTIVE, UNWARY
un·vindicated \"+\ *adj* [1*un-* + *vindicated*, past part. of *vindicate*] : not vindicated
un·vindictive \"+\ *adj* : not vindictive : FORGIVING, MERCIFUL
un·violated \ˌən+\ *adj* [1*un-* + *violated*, past part. of *violate*] : not violated : INTACT, UNBROKEN
un·violent \"+\ *adj* : not violent : MILD, SUBDUED
un·virtuous \"+\ *adj* [ME *unvertuous*, fr. 1*un-* + *vertuous* virtuous] : lacking in honor or integrity : IMMORAL, WICKED — **un·vir·tu·ous·ly** *adv*
un·visited \"+\ *adj* [1*un-* + *visited*, past part. of *visit*] **1** : not attracting visitors : BYPASSED, NEGLECTED ⟨remains astonishingly ~ by Americans —S.P.B.Mais⟩ **2** : not attended : UNACCOMPANIED — usu. used with *by* ⟨many a night ~ by sleep —W.C.Bryant⟩
un·visored \"+\ *adj* : not having or wearing a visor ⟨an ~ helm⟩ ⟨see the face of an ~ foe⟩
un·vital \"+\ *adj* **1** : not vital : INANIMATE **2** : INCONSEQUENTIAL
un·vitiated \"+\ *adj* [1*un-* + *vitiated*, past part. of *vitiate*] *archaic* : not vitiated : UNCONTAMINATED
un·vit·ri·fi·a·ble \ˌənˈvi·trəˌfīəbəl\ *adj* [1*un-* + *vitrify* + *-able*] : incapable of being vitrified
un·vitrified \ˌən+\ *adj* [1*un-* + *vitrified*, past part. of *vitrify*] : not vitrified
un·vocal \"+\ *adj* : not eloquent or outspoken : INARTICULATE ⟨plight of the ~ agricultural worker —H.L.Hoskins⟩; *esp* : UNMUSICAL ⟨~ progressions —M.F.Bukofzer⟩
un·vocalized \"+\ *adj* [1*un-* + *vocalized*, past part. of *vocalize*] : not vocalized
un·voice \"+\ *vt* [2*un-* + *voice*] : DEVOICE
un·voiced \"+\ *adj* [1*un-* + *voiced*, past part. of *voice*] **1** : not verbally expressed : SILENT, STIFLED ⟨an ~ pact between us —H.V.Gregory⟩ ⟨this ~ aspect of Italy has made itself heard in our days through . . . poetry —Serge Hughes⟩ **2** : VOICELESS 2
un·vouched \"+\ *adj* [1*un-* + *vouched*, past part. of *vouch*] : not attested : UNVERIFIED
un·vowed \"+\ *adj* [1*un-* + *vowed*, past part. of *vow*] : not bound by an oath : UNSWORN
un·vowelled \"+\ *adj* : having no vowel sounds or signs
un·voy·age·able \ˌənˈvȯiijəbəl\ *adj* [1*un-* + *voyage* + *-able*] : incapable of being traversed : IMPASSABLE, UNNAVIGABLE
un·vulcanized \ˌən+\ *adj* [1*un-* + *vulcanized*, past part. of *vulcanize*] : not vulcanized
un·vulgar \"+\ *adj* : free from crudity : REFINED
un·waked *or* **un·wakened** \ˌən+\ *adj* [1*un-* + *waked* (past part. of *wake*) or *wakened* (past part. of *waken*)] : not awakened
un·walked \"+\ *adj* [1*un-* + *walked*, past part. of *walk*] **1** : not walked **2** *of a gamecock* : not having the leg muscles hardened by roadwork
un·wall \"+\ *vt* [2*un-* + *wall*] : to expose by demolishing a wall ⟨~ a bricked-up fireplace⟩
un·walled \"+\ *adj* [ME, fr. 1*un-* + *walled*, past part. of *wallen* to wall] : not enclosed by or as if by a wall : OPEN, EXPOSED ⟨an ~ garden⟩ ⟨the round ~ horizon of the open sea —O.W.Holmes †1894⟩
un·wandered \"+\ *adj* [1*un-* + *wandered*, past part. of *wander*] : UNTRAVELED
un·wandering \"+\ *adj* [1*un-* + *wandering*, pres. part. of *wander*] : not devious or vagrant : FIXED, UNSWERVING
un·waning \"+\ *adj* [1*un-* + *waning*, pres. part. of *wane*] : not diminishing : CONSTANT, PERPETUAL ⟨the miracle of the ~ oil in the temple —Israel Zangwill⟩
un·wanted \"+\ *adj* [1*un-* + *wanted*, past part. of *want*] **1** : not wanted ⟨sits at home ~⟩ **2** : not needed or useful : SUPERFLUOUS, UNNECESSARY ⟨give away ~ kittens⟩ ⟨ignore ~ advice⟩ **3** : detrimental in character : FAULTY, UNDESIRABLE ⟨not likely to leave descendants to preserve his . . . ~ qualities —S.A.Coblentz⟩ ⟨~ shadows distort the picture⟩
un·ware \ˌənˈwa(a)(ə)r, -we(ə)r\ *adv* [ME *unwar*, fr. OE *unwær*, fr. *unwær*, adj., unaware, fr. 1*un-* + *wær* wary — more at WARY] *obs* : UNAWARES
un·wares \-rz\ *adv* [ME, fr. *unwar*, adj., unaware (fr. OE *unwær*) + *-es*, adv. suffix (fr. *-es*, gen. sing. ending of nouns) — more at 's] *archaic* : UNAWARES
un·warily \ˌən+\ *adv* : in an unwary manner : CARELESSLY, INCAUTIOUSLY
un·wariness \"+\ *n* : the quality or state of being unwary : HEEDLESSNESS, INDISCRETION
un·warlike \"+\ *adj* : disinclined to wage war : NONBELLIGERENT, PACIFIC
un·warmed \"+\ *adj* [1*un-* + *warmed*, past part. of *warm*] : not subjected to heat or stimulation ⟨~ rolls⟩ ⟨a heart ~ by affection⟩
un·warming \"+\ *adj* [1*un-* + *warming*, pres. part. of *warm*] : not exuding warmth : COLD ⟨the moon's ~ light⟩
un·warned \"+\ *adj* [ME, fr. OE *unwarnod*, fr. 1*un-* + *warnod*, past part. of *warnian* to warn] : receiving no warning : not cautioned or rebuked ⟨stepped ~ into the path of an oncoming car⟩ ⟨wickedness ~ and wrong unredressed —Margaret Oliphant⟩
un·warp \"+\ *vt* [2*un-* + *warp*] : to straighten out : UNTWIST
un·warped \"+\ *adj* [1*un-* + *warped*, past part. of *warp*] : not warped : UNDISTORTED
un·warrantable \"+\ *adj* [1*un-* + *warrant* + *-able*] : not justifiable : INEXCUSABLE ⟨~ liberties . . . taken with ancient works of art —Norman Douglas⟩ — **un·war·rant·ably** \-blē\ *adv*
un·war·rant·able·ness *n* : the quality or state of being unwarrantable
un·warranted \ˌən+\ *adj* [1*un-* + *warranted*, past part. of *warrant*] : lacking adequate or official support : UNJUSTIFIED, UNAUTHORIZED ⟨an ~ restriction of personal freedom —J.V.L. Casserley⟩ ⟨leap to sensational and ~ conclusions —R.W. Murray⟩ ⟨~ search and seizure⟩ — **un·war·rant·ed·ly** *adv*
un·wary \"+\ *adj* **1** *obs* : UNEXPECTED **2 a** : not alert : easily fooled or surprised : HEEDLESS, GULLIBLE ⟨seduce the ~ reader into easy acquiescence —O.J.Campbell⟩ **b** : careless of consequences : IMPRUDENT, RASH ⟨an ~ step may plunge them waist deep into a hidden hole —Hugh Cave⟩
1un·washed \"+\ *adj* [ME *unwasched*, fr. 1*un-* + *wasched*, past part. of *waschen* to wash] **1** : not cleaned with or as if with soap and water ⟨a sink full of ~ dishes⟩ **2** : belonging to or characteristic of the common herd : IGNORANT, PLEBEIAN ⟨the country is intellectually ~ —George Moore⟩ ⟨popular support . . . lay in the ~ social stratum —*Time*⟩
2unwashed \"\ *n* -s : an ignorant or underprivileged group : RABBLE ⟨spreading . . . sunshine among the ~ as well as the nobility —C.W.Ferguson⟩ — often used in the phrase *the great unwashed* ⟨from the society woman down to numbers of the great ~ —*Sydney (Australia) Mail*⟩
un·washen \"+\ *adj* [ME *unwaschen*, fr. OE *unwæscen*, fr. 1*un-* + *wæscen*, past part. of *wascan* to wash] *archaic* : UNWASHED
un·wasted \"+\ *adj* [ME, fr. 1*un-* + *wasted*, past part. of *wasten* to waste] **1** *archaic* : not decreased by consumption or erosion : UNDIMINISHED **2** *archaic* : not sacked : UNRAVAGED
un·wasteful \"+\ *adj* : not wasteful : FRUGAL — **un·wastefully** \"+\ *adv*
un·wasting \"+\ *adj* [ME, fr. 1*un-* + *wasting*, pres. part. of *wasten* to waste] *archaic* : not diminishing : remaining constant
un·watched \"+\ *adj* [ME *unwached*, fr. 1*un-* + *wached*, past part. of *wachen*, *wacchen* to watch] : not watched : NEGLECTED, UNATTENDED ⟨that applied science, ~, improperly handled, and not understood by men —Harrison Brown⟩
un·watchful \"+\ *adj* : not watchful : INATTENTIVE, UNOBSERVANT — **un·watchfully** \"+\ *adv*
un·watch·ful·ness *n* : the quality or state of being unwatchful
un·water \ˌən+\ *vt* [2*un-* + *water*] : to draw off water from : empty of moisture : DRAIN ⟨~ a mine shaft by bucket or pump⟩ ⟨~ a rice field for harvesting⟩
un·watered \"+\ *adj* [ME *unwattred*, fr. 1*un-* + *wattred*, past part. of *wattren*, *wateren* to water] **1 a** : not supplied with water either naturally or artificially : ARID, DRY ⟨~ desert⟩ ⟨an ~ lawn⟩ **b** : emptied of moisture ⟨an ~ mine⟩ **2** : not diluted with water ⟨~ alcohol⟩
un·watermarked \"+\ *adj* [1*un-* + *watermarked*, past part. of *watermark*] : not watermarked
un·waved \"+\ *adj* [1*un-* + *waved*, past part. of *wave*] : not waved : STRAIGHT ⟨~ hair⟩
un·wavering \"+\ *adj* [1*un-* + *wavering*, pres. part. of *waver*] : characterized by absence of fluctuation : FIXED, STEADFAST ⟨an ~ gaze⟩ ⟨~ concentration⟩ ⟨~ faith in God⟩ ⟨complexity of form is handled with ~ conviction and taste —J.T.Soby⟩ — **un·wa·ver·ing·ly** *adv*
un·waving \"+\ *adj* [1*un-* + *waving*, pres. part. of *wave*] : not waving
un·waxed \"+\ *adj* [1*un-* + *waxed*, past part. of *wax*] : not waxed ⟨an ~ floor⟩
un·weakened \"+\ *adj* [1*un-* + *weakened*, past part. of *weaken*] : not weakened
un·wealthy \"+\ *adj* [ME *unwelthy*, fr. 1*un-* + *welthy* wealthy] : not wealthy : POOR
un·weaned \"+\ *adj* [1*un-* + *weaned*, past part. of *wean*] : not weaned
unweapon *vt* [2*un-* + *weapon*] *obs* : DISARM
un·weaponed \ˌən+\ *adj* [ME *unwepned*, fr. 1*un-* + *wepned*, past part. of *wepnen* to arm — more at WEAPON] *archaic* : not armed with or as if with a weapon
un·wearable \"+\ *adj* [1*un-* + *wear* + *-able*] : not wearable : UNBECOMING, WORN-OUT ⟨an ~ style⟩ ⟨shoes so dilapidated as to be ~⟩
un·wea·ri·a·ble \ˌənˈwirēəbəl\ *adj* [1*un-* + *weary* + *-able*] : incapable of being wearied : persevering despite fatigue : INDEFATIGABLE, TIRELESS — **un·wea·ri·a·bly** \-blē\ *adv*
un·wearied \ˌən+\ *adj* [1*un-* + *wearied*, past part. of *weary*] : not tired or jaded : FRESH, DILIGENT ⟨must be skilled, persistent, and ~ —J.B.Gallagher⟩ — **un·wea·ried·ly** *adv*
un·wea·ried·ness *n* : the quality or state of being unwearied : DILIGENCE, ENDURANCE
un·weary \ˌən+\ *adj* [ME *unwery*, fr. OE *unwērig*, fr. 1*un-* + *wērig* weary] : UNWEARIED
un·wearying \ˌən+\ *adj* [1*un-* + *wearying*, pres. part. of *weary*] **1** : UNWEARIABLE **2** : not causing fatigue or boredom — **un·wea·ry·ing·ly** *adv*
un·weathered \"+\ *adj* : not showing the effects of exposure to the weather ⟨~ stone⟩ ⟨~ shingles⟩
un·weave \"+\ *vt* [2*un-* + *weave*] : to dismantle or extract from or as if from a mesh : DISENTANGLE, RAVEL ⟨~ a knot⟩ ⟨cannot be *unwoven* and analyzed independently —S.L.Payne⟩
un·webbed \"+\ *adj* [1*un-* + *webbed*, past part. of *web*] : not webbed
un·wed *or* **un·wedded** \"+\ *adj* [*unwed* fr. 1*un-* + *wed*, past part. of *wed*; *unwedded* fr. ME, fr. 1*un-* + *wedded*, past part. of *wedden* to wed] : not married
un·wedge \"+\ *vt* [2*un-* + *wedge*] **1** : to remove a wedge from ⟨~ a door and let it swing shut⟩ **2** : to release from a tight position ⟨*unwedged* his bulk from the telephone booth⟩

un·wedge·able \"+əbəl\ adj [¹un- + wedge + -able] : impervious to wedges : HARD, IMPENETRABLE ⟨the ~ and gnarled oak —Shak.⟩
un·weeded \ˌən+\ adj [¹un- + weeded, past part. of weed] : not weeded or culled
un·weeting \"+\ adj [ME unweting, fr. ¹un- + weting, pres. part. of weten to know — more at WEET] archaic : UNWITTING — **un·weet·ing·ly** adv, archaic
un·weighed \"+\ adj [ME unweyed, fr. ¹un- + weyed, past part. of weyen to weigh] : not weighed on or as if on a scale : INJUDICIOUS ⟨what an ~ behavior hath this . . . drunkard —Shak.⟩
un·weighted \"+\ adj [¹un- + weighted, past part. of weight] 1 : not encumbered : UNBURDENED ⟨to change . . . direction the ~ ski is turned —George Gallowhur⟩ ⟨plots . . . ~ by great profundity of thought —Americana Annual⟩ 2 : obtained from statistical data not distinguished as to relative importance ⟨~ mean⟩
¹un·welcome \"+\ adj [ME, fr. ¹un- + welcome, adj.] : not welcome : DISTASTEFUL, UNWANTED ⟨~ disturbance of routine —J.H.Robinson †1936⟩ ⟨in the city you are more free from ~ intimacy —M.R.Cohen⟩ ⟨forced the ~ truth out of his mind —Gordon Merrick⟩ — **un·wel·come·ly** adv
²unwelcome \"\ n [¹un- + welcome, n.] : lack of cordiality ⟨unmeant smiles . . . strengthened the irritant feeling of ~ —Richard Llewellyn⟩
³unwelcome \"\ vt [²un- + welcome] : to receive without enthusiasm ⟨plowing through his manuscripts unwelcomed —H.J.Laski⟩
un·wel·come·ness n : the quality or state of being unwelcome
un·welded \ˌən+\ adj [¹un- + welded, past part. of weld] : not welded
un·well \"+\ adj [ME unwel, fr. ¹un- + wel well] 1 : being in poor health : AILING, SICK ⟨felt ~ . . . and went to bed —N. Y. Times⟩ 2 : undergoing menstruation
un·well·ness n : the quality or state of being unwell
unwemmed adj [ME, fr. OE, fr. ¹un- + wemman to stain — more at WEM] obs : having no stain or blemish : FLAWLESS, PURE
un·wept \ˌən+\ adj [¹un- + wept, past part. of weep] : not mourned : UNLAMENTED ⟨go down to the vile dust . . . ~, unhonored, and unsung —Sir Walter Scott⟩
un·wet \"+\ adj [ME, fr. ¹un- + wet, adj.] : not wet; esp : not suffused with tears ⟨with eyes ~ —John Dryden⟩
un·wetted \"+\ adj [¹un- + wetted, past part. of wet] : UNWET
un·wheel \"+\ vt [²un- + wheel] : to deprive of wheels
un·whetted \"+\ adj [¹un- + whetted, past part. of whet] : not whetted
un·whipped \"+\ adj [¹un- + whipped, past part. of whip] : not whipped : UNPUNISHED ⟨crimes ~ of justice —Shak.⟩
un·whiskered \"+\ adj : not having whiskers
un·whispered \"+\ adj [¹un- + whispered, past part. of whisper] : not whispered ⟨something that passed ~ with his breath —E.A.Robinson⟩
un·whitewashed \"+\ adj [¹un- + whitewashed, past part. of whitewash] : not whitewashed
un·wholesome \"+\ adj [ME unholsum, fr. ¹un- + holsum wholesome] 1 : detrimental to physical, mental, or moral well-being : UNHEALTHY ⟨~ food⟩ ⟨~ pastimes⟩ ⟨keep your soul perpetually in the ~ region of remorse —Nathaniel Hawthorne⟩ 2 a : marked by lack of integrity or dependability : CORRUPT, UNSOUND ⟨the people muddied . . . ~ in their thoughts and whispers —Shak.⟩ ⟨wild speculation and ~ overexpansion —Amer. Guide Series: N. C.⟩ b : offensive to the senses : LOATHSOME, REPULSIVE ⟨bluebottles, swollen and ~, crawled and buzzed —Mary Webb⟩
syn UNWHOLESOME, MORBID, SICKLY, DISEASED, and PATHOLOGICAL apply to what is unhealthy in various ways; UNWHOLESOME applies not only to what is physically and mentally unhealthy but also to what is morally corruptive ⟨an unwholesome diet⟩ ⟨an unwholesome environment for children⟩ ⟨an aura about him of unwholesome cleverness —J.V.Baker⟩ ⟨unwholesome thoughts⟩ ⟨an unwholesome exaltation and relaxing revery —P.E.More⟩ MORBID applies not only to what is diseased, markedly unwholesome, deranged or similarly abnormal, or notably decadent but also to the fancies, feelings, or behavior resulting from or suggesting such conditions ⟨a morbid condition of the liver⟩ ⟨the morbid mental habit of dwelling on death and physical decay⟩ ⟨a morbid fascination for crime and violence⟩ SICKLY applies to what is a sign of or shows signs of marked lack of health, typically wanness, weakness, and marked general and often chronic absence of vigor, robustness, virility; it applies widely, for example to persons, animals, plants, feelings, behavior, and colors ⟨the child was puny, white and sickly, so they sent continually for the doctor —Samuel Butler †1902⟩ ⟨movie attendance is at the sickliest level in four years —Wall Street Jour.⟩ ⟨a dark, tunnellike passage, through which came a deathly, sickly odor —Bram Stoker⟩ ⟨the sickly yellow of the sea lamps —Jack London⟩ ⟨a sickly smile⟩ ⟨sickly vines withering on the trellis⟩ DISEASED applies not only to what has been attacked by disease but, like MORBID, also to what is deranged or similarly abnormal, or markedly unwholesome ⟨a diseased liver⟩ ⟨a diseased mind subject to self-deception⟩ ⟨the paralysis of a diseased will⟩ PATHOLOGICAL applies to physical, mental, or moral conditions which have their origin in disease or marked abnormality ⟨a pathological wasting away⟩ ⟨pathological moods of depression⟩ ⟨a pathological fear of crowds⟩ ⟨almost pathological desire to cling to the ideal of unstained innocence —Charles Weir⟩
un·whole·some·ly adv [ME unholsumly, fr. unholsum + -ly] : in an unwholesome manner : INJURIOUSLY, NOXIOUSLY ⟨air . . . ~ close and foul —Florence Nightingale⟩ ⟨the vegetation was . . . ~ green —Mary S. Watts⟩
un·whole·some·ness n : the quality or state of being unwholesome
un·wield·i·ly \ˌənˈwēldəlē, -li\ adv : in an unwieldy manner
un·wield·i·ness \-dēnəs, -din-\ n -ES : the quality or state of being unwieldy : AWKWARDNESS
un·wieldy \-dē, -di\ also **un·wield·ly** \-dlē, -li\ adj [unwieldy fr. ME unweldy, fr. ¹un- + weldy wieldy; unwieldly alter. (influenced by -ly) of unwieldy] 1 obs : characterized by debility : FEEBLE, INFIRM ⟨time the taste destroys, with sickness and ~ years —John Dryden⟩ 2 a : hard to handle or control : AWKWARD, CUMBERSOME ⟨the increasingly ~ colonial organization —Marjory S. Douglas⟩ ⟨on the ~ circus train the going is tedious and filled with fits and starts —R.L. Taylor⟩ b : not useful or workable : INVOLVED, IMPRACTICAL ⟨some of its rules are so ~ that many of the simplest things . . . are often the most difficult to prove —B.N.Cardozo⟩ ⟨brilliant hypotheses and all too often ~ ideas —D.M.Schneider⟩ 3 a : disproportionately large or clumsy : UNGAINLY ⟨his ~ mouth wearing the jealous leer proper to his profession —Herbert Gold⟩ ⟨any word becomes ~ . . . when its spread of emotional sail overbalances the lead and oak that ought to carry cargo —Archibald MacLeish⟩ b : massive in size : HUGE, HULKING ⟨heaved his ~ figure out of his chair —Moray Firth⟩ ⟨discourage ~ . . . corporate surpluses —F.D.Roosevelt⟩
un·wifely \ˌən+\ adj : not wifely
un·wig \"+\ vt [²un- + wig] : to divest of a wig
un·wigged \"+\ adj [¹un- + wigged, adj.] : not wearing a wig
un·will \"+\ vt -ED/-ING/-S [²un- + will] : to change the mind with regard to : CONTRADICT ⟨~s what he willed —J.A. Carlyle⟩
un·willed \"+\ adj [¹un- + willed, past part. of will] : not willed : INVOLUNTARY, UNINTENTIONAL ⟨my heart with ~ love grew warm —George Macdonald †1905⟩
un·willing \"+\ adj 1 a : withholding consent : AVERSE, OPPOSED ⟨the radicals were ~ to this —R.W.Winston⟩ ⟨the judge was ~ that the witness be recalled⟩ b : UNWILLED ⟨'twas a fault ~ —Shak.⟩ ⟨the ~ honor of being the most talked-of man in the musical world —George Copeland⟩ c : not favorably inclined : LOATH, RELUCTANT ⟨pride makes them ~ to appear to be in any way subordinate —James Bryce⟩ ⟨could not dance and was ~ to learn⟩ ⟨his ~ accomplice from beginning to end —G.G.Coulton⟩ 2 : offering opposition : OBSTINATE, REFRACTORY ⟨two horses, one of which is . . . sluggish, lazy and ~ —Rex Warner⟩ ⟨fought against nature and an ~ soil —W.C.Dickinson⟩ — **un·will·ing·ly** adv

un·will·ing·ness n : the quality or state of being unwilling : DISINCLINATION, REFUSAL
un·wilted \ˌən+\ adj [¹un- + wilted, past part. of wilt] : not wilted
un·wily \"+\ adj [ME, fr. ¹un- + wily] : not wily : GUILELESS, SIMPLE
un·wincing \"+\ adj [¹un- + wincing, pres. part. of wince] : not marked by hypersensitivity : FEARLESS, UNFLINCHING ⟨a veteran without hands . . . and his story is told with ~ documentary touches —Parker Tyler⟩
un·wind \"+\ vb [ME unwinden, fr. ²un- + winden to wind] vt 1 a : to free from convolution or cause to uncoil : wind off : UNROLL ⟨~ a bedroll⟩ ⟨unwound her arms from his neck⟩ ⟨~ thread from a spool⟩ b : to free from or as if from a binding or knot : DISENGAGE, UNDO ⟨~ a bandaged arm⟩ ⟨unwound himself from his machine only to fall . . . into an exhausted sleep —W.B.Ready⟩ ⟨an awful lot of red tape to ~ —S.E. White⟩ c : to release from tension : RELAX ⟨try to let yourself go . . . ~ yourself —Claud Cockburn⟩ 2 archaic : to traverse in the opposite direction : RETRACE ⟨~ing the labyrinth and bringing the hero . . . to a state of rest —Laurence Sterne⟩ ~ vi 1 a : to become uncoiled or disentangled : UNFOLD, UNREEL ⟨the dance record went on and on . . . as the machine unwound —Millen Brand⟩ ⟨the narrative ~s slowly⟩ ⟨a vague, unraveling, final tune like a long ~ing silk cocoon —Vachel Lindsay⟩ b : to throw off restraint : cut loose ⟨wanted to be ready to ~ with the race of his life —Time⟩ 2 : to become released from tension : RELAX ⟨this ability to block official worries out of his range of thought . . . enables him to ~ —Russell Baker⟩
un·winder \"+\ n : UNREELER
un·windy \"+\ adj : not windy : CALM, STILL
un·winged \"+\ adj [¹un- + winged, past part. of wing] : not having wings : WINGLESS
un·winking \"+\ adj [¹un- + winking, pres. part. of wink] : not winking : UNWAVERING ⟨an ~ stare⟩ — **un·wink·ing·ly** adv
un·winnable \"+\ adj [¹un- + win + -able] : incapable of being won ⟨an ~ contest⟩; esp : IMPREGNABLE ⟨an ~ fortress⟩
un·winnowed \"+\ adj [¹un- + winnowed, past part. of winnow] : not winnowed
un·wiped \ˌən+\ adj [¹un- + wiped, past part. of wipe] : not wiped : SMEARY
un·wired \"+\ adj [¹un- + wired, past part. of wire] : not wired; esp : not equipped with electric circuits ⟨a totally unheated, ~ and bathroomless house —Joanna Spencer⟩
un·wisdom \"+\ n [ME, fr. OE unwīsdōm, fr. ¹un- + wīsdōm wisdom] : lack of wisdom : FOOLISHNESS, RECKLESSNESS ⟨aesthetically vital but unsound . . . a superb expression of ~ —Norman Foerster⟩ ⟨regarded the attack . . . as almost inept in its ~ —Country Life⟩
un·wise \"+\ adj [ME, fr. OE unwīs, fr. ¹un- + wīs wise] 1 : lacking in wisdom or good sense : FOOLISH, IMPRUDENT ⟨~ to pass another car on a curve⟩ ⟨an ~ investor is soon impoverished⟩ 2 : characterized by lack of wisdom : ILL-ADVISED, SENSELESS ⟨held that the action was "hasty" and "~" at a time of great tension —George Dugan⟩ ⟨these revolting and most ~ persecutions —Anne Marsh⟩ — **un·wise·ly** adv
un·wise·ness n : UNWISDOM
un·wish \ˌən+\ vt [²un- + wish] 1 : to revoke as a wish : CANCEL, WITHDRAW ⟨~ a wish⟩ 2 obs : to wish away : obliterate by wishing ⟨now thou hast ~ed five thousand men —Shak.⟩
un·wished \"+\ adj [¹un- + wished, past part. of wish] : UNWANTED, UNWELCOME
un·wished-for \ˌənˈwisht,fō(ə)r, -ō(ə)\ adj [¹un- + wished for, past part. form of the phrase wish for] : UNWISHED ⟨unwished-for men —Shak.⟩
un·wishful \ˌən+\ adj : not wishful : RELUCTANT
un·wist \ˌənˈwist\ adj [ME, fr. ¹un- + wist, past part. of witen to know] archaic : not known : UNDETECTED, UNRECOGNIZED
un·wit \"+\ vt [²un- + wit, n.] obs : to deprive of wit : DERANGE ⟨as if some planet had unwitted men —Shak.⟩
un·witch \"+\ vt [²un- + witch] : to free from or as if from a magic spell : UNBEWITCH
un·withdrawn \"+\ adj : not withdrawn
un·withered \"+\ adj [¹un- + withered, past part. of wither] : not withered : FRESH, VIGOROUS
un·withering \"+\ adj [¹un- + withering, pres. part. of wither] : remaining fresh and unfaded
un·withstood \"+\ adj [¹un- + withstood, past part. of withstand] : not withstood : VICTORIOUS
un·witnessed \"+\ adj [ME, fr. ¹un- + witnessed, past part. of witnessen to witness] 1 : not discerned by the senses : UNPERCEIVED ⟨trifles, ~ with eye or ear —Shak.⟩ 2 : not bearing the signature of a witness ⟨an ~ legal document⟩
un·witting \"+\ adj [ME, fr. ¹un- + witting, pres. part. of witen, wi̇ten to know — more at WIT] 1 : not intended : ACCIDENTAL, INADVERTENT ⟨probable that any ~ mistake may be overlooked or regarded as ignorance on the part of a stranger —Notes & Queries on Anthropology⟩ 2 a : being unaware : OBLIVIOUS ⟨carried home washings to the best families and also, her father ~, to . . . the parlor houses on alleys —Mary Ross⟩ b : exhibiting lack of knowledge or awareness : IGNORANT, UNCONSCIOUS ⟨man is born the most helpless and ~ of animals —R.M.MacIver⟩ ⟨the lyrical impulse swollen to epical proportions produces either conscious irony or ~ absurdity —L.A.Fiedler⟩ — **un·wit·ting·ly** adv
un·wit·ting·ness n -ES : the quality or state of being unwitting
un·witty \ˌən+\ adj [ME, fr. OE unwittig, fr. ¹un- + wittig witty] : not wise or clever : SENSELESS, SILLY
un·wive \"+\ vt [²un- + wive] : to deprive of a wife
un·wived \"+\ adj [¹un- + wived, past part. of wive] : being without a wife : WIFELESS
unwmkd abbr unwatermarked
un·woman \ˌən+\ vt [²un- + woman] : to deprive of womanly qualities
¹un·womanly \"+\ adv [ME, fr. ¹un- + womanly, adv.] : in an unwomanly manner
²unwomanly \"\ adj [¹un- + womanly, adj.] : not womanly : MANNISH, UNGENTLE
un·won \"+\ adj [¹un- + won, past part. of win] : not won; esp : courted unsuccessfully ⟨the lost dinner and ~ lady —William Maginn⟩
un·wont \"+\ adj [ME unwount, fr. ¹un- + wount, wunt wont] archaic : UNWONTED, UNACCUSTOMED
un·wonted \"+\ adj 1 : being out of the ordinary : RARE, UNUSUAL ⟨an ~ softness had invaded her face —William McFee⟩ ⟨this ~ substitution of warm for cool waters had disastrous effects upon the fish —R.E.Coker⟩ 2 archaic : not accustomed by experience : UNUSED ⟨boys ~ to the tasks of war —W.C.Bryant⟩ — **un·wont·ed·ly** adv
un·wont·ed·ness n : the quality or state of being unwonted : SINGULARITY, STRANGENESS
un·wooded \ˌən+\ adj [¹un- + wooded, past part. of wood] : not wooded : TREELESS
un·wooed \"+\ adj [¹un- + wooed, past part. of woo] : not wooed
un·wordable \"+\ adj [¹un- + word + -able] : inexpressible in words
un·wordy \ˌənˈwərdi\ adj [by alter.] Scot : UNWORTHY
un·workability \ˌən+\ n : the quality or state of being unworkable : IMPRACTICALITY
un·workable \"+\ adj : not workable : IMPRACTICAL
un·work·able·ness n : UNWORKABILITY
un·worked \"+\ adj [¹un- + worked, past part. of work] 1 : not shaped by working : CRUDE, RAW ⟨one single ~ flint —John Lubbock⟩ 2 : not put to use : UNEXPLORED, UNTAPPED ⟨allowing so important a clue to remain ~ —F.W.Crofts⟩ ⟨an ~ inventory⟩ ⟨an ~ mine⟩
un·working \"+\ adj [¹un- + working, pres. part. of work] : not working : IDLE
un·workmanlike \"+\ adj [¹un- + workman + like] : not characteristic of or suited to a good workman : INCOMPETENT, INEFFICIENT ⟨an ~ result⟩ ⟨an ~ tool⟩
un·worldliness \"+\ n : the quality or state of being unworldly
un·worldly \"+\ adj 1 : not of this world : UNEARTHLY ⟨an ~ stillness in the cloud —Ira Wolfert⟩; specif : SPIRITUAL 2 a : not wise in the ways of the world : NAÏVE, UNSOPHISTICATED ⟨this helplessly ~ woman —Kate O'Brien⟩ b : not swayed by mundane considerations ⟨as of wealth⟩ ⟨was ~, and did not greatly miss worldly rewards —Sheldon Cheney⟩
un·worn \"+\ adj 1 : unimpaired by use : not eroded or worn away 2 a : not jaded : FRESH, ORIGINAL b : not worn : NEW, PRISTINE
un·worried \"+\ adj [¹un- + worried, past part. of worry] : not worried
un·worshiped \"+\ adj [ME unworschiped, fr. ¹un- + worschiped, past part. of worschipen to worship] : not worshiped
¹un·worth \"+\ adj [¹un- + worth, adj.] : UNWORTHY
²unworth \"\ n [¹un- + worth, n.] : lack of value or merit : POVERTY, UNWORTHINESS
un·wor·thi·ly \ˌənˈwərthəlē, -li\ adv [ME, fr. unworthy + -ly] : in an unworthy manner
un·wor·thi·ness \-thēnəs, -thin-\ n [ME unworthines, fr. unworthy + -nes -ness] : the quality or state of being unworthy
¹un·worthy \ˌən+\ adj [ME, fr. ¹un- + worthy] 1 a : lacking in excellence or value : POOR, WORTHLESS ⟨the precincts of the Minister are quite clear of any ~ building —S.P.B.Mais⟩ ⟨the tremendous advances of science and technology have somehow led us to believe that other kinds of knowledge are ~ —C.S.Kilby⟩ b : of a contemptible nature : BASE, DISHONORABLE ⟨no right to employ other men on ~ tasks, whether we pay them well or not —W.R.Inge⟩ ⟨the right to dismiss or expel . . . a student whose conduct is deemed ~ —Villanova College Cat.⟩ 2 : not meritorious : UNDESERVING ⟨ration cards to citizens previously held politically ~ —Frank Gorrell⟩ — often used with of or to ⟨~ of continued confidence —H.S.Drinker⟩ ⟨a vile man . . . deemed ~ to discharge the duty —J.G. Frazer⟩ 3 : not corresponding to desert : UNMERITED, UNJUSTIFIED ⟨an ~ treatment of a potentially fine subject —Anthony Boucher⟩ 4 : UNBECOMING — usu. used with of ⟨such bargaining seemed ~ of a self-respecting nation —S.E.Morison & H.S.Commager⟩
²unworthy \"\ n : an unworthy person ⟨a whole gallery of . . . worthies and unworthies come to life —Times Lit. Supp.⟩
³unworthy \"\ adv, archaic : UNWORTHILY
un·wound \"+\ adj [¹un- + wound, past part. of wind] 1 : not wound ⟨an ~ clock⟩ 2 : released from a coiled state ⟨the bobbin has come ~⟩
un·wound·able \"+əbəl\ adj [¹un- + wound + -able] : incapable of being wounded : INVULNERABLE
un·wounded \ˌən+\ adj [ME unwunded, fr. OE unwundod, fr. ¹un- + wundod, past part. of wundian to wound] : not wounded : INTACT, WHOLE
un·woven \"+\ adj [ME, fr. ¹un- + woven, past part. of weven to weave] : not woven ⟨~ fabrics are made by combining textile fibers . . . with a binder by means of heat and pressure —Amer. Fabrics⟩
un·wrap \"+\ vt [ME unwrappen, fr. ²un- + wrappen to wrap] 1 : to open to view by or as if by removing a wrapping : DISCLOSE, REVEAL ⟨~ a package⟩ ⟨~ . . . the evidence in a criminal case —Newsweek⟩ 2 : UNFOLD, UNROLL ⟨unwrapped his blankets, spread them on the bed —Andrew Robertson⟩
un·wreaked \"+\ adj [¹un- + wreaked, past part. of wreak] : not wreaked : UNAVENGED
un·wreathe \"+\ vt [²un- + wreathe] : UNCOIL, UNTWIST
un·wreathed \"+\ adj [¹un- + wreathed, past part. of wreathe] : lacking or divested of a wreath ⟨the Empire's ~ laureate —Time⟩
un·wrench \"+\ vt [²un- + wrench] archaic : to yank off or open
un·wrinkle \"+\ vt [²un- + wrinkle] : to free from wrinkles : smooth out
un·wrinkled \"+\ adj [¹un- + wrinkled, past part. of wrinkle] : not wrinkled : SMOOTH
un·writable \"+\ adj : incapable of being put into writing ⟨an ~ sound⟩
un·write \"+\ vt [²un- + write] : to obliterate from writing : EXPUNGE, RESCIND ⟨it is easier to unsay than to ~ cross words —Court Life at Naples⟩
un·written \"+\ adj [ME unwriten, fr. ¹un- + writen, past part. of writen to write] 1 : not reduced to writing : ORAL, TRADITIONAL ⟨an ~ code⟩ ⟨rites . . . so ancient that they well might have had their ~ origins in Aurignacian times —J.L.T.C. Spence⟩ 2 : containing no writing : BLANK ⟨an ~ page⟩
unwritten constitution n : a constitution not embodied in a single document but implied in the institutions and customs of the country as expressed in long-accepted statutes and the body of the common law — called also customary constitution
unwritten law n 1 : law (as the common law of England or the U.S.) originating in custom or otherwise than as formally made and declared by the sovereign legislative power and not committed to writing at its origin 2 : the custom of granting a measure of immunity to persons guilty of certain criminal acts justified in the eyes of the public esp. in avenging injury to family honor arising from seduction or adultery — usu. used with the
un·wronged \ˌən+\ adj [¹un- + wronged, past part. of wrong] : not wronged
un·wrought \"+\ adj [ME, fr. ¹un- + wrought] 1 : not shaped into finished form : ROUGH ⟨~ steel⟩ ⟨the mass of notes he had made remained ~ —Isabel Paterson⟩ 2 a : not processed for use : still in a natural state : RAW, VIRGIN ⟨~ rock⟩ ⟨~ land⟩ b : not worked : UNDEVELOPED ⟨an ~ mine⟩
un·wrung \"+\ adj [¹un- + wrung, past part. of wring] : not painfully affected : UNMOVED ⟨let the gall'd jade winch; our withers are ~ —Shak.⟩
un·yeaned \"+\ adj [¹un- + yeaned, past part. of yean] : UNBORN — used esp. of a lamb
un·yielded \"+\ adj [¹un- + yielded, past part. of yield] : not yielded : not surrendered
un·yielding \"+\ adj [¹un- + yielding, pres. part. of yield] 1 a : characterized by lack of softness or flexibility : HARD, STIFF ⟨an ~ horsehair sofa⟩ b : refusing to give way : RESOLUTE, OBSTINATE ⟨remove your siege from my ~ heart —Shak.⟩ ⟨the steady, swift, ~ stream of parkway traffic —E.J.Kahn⟩ c : not subject to amelioration or development : FIXED, RIGID ⟨the music was . . . acrobatic, ~ and overdissonant —Time⟩ ⟨the farms look ~, the buildings drab —Amer. Guide Series: Vt.⟩ 2 : characterized by firmness or obduracy : ADAMANT, FLINTY ⟨~ determination⟩ ⟨looks strong-minded and dignified . . . with his ~ mouth and glassy eyes —Marchette Chute⟩ — **un·yield·ing·ly** adv
un·yield·ing·ness n : the quality or state of being inflexible : PERTINACITY, RIGIDITY
un·yoke \ˌən+\ vb [ME unyoken, fr. OE ungeocian, fr. ²un- + geocian to yoke] vt 1 a : to free (a draft animal) from a yoke or harness : OUTSPAN, UNHITCH b obs : to liberate as if from a yoke : RELEASE ⟨the property of truth is . . . to ~ and set free the minds and spirits of a nation —John Milton⟩ 2 : to take apart : DISJOIN, UNLINK ⟨at the rapids the large rafts are . . . unyoked, and divided into small portions —Anthony Trollope⟩ ~ vi 1 archaic : to unharness a draft animal 2 archaic : to stop work : slack off
un·yoked \"+\ adj [in sense 1, fr. ¹un- + yoked, past part. of yoke; in sense 2, fr. past part. of unyoke] 1 : not yoked : UNRESTRAINED 2 : freed from or as if from a yoke
un·zealous \"+\ adj : not zealous — **un·zeal·ous·ly** adv
un·zip \"+\ vb [²un- + zip] vt : to zip open ⟨~ a zipper⟩ ⟨unzipped a pocket in his black nylon parka —E.S.Hatch⟩ ~ vi : to open by means of a zipper ⟨~s to hold full pack —Mademoiselle⟩
un·zipper \"+\ vb : UNZIP
un·zoned \"+\ adj [¹un- + zoned, past part. of zone] 1 : not zoned : UNRESTRICTED 2 archaic : not cinctured
¹up \ˈ(,)əp\ adv [partly fr. ME up upward, fr. OE ūp; partly fr. ME uppe on high, fr. OE; both akin to OHG ūf up, ON upp up, upward, uppi on high, Goth iup upward, uf under, L sub under, below, Gk hypo under, Skt upa towards, near to, at, under, upari over — more at OVER] 1 a (1) : toward the sky : toward a higher position : away from the center of the earth ⟨pushes the boy ~ to the top of the fence so he can see⟩ ⟨the oil shoots ~ 200 feet⟩ ⟨has breakfast brought ~ to her bedroom⟩ ⟨ordered ~ searchlights to stab the sky —Noel Houston⟩ — often used as an intensive ⟨lift ~ your eyes⟩ ⟨raised ~ the ceiling a few feet⟩; often used in commands or exclamations calling for upward motion ⟨hands ~⟩ ⟨~ periscope —E.L.Beach⟩; formerly used in combination with a verb, esp. an

auxiliary ⟨we will, fair Queen, ~ to the mountain's top —Shak.⟩ (2) **:** from beneath the ground or water to the surface ⟨digs ~ arrowheads in his backyard⟩ ⟨the fish swim ~ for crumbs⟩ (3) **:** from below the horizon ⟨sees the moon come ~⟩ (4) **:** toward a slightly higher level ⟨fishermen pulling boats ~ onto a beach⟩; *specif* **:** to or near the putting green of a golf course ⟨hits the ball well ~⟩ (5) **:** toward a point (as on a river) that is farther away from the ocean ⟨must time everything exactly — ~ with the flood tide, arriving . . . precisely at slack water —C.S.Forester⟩ (6) **:** from a prone, sitting, slanting, or stooped position to an upright position ⟨helps ~ a man who has fallen⟩ ⟨draws himself ~ to his full height⟩; *specif* **:** out of bed ⟨stayed ~ all night long⟩ — sometimes used in commands or exclamations ⟨~, ~, my friend, and quit your books —William Wordsworth⟩ **b :** upward from the ground or other surface so as to be detached ⟨pulls ~ all the tulips⟩ **c** *archaic* **:** to a condition of being open ⟨have broken ~ my packet again to insert this letter —Edmund Verney⟩ **d :** so as to expose fully a particular side or surface ⟨turns the ace of spades ~⟩ **2 a :** in a relatively high position ⟨~ in the mountains⟩ ⟨brings in a mirror-sharp picture 35,000 feet ~ —*advt*⟩ ⟨wants to see her name ~ in lights⟩ ⟨only a kid . . . with that flaming hair of hers just ~ —Mary Deasy⟩ ⟨the ball is ~ on the green⟩ **b :** at a point (as on a river) that is farther away from the ocean ⟨camps ~ above the rapids⟩ **c :** in an upright position; *specif* **:** on one's feet ⟨standing ~ in front of a judge —Kay Boyle⟩ **3 a :** so as to cause sound to rise in volume or to be heard ⟨speak ~ so that she can hear⟩ ⟨turns ~ the radio too loud⟩ **b :** so as to cause light to become brighter ⟨turns ~ the lamp on the desk⟩ **4 a :** to or in a higher or better condition or status ⟨on his way ~ as a junior member of a law firm —Sara H. Hay⟩ ⟨pressure on manufacturers to keep quality ~ —*Current Biog.*⟩ ⟨keeps him ~ out of sentimental estheticism —Clive Bell⟩ — sometimes used in exclamations ⟨~ the workers —Liam O'Flaherty⟩ **b :** to or toward an advanced state (as of maturity or skill) ⟨grew ~ in the city⟩ **c :** to or in a state of greater resolution or cheerfulness ⟨brace ~ and keep going⟩ ⟨only buoyed ~ by the hope . . . of seeing a junk —Osbert Lancaster⟩ — sometimes used in commands or exclamations **d** (1) **:** to or in a state of greater activity or excitement ⟨stirs ~ crowds⟩ ⟨the type that boiled ~ inside sometimes —E.V.Roberts⟩ (2) — used as a function word usu. in combination with *it* to indicate marked or intense activity ⟨singing and laughing it ~ with the boys —Arthur Godfrey⟩ **e :** to or at a greater speed, rate, or amount ⟨an effort to bring military plane production ~ —*Current Biog.*⟩ ⟨rents would move ~ or down —S.L.Payne⟩ **f :** to or at a higher musical pitch ⟨transposes the melody ~ a fifth⟩ ⟨singing easily ~ above high C⟩ **g :** in continuance (as in time or a series) ⟨indefatigable labors from youth ~ —D.S. & Jessie K. Jordan⟩ ⟨boys from fourth grade ~ —Gladys Skelley⟩ ⟨rent from $50 ~ —Warner Olivier⟩ ⟨highly alert during the night and ~ through dawn—P.W.Thompson⟩ ⟨from early childhood ~ until the age of 20⟩ **h :** into greater prominence or a higher status or estimation (as by means of a specific action) ⟨talks ~ all the new styles⟩ ⟨the quality of the beef is what counts, and the brown sugar is the touch to point it ~ —C.H.Baker⟩ **i :** to or in a state of expansion ⟨a fish that puffs itself ~⟩ ⟨the ingenious folly of pumping ~ a poem till it means everything —N.E. Nelson⟩ **5 a :** into existence, evidence, prominence, or prevalence **:** into operation or practical form ⟨drawings . . . worked ~ in the office by several draftsmen —F.J.Mather⟩ ⟨saloons went ~ rapidly —D.D.Martin⟩ ⟨a skillful building ~ of suspense —C.W. Shumaker⟩ ⟨the money will turn ~ somewhere⟩ ⟨stokes the fire to get steam ~⟩ **b :** to the consideration or attention of a person so that a decision or disposition can be made ⟨put the problem squarely and finally ~ to the states and cities whose immediate concern it is —F.E. Johnson⟩ ⟨senators come ~ for reelection —T.R.Ybarra⟩ ⟨the unmanageable gelding went ~ for raffle —*Time*⟩ **c :** to or at bat ⟨comes ~ twice in the same inning⟩ **6 a :** into the hands of another ⟨yielded himself ~ a prisoner —Maria Edgeworth⟩ **b :** into one's possession ⟨their licenses can be taken ~ and returned to authorities in their own state —*Birmingham (Ala.) News*⟩ **c :** in disclosure or confession — used with *own, show,* or *give* **7 a :** to or toward a total number or quantity ⟨counts ~ all the factors⟩ ⟨ran ~ a big bill⟩ ⟨sums ~ the whole situation⟩ **b** (1) **:** to a state of completeness or finality ⟨eats ~ the cake⟩ ⟨finds that the land he is interested in is leased ~ —J.L.Harnon⟩ ⟨charge it ~ to experience⟩ — often used as a function word for emphasis with little addition of meaning ⟨might wake even the bomber boys ~ —J.G.Cozzens⟩ ⟨the pipe is stopped ~ with dirt⟩ ⟨the black water had swallowed me ~ —O.S.J.Gogarty⟩ ⟨to fright the animals and to kill them ~ —Shak.⟩ (2) **:** to a degree approaching completeness **:** to a marked degree ⟨show houses were being bought ~ by the moving picture interests —C.F.Wittke⟩ ⟨clean ~ the house⟩ ⟨softening ~ the enemy with artillery before making the final attack⟩ — often used as a function word for emphasis ⟨the plane's fueling ~ —Kay Boyle⟩ ⟨the roads empty magically while the drivers chow ~ —Barrett McGurn⟩ **8 a :** in or into a storage place ⟨lays ~ supplies for the winter⟩ ⟨putting ~ preserves⟩ **b :** in or into a condition of closure or confinement ⟨buttoned himself ~ —John Buchan⟩ ⟨wrapped ~ in a dressing gown —H.A.L.Craig⟩ ⟨a fine time to pot ~ bulbs for forcing —*Catalog: Holland Bulb Gardens*⟩ ⟨cork the bottle ~⟩ ⟨have locked ~ and gone home —Brooks Atkinson⟩ **c :** in or into a condition of union or combination ⟨sews ~ the rip⟩ ⟨joins ~ with his friends⟩ **d :** by way of remedying or eliminating a defect (as a break) ⟨patched ~ his old pants⟩ ⟨a rather battered sign . . . we ought to paint it ~ —*Holiday*⟩ **9 a :** so as to arrive or approach ⟨comes driving ~ in a new car⟩ ⟨an avenue of trees leads ~ to the house⟩ **b :** in a direction that is conventionally the opposite of *down* regardless of difference in elevation **:** toward, to, or at a place that is regarded as higher: as (1) *chiefly Brit* **:** toward or in a more important place (as a large city, university, or headquarters) ⟨went ~ to London as professor of surgery —Harvey Graham⟩ (2) **:** toward the direction from which the wind is blowing **:** to windward (3) **:** toward or in the north ⟨peach cultivation is slowly extending ~ from the south —*Amer. Guide Series: Ark.*⟩ (4) **:** toward or near the top (as of a sheet of paper) ⟨your rapid pen moved ~ and down —Edna S.V. Millay⟩ (5) **:** toward or in an outlying district ⟨went ~ to the farm for a rest⟩ (6) **:** toward or at the rear of a theatrical stage — used chiefly in stage directions ⟨offended, walks ~ —W.S.Gilbert⟩ (7) **:** to prison ⟨went ~ in the 1920's . . . for 20 years —D.W.Maurer⟩ **c :** toward or at a forward position ⟨hold their positions ~ in the trenches⟩ **d :** so as to be even with, overtake, find, or arrive at ⟨his horse was fourth but then came ~ and won⟩ ⟨may be traced ~ to the first beginnings of Greek speculation —Walter Pater⟩ **10 :** in or into separated parts ⟨break ~ the road before widening it⟩ ⟨tears ~ newspapers⟩ — often used as a function word for emphasis ⟨the country was divided ~ into two spheres of interest —A.T. Bouscaren⟩ **11 a :** to a stop — usu. used with *draw, bring, fetch,* or *pull* **b :** without delay **:** PROMPTLY ⟨didn't wait for recognition but spoke right ~⟩ ⟨answers ~ to every question⟩ **12 a :** in advance (as of one's opponent) **:** AHEAD ⟨on the next hole he shot a birdie three to go two ~ —*Time*⟩ ⟨the intellectual's game of being one ~ on the prevailing interpretation —W.L.Miller⟩ **b :** for each side **:** EACH ⟨the score is 15 ~⟩ **13 a :** in multiples (as copies printed on a single sheet from identical plates at a single impression) ⟨when circulars are ordered in large quantities, it is common to print them two ~ or four ~ —Daniel Melcher & Nancy Larrick⟩ — compare [1]GANG 3a(2) **b :** in capital letters **:** with a capital initial letter ⟨put all of these words ~⟩ **c :** on a recto page and with the head next to the binding edge — used of the facing of an illustration; compare [2]FACE 9

[2]**up** \ˈəp\ *adj* [ME *uppe*, fr. OE, fr. *uppe*, adv.] **1 a :** risen above the horizon esp. so as to be visible **:** present in the sky ⟨the sun is still ~⟩ **b** (1) **:** standing on one's feet (2) *chiefly Brit* **:** standing and delivering a speech ⟨the chancellor of the exchequer's ~ —Charles Dickens⟩ **c :** risen from bed **:** being out of bed ⟨is ~ every morning at six⟩ ⟨a man who was just ~ from an attack of the measles —A.W.Long⟩ ⟨was ~ all last night —Kay Boyle⟩ **d :** high with respect to the bank of a stream or a shore ⟨the river is dangerously ~⟩ **e :** being in a raised position **:** RAISED, LIFTED ⟨all the windows are ~⟩ ⟨with the thumbscrew in the ~ position —H.G.Armstrong⟩ ⟨her defenses were ~ —Ethel Wilson⟩ **f :** standing above the ground **:** CONSTRUCTED, BUILT ⟨the two temporary bridges are ~ —Kay Boyle⟩ **g** (1) **:** having the face uppermost and exposed **:** facing upward (2) **:** fried on one side ⟨ordered two eggs ~⟩ **h :** mounted on the back of a horse ⟨with a new jockey ~⟩ ⟨is ~ on a long shot —Walter Bernstein⟩ **i :** grown or moved above a surface (as of the ground) so as to be visible ⟨the corn is ~ now⟩ **j :** cut and placed suitably (as in storage) ⟨the hay is ~, and the turnips thinned —Padraic Fallon⟩ **k** (1) **:** having the surface broken (as for repairs) ⟨began to unload poles and warning notices of "Road *Up*" —Adrian Bell⟩ (2) **:** REMOVED ⟨finds the track ~ for several hundred feet⟩ **l :** moving, inclining, or directed upward ⟨the ~ escalator⟩ ⟨looked at him with an ~ glance⟩ **m** (1) **:** set with a capital initial letter or all in capitals ⟨all genus names are ~⟩ (2) **:** marked by the use of more capital letters than is usual ⟨the style of this magazine is ~⟩ **n :** held or brushed up toward the top of the head ⟨a new ~ hairdo, a little fancy for daytime —Budd Schulberg⟩ **2 a** (1) **:** marked by a state of revolt, agitation, or excitement ⟨they say the tribes are ~ —John Masefield⟩ ⟨their fighting blood was ~ —S.H.Adams⟩ (2) **:** marked by activity **:** ACTIVE ⟨let's be ~ and doing⟩ **b :** marked by confidence and good spirits ⟨in his ~ periods he joked and talked —Cyril Connolly⟩ **c :** increased above a former level (as of quantity or price) ⟨bank loans were ~ six percent —Harvey Walker⟩ ⟨Sunday school enrollment is ~ —Ben Bradford⟩ ⟨fever was down, appetite was ~ —G.W.Gray b. 1886⟩ **d** (1) **:** marked by greater than usual power or strength ⟨haunts the sandbar now and growls when the wind is ~ —Laurence Critchell⟩ ⟨the lights in the drawing room on the first floor . . . were ~ —Margery Allingham⟩ (2) **:** exerting enough force or power (as for operation) ⟨the ship will sail as soon as steam is ~⟩ ⟨I'll make a pot of tea. The fire is just ~ —Katharine Shattuck⟩ **e :** sailing on the way **:** BOUND ⟨a ship now ~ for the tropics⟩ **f :** EFFERVESCENT ⟨took a sip to see if the champagne was still ~⟩ **g :** READY ⟨was ~ to any party of pleasure —W.M.Thackeray⟩; *specif* **:** marked by a high degree of physical and psychological preparedness ⟨players will be ~ for the conference opponents and traditional rivals —H.O. Crisler⟩ **h** (1) **:** going on **:** taking place ⟨went out to see what was ~ —Francis Shean⟩ ⟨begins to realize something is ~ —Anne Brooks⟩ (2) **:** WRONG, AMISS ⟨there was something ~ with her voice —Richard Llewellyn⟩ **3 a :** come to an end **:** COMPLETED, ENDED, TERMINATED ⟨the ringing of a bell in the classroom means that the hour is ~ —Ralph Linton⟩ ⟨his term of duty is nearly ~ —A.H.Townsend⟩ ⟨the game is ~ at 15 points⟩ **b** *Brit* **:** ADJOURNED ⟨Parliament was ~ —C.E. Robinson⟩ **c :** come to an undesired end ⟨the game's all ~ with him⟩ ⟨the hunt was now fairly ~ and a crowd nearly 50 strong was racing down the wharf after them —Max Peacock⟩ **d :** set in type ⟨the editorial is all ~⟩ **4 a :** standing high (as in status or fortune) **:** having risen from a lower position ⟨at graduation he was well ~ in his class⟩ ⟨can almost tell which industries are down and which are ~, from the gifts —Sanford Brown⟩ ⟨choose management material not from men ~ from the bench but from young college-trained technicians —*Time*⟩ **b :** situated forward with respect to others ⟨his horse is well ~⟩ **c** *archaic* **:** much spoken about **d :** being or having arrived on the same level or at the same point **:** EQUAL, EVEN ⟨there were no dragging ends in the rear . . . nobody complaining that food or ammunition was not ~ —*Everybody's Mag.*⟩ — often used with *to* or *with* ⟨was well ~ to the average of her class —F.W. Crofts⟩ ⟨did not feel quite ~ to par and proposed to rest —Alexander MacDonald⟩ ⟨discovers he is ~ with the best of them⟩ **e :** advanced in age ⟨lived until she was ~ in the eighties⟩ **f** (1) **:** well informed through study or experience **:** quite familiar **:** ABREAST — usu. used with *on* ⟨his friends are ~ on the very latest things in the arts —Geoffrey Gorer⟩; also used with *in* or *to* ⟨well ~ in these things —J.B.Smyth⟩ (2) **:** being on schedule **:** not fallen behind — usu. used with *on* or *in* ⟨said he was ~ on his homework⟩ **g :** ahead of one's opponent (as in a game) ⟨in spite of being set four tricks they were still ~⟩ ⟨was three ~ on the second hole⟩ ⟨black is a pawn ~⟩ **h :** being at or near the top (as of a list) ⟨rehashing . . . the rumors of names ~ for rotation —T.H.Phillips⟩ **i :** being the higher pair in a poker hand consisting of two pairs ⟨queens ~⟩ **5 a** (1) **:** bound in a direction regarded as up (as toward the north, an important city, or the source of a river) ⟨caught the ~ train to town⟩ ⟨a very small fraction of the ~ traffic —Werner Mangold⟩ (2) **:** of or relating to traffic bound in a direction regarded as up ⟨checked his suitcase on the ~ side of the station⟩ **b** *chiefly Brit* (1) **:** staying temporarily in a more important place (as London) (2) **:** resident at a university or a school ⟨was ~ . . . with my wife as an undergraduate —W.B.Millen⟩ ⟨was still the depth of the vacation, and there were only a few scholars ~ —C.P.Snow⟩ **c :** placed so as to hold the rudder far to leeward ⟨the tiller is ~⟩ **d :** blowing from a mark used in archery toward the shooter ⟨a strong ~ wind⟩ **e :** confined to prison **6 a** (1) **:** being under consideration (as for the making of a decision) ⟨the bill is now ~ before Congress⟩ ⟨the question is now ~ to the full cabinet and a decision is expected —H.T.Simmons⟩ (2) **:** presented for consideration (as for the making of a decision) **:** due to be considered ⟨is ~ for reelection —Elmer Davis⟩ ⟨is now ~ for sale —S.P.B.Mais⟩ ⟨a labor contract is ~ for negotiation —*Securities Outlook*⟩; *specif* **:** present (as in a court) and charged with an offense ⟨is ~ for rape —Charles Oldfather⟩ **b :** placed at stake **:** BET, WAGERED ⟨many thousands of dollars were ~ on the match⟩ — **up against :** confronted with **:** face-to-face with ⟨realized that they were *up against* a major difficulty —Nevil Shute⟩ ⟨really took a professional to understand what he was *up against* —Robertson Davies⟩ — **up against it :** face-to-face with a seemingly insuperable obstacle **:** in desperate straits ⟨a first-rate story of people who happen to be *up against it* —J.R.Chamberlain⟩ — **up to 1 a :** capable of performing or dealing with **:** competent or able to cope with **:** capable of ⟨feels she is *up to* her role in the play⟩ ⟨is now *up to* seeing visitors⟩ ⟨was *up to* doing the job in a little over six days —Robert Bendiner⟩; *specif* **:** capable of carrying without strain ⟨require a horse *up to* 13 stone —F.C.Hitchcock⟩ **b :** aware of and prepared for ⟨should certainly be *up to* his tricks by this time⟩ **2 :** engaged in esp. secretly and with intentions that are bad or not altogether good ⟨ferreting out clues as to what he was *up to* —R.H.Popkin⟩ ⟨was always *up to* something —H.G.Wells⟩ **3 :** incumbent on **:** devolving on **:** being the responsibility of ⟨it was *up to* the parent to educate his child —Benjamin Fine⟩ ⟨left the next move *up to* the Russians —*Current History*⟩ ⟨the amount you give is entirely *up to* you —Agnes M. Miall⟩

[3]**up** \"\ *vb* **upped** *or in vi 1* **up; upped; upping; ups** *or in vi 1* **up** [[1]*up*] *vi* **1 :** to act abruptly or surprisingly — usu. followed by *and* and another verb ⟨he ~ and married a show girl —Michael Mackay⟩ ⟨the jackass *upped* and died —*Springfield (Mass.) Union*⟩ ⟨no sooner is a girl qualified to be a doctor than she ~*s* with some white-jacketed junior bandage wrapper and is off with him to a suburban villa —R.P.Lister⟩ **2 :** to rise from a lying or sitting position **:** get up **3 :** to move upward **:** RISE, ASCEND **4 :** to raise one's hand or arm esp. quickly and aggressively — followed by *with* ⟨*upped* with a shotgun and opened some rain holes in the cloth top —F.B. Gipson⟩ ~ *vt* **1 :** to catch a swan in order to put the owner's mark on the beak **2 a :** to move to a physically higher position **:** RAISE, LIFT ⟨~*s* flukes and goes down again —W.J.Hopkins⟩ ⟨*upped* sail —John Buchan⟩ **b** (1) **:** to raise to a higher level **:** INCREASE, ADVANCE ⟨*upped* the fare from 10 cents to 15 cents a ride —Gus Tyler⟩ ⟨cattle growers *upped* meat production —*N.Y.Times*⟩ (2) **:** to put into a higher occupational position **:** PROMOTE ⟨has been *upped* to general merchandising director —Bennett Cerf⟩ (3) **:** RAISE 17 **3 :** to put (the helm) up

[4]**up** \(ˌ)əp\ *prep* [[1]*up*] **1 a :** from a lower to a higher place on or along **:** to, toward, or at a higher point of ⟨climbing ~ a tree⟩ ⟨building a cogwheel railway ~ the mountain —*Amer. Guide Series: N.H.*⟩ ⟨the heat which is normally wasted ~ the chimney —Ronald Robson⟩ ⟨a child can be shifted horizontally as he progresses ~ the school —G.B.Jeffery⟩ ⟨it might be snowing ~ the mountain —J.M.Brinnin⟩ **b :** up into or in the ⟨go ~ garret and play —B.F.Taylor⟩ ⟨asked was there anything ~ attic —Robert Frost⟩ **2 :** in a direction regarded as being toward or near the upper end or part of ⟨a journey ~ one of the valleys —L.D.Stamp⟩: as **a :** toward or at a point that is closer to the source or beginning of ⟨a steamer groping her way ~ river —Cicely F. Smith⟩ ⟨these fish winter ~ the river —*Biol. Abstracts*⟩ **b :** toward or near the inner part of ⟨walks ~ the walk —Edna S.V.Millay⟩ ⟨advanced ~ the room —J.G.Cozzens⟩ ⟨will find himself trapped ~ a dead end —H.A.Burr⟩ **c :** to, toward, or in the interior of (as a region) ⟨traveling ~ the country⟩ ⟨~ country in the coffee and cotton plantations . . . life is rougher — William Tate⟩ **d :** toward the north along or through ⟨lives a few miles ~ the coast⟩ ⟨withdrew his army ~ the island — H.E.Scudder⟩ — often used in combination with a following noun to form adjectives and adverbs ⟨an auction of *up*county farm land —Lonnie Coleman⟩ ⟨the water would then flow *up*dip through the more porous strata —C.G.Lalicker⟩ **3 :** in the direction opposite to **:** AGAINST ⟨~ the wind⟩ **4 a :** in a direction parallel to the length of **:** ALONG ⟨took his arm and they began to walk together ~ the street —William Fay⟩ **b :** nearby on ⟨as familiar as the man who lives ~ the street⟩

[5]**up** \ˈəp\ *n* -S [[1]*up* & [2]*up*] **1 :** one that is in a high or advantageous position ⟨the savor of the book lies in . . . figures in the crowd, in the downs as well as the ~*s* —Ernestine Evans⟩ **2 :** an upward slope **3 :** a period or state of prosperity or success ⟨unions always thrive most in times of business ~*s* or business downs —*Kiplinger Washington Letter*⟩ ⟨has had downs as well as ~*s* since he became . . . commander of the northern expeditionary forces —*New Republic*⟩ **4 :** a rise in value or price — **in two ups** *Austral* **:** in a jiffy — **on the up :** moving upward ⟨is *on the up* in any case. Thirteen miles away . . . the world's largest molybdenum mine is booming —*Time*⟩ ⟨the curve is steadily *on the up* —B.M.Beck⟩

up *abbr* upper

UP *abbr* underproof

up-a-daisy *var of* UPSY-DAISY

upaith·ric \(ˈ)yü¦pīthrik\ *adj* [irreg. fr. Gk *hypaithros* in the open air, uncovered + E *-ic* — more at HYPAETHRAL] **:** HYPAETHRAL

up-anchor \¦=¦==\ *vi* [[3]*up* + *anchor*, n.] **:** to pull up the anchor esp. before getting under way ⟨we *up-anchored*, southbound for the canal —*Blue Bk.*⟩

up-and-comer \ˈ==ˈ==\ *n* [*up-and-coming* + *-er*] **:** COMER 2

up-and-coming \¦==¦==\ *adj* [[2]*up*] **:** alertly active and likely to advance or succeed **:** ENTERPRISING, PROMISING ⟨gave encouragement, contracts, and advances to *up-and-coming* young songwriters —Hal Levy⟩ ⟨an *up-and-coming* new town⟩

[1]**up and down** *adv* [ME *up and down*] **1 :** to and fro **:** backward and forward ⟨spent the night pacing *up and down*⟩ **2 :** here and there esp. throughout an area ⟨looking for him *up and down*⟩ **3 a :** with regard to every particular **:** THOROUGHLY, COMPLETELY ⟨his home state which he knows *up and down*⟩ ⟨looked her *up and down* before speaking⟩ **b :** without holding back **:** BLUNTLY, DIRECTLY ⟨told him *up and down* he was a fool⟩ **4 :** into or in a vertical position — used of a cable when the anchor is under or nearly under the bow

[2]**up and down** *n, pl* **ups and downs 1** *ups and downs pl* **a :** alternating rise and fall esp. in fortune or degree of success **:** ALTERNATION, FLUCTUATION, VICISSITUDE ⟨jogging along with *ups and downs* and plenty of worries and some satisfactions —F.M.Ford⟩ ⟨a little weary of the perpetual *ups and downs* of her mood —J.W.Krutch⟩ **b :** an undulation or irregularity (as on the surface of the ground) ⟨a difficult route with many *ups and downs*⟩ **2 :** a quick examining look ⟨gave me the *up and down*, and I saw that he remembered me —*Popular Mag.*⟩ **3 :** a design or texture that changes in appearance when the material is viewed from a different angle and that must be placed upright in order to obtain the desired effect ⟨the pieces of a pattern can be placed closely on this solid-color fabric because it has no *up and down*⟩

up-and-down \¦==¦=\ *adj* [[1]*up and down*] **1 :** marked by alternate upward and downward movement or action ⟨an odd *up-and-down* gait⟩ ⟨in his natural *up-and-down* voice —I.S. Cobb⟩ ⟨many such *up-and-down* years —Thomas Hughes⟩ **2 a :** very steep **:** PERPENDICULAR ⟨in the deep sand about a foot from a straight *up-and-down* bank —Ring Lardner⟩ **b :** DIRECT, DOWNRIGHT ⟨an *up-and-down* quarrel⟩ **3 :** marked by irregularity of surface; *esp* **:** having an irregular terrain **:** HILLY, MOUNTAINOUS ⟨an *up-and-down* place where the hotel has seven main entrances, each on a different floor —*Geog. School Bull.*⟩ **4** *Brit* **:** ROUGH-AND-TUMBLE ⟨savage, desperate, *up-and-down* fighting —Charles Kingsley⟩ — **up-and-downness** *n* -ES

up-and-down indicator *n* **:** a device for showing to what extent a timepiece has run down

up-and-up \ˈ==ˈ=\ *n* [[1]*up*] **1 :** an honest or respectable course — used chiefly in the phrase *on the up-and-up* ⟨it's on the *up-and-up*. Go ahead and start your investigation —Erle Stanley Gardner⟩ ⟨an occupation of free love considered strictly on the *up-and-up* —Hendrik de Leeuw⟩ **2 :** an upward course esp. toward an improved state — used chiefly in the phrase *on the up-and-up* ⟨business was on the *up-and-up* all through 1936 —Benjamin Stolberg⟩

upan·i·shad *also* **upan·i·sad** \üˈpänēˌshäd, üˈpanēˌshad\ *n* -S *usu cap* [Skt *upaniṣad* act of sitting down near something, secret session, secret doctrine, fr. *upa* toward, near to, under + *ni* down + *sīdati* he sits — more at UP, NETHER, SIT] **:** one of a late class of Vedic treatises dealing with broad philosophic problems (as the nature of ultimate reality, man, and the universe) — **upan·i·shad·ic** *also* **upan·i·sad·ic** \=¦==¦shädik, -shad-\ *adj, usu cap*

upa·pu·ra·na \¦üpəpü¦ränə\ *n* -S *often cap* [Skt *upapurāṇa* secondary purana, fr. *upa* toward, near to, under, secondary + *purāṇa* — more at PURANA] **:** a minor purana

uparching \¦=¦==\ *n* [[1]*up* + *arching*, pres. part. of *arch*] **:** the bending of rocks into an anticline or a dome

upas \ˈyüpəs\ *n* -ES [Malay (*pohon*) *upas*, fr. *pohon* tree + *upas* poison, fr. Jav] **1 a** *or* **upas tree :** a very large evergreen tree (*Antiaris toxicaria*) formerly believed to be so poisonous as to destroy any living thing in its vicinity that grows in lowland areas of southeastern Asia and eastward to the Philippines, that is closely related to the breadfruits, that yields a latex containing poisonous glucosides which act on the heart and are used in arrow and dart poisons, and that has an inner bark which is a locally important source of bark cloth **b :** any of various poisonous plants of the genus *Strychnos* that are used with or similarly to the upas in arrow poisons; *esp* **:** a Javanese vine (*S. tieute*) **2 :** a poisonous mixture that usu. contains the juice or latex of a upas, is commonly boiled down to a thick tarry consistency, and is used esp. on arrows or darts **3 :** a poisonous or harmful influence or institution ⟨the ~ of contemporary public life —W.R.Thayer⟩

upbank thaw \ˈ=ˌ=-\ *n* [[4]*up* + *bank*] **:** a thaw on hills while the frost is unbroken in the valley below

upbear \¦=¦=\ *vt* [ME *upberen*, fr. *up* + *beren* to bear — more at BEAR] **:** to bear up **:** SUPPORT, RAISE

[1]**upbeat** \ˈ=ˌ=\ *n* [[2]*up* + *beat*] **1 a :** an unaccented beat in a musical measure; *specif* **:** the last beat of the measure **b :** PICKUP 4g **2 a :** ANACRUSIS 1 **b :** a weak or slack element or syllable in a metrical foot **:** THESIS **3 :** an increase in activity or prosperity ⟨find the town on the ~ after a local recession —S.W.Taylor⟩

[2]**upbeat** \"\ *adj* **:** marked by optimism **:** OPTIMISTIC, CHEERFUL, HAPPY ⟨there is no reason why realistic drama must invariably have a downbeat ending — especially in so ~ an era —Walter Goodman⟩

upbend \ˈ=ˌ=\ *n* [[2]*up* + *bend*] **:** the fore part of a ski that curves upward and terminates at the point

upblast \ˈ=ˌ=\ *n* [[2]*up* + *blast*] **:** a blast that exerts force upward

upblown \¦=¦=\ *adj* [[1]*up* + *blown*, past part. of *blow* (after *blow up*)] **:** blown up; *esp* **:** INFLATED

upboil \¦=¦=\ *vi* [ME *upboilen*, fr. [1]*up* + *boilen* to boil — more at BOIL] **:** to boil up

upbound \ˈ=¦=\ *adj* [[1]*up* + *bound*] **:** traveling or leading in a direction that is regarded as up ⟨~ freighters⟩ ⟨~ shipping lanes⟩

up-bow \ˈ=ˌbō\ *n* [[1]*up* + *bow*] **:** a stroke in playing a bowed instrument (as a violin) made toward the heel of the bow — contrasted with *down-bow;* symbol V

up·braid \¦əp¦brād *sometimes* ˌəpˈb-\ *vt* -ED/-ING/-S [ME *upbreyden*, fr. OE *ūpbregdan*, prob. fr. *ūp* up + *bregdan* to

move suddenly, snatch, weave together — more at UP, BRAID] **1** *obs* **:** to bring forth as a cause for censure ⟨there will come a time when this shall be ~*ed* to us —Jeremy Taylor⟩ **2 a :** to criticize severely **:** find fault with ⟨~*s* all forms of ceremony —W.B.Yeats⟩ **b :** to reproach severely **:** scold vehemently ⟨saw the priest go over to the parents and ~ them for bringing their children to such a place —Francis Stuart⟩ **3** *archaic* **:** to make queasy **:** NAUSEATE **syn** see SCOLD

up·braid·er \-də(r)\ *n* -s **:** one that upbraids

up·braid·ing·ly *adv* **:** in an upbraiding manner

¹upbreak \ˈ=ˌ=\ *vb* [ME *upbreken*, fr. *up* + *breken* to break — more at BREAK] *vt* **:** to break up or open ~ *vi* **:** to force a way up (as through the surface)

²upbreak \ˈ=ˌ=\ *n* **:** an act or instance of breaking up; *esp* **:** ERUPTION, OUTBURST

upbreathe \ˌ=ˈ=\ *vt* [¹*up* + *breathe*] *archaic* **:** to breathe up or out **:** EXHALE

upbringing \ˈ=ˌ==\ *n* -s [fr. gerund of obs. *upbring* to bring up fr. ME *upbringen*, fr. *up* + *bringen* to bring] **:** the process of bringing up **:** early training ⟨by ~ and temperament he is at home in high politics —Alan Campbell-Johnson⟩; *esp* **:** a particular way of bringing up a child ⟨had a strict old-fashioned ~ —A.W.Barkley⟩

upbuild \ˌ=ˈ=\ *vt* [¹*up* + *build*] **:** to build up ⟨man . . . who can ~ or destroy his home, the earth —Van Wyck Brooks⟩ ⟨an atmosphere favorable to the development of a sense of responsibility and the ~*ing* of character —*Villanova College Cat.*⟩ — **up·build·er** \"+ə(r)\ *n*

up·by *also* **up·bye** \ˌəpˈbī\ *adv* [¹*up* + *by*] *chiefly Scot* **:** up there

upcard \ˈ=ˌ=\ *n* [²*up* + *card*] **1 a :** the card turned up to start the play (as in rummy and stops games) — called also *starter, turnup* **b :** the card at the top of a discard pile or talon **2 :** any card properly dealt faceup; *specif* **:** the first card dealt faceup to a player in stud poker

¹upcast \ˌ=ˈ=\ *vt* [ME *upcasten*, fr. *up* + *casten* to cast — more at CAST] **:** to cast up

²upcast \ˈ=ˌ=\ *adj* [ME, fr. past part. of *upcasten*] **1 :** turned or directed upward ⟨saw that she was blind, her face slightly ~ to her companion's —Lawrence Durrell⟩ **2 :** having an upward draft (as in a mine) ⟨the proposed ~ airway —*Economist*⟩

³upcast \"\ *n* [¹*upcast*] **1 :** ACCIDENT, CHANCE ⟨kissed the jack upon an ~ —Shak.⟩ **2** *chiefly Scot* **:** REPROACH, TAUNT **3 :** an upward dislocation of a stratum **4 :** the ventilating shaft (as in a mine) up which the air passes after circulation **5 :** material that has been thrown up (as by digging)

upcheck \ˈ=ˌ=\ *n* [²*up* + *check*] **:** a satisfactory mark in a test and esp. in a check flight

upchuck \ˈ=ˌ=\ *vb* [¹*up* + *chuck*] **:** VOMIT

upclimb \ˌ=ˈ=\ *vb* [¹*up* + *climb*] **:** to climb up **:** ASCEND — **up·climb·er** \"+ə(r)\ *n*

upclose \ˌ=ˈ=\ *vb* [ME *upclosen*, fr. *up* + *closen* to close — more at CLOSE] **:** to close up **:** SHUT

upcoast \ˈ=ˌ=\ *adj* [⁴*up* + *coast*] **:** situated or going up the coast ⟨the isolated ~ cannery will soon be a thing of the past —*Canadian Geog. Jour.*⟩

upcome \ˈ=ˌ=\ *n* [²*up* + *come*] **1** *Scot* **:** the outward appearance of a person **2** *Brit* **:** RESULT, PRODUCT

¹upcoming \ˈ=ˌ==\ *n* -s [ME, fr. *up* + *coming*, gerund of *comen* to come (after *comen up* to come up)] **:** the action or process of coming up

²upcoming \ˌ=ˈ==\ *adj* [¹*up* + *coming*, pres. part. of *come* (after *come up*, v.)] **:** coming up; *esp* **:** being in the near future **:** FORTHCOMING, APPROACHING ⟨the ~ musicals and plays —J.E.Booth⟩

¹up-country \ˈ=ˌ==\ *adj* [⁴*up* + *country*, n.] **:** of, relating to, or characteristic of the interior of a country or a region ⟨lying out there in that *up-country* hospital —John Galsworthy⟩ ⟨the representatives of the *up-country* interests —C.H.Wesley⟩ ⟨the great *up-country* fireplace —Miles Franklin⟩

²up–country \"\ *adv* [⁴*up* + *country*, n.] **:** to or in the interior of a country or a region ⟨marched *up-country* with Indian guides —S.E.Morison⟩ ⟨live *up-country* in comparative isolation —R.J.G.Boothby⟩

³up–country \"\ *n* [²*up* + *country*] **:** the interior of a country or a region

upcropping \ˈ=ˌ==\ *n* [²*up* + *cropping*, gerund of *crop* (after *crop up*, v.)] **:** an act or instance of cropping up **:** APPEARANCE, OUTCROP ⟨the healthy ~ of sizable plants in modest towns —B.M.Bowie⟩

upcurl \ˌ=ˈ=\ *vb* [¹*up* + *curl*] **:** to curl up ⟨his boots . . . had ~*ing* toes —T.B.Costain⟩

upcurve \ˈ=ˌ=\ *n* [²*up* + *curve*] **:** an upward curve

upcurved \ˌ=ˈ=\ *adj* [¹*up* + *curved*, past part. of *curve*] **:** curving upward ⟨has an ~ bill, which he sweeps back and forth through the shallows —*Amer. Guide Series: Wash.*⟩

¹upcut \ˌ=ˈ=\ *vt* [¹*up* + *cut*, v.] **:** to cut (machine work) while the tool is moving upward

²upcut \ˈ=ˌ=\ *n* [²*up* + *cut*, n.] **:** an upward cut

update \ˌ=ˈ=\ *vt* [¹*up* + *date*] **:** to bring up to date ⟨the last four chapters read like filler designed to round out, ~, and lengthen a longish article —Carlos Baker⟩ ⟨the motel is like the roadside inn of old, *updated* and lavished with glamour —C.L.Biemiller⟩ — **up·dat·er** \"+ə(r)\ *n*

up·do \ˈəpˌdü\ *n* -s [*upswept hairdo*] **:** an upswept hairdo

updraft \ˈ=ˌ=\ *n* [²*up* + *draft*] **:** an upward movement of air or other gas

updraft kiln *n* **:** a vertical kiln in which the heat is blown or directed upward through the kiln

¹updraw \ˌ=ˈ=\ *vb* [ME *updrawen*, fr. *up* + *drawen* to draw] **:** to draw up **:** pull up

²updraw \ˈ=ˌ=\ *n* **:** an act or process of drawing up ⟨with a quick ~ of his knees to the other's chest, broke the grip —Jack London⟩

upend \ˌəˈ=\ *vb* -ED/-ING/-S [¹*up* + *end*, n.] *vt* **1 :** to set on end **:** turn up an end of ⟨~*ed* a reed basket and sat down —L.C. Douglas⟩ ⟨was caught by a giant wave which ~*ed* him —Leonard Lyons⟩ **2 a :** to affect radically **:** turn upside down ⟨a painstakingly executed literary shocker, designed to ~ the credulous matrons —Wolcott Gibbs⟩ **b :** BEAT 4a, 4b ⟨one world record and one world champion were ~*ed* during the . . . championships —*Newsweek*⟩ ~ *vi* **:** to rise on an end **:** move so as to expose an end ⟨the great fish would then ~ — head up, tail straight down in mid-water —William Beebe⟩ ⟨would ~ like ducks and begin to graze —William Beebe⟩

upey·gan \ü̇ˈpāgən\ *n* -s [Shona] **:** BLACK RHINOCEROS

upfeed \ˌ=ˈ=\ *adj* [¹*up* + *feed*, v.] **:** supplied with a material (as hot water) that is forced upward ⟨an ~ heating system⟩

upfill \ˌ=ˈ=\ *vt* [ME *upfillen*, fr. *up* + *fillen* to fill] *archaic* **:** to fill up

upfitter \ˈ=ˌ==\ *n* [²*up* + *fitter* (after *fit up*, v.)] **1 :** one that attaches hardware and trim to wooden furniture — called also *fitter* **2 :** one that fits and assembles tops to casket bodies and puts in the hinges and other hardware — called also *fitter* **3 :** an assembly line worker who installs door handles and other hardware in automobile bodies

upflare \ˈ=ˌ=\ *n* [²*up* + *flare* (after *flare up*, v.)] **:** FLARE-UP

upfling \ˌ=ˈ=\ *vt* [¹*up* + *fling*] **:** to fling up

upflow \ˈ=ˌ=\ *n* [²*up* + *flow* (after *flow up*, v.)] **:** an upward flow

upfly \ˌ=ˈ=\ *vi* [¹*up* + *fly*] **:** to fly up

¹upfold \ˌ=ˈ=\ *vt* [ME *upfolden*, fr. *up* + *folden* to fold] **:** to fold up

²upfold \ˈ=ˌ=\ *n* [²*up* + *fold*, n.] **:** stratified rocks that are folded upward to a crest **:** ANTICLINE

upfurled \ˌ=ˈ=\ *adj* [¹*up* + *furled*, past part. of *furl* (after *furl up*, v.)] **:** furled upward

up·gang \ˈəpˌgaŋ\ *n* [ME (Sc), fr. *up* + *gang* (going)] *chiefly Scot* **:** ASCENT

upgather \ˌ=ˈ==\ *vb* [¹*up* + *gather*] **:** to gather up

upglide \ˈ=ˌ=\ *n* [²*up* + *glide*] **:** an upward glide

upgliding \ˌ=ˈ==\ *adj* [¹*up* + *gliding*, pres. part. of *glide* (after *glide up*, v.)] **:** outgliding with an upward glide (as the vocalic parts of *day* and *dough* when these parts are diphthongal)

¹upgo \ˌ=ˈ=\ *vi* [ME *upgon, upgan*, fr. *up* + *gon, gan* to go — more at GO] **:** to go up **:** ASCEND

²upgo \ˈ=ˌ=\ *n* **:** ASCENT

¹upgrade \ˈ=ˌ=\ *n* [²*up* + *grade*, n.] **1 :** an upward grade (as of a road) ⟨ran beside his dogs on the ~*s* —Farley Mowat⟩ **2 a :** INCREASE ⟨thefts and forgeries have been on the ~ —*New Orleans (La.) Times-Picayune*⟩ **b :** a rise toward a better state ⟨on the ~ with nothing more than the occasional discomfort —O.W.Holmes †1935⟩

²upgrade \ˈ=ˌ=\ *adv* [⁴*up* + *grade*, n.] **:** toward a higher level on an incline ⟨a locomotive going ~ —Danforth Ross⟩

³upgrade \ˈ=ˌ=\ *vt* [¹*up* + *grade*, v.] **:** to raise the grade of: as **a :** to improve (as livestock) by the use of purebred sires **b :** to advance to a job requiring a higher level of skill esp. as part of a training program **:** advance in professional rank **c :** to raise the quality of (as a manufactured product) **d :** to raise the classification and usu. the price of (a product) without improving the quality — **up·grad·er** \"+ə(r)\ *n*

upgrow \ˌ=ˈ=\ *vi* [ME *upgrowen*, fr. *up* + *growen* to grow] **:** to grow up

upgrowth \ˈ=ˌ=\ *n* **1 :** the process of growing up **:** upward growth **:** DEVELOPMENT ⟨the ~ of the atolls during a rising sea level —F.P.Shepard⟩ ⟨a tremendous ~ of science and practical arts —I.J.Fellner⟩ **2 :** a result of upward growth or development; *specif* **:** PROCESS 4

¹upgushing \ˌ=ˈ==\ *adj* [¹*up* + *gushing*, pres. part. of *gush*] **:** gushing upward

²upgushing \ˈ=ˌ==\ *n* -s [²*up* + *gushing*, gerund of *gush*] **:** an act or instance of gushing upward

uphang \ˌ=ˈ=\ *vt* [ME *uphongen*, fr. *up* + *hangen, hongen* to hang — more at HANG] **:** to hang up

up-haud \ˌəˈpȯd\ *chiefly Scot var of* UPHOLD

up–headed \ˌ=ˈ==\ *adj* [¹*up* + *headed*] **:** holding the head upright

upheaped \ˌ=ˈ=\ *adj* [ME *upheped*, fr. *up* + *heped*, past part. of *hepen* to heap — more at HEAP] **:** heaped up **:** ACCUMULATED

up·heav·al \ˌəpˈhēvəl, (ˌ)əˈpē- *sometimes* ˌəpˈhē-\ *n* -s **1 a :** the action of upheaving esp. of part of the earth's crust (as by volcanic action) **b :** an instance of upheaving esp. of the earth's crust **2 a :** extreme agitation and disorder (as of society) **:** radical change **:** CONVULSION ⟨unless immediate steps are taken . . . the seven-year-old federation will succumb to violent ~ —Leonard Ingalls⟩ **b :** an instance of extreme disorderly agitation or radical change ⟨the world's peoples are churning in one of history's greatest ~*s* —A.E.Stevenson †1965⟩ ⟨lived through an emotional ~ as shattering as an earthquake —Elizabeth Goudge⟩ **syn** see COMMOTION

up·heav·al·ist \-ləst\ *n* -s **:** an advocate of the theory that upheaval explains geological changes

up·heave \-ēv\ *vb* [ME *upheven*, fr. *up* + *heven* to heave — more at HEAVE] *vt* **1 a :** to heave up **:** LIFT, RAISE ⟨great boulders were *upheaved* by the gold-seekers in their first eager rush —Mary S. Broome⟩ **b :** to force or throw upward with great power or violence ⟨other parts of the coast . . . may be *upheaved* by deep-seated geologic forces —R.W.Miner⟩ **2 :** to disturb extremely **:** throw into disorder ⟨the coming of the troops *upheaved* the whole province⟩ ~ *vi* **:** to move upward esp. with power ⟨the surface of the bay . . . *upheaved* with a slow majestic movement —Bayard Taylor⟩ — **up·heav·er** \-və(r)\ *n*

up·heave·ment \-vmənt\ *n* -s **:** UPHEAVAL

up–hel·ly–aa \ˈəpˌheləˌä\ *n* -s *usu cap U & H & A* [ME *uphaliday*, fr. *up* + *haliday, holiday* holiday] **:** a festival held in Shetland usu. on the last Tuesday night of January to mark the end of the yule season

¹uphill \ˈ=ˌ=\ *n* [⁴*up* + *hill*, n.] **:** rising ground **:** ASCENT ⟨on the ~ our pace was dragging and stiff —Eve Langley⟩

²uphill \ˈ=ˌ=\ *adv* [⁴*up* + *hill*, n.] **1 :** upward on a hill or incline ⟨the heavy material . . . is guided ~ —A.M.Gaudin⟩ ⟨these side streets lay ~ —Sacheverell Sitwell⟩ **2 :** against difficulties ⟨seemed to be talking ~ —Willa Cather⟩

³uphill \"\ *adj* **1 :** situated on elevated ground ⟨an ~ city⟩ **2 :** ascending or directed toward higher ground **:** going up ⟨the trail was ~ and steep —Zane Grey⟩ **3 a :** presenting difficulties **:** requiring much effort **:** DIFFICULT, LABORIOUS ⟨the ~ fight for the abolition of slavery —*London Calling*⟩ ⟨the conversation was all ~ —Irwin Shaw⟩ **b :** struggling against difficulties

uphlstg *abbr* upholstering

uphoard *vt* [¹*up* + *hoard*] *obs* **:** to hoard up

uphol *abbr* upholsterer; upholstering; upholstery

¹up·hold \ˈəˌpōd\ *n* [ME (Sc) *uphald*, fr. OE *ūpheald*, fr. *ūp* up + *heald* hold — more at UP, HOLD] *chiefly Scot* **:** SUPPORT, STAY

²up·hold \ˌəpˈhōld, (ˌ)əˈpō- *sometimes* ˌəpˈhō-\ *vt* **up·held** \ˌəpˈheld, (ˌ)əˈpe- *sometimes* ˌəpˈhe-\ **upheld; upholding; upholds** [ME *uphalden, upholden*, fr. *up* + *halden, holden* to hold — more at HOLD] **1 a :** to give support to (as by help or action) **:** SUSTAIN, MAINTAIN ⟨tried to ~ the morale of the occupied capital —F.L.Paxson⟩ ⟨the patrol went on . . . after the earthquake, thus ~*ing* the finest traditions of this force —Francis Kingdon-Ward⟩ **b** (1) **:** to support against an opponent **:** DEFEND ⟨enough to ~ . . . the air generals against a strong and well-seated opposition —J.G.Cozzens⟩ (2) *dial Brit* **:** AFFIRM, WARRANT, GUARANTEE ⟨will ~ that you are the coolest hand that I ever came nigh —George Borrow⟩ (3) **:** to adjudge constitutional or legally valid ⟨his language toward a witness was censured by the court of appeals but his decision *upheld* —*Current Biog.*⟩ **c** *chiefly Brit* **:** to keep in good repair **:** keep on the same level **2 a :** to give physical support to **:** keep elevated ⟨slender Corinthian columns ~ the hipped roof —*Amer. Guide Series: La.*⟩ **b :** to lift up **:** RAISE ⟨*upheld* their clenched hands —F.W.Farrar⟩

up·hold·er \-də(r)\ *n* [ME *upholdere*, fr. *upholden* (to repair) + *-ere* -er] **1** *archaic* **a** (1) **:** a dealer in small goods (2) **:** a repairer or maker of small goods **b :** UPHOLSTERER **c :** UNDERTAKER 4 **2 :** one that upholds: as **a :** a physical support **b :** SUPPORTER, MAINTAINER, DEFENDER ⟨a stout ~ of authority —V.L.Parrington⟩

¹up·hol·ster \(ˌ)əpˈhōlztə(r), (ˌ)əˈpō-, -l(t)st-\ *n* -s [ME *upholdester*, fr. *upholden* to uphold (repair) + *-estere, -ester* -ster] **1** *archaic* **a :** one who deals in small goods **b :** one who repairs or makes small goods **2** *obs* **:** UPHOLSTERER

²upholster \"\ *vt* **upholstered; upholstered; upholstering** \-t(ə)riŋ\ **upholsters** [back-formation fr. *upholsterer* & *upholstery*] **:** to furnish with or as if with upholstery ⟨the classic broadcloths . . . that were used to ~ carriages —*Amer. Fabrics*⟩ ⟨a very fat woman ~*ed* in pink satin —S.E.White⟩; *esp* **:** to cover (a seat) with padding and fabric that is fastened over the padding

up·hol·stered \-(r)d\ *adj* **:** furnished with or as if with upholstery: as **a** (1) **:** containing furniture or fittings that are padded and covered with fabric (2) **:** marked by a high degree of comfort **:** providing luxury **:** LUXURIOUS ⟨crossed on the ~ route —Horace Sutton⟩ **b :** marked by fullness of style ⟨the more lightly and swiftly moving writers of the 17th century rather than the more heavily ~ ones of the earlier Renaissance —Edmund Wilson⟩ **c :** FAT, FLESHY ⟨~ old dowagers —*Harper's*⟩

up·hol·ster·er \-t(ə)rə(r)\ *n* -s [¹*upholster* + *-er*] **:** one that upholsters; *specif* **:** one whose occupation is the making or supplying of upholstery

upholsterer bee *n* **:** LEAF-CUTTING BEE

up·hol·ster·ess *also* **up·hol·stress** \-t(ə)rə̇s\ *n* -ES **:** a female upholsterer

upholstering *n* -s **:** UPHOLSTERY

up·hol·stery \-t(ə)rē, -ri\ *n* -ES [¹*upholster* + *-y*] **:** the materials (as fabric, padding, and springs) used to make a soft covering esp. for a seat; *specif* **:** the fabric used to cover a seat

upholstery leather *n* **:** leather made from cattlehides tanned in the whole hide and used esp. for upholstering furniture, automobiles, or airplanes

uphung \ˌ=ˈ=\ *adj* [¹*up* + *hung*, past part. of *hang*] **:** hung up **:** SUSPENDED

up jen·kins \-ˈjeŋkənz\ *n, usu cap J* [*Jenkins* fr. the name *Jenkins*] **:** a game in which the players seated on one side of a table pass a coin along under the table and the captain of the opposing team seated on the other side of the table commands them with the words *up Jenkins* and *down Jenkins* to show their hands and tries to guess which hand holds the coin

¹upkeep \ˈ=ˌ=\ *n* [²*up* + *keep* (after *keep up*, v.)] **1 a :** the act of maintaining in good condition **:** MAINTENANCE ⟨the building and ~ of roads⟩ **b :** the state of being maintained in good condition **2 :** the cost of maintaining in good condition or supporting ⟨his parents had no feeling that he ought to contribute to their ~ —Rebecca West⟩

²upkeep \ˌ=ˈ=\ *vt, chiefly Brit* **:** to maintain in good condition **:** keep up ⟨found it hard to ~ his family seat — a 45-room twin-turreted castle —*Irish Digest*⟩

¹up·land \ˈəplənd, -ˌland, -ˌlaa(ə)nd\ *n* [ME *uppeland, upland*, fr. *uppe land* in the country, fr. *uppe* on (fr. OE, fr. *uppe*, adv., on high) + *land* — more at UP, LAND] **:** the rural parts of a country **:** COUNTRY

²upland \"\ *adj* [ME *upland*, fr. *uppeland, upland*, n.] *archaic* **:** of or relating to the country **:** RUSTIC, PROVINCIAL ⟨Christianity was still an exotic religion, professed by the court, but resisted by a stubborn ~ heathenism —F.M.Stenton⟩

³upland \"\ *n* [⁴*up* + *land*] **1 a :** high land esp. far from the sea **:** PLATEAU **b :** a region of high land **2 a :** ground elevated above the lowlands along rivers or between hills **:** land above flood level **b :** an area of land above flood level **3 :** UPLAND COTTON — usu. used in pl. but sing. or pl. in constr.

⁴upland \"\ *adj* **:** of or relating to high land: as **a :** situated on high land esp. away from the sea ⟨an ~ village⟩ ⟨~ provinces⟩ **b** (1) **:** living in a relatively high region esp. away from water **:** frequenting high ground ⟨the woodcock is considered an ~ bird though in reality he belongs to the shore bird family —*Handbk. on Shotgun Shooting*⟩ (2) **:** of or relating to upland game ⟨~ hunting⟩ ⟨used their favorite ~ guns —*Catalog: Remington Trap & Skeet Equipment*⟩ **c :** growing, occurring, or developed on high land ⟨~ floras —*Jour. of Geol.*⟩ ⟨pollens seem likely to bring into a deposit a representation of forms farther from the sedimentary basin and more ~ to it —S.A. Cain⟩

⁵upland \"\ *adv* [⁴*up* + *land*] **:** in the interior or higher regions

upland boneset *n* **:** a boneset (*Eupatorium sessilifolium*) of eastern No. America with slender stems and nearly sessile and usu. opposite leaves

upland cotton *n, often cap U* **:** any of various usu. short-staple cottons that are cultivated esp. in the U.S. and derived chiefly from a prob. tropical American wild cotton (*Gossypium hirsutum*) — called also *American upland cotton*

upland cranberry *n* **:** BEARBERRY 1

upland cress *n* **:** WINTER CRESS

up·land·er \-də(r)\ *n* -s [³*upland* + *-er*] **:** a native or an inhabitant of an upland

upland goose *n* **:** a wild goose (*Chloëphaga leucoptera*) of Patagonia and the Falkland islands

upland hickory *n* **:** SHAGBARK HICKORY 1

¹up·land·ish \ˌəpˈlandish, -aan-, -dēsh\ *adj* [ME *uplondish*, fr. *up* + *land, lond* land, country + *-ish*] *archaic* **:** ⁴UPLAND a

²uplandish \"\ *adj* [ME, fr. *uppeland, upland* + *-ish*] **1** *obs* **:** PROVINCIAL, RUSTIC, CRUDE ⟨the rude and ~ plowmen —Thomas More⟩ **2** *obs* **:** OUTLANDISH

upland moccasin *n* **:** a snake of the southern U. S. that is prob. a dark variety of the copperhead

upland plover *also* **upland sandpiper** *n* **:** a large sandpiper (*Bartramia longicauda*) of eastern No. America that frequents fields and uplands, resembles a plover in habits and in appearance esp. in its short bill, is a fine game bird, and has been nearly exterminated in some states

upland rice *n* **:** any of several rices that can be grown (as in high-rainfall areas) without irrigation — called also *dry rice;* compare LOWLAND RICE

upland speedwell *n* **:** a speedwell (*Veronica officinalis*)

upland white aster *n* **:** a tufted rigid No. American perennial herb (*Aster ptarmicoides*) with rather open loose clusters of white-rayed heads

upland willow oak *n* **:** BLUEJACK

uplay \ˌ=ˈ=\ *vt* [¹*up* + *lay*] **:** to lay up **:** STORE

¹upleap \ˌ=ˈ=\ *vi* [ME *uplepen*, fr. *up* + *lepen* to leap — more at LEAP] **:** to leap up

²upleap \ˈ=ˌ=\ *n* **:** an upward leap

¹uplift \ˌ=ˈ=\ *adj* [ME, fr. *up* + *lift*, past part. of *liften* to lift] *archaic* **:** UPLIFTED

²up·lift \ˌəpˈlift *sometimes* ˌəpˈl-\ *vb* [ME *upliften*, fr. *up* + *liften* to lift] *vt* **1 :** to raise to a higher physical position **:** lift up; *specif* **:** to push up (a part of the earth's surface) above the surrounding area **2 :** to improve or attempt to improve the condition of esp. spiritually, socially, culturally, or intellectually ⟨love ~*s* the lover's being —H.O.Taylor⟩ ⟨stirring to ~ their masses from age-old conditions of squalor and ignorance —Howard M. Jones⟩ **3** *Scot* **:** to take (as money that is owed) into one's possession **:** COLLECT **4 :** RAISE 5 ⟨~*ed* their voices in song⟩ ~ *vi* **:** to rise esp. because of geologic forces

³uplift \ˈ=ˌ=\ *n, often attrib* **:** an act, process, result, or cause of uplifting: as **a** (1) **:** the uplifting of a part of the earth's surface either uniform throughout a region or differential (as in tilting) ⟨the ~ of continents drained vast areas of land —W.E.Swinton⟩ (2) **:** an uplifted mass of land ⟨beyond the desert rise the mountains, the first outlying ranges of that vast ~ —Douglas Carruthers⟩ **b :** the upward pressure of water (as on the base of a structure) **c :** an elevation of spirit or emotion ⟨should have brought a larger mentality, a more vital ~ —*Cosmopolitan*⟩ **d :** a bettering of condition **:** IMPROVEMENT ⟨did for their ~ all that the custom of the times permitted —C.G. Woodson⟩ **e** (1) **:** influences that are intended to improve esp. morally or culturally **:** the ideas of active participants in programs for improvement esp. of moral and cultural standards ⟨night life . . . is conducted in an atmosphere of furious rectitude, fashionable economy, and intellectual ~ —Gilbert Millstein⟩ ⟨all this bosh sounds like ~; I teach my students English —W.G.Perry⟩ ⟨had been delighted when his daily poem and his ~ editorials first proved successful —Willa Cather⟩ (2) **:** a social movement to improve esp. morally or culturally **:** the work or cause of uplifting ⟨goes in for public things — very strong on woman suffrage, charities, ~, and pacifism —O.M.Johnson⟩ ⟨owns all the ~ papers —John Buchan⟩ **f :** a brassiere designed to hold the breasts up

uplifted \ˌ=ˈ==\ *adj* [ME, fr. *up* + *lifted*, past part. of *liften* to lift] **1 :** RAISED, ELEVATED, IMPROVED **2** *archaic* **:** ELATED, PROUD — **up·lift·ed·ness** *n* -ES

up·lift·er \ˌəpˈliftə(r)\ *n* **:** one that uplifts; *esp* **:** a person engaged in or devoted to the improvement of society

up·lift·ment \-tmənt\ *n* -s **:** UPLIFT c, d

uplock *vt* [¹*up* + *lock*] **:** to lock up

up lock *n* [¹*up*] **:** a locking device in airplanes that keeps the landing gear up in the retracted position

¹uplook \ˌ=ˈ=\ *vi* [ME *uploken*, fr. *up* + *loken, looken* to look — more at LOOK] **:** to look upward — **up·look·er** \"+ə(r)\ *n*

²uplook \ˈ=ˌ=\ *n* [²*up* + *look*, n.] **:** an upward look

uplying \ˌ=ˈ==\ *adj* [¹*up* + *lying*, pres. part. of *lie*] **:** situated or growing on high land

¹upmaking \ˈ=ˌ==\ *n* [fr. gerund of obs. Sc *upmake* to make up, fr. ME (Sc) *upmaken*, fr. *up* + *maken* to make — more at MAKE] **:** an act or action of making up

²upmaking \"\ *adj* [fr. pres. part. of obs. Sc *upmake* to make up] *Scot* **:** making up for a shortcoming **:** COMPENSATING

up·most \ˈəpˌmōst *also chiefly Brit* -məst\ *adj* **:** UPPERMOST

up·ness \ˈəpnə̇s\ *n* -ES **:** the state or quality of being up

up north *adv, often cap N* [⁴*up*] **:** in or into a more northerly location; *esp* **:** in or into the part of the U.S. that lies north of Mason and Dixon's Line and the Ohio river

upo \əˈpō\ *prep* [ME *upo, ipo*, fr., *uppe* & *up* up + *o* on — more at o'] *archaic* **:** UPON

upon \əˈpȯn, əˈpän, ə(ˌ)pən *sometimes* ˌəˈp-\ *prep* [ME *uppon, upon*, fr. *uppe* & *up* up + *on*, prep. — more at UP, ON] **1 :** ON **2 a :** upward so as to be on ⟨jumped ~ the horse⟩ **b :** in a high position on ⟨built a house ~ the hill⟩ **3 :** having a powerful influence on **:** lying heavily on ⟨the enchantment of the beautiful scenery was still ~ me —Scott Fitzgerald⟩ ⟨the hush ~ the dinner table —Maurice Hewlett⟩ **4** — used as a function word to indicate the one by which an oath is taken or by which one swears ⟨~ my word⟩ **5** *obs* **:** IN 3b ⟨was ~ this fashion bequeathed me by will —Shak.⟩ **6 a** (1) **:** in or into close proximity or contact with by way of or as if by way of attack ⟨the enemy is ~ us⟩ ⟨despondency fell ~ me —O.S.J. Gogarty⟩ ⟨summer holidays are ~ us —Alex Atkinson⟩ (2) **:** into sudden esp. unexpected contact with ⟨came ~ the letter in an old desk⟩ ⟨hits ~ a solution⟩ **b** *archaic* (1) **:** on the point of ⟨talk with him on this subject, for I see he is ~ settling one —Thomas Gray⟩ (2) **:** coming close to a specified number ⟨has the largest single group . . . in the world (just ~

70 millions) —*Spectator*〉 **7 :** against in vengeance or punishment 〈perform ~ the unguarded —Shak.〉 **8** — used as a function word to indicate (1) a beginning course of action or an action or condition that is beginning 〈students desiring to enter ~ graduate training —*College of William & Mary Cat.*〉 or (2) an area of activity or being 〈a dashing young ensign just come ~ the town —Washington Irving〉 **9 a :** at the risk of 〈are hereby charged, ~ your peril, to pay strict attention —C.S.Forester〉 **b** *obs* **:** on the condition of 〈~ my blessing I command thee go —Shak.〉 **10 a** (1) **:** immediately following on **:** very soon after 〈~ his death, she went on the . . . stage —Marie A. Kasten〉 (2) **:** in answer to **:** in satisfaction of 〈~ the demand of government leaders . . . arrangements were made this year —Wheeler McMillen〉 〈transcripts are sent ~ the request of the particular student —*Bull. of Meharry Med. Coll.*〉 **b :** on the occasion of **:** at the time of 〈tells us what combinations of traits occur ~ the mixture of two racial types —Ruth Benedict〉 〈a yoke which men of spirit will throw off ~ the first favorable opportunity —*Harper's*〉 **11** *archaic* **:** by means of 〈to die ~ the hand I love so well —Shak.〉 **12** *chiefly Scot* **:** TO 〈was married . . . ~ my Uncle Robin —R.L.Stevenson〉

²**upon** \"\ *adv* [ME *uppon, upon,* fr. *uppon, upon,* prep.] **1 a** *obs* **:** on the surface **:** on it 〈a coin that bears the figure of an angel stamped in gold, but that's insculped ~ —Shak.〉 **b** *archaic* **:** on the body or something that resembles a body **2** *obs* **:** THEREAFTER, THEREON 〈followed hard ~ —Shak.〉

upped *past of* UP

¹**up·per** \ˈəpə(r)\ *adj* [ME, fr. *uppe* up + *-er* — more at UP] **1 :** relatively high in physical position: as **a** (1) **:** occupying high ground 〈keep the hills and ~ regions —Shak.〉 (2) **:** farther inland 〈the ~ Mississippi〉 〈carried squared timbers from the ~ lakes lumber ports to the St. Lawrence —*Amer. Guide Series: Mich.*〉 (3) *usu cap* **:** living on higher ground, farther inland, farther upstream, or farther north than others of the same group 〈the *Upper* Creek〉 **b** (1) **:** being a higher part esp. of a pair or a set 〈~ lip〉 〈the ~ stories of the building〉 (2) **:** worn over a part of the body above the waist 〈his ~ clothes were black and his lower clothes red —J.G.Frazer〉 **c :** directed upward **d :** being above or on the earth's surface rather than below it or in nether regions 〈those appointed to sit there had . . . flown to the ~ world —John Milton〉 **e** (1) **:** being or occurring on a higher level with respect to the earth's surface 〈the ~ atmosphere〉 〈~ plankton —R.E.Coker〉 (2) **:** constituting a stratum relatively near the earth's surface (3) *usu cap* **:** being a later epoch or series of the period or series named 〈*Upper* Carboniferous〉 〈*Upper* Cretaceous〉 〈*Upper* Permian〉 〈*Upper* Silurian〉 — contrasted with *Lower* **2 a :** higher in rank or order **:** superior in position 〈senates were substituted for councils as the ~ house —Harvey Walker〉 〈the . . . club was generally restricted to the ~ social brackets —*Current Biog.*〉; *specif* **:** being on a more advanced level in an educational system 〈the ~ school〉 〈~ freshmen〉 **b :** being of superior quality 〈the ~ grades of lumber〉 **3** *archaic* **:** worn on top of another garment **:** OUTER **4 :** situated farther from the door **:** INNERMOST 〈the ~ end of the hall〉 **5 :** of or relating to higher musical pitch 〈although entirely different in their ~ parts, they share the same bass —P.H. Lang〉 〈the most securely brilliant ~ registers heard in the vast house in many years —*Newsweek*〉 **6 :** EARLIER 〈determines the ~ limit of date〉 **7 :** being the northern part of an area 〈cut across ~ New York to the Vermont state line —Budd Schulberg〉 〈~ Manhattan〉

²**upper** \"\ *n* -s **:** one that is upper: as **a :** the parts of a shoe or boot that are above the sole **b uppers** *pl but sometimes sing in constr* **:** the best grade of lumber **:** FINISH **c** (1) **:** an upper tooth 〈has two ~*s* missing〉 (2) **:** an upper denture **d :** an upper berth **e :** a drill hole driven upward in a mine **f :** a piece of clothing worn above the waist **:** TOP 〈were allowed to remove their pink pajama ~*s* —Earle Birney〉 — **on one's uppers :** in straitened circumstances **:** at the end of one's means 〈doing his own laundry, and that . . . indicates he was *on his uppers* —Hal White〉

³**upper** \"\ *n* -s [¹*up* & ³*up* + *-er*] **:** one that ups — sometimes used in combination 〈*builder-upper*〉 〈coffee, which he finds the best of all toner-*uppers* —H.W.Wind〉

upper alveolar index *n* **:** the ratio of the maximum external breadth to the external length of the upper jaw multiplied by 100

upper angle *n* **:** FIRST ANGLE

upper austral *adj, usu cap U&A* **:** of, relating to, or being a division of the Austral zone comprising the Carolinian and Upper Sonoran areas

upper bench *n, usu cap U&B* **:** COURT OF KING'S BENCH — used during the Cromwellian period

upper bridge *n* **:** the higher platform of a ship's bridge having two levels

upper case *n* **:** the upper one of a pair of type cases that contains capitals and usu. also small capitals, fractions, symbols, accents — compare LOWER CASE

¹**uppercase** \ˈ≈≈¦≈\ *adj* [*upper case*] **1** *of a letter* **:** having as its typical form AFG or *BNI* or **QZR** rather than afg or *bni* or **qzr** — abbr. *uc;* compare CAPITAL **2 :** set, printed, written, or otherwise rendered in uppercase letters — abbr. *uc*

²**uppercase** \"\ *n* **:** uppercase letters — abbr. *uc;* compare LOWERCASE

³**uppercase** \"\ *vt* **:** to print or set in uppercase; *also* **:** to change (as a lowercase letter) to an uppercase letter — abbr. *uc*

upper chinook *n, usu cap U&C* **:** a Chinookan language of the Clackamas, Wasco, Wishram, and neighboring peoples

upper class *n* **1 :** the highest stratum of society usu. composed of people with the greatest wealth, education, and prestige **2 upper classes** *pl* **:** an aggregate of social groupings comprising subdivisions of the upper class

upper-class \ˈ≈≈¦≈\ *adj* [*upper class*] **1 a :** of or relating to the upper class **b :** belonging to or having the characteristics of the upper class 〈frightfully *upper-class* and having all the glorious self-confidence that comes of having been born rich —Aldous Huxley〉 — compare LOWER-CLASS, MIDDLE-CLASS **2 :** of or relating to the junior or senior class in a college or a high school

up·per·class·man \ˌ≈≈ˈ≈mən\ *n, pl* **upperclassmen** [fr. the phrase *upper class* "junior or senior class" + *man*] **:** a member of the junior or senior class in a college or a high school

upper crust *n* [ME] **1 :** the top crust (as of a loaf of bread or a pie) **2 :** the highest segment of a social class or group 〈the *upper crust* of the underworld —D.W.Maurer & V.H.Vogel〉; *esp* **:** the highest circle of the upper classes 〈a smart specialty shop for the *upper crust* —McKenzie Porter〉

upper-crust \ˈ≈≈¦≈\ *adj* [*upper crust*] **:** of, relating to, or having the characteristics of the highest class of society 〈one was of low condition, the other, *upper-crust* —W.S.Gilbert〉 〈her best *upper-crust* voice —Marian Castle〉

upper-crust·er \"+ə(r)\ *n, pl* **upper-crusters** [*upper crust* + *-er*] **:** a member of the upper crust

¹**uppercut** \ˈ≈≈ˌ≈\ *n* [*upper* + *cut*] **:** a swinging blow (as in boxing) directed upward with a bent arm

²**uppercut** \"\ *vt* **:** to hit with an uppercut ~ *vi* **:** to deliver or attempt to deliver an uppercut

upper deck *n* **1 :** the topmost full-length deck of a ship **:** a full-length deck above the main deck — see DECK illustration **2 :** a partial deck above the main deck in a naval vessel

upperdog \ˈ≈≈ˌ≈\ *n* **:** TOP DOG

upper facial index *n* **:** the ratio of the distance between nasion and prosthion to the bizygomatic breadth multiplied by 100

upper german *n, usu cap U&G* **:** the southern dialects of High German including Alemannic and Bavarian

upper hand *n* **1 :** CONTROL, MASTERY, ADVANTAGE 〈finally got the *upper hand* of the situation〉 〈at first the Liberals held the *upper hand* —C.L.Jones〉 **2** *archaic* **:** the position of honor or authority

upper house *or* **upper chamber** *n* **:** the house of more restricted membership in a legislative body having two chambers

upper jewel *n* **:** a jewel bearing set into the bridge, cock, or upper plate of a watch

upper leather *n* **1 a :** the leather that forms the upper of a shoe or boot **b :** ²UPPER a **2 :** leather suitable for making uppers

upper limb *n* **:** the edge of a celestial body that is nearest the zenith 〈the *upper limb* of the rising sun〉

upper mars *n, usu cap U&M* **:** a Mount located on the percussion below the Mount of Mercury and above the Mount of Luna that when well developed is usu. held by palmists to indicate passive courage, strength of resistance, and self-control — compare LOWER MARS

upper mordent *n* **:** PRALLTRILLER

up·per·most \ˈəpə(r)ˌmōst *also chiefly Brit* -məst\ *adv* [ME, fr. *upper* + *most*] **1 :** in or into the highest physical position 〈the blade turned ~〉 **2 :** in or into the most prominent position (as in the mind) 〈says whatever comes ~〉

²**uppermost** \"\ *adj* **1 a :** situated in the highest physical position **:** farthest up 〈the ~ falls of the river〉 **b :** OUTERMOST 〈the ~ skin〉 **2 a :** highest in rank or power 〈prominent in its ~ councils —*Current Biog.*〉 〈whatever faction happens to be ~ —Jonathan Swift〉 **b :** occupying the most prominent or most important position 〈the thoughts that were ~ in my mind —R.B.Merriman〉 〈essays in which philosophical considerations are ~ —J.E.Smith〉

upperpart \ˈ≈≈ˌ≈\ *n* **:** a part lying on the upper side esp. of an animal

upper partial *n* **:** OVERTONE 1

upper pharyngeal *n* **:** PHARYNGOBRANCHIAL

upper republican *adj, usu cap U&R* [*Upper Republican,* river in Kansas and Nebraska] **:** of or relating to a culture of the plains and esp. of Kansas and Nebraska about 1300–1600 characterized by earth-covered pit houses, cultivation of gardens in creek bottoms, and hard gray pottery decorated externally by the application of a cord-wrapped paddle and on the rims with incised geometric designs

uppers *pl of* UPPER

upper sonoran *adj, usu cap U&S* **:** of, relating to, being, or native to the cooler part of the Sonoran life zone that adjoins the Transition zone — compare LOWER SONORAN

upperstock \ˈ≈≈ˌ≈\ *n* **:** STOCKING; *specif* **:** a 16th century stocking reaching below the knee and worn with netherstocks and trunk hose

upper story *n* **1 :** a story (as of a house) that is above the ground floor **2** *slang* **:** BRAIN 〈a little off in the *upper story* —Erle Stanley Gardner〉

upper ten *or* **upper ten thousand** *n* **:** the members of the highest social class **:** UPPER CLASS

up·per·ten·dom \ˌəpə(r)ˈtendəm\ *n* -s **:** the highest social class

upper transit *also* **upper culmination** *n* **:** the passage of a celestial body over the celestial meridian at the higher of its two crossings; *also* **:** the point at which such a crossing takes place

upper vol·ta \ˌ≈≈ˈvōltə, -ˈväl-\ *adj, usu cap U&V* [*Upper Volta,* republic in western Africa] **:** of or relating to the Republic of Upper Volta **:** of the kind or style prevalent in Upper Volta

upperworks \ˈ≈≈ˌ≈\ *n pl* **1 a :** all the parts of the hull of a ship that are above the load waterline **b** (1) **:** the sides of a ship from the waterline to the plank-sheer of the upper deck (2) **:** SUPERSTRUCTURE 1b **2** *slang* **:** BRAINS

upperworld \ˈ≈≈ˌ≈\ *n* **:** the respectable law-abiding part of society — contrasted with *underworld*

upping *pres part of* UP

up·pish \ˈəpish, -pēsh\ *adj* [¹*up* + *-ish*] **1** *archaic* **:** being in high spirits **:** ELATED **2 :** UPPITY 〈very full of himself, ~ —A. J.Cronin〉 **3** *archaic* **:** taking offense easily **4 :** somewhat up in position or direction — **up·pish·ly** *adv* — **up·pish·ness** *n* -ES

up·pi·ty \ˈəpəd·ē, -ətē, -i\ *adj* [prob. fr. ¹*up* + *-ity* (as in *biggity,* var. of *biggety*)] **:** marked by airs of superiority **:** ARROGANT, PRESUMPTUOUS, PUSHING 〈were so rich and ~ because the government was trying to make everybody equal —Marya Mannes〉 〈her family laughed at her ~ notions —Peter Cansdale〉 — **up·pi·ty·ness** *n* -ES

up·po·woc \ˌəˈpōˌwäk\ *n* [fr. *uppówoc, uhpooc* (in some Algonquian language of Virginia)] *archaic* **:** TOBACCO

upputting \ˈ≈ˌ≈≈\ *also* **upput** \ˈ≈ˌ≈\ *n* [²*up* + *putting* (gerund of *put*) or *put* (after *put up,* v.)] *Scot* **:** LODGING

¹**upraise** \ˌ≈ˈ≈\ *vt* [ME *upreisen, upraisen,* fr. *up* + *reisen, raisen* to raise — more at RAISE] **1 :** to raise up **:** LIFT, ELEVATE; *specif* **:** to raise by geologic upheaval **2 :** to raise from a depressed state **:** CHEER — **up·rais·er** \"+ə(r)\ *n*

²**upraise** \ˈ≈ˌ≈\ *n* **:** RAISE 4

uprear \ˌ≈ˈ≈\ *vb* [ME *upreren,* fr. *up* + *reren* to raise — more at REAR] *vt* **1 a :** to lift up **:** RAISE 〈commands that . . . be ~*ed* his mighty standard —John Milton〉 **b :** ERECT 〈by adding stone to stone had ~*ed* this monument —Arnold Bennett〉 **2 :** to raise the dignity of **:** EXALT ~ *vi* **:** RISE

¹**upright** \ˈ≈ˌ≈\ *adj* [ME, fr. OE *ūpriht,* fr. *ūp* up + *riht* right — more at UP, RIGHT] **1 a :** standing up straight on the feet or on one end **:** being in a vertical position **:** PERPENDICULAR, ERECT 〈Sinanthropus was of medium stature and certainly ~ —R.W. Murray〉 **b :** marked by erectness of carriage **:** having good posture 〈a tall dark girl with that bold ~ well-poised figure —Anthony Trollope〉 **c** (1) **:** having the main axis or a main part perpendicular 〈designs of freezers . . . center around the alternatives of chest and ~ freezers —J.A.Mixon & H.D. Johnson〉 〈the scribe wrote a large flowing hand . . . with the individual letters ~ and square in formation —Jack Finegan〉 (2) **:** not slanting or upside-down **:** having the right side up 〈had to have a gyroscope . . . inside it in order to keep it ~ —Edward Sackville-West & Desmond Shawe-Taylor〉 **2** *obs* **:** SUPINE 1 **3 :** marked by strong moral rectitude **:** morally correct 〈~ women shall associate with no men who drink alcohol —Waldo Frank〉 〈his unquestioned integrity and ~ innocence —J.G.Cozzens〉 **4** *archaic* **:** BIG, STRONG — used chiefly of a vagrant **5** *obs* **:** straight so as to fit either foot 〈an ~ shoe —Robert Burton〉 **6 :** having a vertical or upward course **7 :** having greater height than width 〈a very decorative antique Sheraton ~ wall mirror —*Antiques*〉 〈~ books〉

syn HONEST, JUST, CONSCIENTIOUS, SCRUPULOUS, HONORABLE: UPRIGHT may imply strict regard for the right and resolute, thoughtful adherence to high moral principles 〈they hate all chicanery, all evasiveness and slipperiness. They are *upright* and downright —H.S.Commager〉 〈best described by the old-fashioned word *upright.* It's a good word, comprises a good many things—all the straight qualities, like loyalty, truthfulness, the right sort of pride —Elizabeth Goudge〉 HONEST may describe adherence to truth, candor, straightforwardness, sincerity, fairness, and freedom from fraud and duplicity 〈the idealism that would build peace and content on *honest* foundations, and would deny them to none —V.L.Parrington〉 〈only a careful study of the evidence will enable us to give an *honest* answer —M.R.Cohen〉 〈the *honest* heart that's free frae a' intended fraud or guile —Robert Burns〉 JUST may stress choice of the righteous and equitable 〈a life unblamable and *just* —William Cowper〉 〈nor shall private property be taken for public use without *just* compensation —*U.S.Constitution*〉 〈crime sometimes pays. The *just* man . . . continues unaccountably to suffer, and the wicked to flourish like the green bay tree —Weston La Barre〉 CONSCIENTIOUS may indicate habitual painstaking dutiful effort to accord with moral law 〈the skillful, *conscientious* schoolmistresses whose lives were spent in trying to inculcate real knowledge —C.H.Grandgent〉 〈she took to religion, and her *conscientious* Christian virtues, practiced with stern inclemency, were the canker of the family —Arnold Bennett〉 SCRUPULOUS describes a very careful, meticulous, and sometimes even anxious adherence to dictates of morality and conscience 〈not one word that I have said runs counter to the demands of delicate and penetrating accuracy of observation, or of *scrupulous* fidelity to fact as it appears —J.L.Lowes〉 〈the delicate equipoise and *scrupulous* objectivity which the judge must try to preserve at all times —R.M.Dawson〉 HONORABLE indicates a holding to codes of honor and sanctioned proprieties 〈too *honorable* to lend himself to an accusation which he knew to be false —J.A.Froude〉 〈he avoided the mean and tricky: he was always an *honorable* foe —W.C.Ford〉

²**upright** \ˈ≈ˌ≈\ *vt* [ME *uprighten,* fr. *upright,* adj.] **:** to make upright

³**upright** \ˈ≈ˌ≈\ *adv* [¹*upright*] *archaic* **:** vertically upward 〈for all beneath the moon would I not leap ~ —Shak.〉

⁴**upright** \ˈ≈ˌ≈\ *n* [¹*upright*] **1 a** *obs* **:** a vertical face (as of a building) **b** *archaic* **:** ELEVATION 5 **2 :** the state of being upright **:** PERPENDICULAR 〈a pillar out of ~〉 **3 :** something that stands upright: as **a :** a vertical piece of timber in a building **b :** a perpendicular stone, post, or stake **c :** a vertical structural member of a piece of furniture (as a chair) — usu. used in pl. **d :** the wall down the middle of a brick clamp **e :** a goalpost esp. on a football field — usu. used in pl. **4 :** an upright geologic stratum **5 :** UPRIGHT PIANO

upright drill *n* **:** a drilling machine with a vertical spindle

uprighteously *adv* [blend of ¹*upright* and *righteously*] **:** in a morally correct manner **:** UPRIGHTLY

up·right·eous·ness \ˌəpˈrīchəsnəs\ *n* [blend of ¹*upright* and *righteousness*] **:** the state or quality of being morally correct **:** UPRIGHTNESS

uprighting *n* -s **:** the process of placing the pivot holes in the plates of a timepiece so that the arbors will be perpendicular to the plates

up·right·ly *adv* **:** in an upright manner or position

up·right·ness *n* **:** the state or quality of being upright

upright piano *n* **:** a piano whose strings run vertically — contrasted with *grand piano*

upright tomato *n* **:** any of various stout erect compact tomatoes with the leaves crowded and curled that prob. have developed in cultivation and are usu. considered a distinct variety (*Lycopersicon esculentum validum*)

upright yellowwood *n* **:** a tall tree (*Podocarpus latifolius* syn. *P. thunkergii*) widely distributed in southern Africa where it is an important timber tree

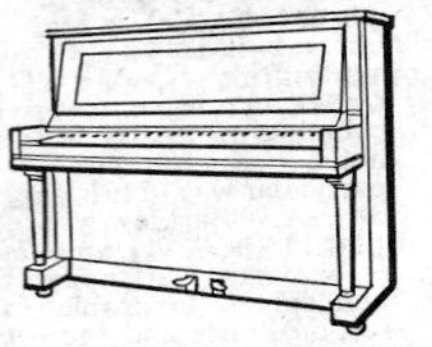

upright piano

up·ris·al \ˌəpˈrīzəl\ *n* **:** an act or instance of rising up **:** UPRISING

¹**up·rise** \ˌəpˈrīz\ *vi* **up·rose** \-ˈrōz\ *also archaic* **up·rist** \-ˈrist\ **up·ris·en** \-ˈrizᵊn\ *also archaic* **uprist; uprising; uprises** [ME *uprisen,* fr. *up* + *risen* to rise — more at RISE] **1 a :** to rise to a higher position 〈the lands were *uprising* and new mountains were rearing their heads —W.E.Swinton〉 **b** (1) **:** to get up on one's feet **:** stand up (2) **:** to get out of bed **c :** to come into view from below; *esp* **:** to come into view from below the horizon 〈the glorious sun *uprist* —S.T.Coleridge〉 **2 :** to rise from the dead or the underworld **3 :** to rise up in or as if in rebellion **4 :** to become existent 〈since earth *uprose* —P.B.Shelley〉 **5 :** to rise up in sound 〈the whisper of gongs and trumpets *uprose* again —James Hilton〉 — **up·ris·er** \-zə(r)\ *n*

²**uprise** \ˈ≈ˌ≈\ *n* **1 :** an act or instance of uprising: as **a :** the rising of a celestial body (as the sun) **:** DAWN **b :** an act or instance of rising to a higher position 〈the ~ of the flood waters〉 **c :** an act or instance of becoming existent or prominent **:** RISE 〈the ~ of a new school of painters〉 **d :** a direct rise from the end of a backward swing to a position of rest on a gymnastic apparatus (as the horizontal bar or flying rings) **2 :** the beginning of a rise in the land **:** an increase in elevation 〈the horizon at which the plains end and, with a swift dramatic ~, the world of the mountains begins —Wynford Vaughan-Thomas〉

uprising \ˈ≈ˌ≈≈\ *n* [ME, fr. *up* + *rising,* gerund of *risen* to rise (after *risen up* to rise up)] **:** an act or instance of rising up; *esp* **:** INSURRECTION, REVOLT **syn** see REBELLION

upriver \ˈ≈¦≈≈\ *adv* (*or adj*) [⁴*up* + *river*] **:** toward, at, or from a point nearer the source of a river 〈proceeded ~ —R.P.Warren〉 〈an ~ voyage —John Hersey〉

up·roar \ˈəpˌrō(ə)r, -ˌrȯ(ə)r, -ōə, -ȯ(ə)\ *n* -s [by folk etymology fr. D *oproer,* fr. MD, fr. *op* up + *roere, roer* motion; akin to OE *ūp* up and to OE *hrēran* to stir — more at UP, CRATER] **1** *archaic* **:** INSURRECTION, REVOLT **2 a :** a loud roaring usu. disorderly noise of some duration 〈the students were making a terrific ~ in the hall〉 〈storms and ~*s* and all such movie wonderments —John McCarten〉 **b :** a state of commotion or excitement **:** violent disturbance **:** TUMULT, TURMOIL 〈the recent ~ created by war-scare statements —*Newsweek*〉

syn see DIN

²**uproar** \ˌ≈ˈ≈\ *vt* -ED/-ING/-S **:** to throw into an uproar

up·roar·i·ous \ˌəpˈrōrēəs, -ˈrȯr- *sometimes* əpˈr-\ *adj* [¹*uproar* + *-ious*] **1 :** marked by a great deal of noise and disorder 〈fights between heavyweight personalities fought to a finish ~ with the shouts of attendant partisans —*Times Lit. Supp.*〉 **2 :** very noisy and full 〈burst into the most ~ laughter —R.H. Davis〉 〈an ~ cough —Frank O'Connor〉 **3 :** productive of loud laughter **:** extremely funny 〈an ~ comedy〉 — **up·roar·i·ous·ly** *adv* — **up·roar·i·ous·ness** *n* -ES

uproll \ˌ≈ˈ≈\ *vb* [¹*up* + *roll*] *vt* **1 :** to move upward by rolling **2 :** to form into a roll **:** wind up ~ *vi* **:** to roll up

¹**uproot** \ˌ≈ˈ≈\ *vb* [¹*up* + *root,* n.] *vt* **1 :** to pull up by or as if by the roots 〈~*ed* the vine —V.L.Parrington〉 〈one signal light tower was ~*ed* when struck by the flying truck —*Springfield (Mass.) Daily News*〉 **2 :** to remove as if by pulling up the roots **:** ERADICATE, DESTROY 〈all vestiges of political democracy were soon ~*ed* —C.E.Black & E.C.Helmreich〉 〈the vulgarity of his age . . . is what he has violently ~*ed* from his own being —Albert Dasnoy〉 **3 :** to displace from a country or traditional habitat **:** tear away from established cultural patterns and values 〈millions of people were ~*ed* by the war〉 〈automation would ~ millions of laborers —John Lear〉 ~ *vi* **:** to change one's place of residence and way of life 〈he's nearly 60, and that's awfully old to ~ and leave everything and everyone you know —Nevil Shute〉 **syn** see EXTERMINATE

²**uproot** \"\ *vt* [¹*up* + *root* (to dig up)] **:** to dig up with the snout

up·root·ed·ness *n* **:** the state or quality of being uprooted 〈a sense of insecurity and ~ —Dixon Wecter〉

up·root·er \"+ə(r)\ *n* **:** one that uproots

uprouse \ˌ≈ˈ≈\ *vt* [¹*up* + *rouse*] **:** to rouse up

¹**uprush** \ˌ≈ˈ≈\ *vi* [¹*up* + *rush*] **:** to rush upward

²**uprush** \ˈ≈ˌ≈\ *n* **1 :** an upward rush of gas or liquid 〈that vigorous ~ of the atmosphere essential to the thunderstorm —W.J.Humphreys〉 **2 a :** a sudden rising esp. from the subconscious 〈an ~ of fear —J.M.Cohen〉 〈was the triumph of irrationalism and betokened an ~ of forces from the psychic underworld —Walter Moberly〉 **b :** a sudden increase 〈an ~ in government debt —Stuart Chase〉

ups *pres 3d sing of* UP, *pl of* UP

ups–a–daisy *var of* UPSY-DAISY

up-saddle \ˌ≈ˈ≈≈\ *vi* [¹*up* + *saddle*] **:** to saddle a horse or a mule 〈sleepy muleteers . . . *up-saddled,* thinking dawn had come —*Spectator*〉

ups and downs *pl of* UP AND DOWN

upscuddle \ˌ≈ˈ≈≈\ *n* -s [²*up* + *scuddle* (origin unknown)] *South* **:** QUARREL

upsee–daisy *var of* UPSY-DAISY

upseeking \ˈ≈ˌ≈≈\ *adj* [¹*up* + *seeking,* pres. part. of *seek*] **:** seeking by looking upward

upsend \ˌ≈ˈ≈\ *vt* [¹*up* + *send*] **:** to send upward

¹**up·set** \ˌəpˈset *sometimes* ˈəpˈs-; *usu* -ed·+V\ *adj* [ME, fr. *up* + *set,* past part. of *setten* to set — more at SET] **1** *archaic* **:** set up **:** RAISED, ERECTED **2** [fr. past part. of ²*upset*] **:** emotionally disturbed **:** affected by an emotional disturbance 〈was too ~ to say anything —Frank Sargeson〉 〈her nerves were more ~ than usual —Arnold Bennett〉

²**upset** \ˌəpˈset *sometimes* ˌəpˈs-; *usu* -ed·+V\ *vb* **upset; upset; upsetting; upsets** *see vt 1b* [ME *upsetten,* fr. *up* + *setten* to set] *vt* **1 a** *obs* **:** to set up **:** put upright **:** RAISE **b** *also past & past part* **upsetted** (1) **:** to turn the outer ends of (stakes) upward so as to make a foundation (as for the side of a basket) (2) **:** to form (the side of a basket) by upsetting the stakes **2 a :** to thicken and shorten (as a heated bar of iron) by the application of pressure on an end (as by hammering) **:** SWAGE **b :** to shorten (a metal tire on a wooden wheel) by cutting and hammering on the ends or by treating in a special machine without cutting **3 :** to force out of the usual upright, level, or proper position **:** CAPSIZE 〈~ his chair —John Buchan〉 〈the winds have torn and ~ the mossy structures in the bushes —Richard Jefferies〉 **4 a :** to disturb the equilibrium of **:** cause an emotional disturbance in **:** DISCOMPOSE 〈the least little thing ~ her —Elizabeth Schutt〉 **b :** to throw into disorder **:** put out of kilter **:** DISARRANGE 〈any effort that ~*s* the routine of daily life may bring about a restless night —Morris Fishbein〉 〈the financial stability of the country was ~ —P.E.James〉 **c** (1) **:** to make invalid by or as if by intervention 〈have enough pigheaded individual ways of their own to ~ any calculation that they will give a certain exact response —C.E.Montague〉 〈induced the jury to ~ a will under unusual circumstances —H.W.H.Knott〉 (2) **:** to defeat unexpectedly (as in an

athletic or political contest) ⟨strong enough to ~ the candidates of the major parties —I.G.Blake⟩ **5 :** to cause a physical disorder in **:** make somewhat ill esp. in the digestive tract ⟨some children are unable to eat certain foods without being ~ by them —H.R.Litchfield & L.H.Dembo⟩ **~ *vi* 1 :** to turn over **:** CAPSIZE ⟨a chafing dish . . . which may be held in the hands yet cannot possibly ~ —G.G.Coulton⟩ **2** *of a bullet* **:** to expand laterally while moving through a rifled bore and upon striking an object **3 :** to upset the stakes in making a basket **syn** see DISCOMPOSE, OVERTURN

³upset \ˈ⸗ˌ⸗\ *n* -S **1 :** a physical overturning **:** OVERTURN ⟨bruised by the ~ of his gig while viewing lands —W.L.Whittlesey⟩ **2 a** (1) **:** an act of throwing into disorder **:** DERANGEMENT, OVERTHROW ⟨the ~ of price levels in the inflation period —C.L.Jones⟩ ⟨a radical innovation, an ~, a reversal of patterns in American domestic life —*Harper's*⟩ (2) **:** a state of disorder **:** CONFUSION ⟨produced less profound changes . . . but also much less ~ and clash —A.L.Kroeber⟩ **b :** QUARREL **c :** an unexpected defeat (as in an athletic or political contest) ⟨cut loose with a dazzling passing attack today to effect one of the most startling ~*s* of the college football season —*N.Y. Times*⟩ ⟨ran for mayor a second time . . . and scored an ~ victory —*Current Biog.*⟩ **3 a :** a physical disorder **:** a slight illness ⟨a stomach ~⟩ ⟨would become disturbed about every single ~ as if it were a major illness —Evelyn Barkins⟩ **b :** an emotional disturbance ⟨went through a big ~ after her father's death⟩ **4 a :** a part of a rod or similar object (as the head on a bolt) that is upset **b :** the buckling of wood fibers due to crushing **c :** the expansion of a bullet that is the result of upsetting **5 :** the rods plaited or woven around the bottoms of the stakes of a basket immediately after upsetting so that they will stay in position — see BASKET illustration **6 :** a swage used in upsetting

upset butt welding *n* **:** butt welding in which a continuous pressure is applied until the work is plastic and is then followed by a pressure high enough to produce an upset joint

upset price *n* **:** the minimum price set by a seller or auctioneer at which property will be offered or sold at auction or public sale

up·set·ter \ˌəpˈsed·ə(r)\ *n* -S **:** one that upsets: as **a :** a person who causes upsets ⟨the businessman . . . is the great ~ on the contemporary scene —M.S.Rukeyser⟩ **b :** an upsetting machine **c :** a forging press operator who increases the breadth of a piece of metal by heating and pressing it so that it spreads

up·set·ter·man \-(r)mən\ *n, pl* **upsettermen :** UPSETTER c

upsetting *adj* **1** *Scot* **:** PRESUMPTUOUS, CONCEITED, ASSUMING **2 :** producing an upset; *esp* **:** causing an emotional disturbance **:** DISTURBING ⟨the hurly-burly of politics is ~ to a sensitive mind and nature —John Lodge⟩ — **up·set·ting·ly** *adv*

¹upshift \ˈ⸗ˌ⸗\ *vi* [¹*up* + *shift*] **:** to shift into a higher automotive gear ⟨the car . . . automatically ~*s* to the cruising range as speed increases —*Report: General Motors Corp.*⟩ ⟨the driver ~*ed* into second⟩

²upshift \ˈ"\ *n* **:** a shift into a higher automotive gear ⟨the ~ to second speed in the low range is produced by the automatic controls —Joseph Heitner⟩

¹upshoot \ˈ⸗ˌ⸗\ *n* [²*up* + *shoot*, n.] **1** *archaic* **:** OUTCOME, UPSHOT **2 :** an act or result of shooting up ⟨the volcanic ~ of fire lasted but a second or two —Russell Grenfell⟩

²upshoot \ˌ⸗ˈ⸗\ *vb* [¹*up* + *shoot*, v.] *vi* **:** to shoot upward **:** grow upward **~ *vt* :** to send up **:** RAISE

upshot \ˈ⸗ˌ⸗\ *n* [²*up* + *shot*] **1 a :** a final shot in an archery match **b :** the best shot up to the moment in an archery match **2 a :** the final result (as of a series or group of actions or events) **:** OUTCOME ⟨the ~ of all this has been a growth of hostility —Sidney Hook⟩ ⟨in the ~ his ideal white man's country . . . has been overtaken by the march of world events —W.M.Macmillan⟩ **b :** the conclusion reached in a reasoning process (as a discussion or an analysis) **:** GIST, ESSENCE ⟨the ~ of the argument⟩ ⟨the ~ of these paragraphs —A.L.Kroeber⟩ **c** *archaic* **:** LIMIT **syn** see EFFECT

upsidaisy *var of* UPSY-DAISY

upside \ˈ⸗ˌ⸗\ *n* [²*up* + *side*] **1 :** the upper side or part **2 :** an upward trend (as of prices) ⟨this issue has emerged on the ~ —*Stock Trend Service*⟩ ⟨appreciable ~ progress —*Wall Street Jour.*⟩

upside down *adv* [by folk etymology fr. earlier *up so down*, *upsedown*, fr. ME *up so doun*, *upsedoun*, fr. *up* + *so* + *doun* down] **1 :** in such a way that the upper and the lower parts are reversed in position ⟨turned the table *upside down*⟩ **2 :** in or into a state of great disorder ⟨turned the world *upside down* —Dorothy Witton⟩

upside-down \ˌ⸗⸗ˈ⸗\ *adj* [*upside down*] **1 :** having the upper and the lower parts reversed in positon **:** INVERTED ⟨*upside-down* letters⟩ **2 :** marked by confusion; *esp* **:** marked by an inversion of the usual or the reasonable ⟨that *upside-down* snobbery of the café chantant —Edmund Wilson⟩ ⟨a fine case of *upside-down* logic —Janet Flanner⟩ — **upside-down·ness** *n*

upside-down cake *n* **:** a cake baked with its batter covering a close arrangement of pieces of fruit in a syrup in the bottom of the pan and served fruit side up

up·sides \ˌəpˈsīdz\ *adv (or adj)* [*upside* + *-s*] **1** *dial Brit* **:** on the same level (as in retaliation) **:** EVEN, SQUARE — usu. used with *with* **2** *Brit* **:** in an equally advanced position (as in a horse race)

up·si·lon \ˈyüpsəˌlän, ˈəp-, -lən, *Brit* yüpˈsīlən\ *n* -S [MGk *y psilon*, *ypsilon*, lit., simple upsilon, fr. Gk *y* upsilon + *psilon*, neut. of *psilos* simple, mere, bare; fr. the desire to distinguish between graphic *y* and graphic *oi*, pronounced the same in later Greek — more at PSIL-] **:** the 20th letter of the Greek alphabet — symbol Υ or υ; see ALPHABET table

upsitten \ˈ⸗ˌ⸗\ *adj* [¹*up* + *sitten*, archaic past part. of *sit*] *Scot* **:** INDIFFERENT

upsitting \ˈ⸗ˌ⸗⸗\ *n* [²*up* + *sitting*, gerund of sit (after *sit up*, v.)] **1 a** *archaic* **:** the first time a woman sits up to receive company after having a baby **b** *obs* **:** the first time one sits up after an illness **2** *chiefly Africa* **:** the act of sitting up at night in courtship

upski \ˈ⸗ˌ⸗\ *n* [¹*up* + *ski*] **:** a ski lift that is pulled uphill like a sled by a cable

upslip \ˈ⸗ˌ⸗\ *n* [²*up* + *slip*] **:** an upward displacement on one side of a fault without there being a downward slip on the other side to the full extent of the total displacement

¹upslope \ˈ⸗ˌ⸗\ *n* [²*up* + *slope*] **:** a slope that lies upward **:** UPHILL

²upslope \ˈ⸗ˌ⸗\ *adv* [⁴*up* + *slope*, n.] **:** in an upward direction **:** UPHILL ⟨the fire . . . was working ~ toward us —G.R.Stewart⟩

upslope fog *n* **:** fog produced by the flow of moist air along upward sloping terrain

upsoar \ˌ⸗ˈ⸗\ *vi* [¹*up* + *soar*] **:** to soar upward

¹upspring \ˈ⸗ˌ⸗\ *n* [ME, fr. OE *ūpspring*, fr. *ūp* up + *spring*] **1** *archaic* **:** an act or instance of springing up; *esp* **:** ORIGIN, DEVELOPMENT, GROWTH **2** *obs* **:** a wild dance

²upspring \ˌ⸗ˈ⸗\ *vi* [ME *upspringen*, fr. *up* + *springen* to spring — more at SPRING] **1 a :** to spring up (as of a plant) **:** GROW **b :** to come into existence **:** ARISE ⟨a little corps of heroes has *upsprung* among us —*Lippincott's Mag.*⟩ **2 :** to spring upward **:** RISE; *specif* **:** to jump to one's feet

¹upstage \ˈ⸗ˈ⸗\ *adv* [⁴*up* + *stage*] **:** toward or at the rear of a theatrical stage or the part away from the footlights — compare DOWNSTAGE, LEFT STAGE, RIGHT STAGE

²upstage \ˈ"\ *adj* **1 :** of or relating to the rear of a theatrical stage **2 a :** occupying the rear of a theatrical stage esp. in such a way as to cause other actors to turn their backs to the audience **b :** marked by superiority of manner **:** HAUGHTY, SNOBBISH, HIGH-CLASS ⟨still thinks he's someone and is very ~ if you start to kid him —H.L.Wilson⟩

³upstage \ˈ⸗ˌ⸗\ *n* **:** the part of a theatrical stage away from the footlights

⁴upstage \ˈ⸗ˈ⸗\ *vt* **1 :** to put (an actor) at the disadvantage of having to face away from the audience by staying upstage ⟨two men and a ballerina maneuver to ~ each other —*Time*⟩ **2 :** to steal the show from ⟨the . . . chimpanzee who has been *upstaging* human actors —*Newsweek*⟩ **3 :** to treat snobbishly **:** put in one's place ⟨properly *upstaged* me by showing me how to shut the door —John Logan⟩

¹upstairs \ˈ⸗ˈ⸗\ *adv* [⁴*up* + *stairs*, pl. of *stair*] **1 a :** up the stairs **:** to or on a higher floor or level **b :** up into or up in the air; *esp* **:** to or at a high altitude ⟨take a new fighter plane ~ —*Business Week*⟩ **2 :** to or in a higher position; *esp* **:** to or in a technically or ostensibly higher position that is less desirable esp. because of diminished authority ⟨began organizing for victory by kicking the commander . . . ~ to the viceroyalty —O.S.J.Gogarty⟩ ⟨quietly moved him ~ to board chairman —*Newsweek*⟩ **3** *slang* **:** in the head ⟨she's all vacant ~ —J.T. Farrell⟩

²upstairs \ˈ"\ *adj* **1** *also* **upstair** \ˈ"\ **a :** situated above the stairs esp. on an upper floor ⟨an ~ room⟩ **b :** of or relating to the upper floors ⟨an ~ maid⟩ **2 :** placed at or occupying a higher level ⟨skilled in ~ politics —C.S.Bluemel⟩ ⟨the ~ ultra-high-frequency area allocated to television —*Telephone Engineer & Management*⟩

³upstairs \ˈ⸗ˈ⸗\ *n pl but sing or pl in constr* **:** the part of a building that is above the ground floor

upstairs man *n* **:** a dining-car waiter who serves meals outside the diner

¹upstand \ˌ⸗ˈ⸗\ *vi* [ME *upstanden*, fr. *up-* + *standen* to stand — more at STAND] **:** to stand up on one's feet **:** rise to a standing position

²upstand \ˈ"\ *n, Brit* **:** one that stands up; *esp* **:** an upright structural part

up·stand·er \ˈ"+ə(r)\ *n* **:** one of the handlebars of an Eskimo sledge

up·stand·ing \ˌəpˈstandiŋ, -aan-, -deŋ\ *adj* [ME, fr. pres. part. of *upstanden*] **1 :** standing up esp. so as to project **:** ERECT ⟨kept his ~ hair and the grin —Edmund Wilson⟩ ⟨one of the most ~ collars in town surmounts a straight coat —Lois Long⟩ **2 :** marked by erect carriage **:** UPRIGHT ⟨a rather ~ horse with strong closely coupled body —G.M.Rommel⟩ ⟨an ~ stalwart figure of a man —*Boston Sunday Herald*⟩ **3 :** marked by integrity and independence **:** STRAIGHTFORWARD ⟨a fine ~ gentleman of the old school —Sinclair Lewis⟩ — **up·stand·ing·ness** *n* -ES

upstaring \ˌ⸗ˈ⸗⸗\ *adj* [¹*up* + *staring*, pres. part. of *stare*] *obs* **:** standing up on end ⟨the king's son . . . with hair ~ —Shak.⟩

¹upstart \ˌ⸗ˈ⸗\ *vi* [ME *upsterten*, fr. *up* + *sterten* to start — more at START] **1 :** to start up **:** jump up (as to one's feet) **2** *obs* **:** to rise up on end **3 :** to come into being or notice

²upstart \ˈ⸗ˌ⸗\ *n* **1 :** one that has risen suddenly (as from a low position to wealth or power); *esp* **:** one that has risen from a lower position and presumes on his success **:** PARVENU **2 :** ⁵KIP 1a

³upstart \ˈ"\ *adj* [²*upstart*] **1 :** recently come into existence **:** NEW ⟨all this material was of neolithic antiquity . . . By comparison the taking of peyote was an ~ ceremony —Alice Marriott⟩ **2 a :** recently or suddenly risen to a higher position or greater prominence ⟨a mésalliance with a little nobody — a little ~ governess —W.M.Thackeray⟩ **b :** characteristic of an upstart **:** FORWARD, PRESUMPTUOUS ⟨the ~ pretensions of a young woman without family, connections, or fortune —Jane Austen⟩ — **up·start·ness** *n* -ES

¹upstate \ˈ⸗ˈ⸗\ *adv* [⁴*up* + *state*, n.] **:** in or to a part of a state designated as upstate ⟨must run ~ and see her —Zona Gale⟩

²upstate \ˈ"\ *adj* **:** of, relating to, originating or being in, or characteristic of a part of a state designated as upstate ⟨~ New York⟩ ⟨an ~ resort —William Peden⟩ ⟨his ~ political organization —Hastings Lyon⟩ ⟨~ pronunciation —H.L. Mencken⟩

³upstate \ˈ"\ *n* **:** the more northerly part of a state of the U.S. as distinguished from a southerly part conventionally designated as *downstate* ⟨the state was again divided: . . . downstate versus ~ —*Our State & Local Gov't of N.Y.*⟩

up·stat·er \ˈ⸗ˈstād·ə(r)\ *n* -S [¹*upstate* + *-er*] **:** an inhabitant or a native of an upstate region

upstay \ˌ⸗ˈ⸗\ *vt* [¹*up* + *stay*] **:** SUSTAIN, SUPPORT

upstir \ˌ⸗ˈ⸗\ *vt* [¹*up* + *stir*] **:** to stir up **:** INCITE, STIMULATE

upstraight \ˌ⸗ˈ⸗\ *adj* [¹*up* + *straight*] **:** ERECT

¹upstream \ˈ⸗ˈ⸗\ *adv* [⁴*up* + *stream*, n.] **:** in a direction nearer the source of a stream ⟨traveled ~⟩ ⟨an extensive tract a few miles ~ —*Amer. Guide Series: La.*⟩

²upstream \ˈ"\ *adj* **1 :** directed upstream ⟨an ~ course⟩ **2 :** situated or occurring upstream ⟨the ~ countries —F.W. Morgan⟩

upstreet \ˈ⸗ˈ⸗\ *adv* [⁴*up* + *street*] **:** up the street

upstretched \ˌ⸗ˈ⸗\ *adj* [¹*up* + *stretched*, past part. of *stretch*] **:** stretched upward

upstroke \ˈ⸗ˌ⸗\ *n* [²*up* + *stroke*] **:** an upward stroke esp. of a pen

¹upsun \ˈ⸗ˌ⸗\ *n* [ME (Sc) *upson*, fr. *up* + *sunne*, *sonne*, *son* sun — more at SUN] *Scot* **:** the time between sunrise and sunset — **with upsun** *adv, Scot* **:** while the sun is up

²upsun \ˈ⸗ˈ⸗\ *adv* [⁴*up* + *sun*, n.] **:** in a direction toward the sun **:** with the sun in one's eyes

¹upsurge \ˌ⸗ˈ⸗\ *vi* [¹*up* + *surge*] **:** to surge up **:** RISE, INCREASE

²upsurge \ˈ⸗ˌ⸗\ *n* **:** an act or instance of surging up; *esp* **:** a rapid increase **:** a sudden rise ⟨a big ~ of wage claims —Margaret Stewart⟩ ⟨the present ~ of concern for the quality of . . . teaching —Ellsworth Barnard⟩

up·sur·gence \ˌəpˈsərjən(t)s\ *n* -S **:** UPSURGE

¹upsweep \ˌ⸗ˈ⸗\ *vi* [¹*up* + *sweep*] **:** to sweep upward

²upsweep \ˈ⸗ˌ⸗\ *n* **:** an upward sweep: as **a :** the upward curving of the underjaw of an animal (as the bulldog) **b :** an increase in elevation; *esp* **:** a steep slope ⟨the thousand-foot ~ of usually frowning scree and cliff on the other side of the water —F.W.Rothwell⟩ **c :** a hairdo in which the hair is brushed up to the top of the head and held in position by pins or combs **d :** a marked increase of activity ⟨this ~ continues to the end of the base period —*Jour. of Accountancy*⟩

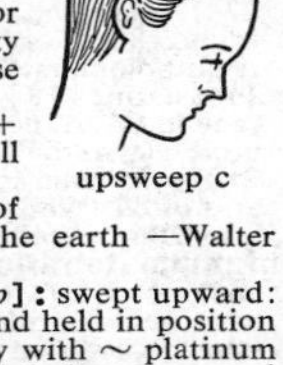

upsweep c

upswell \ˌ⸗ˈ⸗\ *vb* [ME *upswellen*, fr. *up* + *swellen* to swell — more at SWELL] **:** to swell up

upswelling \ˈ⸗ˌ⸗(ˌ)⸗\ *n* **:** an act or instance of swelling upward ⟨the ~ of the seed in the earth —Walter Pater⟩

upswept \ˌ⸗ˈ⸗\ *adj* [fr. past part. of *upsweep*] **:** swept upward: as **a :** brushed up to the top of the head and held in position by pins or combs ⟨a statuesque young lady with ~ platinum hair —Douglas Watt⟩ **b :** curved upward **:** sloped upward ⟨an ~ flourish of mustachios —Frank Yerby⟩ ⟨~ rear fenders⟩

upswing \ˈ⸗ˌ⸗\ *n* [²*up* + *swing*] **:** an upward swing; *esp* **:** an upward movement of considerable strength (as in activity or prices) **:** a marked increase ⟨business activity is still on the ~ —*Amer. Guide Series: Maine*⟩ ⟨a marked ~ in technological progress —H.C.Curtice⟩

up·sy-dai·sy \ˈəpsēˌdāzē\ *also* **up-a-dai·sy** \-pə,-\ *or* **ups-a-dai·sy** \-psə,-\ *or* **up·see-dai·sy** *or* **up·si·dai·sy** \-sē,-\ *interj* [irreg. fr. ¹*up*] — used to express reassurance typically to a small child when it is being lifted

up·sy-down \ˈəpsēˈdau̇n\ *archaic var of* UPSIDE DOWN

upsy dutch *adv, usu cap D, obs* **:** UPSY FREEZE

upsy freeze *adv* [D *op zijn Fries*, lit., in the Frisian manner] *obs* **:** to an excessive degree (as in drinking) **:** HEAVILY

¹uptake \ˌ⸗ˈ⸗\ *vt* [ME *uptaken*, fr. *up* + *taken* to take — more at TAKE] **1** *obs* **:** to take up **:** LIFT, RAISE **2** *chiefly Scot* **:** UNDERSTAND, COMPREHEND

²uptake \ˈ⸗ˌ⸗\ *n* **1 :** UNDERSTANDING, COMPREHENSION ⟨quick on the ~⟩ ⟨slow in the ~ —Arnold Bennett⟩ ⟨prided herself upon being sharp at the ~ —Victoria Sackville-West⟩ **2 a :** the pipe leading upward from the smokebox of a steam boiler to the chimney or smokestack **:** a flue leading upward **b :** a shaft or tube up which a current of air passes esp. for ventilation **:** UPCAST **3 :** TAKE-UP ⟨the loom's ~⟩ **4 :** an act or instance of absorbing and incorporating esp. into a living organism ⟨the ~ of inorganic phosphate normally associated with respiration —P.A.Harvey & Wei Yang⟩ ⟨thyroid function should be determined by radioiodine ~ studies —*Jour. Amer. Med. Assoc.*⟩

uptear \ˌ⸗ˈ⸗\ *vt* [¹*up* + *tear*] **:** to tear up by or as if by the roots **:** DESTROY

up-tempo \ˈ⸗ˌ⸗(ˌ)⸗\ *n* [²*up* + *tempo*] **:** a fast-moving tempo (as in jazz or popular music)

¹upthrow \ˌ⸗ˈ⸗\ *vt* [¹*up* + *throw*] **:** to throw upward **:** cast up

²upthrow \ˈ⸗ˌ⸗\ *n* **1 a :** an upward displacement (as of a stratum or a seam in a mine) **b :** the body of rock on the side of a fault that has moved or appears to have moved upward during the faulting in relation to that on the other side of the fault **c :** an upheaval of the earth's crust **2 :** the amount of upward displacement in a fault — compare THROW

upthrown \ˌ⸗ˈ⸗\ *adj* [fr. past part. of ¹*upthrow*] **:** thrown upward; *specif* **:** displaced upward in a geologic fault

¹upthrust \ˌ⸗ˈ⸗\ *vb* [¹*up* + *thrust*] *vt* **:** to thrust up; *specif* **:** to push up in an upthrust ⟨before the mountains were ~ —E.E. Slosson⟩ **~ *vi* :** to rise with an upward thrust

²upthrust \ˈ⸗ˌ⸗\ *n* **:** an upward thrust; *specif* **:** an uplift of part of the earth's crust commonly with faulting

uptie \ˌ⸗ˈ⸗\ *vt* [ME *uptien*, fr. *up* + *tien* to tie — more at TIE] **:** to tie up

up till *prep* [ME] **1** *obs* **:** up to **:** AGAINST **2 :** TILL, UNTIL ⟨*up till* the moment when bullets and stones began to fly —*Contemporary Rev.*⟩

uptilt \ˌ⸗ˈ⸗\ *vt* [¹*up* + *tilt*] **:** to tilt upward

up to *prep* [ME] **1 :** as far as a designated part (as of the body or a weapon that penetrates) ⟨sank in quicksand *up to* his armpits⟩ ⟨pushed the knife in *up to* the hilt⟩ ⟨was walking right into hot water . . . *up to* her neck —Elizabeth Headley⟩ **2 :** to or in fulfillment of **:** in complete accordance with **:** so as to make full use of ⟨unable to write *up to* their high standards⟩ ⟨practices *up to* his knowledge⟩ **3 a :** to the limit of ⟨guesses on the size of his wealth ran *up to* $2 billion —Joseph Nolan⟩ ⟨sick leave may be accumulated *up to* 150 days —*Careers for College Graduates*⟩ ⟨golden perch, *up to* a few pounds in weight, bit readily —Francis Birtles⟩ ⟨come in sizes *up to* 10 cups —Jane Nickerson⟩ **b :** as many as **:** as much as ⟨freighters carry *up to* 12 passengers —Richard Joseph⟩ ⟨would exempt tickets costing *up to* 60 cents —*Wall Street Jour.*⟩ ⟨carelessness may mean great agony and *up to* weeks in bed —J.L.B.Smith⟩ **4 :** TILL, UNTIL ⟨*up to* that date they had been generally successful —*Amer. Guide Series: Mich.*⟩ ⟨*up to* the war rural areas were always the dwelling place of the surplus population —S. E.Harris⟩ **5 :** as far as a designated point ⟨painted the wall green *up to* the side door⟩ ⟨*up to* this point we have discussed chiefly the material factors —W.C.Huntington⟩

up-to-date \ˌ⸗⸗ˈ⸗\ *adj* **1 :** extending up to the present time **:** including the latest facts ⟨the new 10th edition is *up-to-date* —*Infantry Jour.*⟩ ⟨*up-to-date* maps —George Milburn⟩ **2 :** abreast of the times (as in style or technique) **:** MODERN ⟨the stores . . . are as *up-to-date* as those of any big city —Corey Ford⟩ ⟨the most *up-to-date* methods of cultivation —J.H.Plumb⟩ ⟨a curiously *up-to-date* malaise —Frederic Morton⟩ — **up-to-date·ly** *adv* — **up-to-date·ness** *n* -ES

up-to-the-minute \ˌ⸗⸗⸗ˈ⸗⸗\ *adj* **1 :** extending up to the immediate present **:** including the very latest information ⟨the facts are *up-to-the-minute* —*New Republic*⟩ **2 :** marked by complete up-to-dateness **:** entirely modern ⟨will be remodeled into an *up-to-the-minute* flour mill —*Nat'l Miller*⟩

¹uptown \ˈ⸗ˈ⸗\ *adv* [⁴*up* + *town*, n.] **1 :** toward, to, or in the upper part of a town or city ⟨walked ~ behind two strangers —Sinclair Lewis⟩ **2 :** toward, to, or in the residential section of a city

²uptown \ˈ"\ *adj* **1 :** situated in or belonging to the upper part of a town or city ⟨~ streets⟩ ⟨~ theaters⟩ ⟨~ society⟩ **2 :** situated in or belonging to the residential section of a city

³uptown \ˈ"\ *n* **1 :** the upper part of a town or city **2 :** the residential section of a city

up·town·er \ˈ⸗ˈtau̇nə(r)\ *n* [¹*uptown* + *-er*] **:** one who lives uptown

uptrain *vt* [¹*up* + *train*] *obs* **:** to train up **:** bring up **:** REAR

uptrend \ˈ⸗ˌ⸗\ *n* [²*up* + *trend*] **:** a tendency upward esp. in the development of economic factors

¹upturn \ˌ⸗ˈ⸗\ *vb* [¹*up* + *turn*] *vt* **1 a :** to turn up **:** turn upside down **:** OVERTURN ⟨his plate had been ~*ed* —Marguerite Young⟩ **b :** to throw into great disorder **:** UPHEAVE ⟨a treeless volcanic ~*ed* region —A.W.Greely⟩ **2 :** to direct upward ⟨~*ed* his nostril —John Milton⟩ **~ *vi* :** to turn upward

²upturn \ˈ⸗ˌ⸗\ *n* **1 :** extreme disorder (as of society) **:** CONVULSION, UPHEAVAL ⟨a truth about violent social ~ —Richard Watts⟩ **2 :** an upturned part **3 :** an upward turn esp. toward better conditions or higher prices ⟨an ~ in the economy —*Wall Street Jour.*⟩ ⟨a gradual ~ in living standards —B.M.Jones⟩ ⟨the exceptional ~ of strikes —A.E.Rees⟩

up-twister \ˈ⸗ˌ⸗⸗\ *n* **:** a textile machine with upward feeds that is used to add twist to single yarns without plying them — compare DOWN-TWISTER

upu·pa \ˈyüpyəpə\ *n, cap* [NL, fr. L, hoopoe, prob. of imit. origin] **:** a small genus (the type of the family Upupidae of the order Coraciiformes) of nonpasserine birds comprising the typical hoopoes

¹up·ward \ˈəpwə(r)d\ *or* **up·wards** \-dz\ *adv* [*upward* fr. ME, fr. OE *ūpweard*, fr. *ūp* up + *-weard* -ward; *upwards* fr. ME *upwardes*, fr. OE *ūpweardes*, fr. *ūpweard* + *-es* (adverbially functioning gen. sing. ending of nouns) — more at UP, ¹-S] **1 a :** toward a higher position **:** in a direction from a lower to a higher place ⟨the land gradually rose ~ —J.P.Marquand⟩ ⟨his hands were groping ~ —James Hilton⟩ **b :** toward the source of a stream or the interior of a region ⟨an explorer moving ~ from a river mouth finds a place at which the stream divides —A.A.Hill⟩ **c :** in a higher or the highest relative position ⟨holding out her right hand, palm *upwards* —*Tomorrow*⟩ **d :** in the upper parts esp. of the body **:** toward the head **:** ABOVE ⟨from the waist ~⟩ ⟨sea monster, ~ man and downward fish —John Milton⟩ **2** *archaic* **:** toward the past **3 :** toward a higher or better condition, status, or level ⟨forced his way steadily *upwards* by his mere soldierlike qualities —J.A.Froude⟩ ⟨both man and the manlike apes have developed *upwards* from a common prehistoric ancestral stock —R.W.Murray⟩ ⟨the Senate has amended its opinion of him ~ —*Time*⟩ **4 a :** to an indefinitely greater amount, figure, or rank ⟨from $5 ~⟩ ⟨each claiming as his own anywhere from 100 head ~ —Agnes M. Cleaveland⟩ **b :** toward a greater amount or higher number, degree, or rate ⟨family incomes shot swiftly ~ —Oscar Handlin⟩ ⟨building costs have proved flexible ~ but not downward —T.W.Arnold⟩ **5 :** toward or into later years ⟨from his youth ~⟩ **6 :** toward a large city **7 :** toward the top (as of a sheet of paper) ⟨this stroke . . . is written ~ —Dwight McEwen⟩

²upward \ˈ"\ *prep* [ME, fr. *upward*, adv.] *archaic* **:** up along ⟨~ ragged precipices flit to save poor lambkins —John Keats⟩

³upward \ˈ"\ *adj* [¹*upward*] **1 a :** directed toward a higher place **:** ASCENDING ⟨the drive along that winding ~ track —Norman Douglas⟩ ⟨a general ~ movement of fish⟩ **b :** situated in a higher place or position ⟨scaling the ~ sky —P.B. Shelley⟩ **2 :** marked by improvement or progress ⟨the line of ~ development which led to the anthropoid —R.W.Murray⟩ **3 :** UPSTREAM ⟨discovered and named the falls . . . which they had barely missed on the ~ journey —*Amer. Guide Series: Minn.*⟩ **4 :** rising to a higher pitch ⟨her words had an ~ inflection —Ethel Wilson⟩ **5 :** marked by an increase **:** RISING ⟨prices . . . continued their ~ movement —N.H.Brown⟩ ⟨struggling . . . against the ~ trend of wages —Alzada Comstock⟩ ⟨look forward to an unending ~ market —K.D. Burke⟩ **6 :** directed toward the top (as toward the top of a sheet of paper) ⟨an ~ stroke —J.R.Gregg⟩ — **up·ward·ly** *adv* — **up·ward·ness** *n* -ES

⁴upward \ˈ"\ *n, obs* **:** TOP, CROWN ⟨extremest ~ of thy head —Shak.⟩

upwards of *also* **upward of** *adv* **1 :** more than **:** in excess of ⟨signed *upwards of* 10,000 bills into law and vetoed more than 1500 —Beverly Smith⟩ **2 :** a little less than **:** not quite **:** ALMOST, APPROXIMATELY, ABOUT ⟨outlined *upwards of* a thousand words by means of which he maintained almost anything could be expressed —Louise Pound⟩

¹upwarp \ˈ⸗ˌ⸗\ *n* [²*up* + *warp*, n.] **:** a very broad anticline with gently dipping limbs that is due to differential uplift

²upwarp \ˌ⸗ˈ⸗\ *vt* [¹*up* + *warp*, v.] **:** to uplift differentially so as to produce an upwarp or a broad low arching of the surface ⟨the land to the northward had been ~*ed* —*Jour. of Geol.*⟩

upwash \ˈ⸗ˌ⸗\ *n* [²*up* + *wash*] **:** the upward flow of air directly ahead of the leading edge of a moving airfoil

upwell \ˌ⸗ˈ⸗\ *vi* [¹*up* + *well*] **:** to well up; *specif* **:** to move or flow upward

upwent *past of* UPGO

upwhirl \ˌ⸗ˈ⸗\ *vb* [¹*up* + *whirl*] *vt* **:** to cause to whirl upward **~ *vi* :** to whirl upward

¹upwind \ˌ⸗ˈ⸗\ *vb* [¹*up* + *wind*] *vt, obs* **:** to wind up **:** ROLL, COIL **~ *vi* :** to wind upward

2upwind \ˈ=ˌ=\ *adv* [4*up* + *wind*, n.] **1 :** with face or course against the wind ⟨stalked cautiously ~⟩ ⟨the slim and beautiful jets . . . roared ~ —J.A.Michener⟩ **2 :** in a position toward the direction from which the wind is blowing ⟨are dropped ~ and will drift down upon the survivors —*Nat'l Geographic Mag.*⟩

3upwind \ˈ=ˌ=\ *n* [2*up* + *wind*, n.] **1 :** a wind blowing against one's course **2 :** a wind blowing up a slope

4upwind \ˈ=ˈ=\ *adj* [2*upwind*] **:** being toward or in the direction from which the wind is blowing ⟨the infamous ~ turn which calls for the most precise piece of instrument flying —G.G. O'Rourke⟩ ⟨sent to the ~ side —James Stevenson-Hamilton⟩

1up·with \ˈəpˌwith\ *adv* [1*up* + obs. *with*, adv., together, fr. ME — more at DOWNWITH] *chiefly Scot* **:** UPWARD

2upwith \ˈ"\ *adj, chiefly Scot* **:** sloping upward **:** RISING

1ur \(ˈ)ü(ə)r, (ˈ)ür\ *dial var of* OUR

2ur *like* ER\ *interj* **:** ER

1ur- *or* **uro-** *comb form* [NL, fr. Gk *our-, ouro-*, fr. *ouron* urine — more at URINE] **1 :** urine ⟨*ur*analysis⟩ ⟨*uro*bilin⟩ **2 :** urinary tract ⟨*uro*gram⟩ **3 :** urination ⟨*uro*lagnia⟩ **4 :** urinal and ⟨*uro*genital⟩ **5 :** urea ⟨*ur*ethane⟩ ⟨*ur*acil⟩ **6 :** uric acid ⟨*ur*oxanic⟩

2ur- *or* **uro-** *comb form* [NL, fr. Gk *our-, ouro-*, fr. *oura*, akin to Gk *orrhos* buttocks — more at ASS] **1 :** tail **:** taillike ⟨*uro*steon⟩ ⟨*Uro*glena⟩ ⟨*uro*pod⟩ **2 :** posterior segment, region, or process **:** caudal ⟨*ur*ite⟩ ⟨*uro*hyal⟩ ⟨*uro*some⟩

ur *abbr* urinal; urine

UR *abbr* **1** uniform regulations **2** unsatisfactory report **3** upper right

-u·ra \(y)u̇rə, (y)ürə\ *n comb form, pl* **-ura** [NL, fr. fem. sing. and neut. pl. of *-urus* -urous] **:** one having (such) a tail ⟨Chel*ura*⟩ **:** ones having (such) a tail ⟨Brachy*ura*⟩ — in taxonomic names in zoology

ura·chal \ˈyu̇rəkəl\ *adj* [NL *urachus* + E *-al*] **:** of, relating to, or being a urachus

ura·chus \-kəs\ *n* -ES [NL, fr. Gk *ourachos*, fr. *our-* 1ur- + *-achos* (fr. *echein* to hold) — more at SCHEME] **:** a cord of fibrous tissue extending from the bladder to the umbilicus and constituting the functionless remnant of a part of the duct of the allantois of the embryo

ura·cil \ˈyu̇rəˌsil\ *n* -S [ISV 1*ur-* + *acetic* + *-il*] **:** a crystalline heterocyclic compound $C_4H_4N_2O_2$ that is capable of salt formation with sodium hydroxide and is obtained by hydrolysis of ribonucleic acid or by reaction of urea with ethyl formyl-acetate; 2,4-dihydroxy-pyrimidine; *also* **:** any of various derivatives of this compound — compare THYMINE

urad \ˈu̇rəd\ *n* -S [Hindi *urd, urad*] **:** a small-seeded Indian pulse (*Phaseolus radiatus*) resembling the related mung bean and often cultivated as a small grain crop

uraemia *var of* UREMIA

urae·us \yəˈrēəs, yüˈr-\ *n, pl* **uraei** \-ēˌī\ [NL, fr. LGk *ouraios*, a snake, perh. asp] **:** a stylized representation of the sacred asp (*Naja haje*) appearing on the headdress of ancient rulers esp. just over the forehead and serving as a symbol of sovereignty

uraeus

u rail *n, cap U* **:** a U-shaped rail

ural \ˈyu̇rəl, ˈyürəl, *Russian* üˈrälʹ\ *adj, usu cap* [fr. *Ural* mountains & *Ural* river, western Asia] **:** of, relating to, or constituting the Ural mountain range running north and south and forming for the most part the eastern boundary of the U.S.S.R. in Europe or the Ural river of southern Russia and Asia

1ural-altaic \ˌ==ˌ=ˈ==\ *adj, usu cap U&A* **:** of, relating to, or constituting Uralic, Altaic, or other agglutinating languages

2ural-altaic \ˈ"\ *n* -S *cap U&A* **1 :** a postulated language group comprising the Uralic and Altaic languages **2 :** a language type showing agglutination and vowel harmony and occurring esp. in languages of Eurasia

urali *var of* OORALI

urali·an \yəˈrālēən, yüˈr-, -ral-\ *adj, usu cap* [*Ural* mountains, northwestern Asia + E *-an*] **1 :** of or relating to the Ural mountains or to the people dwelling in or near them **2 :** constituting or relating to the Finno-Ugric or the Finno-Ugric and Samoyed languages

uralian emerald *n, usu cap U* **:** DEMANTOID

1ural·ic \-ralik\ *adj, usu cap* [*Ural* mountains + E *-ic*] **:** URALIAN

2uralic \ˈ"\ *n, cap* **:** a language family comprising the Finno-Ugric and Samoyed languages

URALIC LANGUAGES

SUBFAMILY	BRANCH	LANGUAGES	CHIEF LOCALITIES
FINNO-UGRIC	Finnic	Lapp	northern Scandinavia, Finland, the Kola peninsula of Russia
		Finnish, Karelian, Estonian, Livonian, Veps	Finland, Estonia, Latvia, adjacent parts of Russia
		Mordvin	middle Volga region
		Cheremis	middle Volga region
		Votyak, Zyrian	northeastern European Russia
	Ugric	Ostyak, Vogul	Ob valley of northwestern Siberia
		Magyar	Hungary, Romania
SAMOYED		Kamasin, Tavgi, Yenisei, Yurak, Ostyak Samoyed	northwestern Siberia

ural·ite \ˈyu̇rəˌlīt\ *n* -S [G *uralit*, fr. *Ural* mountains, its locality + G *-it* -ite] **:** a usu. fibrous and dark-green amphibole resulting from alteration of pyroxene — **ural·it·ic** \ˌ==ˈlid·ik\ *adj*

ural·i·ti·za·tion \yəˌralə̇d·əˈzāshən, yüˌr-, -ləˌtīˈz-\ *n* -S [ISV *uralitize* + *-ation*] **:** the development of amphibole from pyroxene

ural·i·tize \ˈ=ˈləˌtīz\ *vt* -ED/-ING/-S [*uralite* + *-ize*] **:** to alter (pyroxene) so as to form uralite

ura·mil \ˈyu̇rəˌmil, yəˈramə̇l\ *n* -S [ISV 1*ur-* + *-am* + *-il*; prob. orig. formed in G] **:** a nitrogenous cyclic compound $CO(NHCO)_2CHNH_2$ obtained from alloxantin and other derivatives of uric acid or urea in colorless crystals that redden on exposure; 5-amino-barbituric acid — called also *murexan*

uran \(y)əˈran\ *n* -S [F *ouran, varan*, fr. Ar *waran*] **:** a monitor lizard

1uran- *or* **urano-** *comb form* [NL, fr. L, fr. Gk *ouran-, ourano-*, fr. *ouranos* sky, heaven, roof of the mouth] **1 :** sky **:** heaven ⟨*urano*graphy⟩ **2 :** palate ⟨*urano*plasty⟩ ⟨brachy*uran*ic⟩

2uran- *or* **urano-** *comb form* [F, fr. NL *uranium*] **:** uranium ⟨*urano*thorite⟩ ⟨*uran*yl⟩

uranalysis *var of* URINALYSIS

ura·nate \ˈyu̇rəˌnāt\ *n* -S [ISV 2*uran-* + *-ate*] **:** a compound [as calcium uranate $CaUO_4$ or ammonium di-uranate $(NH_4)_2U_2O_7$] formed by reaction of a uranyl salt with a base or by fusion of uranium trioxide or tri-uranium oct-oxide with a metal chloride

ura·nia \yəˈrānēə, yüˈr-, -nyə\ *n, cap* [NL, fr. Gk *ourania*, fem. of *ouranios* heavenly, fr. *ouranos* heaven] **:** a genus (the type of the family Uraniidae) of large brilliantly colored moths that are native to the West Indies and So. America and have tailed hind wings and diurnal flight which cause them to resemble butterflies — **ura·ni·id** \-ēə̇d\ *n or adj*

1ura·nian \-nēən,-nyən\ *adj, usu cap* [n sense 1, fr. ML *uranius* heavenly, celestial (fr. Gk *ouranios*) + E *-an*; in sense 2, fr. L *Urania* (fr. Gk *Ourania*, one of the muses, fr. fem. of *ouranios*) + E *-an*] **1 :** of, relating to, or concerned with the heavens **:** HEAVENLY, CELESTIAL **2 a :** relating or dedicated to Urania, the muse of astronomy **b :** of or relating to the science of astronomy **:** ASTRONOMICAL

2uranian \ˈ"\ *adj, usu cap* [*Uranus*, seventh planet from the sun + E *-an* — more at URANIUM] **:** of or relating to the planet Uranus

3uranian \ˈ"\ *n* -S *usu cap* **:** a hypothetical inhabitant or native of the planet Uranus

4uranian \ˈ"\ *adj or n* [*Urania*, the Greek goddess of love Aphrodite + E *-an*] **:** HOMOSEXUAL

1uran·ic \yəˈranik, yüˈr-\ *adj* [ISV 2*uran-* + *-ic*] **:** of, relating to, or containing uranium — used esp. of compounds in which this element has a valence higher than in uranous compounds

2uranic \ˈ"\ *adj* [1*uran-* + *-ic*] **:** URANIAN 2b

urani·cen·tric \ˌyu̇rənəˈsen·trik, yəˌran-, yüˌr-, -ˌran-\ *adj, often cap* [*Uranus* + *-i-* + *-centric*] **:** referred to the planet Uranus as a center

ura·nide \ˈyu̇rəˌnīd\ *n* -S [2*uran-* + *-ide*] **1 :** URANIUM **2 :** a transuranium element — compare ACTINIDE

ura·nif·er·ous \ˌyu̇rəˈnif(ə)rəs\ *adj* [ISV 2*uran-* + *-iferous*] **:** containing uranium

ura·nin \ˈyu̇rənən, yəˈrān-, yüˈran-\ *n* -S [2*uran-* + *-in, -ine*; fr. its fluorescence resembling that of uranium glass] **:** the sodium salt of fluorescein — see DYE table I (under *Acid Yellow 73*)

ura·nin·ite \-əˌnīt, yəˈranə-, yüˈr-\ *n* -S [G *uranin* uraninite (fr. 2*uran-* + *-in*) + E *-ite*] **:** a mineral UO_2 that is a black octahedral or cubic oxide of uranium, that contains also thorium, the cerium and yttrium metals, and lead, that often yields when heated a gas consisting chiefly of helium, and that is the chief ore of uranium (hardness 6.6, sp. gr. 9.7 when unaltered) — called also CLEVEITE; see BRÖGGERITE, NIVENITE, PITCHBLENDE

ura·nism \ˈyu̇rəˌnizəm\ *n* -S [G *uranismus*, fr. *Urania*, the Greek goddess of love Aphrodite (fr. Gk *Ourania*, fr. fem. of *ouranios* heavenly) + G *-ismus* -ism] **:** a homosexual condition esp. when involving physically normal males

ura·nist \-nəst\ *n* -S [ISV *uran-* (in *uranism*) + *-ist*] **:** HOMOSEXUAL

ura·nium \yəˈrānēəm, yüˈr- *also* -nyəm\ *n* -S [NL, fr. *Uranus*, seventh planet from the sun discovered in the same decade as uranium (after *Uranus*, in Greco-Roman mythology the personification of heaven and husband of Earth, fr. L, fr. Gk *Ouranos*, fr. *ouranos* sky, heaven) + NL *-ium*] **:** a lustrous silvery heavy radioactive polyvalent metallic element of the actinide series that occurs in concentrated form in pitchblende, carnotite, and autunite and in traces of 0.2 to 200 parts per million in most igneous rocks, phosphate rocks, lignites, and oil shales, that is prepared from its halides by reduction with alkali or alkaline earth metals or from its oxides by reduction with hot carbon, aluminum, or calcium, that exists naturally as a mixture of three isotopes of mass numbers 238, 235, and 234 in the proportions 99.28 percent, 0.71 percent, and 0.006 percent respectively, that undergoes very slow radioactive decay and captures neutrons in a nuclear reactor to produce a heavier isotope of mass number 239 which decomposes by beta emissions into neptunium and then plutonium, and that is used primarily in atomic energy programs to sustain chain-reaction piles, to provide a source of the light isotope uranium 235, and to make plutonium — symbol *U*; see THORIUM, URANIUM SERIES; ELEMENT table

ura·nium·aire \ˌ=ˌrānēəˈma(a)(ə)r, -nyəˈm-, =ˈ=(=)=ˌ=\ *n* -S [*uranium* + *-aire* (as in *millionaire*)] **:** a person making a fortune from uranium and esp. from the discovery of new deposits

uranium fluoride *n* **:** a fluoride of uranium: as **a :** URANIUM TETRAFLUORIDE **b :** URANIUM HEXAFLUORIDE

uranium glass *n* **:** a fluorescent yellow glass colored by adding uranium compounds

uranium hexafluoride *n* **:** a pale yellow deliquescent crystalline compound UF_6 that sublimes at 56.5°C, that is made usu. from uranium tetrafluoride or uranium by direct action of fluorine, and that is used in the gaseous diffusion process for separation of uranium 235 from ordinary uranium

uranium lead *n* **:** lead consisting essentially of the isotope of mass number 206 formed as the final product of the uranium series

uranium nitrate *n* **:** URANYL NITRATE

uranium-ocher \ˈ=ˈ=(=)=ˈ==\ *n* **:** GUMMITE

uranium oxide *n* **:** any of a series of oxides of uranium that are usu. regarded as definite compounds but are better considered phases with a range of compositions: as **a :** the dioxide UO_2 or approximately $UO_{2.0\text{-}2.6(?)}$ obtained as a brown to black crystalline powder by heating uranium trioxide or tri-uranium oct-oxide in hydrogen or carbon monoxide and formerly used in gas mantles and in ceramic glazes — compare URANINITE **b :** the most stable of the oxides U_3O_8 that occurs in pitchblende, that is obtained as a green to black crystalline compound by treating pitchblende successively with acids, bases, and dilute acids or by igniting other uranium oxides or most other uranium compounds in air, that is reduced to metallic uranium by heating with carbon or aluminum, and that is a primary source of uranium for atomic energy work **:** tri-uranium oct-oxide **c :** the trioxide UO_3 that is obtained as a light yellow to orange to brick-red amorphous or crystalline substance usu. by heating uranyl nitrate or ammonium di-uranate, that loses oxygen on heating to form tri-uranium oct-oxide, and that is sometimes used as a pigment for green-yellow colors in glass

uranium ray *n* **:** BECQUEREL RAY

uranium series *or* **uranium-radium series** *n* **:** a radioactive series beginning with uranium I of mass number 238 and ending with radium G constituting the nonradioactive isotope of lead of mass number 206: uranium I, at. no. 92→ uranium X_1 at. no. 90 (syn. thorium 234) → uranium X_2, at. no. 91 (syn. protactinium 234) → uranium II, at. no. 92 (syn. uranium 234) → ionium, at. no. 90 (syn. thorium 230) → radium 226, at. no. 88 → radon 222, at. no. 86 → radium A, at. no. 84 (syn. polonium 218) → radium B, at. no. 82 (syn. lead 214) [or astatine 218] → radium C, at. no. 83 (syn. bismuth 214) → radium C′, at. no. 84 (syn. polonium 214) [or radium C″, at. no. 81 (syn. thallium 210)] → radium D, at. no. 82 (syn. lead 210) → radium E, at. no. 83 (syn. bismuth 210) → radium F, at. no. 84 (syn. polonium 210) → radium G, at. no. 82 (syn. lead 206) — called also *radium series*

uranium tetrafluoride *n* **:** a green crystalline nonvolatile compound UF_4 that is usu. made from uranium dioxide and hydrogen fluoride above 500°C or from uranium metal and fluorine and that is used in making uranium hexafluoride

uranium 235 *n* **:** a light isotope of uranium of mass number 235 that is physically separable from natural uranium or is formed from plutonium by emission of a helium nucleus, that as the parent of the actinium series undergoes very slow radioactive disintegration, and that when bombarded with slow neutrons undergoes rapid fission into smaller atoms (as strontium and xenon or barium and krypton) together with release of much radiation and atomic energy, and that is used in power plants and atom bombs — symbol U^{235} or ^{235}U; called also ACTINOURANIUM

uranium yellow *n* **:** a yellow salt $Na_2U_2O_7.6H_2O$ used esp. formerly in ceramic glazes and fluorescent glass **:** sodium di-uranate

urano- — see URAN-

ura·no·cir·cite \ˌyu̇rənōˈsərˌsīt, yəˌrān-\ *n* -S [G *uranocircit*, fr. 2*uran-* + Gk *kirkos* hawk (trans. of G *falken* in *Falkenstein*, city in central Germany, its locality) + G *-it* -ite — more at CIRCAETUS] **:** a mineral $Ba(UO_2)_2(PO_4)_2.8H_2O$ that is a hydrous barium uranium phosphate in yellow-green crystals and is isomorphous with torbernite, autunite, saléeite, zeunerite, and uranospinite

ura·nog·ra·pher \ˌyu̇rəˈnägrəfə(r)\ *also* **ura·nog·ra·phist** \-fə̇st\ *n* -S **:** an expert in or student of uranography

ura·no·graph·ic \ˌyu̇rənōˈgrafik\ *or* **ura·no·graph·i·cal** \-fə̇kəl\ *adj* **:** of or relating to uranography

ura·nog·ra·phy \ˌyu̇rəˈnägrəfē\ *n* -ES [Gk *ouranographia*, fr. *ouran-* 1uran- + *-graphia* -graphy] **1 :** description of the celestial regions and the divine abode **2 a :** a branch of science dealing with the description of the heavens and the celestial bodies **:** URANOLOGY **b :** the construction of celestial representations (as maps or globes)

ura·no·log·i·cal \ˌyu̇rənəˈläjəkəl\ *adj* **:** of or relating to uranology

ura·nol·o·gy \ˌyu̇rəˈnäləjē\ *n* -ES [prob. fr. (assumed) NL *uranologia*, fr. NL 1*uran-* + *-logia* -logy] **1 :** the study of the heavens **:** ASTRONOMY **2 :** a discourse or treatise on the heavens and the celestial bodies

ura·no·met·ri·cal \ˌyu̇rənōˈme·trəkəl\ *adj* [NL *uranometria* uranometry + E *-ical*] **:** of or relating to uranometry

ura·nom·e·try \ˌyu̇rəˈnämə·trē\ *n* -ES [NL *uranometria*, fr. 1*uran-* + *-metria* -metry] **1 :** a chart or catalog of celestial bodies and esp. of visible fixed stars **2 :** the measurement of the heavens

uran·o·phane \yəˈranəˌfān\ *n* -S [G *uranophan*, fr. 2*uran-* + *-phan* -phane] **:** a mineral $Ca(UO_2)_2Si_2O_7.6H_2O$ that is a hydrous uranium calcium silicate, occurs in yellow fibrous masses, and is possibly identical with uranotil (sp. gr. 3.81–3.90)

ura·nopi·lite \ˌyu̇rənōˈpīˌlīt, -ˈnäpəˌlīt\ *n* -S [G *uranopilit*, fr. 2*uran-* + Gk *pilos* felt + G *-it* -ite — more at PILE (hair)] **:** a mineral $(UO_2)_6(SO_4)(OH)_{10}.12H_2O$ that is a hydrous basic sulfate of uranium and occurs in yellow velvety incrustations composed of microscopic needlelike crystals

ura·nos·co·pid \ˌyu̇rəˈnäskəpə̇d\ *adj* [NL *Uranoscopidae*] **:** of or relating to the Uranoscopidae

ura·no·scop·i·dae \ˌyu̇rənōˈskäpəˌdē\ *n pl, cap* [NL, fr. *Uranoscopus*, type genus (fr. L *uranoscopus*, a fish, fr. Gk *ouranoskopos*, fr. *ouranoskopos*, adj., observing the heavens, fr. *ouranos* sky, heaven + *-skopos* observing, fr. *skopein* to observe, look at) + *-idae* — more at SPY] **:** a family of percoid fishes comprising the stargazers

uranoso- *comb form* [ISV, fr. NL *uranosus* uranous] **:** uranous ⟨*uranoso*potassic⟩

ura·no·so·uranic oxide \ˌyu̇rəˈnō(ˌ)sō + . . .-\ *n* [*uranoso-* + 1*uranic*] **:** URANIUM OXIDE b

ura·no·sphae·rite *also* **ura·no·sphe·rite** \ˌyu̇rənōˈsfiˌrīt\ *n* -S [G *uranosphaerit*, fr. 2*uran-* + *sphaer-* + *-it* -ite] **:** a mineral $(BiO)_2U_2O_7.3H_2O$ that is a hydrous bismuth uranate and occurs in orange-yellow to brick-red half-globular aggregates

ura·nos·pi·nite \ˌyu̇rəˈnäspəˌnīt\ *n* -S [G *uranospinit*, fr. 2*uran-* + Gk *spinos* chaffinch (taken to mean siskin) + G *-it* -ite; fr. its color resembling that of the siskin — more at FINCH] **:** a mineral $Ca(UO_2)_2(AsO_4)_2.8H_2O$ that is a hydrous calcium uranium arsenate, occurs in green tabular crystals, and is isomorphous with zeunerite, torbernite, autunite, saléeite, and uranocircite

ura·no·tan·ta·lite \ˌyu̇rənōˈtantᵊlˌīt\ *n* [G *uranotantal* uranotantalite (fr. 2*uran-* + *tantal* tantalite) + E *-ite*] **:** SAMARSKITE

ura·no·thal·lite \-ˈthaˌlīt\ *n* -S [G *uranothallit*, fr. 2*uran-* + *thall-* + *-it* -ite; fr. its color] **:** LIEBIGITE

ura·no·thorianite \ˌyu̇rənō+\ *n* [2*uran-* + *thorianite*] **:** a mineral that is an intermediate member in the isomorphous series from uraninite to thorianite

ura·no·thorite \ˈ"+\ *n* [2*uran-* + *thorite*] **:** a uraniferous variety of thorite

uran·o·til \yəˈranəˌtil\ *or* **uran·o·tile** \-ˌtīl\ *n* -S [G *uranotil*, fr. 2*uran-* + Gk *tilos* fiber] **:** URANOPHANE

ura·nous \ˈyu̇rənəs, yəˈrān-\ *adj* [NL *uranosus*, fr. 2*uran-* + L *-osus* -ose] **:** of, relating to, or containing uranium — used esp. of compounds in which this element has a lower valence than in uranic compounds

ura·nyl \ˈyu̇rəˌnil\ *n* -S [ISV 2*uran-* + *-yl*] **:** the bivalent radical UO_2 or ion UO_2^{++} formed by uranium trioxide in acid solution; di-oxo-uranium(VI)

uranyl nitrate *n* **:** a yellow salt $UO_2(NO_3)_2$ that is soluble in many organic solvents as well as in water, that is obtained by reaction of uranium oxides with nitric acid, and that is now used chiefly in the purification of uranium and in nuclear reactions

1ura·re *or* **ura·ri** \(y)üˈrärē\ *n* -S [Carib *urari*] **:** CURARE

2urare \ˈ"\ *n* -S [AmerSp] **:** SPINY RAT 1

urate \ˈyu̇ˌrāt\ *n* -S [F, fr. *ur-* (in *urique* uric, fr. E *uric*) + *-ate*] **:** a salt of uric acid

urate cell *n* **:** a specialized cell in an insect fat body containing uric acid salts

urat·ic \yəˈrad·ik\ *adj* [ISV *urate* + *-ic*] **:** of, relating to, or containing urates

ura·wa \üˈräwə, -ˌwä\ *adj, usu cap* [fr. *Urawa*, Japan] **:** of or from the city of Urawa, Japan **:** of the kind or style prevalent in Urawa

ura·zine \ˈyu̇rəˌzēn, -ˌzən\ *n* -S [ISV 1*ur-* + *az-* + *-ine*; orig. formed as G *urazin*] **1 :** a crystalline compound $C_2H_4N_4O_2$ that is an amino derivative of urazole **2 :** an isomeric crystalline compound $C_2H_4N_4O_2$ derived from tetrazine or theoretically as a condensation product of two molecules of urea — called also *para-urazine*

ura·zole \ˈyu̇rəˌzōl\ *n* -S [ISV 1*ur-* + *az-* + *-ole*, orig. formed as G *urazol*] **:** a crystalline acidic compound $C_2H_3N_3O_2$ derived from triazole and made esp. by heating urea with hydrazine sulfate; *also* **:** a derivative of it

ur·ban \ˈərbən, ˈəb-, ˈəib-\ *adj* [L *urbanus*, fr. *urb-, urbs* city + *-anus* -an] **1 a :** of, relating to, characteristic of, or taking place in a city ⟨~ affairs⟩ ⟨~ manners⟩ ⟨~ life⟩ **b :** constituting or including and centered on a city ⟨an ~ area⟩ **c :** of, relating to, or concerned with an urban and specif. a densely populated area ⟨~ sociology⟩ ⟨~ biology⟩ **2 :** having authority, property, or residence in a city or urban area ⟨an ~ magistrate⟩ ⟨~ property owners⟩ **3 :** belonging or having relation to buildings that are characteristic of cities ⟨an ~ lease⟩

urban district *n* **:** a subdivision of an administrative county esp. in England, Wales, and Northern Ireland comprising thickly populated communities, distinguished from a borough in not possessing a borough charter, and governed by an urban district council with local jurisdiction in matters of roads, housing, and policing and to some extent sanitation and education — compare RURAL DISTRICT

ur·bane \ˌərˈbān, (ˈ)əˈb-, (ˈ)əiˈb-\ *adj, sometimes* -ER/-EST [L *urbanus*] **1** *archaic* **:** URBAN 1, 2 **2 :** evincing the polish and suavity characteristic of social life in large cities **:** smoothly courteous **:** notably polite or finished in manner **syn** see SUAVE

ur·bane·ly *adv* **:** in an urbane manner **:** with urbanity

ur·ban·ism \ˈərbəˌnizəm, ˈəb-, ˈəib-\ *n* -S [F *urbanisme*, fr. L *urbanus* urban + F *-isme* -ism] **1 :** the condition or characteristic way of life of those who live in an urban area **2 :** the study and theory of building and other physical needs in cities or predominantly urban cultures **:** city planning **3 :** URBANIZATION

ur·ban·ist \-nəst\ *n* -S [ISV *urban* + *-ist*] **:** a specialist in city planning — compare URBANISM 2

ur·ban·is·tic \ˌ=bəˈnistik\ *adj* [fr. *urbanism*, after such pairs as E *optimism: optimistic*] **:** of or relating to urbanism — **ur·ban·is·ti·cal·ly** \-tək(ə)lē\ *adv*

ur·ban·ite \ˈ=bəˌnīt\ *n* -S **:** one who lives in a city

ur·ban·i·ty \ˌərˈbanəd·ē, əˈb-, əiˈb-, -nətē, -i\ *n* -ES [MF & L; MF *urbanité* quality of being urbane, fr. L *urbanitat-, urbanitas* urban life, fr. *urbanus* urban + *-itat-, -itas* -ity] **1 a :** the quality or state of being urbane **b urbanities** *pl* **:** suavely gracious acts or conduct **2 :** the condition of being urban; *also* **:** urban life **3 :** well-bred and polished conversation esp. when light and witty

ur·ban·iza·tion \ˌərbənəˈzāshən, ˌəb-, ˌəib-, -ˌnīˈz-\ *n* -S **:** the quality or state of being or becoming urbanized

ur·ban·ize \ˈ=bəˌnīz\ *vt* -ED/-ING/-S *see -ize in Explan Notes* [ISV *urban* + *-ize*] **1 :** to cause (as a rural area) to take on urban characteristics **:** convert to or incorporate into an urban area ⟨the eastern states were gradually *urbanized*⟩ **2 :** to impart to or force upon (as persons) urban habits, ways of life, or responsibilities ⟨the need to ~ a peasant population is a factor in delaying industrialization⟩

urban quaestor *n* **:** an ancient Roman quaestor in charge of the public treasure

urban revolution *n* **:** a period in the growth of a culture characterized by the development of cities **:** an initial period of urbanization

urban servitude *n* **:** a servitude under Roman, civil, and Scots law affecting a building wherever located with respect to various rights (as of inserting a beam in another's wall, of support by another's wall, of eavesdrip, of drainage of rainwater collected and drained onto another's land, and of light and prospect)

urban society *or* **urban culture** *n* **:** a society that is typical of modern industrial civilization and heterogeneous in cultural tradition, that emphasizes secular values, and that is individualized rather than integrated — contrasted with *folk society*

urban sociology *n* **:** a branch of sociology dealing with the development of urban communities and their effect upon society — compare RURAL SOCIOLOGY

ur·bi·car·i·an \ˌərbiˈka(a)rēən\ *adj* [LL *urbicarius* of the city + E *-an* — more at SUBURBICARIAN] : SUBURBICARIAN

ur·bic·o·lae \ˌərˈbikəˌlē\ *n, pl* [NL, fr. pl. of *urbicola* city dweller, fr. L *urb-, urbs* city + NL *-i- -i- -cola*] syn of HESPERIIDAE

ur·bi·cul·ture \ˈərbəˌkəlchər\ *n* [L *urb-, urbs* city + E *-i- -i- culture*] : the practices and problems peculiar to cities or to urban life

URC *abbr* upper right center

ur·cei·form \ˈərsēəˌfȯrm\ *adj* [F *urcéiforme*, fr. L *urceus* + *-iforme* -iform] : shaped like an urceus

ur·ce·o·lar \ˈərˈsēəˌlär\ *adj* [ISV *urceol-* (fr. NL *urceolus*) + *-ar*] : URCEOLATE

ur·ce·o·late \ˈərˈsēəˌlāt\ *adj* [NL *urceolatus*, fr. L *urceolus* little pitcher + *-atus* -ate] : swollen below and contracted toward the orifice : shaped like an urn

ur·ce·ole \ˈərsēˌōl\ *n* [L *urceolus* little pitcher, dim. of *urceus* jar, pitcher] : a vessel for water for washing the hands (as after consecration of the Host in Roman Catholic mass); *also* : one to hold wine or water : CRUET

ur·ce·o·li·na \ˌ.ˌ.or(ˌ)ˈlīnə, -lēnə\ *n, cap* [NL, fr. L *urceolus* little pitcher + NL *-ina*; fr. the shape of the flowers] : a small genus of So. American herbs (family Amaryllidaceae) that are often cultivated as ornamentals and that have usu. yellow and green urceolate flowers and broad leaves produced from a bulb

ur·ce·o·lus \ˈərˈsēələs\ *n, pl* **urceo·li** \-ˌlī\ [NL, fr. L, little pitcher] **1** : an urn-shaped organ or part of a plant **2** : the external tube of some rotifers

ur·ce·us \ˈərsēəs\ *n, pl* **ur·cei** \-ē,ī\ [L — more at URN] : an ancient Roman jug or pitcher with one handle

¹ur·chin \ˈərchən, ˈch-,ˈȯch-\ *n* -s [ME *urchin, urchon, hurcheoun, hirchoun* hedgehog, fr. MF *herichon, hericon*, fr. L *ericius*, fr. *er, eris*; akin to Gk *chēr* hedgehog — more at HORROR] **1** : HEDGEHOG **2** *dial* : HUNCHBACK **3** : a pert or roguish youngster; *esp* : a mischievous boy **4** *obs* : a mischievous elf that sometimes takes the form of a hedgehog **5** : SEA URCHIN **6** : either of two small card cylinders around the large drum of a carding machine

²urchin \"\ *adj* **1** *obs* : inclined to make mischief : ELFISH **2** : of, relating to, or like an urchin; *esp* : PRICKLY

ur·chin·ess \-ˌȯnəs\ *n* -es : a female urchin (sense 3)

urchin fish *n* : PORCUPINE FISH

ur·chin·ly \-ȯnlē\ *adj* : of, relating to, having the character of, or being an urchin

urd \ˈu̇(ˌ)rd, ˈȯrd\ *or* **urd bean** *n* -s [Hindi *urd, uṛad*] : a spreading hairy annual bean (*Phaseolus mungo*) that is native to India, is widely cultivated in warm regions for its edible blackish seed, for green manure, or for forage, and is closely related to but less erect in growth than the mung bean — called also *black gram, woolly pyrol*

ur·dée *also* **ur·dé** \ˈərdē, ˌȯrˈdā\ *or* **ur·dy** \ˈərdē\ *adj* [origin unknown] *of a cross* : having each arm expanding at the end into a form like a lozenge with slightly concave edges

ur·du \ˈu̇(ˌ)rdü, ˈər- *sometimes* ˈu̇r-\ *n* -s *cap* [Hindi *urdū, urdū-* (in *zabān-i-urdū, urdū-zabān* language of the camp, fr. Per *zabān* language + *urdū* camp, army, fr. Turk *ordu*; akin to Mongolian *ordu, orda* court, camp, horde — more at HORDE] : an Indic language that is an official literary language of Pakistan and widely used particularly by Indians in India, has a colloquial basis very similar to that of Hindi but has developed under strong Persian rather than Sanskrit influence, and is generally written in Persian script

¹ure *n* -s [ME, fr. MF *uevre, oeuvre* work, practice, fr. L *opera* — more at OPERA] : USE, CUSTOM, PRACTICE, EXERCISE

²ure \ˈu̇r\ *n* -s [of Scand origin] : old unit of land area used in the Shetland and Orkney islands equal to the area rentable for ⅛ mark : ⅛ markland

³ure \"\ *n* [of Scand origin] : old unit of land area used in the Shetland and Orkney islands equal to the area rentable for ⅛ mark : ⅛ markland

ure- *or* **ureo-** *comb form* [ISV, fr. NL urea] : urea (*ureide*)

-ure \ə(r), (ˌ)ü(ˌ)ə(r), -u̇ə\ *n suffix* -s [ME, fr. OF, fr. L *-ura*] **1** : act : process : being (*tubulature*) (*exposure*) (*composure*) **2 a** : office : function (*judicature*) **b** : body for (such) an activity (*legislature*)

urea \yu̇ˈrēə, ˈyu̇rēə, yu̇ˈr- *sometimes* ˈyu̇rēə *or* ˈyu̇r-\ *n* -s [NL, fr. F *urée*, fr. *urine*, fr. MF — more at URINE] **1** : a highly soluble crystalline nitrogenous compound $CO(NH_2)_2$ that is formed in nature by the decomposition of protein and synthesized commercially usu. by heating ammonia and carbon dioxide under pressure, constitutes the chief solid component of the urine of man and other mammals and is also present in the urine of various lower animals and in small quantities in the blood and other body fluids and in the liver, is a very weak base and forms salts only with strong acids, and is used esp. in various chemical syntheses and in fertilizers and animal rations — called also *carbamide*; compare BIURET, ORNITHINE, PSEUDOUREA **2** : any of various derivatives of urea — usu. used in combination (*alkylated ~s*)

urea form \-ˌfȯrm\ *n* -s [*urea* + *formaldehyde*] : a synthetic fertilizer compounded of urea and formaldehyde and designed to release nitrogen slowly in usable form through the action of soil bacteria

urea–formaldehyde resin *n* : a thermosetting synthetic resin made by condensing urea with formaldehyde and used esp. in wood-bonding adhesives, colored molded articles, and for finishes (as of textiles, paper, and metals)

ure·al \yu̇ˈrēəl *sometimes* ˈyu̇rē-\ *adj* [*ure-* + *-al*] : of or relating to urea : containing or consisting of urea

ure·am·e·ter \ˌyu̇rēˈaməd·ə(r)\ *n* [by alter.] : UREOMETER

urea peroxide *n* : a crystalline addition compound $CO(NH_2)_2$·H_2O_2 of urea and hydrogen peroxide used chiefly as a solid source of hydrogen peroxide

urea resin *n* : a resin made from urea and an aldehyde; *esp* : UREA-FORMALDEHYDE RESIN

ure·ase \ˈyu̇rēˌās, -ˌāz\ *n* -s [ISV *ure-* + *-ase*] : a crystallizable enzyme that promotes the hydrolysis of urea into ammonia and carbon dioxide, is present in the alkaline fermentation of urine, and is produced by many bacteria and found in various seeds (as the jack bean and soybean)

ure·chis \ˈyu̇rəkəs, yu̇ˈrek-\ *n, cap* [NL, fr. ²*ur-* + Gk *echis* viper — more at ECHIS] : a genus (the type of the family Urechidae) of large echiuroid worms which are common in mud along the California seacoast and in which a circulatory system is completely lacking so that the blood corpuscles float free in the coelomic fluid

uredia *pl of* UREDIUM

ure·di·al \yu̇ˈrēdēəl\ *adj* [NL *uredium* + E *-al*] : of, relating to, or constituting a uredium (~ *stages*)

uredi·na·les \yu̇ˌredᵊnˈāˌlēz, -nˈ‑\ *n pl, cap* [NL, fr. *Uredin-, Uredo* + *-ales*] : an order of parasitic fungi (class Basidiomycetes) that cause rusts in plants, have complex life cycles involving usu. pycnial, aecial, uredinial, and telial stages often on different hosts, and are distinguished from the smuts by producing on a sterigma basidiospores which germinate not by budding but by growing out into an infective hypha

uredinales im·per·fec·ti \-ˌimpə(r)ˈfekˌtī\ *n pl, cap U & sometimes cap I* [NL, lit., imperfect Uredinales *in some classifications*] : a group of form genera of rust fungi including those in which the telial stage is unknown or cannot be definitely predicted

ure·din·e·ae \yu̇rəˈdinēˌē\ *n pl, cap* [NL, fr. *Uredin-, Uredo* + *-eae*] syn of UREDINALES

ure·din·i·al \ˌyu̇rəˈdinēəl\ *adj* [NL *uredinium* + E *-al*] : of, relating to, or being a uredinium (~ *stages*)

ure·din·i·op·sis \ˌyu̇rəˌdinēˈäpsəs\ *n, cap* [NL, fr. *uredinium* + *-opsis*] syn of UREDINIOPSIS

ure·din·i·um \ˌyu̇rəˈdinēəm\ *n, pl* **uredin·ia** \-ēə\ [NL, fr. *uredin-, uredo* blast, blight + NL *-ium*] : the crowded usu. yellow or brownish aggregation of spore-bearing hyphae and urediospores of a rust forming pustules or sori that become exposed by rupture of the host's cuticle or epidermis beneath which they develop

uredi·noid \yu̇ˈrēdᵊnˌȯid, -ˌred‑\ *adj* [NL *Uredin-, Uredo* + E *-oid*] **1** : resembling or related to the Uredinales **2** [NL *uredinium* + E *-oid*] : similar to or having the form or function of a uredinium

uredi·nol·o·gy \ˌ.ˌ.nˈläləjē\ *n* -es [NL *Uredin-, Uredo* + E *-o- + -logy*] : a branch of mycology dealing with the rusts

---

uredi·nop·sis \-ˈäpsəs\ *n, cap* [NL, fr. *uredinium* + *-opsis*] : a genus of rusts that is related to *Melampsora* and has solitary sessile teliospores formed within the mesophyll of the leaves of the host

uredi·nous \yu̇ˈred·ᵊnəs, -ˌred‑\ *adj* [NL *Uredin-, Uredo* + E *-ous*] : of, relating to, or being fungi of the order Uredinales

ure·dio·spore \yu̇ˈrēdēəˌspȯ(ə)r\ *or* **ure·do·spore** \-dəˌs-\ *or* **ure·din·io·spore** \yu̇ˌrēdᵊnēōˌs-\ *n* [*urediospore* alter. (influenced by NL *uredium*) of *uredospore*; *uredospore* fr. NL *Uredin-, Uredo* + E *-spore*; *urediniospore* alter. (influenced by NL *uredinium*) of *uredospore*] : one of the thin-walled yellow, orange, or reddish spores that are usu. produced by the uredinia of rust fungi in repeated crops, are readily disseminated and quickly germinate to produce a vegetative mycelium which may give rise to other urediospores and thus further rapid spread of the fungus or esp. later in the growing season may produce telia

ure·di·um \yu̇ˈrēdēəm\ *n, pl* **ure·dia** \-ēə\ [NL, fr. *Uredo* + *-ium*] : UREDINIUM

ure·do \yu̇ˈrē(ˌ)dō\ *n* [NL, fr. L, blast, blight, burning itch, fr. *urere* to burn — more at EMBER] **1** : the uredostage of a rust formerly regarded as a distinct genus **2** *cap* : a form genus of rusts including forms having either a uredostage only or having a uredostage together with pycnial and aecial stages

ure·do·so·rus \yu̇ˌrēdə+\ *n, pl* **uredosori** [NL, fr. *Uredin-, Uredo* + *sorus*] : UREDINIUM

ure·do·stage \yu̇ˈrēdō+ˌ-\ *n* [NL *uredo* + E *stage*] : the uredinial stage of a rust

ure·ic \yu̇ˈrēik\ *adj* [ISV *ure-* + *-ic*] : of, relating to, or containing urea

ure·ide \ˈyu̇rēˌīd, -ēəd\ *n* -s [ISV *ure-* + *-ide*] : an acyl derivative of urea whether acyclic (as acetyl-urea) or cyclic (as parabanic acid, alloxan, or barbituric acid)

ure·ido \yu̇ˈrēəˌdō\ *or* **ureido-** : containing the radical NH_2CONH-

ureido- *comb form* [*ureide* + *-o-*] : UREYLENE **2** : containing the univalent radical NH_2CONH- (*ureido-benzene-arsonic acid*)

ure·mia *or* **urae·mia** \yu̇ˈrēmēə, yu̇ˈr-, -mya\ *n* -s [NL, fr. *¹ur-* + *-emia*] : accumulation in the blood of constituents normally eliminated in the urine producing a toxic condition marked by headache, gastrointestinal disorders and esp. vomiting, coma, and convulsions and commonly associated with severe kidney disorder — **ure·mic** *or* **urae·mic** \-mik,-mēk\ *adj*

ure·na \yu̇ˈrēnə\ *n* [NL, fr. Malayalam *uren urena*] **1** *cap* : a small genus of tropical herbs or shrubs (family Malvaceae) having small yellow flowers with five connate bracts, bearing fruit with hooked bristles, yielding a medicinal mucilaginous juice, and including a coarse weedy herb (*U. lobata*) sometimes cultivated for its fiber which is comparable to jute **2** -s **a** : any plant of the genus *Urena* (esp. *U. lobata*) **b** *or* **urena lo·ba·ta** \-lōˈbäd·ə, -bäd·ə\ : the cordage fiber derived from the urena (*U. lobata*)

ureo- — see URE-

ure·om·e·ter \ˌyu̇rēˈäməd·ə(r)\ *n* [ISV *ure-* + *-meter*] : an apparatus for the detection and measurement of urea (as in blood or urine)

ureo·secretory \ˌyu̇rēˌō, ˌyu̇rē(ˌ)ō+\ *adj* [ISV *ure-* + *secretory*] : of or relating to the secretion of urea

ure·ox \ˈyu̇r(ə)ˌräks\ *n, pl* **ure·oxen** [part trans. of obs. G *urochs* (now *auerochs*) — more at AUROCHS] : URUS

ures *pl of* URE

-ures *pl of* -URE

ure·sis \yu̇ˈrēsəs\ *n* -es [NL, fr. Gk *ourēsis*, fr. *ourein* to urinate] : excretion of urine : URINATION

-u.ret \(y)əˌret, usu |d-+V; in "carburet" often -ˌrā\ *n comb form* -s [NL *-uretum*, fr. F *-ure*, fr. L *-ur* (in *sulfur*)] : -IDE **1** (*carburet*) (*biuret*)

ure·ter \yu̇ˈrēd·ə(r), yu̇ˈrē|, |tə- *also* ˈyu̇rəd *or* ˈyu̇rəd-\ *n* -s [NL, fr. Gk *ourētēr*, fr. *ourein* to urinate — more at URINE] : either of the paired ducts that carry away urine from a kidney to the bladder or cloaca, that in man are slender membranous epithelium-lined flat tubes about sixteen inches long which open above into the pelvis of a kidney and below into the back part of the same side of the bladder at a very oblique angle and in other mammals except monotremes open into the bladder and in lower vertebrates into the cloaca, and that in the lower vertebrates are mesonephric ducts and often serve also as sperm ducts in the male — **ure·ter·al** \yu̇ˈrēd·ərəl, yu̇ˈr-, -ētə-\ *or* **ure·ter·ic** \ˌyu̇rəˈterik, -yu̇r-, -erek; yə-rēd-ərik, yu̇ˈr-, -ētə-\ *adj*

ure·ter·itis \ˌyu̇rēd·əˈrīd·əs *also* ˌyu̇rēd-\ *n* -es [NL, fr. *ureter* + *-itis*] : inflammation of the ureter usu. secondary to pyelonephritis

uretero- *comb form* [ISV *ureter* + *-o-*] **1** : ureter (*ureterography*) **2** : ureteral and (*ureterocervical*)

ure·ter·o·gram \yu̇ˈrēd·ərəˌgram\ *n* [ISV *uretero-* + *-gram*] : an X-ray photograph of the ureters after injection of a radiopaque substance

ure·ter·o·graph \-ˌgraf, -ˌgráf\ *n* [*uretero-* + *-graph*] : URETEROGRAM

ure·ter·og·ra·phy \ˌyu̇ˌrēd·əˈrägrəfē *also* ˌyu̇rəd-\ *n* [ISV *uretero-* + *-graphy*] : the art, practice, or act of making ureterograms

ure·tero·intestinal \ˌyu̇ˌrēd·ə(ˌ)rō+\ *adj* [*uretero-* + *intestinal*] : of, relating to, or involving both the intestine and a ureter

ure·tero·lithotomy \"+\ *n* [ISV *uretero-* + *lithotomy*] : removal of a calculus by incision of a ureter

ure·tero·pelvic \"+\ *adj* [*uretero-* + *pelvic*] : of, relating to, or involving a ureter and the adjoining renal pelvis (~ *obstruction*)

ure·tero·pyelogram \"+\ *n* [*uretero-* + *pyelogram*] : an X-ray photograph of the pelves of the kidneys and the ureters made after filling them by injection with a radiopaque substance

ure·tero·pyelography \"+\ *n* [ISV *uretero-* + *pyelography*] : the making of pyelograms

ure·tero·stenosis \"+\ *n* [NL, fr. *uretero-* + *stenosis*] : stricture of a ureter

ure·thane \ˈyu̇rəˌthān, yə-re,th-\ *or* **ure·than** \-an\ *n* -s [F *uréthane*, fr. *¹ur-* + *éth-* eth- + *-ane* -ane, -an] **1 a** : a crystalline ester-amide $NH_2COOC_2H_5$ made usu. by the action of ammonia on ethyl carbonate or ethyl chloroformate or by heating urea nitrate and ethyl alcohol and used chiefly in medicine, for anesthetizing laboratory animals, and as a gelatinizing agent for cellulose acetate or cellulose nitrate — called also *ethyl carbamate* **b** : an ester of carbamic acid other than the ethyl ester **2 a** : an ester (as phenylurethane or other ethyl esters) of a substituted carbamic acid — compare PHENYLURETHANE **b** : POLYURETHANE (~ *foams*)

ure·than·ize \-ˌā,nīz, -a,n-\ *vt* -ED/-ING/-s : to treat esp. to anesthetize with urethane

urethr- *or* **urethro-** *comb form* [NL, fr. LL *urethra*] : urethra (*urethrectomy*)

ure·thra \yu̇ˈrēthrə, yu̇ˈr-\ *n, pl* **urethras** \-thrəz\ *or* **ure·thrae** \-(ˌ)thrē\ [LL, fr. Gk *ourēthra*, fr. *ourein* to urinate — more at URINE] : the canal that in most mammals carries off the urine from the bladder and in the male serves also as a genital duct — **ure·thral** \-thrəl\ *adj*

ure·thri·tis \ˌyu̇rəˈthrīd·əs\ *n, pl* **ure·thrit·i·des** \-thridˌdēz\ [NL, fr. *urethr-* + *-itis*] : inflammation of the urethra

ure·thro·cele \yə-rēthrəˌsēl\ *n* -s [ISV *urethr-* + *-cele*] : a pouched protrusion of urethral mucous membrane in the female

ure·thro·gram \-thrəˌgram\ *n* [ISV *urethr-* + *-gram*] : a roentgenogram of the urethra made after injection of a radiopaque substance

ure·thro·graph \-raf, -ráf\ *n* [*urethr-* + *-graph*] : URETHROGRAM

ure·thro·scope \-thrəˌskōp\ *n* [ISV *urethr-* + *scope*] : an instrument designed to permit visual inspection of the urethra by means of lighting and optical attachments — **ure·thro·scop·ic** \ˌ.ˌ.ˈskäpik\ *adj*

ure·throt·o·my \ˌyu̇rəˈthräd·əmē, ˌyu̇,rē·th-, yə-rēˌth-\ *n* -es [ISV *urethr-* + *-tomy*] : surgical incision into the urethra esp. for the relief of stricture

uret·ic \yə-rēd·ik\ *adj* [LL *ureticus*, fr. Gk *ourētikos*, fr. (assumed) *ourētos* (verbal of *ourein* to urinate) + *-ikos* -ic]

: more at URINE] : of, relating to, or occurring in the urine : URINARY (~ *solids*) *esp* : DIURETIC (~ *medicine*)

ure·yl·ene \yə-rēəˌlēn\ *n* -s [*ure-* + *-ylene*] : a bivalent radical —$NHCONH$— derived from urea

'urf \ˈu̇(ə)rf\ *n* -s [Ar, custom] : Persian customary law — compare ADAT

ur·fir·nis \ˈu̇(ˌ)ə)rˌfirnəs\ *n* -es [G, fr. *ur-* primitive, original (fr. OHG *ur-, ur* out of) + *firnis* varnish, fr. MHG *vernis*, MF *vernis* — more at ABEAR, VARNISH] : a lustrous paint varying from black to red and found on some prehistoric Greek pottery

ur·ga \ˈu̇rgə, -ˌgä\ *n, usu cap* [fr. *Urga*, Outer Mongolia] : of or from Urga, the capital of Outer Mongolia : of the kind or style prevalent in Urga

'urge \ˈərj, ˈȯj, ˈȯij\ *vb* -ED/-ING/-s [L *urgēre* to press, drive, urge — more at WREAK] *vt* **1** : to present in an earnest or pressing manner : press upon attention : insist upon : plead or allege in or as if in argument or justification : advocate or demand with importunity (the psychiatrist *urged* greater cooperation between the psychiatrist and the general practitioner —*Current Biog.*) (opportunity to ~ her point of view —Samuel Van Valkenburg & Ellsworth Huntington) (alert observers *urged* more forcefully that our country must hurry to develop its military power —Herbert Feis) (let me ~ this thought upon you —Dean Acheson) **2** : to undertake the accomplishment of with energy, swiftness, or enthusiasm : prosecute vigorously (the attack . . . is being violently *urged* wherever the winter conditions permit —*Manchester Guardian Weekly*) **3 a** : to press the mind or will of : ply with motives, arguments, persuasions, or importunity : solicit or entreat earnestly (they ~ us to stop thinking and do something —M.R.Cohen) **b** : to be a compelling, impelling, or constraining influence upon : serve as a motivating impulse or reason for (men . . . living in much the same way, *urged* by the same hungers —Marjory S. Douglas) (three general purposes have *urged* me to the task —R.E.Coker) **4 a** : to force or impel in an indicated direction or to an indicated place (*urged* on by a pair of automatic pistols —Eric Linklater) (mustered the ladies together and *urged* them into another room —Maurice Cranston) (wedges are driven in to ~ the trunk in the required direction —F.D.Smith & Barbara Wilcox) **b** (1) : to accelerate or urgently maintain the speed of : HASTEN (through the thick deserts headlong *urged* his flight —Alexander Pope) (2) *archaic* : to travel rapidly or diligently upon or over ~ : to force or impel to motion or to greater speed (red-jacketed dragoons *urged* their horses in furious pursuit —F.V.W.Mason) **5** : to rouse from a dormant state or into life, expression, or action : STIMULATE, PROVOKE (~ not my father's anger —Shak.) (men *urged* their land with perpetual stinking fertilizing —Pearl Buck) *vi* **1** : to declare, advance, or press earnestly a statement, argument, charge, or claim (appeared before the House Banking Committee to ~ against the adoption of an amendment —*Current Biog.*) **2** : to advance with speed or force : HASTEN (she *urged* toward him —Maurice Hewlett) **3** : to exercise an inciting, constraining, or stimulating influence

syn EGG, EXHORT, GOAD, PROD, SPUR, PRICK, SIC: URGE indicates a pressing, impelling, seeking to influence, or overcoming some obstacle, check, or drawback to a certain course (the American tendency to *urge* youngsters to early independence was contrasted with the French practice of encouraging the young to remain dependent for a longer time upon parental guidance —Dorothy Barclay) (the old president *urged* the new president to take it easy, not to destroy himself with zeal —H.F.Wilkins) EGG suggests encouraging, stimulating, or whetting a will or inclination that is hesitant, laggard, or dull (*egged* me to borrow the money —Rudyard Kipling) (*egg* on one of their number to sing —Edmund Wilson) EXHORT may suggest the ardent urging or admonishing of an orator or preacher (*exhorted* his friend to confess, and not to hide his sin any longer —George Eliot) (the situation was of the strangest and gravest description, but the public was *exhorted* to avoid and discourage panic —H.G.Wells) GOAD may suggest an exciting, driving, or irritating to action suggestive of driving animals with pointed sticks (the harsh ruling only *goaded* the Indians into fiercer resistance —R.A.Billington) (must *goad* the slack part of his orchestra by the constant implied threat of dismissal —J.N.Burk) PROD may suggest a driving to action as if with a stick or rod but is gentler in suggestion than GOAD (Indians grew hungry and hatred of the white man *prodded* them into open hostilities —Julian Dana) (enough public support to *prod* congressmen on both sides to furnish the necessary votes —*Newsweek*) SPUR often suggests the use of a spur or sharp spike on the flanks of a lagging horse (*spurred* to earnest effort —M.L.Bonham) (an aching conscience was the chief thing that *spurred* me on —John McNulty) PRICK, similar to SPUR, may refer to inciting or impelling as if by something with a sharp point (tries only to *prick* the student into a desire for the truth —Barbara Buckley) (rely on their animal instinct and developed reflexes to *prick* them into awareness when danger threatened —Fred Majdalany) SIC, orig. used as a command to a dog, may indicate an inciting to attack or worry (a civilized nation *sicced* on the Barbary whelps to tear the peaceful passerby —J.R.Spears)

²urge \"+\ *n* -s **1** : the act or process of urging **2** : a force or impulse that urges (many young men had the ~ to participate in the new venture —R.J.Dubos); *esp* : a continuing impulse or tendency toward some activity or goal (that almost mystic ~ to climb can dominate your whole life —Wynford Vaughan-Thomas) syn see DESIRE

urged *past of* URGE

ur·gence \-jən(t)s\ *n* -s [MF, fr. LL *urgentia* pressure]

ur·gen·cy \ˈərjənsē, ˈȯj-, ˈȯij-, -si\ *n* -es [LL *urgentia* pressure, urgency, fr. L *urgent-, urgens*, pres. part. + *-ia -y*] **1** : the quality or state of being urgent : INSISTENCE, PRESSURE (the ~ of a petitioner) (the ~ of his need) **2** : an urgent stress (as of wind or need) **3** : a force or impulse that impels or constrains : URGE; *esp* : a compelling desire to urinate or defecate due to some abnormal stress (as inflammation or infection) **4** : IMPORTUNITY, ENTREATY

ur·gent \-nt\ *adj* [ME, fr. MF, fr. L *urgent-, urgens*, pres. part. of *urgēre* to press, urge — more at WREAK] **1 a** : calling for or demanding immediate attention : of a kind to urge to action (~ appeals for help) (problems of an ~ nature) **b** : conveying a sense of urgency (an ~ and determined manner) **2** : impelling onward (borne by the mastery of its ~ wings —Robert Bridges †1930) **3** *obs* : passing quickly **4** : SOLICITOUS, IMPORTUNATE (an ~ lover) **5** : serving to impel or constrain (~ affections) **6** *obs* : OPPRESSIVE syn see PRESSING

ur·gent·ly *adv* : in an urgent manner : with urgency

urg·er \ˈərjər, ˈȯj-(ˌ)r\ *n* -s : one that urges

urges *pres 3d sing of* URGE, *pl of* URGE

ur·gin·ea \ˌərˈjinēə\ *n* [NL, fr. Ben *Urgin*, Arab tribe near Bône, northeastern Algeria, where plants of the genus were orig. found] **1** *cap* : a genus of bulbous herbs (family Liliaceae) native to the Old World and esp. to the Mediterranean region with a deciduous perianth and 3-angled capsule — see SQUILL **2** -s *a* often *cap* : the younger bulbs of a plant (*Urginea indica*) that have action and uses which are the same as those of squill — used in the British Pharmacopoeia **b** : any plant of the genus *Urginea*

urging *pres part of* URGE

urg·ing·ly *adv* : so as to urge : in an urging manner

ur·grund \ˈu̇(ə)rˌgru̇nt\ *n* -s [G, fr. *ur-* primal, original (fr. OHG *ur-, ur* out of) + *grund* ground, bottom, foundation, cause, fr. OHG *grunt* ground, bottom — more at ABEAR, GROUND] : a primal cause or ultimate cosmic principle

-ur·gy \ə(r)jē, ˌərj-, ȯj-, ȯij-, -ji *sometimes* 'ə‑\ *n comb form* -es [NL *-urgia*, fr. Gk *-ourgia* to work (fr. *ergon* work) + -ia -y —more at WORK] : technique or art of dealing or working with (such) a product, matter, or tool (*chemurgy*) (*micrurgy*)

ur·heen *or* **urh·heen** \ˈu̇əˈhē(ə)n\ *n* -s [modif. of Chin (Pek) *êr⁴-hsien²*, lit., two strings] : a Chinese fiddle consisting of two tubes usu. of silk tuned a fifth apart, stretched across a small mallet-shaped hollow block, and fastened at the other end to tuning pegs set in a long stick

uria \ˈyu̇rēə\ *n, cap* [NL, fr. Gk *ouria*, a water bird; akin to Gk *ouron* urine] : a genus of guillemots comprising the murres

-uria \(y)u̇rēə, ˈ(y)u̇r-\ *n comb form* -s [NL, fr. Gk *-ouria*, fr.

ouron urine + *-ia* -y — more at URINE] **1 :** presence of (a specified substance) in urine ⟨aceton*uria*⟩ ⟨albumin*uria*⟩ **2 :** condition of having (such) urine ⟨poly*uria*⟩; *esp* **:** abnormal or diseased condition that is marked by the presence of (a specified substance) ⟨py*uria*⟩

uri·al *or* **oo·ri·al** \'u̇rēəl, -ē,äl\ *n* -s [Panjabi *hureāl*] **:** a wild sheep (*Ovis vignei*) of the uplands of southern and central Asia that is possibly one of the ancestors of domesticated breeds of sheep and is reddish brown with a white neck and a dark beard from the chin to the chest

uric \'yu̇rik, -rēk\ *adj* [¹*ur-* + *-ic*] **1 :** of or relating to urine **2 :** obtained from or occurring in urine

uric- *or* **urico-** *comb form* [*uric* (in *uric acid*)] **:** uric acid ⟨*urico*lytic⟩

-u·ric \¦(y)u̇rik, ¦(y)ůr-, -rēk\ *adj suffix* [*uric*] **1 :** related to uric acid, urea, or both uric acid and urea ⟨allanto*uric*⟩ **2 :** occurring in urine ⟨hipp*uric*⟩

uric acid *n* **:** a white odorless tasteless nearly insoluble dibasic acid $C_5H_4N_4O_3$ that is present in small quantity in the urine of man and most mammals and abundantly in the form of urates in the excrement of birds, reptiles, and invertebrates in whom it constitutes the chief nitrogenous excretion product, that is a common component either as the free acid or as a urate of urinary or renal calculi and of the so-called gouty concretions, and that is capable of being made synthetically; 2,6,8-trihydroxy-purine

uri·case \'yu̇rə,kās, -āz\ *n* -s [ISV *uric-* + *-ase*] **:** an enzyme that promotes oxidation of uric acid to allantoin, carbon dioxide, and other products and that is found esp. in the liver, kidney, and brains of most animals other than primates

uri·col·y·sis \,yu̇rə'käləsəs\ *n* [NL, fr. *uric-* + *-lysis*] **:** breakdown of uric acid esp. in the animal body

uri·co·lyt·ic \¦yu̇rəkō¦lid·ik\ *adj* [*uric-* + *-lytic*] **:** of, relating to, or functioning in uricolysis ⟨a ~ enzyme⟩

uri·co·su·ric \¦yu̇rəkō¦su̇rik\ *adj* [*uric-* + connective *-s-* + *-uric*] **:** relating to or promoting the excretion of uric acid in the urine

uri·dine \'yu̇rə,dēn, -,dən\ *n* -s [ISV ¹*ur-* + *-idine*] **:** a crystalline nucleoside $C_9H_{12}N_2O_6$ that is obtained by hydrolysis of ribonucleic acid and uridylic acid and that in the form of phosphate derivatives (as the coenzyme uridine diphosphate glucose) plays an important role in carbohydrate metabolism; 1-D-ribosyl-uracil

uri·dyl·ic acid \,yu̇rə¦dilik-\ *n* [ISV *uridine* + *-yl* + *-ic*] **:** a crystalline nucleotide $C_9H_{13}N_2O_9P$ known in three isomeric forms obtained by hydrolysis of ribonucleic acid **:** uridine mono-phosphate

urim and thum·mim \¦(y)u̇rəmən'thəməm, ¦u̇,rēmən'tü,mēm\ *n pl, usu cap U&T* [part trans. of Heb *ūrīm wĕthummīm*] **:** sacred lots possibly in the form of precious stones mentioned in the Old Testament as objects cast by a priest for the purpose of obtaining an oracle interpreted as the will of God

urin \'u̇rən\ *n* -s [Panjabi *huren*] **:** URIAL

urin- *or* **urino-** *comb form* [ME, fr. OF, fr. L, fr. *urina* urine — more at URINE] **:** urine **:** ¹UR- ⟨*urino*genital⟩ ⟨*urino*logy⟩

uri·nal \'yu̇rənᵊl, 'yůr-\ *n* -s [ME, fr. OF, fr. LL, fr. L *urinalis* of urine, fr. *urina* urine + *-alis* -al] **1 a :** a vessel so constructed that it can be used for urination by a bedfast patient **b :** a container worn by one with urinary incontinence **2 a :** a building, enclosure, or fixture for urinating purposes

uri·nal·y·sis *also* **uranalysis** \,yu̇rə'naləsəs, ,yůr-\ *n* [*urinalysis* fr. NL, irreg. fr. *urin-* + *analysis*; *uranalysis* fr. NL, fr. ¹*ur-* + *analysis*] **:** chemical analysis of urine

uri·nant \'yu̇rənənt\ *adj* [L *urinant-, urinans*, pres. part. of *urinari* to plunge under water, dive — more at URINE] *heraldry, of a fish or water animal* **:** being in pale with the head down — compare HAURIANT

uri·nar·i·um \,yu̇rə'nerēəm\ *n* -s [ML, fr. L *urin-* + *-arium* -ary] **:** a reservoir into which urine drains from a stable and from which it is drawn to fertilize a field

¹**uri·nary** \'yu̇rə,nerē, 'yůr-, -eri\ *adj* [NL *urinarius*, fr. *urin-* + *-arius* -ary] **1 :** relating to, occurring in, or constituting the organs concerned with the formation and discharge of urine **2 :** of, relating to, or for urine **3 :** excreted as or in urine ⟨~ nitrogen⟩

²**urinary** \"\ *n* -ES [*urin-* + *-ary*, n. suffix] **:** URINAL 2

urinary bladder *n* **:** a distensible membranous sac in many vertebrates that serves for the temporary retention of the urine, that in man is situated in the pelvis in front of the rectum, receives the urine from the two ureters and discharges it at intervals into the urethra through an orifice closed by a sphincter, is lined with transitional hypoblastic epithelium, and develops from the proximal part of the allantois of the embryo, that in the lowest mammals and in birds, reptiles, and amphibians opens separately into the cloaca, and that in fishes if present is not homologous with that of the higher vertebrates but is a dilatation of a ureter or of the united ureters

urinary calculus *n* **:** a calculus occurring in any portion of the urinary tract and esp. in the pelvis of the kidney

urinary pigment *n* **:** any of several coloring materials (as urochrome and urobilin) present in the urine together with indican

urinary tract *n* **:** the tract conducting urine **:** the renal tubules and pelvis of the kidney, the ureters, the bladder, and the urethra

uri·nate \'yu̇rə,nāt, 'yůr-, *usu* -ād.+V\ *vb* -ED/-ING/-S [ML *urinatus*, past part. of *urinare* to urinate, fr. L *urina* urine] *vi* **:** to discharge urine **:** make water **:** MICTURATE ~ *vt* **1 :** to wet with urine **2 :** to pass as or in the urine ⟨*urinated* a bloody fluid⟩ — **uri·na·tion** \,==¦nāshən\ *n* -s

urinator *n* -s [L, fr. *urinari* to plunge under water + *-ator*] *obs* **:** one who dives under water for something **:** DIVER

urine \'yu̇rən, 'yůr-\ *n* -s [ME, fr. MF, fr. L *urina*; akin to Gk *ouron* urine, *ourein* to urinate, L *urinari* to plunge under water, dive, Skt *vār* water, ON *ūr* drizzle, *ver* sea, OE *wær* sea, *wæter* water — more at WATER] **:** liquid to semisolid matter that is produced in the kidney and discharged through the urinary organs, that is typically (as in normal man) a clear transparent amber-colored slightly acid fluid which is essentially a watery solution of end products (as urea, uric acid, and creatinine) of protein metabolism, inorganic salts, and complex pigments, and that constitutes the major true excretion of the vertebrate body

uri·nif·er·ous tubule \,yu̇rə¦nif(ə)rəs-\ *n* [*uriniferous* fr. *urin-* + *-iferous*] **:** a vertebrate nephron

urino- — see URIN-

uri·no·genital ridge \¦yu̇rənō+ . . . -\ *n* [*urinogenital* fr. *urin-* + *genital*] **:** a pair of dorsolateral mesodermal ridges in the vertebrate embryo out of which the urogenital organs are developed

urinogenital sinus *n* **:** a pouch or cavity communicating with the exterior or with the cloaca of which it may be a part and receiving the urinary and genital canals

uri·nom·e·ter \,yu̇rə'nämәd·ə(r)\ *n* [ISV *urin-* + *-meter*] **:** a small hydrometer for determining the specific gravity of urine — **uri·no·met·ric** \¦yu̇rənō¦me·trik\ *adj* — **uri·nom·e·try** \,yu̇rə'nämə·trē\ *n* -ES

uri·nous \'yu̇rənəs, 'yůr-\ *adj* [NL *urinosus*, fr. L *urin-* + *-osus* -ous] **:** of, relating to, like, or having the qualities or odor of urine

urins *pl of* URIN

urisk \'u̇risk\ *n* -s [ScGael *ūruisg*, fr. *uisge* water; akin to OIr *uisce* water — more at WHISKEY] **:** a brownie held in Scottish folklore to frequent sequestered places and waterfalls

urite \'yu̇,rīt\ *n* -s [ISV ²*ur-* + *-ite*] **:** one of the segments of the abdomen or postabdomen of an arthropod

ur·man \(')u̇r¦män, -man\ *n* -s [Russ, fr. Kazan Tatar, forest] **:** TAIGA 1

¹**urn** \'ərn, 'ən, 'əin\ *n* -s [ME *urne*, fr. L *urna*, prob. of non-IE origin; akin to the source of L *urceus* pitcher, ewer, Gk *hyrchē* jar] **1 a :** a vessel (as a vase) of various forms usu. furnished with a foot or pedestal and employed for holding liquids, for ornamental uses, for preserving the ashes of the dead after cremation, for holding lots to be drawn, for receiving ballots, or for other purposes **b :** a closed vessel usu. with a heating device and a spigot used in making and serving a hot beverage ⟨coffee ~⟩ ⟨tea ~⟩ **2 :** a sculptured ornament or decoration in the shape of a footed and usu. covered urn **3** *archaic* **:** a spring, fountain, or watercourse that is the source of a flow of liquid **4 :** the theca of a moss

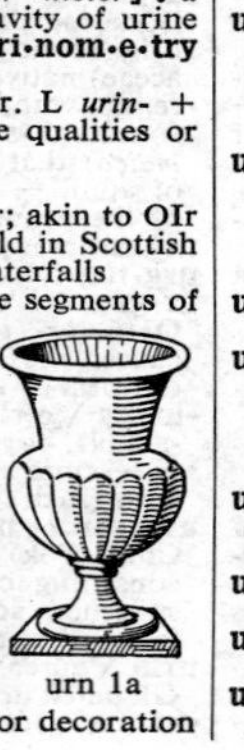

urn 1a

²**urn** \"\ *vt, archaic* **:** INURN

ur·na·tel·la \,ərnə'telə\ *n, cap* [NL, irreg. fr. L *urna* urn + *-ella*] **:** a genus (the type of a family Urnatellidae) of eastern No. American colonial freshwater entoproctans that form small colonies of bell-shaped zooids on the underside of stones in running water

urn burial *n* **:** burial in which a pottery vessel is used as a grave repository for the ashes and bones of the corpse

urnfield \'=,=\ *n* **:** a Bronze Age cemetery of urn burials

urnflower \'=,==\ *n* **:** a plant of the genus *Urceolina*

ur·ning \'u̇rniŋ\ *n* -s [G, irreg. fr. *Urania*, the love goddess Aphrodite (fr. Gk *Ourania*) + G *-ing* ²-ing — more at URANISM] **:** a male homosexual

ur·ning·ism \-ŋ,izəm\ *n* -s **:** male homosexuality

urn moss *n* **:** any of several mosses (as members of the genus *Physcomitrium* and esp. *P. turbinatum*) having an urn-shaped theca

urn schemata *n pl* **:** the representation of frequency distributions by means of withdrawals of different-colored balls from one or more vessels or urns containing the balls in various numbers and proportions

uro- — see UR-

uro·bi·lin \,yu̇rə'bīlən\ *n* -s [ISV ¹*ur-* + *-bilin* (as in *stercobilin*)] **:** any of several brown bile pigments formed from urobilinogens and found in normal feces, in normal urine in small amounts, and in pathological urines in larger amounts — compare STERCOBILIN

uro·bi·lin·o·gen \-,bī'linəjən, -,jen\ *n* -s [ISV *urobilin* + *-ogen* (as in *stercobilinogen*)] **:** any of several chromogens that are reduction products of bilirubin and yield urobilins on oxidation — called also *stercobilinogen*

uro·bi·lin·o·gen·uria \-,linəjə'n(y)u̇rēə\ *n* -s [NL, fr. ISV *urobilinogen* + NL *-uria*] **:** the presence of urobilinogen in the urine esp. in excess

uro·bi·lin·uria \-,bīlə'n(y)u̇rēə\ *n* -s [NL, fr. ISV *urobilin* + NL *-uria*] **:** the presence of urobilin in the urine esp. to an excessive degree

uro·canic acid \¦yu̇rə¦kanik-, -kānik-\ *n* [¹*ur-* + *canine* + *-ic*] **:** a crystalline acid $C_3H_3N_2CH{=}CHCOOH$ obtained first from the urine of a dog and formed by the enzymic deamination of histidine; 4(or 5)-imidazole-acrylic acid

¹**uroc·er·id** \yə'räsərəd\ *adj* [NL *Uroceridae*] **:** SIRICID

²**urocerid** \"\ *n* -s **:** SIRICID

uro·cer·i·dae \,yu̇rə'serə,dē\ [NL, fr. *Urocerus*, genus of siricids (fr. ²*ur-* + *-cerus*) + *-idae*] *syn of* SIRICIDAE

uro·chlo·ral·ic acid \¦yu̇rə(,)klō¦ralik-\ *n* [ISV ¹*ur-* + *chloral* + *-ic*] **:** a crystalline glycoside $C_8H_{11}Cl_3O_7$ of trichloro-ethyl alcohol and glucuronic acid found in the urine after administering chloral hydrate

uro·chord \'yu̇rə,kȯrd\ *n* [²*ur-* + *chord*; fr. its being chiefly confined to the tail region] **1 :** the notochord of larval ascidians and of various adult tunicates **2** [NL *Urochorda*] **:** an animal of the group Urochorda **:** TUNICATE

uro·chor·da \,==¦kȯrdə\ *n pl, cap* [NL, fr. ²*ur-* + *chorda*] **:** a subphylum or sometimes a class of marine animals (phylum Chordata) comprising the tunicates, including the orders Ascidiacea, Thaliacea, and Larvacea, and being distinguished by clefts in the vascular walls of the pharyngeal gills, by the secretion of a thick outer covering of tunicin for the body, by the reduction of the nervous system to little more than a single dorsally placed ganglion, and by a heart that so changes its contractions as to reverse the direction of the blood flow at intervals

uro·chor·dal \¦==¦kȯrdᵊl\ *adj* [NL *Urochorda* + E *-al*] **1 :** of or relating to the Urochorda **2** [*urochord* + *-al*] **:** having a notochord in the tail region only

uro·chordata \¦yu̇rə+\ [NL, fr. ²*ur-* + *Chordata*] *syn of* UROCHORDA

¹**uro·chor·date** \¦yu̇rə¦kȯrdət, -,dāt\ *adj* [*urochord* + *-ate*] **:** having a urochord

²**urochordate** \"\ *n* -s [NL *Urochordata*] **:** UROCHORD 2

uro·chrome \'yu̇rə,krōm\ *n* -s [¹*ur-* + *-chrome*] **:** a yellow pigment to which the yellow color of normal urine is principally due

urochs \'(y)u̇,räks\ *n* [obs. G *urochs* (now *auerochs*), fr. MHG *ūrochse*, fr. OHG *ūrohso* — more at AUROCHS] **1** *archaic* **:** URUS **2** *archaic* **:** WISENT

¹**uro·cop·tid** \¦yu̇rə¦käptəd\ *adj* [NL *Urocoptid-, Urocoptis*] **:** of or relating to the genus *Urocoptis* or the family Urocoptidae

²**urocoptid** \"\ *n* -s **:** a land snail of the genus *Urocoptis* or the family Urocoptidae

uro·cop·tis \,==¦=təs\ *n, cap* [NL, fr. ²*ur-* + *-coptis* (fr. Gk *koptein* to cut off) — more at CAPON] **:** a large genus (the type of the family Urocoptidae of the order Pulmona) of land snails of southern Florida, the West Indies, and Mexico found only on limestone cliffs and outcrops

uroc·y·on \yə'räsēən, -ē,än\ *n, cap* [NL, fr. ²*ur-* + Gk *kyōn* dog — more at HOUND] **:** a genus of mammals (family Canidae) comprising the American gray foxes

uro·cyst \'yu̇rə,sist\ *n* [¹*ur-* + *-cyst*] **:** the urinary bladder — **uro·cys·tic** \¦==¦sistik\ *adj*

uro·cys·tis \,==¦sistəs\ *n, cap* [NL, fr. ²*ur-* + *-cystis*] **:** a genus of smuts (family Tilletiaceae) having compound chlamydospores with the dark central cells fertile and the outer sterile — see FLAG SMUT, ONION SMUT

uro·dae·al *or* **uro·de·al** \¦yu̇rə¦dēəl\ *adj* [NL *urodaeum* + E *-al*] **:** of or relating to the urodaeum

uro·dae·um \,==¦dēəm\ *n* -s [NL, fr. ²*ur-* + *-odaeum* (fr. Gk *hodaion*, neut. of *hodaios* on the way, fr. *hodos* way) — more at CEDE] **:** the part of the cloaca (as of a bird) into which the ureters and genital ducts empty

uro·de·la \,yu̇rə'dēlə\ [NL, fr. ²*ur-* + Gk *dēlos* visible — more at ADEL-] *syn of* CAUDATA

¹**uro·dele** \'==,dēl\ *also* **uro·de·lan** \,==¦dēlən\ *n* -s [*urodele* fr. F *urodèle*, fr. NL *Urodela*; *urodelan* fr. NL *Urodela* + E *-an*] **:** CAUDATE

²**urodele** *also* **uro·de·lous** \¦==¦dēləs\ *adj* [*urodele* fr. ¹*urodele*; *urodelous* fr. ¹*urodele* + *-ous*] **:** of or relating to the Caudata

uro·erythrin \¦yu̇rō+\ *n* [¹*ur-* + *erythrin*] **:** a pink or reddish pigment found in many pathological urines and also frequently in normal urine in very small quantity

uro·gas·ter \¦yu̇rə¦gastə(r)\ *n* -s [NL, fr. ¹*ur-* + *-gaster*] **1 :** the urinary tract (as of the embryo) including the allantoic cavity **2** [NL, fr. ²*ur-* + *-gaster*] **:** the posterior division of the gastric region of a crustacean (as a crab) — **uro·gas·tric** \-strik\ *adj*

uro·gas·trone \,yu̇rə'ga,strōn\ *n* -s [¹*ur-* + *-gastrone* (as in *enterogastrone*)] **:** a substance obtained from the urine of man and other mammals as an amorphous buff-colored powder resembling enterogastrone in physiological activity

uro·gen·i·tal \¦yu̇rə¦jenəd·ᵊl, ¦yůr-, -rō¦-, -nət·ᵊl\ *also* **uro·gen·i·tary** \-nə,terē, -ri\ *adj* [*urogenital* ISV ¹*ur-* + *genital*; *urogenitary* fr. ¹*ur-* + L *genitalis* genital + E *-ary*] **:** of, relating to, or being the organs or functions of excretion and reproduction

urogenital trigone *n* **:** a double layer of pelvic fascia between the ischial and pubic rami supporting the prostate in the male and traversed by the vagina in the female, giving passage to the membranous part of the urethra, and enclosing the urethral sphincter muscle

urog·e·nous \yə'räjənəs\ *adj* [ISV ¹*ur-* + *-genous*] **:** derived from or occurring in urine ⟨~ salts⟩

uro·gle·na \,yu̇rə'glēnə\ *n, cap* [NL, fr. ²*ur-* + Gk *glēnē* socket of a joint — more at GLENOID] **:** a genus of colonial plantlike flagellates (order Chrysomonadina) with numerous biflagellate individuals united in a spherical colony by gelatinous strands

uro·gom·phus \,yu̇rə'gäm(p)fəs\ *n, pl* **urogom·phi** \-m,fī, -m,fē\ [NL, fr. ²*ur-* + L *gomphus* nail, peg, fr. Gk *gomphos* tooth, bolt, peg — more at COMB] **:** PSEUDOCERCUS

uro·gram \'yiuə,gram\ *n* [¹*ur-* + *-gram*] **:** a roentgenogram made by urography

uro·graph·ic \¦==¦grafik\ *adj* [*urography* + *-ic*] **:** of or relating to urography of a part of the urinary tract

urog·ra·phy \yə'rägrəfē\ *n* -ES [ISV ¹*ur-* + *-graphy*] **:** roentgenography of a part of the urinary tract (as a kidney or ureter) after injection of an opaque medium — compare CYSTOGRAPHY, PYELOGRAPHY, RETROGRADE PYELOGRAM

¹**uro·hy·al** \¦yu̇rō¦hīəl\ *adj* [ISV ²*ur-* + *hy-* + *-al*] **1 :** of, relating to, or being a median posterior bony element of the hyoid arch attached between the hypohyals of a fish **2 :** of, relating to, or being a median posterior process or a separate piece extending backward from the basihyal and forming a basibranchial element of a bird

²**urohyal** \"\ *n* -s **:** a urohyal element

urol *abbr* urological; urology

uro·lag·nia \,yu̇rō'lagnēə\ *n* -s [NL, fr. ¹*ur-* + *-lagnia*] **:** sexual excitement associated with urine or with urination

uro·leu·cic acid \¦yu̇rō¦lüsik-\ *or* **uro·leu·cin·ic acid** \¦yu̇rō¦lü¦sinik-\ *n* [*uroleucic* fr. ¹*ur-* + *leuc-* + *-ic*; *uroleucinic* fr. G *uroleucin* (fr. ¹*ur-* + *leuc-* + *-in*) + E *-ic*; fr. its color] **:** a crystalline acid $C_9H_{10}O_5$ that is found in abnormal urine and is similar to homogentisic acid

uro·lith \'yu̇rə,lith\ *n* -s [ISV ¹*ur-* + *-lith*] **:** URINARY CALCULUS — **uro·lith·ic** \¦==¦lithik\ *adj*

uro·li·thi·a·sis \,yu̇rələ'thīəsəs\ *n* [NL, fr. ¹*ur-* + *lithiasis*] **:** the condition characterized by the formation or presence of calculi in any part of the urinary tract

uro·log·ic \¦yu̇rə¦läjik, ¦yůr-, -jēk\ *also* **uro·log·i·cal** \-jəkəl, -jēk-\ *adj* [*urologic* ISV *urology* + *-ic*; *urological* fr. *urology* + *-ical*] **:** of or relating to the urinary tract or to urology

urol·o·gist \yə'räləjəst, yü'r-\ *n* -s [ISV *urology* + *-ist*] **:** a physician who specializes in urology

urol·o·gy \-jē, -ji\ *n* -ES [¹*ur-* + *-logy*] **:** a branch of medicine that concerns itself with the urogenital tract in the male and the urinary tract in the female

uro·mere \'yu̇rə,mi(ə)r\ *n* -s [²*ur-* + *-mere*] **:** an abdominal segment of an arthropod — **uro·mer·ic** \¦==¦merik, -¦mir-\ *adj*

uro·my·ces \,yu̇rə'mī(,)sēz\ *n, cap* [NL, fr. ²*ur-* + *-myces*] **:** a genus of rusts (family Pucciniaceae) having one-celled teliospores — see CARNATION RUST

uro·my·cla·di·um \-,mī'klādēəm\ *n, cap* [NL, fr. *Uromyces* + *clad-* + *-ium*] **:** a genus of chiefly Australian rusts (family Pucciniaceae) distinguished by teliospores clustered at the top of a stalk with usu. a colorless cyst just below and including several forms (as *'U. tepperianum*) that disfigure and destroy wattles in Australia

uro·mys \'yu̇rə,mis\ *n, cap* [NL, fr. ²*ur-* + *-mys*] **:** a genus of murid rodents of Southeastern Asia and Australia — see MOSAIC-TAILED RAT

-u·ron·ic \(y)ə¦ränik, (y)ů¦r-, -nēk\ *adj suffix* [Gk *ouron* urine + ISV *-ic* — more at URINE] **:** urine — in names of certain aldehyde-acids derived from sugars or compounds of such acids ⟨ald*uronic*⟩ ⟨hyal*uronic*⟩

uron·ic acid \yə¦ränik-, yů¦, -nēk\ *n* [*uronic* ISV, fr. *-uronic*] **:** any of a class of aldehyde-acids $HOOC(CHOH)_nCHO$ that are oxidation products of sugars and that occur combined in many polysaccharides and in urine — see HEXURONIC ACID, POLYURONIC ACID, POLYURONIDE

uro·nide \'yu̇rə,nīd, -,nəd\ *n* -s [*uronic* (in *uronic acid*) + *-ide*] **:** a glycosidic compound that yields a uronic acid on hydrolysis; *esp* **:** POLYURONIDE

uro·patagium \¦yů(,)rō+\ *n* [NL, fr. ²*ur-* + *patagium*] **1 :** the membrane that extends between the thighs of a bat and commonly includes the tail **2 :** one of two plates bounding the sides of the anus in insects

uro·path·ic \¦yu̇rə¦pathik\ *adj* **:** of or relating to uropathy

urop·a·thy \yə'räpəthē\ *n* -ES [¹*ur-* + *-pathy*] **:** a disease of the urinary or urogenital tract

¹**uro·pel·tid** \¦yu̇rə¦peltəd\ *adj* [NL *Uropeltidae*] **:** of or relating to the Uropeltidae

²**uropeltid** \"\ *or* **uro·pelt** \'yu̇rə,pelt\ *n* -s [*uropeltid* fr. NL *Uropeltidae*; *uropelt* fr. NL *Uropeltis*] **:** a snake of the family Uropeltidae

uro·pel·ti·dae \,yu̇rə'peltə,dē\ *n pl, cap* [NL, fr. *Uropeltis*, type genus (fr. ²*ur-* + Gk *peltē* shield) + *-idae* — more at PELTA] **:** a family of small harmless Oriental burrowing snakes distinguished by an enlarged scale or shield at the end of the tail

uro·pepsin \¦yu̇rə+\ *n* [¹*ur-* + *pepsin*] **:** a proteolytic hormone found in urine esp. in cases of peptic ulcers and other disorders of the digestive tract

uro·phlyc·tis \,yu̇rə'fliktəs\ *n, cap* [NL, fr. ²*ur-* + Gk *phlyktis* blister, boil, fr. *phlyein, phlyzein* to boil over — more at FLUID] **:** a genus of lower fungi (order Chytridiales) having a thallus made up of a series of top-shaped cells each with a crown of fingerlike haustoria and connected by slender hyphae — see CROWN WART

uro·pod \'yu̇rə,päd\ *n* -s [ISV ²*ur-* + *-pod*] **:** either of the flattened leaflike appendages of the last abdominal segment of various crustaceans (as the lobster) that with the telson forms the tail fan; *sometimes* **:** any abdominal appendage of a crustacean — **urop·o·dal** \yə'räpədᵊl\ *or* **urop·o·dous** \-dəs\ *adj*

uro·poi·e·sis \,yu̇rə,pȯi'ēsəs\ *n* [NL, fr. ¹*ur-* + *-poiesis*] **:** production of urine

uro·poi·et·ic \¦==¦pȯi¦ed·ik\ *adj* [ISV ¹*ur-* + *-poietic*] **:** of or relating to uropoiesis

uro·por·phy·rin \¦yu̇rō+\ *n* [ISV ¹*ur-* + *porphyrin*] **:** any of four isomeric porphyrins $C_{20}H_6N_4(CH_2COOH)_4(CH_2CH_2COOH)_4$ which contain acetic acid and propionic acid groups on the porphin nucleus and are closely related to the coproporphyrins and of which types I and III are found in urine esp. in porphyria and type III is found also as the copper complex turacin

uro·py·gi \,yu̇rə'pī,jī\ *n pl, cap* [NL, fr. ²*ur-* + Gk *pygē* rump, buttocks] **:** a division of Pedipalpida including those (as the whip scorpions) with a tail

¹**uro·pyg·i·al** *also* **uro·pyg·e·al** \¦yu̇rə¦pijēəl\ *adj* [*uropygial* ISV *uropyg-* (fr. NL *uropygium*) + *-ial*; *uropygeal* irreg. fr. NL *uropygium* + E *-al*] **:** of or relating to the uropygium ⟨~ fat⟩

²**uropygial** \"\ *n* -s **:** a uropygial feather **:** a tail feather

uropygial gland *n* **:** a large gland that opens on the back at the base of the tail feathers in most birds, secretes an oily fluid which the bird uses in preening its feathers, and is esp. developed in waterfowl and helps to make the plumage shed water — called also *preen gland*

uro·pyg·i·um \,yu̇rə'pijēəm\ *n* -s [NL, fr. Gk *ouropygion*, fr. *ouro-* ²ur- + *pygē* rump, buttocks — more at FOG] **:** the fleshy and bony prominence at the posterior extremity of a bird's body that supports the tail feathers and contains the free caudal vertebrae and the pygostyle

uro·pyloric \¦yu̇rō+\ *adj* [²*ur-* + *pyloric*] **:** of, relating to, or being a posterior division of the stomach in various crustaceans

uro·sacral \"+\ *adj* [²*ur-* + *sacral*] **:** of or being the caudal and sacral parts of the vertebral column; *specif* **:** of, relating to, or being the anterior caudal vertebrae of a bird that is consolidated with the true sacral vertebrae and pelvic bones

uro·sal·pinx \,yu̇rō'sal(,)piŋ(k)s\ *n, cap* [NL, fr. ²*ur-* + Gk *salpinx* trumpet] **:** a genus of small carnivorous gastropod mollusks (family Muricidae) comprising the oyster drill (*U. cinerea*) and related forms

uros·co·py \yə'räskəpē\ *n* -ES [NL *uroscopia*, fr. ¹*ur-* + *-scopia* -scopy] **:** examination or analysis of the urine (as for the purpose of medical diagnosis)

uro·somite \¦yu̇rō+\ *n* [²*ur-* + *somite*] **:** UROMERE

uroste·gal \yə'rästigəl, ¦yu̇rə¦stēg-\ *adj* [*urostege* + *-al*] **:** of or relating to a urostege

uro·stege \'yu̇rə,stēj\ *also* **uros·te·gite** \yə'rästə,jīt\ *n* -s [*urostege* fr. ²*ur-* + *-stege*; *urostegite* fr. ²*ur-* + *-stege* + *-ite*] **:** a scale on the underside of the tail of a snake

uros·te·on \yə'rästē,än\ *n, pl* **uros·tea** \-ēə\ [NL, fr. ²*ur-* + *-osteon*] **:** a median ossification at the back of the lophosteon in the sternum of some birds

uro·sternite \¦yu̇rō+\ *n* [²*ur-* + *sternite*] **:** the sternite of a uromere

uro·sty·lar \¦yu̇rə¦stīlə(r)\ *adj* **:** of or relating to a urostyle

uro·style \'==,stīl\ *n* -s [ISV ²*ur-* + *-style*] **1 :** a long rodlike unsegmented bone representing a number of fused vertebrae that forms the posterior part of the vertebral column of frogs and toads **2 a :** the hypural bone of a fish **b :** a similar bone formed by the fusion of two or more caudal vertebrae at the end of the tail in various extinct turtles

uro·toxic \ˌyu̇rə+\ *adj* [ISV ¹*ur-* + *toxic*, orig. formed as F *urotoxique*] : of or relating to the toxicity or the toxic constituents of urine

urot·ro·pine \yəˈrä·trəˌpēn, -pən\ *n* [ISV ¹*ur-* + *tropine*] : HEXAMETHYLENETETRAMINE

-u·rous *or* **-ou·rous** \ˈ(y)u̇rəs, ˈ(y)ürəs\ *adj comb form* [NL *-urus, -ourus*, fr. Gk *-ouros*, fr. *oura* tail; akin to Gk *orrhos* buttocks — more at ASS] : tailed ⟨*xiphurous*⟩ ⟨*anourous*⟩

urox·an·ic acid \ˌyu̇ˌräkˈsanik\ *n* [ISV ¹*ur-* + *alloxan* + *-ic*] : a crystalline acid $C_5H_8N_4O_6$ derived from imidizole and obtained by the slow oxidation of uric acid in alkaline solution

¹ur·sid \ˈərsəd\ *adj* [NL *Ursidae*] : of or relating to the Ursidae

²ursid \"\ *n* -s : a mammal of the family Ursidae

ur·si·dae \-səˌdē\ *n pl, cap* [NL, fr. *Ursus*, type genus + *-idae*] : a family of large powerful plantigrade carnivores including the bears and extinct related forms

ur·si·form \-səˌfȯrm\ *adj* [L *ursus* bear + E *-iform*] : having the shape of a bear

ur·si·gram \-səˌgram\ *n* [ISV *ursi-* (fr. F Union Radiophonique Scientifique Internationale, organization which inaugurated the broadcast in 1930) + *-gram*] : a message broadcast by radio or otherwise giving scientific data (as on terrestrial magnetism, radio transmission, or sunspots)

ur·sine \ˈərˌsīn, -ˌsēn, -sᵊn, -ˌsin\ *adj* [L *ursinus*, fr. *ursus* bear + *-inus* -ine — more at ARCTIC] **1** : of, relating to, or characteristic of a bear or the Ursidae **2** : resembling a bear or that of a bear ⟨the ~ indignation that set him on the path toward his final intellectual disaster —*Time*⟩

ursine baboon *n* : CHACMA

ursine dasyure *n* : TASMANIAN DEVIL

ursine howler *n* : HOWLER MONKEY

ursine seal *n* : FUR SEAL b

ur·sin·ia \ˌərˈsinēə\ *n* [NL, fr. Johann Heinrich *Ursinus* (Latinization of G *Bär*) †1667 Ger. theologian + NL *-ia*] **1** *cap* : a genus of annual or perennial southern African herbs or subshrubs (family Compositae) used as ornamentals with usu. yellow flowers and fruit with a white enlarged pappus **2** -s : any plant of the genus *Ursinia*

ur·soid \ˈərˌsȯid\ *adj* [L *ursus* bear + E *-oid*] : resembling a bear or that of a bear

ur·solic acid \ˌərˈsälik-, -sōl\ *n* [¹*uva-ursi* + *-ol* + *-ic*] : a crystalline triterpenoid acid $C_{30}H_{48}O_3$ found in various esp. ericaceous plants (as the bearberry)

ur·sprache \ˈu̇(ə)rˌshpräkə\ *n* -s *usu cap* [G, fr. *ur-* primitive, original (fr. OHG *ur-, ur* out of) + *sprache* language, fr. OHG *sprāhha* speech — more at ABEAR, SPEECH] : a parent language; *esp* : one reconstructed from the evidence of later languages

ur·su·la butterfly \ˈərsələ-\ *n, usu cap U* [fr. *Ursula*, feminine name] : a No. American butterfly (*Limenitis arthemis astyanax*) having purplish black wings with red and blue slight markings

ur·su·line \-lən, -ˌlīn, -ˌlēn\ *n* -s *usu cap* [NL *ursulinus*, fr. *Ursula* St. Ursula 3d or 5th cent. A.D. legendary Christian martyr + L *-inus* -ine] : a member of a teaching order of nuns founded by St. Angela Merici at Brescia, Italy, about 1537

ur·sus \ˈərsəs\ *n, cap* [NL, fr. L, bear — more at ARCTIC] : a genus (the type of the family Ursidae) of bears held by some authorities to include all recent bears except the sloth bear and restricted by others to the European brown bear and immediately related forms or subdivided in various ways — compare SELENARCTOS, THALARCTOS

urta-juz \ˌu̇rdəˈjüz\ *n pl, usu cap U&J* [Kirghiz] : MIDDLE HORDE

ur·ti·ca \ˈərd·əkə\ *n* [NL, fr. L, nettle; prob. akin to L *urere* to burn; fr. its sting — more at EMBER] **1** *cap* : a genus (the type of the family Urticaceae) of widely distributed plants having opposite stipulate leaves with stinging hairs and small greenish tetramerous flowers **2** -s : any plant of the genus *Urtica*

ur·ti·ca·ce·ae \ˌərd·əˈkāsēˌē\ *n pl, cap* [NL, fr. *Urtica*, type genus + *-aceae*] : a family of herbs, shrubs, and trees (order Urticales) including many with stinging hairs and having small monoecious, dioecious, or polygamous apetalous flowers followed by fruits that are usu. achenes — see STRAWBERRY NETTLE — **ur·ti·ca·ceous** \ˌ==ˈkāshəs\ *adj*

ur·ti·ca·les \ˌ==ˈkā(ˌ)lēz\ *n pl, cap* [NL, fr. *Urtica* + *-ales*] : an order of dicotyledonous plants usu. including the Urticaceae, Ulmaceae, and Moraceae and being characterized mainly by the free apetalous perianth and one-celled superior ovary

ur·ti·cant \ˈərd·əkənt\ *adj* [F, fr. ML *urticant-, urticans*, pres. part. of *urticare* to sting] : producing itching or stinging : URTICATING, STINGING; *esp* : producing an itching swelling ⟨a caterpillar with ~ hairs⟩

ur·ti·car·ia \ˌərd·əˈka(a)rēə\ *n* -s [NL, fr. L *urtica* nettle] : a transient skin eruption characterized by itching red or pale smooth slightly raised patches and caused by irritation (as by food or an inhalant) of the gastrointestinal, pulmonary, or urinary mucous membranes or from contact with an external agent (as a plant, sun, or cold) and found in individuals with a peculiar sensitivity — called also *hives*; compare DERMOGRAPHIA — **ur·ti·car·i·al** \ˌ==ˈ==ēəl\ *adj*

ur·ti·cate \ˈərd·əˌkāt\ *vb* -ED/-ING/-S [ML *urticatus*, past part. of *urticare* to sting, fr. L *urtica* nettle] *vi* : to sting in the manner of a nettle; *specif* : to produce urticaria ⟨an *urticating* caterpillar⟩ ~ *vt* : to afflict with urtication or urticaria : cause nettle rash

ur·ti·ca·tion \ˌ==ˈkāshən\ *n* -s [ML *urtication-, urticatio*, fr. *urticatus* (past part.) + L *-ion-, -io* -ion] **1** : an itching and stinging sensation (as from contact with nettles) **2** [*urtic-* (in NL *urticaria*) + *-ation*] : wheal formation in urticaria

ur·ti·cose \ˈərd·əˌkōs\ *adj* [NL *urticosus*, fr. L *urtica* nettle + *-osus* -ose] : abounding with nettles

uru·bu \ˌu̇rəˈbü\ *n* -s [Sp & Pg *urubu, urubú*, fr. Tupi *urubú*] : BLACK VULTURE

uru·cú \ˌu̇rəˈkü\ *n* -s [Pg, fr. Tupi] : ANNATTO 1

urucu-rana \ˌu̇rəkəˈranə\ *n* -s [Pg *urucurana*, fr. Tupi, fr. *urucú* annatto + *rana* false] **1** : a tropical So. American timber tree (*Hieronyma alchorneoides*) of the family Euphorbiaceae **2** : the deep reddish brown hard wood of the urucurana used for construction and cabinet work

uru·cu·ri iba \ˌu̇rəkəˌrēˈēbə\ *n* -s [Tupi, lit., ouricury tree] : OURICURY 1

uru·guay \ˈu̇rəˌgwī, ˈyu̇rəˌgwā *also* ˈyu̇rəˌgwī *sometimes* ˈu̇rəˌgwā\ *adj, usu cap* [fr. *Uruguay*, country in So. America] : of or from Uruguay : of the kind or style prevalent in Uruguay : URUGUAYAN

¹uru·guay·an \ˌ==ˈgwīən, -ˈgwāən\ *adj, usu cap* [Sp *uruguayano*, adj. & n., fr. *Uruguay*, country in So. America + Sp *-ano* -an] : of or relating to Uruguay or its inhabitants

²uruguayan \"\ *n* -s *cap* [Sp *uruguayano*] : a native or inhabitant of Uruguay

uruguay potato *n, usu cap U* **1** : a So. American plant (*Solanum commersonii*) **2** : the tuber of the Uruguay potato resembling the common potato

uruk \ˈu̇rək\ *adj, usu cap* [fr. *Uruk* (Erech), ancient Sumerian city on the Euphrates in Babylonia (now *Warka*, locality in southeastern Iraq), site of the culture's remains] : of or relating to a Sumerian early Bronze Age culture characterized by temples of stone, sculpture in the round, writing on clay, engraved cylinder seals, and plain red or gray pottery often having a polished surface

urun·day \ˌu̇rənˈdī\ *n* -s [Sp, fr. Guarani *urundai*] : any of several timber trees (as *A. urundeuva*) of the genus *Astronium* (family Anacardiaceae) of southern So. America that have hard fine wood used for a variety of purposes

urus \ˈyu̇rəs\ *n* -ES [L, of Gmc origin; akin to OHG *ūrohso* urus — more at AUROCHS] : an extinct large longhorned wild ox (*Bos primigenius*) of the German forests believed to be a wild ancestor of domestic cattle

-u·rus \ˈ(y)u̇r-\ *n comb form* [NL, fr. Gk *oura* — more at -UROUS] : tail — in generic names ⟨*Brachyurus*⟩ ⟨*Dasyurus*⟩ ⟨*Saururus*⟩

uru·shi \əˈrüshē\ *n* -s [Jap] : LACQUER

uru·shic acid \əˌrüshik-\ *or* **uru·shin·ic acid** \ˌu̇rəˌshinik-\ *n* [*urushic* ISV *urushi* (fr. Jap) + *-ic*; *urushinic* fr. *urushi* + *-in* + *-ic*] : URUSHIOL

uru·shi·ol \əˈrüshēˌȯl, -ēˌōl\ *n* -s [ISV *urushi* + *-ol*] : a poisonous oily liquid phenolic compound $C_{15}H_{27}C_6H_3(OH)_2$ in the sap of Oriental lacquer trees (*Rhus verniciferi* and *R. succedanea*) and present also as one of the principal blistering substances in poison ivy, poison oak, and poison sumac that hardens and becomes colored by atmospheric oxidation and serves as the chief component of Japanese and Chinese lacquers; 3-pentadeca-trien-yl-pyrocatechol

uru·shi·ye \əˈrüshē(ˌ)yā\ *n* -s [Jap] : a Japanese color print in which the dark colors are printed with a lustrous medium commonly considered to be lacquer

uru·tu \ˌu̇rəˈtü\ *n* -s [Pg, fr. Tupi] : any of several So. American pit vipers; *esp* : a showy viper (*Bothrops alternatus*) with a series of dark brown lateral crescents on a cream ground

ur·va \u̇rˈvä, ər-\ *n* -s [Nepali *urvā, arvā*] : a common mongoose (*Herpestes urva*) of southeastern Asia having fur like that of the badger in appearance with a white stripe extending from throat to shoulder, the back grizzled black and white, and the feet and chest black

us \(ˌ)əs\ *pron, objective case of* WE [ME, fr. OE *ūs*; akin to OHG & Goth *uns* us, ON *oss*, L *nos*, Gk *hēmas* (Aeolic *amme*), Skt *nas, asmān*] **1** : ¹WE 1: **a** (1) — used as indirect object of a verb ⟨give ~ this day our daily bread —Mt 6:11 (AV)⟩ (2) *obs* — used as a vague indirect object simply to suggest the concern or involvement of a group including the one speaking or writing ⟨they wounded ~ only one man —*London Gazette*⟩ **b** — used as object of a preposition ⟨walking away from ~⟩ ⟨men, women, all of ~, just because we are human —Walter de la Mare⟩ **c** — used as direct object of a verb ⟨they were visiting ~⟩ **d** — used in comparisons after *than* and *as* when the first term in the comparison is the direct or indirect object of a verb or the object of a preposition ⟨the march tired the other platoon more than ~⟩ ⟨the bank would rather give you a loan than ~⟩ ⟨time has dealt as harshly with them as ~⟩ **e** — used in absolute or elliptical constructions ⟨who, ~⟩ esp. together with a prepositional phrase, adjective, or participle ⟨it is best not to speak to him, ~ not knowing to what ideology his loyalty might or might not belong —Peggy Bennett⟩ **f** — used by speakers on all educational levels and by many reputable writers though disapproved by some grammarians in the predicate after forms of *be*, in comparisons after *than* and *as* when the first term in the comparison is the subject of a verb, and in other positions where it is itself neither the subject of a verb nor the object of a verb or preposition ⟨the miraculous generation which is ~ —Arnold Bennett⟩ ⟨you are bigger and stronger than ~ women —K.A.Menninger⟩ ⟨~ and our little problems⟩ **g** (1) — used chiefly in substandard speech and formerly also by reputable writers as part of the compound subject of a verb or esp. with an immediately following appositive noun as the subject of a verb which it does not immediately precede ⟨our neighbors and ~ don't like that⟩ ⟨~ kids were always given a swallow —Walter Karig⟩ (2) *chiefly dial* — used as the subject of a verb from which it is not separated by other words ⟨~ lived in a two-story house —Ralph Ellison⟩ **h** — used like the adjective *our* with a gerund by speakers and writers on all educational levels though disapproved by some grammarians ⟨she approved of ~ getting summer jobs⟩ **2** : OURSELVES, OURSELF — used reflexively as indirect object of a verb ⟨we built ~ a shack by the lake⟩, object of a preposition ⟨we'll take you with ~⟩, or direct object of a verb ⟨now we will divest ~ of rule, interest of territory, cares of state —Shak.⟩ **3 a** : ¹ME 1 — used by kings and other sovereigns and by editors and other writers when *we* is used instead of *I* ⟨what touches ~ ourself shall be last served —Shak.⟩; compare ¹WE 2 **b** : ¹ME 1 — used in ordinary situations by a speaker of any kind in reference to himself ⟨give ~ a goodnight kiss —Richard Llewellyn⟩ **4** : our ship ⟨about to board ~⟩

US *abbr* **1** *often not cap* [L *ubi supra*] where above mentioned **2** undersecretary **3** united service **4** unserviceable **5** *often not cap* [L *ut supra*] as above

u's *or* **us** *pl of* U

us·abil·i·ty \ˌyüzəˈbiləd·ē, -lətē, -i\ *n* : the quality or state of being usable

us·able *also* **use·able** \ˈyüzəbəl\ *adj* [ME, fr. MF *usable*, fr. *user* to use + *-able*] **1** : that can be used ⟨a small lake comprises approximately 20 acres, leaving 140 acres ~ for burial purposes —*U.S.Code*⟩ **2** : that is convenient and practicable for use ⟨the short story, as a ~ form of art, will nevertheless survive —G.H.Genzmer⟩ — **us·able·ness** *n* -ES — **us·ably** \-blē, -li\ *adv*

us·age \ˈyüsij, ǀēj *also* -üz\ *n* -s [ME, fr. OF, fr. *user* to use + *-age*] **1** : habitual or customary practice or use: **a** (1) : the prevailing mode of procedure (as of a craft, business, liturgical tradition) : a principle or method of action or body of these commonly followed within a group ⟨these principles and rules grew up entirely on the basis of ~ (sometimes reenforced by judicial decision), and were never enacted by Parliament —F.A.Ogg & Harold Zink⟩ ⟨the chapel services follow the ~ of the Episcopal church —*Bard College Bull.*⟩ (2) : a uniform certain reasonable practice not contrary to law which exists in a particular locality or among those engaged in a particular occupation or business and by which those entering into consensual transactions are bound either by express assent or by implied acquiescence on the basis of presumed familiarity — compare CUSTOM, PRESCRIPTION **b** : the habitual practice of a person : usual behavior : HABIT ⟨propping oneself on one's elbows to drink a cup of tea . . . is still an ill-bred ~ —Agnes M. Miall⟩ **c** : the way in which words and phrases are actually used (as in a particular form or sense) generally or among a community or group of persons : customary use of language ⟨like all grammarians, he professed to base his work on actual ~; in fact, however, he . . . gave his approval only to such constructions as met his rigid notions of logic and propriety —G.H.Genzmer⟩ ⟨instruct pupils in the rules of good ~⟩ **2 a** : the action, amount, or mode of using : USE ⟨the corners somewhat smashed and broken as by long, rough ~ —R.L.Stevenson⟩ ⟨steadily increasing ~ of the nation's highways —J.C.Nelson⟩ ⟨freshmen students are given a brief period of instruction in library ~ —*Bull. of Meharry Med. Coll.*⟩ **b** : manner of conduct toward a person : TREATMENT ⟨complained of ill ~ at the hands of his jailors — threats, scanty food, beatings⟩ **3** : UTILITY, ADVANTAGE ⟨we can fell trees and put them to our ~ —George Moore⟩ **syn** see FORM, HABIT

us·ag·er \ˈyüzijə(r)\ *n* -s *usu cap* [*usage* + *-er*] : a member of a party of nonjurors in the Church of England and Scottish Episcopal Church accepting the ritual usages of a Communion service published in 1718 including dilution of the Eucharistic wine, a prayer for the descent of the Holy Spirit on the consecrated elements, an oblatory prayer, and prayers for the dead

usam·ba·ra violet \ˌüsämˈbärə-\ *n, usu cap U* [fr. *Usambara*, district of northeast Tanganyika Territory, Africa] : AFRICAN VIOLET

us·ance \ˈyüzᵊn(t)s\ *n* -s [ME *usaunce*, fr. ML *usantia*, fr. *usant-, usans* (pres. part. of *usare* to use) + L *-ia* -y] **1** : USAGE 1a,1b **2** : the action of using or fact of being used : USE **3 a** *obs* : USURY ⟨many a time . . . you have rated me about my monies and my ~s —Shak.⟩ **b** : INTEREST ⟨make an investment of any spare monies as may render some ~ —Lord Byron⟩ **4** : the time allowed exclusive of grace for the payment of a bill of exchange or note as fixed by custom or by law

usar \ˈüˌsär\ *n* -s [Hindi *ūsar*, fr. Skt *ūṣara* fr. *ūṣa* containing salt] : REH

usara root *var of* UZARA ROOT

usar grass *n* : an East Indian perennial grass (*Sporobolus orientalis*) useful for forage in alkali or saline situations

u. s. army black \ˈyüˈes-\ *n, usu cap U&S&A* : a nearly neutral very slightly bluish black

u. s. army brick red *n, usu cap U&S&A* : a dark red

u. s. army brown *n, usu cap U&S&A* : a moderate brown

u. s. army buff *n, usu cap U&S&A* : a light yellowish brown

u. s. army cobalt blue *n, usu cap U&S&A* : a dark blue that is redder and stronger than U.S. Army sky blue

u. s. army color *n, usu cap U&S&A* : a color standardized for the United States Army by the Textile Color Card Association of the U.S. and calibrated by measurements in the National Bureau of Standards

u. s. army crimson *n, usu cap U&S&A* : a deep purplish red

u. s. army dark blue *n, usu cap U&S&A* : a slightly bluish black

u. s. army golden orange *n, usu cap U&S&A* : a strong orange

u. s. army golden yellow *n, usu cap U&S&A* : a vivid yellow

u. s. army green *n, usu cap U&S&A* : a dark yellowish green

u. s. army light blue *n, usu cap U&S&A* : a moderate greenish blue to grayish blue

u. s. army maroon *n, usu cap U&S&A* : a dark grayish red

u. s. army mosstone *n, usu cap U&S&A* : a moderate yellow green

u. s. army old gold *n, usu cap U&S&A* : a moderate yellow

u. s. army orange *n, usu cap U&S&A* : a vivid reddish orange that is redder and paler than international orange, redder and darker than chrome orange, and redder and duller than golden poppy

u. s. army pansy *n, usu cap U&S&A* : a strong violet

u. s. army scarlet *n, usu cap U&S&A* : a strong red

u. s. army silver gray *n, usu cap U&S&A* : a medium slightly yellowish gray

u. s. army sky blue *n, usu cap U&S&A* : a dark blue

u. s. army ultramarine blue *n, usu cap U&S&A* : a vivid blue to purplish blue

u. s. army white *n, usu cap U&S&A* : a yellowish gray to yellowish white

u. s. army yellow *n, usu cap U&S&A* : a strong orange yellow that is redder and deeper than Spanish yellow, bright maize, or nasturtium yellow (sense 2)

usbek *or* **usbeg** *cap, var of* UZBEK

USC *abbr* under separate cover

¹use \ˈyüs\ *n* -s [ME *us*, use, fr. OF *us*, fr. L *usus* use, employment, custom, fr. *usus*, past part. of *uti* to use, employ] **1 a** : the act or practice of using something : EMPLOYMENT ⟨a ~ of his public post to secure a favor for a friend⟩ ⟨become familiar with algebra through the ~ of a good text⟩ ⟨an increase in the ~ of intoxicating liquors⟩ ⟨the ~ of subsidies to hold food prices down —*Current Biog.*⟩ : APPLICATION ⟨knowledge . . . to be valuable must be ready for ~ —C.H.Grandgent⟩ **b** : the fact or state of being used ⟨a lamp in daily ~ for over 50 years⟩ ⟨put the new broom to ~⟩ ⟨expressions out of ~ except in dialect⟩ ⟨when fountain pens first came into ~⟩ **c** : continued or repeated exercise or employment ⟨worn out through long ~⟩ **d** : a method or manner of using something ⟨the water in the font, having once been consecrated, tempted folk to superstitious ~s —G.G.Coulton⟩ ⟨gain proficiency in the ~ of the typewriter⟩ **2 a** (1) : habitual or customary practice : accustomed or usual procedure (2) : an individual habit or group custom ⟨it had been a family ~ . . . to make a point of saving for him anything which he might possibly eat —Mary Austin⟩ **b** : a liturgical form or observance ⟨ferial ~⟩ ⟨festal ~⟩; *esp* : a liturgy having modifications peculiar to a local church or diocese (as in England before the Reformation) or a religious order ⟨the celebration of Mass in those religious orders . . . whose ~ differs from the standard Roman rite —*advt*⟩ ⟨from henceforth all the whole realm shall have but one ~ —*Bk. of Com. Prayer*⟩ **c** *obs* : common occurrence : ordinary experience ⟨these things are beyond all ~ —Shak.⟩ **3 a** : the privilege or benefit of using something ⟨offered him the ~ of his pen for signing⟩ ⟨had the ~ of the usual class time for study⟩ ⟨nor shall private property be taken for public ~ without just compensation —*U.S.Constitution*⟩ ⟨the Lord bless this food to our ~, and us to His service —*Bk. of Com. Worship*⟩ **b** : the ability or power to use something (as a limb or faculty) ⟨regained the ~ of his arm⟩ ⟨still has the ~ of his speech⟩ **c** : the legal enjoyment of property that consists in its employment, occupation, exercise, or practice ⟨~ of the automobile is covered by insurance⟩ **d** : a personal servitude under Roman and civil law consisting in a jus utendi as distinguished from the usufruct **4 a** : a particular service or end : PURPOSE, OBJECT, FUNCTION ⟨put his learning to a good ~⟩ ⟨the river waters were dammed for power ~ —*Amer. Guide Series: Mich.*⟩ ⟨develop the industrial ~s of atomic energy⟩ **b** (1) : the quality of being suitable for employment : capability of filling a need or promoting an advantage : USEFULNESS, UTILITY ⟨being ready first was of little ~, since you were then called on to button the others —Natacha Stewart⟩ ⟨old clothes that might be of some ~ to refugees⟩ (2) : something that fills a need or gives a benefit or advantage — used predicatively ⟨the thing that any artist must have to go on: the feeling . . . that he's some ~ in the world —Deems Taylor⟩ ⟨small ~ to argue if he's already made up his mind⟩ esp. in negative constructions ⟨it is no ~ reading this article any further until you have settled this first point for yourself —J.B.Nettleship⟩ **c** : the occasion or need to employ : NECESSITY, DEMAND ⟨took only what he had ~ for⟩ ⟨found little ~ for his rifle⟩ **5 a** : the benefit in law of one or more persons; *specif* : the benefit or of the profit arising from lands and tenements to which legal title is held by a person in whom a trust or confidence is reposed that another person should take and enjoy — compare CESTUI QUE USE **b** : a legal arrangement that is a right in equity by which such benefits and profits are established in one other than the legal possessor of the property — compare TRUST **6** *chiefly dial* : money paid for the use of a loan : INTEREST **7** : a part of a sermon in which a doctrine is applied to life : practical application ⟨the discourse . . . was divided into fifteen heads, each of which was garnished with seven ~s of application —Sir Walter Scott⟩ **8** : a rough block of iron or steel suitable for working up into small forgings or for welding in making large ones **9** : a favorable attitude toward a person or thing as having worth or use : ESTEEM, LIKING — used with *for* in negative constructions ⟨had no ~ for most sales managers —*Time*⟩ ⟨had very little ~ for the music of most of his contemporaries —Deems Taylor⟩

syn SERVICE, ADVANTAGE, PROFIT, ACCOUNT, AVAIL, and USE have in common a sense of a useful or valuable end, result, or purpose. USE stresses the practicality of the end, result, or purpose for which something is employed ⟨a tool with many *uses*⟩ ⟨put a gift of money to good *use* in paying off debts⟩ SERVICE is used more frequently of persons or animals or their work or activities than of inanimate things; in relation to persons it usu. suggests self-abnegation ⟨a man of great *service* to the community⟩ ⟨put a horse to good *service* in hauling logs⟩ ADVANTAGE puts stress upon improvement of one's position or enhancement of something one considers of value, esp. personal value ⟨gain the *advantage* of a steady income⟩ ⟨offer valuable educational *advantages* —*Amer. Guide Series: Minn.*⟩ ⟨find some *advantage* in even the worst circumstances⟩ PROFIT is more particular in usu. implying reward, often the rewarding character of what is attained but commonly pecuniary gain ⟨whether or not they found the sources of the gold they were seeking, they certainly drew other *profits* from their venture —*Brit. Bk. News*⟩ ⟨pursue graduate studies with *profit* —*Official Register of Harvard Univ.*⟩ ⟨coal and steel interests were merging with mutual *profit* —*Amer. Guide Series: Pa.*⟩ ACCOUNT usu. suggests a calculated value; it occurs commonly in fixed phrases ⟨turn every talent to good *account*⟩ ⟨consider a small loss of no *account* in the long run⟩ AVAIL strongly suggests effectualness or effectiveness, occurring usu. in idiomatic phrases mostly in the negative ⟨medicine that is of no *avail* in curing a given disease⟩ ⟨of what *avail* is it to spend time dreaming⟩ **syn** see in addition HABIT

— in use *or* **into use** : in heat ⟨conception can only occur at the precise time when the mare is fully *in use* —Henry Wynmalen⟩

²use \ˈyüz, *in vi sense 1* ˈyüs *sometimes* ǀyüz\ *vb* **used** \ˈyüzd, *in vi sense 1* ˈyüst (*is* ˈyüs *when "to" follows immediately*) *sometimes* ǀyüz(d)\ **used; using; uses** [ME *usen*, fr. OF *user*, fr. ML *usare*, fr. L *usus*, past part. of *uti* to use, employ, enjoy; akin to Oscan *úíttiuf* uses (acc. pl.)] *vt* **1 a** *archaic* : to observe or follow as a custom ⟨the like custom is *used* throughout the dominions —Samuel Purchas⟩ ⟨it was in old times *used* . . . for men to shave themselves —Richard Montagu⟩ **b** *archaic* : to follow or practice regularly as a mode of life or action ⟨then let them ~ the office of a deacon —1 Tim. 3:10 (AV)⟩ **c** : to make familiar by repeated or continued practice or experience : ACCUSTOM, HABITUATE, INURE ⟨spoke near the sea in storms . . . to ~ himself to speak aloud —Earl of Chesterfield⟩ **d** *chiefly dial* : to resort to regularly : FREQUENT ⟨it ~s more the low sandy inland parts than the plovers —Hans Sloane⟩ **2** : to put into action or service : have recourse to or enjoyment of : EMPLOY ⟨the pronunciations that people from different parts of the country ~⟩ ⟨wondered whether he would ever actually ~ the tie she had given him⟩ : EXERCISE ⟨examiners will ~ judgment and discretion in applying the exercise test —H.G.

Armstrong⟩ ⟨~ his political influence to get the job⟩: as **a** : to speak or write in (a language) ⟨they speak little Welsh — only forty or so in a thousand ~ the tongue —Wilfred Goatman⟩ **b** : to consume or take (as liquor or drugs) regularly ⟨does not give scholarships to students who ~ tobacco⟩ ⟨do you ~ sugar in your coffee⟩ **c** *archaic* : to have sexual relations with ⟨... did carnally know and ~ his wife —Francis Hackett⟩ **d** *archaic* : to practice or exercise upon or toward others ⟨I guess by the ... waspish action which she did —Shak.⟩ ⟨with their tongues they have *used* deceit —Rom 3:13 (AV)⟩ **3** : to carry out a purpose or action by means of : make instrumental to an end or process : apply to advantage : turn to account : UTILIZE ⟨carried air mail *using* two small single-engined planes and five employees —*Current Biog.*⟩ ⟨some of the best tests ... can be *used* only by professional psychologists —Bruce Payne⟩: as **a** : to spend (time) in some occupation, interest, or activity : PASS ⟨they ~ 30 days in traveling ... about 1,000 miles —F.C.Lincoln⟩ ⟨stop by the way ... to chase a rabbit, or merely to ~ time —Joyce Cary⟩ **b** : to make an involuntary or concealed means to one's own ends ⟨he is being *used* and manipulated by the knowing men around him —T.R.Ybarra⟩ ⟨juries ... may be *used* to suppress writings in opposition to the government —Zechariah Chafee⟩ **c** : to employ a word, phrase, or sentence to refer ⟨to say "*life* is a short word" is to mention the word *life* ... but to say "Life is short" is to ~ it —R.G.F.Robinson⟩ **4** : to expend or consume by putting to use ⟨percent of the world's population ... produces and ~s almost one half of the industrial goods and services —C.C.Furnas⟩ **5 a** *archaic* : to bear (oneself) in relations with others : BEHAVE, CONDUCT ⟨the *used* himself more like a fellow to your Highness than like a subject —Edward Herbert⟩ **b** : to behave toward : act with regard to : TREAT ⟨had been taken prisoner by ... partisans, who had *used* him with some brutality —Eric Linklater⟩ **6** : to apply or have applied as the usual designation (as a title or surname) of a person ⟨took his friends a while to acquire the habit of *using* the "*doctor*" after he received his Ph.D.⟩ ⟨a woman who ~s her maiden name professionally⟩ **7** : to benefit from the use of ⟨houses that could ~ a paint job —J.W.Ellison b. 1929⟩ ⟨I can ~ some of that gold —E.B.Lung⟩ ~ *vi* **1 a** : to be in the habit or custom : make a practice of doing something : be wont ⟨sit here by the window with your hand in mine ... both of one mind, as married people ~ —Robert Browning⟩ ⟨he do not ~ to be last on these occasions —George Lillo⟩ ⟨the black coachman, who had *used* to drive ... the carriage —Marguerite Young⟩ ⟨patrons who *used* to do their banking on Friday⟩ ⟨~ to have tallyho parties out on the ... pike when we were young —Anne G. Winslow⟩ ⟨*used* you to beat your mother —G. B.Shaw⟩ **b** — used in the past with *to* to indicate a former fact or state ⟨claims the winters *used* to be harder⟩ ⟨isn't going to take as long as it *used* to⟩ ⟨didn't ~ to have a car⟩ **2** *chiefly dial* **a** : to make a practice of going to a place : resort to : frequent ⟨go regularly ⟨if he didn't quit *using* around there she would make trouble for him —Mark Twain⟩ **b** : to occupy a place as a settled residence or habitat : DWELL, LIVE — usu. used of an animal ⟨I know where the gray fox ~s up yonder —R.A.Helton⟩

syn EMPLOY, UTILIZE, APPLY, AVAIL: USE is general and indicates any putting to service of a thing, usu. for an intended or fit purpose or person, in this latter reference with implications of inconsiderate or high-handed treatment ⟨use a jack to raise a car⟩ ⟨use a knife blade to pry up a lid⟩ ⟨use money wisely⟩ ⟨used his business experience to place the country in a better financial position —S.G.Inman⟩ ⟨his sense of being *used* rose suddenly above the treacherous sympathy he had begun to feel for her —Booth Tarkington⟩ EMPLOY may imply purposive selection, continued use or utilization, or smart turning to account ⟨by the dialect which he *employs* the author betrays that he was an Ionian Greek —Benjamin Farrington⟩ ⟨frequently lotteries were *employed* to raise funds for channel clearing —*Amer. Guide Series: Tenn.*⟩ UTILIZE may indicate finding a new, profitable, or practical use for something ⟨it was now charged against him that he *utilized* his military office for private gain —R.G.Adams⟩ ⟨all civilized governments have *utilized* the Indians as military allies —M.M.Quaife⟩ ⟨a huge wine bottle, *utilized* as a pivot for the rooster weather vane when no other instrument would hold —*Amer. Guide Series: Mich.*⟩ APPLY may imply a using or employing especially for a particular purpose or in a particular situation, sometimes with the suggestion of bringing into contact or relationship ⟨apply salve to a burn⟩ ⟨apply pressure at a crucial point⟩ ⟨the value of *applying* statistical methods to the data⟩ ⟨undertakes to *apply* the findings of science to personal problems —*Amer. Guide Series: Mich.*⟩ AVAIL in reflexive uses applies to a using or taking advantage of something one might waive or leave untouched ⟨I doubt if I should abuse the permission. It is a hundred to one if I should *avail* myself of it four times a year —Charles Dickens⟩ ⟨takes us thus directly into the consciousness of his characters, and in order to do so, he has *availed* himself of methods of which Flaubert never dreamed —Edmund Wilson⟩ — **use language** : to use profanity : SWEAR ⟨her husband's *using language* before ladies showed him to be in high good humor —Edith Wharton⟩

useable *var of* USABLE

use and occupancy insurance *n* [¹*use*] : BUSINESS INTERRUPTION INSURANCE

use and occupation *n* : a legal action of the character of an assumpsit that may be maintained by the owner of real property against a person who has had the use and occupation of it under express or implied contract to pay therefor but without a written lease or beyond the term of the written lease

use and wont *n* : USE 2a(1) ⟨life is an affair of *use and wont* and persists substantially unchanged —Walter Moberly⟩

used \'yüzd, *in sense 3* 'yüst (.'yüs *when "to" follows immediately*) *sometimes* 'yüz(d)\ *adj* [ME, fr. past part. of *usen* to use] **1** : employed in accomplishing something ⟨his most ~ name⟩ ⟨the principle of surprise is the most ~ and misused of all the principles of war —H.H.Arnold & I.C.Eaker⟩ **2** : that has endured considerable use : that has been utilized according to its nature or purpose: as **a** : partly worn-out : SECONDHAND ⟨bought a ~ car because he couldn't afford a new one⟩ ⟨collect ~ clothing for overseas relief⟩ **b** *of a stamp* : that has served as postage on a piece of mail **3** : ACCUSTOMED, HABITUATED, EXPERIENCED ⟨showing how ~ he was to papers with lies on them —Gilbert Millstein⟩

use district *n* [¹*use*] : a zone or area in a city or town within which the types of usage to which buildings are put are regulated by law

used·n't *or* **use·n't** \'yüz°n(t)\ [by contr.] *chiefly Brit* : used not

used to \,yüs *sometimes* 'yüz + *pronunc at* TO\ *adv* [fr. the verb phrase *used to*, fr. *used*, past of ²*use* + *to*, function word normally indicating that the following verb is an infinitive] *dial* : FORMERLY, ONCE ⟨he ain't as popular now as he *used to* was —Mark Twain⟩ ⟨I can't do the hard day's work I *used to* could —Erskine Caldwell⟩ ⟨*used to* Pa wouldn't a done a thing like this —J.H.Stuart⟩

use·ee \.yü'zē, -ä\ *n* [²*use* + -*ee*] : one to or for whose use a thing is done or given; *esp* : one for whose benefit a suit is brought : use plaintiff

use·ful \'yüsfəl\ *adj* [¹*use* + -*ful*] : capable of being put to use : having utility : ADVANTAGEOUS ⟨the Communists find him just as ~ as an opponent —*Time*⟩; *esp* : producing or having the power to produce good : serviceable for a beneficial end or object ⟨all sorts of ~ implements such as axes, chisels, gouges, arrowheads —*Amer. Guide Series: R.I.*⟩ ⟨~ to remind ourselves occasionally of our limitations ⟨no ~ rain had fallen for five or six months —*Sydney (Australia) Bull.*⟩

useful load *n* : the excess of the full load including the crew and passengers, oil and fuel, auxiliary power system, and communication, navigation, and other equipment over the dead weight of an aircraft itself — compare DEAD LOAD

use·ful·ly \-fəlē, -li\ *adv* : in a useful manner

use·ful·ness *n* -ES : the quality or state of being useful : conduciveness to an end : UTILITY

use inheritance *n* [¹*use*] : supposed inheritance by offspring of characters acquired by the parent through use or disuse of structures — compare LAMARCKISM

use·less \'yüsləs\ *adj* [¹*use* + -*less*] : having or being of no use : producing no good end : answering no desired purpose

---

: INEFFECTUAL, INEFFICIENT, UNSERVICEABLE ⟨attempts ... to sterilize the seawater at swimming beaches are ~ because the seawater itself is a sterilizing agent —G.E. & Nettie Mac-Ginitie⟩ — **use·less·ly** *adv* — **use·less·ness** *n* -ES

us·en \'yüs°n\ *dial var of* USED

¹us·er \'yüzə(r)\ *n* -s [ME, fr. *usen* to use + -*er*] : one that uses; *specif* : a person who uses alcoholic beverages or narcotics

²user \"\ *n* -s [back-formation fr. ¹*non-user*] : enjoyment of a right of use : a right to use resulting from long-continued use ⟨claims to arms by ~ could be allowed only if they went back before 1530 —L.G.Pine⟩

uses *pl of* USE, *pres 3d sing of* USE

use tax *n* [¹*use*] : a supplement to a retail sales tax designed to reach goods purchased in a state that does not tax them and brought or shipped in to the taxing jurisdiction for use, storage, or consumption

use up *vt* [²*use*] **1** : to leave nothing of as a result of continued expenditure : consume completely ⟨soon *used up* his supplies and had nothing to eat⟩ **2** : to leave no capacity of force or use in : exhaust of strength or useful properties ⟨who at the age of 53 was pretty well *used up* by fighting —S.E.Morison & H.S.Commager⟩ **3** : to subject to thorough and abusive treatment : attack physically or verbally : work over ⟨the summary and effectual manner in which the argument is put and his opponent *used up* —P.T.Barnum⟩

ush \'osh\ *vi* -ED/-ING/-ES [back-formation fr. ¹*usher*] *slang* : USHER

ushab·ti \(y)ü'shäbtē\ *also* **sha·wab·ti** \shə'wä-\ *n, pl* **ushab·ti** \-tē\ *or* **ushab·tis** \-tēz\ *or* **ushab·tiu** \-tē,ü\ [Egypt *wšbty*, lit., answerer] : a small figure deposited in an ancient Egyptian tomb with the mummy generally bearing inscriptions from the Book of the Dead and representing servants expected to do certain agricultural labors required of the deceased in the land of the dead

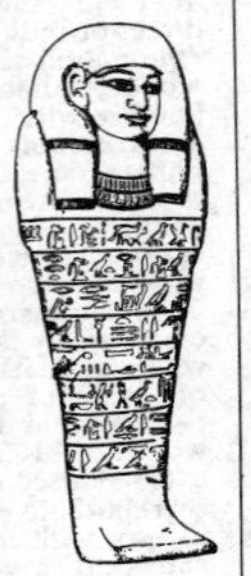

ushak *or* **ou·shak** \ü'shäk\ *n* -s *usu cap* [fr. *Ushak, Oushak* (Usak), manufacturing town of western Turkey in Asia] : a heavy woolen oriental rug tied in Ghiordes knots and characterized by bright primary colors and an elaborate medallion pattern

u-shaped \'∴∷-\ *adj, cap U* : having the shape of a capital U ⟨a *U-shaped* statistical curve⟩; *specif* : resembling a broad U in cross profile ⟨a *U-shaped* valley⟩

ushabti

¹ush·er \'oshə(r)\ *n* -s [ME *ussher*, fr. MF *ussier*, fr. (assumed) VL *ustiarius* doorkeeper, fr. L *ostium, ustium* door, mouth of a river + -*arius* -ary; akin to Skt *oṣṭha* lip, Lith *uostas* mouth of a river, L *or*-, *os* mouth — more at ORAL] **1 a** : an officer or servant who has the care of the door of a court, hall, or chamber **b** (1) : an officer whose business it is to introduce strangers or to walk before a person of rank ⟨various ~s attached to the royal household in England including the Gentleman-Usher of the Black Rod⟩ (2) *obs* : something that precedes or gives indication of the approach of a person or thing : HARBINGER **c** : a minor official of an English court of law (as formerly the Court of Chancery) charged with maintaining silence and order **d** : one who escorts persons to seats at an assemblage (as in a theater, church, or hall) **e** : one employed to direct or assist patrons (as of a store) or visitors (as to a public building) **2** *archaic* : an assistant teacher in a private school **3** *obs* : a male attendant accompanying a lady

²usher \"\ *vb* **ushered; ushered; ushering; ushers** *vt* **1** : to conduct to a place ⟨~ the bride's mother to her seat⟩ **2** : to precede as a herald or harbinger **3** : to serve as introduction for (as a discourse, essay, book) : PREFACE **4** : to cause to enter : INTRODUCE ⟨even before the child was ~ed into the world —J.H.Cornyn⟩ ~ *vi* : to serve as an usher ⟨asked him to ~ at his wedding⟩

ush·er·er \-shərə(r)\ *n* -s [²*usher* + -*er*] : one that ushers : USHER

ush·er·ette \,oshə'ret, *usu* -ed-+V\ *n* -s [¹*usher* + -*ette*] : a woman employed to show patrons to seats (as in a theater) : female usher

usher in *vt* [²*usher*] **1** : to serve to bring into being : INAUGURATE ⟨a truce would *usher in* a period of great uncertainty —*N.Y.Times*⟩ **2** : to bring in or observe the entry of with ceremony ⟨already the town boys were *ushering in* the month of May —A.T.Quiller-Couch⟩ **3** : to mark the beginning or occurrence of ⟨1879 did indeed *usher in* a renaissance —W.V. Quine⟩

ush·er·less \'oshə(r)ləs\ *adj* : having no usher

usher of the black rod : BLACK ROD

ush·er·ship \-(r),ship\ *n* **1** : the office of an usher **2** : a position as an usher

using *adj* [fr. gerund of ²*use*] *of a saddle horse* : trained for utility service (as herding or roping) rather than as a pleasure mount

using-ground \'∷∷-\ *n* : a place frequented by game (as wild fowl)

us·kok \'ü,skäk\ *n* -s *cap* : a Slav of Dalmatian origin orig. fugitive from Turkish rule

us·nea \'əsnēə\ *n* [NL, fr. Ar *ushnah* moss] **1** *cap* : a genus of widely distributed lichens of the family Usneaceae usu. having a grayish or yellow pendulous freely branched thallus — see BEARD LICHEN **2** -s : any lichen of the genus *Usnea*

us·ne·a·ceae \,əsnē'āsē,ē\ *n pl, cap* [NL, fr. *Usnea*, type genus + -*aceae*] : a family of fruticose lichens characterized by prostrate, erect, or pendulous thalli that are generally radially symmetrical and including the genera *Usnea, Evernia, Ramalina,* and *Alectoria* — **us·ne·a·ceous** \,'āshəs\ *adj*

us·ne·oid \'əsnē,öid\ *adj* [NL *Usnea* + E -*oid*] : resembling or related to the genus *Usnea*

us·nic acid \'əsnik-\ *n* [NL *Usnea* + E -*ic*] : a yellow crystalline antibiotic $C_{18}H_{16}O_7$ that is a heterocyclic keto phenol related to dibenzo-furan and that is obtained from various lichens (as of the genera *Usnea* and *Parmelia*)

us·pan·tec \ü'span,tek\ *n, pl* **uspantec** *or* **uspantecs** *usu cap* **1 a** : an Indian people of Uspantan in central Guatemala **b** : a member of such people **2** : a Mayan language of the Uspantec people

us·que ad coe·lum \'üskwäd'köiləm, ,əskwēad'seləm\ [NL] : up to the heavens : as far as heaven — referring to a rule in law that the owner of land owns the air space above it indefinitely upward ⟨the Swiss Government announced that it adopted the principle of territoriality *usque ad coelum* —*Times Hist. of the War*⟩

usque ad fi·lum aquae \-'fēlə'mä,kwī, 'fīlə'mä,kwē\ [ML, lit., as far as the thread of water] : as far as the middle of the stream — referring to a rule in law that when a boundary of a real property is formed by a nontidal stream, unless otherwise evident, the title extends to an imaginary line along the middle of the stream subject to the rights of the public

us·que·baugh *also* **us·que·bagh** \'oskwə,bả, -bô⟩ *or* **us·qua·bae** *or* **us·que·bae** \-bä\ *n* -s [Ir, lit., water of life, fr. IrGael *uisce beathadh*; *usquabae, usquebagh* fr. ScGael *uisge beatha* — more at WHISKEY] **1** *Irish & Scot* : WHISKEY **2 a** : a strong Irish cordial flavored with spice (as cinnamon or clove)

us·ta·ra·na *also* **ush·ta·ra·na** \'üshtərənə\ *n, pl* **ustarana** *or* **ustaranas** *usu cap* **1** : a Pathan people on the west side of the middle Indus in Pakistan **2** : a member of the Ustarana people

us·ti·la·gi·na·ce·ae \,əstə,lajə'nāsē,ē\ *n pl, cap* [NL, fr. *Ustilagin-, Ustilago*, type genus + -*aceae*] : a large and economically important family of smut fungi (order Ustilaginales) that produce chlamydospores which germinate to form a

---

several-celled promycelium either bearing terminal and lateral sporidia or forming an infection hypha — **us·ti·lag·i·na·ceous** \,∷∷-'nāshəs\ *adj*

us·ti·lag·i·na·les \,∷∷-'nā(,)lēz\ *n pl, cap* [NL, fr. *Ustilagin-, Ustilago* + -*ales*] : an order of parasitic basidiomycetous fungi that cause smuts of various plants and esp. of cereal grasses and have a complex life cycle which may include conidia production and in which sessile haploid basidiospores ultimately yield thick-walled dark-colored chlamydospores which typically replace the ovaries of an infected plant in a smutty mass and germinate with a meiosis to form a promycelium and begin a new basidial generation — compare UREDINALES, USTILAGO; see TILLETIACEAE

us·ti·lag·i·noi·dea \-'nöidēə\ *n, cap* [NL, fr. *Ustilagin-, Ustilago* + -*oidea*] : a genus of imperfect fungi (family *Dematiaceae*) forming conidia-bearing sclerotia which replace the grain in grasses and later produce ascigerous heads similar to those in *Claviceps* — see GREEN SMUT

us·ti·la·go \,əstə'lā(,)gō\ *n, cap* [NL *Ustilagin-, Ustilago*, fr. LL, a thistle, fr. L *ustus*, past part. of *urere* to burn; so called from its scorched appearance — more at EMBER] : a genus (the type of the family Ustilaginaceae) of smut fungi comprising the loose smuts — compare TILLETIA

us·tion \'əs(h)chən\ *n* -s [MF, fr. L *ustion-, ustio*, fr. *ustus* (past part. of *urere* to burn) + -*ion-, -io* -ion] **1** : the action of burning **2** *obs* : CAUTERIZATION

u-stirrup \'∷,∷-\ *n, cap U* : a stirrup for reinforced concrete bent in the form of a U

us·tu·la·tion \,əs(h)chə'lāshən\ *n* -s [ML *ustulation-, ustulatio*, fr. L *ustulatus* (past part. of *ustulare* to burn slightly, scorch, fr. assumed L *ustulus* slightly burned, fr. L *ustus*, past part. of *urere* to burn) + -*ion-, -io* -ion] **1** : the action of burning or searing **2** : an operation formerly used in chemistry of expelling one substance from another (as sulfur from an ore) by heat in a muffle

us·tu·li·na \,əs(h)chə'līnə\ *n, cap* [NL, fr. L *ustulare* to scorch + NL -*ina*] : a genus of fungi (family Xylariaceae) distinguished by stromata indefinite in form and often spreading and undulate and including a fungus (*U. zonata*) that causes a common root disease of tea

usu *abbr* usual; usually

¹usu·al \'yüzh(ə)wəl, -zhəl\ *adj* [ME, fr. MF or L; MF *usuel*, fr. LL *usualis* that is for use, usual, fr. L *usus* use, custom + -*alis* -al] **1** : such as accords with usage, custom, or habit : of the character or amount in common use : PREVALENT, ACCUSTOMED ⟨it is ~ to give way to the vehicle on one's right —Richard Joseph⟩ ⟨charged only half his ~ fee in view of their poverty⟩ **2** : commonly or ordinarily employed ⟨tried a short cut instead of following the ~ route⟩ ⟨sent someone strange instead of the ~ substitute⟩ **3** : such as occurs in ordinary practice or in the ordinary course of events : ORDINARY, COMMON ⟨the characters are better drawn than is ~ in romantic drama —A.H.Quinn⟩ ⟨all the facilities ~ to a military base — Amer. Guide Series: Nev.⟩

syn CUSTOMARY, HABITUAL, WONTED, ACCUSTOMED: USUAL describes that which happens frequently in the normal course of events and lacks any element of strangeness ⟨it is with the domestic artist as with artists at large — painters, architects, and others — the *usual* error lies in excess prompted by undue desire for admiration —Herbert Spencer⟩ ⟨it is *usual*, when visiting a new mother for the first time, to take a little present for the baby —Agnes M. Miall⟩ CUSTOMARY describes what characteristically accords with the practices or usages of a particular individual or community ⟨no idea how men behave when their *customary* way of life is disrupted and their familiar habits are disordered —Walter Lippmann⟩ ⟨settle down to his *customary* occupations or amusements —W.M.Thackeray⟩ ⟨the *customary* arts of the pleader, the appeal to the sympathies of the public, the introduction into court of weeping wife and children —G.L.Dickinson⟩ HABITUAL applies to what is settled by long repetition into a habit, followed or conformed to without thoughtful intent ⟨the appearance of self-possession or poise that comes from an *habitual* attention to what is graceful and becoming —D.C.Hodges⟩ ⟨then I stop ashamed, for I am talking *habitual* thoughts, and not adapting them to her ear, forgetting beauty in the pursuit of truth —W.B.Yeats⟩ WONTED may apply to that favored, sought, or purposefully cultivated ⟨his nerve steadied itself back into its *wonted* control —C.G.D.Roberts⟩ ⟨threw himself with his *wonted* zest into appreciating the thoughts and feelings of his artistic friends — R.F.Harrod⟩ ACCUSTOMED may refer to that long practiced, now habitual or customary, and noticed, looked for, or expected by others ⟨will be long before I recover my *accustomed* cheerfulness —W.S.Gilbert⟩ ⟨pausing to fling out an arm with some familiar *accustomed* gesture in a House of Commons — A.T.Quiller-Couch⟩

— as usual *adv* : in the accustomed or habitual way ⟨as usual he was late⟩

²usual \"\ *n* -s : something usual ⟨old tabbies would begin asking questions of me, like what my name was, where was my folks, and the ~ —Helen Eustis⟩ ⟨a reserve of available funds in case their customers should happen to require more than their ~ —J.A.Todd⟩

usual covenant *n* **1** : one of the covenants for title usu. inserted in a deed conveying land to secure to the grantee the benefit of the title purported to be conveyed **2** : a covenant by the lessor for quiet enjoyment so far as concerns his own acts and those of persons claiming under or through him, or one of the covenants by the lessee to pay rent, to pay taxes except those expressly payable by the lessor, to keep and deliver up the premises in repair, and to allow the lessor to enter and view the state of repair

usu·al·ly \'yüzh(ə)lē, -zh(ə)wəlē, -li *sometimes* -üz(ə)l-\ *adv* [ME, fr. *usual* + -*ly*] **1** : by or according to habit or custom : HABITUALLY, CUSTOMARILY ⟨a banqueting house is ~ secluded from the street —Lafcadio Hearn⟩ **2** : more often than not : most often : as a rule : ORDINARILY ⟨the dragonfly is ~ seen near small streams —*Word-List From South Carolina*⟩ ⟨delivered from more than ~ black thoughts —R.L.Stevenson⟩

usu·al·ness *n* -ES : the quality or state of being usual

usu·ary \'yüzhə,werē\ *n* -ES [LL *usuarius*, fr. L *usus* use + -*arius* -ary] *Roman & civil law* : the beneficiary of a use

usu·ca·pi·ent \,yüzə'kāpēənt, ,yüsə-\ *n* -s [L *usucapient-, usucapiens*, pres. part. of *usucapere* to usucapt] *Roman law* : one who claims title by usucaption — called also *usucaptor*

usu·ca·pio \-ē,ō\ *n* -s [L *usucapion-, usucapio*] : USUCAPTION

usu·ca·pi·on \-ē,än\ *also* **usu·cap·tion** \-'kapshən\ *n* -s [usucapion-, usucapio; *in sense 2* fr. *usucapere* to usucapt, alter. (influenced by *caption*) of *usucapion*] *Roman law* : a mode of acquiring title to property by uninterrupted possession of it for a definite period (as one year for movables or two for immovables) under a title acquired in good faith — **usu·ca·pi·on·ary** \-,∷∷,käpēə,nerē\ *adj*

usu·capt \-∷,kapt\ *vt* -ED/-ING/-s [L *usucaptus*, past part. of *usucapere* to usucapt, fr. *usu capere*, lit., to take by use, fr. *usu* (abl. sing. of *usus* use) + *capere* to take — more at HEAVE] : to claim or acquire the title to by usucaption

usu·capt·able *or* **usu·capt·ible** \,∷'kaptəbəl\ *adj* [usucapt + -*able* or -*ible*] : capable of being acquired by usucaption

usu·cap·tor \,∷'kaptə(r)\ *n* -s [usucapt + -*or*] : USUCAPIENT

¹usu·fruct \'yüzə,frəkt, 'yüsə-\ *n* -s [L *ususfructus*, fr. *usus* (et) *fructus* use and enjoyment, fr. *usus* use + *et* and + *fructus* (et) *fructus* use and enjoyment, fr. *usus* use + *et* and + *fructus* use and enjoyment, fr. *usus* use + et and + *fructus* use and enjoyment, fr. *usus* use + *et* and + *fructus*] **1** : the right of using and enjoying the fruits or profits of an estate or other thing belonging to another generally treated as a personal servitude ⟨the land is held to be the property of the tribe ... the individual only enjoys the ~ of a certain piece as long as he continues to cultivate it —G.B.Masefield⟩ ⟨an estate given in ~ — see IMPERFECT USUFRUCT, PERFECT USUFRUCT **2** : the right to use or enjoy something ⟨like the skeptical miser you lost the ~ of heaven —Denis Devlin⟩

²usufruct *vt* -ED/-ING/-s : to hold (property) in usufruct

¹usu·fruc·tu·ary \,∷'frəkchə,werē, -ksh-\ *n* -ES [LL *usufructuarius*, fr. *usufructus* usufruct + -*arius* -ary] **1** : one having the usufruct of property **2** : one having the use or enjoyment of something

²usufructuary \,∷∷∷∷\ *adj* : of or relating to a usufruct : having the character of or possessing in the character of a usufruct

usun \'ü'su̇n\ *n, pl* **usun** *or* **usuns** *usu cap* **:** a member of an ancient people of central Asia said to have been blond and blue-eyed

usu·ra \yü'su̇rə\ *n, pl* **usurae** [L] **:** interest paid on borrowed money

usu·rae usu·ra·rum \yü'su̇,rī,yüsə'rärəm, -rē...'rārəm\ *n pl* [NL, lit., interests on interests] *Roman law* **:** COMPOUND INTEREST

usure *n* -s [ME, fr. MF, fr. L *usura* use, interest, usury — more at USURY] *obs* **:** USURY

usu·rer \'yüzhərə(r)\ *n* -s [ME, fr. AF, fr. ML *usurarius*, fr. L *usura* interest, usury + *-arius* -ary] **:** one that lends money and takes interest for it **:** MONEYLENDER; *specif* **:** one that lends money at a rate of interest beyond that established by law or at an exorbitant rate

usu·ri·ous \yü'zhu̇rēəs\ *adj* [*usury* + *-ous*] **1 :** practicing usury **:** taking illegal or exorbitant interest for the use of money ⟨a ~ old pawnbroker⟩ **2 :** involving usury **:** of the character of usury ⟨a ~ rate of interest⟩ — **usu·ri·ous·ly** *adv* — **usu·ri·ous·ness** *n* -ES

usu·rous \'yüzhərəs\ *adj* [*usure* + *-ous*] *obs* **:** USURIOUS

usurp \yü's|ərp, -|ə̄p, -|əip *sometimes* -'z|\ *vb* -ED/-ING/-S [ME *usurpen*, fr. MF *usurper*, fr. L *usurpare* to take possession of by use, employ, usurp, fr. *usu* (abl. of *usus* use) + *rapere* to seize — more at USE, RAPID] *vt* **1 :** to seize and hold (as office, place, functions, powers, or rights) in possession by force or without right ⟨~ a throne⟩ ⟨by use of the treaty-making power, the president can ~ legislative powers that do not belong to him —J.J.Del Castillo⟩ **2 :** to occupy (as land or a city) by or as if by force **:** take possession of ⟨the bogs, like inland seas, ~ the earth —Sacheverell Sitwell⟩ **3 :** to employ wrongfully **:** use without authority **4 :** to take the place of by or as if by force **:** SUPPLANT ⟨gloom was beginning to ~ mirth —O.S.J. Gogarty⟩ **5** *archaic* **:** to appropriate (a word or expression) for use ~ *vi* **:** to act as a usurper: **a :** to seize or exercise authority or possession wrongfully **b :** to practice usurpation upon a person — used with *on* or *upon* **c :** to encroach or infringe upon a right or privilege — used with *on* or *upon* **syn** see APPROPRIATE

usur·pa·tion \,yüsə(r)'pāshən *sometimes* ,yüzə(-\ *n* -s [ME, fr. MF, fr. L *usurpation-*, *usurpatio* act of using, fr. *usurpatus* (past part. of *usurpare* to use) + *-ion-*, *-io* -ion] **1 :** the act of usurping **:** unauthorized arbitrary assumption and exercise of power esp. as infringing on others' rights ⟨dictatorial ~ of Congressional power —*Current History*⟩; *specif* **:** the illegal seizure of sovereign power — usu. used with *of* or sometimes with *on* or *upon* **2 :** an act or an instance of encroachment ⟨protect the executive branch from any legislative ~*s* —Sidney Hyman⟩ **3 :** the dispossession of the patron of a church by a stranger presenting to a vacant benefice a clerk who is thereupon admitted and instituted **4** *Roman law* **:** an interruption of use or possession (as in usucapion or in cohabitation)

usur·pa·tive \yü'sərpəd·iv *sometimes* -'zər-\ *adj* [LL *usurpativus* wrongly used, fr. L *usurpatus* (past part. of *usurpare* to usurp) + *-ivus* -ive] **:** of or constituting usurpation **:** USURPING ⟨the tyranny of some ~ minority —*Nineteenth Century & After*⟩

usur·pa·to·ry \-pə,tōrē\ *adj* [LL *usurpatorius*, fr. L *usurpatus* + *-orius* -ory] **:** USURPATIVE

usurp·a·ture \-pə,chu̇(ə)r, ,yüzər'pā,-\ *n* -s [L *usurpatus* + E *-ure*] **:** USURPATION

usurp·er \yü's|ərpər, -|ə̄pə(r, -|əipə(r *sometimes* -'z\ *n* -s [ME, fr. *usurpen* to usurp + *-er*] **:** one that usurps: as **a :** one that seizes illegally on sovereign power ⟨a ~ who should make himself master of the relics would be acknowledged king without dispute —J.G.Frazer⟩ **b :** one that infringes or encroaches upon the rights or property of another **c :** one that without proper authority assumes public office and performs official acts

usurp·ing·ly *adv* [*usurping* (pres. part. of *usurp*) + *-ly*] **:** by usurpation

usur·press \-prə̇s\ *n* -ES [*usurper* + *-ess*] *archaic* **:** a woman usurper

usu·ry \'yüzh(ə)rē, -ri\ *n* -ES [ME, fr. ML *usuria*, fr. L *usura* use, interest, usury (fr. *usus* — past part. of *uti* to use — + *-ura* -ure) + *-ia* -y — more at USE] **1** *archaic* **:** a premium or increase paid or stipulated for a loan of money or goods **:** INTEREST ⟨thou shalt not lend upon ~ to thy brother —Deut. 23:19 (AV)⟩ **2 :** the lending out of money with an interest charge for its use **:** the taking or practice of taking interest **3 :** an unconscionable or exorbitant rate or amount of interest; *specif* **:** interest in excess of a legal rate charged to a borrower for the use of money

usus \'yüsəs\ *n* -ES [L — more at USE] **1** *Roman law* **:** the act of making use of something **:** USE **2** *Roman law* **:** the personal and inalienable servitude of the usuary of making the bare use of real or personal property without enjoying its income, profit, or produce

USW *abbr* **1** ultrashort wave **2** *often not cap* [G *und so weiter*] and so forth

us·ward \'əswə(r)d\ *adv* [ME (*to*) *usward*, fr. *to* + *us* + *-ward*] **:** toward us ⟨bending ~ with memorial urns the most high Muses . . . weep —A.C.Swinburne⟩ ⟨the Lord . . . is long-suffering to ~ —2 Pet 3:9 (AV)⟩

ut \'ət, 'üt\ *n* -s [ME, lowest note of Guido's scale, fr. ML, fr. L, that, in order that, a word sung to this note in a medieval hymn to St. John the Baptist] **:** the musical tone *C* in the French fixed-do system replaced in solmization by *do*

ut *abbr* utility

UT *abbr* universal time

[1]**uta** \'yüd·ə\ *n* [NL, fr. E [1]*ute*] **1** *cap* **:** a large genus of iguanid lizards found from New Mexico to Lower California — compare SWIFT 1a **2** -s **:** any lizard of *Uta* or a related genus

[2]**uta** \'üd·ə\ *n* -s [fr. native name in Peru] **:** a leishmaniasis of the skin occurring in Peru **:** ESPUNDIA

[1]**utah** \'yü,tȯ, -tä\ *n, pl* **utah** *or* **utahs** *usu cap* **:** [1]UTE

[2]**utah** \"\ *adj, usu cap* [fr. *Utah*, state in the western U.S. fr. Ute *Yuta* Ute] **:** of or from the state of Utah ⟨*Utah* mines⟩ **:** of the kind or style prevalent in Utah **:** UTAHAN

[1]**utah·an** \-ȯən, -äən\ *adj, usu cap* [*Utah*, state in the western U.S. + E *-an*] **1 :** of, relating to, or characteristic of the state of Utah **2 :** of, relating to, or characteristic of the people of Utah

[2]**utahan** \"\ *also* **utahn** \-ȯn, -än\ *n* -s *cap* **:** a native or resident of the state of Utah

utah juniper *n, usu cap U* **:** a small tree (*Juniperus osteosperma*) of the midwestern and Rocky Mountain regions of No. America with gray fibrous shreddy bark and yellow-green leaves

utah·lite \-ȯ,līt, -ä,-\ *n* -s [fr. *Utah*, state + *-lite*] **:** VARISCITE

utas \'yü,tas\ *n* -ES [ME, contr. of *utaves*, fr. MF *huitaves*, pl. of *huitave* octave, fr. ML *octava* — more at OCTAVE] *archaic* **:** the octave of a church feast

ut dict \'ət'dikt\ *abbr* [L *ut dictum*] as directed

[1]**ute** \'yüt, *usu* -üd·+V; 'yüd·|ē, -üt|, |i\ *n, pl* **ute** *or* **utes** *usu cap* [Ute *Yuta*] **1 a :** a group of Shoshonean peoples of Colorado, Utah, and New Mexico **b :** a member of any of such peoples **2 :** the language of the Ute people

[2]**ute** \'yüt\ *n* -s [by shortening & alter.] **:** a truck adaptable to numerous uses **:** a utility truck ⟨while I'm loading the ~ —R.M.Daw⟩

uten·sil \yü'ten(t)sə̇l\ *n* -s [ME *utensele*, *utensil* collection of domestic articles, fr. MF *utensile*, fr. L *utensilia* utensils, fr. neut. pl. of *utensilis* useful, fr. *uti* to use — more at USE] **1 a :** an article useful or necessary in a household; *esp* **:** an implement, instrument, or vessel used in a kitchen ⟨household ~*s*⟩ **b :** an article (as a tool, implement, or vessel) serving a useful purpose ⟨providing his chums with the ~*s* of smoking —Arnold Bennett⟩ ⟨writing ~*s*⟩ ⟨farming ~*s*⟩ **2 :** a vessel, ornament, or furnishing belonging to a church; *esp* **:** one used in religious service ⟨consecration of the altar and its ~*s*⟩ **3 :** a person that is useful or is made use of ⟨a lackey and serf, the merest ~ of his master's will —Sir Winston Churchill⟩ **4** *archaic* **:** CHAMBER POT **syn** see IMPLEMENT

uter- *or* **utero-** *comb form* [L *uterus*] **1 :** uterus ⟨*uter*algia⟩ ⟨*uter*ectomy⟩ ⟨*utero*cele⟩ ⟨*utero*logy⟩ **2 :** uterine and ⟨*utero*abdominal⟩ ⟨*utero*ovarian⟩ ⟨*utero*vaginal⟩

uteri *pl of* UTERUS

uter·ine \'yüd·ərə̇n, -ütə-, -ə,rīn\ *adj* [ME, fr. LL *uterinus*, fr. L *uterus* + *-inus* -ine] **1 a :** born of the same mother but by a different father ⟨~ brothers⟩ **b** (1) **:** related by blood through the mother **:** having relationship traced entirely through females ⟨~ uncle⟩ ⟨~ kin⟩ (2) **:** based upon such relationship ⟨a ~ system of descent⟩ **2 :** suited for use in or on the uterus ⟨~ probe⟩ ⟨~ speculum⟩ **3 :** of, relating to, or situated in the uterus **:** affecting or taking place in the uterus ⟨~ diseases⟩

uterine artery *n* **:** an artery that is derived from the hypogastric artery and that following a course between the layers of the broad ligament reaches the uterus at the cervix and supplies the uterus and adjacent parts and during pregnancy the placenta — see UTERINE PLEXUS

uterine gland *n* **:** any of the branched tubular glands in the mucous membrane of the uterus

uterine milk *n* **:** a nutritive secretion that is produced by uterine glands esp. during early phases of mammalian gestation and that nourishes the young mammalian embryo prior to implantation

uterine plexus *n* **:** a plexus of veins tributary to the hypogastric vein by which blood is returned from the uterus — compare UTERINE ARTERY

uterine tube *n* **:** FALLOPIAN TUBE

utero·gestation \¦yüd·ə(,)rō+\ *n* [*uter-* + *gestation*] **1 :** the part of the gestation period that is passed within the uterus **2 :** the entire normal mammalian gestation period

uter·o·gram \'yüd·ərə,gram\ *n* [*uter-* + *-gram*] **:** an X-ray photograph of the uterine cavity made after the injection of a radiopaque substance

uter·og·ra·phy \,yüd·ə'rägrəfē\ *n* -ES [ISV *uter-* + *-graphy*] **:** the art, practice, or action of making uterograms

utero·ma·nia \,yüd·ərō'mānēə\ *n* [NL, fr. *uter-* + *mania*] **:** NYMPHOMANIA

uter·o·sal·pin·gog·ra·phy \,≈≈≈,sal,piŋ'gägrəfē\ *n* [ISV *uter-* + *salping-* + *-graphy*] **:** HYSTEROSALPINGOGRAPHY

uter·o·tub·al \¦≈≈≈¦tübəl, --¦tyü-\ *adj* [*uter-* + *tube* + *-al*] **:** of or relating to the uterus and Fallopian tubes ⟨a ~ insufflation of air in which air injected into the uterus is forced through the tubes⟩

uter·us \'yüd·ərəs, -ütər-\ *n, pl* **uteri** \-ə,rī\ [L, womb, belly; perh. akin to Gk *hoderos* belly, Skt *udara*] **1 :** an organ in female mammals for containing and usu. for nourishing the young during development previous to birth that consists of a greatly modified and enlarged section of an oviduct or of the two oviducts united, that has thick walls consisting of an external serous coat, a very thick muscular coat of nonstriated muscle, and a mucous coat containing numerous glands, and that during pregnancy undergoes remarkable increase in size and change in the condition of its walls **:** WOMB — compare CERVIX, FALLOPIAN TUBE, PLACENTA **2 a :** a section or diverticulum of an oviduct of any of various vertebrate or invertebrate animals other than the mammals that is enlarged or modified to serve as a place of development of the eggs or of the young **b :** the glandular part of the oviduct that secretes the eggshell

utes *pl of* UTE

ut·fang·thief *or* **ut·fang·thef** \'ətfəŋ,thēf\ *n* [OE *ūtfangenethēof* — more at OUTFANGTHIEF] **:** OUTFANGTHIEF

utia \ü'tēə\ *n* -s [Sp *hutía* — more at HUTIA] **:** HUTIA

uti·ca \'yüd·|ə̇kə, -üt|, |ēkə\ *adj, usu cap* [fr. *Utica*, manufacturing city of central New York] **:** of or from the city of Utica, N.Y. ⟨*Utica* knitting mills⟩ **:** of the kind or style prevalent in Utica

utick \'yütik\ *n* -s [prob. of imit. origin] *dial Eng* **:** WHINCHAT

util *or* **utile** \'yüd·ᵊl, -ütᵊl, -ü(,)til\ *n* -s [back-formation fr. [1]*utility*] **:** a hypothetical unit of utility

utile \"\ *adj* [MF, fr. L *utilis* — more at UTILITY] **:** having utility **:** productive of profit or advantage **:** PRACTICAL, USEFUL ⟨~ metals such as copper and tin —R.E.M.Wheeler⟩ ⟨ready-made and ~ substitutes —Parker Tyler⟩ ⟨a ~ agent⟩

[1]**util·i·tar·i·an** \(,)yü,tilə'terēən, -'ta(a)r-, -'tär-\ *n* -s [*utility* + *-arian*] **1 :** one that believes in, advocates, or follows the doctrine of utilitarianism ⟨the original ~*s* . . . believed that each individual was the best judge of his own welfare —E.S. Griffith⟩ **2 :** a person who has a utilitarian outlook

[2]**utilitarian** \(¦)≈¦≈≈¦≈≈≈\ *adj* **1 a :** of, relating to, or based upon the doctrine of utilitarianism ⟨on the ~ theory of obligation all duties are subordinate to one: maximize good consequences —O.A.Johnson⟩ ⟨first exponent of ~ political theory —*Times Lit. Supp.*⟩ **b :** believing in, advocating, or supporting the doctrine of utilitarianism ⟨~ philosophers⟩ **2 :** marked by a prevalence of the doctrines, principles, or views of utilitarianism ⟨love of truth for its own sake is . . . becoming rarer in this hasty ~ age —M.R.Cohen⟩ ⟨a ~ culture⟩ **3 a :** of or relating to utility **:** concerned with practical things or material interests ⟨humanistic vs. ~ education —J.E.Tobin⟩ ⟨a ~ point of view⟩ **b** (1) **:** characterized by or aiming at utility as distinguished from beauty or ornament ⟨her dark abundant hair was skewered into a ~ knob —Edna Ferber⟩ ⟨an essentially ~ and only accidentally aesthetic end —Stanley Morison⟩ ⟨~ steel tables⟩ (2) **:** evincing or characterized by a regard for utility of a lower kind **:** marked by a sordid spirit ⟨~ narrowness⟩ ⟨a ~ indifference to art⟩ **c :** preferring such utility ⟨a ~ people who are concerned more with getting on in the world and seducing women than with theology and a decent meal —Thomas Sugrue⟩

util·i·tar·i·an·ism \(,)≈,≈≈'terēə,nizəm, -ta(a)r-, -tär-\ *n* -s [[1]*utilitarian* + *-ism*] **1 a :** a doctrine that the useful is the good and that the determining consideration of right conduct should be the usefulness of its consequences; *specif* **:** a theory elaborated by Jeremy Bentham and James and John Stuart Mill that the aim of moral, social, and political action should be the largest possible balance of pleasure over pain or the greatest happiness of the greatest number — compare BENTHAMISM, HEDONISM 1 **b :** one of a group of primarily 20th century ethical theories based not or not only on a conception of pleasure as an intrinsic good but on other intrinsic goods (as beauty, harmony, or affection) ⟨enunciates the general principle of ~ in the formula that it is right to aim at whatever will promote the increasingly full realization of increasingly high values —C.D.Broad⟩ — called also *ideal utilitarianism* **2 :** utilitarian character, spirit, or quality ⟨the ~ of commercial industry —Bertrand Russell⟩ ⟨the forthright ~ of the superb . . . aqueduct —*Amer. Guide Series: N.Y.*⟩

[1]**util·i·ty** \yü'tiləd·ē, -ətē, -i\ *n* -ES [ME *utilite*, fr. MF *utilité*, fr. L *utilitat-*, *utilitas*, fr. *utilis* useful (fr. *uti* to use + *-ilis* -ile) + *-itat*, *-itas* -ity — more at USE] **1 :** the quality or state of being useful **:** fitness for some purpose **:** profitability to some desired end **:** SERVICEABLENESS, USEFULNESS ⟨demonstrated the ~ of hard coal as a domestic fuel —*Amer. Guide Series: Pa.*⟩ ⟨the design . . . is based on ~ rather than artistic embellishment —*Amer. Guide Series: Minn.*⟩ ⟨a road whose ~ was proved —*Amer. Guide Series: Ark.*⟩ — sometimes used with *of* ⟨more of ostentation than of real ~ in ships of this . . . burthen —Henry Fielding⟩ **2 :** something useful or designed primarily for use: as **a :** a useful factor or feature ⟨their views of the relative *utilities* of . . . democracy and communism —H.A.Steiner⟩ ⟨many of the admitted *utilities* and amenities from social services —J.A.Hobson⟩ **b :** a tool, device, or other implement; *esp* **:** one used as an adjunct to a more important machine **c :** a service provided by a public utility **d** *chiefly Austral* **:** a versatile motor vehicle **:** one having or adaptable to a number of uses (as both a truck and a car) **e :** a unit composed of one or more pieces of equipment usu. connected to or part of a structure and designed to provide a service (as heat, light, power, water, or sewage disposal) ⟨the price of the house included all *utilities*⟩ **3 :** the capacity to satisfy human wants or desires — see MARGINAL UTILITY, SUBJECTIVE UTILITY **4 a :** PUBLIC UTILITY 1 ⟨the *utility's* regular residential . . . customers —*N.Y. Times*⟩ ⟨effective public regulation of *utilities* —*Amer. Polit. Sci. Rev.*⟩ **b utilities** *pl* **:** stocks or bonds of utility companies ⟨*utilities* . . . displayed an easier tone —*Brookmire Investment Reports*⟩

[2]**utility** \"\ *adj* **1 :** capable of serving as a substitute in any of various roles or positions ⟨a ~ actor⟩ ⟨~ workers⟩ — compare UTILITY MAN **2 a :** kept for the production of an economically valued product (as meat, eggs, or milk) rather than for show or as pets ⟨~ livestock⟩ ⟨~ poultry⟩ ⟨~ sheep⟩ **b :** of, belonging to, or constituting an inferior grade of market cattle ⟨~ cows⟩ **c :** of, belonging to, or constituting a low grade of meat or other food products ⟨~ beef⟩ ⟨~ grades of lamb⟩ **3 :** serving primarily for utility rather than beauty **:** designed primarily for usefulness often at the expense of beauty, taste, or good quality **:** FUNCTIONAL, UTILITARIAN ⟨~ furniture⟩ ⟨~ clothes⟩ ⟨~ art⟩ ⟨~ goods⟩ **4 :** having or designed for a number of useful and practical purposes **:** adapted or adaptable for general use esp. in place of something specialized ⟨~ bag⟩ ⟨~ knife⟩ ⟨~ chair⟩ ⟨~ boat⟩ **5 :** of, relating to, or based upon philosophical utility ⟨~ calculus⟩ ⟨~ concepts⟩ **6 :** playing a usu. minor part incidental to the plot but often of considerable technical or expository usefulness ⟨a ~ character in a story or play⟩ **7 a :** of, relating to, or constituting a public utility ⟨~ companies⟩ ⟨~ regulation⟩ ⟨~ mergers⟩ ⟨a ~ meter⟩ **b :** of, relating to, or based on the prices of shares of public utility stocks ⟨the ~ average climbed 1.2 points in heavy trading⟩

utility man *n* **:** a man available for service in various positions: as **a :** an actor who performs minor parts and does odd jobs in a theater **b :** a member of a baseball team who plays various positions in the absence of regular players **c :** a kitchen helper or busboy on a ship — called also *galley man* **d :** JUMPER 1f **e :** one (as a handyman, houseman, or man-of-all-work) who is available for a variety of jobs

utility pole *n* **:** one of a series of poles usu. located at the side of a street or road and used to support wires and other equipment used by utilities (as telephone and electric companies) ⟨his car sideswiped a *utility pole* —*Springfield* (*Mass.*) *Union*⟩

utility principle *n* **:** GREATEST HAPPINESS PRINCIPLE

utility room *n* **:** a room (as in a dwelling) designed or used to house heating, laundry, or general maintenance equipment

uti·liz·able \'yüd·ᵊl,īzəbəl, -ütᵊl-, ,≈≈'≈≈≈\ *adj* **:** capable of being utilized ⟨a two-seated bomber . . . ~ for the launching of torpedoes —*New Republic*⟩

uti·li·za·tion \,yüd·ᵊlə̇'zāshən, -ütᵊl-, -ᵊl,ī'-\ *n* -s [F *utilisation*, fr. *utiliser* to utilize + *-ation*] **:** the action of utilizing or the state of being utilized ⟨the ~ of quotations from archives —C.H.Driver⟩ ⟨~ of glucose in the liver⟩ ⟨the disparity between the established drawing rights and their rate of ~ —R.F.Mikesell⟩

utilization coefficient *n* **:** the fraction of the total luminous flux from the lighting equipment of a room or office that falls upon areas (as desks or tables) where it is actually utilized

utilization factor *n* **:** the ratio of the maximum demand on a generator or generating station to the capacity of the generators

uti·lize \'yüd·ᵊl,īz, -ütᵊl-\ *vt* -ED/-ING/-S *see -ize in Explan Notes* [F *utiliser*, fr. *utile* useful (fr. L *utilis*) + *-iser* -ize — more at UTILITY] **:** to make useful **:** turn to profitable account or use **:** make use of **:** convert to use ⟨a cheese factory ~*s* milk from scores of farms —*Amer. Guide Series: Ark.*⟩ ⟨the ability of an organism to ~ oxygen —H.G.Armstrong⟩ ⟨~ the services of existing agencies —Frederick Graham⟩ **syn** see USE

uti·liz·er \-zə(r)\ *n* -s **:** one that utilizes

uti pos·si·de·tis \'ü,tē,päsə'dād·əs, 'yü,tī,päsə'dēd·ə̇s\ *n* [L, as you (now) possess (fr. the wording of the formula of interdiction)] **1 :** an interdict in Roman and civil law for deciding the right to the possession of immovables and preserving things in statu quo pending the decision — compare UTRUBI **2 :** a principle in international law that a conclusion or treaty of peace between belligerents vests in them respectively as absolute property the territory under their actual control and the things attached to it and the movables then in their possession except as otherwise stipulated (as by treaty)

ut·man khel \'u̇tmən'kā(ə)l\ *n, pl* **utman khel** *or* **utman khels** *usu cap U&K* **1 :** an independent Pathan people in the country southwest of the junction of the Swat and the Panjkora **2 :** a member of the Utman Khel

[1]**ut·most** \'ət,mōst *also chiefly Brit* -məst\ *adj* [ME, alter. (influenced by *most*) of *utmest*, fr. OE *ūtmest*, superl. adj. fr. *ūt* out (adv.) — more at OUT] **1 :** situated at the farthest point or extremity **:** most distant or remote in location **:** EXTREME ⟨the ~ point of the earth —John Hunt⟩ ⟨the ~ island⟩ **2 :** of the greatest or highest degree **:** of the largest quantity, number, or amount ⟨a matter calling for the ~ secrecy —E.S. McCartney⟩ ⟨living in the ~ misery —Angélica Mendoza⟩ ⟨separated with the ~ clearness of distinction —R.M.Weaver⟩ **3 :** final in order or time **:** LAST ⟨obtain the ~ penny of his debt —Maria Edgeworth⟩ **4** *archaic* **:** furthest extended **:** greatest in length, measure, or extent ⟨put forth your hand to the ~ stretch —Henry Felton⟩

[2]**utmost** \"\ *n* [ME, fr. OE *ūtmest*, fr. *ūtmest*, adj.] **1** *archaic* **:** something that is most outward, distant, or remote **:** the farthest limit, part, or district (as of an extent or area) ⟨a city . . . on the ~ of the ridge of a hill —George Sandys⟩ **2 a :** the most possible **:** the extreme limit **:** the highest attainable point or degree ⟨designed to provide the ~ in comfort —*advt*⟩ ⟨the modeling of individual figures was . . . the ~ they attempted —O. Elfrida Saunders⟩ — used esp. in the phrase *to the utmost* ⟨decentralizing authority . . . to the ~ —A.L. Nickerson⟩ ⟨taxing my resources to the ~ —E.S.McCartney⟩ **b :** the highest, greatest, or best of one's abilities, powers, and resources ⟨doing his ~ for a woman confided to his protection —Thomas De Quincey⟩ ⟨after society and culture have done their ~ —Ralph Linton⟩

uto-aztecan \'yü(,)tō+\ *n, usu cap U&A* [*Ute* + *-o* + *Aztec* + *-an*] **1 :** a language phylum comprising the Nahuatlan, Taracahitian, Piman, and Shoshonean families **2 a :** a people speaking a Uto-Aztecan language **b :** a member of such people

uto·pia \yü'tōpēə\ *n* -s [fr. *Utopia* an imaginary country with ideal laws and social conditions (fr. Gk *ou* not, no + *topos* place) described in the book *Utopia* (1516) by Sir Thomas More †1535 English statesman and author — more at TOPIC] **1 :** a place (as a region, island, country, or locality) that is imaginary and indefinitely remote **2** *often cap* **:** a place, state, or condition of ideal perfection esp. in laws, government, and social conditions ⟨that workers' ~ . . . in which there are more jobs than men seeking them —S.E.Harris⟩ — often used without article ⟨many were persuaded that independence would usher in ~ —A.E.Stevenson b. 1900⟩ **3 :** an impractical and usu. impossibly ideal scheme esp. for social improvement **4 :** a romance or other work describing a utopia ⟨a ~ written for girls —Emory Holloway⟩

[1]**uto·pi·an** \(')yü¦tōpēən\ *adj, often cap* [NL *utopianus*, fr. *Utopia*, Sir Thomas More's imaginary country + L *-anus* -an] **1 :** of, relating to, or having the characteristics of a utopia; *specif* **:** having impossibly ideal conditions (as in politics, economics, and social customs and organization) ⟨the dim ~ future —J.G.Colton⟩ ⟨a ~ commonwealth⟩ **2 :** proposing or advocating visionary and usu. impractically ideal schemes esp. for the perfection of social and political conditions ⟨~ idealists⟩ **3 :** involving or founded upon imaginary perfection **:** impossibly ideal **:** CHIMERICAL, VISIONARY ⟨those who react adversely to secrecy often propose ~ alternatives —R.A. Dahl⟩ ⟨branded as a ~ objective —M.K.Dziewanowski⟩ ⟨recognized the ~ nature of his hopes —C.S.Kilby⟩ **4 :** believing in, advocating, or having the characteristics of utopian socialism ⟨~ socialists⟩ ⟨~ doctrines⟩

[2]**utopian** \≈'≈≈≈\ *n* -s *sometimes cap* **1 :** a native or inhabitant of a utopia **2 a :** one that believes in the perfectibility of human society **:** IDEALIST, VISIONARY ⟨a consistent ~, expecting the future to realize her hopes —Van Wyck Brooks⟩ **b :** one that proposes or advocates plans usu. of an impractical kind for social improvement and esp. toward ideal social and political conditions ⟨the attempts of ~*s* to impose an impossible social order —N.S.Timasheff⟩ **c :** one that believes in or advocates utopian socialism

uto·pi·an·ism \-ēə,nizəm\ *n* -s **1 :** a utopian idea or theory ⟨mixes a good deal of hard sense with some curious ~*s* —*New Republic*⟩ **2** *often cap* **:** the body of ideas, views, or aims of a utopian **:** impracticable and usu. impossibly ideal schemes of human perfection or social improvement ⟨the somewhat impractical ~ . . . naturally found among socialists —Woodrow Wyatt⟩

uto·pi·an·ist \-ənə̇st\ *n* -s *often cap* [[1]*utopian* + *-ist*] **:** UTOPIAN 2

uto·pi·an·ize \-ēə,nīz\ *vt* -ED/-ING/-S *sometimes cap* **:** to render utopian **:** make a utopia of ⟨~ society⟩

utopian socialism *n, sometimes cap U&S* **:** socialism based on a belief that elimination of unemployment and the attainment of economic security by means of social ownership of the means of production could be achieved by a voluntary and

peaceful surrender of their holdings by propertied groups — compare MARXIAN SOCIALISM

uto·pism \'yüd·ə,pizəm\ *n* -s [*utop*ia + *-ism*] : UTOPIANISM 2 ⟨unrealistic ~ . . . dominated Italian ideals in the nineteenth and twentieth centuries —R.A.Hall b. 1911⟩

uto·pist \-,pəst\ *n* -s [*utop*ia + *-ist*] : UTOPIAN ⟨that world directorate of which ~s dream —Elmer Davis⟩

uto·pis·tic \¦==¦pistik\ *adj* : having a utopian quality or character ⟨a ~ dream of a federated Italy —R.A.Hall b. 1911⟩ ⟨such idealistic ~ . . . self-righteousness —Violet Paget⟩

u trap *n, cap U* : a U-shaped running trap

utra·quism \'yü·trə,kwizəm\ *n* -s *usu cap* [*utraqu*ist + *-ism*] : the doctrines or practices of the Calixtins

utra·quist \-,kwəst\ *n* -s *usu cap* [NL *utraquista*, fr. L *utraque* (abl. sing. fem. of *uterque* each of two, both, fr. *uter* which of two + *-que* generalizing particle akin to L *-que* and) (in the ML phrase *sub utraque specie* under each kind) + *-ista* -ist — more at WHETHER, SESQUI-] : CALIXTIN

utrecht \'yü·,trekt\ *adj, usu cap* [fr. *Utrecht*, city of western Netherlands] : of or from the city of Utrecht, Netherlands : of the kind or style prevalent in Utrecht

utrecht velvet *n, usu cap U* : a velvet consisting primarily of cotton and mohair and used for upholstery ⟨two large armchairs upholstered in shabby *Utrecht velvet* —Dorothy M. Richardson⟩

utri·cle \'yü·trəkəl, -rēk-\ *n* -s [L *utriculus* small bag, dim. of *uter* leather bag] : any of various small pouches or saccate parts of an animal or plant body: as **a** (1) : an air cell of a fucoid seaweed (2) : one of the bladders of a bladderwort (3) : a saclike terminal branch of an alga of the genus *Codium* **b** (1) : the part of the membranous labyrinth of the ear into which the semicircular canals open — compare SACCULE (2) : UTRICULUS b **c** : a small one-celled usu. indehiscent one-seeded or few-seeded achene (as that of a goosefoot or amaranth) with thin membranous pericarp — see FRUIT illustration

utricul- *or* **utriculo-** *comb form* [L *utriculus* small bag] : utricle ⟨*utriculo*plastic⟩ ⟨*utriculo*plasty⟩ ⟨*utriculi*ferous⟩ : utricular and ⟨*utriculo*saccular⟩

[1]**utric·u·lar** \(')yü·¦trikyələ(r)\ *adj* [L *utricul*us small bag + E *-ar*] **1 a** : of or relating to a utricle **b** : containing one or more utricles **2** : resembling a utricle — used esp. of such substances as sulfur and selenium when condensed from vapor and deposited on cold bodies in small globules filled with liquid

[2]**utricular** \"\ *adj* [L *utricul*us (dim. of *uterus* womb) + E *-ar*] : UTERINE 3 ⟨~ glands⟩

utric·u·lar·ia \yü·,trikyə'la(a)rēə\ *n* [NL, fr. L *utriculus* small bag + NL *-aria*] **1** *cap* : a large widely distributed genus of aquatic plants (family Lentibulariaceae) having saclike ascidia that serve as animal traps, floating stems with finely dissected leaves, and scapose often showy flowers with a very irregular spurred bilabiate corolla **2** -s : any plant of the genus *Utricularia*

utric·u·lar·i·a·ce·ae \=,==,la(a)rē'āsē,ē\ [NL, fr. *Utricularia* + *-aceae*] *syn of* LENTIBULARIACEAE

utric·u·lif·er·ous \(¦)yü·¦trikyə¦lif(ə)rəs\ *adj* [*utricul-* + *-iferous*] : bearing or producing utricles

utric·u·li·form \(')yü·¦trikyələ,fȯrm\ *adj* [ISV *utricul-* + *-iform*] **1** : resembling a utricle **2** : UTRICULOID

utric·u·loid \-yə,lȯid\ *adj* [*utricul-* + *-oid*] : resembling a bladder

utric·u·lo·saccular \yü·¦trikyə(,)lō+\ *adj* [*utricul-* + NL *saccul*us + E *-ar*] : of or relating to the utriculus and sacculus of the inner ear; *specif* : constituting a duct connecting the two

utric·u·lose \(')yü·¦trikyə,lōs\ *adj* [*utricul-* + *-ose*] : UTRICULOID

utric·u·lus \yü·'trikyələs\ *n, pl* **utricu·li** \-yə,lī\ [L, small bag; in sense b, partly fr. L *utriculus* small uterus — more at UTRICULAR] : UTRICLE: as **a** : the utricle of the ear **b** : a small blind pouch directed dorsally from the urethra into the prostate and regarded as a vestige of the fused lower ends of the Müllerian ducts and therefore the homologue in the male of the uterus and vagina in the female

ut·ru·bi \'ə·trə,bī\ *n* -s [L, in which of two places, fr. *uter* which of two + *ubi* where, in what place; fr. the wording of the interdict — more at WHETHER, UBIQUITY] : an interdict in Roman and civil law for deciding the right of possession of movables and preserving things in statu quo pending the decision — compare UTI POSSIDETIS

uts *pl of* UT

UTS *abbr* ultimate tensile strength

[1]**ut·ter** \'əd·ə(r), 'ətə-\ *adj* [ME, fr. OE *ūtera ūterra* outer, compar. adj. fr. *ūt* out, adv. — more at OUT] **1** : situated on the outside or extreme limit : remote and often most remote from the center ⟨through ~ and through middle darkness borne —John Milton⟩ **2** : carried to the utmost point or highest degree : ABSOLUTE, COMPLETE, ENTIRE, TOTAL ⟨a scene of ~ destruction —F.D.Roosevelt⟩ ⟨the ~ clarity of these winter dawns —Florence Jaques⟩ ⟨an ~ impossibility⟩ ⟨~ strangers⟩ **3** : extreme to the point of strangeness or abnormality : UNUSUAL

[2]**utter** \"\ *vb* -ED/-ING/-S [ME *uttren*, fr. *utter* outside, adv., fr. OE *ūtor*, compar. of *ūt* out] *vt* **1** : to place on the market : offer for sale or barter : dispose of in trade : SELL, VEND **2 a** : to send forth as a sound : give out in an audible voice : give vent or expression to : burst out with ⟨the meadowlark ~*ed* her strong but tender note —John Burroughs⟩ ⟨~*ed* a contemptuous laugh —Zane Grey⟩ ⟨~*ed* a wolf whistle —F.V.W.Mason⟩ **b** : to give utterance to : PRONOUNCE, SAY, SPEAK ⟨beyond all the words she could ~ —William Black⟩ ⟨if I could ~ his name on this occasion —Edmund Burke⟩ **c** : to give public expression to : express, describe, or report in words : speak of or about ⟨would ~ opinions on all passing affairs —R.W.Emerson⟩ ⟨visions of splendor which it is not lawful to ~ —W.L.Sullivan⟩ ⟨if one had to ~ any criticism of her book —Sean O'Faolain⟩ **3** *obs* : to make known or manifest (something unknown, secret, or hidden) : DISCLOSE, DIVULGE, REVEAL ⟨his tongue and pen ~*ed* heavenly mysteries —Izaak Walton⟩ **4** : to put (as notes or currency) into circulation; *specif* : to circulate (as a forged or counterfeit note) as if legal or genuine ⟨having possession of 745 counterfeit sovereigns, with intent to ~ them —*Numismatist*⟩ **5** : to put forth or out : pour, thrust, or shoot out : DISCHARGE, EJECT, EMIT, EXHALE ⟨fountains that ~*ed glittering* streams of water⟩ **6** : to express (oneself) in words ⟨meant . . . to ~ himself upon that theme —Nathaniel Hawthorne⟩ ~ *vi* **1** : to exercise the faculty of speech : make a statement or sound : SPEAK, TALK ⟨give me the liberty to know, to ~, and to argue freely —John Milton⟩ ⟨the parrot would never ~ —Osbert Sitwell⟩ **2** : to undergo utterance : become spoken ⟨words that will not ~ —James Hamilton⟩ **syn** see EXPRESS

ut·ter·able \-ərəbəl-\ *adj* : capable of being uttered (as in words or statements)

[1]**ut·ter·ance** \'əd·ərən(t)s, 'ətər- *sometimes* 'ə·trən-\ *n* -s [ME *utteraunce*, *uttraunce*, modif. (influenced by [1]*utter*) of MF *outrance* — more at OUTRANCE] : an extreme degree : the last extremity : BITTER END ⟨come, Fate, . . . champion me to th' ~ —Shak.⟩

[2]**utterance** \"\ *n* -s [ME, fr. *utteren* to utter + *-ance*] **1** *obs* : the sale or disposal (as of goods or commodities) to the public **2** : something that is uttered: **a** : an oral or written statement : a stated or published expression : an articulated sound ⟨seditious oral ~*s* —J.L.O'Brian⟩ ⟨delivers some gemlike ~*s* —Anthony Quinton⟩ ⟨the speech will rank as one of his greater ~*s* —*Manchester Guardian Weekly*⟩ **b** : a continuous stretch of speech activity esp. when regarded as grammatically independent of preceding and following stretches whether by the same or another speaker ⟨a sequence of ~*s* by the same speaker is often called a discourse⟩ **3** : the action of uttering with the voice : vocal expression : ARTICULATION, SPEECH ⟨at length gave ~ to these words —John Milton⟩ ⟨gave ~ to a yell —Rachel Henning⟩ **4 a** : the faculty or power of speech ⟨one who had no gift of ~ —John Buchan⟩ **b** : the style or manner of speaking ⟨a model . . . of beautiful English ~ —George Sampson⟩ ⟨a tall thin man with . . . a sententious ~ —Donn Byrne⟩

utter barrister *n* : a barrister of the outer bar — compare BENCHER b

ut·ter·er \'əd·ərə(r), 'ətər-\ *n* -s : one that utters ⟨~*s* of unknown tongues —H.H.Johnston⟩ ⟨the ~ of a bad note was put to death —Charles Dickens⟩

ut·ter·less \'==ləs\ *adj* [[2]*utter* + *-less*] : incapable of being uttered ⟨pangs of ~ desire —Christina Rossetti⟩ ⟨~ dishonor⟩

ut·ter·ly *adv* [ME, fr. [1]*utter* + *-ly*] : in an utter manner : to an absolute or extreme degree : to the full extent : ABSOLUTELY, ALTOGETHER, ENTIRELY, FULLY, THOROUGHLY, TOTALLY ⟨Congress defeated ~ the administration civil rights program —T.K.Finletter⟩ ⟨this whole harmony . . . is ~ destroyed —P.E.James⟩ ⟨an ~ fantastic notion⟩

[1]**ut·ter·most** \'əd·ə(r),mōst, 'ətə- *also chiefly Brit* -,məst\ *adj* [ME, alter. (influenced by *most*) of *uttermest*, fr. [1]*utter* + *-mest* (as in *utmest* utmost)] **1** : farthest out : most remote : OUTERMOST ⟨to the ~ parts of the earth —Kemp Malone⟩ ⟨from the extreme west to the ~ east —Douglas Carruthers⟩ **2** : being in the farthest, greatest, or highest degree : EXTREME, UTMOST 2 ⟨she had the ~ confidence in the rogue —O.S.J.Gogarty⟩ ⟨reach the ~ peak of position —Irving Stone⟩ ⟨in the ~ distress⟩ **3** *archaic* : LAST — used chiefly in the phrase *the uttermost farthing*

[2]**uttermost** \"\ *n* [ME, fr. [1]*uttermost*] : UTMOST ⟨done her ~ to encourage him —Edith Sitwell⟩ ⟨to the ~ of our capacity —H.S.Truman⟩

ut·ter·ness *n* -ES : the quality or state of being utter : ABSOLUTENESS, COMPLETENESS

utu \'ü,tü\ *n* -s [Maori] : satisfaction for injuries received (as by retaliation in kind or by payment) in Maori law and custom

u-tube \'=,=\ *n, cap U* : a U-shaped tube

u-turn \'=¦=\ *n, cap U* **1** : a turn resembling the letter U; *specif* : one made by a vehicle traveling along one side of a way by crossing the lane of oncoming traffic and turning into and proceeding along a lane on the other side of the way in a direction exactly opposite to the direction of movement at the start of the turn **2** : something held to resemble a U-turn (as a reversal of policy) ⟨stated that the Administration is making an economic *U-turn* —T.R. Ybarra⟩

U-tube

UV *abbr* **1** ultraviolet **2** under voltage

uva \'yüvə\ *n, pl* **uvas** \-əz\ *or* **uvae** \-,vē\ [NL, fr. L, grape, bunch of grapes — more at UVULA] : a pulpy indehiscent fruit (as a grape) with a central placenta

uva grass \'üvə-\ *n* [AmerSp, fr. Tupi *ubá*, *uibá*] : an ornamental tropical American grass (*Gynerium sagittatum*) reaching a height of 30 feet or more and having huge pale tan or cream-colored panicles resembling plumes — called also *cana brava*

uva·la \'üvələ\ *n* -s [Serbo-Croatian] : a large elongate sinkhole resulting from enlargement and coalescence of a linear group of small sinkholes

u-valley \'=,==\ *n, cap U* : a valley of U-shaped cross section such as results from erosion by a valley glacier

uvan·ite \'yüvə,nīt\ *n* -s [*u*ranium + *van*adium + *-ite*] : a hydrous uranium vanadate $U_2V_6O_{21}.15H_2O$ occurring as a brownish yellow powder

uva·rov·ite *also* **uwa·rowite** *or* **ouva·rovite** \ü'värə,vīt, yü-\ *n* -s [G *uwarowit*, fr. Count Sergei S. *Uvarov* †1855 Russ. statesman + G *-it* -ite] : an emerald green calcium-chromium garnet $Ca_3Cr_2(SiO_4)_3$

[1]**uva-ur·si** \¦yüvə'ərsē\ [NL, fr. *uva ursi* bearberry] *syn of* ARCTOSTAPHYLOS

[2]**uva-ursi** \"\ *n* -s [NL *uva ursi*, lit. bear's grape] : BEARBERRY

[1]**uvea** \'yüvēə\ *n* -s [ML, fr. L *uva* grape, bunch of grapes — more at UVULA] **1** : the posterior pigmented layer of the iris of the eye **2** : the portion of the eye composed of the iris and ciliary body together with the choroid coat

[2]**uvea** \ü'vāə\ *n* -s *usu cap* [fr. *Uvea*, main island of Wallis islands] : the Polynesian language of the Wallis islands

uve·al \'yüvēəl\ *adj* [[1]*uvea* + *-al*] : of, relating to, or affecting the uvea : constituting or consisting of the uvea ⟨~ layer⟩ ⟨~ tract⟩

[1]**uve·an** \ü'vāən\ *adj, usu cap* [*Uvea*, main island of the Wallis islands + E *-an*] **1** : of or relating to Uvea Island **2** : of or relating to the people of Uvea Island **3** : of or relating to Uvea

[2]**uvean** \"\ *n* -s *usu cap* **1** : a Polynesian of Uvea Island **2** : [2]UVEA

uve·i·tis \,yüvē'īd·əs\ *n* -ES [NL, fr. [1]*uvea* + *-itis*] : inflammation of the uvea of the eye

uveo·parotid fever \¦yüvē(,)ō+. . .-\ *n* [[1]*uvea* + *-o-* + *parotid*] : chronic inflammation of the parotid gland and uvea marked by low-grade fever, lassitude, and bilateral iridocyclitis and often associated with sarcoidosis or other conditions

uveo·parotitis \"+\ *n* -ES [NL, fr. [1]*uvea* + *parot*is + *-itis*] : UVEOPAROTID FEVER

uveous *adj* [[1]*uvea* + *-ous*] *obs* : UVEAL

uvi·ol glass \'yüvē,ȯl-, -,ōl-\ *n* [fr. *Uviol*, a trademark] : a glass particularly transparent to ultraviolet rays

uvit·ic acid \(')yü¦vid·ik-\ *n* [L *uva* grape + ISV *-itic*; fr. its being producible from tartaric acid] : a crystalline acid CH_3-$C_6H_3(COOH)_2$ obtained esp. by partial oxidation of mesitylene; 5-methyl-isophthalic acid

uvi·ton·ic acid \¦yüvə¦tänik-\ *n* [*uvit-* (as in *uvitic*) + *-onic*] : a crystalline acid $CH_3C_5H_2N(COOH)_2$ obtained by the action of ammonia on pyruvic acid; 6-methyl-2, 4-pyridine-dicarboxylic acid

uvu·la \'yüvyələ\ *n, pl* **uvulas** \-ləz\ *or* **uvu·lae** \-yə,lē\ [ML, dim. of L *uva* grape, bunch of grapes, uvula; akin to Gk *oa* (Ionic *oiē*) service tree, OE *īw* yew — more at YEW] **1** : the pendent fleshy lobe in the middle of the posterior border of the soft palate **2** : an elevation of the mucous membrane lining the lower anterior part of the bladder **3** : a lobe of the vermiform process of the lower surface of the cerebellum located in front of the pyramid

[1]**uvu·lar** \-lə(r)\ *adj* [NL *uvularis*, fr. ML *uvula* + L *-aris* -ar] : of or relating to the uvula ⟨~ glands⟩; *specif* : produced with the aid of the uvula — **uvu·lar·ly** *adv*

[2]**uvular** \"\ *n* -s : a uvular sound

uvu·lar·ia \,yüvyə'la(a)rēə\ *n* [NL, fr. *uvula* + *-aria*] **1** *cap* : a genus of No. American herbs (family Liliaceae) having erect stems, sessile or perfoliate leaves, and yellowish drooping bell-shaped flowers **2** -s : any plant of the genus *Uvularia*

uvular r *n* : a sound formed by trilling the uvula against the back of the tongue or by friction of the breath between the back of the tongue and the uvula or the velum

UW *abbr* underwriter

uwarowite *var of* UVAROVITE

ux *abbr* [L *uxor*] wife

UXB *abbr* unexploded bomb

ux·o·ri·al \¦ək¦s|ōrēəl, ¦əg¦z|, |ȯr-\ *adj* [L *uxori*us uxorial + E *-al* — more at UXORIOUS] : of, relating to, or having the characteristics of a wife

[1]**ux·or·i·cide** \,ək's|ōrə,sīd, ,əg'z|, |ȯr-\ *n* -s [ML *uxoricidium*, fr. L *uxor* wife + *-i-* + *-cidium* -cide (killing) — more at UXORIOUS] : the murder of a wife by her husband

[2]**uxoricide** \"\ *n* -s [L *uxor* + *-i-* + E *-cide* (killer)] : one that murders his wife

ux·ori·local \¦ək¦sōrə+\ *adj* [L *uxor* + *-i-* + E *local*] : MATRILOCAL ⟨the Yao are matrilineal and predominantly ~ —*African Abstracts*⟩ — contrasted with *virilocal*

ux·o·ri·ous \¦ək¦sōrēəs, ¦əg¦z|, |ȯr-\ *adj* [L *uxorius* uxorial, uxorious, fr. *uxor* wife; prob. akin to Skt *ukṣati* he sprinkles — more at HUMOR] : characterized by doting and usu. excessive fondness for and often submission to a wife ⟨an ~ husband⟩

ux·o·ri·ous·ly *adv* : in an uxorious manner : to an uxorious degree

ux·o·ri·ous·ness *n* -ES : the quality or state of being uxorious ⟨a prince whose manhood was . . . molten down in mere ~ —Alfred Tennyson⟩

uza·ra root \ü'zärə-\ *or* **u·sa·ra root** \ü'särə-\ *n* [origin unknown] : the root of a So. African woody herb (*Dicoma anomala*) of the family Compositae that yields uzarin and that is dried and used by the natives as a masticatory for dysentery

uzar·i·gen·in \ü,zärə'jenən\ *n* -s [*uzarin* + *-genin*] : a crystalline steroid lactone $C_{23}H_{34}O_4$ that is the aglucon of uzarin and is structurally similar to digitoxigenin

uza·rin \ü'zärən\ *n* -s [ISV *uzara* + *-in*] : a crystalline glucoside $C_{35}H_{54}O_{14}$ that constitutes the active principle of uzara root and is used as an arrow poison by some southeast African peoples

uz·bek \'u̇z,bek, 'əz-\ *or* **uz·beg** \-eg\ *also* **uz·bak** \-bak\ *or* **us·bek** \'u̇s,bek, 'əs-\ *or* **us·beg** \-eg\ *n, pl* **uzbek** *or* **uzbeks** *or* **uzbeg** *or* **uzbegs** *usu cap* **1 a** : a Turkic people of Turkistan and esp. of the Uzbek Republic of the U.S.S.R. that are Sunnite Muslims and are characterized chiefly by agricultural pursuits and life in towns rather than being nomads **b** : a member of such people **2** : the Turkic language of the Uzbek people

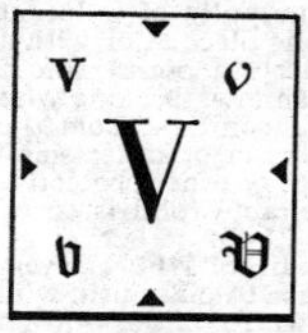

[1]v \'vē\ *n, pl* **v's** *or* **vs** \'vēz\ *often cap, often attrib* **1 a :** the 22d letter of the English alphabet **b :** an instance of this letter printed, written, or otherwise represented **c :** a speech counterpart of orthographic *v* (as *v* in *vivid, hive,* or Spanish *vivo*) **2 :** FIVE — see NUMBER table **3 :** a printer's type, a stamp, or some other instrument for reproducing the letter *v* **4 :** someone or something arbitrarily or conveniently designated *v* esp. as the 21st or when j is used for the 10th the 22d in order or class **5 :** something having the shape of the letter V: as **a :** a V-shaped neck of a dress, sweater, or blouse **b :** a rib, guiding strip, or groove having sloping sides like a V ⟨the *V's* on the bed of a turning lathe on which the carriage slides⟩

[2]**v** *abbr, often cap* **1** vacuum tube **2** vagabond **3** value **4** valve **5** van **6** vapor **7** variable; variation **8** vector **9** vein **10** velocity **11** venerable **12** vent **13** ventilator **14** ventral **15** Ventzke **16** verb **17** verse **18** versicle **19** version **20** verso **21** versus **22** [L *verte*] turn over **23** vertex **24** vertical **25** very **26** vicar **27** vice **28** vicinal **29** victory **30** [L] vide **31** village **32** violin **33** virgin **34** viscosity **35** viscount **36** visibility **37** vision **38** visual acuity **39** vocative **40** voice **41** volt; voltage **42** [It *volti*] turn **43** voltmeter **44** volume **45** volunteer **46** von **47** vowel

[3]**v** *symbol, cap* **1** vanadium **2** potential difference

va *abbr* **1** variance **2** viola

VA *abbr* **1** *often not cap* verb active **2** *often not cap* verbal adjective **3** vicar apostolic **4** vice admiral **5** visual aid **6** [L *vixit annas*] he (she) lived . . . years **7** *often not cap* volt-ampere

va·ad \'vä,äd, ‚=ˈ=\ *n, pl* **vaa·dim** \,vä,ä'dēm, ‚=‚=ˈ=\ [LHeb *wa'ad*] **:** an authorized Jewish representative body that serves in an advisory or supervisory capacity for activities (as the production and sale of kosher food products) of the Jewish community

vaal \'väl\ *n* -s [Afrik, lit., fallow, fr. MD *vale*; akin to OHG *falo* pale, fallow — more at FALLOW] **:** RHEBOK

vaal·haai \'väl,hī\ *n* -s [Afrik, fr. *Vaal*, river in So. Africa + Afrik *haai* shark, fr. D] *southern Africa* **:** TOPE

vac \'vak\ *n* -s [by shortening] *Brit* **:** VACATION 3c

vac *abbr* **1** vacant **2** vacation **3** vacuum

va·cance \'vākən(t)s\ *n* -s [MF, fr. ML *vacantia*] *Scot* **:** VACATION

va·can·cy \'vākənsē, -si\ *n* -ES [ML *vacantia*, fr. L *vacant-, vacans* (pres. part. of *vacare* to be empty, be free) + *-ia* -y] **1** *archaic* **:** time of freedom from occupation **:** an interval of leisure **:** LEISURE, VACATION ⟨those little *vacancies* from toil are sweet —John Dryden⟩ **2 :** the state or fact of being free from occupation or from mental preoccupation **:** physical or mental inactivity or relaxation **:** IDLENESS **3 a :** a vacating of an office, post, or piece of property **b :** the state of such when vacated or vacant **c :** the time such office or property is vacant ⟨the death of the incumbent has caused a ~⟩ ⟨in case of ~ of the property⟩ **4 :** a vacant office, post, or tenancy ⟨three *vacancies* in this apartment house⟩ ⟨the president shall have power to fill up all *vacancies* that may happen during the recess of the senate —*U.S. Constitution*⟩ **5 :** empty space **:** VOID, VACUUM, BLANK **6 :** the state of being vacant **:** BARRENNESS, LONELINESS, VACUITY ⟨a ~ of sound after the train had left —J.P.Marquand⟩ **7 :** a defect existing in a crystal due to the absence of an atom or ion from a normal lattice position — called also *hole*

vacancy clause *or* **vacancy permit** *n* **:** a special endorsement in property insurance permitting premises to be vacant or unoccupied beyond the period stipulated in the original contract and insured during the extension period either for the full or a reduced amount

va·cant \'vākənt\ *adj* [ME, fr. OF, fr. L *vacant-, vacans*, pres. part. of *vacare* to be empty, be free; perh. akin to L *vanus* empty, vain — more at WANE] **1 :** not filled or occupied by an incumbent, possessor, or officer ⟨appointed to the ~ office⟩ **2 :** being without content or occupant ⟨a ~ seat in a bus⟩ ⟨a ~ room⟩ **3 :** DEVOID, DESTITUTE — usu. used with *of* ⟨the past, the future, majesty, love . . . you are ~ of them —Walt Whitman⟩ **4 :** free from activity ⟨amid the stillness of the ~ night —William Cowper⟩ **:** free from work or occupation **:** UNOCCUPIED ⟨obliged to spend his ~ hours in a comfortless hotel —Jane Austen⟩ **5 :** characterized by absence of thought and reflection: as **a :** STUPID, FOOLISH, SILLY, DULL **b :** EXPRESSIONLESS ⟨she would forget altogether what she was about, and would sit down with a peculiarly ~ look on her face —O. E.Rölvaag⟩ ⟨~ serenity of a . . . marble athlete —Edith Wharton⟩ **c :** marked by a respite from coherent purposive thought and reflection or by freedom from care ⟨when on my couch I lie in ~ or in pensive mood —William Wordsworth⟩ **6 :** of, relating to, or being premises which are not lived in and from which the furniture and fixtures have been removed — compare UNOCCUPIED **7 a :** not occupied or put to use ⟨~ land⟩ **b :** having no heir or claimant **:** ABANDONED ⟨a ~ estate⟩ **c :** not granted away — used esp. of state lands **syn** see EMPTY

va·can·tia \vā'kanshēə\ *or* **vacantia bo·na** \-'bōnə\ *n pl but sing or pl in constr* [*vacantia* short for *vacantia bona; vacantia bona* fr. NL, lit., vacant goods] **:** goods without an owner or claimant; *specif* **:** the inheritance of a deceased person when there is no one able and willing to enter

va·cant·ly *adv* **:** in a vacant manner **:** IDLY, INANELY

va·cant·ness *n* -ES **:** the quality or state of being vacant

va·cat·able *pronunc at* VACATE + əbəl\ *adj* **:** that can be vacated

va·cate \'vā,kāt, ‚=ˈ=, *usu* -kād.+V; *chiefly Brit* və'k-\ *vb* -ED/-ING/-S [L *vacatus*, past part. of *vacare* to be empty, be free] *vt* **1 :** to make of no authority or validity **:** make void **:** ANNUL ⟨~ a charter⟩ **2 :** to make useless, ineffectual, or without force or significance ⟨he ~*s* my revenge —John Dryden⟩ **3 :** to make vacant (as an office, post, or house) **:** deprive of an incumbent or occupant; *also* **:** to give up the incumbency or occupancy of ⟨the throne was *vacated* by the exile of the royal family⟩ ⟨*vacated* his seat in Congress by resignation⟩ **4 :** to make free (as from care) ⟨its problems, indeed, *vacated* my mind of her —Edgar Saltus⟩ **~** *vi* **1 :** to vacate an office, post, or tenancy **2 :** to give one's time **:** devote oneself **3** *slang* **a :** to go away **:** LEAVE **b :** to take a vacation

[1]**va·ca·tion** \vā'kāshən, və'k-\ *n* -s *often attrib* [ME *vacacioun*, fr. MF *vacation*, fr. L *vacation-, vacatio* freedom, exemption, immunity, fr. *vacatus* (past part. of *vacare*) + *-ion-, -io* -ion — more at VACANT] **1 :** a respite or a time of respite from something **:** INTERMISSION, REST ⟨on a ~ from acting on the screen, she appeared as a singing and dancing star in . . . vaudeville —*Current Biog.*⟩ **2** *obs* **a :** freedom from work or cares **:** LEISURE **b :** time free for something else; *specif* **:** time for contemplation **3 a :** a scheduled period during which activity or work is suspended **:** RECESS **b :** a period of exemption from work granted to each employee of an industry or business **:** a leave of absence for rest and relaxation ⟨students hired to fill in for workers on ~⟩ ⟨allowed to take two weeks of ~ with pay annually⟩ **c :** an intermission in the regular teaching and studying at an educational institution (as between terms) **d :** intermission of judicial proceedings **:** the interval between the end of one term and the beginning of the next **:** NONTERM, RECESS **4 :** a period spent away from home or business in travel or recreation **:** HOLIDAYS ⟨had a restful ~ at the beach⟩ **5 :** an act or an instance of vacating (as an office, post, or house) ⟨the chief of staff, while holding office as such, shall have the grade of general, without ~ of his permanent grade in the Air Force —*U.S. Code*⟩ **6 :** the act of vacating an order or legal proceeding **:** ANNULMENT

[2]**vacation** \"\ *vi* **vacationed; vacationed; vacationing** \-sh(ə)niŋ\ **vacations :** to take a vacation **:** pass one's vacation ⟨~*ed* in Europe last summer⟩

vacation church school *or* **vacation bible school** *n, usu cap V&C&B&S* **:** a weekday program of Christian education for children featuring religious study courses, arts and crafts, and recreation conducted by local Protestant Christian churches for one or more weeks during the summer vacation — called also *Daily Vacation Bible School*

va·ca·tion·er \-sh(ə)nə(r)\ *n* -s **:** VACATIONIST

va·ca·tion·ist \-nəst\ *n* -s **:** a person taking a vacation; *esp* **:** one traveling for pleasure or passing a vacation at a summer resort

vacationland \=ˈ==‚=\ *n* **:** an area with recreational attractions and facilities for vacationists

va·ca·tion·less \-ləs\ *adj* **:** having no vacation

va·ca·tur \va'kād.ər\ *n* -s [NL, it is vacated, 3d pers. pres. indic. pass. of *vacare* to be empty] **:** an order of court vacating a legal proceeding

vac·car·ia \va'ka(a)rēə\ *n, cap* [NL, fr. ML, cow pasture; fr. its value as fodder] *in some classifications* **:** a small genus of Eurasian annual herbs (family Caryophyllaceae) having opposite acute leaves and rather small red or pink flowers in terminal cymes followed by 5-angled much inflated capsules and including the genus *Saponaria*

vac·ca·ry \'vakərē\ *n* -ES [ME *vaccarie*, fr. ML *vaccaria*, fr. L *vacca* cow + *-aria* -ary — more at VACCINE] **:** a place where cows or cattle are kept **:** cow pasture **:** dairy farm

vac·cen·ic acid \(')vak¦senik-\ *n* [L *vacca* cow + E *-en* (in *octadecenoic*) + *-ic*] **:** a crystalline unsaturated acid C_6H_{13}-$CH{=}CH(CH_2)_9COOH$ that is isomeric with elaidic acid and oleic acid and that is obtained esp. in the trans form from beef fat and other animal fats and in the cis form from bacterial fats; 11-octadecenoic acid

vac·ci·nal \'vaksənəl\ *adj* [ISV [2]*vaccine* + *-al*; orig. formed in F] **:** of or relating to vaccine or vaccination ⟨~ control of a disease⟩

[1]**vac·ci·nate** \'vaksə,nā|t, *usu* |d.+V\ *vb* -ED/-ING/-S [back-formation fr. *vaccination*] *vt* **1 :** to inoculate (a person) with cowpox virus in order to produce immunity to smallpox **2 :** to administer a vaccine to (a person or animal) usu. by injection **~** *vi* **:** to perform or practice vaccination

[2]**vac·ci·nate** \", -,nə|\ *n* -s [[2]*vaccine* + *-ate*] **:** a vaccinated individual

vac·ci·na·tion \,==ˈnāshən\ *n* -s [F, fr. *vaccine*, adj. (fr. NL *vaccinus*) + *-ation*] **:** the introduction into man or domestic animals of microorganisms that have previously been treated to make them harmless for the purpose of inducing the development of immunity ⟨oral ~⟩ ⟨~ against smallpox⟩ ⟨~ for whooping cough⟩

vac·ci·na·tor \'==,nād.ə(r), -ātə-\ *n* -s [ISV *vaccine* + *-ator*] **:** one that vaccinates

[1]**vac·cine** \(')vak¦sēn *sometimes* 'vaksən\ *adj* [L *vaccinus* of or from cows, fr. *vacca* cow + *-inus* -ine; akin to Skt *vaśa* cow] **1 :** of, relating to, or derived from cows; *esp* **:** derived from cows infected with cowpox or inoculated with its virus ⟨~ lymph⟩ **2** [NL *vaccinus*, fr. L] **:** of or relating to vaccinia or vaccination ⟨a ~ pustule⟩

[2]**vaccine** \"\ *n* -s **1 :** matter or a preparation containing the virus of cowpox or vaccinia in a form used for vaccination **2 :** a preparation of killed microorganisms, living attenuated organisms, or living fully virulent organisms that is administered to produce or artificially increase immunity to a particular disease — compare ANTIGEN, SERUM

vac·cin·ia \vak'sinēə\ *n* -s *often attrib* [NL, fr. *vaccinus* + *-ia*] **:** COWPOX; *esp* **:** the mild systemic reaction of a human being to cowpox virus constituting the take that signals immunization following vaccination against smallpox

vac·cin·i·a·ce·ae \(,)vak,sinē'āsē,ē\ *n pl, cap* [NL, fr. *Vaccinium* + *-aceae*] *in some classifications* **:** a family of widely distributed shrubs and trees (order Ericales) including among its genera *Vaccinium, Gaylussacia,* and *Oxycoccus,* comprising the huckleberries, blueberries, and cranberries, and set off from the Ericaceae chiefly on the basis of the inferior ovary which forms in fruit a many-seeded berry or drupe — **vac·cin·i·a·ceous** \(¦)=¦==ˈāshəs\ *adj*

vac·cin·i·al \(')vak¦sinēəl\ *adj* **:** of, relating to, or characteristic of vaccinia

vac·cin·iform \(')vak¦sinə,fȯrm\ *adj* **:** resembling vaccinia

vac·cin·i·um \vak'sinēəm\ *n* [NL, fr. L, blueberry, whortleberry, prob. of non-IE origin; akin to the source of Gk *hyakinthos* hyacinth] **1** *cap* **:** a large widely distributed genus of shrubs (family Ericaceae) including the blueberries and cranberries and distinguished by the 4- to 5-celled ovary and the usu. many-seeded baccate fruit — compare OXYCOCCUS **2** -s **:** any plant of the genus *Vaccinium*

vac·ci·noid \'vaksə,nȯid\ *adj* [ISV *vaccin-* (fr. NL *vaccinia*) + *-oid*] **:** VACCINIFORM

va·chette clasp \(')va¦shet-\ *n* [*vachette* prob. fr. F, cowhide leather (used for ligatures), lit., small cow, fr. *vache* cow + *-ette*] **:** a piece of strong steel wire with the ends curved and pointed used on toe or quarter cracks of a horse's hoof to bind the edges together and facilitate healing

vac·il·lan·cy \'vasələnsē\ *n* -ES [L *vacillare* to sway, waver + E *-ancy*] **:** VACILLATION

vac·il·lant \-nt\ *adj* [L *vacillant-, vacillans*, pres. part. of *vacillare*] **:** VACILLATING

vac·il·late \'vasə,lāt, *usu* -ād.+V\ *vi* -ED/-ING/-S [L *vacillatus*, past part. of *vacillare* to sway, waver; akin to MIr *feccaid* he kneels, Skt *vañcati* he goes crooked — more at PREVARICATE] **1 a :** to sway through lack of equilibrium **:** WAVER, TOTTER **b** FLUCTUATE, OSCILLATE **2 :** to waver in mind, will, or feeling **:** hesitate in choice of opinions or courses **:** be variable in one's emotions or judgments ⟨faced this choice, *vacillated*, and plunged for one or other disagreeable alternative —Peter Wiles⟩ ⟨throughout the book the professor ~*s* between humility and arrogance —Therese Pol⟩ **syn** see HESITATE

vac·il·lat·ing·ly *adv* **:** in a vacillating manner

vac·il·la·tion \,==ˈlāshən\ *n* -s [F, fr. L *vacillation-, vacillatio* action of swaying, fr. *vacillatus* (past part.) + *-ion-, -io* -ion] **1 :** an act or instance of vacillating (as in conduct, purpose, policy) **:** WAVERING **2 :** the quality or state of one that vacillates **:** inability to take a stand **:** IRRESOLUTION, CHANGEABLENESS, INDECISION

vac·il·la·tor \'==,lād.ə(r)\ *n* -s **:** one that vacillates

vac·il·la·to·ry \'==lə,tōrē, -tȯrē, -ri\ *adj* **:** manifesting vacillation

va·coa \və'kōə\ *n* -s [native name in Mauritius] **:** a screw pine (*Pandanus utilis*)

vac·re·a·tion \,vakrē'āshən\ *n* -s **:** the act or process of using a Vacreator machine

Vac·re·a·tor \'==,ād.ə(r)\ *trademark* — used for a machine by means of which dairy fats are pasteurized by a vacuum process

vacua *pl of* VACUUM

vac·u·ate \'vakyə,wāt\ *vt* -ED/-ING/-S [L *vacuatus*, past part. of *vacuare* to empty, fr. *vacuus* empty] *archaic* **:** EVACUATE

vac·u·ist \-yəwəst\ *n* -s [NL *vacuista*, fr. L *vacuum* + *-ista* -ist] **:** one who maintains that there are vacuums in nature ⟨by 1660 learned men were lining up on two opposing sides, the ~*s* and the plenists —*Amer. Scientist*⟩ — compare PLENIST

va·cu·i·ty \va'kyüəd.ē, və'-, -ətē, -i\ *n* -ES [L *vacuitas*, fr. *vacuus* empty + *-itas* -ity — more at VACUUM] **1 a :** an empty space: **a :** an unfilled cavity, interstice, or hollow within a body or substance **b :** an empty open space **:** VOID, GAP **c :** an extent devoid throughout of content, substance, or activity **:** a dull or monotonous stretch ⟨the long ~ of an arctic night⟩ ⟨smoking fills the *vacuities* of life —Bergen Evans⟩ **2 :** space wholly or approximately devoid of matter **:** VACUUM **3 :** the condition, fact, or quality of being empty or unfilled either physically or spiritually **:** VACANCY, EMPTINESS, HOLLOWNESS ⟨the ~ of the arteries after death⟩ ⟨the ~ of a desert⟩ **4 :** vacancy of mind **:** the state or fact of being temporarily or characteristically free of ideas, reflections, cares **:** mental emptiness or inactivity ⟨fatigued his mind into an agreeably grave ~ —Arnold Bennett⟩ ⟨a cunning gravity of manner concealing mere ~ —J.A.Froude⟩ **5 :** INANITY, BLANKNESS, VACUOUSNESS ⟨the ~ of his face⟩ **6 :** a vacuous or inane thing ⟨fill up a speech with *vacuities*⟩ **7 :** the quality or state of being completely free from or devoid of something ⟨his lesser verse seems . . . full of empty conceits whose virtuosity and lavish display only emphasize their intellectual and emotional ~ —R.A.Hall b. 1911⟩ **8 :** NIHILITY, NOTHINGNESS

vac·u·o·lar \¦vakyə¦wōlə(r), 'vakyə(w)ə)l-\ *adj* [ISV *vacuole* + *-ar*] **:** of, relating to, or of the character of a vacuole

vacuolar membrane *n* **1 :** TONOPLAST **2 :** any differentiated layer surrounding a vacuole (as the osmophilic surface of a protozoan contractile vacuole)

vacuolar system *n* **:** the vacuole of the plant cell with all identifiable precursors and derivatives that constitute a fundamental system of organelles comparable to the plastids — compare VACUOME

[1]**vac·u·o·late** \'vakyə(wə),lāt, ¦vakyə¦wōlət\ *or* **vac·u·o·lat·ed** \'vakyə(wə),lād.əd, -yə,wō,l-\ *adj* [*vacuole* + *-ate* or *-ate* + *-ed*] **:** containing one or more vacuoles

[2]**vac·u·o·late** \'vakyə(wə),lāt\ *vi* -ED/-ING/-S [*vacuole* + *-ate*, vb. suffix] **:** to form vacuoles

vac·u·o·la·tion \,==(=)ˈlāshən\ *n* -s [*vacuole* + *-ation*] **:** the development or formation of vacuoles

vac·u·ole \'vakyə,wōl\ *n* -s [F, fr. F, lit., small vacuum, fr. L *vacuum* + F *-ole*] **1 :** a small space in the tissues of an organism containing air or fluid **2 :** a cavity in the cytoplasm of a cell that is bounded by a distinct membrane, that is characteristic of plant cells and protozoans but may occur in higher animals, that in higher plant cells occupies most of the space of the cell, contains cell sap, and is often interpreted as a droplet of fluid enclosed by a membrane rather than as a vacuity, and that in protozoans is one of the most prominent organelles, performs various digestive, excretory, hydrostatic, and secretory functions, and may be either a transitory or an essentially permanent part of the protoplast — see CONTRACTILE VACUOLE, FOOD VACUOLE, TONOPLAST; AMOEBA illustration, CELL illustration

vac·u·ol·iza·tion \,==,wōlə'zāshən, -,lī'z-\ *n* -s [*vacuole* + *-ization*] **:** VACUOLATION

vac·u·ome \'vakyə,wōm\ *n* -s [F, fr. *vacu-* (in *vacuole*) + *-ome*] **1 :** VACUOLAR SYSTEM **2 :** any of various substances or structures in plant or animal cells that resemble the vacuolar system in segregating vital dyes (as neutral red): as **a :** GOLGI APPARATUS **b :** CHONDRIOME

vac·u·om·e·ter \,vakyə'wämәd.ə(r)\ *n* [ISV *vacuum* + *-o-* + *-meter*] **:** an apparatus for measuring low pressures

vac·u·ous \'vakyəwəs\ *adj* [L *vacuus*] **1 :** emptied of or lacking content (as of air or gas) ⟨~ spaces⟩ **2 :** marked by or indicative of mental vacuity or lack of ideas or intelligence **:** lacking substance **:** thin in intellectual content **:** DULL, STUPID, INANE ⟨a ~ mind⟩ ⟨a ~ expression⟩ ⟨a ~ play⟩ **3 :** devoid of serious occupation **:** spent in inanities or frivolity **:** IDLE **4 :** containing no element, point, or member **:** NULL — used of a class in mathematics or logic **syn** see EMPTY

vac·u·ous·ly *adv* **:** in a vacuous manner

vac·u·ous·ness *n* -ES **:** the quality or state of being vacuous

[1]**vac·u·um** \'vakyə(w)əm, -(,)yüm\ *n, pl* **vacuums** \-mz\ *or* **vac·ua** \-yəwə\ [L, fr. neut. of *vacuus* empty; akin to L *vacare* to be empty — more at VACANT] **1 :** emptiness of space ⟨flames . . . mounting on high into ~, into nonentity —William Blake⟩ **2 a :** a space absolutely devoid of matter — opposed to *plenum* **b :** a space (as the interior of a closed vessel) partially exhausted (as to the highest degree possible) by an air pump or by any of various other artificial means ⟨a reaction carried out in ~⟩ **c :** a degree of rarefaction below atmospheric pressure **:** NEGATIVE PRESSURE ⟨a ~ of two millimeters of mercury⟩ ⟨pumps that pull too high a ~ for gages to measure⟩ ⟨spray milk under ~ into a pan⟩ **3 a :** an unfilled or empty space or extent **:** something devoid of content **:** VOID, GAP ⟨his death has left a ~ in their lives⟩ ⟨the music stopped and the voices rose into the ~ it left —Hamilton Basso⟩ **b :** a state of isolation from outside influences or factors ⟨people who live in a ~ . . . so that the world outside them is of no moment —W.S. Maugham⟩ **4 :** a device creating or utilizing a partial vacuum; *specif* **:** VACUUM CLEANER

[2]**vacuum** \"\ *adj* **1 :** of, relating to, or associated with a vacuum or vacuum system ⟨~ pressure⟩ ⟨~ controls⟩ ⟨~ hose⟩ **2 :** used in producing a vacuum ⟨~ equipment⟩ ⟨~ sealing grease⟩ **3 a** (1) **:** partly exhausted of air or gas **:** containing a vacuum ⟨a ~ cylinder⟩ ⟨a ~ oven⟩ (2) **:** made nonconducting by means of a vacuum; *esp* **:** being or containing a usu. glass vessel or casing with double walls enclosing a vacuum for temperature insulation (as of liquids) ⟨a ~ flask⟩ ⟨a ~ jug⟩ ⟨*vacuum*-jacketed apparatus⟩ ⟨a ~ pitcher⟩ **b :** carried on under partial vacuum or by means of suction ⟨~ distillation⟩ ⟨~ metallurgy⟩ ⟨~ spectroscopy⟩ ⟨~ filling of milk bottles⟩ **c :** being or used in a canning, bottling, or packaging process in which much of the air in the container is extracted before sealing for better preservation of contents ⟨~ canning⟩ ⟨a ~ jar⟩ **d :** mounted in a vacuum ⟨a ~ filament lamp⟩ ⟨~ contacts⟩ **4 :** being or incorporating a device producing a partial vacuum (as for drawing off or holding fast) ⟨a ~ dryer⟩ ⟨a ~ filter⟩ ⟨a ~ ash conveyer⟩ ⟨a ~ chuck for holding delicate materials on a lathe⟩ ⟨a ~ pad for hoisting concrete slabs⟩ ⟨~ impregnating apparatus⟩ **5 :** produced by a process utilizing a vacuum (as for evaporation) ⟨~ salt⟩

[3]**vacuum** \"\ *vb* -ED/-ING/-S *vt* **1 :** to use a vacuum device upon **2** *or* **vacuum-clean :** to clean or remove by means of a vacuum cleaner ⟨~ the rug⟩ ⟨~ the crumbs⟩ **~** *vi* **1 :** to operate a vacuum device (as a vacuum drier) **2** *or* **vacuum-clean** \'=(=)=¦=, '=(,)=¦=\ **:** to clean a surface with a vacuum cleaner ⟨hired a woman to scrub, dust, and ~⟩

vacuum back *n* **:** a vacuum platen used in the focal plane of a camera to hold the film during exposure

vacuum booster *n* **:** a piston actuated by the vacuum of the intake manifold and attached to the brake pedal of an automotive vehicle to apply added pressure on the brake cylinder

vacuum bottle *n* **:** a cylindrical container having a usu. glass liner made on the principle of the Dewar vessel for keeping liquids either hot or cold for several hours

vacuum brake *n* **:** a brake using a partial vacuum in its operation; *specif* **:** an automobile brake in which the braking pressure applied by the operator is augmented by the negative pressure of the suction on the intake manifold

vacuum breaker *n* **:** a device admitting (as into a water supply line) air or other gas to vitiate a vacuum (as for preventing back siphonage)

vacuum cleaner *also* **vacuum sweeper** *n* **:** an electrical appliance for cleaning (as floors, carpets, tapestry, or upholstered work) by suction

vacuum coffee maker *n* **:** a coffee maker consisting of an upper bowl that holds ground coffee and a filtering device and is fitted by a tight seal into a lower bowl that holds water which on boiling rises into the upper bowl from which it is drawn through the coffee back into the lower bowl by the suction caused by the reduced pressure upon removal of the heat

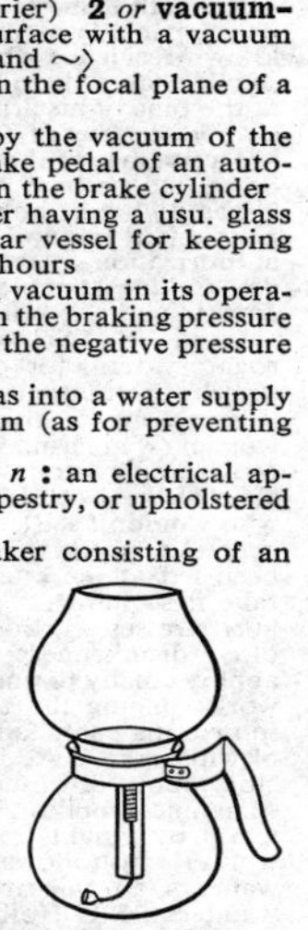

vacuum coffee maker

vacuum concrete *n* **:** concrete that has had a vacuum applied through special mats, pads, or forms shortly after placement for the purpose of removing a portion of the mixing water not needed for the hydration of the cement

vacuum cup *n* **:** a hollow hemisphere (as of rubber) that can adhere to a smooth surface or agitate a fluid by suction **:** SUCTION CUP ⟨*vacuum cups* for hanging suits on car windows⟩

vacuum distillation *n* **:** distillation carried on under reduced pressure so that the liquid being distilled boils at a lower temperature than under atmospheric pressure and consequently with less chance of decomposition — compare MOLECULAR DISTILLATION

vacuum filter *n* **:** a filter in which the pressure on the outlet side of the filter medium is less than that of the atmosphere

vacuum frame *n* **:** a contact printing device using a vacuum to create a uniform pressure during exposure of a photographic film or paper

vacuum gauge *n* **:** a gauge indicating degree of negative pressure

vac·u·um·ize *pronunc at* VACUUM + ,īz\ *vt* -ED/-ING/-S **1 :** to produce a vacuum in **2 :** to clean, dry, or pack by a vacuum mechanism or in a vacuum container

vacuum-packed *adj* **:** packed in a container that has much of the air removed before being hermetically sealed ⟨*vacuum-packed* coffee⟩

vacuum pan *n* **:** a tank with a vacuum pump and condenser for rapid evaporation and condensation (as of salt brine, sugar syrup, milk) by boiling at a low temperature ⟨vacuum pans . . . enable the sugar solution to boil at a low temperature, without burning —*Story of Cane Sugar*⟩

vacuum pump *n* **1 :** PULSOMETER **2 :** a pump for exhausting air or other gas from an enclosed space to a desired degree of vacuum

vacuum tank *n* **:** a tank which is used with some internal-combustion engines, into which the fuel (as gasoline) is sucked from the main tank, and from which it flows by gravity to the carburetor usu. directly below

vacuum tube *n* **:** an electron tube evacuated to a high degree of vacuum

vacuum-tube voltmeter *n* **:** a voltmeter employing vacuum tubes and useful because of its very high input impedence for measurements in circuits (as vacuum-tube circuits) from which only very small currents can be drawn without altering the voltages being measured

vacuum valve *n* **1 :** SAFETY VALVE 1b **2** *chiefly Brit* **:** VACUUM TUBE **3 :** a vacuum-tube rectifier

vacuum ventilation *n* **:** ventilation using an exhaust fan so that air is drawn in from outside

vacuum weight *n* **:** a weight equivalent to the one obtained by weighing a body in a vacuum but actually computed from ordinary weighing by vacuum correction using the known volume of body and weights and the known density of the air

VAD *abbr* voluntary aid detachment

vade *vi* -ED/-ING/-S [ME *vaden*, alter. (prob. influenced by L *vadere* to go) of *faden* to fade — more at WADE, FADE] *obs* **:** FADE

va·de me·cum \ˌvādēˈmēkəm, ˌväd-\ *n, pl* **vade mecums** [L, go with me] **1 :** a book for ready reference **:** HANDBOOK, MANUAL ⟨his first treatise . . . became a *vade mecum* for the local magistrates —V.L.Wilkinson⟩ **2 :** something regularly carried about by a person ⟨the small wooden bowl, the indispensable *vade mecum* of all Tartars —William Hazlitt †1893⟩

vades *pl of* VAS

vad·i·mo·ni·um \ˌvadəˈmōnēəm\ *n, pl* **vadimo·nia** \-ēə\ [L, fr. *vad-, vas* bail, pledge, security — more at WED] **:** any of several legal pledges or securities: as **a :** a contract of suretyship in Roman and civil law used in sales to secure the payment of the purchase price **b :** a bond or pledge in early English law for appearance before a judge on a certain day

vad·i·mo·ny \ˈ==ˌmōnē\ *n* -ES [L *vadimonium*] **:** VADIMONIUM b

vadium mortuum *n* [ML, lit., dead pledge] **:** MORTUUM VADIUM

va·di·um vi·vum \ˈwädēˌu̇mˈwīˌwu̇m\ *n* [ML] **:** LIVING PLEDGE

va·dose \ˈvāˌdōs\ *adj* [L *vadosus* shallow, fr. *vadum*, n., shallow, ford + *-osus* -ose; akin to L *vadere* to go, walk — more at WADE] **:** of, relating to, or resulting from water or solutions in the part of the earth's crust that is above the permanent groundwater level ⟨~ circulation⟩ ⟨~ deposits⟩

vadose water *n* **:** groundwater suspended or in circulation above the water table

vaes·ite \ˈväˌsīt\ *n* -S [Johannes *Vaes*, 20th cent. Belgian mineralogist + E *-ite*] **:** a mineral NiS_2 consisting of sulfide of nickel and belonging to the pyrite group

¹**vag** \ˈvag, -aa(ə)g, -aig\ *n* -S [by shortening] **:** VAGRANT ⟨a society of homeless men . . . the ~s and strays —J.J.Maloney⟩

²**vag** \"\ *vt* **vagged; vagged; vagging; vags :** to arrest as a vagrant ⟨have them all *vagged* . . . in a week —John Lardner⟩

vag- *or* **vago-** *comb form* [ISV, fr. NL *vagus*] **1 :** vagus nerve ⟨*vago*gram⟩ ⟨*vag*olysis⟩ **2 :** vagal and ⟨*vago*accessorius⟩ ⟨*vago*glossopharyngeal⟩

¹**vag·a·bond** \ˈvagəˌbänd, ˈvaig-, *chiefly Brit* -ˌbənd\ *adj* [ME *vagabond*, fr. MF *vagabond*, fr. L *vagabundus*, fr. *vagari* to move about, wander — more at VAGARY] **1 :** moving from place to place without a fixed home **:** WANDERING, NOMADIC ⟨~ minstrels⟩ ⟨a ~ people⟩ **2 a :** of, relating to, or characteristic of a wanderer ⟨those ~ moods that visit husbands in April and November —Ellen Glasgow⟩ **b :** leading an unsettled, irresponsible, or disreputable life **:** WORTHLESS ⟨a thoroughly ~ outcast —Bret Harte⟩ **3 :** not having a fixed course **:** following an irregular or vagrant course ⟨runs ~ sailings out of Montreal —*N.Y.Times*⟩

²**vagabond** \"\ *n* -S [ME *vagabound*, fr. *vagabound*, adj., vagabond] **1 a :** one who wanders about from place to place ⟨a fugitive and a ~ shalt thou be in the earth —Gen 4:12 (AV)⟩ **b** (1) **:** one who wanders from place to place with no fixed dwelling or if he has one not abiding in it and who is without visible means of support (2) **:** one who is by statute declared a vagabond; *esp* **:** one other than a rogue accountable under British vagrancy statutes for specific offenses **c** (1) **:** an idle beggar **:** TRAMP (2) **:** an idle carefree roamer **2 :** an irresponsible, worthless, or disreputable person ⟨such a ~ of a husband —Hall Caine⟩ **3** *or* **vagabond green :** DUCK GREEN

syn VAGABOND, VAGRANT, TRUANT, TRAMP, HOBO, BUM, STIFF, SWAGMAN, and SUNDOWNER designate a person who wanders at will or habitually. VAGABOND usu. implies only a carefree fondness for a roaming life ⟨militiamen fleeing from Washington's army wandered like homeless *vagabonds* on all the roads —Kenneth Roberts⟩ VAGRANT implies disreputableness and in its common legal use applies to a person with no fixed or known residence who is likely to become a public menace or public charge ⟨by no means a *vagrant* but he was an itinerant: at the time of his arrest he peddled fish from a pushcart in the poorer sections of Boston —Phil Stong⟩ ⟨the depression had left a number of them indigent, without state or federal relief. Some had become *vagrants*, tramping the highways of South Texas, living in hobo jungles —Green Peyton⟩ TRUANT applies chiefly to pupils absent from school without permission or authorization ⟨played *truant* from their Dublin school —*London Calling*⟩ ⟨employers were now obliged . . . to discharge *truants* without notice; and one day of unjustified absence sufficed —S.M.Schwarz⟩ TRAMP is the ordinary, generally derogatory term for one who lives by wandering whether in search of transient work or engaged in beggary or petty thievery, and is also often applied to a morally disreputable woman ⟨wandering fruit *tramps* who drift through California's central valley, following the crop seasons —*Time*⟩ ⟨a distinct class of these gentlemen *tramps*, young men no longer young, who wouldn't settle down, who disliked polite society and the genteel conventions —George Santayana⟩ ⟨*tramps* who had been fed at the kitchen door —Sherwood Anderson⟩ ⟨don't take it so hard . . . she's just a *tramp* —Chandler Brossard⟩ BUM stresses worthlessness with implications of laziness and often drunkenness or general moral disreputableness and applies chiefly to one who would rather sponge on others than work ⟨paging the town *bum*, and soon he appeared, barefooted, his pants falling away from his hips, his face a thicket of whiskers —J.A.Michener⟩ ⟨a young reporter working on a story about down-and-out *bums* —J.A.Morris b.1904⟩ HOBO sometimes implies a willingness to work, sometimes suggests travel by freight trains, and is often applied to a migratory worker who follows seasonal occupations ⟨a *hobo* works and wanders, a tramp dreams and wanders, and a bum drinks and wanders —S.H.Holbrook⟩ ⟨a swarm of crop *hoboes* had come in on it to work in the back-country lambing camps —H.L. Davis⟩ ⟨a piano *hobo*, knocking around the Mexican border with a four-piece band —*Lamp*⟩ ⟨most distressing of all was the large number of young people who had virtually become *hoboes* —F.D.Roosevelt⟩ STIFF applies chiefly to workers, esp. migratory workers or roustabouts; the term is usu. limited by a modifier ⟨the pay envelopes of the working *stiffs* of the smoky little towns of western Pennsylvania, Ohio and Indiana —E.A. Lahey⟩ ⟨after sixteen years of being homeless, of working with harvest *stiffs*, hockey players and sailors —Hugh MacLennan⟩ ⟨a cattle *stiff*⟩ ⟨a bindle *stiff*⟩ SWAGMAN is Australian for a hobo or migratory worker in the bush who carries his clothing and bedding with him and SUNDOWNER is Australian and South African for a bum or swagman who makes a practice of arriving at a bush station at sundown to ask for free food and shelter, traditionally unrefusable ⟨bundle of belongings *swagmen* carry as they tramp about the land —*Time*⟩ ⟨the *swagman*, a born wanderer who moves steadily on and occasionally takes a casual job —*Times Lit. Supp.*⟩ ⟨some swagmen were known as *sundowners*, because they arrived in time to eat the evening meal but not to earn it —William Power⟩

³**vagabond** \"\ *vi* -ED/-ING/-S **:** to wander in the manner of a vagabond **:** roam about ⟨a young ex-typist ~*ing* in the Far East —Ida Hurst⟩

vag·a·bond·age \-ˌbändij, -dēj\ *n* -S [F, fr. *vagabond* + *-age*] **1 :** the act, condition, or practice of a vagabond **:** the state or habit of wandering about ⟨winter cruising . . . was the nature of our ~ —*Everybody's Mag.*⟩ **2 :** VAGABONDS ⟨roads were thronged with ~ —John Buchan⟩

vag·a·bon·dia \ˌ==ˈbändēə\ *n* -S [*vagabond* + *-ia* (as in *bohemia*)] **:** the life of a vagabond **:** VAGABONDAGE ⟨his departure from Leyden on the road to ~ —*No. Amer. Rev.*⟩

vag·a·bond·ish \-ˌbändish, -dēsh\ *adj* **:** of, resembling, or characteristic of a vagabond ⟨a lazy ~ itinerant farmer moving from one failure to another —B.J.Hendrick⟩

vag·a·bond·ism \-ˌbänˌdizəm, *chiefly Brit* -ˌbən-\ *n* -S **:** VAGABONDAGE

vag·a·bond·ize \-ˌdīz\ *vi* -ED/-ING/-S **:** VAGABOND

vagabonds *pl of* VAGABOND, *pres 3d sing of* VAGABOND

vagabonds' disease *n* **:** a condition of pigmentation of the skin caused by long continued exposure, uncleanliness, and esp. by scratch marks and other lesions due to the presence of body lice

va·gal \ˈvāgəl\ *adj* [ISV *vag-* + *-al*] **:** of, relating to, involving the action of, or being the vagus nerve ⟨~ inhibition⟩ ⟨~ impulses⟩

va·gar·i·ous \vāˈgerēəs, vəˈg-, -ga(a)r-, -gär-\ *adj* **:** marked by vagaries **:** CAPRICIOUS, WHIMSICAL ⟨a ~ American leadership dependent upon the clash of domestic interests —Herbert Elliston⟩ — **va·gar·i·ous·ly** *adv*

va·gary \ˈvāgərē, -ri; vəˈger-, vāˈg-, -ˈga(a)r-, -ˈgär- *sometimes* ˈvä,g-; *sometimes* ˈvagər- *or* ˈvaigər-\ *n* -ES [prob. fr. L *vagari* to move about, wander; akin to L *vagus* wandering, OIr *fān* slope, bend, Skt *vañcati* he goes crooked — more at PREVARICATE] **1** *archaic* **:** JOURNEY, EXCURSION, TOUR ⟨permitted to make a walking ~ throughout all London —W.E.Andrews⟩ **2** *archaic* **:** an aimless digression ⟨presently would fall into a wordy ~ —Richard Baxter⟩ **3 a** *obs* **:** a departure from the regular, lawful, or proper course of conduct **b :** CAPER, FROLIC ⟨into strange *vagaries* fell, as they would dance —John Milton⟩ **4 :** a departure from an expected, normal, or logical order or course: as **a :** a capricious, eccentric, or unpredictable action ⟨fearing to entrust his person to the *vagaries* of some erratic cabdriver —David Walden⟩ **b :** a change that is hard to predict or explain ⟨dependence of the schooner men upon the *vagaries* of weather —*Amer. Guide Series: Mich.*⟩ ⟨made the best of the *vagaries* of circumstance —Rose Macaulay⟩ ⟨these prospects . . . hinge on the *vagaries* of politics —*Fortune*⟩ ⟨independent of the *vagaries* of the international market —Vicki Baum⟩ ⟨passes through a series of *vagaries* and vicissitudes —John Barkham⟩ **c :** a whimsical, fanciful, or extravagant idea or notion ⟨his mind seemed . . . to be abandoned to *vagaries* —S.H.Adams⟩

vagation *n* -S [ME *vagacion*, fr. MF *vagation*, fr. L *vagation-, vagatio* action of wandering, fr. *vagatus* (past part. of *vagari*) + *-ion-, -io* -ion] *obs* **:** an act or instance of departing from an expected or regular course

vagged *past of* VAG

vagging *pres part of* VAG

vagi *pl of* VAGUS

vag·ile \ˈvajəl, -aˌjīl, -a(ˌ)jil\ *adj* [ISV *vag-* (fr. L *vagus* wandering) + *-ile*; prob. orig. formed as G *vagil*] **:** free to move about ⟨~ aquatic animals⟩ — compare SESSILE

va·gil·i·ty \vəˈjiləd·ē, -ətē, -i\ *n* -ES **:** the quality or state of being vagile; *broadly* **:** the capacity of an organism to compete successfully in the struggle for existence

vagin- *also* **vagini-** *comb form* [NL, fr. L *vagina*] **:** vagina ⟨*vagin*ectomy⟩ ⟨*vagini*coline⟩

va·gi·na \vəˈjīnə\ *n, pl* **vagi·nae** \-ī(ˌ)nē\ *or* **vaginas** [L, scabbard, sheath, vagina; prob. akin to Lith *vožti* to cover over with something hollow] **1 a :** a canal that leads from the uterus of a female mammal to the external orifice of the genital canal **b :** a canal of similar function or location in any of various other animals **2 :** a sheathlike part **:** SHEATH; *specif* **:** the expanded or ensheathing part of the base of a leaf **3 :** the upper part of the shaft of a terminus from which the bust or figure seems to rise

¹**vagi·nal** \ˈvajənᵊl, vəˈjīnᵊl\ *adj* [NL *vaginalis*, fr. L *vagina* + *-alis* -al] **1 :** of, relating to, or resembling a vagina **:** THECAL ⟨a ~ synovial membrane surrounding a tendon⟩ ⟨the ~ branches of the hepatic artery⟩ **2 :** of, relating to, or affecting the vagina of the genital canal ⟨the ~ plexus of nerves or veins⟩

²**vaginal** \"\ *n* -S **:** a vaginal artery or muscle

vaginal artery *n* **:** any of the several branches of the iliac artery supplying the vagina

vaginal process *n* **1 :** a projecting lamina of bone on the inferior surface of the petrous portion of the temporal bone that is continuous with the tympanic plate and surrounds the root of the styloid process **2 :** either of a pair of projecting laminae on the inferior surface of the sphenoid that articulate with the alae of the vomer

vaginal smear *n* **:** a smear taken from the vaginal mucosa for cytologic diagnosis

vag·i·nant \ˈvajənənt\ *adj* [NL *vaginant-, vaginans*, fr. *vagin-* + L *-ant-, -ans* -ant] **:** SHEATHING ⟨~ culm of grass⟩

vagina syn·o·vi·a·lis \-səˌnōvēˈaləs, -ˈāl-, -ˈal-\ *n* [NL, synovial sheath] **:** VAGINA TENDINIS

vag·i·nate \ˈvajəˌnāt, -nət\ *or* **vag·i·nat·ed** \-ˌnād·əd\ *adj* [*vaginate* prob. fr. (assumed) NL *vaginatus*, fr. NL *vagin-* + L *-atus* -ate; *vaginated* prob. fr. (assumed) NL *vaginatus* + E *-ed*] **:** invested with or as if with a sheath

vagina ten·di·nis \-ˈtendənəs\ *n* [NL, tendinous sheath] **:** the synovial sheath of a tendon esp. of the hand or foot

vag·i·nic·o·la \ˌvajəˈnikələ\ *n, cap* [NL, fr. *vagin-* + *-cola*] **:** a genus of ciliate protozoans that form minute vaselike or tubular cases in which they dwell

vag·i·nic·o·lous \ˌ==ˈnikələs\ *adj* [*vagin-* + *-colous*] **:** secreting and inhabiting a theca

vag·i·nif·er·ous \-if(ə)rəs\ *adj* [ISV *vagin-* + *-ferous*] **:** THECATE

vag·i·nis·mus \ˌvajəˈnizməs\ *n* -ES [NL, fr. *vagin-* + L *-ismus* -ism] **:** a painful spasmodic contraction of the vagina

vag·i·ni·tis \-ˈnīd·əs\ *n* -ES [NL, fr. *vagin-* + *-itis*] **1 :** inflammation of the vagina **2 :** inflammation of a sheath (as a tendon sheath)

va·ginu·la \vəˈjinyələ, -jīn-\ *n, pl* **vaginu·lae** \-ˌlē\ [NL, fr. L, dim. of *vagina* sheath, vagina] **1 :** the part of the archegonium of a moss enveloping the base of the embryo or seta after the upper part has been torn away **2 :** a small theca — **va·ginu·late** \-ˌlāt, -lət\ *adj*

vag·i·nule \ˈvajəˌn(y)ül\ *n* -S [NL *vaginula*] **:** VAGINULA

vag·nera \ˈvagnərə\ [NL, prob. modif. of the name *Wagner*] *syn of* SMILACINA

vago- — see VAG-

va·go·depressor \ˌvāgə+\ *adj* [*vag-* + *depressor*] **:** depressing to the vagus nerve — used chiefly of drugs or their action

va·go·sympathetic \"+\ *n* [*vag-* + *sympathetic*] **:** the vagus and a cervical sympathetic nerve when enclosed in the same sheath (as in a dog)

va·got·o·mize \vāˈgäd·əˌmīz\ *vt* -ED/-ING/-S **:** to perform a vagotomy on

va·got·o·my \-ˌmē, -mi\ *n* -ES [ISV *vag-* + *-tomy*] **:** surgical division of the vagus nerve

va·go·to·nia \ˌvāgəˈtōnēə\ *also* **va·goto·ny** \ˈvāgəˌtōnē, vāˈgätᵊnē\ *n, pl* **vagotonias** *also* **vagotonies** [*vagotonia* fr. NL, fr. *vag-* + *-tonia*; *vagotony* ISV *vag-* + *-tony*] **:** excessive excitability of the vagus nerve resulting typically in vasomotor instability, constipation, and sweating — **va·go·ton·ic** \ˌvāgəˈtänik\ *adj*

va·go·trop·ic \ˌvāgəˈträpik\ *adj* [*vag-* + *tropic*] **:** acting selectively upon the vagus nerve ⟨~ drugs⟩

vagous *adj* [L *vagus* — more at VAGARY] *obs* **:** WANDERING, UNSETTLED

va·grance \ˈvāgrən(t)s\ *n* -S **:** VAGRANCY

va·gran·cy \-nsē, -si\ *n* -ES **1 :** VAGARY 4 ⟨the *vagrancies* of the heart —John Tulloch⟩ **2 :** the state or action of wandering about from place to place ⟨happier life I cannot imagine than this ~ if the weather were but tolerable —Thomas De Quincey⟩ **3 :** the state or offense of being a vagrant

¹**va·grant** \-nt\ *n* -S [ME *vagraunt*, prob. modif. (influenced by MF *vagant* vagrant, fr. pres. part. of *vaguer* to wander) of MF *waucrant, wacrant* wandering, fr. OF, fr. pres. part. of *waucrer, wacrer, walcrer* to roll, roam, wander, of Gmc origin; akin to OE *wealcan* to roll, turn, revolve — more at VAGUE, WALK] **1 a** (1) **:** a person who has no established residence and wanders idly from place to place without lawful or visible means of support (2) **:** one whose conduct constitutes statutory vagrancy; *esp* **:** one (as an itinerant peddler trading without a license, a common prostitute wandering in the public streets, one begging in a public place, a fortune teller, one exhibiting an obscene picture in a public place, one guilty of indecent exposure, one playing or betting in a public place at or with a gambling table or instrument, and formerly a pimp) whose conduct constitutes vagrancy under British law **b :** one who leads a wandering life **:** WANDERER ⟨a chronic ~ from the spirit's home —Edward Sapir⟩ **2 :** an insect or other small arthropod that produces no web, nest, gall, or other protective structure but wanders at large where suitable food is to be found **syn** see VAGABOND

²**vagrant** \"\ *adj* [ME *vagraunt*, prob. modif. of MF *waucrant, wacrant*] **1 a :** wandering about from place to place usu. with no means of support ⟨his house was known to all the ~ train —Oliver Goldsmith⟩ **b :** tied to or as if to no home or country **:** ROVING ⟨administer the government in the name of ~ and mendicant Kings —T.B.Macaulay⟩ **2 a :** having a fleeting, wayward, or inconstant quality ⟨had cleared my soul of sundry ~ impulses —Mary Austin⟩ ⟨his ~ attention was caught —Dorothy Sayers⟩ ⟨hummed snatches of some ~ melody —H.A.Sinclair⟩ **b :** having no fixed course, direction, or aim **:** RANDOM ⟨the ~ breeze . . . died down again —Ellen Glasgow⟩ ⟨a ~ shaft of sunlight struck the ocean —Jack London⟩ **3 :** of, relating to, or characteristic of a wanderer ⟨go down to the seas again to the ~ gypsy life —John Masefield⟩

va·grant·ly *adv* **:** in the manner of a vagrant

va·grom \ˈvāgrəm\ *adj* [by alter.] **:** VAGRANT ⟨a ~ . . . thought ran through my head —H.L.Mencken⟩

vags *pl of* VAG, *pres 3d sing of* VAG

¹**vague** \ˈvāg\ *vi* -ED/-ING/-S [ME (Sc) *vagen*, fr. MF *vaguer*, fr. L *vagari* — more at VAGARY] *archaic* **:** WANDER, ROAM

²**vague** \"\ *adj* -ER/-EST [MF, fr. L *vagus* wandering, unsettled, uncertain, vague — more at VAGARY] **1 a :** not clearly expressed **:** stated in general or indefinite terms ⟨sign a very ~ treaty of friendship —William Clark⟩ ⟨~ chatter about the higher things —D.W.Brogan⟩ ⟨distrust of ~ beliefs in social service —M.R.Cohen⟩ **b :** not having an exact or precise meaning ⟨a ~ term of abuse for any style that is bad —T.S. Eliot⟩ ⟨statement . . . is so ~ as to be really meaningless —Havelock Ellis⟩ **2 a :** not clearly defined, grasped, or understood **:** INDISTINCT ⟨owed only ~ allegiance to some overlord —Roger Burlingame⟩ ⟨knows . . . in a ~ way what he wants from a book —Bliss Perry⟩ ⟨a ~ idea of the existence of an all-powerful spirit —P.T.Etherton⟩ **b :** not clearly or sharply felt or sensed **:** somewhat subconscious ⟨a ~ longing for common deliverance —J.R.Green⟩ ⟨the ~ unrest of a husband whose infidelities are imaginary —Ellen Glasgow⟩ ⟨a ~ desire for change —Will Irwin⟩ **3 :** not thinking or expressing one's thoughts clearly or precisely **:** characterized by looseness or haziness of thought or expression ⟨was very ~ about when he could see her again —Irwin Shaw⟩ ⟨somewhat ~ but possessing her own peculiarly feminine brand of common sense —C.V.Woodward⟩ ⟨kept no diary . . . was ~ about dates —Valentine Williams⟩ **4 :** lacking expression **:** VACANT ⟨danced along with ~ regardless eyes —John Keats⟩ **5 :** not sharply outlined **:** dim or indistinct in form or character **:** SHADOWY, HAZY ⟨met by ~ figures with shaded torchlights —Earle Birney⟩ ⟨the pattern is ~ and indecisive —A.N.Whitehead⟩ ⟨the ~ world of sleep —Edmund Wilson⟩ **syn** see OBSCURE

³**vague** \"\ *n* -S **1 :** an indefinite or unsettled state — often used in the phrase *in the vague* ⟨plans are still in the ~ —Jane W. Carlyle⟩ **b :** a haze of thoughts or sensations ⟨am wondering in a vast ~ about her —Thomas Wolfe⟩ **2 :** an indefinite expanse ⟨the gray ~ of unsympathizing sea —J.R.Lowell⟩

⁴**vague** \"\ *adv* **:** VAGUELY — usu. used in combination ⟨*vague*-shining⟩

vague·ly *adv* **:** in a vague manner or form

vague·ness *n* -ES **1 :** the quality or state of being vague ⟨the ~ of a dream that is half forgotten —Elizabeth Goudge⟩ **2 :** something that is vague ⟨paintings . . . grew touch by touch into ~*es* at which I shuddered —E.A.Poe⟩

vague year *n* [prob. so called fr. the fact that in a cycle of 1507 vague years any date in it passed through all the seasons] **:** a year of 365 days used by the ancient Egyptians before the Roman conquest

va·guish \ˈvāgish, -gēsh\ *adj* **:** somewhat vague

va·gus nerve \ˈvāgəs-\ *also* **va·gus** *n, pl* **vagus nerves** *also* **vagi** [*vagus nerve* part trans. of NL *vagus nervus*, lit., wandering nerve; *vagus* fr. NL, fr. L, wandering; fr. its length and wide distribution in the brain — more at VAGARY] **:** either of the 10th pair of cranial nerves being a mixed nerve with sensory fibers that have cell bodies in the ganglion nodosum and jugular ganglion and central connections through the lateral wall of the medulla and with motor fibers that pass from the medulla in company with those of the 9th nerve and supplying chiefly the viscera esp. with autonomic fibers

va·hi·ne \väˈhē(ˌ)nā\ *n* -S [Tahitian] **:** a woman of Central Polynesia

vai *also* **vei** \ˈvī\ *n, pl* **vai** *or* **vais** *usu cap* **1 a :** a Negro people of Liberia **b :** a member of such people **2 :** a Mande language of the Vai people **3 :** a syllabic script invented about 1834 for use with the Vai language

vai·bha·si·ka \vīˈbäs(h)əkə\ *n* -S *usu cap* [Skt *vaibhāṣika*, fr. *Vibhāṣā*, a commentary on the Buddhist scriptures, fr. *vibhāṣate* it shines brightly, fr. *vi* apart, asunder + *bhāṣate* it shines; akin to Skt *bhāti* it shines — more at WITH, FANCY] **:** a Hinayana Buddhist philosophical school of realism derived from the Sarvastivadin and found chiefly in Gandhara and Kashmir

¹**vail** \ˈvāl, *esp before pause or consonant* -āəl\ *vb* -ED/-ING/-S [ME *vailen*, fr. OF *vail-, vaill-*, stem of *valoir* to be of worth, fr. L *valēre* to be strong, be of worth — more at WIELD] *archaic* **:** AVAIL

²**vail** \"\ *vb* -ED/-ING/-S [ME *valen*, partly fr. MF *valer* (short for *avaler* to fall, let fall) & partly short for ME *avalen* to fall, let fall — more at AVALE] *vt* **1 a :** to let fall **:** cause to descend or sink ⟨~*ed* her handkerchief and drew a breath of air —Aldous Huxley⟩ **b :** to lower as a sign of respect or submission ⟨had no intention of ~*ing* their crest —Louis Golding⟩ **2** *archaic* **:** to take off esp. as a sign of respect or submission **:** DOFF ⟨acknowledged their greeting by ~*ing* his plumed cap —E.G.Bulwer-Lytton⟩ **3** *obs* **a :** HUMBLE, ABASE ⟨now ~ your pride . . . and kneel for mercy —Christopher Marlowe⟩ **b :** YIELD, SUBMIT ⟨~ their faith and understanding to his dictates —John Owen⟩ **~** *vi* **1 a** *archaic* **:** to become lowered esp. as a sign of respect or submission **b** *obs* **:** to lower a sail as a sign of respect or submission **2** *archaic* **:** to take off one's hat esp. as a sign of respect or submission **3** *archaic* **:** YIELD

³**vail** \"\ *n* -S [ME, fr. *vailen* to avail — more at ¹VAIL] **1 a** *archaic* **:** an occasional fee or offering usu. attached to an office ⟨his revenue besides ~*s* amounted to about thirty pounds —Jonathan Swift⟩ **b vails** *pl* **:** a perquisite held or claimed as a customary right or possession ⟨the upper garment is the ~*s* of the executioner —John Cleveland⟩ **2** *also* **vale :** a gratuity given esp. to a servant **:** TIP

¹**vain** \ˈvān\ *adj* -ER/-EST [ME *vain, vein*, fr. OF, fr. L *vanus* empty, vain — more at WANE] **1 :** having no real value, meaning, or foundation **:** EMPTY, IDLE, WORTHLESS ⟨~ pomp and glory of this world —Shak.⟩ ⟨~ pretensions⟩ ⟨~ promises⟩ **2 :** marked by futility or ineffectualness **:** FRUITLESS, UNSUCCESSFUL ⟨our ~ quest for a utopian equilibrium —W.H.Whyte⟩ ⟨a ~ effort to stop the decay —H.I.Priestley⟩ **3** *archaic* **:** having or showing little sense or wisdom **:** FOOLISH, SILLY ⟨all that ~ men imagine or believe —P.B.Shelley⟩ **4 :** having or showing undue or excessive pride esp. in one's appearance or achievements **:** CONCEITED ⟨was ~ about his clothes —Hugh Walpole⟩ ⟨~ of the honor which he had won —J.A. Froude⟩ ⟨~ of his family's long history —P.L.Fermor⟩

syn NUGATORY, OTIOSE, IDLE, EMPTY, HOLLOW: VAIN describes that which is either absolutely lacking in value and worth or relatively insignificant and unavailing in comparison or contrast to other things vastly more significant, valuable, or powerful ⟨a good deal of the older speculation on life and destiny was *vain* and insipid because of the theologic bias —M.R.Cohen⟩ ⟨unless the forces of destruction now set loose in the world are brought under control, it is *vain* to plan for the future —Clement Attlee⟩ NUGATORY may apply to the completely insignificant or to the inoperative, ineffective, void, or null ⟨this book is so one-sided that as a constructive contribution it is *nugatory* —*Times Lit. Supp.*⟩ ⟨make the indictment void and *nugatory*⟩ OTIOSE describes that which is purposeless, profitless, or useless and is therefore at best

superfluous and at worst encumbering and productive of unnecessary expense or difficulty ⟨what kinds of criticism are useful and what are *otiose* —T.S.Eliot⟩ ⟨mummified customs that have long outlasted their usefulness, and *otiose* dogmas that have long lost their vitality —W.R.Inge⟩ IDLE may suggest lack of basis or solid foundation and hence may describe that which is incapable of use or effect ⟨in the light of our present very limited knowledge of psychological processes it seems *idle* to speculate as to the origins of this need —Ralph Linton⟩ ⟨living in an age of transition in everything and it is *idle* to deny that it is uncomfortable —S.P.B.Mais⟩ EMPTY applies to what lacks content or substance and hence significance although perhaps apparently consequential ⟨if the right of the states to tax the means employed by the general government be conceded, the declaration that the constitution, and the laws made in pursuance thereof, shall be the supreme law of the land, is *empty* and unmeaning declamation —John Marshall⟩ ⟨they have offered not a shred of evidence — nothing but bald assertion. And on the basis of this *empty* vociferation school programs and college admission requirements are overturned —C.H.Grandgent⟩ HOLLOW may suggest a deceiving lack of substance perceptible after examination or trial ⟨the fight for the extension of the franchise is one of the most thrilling chapters in the history of political liberties, but its final triumph in the extension of the franchise to women came too late to conceal the fact that the victory was a *hollow* one, since political reforms could have little or no efficacy without corresponding economic reforms —F.B.Millett⟩ ⟨the old Georgian mansions were converted into rooming houses. Trees were chopped down, so that the streets could be widened. The title of "most beautiful city" became *hollow* —*Amer. Guide Series: Mich.*⟩

—in vain *adv* [ME; trans. of OF *en vein* & ML *in vanum*] **1 :** to no end : without success or result ⟨protests made *in vain* by county councils —S.P.B.Mais⟩ **2 :** in an irreverent, disrespectful, or blasphemous manner ⟨the Lord will not hold him guiltless who takes his name *in vain* —Deut 5:11 (RSV)⟩

²vain *n* -S [ME *vein*, fr. OF, fr. *vain*, adj., vain] *obs* **:** VANITY

vainglorious \(ˈ)⸗¦⸗⸗⸗\ *adj* [ME *vanegloreous*, fr. MF, fr. ML *vaniglorius*, fr. L *vanus* vain + *gloria* glory, vainglory] **:** marked by vainglory **:** BOASTFUL, VAIN ⟨was rather ~ about his own war record —Gideon Tode⟩ ⟨had a bombastic almost ~ air —*New Yorker*⟩ — **vaingloriously** *adv* — **vaingloriousness** *n*

¹vainglory \ˈ⸗¦⸗⸗ *also* ⸗ˈ⸗⸗⸗\ *n* [ME *vain glory*, *vein glory*, fr. OF *vaine glorire*, *veine gloire*, fr. *vaine*, *veine* (fem. of *vain*, *vein* vain) + *gloire* glory, vainglory, fr. L *gloria*] **1 :** excessive or ostentatious pride esp. in one's achievements ⟨is neither ~ nor vaunting in this little chronicle —J.T.Winterich⟩ **2 :** vain display or show **:** VANITY ⟨these feasts, pomps, and *vainglories* —Shak.⟩ **syn** see PRIDE

²vainglory \"\ *vi* **:** to indulge in or show vainglory

vain·ly *adv* [ME *vainly*, *veinly*, fr. *vain*, *vein* vain + *-ly* — more at VAIN] **:** in a vain manner **:** in vain

vain·ness *n* -ES **:** the quality or state of being vain

¹vair \ˈva(a)|(ə)r, ˈvel, |ə\ *n* -S [ME *veir*, fr. OF *vair*, fr. *vair*, adj., variegated, fr. L *varius* variegated, various — more at VARIOUS] **1 :** a squirrel skin widely used in medieval times as fur trimming or lining for the garments of kings, nobles, and prelates — see MINIVER **2 a** *obs* **:** VAIR ANCIENT **b :** a heraldic fur consisting of rows of interlocking upright and inverted shield-shaped or bell-shaped panes alternately argent and azure unless other tinctures are specified with the rows being so placed one beneath another that each pane stands broad edge to broad edge or point to point with one of the opposite tincture **c** (1) **:** a fur made up of panes typically found in vair — see COUNTERVAIR, VAIR IN PALE, VAIR UNDY (2) **:** a fur or other repeat pattern known or believed to be historically a variety, variant, or modification of vair in its original medieval form

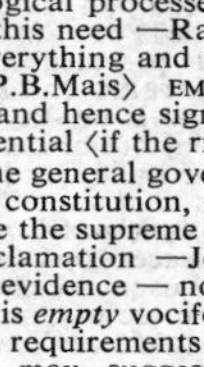

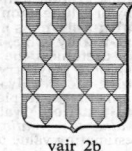

vair 2b

²vair \"\ *adj* **1 :** of the heraldic vair **2 :** VAIRÉ

¹vair ancient *n* [part trans. of F *vair ancien*] **:** a heraldic vair consisting of horizontal bands each of which is divided per fess wavy argent and azure unless other tinctures are specified

²vair ancient *adj* **:** of the heraldic vair ancient

¹vairé *or* **vairy** \ˈva(a)(ə)rē, -erē\ *adj* [*vairé* fr. F, fr. OF *vair*; *vairy* fr. ME *varri*, fr. MF *vairy*, fr. OF *vair*] **1 :** having the pattern of a heraldic vair — used when the tinctures are other then argent and azure ⟨a fess ~ or and gules⟩ **2 :** VAIR 1

²vairé *or* **vairy** \"\ *n* -S **:** a heraldic vair consisting of tinctures other than argent and azure

vair–en–point \ˌ⸗ən¦⸗\ *n* [F, lit., vair in point] **:** VAIR IN PALE

vair in pale *n* **:** a heraldic vair in which each pane stands broad edge to point or point to broad edge with one of the same tincture above or below it

vair undy *n* **:** a heraldic vair in pale in which each pane stands broad edge to point or point to broad edge with one of the other tincture above or below it

vais *usu cap*, *pl of* VAI

vai·she·shi·ka *also* **vai·se·si·ka** \vīˈshāshəkə, -ˈsāsə-\ *n* -S *usu cap* [Skt *vaiśeṣika* distinction, distinct nature of the eternal substances, fr. *viśeṣa* distinction, fr. *viśiṣyate* it is distinguished, fr. *vi* apart, asunder + *śiṣyate* it is left — more at WITH] **:** an orthodox philosophical system in Hinduism distinguished by its atomic theory of cosmology

vaish·na·va *also* **vais·na·va** \ˈvīs(h)nəvə\ *n* -S *usu cap* [Skt *vaiṣṇava* of Vishnu, fr. *Viṣṇu*, second god of the supreme triad of Hindu gods consisting of Brahma, Vishnu and Siva] **:** a worshiper of Vishnu in any of his forms or incarnations

vaish·na·vism *also* **vais·na·vism** \-ə,vizəm\ *n* -S *usu cap* **:** the worship of Vishnu

vaish·na·vite \-ˌvīt\ *n* -S *usu cap* [Skt *vaiṣṇava* + E *-ite*] **:** VAISHNAVA

vais·ya *also* **vaish·ya** \ˈvīs(h)yə\ *n* -S *usu cap* [Skt *vaiśya*, fr. *viś* settlement — more at VICINITY] **1 :** a twice-born Hindu of the third ancient varna assigned by classical law to an agricultural or commercial occupation **2 :** a twice-born Hindu belonging to one of a large group of modern upper castes traditionally derived from the ancient Vaisya varna — compare BRAHMAN, KSHATRIYA, SUDRA

vai·vode \ˈvī,vōd\ *or* **voi·vode** \ˈvȯi,-\ *n* -S [*vaivode* fr. NL & It *vaivoda*, fr. obs. Hung *vajvoda*, fr. Serb & Slovene *vojvoda*, fr. OBulg *vojevoda*, lit., chieftain, fr. *voinŭ* warrior, soldier (akin to Lith *vyti* to pursue, hunt) + *voditi* to lead; *voivode* fr. Russ *voevoda*, fr. OBulg — more at VIM] **:** a military commander or governor of a town or province in various Slavic countries

vaj·ra·ya·na \ˌvəjrəˈyänə, -rēˈä-\ *n* -S *usu cap* [Skt *vajrayāna*, lit., vehicle of thunderbolt, fr. *vajra* thunderbolt + *yāna* vehicle] **:** tantric Buddhism **:** TANTRISM 2

va·kass \vəˈkäs\ *n* -ES [Arm *vagas*] **:** an amice worn by priests of the Armenian Church

va·keel *or* **va·kil** \vəˈkē(ə)l\ *n* -S [Hindi *vakel*, fr. Ar *wakīl*] **1 :** an agent or representative esp. of a person of political importance in India **2 :** an authorized public pleader in a court of justice in India

val \ˈval\ *or* **val lace** *n* -S *often cap V* [by shortening] **:** VALENCIENNES

val *abbr* **1** valentine **2** valuation **3** value; valued

val·ance *also* **val·lance** \ˈvalən(t)s, ˈväl-\ *n* -S [ME *valaunce*, *vallance*, perh. fr. *Valence*, textile manufacturing commune of southeast France] **1 a :** a usu. gathered or pleated drapery attached along the edge of a bed, table, altar, canopy, or shelf and hanging straight and loosely often to the floor for concealment and decoration **b :** a similar decoration of leather, metal, wood esp. on furniture **c :** a short usu. shaped or pleated drapery or a short wood or metal frame used as a decorative heading to conceal the top of curtains and fixtures **2 :** something resembling a valance: as **a :** a flap on the back of a cap **b :** a fringe of hair (as a mustache) **c :** a decorative treatment in the form of balancing scrolls that resemble a drapery valance

val·anced \-st\ *adj* [*valance* + *-ed*] **:** provided or decorated with a valance ⟨an old set-stitched chair, ~ and fringed around —Laurence Sterne⟩

valdenses *usu cap*, *var of* WALDENSES

val·de·pe·nas \ˌväldəˈpānyəs\ *n*, *usu cap* [fr. *Valdepeñas*, commune of south central Spain] **:** a table wine usu. red but occas. white from the village of Valdepeñas south of Madrid, Spain

¹vale \ˈvāl, *esp before pause or consonant* -āəl\ *n* -S [ME, fr. OF *val*, fr. L *valles*, *vallis* valley; akin to L *volvere* to roll — more at VOLUBLE] **1 :** a low-lying country or tract usu. containing a brook or a stream ⟨a prospect of the city in the ~ below —Thomas Gray⟩ ⟨the pattern of parallel strips made by the alternation of ~*s* and cuesta ridges —O.D.Von Engeln⟩ **2 a :** the earth, world, or earthly life in contrast to heaven or eternity ⟨this ~ of tears⟩ ⟨this mortal ~⟩ ⟨the tortured route through the ~ of foreign policy —E.E.Morison⟩ **b :** the scene or place of life ⟨the ~ of time⟩ ⟨the cool sequestered ~ of life —Thomas Gray⟩

²vale *var of* VAIL

³va·le \ˈv|ä(ˌ)lā, ˈw|, |ā(-\ *n* -S [L, farewell, interj., fr. 2d sing. imper. of *valēre* to be strong, be well — more at WIELD] **:** a salutation of leave-taking — often used interjectionally

val·e·dic·tion \ˌvaləˈdikshən\ *n* -S [L *valedictus* (past part. of *valedicere* to say farewell, fr. *vale* farewell + *dicere* to say) + E *-ion* — more at DICTION] **1 :** an act or instance of bidding farewell ⟨each departing with a brief ~⟩ **2 :** VALEDICTORY

¹val·e·dic·to·ri·an \ˌvalə,dikˈtōrēən, -tȯr-\ *n* -S [²*valedictory* + *-an*] **:** the student usu. of the highest rank in a graduating class who delivers the valedictory oration at the commencement exercises

²valedictorian \¦⸗⸗¦⸗⸗⸗\ *adj* **:** of, relating to, or having the characteristics of a valedictory or valedictorian ⟨the ~ speech⟩ ⟨~ gush about gleams, goals, ideals —H.N.Fairchild⟩

¹val·e·dic·to·ry \¦valə¦dikt(ə)rē, -ri\ *adj* [L *valedictus* (past part. of *valedicere*) + E *-ory*] **1 :** spoken or given at a time or ceremony of farewell or leave-taking esp. from an office or an educational institution ⟨a ~ address⟩ ⟨~ praise for his courtesy and uniformly manly course —Dixon Wecter⟩ **2 :** performed or carried out by way of valediction ⟨has settled his hopes on a spectacular Asian compromise as a suitable ~ gesture —*Time*⟩

²valedictory \"\ *n* -ES **:** a valedictory oration or statement; *specif* **:** the speech of farewell usu. given at the commencement exercises of a school or college

va·lence \ˈvālən(t)s\ *n* -S [LL *valentia* power, capacity, fr. L *valent-*, *valens* (pres. part. of *valēre* to be strong) + *-ia* -y — more at WIELD] **1 a :** the degree of combining power of an element or radical **:** the number of atoms of hydrogen, sodium, fluorine, or other univalent element with which an atom of the element or a molecule of the radical will combine by means of bonds or for which it can be substituted or with which it can be compared **:** the oxidation state of an element in a compound ⟨potassium has a ~ of one because a gram atom combines with a gram atom of hydrogen to form potassium hydride KH or with a gram atom of fluorine to form potassium fluoride KF⟩ ⟨iron has a variable ~: two in ferrous chloride $FeCl_2$ and three in ferric chloride $FeCl_3$⟩ — see COVALENCE, ELECTROVALENCE; compare COORDINATE BOND, POLAR VALENCE 2 **b :** a unit of valence ⟨the four ~*s* of carbon⟩ **2 a :** relative capacity to unite, react, or interact (as with antigens or a biological substrate) **b :** the degree of attractiveness an individual, activity, or object possesses as a behavioral goal ⟨the group may have a positive ~ for member A because he has friends in it —Neal Gross & W.E.Martin⟩

valence electron *n* **:** a single electron or one of two or more electrons contained in the outer incomplete shell of an atom and responsible for the chemical properties of the atom ⟨sodium and other alkali metals have only one *valence electron*⟩

valence number *n* **:** OXIDATION STATE

valence shell *n* **:** the outermost shell of an atom containing the valence electrons

va·len·cia \vəˈlench(ē)ə, -n(t)sēə\ *adj*, *usu cap* **1** [fr. *Valencia*, commune of eastern Spain] **:** of or from the city of Valencia, Spain **:** of the kind or style prevalent in Valencia **2** [fr. *Valencia*, commercial city of northern Venezuela] **:** of or from the city of Valencia, Venezuela **:** of the kind or style prevalent in Valencia

valencia cocktail *n*, *usu cap V* **:** a cocktail made from apricot brandy and orange juice and flavored with several dashes of orange bitters

¹va·len·cian \-nch(ē)ən, -n(t)sēən\ *adj*, *usu cap* [*Valencia*, province & commune of eastern Spain + E *-an*] **1 :** of, relating to, or characteristic of Valencia province or city **2 :** of, relating to, or characteristic of the Valencians

²valencian \"\ *n* -S *cap* **:** a native or resident of Valencia province or city in Spain

va·len·ci·ennes \vəˌlen(t)sēˈen(z) *sometimes* ¦valənsē¦en(z) *or* ¦valən¦sēnz\ *also* **valenciennes lace** *n*, *usu cap V* [fr. *Valenciennes*, industrial city of northern France] **:** a fine bobbin lace having a ground with a square or diamond-shaped mesh which is plaited rather than twisted and a pattern made together with the ground and of the same kind of thread

va·len·cy \ˈvālənsē, -si\ *n* -ES [LL *valentia* power, capacity — more at VALENCE] *chiefly Brit* **:** VALENCE

va·lent \ˈvālənt *sometimes* ˌvalənt; *the second pronunc is not shown at the entries of compounds*\ *adj* [back-formation fr. *valence* or *valency*] **:** having valence — usu. used in combination ⟨bi*valent*⟩ ⟨multi*valent*⟩

val·en·tine \ˈvalən,tīn, *dial* ˈväl- *or* ˈvȯl-\ *n* -S [ME, after Saint *Valentine's* Day] **1 :** a sweetheart chosen or complimented on St. Valentine's Day **:** one's beloved **2** *dial Brit* **:** one of a number of folded papers containing a name to be drawn as a valentine **3 a :** something sent or given esp. to a sweetheart on St. Valentine's Day; *specif* **:** an ornamental engraved or printed greeting of a mock sentimental or comic character sent often anonymously on this day **b :** a piece of writing or a literary work expressing praise or affection for something ⟨toss a nostalgic ~ to his Bronx boyhood in his novel —*Time*⟩ — usu. used with *to* ⟨one of the finest American plays . . . is a radiant personal mirror of life and a ~ to humanity —T.J.Panter⟩ ⟨this ~ to the pioneer jazz-makers of the Twenties —Lee Rogow⟩ **4** *usu cap* **:** LOVE SONG

valentine day *or* **valentine's day** *n*, *usu cap V&D* **:** SAINT VALENTINE'S DAY

¹val·en·tin·i·an \ˌvalən·ˈtinēən\ *n* -S *usu cap* [ME, fr. *Valentinus* 2nd cent. A.D. Roman Gnostic philosopher and teacher + ME *-an*] **:** an adherent of Valentinianism

²valentinian \¦⸗⸗¦⸗⸗⸗\ *adj* **:** of or relating to Valentinus or his system of gnosticism

val·en·tin·i·an·ism \ˌ⸗⸗ˈ⸗⸗ə,nizəm\ *n* -S *usu cap* [*valentinian* + *-ism*] **:** gnosticism in which the divine pleroma is conceived as being made up of aeons that are held to be aspects of the nature and activity of God

val·en·ti·nite \ˈvalən·ˌtē,nī+\ *n* -S [G *valentinit*, fr. Basil *Valentine* 15th cent. Ger. alchemist + G *-it* -ite] **:** a mineral Sb_2O_3 consisting of antimony oxide in orthorhombic crystals polymorphous with senarmontite

val·en·tin's knife \ˈvalən·ˌtēnz-\ *n*, *usu cap V* [prob. after Gabriel G. *Valentin* †1883 Ger. physiologist] **:** a knife made with two parallel adjustable blades and used to cut thin slices of fresh tissues

vale of years [¹*vale*] **:** the declining years of life

valer- *or* **valero-** *comb form* [*valeric (acid)*] **:** valeric acid ⟨*valer*aldehyde⟩ ⟨*valero*lactone⟩

val·er·aldehyde \¦valər+\ *n* [ISV *valer-* + *aldehyde*] **:** any of four isomeric liquid aldehydes C_4H_9CHO corresponding to the valeric acids; *esp* **:** the normal aldehyde $CH_3(CH_2)_3CHO$

val·er·amide \"+\ *n* [ISV *valer-* + *-amide*] **:** any of four crystalline amides $C_4H_9CONH_2$ derived from the valeric acids; *esp* **:** the normal amide $CH_3(CH_2)_3CONH_2$

val·er·ate \ˈvalə,rāt\ *n* -S [ISV *valer-* + *-ate*] **:** a salt or ester of valeric acid

va·le·ri·an \vəˈlirēən\ *n* -S [ME, fr. MF or ML; MF *valeriane*, fr. ML *valeriana*, prob. fr. fem. of *valerianus* of Valeria, fr. *Valeria*, Roman province formerly part of Pannonia + L *-anus* -an] **1 :** a plant of the genus *Valeriana* (esp. *V. officinalis*) — compare GREEK VALERIAN **2 a :** a drug consisting of the dried rhizome and roots of the garden heliotrope (*Valeriana officinalis*) formerly used as a carminative and sedative esp. in nervous conditions **b :** the dried rhizome and roots of an East Indian valerian (*V. wallichii*) used in incense and perfumes

va·le·ri·ana \vəˌlirēˈanə, -ˈä-, -ˈā-\ *n* [NL, fr. ML, valerian] **1** *cap* **:** a large genus of widely distributed perennial herbs (family Valerianaceae) having lobed or dissected leaves and cymose white or pink flowers with spurless corollas **2** -S **:** any plant of the genus *Valeriana*

va·le·ri·a·na·ce·ae \və,lirēəˈnāsē,ē\ *n pl*, *cap* [NL, fr. *Valeriana*, type genus + *-aceae*] **:** a family of herbs (order Rubiales) chiefly of temperate regions having opposite leaves and mostly cymose flowers, a regular or irregular corolla and free anthers, and an achene fruit crowned with a persistent calyx border — **va·le·ri·a·na·ceous** \⸗¦⸗⸗⸗¦nāshəs\ *adj*

va·le·ri·a·na·les \-ā(ˌ)lēz\ *n pl*, *cap* [NL, fr. *Valeriana* + *-ales*] *in some classifications* **:** an order of dicotyledonous plants consisting of the two families Valerianaceae and Dipsacaceae characterized by a gamopetalous corolla and an inferior ovary

va·le·ri·a·nel·la \-ˈnelə\ *n*, *cap* [NL, fr. *Valeriana* + *-ella*] **:** a genus of annual herbs (family Valerianaceae) that are natives of the Old World but naturalized widely (as in the U. S.) and are distinguished by the variously appendaged but not pappose calyx — compare CORN SALAD

valerian family *n* **:** VALERIANACEAE

valerian oil *n* **:** a yellowish green to brownish essential oil that has an unpleasant odor and is obtained from the roots and rhizomes of the garden heliotrope

va·le·ric acid \vəˈlirik-, -lerik-\ *also* **va·le·ri·an·ic acid** \-¦lirē¦anik-\ *n* [*valerian* + *-ic*; fr. its occurrence in the root of valerian] **:** any of four isomeric fatty acids C_4H_9COOH or a mixture of two or more of them: **a :** a liquid normal acid $CH_3(CH_2)_3COOH$ that has a disagreeable odor, that is found in pyroligneous acid and petroleum distillates, that is made synthetically (as by oxidation of normal pentyl alcohol or by fermentation), and that is used in organic synthesis — called also *pentanoic acid* **b :** ISOVALERIC ACID **c :** a liquid acid $CH_3CH_2CH(CH_3)COOH$ existing in three optically isomeric forms and occurring usu. in the dextrorotatory form in a few essential oils; α-methyl-butyric acid **d :** PIVALIC ACID

va·le·ro·lactone \vəˈli(ˌ)rō, ˈvalərō+\ *n* [ISV *valer-* + *lactone*] **:** the lactone $C_5H_8O_2$ of any hydroxy derivative of valeric acid; *esp* **:** the γ-lactone found in pyroligneous acid, made synthetically, and used chiefly as a solvent

va·le·ryl \vəˈlirəl, ˈvalə,ril\ *n* -S [ISV *valer-* + *-yl*] **:** the univalent radical C_4H_9CO of a valeric acid; *esp* **:** the normal radical $CH_3(CH_2)_3CO—$

vales *pl of* VALE

¹valet \ˈvalət (*usu* -əd·+V) *also* ˈva,lā *or* vaˈlā *sometimes* vəˈlā *or* ˈvalē *or* ˈvali\ *n* -S [MF *vaslet*, *vallet*, *valet*, *varlet* young nobleman, page, squire, domestic servant, fr. (assumed) ML *vassellittus*, dim. of *vassus* servant, vassal — more at VASSAL] **1 a :** a man's male servant who performs personal services (as taking care of clothing and doing errands) for his employer — called also *manservant* **b :** an employee of a hotel, ship, or other public facility who performs personal services (as the cleaning and repair of clothing) for guests **2 :** a goad or stick with a point of iron **3 :** any of various contrivances usu. of a metal framework designed for holding clothing or personal effects

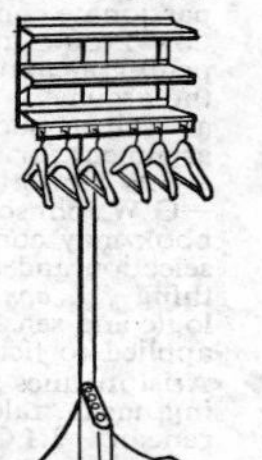

valet 3

²valet \"\ *vt* -ED/-ING/-S **:** to serve as a valet ⟨he . . . was waited upon and ~*ed* by the staff —Dorothy Sayers⟩

va·let de cham·bre \ˌva,lādəˈshäⁿbr(ᵊ), -b(rə)\ *n*, *pl* **valets de chambre** \-ā(z)d-\ [F, lit., chamber valet] **:** VALET 1a

valet de place \-dəˈplàs, -las\ *n*, *pl* **valets de place** \-ā(z)d-\ [F, lit., valet of the locality] **:** a valet who serves transient travelers or strangers by acting as guide ⟨the people the traveler naturally sees most — the tavern keepers, *valets de place*, and postilions —C.G.Bowers⟩

val·et·ry \ˈvalətrē\ *n* -ES [*valet* + *-ry*] **:** the occupation or service of a valet; *also* **:** VALETS

¹val·e·tu·di·nar·i·an \ˌvalə,tüdᵊnˈerēən, -lə·ˌtyü-, -ˈa(a)r-, -ˈär-\ *n* -S [¹*valetudinary* + *-an*] **:** a person of a weak or sickly constitution; *esp* **:** one whose chief concern is his invalidism ⟨was a ~ and believed that no other physician could keep him in health —Bertrand Russell⟩

²valetudinarian \¦⸗⸗,⸗⸗¦⸗⸗⸗\ *adj* **:** of, relating to, or characteristic of a valetudinarian **:** SICKLY, WEAK, INFIRM ⟨become slight-limbed, puny, and ~ —William Cowper⟩ ⟨the virtue which the world wants is a healthful virtue, not a ~ virtue —T.B.Macaulay⟩

val·e·tu·di·nar·i·an·ism \ˌ⸗⸗,⸗⸗ˈ⸗⸗ə,nizəm\ *n* -S [¹*valetudinarian* + *-ism*] **:** the condition or state of mind of a valetudinarian

¹val·e·tu·di·nary \¦valə¦tüdᵊn,erē, -lə·¦tyü-, -ri\ *adj* [L *valetudinarius*, fr. *valetudin-*, *valetudo* health, state of health, sickness (fr. *valēre* to be well + *-tudin-*, *-tudo* -tude) + *-arius* -ary — more at WIELD] **:** VALETUDINARIAN

²valetudinary \"\ *n* -ES **:** VALETUDINARIAN

val·gus \ˈvalgəs\ *n* -ES [NL, adj., turned outward to an abnormal degree, fr. L, bowlegged — more at WALK] **:** a position of a joint's being turned outward to an abnormal degree ⟨the heel is in ~ —*Yr. Bk. of Orthopedics & Traumatic Surgery*⟩

val·hal·la \valˈhalə, välˈhälə, vålˈhålə\ *also* **wal·hal·la** \wȯl-, wäl-\ *n* -S *usu cap* [fr. *Valhalla*, *Walhalla*, in Norse mythology the hall of Odin into which he receives the souls of heroes slain in battle, fr. G & ON; G *Walhalla*, fr. ON *Valhöll*, lit., hall of the slain, fr. *valr* the slain + *höll* hall; akin to OE *wæl* slaughter, the slain, OHG *wal*, OIr *fuil* blood — more at HALL] **:** a place of honor or glorification **:** SHRINE ⟨announced that later a pantheon will replace the present tomb . . . as a *Valhalla* for all the fallen heroes —*Newsweek*⟩ ⟨has made the . . . city a gourmet's *Valhalla* and lures lovers of fine food from all over the world —J.A.Maxwell⟩

va·li \ˈvälē\ *n* -S [Turk *vali*, fr. Ar *walīy* wali] **1 :** a governor general of a vilayet **2 :** WALI 1

val·iance \ˈvalyən(t)s\ *n* -S [ME *valiaunce*, fr. MF *vaillance*, fr. OF, fr. *vaillant* valiant] **:** VALIANCY ⟨on that . . . day there were terror and ~ and devotion —Adria Langley⟩

val·ian·cy \-nsē, -nsi\ *n* -ES [*valiant* + *-cy*] **:** the quality or state of being valiant **:** BRAVERY, VALOR

¹val·iant \ˈvalyənt\ *adj* [ME *valiaunt*, fr. MF *vaillant*, fr. OF, fr. pres. part. of *valoir* to be strong, be worth, fr. L *valēre* — more at WIELD] **1** *obs* **:** FIRM, STRONG, ROBUST **2 :** possessing or acting with bravery or boldness **:** COURAGEOUS, INTREPID, STOUTHEARTED ⟨~ he was, cunning and skilled in war —Charles Kingsley⟩ ⟨a ~ and energetic lot whose legends described their long migration —Marjory S. Douglas⟩ ⟨was . . . an ardent lover of mankind and a passionate and ~ idealist —J.H. Holmes⟩ — sometimes used ironically ⟨became this chieftain's guest, crony, and ~ drinking companion —Alan Devoe⟩ ⟨was as ~ a trencherman —B.A.Williams⟩ **3 :** marked by, exhibiting, or carried out with courage, persistence, or determination **:** HEROIC ⟨had a ~ war record —F.C.Brady⟩ ⟨is prepared to make a ~ fight —Douglass Cater⟩ ⟨made a ~ effort to relieve the distress of the people —Hallie Farmer⟩ ⟨against all these . . . forces the critic and the historian must make a ~ struggle —L.P.Smith⟩ — sometimes used ironically ⟨his contribution had been a ~ plan to send a thousand men to die gloriously in a futile attack —Leslie Rees⟩ **4 :** possessing merit or worth **:** EXCELLENT, NOTEWORTHY ⟨wrote two most ~ and revelatory works of realism —Sinclair Lewis⟩ ⟨the six-volume series began . . . with his ~ and lovely impressions of childhood —Brooks Atkinson⟩ **syn** see BRAVE

²valiant \"\ *n* -S **:** a valiant person ⟨the first white comers . . . were two ~*s* of Cortez's band —Julian Dana⟩

val·iant·ly *adv* **:** in a valiant manner **:** BRAVELY, COURAGEOUSLY, DETERMINEDLY

val·iant·ness *n* -ES [ME *valiauntnesse*, fr. *valiaunt* valiant + *-nesse* -ness] *obs* **:** the quality or state of being valiant

val·id \ˈvaləd\ *adj* [MF or ML; MF *valide*, fr. ML *validus*, fr. L, strong, fr. *valēre* to be strong — more at WIELD] **1 a :** having legal strength or force **:** incapable of being rightfully overthrown or set aside **:** sanctioned or authorized by sovereign temporal or spiritual power ⟨a ~ deed⟩ ⟨a ~ covenant⟩ ⟨a ~ title⟩ ⟨where a client has no ~ ground for divorce —H.S. Drinker⟩ ⟨exempt from the natural laws which may be ~ for lesser creatures —Ritchie Calder⟩ **b :** conforming to conditions essential to sacramental efficacy ⟨the synod also declared that the only ~ baptism was by immersion —K.S.Latourette⟩ **2 a :** well grounded or justifiable **:** applicable to the matter at

hand : PERTINENT, SOUND ⟨the above theory was tested experimentally . . . and was proved to be ~ —H.G.Armstrong⟩ ⟨particular grievances call . . . for the formulation of universally ~ reasons why they should be redressed —Aldous Huxley⟩ ⟨find no ~ evidence for such suspensions —W.R.Inge⟩ ⟨a ~ argument⟩ ⟨a ~ purpose⟩ **b** *of an inference* : correctly derived from its premises; *specif* : true in terms of the logical principles of the logistic system to which the inference belongs **3 a** : able to effect or accomplish what is designed or intended : EFFECTIVE, EFFICACIOUS ⟨literary scholarship has its own ~ methods —René Wellek & Austin Warren⟩ ⟨the written word was no longer a ~ medium, the motion picture having supplanted it —Alexander Klein⟩ ⟨in finally finding her courage ~ it had in the same moment vanished —Janet Terrace⟩ **b** : capable of measuring, predicting, or representing according to intention or design ⟨if the results of university matriculation examinations are a ~ test —B.K.Sandwell⟩ — compare RELIABLE **4 a** : STRONG, POWERFUL **b** : HEALTHY, ROBUST **5 a** *of a taxon* : based on distinctive characters of recognized importance : founded on an adequate basis of classification; *also* : validly published **b** *of the publication of a taxon* : effective and accompanied by a description of the taxon or a reference to a previous description

syn SOUND, COGENT, CONVINCING, TELLING may be compared with VALID in being applied to arguments, reasonings, principles, ideas which have such force that they compel acceptance. Both VALID and SOUND imply that the force is inherent in the rationality of the thought apart from its presentation. A VALID argument or principle is supported either by objective truth or a generally accepted standard or authority ⟨mathematical symbols, which are *valid* whether there is anything corresponding to them in nature or not —W.R.Inge⟩ ⟨charges always *valid* in every age and country —J.A.Hobson⟩ although a VALID concept may have certain especially psychological limits ⟨a "psychological fact" is *valid* for the person who holds it if for no other —F.J.Hoffman⟩ SOUND, which may be applied to both persons and concepts, implies avoidance of fallacies, insufficient evidence, and hasty conclusions, and stresses solid foundation in fact or in reason or both, as well as the habit of clear and deliberate thought, often with an admixture of shrewd practical sense ⟨much too *sound* a political thinker and too sagacious a party leader to rest his case upon abstract theory —V.L.Parrington⟩ ⟨good, *sound* reasons against the passionate conclusions of love —Joseph Conrad⟩ COGENT and CONVINCING apply to ideas (less frequently, to persons) compelling mental assent, but COGENT stresses a force resident in the argument or reasoning, as inevitability or conclusiveness, as well as succinct and lucid presentation ⟨the most *cogent* argument for freedom — man's tremendous innate variability —E.W.Sinnott⟩ ⟨the most *cogent* political comment of the year —G.W.Johnson⟩ whereas a convincing argument, speaker, or book may convince by either sound reasoning or by skillful selection and presentation ⟨there are other ways of making a thing . . . *convincing* . . . besides merely appealing to one's logic and sense of fact —Irving Babbitt⟩ CONVINCING is often applied to fictional creations having the flavor of reality ⟨in Aristophanes you have the *convincing* hurly-burly, the sweating, mean, talented, scrambling, laughing life of the Mediterranean —J.J.Chapman⟩ TELLING suggests an immediate and crucial effect striking at the essence of the point, idea, or sentiment to be conveyed regardless of the validity of the cause ⟨certainly makes some *telling* points . . . with a deftness that will disarm orthodox heresy-hunters —M.R.Cohen⟩ ⟨paused as if to edit his woes and select the most *telling* ones —Norman Mailer⟩

val·i·date \ˈvalə,dāt, *usu* -ād·+V\ *vt* -ED/-ING/-S [ML *validatus*, past part. of *validare* to validate, fr. *validus* valid] **1 a** : to make legally valid : confirm or declare formally or officially : RATIFY ⟨requires legislation by the whole Congress to ~ every treaty —*Civil Liberties*⟩ ⟨*validated* the marriages of former slaves —*Amer. Guide Series: N. C.*⟩ **b** : to grant official sanction to by or as if by stamping or marking ⟨the Coast Guard would ~ seamen's papers —Frank O'Leary⟩ **c** : to confirm the validity of (an election); *also* : to declare (a person) elected **2** : to corroborate or support on a sound basis or authority : VERIFY, SUBSTANTIATE ⟨true ideas are those that we can assimilate, ~, corroborate —William James⟩ ⟨the freedom . . . to worry through with a theory until it is *validated* or disproved —*Science*⟩ ⟨describe, define, and ~ the doctrinal distinctions between church and chapel —W.L.Sperry⟩ **syn** see CONFIRM

val·i·da·tion \,valəˈdāshən\ *n* -S [*validate* + *-ion*] : an act, process, or instance of validating ⟨meeting to discuss ~ of the contract⟩ ⟨stamping the ~ on the passport⟩; *specif* : the process of determining the degree of validity of a measuring device ⟨many . . . criteria require almost as much ~ as the tests they are supposed to validate —Herbert Goldhamer⟩

val·i·da·to·ry \ˈvaləda,tōrē\ *adj* [*validate* + *-ory*] : of or relating to validation

va·lid·i·ty \vəˈlidəd·ē, -idətē, -i *sometimes* vaˈl-\ *n* -ES [MF or ML; MF *validité*, fr. ML *validitat-, validitas*, fr. L, strength, fr. *validus* strong + *-itat-, -itas* -ity — more at VALID] : the quality or state of being valid ⟨the ~ of marriages celebrated in accordance with polygamous forms . . . is a question of considerable difficulty —J.H.C.Morris⟩ ⟨you can travel any time . . . during the nine-day ~ of the ticket —Richard Joseph⟩ ⟨a defender of the ~ of Presbyterian ordination —H.E.Starr⟩ ⟨dared question the ~ of the esthetic or moral principles —Manès Sperber⟩ ⟨the ~ of a test is a relative matter, depending upon the criterion used —J.B.Carroll⟩

val·id·ly *adv* : in a valid manner : with validity ⟨to do by exposure and publicity what . . . may not ~ be done by legislation —*New Republic*⟩ ⟨could not ~ oppose the journey —Arnold Bennett⟩ ⟨a name that has not been ~ published has no standing in nomenclature —*Internat'l Bull. of Bacteriological Nomenclature & Taxonomy*⟩

val·id·ness *n* -ES : VALIDITY

val·i·en·te \,valēˈentē\ *n, pl* **valiente** *or* **valientes** *usu cap* **1 a** : a Chibchan people of western Panama **b** : a member of such people **2** : a language of the Valiente people

valine \ˈva,lēn, ˈvā,-, -lən\ *n* -S [ISV *val-* (fr. iso*valeric* acid) + *-ine*] : a crystalline amino acid $(CH_3)_2CHCH(NH_2)COOH$ that in the dextrorotatory L form is essential in the nutrition of lower animals and man and that is obtained in this form by the hydrolysis of proteins (as casein or zein) and in the racemic form by synthesis; α-amino-isovaleric acid

valis *pl of* VALI

va·lise \vəˈlēs, *chiefly Brit* -ēz\ *n* -S [F, fr. It *valigia*] : TRAVELING BAG

val·kyr \ˈvalkə(r)\ *n* -S *usu cap* [by shortening] : VALKYRIE

val·kyri·an \(ˈ)valˈkirēən, -kir-\ *adj, usu cap* [*valkyrie* + *-an*] : of or relating to the Valkyries or to battle ⟨like some *Valkyrian* hero lighting a fire in a black forest —Anais Nin⟩

val·kyrie \valˈkirē, -ˈkīr, -ri, ˈ=,==; ˈvalkər-\ *also* **wal·kyrie** \wȯl-,wäl-\ *n* -S *usu cap* [G & ON; G *walküre*, fr. ON *valkyrja*, lit., chooser of the slain; akin to OE *wælcyrige* witch, sorceress; both fr. a prehistoric WGmc-NGmc compound whose first constituent is represented by ON *valr* the slain and whose second constituent is akin to ON *kjōsa* to choose — more at VALHALLA, CHOOSE] : one of the maidens of the mythological Norse god Odin who hover over the field of battle choosing those to be slain and conducting the worthy heroes to Valhalla

valla *pl of* VALLUM

val·la·bha·char·ya \,valəˌbäˈchärya\ *n* -S *usu cap* [Skt *vallabhācārya*, fr. *Vallabha fl*1520 Hindu religious leader + *ācārya* teacher — more at ACHARYA] : one of a Hindu Vaishnava sect founded by the Brahmin Vallabha

val lace *often cap V, var of* VAL

val·la·do·lid \ˌvaləˈdəˌlid -ˌlē; ˌvä(l)yədəˈlē, -yəthə-\ *adj, usu cap* [fr. *Valladolid*, commune of northwest central Spain] : of or from the city of Valladolid, Spain : of the kind or style prevalent in Valladolid

vallance *var of* VALANCE

val·la·ry *also* **val·lery** \ˈvalərē\ *adj* [L (*corona*) *vallaris* mural crown, fr. *vallum* wall, rampart + *-aris* -ar] *heraldry* : formed of a gold circlet surmounted by flat pointed or curved strips

val·late \ˈva,lāt\ *adj* [L *vallatus*, past part. of *vallare* to surround with a wall, fr. *vallum* wall, rampart — more at WALL] : having a raised edge surrounding a depression

vallate papilla *n* : CIRCUMVALLATE PAPILLA

val·la·tion \vaˈlāshən\ *n* -S [LL *vallation-, vallatio*, fr. L *vallatus* + *-ion-, -io* -ion] *archaic* : an earthwork wall : RAMPART, ENTRENCHMENT

val·lec·u·la \vəˈlekyələ, vaˈl-\ *n, pl* **vallecu·lae** \-yə,lē, -lī\ [NL, fr. LL, little valley, depression, dim. of *valles* valley — more at VALE] : an anatomical groove, channel, or depression: as **a** (1) : a groove on the stem of a plant of the genus *Equisetum* (2) : a groove on the fruit of a various plant of the family Ammiaceae **b** : a groove between the base of the tongue and the epiglottis **c** : a fossa on the underside of the cerebellum separating the hemispheres and including the inferior vermis

val·lec·u·lar \-yələ(r)\ *adj* [NL *vallecula* + E *-ar*] : of or relating to a vallecula

vallecular canal *n* : one of the large intercellular passages of the cortical parenchyma alternating with the vascular bundles in the stems of plants of the genus *Equisetum*

vallecula syl·vii \-ˈsilvē,ī, -vē,ē\ *n, usu cap S* [NL, lit., vallecula of Sylvius, after Franciscus *Sylvius* (Franz de la Boë) †1672 Ger. anatomist] : the depression in the brain in which the lateral fissure begins

val·lec·u·late \-lət, -,lāt\ *adj* [NL *vallecula* + E *-ate*] : having valleculae

val·le·ri·ite \vəˈlirē,īt\ *n* -S *usu cap* [Sw, *valleriit*, fr. G. *Wallerius* (*Vallerius*) †1742 Swed. mineralogist + Sw *-it* -ite] : a mineral $Cu_2Fe_4S_7$ consisting of sulfide of copper and iron perhaps identical with the artificial compound $Cu_3Fe_4S_6$

val·ley \ˈvalē, -li\ *n, pl* **valleys** *often attrib* [ME *valeie, valey*, fr. OF *valee*, fr. *val* valley, vale — more at VALE] **1 a** : an elongate depression of the earth's surface commonly situated between ranges of hills or mountains and often comprising a drainage area — compare CANYON, GULLY, RAVINE; see RIFT VALLEY, SYNCLINAL VALLEY **b** : an area of generally flat land extending many miles inland and drained or watered by a large river and its tributary streams **2 a** : a low, gloomy, or fearsome place or situation ⟨the ~ of the shadow of death⟩ ⟨a ~ of misery without parallel in industrial history —Roger Burlingame⟩ **b** : a low point in a course of development esp. as represented or capable of being represented on a graph ⟨peaks of inflation and . . . ~*s* of extreme depression —F.D.Roosevelt⟩ ⟨a sequence of sounds . . . is therefore characterized by successive peaks and ~*s* of sonority —Bernard Bloch & G.L.Trager⟩ **3** : a hollow or depression resembling or suggestive of a valley: as **a** : a trough between waves **b** : the place of meeting of two slopes of a roof that form on the plan a reentrant angle; *also* : the material (as sheet metal or tile) placed in a roof valley to shed water **c** : VALLECULA **4** : LILY OF THE VALLEY

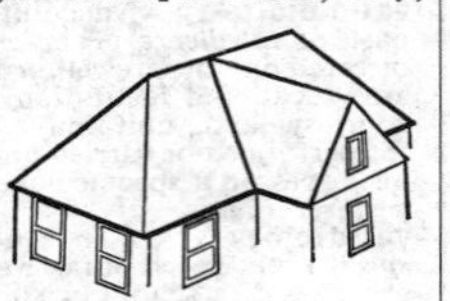

valley 3b

valley board *n* : a board placed for the reception of the lead gutter in the valley of a roof

valley breeze *n* : a breeze that blows up valleys or mountain slopes on clear days

valley fever *n* [so called fr. its prevalence in the San Joaquin valley of central California] : COCCIDIOIDOMYCOSIS

valley flat *n* : the low flat land bordering the channel of a stream

valley glacier *n* : a glacier usu. originating in a cirque at a valley head or in a plateau ice cap and flowing downward between the walls of a valley

valley lily *n* : LILY OF THE VALLEY

valley oak *n* : CALIFORNIA WHITE OAK

valley quail *also* **valley partridge** *n* : CALIFORNIA QUAIL; *esp* : a bird of a distinct variety (*Lophortyx californica californica*) that is distinguished by pale plumage and is found chiefly in dry interior valleys below 5000 feet

valley rafter *n* : the rafter running from the wall plate to the ridge and along the valley of a valley roof

valley tile *n* : roofing tile shaped to fit in the valley of a roof

valley train *n* : a deposit of glaciofluvial sand and gravel extending along the floor of a valley : TRAIN

valley white oak *n* : CALIFORNIA WHITE OAK

valley wind *n* : a breeze of diurnal period depending on the unevenness of land surfaces that blows up the slope by day — compare MOUNTAIN WIND

val·lis \ˈvaləs\ *n* -ES [NL, fr. L, valley — more at VALE] : VALLECULA

val·lis·ne·ria \,valəsˈnirēə, -ləzˈn-\ *n, cap* [NL, fr. Antonio *Vallisnieri* †1730 Ital. naturalist + NL *-ia*] : a genus of submerged aquatic plants (family Hydrocharitaceae) with ribbonlike leaves and pistillate spathes on long finally spiral scapes

val·lis·ne·ri·a·ce·ae \,==,==ˈāsē,ē\ *n pl, cap* [NL *Vallisneria*, type genus + *-aceae*] *in some classifications* : a family comprising monocotyledonous aquatic herbs (order Naiadales) that are distinguished by having flowers with the tube of the perianth more or less adnate to the ovary and the carpels united in fruit and that are now usu. included in Hydrocharitaceae — **val·lis·ne·ri·a·ceous** \;==,==;āshəs\ *adj*

val·lo·ta \vəˈlōd·ə, vaˈ-\ *n, cap* [NL, after Antoine *Vallot* †1671 Fr. physician and botanist] : a genus of southern African bulbous herbs (family Amaryllidaceae) with a long funnel-shaped perianth tube and winged seeds — see SCARBOROUGH LILY

val·lum \ˈvaləm, ˈwä,lu̇m\ *n, pl* **val·la** \-lə, -(,)lä\ *or* **vallums** [L — more at WALL] : a defensive wall of earth, sod, or stone : RAMPART; *specif* : an earthwork surmounted by a palisade esp. as constructed by the ancient Romans from dirt thrown up from a surrounding fosse

valn *abbr* valuation

va·lois \ˈval,wä, =ˈ=\ *adj, usu cap* [*Valois*, French royal house] : of or relating to a French royal family furnishing the rulers of France from 1328 to 1589

¹va·lo·nia *also* **va·lo·nea** *or* **val·lo·nia** \vəˈlōnēə\ *n* -S [It *vallonia, vallonea*, fr. MGk *balanidia*, pl. of *balanidion*, dim. of Gk *balanos* acorn — more at GLAND] : dried acorn cups that are obtained from the valonia oak or sometimes various other oaks, contain from 20 to 40 percent of tannin, and are used esp. in tanning or dressing leather — compare CAMATA

²valonia \"\ *n, cap* [NL] : a genus (coextensive with the family Valoniaceae) of marine green algae having a thallus that is a single oval or cylindrical multinucleate cell often an inch long — compare SEA BOTTLE

va·lo·ni·a·ce·ae \və,lōnēˈāsē,ē\ *n pl, cap* [NL *Valonia*, type genus + *-aceae*] : a family of coenocytic green algae usu. classed among the Siphonocladales but sometimes esp. formerly among the Siphonales — see ²VALONIA — **va·lo·ni·a·ceous** \və;lōnē;āshəs\ *adj*

valonia oak *n* [¹*valonia*] : a tall evergreen oak (*Quercus aegilops*) of southwestern Europe and Asia Minor whose immature fruit yields valonia and camata and whose wood is used for furniture

val·or \ˈvalə(r)\ *n* -S *see -or in Explan Notes* [ME *valour, valor*, fr. MF *valor, valour, valeur*, fr. ML *valor*, fr. L *valēre* to be strong, be worth — more at WIELD] **1** *obs* : VALUE, WORTH **2** : the quality or state of mind with which a person faces danger or hardship boldly or firmly : BRAVERY, COURAGE ⟨the fortitude and ~ of her sons —William Laurence⟩ ⟨to stay there . . . required a ~ which is an essential part of sheer nobility and integrity —*advt*⟩ ⟨perhaps it would have been the better part of ~ to have come back later —John Cogley⟩

val·o·ri·za·tion \,valərəˈzāshən, -,rīˈz-\ *n* -S [Pg *valorização*, fr. *valorizar* to valorize, boost prices (fr. *valor* value, price— fr. ML — + *-izar* -ize, fr. LL) + *-ação* -ation, fr. L *-ation-, -atio*] : the act or process of attempting to give an arbitrary market value or price to a commodity usu. by governmental intervention (as by maintaining a purchasing fund to buy up surpluses or making loans to producers to enable them to store their products); *specif* : price fixing by cartels or agreements — compare TRUST

val·o·rize \ˈvalə,rīz\ *vt* -ED/-ING/-S [back-formation fr. *valorization*] : to determine or set the price of by valorization ⟨the coffee crisis came, and our main product was *valorized*; we tried to protect its price —G.D.Vargas⟩

val·or·ous \ˈvalərəs\ *adj* [ML *valorosus*, fr. *valor* + L *-osus* -ous] **1** : possessing or exhibiting valor : BRAVE, COURAGEOUS ⟨~ men continued the struggle against overwhelming odds⟩ **2** : characterized by or performed with valor ⟨his thoughts would be full of ~ deeds —Joseph Conrad⟩ ⟨the ~ days of 1945 —Byron Price⟩ **syn** see BRAVE

val·or·ous·ly *adv* : in a valorous manner : with valor

val·or·ous·ness *n* -ES : the quality or state of being valorous

val·pa·rai·so *or* **val·pa·ra·i·so** \ˌvalpəˈrī(,)zō, -pəˈrä(-, ˌval,pärəˈē(,)sō\ *adj, usu cap* [fr. *Valparaiso*, seaport of central Chile] : of or from the city of Valparaiso, Chile : of the kind or style prevalent in Valparaiso

valparaiso oak *n, usu cap V* : CANYON LIVE OAK

val·po·li·cel·la \ˌväl,pōləˈchelə\ *n, usu cap* [fr. *Valpolicella*, valley of northern Italy] : a dry red table wine from vineyards near Lake Garda in Venetia in Italy

vals *pl of* VAL

val·sa \ˈvalsə\ *n, cap* [NL] : a genus (the type of the family Valsaceae) of fungi having perithecia immersed in a stroma and usu. with elongated necks converging toward the center — compare DIAPORTHE

val·sa·ce·ae \valˈsāsē,ē\ *n pl, cap* [NL, fr. *Valsa*, type genus + *-aceae*] : a family of ascomycetous fungi (order Sphaeriales) sharing the characters of the genus *Valsa*

val·sal·va maneuver \(,)valˈsalvə-\ *n, usu cap V* [after Antonio *Valsalva* †1723 Ital. anatomist] : the inflation of the middle ear by closing the mouth and nostrils and blowing so as to puff out the cheeks

valse \ˈväls\ *n* -S [F, fr. G *walzer* — more at WALTZ] : WALTZ; *specif* : a concert waltz

val·soid \ˈval,sȯid\ *adj* [NL *Valsa* + E *-oid*] : of, resembling, or having perithecia like fungi of the genus *Valsa*

¹val·u·able \ˈvalyəbəl *also* -yəwəbəl\ *adj* [²*value* + *-able*] **1** : possessing monetary value in use or exchange ⟨disposing of a ~ store of furs —I.B.Richman⟩ ⟨contains the most ~ minerals in a profuse variety —H.T.Buckle⟩ ⟨started the very ~ ostrich feather industry —Carveth Wells⟩ **2 a** : having or exhibiting desirable or esteemed characteristics or qualities esp. of an intrinsic nature : VALUED ⟨another human being equally ~ in the sight of . . . God —W.R.Harris⟩ ⟨both are unquestionably ~ as literature —*Americas*⟩ ⟨a continual surrender of himself . . . to something which is more ~ —T.S. Eliot⟩ **b** : characterized by usefulness, worth, or serviceableness usu. for a specific purpose ⟨experience . . . made him a ~ member of committees —*Current Biog.*⟩ ⟨food is ~ to the animal and moisture to the plant —Samuel Alexander⟩ ⟨the author's illustrations are highly ~ to the text —Irene Smith⟩ ⟨~ information⟩ ⟨~ advice⟩ ⟨~ contributions⟩ **3** *obs, of a person* : ESTIMABLE, WORTHY **syn** see COSTLY 2

²valuable *n* -S : something of worth or value usu. of the nature of personal effects — usu. used in pl. ⟨the man . . . told me to check my ~*s* —Andy Logan⟩ ⟨they contracted to carry ~*s*, securities, and bundles —R.J.Purcell⟩

valuable consideration *n* : an equivalent or compensation having value that is given for something (as money, marriage, services) acquired or promised and that may consist either in some right, interest, profit, or benefit accruing to one party or some responsibility, forbearance, detriment, or loss exercised by or falling upon the other party — compare CONSIDERATION 8

val·u·able·ness *n* -ES : the quality or state of being valuable

val·u·ably \-blē,-bli\ *adv* : in a valuable manner : with value or usefulness ⟨he adds ~ to the record of our national life —George Mayberry⟩

val·u·ate \ˈvalyə,wāt\ *vt* -ED/-ING/-S [back-formation fr. *valuation*] : to place a value on : VALUE, APPRAISE

val·u·a·tion \,valyəˈwāshən\ *n* -S [MF, fr. *valuer* to value (fr. *value*, n.) + *-ation*] **1** : the act or process of valuing or of estimating value or worth: as **a** : the act or process of setting or determining the price of something : APPRAISAL **b** : the determination of the present value of a life insurance policy as measured by the difference between the present value of the benefits promised and the present value of all the premiums expected to be received on the policy **2** : the value or price set upon something as its estimated or determined market value ⟨if the final bid is below the reserve ~ of the wool, the sale may be closed⟩ ⟨the property is valued by local assessors . . . to determine the ~ on which the owners' tax obligations shall be computed —F.A.Ogg & P.O.Ray⟩ **3** : the appreciation or usu. personal estimation of the merit, excellence, or character of something ⟨the private ~ of a person's worth —M.O.Purcell⟩ ⟨children whose ~ of fighting is simple and absolute —Margaret Mead⟩ ⟨the traditional British ~ of high scholastic attainment —A.T.M.Wilson⟩

valuation account *n* : RESERVE ACCOUNT 1

val·u·a·tion·al \ˌvalyəˈwāshənᵊl, -shnəl\ *adj* : of, relating to, or concerned with valuation ⟨all judgments are ~ —Herbert Fingarette⟩ ⟨advances a number of ~ and moral arguments —Frank Thilly⟩ ⟨aspects which determine . . . our ~ attitudes —Eliseo Vivas⟩ — **val·u·a·tion·al·ly** \-ᵊlē, -əlē\ *adv*

valuation survey *n* : the survey of the stand of trees upon an average area of forest selected for detailed measurement and valuation

val·u·a·tive \ˈvalyə,wād·iv, -,wəd· -\ *adj* [²*value* + *-ative*] : VALUATIONAL, EVALUATIVE — **val·u·a·tive·ly** \-d·əvlē\ *adv*

val·u·a·tor \-,wād·ə(r)\ *n* -S [²*value* + *-ator*] : one that valuates; *specif* : APPRAISER

¹val·ue \ˈval(,)yü, -yə (*this pronunc before a vowel or pause is esp South*); *often* -yəw+V; *dial* -lē *or* -li\ *n* -S *often attrib* [ME, fr. MF, fr. (assumed) VL *valuta*, fr. fem. of (assumed) VL *valutus*, past part. of L *valēre* to be worth — more at WIELD] **1 a** : the amount of a commodity, service, or medium of exchange that is the equivalent of something else : a fair return in goods, services, or money ⟨the method of merchandising is to give the buyer good ~ at the right price —*Wall Street Jour.*⟩ ⟨I take his wages because I give good ~ for them —John Buchan⟩ — often used in pl. ⟨priced at levels that reflect . . . policy of passing on to the customer the ever greater ~*s* resulting from technological progress —A.P.Sloan & H.H. Curtice⟩ ⟨the store advertises great ~*s* at large savings⟩ **b** : VALUABLE CONSIDERATION ⟨for ~ received⟩ ⟨a holder or purchaser for ~⟩ **2** : the monetary worth of something : marketable price usu. in terms of a medium of exchange ⟨his holdings increase in ~⟩ ⟨has the same ~ as the U.S. dollar —S.G.Inman⟩ ⟨fool's gold is of practically no ~⟩ ⟨having a ~ of $5⟩ **3 a** : relative worth, utility, or importance : degree of excellence : status in a scale of preferences ⟨we know the ~ of a thing by the way it is sought, shunned, protected —H.N. Wieman⟩ ⟨he knew the precise ~ of men and could marshal them —A.H.Meneely⟩ ⟨learned the ~ of rest in the treatment of . . . tuberculosis —J.F.Fulton⟩ ⟨the physicist has become a military asset of such ~ —I.I.Rabi⟩ ⟨only a few . . . have anything of ~ to say —Edward Clodd⟩ **b** : a liking or regard for a person or thing ⟨she had a ~ for rank and consequence —Jane Austen⟩ ⟨a sad man who, for all his gaiety . . . had little ~ for life —Joyce Cary⟩ **4 a** : a particular quantitative determination in mathematics ⟨as the ~ of *a* increases, *b* decreases⟩ ⟨the ~*s* of the angles vary proportionately⟩ **b** : the amount or extent of a specified measurement of time, space, or quantity ⟨~*s* of the age of the earth determined by the geologists —S.F.Mason⟩ ⟨gives a fairly exact ~ of the constant temperature deeper down —Valter Schytt⟩ ⟨pressure maintained at sea level ~*s* —H.G.Armstrong⟩ **5** : the relative length or duration of a musical tone or note ⟨a quarter note has the ~ of two eighth notes⟩ **6** : the relative rank, importance, or numerical worth of a playing card, chessman, or other game component ⟨the ace is often given a different ~ in different forms of rummy⟩ **7 a** : ¹LIGHTNESS 2 **b** : value in the Munsell system — used in psychophysics; see the Color Charts explanation at COLOR **c** : the relation of one part or detail in a picture to another with respect to lightness and darkness **8** : something (as a principle, quality, or entity) intrinsically valuable or desirable ⟨may call food a ~ for the animal —Samuel Alexander⟩ ⟨the devotee of . . . education and religion was keenly aware of ~ —A.H.Johnson⟩ — often used in pl. ⟨defending the ~*s* of the classical . . . tradition —*Current Biog.*⟩ ⟨all ~*s* are only relative to a given culture —Erich Fromm⟩ ⟨the business world with its regulated system of ~*s* —D.H.Lawrence⟩ ⟨for the sensate mentality . . . human ~*s* are hedonistic and utilitarian —David Bidney⟩ **9** : the precious metals contained in rock, gravel, or earth — usu. used in pl. ⟨the vein carries good ~*s*⟩ ⟨~*s* were discovered here in 1864 and a 10-stamp mill was soon at work —*Amer. Guide*

Series: Nev.⟩ **10** : DENOMINATION 4 ⟨a new airmail ~ is to be issued here soon —*Nat'l Stamp News*⟩ **11** : the distinctive character or quality of a speech sound ⟨an alphabet made up of letters with phonetic ~s —Charlton Laird⟩ ⟨in . . . *Elhua* the *h* really has the ~ of *ch* in the Scottish word *loch* —T.H. Gaster⟩ **12** : a term or an expression in logic that may replace a variable in a propositional function so that the resultant is a true or false statement ⟨*man* is a ~ for *x* in the function *x is rational*⟩

syn WORTH: VALUE and WORTH are frequently differentiated more often by the demands of idiom than by differences in meaning or connotation. VALUE may sometimes suggest an evaluation made from an individual or specific point of view or in an individual or special situation ⟨have to comprehend the artist's own *values* —Havelock Ellis⟩ ⟨the ability of an ordinary Englishman to measure up to the times even though he must change his *values* —J.D.Hart⟩ WORTH may suggest more lasting genuine merit resting on deeper, intrinsic, and enduring qualities ⟨those qualities of the human personality which have an abiding *worth* under the tests of our civilization —Henry Suzzallo⟩ ⟨having gained a more judicious knowledge of the *worth* and dignity of individual man —William Wordsworth⟩ ⟨this book on navigation has chapters of varying *worth*⟩

— **at value** *adv* : at the value fixed by the ruling or current market price — used where goods are sold subject to the price being fixed at some time later than the sale or when shipment is made

²**value** \"\ *vt* -ED/-ING/-S **1 a** : to estimate or assign the monetary worth of : APPRAISE ⟨gave me a piece of his amethyst and I planned to have it properly *valued* —Edwin Corle⟩ ⟨merchandise inventories will be *valued* at the end of the year⟩ — often used with *at* ⟨~s his holdings at $3,000,000⟩ ⟨the institution ~s its plant and endowment at several million⟩ **b** : to rate or scale in usefulness, importance, or general worth : EVALUATE ⟨impresssions which she had long since arranged and *valued* in her mind —Mary Deasy⟩ ⟨search and ~ every element in the conflict before him —Thomas De Quincey⟩ **2** : to consider or rate highly : PRIZE, ESTEEM ⟨from his parents . . . he learned to ~ education —*Current Biog.*⟩ ⟨responded to and *valued* pleasant friendships —Ruth P. Randall⟩ ⟨*valued* himself on his tolerance of heresy in great thinkers —Robert Frost⟩ **3** *archaic* : to show concern for : HEED **syn** see APPRECIATE, ESTIMATE

value added *n* : the value added to or created in a product or commodity by the manufacturing or marketing process exclusive of the cost of materials, supplies, packaging, or overhead

val·ued \ˌval(ˌ)yüd, -yəd\ *adj* [¹*value* + *-ed*] : having such or so many values — usu. used in combination ⟨multi*valued*⟩ ⟨two-*valued*⟩

value date *n, chiefly Brit* : the date when the proceeds of a credit instrument (as a check) or of a foreign exchange transaction (as the sale of dollars for sterling) become available for use

valued policy *n* [fr. past part. of ²*value*] : an insurance policy in which the insurer and insured agree upon a stated value in advance of a loss to be accepted as the measure of liability in case of a total loss

valued policy law *n* : a law requiring insurance companies to pay to the insured in case of total loss the full amount of the insurance regardless of the actual value of the property at the time of the loss

value judgment *n* : a judgment attributing a value (as good, evil, beautiful, desirable) to a thing, action, or entity ⟨even where there are protestations of tolerance and avowed lack of prejudice, *value judgments* creep in —F.J.Brown & J.S.Roucek⟩

val·ue·less \ˈvalyüləs, -yəl-\ *adj* **1** : having no value : WORTHLESS ⟨hemlock, at first considered ~, was ruthlessly destroyed —*Amer. Guide Series: Pa.*⟩ **2** : lacking in values — **val·ue·less·ness** *n* -ES

value of service : the highest sum in transportation charges that any particular class of shippers can afford or will consent to pay

val·u·er \ˈvalyəwə(r)\ *n* -S : one that values: as **a** *Brit* : APPRAISER **b** : CRUISER 4a

values *pl of* VALUE, *pres 3d sing of* VALUE

value system *n* : the system of established values, norms, or goals existing in a society

va·lu·ta \vəˈlüd·ə\ *n* -S [It, value, coin, commercial paper, fr. (assumed) VL *valuta* value — more at VALUE] **1** : the value of a currency (as of a European country) as agreed upon or its exchange value with reference to the currency of another country **2** : foreign exchange in available or usable form

val·va \ˈvalvə\ *n, pl* **val·vae** \-lˌvē, -lˌvī\ [NL, fr. L, leaf of a double door — more at VALVE] : VALVE 2a,3,4

val·val \ˈvalvəl\ *or* **val·var** \-alvə(r)\ *adj* [*valve* + *-al* or *-ar*] : VALVULAR

valvasor *or* **valvassor** *var of* VAVASOR

val·va·ta \valˈväd·ə, -ˈvād·ə\ *n* [NL, fr. fem. of *valvatus* valvate] **1** *cap* : a genus of freshwater operculate snails (suborder Taenioglossa) having the gill attached only by the base so that it forms a process like a feather outside the shell when extended **2** -S : any snail of the genus *Valvata*

val·vate \ˈvalˌvāt\ *adj* [NL *valvatus*, fr. L, having folding doors, fr. *valva* leaf of a folding door + *-atus* -ate — more at VALVE] : having valves or parts resembling a valve: as **a** : meeting at the edges without overlapping ⟨~ sepals⟩ ⟨~ leaves⟩ **b** : opening as if by doors or valves ⟨~ capsules⟩ ⟨~ anthers⟩

valve \ˈvalv, ˈvaüv\ *n* -S *often attrib* [L *valva* leaf of a folding or double door; akin to L *volvere* to roll, turn around — more at VOLUBLE] **1 a** *archaic* : a leaf or a half of a folding or double door **b** : the door or gate used for regulating the flow of water in a sluice **2** : something resembling or suggestive of a valve or stop esp. in regulating, checking, or permitting flow or movement through a passage: as **a** [NL *valva*] : any of various bodily structures esp. in the veins and lymphatics whose function is to close temporarily a passage or orifice or permit a movement of fluid in one direction only and that may consist of a sphincter muscle or of two or sometimes three membranous folds inclined in the normal direction of flow — see MITRAL VALVE, SEMILUNAR VALVE, TRICUSPID VALVE **b** (1) : any of numerous mechanical devices by which the flow of liquid, air or other gas, or loose material in bulk may be started, stopped, or regulated by a movable part that opens, shuts, or partially obstructs one or more ports or passageways; *also* : the movable part of such a device — compare COCK 2; see CHECK VALVE, GATE VALVE, PISTON VALVE, SAFETY VALVE (2) : such a device in a brass wind instrument that is designed for quickly varying the tube length in order to change the fundamental tone by some definite interval and usu. consists of a piston or rotary valve **c** *chiefly Brit* : ELECTRON TUBE, VACUUM TUBE **3** [NL *valva*] **a** : one of the distinct and usu. movably articulated pieces of which the shell of lamellibranch mollusks, brachiopods, barnacles, and some other shell-bearing animals consists **b** : one of the pieces forming the sheath of the ovipositor or external genital organs of many insects **4** [NL *valva*] **a** : one of the segments or pieces into which a dehiscing capsule or legume separates **b** : the portion of various anthers (as of the barberry) resembling a lid **c** : one of the two silicified shells or encasing membranes of a diatom **5** : one of the two halves of a stone or clay mold used by primitive or ancient people for casting bronze objects

valve chest *also* **valve box** *n* : a chamber in which a valve works; *specif* : STEAM CHEST

valved \-vd\ *adj* [*valve* + *-ed*] **1** : VALVATE **2** : provided or equipped with valves ⟨~ outlets⟩ ⟨~ musical instruments⟩

valve gear *n* : any of numerous gears by which motion is given to the valves of an engine and esp. a steam engine; *specif* : such a gear for a steam engine by which the cutoff may be varied while the engine is running and the engine started, stopped, or reversed

valve-in-head engine \ˈ=,=,=-\ *n* : an internal-combustion engine in which both inlet and exhaust valves are located in the cylinder head

valve·less \ˈ=ləs\ *adj* : having no valves; *specif* : having no separate valve ⟨a ~ engine⟩

valve lifter *n* : a device used esp. in the internal-combustion engine for opening the valve of a cylinder

valve·man \ˈ=mən, -ˌman\ *n, pl* **valvemen** : a valve operator

valve motion *n* : VALVE GEAR

valve of bau·hin \-bōˈaⁿ\ *usu cap B* [after Gaspard *Bauhin* †1624 Swiss botanist and anatomist] : ILEOCECAL VALVE

valve of ger·lach \-ˈgerˌläk\ *usu cap G* [after Joseph *Gerlach* †1896 Ger. anatomist] : an inconstant fold of mucous membrane resembling a valve at the cecal end of the vermiform appendix

valve of has·ner \-ˈhäsnə(r), -äz-\ *usu cap H* [after Joseph Ritter von Artha *Hasner* †1892 Austrian oculist] : an imperfect valve at the opening of the nasolacrimal duct into the inferior meatus of the nose

valve of hei·ster \-ˈhīstə(r)\ *usu cap H* [after Lorenz *Heister* †1758 Ger. surgeon] : VALVULA SPIRALIS

valve of hous·ton \-ˈ(h)yüstən, -ˈhüs-,-ˈhaùs-\ *usu cap H* [after John *Houston* †1845 Irish physician] : RECTAL VALVE

valve of kerck·ring \-ˈkerkriŋ\ *usu cap K* [after Theodor *Kerckring* †1693 Du. anatomist] : PLICA CIRCULARIS

valve of the·be·si·us \-təˈbāzēəs\ *usu cap T* [after Adam C. *Thebesius* †1732 Ger. physician] : CORONARY VALVE

valve of vieus·sens \-ˌvyə(r)ˈsäⁿs, -vyəˈs-\ *usu cap 2d V* [after Raymond *Vieussens* †1716 Fr. anatomist] : the anterior medullary velum

valve pilot *n* : a device used on a steam locomotive to inform the engineman by visual indication on a dial the proper percentage of cutoff to use in admitting steam to the cylinders

valve ring *n* : RELIEF FRAME

valve seat *n* : a circular ring of heat-resistant bronze or steel on which a valve of an internal-combustion engine rests when closed

valve snail *n* : a snail of the genus *Valvata*

valve trombone *n* : a trombone having three piston valves instead of a slide to alter the tone or pitch

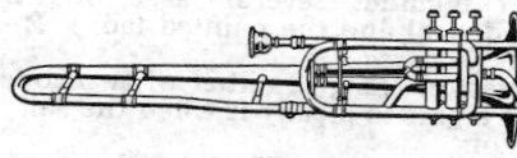
valve trombone

val·vi·fer \ˈvalvəfə(r)\ *n* -S [NL, fr. *valva* + *-i-* + *-fer*] : any of the basal plates of an insect's ovipositor arising from the eighth and ninth abdominal segments — compare VALVULA 2

val·vif·er·ous \(ˈ)valˈvif(ə)rəs\ *adj* [*valve* + *-iferous*] : having valves

val·vi·form \ˈvalvəˌfȯrm\ *adj* [*valve* + *-iform*] : shaped or formed like a valve

valv·ing \ˈvalviŋ\ *n* -S [*valve* + *-ing*] : a system or arrangement of valves ⟨changed the angle and the ~ on the rear shocks —Walt Woron⟩ ⟨the ~ can be opened to the pump line —George Hofferkamp & John Zich⟩

val·vot·o·my \valˈväd·əmē\ *n* -ES [*valve* + *-o-* + *-tomy*] : VALVULOTOMY

valvul- *or* **valvulo-** *comb form* [NL *valvula*] : small valve : valvule : fold ⟨*valvul*itis⟩ ⟨*valvulo*tome⟩

val·vu·la \ˈvalvyələ\ *n, pl* **valvu·lae** \-ˌlē, -ˌlī\ [NL, dim. of *valva*] **1** : a small valve or fold **2** : any of the six processes forming the blades and enclosing the lobes of an insect's ovipositor

valvula co·li \-ˈkōˌlī, -ˈkōˌlē\ *n* [NL, lit., valvula of the colon] : ILEOCECAL VALVE

valvula con·ni·vens \-kəˈnīˌvenz, -nēˌven(t)s\ *n, pl* **valvulae conniven·tes** \-ˌkänəˈvenˌtēz, -enˌtäs\ [NL, lit., closing valvula] : PLICA CIRCULARIS

val·vu·lar \ˈvalvyələ(r)\ *adj* [*valve* + *-ular*] **1** : resembling or having the function of a valve esp. of a plant or animal body ⟨a ~ opening⟩ ⟨~ divisions of the heart⟩ **2** : of or relating to a valve esp. of the heart ⟨~ defect⟩ ⟨~ disease⟩ ⟨~ stenosis⟩

valvula spi·ra·lis \-ˌspīˈralǝs, -räl-; spəˈräl-\ *n, pl* **valvulae spira·les** \-ä(ˌ)lēz, -ä(ˌ)lēz, -ä(ˌ)läs\ [NL, lit., spiral valvula] : a series of crescentic folds of mucous membrane somewhat spirally arranged on the interior of the gallbladder and continuing into the cystic duct — called also *valve of Heister*

val·vu·late \ˈvalvyəˌlāt, -ˌlət\ *adj* [*valvul-* + *-ate*] : having valvules

val·vule \ˈval(ˌ)vyül\ *n* -S [NL *valvula*] : a small valve or structure resembling a valve

val·vu·li·tis \ˌvalvyəˈlīd·əs\ *n* -ES [NL, fr. *valvul-* + *-itis*] : inflammation of a valve esp. of the heart ⟨mitral ~⟩

val·vu·lo·plas·ty \ˈvalvyəlōˌplastē\ *n* -ES [*valvul-* + *-plasty*] : VALVULOTOMY

val·vu·lo·tome \ˈvalvyəlōˌtōm\ *n* -S [*valvul-* + *-tome*] : a surgical blade designed for valvulotomy or commissurotomy

val·vu·lot·o·my \ˌvalvyəˈläd·əmē\ *n* -ES [*valvul-* + *-tomy*] : the operation of enlarging a narrowed heart valve by cutting through the mitral commissures to relieve the symptoms of mitral stenosis — compare COMMISSUROTOMY

valyl \ˈvaləl, ˈvāləl\ *n* -S [ISV *valine* + *-yl*] : the univalent acyl radical $(CH_3)_2CHCH(CH_2)CO$— of valine

vam·brace \ˈvamˌbrās\ *n* [ME *vambras, vambrace*, fr. AF *vauntbras*, fr. *vaunt-* fore- (fr. OF *avant-*) + *bras* arm (fr. OF) — more at VANGUARD, BRACELET] : a piece of medieval armor designed to protect the forearm

vam·braced \-st\ *adj* [*vambrace* + *-ed*] : wearing a vambrace — used chiefly in heraldic description

va·moose \vaˈmüs, vəˈm- *sometimes* -mōs\ *vb* -ED/-ING/-S [Sp *vamos* let us go, suppletive 1st pl. imper. (fr. L *vadere* to go) of *ir* to go — more at WADE] *vi, slang* : to depart quickly : DECAMP ~ *vt, slang* : to depart from ⟨~ the ranch⟩

¹**vamp** \ˈvamp, -aa(ə)-, -ai-\ *n* -S [ME *vaumpe, vampe*, fr. OF *avantpiè*, fr. *avant-* fore- + *pié* foot, fr. L *ped-, pes* — more at VANGUARD, FOOT] **1** *dial* : a short hose coming to the calf formerly sometimes worn over a stocking : SOCK **2** : the part of a shoe upper or boot upper covering esp. the forepart of the foot and sometimes also extending forward over the toe or backward to the back seam of the upper — see BROGUED VAMP, CIRCULAR VAMP, THREE-QUARTER VAMP, WHOLE VAMP; SHOE illustration **3** [²*vamp*] **a** : a simple musical accompaniment improvised for the occasion **b** : an introductory section of two or four measures often played several times (as in vaudeville) before a solo or between verses while the soloist is preparing to sing or is indulging in byplay **4** [²*vamp*] : something vamped or patched up; *esp* : a literary composition based on old material

²**vamp** \"\ *vb* -ED/-ING/-S *vt* **1 a** : to provide (a shoe) with a new vamp : REVAMP **b** : to piece (something old) with a new part : PATCH — used often with *together* or *up* ⟨~ up old sermons⟩ ⟨a ~*ed* play⟩ **2** : INVENT, CONCOCT, FABRICATE — usu. used with *up* ⟨~ up an excuse⟩ ⟨hastily *vamped*-up pretext⟩ **3** *obs* : to make or present (one) as something else **4** *dial* : to walk or tramp over or along **5** : to make a vamp to : improvise (an accompaniment) for a solo ~ *vi* **1** *dial* : to go on foot : TRAMP, PLOD **2** : to play a vamp or a vamped accompaniment

³**vamp** \"\ *n* -S [origin unknown] : a volunteer fireman

⁴**vamp** \"\ *n* -S [short for *vampire*] : a woman who uses her charm or wiles to seduce and exploit men : FLIRT, ADVENTURESS ⟨uncle who confronts a ~ to rescue a foolish nephew from her clutches —*Theatre Arts*⟩

⁵**vamp** \"\ *vt* -ED/-ING/-S : to practice seductive wiles on : capture or seduce by coquetry

vamped \-m(p)t\ *or* **vamped-up** \ˈ=ˌ=\ *adj* [fr. past part. of ²*vamp*] **1** : patched up : REPAIRED **2** : made up of old materials : not fresh or original ⟨~ adventure story⟩ **3** : trumped-up : FABRICATED

vamp·er \-mpə(r)\ *n* -S **1** [²*vamp* + *-er*] : one that vamps **2** [¹*vamp* + *-er*] : a shoe worker who stitches vamps to quarters

vamphorn \ˈ=ˌ=\ *n* [²*vamp* + *horn*; fr. its use by the choir leader to amplify his voice as an accompaniment to the rest of the choir] : a megaphone used in churches during the 18th and early 19th centuries

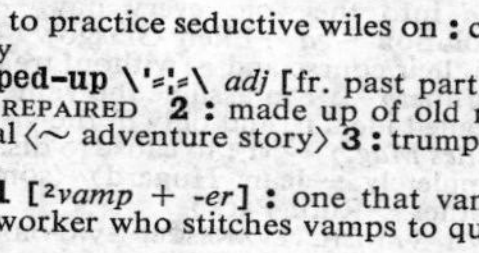
vamphorn

vam·pire \ˈvamˌpī(ə)r, ˈvaam-, -īə\ *n* -S [F, fr. G *vampir*, of Slav origin; akin to Serb *vampir* vampire, Russ *upyr*] **1** : a bloodsucking ghost or reanimated body of a dead person believed to come from the grave and wander about by night sucking the blood of persons asleep and causing their death **2 a** : one who lives by preying mercilessly on others : EXTORTIONER, BLOODSUCKER **b** : a mercenary unscrupulous woman who seduces, exploits, and ruins her lover: as (1) : a stage character of this kind (2) : an actress playing such roles **3** *also* **vampire bat** : any of various bats reputed to feed on blood: as **a** : any of several large So. and Central American leaf-nosed bats (as a false vampire or spearnose bat) that in fact feed on insects rather than blood **b** : any of various So. American bats constituting the genera *Desmodus* and *Diphylla* of the family Desmodontidae that are structurally adapted for subsisting on blood with incisor and canine teeth modified for slitting the skin, with the stomach small and tubular, and with the intestine short and are dangerous to man and domestic animals esp. because they are vectors of equine trypanosomiasis and of rabies in some regions **c** : any large bat (as a fruit bat) of the Old World supposed to suck blood but actually either insectivorous or frugivorous **4** : a stage trapdoor for sudden disappearances

vam·pir·ic \(ˈ)=ˈpirik\ *adj* [*vampire* + *-ic*] : BLOODSUCKING, PARASITIC

vam·pir·ish \ˈ=ˌpī(ə)rish, -rēsh\ *adj* : of, relating to, resembling, or characteristic of a vampire ⟨a mischievous flirtatious girl rather than a ~ woman of the world —W.C.Smith⟩

vam·pir·ism \-ˌrizəm\ *n* -S **1** : belief in vampires **2** : the actions of a vampire : the act or practice of bloodsucking : the practice of preying upon another (as a lover)

vam·pir·ize \-ˌrīz\ *vb* -ED/-ING/-S *vi* : to play the vampire ~ *vt* : to exhaust or prey upon in the manner of a vampire ⟨parents who ~ their children⟩

vamp·ish \ˈvampish\ *adj* [⁴*vamp* + *-ish*] : having the characteristics of a vamp ⟨~ actress⟩

vam·plate \ˈvamˌplāt\ *n* [ME, *vaunplate*, fr. AF *vaunt-* fore- (fr. OF *avant-*) + *plate* — more at VANGUARD] : a round plate of iron mounted on the shaft of a lance or tilting spear to protect the hand

vamps *pl of* VAMP, *pres 3d sing of* VAMP

vamp trap *n* [*vamp* (short for *vampire*) + *trap*] : VAMPIRE 4

vam·py·rel·la \ˌvampəˈrelə, -ˌpīˈr-\ *n, cap* [NL, fr. *vampyrus* vampire + *-ella* — more at VAMPYRUM] : a genus of protozoans (order Amoebina) comprising small amoeboid forms that are ectoparasitic on algae

vam·py·rum \(ˈ)vamˌpīrəm\ *n, cap* [NL, fr. *vampyrus* vampire, fr. F *vampire*] : a genus of So. and Central American bats (family Phyllostomatidae) that includes various harmless insectivorous usu. spearnose bats — compare VAMPIRE 3a

¹**van** \ˈvan, ˈvaa(ə)n\ *n* -S [ME, fr. MF, fr. L *vannus* — more at WINNOW] **1** *dial Eng* : a fan or other winnowing device **2 a** : the wing of a bird or insect ⟨the bird . . . leant on the wind and then swung into it on taut ~s —Alan Duncan⟩ **b** : a windmill's sail **3 a** : a shovel used in dressing ore **b** *dial Eng* : the process of testing ore on such a shovel

²**van** \"\ *n* -S [short for *vanguard*] **1** : the leading unit or division of an advancing army, fleet, or other group ⟨battling its way . . . through the high steep seas of a levanter with the red-crossed admiral's flag in the ~ —C.S.Forester⟩ **2** : the group taking the lead or occupying the front position in a moving company : the first part of a procession : HEAD ⟨the paper would be in the ~ of progressive thought —John Buchan⟩ ⟨led the ~ in solving problems —G.C.Sellery⟩ ⟨stocks . . . which have been in the ~ of the market —*Wall Street Jour.*⟩

³**van** \"\ *n* -S [short for *caravan*] **1** : a wagon or motortruck usu. enclosed and used for transportation of goods or animals ⟨route ~⟩ ⟨horse ~⟩ ⟨great ~s carrying enormous piled-up loads advanced swaying through little mountains —Joseph Conrad⟩ **2** *chiefly Brit* : an enclosed railroad freight or baggage car ⟨the train, consisting of three carriages and a ~ —G.B.Shaw⟩ **3** : a small general store in a lumber camp and sometimes on wheels at which clothing, tobacco, and other small articles for the crew are kept for sale

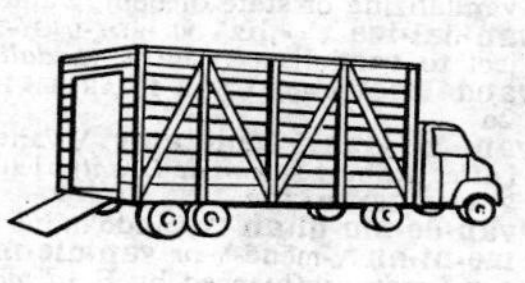
livestock van

⁴**van** \"\ *vt* **vanned; vanned; vanning; vans** : to carry or forward in a van ⟨it would be possible to ~ the horses each day from one track to the other —*Springfield (Mass.) Union*⟩

⁵**van** \"\ *n* -S [by shortening] *Brit* : ADVANTAGE 5

vanad- *or* **vanado-** *comb form* [NL *vanadium*] : vanadium ⟨*vanad*yl⟩ ⟨*vanado*silicate⟩

van·a·date \ˈvanəˌdāt\ *n* -S [ISV *vanad-* + *-ate*] : a salt or ester derived from vanadium pentoxide and containing pentavalent vanadium — compare METAVANADATE

va·nadic \vəˈnādik, -nad-\ *adj* [NL *vanadium* + ISV *-ic*] : of, relating to, or containing vanadium — used esp. of compounds in which this element has a relatively higher valence than in vanadous compounds

vanadic acid *n* **1** : any of various acids that are hydrates of vanadium pentoxide or known esp. in the form of salts and esters — compare METAVANADIC ACID **2** : VANADIUM PENTOXIDE — not used systematically

vanadic oxide *n* : VANADIUM PENTOXIDE

van·a·dif·er·ous \ˌvanəˈdif(ə)rəs\ *adj* [ISV *vanad-* + *-iferous*] : containing or yielding vanadium

va·na·di·nite \vəˈnādᵊnˌīt; ˌvanəˈdēˌnīt, ˈvanədə̇ˌn-\ *n* -S [G *vanadinit*, fr. *vanadin* vanadium (fr. NL *vanadium* + G *-in* -ine) + *-it* -ite] : a mineral consisting of a lead vanadate and chloride of the opatite group and occurring in yellowish, brownish, or ruby-red hexagonal crystals (hardness 2.75–3, sp. gr. 6.66–7.10)

van·a·dite \ˈvanəˌdīt\ *n* -S [G *vanadit*, fr. *vanad-* + *-it* -ite] : HYPOVANADATE

va·na·di·um \vəˈnādēəm\ *n* -S [NL, fr. ON *Vanadís* (Freya, Scandinavian goddess) + NL *-ium*] : a gray or white malleable ductile polyvalent metallic element that is resistant to air, seawater, alkalies, and reducing acids except hydrofluoric acid, that occurs widely but for the most part in small amounts in combination in minerals (as vanadinite, patronite, carnotite, roscoelite), in the ashes of many plants, in coals, petroleums, and asphalts, and in the blood of tunicates and other marine animals, that is usu. obtained in the form of ferrovanadium or other alloys or in almost pure metallic form containing small amounts of oxygen, carbon, or nitrogen by reduction of ores, slags, or vanadium pentoxide, and that is used chiefly as a constituent of vanadium steel — symbol *V*; see ELEMENT table

vanadium bronze *n* : any of various yellow or orange pigments said to be metavanadic acid or a salt containing vanadium in the anion

vanadium oxide *n* : an oxide of vanadium: as **a** : the sesquioxide V_2O_3 obtained as a black crystalline powder by reducing vanadium pentoxide : di-vanadium trioxide **b** : the dioxide VO_2 or V_2O_4 obtained as blue-black crystals by partially reducing vanadium pentoxide **c** : VANADIUM PENTOXIDE

vanadium pentoxide *n* : a yellowish red crystalline compound V_2O_5 that forms yellow colloidal solutions, that is obtained by roasting ammonium metavanadate in oxygen or as a by-product of smelting operations or from the soot of some petroleum fuel oils, and that is used in glass manufacture and as a catalyst for oxidations and other reactions; di-nitrogen pentoxide

vanadium steel *n* **1** : steel alloyed with vanadium which strengthens the steel and serves to remove oxygen and possibly nitrogen **2** : steel alloyed with vanadium and other elements (as chromium)

va·na·do·an \vəˈnādəwən\ *adj* [obs. E *vanado*-magnetite coulsonite (fr. E *vanad-* + *magnetite*) + E *-an*] : containing vanadous vanadium and esp. bivalent vanadium

vana·dous \vəˈnādəs, ˈvanəd-\ *adj* [*vanad-* + *-ous*] : of, relating to, or containing vanadium — used esp. of compounds in which this element has a lower valence than in vanadic compounds

vana·dyl \vəˈnadᵊl, ˈvanəˌdil\ *n* -S [*vanad-* + *-yl*] : either of two radicals composed of vanadium and oxygen: **a** : the univalent, bivalent, or trivalent radical VO ⟨~ sulfate $VOSO_4$⟩ **b** : the univalent radical VO_2

van al·len radiation belt \vaˈnalən-, vəl\ *n, usu cap V&A* [after James A. *Van Allen b*1914 Am. physicist] : a belt of

intense ionizing radiation that surrounds the earth in the outer atmosphere, has particles carrying energies of from approximately 20,000 electron volts to several million electron volts or more, and has an outer zone that extends into space to a distance of about 55,000 kilometers

va·na·pras·tha \ˌvänəˈprəstə\ *n* -s [Skt, lit., one who departs to the forest, fr. *vana* forest + *pratiṣṭhati* he sets forth, fr. *pra-* forward, forth + *tiṣṭhati* he stands — more at BANDAR, FOR, STAND] **:** a forest-dwelling Hindu hermit; *esp* **:** one in the third stage of the Brahmanic scheme of life

va·nas·pa·ti \vəˈnəspəd-ē\ *n* -s [Skt *vanaspati* forest tree, soma plant, lit., lord of the forest, fr. *vana* forest + *pati* lord, master — more at BANDAR, POTENT] **:** a hydrogenated vegetable fat used as a butter substitute in India

van·courier \(ˈ)van + *pronunc at* COURIER\ *n* [modif. (influenced by *courier*) of MF *avant-coureur*, fr. *avant-* fore- + *coureur* runner, fr. OF *courre* to run + *-eur* -or — more at VANGUARD, CURRENT] **:** a scout or herald sent in advance **:** FORERUNNER, PRECURSOR

van·cou·ver \(ˈ)vanˈküvə(r), (ˈ)vaan-\ *adj, usu cap* [fr. *Vancouver*, city of southern British Columbia, Canada] **:** of or from the city of Vancouver, B.C. **:** of the kind or style prevalent in Vancouver

van·cou·ve·ria \ˌvankülˈvirēə\ *n, cap* [NL, prob. fr. George *Vancouver* †1798 Eng. navigator + NL *-ia*] *in some classifications* **:** a genus of western No. American herbs (family Berberidaceae) that have dissected basal leaves and small panicled white flowers with numerous sepals and six petals and are usu. included in the genus *Epimedium*

van·cou·ver·ite \-ˈküvəˌrīt\ *n* -s *cap* [*Vancouver*, British Columbia + E *-ite*] **:** a native or resident of Vancouver, B.C.

van·da \ˈvandə\ *n* [NL, fr. Hindi *vandā* mistletoe, fr. Skt, a parasitic plant] **1 a** *cap* **:** a genus of Indo-Malayan epiphytic orchids having loose racemes of large flowers with spreading perianth and a lip saccate at the base **b** -s **:** any plant of the genus *Vanda* **2** -s **:** a pale purple to pale reddish purple

¹van·dal \ˈvandᵊl, ˈvaan-\ *n* -s [L *Vandalus* (sing.), *Vandalii* (pl.), of Gmc origin] **1** *usu cap* **:** one of a Germanic people anciently dwelling south of the Baltic between the Vistula and the Oder, overrunning Gaul, Spain, and northern Africa in the 4th and 5th centuries A.D. and in 455 entering Italy, sacking Rome, and destroying many monuments of art and literature, and being overthrown in their final stronghold in No. Africa by Belisarius in 534 — see HERMINONES **2 a :** one who willfully destroys or mars something beautiful (as a work of art) **b :** a wanton or ignorant destroyer or defacer of a building or monument that should be preserved ⟨although abandoned and exposed to the elements and to ~*s* for centuries, the walls of these buildings stand strong —R.W.Murray⟩

²vandal \"\ *adj* **1** *usu cap* **:** of, relating to, or characteristic of the Vandals **2 :** carelessly or ignorantly destructive **:** given to vandalism

van·dal·ic \(ˈ)=ˈdalik\ *adj* [¹*vandal* + *-ic*] **1 :** VANDAL 2 **2** *usu cap* **:** VANDAL 1

van·dal·ish \ˈ= dəlish\ *adj* [¹*vandal* + *-ish*] **:** VANDALISTIC

van·dal·ism \-ˌlizəm\ *n* -s [F *vandalisme*, fr. *vandale* vandal, Vandal (fr. L *Vandalus*) + *-isme* -ism] **:** willful or malicious destruction or defacement of things of beauty or of public or private property

van·dal·is·tic \ˌ==ˈlistik, -tēk\ *adj* [¹*vandal* + *-istic*] **:** of, relating to, or perpetrating vandalism

van·dal·iza·tion \ˌ=dələˈzāshən, -ˌlīˈz-\ *n* -s **:** the act of vandalizing or state of being vandalized

van·dal·ize \ˈ==ˌlīz\ *vt* -ED/-ING/-S [¹*vandal* + *-ize*] **:** to subject to vandalism ⟨youths *vandalized* the shop —*N.Y.Times*⟩

vandalroot \ˈ==ˌ=\ *n* **1 :** GARDEN HELIOTROPE 1 **2 :** VALERIAN 2a

van de graaff generator \ˈvandəˌgraf-\ *n, usu cap V&G* [after Robert J. *Van de Graaff* b1901 Am. physicist] **:** ELECTROSTATIC GENERATOR

¹van·de·mo·ni·an \ˌvandəˈmōnēən, -dēˈm-\ *also* **van·die·me·ni·an** \-ˈmēnē-\ *or* **van·die·mo·ni·an** \-ˈmōnē-\ *n* -s *usu cap* [irreg. (influenced by E ¹*demon*) fr. *Van Diemen's Land* (now Tasmania) (fr. Anton *Van Diemen* †1645 Du. statesman) + E *-an*] **:** a white inhabitant of Tasmania; *esp* **:** one penally transported there before 1853

²vandemonian \ˌ==ˈ===\ *adj, usu cap* **1 :** of or relating to a Vandemonian **2 :** RUFFIANLY, VIOLENT

van den bergh test \ˈvandənˌbərg-\ *n, usu cap B* [after A. A. H. *van den Bergh* †1943 Du. physician] **:** a test indicating presence of bilirubin in the blood when a diazotizing reagent added to blood serum turns it red (as in jaundice and destructive diseases of the liver)

van·den·brande·ite \ˌvandənˈbrandēˌīt\ *or* **van·den·bran·dite** \-branˌdīt\ *n* -s [F *vandenbrandeite*, fr. P. *Van den Brande*, 20th cent. Belg. geologist + F *-ite*] **:** a mineral $CuUO_4.2H_2O$ consisting of a hydrous uranium and copper oxide in very dark green flattened crystals

van·der·bilt club convention \ˈvaˌndə(r)ˌbilt-, ˈvaa\ *n, usu cap V* [after Harold S. *Vanderbilt* b1884 Am. capitalist, its inventor] **:** CLUB CONVENTION

van der waals adsorption \ˈvandə(r)ˌwȯlz-\ *n, usu cap W* **:** adsorption due to van der Waals forces between the adsorbed molecules and the adsorbing material — opposed to *chemisorption*

van der waals equation *n, usu cap W* [after Johannes D. *van der Waals* †1923 Dutch physicist] **:** an equation that defines the physical state of a homogeneous gas, is a modification of the ideal-gas equation, and more nearly describes the properties of actual gases: $(p+\frac{a}{v^2})(v-b)=RT$ where *p* is the pressure, *v* the specific volume, *R* the gas constant, *T* the absolute temperature, and *a* and *b* are constants depending respectively on the cohesion between the molecules and the volume occupied by the molecules — compare GAS LAW c

van der waals forces *n pl, usu cap W* [after Johannes D. *van der Waals* †1923 Du. physicist] **:** the relatively weak attractive forces operative between neutral atoms and molecules, arising because of the electric polarization induced in each of the particles by the presence of other particles, and effective at relatively great distances

V and M *abbr* virgin and martyr

V and T *abbr* volume and tension

¹van·dyke *or* **van·dyck** \(ˈ)vanˈdīk, (ˈ)vaan- *also* vənˈd-\ *n* -s [after Sir Anthony *Vandyke* or *Van Dyck* †1641 Flem. painter] **1** *usu cap* [so called fr. its frequent appearance in paintings by Vandyke] **a :** a wide collar made to resemble that of a cape with a deeply indented edge and worn by men and women in the 17th century and later by women only **b :** one of several deeply indented, pointed, or scalloped sections of a decorative edging (as on a collar) **c :** a border or edging with such indentations **2** *usu cap* **:** VANDYKE BEARD **3** [prob. fr. *vandyke brown*] **:** a photographic print similar to a blueprint but in white and brown; *esp* **:** one that has white translucent lines on a brown opaque background and is used as a master print from which blueprints with blue lines on a white background are made

²vandyke \"\ *vb* -ED/-ING/-S *vt* **:** to finish (an edge) with vandykes **:** make or shape with deep indentations ⟨a *vandyked* apron⟩ ~ *vi* **:** to stagger, weave, or wander in the zigzag course of one drunken or irresolute

vandyke beard *n, often cap V* [so called from its frequent appearance in paintings by Vandyke] **:** a trim pointed beard

vandyke brown *n* [so called from its use by Vandyke] **1** *usu cap V* **a :** a deep-brown pigment of uncertain identity **b :** a natural brown-black pigment of poor light fastness obtained from bog earth or peat or lignite deposits, composed chiefly of organic matter with a small amount of ferric oxide, and used chiefly as an artist's color and stain — called also *Cassel brown*, *Cologne brown* **c :** any of various synthetic brown pigments (as a mixture of a carbon black with an iron-oxide red) **2** *often cap V* **:** a moderate brown that is redder, lighter, and slightly stronger than coffee, slightly redder, lighter, and stronger than chestnut brown, slightly yellower than auburn, and yellower and paler than bay — called also *Cassel brown*, *Cologne brown*, *Cullen earth*, *Roman sepia*, *Verona brown*

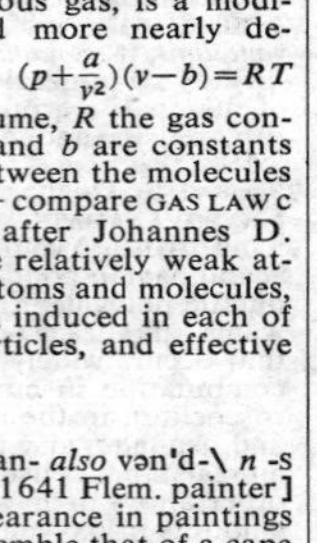

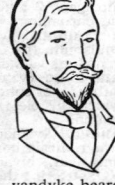

vandyke beard

vandyke red *n* [after Sir Anthony *Vandyke* †1641 Flem. painter] **1** *often cap V* **:** a grayish red that is bluer and deeper than Pompeian red, bluer and darker than bois de rose, and yellower and deeper than appleblossom — called also *Florence brown* **2 :** a synthetic red to brown pigment consisting of copper ferrocyanide $Cu_2Fe(CN)_6$

vane \ˈvān\ *n* -s [ME (southern) *vane*, fr. OE *fana* flag, banner; akin to OHG *fano* cloth, gund*fano* war flag, gonfalon, ON gunn*fani*, Goth *fana* piece of cloth, rag, L *pannus*, Gk *pēnē* thread on a bobbin, woof, web] **1 a :** a movable device attached to a spire, mast, or other elevated object for showing the direction of the wind **b :** one that is changeable or inconstant **2 :** a flat or curved surface exposed to a flow of air, gas, or liquid so as to be impelled to move or to rotate about an axis, to redirect the flow (as in a turbine), or itself to be the impeller ⟨the ~*s* of a windmill⟩ ⟨the ~*s* of a fan blower⟩ ⟨the ~*s* of a ship's screw⟩ ⟨the ~*s* of a washing machine agitator⟩ ⟨the ~*s* of an aerial bomb⟩ **3 :** the web or flat expanded part of a feather formed of the barbs and their appendages **4 :** a feather fastened to the shaft near the nock of an arrow **5 a :** the target of a leveling staff **b :** one of the sights of a compass or quadrant

vaned \ˈvānd\ *adj* [*vane* + *-ed*] **:** having vanes

va·nel·lus \vəˈneləs\ *n, cap* [NL, fr. F *vanneau* lapwing, fr. OF *vaniel*, fr. *van* winnowing fan — more at VAN] **:** a genus of birds (family Charadriidae) including the Eurasian lapwing

va·nes·sa \vəˈnesə\ *n* [NL] **1** *cap* **:** a cosmopolitan genus of nymphalid butterflies that includes several large brightly colored forms (as the red admiral and the painted lady) **2** -s **:** any butterfly of the genus *Vanessa*

vang \ˈvaŋ, ˈvaiŋ\ *n* -s [alter. of ²*fang*] **:** either of two ropes extending from the peak of a gaff to steady it when the sail is not set — see SHIP illustration

van·guard \ˈvanˌgärd, ˈvaan-, -ˌgȧd\ *n* [ME *avaunt garde*, *vantgard*, fr. MF *avant-garde*, fr. OF *avant-* fore- (fr. *avant*, before, forward, fr. L *abante*) + *garde* guard — more at ADVANCE, GUARD] **1 :** the troops who march at the head of an army **:** VAN **2 :** the leaders of thought, taste, or opinion in a field (as art, letters, or politics) **:** the forefront of a school or movement ⟨men whose claim to attention is that they lead the ~ —*Times Lit. Supp.*⟩ ⟨the educators may be in the ~, but . . . they are bucking no trends —W.H.Whyte⟩

van guard \"\ *n* [³*van* + *guard*] **:** a guard for a railway van or a motortruck

van·guard·ism \-ˌdizəm\ *n* -s **:** the attitudes, ideas, or activities of persons regarding themselves as members of a vanguard

van·guard·ist \-ˌdəst\ *n* -s **:** a member of a vanguard

van·gue·ria \vanˈg(w)irēə\ *n, cap* [NL, fr. Malagasy *voavanguer*, a tree of the genus + NL *-ia*] **:** a genus of tropical African and Asiatic trees or shrubs (family Rubiaceae) having axillary clusters of small whitish flowers with five stamens and a 3- to 5-celled ovary and drupaceous fruit

van hoorne's canal \vaˈnˈhō(ə)rnz- *also* və\ *n, usu cap H* [after Jean *van Hoorne* †1670 Du. anatomist] **:** THORACIC DUCT

va·nil·la \vəˈnilə, -nelə\ *n* -s *often attrib* [in sense 1a, fr. NL, fr. Sp *vainilla* vanilla; in other senses fr. Sp *vainilla* pod, vanilla, dim. of *vaina* sheath, fr. L *vagina* — more at VAGINA] **1 a** *cap* **:** a genus of tropical American climbing orchids (family Orchidaceae) having fleshy distichous leaves, numerous aerial roots, and flowers in axillary racemes with a spreading perianth and the labellum united to the column **b** -s **:** any plant of this genus **2** -s **a :** a capsule that is the fruit of a vanilla (*Vanilla planifolia*) widely distributed from Florida southward throughout tropical America, that has the form of an elongated pod, and that is an important article of commerce for the flavoring extract that it yields; *broadly* **:** any of several capsules that are the fruits of other vanillas — compare VANILLON **b :** a flavoring extract made by soaking comminuted vanilla pods in a mixture of water and grain alcohol **3** -s **:** WILD VANILLA

vanilla bean *n* **:** VANILLA 2a

vanilla grass *n* **:** SWEET GRASS 1b(1)

vanill·aldehyde \ˌvanᵊl, vəˈnil+\ *n* [*vanilla* + *aldehyde*] **:** VANILLIN

vanilla leaf *n* **:** WILD VANILLA

vanilla plant *n* **1 :** a plant (*Vanilla planifolia*) that occurs in Florida and tropical America and is widely cultivated **2 :** WILD VANILLA

vanil·late \ˈvanᵊlˌāt; vəˈnilət, -ˌlāt\ *n* -s [ISV *vanillic* (*acid*) + *-ate*] **:** a salt or ester of vanillic acid

va·nille \vaˈnē, vəˈnē\ *n* -s [F, fr. Sp *vainilla*] **1 :** VANILLA 2b **2** *or* **vanille ice :** vanilla ice cream

va·nil·lery \vəˈnilərē\ *n* -ES [F *vanillerie*, fr. *vanille* vanilla + *-erie* -ery] **:** a plantation of vanilla

va·nil·lic acid \vəˈnilik-\ *n* [ISV, fr. *vanilla* + *-ic*] **:** an odorless crystalline phenolic acid $CH_3O(OH)C_6H_3COOH$ found in some varieties of vanilla, formed by oxidation of vanillin, and used chiefly in the form of esters as food preservatives

vanil·lin \vəˈnilən, ˈvanᵊl-; *the second is the usual pronunc among chemists*\ *n* -s [ISV, fr. *vanilla* + *-in*] **:** a crystalline phenolic aldehyde $CH_3O(OH)C_6H_3CHO$ that is the principal fragrant component of vanilla and occurs in many other plants (as the tonka bean), that is usu. made synthetically, and that is used chiefly in flavoring and in perfumery; 4-hydroxy-3-methoxy-benzaldehyde **2 :** an aldehyde isomeric with vanillin; *esp* **:** the ortho isomer; 2-hydroxy-3-methoxy-benzaldehyde

vanil·lism \vəˈniˌlizəm, ˈvanᵊlˌi-\ *n* -s [*vanilla* + *-ism*; fr. its being caused by excessive handling of vanilla] **:** GROCER'S ITCH

va·nil·lon \ˌvaneˈyōⁿ\ *n* -s [F, fr. *vanille* vanilla] **:** any of various usu. large coarse vanillas of inferior flavor and aroma that are obtained esp. from uncultivated vanilla vines

va·nil·lo·yl \vəˈniləˌwil\ *n* -s [*vanillic* (*acid*) + *-oyl*] **:** the univalent radical $CH_3O(OH)C_6H_3CO—$ of vanillic acid

vanil·lyl \ˈvanᵊlˌil, vəˈnilᵊl\ *n* -s [*vanillin* + *-yl*] **:** the univalent radical $CH_3O(OH)C_6H_3CH_2—$ derived from vanillyl alcohol

vanillyl alcohol *n* **:** a crystalline phenolic alcohol $CH_3O(OH)C_6H_3CH_2—$ obtained by reducing vanillin

¹van·ish \ˈvanish, -nēsh, *esp in pres part* -nəsh\ *vb* -ED/-ING/-ES [ME *vanisshen*, fr. MF *evaniss-*, stem of *esvanir*, *evanir*, fr. (assumed) VL *exvanire*, alter. of L *evanescere* to evaporate, die away, vanish, fr. *e-* + *vanescere* to vanish, fr. *vanus* empty — more at WANE] *vi* **1 a :** to disappear entirely **:** pass altogether out of sight **:** become invisible ⟨straightway ~*ed* beneath his blankets —John Muir †1914⟩ ⟨the last traces of respectability had ~*ed* —Marcia Davenport⟩ **b :** to disappear by departing **:** go away ⟨he ~*ed* into the bathroom —Scott Fitzgerald⟩ ⟨as each member of our family finished eating dinner he would excuse himself and ~ —*Parents' Mag.*⟩ ⟨takes her to a social and ~*es* with the boys to the bar —Marjorie Proops⟩ **c :** to disappear by passing out of existence **:** cease to be ⟨two dozen cheeses, as big as cartwheels, ~*ed* into the void every day —Van Wyck Brooks⟩ ⟨her resolution ~*ed* —Ellen Glasgow⟩ ⟨many human ills . . . will run their course and ~ without treatment of any sort —Martin Gardner⟩ **2 :** to assume the value zero ⟨by definition a fluid is called ideal if, and only if, the viscosity tensor ~*es* —*Mathematics Mag.*⟩ ~ *vt* **:** to cause to disappear ⟨you can ~ the coin completely —Jean Hugard⟩ ⟨someone had ~*ed* her little brother —Ruth Park⟩

syn VANISH, EVANESCE, EVAPORATE, DISAPPEAR, and FADE agree in meaning to pass from view or out of existence. VANISH usu. suggests a total, often mysterious, sudden passing, commonly leaving no trace ⟨his grandmother's fortune *vanished* in a bank failure —Catharine Brody⟩ ⟨many of the wild creatures of early times have *vanished* or are almost extinct —*Amer. Guide Series: Texas*⟩ ⟨his smile quickly *vanished* —Kenneth Roberts⟩ ⟨the apparition appeared for a moment, then *vanished*⟩ EVANESCE usu. suggests a gradual effacement or dissipation to a final complete dissolution ⟨their hopes *evanesced* as money and food became scarcer⟩ ⟨the beauty of youth *evanesced* before the hardships of existence⟩ EVAPORATE suggests a vanishing as silently and inconspicuously as that of a vapor ⟨nothing can insure the continuance of love. It will *evaporate* like a spirit —Thomas Hardy⟩ ⟨his anger did not *evaporate* in words —George Meredith⟩ ⟨invested capital *evaporates* even with watchful care —W.C.Allee⟩ DISAPPEAR usu. suggests only the passing from sight or thought, other implications depending on context, although it is often interchangeable with VANISH ⟨the man seemed to *disappear* before his eyes⟩ ⟨what caused the Hohokam culture to *disappear* suddenly around 1400 . . . is a mystery —R.W.Murray⟩ ⟨farming is rapidly *disappearing* because of poor marketing conditions —*Amer. Guide Series: N.H.*⟩ ⟨this document has *disappeared* from the files — R.M.Lovett⟩ FADE, often with *out* or *away*, stresses a gradual diminution in clearness or distinctness, usu. to an ultimate disappearance ⟨the old myth . . . had *faded* from the minds of men —Agnes Repplier⟩ ⟨the shouting on shore *faded* to a whispering —Kenneth Roberts⟩ ⟨the trade routes fell into disuse and the towns *faded* out of existence —Anne Dorrance⟩ ⟨the earlier beauty of the piece had *faded* away over the years⟩

²vanish \"\ *n* -ES **1 :** a disappearance or an act of causing something to disappear ⟨this ~ . . . has been used by generations of magicians —Jean Hugard⟩ **2 :** the relatively faint latter part of a speech sound (as a falling diphthong)

vanished *past of* VANISH

vanishes *pres 3d sing of* VANISH

vanishing *pres part of* VANISH

vanishing cream *n* [*vanishing* (pres. part. of ¹*vanish*) + cream] **:** a cosmetic preparation that is less oily than cold cream, that typically contains an excess of stearic acid emulsified by a stearate soap in a high percentage of water, and that is used chiefly as a foundation for face powder ⟨*vanishing creams* do not actually disappear into the skin, but simply spread a thin smooth film over it —Florence E. Wall⟩ — compare COLD CREAM

vanishing line *n* **:** one of the lines converging to a vanishing point in a pictorial perspective

van·ish·ing·ly *adv* **:** in a vanishing manner **:** so as to disappear or to approach or become zero ⟨their mass is ~ small in proportion to their bulk —Agnes M. Clerke⟩

vanishing point *n* [*vanishing* (gerund of ¹*vanish*) + *point*] **1 :** a point at which a group of receding parallel lines seems to meet when represented in linear perspective **2 :** a point at which something disappears or ceases to exist ⟨cut down the incidence of tuberculosis in cattle to the *vanishing point* —Morris Fishbein⟩

vanishing trace *n* **:** a line containing the vanishing points of all systems of parallels in a picture in linear perspective

van·ish·ment \-mənt\ *n* -s [¹*vanish* + *-ment*] **:** an act of vanishing or state of having vanished

van·ist \ˈvānəst\ *n* -s *usu cap* [Sir Henry *Vane* †1662 governor of Massachusetts (1636–37) + E *-ist*] **:** a follower of Sir Henry Vane who as governor of Massachusetts colony defended Anne Hutchinson on charges of antinomianism

van·i·to·ry \ˈvanəˌtōrē\ *n* -ES [fr. *Vanitory*, a trademark] **:** a combined bathroom lavatory basin and dressing table ⟨full room-size master bathroom with dressing ~ —*advt*⟩

van·i·tous \ˈvanəd-əs\ *adj* [*vanity* + *-ous*] **:** INFLATED, VAIN

van·i·ty \ˈvanəd-ē, -ətē, -i\ *n* -ES [ME *vanite*, fr. OF *vanité*, fr. L *vanitat-*, *vanitas* quality of being empty or vain, fr. *vanus* empty, idle, vain + *-itat-*, *-itas* -ity — more at WANE] **1 a :** something that is empty, vain, or valueless **:** something idle, objectless, or unprofitable ⟨the powerlessness of man before the blind hurry of the universe from ~ to ~ —Bertrand Russell⟩ ⟨he had ceased then to be an egotism, a ~ —H.G.Wells⟩ ⟨the pomps and *vanities* of the great world —C.E.Montague⟩ **b** *obs* **:** trivial or unprofitable activity **:** blind frittering away of time **c :** the quality of being vain or empty **:** HOLLOWNESS, WORTHLESSNESS ⟨knew the ~ of her own attainments —G.B. Shaw⟩ **2 a :** exaggerated self-love **:** inflated pride in oneself or in one's appearance, attainments, performance, possessions, or successes **:** hunger for praise or admiration **:** CONCEIT, VAINGLORY ⟨love of the good opinion of others (which we may call ~) is a desire which man shares with many animals —Bertrand Russell⟩ ⟨the epitome of maleness with all its ~ and self-importance —Carl Van Vechten⟩ ⟨his wounded ~ turned and turned upon itself —J.C.Powys⟩ **b :** an instance or example of such vanity **:** something of which one is proud or which exhibits his self-love ⟨one of his hidden *vanities* was to be the first man on the subscription paper with the largest donation —W.A.White⟩ **3 :** the ostentation of fashion, wealth, or power regarded as an occasion of empty pride or a vain show ⟨takes for granted . . . all the privileges and appurtenances of wealth, and there emerges the 16-year-old boy caught up in *vanities* —Gene Baro⟩ **4 :** a fashionable trifle or knickknack **:** GAUD ⟨such *vanities* as gloves, a wristwatch, a silver cigarette case —John Morrison⟩ **5 a :** ³COMPACT 2 **b :** a small case or handbag for toilet articles used by women ⟨room beneath your chair for small luggage like a briefcase or ~ —*Welcome Aboard*⟩ **6 :** DRESSING TABLE **7 :** SANDUST **syn** see PRIDE

vanity bag *or* **vanity case** *n* **:** VANITY 5b

vanity fair *n, often cap V&F* [fr. *Vanity-Fair*, a fair held in the frivolous town of Vanity in *Pilgrim's Progress* (1678) by John Bunyan †1688 Eng. preacher and writer] **:** a place of busy pride and empty ostentation ⟨a meretricious *vanity fair* of the gaudy commonplace —Rose Macaulay⟩ ⟨the *Vanity Fair* of Washington society —C.G.Bowers⟩

vanity press *or* **vanity publisher** *n* **:** a press that publishes books at the authors' expense — compare AUTHOR'S EDITION

van·john \(ˈ)vanˈjän\ *n* [modif. of F *vingt-et-un*] *Brit* **:** ³TWENTY-ONE 5

van·man \ˈvanˌman, -ˌmən\ *n, pl* **vanmen** [³*van* + *man*] **:** a van driver

van·nal \ˈvanᵊl\ *adj* [NL *vannus* + E *-al*] **:** of, relating to, or constituting a vannus and esp. a fold between the remigium and vannus of the wings of some insects

vanned *past of* VAN

¹van·ner \ˈvanə(r)\ *n* -s [E dial. *van* to separate ore with a van (fr. ¹*van*) + E *-er*] **1 :** a miner who separates ore with a shovel or pan **2 :** SHAKING TABLE

²vanner \"\ *n* -s [³*van* + *-er*] *chiefly Brit* **:** a horse used or suitable for use in hauling vans

van·ner·man \-mən\ *n, pl* **vannermen** [¹*vanner* + *man*] **:** one who operates an ore vanner

vanning *pres part of* VAN

van·nus \ˈvanəs\ *n* -ES [NL, fr. L, winnowing fan — more at WINNOW] **:** the anal lobe of an insect's wing esp. when large and fanlike

van·ox·ite \(ˈ)vaˈnäkˌsīt\ *n* -s [*vanadium oxide* + *-ite*] **:** a mineral $V_6O_{13}.8H_2O(?)$ consisting of a hydrous oxide of vanadium

¹van·quish \ˈvaŋkwish, -ank-, -wēsh, *esp in pres part* -wəsh\ *vb* -ED/-ING/-ES [ME *venquissen*, *vainquisshen*; *venquissen* fr. MF *venquis*, preterit of *veintre* to conquer, fr. OF, fr. L *vincere*; ME *vainquisshen* fr. MF *vainquiss-*, stem of *vainquir* to conquer, fr. OF *vainkir*, alter. of *veintre* — more at VICTOR] *vt* **1 :** to conquer or overcome in battle **:** win dominion over **:** SUBJUGATE **2 :** to defeat (an antagonist) in a conflict or contest of any kind **:** emerge as victor over **3 :** to gain mastery over (an emotion, passion, or temptation) **:** CONTROL, SUBDUE ~ *vi* **:** to be victorious **syn** see CONQUER

²vanquish \"\ *n* -ES *Scot* **:** ¹PINE 3

van·quish·able \-shəbəl\ *adj* **:** capable of being vanquished **:** VINCIBLE

van·quish·er \-shə(r)\ *n* -s [ME *vainquissheur*, fr. *vainquisshen* to vanquish + *-eur* -or] **:** one that vanquishes **:** CONQUEROR

van·quish·ment \-shmənt\ *n* -s [¹*vanquish* + *-ment*] **1 :** an act of vanquishing **:** CONQUEST, VICTORY **2 :** the state of being vanquished **:** DEFEAT

vans *pl of* VAN, *pres 3d sing of* VAN

van·sit·tart·ism \vanˈsid-ə(r)d-ˌizəm *also* van-\ *n* -s *usu cap* [Sir Robert *Vansittart*, 1st Baron Vansittart of Denham †1957 Brit. diplomat + E *-ism*] **:** a doctrine holding that the conduct of German war leaders from the Franco-Prussian war on has had the wholehearted support of the majority of Germans and that Germany must be demilitarized during a protracted period of occupation and reeducation to insure against her undertaking further wars of conquest

van slyke method \vaˈnˈslīk- *also* və\ *n, usu cap V&S* [after Donald D. *Van Slyke* b1883 Am. biochemist] **:** any of several analytical methods; *esp* **:** the determination of free amino groups (as in amino acids, peptides, or proteins) by measuring

the volume or pressure of nitrogen gas formed by reaction with nitrous acid

[1]van·tage \'vantij, -aan-,-ain-,-ȧn-, -tēj\ *n* -s [ME, fr. AF, fr. MF *avantage* — more at ADVANTAGE] **1** *archaic* : BENEFIT, GAIN **2 a** : an advantage in a contest : SUPERIORITY **b** : something (as strategic position or superior force) that gives an advantage to one of two contenders ⟨attempts to secure ~ ground south of the river —*Amer. Guide Series: Va.*⟩ ⟨manipulation of the machinery of the convention from his ~ point as chairman —C.R.Erdman⟩ **c** : a place esp. suited to give a comprehensive view or a commanding perspective : COIGN OF VANTAGE ⟨looking back on her life from the ~ of her 80th birthday —*Newsweek*⟩ ⟨from the ~ point of a window seat, one surveys the slums —*Amer. Guide Series: N.Y. City*⟩ **3** : something thrown in for good measure : an additional sum or quantity : BOOT **4** [by shortening] *Brit* : ADVANTAGE 5 — **to the vantage** *adv* : in addition : to boot

[2]vantage \"\ *vt* -ED/-ING/-S [ME *vantagen*, fr. [1]*vantage*] : ADVANTAGE, PROFIT

vantguard *n* [ME *avaunt garde, vantgard* — more at VANGUARD] *obs* : VANGUARD

vant·hoff·ite \vant'hȯ,fīt, vän-, -hä,f-\ *n* -s [Jacobus H. *van't Hoff* †1911 + E *-ite*] : a mineral consisting of a sulfate of sodium and magnesium that occurs in granular or layered aggregates

van't hoff's law \-ȯfs-,-äfs-\ *n, usu cap H* [after Jacobus H. *van't Hoff* †1911 Du. physical chemist] : a statement in physical chemistry: for a system in equilibrium an increase in temperature increases the rate of the reaction absorbing heat — compare LE CHATELIER'S LAW

van tie·ghem cell \van·'tēgəm-, ¦van·(,)tyä¦gem-\ *n, usu cap V&T* [after P.E.L. *Van Tieghem* †1914 Fr. botanist] : a device used for the microscopic observation of microorganisms usu. in hanging-drop cultures and consisting of a ring or short tube fixed to a glass slide or Petri dish and capped with a cover glass

[1]van·ward \'vanwə(r)d, 'vaan-\ *adj* [[2]*van* + *-ward*, adj. suffix] : located in the van : taking the lead : ADVANCED ⟨a ~ woman —George Meredith⟩

[2]vanward \"\ *adv* [[2]*van* + *-ward*, adv. suffix] : to or toward the van : FORWARD

van–winged hawk \'=,=-\ *n* [[1]*van* + *winged*] *dial Eng* : [3]HOBBY

vap·id \'vapəd *also* 'väp-\ *adj* [L *vapidus* flat tasting, spiritless; akin to L *vappa* vapid wine and prob. to L *vapor* steam — more at COVET] : lacking flavor, zest, animation, or spirit : having lost the appeal of liveliness, tang, briskness, or force : FLAT, INSIPID, UNINTERESTING, POINTLESS, TRITE ⟨~ beer⟩ ⟨a fixed, ~ smile —Roger Eddy⟩ ⟨expressed a mild, ~ surprise at things told her —Arnold Bennett⟩ **syn** see INSIPID

va·pid·i·ty \və'pidəd·ē, va'-, -ətē, -i\ *n* -ES [*vapid* + *-ity*] **1** : VAPIDNESS ⟨unblushing acceptance of a total ~ of soul —Albert Dasnoy⟩ **2** : something vapid ⟨the *vapidities* of everyday conversation⟩

vap·id·ly *adv* : in a vapid manner ⟨~ smiling little man —Richard Blaker⟩

vap·id·ness *n* -ES : the quality or state of being vapid ⟨the ~ of the entertainments⟩

vapo- *comb form* [*vapor*] : vapor ⟨*vapocauterization*⟩ ⟨*vapography*⟩

va·po–dusting \'vāpō+,-\ *n* [*vapo-* + *dusting*, gerund of *dust*] : a method of dispersing insecticides in which the insecticide solution is broken up into fine particles and carried to the foliage in an air stream

va·pog·ra·phy \vā'pägrəfē\ *n* -ES [*vapo-* + *-graphy*] : the process of obtaining a developable image by permitting a sensitive film or plate to remain in contact with a substance (as zinc or printer's ink) that gives off vapors or emanations affecting it without exposure to light

[1]va·por \'vāpə(r)\ *n* -s *see -or in Explan Notes* [ME *vapour*, fr. MF *vapeur*, fr. L *vapor* steam, vapor — more at COVET] **1** : diffused matter (as smoke, fog, mist, steam, or an exhalation) suspended floating in the air and impairing its transparency ⟨cold motors turning over and the ~ from the exhausts steaming —R.H.Newman⟩ **2 a** : a substance in the gaseous state as distinguished from the liquid or solid state : a gasified liquid or solid : a gaseous substance that is at a temperature below its critical temperature and therefore liquefiable by pressure alone **b** : a substance (as gasoline, alcohol, mercury, or benzoin) vaporized for industrial, therapeutic, or military uses; *also* : a mixture (as in an internal-combustion engine) of such a vapor with air **3 a** *archaic* : something unsubstantial or transitory : PHANTASM ⟨beyond the ~s of her sleep she would hear a night-passer —Elizabeth M. Roberts⟩ **b** : a foolish or fanciful notion : a fantastic idea ⟨his realities may seem most impalpable ~s —G.W.Brace⟩ ⟨what amazing ~s a lonely man may get into his head —H.G. Wells⟩ **4 vapors** *pl* **a** *archaic* : exhalations of bodily organs (as the stomach) held to affect the physical or mental condition **b** : a depressed or hysterical nervous condition formerly held to be caused by bodily exhalations ⟨neurotic women subject to the ~s —Lois & Don Thorburn⟩ ⟨had a fit of the ~s shortly after breakfast —James Reynolds⟩ **5** : a medicinal agent designed for administration in the form of inhaled vapor

[2]vapor \"\ *vb* -ED/-ING/-S [ME *vapouren*, fr. *vapour* vapor] *vt* **1** : to send in or as if in vapor : cause to evaporate : reduce to vapor ⟨~ away a heated fluid⟩ **2 a** : to assert or boast loudly or foolishly : utter in highflown language **b** *archaic* : to overcome by highflown or bombastic language : BULLY **3** *archaic* : to affect with the vapors : DEPRESS, BORE ~ *vi* **1 a** : to rise in vapor : pass off as vapor : EVAPORATE ⟨could see his breath and my own ~ing . . . in the freezing air —H.E.Bates⟩ **b** : to emit vapor : FUME, STEAM ⟨running waters ~ not so much as standing waters —Francis Bacon⟩ **2** : to indulge in bragging, blustering, or idle talk : speak or write in a pompous or inflated style

va·por·abil·i·ty \,vāpərə'biləd·ē\ *n* : the quality of being vaporable

va·por·able \'vāpərəbəl\ *adj* [ME, fr. ML *vaporabilis*, fr. L *vaporare* to steam (fr. *vapor* steam, vapor) + *-abilis* -able] : that can be vaporized : VAPORIZABLE

vapor barrier *n* : a layer of material (as of paint, building paper, or felt) used to retard or prevent the absorption of moisture (as into a wall or floor) and its subsequent condensation therein

vapor density *n* : the relative density of a gas or vapor as compared with some specific standard (as hydrogen)

vapor engine *n* : an engine in which the working fluid is a vapor esp. other than steam

va·por·er \'vāpərə(r)\ *n* -s [[2]*vapor* + *-er*] : one that vapors; *esp* : BRAGGART

vaporer moth \"+\ *n* : TUSSOCK MOTH

va·po·ret·to \,vāpə'red·(,)ō\ *n* -s [It, dim. of *vapore* steamboat, fr. F *vapeur*, fr. *bateau à vapeur* steamboat, fr. *bateau* boat + *à* to (fr. L *ad*) + *vapeur* steam, fr. L *vapor* — more at BATEAU, AT, COVET] : a small steamboat used as a canal bus in Venice, Italy

vapor heating *n* : steam heating in which the steam has a pressure slightly above that of the atmosphere : very low-pressure steam heating

vapori- *comb form* [L *vapor*] : vapor ⟨*vaporiform*⟩ ⟨*vaporimeter*⟩

va·por·if·ic \,vāpə¦rifik\ *adj* [*vapori-* + *-fic*] : producing vapor : tending to pass or to cause to pass into vapor : VAPOROUS

va·por·im·e·ter \,vāpə'rimǝd·ə(r)\ *n* [ISV *vapori-* + *-meter*; orig. formed in G] : an instrument for measuring the volume or the pressure of a vapor; *specif* : one used in alcoholometry

[1]vaporing *n* -s [fr. gerund of [2]*vapor*] : the act or speech of one that vapors : an idle, extravagant, or high-flown expression or speech : a vapid remark or statement ⟨a minimum of nationalistic ~ —*Newsweek*⟩ ⟨not mere academic ~ —Raymond Moley⟩ — usu. used in pl. ⟨like the juvenile ~s of an immature mind —Mary R. Rinehart⟩ ⟨unmistakable warnings against grandiose ~s —E.H.Eby⟩

[2]vaporing *adj* [fr. pres. part. of [2]*vapor*] : that vapors : spouting forth vapors : VAUNTING — **va·por·ing·ly** *adv*

va·por·ish \'vāpərish, -rēsh\ *adj* [[1]*vapor* + *-ish*] **1** : resembling or suggestive of vapor : VAPOROUS, MISTY, THIN ⟨her pure white and ~ hair —Antonio Barolini⟩ ⟨an old man's ideas were apt to be wild and ~ —H.L.Davis⟩ ⟨stories . . . are ~ and sad, without much core —*New Yorker*⟩ **2** : affected by the vapors : given to fits of depression or hysteria — **va·por·ish·ness** *n* -ES

va·por·iz·able \'vāpə,rīzəbəl, ,==¦===\ *adj* : capable of being vaporized

va·por·iza·tion \,vāpərə'zāshən, -,rī'-\ *n* -s [*vaporize* + *-ation*] : the act or process of vaporizing or state of being vaporized : artificial formation of vapor; *specif* : conversion of water into steam (as in a steam boiler)

va·por·ize \'vāpə,rīz\ *vb* -ED/-ING/-S [[1]*vapor* + *-ize*] *vt* **1** : to convert into vapor either naturally or artificially (as by the application of heat or by spraying) **2** : to reduce to a vaporous state or form : cause to become ethereal or dissipated ⟨*vaporized* by a nuclear explosion⟩ ~ *vi* **1** : to become converted into vapor or reduced to a vaporous state **2** : to indulge in vaporing

va·por·iz·er \-zə(r)\ *n* -s : one that vaporizes: as **a** : ATOMIZER **b** : an apparatus for vaporizing a heavy oil (as petroleum) for the explosive charge of an internal-combustion engine; *also* : a simple form of carburetor **c** : a device for converting a medicated liquid into a vapor for inhalation **d** : one who prepares plastics material for finishing by treating it with solvent vapors in a vaporizing machine

vaporizing *n* -s [fr. gerund of *vaporize*] : VAPORING ⟨the ~s of latter-day romancers —*New Yorker*⟩

vapor jacket *n* : a closed glass or metal case surrounding a bulb or other apparatus and often containing a vapor at a known temperature

vapor lamp *n* **1** : a lamp burning a vapor (as of alcohol) **2** : a lamp in which an electric discharge takes place through a metallic vapor — compare MERCURY-VAPOR LAMP

va·por·less \'vāpə(r)ləs\ *adj* : devoid of vapor

vapor lock *n* : partial or complete interruption of fuel flow in an internal-combustion engine caused by the formation of bubbles of vapor or gas in the fuel-feeding system

va·por·ous \'vāp(ə)rəs\ *adj* [L *vaporosus* full of steam or vapor, fr. *vapor* + *-osus* -ous] **1** : consisting or characteristic of vapor : having the form or nature of vapor ⟨a ~ substance⟩ ⟨~ consistency⟩ **2 a** *obs* : causing flatulence ⟨~ foods⟩ **b** : producing vapors : VOLATILE ⟨a ~ paint⟩ **3** : full of vapor : containing or obscured by vapors : FOGGY, MISTY ⟨a ~ atmosphere⟩ ⟨shady vales between the ~ mountains —H.D. Thoreau⟩ ⟨faint beacon, ~ in the rainy darkness —A.J.Cronin⟩ **4 a** : ETHEREAL, UNSUBSTANTIAL, VAGUE ⟨a score of ~ twilight landscapes —*Time*⟩ **b** : FILMY ⟨~ silks⟩ **c** : consisting of or indulging in vaporings ⟨such ~ speculations were inevitable —Thomas Carlyle⟩ ⟨~ realms of conjecture and hyperbole —H.E.Clurman⟩ ⟨give himself up to ~ dreams —Sherwood Anderson⟩ — **va·por·ous·ly** *adv* — **va·por·ous·ness** *n* -ES

vapor pressure *or* **vapor tension** *n* : the pressure exerted by a vapor that is in equilibrium with a solid or liquid

vapor–pressure thermometer *n* : a thermometer in which the variable saturated vapor pressure of a volatile liquid is used as a measure of the temperature and which thus has the advantage over some other types of thermometers of being free from errors due to bulb expansion

vaporproof \'==,=\ *adj* : impervious to the penetration of vapor

vapors *pl of* VAPOR, *pres 3d sing of* VAPOR

vapor seal *n* : VAPOR BARRIER

vapor trail *n* : CONTRAIL

va·pory \'vāp(ə)rē, -ri\ *adj* [[1]*vapor* + *-y*] : consisting of, full of, characterized by, or resembling vapor : VAPOROUS, MISTY, VAGUE ⟨~ outlines⟩

va·que·ro \vä'ke(,)rō, vȧ'-\ *n* -s *see sense 2* [Sp — more at BUCKAROO] **1** : HERDSMAN, COWBOY **2** *or pl* **vaquero** *usu cap* : APACHE; *esp* : QUERECHO

va·quez's disease \vä'kezəz-\ *n, usu cap V* [after Louis Henri *Vaquez* †1936 Fr. physician] : POLYCYTHEMIA

va·qui·ta \vä'kēd·ə\ *n* -s [AmerSp, dim. of Sp *vaca* cow, fr. L *vacca* — more at VACCINE] : a West Indian weevil (*Diaprepes abbreviatus*) of which the larvae feed on the roots esp. of trees and the adults on the leaves

var \'vär\ *n* -s [*v*olt-*a*mpere *r*eactive] : the reactive volt-ampere unit

var *abbr* **1** variable **2** variant **3** variation **4** variegated **5** variety **6** variometer **7** various

VAR *abbr* **1** visual-aural radio range; visual-aural range **2** volt-ampere reactive

va·ra \'värə\ *n* -s [Sp & Pg, rod, pole, a unit of length, fr. L, forked pole, fr. fem. of *varus* bent, crooked — more at PREVARICATE] **1** : any of various Spanish and Portuguese units of length used in Latin America and southwestern U. S. equal to between 31 and 34 inches; *esp* : a Texas unit equal to 33.33 inches **2** : a staff or cane used in Spanish-American countries as a badge of office **3** : [5]PIC 1

var·an \'varən\ *n* -s [NL *Varanus*] : MONITOR LIZARD

[1]va·ran·gi·an \və'ranjēən\ *adj, usu cap* [MGk *Barangoi*, pl. + E *-an*, adj. suffix] : of, relating to, or characteristic of the Varangians

[2]varangian \"\ *n* -s *cap* [MGk *Barangoi*, pl., Varangians (of Scand origin; akin to ON *Væringjar* Varangians, fr. pl. of *væringi* confederate, fr. *vārar*, pl., pledge) + E *-an*, n. suffix — more at VERY] **1** : one of the Scandinavians who founded a dynasty in Russia in the 9th century **2** : a member of the bodyguard of the Byzantine emperors esp. in the 11th and 12th centuries composed chiefly of Russians or later of Scandinavians or other northern Europeans

[1]var·a·nid \'varənəd\ *adj* [NL *Varanidae*] : of or relating to the Varanidae

[2]varanid \"\ *n* -s : a lizard of the family Varanidae

va·ran·i·dae \və'ranə,dē\ *n pl, cap* [NL, fr. *Varanus*, type genus + *-idae*] : a family of large tropical Old World lizards comprising the monitors, having an elongated neck and tail and well-developed limbs, and being terrestrial or semiaquatic and voraciously carnivorous — compare KOMODO DRAGON

var·a·nus \'varənəs\ *n, cap* [NL, fr. Ar *waran, waral* monitor lizard] : a genus (the type and sole recent genus of the family Varanidae) of Old World lizards

vardapet *var of* VARTABED

vare \'va(a)(ə)r\ *n* -s [ME *veir* squirrel fur, weasel — more at VAIR] *dial Eng* : WEASEL

var·ec *also* **var·ech** \'va,rek\ *n* -s [F, fr. AF *warec* wreck, seaweed — more at WRECK] **1** : SEAWEED **2** : the calcined ashes of coarse seaweeds used for the manufacture of iodine, potash, and formerly soda : KELP 2

var·gue·no \vär'gān(,)yō\ *n* -s [Sp *bargueño*, fr. *bargueño* of Bargas, fr. *Bargas*, village near Toledo, Spain] : a decorative writing cabinet of a form originating in Spain, composed of a rectangular chest supported on legs or a decorative framework, and having the front opening downward on hinges to serve as a writing desk

va·ri \'vä'rē\ *n* -s [Malagasy *varika*] : RUFFED LEMUR

vari- *or* **vario-** *comb form* [L *varius* — more at VARIOUS] : varied : diverse ⟨*variform*⟩ ⟨*variocoupler*⟩

var·ia \'va(a)rēə\ *n pl* [NL, fr. L, neut. pl. of *varius* various] : various things : MISCELLANY; *esp* : a literary miscellany

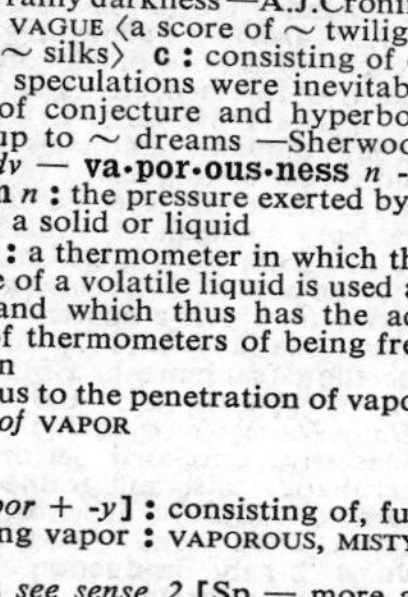

vargueno

var·i·a·bil·i·ty \,verēə'biləd·ē, ,va(a)r-, ,vär-, -lətē, -i\ *n* **1** : the quality or fact of being variable or subject to variation : VARIABLENESS ⟨apparently unlimited ~ of individual behavior —Edward Sapir⟩ ⟨free intellectual ~ which is the source of genuine progress in science —M.R.Cohen⟩ **2** : the quality or attribute of animals and plants that causes them to exhibit variation : the ability to vary from whatever cause — compare VARIATION 6a **3** : DISPERSION 2a

[1]var·i·a·ble \'verēəbəl, 'va(a)r-, 'vär-\ *adj* [ME, fr. MF, fr. L *variabilis*, fr. *variare* to vary + *-abilis* -able] **1 a** : able or apt to vary or change : susceptible or subject to variation or changes : CHANGEABLE, SHIFTING ⟨~ winds⟩ ⟨a ~ climate⟩ ⟨a ~ speech habit —Stanley Newman⟩ ⟨~ manufacturing expenses —*Cost Accounting*⟩ **b** : FICKLE, UNSTEADY, INCONSTANT ⟨lest thy love prove likewise ~ —Shak.⟩ **2** : characterized by variations or by varying : marked by diversity or difference ⟨nature is infinitely ~ —John Burroughs⟩ ⟨the ~ and tuneful warblings of the nonpareil —William Bartram⟩ **3** : admitting change or variation : ALTERABLE ⟨a ~ period of three days to two weeks⟩ ⟨the annual fair begins on a ~ date in October⟩ ⟨a ~ angle⟩ **4** : being or having the characteristics of a variable ⟨a ~ number⟩ **5** : not true to type : ABERRANT, INCONSTANT — used of a biological group or a biological character

[2]variable \"\ *n* -s **1** : something that is variable : something that varies, may vary, or is liable to vary : something subject to change **2 a** : a quantity that may assume any one of a specified set of values — see DEPENDENT VARIABLE, INDEPENDENT VARIABLE, STATISTICAL VARIABLE **b** (1) : a symbol in a mathematical formula representing a variable : PLACEHOLDER ⟨the value of the function $f(x)$ is determined by the value of the ~ x⟩ (2) : a symbol in a logistical formula that stands for any one of a class of things; *esp* : FREE VARIABLE — see BOUND VARIABLE, INDIVIDUAL VARIABLE, PREDICATE VARIABLE **3 variables** *pl* : an area or belt of ocean where the winds do not usu. blow steadily : a region of calm; *specif* : DOLDRUMS **4** : VARIABLE STAR **5** : a course in a school curriculum that may or may not be included in a pupil's program — contrasted with *constant*

variable–area \¦====¦===\ *adj* : being or relating to a motion-picture sound track in which the sounds are represented by an opaque line of varying width that runs parallel to the length of the film ⟨*variable-area* track⟩ — compare VARIABLE-DENSITY

variable condenser *or* **variable capacitor** *n* : a condenser whose capacitance may be varied for circuit-tuning or other purpose

variable cost *n* : cost that fluctuates directly with changes in output — compare FIXED COST

variable–density \¦====¦===\ *adj* : being or relating to a motion-picture sound track in which the sounds are represented as parallel lines that are at right angles to the length of the film and that vary in density in accordance with the volume and pitch of the recorded sound ⟨*variable-density* track⟩ — compare VARIABLE-AREA

variable error *n* : the variability of a subject's estimates of an objective magnitude measured by their average deviation

variable gear *or* **variable gearing** *n* : a gear wheel of irregular outline gearing with a corresponding wheel so that the velocity ratio changes one or more times throughout a single revolution

variable inductor *n* : an inductor or reactor whose inductance is continuously adjustable

variable nebula *n* : a nebula whose light is subject to fluctuations

var·i·able·ness *n* -ES [ME *variablenesse*, fr. [1]*variable* + *-nesse* -ness] : the quality of being variable : tendency to vary : CHANGEABLENESS

variable oak leaf caterpillar *n* : a caterpillar that is the larva of a notodontid moth (*Heterocampa manteo*) and that feeds on many deciduous trees in the eastern U.S.

variable spacer *n* : a control on the left-hand platen knob of a typewriter that disengages the line space lever to allow writing at positions other than those normally turned up by the ratchet

variable–speed gear *n* : CHANGE GEAR

variable star *n* : a star whose brightness changes usu. in more or less regular periods — compare CEPHEID, ECLIPSING VARIABLE, PULSATING STAR

variable time fuze *n* : PROXIMITY FUZE

variable toad *n* : GREEN TOAD

var·i·a·bly \'verēəblē, 'va(a)r-, 'vär-, -li\ *adv* [[1]*variable* + *-ly*] : in a varying manner : with frequent variation ⟨~ strong winds⟩ ⟨highway is . . . ~ macadam, concrete, and blacktop —*Amer. Guide Series: Vt.*⟩

Var·i·ac \'verē,ak, 'va(a)r-\ *trademark* — used for an adjustable-ratio transformer for test and calibration work

var·i·ad \-,ad\ *n* -s [*vari-* + *-ad*] : one of the slightly differentiated subforms that make up a phylogenetic stock or species

va·ri·ag \'värē,äg\ *n, cap* [Russ *Varyag*, of Scand origin; akin to ON *Væringjar* Varangians — more at VARANGIAN] : VARANGIAN

var·i·ance \'verēən(t)s, 'va(a)r-, 'vär-\ *n* -s [ME *variaunce*, fr. MF, fr. L *variantia*, fr. *variant-, varians* (pres. part. of *variare*) + *-ia* -y] **1 a** : the fact, quality, or state of being variable or variant : VARIATION, DIFFERENCE, DEVIATION ⟨account for the ~ in crops⟩ ⟨a daily ~ of one degree Fahrenheit⟩ ⟨the ~ between reports⟩ **b** : an instance of variableness : a degree of difference : DISCREPANCY ⟨a ~ in the testimony⟩ ⟨send the bill to conference to iron out ~s in House and Senate bills —*Springfield (Mass.) Union*⟩ **c** : a difference between what has been expected or predetermined and what actually occurs; *specif* : a difference between a standard and an historical cost or between a budgeted and an actual expense **2 a** : the fact or state of being in disagreement : a difference of opinion producing dispute or controversy : DISSENSION, DISCORD ⟨forestall ~ among the heirs⟩ **b** : an instance of this ⟨friends who have never had a ~⟩ **3 a** : a disagreement or difference between two parts (as the writ and the declaration, or the allegation and the proof) of the same legal proceeding that to be effectual ought to agree **b** : a permission or license to do some act contrary to the usual rule and used esp. of grants of permission or authorizations to build contrary to the provisions of an otherwise applicable zoning ordinance or building code **4** : the number of degrees of freedom possessed by a physical-chemical system esp. when it is in equilibrium — compare PHASE RULE **5** : the square of the standard deviation : the mean square of the deviations from the arithmetic mean of a frequency distribution — symbol σ^2 **syn** see DISCORD — **at variance 1** : in a state of difference : not in harmony or agreement ⟨may find his pecuniary advantage *at variance* with his professional duty —R.M.MacIver⟩ **2** : in a state of dissension or controversy ⟨*at variance* with himself —John Milton⟩

[1]var·i·ant \-nt\ *adj* [ME, fr. MF, fr. L *variant-, varians*, pres. part. of *variare* to vary] **1** *obs* : tending to, undergoing, or exhibiting change : not constant, unchanging, or uniform : VARIABLE, FICKLE **2** : manifesting variety : marked by diversity : VARIEGATED, VARIED ⟨long strip of ~ country —M.H.Ellis⟩ **3 a** : different from others of its kind or class : exhibiting slight difference, alteration, or disagreement ⟨the principal ~ points of view —A.T.Weaver⟩ ⟨a phrase . . . subject to ~ interpretation by successive scholars —*Language*⟩ ⟨development of these ~ religious groups —E.T.Thompson⟩ **b** : not definitive, generally accepted, or commonly found : MODIFIED ⟨an appendix which contains some ~ readings —B.R.Redman⟩ ⟨rare and elusive ~ editions —L.C.Wroth⟩

[2]variant \"\ *n* -s **1 a** : one of two or more persons or things exhibiting usu. slight differences : VARIATION ⟨~s of a folk song⟩ ⟨that all societies are but ~s of one another —Thornton Wilder⟩ **b** : one that varies from the original or archetype ⟨most military campaigns are . . . ~s on a historical pattern —*New Republic*⟩ **c** : one that exhibits variation from a type or norm : MUTATION; *often* : one whose behavior is at variance with societal norms — compare DEVIANT **2 a** : one of two or more different spellings (as *labor* and *labour* or *indexes* and *indices*) or pronunciations (as of *economics* \ek-, ēk-\) of the same word **b** : one of two or more words or word elements (as *biologic* and *biological* or *stomat-* and *stomato-*) of essentially the same meaning differing only in the presence or absence of an affix **3** : ALLOPHONE **4** : a cipher element or code group having the same significance as another and used to impede cryptanalysis

[1]var·i·ate \-ē,āt\ *vt* -ED/-ING/-S [L *variatus*, past part. of *variare* to vary] : to make varied or irregular : BREAK ⟨the *variated* melody of the first three measures —*Down Beat*⟩ ⟨a *variated* ceiling⟩

[2]var·i·ate \-ēət, -ē,āt\ *n* -s [L *variatus*, past part. of *variare* to vary] **1** : VARIANT **2 a** : a particular value of a mathematical variable : the quantitative measure of a characteristic **b** : VARIABLE : a variable that has a probability density function

var·i·a·tion \,verē'āshən, ,va(a)r-, ,vär-\ *n* -s [L *variation-, variatio*, fr. *variatus* (past part. of *variare* to vary) + *-ion-, -io* -ion] **1 a** : the act of varying : the process, state, or fact of being varied : change in the form, position, state, or quality of something : MODIFICATION, ALTERATION, MUTATION, DIVERSIFICATION ⟨things incapable of ~⟩ **b** : an instance of varying ⟨long for a ~ in our routine⟩ ⟨an agreeable ~ in weather⟩

c : an embellishing change ⟨telling his story again with ~s⟩ **d** : extent to which or range in which a thing varies : degree of departure from norm or type : amount or rate of change ⟨great ~s in speed⟩ ⟨within the limits of barometric ~⟩ **2 a** : the compass error caused by the earth's magnetic field and measured as the angle between true north and north as indicated by a compass needle unaffected by any other influence **b** : DECLINATION 6 **3** : a change in the mean motion or mean orbit of a planet or other celestial body ⟨the ~ of the moon depending on its angular distance from the sun⟩ **4 a** : PERMUTATION 3b **b** : the sequence + − or − + in a row of such signs or of terms affected by them — opposed to *permanence* **c** : lack of uniformity in statistical observations or measures **5 a** : the repetition of a theme or melody with embellishments or modifications in rhythm, tune, harmony, or key **b variations** *pl* : the varied repetitions of a theme in a theme and variations **6 a** : divergence in structural or functional qualities of an organism or biotype from those typical or usual to the group of which it is a part (as divergence of offspring from parent) usu. including fundamental hereditary changes through which natural selection works to induce evolutionary development as well as purely individual fluctuations that lack evolutionary significance — compare ADAPTATION, MUTATION **b** : an individual or group exhibiting variation : VARIANT **7 a** : a continuation (as in notes to a tournament game) from a given position different from that actually played in a chess game **b** : one of a family of opening continuations branching off from an initial common sequence **8** : the maximum angular displacement in electrical degrees between the voltage wave of an alternating-current circuit or machine and a wave whose constant frequency is the average frequency of the circuit or machine **9** : the maximum angular or phase displacement of the revolving member or armature of a machine from the position of uniform rotation — compare PULSATION 3 **10 a** : a solo dance in ballet **b** : a repetition in modern dance composition of a movement sequence with changes

var·i·a·tion·al \¦==¦āshənᵊl, -shnəl\ *adj* : of or relating to variation : characterized by variation — **var·i·a·tion·al·ly** \-shənᵊlē, -shnəlē, -i\ *adv*

var·i·a·tion·ist \,==ˈāshənəst\ *n* -s : a composer of musical variations

variation of latitude : a small periodic change in the observed latitude of any place resulting from wandering of the poles

variation of parameters : a method for solving a differential equation by first solving a simpler equation and then generalizing this solution properly so as to satisfy the original equation by treating the arbitrary constants not as constants but as variables

var·i·a·tive \ˈverē,ād·iv, ˈva(a)r-, -ēəd·iv\ *adj* [L *variatus* (past part. of *variare* to vary) + E *-ive*] : of, relating to, or showing variation — **var·i·a·tive·ly** \-d·əvlē\ *adv*

var·i·a·tor \-ē,ād·ə(r)\ *n* -s [NL *variatus* + E *-or*] : one that variates ⟨a speed ~⟩; *specif* : a joint that compensates for variations in length due to temperature changes : EXPANSION JOINT

var·i·a·tus \,verēˈād·əs, ,va(a)r-\ *n* -ES [NL *variatus* (specific epithet of *Platypoecilus variatus*), fr. L, past part. of *variare* to vary] : a fish (*Platypoecilus variatus*) related to the common platy and often kept in the tropical aquarium

varic- *or* **varico-** *comb form* [L *varic-, varix* — more at VARICOSE] : varix ⟨*varicosis*⟩ ⟨*varicocele*⟩

var·i·cel·la \,varəˈselə\ *n* -S [NL, irreg. dim. of *variola*] : CHICKEN POX — **var·i·cel·lar** \¦==ˈselə(r)\ *adj*

var·i·cel·late \¦==ˈselət, -e,lāt\ *adj* [NL *varicella* (dim. of *varic-, varix*) + E *-ate*] *of a shell* : having small or indistinct varices

var·i·cel·li·form \¦==ˈseləˌfȯrm\ *adj* [NL *varicella* chicken pox + ISV *-iform*] : resembling chicken pox

varices *pl of* VARIX

var·i·co·cele \ˈvarəkō,sēl\ *n* -S [NL, fr. *varic-* + *-cele*] : a varicose enlargement of the veins of the spermatic cord producing a soft compressible tumor mass in the scrotum

var·i·coid \ˈvarə,kȯid\ *adj* [*varic-* + *-oid*] : resembling a varix

vari·colored \ˈverē,kələ(r)d, ˈva(a)r-, -ri,-\ *adj* [*vari-* + *colored*] : having various colors : VARIEGATED ⟨~ marble⟩

var·i·cose \ˈvarə,kōs, ˈver-\ *adj* [L *varicosus* full of dilated veins, fr. *varic-, varix* dilated vein + *-osus* -ose; prob. akin to L *varus* pimple, *verruca* wart — more at WART] **1 a** *also* **var·i·cosed** \-st\ : abnormally swollen or dilated ⟨~ veins⟩ ⟨~ lymph vessels⟩ **b** : causing abnormal swelling ⟨~ stasis⟩ **2** : of, relating to, or exhibiting varices ⟨~ mollusks⟩ ⟨puffy and ~ men —C.W.Ferguson⟩

var·i·cose·ness *n* -ES : the condition of being varicose

varicose vein *n* : VARIX 1b

var·i·co·sis \,==ˈkōsəs\ *n, pl* **varico·ses** \-ō,sēz\ [NL, fr. *varic-* + *-osis*] **1** : the condition of being varicose **2** : VARIX

var·i·cos·i·ty \,==ˈkäsəd·ē, -ətē, -i\ *n* -ES [*varicose* + *-ity*] **1** : the quality, state, or condition of being varicose **2** : VARIX ⟨a hemorrhoid is a ~ within the anal canal⟩

var·ied \ˈverēd, ˈva(a)r-, ˈvär-, -rid\ *adj* [fr. past part. of *vary*] **1** : CHANGED, ALTERED **2** : having numerous forms or types : VARIOUS, DIVERSIFIED, DIVERSE ⟨a ~ experience⟩ ⟨~ interests⟩ ⟨~ scenery⟩ **3** : marked conspicuously or contrastingly with several colors : VARIEGATED

varied bunting *n* : a bunting (*Passerina versicolor*) of eastern Mexico and southern Texas the male of which is handsomely colored with the plumage largely of shades of purple and red

varied carpet beetle *n* : a mottled brown and white dermestid beetle (*Anthrenus verbasci*) that feeds as both larva and adult on dry organic matter (as wool, skin, or hair) and is often a household pest

var·ied·ly *adv* : in a varied manner

varied thrush *n* : a thrush (*Ixoreus naevius*) of western No. America similar in form and size to the robin but reddish or orange brown underneath and with a black mark on the breast

var·ie·gate \ˈver(ē)ə,gāt, ˈva(a)r-, ˈvär-, -rē,-, -ri,-, *usu* -gād·+V\ *vt* -ED/-ING/-S [L *variegatus*, past part. of *variegare* to variegate, fr. *varius* varied, various + *-egare* (akin to L *agere* to drive) — more at VARIOUS, AGENT] : to diversify esp. in external appearance (as with different colors) : enliven or impart interest to by means of variety ⟨as a woman saves odd moneys to ~ her wardrobe with a gown —Freya Stark⟩ ⟨the irresolution, precipitation, regret and so on that ~ a character through its forties and fifties —Donald Sutherland⟩

var·ie·gat·ed \-gād·əd, -gātəd\ *adj* [fr. past part. of *variegate*] : VARIED ⟨a ~ throng —Adrian Bell⟩; *esp* : marked with different colors or tints in spots, streaks, or stripes ⟨a ~ tulip⟩

syn PARTI-COLORED, MOTLEY, CHECKERED, CHECKED, PIED, PIEBALD, SKEWBALD, DAPPLED, FREAKED: VARIEGATED indicates only variation in the color of a single piece, object, or specimen without indication of what colors or what forms — spots, streaks, blotches — are involved ⟨disliked the *variegated* hues of the buildings — they reminded him of the garish brilliance in the lower town —Norman Douglas⟩ PARTI-COLORED may stress not so much the presence of different colors as their clear and distinct presentation. MOTLEY in most uses is likely to suggest presence of three or more colors in very noticeable diversity in a chance or very capricious arrangement ⟨birds of *motley* colors and varied cries —G.K.Chesterton⟩ ⟨the *motley* dress of a court jester⟩ CHECKERED indicates a regular alternation of rectangular shapes different in color or shade like a checkerboard, esp. an alternation between black and white or dark and light ⟨the *chequered* fabric of Constable's pictures, their deep undertones overlaid with variegated passages of crumbling impasto and strewn with particles of white light —Robin Ironside⟩ CHECKED indicates much the same thing but is admissible in situations where figures are less certainly rectangular; it is common in reference to fabrics ⟨a gambler's *checked* vest⟩ PIED suggests patches, blotches, or spots of colors on a contrasting background, esp. the white on black of a magpie's plumage. PIEBALD suggests the same coloration, esp. in reference to the markings of a horse or dog, and SKEWBALD indicates an arrangement of spots and background involving white and some color other than black ⟨*piebald* strictly means spotted white and black and *skewbald* white and any color but black —G.G.Simpson⟩ DAPPLED describes a marking with small spots, patches, or specks of color or shade differing from that of the background ⟨it lay *dappled* with sun and shade, still, clear, and irresistible —Susan Ertz⟩ FREAKED may suggest bold streaks of contrasting color ⟨tall bare fells, capped and *freaked* with snow —John Brophy⟩ ⟨the woods were *freaked* and pied with fresh transparent leaves and flowers —Elinor Wylie⟩

variegated copper ore *n* : BORNITE

variegated cutworm *n* : a widespread and destructive cutworm (*Peridroma saucia*)

variegated grass *n* : RIBBON GRASS

variegated sheldrake *n* : PARADISE DUCK

variegated spider monkey *n* : a black, white, and yellow So. American spider monkey (*Ateles variegatus*)

variegated spurge *n* : SNOW-ON-THE-MOUNTAIN 2

variegated thistle *n, NewZeal* : MILK THISTLE 1

var·ie·ga·tion \,==(=)ˈgāshən\ *n* -S [*variegate* + *-ion*] **1** : the act of variegating or state of being variegated; *esp* : diversity of colors or tints **2** : the presence of two or more colors in leaves, flowers, or stems due to localized distribution of pigments or to absence of pigments in some areas

var·ie·ga·tor \ˈ==(=),gād·ə(r)\ *n* -S [*variegate* + *-or*] : one that variegates

var·i·er \ˈverēə(r), ˈva(a)r-\ *n* -S : one that varies

varies *pres 3d sing of* VARY

va·ri·e·tal \vəˈrīəd·ᵊl, -ətᵊl\ *adj* [*variety* + *-al*] : of, relating to, or characterizing a variety ⟨~ name⟩ : being a variety in distinction from an individual or species : SUBSPECIFIC — **va·ri·e·tal·ly** \-ᵊlē, -ᵊli\ *adv*

varietal wine *also* **varietal** *n* -S : a wine bearing the name of the principal grape from which it is produced ⟨Cabernet is a California *varietal wine*⟩ — compare GENERIC WINE

va·ri·e·tas \vəˈrīə,tas\ *n, pl* **varieta·tes** \=,==ˈtäd·,ēz\ [L *varietat-, varietas*] : VARIETY

va·ri·e·tist \vəˈrīəd·əst\ *n* -S [*variety* + *-ist*] : one who varies from the norm (as in aptitudes, desires, or appetites)

va·ri·e·ty \vəˈrīəd·ē, -ətē, -i\ *n* -ES [MF or L; MF *varieté*, fr. L *varietat-, varietas*, fr. *varie-* (fr. *varius* various) + *-tat-, -tas* -ty] **1** : the quality or state of having numerous forms or types : the quality or state of being various or varied : MULTIFARIOUSNESS ⟨astonishing grasp of the multiplicity and ~ of life —René Wellek⟩ ⟨his imagination is ensnared by her endless ~ —Edwin Mims⟩ ⟨the ~ of the city's musical life⟩ **2** : an intermixture or succession of different things, forms, or qualities : a number or collection of different things esp. of a particular class : ASSORTMENT ⟨worked at a ~ of occupations —*Current Biog.*⟩ ⟨fought for a ~ of local improvements —Frank Monaghan⟩ ⟨region has a wide ~ of plant life —*Amer. Guide Series: Ark.*⟩ **3** : something differing from others of the same general kind : one of a number of things that are related : SORT ⟨army of foremen, clerks, shopkeepers and middlemen of every ~ —G.M.Trevelyan⟩: as **a** : any of various infraspecific groups of plants or animals: as (1) *archaic* : a group or kind of individual distinguished by characters too inconstant or too trivial to justify specific rank (2) : SUBSPECIES a (3) : a category immediately inferior to a subspecies and not resulting from geographic isolation (4) : a specified biotype (as a color phase) (5) : HORTICULTURAL VARIETY **b** : one of the forms in which a species of mineral may occur differing in minor characteristics esp. of structure, color, or purity of composition ⟨sapphire is a blue ~ of corundum⟩ **4** : VARIETY STORE ⟨operates a ~ and luncheonette —*Springfield (Mass.) Daily News*⟩ ⟨a ~ chain⟩ **5 a** : entertainment consisting of successive unrelated performances (as songs, dances, skits, acrobatic feats, and trained animal acts) ⟨~ program⟩ ⟨~ turn⟩ ⟨~ house⟩ ⟨the wireless blares out ~ and swing music —Flora Thompson⟩ — see VARIETY SHOW; compare VAUDEVILLE **b** : the production of or performance in variety shows : variety performances **6** : the effect of multiplicity and continuous discovery in form as opposed to aesthetic monotony

syn SUBSPECIES, RACE, BREED, STRAIN, STOCK: these words show variable uses according to the period of scientific writing in which they appear and have been used to designate closely related groups of plants or animals narrower in scope than a species. VARIETY and SUBSPECIES often apply to a group distinguished from others in a general class by characteristics too minor to constitute criteria of a species. Sometimes VARIETY designates a group produced by human research and control ⟨a new *variety* of apples⟩ SUBSPECIES indicates a subdivision of a species set off from the rest by minor or unstable differences. RACE, often a bitterly controversial word in both scientific and lay discussions, may designate a group whose distinctive characteristics set it off from other groups of the same ancestry and are likely to be inherited from generation to generation with a degree of stability ⟨the darker *races* of mankind are made up of those having skins rich in melanin⟩ BREED may refer to an established group within a species sharing inheritable characteristics and usu. developed or maintained through human control (as Jersey cows or beagle dogs). STRAIN may refer to a group smaller than a breed and linked by common quite specific ancestry or identifying characteristic ⟨a *strain* of Shorthorn cattle known as the Milking Shorthorn⟩ ⟨a resistant *strain* of bacteria⟩ STOCK may suggest a genetically close relationship and a general similarity of origin, environment, and development, but its range of reference is not clearly defined ⟨coming from a healthy *stock*⟩

syn VARIETY, DIVERSITY: VARIETY usu. applies to a multiplicity of things within the same class or category that can be distinguished, often by marked differences ⟨the *variety* of feelings which bore me onward —Mary W. Shelley⟩ ⟨a *variety* of competing sects —Stringfellow Barr⟩ ⟨a *variety* of styles⟩ ⟨a *variety* of pleasures⟩ DIVERSITY, though often interchangeable with VARIETY, more usu. stresses a marked difference or divergence among individuals, parts, or elements, seldom implying also or putting much stress on a class likeness ⟨the range and *diversity* of their interests and activities —Dumas Malone⟩ ⟨man's genetic *diversity* —Curt Stern⟩ ⟨has a better eye for similarities among cultures than for *diversities* —Raphael Demos⟩ ⟨absorbed in the *diversity* resulting where immigration plays an important role, as in religion and personal names —B.A.Botkin⟩

variety meat *n* : an edible part of a slaughter animal other than skeletal muscle usu. including organ meats (as liver, heart, tripes, or kidneys) and various other organ structures (as tongues, ears, or skin); *broadly* : any of various edible meat products or meat by-products that do not consist predominantly of skeletal muscle (as feet) and that are often sold partially processed (as in sausage)

variety show *n* : a theatrical entertainment of successive separate performances (as of songs, dances, comic routines, and acrobatic feats, short dramatic sketches) ⟨*variety shows* on television⟩

variety store *also* **variety shop** *n* : a retail establishment dealing in a large variety of merchandise esp. of low unit value — compare FIVE-AND-TEN, GENERAL STORE

vari·focal lens \¦verē, ¦va(a)rē+ . . . -\ *n* [*vari-* + *-focal*] : ZOOM LENS

var·i·form \ˈva(a)rə,fȯrm, ˈver-, -fō(ə)m\ *adj* [*vari-* + *-form*] : having various forms : varied or different in form : DIVERSIFORM — **var·i·form·ly** *adv*

vario- — see VARI-

var·io·coupler \¦verē(,)ō, ¦va(a)rē(,)ō+\ *n* [*vari-* + *coupler*] : an inductive coupler the mutual inductance of which is adjustable by moving one coil with respect to the other

va·ri·o·la \vəˈrīələ\ *n* -S [NL, fr. ML, pustule, pox, fr. LL, pustule; prob. akin to L *varus* pimple — more at VARICOSE] : any of several virus diseases marked by a pustular eruption: as **a** : SMALLPOX 1 **b** : COWPOX 1 **c** : HORSEPOX **d** : FOWL POX a

variola equi·na \-ēˈkwīnə\ *n* [NL] : HORSEPOX

va·ri·o·lar \vəˈrīələ(r)\ *adj* [NL *variola* + E *-ar*] : VARIOLOUS

var·i·o·late \ˈverēələt, ˈva(a)r-, -ə,lāt\ *adj* [NL *variola* + E *-ate*] : having lesions or marks resembling those of smallpox

variola vac·cin·ia \-vakˈsinēə\ *n* [NL] : COWPOX

var·i·ole \ˈverē,ōl, ˈva(a)r-\ *n* -S [ML *variola* pustule, pox] **1** : FOVEOLA **2** : a spherule of a variolite

var·i·ol·ic \¦==¦älik\ *adj* [NL *variola* + E *-ic*] : VARIOLOUS

var·i·ol·i·form \¦==¦äləˌfȯrm\ *adj* [NL *variola* + ISV *-iform*] : resembling smallpox

var·i·o·lite \ˈverēə,līt, ˈva(a)r-\ *n* -S [prob. fr. NL *variolites*, fr. ML *variola* pustule, pox + L *-ites* -ite] : a basic rock embedded with whitish spherules

var·i·o·lit·ic \¦===¦lid·ik\ *adj* [ISV *variolite* + *-ic*] : of, relating to, or resembling variolite

var·i·o·lit·iza·tion \,===,lid·əˈzāshən\ *n* -S [*variolite* + *-ization*] : conversion into variolite : production of variolitic structure

var·i·o·loid \ˈverēə,lȯid, ˈva(a)r-\ *n* -S [NL *variola* + E *-oid*] : a modified mild form of smallpox occurring in persons who have been vaccinated or who have had smallpox

va·ri·o·lous \vəˈrīələs\ *adj* [in sense 1, fr. NL *variola* smallpox + L *-osus* -ous; in sense 2, fr. ML *variolosus* pockmarked, fr. *variola* pustule, pox + L *-osus* -ous] **1** : of or relating to smallpox **2** : FOVEATE

var·i·om·e·ter \,verēˈämədˌə(r), ,va(a)r-\ *n* [*vari-* + *-meter*] **1** : VARIOCOUPLER; *esp* : one provided with an arbitrary scale **2** : DECLINOMETER **3** : an aeronautical instrument for indicating rate of climb

¹**var·i·o·rum** \,verēˈōrəm, ,va(a)rē-, ,värē-, -ˈȯr-\ *or* **variorum edition** *n* -S [L *variorum* of various persons (gen. pl. masc. of *varius* various), in the phrase *cum notis variorum* with the notes of various persons] **1** : an edition or text esp. of a classical author with notes by different persons **2** : an edition of a publication containing variant readings of the text ⟨a *variorum edition* is indicated whenever a great literary work has had a long and complex editorial history —L.P.G.Peckham⟩

²**variorum** \¦==¦==\ *adj* **1** : relating to or being an edition or text containing notes of various commentators and editors ⟨The Dunciad *Variorum*⟩ **2** : drawn or derived from various sources ⟨~ illustrations⟩ ⟨this last charge, as it flew from tongue to tongue, acquired ~ readings —H.L.Mencken⟩

¹**var·i·ous** \ˈverēəs, ˈva(a)r-, ˈvär-\ *adj* [L *varius*; prob. akin to L *varus* bent, crooked — more at PREVARICATE] **1** *archaic* : subject to change or undergoing changes : VARIABLE, CHANGEABLE, INCONSTANT **2** : of varied color : VARICOLORED ⟨birds of ~ plumage —H.W.Longfellow⟩ **3 a** : of differing kinds : being a varied assortment : MULTIFARIOUS ⟨doors had been blocked open with ~ mine equipment —J.E.Summers⟩ ⟨engaging at times in ~ business enterprises —E.E.Dale⟩ **b** : UNLIKE ⟨animals as ~ as the jaguar, the cavy, and the sloth⟩ **4** : having or manifesting a number of different aspects or characteristics ⟨a most ~ genius —F.J.Mather⟩ ⟨the story is lively and ~ —James Gray⟩ ⟨ready, cheerful, ~, and illuminating conversation —J.B.Holroyd⟩ **5** : VARIANT ⟨~ readings of the Bible⟩ **6** : consisting of an indefinite number greater than one : SUNDRY, DIVERS ⟨inspection trips to ~ manufacturing plants —*Current Biog.*⟩ **7** : being one of a group : INDIVIDUAL, SEPARATE ⟨refunds to the ~ club members⟩ ⟨distribute taxes equitably among the ~ economic groups —R.G.Woolbert⟩ ⟨the twelve ~ departments of the Clinic —Terry Southern⟩ **syn** see DIFFERENT

²**various** \"\ *pron, pl in constr* : several different ones ⟨I questioned ~ of them⟩

var·i·ous·ly *adv* **1** : in various ways : at various times : DIVERSELY ⟨was ~ occupied teaching school, farming, clerking in a store⟩ ⟨the family name is ~ spelled —*Current Biog.*⟩ ⟨artists speaking languages ~ alien to our own —Irwin Edman⟩ ⟨the most ~ stored mind of his age —Robert Lynd⟩ **2** : by various designations ⟨insects ~ known as sandflies, biting midges, punkies —*Jour. of Economic Entomology*⟩ **3** : in a varied selection or arrangement ⟨scattered on top of the outmoded square piano, I could see ~: a large family album, several daguerreotypes, an assortment of seashells —Ruby Tartt⟩

var·i·ous·ness *n* -ES : the quality or state of being various ⟨the infinite ~ of the world —John Buchan⟩

var·is·cite \ˈvarə,sīt\ *n* -S [G *variscit*, fr. ML *Variscia*, ancient name of the Vogtland district, Saxony, Germany + G *-it* -ite] : a bluish to greenish gem mineral sometimes confused with or substituted for turquoise — called also *utahlite*; see AMATRICE

variscite green *n* : a light green that is yellower and less strong than average mint green and yellower and paler than serpentine

vari-sized \ˈverē,sīzd, ˈva(a)r-, ˈvär-, -ri\ *adj* [*vari-* + *sized*] : of various sizes ⟨swirls of ~ navy polka dots —*New Yorker*⟩

var·is·tor \vaˈristə(r), ve'-\ *n* -S [*vari-* + *resistor*] : an electrical resistor whose resistance depends on the applied voltage

¹**var·i·type** \ˈverē,tīp, ˈva(a)r-, ˈvär-, -rə,-\ *n* [back-formation fr. *VariTyper*] **1** : VariTyper machine **2** : the process of composing text matter by means of a VariTyper machine

²**varitype** \"\ *vt* : to set by varitype ~ *vi* : to operate a VariTyper machine

Var·i·Typ·er \-pə(r)\ *trademark* — used for a machine for composing text matter often in justified lines that is similar in operation to a typewriter but has changeable type

var·i·typ·ist \-pəst\ *n* [¹*varitype* + *-ist*] : an operator of a VariTyper machine

var·ix \ˈva(a)riks, ˈver-, -rēks\ *n, pl* **vari·ces** \-rə,sēz\ [L *varic-, varix* — more at VARICOSE] **1 a** : an abnormally dilated and lengthened vein, artery, or lymph vessel ⟨esophageal ~⟩ **b** : an abnormal swelling and tortuosity esp. of the superficial veins of the legs **2** : one of the prominent ridges across each whorl of various univalves showing a former position of the outer lip of the aperture

var lect *abbr* [L *varia lectio*] variant reading

var·let \ˈvärlət, ˈväl-, *usu* -əd·+V\ *n* -S [ME, fr. MF *vallet*, *varlet, vaslet* young nobleman, page, squire — more at VALET] **1** *archaic* **a** : ATTENDANT, MENIAL, SERVANT **b** : a knight's page **2** : a low fellow : a base unprincipled person ⟨some ~ put a parking ticket on the . . . car —Claudia Cassidy⟩

var·let·ry \-trē\ *n* -ES [*varlet* + *-ry*] *archaic* : a group of menials : RABBLE, CROWD, MOB

var·ley loop \ˈvärlē-\ *n, usu cap V* [after C. F. Varley †1883 Eng. electrical engineer] : a bridge circuit in wire line work to determine the distance to a fault on the line

var·ley's gray \ˈvärlēz-\ *n, usu cap V* [after John Varley †1842 Eng. landscape painter] : a purplish gray to grayish purple

var·meter \ˈvär,mēd·ər\ *n* [²*var* + *-meter*] : an instrument for indicating volt-amperes reactive

¹**var·mint** *also* **var·ment** \ˈvärmənt, ˈvȧm-\ *n* [alter. of *vermin*] **1** *pl* **varmints** *also* **varmint a** *dial* : VERMIN **b** : an animal classed as vermin and unprotected by game laws ⟨coyotes, prairie dogs, or other hard-to-stalk ~s —*Amer. Rifleman*⟩ **c** *dial* : an esp. wild animal or bird considered as a pest or nuisance ⟨old dog running out to bark at some ~ above in the brush —*Amer. Mercury*⟩ **2** -S : an obnoxious, vexing, or contemptible person : RASCAL, ROGUE; *broadly* : PERSON, FELLOW, CHAP

²**varmint** *or* **varment** \"\ *adj* [fr. obs. *varmint, varment* an amateur in sports with professional skill, of unknown origin] **1** *archaic* : SPORTING, DASHING **2** *dial* : CLEVER, SHARP, CUNNING

var·mint·er \-t(ə)r\ *n* -S [¹*varmint* + *-er*] : a rifle designed esp. for hunting varmints

varmint gun *or* **varmint rifle** *n* : VARMINTER

var·na \ˈvərnə\ *n* -S [Skt *varṇa*, lit., color, sort, class, fr. *vṛnoti* he covers, envelops — more at WEIR] **1** : one of the four ancient Hindu social groups assigned by classical law to specific occupational duties and including the twice-born Brahmans, Kshatriyas, and Vaisyas and the chiefly aboriginal Sudras **2** : one of four groupings of modern Hindu castes traditionally derived from the ancient varnas : CLASS

var·nash·ra·ma \,vərˈnäshrəmə\ *n* -S [Skt *varṇāśrama*, lit., caste and stage of life, fr. *varṇa* varna + *āśrama* ashrama] : the institution of caste

¹**var·nish** \ˈvärnish, ˈvȧn-, -nēsh\ *n* -ES *see sense 4* [ME *vernisch*, fr. MF *vernis*, fr. OIt or ML; OIt *vernice*, fr. ML *veronice, veronic-, veronix* sandarac (resin), fr. Gk *berenikē*, prob. fr. *Berenikē* Berenice (now Benghazi), city in Cyrenaica] **1 a** : a liquid preparation that when spread upon a surface dries by evaporation or oxidation forming a hard lustrous coating that is more or less transparent unless pigments have been added and serves for decoration and protection — see OIL VARNISH, SPIRIT VARNISH; JAPAN, LACQUER, SHELLAC; compare ENAMEL 3 **b** : the covering, coating, or glaze given by the application of varnish ⟨seemed to be like a painting cleaned of later restorations and ~es —Erwin Rosenthal⟩ **c** : the act of applying this substance to a surface **d** : something that resembles or suggests varnish by its gloss ⟨the ~ of the holly and ivy —T.B.Macaulay⟩ **2** : an artificial covering to

give a pleasing or conventional appearance to action or conduct : an embellishing feature : outside show ⟨GLOSS ⟨absence of literary ~ —Frederic Morton⟩ ⟨concealed, under a ~ of conventionality ... a nature throbbing with passion —Norman Douglas⟩ **3 a** : thickened linseed oil with which pigments are ground to form the ink used in lithography **b** : GROUND 3g **4** *pl* **varnish** *slang* **a** : a through passenger train or car ⟨ride the ~⟩ ⟨a ~ conductor⟩ **b** : a highly varnished wooden passenger car ⟨the last such ~ ever to roll over the Carson meadows —Lucius Beebe & C.M.Clegg⟩ **5** *chiefly Brit* : NAIL POLISH **6** : a deposit formed in engines by oxidation and polymerization of fuels and lubricants

²**varnish** \"\, *esp in pres part* -nǝsh\ *vb* -ED/-ING/-ES [ME *vernischen*, fr. MF *vernisser*, fr. *vernis* varnish] *vt* **1** : to apply varnish to : cover with a thin coating of a liquid that when dry produces a hard glossy surface ⟨~ a table⟩ ⟨~ a painting⟩ — often used with *over* ⟨~ over a surface⟩ **2** : to coat over with something resembling or likened to varnish : cover or conceal with something that gives a fair appearance : gloss over ⟨a manner highly ~ed, a blend of cool bluff and right thinking —Francis Hackett⟩ ⟨never imagine that anything you can say yourself will ~ your defects —Earl of Chesterfield⟩ ⟨one that degraded art, and ~ed vice —Robert Bridges †1930⟩ **3** : ADORN, EMBELLISH ⟨beauty doth ~ age —Shak.⟩ ~ *vi* : to apply varnish

varnished *adj* [fr. past part. of ²*varnish*] **1** : covered with or as if with varnish ⟨a ~ table⟩ ⟨a ~ reputation⟩ **2** : VERNICOSE

varnished willow *n* : CRACK WILLOW 1

varnish.er \-shǝ(r)\ *n* -s : one that varnishes varnish

varnish gum *n* : a natural or synthetic resin used in making varnishing

varnishing day *n* [*varnishing* (gerund of ²*varnish*) + *day*] **1** : a day before the opening of an exhibition of paintings reserved for the painters to varnish or put on finishing touches **2** : the opening day of an art exhibition

varnish tree *n* : any of various trees yielding a milky juice from which in some cases varnish or lacquer is prepared: as **a** : JAPANESE VARNISH TREE 1 **b** : LACQUER TREE **c** : BLACK-VARNISH TREE **d** : MARKING NUT **e** : AILANTHUS 1 **f** : GOLDENRAIN TREE **g** : CANDLENUT 2

var.nishy \-shē\ *adj* [*varnish* + -*y*] : of, relating to, or resembling varnish : having a varnished surface ⟨a ~ smell⟩ ⟨a ~ appearance⟩

va.ro.hio \vä'rō'hē(,)ō\ *n*, *pl* **varohios** *usu cap* **1** : a Tarachitian people of the Río Mayo valley between the states of Chihuahua and Sonora, Mexico **2** : a member of the Varohío people

va.ro.li.an \vä'rōlēǝn\ *adj*, *usu cap* [NL (*pons*) *varolii* + E -*an*] : of or relating to the pons Varolii

var.ro.nia \vǝ'rōnēǝ\ *n*, *cap* [NL, fr. *Varron-*, *Varro* (Marcus Terentius *Varro* †27 B.C. Roman scholar) + NL -*ia*] : a large genus of tropical American shrubs and trees (family Boraginaceae) having pubescent or scabrous foliage and small usu. white flowers with a 4-lobed or 5-lobed limb followed by fruit that is a small slightly fleshy drupe

var.ro.ni.an \-ēǝn\ *adj*, *usu cap* [L *varronianus*, fr. the Roman surname *Varron-*, *Varro*] : of or relating to a person having the surname Varro (as Marcus Terentius Varro)

varronian satire *n*, *usu cap V* : a form of dramatic satire practiced by Marcus Terentius Varro

vars *pl of* VAR

var.sha \'vorshǝ\ *n* -s [Skt *varṣa* rain, rainy season; akin to Skt *varṣati* it rains, *vār* water — more at URINE] *India* : the rainy season : MONSOON

var.si.ty \'värsǝtē, -'vás-, -ǝtē, -i\ *n* -ES *often attrib* [by shortening & alter. fr. *university*] **1** *chiefly Brit* : UNIVERSITY **2** : a first team or group of players capable of playing on the first team representing a university, college, school, or club in a sport or other form of competition in contests with teams of equal standing from other universities, colleges, schools, or clubs

¹**var.so.vi.an** \(')vär,sōvēǝn\ *adj*, *usu cap* [fr. (assumed) ML *varsovianus*, fr. *Varsovia* Warsaw, capital of Poland + L -*anus*] : of, relating to, or characteristic of Warsaw, Poland

²**varsovian** \"\ *n* -s *cap* : a native or resident of Warsaw, Poland

var.so.via.na *also* **var.sou.via.na** \,värsō'vyänǝ\ *n* -s [prob. fr. Sp *varsoviana*, fr. fem. of *varsoviano* Varsovian, fr. (assumed) ML *varsovianus*] **1** : a graceful dance similar to a mazurka and popular in many European countries, Mexico, and the U.S. **2** : music for the varsoviana characterized by a slow triple meter and a strong initial accent in every second measure

var.so.vienne \-'vyen\ *n* -s [F, fr. fem. of *varsovien* Varsovian, fr. (assumed) ML *varsovianus*] : VARSOVIANA

var.ta.bed \'värtǝ,bed\ *or* **var.da.pet** \-dǝ'pet\ *or* **var.ta.bet** \-tä,'bet\ *n* -s [Arm *vartabed*, lit., teacher] : a member of an order of celibate preachers in the Armenian clergy corresponding to the archimandrite in the Greek church

va.ru.lite \'värǝ,līt\ *n* -s [Sw *varulit*, fr. *Varuträsk*, locality in northern Sweden + Sw -*lit* -lite] : a mineral $(Na,Ca)(Mn,Fe)_2(PO_4)_2$ consisting of manganese, sodium, and calcium with minor amounts of iron, isomorphous with hühnerkobeite, and isostructural with triphylite and lithiophilite

var.us \'va(ǝ)rǝs, 'ver-\ *n* -ES [NL, adj., turned inward to an abnormal degree, fr. L, knock-kneed — more at PREVARICATE] : the position of a joint's being turned inward to an abnormal degree ⟨the foot must turn ~ to keep in line with the knee joint —*Yr. Bk. of Orthopedics & Traumatic Surgery*⟩

varve \'värv, 'vȧv\ *n* -s [Sw *varv* turn, revolution, layer; akin to OE *hweorfan* to turn — more at WHARF] : a pair of layers of alternately finer and coarser silt or clay believed to comprise an annual cycle of deposition in a body of still water (as a glacial lake) and used to measure the time involved in the deposition of the entire group of sediments and to construct a time scale in a manner similar to that employed in the study of annual rings in trees ⟨~ chronology⟩

varved \-vd\ *adj* [*varve* + -*ed*] : stratified in paired layers of annual deposition ⟨~ clays⟩

varvel *var of* VERVEL

var.vi.ty \'värvǝd-ē\ *n* -ES [*varve* + -*ity*] : stratification in varves

vary \'verē, 'va(ǝ)r-, 'vār-, -ri\ *vb* -ED/-ING/-ES [ME *varien*, fr. MF or L; MF *varier*, fr. L *variare*, fr. *varius* diverse, various — more at VARIOUS] *vt* **1** : to bring about differences in: **a** : to make an esp. minor or partial change in : make different in some attribute or characteristic ⟨this is not a proceeding which may be *varied* —John Marshall⟩ **b** : to make differences between items in : insure variety in : make unlike in some particular : VARIEGATE, DIVERSIFY ⟨a program that was *varied* enough to avoid monotony —Katharine Amend⟩ ⟨the days were not crowded, but they were enviably *varied* —Virginia Woolf⟩ **2** : to present under new aspects ⟨~ the rhythm and harmonic treatment⟩ ~ *vi* **1** : to exhibit or undergo change : break from sameness or uniformity : DIFFER ⟨a constantly ~*ing* terrain —Shipley Thomas⟩ ⟨chapters of ~*ing* worth —F.N.Robinson⟩ ⟨historical allusions of ~*ing* degrees of accuracy —T.D.McCormick⟩ **2** : DEVIATE, DEPART, SWERVE ⟨~ from the law⟩ ⟨~ from the mean⟩ **3** : to exhibit differing qualities or attributes in alternation or succession with something else ⟨one mathematical quantity may ~ inversely with another⟩ **4** : to exhibit divergence in structural or physiological characters from those typical or usual in the group *syn* see CHANGE, DIFFER

varying hare *n* [*varying* (pres. part. of *vary*) + *hare*] : any of several hares having white fur in winter; *esp* : SNOWSHOE RABBIT

varying lemming *n* : an arctic lemming esp. of the genus *Dicrostonyx* in which the pelage is more or less completely white in winter

vary.ing.ly *adv* : in a varying manner

¹**vas** \'vas\ *n*, *pl* **vasa** \'väsǝ, 'väsǝ, 'väzǝ, 'väzǝ\ [NL, fr. L, vessel — more at VASE] : an anatomical vessel : DUCT

²**vas** \'wäs, 'vas\ *n*, *pl* **va.des** \'wä(,)dēz, 'va(,)dēz\ [L — more at WED] *Roman & civil law* : a pledge or surety for another's appearance in court

vas- *or* **vasi-** *or* **vaso-** *comb form* [NL, fr. L *vas*] **1** : duct : channel : vessel ⟨*vasicentric*⟩: as **a** : blood vessel ⟨*vaso-formative*⟩ ⟨*vasoconstriction*⟩ **b** : vas deferens ⟨*vasectomy*⟩ **2** : vascular and ⟨*vasovagal*⟩ **3** : vasomotor ⟨*vasoinhibitor*⟩

vasa *n* -s [L, pl., vessels] *obs* : VASE

vas ab.er.rans \'va'sabǝ,ranz\ *n*, *pl* **vasa aberran.tia** \,=ǝ,ab'ranch(ē)ǝ\ [NL, lit., deviating vessel] **1** : a blind tube that is occas. present parallel to the first part of the vas deferens with which or with the epididymis it may communicate **2** *vasa aberrantia pl* : slender arteries that are only occas. present and that connect the axillary or brachial artery and the radial or other artery of the forearm or the subclavian artery and the thoracic aorta

vasa bre.via \,=ǝ'brēvēǝ\ *n pl* [NL, lit., short vessels] : short vessels of the splenic artery and vein that run to the greater curvature of the stomach

vasa deferentia *pl of* VAS DEFERENS

vasa ef.fer.en.tia \-,efǝ'rench(ē)ǝ\ *n pl* [NL, lit., efferent vessels] : the 12 to 20 tubes that lead from the rete of the testis to the vas deferens and except near their commencement are greatly convoluted and form the compact head of the epididymis

vasal \'väsǝl, 'väzǝl, 'vasǝl\ *adj* [*vas-* + -*al*] : of, relating to, or constituting an anatomical vessel

vasa mur.rhi.na \-mǝ'rīnǝ, -'rēnǝ\ *n*, *usu cap V&M* [NL, lit., murrhine dish] : a late 19th century American glassware of variegated color and often with metallic flecking

va.sa parrot \'väsǝ-, -äzǝ-\ *n* [Malagasy *vaza* vasa parrot, lit., loud-voiced] : any of several blackish brown Madagascan parrots of the genus *Coracopsis* (esp. *C. vasa*)

va.sa.tes \vǝ'sād-(,)ēz\ *n*, *cap* [NL] : a genus of plant-feeding mites containing some that are destructive to many crop plants — see TOMATO RUSSET MITE

vasa va.so.rum \-,vä'sōrǝm, -,vā\, -,vȧ\, -|'zō-\ *n pl* [NL, lit., vessels of vessels] : small blood vessels that are distributed to the walls of the larger arteries and veins and arise from a branch of the same vessel or from a neighboring vessel

vas.con \'vaskǝn, -,skän\ *n*, *pl* **vascons** \-nz\ *or* **vasco.nes** \-,skä,nēz\ *cap* [L *Vascon-*, *Vasco*] : BASQUE 1

vascul- *or* **vasculo-** *comb form* [NL, fr. L *vasculum* small vessel; *esp* : blood vessel ⟨*vasculomotor*⟩

vas.cu.lar \'vaskyǝlǝ(r), 'vaas-\ *adj* [NL *vascularis*, fr. L *vasculum* small vessel (dim. of *vas* vessel) + -*aris* -ar — more at VASE] **1 a** : of, relating to, or affecting a tube for the conveyance of a body fluid (as the blood of an animal or the sap of a plant); *often* : of, relating to, or constituting a system of such tubes ⟨lymph ~ degeneration⟩ — compare WATER-VASCULAR SYSTEM **b** : supplied with or containing ducts and esp. blood vessels ⟨a ~ tumor⟩ ⟨the ~ layer of the skin⟩ **2** : marked by vigor and ardor : SPIRITED, PASSIONATE ⟨writing must be done with gusto, must be ~ —S.E.Hyman⟩ ⟨the most ~ and virile thus far printed —Mark Sullivan⟩

vascular bed *n* : the intricate meshwork of minute blood vessels that ramifies through the tissues of the body or of one of its parts

vascular bundle *also* **vascular strand** *n* : a unit strand of the vascular system of a higher plant consisting usu. of vessels and sieve tubes commonly in association with elongated parenchyma cells and fibers that may surround the strand as a sheath — called also *fibrovascular bundle*; see AMPHICRIBRAL, AMPHIVASAL; compare STELE

vascular cambium *n* : the lateral meristem from which vascular tissue is differentiated and which is distinguished from phellogen

vascular cryptogam *n* : a cryptogamic plant (as a fern or moss) that has a vascular system — compare CELLULAR CRYPTOGAM

vascular cylinder *n* : the cylinder of vascular tissue between cortex and pith of a vascular plant : STELE

vas.cu.lar.i.ty \,=ǝ'larǝd-ē\ *n* -ES [ISV *vascular* + -*ity*] : the quality or state of being vascular

vas.cu.lar.iza.tion \,=ǝ,lǝrǝ'zāshǝn, -,rī'z-\ *n* -s [ISV *vascular* + -*ization*] : the process of becoming vascular; *often* : abnormal or excessive formation of blood vessels (as in the retina or the body)

vas.cu.lar.ize \'=ǝ,rīz\ *vt* -ED/-ING/-s [*vascular* + -*ize*] : to make vascular ⟨gradually *vascularizing* the yolk sac⟩

vas.cu.lar.ly *adv* : in a vascular manner : by vessels

vascular plant *n* : a plant having a specialized conducting system that includes xylem and phloem : TRACHEOPHYTE

vascular ray *n* : a ray of cambial origin that occurs in the stele of many vascular plants and often separates the vascular bundles — see PHLOEM RAY, XYLEM RAY; compare MEDULLARY RAY

vascular system *n* : the part of the body of a vascular plant that is made up of vascular tissue

vascular tissue *n* : tissue concerned mainly with conduction in plants; *esp* : the highly specialized tissue found in the higher plants consisting essentially of phloem and xylem and forming a continuous system throughout the plant body — compare VASCULAR BUNDLE

vas.cu.la.tion \,vaskyǝ'lāshǝn\ *n* -s [*vascul-* + -*ation*] : formation or arrangement of vessels in a plant

vas.cu.la.ture \'vaskyǝlǝ,chu̇(ǝ)r, -,chǝr\ *n* -s [*vascul-* + -*ature* (as in *musculature*)] : the disposition or arrangement of blood vessels in an organ or part

vas.cu.lo.genesis \,vaskyǝlō+\ *n* [NL, fr. *vascul-* + *genesis*] : embryonic formation and differentiation of the blood-vascular system

vas.cu.lum \'vaskyǝlǝm\ *n*, *pl* **vascu.la** \-lǝ\ [NL, fr. L, small vessel — more at VASCULAR] **1** : ASCIDIUM **2** : a usu. metal and commonly cylindrical or flattened box with a cover opening lengthwise that is used in collecting plants

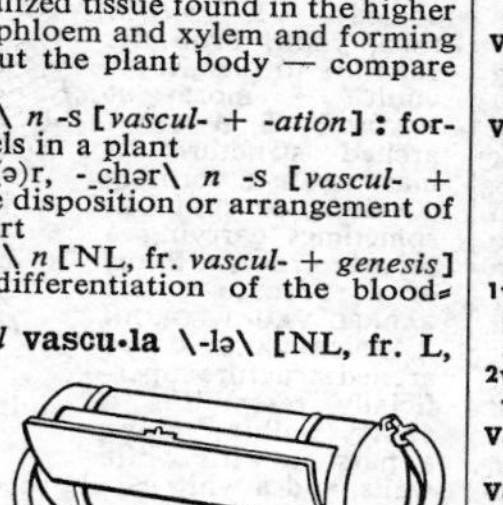

vas defer.ens \'defǝrǝnz, -,renz\ *n*, *pl* **vasa deferen.tia** \-,defǝ'rench(ē)ǝ\ [NL, lit., deferent vessel : a spermatic duct esp. of a higher vertebrate that in man is a small but thick-walled tube about two feet long formed by the union of the vasa efferentia, is greatly convoluted in its proximal portion where it forms the body and tail of the epididymis, runs in the spermatic cord through the inguinal canal, and descends into the pelvis where it joins the duct of the seminal vesicle to form the ejaculatory duct

vasculum 2

vase \'vās also 'vāz sometimes 'vȧ|z *or* 'vȧ| *or* |s, archaic Brit 'vȯz\ *n* -s [F, fr. L *vas*; akin to Umbrian *vasor* vessels] **1** : a vessel that is usu. rounded and of greater depth than width, is commonly decorative, and is used chiefly for ornament or for flowers though also adapted for various domestic purposes and used anciently in religious rites ⟨a porcelain ~⟩ ⟨a Grecian ~⟩ **2** : an ornament (as on furniture) having the form of a vase

vase clock *n* : a clock whose decorative case has the general form of a vase; *one* in which there is no dial of the usual form but in which a part of a vase revolves while a single stationary indicator serves as a hand

vas.ec.to.mize \va'sektǝ,mīz, va'ze-, vā'ze-, vā'se-\ *vt* -ED/-ING/-s to perform a vasectomy on

vas.ec.to.my \-,mē\ *n* -ES [ISV *vas-* + -*ectomy*] : surgical excision of the vas deferens usu. to produce permanent sterility

vase.ful *pronunc at* VASE +,ful\ *n* -s : as much as a vase will hold

vaselike \'=,=\ *adj* : resembling or suggesting a vase esp. in outline

vas.e.line \'vasǝ,lēn, ,=ǝ'=\, *sometimes* -azǝ-\ *vt* -ED/-ING/-s [*Vaseline*] : to apply petrolatum to

Vas.e.line \"\ *trademark* — used for petrolatum

vase rug *n* : an uncommon 16th century Persian rug woven over a double warp in striking and severe floral designs with which a vase motive is often combined

vase splat *n* : a splat of a chair back having the outline of a vase and being common in the Queen Anne period

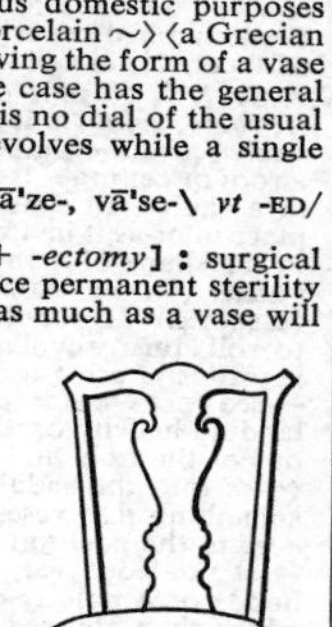

vase-vine \'=,=\ *n* : LEATHERFLOWER

va.sey grass \'vāsē-\ *n*, *usu cap V* [after George *Vasey* †1893 Am. physician and botanist] : an erect perennial grass (*Paspalum urvillei*) native to Argentina and grown for pasture from No. Carolina to Texas

vas.hegy.ite \'väsh,he,jīt, 'vȯsh-\ *n* -s [G *vashegyit*, fr. *Vashegy*, village formerly in Hungary, now in southern Czechoslovakia, its locality + G -*it* -ite] : a mineral $2Al_2(PO_4)_3(OH)_3.27H_2O$ (?) that is hydrated basic aluminum phosphate and occurs in white to yellow masses (hardness 2–3, sp. gr. 1.96)

vasi- — see VAS-

vasi.cen.tric \'väzǝ|sen,trik, 'väsǝ-, 'vasǝ-, 'vazǝ-\ *adj* [*vas-* + -*centric*] : forming a distinct round to oval sheath about a vessel in wood ⟨~ parenchyma⟩ — see VASICENTRIC TRACHEID; compare APOTRACHEAL, METATRACHEAL, PARATRACHEAL

vasicentric tracheid *n* : any of the short tracheids found in the vicinity of wood vessels and not arranged in definite longitudinal rows

vas.i.cine \'vasǝ,sēn, -azǝ-\ *n* -s [ISV *vasic-* (fr. NL *vasica* — specific epithet of the Malabar nut *Adhatoda vasica*, — fr. Skt *vāsikā*, *vāsaka* Malabar nut, fr. *vāsayati* it perfumes, makes fragrant) + -*ine*] : a crystalline alkaloid $C_{11}H_{12}N_2O$ that is found in the leaves of the Malabar nut and seeds of the harmal and is thought to poison lower plants and animals but not higher animals

vasi.fac.tive \'väzǝ|faktiv, 'väsǝ-, |vas|, |vaz|\ *or* **vaso.fac.tive** \|ō,f-\ *adj* [*vas-* + -*factive*] : VASOFORMATIVE

vasi.form \'väzǝ,form, 'väsǝ-, 'vasǝ-, 'vazǝ-\ *adj* [NL *vasiformis*, fr. L *vas* + -*iformis* -iform — more at VASE] **1** : having the form of a hollow tube : resembling or consisting of a duct **2** : having the form of a vase ⟨porcelain ~ lamp, with shade —Parke-Bernet Galleries Cat.⟩

vaso- — see VAS-

vaso.con.strict.ing \|vȧ|zō, 'vȧ|,zō, 'vȧ|,sō, 'va(,)zō+\ *adj* [*vasoconstriction* + -*ing*] : VASOCONSTRICTIVE

vaso.con.striction \"+\ *n* [ISV *vas-* + *constriction*] : narrowing of the lumen of blood vessels esp. as a result of vasomotor nervous action

vaso.con.strict.ive \"+\ *adj* [*vas-* + *constrictive*] : inducing vasoconstriction

vaso.con.strict.or \"+\ *n* [ISV *vas-* + *constrictor*] : an agent (as a sympathetic nerve fiber or a drug) that induces or initiates vasoconstriction

vaso.corona \"+\ *n* [NL, fr. *vas-* + *corona*] : the system of peripheral blood vessels of the spinal cord sending branches toward the central canal

vaso.dentin \"+\ *n* [*vas-* + *dentin*] : a modified dentin permeated by blood capillaries and common in the teeth of the lower vertebrates

vaso.depressor \"+\ *n*, *often attrib* [*vas-* + *depressor*] : VASODILATOR

vaso.dilatation \"+\ *n* [ISV *vas-* + *dilatation*] : widening of the lumen of blood vessels whether due to vasodilator action or to the failure of vasoconstrictor activity

vaso.dil.a.tin \"+'dilǝtǝn\ *n* -s [ISV *vasodilation* + -*in*] : a substance (as acetylcholine) that induces vasodilation

vaso.dilating \"+\ *adj* [*vasodilation* + -*ing*] : inducing or initiating vasodilation

vaso.dilation \"+\ *n* [*vas-* + *dilation*] : VASODILATATION

vaso.dilator \"+\ *n* [*vas-* + *dilator*] : VASODILATATION

vaso.dilator \"+\ *n* [*vas-* + *dilator*] : an agent (as a parasympathetic nerve fiber or a drug) that induces or initiates vasodilatation

vaso.excitor \"+\ *n* : VASOCONSTRICTOR

vaso.formative \"+\ *adj* [ISV *vas-* + *formative*] : functioning in the development and formation of vessels and esp. blood vessels ⟨~ cells⟩

vaso.ganglion \"+\ *n* [NL, fr. *vas-* + *ganglion*] : a dense knot of blood vessels

vaso.inhibitor \"\ *n* [*vas-* + *inhibitor*] : an agent (as a drug) that depresses or inhibits the vasomotor and esp. the vasoconstrictor nerves — **vaso.inhibitory** \"+\ *adj*

vaso.ligation \"+\ *n* [*vas-* + *ligation*] : surgical ligation of a vessel and esp. of the vas deferens

vaso.motion \"+\ *n* [*vas-* + *motion*] : alteration in the caliber of blood vessels

vaso.motor \"+\ *adj* [ISV *vas-* + *motor*] **1** : controlling the size of blood vessels **2** : of, relating to, affecting, or being those nerves or the centers (as in the medulla and spinal cord) from which they arise that supply the muscle fibers of the walls of blood vessels, include sympathetic vasoconstrictors and parasympathetic vasodilators, and by their effect on vascular diameter regulate the amount of blood passing to a particular body part or organ

vasomotor rhinitis *n* : allergic rhinitis

vaso.neurosis \,vä(,)zō, 'vä(,)sō, 'vȧ(,)zō, 'va(,)zō+\ *n* [NL, fr. *vas-* + *neurosis*] : a disorder of blood vessels (as a vascular spasm) that is of basically neural origin : pathology arising in the vasomotor structures

vaso.neurotic \"+\ *adj* [fr. NL *vasoneurosis*, after NL *neurosis*; E *neurotic*] : of, relating to, or constituting a vasoneurosis

vaso.pres.sin \,vȧzō'pres°n, -,āsō-, ,vazo-, ,vasō-\ *n* -s [fr. *Vasopressin*, a trademark] : a polypeptide hormone that is secreted together with oxytocin by the posterior lobe of the pituitary, that is also obtained synthetically, that increases blood pressure in mammals and exerts an antidiuretic effect, and that is used esp. in treating diabetes insipidus

¹**vaso.pressor** \,vä(,)zō, 'vä(,)sō, 'vȧ(,)zō, 'va(,)zō+\ *adj* [*vas-* + *pressor*] : causing a rise in blood pressure : exerting a vasoconstrictor effect

²**vasopressor** \"\ *n* -s : a vasopressor agent : VASOCONSTRICTOR

vaso.reflex \,vä(,)zō, 'vä(,)sō, 'vȧ(,)zō, 'va(,)zō+\ *n* [*vas-* + *reflex*] : a reflex reaction of a blood vessel

vaso.spasm \,=,+,-\ *n* [ISV *vas-* + *spasm*] : sharp and often persistent contraction of a blood vessel resulting in a reduction of its caliber and blood flow : ANGIOSPASM

vaso.spastic \,-|,+-\ *adj* [fr. *vasospasm*, after E *spasm*: *spastic*] : of, relating to, or tending to induce vasospasm

vaso.tonic \"+\ *adj* [*vas-* + *tonic*] : of, relating to, or promoting tone of blood vessel walls

vaso.vagal \"+\ *adj* [*vas-* + *vagal*] : of, relating to, or involving both vascular and vagal factors

vasovagal syncope *n* : a usu. transitory condition marked by anxiety, nausea, and respiratory distress and believed due to joint vasomotor and vagal disturbances

¹**vas.sal** \'vasǝl, 'vasǝl\ *n* -s [ME, fr. MF, fr. ML *vassallus*, fr. *vassus* servant, vassal, of Celt origin; akin to W *gwas* boy, servant, Bret *gwaz* man, OIr *foss* servant] **1 a** : a person who is under the protection of another as his feudal lord and is bound to homage and fealty to that other : a feudal tenant : FEUDATORY **b** *Scots law* : a tenant entitled to the beneficial enjoyment of land and holding of a lord or other superior owning the legal title thereto conditionally upon the rendering of an annual service or payment — compare FEU-DUTY **2** : one in a position or status felt to resemble that of a feudal vassal to his lord : one who owes or is forced to give allegiance and service to another ⟨as a superior (the Baltic states that became ~s of Russia⟩ **3 a** : a person in a humble and subordinate or suppliant position : DEPENDENT, SERVANT, SLAVE **b** : one wholly subordinated to some controlling influence ⟨a ~ to his fears⟩ ⟨interest rates became the ~ of central banking and treasury policy —R.I.Robinson⟩

²**vassal** \"+\ *adj* **1** : of, relating to, or typical of a vassal **2** : occupying the position or relation of a vassal; *broadly* : SERVILE SUBSERVIENT ⟨a tenuous ~ relationship to the Chinese court —J.F.Cady⟩

³**vassal** \"\ *vt* **vassaled** *or* **vassalled**; **vassaled** *or* **vassalled**; **vassaling** *or* **vassalling**; **vassals** *archaic* : VASSALIZE ⟨~ed themselves to the great Mongol —Peter Heylin⟩

vas.sal.age \-ij\ *n* -s [ME, fr. MF, fr. *vassal* + -*age*] **1 a** *archaic* : conduct becoming to a vassal; *esp* : courage and prowess under difficulties (as on the field of battle) **b** *obs* : a valiant or chivalrous act **2** : the condition or status of a vassal : the relation of a vassal to his lord; *also* : the specific homage, fealty, or services due from vassal to lord **3** : a position of subordination or submission (as to a political power or a detrimental influence) : SERVITUDE, SUBJECTION ⟨~ of the states through increasing centralization of power in the federal government ⟨a mind in ~ to passion⟩ **4** : vassals as a group or of a particular lord : VASSALRY

vas.sal.ic \va'salik, vǝ-\ *adj* : of or relating to or having the nature of a vassal or the vassal system

vas.sal.ize \'vasǝ,līz, 'vaas-\ *vt* -ED/-ING/-s : to make a vassal

of **:** bring into a condition of subordination to someone or something ⟨~ a people⟩
vas·sal·ry \-səlrē, -ri\ *n* -ES **:** the whole body or estate of vassals
vassal state *n* **:** a state with varying degrees of independence in its internal affairs but dominated by another state in its foreign affairs and potentially wholly subject to the dominating state
vas·sar rose \ˌvasəˌrōz, ˈvaas-\ *n, often cap V* [fr. *Vassar* College, Poughkeepsie, N.Y.] **1 :** a dark pink to grayish red **2** *of textiles* **:** a moderate purplish pink that is redder and paler than fuchsia pink
vassar tan *n, often cap V* [fr. *Vassar* College] **:** a moderate to strong brown that is redder and slightly lighter than oak, lighter than Arabian brown, and redder and slightly lighter than Sudan brown
¹vast \ˈvast, -aa(ə)-, -ai-, -ȧ-\ *adj* -ER/-EST [L *vastus;* akin to OIr *fot, fut* length] **:** characterized by greatness in size, bulk, amount, numbers, degree, intensity, or esp. in extent, range, and comprehensiveness ⟨stimulate consumption in these ~ areas of low-paid labor, China, India, Russia, Africa —J.A. Hobson⟩ ⟨the ~ accumulation of knowledge, and of mechanical appliances, which we call civilization —W.R.Inge⟩ ⟨the dog with ~ unconcern, curled up on the floor and went to sleep —Jan Struther⟩ **syn** see HUGE
²vast \"\ *n* -S **1 :** a boundless compass or space **:** IMMENSITY ⟨the ~ of heaven —John Milton⟩ ⟨the dead ~ and middle of the night —Shak.⟩ **2** *chiefly dial* **:** a great quantity, amount, or number ⟨took a ~ of pains to have everything ready for the fair⟩
³vast \"\ *adv, chiefly dial* **:** VASTLY
vas·ta·tion \vaˈstāshən\ *n* -S [L *vastation-, vastatio,* fr. *vastatus* (past part. of *vastare* to lay waste, fr. *vastus* empty, waste) + *-ion-, -io* -ion — more at WASTE] **1** *obs* **:** DEVASTATION **2 :** a renewal or purification through the burning away or destruction of evil attributes
vas·tid·i·ty \vaˈstidədē\ *n* -ES [alter. of *vastity*] *archaic* **:** VASTNESS ⟨through all the world's ~ —Shak.⟩
vas·ti·tude \ˈvastəˌtüd, ˈvaas-,ˈvais-,ˈvȧs-, -stə-,tyüd\ *n* -S [L *vastitudo,* fr. *vastus* vast + *-tudo* -tude] **1 :** the quality or state of being vast **:** IMMENSITY ⟨the ~ of the concept held him spellbound⟩ **2 :** a vast extent or space ⟨all that ~ of wilderness —Walter O'Meara⟩
¹vas·ti·ty \-stəd·ē, -ti\ *n* -ES [MF *vastité,* fr. L *vastitat-, vastitas,* fr. *vastus* empty, waste + *-itat-, -itas* -ity] *archaic* **:** a waste or desolate condition ⟨all the ~ of the Arabian peninsula —C.M.Doughty⟩
²vastity \"\ *n* -ES [L *vastitas,* fr. *vastus* vast + *-itas* -ity] **:** VASTITUDE ⟨the dreadful ~ of the stars —Rose Macaulay⟩
vast·ly *adv* **:** to a vast extent or degree **:** IMMENSELY; *often* **:** very greatly ⟨I shall be ~ obliged⟩
vast·ness \-s(t)nəs\ *n* -ES **1 :** the quality or state of being vast **2 :** a vast expanse or region ⟨watching the ~*es* of the mountains unfold⟩
vas·tus ex·ter·nus \ˌvastəˌsekˌstərnəs\ *n* [NL, lit., great external (muscle)] **:** VASTUS LATERALIS
vastus in·ter·me·di·us \-ˌsintərˈmēdēəs\ *n* [NL, lit., great intermediate (muscle)] **:** the division of the quadriceps muscle that arises from and covers the front of the shaft of the femur
vastus in·ter·nus \-ˌsinˈtərnəs\ *n* [NL, lit., great internal (muscle)] **:** VASTUS MEDIALIS
vastus lat·er·alis \-ˌslad·əˈralės, -rāl-,-räl-\ *n* [NL, lit., great lateral (muscle)] **:** a division of the quadriceps muscle covering the outer anterior aspect of the femur, arising chiefly from that bone and inserted into the outer border of the patella by a flat tendon which blends with that of the other divisions of the muscle and sends an expansion to the knee capsule
vastus me·di·alis \-ˌsmēdēˈalės, -ˈāl-,-ˈäl-\ *n* [NL, lit., great medial (muscle)] **:** a division of the quadriceps muscle covering the inner anterior aspect of the femur, arising chiefly from that bone and the adjacent intermuscular septum, inserted into the inner border of the patella and into the tendon of the other divisions of the muscle, sending also a tendinous expansion to the capsule of the knee joint and being closely united and in the upper part often inseparably with the vastus intermedius
vasty *pronunc at* ˈvast + ē *or* i\ *adj* -ER/-EST [¹*vast* + *y*] **:** VAST, IMMENSE ⟨call spirits from the ~ deep —Shak.⟩
va·su \ˈvä(ˌ)sü, -)zü\ *n* -S [Fijian] **:** a child of a sister of a Fijian male upon whom the child has particular claims (as for food, portable property, or land); *also* **:** the peculiar right or claim of a vasu
¹vat \ˈvat, *usu* -ad·+V\ *n* -S [ME *vat, fat,* fr. OE *fæt;* akin to OHG *vaz* vessel, cask, vat, ON *fat* vessel, Lith *puodas* pot and perh. to Skt *palla* granary, barn] **1 a :** a large cistern, tub, barrel, or other vessel; *esp* **:** one used to hold or store liquids ⟨soups fresh from the big fifty-gallon soup ~*s* —Jack Alexander⟩ **2 a :** a large vessel for holding preparations for dyeing **b :** a liquor or bath containing a dye that has been converted by reduction usu. with sodium hydrosulfite and alkali into a soluble leuco form that does not dye **3 :** TAN VAT **4 a :** a tank used in papermaking that contains the stock from which handmade papers are dipped by a mold **b :** one of the tanks in which the cylinders of a cylinder machine rotate **c :** a tank used to hold tub sizing **d :** a tank in which paper stock is bleached **5 :** a wooden tub in which to wash ores and minerals **6 a :** SALT PIT **b** *Southwest* **:** an incrusted dried margin around a water hole
²vat \"\ *vt* **vatted; vatted; vatting; vats 1 :** to put into or treat in a vat **2 :** to prepare a vat (sense 2b) **:** reduce (a vat dye) to form a solution of a leuco compound
va·tair·eop·sis \vəˌta(a)rēˈäpsəs\ *n, cap* [NL, fr. *Vatairea,* genus of unarmed trees (perh. alter. of *Vateria*) + *-opsis*] **:** a small genus of unarmed Brazilian trees (family Leguminosae) with large panicles of violet flowers — see GOA POWDER
vat dye *or* **vat color** *n* **:** any of a large and widely used class of water-insoluble generally fast dyes (as indigoid dyes and many anthraquinone dyes) that are formed on and in textile fibers by oxidation of a soluble reduced leuco form either prepared previously in a vat (sense 2b) or produced on the fibers by treating with a suspension or paste containing the unreduced dye and then reducing — see DYE table I, SOLUBILIZED VAT DYE
vat–dyed \ˈ=ˌ=\ *adj* **:** dyed with one or more vat dyes
va·te·ria \vəˈtirēə\ *n, cap* [NL, fr. Abraham *Vater* †1751 Ger. anatomist and botanist + NL *-ia*] **:** a genus of Asiatic trees (family Dipterocarpaceae) having entire small coriaceous leaves and white or yellow flowers with about 15 stamens — see PINEY TREE
va·ter·ite \ˈväd·əˌrīt, ˈfä-\ *n* -S [Heinrich *Vater,* 20th cent. Ger. mineralogist + E *-ite*] **:** a mineral $CaCO_3$ that consists of a relatively unstable form of calcium carbonate and is polymorphous with calcite and aragonite
vater's ampulla *n, usu cap V* **:** AMPULLA OF VATER
va·ter's corpuscle \ˈfä|tə(r)z-, -ä|\ *n, usu cap V* [after Abraham *Vater* †1751] **:** PACINIAN CORPUSCLE
vat·ic \ˈvad·ik\ *adj* [L *vates* seer, prophet + E *-ic;* akin to OIr *fāith* seer, poet, OE *wōth* voice, song, poetry, *wōd* mad, raging, OHG *wuot* frenzy, madness, ON *ōthr,* n., song, poetry, *ōthr,* adj., frantic, mad, Goth *woths* possessed] **:** of, relating to, or characteristic of a prophet **:** PROPHETICAL, ORACULAR ⟨any poet . . . has his stuffy moments, especially when he is being consciously ~ —Dudley Fitts⟩
vat·i·can \ˈvad·|əkən, -at|, |ēk-\ *adj, usu cap* [fr. The *Vatican,* official residence of the pope situated upon Vatican Hill in Vatican City, Rome, fr. ML *Vaticanus,* fr. L, Vatican Hill] **:** of or relating to the Vatican esp. as symbolizing the Papacy or its policies ⟨a *Vatican* announcement⟩
vatican city *adj, usu cap V&C* [fr. *Vatican City,* independent papal state within Rome, Italy] **:** of or relating to Vatican City
vat·i·can·ism \-kəˌnizəm\ *n* -S *usu cap* **:** the doctrine of absolute papal supremacy
vat·i·can·ist \-ˌnəst\ *n* -S *usu cap* **:** a supporter of Vaticanism
vat·i·cide \ˈvad·əˌsīd\ *n* -S [L *vates* prophet + E *-cide*] **:** the murderer of a prophet
va·tic·i·nal \vəˈtisᵊnᵊl, vaˈt-\ *adj* [L *vaticinus* prophetic (fr. *vaticinari* to prophesy) + E *-al*] **:** of, relating to, or containing prophecy **:** PROPHETIC ⟨credited with very solid ~ powers —Wilder Hobson⟩
va·tic·i·nate \-ᵊnˌāt\ *vb* -ED/-ING/-S [L *vaticinatus,* past part. of *vaticinari* to prophesy, fr. *vates* prophet + *-cinari* (akin to L *canere* to sing, prophesy) — more at CHANT] *vi* **:** to prophesy things to come **:** behave like a seer and a prophet ⟨it is very seldom that we can . . . ~ on such subjects —George Saintsbury⟩ ~ *vt* **:** to predict about **:** FORETELL ⟨the revolution *vaticinated* by Marx —R.M.MacIver⟩
va·tic·i·na·tion \vəˌtisᵊnˈāshən, (ˌ)vaˌt-\ *n* -S [L *vaticination-, vaticinatio,* fr. *vaticinatus* (past part.) + *-ion-, -io* -ion] **1 :** something foretold **:** PREDICTION, PROPHECY ⟨had been wont to smile at these annual ~*s* of his mother's —Edith Wharton⟩ **2 :** the act of prophesying ⟨rejected ~ along with the Victorian tendency to preach —Van Wyck Brooks⟩
va·tic·i·na·tor \-ˈ==ˌād·ə(r)\ *n* -S [L, fr. *vaticinatus* (past part. of *vaticinari* to prophesy) + *-or*] **:** one that vaticinates **:** PROPHET
vat jade green *n, usu cap V&J&G* **:** an anthraquinone vat dye — see DYE table I
vat–lined \ˈ=ˌ=\ *adj* **:** having liners affixed by a cylinder machine
vat machine *n, Brit* **:** CYLINDER MACHINE
vat·man \ˈvatmən\ *n, pl* **vatmen :** a worker who washes, dyes, cooks, or chemically treats products in a vat: as **a :** a workman who forms sheets of handmade paper by dipping a mold into a vat of stock **b :** one who saturates logs and flitches with hot water or steam to soften the fibers prior to veneer cutting — called also *wood cooker* **c :** an operator of a dye reel or jig **:** JIGGER **d :** PLATER 1a(2) **e :** one who pasteurizes and ripens cream for use in making butter
vat paper *n* **:** handmade paper
vats *pl of* VAT, *pres 3d sing of* VAT
vatted *past of* VAT
vatting *pres part of* VAT
vau \ˈvau̇, ˈvȯ\ *n* -S [L, fr. Gk *wau,* of Sem origin; akin to Heb *wāw* waw] **:** DIGAMMA
vau·che·ria \vōˈshirēə, vōˈsh-\ *n* [NL, fr. Jean Pierre Étienne *Vaucher* †1841 Swiss botanist + NL *-ia*] **1** *cap* **:** a genus of green algae (family Vaucheriaceae) that have a thallus consisting of a single elongated irregularly branched multinucleate cell attached to the substratum by rhizoids, reproduce both sexually and asexually, and live in fresh or brackish water or on damp ground where they often form a green tangled mat **2** -S **:** any green alga of the genus *Vaucheria*
vau·che·ri·a·ce·ae \(ˌ)=ˌ==ˈāsēˌē\ *n pl, cap* [NL, fr. *Vaucheria,* type genus + *-aceae*] **:** a family of oogamous green algae (order Siphonales) of which *Vaucheria* is the chief and type genus — **vau·che·ri·a·ceous** \(ˌ)=ˌ==ˈāshəs\ *adj*
vaude \ˈvȯd *also* ˈvōd *or* ˈväd\ *n* -S [by shortening] **:** VAUDEVILLE
vaude·ville \ˈvȯd(ə)vəl, -)ˌvil *also* ˈvōd- *or* ˈväd-\ *n* -S [F, fr. MF, alter. (influenced by *ville* town, city, fr. L *villa* village) of *vaudevire* popular satirical song, fr. *vau-de-Vire* valley of Vire, locality near Vire, town in northwestern France where such songs were first composed in the 15th century, fr. *vau, val* valley + *de* from, of (fr. L) + *Vire* — more at VILLAGE, DE-, VALE] **1 a :** a popular song often satirical in character **2 :** a light often comic theatrical piece frequently combining pantomime, dialogue, dancing, and song ⟨an aria apiece for the rival ladies . . . and a concluding ~ in which all express their desire to cooperate for the greater glory of art —Edward Sackville-West & Desmond Shawe-Taylor⟩ **3 a :** a stage entertainment esp. popular in theaters in the early decades of the 20th century that consisted of various unrelated acts following one another in succession and that might include performing animals, acrobats, comedians, dancers, singers, or magicians **b :** something resembling the lightness and frivolity of vaudeville ⟨I have also written three novels . . . but they are none of them ~ —Sinclair Lewis⟩
¹vaude·vil·lian \(ˈ)vōdˌvilyən, ˌvȯdəˈv- *also* -vōd- *or* -väd-\ *also* **vaude·vill·ist** *pronunc at* VAUDEVILLE + əst\ *n* -S [*vaudevillian* fr. *vaudeville* + *-an,* n. suffix; *vaudevillist* fr. F *vaudevilliste* vaudeville writer, fr. *vaudeville* + *-iste* -ist] **:** a vaudeville writer, actor, singer, or performer ⟨never ceased to wonder at the showmanship of the old-time ~*s* —Philip Hamburger⟩
²vaudevillian \"\ *adj* [*vaudeville* + *-an* (adj. suffix)] **:** of, relating to, or characteristic of vaudeville ⟨a certain ~ flavor has crept in —Amy Lowell⟩
¹vau·dois \(ˈ)vōˌdwä\ *n pl, usu cap* [MF *Vaudois, Valdois,* fr. ML *Valdenses* — more at WALDENSES] **:** WALDENSES
²vaudois \"\ *n, pl* **vaudois** *cap* [F, fr. *Vaud,* Switzerland + F *-ois* -ese (fr. L *-ensis*)] **1 :** a native or inhabitant of the Swiss canton of Vaud **2 :** the French dialect of Vaud
vau·dy \ˈvȯdi\ *adj* [origin unknown] **1** *Scot* **:** CHEERFUL, ELATED **2** *Scot* **:** gaudy in appearance
¹vault \ˈvȯlt, *chiefly Brit* ˈvält\ *n* -S [ME *vout, voute,* fr. MF *voute, volte,* fr. (assumed) VL *volvita* turn, vault, prob. fr. *volvitare* to turn, leap, vault — more at ³VAULT] **1 a :** an arched structure of masonry usu. forming a ceiling or roof but sometimes carrying a separate roof, a floor, or a staircase — see BARREL VAULT, GROIN 2, RIBBED VAULT **b :** an arched structure superficially resembling a vault ⟨walking along a passage with white walls, and a white ~ above —W.C.Bryant⟩ **2 a :** a room or space covered by an arched structure esp. when underground **b (1) :** a part of a cellar usu. devoted to a special purpose (as the storage of wine or valuables) **(2) :** such a compartment even when not covered by a vault (as below the street pavement in front of a building) **c (1) :** a room for the safekeeping of valuables and commonly built of steel **(2) :** a special compartment usu. in a piece of office equipment for the safekeeping of money **3 :** a place (as a cavern, the crater of a volcano, a great pit) resembling or suggesting a vault ⟨the ~*s* of Mt. Vesuvius⟩ **4 a :** a burial chamber with or without an arched roof esp. when partially or entirely underground **b :** a prefabricated container typically of metal or concrete into which a casket is placed at burial **5 :** the canopy of heaven **:** SKY ⟨a falling star streamed down the blue ~ —O.S.J.Gogarty⟩ **6 :** an arched or dome-shaped anatomical structure: as **a :** SKULLCAP, CALVARIUM **b :** the arched roof of the nasopharynx **c :** the combined hard and soft palate forming the roof of the mouth **d :** FORNIX 1d **7 :** the pit of a privy **8 :** an arched covering of calcareous plates between the arms of Paleozoic crinoids

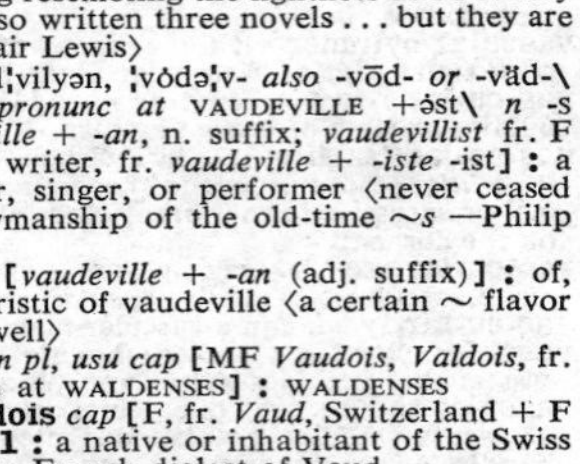

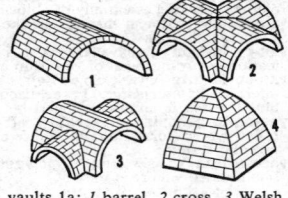

vaults 1a: *1* barrel, *2* cross, *3* Welsh, *4* cloister

²vault \"\ *vb* -ED/-ING/-S [ME *vouten,* fr. MF *vouter, volter,* fr. *voute, volte* vault] *vt* **1 a :** to form with or to cover with a vault **:** give the shape or the character of a vault to **:** ARCH ⟨~ a roof or ceiling⟩ **b :** to overarch or extend over in the fashion of a vault ⟨tall elms ~*ed* the quiet street⟩ **2** *chiefly dial* **:** to place in or as if in a vault **:** BURY ~ *vi* **:** to arch, bend, or curve in the shape of a vault
³vault \"\ *vb* -ED/-ING/-S [MF *volter,* fr. OIt *voltare,* fr. (assumed) VL *volvitare* to turn, leap, vault, freq. of L *volvere* to roll, turn, revolve — more at VOLUBLE] *vi* **1 :** to bound vigorously; *esp* **:** to execute a leap using the hands or a pole — see POLE-VAULT ⟨put his hand on the counter and ~*ed* over, landing heavily on the other side —Josephine Johnson⟩ ⟨~*ed* out of the hole and moved across the clearing —W.F.Davis⟩ ⟨~*ed* into the saddle —L.C.Douglas⟩ **2 :** to do or achieve something that resembles a leap ⟨the rapidity with which we ~*ed* to the position of world leadership —Reinhold Niebuhr⟩ ~ *vt* **:** to leap over; *esp* **:** to leap over by or as if by aid of the hands or a pole ⟨~ a fence⟩ ⟨have ~*ed* price levels beneath which they hovered for . . . years —J.T.Soby⟩ **syn** see JUMP
⁴vault \"\ *n* -S [MF *volte* turn, vault, fr. OIt *volta,* fr. *voltare* to turn, vault] **1 :** an unusually vigorous leap **:** BOUND; *esp* **:** a leap over or upon something made by aid of the hands or of a pole **2 :** the leap of a horse **:** CURVET **syn** see JUMP
vault·age \-ij\ *n* -S **:** a vaulted place **:** an arched cellar
vaulted *adj* [fr. past part. of ²*vault*] **1 a :** built in the form of a vault **:** ARCHED ⟨a ~ roof⟩ ⟨on its ~ blue dome are gold stars —*Amer. Guide Series: La.*⟩ **b :** having a form resembling a vault ⟨the spacious ~ reaches of the sky⟩ **2 :** covered with a vault ⟨~ centrally planned buildings of Christian practice —J.B.Ward-Perkins⟩
vault·er \ˈvȯltə(r)\ *n* -S [³*vault* + *-er*] **:** one that vaults; *esp* **:** POLE-VAULTER
¹vaulting *n* -S [fr. gerund of ²*vault*] **1 :** the act, practice, or art of building vaults ⟨method of ~⟩ **2 :** vaulted construction ⟨arches and ~⟩
²vaulting *adj* [fr. pres. part. of ³*vault*] **1 :** leaping upwards **:** reaching or stretching for the heights ⟨achieve a quiet serenity if not a ~ happiness —D.L.Cohn⟩ ⟨the calm aggressive flash . . . of ~ ambition —Liam O'Flaherty⟩ **2** [fr. gerund of ³*vault*] **:** designed for use in vaulting or in gymnastic exercises ⟨a ~ block⟩ ⟨a ~ bar⟩
vaulting capital *n* **:** the capital of a vaulting shaft
vaulting cell *n* **:** a compartment of a vault contrived (as in ribbed structure) to permit the building of an entire part at a time
vaulting course *n* **:** a course consisting of the springers of a vault usu. set with horizontal beds and in projection or corbeled out
vaulting horse *n* **1 :** LONG HORSE 1 **2 :** SIDE HORSE
vaulting shaft *or* **vaulting pillar** *n* **:** an upright member (as a pilaster or column) from which springs a rib of a vault and that is commonly one of a cluster or forms part of a larger pier
vault·man \ˈ=mən, -ˌman\ *n, pl* **vaultmen** [¹*vault* + *man*] **1 :** a boxman in an ice or dairy products plant who removes goods as needed for delivery **2 :** a custodian of the vault in which motion-picture negatives are kept
vault mount *n* **:** a leap in gymnastics onto a piece of apparatus made by aid of the hands
vault rib *n* **:** one of the arches carrying a vault
vaults *pl of* VAULT, *pres 3d sing of* VAULT
vaulty \ˈvȯltē\ *adj, sometimes* -ER/-EST **:** resembling a vault **:** ARCHED, CONCAVE ⟨the ~ heaven so high above our heads —Shak.⟩
¹vaunt \ˈvȯnt, -ä-,-ȧ-\ *vb* -ED/-ING/-S [ME *vaunten,* fr. MF *vanter,* fr. LL *vanitare,* fr. L *vanitas* vanity — more at VANITY] *vi* **:** to make a vain display esp. of one's own worth or attainments **:** talk vaingloriously **:** BRAG ⟨strutted and ~*ed* before the girls⟩ ~ *vt* **:** to boast of **:** make a vainglorious display of **:** put forward boastfully ⟨propaganda literature ~*ed* the successes of . . . scientists —F.L.O'Dea⟩ ⟨ye ~*ed* your fathomless power, and ye flaunted your iron pride —Rudyard Kipling⟩ **syn** see BOAST
²vaunt \"\ *n* -S **1 :** a vainglorious display of what one is or has or has done **:** OSTENTATION **2 :** a bragging assertive speech **:** loud boast ⟨may the ~*s* and menace of the vengeful enemy pass like the gust —S.T.Coleridge⟩
³vaunt \"\ *n* -S [MF *avant* before, forward — more at AVAUNT (hence)] **1** *obs* **:** the front part **2** *obs* **:** the foremost ranks of an army **:** VAN
vaunt–courier \(ˈ)=+\ *n* [MF *avant-courrier,* lit., advance courier] **1** *obs* **:** AVANT COURIER 1 **2 :** one sent in advance **:** FORERUNNER
vaunted *adj* [fr. past part. of ¹*vaunt*] **:** boasted about **:** praised to the skies ⟨the ~ Southern hospitality —Marjorie K. Rawlings⟩ ⟨our ~ industrial economy which makes this population possible —Marston Bates⟩
vaunt·er \ˈvȯntə(r), ˈvän-,ˈvȧn-\ *n* -S [ME *vauntour,* fr. MF *vanteur,* fr. *vanter* to boast + *-eur* -or] **:** one that boasts ⟨men are . . . ~*s* about what they can't do —Bruce Marshall⟩
vaunt·ery \-tərē\ *n* -ES [¹*vaunt* + *-ery*] **1 :** an overweening vaunting **2** *obs* **:** BOAST
vaunt·ful \ˈvȯntfəl, ˈvän-,ˈvȧn-\ *adj* **:** BOASTFUL, VAINGLORIOUS
¹vaunting *n* -S [ME, fr. gerund of *vaunten* to vaunt] **:** the act of boasting **:** BRAGGING ⟨make your ~ true —Shak.⟩
²vaunting *adj* [fr. pres. part. of ¹*vaunt*] **1 :** inclined or given to vainglorious boasting ⟨a ~ Spaniard —Francis Hackett⟩ **2 :** of or characterized by boastfulness ⟨~ smile appeared on his lips —Mary McCarthy⟩
vaunt·ing·ly *adv* **:** in a vaunting manner
vaunt·lay \ˈvȯntˌlā, ˈvän-,ˈvan-\ *n* -S [³*vaunt* + *-lay* (as in *relay*)] **:** the releasing of a relay of hunting dogs after the quarry has passed and before the rest of the pack has come up; *also* **:** the relay of dogs released in this manner
vaunty *also* **vaunt·ie** \-ti\ *adj, Scot* **:** BOASTFUL, PROUD, VAIN ⟨your letter made me ~ —Robert Burns⟩
vau·que·lin·ite \ˈvȯk(ə)lə,nīt\ *n* -S [Sw *vauquelinit,* fr. Louis N. *Vauquelin* †1829 Fr. chemist + Sw *-it* -ite] **:** a mineral $(Pb,Cu)_3(CrO_4,PO_4)_2(?)$ consisting of a green to brown lead copper phosphate and chromate
vaux·ite \ˈvȯkˌsīt, ˈväk-\ *n* -S [George *Vaux* †1927 Am. lawyer and naturalist + E *-ite*] **:** a mineral $FeAl_2(PO_4)_2(OH)_2.7H_2O$ consisting of a hydrous basic phosphate of iron and aluminum in triclinic crystals
vav *var of* WAW
vav·a·sor *or* **vav·a·sour** *also* **vav·as·sor** \ˈvavəˌsȯ(ə)r, -sü(-, -sō(-\ *or* **val·va·sor** *or* **val·vas·sor** \ˈvalv-\ *n* -S [ME *vavasour,* fr. OF *vavassor, vavassour,* prob. fr. ML *vassus vassorum* vassal of vassals, fr. *vassus* vassal + *vassorum* of vassals, gen. pl. of *vassus* — more at VASSAL] **:** a feudal tenant ranking directly below a peer or baron
vav·a·so·ry \-sōrē\ *n* -ES [OF *vavassourie,* fr. *vavassour* + *-ie* -y] **:** the tenure of a fee or the lands held by a vavasor
va·ward \ˈvau̇,(w)ȯrd\ *n* -S [ME *vauntwarde, vaward,* fr. ONF *avantwarde,* fr. *avant* forward, before (fr. L *abante*) + *warde* guard, guardian, fr. *warder* to guard — more at AVAUNT, REWARD] **:** the foremost part **:** FOREFRONT ⟨the ~ of our youth —Shak.⟩
vb *abbr* verb; verbal
VB *abbr* **1** valve box **2** vertical beam **3** volunteer battalion
v–beam radar \ˈ=ˌ=-\ *n, cap V* **:** a height-finding radar emitting a vertical beam and another beam at a 45-degree angle each of which receives separate signals that can be measured against the range of target to obtain an accurate measurement of its height
v–belt \ˈ=ˌ=\ *cap V, also* **vee belt** \"\ *n* **:** a belt of V-shaped cross section engaging a V-shaped groove in a pulley for wedging and better traction
vbl *abbr* verbal
v–block \ˈ=ˌ=\ *n, cap V* **:** a steel block having a V-shaped groove in one side and used in machine tooling esp. as a support for round work
v–bob \ˈ=ˌ=\ *n, cap V* **:** a strong frame shaped like an isosceles triangle, turning on a pivot at its apex, and used as a bell crank to change the direction of a main pump rod
v–bomb \ˈ=ˌ=\ *n, usu cap V* [*v* (as in *V-1, V-2*) + *bomb*] **:** a V-1, V-2, or similar weapon used esp. by the Germans in World War II

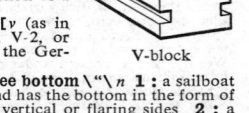

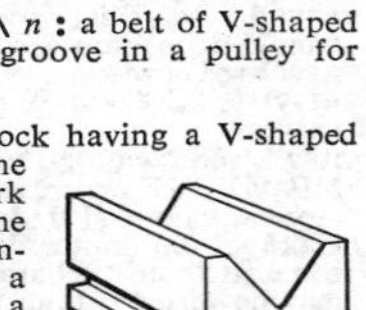
V-block

v–bottom \ˈ=ˌ=\ *cap V, also* **vee bottom** \"\ *n* **1 :** a sailboat that is usu. broad and shoal and has the bottom in the form of a flat V joined by a chine to vertical or flaring sides **2 :** a usu. high-speed powerboat developed from the sailing type of V-bottom
vc *abbr* violoncello
VC *abbr* **1** valuable cargo **2** valuation clause **3** veterinary corps **4** vice-chairman **5** vice-chancellor **6** vice-consul **7** vigilance committee **8** visible capacity **9** [vision color] color vision **10** volunteer corps
v–connection \ˈ=ˌ==ˌ=\ *n, cap V* **:** OPEN-DELTA CONNECTION
vct *abbr* victor
VD \ˈ=ˈ=\ *abbr or n* -S *sometimes not cap* venereal disease
VD *abbr* **1** vapor density **2** various dates
v–day \ˈ=ˌ=\ *n, usu cap V* [*v* (abbr. for *victory*)] **:** a day of victory — compare D DAY, M-DAY
VDH *abbr* valvular disease of the heart
VDM *abbr* vasodepressor material
ve *var of* VEE
VE *abbr* vesicular exanthema
've \(ə)v\ *vb* [by contr.] **:** HAVE ⟨we've been there⟩ ⟨I've the book⟩
ve·adar *or* **we–adar** \ˌvāˈ(ˌ)äˌdär\ *n* -S *usu cap V&W&A* [Heb *wĕ-ădhār,* lit., and Adar (i.e., the second Adar)] **:** the intercalary month of the Jewish year having 29 days and in leap years following Adar — called also *Adar Sheni;* see MONTH table

¹veal \'vēl, *esp before pause or consonant* -ēəl\ *n* -s *often attrib* [ME *vel, veel,* fr. MF *veel,* fr. L *vitellus* small calf, dim. of *vitulus* calf — more at WETHER] **1 :** CALF; *esp* **:** one suitable for or used for food **2 :** the flesh of a calf a few days to 12 or 14 weeks of age — see BOB VEAL, VEALER

²veal \"\ *vt* -ED/-ING/-S **:** to kill and dress (a calf) for veal

veal bird *n* **:** a small thin slice of veal rolled around stuffing, seared, and stewed

veal cutlet *n* **:** a slice from a leg of veal cut into small portions and fried plain or breaded

veal·er \'vēlə(r)\ *n* -s **:** a calf suitable for veal; *esp* **:** one less than three months old and largely or wholly milk-fed

veal·i·ness \-lēnəs\ *n* -ES **:** the quality or state of being vealy **:** IMMATURITY

vealskin \'ₛ,ₛ\ *n* **:** a large calfskin — compare KIP 2

vealy \'vēlē\ *adj* -ER/-EST **:** resembling or suggesting veal or a calf ⟨white ~ face —John Dos Passos⟩; *esp* **:** IMMATURE ⟨a ~ graduate⟩

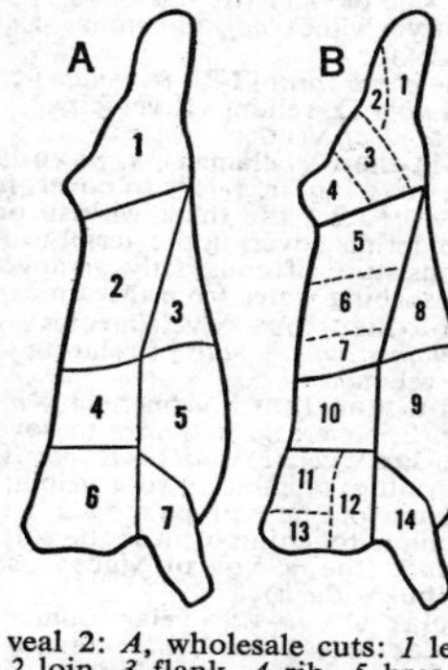

veal 2: *A,* wholesale cuts: *1* leg, *2* loin, *3* flank, *4* rib, *5* breast, *6* shoulder, *7* shank; *B* retail cuts: *1* hind shank, *2* heel of round, *3* round, *4* rump roast, *5* sirloin steak, *6* loin chops, *7* kidney chops, *8* flank, *9* breast, *10* rib roast, *11* blade steak, *12* arm steak, *13* shoulder roast, *14* fore shank

veatch·ite \'vē,chīt\ *n* -s [John A. *Veatch,* 19th cent. Am. mineralogist + E *-ite*] **:** a mineral $Sr_3B_{16}O_{27}.5H_2O$(?) consisting of a hydrous strontium borate but orig. thought to be a calcium borate

veb·le·ni·an \(')ve¦blēnēən\ *adj, usu cap* [Thorstein B. *Veblen* †1929 Am. social scientist + E *-an*] **:** of or relating to the social scientist Veblen or his theories

veb·len·ism \'vebla,nizəm\ *n* -s *usu cap* [Thorstein *Veblen* + E *-ism*] **:** the theories of Veblen

veb·len·ite \-,nīt\ *n* -s *usu cap* [Thorstein *Veblen* + E *-ite*] **:** a supporter of Veblen

vec·to·graph \'vektə,graf, -rāf\ *n* [*vector* + *-graph*] **:** a picture composed of two superposed stereoscopic images polarized at right angles to each other and giving a three-dimensional effect when viewed through appropriate polarizing spectacles — compare STEREOGRAPH — **vec·to·graph·ic** \¦ₛₛ¦grafik\ *adj*

¹vec·tor \'vektə(r) *sometimes* -,tō(ə)r *or* -ō(ə)\ *n* -s [NL, fr. L, carrier, fr. *vectus* (past part. of *vehere* to carry) + *-or* — more at WAY] **1 a :** RADIUS VECTOR 2 **b** *or* **vector quantity :** a quantity that requires for its complete specification a magnitude, direction, and sense and that is commonly represented by a line segment the length of which designates the magnitude of the vector, the orientation of which designates the direction of the vector, and the sense of which is designated by an arrowhead at one end of the segment **:** a quantity having both magnitude and direction **c :** a course or compass direction esp. of an airplane **2 :** an agent capable of transmitting a pathogen from one organism to another either mechanically as carrier (as houseflies that transport typhoid bacteria) or biologically by playing a specific role in the life cycle of the pathogen (as mosquitoes in relation to the malaria parasite) ⟨fleas are ~s of plague⟩ ⟨aphids are ~s of plant viruses⟩ **3 :** a behavioral field of force toward or away from the performance of various acts; *broadly* **:** DRIVE

²vector \"\ *vt* -ED/-ING/-S **:** to guide (as an airplane or a missile) in flight by means of a radioed vector ⟨system to ~ night fighters to attack approaching airplanes —*Flying*⟩ ⟨was ~*ed* into radar contact with these aircraft —Guy Bordelon⟩ ⟨the pilots were ~*ed* through the storm by the flight controller —*Science*⟩

vector addition *n* **:** the process of finding the geometric sum of a number of vectors by repeated application of the parallelogram law

vector algebra *n* **:** an algebra for which the elements involved may represent vectors and the assumptions and rules are based on the behavior of vectors

vector analysis *n* **:** a branch of mathematics that treats of vectors

vector calculus *n* **:** the application of the calculus to vectors

vec·tor·cardiogram \¦ₛ(,)ₛ+\ *n* [*vector* + *cardiogram*] **:** the graphic record made by vectorcardiography

vec·tor·cardiographic \"+\ *adj* [*vectorcardiography* + *-ic*] **:** relating to, employing, or obtained by means of vectorcardiography ⟨~ systems that employ a limited number of body surface electrodes —D.A.Brody⟩

vec·tor·cardiography \"+\ *n* [*vector* + *cardiography*] **:** a method of recording the direction and magnitude of the electrical forces of the heart by means of a continuous series of vectors that form a curving line around a center

vector diagram *n* **:** a diagram involving vectors

vector field *or* **vector point** *n* **:** an aggregate of vectors which is defined at the various points of a curve or surface or region of space and in which one of the aggregate is associated with each point of the curve, surface, or region

vec·to·ri·al \(')vek¦tōrēəl\ *adj* [ISV *vector* + *-ial*] **:** of or relating to a vector or vector quantity

vectorial angle *n* **:** the angle from the polar axis to the radius vector

vec·to·ri·al·ly \-ēəlē\ *adv* **:** in a vectorial way

vector multiplication *n* **:** the product of vectors

vector potential *n* **:** a vector field so distributed in space as to represent by means of its curl some physically important vector

vector product *also* **vector cross product** *n* **:** a vector that is the product of the magnitude of two vectors A and B and the sine of the included angle and that has a direction perpendicular to the plane of the two vectors A and B and a sense that is determined by the right-handed screw convention

vector psychology *n* **:** TOPOLOGICAL PSYCHOLOGY

vector sum *n* **:** the sum obtained in vector addition

vec·tu·rist \'vekchərəst\ *n* -s [L *vectura* vehicle (fr. *vectus* + *-ura* -ure) + E *-ist* — more at VECTOR] **:** a collector of transportation tokens

ve·da \'vādə *sometimes* 'vēdə\ *n* -s *usu cap* [Skt, knowledge, sacred lore, Veda; akin to Skt *veda* I know — more at WIT] **:** any of a class of the most ancient sacred writings of the Hindus; *specif* **:** any of the four Samhitas — compare ARANYAKA, BRAHMANA, SUTRA, UPANISHAD

ve·da·ic \vəˈdāik, vä'd-\ *adj, usu cap* **:** of or relating to the Vedas **:** VEDIC

¹ve·da·lia \və'dālyə, -lēə\ [NL] *syn of* RODOLIA

²vedalia \"\ *n* -s [NL] **:** an Australian ladybug (*Rodolia cardinalis*) that has been introduced to many countries to control scale (as the cottony-cushion scale)

ve·dan·ga \vä'däŋgə\ *n* -s *usu cap* [Skt *vedāṅga,* lit., limb of the Veda, fr. *veda* + *aṅga* limb — more at ANGLE] **:** any one of six classes of Sanskrit works written in the sutra style including phonetics, meter, grammar, etymology, religious ceremony, and the ritualistic calendar and designed to teach how to recite, understand, and apply Vedic texts

ve·dan·ta \vä'däntə, və'dan-\ *n* -s *usu cap* [Skt *vedānta,* lit., end of the Veda, fr. *veda* + *anta* end — more at END] **:** an orthodox Hindu philosophy based on the latter part of the Vedas as concerned with the ultimate goal of contemplation — compare BRAHMAN, MIMAMSA

ve·dan·tic \-tik\ *adj, usu cap* **1 :** of or relating to the Vedanta philosophy **2 :** VEDIC

ve·dan·tism \-n·,tizəm\ *n* -s *usu cap* **:** Vedantic philosophy

¹ve·dan·tist \-ntəst\ *adj, usu cap* **:** VEDANTIC

²vedantist \"\ *n* -s **:** an adherent of Vedantism

ved·da *also* **ved·dah** \'vedə\ *n, pl* **vedda** *or* **veddas** *usu cap* [Sinhalese *vedda* hunter] **1 :** an aboriginal people of Ceylon characterized by slender build, small stature, dark complexion, and profuse wavy hair and often held to be intermediate between the Australian blacks and the Dravidians of Hindustan **2 :** a member of the Vedda people

¹ved·doid \'ve,dȯid\ *adj, usu cap* [*Vedda* + E *-oid*] **1 :** resembling or related to the Veddas **2 :** of or relating to the Veddoids

²veddoid \"\ *n* -s *usu cap* **:** a member of an ancient race of southern Asia characterized by wavy to curly hair, chocolate-brown skin color, linear build, and fine features and represented by the Vedda of Ceylon, the Shom Pen of the Nicobars, the Toala of Celebes, and aborigines of northern Australia

veddoid-australoid \¦ₛₛ¦ₛₛₛ\ *n* -s *usu cap V&A* **:** VEDDOID

ve·dette *or* **vi·dette** \və'det\ *n* -s [F, fr. It *vedetta,* alter. (influenced by *vedere* to see, fr. L *vidēre*) of *veletta,* prob. fr. Sp *vela* watch (fr. *velar* to keep watch, fr. L *vigilare* to wake, watch, fr. *vigil* awake, watchful) + It *-etta* -ette (fr. LL *-ita*) — more at WIT, VIGIL] **:** a mounted sentinel stationed in advance of pickets to watch an enemy and give notice of danger

vedette post *n* **:** an outpost of two or more vedettes one of whom is constantly on the alert

¹ve·dic \'vādik *sometimes* 'vēd-\ *adj, usu cap* [*Veda* + *-ic*] **:** of or relating to the Vedas, the language in which they are written, or the period and culture that they represent

²vedic \"\ *or* **vedic sanskrit** *n, cap V&S* **:** the Indic language of the Vedas

ve·dro \və'drō, -rō\ *n* -s [Russ, lit., bucket] **:** a Russian unit of liquid capacity equal to 3.25 U.S. gallons or 2.71 imperial gallons

¹vee *also* **ve** \'vē\ *n* -s *often attrib* **1 :** the letter *v* **2 a :** something having the shape of the letter V ⟨~ formation of flying geese⟩ ⟨make the sign ~ for victory⟩ ⟨dropped it inside the ~ of his shirt —Howard Hunt⟩ ⟨~ neck of a sweater⟩ ⟨the vast, gloomy ~ of the gorge —John Hersey⟩ **b :** a groove with a V-shaped section

²vee \"\ *vt* -ED/-ING/-S **:** to form into a vee ⟨~ boards to make a trough⟩

vee belt *var of* V-BELT

vee bottom *var of* V-BOTTOM

vee engine *var of* V-ENGINE

veep \'vēp\ *n* -s [fr. *v.p.* (abbr. for *vice-president*)] **:** VICE-PRESIDENT

¹veer \'vi(ə)r, -iə\ *vt* -ED/-ING/-S [ME *veren,* of LG or D origin; akin to MD *vieren* to let out, slacken, MLG *vīren* to slacken; prob. akin to OHG *fiaren* to give direction to, OFris *firia* to be far and prob. to OE *feorr* far — more at FAR] **:** to let or pay out (as a rope or anchor chain) ⟨~ the mainsheet⟩ — **veer and haul :** to pay out and haul in alternately or to pay out and haul in simultaneously on various parts

²veer \"\ *vb* -ED/-ING/-S [MF *virer,* prob. of Celt origin; akin to W *gwyro* to shift, deviate, Bret *goara* to curve, OIr *fiar* slanting, oblique; akin to OE *wīr* wire — more at WIRE] *vi* **1 :** to change direction **:** shift from one direction, position, condition, or inclination to another **:** be variable **:** TURN ⟨the highway ~s inland at this point⟩ ⟨his ~*ing* gait —William Wordsworth⟩ ⟨he ~*ed* aside when he heard the train moving —J.C.Powys⟩ ⟨my attention ~*ed* aimlessly around —Anne S. Mehdevi⟩ ⟨his mind ~*ed* away from the memory —Marcia Davenport⟩ **2** *of the wind* **:** to shift in a clockwise direction — opposed to *back* **3 :** to wear ship **:** alter course by turning away from the direction of the wind **~** *vt* **1 :** to direct to a different course ⟨pressures ~*ing* him from his purpose⟩ **:** TURN, SHIFT; *specif* **:** WEAR 8 ⟨~ a ship⟩ **syn** see SWERVE — **veer and haul :** to vary the course or direction ⟨a wind that *veers* aft *and hauls* forward⟩

³veer \"\ *n* -s **:** an act of veering **:** a change in course, direction, or inclination ⟨took a sharp ~ to the left⟩ ⟨a ~ toward ultraconservatism⟩ ⟨a ~ in our policy —*Kiplinger Washington Letter*⟩

veer away *or* **veer out** *vt* **1 :** to let out **:** slacken and let run **:** pay out ⟨*veer away* the cable⟩ ⟨*veer out* a rope⟩ **2 :** to permit to drift off by letting out a line ⟨*veer* the ship *away*⟩

¹veering *adj* [fr. pres. part. of ²*veer*] **:** TURNING, SHIFTING, VARIABLE ⟨snakelike, ~ dances —Richard Wright⟩ ⟨such a ~ record . . . would seem to support the charges of inconsistency often brought against him —John Mason Brown⟩; *esp* **:** shifting in a clockwise direction ⟨a ~ wind⟩

²veering *n* -s [fr. gerund of ²*veer*] **:** a shifting esp. in a clockwise direction; *specif* **:** an altering of a ship's course by turning away from the direction of the wind

veer·ing·ly *adv* **:** in a veering manner

vee·ry \'virē, -ri\ *n* -ES [perh. imit. of one of its notes] **:** a thrush (*Hylocichla fuscescens*) common in the eastern U.S. that is light tawny brown above, pale buff below, rather indistinctly spotted with brown, and grayish white on the sides — called also *tawny thrush, Wilson's thrush*

vee tail *also* **v tail** *n, cap 2d V* **:** an airplane tail in which longitudinal and directional stability and control are provided by two surfaces inclined to each other and to the plane of symmetry so that in section they form a V — see RUDDERVATOR

vee thread *var of* V THREAD

ve·ga \'vāgə\ *n* -s [Sp, prob. of Basque origin; akin to Basque *ibaiko* of the river, *ibai* river] **:** an open tract of ground **:** PLAIN; *esp* **:** a moist or boggy meadow

¹veg·e·ta·ble \'vejtəbəl *also* -jəd·əb- *or* -jətəb-\ *adj* [ME, fr. ML *vegetabilis* capable of growth, vegetative, fr. *vegetare* to grow, flourish (fr. L, to enliven, animate, fr. *vegetus* lively, animated, fr. *vegēre* to rouse, excite, be active) + L *-abilis* -able — more at WAKE] **1** *obs* **:** living or growing in the manner of simple living things (as plants) **:** VEGETATIVE **2 a :** of or relating to plants **:** having the nature of or produced by plants **:** growing in the manner of a plant ⟨~ growths⟩ ⟨~ matter⟩ ⟨high pointed tower . . . seems . . . to have grown up in an inevitable, ~ way from the three tall arches —Eleanor Clark⟩ **b :** consisting of plants **:** VEGETATIONAL ⟨~ cover⟩ **3 :** made from plant matter ⟨~ color⟩ ⟨insulation used in houses can be grouped into three general classes, ~, mineral, and metallic —*Building, Estimating & Contracting*⟩; *often* **:** made chemically from plant tissue or substance to resemble an animal product ⟨~ wool⟩ ⟨~ fat⟩ **4 :** resembling or suggesting a plant (as in lowliness, monotony of existence attached to one place, or inexpressiveness) **:** MONOTONOUS, DULL, STUPID ⟨great stretch of empty time . . . in which I lived an essentially ~ existence —J.P.Roche⟩ ⟨gossip, the necessary continuum of corruption and violence in otherwise ~ lives —Harvey Manning⟩

²vegetable \"\ *n* -s **1 a :** PLANT 1c — not used technically **b :** a usu. herbaceous plant (as the cabbage, potato, bean, or turnip) that is cultivated for an edible part which is used as a table vegetable **2 :** an edible part of a plant (as seeds, leaves, or roots) that is used for human food and usu. eaten cooked or raw during the principal part of a meal rather than as a dessert — contrasted with *fruit* ⟨the tomato though botanically a fruit is usu. eaten as a ~⟩

vegetable bezoar *n* **:** a concretion formed of the hairs of crimson clover, the awns of oats, or similar vegetable matter in the stomach of a ruminating animal to which it is sometimes fatal

vegetable black *n* **1 :** a fine lampblack made by the combustion of vegetable oils **2 :** any of various black pigments resembling lampblacks but made by charring vegetable matter (as vine twigs, willow wood, or wood-pulp waste) and used chiefly in printing inks, cements, and mortars — compare CARBON BLACK, VINE BLACK

vegetable brain *n* **:** the aril of the akee

vegetable butter *n* **1 :** a vegetable fat (as cocoa butter or shea butter) that resembles butter or lard in consistency — compare VEGETABLE TALLOW **2 :** AVOCADO

vegetable caterpillar *n* **:** AWETO

vegetable color *n* **:** a coloring matter of plant origin

vegetable dye *n* **:** a natural dye (as logwood) obtained from a plant

vegetable egg *n* **1 :** EGGPLANT **2 :** the fruit of the marmalade tree

vegetable fat *n* **:** a fat of vegetable origin that is obtained naturally from plants or by hydrogenation of a vegetable oil

vegetable glue *n* **:** an adhesive made from vegetable material; *esp* **:** one made by treating starch (as from cassava root) with alkali and used in plywood and veneered products

vegetable hair *or* **vegetable horsehair** *n* **:** a fiber from a European dwarf fan palm (*Chamaerops humilis*) used for furniture stuffing

vegetable ivory *n* **1 :** the hard white opaque endosperm of the ivory nut that takes a high polish and is used as a substitute for ivory esp. in the manufacture of buttons **2 :** IVORY NUT

vegetable kingdom *n* **:** PLANT KINGDOM

vegetable lamb *n* **1 :** SCYTHIAN LAMB 1 **2 :** the cotton plant

vegetable leather *n* **:** a shrubby West Indian spurge (*Euphorbia punicea*) having leathery foliage and crimson bracts

vegetable marrow *n* **:** any of various smooth-skinned cylindrical to oval summer squashes (as a cocozelle or zucchini) that usu. have creamy white to deep green skins often mottled or streaked with darker color

vegetable mold *n* **:** HUMUS

vegetable oil *n* **:** an oil obtained from a plant; *esp* **:** a fatty oil obtained usu. from seeds or nuts — compare DRYING OIL, ESSENTIAL OIL

vegetable orange *n* **:** MANGO MELON

vegetable oyster *n* **1 :** SALSIFY **2 :** BLACK SALSIFY

vegetable parchment *n* **:** a highly grease-resistant and water-resistant paper resembling parchment, often used as a food wrapper, and made by passing unsized paper through sulfuric acid to gelatinize its surface and then washing and drying it — called also *parchment paper*

vegetable pathology *n* **:** PLANT PATHOLOGY

vegetable pear *n* **:** CHAYOTE

vegetable plate *n* **:** a main course without meat consisting of several vegetables cooked separately and served on one plate

vegetable rennet *n* **:** a plant that has the power of coagulating milk: as **a :** BUTTERWORT **b :** a shrub (*Withania coagulans*) of Afghanistan whose seeds are used in place of rennet

vegetable rouge *or* **vegetable red** *n* **:** CARTHAMUS RED

vegetable satyr *n* **:** SATYR ORCHID

vegetable sheep *n* **:** SHEEP PLANT

vegetable silk *n* **:** a cottony fibrous material obtained from the coating of the seeds of any of various trees (as the floss-silk) and used esp. for stuffing cushions — compare SILK COTTON

vegetable soul *n* **:** the soul that in the scholastic tradition controls the nutritive and reproductive functions of human life and is held to be lower or less complete than the animal soul and rational soul

vegetable sponge *n* **:** LUFFA 3

vegetable stock *n* **:** vegetable pot liquor

vegetable sulfur *n* **:** LYCOPODIUM POWDER 2

vegetable tallow *n* **:** a fatty substance (as Chinese tallow) that is obtained from plants and resembles tallow in consistency

vegetable-tallow tree *or* **vegetable tallow** *n* **:** WAX MYRTLE

vegetable tanning *n* **:** the process of tanning by impregnating (an animal skin) with plant infusions

vegetable wax *n* **:** a waxy product (as Japan wax) that is secreted by various plants commonly in thin flakes by the walls of the epidermal cells and that sometimes forms a bloom

vegetable weevil *n* **:** a So. American weevil (*Listroderes obliquus*) that has been introduced into No. America, Australia, Africa, and Hawaii and is very destructive to many vegetable and other crop plants

veg·e·ta·blize \'vejtəbə,līz *also* -jəd·əb- *or* -jətəb-\ *vt* -ED/-ING/-S **:** to transform into or cause to take the properties of a vegetable

veg·e·ta·bly \'vejtəblē, -bli *also* -jəd·əb- *or* -jətəb-\ *adv* **:** in the manner of or like a vegetable **:** with the characteristics of a vegetable ⟨living ~ and intuitively —Aldous Huxley⟩

¹vegetal *n* -s [MF, fr. ML *vegetare* to grow as a plant, fr. ML *vegetare* to grow, flourish] *obs* **:** VEGETABLE

²veg·e·tal \'vejəd·ᵊl, -jətᵊl\ *adj* [ML *vegetare* to grow, flourish + E *-al*] **1** *obs* **:** having or showing plantlike life and growth **2 :** relating to vegetables or to vegetation **:** of the nature of a vegetable (as in growth and development) as contrasted with that of an animal **:** VEGETABLE **3 :** composed of or derived from vegetables ⟨a ~ diet⟩ ⟨a ~ remedy⟩ ⟨regions rich in ~ and mineral products —*Canadian Mining Jour.*⟩ **4 :** VEGETATIVE 1 **5 :** of or relating to the vegetal pole of an egg or to that part of an egg from which the endoderm normally develops — compare ANIMAL 5

veg·e·tal·ize \-,īz\ *vb* -ED/-ING/-S *vt* **:** to cause (embryonic cells) to exhibit vegetal characters **~** *vi, of embryonic cells* **:** to exhibit vegetal characters

vegetal pole *n* **:** the point on the surface of an egg that is diametrically opposite to the animal pole and usu. marks the center of the protoplasm containing more yolk, dividing more slowly and forming larger blastomeres than that about the animal pole, and giving rise to the hypoblast of the embryo — see BLASTULA illustration

¹veg·e·tar·i·an \,vejə'terēən, -ta(a)r-, -tār-\ *n* -s [²*vegetable* + *-arian*] **1 :** one who believes in or practices vegetarianism **2 :** a phytophagous animal **:** HERBIVORE

²vegetarian \¦ₛₛₛ¦ₛₛ\ *adj* **1 :** of or relating to vegetarianism **2 :** consisting wholly of vegetables ⟨a ~ diet⟩

veg·e·tar·i·an·ism \,ₛₛ'ₛₛₛə,nizəm\ *n* -s **:** the theory or practice of living solely upon vegetables, fruits, grains, and nuts

veg·e·tate \'vejə,tāt, *usu* -ād·+V\ *vb* -ED/-ING/-S [ML *vegetatus,* past part. of *vegetare* to grow, flourish — more at VEGETABLE] *vi* **1 a :** to grow as a plant or after the fashion of plants ⟨the algae usually ~ vigorously —Florence Chase⟩ **b :** to produce vegetation ⟨fields permitted to ~ for a given time⟩ **c :** to propagate vegetatively as distinguished from sexually ⟨a bacterial growth . . . was *vegetating* along with the fungus —*Chronica Botanica*⟩ **2 :** to lead a passive existence without initiative or exertion of body or mind **:** do little but eat and grow ⟨a dull, ambitionless, *vegetating* individual —J.A.Brussel⟩ ⟨left to ~ back to a robust physical health —William Manchester⟩ ⟨~ in luxurious subtropical surroundings —Jack Westeyn⟩ ⟨perfectly content to ~, to continue leading a humdrum, uneventful life —A.H. & Ruth Verrill⟩ **3 :** to grow exuberantly **:** produce fleshy or warty outgrowths ⟨a *vegetating* tumor⟩ **~** *vt* **1** *obs* **:** to cause to grow **2 :** to establish vegetation in or on **:** provide the vegetation of ⟨~ a hillside or ravine⟩ ⟨~ a meadow with native grasses⟩ ⟨dominant types of trees that ~ a coral island —T.C.Roughley⟩

veg·e·ta·tion \,vejə'tāshən\ *n* -s [ML *vegetation-, vegetatio,* fr. *vegetatus* (past part. of *vegetare* to grow, flourish) + L *-ion-, -io* -ion] **1 :** the act or process of growing as a plant does **:** vegetable growth, development, or activity **2 :** inert existence **:** life removed from the stimulation of social and intellectual activity **:** dull and stagnant living ⟨lived a life of serene ~ —William Faulkner⟩ **3 :** plant life or total plant cover (as of an area, forest, or prairie) ⟨all life depends on the photosynthetic action of ~⟩ — sometimes distinguished from *flora* as concerned with mass effects or individuals rather than kinds of plants ⟨though the flora was small at this time it formed a heavy ~ chiefly of tree ferns and primitive gymnosperms⟩ **4 :** an abnormal outgrowth upon a part resembling in form a plant or sponge; *specif* **:** one of the warty excrescences on the valves of the heart that are composed of fibrin, collagen, and other tissue elements and are typical of endocarditis

veg·e·ta·tion·al \¦ₛₛ¦tāshənᵊl, -shnəl\ *adj* **:** relating to, composed of, or suggesting vegetation ⟨~ cover⟩

veg·e·ta·tion·less \¦ₛₛ'tāshənləs\ *adj* **:** destitute of or free from vegetation

vegetation type *also* **vegetational type** *n* **:** the life form (as grass, shrub, submerged aquatic) that gives its character to a plant community

veg·e·ta·tive \'vejə,tād·|iv, -āt|, |ēv *also* |əv, *chiefly Brit* -jətətiv\ *adj* [ME *vegetatif,* fr. ML *vegetativus,* fr. *vegetatus* (past part. of *vegetare*) + L *-ivus* -ive] **1 a :** growing or having the power of growing **:** of, relating to, or engaged in nutritive and growth functions (as of a plant) as contrasted with reproductive functions ⟨a ~ stage in the life history of a plant⟩ ⟨a ~ nucleus⟩ ⟨roots, stems, and leaves are termed the ~ organs of a seed plant's body —H.J.Fuller & Oswald Tippo⟩ ⟨concerned with the ~ activities of the plant —E.W. Sinnott⟩ **b :** having the power to induce growth in plants **:** PRODUCTIVE ⟨the ~ properties of soil⟩ **c :** of or relating to the propagation esp. of plants by nonsexual processes (as gemmation or the formation of runners or tubers) or methods (as division, cuttings, or grafting) **2 :** VEGETATIONAL ⟨~ cover⟩ ⟨the ~ layer of forest duff —Russell Lord⟩ **3 :** of or relating to the division of nature comprising the vegetable kingdom ⟨the ~ as contrasted with the animal world⟩ **4 :** affecting, arising from, or relating to involuntary bodily functions or esp. the parasympathetic nervous system **:** AUTONOMIC ⟨a ~ neurosis⟩ ⟨~ symptoms⟩ ⟨circulation, respiration, digestion, excretion, and related ~ functions —F.A.Geldard⟩ **5 :** leading a secluded or passive existence without social or intellectual

activity : VEGETABLE 4 — **veg·e·ta·tive·ly** *adv* — **veg·e·ta·tive·ness** *n* -ES

vegetative cell *n* : SOMATIC CELL; *specif* : TUBE CELL

vegetative cone *n* : the conical protuberance that commonly forms the apex of a growing shoot : the apical point of a shoot

vegetative mutation *n* : SOMATIC MUTATION

vegetative nervous system *n* : SYMPATHETIC NERVOUS SYSTEM

vegetative pole *n* : VEGETAL POLE

ve·gete \və'jēt\ *adj* [L *vegetus* — more at VEGETABLE] *archaic* : LIVELY, HEALTHY, FLOURISHING ⟨when my brain is ~ and apt for thought —R.W.Emerson⟩

veg·e·tive \'vejəd·iv\ *adj* [ML *vegetare* to grow + E *-ive* — more at VEGETABLE] : VEGETABLE, VEGETATIVE

ve·he·mence \'vēəmən(t)s *sometimes* 'vēhəm- *or* 'vāəm-, *chiefly in substand speech* və'hēm- *or* vē'h-, *in substand speech* -'hēəm-\ *n* -S [MF, fr. L *vehementia*, fr. *vehement-, vehemens* impetuous, vehement + *-ia* -y] : the quality or state of being vehement : INTENSITY, VIOLENCE

ve·he·men·cy \-nsē, -nsi\ *n* -ES [L *vehementia*] *archaic* : VEHEMENCE

ve·he·ment \-nt\ *adj* [MF, fr. L *vehement-, vehemens*; akin to L *vehere* to carry — more at WAY] **1 a** *archaic* : immoderate in strength or degree : INTENSE, SEVERE ⟨his pain was very ~ —Nicholas Robinson⟩ ⟨requires a ~ fire to flux it —Robert Boyle⟩ **b** *archaic* : marked by excessive vigor or turbulence : FURIOUS, VIOLENT ⟨~ deluges of rain —John Morgan⟩ **c** : having a strong physical effect : POTENT ⟨produces a ~ kind of whiskey known as tanglefoot —Joseph Mitchell⟩ **2** : strongly entertained : EMPHATIC, PRONOUNCED ⟨any denial . . . was thenceforward sufficient to justify ~ suspicion of heresy —G.G.Coulton⟩ **3 a** : warmly emotional : ARDENT, PASSIONATE ⟨the affections of an only child of fourteen are as concentrated as they are ~ —Ngaio Marsh⟩ ⟨~ patriotism and poetic style —E.E.Allen⟩ **b** : scathingly hostile : RANCOROUS, TRUCULENT ⟨that ~, that furious obsession of animosity —Van Wyck Brooks⟩ **4 a** : full of energy : LIVELY, STRENUOUS ⟨~ applause⟩ ⟨against his ~ opposition, the war . . . was precipitated —U.B.Phillips⟩ **b** : strikingly colorful : SHOWY, VIVID ⟨a tall, pale apparition, equipped with a ~ red wig and a police whistle —Wolcott Gibbs⟩ **5 a** : expressive of strong emotion or conviction : IMPASSIONED ⟨~ utterances in opposition to slavery —H.A.Bridgman⟩ **b** : characterized by active conviction or enthusiasm : FERVENT, ZEALOUS ⟨a ~ extremist⟩ ⟨a fine . . . scholar and ~ teacher —W.B.Yeats⟩ **c** : characterized by bitter antagonism : HEATED ⟨a ~ debate⟩ — **ve·he·ment·ly** *adv*

ve·hi·cle \'vē,ikəl *also* 'vē,hik- *or* 'vēək- *sometimes* vē'hik- *or* vi'h-\ *n* -S *often attrib* [F *véhicule* transmitting agent, vehicle, fr. L *vehiculum* carriage, conveyance, fr. *vehere* to carry — more at WAY] **1 a** : an inert substance (as syrup, lard, or liquid petrolatum) in a medicinal compound through which an active agent is administered or by which other ingredients are held together : DILUENT, EXCIPIENT **b** : a liquid ingredient of other mixtures: as (1) : a fluid in which something is dissolved or held in suspension ⟨filled his glass of tomato juice half full of salt so that . . . the juice became scarcely more than a ~ for the salt —C.P.Richter⟩ ⟨lapping abrasive has been used successfully with ~*s* of all kinds: water, soluble oils, cottonseed oil —E. Leslie Anderson⟩ (2) : the binder and volatile thinners of a finishing material (as paint or lacquer) (3) : the varnish in printing ink (4) : a fluid or other substance in which light-sensitive salts for coating photographic plates are contained **c** : MEDIUM 9b **2 a** : an agent of transmission : CARRIER ⟨water, food, insects, and inanimate objects may be ~*s* of infection —V.M.Ehlers & E.W.Steel⟩ ⟨the conception of blood as the ~ of life —J.G.Frazer⟩ ⟨man . . . as a ~ of culture —A.L. Kroeber⟩ **b** : the literal content of a metaphorical statement — compare TENOR 1c **3 a** : a mode of expression : FORM, STYLE ⟨words, pictures, and other ~*s* of expression —H.O.Taylor⟩ ⟨find a new form of verse which shall be as satisfactory a ~ for us as blank verse was for the Elizabethans —T.S.Eliot⟩ **b** : MEDIUM 3c ⟨the organ had been for centuries the ~ of sacred music —A.E.Wier⟩ ⟨public schools remain the primary ~ for the education of our youth —J.B.Conant⟩ ⟨using a program of slum clearance as a ~ . . . to secure the adoption of other and extraneous legislation —*New Republic*⟩ ⟨the United Nations as the principal ~ by which world peace may . . . be reached —Patrick McMahon⟩; *specif* : an artistic composition serving to convey a particular conception ⟨these pictures are the ~*s* of this spirit —Herbert Read⟩ **c** : a Buddhist path to salvation — compare HINAYANA, MAHAYANA **d** : an outlet for artistic talent ⟨the American minstrel show . . . as a ~ for amateurs —C.F.Wittke⟩; *specif* : a work created esp. to display the powers of a particular performer ⟨a play intended as a starring ~ for an actress⟩ ⟨a piano concerto composed as a ~ for a famous virtuoso⟩ **4** : a material embodiment or repository ⟨capable of exercising choice in the matter of reincarnation ~*s* —H.B.Piper⟩ **5** : a means of carrying or transporting something : CONVEYANCE: as **a** : a carrier of goods or passengers ⟨the most used ~ was the mule —James Bird⟩ ⟨the locomotive is well under way by the time the last ~*s* are started from rest —O.S.Nock⟩ ⟨aerial ~*s* such as airplanes, and submerged ~*s* such as . . . submarines —Fritz Zwicky⟩ ⟨for summer hunting . . . the kayak is their indispensable ~ —C.D.Forde⟩; *specif* : MOTOR VEHICLE ⟨exhaust from road ~*s*⟩ ⟨the turning radii of the transit ~ determines the length of the bus stop —B.H. Sexton⟩ **b** : a container in which something is conveyed ⟨the research ~*s* — the satellites and the lunar probes —H.H.Martin⟩ ⟨have the space ~ tracked from the earth —L.S.Brown⟩ **c** : a piece of mechanized equipment ⟨tractors and farm ~*s* —*Statesman's Yr. Bk.*⟩ ⟨tanks, half-tracks and other combat ~*s* —*Time*⟩ **d** : a propulsive device ⟨launching ~ lifts the satellite into orbit —*Space Talk*⟩ **syn** see MEAN

ve·hic·u·lar \(')vē¦hikyələ(r) *sometimes* -ē¦i-\ *adj* [LL *vehicularis*, fr. L *vehiculum* vehicle + *-aris* -ar] **1 a** : of, relating to, or designed for vehicles and esp. for motor vehicles ⟨~ traffic volume⟩ ⟨a ~ tunnel⟩ **b** : transported by vehicle ⟨~ . . . public address systems —*Armed Forces Talk*⟩ **2** : serving as a vehicle ⟨speak . . . at least one of the three ~ languages —*N. Y. Herald Tribune*⟩

vei *usu cap, var of* VAI

v-eight \'=,=\ *n, cap V* : an internal-combustion engine (as in an automobile) having two banks of four cylinders each with the banks at an angle to each other; *also* : an automobile having such an engine

¹veil \'vāl, *chiefly before pause or consonant* -āəl\ *n* -S [ME *veile*, fr. ONF, fr. L *vela*, neut. pl. of *velum* covering, curtain, veil] **1 a** (1) : a length of cloth worn by women from ancient times as a covering for the head and shoulders and often used also in eastern countries to conceal the face esp. of a married woman ⟨Jewish women wore ~*s* . . . in token of reverence and submission —Mary B. Eddy⟩; *specif* : the outer covering of a nun's headdress (2) : the cloistered life of a nun ⟨make a choice between the world and the ~ —Sir Walter Scott⟩ **b** : a length of veiling or netting worn over the head or face or attached for protection or ornament to a hat or headdress ⟨bridal ~⟩ ⟨tiny black velvet hat has a visor ~ ending at the temples —*Women's Wear Daily*⟩ **2 a** (1) : a hanging used to curtain off a sacred enclosure ⟨~ of the sanctuary⟩ (2) : the limit of sense perception dividing the living from the dead ⟨when you and I behind the ~ are past —Edward FitzGerald⟩ (3) : a hidden sanctuary; *esp* : the mysterious realm of the dead ⟨passed on within the ~ —A.J.Ross⟩ **b** : a liturgical cloth used to cover or shroud a religious object (as a crucifix or chalice) esp. during Lent : PALL **c** : HUMERAL VEIL **3 a** : a deceptive appearance or masking layer : CLOAK, COVER ⟨expressing daring criticism under the ~ of . . . buffoonery —R.A.Hall b. 1911⟩ ⟨against the first ~*s* of twilight the flashing of the guns was faintly . . . orange —Eric Linklater⟩ ⟨tear away the ~ of mystery that shrouds human sleep —Webb Garrison⟩ **b** : a curtain of silence or reticence ⟨the few sketches of his career draw a ~ over the nature of his pranks —Lindsay Rogers⟩ ⟨the first lifting of the ~ on the privacy of . . . royalty —Sheila O'Callaghan⟩ **c** : a slight obscuration of the voice in singing (as from a peculiarity of the larynx or a natural huskiness) ⟨sang . . . handsomely, though her voice has a ~ on it —Virgil Thomson⟩ **d** : a slight darkening of the lighter portions of a photographic image and the unexposed areas usu. due to chemical fog and resulting in loss of contrast **4 a** (1) : PARTIAL VEIL (2) : UNIVERSAL VEIL **b** : CALYPTRA 1 **c** : VELUM **d** : a part of the amnion sometimes covering the face of a newborn child : CAUL

²veil \"\ *vb* -ED/-ING/-S [ME *veilen*, fr. *veile* veil] *vt* **1 a** : to conceal or curtain off with or as if with a veil : HIDE, OBSCURE ⟨lace appliqués . . . ~*ed* by nylon tulle —*Women's Wear Daily*⟩ ⟨evasiveness . . . ~*ed* her face —Marcia Davenport⟩ ⟨rain and mist often ~*ed* the passage —Elsie M. B. Grosvenor⟩ ⟨~*s* his toughness with soft speech —*Newsweek*⟩ **b** : to withhold from public knowledge ⟨profound secrecy ~*ed* this undertaking —C.F.Cochran⟩ **2** *archaic* : to admit into membership in a convent ⟨she had surely been sainted if ~*ed* —Thomas Fuller⟩ ~ *vi* : to put on or wear a veil : become veiled ⟨many eastern women ~ in the presence of men⟩ ⟨his ice-clear eye gradually ~*ed* . . . his powers slipped —*Time*⟩

veiled \'vā(ə)ld\ *adj* [fr. past part. of ²*veil*] **1 a** : having or wearing a veil or concealing cover ⟨a ~ hat⟩ ⟨a ~ dancer⟩ ⟨a rose-*veiled* five-room cottage —Sinclair Lewis⟩ ⟨snowflakes from the ~ immensity of the sky —Ellen Glasgow⟩ **b** : characterized by a softening tonal distortion : BLURRED, MUFFLED ⟨strive for a little more sharpness of detail; the sound here is sometimes a bit ~ —Irving Kolodin⟩ **c** : lacking in contrast : CLOUDY ⟨if negative appears ~ or fogged —*Map Reproduction in the Field*⟩ **2** : obscured as if by a veil : DISGUISED, HIDDEN ⟨announcement of the capabilities of the new missile constitutes a ~ threat⟩ ⟨penned a ~ letter . . . hinting that French traders would be kindly received —R.A.Billington⟩ ⟨~ by this genial brogue . . . was a cold and analytical mind —*Irish Digest*⟩ — **veil·ed·ly** \'vālədlē\ *adv*

veiled medusa *n* : a velate typically Hydrozoan jellyfish having a diaphragm that partially closes the subumbrellar cavity

veiling *n* -S [fr. gerund of ²*veil*] **1 a** : VEIL ⟨no jungle tree . . . can withstand the blasting of violent sun after the ~ of emerald foliage is torn away —William Beebe⟩ **b** : an act or instance of covering with or as if with a veil ⟨the ~ of the cross on Good Friday⟩ ⟨color can be applied by . . . spray ~ —S.W.Menefee⟩ **2** : any of various light sheer fabrics (as net, lace, or chiffon) suitable for veils and used also for making dresses, hats, and scarves

veil·less \'vā(ə)lləs\ *adj* : not veiled : EXPOSED, UNSCREENED ⟨drove the dust against her ~ eyes —Alfred Tennyson⟩ ⟨the sun's hard ~ stare —Rhoda Broughton⟩

veillike \'=,=\ *adj* : resembling a veil

veiltail \'=,=\ *n* : a variety of domesticated goldfish with a very long, nearly transparent, veillike tail

¹vein \'vān\ *n* -S [ME *veine*, fr. OF, fr. L *vena* blood vessel, watercourse, natural bent, trait, vein] **1 a** (1) : a narrow water channel in rock, earth, or ice ⟨shooting, more often than not, collapses the ceiling and sides of the water ~ —Gaston Burridge⟩ (2) : a stream of water flowing through such a channel ⟨learned that several ~*s* of water . . . originated from one central dome and spread out in all directions —Kenneth Roberts⟩ **b** : a venous sinus of an invertebrate animal **c** : BLOOD VESSEL — not used technically ⟨had ice water in his ~*s*⟩ **d** : something likened to a vein or system of veins ⟨across the face of the . . . new map of the United States runs a significant network of fine scarlet ~*s* —*Nat'l Geographic*⟩ **2 a** : one of the tubular branching vessels that carry blood from the capillaries towards the heart in man and other vertebrates and have thinner walls than the arteries and often valves at intervals to prevent reflux of the blood which flows in a steady stream and is in most cases dark-colored due to the presence of reduced hemoglobin — compare CIRCULATION, PORTAL VEIN, VENAE COMITES **b** (1) : a body of ore filling a rock fissure and usu. deposited there from solution by underground water : LODE — compare DIKE (2) : a mineral bed or deposit ⟨a ~ of coal⟩ **c** : something that resembles a lode ⟨this . . . novel is by no means a pursuit of a worn-out ~; the author has discovered a new gold mine —Harrison Smith⟩ **d** : a strip of land differentiated by quality (as by special fertility) from its surroundings **e** *archaic* : the channel or flow of a stream : CURRENT, LANE ⟨whales . . . mostly swim in ~*s* —Herman Melville⟩ ⟨a whirlwind . . . directed its course toward the east, in a ~ of near half a mile wide —Jeremy Belknap⟩ **3 a** : one of the vascular bundles forming the framework of fibrous tissue of a leaf — called also *nerve, rib* **b** : a line of a different color or texture from the main body : STREAK, STRIPE; *esp* : a wavy variegation in marble and other stones **c** : one of the thickened cuticular ribs that serve to stiffen the wings of an insect **d** : the intestine and associated structures of a shrimp or prawn that appear as a dark line on the convex surface of the shellfish after it has been cooked and shelled **4 a** : a distinctive mode of expression : MANNER, STYLE ⟨produced some fifty ballets . . . in the romantic ~ characteristic of his generation —Anatole Chujoy⟩ ⟨a small masterpiece . . . in his best ~ —Mary A. Hamilton⟩ ⟨written . . . in the appropriate ~ for commercial correspondence —G.B.Shaw⟩ **b** : a distinctive thread : STRAIN ⟨a ~ of comedy weaves in and out of a great tragedy —R.M.Weaver⟩ **c** : a predominant line : general direction : TENOR ⟨statesmen whose hopes ran in this ~ —Oscar Handlin⟩ ⟨have no intention of continuing my comment . . . in this ~ —A.P.d'Entrèves⟩ **5 a** : a quality of character : TRAIT ⟨in the mother there was a deep ~ of mystical piety —Stewart Means⟩ **b** : a special aptitude : TALENT ⟨in her youth had no comedy ~ —Athene Seyler & Stephen Haggard⟩ **c** (1) : a frame of mind : HUMOR ⟨in your happiest ~ —H.J.Laski⟩ ⟨seemed to feel in the ~ to justify himself —Maurice Hewlett⟩ (2) : top form : FETTLE ⟨I am in ~ tonight . . . I have just got a third good idea —Angela Thirkell⟩ ⟨in the ~, there is probably no one . . . who can match the power and splendor of her singing —*N.Y. Post*⟩ **syn** see MOOD

²vein \"\ *vt* -ED/-ING/-S **1** : to pattern with or as if with veins : STRIATE ⟨the backs of her hands . . . were ~*ed* and worn —Kay Boyle⟩ ⟨goat paths ~*ing* its slopes —Josephine Pinckney⟩ ⟨was ~*ed* by railroads —W.A.White⟩ ⟨their works are ~*ed* with insinuations —Laurent Le Sage⟩ **2** : to diffuse in ramified form : SPREAD ⟨quartz crystals ~*ed* abundantly through its sandstone —*Amer. Guide Series: Ark.*⟩

vein·al \'vān°l\ *adj* : of or relating to the veins ⟨leaves affected with ~ mosaic⟩

veinbanding \'=,==\ *n* [¹*vein* + *banding*] **1** : an evanescent abnormality of leaves commonly associated with virus diseases and characterized by veins standing out clearly because of either a chlorotic or a dark green bounding band that often sets off more clearly the adjacent interveinal tissue **2** : a plant disease of which veinbanding is a symptom — compare RUGOSE MOSAIC, VEINCLEARING

veinclearing \'=,==\ *n* [¹*vein* + *clearing*] : an early and usu. evanescent symptom of plant diseases esp. of virus origin in which the veins stand out clearly because the tissue close to them is more or less translucent — compare VEINBANDING

veined \'vānd\ *adj* [¹*vein* + *-ed*] : marked or shot through with or as if with veins ⟨black hair, ~ with silver —Gordon Bottomley⟩ ⟨the terrain is finely ~ with roads —A.J.Liebling⟩ ⟨a beautiful book; heartbreaking, and at the same time ~ with humor —C.J.Rolo⟩; *specif* : showing venation ⟨a ~ leaf⟩

vein ending *n* : VEINLET

vein·er \'vānə(r)\ *n* -S : one that veins; *specif* : a small V gouge used in wood carving

veining *n* -S [fr. gerund of ²*vein*] **1** : the act or process of marking with or as if with veins ⟨use it for . . . mortising, ~, beading and for hundreds of other different cuts —*advt*⟩ **2 a** : a vein or pattern of veins ⟨an enchanting . . . watercolor, all delicate ~ and spongy texture —Carlyle Burrows⟩; *specif* : VENATION **b** : BEADING c

vein islet *n* : AREOLA a

vein·less \'vānləs\ *adj* : having no veins

vein·let \'vānlət\ *n* -S : a small vein; *specif* : the smallest or terminal branch of a vein (as of a leaf) — compare VENULE

veinlike \'=,=\ *adj* : resembling a vein

vein of galen *usu cap G* : GALEN'S VEIN 1

vein·ous \'vānəs\ *adj* **1** : having veins that are esp. prominent : VEINED ⟨clasped her ~ and knotted hands —Charles Dickens⟩ **2** : VENOUS ⟨less evidence of a ~ stasis —*Diseases of the Nervous System*⟩

vein quartz *n* : quartz occurring as gangue in a vein

vein rot *n* : a pole rot of tobacco involving principally the main veins and larger lateral veins

veins *pl of* VEIN, *pres 3d sing of* VEIN

veinstone \'=,=\ *n* [¹*vein* + *stone*] : GANGUE

veinstuff \'=,=\ *n* [¹*vein* + *stuff*] : GANGUE

vein·ule \'vā(,)nyül\ *also* **vein·u·let** \'vānyələt\ *n* -S [¹*vein* + *-ule* or *-ulet* (fr. *-ule* + *-et*)] : VEINLET

veiny \'vānē\ *adj, sometimes* -ER/-EST : full of veins : VEINED, VEINOUS

vel- *comb form* [NL, fr. *velum*] : velum ⟨*veliform*⟩

vel *abbr* **1** vellum **2** velocity

vela *pl of* VELUM

ve·la·men \və'lāmən\ *n, pl* **ve·lam·i·na** \-lamənə\ [NL, fr. L, covering, fr. *velare* to cover, fr. *velum* veil] **1** : MEMBRANE, VELUM **2** : the thick whitish or greenish multiseriate corky epidermis covering the aerial roots of an epiphytic orchid and consisting of compactly arranged nonliving cells capable of absorbing water from the atmosphere

vel·a·men·tous \¦velə¦mentəs\ *adj* [ISV *velament-* (fr. NL *velamentum*) + *-ous*] : relating to, resembling, or constituting a velamen

vel·a·men·tum \,==ˈmentəm\ *n, pl* **velamen·ta** \-tə\ [NL, fr. L, covering, fr. *velare* to cover] : MEMBRANE

¹ve·lar \'vēlə(r)\ *adj* [NL *velaris*, fr. *velum* + *-aris* -ar] **1** : of, forming, or relating to a velum; *specif* : of or relating to the velum of the soft palate **2** : formed with the back of the tongue touching or near the soft palate ⟨the ~ \k\ of \'kül\ *cool*⟩ ⟨the ~ \g\ of \'güs\ *goose*⟩ ⟨the ~ \k̲\ of German \'bük̲\ *Buch*⟩

²velar \"\ *n* -S : a velar sound

ve·lar·ic \və'larik\ *adj* : having velar inner closure — used of a stop or stop articulation; compare GLOTTALIC, PULMONIC

ve·lar·i·um \və'la(a)rēəm\ *n, pl* **velar·ia** \-ēə\ [L, fr. L *velum* veil] **1** : an awning over an ancient Roman theater or amphitheater **2** [NL, fr. L] : the velum that occurs in various scyphozoans and cubomedusans and that differs from that of hydrozoa in containing endoderm-lined canals

ve·lar·iza·tion \,vēlərə'zāshən, -,rī'-\ *n* -S : the act of velarizing

ve·lar·ize \'vēlə,rīz\ *vt* -ED/-ING/-S [¹*velar* + *-ize*] : to modify (as the \l\ of \'pül\ *pool*) by a simultaneous velar articulation as a result of the assimilative influence of the vowel

velar r *n* : UVULAR R; *specif* : uvular r formed by friction

ve·late \'vēlət, -ē,lāt, *usu* -d·+V\ *adj* [partly fr. L *velatus*, past part. of *velare* to veil & partly fr. NL *velatus*, fr. *vel-* + L *-atus* -ate] : having a veil or velum

ve·lat·ed \-ē,lād·əd\ *adj* [L *velatus* & NL *velatus* + E *-ed*] : VEILED, VELATE

ve·la·tion \və'lāshən\ *n* -S [L *velation-, velatio* action of veiling, fr. *velatus* (past part. of *velare* to veil) + *-ion-, -io* -ion] **1** : the act or process of veiling or the state of being veiled **2** : the formation of a velum

veld *or* **veldt** \'velt, *in S. Africa* 'fe-\ *n* -S [Afrik *veld*, fr. MD *velt, veld* field; akin to OE & OHG *feld* field — more at FIELD] **1** : African grassland that is usu. nearly level, is often intermixed with scattered shrubs or trees, and is chiefly located in eastern and southern Africa — see SOURVELD, SWEETVELD; compare TREE STEPPE **2** : grassland similar to African veld (as in parts of California or elevated plains of the Russian steppes)

veld grass *n* : a southern African grass (*Leersia calycina*) naturalized in western Australia and used in the southwestern U.S. esp. for anchorage of light soils

veld·schoen \'velt,skün, 'fe-\ *n, pl* **veldschoens** \-nz\ *or* **veldschoen** \-n\ [modif. of Afrik *velskoen*, fr. *vel* skin (fr. MD) + *skoen* shoe, fr. MD *schoe, schoen*; akin to OHG *fel* skin and to OE *scōh* shoe — more at FELL (skin), SHOE] : a heavy rawhide shoe made without nails and usu. without insole

veld sore *n* : DESERT SORE

veldt·schoen *Brit var of* VELDSCHOEN

ve·le·la \və'lelə\ *n* [NL, fr. L *velum* sail + *-ella*] **1** *cap* : a genus of floating oceanic siphonophores widely distributed in warm seas and closely related to those of the genus *Porpita* but having an oblique crest which acts as a sail and often causes the animal to be drifted to coasts remote from its native habitat **2** -S : any animal of the genus *Velella* — **ve·lel·li·dous** \-elədəs\ *adj*

ve·le·ta \vä'läd·ə\ *n* -S [Sp, weathervane, fr. *vela* cloth, veil, fr. L *vela*, pl. of *velum* veil] : a ballroom round dance of English origin in waltz time

ve·lic \'vēlik\ *adj* [*vel-* + *-ic*] : being or relating to the narrow passage located between the pharynx and the nasal passages and closable by raising the velum

ve·li·form \'vēlə,fȯrm, 'vel-\ *adj* [ISV *vel-* + *-iform*] : resembling a velum in form

ve·li·ger \'veləjə(r), 'vel-\ *n* -S [NL, fr. *vel-* + L *-iger* -igerous] : a larval mollusk in the stage when it has developed the velum

ve·li·idae \və'līə,dē\ *n pl, cap* [NL, fr. *Velia*, type genus + *-idae*] : a family of aquatic bugs that is closely related to Gerridae and is distinguished chiefly by details of the form and placement of the legs and by a 3-jointed proboscis — see WATER STRIDER

vel·i·ta·tion \,velə'tāshən\ *n* -S [L *velitation-, velitatio*, fr. *velitatus* (past part. of *velitari* to skirmish, fr. *velit-, veles* light-armed foot soldier) + *-ion-, -io* -ion — more at VELOCITY] : a dispute or slight contest : SKIRMISH

¹vell \'vel\ *vt* -ED/-ING/-S [E dial. *vell*, n. fleece, skin, var. of ¹*fell*] *dial Eng* : to cut the turf from (as for burning)

²vell \"\ *n* -S [origin unknown] *Brit* : the stomach of a calf used in making rennet

vel·la·la *or* **vel·lal·la** \və'lälə\ *n, pl* **vellala** *or* **vellalas** *or* **vellalla** *or* **vellallas** *usu cap* [Tamil *veḷḷāḷan*] : a member of a Tamil caste of the highest Sudra rank whose members are numerous in Madras and consist chiefly of landowners and cultivators

vel·le·da moth \'veləda-\ *n* [NL *velleda*, fr. *Veleda, Velleda*, legendary German prophetess of the 1st cent. A.D. fr. L] : a lappet moth (*Tolype velleda*) having the body chiefly white and wings dusky gray with white markings and having a larva that feeds on the apple, poplar, and other trees

vel·le·i·ty \və'lēəd·ē, ve'-, -lēətē, -i\ *n* -ES [NL *velleitas*, fr. L *velle* to wish, will + *-itas* -ity — more at WILL] **1** : the lowest degree of desire : imperfect or incomplete volition ⟨~, which is only a . . . faint, imperfect volition of an end, without regard to the means —Theophilus Gale⟩ **2** : a slight wish : a faint hope : DESIRE, INCLINATION ⟨every wish, every ~ of his had only to be expressed to be at once Victoria's —Lytton Strachey⟩ ⟨I have a secretary who has socialistic *velleities* —O.W. Holmes †1935⟩ ⟨his *velleities* toward the good life, true taste, beautiful women . . . weakened as he drew on toward middle age —*Time*⟩

vel·li·cate \'velə,kāt, *usu* -ād·+V\ *vb* -ED/-ING/-S [L *vellicatus*, past part. of *vellicare* to twitch, fr. *vellere* to pluck, pull — more at VULNERABLE] *vt* **1** : TWITCH, NIP, PINCH; *also* : to cause to twitch **2** : TICKLE, TITILLATE ~ *vi* : to move spasmodically : TWITCH

vel·li·ca·tion \,==ˈkāshən\ *n* -S [L *vellication-, vellicatio*, fr. *vellicatus* (past part.) + *-ion-, -io* -ion] : the act of twitching or of causing to twitch; *also* : a local twitching of a group of muscle fibers

vel·linch \'velinch\ *n* -ES [alter. of earlier *valinch*, alter. of *valentia*, modif. of Sp *venencia* fr. *avenencia* agreement, transaction, fr. *avenir* to come to (fr. L *advenire*) + *-encia* -ency (fr. L *-entia*) — more at ADVENE] : an instrument for drawing a sample from a cask through the shive hole — called also *flincher*

ve·llon \ve(l)'yōn\ *n* -S [Sp *vellón*, modif. (influenced by *vellón* fleece) of F *billon* — more at BILLON] : debased silver esp. when alloyed with considerable copper : BILLON

ve·llo process \'vel(,)yō-\ *n, usu cap V* [after Leopoldo Sanchez-*Vello*, 20th cent. Span. inventor] : a process for producing glass tubing by dropping molten glass through an annular space surrounding a rotating hollow pipe, the diameter of the tubing being determined by pressure of the air passed through the pipe, drawing speed, and temperature of the glass

vel·lo·zia \və'lōzēə\ *n, cap* [NL, fr. José *Velloso* Xavier †1811 Brazilian botanist + NL *-ia*] : a genus (the type of the family Velloziaceae) of Brazilian plants having branching stems clothed with the bases of the stiff linear pointed leaves and including some that are cultivated for their bell-shaped flowers

vel·lo·zi·a·ce·ae \və,lōzē'āsē,ē\ *n pl, cap* [NL, fr. *Vellozia*, type genus + *-aceae*] : a family of African and Brazilian plants (order Liliales) distinguished from Amaryllidaceae

by woody stems, one-flowered peduncles, commonly persistent perianth, and more numerous stamens — **vel·lo·zi·a·ceous** \¦=,==¦āshəs\ *adj*

¹vel·lum \'veləm\ *n* -s [ME *velim*, fr. MF *velin*, *veelin*, fr. *velin*, *veelin*, adj., of a calf, fr. *veel* calf — more at VEAL] **1 a :** a thin calfskin specially prepared for uses similar to those of parchment (as for writing upon and binding books) **b :** a fine-grained unsplit lambskin, kidskin, or calfskin prepared for these uses **2 :** a manuscript written or printed on vellum **3 a :** VELLUM PAPER **b :** VEGETABLE PARCHMENT **c :** paper that has been made sufficiently translucent for tracing purposes ⟨a blueprint made from a drawing on ~⟩ **d :** a usu. glazed and embossed cotton book cloth made to imitate calfskin parchment **4 :** MEMBRANE

²vellum \"\ *adj* **1 :** of, resembling, or bound in vellum **2 :** resembling the finish of eggshell paper but having a finer grain ⟨paper having a ~ finish⟩

vellum paper *n* **:** a strong cream-colored paper resembling parchment from calfskin in appearance but not parchmentized

vel non \'vel'nän\ *adv* [L, or not] **:** whether or not — used to express a legal situation where something must be done or a given determination must be made or not with no third alternative; see DEVISAT VEL NON

ve·lo \'vē(,)lō\ *n* -s [F *vélo*, short for *vélocipède* velocipede] **:** VELOCIPEDE; *specif* **:** TRICYCLE ⟨bikes and ~s⟩

ve·lo·ce \və'lōchē\ *adj* [It, fr. L *veloc-*, *velox* quick — more at VELOCITY] **:** rapid in tempo — used as a direction in music

ve·loc·i·man \və'läsəmən\ *n* -s [F *vélocimane*, fr. *véloci-* (as in *vélocipède*) + L *manus* hand — more at MANUAL] **:** an obsolete hand-driven vehicle like a velocipede

vel·o·cim·e·ter \,velə'simәd·ə(r)\ *n* [*velocity* + *-meter*] **:** an apparatus for measuring speed (as of machinery, vessels, projectiles, or sound)

ve·lo·cious \və'lōshəs\ *adj* [L *veloc-*, *velox* quick + E *-ious*] **:** SPEEDY, FAST

¹ve·loc·i·pede \və'läsə,pēd\ *n* -s [F *vélocipède*, fr. *véloci-* (as in *vélocité* velocity) + L *ped-*, *pes* foot — more at FOOT] **:** a lightweight wheeled vehicle propelled by the rider: as **a :** DANDY HORSE **b :** BICYCLE — used of early forms **c :** TRICYCLE a(2)

²velocipede \"\ *vi* -ED/-ING/-S **:** to ride on a velocipede

velocipede car *n* **:** a lightweight hand-propelled 3-wheeled railway inspection car used mainly by telegraph linemen and maintenance personnel

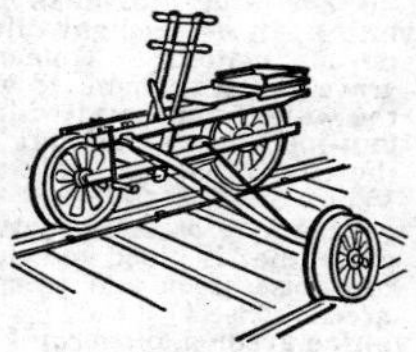

velocipede car

ve·loc·i·ped·ist \-dəst\ *n* -s **:** one who rides a velocipede

ve·loc·i·tize \və'läsə,tīz\ *vt* -ED/-ING/-S [*velocity* + *-ize*] **:** to cause (an automobile driver) to misjudge or become unaware of true speed or to become drowsy as a result of prolonged traveling at a high speed (as on an open highway)

ve·loc·i·ty \və'läsəd·ē, -ətē, -i\ *n* -ES [MF *velocité*, fr. L *velocitat-*, *velocitas*, fr. *veloc-*, *velox* quick + *-itat-*, *-itas* -ity; akin to L *veles* light-armed foot soldier, *vehere* to carry, convey — more at WAY] **1 :** quickness of motion **:** SWIFTNESS, SPEED, CELERITY, RAPIDITY — used chiefly of inanimate things ⟨the ~ of a bullet⟩ ⟨the ~ of flow of water⟩ ⟨~ of a train⟩ ⟨the ~ of sound⟩ **2 a** (1) **:** time rate of linear motion in a given direction **:** a vector quantity equal to speed in a particular direction and relative to a stated frame of reference — compare SPEED 2b (2) **:** ANGULAR VELOCITY **b :** the rate at which a chemical reaction progresses **3 :** rate of occurrence or action **:** RAPIDITY ⟨*velocities* of inhibition of bacterial growth by sulfonamide —*Jour. Amer. Med. Assoc.*⟩ ⟨if the blood vessels were in a dilated condition the ~ of heat transfer was reduced —F.A.Geldard⟩ ⟨a book having a high sales ~⟩ **:** rate of turnover ⟨~ of money⟩

velocity function *n* **:** the distribution of the velocities of the stars in a given region of space

velocity head *n* **:** the vertical distance through which a liquid would have to fall to attain a given velocity

velocity microphone *n* **:** a microphone (as the ribbon microphone) whose very light and flexible diaphragm follows almost without phase lag the air movements in the sound waves that actuate it

velocity modulation *n* **:** modification of the velocity of a stream of electrons by imparting alternate accelerations and decelerations to the electrons in such a way that they are caused to bunch together with the result that each bunch causes a cycle of current as it passes an output electrode

velocity of circulation : the average number of times that a unit of currency circulates during a given period of time **:** the rate of turnover of money

velocity of escape : a velocity that if attained by a moving body (as a rocket) would enable it to escape from the gravitational field of the earth or a celestial body and move outward in space ⟨the ability of a celestial body to retain an atmosphere around it depends on the *velocity of escape* at its surface —R. H.Baker⟩ ⟨this critical speed of seven miles a second is known as the earth's *velocity of escape* —P.A.Moore⟩

velocity of light : a fundamental constant that represents the speed of electromagnetic radiation in a vacuum and equals approximately 2.9979×10^{10} centimeters per second

velocity potential *n* **:** the scalar quantity whose negative gradient equals the velocity in the case of irrotational flow of a fluid

velocity ratio *n* **:** the ratio of the distance through which any part of a machine moves to that through which the driving part moves during the same time

velocity stage *n* **:** the stage in the process of expansion and of energy transformation in which there is no pressure drop and in which the velocity of steam flow in a steam turbine decreases the kinetic energy of the steam being imparted to the moving blades — compare PRESSURE STAGE

ve·lo·drome \'vēlə,drōm, 'vel-\ *n* -s [F *vélodrome*, fr. *vélo* velo + *-drome*] **:** a building containing a track designed for cycling

Ve·lom·e·ter \və'lämәd·ə(r)\ *trademark* — used for a meter for measuring the velocity of air

velos *pl of* VELO

ve·lour *or* **ve·lours** \və'lů(ə)r, -ů(ə)\ *n, pl* **velours** \-ů(ə)r(z), -ů(ə)(z)\ *often attrib* [F *velours* velvet, velour, fr. MF *velours*, *velour* — more at VELURE] **1 :** any of various fabrics with a pile or napped surface resembling velvet made usu. of cotton, rayon, silk, or wool and used in heavy weights for upholstery and curtains and in light weights for coats and jackets **2 :** a fur felt usu. of rabbit, hare, beaver, or nutria finished with a long velvety nap and used esp. for hats

ve·lou·té \və,lü'tā\ *also* **velouté sauce** *n* -s [F *velouté*, lit., velvety, fr. MF, fr. *velours* velvet] **:** a white sauce made of chicken or veal stock and cream and thickened with butter and flour — compare BÉCHAMEL, POULETTE

velt-marshal \'felt+,-\ *n* [part trans., part modif. (influenced by obs. D *velt* field, fr. MD) of G *feldmarschall* (trans. of F *maréchal de camp*), fr. *feld* field (fr. OHG) + *marschall* marshal, fr. OHG *marahscalc* — more at VELD, MARSHAL] **:** FIELD MARSHAL

ve·lum \'vēləm\ *n, pl* **ve·la** \-lə\ [NL, fr. L, covering, curtain, veil] **:** a membrane or membranous part likened to a veil or curtain: as **a :** SOFT PALATE **b :** an annular membrane projecting inward from the margin of the umbrella in hydromedusans and a few other jellyfishes **c :** a delicate membranelle bordering the mouth of various infusorians **d** (1) **:** PARTIAL VEIL (2) **:** UNIVERSAL VEIL **e :** the thin membrane that envelops a sporocarp in plants of the genus *Isoetes* **f :** a larval swimming organ that is esp. well developed in the later larval stages of many marine gastropods but occurs also in those of many lamellibranchs, that is developed from the preoral ciliate ring of the trochophore with the ring of cilia becoming raised on a more or less prominent and contractile collar-shaped ridge which in typical cases is produced into large lateral lobes bordered with long cilia, and that prob. serves also for respiration

ve·lu·men \və'lümən\ *n, pl* **velumi·na** \-mənə\ [L, fleece; prob. akin to L *vellere* to pluck, pull — more at VULNERABLE] **:** the velvety covering of various parts of plants or animals

velure *n* -s [modif. (influenced by *-ure*) of MF *velours*, *velour*, fr. OF *velous*, *velos*, fr. L *villosus* hairy, shaggy, fr. *villus* hair + *-osus* -ose — more at VELVET] *obs* **:** velvet or a fabric resembling it

ve·lu·ti·na \,velə'tīnə\ *n* [NL, fr. fem. of *velutinus* velutinous] **1** *cap* **:** a genus of marine gastropods related to the moon shells but having a shell with few whorls and a thick periostracum **2** -s **:** any member of the genus *Velutina*

ve·lu·ti·nous \və'lütᵊnəs\ *adj* [NL *velutinus*, fr. ML *velutum* velvet (prob. fr. OIt *velluto* shaggy, fr. — assumed — VL *villutus*) + L *-inus* -ine] **:** covered with a fine and dense silky pubescence **:** VELVETY

vel·ver·et \¦velvə¦ret\ *n* -s [alter. of ¹*velvet*] **:** a velveteen often having printed designs

¹vel·vet \'velvət, *usu* -əd·+V\ *n* -s [ME *veluet*, *velvet*, fr. MF *velu* shaggy (fr. — assumed —VL *villutus*, fr. L *villus* shaggy hair) + ME *-et*; akin to L *vellus* fleece — more at WOOL] **1 :** a clothing and upholstery fabric in a wide range of constructions and weights made of silk, rayon, cotton, nylon, or wool and characterized by a short soft dense pile produced by weaving into a single cloth an extra warp which is looped over wires and later cut or by weaving a double cloth with an extra warp connecting the two fabrics which are later cut apart — see UNCUT VELVET **2 a :** something like or suggesting velvet (as in softness or luster) **b :** a characteristic of velvet: as (1) **:** SOFTNESS ⟨the stars are studded in the warm intimate ~ of the night —Norman Mailer⟩ (2) **:** SMOOTHNESS ⟨fine old cognac loses its ~ when chilled —Jerry Thomas⟩ **3 :** the soft and highly vascular hairy skin that envelops and nourishes the antlers of deer during their rapid growth but later peels off or is rubbed off by the animal **4 a :** the cash or chips a player is ahead in a gambling game **:** WINNINGS **b :** a profit or gain esp. when beyond ordinary expectation ⟨the rest of the collection . . . would cost him nothing; whatever he could sell it for would be ~ —S.N.Behrman⟩ ⟨if one of them is real lucky and has the breaks and finally gets to be well known and makes some money, well, it's so much ~ then —Louis Armstrong⟩ **5 :** a drink that is half champagne and half porter — compare BLACK VELVET 2 **6 :** VELVET SPONGE — **on velvet 1 :** in the position of having or operating with money previously won (as in gambling or speculating) **2 :** in an easy, safe, prosperous, or otherwise desirable position ⟨we were *on velvet* financially —J.C.Snaith⟩

²velvet \"\ *adj* **1 :** made of or covered with velvet; *sometimes* **:** clad in velvet **2 :** resembling or suggesting velvet **:** VELVETY ⟨the callous soles of the passersby made the merest ~ shuffling —William Beebe⟩ ⟨the horse had a ~ gait —Edna Ferber⟩ ⟨the apple-green twilight deepened into emerald and then into a ~ darkness —John Buchan⟩ ⟨~ lawns⟩

³velvet \"\ *vt* -ED/-ING/-S [ME, fr. *velvet*, n.] **:** to make like or cover with velvet ⟨bald mountains that ~ their own sides with shadows —*New Republic*⟩

velvet ant *n* **:** any of various solitary fossorial wasps that constitute the family Mutillidae, have a wingless female and a body usu. covered with fine soft hair often of bright red or some other conspicuous color, are able to sting, in many cases are parasitic in the nests of bees or other hymenopterous insects and in such cases feed while young on the larvae of the host

velvet ash *n* **:** a forest tree (*Fraxinus velutina*) of New Mexico and Arizona

velvet bean *n* **1 :** an annual legume (*Stizolobium deeringianum* syn. *Mucuna deeringiana*) that is related to the cowage and cultivated esp. in the southern U. S. for green manure and grazing **2 :** the seed of the velvet bean which is often used as cattle and hog feed — called also *Florida velvet bean*

velvet bean caterpillar *n* **:** a caterpillar that is the larva of a noctuid moth (*Anticarsia gemmatilis*) and feeds on velvet beans, soybeans, and other leguminous crops in southern U. S.

velvet bent *n* **:** DOG BENT

velvetbreast \'==,=\ *n* -s **:** AMERICAN MERGANSER

velvet brown *n* **:** BURNT UMBER 2

velvet bur *n* **:** a tropical American perennial herb (*Priva lappulacea*) of the family Verbenaceae whose fruiting calyx is beset with small hooked bristles

velvet carpet *or* **velvet rug** *n* **:** a carpet or rug having a cut pile; *esp* **:** TAPESTRY VELVET CARPET

velvet crab *n* **:** a small stoutly built Australian spider crab (*Paratymolus latipes quadridentata*) that is densely covered with short velvety hairs

velvet dock *n* **1 :** a common mullein (*Verbascum thapsus*) **2 :** ELECAMPANE

velveted *adj* **:** covered with velvet **:** having the texture of velvet **:** made to resemble velvet (as in softness or smoothness)

vel·vet·een \¦velvə¦tēn\ *n* -s *often attrib* [¹*velvet* + *-een*] **1 :** a clothing fabric usu. of cotton in twill or plain weaves made with a short close weft pile in imitation of velvet **2 velveteens** *pl* **:** clothes made of velveteen; *esp* **:** trousers made of it

velvet fish *n* **:** any of various Australian fishes having a velvety skin; *esp* **:** a fish (*Aploactis milesii*) related to the scorpion fishes

velvet flower *n* **:** SALPIGLOSSIS 2

velvet glove *n* **:** superficial gentleness and courtesy masking a strong and unyielding will or determination ⟨the communists were on the . . . Peninsula only six months in any force, so the people did not have a chance to feel the iron beneath their *velvet glove* —Darrell Berrigan⟩

velvet grass *n* **:** a tall European grass (*Holcus lanatus*) having a velvety stem, naturalized in the U. S., and used for forage

velvet green *n* **:** a moderate olive green that is yellower, lighter, and stronger than cypress green, greener and stronger than holly green (sense 2), and greener, lighter, and stronger than Lincoln green

velvet groundsel *n* **:** CALIFORNIA GERANIUM

velvet guard *n, obs* **:** velvet trimming or one wearing it

vel·vet·i·ness \'velvəd·ēnəs\ *n* -ES **:** quality of velvet **:** velvety appearance, feeling, or taste

velveting *pres part of* VELVET

velvetleaf \'==,=\ *n* **:** any of various plants that have soft velvety leaves: as **a :** a tropical vine (*Cissampelos pareira*) with roots that constitute the false pareira of commerce **b :** INDIAN MALLOW 1 **c :** TREE MALLOW **d :** MULLEIN

velvet loom *n* **1 :** a loom for weaving velvet fabric **2 :** a loom for weaving velvet carpet

velvet moss *n* **:** a northern European lichen (*Gyrophora murina*) used in dyeing

velvet osier *n* **:** OSIER 1a

velvet plant *n* **1 :** GREAT MULLEIN **2** *also* **velvet tree :** a Javanese foliage plant (*Gynura aurantiaca*) with handsome velvety leaves with violet-purple hairs

velvets *pl of* VELVET, *pres 3d sing of* VELVET

velvet scoter *or* **velvet duck** *n* **1 :** a large scoter (*Melanitta fusca*) of northern Europe and Asia closely resembling the white-winged scoter of America **2 :** WHITE-WINGED SCOTER

velvetseed \'==,=\ *n* **1 :** a shrub or small tree (*Guettarda elliptica*) of the family Rubiaceae of the West Indies and Florida with yellowish white flowers and black fruit **2 :** SEVEN-YEAR APPLE 1

velvet shell *n* **:** a marine gastropod of *Velutina* or a related genus

velvet sponge *n* **:** a fine soft commercial sponge (*Hippiospongia equina meandriformis*) typically of flat rounded form occurring in the Gulf of Mexico and off the West Indies

velvet sumac *n* **:** STAGHORN SUMAC

velvet tamarind *n* **:** a western African tree (*Dialium guineënse*) of the family Leguminosae with velvety black pods containing an acid pulp that is chewed to relieve thirst or macerated in water to form a beverage — called also *black tamarind*

velvet violet *n* **:** PANSY VIOLET 1

velvetweed \'==,=\ *n* **:** INDIAN MALLOW

velvet willow *n* **:** SITKA WILLOW

vel·vety \'velvəd·ē, -ətē, -i\ *adj* **1 :** having the character of velvet **:** soft and smooth (as in appearance or to the sight, hearing, touch) ⟨the shadows in the valleys and gorges of ~ blackness —Bram Stoker⟩ ⟨his tone is not as ~ as that of some other cellists —*N.Y. Times*⟩ ⟨how I loved the ~ highway dust —W.A.White⟩ **2 a :** smooth to the taste **:** MILD ⟨~ rum⟩ **b :** giving a contact like that of velvet ⟨the ~ touch of a piano player⟩

VEM *abbr* vasoexcitor material

ven \'ven\ *chiefly dial var of* FEN

ven- *or* **veni-** *or* **veno-** *comb form* [L *vena*] **1 :** vein ⟨*venipuncture*⟩ ⟨*venoclysis*⟩ ⟨*venisection*⟩ **2 :** of or relating to the vena cava **:** caval and ⟨*venoatrial*⟩

ven *abbr, often cap* venerable

ve·na \'vēnə\ *n, pl* **ve·nae** \-,nē, -,nī\ [ME, fr. L] **:** VEIN

ve·na ca·va \,vēnə'kāvə\ *n, pl* **ve·nae ca·vae** \,vēnē'kā(,)vē\ [NL, fr. L, hollow vein] **:** one of the large veins by which in air-breathing vertebrates the blood is returned to the right atrium of the heart, which develop in part from and replace in function the cardinal veins and ducts of Cuvier of the embryo, and which commonly occur as two anterior venae cavae returning blood from the head and forelimbs and one posterior vena cava returning blood from the posterior parts of the body and the viscera

vena co·mes \-'kō,mēz, -mes\ *n, pl* **venae com·i·tes** \-'kämə,tēz, -tās\ [NL, companion vein] **:** a vein accompanying an artery

vena con·trac·ta \-kən'traktə\ *n, pl* **venae contrac·tae** \-k,tē, -,tī\ [NL, contracted vein] **:** any of the contracted parts of minimum cross section of a jet of fluid discharging from an orifice; *esp* **:** the one nearest the orifice

venae vor·ti·co·sae \-,vȯ(r)d·ə'kō,sē, -,sī\ *n pl* [NL, lit., eddying veins] **:** the veins of the outer layer of the choroid coat of the eye

¹ve·nal \'vēnᵊl\ *adj* [L *vena* + E *-al*] *archaic* **:** VENOUS

²venal \"\ *adj* [L *venalis*, fr. *venus*, *venum* sale + *-alis* -al; akin to Gk *ōnos* price, Skt *vasna*] **1 :** capable of being bought or obtained for money or other valuable consideration **:** made matter of trade or barter **:** PURCHASABLE; *esp* **:** open to corrupt influence and esp. bribery ⟨a ~ legislator⟩ ⟨~ services⟩ ⟨~ votes⟩ **2 :** originating in, characterized by, or associated with corrupt bargaining ⟨a ~ throne⟩ ⟨a ~ arrangement with the police⟩

ve·nal·i·ty \vē'naləd·ē, və'-, -lətē, -i\ *n* -ES [F or LL; F *venalité*, fr. LL *venalitat-*, *venalitas*, fr. L *venalis* venal + *-itat-*, *-itas* -ity] **:** the quality or state of being venal esp. in the prostitution of talents, offices, or services for reward **:** willingness to be influenced improperly (as by bribery or corrupt measures) ⟨the ~ of a judge⟩

ve·nal·ly \'vēnəlē, -li\ *adv* [²*venal* + *-ly*] **:** in a venal manner **:** so as to be venal

ve·nal·ness *n* -ES **:** VENALITY

ve·nan·tes \və'nan,(,)tēz\ *n pl, cap* [NL, fr. L *venant-*, *venans*, pres. part. of *venari* to hunt] *in some classifications* **:** a group comprising the hunting spiders

vena sal·va·tel·la \-,salvə'telə\ *n, pl* **venae salvatel·lae** \-e(,)lē,-,lī\ [NL, lit., little saver vein; fr. the former belief that bleeding from it saved one from disease] **:** a superficial vein on the back of the hand coming from the little finger

ve·nat·ic \və'nad·ik, vē'-\ *also* **ve·nat·i·cal** \-d·əkəl\ *adj* [*venatic* fr. L *venaticus*, fr. *venatus* (past part. of *venari* to hunt) + *-icus* -ic; *venatical* fr. L *venaticus* + E *-al* — more at VENISON] **1 :** of, relating to, or used in hunting ⟨the ~ sport⟩ ⟨~ equipment⟩ **2 :** fond of or living by hunting ⟨the ~ tribes of ancient Europe⟩ — **ve·nat·i·cal·ly** \-k(ə)lē\ *adv*

¹ve·na·tion \vē'nāshən, və'-\ *n* -s [L *venation-*, *venatio*, fr. *venatus* (past part.) + *-ion-*, *-io* -ion] *archaic* **:** HUNTING

²venation \"\ *n* -s [*ven-* + *-ation*] **:** an arrangement or system of veins ⟨the ~ of the hand⟩: as **a :** the arrangement of veins in the tissue of a leaf blade **b :** the arrangement of veins in the wing of an insect

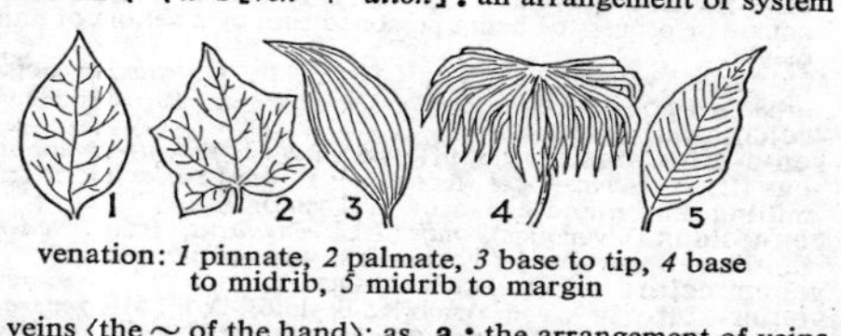

venation: *1* pinnate, *2* palmate, *3* base to tip, *4* base to midrib, *5* midrib to margin

ve·na·tion·al \-shənᵊl, -shnəl\ *adj* [²*venation* + *-al*] **:** of or relating to venation

ven·a·to·ri·al \¦venə¦tōrēəl, -tȯr-\ *or* **ven·a·to·ry** \'==,tōrē, -tȯrē, -ri\ *adj* [*venatorial* fr. L *venatorius* venatic (fr. *venatus*, past part. + *-orius* -ory) + E *-al*; *venatory* fr. L *venatorius*] **:** VENATIC

ven·co·la \veŋkələ\ *n* -s [AmerSp] **:** QUIRA

¹vend \'vend\ *vb* -ED/-ING/-S [L *vendere*, contr. of *venumdere*, fr. *venum* sale + *-dere* (fr. *dare* to give) — more at VENAL, DATE] *vi* **:** to become an object of commerce **:** change hands through sale ⟨a product that should ~ well⟩; *also* **:** to engage in selling ⟨merchants planning to ~ abroad⟩ ~ *vt* **1 a :** to transfer to another for a pecuniary equivalent ⟨planned to ~ his household goods **b :** to engage in the sale of often by hawking or peddling ⟨~*ed* fruit on that corner for many years⟩ ⟨developed a machine for ~*ing* hot coffee⟩ **2 :** to put forth in or as a statement **:** utter publicly **:** publish abroad ⟨uttering such comments as ought not to have been ~*ed* from a pulpit⟩

²vend \"\ *n* -s *Brit* **:** an occasion or act of vending **:** SALE; *esp* **:** the total sales of a colliery esp. as restricted by annual agreement

³vend \"\ *or* **ve·ned** \və'ned\ *n, pl* **vends** \-n(d)z\ *or* **ve·ne·di** \və'nedē\ *cap* [*vend* alter. (influenced by L *Venedi* Vends) of ²*wend*; *vened* fr. L *Venedi*, *Veneti*, pl., Vends] **:** WEND

ven·da \'vendə\ *n, pl* **venda** *or* **vendas** *usu cap* **1 a :** a people of the northern Transvaal, Africa **b :** a member of such people **2 :** a Bantu language of the Venda people

ven·dace \'vendəs *also* -,dās\ *n, pl* **vendace** *also* **vendaces** [NL *vandesius*, fr. MF *vandoise*, prob. of Celt origin; akin to OIr *find* white — more at FINNOCK] **:** a whitefish (*Coregonus vandesius*) native to various lakes of Scotland and England

ven·dage \'vendij\ *n* -s [ME — more at VINTAGE] **:** the harvesting or harvest time of grapes **:** VINTAGE

ven·da·val \,vendə'val, -väl\ *n* -s [Sp, fr. F *vent d'aval* westerly wind, lit., downstream wind, fr. *vent* wind (fr. L *ventus*) + *d'* of (contr. of *de*, fr. L) + *aval* downstream, downward — more at WIND, DE-, AVALE] **1 :** a gusty southwest wind occurring chiefly in winter about the strait of Gibraltar **2 :** an autumnal thundersquall on the coast of Mexico

¹ven·de·an \(')ven¦dēən\ *adj, usu cap* [La *Vendée*, region in western France + E *-an*] **:** of or relating to La Vendée, France

²vendean \"\ *n* -s *usu cap* **:** one of the people of La Vendée; *esp* **:** one of those taking part in the Wars of the Vendée during the French Revolution

vend·ee \(')ven¦dē\ *n* -s [¹*vend* + *-ee*] **:** one to whom a thing is sold **:** BUYER, PURCHASER

vend·er \'vendə(r)\ *n* -s [by alter.] **:** VENDOR

ven·det·ta \ven'ded·ə, -etə\ *n* -s [It, lit., revenge, fr. L *vindicta*, fr. *vindicare* to avenge — more at VINDICATE] **1 :** BLOOD FEUD ⟨should have disappeared from civilized society along with ~*s* and black magic —Lucius Garvin⟩ **2 :** a prolonged feud marked by bitter hostility ⟨waging a literary ~ of his own —C. I.Glicksberg⟩ ⟨would neither conduct partisan ~*s* nor indulge in political patronage —*Newsweek*⟩

ven·deuse \(')vä¦də(r)z, -dəz, 'vän¦düz, *F* vändœ̄z\ *n* -s [F, fem. of *vendeur* salesman — more at VENDOR] **:** SALESWOMAN

vend·ibil·i·ty \,vendə'biləd·ē\ *n* -ES **:** the quality or state of being vendible

¹vend·ible *or* **vend·able** \'=dəbəl\ *adj* [*vendible* fr. ME, fr. L *vendibilis*, fr. *vendere* to sell + *-ibilis* -ible; *vendable* fr. ME, fr. MF, fr. *vendre* to sell (fr. L *vendere*) + *-able* — more at VEND] **1 :** available or suitable for sale ⟨~ produce⟩ **:** of a kind to command a cash return ⟨~ beauty⟩ **2** *obs* **:** open to corrupt bargaining **:** VENAL **3 :** generally acceptable **:** passing as current

²vendible \"\ *n* -s **:** a vendible article — usu. used in pl.

vending *pres part of* VEND

vending machine *n* **:** a slot machine for vending merchandise mechanically

ven·di·tion \ven'dishən\ *n* -s [L *vendition-*, *venditio*, fr. *venditus* (past part. of *vendere* to sell) + *-ion-*, *-io* -ion] **:** the act of selling **:** SALE

ven·dor \'vendə(r); (')ven¦dȯ(ə)r, -ȯ(ə)\ *n* -s [MF *vendeor*, *vendeur*, fr. *vendre* to sell (fr. L *vendere*) + *-eor*, *-eur* -or] **:** one that offers goods for sale esp. habitually or as a means of liveli-

hood : SELLER: **a** (1) : an independent seller in a small way of business; *esp* : PEDDLER (2) : a person that hawks and sells merchandise (as refreshments, programs, or souvenirs) to patrons of a public gathering **b** : VENDING MACHINE

vendor's lien *n* : an implied lien given in equity to a vendor of lands for unpaid purchase money as against the vendee and volunteers under him

vendor's share *n* : a security taken instead of cash payment by one transferring property to a corporation

vends *pres 3d sing of* VEND, *pl of* VEND

ven·due \(ˈ)ven¦d(y)ü, (ˈ)van-, (ˈ)vän-\ *n* -s [obs. F, fr. MF, fr. *vendu*, past part. of *vendre* to sell] : a public sale at which goods are sold to the highest bidder : AUCTION

vendue crier *or* **vendue master** *n* : AUCTIONEER

vened *usu cap, var of* VEND

¹**ve·neer** \vəˈni(ə)r, -iə\ *n* -s [G *furnier*, fr. *furnieren* to veneer] **1 a** : a thin sheet of wood cut or sawed from a log and adapted for adhesion to a smooth surface (as of wood) ⟨cut the log into ~*s*⟩: as (1) : a layer of wood of superior value or excellent grain for overlaying an inferior wood (as in cabinetmaking) usu. by gluing (2) : any one of the thin layers that are glued or otherwise bonded together to form plywood **b** : material (as sheets of wood) for veneering; *sometimes* : thin highly glazed colored paperboard for such use **2** : something felt to resemble or functioning in the manner of a veneer of wood esp. in forming a superficial layer: as **a** : a superficial or meretricious show : GLOSS **b** : a protective or ornamental facing (as of brick or stone) for a wall **c** (1) : a thin but extensive covering of an older geologic formation or surface ⟨a ~ of till⟩ (2) : a weathered or otherwise altered surficial part of a rock ⟨an indurated ~⟩

²**veneer** \"\ *vt* -ED/-ING/-S [earlier *fineer*, fr. G *furnieren*, fr. F *fournir* to furnish, fr. MF *furnir, fournir* to complete, equip — more at FURNISH] **1 a** : to overlay or plate (as a common sort of wood) with a thin layer of finer wood for outer finish or decoration ⟨~ gumwood furniture with mahogany⟩; *broadly* : to face with a material giving a superior surface ⟨a wall ~*ed* with brick⟩ **b** : to glue together (thin pieces of wood) into plywood **2** : to cover like a veneer of wood : give an attractive surface appearance to; *esp* : to conceal (as a defect of character) under a superficial and specious attractiveness

ve·neer·er \vəˈnirə(r)\ *n* -s : one that veneers

veneer graft *n* : a plant graft made by chamfering the surfaces of scion and stock and applying the one to the other

ve·neer·ing \-riŋ, -rēŋ\ *n* -s [¹*veneer* + *-ing*] **1** : VENEER 1b **2** : a surface covered by veneer : a veneered surface

veneer moth *n* : any of various small moths of the family Pyralididae with mottled colors that suggest those of some veneering

¹**ven·e·nate** \ˈvenə,nāt\ *vb* -ED/-ING/-S [L *venenatus*, past part of *venenare* to poison, fr. *venenum* poison — more at VENOM] *vt* : POISON; *specif* : to inject a toxic substance into ⟨blood-sucking insects that ~ the wounds they form⟩ ~ *vi* : to use a toxic substance in preying or feeding ⟨*venenating* arthropods⟩

²**ven·e·nate** \-.nət, -,nāt\ *adj* [L *venenatus*, past part. of *venenare*] : POISONED, POISONOUS ⟨a ~ zone surrounding the primary lesion in the leaf⟩

ven·e·na·tion \,==ˈnāshən\ *n* -s [L *venenatus* + E *-ion*] : the course or process of being poisoned esp. by a venom of animal origin

¹**ve·nene** \vəˈnēn, veˈn-\ *adj* [irreg. fr. L *venenum* poison] *archaic* : POISONOUS

²**venene** *var of* VENIN

ven·e·nif·er·ous \¦venə¦nif(ə)rəs\ *adj* [L *venenifer* veneniferous (fr. *venenum* + *-fer* -ferous) + E *-ous*] : bearing or transmitting poison and esp. a natural venom

ven·e·nous \ˈvenənəs\ *adj* [LL *venenosus*, fr. L *venenum* poison + *-osus* -ose] : POISONOUS, VENOMOUS

venepuncture *var of* VENIPUNCTURE

ven·er·abil·i·ty \,ven(ə)rəˈbiləd·ē, -lətē, -i\ *n* [ML *venerabilitas*, fr. L *venerabilis* venerable + *-itas* -ity] : the quality or state of being venerable

¹**ven·er·able** \ˈvenər(ə)bəl, -nrəb-\ *adj* [ME, fr. L *venerabilis*, fr. *venerari* to venerate + *-abilis* -able] **1** : deserving to be venerated : worthy of honor and respect usu. by reason of prolonged testing (as of character or in office) ⟨a ~ judge⟩ — used as a title or in a respectful form of address to an archdeacon of a church of the Anglican Communion or a person recognized by Roman Catholics as having attained the lowest of three degrees of sanctity **2** : made sacred by religious, historic, or other associations : meriting to be regarded with awe and treated with reverence ⟨the ~ walls of a church⟩ ⟨~ relics of our forefathers⟩ ⟨the ~ silence of the library —Ernst Krenek⟩ **3 a** : calling forth respect through age, character, and attainments ⟨~ sages⟩ ⟨a ~ leader⟩; *broadly* : conveying an impression of aged goodness and benevolence ⟨his ruddy features and snow-white hair gave him a ~ appearance⟩ **b** : impressive by reason of age ⟨under ~ pines⟩ ⟨that ~ coat had sheltered three generations⟩ **4** *obs* : showing or giving deep respect : REVERENTIAL **syn** see OLD

²**venerable** \"\ *n* -s : a venerable individual; *esp* : one entitled (as by position) to the title of venerable

ven·er·able·ness *n* -ES : VENERABILITY

ven·er·ably \-blē, -li\ *adv* : in a venerable manner : so as to be venerable

ven·er·a·cea \,venəˈrāshēə\ *n pl, cap* [NL, fr. *Vener-, Venus*, included genus + *-acea*] : a suborder of Eulamellibranchia comprising bivalve mollusks with the foot compressed, the siphons generally short, and both adductor muscles present and including the families Veneridae and Petricolidae — **ven·er·a·cean** \¦==¦āshən\ *adj or n* — **ven·er·a·ceous** \-shəs\ *adj*

ven·er·ate \ˈvenə,rāt, *usu* -ād·+V\ *vt* -ED/-ING/-S [L *veneratus*, past part. of *venerari* to venerate — more at WIN] : to regard with reverential respect or with admiration and deference as being hallowed or as having nobility esp. if accompanied with age : REVERE ⟨we ~ noble parents⟩ ⟨do not know a man more to be *venerated* for uprightness of heart and loftiness of genius —Sir Walter Scott⟩ **syn** see REVERE

ven·er·a·tion \,==ˈrāshən\ *n* -s [ME *veneracion*, fr. L *veneration-, veneratio*, fr. *veneratus* (past part. of *venerari*) + *-ion-, -io* -ion] **1** : a feeling of respect mingled with awe excited by the dignity, wisdom, or superiority of a person, by sacredness of character, by consecrated state, or by hallowed association ⟨the tremendous ~ in which art and artists have been held —Huntington Hartford⟩ ⟨regarded their teachers and institutions with the deepest ~⟩ **2 a** : the act of venerating esp. by the expressing of deeply revent feeling — compare ADORATION **b** : the act of admiring humbly and respectfully **3** : the condition of one that is venerated ⟨hoping to attain ~ from his subjects⟩ **4** : the phrenologic faculty of reverence — **ven·er·a·tion·al** \¦==¦rāshənᵊl, -shnəl\ *adj*

ven·er·a·tor \ˈ==,rād·ə(r), -ātə-\ *n* -s [L, fr. *veneratus* (past part.) + *-or*] : one that venerates ⟨a ~ of tradition⟩

ve·ne·re·al \vəˈnirēəl\ *adj* [ME *venereall*e, fr. L *venereus* venereal (fr. *vener-, venus* love, sexual desire) + ME *-alle, -al* -al — more at WIN] **1 a** : of or relating to sexual pleasure or indulgence : of, relating to, or preoccupied with sexual intercourse **b** *obs, of persons* : inclined to be lascivious **2** : adapted or likely to excite sexual desire : APHRODISIAC **3 a** : resulting from or contracted during sexual intercourse ⟨a ~ inflammation⟩ ⟨~ transmission of disease⟩ ⟨~ infections⟩ **b** (1) : of or relating to venereal disease ⟨a ~ clinic⟩ ⟨a high ~ rate⟩ ⟨newer ~ treatments⟩ (2) : affected with venereal disease ⟨the ~ patient⟩ **c** : occurring on or affecting the genital organs ⟨a ~ sarcoma⟩

venereal disease *n* : a contagious disease that is typically acquired in sexual intercourse ⟨cloacitis of fowls is a *venereal disease*⟩ — compare CHANCROID, GONORRHEA, GRANULOMA INGUINALE, LYMPHGRANULOMA, SYPHILIS

venereal wart *n* : CONDYLOMA

ve·ne·re·an \-rēən\ *adj* [L *venereus* venerean (fr. *Vener-, Venus*, Roman goddess of love, 2d planet from the sun — fr. *vener-, venus* love, sexual desire — + *-eus* -eous) + E *-an*] **1** : of or relating to the ancient goddess Venus or to the planet Venus : VENUSIAN ⟨the strange ~ landscape⟩ **2** *obs* : VENEREAL

ve·ne·re·ol·o·gist \və,nirēˈäləjəst\ *n* -s [*venereology* + *-ist*] : a physician specializing in venereal diseases

ve·ne·re·ol·o·gy \-jē\ *or* **ven·er·ol·o·gy** \,venəˈräləjē\ *n* -ES [*venereology* ISV *venereal* + *-o-* + *-logy*; *venerology* ISV *venereal* venereal (fr. ML *veneralis*, fr. L *vener-, venus* love, sexual desire + *-alis* -al) + *-o-* + *-logy*] : a branch of medical science concerned with venereal diseases

ve·ne·re·ous \vəˈnirēəs\ *adj* [L *venereus*] : VENEREAL; *esp* : LASCIVIOUS

ven·er·er \ˈvenərə(r)\ *n* -s [¹*venery* + *-er*] : HUNTER 1

veneres *pl of* VENUS

¹**venerian** *adj* [ME *venerien*, fr. MF, fr. L *venerius, venereus* venerean + MF *-en* -an] *obs* : VENEREAN

²**ve·ne·ri·an** \vəˈnirēən\ *n* -s *usu cap* [L *Vener-, Venus*, 2d planet from the sun + E *-an*] : VENUSIAN 2

ve·ner·i·dae \vəˈnerə,dē\ *n pl, cap* [NL, fr. *Vener-, Venus*, type genus + *-idae*] : a family of bivalve mollusks (order Eulamellibranchia) mostly having a solid equivalve shell, short siphons, and a narrow foot and sometimes a strikingly sculptured shell

ve·ner·i·form \-rə,fȯrm\ *adj* [NL *Vener-, Venus* + E *-iform*] : resembling a mollusk of the family Veneridae

¹**ven·ery** \ˈvenərē, -ri\ *n* -ES [ME *venerie*, fr. MF, fr. *vener* to hunt (fr. L *venari*) + *-ie* -y — more at VENISON] **1** : the activity or practice of hunting esp. when developed into or carried out as a highly stylized art (as during the middle ages in Europe) or when forming a professional craft **2** : animals that are hunted : GAME; *specif* : BEASTS OF VENERY

²**ven·ery** \" *sometimes* ˈvēn-\ *n* -ES [ME *venerie*, fr. ML *veneria*, fr. L *vener-, venus* love, sexual desire, venery + *-ia* -y — more at WIN] : sexual intercourse : COITUS; *often* : pursuit of or indulgence in sexual pleasures

ven·e·sect \ˈvenə,sekt, ,==ˈ=\ *vt* -ED/-ING/-S [back-formation fr. *venesection*] : to perform venesection on

ven·e·sec·tion *or* **ven·i·sec·tion** \,==ˈsekshən\ *n* [*venesection* fr. L *venae* (gen. of *vena* vein) + E *section*; *venisection* fr. *ven-* + *section*] : the operation of opening a vein for letting blood : PHLEBOTOMY

ven·e·ti \ˈvenə,tī\ *also* **ven·e·tes** \-ə,tēz\ *n pl, usu cap* [L] **1** : an ancient people in Gaul conquered by Caesar 56 B.C. **2** : an ancient people in northeastern Italy allied politically to the Romans

¹**ve·ne·tian** \vəˈnēshən *sometimes* -nish-\ *n* -s [alter. (influenced by L *Venetia*) of ME *venicien*, fr. MF, fr. ML *venetianus*, fr. *Venetia* Venice, city in northeastern Italy (fr. L, land of the Veneti in northern Italy) + L *-anus* -an] **1** *cap* **a** : a native or resident of Venice **b** : the Italian dialect of Venice **2** *or* **venetian cloth** [F *vénitienne*, fr. fem. of *vénitien* native of Venice, fr. MF *venicien*] **a** : a fine worsted fabric used esp. for suits, coats, or dresses and made in twill or satin weave with a napped or clear surface and a lustrous finish **b** : a lustrous sateen used esp. for linings **3** : VENETIAN BLIND

²**venetian** \"\ *adj, usu cap* [ML *venetianus*, fr. *Venetia* Venice + L *-anus* -an] : of or relating to Venice in Italy : of the kind or style typical of Venice

venetian arch *n, usu cap V* : a usu. pointed arch with a band wider at the peak than at the spring

venetian ball *n, usu cap V* : a ball of glass made decorative by colored patterns or by objects enclosed within its mass and used esp. as a toy or paperweight

venetian blind *n, sometimes cap V* : a blind (as for a window) made of numerous horizontal slats suspended one above another so that they may be set simultaneously at one of several angles permitting various degrees of overlapping or may be drawn together and raised

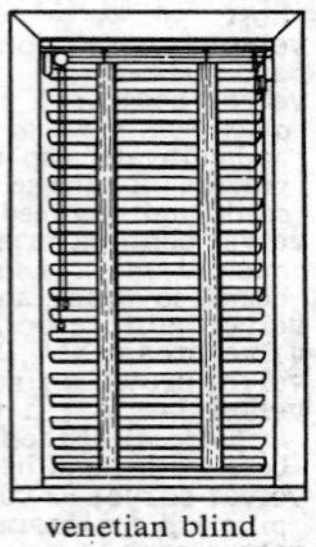

venetian blind

venetian blue *n, often cap V* : COBALT BLUE 2

venetian carpet *n, usu cap V* : an inexpensive carpet having a worsted warp which conceals the weft and a pattern commonly made up of simple stripes and used esp. formerly for passages and stairs

venetian chalk *n, usu cap V* : a white compact talc or steatite used esp. for marking on cloth

venetian dentil *n, usu cap V* : one of a series of cubical projections alternating with splayed surfaces that may be formed along the edge of a projecting band by cutting bevels at intervals to produce notches with the dentils between; *also* : the ornament or ornamentation so produced

venetian door *n, sometimes cap V* : a door with sidelights like those of a Palladian window

ve·ne·tianed \-nd\ *adj, sometimes cap* : having or furnished with venetian blinds

venetian glass *n, often cap V* **1** : a dainty delicate and artistic glassware made at Murano near Venice **2** : a decorative glass made by the combination of pieces of glass of different colors fused together and wrought into various ornamental patterns

venetian green *n, often cap V* : a moderate bluish green that is greener and darker than porcelain green and greener and duller than sea blue

venetian lake *n, often cap V* : CARMINE 2

venetian pearl *n, often cap V* : an imitation pearl made of solid glass

venetian pink *n, often cap V* : BLOSSOM 5

venetian point *n, often cap V* : needlepoint lace (as raised point or rose point) of Venetian origin

venetian red *n* **1** *usu cap V* **a** : an earthy hematite used as a pigment **b** : a synthetic iron oxide pigment that is made usu. by calcining copperas with lime and consists essentially of ferric oxide and calcium sulfate — compare INDIAN RED 1 **2** *often cap V* **a** : a strong reddish brown that is yellower and slightly lighter than Indian red and yellower, stronger, and very slightly darker than Morocco red — called also *Siena, Sierra* **b** : a moderate reddish brown that is yellower and deeper than mahogany (sense 5)

venetian rose *n, often cap V* : a moderate to deep red that is bluer than cadmium purple or burnt carmine

venetian scarlet *n, often cap V* : SCARLET 2b

venetian soap *n, usu cap V* : a soap made from olive oil — compare CASTILE

venetian sumac *n, usu cap V* : SMOKE TREE 1a

venetian swell *n, often cap V* : a swell organ with blinds patterned on venetian blinds closing the swell box

venetian turpentine *n, usu cap V* : VENICE TURPENTINE

venetian white *n, usu cap V* : a pigment consisting of a mixture of white lead and barium sulfate usu. in equal parts

venetian window *n, sometimes cap V* : PALLADIAN WINDOW

venetian yellow *n, often cap V* : AMBER YELLOW

¹**ve·net·ic** \vəˈned·¦ik, -et¦, ēk\ *adj, often cap* [L *veneticus*, fr. *Veneti* + L *-icus* -ic] : of or relating to the ancient Veneti of Italy or their language

²**venetic** \"\ *n* -s *usu cap* : the Italic language of the Venetic people known from a small body of inscriptions and formerly classified as Illyrian

ve·neur *R* vəˈnər, + *vowel* -ˈnər·; –*R* -ˈnə̄, + *vowel in a word following without pause* -ˈnər· *or* -ˈnə̄ *also* -ˈnər\ *n* -s [MF, fr. OF, hunter, fr. L *venator*, fr. *venatus* (past part. of *venari* to hunt) + *-or* — more at VENISON] : a person acting as superintendent of the chase and esp. of hounds in French medieval venery and being an important officer of the royal household

ven·e·zu·e·la \,venəz(ə)ˈwālə, -wēlə\ *adj, usu cap* [fr. *Venezuela*, republic of So. America] : of or from Venezuela : of the kind or style prevalent in Venezuela : VENEZUELAN

venezuela grass *n, usu cap V* : MOLASSES GRASS

¹**ven·e·zu·e·lan** \¦venəz(ə)¦wālən, -wēl-\ *adj, usu cap* [*Venezuela* + E *-an*] : of or relating to Venezuela or its people : VENEZUELA

²**venezuelan** \"\ *n* -s *cap* : a native or inhabitant of Venezuela

venge \ˈvenj\ *vb* -ED/-ING/-S [ME *vengen*, fr. OF *venger, vengier*] : AVENGE

venge·able *or* **veng·ible** \ˈvenjəbəl\ *adj* [*vengeable* fr. ME, fr. *vengen* to avenge + *-able*; *vengible* fr. *venge* + *-ible*] **1** *chiefly dial* **a** : able, apt, or of a kind to take vengeance **b** : MISCHIEVOUS, DESTRUCTIVE **2** *obs* : very great : TREMENDOUS, EXTRAORDINARY

ven·geance \ˈvenjən(t)s\ *n* -s [ME, fr. OF, fr. *venger, vengier* to avenge (fr. L *vindicare* to lay claim to, avenge) + *-ance* — more at VINDICATE] **1 a** : the taking of revenge : infliction of punishment in return for an injury or offense : retributive action ⟨to me belongeth ~ and recompense —Deut 32:35 (AV)⟩ **b** : a particular act or instance of such vengeance ⟨plagued with petty spites and ~*s*⟩ **2** *obs* : HARM, MISCHIEF, EVIL ⟨do no ~ to me —Shak.⟩ **3** *archaic* : a harsh or blasphemous utterance : CURSE, OATH, IMPRECATION ⟨a ~ on't —Shak.⟩ — usu. used with *with* — **with a vengeance** *adv* (*or adj*) **1** : in a markedly violent, forceful, or urgent manner ⟨the wind blew *with a vengeance*⟩ ⟨finally beat him *with a vengeance*⟩ **2** : in an abundant or excessive amount or to such a degree ⟨leading a double life *with a vengeance* —John McCarten⟩ ⟨this was understatement *with a vengeance*⟩

ven·geant \ˈvenjənt\ *adj* [ME *vengaunt*, fr. MF *vengant*, pres. part. of *venger* to avenge] : AVENGING

venge·ful \ˈvenjfəl\ *adj* [obs. E *venge* revenge (fr. E *venge*, v.) + E *-ful*] : REVENGEFUL: as **a** : seeking to avenge **b** : serving to gain vengeance **c** : caused by the desire to gain vengeance : inspired by desire to avenge **syn** see VINDICTIVE

venge·ful·ly \-fəlē\ *adv* : in a vengeful manner : so as to be vengeful : REVENGEFULLY

venge·ful·ness *n* -ES : the quality or state of being vengeful

veng·er \ˈvenjə(r)\ *n* -s [ME, modif. (influenced by *-er*) of MF *vengeor, vengeur*, fr. *venger* to avenge + *-eor, -eur* -or] : AVENGER

v–engine *cap V, also* **vee engine** \ˈvē-\ *n* : an internal-combustion engine the cylinders of which are arranged in two banks forming an acute angle

veni- — see VEN-

ve·nia ae·ta·tis \ˈvēnēəēˈtād·əs\ *n* [L, lit., privilege of age] : the privilege of age sometimes granted a minor under Roman or civil law, entitling him to the rights and liabilities of a person of full age, and resembling emancipation in modern law

ve·nial \ˈvēnēəl, -nyəl\ *adj* [ME, fr. OF, fr. LL *venialis*, fr. L *venia* indulgence, grace, privilege, pardon + *-alis* -al; akin to L *venus* love — more at WIN] **1 a** : of a kind that can be forgiven or remitted : not heinous nor damning — see VENIAL SIN **b** : meriting no particular censure or notice : minor or trivial in comparison with the whole in question : EXCUSABLE, INSIGNIFICANT ⟨the faults of this book . . . are few and ~ —Dudley Fitts⟩ ⟨the fastidious could carp at many minor slips . . . but they seem fairly ~ —R.H.Bowers⟩ **2** *obs* : of a kind to be permitted : ALLOWABLE, UNOBJECTIONABLE — **ve·nial·ly** \-əlē, -li\ *adv* — **ve·nial·ness** *n* -ES

venial sin *n* : a slight offense against divine law in less important matters of Roman Catholic belief or an offense in grave matters committed without reflection or full consent of the will — contrasted with *mortal sin*

¹**ven·ice** \ˈvenəs\ *adj, usu cap* [fr. *Venice*, Italy] : of or from the city of Venice, Italy : of the kind or style prevalent in Venice : VENETIAN

²**venice** \"\ *or* **venice blue** *n* -s *often cap V* : a light bluish green that is bluer and duller than Venice green or average turquoise green and greener and deeper than average aqua green (sense 1)

venice green *n, often cap V* : a light bluish green that is greener and deeper than average aqua green (sense 1), deeper and slightly bluer than robin's-egg blue (sense 2), and greener, stronger, and slightly darker than average turquoise green

venice red *n, often cap V* : BOLE 3

venice treacle *n, usu cap V* : a long-disused universal antidote or cure-all : THERIACA 1

venice turpentine *n, usu cap V* **1** : a yellowish or yellowish green viscous oleoresin from the European larch (*Larix decidua*) used chiefly for lithographic work, in sealing wax, and in varnishes — called also *larch turpentine, Venetian turpentine* **2** : a mixture of rosin and turpentine oil — called also *artificial Venice turpentine*

ve·nid·i·um \vəˈnidēəm\ *n* [NL, fr. *ven-* + *-idium*; prob. fr. the veined achenes] **1** *cap* : a genus of southern African annual or perennial tomentose herbs (family Compositae) that are used as ornamentals and have solitary chiefly yellow or creamy flower heads with involucral bracts in several rows **2** -s : any plant of the genus *Venidium*

ven·in \ˈvenən\ *also* **ven·ene** \ˈve,nēn\ *n* -s [*venin* fr. ¹*venom* + *-in*; *venene* fr. L *venenum* poison] : any of various toxic substances in snake venom

veni·puncture *also* **vene·puncture** \ˈvenə, ˈvēnə, ˈvānə+,-\ *n* [*venipuncture* fr. *ven-* + *puncture*; *venepuncture* fr. *vene-* (as in *venesection*) + *puncture*] : surgical puncture of a vein usu. with a hypodermic needle for the purpose of withdrawing blood or for intravenous injection of medication

ve·nire \vəˈnīrē, -nirē\ *n* -s [NL, lit., to come, short for ML *venire facias*, lit., that you should cause to come, fr. L *venire* to come + *facias* you should cause, should make, 2nd pers. sing. pres. subj. of *facere* to make, do, cause; fr. the words in the writ — more at COME, DO] **1** *or* **venire fa·ci·as** \-ˈfāshē,as\ [ME, fr. ML] **a** : a judicial writ directed to a sheriff and requiring him to cause an indicated number of qualified persons to appear in court at a specified time for service as jurors **b** : a writ under English law that is a summons to a person indicted on a penal statute to appear in court **2** : an entire panel which is drawn for jury duty and from which a jury is to be selected

venire facias de novo *also* **venire de novo** *n* [*venire facias de novo* fr. NL, lit., you cause to come anew; *venire de novo* fr. NL, lit., to come anew] : a new writ of venire issued to summon a jury anew on some irregularity or defect in the proceeding under the first venire; *also* : an order granting a new trial for any reason

venire·man \=ˈ==,mən\ *n, pl* **veniremen** [*venire* + *man*] : a member of a venire : JUROR

venisection *var of* VENESECTION

ve·nise lace \vəˈnēs, ˈvenəs-\ *also* **venise** *n* -s *usu cap V* [*venise* fr. F, fr. *Venise* Venice, fr. It *Venezia*, fr. L *Venetia*] **1** : VENETIAN POINT **2** : a machine-made imitation of Venetian point made by the burnt-out process

ven·i·son \ˈvenəsən, -əzən *chiefly Brit* -nzən\ *n, pl* **venisons** *also* **venison** *often attrib* [ME *venison, veneison*, fr. OF *veneison*, fr. L *venation-, venatio* hunt, chase, quarry, prey, fr. *venatus* (past part. of *venari* to hunt, pursue) + *-ion-, -io* -ion; akin to Skt *vanati* he loves, desires — more at WIN] **1 a** : the edible flesh of a wild mammal or sometimes bird or one taken by hunting (as in the chase); *esp* : the edible flesh of a beast of venery **b** : the flesh of a deer ⟨elk ~⟩ **2 a** *archaic* : a game animal (as a beast of chase or beast of venery) **b** : a mammal of the family Cervidae : DEER ⟨bought ~ skins for glovemaking⟩

venison bird *or* **venison hawk** *n* : CANADA JAY

venn \ˈven\ *dial var of* FEN

venn diagram \ˈven-\ *or* **venn's diagram** *n, usu cap V* [after John *Venn* †1923 Eng. logician] : a graphic method employing circles or ellipses to represent relations in logic between and operations on classes and the terms of propositions by the inclusion, exclusion, or intersection of these figures and by the use of shading to indicate empty areas, crosses for those that are not empty and blank spaces for those that may be either

ven·nel \ˈvenᵊl\ *n* -s [ME, fr. MF *vanelle, venelle*, fr. ML *venella*, fr. L *vena* vein, duct + *-ella*] **1** *chiefly Scot* : a narrow urban passage (as a lane or alley) **2** *dial Brit* : GUTTER, SEWER

veno- —see VEN-

veno·clysis \¦vēnə, ¦venə+\ *n* [NL, fr. *ven-* + *clysis*] : clysis into a vein

veno·gram \ˈ==,gram\ *n* [ISV *ven-* + *-gram*] : a roentgenogram after the injection of an opaque substance into a vein

veno·graph·ic \¦==¦grafik\ *adj* : of or relating to venography or a venogram

ve·nog·ra·phy \vēˈnägrəfē, vəˈ-\ *n* -ES [ISV *ven-* + *-graphy*] : roentgenography of a vein after the injection of an opaque substance

¹**ven·om** \ˈvenəm\ *n* -s [ME *venom, venum, venim*, fr. OF *venim*, fr. (assumed) VL *venimen*, alter. of L *venenum* drug, poison, magic potion, charm; akin to L *venus* love, sexual desire — more at WIN] **1** : poisonous matter normally secreted by some animals (as snakes, scorpions, or bees) used chiefly in the taking of prey and in defense and communicated chiefly by biting or stinging; *broadly* : material that is poisonous : matter fatal or injurious to life **2** : something that embitters or blights the mind or spirit as a poison blights the body: as **a** : a spiteful malicious feeling or state of mind : MALIGNITY ⟨their belief in ~ and jealousy behind the war

—F.L.Paxson⟩ **b** : a venomous utterance ⟨spouting ~ —Kenneth Roberts⟩ **syn** see POISON

2venom \"\ *vb* -ED/-ING/-S [ME *venomen, venimen*, fr. MF *venimer*, fr. OF, fr. *venim* venom] *vt* **1** : to inject or injure with venom : CORRUPT, POISON **2** *archaic* : to make venomous by or as if by application of a venom ~ *vi, obs* : to become envenomed

ven·om·ness *n* -ES : the quality or state of being venomous

ven·o·mo·salivary \ˌvenəmō+\ *adj* [1*venom* + *-o-* + *salivary*] **1** : of or relating to venom and saliva **2** *of a salivary gland* : modified to secrete venom instead of saliva

ven·om·ous \ˈvenəməs\ *adj* [ME *venimous*, fr. OF *venimos, venimeux*, fr. *venim* venom + *-os, -eux* -ous] **1 a** : full of venom : noxious to animal life by means of venom ⟨a ~ sting⟩; *broadly* : POISONOUS **b** : VIRULENT, BANEFUL ⟨a ~ doctrine⟩ **2** : characterized by or having the nature of venom; *often* : MISCHIEVOUS, MALIGNANT, SPITEFUL ⟨a ~ writer⟩ ⟨~ criticism⟩ **3** : having a gland for the secretion of venom : able to inflict a poisoned bite, sting, or wound **4** : tipped with or dipped in poison : POISONED, ENVENOMED ⟨~ darts⟩ — **ven·om·ous·ly** *adv* — **ven·om·ous·ness** *n* -ES

ven·om·some \ˈ==səm\ *adj* [1*venom* + *-some*] *dial Eng* : VENOMOUS

ve·no·pressor \ˌvēnə, ˌvenə+\ *adj* [*ven-* + *pressor*] : of, relating to, or controlling venous blood pressure

ve·nose \ˈveˌnōs\ *adj* [L *venosus*] : VENOUS; *esp* : having numerous or conspicuous veins ⟨insects with ~ wings⟩

ve·nos·i·ty \vēˈnäsəd·ē, vəˈ-\ *n* -ES : the quality or state of being venous

ve·nos·ta·sis \vēˈnästəsəs, vəˈ-\ *n* [NL, fr. *ven-* + *-stasis*] : an abnormal slowing or stoppage of the flow of blood in a vein

ve·nous \ˈvēnəs\ *adj* [L *venosus*, fr. *vena* vein + *-osus* -ose] **1 a** : full of or characterized by veins : VEINY, VEINED ⟨a ~ rock⟩ **b** : made up of or carried on by veins ⟨the ~ circulation⟩ ⟨an open ~ system⟩ **2** : of, relating to, or performing the functions of a vein ⟨a ~ inflammation⟩ ⟨~ arteries⟩ **3** *of blood* : having passed through the capillaries and given up oxygen for the tissues and become charged with carbon dioxide and ready to pass through the respiratory organs to release its carbon dioxide and renew its oxygen supply : dark red from reduced hemoglobin : UNOXYGENATED — compare ARTERIAL — **ve·nous·ly** *adv*

venous sinus *n* **1 a** : a large vein or passage (as in the dura mater) for venous blood **b** : SINUS VENOSUS **2** : one of the ill-defined spaces among the tissues of many invertebrates that is functionally equivalent to a vertebrate vein

1vent \ˈvent\ *vb* -ED/-ING/-S [ME *venten*, prob. fr. MF *eventer, esventer*, fr. *e-, es-* out, forth (fr. L *ex-* 1ex-) + *venter* to blow, fr. (assumed) VL *ventare* to blow, be windy, fr. L *ventus* wind — more at WIND] *vt* **1** : to provide with an opening for the discharge of gases or the relief of pressure ⟨~ a plumbing system⟩ : equip with a vent or venting **2 a** : to serve as a vent for ⟨tall chimneys ~*ed* the smoke⟩ **b** (1) : to cause to flow or drain away : cast out : EXPEL ⟨~*ing* off the excess fluid through a series of conduits⟩ (2) *archaic* : to eject from the body : EVACUATE **c** (1) : to give expression to : release by expressing : LOOSE ⟨~*ed* his fury on the hapless dog⟩ (2) : to give utterance to : make public ⟨~*ing* his grievance before them all⟩ **3** : to relieve by venting ⟨some could ~ themselves in grief⟩ ⟨a valve to ~ the pressure in the boiler⟩ ~ *vi* **1** : to issue forth by or as if by a vent : go away or out through a vent **2** : to come to the surface to breathe — used esp. of an otter **3 a** : to have a vent (as for the escape of gases) ⟨an old-fashioned toilet ~*ing* through the chimney⟩ **b** *chiefly Scot* : to have draft : DRAW ⟨the chimney ~*s* well⟩ **syn** see EMIT, EXPRESS

2vent \"\ *n* -S [ME *vente*, alter. (prob. influenced by MF *vent* wind, fr. L *ventus*) of *fente, fent*, fr. MF *fente* slit, fissure, fr. *fendre* to split, fr. L *findere* — more at BITE] : a slit in a garment; *specif* : an opening in the lower part of a seam (as of a jacket, coat, skirt, or sleeve)

3vent \"\ *vb* [ME *venten*, fr. MF *vente* sale — more at 5VENT] *archaic* : VEND, SELL

4vent \"\ *n* -S *often attrib* [partly fr. 1*vent* & partly fr. MF *event, esvent* opening, vent, fr. *eventer, esventer* to blow out, vent — more at 1VENT] **1** *obs* : the act or fact of emitting something (as words) **2 a** : an opportunity or way of escape or passage : OUTLET ⟨the gases found ~ through fissures in the rock⟩ ⟨his writing gives ~ to his unused talents⟩ **b** : an opening or hole for the escape or passage of something (as of a gas or liquid) or for the relief of pressure within something (as a boiler) ⟨the ~ of a cask⟩ ⟨a hot-water system with a relief tank as ~⟩: as (1) : the external opening of the rectum or cloaca : ANUS — used esp. of a nonmammalian vertebrate (as a fish or bird) (2) : PIPE 3b(3), FUMAROLE (3) : an opening at the breech of a gun through which fire is communicated to the powder (as a hole from the top of the breech to the chamber of a muzzle-loading gun or a hole in the axis of the breechblock of a breech-loading gun) (4) *chiefly Scot* : CHIMNEY, FLUE (5) : an opening (as in a room or building) for ventilation esp. when not such as would ordinarily be classed as a window or door ⟨a poultry house with adjustable ~*s* under the eaves⟩ **3** : the coming of an otter to the surface of the water in order to breathe

5vent \ˈvent\ *n* -S [MF *vente*, fr. (assumed) VL *vendita*, fr. fem. of L *venditus*, past part. of *vendere* to sell — more at VEND] *archaic* : SALE: as **a** : the act of selling **b** : opportunity to sell : MARKET

6vent *or* **vent brand** \"\ *n* -S [Sp *venta* sale, inn, fr. (assumed) VL *vendita* sale] *West* : a brand indicating the sale of the animal branded that sometimes takes the form of a special mark but is commonly a bar across the seller's brand

7vent \"\ *vt* -ED/-ING/-S *West* : to cancel (a brand) by a vent

vent *abbr* ventilate; ventilating; ventilation; ventilator

ven·ta \ˈventə\ *n* -S [Sp] : a rural inn esp. in a Spanish-speaking area

vent·age \ˈventij\ *n* -S [4*vent* + *-age*] **1** : a small hole (as a flute stop) : VENT **2** : arrangement for or means of venting something

ven·tail \ˈven·ˌtāl\ *n* -S [ME, fr. MF *ventaille* sluice, ventail, fr. *vent* wind, air] : the lower movable front of a medieval helmet designed for the admission of air and usu. restricted to the part below the visor but sometimes including the visor

vent disease *n* : RABBIT SYPHILIS

vent drill *or* **vent gimlet** *n* : an instrument for freeing the vent of a cannon from obstructions — called also *vent punch*

vented *past of* VENT

1ven·ter \ˈventə(r)\ *n* -S [AF, fr. L, abdomen, womb; akin to L *vensica, vesica* bladder, OHG *wanast, wenist* paunch, Icel *vinstr* omasum, Skt *vasti* bladder] **1** : a wife or mother that is a source of offspring ⟨had a son by one ~ and two daughters by another⟩ ⟨children of the same ~⟩ **2** : an anatomical structure that is protuberant and often hollow: as **a** : ABDOMEN; *also* : a large bodily cavity (as in the head, thorax, or abdomen) containing organs **b** : BELLY 5c ⟨a muscle with a double ~⟩ **c** : the undersurface of the abdomen of an arthropod **d** : a broad shallow concavity of a bone ⟨the ~ of the scapula⟩ **e** : the outer and convex part of the shell of a curved or coiled cephalopod or gastropod **f** : the swollen basal portion of an archegonium in which the egg of a vascular cryptogam is developed

2vent·er \ˈventə(r)\ *n* -S [1*vent* + *-er*] : one that vents; *esp* : one that gives utterance or publicity to personal ideas, doctrines, or grievances

vent feather *n* : a crissal feather

vent gleet *n* : CLOACITIS

venthole \ˈ=ˌ=\ *n* [4*vent* + *hole*] : an opening that is a vent or is used for venting ⟨an otter's ~ in the ice⟩

venti- *or* **vento-** *comb form* [L *ventus* wind + E *-i-* or *-o-*] : wind ⟨*venti*fact⟩

ven·ti·duct \ˈventəˌdəkt\ *n* [*venti-* + *-duct* (as in *aqueduct*)] : a passage for wind or air (as for ventilating an apartment)

ven·ti·fact \-ˌfakt\ *n* [*venti-* + *-fact* (as in *artifact*)] : a stone worn, polished, or faceted by windblown sand — called also *glyptolith, rillstone*

ven·til \ˈventᵊl\ *n* -S [G, prob. fr. F *ventelle* small valve, sluice, fr. MF *ventaille* sluice — more at VENTAIL] : a valve in various wind musical instruments

ven·tila·gin \ven·ˈtiləjən; ˌventᵊlˈāj-, -ᵊlˈaj-\ *n* -S [ISV *ventilag-* (fr. NL *Ventilago* — genus name of *Ventilago maderaspatana* —, irreg. fr. L *ventulus* + *agere* to drive) + *-in* — more at AGENT] : a reddish brown resinous coloring matter $C_{15}H_{14}O_6$ derived from anthraquinone and obtained from the root bark of an East Indian woody vine (*Ventilago maderaspatana*) of the family Rhamnaceae

ven·ti·late \ˈventᵊlˌāt, *usu* -ād·+V\ *vb* -ED/-ING/-S [LL *ventilatus*, past part. of *ventilare* to ventilate, fr. L, to toss, brandish in the air, winnow, fan, fr. *ventulus* slight wind, breeze, fr. *ventus* wind + *-ulus* — more at WIND] *vt* **1 a** : to open for consideration and discussion : examine, discuss, or investigate freely, fully, and usu. publicly ⟨*ventilating* family quarrels before strangers⟩ **b** : to make public or known to others : give expression to : UTTER ⟨continued to ~ his complaints⟩ **2 a** *archaic* : to free (as grain) from chaff by fanning or winnowing **b** *obs* : to enliven (as a fire) by or as if by blowing or fanning **c** *archaic* : to cause (air) to move as by fanning or blowing **3** : to expose to air and esp. to a current of fresh air (as for cooling, purifying, or refreshing): as **a** : to expose (blood) to air (as in a lung or gill) to permit uptake of oxygen and release of carbon dioxide : OXYGENATE, AERATE **b** : to expose (as grain or hay) to a current of air usu. to dry or cure **4 a** *of a current of air* : to pass or circulate through so as to freshen and to dissipate vitiated or contaminated air **b** : to cause fresh air to circulate through and vitiated or contaminated air to be simultaneously withdrawn from (as a room or mine) ⟨powerful blowers ~ the long passages⟩ **5 a** : to plan the ventilation of or provide with vents or other openings through which air or other gas may pass or circulate ⟨an attic *ventilated* with louvers under the eaves⟩ ⟨diagrams showing how to ~ a founder's mold⟩ **b** : to induce ventilation of by manipulation of facilities provided ⟨threw open the windows and *ventilated* the long-closed house⟩ **c** : to make (as a wig) by knotting individual hairs to a lace net foundation **d** : to provide an opening in (a burning structure) to permit escape of smoke and heat ~ *vi* : to undergo ventilation : become ventilated ⟨surfacing at night to recharge her batteries and ~ —J.P.Baxter b.1893⟩ **syn** see EXPRESS

ventilated car *n* : a boxcar having openings at the top, sides, and often ends for ventilation

ventilated rib *n* : a shotgun rib that is supported over the barrel by a series of fastenings to provide better cooling as well as a straight sighting plane

ventilating *adj* : serving to ventilate : used in the provision or production of ventilation ⟨~ skylights⟩ ⟨~ devices⟩

ventilating brick *n* : a cored-out brick providing an air passage (as for ventilation)

ventilating jack *n* : a sheet-metal hood placed over the inlet of a ventilating pipe to cause the induction of an increased air volume into the pipe

ventilating millstone *n* : a millstone having a device for inducing a strong current of air through its grooves

ven·ti·la·tion \ˌventᵊlˈāshən\ *n* -S [ME *ventulacioun*, modif. (influenced by L *ventulus* breeze) of L *ventilation-, ventilatio*, fr. *ventilatus* (past part. of *ventilare* to brandish in the air) + *-ion-, -io* -ion] **1** *obs* : a current of air (as a breeze) **2** : an act or instance of ventilating: as **a** *archaic* : an act or action of fanning or blowing; *esp* : the winnowing of grain **b** : a movement and esp. a circulation of air (as in an enclosed space) ⟨a mine with poor ~⟩; *often* : the circulation and exchange of gases in the lungs that is basic to respiration **c** (1) : a making public or openly uttering : VENT ⟨his ~ of these views alienated popular sympathy⟩ (2) : free and open discussion (as of a matter of public interest) ⟨such a proposal deserves thorough ~⟩ (3) : verbal expression of mental or emotional conflicts leading to reduction of inner tensions — compare CATHARSIS 3a **3** : provision of facilities or the facilities available to ensure an adequate or a particular sort of circulation (as of air) ⟨a cave with good natural ~⟩ ⟨planned a complex ~ system of blowers and ducts⟩ ⟨the ~ broke down⟩

ven·ti·la·tive \ˈ==ˌād·iv\ *adj* : of or relating to ventilation : adapted to secure ventilation

ven·ti·la·tor \-ˌād·ə(r)\ *n* -S : one that ventilates: as **a** : a contrivance (as a shutter device forming an adjustable aperture or a machine causing movement of air) used for introducing fresh air or expelling foul or stagnant air to or from an enclosed space (as a building) **b** : one responsible for ventilating some place

ven·ti·la·to·ry \-_əˌtōrē, -tȯrē, -ri\ *adj* **1** : provided with ventilation **2** : of, relating to, or involved in pulmonary ventilation ⟨the ~ response to carbon dioxide⟩ ⟨~ efficiency⟩ ⟨~ thoracic pressure changes⟩

ven·tile \ˈventᵊl, -n·ˌtīl\ *adj* [back-formation (influenced by *-ile*) of *ventilation*] *of a textile* : designed to exclude water while permitting a free circulation of air ⟨a light raincoat of finely woven ~ cotton fabric⟩

venting *pres part of* VENT

vent·less \ˈventləs\ *adj* [4*vent* + *-less*] : having no vent

vento- — see VENTI-

ven·tom·e·ter \ven·ˈtämәd·ə(r)\ *n* [*venti-* + *-meter*] : an instrument for indicating the velocity of the wind esp. as designed for use on target ranges — compare ANEMOMETER

ven·tose \ˈven·ˌtōs, =ˈ=\ *adj* [L *ventosus*, fr. *ventus* wind + *-osus* -ose — more at WIND] *archaic* : FLATULENT, WINDY

ven·tos·i·ty \ven·ˈtäsəd·ē\ *n* -ES [ME *ventosite*, fr. MF *ventosité*, fr. LL *ventositat-, ventositas*, fr. L *ventosus* windy, flatulent + *-itat-, -itas* -ity] **1** *obs* : flatulence or its cause **2** : pompous inflated conceit or boasting

vent punch *n* : VENT DRILL

ventr- *or* **ventri-** *or* **ventro-** *comb form* [F, fr. L *ventr-, venter* — more at VENTER] **1** : abdomen : ventral ⟨*ventr*ic⟩ ⟨*ventro*tomy⟩ ⟨*ventri*columna⟩ **2** : ventral and ⟨*ventro*dorsal⟩ **3** : ventricose : round ⟨*ventri*pyramid⟩

ven·trad \ˈven·ˌtrad\ *adv* [*ventr-* + *-ad*] : toward the ventral side : VENTRALLY ⟨tracing the nerve ~⟩

1ven·tral \ˈven·trəl\ *adj* [F, fr. L *ventralis*, fr. *ventr-, venter* + *-alis* -al] **1** : of or relating to the belly : ABDOMINAL; *usu* : belonging to or situated near or on the anterior or lower surface of an animal or one of its parts that is opposite the back — opposed to DORSAL ⟨a ~ scale of a snake⟩ ⟨the liver is somewhat ~ in position⟩ ⟨the ~ aspect of the body⟩ **2 a** : AXIAL **b** : belonging to or located on the lower surface usu. of a creeping dorsiventral structure (as a thallus)

2ventral \"\ *n* -S : a ventral part (as a scale or plate); *esp* : VENTRAL FIN

ventral canal cell *n* [trans. of G *bauchkanalzelle*] : a small cell that is cut off from the central cell of an archegonium just below the neck and above the oosphere

ventral column *n* : either of a pair of gray columns situated one on each side in the ventral aspect of the spinal column and containing neurons that give rise to motor fibers of the ventral roots of spinal nerves

ventral diaphragm *n* : a muscular membrane present in the ventral part of the abdomen of some insects

ventral fin *n* **1 a** : either of the pair of fins of a fish that correspond to the hind limbs of quadrupeds : PELVIC FIN **b** : ANAL FIN **2** : a fixed stabilizing surface attached to the rear undersurface of an airplane

ven·tral·ly \ˈven·trəlē, -li\ *adv* : in a ventral direction or position ⟨attached ~ to the mesentery⟩ — see VENTRAD

ventral nerve cord *n* : a chain of connected segmental ganglia lying against the body wall in the body of an arthropod or annelid

ventral plate *n* : a thickening of the blastoderm in an early embryo of an insect or other arthropod on the underside of the egg that is destined to develop into the body of the embryo proper

ventral root *n* : the one of the two roots of a spinal nerve that passes ventrally from the spinal cord and consists of motor fibers — compare DORSAL ROOT

ventral segment *n* : the portion of a vibrating medium between two successive nodes

ventral sinus *n* : a cavity of the abdomen of an insect between the ventral diaphragm and the ventral body wall

ventral tube *n* : COLLOPHORE

ventral·ward \ˈ==wə(r)d\ *also* **ventral·wards** \-dz\ *adv* [1*ventral* + *-ward, -wards*] : toward the ventral aspect or surface

ven·tri·cle \ˈven·trəkəl, -rēk-\ *n* -S [ME, fr. L *ventriculus* stomach, ventricle of the heart, dim. of *venter* abdomen — more at VENTER] : a cavity of a bodily part or organ: as **a** : a chamber or one of the chambers of the heart which receives blood from a corresponding atrium and from which blood is forced into the arteries **b** : one of the system of communicating cavities in the brain that are continuous with the central canal of the spinal cord, that like it are derived from the medullary canal of the embryo, that are lined with an epithelial ependyma, and that contain a serous fluid **c** : a fossa or pouch on each side of the larynx between the false vocal cords above and the true vocal cords below — called also *ventricle of Morgagni* **d** : STOMACH, VENTRICULUS **e** *obs* : BELLY, WOMB

ven·tri·columna \ˌven·trə+\ *n* [NL, fr. *ventr-* + *columna*] : VENTRAL COLUMN — **ven·tri·columnar** \"+\ *adj*

ven·tri·cornu \"+\ *n* [NL, fr. *ventr-* + *cornu*] : VENTRAL COLUMN

ven·tri·cose \ˈven·trəˌkōs\ *adj* [NL *ventricosus*, fr. (assumed) NL *ventricus* of the abdomen (fr. L *ventr-, venter* + *-icus* -ic) + L *-osus* -ose] : DISTENDED, INFLATED; *esp* : markedly swollen on one side

ventricose shell *n* **1** : a spiral shell having the body whorls rounded or swollen in the middle **2** : a bivalve shell in which the valves are strongly convex

ven·tri·cos·i·ty \ˌ==ˈkäsəd·ē\ *n* -ES : the quality or state of being ventricose : CONVEXITY

ven·tric·u·lar \(ˈ)ven·ˈtrikyələ(r)\ *adj* [NL *ventricularis*, fr. L *ventriculus* stomach, ventricle + *-aris* -ar] **1 a** : of or relating to the stomach or belly : ABDOMINAL **b** : of, relating to, or constituting a ventriculus **2** : of or relating to a ventricle (as of the heart or brain)

ventricular fibrillation *n* : very rapid uncoordinated contractions of the ventricles of the heart resulting in loss of synchronization between heartbeat and pulse beat

ventricular fold *n* : FALSE VOCAL CORD

ven·tric·u·lar·is \(ˌ)ven·ˌtrikyəˈla(a)rəs\ *n* -ES [NL, fr. *ventricularis* ventricular] : a part of the thyroarytenoideus that enters the false vocal cord on either side

ven·tric·u·lite \ven·ˈtrikyəˌlīt\ *n* -S [NL *Ventriculites*] : a fossil sponge of *Ventriculites* or related genus — **ven·tric·u·lit·ic** \(ˈ)=ˌ==ˌlid·ik\ *adj*

ven·tric·u·li·tes \=ˌ==ˈlīd·ˌēz\ *n, cap* [NL, fr. L *ventriculus* ventricle + NL *-ites*] : a genus (the type of the family Ventriculitidae of the class Hyalospongiae) of fossil often vase-shaped or mushroom-shaped chiefly Cretaceous sponges having a latticed skeleton in which the nodes formed by the crossing of the spicular threads are perforated

ven·tric·u·lo·gram \=ˈ==_ləˌgram\ *n* [ISV *ventriculo-* (fr. L *ventriculus* ventricle) + *-gram*] : an X-ray photograph of the ventricles of the brain made after withdrawing fluid from the ventricles and replacing it with air or a radiopaque substance

ven·tric·u·log·ra·phy \=ˌ==ˈlägrəfē\ *n* -ES [ISV *ventriculo-* + *-graphy*] : the act or process of making ventriculograms

ven·tric·u·lus \=ˈ==_ləs\ *n, pl* **ventricu·li** \-ˌlī\ [NL, fr. L, stomach, ventricle of the heart — more at VENTRICLE] : a ventricle that functions or is viewed as functioning in digestion: as **a** : STOMACH **b** : GIZZARD 1a **c** : the digestive part of an insect's stomach usu. immediately behind the proventriculus

ven·tri·lo·qui·al \ˌven·trəˈlōkwēəl\ *adj* : of, relating to, resembling, or using ventriloquism — **ven·tri·lo·qui·al·ly** \-əlē, -li\ *adv*

ven·tril·o·quism \ven·ˈtriləˌkwizəm\ *n* -S [LL *ventriloquus* ventriloquist (fr. L *ventr-, venter* abdomen + *loqui* to speak) + E *-ism*; fr. the belief that the voice is produced in the ventriloquist's stomach — more at VENTER] : the act, art, or practice of speaking in such a manner that the voice appears to come from some source other than the vocal organs of the speaker and esp. with little or no movement of the lips so as to create the illusion that the voice may be coming from a source other than the speaker (as from a dummy whose lip movements are produced mechanically by the speaker)

ven·tril·o·quist \-_kwəst\ *n* -S [*ventriloquy* + *-ist*] : one who uses or is skilled in ventriloquism; *esp* : one who entertains by ventriloquism usu. through holding a wooden dummy and apparently carrying on a conversation with it

ven·tril·o·quis·tic \(ˌ)=ˌ==ˈkwistik\ *adj* **1** : of or relating to ventriloquism or ventriloquists : practicing ventriloquism **2** *of a sound* : seeming to originate at other than the actual point of origin

ven·tril·o·quize \=ˈ==ˌkwīz\ *vb* -ED/-ING/-S [*ventriloquy* + *-ize*] *vi* : to use ventriloquism ~ *vt* : to utter (as a speech or opinion) in the manner of a ventriloquist

ven·tril·o·quous \=ˈ==kwəs\ *adj* [LL *ventriloquus* + E *-ous*] : VENTRILOQUISTIC

ven·tril·o·quy \ven·ˈtriləkwē\ *n* -ES [LL *ventriloquus* + E *-y*] : VENTRILOQUISM

ven·trip·o·tent \ven·ˈtripəd·ənt, -ətənt *also* -ətᵊnt\ *adj* [F, fr. *ventri-* (fr. L, fr. *ventr-, venter* abdomen) + L *potent-, potens*, pres. part. of (assumed) OL *potēre* to be powerful — more at POTENT] : having a large belly; *also* : GLUTTONOUS

ven·tri·pyramid \ˌven·trə+\ *n* [*ventr-* + *pyramid*] : the pyramid of the medulla oblongata

ventro- — see VENTR-

ven·tro·lateral \ˌven·(ˌ)trō+\ *adj* [*ventr-* + *lateral*] : ventral and lateral; *usu* : situated or occurring ventrally and somewhat laterally — **ven·tro·laterally** \"+\ *adv*

ven·tro·medial \"+\ *also* **ven·tro·median** \"+\ *adj* [*ventr-* + *medial* or *median*] : ventral and medial : situated or occurring in the median ventral line — **ven·tro·medially** \"+\ *adv*

ven·tro·mesial \"+\ *adj* [*ventr-* + *mesial*] : ventral and mesial

1vents *pres 3d sing of* VENT, *pl of* VENT

2vents \ˈvents\ *var of* FEN

vent stack *n* : a pipe placed vertically or nearly so and connected to the traps of plumbing fixtures in such a manner as to ventilate them and prevent the water seal from being siphoned out of them

vent tank *n* : a primary still used in the manufacture of natural gasoline to remove absorbed gases that are too volatile for gasoline

1ven·ture \ˈvenchə(r)\ *vb* -ED/-ING/-S [ME *venteren*, by shortening & alter. fr. *aventuren* to venture — more at ADVENTURE] *vt* **1** : to expose to risk or hazard: as **a** : to lay (as oneself) open to danger **b** : to put or send on a venture esp. when involving unusual risks : gamble or speculate with : HAZARD ⟨~ a ship in the coastal trade⟩ ⟨*ventured* more than he could afford on speculative stocks⟩ **2 a** : to face or undertake the risks and dangers of : dare to encounter, undertake, or embark on : BRAVE ⟨a band of Puritans . . . *ventured* in 1620 a settlement at Plymouth —Stringfellow Barr⟩ ⟨unwilling to ~ the elements in such a storm⟩ **b** *archaic* : to risk giving one's confidence to : rely on : TRUST **3** : to dare or have the courage or boldness to advance, offer, or put forward esp. when rebuff, rejection, or censure seems likely to ensue ⟨*ventured* a hint of doubt —H.J.Laski⟩ ⟨upon the irresponsible taxation he does ~ to speak plainly —G.G.Coulton⟩ ⟨I ~ to say that 5000 people were present⟩ ~ *vi* : to proceed accepting risks : go ahead with something uncertain or risky despite danger and trepidation : dare or show the courage to go ⟨explorers by sea, *venturing* uneasily northward along the shores in pygmy galleons —*Amer. Guide Series: Calif.*⟩ ⟨strikebreakers were compelled to remain in the shops for weeks before *venturing* to their homes —*Amer. Guide Series: Del.*⟩ ⟨too old to ~ on a new way of life⟩

syn HAZARD, RISK, CHANCE, ENDANGER, IMPERIL, JEOPARDIZE: VENTURE indicates an exposing to risk of losing in speculation, gambling, or other matters of chance either boldly or timorously ⟨*venture* one's capital⟩ and it may suggest a proceeding that calls for caution or an offering liable to rejection or contradiction ⟨hazardous to approach too near to the snow or *venture* beneath it —*Amer. Guide Series: N.H.*⟩ ⟨I *venture* to predict —F.D.Roosevelt⟩ HAZARD may occas. more strongly suggest utter chance, as of the turn of a card or spin of a wheel, as a determining factor, and consequently suggest more uncertainty and less calculation than VENTURE ⟨able young men have been willing to *hazard* their chances of professional advancement in order to engage in academic experiments —G.F. Whicher⟩ RISK may stress the fact of danger of loss, damage, or defeat without undue implication of reasons, motives, degrees of danger ⟨Poland did not hesitate . . . to *risk* all the progress she had made —Sir Winston Churchill⟩ ⟨not *risking* a landing because of the fierce aspect of the natives —V.G.Heiser⟩ CHANCE may suggest more inclination to trust to luck and less

considering or reckoning. ENDANGER, IMPERIL, and JEOPARDIZE heighten notions of exposure to danger. IMPERIL may occas. suggest exposure to greater or inseparable danger and may be preferred in figurative uses ⟨floods *endangering* the building in 1866, Fort Lyon was moved up the river —L.R.Hafen⟩ ⟨kings in Europe were sometimes shot at by passersby, there being hardly a monarch who had not been so *imperiled* —G.B. Shaw⟩ JEOPARDIZE may be somewhat stronger and imply even chances of success or failure, preservation or loss, or suggest greater imminence of danger or inexorability of decision ⟨to settle for merely another temporary respite would surely *jeopardize* the future security of all the world —H.S.Truman⟩

²**venture** \"\ *n* -s [ME, short for *aventure* adventure — more at ADVENTURE] **1** *obs* **:** FORTUNE, HAP, CONTINGENCY; *also* **:** PERIL, JEOPARDY **2 a :** an undertaking involving chance, risk, or danger **:** an undertaking of uncertain outcome or unforeseen conditions; *esp* **:** a business enterprise of speculative nature **:** SPECULATION ⟨a trading ~⟩ ⟨took a ~ in oil⟩ **b :** an act of venturing (as in speech or action) **:** venturesome conduct ⟨his ~ into honest living⟩ ⟨this ~ in plain speaking cost us dear⟩ **c :** an entire voyage (as of a trading ship) from home port to home port **3 :** something at hazard in a speculative venture (as of trade by sea) ⟨lost his first ~ in the China trade⟩; *usu* **:** the property, money, or other thing of value that is risked in a business enterprise or speculation ⟨my ~s are not in one bottom trusted —Shak.⟩ **4** *dial Brit* **:** an adventurous spirit **:** a willingness to take risks or run dangers **:** COURAGE ⟨what in the world wide put ~ into you that made you go face the dog —Augusta Gregory⟩ — **at a venture** *adv* **:** at hazard or random **:** without seeing the mark or foreseeing the issue

venture capital *n* **:** money invested or available for investment in stocks; *esp* **:** funds invested in stock of newer unseasoned enterprises — called also *equity capital, risk capital*

ven·tur·er \ˈvenchərər, -ch(ə)rə\ *n* -s **:** one that ventures or puts to hazard **:** ADVENTURER; *specif* **:** a person (as a merchant) who engages in business ventures

ven·ture·some \-chə(r)səm\ *adj* **1 :** disposed to court or incur risk or danger **:** inclined to undertake hazardous ventures **:** bold or daring in new enterprises ⟨a ~ hunter⟩ ⟨a chance for ~ investors⟩ ⟨a ~ outlook on life⟩ **2 :** resembling or characteristic of a venture involving risk **:** HAZARDOUS ⟨a ~ journey in wintertime⟩ ⟨planned to do something ~⟩ **syn** see ADVENTUROUS

ven·ture·some·ly *adv* **:** in a venturesome manner **:** so as to be venturesome

ven·ture·some·ness *n* -ES **:** the quality or state of being venturesome

ven·tu·ri \venˈtu̇rē\ *or* **venturi tube** *n* -s *sometimes cap V* [after G. B. *Venturi* †1822 Ital. physicist] **:** a short tube that is inserted in a pipeline, that has flaring ends connected by a constricted middle section forming a throat, that depends for operation upon the fact that as the velocity of flow of a fluid increases in the throat the pressure decreases, that is used for measuring the quantity of a fluid flowing, in connection with other devices for measuring airspeed, and for producing suction esp. for driving aircraft instruments by means of a branch tube joined at the throat

ven·tu·ria \venˈt(y)u̇rēə\ *n, cap* [NL, fr. A. *Venturi*, 19th cent. Ital. botanist + NL *-ia*] **:** a genus of fungi (family Mycosphaerellaceae) having generally sunken dark-colored perithecia with a bristly apex and olive green unequally 2-celled ascospores — see APPLE SCAB, PEAR SCAB

ven·tu·rine \ˈvenchəˌrēn, -ˌrən\ *n* -s [F *aventurine* — more at AVENTURINE] **:** a gold powder for varnished surfaces

venturing *pres part of* VENTURE

ven·tur·ous \ˈvench(ə)rəs\ *adj* [short for *adventurous*] **1 :** courting or oblivious of danger **:** ready to meet risks **:** DARING, BOLD, VENTURESOME, ADVENTUROUS ⟨a ~ spirit⟩ **2 :** involving danger or risk **:** HAZARDOUS, DANGEROUS, RISKY ⟨a ~ enterprise⟩ **syn** see ADVENTUROUS

ven·tur·ous·ly *adv* **:** in a venturous manner

ven·tur·ous·ness *n* -ES **:** the quality or state of being venturous

vent wire *n* **:** a pointed wire for making vents in foundry molds

ven·ue \ˈven(ˌ)yü *also* ˈve(ˌ)nü *sometimes* ˈvā(-\ *n* -s [MF, fr. fem. of *venu*, past part. of *venir* to come, fr. L *venire* — more at COME] **1** *obs* **a :** a thrust, hit, or lunge in or as if in fencing **b :** an encounter, bout, or match in or as if in fencing or cudgel play **2 a** (1) **:** a place (as a county) in which alleged events from which a legal action arises take place (2) **:** the place from which the jury is drawn and in which trial is held in such an action **b :** the locale of a past or projected real or imaginary event; *esp* **:** a place designated to be the scene of a proposed gathering (as for a sports event or a political conference) **c :** the position, side, or line of argument assumed by an individual in debate or discussion **:** GROUND **3 a :** a statement forming part of a declaration at law and alleging the residence of the parties, where the injury occurred, or other information that shows the case to be brought to the proper court or authority **b :** a clause or acknowledgment in an affidavit indicating the locality of execution

ven·u·la \ˈvenyələ\ *n* -s [L] **:** a small vein **:** VENULE

ven·u·lar \-lə(r)\ *adj* **:** of, relating to, or involving venules ⟨~ disorders⟩

ven·ule \ˈven(ˌ)yül\ *n* -s [L *venula*, dim. of *vena* vein] **:** a small vein: as **a :** one of the small branches of a vein of an insect's wing **b :** a minute vein connecting the capillary bed with the larger systemic veins

ven·u·lose \ˈvenyəˌlōs\ *or* **ven·u·lous** \-ləs\ *adj* [*venule* + *-ose* or *-ous*] **:** full of venules

ve·nus \ˈvēnəs\ *n* [after *Venus*, Roman goddess of love, 2d planet from the sun, fr. L *Vener-*, *Venus*, fr. *vener-*, *venus* love — more at WIN] **1** -ES *usu cap* **:** a woman felt to resemble the Roman goddess of love and beauty; *broadly* **:** a beautiful and charming woman or one who exemplifies feminine grace and charm **2** -ES *usu cap* [ME *Venus*, 2d planet from the sun, fr. L *Vener-*, *Venus*] **:** the lesser astrological fortune **:** a feminine temperately cold and moist nocturnal planet the mansions of which are Taurus and Libra, the exaltation 27 degrees Pisces, the depression 27 degrees Virgo, and the orb 7 degrees **3** -ES [ME *Venus*, fr. ML *Vener-*, *Venus*, fr. L, 2d planet from the sun] **:** COPPER **4** [NL, fr. L] **a** *cap* **:** a large genus of marine bivalve mollusks (family Veneridae) having a thick oval usu. inflated shell with often prominent concentric ridges and with the internal margins finely denticulate **b** *pl* **venuses** \-əsəz\ *also* **ven·er·es** \ˈvenəˌrēz\ **:** any mollusk of *Venus* or a related genus

venus and adonis stanza *usu cap V & 2d A* [fr. *Venus and Adonis* (1593), poem in this stanza by William Shakespeare †1616 Eng. dramatist and poet] **:** a stanza consisting of an iambic pentameter quatrain and couplet with the rhyme scheme *ababcc*

venus calendar *n, usu cap V* [*Venus*, 2d planet from the sun] **:** a Maya ritualistic calendar based on the lowest common factor of the synodical revolution of the planet Venus reckoned as 584 days and the year of 365 days

venus clam *n, often cap V* [NL *Venus*] **:** a bivalve mollusk of the family Veneridae

venus flytrap *n, sometimes cap V* **:** VENUS'S-FLYTRAP

venushair \ˈ==ˌ=\ *or* **venus'-hair fern** *n, usu cap V* [*Venus*, Roman goddess of love + *hair*] **:** a delicate maidenhair fern (*Adiantum capillus-veneris*) having a slender black and shining stipe and branches

¹**ve·nu·sian** \vəˈn(y)üsēən, -sh(ē)ən\ *adj, usu cap* [*Venus*, 2d planet from the sun + E *-an*] **:** relating to the planet Venus **:** of or belonging to the planet Venus

²**venusian** \"\ *n* -s *usu cap* [*Venus*, Roman goddess of love + E *-an*] **1 :** one that has a prominent and well-developed Mount of Venus often marked with many lines and that is usu. held by palmists to be characterized by warmth of personality, strong sexual attraction, and personal attractiveness and beauty **2** [¹*venusian*] **:** a hypothetical native or inhabitant of the planet Venus

venus's-basket \ˈvēnəs(əz)ˈ=ˌ=\ *n, pl* **venus's-baskets** *usu cap V* **:** VENUS'S-FLOWER-BASKET

venus's-chariot *n, pl* **venus's-chariots** *usu cap V* **:** a monkshood (*Aconitum napellus*)

venus's-comb *also* **venus comb** *n, pl* **venus's-combs** *usu cap V* **1 :** LADY'S-COMB **2 :** a marine snail (*Murex tenuispina*) having a long tubular canal with a row of long slender spines along both of its borders and rows of similar spines on the body of the shell

venus's-cup *n, pl* **venus's-cups** *usu cap V* **1 :** a yellow lady's slipper (*Cypripedium parviflorum*) **2 :** WILD TEASEL

venus's-ear *n, pl* **venus's-ears** *usu cap V* **:** ABALONE

venus's-fan *n, pl* **venus's-fans** *usu cap V* **:** a reticulated fan-shaped gorgonian (*Gorgonia flabellum*) native to Florida and the West Indies commonly purple or yellow or a mixture of the two while living

venus's-flower-basket *n, pl* **venus's-flower-baskets** *usu cap V* **:** a delicate tubular or cornucopia-shaped hexactinellid sponge (genus *Euplectella*) native to the East Indies and the eastern coast of Asia and having a skeleton of glassy transparent siliceous fibers interwoven into a firm network with long slender divergent anchoring fibers at the base by means of which the sponge stands erect in the soft mud at the bottom of the sea

venus's-flytrap *n, pl* **venus's-flytraps** *usu cap V* **:** an insectivorous plant (*Dionaea muscipula*) of the family Droseraceae found on the coast of the Carolinas and having the leaf apex modified into a ciliate margined insect trap of which the inner surface is provided with hairs that are sensitive to contact and cause the halves of the leaf to come together when touched

venus's-girdle *n, pl* **venus's-girdles** *usu cap V* **:** any of various ctenophores constituting the genus *Cestum* and having the body greatly compressed transversely and elongated in a sagittal plane so that it is ribbonlike with the mouth at the middle of one border

venus's-hairstone *or* **venus hairstone** *n, pl* **venus's-hairstones** *usu cap V* **:** quartz penetrated by acicular crystals of rutile

venus's looking-glass *n, usu cap V* **:** a plant of the genus *Specularia* (esp. *S. speculum-veneris*)

venus's-navelwort *n, pl* **venus's-navelworts** *usu cap V* **:** NAVELWORT 1,2

venus's-pride *n, pl* **venus's-prides** *usu cap V* **:** a bluet of the genus *Houstonia*

venus's-shell *n, pl* **venus's-shells** *usu cap V* **1 :** COWRIE **2 :** VENUS'S-COMB 2 **3 :** a mollusk of the family Veneridae; *also* **:** its shell

venus's-shoe *or* **venus's-slipper** *n, pl* **venus's-shoes** *or* **venus's-slippers** *usu cap V* **:** an American orchid of the genus *Cypripedium* — compare LADY'S SLIPPER

ve·nust \vəˈnəst\ *adj* [L *venustus*; akin to L *vener-*, *venus* love, charm — more at WIN] *archaic* **:** BEAUTIFUL, COMELY, GRACEFUL, ELEGANT

ve·nu·tian \vəˈn(y)üshən\ *n* -s *usu cap* [*Venus*, 2d planet from the sun + E *-tian* (as in *Martian*)] **:** VENUSIAN 2

ven·ville \ˈvenˌvil\ *n* -s [alter. (influenced by *-ville*, suffix of place names, fr. OF *ville* town, village) of ME *vennefeld*, *wengefeld*, fr. *venne*, *wenge* (of unknown origin) + *feld* field — more at VILLAGE, FIELD] **:** a tenure under English law peculiar to the neighborhood of Dartmoor forest by which the tenants have some rights in the forest

veny *obs var of* VENUE

veps \ˈveps\ *also* **vep·se** \ˈvepsə\ *n, pl* **veps** *also* **vep·ses** *cap* [Finn *vepsä*] **1 a :** a Finnish people of Russia now merged in the general population of the area between the Dnieper and the Volga **b :** a member of such people **2 :** a Finno-Ugric language of the Veps people — see URALIC LANGUAGES table

vep·si·an \ˈvepsēən\ *n* -s *usu cap* [*Veps* + *-ian*] **:** VEPS 2

ver *n* -s *usu cap* [ME, fr. L — more at VERNAL] *obs* **:** SPRINGTIME

ver *abbr* **1** verse **2** version **3** vertex

¹**vera** \ˈverə, ˈvarə, ˈvərə\ *Scot var of* VERY

²**ve·ra** \ˈvārə\ *n* -s [AmerSp, prob. fr. Sp, edge, border, fr. Pg *beira*] **1 :** a timber tree (*Bulnesia arborea*) of the family Zygophyllaceae of northwestern So. America **2 :** the very hard brownish yellow wood of the vera tree that is used as a substitute for lignum vitae

ve·ra·cious \vəˈrāshəs\ *adj* [L *verac-*, *verax* + E *-ious*] **1 :** observant of the truth **:** habitually speaking the truth **:** TRUTHFUL ⟨fish, flesh, and fowl . . . have been picked up by ~ people after a storm —John Burroughs⟩ **2 a :** marked by truth **:** ACCURATE, TRUE ⟨efforts to call up before us ~ images of a bedroom, a bed, pillows, a lighted candle —C.E.Montague⟩ ⟨a striving toward the ~ depiction of reality —*Encyc. Americana*⟩ **b :** not deceitful **:** DIRECT, HONEST, SINCERE ⟨the clear ~ glance of the brown eyes —George Eliot⟩ — **ve·ra·cious·ly** *adv* — **ve·ra·cious·ness** *n* -ES

ve·rac·i·ty \vəˈrasəd-ē, -raas-, -sətē, -i\ *n* -ES [NL *veracitas*, fr. L *verac-*, *verax* true, truthful + *-itas* -ity — more at VERY] **1 :** devotion to the truth **:** TRUTHFULNESS ⟨have no confidence in the ~ of this witness⟩ **2 :** power of conveying or perceiving truth **:** CORRECTNESS ⟨the ~ of his vision⟩ **3 :** conformity with truth or fact **:** ACCURACY ⟨any fool may write a most valuable book by chance, if he will only tell us what he heard and saw with ~ —Thomas Gray⟩ **4 :** something that is true ⟨a convincing speaker who can make lies sound like *veracities*⟩ **syn** see TRUTH

ve·ra·cruz \ˌverəˈkrüz\ *adj, usu cap* [fr. *Veracruz*, Mexico] **:** of or from the city of Veracruz, Mexico **:** of the kind or style prevalent in Veracruz

ve·ra·cru·za·no \ˌ==ˌkrüˈzä(ˌ)nō\ *n* -s *cap* [Sp, fr. *Veracruz*, Mexico + Sp *-ano* -an (fr. L *-anus*)] **:** a native or resident of Veracruz, Mexico

ve·ran·da *or* **ve·ran·dah** \vəˈrandə, -raan-\ *n* -s [partly fr. Hindi *varanda*, *baranda*; akin to Beng *bārāndā* veranda, lexical Skt *varanda*; partly fr. Pg *varanda*; akin to Sp *baranda* railing, balustrade, Prov *barando*, Catal *barana*] **:** a usu. roofed open gallery or portico attached to the exterior of a building and used for sitting out of doors **:** PIAZZA, PORCH — compare LOGGIA **syn** see BALCONY

ve·ran·daed *also* **ve·ran·dahed** \-dəd\ *adj* **:** having a veranda ⟨an old-fashioned wide ~ house —*Living Church*⟩

ver·a·scope \ˈverəˌskōp\ *n* [ISV *vera* (fem. of L *verus* true) + *-scope* — more at VERY] **:** a small stereoscopic camera made of metal and taking plates 45 to 107 millimeters in size

veratr- *or* **veratro-** *comb form* [NL, fr. *Veratrum*] **:** veratrine ⟨*veratrize*⟩ ⟨*veratroyl*⟩ **:** veratric acid ⟨*veratrole*⟩

ver·a·tral·de·hyde \ˌverəˈtraldəˌhīd\ *n* [*veratr-* + *aldehyde*] **1 :** a crystalline compound $(CH_3O)_2C_6H_3CHO$ made usu. by methylating vanillin; 3,4-dimethoxy-benzaldehyde **2 :** a crystalline compound isomeric with veratraldehyde; 2,3-dimethoxy-benzaldehyde — called also *ortho-veratraldehyde*

ver·a·tram·ine \-ˈtraˌmēn, -mən, vəˈratrəmən\ *n* [*veratr-* + *amine*] **:** a crystalline alkaloid $C_{27}H_{39}NO_2$ obtained from hellebore and esp. American hellebore

vera·trate \ˈverəˌtrāt\ *n* -s [ISV *veratr-* + *-ate*] **:** a salt or ester of veratric acid

ve·rat·ric acid \vəˈra·trik-\ *n* [ISV *veratr-* + *-ic*] **1 :** a crystalline acid $(CH_3O)_2C_6H_3COOH$ occurring in sabadilla seed and also formed by decomposition of veratridine and other alkaloids; 3,4-dimethoxy-benzoic acid **2 :** a crystalline acid isomeric with veratric acid; 2,3-dimethoxy-benzoic acid — called also *ortho-veratric acid*

ve·rat·ri·dine \-rəˌdēn, -dən\ *n* -s [*veratr-* + *-idine*] **:** a poisonous amorphous alkaloid $C_{36}H_{51}NO_{11}$ occurring in sabadilla seed and in some hellebores (as American hellebore)

ver·a·trine \ˈverəˌtrēn, -trən\ *n* -s [NL *veratrina*, fr. *Veratrum* + *-ina* -ine] **1 :** a mixture of alkaloids including cevadine, veratridine, and cevine that is obtained as a white or grayish powder from sabadilla seeds, that is an intense local irritant and a powerful muscle and nerve poison, and that has been used as a counterirritant in neuralgia and arthritis **2 a :** VERATRIDINE **b :** CEVADINE

ver·a·trole \-ˌtrōl\ *n* -s [ISV *veratr-* + *-ole*] **:** a crystalline or liquid ether $C_6H_4(OCH_3)_2$ made by methylating guaiacol or pyrocatechol; *ortho*-dimethoxy-benzene

ve·rat·ro·yl \vəˈra·trəˌwil\ *n* -s [ISV *veratr-* + *-yl*] **:** the univalent radical $(CH_3O)_2C_6H_3CO-$ of veratric acid

ve·ra·trum \vəˈrā·trəm\ *n* [NL, fr. L, hellebore] **1 a** *cap* **:** a genus of coarse herbs (family Liliaceae) having short poisonous rootstocks, large plicate clasping leaves in three vertical ranks, and panicled flowers with the perianth segments adnate to the ovary — compare VERATRINE **b** -s **:** any plant of the genus *Veratrum* **2** -s **:** the dried rhizome and roots of the American hellebore (*Veratrum viride*) or the European white hellebore (*V. album*) used in the treatment of hypertension

ver·a·tryl \ˈverəˌtril, -ēl\ *n* -s [*veratr-* + *-yl*] **:** the univalent radical $(CH_3O)_2C_6H_3CH_2-$ of the alcohol corresponding to veratraldehyde and veratric acid; 3,4-dimethoxy-benzyl

ver·a·tryl·i·dene \ˌ==ˈtriləˌdēn\ *n* -s [*veratryl* + *-idene*] **:** the bivalent radical $(CH_3O)_2C_6H_3CH=$ derived from veratraldehyde by removal of the aldehydic oxygen

verb \ˈvərb, ˈvəb, ˈvəib\ *n* -s *often attrib* [ME *verbe*, fr. MF, fr. L *verbum* word, verb; trans. of Gk *rhēma* — more at WORD] **:** a word belonging to that part of speech that characteristically is the grammatical center of a predicate and expresses an act, occurrence, or mode of being and that in various languages is inflected for agreement with the person and number of the subject, for tense, for voice, for mood, or for aspect and that typically has rather full descriptive meaning and characterizing quality but is in some instances nearly devoid of such meaning and quality esp. in use as an auxiliary or copula

¹**ver·bal** \ˈvərbəl, ˈvəb-, ˈvəib-\ *adj* [MF or LL; MF *verbal*, fr. LL *verbalis*, fr. L *verbum* word, verb + *-alis* -al] **1 a :** expert or facile in the use of words ⟨the most painstaking and elaborate ~ artist among the . . . poets of today —H.M.Green⟩ **b :** concerned with or using words for effect rather than meaning ⟨a merely ~ writer who sacrifices content to sound⟩ **c** *obs* **:** VERBOSE, WORDY ⟨you put me to forget a lady's manners by being so ~ —Shak.⟩ **2 a :** of or relating to words **:** consisting in or having to do with words ⟨few poets of the twentieth century have written ~ music with deeper sensibility —H.V. Gregory⟩ ⟨a table of proportional dimensions for various widths is reproduced, and detailed ~ instructions are given —*Experiment Station Record*⟩ **b :** of, relating to, or involving words only **:** having to do with words rather than meaning or substance ⟨a consistency that is merely ~ and scholastic —B.N.Cardozo⟩ ⟨an outward conformity with its precepts and a ~ profession of its tenets —J.G.Frazer⟩ **c :** consisting of or using words only and not effective action ⟨confined himself to a mere ~ protest⟩ **3 :** of, relating to, or formed from a verb ⟨occurs not less than ten times (eight times as a noun and twice in its ~ form) —*Lutheran Quarterly*⟩ ⟨a ~ adjective⟩ **4 :** spoken rather than written **:** ORAL ⟨invitations to them may be ~ or by way of a short, informal note —Noreen Routledge⟩ ⟨the employer's consent, ~ or written —Jacob Loft⟩ **5 :** word for word **:** LITERAL, VERBATIM ⟨a ~ translation⟩ **6 a :** of or relating to facility in the use and comprehension of words ⟨~ aptitude⟩ ⟨the ~ factor of a test⟩ — compare NUMERICAL 1e **b :** depending on the medium of words ⟨~ communication⟩ ⟨~ arts⟩ **7 a :** involving the use of words rather than action or performance ⟨the ~ IQ⟩ **b :** expressed merely through words **:** lacking in conceptual or emotional grasp — **ver·bal·ly** \-bəlē, -li\ *adv*

²**verbal** \"\ *n* -s **:** a word that combines characteristics of a verb with those of a noun or adjective — compare GERUND, INFINITIVE, PARTICIPLE

verbal auxiliary *n* **:** an auxiliary verb

verbal definition *n* **:** NOMINAL DEFINITION

verbal fallacy *n* **:** unsound reasoning that uses words ambiguously or otherwise violates a condition for the proper use of language in argument — compare AMPHIBOLOGY, FALLACY OF COMPOSITION, FALLACY OF DIVISION, FORMAL FALLACY

verbal image *n* **:** a mental image representing a word as heard, as seen, or as felt when pronounced

verbal inspiration *n* **:** the theological doctrine that a divine inspiration extends to every word of a particular text ⟨those who defend the *verbal inspiration* of the Bible⟩

ver·bal·ism *pronunc at* ¹VERBAL + ˌizəm\ *n* -s **1 a :** something expressed verbally **:** TERM, WORD ⟨the ~s so frequently considered amusing in published lists of pupils' boners —*Textbooks in Education*⟩ **b :** PHRASING, WORDING ⟨himself reasonably discriminating in his ~, he is apt to quote less carefully phrased expressions from the writings of others —*Times Lit. Supp.*⟩ **2 :** words used as or as if a substitute for or more significant than things **:** the equating of verbal quality with reality ⟨the emancipation of science from ~ —G.A.L.Sarton⟩ ⟨for the normal person every experience, real or potential, is saturated with ~ —Edward Sapir⟩ **3 a :** an empty form of words **:** a wordy expression of little meaning ⟨has produced grandiose theories and pretentious ~s —Austin Warren & René Wellek⟩ **b :** WORDINESS ⟨no time is wasted with superfluous ~ —M.W.Smith⟩

ver·bal·ist \-ləst\ *n* -s **1 :** one who places a special or undue emphasis on words ⟨we ~s and theorists often lack the simple faith of the concretizing mind —R.L.Shayon⟩ **2 :** a person skilled in the use of words ⟨the best ~ in his class⟩ — **ver·bal·is·tic** \ˌ==ˈlistik, -tēk\ *adj*

ver·bal·i·ty \ˌvərˈbaləd-ē, -lətē, -i\ *n* -ES **1 :** VERBIAGE ⟨prolix, drawling stuff, full of stale, puling ~ —G.T.Buckley⟩ **2 :** a verbal statement or formulation ⟨if they agree with these *verbalities* and effects, we can know that our ideas of the past are true —William James⟩ **3 :** the quality or nature of a verb

ver·bal·iza·tion \ˌvərbələˈzāshən, ˌvəb-, ˌvəib-, -əˌlīˈz-\ *n* -s **:** the act or an instance of verbalizing

ver·bal·ize \ˈ==ˌlīz\ *vb* -ED/-ING/-S [*verbal* + *-ize*] *vi* **1 :** to speak or write verbosely **2 :** to state something in words **:** make a verbal statement ⟨this wondrous ability of each character to ~, to articulate so clearly and precisely his point of view —Arthur Knight⟩ ~ *vt* **1 :** to convert into a verb **:** VERBIFY ⟨a language in which nouns are freely *verbalized*⟩ **2 :** to express in speech **:** name or describe in words ⟨doesn't ~ his cockiness, but he has a kind of negative confidence —A. J.Liebling⟩ ⟨difficult to ~ these pain experiences —Fredric Wertham⟩

ver·bal·iz·er \-zə(r)\ *n* -s **:** one that verbalizes

verbal note *n* **:** an unsigned diplomatic memorandum serving as an informal reminder of an unanswered question or request

verbal noun *n* **:** a noun derived directly from a verb or verb stem and in certain uses partaking of the sense and constructions of a verb — see GERUND

verbal proposition *n* **:** a proposition in which the subject and predicate are only verbally different and which conveys no real information unless about the meaning of words

ver·bar·i·um \(ˌ)vərˈba(a)rēəm\ *n* -s [NL, fr. L *verbum* + *-arium*] **:** ANAGRAMS

ver·bas·cose \(ˌ)=ˈbaˌskōs\ *n* -s [ISV *verbasc-* (fr. NL *Verbascum*) + *-ose*] **:** a crystalline sugar $C_{30}H_{56}O_{26}$ obtained from mullein root

ver·bas·cum \-ˌskəm\ *n, cap* [NL, fr. L, mullein] **:** a genus of coarse widely distributed herbs (family Scrophulariaceae) having large often woolly leaves and terminal spikes of yellow, white, or purplish flowers with a rotate corolla and five perfect stamens — see MULLEIN

¹**ver·ba·tim** \və(r)ˈbā|d·əm, ˌvərˈb-, vəˈb-, vəiˈb-, |təm *sometimes* -ba|\ *adv* [ME, fr. ML, fr. L *verbum* word — more at WORD] **1 :** word for word **:** in the same words ⟨that irritating and unforgivable habit of reporting conversations ~ —*Times Lit. Supp.*⟩ **2 :** note for note ⟨in ragtime are often repeated ~ or else varied by slight changes in figuration —Rudi Blesh⟩

²**verbatim** \"\ *adj* **1 :** reproduced from or repeating an original source word for word **:** following the original exactly ⟨the stenographers who take down the ~ record —J.F.J.Gillen⟩ **2 :** skilled in taking down a speech, report, or proceedings word for word ⟨a ~ reporter⟩

³**verbatim** \"\ *n* -s **:** an account, translation, or report that follows an original word for word

ver·be·na \və(r)ˈbēnə, ÷ -nyə\ *n* [NL, fr. L, sing. of *verbenae* sacred boughs of laurel or olive or myrtle, class of medicinal plants — more at VERVAIN] **1** *cap* **:** a genus (the type of the family Verbenaceae) of chiefly American herbs or subshrubs having bracted flowers in heads or spikes, a regular corolla with a 5-lobed limb, and four one-seeded nutlets **2** -s **a :** VERVAIN 1; *esp* **:** any of numerous garden plants of hybrid origin but treated as a hybrid species (*Verbena* × *hybrida*) that are widely cultivated usu. as annuals for their showy spikes of white, pink, red, or blue flowers which are borne in profusion over a long season — see BLUE VERVAIN **b :** any of various plants felt to resemble verbenas — usu. used in combination; see LEMON VERBENA, SAND VERBENA **3** *or* **verbena violet** -s **:** a pale violet to pale purple — called also *vervain*

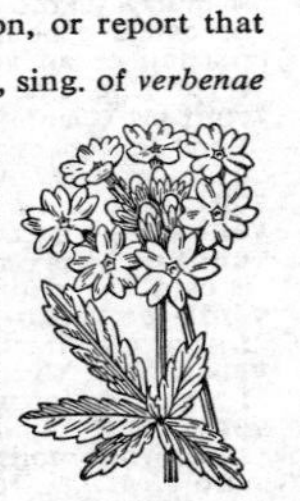
verbena

ver·be·na·ce·ae \ˌvərbəˈnāsēˌē\ *n pl, cap* [NL, fr. *Verbena*,

type genus + *-aceae*] : a family of herbs, shrubs, and trees (order Polemoniales) having opposite leaves, chiefly irregular flowers, and entire ovary — **ver·be·na·ceous** \¦==¦nāshəs\ *adj*

verbena family *n* : VERBENACEAE

ver·be·na·lin \və(r)ˈbēnᵊlən\ *n* -S [ISV *verben-* (fr. NL *Verbena*) + *-alin* (as in *digitalin*)] : a bitter crystalline glucoside $C_{17}H_{24}O_{10}$ in the flowers of the common vervain (*Verbena officinalis*)

verbena oil *n* **1** : a fragrant essential oil obtained esp. from lemon verbena and used in perfumery **2** : LEMONGRASS OIL

ver·be·none \ˈvərbə,nōn\ *n* -S [ISV *verben-* (fr. NL *Verbena*) + *-one*] : a liquid ketone $C_{10}H_{14}O$ found in verbena oil from Spain; 2-pinen-4-one

ver·ber·ate \ˈvərbə,rāt\ *vt* -ED/-ING/-S [L *verberatus*, past part. of *verberare* to lash, whip, beat — more at REVERBERATE] : BEAT, STRIKE

ver·ber·a·tion \,==ˈrāshən\ *n* -S [LL *verberation-, verberatio*, fr. L *verberatus* (past part.) + *-ion-, -io* -ion] : the act or action of beating or striking; *specif* : the impulse or vibration of a body that causes sound

ver·be·si·na \,vərbəˈsīnə, -sēnə\ *n* [NL, modif. (influenced by *Verbena*) of It dial. *forbesina* verbesina] **1** *cap* : a small genus of herbs (family Compositae) having yellow or white heads of tubular and radiate flowers — see GRAVELWEED, VIRGINIA CROWNBEARD **2** -S : any plant of the genus *Verbesina* — called also *crownbeard*

ver·bi·age \ˈvərbēij, ˈvə̄b-, ˈvəib- *sometimes* -bij *or* -bēj\ *n* -S [F, fr. MF *verbier* to chatter (fr. *verbe* word) + *-age* — more at WORD] **1** : excessive use of words : superfluity of language in proportion to sense or content : PROLIXITY, VERBOSITY, WORDINESS ⟨his concise and well-informed speeches were welcomed amid the common ~ of debate —John Buchan⟩ **2** : manner of expressing oneself in words : DICTION, WORDING ⟨messages and orders must use concise military ~ —G.S.Patton⟩

ver·bi·cide \-bə,sīd\ *n* -S [L *verbi-* (fr. *verbum* word) + E *-cide*] **1** : deliberate distortion or destruction of the sense of a word (as in punning) ⟨raises the humor above the exasperation of sheer ~ —P.E.More⟩ **2** : one who distorts or destroys the sense of a word ⟨is not a true humorist but a dull ~⟩

ver·bid \ˈvərbəd\ *n* -S [*verb* + *-id*] : VERBAL

verb·ifi·ca·tion \,vərbəfəˈkāshən\ *n* -S [fr. *verbify*, after such pairs as E *ossify: ossification*] : the act of making into a verb

verb·ify \ˈ==,fī\ *vb* -ED/-ING/-ES [*verb* + *-ify*] *vt* : to make into a verb : use as a verb ⟨elements used to ~ nouns are suffixed to noun stems —Edward Sapir⟩ ~ *vi* : to create a verb

ver·big·er·ate \(,)vərˈbijə,rāt\ *vi* -ED/-ING/-S [L *verbigeratus*, past part. of *verbigerare* to talk, fr. *verbum* word + *-gerare* (fr. *gerere* to carry) — more at CAST] : to repeat a word or sentence endlessly and meaninglessly ⟨never varied his ideas, seldom his expressions . . . he went on stubbornly *verbigerating* in the face of history —Vincent Sheean⟩

ver·big·er·a·tion \(,)=,==ˈrāshən\ *n* -S [ISV *verbigerate* + *-ion*] : continual repetition of stereotyped phrases (as in schizophrenia)

ver·bile \ˈvər,bīl\ *n* -S [L *verbum* word + E *-ile* (as in *audile*)] : one whose mental imagery consists of words — compare AUDILE

verb·less \ˈ=ləs\ *adj* : lacking a verb

ver·bo·mania \,vərbə+\ *n* [NL, fr. *verbo-* (fr. L *verbum* word) + *mania*] : a mania for words : excessive use of or obsession with words

ver·bo·maniac \¦==+\ *n* [ISV, fr. NL *verbomania*, after LL *mania*: ISV *maniac*] : one afflicted with verbomania

ver·bose \və(r)ˈbōs, ,vərˈb-,və̄ˈb-,vəiˈb-\ *adj* [L *verbosus*, fr. *verbum* word + *-osus* -ose — more at WORD] **1** : abounding in words : containing more words than necessary : PROLIX, TEDIOUS ⟨his arguments, clear, logical, never ~ —H.W.H. Knott⟩ **2** : given to wordiness : using words excessively : tediously long in speaking or writing ⟨a ~ orator⟩ **syn** see WORDY

ver·bose·ly *adv* : in a verbose manner

ver·bose·ness *n* -ES : VERBOSITY

ver·bos·i·ty \-ˈbäsəd·ē, -ətē, -i\ *n* -ES [MF or LL; MF *verbosité*, fr. LL *verbositat-, verbositas*, fr. L *verbosus* verbose + *-itat-, -itas* -ity] : the quality or state of being verbose : PROLIXITY, WORDINESS ⟨produced fifty-nine volumes of lachrymose ~ —*Amer. Guide Series: Conn.*⟩

[1]**ver·bo·ten** \və(r)ˈbōtᵊn, fə(r)ˈb-, ferˈb-, feəˈb-\ *adj* [G, fr. OHG *farbotan*, past part. of *farbiotan, firbiotan* to forbid — more at FORBID] : FORBIDDEN; *esp* : prohibited by dictate ⟨hanging onto the steps is ~ —J.F.Dobie⟩

[2]**verboten** \"\ *n* -S : something forbidden by authority ⟨the duties are mostly negative, in the form of standard, well-understood ~*s* —*Commonweal*⟩

verbs *pl of* VERB

verb sap \¦vərbˈsap\ *or* **ver·bum sap** \,vərbəmˈs-\ [short for L *verbum sapienti sat est* a word to the wise is sufficient] : enough said — used terminally and often responsively to indicate that something left unsaid may or should be inferred

verd \ˈvərd\ *n* -S [obs. F *verd* (now *vert*), fr. OF, fr. L *viridis*] *archaic* : GREEN, GREENNESS

verd- *or* **verdo-** *comb form* [MF *verd-*, fr. OF *verd, vert* green] : green-colored ⟨*verdo*hemoglobin⟩

ver·dac·cio \verˈdä(,)chō, -,chē,ō\ *n* -S [It, fr. *verde* green (fr. L *viridis*) + *-accio* (fr. L *-aceus* -aceous)] : a green color popular in late medieval Italy for fresco painting

ver·dan·cy \ˈvərdᵊnsē, ˈvə̄d-,ˈvəid-, -si\ *n* -ES : the quality or state of being verdant

ver·dant \-nt\ *adj* [MF *verdoyant*, fr. pres. part. of *verdoyer* to be verdant, to grow green, fr. OF *verdier, verdoier*, fr. *verd, vert* green, fr. L *viridis*, fr. *virēre* to be green] **1 a** : green in tint or color ⟨~ grass⟩ **b** : green with growing plants : covered with fresh vegetation ⟨~ fields⟩ **2** : unripe in knowledge or judgment : UNSOPHISTICATED, RAW — **ver·dant·ly** *adv*

verdant green *n* : a moderate yellow green that is yellower and less strong than average pea green, yellower and duller than apple green (sense 1), and greener and lighter than average moss green

verd an·tique *or* **verde antique** \¦vər,dan·¦tēk\ *n* [It *verde antico*, lit., ancient green] **1** : a green mottled or veined serpentine marble or calcareous serpentine much used for indoor decoration esp. by the ancient Romans : OPHICALCITE **2** : an andesite porphyry showing crystals of feldspar in a dark green groundmass

verdant zone *n* : THERMAL BELT

ver·der·er *or* **ver·der·or** \ˈvərdərər, ˈvə̄dərə(r, ˈvəidərə(r\ *n* -S [AF *verderer*, fr. OF *verdier* (fr. *verd* green + *-ier* -er) + E *-er*] : an English judicial officer having charge of the king's forest who is sworn to preserve the vert and venison, keep the assizes, and to view, receive, and enroll attachments and presentments of all manner of trespasses

ver·der·er·ship \-,ship\ *n* : the office or position of a verderer

ver·det \,vərˈdā, -det\ *n* -S [MF, fr. *verd* green + *-et*] : VERDIGRIS 4

ver·det constant \,vərˈdā-\ *n, usu cap V* [after Marcel Emile *Verdet* †1866 Fr. mathematician] : a constant that expresses the effect of a magnetic field in rotating the plane of polarization of plane polarized light when it traverses a transparent substance placed in the field and that is equal to the rotation produced in one centimeter length of the substance by a magnetic field of one gauss

verd gay \ˈvərdˈgā\ *n* [F *vert gai*] : PARROT GREEN

ver·dict \ˈvər|(,)dikt, ˈvə̄|, |ˈvəi|, |,dēkt\ *n* -S [alter. (influenced by ML *verdictum, veredictum* verdict, fr. L *vere dictum* truly said, fr. *vere* truly — fr. *verus* true — + *dictum* something said, saying) of ME *verdit*, fr. AF, fr. OF *ver, veir* true (fr. L *verus*) + *dit* saying, fr. past part. of *dire* to say, fr. L *dicere* — more at DICTUM, VERY, DICTION] **1** : the answer of a jury given to a court concerning a matter of fact in a civil or criminal cause committed to their examination and determination : the finding or decision of a jury on the matter legally submitted to them in the course of the trial of a cause that ordinarily in civil actions is for the plaintiff or for the defendant and in criminal actions guilty or not guilty — see DIRECTED VERDICT, SCOTCH VERDICT, SEALED VERDICT, SPECIAL VERDICT **2** : an opinion pronounced or felt : DECISION, JUDGMENT ⟨rejected the general ~ on her looks —Edith Wharton⟩ ⟨that a given novel satisfies the criterion entails a favorable critical ~ —C.W.Shumaker⟩

[1]**ver·di·gris** \ˈvərdə,grēs, ˈvə̄d-,ˈvəid-, -,gris *sometimes* -,grē\ *n* -ES [alter. (influenced by MF *verdegris*, alter. — influenced by *gris* gray — of OF *verte grez*) of ME *vertegrez*, fr. OF *verte grez, vert de Grice*, lit., green of Greece, fr. *vert* green + *de* of, from (fr. L) + *Grice, Grece* Greece, fr. L *Graecia* — more at GRIZZLE, VERDANT, DE-, GRECIAN] **1** : a green or greenish blue poisonous pigment obtained by the action of acetic acid on copper and used chiefly in antifouling paints and formerly in medicine: as **a** : a light blue powder or silky blue crystalline product $Cu(C_2H_3O_2)_2.CuO.6H_2O$ — called also *blue verdigris* **b** : a green product $2Cu(C_2H_3O_2)_2.CuO.6H_2O$ — called also *green verdigris* **2** : the poisonous normal copper acetate $Cu(C_2H_3O_2)_2.H_2O$ obtained as a green powder or dark green efflorescent crystals (as by the action of acetic acid on copper oxide [sense b]) and used chiefly in making Paris green — called also *crystallized verdigris, neutral verdigris* **3** : a green or bluish deposit esp. of copper carbonates formed on copper, brass, or bronze surfaces — compare PATINA 2 **4** *or* **verdigris green** : a moderate yellowish green that is greener, lighter, and stronger than tarragon or average almond green and paler and slightly greener than malachite green — called also *distilled green, Montpellier green, Spanish green, verdet*

[2]**verdigris** \"\ *vb* -ED/-ING/-ES *vt* : to cover or coat with verdigris ⟨a rusty lantern or a ~*ed* cannonball —Nike Anderson⟩ ~ *vi* : to become spotted or stained with verdigris — used of an insect mounted on a pin

ver·di·grisy \-ēsē, -isē, -si\ *adj* : resembling or suggesting verdigris (as in color)

ver·din \ˈvərdᵊn, vərˈdan\ *n* -S [F, yellowhammer] : a very small yellow-headed titmouse (*Auriparus flaviceps*) found from Texas to California and southward that builds a large globular nest

ver·dit \ˈvərdət, ˈvär-\ *dial var of* VERDICT

ver·di·ter \ˈvərdəd·ə(r), ˈvə̄d-,ˈvəid-, -dətə-\ *n* -S [MF *verd de terre*, lit., green of earth] **1** : BLUE VERDITER **2** : GREEN VERDITER

verditer blue *n* : AZURITE BLUE

verditer green *n* : MALACHITE GREEN 3

verdo- — see VERD-

ver·do·globin \¦vərdə+\ *n* [*verd-* + *globin*] : any of several green compounds (as choleglobin and sulfhemoglobin) derived from hemoglobin or related compounds by cleavage of the porphyrin ring

ver·do·la·ga \,vərdəˈlägə, ,ver-\ *n* -S [Sp, fr. Ar *bardilāga*, fr. L *portulaca* purslane — more at PORTULACA] : a common purslane (*Portulaca oleracea*)

ver·do·peroxidase \¦vərdə+\ *n* [*verd-* + *peroxidase*] : a green-colored peroxidase obtained from leukocytes

verds *pl of* VERD

ver·dure \ˈvərjər, ˈvə̄jə(r, ˈvəijə(r\ *n* -S [ME, fr. MF, fr. *verd* green + *-ure* — more at VERDANT] **1** : the greenness and freshness of growing vegetation; *also* : such vegetation itself : a green growth **2** : a tapestry having a design made up of foliage, trees, or flowers often in the form of formal gardens **3** : a dark to deep yellowish green **4** : a vigorous condition suggesting fresh growth of vegetation : good health : freshness and strength

ver·dured \-jə(r)d\ *adj* : covered with verdure

ver·dure·less \ˈ==ləs\ *adj* : having no verdure : lacking vegetation

ver·dur·ous \-jərəs\ *adj* : clothed with the fresh green of vegetation : VERDURED, VERDANT

verd ves·sie \-ˈvesē\ *n* [F *vert de vessie*] : SAP GREEN 2b

ver·ein \vəˈrīn, fə-\ *n* -S [G, fr. MHG *vereine* union, association, fr. *vereinen* to unite, fr. *ver-* for- (fr. OHG *far-*) + *einen* to make one, fr. *ein* one, fr. OHG — more at FOR-, ONE] : a usu. social or political organization or association

ver·ek \ˈfe,rek\ *n* -S [NL (specific epithet of *Acacia verek*, syn. of *Acacia senegal*), fr. Berber *afarak*, fr. Hausa *farak k'aya*, fr. *farar* white + *k'aya* thorn] : an acacia (*Acacia senegal*)

ver·e·til·lum \,verəˈtiləm\ *n* [NL, fr. L, dim. of *veretrum* genitals; akin to L *vereri* to fear — more at WARY] **1** *cap* : a genus of club-shaped pennatulaceans with zooids distributed irregularly all round the rachis that occur at moderate depths in the Mediterranean and Atlantic **2** -S : any animal of the genus *Veretillum*

[1]**verge** \ˈvərj, ˈvə̄j, ˈveij\ *n* -S [ME, fr. MF, fr. L *virga* twig, rod, streak, stripe — more at WHISK] **1 a** (1) : a rod or staff carried as an emblem of authority or as a symbol of office (2) *obs* : a stick or wand held by a person being admitted to tenancy while he swears fealty **b** (1) : the spindle of a watch balance; *esp* : a spindle with pallets in an old vertical escapement (2) *or* **verge watch** : a watch with a vertical escapement **c** : the male intromittent organ of any of various invertebrates **d** (1) : a needle guide in a stocking machine (2) : a bobbin guide in a lace machine **2 a** : something that borders, limits, or bounds: as (1) : an outer often decorated or inscribed margin of an object or structural part ⟨electric candles . . . around the ~ between walls and ceiling —Clifton Daniel⟩ (2) *obs* : an enclosing band : CIRCLET, RING ⟨the inclusive ~ of golden metal that must round my brow —Shak.⟩; *also* : RIM, BRIM (3) : the outermost edge or a part of the edge of an extended area ⟨a row of white palings, which marked the ~ of the heath —Thomas Hardy⟩ ⟨the southern ~ of the Lake District —E.B. Ford⟩ ⟨the ~ of the sea⟩ (4) : the bottom or usu. the upper margin of a precipice ⟨the child crept to the edge, and was balanced on the very ~ —Richard Jefferies⟩ (5) : the edge of a bed or border esp. of flowers (6) : a strip of vegetation adjoining a walk, road, or railway line ⟨grass ~*s* also lose their correct level above the path —*Gardeners' Chronicle*⟩ (7) : HORIZON ⟨the sky was clear from ~ to ~ —Thomas Hardy⟩ (8) : the edge of the tiling projecting over the gable of a roof (9) *Brit* : the paved, unpaved, or planted shoulder of a road or walk ⟨the graveled ~*s* of the path —Lionel Shapiro⟩ ⟨the road narrows and . . . the edges of the ~*s* are not surfaced —R.J.P. Mortished⟩ **b** : the point marking the beginning of a new or different state, condition, or action : BRINK, THRESHOLD ⟨the country was on the ~ of bankruptcy —*London Calling*⟩ ⟨on the ~ of asking to be relieved —John Mason Brown⟩ ⟨vocabulary and grammar are both bad to the ~ of illiteracy —M.M. Rossi⟩ **c** : the outermost margin or marginal area of a state, concept, class, or jurisdiction : FRINGE ⟨the mob operates on the ~ of the confidence rackets —D.W.Maurer⟩ ⟨not enough that a statute goes to the ~ of constitutional power —O.W. Holmes †1935⟩ **3 a** (1) : the area or limit within 12 miles of the place of the court of an English sovereign formerly delimited as under the king's peace (2) : either of two former English courts under the special jurisdiction of the lord steward and marshal of the king's household **b** (1) *obs* : the area of application of a category or concept : RANGE, SCOPE (2) *obs* : the entities that fall within the area of a category or concept : CLASS (3) *obs* : CONTROL, JURISDICTION **c** : the actual area covered by or the immediate environs of a place **4** : the scope permitted by a limiting line or condition ⟨anyone who has figured prominently in the social consciousness . . . should be given ~ and room —Allan Nevins⟩ **syn** see BORDER

[2]**verge** \"\ *vb* -ED/-ING/-S *vt* **1** : to provide with a verge : BORDER, EDGE, TRIM ⟨shores . . . *verged* with floating lawns of . . . aquatic plants —William Bartram⟩ **2** : to constitute the verge of : act as a border for ⟨a file of trees *verging* the road —Richard Wilbur⟩ ~ *vi* **1** : to be in the next or neighboring place : be contiguous **2** : to be on the verge : be at or approach the border or start of condition, state, or event ⟨a personality who at least *verged* on greatness —George Woodcock⟩ ⟨a courage that *verged* on foolhardiness —Agnes M. Cleaveland⟩ ⟨already *verging* on old age —W.H.Hudson †1922⟩

[3]**verge** \"\ *vi* -ED/-ING/-S [L *vergere* to bend, incline — more at WRENCH] **1 a** *of the sun* : to incline toward the horizon : SINK **b** : to move, extend, or incline in a particular direction or toward a point, goal, or condition ⟨the hill ~*s* to the north⟩ ⟨the declining civilization ~*s* to its fall —A.J.Toynbee⟩ **2** : to be in or as if in transition from one state to another : be in the process of changing or merging ⟨gradations from azures to hues *verging* on black —H.E.Riesebery⟩

vergeboard \ˈ=,=\ *n* [by alter.] : BARGEBOARD

ver·gence \ˈvərjən(t)s\ *n* -S [[3]*verge* + *-ence*] : a turning movement of the eyeballs

ver·gen·cy \-nsē, -si\ *n* -ES [[3]*verge* + *-ency*] **1** *obs* : the act or process of verging, approaching, or bordering on something : TENDENCY, INCLINATION **2** : a measure of convergence or divergence of a pencil of rays entering or issuing from a lens or mirror that is expressed as the reciprocal of the distance from lens or mirror to the focus of the rays and for rays through a principal focus is equal to the focal power of the lens or mirror

verg·er \ˈvərjər, ˈvə̄jə(r, ˈvəijə(r\ *n* -S [ME, fr. MF *verge* + ME *-er* — more at VERGE] **1** *Brit* : an attendant that carries a verge before a bishop, dean, or other official **2** : a church official who serves as a sacristan, as an attendant who keeps order during services, or as an usher

verge rafter *n* [*verge* short for *vergeboard*] : BARGEBOARD

verges *pl of* VERGE, *pres 3d sing of* VERGE

verge watch *n* : VERGE 1b(2)

ver·gi·form \ˈvərjə,fȯrm\ *adj* [[1]*verge* + *-iform*] : RODLIKE

ver·gil·ian *or* **vir·gil·ian** \,vərˈjilēən, vəˈj-, vəiˈj-, -lyən\ *adj, usu cap* [*vergilian* fr. L *vergilianus*, fr. Publius *Vergilius* Maro †19 B.C. Roman poet + L *-anus* -an; *virgilian* fr. LL *virgilianus*, alter. of L *vergilianus*] : of or relating to Vergil; *esp* : characteristic of the style of Vergil

ver·glas \(ˈ)ver¦glä\ *n, pl* **verglases** \-ä(z)\ [F, fr. MF, fr. OF *verre-glaz* lit., glass-ice, fr. *verre* glass (fr. L *vitrum* glass, woad) + *glaz, glace* ice, fr. LL *glacia* — more at WOAD, GLACIER] : a thin film of ice on rock

veridian *var of* VIRIDIAN

ve·rid·i·cal \vəˈridəkəl, -dēk-\ *adj* [L *veridicus* veracious (fr. *verus* true + *-dicus*, fr. *dicere* to say) + E *-al* — more at VERY, DICTION] **1** : conforming to the truth : TRUTHFUL, VERACIOUS ⟨tried . . . to supply . . . a ~ background to the events and people portrayed —Laura Krey⟩ **2** : not illusory : GENUINE, REAL, ACTUAL, TRUE ⟨perceptual error . . . has a surprising resemblance to ~ perception —F.A.Olafson⟩ — **ve·rid·i·cal·ly** \-k(ə)lē, -li\ *adv*

veridical hallucination *n* : a hallucination corresponding to a real event (as when the apparition of an image of an absent person is coincident with his death)

ve·rid·i·cal·i·ty \və,ridəˈkaləd·ē\ *n* -ES : the quality or state of being veridical : TRUTHFULNESS, GENUINENESS

verier *comparative of* VERY

veriest *superlative of* VERY

ver·i·fi·abil·i·ty \,verə,fīəˈbiləd·ē, -lətē, -i\ *n* : the quality or state of being confirmable

verifiability principle *or* **verifiability theory** *n* : a proposal or claim of early logical positivists according to which a requirement or criterion for the meaningfulness of a factual statement is its susceptibility to the possibility of being either theoretically or actually proved true or false by reference to empirical facts — compare CONFIRMABILITY THEORY

ver·i·fi·able \ˈverə,fīəbəl\ *adj* **1** : capable of being verified **2** : susceptible to the possibility of being either theoretically or actually proved true or false by reference to empirical facts — compare CONFIRMABLE 2 — **ver·i·fi·able·ness** *n* -ES

ver·i·fi·ca·tion \,verəfəˈkāshən\ *n* -S [MF, fr. ML *verification-, verificatio*, fr. *verificatus* (past part. of *verificare* to verify) + L *-ion-, -io* -ion] **1 a** : the act or process of verifying or the state of being verified : the authentication of truth or accuracy by such means as facts, statements, citations, measurements, or attendant circumstances **b** (1) : confirmation by evidence in law (2) : confirmation by oath or affidavit **c** : the procedure required for the establishment of the truth or falsity of a statement **2** : an averment used in concluding a plea that states that the pleader is prepared to prove his allegations **3** : an oath to the truth of a pleading in code pleading **4** : the ceremony of subscribing statements as true under oath and the certification of the ceremony by the notary or other officer administering the oath **5** : RATIFICATION

verification principle *or* **verification theory** *n* : VERIFIABILITY PRINCIPLE

ver·i·fi·ca·to·ry \ˈverəfə,kād·ərē, -ātərē, -ā·trē, -i\ *adj* [*verification* + *-ory*] : that is capable of verification or serves to verify : VERIFYING, AUTHENTICATING, CONFIRMING

ver·i·fied \ˈverə,fīd\ *adj* [ME, fr. past part. of *verifien* to verify] **1** : authenticated by affidavit ⟨a ~ motion⟩ **2** : substantiated by competent proof ⟨a ~ case⟩ ⟨a ~ claim⟩

ver·i·fi·er \-,fī(ə)r, -īə\ *n* -S **1** : one that searches for or discovers verification **2** : one that serves as verification ⟨the problem of verifying beliefs . . . where the ~ lies beyond experience —J.W.Yolton⟩ **3** : a machine used to check the correctness of the previous recording of data (as by punching cards or magnetizing tape)

ver·i·fy \-,fī\ *vt* -ED/-ING/-ES [ME *verifien*, fr. MF *verifier*, fr. ML *verificare*, fr. L *verus* true + *-ficare* -fy — more at VERY] **1 a** : to confirm or substantiate in law by oath or proof : add the legal verification to (a pleading or petition) **b** (1) : to swear to or affirm the truth of (2) *obs* : to second the testimony of : affirm the truthfulness of **2** : to prove to be true : establish the truth of : conclusively demonstrate by presentation of facts or by sound reasoning or argument ⟨have continually *verified* their own position by an appeal to the arts of the past —Bernard Smith⟩ **3** : to serve as conclusive evidence, argument, proof, or demonstration of ⟨observations of the research team *verified* the foreman's statement —*Management Behavior & Foreman Attitude*⟩ ⟨admirably adapted to an aquarium life, as the following account will ~ —G.E. & Nettie MacGinitie⟩ **4** : to check or test the accuracy or exactness of : confirm the truth or truthfulness of by or as if by comparison with known data or a recognized standard or authority ⟨sought out and *verified* the scientific names of birds mentioned in the text —E.A.Armstrong⟩ ⟨a government survey party was ~*ing* the neighboring landmarks —Joseph Furphy⟩ **5** : to confirm or establish the authenticity or existence of by examination, investigation, or competent evidence **syn** see CONFIRM

ver·i·ly \ˈverəlē, -li\ *adv* [ME *verraily*, fr. *verray* very + *-ly* — more at VERY] **1** : in very truth : beyond doubt or question : in fact : CERTAINLY ⟨trust in the Lord and do good . . . and ~ thou shalt be fed —Ps 37:3 (AV)⟩ **2** : TRULY, CONFIDENTLY, REALLY ⟨I ~ think so⟩

veri·sim·i·lar \¦verə¦siməlә(r)\ *adj* [L *verisimilis* verisimilar + E *-ar*] : having the appearance of truth : PROBABLE, LIKELY — **veri·sim·i·lar·ly** *adv*

veri·si·mil·i·tude \,==səˈmilə,tüd, -ə·,tyüd\ *n* [L *verisimilitudo*, fr. *verisimilis, veri similis* having the appearance of truth (fr. *veri* — gen. of *verum*, neut. of *verus* true — + *similis* like, similar) + *-tudo* -tude — more at VERY, SAME] **1** : the quality or state of being verisimilar : the appearance of truth : PROBABILITY, LIKELIHOOD ⟨the dialogue is too abstract and self-conscious for ~ —Paul Pickrel⟩ **2** : that which is verisimilar : a statement apparently true **syn** see TRUTH

veri·si·mil·i·ty \-əd·ē\ *n* -ES [L *verisimilis* + E *-ity*] : VERISIMILITUDE

veri·sim·i·lous \¦==¦siməl əs\ *adj* [L *verisimilis* + E *-ous*] : VERISIMILAR

ve·rism \ˈvi,rizəm, ˈve,r-\ *n* -S [It *verismo*, fr. *vero* true (fr. L *verus*) + *-ismo* -ism] **1** : artistic use of contemporary everyday material esp. in opera in preference to the heroic, the mythical and legendary, or the historical **2** : a realistic or objective style of musical composition or of painting appropriate to the treatment of everyday material

[1]**ve·rist** \-,rəst\ *n* -S [It *verista*, fr. *vero* true + *-ista* -ist] : one who practices or advocates verism

[2]**verist** \"\ *or* **ve·ris·tic** \vəˈristik\ *adj* [*verist* fr. F *vériste*, fr. It *verista* verist, n.; *veristic* fr. [1]*verist* + *-ic*] : having the qualities or character of verism

ver·i·ta·ble \ˈverəd·əbəl, -rətə-\ *adj* [MF *veritable*, fr. *verité* verity + *-able*] : being actually that which is named : possessing the characteristics applied : not false, unreal, imaginary, or metaphorical ⟨shots taken in a ~ bull ring —John McCarten⟩ ⟨the only guts that are mentioned . . . are the ~ entrails of a fish —Mark Schorer⟩ ⟨spiritual heights which may be just as ~ as the streets and gutters —H.O.Taylor⟩ — often used to stress the aptness of a metaphor ⟨whose conversation was a ~ memo pad of given names, connections, ties, appointments —Mary McCarthy⟩ ⟨a ~ mountain of newspaper material —T.D.Clark⟩ **syn** see AUTHENTIC

ver·i·ta·ble·ness *n* -ES : the quality or state of being veritable

ver·i·ta·bly \-blē, -li\ *adv* : in a veritable manner : TRULY

ver·i·tism \ˈverə,tizəm\ *n* -S [*verity* + *-ism*] : VERISM

ver·i·tist \-rəd·əst\ *n* -S [*verity* + *-ist*] : VERIST

ver·i·ty \ˈverəd·ē, -rətē, -i\ *n* -ES [ME *verite*, fr. MF *verité*, fr. L *veritat-, veritas*, fr. *verus* true + *-itat- -itas* -ity — more at VERY] **1 a** : the quality or state of being true or real: (1) : the consonance of a statement, proposition, or representation with fact ⟨the ~ of his recollection of the castle⟩ (2) : faith-

fulness or correspondence to aesthetic truth ⟨the ~ of a symphony to the composer's conception⟩ **b** : the quality or state of being eternally or necessarily true and not merely true as a matter of fact **2** : something that is true : a true fact or statement; *esp* : a statement true in all circumstances : a necessary esp. ethical, religious, or aesthetic truth **3** : HONESTY, VERACITY **syn** see TRUTH

¹**ver·juice** \'vər.jüs\ *n* [ME *verjuis, verjus*, fr. MF *verjus, vert jus*, lit., green juice, fr. OF, fr. *vert* green + *jus* juice — more at VERDANT, JUICE] **1** : the sour juice of crab apples or of green or unripe grapes, apples, or other fruit; *also* : an acid liquor made from verjuice **2** : acidity of disposition, manner, or temperament

²**verjuice** \"\ *vt* : to acidify as if with verjuice : EMBITTER

ver macaque \"\ *n* [F, lit., macaque worm] : TORSALO

¹**ver·meil** \'vərməl, -ˌmāl, vər'mā(ə)l\ *adj* [ME *vermail*, fr. OF — more at VERMILION] : bright red

²**vermeil** \"\ *n* -s [MF, fr. *vermeil*, adj.] **1** : VERMILION **2 a** : an orange-red garnet **b** : SPINEL **c** : RUBY **3** : a red varnish applied to a gilded surface to give luster **4** : gilded silver, bronze, or copper

³**vermeil** \"\ *vt* -ED/-ING/-s : to color or stain with or as if with vermilion

¹**ver·mes** \'vər(ˌ)mēz\ *n pl, cap* [NL, fr. pl. of L *vermis* worm] : any of several major divisions of the animal kingdom: as **a** *in former classifications* : a group containing all invertebrates with the exception of the arthropods **b** *in some esp former classifications* : a group comprising the typically soft-bodied and more or less vermiform invertebrates, including the flatworms, roundworms, annelid worms, and minor forms, and usu. held to be a purely artificial assemblage

²**vermes** *pl of* VERMIS

¹**ver·me·tid** \'vərmətəd\ *adj* [NL *Vermetidae*, family of mollusks, fr. *Vermetus*, type genus + *-idae*] : of or relating to the Vermetidae

²**vermetid** \"\ *n* -S [NL *Vermetidae*] : a mollusk of the family Vermetidae — WORM SHELL

ver·met·i·dae \vər'metəˌdē\ *n pl, cap* [NL, fr. *Vermetus*, type genus + *-idae*] : a small family of marine mollusks (suborder Taenioglossa) comprising *Vermetus* and closely related genera — see SILIQUARIA

ver·me·tus \-'mēd·əs\ *n* [NL, fr. L *vermis* worm] **1** *cap* : a genus (the type of the family Vermetidae) of marine gastropod mollusks having when young regularly spiral shells and being free to creep about and later becoming permanently attached to an object and developing separate whorls often irregularly bent and contorted like a worm tube **2** -ES : VERMETID

vermi- *comb form* [NL, fr. LL, fr. L *vermis* — more at WORM] : worm ⟨*vermiform*⟩ ⟨*vermiparous*⟩

ver·mi·an \'vərmēən\ *adj* [ISV *vermi-* + *-an*] **1** : of, relating to, or resembling the worms **2** : of or relating to the worms of the cerebellum

¹**ver·mi·cel·li** \ˌvərmə'selē, -ˌvōm-, -ˌvəim-, -mə'che-\ *n* -S [It, fr. pl. of *vermicello*, dim. of *verme* worm, fr. L *vermis*] : alimentary paste made in long thin solid strings smaller in diameter than spaghetti — compare MACARONI

²**vermicelli** \"\ *adj* **1** : composed of or containing vermicelli ⟨~ soup⟩ **2** : suggestive of or resembling vermicelli ⟨~ braids⟩ ⟨~ designs⟩

ver·mi·ci·dal \ˌvərmə'sīd²l\ *adj* **1** : destroying worms **2** : of or relating to a vermicide

ver·mi·cide \'vərməˌsīd\ *n* -S [*vermi-* + *-cide*] : an agent that destroys worms, esp. those that are intestinally parasitic — compare ANTHELMINTIC

ver·mi·cle \'vərməkəl\ *n* -S [L *vermiculus*] : a small worm or wormlike larva

ver·mic·u·lar \(ˌ)vər'mikyələr\ *adj* [NL *vermicularis*, fr. L *vermiculus* little worm + *-aris* -ar] **1 a** : resembling a worm in form or motion : VERMIFORM **b** : VERMICULATE **2** : of, relating to, or caused by worms

ver·mic·u·lar·ia \(ˌ)vər.mikyə'la(ə)rēə\ *n, cap* [NL, fr. L *vermiculus* + NL *-aria*] : a genus of imperfect fungi (family Melanconiaceae) characterized by setose pycnidia and unicellular vermiform pycnospores

ver·mic·u·late \vər(r)'mikyələt, -ˌlāt, usu -ə.+V\ *adj* [L *vermiculatus*, past part. of *vermiculari* to be wormy, fr. *vermiculus* little worm — more at VERMILION] **1 a** : wormlike in shape **b** : covered with wormlike elevations : marked with irregular fine lines of color or with irregular wavy impressed lines like worm tracks ⟨a ~ nut⟩ **2** : TORTUOUS, INVOLUTE **3** : full of worms : WORM-EATEN

ver·mic·u·lat·ed \-ˌlād·əd, -ātəd\ *adj* [L *vermiculatus* + E *-ed*] : VERMICULATE

vermiculated work *or* **vermicular work** *n* : stonework wrought to have the appearance of convoluted worms or of having been eaten into by or covered with tracks of worms

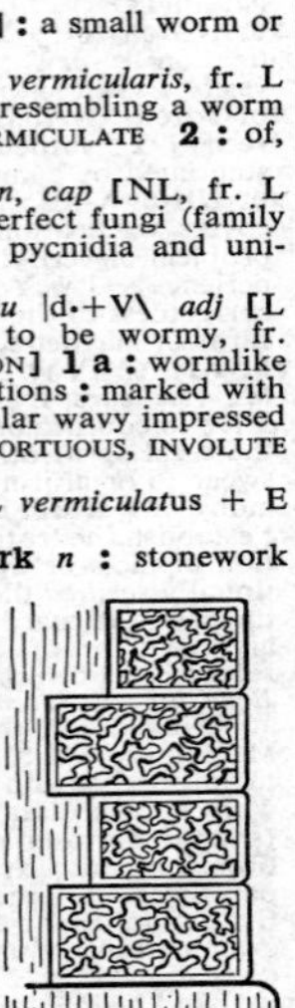

ver·mic·u·la·tion \ˌ.ˌlāshən\ *n* -s [L *vermiculation-, vermiculatio*, fr. *vermiculatus* (past part. of *vermiculari*) + *-ion, -io* ion] **1** : penetration by worms : the state of being worm-eaten **2** : the act or process of moving like a worm : WRITHING, TWISTING ⟨the ~ of the intestines⟩ **3** : an esp. ornamental narrow and wavy or tortuous marking or system of markings

ver·mi·cule \'vərmə.kyül\ *n* -s [L *vermiculus* little worm] : a wormlike body; *specif* : OOKINETE

ver·mic·u·lite \və(r)'mikyə.līt, usu -īd·+V\ *n* -s [L *vermiculus* + E *-ite*] : any of a number of micaceous minerals (as maconite) that are hydrous silicates derived generally from the alteration of mica which do not burn, are not harmed by water, and whose granules expand greatly at high temperatures to give a lightweight highly water-absorbent material that is used in seedbeds as a mulch, in plaster, mortar, and concrete as a substitute for sand, and as an insulating material in walls, floors, and ceilings

ver·mi·form \'vərmə.fȯrm\ *adj* [NL *vermiformis*, fr. *vermi-* + *-formis* -form] : WORMLIKE, VERMICULAR

vermiform appendix *n* [trans. of NL *appendix vermiformis*] : a narrow blindly ending tube usu. about three or four inches long that extends from the cecum in the lower right-hand part of the abdomen in a direction which varies in different individuals, that has much lymphoid wall tissue, that normally communicates with the cavity of the cecum, and that represents an atrophied terminal part of the cecum — called also *vermiform process*; compare APPENDICITIS; see DIGESTION illustration

ver·mi·for·mis \ˌvərmə'fȯrməs\ *n* -ES [NL, short for *appendix vermiformis*] : VERMIFORM APPENDIX

vermiform process *n* : the vermis of the cerebellum **2** : VERMIFORM APPENDIX

ver·mif·u·gal \ˌvər'mifyəgəl, 'vərmə.fyüg-\ *adj* [²*vermifuge* + *-al*] : VERMIFUGE

¹**ver·mi·fuge** \'vərmə.fyüj\ *adj* [prob. fr. (assumed) NL *vermifugus*, fr. NL *vermi-* + (assumed) NL *-fugus* expelling (fr. L *fugare* to put to flight) — more at *-FUGE] : serving to destroy or expel parasitic worms esp. of the intestine : ANTHELMINTIC

²**vermifuge** \"\ *n* -s [*vermi-* + *-fuge*] : a vermifuge agent

ver·mi·lin·gua \ˌvərmə'lingwə\ *n pl, cap* [NL, fr. *vermi-* + L *lingua* tongue — more at TONGUE] *in some esp former classifications* : a superfamily comprising the American anteaters or sometimes these together with the pangolins and aardvark

¹**ver·mil·in·gua** \-gwēə\ *also* **vermil·in·gues** \-ˌ)gwēz\ *n* [NL, fr. *vermi-* + *-lingua* or *-lingues* (fr. L *lingua* tongue)] : syn of VERMILINGUA

²**vermilingua** \"\ *n pl, cap* [NL, fr. *vermi-* + *-lingua* (fr. L *lingua* tongue)] : a division of lizards consisting of the chameleons — **ver·mi·lin·gui·al** \-ˌ.ˌgwēəl\ *adj*

¹**ver·mil·ion** *or* **ver·mil·lion** \və(r)'milyən\ *n* -s [ME *vermilioun*, fr. OF *vermeillon*, fr. *vermeil*, adj., bright red, fr. LL *vermiculus* kermes (scale insect from which the red dyestuff is derived), fr. L, little worm, dim. of *vermis* worm — more at WORM] **1 a** : a bright red pigment consisting of mercuric sulfide formerly obtained from the mineral cinnabar but now

always prepared synthetically (as by reaction of mercury, sulfur, and sodium hydroxide), that varies from crimson to orange when finely divided, and that is coarse-grained to nearly orange when finely divided, and that is used chiefly as an artist's color and in rubber — called also *Chinese vermilion*; see ENGLISH VERMILION **b** : any of various other red pigments: as (1) : AMERICAN VERMILION (2) : ANTIMONY VERMILION **2 a** : GOYA **b** : a variable color averaging a vivid reddish orange that is redder, darker, and slightly stronger than chrome orange, redder and darker than golden poppy, and redder and lighter than international orange **3** : VERMEIL 2a **4** : AMBOYNA 1

²**vermilion** *or* **vermillion** \"\ *vt* -ED/-ING/-s : to color or tint with or as if with vermilion

ver·mil·ion·ette \ˌ.ˌ'net\ *n* -s [ISV *vermilion* + *-ette*] : any of various brilliant red organic pigments made by precipitating eosin or a similar dye upon a base (as barium sulfate or white lead)

vermilion flycatcher *n* : any of several American flycatchers of the genus *Pyrocephalus* which have in the adult male bright scarlet and brownish gray or black plumage and one (*P. rubinus mexicanus*) of which is found as far north as southern Texas and Arizona

ver·mil·ion·ize \və(r)'milyə.nīz\ *vt* -ED/-ING/-s : to make vermilion in color

vermilion rockfish *n* : a common commercially important red rock cod (*Sebastodes miniatus*) of the Pacific coast of No. America that is vermilion to brick red above shading to pink and light red on the sides and belly and liberally speckled with black on the back and sides

ver·min \'vərmən, 'vȯm-, 'vəim-\ *n, pl* **vermin** *usu pl in constr* [ME, fr. MF *vermin, vermine*, fr. L *vermis* worm] **1** : animals obnoxious to man: as **a** : small animals (as lice, bedbugs, mice) that tend to occur in great numbers, are difficult to control, and are offensive as well as injurious **b** : birds and mammals (as owls and weasels) that prey upon game **c** : animals that at a particular time and place compete with man or his domestic animals (as for food) (deer are considered ~ in New Zealand) **2** : a noxious or offensive person or persons

²**vermin** \"\ *vi* -ED/-ING/-s [L *verminatus*, past part. of *verminare* to have worms, fr. *vermis* worm] **1** *archaic* : to breed vermin **2** : to become infested with vermin

ver·mi·na·tion \ˌ.ˌ'nāshən\ *n* -s [L *vermination-, verminatio* disease caused by botflies or worms, fr. *verminatus* (past part.) + *-ion-, -io* ion] *obs* : the growth of vermin : the multiplication of vermin by breeding

ver·mi·no·sis \ˌvərmə'nōsəs\ *n, pl* **vermino·ses** \-ˌōˌsēz\ [NL, fr. L *vermin-* (as in *verminare*) + *-osis*] : infestation with or disease caused by parasitic worms

ver·min·ous \'vərmənəs, 'vȯm-, 'vəim-\ *adj* [L *verminosus*, fr. *vermin-* (as in *verminare*) + *-osus -ous*] **1** : consisting of vermin : being vermin : NOXIOUS ⟨a ~ brood⟩ **2** : tending to be a breeding place of vermin; *also* : infested by vermin : FILTHY, OFFENSIVE ⟨~ garbage⟩ ⟨a dirty ~ cellar⟩ **3** : caused by or characterized by the presence of vermin ⟨~ disease⟩ — **ver·min·ous·ly** *adv*

ver·mip·a·rous \(ˌ)vər'mipərəs\ *adj* [prob. fr. (assumed) NL *vermiparus*, fr. LL *vermi-* (fr. L *vermis*) + L *-parus* -parous] : producing wormlike young (blowflies are ~)

ver·mis \'vərməs\ *n, pl* **ver·mes** \-r,mēz\ [NL, fr. L, worm] **1** : either of two parts of the median lobe of the cerebellum: **a** : one slightly prominent on the upper surface — called also *superior vermis* **b** : one on the lower surface sunk in the vallecula — called also *inferior vermis* **2** : the median lobe or part of the cerebellum

ver·miv·o·rous \(ˌ)vər'mivərəs\ *adj* [ISV *vermi-* + *-vorous*] : feeding on worms

ver·mix \'vərmiks\ *n* -ES [*vermiform appendix*] : VERMIFORM APPENDIX

¹**ver·mont** \və(r)'mänt *also* ˌvər'm- *or* vō'm- *or* vəi'm- *sometimes* -mänt *in* NE\ *geog, usu cap* [F *Vert*, state in the northeastern U.S., irreg. fr. F *vert* green + *mont* mountain; intended as trans. of E *Green Mountains* — more at VERDANT, MOUNT] : of or from the state of Vermont ⟨*Vermont* marble⟩ : of the kind or style prevalent in Vermont ⟨*Vermontese*⟩

²**vermont** \"\ *n* -s *usu cap* [so called fr. its having been orig. imported into Vermont and bred there] : a Merino sheep having the skin folds greatly exaggerated

ver·mont·er \-nä(r)\ *n* -s *cap* [*Vermont*, state in the northeastern U.S. + E *-er*] : a native or resident of the state of Vermont

¹**ver·mont·ese** \(ˌ)ˌ'mänt.'ēz, -mòn-, -ēs\ *adj, usu cap* [*Vermont* state + E *-ese*] **1** : of, relating to, or characteristic of the state of Vermont **2** : of, relating to, or characteristic of the people of Vermont

²**vermontese** \"\ *n, pl* **vermontese** *cap*

vermont snakeroot *n, usu cap* V : WILD GINGER 2a

ver·mo·rel \ˌvərmə'rel, 'vərm-\ *adj* [after Victor B. *Vermorel* †1927 Fr. industrialist and author] : of, relating to, or being a spray nozzle for projecting liquid insecticides in a fine spray with considerable force

ver·mouth *also* **ver·muth** \və(r)'müth\ *n* -s [modif. of F *vermout*, fr. G *wermut* wormwood, absinthium, fr. MHG *wermuot, wermuote* wormwood, fr. OHG *wermuota* — more at WORMWOOD] : a white wine flavored esp. with herbs (as coriander, orris root, cinchona, calamus, elder flowers, angelica, cloves, nutmeg, or sage) that is used principally as an aperitif or in mixed drinks and that is produced chiefly in (1) a pale amber and dry variety and in (2) a dark amber and sweet variety — called also respectively (1) *French vermouth*, (2) *Italian vermouth*

vermouth cassis *n* : a mixed drink consisting of French vermouth, crème de cassis, and carbonated water

vernacle *var of* VERNICLE

¹**ver·nac·u·lar** \R və(r)'nakyələr, -R və'nakyələ(r\ *adj* [L *vernaculus* homeborn, native (fr. *verna* homeborn slave, native) + E *-ar*] **1 a** : using a language or dialect native to a region or country rather than a literary, cultured, or foreign language ⟨~ speakers⟩ ⟨Ceylon had 336 English and 4701 ~ schools — *Origins & Purpose*⟩ ⟨in ... poetry, the effect of Latin verse forms appears —H.O.Taylor⟩ **b** : belonging to or being a language or dialect developed in and spoken and used by the people of a particular place, region, or country in a form (as a dialect or a variety of cant, slang, jargon, or argot) considered nonstandard or substandard usu. as contrasted with a literary or cultured form ⟨his freedom from eccentricity, his gumption, to use the ~ word —William James⟩ ⟨only when a language ... has ceased to grow, does it become unchanging — L.H.Gray⟩ ⟨slang widely used by ... adults in the ~ speech of the street and country —H.D.Rinsland⟩ ⟨Hebrew ... translated into the ~ Aramaic —J.R.Dummelow⟩ ⟨the various ~ languages of the region —Cecil Hobbs⟩ **c** : of, relating to, expressed in, or being a dialect or variety of a language normally or naturally spoken by all the speakers of a language ⟨crudely written, in a ~ style that is often tiring —Granville Hicks⟩ **d** : being the name of a plant or animal in the vernacular language or common native speech as distinguished from the Latin nomenclature of scientific classification ⟨black alder and winterberry are ~ names of *Ilex verticillata*⟩ **2** : of, relating to, characteristic of, or expressed in the style of a place, period, or group ⟨the ~ culture of our people —L.R. Beltran⟩; *esp* : of, relating to, or being the common building style of a period or place : employing the commonest or most typical architectural forms and decoration ⟨thatch and half-timber construction ... of English ~ building —Harry Batsford & Charles Fry⟩ — **ver·nac·u·lar·ly** *adv*

²**vernacular** \"\ *n* -s **1** : a vernacular language, expression, or mode of expression: as **a** : the native language or dialect of a country, region, or person ⟨autobiography of a Nigerian woman was dictated in the ~ —*Brit. Bk. News*⟩ ⟨the English ~ of Ireland⟩ **b** : a language that is spoken or written naturally at a particular period ⟨LIVING LANGUAGE ⟨read Greek and Latin as energetically as he read Italian and French and other ~ —Gilbert Highet⟩ ⟨an imported ~ was widely current — Ruth Dean⟩ **c** : an expression or mode of expression natural to or used by a group or class ⟨has become a part of ethnological, even ... of literary ~ —Gladys A. Reichard⟩ ⟨the findings of accredited biblical psychologists are translated into the ~s of childhood and youth —W.L.Sperry⟩ ⟨believed signs were the ~ of the deaf —J.S.Long⟩ **d** : the variety of a lan-

guage or an expression in this variety commonly spoken by all or a part of the users of the language as distinguished from a written, literary, or cultured variety ⟨state the problem in simple ~ —Anthony Leviero⟩ ⟨in the inelegant ~, "So what?" —C.R.Rogers⟩ **e** : a vernacular name of a plant or animal **2** : a style of artistic or technical and esp. architectural expression employing the commonest forms, materials, and decorations of a place, period, or group ⟨an impressive structure of white marble, expressed in a Renaissance ~ —*Amer. Guide Series: Minn.*⟩ ⟨builders, masons, and thatchers developed their forms ... in response to climatic conditions —Norman Wymer⟩ **syn** see DIALECT

ver·nac·u·lar·ism \-lə.rizəm\ *n* -s : a vernacular word or idiom

ver·nac·u·lar·i·ty \ˌ.ˌ'larəd·ē\ *n* -ES **1** : the use of or adherence to the vernacular in literary composition **2** : VERNACULARISM

ver·nac·u·lar·ize \ˌ.ˌ'ˌrīz\ *vt* -ED/-ING/-s : to render into or express in a vernacular

ver·nad·skite \və(r)'nadˌskīt, -dˌsk-\ *n* -s [Vladimir I. *Vernadsky* †1945 Russ. geologist + E *-ite*] : a mineral $Cu_4(SO_4)_3(OH)_2 \cdot 4H_2O$ consisting of a hydrous basic sulfate of copper

ver·nal \'vərn²l, 'vȯn-, 'vəin-\ *adj* [L *vernalis*, fr. *vernus* vernal (fr. *ver* spring) + *-alis* -al; akin to Gk *ear* spring, OIr *errach*, OSlav *vesna*, Skt *vasanta* and prob. to ON *vár* spring and perh. to L *aurora* dawn — more at EAST] **1 a** : appearing or occurring in the spring ⟨~ flora⟩ ⟨~ catarrh⟩ **b** *of migratory birds* : arriving at the breeding range in spring **2** : of, relating to, or characteristic of the spring ⟨~ sunshine⟩ ⟨the ~ softness of first bloom —Claudia Cassidy⟩ **3** : resembling or suggesting the spring of the year esp. in freshness, greenness, or newness : SPRINGLIKE ⟨~ freshness of a child —Coulton Waugh⟩ — **ver·nal·ly** \-n²lē, -li\ *adv*

vernal grass *n* : SWEET VERNAL GRASS

ver·nal·i·za·tion \ˌvərn²lə'zāshən, -nˌ²lˌīz-\ *n* -s [ISV ²*vernalize* + *-ation*] : the act or process of vernalizing

¹**ver·nal·ize** \ˌ'ˌ.ˌīz\ *vt* -ED/-ING/-s : to make vernal : give freshness to

²**vernalize** \"\ *vt* -ED/-ING/-s [ISV *vernal* + *-ize*] : to hasten the flowering and fruiting of (plants) by treating seeds, bulbs, or seedlings by a method (as exposing sometimes partially sprouted seed to low or high temperatures for a period) that induces a shortening of the vegetative period : JAROVIZE

vernal sedge *n* : a Eurasian sedge (*Carex caryophyllea*) with stoloniferous habit and early-blooming spikes that is naturalized in the eastern U.S. — called also *iron grass*

vernal witch hazel *n* : a fragrant witch hazel (*Hamamelis vernalis*) native to the lower Mississippi valley with very small flowers that appear from midwinter to spring

ver·nant \'vərnənt\ *adj* [ME *vernand*, fr. L *vernant-, vernans*, pres. part. of *vernare* to flourish, be verdant, fr. *ver* spring] *archaic* : VERNAL

ver·na·tion \vər'nāshən\ *n* -s [NL *vernation-, vernatio*, fr. L *vernatus* (past part. of *vernare* to flourish, be verdant) + *-ion-, -io* ion] : the arrangement of foliage leaves within the bud — compare AESTIVATION

ver·ner's law \'ver|nərz-, 'vər|\ *n, usu cap V* [after Karl A. *Verner* †1896 Dan. philologist, its formulator] : a statement in historical linguistics: in medial or final position in voiced environments and when the immediately preceding vowel did not bear the principal accent in Proto-Indo-European, the Proto-Germanic voiceless fricatives f, $þ$, and χ which came from the Proto-Indo-European voiceless stops p, t, and k respectively, and the Proto-Germanic voiceless fricative s which came from Proto-Indo-European s, became the voiced fricatives $ð$, $ð$, g, and z respectively, represented in many of the recorded Germanic languages by b, d, g, and r respectively ⟨the b of Gothic *thaurbum* "we need" as contrasted with the f of Gothic *tharf* "I need," the final d of English *dead* as contrasted with the final *th* of English *death*, the g of Old High German *zugum* "we pulled" as contrasted with the h of Old High German *ziohan* "to pull," and the r of English *were* as contrasted with the s of English *was*, are examples of *Verner's law*⟩ — see GRAMMATICAL CHANGE; compare GRIMM'S LAW

ver·neuil process *or* **verneuil method** \(ˌ)ver|nər, -nˌŏ, F vernœuy\ *n* [after A. V. L. *Verneuil*, 19th cent. Fr. mineralogist] : a procedure for growing large crystals (as of sapphire, ruby, spinel, or rutile) by adding the powdered material to the top of a rod the end of which is maintained at or close to the melting point by a flame directed vertically downward upon it

ver·neuk \və(r)'nük\ *vt* [Afrik, fr. D dial. *verneuken* to hinder, cheat, fr. D *ver-* for- (akin to OHG *far-, fir-*) + D dial. *neuken* to nag — more at FOR-] *southern Africa* : HUMBUG, CHEAT, SWINDLE

ver·ni·cle *or* **ver·na·cle** *n* -s \'vərnəkəl\ [ME *vernicle*, fr. MF *vernicle, veronique*, fr. ML *veronica* — more at VERONICA] : VERONICA

ver·ni·cose \'vərnəˌkōs\ *adj* [ML *vernic-, vernix, veronic-, veronix* varnish + E *-ose* — more at VARNISH] : brilliantly polished ⟨~ leaves⟩

¹**ver·ni·er** \'vərnēər, 'vənēə(r, 'vəinēə(r\ *also* **vernier scale** *n* -s [after Pierre *Vernier* †1637 Fr. mathematician] **1** : a short scale made to slide along the divisions of a graduated instrument (as the limb of a sextant or the scale of a barometer) for indicating parts of divisions and so graduated that a convenient number of its divisions are just equal in length to a number (either one less or one more) of the divisions of the instrument and so that parts of a division are determined by observing what line on the vernier coincides with a line on the instrument **2** : a small auxiliary device (as a variable condenser of very small capacity in parallel with another condenser) used with a main device to obtain fine adjustment

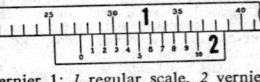
vernier 1: *1* regular scale, *2* vernier scale indicating measurement of 27.4

²**vernier** \"\ *adj* : having or comprising a vernier ⟨~ comparator⟩

vernier caliper *or* **vernier micrometer** *n* : a caliper rule with vernier attachment and adjusting screw for very fine measurement

vernier compass *n* : a surveyor's compass with a vernier by means of which a compensating adjustment may be made for magnetic variation to enable the reading of the correct bearings directly from the compass

vernier gage *n* : an adjustable gage (as a height or depth gage) having a vernier scale on it

ver·nis mar·tin \ˌver'nē.mär'tan\ *n, usu cap M* [F, lit., Martin varnish, after Robert *Martin* †1765 and his brothers Guillaume, Simon-Étienne, & Julien *Martin*, 18th cent. Fr. furniture makers and decorators] : a preparation of green varnish with gold powder used to finish furniture; *also* : furniture finished with vernis Martin

ver·nis·sage \ˌvern(ˌ)nēˌsäzh\ *n* -s [F, *vernis* varnish + *-age* — more at VARNISH] : VARNISHING DAY

ver·nix \'vərniks\ *or* **vernix ca·se·o·sa** \ˌˌkāsē'ōsə\ *n* -Es [NL *vernix*, short fr. *vernix caseosa*, lit., cheesy varnish] : a pasty covering chiefly of dead cells and sebaceous secretions that protects the skin of the fetus

ver·no·nia \vər'nōnēə\ *n* [NL, fr. William *Vernon* †1711 Eng. botanist + NL *-ia*] **1** *cap* : a genus of chiefly tropical herbs or shrubs (family Compositae) occurring chiefly in So. America but including some that are native to No. America and having alternate leaves mostly red or purple and terminal cymose heads of perfect tubular flowers — see IRONWEED **2** : any plant of the genus Vernonia

vernonia purple *n* [NL *Vernonia*] : a grayish purplish red that is redder and deeper than average rose plum, bluer, stronger, and slightly lighter than Aztec maroon, and redder and darker than tourmaline pink

ver·no·nin \'vərnōnən, -ˌnin, vər'nōnən\ *n* -s [*vernon-* (fr. NL *Vernonia*) + *-in*] : a poisonous glucoside $C_{16}H_{24}O_7$ extracted from batiator root (*Vernonia nigritiana*) as a deliquescent powder

ver·nunft \fer'nùnft, fər-, -ùm(p)ft\ *n* *usu cap* [G, fr. OHG *firnunft* perception, understanding, fr. *firneman* to per-

ceive, understand, fr. *fir-* for- + *neman* to take — more at NIMBLE] **:** REASON 2f — distinguished from *verstand*

ve·ro·na \və'rōnə\ *adj, usu cap* [fr. *Verona*, Italy] **:** of or from the city of Verona, Italy **:** of the kind or style prevalent in Verona

verona brown *n, often cap V* **:** VANDYKE BROWN 2

verona earth *n, often cap V* **:** GREEN EARTH 2

verona green *n, often cap V* **:** TERRE VERTE

Ver·o·nal \'verə,nȯl, -,nᵊl, -,nal\ *trademark* — used for barbital

verona orris *n, usu cap V* **:** orrisroot from a German iris (*Iris germanica*) grown in central and southern Europe or from an iris (*Iris pallida*) indigenous to the eastern Mediterranean countries

verona yellow *n* **1** *usu cap V* **:** CASSEL YELLOW 1 **2** *often cap V* **:** ORPIMENT 2

¹ver·o·nese \¦verə¦nēz, -nēs\ *adj, usu cap* [It, fr. (assumed) VL *veronesis*, fr. L *veronensis*, fr. *Verona*, city in northeastern Italy + L *-ensis* -ese] **:** of or relating to Verona, Italy

²veronese \"\ *n, pl* **veronese** *cap* [It, fr. *veronese*, adj.] **:** a native or resident of Verona

veronese green *n, often cap V* [*veronese* in sense 1, fr. ¹*veronese*; in sense 2, after Paolo *Veronese* †1588 Ital. painter born in Verona; trans. of F *vert véronèse*] **1 :** VIRIDIAN 2 **2 :** EMERALD 2a

veronese yellow *n, often cap V* **:** ORPIMENT 2

¹ve·ron·i·ca \və'ränəkə\ *n* [NL, prob. modif. (influenced by the feminine name *Veronica*) of LGk *berenikion*, a plant, fr. Gk *Berenikē, Pherenikē* Berenice, feminine name] **1** *cap* **:** a genus of herbs and sometimes shrubs or trees (family Scrophulariaceae) of wide distribution, with small pink, white, blue, or purple flowers with a 4-lobed rotate corolla, two stamens, and a compressed capsule — see HEBE, SPEEDWELL **2** -s **:** any plant of the genus *Veronica*

²veronica \"\ *n* -s *sometimes cap* [ML, fr. *Veronica* St. Veronica, legendary saint of the 1st cent. A.D.] **:** a portrait or representation of the image of Christ's face said to have been impressed on the handkerchief that St. Veronica gave him to wipe his face as he passed on the way to his crucifixion; *also* **:** a handkerchief or cloth resembling the legendary one of St. Veronica — called also *vernicle*

³veronica \"\ *n* -s [Sp, fr. *Veronica*, feminine name] **:** a pase in bullfighting in which the cape is swung slowly away from the charging bull while the matador keeps his feet in the same position

ve·ron·i·cas·trum \=,=nə'kastrəm\ *n, cap* [NL, fr. *Veronica* + L *astrum* star, fr. Gk *astron* — more at STAR] **:** a small genus of tall herbs (family Scrophulariaceae) that resemble speedwells — see CULVER'S ROOT

ve·ron·i·cel·la \və,ränə'selə\ *n, cap* [NL, prob. fr. the name *Veronica* + NL *-ella*] **:** a genus (the type of the family Veronicellidae) of sluglike pulmonate gastropods having the body covered by a thick coriaceous mantle beneath which the head may be retracted

ver·pa \'vərpə\ *n, cap* [NL, fr. L, penis] **:** a genus of fungi (family Helvellaceae) with a bell-shaped cap attached only at the top of the stipe

ver·ra \'verə\ *Scot var of* VERY

ver·rel \'verəl\ *archaic var of* FERRULE

ver·ric·u·late \və'rikyələt, ve'-, -,lāt\ *or* **ver·ric·u·lat·ed** \-,lād·əd\ *adj* [L *verriculum* dragnet, seine + E *-ate* or *-ated* (fr. *-ate* + *-ed*)] **:** having verricules

ver·ri·cule \'verə,kyül\ *n* -s [L *verriculum* dragnet, fr. *verrere* to sweep — more at WAR] **:** a close tuft of nearly parallel upright hairs, bristles, or other slender filaments

¹ver·ru·ca \və'rükə, ve'r-\ *n, pl* **ver·ru·cae** \-ü(,)kē, -ü,kī, -ü(,)sē\ [L — more at WART] **1 a :** WART **b :** any of numerous warty skin lesions — usu. used in combination **2 a :** a warty elevation on a plant or animal surface; *specif* **:** a large tubercle bearing a tuft of bristles or spines in some caterpillars

²verruca \"\ *n, cap* [NL, fr. L, wart] **:** a nearly cosmopolitan genus (the type of the family Verrucidae) of sessile barnacles

verruca acu·mi·na·ta \-ə,kyümə'nād·ə, -nād·ə\ *n* [NL, acuminate wart] **:** a venereal wart

ver·ru·car·ia \,ver(y)ə'ka(a)rēə\ *n, cap* [NL, fr. L *verruca* wart + NL *-aria*] **:** a genus (the type of the family Verrucariaceae) of chiefly rock-inhabiting crustose lichens having small immersed globular apothecia

ver·ru·cat·ed \'ver(y)ə,kād·əd\ *adj* [NL *verrucatus* (fr. L *verruca* + *-atus* -ate) + E *-ed*] **:** VERRUCOSE

verruca vul·ga·ris \-,vəl'ga(a)rəs\ *n* [NL] **:** WART 1a

ver·ru·cose \'ver(y)ə,kōs\ *adj* [L *verrucosus*, fr. *verruca* wart + *-osus* -ose] **:** covered with wartlike elevations **:** WARTY ⟨a ~ capsule⟩ — **ver·ru·cose·ness** *n* -es

ver·ru·co·sis \,==¦kōsəs\ *n, pl* **verruco·ses** \-ō,sēz\ [NL, fr. L *verruca* + *-osis*] **:** CITRUS SCAB

ver·ru·cous \və'rükəs, ve'r-\ *adj* [L *verruca* + E *-ous*] **:** of, relating to, or resembling a wart **:** characterized by warts

verrucous endocarditis *n* **:** endocarditis marked by the formation or presence of warty nodules of fibrin on the lips of the heart valves

ver·ru·cu·lose \və'rükyə,lōs, ve'r-\ *adj* [NL *verruculosus*, fr. L *verrucula* (dim. of *verruca* wart) + *-osus* -ose] **:** minutely verrucose

ver·ru·ga \və'rügə, ve'r-\ *n* -s [Sp, fr. L *verruca* — more at WART] **1 :** VERRUCA **2 :** VERRUGA PERUANA

verruga per·u·a·na \-,perə'wänə\ *also* **verruga pe·ru·vi·ana** \-pə,rüvē'anə, -'änə, -'änə\ *n* [*verruga peruana* fr. Sp, lit., Peruvian wart; *verruga peruviana* fr. NL, part trans. of Sp *verruga peruana*] **:** the second stage of bartonellosis characterized by warty nodules tending to ulcerate and bleed

ver·ry \'verē\ *archaic var of* VAIRÉ

vers *abbr* versed sine

ver·sa·bil·i·ty \,vərsə'bilәd·ē\ *n* [LL *versabilitat-, versabilitas*, fr. L *versabilis* capable of being turned, changeable (fr. *versare, versari* to turn + *-bilis* capable of being acted upon) + *-tat-, -tas* -ty — more at -ABLE] *archaic* **:** capability of being turned

¹ver·sal \'vərsəl\ *adj* [short for *universal*] *archaic* **:** ENTIRE, UNIVERSAL ⟨looks as pale as any clout in the ~ world —Shak.⟩

²ver·sal \"\ *n* -s [¹*verse* + *-al*] **:** an often elaborate and ornate capital letter used (as in illuminated manuscripts) at the beginning of a verse, paragraph, section, or chapter

¹ver·sant \'vərsᵊnt, 'vəs-, 'vəis-\ *adj* [L *versant-, versans*, pres. part. of *versare, versari* to turn, occupy oneself, meditate, be busy with] **1 :** mentally engaged or occupied **:** CONCERNED, INTERESTED **2 :** EXPERIENCED, PRACTICED **3 :** closely acquainted **:** CONVERSANT ⟨men not ~ with courts of justice will believe it —Sydney Smith⟩

²versant \"\ *n* -s [F, fr. pres. part. of *verser* to turn, incline, fr. L *versare* to turn] **1 :** the slope of a side of a mountain chain **2 :** the general slope of a country **:** INCLINATION

ver·sa·tile \'vərsəd·ᵊl, 'vəs-, 'vəis-, -sət ᵊl, -sə(,)til *sometimes* -stᵊl *or* -(,)stil, *chiefly Brit* -sə,tīl\ *adj* [F or L; F *versatile*, fr. L *versatilis*, fr. *versatus* (past part. of *versare, versari* to turn, change, overturn, occupy oneself, be busy with, freq. of *vertere* to turn) + *-ilis* -ile — more at WORTH] **1 a :** marked by a tendency to change **:** fluctuating readily **:** CHANGEABLE, VARIABLE ⟨a ~ disposition⟩ **b :** easily swayed **:** FICKLE ⟨a ~ faction⟩ **2 a :** adapted to or embracing a variety of subjects, fields, or skills ⟨his steady political wisdom and his vast and ~ erudition —*Amer. Guide Series: Ind.*⟩ **b :** having a capacity for turning with ease from one thing to another **:** having a wide range of skills, aptitudes, or interests **:** MANY-SIDED ⟨extremely ~ in the sense that he was a painter of portraits, of genre, of still life, and of landscape —Eliot Clark⟩ ⟨the most ~ soprano now active —Irving Kolodin⟩ **3 a (1) :** capable of turning forward or backward **:** REVERSIBLE ⟨a ~ toe of a bird⟩ **(2) :** capable of moving laterally and up and down ⟨~ antennae⟩ **b** *of an anther* **:** having the filaments attached at or near the middle so as to swing freely — compare BASIFIXED **4 a :** having many uses or applications ⟨a handy, ~ material which you will find as veneer base and drawers in furniture, as cabinets and shelving —*Monsanto Mag.*⟩ **b :** capable of being worn in varied combinations or ways ⟨~, packable separates —*Woman's Home Companion*⟩ ⟨has evolved a ~ topcoat for a man who does a lot of traveling —*New Yorker*⟩ **5 :** DIVERSIFIED ⟨a ~ line of over 100 different papers —*advt*⟩

syn VERSATILE, MANY-SIDED, and ALL-AROUND can all suggest being marked by or showing skill or ability or capacity or usefulness of many different kinds. When applied to persons, VERSATILE stresses aptitude and facility in many different activities requiring skill or ability, esp. the ability to turn with no diminution in skill from one activity to another without a hitch; applied to things, it stresses their multiple and diverse qualities, uses, or possibilities ⟨a *versatile* student⟩ ⟨a *versatile* athlete⟩ ⟨*versatile* interests⟩ ⟨a *versatile* combat weapon⟩ ⟨a *versatile* building material⟩ MANY-SIDED applied to persons stresses breadth or diversity of interests or accomplishments; applied to things, their diversity of aspects, attributes, or uses ⟨a *many-sided* scholar and citizen⟩ ⟨a *many-sided* and truly civilized life —G.M.Trevelyan⟩ ⟨a *many-sided* personality⟩ ⟨a *many-sided* agreement —*Manchester Guardian Weekly*⟩ ALL-AROUND implies completeness or symmetry in development, generally or within a single activity with many phases, not necessarily implying any special or great attainments but rather a general ability to do oneself credit; when applied to things, it implies an analogous general usefulness ⟨many observers have called him the best *all-around* reporter in the country —Stanley Walker⟩ ⟨the *all-around* adaptability and quality of our men —A.B.Vosseller⟩

ver·sa·tile·ly \-l(l)ē, -i\ *adv* **:** in a versatile manner

ver·sa·tile·ness *n* -es **:** VERSATILITY

ver·sa·til·i·ty \,==¦tilәd·ē, -lәtē, -i\ *n* -es [F *versatilité*, fr. *versatile* + *-ité* -ity] **:** the quality or state of being versatile ⟨a man of great ~, an explorer in all the sciences underlying agriculture —R.H.Chittenden⟩ ⟨a metal valued for its ~⟩

ver·sa·tion \,vər'sāshən\ *n* -s [L *versation-, versatio*, fr. *versatus* (past part. of *versare* to turn) + *-ion-, -io* -ion] *archaic* **:** the act or action of turning something over

vers de so·cié·té \,verdə,sōs,yā'tā, -ōsēə'tā\ *n* [F, society verse] **:** witty and typically ironic light verse written to amuse a sophisticated circle of readers

¹verse \'vərs, 'vəs, 'vəis\ *n* -s [ME *vers, fers*, fr. OF *vers* & OE *fers*, both fr. L *versus* row, line, verse; akin to L *vertere* to turn — more at WORTH] **1 :** a line of metrical writing ⟨in English the caesura . . . can occur after any syllable, even the first or the ninth of a ten-syllable ~ —Malcolm Cowley⟩ **2 :** VERSICLE 1 **3 a (1) :** metrical language **:** speech or writing distinguished from ordinary language by its distinctive patterning of sounds and esp. by its more pronounced or elaborate rhythm **(2) :** metrical writing that is distinguished from poetry esp. by its lower level of intensity and its lack of essential conviction and commitment ⟨many writers of ~ who have not aimed at writing poetry —T.S.Eliot⟩ **(3) :** POETRY 2 ⟨~ that gives immortal youth to mortal maids —W.S.Landor⟩ **b :** a particular example of metrical writing **:** POEM ⟨using some of her ~s as exercises in one of his textbooks —Antony Alpers⟩ **c :** a body of metrical writing (as of a single author, a period, or a country) ⟨Shakespearean ~⟩ ⟨Renaissance ~⟩ ⟨English ~⟩ **4 a (1) :** a unit of metrical writing larger than a single line **:** STANZA **(2) :** the portion of a song preceding the refrain or chorus and excluding any introduction ⟨sing the first and last ~s only⟩ **b :** a portion of an anthem or musical service to be performed by a single voice to each part **5 :** one of the short divisions into which a chapter of the Bible is traditionally divided ⟨the first ~ of the first chapter of Genesis⟩

²verse \"\ *adj* **:** of, relating to, or written in verse ⟨~ technique⟩ ⟨a ~ drama⟩

³verse \"\ *vb* -ED/-ING/-S [ME *versen*, partly fr. *vers, fers* verse & partly fr. OE *fersian* to versify, fr. *fers* verse] *vi* **:** to make verse **:** write poetry **:** VERSIFY ~ *vt* **1 :** to tell or celebrate in verse **2 :** to turn into verse

⁴verse \"\ *vt* -ED/-ING/-S [back-formation fr. *versed*] **:** to familiarize by close association, study, or experience ⟨*versed* himself in the theater⟩

verse anthem *n* [¹*verse*] **:** an anthem in use in the English Church for solo voices or having a passage for solo voices — compare FULL ANTHEM

versecraft \'=,=\ *n* **:** the art or practice of writing verse

versed \'vərst, 'vəst, 'vəist\ *adj* [L *versatus* (past part. of *versare, versari* to turn, overturn, occupy oneself, be busy with) + E *-ed* — more at VERSATILE] **:** acquainted or familiar from experience, study, or practice **:** PRACTICED, SKILLED — usu. used with *in* ⟨~ in magnetism and familiar with compasses —K.K.Darrow⟩ ⟨was better ~ in diplomatic usage than any of his colleagues —F.A.Ogg & Harold Zink⟩

versed sine *n* [*versed* fr. NL *versus* turned (fr. past part. of L *vertere* to turn) + E *-ed*] **:** 1 minus the cosine of an angle

verse·let \'=lət\ *n* -s **:** a little verse

verse·man \'=mən\ *n, pl* **versemen :** a maker of verses **:** VERSIFIER

versemonger \'=,==\ *n* [¹*verse* + *monger*] **:** POETASTER

vers·er \'vərsə(r), 'vəsə(r, 'vəisə(r\ *n* -s **:** VERSIFIER

verse service *n* **:** a service in the English Church sung by solo voices

versesmith \'=,=\ *n* [¹*verse* + *smith*] **:** VERSIFIER

verse–speaking choir \'=¦==-\ *n* **:** a group organized for the choral speaking of poetry

vers·et \'vərsət, ¦vər¦set\ *n* -s [ME, fr. OF, fr. *vers* verse + *-et* — more at VERSE] **1 a** *archaic* **:** VERSICLE **b :** a short verse esp. from a sacred book ⟨sat . . . with an open Koran on his knees and chanted the ~s —Joseph Conrad⟩ **2 :** a short interlude or prelude for the pipe organ

ver·si·cle \'vərsəkəl\ *n* -s [ME, fr. L *versiculus* short line, dim. of *versus* line, verse — more at VERSE] **1 a :** a short verse or sentence said or sung in public worship by a priest or minister and followed by a response from the people — symbol ℣ **b :** a suffrage taken from the Psalms in the Anglican Communion **2 :** a little verse: as **a :** a line of verse ⟨here are some ~s, which I made one sleepless night —Lord Byron⟩ **b :** a brief poem or set of verses ⟨a little ~ that most of us learned when we were very young —Kenneth MacKenzie⟩

ver·si·color *or* **ver·si·colored** \¦vərsə+\ *adj* [*versicolor* fr. L, fr. *versus* (past part. of *vertere* to turn, change) + *color*; *versicolored* fr. L *versicolor* + E *-ed* — more at WORTH] **1 :** having various colors **:** PARTI-COLORED, VARIEGATED ⟨~ flowers⟩ **2 :** changeable in color **:** IRIDESCENT ⟨~ silk⟩

ver·sic·u·lar \(¦)vər¦sikyələr\ *adj* [L *versiculus* + E *-ar*] **:** of or relating to verses or versicles; *esp* **:** of or relating to biblical verses

ver·si·cule \'vərsə,kyül\ *n* -s [F, fr. L *versiculus*, dim. of *versus* line, verse] **:** a short poem **:** VERSICLE

ver·sic·u·lus \,vər'sikyələs\ *n, pl* **versicu·li** \-ə,lī\ [L] **:** VERSICLE

ver·si·fi·ca·tion \,vərsəfə'kāshən, ,vəs-, ,vəis-\ *n* -s [L *versification-, versificatio*, fr. *versificatus* (past part. of *versificare* to versify) + *-ion-, -io* -ion] **1 :** the making of verses **:** the act, art, or practice of metrical composition ⟨~ based on . . . strict rules —H.A.Grubbs⟩ **2 a :** metrical structure **b :** a particular metrical structure or style ⟨commending her poem . . . for its ~ —Bertha Stearns⟩ **3 :** a version in verse of something orig. in prose

ver·si·fi·ca·tor \'==fə,kād·ə(r)\ *n* -s [L, fr. *versificatus* (past part.) + *-or*] **:** VERSIFIER

ver·si·fi·er \'==,fī(ə)r, -īə\ *n* -s [ME, fr. *versifien* to versify + *-er*] **1 :** one that makes verses; *esp* **:** a writer of light or poor verse ⟨the art of putting words on the line so that they create rhythms independent of the steady beat . . . distinguishes the poet from the ~ —Ronald McCraig⟩ **2 :** one that converts into verse; *esp* **:** one that versifies prose

ver·si·fy \'==,fī\ *vb* -ED/-ING/-S [ME *versifien*, fr. MF *versifier*, fr. L *versificare*, fr. *versus* line, verse + *-ficare* -fy — more at VERSE] *vi* **:** to make verses **:** write poetry ~ *vt* **1 :** to relate or describe in verse **:** compose in verse **2 :** to turn into verse **:** render into metrical form

ver·sine *or* **ver·sin** \'vər,sīn\ *n* -s [by contr.] **:** VERSED SINE

versing *pres part of* VERSE

¹ver·sion \'vər¦zhən, 'vəˌ, 'vəi¦ *also* ¦shən\ *n* -s [MF, fr. ML *version-, versio* action of turning, fr. L *versus* (past part. of *vertere* to turn) + *-ion-, -io* -ion — more at WORTH] **1 a :** something rendered from another language **:** TRANSLATION ⟨comparison of the original text with the English ~ —Milton Hindus⟩; *esp* **:** a free rendering of a literary work and esp. a poem into another language that endeavors to express the spirit rather than the literal sense of the original **b :** a translation or rendering of the Bible or a part of it **2 a :** an account or description from a particular point of view esp. as contrasted with another account ⟨each came . . . to give his separate ~ of the event —H.J.Laski⟩ ⟨their ~ of economic history —W.H.Whyte⟩; *broadly* **:** one of a set of related intellectual constructions ⟨the senate . . . passed its ~ of the excise-tax bill —*Wall Street Jour.*⟩ ⟨his fictional ~ of what he saw —*Yankee*⟩ ⟨the printed problem or the teacher's blackboard ~ —I.G.Ellson⟩ ⟨the full ~ of the journals —Bernard De Voto⟩ **b :** one from a set of related artistic productions without out one among them having a special status or with an original excluded from the set or with an original included among the set: as **(1) :** an adaptation of a literary work ⟨a stage ~ of the novel⟩ **(2) :** a distinct form of something regarded by its creator or others as one work ⟨published a shortened ~ myself —G.W.Knight⟩ ⟨the original ~s written piecemeal for a monthly publication —Peter Blake⟩ **(3) :** a musical composition adapted or arranged for a new purpose ⟨a ~ of a symphony arranged as a ballet suite⟩ ⟨a concert ~ of an opera⟩ **(4) :** a performance or interpretation of a work of art esp. when thought to have a marked character or excellence ⟨several recorded ~s of the opera⟩ ⟨his ~ of the role has matured⟩ **(5) :** an artistic production expressing an artist's or period's interpretation of a theme or style ⟨a modern ~ of Italian Renaissance architecture —*Amer. Guide Series: N.Y.*⟩ ⟨a swing ~ of a blues tune⟩ **(6) :** EDITION 2 **3 :** a form, variant, species, or copy of a type or original ⟨an experimental night-fighter ~ of the plane⟩ ⟨the emery wheel — an improved ~ of the age-old grindstone —Howell Walker⟩ ⟨modern ~s of old-time medicine shows —*Amer. Guide Series: Texas*⟩ ⟨radioactive ~s of the ordinary elements —S.F.Mason⟩ ⟨in front of the three-folded mirror so that she could see three separate ~s of her . . . face—Virginia Woolf⟩ **4 a :** a condition of an organ or part (as the uterus) of being turned from its normal position **b :** the manual operation of turning a fetus in the uterus to aid delivery

²version \"\ *vt* -ED/-ING/-S **:** to make a translation of

ver·sion·al \¦zhənᵊl, ¦zhnəl, ¦sh-\ *adj* **:** of or relating to a version of the Bible

vers li·bre \ver'lēbr(ᵊ), -b(rə)\ *n, pl* **vers libres** \", -b(rə)z\ [F] **:** FREE VERSE

vers–librist \-brəst\ *also* **vers–libriste** \", ¦verlē¦brēst\ *n* -s [F *vers-libriste*] **:** a writer of free verse

ver·so \'vər(,)sō, 'və(-, 'vəi(-\ *n* -s [NL *verso (folio)* the page being turned] **1 :** the side of a leaf (as of manuscript) that is to be read second — contrasted with *recto* **2 :** a left-hand page (as of a book) usu. carrying an even page number **3 :** the back cover of a book and esp. the outside back cover; *also* **:** the corresponding part of a book jacket

verst *also* **verste** *or* **werst** \'vərst\ *n* -s [F *verste* & G *werst*, fr. Russ *versta* row, line, verst; akin to Lith *versti* to turn — more at WORTH] **:** a Russian unit of distance equal to 500 sagenes or 0.6629 miles

ver·stand \fer'shtänt, fər-\ *n* -s [G, fr. MHG *verstant*, fr. *verstan* to understand, fr. OHG *farstān*, fr. *far-* for- + *stān* to stand — more at FOR-, STAND] **:** UNDERSTANDING 3c — distinguished from *vernunft*

ver·ste·hen \fer'shtāən, fər-\ *n* -s *usu cap* [G, fr. *verstehen* to understand, fr. MHG *versten, verstan*] **:** an intuitive doctrine or method of interpreting human culture esp. in its subjective motivational and valuational aspects through the understanding of symbolic relationships

ver·sus \'vərsəs, -vəs-,'vəis-, -səz\ *prep* [L, towards, fr. *versus*, past part. of *vertere* to turn] **1 :** AGAINST ⟨John Doe ~ Richard Roe⟩ ⟨the varsity ~ the scrubs⟩ ⟨the champion ~ the challenger⟩ **2 :** in contrast to or as the alternative of ⟨free trade ~ protection⟩ — *abbr.* v, *vs*

ver·sus cau·da·ti \'vərsə,skaù'dä d·(,)ē\ *n* [NL] **:** TAIL RHYME

¹vert \'vərt, 'vət, 'vəit, *usu* -d·+V\ *n* -s [ME *veert, verte*, fr. MF *vert* green, fr. L *viridis* — more at VERDANT] **1 a :** the green and growing things of a forest esp. when forming cover or providing food for deer **b :** the right or privilege (as in England) of cutting living wood or sometimes of pasturing animals in a forest **2 :** the color green esp. as an heraldic tincture

²vert \"\ *vt* -ED/-ING/-S [L *vertere*] **:** to cause to turn or bend from one direction to another

³vert \"\ *n* -s [short for *convert*] **:** one who changes his affiliation or orientation esp. in religion

⁴vert \"\ *vi* -ED/-ING/-S **:** to become a convert

vert *abbr* **1** vertebra; vertebrate **2** vertical

vertebr- *or* **vertebro-** *comb form* [NL, fr. L *vertebra*] **1 :** vertebra **:** vertebrae ⟨*vertebri*form⟩ ⟨*vertebr*ectomy⟩ **2 :** vertebral and ⟨*vertebro*femoral⟩

ver·te·bra \'vər¦d·əbrə, 'və¦, 'vəi¦, ¦təb-, ÷ -,brā\ *n, pl* **vertebrae** \-(,)brē, ÷ -,brā\ *also* **vertebras** [L, joint, vertebra; akin to L *vertere* to turn — more at WORTH] **1 :** one of the bony or in young or primitive individuals more or less cartilaginous elements that together make up the spinal column of a vertebrate, that in lower forms consists of several imperfectly fused elements, and that in higher vertebrates is a solidly fused structure consisting of a cylindrical centrum articulated with adjacent centra by cartilaginous or elastic pads, a dorsal arch arising from the centrum and providing a protected passage for the spinal cord, and various spinous and articular processes by which the spinal column is stiffened and attached to muscles and other bones (as the ribs) **2** *vertebrae pl* **:** SPINAL COLUMN, BACKBONE **3 :** any of a series of ossicles that resemble the centrum of a vertebra and form the axis of the arm in most ophiurans

¹ver·te·bral \-brəl, (,)vər¦tēb-, vē-, vəi'-\ *adj* [NL *vertebralis*, fr. L *vertebra* + *-alis* -al] **1 :** of, relating to, or constituting vertebrae or the vertebral column **:** SPINAL **2 :** composed of or having vertebrae **3 :** situated near or in the median dorsal plane of a vertebrate animal

²vertebral \"\ *n* -s **:** a vertebral part or element (as an artery or a vein or plate); *esp* **:** a median dorsal plate in the carapace of a turtle

vertebral aponeurosis *n* **:** a fascia of the back separating the muscles that hold erect the spinal column and head from those that move the arm and shoulders and extending from the spinous processes to the angles of the ribs

vertebral artery *n* **:** a large branch of the subclavian artery that ascends through the foramina in the transverse processes of each of the cervical vertebrae except the last one or two, enters the cranium through the foramen magnum, and unites with the corresponding artery of the opposite side to form the basilar artery

vertebral canal *n* **:** SPINAL CANAL

vertebral column *n* **:** SPINAL COLUMN

ver·te·bral·ly \-brəlē\ *adv* **:** toward, upon, or with the vertebrae

vertebral plate *n* **1 :** the part of the mesoblast that in most craniate vertebrate embryos lies near the notochord and forms somites **2 :** a vertebral plate of a turtle

vertebral rib *n* **:** FLOATING RIB

vertebral vein *n* **:** a tributary of the innominate vein formed by the union of branches which originate in the occipital region and form a plexus about the vertebral artery in its passage through the foramina of the cervical vertebrae and receiving various branches which join it near its termination

ver·te·brar·ia \,vərd·ə'bra(a)rēə\ *n, cap* [NL, fr. *vertebr-* + *-aria*] **:** a genus of fossil plants based upon rootlike remains of Triassic age that resemble a vertebral column

ver·te·bra·ta \,==¦brād·ə, -rād·ə\ *n pl, cap* [NL, fr. neut. pl. of *vertebratus* vertebrate] **1 :** a major division of animals that is usu. a subphylum of Chordata, that comprises bilaterally symmetrical animals with a segmented spinal column or in primitive forms with a persistent notochord, a tubular dorsal nervous system divisible into brain and spinal cord, an anterior head bearing a mouth and the major sense organs, an internal articulated skeleton of bone or cartilage, respiration by gills or lungs, and not more than two pairs of limbs which may be modified as grasping, walking, swimming, or flying organs in different members of the division, and that includes the mammals, birds, reptiles, amphibians, fishes, elasmobranchs, and cyclostomes and sometimes the lancelets — compare ACRANIA **2** *in some classifications* **:** CHORDATA

¹ver·te·brate \'==,brət, -,brāt, *usu* ¦d·+V\ *adj* [NL *vertebratus*, fr. L, jointed, fr. *vertebra* joint, vertebra + *-atus* -ate] **1 a :** having a spinal column **b (1) :** of or relating to the Vertebrata **(2) :** characteristic of or found in an animal belonging to the Vertebrata **2 :** having a strong framework suggesting vertebrae **3 :** organized or constructed in orderly or developed form ⟨a ~ piece of composition⟩

²ver·te·brate \-,brāt, *usu* -əd-+V\ *vt* -ED/-ING/-S : to link together in a manner suggesting vertebrae
³vertebrate *same as* ¹VERTEBRATE\ *n* -S [NL *Vertebrata*] : a vertebrate animal
ver·te·brat·ed \'∗∗,brād-əd\ *adj* [NL *vertebratus* + E -ed] 1 : VERTEBRATE 2 : composed of or having vertebrae or segments resembling vertebrae ⟨a fish with a ∼ tail⟩
ver·te·bra·tion \,∗∗'brāshən\ *n* -s [¹vertebrate + -ion] : strength as if from a firm spinal column : FIRMNESS ⟨the solid ∼ of his logic⟩
ver·te·bre \'vərd-əbə(r)\ *n* -s [MF, fr. L *vertebra*] *archaic* : VERTEBRA
vertebro- — see VERTEBR-
ver·te·bro·chondral \,vərd-əbrō-+\ *adj* [*vertebr-* + *chondral*] : of, relating to, or involving a vertebra and a costal cartilage
ver·te·bro·ster·nal \"+\ *adj* [*vertebro-* + *sternal*] : of, relating to, or extending between the vertebrae and the sternum
vert·ed *past of* VERT
ver·tep \'vər'tep\ *n* -s [Russ., lit., cavern, den] : an early Russian puppet show
ver·tex \'vər,teks, 'vəl\, 'vəl\ *n, pl* **verti·ces** \,tə-\ *also* **vertexes** \,teksəz\ [L *vertex, vortex* whirl, whirlpool, highest point, peak, fr. L *vertere* to turn — more at WORTH] **1 a** : the point opposite to and farthest from the base in any figure having a base : the terminating point ⟨as where the sides of an angle meet or where a curve or surface meets its axis⟩ of some particular lines in a figure or a curve — see ANGLE illustration of a conic and its principal axis **b** : the point of intersection of an axially symmetrical optical surface with its axis of symmetry **c** (1) : ZENITH 1; *also* : the point on the limb of a celestial body nearest the horizon (2) : a point on the celestial sphere toward which star streaming is directed **2** : the top of the head: as **a** : the upper part of the head of an insect in front above the antennae and between the compound eyes **b** (1) : the highest point of the human skull when held in the eye-ear plane (2) : the highest median point of the head of the living human when in a natural position **3** : a principal or highest point : SUMMIT, APEX ⟨a monument on the ∼ of the hill⟩; *often* : the high point of an arch ⟨CROWN, KEYSTONE⟩
¹ver·ti·cal \'vər|d-ə|kəl, 'vəl, 'vəl, |ek-\ *adj* [MF or LL; MF *vertical*, fr. LL *verticalis*, fr. L *vertic-, vertex* peak + *-alis -al*] **1 a** : of or relating to the vertex : situated at the highest point : directly overhead or in the zenith **b** *obs* : being or relating to a high point ⟨as of a life, of eminence, or of excellence⟩ **c** : of or relating to the vertex of the head **d** : of, relating to, or being an aerial photograph taken with the camera pointing straight down or nearly so **2 a** : perpendicular to the plane of the horizon or to a primary axis : UPRIGHT, PLUMB ⟨a ∼ line⟩ **b** (1) : located at right angles to the plane of a supporting surface (2) : lying in the direction of an axis : LENGTHWISE **c** : directed upward or downward at a right angle to the plane of the body or part of the surface of the earth ⟨∼ fins of a fish⟩ **3** : relating to, involving, or integrating discrete elements ⟨as from lowest to highest or from first to last⟩: as **a** : consisting of two or more economic units on different levels of production or distribution ⟨a ∼ business organization⟩ ⟨a completely ∼ manufacturing operation —*N.Y. Times*⟩ **b** : of, relating to, or comprising persons of different status ⟨the ∼ arrangement of society⟩ ⟨race, religion, and nation are examples of ∼ groups —C.M.Panunzio⟩ — compare INDUSTRIAL UNION **4** : relating to harmony esp. in a homophonic composition as contrasted with a contrapuntal one — compare HORIZONTAL 2b(3) **5** *of a stamp* : having a rectangular shape with the shorter sides forming the top and bottom **6** : coming from or involving action from above and specif. from the air ⟨∼ warfare⟩; *esp* : constituting aerial bombing from a craft flying parallel with the earth
syn PERPENDICULAR, PLUMB: VERTICAL in general nontechnical use may suggest a line or direction rising upward toward a zenith ⟨the design is the characteristic American perpendicular skyscraper style, with horizontal lines subdued and the *vertical* lines emphasized —*Amer. Guide Series: Minn.*⟩ ⟨the *vertical*, or conventional, approach, was to begin at a designated place and time in history, and then climb the chronological ladder until you reached the present —Norman Cousins⟩ and it may also be applied to a straight downward direction but is so used less frequently ⟨face, as many have done and are doing, the level as opposed to the *vertical* fire of the enemy —Sir Winston Churchill⟩ PERPENDICULAR may suggest a stiff straightness; it is somewhat more likely than VERTICAL to suggest a downward line or straight drop or descent ⟨it appears that the water is broken nowhere by striking against the rocks, and that therefore the descent is *perpendicular* —Anthony Trollope⟩ ⟨the trail led under the foot of a high, almost *perpendicular* rock —C.G.D.Roberts⟩ PLUMB in this sense is mainly an artisan's or builder's term indicating exact verticality capable of being ascertained by plumb line ⟨the wall was not *plumb*⟩
²vertical \"\ *n* -s : something that is vertical: as **a** *obs* : VERTEX, HEIGHT, SUMMIT **b** : a vertical line, plane, or circle; *esp* : PERPENDICULAR **c** : a vertical member in a truss **d** : a vertical photograph : an aerial photograph taken with the camera pointed straight downward **e** : UPRIGHT PIANO
vertical angle *n* **1** : an angle measured on a vertical circle either upward or downward from the horizon **2** : either of two angles lying on the opposite sides of two intersecting lines or planes
vertical bank *n* : a flight maneuver in which an airplane is so steeply banked that its longitudinal axis approaches the vertical
vertical circle *n* **1 a** : a great circle of the celestial sphere whose plane is perpendicular to that of the horizon : AZIMUTH CIRCLE **b** : an astronomical observational circle so mounted as to turn to any azimuth **2** : a theodolite having a finely divided circle on its horizontal axis and used for measuring altitudes
vertical combination *or* **vertical integration** *n* : a combining of business firms engaged in different phases of the manufacture and distribution of a product into an interacting whole
vertical curve *n* : an easement curve in railroad track to connect intersecting grade lines
vertical engine *n* : an engine in which the piston moves vertically up and down and the crankshaft is usu. below the cylinder
vertical envelopment *n* : envelopment of a military enemy from the air (as with troops dropped by parachute or landed by gliders, helicopters, or airplanes) usu. to seize key objectives in the enemy's rear
vertical-fiber brick *n* : a wire-cut vitrified paving brick laid in a pavement with a wire-cut face up
vertical file *n* **1** : a file the records of which are placed upright or on edge **2** : a collection of pamphlets, clippings, and ephemera (as in a library) that is maintained to answer brief questions quickly or to provide points of information not easy to locate elsewhere
vertical fin *n* : any of the median fins of a fish : a dorsal, anal, or caudal fin
vertical flute *n* : RECORDER
vertical gradient *n* : LAPSE RATE
vertical grain *n* : quarter-sawed lumber
vertical-grained \,∗∗∗'∗∗∗\ *adj* : QUARTER-SAWED
vertical index *n* : the ratio of the height of the cranium to its length multiplied by 100
vertical interval *or* **vertical distance** *n* : CONTOUR INTERVAL
ver·ti·cal·ism \'∗∗∗∗,lizəm\ *n* -s [ISV *vertical* + *-ism*] : VERTICALITY
ver·ti·cal·i·ty \∗∗∗∗'kalēd-ē\ *n* -ES : the quality or state of being vertical : PERPENDICULARITY
vertical keel *n* **1** : KEELSON b **2** : ³KEEL 1a(2)
vertical lift bridge *n* : a drawbridge of which the moving parts rise vertically
vertical-lift mower *n* : a mowing machine so designed that the cutter bar can be lifted to nearly a vertical position permitting the machine to pass close to an obstacle

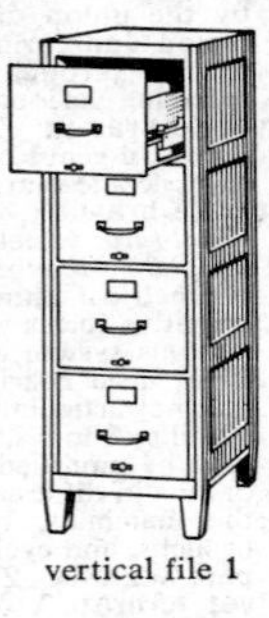

vertical file 1

vertical limb *n* : a graduated arc attached to an instrument (as a theodolite), for measuring vertical angles
vertical line *n* : a line perpendicular to a surface or to another line considered as a base: as **a** : a line perpendicular to the horizon **b** : a line parallel to the sides of a page or sheet as distinguished from a horizontal line **c** : the direction of a plumb line : a line normal to the surface of still water
ver·ti·cal·ly \∗∗k(ə)lē, -li\ *adv* : so as to be vertical : in respect to the vertical
ver·ti·cal·ness \∗∗∗ -ES : VERTICALITY
vertical plane *n* **1** : a plane that passes through a vertical line **2** : a plane of perspective passing through the point of sight and perpendicular to the ground plane and to the picture
vertical renversement *n* : an air maneuver in which an airplane reverses its direction of flight by pulling up in a vertical climb until stall, dropping the nose in a wingover, and doing a half-roll
vertical sash *n* : a sash sliding up and down — compare FRENCH SASH
vertical saw *n* **1** : a saw (as a muley saw) whose supporting frame moves in vertical guides **2** : a circular saw operating in a vertical plane
vertical section *n* : a mechanical drawing showing an interior, wall thicknesses, and similar relations as if made on a vertical plane passing through the object (as a building) depicted
vertical south dial *n* : a sundial (as on the south wall of a building) in the vertical plane facing south
vertical structure *n* : music composed or viewed as a succession of harmonies or chordal units in contrast to simultaneous independent melodies — compare HORIZONTAL STRUCTURE
vertical trust *n* : a trust formed by vertical combination
vertical union *n* : INDUSTRIAL UNION
vertices *pl of* VERTEX
ver·ti·cil \'vərd-ə,sil\ *n* -S [NL *verticillus*, fr. L, whorl of a spindle] : a circle or whorl of similar body parts (as flowers about a point on an axis or sensory hairs about an antennal joint)
verticill- *comb form* [NL, fr. *verticillus*, fr. L, whorl of a spindle, dim. of *vertic-, vertex* whirl — more at VERTEX] : whorl : verticil ⟨*verticillary*⟩
ver·ti·cil·las·ter \,vərd-əsə'lastə(r)\ *n* -S [NL, fr. *verticill-* + *-aster*] : a mixed inflorescence (as in many labiates) consisting of a pair of much-condensed nearly sessile cymes arranged around an axis like a true verticil — see INFLORESCENCE illustration
ver·ti·cil·las·trate \,∗∗∗'la,strāt, -astrət\ *adj* [NL *verticillaster* + E *-ate*] : bearing or arranged in verticillasters
ver·ti·cil·la·tae \,vərd-əsə'llād-(,)ē, (,)vər,tis-\ [NL, fr. fem. pl. of *verticillatus* verticillate] *syn of* CASUARINALES
ver·ti·cil·late \,vərd-ə'silət, (,)vər'tisə,lāt\ *adj* [NL *verticillatus*, fr. *verticillus* + L *-atus -ate*] : arranged in verticils : WHORLED ⟨ esp : arranged in a transverse whorl like the spokes of a wheel ⟨∼ leaves⟩ ⟨a ∼ shell⟩ — **ver·ti·cil·late·ly** \-'lē\ *adv* — **ver·ti·cil·la·tion** \,vərd-əsə'lāshən, (,)vər,tisə'l-\ *n* -s
ver·ti·cil·lat·ed \∗∗,lād-əd\ *adj* [NL *verticillatus* + E *-ed*] : VERTICILLATE
verticilli- *comb form* [NL *Verticillium*] : Verticillium ⟨*verticilliosis*⟩
ver·ti·cil·li·ose \,vərd-ə'silē,ōs\ *n* -S [ISV *verticilli-* + *-ose*] : VERTICILLIOSIS
ver·ti·cil·li·o·sis \,∗∗∗,silē'ōsəs\ *n, pl* **verticillio·ses** \-ō,sēz\ [NL, fr. *verticilli-* + *osis*] : a wilt disease of various plants caused by soil-borne fungi of the genus *Verticillium*
ver·ti·cil·li·um \∗∗∗'silēəm\ *n* [NL, fr. *verticill-*] **1** *cap* : a genus of imperfect fungi (order Moniliales) having conidia borne singly at the apex of whorled branchlets and including several that cause destructive wilts in plants — see VERTICILLIOSIS **2** -S : a fungus of the genus *Verticillium*
verticillium wilt *n* : VERTICILLIOSIS
ver·tic·i·ty \vər'tisəd-ē\ *n* -ES [NL *verticitat-, verticitas*, fr. L *vertic-, vertex* highest point, peak + *-itat-, -itas -ity* — more at VERTEX] : a tendency (as shown by a magnetized needle) to turn toward a magnetic pole ⟨the old window stanchions had become magnetic, proving, as he thinks, that iron acquires ∼ —Walter Pater⟩
ver·tig·i·nate \,vər'tijə,nāt\ *vi* -ED/-ING/-S [LL *vertiginatus*, past part. of *vertiginare* to whirl around, fr. L *vertigin-, vertigo* action of whirling] : to whirl dizzily around : TWIRL
ver·tig·i·nous \-nəs\ *adj* [L *vertiginosus* one suffering from dizziness, vertiginous, fr. *vertigin-, vertigo* + *-osus -ose*] **1** : characterized or accompanied by vertigo ⟨a ∼ dream⟩ ⟨∼ disorders⟩ **2 a** : suffering from vertigo : afflicted with dizziness : GIDDY **b** : having a light or silly mind : deficient in steadfastness or constancy : inclined to frequent and often pointless or foolish change **3** : causing or tending to cause dizziness : of a kind likely to cause vertigo ⟨∼ heights⟩ ⟨a ∼ speed⟩ **4** : involving or marked by turning : ROTARY ⟨the motion of the earth⟩ — **ver·tig·i·nous·ly** *adv*
ver·ti·go \'vərt|ə,gō, 'vəl, |vəl, |tl, (t)gō\ *n, pl* **vertigoes** *sometimes* \∗∗,gō\ *or* \vər'tī(,)gō\ *or* **vertig·i·nes** \vər'tijə,nēz\ *or* **vertigos** \-,ōz\ *or* **vertig·i·nes** \vər'tijə,nēz\ *n* [L, action of whirling, fr. *vertere* to turn — more at WORTH] **1** *pl* **vertigoes** or **vertig·i·nes** \vər'tijə,nēz\ **a** (1) : a disturbance which is associated with various known diseases or due to unknown causes and in which the external world seems to revolve around the individual or in which the individual seems to revolve in space — called also respectively *objective vertigo, subjective vertigo* (2) : DIZZINESS **b** : a dizzy confused condition of mind : a state in which all things seem to be whirling around : mental bewilderment or confusion **c** : disordered equilibration or vertiginous movements in a lower animal often forming a symptom of a specific disease; *also* : a disease (as gid or staggers) marked by such vertigo **2** *cap* [NL, fr. L] : a genus that comprises very small cylindrical land snails usu. found under stones and dead wood and is included in the family Pupillidae or made the type of a separate family
verting *pres part of* VERT
vert russe \,ver,'rüs\ *n* [F] : RUSSIAN GREEN
verts *pl of* VERT, *pres 3d sing of* VERT
vertu *var of* VIRTU
ver·u·la·mi·an \,∗∗∗'lāmēən\ *adj, usu cap* [Baron *Verulam* (title of Francis Bacon †1626 Eng. philosopher and author) + E *-an*] : of, relating to, or like that of Francis Bacon
ver·u·mon·ta·num \,verə,män'tānəm\ *n* -S [NL, fr. L *veru* spit, dart + *montanum*, neut. of *montanus* mountainous — more at SAUERKRAUT, MOUNTAIN] : an elevation in the floor of the prostatic portion of the urethra where the seminal ducts enter
ver·vain \'vər,vān\ *n* -s [ME *verveine*, fr. MF, fr. L *verbena*, sing. of *verbenae* sacred boughs of laurel, olive, or myrtle, class of medicinal plants; akin to L *verber* rod, Gk *rhabdos* rod, *rhamnos* buckthorn and prob. to Gk *rhembein* to whirl, OHG *werfan* to throw — more at WARP] **1** : a plant of the genus *Verbena*; *esp* : one having small spicate flowers — see BLUE VERVAIN **2** : VERBENA 3
vervain family *n* : VERBENACEAE
vervain hummingbird *n* : a very small hummingbird (*Mellisuga minima*) of Hispaniola and Jamaica
vervain mallow *n* : a European mallow (*Malva alcea*) often cultivated for its rose-colored flowers
vervain sage *n* : WILD SAGE 1
vervain thoroughwort *n* : a rough-foliaged perennial herb (*Eupatorium pilosum*) of the eastern U.S. having opposite mostly oblong leaves and an open cymose cluster of white flower heads
verve \'vərv, 'vəv, 'vəiv, 've(ə)rv, 'veəv\ *n* -S [F, fr. MF, caprice, fantasy, fr. OF, proverb, delivery, verbosity, fr. L *verba*, pl. of *verbum* word — more at WORD] **1** *archaic* : special ability or talent **2 a** : a forceful and lively quality or manner of composition or performance (as of a poem, painting, musical work) : DASH, VIVACITY ⟨the animals were drawn with such ∼ that they seemed ready to leap straight out of the scroll —New Yorker⟩ ⟨performing with matchless ∼ and gusto —Barry Carman⟩ **b** : ENERGY, VITALITY ⟨with the ∼ of a girl under twenty, she recovered her spirits —Francis Hackett⟩ **syn** see VIGOR
ver·veine \'vər,vān\ *n* -s [F, fr. MF] : VERVAIN
ver·vel \'vərvəl\ *also* **var·vel** \'värvəl\ *n* -S [MF *vervelle*, fr. LL *vertibulum* joint of the spine; akin to L *vertebra* — more at VERTEBRA] : a ring or one of several rings attached to a bird's leg for securing the bird to its perch

ver·velle \,vər'vel\ *n* -S [obs. F, fr. MF, vervelle, vervel] : a staple or small loop used in medieval armor esp. for lacing a camail to the headpiece
ver·ver \(')vā;rvā, (')və;vā\ *n* -s [Haitian Creole] : a voodooistic ritual design commonly traced on the ground
ver·vet \'vərvət\ *n* -S [F, fr. *vert* green + *-vet* (as in *grivet*); fr. its color — more at VERT] : a southern and eastern African guenon monkey (*Cercopithecus pygerythrus*) related to the grivet but having the face, chin, hands, and feet black
¹very \'verē, -ri\ *adj* -ER/-EST [ME *verray, verrai* true, truthful, fr. (assumed) VL *veracus*, fr. L *verac-, verax* true, truthful, fr. *verus* true; akin to OE *wǣr* true, correct, *wǣr* faith, care, bond of friendship, OHG *wāra* bond, trust, care, ON *vārar* pledge, OIr *fír* true, Gk *ēra* (acc.) favor, OSlav *věra* faith; basic meaning: care, loyalty] **1 a** : properly entitled to the name or designation : TRUE ⟨∼ God of ∼ God, begotten not made —Nicene Creed⟩ ⟨the fierce hatred of a ∼ woman —J.M. Barrie⟩ **b** : ACTUAL, REAL, VERITABLE ⟨whether thou be my ∼ son . . . or not —Gen 27:21 (AV)⟩ ⟨the ∼ blood and bone of our grammar —H.L.Smith b. 1913⟩ **c** : SIMPLE, PLAIN ⟨in ∼ truth, life is short —Benjamin Farrington⟩ **2 a** : EXACT, PRECISE ⟨might be the ∼ condition we seek —Gerard MacGowan⟩ **b** : exactly suitable or necessary ⟨may be the ∼ thing for the purpose —C.K.Ogden⟩ **3** : ABSOLUTE, UTTER ⟨the *veriest* idiot that ever lived —Joseph Conrad⟩ **b** : SHEER, UNQUALIFIED ⟨the sailors mutinied from ∼ hunger —T.B.Macaulay⟩ **4** — used as an intensive esp. to emphasize identity ⟨my ∼ chains and I grew friends —Lord Byron⟩ ⟨cause the ∼ rocks to tremble —Amer. Guide Series: Maine⟩ ⟨the ∼ language of the churches is becoming unintelligible to them —W.R.Inge⟩ **5** : MERE, BARE ⟨the *veriest* shadow of a mighty dynasty —W.E. Swinton⟩ ⟨the ∼ thought of thee with sweetness fills the breast —Edward Caswall⟩ **6** : SELFSAME, IDENTICAL ⟨her own mother had once said that ∼ word —Helen Howe⟩ **7** : SPECIAL, PARTICULAR ⟨the path that led across the roots of his ∼ tree —Nathaniel Hawthorne⟩ **syn** see SAME
²very \"\ *adv* [ME *verray*, fr. *verray*, adj.] **1** : to a high degree : to a considerable extent : EXTREMELY, EXCEEDINGLY ⟨a ∼ hot day⟩ ⟨sun is ∼ bright⟩ ⟨is ∼ much a believer in reason —F.A. Pottle⟩ ⟨saw the four of them ∼ plainly —Carson McCullers⟩ ⟨is ∼ pleased to edit the ... magazine —H.M.McLuhan⟩ ⟨towns were ∼ separated from one another —L.D.Stamp⟩ ⟨round the corner came a ∼ ∼ nice old lady —Lilian Balch⟩ **2** : in actual fact : REALLY, TRULY ⟨the ∼ best store in town⟩ ⟨on the ∼ next page⟩ ⟨told the ∼ same story⟩ ⟨expected the ∼ opposite result⟩ **3** *archaic* : EXACTLY, PRECISELY ⟨looked as though in her heart she was now, ∼ now, singing the old lines —Llewelyn Powys⟩
very high frequency *n* **1** : a radio frequency in the range of the radio spectrum above high frequency — see RADIO FREQUENCY table **2** : a radio frequency in the part of the very high frequency band between 100 and 156 megacycles used for radio aids to airplane navigation and communication
very-high-frequency *adj* : of or relating to very high frequency or to a radio wave having such a frequency
very light \'verē, -ri-\ *n, usu cap V* [after Edward W. *Very* †1910 Am. naval officer] : one of the flares used in the Very system of signaling — compare STAR SHELL, VERY'S NIGHT SIGNALS
very low frequency *n* : a radio frequency in the lowest range of the radio spectrum — see RADIO FREQUENCY table
very-low-frequency *adj* : of or relating to very low frequency or to a radio wave having such a frequency
very pistol *n, usu cap V* [after Edward W. *Very* †1910] : a pistol designed to fire Very lights
very reverend — used as a courtesy title for various ecclesiastical officials (as Roman Catholic and Anglican deans, rectors of Roman Catholic colleges and seminaries, superiors of religious houses, monsignor with the rank of papal chamberlain)
very's night signals *also* **very night signals** *n pl, usu cap V* [after Edward W. *Very* †1910 Am. naval officer] : a system of signaling in which balls of red and green fire are fired from a pistol and their arrangement in groups denotes numbers having a code significance
ves *pl of* VE
ves abbr **1** [L *vesica*] bladder **2** vesicular **3** vessel **4** vestry
ve·si \'vāsē, -āzē\ *n* -s [Fiji] : IPIL
vesic abbr [L *vesicula*] blister
vesi·ca \və'sēkə, və'sīkə, 'vēsəkə\ *n, pl* **vesi·cae** \-ē,kī, -ī(,)kē, -ī(,)sē, -ə,kē, -ə,kī, -ə,sē\ [L *vesica, vensica*] : akin to L *venter* belly — more at VENTER] **1** : BLADDER **2** *obs* : a large vessel for distilling liquor **3** : VESICA PISCIS ⟨the ∼ and festoons common in Irish cut glass⟩
ves·i·cal \'vesəkəl, -sēk-\ *adj* [F *vesical*, fr. MF *vesical*, fr. L *vesica* + MF *-al*] **1** : of or relating to a bladder; *esp* : of or relating to the urinary bladder **2** : of the shape of a bladder : having the form of a pointed oval
vesical artery *n* : any of several arteries derived from the anterior trunk of the hypogastric artery and distributed to the urinary bladder and adjacent parts
vesical neck *n* : the part of the urinary bladder immediately surrounding the internal orifice of the urethra
vesical plexus *n* **1** : a plexus of nerves at the base of the bladder comprising preganglionic fibers chiefly from the hypogastric plexus and lodging postganglionic neurons whose fibers are distributed to the bladder **2** : a venous plexus between the muscular wall of the bladder and the overlying peritoneum draining into the pudendal plexus
¹ves·i·cant \'vesəkənt\ *n* -S [L *vesican-, vesicans*, blister + E *-ant*, n. suffix] **1** : an agent (as a drug or a plant substance) that induces blistering **2** : a vesicant war gas (as mustard gas or lewisite) — called also *blister gas*
²vesicant \"\ *adj* [L *vesica* + E *-ant*, adj. suffix] : producing or tending to produce blisters
vesica pis·cis \-'piskəs, 'pisəs, 'pīsəs, 'pēsəs\ *n* [NL, lit., fish bladder] : a pointed oval figure typically composed of two intersecting arcs; *specif* : an aureole of this shape surrounding a representation of a sacred personage
ves·i·car·ia \,vesə'ka(a)rēə\ *n, cap* [NL, fr. L *vesica* + NL *-aria*] : a small genus of chiefly Mediterranean annual or perennial herbs (family Cruciferae) with inflated seed pods
ves·i·cate \'vesə,kāt\ *vb* -ED/-ING/-S [back-formation fr. *vesication*] : BLISTER
ves·i·ca·tion \,vesə'kāshən\ *n* -s [MF, fr. L *vesica* bladder, blister + MF *-ation*] **1** : an instance or the process of blistering **2** : BLISTER
ves·i·ca·to·ry \'vesəkə,tōrē, və'sik-\ *adj or n* [MF *vesicatoire*, fr. *vesication* + *-oire -ory*] : VESICANT
vesicatory gas *n* : a war gas that causes blistering
ves·i·cle \'vesəkəl, -sēk-\ *n* -S [MF *vesicule*, fr. L *vesicula* small bladder, small blister, dim. of *vesica* bladder, small blister — more at VESICA] : a body felt to resemble a bladder esp. in constituting a small thin-walled cavity: as **a** : a plant or animal structure (as a cyst, vacuole, or cell) having the general form of a membranous cavity : a thin sac esp. when filled with fluid **b** : minute bubbles formerly held to make up the substance of a cloud or fog **c** : a small and more or less circular elevation of the cuticle of the skin containing a clear watery fluid : BLISTER **d** : a small cavity in a mineral or rock and esp. in a basaltic lava produced ordinarily by the expansion of vapor in the molten mass

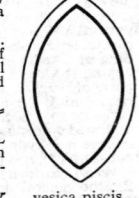
vesica piscis

vesicul- *or* **vesiculo-** *comb form* [NL *vesicula*] : vesicle ⟨*Vesicularia*⟩ : vesicular and ⟨*vesiculopapular*⟩
ve·sic·u·la \və'sikyələ\ *n, pl* **vesicu·lae** \-,lē, -,lī\ *also* **vesiculas** [NL, fr. L, small bladder, small blister — more at VESICLE] : VESICLE
ve·sic·u·lar \-lə(r)\ *adj* [*vesicul-* + *-ar*] **1 a** : formed or constructed like a vesicle : constituting a vesicle ⟨a ∼ cavity⟩ **b** : containing, made up of, or characterized by the presence of vesicles ⟨∼ lava⟩ ⟨a ∼ texture in rock⟩ **2 a** : of, relating to, or involving a vesicular structure (as the alveoli of the lungs or the presence or formation of vesicles ⟨a ∼ eczema⟩ ⟨normal ∼ breathing in which air has free access to the individual alveoli **3** *of a cell nucleus* : appearing to have the chromatin in discrete

stainable particles embedded in a clear nuclear sap — **ve·sic·u·lar·ly** *adv*
vesicular exanthema *n* : an acute virus disease of swine that closely resembles foot-and-mouth disease but is not transmissable to cattle, sheep, or goats and may occur in epizootic proportions in outbreaks which are usu. traceable to the feeding of contaminated garbage
vesicular gland *n* : a subepidermal gland in a plant containing essential oil
ve·sic·u·lar·ia \və̇ˌsikyəˈla(a)rēə\ *n, cap* [NL, fr. *vesicul-* + *-aria*] : a genus of marine bryozoans (order Ctenostomata) that have delicate tubular cells clustered on slender flexible stems
vesicular stomatitis *n* : an acute virus disease of horses and mules and sometimes also of cattle or rarely of swine much resembling foot-and-mouth disease and marked by erosive blisters in and about the mouth and esp. on the tongue which may prevent eating
1ve·sic·u·late \və̇ˈsikyəˌlāt, -ˌlə̇t, *usu* -d.+V\ *adj* [*vesicul-* + *-ate*, adj. suffix] **1** : containing or covered with vesicles **2** : VESICULAR 1a
2ve·sic·u·late \-ˌlāt, *usu* -ād.+V\ *vb* -ED/-ING/-S [*vesicul-* + *-ate*, v. suffix] *vt* : to cause to become vesicular ~ *vi* : to become vesicular ⟨chromosome fragments ~ at metaphase —*Amer. Naturalist*⟩
ve·sic·u·la·tion \=ˌ==ˈlāshən\ *n* -S **1** : the condition of having or process of forming vesicles : the presence or formation of vesicles **2** : distribution or arrangement of vesicles ⟨a saclike ~ of the affected skin⟩ ⟨~ of the two types of lava differs considerably —G.W.Tyrrell⟩
ve·sic·u·li·na \-ˈlīnə\ *n, cap* [NL, fr. *vesicul-* + *-ina*] *in some classifications* : a genus of American herbs comprising New World forms (as the purple bladderwort) that are usu. assigned to the genus *Utricularia*
ve·sic·u·lo·papular \və̇ˈsikyəlō+\ *adj* : of, relating to, or marked by both vesicles and papules ⟨a ~ inflammation⟩
ve·sic·u·lo·pustular \"+\ *adj* : of, relating to, or marked by both vesicles and pustules ⟨a ~ eruption⟩
ve·sic·u·lose \və̇ˈsikyəˌlōs\ *adj* [*vesicul-* + *-ose*] : VESICULATE
ve·sic·u·lus \-ləs\ *n, pl* **vesicu·li** \-ˌlī, -ˌlē\ [NL, alter. of *vesicula*] : VESICLE
ves·kit \ˈveskə̇t, *usu* -ə̇d.+V\ *dial var of* WAISTCOAT
ves·pa \ˈvespə\ *n, cap* [NL, fr. L, wasp — more at WASP] **1** *cap* : the type genus of Vespidae including various hornets and yellowjackets **2** -S : any insect of the genus *Vespa*
ves·pa·cide \-ˌsīd\ *n* -S [L *vespa* wasp + E *-cide*] : one that kills wasps
ves·pal \ˈvespəl\ *adj* [L *vespa* wasp + E *-al*] : of or relating to wasps
1ves·per \ˈvespə(r)\ *n* -S [ME, fr. L, evening, evening star — more at WEST] **1** *usu cap* : EVENING STAR 1 **2 vespers** *pl* [modif. of ML *vesperia*, fr. L *vesper* evening + *-ia* -y] : public ceremonies or disputations formerly preceding commencement at an English university; *also* : the time of such ceremonies : the eve of commencement **3 vespers** *pl, often cap* [F *vespres*, fr. ML *vesperae*, fr. pl. of L *vespera* evening — more at WEST] **a** : the sixth and next to the last of the canonical hours **b** : a religious office or service for this time: as (1) : an office formerly said or sung before nightfall (2) : the evening prayer or evensong of churches of the Anglican communion compiled from the ancient offices of vespers and compline (3) *or* **vesper service** : a late afternoon or evening religious service that is often largely musical **4** : a vesper bell **5** *archaic* : EVENING, EVENTIDE
2vesper \"\ *adj* **1** : of, relating to, or used in connection with religious vespers ⟨~ music⟩ **2** : of or relating to the evening : VESPERTINE
1ves·per·al \-p(ə)rəl\ *adj* [LL *vesperalis*, fr. L *vesper* evening + *-alis* -al] : VESPER ⟨a ~ breeze⟩; *esp* : CREPUSCULAR 2 ⟨~ insects⟩
2vesperal \"\ *also* **ves·per·a·le** \ˌvespəˈra(ˌ)lē, -rāl-, -räl-\ *n* -S [F *vespéral*, fr. LL *vesperalis*, adj.] **1** : a book containing the office and music for vespers **2** : a generally colored altar cover that is used to protect the white altar cloths between ceremonies
ves·per·ing \ˈvesp(ə)riŋ, -rēŋ\ *adj* [*1vesper* + *-ing*] : singing vesper songs ⟨a hush of ~ birds —Thomas Moult⟩
vesper iris *n* : a late-flowering and very free-blooming Asiatic fibrous-rooted iris (*Iris dichotoma*) that is sometimes cultivated for its predominantly lavender and white flowers which open only toward dusk
vesper mouse *n* : WHITE-FOOTED MOUSE
vesper sparrow *also* **vesper bird** *n* : a common American sparrow (*Pooecetes gramineus*) having the outer tail feathers white and singing esp. in the evening
vespertide \ˈ==ˌ=\ *n* : the time of vespers
ves·per·til·ian \ˌvespə(r)ˈtilēən, -lyən\ *adj* [L *vespertilio* bat + E *-an*] : of, relating or suitable to, or resembling a bat ⟨~ habits⟩ ⟨~ anatomy⟩
ves·per·til·io \ˌ==ˈtilē(ˌ)ō\ *n* [NL, fr. L, bat, fr. *vesper* evening — more at WEST] **1** *cap* : the type genus of Vespertilionidae formerly comprehensive but now comprising solely the frosted bat (*V. murinus*) or slightly extended to include the serotine and the American brown bats which are more often placed in the genus *Eptesicus* **2** -S : any bat of the genus *Vespertilio*; *broadly* : BAT
1ves·per·til·i·o·nid \ˌ==ˈtilēəˌnid\ *adj* [NL *Vespertilionidae*] : of or related to the Vespertilionidae
2vespertilionid \"\ *n* -S : a bat of the family Vespertilionidae
ves·per·til·i·on·i·dae \ˌ==ˌtilēˈänəˌdē\ *n pl, cap* [NL, fr. *Vespertilion-*, *Vespertilio*, type genus + *-idae*] : a very large family of bats (suborder Microchiroptera) found in most parts of the world, including the majority of the common bats of temperate regions, and having separate ears with well-developed tragal lobes, a simple nose without appendages, and a tail that extends to the border of the posterior part of the volar membrane which stretches between the thighs — see VESPERTILIO
ves·per·ti·nal \ˌ==ˈtīnᵊl\ *adj* [LL *vespertinalis*, fr. L *vespertinus* + *-alis* -al] : VESPERTINE ⟨became purely ~, never stirring abroad till after dark —J.R.Lowell⟩
ves·per·tine \ˈ==ˌtīn, -ˌtēn\ *adj* [L *vespertinus*, fr. *vesper* evening + *-tinus* (as in *matutinus* of the morning) — more at WEST] **1** : of, relating to, or occurring in the evening : resembling that of evening ⟨~ shadows⟩ **2** *of a planet* : setting with or just after the sun **3** : active or flourishing in the evening : CREPUSCULAR: as **a** : feeding or flying in early evening **b** : blossoming in the evening
ves·pe·tro \ˈvespəˌtrō\ *n* -S [F *vespétro*, fr. *vesser* to break wind noiselessly + *péter* to break wind + *roter* to belch] : a liqueur consisting of brandy flavored with anise, fennel, coriander, and angelica and sweetened with sugar
ves·pi·ary \ˈvespēˌerē\ *n* -ES [L *vespa* wasp + E *-iary* (as in *apiary*) — more at WASP] : a nest of social wasps; *also* : a colony of wasps inhabiting such a nest
1ves·pid \ˈvespə̇d\ *adj* [NL *Vespidae*] : of or relating to the Vespidae
2vespid \"\ *n* -S : a wasp of the family Vespidae
ves·pi·dae \-pəˌdē\ *n pl, cap* [NL, fr. *Vespa*, type genus + *-idae*] : a widely distributed family of wasps (superfamily Vespoidea) containing the social wasps that live in colonies like bees, produce workers as well as perfect females and males, feed on various animal or vegetable matter but usu. do not store up supplies since their colonies are destroyed by the cold season, and build nests which generally consist of or contain one or more combs of papery material that is usu. horizontally placed so that the cells are vertical and with the open end down — compare POLISTES, VESPA, VESPULA; HORNET, YELLOW JACKET
ves·pine \ˈveˌspīn, -ˌspə̇n\ *adj* [L *vespa* wasp + E *-ine* — more at WASP] : of, relating to, characteristic of, or resembling wasps esp. of the family Vespidae
ves·poid \ˈveˌspȯid\ *adj* [L *vespa* wasp + E *-oid*] **1** : resembling or related to the wasps **2** [NL *Vespoidea*] : of or relating to the Vespoidea
ves·poi·dea \veˈspȯidēə\ *n pl, cap* [NL, fr. *Vespa* + *-oidea*] : a superfamily of Hymenoptera comprising the true wasps, hornets, and related insects and consisting of the family Vespidae often together with other families (as Pompilidae and Mutillidae)
ves·pu·la \ˈvespyələ\ *n, cap* [NL, fr. *Vespa* + *-ula*] : a genus of social wasps that includes various hornets and yellow jackets and is sometimes treated as a subgenus of *Vespa*
1ves·sel \ˈvesəl\ *n* -S [ME *vessel*, *vesselle*, fr. OF *vassel*, *vaissel*, *vessel* receptacle, container (fr. LL *vascellum*, dim. of L *vas* vessel, vase) & *vassele*, *vaissele*, *vessele* domestic receptacles collectively, fr. (assumed) VL *vascella*, fr. LL, pl. of *vascellum* — more at VASE] **1 a** *obs* : domestic containers or utensils; *specif* : PLATE 3a **b** *dial Brit* : cutlery, dishes, and other table furnishing ⟨had to wash up the ~ before she could leave⟩ **2 a** : a hollow and usu. cylindrical or concave utensil (as a hogshead, bottle, kettle, cup, or bowl) for holding something and esp. a liquid : a receptacle of tight construction sometimes as distinguished from one (as a basket) of slack or open construction ⟨set a large copper ~ over the fire⟩ ⟨alchemists' flasks and similar ~*s*⟩ **b** : a person that is the receptacle of something; *esp* : one in whom a divine action is manifested **c** *dial Eng* : the udder of a cow **3 a** : a usu. hollow structure used on or in the water for purposes of navigation : a craft for navigation of the water; *esp* : a watercraft or structure with its equipment whether self-propelled or not that is used or capable of being used as a means of transportation in navigation or commerce on water and that usu. excludes small rowboats and sailboats **b** : any of various aircraft; *esp* : an airplane (as a hydroplane) that is capable of being used on water **4 a** : a tube or canal (as an artery, vein, or lymphatic) in which a body fluid (as blood or lymph) is contained and conveyed or circulated **b** : a conducting tube in a vascular plant formed in the xylem by the fusion and loss of end walls of a series of cells — compare TRACHEID
2ves·sel \ˈvesəl\ *n* -S [origin unknown] : a piece of paper ⅛ of a sheet of foolscap (about 7 in. x 4½ in.)
vessel element *or* **vessel member** *n* : one of the individual cells making up a vessel of the plant vascular system
vessel ton *n* : TON 2a
1vest \ˈvest\ *vb* -ED/-ING/-S [ME *vesten*, fr. MF *vestir* to clothe, invest with ecclesiastical vestments, fr. L *vestire* to clothe, fr. *vestis* garment, attire — more at WEAR] *vt* **1 a** : to place or give into the possession or discretion of some person or authority ⟨the regulation of the waterways . . . was ~*ed* in the corporation —Edwin Benson⟩; *esp* : to give to a person a legally fixed immediate right of present or future enjoyment of (as an estate) ⟨a deed that ~*s* a life estate in the grantee and a remainder in his children⟩ **b** : to grant, endow, or clothe with a particular authority, right, or property ⟨~ a court with the right to try criminal cases⟩ ⟨the retirement plan ~*ed* the workers absolutely with the company's contribution after 10 years of continuous employment⟩ **c** : to put (a person) in possession of land by the feudal ceremony of investiture : ENFEOFF **2** : to clothe with or as if with a garment; *esp* : to garb in ecclesiastical vestments ⟨came ~*ed* all in white, pure as her mind —John Milton⟩ **3** : to lay out (money) : INVEST ~ *vi* **1** : to become legally vested ⟨normally title to real property ~*s* in the holder of a properly executed deed⟩ **2** : to put on garments; *esp* : to robe formally for or as if for a ceremonial occasion ⟨the little room where the priests ~*ed* for mass⟩
2vest \"\ *n* -S [F *veste*, fr. It, fr. L *vestis* garment, attire] **1** *archaic* **a** (1) : a loose outer garment worn by men (as in ancient times or eastern countries) : ROBE, GOWN (2) : a similar garment worn by women **b** : VESTURE, CLOTHING, GARB **c** : an ecclesiastical vestment **2 a** : a man's garment for wear under a coat made in varying styles and lengths; *esp* : a sleeveless collarless close-fitting coat reaching just below the waist, having four small pockets, and buttoned up to a V neck **b** : a garment of similar design for women : WAISTCOAT **c** : a protective or safety garment shaped like a man's vest and worn esp. by military personnel on active duty or people in or on the water **3 a** *chiefly Brit* : a man's undershirt **b** : a knitted sleeved or sleeveless undershirt for women or sometimes children **4** : a plain or decorative piece used to fill in the front neckline of a woman's outer garment (as a waist, coat, or gown) — compare DICKEY

vest 2a

vest *abbr* vestibule
ves·ta \ˈvestə\ *n* -S [after *Vesta*, ancient Roman goddess of the hearth, fr. L] : a short match with a shank of wax coated threads; *also* : a short wooden match
1ves·tal \ˈvestᵊl\ *adj* [ME *vestalle*, fr. L *vestalis*, fr. *Vesta* + L *-alis* -al] **1** : of or relating to the Roman goddess Vesta **2 a** : of or relating to a vestal virgin **b** : CHASTE ⟨who, even in pure and ~ modesty, still blush —Shak.⟩ — **ves·tal·ly** \-tᵊlē, -li\ *adv*
2vestal \"\ *n* -S [L *vestalis*, fr. *vestalis*, adj.] **1** *or* **also vestal virgin** [*vestal virgin* part trans. of L *vestalis virgo*] **a** : a virgin consecrated to the Roman goddess Vesta and to the service of watching the sacred fire perpetually kept burning upon her altar **b** : a pure and chaste woman (as a virgin or nun) **2** : a grayish purple to grayish reddish purple
vested interest *n* **1 a** : an interest (as a right or title to an estate) carrying a legal right of present or future enjoyment and of present alienation **b** : an interest (as in an existing political, economic, or social arrangement) in which the holder has a strong personal commitment as a result sometimes of long association but more often of present or future benefits ⟨those who have a *vested interest* in the educational status quo —A.E.Bestor⟩ ⟨to continue in existence it must create *vested interests* in its survival —Paul Johnson⟩ **c** : a right vested in an employee under a pension plan **2** : one having a vested interest in something; *specif* : a group closely associated with and enjoying benefits from an existing economic or political privilege ⟨vacant land . . . is bought up by speculators or held by *vested interests* —A.J.Bruwer⟩ ⟨the free press, so integral to the self-maintenance and growth of free society, was brought into subservience to the *vested interests* —H.M.Kallen⟩
vested remainder *n* : a remainder granted or devised by the owner of a fee to a then ascertainable existing person who has or whose heirs or devisees have the present legal right to enter into possession and enjoy the estate upon the termination of a preceding freehold estate (as a life estate fee tail)
vested right *n* : a right belonging so absolutely, completely, and unconditionally to a person that it cannot be defeated by the act of any private person and that is entitled to governmental protection usu. under a constitutional guarantee ⟨the contract clause remained extremely important for the protection of *vested rights* against state legislation —C.B.Swisher⟩
vest·ee \(ˈ)vesˈtē\ *n* -S [*2vest* + *-ee*] **1** : DICKEY; *esp* : one that is made to resemble a vest and is worn under a coat **2** : VEST 4
ves·ti·ar·i·an \ˌvesteˈa(a)rēən\ *adj, often cap* [L *vestiarius* vestiary + E *-an*] : of, relating to, or constituting a controversy over ecclesiastical vestments in 16th century England ⟨at present a refugee in consequence of the *Vestiarian* controversy —J.Y.Evans⟩
1ves·ti·ary \ˈvestēˌerē, -ri\ *n* -ES [ME *vestiarie*, fr. OF *vestiaire*, *vestiarie*, fr. ML *vestiarium*, fr. L *vestire* to clothe, put on + *-arium* -ary, n. suffix — more at VEST] **1 a** : a robing room (as of a church) : VESTRY **b** : a room (as in a monastery) where clothing is stored and attended; *also* : CLOAKROOM **c** : a storage chest (as for clothing) **2** : CLOTHING, RAIMENT; *esp* : a set of clerical vestments **3** : any of various medieval officials or household officers; *specif* : an ecclesiastical dignitary who is charged in some cathedrals with the robing of the canons
2vestiary \"\ *adj* [L *vestiarius*, fr. *vestis* garment, attire + *-arius* -ary, adj. suffix — more at WEAR] : of or relating to clothes and esp. vestments
ves·tib·u·lar \(ˈ)veˈstibyələ(r)\ *adj* [*vestibule* + *-ar*] **1** : of or relating to a vestibule : resembling or sharing the nature of a vestibule **2** : of, relating to, mediating, constituting, or affecting the vestibular sense
vestibular apparatus *n* : the vestibule of the inner ear together with the end organs and nerve fibers that mediate the vestibular sense
vestibular nerve *n* : a branch of the auditory nerve that supplies the vestibule of the inner ear and the ampullae of the semicircular canals
vestibular nucleus *n* : a neural nucleus in which the fibers of the vestibular nerve terminate and of which the upper part is continuous with Deiters' nucleus
vestibular sense *n* : a sense mediated by end organs in the vestibule of the internal ear that contain otoliths and are stimulated by the pull of gravity and by the starting and stopping of rectilinear head movements; *broadly* : LABYRINTHINE SENSE
ves·tib·u·late \(ˈ)veˈstibyələt, -ˌlāt\ *adj* [*vestibule* + *-ate*] : having or resembling a vestibule
1ves·ti·bule \ˈvestəˌbyül\ *n* -S [F & L; F *vestible*, *vestibule*, fr. L *vestibulum*] **1 a** : an entrance court (as of an ancient Roman building) **b** : a passage, hall, or chamber between the outer door and the interior of a building : a porch or entrance into a house : LOBBY, NARTHEX **c** : an enclosed entrance to a railway passenger car fitted with side doors for ingress to and egress from the train and with a flexible side wall and roof attached to the end of the car **2** : any of various bodily cavities esp. when serving as or resembling an entrance to some other cavity or space: as **a** (1) : the central cavity of the bony labyrinth of the ear (2) : the parts of the membranous labyrinth comprising the utricle and the saccule and contained in the cavity of the bony labyrinth — see EAR illustration **b** : the space between the labia minora containing the orifice of the urethra **c** : the part of the left ventricle of the heart immediately below the aortic orifice **d** : the part of the mouth cavity outside the teeth and gums **e** : the part of the larynx above the false vocal cords **f** : a more or less tubular depression leading to the mouth of an infusorian **g** : the space within the circle of tentacles in bryozoans esp. of the group Entoprocta
2vestibule \"\ *vt* -ED/-ING/-S **1** : to furnish with a vestibule **2** : to join (railroad cars) by vestibules
vestibule car *n* : a railway car with a vestibule at each end
ves·ti·buled \-ld\ *adj* : having a vestibule
vestibule latch *n* : a lock actuated from outside by a key and from inside by a knob and having no dead bolt
vestibule school *n* : a school organized in an industrial plant to train new workers in specific skills before starting them on the actual working routine
vestibule train *n* : a railway train that is made up of vestibule cars
vestibule training *n* : in-service training in a vestibule school
ves·ti·bu·li·tis \ˌvestəbyəˈlīd.ə̇s\ *n* -ES [NL, fr. *vestibulum* + *-itis*] : inflammation of a bodily vestibule
ves·tib·u·lo·spinal \veˈstibyəlō+\ *adj* [*vestibule* + *-o-* + *spinal*] : of, relating to, or being a nerve tract passing from the nuclei of the vestibular nerve in the medulla down the spinal cord
vestibulo-urethral \"+\ *adj* [*vestibule* + *-o-* + *urethral*] : of or relating to the vestibule of the vagina and the urethra
ves·tib·u·lum \veˈstibyələm\ *n, pl* **vestibu·la** \-lə\ [NL & L; NL (in anatomical senses), fr. L (in other senses)] : VESTIBULE
ves·tige \ˈvestij, -tēj\ *n* -S [F, fr. L *vestigium*] **1 a** : a trace, mark, or visible sign left by a material thing (as a building) formerly present but now otherwise lost or unknown ⟨digging for the ~*s* of past civilizations⟩ ⟨fossil bones and other ~*s*⟩ **b** : the mark of a foot left on the earth : FOOTSTEP, TRACK **2 a** : a remaining bit that constitutes a memorial or trace of something formerly present or assumed to be present ⟨a manner showing ~*s* of past culture⟩ ⟨could detect ~*s* of beauty in her aging face⟩; *broadly* : a minute amount : the smallest quantity or trace ⟨lost all remaining ~*s* of self-control —Evelyn Barkins⟩ ⟨the lack of a ~ of hair on his pate —Leonard Wibberley⟩ ⟨not a ~ of sugar in the house⟩ **b** : a small and degenerate or imperfectly developed bodily part or organ that remains from one more fully developed in an earlier stage of the individual, in a past generation, or in closely related forms
ves·tig·ial \(ˈ)veˈstij(ē)əl\ *adj* [L *vestigium* + E *-al*] : of, relating to, or being a vestige : resembling or having the form of a vestige — **ves·tig·ial·ly** \-ēlē, -li\ *adv*
vestigial side band *n* : the transmitted portion of a partially suppressed side band utilized with the corresponding unsuppressed side band in signal transmission
ves·tig·i·um \veˈstijēəm\ *n, pl* **vestig·ia** \-jēə\ [L] : VESTIGE
ves·ti·ment \ˈvestəmənt\ *archaic var of* VESTMENT
vesting *n* -S [fr. gerund of *1vest*] **1** : the conveying to an employee of inalienable rights to share in a pension fund and esp. to recover his own and his employer's contribution on his behalf in the event of termination of employment prior to the normal retirement age; *also* : the right so conveyed **2** : the taking over of private property by a government usu. in return for compensation ⟨~ of foreign security holdings in time of war⟩
vesting order *n* : an order of a court, an administrative agency, or public officer passing the legal title in lieu of a legal conveyance
ves·ti·ni \veˈstīˌnī, -tē(ˌ)nē\ *n pl, usu cap* [L] : an ancient Sabine people of central Italy allied with the Romans about 300 B.C.
ves·tin·i·an \veˈstinēən\ *n* -S *usu cap* : a Sabellian dialect
ves·ti·ture \ˈvestəˌchü(ə)r, -ˌchu̇ə, -ˌch(ə)r, -tə̇ˌtü-, -tə̇ˌtyü-\ *n* -S [ML *vestitura*, fr. L *vestitus* (past part. of *vestire* to clothe, put on) + *-ura* -ure — more at VEST] **1** : INVESTITURE ⟨a ~ of power in the proletariat —Philip Wylie⟩ **2** : CLOTHING, GARB, DRESS **3** : something that covers a surface like a garment; *esp* : a covering (as of scales, hairs, or spines) on an insect's body or wings
vest·less \ˈ=lə̇s\ *adj* : having no vest
vest·let \-lə̇t\ *n* -S [*2vest* + *-let*] : any of various actinians (genus *Cerianthus*) that secrete a tough tube about the body
vestlike \ˈ=ˌ=\ *adj* : resembling a vest
vest·ment \ˈves(t)mənt\ *n* -S [ME *vestement*, *vestiment*, fr. OF, fr. L *vestimentum*, fr. *vestire* to clothe, put on + *-mentum* -ment — more at VEST] **1 a** : a covering or outer garment; *esp* : a garment or robe of ceremony or office **b vestments** *pl* : CLOTHING, GARB, DRESS **2** : a covering felt to resemble a garment ⟨the verdant ~ which spring spreads over the land⟩ **3** : a liturgical garment : an article of the ceremonial attire and insignia that are worn by ecclesiastical officiants and assistants during divine service as appropriate to the rite and indicative of their hierarchical rank — **vest·men·tal** \(ˈ)=ˈmentᵊl\ *adj*
vest·ment·ed \ˈ=məntə̇d\ *adj* **1** : arrayed in vestments **2** *of a ceremony or service* : conducted by clergy in vestments
ves·to·ri·an blue \(ˈ)veˈstōrēən, -tȯr-,-\ *n, usu cap V* [part trans. of L *caeruleum vestorianum*, fr. *caeruleum* blue + *vestorianum*, neut. of *vestorianus* of Vestorius, perh. fr. *Vestorius fl* 44 B.C. Roman banker + L *-anus* -an] : EGYPTIAN BLUE
vest-pocket \ˈ=ˈ==\ *adj* : adapted to fit into the vest pocket : of very small size or scope ⟨a *vest-pocket* edition of a book⟩ ⟨a *vest-pocket* political party⟩
vest-pocket camera *n* : a camera taking pictures 1⅝ by 2½ inches in size
vest-pocket veto *n* : POCKET VETO
ves·tral \ˈvestrəl\ *adj* [*vestry* + *-al*] : of or relating to a vestry
ves·try \-trē, -ri\ *n* -ES [ME *vestrie*, prob. modif. of MF *vestiarie*, *vestiaire* — more at VESTIARY] **1** *or* **vestry room a** (1) : a room within or attached to a church building in which the vestments of the clergy, the altar linen and hangings, and the sacred vessels and often church records are kept — called also *sacristy* (2) : a room corresponding to a church vestry in a non-Christian temple **b** : a storage place (as a room or closet) for clothing or formerly other valuables **c** : a room within or a building attached to a church building used variously as a chapel, church-school room, or prayer-meeting room **2** : a body of persons entrusted with the administration of the temporal affairs of a parish in the Church of England or in the Protestant Episcopal Church; *also* : a parish meeting or a meeting of a vestry esp. in England

ves·try·man \ˈ==mən\ *n, pl* **vestrymen** **:** one of a vestry
vests *pres 3d sing of* VEST, *pl of* VEST
ves·tur·al \ˈveschərəl\ *adj* **:** of or relating to vesture or clothing
¹ves·ture \ˈveschə(r)\ *n* -s [ME, fr. MF, fr. *vestir* to clothe + *-ure* — more at VEST] **1 :** something that covers the body: **a :** a covering garment (as a robe or vestment) **b :** CLOTHING, APPAREL, COSTUME **2 :** something that covers like a garment: as **a :** the covering vegetation (as crops) other than trees on land **b :** a covering (as of data, style, and language) in which a theme or topic is enveloped in being developed or elaborated **3 :** INVESTITURE, SEISIN
²vesture \"\ *vt* -ED/-ING/-S **:** to cover with vesture **:** CLOTHE, ENVELOP
vestured pit *n* **:** a bordered pit with minute outgrowths projecting into the pit cavity from the secondary wall around the pit
ves·tur·er \-chərə(r)\ *n* -s **:** SEXTON; *esp* **:** one in charge of church vestments and ornaments
¹ve·su·vian \vəˈsüvēən, -vyən\ *adj, usu cap* [*Vesuvius*, volcano near Naples, Italy + E *-an*] **1 :** of, relating to, or resembling the volcano Vesuvius **2 :** marked by uncertainty or sudden outbursts **:** FURIOUS ⟨a *Vesuvian* rage⟩ ⟨*Vesuvian* language⟩
²vesuvian \"\ *n* -s [in sense 1, fr. G, fr. *Vesuv* Vesuvius + G *-ian* (fr. L *-ianus* -ian); in sense 2, fr. ¹*vesuvian*] **1 :** IDOCRASE **2 :** a match or fusee used esp. formerly for lighting cigars
ve·su·vi·an·ite \-ə,nīt\ *n* -s [²*vesuvian* + *-ite*] **:** IDOCRASE
ve·su·vin \vəˈsüvən\ *n* -s [G, fr. *Vesuv* Vesuvius + G *-in*] **:** BISMARCK BROWN
ve·szel·yite \ˈvesəl,yīt, ˈvesē,īt; vəˈs|ālē,īt, ˈz|, |el-\ *n* -s [G *veszelyit*, fr. A. *Veszely*, 19th cent. Hung. mining engineer + G *-it* -ite] **:** a mineral $(Cu,Zn)_3PO_4(OH)_3.2H_2O$ that is a hydrous basic copper zinc phosphate occurring mostly in greenish blue incrustations (hardness 3.5–4, sp. gr. 3.5)
¹vet \ˈvet, *usu* -ed·+V\ *n* -s [by shortening] **:** VETERINARIAN, VETERINARY
²vet \"\ *vb* **vetted; vetted; vetting; vets** *vt* **1 a :** to provide veterinary care for (an animal) **:** subject to veterinary examination and care and esp. to a general physical examination **b :** to provide (a person) with medical care; *esp* **:** to subject to a physical examination or checkup **2 :** to inspect or examine with careful thoroughness and esp. in the quality of an expert ⟨spent the evening *vetting* the report⟩ ⟨it is wise to have an experienced person ~ old silver before you buy⟩ **~** *vi* **:** to practice as a veterinarian ⟨*vetted* for the track since its opening season⟩
³vet \"\ *adj or n* [by shortening] **:** VETERAN
ve·ta \ˈvād·ə\ *n* -s [AmerSp] **:** MOUNTAIN SICKNESS
¹vetch \ˈvech\ *n* -ES [ME *fecche, vecche*, fr. ONF *veche*, fr. L *vicia*; akin to OE *wicga* insect, MHG *gewige* antlers, Goth *waihsta* corner, L *vincire* to bind, tie, Gk *eikein* to yield, retreat, Skt *vejate, vijate* he flees from, retreats, OE *wīr* wire — more at WIRE] **1 :** any of various annual, biennial, or perennial herbaceous twining plants constituting the genus *Vicia* and including valuable fodder and soil-building plants as well as a few that are toxic; *also* **:** any of several other herbaceous legumes that resemble or are used like vetch — often used with a qualifying term; see BITTER VETCH, HORSESHOE VETCH, KIDNEY VETCH, MILK VETCH **2 :** the seed of a vetch; *esp* **:** the small edible dark brown seed of a Eurasian vetch (*Vicia sativa*)
²vetch \"\ *dial Eng var of* FETCH
vetch bruchid *n* **:** a widely distributed bruchid weevil (*Bruchus brachialis*) that is destructive to the seeds of various vetches
vetch·ling \ˈvechliŋ, -lēŋ\ *n* -s [¹*vetch* + *-ling*] **:** any of various small plants of the genus *Lathyrus* (esp. *L. pratensis*)
vetchworm \ˈ=,=\ *n* **:** CORN EARWORM
¹vet·er·an \ˈved·ərən, ˈve·trən, ˈved·ərn, ˈvetərən\ *n* -s [L *veteranus*, fr. *veteranus*, adj.] **1 a** (1) **:** a person with long experience in military service **:** an old soldier (2) **:** a former member of armed forces who by length and type of service, honorable discharge or release, or degree of disablement qualifies under a statute (as of the U. S. or one of its states) for benefits or privileges provided by law for ex-servicemen **b :** one grown old in service (as in politics, a profession, or an industry or art) or experienced through length of service ⟨depended on the ~s to help the novices on the assembly line⟩ ⟨a ~ of 20 years' service⟩ **c :** one seasoned by intensity of experience or service however brief either in or out of military life ⟨the ~s of a battle⟩ **2 :** an old tree (as from a former stand); *specif* **:** a tree over two feet in diameter breast high
²veteran \"\ *adj* [L *veteranus* old, veteran, fr. *veter-, vetus* old + *-anus* -an — more at WETHER] **1 :** grown old and skilled through experience **:** attained to competence through long practice (as of military life) ⟨a ~ officer⟩ ⟨the team depended on its ~ fielder⟩ **2 :** extending over a great period **:** PROLONGED ⟨~ service to his country⟩ **3 :** of, relating to, or characteristic of a veteran **:** available to veterans **:** dealing with veterans ⟨~ steadiness⟩ ⟨a ~ administrator⟩ ⟨~ benefits⟩ ⟨a ~ camp⟩
vet·er·an·ize \-ə,nīz\ *vb* -ED/-ING/-S *vi* **:** to make a veteran of oneself by reenlisting in a military service **~** *vt* **:** to cause (as soldiers) to become seasoned usu. by exposure to active service
veterans day *n, usu cap V&D* **:** ARMISTICE DAY
veterans' preference *n* **:** preferential treatment (as in employment, securing of housing, or credit) given qualified veterans (as of the U. S. armed forces) under a federal or state statute; *specif* **:** special consideration (as by allowance of points) on a civil service examination
vet·er·i·nar·i·an \,ved·ərəˈner|ēən, ,vetərəˈn|, ,ve·trəˈn|, ÷,ved·ə(r)ˈn|, ÷,vetəˈn|, ÷,vetᵊnˈ|, |a(a)r-, |ār-\ *n* -s [L *veterinarius* veterinarian + E *-an*] **:** one skilled in or treating diseases and injuries of animals **:** one qualified and duly authorized to treat diseases of animals **:** a doctor of veterinary medicine
¹vet·er·i·nary \ˈved·ərə,nerē, ˈvetərə,ne-, ˈve·trə,ne-, ÷ˈved·ə(r)ne-, ÷ˈvetə(r),ne-, ÷ˈvetᵊn,e-, -eri\ *adj* [L *veterinarius*, fr. *veterinae, veterina* beasts of burden, domestic animals (fr. fem. pl. & neut. pl. respectively of *veterinus* suitable for a beast of burden, of a beast of burden) + *-arius* -ary; akin to L *veter-, vetus* old — more at WETHER] **:** of, relating to, or constituting a branch of science and art dealing with the prevention, cure, or alleviation of disease and injury in animals and esp. domestic animals and including the normal biology (as anatomy and physiology) as well as the pathology of such animals
²veterinary \"\ *n* -ES [L *veterinarius*, fr. *veterinarius*, adj.] **:** VETERINARIAN
veterinary surgeon *n, Brit* **:** VETERINARIAN
vet·i·vene \ˈved·ə,vēn\ *n* -s [ISV *vetiver* + *-ene*] **:** a liquid mixture of sesquiterpenes $C_{15}H_{24}$ obtained from vetiver oil
vet·i·ven·ol \-,nōl, -,nōl\ *n* -s [ISV *vetivene* + *-ol*] **:** VETIVEROL
vet·i·ver \ˈved·əvə(r)\ *also* **vet·i·vert** \-və(r)t\ *n* -s [F *vétiver, vétyver*, fr. Tamil *veṭṭivēr*, fr. *veṭṭi* khuskhus + *vēr* root] **:** KHUSKHUS
vetiver green *n* **:** a light grayish olive color that is deeper than Quaker gray or twine, greener and slightly duller than hemp, and redder and deeper than average citron gray
vet·i·ve·ria \,==ˈvirēə\ *n, cap* [NL, fr. ISV *vetiver* + NL *-ia*] *in some classifications* **:** a small genus of perennial grasses found in the Old World tropics, having narrow panicles of slender spikelike racemes, including some cultivated for the aromatic roots or oil, and being usu. placed in the genus *Andropogon*
vetiver oil *also* **vetivert oil** *n* **:** a brown to reddish brown essential oil obtained from the roots of khuskhus and used in perfumes, cosmetics, and soaps
vet·i·ver·ol \,ved·əˈve,rōl, -,rōl\ *n* -s [ISV *vetiver* + *-ol*] **:** a liquid mixture of sesquiterpenoid alcohols $C_{15}H_{23}OH$ obtained from vetiver oil and used often in the form of the acetate in perfumes — called also *vetivenol*
vet·i·vone \ˈved·ə,vōn\ *or* **vet·i·ver·one** \,==ˈve,rōn\ *n* -s [*vetivone* fr. *vetiver* + *-one*; *vetiverone* ISV *vetiver* + *-one*] **:** a bicyclic sesquiterpenoid ketone $C_{15}H_{22}O$ that is an odorous component of vetiver oil and is known in two crystalline stereoisomeric forms
vet·kou·sie \ˈfet,kōsē\ *n* -s [Afrik, lit., fat wick, fr. *vet* fat, grease (fr. MD) + *kousie* wick, fr. D *kousje*, dim. of *kous* stocking, fr. MD *couse* chausses, fr. OF dial. (Picardy) *cauce*, fr. ML *calcea*; akin to OE *fǣtt* fat — more at FAT, CHAUSSES] **:** a southern African fig marigold (*Mesembryanthemum pomeridianum*) the young foliage of which is used like spinach
¹ve·to \ˈvē(,)tō, -ēd·(,)ō *sometimes* -ēd·ə *or* (+V) -ēd·əw\ *n* -ES [L, I forbid, 1st pers. sing. pres. indic. of *vetare* to forbid] **1 :** an authoritative prohibition or negative **:** an act or instance of forbidding something proposed ⟨mother's ~ of our plans⟩ **2 a** *or* **veto power :** a right or power possessed by one department or branch of a government to forbid or prohibit finally or provisionally the carrying out of projects attempted by another department; *esp* **:** a power vested in a chief executive to prevent permanently or temporarily the enactment of measures passed by a legislature — see POCKET VETO, SUSPENSIVE VETO **b** (1) **:** the exercise of such authority **:** an act of prohibition or prevention ⟨a ~ is probable if the bill passes⟩ (2) *or* **veto message :** a document or message communicating the reasons of an executive (as the president of the U. S.) for not officially approving a proposed law
²veto \"\ *vt* -ED/-ING/-ES **:** to refuse to admit or approve **:** NEGATIVE, PROHIBIT; *also* **:** to refuse assent to (a legislative bill) so as to prevent enactment or cause reconsideration
ve·to·er \-ōə(r) *sometimes* -əwə-\ *n* -s **:** one that vetoes
vets *pl of* VET, *pres 3d sing of* VET
vetted *past of* VET
vetting *pres part of* VET
vet·tu·ra \veˈtürə\ *n, pl* **vettu·re** \-ü(,)rā\ [It, fr. L *vectura* transportation, conveyance, fr. *vectus* (past part. of *vehere* to carry, convey) + *-ura* -ure — more at WAY] **:** an Italian four-wheel carriage usu. for hire
vet·tu·ri·no \,ved·əˈrē(,)nō\ *n, pl* **vetturi·ni** \-nē\ [It, dim. of *vettura*] **:** one who lets or drives a vettura
veuve \vœœv\ *n, pl* **veuves** \"\ *n* -s [F, lit., widow, fr. L *vidua*; fr. the somber plumage — more at WIDOW] **:** WHYDAH
¹vex \ˈveks\ *vb* **vexed** *also* **vext** \ˈvekst\; **vexed** *also* **vext; vexing; vexes** [ME *vexen*, fr. MF *vexer*, fr. L *vexare* to shake, injure, annoy, prob. fr. *vehere* to carry, convey — more at WAY] *vt* **1 :** to bring trouble or distress to: as **a :** to subject to mental suffering **:** cause agitation or anxiety to **:** interfere with the peace and quiet of by or as if by encroachment ⟨~*ing* his mind to recall the address⟩ ⟨~*ed* by a restless desire for change⟩ ⟨tasks that ~ our quiet days⟩ **b :** to bring physical distress to **:** cause bodily pain or anguish ⟨~*ed* with a rheumatic disorder⟩ ⟨a headache had ~*ed* him all day⟩ **c :** to irritate or annoy by or as if by petty provocations **:** harass to anger **:** PLAGUE ⟨a lazy stubborn boy who ~*ed* his father daily⟩ ⟨was ~*ed* with the heedless crowds⟩ **d :** to cause difficulty to in respect to finding a solution or answer ⟨a puzzle to ~ the keenest wit⟩ **e :** TEASE, TORMENT ⟨don't ~ the cat⟩ **2 :** to go over in careful and minute detail **:** debate or discuss at length ⟨many men have ~*ed* this question without reaching a solution⟩ **3 :** to perturb by physical agitation **:** shake or toss about **:** BATTER, BELABOR ⟨wintry winds ~*ing* the forest giants⟩ ⟨a coast ~*ed* by waves⟩ **~** *vi* **:** to suffer distress (as of mind) **:** become irritated **:** FRET, WORRY ⟨how foolish to ~ over such trivia⟩ **syn** see ANNOY
²vex \"\ *n* -ES *Scot* **:** VEXATION, ANNOYANCE, DISTURBANCE
vex·a·tion \vekˈsāshən\ *n* -s [ME *vexacioun*, fr. MF *vexation*, fr. L *vexation-, vexatio* shaking, agitation, annoyance, fr. *vexatus* (past part. of *vexare*) + *-ion-, -io* -ion] **1 :** the quality or state of being vexed **:** IRRITATION ⟨have found continual ~ in my work⟩ **2 :** the act of harassing or vexing **:** TROUBLING; *esp* **:** harassment by process of law **3 :** a cause of trouble or disquiet **:** AFFLICTION ⟨your children were ~ to your youth —Shak.⟩
vex·a·tious \(ˈ)vekˈsāshəs\ *adj* [*vexation* + *-ous*] **1 a :** causing or likely to cause vexation **:** DISTRESSING, AFFLICTIVE ⟨a ~ child⟩ ⟨nothing is more ~ than to find that one is wrong⟩ **b :** lacking justification and intended to harass ⟨the company's ~ refusal to pay a patently valid claim⟩ ⟨a ~ suit at law⟩ **2 :** lacking in peace or calm **:** full of disorder or stress **:** UNQUIET, DISORDERED, TROUBLED ⟨a ~ period in his life⟩ ⟨a very ~ interview⟩ — **vex·a·tious·ly** *adv* — **vex·a·tious·ness** *n* -ES
vex·ed·ly \ˈveksədlē, -li\ *adv* **:** in a vexed manner **:** with vexation
vex·ed·ness \-nəs\ *n* -ES **:** the quality or state of being vexed
vex·er \ˈveksə(r)\ *n* -s **:** one that vexes
¹vex·il·lary \ˈveksə,lerē, -ri\ *n* -ES [L *vexillarius*, fr. *vexillum* + *-arius* -ary, n. suffix] **1 :** a veteran under a special standard in an ancient Roman army **2 :** STANDARD-BEARER
²vexillary \"\ *adj* [L *vexillum* + E *-ary*, adj. suffix] **1 :** of or relating to an ensign or standard **2 :** relating to or constituting a vexillum
vexillary aestivation *n* **:** aestivation (as in most pea flowers) in which one large upper petal folds over and covers the other smaller petals
vex·il·late \ˈveksə,lāt, vekˈsilət, ˈveksələt\ *adj* [NL *vexillum* + E *-ate*] **:** having a vexillum
vex·il·la·tion \,veksəˈlāshən\ *n* -s [L *vexillation-, vexillatio*, fr. *vexillum* + *-ation-, -atio* -ation] **1 :** a company of ancient Roman troops under one vexillum and detached for special service from a main body of soldiers **2 :** a regular troop of Roman cavalry; *also* **:** a company of veterans of a legion
vex·il·lum \vekˈsiləm\ *n, pl* **vexil·la** \-lə\ [L, prob. fr. *velum* cloth, sail, veil — more at VEIL] **1 a :** a square flag hanging transversely by a wooden crosspiece from a spear and used esp. by ancient Roman cavalry **b :** a processional standard, banner, or cross **2 :** STANDARD 16a **3** [NL, fr. L] **:** the web or vane of a feather **4 :** a company of ancient Roman troops and esp. of vexillaries serving under one standard
vex·ing·ly *adv* **:** so as to vex **:** in a manner designed or likely to produce vexation
vext *past of* VEX
VF *abbr* **1** vertical file **2** very fair; very fine **3** vicar forane **4** video frequency **5** visual field **6** voice frequency
VFO *abbr* variable frequency oscillator
VFR *abbr* visual flight rules
VG *abbr* **1** *often not cap* [L *verbi gratia*] for example **2** vertical grain **3** very good **4** vicar-general
v-girl *n, usu cap V* [*victory girl*] **:** VICTORY GIRL
VHC *abbr* very highly commended
VHF *abbr, often not cap* very high frequency
v-hut \ˈ=,=\ *n, cap V* **:** a primitive hut having a cross section like an inverted letter V
vi *var of* VI APPLE
VI *abbr* **1** *often not cap* verb intransitive **2** vertical interval **3** *often not cap* [L *vide infra*] see below **4** viscosity index **5** volume indicator
¹via \ˈvīə *also* ˈvēə\ *prep* [L, abl. of *via* way; akin to Gk *hiesthai* to hurry — more at VIM] **1 :** by way of **:** by a route passing through ⟨shipped to New York ~ the Panama Canal⟩ ⟨arrived ~ the back door of the inn —Adrian Bell⟩ ⟨excretion of absorbed aluminum is ~ liver and kidney —C.H.Thienes⟩ **2 :** through the medium of ⟨an increase in number of shareholders ~ lower-priced stock —*Wall Street Jour.*⟩ ⟨the central role which communication, especially ~ the mass media, plays —F.S.Fearing⟩ **:** by means of ⟨ability to harness . . . neighbor states to its war machine ~ blitz attack —S.L.A. Marshall⟩ ⟨gets ~ two his reader, ~ heavy humor —Frances Keene⟩
²via \ˈvīə; ˈvēə\ *n, pl* **vias** \-əz\ *or* **vi·ae** \-ī,ē; -ē,ī\ [L] **1 a :** ROAD, PASSAGE, RIGHT-OF-WAY **b** *pl* **viae** [NL, fr. L] **:** an anatomical passage (as a blood vessel or lymph channel) **2 :** a right under Roman law to pass over the land of another in any manner — compare ACTUS
vi·a·bil·i·ty \,vīəˈbiləd·ē, -lətē, -i\ *n* [F *viabilité*, fr. *viable* + *-ité* -ity] **:** the quality or state of being viable **:** the ability to live, grow, and develop ⟨the ~ of seeds under dry conditions⟩ ⟨~ of a fetus⟩ ⟨the ~ of small, new states is uncertain —R.A. Newhall⟩ ⟨serious questions as to the ~ of the economic plans —Vera M. Dean⟩
vi·a·ble \ˈvīəbəl\ *adj* [F, fr. MF, fr. *vie* life (fr. L *vita*) + *-able* — more at VITAL] **1 a :** capable of living ⟨the skin graft was ~⟩ ⟨~ cancer cells⟩ ⟨a ~ infant⟩ **b** *of a fetus* **:** having attained such form and development of organs as to be normally capable of living outside the uterus ⟨a 7-month ~ fetus⟩ **2 :** capable of growing or developing ⟨~ seeds⟩ ⟨~ eggs⟩ **3 :** affecting the imagination, mind, or senses as real, genuine, artistically whole, or important **:** LIVING ⟨make the life of industry and the city ~ to the imagination —L.A.Fieldler⟩ ⟨make ~ for their students the great cultural heritage —J.W. Dodds⟩ ⟨the poet . . . is to make philosophic content more ~ by addition of sensuous and emotional qualities —John Dewey⟩ **4 a :** capable of being put into practice **:** WORKABLE ⟨a ~ middle road . . . between the grim alternatives of appeasement and all-out war —F.W.Riggs⟩ ⟨even brigands can make a ~ agreement provided it embodies a common purpose —*New Republic*⟩ **b :** not self-contradictory **:** not lacking significance or consequences **:** capable of conceptual or aesthetic development ⟨offers a ~ alternative to other world views —J.W.Nixon⟩ ⟨anthropology is a ~ science —E.A. Hoebel⟩ ⟨if skepticism is a ~ enterprise —F.A.Olafson⟩ ⟨the novel is the only major art form that has come down to us from the nineteenth century in a ~ condition —Arnold Hauser⟩ **5 :** capable of existence and development as a relatively independent social, economic, or political unit ⟨adopted the politically and economically superior culture . . . and set about transforming it into a ~ tropical civilization —Gilberto Freyre⟩ ⟨an artificial and hardly ~ state —E.K. Lindley⟩ ⟨reapportioning the country into 14 large and ~ states —*Time*⟩ — **vi·a·bly** \-blē, -li\ *adv*
via do·lo·ro·sa \-,dāləˈrōsə, -,dōl-\ *n* [fr. *Via Dolorosa* (fr. L, lit., sorrowful road), Jesus' route from Pilate's judgment hall to Golgotha to be crucified] **:** a painfully difficult route, passage, or series of experiences ⟨an epoch which condemns its children to a *via dolorosa* of examinations —Herbert Read⟩
vi·a·duct \ˈvīə,dəkt *sometimes* ˈvēə,\ *n* [L *via* way, road + E *-duct* (as in *aqueduct*)] **1 :** a bridge esp. when resting on a series of narrow reinforced concrete or masonry arches, having high supporting towers or piers, and carrying a road or railroad over a valley, river, road, or other low-lying obstruction — compare TRESTLE **2 :** a steel bridge made up of short spans carried on high steel towers

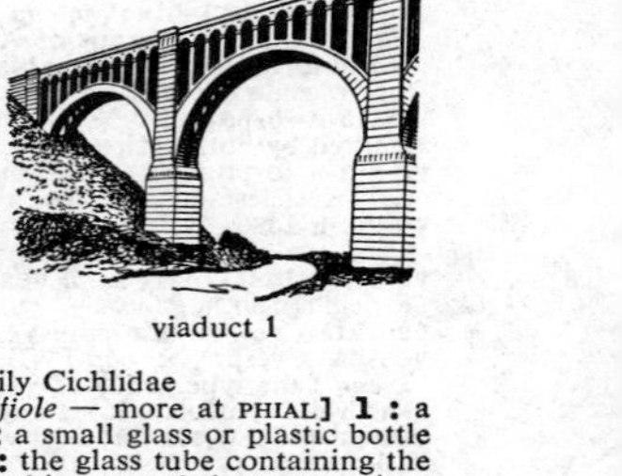
viaduct 1

via·ja·ca \vyəˈhäkə\ *n* -s [AmerSp (Cuba) *viajaca, biajaca*, modif. of Carib *diahaca*] **:** a small Cuban freshwater food fish (*Parapetenia tetracantha*) of the family Cichlidae
vi·al \ˈvī(ə)l\ *n* -s [ME *viole, fiole* — more at PHIAL] **1 :** a small vessel for liquids: as **a :** a small glass or plastic bottle for a medicine or chemical **b :** the glass tube containing the liquid in a spirit level **2 :** something regarded as a container or receptacle esp. of something immaterial ⟨pour out the ~*s* of the wrath of God upon the earth —Rev 16:1 (AV)⟩
via lac·tea \-ˈlaktēə\ *n, usu cap V&L* [L] **:** MILKY WAY
via la·sci·via \-ləˈsivēə\ *n, usu cap V&L* [NL, lit., lascivious path] **:** a line on the palm that appears as a sister line to the line of Mercury and is usu. held by palmists to indicate intensity of sentiments and sometimes sensuality
via me·dia \-ˈmēdēə, -ˈmādēə\ *n* [L] **:** a middle way or ground **:** a mediating conception ⟨a *via media* between dogmatism and skepticism —W.T.Jones⟩
vi·and \ˈvīənd *sometimes* ˈvēə-\ *n* -s [ME *viaunde*, fr. MF *viande*, fr. (assumed) VL *vivanda*, alter. of L *vivenda*, neut. pl. of *vivendus*, gerundive of *vivere* to live — more at QUICK] **1 :** an article of food **2 : viands** \-n(d)z\ *pl* **:** PROVISIONS, FOOD, FARE
vi antigen \ˈvē,ī-\ *n, usu cap V* [*virulent antigen*] **:** a heat-labile somatic antigen associated with virulence in some bacteria (as of the genus *Salmonella*) and esp. in the typhoid fever bacterium and used to detect typhoid carriers through the presence in their serum of agglutinins against this antigen
vi apple \ˈvē-\ *also* **vi** *n* -s [*vi* fr. Tahitian] **:** OTAHEITE APPLE 1
vias *pl of* VIA
vi·at·i·cum \vīˈad·|ēkəm, -at|, |ēk-\ *n, pl* **viaticums** \-mz\ *or* **viati·ca** \-kə\ [L — more at VOYAGE] **1 a :** an allowance (as of transportation or supplies and money) for traveling expenses **b :** provisions for a journey ⟨prepared for me a ~ in the shape of a small loaf —C.B.Fairbanks⟩ **2** [LL, fr. L] **:** the Christian Eucharist or communion given to a person in danger of dying — compare EXTREME UNCTION
vi·a·tor \vīˈād·ə(r)\ *n* -s [L, fr. *viatus* + *-or*] **:** TRAVELER, WAYFARER
vib *abbr* vibrate; vibration
vibes \ˈvībz\ *n pl but usu sing in constr, also* **vibe** \-b\ [by shortening & alter.] **:** VIBRAPHONE
vi·bex \ˈvī,beks\ *n, pl* **vibi·ces** \-ībə,sēz\ [L, mark of a blow, weal; prob. akin to Latvian *wībele* weals, *wile* seam, weal, scar, and perh. to L *vibrare* to shake, vibrate — more at WIPE] **:** a linear subcutaneous extravasation of blood
vib·ist \ˈvībəst\ *n* -s [*vibes* + *-ist*] **:** VIBRAPHONIST
vi·brac·u·lar \vīˈbrakyələ(r)\ *adj* [NL *vibraculum* + E *-ar*] **:** of, relating to, or furnished with vibracula
vi·brac·u·lar·i·um \vī,brakyəˈla(a)rēəm\ *n* -s [NL, fr. *vibraculum* + *-arium*] **1 :** VIBRACULUM **2 :** a cell containing the motive cells of a vibracularium
vi·brac·u·loid \=ˈ==,lȯid\ *adj* [NL *vibraculum* + E *-oid*] **:** of, relating to, or resembling a vibraculum
vi·brac·u·lum \-yələm\ *n, pl* **vibracula** [NL, fr. L *vibrare* to shake, vibrate + *-culum* -cle] **:** one of the movable slender spinelike organs or parts with which bryozoans are furnished and which are specially modified zooids of nearly the same nature as avicularia
vi·brance \ˈvībrən(t)s\ *n* -s **:** VIBRANCY
vi·bran·cy \-nsē, -si\ *n* -ES **:** the quality or state of being vibrant **:** RESONANCE, VIBRATION
vi·brant \-nt\ *adj* [L *vibrant-, vibrans*, pres. part. of *vibrare* to shake, vibrate — more at WIPE] **1 a** (1) **:** oscillating or pulsating rapidly **:** VIBRATING, PULSING ⟨~ quivering telegraph wires —J.C.Powys⟩ (2) **:** pulsating with life, vigor, or activity **:** ALIVE, VITAL ⟨the ~ atmosphere of a new age and a new world —I.M.Price⟩ ⟨a ~, active force, refusing to cede the dominion he had won —E.M.Lustgarten⟩ ⟨his ~ personality⟩ (3) **:** actively affected by an influence ⟨enfeebled but still ~ with her memories —*Newsweek*⟩ **b** (1) **:** readily set in vibration (2) **:** open and responsive to or easily affected by environment, events, other people, or stimuli **:** SENSITIVE ⟨hungry for ideas, intellectually and emotionally ~ —V.L.Parrington⟩ ⟨mind was ~ rather than deeply original —L.H.Butterfield⟩ **2 a :** sounding as a result of vibration **b :** having, exhibiting, or being a vital resonant sound **:** SONOROUS, RESONANT, RESOUNDING ⟨~ baritone voice —William Fifield⟩ **c :** resonant or echoing with the sounds of life and activity **3 :** having the effect of or enlivened by sparkling light, color, or texture ⟨a painting ~ with color and action —F.J.Mather⟩ **syn** see RESONANT
vi·brant·ly *adv* **:** in a vibrant manner
vi·bra·phone \ˈvībrə,fōn\ *n* [ISV *vibra-* (fr. L *vibrare* to shake, vibrate) + *-phone*] **:** a percussion musical instrument resembling the xylophone but having metal bars and motor-driven resonators for sustaining the tone and producing a vibrato effect
vi·bra·phon·ist \-nəst\ *n* -s **:** one that plays the vibraphone
vi·brate \ˈvī,brāt, *usu* -ād·+V\ *vb* -ED/-ING/-S [L *vibratus*, past part. of *vibrare* to shake, vibrate — more at WIPE] *vt* **1 :** THROW, CAST, LAUNCH **2 :** to emit with or as if with a vibratory motion **3 :** to mark or measure by oscillation ⟨a pendulum *vibrating* seconds⟩ **4 :** to set in vibration ⟨*vibrated* their open hands in imitation of the quivering sunlight —Philippa Pollenz⟩ **5 :** to treat by vibration; *specif* **:** to compress or compact by vibration **~** *vi* **1 a :** to move to and fro or from side to side **:** OSCILLATE **b :** ALTERNATE ⟨*vibrated* for some years between art and literature —G.F.Whicher⟩ **2 :** to have an effect or move by or as if by vibration **3 a :** to be in a state of vibration **:** oscillate very rapidly **:** QUIVER ⟨the eardrum ~*s* and transmits the vibrations —Morris Fishbein⟩ ⟨the lower lip *vibrated* with a delicate flabbiness —R.P. Warren⟩ **b :** to act in or as if in acoustic sympathy ⟨strings . . . which ~ when a chord is struck —R.W.Sockman⟩ ⟨an intellectual who ~*s* intuitively to ideas —William Barrett⟩ ⟨the scrapbook fairly ~*s* with enthusiasm —Virginia D. Dawson & Betty D. Wilson⟩ **syn** see SWING
vibrated concrete *n* **:** concrete that has been vibrated either

internally or externally after it has been placed in order to produce a denser mass

vi·bra·tile \'vībrəd·ᵊl, -ət²l, -ə,tīl, -ə(,)til\ *adj* [F, fr. L *vibratus* + F *-ile*] **1 :** characterized by vibration : VIBRATORY, OSCILLATING **2 :** adapted to or used in vibratory motion ⟨~ organs of insects⟩ — **vi·bra·til·i·ty** \,vībrə'tiləd·ē, -lətē, -i\ *n* -ES

vi·brat·ing·ly *adv* : in a vibrating manner

vibrating screen *n* : a device made with a screening surface vibrated mechanically at high speeds and used esp. for screening ore, coal, or other fine dry materials

vi·bra·tion \vī'b·āshən\ *n* -S [L *vibration-, vibratio*, fr. *vibratus* (past part. of *vibrare* to shake, vibrate) + *-ion-, -io* -ion — more at WIPE] **1 a :** a periodic motion of the particles of an elastic body or medium in alternately opposite directions from the position of equilibrium when that equilibrium has been disturbed (as when a stretched cord or other body produces musical tones or particles of air transmit sounds to the ear) **b :** the action of vibrating or the state of being vibrated or in vibratory motion: as (1) : OSCILLATION (2) : a quivering or trembling motion : QUIVER **2 :** an instance of vibration: as **a :** the complete movement described by a particle of an elastic body or medium until the periodic motion begins to repeat itself **b :** one half of the periodic motion of a particle **c** *obs* : a hypothetical motion of the nerves serving as a means of transmission of sensory impressions **d :** an occult or supernatural entity that exerts a harmful or beneficial influence and is sensible to a person psychically attuned to it ⟨the evil act has set millions of ~s going —Margery Allingham⟩ ⟨got ~s that you fellows were close —W.T.Brannon⟩ **3 :** vacillation in opinion, doctrine, or conduct **4 a :** a characteristic emanation, aura, or spirit that infuses or vitalizes and that can be intuitively sensed or experienced ⟨what was most stimulating . . . depended largely on the ~s of his time and country —Sean O'Faolain⟩ ⟨the ~ of human kinship —Jean S. Untermeyer⟩ **b :** a psychological response esp. to aesthetic or emotional stimuli ⟨could . . . the memory of his smile awake the familiar ~s —Ellen Glasgow⟩

vi·bra·tion·al \(')vī¦brāshənᵊl, -shnəl\ *adj* **1 :** of or relating to vibration **2 :** having a periodic or harmonic motion

vibrational quantum number *n* : a scalar quantum number that defines the energy state of a harmonic or approximately harmonic vibrating atomic system

vibrational specific heat *n* : the contribution made by the energy of internal vibration of the molecules of a substance to the total specific heat of the substance — compare ROTATIONAL SPECIFIC HEAT

vibrational spectrum *or* **vibration spectrum** *n* : the part of a molecular spectrum in which the bands arise from quantized changes in the energy of mutual atomic vibrations within the molecule — compare ROTATIONAL SPECTRUM

vi·bra·tion·less \-shənləs\ *adj* : having no vibration

vibration number *or* **vibrational number** *n* : the number of vibrations per second of a musical tone — compare ⁴PITCH 4b(1)

vi·bra·ti·un·cle \vī'brāshē,əŋkəl\ *n* -S [*vibration* + *-uncle* (fr. L *-uncula*, dim. suffix)] : a slight vibration

vi·bra·tive \'vībrəd·iv\ *adj* [*vibrate* + *-ive*] : VIBRATORY

vi·bra·to \vē'bräd·(,)ō, vī'-, -ä(,)tō\ *n* -S [It, past part. of *vibrare* to vibrate, fr. L, to shake, vibrate — more at WIPE] **1 :** a slightly tremulous effect imparted to vocal or instrumental tone for added warmth and expressiveness and consisting of slight and rapid variations in the pitch of the tone being produced **2 :** TREMOLO 1b **3 :** a periodic fluctuation of sustained tones or of tones of steadily changing pitch in speech and in emotional speech

vi·bra·tor \'vī,brād·ə(r), -ātə-\ *n* -S **1 :** a device, instrument, mechanism, attachment, or organ that vibrates or causes vibration or oscillation: as **a :** a vibrating object (as a violin string or a reed in an organ) that produces a tone **b :** an ink-distributing roller in a printing press that has end-to-end vibratory motion as well as rotary motion **c :** a vibrating electrical apparatus used in massage **d :** a usu. pneumatic attachment in a molding machine to shake the pattern or match plate loose **e :** a vibrating device (as in an electric bell or buzzer) for opening or closing an electric circuit **f :** a device for vibrating concrete **2 :** a device that consists of a standard balance and standard balance spring and is used for determining the strength of balance springs by a comparison of the vibrations **3 :** an electromagnetic device that converts low direct current to pulsating direct current or alternating current

vi·bra·to·ry \'vībrə,tōrē, -tȯr-, -ri\ *adj* [*vibrate* + *-ory*] **1 a :** consisting in, capable of, or causing vibration or oscillation **b :** characterized by vibration : VIBRANT, VIBRATING **2 :** of, relating to, affecting, or constituting a sense responsive to vibrations and believed by some to be distinct from the sense of touch

vib·rio \'vibrē,ō\ *n* [NL, fr. L *vibrare* to shake, vibrate — more at WIPE] **1** *cap* : a genus of short rigid motile bacteria (family Spirillaceae) having a polar flagellum or sometimes two or three, being typically shaped like a comma or an S that occur singly or united into spirals, and including various saprophytes and a few important pathogens (as *V. comma* and *V. fetus* that are the cause of Asiatic cholera and of abortion in cattle and sheep respectively) — compare SPIRILLUM **2** -S : any bacterium of the genus *Vibrio*; *broadly* : a curved rod-shaped bacterium — **vib·ri·oid** \-ē,ȯid\ *adj*

vib·ri·on \-ē,än\ *n* -S [NL *Vibrion-, Vibrio*] : VIBRIO; *also* : a motile bacterium

vib·ri·on·ic \¦==¦änik\ *adj* [NL *Vibrion-, Vibrio* + E *-ic*] : caused by a vibrio ⟨~ dysentery⟩

vibrionic abortion *n* : abortion in sheep and cattle caused by a bacterium (*Vibrio fetus*) that invades the uterine and placental capillaries, interferes with fetal nutrition, and causes the death of the developing fetus

vib·ri·o·sis \,==ō'sə̇s\ *n, pl* **vibrio·ses** \-ō,sēz\ [NL, fr. *Vibrio* + *-osis*] : infestation with or disease caused by bacteria of the genus *Vibrio*; *specif* : VIBRIONIC ABORTION

vi·bris·sa \vī'brisə\ *n, pl* **vibris·sae** \-i,sē\ [NL, fr. L *vibrissae*, pl., hairs in the nostrils, prob. fr. *vibrare* to shake, vibrate — more at WIPE] **1 :** one of the stiff hairs that grow about the nostrils or on other parts of the face in many mammals (as the whiskers of a cat or the hairs of the nostrils of man) and that are not themselves sensitive but often serve as tactile organs; *also* : a similar stiff tactile hair growing elsewhere on some mammals (as in a small tuft at the wrist) **2 :** one of the feathers that resemble bristles near the mouth of many birds and esp. of some insectivorous birds and that may help to prevent the escape of insects **3 :** either of a pair of stout bristles situated on either side of the mouth of some two-winged flies

vi·bris·sal \-səl\ *adj* [NL *vibrissa* + E *-al*] : of or relating to a vibrissa

vibro- *comb form* [ISV, fr. L *vibrare* to shake, vibrate] : vibration ⟨*vibro*massage⟩

vi·bro·graph \'vībrə,graf, -råf\ *n* [ISV *vibro-* + *-graph*] : an instrument to observe, measure, and record vibrations

vi·brom·e·ter \vī'brämə̇d·ə(r)\ *n* [*vibro-* + *-meter*] : VIBROGRAPH

vi·bur·num \vī'bərnəm, -'bən-, -'bəin-\ *n* [NL, fr. L, wayfaring tree] **1** *cap* : a large genus of widely distributed shrubs or trees (family Caprifoliaceae) having simple leaves and white or rarely pink cymose flowers with a regular 5-lobed corolla, a 3-lobed style, and a 1- to 3-celled ovary that becomes in fruit a one-seeded drupe — see BLACK HAW, CRANBERRY BUSH, DOCKMACKIE, LAURUSTINE, WAYFARING TREE, WITHE ROD **2** -S : any plant of the genus *Viburnum*

¹vic \'vik\ *n* -S [short for *victrola*] : PHONOGRAPH

²vic \"\ *n* -S [fr. British signalmen's telephone pron. of the letter *V*] *Brit* : a V-shaped formation of airplanes

vic- *comb form, usu ital* [*vicinal*] : vicinal — in names of organic chemical compounds ⟨*vic*-triazine or 1,2,3-triazine⟩ ⟨*vic-, as-*, or 1,2-dinitro-ethane⟩

vic abbr 1 vicar; vicarage 2 vicinity

vic·ar \'vikə(r)\ *n* -S [ME *vicar, vicair, viker*, fr. LL *vicarius*, fr. L, substitute, deputy, fr. *vicarius*, adj., substituting, delegated, vicarious — more at VICARIOUS] **1 :** a human representative or agent of God on earth ⟨those who regard the pope as being God's ~⟩ **2 a :** the incumbent of an impropriated or formerly appropriated benefice of the Church of England : the priest of a parish of which the tithes are owned by a layman or formerly a spiritual corporation : an incumbent of a Church of England parish not a rector **b :** a Protestant Episcopal clergyman in charge of a dependent chapel as the deputy of another clergyman **c :** an ecclesiastic who acts as the substitute or representative of another in the Roman Catholic Church **3 a :** an administrative deputy : VICEGERENT **b :** someone or something that serves as a substitute ⟨there is no ~ for poetry on earth —R.P.Blackmur⟩

Vi·cara \vī'karə\ *trademark* — used for a woolly protein textile fiber from corn zein used esp. in blends with other fibers

vic·ar·age \'vikərij, -rēj\ *n* -S [ME *vicarage, vikerage*, fr. *vicar, vicair, viker* vicar + *-age*] **1 a :** the benefice of a vicar **b** *Scot* : tithes or dues paid to a vicar **2 :** the house or household of a vicar **3 :** the office, function, or duty of a vicar : VICARSHIP

vicar apostolic *n, pl* **vicars apostolic** : a titular bishop who acts as a delegate of the Roman Catholic pope in administering an ecclesiastical district in a missionary region

vic·ar·ate \-kərə̇t, -kə,rāt\ *n* -S : VICARIATE

vicar capitular *n, pl* **vicars capitular** : an ecclesiastic selected by a Roman Catholic cathedral chapter to administer the affairs of a vacant see until a new bishop is appointed

vicar choral *n, pl* **vicars choral** : one of a number of clergy or laymen in an Anglican cathedral whose duty is to sing a portion of the music of the services

vic·ar·ess \-kərə̇s\ *n* -ES **1 :** a nun whose official rank is immediately below that of the superior of a convent **2 :** a woman who is the representative or vicegerent of someone else **3 :** a vicar's wife

vicar fo·rane \-fō'rān\ *n, pl* **vicars forane** [*forane* fr. LL *foranus* situated on the outside — more at FOREIGN] : DEAN 2c

vicar–general \'==¦(=)=\ *n, pl* **vicars–general** [ME; trans. of ML *vicarius generalis*] **1 a :** the deputy of a Roman Catholic or Anglican bishop assisting in the jurisdiction of the diocese **b :** an administrative deputy of the head of a religious order **2 :** a lay legal officer who is deputy of a bishop of the Church of England in some matters

vicar–general·ship \"+,ship\ *n* : the office of vicar-general

vi·car·i·al \(')vī¦ka(a)rēəl, və'k-, -ker-, -kär-\ *adj* [L *vicarius* + E *-al*] **1 :** DELEGATED, DEPUTED **2 :** of or relating to a vicar ⟨~ duties⟩

¹vi·car·i·ate \-ēə̇t, -ē,āt, *usu* -d·+V\ *n* -S [ML *vicariatus*, fr. LL *vicarius* vicar + L *-atus* -ate, n. suffix — more at VICAR] **1 a :** the office, authority, or jurisdiction of a vicar : VICARSHIP **b :** the period of a vicar's incumbency **2 a :** a governmental or administrative office held by a deputy **b :** a district governed or administered by a deputy **3 :** SUBSTITUTION ⟨the ~ seemingly exercised by the sharpened remaining senses of a blind man⟩

²vicariate \"\ *adj* [L *vicarius* + E *-ate*, adj. suffix] : having delegated power : VICARIOUS

vicariate apostolic *n, pl* **vicariates apostolic** : a Roman Catholic missionary district over which a vicar apostolic exercises jurisdiction

vi·cari·ism \vī'ka(a)rē,izəm\ *n* -S [*vicarious* + *-ism*] : the quality or state of being vicarious ⟨the tendency of some genera to exhibit ~⟩

vi·car·i·ous \(')vī¦ka(a)rēəs, -ker-, -kär- *sometimes* və'k-\ *adj* [L *vicarius*, fr. *vicis* change, alternation, stead + *-arius* -ary — more at WEEK] **1 :** having the function of a substitute : serving instead of someone or something else : acting for a principal : representing or taking the place of something primary or original : DELEGATED ⟨memory is ~ experience in which there is all the emotional value of actual experience —John Dewey⟩ **2 :** performed or suffered by one person as a substitute for another or to the benefit or advantage of another : SUBSTITUTIONARY ⟨~ sacrifice⟩ **3 :** experienced or realized through imaginative or sympathetic participation in the experience of another ⟨was getting a ~ kick out of watching a fellow female preening herself over the capitulation of the male —Helen Howe⟩ **4 :** occurring in an unexpected or abnormal part of the body instead of the usual one ⟨bleeding from the gums sometimes replaces the discharge from the uterus in ~ menstruation⟩ **5 a :** of, relating to, or being closely related kinds of organisms that occur in similar environments or as fossils in corresponding strata but in distinct and often widely separated areas **b :** made up of or characterized by the presence of such organisms ⟨~ pairs⟩ ⟨a ~ area⟩

vi·car·i·ous·ly *adv* : in a vicarious manner : as, by, or through a substitute ⟨we want ~ and temporarily to be other people in other worlds —C.A.Smart⟩

vi·car·i·ous·ness *n* -ES : the quality or state of being vicarious

vicar of bray \-'brā\ *usu cap B* [after the *Vicar of Bray*, semilegendary 16th cent. Eng. vicar of the village of Bray, Berkshire county, England, who gave allegiance to Protestantism or Roman Catholicism according to the religion of the reigning monarch, and is said to have been twice a Protestant and twice a Roman Catholic vicar] : a man of changeable allegiance : OPPORTUNIST, TURNCOAT

vicar of christ *cap C* : a Roman Catholic pope

vicars *pl of* VICAR

vic·ar·ship \'vikə(r),ship\ *n* : the office or tenure of a vicar

vi·cat apparatus \(')vē¦kä-\ *n, usu cap V* [after Louis J. *Vicat* †1861 Fr. engineer] : a device for determining the normal consistency and time of setting of portland cements that consists of a rod weighing 300 grams, having a needle in each end, and supported in a frame with a graduated scale to measure the distance to which the needle penetrates the cement

¹vice \'vīs\ *n* -S [ME, fr. OF, fr. L *vitium* fault, blemish, crime, vice — more at WITH] **1 a :** moral depravity or corruption : evil conduct or habits : indulgence of degrading appetites : WICKEDNESS ⟨the true lover of the human race is surely he who can put up with it in all its forms, in ~ as well as in virtue —John Galsworthy⟩ **b :** a wrong, depraving, or immoral habit or practice : evil behavior of a particular or accustomed kind ⟨tainted with the ~ of homosexuality —R.A.Hall b. 1911⟩ **c :** a fault or shortcoming that becomes a foible : a constitutional failing : a moral flaw ⟨the local ~ of overstatement —W.L.Sperry⟩ **2 a :** a blemish or imperfection in something : DEFECT ⟨the ~ of his conception is that it overlooks the serious consequences⟩ **b** (1) : an imperfection in merchandise or in a contract serious enough to invalidate the contract or a sale of the goods (2) : a fault or imperfection which because inherent in the nature of the goods or material often cannot be insured against **3 :** a physical imperfection, deformity, or taint **4 a** *often cap* : a character representing one of the vices in an English morality play **b :** BUFFOON, JESTER **5 :** habitual undesirable conduct in a domestic animal; *specif* : an abnormal behavior pattern (as in cannibalism of poultry or the sucking vice of calves) detrimental to the health or usefulness of an individual or group and commonly representing perversion or overdevelopment of normal instincts or reflexes — compare CRIB-BITING **6 :** injurious capacity : HARMFULNESS **7 :** sexual immorality; *esp* : PROSTITUTION **syn** see FAULT

²vice \"\ *n* -S [ME *vis, vice*, fr. MF *vis, viz* — more at VISE] **1 :** a winding stairway **2** *obs* **a :** a mechanical device working an apparatus **b :** SCREW **c :** a stopper that screws into an opening (as of a cask) **3** *chiefly Brit* : VISE **4 :** a device for making the leads for leaded windows

³vice \"\ *vt* -ED/-ING/-S *chiefly Brit* : VISE

⁴vice \"\ *n* -S [*vice-*] : PROXY, SUBSTITUTE

⁵vi·ce \'vīsē, -si\ *n* -S [L, abl. of *vicis* change, alternation, stead — more at WEEK] **1** *chiefly Scot* : PLACE, STEAD **2** *chiefly Scot* : a turn in sequence

⁶vice \"\ *prep* [L, abl. of *vicis*] : in the place of : in the stead of : SUCCEEDING ⟨John Doe was appointed postmaster ~ Richard Roe, resigned⟩

vice- *prefix* [ME *vis-, vice-*, fr. MF, fr. LL *vice-*, fr. L *vice*, abl. of *vicis*] : one that takes the place of ⟨*vice*-consul⟩ ⟨*vice*-chairman⟩ ⟨*vice*-principal⟩

vice admiral \'vīs+\ *n* [MF *visamiral*, fr. *vis-* vice + *amiral* admiral — more at ADMIRAL] **1 :** a commissioned naval officer ranking just below an admiral and above a rear admiral — abbr. *VA* **2** *obs* : a ship of war commanded by a vice admiral

vice admiralty \"+\ *n* **1 :** the office of a vice admiral **2 :** the district under the jurisdiction of a vice admiral

vice–admiralty court *n* : a British Admiralty court established in a colony beyond the seas in which the governor of the colony in his capacity as vice admiral exercises his judicial authority for the trial of maritime cases of a civil nature including prize cases

vice–chairman \'vīs+\ *n* [*vice-* + *chairman*] : one that assists a chairman or acts as his deputy in his absence

vice–chamberlain \"+\ *n* [*vice-* + *chamberlain*] : a deputy of a chamberlain

vice–chancellor \"+\ *n* [ME *vichauncellor*, fr. MF *vischancelier*, fr. *vis-* vice- + *chancelier* chancellor — more at CHANCELLOR] : an officer ranking next below a chancellor : a chancellor's deputy ⟨the *vice-chancellor* of a university⟩; *esp* : a judge appointed to act for or to assist a chancellor

vice–chancellorship \"+\ *n* : the office or term of a vice-chancellor

vice–consul \"+\ *n* [*vice-* + *consul*] : a consular officer subordinate to a consul general or to a consul

vice–count *n* [ME *viscounte, vicecount* — more at VISCOUNT] *obs* : VISCOUNT

vice–county \'vīs+\ *n* [*vice-* + *county*] *Brit* : a subdivision of a county

viced *past of* VICE

vice·ge·ren·cy \vīs'jirənsē, -si\ *also* **vice·ge·rence** \-n(t)s\ *n, pl* **vicegerencies** *also* **vicegerences** : the office or jurisdiction of a vicegerent

vice·ge·rent \-nt\ *n* [ML *vicegerent-, vicegerens*, fr. L *vice-* + *gerent-, gerens*, pres. part. of *gerere* to bear — more at CAST] **1 :** an administrative deputy : a person appointed to perform functions of a king or magistrate : DEPUTY, LIEUTENANT **2 :** a person deputed by God to exercise his authority in government or in religious matters ⟨kings who considered themselves God's ~s in their dominions⟩ **3 :** someone or something that substitutes for another

vice–god \'vīs+\ *n, often cap V&G* [*vice-* + *god*] : a deputy of God — usu. used disparagingly

vice–governor \"+\ *n* [*vice-* + *governor*] : a governor's assistant or deputy

vice–king \"+\ *n* [*vice-* + *king*] : VICEROY

vice–legate \"+\ *n* [*vice-* + *legate*] : the deputy of a legate

vice·less \'vīslə̇s\ *adj* [¹*vice* + *-less*] : having no vices

vicelike \'=,=\ *adj* [²*vice* + *-like*] : VISELIKE

vice–master \'vīs+\ *n* [*vice-* + *master*] : a master's deputy or assistant

vic·e·nary \'visə,nerē, -ri\ *adj* [L *vicenarius*, fr. *viceni* twenty each + *-arius* -ary; akin to L *viginti* twenty; akin to OIr *fiche* twenty, Gk *eikosi* (Doric *ϝikati*), Skt *viṁśati*; all fr. an IE compound whose 1st constituent was an IE word meaning "two" (represented by Skt *vi* apart), and whose 2d constituent is represented by L *decem* ten — more at WITH, TEN] **1 :** containing 20 **2 :** based on the number 20 : VIGESIMAL

vi·cen·ni·al \(')vī¦senēəl\ *adj* [LL *vicennium* period of 20 years (fr. L *vicies* 20 times + *-ennium*, fr. *annus* year) + E *-al*; akin to L *viginti* twenty — more at ANNUAL] : occurring once every 20 years

vice–premier \'vīs+\ *n* [*vice-* + *premier*] : a premier's deputy or assistant

vice–presidency \"+\ *n* : the office of vice-president

vice–president \"+\ *n* [*vice-* + *president*] **1 :** an officer next in rank below a president and acting as president in case of that officer's absence or disability **2 :** one of several officers serving as a president's deputies in charge of particular locations or functions ⟨eastern regional *vice-president*⟩ ⟨*vice-president* and plant manager⟩ ⟨*vice-president* in charge of sales⟩ ⟨*vice-president* in charge of engineering⟩ — **vice–presidential** \"+\ *adj*

vice–queen \"+\ *n* [*vice-* + *queen*] **1 :** VICEREINE 2 **2 :** a viceroy's wife

viceregal \"+\ *adj* [*vice-* + *regal*] : of or relating to a viceroy

vice–regent \"+\ *n* [*vice-* + *regent*] : a regent's deputy or assistant

vice·reine \'vīs,rān\ *n* -S [F, fr. *vice-* + *reine* queen, fr. L *regina* — more at REINA] **1 :** the wife of a viceroy **2 :** a woman viceroy

vice·roy \'vīs,rȯi\ *n* -S [MF *vice-roi*, fr. *vice-* + *roi* king, fr. L *reg-, rex* — more at ROYAL] **1 :** the governor of a country or province who rules as the representative of his king or sovereign and has power to act generally in the name and behalf of his sovereign **2 :** a showy American butterfly (*Limenitis archippus*) closely mimicking the monarch butterfly in coloration but smaller and having larvae that feed on willow, poplar, and apple trees

vice·royalty \'vīs+¦-\ *n* [*vice-* + *royalty*; trans. of F *vice-royauté*] : the office, jurisdiction, or term of service of a viceroy

vice·roy·ship \'==,ship\ *n* [*viceroy* + *-ship*] : VICEROYALTY

vices *pl of* VICE, *pres 3d sing of* VICE

vicesimo–quarto *var of* VIGESIMO-QUARTO

vice–skip \'vīs+\ *n* [*vice-* + *skip*] : the third man on a curling team

vice squad *n* : a police squad charged with enforcement of laws concerning vice

vice–treasurer \'vīs+\ *n* [*vice-* + *treasurer*] : a treasurer's deputy or assistant

vice–treasurer·ship \"+,ship\ *n* : the office or tenure of a vice-treasurer

vice ver·sa \¦vīsə'vərsə, -sē'-, -si'-, -'vəsə, -'vəisə, (')vīs'-\ *adv* [L] : with the alternation or order changed : with the relations reversed : CONVERSELY ⟨it was with vast relief that we came upon a man pretending to be a machine, rather than *vice versa* —*New Yorker*⟩

vice–warden \'vīs+\ *n* [*vice-* + *warden*] : a warden's deputy or assistant

vich·i·an \'vikēən\ *adj, usu cap* [It *vichiano*, fr. G. B. *Vico* + It *-iano* -ian — more at VICONIAN] : VICONIAN

vi·chy·ite \'vishē,īt, 'vēsh-, -shi,-, *usu* -īd·+V\ *n* -S *usu cap* [fr. *Vichy*, France, capital of unoccupied France in World War II + E *-ite*] : a member or supporter of the authoritarian regime of Marshal Henri Pétain governing unoccupied France during the earlier part of World War II under an agreement calling for economic collaboration with the Nazis

vi·chys·soise \,vishē'swäz, ,vēsh-, -shi'-\ *n* -S [F (short for *crème vichyssoise glacée*, lit., iced-cold Vichy cream), fr. fem. of *vichyssois* of Vichy, fr. *Vichy*, France] : a soup made of pureed leeks or onions and potatoes, cream, chicken stock, and seasoning and usu. served cold

vi·chy water \'vi¦shē- 'vē¦, -shi-\ *n, often cap V* [fr. *Vichy*, France] : SODA WATER 2a

Vi·ci \'vī,sī\ *trademark* — used for leather used esp. for the uppers of shoes

vi·cia \'vis(h)ēə\ *n, cap* [NL, fr. L, vetch — more at VETCH] : a widely distributed genus of often climbing herbs (family Leguminosae) having pinnate leaves and blue, purple, or yellow flowers either solitary or in axillary racemes, the style usu. beaked or tufted, and the ovary containing numerous ovules — see HAIRY VETCH, VETCH

vi·ci·a·nin \-ənə̇n\ *n* -S [ISV *vician-* (fr. NL *Vicia angustifolia*) + *-in*] : a crystalline glycoside $C_{19}H_{25}NO_{10}$ found in the seeds of a vetch (*Vicia angustifolia*) that yields vicianose, benzaldehyde, and hydrogen cyanide on hydrolysis

vi·ci·a·nose \-ə,nōs\ *n* -S [ISV *vicianin* + *-ose*] : a crystalline disaccharide sugar $C_{11}H_{20}O_{10}$ that is obtained by hydrolysis of vicianin and that yields L-arabinose and D-glucose on hydrolysis

vic·i·lin \'visələn\ *n* -S [L *vicia* vetch + E *globulin*] : a globulin associated with legumin (as in the pea, lentil, or broad bean)

vic·i·nage \'vis(ᵊ)nij, -(ᵊ)nēj\ *n* -S [ME *vesinage*, fr. MF *vesinage, vicenage, voisinage*, fr. *vesin, vicin, voisin* neighboring (fr. L *vicinus*) + *-age* — more at VICINITY] **1 a :** an adjacent, neighboring, or surrounding district : a limited nearby area : NEIGHBORHOOD, VICINITY **b :** the residents of a vicinage **2 :** a right of common arising to neighboring tenants of the same barony and fee

vic·i·nal \-(ᵊ)nəl\ *adj* [L *vicinalis*, fr. *vicinus* neighbor (fr. *vicinus* neighboring) + *-alis* -al] **1 :** of, relating to, or confined to a limited district or neighborhood : belonging to or restricted to a vicinity : LOCAL ⟨~ roads are distinguished from through highways⟩ **2 :** of, relating to, or being the subordinate forms or faces on a crystal which sometimes take the place of the fundamental ones, approach them very closely in angle, and have in general very complex symbols **3 :** relating to,

characterized by, or being adjoining positions in an organic chemical compound ⟨the three ~ 1,2,3-positions in benzene⟩ — abbr. *v;* compare NEIGHBORING 2, ¹ORTHO 2

vic·ine *also* **vic·in** \ˈvisən\ *n* -s [L *vicia* vetch + ISV *-ine*] : a crystalline glucoside $C_{10}H_{16}N_4O_7$ obtained esp. from seeds of vetches (genus *Vicia*) and beets that yields glucose and a pyrimidine on hydrolysis

vicing *pres part of* VICE

vic·i·nism \ˈvisə,nizəm\ *n* -S [ISV *vicin-* (fr. L *vicinus* neighbor) + *-ism*] : natural cross-pollination between two species or two varieties of a plant

vi·cin·i·ty \və̇ˈsinəd·ē, -ōt·ē, -i *sometimes chiefly Brit* vī¹-\ *n* -ES [MF *vicinité,* fr. L *vicinitat-, vicinitas,* fr. *vicinus* neighboring (fr. *vicus* row of houses, village + *-inus* -ine) + *-itat-, -itas* -ity; akin to Goth *weihs* village, Gk *oikos* house, dwelling, Skt *viś* settlement, dwelling, house] **1** : the quality or state of being near : NEARNESS, PROPINQUITY, PROXIMITY ⟨might well dread the immediate ~ of a monarch so great, so ambitious, and so unscrupulous —T.B.Macaulay⟩ ⟨so near a ~ to her mother . . . was not desirable —Jane Austen⟩ **2** *obs* : close relationship or resemblance **3** : a surrounding area or district : LOCALITY, NEIGHBORHOOD ⟨in the ~ of his home⟩ ⟨old residents of the ~ —John DeMeyer⟩ **4** : NEIGHBORHOOD 3b ⟨invitations which he receives average in the ~ of 300 a month —Philip Hamburger⟩

vi·cious \ˈvishəs\ *adj* [ME, fr. MF *vicieus,* fr. L *vitiosus* full of faults, bad, corrupt, fr. *vitium* blemish, crime, vice + *-osus* -ous — more at WITH] **1 a** : having the nature or quality of vice : violative of moral rectitude : contrary to accepted standards of right or good : DEBASED, DEPRAVED ⟨a great university, in a few months, became a ~ political tool —R.A.Smith⟩ **b** : addicted to vice, immorality, or depravity : corrupt or dissolute in conduct : EVIL, REPROBATE ⟨a family with a good mother can withstand a feckless or even a ~ father —*Times Lit. Supp.*⟩ **2 a** : missing or incompatible with a norm of excellence : failing to meet a test or criterion : BAD, FAULTY, POOR, REPREHENSIBLE ⟨discriminate between thoroughly ~ ideas and those which should have a chance to be heard —Zechariah Chafee⟩ ⟨criticism at its most ~ —C.D.Lewis⟩ **b** : marred or nullified by imperfection : voided before the law by inherent defect : UNLAWFUL ⟨a badly drawn or ~ bill —Allan Nevins⟩ **c** : ruined or invalidated by defect ⟨a ~ argument⟩ : inferior in form or taste : stunted in development : IMPAIRED, TRIVIAL ⟨a ~ line of reasoning⟩ ⟨~ and ephemeral light verse⟩ ⟨~ spelling⟩ **3 a** : FOUL, IMPURE, NOXIOUS **b** : DISEASED, MALIGNANT, MORBID ⟨a gastric carcinoma is a very ~ tumor —W.H.Cole⟩ **4 a** : having dangerous or refractory habits : SAVAGE, UNTAMED ⟨a particularly ~ dog which snapped at every passerby —*Amer. Guide Series: R.I.*⟩ **b** : marked by violence or ferocity : FIERCE, SHARP, WILD ⟨took a ~ swing at him with the pick —Rex Ingamells⟩ ⟨~ animosity of political opponents —*Amer. Guide Series: Tenn.*⟩ **c** : of or relating to perverse or abnormal behavior of domestic animals ⟨the ~ habit of picking feathers —*Poultry Science*⟩ **5** : MALICIOUS, SPITEFUL ⟨ugly and ~ stories invented and repeated by respectable lawyers and college professors —A.M. Schlesinger b. 1917⟩ **6** : INTENSE, SEVERE ⟨there have been unusually ~ windstorms —Janet Flanner⟩ **7** : painfully strenuous or extreme ⟨the alternative of a ~ tightening of . . . strenuous or extreme ⟨the alternative of a ~ tightening of . . . belts later in the year —*Economist*⟩ **8** : having a sequence or progression analogous to that of a vicious circle : intensified, worsened, or accelerated by internal causes that reciprocally aggravate each other's bad effects ⟨you can see in all this wage business the ~ spiral at work. The miners got more pay, so coal prices went up, so the railways raised their freight charges, so coal prices went up again to meet dearer transport, so the miners asked for more pay to meet the higher cost of living —Margaret Stewart⟩ ⟨a ~ cycle⟩

syn VILLAINOUS, INIQUITOUS, NEFARIOUS, FLAGITIOUS, INFAMOUS, CORRUPT, DEGENERATE: VICIOUS may suggest addiction to or exemplification of vice, immorality, or depravity; it may connote violence, deliberate cruelty, or effective malignancy ⟨she had been *vicious* and unnatural; she had thriven on hatred, and had made life a hell for everyone about her —W.H. Wright⟩ ⟨protect the community from even its thoroughly *vicious* young criminals —Bruce Smith⟩ ⟨*vicious* accusations in the press that Jews had poisoned water supplies —Shlomo Katz⟩ VILLAINOUS is a forceful general descriptive term for anything depraved, scoundrelly, evil, or vile ⟨certain *villainous* government officials had plotted to murder the Count —Edmund Wilson⟩ ⟨nor does great creative Nature pause for one minute to discourage such scoundrels in their *villainous* malpractice —J.C.Powys⟩ INIQUITOUS applies to an utter lack of justice or fairness, a callous disregard for decent conduct or procedure ⟨they now appeared to him everything that was *iniquitous* and bad. Secret murder was their object — black, foul, midnight murder —Anthony Trollope⟩ ⟨that quenchless hunger for raw, quick, dirty money in American politics, which hardly sugarcoats its bribes, which glazes over its most *iniquitous* corruption —W.A.White⟩ NEFARIOUS sometimes suggests impiety or flagrantly countering established laws and social principles ⟨he kills devotion with an almost infallible aim. Charity turns into a lump of ice under his *nefarious* gaze —Julien Green⟩ ⟨our politicians would not dare to sacrifice the life and happiness of innumerable children to their *nefarious* schemes of bloodshed and oppression —Bertrand Russell⟩ FLAGITIOUS may describe whatever is disgracefully or scandalously wicked ⟨the most *flagitious* villain upon earth —Henry Fielding⟩ INFAMOUS is a general adjective for anything very bad, abhorrent, base, and deserving of evil fame ⟨this man is of a character so *infamous* that he will stick at no falsehood, or hesitate at no crime —W.M.Thackeray⟩ ⟨the *infamous* Luboff, who, as chief of the secret police at Odessa after the defeat of Denikin's army, put thousands of innocent people to death —Valentine Williams⟩ CORRUPT applies to what has lost integrity, honesty, and virtue and become degraded and depraved ⟨now known to have been a traitor to the United States, a pensioner of Spain, and an accomplice of Aaron Burr: corrupt, profligate, and insubordinate —Allan Nevins & H.S.Commager⟩ ⟨a disordered and competitive mob, bent only on turning each to his own personal advantage the now *corrupt* machinery of administration and law —G.L. Dickinson⟩ DEGENERATE may suggest retrogression and corruption into an especially vicious or enervated condition ⟨the *degenerate* practices of the court of the Caesars⟩ ⟨the *degenerate* physique as a whole is often marked by diminished stature and inferior vigor —H.G.Armstrong⟩

vicious circle *n* **1** : a chain of circumstances constituting a situation in which the process of solving one difficulty creates a new problem involving increased difficulty in the original situation **2** : an argument or definition that is valueless because it either overtly or covertly assumes as true or as established something which is to be proved or defined **3** : a chain of abnormal processes in which a primary disorder leads to a second which in turn aggravates the first one ⟨the *vicious circle* of fatigue-anxiety-fatigue⟩

vicious circle principle *n* : a principle in logic : whatever is defined in terms of all of a collection or of a totality cannot be a member thereof — compare RUSSELL'S PARADOX

vicious intromission *n* : an intromission made unjustifiably under Scots law by an heir with his ancestor's movable estate — compare EXECUTOR DE SON TORT, LEGAL INTROMISSION

vi·cious·ly *adv* [ME, fr. *vicious* + *-ly*] : in a vicious manner

vi·cious·ness *n* -ES [ME *viciousnesse,* fr. *vicious* + *-nesse* -ness] : the quality or state of being vicious

vi·cis·si·tude \və̇ˈsisə,t(y)üd, və̇ˈsisə,tüd sometimes chiefly Brit vī¹-\ *n* -S [MF, fr. L *vicissitudo,* fr. *vicissim* in turn (fr. *vicis* change, alternation, stead) + *-tudo* -tude — more at WEEK] **1 a** : the quality or state of being changeable or in flux : MUTABILITY ⟨the ~ of human condition⟩ **b** : natural change or mutation : the rise and decline of phenomena : the successive alterations visible in nature or in human affairs ⟨~s of time and chance have left only 9 of the 30 trees —*Amer. Guide Series: Mich.*⟩ **2 a** : an accident of fortune : a shift of luck or vagary of chance : a fluctuation in state ⟨as of wealth, prosperity, or fortune⟩ ⟨lovers not only faithful but patient in the face of remarkable ~s —Claudia Cassidy⟩ **b** : alternating change : SUCCESSION ⟨such alternations of energy and inertia, such sudden ~s of greatness and decay —Irving Babbitt⟩

syn see DIFFICULTY

---

vi·cis·si·tu·di·nous \və̇¦sisə¦t(y)üd·ə̇nəs, -ˌtyü-\ *adj* [L *vicissitudin-, vicissitudo* + E *-ous*] : marked by or filled with vicissitudes : undergoing alternations of fortune or condition

Vick·ers hardness test \ˈvikə(r)z-\ *n, usu cap V* [prob. fr. Vickers Armstrong Ltd., Brit. steel-manufacturing concern] : an indentation hardness test for metals in which a 136-degree diamond pyramid is pressed onto the surface of the metal being tested by a load of 5 to 120 kilograms

vi·co·ri·an \vēˈkōrēən\ *adj, usu cap* [fr. Giovanni Vico †1744 Ital. philosopher + connective *-ie-* + E *-ian*] : of, relating to, or typical of the philosopher Vico or his cyclical theory of history

vi·con·ti·el \(ˌ)vīˈkäntēəl\ *adj* [AF *viscontiel, vicontiel,* fr. MF *visconte* viscount + *-iel* -ial — more at VISCOUNT] : of or relating to a viscount or sheriff

vicontiel rents *n pl* : royal farm rents collected and paid by a viscount or sheriff

vi·con·ti·els \vīˈkäntēəlz\ *n pl* : money payable by a viscount or sheriff to the English crown; *esp* : VICONTIEL RENTS

vicontiel writs *n pl* : writs triable in the old county court before the sheriff

vics *pl of* VIC

vic·tim \ˈviktəm\ *n* -S [L *victima;* akin to OE *wīh, wēoh, wīg* idol, image, OHG *wīh, wīhi* holy, ON *vē* temple, Goth *weihs* holy, Skt *vinakti* he separates, sets apart; basic meaning: to set apart, single out] **1** : a living being sacrificed to some deity or in the performance of a religious rite **2** : someone put to death, tortured, or mulcted by another : a person subjected to oppression, deprivation, or suffering ⟨a ~ of war⟩ ⟨a ~ of intolerance⟩ ⟨fell a ~ to prohibition era gangsters⟩ **3** : someone who suffers death, loss, or injury in an undertaking of his own ⟨became a ~ of his own strenuous ambition⟩ **4** : someone tricked, duped, or subjected to hardship : someone badly used or taken advantage of ⟨felt himself the ~ of his brother's shrewdness —W.F.Davis⟩ ⟨little boys, as well as adolescent girls, became the willing ~s of sailors and marines —R.M. Lovett⟩

syn PREY, QUARRY: VICTIM applies to anyone who suffers either as a result of ruthless design or incidentally or accidentally ⟨the *victim* sacrificed on these occasions is a hen, or several hens —J.G.Frazer⟩ ⟨was the girl born to be a *victim;* to be always disliked and crushed as if she were too fine for this world —Joseph Conrad⟩ ⟨lest such a policy precipitate a hot war of which western Europe would be the *victim* —Quincy Wright⟩ PREY may designate a victim clutched, seized, captured by or as if by an enemy, hunter, or wild beast ⟨others hold the battleship to be an obsolete arm, expensive beyond its worth, useful only for fighting other battleships and the easy *prey* of the submarine and the airplane —R.L.Buell⟩ ⟨an old castle from which the robber barons in the old days could see their *prey* coming and rush down upon the caravan to overpower it —W.A.White⟩ ⟨she still went recklessly on, her eyes confused by the rain, her brain a *prey* to wild and despairing thoughts —William Black⟩ QUARRY is applicable to the object of a chase, esp. by hounds, or to a person or thing relentlessly pursued or vigorously quested after ⟨with grain in their storerooms, and mountain sheep and deer for their *quarry,* they rose gradually from the condition of savagery —Willa Cather⟩ ⟨government agents tracking their *quarry* through the underworld of several cities⟩

vic·tim·hood \ˈviktəm,hu̇d\ *n* : the state or condition of being a victim

vic·tim·iza·tion \ˌviktəmə̇ˈzāshən, -tə,mī¹-\ *n* -S : the act or process of victimizing or the state of being victimized

vic·tim·ize \ˈviktə,mīz\ *vt* -ED/-ING/-S *see -ize in Explan Notes* [*victim* + *-ize*] **1 a** : to make a victim of : SACRIFICE ⟨as a family they were flogged, defrauded, *victimized* —Ann Petry⟩ **b** : to slaughter as a sacrificial victim **2** : to subject to deception or fraud : CHEAT, DUPE, TRICK ⟨fearing to be *victimized* we are inclined not to believe at all —N.M.Pusey⟩ ⟨relentlessly *victimized* by every piece of mischief known to the young —Paul Pickrel⟩ **3** : to destroy ⟨plants⟩ entirely ⟨the red spores of the parasite . . . ~ winter wheat —*Current Biog.*⟩

vic·tim·iz·er \-,zə(r)\ *n* -S : one that victimizes

¹vic·tor \ˈviktə(r)\ *n* -S [ME, fr. L, fr. *victus* (past part. of *vincere* to conquer) + *-or;* akin to OE & OHG *wīgan* to fight, ON *vīg* fight, Goth *weihan* to fight, OIr *fichid* he fights, OSlav *vēkŭ* strength, power; basic meaning: strength, manifestation of strength] **1** : one that defeats an enemy : the winner in a battle, war, or fight **2** : the winner in a conflict or struggle : a successful contender ⟨emerged ~ at the polls⟩ ⟨~ in a series of intramural contests⟩

²victor \"\ *adj* : VICTORIOUS, TRIUMPHANT

³victor \"\ *n, usu cap* : a communications code word for the letter *v*

victorfish \ˈ¦ˌ¦¦\ *n* : OCEANIC BONITO

¹vic·to·ria \vikˈtōrēə, -tȯr-\ *n* -s [after *Victoria* †1901 queen of England] **1 a** : a low four-wheel pleasure carriage for two with a calash top and a raised seat in front for the driver **b** : an open passenger automobile with a calash top that usu. extends over the rear seat only **2** [NL, after Queen *Victoria*] **a** *cap* : a genus of immense So. American aquatic plants (family Nymphaeaceae) with large spreading leaves that are often over 5 feet in diameter and have a rim from 3 to 8 inches high, extremely large rose-white flowers opening for several successive evenings, and edible seeds **b** -s : any plant of this genus — see VICTORIA REGIA

victoria 1a

²victoria \(¹)¦¦¦¦\ *adj, usu cap* [fr. *Victoria,* Australia & *Victoria,* British Columbia] **1** : of or from the state of Victoria, Australia : of the kind or style prevalent in the state of Victoria **2** : of or from Victoria, the capital of British Columbia : of the kind or style prevalent in Victoria, B. C.

victoria blight *n, usu cap V* [fr. *Victoria,* a variety of oats, after Queen *Victoria*] : a fungous disease that is peculiar to oats which have Victoria variety in their parentage, is caused by a fungus (*Helminthosporium victoriae*), and is characterized by seed and root rot, seedling stunt, and orange or orange-brown streaking esp. of the leaf margins and blackening and breaking at the nodes

victoria blue *n* [after Queen *Victoria*] **1** *usu cap V* & *often cap B* : any of several basic dyes derived from diphenylnaphthyl-methane that dye wool and silk royal blue and are used also as biological stains and organic pigments: as **a** *or* **victoria blue B** : a dye made from Michler's ketone and N-phenyl-alpha-naphthylamine — see DYE table I (under *Basic Blue 26, Pigment Blue 2, Solvent Blue 4*) **b** *or* **victoria blue R** : a dye made from Michler's ketone and N-ethyl-alpha-naphthylamine — see DYE table I (under *Basic Blue 11, Solvent Blue 6*) **c** : VICTORIA PURE BLUE B **2** *often cap V* : a strong blue that is redder and duller than Sèvres, cerulean blue (sense 1b), or victoria blue (sense 1a)

victoria day *n, usu cap V&D* [after Queen *Victoria*] **1** : May 24 observed in Canada as a legal holiday **2** : EMPIRE DAY

victoria fast violet RR *n, usu cap both Vs & F* [after Queen *Victoria*] : an acid dye — see DYE table I (under *Acid Violet I*)

victoria green *n, usu cap V* & *often cap G* [after Queen *Victoria*] : MALACHITE GREEN 2

victoria lake *n, often cap V* [fr. *Victoria Lake,* east-central Africa] : PUCE

victoria lily *n, usu cap V* [after Queen *Victoria*] : VICTORIA 2b

¹vic·to·ri·an \(¹)vikˈtōrēən, -tȯr-\ *adj, usu cap* [Queen *Victoria* + E *-an*] **1** : of or relating to the reign of Queen Victoria of England : representative of the art, letters, or taste of Victoria's reign ⟨*Victorian* novels⟩ **2** : typical of the moral standards or conduct of the age of Victoria esp. when stuffy or hypocritical ⟨the bohemian was always at war with him with the *Victorian* gentleman —G.S.Haight⟩

²victorian \"\ *n, usu cap* : a person living during Queen Victoria's reign; *esp* : a representative author of that time

³victorian \"\ *adj, usu cap* [fr. *Victoria,* Australia & *Victoria,* British Columbia + E *-an*] **1** : of, relating to, or characteristic of the state of Victoria, Australia, or the city of Victoria, British Columbia **2** : of, relating to, or characteristic of the

people of Victoria, Australia, or Victoria, B. C.

⁴victorian \"\ *n -s cap* : a native or inhabitant of Victoria

victorian box *or* **victorian laurel** *n, usu cap V* [³*Victorian* (of Victoria, Australia)] : NATIVE LAUREL 1

victorian gothic *n, usu cap V&G* [¹*Victorian*] : an architectural style belonging to the later Gothic Revival of Victoria's reign and combining French, Italian, and English elements with a free use of parti-colored materials

victorian hazel *n, usu cap V* [³*Victorian* (of Victoria, Australia)] : a shrub of the genus *Pomaderris*

vic·to·ri·an·ism \vikˈtōrēə,nizəm, -tȯr-\ *n* -s *usu cap* [¹*Victorian* + *-ism*] **1** : the quality or state of being Victorian esp. in taste, habits of thought, or conduct **2** : a typical instance or product of Victorian expression, taste, or conduct ⟨a scrolly piece of ~ just big enough to hold his papers and his typewriter —Clemence Dane⟩

vic·to·ri·an·ize \-,nīz\ *vt* -ED/-ING/-S *often cap* [¹*Victorian* + *-ize*] : to make Victorian (as in style or taste)

victorian rosemary *n, usu cap V* [³*Victorian* (of Victoria, Australia)] : an Australian shrub (*Westringia rosmariniformis*) of the family Labiatae with silvery-white fragrant foliage and small axillary flowers

victoria pigeon *n, usu cap V* [fr. *Victoria,* Australia] : a crowned pigeon (*Goura victoria*)

victoria pure blue B *or* **victoria pure blue BO** *n, usu cap V&P&B* [after Queen *Victoria*] : a Victoria blue dye made from the ethyl analogue of Michler's ketone and N-ethyl-alpha-naphthylamine — see DYE table I (under *Basic Blue 7, Pigment Blue 1, Solvent Blue 5*)

victoria red *n, often cap V* [after Queen *Victoria*] : vermilion or a color resembling it

victoria re·gia \-ˈrējēə\ *n* [NL, lit., royal Victoria; after Queen *Victoria*] : ROYAL WATER LILY

victorias *pl of* VICTORIA

vic·to·ri·ate \vikˈtōrēət, -tȯr-, -ēāt\ *n* -S [L *victoriatus,* fr. *victoria* victory + *-atus* -ate — more at VICTORY] : a silver coin of the ancient Roman republic orig. worth ¾ denarius, having on the reverse a figure of Victory crowning a trophy, and struck for use in foreign trade

victoria violet 4BS *n, usu cap both Vs* [after Queen *Victoria*] : an acid dye — see DYE table I (under *Acid Violet 3*)

¹vic·to·rine \ˈviktə,rēn\ *n* -s [prob. fr. Queen *Victoria* + E *-ine*] : a woman's fur tippet with long ends

²Victorine \"\ *n, usu cap* [F *victorin,* fr. the Abbey of St. *Victor* near Paris, France + F *-in -ine*] : a canon regular of the Order of St. Victor founded in Paris in 1110, widespread during the medieval period, famous for its learning, and extinct since the French Revolution

vic·to·ri·ous \(¹)vikˈtōrēəs, -tȯr-\ *adj* [ME, fr. MF *victorieus,* fr. L *victoriosus,* fr. *victoria* victory + *-osus* -ous] **1 a** : having defeated an enemy or antagonist : having won a battle or contest : CONQUERING, TRIUMPHANT ⟨a ~ army⟩ ⟨a fighter⟩ ⟨a ~ candidate⟩ **b** : of, relating to, or characteristic of victory : emblematic or suggestive of a winner or a success ⟨a ~ flag⟩ ⟨a ~ air⟩ **2** : having displaced a rival : having won approval or acceptance instead of another ⟨an urban industrial society was ~ over historic agrarian forms⟩ **3 a** : evincing moral harmony or other attainment : consummating an endeavor : FULFILLED ⟨a robust, thoroughly healthy, and withal, very prosperous and ~ man —Thomas Carlyle⟩ **b** : achieving a perfection of form, grace, or vision ⟨as in artistic performance⟩

vic·to·ri·ous·ly *adv* : in a victorious manner

vic·to·ri·ous·ness *n* -ES : the quality or state of being victorious

victors *pl of* VICTOR

vic·to·ry \ˈvikt(ə)rē, -ri\ *n* -ES [ME, fr. MF *victorie,* fr. L *victoria,* fr. fem. of (assumed) L *victorius* victorious, fr. L *victus* (past part. of *vincere* to conquer) + *-orius -ory* — more at VICTOR] **1** : the overcoming of an enemy in battle or of an antagonist in a contest ⟨won ~ at last in a protracted war⟩ ⟨scored a knockout ~⟩ ⟨earned a significant political ~⟩ — opposed to *defeat* **2 a** : the gaining of superiority or success in any struggle or endeavor ⟨his new model represented a ~ of constructive imagination⟩ **b** : a moral or spiritual triumph of any kind ⟨yet his mental ~ over this cruel illness is complete as well as inspiring —Ellen Patterson⟩

syn CONQUEST, TRIUMPH: although VICTORY can be used to imply no more than the defeat of an opponent in a contest or struggle, in applying to certain kinds of struggle it often inevitably suggests a certain satisfaction or praise accruing to the victor ⟨a new concept of *victory* in war —R.J.Bunche⟩ ⟨*victory* without peace —Archibald MacLeish⟩ ⟨the *victory* over Everest was a fit coronation present for the Queen —W.O.Douglas⟩ CONQUEST implies a mastery over or subjugation of the opponent, whether a group of human beings or a difficult undertaking ⟨the Roman *conquest* of the Greeks⟩ ⟨the *conquest* of the Atlantic by air —*Irish Digest*⟩ ⟨the education of women was in large part a feminine *conquest* —H.M. Parshley⟩ TRIUMPH suggests great acclaim or personal satisfaction accruing to the victor as from a brilliant or decisive victory or an overwhelming conquest ⟨it is surely questionable whether we as noncombatant individuals should desire their *triumph,* a degree of success that clearly implies the full accomplishment of all their ends, good and bad —*Commonweal*⟩ ⟨the battle . . . marked the beginning of final Union *triumph* in the Chattanooga campaign —A.P.James⟩ ⟨achieved a diplomatic *triumph* in bringing about the adoption of treaties —G.E. Rines⟩ ⟨that she did as well as she did was a *triumph* of experience over inadequate means —Irving Kolodin⟩

victory garden *n, often cap V* : a wartime vegetable garden developed to increase food production esp. by home gardeners

victory girl *n, often cap V* : a wartime amateur camp follower or pickup girl — called also *V-girl*

vic·tress \ˈviktrəs\ *n -ES* [*victor* + *-ess*] : a female victor

vic·trix \-riks\ *n, pl* victri·ces \-rə,sēz\ [L, fem. of *victor*] : VICTRESS

Vic·tro·la \vikˈtrōlə\ *trademark* — used for a phonograph

¹vict·ual \ˈvid·ᵊl, -it²l\ *n -s* [alter. (influenced by LL *victualia*) of ME *vitaille, vitaille,* fr. MF, fr. LL *victualia,* pl., provisions, victuals, fr. neut. pl. of *victualis* of nourishment, fr. L *victus* nourishment, sustenance (fr. *victus,* past part. of *vivere* to live) + *-alis* -al — more at QUICK] **1 a** : food usable by man ⟨drinks and cakes and pastry, but . . . no substantial ~ — Nathaniel Hawthorne⟩ **b** *archaic* : vegetable produce **c** *Scot* : GRAIN **2** victuals *pl* : supplies of food : PROVISIONS ⟨the navy's ships provided artillery support 10 miles deep, besides ~s and supplies for the advancing army —Walter Karig⟩ ⟨worker's wives switching to the less costly kinds of ~s —J.A. Lack⟩ ⟨tempting tales of appetizing ~s —Green Peyton⟩

²victual \"\ *vb* **victualed** *or* **victualled; victualed** *or* **victualled; victualing** *or* **victualling** \-d²liŋ, -it²l-, -t(²)l-\ **victuals** [ME *vitaillen,* vitaille, fr. MF *vitailer, vitailler,* fr. *vitaille, vitaille,* n.] *vt* : to supply with food ⟨this population was ~ed with goods brought by rail —H.W.H.King⟩ ~ *vi* **1 a** : EAT **b** : FEED, PASTURE — used of domestic animals **2** : to lay in provisions ⟨the ship was ~ing⟩

vict·ual·age \-ᵊlij\ *n -s* : VICTUALS

victualing bill *n* : a list of bonded or drawback goods taken aboard for use as ship's stores that when signed by a customs officer becomes one of the master's clearance papers

vict·ual·ler *or* **vict·ual·er** \ˈvid·ᵊlə(r), -it²l-\ *n -s* [ME *vitailler, vitailler,* fr. MF *vitailler, vitailler,* fr. *vitaille, vitaille* + *-ier*] **1** : the keeper of a restaurant or tavern : one who serves meals or liquors in a public house ⟨held a common ~'s license⟩ **2** : one that provisions an army, a navy, or a ship with supplies of food : SUTLER **3** : an army or navy provision ship

vi·cu·ña *or* **vi·cu·na** *also* **vi·cu·gna** \vī¹k(y)ünə, vȧ¹-, vȧ¹künyə\ *n -s* [Sp *vicuña,* fr. Quechua *wikúña*] **1** : a wild ruminant (*Lama vicugna*) of the Andes from Ecuador to Bolivia that is related to the domesticated llama and alpaca,

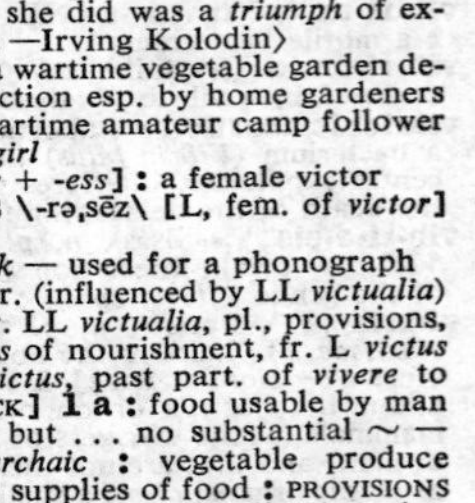

vicuña

is light brown, paler on the underparts and with light markings on legs and head, is smaller than the guanaco but like it lives in herds and is fleet-footed, and has been much hunted for its wool and fur **2 a** : the woollike fiber from the vicuña's fine lustrous undercoat **b** (1) : a fabric made of vicuña fiber (2) : woolen fabric made to imitate this
vid *abbr* **1** [L *vide*] see **2** video **3** [L *vidua*] widow
vida finch \ˈvīdə-\ *n* [*vida* modif. of NL *Vidua*] : WHYDAH
vi·dame \vēˈdam\ *n* -s [MF, fr. ML *vice-dominus*, fr. LL *vice-* + L *dominus* lord, master — more at DAME] : one of a class of French feudal temporal officers or advocates who orig. represented the abbeys or bishops but later erected their offices into fiefs — used as an hereditary title of nobility which was recognized to the end of the ancien régime
vid·dhal \vəˈdäl\ *n, pl* **viddhal** *or* **viddhals** *usu cap* : a member of a Turkoman people on the east shore of the Caspian sea
vid·dui \vəˈdüē\ *n* [Heb *widdūy*] *Jewish relig* : a confession of sin alphabetically arranged and recited as part of the Yom Kippur liturgy in the synagogue; *also* : a confession of sin recited privately by a person approaching death
¹vi·de \ˈvīdē, -di, ˈvēdā\ *v imper* [L, 2d pers. sing. imper. of *vidēre* to see] : SEE — used to direct a reader to another item
²vide \ˈvēd\ *adj* [F, fr. OF *vuit, voit* — more at VOID] **1** : OPEN, EMPTY — used of strings on musical instruments **2** : CUT, OMITTED — used as a direction on musical scores with *vi* indicating the beginning and *de* its close
vi·de·li·cet \vəˈdeləˌset, -ˌsət; vəˈdāləˌket, wēˈd-\ *adv* [L, fr. *vidēre* to see + *licet* it is permitted, 3d pers. sing. pres. indic. of *licēre* to be permitted — more at WIT, LICENSE] : that is to say : NAMELY — abbr. *viz.*
¹vid·eo \ˈvidēˌō\ *adj* : relating to or used in the transmission or reception of the television image ⟨~ channel⟩ ⟨~ frequency⟩ — compare AUDIO
²video \"\ *n* -s [L *vidēre* to see + E *-o* (as in *audio*)] : TELEVISION
vid·e·o·gen·ic \ˌvidēōˈjenik\ *adj* [*video* + *-genic*] : TELEGENIC
video recording *n* **1** : a motion picture of a television production made by photographing the kinescope tube **2** : VIDEO TAPE RECORDING
video signal *n* : PICTURE SIGNAL
video tape recording *n* : a recording of a television production made by recording sound and video signals on magnetic tape
vi·dette \vəˈ-\ *var of* VEDETTE
vid·i·an \ˈvidēən\ *adj, usu cap* [Vidus *Vidius* (Guido Guidi) †1569 Ital. anatomist + E *-an*] : of or relating to the anatomist Guidi
vidian artery *n, usu cap V* : a branch of the internal maxillary artery passing through the pterygoid canal of the sphenoid bone
vidian canal *n, usu cap V* : PTERYGOID CANAL
vidian nerve *n, usu cap V* : a nerve formed by the union of the greater superficial petrosal and the deep petrosal nerves and passing forward through the pterygoid canal in the sphenoid bone and joining the sphenopalatine ganglion
vid·i·con \ˈvidəˌkän\ *n* -s *often cap* [*video* + *iconoscope*] : a small camera tube containing an electron gun and a photoconductor on which an optical image is focused so that a beam of electrons from the gun is collected by the photoconductor and transformed into current whose rapid fluctuations representing the light and shade of the image are subsequently amplified and transmitted as television picture signals
vi·di·mus \ˈvidəməs, ˈvīd-\ *n* -ES [L, we have seen, 1st pers. pl. perf. indic. of *vidēre* to see] : an official or legal inspection (as of a document); *also* : an attested copy of a document
vid·ua \ˈvijəwə\ *n, cap* [NL, fr. L, widow] : a genus of African weaverbirds comprising various typical whydahs
vidual *adj* [LL *vidualis*, fr. L *vidua* widow + *-alis* -al] *obs* : of or relating to widowhood or widows
vi·du·i·ty \vəˈd(y)üəd-ē\ *n* -ES [ME (Sc) *viduite*, fr. MF *viduité*, fr. L *viduitat-, viduitas*, fr. *vidua* widow + *-itat-, -itas* -ity] : WIDOWHOOD
¹vie *n* -s [modif. of MF *envi*, fr. OF, invitation, challenge, wager, fr. *envier* to invite, challenge, wager a sum at cards] *obs* : CHALLENGE, WAGER
²vie \ˈvī\ *vb* **vied; vied; vying; vies** [modif. of MF *envier*, fr. OF, to invite, challenge, wager a sum at cards, fr. L *invitare* to invite, challenge — more at INVITE] *vi* : to strive for superiority : CONTEND ⟨politicians *vying* with each other⟩ ⟨nations *vying* for international trade⟩ ~ *vt* : to hazard, stake, or wager ⟨~ money on the turn of a card⟩; *also* : to exchange in rivalry : MATCH ⟨~ accusation against accusation⟩
vie·ji·tos \vyäˈhēˌtōs\ *n pl but sing in constr* [MexSp, fr. Sp, little old men, pl. of *viejito* old man, dim. of *viejo* old man, fr. *viejo*, adj., old, fr. L *vetulus*, fr. *vetus* old — more at WETHER] : a comic dance of the Tarascan Indians performed by young men dressed and masked as old men
vielle \ˈvyel\ *n* -s [F — more at VIOL] **1** : a large medieval viol of the 12th and 13th centuries **2** : HURDY-GURDY 1
vi·en·na \vēˈenə\ *adj, usu cap* [fr. *Vienna*, Austria] : of or from Vienna, the capital of Austria : of the kind or style prevalent in Vienna
vienna brown *n, often cap V* : GOLD BRONZE 2
vienna coup *n, usu cap V* : a squeeze in bridge or whist that is introduced by the cashing of a winning card that establishes an opponent's card
vienna green *n, often cap V* : EMERALD 2a
vienna lake *n, often cap V* : CARMINE 2
vienna lime *n, usu cap V* : a high-magnesia lime specially prepared from calcined dolomite for use as a buffing and polishing material esp. for metals, plastics, and glass
vienna red *n, often cap V* : vermilion or a color resembling it
vienna sausage *n, usu cap V* : a short slender frankfurter in a thin casing usu. having the ends cut off
vienna smoke *n, often cap V* : SMOKE BROWN
vienna system *n, usu cap V* : a method of bidding in contract bridge that is a modification of the club convention
¹vi·en·nese \ˌvēəˈnēz, -nēs\ *adj, usu cap* [*Vienna*, Austria + E *-ese*] **1** : of or belonging to Vienna, Austria **2** : characteristic of Vienna or the Viennese
²viennese \"\ *n, pl* **viennese** *cap* **1** : a native or resident of Vienna, Austria **2** : the dialect of German spoken in Vienna
vien·tiane \(ˈ)vyenˈtyän\ *adj, usu cap* [fr. *Vientiane*, Laos] : of or from Vientiane, the capital of Laos : of the kind or style prevalent in Vientiane
vi·er \ˈvī(ə)r\ *n* -s [²*vie* + *-er*] : one that vies (as for supremacy)
vie·ren·deel truss \ˈvirənˌdāl-\ *or* **vierendeel girder** *n, usu cap V* [after M. *Vierendeel*, Belgian engineer who invented it in 1896] : an open-web truss with vertical members but without diagonals and with rigid joints
viet \vēˈet, ˈvyet\ *n* -s *usu cap* [short for *Vietminh*] : a member of the Vietminh
vi et armis \ˈvīēˈtärməs\ *adv* [L] : with force and arms — used of a trespass to person or property which is the immediate cause of damage; compare MANU FORTI
viet·cong \vēˈetˈkäŋ, ˈvyet-, -ˈkȯŋ, *also* ¦vēət- *or* ˈvēt-\ *n, pl* **vietcong** *usu cap* : an adherent of the Vietnamese communist movement supported by North Vietnam and engaged esp. in guerrilla warfare in South Vietnam
viet·minh \vēˈetˈmin, ˈvyet-, *also* ¦vēət- *or* -mēn *or* ˈvētˈmin\ *n, pl* **vietminh** *or* **vietminhs** *usu cap* : an adherent of the Vietnamese communist movement
viet·nam \-¦näm, -nam, -nȧm\ *adj, usu cap* [fr. *Vietnam*, country in Indochina] : of or from Vietnam : of the kind or style prevalent in Vietnam : VIETNAMESE
¹viet·nam·ese \vēˌetnəˈmēz, ¦vyet-, -t(ˌ)naˈm-, -t(ˌ)näˈm-, -mēs *also* ¦vēət- *or* ¦vēt-\ *adj, usu cap* [*Vietnam* + E *-ese*] **1 a** : of, relating to, or characteristic of Vietnam **b** : of, relating to, or characteristic of the people of Vietnam **2** : of, relating to, or characteristic of the Vietnamese language
²vietnamese \"\ *n, pl* **vietnamese** *cap* **1** : a native or inhabitant of Vietnam **2** : the language of the largest group in Vietnam and the official language of the country — compare MUONG
¹view \ˈvyü\ *n* -s [ME *vewe*, fr. MF *veue, vue*, fr. OF, fr. fem. of *veu, vu*, past part. of *veeir, veoir, voir* to see, fr. L *vidēre* — more at WIT] **1** : the act of seeing or beholding; *specif* : an inspection by the jury of a court of law of a place where a litigated transaction (as a crime or tort) occurred or of premises or some other object (as a corpse) involved in a legal proceeding **2** : a formal examination : INSPECTION ⟨a close ~ of all details⟩ : SURVEY ⟨a ~ of German literature⟩ **3** : mode or manner of looking at or regarding something : CONCEPTION, GRASP ⟨an imperfect ~ of parliamentary government⟩ **4** : an overall survey : complete summary ⟨a columnist's ~ of the world crisis⟩ **5** : what is revealed to the vision or can usu. be seen ⟨the ~ from a picture window⟩; *also* : an extensive or imposing prospect : PANORAMA ⟨Alpine ~*s*⟩ **6** : extent or range of vision : SIGHT ⟨no ships in ~⟩ **7 a** : something that is looked toward or kept in sight : OBJECT, AIM ⟨with no ~ in mind⟩ ⟨diplomatic maneuvers with a ~ to establishing a clear case⟩ **b** : something that is expected : PROSPECT ⟨no hope in ~⟩ **8 a** : a pictorial representation : SKETCH ⟨a photographic ~ of the local town hall⟩; *also* : DIAGRAM **b** : the graphic projection of an object upon a plane obtained by finding the intersections with the plane of parallel lines drawn through the points of the object **9** *dial* : APPEARANCE, ASPECT ⟨if you're an ugly man to be looking at, I'm thinking your tongue's worse than your ~ —J.M.Synge⟩ **10** : intellectual makeup : spiritual and cultural nature ⟨literary themes which reveal the ~ of their author⟩ **syn** see OPINION — **at the view** *adv* : by sight — usu. used in the phrase *hunt at the view* — **in view of** *prep* : in regard to : in consideration of ⟨a failure *in view of* financial returns⟩ — **on view** : on exhibition : open to public inspection ⟨model homes *on view*⟩
²view \"\ *vt* -ED/-ING/-S **1 a** : to examine carefully or officially : INSPECT ⟨~ evidence⟩ ⟨~ records⟩ **b** *archaic* : EXPLORE **2** : to look at attentively : SCRUTINIZE, OBSERVE ⟨~ a landscape⟩ **3** : to consider esp. with earnest attention or with an attempt at wide or overall comprehension ⟨~ a problem⟩ : take under consideration ⟨~ applications for membership⟩ **syn** see SEE
view·able \-üəbəl\ *adj* **1** : capable of being seen or inspected ⟨~ evidence⟩ **2** : likely to be or possessing enough appeal to be viewed ⟨a ~ television show⟩
view angle *n* : the angle included by a photographic lens as determined from the ratio of the focal length to the diameter of the field : ANGLE OF VIEW
view camera *n* : a camera having a rising, tilting, and swinging front, a removable lens board, a long bellows, a focusing cloth, a ground-glass focusing screen, a tilting and swinging back, a plate or film holder, and a rack-and-pinion adjustment
view·er \ˈvyüə(r), -yü(ə)r, -yüə\ *n* -s [ME *vewer*, fr. *vewe* view + *-er* — more at VIEW] : one that views: as **a** : a person legally appointed to inspect and report on property (as highways) **b** : an optical device of any of several forms used to assist in viewing (as photographic transparencies) **c** : a person who watches television
viewfinder \ˈ=,==\ *n* : FINDER 5
view halloo *also* **view hallo** *or* **view halloa** *n* : a shout uttered by a hunter on seeing a fox break cover; *also* : a shout indicating or announcing the appearance of something
viewing *n* -s [fr. gerund of ²*view*] **1** : an act of seeing or taking a look (as at scenery or an exhibition) ⟨the ~ of the new models⟩; *specif* : a period when visitors may view a body in a funeral parlor **2** : the watching of television
viewing glass *n* : a colored filter used in viewing the scene to be photographed in order to anticipate how the scene will be reproduced
view·less \ˈvyüləs\ *adj* **1** : affording no view **2** : expressing no views or opinions **3** : not perceivable : INVISIBLE
view·less·ly *adv* [*viewless* + *-ly*] : INVISIBLY
view of frankpledge [ME, trans. of AF *vewe de fraung plege*] : the gathering and inspection in the court leet at least once a year of all the men who were or ought to be in frankpledge
viewpoint \ˈ=,=\ *n* **1** : an attitude of mind from which something is considered ⟨incapable of comprehending another person's ~ —Ruth Park⟩ **2** : a position from which something is observed ⟨describes his own method of photographing motor races, and gives hints on the choice of subjects and ~*s* —*Eastman Kodak Monthly Abstract Bull.*⟩
views *pl of* VIEW, *pres 3d sing of* VIEW
view window *n* : PICTURE WINDOW
viewy \ˈvyüē, -üi\ *adj* -ER/-EST **1** : possessing visionary, impractical, or fantastic views **2** : spectacular or arresting in appearance : SHOWY ⟨a ~ little socialite⟩
vi·ga \ˈvēgə\ *n* -s [Sp, beam, rafter] : one of the heavy rafters that is often a log and that supports the roof in the native Indian and Spanish colonial architecture of the Southwest
vi·ge·nère cipher \ˌvēzhəˈne(ə)r-\ *n, usu cap V* [after Blaise de *Vigenère* †1596 Fr. diplomat and student of cryptography] : polyalphabetic substitution with alphabets derived from one pair of primary alphabets by sliding (as in the Vigenère tableau) for which the usual keying formula is P+K=C where P is the position of the plaintext letter in the plain component, C that of the ciphertext letter in the cipher sequence, and K that of the key letter in the normal alphabet and where positions are numbered from 0 to 25 and 26 is subtracted from sums above 25 — compare BEAUFORT CIPHER, PROGRESSIVE-ALPHABET CIPHER
vigenère tableau *also* **vigenère table** *or* **vigenère square** *n, usu cap V* [after B. de *Vigenère*] : a square cipher table formed by placing the same normal or mixed primary alphabet one step farther to the left on each successive line and used by reading the ciphertext letter within the table in the row and column defined by key and plaintext letters in alphabets in the left and top margins respectively
¹vi·gen·ten·ni·al \ˌvījenˈtenēəl\ *adj* [L *vigeni, viceni* twenty each + E *-tennial* (as in *centennial*) — more at VICENARY] : occurring once every 20 years : relating to a 20th anniversary
²vigentennial \"\ *n* -s : a 20th anniversary or its celebration
vi·ges·i·mal \(ˈ)vīˈjesəməl\ *adj* [L *vigesimus, vicesimus* twentieth + E *-al*; akin to L *viginti* twenty — more at VICENARY] : based on the number 20
vi·ges·i·mo-quarto \(ˈ)vīˌjesə(ˌ)mō+\ *or* **vi·ces·i·mo-quarto** \-ˈīˌse-+\ *n* [L, abl. of *vigesimus-quartus, vicesimus-quartus* twenty-fourth, fr. *vigesimus, vicesimus* twentieth + *quartus* fourth — more at QUART] : TWENTY-FOURMO — see BOOK tables
vi·gia \vəˈjēə, vēˈhēə\ *n* -s [Sp *vigía* watch, vigil, rock, reef, fr. Pg *vigia*, fr. *vigiar* to watch, keep vigil, fr. L *vigilare* — more at VIGILANT] : a mark made on a nautical chart indicating a dangerous rock or shoal and used chiefly on Spanish charts
vig·il \ˈvijəl\ *n* -s [ME *vigile*, fr. OF, fr. LL & L; LL *vigilia* watch on the eve of a religious festival, fr. L, wakefulness, watch, fr. *vigil* awake, alert; akin to L *vigēre* to be vigorous, flourish, *vegēre* to rouse, excite, be active — more at WAKE] **1 a** : a watch formerly kept on the night before a religious feast and customarily spent in prayer or other devotions **b** : the day before a religious feast observed as a day of spiritual preparation **c** : a religious service on the morning of the day before a holy day **2 a** : evening or nocturnal devotions or prayers — usu. used in pl. **b** : devotional watching ⟨nobles standing ~ by the coffin of their dead monarch⟩ **3 a** : the act or action of keeping awake esp. at times when sleep is customary; *also* : a period of wakefulness ⟨an all-night ~ spent awaiting the arrival of a celebrity⟩ **b** : unrelenting, hostile, or oppressive observation ⟨guards keeping ~ over a noisy mob⟩; *also* : a steady gaze or stare **4 a** : an act or action of wakeful watching : WATCH ⟨keep ~ all night beside a sickbed⟩; *also* : the period spent in wakeful watching **b** : a protracted and usu. lonely stay or sojourn ⟨a five-month ~ near the polar ice pack⟩
vig·i·lance \ˈvijələn(t)s\ *n* -s [MF, fr. L *vigilantia* wakefulness, vigilance, fr. *vigilant-, vigilans* + *-ia* -y] **1** : the quality or state of being vigilant : watchfulness in respect of danger or hazard ⟨constant ~ against the spread of disease⟩ **2** : readiness or alertness esp. to respond to stimuli ⟨the ~ of a person's nerves⟩
vigilance committee *n* : a volunteer committee of citizens for the oversight and protection of an interest; *esp* : a committee organized to suppress and punish crime summarily (as when the processes of law appear inadequate) — compare VIGILANTE
vig·i·lant \-nt\ *adj* [ME, fr. MF, fr. L *vigilant-, vigilans*, fr. pres. part. of *vigilare* to be awake, watch, keep vigil, fr. *vigil* awake, alert — more at VIGIL] : alertly or watchfully awake; *esp* : alert or watchful to discover and avoid danger ⟨a ~ mountain climber⟩ ⟨a ~ treasurer⟩ **syn** see WATCHFUL
vig·i·lan·te \ˌvijəˈlantē, -län-, -ti\ *n* -s *often attrib* [Sp, watchman, guard, fr. *vigilante*, adj., watchful, vigilant, fr. L *vigilant-, vigilans*] : a member of a vigilance committee ⟨~ work⟩ ⟨a ~ system⟩
vig·i·lan·tism \-nˌtizəm\ *n* -s [*vigilante* + *-ism*] : the policy or practice of vigilantes
vig·i·lant·ly *adv* : in a vigilant manner : ALERTLY, WATCHFULLY
vig·i·lant·ness *n* -ES : the quality or state of being vigilant
vigil light *n* **1** : a candle lighted by a worshiper in a Roman Catholic church for a specific religious purpose (as the veneration of a saint) **2** : a candle or small lamp burning before a shrine, memorial, statue, or image
vi·gin·ten·ni·al \ˌvījinˈtenēəl\ *adj or n* [L *viginti* twenty + E *-ennial* (as in *centennial*) — more at VICENARY] : VIGENTENNIAL
vi·gin·til·lion \ˌ==ˈtilyən\ *n* -s *often attrib* [L *viginti* twenty + E *-illion* (as in *million*)] — see NUMBER table
vig·na \ˈvignə\ *n, cap* [NL, after Domenico *Vigna* †1647 Ital. botanist] : a genus of vines or erect herbs (family Leguminosae) found in warm or tropical regions and having trifoliolate leaves, yellowish or purplish flowers with an eared vexillum, and a linear and 2-valved pod — see COWPEA
vi·gne·ron \ˌvēnyəˈrōn\ *n* -s [ME *vigneroun*, fr. MF *vigneron*, fr. OF *vineron*, fr. *vine, vigne* vine, vineyard — more at VINE] : WINEGROWER, VITICULTURIST
¹vi·gnette \(ˈ)vinˈyet, (ˈ)vēn-, *usu* -ed·+V\ *n* -s [F, fr. MF *vignete* young vine, vignette, dim. of *vigne* vine — more at VINE] **1** : a running ornament (as of vine leaves, tendrils, and grapes) put on or just before the title page or at the beginning or end of a chapter of a manuscript or book; *also* : a small decorative design or picture so placed **2 a** : a picture (as an engraving or photograph) that shades off gradually into the surrounding ground or the unprinted paper; *also* : the rough or serrated edged mask used to print the picture **b** : a picture on a postage stamp : the pictorial part of a stamp design as distinguished from the frame and lettering **3** : a short literary sketch chiefly descriptive and characterized usu. by delicacy, wit, and subtlety
²vignette \"\ *vt* -ED/-ING/-S **1** : to apply a vignette to ⟨*vignetted* plates⟩ **2** : to finish (as a photograph) in the manner of a vignette **3** : to describe or sketch delicately or subtly
vi·gnet·ter \-ed·ə(r)\ *n* -s **1** : one who makes vignettes : VIGNETTIST **2** : a photographic device for vignetting (as a screen with an aperture the edges of which insensibly become opaque)
vignetting *n* -s **1** : a reduction in intensity of illumination at the edges of a field of view of an optical instrument due to the restrictive action of the edge of the aperture for rays that are not axial **2** : the progressive reduction in the illumination falling on a photographic film towards the corners of the picture due to the obstruction of oblique light beams by the lens mount
vi·gnet·tist \-ed·əst\ *n* -s : an artist, designer, or author who produces vignettes
vi·gnoles rail \(ˈ)vinˈyōlz-\ *n, usu cap V* [after Charles B. *Vignoles* †1875 Eng. engineer] : T RAIL
vi·gogne yarn \vēˈgōnʸ-, -ōn-\ *n* [*vigogne* fr. F, vicuña, fabric made from vicuña wool, fr. Sp *vicuña* — more at VICUÑA] : a yarn spun from a blend of cotton and wool and used chiefly for clothing fabrics
vig·or \ˈvigə(r)\ *n* -s *see -or in Explan Notes* [ME *vigour*, fr. MF *vigeur*, fr. L *vigor*, fr. *vigēre* to be vigorous, flourish + *-or* — more at VIGIL] **1** : active strength or force of body or mind : capacity for physical, intellectual, or moral exertion : effective energy or power ⟨the ~ of youth⟩ ⟨the ~ of a storm⟩ **2** : strength or force in animal or vegetable nature or action ⟨a plant grows with ~⟩ **3** : intensity of action or effect : FORCE, ENERGY ⟨the ~ of an argument⟩ ⟨commanding a troop with ~⟩ ⟨a drug that acts with ~⟩ **4** : effective legal status : VALIDITY ⟨laws that are still in ~⟩
syn VIGOR, VIM, SPIRIT, DASH, ESPRIT, VERVE, PUNCH, ÉLAN, and DRIVE denote, in common, a quality of force, forcefulness, or energy. VIGOR implies active good health and native robustness or a display of energy or forcefulness deriving from it or befitting it ⟨the physical and intellectual *vigor* and toughness which the trial lawyer needs —Robert Hale⟩ ⟨the *vigor* and inventiveness that American business has shown in many other fields —*Defense Against Recession*⟩ ⟨burst into leaf with exceptional *vigor* —*Amer. Guide Series: Md.*⟩ ⟨a wonderfully witty book, with an intellectual *vigor* —Paul Pickrel⟩ VIM stresses the display of usu. enthusiastic energy in doing or making something ⟨enter into an enterprise with a good deal of *vim*⟩ ⟨the *vim* and energy with which he spoke was exhausting to the audience⟩ SPIRIT stresses a driving vivacity, liveliness, or animated interest usu. deriving from disposition or temperament ⟨enter into a campaign with *spirit*⟩ ⟨on the eve of a match the players worked up *spirit* by celebrations —*Amer. Guide Series: Fla.*⟩ DASH implies a bold, devil-may-care force, often tending to stress the impact upon the observer, reader, or listener ⟨the picture really captures the obsessive *dash* of professional airmen —*Time*⟩ ⟨their lineaments and general contours to be drawn with Düreresque vigor and *dash* —Thomas Hardy⟩ ⟨his study . . . aspiring to make up in liveliness, *dash*, and clarity what it is bound to lack in analytical rigor —Clifton Fadiman⟩ ⟨lack of oratorical *dash* —N.F.Busch⟩ ESPRIT is a quality of interest or energy of mind or disposition more subtly manifest than spirit and often strongly implying active cleverness or wit ⟨there are men of *esprit* who are excessively exhausting to some people —O.W.Holmes †1894⟩ ⟨acquire the industrial *esprit* that could spark general economic advance —David Riesman⟩ VERVE suggests strongly a characteristic or peculiar active energy or interest ⟨writing with the *verve* and gusto dear to the mid-nineteenth century —Mary Ross⟩ ⟨both sing with shattering *verve* —Herbert Weinstock⟩ ⟨the dancers performed with *verve* —Douglas Watt⟩ ⟨tells his story . . . with unquenchable *verve* and enthusiasm —*Times Lit. Supp.*⟩ ⟨recited King Henry V's speech before the battle of Agincourt with such *verve* that she brought the house down —Bruce Marshall⟩ PUNCH stresses forcefulness of impact or immediate effectiveness ⟨a speech with very little *punch*⟩ ⟨the poem which I have chosen seems to me . . . to be crisp in its language and also to carry a considerable *punch* —Louis MacNeice⟩ ⟨coconut sap is poured to make toddy — which looks like milk but has a *punch* —*N. Y. Times Mag.*⟩ ÉLAN stresses a spirit or quality marked by ardor or spiritedness in action ⟨marching in perfect formation and with military *élan* —Philip Hamburger⟩ ⟨clears his hurdles with agility and *élan* —*Times Lit. Supp.*⟩ ⟨a real victory would give them a great *élan* for the sterner tests yet to come —D.D.Eisenhower⟩ DRIVE stresses an unremitting purposive action or forcefulness resulting from a large reservoir of energy ⟨lack the *drive*, the initiative, and the sense of aggression necessary to carry out a planned crime of violence —D.W.Maurer & V.H.Vogel⟩ ⟨this titan's spirit which gave such *drive* and strength to the mightiest of his plays —John Mason Brown⟩ ⟨enough *drive* to achieve success in almost any field⟩
vig·or·ish \ˈvigərish\ *n* -ES [prob. fr. Yiddish, fr. Russ *vyigrysh* winnings, profit] **1** : a charge taken (as by a bookie or gambling house) on bets; *also* : the degree of such a charge ⟨a ~ of 5 percent⟩ **2** : interest paid to a moneylender
vig·or·less \ˈvigə(r)ləs\ *adj* : lacking vigor : LISTLESS, WEAK
vi·go·ro·so \ˌvēgəˈrō(ˌ)sō\ *adj (or adv)* [It, vigorous, fr. OIt, fr. MF *vigorous*] : energetic in style — used as a direction in music
vig·or·ous \ˈvig(ə)rəs\ *adj* [ME, fr. MF, fr. OF, fr. *vigour, vigeur* vigor + *-ous*] **1** : possessing vigor : full of physical or mental strength or active force : STRONG ⟨a ~ youth⟩ ⟨a ~ plant⟩ **2** : exhibiting strength either of body or mind : POWERFUL, STRONG ⟨~ exertions⟩ ⟨a ~ prosecution of a war⟩ ⟨a ~ protest⟩ **3** : done with vigor : carried out forcefully and energetically : enforced strictly ⟨took ~ measures to stop the practice⟩ ⟨~ enforcement of the country's laws⟩
syn ENERGETIC, STRENUOUS, LUSTY, NERVOUS: VIGOROUS suggests active strength, force, reserve vitality, and undiminished or pulsing robustness of body or freshness and ability of mind ⟨the *vigorous* mother of a large family⟩ ⟨his *vigorous* industry that produced so many full-bodied books before his death at forty-four —H.T.Moore⟩ ⟨a *vigorous* critic of materialism, complacency, and hazy thinking —*Current Biog.*⟩ ENERGETIC may apply to display of or capacity for great activity, sometimes bustling or ambitious ⟨displayed a highly cultivated and *energetic* mind, full of impassioned schemes of liberty, and impatience of masculine usurpation —T.L. Peacock⟩ ⟨restless, *energetic*, impetuous, temperamental, and at times a little irascible —A.W.Long⟩ STRENUOUS suggests the constantly energetic; used of persons and their inclinations, it

may indicate a pleasure in or preference for coping with the arduous or vigorous ⟨if you want an incentive to act, if you want to live the *strenuous* life —Alfred Buchanan⟩ ⟨attribute the winning of the West principally to the *strenuous* virtues of Teutonic males —Howard M. Jones⟩ ⟨a *strenuous* and sometimes violently abusive opponent of every political movement that threatens to curtail her leisure —G.B.Shaw⟩ LUSTY suggests a healthy vitality and exuberant energy, with a robust and unrestrained inclination for enjoyment ⟨the native men and half a dozen *lusty* girls shouting and laughing as they put their backs into the work —C.B.Nordhoff & J.N.Hall⟩ ⟨the *lusty* American spirit of active, vigorous living —Bud Wilson⟩ NERVOUS may suggest continuing activity, often forceful, arising from an energetic temperament ⟨his rhythm has a pulsating and *nervous* vitality —Robert Collet⟩ ⟨the suppleness of youthful fingers, the *nervous* alertness of youthful brains, and the stamina of youthful bodies —*Amer. Guide Series: Mich.*⟩ ⟨the *nervous* new civilization of the Texas cities —T.H.White b. 1915⟩

vig·or·ous·ly *adv* [ME, fr. *vigorous* + *-ly*] **:** in a vigorous manner **:** FORCEFULLY

vig·or·ous·ness *n* -ES [ME *vigorousnesse*, fr. *vigorous* + *-nesse* -ness] **:** the quality or state of being vigorous **:** FORCEFULNESS

vigour *chiefly Brit var of* VIGOR

vi·gou·reux \ˌvēgəˈrə\ *n*, *pl* **vigoureux** \"\ *often attrib* [*vigoureux* (*printing*)] **:** a yarn or fabric colored by vigoureux printing

vigoureux printing *n* [after *Vigoureux*, 19th cent. Fr. textile printer who invented it] **:** a method of printing woolen sliver before spinning to produce a mixed usu. black and white color effect in yarn and fabric

vi·greux column \vēˈgrə-\ *n*, *usu cap V* [prob. after Léon *Vigreux* †1891 Fr. hydraulic engineer] **:** a long unpacked glass tube for use in laboratory fractional distillation that is characterized by many deep pointed indentations in its sidewall and has an opening at the top for a thermometer and a side arm near the top for attachment to a condenser

vi·ha·ra \vəˈhärə\ *n* -S [Skt *vihāra*, lit., place of recreation, fr. *viharati* he spends time, he walks about for pleasure, fr. *vi* apart, asunder + *harati* he takes, carries — more at WITH, YARD] **:** a Buddhist monastery or temple

vi·hue·la \vēˈwālə\ *n* -S [Sp] **1 :** the early Spanish viol **2 :** the Spanish lute

vi·jao \vēˈhä(ˌ)ō\ *n* -S [Sp *vijao*, *bijao*, *vihao*, *bihao*, fr. Taino *bihao*] **:** a tropical herb (*Amomum exaltatum*) whose seeds are used in Puerto Rico as a source of black coloring matter

vij·na·na·va·da \vijˌnänəˈvädə\ *n* -S *usu cap* [Skt *vijñānavāda*, fr. *vijñāna* discrimination, intelligence (fr. *vijānāti* he distinguishes, understands, fr. *vi-* apart + *jānāti* he knows) + *vāda* speech, discourse, doctrine, fr. *vadati* he speaks, says — more at WITH, KNOW, ODE] **:** the subjective idealism taught by the Yogacara school of Buddhist philosophy

vi·king \ˈvīkiŋ, -kēŋ\ *n* -S [ON *víkingr*, prob. fr. *vík* small inlet, creek, bay + *-ingr* -ing — more at WICK (creek)] **1 a** *usu cap* **:** one belonging to the pirate crews from among the Northmen plundering the coasts of Europe in the 8th to 10th centuries **b :** SEA ROVER **2** *usu cap* **:** SCANDINAVIAN

vil *abbr* village

vi·la \ˈvēlə\ *n*, *pl* **vilas** \-əz\ *or* **vi·ly** \-lē\ [Slovenian & Serbo-Croatian; akin to ORuss & Bulg *vila* and perh. to Lith *vyti* to chase, pursue, Skt *veti* he goes, advances — more at VIM] **:** a supernatural being of Slavonic lands sometimes held to inhabit hills and woods and appear in the form of a beautiful young woman **:** FAIRY

vi·la·yet \vēˈläˌyet, ˌvēləˈyet\ *n* -S [Turk *vilâyet*, fr. Ar *wilāyat*, fr. *walīy* governor] **:** one of the chief administrative divisions of Turkey having as head a vali who represents the government and is assisted by an elective council and being subdivided into cazas

vild \ˈvīld\ *adj* [by alter.] *archaic* **:** VILE

¹vile \ˈvīl, *esp before pause or consonant* -īəl\ *adj* -ER/-EST [ME *vil*, *vile*, fr. OF *vil*, fr. L *vilis* cheap, base, vile; perh. akin to L *venus*, *venum* sale — more at VENAL] **1 :** of small worth or account ⟨the sea, wherein he counts not one inch of ~ dominion —Robert Browning⟩ **:** of inferior quality or state **:** COMMON ⟨Savior . . . shall change our ~ body, that it may be fashioned like unto his glorious body —Phil 3:21 (AV)⟩ **:** MEAN ⟨wrapped in a ~ disguise —P.B.Shelley⟩ **2 a :** morally despicable or abhorrent ⟨instills ~ suspicions into her confiding soul —Karl Polanyi⟩ ⟨the *vilest* specimens of human nature are to be found among demagogues —T.B.Macaulay⟩ **b :** physically repulsive (as from filth or corruption) **:** FOUL ⟨the plagues that came from the ~ unsanitary quarters of the industrial city —Lewis Mumford⟩ **3 :** tending to degrade a person **:** HUMILIATING, IGNOMINIOUS ⟨a slave, in the *vilest* of all positions —F. W.Farrar⟩ **4 a :** disgustingly bad or inferior **:** highly objectionable ⟨in a ~ temper⟩ **:** CONTEMPTIBLE ⟨the ~ habit of thinking that the latest is always the best —M.R.Cohen⟩ ⟨a ~ climate⟩ ⟨~ handwriting⟩ ⟨writes ~ verse⟩ **b :** GREAT, EXTREME — used intensively with nouns denoting a bad quality or state ⟨protecting her against the *vilest* evil Europe has yet produced —Beverley Nichols⟩ **syn** see BASE

²vile \"\ *adv* [ME *vil*, *vile*, fr. *vil*, *vile*, adj.] **:** VILELY — used chiefly in combination ⟨*vile*-smelling⟩

vi·le·la \vēˈlālə\ *n*, *pl* **vilela** *or* **vilelas** *usu cap* [Sp, of Amer-Ind origin] **1 :** a group of peoples of northwestern Argentina **2 :** a member of a Vilela people

vile·ly \ˈvī(ə)llē, -iˌ\ *adv* [ME *vily*, fr. *vil*, *vile* + *-ly*] **:** in a vile manner ⟨the suit was ~ botched and skimped —Thomas Wolfe⟩

vile·ness *n* -ES **1 :** the quality or state of being vile **2 :** an instance of vileness **3 :** something vile ⟨addressed a final ~ at the caricaturer —D.C.Loughlin⟩

vil·i·fi·ca·tion \ˌviləfəˈkāshən\ *n* -S [ML *vilification-*, *vilificatio*, fr. LL *vilificatus* (past part. of *vilificare*) + L *-ion-*, *-io* -ion] **1 :** the act of vilifying **:** ABUSE **2 :** an instance of vilifying **:** defamatory utterance

vil·i·fi·er \ˈviləˌfī(ə)r, -īə\ *n* -S **:** one that vilifies

vil·i·fy \-ˌfī\ *vb* -ED/-ING/-ES [ME *vilifien*, fr. LL *vilificare*, fr. L *vilis* cheap, base, vile + *-ficare* -fy — more at VILE] *vt* **1 a :** to make less valuable or important **:** lower in estimation ⟨declare that opposition to the established system was an effort to destroy and ~ religion —C.L.Jones⟩ **b** *obs* **:** to make morally despicable or abhorrent **:** DEGRADE ⟨themselves they *vilified* to serve ungoverned appetite —John Milton⟩ **2 a** *obs* **:** to speak slightingly or contemptuously of ⟨the disposition of vulgar minds to ridicule and ~ what they cannot comprehend —Samuel Johnson⟩ **b :** to utter slanderous and abusive statements against **:** denounce unjustly or abuse as hateful or vile **:** DEFAME, TRADUCE ⟨his policies . . . attacked; his personal character *vilified* —William Peden⟩ ~ *vi* **1 :** to cause a person to become vile ⟨nothing *vilifies* and degrades more than pride —Earl of Chesterfield⟩ **2 :** to utter or publish slander **syn** see MALIGN

vil·i·fy·ing·ly *adv* **:** in a vilifying manner

vil·i·pend \ˈviləˌpend\ *vb* -ED/-ING/-S [ME *vilipenden*, fr. MF *vilipender*, fr. ML *vilipendere*, fr. L *vilis* cheap, base, vile + *pendere* to weigh, estimate — more at PENDANT] *vt* **1 :** to hold or treat as of small worth or account **:** CONTEMN ⟨that petulant volatility which . . . ~s the conversation and advice of seniors —Sir Walter Scott⟩ **2 :** to speak of slightingly or disparagingly **:** express a low opinion of **:** DEPRECIATE ⟨a censorious critic might ~ it . . . as want of imagination —Frederick Pollock⟩ ~ *vi* **:** to be disparaging or depreciatory

vil·i·ty \ˈviləd·ē\ *n* -ES [ME *vilite*, fr. MF *vilité*, fr. L *vilitat-*, *vilitas* cheapness, baseness, vileness, fr. *vilis* cheap, base, vile + *-itat-*, *-itas* -ity — more at VILE] **1** *archaic* **:** VILENESS, BASENESS **2** *obs* **:** lowness of estate or value

vill \ˈvil\ *n* -S [AF *vill*, *vile*, fr. OF *ville*, *vile* farm, village — more at VILLAGE] **1 :** a division of a hundred for purposes of administration and taxation in English feudal law orig. equivalent to a manor and superseded by the parish **:** TOWNSHIP **2 :** VILLAGE

vill *abbr* village

vil·la \ˈvilə\ *n* -S [It, fr. L, country house, country estate; akin to L *vicus* row of houses, village — more at VICINITY] **1 :** a country estate: **a :** a pretentious rural or suburban residence with extensive grounds maintained as a pleasurable retreat from city life by a person of wealth **b** *Brit* **:** a detached or semidetached urban residence with yard and garden space **2** *pl also* **vil·lae** \-iˌlē\ [L] **:** an agricultural estate of Roman or early medieval times

vil·la·dom \-lədəm\ *n* -S [*villa* + *-dom*] *Brit* **:** the world constituted by villas and their occupants **:** SUBURBIA

vil·lage \ˈvilij, -lēj\ *n* -S *often attrib* [ME, fr. MF, fr. OF, fr. *ville*, *vile* farm, village (fr. L *villa* country house, country estate, village) + *-age*] **1 a :** a unit of compact settlement varying in size but usu. larger than a hamlet and smaller than a town and distinguished from surrounding rural territory **:** a small cluster of houses and other buildings (as stores and churches) forming a unit distinct from a surrounding rural area **b (1) :** one incorporated and given definite boundaries and powers by law **:** a minor municipality ⟨the distinction between cities and ~*s* is not one of size and population, but rather one of powers —F.A.Ogg & P.O.Ray⟩ **(2) :** an incorporated municipal unit in some states (as New York) having a separate status and some independent powers although still constituting part of the parent town ⟨a thickly settled area in a town, faced with some problems of living close together, may be incorporated into a ~ —*Our State & Local Gov't of N. Y.*⟩ **(3) :** an incorporated municipal unit in a Canadian province varying in population but usu. smaller than a town **c :** a unit of settlement having or held to have the status of a village but differing from the traditional village in some important respect: as **(1) :** one having a large population ⟨Spanish agricultural ~*s* of 10,000 or more inhabitants⟩ **(2) :** one constituting a unit in a predominantly urban rather than rural territory **2 a :** the citizens or inhabitants of a village ⟨the entire ~ turned out to welcome him⟩ **b :** the qualified voters of a village ⟨the ~ elects a council of five members⟩ **c :** the governing officials of a village acting on behalf of the village as a corporation or of the whole body of inhabitants ⟨the ~ purchased land for a new school⟩ **3 :** something (as an aggregation of burrows) resembling or suggesting a village ⟨a prairie dog ~⟩ **4 a :** a territorial area having the status of a village esp. as a unit of local government ⟨paved streets in the ~ but not in the rest of the town⟩ **b :** a section or district of a larger municipality (as a city) having characteristics that set it apart as an individual unit resembling a village ⟨Greenwich ~ in New York⟩ **5 :** a relatively small group of people organized chiefly in families that constitutes a distinct social unit and usu. forms a community **6 :** any of various groups of residential and related buildings; *specif* **:** an institution (as for children requiring special care) providing residence in small groups occupying separate cottages

village cart *n* **:** CART 3b

village economy *n* **:** a stage in economic history following that in which agriculture is the principal pursuit and having for its characteristic features the village, barter trading, and little division of labor

vil·lage·less \-jləs\ *adj* **:** having no village

vil·lage·ous \-jəs\ *adj* **:** of or relating to a village or villagers

vil·lag·er \-jə(r)\ *n* -S **:** an inhabitant or resident of a village

vil·lage·ry \-jrē\ *n* -ES [*village* + *-ery*] **:** VILLAGES

vil·lagey *or* **vil·lagy** \-jē\ *adj* **:** resembling or suggesting a village (as in size, appearance, or habits)

vil·lag·ism \-ˌjizəm\ *n* -S **:** a word, form, or expression characteristic of village or rural speech as contrasted with urban

¹vil·lain \ˈvilən\ *n* -S [ME *vilein*, *vilain*, fr. MF, fr. ML *villanus*, fr. L *villa* country house, country estate, village + *-anus* -an — more at VILLA] **1 :** VILLEIN **2 :** a person of uncouth mind and manners **:** BOOR **3 :** a person of depraved and malevolent character devoted to base or evil acts **:** one who deliberately plots and does serious harm to others **4 :** a character in a story or play who opposes the hero **5 :** a person or thing blamed for a particular evil or difficulty ⟨the ~ of the Government's case . . . is the paper's advertising director —*Time*⟩ ⟨ozone, a form of oxygen, has been previously reported as a chief and elusive ~ in the . . . smog problem —*N.Y.Times*⟩

syn SCOUNDREL, BLACKGUARD, KNAVE, RASCAL, ROGUE, SCAMP, RAPSCALLION, MISCREANT: these words as here considered all describe low, mean, and reprehensible characters. VILLAIN describes one utterly given to crime, evil, and baseness ⟨were not made *villains* by the commission of a crime, but were *villains* before they committed it —John Ruskin⟩ SCOUNDREL may suggest blended worthlessness, meanness, and unscrupulousness ⟨a crew of pirates . . . will elect a boatswain to order them about and a captain to lead them and navigate the ship, though the one may be the most insufferable bully and the other the most tyrannical *scoundrel* on board —G.B.Shaw⟩ BLACKGUARD may suggest inveterate depravity; sometimes it is used as the antithesis of *gentleman* ⟨you must employ either *blackguards* or gentlemen, or, best of all, *blackguards* commanded by gentlemen, to do butcher's work with efficiency and dispatch —Rudyard Kipling⟩ KNAVE may suggest sly trickery and deceit ⟨cheating *knaves* gathered at the taverns⟩ ⟨more fool than *knave*⟩ RASCAL may suggest base dishonesty ⟨your true *rascal* is today your only true citizen of the world. He plunders all nations without pride in one or prejudice against another —Eric Linklater⟩ ROGUE may suggest the blended roughness and wiliness of a vagabond ⟨sturdy *rogues* taking to the roads as highwaymen⟩ SCAMP may describe one given to artful cheating, clever robbery, or interesting escapades ⟨a *scamp* who had pinched pennies out of the teacups of the poor by various shenanigans, who was distributing his largess to divert attention from his rascality —W.A.White⟩ RAPSCALLION may refer to an ill-dressed rogue or rascal rarely successful ⟨the *rapscallions* of the river, the Black Gangs —Meridel Le Sueur⟩ MISCREANT may refer to a singularly conscienceless villain ⟨a sordid glamour about imprisonment which makes the young *miscreant* feel important; he has the inverted satisfaction of being treated like a grown-up gangster —*Times Lit. Supp.*⟩

²villain \"\ *adj* [ME *vilein*, *vilain*, fr. MF, fr. *vilein*, *vilain*, adj.] **:** of, being, or befitting a villain: **a :** of a base or depraved character **:** WICKED, DASTARDLY **b :** of low or common birth or origin

villainage *var of* VILLENAGE

vil·lain·ess \ˈvilənəs\ *n* -ES [¹*villain* + *-ess*] **:** a female villain

vil·lain·ize \-ləˌnīz\ *vb* -ED/-ING/-S [¹*villain* + *-ize*] *vt* **:** VILIFY ~ *vi* **:** to play the role of a villain

¹vil·lain·ous \ˈvilənəs\ *adj* [ME *villenouse*, fr. MF *vileneus*, fr. *vilein*, *villain* + *-eus* -ous] **1 :** befitting a villain **:** proceeding from or revealing great depravity ⟨a ~ assault⟩ **2 :** having the character of a villain **:** DEPRAVED ⟨the ~ foe⟩ **3 :** highly objectionable **:** MEAN, BAD, WRETCHED, VILE, DETESTABLE ⟨~ weather⟩ ⟨a ~ jargon⟩ **syn** see VICIOUS

²villainous \"\ *adv* **:** VILLAINOUSLY ⟨apes with foreheads ~ low —Shak.⟩

vil·lain·ous·ly *adv* **:** in a villainous manner ⟨did the difficult, ~ fatiguing job —James Cameron⟩

vil·lain·ous·ness *n* -ES **:** the quality or state of being villainous **:** VILLAINY

vil·lainy \-nē, -ni\ *n* -ES [ME *vileinie*, *vilainie*, *vilenie*, fr. OF, fr. *vilein*, *vilain* villain, villein + *-ie* -y — more at VILLAIN] **1 a :** villainous action or conduct ⟨his master crime, a singular piece of atrocious ~ —George Borrow⟩ **b :** the quality or state of being villainous **:** extreme depravity or wickedness ⟨the ~ of a seducer⟩ ⟨a power of ~ walking in the world —J.M. Synge⟩ **2 :** a villainous act **:** a deed of an evil or objectionable character ⟨is not a brutal revelation of fact often a consummate ~ —Cecil Sprigge⟩

vil·lan \ˈvilən\ *n* -S [ML *villanus* — more at VILLAIN] **:** VILLEIN

vil·lan·ci·co \ˌvēlyənˈthē(ˌ)kō\ *n* -S [Sp, fr. obs. Sp *villán* peasant, villein, fr. ML *villanus* — more at VILLAIN] **1 :** a Spanish part-song resembling the madrigal **2 :** a cantata or anthem sung in the churches

vil·la·nel·la \ˌviləˈnelə\ *n*, *pl* **villanel·le** \-elē\ [It, fr. *villano* rustic laborer, peasant, fr. ML *villanus*] **1 :** a 16th century Italian part-song unaccompanied and in free form and clownish and often parodistic in nature in sharp contrast to the sophistication of the contemporary madrigal **2 :** an instrumental piece in the style of a rustic dance

vil·la·nelle \ˌviləˈnel\ *n* -S [F, fr. It *villanella*] **:** a chiefly French poem having typically five tercets and a quatrain with the second lines having one rhyme and the remaining lines another and with the first and third lines of the first tercet repeated in alternation as the last line of the succeeding tercets and together as the closing couplet of the quatrain — compare VIRELAY

vil·la·no·va \ˌviləˈnōvə, ˌvēl-\ *adj*, *usu cap* [fr. *Villanova*, town in northeastern Italy] **:** VILLANOVAN

¹vil·la·no·van \-vən\ *adj*, *usu cap* [*Villanova*, town in northeastern Italy, its type station + E *-an*] **:** of or relating to an early Iron Age culture of northern Italy characterized by lake dwellings and urn burials in well tombs

²villanovan \"\ *n* -S *usu cap* **:** a member of the Villanovan people

vil·la·ri effect \vəˈlärē-\ *n*, *usu cap V* [after E. *Villari*, 19th cent. Ital. physicist] **:** change of magnetization as a result of longitudinal stress

villas *pl of* VILLA

vil·lat·ic \viˈlad·ik\ *adj* [L *villaticus*, fr. *villa* country house, country estate, village + *-aticus* (fr. *-atus* -ate + *-icus* -ic) — more at VILLA] **:** of or relating to a villa or a village **:** RURAL ⟨tame ~ fowl —John Milton⟩

vil·leg·gia·tu·ra \vəˌlejəˈtürə\ *also* **vil·le·gia·ture** \vəˌlāzhəˈtü(ə)r\ *n* -S [*villeggiatura* fr. It, fr. *villeggiato* (past part. of *villeggiare* to reside in a country villa, fr. *villa*) + *-ura* -ure; *villegiature* fr. F *villégiature*, fr. It *villeggiatura* — more at VILLA] **1 :** residence in the country for a holiday **:** a country holiday ⟨go into ~ at the farm —W.J.Locke⟩ **2 :** a place that is suitable for a holiday from the city **:** rural or suburban retreat

vil·lein \ˈvilən, -iˌlān, viˈlān\ *n* -S [ME *vilein*, *vilain* — more at VILLAIN] **1 :** a free common villager or village peasant of any of the feudal classes lower in rank than the thane **2 :** a free peasant of a feudal class lower than a sokeman and higher in rank than the cotters and bordars and colliberts having property rights in both real and personal property and not adscript to the soil **3 :** an unfree peasant that is a slave as regards his feudal lord but free in his legal relations with respect to all others, that has no rights against the lord except that of protection from being maimed or killed, and that is subject to be sold by the lord or removed from his lands at will

vil·lein·hold \-nˌhōld\ *n* -S [*villein* + *-hold* (as in *freehold*)] **:** a tenement held by villein socage

villein socage *n* **:** a tenure of land held by a tenant villein owing by custom a duty to render to the feudal lord fixed and definite services of a base and servile nature

vil·len·age *also* **vil·lein·age** *or* **vil·lain·age** \-nij\ *n* -S [ME *vilenage*, fr. MF, fr. OF, fr. *vilein*, *vilain* villein + *-age* — more at VILLAIN] **1 :** tenure on the terms by which a villein held of his feudal lord **:** tenure at the will of the lord by villein services **2 :** the status of a villein

vi·lliaum·ite \vēˈyōˌmīt\ *n* -S [F *villiaumite*, fr. *Villiaume*, 20th cent. French explorer in Africa + F *-ite*] **:** a mineral (NaF) consisting of a sodium fluoride and occurring in small carmine to colorless isometric crystals (sp. gr. 2.8)

vil·li·cus \ˈviləkəs\ *n*, *pl* **vil·li·ci** \-ləˌsī\ [L *vilicus*, *villicus*, fr. *villa* country house, country estate + *-icus* -ic — more at VILLA] **1 :** the steward and overseer of a large farm or of farmlands in Roman and early medieval times **2 :** a member of a privileged class of feudal landless tillers holding a farm of a landlord for a part of the harvest or for a fixed fee

vil·lif·er·ous \(ˈ)viˈlif(ə)rəs\ *adj* [NL *villus* + E *-iferous*] **:** VILLOUS 1a

vil·li·form \ˈviləˌfȯrm\ *adj* [ISV *villi-* (fr. NL *villus*) + *-iform*] **:** having the form or appearance of villi **:** resembling the pile of velvet; *often* **:** resembling bristles in a brush ⟨a fish with ~ teeth⟩

vil·li·no \viˈlē(ˌ)nō\ *n*, *pl* **villi·ni** \-ēnē\ [It, dim. of *villa* — more at VILLA] **:** a residence for a single household separated from other houses by a yard **:** a detached house

vil·li·pla·cen·tal \ˌviləpləˈsentᵊl\ *adj* [NL *Villiplacentalia*] **:** of or relating to the Villiplacentalia

vil·li·plac·en·ta·lia \ˌviləˌplasᵊnˈtālēə\ *n pl*, *cap* [NL, fr. *villus* + *-i-* + *Placentalia*] **:** mammals having a nondeciduate villous placenta and comprising the cetaceans, sirenians, and ungulates

vil·lose \ˈviˌlōs\ *adj* [L *villosus* hairy, shaggy — more at VILLOUS] **:** VILLOUS

vil·los·i·ty \viˈläsəd·ē\ *n* -ES [*villose* + *-ity*] **1 :** the state of being villous **2 a :** VILLUS **b :** a villous patch or area **3 :** a coating of long slender hairs

vil·lo·ta \viˈlōtə\ *n*, *pl* **villo·te** \-tā\ [It *villotta*, fr. *villa* villa, village — more at VILLA] **:** a folk dance song of the 16th century that is homophonic in style and of northern Italian origin

vil·lous \ˈviləs\ *adj* [ME, fr. L *villosus* rough, shaggy, fr. *villus* shaggy hair, tuft of hair + *-osus* -ous — more at VELVET] **1 a :** covered or furnished with villi ⟨two ~ normal human ova⟩ **b :** of the character of a villus ⟨a ~ filament⟩ **2 :** having soft long hairs ⟨leaves ~ underneath⟩ — compare PUBESCENT — **vil·lous·ly** *adv*

vills *pl of* VILL

vil·lus \ˈviləs\ *n*, *pl* **vil·li** \-iˌlī\ [NL, fr. L, shaggy hair, tuft of hair — more at VELVET] **1 :** a small slender vascular process: as **a :** one of the minute fingerlike processes which more or less thickly cover and give a velvety appearance to the surface of the mucous membrane of the small intestine and serve in the absorption of nutriment and of which each has a central blindly ending lacteal surrounded by blood capillaries and covered with epithelium **b :** one of the branching processes of the surface of the chorion of the developing egg or blastodermic vesicle of most mammals that are restricted to particular areas or diffusely arranged and over parts of the surface become vascular and help to form the placenta **2 :** TROPHONEMA

vil·na \ˈvilnə\ *or* **vil·no** \-l(ˌ)nō\ *adj*, *usu cap* [fr. *Vilna*, *Vilno* (Vilnyus), Lithuania] **:** VILNYUS

vil·ny·us *or* **vil·ni·us** \ˈvilnēəs\ *adj*, *usu cap* [fr. *Vilnyus*, *Vilnius*, Lithuania] **:** of or from Vilnyus, the capital of Lithuania **:** of the kind or style prevalent in Vilnyus

vily *pl of* VILA

vim \ˈvim\ *n* -S [L, accus. of *vis* strength; akin to Gk *is* strength, Skt *vayas* strength, OE *wāth* wandering, pursuit, hunt, *wǣthan* to wander, hunt, OHG *weida* fodder, pasture, catch, *weidōn* to seek fodder, hunt, ON *veithr* catch, *veitha* to hunt, Gk *hiesthai* to hurry, Lith *vyti* to pursue, hunt, Skt *veti* he goes, advances] **:** robust energy and enthusiasm **:** VITALITY, ZIP ⟨the ~ . . . generally absent from more civilized gatherings —R.H. Croll⟩ ⟨woke up full of ~ and optimism⟩ **syn** see VIGOR

vi·ma·na \vəˈmänə\ *n* -S [Skt *vimāna*, lit., measuring out, traversing, fr. *vimāti* he measures, fr. *vi* apart + *māti* he measures — more at WITH, MEASURE] **:** a pyramidal tower built over the central shrine of a temple in India — compare GOPURA, SHIKARA

vim·i·nar·ia \ˌviməˈna(a)rēə\ *n*, *cap* [NL, fr. L *vimin-*, *vimen* withe + NL *-aria*] **:** a genus of Australian leafless shrubs (family Leguminosae) that resemble the brooms and have small orange-yellow flowers with a broad vexillum and connate keel petals and a one-seeded pod — see SWAMP OAK

vi·min·e·ous \vəˈminēəs\ *adj* [L *vimineus*, fr. *vimin-*, *vimen* pliant twig, withe + *-eus* -eous; akin to L *viēre* to plait — more at WITHY] **1** *obs* **:** woven of pliant twigs ⟨a ~ texture like a birdcage —Richard Tomlinson⟩ **2 :** of or producing long slender twigs or shoots ⟨a shrub of ~ habit⟩

vim·pa \ˈvimpə\ *n* -S [ML, fr. OIt *vimpa*, *glimpla*, fr. OF *guimple*, *wimple* veil, pennant, wimple — more at GUIMPE] **:** a veil of silk worn over the shoulders and hands of acolytes carrying the crosier and the miter in Roman Catholic pontifical services — compare HUMERAL VEIL

vi·na \ˈvēnə\ *also* **bi·na** \ˈbē-\ *n* -S [Skt & Hindi; Hindi *bīnā*, fr. Skt *vīṇā*] **:** a musical instrument of India having usu. four strings and a long bamboo fingerboard with movable frets and a gourd resonator at each end

vi·na·ceous \(ˈ)vīˈnāshəs\ *adj* [L *vinaceus* of wine, fr. *vinum* wine + *-aceus* -aceous — more at WINE] **1 :** of the color wine **2 :** of the color wine red

vin·age \ˈvīnij\ *n* -S [F, fr. *vin* wine + *-age* — more at VINEGAR] **:** the adding of alcohol to wine

vi·na·gron \ˌvēnəˈgrōn\ *n* -S [MexSp *vinagrón* — more at VINEGARROON] **:** VINEGARROON

¹vin·ai·grette \ˌvinəˈgret, *usu* -ed+V\ *n* -S [F, fr. *vinaigre* vinegar + *-ette* — more at VINEGAR] **1** [so called fr. its resemblance to vehicles used by French vinegar merchants] **:** a small 2-wheeled vehicle designed to be drawn or pushed ⟨sat in a ~, but the donkey refused to budge —O.S.J.Gogarty⟩ **2 :** VINAIGRETTE SAUCE **3 :** a small ornamental box or bottle

that has a perforated top and is used for holding an aromatic preparation (as smelling salts)

²vinaigrette \ˈ⸗⸗⸗\ *adj* : made or served with vinaigrette sauce ⟨~ salad dressing⟩ ⟨asparagus ~⟩

vinaigrette sauce *n* : a sauce made typically of vinegar, oil, onions, parsley, and herbs and used esp. on cold meats or fish

¹vi·nal \ˈvīnᵊl\ *adj* [L *vinalis*, fr. *vinum* wine + *-alis* -al] : of or from wine : VINOUS

²vinal \ˈ"\ *n* -S [polyvinyl alcohol] : any of various synthetic textile fibers that are long-chain polymers composed of at least 50 percent by weight of vinyl alcohol units —CH_2CHOH— and at least 85 percent by weight of vinyl alcohol units together with polyvinyl acetal units

vi·nasse \vəˈnas\ *n* -S [F, fr. L *vinacea*, fem. of *vinaceus* vinaceous] : a residual liquid remaining from the fermentation and distillation of alcoholic liquors

vin·a·ya \ˈvinəyə\ *n* -S *usu cap* [Skt, discipline, lit., leading apart, separating, fr. *vi* apart, asunder + *nayati* he leads — more at WITH] : a code of monastic disciplinary rules in Buddhism

vin·ca \ˈviŋkə\ *n, cap* [NL, short for L *pervinca* periwinkle — more at PERIWINKLE] : a genus of often prostrate woody herbs (family Apocynaceae) comprising the Old World periwinkles and having solitary axillary blue, red, or white flowers with a plumose stigma

¹vin·cen·tian \vinˈsenchən\ *n* -S *usu cap* [Saint *Vincent* de Paul †1660 Fr. Roman Catholic priest + E *-an*, n. suffix] **1** : a member of a Roman Catholic society of priests founded in 1625 by St. Vincent de Paul and devoted to conducting missions and clerical seminaries — called also *Lazarist* **2** : SISTER OF CHARITY

²vincentian \(ˈ)⸗¦⸗⸗\ *adj, usu cap* [Saint *Vincent* de Paul †1660 + E *-an*, adj. suffix] **1** : of, relating to, or founded by St. Vincent de Paul **2** : of or relating to the Vincentians

vin·cent's angina \ˈvin(t)sənts-\ *n, usu cap V* [after Jean Hyacinthe *Vincent* †1950 Fr. bacteriologist] : Vincent's infection of the tonsils, pharynx, and throat — called also *trench mouth*

vincent's infection *also* **vincent's stomatitis** *n, usu cap V* [after Jean H. *Vincent* †1950 Fr. bacteriologist] : infection of the respiratory tract and mouth by the fusiform bacillus often in association with a spirochete (*Borrelia vincentii*) producing destructive ulceration esp. of the mucous membranes of the cheeks, gums, and throat

vin·ce·tox·i·cum \ˌvin(t)səˈtäksəkəm\ *n, cap* [NL, fr. L *vincere* to conquer + *toxicum* poison; fr. the former belief that it was a counterpoison — more at TOXIC] : a large genus of chiefly tropical American vines (family Asclepiadaceae) having cordate leaves and large purple or greenish cymose flowers with the corolla rotate and 5-parted and an entire or lobed crown — see NEGRO VINE

vin·chu·ca \vinˈchükə\ *n* -S [Sp, fr. Quechua *wihchuykuk*] : any of several bugs of the genus *Triatoma* (esp. *T. infestans*)

vin·ci·ble \ˈvin(t)səbəl\ *adj* [L *vincibilis*, fr. *vincere* to conquer + *-ibilis* -ible — more at VICTOR] **1** : capable of being overcome or subdued : SURMOUNTABLE ⟨powerful governments showing signs of being ~⟩ ⟨our boys were plenty ~ in the . . . track events —*New Yorker*⟩ **2** : being within an individual's control and therefore involving moral responsibility — used esp. of lack of knowledge about theological concepts ⟨~ ignorance⟩

vin·cu·lum \ˈviŋkyələm\ *n pl* **vinculums** \-mz\ *or* **vincu·la** \-lə\ [L, fr. *vincire* to bind, tie — more at VETCH] **1** : a unifying bond : LINK, TIE ⟨the strong ~ between the candidate and his supporters⟩ **2** : a uniting band or bundle of fibers (as a commissure uniting the two main tendons of the foot in a bird) : FRENUM **3** : a straight horizontal mark in mathematics placed over two or more members of a compound quantity and equivalent to parentheses or brackets about them (as in a—b—c=a—[b—c])

vin·di·ca·ble \ˈvindəkəbəl, -dēk-\ *adj* [L *vindicare* + E *-able*] : capable of being vindicated : JUSTIFIABLE ⟨think every work of God ~ —S.J.Pratt⟩

vin·di·cate \ˈvindəˌkāt, *usu* -ād.+V\ *vt* -ED/-ING/-S [L *vindicatus*, past part. of *vindicare* to lay claim to, set free, avenge, fr. *vindic-*, *vindex* claimant, protector, avenger, fr. a prehistoric compound whose first constituent is of unknown origin and whose second constituent is the same as L *-dic-*, *-dex* (fr. *dicere* to determine, say) — more at DICTION] **1** *obs* : to set free : DELIVER ⟨~ ourselves into perfect liberty —Edmund Burke⟩ **2** : to take vengeance for : AVENGE ⟨~ the laws which have been breached —W.E.Jackson b. 1919⟩ **3 a** : to free from any question of error, dishonor, guilt, or negligence : EXONERATE, ABSOLVE ⟨the . . . politicians were *vindicated* on all counts —R.H.Rovere⟩ ⟨~ his official honor —Dumas Malone⟩ **b** (1) : to show to be true, reasonable, just, or acceptable against denial, disbelief, or criticism : PROVE, CONFIRM, SUBSTANTIATE ⟨many of his insights have been *vindicated* —G.C.Sellery⟩ ⟨efforts . . . to ~ their position as gentlefolk —Edmund Wilson⟩ ⟨the right . . . has been *vindicated* by the Supreme Court —R.J.Slavin⟩ (2) : to provide justification or defense for : JUSTIFY ⟨his negative attitude ~*s* resentment⟩ **c** : to protect from attack or encroachment : PRESERVE, DEFEND ⟨~ the glory of his name against all competition —John Milton⟩ **4** : to lay claim to : maintain a right to : ASSERT ⟨no one can ~ to himself . . . exclusive prerogative —*U.S. Code*⟩ ⟨~ their right to a place in the university —Walter Moberly⟩ **syn** see EXCULPATE, MAINTAIN

vin·di·ca·tion \ˌ⸗⸗ˈkāshən\ *n* -S [L *vindication-*, *vindicatio*, fr. *vindicatus* (past part.) + *-ion-*, *-io* -ion] **1 a** : an act or instance of vindicating: as (1) : EXONERATION ⟨the ~ of a man falsely convicted of murder —*Current Biog.*⟩ (2) : JUSTIFICATION, DEFENSE ⟨undertook a successful ~ of democratic principles⟩ ⟨called on to say something in ~ of his behavior —Jane Austen⟩ (3) : SUBSTANTIATION, SUPPORT ⟨considered the event to be a ~ of the law of chance⟩ **b** : the state or condition of being vindicated ⟨sought ~ for being unjustly charged with subversion⟩ **2** : a means of gaining exoneration, justification, or support ⟨used his unhappy childhood as a ~ of his crimes⟩ ⟨discern a new ~ for poetry . . . and religion as revealers of reality —W.L.Sullivan⟩

vin·di·ca·tive \vinˈdikəd-iv, -ndəkəl, -ndēkəl, (ˈ)vin¦dikəl, |t|, |ēv *also* |əv\ *adj* [ML *vindicativus*, fr. L *vindicatus* (past part. of *vindicare*) + *-ivus* -ive] **1** *obs* : VINDICTIVE, VENGEFUL ⟨more ~ than jealous love —Shak.⟩ **2** *archaic* : of or related to punishment or discipline : PUNITIVE ⟨~ power . . . belongs not to the church —George Carleton⟩

vin·di·ca·tor \ˈvindəˌkād·ə(r), -ātə-\ *n* -S [LL, fr. L *vindicatus* + *-or*] : one that vindicates

vin·di·ca·to·ry \ˈvindəkəˌtōrē, -dēk-, (ˈ)vin¦dikə, -tōr-, -ri\ *adj* **1** : providing vindication : JUSTIFICATORY ⟨writing urgent ~ letters . . . on his behalf —George Eliot⟩ **2** : providing punishment : PUNITIVE, RETRIBUTIVE ⟨~ justice⟩ **3** : providing sanctions esp. in law

vin·dic·tive \(ˈ)vinˈdiktiv, -tēv *also* -təv\ *adj* [L *vindicta* revenge, vindication (fr. *vindicare* to defend, avenge) + E *-ive*] **1 a** (1) : having a bitterly vengeful character : disposed to seek revenge ⟨a ~ man will look for occasions of resentment —James Martineau⟩ (2) : intended for or involving revenge ⟨punishments . . . essentially ~ in their nature —M.R.Cohen⟩ **b** : characterized by an intent to cause unpleasantness, damage, or pain : NASTY, VICIOUS, SPITEFUL ⟨letters . . . with rather ~ comments upon the people —Martha T. Stephenson⟩ ⟨a priggish and even ~ poem —Cyril Connolly⟩ **2** : intended for or involving retribution : PUNITIVE ⟨a ~ purpose, — a purpose to punish you for your suspicion —William Cowper⟩

syn REVENGEFUL, VENGEFUL: VINDICTIVE applies to a desire to see another suffer or a disposition to revenge oneself for real or imagined wrong or slight, sometimes with implacable malevolence, sometimes with spiteful malice ⟨his dark, handsome, aquiline features were convulsed into a spasm of *vindictive* hatred, which had set his dead face in a terribly fiendish expression —A. Conan Doyle⟩ ⟨the Muses are *vindictive* virgins, and avenge themselves without mercy on those who weary of their charms —L.P.Smith⟩ REVENGEFUL and VENGEFUL suggest truculent readiness to take vengeance on the part of one provoked ⟨the sorrow through the villages spread by triumphant cruelties of *vengeful* military force and punishments without remorse —William Wordsworth⟩ ⟨to some *vengeful* people the treaty seemed too easy upon Germany; to many liberals it seemed too harsh —Allan Nevins & H.S.Commager⟩ ⟨*revengeful* Nature grudged him the crops which she granted to more liberal husbandmen —W.M. Thackeray⟩

vindictive damages *n pl* : PUNITIVE DAMAGES

vin·dic·tive·ly \-təvlē, -li\ *adv* : in a vindictive manner ⟨~ plotted against his superiors⟩

vin·dic·tive·ness \-tivnəs, -tēv *also* -təv-\ *n* -ES : the quality or state of being vindictive ⟨a refusal that suggested . . . puritanical ~ —Alan Gregg⟩

¹vine \ˈvīn\ *n* -S *often attrib* [ME, fr. OF *vine*, *vigne*, fr. L *vinea* vine, vineyard, fr. fem. of *vineus* of wine, fr. *vinum* wine + *-eus* -eous — more at WINE] **1 a** : GRAPE 2 **b** : a plant having a woody or herbaceous stem that is too slender, flexible, or weak to hold itself erect and that supports itself in nature by climbing over an object (as a wall, fence, or trellis) or other plants by tendrils or by twining or that extends itself horizontally by running along the ground ⟨honeysuckle ~⟩ ⟨cucumber ~⟩ **c** : any of various lax sprawling herbaceous plants (as a tomato or potato plant) that lack modification for climbing — not used technically **2** *archaic* : VINEA

²vine \ˈ"\ *vb* -ED/-ING/-S *vi* : to form a vine : grow in the manner of a vine ⟨the grapes began to ~ soon after planting⟩ ⟨morning glories *vining* up the corn —J.H.Stuart⟩ ~ *vt* : to harvest (as peas) by means of a mechanical viner

vin·ea \ˈvinēə\ *n, pl* **vin·eae** \-ēˌē\ [L, vine, vinea] : a shedlike structure used in ancient Rome to protect besiegers

vin·e·al \ˈvinēəl\ *adj* [L *vinealis*, fr. *vinea* vine + *-alis* -al] **1** : of or relating to grapes or grapevines ⟨~ plantations —Sir Thomas Browne⟩ **2** : of or relating to wine ⟨importing of ~ spirits⟩

vine beetle *n* : any of several beetles injurious to the leaves, branches, or roots of the grapevine — compare GRAPE LEAFHOPPER, GRAPE ROOTWORM, SPOTTED PELIDNOTA

vine black *n* : a vegetable black pigment made by charring vine twigs, the lees of wine, old wine casks, or similar materials — compare FRANKFORT BLACK

vine borer *n* **1** : any of several beetles whose larvae bore in the wood or pith of the grapevine: as **a** : a small beetle (*Xylobiops basilaris*) whose larva bores in the stems **b** : a small reddish brown weevil (*Ampeloglypter sesostris*) that produces galls on the branches — see WOUND GALL **2** : a clearwing moth (*Memythrus polistiformis*) whose larva bores often destructively in the roots of the grapevine

vine cactus *n* : OCOTILLO 1

vine chafer *n* **1** : ROSE CHAFER **2** : SPOTTED PELIDNOTA

vined \ˈvīnd\ *adj* [in sense 1, fr. past part. of ²*vine*; in sense 2, fr. ¹*vine* + *-ed*] **1** : separated from the shells ⟨~ peas⟩ **2** : covered with vines ⟨a little ~ cottage⟩

vinedresser \ˈ⸗,⸗⸗\ *n* : one that cultivates and prunes grapevines

vine forester *n* : any of several moths of the genus *Alypia* having larvae that feed on the leaves of the grapevine

vine fretter *n* : a plant louse (esp. *Phylloxera vitifoliae*) that injures the grapevine — called also *vine louse*

¹vin·e·gar \ˈvinigə(r), -nēg-\ *n* -S *often attrib* [ME *vinegre*, fr. OF *vinaigre*, lit., sour wine, fr. *vin* wine (fr. L *vinum*) + *aigre* sharp, sour — more at WINE, EAGER] **1** : a sour liquid used as a condiment or a preservative that is obtained by acetic fermentation of dilute alcoholic liquids (as fermented cider, malt beer, or wine) or of dilute distilled alcohol and is often seasoned esp. with herbs ⟨tarragon ~⟩ **2** : disagreeableness of speech, disposition, or attitude : SOURNESS ⟨the smile couldn't disguise the ~ in her voice⟩ **3** : a pharmaceutical solution of the active principles of drugs in dilute acetic acid usu. prepared by maceration ⟨aromatic ~⟩ — see VINEGAR OF OPIUM **4** : vigorous strength and spirits : VIM ⟨just a kid, full of ~ —Eddie Krell⟩

²vinegar \ˈ"\ *vt* -ED/-ING/-S : to treat with vinegar : apply vinegar to ⟨proceeded to ~ the forehead . . . of the spinster aunt —Charles Dickens⟩

vinegar eel *also* **vinegar worm** *n* : a minute nematode worm (*Turbatrix aceti*) often found in great numbers in vinegar, sour paste, and other acid fermenting vegetable substances

vinegar fly *n* : any of various fruit flies (esp. *Drosophila melanogaster*) that often become pests by breeding in imperfectly sealed preserves and in pickles

vin·e·gar·ish \-rish, -rēsh\ *adj* : sour or sullen in disposition, speech, or manner : given to caustic comment : ACIDULOUS, WASPISH ⟨a ~, aggressive-mannered woman —*Wall Street Jour.*⟩

vinegar maker *n* : VINEGARROON

vinegar mother *n* : ⁴MOTHER 2

vinegar of lead : GOULARD'S EXTRACT

vinegar of opium : a solution of opium in diluted acetic acid — called also *black drop*

vinegar pie *n* : a pie consisting of a flour-thickened filling of water, vinegar, and butter sweetened with brown sugar and baked in a pastry shell

vin·e·gar·roon \ˌvinigəˈrün, -nēg-, -ˈrōn\ *n* -S [MexSp *vinagrón*, aug. of Sp *vinagre* vinegar, fr. OSp, fr. OF *vinaigre* — more at VINEGAR] : a large whip scorpion (*Mastigoproctus giganteus*) of the southern U. S. and Mexico that emits a vinegary odor when disturbed and is inaccurately held to be very venomous

vinegar rot *n* : a soft rot of sweet potatoes caused by any of several fungi of the genus *Rhizopus*

vinegar tree *n* : a sumac with acid berries sometimes used to intensify the sourness of vinegar; *esp* : STAGHORN SUMAC

vinegarweed \ˈ⸗⸗⸗,⸗\ *n* : a Californian mint (*Trichostema lanceolatum*) that has light blue flowers and is a common bee plant

vin·e·gary \ˈvinig(ə)rē, -nēg-, -ri\ *adj* **1** : resembling vinegar esp. in taste : TART, SOUR ⟨munched bread and dark, ~ . . . olives —*New Yorker*⟩ **2 a** : having a disagreeable, bitter, or coldly severe character or manner : ACERBIC, CRABBED, ASTRINGENT ⟨a ~ unpleasant person —W.H.Wright⟩ ⟨gave him a thin ~ greeting —G.W.Brace⟩ **b** : easily moved to irascibility : PEPPERY, CHOLERIC ⟨~ but lovable old village practitioner —*Newsweek*⟩

vine hawk moth *n* : any of several hawk moths (esp. *Pholus achemon* and *Ampelophaga myron*) whose larvae feed on grape leaves

vine hopper *n* : GRAPE LEAFHOPPER

vi·ne·i·ty \vəˈnēəd·ē\ *n* -ES [L *vineus* of wine + E *-ity* — more at VINE] : the quality or state of being wine ⟨the ~ of the eucharistic wine⟩

vineland \ˈ⸗,⸗\ *n* : land adapted esp. to the cultivation of vines ⟨rich ~s producing grapes of fine quality⟩

vine leaf folder *or* **vine leaf roller** *n* : GRAPE LEAF FOLDER

vine leek *n* : a Eurasian plant (*Allium ampeloprasum*) that is probably the ancestor of the leek

vine·let \ˈvīnlət\ *n* : a young undeveloped vine

vine louse *or* **vine pest** *n* : VINE FRETTER

vine maple *n* **1** : a maple (*Acer circinatum*) of northwestern No. America having often prostrate stems that root freely and form dense thickets **2** : CANADA MOONSEED

vine mesquite *n* : a wiry stoloniferous perennial grass (*Panicum obtusum*) that grows esp. in sandy soil and along watercourses of the western U. S. and Mexico

vine mite *n* : a mite (*Tenuipalpus californicus*) that damages lemons and grapes

vine moth *n* : any of several moths whose larvae feed on grapevine

vine peach *n* : MANGO MELON

vin·er \ˈvīnə(r)\ *n* -S **1** : a machine in which fresh peas are separated from the pods and vines **2** : a mechanical pea harvester

vin·ery \ˈvīnərē\ *n* -ES : an area or building in which vines are grown ⟨grape ~⟩ ⟨pea ~⟩

vines *pl of* VINE, *pres 3d sing of* VINE

vine sawfly *n* : a small black sawfly (*Erythraspides pygmaea*) whose larva feeds on the leaves of the grapevine

vine scale *n* : any of several scales that attack grapevines: as **a** : a brown No. American unarmored scale (*Pulvinaria vitis*) that deposits its eggs in a cottony mass **b** : GRAPE SCALE

vine slug *n* : the black larva of the vine sawfly

vine sorrel *n* : SORREL VINE

vinestock \ˈ⸗,⸗\ *n* : the main stem of a vine

vinet *n* -S [ME *vinnet*, fr. MF *vignete* — more at VIGNETTE] *obs* : VIGNETTE 1

vine weevil *n* : any of various weevils feeding on grape and often other plants; *esp* : BLACK VINE WEEVIL — compare VINE BORER 1b

vine wilt *n* : a stem rot of sweet potatoes that is caused by either of two fungi (*Fusarium batatatis* and *F. hyperoxysporum*)

vine·yard \ˈvinyə(r)d *sometimes* -nˌyärd *or* -yäd\ *n* [ME *vineyard*, *vineyerd*, fr. ¹*vine* + *yard*, *yerd* yard] **1** : a field of grapevines ⟨apple and peach orchards . . . mingle with farms and ~s —*Amer. Guide Series: Va.*⟩ **2** : an area or category of physical or mental occupation ⟨a . . . minister whose ~ was in the slums —*Brit. Books of the Month*⟩ ⟨beginning his labors in the ~ of gossip —*Time*⟩

vine·yard·ist \-dəst\ *n* -S : one who owns or cultivates a vineyard

vineyard plow *n* : a moldboard plow with a relatively small bottom used for plowing in orchards and vineyards

vingt-et-un \¦vanˈtāˈtən, ¦vaⁿtāˈtəⁿ\ *n* -S [F, fr. L, lit., twenty-one (number)] : ³TWENTY-ONE 5

vingt-un \(ˈ)vanˈtən, (ˈ)vaⁿˈtəⁿ\ *n* -S [by contr.] : VINGT-ET-UN

vin·ha·ti·co \ˌvēnˈyäd·əˌkō\ *n* -S [Pg, prob. fr. *vinha* vineyard, fr. L *vinea* — more at VINE] **1 a** : any of several So. American leguminous timber trees of the genera *Plathymenia* and *Pithecolobium* **b** : the yellowish wood of any of these trees **2 a** : an ornamental tree (*Persea indica*) of the Azores and the Canary islands **b** : the coarse dark-colored wood of this tree

vi·nic \ˈvīnik, ˈvin-, -nēk\ *adj* [ISV *vin-* (fr. L *vinum* wine) + *-ic* — more at WINE] : of, relating to, or derived from wine or alcohol ⟨~ ether⟩ ⟨enchant the intellect . . . in a ~ drowsiness —J.P.Bishop⟩

vini·cul·tur·al \¦vinə¦kəlch(ə)rəl\ *adj* [*viniculture* + *-al*] : VITICULTURAL

vini·cul·tur·al·ist \-rələst\ *n* : a person engaged in viticulture ⟨wines selected by . . . ~s and tasters —Roger Angell⟩

vini·cul·ture \ˈ⸗⸗ˌkəlchə(r)\ *n* [ISV *vini-* (fr. L *vinum* wine) + *culture*] : VITICULTURE

¹vi·nif·era \(ˈ)vī¦nif(ə)rə\ *adj* [NL (specific epithet of *Vitis vinifera*), fr. L *vinifer* wine-producing] : of, relating to, or derived from a common European grape (*Vitis vinifera*) that is the chief source of Old World wine grapes and table grapes ⟨Delaware grapes contain both labrusca and ~ blood⟩ ⟨several new ~ hybrids⟩ ⟨a seedless ~ grape⟩

²vinifera \ˈ"\ *n* -S : a vinifera grape

vi·nif·er·ous \-rəs\ *adj* [L *vinifer*, fr. *vinum* wine + *-ifer* -iferous] **1** : yielding or grown for the production of wine ⟨the grape is the chief ~ fruit⟩ **2** [NL *vinifera* + E *-ous*] : VINIFERA

vin·i·fi·ca·tion \ˌvinəfəˈkāshən\ *n* -S [F, fr. *vin* wine + *-i-* + *-fication* — more at VINEGAR] : the conversion of a fruit juice or other saccharine solution into alcohol by fermentation

vining *pres part of* VINE

vi·no \ˈvē(ˌ)nō\ *n* -S [It & Sp, fr. L *vinum*] : WINE

vi·nos·i·ty \vīˈnäsəd·ē, -ətē, -i\ *n* -ES [LL *vinositas*, fr. L *vinosus* of wine + *-itas* -ity] : the characteristic body, flavor, and color of a wine ⟨similar in ~ . . . but with a distinctive bouquet —A.L.Simon⟩

vi·nous \ˈvīnəs\ *adj* [L *vinosus*, fr. *vinum* wine + *-osus* -ose] **1 a** : of, relating to, or having the characteristics of wine ⟨villages redolent with ~ aroma —Richard Ford⟩ ⟨~ and amorous verse —Douglas Bush⟩ ⟨~ liquid⟩ **b** : made with or containing wine ⟨~ medications⟩ **2** : caused by or resulting from drinking wine : showing the effects of the use of wine ⟨the hubbub of ~ political fervor —William Black⟩ ⟨~ bloodshot eyes⟩ **3** *of a bird* : VINACEOUS — **vi·nous·ly** *adv*

vin·quish \ˈviŋkwish\ *n* -ES [alter. of ²*vanquish*] *Scot* : ¹PINE 3

vin ro·sé \ˌvaⁿrōˈzā\ *n, pl* **vins rosés** \ˈ"\ [F, rosy wine] : WILD CHERRY 3

¹vint \ˈvint\ *vt* -ED/-ING/-S [prob. back-formation fr. *vintage*] : to make (wine) from fruit ⟨cherry-wine ~*ed* in the . . . forest —O.E.Schniebs⟩

²vint \ˈ"\ *n* -S [Russ, prob. fr. Yiddish, lit., wind, fr. MHG *wint*, fr. OHG — more at WIND] : a card game resembling whist and similar to auction bridge in its bidding that has every trick scored and on a failed bid has the declarer score as usual while the adversaries score 100 times the value for their tricks — called also *Russian whist*

vin·ta \ˈvēntə\ *n* -S [PhilSp] : a dugout canoe with double outriggers used in the Philippines — compare BANCA, BAROTO

¹vin·tage \ˈvintij, -tēj\ *n* -S [ME, alter. (influenced by *vineter*, *vintener* vintner) of *vindage*, *vendage*, fr. MF *vendenge*, *vendeigne*, fr. L *vindemia*, fr. *vinum* wine, grapes + *demere* to take off, fr. *de-* + *emere* to take — more at WINE, REDEEM] **1 a** (1) : the yield of grapes or wine from a vineyard during a single season ⟨never did . . . the vines yield a more luxuriant ~ —Mary W. Shelley⟩ ⟨half bottles . . . of the 1947 ~ —*New Yorker*⟩ (2) : WINE ⟨the ~ flowed freely during the reception⟩ (3) *or* **vintage wine** : a wine of a particular type, region, and year and usu. of superior quality that is dated and allowed to mature ⟨several ordinary wines and a bottle of ~⟩ ⟨sampled every ~ and kickshaw of the gourmet's art —S.J.Perelman⟩ **b** : a collection of persons or things that are contemporaneous with each other and share similar or identical characteristics : CROP ⟨the book is not of this season's ~ —Muna Lee⟩ ⟨was of the ~ of comfortably well-off intellectuals —Janet Flanner⟩ **2 a** : the activity or process of harvesting and pressing grapes, fermenting the juice, and caring for the new wine ⟨nearly time for the annual ~⟩ **b** : the season when this activity or process takes place ⟨the ~ . . . is a time of gaiety and . . . hard work —P.M.Wagner⟩ **3 a** : a period of origin or manufacture ⟨term of Edwardian ~ —*N.Y. Times Mag.*⟩ ⟨a small coupé of rather ancient ~ —Leslie Charteris⟩ **b** : length of existence : MATURITY, AGE ⟨preserved . . . shark's fins of twenty years' ~ —Eve Langley⟩ ⟨many of us, of a certain ~, have been forced to think back —John Mason Brown⟩

²vintage \ˈ"\ *vb* -ED/-ING/-S *vt* : to harvest (grapes) for making wine ⟨if . . . a first growth is *vintaged* a little too late —H.J. Newman⟩ ~ *vi* : to engage in the harvesting of grapes ⟨illustrations . . . of a winged Eros *vintaging* —Nelson Glueck⟩

³vintage \ˈ"\ *adj* **1 a** (1) : of or relating to a vintage ⟨prepared for the ~ activities in the vineyards⟩ (2) : unblended and dated with the year of vintage ⟨a ~ wine⟩ — compare NONVINTAGE **b** : having a fine mellowed character ⟨drink a health in ~ vodka⟩ ⟨turning leaves make fall a ~ season⟩ **c** : of old, recognized, and enduring interest, importance, or quality : CLASSIC, VENERABLE ⟨~ comedy from the silent era —Arthur Knight⟩ ⟨collectors who . . . cherish ~ automobiles —Beverly Kelley⟩ ⟨an album of ~ tunes —Wilder Hobson⟩ **2 a** : marked by an advanced age : dating from the past : OLD, ARCHAIC ⟨a ~ actress but still thin and chic —Janet Flanner⟩ ⟨failing to answer seventy-two ~ traffic tickets —Robert Rice⟩ **b** : not fashionable or up-to-date : OLD-FASHIONED, OUTMODED ⟨~ plays of no merit whatsoever —Wolcott Gibbs⟩ ⟨a rumpled tweed suit of ~ cut —Jacob Hay⟩ **3** : of the best and most characteristic : having the typical and most admirable characteristics — used with a proper noun ⟨~ Shaw: a wise and winning comedy, beautifully played —*Time*⟩ ⟨seemed to be fine . . . but not absolutely first-rate ~ Old Vic —Mollie Panter-Downes⟩

vintage port *n* : a port wine that has a fruitier flavor and heavier body and is deeper red than either ruby or tawny port

vin·tag·er \-jə(r)\ *n* -S : one that takes part in a vintage ⟨green grapes . . . the ~*s* ought not to gather —Philip Miller⟩

vintage year *n* **1** : a year in which a vintage wine is produced ⟨the date of the *vintage year* is marked on the bottle⟩ **2** : a year of outstanding distinction or success ⟨not a *vintage year* in English scholarship —C.J.Sisson⟩ ⟨proved a *vintage year* from the radio engineer's point of view —*Wireless Engineer*⟩

vinted *past of* VINT

vin·tem \vēⁿˈtāⁿ\ *n* -S [Pg *vintém*, fr. *vinte* twenty, fr. L *viginti* — more at VICENARY] : an old Portuguese coin orig. of silver and later bronze and worth 20 reals

vinting *pres part of* VINT

vint·ner \ˈvintnə(r)\ *n* -S [ME *vineter*, *vintener*, fr. OF *vinetier*, fr. ML *vinetarius*, fr. L *vinetum* vineyard (fr. *vinum* wine, grapes) + *-arius* -ary] **1** : a person who sells wine : a wine merchant **2** : a person who makes wine ⟨collected wine-

making tips from leading amateur and professional ~s —*Packer*⟩
vints *pres 3d sing of* VINT, *pl of* VINT
viny \ˈvīnē, -ni\ *adj* **1 :** of, relating to, or resembling vines **:** covered with or abounding in vines ⟨~ low-lying plants⟩ ⟨~ hillsides and forests⟩ **2 :** having notably long vigorous prostrate stems ⟨a ~ but very productive sweet potato⟩
vi·nyl \ˈvīnᵊl *sometimes* ˈvin-\ *n* -S *often attrib* [ISV *vin-* (fr. L *vinum* wine) + *-yl*] **1 :** a univalent radical $CH_2{=}CH{-}$ derived from ethylene by removal of one hydrogen atom **2 :** a polymer of a vinyl compound or product made from one: as **a :** VINYL RESIN **b :** VINYL PLASTIC
vinyl acetal *n* **:** POLYVINYL ACETAL
vinyl acetate *n* **:** a flammable polymerizable liquid ester $CH_3COOCH{=}CH_2$ with a sharp odor that is prepared by catalytic addition of acetic acid to acetylene and that is used chiefly for the production of vinyl resins and in making other vinyl esters by reaction with other acids — see POLYVINYL ACETATE
vi·nyl·acetylene \¦≈≈+\ *n* [*vinyl* + *acetylene*] **:** a sweet-smelling gaseous or low-boiling liquid unsaturated hydrocarbon $CH_2{=}CHC{\equiv}CH$ formed by dimerization of acetylene as an intermediate in making chloroprene and neoprene; 1-buten-3-yne
vinyl alcohol *n* **:** an unstable compound $CH_2{=}CHOH$ known only in the form of its polymers or derivatives (as vinyl acetate or vinyl chloride) because attempts to prepare it yield its tautomer acetaldehyde — see POLYVINYL ALCOHOL
vi·nyl·ate \ˈvīnᵊl,āt *sometimes* ˈvin-\ *vt* -ED/-ING/-S [back-formation fr. *vinylation*] **:** to subject to vinylation
vi·nyl·a·tion \,≈≈ˈāshən\ *n* -S [*vinyl* + *-ation*] **:** the introduction of the vinyl radical into a compound usu. by catalytic addition of the compound to acetylene ⟨~ of alcohols yields vinyl ethers⟩
vi·nyl·benzene \¦vīnᵊl+\ *n* [ISV *vinyl* + *benzene*] **:** STYRENE 1a
vinyl butyral *n* **:** POLYVINYL BUTYRAL
vinyl chloride *n* **:** a flammable gaseous compound $CH_2{=}CHCl$ with an ethereal odor prepared by catalytic addition of hydrogen chloride to acetylene or by pyrolysis of ethylene dichloride and used chiefly for making vinyl resins **:** chloroethylene — see POLYVINYL CHLORIDE
vinyl compound *n* **:** a compound containing the vinyl radical esp. in halides, esters, and ethers; *broadly* **:** any of the class of compounds including styrene and its derivatives and acrylic compounds — compare POLYVINYL
vinyl cyanide *n* **:** ACRYLONITRILE
vi·nyl·ene \ˈvīnᵊl,ēn *sometimes* ˈvin-\ *n* -S [ISV *vinyl* + *-ene*] **:** a bivalent radical $-CH{=}CH-$ derived from ethylene by removal of one hydrogen atom from each carbon atom
vinyl ether *n* **1 :** a volatile flammable liquid unsaturated ether $(CH_2{=}CH)_2O$ that is made by removal of hydrogen and chlorine from dichloroethyl ether, that polymerizes on standing unless protected by an antioxidant, and that is used as an inhalation anesthetic for short operative procedures **2 :** an ether in which one of the radicals united to oxygen is vinyl ⟨polymers of *vinyl ethers*⟩
vinyl formal *n* **:** POLYVINYL FORMAL
vi·nyl·i·dene \vīˈniləˌdēn\ *n* -S [ISV *vinyl* + *-idene*] **:** a bivalent radical $CH_2{=}C{<}$ derived from ethylene by removal of two hydrogen atoms from one carbon atom
vinylidene chloride *n* **:** a low-boiling flammable liquid compound $CH_2{=}CCl_2$ prepared usu. from trichloroethane and used in making saran by polymerization; 1,1-dichloro-ethylene — see POLYVINYLIDENE CHLORIDE
vinylidene dinitrile *or* **vinylidene cyanide** *n* **:** a compound $CH_2{=}C(CN)_2$ made from acetic acid and hydrogen cyanide and used chiefly in making nytril fibers
vinylidene resin *or* **vinylidene plastic** *n* **:** any of a group of tough thermoplastic resins or plastics formed by polymerization or copolymerization of a vinylidene compound (as vinylidene chloride with or without vinyl chloride or acrylonitrile) and used esp. for filaments, films, screens, and molded articles — compare POLYVINYLIDENE CHLORIDE, SARAN, VINYL RESIN
Vi·nyl·ite \ˈvīnᵊl,īt *sometimes* ˈvin-\ *trademark* — used for any of a series of vinyl resins
vi·nyl·og \-,ȯg\ *n* -S [*vinyl* + *-log*] **:** a member of a vinylogous series
vi·nyl·o·gous \vīˈniləgəs\ *adj* [*vinylog* + *-ous*] **:** of a related chemical type but differing in having one or more vinylene bridges between functional atoms in an organic molecule ⟨acetaldehyde and crotonaldehyde are ~ compounds⟩
vinyl plastic *n* **:** any of a group of tough durable plastics based on vinyl resins often compounded with other substances (as plasticizers, pigments, fillers, stabilizers, or lubricants) and used esp. in the form of films and sheeting, coatings, tile and flooring, foams, sound records, and other molded and extruded products
vi·nyl·pyridine \¦vīnᵊl+\ *n* [*vinyl* + *pyridine*] **:** any of three liquid isomeric bases $CH_2{=}CHC_5H_4N$ synthesized in various ways and used to introduce basic sites in polymer chains by copolymerizing with other vinyl-containing monomers (as acrylonitrile or styrene)
vi·nyl·pyrrolidone \"+\ *n* [*vinyl* + *pyrrolidone*] **:** a liquid compound $CH_2{=}CHC_4H_6NO$ made by condensation of acetylene and pyrrolidone and used in the manufacture of polyvinylpyrrolidone and in various copolymerizations — called also *N-vinylpyrrolidone*
vinyl resin *n* **1 :** any of a large group of thermoplastic resinous materials containing the recurring group $-CH_2CHX-$ and consisting essentially of polymers or copolymers of vinyl compounds (as vinyl chloride or vinyl acetate) and sometimes including polyvinylidene compounds — compare POLYVINYL ACETAL, POLYVINYL ACETATE, POLYVINYL ALCOHOL, POLYVINYL CHLORIDE **2 :** VINYL PLASTIC
vinyl sulfone *n* **:** a liquid compound $(CH_2{=}CH)_2SO_2$ some of whose derivatives are used as fiber-reactive dyes
vinyl-type polymerization *n* **:** addition polymerization of vinyl compounds or related unsaturated compounds (as vinylidene chloride)
vin·yon \ˈvin,yän\ *n* -S [fr. *Vinyon*, a trademark] **1 :** any of various synthetic textile fibers in filament or staple form that are long-chain polymers composed of at least 85 percent by weight of vinyl chloride units $-CH_2CHCl-$ often together with vinyl acetate units, that show good strength wet or dry, but that have a low softening temperature and can be easily molded **2 :** yarn or fabric made from vinyon fiber and used esp. for industrial filter cloth, fishing lines and nets, and clothing
¹**viol** *obs var of* VIAL
²**vi·ol** \ˈvī(ə)l *sometimes* -ī(,)ōl\ *n* -S [MF *viole* viol, viola, fr. OProv *viola, viula* viol, prob. fr. ML *vitula* fiddle — more at FIDDLE] **1 :** a bowed stringed musical instrument chiefly of the 16th and 17th centuries made with a relatively deep body and flat back and sloping shoulders, usu. six strings tuned in fourths, a fretted fingerboard, and a low-arched bridge, made in treble, alto, tenor, and bass sizes, and played in a vertical position resting on or between the knees of the player — see CONTRABASS, TREBLE VIOL, VIOLA DA BRACCIO, VIOLA DA GAMBA **2 :** a labial pipe-organ stop with string tone
³**vi·ol** \ˈvī(ə)l\ *n* -S [origin unknown] *archaic* **:** a large rope used esp. in weighing anchor
viol- *comb form* [ISV, fr. NL *Viola*] **:** pansy ⟨*viol*aniline⟩
viol *abbr* [L *violaceus*] purple
¹**vi·o·la** \vēˈōlə *sometimes* vī-\ *n* -S [It & Sp, viol, viola, fr. OProv *viola, viula* viol] **1 :** a musical instrument of the violin family that is intermediate in size and compass between the violin and the violoncello, is tuned a fifth lower than the violin with its open string pitches being c, g, d′, a′, and has a somber tone quality when played on its lower strings but a more strident sound on its A string **2 :** a player of the viola **3 :** a string-toned labial pipe-organ stop of 8-foot or 4-foot pitch
²**vi·o·la** \vīˈōlə, ˈvīələ\ *n* [NL, fr. L, violet — more at VIOLET] **1** *cap* **:** a very large genus of acaulescent or leafy-stemmed herbs or undershrubs (family Violaceae) having alternate stipulate leaves and both conspicuous petaliferous mostly vernal flowers and cleistogamous flowers borne on peduncles or stolons and sometimes concealed underground, the former with purple, yellow, or white petals often marked or variegated and with the corolla irregular and often spurred and the sepals eared at the base and the latter without petals, self-fertilized in the bud, and very fruitful — see PANSY, SWEET VIOLET, VIOLET, WILD PANSY **2** -S **:** any plant of the genus *Viola; esp* **:** any of numerous cultivated and sometimes naturalized hybrids orig. developed by crossing the garden pansy and the tufted pansy and having flowers intermediate in size between the garden pansy and the wild pansy
vi·o·la al·ta \vē,ōləˈältə\ *n, pl* **viola altas** [It, tall viola] **:** a large orchestral viola
viola bas·tar·da \-bäˈstärdə\ *n, pl* **viola bastardas** [It, bastard viol] **1 :** a viola da gamba tuned and played according to the lute tablature **2 :** ²LIRA 3
vi·o·la·bil·i·ty \,vīələˈbiləd-ē\ *n* **:** the quality or state of being violable
vi·o·la·ble \ˈvīələbəl\ *adj* [L *violabilis*, fr. *violare* to violate + *-abilis* -able — more at VIOLATE] **:** capable of being or likely to be violated ⟨~ national boundaries⟩ — **vi·o·la·ble·ness** *n* -ES — **vi·o·la·bly** \-blē, -li\ *adv*
vi·o·la·ce·ae \,vīəˈlāsē,ē\ *n pl, cap* [NL, fr. *Viola*, type genus + *-aceae*] **:** a family of herbs, shrubs, and trees (order Hypericales) having pentamerous mostly irregular flowers and a one-celled ovary containing three parietal placentae
vi·o·la·ceous \¦≈≈¦lāshəs\ *adj* [L *violaceus*, fr. *viola* violet + *-aceus* -aceous] **1 :** of the color violet **2** [NL *Violaceae* + E *-ous*] **:** of or relating to the family Violaceae — **vi·o·la·ceous·ly** *adv*
viola clef *n* **:** ALTO CLEF
vi·o·la da brac·cio \vē,ōlədəˈbrä(,)chō\ *n, pl* **vio·le da braccio** \-(,)lād-\ [It, arm viol] **:** a viol having approximately the range of the modern viola
viola da gam·ba \-dəˈgämbə, -ˈgam-, -ˈgȧm-, -ˈgaam-\ *n, pl* **viole da gamba** [It, leg viol] **1 :** a bass member of the viol family having a range approximating the cello and popular esp. in the 17th century **2 :** a string-toned pipe-organ stop of 8-foot pitch
viola d'a·mo·re \-dəˈmōrā\ *n, pl* **viole d'amore** [It, viol of love] **1 :** a tenor viol having usu. seven gut strings with seven or more wire strings passing under the fingerboard and sounding sympathetically as the first are played and producing a sweet tone **2 :** a soft string-toned pipe-organ stop of 8-foot or 4-foot pitch
viola da spal·la \-dəˈspälə\ *n, pl* **viole da spalla** [It, shoulder viol] **:** a cello carried in processions by a shoulder strap
viola di bor·do·ne \-dēbȯrˈdōnā\ *n, pl* **viole di bordone** [It, bass viol] **:** a large viola d'amore
vi·o·lan \ˈvīə,lan\ *or* **vi·o·lane** \-,lān\ *n* -S [G *violan*, fr. L *viola* violet — more at VIOLET] **:** a diopside of a fine blue or violet color
vi·o·lan·in \,vīəˈlanən\ *n* -S [ISV *viol-* + anthocy*anin*] **:** an anthocyanin that is obtained from the pansy as the bluish violet crystalline chloride $C_{36}H_{37}O_{18}Cl$ and yields on hydrolysis delphinidin, *para*-hydroxy-cinnamic acid, and glucosyl-rhamnose
vi·o·lan·throne \,vīəˈlan,thrōn\ *n* [ISV *viol-* + *anthrone*] **:** a vat dye — see DYE table I (under *Vat Blue 20*)
viola pom·po·sa \vē,ōləpämˈpōsə\ *n, pl* **viole pompo·se** \-(,)läpämˈpō(,)sā\ [It, pompous viol] **1 :** an obsolete large viola with five strings **2 :** a string-toned pipe-organ stop usu. of 8-foot pitch
vi·o·la·rite \vīˈōlə,rīt\ *n* -S [L *violaris* of violet (fr. *viola* violet + *-aris* -ar) + E *-ite*; fr. its color] **:** a mineral Ni_2FeS_4 consisting of a sulfide of nickel and iron that is isomorphous with linnaeite, siegenite, carrollite, and polydymite
violas *pl of* VIOLA
¹**vi·o·late** \ˈvīə,lāt, *usu* -ād-+V\ *vt* -ED/-ING/-S [ME *violaten*, fr. L *violatus*, past part. of *violare* to treat with violence, injure, violate; akin to L *vis* strength — more at VIM] **1 :** to fail to keep **:** BREAK, DISREGARD ⟨~ the law⟩ **2 :** to do harm to the person or esp. the chastity of; *specif* **:** to commit rape on ⟨~ a woman⟩ **3 a :** to fail to show the requisite respect for **:** treat or handle in a disrespectful or high-handed manner **:** PROFANE, DESECRATE ⟨~ a shrine⟩ ⟨~ personal liberty⟩ **b** *obs* **:** to damage or destroy esp. by violence **4 :** to interfere with by interruption or disturbance ⟨~ an individual's privacy⟩
²**violate** \"\ *adj* [L *violatus*, past part. of *violare*] *archaic* **:** VIOLATED — **vi·o·late·ly** *adv, archaic*
vi·o·lat·er \-ād-ə(r), -ātə-\ *n* -S [¹*violate* + *-er*] **:** VIOLATOR
vi·o·la·tion \,vīəˈlāshən\ *n* -S [ME *violacion*, fr. L *violation-, violatio*, fr. *violatus* (past part.) + *-ion-, -io* -ion] **:** the act or action of violating or the quality or state of being violated: as **a :** an infringement or transgression ⟨a ~ of law⟩ ⟨~ of promises⟩; *specif* **:** an infringement of the rules in sports that is less serious than a foul and that usu. involves technicalities of play (as a rules infraction in basketball for which the ball is awarded to the opponents out of bounds) **b :** an act of irreverence **:** DESECRATION, PROFANATION ⟨~ of a church⟩ **c :** INTERRUPTION, DISTURBANCE ⟨~ of civil order⟩ ⟨~ of the peace⟩ **d :** RAVISHMENT, RAPE ⟨the ~ of civilian population⟩ **syn** see BREACH
vi·o·la·tion·al \¦≈≈¦lāshənᵊl, -shnəl\ *adj* **:** of or relating to violation
vi·o·la·tive \ˈvīə,lād·iv, -¦ə¦, |t|, |ēv *also* |əv\ *adj* **:** violating or tending to violate ⟨~ gestures⟩ ⟨~ of the principles of liberty⟩
vi·o·la·tor \ˈvīə,lād-ə(r), -ātə-\ *n* -S [ME, ravisher, fr. L, violator, fr. *violatus* (past part. of *violare* to violate) + *-or*] **:** one that commits a violation
vi·o·la·xanthin \vī¦ō¦lə, ¦vīələ+\ *n* [NL *Viola* + E *xanthin*] **:** an orange to red crystalline carotenoid pigment $C_{40}H_{56}O_4$ obtained from yellow pansies and many other plants **:** zeaxanthin di-epoxide
vi·ole d'orchestre \vēˈōldȯ(r)ˈkestr(ᵊ), -t(rə)\ *n, pl* **violes d'orchestre** [F, orchestra viol] **:** an imitative string-toned pipe-organ stop of small scale and incisive quality
vi·o·lence \ˈvīələn(t)s *sometimes* ˈvīl-\ *n* -S [ME, fr. OF, fr. L *violentia*, fr. *violentus* violent + *-ia* -y] **1 a :** exertion of any physical force so as to injure or abuse (as in warfare or in effecting an entrance into a house) **b :** an instance of violent treatment or procedure **2 :** injury in the form of revoking, repudiation, distortion, infringement, or irreverence to a thing, notion, or quality fitly valued or observed ⟨no ~ has been done to expert military opinion —Sir Winston Churchill⟩ ⟨did unconscious ~ to the instincts of the mystic —V.L.Parrington⟩ **3 a :** intense, turbulent, or furious action, force, or feeling often destructive ⟨the ~ of a volcanic eruption —R.W. Livingstone⟩ ⟨hurled himself around the corner . . . with almost drunken ~ —Liam O'Flaherty⟩ **b :** vehement feeling or expression **:** FERVOR, PASSION, FURY ⟨the ~ of a fluent orator whose temper ran away with him —V.A.Froude⟩ ⟨~ such as the normally placid New York art critics seldom resort to —R. M.Coates⟩ **c :** an instance or show of such action or feeling **:** a tendency to violent action ⟨the mounting ~s of the Whig rabble against their Tory neighbors —Margaret Evans⟩ **d :** clashing, jarring, discordant, or abrupt quality ⟨certain freaks and ~s in Mr. Palgrave's criticism —Matthew Arnold⟩ ⟨the ~ of the contrasting colors⟩ **4 :** undue alteration of wording or sense (as in editing or interpreting a text) **syn** see FORCE
¹**vi·o·lent** \-nt\ *adj* [ME, fr. MF, fr. L *violentus*; akin to L *violare* to violate — more at VIOLATE] **1 :** characterized by extreme force ⟨a ~ storm⟩ **:** marked by abnormally sudden physical activity and intensity ⟨a ~ attack⟩ **2 :** furious or vehement to the point of being improper, unjust, or illegal ⟨lay ~ hands on an individual⟩ ⟨a ~ denunciation⟩ **3 :** extremely or intensely vivid or loud ⟨~ colors⟩ ⟨~ noise⟩ **:** unusually intense ⟨~ pain⟩ **:** unnaturally strong ⟨~ passion⟩ **4 :** produced or effected by force **:** UNNATURAL ⟨a ~ death⟩ ⟨come to a ~ end⟩ **5 :** tending to distort or misrepresent ⟨a ~ interpretation⟩ **6 :** extremely excited **:** emotionally aroused ⟨become ~ after an insult⟩ — **vi·o·lent·ly** *adv*
²**violent** *vi, obs* **:** to be violent or act violently ~ *vt, obs* **:** to constrain by or as if by violence
vi·o·lent·ness *n* -ES **:** the quality or state of being violent
violent profits *n pl* **:** rents or profits of an estate in Scots law obtained by a tenant wrongfully holding over after warning and recoverable in a process of removing at double the actual rate for urban land and at the highest possible yield for rural land
vi·o·les·cent \¦vīə¦lesᵊnt\ *adj* [L *viola* violet + E *-escent*] **:** tending to a violet color
vi·ole sor·dine \vēˈōlsȯrˈdēn\ *n, pl* **viole sordines** [prob. modif. of F *viole sourdine* muted viol] **:** a soft string-toned pipe-organ stop imitating a muted violin
¹**vi·o·let** \ˈvīələt *sometimes* ˈvīl-; *usu* -əd-+V\ *n* -S [ME, fr. MF *violete*, dim. of *viole* violet, fr. L *viola*, of non-IE origin; akin to the source of Gk *ion* violet] **1 a :** a plant of the genus *Viola; esp* **:** one of the small-flowered forms as distinguished from the typically larger-flowered violas and pansies **b :** any of several plants (as a dogtooth violet) of genera other than *Viola* **2 a :** any of a group of colors that resemble those of violets (sense 1) and are of reddish blue hue, low lightness, and medium saturation **b :** a reddish blue hue that is evoked in the normal observer under normal conditions by radiant energy of wavelength 420 millimicrons **3 :** cloth or clothing of the color violet **4 :** a pigment or dye that imparts a violet color **5 :** any of numerous small violet-colored butterflies of the family Lycaenidae **6 :** an overly fastidious, modest, or retiring person ⟨a shrinking ~⟩ ⟨a blushing ~⟩
²**violet** \"\ *vt* **violetted; violetted; violetting; violets :** to make violet-hued
³**vi·o·let** \ˈvīə,let\ *n* -S [It *violetta* — more at VIOLETTE] **:** ¹VIOLETTE; *specif* **:** VIOLA D'AMORE
violet aphid *n* **:** a plant louse (*Neotoxoptera violae*) that feeds on violets
violet-bloom \ˈ(≈)≈,≈\ *n* **:** BITTERSWEET 2a
violet carmine *n* **:** a dark reddish purple that is bluer and deeper than royal purple (sense 1), redder, stronger, and slightly lighter than average plum (sense 6a), and redder and less strong than imperial (sense 10)
violet-ear \ˈ≈(≈)≈,≈\ *n* **:** a tropical hummingbird of the genus *Colibri* having violet or bluish purple ear tufts
violet family *n* **:** VIOLACEAE
violet-green swallow *n* **:** a common swallow (*Tachycineta thalassina lepida*) of western No. America that is violet green above and that has white ear coverts, rump patches, and lower side
violet iris *n* **:** a dwarf iris (*Iris verna*) of eastern No. America with purplish blue flowers
vi·o·let·ish \ˈvīələd-ish\ *adj* **:** somewhat of the color violet
violet midge *n* **:** a cecidomyiid fly (*Contarinia violicola*) the larva of which feeds on violets in the eastern U.S.
violet parme *n, often cap P* **:** PARMA VIOLET 2a
violet ray *n* **1 :** an ultraviolet ray — not used technically **2 :** a high-frequency electric discharge from the outer surface of a one-electrode vacuum tube having violet-colored fluorescence and often used in therapeutic treatments
violet root rot *n* **:** a root rot (as of alfalfa, asparagus, and potato) caused by an imperfect fungus (*Rhizoctonia crocorum*) and characterized by a purplish growth of mycelium on the basal parts of the shoot and roots
violet scab *n* **:** a disease of violets and esp. of the sweet violet caused by a fungus (*Sphaceloma violae*) and characterized by brownish warty outgrowths on the leaves which become brittle and crack very easily when handled
violet shift *n* **:** the Doppler effect of recession **:** a shift of the spectrum toward shorter wavelengths
violet snail *or* **violet shell** *n* **:** a mollusk of the genus *Janthina*
¹**vi·o·lette** \¦vīə¦let\ *n* -S [It *violetta*, fr. *viola* viol, viola + *-etta* -ette (fr. F *-ette*)] **:** a small viol
²**violette** \"\ *n* -S [F, violet, violette, fr. MF *violete* — more at VIOLET] **:** a carved ornament resembling or suggesting a violet
violet tip *n* **:** an American butterfly (*Polygonia interrogationis*) the wings of which are mottled with various shades of red and brown and have violet tips
violet wood *n* **1 :** any of several hard purplish or reddish woods; *esp* **:** KINGWOOD **2 :** a tree that yields violet wood **3 :** PURPLEHEART
violet wood sorrel *n* **:** a perennial herb (*Oxalis violacea*) of the eastern U. S. with palmately compound usu. sensitive leaves and rose-purple or rarely white flowers
vi·o·lety \ˈvīələd-ē\ *adj* **:** resembling or suggesting a violet color or violets ⟨a ~ odor⟩ ⟨a ~ color⟩ ⟨a ~ sky⟩
¹**vi·o·lin** \,vīəˈlin *sometimes* ˈvīə,lin *or* -ələn\ *n* -S [It *violino*, dim. of *viola* viol, viola, fr. OProv *viola, viula* viol — more at VIOL] **1 a :** a bowed stringed musical instrument having four strings tuned at intervals of a fifth and a range from G below middle C to the fourth C above or higher which is distinguished from the viol in having a shallower body, shoulders at right angles with the neck, and a more curved bridge and is capable of a richer, more powerful, and more varied tone **b :** an 8-foot labial pipe-organ stop having a tone like a violin **2 :** a violin player ⟨first ~ of an orchestra⟩

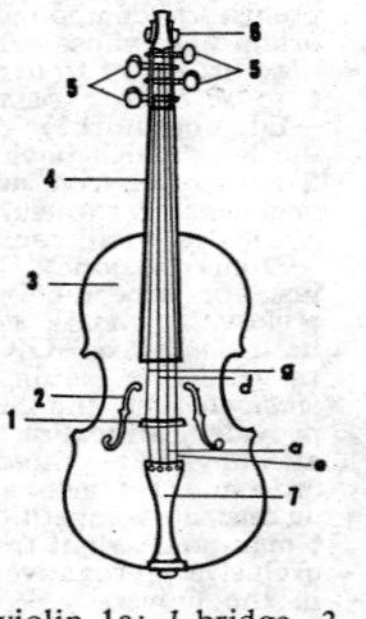

violin 1a: *1* bridge, *2* sound hole, *3* soundboard, *4* fingerboard, *5* pegs, *6* scroll, *7* string holder, *g* G string, *d* D string, *a* A string, *e* E string

²**violin** \"\ *vi* -ED/-ING/-S **:** to play the violin
vi·o·li·na \,vēəˈlēnə\ *n* -S [alter. of ¹*violin*] **:** a string-toned pipe-organ stop of 4-foot pitch
violin clef *n* **:** G CLEF
violin diapason *n* **:** a metal labial pipe-organ stop of 8-foot pitch with a combination of diapason and string-toned quality
vi·o·line \ˈvīə,lēn, -ələn\ *n* -S [F, fr. NL *Viola* + F *-ine*] **:** a moderate to strong violet
violine pink *n* **:** a moderate purplish red that is bluer and deeper than average rose, bluer and paler than magenta rose or average fuchsia rose, deeper than mallow, and bluer, lighter, and stronger than solferino
vi·o·lin·ette \¦vīələ¦net\ *n* -S [¹*violin* + *-ette*] **:** VIOLINO PICCOLO
vi·o·lin·ist \,vīəˈlinəst *sometimes* ˈvīə,lin- *or* -ələn-\ *n* -S [It *violinista*, fr. *violino* violin + *-ista* -ist] **:** one who plays the violin
vi·o·lin·is·tic \¦vīələ¦nistik\ *adj* **:** relating to the violin and violin playing; *specif* **:** particularly suited to playing on the violin — **vi·o·lin·is·ti·cal·ly** \-tək(ə)lē\ *adv*
vi·o·li·no \,vēəˈlē(,)nō\ *n* -S [It] **:** VIOLIN
violino pic·co·lo \-ˈpēkə,lō\ *n, pl* **violino piccolos** [It, little violin] **:** a small violin made with the same proportions as the ordinary violin and usu. tuned a third higher
¹**vi·ol·ist** \ˈvīələst\ *n* -S [²*viol* + *-ist*] **:** one who plays the viol
²**vi·o·list** \vēˈōləst *sometimes* vī-\ *n* -S [¹*viola* + *-ist*] **:** one who plays the viola
violle standard \ˈvyȯl-\ *or* **violle** *n* -S *usu cap V* [after Jules *Violle* †1923 Fr. physicist] **:** a photometric unit that is the luminous intensity of a square centimeter of platinum at the temperature of solidification and equals about 20 candles
vi·o·lon \ˈvīələn, ˈvēəl-, -,län\ *n* -S [MF, aug. of *viole* viol, viola — more at VIOL] **:** VIOLIN
vi·o·lon·cel·list \,vīələnˈcheləst, ,vēəl-, -,län-\ *n* **:** CELLIST
vi·o·lon·cel·lo \-e(,)lō\ *n* -S [It, dim. of *violone*] **1 :** a bass violin that is the modern form of the viola da gamba with four strings tuned an octave lower than the viola and with a pitch compass of C to e″, that is held vertically on the floor between the player's knees while in a sitting position, and that when played produces a sonorous and expressive quality **2 :** a labial pipe-organ stop of similar quality
violoncello pic·co·lo \-ˈpēkə,lō\ *n* [It, little violoncello] **:** a small violoncello having the same shape and tuning
vi·o·lo·ne \,vēəˈlōnā\ *n* -S [It, aug. of *viola* viol, viola — more at VIOLIN] **1 :** a viol of contrabass size and range **2 :** CONTRE BASSE
vi·o·lot·ta \,vēəˈläd-ə\ *n* -S [It *viola* + *-otta* (aug. suffix)] **:** a violin having a range extending to a fourth below the range of the viola
viols *pl of* VIOL
vi·o·lu·ric acid \¦vīə¦lu̇rik-\ *n* [ISV *violet* + *barbituric*] **:** a crystalline monobasic acid $HON(CONH)_2CO$ that is made from nitrous acid and barbituric acid or from hydroxylamine and alloxan, that tautomerizes in water from the isonitroso

form to the violet nitroso form, and that forms characteristic colored salts; 5-isonitroso-barbituric acid
vi·o·my·cin \ˌvīəˈmīsᵊn\ *n* -s [*violet* + *-mycin*; fr. the color of the soil mold] **:** a basic polypeptide antibiotic produced by a soil actinomycete (as *Streptomyces puniceus*) and administered intramuscularly in the form of its sulfate in the treatment of tuberculosis esp. in combination with other antitubercular drugs
vi·or·na \vīˈȯrnə\ *n, cap* [NL, fr. F *viorne* clematis, fr. L *viburnum* wayfaring tree] *in some classifications* **:** a genus of chiefly No. American vines or erect herbs (family Ranunculaceae) that have mostly solitary flowers with erect sepals and stamens and are usu. included in the genus *Clematis*
vi·os·ter·ol \vīˈästəˌrōl, -rȯl\ *n* -s [ultra*violet* + *sterol*] **:** vitamin D_2 esp. when dissolved in an edible vegetable oil for use chiefly in infant nutrition
VIP \ˌvēˌīˈpē\ *n* -s [*very important person*] **:** a person of considerable influence or prestige; *esp* **:** a high official receiving special privileges
vi·per \ˈvīpə(r)\ *n* -s [MF *vipere*, fr. L *vipera* adder, snake, perh. fr. *vivi-* + *-pera* (fr. *parere* to give birth to, produce); fr. an old belief that it is viviparous — more at PARE] **1 a :** a common European venomous snake (*Vipera berus*) that attains a length of two feet, varies in color from red, brown, or gray with dark markings to black, occurs across Eurasia from England to Sakhalin, and that is rarely fatal to man; *broadly* **:** any snake of the venomous Old World family Viperidae and sometimes of the closely related Crotalidae **b :** a venomous or reputedly venomous snake **2 :** a dangerous, malignant, or treacherous person ⟨they forgot that this helpless, shapeless mass of humanity . . . was a ~ they must crush —Liam O'Flaherty⟩
vi·pera \ˈvīpərə\ *n, cap* [NL, fr. L, viper] **:** a genus of Old World snakes that is the type of the family Viperidae
vi·per·an \ˈvīpərən\ *adj* [*viper* + *-an*] **:** VIPERINE
viperfish \ˈ≈≈ˌ≈\ *n* **:** a fish of the family Gonostomatidae or of the related family Chauliodontidae
vi·pe·ri·an \(ˈ)vīˌpirēən\ *adj* [*viper* + *-ian*] **:** VIPERINE
¹vi·per·id \ˈvīpərəd\ *adj* [NL *Viperidae*] **:** of or relating to the Viperidae
²viperid \"\ *n* -s **:** a snake of the family Viperidae
vi·per·i·dae \vīˈperəˌdē\ *n pl, cap* [NL, fr. *Vipera*, type genus + *-idae*] **:** a widely distributed family comprising sluggish heavy-bodied Old World venomous snakes that are characterized by large tubular venom-conducting fangs erected by rotation of the movable premaxillary bone — see VIPER; compare CROTALIDAE
vi·per·i·form \ˈvīpərəˌfȯrm\ *adj* [*viper* + *-iform*] **:** resembling a viper
vi·per·ine \ˈvīpərən, -əˌrīn\ *adj* [L *viperinus*, fr. *vipera* viper + *-inus* -ine] **:** of, relating to, or resembling a viper **:** VENOMOUS
viperine snake *n* **1** *also* **viperine :** a snake of the family Viperidae **2 :** a small harmless snake (*Natrix viperinus*) colored much like the viper and found in southern Europe and northern Africa
vi·per·ish \ˈvīpərish\ *adj* [*viper* + *-ish*] **:** spitefully vituperative **:** VENOMOUS ⟨a fierce ~ tongue on occasion —Peggy Bennett⟩ — **vi·per·ish·ly** *adv*
viperlike \ˈ≈≈ˌ≈\ *adj* [*viper* + *like*] **:** behaving like a viper
vi·per·ling \-ə(r)liŋ\ *n* -s [*viper* + *-ling*] **:** a young viper
vi·per·ous \ˈvīp(ə)rəs\ *adj* [*viper* + *-ous*] **1 :** of, relating to, or composed of vipers **2 a :** characteristic of a viper **:** deliberately treacherous **:** MALIGNANT, VENOMOUS ⟨no punishment is too severe for his ~ act of treason⟩ **b :** possessing qualities attributed to a viper ⟨a ~ murderer⟩
vi·per·ous·ly *adv* **:** in a viperous manner
viper's bugloss *n* **:** BLUEWEED 1
viper's-grass \ˈ≈≈ˌ≈\ *n, pl* **viper's-grasses :** a perennial herb (*Scorzonera hispanica*) with narrow entire leaves, solitary heads of yellow flowers, and long white carrot-shaped roots that are eaten in Spain and elsewhere
viper wine *n* **:** a medicated wine containing a decoction from vipers formerly believed to restore vital powers
vip·i·on·i·dae \ˌvipēˈänəˌdē\ *n pl, cap* [NL, fr. *Vipion-, Vipio*, type genus (fr. L, a small crane) + *-idae*; fr. their long legs] **:** a family of small ichneumon flies that is often included in Braconidae and includes forms which as larvae are parasites of various lepidopterous, hymenopterous, coleopterous, and dipterous insects
VIPs *pl of* VIP
vir *abbr* [L *viridis*] green
vi·rag·i·nous \vəˈrajənəs\ *adj* [L *viragin-, virago* virago + E *-ous*] **:** of, relating to, or characteristic of a virago
vi·ra·go \vəˈrä(ˌ)gō, -rā-, -rä(- *also* ˈvirəˌgō\ *n, pl* **viragoes** *or* **viragos** [L *viragin-, virago* manlike heroic woman, fr. *vir* man, male — more at VIRILE] **1 :** a loud overbearing woman **:** SHREW, TERMAGANT **2 :** a woman of great stature, strength, and courage **:** one possessing supposedly masculine qualities of body and mind
vi·ral \ˈvīrəl\ *adj* [NL *virus* + ISV *-al*] **:** of or belonging to a virus **:** caused by a virus **:** concerned with or involving viruses
vi·ra·les \vīˈrā(ˌ)lēz\ *n pl, cap* [NL, fr. *virus* + *-ales*] **:** an order of parasitic plants consisting of the viruses and comprising three suborders — see PHAGINEAE, PHYTOPHAGINEAE, ZOOPHAGINEAE
viral hepatitis *n* **:** INFECTIOUS HEPATITIS
vi·ra·ma \vəˈrämə\ *n* -s [Skt *virāma*, lit., cessation, stop, fr. *viramati* he ceases, pauses, fr. *vi-* apart, asunder + *ramate* he stands still, rests — more at WITH, RIM] **:** a mark added to a consonant sign in Devanagari and related alphabets to indicate that the consonant sign stands only for a consonant and not for a combination of consonant plus following vowel
vir·e·lay *also* **vir·e·lai** \ˈvirəˌlā\ *n* -s [ME, fr. MF *virelai*, alter. (influenced by *lai* lay) of OF *vireli*, prob. fr. the meaningless refrain *vireli*] **1 a :** an old French verse form having a refrain and composed wholly in two rhymes **b :** a verse form composed of stanzas indeterminate in length and number but usu. repeating one of the two rhymes of the first stanza in the second, the new rhyme of the second stanza in the third, until the last stanza where the unrepeated rhyme of the first stanza takes the place of a new rhyme — compare VILLANELLE **2 :** an old song or poem esp. with a refrain or an intricate or monotonous rhyme scheme
vire·ment \ˈvirmäⁿ\ *n* -s [F, fr. MF, act of turning, fr. *virer* to turn + *-ment* — more at ENVIRON] **:** an administrative transfer of budgetary funds
vi·re·mia *also* **vi·rae·mia** \vīˈrēmēə\ *n* -s [NL, fr. *virus* + *-emia*] **:** the presence of a virus in the blood of a host — **vi·re·mic** \(ˈ)vīˈrēmik\ *adj*
vi·rent \ˈvīrənt\ *adj* [L, fr. *virent-, virens* pres. part. of *virēre* to be green] **1 :** not withered **:** FRESH **2 :** green in color
vir·eo \ˈvirēˌō\ *n* [L *vireon-, vireo*, a small bird, perh. the greenfinch, fr. *virēre* to be green] **1** -s **:** any of various small birds of the family Vireonidae — see RED-EYED VIREO, SOLITARY VIREO **2** *cap* [NL, fr. L] **:** a genus of vireos that is the type of the family Vireonidae
vir·e·on·i·dae \ˌvirēˈänəˌdē\ *n pl, cap* [NL, fr. *Vireon-, Vireo*, type genus + *-idae*] **:** a family of small insectivorous American passerine birds that are plainly but delicately colored chiefly in olivaceous and grayish shades, that are sweet singers, and that usu. build pensile nests
¹vir·e·o·nine \ˈvirēəˌnīn, -ˌnən\ *adj* [L *vireon-, vireo* vireo + E *-ine*] **:** of or relating to the vireos
²vireonine \"\ *n* -s **:** VIREO 1
vires *pl of* VIS
vi·res·cence \vəˈresᵊn(t)s, vīˈ-\ *n* -s [fr. *virescent*, after such pairs as E *intelligent*: *intelligence*] **:** the state or condition of becoming green: as **a :** such a condition due to the development of chloroplasts in organs (as petals) normally white or colored **b** *Austral* **:** BIG BUD
vi·res·cent \-nt\ *adj* [L *virescent-, virescens*, pres. part. of *virescere* to become green, incho. of *virēre* to be green] **:** beginning to be green **:** slightly green **:** developing or displaying virescence **:** GREENISH
virescent gold *n, often cap V&G* **:** an organic pigment — see DYE table I (under *Pigment Green 10*)
virg *abbr* [L *virgo*] virgin
vir·ga \ˈvərgə\ *n* -s [NL, fr. L, branch, rod, streak in the sky suggesting rain] **:** trailing wisps of precipitation falling from the base of a cloud but evaporating before reaching the ground

¹vir·gate \ˈvər|gət, ˈvə̄|, ˈvəi|, |ˌgāt, *usu* -d-+V\ *n* -s [ML *virgata*, fr. *virga*, a land measure, fr. L, rod] **:** any of various old English units of land area equal to one quarter of a hide or one quarter of an acre
²virgate \"\ *adj* [NL *virgatus*, fr. L, made of twigs, striped, fr. *virga* branch, twig, rod, streak + *-atus* -ate — more at WHISK] **1 a :** having the form of a rod **:** shaped like a wand **b :** bearing many small twigs **2 :** slender and slightly toothed — used of the trophi of various rotifers
³vir·gate \|ˌgāt\ *vi* -ED/-ING/-S [back-formation fr. *virgation*] **:** to branch in diverging lines
vir·gat·er \ˈvərˌgād·ər\ *n* -s [¹*virgate* + *-er*] **:** a holder of a virgate
vir·ga·tion \ˌvərˈgāshən\ *n* -s [L *virga* branch + E *-ation*] **:** a branching arrangement of fault lines
vir·gil·ia \(ˌ)vərˈjilēə, və̄-, vəi-\ *n* [NL, fr. LL *Virgilius* (alter. of *Vergilius* — Publius Vergilius Maro †19 B.C. Roman poet) + NL *-ia*] **1** *cap* **:** a genus of southern African trees (family Leguminosae) having pinnate leaves and rose-purple flowers succeeded by a coriaceous 2-valved pod **2** -s **:** any of several trees related to or formerly included in the genus *Virgilia*: as **a :** YELLOWWOOD 1a **b :** KENTUCKY COFFEE TREE
¹virgilian *usu cap, var of* VERGILIAN
²vir·gil·i·an \(ˌ)vərˈjilēən, və̄-, vəi-\ *adj, usu cap* [*Virgil*, town of southeastern Kansas + E *-ian*] **:** of, relating to, or constituting a subdivision of the Pennsylvanian — see GEOLOGIC TIME table
¹vir·gin \ˈvərjən, ˈvə̄j-, ˈvəij-\ *n* -s [ME, fr. OF *virgine*, fr. L *virgin-, virgo* young woman, maiden, virgin, perh. fr. *virga* green branch, twig — more at WHISK] **1 a :** an unmarried or chaste woman noted in the early Christian Church for her piety and steadfast service to her faith and accorded by virtue of these qualities a special place among the members of the Christian community **b :** an unmarried woman devoted to a deity in a celibate life of service within a religious temple ⟨the Inca ~s of the Sun⟩ **2 a :** a usu. young woman noted for purity and chastity **b :** a young unmarried woman **3 :** a person who has not had sexual intercourse **4** *usu cap* **:** VIRGO **5 :** a picture of a madonna **6 :** a female animal that has never copulated
²virgin \"\ *adj* [ME, fr. ¹*virgin*] **1 :** free of impurity or stain **:** not defiled **:** UNSULLIED ⟨all their branches laden with soft . . . ~ snow —Willa Cather⟩ **2 :** being a virgin **:** CHASTE **3 :** made up of virgins ⟨watched his graceful maid as mid the ~ train she strayed —R.W.Emerson⟩ **4 :** of, relating to, characteristic of, or befitting a virgin **:** indicating modesty **:** MODEST ⟨was permitted no greater magnificence than a Greek robe of ~ white —Elinor Wylie⟩ **5 a :** not yet disturbed or made use of **:** FRESH, NEW, UNSPOILED, UNTAPPED ⟨a ~ wilderness of jagged mountains, deep ravines, and swift watercourses —*Amer. Guide Series: Oregon*⟩ **:** not altered by human activity **:** free from artificial alteration ⟨a ~ forest⟩ ⟨~ unplowed turf⟩ **b :** not previously treated or handled **:** not reclaimed or reworked: as (1) **:** of or relating to chemical wood pulp that has not previously been used (2) **:** never treated with dyes or bleaches ⟨~ hair⟩ **6 a** (1) **:** being made use of for the first time ⟨observed that the candles were not ~: both had been burned —Elizabeth Bowen⟩ (2) **:** processed or worked for the first time — see VIRGIN WOOL **b :** INITIAL, FIRST ⟨liked the idea of guiding my ~ steps on the hard road of letters —W.S. Maugham⟩ **7 a** *of a chemical element* **:** occurring naturally uncombined **:** NATIVE ⟨~ sulfur⟩ **b** *of a vegetable oil* **:** obtained from the first light pressing esp. of olives or walnuts in the cold **8 :** produced directly from ore or by primary smelting — used of metal to distinguish it from scrap or from metal obtained by remelting used material **9 :** never captured **:** UNSUBDUED — usu. used of a fortress **10 :** as yet without contact ⟨the second team, ~ to harness —Owen Wister⟩ ⟨absolutely ~ towards such experience —Walter Pater⟩ **syn** see YOUTHFUL
¹vir·gin·al \-nᵊl\ *adj* [ME, fr. MF or L; MF *virginal*, fr. L *virginalis*, fr. *virgin-, virgo* virgin + *-alis* -al] **1 :** of, relating to, or characteristic of a virgin or virginity **2 :** continuing in or maintaining a state of chastity **:** possessing the purity attributed to a virgin **3 :** essentially pure **:** PRISTINE, UNSULLIED, UNTOUCHED ⟨nor is there anything more ~ than the shimmer of young foliage —L.P.Smith⟩ **syn** see YOUTHFUL
²virginal \"\ *n* -s [prob. fr. L *virginalis* of or relating to a virgin; perh. fr. its being played by young girls] **:** a small rectangular spinet having no legs and having only one wire to a note, popular in the 16th and 17th centuries — often used in pl. ⟨plays upon the ~s⟩ ⟨a pair of ~s⟩
³virginal \"\ *vi, obs* **:** to tap with the fingers as if on a virginal
⁴virginal \"\ *n* -s *usu cap* [ML, fr. L *virginale*, neut. of *virginalis* of a virgin] **:** a book of the offices of the Virgin Mary
vir·gin·al·ist \-ᵊləst\ *n* -s [²*virginal* + *-ist*] **:** one who plays a virginal
vir·gin·al·ly \-ᵊlē\ *adv* [¹*virginal* + *-ly*] **:** in a virginal manner
virginal membrane *n* **:** HYMEN
virgin birth *n* **1 :** birth from a virgin **:** PARTHENOGENESIS **2** *sometimes cap V&B* **:** the theological doctrine that Jesus was miraculously begotten of God and born of a virgin mother — compare IMMACULATE CONCEPTION
virgin-born \ˈ≈≈ˌ≈\ *adj* **:** PARTHENOGENETIC
virgin bower *n* **:** VIRGIN'S BOWER
virgin cork *n* **:** cork that is taken from young cork oaks and consists of epidermis, cortical tissue, and periderm
virgin dip *n* **:** the resin obtained during the first year a tree is tapped for turpentine
virgin forest *n* **:** OLD GROWTH 1
virgin honey *n* **:** honey that flows freely from the uncapped comb at ordinary temperature and is produced usu. by a young colony
¹vir·gin·ia \və(r)ˈjinyə, -nēə\ *adj, usu cap* [fr. *Virginia*, eastern state of the U.S., fr. L *virgin-, virgo* virgin; fr. Queen Elizabeth I's familiar appellation "the Virgin Queen"] **:** of or from the state of Virginia ⟨a *Virginia* plantation⟩ **:** of the kind or style prevalent in Virginia **:** VIRGINIAN
²virginia \"\ *n* -s *usu cap* **:** VIRGINIA TOBACCO
virginia cedar *n, usu cap V* **:** RED CEDAR 1a
virginia cowslip *or* **virginia bluebell** *n, usu cap V* **:** a smooth erect herb (*Mertensia virginica*) of eastern No. America having entire leaves and showy blue flowers that are pink in bud
virginia creeper *n, usu cap V* **:** a common No. American tendril-climbing vine (*Parthenocissus quinquefolia*) having palmately 5-foliolate or 7-foliolate leaves and bluish black berries — called also *American ivy, woodbine*
virginia creeper leafhopper *n, usu cap V* **:** a jassid bug (*Erythroneura ziczac*) that is highly destructive to Virginia creeper in parts of the U.S.
virginia crownbeard *n, usu cap V* **:** a tall perennial herb (*Verbesina virginica*) of the eastern U.S. with alternate leaves and paniculate heads of white flowers
virginia deer *n, usu cap V* **:** WHITE-TAILED DEER — used esp. of forms found in the eastern U.S.
virginia dogwood *n, usu cap V* **:** FLOWERING DOGWOOD
virginia false gromwell *n, usu cap V* **:** a false gromwell (*Onosmodium virginianum*)
virginia fence *or* **virginia rail fence** *n, usu cap V* **:** WORM FENCE
virginia goatsbeard *n, usu cap V* **:** a small pale green herb (*Cynthia virginica*) of the family Compositae with yellow flower heads
virginia goat's rue *n, usu cap V* **:** CATGUT 3a
virginia grape fern *n, usu cap V* **:** a rattlesnake fern (*Botrychium virginianum*)
virginia ham *n, usu cap V* **:** a flat lean hickory-smoked ham with dark red meat from a peanut-fed razorback hog
virginia knotweed *n, usu cap V* **:** an erect herb (*Polygonum virginiana*) of the family Polygonaceae of eastern No. America with ovate pointed leaves and spikes of small greenish or rose-colored flowers
virginia mallow *n, usu cap V* **:** a perennial herb (*Sida hermaphrodita*) that is native to the southeastern U.S. and has white flowers and leaves like those of the maple
¹vir·gin·ian \və(r)ˈjinyən, -inēən\ *n* -s *cap* [*Virginia*, eastern state of the U.S. + E *-an*] **:** a native or resident of the state of Virginia
²virginian \"\ *adj, usu cap* [*Virginia*, state of U.S. + E *-an*] **:** of, relating to, or characteristic of Virginia or Virginians

virginian creeper *n, usu cap V* **:** VIRGINIA CREEPER
virginia nightingale *n, usu cap V* **:** CARDINAL 5
virginian stock *n, usu cap V* **:** an erect branching annual cruciferous herb (*Malcolmia maritima*) sometimes cultivated for its loose racemes of white, pink, red, or lilac flowers
virginia opossum *n, usu cap V* **:** the common opossum (*Didelphis virginiana*) of No. America
virginia oyster *n, usu cap V* **:** the common edible oyster of the Atlantic coast of No. America
virginia pine *n, usu cap V* **1 :** LONGLEAF PINE **2 :** LOBLOLLY PINE 1 **3 :** a scrub pine (*Pinus virginiana*)
virginia poke *n, usu cap V* **1 :** a pokeweed (*Phytolacca americana*) **2 :** AMERICAN HELLEBORE 1
virginia quail *n, usu cap V* **:** BOBWHITE
virginia rail *n, usu cap V* **:** an American long-billed rail (*Rallus limicola*) resembling the king rail in color but scarcely larger than the sora
virginia reel *n, usu cap V* **:** an American longways danced usu. by from four to eight couples in which the head and foot couples perform a series of figures and all in turn participate in swinging with the head couple who then go to the foot permitting the dance to continue until each couple has taken part in the figures; *also* **:** the music for the dance
virginia sarsaparilla *n, usu cap V* **:** WILD SARSAPARILLA 1
virginia silk *n, usu cap V* **:** a common milkweed (*Asclepias syriaca*) of eastern No. America
virginia snakeroot *also* **virginia serpentaria** *or* **virginia serpentary** *n, usu cap V* **:** a birthwort (*Aristolochia serpentaria*) of the eastern U. S. with oblong leaves cordate at the base and a solitary basal very irregular flower
virginia stickseed *or* **virginia mouse-ear** *n, usu cap V* **:** a biennial No. American herb (*Lappula virginiana*) with broad oval leaves and prickly-barbed fruit
virginia stock *n, usu cap V* **:** VIRGINIAN STOCK
virginia strawberry *n, usu cap V* **:** a No. American herb (*Fragaria virginiana*) having white flowers and sweet scarlet fruit and being one of the plants used in developing the garden strawberry
virginia sumac *n, usu cap V* **:** STAGHORN SUMAC
virginia thorn *n, usu cap V* **:** WASHINGTON THORN
virginia thyme *n, usu cap V* **:** a fragrant perennial herb (*Pycnanthemum virginianum*) of eastern No. America with opposite linear lanceolate leaves and tiny close heads of flowers in a terminal cluster
virginia tobacco *n, usu cap V* **1 :** tobacco grown in colonial No. America and shipped from Virginia ports **2 a :** tobacco grown east of the Appalachian mountains and flue-cured **b :** any of various fire-cured, sun-cured, or air-cured tobaccos of the eastern U. S. — distinguished from *burley*
virginia wake-robin *n, usu cap V* **:** GREEN ARROW ARUM
virginia waterleaf *n, usu cap V* **:** a showy perennial herb (*Hydrophyllum virginianum*) with white flowers and foliage that is sometimes used as greens in the southeastern U. S. — called also *Shawnee salad, shawny*
virginia willow *also* **virginia tea** *n, usu cap V* **:** a No. American shrub (*Itea virginica*) with simple alternate leaves and small white flowers in simple racemes
virginia winterberry *n, usu cap V* **:** BLACK ALDER 1
virginia yellow pine *n, usu cap V* **:** SHORTLEAF PINE 1
virgin islander *n, cap V&I* [*Virgin Islands*, group of islands in the West Indies + E *-er*] **1 :** a native or inhabitant of the British Virgin Islands **2 :** a native or inhabitant of the Virgin Islands of the U. S.
vir·gin·i·ty \və(r)ˈjinəd·ē, -nətē, -i\ *n* -ES [ME *virginite*, fr. OF *virginité*, fr. L *virginitat-, virginitas* maidenhood, virginity, fr. *virgin-, virgo* virgin + *-itat-, -itas* -ity] **1 :** the quality or state of being chaste; *often* **:** the physical attributes distinguishing a virgin **2 :** the unmarried life **:** CELIBACY, SPINSTERHOOD **3 :** the quality or state of being fresh or new
vir·gin·i·um \və(r)ˈjinēəm\ *n* -s [NL, fr. *Virginia*, state of the U.S. + NL *-ium*] **:** chemical element 87 — superseded by *francium*
virgin moth *n* **:** WHITE MILLER 1b
vir·gin·o·ge·nia \ˌvərjənōˈjēnēə\ *n, pl* **virginogeniae** \-nēˌē\ [NL, fr. L *virgin-, virgo* maiden + NL *-o-* + *-genia* (fr. Gk *-genēs* -gen)] **:** VIRGINOPARA — **vir·gin·o·gen·ic** \ˈ≈≈ˌjenik\ *adj*
vir·gi·nop·a·ra \ˌvərjəˈnäpərə\ *n, pl* **virginopa·rae** \-pəˌrē\ [NL, fr. L *virgin-, virgo* virgin + NL *-o-* + *-para*] **:** one of the polymorphic types of some plant lice; *specif* **:** an apterous parthenogenetic female derived from a parthenogenetic parent — **vir·gi·nop·a·rous** \ˈ≈≈ˈnäpərəs\ *adj*
virgin parchment *n* **:** fine parchment made from the skins of newborn lambs and kids
virgin rosin *n* **:** pale yellow rosin made from the first turpentine that exudes after a tree is boxed
virgins *pl of* VIRGIN
virgin's bower *n* **:** a plant of the genus *Clematis* esp. when small-flowered and climbing: as **a :** the European traveler's-joy **b :** a common clematis (*C. virginiana*) of eastern No. America that sprawls and scrambles over other plants and bears numerous panicles of small creamy white flowers **c :** a rather similar clematis (*C. ligusticifolia*) of the western U.S. with distinctively fragrant flowers
virgin's milk *n, often cap V* **:** a former cosmetic consisting either of the tincture of benzoin or some balsam or of lead subacetate precipitated by addition of water
virgin soil *n* **:** soil that has never been cultivated
virgin spawn *n* **:** mushroom spawn made by mixing the fresh spores directly with the nutritive material making up the bricks
virgin widow *n* **:** one widowed before the consummation of her marriage
virgin wool *n* **1 :** raw wool sheared from live sheep; *specif* **:** wool that has not been worked into yarn or cloth **2 :** WOOL 2a(2)
vir·go \ˈvər(ˌ)gō, ˈvə̄(-, ˈvəi(-\ *n* -s *usu cap* [L *virgin-, virgo* virgin] **:** the sixth sign of the zodiac — see SIGN table, ZODIAC illustration
vir·gu·la \ˈvərgyələ\ *n* -s [NL, fr. L, small rod — more at VIRGULE] **1 :** the axial support of various graptolites **2 :** a bilobate secretory reservoir in various cercariae — **vir·gu·lar** \-lər\ *adj*
vir·gu·lar·ia \ˌvərgyəˈla(a)rēə\ *n, cap* [NL, fr. L *virgula* small rod + NL *-aria*; fr. the rodlike rachis] **:** a genus (the type of the family Virgulariidae) of pennatulaceans having a long rodlike rachis enclosing a slender round or square calcareous axis and having polyps that are arranged in transverse rows or clusters on short fleshy transverse processes borne on each side of the rachis for nearly its whole length
¹vir·gu·lar·i·an \ˈ≈≈ˈla(a)rēən\ *adj* [NL *Virgularia* + E *-an*] **:** of or relating to the genus *Virgularia* or family Virgulariidae
²virgularian \"\ *n* -s **:** a virgularian pennatulacean
vir·gu·late \ˈvərgyələt, -yəˌlāt\ *adj* [L *virgulatus* striped, fr. *virgula* small rod, small stripe + *-atus* -ate] **:** having a shape resembling a rod
vir·gule \ˈvərˌgyül, ˈvə̄-, ˈvəi-,-\ *n* -s [F, fr. L *virgula* small rod, small stripe, obelus, dim. of *virga* branch, rod, stripe — more at WHISK] **1 a :** a short usu. slanting stroke or mark used in medieval manuscripts: as (1) **:** the earliest form of a comma usu. used to indicate a caesura (2) **:** an indication of a division of a word at the end of a line **b :** DIAGONAL 4 **2 :** a form of timepiece escapement that somewhat resembles the verge but has a comma-shaped projection from the balance staff serving as its pallet
vir·i·al \ˈvirēəl\ *n* -s [G, fr. L *vires*, pl., strength, power + G *-ial*; akin to L *vis* strength, force, violence — more at VIM] **:** half the product of the stress due to the attraction or repulsion between two particles in space times the distance between them or in the case of more than two particles half the sum of such products taken for the entire system
virial coefficient *n* **:** one of the coefficients in a series of terms involving inverse powers of specific volume whose sum represents the product of specific volume by pressure for a pure gas ⟨useful form of the equation of state of a real gas is $pv = A + \frac{B}{v} + \frac{C}{v^2} + \ . \ . \ . \ ,$ where A, B, C, etc. are functions of the temperature and are called the *virial coefficients* —F.W.Sears⟩
vi·ri·ci·dal \ˌvīrəˈsīdᵊl\ *adj* [*viricide* + *-al*] **:** of or relating to a viricide **:** acting destructively on viruses
vi·ri·cide \ˈ≈≈ˌsīd\ *n* -s [NL *virus* + E *-i-* + *-cide* (killer)]

: a physical or chemical agent that destroys or inactivates viruses

vir·id \ˈvirəd\ *adj* [L *viridis* green — more at VERDANT] : vividly green : VERDANT ⟨the ~ brilliance of the grass —Mary McCarthy⟩ ⟨distant peaks, ~ vistas, nearby trees and bushes —Joseph Hergesheimer⟩

vir·i·dans \ˈvirə̇ˌdanz\ *adj* [NL, fr. L *viridant-, viridans,* pres. part. of *viridare* to make green, fr. *viridis* green] : ALPHA 3

vir·i·des·cent \ˌvirə̇ˈdesᵊnt\ *adj* [L *viridis* green + E *-escent*] : slightly green : GREENISH

vi·rid·i·an *also* **ve·rid·i·an** \vəˈridēən\ *n* -s [L *viridis* + E *-ian*] **1** : GUIGNET'S GREEN **2** *or* **viridian green** : a strong green that is bluer and duller than average mintleaf (sense 1) or primitive green — called also *chrome green, emeraude, French Veronese green, Veronese green*

vir·i·dig·e·nous \ˌvirə̇ˈdijənəs\ *adj* [L *viridis* green + E *-genous*] : producing greenness

vir·i·din \ˈvirədə̇n\ *n* -s [NL *viride* (specific epithet of *Trichoderma viride*) (fr. L, neut. of *viridis* green) + E *-in*] : a crystalline fungistatic antibiotic $C_{19}H_{16}O_6$ produced by a fungus (*Trichoderma viride*)

vir·i·dine green \ˈvirə̇ˌdēn-, -ˌdə̇n-\ *n* [obs. *viridine* chlorophyll, a green dye, fr. L *viridis* green] : a light yellow green that is greener and stronger than glass green and greener and lighter than sky green

viridine yellow *n* [obs. *viridine*] : a strong yellow green that is greener, lighter, and stronger than parrot green and greener than lovebird

vi·rid·i·ty \vəˈridədē\ *n* -ES [ME *viridite,* fr. MF *viridité,* fr. L *viriditat-, viriditas,* fr. *viridis* green + *-itat-, -itas* -ity — more at VERDANT] **1** : the quality or state of being green : the color of grass or foliage **2** : the quality or state of being or of appearing to be young, fresh, and innocent

vir·ile \ˈvirəl, *chiefly Brit* -iˌrīl\ *adj* [MF or L; MF *viril,* fr. L *virilis,* fr. *vir* man, adult male + *-ilis* -ile; akin to OE & OHG *wer* man, husband, ON *verr,* Goth *waír,* Skt *vīra* man, hero, and prob. to L *vis* strength — more at VIM] **1 a** : having the nature, properties, or qualities of an adult male **b** : characteristic of developed manhood : *specif* : capable of functioning as a male in copulation **2** : characterized by energy and drive considered typically male ⟨existence of a ~ and ever stronger free society in our country —J.E.Allen⟩ ⟨described the inhabitants as an alert ~ efficient people —P.E.James⟩ **3** : characteristically belonging to or associated with men : MASCULINE ⟨considered caps the only ~ form of headgear for a fellow —A.J.Liebling⟩ ⟨frowned around a ~ pipe —Berton Roueché⟩ **4** : marked by unusual strength and vigor : DECISIVE, FORCEFUL ⟨talked with the ~ diction of a Yankee —Margaret Long⟩ ⟨translated into ~ tense American verse —Dudley Fitts⟩ **syn** see MALE

virile member *n* [trans. of L *membrum virile*] : PENIS

vir·i·les·cence \ˌvirəˈlesᵊn(t)s\ *n* -s [*virile* + *-escence*] : the acquiring of characters more or less like those of the male often by a barren or old female — **vir·i·les·cent** \ˌ==ˈlesᵊnt\ *adj*

vir·il·ia \vīˈrilēə\ *n pl* [L, fr. neut. pl. of *virilis* virile] : the male genitals

vir·il·ism \ˈvirəˌlizəm\ *n* -s [ISV *virile* + *-ism*] **1** : precocious development of secondary masculine characters in the male **2** : the appearance of secondary male characters in the female

vi·ril·i·ty \vəˈrilədē, -ətē, -i\ *n* -ES [L *virilitat-, virilitas,* fr. *virilis* virile + *-itat-, -itas* -ity] : the quality or state of being virile: as **a** : the period of developed manhood — compare MULIEBRITY **b** : the capacity to function in copulation **c** : action attributed to masculine strength and drive ⟨to play soccer requires stamina and ~⟩ **d** : a vigorous often dynamic force ⟨literature has lost standards and discipline and at the same time ~ —Irving Babbitt⟩ ⟨industrial ~ in no way mars its gracious and orderly appearance —*Amer. Guide Series: Vt.*⟩

vir·il·iza·tion \ˌvirələ̇ˈzāshən\ *n* -s : the condition of being or process of becoming virilized

vir·il·ize \ˈvirəˌlīz\ *vt* -ED/-ING/-S [*virile* + *-ize*] : to cause or produce virilism in

viri·local \ˌvirə+\ *adj* [L *vir* man + E *-i-* + *local*] : PATRILOCAL — **viri·locally** \"+\ *adv*

virl \ˈvərl\ *n* -s [ME *virole, virell, verelle* — more at FERRULE] *Scot* : FERRULE 1a

¹vi·roid \ˈvīˌrȯid\ *n* -s [NL *virus* + E *-oid,* n. suffix] : a hypothetical viruslike symbiont favorable to the host but tending to mutate to the virus form

²viroid \"\ *adj* [NL *virus* + E *-oid,* adj. suffix] **1** : caused by a virus ⟨~ pneumonia⟩ **2** : of or relating to viroids

vir·o·la \ˈvirələ\ *n, cap* [NL] : a genus of chiefly So. American forest trees (family Myristicaceae) which yield pale to reddish brown wood — see BANAK, UCUUBA

vi·ro·log·i·cal \ˌvīrəˈläjəkəl, -jēk-\ *adj* : of or relating to virology

vi·rol·o·gist \vīˈrälə̇jə̇st\ *n* -s : a specialist in virology

vi·rol·o·gy \-jē, -ji\ *n* -ES [ISV *viro-* (fr. NL *virus*) + *-logy*] : a branch of science that deals with viruses

¹vi·rose \ˈvīˌrōs\ *adj* [L *virosus* poisonous, fr. *virus* poison + *-osus* -ous — more at VIRUS] **1** : having or suggestive of a poisonous quality **2** : FETID, MALODOROUS

²virose \"\ *n* -s [F or G, fr. NL *virosis*] : VIROSIS

vi·ro·sis \vīˈrōsə̇s\ *n, pl* **viro·ses** \-ōˌsēz\ [NL, fr. *virus* + *-osis*] : infection with or disease caused by a virus

vi·rous \ˈvīrəs\ *adj* [NL *virus* + E *-ous*] : caused by a virus

vir·tu *or* **ver·tu** \ˌvərˈtü, vəˈ-, ˌvəiˈ-, ˈ=ˌ=, virˈ-, vəˈ-\ *n* -s [It *virtù* & obs. It *vertù,* lit., virtue, strength, fr. L *virtut-, virtus* — more at VIRTUE] **1** : a love of or a taste for curios or objets d'art **2** : productions of art esp. of a curious or antique nature : OBJETS D'ART **3 a** : an artistic quality **b** : a study of the fine arts

vir·tu·al \ˈvərch(ə)wəl, ˈvəch-, ˈvəich-, -chəl\ *adj* [ME, fr. ML *virtualis,* fr. L *virtus* strength, virtue + *-alis* -al — more at VIRTUE] **1** *obs* : of, relating to, or possessing a power of acting without the agency of matter **2** : notably effective **3** : being functionally or effectively but not formally of its kind ⟨a ~ certainty⟩ ⟨planned the ~ abandonment of the post —Julian Dana⟩ ⟨the ~ abdication of parents from their role as educators —Dorothy Barclay⟩

virtual displacement *n* : an infinitesimal displacement of any point of a mechanical system that may or may not take place but that is compatible with the constraints of the system

virtual focus *n* **1** : a point from which divergent rays (as of light) seem to emanate but do not actually do so (as in the image of a point source seen in a plane mirror) **2** : a point toward which convergent rays are directed but which being intercepted they do not reach

virtual height *n* : the effective height of a layer of ionized gas in the atmosphere by which radio waves are reflected around the earth's curvature

virtual image *n* : an image (as seen in a plane mirror) formed of virtual foci

vir·tu·al·ism \-ˌlizəm\ *n* -s *sometimes cap* : the theological doctrine attributed to John Calvin and other Reformers that though the eucharistic elements remain unchanged in the Lord's Supper the spiritual body, blood, and benefits of Jesus Christ are conveyed through them

vir·tu·al·i·ty \ˌvərchəˈwalədē\ *n* -ES **1** : the essential nature : ESSENCE ⟨the relation between the actuality of the present moment and the *virtualities* of the subsisting past —Milic Capek⟩ **2** : potential existence : POTENTIALITY, EFFICACY

vir·tu·al·ly \ˈvərch(ə)wəlē, ˈvəch-, ˈvəich-, -chəl-, -li\ *adv* [ME, fr. *virtual* + *-ly*] **1** *obs* : in essence : not merely formally **2** : almost entirely : for all practical purposes ⟨unnoticed and ~ unknown —Philip Brady⟩ ⟨was ~ penniless —C.C.Cregan⟩

virtual pitch *n* : the distance a propeller would have to advance in one revolution so that there might be no thrust

vir·tue \ˈvər(ˌ)chü, ˈvə̄(-, ˈvəi(-, *chiefly in southern U.S.* -ˌchə\ *n* -s [ME *vertu, virtu,* fr. OF, fr. L *virtut-, virtus* strength, manliness, virtue, fr. *vir* man — more at VIRILE] **1 a** : moral practice or action : conformity to a standard of right (as divine law or the highest good) : moral excellence : integrity of character : uprightness of conduct : RECTITUDE, MORALITY ⟨~ is not to be considered in the light of mere innocence, or abstaining from harm, but as the exertion of our faculties in doing good —Joseph Butler⟩ ⟨~ is its own reward⟩: as (1) : wisdom based on a knowledge of the good that makes one act in accordance with the good (2) : a habit involving the choice of excellence in conduct with the excellence being realized in a mean between excess and defect **b** : a particular moral excellence ⟨the very ~ of compassion —Shak.⟩ — see CARDINAL VIRTUE, NATURAL VIRTUE, THEOLOGICAL VIRTUE **2 a** *archaic* : supernatural power or influence exerted by a divine being **b virtues** *pl, usu cap* : an order of angels in various medieval descriptions of celestial hierarchies **3** : a particular beneficial quality or efficacy in something ⟨a large spring of unusually fine water . . . credited with unusual ~s —*Amer. Guide Series: Maine*⟩ ⟨certain herbs have greater ~ when they are picked at midnight —Robert Graves⟩ **4** : manly strength or courage : VALOR **5** : a characteristic, quality, or trait known or felt to be excellent : MERIT, VALUE, WORTH ⟨unquestioned faith in the ~ of the cause he served —C.L. Becker⟩ ⟨the house is a graceful structure, built simply when simplicity was not considered a ~ —*Amer. Guide Series: Minn.*⟩ **6** : an active quality or power whether of physical or of moral nature : the capacity or power adequate to the production of a given effect : ENERGY, POTENCY, STRENGTH ⟨the ~ to hold up her head and look the Square in the face —Arnold Bennett⟩ ⟨the rare ~ of being able to face up to any storm without hesitation —M.S.Handler⟩ **7** : an ability or accomplishment **8** : CHASTITY, PURITY; *esp* : the chastity of a woman ⟨the same grim jealousy it shows toward the ~ of its young women —*Newsweek*⟩ **syn** see EXCELLENCE — **by virtue of** *or* **in virtue of** *prep* : through the force of : by authority of ⟨the crossing could succeed only *by virtue of* its boldness —P.W.Thompson⟩ ⟨when technicians . . . assert their authority, it is *in virtue of* their experience —A.L.Guérard⟩

vir·tue·less \ˈ==lə̇s\ *adj* [ME *virtules, vertules,* fr. *virtu, vertu* virtue + *-les* -less] **1** : devoid of excellence or worth **2** : lacking in moral goodness — **vir·tue·less·ness** *n* -ES

vir·tu·o·sa \ˌvərchəˈwōsə, ˌvəch-, ˌvəich-, -ōzə\ *n, pl* **virtuo·se** \-sā, -zā\ *or* **virtuosas** [It, fem. of *virtuoso*] : a female virtuoso

vir·tu·ose \ˌ==ˈwōs\ *adj* [It *virtuoso*] : VIRTUOSIC

vir·tu·osic \-ˈwäsik\ *adj* [ˈ*virtuoso* + *-ic*] : relating to or characteristic of a virtuoso ⟨a vehicle for the display of a ~ performer and his instrument —Robert Evett⟩

vir·tu·os·i·ty \ˌ==ˈwäsədē, -sətē, -i\ *n* -ES [ˈ*virtuoso* + *-ity*] **1** : an often dilettantish interest esp. in one of the fine arts or its products **2 a** (1) : great technical skill in the practice of the fine arts and esp. in the performance of music ⟨performed with ~ on the piano⟩ (2) : technical brilliance of performance without accompanying artistic insight ⟨a period of technical ~ without serious purpose —M.D.Geismar⟩ **b** : technical skill as manifested in the artistic product ⟨struck by the ease and ~ of the writing —Arnold Bennett⟩

¹vir·tu·o·so \ˌvərchəˈwō(ˌ)sō, -)zō\ *n, pl* **virtuosos** \-)sōz, -)zōz\ *or* **virtuo·si** \-ˈwōsē, -ōzē\ [It, fr. *virtuoso,* adj., virtuous, learned, skilled, fr. LL *virtuosus* virtuous — more at VIRTUOUS] **1** : one interested in the pursuit of knowledge : an experimenter or investigator esp. in the arts and sciences : SAVANT ⟨*virtuosi* collected shells, fossils, rocks —C.W.Shumaker⟩ ⟨Christian *virtuosi* who wished to unite the new science and religion against the threat of . . . atheistic mechanism —J.I.Cope⟩ **2** : one devoted to virtu : one skilled in or having a taste for the fine arts : a collector or ardent admirer of curios or objects of art **3** : one who excels in the technique of an art; *esp* : a musical performer (as on the violin or the piano) **syn** see EXPERT

²virtuoso \ˌ==ˈ=(ˌ)=\ *adj* : of, relating to, or characteristic of a virtuoso : having the manner or style of a virtuoso ⟨does not compose for the orchestra in an obviously ~ way —Neville Cardus⟩

vir·tu·ous \ˈvərchəwəs, ˈvəch-, ˈvəich-\ *adj* [ME *virtuous, vertuous,* fr. MF *virtueus, vertueus,* fr. LL *virtuosus,* fr. L *virtus* strength, virtue + *-osus* -ous — more at VIRTUE] **1** *obs* : displaying valor : BRAVE, VALIANT **2** : capable of bringing forth a powerful effect : having potent usu. beneficial qualities : EFFICACIOUS **3** : having or exhibiting virtue : acting in a just way and in accordance with moral laws : devoid of wickedness ⟨a ~ man⟩ **4** : characterized by virtue : morally excellent : RIGHTEOUS ⟨~ indignation is a powerful stimulant but a dangerous diet —G.B.Shaw⟩ ⟨his eyes wild with ~ anger —Joseph Conrad⟩ **5** : CHASTE, PURE ⟨would have known all about those young girls . . . whether they were still ~, what books they read —Aldous Huxley⟩ **syn** see MORAL

vir·tu·ous·ly *adv* [ME *virtuously, vertuously,* fr. *virtuous, vertuous* + *-ly*] : in a virtuous manner

vir·tu·ous·ness *n* -ES [ME *virtuousnesse, vertuousnesse,* fr. *virtuous, vertuous* + *-nesse* -ness] : the quality or state of being virtuous

virtus *pl of* VIRTU

vi·ru \vēˈrü\ *adj, usu cap* [fr. the *Virú* valley, northwestern Peru] : GALLINAZO

vi·ru·ci·dal \ˌvīrəˈsīdᵊl\ *adj* [NL *virus* + E *-cidal*] : tending to kill viruses : acting as a virucide

vi·ru·cide \ˈ==ˌsīd\ *n* -s [NL *virus* + E *-cide*] : an agent that kills viruses

vir·u·lence \ˈvir(y)ələn(t)s\ *or* **vir·u·len·cy** \-nsē, -si\ *n, pl* **virulences** *or* **virulencies** [LL *virulentia* stench, infection, fr. L *virulentus* + *-ia* -y] **1** : extreme bitterness or malignity of temper : RANCOR ⟨old age added ~ to her tongue —Harrison Smith⟩ **2** : the quality or property of being virulent (as an infection) : VENOMOUSNESS, MALIGNANCY **3** : the relative capacity of a microorganism to overcome the body defenses of the host — distinguished from *infectivity*

vir·u·lent \-nt\ *adj* [ME, fr. L *virulentus,* fr. *virus* slimy liquid, poison, stench — more at VIRUS] **1** : characterized by rapid course, severity, and malignancy — used esp. of a disease or infection **2** : extremely poisonous or venomous : DEADLY, NOXIOUS ⟨those mosquitoes must have been particularly ~ —*Farmer's Weekly (So. Africa)*⟩ **3** : bitter in enmity : full of malicious hatred : MALIGNANT ⟨~ hostility . . . thwarted him at every turn —Allen Nevins & H.S.Commager⟩ **4** : objectionably and sometimes intolerably harsh or strong ⟨the zeal for culture was equally ~ —T.S.Eliot⟩ ⟨wearing a *virulent*-purple bathrobe —Harold Brodkey⟩ ⟨a Mexican port stilled with plague . . . beneath the ~ sun —Sinclair Lewis⟩ **5** : exhibiting virulence : able to overcome or break down the defensive mechanism of the host

vir·u·lent·ly *adv* : in a virulent manner ⟨laws ever more ~ isolationist —*President's Commission on Immigration & Naturalization*⟩

vir·u·lif·er·ous \ˌvir(y)əˈlif(ə)rəs\ *adj* [*virulence* + *-iferous*] : containing, producing, or conveying an agent of infection (as a bacterium, virus)

vi·rus \ˈvīrəs\ *n* -ES [L, slimy liquid, poison, stench; akin to OE *wāse* mire, marsh, OFris *wase* mud, ON *veisa* swamp, Gk *ios* poison, Skt *veṣati* it flows away, *viṣa* poison] **1** *archaic* : venom emitted by a poisonous animal **2** [NL, fr. L] **a** : the causative agent of an infectious disease : DISEASE GERM **b** : FILTERABLE VIRUS; *specif* : any of a large group of submicroscopic infective agents that are held by some to be living organisms and by others to be complex autocatalytic protein molecules containing nucleic acids and comparable to genes, that are capable of growth and multiplication only in living cells, and that cause various important diseases in man, animals, or plants (as mumps, rabies, or tobacco mosaic) — see BACTERIOPHAGE, FIXED VIRUS, STREET VIRUS **c** : VIRUS DISEASE 1 ⟨has recovered from a ~ which confined her to her home —*Springfield (Mass.) Daily News*⟩ **3** : a morbid corrupting quality in intellectual or moral conditions : something that poisons the mind or soul ⟨these particular officials affect the public service with an undemocratic ~ —Taylor Cole⟩ ⟨the force of this ~ of prejudice —V.S. Waters⟩ **4** [NL, fr. L] : an antigenic but not infective material (as vaccine lymph) obtainable from a case of an infectious disease **syn** see MICROORGANISM, POISON

virus abortion *n* : abortion in mares caused by a virus possibly identical with that of equine influenza

vi·rus·ci·dal \ˌvīrəˈsīdᵊl\ *adj* [NL *virus* + E *-cidal*] : VIRUCIDAL

vi·rus·cide \ˈ==ˌsīd\ *n* -s [NL *virus* + E *-cide*] : VIRUCIDE

virus disease *n* **1** : a disease caused by a filterable virus (as leaf roll, foot-and-mouth disease, poliomyelitis, the common cold, influenza) **2** : VIROSIS

viruslike \ˈ==ˌ=\ *adj* [NL *virus* + E *like*] : resembling or similar to a virus

virus pneumonia *n* : PRIMARY ATYPICAL PNEUMONIA

vi·rus·tat·ic \ˌvīrəˈstadik\ *adj* [NL *virus* + E *static*] : tending to check the growth of viruses

virus X *n, sometimes cap V & usu cap X* **1** : any of various viruses that are imperfectly identified **2** *or* **virus X disease** : a disease caused by a virus X

¹vis *or* **viss** \ˈvis\ *n, pl* **vis** *or* **viss** [Tamil *vīsai* & Telugu *vīse*] : an old unit of weight used in Burma and southern India equal to 3.65 pounds; *also* : a modern Burmese unit equal to 3.60 pounds

²vis \"\ *n, pl* **vi·res** \ˈvīˌrēz\ [L — more at VIM] : FORCE, POWER

³vis \ˈvē\ *n, pl* **vis** \"\ [by shortening] *archaic* : VIS-À-VIS 2

vis *abbr* **1** viscosity **2** *often cap* viscount **3** visibility; visible **4** visiting **5** visual

¹vi·sa \ˈvēzə *sometimes* -ēsə\ *n* -s [F, fr. L, neut. pl. of *visus,* past part. of *vidēre* to see] **1** : an endorsement made on a passport by the proper authorities (as of the country the bearer wishes to enter) denoting that it has been examined and that the bearer is permitted to proceed **2** : a signature of formal approval by a superior upon a document requiring approval as to form or content

²visa \"\ *vt* **visaed** \-zəd, -səd\ **visaed** \"\ **visaing** \-zəiŋ, -səiŋ\ **visas 1** : to give a visa to (a passport) ⟨provide themselves with passports and . . . have them ~*ed* by the consular officers —A.E.Aspinall⟩ **2** : to give official approval to : RATIFY ⟨a list of topics and speakers must be presented and ~*ed* in advance of every meeting —*Nation*⟩

vis·age \ˈvizij, |ēj *sometimes* -is\ *n* -s [ME, fr. OF, fr. *vis* face (fr. L *visus* sight, vision, fr. *visus,* past part. of *vidēre* to see) + *-age* — more at WIT] **1 a** : the front part of the human head ⟨black hair . . . generally, rather handsome ~ —Charles Dickens⟩ **b** : the corresponding part of the head of a lower animal ⟨the pebble-smooth ~ of a tortoise —*Books of the Month*⟩ **2 a** : a cast of features that express emotion or character : expression of countenance ⟨a monstrous little man . . . with the ~ of a thief —Jean Stafford⟩ ⟨puts on a smiling ~ for the occasion⟩ **b** : APPEARANCE, LOOK, ASPECT ⟨the grimy, gloomy ~ of the mining town⟩ **3** : visible surface — used esp. of the sun or moon ⟨fair moon . . . stoop thy pale ~ through an amber cloud —John Milton⟩ **4** *obs* : outward show : SEMBLANCE ⟨others . . . trimmed in forms and ~s of duty keep yet their hearts attending on themselves —Shak.⟩ **syn** see FACE

vis·aged \-jd\ *adj* [ME, fr. *visage* + *-ed*] : having a visage of a specified kind ⟨he was dour, dark ~, built like the base of an oak tree —Liam O'Flaherty⟩

vi·sam·min \vəˈsamə̇n\ *n* -s [*vis* (prob. abbr. for *viscosity*) + *Ammi* + *-in*] : KHELLIN

vi·sar·ga \vəˈsärgə\ *n* -s [Skt, lit., discharge, fr. *vi* asunder + *sarga* action of letting go, fr. *srjati* he lets go — more at WITH] **1** : a Sanskrit postvocalic sound or group of sounds produced by keeping the vocal organs above the glottis in the same position as for the preceding vowel and continuing to expel air from the lungs but not vibrating the vocal cords **2** : a sign used in writing Sanskrit to represent the visarga sound or sounds — see ALPHABET table

vis a ter·go \ˌvisəˈtər(ˌ)gō\ *n, pl* **vires a tergo** [L] : a force acting from behind ⟨the *vis a tergo* imparted by the heart and transmitted through the arteries —*Science*⟩

¹vis-à-vis \ˌvēzəˈvē, -zä-\ *n, pl* **vis-à-vis** \"\ [F, lit., face to face] **1** : one that is face-to-face with, opposite to, or paired with another: as **a** : one that faces another (as in a folk dance or a parlor game) ⟨each member can ask his *vis-à-vis* in the other team any question —K.M.Willey⟩ **b** : a partner at a social function : ESCORT, DATE ⟨invited . . . to be his *vis-à-vis* at a house party —Jean Stafford⟩ ⟨her *vis-à-vis* was a handsome, balding man —Wolcott Gibbs⟩ **c** : one holding an equal or parallel position : COUNTERPART 3b, OPPOSITE NUMBER 1 ⟨a field representative conferring with his *vis-à-vis* in the home office⟩ ⟨going across to talk with his American *vis-à-vis* —Frederick Simpich †1950⟩ **2** : a carriage in which persons sit face to face **3** : TÊTE-À-TÊTE

²vis-à-vis \"\ *prep* [F] **1** : face-to-face with : OPPOSITE ⟨dining *vis-à-vis* his rival⟩ **2** : in relation to : over against : TOWARD ⟨man's pride *vis-à-vis* the gods —Robert Gordis⟩ **3** : in comparison with : as compared with ⟨traditional logic *vis-à-vis* dialectic —G.L.Kline⟩ ⟨the House, jealous of its powers *vis-à-vis* the Senate —A.J.Liebling⟩

³vis-à-vis \"\ *adv* [F] : in company : FACE-TO-FACE, TOGETHER ⟨found themselves *vis-à-vis* for the first time⟩

vi·sa·yan \vəˈsī(y)ən\ *usu cap, var of* BISAYAN

vis·breaking \ˈvis+ˌ-\ *n* [*vis* (abbr. of *viscosity*) + *breaking*] : VISCOSITY BREAKING

visc *abbr* **1** viscosity **2** *often cap* viscount; viscountess

visc- *or* **visco-** *comb form* [ME, fr. L, fr. *viscum* mistletoe, birdlime — more at VISCOUS] **1** : viscous : viscosity ⟨*visco*gen⟩ ⟨*visco*scope⟩ **2** : viscous and ⟨*visco*elastic⟩

Vis·ca \ˈviskə\ *trademark* — used for an artificial straw made by spinning viscose in a flat filament capable of being braided, woven, or knitted and used esp. for women's hats

vis·cac·cia \viˈskakshēə\ *n* -s [NL, fr. AmerSp *vizcacha*] **1** *syn of* LAGIDIUM **2** *syn of* LAGOSTOMUS

viscacha *or* **viscache** *var of* VIZCACHA

vis·car·ia \viˈska(a)rēə\ *n* [NL, fr. *visc-* + *-aria*] *cap, in some classifications* : a genus of alpine or boreal plants with viscous stems and foliage that are usu. included in the genus *Lychnis*

viscer- *or* **visceri-** *or* **viscero-** *comb form* [LL, fr. L *viscera*] **1** : visceral : viscera ⟨*viscer*algia⟩ ⟨*viscero*ptosis⟩ ⟨*viscero*genic⟩ **2** : visceral and ⟨*visceri*pericardial⟩

viscera *pl of* VISCUS

vis·cer·al \ˈvisərəl\ *adj* [LL *visceralis* intestinal, inguinal, fr. L *viscera* + *-alis* -al] **1** : felt in the viscera : PHYSICAL, BODILY ⟨the ~ sensation of being catapulted down a roller coaster —Gilbert Seldes⟩ ⟨intense ~ delight —F.L.Allen⟩ **2** : felt in the inner being : deep down : INNER ⟨his liberalism . . . is seldom ~ —H.J.Bresler⟩ ⟨had the . . . ~ conviction that he was at home —R.L.Mittenbuhler⟩ **3** : of, relating to, or marked by instinctive or appetitive drives : not intellectual : NONRATIONAL, UNREASONING ⟨the conflict . . . between enlightened conservatives and the more ~ types —Rolfe Humphries⟩ **4** : dealing with crude or elemental emotions : RAW, EARTHY ⟨as emotionally naked and relentlessly ~ a play as our theater has seen —Henry Hewes⟩ **5** : of, relating to, or located on or among the viscera : SPLANCHNIC — compare PARIETAL 1a

visceral arch *n* **1** : one of a series of bony or cartilaginous inverted arches that develop in the walls of the mouth cavity and pharynx of a vertebrate embryo and consist typically of a curved segmented bar or rod on each side meeting its fellow of the opposite side at the ventral end either directly or with the intervention of a median piece — compare BRANCHIAL ARCH, HYOID BONE, MANDIBULAR ARCH **2** : one of the visceral arches together with the structures surrounding and supported by it

visceral bar *n* : one of various cartilaginous rods forming the skeletal frame of the visceral or branchial arches in rays and sharks and in the embryos of higher vertebrates

visceral cleft *n* : one of the clefts that occur on each side of the neck region between successive visceral arches in vertebrates and that may or may not extend through from the exterior to the cavity of the mouth and pharynx — compare BRANCHIAL CLEFT, SPIRACLE 3c

visceral ganglion *n* : either of a pair of ganglia in most mollusks that may lie close to or be fused with the pleural ganglia or may lie much farther back and are connected with the pleural ganglia by pleurovisceral connectives

visceral leishmaniasis *n* : KALA AZAR

visceral loop *n* : a loop that is formed in most mollusks by the visceral ganglia with their commissure and the pleurovisceral connectives and that gives off branches to the gill, osphradium, parts of the mantle, and various viscera

vis·cer·al·ly \-rəlē\ *adv* : in a visceral manner : UNREASONINGLY ⟨thought ~, with his heart and bowels instead of his brain —Malcolm Cowley⟩

visceral nerve *n* : a nerve supplying viscera; *specif* : any of the nerves forming the visceral loop of a mollusk

visceral nervous system *n* : SYMPATHETIC NERVOUS SYSTEM

vis·cer·ate \ˈvisəˌrāt\ *vt* -ED/-ING/-S [by alter.] *archaic* : EVISCERATE

vis·ceri·peri·car·di·al \ˌvisərə+\ *adj* [viscer- + pericardial] : of, relating to, or constituting the body cavity of a cephalopod mollusk that is incompletely divided into an upper cavity containing the heart and a lower one containing the viscera

vis·cero·cra·ni·um \ˌvisərō(ˌ)rō+\ *n* [NL, fr. viscer- + cranium] : SPLANCHNOCRANIUM

vis·cero·gen·ic \ˌvisərōˈjenik\ *adj* [viscer- + -genic] : arising within the body ⟨the common ∼ desires for food, rest, sex, and safety⟩

vis·cero·in·hib·i·tory \ˌvisə(ˌ)rō+\ *adj* [viscer- + inhibitory] : inhibiting functional activity of the viscera ⟨∼ nerves⟩

vis·cero·mo·tor \″+\ *adj* [viscer- + motor] : causing or concerned in the functional activity of the viscera ⟨∼ nerves⟩

vis·cero·pa·ri·etal \″+\ *adj* [viscer- + parietal] : of, relating to, or constituting the visceral ganglia of bivalve mollusks generally situated in contact with the posterior adductor muscles

vis·cer·op·to·sis \ˌvisərˈäpˈtōsəs\ *n* [NL, fr. viscer- + ptosis] : downward displacement of the abdominal viscera

vis·cer·op·tot·ic \ˌ‗‗‗ˈtäd‧ik\ *adj* [fr. NL visceroptosis, after such pairs as NL neurosis: E neurotic] : of, relating to, or affected by visceroptosis ⟨∼ patients⟩

vis·cer·o·to·nia \ˌvisərˈtōnēə\ *n* -s [NL, fr. viscer- + -tonia] : a pattern of temperament that is typical of the endomorphic individual, is marked by predominance of social over intellectual or physical factors, and exhibits conviviality, tolerance, complacency, and love of food — compare CEREBROTONIA, SOMATOTONIA

¹vis·cer·o·ton·ic \ˌ‗‗‗ˈtänik\ *adj* [NL viscerotonia + E -ic] : exhibiting viscerotonia

²viscerotonic \″\ *n* -s : a viscerotonic individual : a typical endomorph

vis·cer·o·trop·ic \ˌvisərəˈträpik\ *adj* [viscer- + -tropic] : turning towards or having an affinity for the viscera — used esp. of a virus

vis·cer·ot·ro·pism \ˌvisəˈrä·trə·pizəm\ *n* : the quality or state of being viscerotropic

vis·cer·ous \ˈvisərəs\ *adj* [L viscera + E -ous] : VISCERAL

vis·cid \ˈvisəd\ *adj* [LL viscidus, fr. L viscum mistletoe, birdlime — more at VISCOUS] **1 a** : having an adhesive quality : GLUEY, STICKY ⟨∼ with resin⟩ **b** : having a glutinous consistency : VISCOUS ⟨a ∼ scum⟩ **c** : covered with a sticky layer ⟨∼ leaves⟩

vis·cid·i·ty \vi'sidəd·ē\ *n* -ES **1** : the quality or state of being viscid : STICKINESS **2** : viscid matter

vis·cid·ly *adv* : in a viscid manner

vis·cin \ˈvisⁿn\ *n* -s [F, fr. visc- + -in] : a clear viscous tasteless substance from the mucilaginous sap of the mistletoe or holly — compare BIRDLIME, VISCUM

visco- — see VISC-

vis·co·elas·tic \ˌviskō+\ *adj* [visc- + elastic] : having both viscous and elastic properties in appreciable degree ⟨∼ cold tar⟩ ⟨∼ asphalt⟩

vis·co·lize \ˈviskəˌlīz\ *vt* -ED/-ING/-s [back-formation fr. Viscolizer] : HOMOGENIZE

Vis·co·liz·er \-zə(r)\ *trademark* — used for a machine similar to a homogenizer but usu. operating at a lower pressure and having smaller openings

vis·com·e·ter \vi'skämət‧ə(r)\ *n* [visc- + -meter] : an instrument with which to measure viscosity

vis·co·met·ric \ˌviskə'me‧trik\ *adj* [visc- + -metric] : of, relating to, or ascertained by a viscometer or viscometry ⟨∼ readings⟩

vis·co·met·ri·cal·ly \-rək(ə)lē\ *adv* [viscometric + -ally (as in metrically)] : in a viscometric manner : by means of a viscometer

vis·com·e·try \vi'skämə‧trē\ *n* -ES [visc- + -metry] : measurement of viscosity

vis·co·scope \ˈviskə‧skōp\ *n* [visc- + -scope] : an instrument for estimating viscosity

¹vis·cose \ˌvi‧skōs\ *adj* [ME, fr. LL viscosus viscous] **1** : VISCOUS ⟨a ∼ solution⟩ **2** [²viscose] : of, relating to, or made from viscose ⟨∼ rayon⟩

²viscose \″\ *n* -s **1** : a viscous sticky golden-brown solution consisting essentially of cellulose xanthate in sodium hydroxide that after ripening from one to several days is usu. extruded through spinnerets or dies and coagulated by means of a bath containing sulfuric acid and salts to form filaments, staple fibers, or films of regenerated cellulose — see CELLOPHANE, VISCOSE RAYON **2** : VISCOSE RAYON

viscose rayon *n* **1** : rayon fiber made from viscose in filament or staple form **2** : rayon yarn or fabric made from viscose rayon fiber

vis·co·sim·e·ter \ˌviskə'simə‧də(r)\ *n* [ISV viscosity + -meter] : VISCOMETER

vis·co·si·met·ric \ˌvi'skäsə'me‧trik\ *adj* [viscosity + -metric] : VISCOMETRIC

vis·co·si·met·ri·cal·ly \-rək(ə)lē\ *adv* : VISCOMETRICALLY

vis·co·sim·e·try \ˌviskə'simə‧trē\ *n* -ES [viscosity + -metry] : VISCOMETRY

vis·cos·i·ty \vi'skäsəd‧ē, -ət‧ē, -i\ *n* -ES [ME viscosite, fr. MF viscosité, fr. ML viscositat-, viscositas, fr. LL viscosus viscous + L -itat-, -itas -ity] **1 a** : the quality or state of being viscous; specif : the physical property of a fluid or semifluid that enables it to develop and maintain a certain amount of shearing stress dependent upon the velocity of flow and then to offer continued resistance to flow — compare COEFFICIENT OF KINEMATIC VISCOSITY, FLUIDITY **b** : COEFFICIENT OF VISCOSITY **c** : the capability possessed by a solid of yielding continually under shearing stress **2** : a viscous substance or mass

viscosity breaking *n* : a process of lowering the viscosity esp. of heavy straight-run residues in petroleum refining by mild cracking

viscosity index *n* : an arbitrary number assigned as a measure of the constancy of the viscosity of a lubricating oil with change of temperature such that a high index indicates that the viscosity changes little with temperature

vis·count \ˈvī‧kaunt\ *n* [ME viscounte, fr. MF visconte, vicomte, fr. ML vicecomit-, vicecomes, fr. LL vice- vice- + comit-, comes count — more at COUNT] **1** : an officer acting as the representative of a count in the administration of a district; specif : a sheriff or high sheriff in England **2** : a member of the fourth grade of the peerage in Great Britain ranking below an earl and above a baron

vis·count·cy \-tsē\ *n* -ES [viscount + -cy] : the rank or dignity of a viscount

vis·count·ess \-təs\ *n* [ME viscountesse, fr. viscounte viscount + -esse -ess] **1** : the wife or widow of a viscount **2** : a woman who holds in her own right the rank of viscount

vis·count·y \-tē\ *n* [viscount + -y] : the territory or jurisdiction of a viscount **2** : VISCOUNTCY

vis·cous \ˈviskəs\ *adj* [ME viscouse, fr. LL viscosus full of birdlime, sticky, viscous, fr. L viscus, viscum mistletoe, birdlime made from berries of mistletoe + -osus -ose; akin to Gk ixos mistletoe, birdlime, Russ vishnya cherry, OHG wīhsila mahaleb cherry and perh. to OE wāse mire, marsh — more at VIRUS] **1 a** : having a ropy or glutinous consistency and the quality of sticking or adhering : VISCID, GELATINOUS, GLUEY ⟨more ∼ than gasoline —Principles of Automotive Vehicles⟩ **b** : having the physical property of viscosity ⟨diesel fuels are more ∼ than gasoline —Principles of Automotive Vehicles⟩ **2** : suggestive of a gluey adhesiveness or mass ⟨a lack of easy movement or fluidity ⟨the ∼ flow of her prose could not cloy a public that feasted on its bright sweetness —J.D.Hart⟩ — vis·cous·ly *adv* : in a viscous manner ⟨few districts in which traffic flows as ∼ as in midtown New York —Harper's⟩

vis·cous·ness *n* -ES archaic : VISCOSITY

vis·cum \ˈviskəm\ *n* [NL, fr. L, mistletoe, birdlime] **1** cap : a genus of Old World semiparasitic plants (family Loranthaceae) distinguished by the clustered axillary bracteate flowers with adnate anthers — see MISTLETOE **2** -s : birdlime made from the berries of the European mistletoe — compare VISCIN

vis·cu·ous \ˈviskyəwəs\ *adj* [visc- + -ous] archaic : VISCOUS

vis·cus \ˈviskəs\ *n*, pl vis·cera \ˈvisərə\ [L] **1** : an internal organ of the body; esp : one (as the heart, liver, or intestine) located in the great cavity of the trunk proper **2** viscera pl : inner or interior matter or contents ⟨the magazine's viscera were arranged in an unusually agreeable order —New Republic⟩ ⟨getting at the viscera of the old sofa⟩

---

¹vise \ˈvīs\ *n* -s [MF vis, viz something winding, winding stairway, screw, fr. L vitis vine — more at WITHY] : any of various tools having two jaws for holding work (as in saw filing) that close usu. by a screw, lever, or cam — see SWIVEL VISE, UNIVERSAL VISE

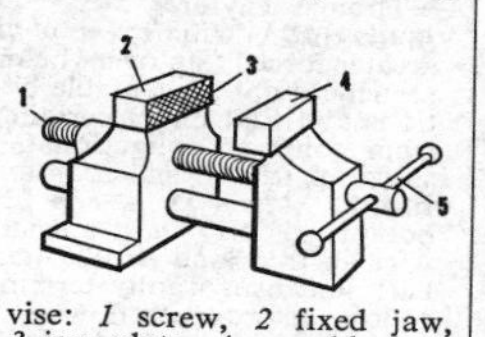

²vise \″\ *vt* -ED/-ING/-s : to hold, force, or squeeze (as work) with or as if with a vise ⟨has a cigar butt vised in his teeth —James Stephens⟩

³vi·sé \'vē‧zā, ‗'‗\ *vt* vis·éd also vis·eed; vis·éd also vis·eed; vis·é·ing; vis·és [F, past part. of viser to put a visa to, examine a visa, fr. visa — more at VISA] : VISA

⁴visé \″\ *n* [F, past part.] : VISA

vise cap *n* : one of the two guards of soft material (as copper) fitting over the jaws of a metalworker's vise

vise coupling *n* : WEDGE COUPLING

vi·sé·ite \'vē‧zā‧ˌīt\ *n* -s [F, fr. Visé, town in Belgium, its locality + F -ite] : a mineral $Ca_8Al_{10}(PO_4)_2(SiO_4)_3(OH)_{10}$-$20-25H_2O$ consisting of a hydrous hydroxide phosphate and silicate of aluminum and calcium

vise·like \'‗‗\ *adj* : acting like a vise ⟨a ∼ grip⟩

vise·man \'vīsmən\ *n*, pl vise·men **1** : a man who works at a vise **2** : an alcohol distillery worker who with a wrench screws plugs and tops on tanks in which gas is held under pressure

vish·nu \ˈvish(ˌ)nü\ *adj*, usu cap [fr. Vishnu's Temple, area on the Colorado river] : of, relating to, or constituting a division of the Archeozoic — see GEOLOGIC TIME table

vish·nu·ism \-ü‧izəm\ *n*, usu cap [Vishnu, second god of the Hindu triad of deities (fr. Skt Viṣṇu) + E -ism] : VAISHNAVISM

vish·nu·ite \-ü‧ˌīt\ *n* -s usu cap [Vishnu + E -ite] : a worshiper of Vishnu : VAISHNAVA

vis·i·bil·i·ty \ˌvizə'biləd‧ē, -lət‧ē, -i\ *n* -ES [LL visibilitas, fr. L visibilis visible + -itas -ity] **1** : the quality or state of being visible ⟨the ∼ of a navigational light⟩ ⟨the need for improving the ∼ of bicycles at night⟩ ⟨stage action with maximum ∼ — Irving Kolodin⟩ **2** archaic a : something visible ⟨modelled . . . into a Shape, a Visibility —Thomas Carlyle⟩ **b** : something worth seeing : a notable sight ⟨have seen all the visibilities of Paris —Samuel Johnson⟩ **3 a** : the degree or extent to which something is visible (as by the degree of clearness of the atmosphere); specif : the mean greatest distance prevailing over the range of more than half of the horizon at which a large object (as a building or ship) may be seen and identified depending upon its size, distance from the observer, the contrast between it and surrounding objects, glare, transparency and illumination of the atmosphere between the object and the observer, and the condition of the observer's eye unaided by special optical devices ⟨up to five miles⟩ ⟨dust storms . . . reducing ∼ to a few yards —Keith Ellis⟩ **b** : capability of being readily noticed ⟨advertising . . . that has the greatest ∼ —Publishers' Weekly⟩ **c** : capability of being distinguished as belonging to a racial, religious, or social group on the basis of either physical or cultural characteristics **d** : capability of affording an unobstructed view ⟨a new car with improved front and rear ∼⟩ ⟨an airplane with good ∼ in the nose⟩ **4** : a measure of the ability of radiant energy to evoke visual sensation : the luminous efficiency of light of a specified wavelength expressed in lumens per watt or usu. as a percentage of its maximum value of about 680 lumens per watt at the green wavelength 5500 angstroms ⟨the ∼ of yellow sodium light is about 76 percent⟩

visibility curve *n* : a curve expressing the values of visibility as a function of wavelength — compare VISIBILITY 4

visibility meter *n* : an instrument for measuring visibility

¹vis·i·ble \ˈvizəbəl\ *adj* [ME, fr. MF or L; MF visible, fr. L visibilis, fr. visus (past part. of vidēre to see) + -ibilis -ible — more at WIT] **1 a** : capable of being seen : perceptible by vision ⟨∼ light⟩ ⟨a ∼ object⟩ ⟨a clearly ∼ stain⟩ ⟨a ship barely ∼ on the horizon⟩ ⟨a cupola ∼ at night for miles — Amer. Guide Series: Minn.⟩ **b** : seen on earth : TEMPORAL ⟨the ∼ church⟩ — compare CHURCH VISIBLE **c** : not subterranean ⟨lagoons with no ∼ outlets⟩ **d** : tangibly present : AVAILABLE ⟨the total of ∼ wheat as of this date⟩ **e** : of or relating to tangible exports and imports ⟨the ∼ items in the balance of payments⟩ **f** : easily seen : impressive to the view ⟨colored slides . . . are both highly ∼ and dramatic —J.K.Blake⟩ **g** : CONSPICUOUS ⟨his highly ∼ neckties —Robert Rice⟩ **h** : possessing cultural visibility ⟨dietary habits may make the foreigner highly ∼ in American culture⟩ **2** : capable of being perceived mentally : DISCOVERABLE, RECOGNIZABLE ⟨serves no ∼ purpose⟩ ⟨had no ∼ means of support⟩ ⟨the ∼ facts of a man's environment —H.O. Taylor⟩ ⟨employees look for . . . a path for advancement —A.S.Igleheart⟩ **3** : willing to receive visitors ⟨was ∼ only to her most intimate friends⟩ **4** : devised in such a way that a particular part or a record made is always in full view or can be readily seen or referred to ⟨a ∼ index⟩ ⟨a ∼ ledger⟩

²visible \″\ *n* -s **1** : something visible ⟨preference for ∼s . . . in teaching —I.A.Richards⟩; specif : the wavelength range of electromagnetic radiation that is perceptible to the human eye — used with the; see LIGHT 1c **2** : a biological mutation determinable by inspection — compare LETHAL 2a

visible church *n* : CHURCH VISIBLE

visible horizon *n* : APPARENT HORIZON

vis·i·ble·ness *n* -ES : VISIBILITY

visible spectrum *n* : the part of the electromagnetic spectrum to which the human eye is sensitive extending from a wavelength of about 3800 angstroms for violet light to about 7600 angstroms for red light

visible speech *n* **1** : a system of phonetic symbols that is intended to represent the positions of the vocal organs in producing speech sounds **2** : a method in which electronic equipment is used for making a spectrographic analysis so that speech is reproduced either as a continuous pattern on a fluorescent screen or as a permanent record on a spectrogram

visible supply *n* : the total of what is known to be available (as of stocks of grain in elevators and on the way to market)

vis·i·bly \ˈvizəblē, -li\ *adv* [ME visibely, fr. visible + -ly] : in a visible manner : OBVIOUSLY, NOTICEABLY ⟨the waters were ∼ diminishing —Rex Ingamells⟩ ⟨the audience was ∼ transported —Virgil Thomson⟩

vis·i·goth \ˈvizə‧gäth, -‧goth sometimes -iso‧-\ *n*, cap [LL Visigothi, pl., of Gmc origin; prob. fr. a Gothic compound whose first constituent is akin to Goth iusiza better, OIr fiu worthy, Gk eus good, brave, Skt vasu good and whose second constituent is the same as the source of LL Gothi Goths — more at GOTH] : a member of the western division of the Goths that invaded the Roman empire beginning in the 4th century and later established kingdoms between the Loire and Gibraltar — called also West Goth; compare OSTROGOTH

¹vis·i·goth·ic \ˌ‗‗‗'gäthik, -goth-, -thēk\ *adj*, usu cap **1** : of or relating to the Visigoths **2** : of or relating to an early medieval Spanish writing developed from the Roman cursive

²visigothic \″\ *n*, usu cap : a Visigothic script

vis·ile \ˈvi‧zīl\ *n* -s [L visus (past part. of vidēre to see) + -ile (as in audile)] : VISUALIZER

vis in·er·ti·ae \‧ə'nərshē‧ē\ *n*, pl vires inertiae [NL, lit., force of inertia] : INERTIA 1a

vi·sion \ˈvizhən\ *n* -s [ME visioun, fr. OF vision, fr. L vision-, visio, fr. visus (past part. of vidēre to see) + -ion-, -io -ion — more at WIT] **1 a** : something seen otherwise than by the ordinary sight : an imaginary, supernatural, or prophetic sight beheld in sleep or ecstasy; esp : one that conveys a revelation ⟨a ∼ of the night, when deep sleep falleth upon men —Job 33:15 (AV)⟩ **b** : a writing (as a poem) purporting to represent something beheld in a revelatory dream, trance, or ecstasy — compare DREAM VISION ⟨the masterpieces of the Middle Ages . . . the story cycle and the allegorical ∼ —Boris Ford⟩ **c** : a vivid concept or object of imaginative contemplation ⟨brought ∼s of wealth to be gained in silk culture —Amer. Guide Series: Del.⟩ **d** : the apparition of a person (as in a dream) : PHANTOM ⟨thus the ∼ spoke —John Dryden⟩ **e** : a visual image without corporeal presence; esp : a manifestation to the senses of something immaterial (as a spiritual being or state) ⟨the baseless fabric of this ∼ —Shak.⟩ ⟨look, not at ∼s, but at realities —Edith Wharton⟩ **2 a** : the act or power of perceiving mental images (as those formed by the imagination) ⟨a listlessness . . . behind a veneer of technical virtuosity — G.A.Wagner⟩ **b** (1) : a mode or way of seeing ⟨trying to express his ∼ in terms of recognizable subject matter —Times Lit. Supp.⟩ ⟨every ∼ of the world implies some sort of philosophy —Walter Lippmann⟩ (2) : unusual discernment or foresight ⟨a man of ∼⟩ ⟨planning that combines realism with ∼ —advt⟩ **c** : direct mystical awareness of the supernatural usu. in visible form ⟨a spirit and a Vision . . . beyond all that the mortal and perishing nature can produce —William Blake⟩ **3 a** : the act or power of seeing : visual sensation or the capacity for it : SIGHT ⟨the ∼ of the audience comprised the speakers and actors of the play —Harley Granville-Barker⟩ ⟨cast out from God and blessed ∼ —John Milton⟩ **b** : the special sense that is concerned with the perception and distinguishing of the qualities of an object (as color, luminosity, shape and size) constituting its appearance, that is mediated by the rods and cones of the retina stimulated by light projected from the object through the lens of the eye, and that is conducted centrally by the optic nerves and is coordinated esp. by centers in the lateral geniculate bodies and the occipital portion of the cerebral cortex **4 a** : something seen : an object of sight ⟨this glorious ∼ of manly strength and beauty —G.B.Shaw⟩ **b** : something seen of such charm as to seem imaginary ⟨she was a ∼ in that dress⟩ ⟨a ∼ of her, of something eager, cleverly active —J.D.Beresford⟩ **5** : a figure of speech by which something present to the imagination (as a person or scene) is represented as actually before the eyes (as in Tennyson's "I see the wealthy miller yet, his double chin, his portly size") — compare APOSTROPHE 1 **6** : a small motion-picture scene photographed by double exposure within a larger one usu. to indicate the thought of an actor at a particular moment — compare DISSOLVE syn see FANCY

²vision \″\ *vt* -ED/-ING/-s **1** : to make evident to the sight : show forth : DISPLAY ⟨the anger of God apparently ∼ed . . . unto thee in the knitting of my brows —Thomas Nash⟩ **2** : to see in or as if in a vision : IMAGINE, ENVISION ⟨∼ed the tiny town as the future metropolis —Amer. Guide Series: Oregon⟩ ⟨∼ed a life of failure stretching before me —David Fairchild⟩

vi·sion·al \-n⁐l\ *adj* **1** : of, relating to, or of the nature of a vision ⟨gave a ∼ interpretation to the biblical episode⟩ **2** : based upon or seen in a vision : UNREAL, IMAGINARY ⟨a ∼ apparition⟩ — vi·sion·al·ly \-l‧ē\ *adv*

vi·sion·ar·i·ness \ˌvizhə‧nerēnəs\ *n* -ES : the quality or state of being visionary

¹vi·sion·ary \-rē, -ri\ *adj* **1 a** : capable of seeing visions : disposed or likely to see visions ⟨a ∼ prophet⟩ ⟨people call you ∼ . . . you see things before they happen —S.M.Crothers⟩ **b** : disposed to indulgence in reverie or fancy : full of imaginative conceptions : apt to accept and act on fancies as if realities : DREAMY, IMPRACTICAL ⟨one ∼ explorer . . . devoted a season to gold digging —Amer. Guide Series: Mass.⟩ ⟨∼ and sentimental persons —Willa Cather⟩ ⟨in expecting . . . enough popular support —E.S.Morgan⟩ **2 a** : having the nature of a vision : beheld or existing in a vision or dream : ILLUSORY, PHANTOM ⟨beheld . . . through so dim a medium that she looked ∼ —Nathaniel Hawthorne⟩ ⟨clutched at some ∼ object in the air —Thomas DeQuincey⟩ **b** : having no basis or justification in reality : incapable of being realized or achieved : UTOPIAN ⟨a ∼ scheme⟩ ⟨discussions of monorail systems seemed academic, if not ∼ —Fortune⟩ **c** : existing only in the imagination by visions ⟨able to endow a rapid sketch of some trees seen by a roadside with . . . power —Stuart Preston⟩ ⟨the ∼ hour —James Thomson †1748⟩ syn see IMAGINARY

²visionary \″\ *n* -ES **1** : a person who sees visions : SEER ⟨too clever to place any faith in the dreams of visionaries . . . knew all the priestcraft and fakery of his kind —Bruce Nelson⟩ **2** : one that relies or tends to rely on dreams and fancies or on imaginary or ideal conceptions or projects having little basis in reality : an impractical person : DREAMER, ENTHUSIAST ⟨ridiculed as a ∼ when he first proposed the plan⟩ ⟨realized what a hopeless ∼ he was —Cosmopolitan⟩

vi·sioned *adj* [partly fr. ¹vision + -ed & partly fr. past part. of ²vision] **1** : seen in a vision ⟨a ∼ face⟩ **2 a** : produced by or experienced in a vision ⟨∼ moods⟩ ⟨∼ agony⟩ **b** : marked by visions ⟨a ∼ sleep⟩ **3** : endowed with vision : INSPIRED ⟨a ∼ experimenter⟩

vi·sion·ing *n* -s [fr. gerund of ²vision] : the act or an instance of seeing visions ⟨such ∼s . . . produced much of the world's misery —Bruce Marshall⟩

vi·sion·ist \-nⁱst\ *n* -s : VISIONARY 1

vi·sion·less \-nləs\ *adj* **1** : SIGHTLESS, BLIND ⟨∼ eyes⟩ **2** : lacking vision or inspiration : UNINSPIRED ⟨a ∼ leader⟩

vision quest *n* : a solitary vigil by an adolescent American Indian boy to seek spiritual power and learn through a vision the identity of his usu. animal or bird guardian spirit

visions pl of VISION, pres 3d sing of VISION

¹vis·it \ˈvizət, usu -zd-+V\ *vb* visited \-zəd‧əd, -z(ə)təd\ OF visiter, fr. L visitare to go to see, visit, freq. of visere to look at, go to see, fr. vidēre to see — more at WIT] *vt* **1 a** archaic : to come to or upon as a spiritual help : COMFORT — used of the deity ⟨∼ us with Thy salvation —Charles Wesley⟩ **b** (1) : to bring trouble or harm to : AFFLICT — usu. used with with ⟨∼ed his people with distempers —Tobias Smollett⟩ (2) : INFLICT, IMPOSE — usu. used with on or upon ⟨∼ed everlasting grief on many people because of a few rash words —T.B.Costain⟩ ⟨the court ∼s all costs on them —H.J.Laski⟩ **c** (1) : to take vengeance for : AVENGE ⟨∼ the sins of the fathers upon the children⟩ (2) obs : to move vengefully against : come at ⟨ere the king dismiss his power, he means to us ∼ —Shak.⟩ (3) : to exact retribution for : PUNISH ⟨now will he . . . ∼ their sins —Hos 8:13 (AV)⟩ ⟨the legislature ∼ed the action with censure⟩ **d** : to present itself to or come over momentarily ⟨∼ed by a strange notion ⟨the surprise which ∼ed me when I saw the blood —R.P.Warren⟩ **2 a** : to go to see and care for as a charitable work : minister to ⟨∼ing the sick of the parish⟩ **b** (1) : to go to attend (a patient) — used esp. of a physician (2) : to go to see (as a physician or dentist) for professional service **3 a** : to make a social call upon ⟨∼ed friends in the early evening⟩ **b** : to reside with temporarily as a guest : stay with ⟨∼ed a colleague for a week at his summer home⟩ **c** : to have sexual relations with **d** : to frequent temporarily ⟨many migratory birds ∼ these shores annually⟩ **4 a** : to go to see or sojourn in (a place) for a particular purpose (as for business, pleasure, or sight-seeing) ⟨what local points of interest they should ∼ —Dana Burnet⟩ ⟨a medicinal spring . . . frequently ∼ed by invalids —Amer. Guide Series: N.H.⟩ **b** : to go to (a place of business) on an errand ⟨enough time to ∼ the stores before dinner⟩ **5** obs : to observe or test the spiritual state — used of the deity ⟨God often descends to ∼ men unseen —John Milton⟩ **b** : to go over or correct the operation of : INSPECT ⟨a bishop ∼ing his diocese⟩ ⟨congressional committee ∼ing a military base⟩ ⟨a department head ∼ing classrooms⟩ **c** : to make an official examination of (as baggage or a ship and its cargo) : SEARCH — *vi* **1** obs : to make an official inspection **2 a** : to make a call ⟨spends most of her afternoons ∼ing⟩ **b** : to stay as a guest ⟨∼s here for a month in every year⟩ **3** : to carry on casual conversation : CHAT ⟨let's sit here and ∼ together for a while⟩ ⟨∼ing with a neighbor on the telephone⟩ **4** : to progress around and about with a figure in square dancing

²visit \″\ *n* -s **1 a** : a short stay (as for sociability or friendship) that usu. longer than a social call ⟨make a ∼⟩ ⟨a ∼ with friends⟩ ⟨pay a ∼⟩ ⟨return a ∼⟩ ⟨suburban housewives spending their afternoons in ∼s and card playing⟩ **b** : a brief residence as a guest ⟨a weekend ∼ with friends⟩ **c** : an extended but temporary stay ⟨his annual summer ∼ abroad⟩ **2 a** : a journey to and stay or short sojourn at a place for a particular purpose ⟨a ∼ to a museum⟩ ⟨a ship's ∼ to a port⟩ ⟨a ∼ to a neighboring town⟩ ⟨an educational ∼ to a

steel mill⟩ ⟨∼s to points of historical interest⟩ **b** : a brief stop on an errand or for a business purpose ⟨telephoned between ∼s to the stores⟩ ⟨a salesman's ∼ to a firm⟩ ⟨repeated ∼s to theatrical agencies⟩ **3 a** (1) : a professional call ⟨as of a physician to treat a patient⟩ ⟨paid the doctor for three home ∼s⟩ (2) : a pastoral call by a clergyman on a parishioner ⟨met the minister returning from his afternoon ∼s⟩ **b** : a call upon a professional man ⟨as a physician or dentist⟩ for consultation or treatment ⟨urged to make regular ∼s to his dentist⟩ **4** : VISITATION ⟨a ∼ by a national officer to the local chapter of a fraternal order⟩ ⟨a committee of trustees on a ∼ to a university⟩ **5** : an official examination or search ⟨as of goods or cargo⟩; *specif* : the act of a naval officer of one state in boarding a neutral merchant vessel of another state in the exercise of the right of search

vis·it·able \'vizəd-əbəl, -z(ə)təb-\ *adj* **1** : subject to visitation or inspection ⟨an institution maintained by the church and ∼ by the bishop⟩ **2** : accessible for visiting : OPEN ⟨a museum ∼ only at certain hours⟩ ⟨∼ countries of the globe —Raymond Walters b. 1912⟩ **3** : socially eligible to receive visits ⟨became known to all the ∼ people here —William Cowper⟩

vis·i·tan·dine \,vizə'tandən, -,dēn\ *n* -s *usu cap* [F, fr. L *visitandum* (gerund of *visitare* to visit) + F -*ine*] : NUN OF THE VISITATION

¹vis·i·tant \'vizəd-ənt, -z(ə)tənt *also* -zət°ənt\ *n* -s [L *visitant-, visitans,* pres. part. of *visitare* to visit] : one that visits: **a** : one that comes for a short or temporary stay : VISITOR, GUEST ⟨a frequent ∼ at the rectory⟩ ⟨a ∼ from the outside world —Clarice Short⟩; *esp* : one thought to come from a spirit world ⟨a ghostly ∼⟩ ⟨heavenly ∼s⟩ **b** : one that visits a place of religious or worship-seeing interest : PILGRIM, TOURIST ⟨collected a small fee from ∼s to the cathedral⟩ **c** : something ⟨as a bodily or mental state⟩ that comes to or over a person for a time ⟨that mood of sadness ... my frequent ∼ —George Eliot⟩ **d** : a bird that is not resident in a given region at all seasons but that appears there at regular or irregular intervals for a limited period ⟨a winter ∼⟩

²visitant \"\ *adj* [L *visitant-, visitans*] : coming as or appearing in the character of a visitor : VISITING ⟨a devil ∼ —Daniel Defoe⟩

vis·i·ta·tion \,vizə'tāshən\ *n* -s [ME *visitacioun,* fr. MF *visitation,* fr. L *visitation-, visitatio,* fr. *visitatus* (past part. of *visitare* to visit) + -*ion-, -io* -ion — more at VISIT] **1 a** : an official visit of a superior or superintending officer to an institution ⟨as a corporation, college, church⟩ to inspect the manner in which it is conducted and see that its laws and regulations are observed and executed ⟨the ∼ of a diocese by a bishop⟩ **b** (1) : a personal inquiry by a visiting officer of arms in Great Britain at different times into the rights of the people within his heraldic province to bear arms (2) : a documentary record of such an inquiry ⟨a ∼ of VISIT 5 **2 a** : a special dispensation of divine favor or wrath ⟨my Celestial Patroness who deigns her nightly ∼ unimplored —John Milton⟩; *esp* : retributive calamity : divine judgment ⟨a ∼ of the plague for the people's sins⟩ **b** : an unusual event likened to a special dispensation; *esp* : a severe trial : AFFLICTION ⟨suffered one ∼ after another of disease and famine⟩ **3 a** : a visit to a place of interest ⟨as on a sightseeing or educational tour⟩ **b** : a visit for a charitable purpose ⟨a ∼ of the sick⟩ **c** (1) : a pastoral call or official visit by a Protestant minister (2) : an official visit by one or more laymen on church business **d** *archaic* : a social call **4** : resort to a place by animals ⟨as birds or mammals⟩ at an unusual time or in unusual numbers **5** : a passing influence ⟨as of something intangible or supernatural⟩ ⟨gentle ∼s of calm thought —P.B.Shelley⟩
syn see TRIAL

vis·i·ta·tor \'∤zə,tād-ə(r)\ *n* -s [LL, fr. L *visitatus* (past part.) + -*or*] : an official visitor or examiner in the Roman Catholic Church ⟨the ∼ visits all the monasteries in succession⟩

vis·i·ta·to·ri·al \,vizəd-ə¦tōrēəl, -ə¦ta¸-, -tōr-\ *adj* [ML *visitatorius* visitatorial (fr. L *visitatus-* + -*orius* -ory) + E -*al*] : of or relating to visitation or to a judicial visitor or superintendent ⟨∼ authority⟩ ⟨∼ jurisdiction⟩

vi·site \vē'zēt\ *n* -s [F, lit., visit, fr. *visiter* to visit] : a cape or short cloak formerly worn by women in summer — compare ³POLKA

visited *past of* VISIT

visiter *var of* VISITOR

¹visiting *n* -s [ME, fr. gerund of *visiten* to visit — more at VISIT] : a fleeting influence ⟨as from a spiritual source⟩ ⟨no compunctious ∼s of Nature shake my fell purpose —Shak.⟩

²visiting *adj* [fr. past part. of ¹*visit*] : giving professional or technical service or advice in the home and for short periods rather than by the day or week ⟨a ∼ housekeeper⟩

visiting book *n* : a book containing a record of visits received, made, and to be made

visiting card *n* : a small card bearing the name and sometimes the address of a person or married couple for presentation ⟨as when visiting or calling⟩ — called also *calling card*

visiting couple *n* : the couple that momentarily is progressing around the set in square dancing

visiting day *n* : a day for receiving callers

visiting fireman *n* **1** : a usu. important or influential visitor ⟨as a high official from the headquarters of an organization or a general on a tour of inspection⟩ whom it is desirable or expedient to show about or entertain impressively ⟨for an aspiring politician ... a fine place to throw parties for *visiting firemen* and local bigwigs —Clare B. Luce⟩ **2** : a visitor to a city ⟨as a convention delegate⟩ who goes out on the town and spends freely ⟨girls who will show your visitors what most *visiting firemen* want to see —Hal White⟩

visiting list *n* : a list of persons whom one visits socially

visiting nurse *n* : a nurse employed by a hospital or social-service agency to visit sick persons or perform other public health services in a community

visiting patrol *n* : a patrol that visits elements of its own command and those of adjacent units ⟨as in an outpost⟩ to maintain liaison

visiting professor *n* : a professor invited to join a college or university faculty for a limited time ⟨as a half year or an academic year⟩

visiting teacher *n* **1** : an educational officer employed by a public school system to go into the homes of pupils in order to effect cooperation between school and family, assist in the solving of social or emotional problems due to home environment, instruct sick or handicapped pupils unable to attend school, or enforce attendance regulations **2** : a social worker whose duty is dealing with behavior problems among school children

visiting ticket *n, archaic* : VISITING CARD

vis·i·tor *also* **vis·it·er** \'vizəd-ə(r), -z(ə)tə-\ *n* -s [ME *visitour, visiter,* fr. MF *visiteur,* fr. OF *visiter* to visit + -*eur* -or — more at VISIT] : one that visits: as **a** : a superior or a person lawfully appointed for the purpose who makes formal visits of inspection or supervision **b** (1) : a member of a board of overseers of an academic institution : TRUSTEE (2) *Brit* : a person of high rank or eminence serving as the highest authority and court of last appeal for a university ⟨if the fellows could not find a clear majority ... for one candidate, it was left for the ∼ to appoint —C.P.Snow⟩ **c** : one that makes charitable visits ⟨took a job as ∼ to Boston's poor —J.S.Redding⟩; *esp* : a social worker assigned to visit clients in their homes **d** : one that makes social visits : CALLER, GUEST ⟨a warm welcome for ∼s⟩ ⟨had no ∼s all day⟩ **e** : one that goes to or stays at a place for a particular purpose ⟨as business or sightseeing⟩ : TOURIST, TRAVELER ⟨∼s to a city for a convention⟩ ⟨∼s at a vacation resort⟩ **f** : VISITANT d

vis·i·to·ri·al \,vizə¦tōrēəl, -tōr-\ *adj* : VISITATORIAL; *specif* : of or relating to the visiting rights of one parent when custody of a child is awarded to the other

visitors' book *n* : a book or register for the signatures and written comments of visitors ⟨as to a museum, a restaurant, or an exposition⟩

vis·i·tress \'vizə̇trə̇s\ *n* -es [*visitor* + -*ess*] *archaic* : a female visitor; *esp* : one who makes visits for social-service work

visits *pres 3d sing of* VISIT, *pl of* VISIT

vi·sive \'visiv\ *adj* [ML *visivus,* fr. L *visus* sight, vision + -*ivus* -ive — more at VISAGE] **1** *archaic* : of, relating to, or serving for vision ⟨the ∼ sense —George Berkeley⟩ **2** *archaic*

: capable of seeing or of being seen ⟨gives vision to ∼ natures —Thomas Taylor⟩

vis ma·jor \-'mājə(r)\ *n, pl* **vires ma·jo·res** \-mə'jō¸rēz\ [L, greater force] : an overwhelming force of nature that has consequences not preventable by any due and reasonable precautions and that under certain circumstances is held to exempt from contract obligations — compare ACT OF GOD, FORCE MAJEURE, INEVITABLE ACCIDENT, UNAVOIDABLE CASUALTY

vis·mia \'vismēə\ *n, cap* [NL, fr. *Visme,* 18th cent. Port. botanist + NL -*ia*] : a small genus of tropical American or African trees and shrubs ⟨family Guttiferae⟩ with a resinous bark and usu. woolly terminal or axillary panicles of white, yellow, or brownish flowers

visne \'vēn(ē)\ *n* -s [ME, fr. MF *visné* neighborhood, fr. *visin, veisin* neighbor, fr. L *vicinus* — more at VICINITY] **1** *archaic* : VICINAGE; *esp* : the place ⟨as the county⟩ of a crime from which the jury is called **2** *archaic* : a jury of the visne

vis·no·my \'viznomē\ *n* -s [alter. of ME *phisnomye, phisonomie* physiognomy — more at PHYSIOGNOMY] *archaic* : PHYSIOGNOMY 2a

vi·son \'vīs°n\ *also* **vison weasel** *n* -s [F *vison,* fr. MF, a marten, perh. of Gmc origin; akin to OHG *wisula* weasel — more at WEASEL] : the American mink

vi·sor *also* **vi·zor** \'vīzə(r)\ *n* -s [ME *viser,* fr. AF, fr. OF *visiere,* fr. *vis* face + -*iere* -*er* — more at VISAGE] **1** : the front piece of a helmet usu. containing openings for seeing and breathing; *esp* : an upper piece lifting or opening to show the face **2 a** : a mask for the face : VIZARD ⟨have worn a ∼ and could tell a whispering tale in a fair lady's ear —Shak.⟩ **b** : something that disguises an evil purpose : outward semblance : MASK ⟨once sure of his ground, he dropped the ∼⟩ **c** *obs* : FACE, COUNTENANCE ⟨give me a case to put my visage in: a visor for a ∼ —Shak.⟩ **3 a** : a projecting front brim on a cap or hat for shading the eyes : PEAK **b** (1) : EYESHADE (2) : a projecting forepiece on an automobile windshield to protect the eyes from glare **c** (1) : an overhang ⟨as for a window⟩ to give shade (2) : a small inclined canvas or metal awning around a ship's pilothouse **d** : FACE GUARD **4** : SUPERCILIARY RIDGE

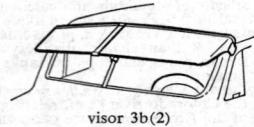
visor 3b(2)

vi·sored *also* **vi·zored** \-(r)d\ *adj* [ME *visered,* fr. *viser* visor + -*ed*] **1** : covered or masked with a visor : DISGUISED ⟨∼ falsehood and base forgery —John Milton⟩ **2** : equipped with a visor ⟨a ∼ helmet⟩ ⟨from under the ∼ cap his glance was sharp —Kay Boyle⟩

vi·sor·less \-(r)ləs\ *adj* : having no visor

vis·pe·red \'vēspə¸red\ *or* **vis·pa·rad** \-rad\ *n* -s [Av *vīspē ratavō* all the lords] : one of the supplementary ritual texts included in the Avestan sacred writings

viss *var of* VIS

vis·ta \'vistə\ *n* -s [It, sight, view, fr. *visto* (past part. of *vedere* to see, fr. L *videre*), fr. L *visus* (past part. of *videre* to see) + It -*to,* past. suffix (fr. L -*tus*)] **1 a** : a more or less distant view through or along an avenue or opening ⟨as between rows of trees⟩ : PROSPECT ⟨garden ... noted for its long ∼s of formal beds between lines of evergreens —*Amer. Guide Series: Md.*⟩ ⟨an ∼ opened among the dancers —Rebecca West⟩ **b** : an extended view afforded by an architectural feature ⟨as a corridor or opening in walls⟩ ⟨galleries extended into ∼s by mirrors⟩ ⟨∼s of stone passages with numbered doors —Christopher Isherwood⟩ **2** : an extensive mental view ⟨as over a stretch of time or a series of events⟩ : a prospect opening out to thought ⟨before us an infinite ∼ of human improvement —*Times Lit. Supp.*⟩ ⟨leading her memories down forgotten ∼s —B.A.Williams⟩

vista dome *n* : DOME 4g(1)

vis·taed \-təd\ *adj* **1** : affording or made to form a vista ⟨the ∼ galleries ... of this palace —Ruth Davidson⟩ **2** : seen in or as if in a vista ⟨the ∼ rooms which he had ∼ I sped —F.J.Thompson⟩

vis·to \'vi(,)stō\ *archaic var of* VISTA

¹vi·su·al \'vizh(ə)wəl, -zhəl\ *adj* [ME, fr. LL *visualis,* fr. L *visus* sight, vision ⟨fr. *visus,* past part. of *videre* to see⟩ + -*alis* -al — more at WIT] **1** : of, relating to, or used in vision : serving as the instrument of seeing ⟨the ∼ nerve⟩ ⟨the ∼ sense⟩ **2** : attained or maintained by sight ⟨∼ impressions⟩ ⟨∼ knowledge⟩ ⟨a language with which he had only a ∼ acquaintance —H.J.Laski⟩ ⟨in the heavy growth ... impossible to keep ∼ contact —H.D.Skidmore⟩ **3** : OPTICAL ⟨the ∼ focus of a lens distinguished from the actinic focus⟩ **4** : capable of being seen : VISIBLE ⟨∼ objects⟩ ⟨a ∼ equivalent for feelings which enrich experience —Michael Kitson⟩ **5** : producing mental images : VIVID ⟨his narratives are stirringly ∼ —John Mason Brown⟩ **6** : done or executed with the aid of direct sight and without assistance ⟨as from instruments or radar⟩ ⟨∼ flying⟩ ⟨∼ bombing⟩ ⟨∼ navigation⟩ **7** : of, relating to, or constituting a means of instruction ⟨as a map, chart, model, perspective drawing, or documentary film⟩ that appeals to the sense of sight ⟨∼ aid⟩ ⟨∼ education⟩ ⟨∼ lesson⟩ — compare AUDIO-VISUAL

²visual \"\ *n* -s **1** *archaic* : VISUAL RAY **2** : VISUALIZER **3** : a roughly sketched advertising layout — compare COMPREHENSIVE **4 visuals** *pl* : the picture images as distinguished from the sounds of a motion picture film ⟨a master film maker ... knows how to keep his action taut, his ∼s alive —Arthur Knight⟩

visual acuity *n* : the relative ability of the visual organ to resolve detail that is a function of sensitivity of a particular retina to light together with the minimum separable and the minimum visible characteristic of the optical system of that eye, that is usu. expressed as the reciprocal of the minimum angular separation in minutes of two lines just resolvable as separate, and that forms in the average human eye an angle of one minute

visual angle *n* : the angle formed by two rays of light or two straight lines drawn from the extreme points of a viewed object to the visual point of the eye

visual aphasia *n* : aphasia in which a person is unable to comprehend written words previously understood

visual area *n* : a sensory area of the occipital lobe of the cerebral cortex receiving afferent projection fibers concerned with the sense of sight

visual-auditory \¦∙¦∙(∙)¦¸∙∙∙\ *adj* : AUDIO-VISUAL

visual-aural radio range *or* **visual-aural range** *n* : a radio aid to air navigation by which a pilot determines if he is on course by either an appropriate aural signal, a meter reading, or both

visual axis *n* : LINE OF VISION

visual binary *n* : a double star in which the components may be distinguished separately in a telescope of sufficient resolving power — compare BINARY STAR

visual communication *n* : any system of signaling in which the signals are received by the eye ⟨as by lamps, wigwag, semaphore, pyrotechnics, or panels⟩

visual control *n* : a remote supervisory control system in which code signals in the form of electric impulses are sent out by a dispatcher and return signals are received through the medium of colored lights

visual field *n* **1** : the entire expanse of space visible at a given instant without moving the eyes — called also *field of vision* **2** : the visual content of a person's mind at a given instant

vi·su·al·ist \'vizhələ̇st, -zh(ə)wəl-\ *n* -s : VISUALIZER

vi·su·al·i·ty \,vizhə'walə̇d-ē\ *n* -es **1** : the quality or state of being visual or visible **2** : a mental image or picture : VIEW, GLIMPSE

vi·su·al·iz·able \'vizhə,līzəbəl, -zh(ə)wə-, -¸ə(⁀)∙∙∙\ *adj* : capable of being visualized

vi·su·al·i·za·tion \,vizhə¸līzə'zāshən, -zh(ə)wəl-, -¸ī'-\ *n* -s [ISV *visualize* + -*ation*] **1** : the act or power of forming mentally visual images of objects not present to the eye ⟨aware of his uncanny gift of ∼ —G.D.Brown⟩ **2** : the act or process of putting into or interpreting in visual terms or in visible form ⟨means of ∼, such as scale models ... colored slides —J.L. Sert⟩ **3 a** : the process of exposing an organ to view by surgery ⟨∼ of the gallbladder by a paramedian incision⟩ **b** : the process of making a viscus visible by injection of a radiopaque

substance followed by roentgenography ⟨∼ of the renal calyces by intravenous pyelography⟩ **4** : a modern dance deriving its patterns entirely from movement equivalents of musical phrases and qualities

vi·su·al·ize \'vizhə¸līz, -zh(ə)wə-\ *vb* -ED/-ING/-S *vt* **1** : to make visual or visible : PICTURE; *esp* : to see a mental image of ⟨something not before the eye⟩ : picture mentally : IMAGE, IMAGINE ⟨∼ a scene in all its concreteness —Herbert Read⟩ ⟨*visualized* atomic scientists as bearded old men⟩ **2 a** : to conceive definitely ⟨as something abstract⟩ : ENVISAGE ⟨a scheme⟩ ⟨*visualizing* anatomy as a living subject⟩ ⟨did not ∼ a third alternative —E.H.Erikson⟩ **b** : FORESEE ⟨had not *visualized* such an attack⟩ **3** : to make ⟨an organ⟩ visible by surgical or roentgenographic visualization — *vi* **1** : to form a visual mental image of something not present before the eye at the time ⟨had the power of *visualizing* in minute detail⟩ **2** : to become visible — used esp. of an internal bodily organ or condition ⟨the worm *visualized* through a bronchoscope —E.C. Faust⟩

vi·su·al·iz·er \-zə(r)\ *n* -s **1** : one whose mental imagery is prevailingly visual — compare AUDILE, MOTILE **2** : VIEWER **3** : one that lays out advertising for a company preferring to have the work done by a newspaper or periodical or by an advertising firm rather than by its own advertising department

visual line *n* : LINE OF VISION

vi·su·al·ly \'vizhəlē, -zh(ə)wəl-, -li\ *adv* in a visual manner: as **a** : with regard to vision ⟨gifted ∼ to ... an unusual degree —Osbert Sitwell⟩ **b** : by visual means ⟨the high points of his career ... were all ∼ recorded —R.W.Murray⟩

visual magnitude *n* : the brightness of a celestial body determined by eye estimation with or without optical aid or by other instrumentation equivalent to the eye in spectral sensitivity

visual plane *n* : a plane passing through the point of sight; *specif* : the plane in which the visual axes of the two eyes lie in binocular vision

visual point *n* : the point taken as the position of the eye in calculations of optical instruments; *specif* : the optical center of the cornea-lens system as backed by the vitreous humor

visual purple *n* : a photosensitive red or purple pigment in the retinal rods of various vertebrates; *esp* : RHODOPSIN — compare PORPHYROPSIN

visual ray *also* **visual beam** *n* : a ray from any point of the object field to the eye; *specif* : any ray that on its way to the retina passes through the visual point

visuals *pl of* VISUAL

visual telescope *n* : a refractor whose objective is designed to be achromatic in the yellow-green region of the spectrum where the human eye has its highest sensitivity

vis vi·va \-'vīvə\ *n, pl* **vires vi·vae** \-¸ī,vē\ [NL, living force] : the force of a moving body calculated as the product of its mass and the square of its velocity : twice the kinetic energy

vit *abbr* **1** vitamin **2** vitreous **3** vitrified

vi·ta \'vīd-ə, 'wē,tä\ *n, pl* **vi·tae** \-ī,tē, ē,tī\ [L, lit., life — more at VITAL] : a brief autobiographical sketch ⟨as in a thesis for a doctorate⟩

Vi·ta \'vīd-ə\ *trademark* — used for glass that does not obstruct ultraviolet rays

vi·ta·ce·ae \vī'tāsē,ē\ *n pl, cap* [NL, fr. *Vitis,* type genus + -*aceae*] *cap* : a family of woody or herbaceous vines ⟨order Rhamnales⟩ having simple, palmate, or pinnate leaves, usu. tendril-bearing stems, and small greenish clustered flowers succeeded by a several-seeded berry — see CISSUS, PARTHENOCISSUS, VITIS — **vi·ta·ceous** \(')vī¦tāshəs\ *adj*

vi·tal \'vīd-°l, -īt°l\ *adj* [ME, fr. MF, fr. L *vitalis* of life, fr. *vita* life + -*alis* -al; akin to L *vivere* to live — more at QUICK] **1 a** : existing as a manifestation of life ⟨∼ powers⟩ ⟨recognizing no mystic ∼ force⟩ **b** : concerned with or necessary to the maintenance of life ⟨blood and other ∼ fluids⟩ ⟨the loss of ∼ heat in shock⟩; *esp* : performing an essential role in the living body ⟨∼ organs⟩ ⟨wounded in a ∼ spot⟩ **2 a** : having or characterized by life : ANIMATE ⟨a ∼ being⟩ **b** : full of life and vigor : ENERGETIC, ANIMATED ⟨spirits that live throughout, ∼ in every part —John Milton⟩ ⟨this whole ∼ world⟩ **3** : characteristic of life or living beings : inhering in the living or organic ∼ activities⟩ ⟨expending ∼ energies⟩ **4 a** : concerned with or affecting life esp. in some fundamental manner: as (1) : tending to renew or refresh the living : INVIGORATING ⟨warmed by the ∼ rays of heaven's sun⟩ (2) : destructive to life : FATAL, MORTAL ⟨a ∼ wound⟩ **b** : of the utmost importance : essential to the continued existence, vigor, efficiency, independence, or value of something expressed or implied ⟨a ∼ point to the argument⟩ ⟨matters ∼ to the national security⟩; *often* : taking priority in consideration over other factors or elements ⟨it is ∼ to know what he plans⟩ **5** *obs* : capable of living : VIABLE **6** : recording the chief data relating to lives ⟨∼ records⟩ — see VITAL STATISTICS **7** : of, relating to, or constituting the staining of living tissues ⟨as by injecting a dye into a living animal⟩ **syn** see ESSENTIAL

vital air *n, archaic* : OXYGEN

vital capacity *n* : the breathing capacity of the lungs expressed as the number of cubic inches or cubic centimeters of air that can be forcibly exhaled after a full inspiration

vital dye *n* : a dye or stain capable of penetrating living cells or tissues and not inducing immediate evident degenerative changes — called also *vital stain*

vital force *n* : ÉLAN VITAL

vital function *n* : a function of the body ⟨as the circulation of the blood, respiration, or digestion⟩ on which life is directly dependent

vital index *n* : the ratio of births to deaths in a human population at any given time

vi·tal·ism \'vīd-°l¸izəm, -īt°l-\ *n* -s [*vital* + -*ism*] **1** : a doctrine that the functions of a living organism are due to a vital principle ⟨as an élan vital or entelechy⟩ distinct from physicochemical forces — compare MECHANISM, ORGANICISM **2** : a doctrine that the processes of life are not explicable by the laws of physics and chemistry alone and that life is in some part self-determining instead of mechanistically determined — compare ORGANICISM, ORTHOGENESIS

vi·tal·ist \-°lə̇st\ *n* -s [*vitalism* + -*ist*] : a believer in vitalism

vi·tal·is·tic \,∤¸∙'istik\ *or* **vi·tal·ist** \'∤¸∙-°st\ *adj* : of, relating to, or characteristic of vitalism or vitalists — **vi·tal·is·ti·cal·ly** \'∤¸∙'istik(ə)lē\ *adv*

vi·tal·i·ty \vī'talə̇d-ē, -lətē, -i\ *n* -es [L *vitalitat-, vitalitas,* fr. *vitalis* of life + -*itat-, -itas* -ity — more at VITAL] **1 a** : the peculiarity distinguishing the living from the nonliving and acting as if a specific force or principle — compare ÉLAN VITAL **b** : capacity to live and develop ⟨the ∼ of a seed⟩; *esp* : physical or mental vigor esp. when highly developed ⟨a man of great ∼⟩ **2 a** : power of enduring or continuing : capacity for survival ⟨the ∼ of an idiom⟩ **b** : lively and animated character : VIGOR ⟨the ∼ of his reasoning⟩ ⟨inspired his helpers with a new ∼⟩ **3** : a manifestation or embodiment of vital force

vi·tal·iza·tion \,vīd-°lə'zāshən, -īt°l-, -¸ī'-\ *n* -s [*vitalize* + -*ation*] : the act or process of vitalizing : the quality or state of being vitalized

vi·tal·ize \'∤¸∙¸īz\ *vb* -ED/-ING/-S *see* -ize *in Explan Notes* [¹*vital* + -*ize*] *vt* **1** : to endow with vitality : give life or animation to : make vigorous or active ⟨∼ the patriotism of a people⟩ **2** : to portray ⟨as in writing or painting⟩ with lifelike effect — *vi* **1** : to give life or animation
syn ENERGIZE, ACTIVATE: VITALIZE signifies to arouse, usu. something more or less inert or lifeless, to vital activity, often by communicating an impetus or force, or to impart significance or interest to ⟨something⟩ or make one aware of its inherent significance or interest, usu. suggesting a vigor, freshness, or health in the effect ⟨a force which can *vitalize* or destroy men —C.W.Cunnington⟩ ⟨a power of description that *vitalizes* his words —*Christian Science Monitor*⟩ ENERGIZE implies an arousing to activity by an imparting of force, heat, or any power that increases capacity for activity, esp. work, or in acting with a vitality presumably induced by such power ⟨oats are, without doubt, the best *energizing* food for horses —Henry Wynmalen⟩ ⟨storage batteries *energize* railroad block-signal circuits —J.A. Orsino & T.C.Lynes⟩ ACTIVATE stresses an arousing to activity by the influence of an external agent, esp. in imparting or arousing a material or integrating activity ⟨breaks contact with the photoelectric cell and *activates* an alarm —Alan Hynd⟩ ⟨the report has done much to crystallize and *activate* official and private opinion —Walter White⟩

vi·tal·iz·er \-zə(r)\ *n* -s : one that vitalizes

Vi·tal·li·um \vīˈtalēəm\ *trademark* — used for a cobalt-chromium alloy of platinum-white color used esp. for cast dentures, prostheses, and industrial castings

vi·tal·ly \ˈvīdᵊlē, -ītᵊl-, -ᵊli\ *adv* **:** in a vital manner or to a vital degree ⟨prefabricated businessmen more ~ interested in present problems —A.W.Long⟩ **:** so as to be vital; *broadly* **:** NOTABLY, EXTREMELY, VERY

vi·tal·ness \-ᵊlnəs\ *n* -ES **:** the quality or state of being vital

vital principle *n* **:** a hypothetical force to which the functions and qualities peculiar to living matter are sometimes ascribed

vital red *n* **:** a disazo acid dye used as a biological stain and in the determination of the volume of blood in the body

vital revolution *n* **:** a marked historical change in the rate of reproduction in a society characterized by the achievement of a stable equilibrium of low death and birth rates

vi·tals \ˈvīdᵊlz, -ītᵊlz\ *n pl* [*vital;* trans. of L *vitalia*] **1 :** organs (as the heart, liver, lungs, and brain) that are most necessary for life **2 :** the parts essential for continued existence, health, or soundness ⟨the ~ of a state⟩ ⟨the ~ of a motor⟩

vital space *n* **:** LEBENSRAUM

vital spirits *n pl, obs* **:** a product held to be derived from the natural spirits by commingling in the heart with respiratory air and to convey heat and life throughout the body by way of the arteries

vital stain *n* **:** VITAL DYE

vital statistics *n pl but sing or pl in constr* **:** statistics relating to births, deaths, marriages, health, and disease — compare DEMOGRAPHY

vi·ta·mer \ˈvīdəmə(r)\ *n* -S [*vitamin* + *isomer*] **:** any of two or more compounds that relieve a particular vitamin deficiency ⟨a D ~⟩ ⟨biotin ~s⟩ — **vi·ta·mer·ic** \¦==¦merik\ *adj*

vi·ta·min *also* **vi·ta·mine** \ˈvīdəmən, -ītəm-\ *n* -S *often attrib* [ISV *vit-* (fr. L *vita* life) + *amine;* prob. orig. formed in G; fr. the former belief that such substances were amines — more at VITAL] **:** any of various organic substances that individually or collectively are as far as is known essential to the nutrition of vertebrates, some invertebrates, many microorganisms, but prob. not most higher plants, that act typically in minute amounts in the regulation of various metabolic processes but do not provide energy or serve as building units, that are present in small amounts in various natural foodstuffs and are sometimes produced within the body (as by the action of intestinal bacteria in the rat) but are not ordinarily synthesized or stored in quantity in the human body, that may be detected as deficient in a particular organism by specific symptoms which can be relieved by administration of the appropriate vitamin, and that are commonly classified according to their water or fat solubility, their physiologic effects, or their chemical structure — see ANTIVITAMIN, AVITAMINOSIS, PROVITAMIN; compare AUXIN, GROWTH FACTOR

vitamin A \,==məˈnā\ *n* **:** any of several fat-soluble vitamins or a mixture of two or more of them whose lack in the animal body causes keratinization of epithelial tissues (as in the eye with resulting nyctalopia and xerophthalmia): as **a** *also* **vitamin** A_1 \,==mə¦nā¦wən\ **:** a pale yellow crystalline highly unsaturated alicyclic alcohol $C_{20}H_{29}OH$ that occurs free or in the form of esters usu. along with smaller amounts of a cis isomer in animal products (as egg yolk, milk, and butter) and esp. in marine fish-liver oils (as of cod, halibut, and shark), that is synthesized biologically from carotene and other carotenoids and commercially, and that is used in various forms in medicine and nutrition (as in fortifying margarine and other foods and in supplementing animal feeds); all-*trans*-vitamin A — see IODOPSIN, RETINENE a, RHODOPSIN **b** *or* **vitamin** A_2 **:** a yellow viscous liquid alicyclic alcohol $C_{20}H_{27}OH$ that contains one more double bond in the molecule than vitamin A_1 and is less active biologically in mammals and that occurs esp. in the liver oil of freshwater fish — see PORPHYROPSIN, RETINENE b

vitamin B *n* **1 :** VITAMIN B COMPLEX **2 :** any of numerous members of the vitamin B complex: as **a** *or* **vitamin** B_1 **:** THIAMINE **b** *or* **vitamin** B_2 **:** RIBOFLAVIN **c** *or* **vitamin** B_6 **:** any or all of the three closely related compounds pyridoxine, pyridoxal, and pyridoxamine that occur widely in combined form (as in liver, cereals, royal bee jelly, and yeast), that prevent rat acrodynia and are considered generally essential in the nutrition of vertebrates including man, and that are interconvertible in mammals and birds but vary in their activity as growth factors for microorganisms; *esp* **:** PYRIDOXINE **d** *or* **vitamin** B_{12} (1) **:** a red crystalline complex cobalt-containing cyano antianemic compound $C_{63}H_{90}CoN_{14}O_{14}P$ that is in part related chemically to porphin and is in part a nucleotide, that occurs in most animal products and esp. liver, kidney, and various seafoods but is usu. obtained commercially by bacterial fermentation, that is essential for normal blood formation, neural function, and growth and maintenance in man, various lower animals, and many microorganisms, and that is used chiefly in the treatment of pernicious anemia and other macrocytic anemias and of neuropathies and as a growth factor esp. for hogs and poultry — called also *antianemic factor, cyanocobalamin;* see ANIMAL PROTEIN FACTOR, EXTRINSIC FACTOR (2) **:** any or all of various compounds having similar biological activity to vitamin B_{12} but differing chemically in containing hydroxyl or other group in place of the cyano group and readily interconvertible with vitamin B_{12} **:** COBALAMIN; *broadly* **:** any of various related compounds differing from vitamin B_{12} in other respects (as in biological activity for higher animals and in the chemical composition of the nucleotide portion of the molecule) and formed in many cases by bacterial fermentation **e** *or* **vitamin** B_c **:** FOLIC ACID 1 **f** *or* **vitamin** B_T **:** CARNITINE

vitamin B complex \-ˈbē,kämˌpleks\ *n* **:** a group of water-soluble vitamins that are found esp. in yeast, the germ of cereals, nuts, eggs, liver, meats, fish, and vegetables, that in addition to those given vitamin B names usu. include *para*-aminobenzoic acid, biotin, carnitine, choline, folic acid, *meso*-inositol, nicotinic acid or nicotinamide, and pantothenic acid, that in a few cases function as coenzymes, and that in some cases are growth factors for bacteria and are formed by bacterial action in the intestinal tract of various animals

vitamin C *n* **:** the antiscorbutic vitamin **:** ASCORBIC ACID 1

vitamin D *n* **:** any or all of several fat-soluble antirachitic vitamins that are related chemically to the steroids, that are essential for normal bone and teeth structure, and that occur esp. in the liver oils of various fishes, in egg yolk, and in milk or are produced by activation of sterols (as by ultraviolet irradiation of individual sterols or of foods containing them): as **a** *or* **vitamin** D_2 **:** a crystalline unsaturated alcohol $C_{28}H_{43}OH$ that is usu. prepared by irradiation of ergosterol and is used as a dietary supplement in human and animal nutrition (as in fortified milk or butter) and medicinally in the treatment and control of rickets, osteomalacia, and other hypocalcemic disorders — called also *calciferol, ergocalciferol;* compare VIOSTEROL **b** *or* **vitamin** D_3 **:** a crystalline unsaturated alcohol $C_{27}H_{43}OH$ that is the predominating form of vitamin D in most fish-liver oils and is formed in the skin of animals on exposure to sunlight or ultra-violet rays and is usu. made commercially by irradiation of dehydrocholesterol and that is used similarly to vitamin D_2 but is preferred for addition to poultry feeds because of its greater activity — called also *cholecalciferol* **c** *or* **vitamin** D_4 **:** a crystalline alcohol $C_{28}H_{45}OH$ isomeric with dihydrotachysterol and obtained by irradiation of a dihydro derivative of ergosterol

vitamine *var of* VITAMIN

vitamin E *n* **:** any or all of a group of fat-soluble vitamins that consist of the tocopherols, are essential in the nutrition of various animals (as some rodents, ruminant mammals, and poultry) in which their absence is associated with infertility, muscular dystrophy, or abnormalities in the vascular system, are found esp. in the leaves of many plants and in oils from seed germs, and are used chiefly in supplementing animal feeds and as antioxidants in foods and pharmaceutical preparations; *esp* **:** TOCOPHEROL a

vi·ta·mined \ˈ==mənd\ *adj* [*vitamin* + *-ed*] **:** full of or as if full of vitamins; *also* **:** vigorously and robustly healthy

vitamin G *n* **:** RIBOFLAVIN

vitamin H *n* **:** BIOTIN

vi·ta·min·ize \ˈvīdəmə,nīz, -ītə-\ *vt* -ED/-ING/-S *see -ize in Explan Notes* [*vitamin* + *-ize*] **1 :** to provide with an optimum or a superior allotment of vitamins; *esp* **:** to introduce supplementary vitamins into (a foodstuff) **2 :** to make vigorous as if by the feeding of vitamins ⟨such ideas ~ his writings⟩

vitamin K *n* [Dan *koagulation* coagulation, fr. L *coagulation-, coagulatio*] **1 :** either of two naturally occurring fat-soluble vitamins that are essential for the clotting of blood because of their role in the production of prothrombin in the liver and that are used in preventing and treating hypoprothrombinemia and hemorrhage: **a** *or* **vitamin** K_1 **:** a yellow oily disubstituted naphthoquinone $CH_3(C_{20}H_{39})C_{10}H_4O_2$ that is obtained esp. from alfalfa or made synthetically (as from phytol and methylnaphthoquinone or their derivatives) and that has a fast, potent, and prolonged biological effect, is effective orally, and is useful esp. in treating hypoprothrombinemia induced by anticoagulant drugs; 2-methyl-3-phytyl-1,4-naphthoquinone — called also *phylloquinone, phytonadione* **b** *or* **vitamin** K_2 **:** a pale yellow crystalline disubstituted naphthoquinone $CH_3(C_{30}H_{49})C_{10}H_4O_2$ that is obtained esp. from putrefied fish meal and is synthesized by various bacteria (as in the intestines of man and higher animals) and that is much more unsaturated than vitamin K_1 and slightly less active biologically **2 :** any of several synthetic compounds that are closely related chemically to vitamins K_1 and K_2 but are simpler in structure and that have similar biological activity but except for menadione are less active than the natural vitamins: as **a** *or* **vitamin** K_3 **:** MENADIONE **b** *or* **vitamin** K_4 **:** a hydroquinone derivative $CH_3C_{10}H_5(OH)_2$ formed from menadione by hydrogenation and used in the form of its crystalline diacetate or the water-soluble crystalline sodium salt of its diphosphate; 2-methyl-1,4-naphthalene-diol **c** *or* **vitamin** K_5 **:** a water-soluble crystalline compound $CH_3C_{10}H_5(OH)NH_2$.HCl that inhibits the growth of various microorganisms and is useful esp. as a food preservative; 4-amino-2-methyl-1-naphthol hydrochloride **d** *or* **vitamin** K_6 **:** a toxic water-soluble crystalline compound $CH_3C_{10}H_5(NH_2)$.2HCl; 2-methyl-1,4-naphthalene-diamine dihydrochloride

vitamin M *n* **:** FOLIC ACID 1

vi·ta·min·ol·o·gy \,vīdəməˈnäləjē\ *n* -ES [ISV *vitamin* + *-logy*] **:** a branch of knowledge dealing with vitamins, their nature, action, and use

vitamin P *n* [partly fr. *p*aprika; partly fr. *p*ermeability] **:** a substance that is obtained from citrus fruits and esp. their peel and from some paprikas and is held to decrease capillary fragility and permeability in various animals but is not a vitamin **:** BIOFLAVONOID — see CITRIN

vitamin PP \,==,pēˈpē\ *n* [*p*ellagra-*p*reventive] **:** a pellagra-preventive vitamin (as nicotinamide or nicotinic acid)

vi·ta·scope \ˈvīdə,skōp\ *n* [L *vita* life + E *-scope* — more at VITAL] **:** an early motion-picture projector — **vi·ta·scop·ic** \¦==¦skäpik\ *adj*

vite \ˈvēt\ *adv* [F, fr. MF, fr. *vite* rapid, swift, fr. OF *viste*] **:** QUICKLY, LIVELY — used chiefly as a direction in music

vi·tebsk \ˈvē,tepsk, -ebzk, -ebsk, vəˈt-\ *adj, usu cap* [fr. *Vitebsk*, city of northeast White Russia, U.S.S.R.] **:** of or from the city of Vitebsk, U.S.S.R. **:** of the kind or style prevalent in Vitebsk

vitel *abbr* vitellus

vitell- *or* **vitello-** *comb form* [L *vitellus*] **1 :** yolk **:** vitellus ⟨*vitell*in⟩ ⟨*vitello*genesis⟩ **2 :** vitelline and ⟨*vitello*intestinal⟩

vi·tel·lar·i·um \,vīdᵊlˈa(a)rēəm, ,vid-\ *n, pl* **vitellar·ia** \-ēə\ [NL, fr. *vitell-* + *-arium*] **1 :** a modified part of the ovary that in many flatworms and rotifers produces yolk-filled cells serving to nourish the true eggs — distinguished from *germarium* **2 :** the part of an insect ovariole in which the egg cells grow to mature size

vi·tel·lary \ˈvīdᵊl,erē, ˈvid-; vīˈtelərē, vəˈt-\ *adj* [L *vitellus* + E *-ary*] **:** VITELLINE

vi·tel·lig·e·nous \¦vīdᵊl¦ijənəs, ¦vid-\ *adj* [L *vitellus* + *-i-* + E *-genous*] **:** producing yolk ⟨~ cells in the ovaries which supply nutriment to the developing ova of many insects⟩

vi·tel·lin \vīˈtelən, vəˈt-\ *n* -S [ISV *vitell-* + *-in*] **:** a phosphoprotein constituting the principal protein in egg yolk and containing lecithin as often prepared — called also *ovovitellin*

vi·tel·line \-lən, -,lēn, -,līn\ *adj* [ME, fr. MF *vitellin*, fr. ML *vitellinus*, fr. L *vitellus* + *-inus* -ine] **1 :** resembling the yolk of an egg esp. in yellow color **2 :** of, relating to, or producing yolk

vitelline artery *n* **:** an artery that arises in a vertebrate embryo from the aorta or one of the aortic trunks of the embryo, is distributed by numerous branches over the yolk sac, and is usu. paired — compare VITELLINE VEIN

vitelline duct *n* **:** the duct by which the yolk sac or umbilical vesicle remains connected with the alimentary tract of the vertebrate embryo

vitelline gland *n* **:** VITELLARIUM

vitelline membrane *n* **:** a membrane enclosing the egg proper and corresponding to the cell wall of an ordinary cell; *esp* **:** a membrane separated from the surface of the egg in many invertebrates immediately the egg is fertilized, thus preventing other spermatozoa from entering

vitelline vein *n* **:** one of the veins in a vertebrate embryo that return the blood from the yolk sac to the heart or later to the portal vein and in mammals have their function of bringing nutriment to the embryo superseded early by that of the umbilical vein

vi·tel·lo·gene \vīˈtelə,jēn, vəˈt-\ *or* **vi·tel·lo·gen** \-jən, -,jen\ *n* -S [*vitell-* + *-gen*] **:** VITELLARIUM

vi·tel·lo·genesis \(,)vī,telə, və,t-+\ *n* [NL, fr. *vitell-* + *genesis*] **:** yolk formation

vi·tel·log·e·nous \¦vīdᵊl¦äjənəs, ¦vid-\ *adj* [*vitell-* + *-genous*] **:** VITELLIGENOUS

vi·tel·lo·intestinal \vī¦te(,)lō, və¦t-+\ *adj* [*vitell-* + *intestinal*] **:** of, relating to, or connecting the intestine and yolk sac

vi·tel·lo·phag \vīˈtelə,fag, vəˈt-\ *also* **vi·tel·lo·phage** \-,fāj\ *n* -S [*vitell-* + *-phage*] **:** any of the cleavage cells or nuclei in a centrolecithal egg that do not participate in embryo formation but remain in and function in the assimilation of the yolk

vi·tel·lus \vīˈteləs, vəˈt-\ *n* -ES [L, lit., little calf — more at VEAL] **:** the yolk of egg; *broadly* **:** the egg cell proper including the yolk but excluding any albuminous or membranous envelopes

vi·tex \ˈvī,teks\ *n* [NL *Vitic-, Vitex*, fr. L, chaste tree — more at WITHY] **1** *cap* **:** a large genus of chiefly tropical shrubs and trees (family Verbenaceae) having divided leaves and forking cymes of small flowers with a short tube and bilabiate limb — see AGNUS CASTUS, PURIRI **2** -ES **:** any plant of the genus *Vitex*

viti- *comb form* [L, fr. *vitis* — more at WITHY] **:** vine ⟨*viti*culture⟩

¹vi·ti·ate \ˈvishēət\ *adj* [ME, fr. L *vitiatus*, past part. of *vitiare* to vitiate] **:** VITIATED

²vi·ti·ate \ˈvishē,āt, *usu* -ād- +V\ *vb* -ED/-ING/-S [L *vitiatus*, past part. of *vitiare* to vitiate, fr. *vitium* fault, vice — more at WITH] *vt* **1 :** to make incomplete, faulty, or defective **:** injure the substance or quality of **:** IMPAIR, CONTAMINATE, SPOIL, CORRUPT ⟨exaggeration ~s a style of writing⟩ ⟨the fox . . . ~s his line of scent with the gas fumes on the macadam highways —George Heinold⟩ **2 a :** to debase in moral or aesthetic standards **:** DEPRAVE, PERVERT ⟨vitiated by luxury⟩ ⟨*vitiating* the public taste⟩ **b** *obs* **:** to violate the chastity of **3 :** to make ineffective either wholly or in part **:** destroy the validity or force of (as an instrument or transaction) **:** INVALIDATE; ⟨fraud ~s a contract⟩ **4 :** to make (air) impure by or as if by the accumulation of the products of respiration **~** *vi* **:** to become vitiated; *also* **:** to cause vitiation **syn** see DEBASE

vi·ti·a·tion \,vishēˈāshən\ *n* -S [L *vitiation-, vitiatio*, fr. *vitiatus* + *-ion-, -io* -ion] **1 :** the quality or state of being vitiated ⟨the air in the room showed marked ~⟩ **2 :** the act of vitiating ⟨protesting his ~ of the agreement⟩

vi·ti·a·tor \ˈ==,ād·ə(r), -,ātə-\ *n* -S [L, fr. *vitiatus* + *-or*] **:** one that vitiates

viti·ce·tum \,vidəˈsēdəm, ,vīd-\ *n, pl* **vitice·ta** \-ēdə\ *also* **viticetums** [irreg. (influenced by L *vitic-, vitex* chaste tree) fr. L *vitis* vine + *-etum* — more at WITHY] **:** a growth or plantation of vines, esp. grapevines

viti·cul·tur·al \¦vidə¦kəlch(ə)rəl, ¦vīd-\ *adj* **:** of, relating to, or used in viticulture

viti·cul·ture \ˈ==,chə(r) *also* ,==ˈ==\ *n* [*viti-* + *culture*] **1 :** the cultivation of vines **:** grape growing **2 :** a branch of agricultural science concerned with the culture and production of grapes esp. for wine and market

viti·cul·tur·ist \¦==¦kəlch(ə)rəst\ *n* **:** a practicer of viticulture **:** a producer of grapes or vineyards

vit·i·lig·i·nous \¦vidᵊl¦ijənəs\ *adj* [NL *vitiligin-*, *vitiligo* + E *-ous*] **:** of, relating to, or characterized by vitiligo

vit·i·li·go \,==ˈī(,)gō\ *n* -S [NL *vitiligin-, vitiligo*, fr. L, tetter; prob. akin to L *vitium* fault, blemish, vice — more at WITH] **:** a skin abnormality characterized by loss of pigment in areas of various shapes and sizes and by producing white patches surrounded by heavily pigmented borders — compare LEUKODERMA

vit·i·li·goid \¦==¦ī,gȯid\ *adj* [NL *vitiligo* + E *-oid*] **:** resembling vitiligo

vi·ti·os·i·ty \,vishēˈäsəd·ē\ *n* -ES [L *vitiositat-, vitiositas*, fr. *vitiosus* faulty, vicious + *-itat-, -itas* -ity — more at VICIOUS] **1 a** *obs* **:** DEFECT **b** *archaic* **:** DEFECTIVENESS **2** *archaic* **:** VICIOUSNESS, DEPRAVITY

vi·tious \ˈvishəs\ *archaic var of* VICIOUS

vi·tis \ˈvīd·əs\ *n, cap* [NL, fr. L, vine — more at WITHY] **:** a large genus (the type of the family Vitaceae) of woody vines having simple often lobed leaves and small polygamously dioecious flowers with the petals united in a cap that falls away entire from the hypogynous disk — see GRAPE 2

vitr- *or* **vitro-** *comb form* [L *vitrum* glass — more at WOAD] **:** glass **:** glassy ⟨*vitro*phyre⟩ ⟨de*vitr*ify⟩

vi·trailed \vəˈtrīd, ˈvi·trəld\ *adj* [F *vitrail* leaded glass window (fr. MF *vitral*, fr. *vitre* pane of glass, fr. L *vitrum* glass) + E *-ed*] **:** fitted with stained glass

vi·trail·list \vəˈtrīəst, ˈvi·trələst\ *n* -S [F *vitrail* + E *-ist*] **:** a maker or designer of work in stained glass

vit·rain \ˈvi,trān\ *n* -S [*vitr-* + *-ain* (as in *fusain*)] **:** a constituent of banded bituminous coal that has a vitreous or glossy fracture — compare CLARAIN, DURAIN, FUSAIN

vi·trel·la \vəˈtrelə\ *n, pl* **vitrel·lae** \-e(,)lē\ [NL, fr. L *vitrum* glass + NL *-ella* — more at WOAD] **:** RETINOPHORE

vit·reo·dentine \¦vi·trē(,)ō+\ *n* [L *vitreus* vitreous + E *-o-* + *dentine*] **:** a dentine characterized by extreme hardness

¹vit·re·ous \ˈvi·trēəs\ *adj* [L *vitreus*, fr. *vitrum* glass — more at WOAD] **1 :** of, relating to, derived from, or consisting of glass **2 a :** resembling glass (as in color, composition, brittleness, or luster) **:** GLASSY ⟨~ rocks⟩ **b** *of a fired clay body* **:** having extremely low porosity because of the presence of a glassy phase **3 :** of, relating to, or constituting the vitreous humor of the eye ⟨the ~ chamber⟩ **4 :** of the color glass green — **vit·re·ous·ly** *adv* — **vit·re·ous·ness** *n* -ES

²vitreous \"\ *n* -ES **:** VITREOUS HUMOR

vitreous aggregate *n* **:** a brilliantly lustrous aggregate made with materials and by processes similar to those of the glass industry and used in the surface layer of ornamental concrete

vitreous china *n* **:** a hard-fired ceramic ware that has a dense, vitrified, but opaque body and is used esp. for plumbing fixtures

vitreous enamel *n* **:** a fired-on opaque glassy coating on steel or other metals — called also *porcelain enamel*

vitreous fusion *n* **:** gradual fusion (as of glass) not showing a sharp melting point

vitreous humor *also* **vitreous body** *n* **:** the clear colorless transparent jelly that fills the eyeball posterior to the lens, is enclosed by a delicate hyaloid membrane, and in the adult is nearly homogeneous but in the fetus is pervaded by fibers with minute nuclei at their points of junction

vitreous silica *n* **:** a chemically stable and refractory glass made of silica alone and when prepared from quartz marked by great transparency to light as well as to ultraviolet and infrared radiation — called also *fused quartz, quartz glass*

vi·tres·cence \vəˈtresᵊn(t)s\ *n* -S [fr. *vitrescent*, after such pairs as E *adolescent: adolescence*] **:** the quality or state of being or becoming vitreous

vi·tres·cent \-nt\ *adj* [*vitr-* + *-escent*] **:** capable of being formed into glass **:** tending to become glassy

vi·tres·ci·ble \vəˈtresəbəl\ *adj* [*vitrescent* + *-ible*] **:** VITRIFIABLE

vit·ric \ˈvi·trik\ *adj* [L *vitrum* glass + E *-ic* — more at WOAD] **:** having the nature or quality of glass **:** resembling glass — distinguished from *ceramic*

vit·ri·fac·tion \¦vi·trə¦fakshən\ *n* -S [*vitrify* + *-faction*] **:** VITRIFICATION

vit·ri·fi·able \ˈvi·trə,fīəbəl, ,==ˈ===\ *adj* **:** of a kind that can be vitrified ⟨~ colors⟩

vit·ri·fi·ca·tion \,vi·trəfəˈkāshən\ *n* -S [*vitrify* + *-fication*] **1 :** an act or instance or the process of vitrifying **2 a :** the condition of being vitrified **b :** a vitrified body

vitrified fort *n* **:** ancient masonry remains apparently of defensive works found esp. in Scotland, Ireland, France, and Germany and characterized by siliceous stones converted into a hard glassy material by the action of fire

vit·ri·form \ˈvi·trə,fȯrm\ *adj* [*vitr-* + *-iform*] **:** having the form or appearance of glass **:** GLASSY

vit·ri·fy \ˈvi·trə,fī\ *vb* -ED/-ING/-ES [F *vitrifier*, fr. MF, fr. L *vitrum* glass + MF *-ifier* -ify — more at WOAD] *vt* **:** to change into glass or a glassy substance by heat and fusion **:** make vitreous; *esp* **:** to produce in (a ceramic ware) enough glassy phase or close crystallization by high firing to make nonporous **~** *vi* **:** to undergo vitrification **:** become vitreous

vi·tri·na \vəˈtrīnə, -rēnə\ *n* [NL, fr. L *vitrum* glass + NL *-ina*] **1** *cap* **:** a genus of land snails (order Pulmonata) having a very thin translucent spiral shell with a large aperture **2** -S **:** VITREOUS HUMOR

vi·trine \vəˈtrēn\ *n* -S [F, fr. *vitre* pane of glass, fr. OF, fr. L *vitrum* glass] **:** a glass showcase for display (as of fine wares or specimens)

vit·ri·nite \ˈvi·trə,nīt\ *n* -S [*vitrin-* (fr. *vitrain*) + *-ite*] **:** the principal maceral of bright coal

¹vit·ri·ol \ˈvi·trēəl, *chiefly in substand speech* -rəl\ *n* -S [ME, fr. MF, fr. ML *vitriolum*, fr. LL *vitreolum*, neut. of *vitreolus* glassy, fr. L *vitreus* vitreous] **1 a :** a sulfate of any of various metals (as copper, iron, zinc); *esp* **:** a hydrate (as the heptahydrate) of such a sulfate having a glassy appearance or luster **b :** OIL OF VITRIOL **c** *obs* **:** any of various salts not sulfates ⟨~ de luna is silver nitrate⟩ **2 :** something felt to resemble vitriol esp. in caustic quality; *esp* **:** virulence of feeling or of speech

²vitriol \"\ *vt* -ED/-ING/-S **:** to expose to the action of vitriol; *esp* **:** to dip (as metal) in dilute sulfuric acid

vit·ri·o·lat·ed \ˈvi·trēə,lād·əd\ *adj* [fr. past part. of obs. E *vitriolate* to convert into or subject to the action of vitriol, fr. E ¹*vitriol* + *-ate*] **:** converted into a vitriol or other sulfate **:** subjected to the action of sulfuric acid

vitriolated tartar *n* **:** POTASSIUM SULFATE a

vit·ri·ol·ic \¦vi·trē¦älik, -lēk, *chiefly in substand speech* vəˈträ-\ *adj* [¹*vitriol* + *-ic*] **1 :** of or relating to vitriol **:** derived from or resembling vitriol ⟨a ~ liquid⟩ **2 :** marked by a caustic biting quality **:** VIRULENT ⟨a ~ denunciation⟩

vitriolic acid *n, archaic* **:** SULFURIC ACID; *esp* **:** OIL OF VITRIOL

vit·ri·ol·ized \ˈvi·trēə,līzd\ *adj* [fr. past part. of obs. E *vitriolize* to subject to the action of vitriol, fr. E ¹*vitriol* + *-ize*] **:** subjected to the action of vitriol and esp. oil of vitriol

vitriol stone *n* **:** a hard crystalline mass that consists chiefly of ferric sulfate and aluminum sulfate, is obtained by exposing pyritic schist to the atmosphere for some years, lixiviating the mass, and evaporating, and is used in manufacturing fuming sulfuric acid

vitro- — see VITR-

vit·ro·basalt \¦vi·(,)trō+\ *n* [*vitr-* + *basalt*] **:** BASALT GLASS

vitro-clarain \"+\ *n* [*vitr-* + *clarain*] **:** ANTHRAXYLON

vi·tro·clas·tic \¦vi·trə¦klastik\ *adj* [*vitr-* + *-clastic*] **:** of, relating to, or characterized by glassy rock fragments ⟨a ~ tuff⟩

vi·tro di tri·na \,vi·(,)trōdəˈtrēnə\ *n* [It *vetro di trina*, lit., lace glass] **:** a Venetian glass or glassware in which white threads are embedded in transparent glass with a lacelike or netted effect

Vit·ro·lite \ˈvi·trə,līt\ *trademark* — used for a thick homogeneous opaque structural glass used esp. for ornamental finish on surfaces exposed to the weather

vit·ro·phyre \ˈvi·trə,fī(ə)r\ *n* -S [ISV *vitr-* + *-phyre;* orig. formed as G *vitrophyr*] **:** porphyritic glassy rock — **vitro·phyric** *adj*

vit·ro·type \ˈvi·trə,tīp\ *n* [*vitr-* + *type*] **:** a photograph on glass or ceramic ware produced orig. about 1860 by a collodion process and burned into the surface

vi·tru·vi·an \vəˈtrüvēən\ *adj, usu cap* [Marcus *Vitruvius*

Pollio, 1st cent. B.C. Roman architect and engineer + E *-an*] : of, relating to, or being in the architectural style of Marcus Vitruvius Pollio

vitruvian scroll *n, usu cap V* : a scroll of convolved undulations used esp. in friezes of the composite order

Vitruvian scroll

vit·ry \'vi·trē\ *n* [F *vitré,* fr. *Vitré,* manufacturing and commercial town of northwest France] *archaic* : a light durable canvas

vit·ta \'vid·ə\ *n, pl* **vit·tae** \'vi,tē, -,tī\ *also* **vittas** [NL, fr. L, fillet, headband; akin to L *viēre* to twist, plait — more at WIRE] **1 a** : one of the oil tubes in the fruits of plants of the family Umbelliferae occurring commonly in the grooves between the ridges and affording by their number and position important diagnostic characters **b** : one of the internal septa in some diatoms (as of the genus *Tabellaria*) **2** : STRIPE, STREAK

vit·ta·din·ia \,vid·ə'dinēə\ *n, cap* [NL, fr. C. *Vittadini* †1865 Ital. physician and botanist + NL *-ia*] : a small genus of composite herbs and subshrubs chiefly of the southern hemisphere that are sometimes cultivated for their flower heads which have yellow disks and white or blue ray florets

vit·tar·ia \və'ta(a)rēə\ *n, cap* [NL, fr. L *vitta* fillet + NL *-aria* — more at VITTA] : a genus of tropical epiphytic ferns (family Polypodiaceae) having narrow grasslike fronds and linear marginal sori in continuous lines — see GRASS FERN, RIBBON FERN

vit·tate \'vi,tāt\ *adj* [L *vittatus* having a fillet, fr. *vitta* fillet + *-atus* -ate] **1** : bearing or containing vittae **2** : striped longitudinally

vit·tle *n* -s [ME *vitaille* — more at VICTUAL] : VICTUAL

vit·u·line \'vichə,līn, -,lən\ *adj* [L *vitulinus,* fr. *vitulus* calf + *-inus* -ine — more at VEAL] : of, relating to, or like a calf or veal

vi·tu·per·ate \vī'tüpə,rāt, vә̇, |·'tyü·\ *vb* -ED/-ING/-S [L *vituperatus,* past part. of *vituperare* to vituperate, fr. *vitium* fault, blemish, vice + *-perare* (fr. *parare* to prepare, make) — more at WITH, PARE] *vt* : to abuse in words : censure severely or abusively : BERATE ~ *vi* : to use abusive language : give vent to abusive utterances **syn** see SCOLD

vi·tu·per·a·tion \(,)vī,tüpə'rāshən, vә̇|, |·,tyü-\ *n* -s [ME, fr. MF, fr. L *vituperation-, vituperatio,* fr. *vituperatus* + *-ion-, -io* -ion] : an act or instance of vituperating : sustained and bitter railing and condemnation : vituperative utterance ⟨something ugly, sly, knowing, and triumphant that was far more evil than . . . any open ~ of abuse —Thomas Wolfe⟩ **syn** see ABUSE

vi·tu·per·a·tive \=ˈ=pə,rāt|d·|iv, -p(ə)rə|, |t|, |ēv *also* |əv\ *adj* [LL *vituperativus,* fr. L *vituperatus* + *-ivus* -ive] : uttering or given to censure : containing or characterized by wordy abuse : SCOLDING, ABUSIVE, RAILING — **vi·tu·per·a·tive·ly** \|ə̇vlē, -li\ *adv*

vi·tu·per·a·tor \-pə,rād·ə(r), -ātə-\ *n* -s [L, fr. *vituperatus* + *-or*] : one that vituperates

vi·tu·per·a·to·ry \-p(ə)rə,tō|rē, -tȯ|, |ri\ *adj* [L *vituperatus* + E *-ory*] : VITUPERATIVE

vi·tu·per·ous \vī'tüp(ə)rəs, vә̇|, |·'tyü-\ *adj* [MF *vitupereux,* fr. ML *vituperosus,* alter. of *vituperiosus*] : VITUPERATIVE

vi·u·va \vē'üvə\ *n* -s [Pg *viúva,* lit., widow, fr. L *vidua* — more at WIDOW] : a California rockfish (*Sebastodes ovalis*) of a reddish olivaceous color with small black spots on the dorsal fins, sides, and back

viv *abbr* vivace

¹vi·va \'vē|və, |(,)vä, |(,)vȧ\ *interj* [It, long live, fr. 3d pers. sing. pres. subj. of *vivere* to live, fr. L — more at QUICK] — used to express good will or approval

²vi·va \'vīvə\ *n* -s *Brit* : ³VIVA VOCE

vi·va·ce \vē'vä(,)chā, -chē\ *adv (or adj)* [It, vivacious, fr. L *vivac-, vivax*] : in a brisk spirited manner — used as a direction in music

vi·va·cious \və'vāshəs, vī'-\ *adj* [L *vivac-, vivax* long-lived, vivacious (fr. *vivere* to live) + E *-ious* — more at QUICK] **1** *archaic* : having vigorous powers of life : tenacious of life : LONG-LIVED ⟨the faith of Christianity is far more ~ than any mere ravishment of the imagination —Isaac Taylor⟩ **2** : lively in temper or conduct : SPRIGHTLY ⟨in contrast to the dour, lethargic . . . orang, the chimpanzee is highly active, ~ —Weston La Barre⟩ ⟨a strong ~ strain, a bright noonday song, full of health and assurance —John Burroughs⟩ **syn** see LIVELY

vi·va·cious·ly *adv* : in a vivacious manner : with vivacity ⟨the texture of the stuff has sparkle; whatever he means to convey at the time is being ~ put —C.E.Montague⟩

vi·va·cious·ness *n* -ES : the quality or state of being vivacious : VIVACITY

vi·va·cis·si·mo \,vēvə'chēsə,mō\ *adv (or adj)* [It, fr. *vivace* vivacious + *-issimo,* superlative suffix (fr. L *-issimus*)] : in a very lively or vivacious manner — used as a direction in music

vi·vac·i·ty \və'vasəd·ē, vī'-, -sətē, -i\ *n* -ES [ME *vivacite,* fr. L *vivacitat-, vivacitas,* fr. *vivac-, vivax* + *-itat-, -itas* -ity] **1** : the quality or state of being vivacious: **a** *obs* : vital force : natural vigor **b** : tenacity of life : LONGEVITY **c** : ANIMATION, LIVELINESS, SPRIGHTLINESS ⟨from languor she passed to the lightest ~; her temper became merry and wild —Elinor Wylie⟩ **d** *of a color* : BRILLIANCE **2** : a vivacious act or expression

vi·va·men·te \,vēvə'mentē\ *adv* [It, lively, quickly, fr. *vivo,* adj., alive, lively, quick — more at VIVO] : QUICKLY — used as a direction in music

vi·van·dier \;vē,vänd;yā\ *n* -s [MF, irreg. (influence of L *vivere* to live) fr. *viande* viand + *-ier* — more at VIAND] : a sutler for a French or some other Continental army

vi·van·dière \;ye(ə)r\ *n* -s [F, fem. of *vivandier*] : a woman formerly accompanying troops to sell provisions and liquor to the soldiers : a female sutler

vi·var·i·um \vī'verēəm, -'va(a)r-,-'vär-\ *n, pl* **vivar·ia** \-ēə\ *or* **vivariums** [L, fr. *vivus* alive + *-arium* -ary — more at QUICK] **1** *archaic* : a place in which living animals are kept for food; *esp* : a fish pond or pool **2** : an enclosure usu. of limited size with glass sides arranged for keeping or raising and observing animals or plants indoors; *esp* : one for terrestrial or partly terrestrial animals — called also *terrarium;* compare AQUARIUM, WARDIAN CASE

vi·va·ry \'vīvərē\ *n* -ES [L *vivarium*] : VIVARIUM

vi·vat \'vī,vat, 'vē,vat, 'vē,vät\ *interj* [L, long live, 3d pers. sing. pres. subj. of *vivere* to live — more at QUICK] : ¹VIVA

¹vi·va vo·ce \¦vīvə¦vō(,)sē, -,si\ *adv* [ML, lit., with the living voice] : by word of mouth : ORALLY ⟨gave an account *viva voce*⟩

²viva voce \"\ *adj* : expressed or conducted by word of mouth : ORAL ⟨*viva voce* voting⟩ ⟨a *viva voce* examination⟩

³viva voce \"\ *n, pl* **viva voces** : an examination conducted viva voce : oral examination

vi·vax \'vī,vaks\ *n* -ES [NL (specific epithet of *Plasmodium vivax*), fr. L, long-lived, vivacious — more at VIVACIOUS] : the tertian malaria parasite (*Plasmodium vivax*)

vivax malaria *n* : malaria caused by a malaria parasite (*Plasmodium vivax*) and marked by recurrence of paroxysms at 48-hour intervals — called also *tertian;* compare FALCIPARUM MALARIA

vive \'vēv\ *adj* [MF *vif* (fem. *vive*), fr. L *vivus* alive — more at QUICK] **1** *chiefly Scot* **a** : LIVELY, BRISK **b** : having active properties : FORCIBLE **2** *chiefly Scot* **a** : LIFELIKE **b** : VIVID **c** : distinctly perceived — **vive·ly** *adv, chiefly Scot*

vi·ver·ra \vī'verə, və'v-\ *n, cap* [NL, fr. L, ferret; akin to OE ācweorna squirrel, OHG *eihhurno, eihhorno,* ON *īkorni,* Lith *vaiverė,* vovėrė squirrel, *vaiveris* male polecat, male marten, Czech *veverka* squirrel] : a genus (the type of the family Viverridae) of civets comprising the common large civet (*V. zibetha*) of India and southeastern Asia

viver·ric·u·la \,vīvə'rikyələ, ,viv-\ *n, cap* [NL, dim. of *Viverra*] : a genus of civets including the common small civet (*V. indica* syn. *V. malaccensis*) of southeastern Asia

¹vi·ver·rid \vī'verə̇d, və'v-\ *adj* [NL *Viverridae*] : of or relating to the Viverridae

²viverrid \"\ *n* -s : a mammal of the family Viverridae

vi·ver·ri·dae \-rə,dē\ *n pl, cap* [NL, fr. *Viverra,* type genus + *-idae*] : a large family of somewhat catlike carnivorous mammals that are widely distributed in the warmer parts of the Old World, are rarely larger than a domestic cat but long, slender, and weasellike in build with short legs, rounded feet, and more or less retractile claws, and include civets, palm civets, genets, mongooses, and related forms

vi·ver·ri·form \-rə,fȯrm\ *adj* [NL *Viverra* + E *-iform*] : resembling or having the structure of a viverrid

vi·ver·rine \-rən, -,rīn\ *adj* [NL *viverrinus,* fr. *Viverra* + L *-inus* -ine] : of, relating to, or resembling the Viverridae

viverrine cat *n* : FISHING CAT

viverrine otter *n* : MAMPALON

vi·vers \'vēvərz\ *n pl* [MF *vivres,* pl. of *vivre* food, victual, fr. *vivre* to live, fr. L *vivere* — more at QUICK] *chiefly Scot* : VICTUALS, FOOD

vi·veur \(')vē;vər(·)\ *n* -s [F, fr. *vivre* to live + *-eur* -or] : one who indulges freely or with habitual excess in the pleasures of life

vivi- *comb form* [MF, fr. L, fr. *vivus* — more at QUICK] : alive : living ⟨*vivi*dialysis⟩ ⟨*vivi*perfuse⟩ ⟨*vivi*section⟩

viv·i·an·ite \'vivēə,nīt\ *n* -s [G *vivianit,* fr. J. G. *Vivian,* 19th cent. Eng. mineralogist + G *-it* -ite] : a mineral $Fe_3(PO_4)_2·8H_2O$ consisting of a hydrous ferrous phosphate that has limited isomorphism with annabergite, erythrite, and koettigite, is colorless when unaltered or blue to green when unaltered but grows darker on exposure, and occurs in monoclinic crystals or fibrous, massive, and earthy (hardness 1.5–2; sp. gr., 2.58–2.68)

viv·id \'vivə̇d\ *adj* -ER/-EST [L *vividus,* fr. *vivere* to live — more at QUICK] **1** : having the appearance of vigorous life or freshness : ANIMATED, SPIRITED, FRESH, LIVELY ⟨figures so ~ that they seemed to breathe and speak before us —L.P. Smith⟩ ⟨an exuberant ~ young girl⟩ **2** *of a color* : very strong : very high in chroma ⟨the whole plant, turning red, is ~ against the alkali —*Amer. Guide Series: Nev.*⟩ **3** : producing a strong or clear impression on the senses : SHARP, KEEN, INTENSE ⟨a ~ sensation of pain⟩ ⟨the first ~ notes of the bugle⟩; *specif* : producing or tending to produce distinct and lifelike mental images ⟨a ~ description⟩ **4** : acting with distinctness and force : ACTIVE — used esp. of a mental faculty ⟨a ~ imagination⟩ ⟨thanks to her ~ eye, she re-creates fourteenth century England with broad strokes —Nardi Campion⟩ ⟨~ emotions⟩ — **viv·id·ly** *adv* — **viv·id·ness** *n* -ES

vi·vid·i·ty \və'vidəd·ē\ *n* -ES : VIVIDNESS

vi·vif·ic \(')vī¦vifik\ *adj* [L *vivificus,* fr. *vivi-* + *-ficus* -fic] : VIVIFYING, REVIVING, ENLIVENING

viv·i·fi·cate \vī'vifə,kāt\ *vt* -ED/-ING/-S [ME *vivificaten,* fr. LL *vivificatus,* past part. of *vivificare,* fr. L *vivificus*] : to give life to : ANIMATE, REVIVE, VIVIFY ⟨God ~s and actuates the whole world —Henry More⟩

viv·i·fi·ca·tion \,vivəfə'kāshən\ *n* -s [LL *vivification-, vivificatio,* fr. *vivificatus* + L *-ion-, -io* -ion] : the act of vivifying or state of being vivified : restoration of life : REVIVAL

viv·i·fi·er \'vivə,fī(ə)r, -īə\ *n* -s : one that vivifies

viv·i·fy \'vivə,fī\ *vb* -ED/-ING/-ES [MF *vivifier,* fr. LL *vivificare*] *vt* **1** : to endue with life : QUICKEN, ANIMATE **2** : to make vivid : make sharper, clearer, or brighter ⟨in the mood when the imagination intensely *vivifies* everything —George Meredith⟩ ~ *vi* **1** : to impart life **2** : to become alive **syn** see QUICKEN

¹vi·vip·a·ra \vī'vipərə\ [NL, fr. L, fem. of L *viviparus* viviparous] *syn of* VIVIPARUS

²vivipara \"\ *n* -s : a mollusk of the genus *Viviparus* or the family Viviparidae

¹vi·vip·a·rid \-rə̇d\ *adj* [NL *Viviparidae* family of snails, fr. *Viviparus,* type genus + *-idae*] : of or relating to the genus *Viviparus* or the family Viviparidae

²viviparid \"\ *n* -s : a snail of the genus *Viviparus* or the family Viviparidae

vi·vip·a·rism \-,rizəm\ *n* -s [ISV *viviparous* + *-ism*] : viviparous reproduction

vivi·par·i·ty \,vīvə'parəd·ē, ,viv-\ *n* -ES [ISV *viviparous* + *-ity*] : the quality or state of being viviparous

vi·vip·a·rous \(')vī¦vip(ə)rəs\ *adj* [L *viviparus,* fr. *vivi-* + *-parus* -parous] **1** : producing living young instead of eggs from within the body in the manner of nearly all mammals, many reptiles, and a few fishes — compare LARVIPAROUS, OVIPAROUS, OVOVIVIPAROUS **2** : germinating while still attached to the parent plant ⟨the ~ seed of the mangrove⟩ — **vi·vip·a·rous·ly** *adv* — **vi·vip·a·rous·ness** *n* -ES

viviparous perch *n* : SURF FISH

vi·vip·a·rus \-p(ə)rəs\ *n, cap* [NL, fr. L, adj., viviparous] : a widely distributed genus (the type of the cosmopolitan family Viviparidae of the suborder Taenioglossa) of freshwater snails that have a turbinate operculate shell which is usu. greenish and more or less banded with brown and that are born alive and with a well-developed shell

vi·vip·a·ry \-pərē\ *n* -ES [ISV *viviparous* + *-y*] **1** : the development of vegetative shoots upon or among the reproductive organs of a plant (as in the proliferous flower clusters of some agaves or the growth of bulblets in the flower cluster of an onion) **2** : VIVIPARITY

vivi·perfuse \¦vivə+\ *vt* [*vivi-* + *perfuse*] : to perfuse (as an organ of the body) during life — **vivi·perfusion** \"+\ *n*

viv·i·sect \'vivə,sekt, ,==ˈ=\ *vb* -ED/-ING/-S [back-formation fr. *vivisection*] *vt* : to perform vivisection on : dissect alive ~ *vi* : to practice vivisection

viv·i·sect·ible \¦==¦sektəbəl\ *adj* : that can be vivisected

viv·i·sec·tion \¦==¦sekshən\ *n* [*vivi-* + *section*] **1** : the cutting of or operation on a living animal usu. for physiological or pathological investigation; *broadly* : any form of animal experimentation esp. if considered to cause distress to the subject **2** : subjection to minute or pitiless examination or criticism — **viv·i·sec·tion·al** \-shən°l,-shnəl\ *adj* — **viv·i·sec·tion·al·ly** \-°lē,-əlē\ *adv*

viv·i·sec·tion·ist \,==ˈseksh(ə)nə̇st\ *n* -s : a practitioner or advocate of vivisection : VIVISECTOR

viv·i·sec·tor \-tə(r)\ *n* -s : one that vivisects

vivi·sepulture \¦vivə+\ *n* [*vivi-* + *sepulture*] : the act or practice of burying alive

vi·vo \'vē(,)vō\ *adv (or adj)* [It, alive, lively, quick, fr. L *vivus* alive — more at QUICK] : VIVACE — used as a direction in music

vi·vres \'vēvə(r)z, *F* vēvr(°) *or* vēv(rə)\ *n pl* [F — more at VIVERS] : FOODSTUFF, PROVISIONS

vi·vum va·di·um \¦vīvəm'vādēəm\ *n* [L] : LIVING PLEDGE

¹vix·en \'viksən\ *n* -s [fr. (assumed) ME (southern dial.) *vixen,* alter. of ME *fixen,* fr. OE *fyxe* (oblique cases *fyxan*), fem. of *fox*] **1** : a female fox **2** : a shrewish ill-tempered woman

²vixen \"\ *adj* : VIXENISH

vix·en·ish \-sənish\ *adj* : resembling a vixen : ILL-TEMPERED, SHREWISH — **vix·en·ish·ly** *adv* — **vix·en·ish·ness** *n* -ES

viz \'nāmlē, -li; 'viz; və'deləˌset, -,sət; və'dālə,ket, wē'd-\ *abbr* [L *videlicet*] namely

¹viz·ard \'vizə(r)d\ *n* -s [alter. (influenced by *-ard*) of earlier *viser,* fr. ME, visor, mask — more at VISOR] **1** : a mask for disguise or protection **2** : DISGUISE, GUISE **3** *obs* : a prostitute wearing a mask in public

²vizard \"\ *vt* -ED/-ING/-S : to hide or disguise with or as if with a mask

vizard mask *n* **1** *archaic* : a mask for hiding the face **2** *archaic* : a person wearing such a mask; *specif* : PROSTITUTE

viz·ca·cha *or* **vis·ca·cha** \vi'skächə\ *or* **vis·ca·che** \-chē\ *also* **bis·ca·cha** \bi-\ *n* -s [Sp *vizcacha,* fr. Quechua *wiskácha*] : any of several So. American burrowing rodents closely related to the chinchilla — see MOUNTAIN VIZCACHA

viz·ca·che·ra \,vi,skä'cherə\ *n* -s [AmerSp, fr. Sp *vizcacha*] : a group of burrows of the plains vizcacha — compare PRAIRIE DOG TOWN

viz·ca·chon \,vi,skä;chōn, -chōn\ *n* -s [AmerSp *vizcachón,* aug. of *vizcacha*] : PLAINS VIZCACHA

vi·zier \və'zi(ə)r, -'ziə *sometimes* 'vizēə(r)\ *also* **vi·zir** \və'zi(ə)r, -'ziə\ *n* -s [Turk *vezir,* fr. Ar *wazīr,* fr. *wazara* to bear a burden] : a high executive officer of various Muslim countries (as of the former Turkish empire) : a minister or councilor of state — compare GRAND VIZIER

vi·zier·ate \və'zirə̇|t, -'zi,rā| *sometimes* 'vizēə,rā|; *usu* |d·+V\ *n* -s **1** : the office, dignity, or authority of a vizier **2** : the term of office of a vizier

vi·zier·ial \və'zirēəl\ *adj* : of, relating to, or issued by a vizier

vi·zier·ship \və'zi(ə)r,ship, -'ziə,sh- *sometimes* 'vizēə(r),sh-\ *n* : VIZIERATE

viznaga *var of* BISNAGA

vizor *var of* VISOR

viz·s·la \'vizhlə\ *n* [fr. *Vizsla,* town in Hungary] **1** *usu cap* : a Hungarian breed of hunting dog resembling the Weimaraner but having a rich deep red coat and brown eyes **2** -s *sometimes cap* : a dog of the Vizsla breed

¹vizy *or* **viz·zy** \'vizi, 'vēzi\ *vb* [ME *visien, vesien,* fr. MF *viser,* fr. (assumed) VL *visare,* intens. of L *vidēre* to see — more at WIT] *vt, Scot* : to look at closely : EXAMINE ~ *vi, Scot* : to take aim

²vizy *or* **vizzy** \"\ *n* **1** *Scot* : AIM 2 **2** *Scot* : a careful look

vl *abbr* violin

VL *abbr, often not cap* [L *varia lectio*] variant reading

vla *abbr* viola

VLA *abbr* very low altitude

vlach \'vläk, -lak\ *n* -s *cap* [Czech, Slovak, or Bulg, of Gmc origin; akin to OHG *Walah, Walh* Celt, Roman, OE *Wealh* Celt, Welshman — more at WELSH] : a member of a people scattered through southeastern Europe originating in the early middle ages prob. in the Balkans, speaking a Romanian dialect, and including chiefly mountain herdsmen (as in northwestern Greece) — called also *Wallach, Wallachian*

vlad·i·vos·tok \¦vladə¦vä¦stäk, -dəvə¦s-, -¦stȯk, ,==ˈvä,stäk, *stress in Russian* ===ˈ=\ *adj, usu cap* [fr. *Vladivostok,* U.S.S.R.] : of or from the city of Vladivostok, U.S.S.R. : of the kind or style prevalent in Vladivostok

vlei *also* **vlaie** *or* **vly** \in *sense 1* 'f|lā *or* 'v| *or* |lī *or Afrik* 'fləi, *in sense 2* 'vlī *or* 'flī\ *n* -s [in sense 1, fr. Afrik *vlei* meadow, valley, vlei, fr. MD *valeye* valley, field, fr. OF *valee;* in sense 2, fr. obs. D dial. (Hudson valley) *vlei,* fr. MD *valeye* — more at VALLEY] **1** *also* **vley** *southern Africa* : a marshy depression in which water collects in the wet season : a temporary lake : PAN **2** *North* : MARSH

vlei rat *n* : a southern African murid rodent (*Otomys irroratus*) that has long shaggy grizzled pelage, broad ears, and a short scaly tail and is often destructive to young conifers

vlem·inckx' solution \'vlemiŋ(k)s-\ *also* **vleminckx' lotion** *n, usu cap V* [after Jean F. *Vleminckx* †1876 Belg. physician] : an orange-colored solution containing calcium sulfides made by boiling a mixture of hydrated lime and sublimed sulfur in water and applied externally in the treatment of acne and other skin diseases

v-letter \'=,==\ *n, usu cap V* : a letter sent by or prepared for V-mail

VLF *abbr, often not cap* very low frequency

VLR *abbr* very long range

vm *abbr* voltmeter

¹v-mail \'=,=\ *n, usu cap V* [*V* abbr. for *victory* (in the World War II slogan *V for victory*)] : a system of mail transmission in which a letter written on a letter sheet is reproduced on photographic microfilm and forwarded in this form to be enlarged on photographic paper for delivery; *also* : mail or a letter prepared for or sent by this method of transmission

²v-mail \"\ *vt, usu cap V* : to send by V-mail

VMT *abbr* very many thanks

vn *abbr* violin

VN *abbr* **1** *often not cap* verb neuter **2** visiting nurse

v neck *n, cap V* : a V-shaped neck of a garment

V neck

vo *abbr* verso

VO *abbr* **1** verbal order **2** very old

vo-ag \(')vō¦ag, -a(a)g, -aig\ *adj* [vocational agriculture] : of or relating to vocational agriculture ⟨a *vo-ag* instructor⟩

vo·and·ze·ia \,vō,an(d)'zēyə\ *n, cap* [NL, fr. Malagasy *voandzou*] : a genus of tropical creeping herbs (family Leguminosae) with trifoliolate leaves and small axillary flowers

voc *abbr* **1** vocational **2** vocative

vocab *abbr* vocabulary

¹vo·ca·ble \'vōkəbəl\ *n* -s [MF, fr. L *vocabulum* designation, name, fr. *vocare* to call — more at VOICE] **1** : TERM, NAME; *specif* : a word composed of various sounds or letters without regard to its meaning **2** : an individual sound **syn** see WORD

²vocable \"\ *adj* [L *vocare* to call + E *-able*] **1** : that may be voiced or uttered aloud **2** : capable of utterance — **vo·ca·bly** \-blē, -li\ *adv*

vo·cab·u·lar \vō'kabyələ(r), və'k-\ *adj* [L *vocabulum* + E *-ar*] : of or relating to words or phraseology : VERBAL ⟨a developing science frequently inherits its first ~ wardrobe from older relatives —G.L.Jepsen⟩

vo·cab·u·lary \=ˈ==,lerē, -ri\ *n* -ES *often attrib* [MF *vocabulaire,* prob. fr. ML *vocabularium,* fr. neut. of *vocabularius* vocabular, fr. L *vocabulum* designation, name + *-arius* -ary] **1** : a list or collection of words or of words and phrases usu. alphabetically arranged and explained or defined; *specif* : a list in a foreign language textbook of the words and phrases taught or used ⟨study the ~ at the end of each chapter⟩ : LEXICON **2 a** : a sum or stock of words employed by a language, group, individual, or work, or in relation to a subject : scope of language ⟨Latin contributions to the ~ of English⟩ ⟨words peculiar to the educationists' ~⟩ ⟨estimates his English speaking ~ at from 25,000 to 30,000 words —*Current Biog.*⟩ ⟨the ~ of nostalgia⟩ ⟨color *vocabularies* we acquire in the course of . . . experiences with colored objects —F.A.Geldard⟩ **3** : a set or list of nonverbal symbols (as shorthand signs, sign language positions, marine alphabet flag signals) **4** : a set of expressive forms used in an art : the range of elements composing a formal medium of artistic creation ⟨the Georgian and Federal styles . . . both used the classical ~ of columns, pilasters, pediments —H.S.Morrison⟩ ⟨the complex rhythms and brilliant effects . . . are the natural means of a man who has immense vitality and an enormous musical ~ —*New Yorker*⟩; *specif* : the code of set movements that form the basis of expression for a dance composer and his art product ⟨a rigid dance ~ based on five fundamental positions —*Newsweek*⟩ ⟨a considerable difference between ballet, which has a set ~ of movements, and modern dance, which . . . finds its pattern as it goes along —Philip Hamburger⟩ **5** : a range of means by which one can apprehend experiences or express ideas or feelings ⟨dancing is but a part of her ~ of expression; by face, gesture, and exquisite movement, she is, by turn, the playful child, the joyful maiden, and the awakened woman —*Newsweek*⟩

vocabulary entry *n* : a word (as the noun *book*), hyphened or open compound (as the verb *book-match* or the noun *book review*), word element (as the affix *pro-*), abbreviation (as *agt*), verbalized symbol (as *Na*), or term (as *man in the street*) entered alphabetically in a dictionary for the purpose of definition or identification or expressly included as an inflectional form (as the noun *books* or the verbs *booked* and *saw*) or as a derived form (as the noun *godlessness* or the adverb *globally*) or related phrase (as *one for the book*) run on at its base word and usu. set in a type (as boldface or small capitals) readily distinguishable from that of the running text which defines, explains, or identifies the entry

vocabulary test *n* : a test for knowledge (as of meaning or use) of a selected list of words that is often used as part of an intelligence test

¹vo·cal \'vōkəl\ *adj* [ME, fr. L *vocalis,* fr. *voc-, vox* voice + *-alis* -al — more at VOICE] **1 a** : uttered by the voice (as in speech or song) : ORAL ⟨silent and ~ prayers⟩ ⟨by gestures or ~ communication⟩ **b** : consisting of or characterized by tone produced in the larynx : uttered with voice rather than breath : VOICED, SONANT, INTONATED **2 a** : relating to, composed or arranged for, or sung by the human voice with or without accompaniment ⟨~ music⟩ ⟨~ technique⟩ — compare INSTRUMENTAL **b** : of or devoted to singing ⟨a recital of ~ students⟩ ⟨organized a ~ group to sing his compositions⟩ **3** : VOCALIC **4 a** : having or exercising the power of producing voice, speech, or sound ⟨all ~ beings hymned their equal God —Alexander Pope⟩ ⟨our harps, no longer ~ now —Charles Wesley⟩ ⟨the brook ~, with here and there a silence —Alfred Tennyson⟩ **b** : expressive as if by speech ⟨not that she made a fuss, but her back was most extraordinarily ~ —Willa Cather⟩ **c** : full of the sound of voices : RESOUNDING ⟨forests, ~ with the songs of many birds —*Amer. Guide Series: Wash.*⟩ **d** : given to expressing oneself freely or insistently : OUTSPOKEN ⟨the islanders are, by nature, highly ~, and quite a few have reputations . . . as street-corner orators —*New Yorker*⟩ ⟨~ in support of his party's candidate⟩ ⟨one way of proving that you are a good security risk is to be ~ and aggressive about your

patriotism —H.S.Commager〉 **e :** formulated and expressed in words 〈make ~ the aspiration of decent Americans for a just and lasting peace —Bruce Bliven b. 1889〉 〈the demand for special-training courses has not yet become ~ —H.P.Hammond〉 **5 :** of, relating to, or resembling the voice 〈~ dysfunction due to a throat infection〉 〈~ tone〉 〈the organ had been . . . the vehicle of sacred music because of the sustained and ~ character of its tone —A.E.Wier〉 **6 :** concerned with the production of voice 〈the ~ tract〉

syn ARTICULATE, FLUENT, ELOQUENT, VOLUBLE, GLIB: VOCAL applies to freely speaking out, usu. forcefully, insistently, or emphatically 〈our most *vocal* theologians — one might almost say, most vociferous — are either at the humanist left or the neoorthodox right —W.L.Sperry〉 〈this instantaneous indignation of the most impulsive and *vocal* of men —H.L.Mencken〉 ARTICULATE may suggest exact, distinct, or fluent and unmistakable expression in words 〈the deepest intuitions of a race are deposited in its art; no criticism can make these wholly *articulate* —Laurence Binyon〉 〈perhaps the most *articulate* and effective champion of human freedom in post-Waterloo Europe —P.G.Trueblood〉 FLUENT suggests, sometimes depreciatively, a facile, copious flow of words 〈rage was making him *fluent;* the words came easily, in a rush —Aldous Huxley〉 〈not a *fluent* talker. He seemed to express himself with difficulty —W.S.Maugham〉 ELOQUENT may suggest easy expressive delivery of fervent, moving, or persuasive language 〈the *eloquent* arguments delivered about the wording of each phrase of the Constitution〉 VOLUBLE suggests fast utterance, sometimes inspired by protest or enthusiastic interest, that is hard to stop 〈a *voluble* person, but at last the flow of words stopped —Ellen Glasgow〉 〈she was *voluble,* however, on the subject of divine punishment, and it was with difficulty that Vance stemmed her oracular stream of words —W.H.Wright〉 GLIB suggests ready facile utterance unembarrassed by the speaker's lack of depth, knowledge, wisdom, sincerity, or honesty 〈in some colonies any *glib*-tongued man with a pleasing personality could induce men to enlist under him as captain —Allan Nevins & H.S.Commager〉 〈a suspect who is a *glib* talker, who runs wild with his tongue and apparently gives out with all sorts of information —Lou Richter〉

²vocal \"\ *n* -s **1 :** a vocal sound **2 :** a musical composition for or performance by the human voice with or without accompaniment **:** SONG 〈arranges his own ~*s*〉 〈puts down his horn and takes the ~*s* —Wilder Hobson〉 — compare INSTRUMENTAL

vocal chink *n* **:** GLOTTIS

vocal cords *also* **vocal bands** *n pl* **:** either of two pairs of folds of mucous membrane that project into the cavity of the larynx and have free edges extending dorsoventrally toward the middle line: **a :** FALSE VOCAL CORDS **b** *or* **vocal folds :** TRUE VOCAL CORDS

¹vo·cal·ic \vō'kalik, və'-, -lēk\ *adj* [prob. fr. (assumed) NL *vocalicus,* fr. L *vocalis* vowel (fr. fem. of *vocalis* sounding, sonorous, vocal) + *-icus* -ic] **1 :** marked by or consisting of vowels 〈the Gaelic language being uncommonly ~ —Sir Walter Scott〉 **2 a :** being or functioning as a vowel 〈~ and consonantal sounds〉 **b :** of, relating to, or associated with a vowel 〈a ~ sign〉 〈the ~ ablaut〉 **3 :** having the character or some of the characteristics of a vowel sound 〈the ~ nature of *r* —John Peile〉 **4 :** characterized by vowel change 〈~ preterits〉 — **vo·cal·i·cal·ly** *adv*

²vocalic \"\ *n* -s **:** a vowel sound or phoneme or a diphthong or triphthong that functions as the peak of syllables **:** a syllabic nucleus

vocalic harmony *n* **:** VOWEL HARMONY

vo·ca·lise \,vōkə'lēz, ˌ=ˌ=ˈ=\ *n, pl* **vocalises** \-z(əz)\ [F, fr. *vocaliser* to vocalize] **1 :** an exercise for singers, commonly using vowels or Italian syllables designed to develop vocal beauty or agility — compare SOLFÈGE **2 :** a vocalized melody or passage without words 〈long and haunting series of unaccompanied Oriental ~*s* —Edward Sackville-West & Desmond Shawe-Taylor〉

vo·cal·ism \'vōkə,lizəm\ *n* -s [ISV ¹*vocal* + *-ism*] **1 :** the exercise of the vocal organs in song or speech **:** VOCALIZATION **2 :** vocal art or technique **:** SINGING 〈mistresses of ~ and . . . intelligent interpreters of songs —Virgil Thomson〉 〈singing with fervor and appeal and accomplishing her best ~ of the season —*N.Y.Times*〉 **3 a :** the vowel system (as of a language or dialect) 〈a ~ richer than that of Greek —André Martinet〉 — compare CONSONANTISM **b :** the vowel or sequence of vowels or quality peculiar to the vowel of a word, syllable, or group of related words

vo·cal·ist \-ələ̇st\ *n* -s **:** a vocal artist **:** SINGER 〈trumpeter and ~ in a jazz band〉

vo·cal·i·ty \vō'kalәd·ē, -ətē, -i\ *n* -ES **1 :** possession or exercise of vocal powers 〈the orator accompanied his fine ~ with a series of six gestures —S.H.Adams〉 **2 :** the quality or state of being vocal; *specif* **:** the quality or state of being voiced or vocalic 〈simple tones do have vowel quality, and ~ should be added to the list of tonal dimensions —R.S.Woodworth〉

vo·cal·iza·tion \,vōkələ̇'zāshən, -ə,lī'z-\ *n* -s [ISV *vocalize* + *-ation*] **1 :** the act or process of vocalizing: as **a :** utterance with the voice 〈among the anthropoids, ~ seems . . . to serve social purposes —Weston La Barre〉 **b :** the change of a consonant to a vowel 〈the ~ of *g* in Old English *plegere* to *y* in *player*〉 **2 a :** a reading with the vowels supplied sometimes conjecturally of a word orig. written (as in Hebrew or Arabic) with only consonants **:** a vocalized form of a word in a consonantal text 〈prefers *Yahweh* to *Jehovah* as the ~ of the Hebrew tetragrammaton *Yhwh*〉 **b :** the insertion of vowels (as in reading or writing script customarily written only with consonants) 〈the first step toward the ~ of the text had appeared in the use of . . . vowel letters —W.A.Jeffery〉 **c :** a manner or system of vocalizing 〈fix the Hebrew ~ . . . in consonance with the traditional pronunciation —William Chomsky〉 **3 :** an instance or product of vocalizing

vo·cal·ize \'==,līz\ *vb* -ED/-ING/-S *see -ize in Explan Notes* [in sense 1, prob. fr. F *vocaliser,* fr. *vocal,* adj. (fr. L *vocalis*) + *-iser* -ize; in other senses, ISV ¹*vocal* + *-ize*] *vt* **1 :** to give voice to **:** execute vocally **:** UTTER; *specif* **:** SING **2 a :** to make voiced rather than voiceless **:** VOICE **b :** to convert (as from a consonant) to a vowel 〈*w* . . . after consonants became *vocalized* to *u* —Joseph Wright〉 **3 :** to furnish (as a consonantal Hebrew or Arabic text) with vowels or vowel points or signs 〈the Akkadian texts . . . ~ *spl* with *a; sapl*- —C.H. Gordon〉 〈if it is necessary to indicate in your shorthand notes that a longhand abbreviation is to be used, write a fully *vocalized* outline —*Pitman Shorthand*〉 ~ *vi* **1 :** to utter vocal sounds 〈the gorilla is just as likely to thump upon the upper chest . . . as he is to ~ —Weston La Barre〉 **2 :** SING; *specif* **:** to sing without words (as in practicing vowel sounds) 〈with the spirituals she started singing words . . . instead of *vocalizing* —Virgil Thomson〉

vo·cal·iz·er \-zə(r)\ *n* -s **:** one that vocalizes

vo·cal·ly \'vōkəlē, -li\ *adv* **1 :** in a vocal manner 〈protested long and ~〉 **2 :** as regards voice 〈visually and ~ appealing〉

vo·cal·ness *n* -ES **:** the quality or state of being vocal

vocal process *n* **:** the anterior angle of an arytenoid cartilage to which the true vocal cords of the corresponding side are attached

vocal qualifier *n* **:** VOICE QUALIFIER

vocals *pl of* VOCAL

vocal sac *also* **vocal pouch** *n* **:** one of a pair of inflatable resonating sacs in the mouth of various frogs; *also* **:** the unpaired sac in the true toads of the genus *Bufo*

vo·ca·tion \vō'kāshən\ *n* -s [ME *vocacioun,* fr. LL *vocation-, vocatio,* fr. L, summons, bidding, invitation, fr. *vocatus* (past part. of *vocare* to call) + *-ion-, -io* -ion — more at VOICE] **1 a :** a summons from God to an individual or group to undertake the obligations and perform the duties of a particular task or function in life **:** a divine call to a place of service to others in accordance with the divine plan 〈does not the sense of divine ~ . . . need to be reintroduced as motivation into the profession of teaching —Gordon Poteat〉; *specif* **:** a divine call to a religious career (as the priesthood or monastic life) as shown by one's fitness, natural inclinations, and often a conviction of divine summons 〈resolve not to leave the seminary until someone in authority . . . tells him he has no ~ —J.H.Wilson〉 **b :** the divine act by which an individual is invited or brought to accept salvation through the gospel — compare EFFECTUAL CALLING 〈I press towards the mark, to the prize of the supernal ~ of God in Christ Jesus —Phil 3:14 (DV)〉 **c :** an official invitation to a particular ecclesiastical office; *esp* **:** CALL 2d(1) **2 a** (1) **:** a task or function to which one is called by God 〈the asceticism of the Middle Ages . . . regarded the religious calling as the only true ~ —E.G.Homrighausen〉 〈getting married is an answer to an invitation from God; and . . . marriage is a ~ —M.J.Huber〉 (2) **:** the responsibility of an individual or group to serve the divine purposes in every condition, work, or relationship of life **:** one's obligations and responsibilities (as to others) under God 〈~ involves the total orientation of a man's life and work in terms of his ultimate sense of mission —R.F.West〉 〈domination of physical nature is part of the ~ of man —*New Scholasticism*〉 **b :** the work in which a person is regularly employed usu. for pay **:** line of work **:** OCCUPATION 〈~: carpenter〉 〈soon made art his ~, although he had intended to follow it only as a sideline —*Americas*〉 〈those who are philosophers by ~ will . . . leave it to the amateur philosophizing of scientists and men of letters —R.B.Perry〉 — opposed to *avocation* **c :** the special function of an individual or group within a larger order (as society) **:** ROLE 〈being a husband and father is only one of many ~*s* of a married man —Margaret Deland〉 **:** TASK 〈it is not the ~ of the philosopher . . . to devise and furnish formulae that will define what are in all cases reasonable decisions —F.L.Will〉 **3** *archaic* **:** the position in life in which God has placed a person **:** ESTATE, STATION 〈walk worthy of the ~ wherewith ye are called, with all lowliness and . . . long suffering —Eph 4:1 (AV)〉 **4 :** the membership of a particular occupational group **:** the persons engaged in a field of business, profession, or trade 〈the ~ of politics contains probably more than its share of brave and conscientious men —John Lodge〉 **5 :** a strong inclination toward a particular type of work or course of action 〈moved by a deep messianic ~ —John Bright b. 1908〉 〈though an earnest devotee, she felt no ~ for the cloister —Francis Parkman〉 〈one who is not a dissenter by ~ —M.W.Straight〉 〈a personage whom I might describe minutely, but I feel no ~ for the task —Charlotte Brontë〉 **6 :** an entry into preparation for the priesthood or a religious order 〈all religious communities, he said, are praying and hoping for ~*s* . . . to staff educational, charitable and other institutions —H.C.Bezou〉

vo·ca·tion·al \(')=ˈ=shən°l, -shnəl\ *adj* **1 a :** of, relating to, or concerned with a vocation **b :** pursued as a vocation 〈~ experience〉 **2 :** of, relating to, or being in training in a specific skill or trade usu. with a view to gainful employment soon after completion of the course 〈~ school〉 〈~ guidance〉

vocational agriculture *n* **:** agriculture as taught in high schools in the U.S.

vocational bureau *or* **vocational office** *n* **:** a placement service

vocational education *n* **:** training for a specific occupation in agriculture, trade, or industry through a combination of theoretical teaching and practical experience provided by many high schools in their commercial and technical divisions, and by special institutions of collegiate standing (as a college of agriculture, a school of engineering, or a technical institute)

vo·ca·tion·al·ism \=ˈ=shən°l,izəm, -shnə,li-\ *n* -s **:** emphasis on vocational training in education

vo·ca·tion·al·ist \-shən°ləst, -shnəl-\ *n* -s **:** an adherent or advocate of vocationalism

vo·ca·tion·al·ize \-shən°l,īz, -shnə,līz\ *vt* -ED/-ING/-S **:** to make vocational

vo·ca·tion·al·ly \(')=ˈ=shən°lē, -shnəlē, -li\ *adv* **1 :** with respect to a vocation 〈~ valuable experience〉 **2 :** in a vocational manner 〈~ oriented curricula〉

vocational psychology *n* **:** the application of psychological principles to the problems of vocational choice, selection, and training

¹voc·a·tive \'väkəd·iv, -ətiv\ *adj* [ME *vocatif,* fr. MF, fr. L *vocativus,* fr. *vocatus* (past part. of *vocare* to call) + *-ivus* -ive — more at VOICE] **1 a :** of, relating to, or being a grammatical case marking the one addressed — used esp. in the grammar of languages that have relatively full inflection 〈Latin *Domine* in *miserere, Domine* "have mercy, O Lord" is in the ~ case〉 〈a ~ ending〉 **b** *of a word or word group* **:** marking the one addressed even when this relation is not marked by an inflectional element 〈*mother* in "mother, come here", *beautiful* in "hello, beautiful", and *my beloved* in "be assured, my beloved, that I will come" are ~ expressions〉 **2 :** characterized by fluent address toward others **:** VOLUBLE, GARRULOUS — **voc·a·tive·ly** \-əd·əvlē, -ətəv-, -li\ *adv*

²vocative \"\ *n* -s **1 :** the vocative case of a language **2 :** a form in the vocative case

vo·ce pi·ena \,vō(,)chäpē'enə\ *adv (or adj)* [It] **:** with full voice — used as a direction in music

voce ve·la·ta \-və'läd·ə\ *adv (or adj)* [It] **:** with veiled voice — used as a direction in music

vo·chys·ia \vō'kizh(ē)ə, -izēə, -is-\ *n, cap* [NL, irreg. fr. Galibi *vochy,* a tree of the genus Vochysia + NL *-ia*] **:** a genus (the type of the family Vochysiaceae) of tropical American trees and shrubs having showy fragrant flowers with a single stamen — see COPAIYÉ WOOD

vo·chys·i·a·ce·ae \=,==ˈāsē,ē\ *n pl, cap* [NL, fr. *Vochysia,* type genus + *-aceae*] **:** a family of tropical American trees and shrubs (order Geraniales) having large irregular flowers often with a single petal or stamen and a 3-angled capsular fruit — **vo·chys·i·a·ceous** \=,==ˈāshəs\ *adj*

vo·cif·er·ance \vō'sifərən(t)s, və'-\ *n* -s **:** VOCIFERATION, VOCIFEROUSNESS

vo·cif·er·ant \-nt\ *adj* [L *vociferant-, vociferans,* pres. part. of *vociferari* to cry out] **:** crying out noisily **:** CLAMOROUS, VOCIFEROUS

vo·cif·er·ate \-ə,rāt, *usu* -ād·+V\ *vb* -ED/-ING/-S [L *vociferatus,* past part. of *vociferari* to cry out, vociferate, fr. *voc-, vox* voice + *-ferari* (fr. *ferre* to carry) — more at VOICE, BEAR] *vi* **:** to cry out with quick noisy insistent vehemence 〈purists have long *vociferated* against *mad* in the meaning "angry" —Thomas Pyles〉 ~ *vt* **:** to utter with a loud voice **:** shout out 〈an atmosphere of shrieks and moans; prayers *vociferated* like blasphemies —Joseph Conrad〉 **syn** see ROAR

vo·cif·er·a·tion \=,==ˈrāshən\ *n* -s [ME *vociferacion,* fr. MF *vociferation,* fr. L *vociferation-, vociferatio,* fr. *vociferatus* (past part.) + *-ion-, -io* -ion] **:** the act of vociferating **:** OUTCRY, CLAMOR 〈the perpetual ~ of inflammatory opinion by all sorts of periodicals —George Sampson〉

vo·cif·er·a·tor \=ˈ==,rād·ə(r)\ *n* -s **:** one that vociferates

vo·cif·er·ous \(')vō;sif(ə)rəs, və'-\ *adj* [LL *vocifer* (fr. L *vociferari*) + E *-ous*] **:** marked by or given to ready vehement insistent outcry 〈adult newsboys hawk their papers and racing forms like sideshow barkers . . . a ~ performance —*Amer. Guide Series: Fla.*〉 〈the Northern press and people were ~ for action —S.E.Morison & H.S.Commager〉

syn CLAMOROUS, BOISTEROUS, OBSTREPEROUS, STRIDENT, BLATANT: VOCIFEROUS suggests ready, insistent, or vehement loud outcry 〈the first California booster, the founder of a long line of *vociferous* enthusiasts whose clamor has resounded throughout the land —Herbert Asbury〉 CLAMOROUS may add to VOCIFEROUS notions of sustained din or confused turbulence often in demand or protest 〈the district had been *clamorous* with trucks arriving, backing in and out . . . the drivers bawling and cursing —Peggy Bacon〉 〈the Federalists fairly overwhelmed the silent majority with *clamorous* argument —V.L. Parrington〉 BOISTEROUS suggests unrestrained noise and noisy activity occasioned by rowdy high spirits or disdain or defiance of authority 〈from the distant halls the *boisterous* revelry floated in broken bursts of faint-heard din and tumult —J.K. Jerome〉 〈wild and *boisterous* factory girls —George Sampson〉 OBSTREPEROUS suggests noisy, truculent unruliness in activity directed against control or authority 〈disrespectful of Parliamentary decorum, they are so *obstreperous* that sittings sometimes have to be suspended to stop their hubbub —Janet Flanner〉 STRIDENT suggests an insistent continuing harsh grating, jangling, or other unpleasant noise 〈*strident* tones〉 〈a *strident* electric gong kept ringing above the noise of the crowd —Louis Bromfield〉 BLATANT, orig. suggesting an angry bellowing, now indicates any loud or vulgar obtrusiveness 〈a *blatant* child . . . thoughtless, headstrong, jealous, and filled with a tinsel courage —Stephen Crane〉 〈every dictator in history has been a notorious exhibitionist, tub-thumper, and *blatant* publicity hound —J.D.Voelker〉

vo·cif·er·ous·ly *adv* **:** in a vociferous manner 〈the young chirped ~ as I approached the nest —John Burroughs〉

vo·cif·er·ous·ness *n* -ES **:** the quality or state of being vociferous

vo·cod·er \(')vō¦kōdə(r)\ *n* [*voice coder*] **:** an electronic mechanism that reduces speech signals to slowly varying signals which can be transmitted over communication systems of limited frequency band width incapable of transmitting the original speech signals and that then can reconstruct a fair approximation of the original speech signals

vo·coid \'vō,kȯid\ *n* -s [*vocal* + *-oid*] **:** a vowel or vowel glide completely devoid of oral friction 〈consider certain weak ~*s* as constituting nonsignificant transition sounds —K.L.Pike〉

vo·der \'vōdə(r)\ *n* -s [*voice operation demonstrator*] **:** an electronic device that is capable of producing a recognizable approximation of speech

vod·ka \'vädkə *also* 'vȯd-\ *n* -s [Russ, fr. *voda* water; akin to Skt *udan* water — more at WATER] **:** a colorless and unaged liquor of neutral spirits distilled from a mash (as of rye or wheat) and treated so as to be without distinctive aroma or taste

vo·dun *also* **vo·doun** \vō'dün\ *n* -s [Haitian Creole *vodou, vodun,* of African origin; akin to Fon *vodũ* spirit — more at VOODOO] **:** VOODOOISM 1

voe \'vō\ *n* -s [of Scand origin; akin to Norw *vaag* bay, inlet, ON *vāgr* creek, bay; akin to OE *wǣg* wave, sea, OHG *wāg* wave, sea, ON *vega* to move — more at WEIGH] **:** an inlet or narrow bay of the Orkney and Shetland islands

voet·gang·er \'füt,gäŋər\ *n* -s [Afrik, lit., pedestrian, fr. MD, fr. *voet* foot + *ganger* walker, fr. *ganc* act of going, walk; akin to OE *fōt* foot and to OHG *gang* act of going — more at FOOT, GANG] **:** one of the immature wingless young of a southern African locust (*Locustana pardalina*) which migrate in huge devastating swarms

¹vo·ë·tian \(')vō¦ēshən\ *adj, usu cap* [Gysbertus *Voëtius* (Latinized name of Gisbert Voët) †1676 Dutch theologian + E *-an*] **:** of or relating to Voëtius the Calvinist opponent of Arminianism, Cocceianism, and Cartesianism

²voëtian \"\ *n* -s *usu cap* **:** a follower of Voëtius

voeu \'vᵫ, |ər(·),|ɜ̄, F|œ\ *n, pl* **voeux** \|ə(z), |ərz, |ər(·), |ɜ̄(z), |œ\ [F *vœu* vow, wish, fr. OF *vou* — more at VOW] **:** a proposal or recommendation made by a country to an international body or conference

vo·ges-pros·kauer reaction \,fōgə¦sprə̇,skau̇(ə)r-\ *or* **voges-proskauer test** *n, usu cap V&P* [after Otto *Voges* and Bernhard *Proskauer,* 19th cent. Ger. physicians] **:** a method for detecting the presence of acetyl methyl carbinol in a bacterial broth culture by adding a concentrated solution of sodium hydroxide whereupon the presence of the substance is indicated by a red color

vo·gie \'vōgi\ *adj* [origin unknown] **1** *Scot* **:** PROUD, VAIN **2** *Scot* **:** ELATED, MERRY

vo·glite \'vō,glīt\ *n* -s [G *voglit,* fr. J. F. *Vogl,* 19th cent. Ger. mineralogist + G *-it* -ite] **:** a mineral $Ca_2CuU(CO_3)_5.6H_2O$ consisting of a green hydrous carbonate of uranium, calcium, and copper

¹vogue \'vōg\ *n* -s [MF, action of rowing, course, fashion, vogue, fr. OIt *voga,* fr. *vogare* to row, sail; akin to OSp *bogar* to row, sail, OPg & OProv *vogar*] **1** *archaic* **:** the leading place in popularity or acceptance **2 a :** popular acceptation or favor **:** POPULARITY 〈scheme for economic regeneration . . . enjoyed a great ~ a few years ago —H.P.Fairchild〉 〈its ~ has gradually spread among the lovers of books —William McFee〉 〈the slender, undeveloped figure then very much in ~ —Willa Cather〉 **b :** a period of popularity 〈in spite of the recent ~ of the Marxist theory —John Dewey〉 **3 :** something or someone in fashion at a particular time 〈strange genius . . . now taking posthumous revenge by making himself a ~ —Brand Blanshard〉 〈when the bicycle ~ engulfed the country —Alfred Lief〉 〈plaids were the ~ that season〉 **4** *obs* **a :** general trend, current, or temper **b :** general character **syn** see FASHION

²vogue \"\ *adj* **:** being currently or temporarily in vogue **:** FASHIONABLE 〈~ words and current cant —J.M.Barzun〉

vogu·ish *also* **vogue·ish** \'vōgish, -gēsh\ *adj* **1 :** FASHIONABLE, SMART 〈~ suit〉 **2 :** suddenly or temporarily very popular 〈their ~ meanings show a considerable extension of the earlier technical meanings of these terms —Thomas Pyles〉

vo·gul \'vōgül\ *n, pl* **vogul** *or* **voguls** *cap* [Russ, fr. Ostyak *Uogal*] **1 a :** a hunting and herding people of the northern Ural mountains akin to the Votyaks and Magyars and forming an autonomous district of the Soviet Union — called also *Mansi* **b :** a member of such people **2 :** the Finno-Ugric language of the Vogul people — see URALIC LANGUAGES table

¹voice \'vȯis\ *n* -s [ME *voice, vois,* fr. OF *vois, voiz,* fr. L *voc-, vox;* akin to L *vocare* to call, OHG *giwahanen* to mention, remember, *giwaht* mention, fame, ON *vāttr* witness, *vātta* to witness, affirm, Gk *epos* word, *opa* (acc.) voice, Skt *vāk* voice, *vakti* he says] **1 a :** sound produced by vertebrates by means of lungs, larynx or syrinx, and various buccal structures 〈the chorused ~*s* of the birds〉; *esp* **:** sound so produced by human beings (as in speaking, singing, crying, or shouting) **b** (1) **:** the musical sound produced by the vocal cords and resonated by the various cavities of head and throat and differing chiefly from voice in speaking in the greater prolongation of vowel sounds on definite pitches (2) **:** the power or ability to produce musical tones 〈have a ~〉 〈train the ~〉 (3) **:** SINGER 〈the great ~*s* of an age〉 (4) *also* **voice part :** one of the melodic parts in a vocal or instrumental composition 〈the bass ~ of a fugue〉 (5) **:** condition of the vocal organs with respect to the production of esp. musical tones 〈be in good ~〉 (6) **:** the use of the voice in singing, acting, public speaking 〈study ~〉 〈classes in ~〉 **c :** expiration of air with the vocal cords drawn close so as to vibrate audibly (as in uttering vowels and such consonant sounds as \v\ or \z\) — compare BREATH 7, VOICELESS, WHISPER **d :** the organs by which uttered sound is produced 〈strained her ~ with coughing〉 **e :** the faculty or power of utterance **:** SPEECH 〈fear took away his ~〉 **2 a :** characteristic sound produced by animals using other than vocal mechanisms (as stridulation) 〈cheerful ~ of the cricket〉 **b :** a sound resembling or suggesting vocal utterance 〈distant ~ of a waterfall〉 〈silvery ~*s* of bells〉 〈hoarse ~ of a foghorn〉 〈wailing ~*s* of sirens〉 **3 :** something resembling human speech in being an instrument or medium of expression 〈majestic ~ of the law〉 〈~ of conservatism〉 **4 a :** wish, choice, or opinion openly or formally expressed 〈policy adopted despite many dissenting ~*s*〉 **b :** the right to express a wish, choice, or opinion **:** SAY, SUFFRAGE 〈every member of the family had a ~ in making the plan〉 **5** *obs* **:** RUMOR, FAME **6 :** one that speaks **:** one that warns, urges, prompts, or commands 〈guided by an inner ~〉 〈ancestral ~*s* prophesying war —S.T.Coleridge〉 〈~ of doom〉 〈saw visions and heard ~*s*〉 **7 :** distinction of form or a particular system of inflections of a verb to indicate the relation of the subject of the verb to the action which the verb expresses — see ACTIVE, MIDDLE, PASSIVE — **with one voice** *adv* **:** UNANIMOUSLY

²voice \"\ *vb* -ED/-ING/-S [ME *voicen, voisen,* fr. *voice, vois*] *vt* **1 a :** to give utterance to **:** UTTER 〈a chance to ~ his objections〉 〈has *voiced* the sentiments of the whole group〉 **b** *obs* **:** REPORT, RUMOR **2** *obs* **:** to appoint by or as if by voting **:** ELECT **3 :** to adjust for producing the proper musical sounds **:** regulate the tone of 〈to ~ the pipes of an organ〉 **4 :** to utter with sonant or vocal tone produced by vibration of the vocal cords **:** pronounce with voice 〈the vowels and such consonants as \b\, \v\, \j\ are *voiced* in contrast with \p\, \f\, \ch\〉 ~ *vi* **:** to pronounce a sound with voice **syn** see EXPRESS

voice box *n* **:** LARYNX

voicecast \'=,=\ *n* [¹*voice* + *-cast* (as in *broadcast*)] **:** radio broadcast of the speaking voice

voice coil *n* **:** a coil in an electro-acoustic instrument (as a microphone or a loudspeaker) that carries the audio frequency currents corresponding to the sound waves

voiced \'vȯist\ *adj* [in sense 1, fr. ¹*voice* + *-ed;* in sense 2, fr. past part. of ²*voice*] **1 a :** furnished with a voice or with a specified voice — used often in combination 〈soft-*voiced*〉 **b :** expressed by the voice 〈a frequently ~ opinion〉 **2 :** uttered with vocal cord vibration 〈~ consonant〉 — **voiced·ness** \'vȯisəd-nə̇s, -stnə̇s\ *n* -ES

voiced t *n* **:** a *t* or *tt* that is in some contexts articulated by many speakers of English as a flap rather than as a stop and is accompanied by voice with absence or reduction of the distinction commonly heard in other dialects (as Southern British) between pairs like *latter* and *ladder, hearty* and *hardy, leader* and *liter, let on* and *led on, metal* and *medal*

voice·ful \ˈvȯisfəl\ *adj* **:** having a voice or vocal quality **:** having a loud voice or many voices ⟨busy, ~ world —Odell Shepard⟩ — **voice·ful·ness** *n* -ES

voice glottis *n* **:** CORD GLOTTIS

voice key *n* **:** an electric key arranged to be opened or closed by speaking against it and used for measuring speech reaction time

voice leading *n* **:** the progression of the individual parts or voices in a vocal or instrumental composition

voice·less \ˈvȯislə̇s\ *adj* **1 :** having no voice, utterance, or vote **:** SILENT, MUTE, DUMB ⟨because native labor was ~ and constrained —C.W. de Kiewiet⟩ **2 :** uttered or pronounced without voice **:** not voiced **:** SURD ⟨~ fricative⟩ ⟨~ glide⟩ — **voice·less·ly** *adv* — **voice·less·ness** *n* -ES

voice part *n* **:** VOICE 1b(4)

voice pipe *or* **voice tube** *n* **:** SPEAKING TUBE

voice qualifier *n* **:** one of the manners of speaking (as whining, chuckling, loud tone of voice, rasp, general high pitch) that may accompany the articulation of the vowels and consonants of an utterance and convey a meaning of social relationship and emotion

voic·er \ˈvȯisə(r)\ *n* -S **:** one that voices; *specif* **:** one that voices organ pipes

voices *pl of* VOICE, *pres 3d sing of* VOICE

voice vote *n* **:** a parliamentary vote taken by calling for ayes and noes and estimating which response is stronger instead of by individual ballot or roll call — compare RISING VOTE, DIVISION 17

voicing *n* -S [fr. gerund of ²*voice*] **1 a :** final regulation of the pitch and tone of the pipes of an organ **b :** the tone resulting from such regulation **2 :** adjustment of the hardness of the felts of a piano for securing the desired quality and evenness of all the tones

¹**void** \ˈvȯid\ *adj* [ME *void, voide,* fr. OF *voide, vuide,* fr. (assumed) VL *vocitus,* fr. (assumed) VL *vocuus* empty, fr. L *vacuus* — more at VACUUM] **1 :** containing nothing ⟨the earth was without form, and ~ —Gen 1:2(AV)⟩ **2 :** unoccupied with work or business **:** IDLE, LEISURE ⟨~ hours⟩ **3 a :** having no holder or occupant **:** UNOCCUPIED, VACANT ⟨~ bishopric⟩ **b :** not occupied by inhabitants or buildings **:** DESERTED **4 a :** being without **:** WANTING, DEVOID — used with *of* ⟨~ of common sense⟩ ⟨~ of malice⟩ ⟨a bridge hand ~ of spades⟩ **b** *of a category, class, or suit* **:** having no members or examples ⟨bid a ~ suit as a slam signal⟩ **5** *obs* **:** wanting good qualities **:** FOOLISH, WORTHLESS ⟨idol ~ and vain —Alexander Pope⟩ **6 :** not producing any effect **:** VAIN, USELESS ⟨dull and ~ as a work of art —C.E.Montague⟩ **7 a :** of no legal force or effect and so incapable of confirmation or ratification **:** NULL ⟨declare a marriage ~⟩ ⟨~ ballot⟩ **b :** VOIDABLE **syn** see EMPTY

²**void** \"\ *n* -S **1 a :** empty or unfilled space **:** EMPTINESS, VACANCY, VACUUM ⟨gazing out into the ~⟩ ⟨wandering about in a ~⟩ **b :** a space not filled by anything solid **:** OPENING, GAP ⟨air-filled ~*s* of the soil⟩ ⟨alternation of solid and ~ that is characteristic of the Japanese house —Lewis Mumford⟩ **2 :** the quality or state of being without or free from something **:** LACK, ABSENCE, WANT ⟨loneliness that was one with the cruel ~ of the prairie sky —Walter O'Meara⟩ **3 :** a feeling of want or hollowness (as from unsatisfied desire) **4 :** SUNYATA 1 **5 :** absence of any card of a particular suit in a hand as orig. dealt ⟨partner has a ~ in spades⟩

³**void** \"\ *vb* -ED/-ING/-S [ME *voiden,* fr. MF *voidier, vuidier,* fr. OF, fr. (assumed) VL *vocitare,* fr. *vocuus* empty] *vt* **1 a :** to make empty or vacant **:** CLEAR ⟨press gallery has been ~*ed* of the customary bulky desks —*Springfield (Mass.) Union*⟩ **b :** VACATE, LEAVE ⟨~ the room⟩ **2 :** to cast out **:** DISCHARGE, EMIT ⟨~ excrement⟩ **3** *obs* **:** EXPEL, DISMISS **4 :** to cause to be of no validity or effect **:** NULLIFY, ANNUL ⟨~ a deed⟩ ⟨~ a pension⟩ ⟨~ an insurance policy⟩ ⟨~ a contract⟩ **5** *archaic* **:** AVOID, SHUN, EVADE, PREVENT ~ *vi* **1** *archaic* **:** to go out or away **:** DEPART **2 :** URINATE

void·able \-dəbəl\ *adj* [ME, fr. *voiden* to void + *-able*] **:** capable of being voided; *specif* **:** capable of being adjudged void, invalid, and of no force ⟨a ~ contract . . . may be set aside usually at the option of one party —S.B.Ackerman⟩ — **void·able·ness** *n* -ES

void·ance \-dᵊn(t)s\ *n* -S [ME *voidaunce,* fr. MF *voidance, vuidance,* fr. OF, fr. *voidier, vuidier* to void + *-ance*] **1 :** the act of voiding, emptying, ejecting, evacuating, casting away, or removing **2** *of a benefice* **:** the condition of being without an incumbent

void·ed \ˈvȯidə̇d\ *adj* **1 :** having a void or opening **2 :** having the inner part cut away or left vacant with a narrow border left at the sides and the tincture of the field seen in the vacant space — compare GAMMADION illustration

void·ee \ˈvȯidē\ *n* -S [ME *voidee, voide,* fr. MF *voidée, voidé,* past part. of *voider, voidier* to void, fr. OF] **:** a serving of wine with comfits or spices after a feast and just before the departure or withdrawal of the company

void end *n* **:** an end in lawn bowls in which neither side scores a cast

void·er \ˈvȯidə(r)\ *n* -S [ME, fr. *voiden* to void + *-er*] **1 :** one that empties, vacates, or annuls **2** *dial* **a :** a tray or basket for clearing away (as a meal); *sometimes* **:** a basket for household articles (as clothes) **b :** a servant whose business is to clear away a table after a meal **3 a** *obs* **:** ARBOR, SCREEN **b :** a contrivance usu. of chain mail for covering any part of the body of an armored knight not protected by plate armor **4 :** a heraldic bearing identical with or narrower than a flasque

voiding *n* -S [ME, fr. gerund of *voiden* to void] **:** something that is voided **:** **a voidings** *pl* **:** EXCREMENT, DUNG **b** *obs* **:** scraps of food from a table

voiding knife *n, obs* **:** a scraper used in gathering fragments of food from the table to put them into a tray or basket

void·ness *n* -ES [ME *voidenes,* fr. *voide* void + *-nes* -ness — more at VOID] **:** the quality or state of being void **:** NULLITY

void-solid ratio *n* **:** the proportion of wall surface pierced by windows and doors

voile \ˈvȯil, *esp before pause or consonant* -ȯiəl, *F* ˈvwȧl\ *n* -S [F, veil, fr. L *vela,* neut. pl. of *velum* curtain, veil] **:** a fine soft sheer fabric with a clear finish made from various fibers in open plain weave and used in solid colors and printed or woven designs for women's summer clothing or curtains

voi·lier \vwȧˈlyā\ *n* -S [F, lit., sailor, sailmaker, fr. *voile* sail (fr. L *vela,* neut. pl. of *velum* sail) + *-ier* -er] **:** SAILFISH

voir dire \ˌvwärˈdi(ə)r\ *n* [AF, fr. OF, to say the truth, fr. *voir* true, truth (fr. L *vera,* neut. pl. of *verus* true) + *dire* to say, fr. L *dicere* — more at VERY, DICTION] **:** an oath given to a witness or to a person drawn as juror requiring him to speak the truth under questioning to ascertain whether he is incompetent to give evidence or serve as juror by reason of having an interest in the cause

voi·ture \vwäˈtü(ə)r, -ä·ˈtyü-, -ùə, -ä'chü-; ˈvwächə(r)\ *n* -S [F, fr. L *vectura* vehicle — more at VECTURIST] **1** *obs* **:** means of travel **:** CONVEYANCE **2 a :** a light carriage **b :** a light open automobile **3 :** a local constituent unit of the Forty-and-Eight division of the American Legion

voi·tu·rette \ˌvwächəˈret\ *n* -S [F, fr. *voiture* + *-ette*] **:** a small usu. two-seater automobile

voivode *var of* VAIVODE

voix cé·leste \ˌvwäsāˈlest\ *n, pl* **voix célestes** [F, lit., heavenly voice] **:** a labial organ stop of 8-foot pitch with its characteristic soft tremulous tone produced either by the stop being used with another stop of slightly different pitch or by its being composed of two or three ranks of pipes tuned sharp or flat with each other

vol \ˈväl\ *n* -S [F, flight, fr. *voler* to fly, fr. MF — more at VOLLEY] **:** a heraldic charge consisting of two wings displayed and conjoined

vol *abbr* **1** volcanic; volcano **2** volume **3** volunteer

vola \ˈvōlə\ *n* -S [L — more at WALE] **:** the palm of the hand or sole of the foot

vo·la·dor \ˌvōləˈdō(ə)r\ *n* -S [Sp, flying fish, lit., flyer, fr. LL *volator,* fr. L *volatus* (past part. of *volare* to fly) + *-or*] **1 :** any of various flying fishes (as *Cypselurus californicus* of California and *Exocoetus mesogaster* and *C. bahaiensis* of the West Indies) **2 :** a widely distributed flying gurnard (*Dactylopterus volitans*) of the Atlantic ocean **3 :** any of various sailfishes (as *Istiophorus volador* of Florida and *I. americanus* of the Gulf Stream)

vo·la·do·ra \-ˈdȯrə\ *n* -S [Sp, fem. of *volador* flying fish] **:** any of several small So. American characin fishes of some importance in mosquito control

vo·lage \vōˈlazh\ *adj* [ME, fr. MF, fr. L *volaticus* flying, volatile, fickle, fr. *volatus* (past part. of *volare* to fly) + *-icus* -ic] **:** FLIGHTY, GIDDY, FICKLE, FLEETING

¹**vo·lant** \ˈvōlənt\ *adj* [MF, fr. L *volant-, volans,* pres. part. of *volare* to fly — more at VOLATILE] **1 :** having the wings extended as if in flight — used of a heraldic bird usu. as viewed from the side or an angle or of a heraldic insect usu. as viewed from the back **2 a :** passing through the air upon or as if upon wings **:** FLYING **b** *obs* **:** passing from place to place **:** CURRENT **3 :** QUICK, NIMBLE **4 :** capable of flying **:** VOLITANT

²**volant** \"\ *n* -S [F, fr. *volant* flying] **:** ⁴FLOUNCE

¹**vo·lan·te** \vōˈläntā\ *adj* [It, lit., flying, fr. L *volant-, volans,* pres. part. of *volare* to fly] **:** moving with light rapidity — used as a direction in music

²**volante** \"\ *n* -S [Sp, lit., flying, fr. L *volant-, volans,* pres. part. of *volare* to fly — more at VOLATILE] **:** a 2-wheeled carriage formerly much used in Cuba, made with the axle behind the body, and driven by a rider on the horse

volante

volant piece *n* **:** an adjustable piece of medieval armor for guarding the throat in a joust

vo·la·pié \ˌvōləpēˈā\ *n* -S [Sp, lit., foot flight, fr. *volar* to fly (fr. L *volare*) + *pie* foot, fr. L *ped-, pes* foot — more at FOOT] **:** a method of killing a bull in which the matador advances head on toward the bull and lunges in over the horns to drive the blade between the shoulders

vo·la·pük \ˈvōləˌpu̇k, ˈväl-, -pu̇k\ *n* -S *usu cap* [Volapük, lit. world speech, fr. *vol* world (modif. of E *world*) + *pük* speech, modif. of E *speak*] **:** an artificial international language based largely on English but built upon some root words from German, French, and Latin

¹**vo·lar** \ˈvōlə(r)\ *adj* [L *vola* palm of the hand, sole of the foot + E *-ar*] **:** relating to the palm of the hand or sole of the foot; *specif* **:** located on the same side as the palm of the hand ⟨the ~ surface of the forearm —R.S.Woodworth⟩

²**volar** \"\ *adj* [L *volare* to fly + E *-ar*] **:** relating to or used in flight

vo·la·ry \ˈvōlərē, ˈväl-, -ri\ *n* -ES [L *volare* to fly + E *-ary*] **1 :** a large birdcage **:** AVIARY **2 :** the birds in an aviary **:** a flight or flock of birds

vo·la·ta \vōˈlädə\ *n* -S [It, fr. *volare* to fly, fr. L] **:** a rapid series of musical notes (as a roulade)

¹**vol·a·tile** \ˈvälədᵊl, -ətᵊl *sometimes* -ə(ˌ)til, *chiefly Brit* -əˌtīl\ *n* -S [ME *volatil,* fr. OF, backformation fr. *volatille, volatilie* group of birds, fr. ML *volatilia,* fr. neut. pl. of L *volatilis* winged, volatile] **1 :** a winged animal **:** BIRD, WILDFOWL **2 :** a volatile substance ⟨coffee ~*s*⟩

²**volatile** \"\ *adj* [F, fr. L *volatilis,* fr. *volatus* (past part. of *volare* to fly) + *-ilis* -ile; prob. akin to Skt *garuda,* a mythical bird, *garut* wing of a bird] **1 :** passing through the air on wings **:** having the power to fly **:** FLYING; *also* **:** moving about as if by flight **2 :** easily passing off by evaporation **:** readily vaporizable at a relatively low temperature ⟨~ matter⟩ ⟨~ solvents⟩ **3 a :** AIRY, LIGHTHEARTED, LIVELY ⟨people think that I am ~ because I dance and go to the movies —Ellen Glasgow⟩ ⟨had a ~ mind and was furiously interested in Indians and geography —Bernard De Voto⟩ **b :** easily aroused or moved **:** easily affected by circumstances ⟨these things annoyed and irritated, even drove her ~ temper to a distraction —Ellis St. Joseph⟩ ⟨if, as mortals, they are violent and ~, it is because their emotions are near the surface —John Mason Brown⟩ ⟨the developments which even my ~ suspicions hadn't allowed me to foresee —Ralph Ellison⟩ **c :** tending to burst forth or erupt into violent action **:** EXPLOSIVE ⟨faced with a highly ~ social situation . . . with the problem of reconciliation in this city of forty-eight different ethnic groups —Jean Burden⟩ ⟨world government . . . could halt rigidly and abruptly whatever danger of war might proceed out of the highly ~ competition for military supremacy between the two —Norman Cousins⟩ **4 a :** characterized by quick or unexpected changes **:** not steady or predictable **:** CHANGEABLE, FICKLE ⟨as giddy and ~ as ever —Jonathan Swift⟩ ⟨the most ~ of men, and what is true today may be quite false before the winter snows . . . have melted —Bruce Bliven b. 1889⟩ ⟨in the midst of an area whose politics are explosively ~ —E.A.Kehr⟩ ⟨this ~ element of reader preference —*Printers' Ink*⟩ **b :** subject to or characterized by wide price fluctuations ⟨~ markets⟩ ⟨~ common stocks⟩ **5 :** difficult to capture or hold permanently **:** EVANESCENT, TRANSITORY ⟨so ~ an essence that he escaped definition —Elinor Wylie⟩ ⟨what we actually traffic in are living ideas; the books are only containers for a more ~ commodity —*Publishers' Weekly*⟩ **syn** see ELASTIC

volatile liniment *n* [so called fr. the ready evaporation of ammonia] **:** a liniment composed of ammonia water and a fixed oil (as sesame, olive, or sweet almond)

vol·a·tile·ness *n* -ES **:** the quality or state of being volatile **:** VOLATILITY

volatile oil *n* **:** an oil that vaporizes readily; *specif* **:** ESSENTIAL OIL — distinguished from *fixed oil*

volatile salt *n* **1 :** AMMONIUM CARBONATE c **2 :** SAL VOLATILE 2

vol·a·til·i·ty \ˌväləˈtiləd·ē, -lətē, -i\ *n* -ES **:** the quality or state of being volatile ⟨high ~ in gasoline is an advantage in the starting of cold engines —H.L.Williams⟩

vol·a·til·iz·able \ˈvälədᵊlˌīzəbəl, ˌ=ˌ=ˈ=ˌ=\ *adj* [ISV *volatilize* + *-able*] **:** capable of being volatilized

vol·a·til·iz·a·tion \ˌvälədᵊlə̇ˈzāshən, -lətᵊl-, -ᵊlˌī-\ *n* -S [prob. fr. (assumed) NL *volatilization-, volatilizatio,* fr. *volatilizare* to volatilize + L *-ation-, -atio* -ation] **1 :** the act or process of volatilizing **2 :** the state of being volatilized

vol·a·til·ize \ˈvälədᵊlˌīz, -ətᵊl-\ *vb* -ED/-ING/-S [prob. fr. (assumed) NL *volatilizare,* fr. L *volatilis* volatile + LL *-izare* -ize] *vt* **:** to make volatile **:** cause to exhale or evaporate **:** cause to pass off in vapor ~ *vi* **:** to become volatile **:** pass off in vapor

vol·a·tize \ˈväləˌtīz\ *vb* -ED/-ING/-S [²*volatile* + *-ize*] **:** VOLATILIZE

vol-au-vent \ˌvōlōˈvän, ˌväl-\ *n* -S [F, lit., flight in the wind] **:** a large patty of puff paste filled with a ragout of meat, fowl, game, or fish

vol·borth·ite \ˈvälˌbȯrˌthīt\ *n* -S [F *volborthite,* fr. Alexander von *Volborth* †1876 Russian paleontologist + F *-ite*] **:** a mineral $Cu_3(VO_4)_2.3H_2O$ consisting of a hydrous vanadate of copper and occurring in small green or yellow 6-sided tabular crystals or in globular forms

volc *abbr* volcanic; volcano

vol·can \ˈvälkən\ *n* -S [Sp *volcán,* fr. Pg *volcão,* fr. L *Volcanus, Vulcanus,* Roman god of fire] **:** VOLCANO

¹**vol·can·ic** \(ˈ)välˈkanik, -nēk *sometimes* -ˈkān-\ *adj* [F *volcanique,* fr. *volcan* volcano (fr. It *volcano, vulcano*) + *-ique* -ic — more at VOLCANO] **1 a :** of or relating to a volcano ⟨~ activity⟩ ⟨~ steam⟩ **b :** characterized by or composed of volcanoes ⟨a ~ region⟩ ⟨a ~ chain⟩ ⟨a ~ range⟩ **c :** produced, influenced, or changed by a volcano or by volcanic agencies **:** made of materials from volcanoes ⟨a ~ mountain⟩ **2 :** resembling a volcano esp. in explosive violence or latent explosive violence **:** characteristic of a volcano **:** VIOLENT, VOLATILE ⟨blurting out a few ~ words, and then relapsing —Thomas Wolfe⟩ ⟨long-oppressed ~ emotions erupt, old family feuds flare up —Vicki Baum⟩ ⟨this ~ tempest of a man, fierce, merciless to the flesh —H.O.Taylor⟩ ⟨the ~ tremors that now convulse civilization —Sumner Welles⟩ ⟨major adjustments of one kind or another are essential to stabilize that politically ~ region —Vera M. Dean⟩ — **vol·can·i·cal·ly** \-nə̇k(ə)lē, -nēk-, -li\ *adv*

²**volcanic** \"\ *n* -S **:** a volcanic rock

volcanic ash *or* **volcanic ashes** *n* **:** ASH 1c

volcanic bomb *n* **:** BOMB 4

volcanic cloud *n* **:** a convoluted rolling mass of partly condensed water vapor and dust that is generally highly charged with electricity and that overhangs a volcano during eruption

volcanic cone *n* **:** a conical mountain or hillock built up of cinders, tuff, breccia, and lava by volcanic eruptions

volcanic dust *n* **:** fine particles of rock powder that are blown out from a volcano and that may remain suspended in the atmosphere for long periods producing red sunsets and climatic modifications thousands of miles away

volcanic foci *n pl* **:** the subterranean centers of volcanic action

volcanic glass *n* **:** natural glass produced by the cooling of molten lava too rapidly to permit crystallization

vol·ca·nic·i·ty \ˌvälkəˈnisəd·ē\ *n* -ES [F *volcanicité,* fr. *volcanique* volcanic + *-ité* -ity] **:** VOLCANISM ⟨results of ~⟩

volcanic mud *n* **:** mud that is formed by the mixture with water of volcanic ash or of other fragmental products of volcanic explosions and that is often initially hot and may flow much like a lava stream

volcanic neck *n* **:** a column of igneous rock that is formed by congelation of lava or the consolidation of volcanic breccia in the conduit of a volcano and that may later be left standing above the adjacent country by the removal of surrounding rocks by erosion

volcanic rock *n* **:** an igneous rock (as basalt or obsidian) solidified on or near the surface — compare EFFUSIVE 3

volcanic water *n* **:** water of volcanic origin or deriving its heat and chemical activity from volcanic sources or volcanism

volcanic wind *n* **:** a wind associated with a volcanic outburst and due to the eruption or to convection currents over hot lava

vol·can·ism \ˈvälkəˌnizəm\ *n* -S [ISV *volcano* + *-ism*] **:** volcanic power or action **:** the quality or state of being volcanic ⟨~ includes all phenomena connected with the movement of heated material from the interior to or toward the surface of the earth —P.G.Worcester⟩ ⟨the craters on the moon appear to have been formed by meteoritic impact rather than ~ —*Jour. of Geol.*⟩

vol·can·ist \-nə̇st\ *n* -S [F *volcaniste,* fr. *volcan* volcano + *-iste* -ist] **1 :** one who specializes in the study of volcanic phenomena **2 :** PLUTONIST

vol·can·ize \-ˌnīz\ *vt* -ED/-ING/-S **:** to subject to or cause to undergo and be affected by volcanic heat

vol·ca·no \välˈkā(ˌ)nō\ *n, pl* **volcanoes** *or* **volcanos** [It *volcano, vulcano,* fr. L *Volcanus, Vulcanus,* Roman god of fire and metalworking represented in Greco-Roman myth as the blacksmith of the gods forging thunderbolts on Mount Etna and other volcanoes] **1 a :** a vent in the earth's crust from which molten or hot rock and steam issue **b :** a more or less conical hill or mountain composed wholly or in part of the material ejected from such a vent and often having a depression or crater at its top **2 :** something suggestive of a volcano esp. in suppressed force or violence of outbursts ⟨~*es* of gunfire erupted —Kenneth Roberts⟩ ⟨chief of foreign correspondents who can only guess which ~ of international antipathies will erupt next —F.L.Mott⟩ ⟨the muttering ~ of . . . politics shot forth a shower of sparks which all but extinguished the life of his father —Barbara Henderson⟩

vol·ca·no·log·ic \ˌvälkənᵊlˈäjik\ *or* **vol·ca·no·log·i·cal** \-jə̇kəl\ *adj* **:** of or relating to volcanology

vol·ca·nol·o·gist \ˌvälkəˈnäləjə̇st\ *n* -S **:** a geophysicist who specializes in volcanology

vol·ca·nol·o·gy \-jē, -ji\ *n* -ES [*volcano* + *-logy*] **:** a branch of science that deals with volcanic phenomena

volcans *pl of* VOLCAN

¹**vole** \ˈvōl\ *n* -S [F, prob. fr. *voler* to fly, fr. MF — more at VOLLEY] **:** GRAND SLAM 1a — **go the vole :** to risk all for great gains; *also* **:** to try everything ⟨he has *gone the vole* — has been soldier, ballad singer, traveling tinker, and is now a beggar —Sir Walter Scott⟩

²**vole** \"\ *n* -S [earlier *vole mouse,* fr. *vole* (of Scand origin) + *mouse;* akin to Norw *voll* meadow, field, ON *vǫllr* — more at WOLD] **:** any of various rodents of the chiefly palaearctic genus *Microtus* that are closely related to the lemmings and muskrats but in general resemble murid mice or rats, typically have a stout body, rather blunt nose, short tail, and short ears, inhabit both moist meadows and dry uplands, and do much damage to crops; *also* **:** any of various other rodents of the family Cricetidae — compare LEMMING MOUSE, RED-BACKED MOUSE, WATER VOLE

American vole

³**vo·lé** \vōˈlā\ *adj* [F, past part. of *voler* to fly] *of a ballet step* **:** executed with the greatest possible elevation

vole bacillus *n* [²*vole;* fr. its having been first described as causing tuberculosis in the wild vole *Microtus agrestis*] **:** a morphologically and culturally distinct strain of the tubercle bacillus that is serologically indistinguishable from the human and bovine strains and that has been used to immunize individuals against the latter strains

vo·le·mic \vōˈlēmik\ *adj* [*volume* + *-emia* + *-ic*] **:** of, relating to, or concerned with the volume of circulating blood or plasma ⟨gelatin and dextrin are used as ~ expanders⟩ — often used in combination ⟨normo*volemic*⟩ ⟨hypo*volemic*⟩

vo·lem·i·tol \vōˈleməˌtȯl, -tōl\ *n* -S [ISV *volem-* (fr. NL *volemus* — specific epithet of *Lactarius volemus* — fr. L *volemum,* a pear) + *-itol*] **:** a slightly sweet crystalline heptahydroxy alcohol $C_7H_9(OH)_7$ found esp. in a mushroom (*Lactarius volemus*)

vo·lent \ˈvōlənt\ *adj* [L *volent-, volens,* pres. part. of *velle* to will, wish — more at WILL] **:** exercising volition

vol·ery \ˈvälərē, -ri\ *n* -ES [modif. (influenced by *-ery*) of F *volière* volary, fr. *voler* to fly + *-ière* -er] **:** VOLARY

vo·let \(ˈ)vōˌlā\ *n* -S [F, lit., kerchief, small veil, fr. *voler* to fly] **:** either of the folding side compartments or wings of a triptych

vol·go·grad \ˈvälgəˌgrad, -ˈvōl-, ˈvȯl-\ *adj, usu cap* [fr. *Volgograd,* city in southeastern U.S.S.R.] **:** STALINGRAD

vol·hard method \ˈfōlˌhärt-\ *n, usu cap V* [after Jakob *Volhard* †1910 Ger. chemist] **:** a method for the determination of chlorine, bromine, and iodine in the form of halides by precipitating them with excess silver nitrate and titrating the excess with a thiocyanate solution

vol·i·tant \ˈväləd·ənt, -lətənt *also* -lətᵊnt\ *adj* [L *volitant-, volitans,* pres. part. of *volitare* to fly about, flutter] **:** able to fly **:** FLYING; *also* **:** moving about

vol·i·tate \ˈväləˌtāt\ *vt* -ED/-ING/-S [L *volitatus,* past part. of *volitare* to fly about] **:** to flutter or fly hither and thither

vol·i·ta·tion \ˌ=ˈtāshən\ *n* -S [LL *volitation-, volitatio,* fr. L *volitatus* (past part. of *volitare* to fly about, flutter, freq. of *volare* to fly) + *-ion-, -io* -ion — more at VOLATILE] **:** the act or power of flying — **vol·i·ta·tion·al** \ˌ=ˈtāshənᵊl\ *adj*

vo·li·tion \vōˈlishən\ *n* -S [F, fr. ML *volition-, volitio,* fr. L *vol-* (stem of *velle* to will, wish) + *-ition-, -itio* (as in L *position-, positio* position) — more at WILL] **1 :** the act of willing or choosing **:** the act of deciding (as on a course of action or an end to be striven for) **:** the exercise of the will ⟨followed my father of my own ~ —C.H.Marshall⟩ ⟨our children do not seek school of their own ~ nor do they remain there willingly —C.H.Grandgent⟩ ⟨without my ~ . . . I have become involved in something malignant —C.B.Kelland⟩ **2 :** the termination of an act or exercise of choosing or willing **:** a state of decision or choice **3 :** the power of willing or determining **:** WILL ⟨she marshaled her ~, all her self-control and strength, to shout —Arnold Bennett⟩ ⟨the exercise of their ~ we construe as revolt —George Meredith⟩ ⟨orders his people not as automatons, but as characters moved by their own ~ —P.E. More⟩

vo·li·tion·al \-shənᵊl, -shnəl\ *adj* **:** of, relating to, or of the nature of volition **:** possessing or exercising volition — **vo·li·tion·al·ly** \-shənᵊlē, -shnəlē, -i\ *adv*

vo·li·tion·less *adj* **:** having no volition **:** lacking volition

¹vo·li·tive \ˈvälәd·iv, -ətiv\ *adj* [ML *volitivus*, fr. L *vol-* (stem of *velle* to will) + *-itivus* (as in L *positivus* positive)] **1 :** of or relating to the will **:** originating in the will **:** having the power to will **2 :** expressing a wish or permission ⟨the Latin ~ subjunctive with *ut*⟩

²volitive \"\ *n* -s **:** a volitive verb form

vol·i·to·ri·al \ˌväləˈtōrēəl\ *adj* [NL *volitor* bird able to fly (fr. L *volitare* to fly about + *-or*) + E *-ial*] **:** able to fly **:** FLYING

völ·ker·wanderung \ˈfəlkə(r),vändə,ruŋ\ *n, pl* **völkerwan·derung·en** \-ŋən\ [G (trans. of L *migratio gentium*), fr. *völker* nations (pl. of *volk* people, nation, fr. OHG *folc*) + *wanderung* wandering, migration, fr. MHG *wanderunge*, fr. *wandern* to wander + *-unge* -ing (fr. OHG *-unga*) — more at FOLK, WANDER] **:** the migration of nations; *esp* **:** the movement into southern and western Europe of the Teutonic peoples, Huns, and Slavs from the 2d century A.D. to about the 11th century reaching the peak in the 5th and 6th centuries and closing with the settling of Norsemen in England and France

volk·mann's canal \ˈfōlkmənz-, ˈvō-\ *n, usu cap V* [after Alfred W. *Volkmann* †1877 Ger. physiologist] **:** one of many nutrient canals transmitting blood vessels from the periosteum into the bone but not forming the center of a Haversian system

volks·deut·scher \ˈfōlks,dòichə(r)\ *n, pl* **volksdeut·sche** \-chə\ *usu cap* [G, fr. *volks* (gen. of *volk* people, nation) + *deutscher*, n., German, fr. *deutsch*, adj., German, fr. OHG *diutisc* — more at DUTCH] **:** a person of German ethnic origin long settled in a central or east European country, repatriated for political reasons by the Nazi regime, and expelled into West Germany after World II

volks·lied \ˈfōlk,slēt\ *n, pl* **volkslie·der** \-ēdə(r)\ *usu cap* [G, fr. *volks* (gen. of *volk* people) + *lied* song — more at LIED] **:** a folk song — compare LIED

volks·raad \ˈfōlks,rät\ *n* -s *usu cap* [Afrik, fr. D *volks* (gen. of *volk* people, fr. MD *volc*, *follc*) + *raad* council; akin to OHG *folc* people — more at FOLK, RAAD] **:** PARLIAMENT, LEGISLATURE: as **a :** the legislative assembly of the So. African Republic before it became the Transvaal province of the Union of So. Africa **b :** the legislative assembly of the Orange Free State before it became a province of the Union of So. Africa **c :** the legislative assembly of the Dutch East Indies

¹vol·ley \ˈvälē, -li\ *n, pl* **volleys** *also* **vollies** [MF *volee* flight, volley, fr. *voler* to fly, fr. L *volare* — more at VOLATILE] **1 a :** a flight of missiles (as arrows or bullets) **:** the simultaneous or nearly simultaneous discharge of a number of missile weapons (as muskets or rifles) ⟨some companies being able to attain three ~*s* per minute —R.K.Sprague⟩ ⟨both were killed by a British ~ a few minutes later —*Amer. Guide Series: Md.*⟩ **b :** one round per gun in an artillery battery fired as soon as each gun is ready without regard to the order of firing **c :** a mining blast consisting of a number of holes fired simultaneously **d** (1) **:** the flight of the ball in tennis or the course of the ball before striking the ground ⟨a ball hit on the ~⟩; *also* **:** a return of the ball before it touches the ground (2) **:** FULL TOSS (3) **:** a kick of the ball in soccer before it rebounds (4) **:** the exchange of the shuttlecock in badminton following the serve **2 a :** a burst or emission of many things at once ⟨every push of the pole against the loose mud of the bottom brought forth ~*s* of bubbles —C.S.Forester⟩ ⟨writing ~*s* of letters —G.B.Shaw⟩ ⟨broke into a ~ of curses —R.H.Davis⟩ **b :** a burst of simultaneous or immediately sequential nerve impulses passing to an end organ, synapse, or center ⟨two distinct ~*s* occur in each heart cycle —Albert Hemingway⟩ **c :** a short response (as *Amen*) said in unison by Salvationists — **at the volley** *or* **on the volley** *adv* (*or adj*) **1 :** at random **:** in passing **2 :** in flight — used of a ball in sports

²volley \"\ *vb* **volleyed** *also* **vollied; volleyed** *also* **vollied; volleying; volleys** *also* **vollies** *vt* **1 a :** to discharge in or as if in a volley **b :** to utter rapidly and vehemently ⟨driver then ~*ed* a string of curses —Marcia Davenport⟩ ⟨she ~*ed* him a string of questions —Maurice Hewlett⟩ **2 :** to propel (an object of play) while in the air and before touching the ground: as **a :** to hit (a tennis ball) on the volley **b :** to kick (a soccer ball) before a rebound ~ *vi* **1 a :** to become discharged in or as if in a volley **b :** to make a volley ⟨their eyes, diminished in mirth, twinkled at each other . . . as if wit had ~*ed* between them —G.D.Brown⟩; *specif* **:** to volley an object of play (as in tennis) **2 :** to make loud sounds continuously or repeatedly ⟨a trickle of water ~*ed* loudly on the tarpaulin —C.S.Forester⟩

volleyball \ˈ≈≈,≈\ *n* **:** a game played on a rectangular court

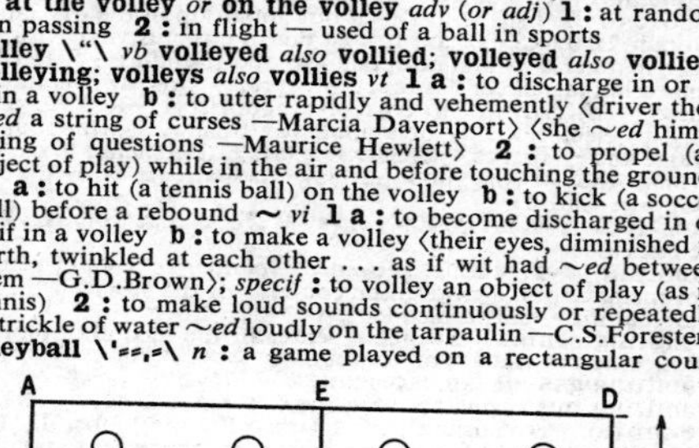

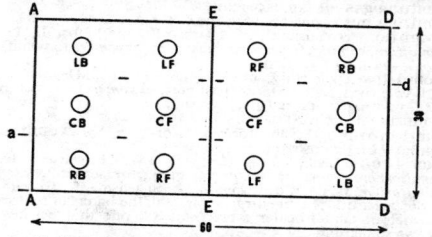

volleyball court: end lines, *AA, DD;* sidelines, *AD, AD;* net, *EE;* serving area, *Aa,* Dd; left back, *LB;* center back, *CB;* right back, *RB;* left forward, *LF;* center forward, *CF;* right forward, *RF*

not exceeding 60 feet in length by 30 feet in width usu. by teams having six players to a side by volleying a large inflated ball with the hands over a net 8 feet high; *also* **:** the ball for use in this game

vol·ley·er \-lēə(r), -liə(r)\ *n* -s **:** one that volleys (as in tennis)

volley fire *n* **1 :** artillery fire in which the pieces included in the command fire the specified number of rounds as rapidly as is consistent with accuracy and without regard to the other pieces **2 :** infantry fire in which the unit fires simultaneously at the word of command

volof *usu cap, var of* WOLOF

¹vol·plane \ˈväl,plān\ *n* [F *vol plané*, fr. *vol* flight (fr. *voler* to fly) + *plané*, past part. of *planer* to glide, soar — more at PLANE] **:** a glide in an airplane

²volplane \"\ *vi* **1 a :** to glide in an airplane **b :** GLIDE 3 **2 :** to sail or coast through the air in the manner of an airplane that glides ⟨these small creatures ~ from tree to tree with the assistance of a membrane joining fore and hind legs —R.T. Littlejohns⟩

vol·sci \ˈväl,sī\ *n pl, usu cap* [L] **:** a people of ancient Italy dwelling between the Latins and Samnites and becoming part of the Roman republic about 373 B.C.

¹vol·sci·an \ˈvälshən\ *n* -s *usu cap* [L *Volsci* + E *-an*] **1 :** a member of the Volsci **2 :** the Italic language of the Volsci

²volscian \"\ *adj, usu cap* **:** of or relating to the Volsci or their language

vol·sel·la \välˈselə\ *n* -s [NL, fr. L, tweezers] **:** VULSELLUM

volsellum \-ləm\ *n, pl* **volsella** \-lə\ [NL, alter. of L *vulsella* tweezers, fr. *vellere* to pluck, pull — more at VULNERABLE] **:** VULSELLUM

vol·stead·ian \(ˈ)välˈstedēən, (ˈ)vōl-, (ˈ)vòl-\ *adj, usu cap* [*Volstead* Act, congressional act passed October 28, 1919 to enforce prohibition (after Andrew J. *Volstead* †1947 Am. legislator and author of the Volstead Act) + E *-an*] **:** of or relating to prohibition ⟨~ days⟩ ⟨~ restrictions⟩

vol·stead·ism \ˈ≈,ste,dizəm\ *n* -s *usu cap* [*Volstead* Act + E *-ism*] **:** the doctrine of or adherence to prohibition

¹volt \ˈvōlt\ *n* -s [F *volte*, fr. It *volta* turn, volt, fr. *voltare* to turn, fr. (assumed) VL *volvitare*, freq. of L *volvere* to roll — more at VOLUBLE] **1 a :** a tread or gait in which a horse going sideways makes a turn round a center **b :** a circle traced by a horse in this movement **c :** the ground marked for the volt **2 :** a leaping movement in fencing to avoid a thrust

²volt \"\ *n* -s [after Alessandro *Volta* †1827 Ital. physicist] **:** the practical mks unit of electrical potential difference and electromotive force that is equal to the difference of potential between two points in a conducting wire carrying a constant current of one ampere when the power dissipated between these two points is equal to one watt, that is equivalent to the potential difference across a resistance of one ohm when one ampere is flowing through it, and that is taken as the standard in the U.S. **2 :** a unit of electrical potential difference and electromotive force equal to 1.00034 volts and formerly taken as the standard in the U.S. — called also *international volt*

vol·ta \ˈvōltə, ˈväl- *or* **vol·te** \-tā\ *n, pl* **volte** [*volta* fr. It, turn, lavolta, fr. *voltare* to turn; *volte* fr. F, fr. It *volta*] **:** LAVOLTA

vol·ta effect \ˈvōltə-, ˈvältə-\ *n, usu cap V* [after Alessandro *Volta* †1827 Ital. physicist] **:** the difference of potential observable between two dissimilar metals when placed in contact with one metal becoming positive and the other negative — called also *contact potential*

volt·age \ˈvōltij, -tēj\ *n* -s [ISV ²*volt* + *-age*] **1 :** electric potential or potential difference expressed in volts **2 :** intensity of feeling **:** EFFECTIVENESS, POWER ⟨the ~ of his verse is praised —J.L.Sweeney⟩ ⟨by slow degrees the author raises the ~ of her story —John Barkham⟩ ⟨she was shocked by the ~ of his rapacious tone —Peggy Bennett⟩

voltage amplification *n* **:** the ratio of the alternating voltage produced at the output terminals of an amplifier to the alternating voltage impressed at the input terminals

voltage divider *n* **:** a resistor or series of resistors that is provided with taps at certain points and that is used to provide various potential differences from a single power source — called also *potential divider*

voltage multiplier *n* **:** an accelerator in which particles (as protons) are propelled by means of high voltages produced by capacitors in series with each capacitor charged to a higher potential than the preceding one

voltage regulator *n* **:** a transformer having its primary winding in shunt and its secondary winding in series with an alternating-current circuit the voltage of which may be regulated by varying the voltage ratio of transformation

¹vol·ta·ic \(ˈ)välˌtāik, (ˈ)vōl-, -ˈāek\ *adj* [Alessandro *Volta* †1827 Ital. physicist + E *-ic*] **:** of, relating to, or producing direct electric current by chemical action (as in a battery) **:** GALVANIC ⟨~ cell⟩

²vol·ta·ic \välˈtāik\ *n, usu cap* [upper *Volta* river valley in Ghana and Upper *Volta*, West Africa + E *-ic*] **:** GUR

³voltaic \(ˈ)≈¦≈≈\ *adj, usu cap* [Upper *Volta*, West Africa + E *-ic*] **1 a :** of, relating to, or characteristic of Upper Volta **b :** of, relating to, or characteristic of the people of Upper Volta **2 :** of, relating to, or characteristic of the Gur language

voltaic couple *n* **:** a pair of substances usu. but not necessarily metals capable of acting together as an electric source when dipped in an electrolyte

voltaic pile *n* **:** ⁵PILE 6a

¹vol·tair·e·an *or* **vol·tair·i·an** \≈ˈta(a)rēən, -ˈter-\ *n, usu cap* [*Voltaire* (F. M. Arouet) †1778 Fr. writer + E *-an*, n. suffix] **:** a follower of Voltaire or an advocate of Voltairianism

²voltairean *or* **voltairian** \(ˈ)≈¦≈≈\ *adj, usu cap* [*Voltaire* + E *-an*, adj. suffix] **:** of, relating to, or typical of Voltaire

vol·taire chair \(ˈ)vōl¦ta(ə)|(ə)r-, (ˈ)vōl-, -tel, |ə *also* (ˈ)väl-\ *n, usu cap V* [prob. after *Voltaire* †1778 Fr. writer] **:** an armchair with a low seat and a high back

vol·tair·i·an·ism \≈ˈ≈rēə,nizəm\ *n* -s *usu cap* [*Voltaire* †1778 Fr. writer + E *-ianism* (as in *trinitarianism*)] **:** the theories or practices of Voltaire characterized by a skeptical but deistic religious attitude, opposition to intolerance, and castigation of bigotry

vol·ta·ism \ˈvältə,izəm\ *n* -s [ISV ¹*voltaic* + *-ism*] **:** GALVANISM 1

vol·ta·ite \ˈvältə,īt\ *n* -s [It *voltaita*, fr. Alessandro *Volta* †1827 Ital. physicist + It *-ita* -ite] **:** a mineral $(K,Fe)_3Fe(SO_4)_3.4H_2O$ or $HK_2Fe_4(Fe,Al)_3(SO_4)_{10}.13H_2O$ consisting of a hydrous sulfate of potassium and iron

vol·tam·e·ter \välˈtamәd·ə(r), vōl-, -mətə-\ *n* [ISV ¹*voltaic* + *-meter*] **:** an apparatus for measuring the quantity of electricity passed through a conductor by the amount of electrolysis produced (as by measuring the gases generated from acidulated water or by weighing the silver deposited from a solution of silver nitrate) — **vol·ta·met·ric** \ˌvältə¦me-trik, ¦vōl-, -rēk\ *adj*

volt–ammeter \ˈ≈ˈ≈,≈≈\ *n* **:** an instrument for indicating one or more ranges of volts and amperes by changing terminal connections

volt–ampere \ˈ≈ˈ≈,≈\ *n* **:** a unit of electric measurement that is equal to the product of a volt and an ampere and that for direct current constitutes a measure of power equivalent to a watt and for alternating current a measure of apparent power

volta's pile *n, usu cap V* [after Alessandro *Volta* †1827 Ital. physicist] **:** ⁵PILE 6a

volt box *n* **:** a resistance box provided with taps, usu. used with a potentiometer for measuring potentials beyond the range of that instrument, and so constructed that by means of the taps a definite fraction (as ¹⁄₁₀ or ¹⁄₁₀₀) of the potential applied to the volt box is made available for potentiometer measurement

¹volte *var of* VOLTA

²volte \ˈvält, ˈvōlt\ *n* -s [F — more at VOLT] **:** ¹VOLT 1

¹volte–face \-t(ə)ˈfäs\ *n* [F, fr. It *voltafaccia*, fr. *volta* turn + *faccia* face, fr. (assumed) VL *facia* — more at VOLT, FACE] **:** a change of front **:** a facing about **:** ABOUT-FACE, REVERSAL ⟨he performed a *volte-face* and attacked his former associates —S.F.Mason⟩ ⟨a *volte-face* in American economic policy —*Foreign Affairs*⟩ ⟨a last-minute *volte-face* against the spearhead of his own clan — the ultramodernists —*Canadian Art*⟩ ⟨not that an instant *volte-face* took place . . . in politics, manners, and customs —R.A.Hall b. 1911⟩

²volte–face \"\ *vi* **:** to perform a volte-face **:** face about

vol·ti·geur \ˌvältəˈzhər\ *n* -s [F, lit., leaper, fr. *voltiger* to leap, vault (fr. It *volteggiare*, freq. of *voltare* to turn) + *-eur* -or — more at VOLT] **:** a member of any of various French organizations of light infantry; *often* **:** a sharpshooter in the French army

vol·tin·ism \ˈvōltᵊn,izəm\ *n* -s [*voltine* (as in *bivoltine*) + *-ism*] **:** the frequency or number of annual broods (as of insects) — compare POLYVOLTINE, UNIVOLTINE

vol·ti su·bi·to \ˈvōltēˈsübəd·(,)ō\ [It, lit., turn quickly] **:** turn the page quickly — used as a direction in music; abbr. *v.s.*

volt·me·ter \ˈvōlt,mēd·ə(r), -ētə-\ *n* [ISV ²*volt* + *-meter*] **:** an instrument (as a galvanometer) for measuring in volts the differences of potential between different points of an electrical circuit

vol·to·li·za·tion \ˌvältələˈzāshən\ *n* -s **:** the process of voltolizing

vol·to·lize \ˈvältə,līz\ *vt* -ED/-ING/-S [²*volt* + *-ol* + *-ize*] **:** to subject (as an oil) to an electric discharge

volts *pl of* VOLT

voltz·ite \ˈvält,sīt\ *n* -s [G *voltzit*, fr. Philippe L. *Voltz* †1840 Fr. mining engineer + G *-it* -ite] **:** a mineral Zn_5OS_4 consisting of a zinc oxysulfide and occurring in implanted spherical globules of a yellowish or reddish color

vol·u·bil·i·ty \ˌvälyəˈbilәd·ē, -ilətē, -i\ *n* -ES [L *volubilitas*, fr. *volubilis* voluble + *-itas* -ity] **:** the quality or state of being voluble ⟨from her ~ of tongue seemed likely to stretch the discourse to an immoderate length —Henry Fielding⟩

vol·u·ble \ˈvälyəbəl\ *adj* [MF or L; MF *voluble*, fr. L *volubilis*, fr. L *volvere* to roll, turn, revolve + *-bilis* capable of being acted upon; akin to Gk *eilyein* to roll, wrap, fold, Goth *-walwjan* to roll, OE *walwian*, *wealwian*, OHG *wellan* to roll, OSlav *valiti* to roll, trundle, Skt *valati* he turns; basic meaning: turning, rolling] **1 a :** easily rolling or turning **:** easily set in motion **:** apt to roll **:** ROTATING, REVOLVING **b :** having the power or habit of twining ⟨a ~ plant stem⟩ **2 :** CHANGEABLE, UNSTABLE, FICKLE **3 :** characterized by ease and smoothness of utterance **:** characterized by ready or rapid speech **:** GLIB, FLUENT ⟨seemed ~, prone to speech as I had never seen him before —Jack London⟩ ⟨that he, who once had been so ~, should have become almost inarticulate —Ellen Glasgow⟩ **syn** see TALKATIVE, VOCAL

vol·u·ble·ness *n* -ES **:** VOLUBILITY

vol·u·bly \-blē, -li\ *adv* **:** in a voluble manner **:** GLIBLY ⟨a boiling pot of enthusiasms and animosities, which he pours out ~, skillfully, and eloquently —Brand Blanshard⟩

vol·u·crine \ˈvälyə,krīn, -əkrən\ *adj* [L *volucris* flying creature, bird (akin to L *volare* to fly) + E *-ine* — more at VOLATILE] **:** of or relating to birds

¹vol·ume \ˈvälyəm *also* -l(,)yüm\ *n* -s [ME *volum*, *volume*, fr. MF, fr. L *volumen* roll of writing, book, volume, fr. *volvere* to roll — more at VOLUBLE] **1 :** a written document (as on parchment) rolled up on a short staff for keeping and unrolled for reading **:** SCROLL **2 a :** a collection of printed sheets bound together whether constituting a single work ⟨a ~ of memoirs⟩, a part of a work ⟨the first ~ of a long biography⟩, or a part in a related series of works ⟨the ~ of Victorian poetry in the series of English poetry⟩ **:** BOOK; *esp* **:** the part of an extended work bound up together in one cover — compare BROCHURE, PAMPHLET, TOME **b :** an arbitrary number of issues of a periodical or the issues printed within a set time (as a year) ⟨each issue of a magazine bears a ~ number and an issue number which are assigned by the publisher and continue in regular sequence from Volume 1, No. 1. —*Theory & Practice of Bookbinding*⟩ **c :** ALBUM 1c ⟨the Russian basso, has done a ~ of lieder —*Harper's*⟩ **3 a :** something that may be studied and interpreted like a book ⟨the ~ of nature⟩ **b :** something having a rounded or swelling form suggestive of a scroll **:** COIL, CONVOLUTION, TURN ⟨imbedded in the ~*s* of her hair —J.F. Cooper⟩ ⟨feminine attributes of even greater value than the curves and ~*s* of the female body —Frank Budgen⟩ **4 :** space occupied or enclosed by cubic units (as inches, feet, quarts, pecks, bushels, gallons) **:** COMPASS, CAPACITY ⟨the ~ of a container⟩; *specif* **:** the number of cubes each with an edge one unit long that can be fitted exactly into a solid (as some rectangular parallelepipeds) when it can be fitted in such a manner or a number that is equally acceptable as a measure of the solid (as a sphere or cone) when it cannot be fitted in this manner

VOLUME FORMULAS

FIGURE	FORMULA	MEANING OF LETTERS
cube	$V=a^3$	a=one of the dimensions
rectangular prism	$V=abc$	a=length; b=width; c=depth
pyramid	$V=\frac{Ah}{3}$	A=area of base; h=height
cylinder	$V=\pi r^2h$	π=3.1416; r=radius of the base; h=height
cone	$V=\frac{\pi r^2h}{3}$	π=3.1416; r=radius of the base; h=height
sphere	$V=\frac{4\pi r^3}{3}$	π=3.1416; r=radius

5 a : AMOUNT, BULK, MASS, QUANTITY ⟨as a composer he produced a considerable ~ of church music —J.T.Howard⟩ ⟨the ~ of employment rose —Oscar Handlin⟩ ⟨the flow of income to individuals was of record dollar ~ —Milton Gilbert⟩ ⟨a large ~ of unclassified technological data has been published —R.A.Tybout⟩ ⟨overwhelmed by the ~ and violence of his dispatches —Pierre Frédérix⟩ ⟨a sales ~ of . . . a million dollars on his books —*Current Biog.*⟩ ⟨shelled clams are bought by the count or by ~ —Marjorie M. Heseltine & Ula M. Dow⟩; *often* **:** a considerable quantity ⟨profits are made by selling ~ at market price —*Wall Street Jour.*⟩ ⟨chance that the snow will fall in ~, and soon —J.M.Vander Voort⟩ ⟨pouring forth a ~ of amiable absurdities —Victoria Sackville-West⟩ **b :** the amount of a substance that occupies a particular volume ⟨one ~ of the material which has been collected is added to 9 ~*s* of normal saline —F.J.Hamilton⟩ ⟨water on electrolysis gives 2 ~*s* of hydrogen to one of oxygen⟩ **c :** the number of vehicles or pedestrians that pass a given point during a specified period of time ⟨the ~ of traffic⟩ **d** (1) **:** a shaped or defined mass in a sculpture or an architectural structure (2) **:** the representation of mass or three-dimensional shape in a drawing or painting **6 a :** the degree of loudness or the intensity of a sound ⟨by the last chorus the ~ of sound was overwhelming —Agnes S. Turnbull⟩ ⟨a desire for ever greater ~ overtook musicians and instrument-makers —Robert Donington⟩; *also* **:** LOUDNESS ⟨a singer who could look pathetic and who had ~ —Jo Sullivan⟩ **b :** the magnitude of an audio frequency wave in an electric circuit **7 :** a characteristic of auditory sensations such that high tones seem small and sharp while low tones appear to fill much space **syn** see SIZE

²volume \"\ *adj* **:** of, dealing with, or involving large quantities ⟨~ production of airplanes⟩ ⟨~ sales of books⟩

³volume \"\ *vb* -ED/-ING/-S *vi* **:** to roll or rise in volume ⟨her dress *volumed* —George Meredith⟩ ⟨a drift of pale, *voluming* smoke arose from the sawdust pile —J.G.Cozzens⟩ ⟨the blood cry went up and *volumed* in a discordant chorus —J.F.Dobie⟩ ~ *vt* **1 :** to collect or gather in or as if in a volume **2 :** to send or give out in volume

volume color *n* **:** BULKY COLOR

vol·umed \-md\ *adj* **1 :** having the form of a roll **:** occurring in rounded masses ⟨~ mist⟩ **2 :** having bulk **:** MASSIVE, GREAT **3 :** having such or so many volumes — used in combination ⟨a three-*volumed* history⟩

volume displacement *n* **:** displacement of a fluid expressed in terms of volume as distinguished from displacement expressed in terms of mass

vol·u·me·nom·e·ter \ˌvälyəmēˈnäməd·ə(r)\ *n* [ISV *volumeno-* (fr. NL *volumen* volume, fr. L, book) + *-meter*] **:** an instrument for measuring the volume and indirectly the specific gravity of a body (as a solid) by means of the difference in pressure caused by its presence and absence in a closed air space — **vol·u·me·nom·e·try** \-ˈnämə-trē\ *n* -ES

volume resistance *n* **:** the electrical resistance of a body to current passing through its bodily substance irrespective of any surface leakage

volume table *n* **:** a tabulated statement of the yield of trees upon the basis of various measurements of diameter and height

vo·lu·me·ter \vəˈlüməd·ə(r), -mətə- *also* vəlˈyü- *or* välˈyü-; ˈvälyə,mēd·ə(r), -ētə-\ *n* [ISV, blend of ¹*volume* and *-meter*] **:** an instrument for measuring volumes (as of gases or liquids) directly or (as of solids) by displacement of a liquid

vol·u·met·ric \ˌvälyə¦me-trik, -rēk\ *also* **vol·u·met·ri·cal** \-rəkəl, -rēk-\ *adj* [ISV, blend of ¹*volume* and *metric*] **:** of or relating to the measurement of volume — **vol·u·met·ri·cal·ly** \-rək(ə)lē, -rēk-,-li\ *adv*

volumetric analysis *n* **1 :** quantitative analysis by the use of definite volumes of standard solutions of reagents **2 :** analysis (as by the eudiometer) of gases by volume

volumetric flask *n* **:** a graduated flask for use in volumetric analysis

volumetric solution *n* **:** a standard solution for use in volumetric analysis

vol·u·mette \ˌvälyəˈmet\ *n* -s [¹*volume* + *-ette*] **:** a small volume ⟨a ~ of poems⟩

volume unit *n* **:** a unit equal to a decibel for specifying the power level of a signal in audio equipment above a value of 1 milliwatt in a 500 ohm circuit

vo·lu·mi·nal \vəˈlümənᵊl\ *adj* [L *volumin-*, *volumen* + E *-al*] **:** of or relating to volume

vo·lu·mi·nos·i·ty \vəˌlüməˈnäsәd·ē\ *n* -ES **:** the quality or state of being voluminous; *also* **:** an instance of this

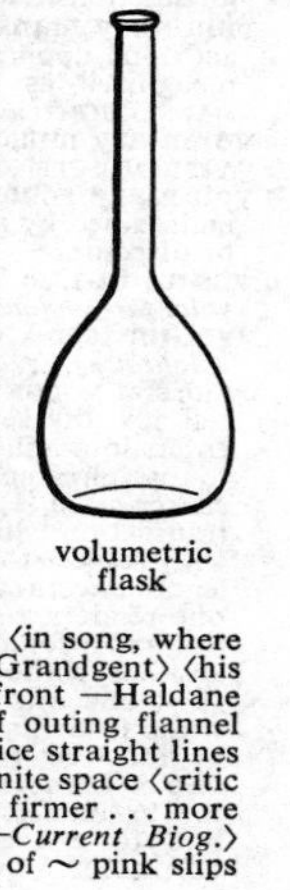

volumetric flask

vo·lu·mi·nous \vəˈlümənəs *also* vəlˈyü-\ *adj* [LL *voluminosus* full of folds, fr. L *volumin-*, *volumen* roll of writing, book + *-osus* -ose — more at VOLUME] **1 :** of or relating to volume **2 :** winding or full of windings **:** consisting of many folds, coils, or convolutions **3 a :** having or marked by great volume **:** BULKY, LARGE, SWELLING ⟨her extremely fair hair very ~ and noticeable —F.M.Ford⟩ ⟨a ~ Negress held him by the hand —P.L.Fermor⟩ ⟨in song, where a more ~ output of air is customary —C.H.Grandgent⟩ ⟨his chin sunk in a billow of his ~ white shirt front —Haldane Macfall⟩; *specif* **:** FULL ⟨a ~ nightgown of outing flannel —Adria Langley⟩ ⟨coats are ~ but hang in nice straight lines —Lois Long⟩ **b :** seeming to fill a large indefinite space ⟨critic who described her voice as "fresher, freer, and firmer . . . more under control and more ~ at the full" —*Current Biog.*⟩ **c :** NUMEROUS ⟨it is more work to keep track of ~ pink slips

than to spend occasional checks —Joanne Wheeler⟩ **4 a :** filling or capable of filling a large volume or several volumes ⟨a ~ correspondence⟩ ⟨~ evidence⟩ ⟨~ notes⟩ ⟨a ~ report⟩ **b :** consisting of or containing many volumes ⟨a ~ publication⟩ **c :** writing or speaking much or at great length ⟨a ~ and energetic writer of letters, memoranda, and diaries —J.T.Flexner⟩ — **vo·lu·mi·nous·ly** *adv* — **vo·lu·mi·nous·ness** *n* -ES

voluntaries *pl of* VOLUNTARY

vol·un·tar·i·ly \ˌvälən¦terəlē, -rəli\ *adv* [ME, fr. ¹*voluntary* + *-ly*] **:** in a voluntary manner **:** of one's own free will **:** SPONTANEOUSLY

vol·un·tar·i·ness \'==,terēnəs, -rin-\ *n* -ES **:** the quality or state of being voluntary **:** SPONTANEOUSNESS; *specif* **:** the quality or state of being free in the exercise of one's will

vol·un·ta·rism \'väləntə,rizəm\ *n* -S [¹*voluntary* + *-ism*] **:** the principle or system of supporting or doing something by voluntary action or of relying upon voluntary action ⟨the essence of democracy is, of course, ~ as opposed to coercion —M.A. Tuve⟩: as **a :** a theory that conceives will to be the dominant factor in experience or in the constitution of the world — compare FICHTEANISM, INTELLECTUALISM, SCHOPENHAUERISM, SCOTISM **b** (1) **:** the principle of supporting a religious system and its institutions by voluntary association and effort rather than by state aid or patronage (2) **:** insistence upon this principle as alone consistent with true religious freedom **c :** a principle calling for development of union labor relations with employers by free choice of the workers and without outside influence, assistance, or interference; *also* **:** the principle of free collective bargaining without governmental imposition of terms — **vol·un·ta·rist** \-rəst\ *n* -S — **vol·un·ta·ris·tic** \¦===¦ristik, -stēk\ *adj*

¹**vol·un·tary** \'välən,terē, -ri\ *adj* [ME, fr. L *voluntarius*, fr. *voluntas* will, choice (fr. *vol-*, stem of *velle* to will, wish) + *-arius* -ary — more at WILL] **1 a :** proceeding from the will **:** produced in or by an act of choice ⟨~ action⟩ **b :** performed, made, or given of one's own free will ⟨a ~ task⟩ ⟨~ services⟩ ⟨~ contributions⟩ ⟨~ efforts⟩ **c** *obs* **:** READY, WILLING **d :** done by design or intention **:** not accidental **:** INTENTIONAL, INTENDED ⟨~ manslaughter⟩ **e :** acting of oneself **:** not constrained, impelled, or influenced by another **:** SPONTANEOUS, FREE ⟨~ worker⟩ ⟨~ or forced labor⟩ **f** *obs* **:** growing spontaneously **g :** acting or done of one's own free will without valuable consideration **:** acting or done without any present legal obligation to do the thing done or any such obligation that can accrue from the existing state of affairs **2 :** of or relating to the will **:** subject to or regulated by the will ⟨~ behavior⟩ ⟨~ control⟩ ⟨~ motions⟩ **3 :** able to will ⟨man is a ~ agent⟩ **4 a :** provided or supported by voluntary action or support ⟨the hospital is a ~ one with 400 beds —*Science*⟩ ⟨the importance of ~ societies in a democracy⟩ **b :** of or relating to voluntarism ⟨sell blanket insurance policies covering medical, dental, and hospital care to the public on a ~ basis —*Current Biog.*⟩

syn VOLUNTARY, INTENTIONAL, DELIBERATE, WILLFUL, and WILLING can agree in meaning done, made, brought about, and so on, of one's own free will. VOLUNTARY implies freedom from any compulsion that could constrain one's choice; often it suggests merely spontaneity, or, in contrast with *involuntary*, stresses the control of the will ⟨a *voluntary* confession of guilt⟩ ⟨a *voluntary* taking of life⟩ ⟨*voluntary* muscle movements⟩ INTENTIONAL contrasts with *accidental* and *inadvertent* in specifying an intention and purpose ⟨an *intentional* insult⟩ ⟨any injury to bystanders at an auto race cannot be considered *intentional*⟩ DELIBERATE carries the idea of full knowledge or full consciousness of the nature of an intended action ⟨a *deliberate* lie⟩ ⟨*deliberate* acts of vandalism⟩ ⟨an organized and *deliberate* attack — carefully planned and calculated —*N.Y. Times*⟩ WILLFUL adds to DELIBERATE the idea of a refusal to be advised or directed in any way and an obstinate determination to act despite all wiser opposing forces or considerations ⟨a *willful* disobedience⟩ ⟨a gigantic glorification of vice and crime, a *willful* inversion of all normal ethical standards —Joseph Frank⟩ WILLING implies such qualities as agreeableness or openmindedness that make one ready or eager to accede to others' wishes or effect an end pleasing to them ⟨my most *willing* activity is listening to my secretary —O. W. Holmes †1935⟩ ⟨no aspect of the world of science to which we cannot find *willing* and thrilling guidance —G.I.Schwartz⟩

²**voluntary** \"\ *adv* [ME, fr. ¹*voluntary*] **:** VOLUNTARILY

³**voluntary** \"\ *n* -ES [¹*voluntary*] **1 a :** a piece of music performed extempore and often improvised usu. serving as a prelude to a set performance **b :** a usu. pipe-organ solo played before, during, or after a religious service and sometimes extemporized **2 :** something done, made, or given voluntarily **:** a voluntary action or piece of work **:** a voluntary contribution **3 :** one who engages in an affair of his own free will **:** VOLUNTEER **4 :** one who advocates voluntarism **5 :** a fall of a horseback rider for which there is insufficient cause

voluntary affidavit *or* **voluntary oath** *n* **1 :** an affidavit or oath not required by law **:** one made in an extrajudicial matter **2 :** an affidavit or oath taken before one not authorized to administer it

voluntary association *n* **:** an unincorporated group associated for some specific purpose — used chiefly of commercial or financial associations

voluntary bankruptcy *n* **:** a bankruptcy declared upon petition of the bankrupt

voluntary chain *n* **:** a voluntary association of independent retailers in a given line of business (as groceries or drugs) for collective action in buying, advertising, and other phases of management

voluntary conveyance *n* **:** a conveyance without valuable consideration

voluntary escape *n* **:** the escape of a prisoner without prison breach and with the custodian's consent — contrasted with *negligent escape*

voluntary hospital *n* **1 :** a hospital that is operated under individual, partnership, or corporation control and provides mainly semiprivate and private care **2** *Brit* **:** a hospital that is supported by voluntary contributions

voluntary improvement *n* **:** an improvement on land serving merely for adornment of the property

vol·un·tary·ism \'välən,terē,izəm\ *n* -S **:** VOLUNTARISM ⟨~ in cultural affairs is an American way which is not defunct —Leland Hazard⟩ — **vol·un·tary·ist** \-ēəst\ *n* -S

voluntary jurisdiction *n* **1 :** jurisdiction in cases not admitting of contentious litigation **2 :** jurisdiction acquired over a person only by virtue of his consent as opposed to compulsory jurisdiction that may be exercised against his will

voluntary manslaughter *n* **:** manslaughter resulting from an act done upon a sudden heat or passion due to provocation recognized as adequate in law — compare INVOLUNTARY MANSLAUGHTER

voluntary muscle *n* **:** muscle under voluntary control **:** STRIATED MUSCLE

voluntary school *n* **:** a usu. denominational English school maintained by a voluntary body and administered by a board of directors — see AIDED SCHOOL, CONTROLLED SCHOOL

vol·un·ta·tive \'välən,tād·iv\ *adj* [ML *voluntativus*, fr. L *voluntat-*, *voluntas* will, choice + *-ivus* -ive] **:** VOLUNTARY

¹**vol·un·teer** \ˌvälən¦ti(ə)r, -iə\ *n* -S [obs. F *voluntaire* (now *volontaire*), fr. *voluntaire*, adj., voluntary, fr. L *voluntarius* — more at VOLUNTARY] **1 :** one who enters into or offers himself for any service of his own free will: as **a :** one who enters into military service voluntarily but who is then subject to discipline and regulations like other soldiers — opposed to *conscript* **b** (1) **:** one who renders a service or takes part in a transaction while having no legal interest, duty, or authority with respect to it **:** an intruder in a transaction who has no legal concern or interest to advance or to protect (as where one renders a service without any express or implied agreement for compensation or seeks to become the servant of another without his assent or pays the debt of a stranger) (2) **:** one who receives a conveyance or transfer of property without giving valuable consideration **:** a gratuitous grantee or transferee **:** DONEE **2 :** a volunteer plant ⟨oats may persist as a ~ for several years⟩ **3** *usu cap* **:** an officer or member of the Volunteers of America organized in 1896 along military lines for evangelistic and philanthropic work

²**volunteer** \"\ *adj* **1 :** of or relating to a volunteer **:** consisting of volunteers **:** VOLUNTARY ⟨a ~ fire department⟩ ⟨~ work⟩ **2 :** growing spontaneously without direct human control or supervision ⟨in some areas there is still an adequate ~ crop of game; in others management is essential⟩; *esp* **:** growing without cultivation from seeds lost from a previous crop ⟨a stand of ~ wheat⟩

³**volunteer** \"\ *vb* -ED/-ING/-S *vt* **:** to offer or bestow voluntarily or without solicitation or compulsion ⟨~ his services⟩ ⟨~ help⟩ ⟨~ information⟩ ⟨~ a donation⟩ ~ *vi* **1 :** to enter into or offer oneself for any service of one's own free will without solicitation or compulsion **:** OFFER ⟨~ in an undertaking⟩ ⟨~ for the army⟩ **2 :** to grow spontaneously **:** form a volunteer crop or stand ⟨many clovers perpetuate themselves indefinitely by ~*ing*⟩

¹**vo·lup·tu·ary** \və'ləpchə,werē, -ri\ *adj* [LL *voluptuarius*, alter. of L *voluptarius*, fr. *voluptas* pleasure + *-arius* -ary] **:** VOLUPTUOUS, LUXURIOUS ⟨when words are turned to purely ~ uses and divorced from rational purpose, the result is not a real advance but rather the beginning of decadence —Irving Babbitt⟩

²**voluptuary** \"\ *n* -ES [modif. (influenced by LL *voluptuarius*, adj.) of L *voluptarius* voluptuous person, fr. *voluptarius*, adj., voluptuous] **:** a voluptuous person **:** one who makes luxury and the gratification of sensual appetites his chief care **:** SENSUALIST ⟨a comprehensiveness of outlook unknown both to the ~ and to the ascetic —Bertrand Russell⟩

vo·lup·tu·ate \-,wāt\ *vi* -ED/-ING/-S [*voluptu*ous + *-ate*] **:** LUXURIATE ⟨second largest sugar producing country in the world, *voluptuated* in crazy wealth —John Gunther⟩

vo·lup·tu·os·i·ty \=,==ˈwäsəd·ē\ *n* -ES [ME *voluptuosite*, fr. ML *voluptuositas*, fr. L *voluptuosus* voluptuous + *-itas* -ity] **:** VOLUPTUOUSNESS

vo·lup·tu·ous \və'ləpchəwəs, -chəs\ *adj* [ME, fr. L *voluptuosus*, fr. *voluptas* pleasure, delight + *-osus* -ose; akin to L *volup* agreeably, pleasurably, Gk *elpis* hope, expectation, L *velle* to will, wish — more at WILL] **1 a :** full of delight or pleasure esp. to the senses **:** ministering to, relating to, inclining to, or arising from sensuous or sensual gratification **:** LUXURIOUS, SENSUOUS ⟨music arose with its ~ swell —Lord Byron⟩ ⟨the kind of sleep which you can feel yourself enjoying with an almost ~ pleasure —Louis Bromfield⟩ ⟨the riotous decor, the ~ ceiling, the flowering dazzle of the chandelier —Claudia Cassidy⟩ ⟨the ~ contortions of dancers —Lewis Mumford⟩ ⟨~ narratives of the far-away South Seas —C.R.Anderson⟩ ⟨anchorites in their cells are at times tormented by ~ visions —Rebecca West⟩ **b :** suggesting sensual pleasure by fullness and beauty of form ⟨she was startlingly good-looking, of ~ build —Ngaio Marsh⟩ **2 :** given to or spent in enjoyments of luxury, pleasure, or sensual gratifications ⟨depiction of the ~ life —J.D.Hart⟩ ⟨a long and ~ holiday —Edmund Wilson⟩

syn see SENSUOUS

vo·lup·tu·ous·ly *adj* [ME, fr. *voluptuous* + *-ly*] **:** in a voluptuous manner ⟨sniffed the scent ~ —James Reynolds⟩ ⟨relatively slim-lipped and less ~ curved —*Time*⟩

vo·lup·tu·ous·ness *n* -ES **:** the quality of being voluptuous ⟨her outlines had lost the ~ which had once made them such an asset —Leslie Charteris⟩

vo·lu·ta \və'lüd·ə, -ütə *also* vəl'yü-\ *n* [L] **1** -S *obs* **:** VOLUTE **2** *cap* [NL, fr. L] **:** the type genus of Volutidae — see VOLUTE 3

vol·u·ta·tion \ˌvälyə'tāshən\ *n* -S [L *volutation-*, *volutatio*, fr. *volutatus* (past part. of *volutare* to roll about, wallow, freq. of *volvere* to roll) + *-ion-*, *-io* -ion] **:** the action of rolling or wallowing

¹**vo·lute** \və'lüt *also* vəl'yüt, *usu* -üd·+V\ *n* -S [L *voluta*, fr. fem. of *volutus*, past part. of *volvere* to roll, turn — more at VOLUBLE] **1 :** a spiral or scroll-shaped form ⟨locks of hair were curled in little flat ~*s* —Herman Goodman⟩ ⟨the bright overturning ~ of a wave —Henry Beston⟩ **2 :** an object or part having a spiral or scroll-shaped form: as **a :** a spiral scroll-shaped ornament that forms the chief feature of the Ionic capital and that also appears in the Corinthian and Composite capitals **b :** the ornamental scroll-shaped bottom end of a stair rail on top of the newel **c :** a turn of a spiral shell **d :** the spiral casing surrounding the impeller of a volute pump; *also* **:** VOLUTE PUMP **3 :** any of numerous marine gastropod mollusks of *Voluta* and related genera of the family Volutidae whose shell is usu. rather thick, has a short spire, wide aperture, conspicuous columellar folds, and usu. is inoperculate — compare MUSIC SHELL

²**volute** \"\ *adj* **1 :** having a spiral or scroll-shaped form **:** rolled up **:** VOLUTED ⟨a ~ ornament⟩ ⟨a ~ termination of a stair rail⟩ **2 :** having a part of spiral form or operating with a rotary action — used esp. of machinery

vo·lut·ed \-üd·əd\ *adj* **:** having a spiral scroll **:** scroll-shaped

vo·lu·tel·la \ˌvälyə'telə\ *n*, *cap* [NL, fr. L *voluta* spiral scroll + *-ella*] **:** a genus of imperfect fungi (family Tuberculariaceae) characterized by setose sporodochia and unicellular ovoid to oblong conidia — see DRY ROT 2b

volute pump *n* **:** a centrifugal pump with a spiral casing

volute spring *n* **:** a spring formed of a conically spiral coil of plate, rod, or wire that is extended or extensible in the direction of the axis of the coil in which direction its elastic force is exerted

vo·lu·ti·dae \və'lüd·ə,dē\ *n pl*, *cap* [NL, fr. *Voluta*, type genus + *-idae*] **:** a family of gastropods (division Rachiglossa) comprising the volutes

vol·u·tin \'välyəd·ən, -ətən\ *n* -S [G, fr. *volut-* (fr. NL *volutans* — specific epithet of the bacterium *Spirillum volutans* in which volutin was first found — fr. L, rolling, tumbling, pres. part. of *volutare* to roll about, wallow) + *-in* (as in *chromatin*) — more at VOLUTATION] **:** a basophilic substance that is probably a nucleic acid compound and that is widely distributed as granules in the cytoplasm or vacuoles of microorganisms

vo·lu·tion \və'lüshən\ *n* -S [L *volutus* (past part. of *volvere* to roll) + E *-ion*] **1 :** a rolling or revolving motion **2 :** a spiral turn **:** TWIST, CONVOLUTION **3 :** a whorl of a spiral shell **:** VOLUTE

¹**vol·u·toid** \'välyə,tȯid\ *adj* [NL *Voluta* + E *-oid*] **:** resembling or related to the Volutidae

²**volutoid** \"\ *n* -S **:** a volutoid gastropod

vol·va \'välvə\ *n* -S [NL, fr. L *volva*, *vulva* covering, integument, womb — more at VULVA] **:** a membranous bulbous sac or cup that surrounds the base of the stipe in many gill fungi (as of the genus *Amanita*) and is formed by the rupture of the universal veil — compare VELUM

vol·var·ia \väl'va(a)rēə\ *n*, *cap* [NL, fr. *volva* + *-aria*] **:** a genus of agarics having pink spores and a distinct volva and including a fungus (*Volvaria bombycina*) that is parasitic on various trees

vol·vate \'välvət, -l,vāt\ *adj* [NL *volva* + E *-ate*] **:** provided with or characterized by a volva

volve *vt* -ED/-ING/-S [L *volvere* to roll, turn over] *obs* **:** CONSIDER

vol·velle *also* **vol·vell** \'väl,vel\ *n* -S [ME *volvelle*, prob. fr. ML *volvella*, fr. L *volvere* to roll, turn + *-ella*] **:** an old contrivance for ascertaining the time of the rising and setting of the moon and sun and the time of high and low tide consisting of one or more movable circles with pointers and figures of the moon and sun which are placed upon several graduated and figured circles drawn on the leaf of a book

vol·vo·ca·ce·ae \ˌvälvə'kāsē,ē\ *n pl*, *cap* [NL, fr. *Volvoc-*, *Volvox*, type genus + *-aceae*] **:** a family of unicellular or colonial biflagellate free-swimming flagellates that are usu. held to be green algae of the class Chlorophyceae — see VOLVOX; compare PHYTOMONADINA — **vol·vo·ca·ceous** \¦==¦kāshəs\ *adj* — **vol·vo·cine** \'==,sīn, -,sən\ *adj*

vol·vo·ca·les \ˌ==ˈkā(,)lēz\ *n pl*, *cap* [NL, fr. *Volvoc-*, *Volvox* + *-ales*] **:** an order of chiefly freshwater green algae (class Chlorophyceae) that are solitary or colonial usu. with a strictly fixed number of cells in the colony — compare HETEROCAPSALES, VOLVOCACEAE

vol·voc·i·dae \väl'väsə,dē\ *n pl*, *cap* [NL, fr. *Volvoc-*, *Volvox*, type genus + *-idae*] **:** a family of flagellates (order Phytomonadina) more or less equivalent to the Volvocaceae

vol·vox \'väl,väks\ *n*, *cap* [NL, fr. L *volvere* to roll — more at VOLUBLE] **:** a genus of minute pale green flagellates that occur in spherical colonies about one fiftieth of an inch in diameter, that are propelled through water by means of minute colorless flagella which rotate the colony about an axis so that one end is constantly anterior, and that are treated as green algae and the type of the family Volvocaceae or as plantlike flagellates and the type of the family Volvocidae

vol·vu·lus \'välvyələs\ *n* -ES [NL, fr. L *volvere* to roll, turn] **:** a twisting of the intestine upon itself that causes obstruction — compare ILEUS

volyer *var of* FOLLYER

¹**vom·ba·tid** \'väm bəd·əd, -ətəd\ *adj* [NL *Vombatidae*] **:** of or relating to the Vombatidae

²**vombatid** \"\ *n* -S **:** a marsupial of the family Vombatidae **:** WOMBAT

vom·bat·i·dae \väm'bad·ə,dē\ *n pl*, *cap* [NL, fr. *Vombatus*, type genus + *-idae*] **:** a family of marsupials including the wombats

vom·ba·tus \'väm'bäd·əs, -bād·əs\ *n*, *cap* [NL, modif. of E *wombat*] **:** a genus of mammals comprising the common Australian and Tasmanian wombats and being the type of the family Vombatidae

vo·mer \'vōmə(r)\ *n* -S [NL, fr. L, plowshare — more at WEDGE] **1 a :** a bone of the skull of most vertebrates that is situated below the ethmoid region, that develops from lateral halves which remain separate in some animals, that in man forms a vertical plate pointed in front and expanding at the upper back part into lateral wings, and that constitutes part of the nasal septum **b :** a corresponding bone in teleost fishes that forms the front part of the roof of the mouth and often bears teeth **2 :** PYGOSTYLE

vomer·ine \'vōmə,rīn, 'väm-, -,rən\ *adj* [NL *vomer* + E *-ine*] **:** of or relating to the vomer

vomerine cartilage *n* **:** JACOBSON'S CARTILAGE

vomero- *comb form* [NL *vomer*] **:** vomerine and ⟨*vomero*palatine⟩

vom·ero·nasal \¦vämərō+\ *adj* [*vomero-* + *nasal*] **:** of or relating to the vomer and the nasal region and esp. to Jacobson's organ or Jacobson's cartilage

vom·ero·palatine \"+\ *n* [*vomero-* + *palatine*] **:** a bone in the roof of the mouth of ganoid fishes and some amphibians formed by the fusion of the vomer and the palatine bones

vom·i·cine \'vämə,sēn, -,sən\ *n* -S [NL *vomica* (in *nux-vomica*, specific epithet of the nux vomica tree *Strychnos nux-vomica*) + ISV *-ine*] **1 :** BRUCINE **2 :** a crystalline alkaloid $C_{22}H_{24}N_2O_4$ occurring with brucine and strychnine

¹**vom·it** \'vämət, *usu* -əd·+V\ *n* -S [ME *vomet*, *vomit*, *vomite*, fr. MF *vomite*, *vomit*, fr. L *vomitus*, fr. *vomitus*, past part. of *vomere* to vomit; akin to ON *vāma* sickness, nausea, Norw *vimla* to be sick, be nauseous, Gk *emein* to vomit, Skt *vamiti*, *vamoti* he vomits] **1 a :** an act or instance of disgorging the contents of the stomach through the mouth **b :** the disgorged contents of the stomach **c :** a disease characterized by vomiting — compare BLACK VOMIT **2** *archaic* **:** a pharmaceutical preparation that causes vomiting **:** EMETIC **3 a :** a disgusting or contemptible person or thing ⟨must not think that nausea and ~ are the ultimate realities of our time —Lewis Mumford⟩ **b :** a violent discharge **:** BELCH, GUSH ⟨an enemy craft hit by a torpedo, breaking in two . . . as the ~ of flame and spray subsides —Alfred Stanford⟩

²**vomit** \"\ *vb* -ED/-ING/-S [ME *vomiten*, fr. L *vomitare*, fr. *vomitus*, past part. of *vomere* to vomit] *vi* **1 :** to bring up the contents of the stomach ⟨the baby who eats too long or too much will tend to regurgitate, or ~ —Morris Fishbein⟩ **2 :** to spew forth **:** BELCH, GUSH ⟨great clouds of steam ~*ing* from their exhausts —Nevil Shute⟩ **3** *archaic* **:** to cause vomiting ⟨emetic tartar, when introduced into the jugular vein, will ~ in one or two minutes —J.M.Good⟩ ~ *vt* **1 a :** to disgorge (the contents of the stomach) through the mouth **:** RETCH ⟨the Lord spoke to the fish, and it ~*ed* out Jonah upon the dry land —Jonah 2:10 (RSV)⟩ **b :** to cast out in a repulsive or vituperative manner ⟨~*s* him out penniless and friendless . . . to renew his criminal career —Maury Maverick⟩ ⟨his own epitaph is here ~*ed* forth in . . . corrosive aphorisms —R.W.Speaight⟩ **2 :** to eject violently or abundantly **:** SPEW, SPOUT ⟨roar and fume and ~ sparks —C.G.D.Roberts⟩ **3** *archaic* **:** to cause to vomit ⟨he is ~*ing* and purging his patients with herbs —George Catlin⟩

vom·it·er \-əd·ə(r), -ətə-\ *n* -S **1 :** one that vomits **2** *obs* **:** EMETIC

vomiting *n* -S [ME, fr. gerund of *vomiten* to vomit] **:** an act or instance of disgorging the contents of the stomach through the mouth — called also *emesis*

vomiting center *n* **:** a nerve center in the medulla oblongata concerned in the act of vomiting

vomiting gas *n* **:** CHLOROPICRIN

vomiting nut *n*, *obs* **:** NUX VOMICA

vo·mi·tion \və'mishən\ *n* -S [obs. F or L; obs. F, fr. L *vomition-*, *vomitio*, fr. *vomitus* (past part. of *vomere* to vomit) + *-ion-*, *-io* -ion] **:** VOMITING

¹**vom·i·tive** \'vämәd·iv, -ətiv\ *adj* [MF or ML; MF *vomitif*, fr. ML *vomitivus*, fr. L *vomitus* (past part. of *vomere*) + *-ivus* -ive] **:** of, relating to, or causing vomiting

²**vomitive** *n* -S *obs* **:** EMETIC

vom·i·to·ri·um \ˌvämə'tōrēəm, -tȯr-\ *n*, *pl* **vomito·ria** \-rēə\ [LL] **:** VOMITORY

¹**vom·i·to·ry** \'vämə,tōrē, -tȯr-, -ri\ *n* -ES [in sense 1, fr. L *vomitorium*, neut. of *vomitorius*, adj.; in sense 2, fr. LL *vomitorium*, fr. neut. of L *vomitorius*; in sense 3, fr. ²*vomitory*] **1** *obs* **:** EMETIC **2 :** an entrance piercing the banks of seats of a theater or amphitheater **:** PORTAL **3 :** one that belches or spews something out

²**vomitory** \"\ *adj* [L *vomitorius*, fr. *vomitus* (past part. of *vomere* to vomit) + *-orius* -ory — more at VOMIT] *archaic* **:** VOMITIVE

vom·i·tous \-məd·əs, -mətəs\ *adj* [¹*vomit* + *-ous*] **:** VOMITIVE — **vom·i·tous·ly** *adv*

vom·i·tu·ri·tion \ˌvämәchə'rishən\ *n* -S [²*vomit* + *-urition* (as in *micturition*)] **:** repeated ineffectual attempts at vomiting **:** RETCHING

vom·i·tus \'vämәd·əs, -ətəs\ *n* -ES [L — more at VOMIT] **:** VOMIT 1b

von baer's law \väṇ'ba(a)(ə)rz-, fə|, vəl, -be(ə)rz-\ *n*, *usu cap B* [after Karl E. *von Baer* †1876 Estonian embryologist] **:** a principle in biology: the development of an organism proceeds from the general to the special and embryos belonging to various classes closely resemble one another in their earlier stages but diverge more and more as development proceeds — compare RECAPITULATION THEORY

von behr trout \-'be(ə)r-\ *n*, *usu cap B* [prob. fr. the name *von Behr*] **:** a European brown trout (*Salmo trutta*)

v-1 *also* **v-one** \'vē'wən\ *n* -S *usu cap V* [*v-1* fr. G, symbol for *V-eins* V-one; *v-one* part trans. of G *V-eins*, abbr. for *vergeltungswaffe eins*, lit., reprisal weapon (No.) one] **:** ROBOT BOMB

von grae·fe's sign \väṇ'grāfəz-, fə|, və|\ *n*, *usu cap G* [after Albrecht *von Graefe* †1870 Ger. ophthalmologist] **:** the failure of the upper eyelid to follow promptly and smoothly the downward movement of the eyeball that is seen in exophthalmic goiter

von mo·na·kow's tract \-'mōnə,kəfs-\ *n*, *usu cap M* [after Konstantin *von Monakow* †1930 Russ. neurologist] **:** a rubrospinal tract

von pir·quet's test \-(')pir¦kāz-\ *n*, *usu cap P* **:** PIRQUET TEST

von reck·ling·hau·sen's disease \-'rekliŋ,haủzənz-\ *n*, *usu cap R* [after Friedrich D. *von Recklinghausen* †1910 Ger. pathologist] **:** NEUROFIBROMATOSIS

¹**voo·doo** *also* **vou·dou** \'vü,dü *sometimes* ,='=\ *n* -S *often attrib* [LaF *voudou*, of African origin; akin to Fon *vodū* spirit, Ewe *vo¹du³* tutelary deity, demon] **1 :** VOODOOISM **2 a :** one who deals in spells and necromancy **:** SORCERER **b** (1) **:** a sorcerer's spell **:** HEX, JINX ⟨put a ~ on an enemy⟩ (2) **:** a hexed object **:** CHARM

²**voodoo** \"\ *vt* -ED/-ING/-S **:** to bewitch by or as if by means of voodoo **:** HEX

voo·doo·ism *also* **vou·dou·ism** \'=,=,izəm\ *n* -S **1 :** a religion originating in Africa as a form of ancestor worship, practiced chiefly by Negroes of Haiti and to some extent other West Indian islands and the U.S., and characterized by propitiatory rites and use of the trance as a means of communicating with animistic deities — called also *vodun*; compare OBEAH **2 :** the practice of black magic **:** CONJURING, WITCHCRAFT

voo·doo·ist \-əst\ *n* -S **1 :** an adherent or practitioner of voodooism ⟨from the animists' viewpoint, it is not contradictory for a ~ in Haiti to regard himself as a good Roman

Catholic —E.A.Nida⟩ **2 :** SORCERER, VOODOO — **voo·doo·is·tic** \¦=,=¦istik\ *adj*

voor·trek·ker \'fōr,trekə(r)\ *n* -S *often cap* [Afrik, fr. *voor* before, in front (fr. MD *vore*) + *trekker* emigrant, fr. *trek* to pull, move, emigrate + *-er;* akin to OHG *fora* before — more at FORE, TREK] **:** a So. African pioneer; *esp* **:** one of the Boers who took part in the trek from Cape Colony to the Transvaal in 1834–37

VOP *abbr, often not cap* valued as in original policy

VOR *abbr* very high-frequency omnirange

-vo·ra \v(ə)rə\ *n pl comb form* [NL, fr. L, neut. pl. of *-vorus* -vorous] **:** ones that eat (something specified) ⟨Insecti*vora*⟩

vo·ra·cious \vȯ'rāshəs, və'r-\ *adj* [L *vorac-, vorax* voracious (fr. *vorare* to devour) + E *-ious;* akin to OHG *querdar* bait, ON *krās* dainty, tidbit, L *gurges* whirlpool, Gk *bora* food, meat, *bibrōskein* to devour, Skt *girati* he swallows] **1 :** having a huge appetite **:** GREEDY, RAVENOUS ⟨the most ~ and demanding of the breakfast-food public — the kiddies —Bennett Cerf⟩ ⟨because so many normal joys had been denied him he was all the more ~ for pleasure —Mary Webb⟩ **2 :** excessively eager **:** AVID, INSATIABLE ⟨a ~ appetite⟩ ⟨his ~ love of life —*Time*⟩ ⟨the ~ reading odysseys of your childhood —J.H.Burns⟩

syn VORACIOUS, GLUTTONOUS, RAVENOUS, RAVENING, and RAPACIOUS agree in meaning excessively greedy. VORACIOUS implies a gorging with anything that satisfies an excessive appetite ⟨a *voracious* shark decimating a school of fish⟩ ⟨pay taxes to *voracious* governments —W.F.Hambly⟩ ⟨a *voracious* reader of poetry —Elinor Wylie⟩ GLUTTONOUS emphasizes greediness and delight in excessive eating ⟨his *gluttonous* appetite for food, praise, pleasure —A.L.Guérard⟩ ⟨his sickness was inflamed by a *gluttonous* debauch —J.R.Green⟩ ⟨*gluttonous* for jewels —John Gunther⟩ RAVENOUS implies abnormally great hunger and suggests violent, grasping methods of dealing with food or whatever satisfies the hunger ⟨a child with a *ravenous* desire for candy⟩ ⟨this fish is remarkably *ravenous;* nothing living that he can seize upon escapes his jaws —William Bartram⟩ ⟨mad hungers that grew more *ravenous* as he fed them —Oscar Wilde⟩ RAVENING comes closer to RAPACIOUS in suggesting a violent, predatory seizing for oneself ⟨the hordes of *ravening* ants —William Beebe⟩ ⟨stood off the other *ravening* creditors —R.L.Taylor⟩ ⟨the jaeger, a *rapacious* tyrant, plays a role as villainous as that of the sparrow hawk and the prairie falcon farther inland —*Amer. Guide Series: Wash.*⟩ ⟨a *rapacious* divorcee on the prowl —Helen Howe⟩ ⟨a mind *rapacious* for all knowledge⟩

vo·ra·cious·ly *adv* **:** in a voracious manner **:** AVIDLY, GREEDILY

vo·ra·cious·ness *n* -ES *archaic* **:** VORACITY

vo·rac·i·ty \vȯ'rasəd·ē, və'r-, -sətē, -i\ *n* -ES [MF *voracité,* fr. L *voracitat-, voracitas,* fr. *vorac-, vorax* voracious + *-itat-, -itas* -ity] **:** the quality or state of being voracious

vo·ra·go \və'rā,gō\ *n* -ES [L, fr. *vorare* to devour — more at VORACIOUS] **:** an engulfing chasm **:** ABYSS

vo·rant \'vōrənt, 'vȯr-\ *adj* [L *vorant-, vorans,* pres. part. of *vorare* to devour] *heraldry* **:** shown in the act of devouring ⟨a serpent crowned ~ a child —Iain Moncreiffe⟩

vorce cell \'vō(ə)rs, -ȯ(ə)rs, -ō(ə)s-\ *n, usu cap V* [after Lafayette Denton *Vorce* †1953 Am. chemical engineer] **:** a cylindrical cell that has graphite anodes and a steel cathode with an asbestos diaphragm and that is used for making sodium hydroxide and chlorine by electrolysis of sodium chloride

-vore \,vō(ə)r, ,vȯ(ə)r, ,vōə, ,vȯ(ə)\ *n comb form* -S [F, fr. *-vore* -vorous, fr. L *-vorus*] **:** one that eats (something specified)

vor·hand \'fōr,hänt\ *n* [G, fr. *vor* fore, before (fr. OHG *fora*) + *hand,* fr. OHG *hant* — more at FORE, HAND] **:** FOREHAND 6

vor·la·ge \-,lägə\ *n* -S [G, lit., forward position, fr. *vor* fore, before + *lage* position, fr. OHG *lāga;* akin to OHG *ligen* to lie — more at LIE] **:** the position of a skier leaning forward from the ankles usu. without lifting the heels from the skis

vor·mela \vȯr'mēlə\ *n, cap* [NL] **:** a genus of carnivorous mammals (family Mustelidae) comprising the tiger weasels and sometimes treated as a subgenus of *Mustela*

vo·ro·nezh \və'rōnish\ *adj, usu cap* [fr. *Voronezh,* U.S.S.R.] **:** of or from the city of Voronezh, U.S.S.R. **:** of the kind or style prevalent in Voronezh

-vo·rous \v(ə)rəs\ *adj comb form* [L *-vorus,* fr. *vorare* to devour — more at VORACIOUS] **:** eating **:** feeding on ⟨carni*vorous*⟩ ⟨pisci*vorous*⟩

vor·spiel \'fōr,shpēl\ *n* [G, fr. *vor* before, fore + *spiel* play, performance, fr. OHG *spil* — more at SPIEL] **:** a musical prelude or overture

vor·tex \'vȯr,teks, -ȯ(ə)\ *n, pl* **vor·ti·ces** \|d·ə,sēz\ *also* **vor·tex·es** \|,teksəz\ [NL, fr. L *vertex, vortex* whirl, whirlpool — more at VERTEX] **1 a :** a supposed collection of particles of very subtle matter endowed with a rapid rotary motion around an axis which is also the axis of a sun or a planet **b :** something resembling such rapid rotary motion ⟨look forward to a time when human beings shall have sloughed off the body and become *vortices* of thought —*Harper's*⟩ **2 :** a region within a body of fluid in which the fluid elements have an angular velocity **3** [L] **a (1) :** a rapidly spiraling column of air **:** TORNADO, WHIRLWIND; *esp* **:** the eye of a cyclone **(2) :** a rapidly spinning current of water **:** MAELSTROM, WHIRLPOOL **(3) :** an eddying current in the slipstream of an airplane **b (1) :** something that resembles a whirlwind or whirlpool **:** SWIRL, WHIRL ⟨the hellish ~ of battle —*Time*⟩ ⟨such a ~ of accepted invitations . . . makes me positively dizzy —Siegfried Sassoon⟩ ⟨created a ~ of speculation wherever she passed —V.L.Parrington⟩ **(2) :** a turbulent center ⟨became the howling ~ of an alarmed hospital —Earle Birney⟩ ⟨politically and commercially it has become the ~ of eastern South Jersey —*Amer. Guide Series: N.J.*⟩ **(3) :** a situation or predicament into which one is irresistibly drawn ⟨the conflict . . . drew into its ~ the best energies of a generation —*Amer. Guide Series: Va.*⟩ ⟨was sucked into the ~ of the . . . scandal —G.H.Genzmer⟩ **(4) :** the spiral arrangement of the muscular fibers at the apex of the heart

vor·ti·cal \'vȯ(r)d·|əkəl, -(t|, |ēk-\ *adj* [L *vortic-, vortex* + E *-al*] **:** of, relating to, or resembling a vortex **:** SWIRLING — **vor·ti·cal·ly** \-k(ə)lē, -li\ *adv*

vortical motion *n* **:** motion of a fluid (as at the boundary between two layers flowing in opposite directions) in which each individual particle rotates about its own axis — called also *rotational motion*

vor·ti·cel·la \,vȯrd·ə'selə\ *n* [NL, fr. L *vortic-, vortex* + NL *-ella*] **1** *cap* **:** a genus (the type of the family Vorticellidae) of stalked bell-shaped peritrichous ciliates with a marginal row of strong cilia about the oral disk **2** *pl* **vorticel·lae** \-e,lē\ *or* **vorticellas :** any ciliate of the genus *Vorticella* or of the family Vorticellidae

¹vor·ti·cel·lid \¦=≠'seləd\ *adj* [NL *Vorticellidae*] **:** of or relating to the Vorticellidae

²vorticellid \"\ *n* -S **:** VORTICELLA 2

vor·ti·cel·li·dae \,=≠'selə,dē\ *n pl, cap* [NL, fr. *Vorticella,* type genus + *-idae*] **:** a family of marine or freshwater free-living or ectocommensal ciliates — see VORTICELLA

vor·ti·cism \'vȯ(r)d·ə,sizəm\ *n* -S [L *vortic-, vortex* + E *-ism*] **:** an offshoot of futurism flourishing in England in the second decade of the 20th century and designed to relate all art forms directly to the machine and modern industrial civilization

vor·ti·cist \-əsəst\ *n* -S **:** an advocate or practitioner of vorticism

vor·tic·i·ty \vȯ(r)'tisəd·ē\ *n* -ES [L *vortic-, vortex* + E *-ity*] **1 :** the state of a fluid in vortical motion **2 :** twice the angular velocity of a small element of fluid around which there is circulation

vor·ti·cose \'vȯ(r)d·ə,kōs\ *adj* [L *vorticosus, verticosus,* fr. *vortic-, vertic-, vortex, vertex* vortex + *-osus* -ose] **:** VORTICAL — **vor·ti·cose·ly** *adv*

vor·tig·i·nous \(')vȯ(r)¦tijənəs\ *adj* [L *vortigin-, vortigo, vertigin-, vertigo* action of whirling + E *-ous* — more at VERTIGO] **1** *archaic* **:** VORTICAL **2** *archaic* **:** moving in a series of eddies **:** SWIRLING

vos·gi·an *also* **vos·ge·an** \'vōzhēən\ *adj, usu cap* [F *Vosgien,* fr. *Vosges* mountains, northeastern France + F *-ien* -ian] **:** of or relating to the Vosges mountains

vot·able \'vōd·əbəl\ *adj* **1 :** eligible to vote ⟨a ~ citizen⟩ **2 :** capable of being voted upon or decided by vote

vo·tal \'vōd·ᵊl\ *adj* [L *votum* vow, wish + E *-al* — more at VOW] *archaic* **:** VOTIVE

vo·ta·ress \'vōd·ərəs, -ōtə-\ *n* -ES [*votary* + *-ess*] **:** a female votary

vo·ta·rist \-rəst\ *n* -S [*votary* + *-ist*] **:** VOTARY

vo·ta·ry \-rē, -ri\ *n* -ES [L *votum* vow + E *-ary* — more at VOW] **1** *archaic* **a :** one pledged by solemn vows to a religious life **:** MONK, NUN ⟨monasteries of *votaries* under special . . . rules —John Owen⟩ **b :** a sworn adherent ⟨the *votaries* . . . that are vow-fellows with this virtuous duke —Shak.⟩ **2 a :** an ardent enthusiast **:** ADDICT, DEVOTEE ⟨it was a paper for the home . . . and the female sex became its faithful *votaries* —John Buchan⟩ ⟨gaming tables, thronged all night by the *votaries* of chance —Bayard Taylor⟩ **b :** a devoted admirer **:** DISCIPLE, FAN ⟨this volume . . . records the scattered yet absorbing talk of master and ~ —Gene Baro⟩ **3 a :** an adherent of a pagan deity ⟨cultivate the goodwill of the gods, and so . . . induce them to bestow their benefits on their *votaries* —E.O.James⟩ **b :** a devout or zealous worshiper ⟨a temple indifferent to the plight of . . . *votaries* below —Charlton Agburn⟩ **c :** a dedicated believer **:** staunch advocate ⟨each religious dogma has its *votaries*⟩ ⟨affluent *votaries* of the status quo —Hodding Carter⟩

¹vote \'vōt, *usu* -ōd·+V\ *n* -S [ME (Sc), fr. L *votum* vow, wish — more at VOW] **1 a :** a usu. formal expression of opinion or will in response to a proposed decision; *esp* **:** one given as an indication of approval or disapproval of a proposal, motion, or candidate for office ⟨proposal was rejected by 5 ~*s* in favor, 51 against, with two abstentions —*U.N.Bull.*⟩ ⟨4000 write-in ~*s* for another candidate —H.H.Martin⟩ — see CASTING VOTE **b :** the total number of such expressions of opinion made known at a single time (as at an election) ⟨to increase its ~ the party must appeal to the farmers⟩ ⟨their aggregate popular ~ in that region fell below 1200 —H.R.Penniman⟩ ⟨polled a large ~⟩ **c :** an expression of opinion or preference that is held to resemble a vote ⟨the consumer, by his ~*s* when he buys or fails to buy, is the ultimate sovereign in a free economy —Eugene Staley⟩ ⟨deserves a ~ of thanks for his hard work⟩ **d :** BALLOT 1 ⟨members . . . who cast their ~ into a single urn —E.S.Stavelay⟩ **2 :** the collective opinion or verdict of a body of persons expressed by voting ⟨the legislative ~ on any issue thus tends to represent . . . the balance of power among the contending groups —Earl Latham⟩ ⟨refused to take a ~ on the question⟩ ⟨chosen by the ~ of the people of the city⟩ **3 :** the right to cast a vote ⟨every member of the community . . . should have a ~ in electing those delegates —William Blackstone⟩; *specif* **:** the right of suffrage **:** FRANCHISE ⟨the 19th Amendment gave American women the ~ in national elections⟩ **4 a :** the act or process of voting ⟨the question came to a ~⟩ ⟨elect judges by popular ~ —F.A.Ogg & P.O.Ray⟩ ⟨put a question to the ~⟩ **b :** a method of voting ⟨roll-call ~⟩ **5** *obs* **a :** a prayer of intercession **:** ENTREATY, PETITION ⟨the heavens consent . . . in answer to the public ~*s* —Ben Jonson⟩ **b :** an earnest desire **:** WISH ⟨the glory of God, is to be the alpha and omega of all our ~*s* and desires —Robert Sanderson⟩ **6** *obs* **:** BELIEF, REPORT ⟨by common ~, reputed the greatest empire in the Orient —Thomas Herbert⟩ **7 :** a decision passed by or carried in an assembly as the result of voting **:** a formal expression of a wish, will, or choice (as in regard to a proposed measure) voted by a meeting ⟨giving the ~*s* of Parliament the authority of laws —Alexander Mudie⟩ — compare CENSURE 6, CONFIDENCE 6d **8 a :** a person who is merely an embodiment of the right to vote ⟨from a patriot of distinguish'd note have . . . purg'd me to a simple ~ —Alexander Pope⟩ **b :** VOTER ⟨took up his challenge in the name of the 39,000 stay-at-home ~*s* —J.J.Chapman⟩ **9 a :** a number of voters or potential voters constituting a group usu. with some common and identifying characteristics ⟨appeals to the Polish ~⟩ **b :** the collective opinion expressed through voting of such a group ⟨elections in which the independent ~ has obviously tipped the balance —John Lodge⟩; *esp* **:** the electoral support of such a group ⟨Democrats need to worry about losing the Negro ~ —Samuel Lubell⟩ **10** *chiefly Brit* **a :** a proposition to be voted upon; *esp* **:** a legislative money item ⟨nearly two hundred ~*s,* covering all branches of administrative expenditure . . . comprise the estimates —T.E.May⟩ **b :** APPROPRIATION ⟨prisons had to be equipped and staff paid out of the annual ~*s* for the naval services —Olive Anderson⟩ **11** *often cap* **:** a daily record of proceedings in the House of Commons — usu. used in pl. ⟨no motion for the issue of a new writ shall be made without previous notice . . . in the ~*s* —T.E.May⟩

²vote \"\ *vb* -ED/-ING/-S *vi* **1 :** to express one's views in response to a poll ⟨~ by a show of hands⟩; *esp* **:** to exercise a political franchise ⟨was interested in politics long before he was old enough to ~⟩ **2 :** to express an opinion ⟨*voted* by acts ranging from sullenness to suicide against the regime —D.W. Treadgold⟩ **~** *vt* **1 a :** to choose or endorse by vote **:** ELECT, RATIFY ⟨~ a straight party ticket⟩ ⟨the resolution was *voted* by a two-thirds majority⟩ — often used with *in* ⟨~ in the whole slate of officers⟩ **b :** to decide the disposition of by vote ⟨one British colony after another . . . was *voting* itself into an American state —Dorothy C. Fisher⟩ ⟨a small membership meeting . . . *voted* the organization out of existence —*Newsweek*⟩ **c :** to defeat by vote ⟨~ down a motion⟩ ⟨~ an incumbent out of office⟩ **d :** to authorize by vote ⟨~ an appropriation⟩ ⟨*voted* an adequate force for the expedition —S.J.Buck⟩ ⟨*voted* the president special emergency powers⟩ **2 a :** to adjudge by general agreement **:** DECLARE ⟨got talking who was the cleverest man . . . and we *voted* it was you —Frances H. Eliot⟩ **b :** to offer as a suggestion **:** MOVE, PROPOSE ⟨I ~ we anchor out here —C.S.Forester⟩ **3 a :** to cause to vote in a given way **:** control the franchise of ⟨mobilize small armies of cheap laborers . . . to be *voted* at the polls for a consideration —C.G.Bowers⟩ ⟨build up a bloc of . . . states which could be *voted* as a unit —*Newsweek*⟩ **b :** to cause to be cast for or against a proposal in accordance with the wishes of the owner ⟨nearly all the . . . stockholders mail proxies to me so I can ~ them at the meetings —Erle Stanley Gardner⟩

vo·teen \vō'tēn\ *n* -S [prob. alter. of *devotee*] *Irish* **:** an uncommonly devout person **:** religious zealot

vote·less \'vōtləs\ *adj* **:** having no vote; *esp* **:** denied the political franchise

vot·er \'vōdə(r), -ōtə-\ *n* -S **1 :** one that votes **2 :** one having the legal right to vote

¹voting *n* -S [fr. gerund of ²*vote*] **:** the act or process of casting a vote esp. in a political election

²voting *adj* [fr. pres. part. of ²*vote*] **1 :** of, relating to, or used in conducting a poll ⟨~ precinct⟩ ⟨~ machine⟩ **2 :** entitling one to vote ⟨~ age⟩ ⟨~ stock⟩

voting trust *n* **:** an arrangement transferring the voting rights of shares in a corporation from stockholders to trustees for a specified period

vo·tive \'vōd·|iv, -ōt|, |ēv *also* |əv\ *adj* [L *votivus,* fr. *votum* vow + *-ivus* -ive] **1 a :** offered or erected in fulfillment of a vow and often in gratitude for deliverance from distress ⟨a hundred ~ tapers burning in receptacles of ruby glass —Herman Smith⟩ ⟨~ gifts from women desiring offspring —Heinrich Zimmer⟩ ⟨on this green bank . . . we set today a ~ stone; that memory may their deed redeem —R.W.Emerson⟩ **b :** undertaken or performed in fulfillment of a vow ⟨a ~ pilgrimage⟩ **2 :** consisting of or expressing a vow, wish, or desire ⟨a ~ prayer or benediction —Robert Sanderson⟩

votive dance *n* **:** a ritual dance performed or sponsored by an individual in fulfillment of a vow to a supernatural being

votive mass *n, often cap M* **:** a mass celebrated in place of the mass appointed for the day except when that takes precedence due to festal rank or identity of intention and offered in special devotion (as in honor of a saint or the angels) or applied for the benefit of a particular purpose (as peace or the spread of the faith) or person (as an invalid) **:** a mass provided in the missal for a special intention, occasion, or devotion: **a :** one of a strict class that must be said on a certain day including masses (as a mass of the Blessed Virgin on Saturdays or a requiem on All Souls' Day) prescribed in the rubrics of the missal, solemn masses ordered by the pope or ordinary for grave occasions (as the election of a bishop or a time of war), masses of the forty hours devotion, and nuptial and some requiem masses **b :** one (as for the private intention of a donor) that may be said at the discretion of the priest

votive office *n* **:** an office of special devotion formerly permitted in the Roman Catholic Church to be celebrated in place of the office appointed for the day unless the festal rank of the day prevented

vo·tress \'vō·trəs\ *n* -ES [by alter.] *archaic* **:** VOTARESS

vo·tyak *or* **vo·ti·ak** \'vōd·ē,ak\ *n, pl* **votyak** *or* **votiak** *also* **votyaks** *or* **votiaks** *cap* [Russ *Votyak* member of the Votyaks, fr. *Vot'* Votyak people, fr. Cheremis *òdə,* fr. Votyak *Udmurt* Votyak man] **1 a :** a Finno-Ugrian people of the Udmurt Republic in eastern Soviet Russia, Europe — called also *Udmurt* **b :** a member of such people **2 :** the Finnic language of the Votyak people

vou *abbr* voucher

vou·a·ca·poua \,vüəkə'püə\ [NL, fr. Galibi *wakápu* angelim] *syn of* ANDIRA

¹vouch \'vau̇ch\ *vb* -ED/-ING/-ES [ME *vochen, vouchen,* fr. MF *vocher, voucher,* fr. L *vocare* to call, summon, fr. *voc-, vox* voice — more at VOICE] *vt* **1 :** to summon (a vouchee) into court to warrant or defend a title — now used esp. in the phrase *vouch to warranty;* compare VOUCH IN **2** *archaic* **a :** AVOUCH 2, 3 ⟨to ~ this, is no proof —Shak.⟩ ⟨be glad to have found this ~*ed* by better authority —Henry Hallam⟩ **b :** to bear witness **:** TESTIFY ⟨the Prior . . . will ~ for me that they are more than half heathen —Sir Walter Scott⟩ **c :** to serve as a sponsor for ⟨want no patrons for to ~ my books —Thomas Pecke⟩ **3** *archaic* **a :** to cite as authority or supporting evidence ⟨~ every man's experience to warrant this truth —Cunelgus Bonde⟩ **b :** to refer to or quote in support of an opinion or statement ⟨~ examples out of the ancient histories —Thomas Drant⟩ ⟨for the truth of this I ~ the mathematicians —William Wollaston⟩ **4 a :** to give tangible support to **:** PROVE, SUBSTANTIATE ⟨~*ed* his words by his deeds —Isaac D'Israeli⟩ **b (1) :** to verify (a business transaction) by examining documentary evidence **(2) :** to attest the necessity of (a payment) **5** *archaic* **:** VOUCHSAFE ⟨means ~*ed* heretofore to some —P.J.Bailey⟩ **~** *vi* **1 :** to give a guarantee **:** become surety ⟨good friends who are willing to ~ for you and give you the old buildup —W.J.Reilly⟩ ⟨no observer can ~ for his own unconscious, and the personality of a field worker inevitably influences his results —Ralph Linton⟩ **2 a :** to supply supporting evidence or testimony ⟨who is going to assemble it and ~ for the names cited —*Saturday Rev.*⟩ ⟨a young man . . . whose very countenance may ~ for your being amiable —Jane Austen⟩ **b :** to give personal assurance ⟨what I didn't see and hear for myself I got from good report and I can ~ for the truth of it —H.E. Giles⟩ ⟨~*ed* for it with his most eloquent oaths —George Meredith⟩

²vouch *n* -ES *obs* **:** a positive assertion **:** ALLEGATION, DECLARATION ⟨my ~ against you . . . will so your accusation overweigh —Shak.⟩

vouch·ee \(,)vau̇¦chē\ *n* -S [ME, fr. *vouchen* to vouch + *-ee*] **1 :** one called into court to warrant or defend a title in a common recovery **2** *archaic* **:** one cited as an authority or sponsor ⟨some respectable names are occasionally attached as ~*s* —*Fraser's Mag.*⟩ **3 :** one for whom another vouches

¹vouch·er \'vau̇chə(r)\ *n* -S [MF *vocher, voucher* to vouch] **1 :** an act of summoning one into court to warrant or defend a title or to undertake the defense of a case in which he is ultimately liable to the person sued **2 a :** a piece of supporting evidence **:** PROOF ⟨destruction of the ~*s* of the cruise . . . the logbooks, the meteorological registers, the surveys, and the journals —E.K.Kane⟩ **b :** a documentary record of a business transaction ⟨canceled checks are often called ~*s* because they offer proof of payment —G.G.Munn⟩ **c :** a written affidavit or authorization **:** CERTIFICATE, CREDENTIAL ⟨servicemen traveling on free ~*s* —S.P.B.Mais⟩

²voucher \"\ *vt* **vouchered; vouchered; vouchering** \-ch(ə)riŋ\ **vouchers 1 :** to establish the authenticity of **:** CERTIFY, VERIFY ⟨every invoice or bill received must be ~*ed* —H.S.Noble⟩ **2 :** to prepare a voucher for ⟨coded, abstracted, indexed, inspected, noted and ~*ed* through 288 separate steps —*Time*⟩ — **vouch·er·able** \-ch(ə)rəbəl\ *adj*

³voucher \"\ *n* -S [¹*vouch* + *-er*] **1** *obs* **:** VOUCHEE 1 **2** *archaic* **a :** one that corroborates **:** AUTHORITY ⟨sayings of the Fathers, whom he quotes as his ~*s* —Jonathan Edwards⟩ **b :** one that sponsors or guarantees **:** SURETY ⟨notwithstanding you are these people's ~, this appears but a scheme —Elizabeth Inchbald⟩ **3 :** a tangible proof **:** EVIDENCE, WITNESS ⟨Indian fighters with ~*s* . . . dangling from their belts —J.F.Dobie⟩

voucher check *n* [¹*voucher*] **:** a check carrying a notation of the invoices or items covered either on its face or on a detachable stub

voucher clerk *n* **1 :** one who makes out vouchers payable and records authorized disbursements in a voucher register **2 :** one who prorates the cost of lost or damaged goods among the railroads over which they were carried

voucher payable *n* **:** ACCOUNT PAYABLE

voucher register *n* **:** a book of original entry for vouchers

voucher system *n* **:** a system of accounting in which a voucher (as for an account payable) is prepared usu. with supporting documents attached for each transaction or a series of transactions affecting a single account and when approved is entered in a voucher register

vouch in *vt* **:** to call into court to defend a lawsuit against another and to be made liable to pay in whole or in part any judgment secured for the plaintiff ⟨a defendant *vouches in* his own liability insurance company to defend a negligence case against him⟩

vouch·safe \(,)vau̇ch'sāf\ *vt* -ED/-ING/-S [ME *vouchen sauf,* fr. *vouchen* to vouch + *sauf* safe — more at VOUCH, SAFE] **1 a :** to furnish often in a gracious or condescending manner **:** ACCORD, SUPPLY ⟨asked no questions . . . *vouchsafed* no information —I.V.Morris⟩ ⟨occasionally a true poet is *vouchsafed* to the world —Rumer Godden⟩ ⟨some of the information *vouchsafed* by colleagues was only imperfectly grasped by him —R.A. Fowkes⟩ ⟨discipline that only a systematic and formal study of language . . . can ~ —H.R.Warfel⟩ **b :** to choose to give by way of reply ⟨know little more . . . than what he has *vouchsafed* in occasional interviews —T.H.White b. 1915⟩ **2 :** to grant as a privilege **:** ALLOW, PERMIT ⟨settle terms for evacuating their 1500 wounded, as *vouchsafed* by the Communists at Geneva —*Time*⟩ ⟨we are seldom *vouchsafed* a glance behind this barrier —J.K.Galbraith⟩ **3 a :** to grant as a special favor **:** CONDESCEND, DEIGN ⟨~, O Lord, to keep us this day without sin —*Bk. of Com. Prayer*⟩ **b** *obs* **:** to accept graciously ⟨~ good morrow from a feeble tongue —Shak.⟩ **syn** see GRANT

vouch·safe·ment \-mənt\ *n* -S *archaic* **:** an act or instance of vouchsafing **:** BOON, CONCESSION ⟨a merciful ~ from God to mankind —Thomas Amory⟩ ⟨the sovereign ~ of mercy to some —R.W.Hamilton⟩

voudou *var of* VOODOO

vouge \'vüzh\ *n* -S [F, fr. ML *vidubium* scythe, of Celt origin; akin to Bret *gwif* two-tined fork, W *gwyddif* scythe] **:** a long-handled pike of the later medieval period resembling a halberd

vous·soir \(')vü¦swär\ *n* -S [F, fr. (assumed) VL *volsorium,* fr. *volsus* (alter. of L *volutus,* past part. of *volvere* to roll, turn) + L *-orium* -ory — more at VOLUBLE] **:** one of the tapering or wedge-shaped pieces forming an arch or vault — compare INTRADOS, KEYSTONE, SPRINGER

vou·vray \vü'vrā\ *n* -S *usu cap* [F, fr. *Vouvray,* village in Loire dept., France, where it is produced] **:** a still or sparkling white wine from the Touraine district in the Loire valley of France

¹vow \'vau̇\ *n* -S [ME *vowe, vow, vou,* fr. OF *vo, vou, vowe,* fr. L *votum,* fr. neut. of *votus,* past part. of *vovēre* to vow; akin to Gk *euchesthai* to pray, vow, Skt *ohate* he praises] **1 a :** a solemn promise **:** PLEDGE ⟨make a ~ to give up smoking⟩; *specif* **:** OATH ⟨makes ~ . . . nevermore to give the assay of arms against your Majesty —Shak.⟩ **b :** a promise of constancy and esp. of marital fidelity ⟨exchange marriage ~*s*⟩ **2 a** *obs* **:** a votive offering ⟨the vast treasures of the abbey . . . crucifixes, and ~*s,* crowns and reliquaries —Thomas Gray⟩ **b :** a promise of dedication to the monastic life — compare SIMPLE VOW, SOLEMN VOW **3 :** an earnest wish or declaration **:** PRAYER ⟨it is customary for a song of lamentation to close with a ~ of gratitude and praise —E.A.Leslie⟩

²vow \"\ *vb* -ED/-ING/-S [ME *vowen, -vouen,* fr. OF *vower, vover,* fr. *vo, vowe, vou,* n.] *vt* **1 a :** to promise solemnly **:** SWEAR ⟨~*ed* never to leave each other —*Amer. Guide Series: Texas*⟩ ⟨leaders ~ . . . filibuster won't derail program —*Wall Street Jour.*⟩ ⟨when a man ~*s* a vow to the Lord . . . he shall

not break his word —Num 30:2(RSV)⟩ **b :** to resolve to bring about : PLEDGE ⟨with rhetorical swagger . . . ~*ing* the death of an aristocrat —F.J.Mather⟩ **2 :** to dedicate to a specified pursuit or service : CONSECRATE ⟨creatures of the Devil, ~*ed* to idolatry —Nevil Shute⟩ ⟨virgins ~*ed* to Heaven —Alfred Austin⟩ ⟨his country . . . was ~*ed* to other quests than that of the Holy Grail —Clifton Fadiman⟩ **~** *vi* **:** to make a solemn promise ⟨the hall was all in tumult — some ~*ing*, and some protesting —Alfred Tennyson⟩

³**vow** \"\ *vb* -ED/-ING/-S [ME *vowen*, short for *avowen* — more at AVOW] **:** AVOW, DECLARE ⟨I ~ there's a heap of stars out tonight —Elizabeth M. Roberts⟩

⁴**vow** \"\ *interj* [(*I*)*vow* (avow)] *chiefly Scot* — used to express an emphatic degree (as of surprise or admiration) ⟨it's long since I saw you, and ~! ye're grown gaudy and grand —William Nicholson⟩

vowed *adj* [fr. past part. of ²*vow*] **1 :** bound by or as if by a vow : PLEDGED, SWORN **2** *archaic* **:** VOTIVE 1b

¹**vow·el** \'vau̇(ə)l\ *n* -S *often attrib* [ME, fr. MF *vouel, voieue*, fr. L *vocalis*, fr. fem. of *vocalis* sounding, sonorous — more at VOCAL] **1 :** one of a class of speech sounds (as of the *o* of English *hot*, the *i* of English *give*, the *u* of English *put*, or the *ü* of German *fünf* "five") in the articulation of which the oral part of the breath channel is not blocked and is not constricted enough to cause audible friction; *broadly* **:** the one most prominent sound in a syllable — compare CONSONANT **2 :** a letter or other symbol representing a vowel ⟨a Hebrew manuscript without ~*s*⟩ — usu. used in English of *a, e, i, o, u*, and sometimes *y*

²**vowel** \"\ *vt* **voweled** *or* **vowelled; voweled** *or* **vowelled; voweling** *or* **vowelling; vowels 1 :** to furnish with vowel signs, points, or letters ⟨distinguish the pointed or ~*ed* from the unpointed text of the Old Testament —J.F.McCurdy⟩ **2 :** to pay with an IOU

vowel declension *n* **:** a declension characterized by the addition of case endings to a stem that ends in a vowel

vowel harmony *n* **:** a structural feature of some languages (as Finnish and Turkish) whereby the vowels of the language are divided into two or more classes and affixed morphemes have vowels that vary so as to belong to the same class as that of the morpheme to which they are affixed

voweling *or* **vowelling** *n* -S [fr. gerund of ²*vowel*] **:** VOCALISM 3b

vow·el·ize \'vau̇ə,līz\ *vt* -ED/-ING/-S **1 :** to produce or cause by means of vowels **2 :** to make vocalic **3 :** ²VOWEL 1

vow·el·less \'⸗⸗ləs\ *adj* **:** having no vowels

¹**vowellike** \'⸗⸗,⸗\ *adj* [¹*vowel* + *like*] **:** resembling a vowel esp. in sonority and freedom from obstruction in utterance ⟨\l\, \m\, \n\, \ŋ\, \r\, \w\, and \y\ are ~⟩

²**vowellike** \"\ *n* **:** a vowellike sound

vowel point *also* **vowel mark** *n* **:** a mark placed below or otherwise adjacent to a consonant in some languages (as Hebrew) and representing the vowel sound that precedes or follows the consonant sound

vowel rhyme *n* **:** ASSONANCE 2b

vowel sign *n* **1 :** VOWEL POINT **2 :** a shorthand symbol for a vowel

vowel system *n* **:** the system of vowels, vowel sounds, or vowel indications of a language or of a group of related languages

vowel triangle *n* **:** a triangular or a trapezoidal or trapeziform figure on which vowels are charted according to the position of the part of the tongue that is highest in their articulation

vow·ely *or* **vow·el·ly** \'vau̇(ə)lē, -li\ *adj* **:** full of or marked by vowels

vow·er \'vau̇(ə)r, -au̇ə\ *n* -S [²*vow* + *-er*] **:** one that vows

vox an·ge·li·ca \,väk,san'jeləkə\ *n, pl* **vox angelicas** [NL, lit., angelic voice] **1 :** VOIX CÉLESTE **2 :** any of various labial and reed pipe-organ stops having a notably refined quality of tone

vox hu·ma·na \,väks,hyü'mänə, -mānə\ *n, pl* **vox humanas** [NL, lit., human voice] **:** a reed pipe-organ stop of usu. 8-foot pitch made to give a sound imitative of the human voice and usu. employing a tremolant

vox po·pu·li \-'päpyə,lī\ *n, pl* **vox populis** [L, lit., voice of the people] **:** popular sentiment ⟨*vox populi* was whooping it up in the galleries . . . and making no impression upon the massed delegates below —S.H.Adams⟩

¹**voy·age** \'vȯi(-)ij, 'vȯiēj, 'vȯ(i)yij, -yēj\ *n* -S [ME *veyage, vayage, voyage*, fr. OF *veiage, vayage, voiage*, fr. LL *viaticum*, fr. L, traveling money, provisions for a journey, fr. neut. of *viaticus* of a journey, fr. *viatus* (past part. of *viare* to travel, fr. *via* way) + *-icus* -ic — more at VIA] **1 a :** an act or instance of traveling : EXCURSION, TOUR ⟨the glee club . . . Christmas trip, a ~ taken annually to advertise the institution —*Scribner's*⟩ ⟨spent the last fortnight in ~*s* through furniture shops —H.J. Laski⟩ **b :** something that resembles a trip ⟨a couple from London, bound . . . on the ~ of matrimony —Tobias Smollett⟩ **2** *obs* **a :** a military expedition ⟨the Simeonites' second ~ against the Amalekites —Thomas Fuller⟩ **b :** a private venture ⟨if he should intend this ~ toward my wife, I would turn her loose to him —Shak.⟩ **3 a :** a journey by water : CRUISE ⟨with a fair sea ~, and a fair land journey —Charles Dickens⟩ ⟨icebergs . . . breaking loose for their long ~ to obliteration —Valter Schytt⟩ **b :** a journey through air or space ⟨the first human balloon ~ —Charles Dimont⟩ ⟨the earth in its annual ~ round the sun —R.S.Ball⟩ ⟨a rocket ~ to the moon⟩ **4 :** an account of a journey and esp. of an exploratory trip by sea ⟨Canto XXVI, the ~ of Ulysses —T.S.Eliot⟩ **5 a :** an expedition undertaken for the collection at sea of a commercial cargo for disposal usu. on return to the home port ⟨a whaling ~⟩ **b** (1) **:** the proceeds of such a nautical enterprise ⟨share a ~⟩ (2) **:** a crew member's share of such proceeds ⟨said . . . he was willing to bet his whole ~ that the ship had overrun her reckoning —H.A.Chippendale⟩

²**voyage** \"\ *vb* -ED/-ING/-S *vi* **:** to take a trip : TRAVEL ⟨~ up the seaway aboard the royal yacht —*Newsweek*⟩ ⟨novelists have *voyaged* in imagination from planet to planet in rockets —Waldemar Kaempffert⟩ **~** *vt* **:** SAIL, TRAVERSE ⟨~ the briny deep⟩ ⟨in a year, Americans *voyaged* 18,059,000,000 scheduled air-passenger-miles —*Time*⟩

voyage charter party *n* **:** a charter party whereby the owner of a ship agrees to transport on his ship with his crew and master in control of the navigation a full shipload of cargo owned or furnished by another person

voyage policy *n* **:** a marine insurance policy covering only a stated voyage

voy·ag·er *pronunc at* VOYAGE + ə(r)\ *n* -S **:** one that voyages : TRAVELER

voy·a·geur \¦vwä¦yä¦zhər(·), ¦vȯi(y)ä-, ¦vȯyä-; ¦vȯi·i¦jər(·), ¦vȯ(i)yi¦-\ *n* -S [CanF, fr. F, traveler, voyager, fr. *voyager* to travel (fr. *voyage*, n.) + *-eur* -or] **:** a man employed by a fur company to transport goods and men to and from remote stations in the Northwest principally by boat ⟨bateaux of the French-Canadian ~*s*, laden with bales of furs, shot its rapids and paddled its smooth waters —*Amer. Guide Series: Oregon*⟩

voy·eur \(')vwä¦yər(·), (')vȯi¦y-\ *n* -S [F, lit., one who sees, fr. MF, fr. *voir* to see (fr. L *vidēre*) + *-eur* -or — more at WIT] **1 :** one whose sexual desire is concentrated upon seeing sex organs and sexual acts — called also *peeping tom* **2 :** an unduly prying observer usu. in search of sordid or scandalous sights ⟨a sordid sideshow for political ~*s* —A.M.Schlesinger b. 1917⟩

voy·eur·ism \-ə,rizəm\ *n* -S **:** the tendencies, act, or looking of a voyeur ⟨~ into neighboring apartment houses —John Lardner⟩ — compare EXHIBITIONISM

voy·eur·is·tic \¦⸗,⸗¦ristik\ *adj* **:** of, relating to, or having the characteristics of a voyeur ⟨~ drives⟩ — **voy·eur·is·ti·cal·ly** \-tək(ə)lē\ *adv*

VP *abbr* **1** vapor pressure **2** variable pitch **3** *often not cap* various pagings **4** *often not cap* various places **5** *often not cap* verb passive **6** verb phrase **7** vest pocket **8** vice-president **9** voting pool **10** vulnerable point

v–particle \'⸗,⸗⸗⸗\ *n, cap V* [so called fr. the shape of its track in a cloud chamber] **:** a charged or uncharged elementary short-lived particle produced by collisions of very high energy particles with nuclei

VPM *abbr, often not cap* **1** vibrations per minute **2** volts per mil

VPP *abbr* value payable by post

VPS *abbr, often not cap* vibrations per second

VR *abbr* **1** *often not cap* variant reading **2** *often not cap* verb reflexive **3** vicar rural **4** vocal resonance **5** voltage regulator **6** voltage relay **6** vulcanized rubber

vrack \'vrak\ *Scot var of* WRACK

vraic \'vrāk\ *n* -S [F dial. (Channel islands), alter. of F *varec* — more at VAREC] **1 :** seaweed found in the Channel islands where it is collected and burned for manure **2 :** the fertilizer obtained in the Channel islands by burning vraic

vraick·ing \-kiŋ, -kēŋ\ *n* -S **:** the gathering of vraic

vrba·ite \'vərbə,īt\ *n* -S [G *vrbait*, fr. Karel *Vrba* †1922 Bohemian mineralogist + G *-it* -ite] **:** a mineral $TlAs_2SbS_5$ consisting of a sulfide of thallium, arsenic, and antimony and occurring in small gray-black to dark-red orthorhombic crystals

vrbl *abbr* variable

vred·en·burg·ite \'vredᵊn,bər,gīt\ *n* -S [*Vredenburg*, Alabama + E *-ite*] **1 :** a mineral consisting of an oriented intergrowth of jacobsite and hausmannite — called also *beta-vredenburgite* **2 :** a homogeneous mineral $(Mn,Fe)_3O_4$ that has the same composition as beta-vredenburgite, is stable at high temperature, and in rare instances is preserved in a metastable state at ordinary temperature — called also *alpha-vredenburgite*

vrg *abbr* veering

vrie·sia \'vrēzh(ē)ə, -zēə\ *n* [NL, fr. W. H. de *Vriese* †1862 Dutch botanist + NL *-ia*] **1** *cap* **:** a genus of chiefly epiphytic herbs (family Bromeliaceae) having densely rosetted leaves, free petals, and basal scales on the inner sides of the petals **2** -S **:** any plant of the genus *Vriesia*

¹**vrille** \'vril\ *n* -S [F, lit., tendril, fr. OF *veille*, fr. L *viticula*, dim. of *vitis* vine — more at WITHY] **:** the nose-first spinning descent of an airplane deliberately induced as a maneuver

²**vrille** \"\ *vi* -ED/-ING/-S [F *vriller*, fr. *vrille*] **:** to execute a vrille

v roof *n, cap V* **:** GABLE ROOF, PEAKED ROOF

vrouw *or* **vrow** \'vr¦au̇, 'fr¦, ¦ō\ *n* -S [D *vrouw* & Afrik *vrou* woman, married woman, wife, fr. MD *vrouwe* lady, woman — more at FROW] **1 :** a Dutch or Afrikaner woman **2 :** MISTRESS — usu. used preceding the name of a Dutch or Afrikaner married woman

vs *abbr* **1** verse **2** versus

VS *abbr* **1** vertical stripes **2** veterinary surgeon **3** vibration seconds **4** *often not cap* [L *vide supra*] see above **5** visible supply **6** visual signaling **7** *often not cap* [It] volti subito **8** volumetric solution

v's *or* **vs** *pl of* v

vsb *abbr* visible

vsby *abbr* visibility

v–shaped \'⸗¦⸗\ *adj, cap V* **:** having the general shape of the letter V or resembling a V in cross section

v–shaped comb *n, cap V* **:** a comb of some domestic fowl with two hornlike sections forming a V — see LA FLÈCHE

v sign *n, cap V* [*v* abbr. for *victory*] **:** a sign made by raising the index and middle fingers in a V and used as a victory salute (as by the allied nations during World War II), a gesture of approval, or an okay

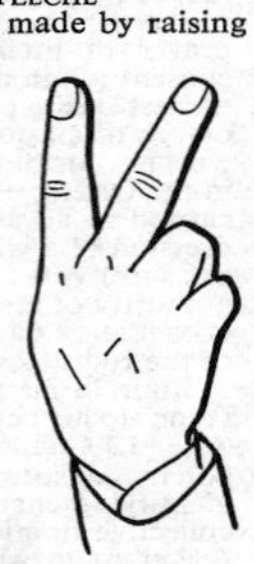

V sign

vsn *abbr* vision

vss *abbr* **1** verses **2** versions

v–stern \'⸗,⸗\ *n, cap V* **:** a square stern with the transom inclined from the vertical

VSW *abbr* very short wave

VT *abbr* **1** vacuum tube **2** variable time **3** *often not cap* verb transitive **4** voice tube

vt *abbr* voting

v tail *cap V, var of* VEE TAIL

VTC *abbr* voting trust certificate; voting trust company

vt fuze \'vē'tē-\ *n, usu cap V&T* [variable *time fuze*] **:** PROXIMITY FUZE

v thread *cap V, also* **vee thread** *n* **:** a screw thread having a thread angle of 60 degrees with the bisector of the angle being perpendicular to the axis of the thread and the crests and roots of the threads being lines formed by the intersections of the sides

VTO *abbr* vertical takeoff

VTR *abbr* video tape recorder

VTVM *abbr* vacuum tube voltmeter

v–2 *also* **v–two** \'vē'tü\ *n* -S *usu cap V* [*v-2* fr. G, symbol for *V-zwei* V-two; *v-two* part trans. of G *V-zwei*, abbr. for *vergeltungswaffe zwei*, lit., reprisal weapon (No.) two] **:** a rocket-propelled bomb of German invention that ascends to an altitude of over 60 miles and descends at a speed far greater than that of sound

v–type engine \'⸗,⸗-\ *n, cap V* **:** an internal-combustion engine in which two sets of cylinders are arranged side by side in two planes making an angle with each other so that a cross section perpendicular to the shaft would be V-shaped

VU *abbr* volume unit

vug *or* **vugg** *or* **vugh** \'vəg, 'vu̇g\ *n* -S [Corn. dial. *vooga, fouga* underground chamber, fr. L *fovea* small pit] **:** a small unfilled cavity in a lode or in rock usu. lined with a crystalline layer of different composition from the surrounding rock

vug·gy \'vəgē, 'vu̇gē\ *adj* **:** of or relating to a vug

vu·gu·sa \və'güsə\ *n, pl* **vugusa** *or* **vugusas** *usu cap* **1 :** a Bantu-speaking people of western Kenya — see BANTU KAVIRONDO **2 :** a member of the Vugusa people

vul·can \'vəlkən\ *n* -S *often cap* [in sense 1, fr. It *vulcano, volcano*; in other senses, after *Vulcan*, ancient Roman god of fire and metalworking — more at VOLCANO] **1** *obs* **:** VOLCANO **2 :** a worker in metals; *esp* **:** BLACKSMITH **3** *obs* **:** FIRE

vulcan fast pigment *n, usu cap V&F* **:** any of several organic pigments — see DYE table I (under *Pigment Orange, Pigment Red, Pigment Yellow*)

vul·ca·ni·an *also* **vul·ca·ne·an** \¦vəl¦kānēən\ *adj* [L *Vulcanius* of Vulcan (fr. *Vulcanus* Vulcan) + E *-an*] **1** *usu cap* **:** of, relating to, or associated with the ancient god Vulcan or to working in iron or other metals **2 a :** VOLCANIC **b :** of or relating to a volcanic eruption in which highly viscous or solid lava is blown into fragments and dust

vul·can·ic \¦vəl¦kanik\ *adj, often cap* **:** VULCANIAN

vul·can·ic·i·ty \,vəlkə'nisəd·ē\ *n* **:** VOLCANICITY

vul·can·ism \'vəlkə,nizəm\ *n* -S **:** VOLCANISM

vul·can·ist \-,nəst\ *n* -S [*Vulcan*, god of fire and metalworking + E *-ist*] **:** VOLCANIST

vul·can·ite \-,nīt\ *n* -S [*vulcan* + *-ite*] **:** a hard vulcanized rubber : EBONITE, HARD RUBBER

vul·can·i·zate \'vəlkənə,zāt, -ə,nī,zāt, *usu* -ād·+V\ *n* -S [*vulcanize* + *-ate*] **:** a vulcanized product

vul·can·iza·tion \,⸗⸗nə'zāshən, -,nī'z-\ *n* -S [ISV *vulcanize* + *-ation*] **1 :** the act or process of treating crude rubber, synthetic rubber, or other plastic rubberlike material with a chemical (as sulfur or a compound of sulfur) to decrease its plasticity, tackiness, and sensitivity to heat and cold and to give it useful properties (as elasticity, strength, and stability) — see ACCELERATOR, COLD CURE, OPEN CURE **2 :** the act or process of treating (as for hardening) various materials in any of various ways — compare VULCANIZED FIBER, VULCANIZED OIL

vul·can·ize \'⸗⸗,nīz\ *vb* -ED/-ING/-S *see -ize in Explan Notes* [ISV *vulcan* + *-ize*] *vt* **:** to subject to the process of vulcanization **~** *vi* **:** to undergo vulcanization

vulcanized fiber *n* [fr. *Vulcanized Fibre*, a trademark] **:** a tough substance that is made both in hard grades with the consistency of horn and in softer flexible grades by treating cellulose (as paper from rags) usu. with a solution of zinc chloride or sulfuric acid and compressing it and that is used chiefly for luggage and for electrical and mechanical applications

vulcanized oil *n* **:** any of various brown or white elastic materials made from unsaturated fatty oils (as rape oil or linseed oil) by heating with sulfur or by reaction with sulfur monochloride and used chiefly in compounding rubber and in coatings

vul·can·iz·er \'vəlkə,nīzə(r)\ *n* -S **:** one that vulcanizes: as **a :** one that cures tires by vulcanization **b :** one that makes a bakelite matrix and from it prepares a vulcanized rubber printing plate — compare STEREOTYPER **a c :** an apparatus in which rubber is vulcanized

vulcano *obs var of* VOLCANO

vul·can·o·log·i·cal \¦vəlkənə¦läjəkəl\ *adj* **:** VOLCANOLOGIC

vul·can·ol·o·gist \,⸗⸗'näləjəst\ *n* -S **:** VOLCANOLOGIST

vul·can·ol·o·gy \-jē, -ji\ *n* -ES [ISV *vulcan* + *-o-* + *-logy*] **:** VOLCANOLOGY

¹**vul·gar** \'vəlgə(r)\ *adj, sometimes* -ER/-EST [ME, fr. L *vulgaris, volgaris* of the mob, of the common people, common, vulgar, fr. *vulgus, volgus* mob, common people + *-aris* -ar; akin to W *gwala* sufficiency, enough, Bret *awalc'h* enough, Toch B *walke* long, Skt *varga* group, body of men, and perh. to Gk *eilein* to press, squeeze] **1 a :** generally used, applied, or accepted **:** found in ordinary practice ⟨the ~ course of events⟩ **b :** usual or customary in sense or interpretation **:** having the common or recognized meaning **:** taken in the ordinary way ⟨they reject the ~ conception of miracle —W.R.Inge⟩ **2 :** of or relating to common speech **:** VERNACULAR ⟨it is quite possible for a language which is no longer the language of ~ communication to remain the language of scholarship for generations and even for centuries —Norbert Wiener⟩ ⟨the ~ languages of Europe⟩ **3 a :** of or relating to the common people **:** belonging to the rank and file of a community or group or to an undistinguished or indistinguishable mass **:** PLEBEIAN ⟨keep their knowledge to themselves, safe from the ~ herd —R.A. Hall b.1911⟩ ⟨vegetarianism is a diet for heroes and saints, not for ~ persons —G.B.Shaw⟩ **b :** widely known **:** generally current **:** PUBLIC ⟨followed the ~ opinion of the day⟩ ⟨must inevitably be . . . a history of ~ errors —J.H.Sledd⟩ **c :** usual, typical, or ordinary in kind **:** of the common sort ⟨paints the objects themselves in all their ~ everydayness —Roger Fry⟩ ⟨conceal the details of a commonplace ~ death —James Joyce⟩ **d** *obs* (1) **:** not developed or refined beyond the ordinary **:** having the qualities or understanding of common people (2) **:** generally comprehensible **:** intelligible to the average mind **4 a :** lacking in cultivation, perception, or taste **:** COARSE, ILL-BRED, ILL-MANNERED, RUDE ⟨an essentially ~ mind, incapable of any real finesse or delicacy —H.J.Laski⟩ ⟨thought the farm hands who ate so greedily were ~ —Sherwood Anderson⟩ ⟨had quitted the ways of ~ men, without light to guide him on a better way —Thomas Hardy⟩ **b :** falling short of an artificial gentility or veneer **:** regarded as common by overrefined, precious, or affected persons ⟨she must neither move nor speak like other women, because it would be ~ —George Savile⟩ **c :** morally crude, undeveloped, or unregenerate **:** SELF-CENTERED, SELF-SEEKING, SELF-AGGRANDIZING, GROSS ⟨no ~ ambition, no morbid lust for material gain at the expense of others, had led us to the field —Sir Winston Churchill⟩ **d :** ostentatious, elaborate, or excessive esp. in expenditure or display **:** lacking simplicity, moderation, or propriety **:** PRETENTIOUS, VAIN ⟨saw so many ~ abuses of money as I grew older that I developed a positive disdain for the ostentatious symbols of wealth —Elsa Maxwell⟩ **5 a :** marked by coarseness of speech or expression **:** crude or offensive in language **:** EARTHY **b :** lewd, obscene, or profane in expression or behavior **:** INDECENT, INDELICATE ⟨names too ~ to put into print —H.A.Chippendale⟩ **6 :** marked by lack of discrimination, coherence, or selection **:** shaped by no unifying viewpoint or conception **:** flashy, congested, or extravagant in execution or performance ⟨the ~ . . . concept of spectacle rather than selective art —Roger Burlingame⟩ ⟨a luridly spectacular, aggressively tawdry, affirmatively ~ novelist of the fourth class —James Gray⟩ **7 :** dominated or prevailingly colored by the material concerns or business of life **:** not relieved by graces, manners, or arts ⟨becoming by giant strides more urban, more commercial and more ~ —*Times Lit. Supp.*⟩ **syn** see COARSE, COMMON

²**vulgar** \"\ *n* -S [ME, fr. *vulgar*, adj.] **1** *obs* **:** VERNACULAR **2 :** a vulgar or common person

vul·gare \,vəl'ga(a)rē, -gārē\ *adj* [NL (specific epithet of *Triticum vulgare*, a species of wheat), fr. L, neut. of *vulgaris* common — more at VULGAR]: of or relating to common wheat

vulgar era *n* **:** CHRISTIAN ERA

vulgar establishment *n* **:** the average interval of time that occurs between the moon's upper transit and the first high water following the transit and that is taken at the time of the full moon or new moon — called also *common establishment, establishment of the port*

vulgar fraction *n* **:** COMMON FRACTION

¹**vul·gar·i·an** \¦vəl¦gerēən, -ga(a)r-, -gār-\ *adj* [L *vulgarius* common, vulgar (fr. *vulgus* mob, common people + *-arius* -ary) + E *-an* — more at VULGAR] **:** of, relating to, or characteristic of a vulgar person **:** marked by vulgarity **:** COARSE, LOW

²**vulgarian** \"\ *n* -S **:** a vulgar person ⟨a juicy old ~ full of loving guile —Stanley Kauffmann⟩

vul·gar·ism \'vəlgə,rizəm\ *n* -S [¹*vulgar* + *-ism*] **1 a :** a word or expression originated or used chiefly by illiterate persons **:** a substandard use **:** BARBARISM, SOLECISM ⟨"he ain't got no sense" is traditionally regarded as a ~⟩ **b :** a lewd, profane, or coarse word or phrase **:** OBSCENITY **2 :** VULGARITY ⟨there is an inherent contradiction between art and ~ —Herbert Read⟩

vul·gar·i·ty \,vəl'garəd·ē, -ətē, -i, *also* -ger-\ *n* -ES [LL *vulgaritas*, fr. L *vulgaris* common, vulgar + *-itas* -ity — more at VULGAR] **1** *obs* **a :** the common people **b :** the run-of-mill average of a class **2** *obs* **:** the quality or state of being widely diffused **3** *obs* **:** the quality or state of being usual or ordinary **:** COMMONNESS **4 a :** the quality or state of being vulgar ⟨the ~ of a picture-postcard scene —Winthrop Sargeant⟩ ⟨would never stoop to the ~ of boasting how frequently he has been right —John Mason Brown⟩ **b :** something vulgar (as an act or display) ⟨some of the elegances were astounding *vulgarities* — for instance, seating a chimpanzee at a formal dinner —Gene Baro⟩

vul·gar·iza·tion \,vəlgərə'zāshən, -ə,rī'z-\ *n* -S **1 :** a making widely familiar **:** POPULARIZATION ⟨the book is unpretentious — a sensible piece of ~ —*New Republic*⟩ ⟨a work of ~ marked by scholarly accuracy —Kemp Malone⟩ **2 :** COARSENING, DEBASEMENT ⟨a general ~ of taste and feeling —August Heckscher⟩

vul·gar·ize \'⸗⸗,rīz\ *vb* -ED/-ING/-S *see -ize in Explan Notes* [¹*vulgar* + *-ize*] *vi* **:** to behave in a vulgar manner **~** *vt* **1 :** to spread widely **:** diffuse generally **:** POPULARIZE **2 :** to make vulgar **:** COARSEN ⟨written and repeated brutalities hit the mind more deeply and ~ the spirit more grossly than those that we see in real life —J.C.Powys⟩

vul·gar·iz·er \-zə(r)\ *n* -S **:** one that vulgarizes

vulgar latin *n, cap V&L* **:** the nonclassical Latin of ancient Rome including both the speech of plebeians and the informal daily speech of educated Romans that is scantily recorded in literature but attested by inscriptions and established by comparative evidence as the chief source of the Romance languages

vulgar law *n* **:** law arising in the time of the Roman Empire from sources (as foreigners in the provinces) other than the Roman law or applicable in places or provinces not under the Roman law

vul·gar·ly *adv* [ME, fr. *vulgar*, adj. + *-ly*] **:** in a vulgar manner

vul·gar·ness *n* -ES *archaic* **:** VULGARITY

vulgar purgation *n* [so called fr. its not having been sanctioned by the church] **:** purgation by combat or by ordeal by fire or water — compare CANONICAL PURGATION

vulgar substitution *n* [trans. of LL *substitutio vulgaris*] **:** SUBSTITUTION 1a(1)

vul·gate \'vəl,gāt, -,gət, *usu* -d·+V\ *n* -S [ML *Vulgata*, fr. LL *vulgata* (*editio*) Septuagint, Latin translation of the Septuagint, fr. L *vulgata* (fem. of *vulgatus* ordinary, common, general, fr. past part. of *vulgare* to make known, publish, fr. *vulgus* mob, common people) + *editio* edition — more at VULGAR] **1** *usu cap* **:** an edition or copy of the Latin Bible authorized and used by the Roman Catholic Church **2 :** any commonly accepted text or reading of an author's work **3 a :** common or informal speech ⟨a remarkable ear for the ~ —M.D.Geismar⟩ **b :** substandard or illiterate speech

¹**vul·gus** \'vəlgəs\ *n* -ES [L — more at VULGAR] **:** the common people

²**vulgus** \"\ *n* -ES [prob. alter. of obs. E *vulgars* English sentences to translate into Latin, fr. pl. of E ²*vulgar*] **:** a short composition in Latin verse formerly common as an exercise in some English public schools

vulned \'vəlnd\ *adj* [L *vulnus* wound + E *-ed*] *heraldry* **:** WOUNDED

vul·ner·a·bil·i·ty \,vəln(ə)rə'biləd·ē, -lətē, -i\ *n* **:** the quality or state of being vulnerable

vul·ner·a·ble \'vəlnər(ə)bəl, -nrəb-\ *adj* [LL *vulnerabilis*, fr.

L *vulnerare* to wound (fr. *vulner-, vulnus* wound) + -*abilis* -able; akin to Goth *wilwan* to rob, *wulwa* robbery, MLG *wlete* wound, L *vellere* to pluck, pull, Gk (Homeric) *oulē* wound, Per *valāna, vālāna* wound, Hitt *ụalḥmi* I battle] **1** : capable of being wounded : defenseless against injury ⟨the problem of protecting the ∼ human body —Lionel Whitby⟩ **2** : open to attack or damage : readily countered : inviting obvious retort, ridicule, or obloquy : ASSAILABLE ⟨a scientific statement is a ∼ statement —M.G.Joos⟩ ⟨weren't charged with anything perverse, simply with some affairs with women that made them ∼ to the new Puritans —W.H.Hale⟩ ⟨the man who can read commercial documents . . . is far less ∼ to fraud —Jerome Ellison⟩ **3** : exposed to capture : likely to be reduced by military assault ⟨a particularly ∼ outpost —*N.Y. Herald Tribune*⟩ **4** : liable to increased penalties but entitled to increased bonuses after winning a game of contract bridge

vul·ner·a·ble·ness *n* -ES : VULNERABILITY

vul·ner·a·bly \'vəlnər(ə)blē, -nrəb-, -li\ *adv* : in a vulnerable manner

¹**vul·ner·ary** \'vəlnə,rerē, -ri\ *adj* [L *vulnerarius*, fr. *vulner-, vulnus* wound + -*arius* -ary] **1** : promoting the healing of wounds : CURATIVE, SANATIVE ⟨a ∼ herb⟩ ⟨a ∼ application⟩ **2** : WOUNDING

²**vulnerary** \"\ *n* -ES : a vulnerary remedy

vul·pe·ci·dal *or* **vul·pi·ci·dal** \,vəlpə̇'sīdᵊl\ *adj* : of, relating to, or committing vulpecide

vul·pe·cide *or* **vul·pi·cide** \'∙∙,sīd\ *n* -S [*vulpecide* irreg. fr. L *vulpes* fox + E -*cide*; *vulpicide* fr. L *vulpes* fox + E -*i-* + -*cide*] **1** : a person killing a fox by means other than those of hunting with hounds **2** : the killing of a fox by means other than those of hunting with hounds

vul·pec·u·la \,vəl'pekyələ\ [NL, fr. L, small fox, a small shark, dim. of *vulpes* fox, a shark] *syn of* ALOPIAS

vul·pe·cu·li·dae \,vəlpə'kyülə,dē\ [NL, fr. *Vulpecula* + -*idae*] *syn of* ALOPIIDAE

vul·pes \'vəl,pēz\ *n, cap* [NL, fr. L, fox — more at VULPINE] : a genus of mammals (family Canidae) including the common red fox and closely related animals — see FOX 1; compare FENNEC, GRAY FOX

vul·pine \'vəl,pīn, -,pə̇n\ *adj* [L *vulpinus*, fr. *vulpes* fox + -*inus* -ine; akin to Gk *alōpēx* fox, Arm *aluēs* fox, Skt *lopāśa* jackal, fox, Lith *vilpišys* wildcat] **1** : of, relating to, or resembling a fox **2** : marked by slyness or predatoriness : CRAFTY ⟨believed the mildest house agent grew ∼ at sight of them —Audrey Barker⟩

vulpine opossum *or* **vulpine phalanger** *n* : a common Australian opossum (*Trichosurus vulpecula*) that is gray above fading to yellowish on the underparts

vul·pin·ic acid \'vəl'pinik-\ *or* **vul·pic acid** \'vəlpik-\ *n* [*vulpinic* ISV *vulpin-* (fr. NL *vulpina* — specific epithet of *Cetraria vulpina* —, fr. fem. of L *vulpinus* vulpine) + -*ic*; *vulpic* fr. NL *vulpina* + E -*ic*] : a yellow crystalline compound $C_{19}H_{14}O_5$ occurring in various lichens (as *Cetraria vulpina*) and also made synthetically : the methyl ester of pulvinic acid

vul·pi·nite \'vəlpə,nīt\ *n* -S [G *vulpinit*, fr. *Vulpino*, Lombardy, Italy + G -*it* -ite] : a mineral consisting of a scaly granular grayish white variety of anhydrite

vul·sel·la \,vəl'selə\ *n* -s [NL, fr. L, tweezers] : VULSELLUM

vul·sel·lum \-ləm\ *n, pl* **vulsel·la** \-lə\ [NL, alter. of L *vulsella* tweezers, fr. *vellere* to pluck, pull — more at VULNERABLE] : a surgical forceps with serrated, clawed, or hooked blades

vul·tur \'vəltər\ *n, cap* [NL, fr. L, vulture] : a formerly comprehensive genus of vultures that is usu. restricted to the Andean condor

¹**vul·ture** \'vəlchə(r)\ *n* -s [ME, fr. L *vultur;* prob. akin to L *vellere* to pull, pluck — more at VULNERABLE] **1** : any of various large raptorial birds of temperate and tropical regions that are related to the hawks, eagles, and falcons but have weaker claws and the head usu. naked, that subsist chiefly or entirely on carrion, and that constitute the families Aegypiidae and Cathartidae and include some of the largest birds of flight — see BLACK VULTURE, CONDOR, EYPTIAN VULTURE, KING VULTURE, LAMMERGEIER, TURKEY BUZZARD **2** : someone or something likened to a vulture: as **a** : an emotion or passion that preys on the mind or body **b** : a rapacious or predatory person or one pursuing vile or base objects ⟨shyster lawyers, crooked photographers and assorted ∼s circling a big cash settlement —*Time*⟩ ⟨a ∼ of an old woman who preyed on her lodgers and boarders⟩

²**vulture** \"\ *vt* **vultured; vultured; vulturing** \-ch(ə)riŋ\ **vultured** the library's reference and guidebooks —*Newsweek*⟩

vultures \"\ : to make prey or loot of : SNATCH, SWIPE ⟨had vultured the library's reference and guidebooks —*Newsweek*⟩

vulture hock *n* : a cluster of stiff feathers growing on the thighs of a domestic fowl and projecting backward

vulture-hocked \,∙∙'häkt\ *adj* : having vulture hocks

vulture-like \'∙∙,∙\ *adj* : resembling a vulture

vulture raven *n* : either of two large ravens of eastern Africa belonging to the genus *Corvultur* and having a thick arched bill

vul·tur·ine \'vəlchə,rīn, -,rə̇n\ *adj* [L *vulturinus*, fr. *vultur* + -*inus* -ine] **1 a** : of or relating to the vultures **b** : characteristic of a vulture ⟨a ∼ taste for offal⟩ **2** : marked by a vile rapacity : PREDATORY ⟨∼ congressmen —John Brooks⟩ ⟨this ∼ essay —E.J.Kahn⟩

vulturine eagle *n* : an eagle (*Aquila verreauxii*), of southern Africa having the lower back and rump white and the rest of the plumage black

vulturine guinea fowl *n* : a large long-tailed guinea fowl (*Acryllium vulturinum*) of eastern Africa with a naked head and lanceolate blue, black, and white feathers on the neck, breast, and shoulders, a back mostly black spotted with white, and a bluish abdomen that becomes purple on the sides

vulturine sea eagle *n* : EAGLE VULTURE

vul·tur·ish \'vəlchərish, -rēsh\ *adj* : VULTUROUS

vul·tur·ous \-rəs\ *adj* : resembling a vulture esp. in rapacity or scavenging habits ⟨∼ expectancy⟩

vulv- *or* **vulvo-** *comb form* [NL *vulva*] **1** : vulva ⟨*vulvitis*⟩ **2** : vulvar and ⟨*vulvovaginal*⟩

vul·va \'vəlvə\ *n* -s [NL, fr. L *vulva, volva* covering, integument, womb; akin to Skt *ulva, ulba* vulva, womb, placenta, L *volvere* to roll, turn — more at VOLUBLE] **1 a** : the external parts of the female genital organs **b** : the opening between the projecting parts of the external organs **2** : the orifice of the oviduct of an insect or other invertebrate

vul·val \-vəl\ *adj* [*vulv-* + -*al*] : VULVAR

vul·var \-və(r)\ *adj* [*vulv-* + -*ar*] : of or relating to the vulva

vul·vate \-,vāt, -,və̇t, usu -d-+V\ *adj* [*vulv-* + -*ate*] : VULVAR, VULVIFORM

vul·vi·form \'vəlvə,fórm\ *adj* [*vulv-* + -*iform*] **1** : having an oval shape with a middle cleft and projecting lips **2** : suggesting a cleft with projecting edges — used of plant forms

vul·vi·tis \,vəl'vīd·əs\ *n* -ES [NL, fr. *vulv-* + -*itis*] : inflammation of the vulva

vul·vo·vaginitis \,vəlvə+∙∙ *n* [NL, fr. *vulv-* + *vaginitis*] : coincident inflammation of the vulva and vagina

vum \'vəm\ *vi* [prob. alter. of ³*vow*] *dial* : AVOW, SWEAR ⟨I ∼, I'd soon put harness on myself as worry along with that lazy mule —Elizabeth M. Roberts⟩

vv *abbr* **1** *often cap both Vs* [L *venerabiles*] venerables **2** verbs **3** verses **4** violins **5** volumes

VV *abbr, often not cap* vice versa

v-value \'∙;∙(,)∙\ *n, usu cap 1st V* : the reciprocal of the dispersive power of an optical medium

VW *abbr* **1** very worshipful **2** vessel wall

vy *abbr* very

vying *pres part of* VIE

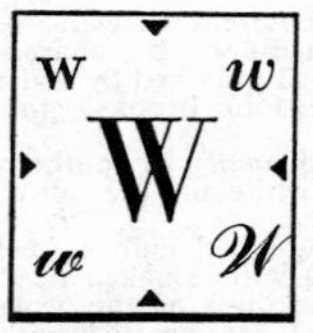

1w \'dəbəl(,)yü, -lyə; *in rapid speech also* -b(ə)yə *or* -byē\ *n, pl* **w's** *or* **ws** *often cap, often attrib* **1 a :** the 23d letter of the English alphabet **b :** an instance of this letter printed, written, or otherwise represented **c :** a speech counterpart of orthographic *w* (as *w* in *woo, watt, sway,* or German *wasser*) **2 :** a printer's type, a stamp, or some other instrument for reproducing the letter *w* **3 :** someone or something arbitrarily or conveniently designated *w* esp. as the 22d or when j is used for the 10th the 23d in order or class **4 :** something having the shape of the letter W

2w *abbr, often cap* **1** wall **2** wanting **3** war **4** warden **5** warehouse; warehousing **6** warm **7** waste **8** water **9** watt **10** weather **11** week **12** weight **13** west; western **14** wet **15** whip **16** white **17** wicket **18** wide **19** widow **20** width **21** wife **22** wind **23** wire **24** with **25** won **26** wood **27** word **28** work **29** wrong

3w *symbol, cap* **1** energy **2** [G *wolfram*] tungsten

1wa \'wä\ *Scot & dial Eng var of* WOE

2wa \"\ *Scot & dial Eng var of* WAY

3wa \"\ *n, pl* **wa** *or* **was** *usu cap* **1 a :** a people in the Wa States of northeastern Burma and adjoining parts of Yunnan province, China who have never been subdued by the Burmese or the Chinese, have preserved ancient cultural traits (as head hunting and the erection of megalithic monuments), are excellent agriculturists in mountain farming, and in the Wild Wa area do not wear clothes — called also *Kawa* **b :** a member of such people **2 :** the Mon-Khmer language of the Wa people

WA *abbr* **1** warm air **2** with average

wa' \'wȯ, 'wä\ *Scot var of* WALL

1waac \'wak\ *n -s usu cap* [*Women's Auxiliary Army Corps*] **:** a member of the Women's Auxiliary Army Corps formed in England during World War I

2waac \"\ *n -s usu cap* [*Women's Army Auxiliary Corps*] **:** a member of the Women's Army Auxiliary Corps formed in the U.S. during World War II — compare WAC

waaf \'waf\ *n -s usu cap* [*Women's Auxiliary Air Force*] **:** a member of the Women's Auxiliary Air Force formed as an auxiliary of the British Royal Air Force during World War II

waahoo *var of* WAHOO

wab \'wab\ *Scot & dial Eng var of* WEB

wabanaki *usu cap, var of* ABNAKI

1wabble *var of* WOBBLE

2wab·ble \'wäbəl\ *n -s* [alter. of *5warble*] **:** the larva of a botfly (*Bogeria emasculator*) that infests squirrels and destroys their testes

wab·by \'wäbē\ *or* **whab·by** \'(h)w-\ *n -es* [origin unknown] **:** RED-THROATED LOON

wa·be·no \wȯ'bē(,)nō\ *n -s* [Ojibwa *wâbanow,* lit., I am a sorcerer] **:** an Ojibwa shaman

wab·ster \'wabztə(r), -bst-\ *Scot & dial Eng var of* WEBSTER

wab·ur *also* **wab·ber** \'wäbə(r)\ *n -s* [Ar *wabr,* fr. *wabar* to be hairy] **:** SYRIAN HYRAX

wac \'wak\ *n -s usu cap* [*Women's Army Corps*] **:** a member of the Women's Army Corps established in the U.S. during World War II as successor to the Women's Army Auxiliary Corps — compare 2WAAC

wac·ca·maw \'wäkə,mȯ\ *n, pl* **waccamaw** *or* **waccamaws** *usu cap* **1 :** a Siouan people of the Waccamaw river valley in eastern So. Carolina **2 :** a member of the Waccamaw people

wach·na \'wäknə\ *or* **wachna cod** *n -s* [Russ *vakhnya*] **:** a cod (*Eleginus nawaga*) of Alaska and Kamchatka

wack \'wak\ *or* **whack** \'(h)wak\ *n -s* [prob. back-formation fr. *wacky*] *slang* **:** a wacky person **:** CRACKPOT, SCREWBALL

wacke \'wakə\ *n -s* [G, fr. MHG, large stone, fr. OHG *waggo*] **:** GRAYWACKE

wack·en·ro·der solution \'väkən,rōdə(r)-\ *n, usu cap W* [prob. after H. W. F. *Wackenroder* †1854 Ger. chemist and apothecary] **:** a solution containing colloidal sulfur and polythionic acids obtained by passing hydrogen sulfide into a saturated aqueous solution of sulfur dioxide

wack·i·ly \'wakəlē\ *adv* **:** in a wacky manner

wack·i·ness \-kēnəs, -kin-\ *n -es* **:** the quality or state of being wacky

wacky \-kē, -ki\ *or* **whacky** \'(h)w-\ *also* **wack·ey** *or* **wack·ie** \'w-\ *adj* **wackier** *or* **whackier; wackiest** *or* **whackiest** [perh. fr. E dial. *whacky* fool, fr. *whack*-head fool, lit., one who has been whacked on the head + E *-y*] **:** eccentric or irrational esp. in an amusing, absurd, or fantastic manner **:** CRAZY, INSANE ⟨his somewhat ~ philosophy pervades the family life —E.E.Calkins⟩ ⟨that explanation was just as ~ as many others —R.M.Blough⟩ ⟨if she kept on with such illogical ideas . . . she would end up as ~ as the other patients —Nancy Hale⟩

wa·co \'wä(,)kō\ *n, pl* **waco** *or* **wacos** *usu cap* [fr. Caddoan *Wehiko* Mexico; fr. their frequent fighting with the Mexicans] **1 :** a Caddo people of Oklahoma and Texas **2 :** a member of the Waco people

1wad \'wad, 'wäd\ *n -s* [ME(Sc), alter. of E *wed*] *Scots law* **:** PLEDGE — **in wad :** PLEDGED

2wad \'wäd *also* 'wȯd\ *n -s* [origin unknown] **1 a :** a usu. small mass, bundle, or tuft ⟨always has with him a ~ of photos —Walter Sullivan⟩ ⟨little ~*s* of mutton —Katherine Mansfield⟩ ⟨spread ~*s* of marmalade —Anthony Powell⟩ ⟨a glowing ~ of fireflies along the ground —William Goyen⟩ **b :** a soft mass (as of a loose fibrous material) variously used (as to stop an aperture, pad a garment, or hold grease around an axle) ⟨replaced cotton ~*s* in vials with a foamed polystyrene plug —*Modern Packaging*⟩ **c** (1) **:** a relatively soft plug used to retain a charge of powder to keep the powder and shot close or to avoid windage esp. in a muzzle-loading cannon or gun (2) **:** a disk of felt or paper used to separate the components of a shotgun cartridge or to retain the powder in a blank cartridge — see CARTRIDGE illustration **d :** a piece of clay used in ceramics for various purposes; *specif* **:** a strip of moist clay laid around the rim of a sagger to form a bed for a superimposed sagger in the kiln **e :** a small mass of a chewing substance ⟨a ~ of tobacco⟩ ⟨a ~ of gum⟩ **2 a :** a considerable amount ⟨bought himself a big ~ of radio time —R.P.Warren⟩ ⟨a whopping ~ of surpluses —*Sydney (Australia) Bull.*⟩ — often used in pl. ⟨has been getting ~*s* of publicity —*New Yorker*⟩ **b :** the amount of which one is capable of expending — usu. used with *shoot* ⟨going to shoot our whole ~ at the carrier —E.L.Beach⟩ **3 a :** a roll of paper money ⟨produced a ~ of dirty notes —T.H.Barnardo⟩ ⟨a ~ on your hip that would choke a coal chute —Raymond Chandler⟩ **b :** a supply of money ⟨bet his ~ on a race⟩ **c :** a large amount of money ⟨idea of making a ~ and setting the folks up in style —Hiram Haydn⟩ ⟨quite a ~, close on two thousand dollars —Nevil Shute⟩

3wad \"\ *vt* **wadded; wadded; wadding; wads 1 :** to form into a wad or into wadding ⟨~ tow⟩; *esp* **:** to roll or crush into a tight wad ⟨they *wadded* their paper napkins into small, round balls —Grace Metalious⟩ ⟨handed the driver a *wadded* bill —Lillian Ross⟩ — often used with *up* ⟨took off my shirt, *wadded* it up —Herbert Passin⟩ **2 a :** to insert or crowd a wad into ⟨~ a gun⟩ **b :** to hold in by a wad ⟨~ a bullet in a gun⟩ **3 :** to stuff or line with some soft substance (as cotton) **:** PAD ⟨long blue gowns over *wadded* coats and trousers —Nora Waln⟩ ⟨let up rowing to ~ the oarlocks so they wouldn't make a noise —H.L.Davis⟩; *broadly* **:** to pack tightly ⟨families . . . were *wadded* closely into the available space —Julian Dana⟩

4wad \'wad, 'wäd\ *n -s* [prob. of Scand origin; akin to ON *vathr* fishing line, measuring line] *dial Eng* **:** LINE; *esp* **:** one marked in land surveying

5wad \", *in sense 2* 'wäd *also* 'wȯd\ *n -s* [origin unknown] **1** *dial Eng* **:** GRAPHITE, BLACK LEAD **2 :** an amorphous dull brown or black mineral substance that occurs usu. in low places, consists chiefly of oxides of manganese with varying amounts of other minerals (as copper, cobalt, and silica) and water, is commonly very soft but sometimes hard and compact, and is used in making chlorine and as a pigment **:** BOG MANGANESE — called also *black ocher;* compare BAUXITE, LIMONITE

6wad \wäd, ,wəd\ *Scot & dial Eng var of* WOULD

wad·able *or* **wade·able** \'wādəbəl\ *adj* **:** capable of being waded ⟨a ~ stream⟩

wadcutter \'=,==\ *n* [*2wad* + *cutter*] **:** a cylindrical bullet having a flat top instead of a pointed or rounded nose or a truncated version of one of the latter

wad·der \'wädə(r) *also* 'wȯd-\ *n -s* **:** one that wads

1wad·ding \-diŋ\ *n -s* [*2wad* + *-ing*] **1 a :** wads or material for making wads **b :** a soft mass or sheet of short loose fibers used for stuffing or padding (as quilts, costumes, upholstery, or packages) **c** (1) **:** a soft absorbent paper used in hospitals and as sanitary napkins (2) **:** a loosely formed crepe paper used for packing **2** *or* **wadding thread :** a stuffer thread

2wad·ding \'wadin\ *Scot var of* WEDDING

1wad·dle \'wäd³l *also* 'wȯd-\ *vi* **waddled; waddled; waddling** \-d(³)liŋ\ **waddles** [freq. of *1wade*] **1 :** to walk with short steps swinging the forepart of the body from side to side ⟨ducks *waddling* to water⟩ ⟨*waddling* around with a fat man's strut —W.A.White⟩ **2 :** to move clumsily in a manner suggesting a waddle ⟨a bulldozer *waddled* up —M.O.Williams⟩ ⟨watched the steamer ~ out into the river —R.J.White⟩

2waddle \"\ *n -s* **:** the act of waddling **:** an awkward clumsy swaying gait **:** TODDLE

wad·dling·ly *adv* [*waddling* (pres. part. of *1waddle*) + *-ly*] **:** in a waddling manner

wad·dly \-d(³)lē\ *adj* **:** having or suggesting a waddle ⟨a ~ person⟩ ⟨watching the small form . . . disappear with its curious ~ walk —John Dos Passos⟩

1wad·dy \'wädē, -di *also* 'wȯd-\ *n -es* [native name in Australia, perh. modif. of E *2wood*] **1 :** a straight tapered throwing-stick used in hunting and war by aborigines esp. of Australia **2 :** a piece of wood **:** STICK, PEG, WALKING STICK

2waddy \"\ *vt -ED/-ING/-ES Austral* **:** to attack or beat with a waddy

3waddy *or* **wad·die** \"\ *n, pl* **waddies** [origin unknown] **1** *West* **:** COWBOY 3 **2** *West* **:** RUSTLER c

4waddy *var of* WADI

1wade \'wād\ *vb -ED/-ING/-S* [ME *waden,* fr. OE *wadan;* akin to OHG *watan* to go, wade, ON *vatha* to go through, wade, L *vadere* to go, OE *wæd* ford, ON *vath,* L *vadum*] *vi* **1** *obs* **:** GO, PASS, PENETRATE **2 :** to step in or through a medium (as water, mud, or sand) that offers more resistance than air ⟨*waded* through a snowdrift —F.V.W.Mason⟩ ⟨burros came *wading* through the corral dust —F.B.Gipson⟩ ⟨*wading* waist-deep in bushes —A.W.Hughes⟩ **3 :** to move or get forward with difficulty or labor **:** proceed slowly among things that constantly hinder or embarrass ⟨have to ~ through twenty pages of dull moralizing —Douglas Stewart⟩ ⟨~ through slaughter to a throne —Thomas Gray⟩ **4 :** to set to work or attack with determination or vigor — used with *in* or *into* ⟨obtained some textbooks and *waded* in⟩ ⟨~ into the morning's mail⟩ ⟨*waded* into his opponent with his bare fists⟩ ⟨*waded* into the reputations of our national heroes —C.V.Woodward⟩ **~** *vt* **:** to pass or cross by wading ⟨~ a stream⟩ ⟨~ mud⟩

2wade \"\ *n -s* **:** an act of wading ⟨go for a ~ in the brook⟩

wadeable *var of* WADABLE

wade·ite \'wā,dīt\ *n -s* [Arthur *Wade* †1951 Eng. geologist + E *-ite*] **:** a mineral $K_2CaZr(SiO_3)_4$ consisting of a silicate of potassium, calcium, and zirconium

wad·er \'wādə(r)\ *n -s* **1 :** one that wades **2 :** WADING BIRD **3 a :** WADING BOOT **b :** a waterproof garment that consists of trousers sometimes reaching to the armpits, has attached socks or waterproof boots or shoes, and is worn (as by anglers or duck hunters) over the regular clothing — often used in pl. ⟨a pair of ~*s*⟩

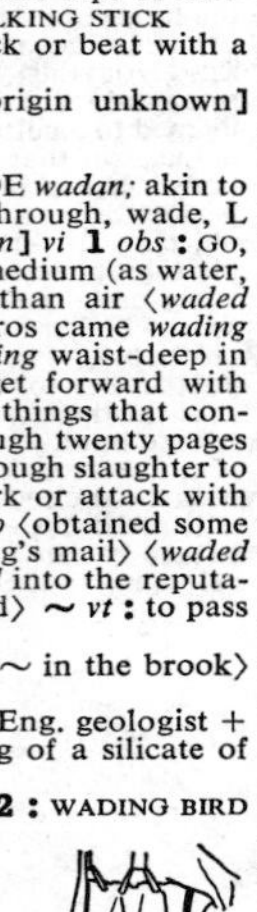
wader 3b

wadge \'waj\ *n -s* [alter. of *1wedge*] *Brit* **:** BUNCH, BUNDLE, SLAB, WEDGE ⟨the ~ of letters was in his hands —Elizabeth Bowen⟩ ⟨twisting a biscuit deep into the thick ~ of yogurt —G.A.Wagner⟩

wad hook *n* [*2wad*] *archaic* **:** WORMER b

wa·di *also* **wa·dy** *or* **wad·dy** \'wädē, -di\ *or* **oued** \'wed\ *n, pl* **wadis** *also* **wadies** *or* **waddies** *or* **oueds** [Ar *wādiy*] **1 :** the bed or valley of a stream in arid regions of southwestern Asia and northern Africa that is usu. dry except during the rainy season and that often forms an oasis **:** GULLY, RAVINE, WASH **2 :** a shallow usu. sharply defined depression in a desert region of poorly developed drainage in southwestern Asia and northern Africa

wading bird *n* [*wading* (pres. part. of *1wade*) + *bird*] **:** any of many long-legged birds including the shorebirds (as sandpipers and snipe) and the inland water birds (as cranes and herons) that wade in water in search of food

wading boot *n* [*wading* (gerund of *wade*) + *boot*] **:** a high waterproof boot worn esp. by fishermen; *esp* **:** HIP BOOT

wading pool *n* **:** a shallow pool of portable or permanent construction used (as in a park) by children for wading

wa·djak man \'wä,jäk-, 'wä,dyäk-\ *n, usu cap W* [fr. *Wadjak,* locality in Java where the skulls were discovered] **:** an extinct large-headed man of primitive proto-Australoid type known from two Javanese skulls that is often set apart as a species (*Homo wadjakensis*) but is probably a primitive form of modern man (*Homo sapiens*) intermediate between Solo man and the modern Australian natives

wad·mal *or* **wad·mol** *or* **wad·mel** \'wädməl\ *n -s* [ME *wadmoll, wadmale,* fr. ON *vathmāl,* lit., standard cloth, fr. *vāth* cloth, clothing + *māl* measure — more at WEED, MEAL] **:** a coarse rough woolen fabric formerly used in the British Isles and Scandinavia for protective coverings and warm clothing

wad·na \'wädnə\ [*6wad* + *na*] *Scot & dial Eng* **:** would not

wads *pl of* WAD, *pres 3d sing of* WAD

1wad·set \'wad,set, 'wäd-\ *vt* [Sc, alter. of ME *wedsetten* to pledge, fr. *1wed* + *setten* to set] *Scots law* **:** MORTGAGE, PLEDGE

2wadset \"\ *n -s* [Sc, alter. of ME *wedset* mortgage, fr. *wedsetten* to pledge] *Scots law* **:** MORTGAGE, PLEDGE, PAWN; *esp* **:** a mortgage of real estate given by a borrower to a lender formerly transferring possession only but later the legal title

wad·set·ter \-tər\ *n* [*1wadset* + *-er*] **1** *Scot* **:** MORTGAGOR **2** *Scot* **:** MORTGAGEE

WAE *abbr* when actually employed

wae·suck \'wā,sək\ *or* **wae·sucks** \-ks\ *interj* [Sc *wae* woe (fr. ME *wa*) + *suck, sucks,* alter. of E *sake, sakes* — more at WOE] *Scot* — used to express grief or pity

waf \'waf\ *n -s usu cap* [*Women in the Air Force*] **:** a member of the women's component of the U. S. Air Force formed after World War II

WAF *abbr, often not cap* with all faults

1wa·fer \'wāfə(r)\ *n -s* [ME *wafre, wafer,* fr. ONF *waufre,* of Gmc origin; akin to MD *wafel, wafer* waffle — more at WAFFLE] **1 a :** a thin crisp cake or cracker **b :** a thin cake or piece of bread usu. unleavened, circular, and stamped with a cross or sacred monogram that is used in a religious service esp. in the celebration of the Eucharist in high liturgical churches — compare ALTAR BREAD **2 :** an adhesive disk of dried paste made of flour mixed with gum or of gelatin, isinglass, or similar material with added coloring matter and used as a seal (as for letters or the attaching of papers) **3** *or* **wafer capsule :** CACHET 3 **4 :** a thin disk or ring resembling a wafer and variously used (as for a valve, diaphragm, or tumbler in a lock)

2wafer \"\ *vt -ED/-ING/-S* **:** to seal, close, or fasten with a wafer

wafer ash *n* **:** HOP TREE

wafer bread *n* **1 :** eucharistic bread in the form of wafers **2 :** corn bread baked in thin sheets esp. by southwestern Indians

wafer iron *n* [ME *wafer iren,* fr. *1wafer* + *iren* iron] **:** a long-handled pair of iron tongs molded with a design that is impressed upon the wafer batter in baking

wafer sheet *n* **:** a very thin sheet of baked dough used in pharmacy for making small envelopes or cachets

wafer-thin \'=;=\ *adj* **:** PAPER-THIN ⟨holding a *wafer-thin* majority on the executive board —J.C.Cort⟩

1waff \'waf\ *vb -ED/-ING/-S* [ME (northern) *waffen,* alter. of ME *waven* to wave] *Scot & dial Eng* **:** WAVE, FLUTTER, WAG, FLAP

2waff \"\ *n -s* **1** *Scot & dial Eng* **:** a waving motion **:** FLAPPING **2** *Scot & dial Eng* **:** PUFF, GUST, WHIFF, ODOR **3** *Scot & dial Eng* **:** GLIMPSE **4** *Scot & dial Eng* **:** WRAITH

3waff \"\ *adj* [alter. of *waif*] *Scot* **:** WORTHLESS, DISREPUTABLE, LOWBORN, PALTRY — **waff·ness** *n -es*

waff·ie \-fi\ *n -s* [*3waff* + *-ie*] *Scot* **:** VAGRANT, VAGABOND

1waf·fle \'wäfəl, 'wȯf-\ *n -s* [D *wafel,* fr. MD *wafel, wafer;* akin to MLG *wafel* waffle, OHG *waba* honeycomb, *weban* to weave — more at WEAVE] **1 :** a crisp cake made of pancake batter baked in a waffle iron ⟨had ~*s* for supper⟩ **2 :** WAFER 1a

2waffle \"\ *also* **waf·fled** \-ld\ *adj* **:** having an indented latticed pattern or form

3waffle \"\ *vi* **waffled; waffled; waffling** \-f(ə)liŋ\ **waffles** [freq. of obs. *waff* to yelp, of imit. origin] *Brit* **:** to talk foolishly **:** BLATHER ⟨the aggressive one becomes nervous and ~*s* —D.E.Morris⟩ ⟨*waffling* fathead —Earle Birney⟩

waffle cloth *n* [*2waffle*] **:** HONEYCOMB 3b(2)

waffle ingot *n* **:** an ingot of aluminum about three inches square and a quarter of an inch thick

waffle iron *n* [*1waffle*] **:** a utensil for cooking waffles that consists of two metal parts hinged together so as to shut upon each other and impress square, round, or oval surface projections on the waffle in baking

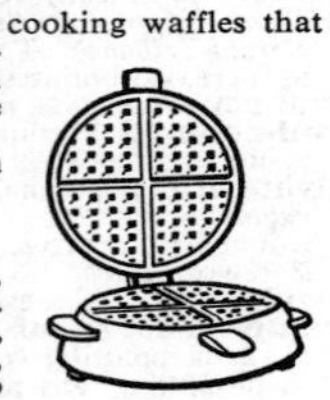
waffle iron

waffle piqué *n* [*2waffle*] **:** a fine cotton usu. printed honeycomb cloth

waffle weave *n* **:** HONEYCOMB 3b(1)

wafs *pl of* WAF

1waft \'wäft, 'waft, 'waa(ə)ft, 'waift, 'wȧft *also* 'wȯft\ *vb -ED/-ING/-S* [fr. (assumed) ME *waughten* to guard, convoy (whence ME *waughter* wafter, convoy), fr. MD or MLG *wachten* to watch, guard; akin to OE *wæccan* to watch — more at WAKE] *vt* **1** *obs* **:** to act as convoy to **:** sail in company with (as for protection) **2** [prob. alter. of *1waff*] *obs* **:** to signal to (as by waving the hand) **:** BECKON ⟨who ~*s* us yonder —Shak.⟩ **3** *archaic* **:** to convey by water **:** transport across a body of water ⟨~ me safely cross the Channel —Shak.⟩ **4 :** to cause to move or go lightly by or as if by the impulse of wind or waves **:** to bear along on or as if on a buoyant medium ⟨a light hot gust of wind ~*ed* the clouds towards other slopes —Anna Seghers⟩ ⟨the aroma of coffee was ~*ed* in —Ellen Glasgow⟩ ⟨milkweed is already ~*ing* silky down across the bog grass —D.C. Peattie⟩ ⟨he ~*ed* the subject aside with the smoke from his cigar —Marguerite Steen⟩ **~** *vi* **:** to become moved or pass on or as if on a buoyant medium ⟨scent of oregano ~*s* from their doors —Franc Shor⟩ ⟨light classical tunes ~ from amplifiers —C.M.Barss⟩ ⟨the waiter . . . nodded and ~*ed* off —Peter De Vries⟩

2waft \"\ *n -s* **1 :** something (as an odor) that is wafted **:** something fleeting **:** something that lingers lightly **:** WHIFF ⟨stale ~ of an exotic perfume —C.D.Lewis⟩ ⟨a ~ of carbolic acid was borne on a warm gust of wind —Cyril Connolly⟩ ⟨fragmentary ~*s* of village gossip floated in at the windows —Richard Church⟩ **2 :** a wafting movement **:** PUFF, GUST ⟨every ~ of the air —H.W.Longfellow⟩ ⟨expresses every whim and ~ of his time —*John o' London's Weekly*⟩ **3 :** the act of wafting; *esp* **:** a signal made by waving something (as a flag) in the air **4** *or* **weft** \'weft\ **a :** a pennant or a stopped or knotted flag used to signal or sometimes to show the direction of the wind to the steersman **b :** the knot in such a flag

3waft \'waft\ *Scot var of* WEFT

waft·age *pronunc at* 1WAFT + ij\ *n -s* [*1waft* + *-age*] **:** the act of wafting or state of being wafted **:** passage or conveyance on or through a buoyant medium; *broadly* **:** CONVEYANCE, CARRIAGE ⟨boats prepared for ~ to and fro —Michael Drayton⟩

waft·er \"+ə(r)\ *n -s* [ME *waughter* convoy, commander of a convoy, fr. (assumed) *waughten* to guard, convoy + *-er* — more at WAFT] **1 :** one that wafts; *specif* **:** a revolving disk or fan for a blower **2** *obs* **:** a transport or passenger boat or its master; *also* **:** a warship serving as a convoy to such a boat

waf·ture \'wäfchə(r), 'waf-\ *n -s* [*1waft* + *-ure*] **1 :** the act of wafting or waving **:** a wavelike motion **:** WAFT, BECKONING **2 :** something wafted or conveyed by or as if by a breeze or the waves of the sea

1wag \'wag, -aa(ə)g, -aig\ *vb* **wagged; wagged; wagging; wags** [ME *waggen;* akin to ON *vagga* cradle, Sw *vagga* to rock, MHG *wacken* to totter; akin to OE *wagian* to move, swing, totter, OHG *wagōn* to move, surge, ON *vaga* to wag; akin to OE *wegan* to move — more at WAY] *vi* **1 :** to be in action or motion **:** MOVE, STIR ⟨see . . . how the world ~*s* —Shak.⟩ **2 :** to move to and fro or up and down esp. repeatedly and with a quick or jerky motion **:** OSCILLATE, SWITCH, WAGGLE, WAVE, WIGWAG **3 :** to keep moving in chatter or gossip ⟨his tongue ~*s* incessantly⟩ ⟨beards *wagged* throughout the scientific world —Webb Garrison⟩ ⟨heads *wagged* for a time —Louis Bromfield⟩ ⟨his lips were still *wagging* —*Time*⟩ **4 a** *archaic* **:** to move from a place **:** pack off **:** DEPART ⟨~ to town⟩ **b** *archaic* **:** to wander from place to place **:** TRAVEL **c** *slang* **:** to play truant from school ⟨the school we both attended — when not *wagging* it —*Sydney (Australia) Bull.*⟩ **5 a :** to move with a wagging or wobbling motion **:** WADDLE ⟨a dog *wagging* down the street⟩ **b** *of an animal* **:** to wag the tail ⟨a pack of dogs — they fawned, they *wagged,* they growled —Helen Howe⟩ **~** *vt* **1 a** *archaic* **:** MOVE, STIR, BUDGE **b** *dial* **:** to carry or haul with difficulty **:** LUG ⟨~ groceries home in a cart⟩ ⟨a small child . . . compelled to ~ her baby brother around with her —Theodore Garrison⟩ **2 a :** to swing to and fro or up and down esp. repeatedly and with a quick or jerky motion **:** SHAKE, SWITCH, WAVE ⟨ducks . . . nonchalantly *wagging* their tails —Edmund Wilson⟩ ⟨formation leaders have telegraphed their dive attacks by *wagging* their wings before coming in —Keith Ayling⟩ ⟨naval vessels . . . would be *wagging* and hoisting flags and blinking lights at one another —Gavin Douglas⟩; *specif* **:** to nod (the head) or shake (a finger) at (as in assent or mild reproof) ⟨don't ~ your finger at me⟩ **b :** to move (as the head) animatedly in conversation ⟨a scandalous event that set the villagers to *wagging* their tongues⟩ ⟨a theory for philosophers to ~ their heads over —Henry Bordeaux⟩ **3 :** to strongly influence or exert control over (a related thing) out of proportion to size or true importance ⟨the tail ~*s* the dog⟩ ⟨instances . . . in which the choirs are *wagging* the church —Maurice Thompson⟩

2wag \"\ *n -s* [prob. short for obs. *waghalter* gallows bird, fr. *1wag* + *halter*] **1** *obs* **a :** a mischievous boy **b :** a young man **:** CHAP **2 :** one full of sport and humor **:** WIT, JESTER, JOKER ⟨we wink at ~*s* when they offend —John Dryden⟩ ⟨many of the most celebrated ~*s* of history —E.J.Kahn⟩ **3 :** an act of wagging **:** SHAKE, NOD ⟨a ~ of the head⟩

wag *abbr* wagon; wagoner

wa·gang *or* **wa'·gang** \'wä,gaŋ\ *or* **wa·gang·ing** \-ŋin\ *or* **wa·gaun** \-,gȯn\ *n -s* [*wagang, wa'gang* fr. *2wa* + *gang* (act of going); *waganging* fr. *2wa* + *ganging,* gerund of *gang* (to go); *wagaun* fr. *2wa* + Sc *gaun,* gerund of *go*] *Scot* **:** DEPARTURE, LEAVE-TAKING, DEATH

wag-at-the-wall *var of* WAG-ON-THE-WALL

1wage \'wāj\ *vb -ED/-ING/-S* [ME *wagen* to pledge, give as security, engage, employ, fr. ONF *wagier,* fr. *wage* pledge] *vt* **1** *dial* **:** to put upon wages **:** ENGAGE, HIRE, EMPLOY ⟨won't be able to ~ them, like you ~ hands, at sixteen shillings a month —John Masefield⟩ **2 :** to bind oneself to **:** agree to abide the event of ⟨~ trial by battle⟩ — compare WAGER OF LAW **3 :** to engage in (as a contest) as if by previous gage or pledge **:** carry on actions that constitute or promote ⟨~ war⟩ ⟨~ a campaign⟩ ⟨~ a filibuster⟩ ⟨farmers still ~ a losing fight with poor, stony land —*Amer. Guide Series: Conn.*⟩ ⟨an intense game of bridge that had been *waged* en route —*N.Y.Times*⟩ ⟨we are now *waging* peace —J.F.Dulles⟩ **4** *obs* **:** to let out for hire or reward **:** hire out **5** [by alter.] **:** WEDGE *vt* 6 **~** *vi* **:** to be in process of occurring ⟨the riot *waged* for several hours —*Amer. Guide Series: Md.*⟩ ⟨controversy ~*s* even more fiercely —O. Elfrida Saunders⟩ ⟨financial splurge that *waged* across promotional circles —Claude Taylor⟩

2wage \"\ *n -s often attrib* [ME, pledge, security, wage, fr. ONF, of Gmc origin; akin to Goth *wadi* pledge — more at WED] **1 a :** a pledge or payment of usu. monetary remuneration by an employer esp. for labor or services usu. according to contract and on an hourly, daily, or piecework basis and often including bonuses, commissions, and amounts paid by the employer for insurance, pension, hospitalization, and other benefits; *esp* **:** such remuneration paid to a skilled or unskilled laborer ⟨pelt . . . would bring about fifty dollars which wasn't a bad ~ for their two days' work —Robert Lund⟩ ⟨the starting ~ was $17.50 a month —J.L.Marshall⟩ ⟨~ freeze⟩ ⟨~ scale⟩

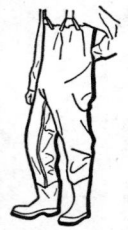

— often used in pl. but sometimes sing. in constr. ⟨a freeman makes himself a servant to another by selling him for a certain time the service he undertakes to do in exchange for ~s he is to receive —John Locke⟩ ⟨work by the day at lower ~s —*Current Biog.*⟩; see LIVING WAGE, MINIMUM WAGE; compare SALARY **b wages** *pl but sing or pl in constr* **:** the share of the annual product or national dividend that is the return to labor as distinct from the remuneration received by capital or land — compare INTEREST, PROFIT, RENT **2 :** RECOMPENSE, REQUITAL, REWARD — usu. used in pl. but sing. or pl. in constr.; used chiefly with *of* ⟨for the ~s of sin is death —Rom 6:23 (RSV)⟩ ⟨loving falsehood, ignorant of the ~s of uprightness —E.J. Goodspeed⟩ ⟨the gods give thee fair ~ and dues of death —A.C.Swinburne⟩

syn WAGE *or* WAGES, SALARY, STIPEND, FEE, PAY, HIRE, and EMOLUMENT can all mean the price paid someone for his labor or services. WAGE or WAGES applies chiefly to an amount paid daily or weekly esp. for chiefly physical labor ⟨earn a day's *wage*⟩ ⟨receives his *wages* in cash once a week⟩ SALARY and STIPEND usu. apply to a fixed compensation commonly paid at longer intervals than wages and usu. for services that require training or special ability, STIPEND often applying specially to the pay of a teacher, magistrate, or clergyman or to money received as from a scholarship or pension, and usu. implying a relatively small sum ⟨an executive's *salary*⟩ ⟨the *salary* of a white-collar worker⟩ ⟨a minister's *stipend* often includes the use of a house⟩ ⟨a modest *stipend* from a retirement policy⟩ FEE applies to the price asked or paid for the services of a physician, lawyer, artist, or other professional ⟨a lawyer's *fee*⟩ ⟨*a fee* for professional services⟩ ⟨pays its authors and illustrators very reasonable *fees* —Lilo Linke⟩ PAY is usu. the equivalent of WAGES, SALARY, or STIPEND ⟨a teacher's *pay*⟩ ⟨a porter's *pay*⟩ ⟨the *pay* scale of workers or executives⟩ ⟨a clergyman's *pay*⟩ HIRE is archaic in the sense of WAGES but occurs sometimes in the sense of *rental fee* ⟨lends his pen for small *hires* —George Meredith⟩ ⟨the films can be had at a reasonable *hire* charge —*Paper & Print*⟩ EMOLUMENT is bookish except in the plural when it often means the rewards, usu. other than pay, of one's work or office ⟨wages include *emoluments* of value, like pension and insurance benefits, which may accrue to employees out of their employment relationship —C.W.Boyce⟩ ⟨old institutions whose prestige, influence and *emoluments* of power depend upon the preservation of the old order —John Dewey⟩ ⟨salary £550 with no *emoluments* —*Farmer & Stock-Breeder*⟩ ⟨on observing women kissing the veteran Franklin, he asked if that was one of the *emoluments* of his office —C.G.Bowers⟩

wage bill *n* **:** the total amount paid in wages by a business establishment or industry usu. figured on an annual basis

wage board *n* **:** a board established by law to investigate wage rates

wage bracket *n* **:** a stipulated wage rate varying from a low limit to a high limit for a particular purpose

waged *adj* [ME, fr. past part. of *wagen* to engage, employ — more at WAGE] **:** receiving wages **:** HIRED ⟨large plots of ground at economic rents, and decently ~ people paying them —John Galsworthy⟩

wage dividend *n* **:** payment of a share of profits in a profit-sharing plan to employees in relation to dividends paid to stockholders and in relation to the proportionate earnings of each employee

wage earner *n* **:** one that works for wages or salary

wage-fund theory *or* **wages-fund theory** *n* **:** a theory in economics: there is at any one time a rigid capital fund available for wage payments, and increases in wage rates to any groups will only redistribute wage payments, not increase the aggregate of wages paid — compare IRON LAW OF WAGES, SUBSISTENCE THEORY

wage home *n* **:** a foster home in which children must earn their board by working

wag·el \ˈwagəl\ *or* **wagel gull** *var of* WAGGEL

wage·less \ˈwājləs\ *adj* **:** having no wages **:** UNPAID ⟨a ~ menial —Holbrook Jackson⟩ — **wage·less·ness** *n* -ES

wage level *n* **:** the approximate position of wages at any given time in any occupation or trade or esp. in industry at large

¹wa·ger \ˈwājə(r)\ *n* -S [ME *wageour*, wager pledge, bet, prize, fr. AF *wageure*, fr. ONF *wagier* to pledge + *-ure* — more at WAGE] **1 a :** something (as a sum of money) that is risked on an uncertain event **:** BET, STAKE, PRIZE ⟨laid a ~ of five dollars on the race⟩ **b :** an act of betting; *specif* **:** WAGERING CONTRACT ⟨the outcome may be sufficiently in doubt to make a true ~ possible —Oswald Jacoby⟩ **c :** something on which bets are laid **:** the subject of a bet **:** GAMBLE ⟨do a stunt as a ~⟩ **2** *archaic* **:** an act of giving a pledge to take and abide by the result of some action: as **a :** TRIAL BY BATTLE **b :** WAGER OF LAW

²wager \ˈ"\ *vb* **wagered; wagered; wagering** \-j(ə)riŋ\ **wagers** *vt* **:** to hazard on the issue of a contest or on a question that is to be decided or on a casualty **:** RISK, VENTURE; *specif* **:** to lay as a gamble ⟨~ five dollars on a horse⟩ ~ *vi* **:** to make a bet **:** lay a wager

³wag·er \ˈ"\ *n* -S **:** one that wages **:** one that engages in a contest or competition **:** COMPETITOR ⟨the great numbers of these fish show that they are successful ~s of life —William Beebe⟩

wage rate *n* **:** the amount of base wage paid to a worker per unit of time (as per hour or day) or per unit of output if on piecework

wage reopening *n* **:** the contractual right of a union or management to seek a change in wage rates at some specified time during the life of the contract

wa·ger·er \ˈwājərə(r)\ *n* -S **:** one that wagers **:** BETTOR

wagering *adj* [fr. gerund of ²*wager*] **:** relating to the act of one who wagers **:** BETTING

wagering contract *n* **:** a contract by which a promisor agrees that upon the occurrence of an uncertain event or condition he will render a performance for which there is no agreed consideration exchanged, and under which the promisee or the beneficiary of the contract is not made whole for any loss caused by such occurrence (as in options, insurance contracts, trading in futures, or betting contracts)

wager of battle [trans. of ML *vadiatio duelli*] **:** TRIAL BY BATTLE ⟨defiant men, accepting the *wager of battle* —D.D.Martin⟩

wager of law [trans. of ML *vadiatio legis*] **:** the act of a party having the negative in an action in early English law in giving a pledge or in binding himself to resort to and abide the event of an attempt to prove his case by the oath of himself and the required number of compurgators

wager policy *n* **:** a marine insurance policy covering property in which the insured does not possess an insurable interest capable of legal proof

wages *pres 3d sing of* WAGE, *pl of* WAGE

wage scale *n* **1 :** a schedule of rates of wages paid for related tasks **2 :** the level of wages paid by an individual employer

wages council *n* **:** TRADE BOARD

wage slave *n* **:** one whose toil for wages is tantamount to slavery

wage structure *n* **:** the schedule of wage differentials among jobs in a plant, industry, or country

wage system *n* **:** an industrial system in which free laborers are hired by capitalists to do a large part of the productive work of society as contrasted with slavery or serfdom on the one hand and small proprietorship on the other

wageworker \ˈ⸗,⸗\ *n* **:** WAGE EARNER

wagged *past of* WAG

wag·gel \ˈwagəl\ *or* **waggel gull** *n* [origin unknown] *Brit* **:** a black-backed gull in immature plumage

wag·ger \ˈwagə(r)\ *n* -S **:** one that wags

wag·gery \ˈwagərē, ˈwaag-, ˈwaig-, -ri\ *n* -ES [²*wag* + *-ery*] **1 :** the manner or action of a wag **:** mischievous merriment **:** PLEASANTRY, JOCULARITY, WAGGISHNESS ⟨witches of the conventional sort are an easy target for ~ —*Times Lit. Supp.*⟩ ⟨fair sample of early wartime radio ~ —*Coronet*⟩ **2 :** a bit of foolery **:** JEST; *esp* **:** PRACTICAL JOKE ⟨man given to little *waggeries* —Anthony Trollope⟩

wagging *pres part of* WAG

wag·gish \-gish, -gēsh\ *adj* [²*wag* + *-ish*] **1 :** resembling or characteristic of a wag **:** sportively or good-humoredly mischievous or roguish **:** FROLICSOME ⟨a company of ~ boys —Roger L'Estrange⟩ ⟨a ~ disposition⟩ **2 :** done or made in waggery or for sport **:** SPORTIVE, HUMOROUS ⟨a ~ trick⟩ — **wag·gish·ly** *adv* — **wag·gish·ness** *n* -ES

¹wag·gle \ˈwagəl, ˈwaig-\ *vb* **waggled; waggled; waggling** \-g(ə)liŋ\ **waggles** [freq. of ¹*wag*] *vt* **1 :** to move back and forth or up and down esp. repeatedly and with a jerky or undulating movement **:** WAG ⟨a bird ~s his tail⟩ ⟨*waggled* his forefinger in the air⟩ ⟨the pilot *waggled* his wings as a signal —F.B.Colton⟩ ⟨we grown-ups ~ our heads when we greet a baby —Benjamin Spock⟩ ⟨clenched a big fist and *waggled* it experimentally —L.C.Douglas⟩ **2 :** to impart a waggle to (a golf club) ~ *vi* **1 :** to move back and forth or up and down esp. repeatedly and with a jerky or undulating movement **:** WAG, WOBBLE ⟨boats were gently *waggling* at their moorings —Sylvia T. Warner⟩ ⟨prancing firmly, her flowered muslin bustle *waggling* as she went —F. Tennyson Jesse⟩ **2 :** to move with a pronounced swinging motion (as of the hips) **:** WADDLE ⟨teaching a maid to ~ provocatively —*New Yorker*⟩

²waggle \ˈ"\ *n* -S **:** an instance of waggling **:** a jerky motion back and forth or up and down **:** WOBBLE ⟨reminds them with a ~ of one gnarled finger —Fulton Oursler⟩; *specif* **:** a preliminary swinging of a golf club head back and forth over the ball in preparing to start the stroke

wag·gly \-g(ə)lē, -li\ *adj* [¹*waggle* + *-y*] **1 :** having a wavering or wobbly course ⟨a ~ path⟩ **2 :** characterized by a waggling movement ⟨a ~ dog⟩

wag·gon \ˈwagən\ *chiefly Brit var of* WAGON

wag·gy \ˈwagē\ *adj* -ER/-EST [¹*wag* + *-y*] **:** having a tendency to wag **:** given to wagging ⟨hounds with ~ tails⟩

wagh *var of* WAUGH

waging *pres part of* WAGE

wag·ner·esque \¦vägnə¦resk\ *adj, usu cap* [Richard *Wagner* †1883 + E *-esque*] **:** resembling or suggesting in style and treatment the work of Wagner

¹wag·ne·ri·an \(ˈ)väg¦nirēən, -¦ner-\ *adj, usu cap* [Richard *Wagner* †1883 Ger. tone poet, composer, and writer on music + E *-ian*] **1 :** relating to, characterized by, or resembling the theories or style of Wagner **2 :** belonging to, characteristic of, or suggestive of the operas of Wagner ⟨a *Wagnerian* singer⟩ ⟨misty, *Wagnerian* mountains —G.A.Wagner⟩ ⟨thunderstorms . . . capable of truly *Wagnerian* effects —Andrew Hamilton & Chandler Harris⟩

²wagnerian \ˈ"\ *n* -S *usu cap* [Richard *Wagner* †1883 + E *-ian*] **:** an admirer of the musical theories and style of Wagner

wag·ne·ri·an·ism \väg'nirēə,nizəm, -ˈner-\ *n* -S *usu cap* [²*wagnerian* + *-ism*] **:** WAGNERISM

wag·ner·ism \ˈvägnə,rizəm\ *n* -S *usu cap* [Richard *Wagner* †1883 + E *-ism*] **1 :** Wagner's theory and practice in the composition of opera **2 :** the influence of the work of Wagner in the world of music

¹wag·ner·ite \ˈvägnə,rit, ˈwag-\ *n* -S [G *wagnerit*, fr. F. M. von *Wagner* †1851 Ger. mining engineer + G *-it* -ite] **:** a mineral $Mg_2(PO_4)F$ consisting of a magnesium fluorophosphate and occurring in yellow monoclinic crystals and also in massive forms

²wag·ner·ite \ˈvägnə,rīt\ *n* -S *usu cap* [Richard *Wagner* †1883 + E *-ite*] **:** an adherent of Wagnerism **:** WAGNERIAN

wag·ner rearrangement \ˈvägnə(r)-\ *or* **wag·ner-meer·wein rearrangement** \-ˈmer,vīn-\ *n, usu cap W&M* [after Georg *Wagner* 19th cent. Russ. chemist] **:** a reaction that is applicable esp. to organic compounds containing a neopentyl or similar grouping, that is thought to proceed by way of a carbonium ion, and that involves change of the carbon skeleton (as from pinene to bornyl chloride by hydrogen chloride, from neopentyl iodide to *tert*-amyl acetate by silver acetate, or from methyl-*tert*-butyl-carbinol to tetramethyl-ethylene by acids) — compare PINACOLONE

wag·ner tuba \ˈvägnə(r)-\ *n, usu cap W* [after Richard *Wagner* †1883 Ger. composer] **:** a brass wind musical instrument between a French horn and a tuba in construction and timbre designed by Wagner and called for in his scores

¹wag·on \ˈwagən, ˈwaig- *sometimes* ˈwaag- *or* -gᵊŋ\ *n* -S *often attrib* [earlier *wagan, wagen, waghen*, fr. D *wagen*, fr. MD — more at WAIN] **1 a :** a heavy four-wheel usu. uncovered vehicle designed esp. for transporting bulky commodities and drawn orig. by animals ⟨ox ~⟩ but now often by a motor vehicle (as a tractor) ⟨freight ~⟩ ⟨farm ~⟩ ⟨~ road⟩ — see COVERED WAGON; compare CART, DRAY, VAN, WAIN

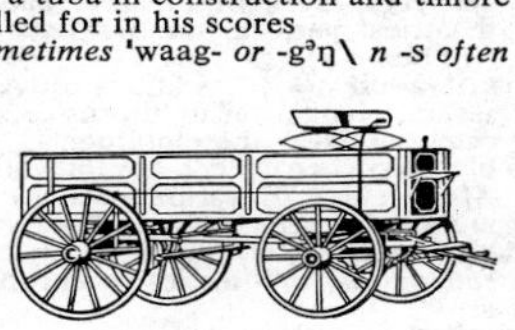
wagon 1a

b : a similar but lighter typically horse-drawn vehicle for transporting goods or passengers — see SPRING WAGON **c :** a four-wheeled cart, trailer, or powered vehicle for hauling men (as a fire-fighting squad, a police detail, or prisoners) or equipment ⟨hose ~⟩ ⟨searchlight ~⟩ ⟨sheriff's ~⟩; *specif* **:** PATROL WAGON ⟨call the ~⟩ **2** *Brit* **:** a vehicle for transporting goods on a railway corresponding in general to the American freight car but usu. of much smaller capacity — compare ³VAN 2 **3 :** a cart, trailer, motortruck, or small wheeled cabin used (as on the street or by a traveling show) esp. to dispense foods or other articles ⟨hotdog ~⟩ ⟨ice-cream ~⟩ ⟨popcorn ~⟩ ⟨ticket ~⟩ ⟨book ~⟩ **4 :** COASTER WAGON **5 :** a tool used by gold-beaters and others to cut and trim gold leaf and formed like a miniature sledge with runners of malacca reed that form the cutting edges **6 :** DINNER WAGON ⟨the waiter appeared . . . with his ~ of hors d'oeuvres —Gwethalyn Graham⟩ **7 :** a delivery truck ⟨bread ~⟩ ⟨milk ~⟩ **8 :** STATION WAGON **9 :** a low sliding or rolling platform used for the quick shifting of scenes on a theater stage — see WAGON STAGE **10 :** a large earth-moving trailer with a dump body — **off the wagon** *adv (or adj)* **:** no longer under pledge or resolution to abstain from alcoholic beverages — **on the wagon** *adv (or adj)* **:** under pledge or resolution to abstain from alcoholic beverages ⟨I do drink . . . but I'm *on the wagon* just now —Dan Wickenden⟩

²wagon \ˈ"\ *vb* -ED/-ING/-S *vi* **:** to travel or transport goods by wagon ⟨like ~*ing* on smooth, silent wheels across a roadless prairie —S.H.Adams⟩ ~ *vt* **:** to transport (goods) by wagon

wag·on·age \-gənij\ *n* -S [¹*wagon* + *-age*] **1** *archaic* **:** transportation by wagon **2** *archaic* **:** money paid for carriage or conveyance in a wagon

wagon boss *n* **1 :** a man in charge of a wagon train **2** *West* **:** a man in charge of a roundup

wagon box *also* **wagon bed** *n* **:** the body of a wagon

wagon breast *n* **:** a breast in a coal mine into which wagons can be taken

wagon ceiling *n* **:** BARREL CEILING

¹wag·on·er \-gənə(r)\ *n* -S [¹*wagon* + *-er*] **:** one that hauls heavy loads in a wagon **:** the driver of a wagon

²wagoner \ˈ"\ *n* -S [after Lucas J. *Waghenaer*, 16th cent. Du. cartographer] *archaic* **:** a book of nautical charts

wag·on·ette \¦wagə¦net\ *n* -S [¹*wagon* + *-ette*] **:** a light wagon having two facing seats along the sides back of a transverse seat in front and designed to carry six or more

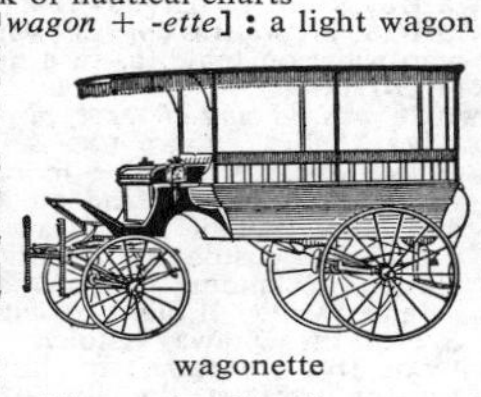
wagonette

wag·on·ful \ˈ⸗,ful\ *n* -S [¹*wagon* + *-ful*] **:** WAGONLOAD

wagon-head \ˈ⸗,⸗\ *or* **wagon-headed** \ˈ⸗,⸗⸗\ *adj* [¹*wagon* + *head* or *headed*] **:** barrel-vaulted ⟨*wagon-head* ceiling⟩

wagon jobber *or* **wagon distributor** *n* **:** a wholesaler or jobber who services retailers with merchandise (as grocery specialties) carried on a truck and thus combines selling with delivery

wa·gon-lit \vagōⁿˈlē\ *n, pl* **wagons-lits** *or* **wagon-lits** \-ē(z)\ [F, fr. *wagon* railroad car (fr. E ¹*wagon*) + *lit* bed, fr. L *lectus* — more at LIE] **1 :** a railroad sleeping car esp. of continental Europe having beds in separate compartments **2 :** a compartment or accommodation in a wagon-lit ⟨had engaged a *wagon-lit* —*Spectator*⟩

wagonload \ˈ⸗,⸗\ *n* **:** the quantity that a wagon contains ⟨~s of people⟩ ⟨a ~ of hay⟩

wagonmaker \ˈ⸗,⸗\ *n* **:** one that makes wagons

wag·on·man \ˈ⸗⸗mən\ *n, pl* **wagonmen 1 :** ¹WAGONER **2 :** FOOTMAN 2d

wagon master *n* **:** a person in charge of one or more wagons esp. for transporting freight

wagon roof *n* **:** BARREL ROOF

wagons *pl of* WAGON, *pres 3d sing of* WAGON

wagon seat *n* **:** a settee usu. in the form of a double chair with slat back and turned posts and used orig. both in the house and in the market wagon

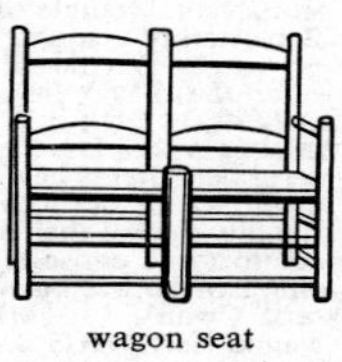
wagon seat

wagon sheet *n* **:** a sheet of canvas used esp. to cover a wagon or a truck bed

wagonsmith \ˈ⸗⸗,⸗\ *n* [¹*wagon* + *smith*] **:** one who builds and repairs wagons and carts

wagon soldier *n, slang* **:** ARTILLERYMAN

wagon stage *n* **1 :** WAGON 9 **2 :** a theater stage equipped with wagons for the quick shifting of scenes

wagon table *n* **:** DINNER WAGON

wag·on-the-wall *or* **wag-on-the-wall clock** \ˈ⸗⸗⸗-ˈ⸗-\ *also* **wag-at-the-wall** \ˈ⸗⸗⸗ˈ⸗\ *n* **:** a wall clock with pendulum and weights exposed

wagon top *n* **:** the enlarged rear part of the shell of a locomotive boiler over the furnace

wagon train *n* **:** a group of wagons (as of settlers or of supplies for a column of troops) traveling overland

wagon vault *n* **:** BARREL VAULT

wagonway \ˈ⸗⸗,⸗\ *n, archaic* **:** TRAMROAD

wagon wheel *n* **:** MILL

wagonwright \ˈ⸗⸗,⸗\ *n* **:** WAINWRIGHT

wagonyard \ˈ⸗⸗,⸗\ *n* **:** an enclosure where wagoners can put up their wagons and teams

wags *pres 3d sing of* WAG, *pl of* WAG

wagtail \ˈ⸗,⸗\ *n* [¹*wag* + *tail*] **1 :** any of numerous chiefly Old World birds (family Motacillidae) related to the pipits and having a trim slender body and a very long tail that they habitually jerk up and down — see PIED WAGTAIL, YELLOW WAGTAIL **2 :** a bird resembling a wagtail (as an American water thrush or an Australian fantail); *esp* **:** WILLIE WAGTAIL

wagtail flycatcher *n* **:** PIED WAGTAIL

¹wah \ˈwä\ *n* -S [fr. native name in Nepal, of imit. origin] **:** PANDA

²wah *var of* WAUGH

wah·ha·bi *or* **wa·ha·bi** \wəˈhäbē, wäˈ-, -bi\ *n* -S [Ar *wahhābīy*, fr. Muḥammad b. ʽAbd al-*Wahhāb* (Abdul-Wahhab) †1787 Arab religious reformer] **1** *cap* **:** a puritanical Muslim sect founded in Arabia in the 18th century by the reformer Muhammad ibn-Abdul Wahhab and revived by Ibn Saʽud in the 20th century **2** *usu cap* **:** a member of the Wahhabi sect

wah·ha·bism *or* **wa·ha·bism** \-ˈhä,bizəm\ *n* -S *cap* [*wahhabi* + *-ism*] **:** the doctrines or practice of the Wahhabi

wah·ha·bite *or* **wa·ha·bite** \-,bīt\ *n* -S *usu cap* [*wahhabi* + *-ite*] **:** WAHHABI 2

¹wa·hi·ne \wäˈhēnä\ *n* -S [Maori & Hawaiian] *Hawaii & NewZeal* **:** WOMAN, WIFE, SWEETHEART, MISTRESS

²wahine \ˈ"\ *adj, Hawaii & NewZeal* **:** FEMALE, FEMININE

wah·len·ber·gia \,wälənˈbərjēə\ *n, cap* [NL, fr. Göran *Wahlenberg* †1851 Swed. botanist + NL *-ia*] **:** a genus of perennial herbs (family Campanulaceae) chiefly of the southern hemisphere that differs from the closely related genus *Campanula* in the loculicidal capsule

¹wa·hoo \¦wä¦hü\ *also* **wha·hoo** \¦(h)w-\ *n* -S [Creek *ûhawhu* cork elm] **:** any of various American trees or shrubs: as **a :** ROCK ELM 1a **b :** WINGED ELM **c :** CASCARA BUCKTHORN **d :** BASSWOOD 1 **e :** UMBRELLA TREE 1

²wahoo *or* **waa·hoo** \ˈ"\ *n* -S [Dakota *wāhu*, lit., arrowwood] **:** either of two No. American spindle trees: **a :** a shrub or small shrubby tree (*Euonymus atropurpureus*) having purple capsules which in dehiscence expose the scarlet-ariled seeds and a root bark with cathartic properties — called also *burning bush* **b :** STRAWBERRY BUSH 1a

³wahoo \ˈ"\ *n* -S [origin unknown] **:** a large vigorous mackerel (*Acanthocybium solanderi*) that is bluish black above fading to gray or silvery below, is cosmopolitan in warm seas, and is highly esteemed for sport and food

⁴wahoo \ˈ"\ *interj, chiefly West* — used to express exuberance or enthusiasm or to attract attention

wah·pe·ku·te \ˈwäpə,küd·ē\ *n, pl* **wahpekute** *or* **wahpekutes** *usu cap* **1 :** a portion of the eastern forest group of the Dakota people **2 :** a member of the Wahpekute division of the Dakota people

wah·pe·ton \ˈwôpətən\ *n, pl* **wahpeton** *or* **wahpetons** *usu cap* **1 :** a portion of the eastern forest group of the Dakota people **2 :** a member of the Wahpeton division of the Dakota people

wah-wah *var of* WOU-WOU

wai·a·ta \ˈwīəd·ə\ *n* -S [Maori] **:** a Maori song usu. commemorative of some important event ⟨a ~ sung at tribal gatherings⟩

wai·cu·ri \wīˈkürē\ *n, pl* **waicuri** *or* **waicuris** *usu cap* **1 a :** an Indian people of southern Baja California in Mexico **b :** a member of such people **2 :** a language of the Waicuri people

waidner-burgess standard \¦wīdnər¦bərjəs-\ *n, usu cap W&B* [after Charles W. *Waidner* †1922 and George K. *Burgess* †1932 Am. physicists] **:** a unit of luminous intensity equal to the luminous intensity of one square centimeter of ideal black-body at the freezing point of platinum or to 60 candles

¹waif \ˈwāf\ *n* -S [ME, fr. ONF, adj., lost, unclaimed, prob. of Scand origin; akin to ON *veif* flapping or waving thing, *veifa* to wave — more at WIFE] **1 a** (1) **:** a piece of property (as something washed up by the sea or a stray animal) whose owner cannot be found — often used in the expression *waifs and strays* (2) **:** the right (as of the lord of the manor in medieval law) to such property **b waifs** *pl* **:** stolen goods thrown away by a thief in his flight claimable by the king or by the lord of the manor if the king has granted him franchise of waif but recoverable by the owner if he prosecutes the thief to conviction **2 a :** something found without an owner; *esp* **:** something that comes along by chance **:** a stray bit ⟨a ~ of travel lore from the mysterious Orient —J.L.Lowes⟩ **b :** a stray person or animal (as a homeless child or a lost sheep) **:** VAGRANT ⟨street ~s . . . were fed —*N. Y. Times*⟩ ⟨a lonely ~ of a cat —Richard Lockridge⟩

²waif \ˈ"\ *adj* **1** *chiefly Scot* **:** VAGRANT **2** *chiefly Scot* **:** CIRCULATING, CURRENT — used of a report or rumor ⟨heard a ~ word . . . that you were a hard man to drive —R.L.Stevenson⟩

³waif \ˈ"\ *n* -S [prob. of Scand origin; akin to ON *veif* waving thing] **1 :** a small flag or other device set to mark the position and establish prior right to the floating body of a harpooned whale **2 :** WAFT 4

⁴waif \ˈ"\ *vt* -ED/-ING/-S **:** to mark or signal the position of (as a harpooned whale) with a waif

wai·il·at·pu·an \(¦)wī¦ilət¦püən\ *or* **wai·lat·pu·an** \¦wīlə-\ *n, pl* **waiilatpuan** *or* **waiilatpuans** *or* **wailatpuan** *or* **wailatpuans** *usu cap* [Cayuse *Wayúletpu* Cayuse men + E *-an*] **1 a :** an American Indian people of northern Oregon comprising the Cayuse and the Molala **b :** a member of such people **2 :** a language family consisting of the languages of the Cayuse and the Molala peoples

¹wail \ˈwāl, *esp before pause or consonant* -āəl\ *vb* -ED/-ING/-S [ME *wailen, weilen*, of Scand origin; akin to ON *væla, vāla* to wail; akin to ON *vei* woe — more at WOE] *vi* **1 :** to express sorrow audibly **:** make mournful outcry **:** LAMENT, WEEP ⟨a child ~*ing* for his mother⟩ **2 :** to make a sound resembling or suggestive of a mournful cry ⟨deep in the grass . . . the curlew ~*ed* —Eve Langley⟩ **3 :** to express dissatisfaction plaintively **:** COMPLAIN ⟨stop ~*ing* about our divisions and emphasize our unity —W.E.Barton⟩ ~ *vt, archaic* **:** to grieve over **:** BEWAIL ⟨~ her wretched fate —William Morris⟩

²wail \ˈ"\ *n* -S [ME, fr. *wailen*] **1 :** the act, process, or practice of wailing **:** loud lamentation **:** KEEN ⟨there was weeping and ~ from young and old —Tom Taylor⟩ **2 a :** a usu. prolonged cry or sound expressing grief or pain ⟨a long broken ~ of pain —Scott Fitzgerald⟩ **b :** a sound suggestive of wailing ⟨the ~ of an air-raid siren⟩ **c :** a querulous expression of grievance **:** COMPLAINT ⟨their ~s penetrated the offices of local officialdom —*N. Y. Times*⟩

wai·la·ki \ˈwīləkē\ *n, pl* **wailaki** *or* **wailakis** *usu cap* [Wintun *wailaka*, lit., northern language] **1 a :** an Athapaskan people of the Eel river basin in northwestern California **b :** a member

of such people **2 :** a dialect of the Kato language spoken by the Wailaki people

wail·er \ˈwālə(r)\ *n* -s **:** one that wails; *specif* **:** a professional mourner

wail·ful \ˈ=fəl\ *adj* **1 :** expressing grief or pain **:** SORROWFUL, MOURNFUL ⟨tangle her desires with ~ sonnets —*Shak.*⟩ **2 :** uttering a sound suggestive of mourning or wailing ⟨the ~ bagpipes⟩ ⟨the ~ sough of the wind through the trees⟩ — **wail·ful·ly** \-fəlē, -li\ *adv*

wail·ing·ly *adv* **:** in a wailing manner

wailing wall *n* [fr. the *Wailing Wall,* ancient wall on Mt. Zion, Jerusalem that is held by Jews to be the remains of the Temple destroyed by the Romans in A.D. 70 and at which they traditionally bewail their loss and seek consolation] **:** a source of comfort and consolation in misfortune ⟨a soldier making the chaplain's office his *wailing wall*⟩

wain \ˈwān\ *n* -s [ME, fr. OE *wægn, wæn;* akin to MD *wagen* wagon, cart, OHG *wagan,* ON *vagn* wagon, cart, OE *wegan* to move, carry, *weg* way — more at WAY] **1 :** a usu. large and heavy vehicle for farm use **:** WAGON, CART ⟨a hay ~ on a meadow —Wolfgang Born⟩ **2** *archaic* **:** CHARIOT

wain·age \-nij\ *n* -s [ONF *waaignage,* fr. *waaignier* to till, earn, gain (of Gmc origin) + *-age;* akin to OHG *weidanōn* to hunt, search for food — more at GAIN] **:** implements of feudal husbandry

wain·man \ˈ=mən\ *n, pl* **wainmen** [ME, fr. ¹*wain* + *man*] **:** ¹WAGONER

¹**wain·scot** \ˈwānzkət, -nsk- *also* -nz,kä| *or* -nz,kō| *or* -n,skä| *or* -n,skō|; *usu* |d·+V; *also chiefly Brit* ˈwen-\ *n* -s [ME, fr. MD *wagenschot,* prob. fr. *wagen* wagon, cart + *schot* shot, crossbar, wooden partition; akin to OE *scot* shot — more at WAIN, SHOT] **1 a** *Brit* **:** a fine grade of oak imported for woodwork **b** (1) **:** a wooden lining of an interior wall usu. paneled (2) **:** a lining of an interior wall irrespective of material ⟨a tile ~⟩ **c :** the lower three or four feet of an interior wall when finished differently from the remainder of the wall (as with wood panels, tile, or marble slabs) **2 :** any of various European and American noctuid moths belonging to the genera *Leucania* and *Cirphis* that are reddish or yellowish and are streaked or lined with black and white and that in the larval stage are army worms

²**wainscot** \"\ *vt* **wainscoted** *also* **wainscotted; wainscoted** *also* **wainscotted; wainscoting** \-ōd·iŋ, |t|, |ēŋ *also* -ə| *or* -ä|\ *also* **wainscotting** \-ə|, -ä|\ **wainscots** \-əts *also* -äts *or* -ōts\ **:** to line (as a wall) with or as if with boards or paneling ⟨~ a hall⟩ ⟨~*ed* with looking glass —Joseph Addison⟩

³**wainscot** \"\ *adj* **1 :** made of wainscot ⟨a ~ door⟩ **2 :** resembling or suggestive of wainscot (as in hardness or color) ⟨a ~ face⟩ **3** *or* **wainscoted :** provided with or lined with a wainscot or with paneling of any sort ⟨a ~ wall⟩ ⟨a ~ seat⟩

wainscot chair *n* **:** a very early Colonial heavy oak chair of framed construction with solid panels in back and seat and sometimes turned posts and carved back

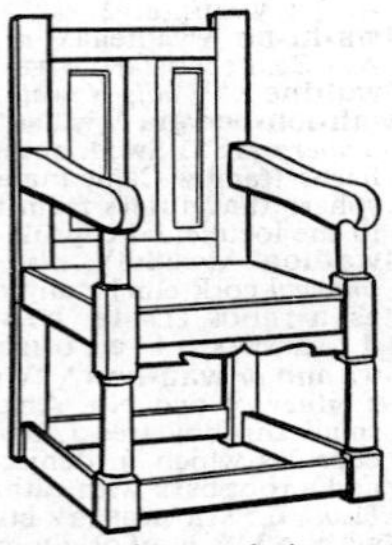
wainscot chair

wain·scot·ing *also* **wain·scot·ting** \-ōd·iŋ, |t|, |ēŋ *also* -ə| *or* -ä|\ *n* -s [fr. gerund of ²*wainscot*] **1 :** the material used to wainscot a house **2 :** WAINSCOT 1b, 1c, PANELING

wainscot oak *n* **:** ¹TURKEY OAK

wainwright \ˈ=,=\ *n* [OE *wægnwyrhta,* fr. *wægn* wagon + *wyrhta* worker, maker — more at WAIN, WRIGHT] **:** a maker and repairer of wagons

wair *Scot var of* ⁶WARE

waist \ˈwāst\ *n* -s [ME *wast, waste,* fr. (assumed) OE *wæst* growth; akin to OE *wæstm* growth, increase, ON *vǫxtr,* Goth *wahstus* growth, increase, OE *weaxan* to grow, increase — more at WAX] **1 a :** the part of the human body immediately below the ribs or thorax **:** the small part of the body between the thorax and hips **b :** the greatly constricted basal part of the abdomen of some insects (as various wasps and flies) **2 :** the part of something that corresponds in position to or in some way resembles the human waist **:** the middle or central part esp. when narrower or less thick than the ends ⟨the ~ of a boiler⟩ ⟨the ~ of a saddle⟩ ⟨the ~ of a violin⟩ ⟨the narrow ~ of a peninsula⟩: as **a :** the part of a vessel's deck between the poop and forecastle **:** the middle part of a sailing vessel between foremast and mainmast **b :** the smallest part of a shoe or last between the ball and instep **c** (1) **:** the narrow after-portion of the fuselage of an airplane (2) **:** the middle section of the fuselage of a bomber **3** *obs* **:** a belt for the waist **:** GIRDLE **4 a :** a garment or the part of a garment covering the body from the neck to the waistline or just below: (1) **:** the upper part of a woman's dress (2) **:** BLOUSE (3) **:** a child's undergarment to which other garments may be buttoned **b :** WAISTLINE

waist anchor *n* **:** SHEET ANCHOR

waist·band \ˈwās(t)+,-\ *n* **:** a band or sash worn around the waist; *specif* **:** a fitted band forming the top edge of trousers, shorts, breeches, or skirt or the lower edge of a sweater, blouse, or jacket

waist board *n* **:** temporary planking in the waist and esp. in the gangway of a ship to protect against seas

waist boat *n* **:** a boat carried in the waist of a whaling vessel on the port side and usu. commanded by the second mate

waistcloth \ˈ=,=\ *n* **1 a waistcloths** *pl* **:** cloths hung about a ship's waist as adornment or as a screen for the men when in action **b :** HAMMOCK CLOTH **2 :** LOINCLOTH

waist·coat \ˈweskə|t, ˈwā,skō|, ˈwāst,kō|, *usu* |d·+V\ *n* **1 :** an ornamental garment worn under a doublet, pulled through at the slashes, and sometimes showing at the neck and cuffs **2 a** *chiefly Brit* **:** a short sleeveless collarless coat for men worn under a jacket **:** VEST **b :** a garment of similar design ⟨a life-saving ~⟩ **3 a** *obs* **:** a woman's garment resembling a man's vest and worn to show underneath a gown **b :** such a short coat worn by a woman as an outer garment **4** *archaic* **a :** a man's undershirt **b :** a woman's camisole

waist·coat·ed \-kə|d·əd, -kō|, |təd\ *adj* **:** having or wearing a waistcoat ⟨a ~ gentleman⟩

waist-deep \ˈ=ˈ=\ *adj* **1 :** rising to the waist **:** WAIST-HIGH ⟨the water was only *waist-deep* at one end of the pool⟩ **2 :** sunk to the waist ⟨stood *waist-deep* in the surf⟩

waist·ed \ˈwāstəd\ *adj* **1 :** having a waist of a specified kind — usu. used in combination ⟨long-*waisted*⟩ ⟨wasp-*waisted*⟩ **2 :** shaped like a waist

waist·er \ˈwāstə(r)\ *n* -s **:** a usu. green or broken-down seaman stationed in the waist of a ship (as a whaling vessel)

waist-high \ˈ=ˈ=\ *adj* **1 :** reaching to or being at the level of the waist ⟨*waist-high* waves⟩ ⟨the batter let a good *waist-high* ball go by⟩ **2 :** reaching only a middle level in quality **:** MEDIOCRE ⟨a *waist-high* culture⟩

waist·less \ˈwāstləs\ *adj* **:** having no waist **:** UNSHAPELY

waistline \ˈ=,=\ *n* **1 :** an arbitrary line encircling the narrowest part of the waist; *specif* **:** the part of a garment that covers this natural line of the waist and that may be above or below it as fashion dictates **2 :** body circumference at the waist or belly **:** GIRTH ⟨dieting to reduce the ~⟩

waist sheet *n* **:** a vertical steel plate that secures the waist of a locomotive boiler to the frames of the locomotive allowing at the same time a small amount of expansion and contraction — compare BELLY BRACE

¹**wait** \ˈwāt, *usu* -ād·+V\ *vb* -ED/-ING/-S [ME *waiten,* fr. ONF *waitier* to watch, of Gmc origin; akin to OHG *wahta* watch, guard, *wahhēn, wahhōn* to watch, be awake — more at WAKE] *vt* **1 a :** to stay in place or remain inactive in expectation of **:** stay for **:** AWAIT ⟨~*ed* his turn to play⟩ ⟨horses . . . ~*ing* their riders —L.C.Douglas⟩ ⟨~*ed* their coming with dignity —Elizabeth Middleton⟩ **b** (1) **:** to hold back in expectation of **:** delay in hope of **:** defer until ⟨~ a favorable opportunity⟩ ⟨~*ed* a better day —*Century Mag.*⟩ ⟨~*ed* her chance —Amelia Walden⟩ (2) **:** to delay in hope of a favorable change in or cessation of ⟨wait out the stock market⟩ ⟨wait out a storm⟩ **2** *archaic* **:** to accompany with ceremony or respect **:** attend on **:** ESCORT ⟨bids him ~ her to her sacred dome —Alexander Pope⟩ **3** *archaic* **:** to be ready or available for ⟨tea and coffee ~ your pleasure in the drawing room —R.S.Surtees⟩ **4 :** to delay serving (a meal) **:** put off **:** HOLD, KEEP ⟨~*ed* dinner for the latecomers to arrive⟩ **5 :** to serve the eaters sitting at ⟨earned a few dollars ~*ing* table —Ralph Ellison⟩ ~ *vi* **1 a :** to remain stationary in readiness or expectation ⟨sat and ~*ed* for the man in charge⟩ ⟨~*ing* in line for hours⟩ ⟨kept us ~*ing* in the rain⟩ **b** *obs* **:** to remain hopeful and trusting ⟨truly my soul *waiteth* upon God —Ps 62:1 (AV)⟩ **c** (1) **:** to linger expectantly at or near a place **:** hang around ⟨~*ing* around hoping to see a celebrity⟩ (2) *of a hawk* **:** to circle above the hunter till the game is sprung **d :** to pause or halt for another to catch up ⟨~*ed* up for me . . . and we went along side by side —Helen Eustis⟩ **e** *South & Midland* **:** to stay expectantly for another to speak or act ⟨come on, we're ~*ing* on you⟩ **f :** to delay going to bed ⟨~*ed* up to see a late show on television⟩ **2 a :** to look forward expectantly ⟨~*ing* to see his rival lose⟩ ⟨~*ing* for the shell to explode⟩ **b :** to hold back expectantly **:** delay until the proper condition has come about ⟨~*ing* for his chance to strike⟩ ⟨a land where wealth ~*ed* on a lot of hard work —J.H.Plumb⟩ ⟨~*ed* till the war's end to get married⟩ **c :** to hold back in a competition (as a race) with the expectation of closing strong to win in the final stage ⟨~*ed* off, well behind the leaders, until the last lap⟩ **3 a** *archaic* (1) **:** to be in readiness to serve or execute orders ⟨they also serve who only stand and ~ —John Milton⟩ (2) **:** to act as an attendant ⟨maids of honor to ~ upon the queen —*Amer. Guide Series: Md.*⟩ (3) *South & Midland* **:** to attend a bride or groom at a wedding ceremony **b :** to supply the wants of another **:** SERVE ⟨~*ed* on her children hand and foot⟩ **c :** to serve at meals **:** be a waiter ⟨specialized either in ~*ing* or in cookery —G.V.Selsey⟩ — usu. used in the phrases *wait at table* or *wait on table* ⟨as a student he ~*ed* at table for two years⟩ ⟨~*s* on tables when the restaurant is crowded⟩ **d :** to serve a customer or client (as in a shop) ⟨looked around for a salesgirl to ~ on her⟩ **e :** to serve as escort ⟨~*ed* upon the visiting dignitaries to their lodgings⟩ **4 :** to make a formal call ⟨a delegation ~*ed* on the commissioners —Meridel LeSueur⟩ **5 a :** to be ready and available ⟨a letter ~*ing* for you on the table⟩ ⟨slippers ~*ed* by the bed —Mary Cable⟩ ⟨ideas . . . ~*ing* for discovery —A.N.Whitehead⟩ **b :** to remain temporarily neglected ⟨your letter has ~*ed* longer than they often do —O.W.Holmes †1935⟩ **c :** to remain unrealized for a time ⟨the establishment of large purses ~*ed* until the seventies —*Amer. Guide Series: N.Y.*⟩ **6** *Brit* **:** PARK 1 **syn** see STAY — **in waiting :** in attendance (as at a royal court) — usu. used in combination ⟨lord-*in-waiting*⟩ ⟨ladies-*in-waiting*⟩

²**wait** \"\ *n* -s [ME *waite* watchman, watchman who sounds watch, public musician, watch, wait, fr. ONF, watchman, watch, of Gmc origin; akin to OHG *wahta* watch, guard] **1 a :** one of a band of public musicians in England employed usu. by a city to play for processions or at official or public entertainments ⟨the ~ who played the bagpipes —*London Calling*⟩ **b** (1) **:** one of a group of street or rustic serenaders who play or sing at night for small gratuities esp. around the Christmas season (2) **:** a piece of music provided by these musicians **c :** SHAWM; *esp* **:** one played by the town musicians of England **2 a :** a position from which a person in concealment can watch usu. with intent to attack or surprise **:** AMBUSH — used chiefly in the expression *lie in wait* ⟨thieves lying in ~ around the bend of the road⟩ **b :** a condition or attitude of watchfulness and expectancy ⟨anchored in ~ for early morning fishing —Fred Zimmer⟩ **3 a :** an act of waiting ⟨endless ~*s* that make up a soldier's life —Dixon Wecter⟩ **b :** a period of waiting ⟨a long ~ in line⟩ ⟨a week's ~ before delivery⟩; *specif* **:** a break or pause (as between the acts) in a theatrical performance **:** INTERMISSION ⟨run off the program without ~*s*⟩

wait-a-bit \ˈ==,=\ *n* [trans. of Afrik *wacht-en-bitje*] **:** any of several plants bearing thorns or stiff hooked appendages that catch and tear the clothing: as **a :** NEW ZEALAND BRAMBLE **b :** GREENBRIER **c :** any of various hawthorns **d** *southern Africa* **:** any of various acacias and mimosas **e :** GRAPPLE PLANT **f :** PRICKLY ASH **g** *West Indies* **:** COCKSPUR 2b

wait-awhile \ˈ==,=\ *n* -s **1 :** an Australian wattle tree (*Acacia colletioides*) that makes an impenetrable thicket **2 :** WAIT-A-BIT

waited *past of* WAIT

wait·er \ˈwād·ə(r), -ātə-\ *n* -s [ME, fr. *waiten* to wait + *-er*] **1 a** *archaic* **:** one that watches (as at a city gate) **:** WATCHMAN, GUARD **b** *Brit* **:** a customs official — compare LANDWAITER **2 :** one that waits or attends upon another: as **a** *obs* **:** a lord-in-waiting or lady-in-waiting **b** *dial South* **:** an attendant of the bride or groom at a wedding **c** *archaic* **:** MANSERVANT **d :** WAITING MAID **e :** a uniformed official attendant on the London stock exchange **f :** a man who waits on table (as in a hotel or restaurant) — compare COUNTERMAN **3 :** a vessel or tray on which something (as a breakfast or tea service) is carried **:** SALVER ⟨bringing a ~ laden with all he could desire —B.A.Williams⟩

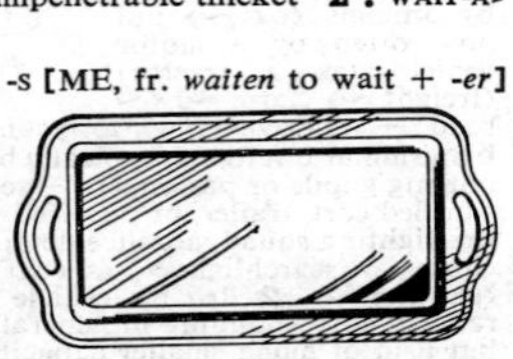
waiter 3

wait·er·ing \ˈwād·əriŋ, -ātər-, -ā·tr-, -rēŋ\ *n* -s **:** service or employment as a waiter ⟨worked at ~ in the evenings⟩

waiting *pres part of* WAIT

waiting game *n* **:** a strategy (as in a game) in which one or more participants withhold action for the time being in the hope of having a favorable opportunity for more effective action at a later period

waiting list *also* **wait list** *n* **:** a list or roster of those waiting (as for a professional or business opportunity, for election to a club, or appointment to a position) ⟨placed on the *waiting list* by the college admissions committee⟩ ⟨a long *wait list* for tourist class accommodations⟩

waiting maid *or* **waiting woman** *n* **:** a maid or woman who waits on another as a personal servant

waiting man *n* **:** a man who waits on another as a personal servant; *esp* **:** VALET

waiting move *n* **:** COUP DE REPOS

waiting period *n* **:** a stated period in various forms of insurance (as accident and health, workmen's compensation and unemployment or idleness insurance) after the beginning of disability during which no benefits are paid

waiting room *n* **:** a room for the use of persons waiting (as at a railroad station or in the office suite of a professional man or official)

waiting table *n* **:** SERVING TABLE

wait·ress \ˈwā·trəs\ *n* -ES [*waiter* + *-ess*] **:** a girl or woman who waits on table (as in a hotel or restaurant) — compare COUNTERGIRL

waits *pres 3d sing of* WAIT, *pl of* WAIT

waive \ˈwāv\ *vt* -ED/-ING/-S [ME *weiven,* fr. ONF *weyver,* fr. *waif* lost, unclaimed — more at WAIF] **1 :** to declare (as a woman failing to defend an accusation) outside the benefit and protection of feudal law **2 a** *archaic* **:** to give up (as a position, custom, or intention) **:** FORSAKE ⟨*waived* his intention of landing on that island, and steered for Ternate —James Mill⟩ **b** *obs* **:** to withdraw (as a motion) formally **3 :** to throw away (stolen goods) **:** ABANDON — compare ¹WAIF 1b **4** *archaic* **:** to shunt aside (as a danger or duty) **:** EVADE, DECLINE ⟨the most effectual mode of . . . *waiving* all discussions —Sir Walter Scott⟩ ⟨'tis still the wiser way to ~ contention with superior sway —Alexander Pope⟩ **5** *obs* **:** to neglect to take advantage of **:** DISREGARD **6 a :** to relinquish voluntarily (as a legal right) ⟨~ a jury trial⟩ ⟨~ fulfillment of certain onerous provisions of a contract⟩ **b :** to refrain from pressing or enforcing (as a claim or rule) **:** dispense with **:** FORGO ⟨~ a portion of the tax due⟩ ⟨~*s* his opposition to the bill⟩ ⟨~ the customary formalities⟩ ⟨*waived* the club rules to admit him⟩ **7 :** to put off from immediate consideration **:** DEFER, POSTPONE ⟨*waiving* this theory for the present, let us resume the inquiry —John Marshall⟩ **8 :** to dismiss (as a person or thought) with or as if with a wave of the hand ⟨evils . . . are not magically *waived* out of existence —John Dewey⟩ ⟨~ the whole business aside —O.S.J.Gogarty⟩ ⟨said "no" and *waived* them off —E.L.Masters⟩ **syn** see RELINQUISH

waiv·er \-və(r)\ *n* -s [AF *weyver,* fr. ONF *weyver* to abandon, waive (taken as a n.)] **1 :** the act of waiving or intentionally relinquishing or abandoning a known right, claim, or privilege ⟨the defendant's ~ of a jury trial⟩ ⟨a ~ of the privilege of immunity from prosecution⟩ ⟨a ~ of a contract provision⟩; *specif* **:** the relinquishment by a team of one professional baseball league of the right to buy the contract of a player at a stipulated price before he can go to a club of any other league ⟨asked for ~*s* on him and he left the big leagues for good —Christopher Mathewson⟩ **2 :** the document or legal instrument evidencing an act of waiving ⟨signed a ~ of immunity⟩

waiver of premium : a clause in an insurance policy providing continued coverage without payment of premiums under stated circumstances

wai·wai \ˈwī,wī\ *also* **woy·a·wai** *or* **woy·a·way** \ˈwȯiə,wī\ *n, pl* **waiwai** *or* **waiwais** *usu cap* **1 a :** a Cariban people of the borderlands of Brazil, British Guiana, and Surinam **b :** a member of such people **2 :** the language of the Waiwai people

wajang *var of* WAYANG

wa·ka \ˈwäkə\ *n* -s [Maori] **:** CANOE; *broadly* **:** a Maori seagoing craft

wa·kan \wäˈkän\ *or* **wa·kan·da** \-ndə\ *or* **wa·kon** \wäˈkän\ *or* **wa·kon·da** \-ndə\ *n* -s [Siouan] **:** a supernatural force similar to mana believed by the Sioux to pervade animate and inanimate objects in varying degrees sometimes giving them extraordinary powers and usu. assumed to be the cause of extraordinary happenings ⟨the eagle has ~, because it can soar higher than any other bird and for a longer time —W.D. Wallis⟩

wa·kash·an \wäˈkashən\ *or* **wa·kash** \-ˈkash\ *n, pl* **wakashan** *or* **wakashans** *or* **wakash** *or* **wakashes** *usu cap* [*wakash* fr. Nootka *waukash* good; *wakashan* fr. *Wakash* + *-an*] **1 :** a language family of British Columbia and Washington comprising Kwakiutl and Bellabella as the two main branches and Nootka **2 a :** a Wakashan-speaking people **b :** a member of any such people

wa·ka·ya·ma \ˌwäkəˈyämə\ *adj, usu cap* [fr. *Wakayama,* Japan] **:** of or from the city of Wakayama, Japan **:** of the kind or style prevalent in Wakayama

¹**wake** \ˈwāk\ *vb* **waked** \ˈwākt\ *or* **woke** \ˈwōk\ **waked** *or* **wok·en** \ˈwōkən\ *or* **woke; waking; wakes** [ME *waken* (past *wok, wook,* past part. *waken*), fr. OE *wacan* to wake, be born (past *wōc,* past part. *wacen*) and ME *waken, wakien* (past & past part. *waked*), fr. OE *wacian* to watch, be awake (past *wacode,* past part. *wacod*); akin to OE *wæccan* to watch, be awake, OHG *wahhēn, wahhōn,* ON *vaka,* Goth *wakan;* akin to OE *weccan* to rouse, stir, waken, OHG *wecchan,* ON *vekja,* Goth *uswakjan* to rouse, waken, L *vegēre* to rouse, excite, be active, Skt *vāja* strength, speed, vigor, contest, prize] *vi* **1 a :** to be or continue awake **:** refrain from sleep ⟨usually asleep, and in our *waking* hours always held back —Sir Winston Churchill⟩ **b** *obs* **:** to work all night **:** stay awake engaged in activity **c :** to remain awake on watch or guard esp. over a sick person or a corpse **d** *obs* **:** to stay up late in revelry ⟨the king doth ~ tonight, and takes his rouse —*Shak.*⟩ **2 a :** to become roused from sleep **:** stop sleeping **:** AWAKE ⟨soon *woke* refreshed —Eudora Welty⟩ ⟨ruffled his hair as if he had just *woken* —Audrey Barker⟩ — often used with *up* ⟨I *waked up* at 3 o'clock in the morning —Joyce Cary⟩ ⟨the boy had *waked* from dreams —Ralph Robin⟩ **b :** to become stirred from a dormant, torpid, or inactive state ⟨*woke* out of his trance —O.S.J.Gogarty⟩ ⟨the old feelings had *woken* —Rumer Godden⟩ — often used with *up* ⟨on national holidays . . . the little place ~*s* up —Tom Marvel⟩ **c :** to enter into a new state of awareness or consciousness **:** become free from misconception or illusion ⟨has *woken* up and . . . rescinded its previous resolution —*Cape Town (So. Africa) Monitor*⟩ — usu. used with *to* ⟨social scientists have *waked* to the story's importance —Roger Burlingame⟩ ⟨*woke* up to the fact that this was a delusion —*Atlantic*⟩ ~ *vt* **1 :** to stand watch over (as a dead body) **:** hold a wake over ⟨will be *waked* at the church rectory —*Springfield (Mass.) Union*⟩ ⟨*waked* the departed term most gloriously over eggs, pie, and cider —W.G.Hammond⟩ **2 a :** to rouse from sleep **:** AWAKEN ⟨was *woken* by raucous bird cries —A.H.Barton⟩ — often used with *up* ⟨a young physicist *woke* up his wife —Laura Fermi⟩ ⟨is partly *waked up* . . . by the crying of one of his children —Edmund Wilson⟩ ⟨snakes are *woken* up by heat —T.H.White b. 1906⟩ **b :** to bring to motion, action, or life **:** STIR, EXCITE ⟨an offense against himself which *woke* his terrible wrath —H.E.Scudder⟩ ⟨his tears *woken* and then held back —H.E.Bates⟩ ⟨*woke* up latent possibilities —Norman Douglas⟩ **c :** to arouse conciousness or interest in **:** ALERT ⟨what ~*s* him up is the horrified refusal of his future wife to be kissed —Anthony Quinton⟩ — usu. used with *to* ⟨*woke* the publishers to the fact that there was an enormous . . . audience —Harrison Smith⟩ **d** (1) *archaic* **:** to break the silence of ⟨no wind *waked* the wood —C.K.D. Patmore⟩ (2) **:** to cause (an echo) to resound ⟨his great laugh *woke* distant echoes in the forest —Irving Bacheller⟩

²**wake** \"\ *n* -s [ME, fr. *waken, wakien* to wake] **1 :** the state of being awake **:** a condition of sleeplessness ⟨making such difference twixt ~ and sleep —*Shak.*⟩ **2** [trans. of ML *vigilia;* fr. the early church custom of preceding certain festivals by services lasting through the night] **a** (1) **:** an annual English parish festival formerly held in commemoration of the church's patron saint either on the saint's day or on a selected Sunday (2) **:** a vigil of fasting and prayer formerly held on the night prior to a wake or other feast day **b :** a period of festivities usu. including a fair or market orig. connected with the wake of an English parish church — usu. used in pl. but sing. or pl. in constr. ⟨fairs, markets, folk dancing and all kinds of amusements characterize *Wakes* Week celebration —Dorothy G. Spicer⟩ **c** *Brit* **:** an annual holiday or vacation from work — usu. used in pl. but sing. or pl. in constr. ⟨the ~*s* . . . had closed the workshops —*Manchester Examiner*⟩ **3 a :** a watch held over the body of a dead person prior to burial and sometimes accompanied by festivity ⟨when the boys gather to hold a ~ . . . they'll have to bring their own drinking —F.B.Gipson⟩ ⟨mourn their dead with the primitive wails of a Corsican ~ —Marguerite Yourcenar⟩ **b :** a gathering or party marking a change of circumstance likened to a wake ⟨the bridal ~ that the villagers gave —*Christian Science Monitor*⟩ ⟨a few old friends . . . hold a brief ~ over old days —J.R. Allan⟩

³**wake** \"\ *adj* [ME, by shortening] **:** AWAKE ⟨whose struggle is to keep the world of ~ men from their sleep world —E.J. Fitzgerald⟩

⁴**wake** \"\ *n* -s [of Scand origin; akin to ON *vǫk* hole, opening in the ice, Sw *vak,* Dan *vaage;* akin to MD *wak* damp, wet — more at HUMOR] **1 :** the track left by a ship or other body in the water ⟨the ~ of a ship showing green and white —Stewart Beach⟩ ⟨beaver ~*s* glistening under the moonlight —R.M. Ormes⟩; *broadly* **:** a turbulent condition of the air or other fluid left behind by a body moving through it ⟨the ~ of an airplane wing⟩ **2 :** the path of light left or apparently left by a moving luminous body or its reflection ⟨staring out over the water at the figure receding beyond the moon's ~ —R.O. Bowen⟩ **3 :** the visible or otherwise detectable trace of a body moving on land ⟨a big red truck passes . . . and a billowing ~ of dust floats toward the house —Helen Upshaw⟩ — **in the wake of 1 a :** in the immediate rear of ⟨when alighting from the train, unless . . . others are getting out *in your wake* —Agnes M. Miall⟩ ⟨*in the wake of* trappers and solitary riflemen came land-hungry settlers —*Amer. Guide Series: Ind.*⟩ ⟨we scrambled *in the wake of* their powerful, barging bodies —Christopher Isherwood⟩ **b :** in the slot or path behind an opening (as in a canvas covering) through which something (as a mast) protrudes **2 :** in the path or territory passed over by ⟨the floods began to recede leaving swamps *in their wake* —V.W.Turner⟩ ⟨sacked and burned as they went, leaving scarcely a cabin *in their wake* —*Amer. Guide Series: La.*⟩ **3 :** as a result of **:** as a consequence of ⟨responsibilities which follow *in the wake of* war —F.D.Roosevelt⟩ ⟨mass immigration . . . brought *in its wake* grave problems of public health and poor relief —*Amer. Guide Series: N.Y.*⟩

wake·ful \ˈwākfəl\ *adj* **1 :** WATCHFUL, VIGILANT **2 :** not sleeping or able to sleep **:** SLEEPLESS, RESTLESS ⟨books for night

reading when ~ —Agnes M. Miall⟩ — **wake·ful·ly** \-fəlē, -li\ *adv* — **wake·ful·ness** \-lnə̇s\ *n* -ES

wake gain *n* **:** an increase in the propeller thrust of a ship due to the forward motion of the wake

wake·less \ˈwāklə̇s\ *adj, of sleep* **:** SOUND, UNBROKEN

wak·en \ˈwākən\ *vb* **wakened; wakened; wakening** \-k(ə)niŋ\ **wakens** [ME *waknen, wakenen,* fr. OE *wæcnan, wæcnian;* akin to ON *vakna* to awaken, Goth *gawaknan;* derivative fr. the root of E ¹*wake*] *vi* **1 :** to become active, aware, or animated ⟨a vigorous artist's shaping spirit may chance to ~ —Warren Beck⟩ ⟨~ to the point about seven minutes after —H.J.Laski⟩ **2 :** to cease to sleep **:** AWAKE ⟨had ~*ed* and heard the lion —Ernest Hemingway⟩ — often used with *up* ⟨pleasant to ~ up in that bed —Willa Cather⟩ ~ *vt* **1 :** to stir or rouse out of sleep **:** WAKE ⟨~*ed* at 5:30 by reveille —*Harper's*⟩ **2 :** to excite into life, activity, or awareness ⟨stained glass in churches always ~*ed* some strange fancy in his mind —T.B.Costain⟩ ⟨~ the reader's sympathy for the man or woman involved —C.B.Tinker⟩ — often used with *up* ⟨~*s* up . . . government agencies to the wanton waste —*Canadian Forum*⟩ **syn** see STIR

wak·en·er \-k(ə)nə(r)\ *n* -S **:** one that causes to waken

wak·en·ing \-k(ə)niŋ, -nēŋ\ *n* -S [ME, fr. gerund of *wakenen* to waken] **1 :** AWAKENING **2** *Scots law* **:** revival of an action or of the process for it

wak·er \ˈwākə(r)\ *n* -S [ME, fr. *waken* to wake + *-er*] **1 :** WAKENER **2 :** one that is wakened

wake·rife \ˈwā,krīf\ *adj* [ME (Sc) *walkryfe,* fr. *walk* awake (fr. *walken, waken* to wake, fr. OE *wacan*) + *ryfe* rife, fr. OE *rȳfe* — more at WAKE, RIFE] *Scot* **:** WAKEFUL, WATCHFUL, ALERT

wake-robin \ˈ=,==\ *n* [prob. fr. ¹*wake* + *robin*] **1** *Brit* **a :** a plant of the genus *Arum; esp* **:** CUCKOOPINT **b :** SPOTTED ORCHIS **2 a :** any of various American plants of the genus *Trillium* **b :** ARROW ARUM **c :** an American plant of the genus *Arisaema; esp* **:** JACK-IN-THE-PULPIT **3 :** any of several tropical American plants of the genera *Anthurium* and *Philodendron*

wakes *pres 3d sing of* WAKE, *pl of* WAKE

¹**wake-up** \ˈ=,=\ *n* -S [fr. *wake up,* v.] **:** FLICKER

²**wake-up** \ˈ"\ *n* -S [fr. *wake up,* v.] *Austral* **:** a person on the alert **:** one not likely to be fooled

wakf *var of* WAQF

wak·hi \wäkˈhē\ *n, pl* **wakhi** *or* **wakhis** *usu cap* **1 :** an Indo-European people of Alpine type on the northern slope of the Hindu Kush **2 :** a member of the Wakhi people

waking *pres part of* WAKE

wakon *or* **wakonda** *var of* WAKAN

wa·kore \wäˈkōr\ *n, pl* **wakore** *or* **wakores** *usu cap* [Songhai] **:** SARAKOLLE

wal *abbr* walnut

WAL *abbr, often not cap* wider all lengths

walach *cap, var of* WALLACH

walachian *usu cap, var of* WALLACHIAN

wa·la·pai *also* **hua·la·pai** \ˈwälə,pī\ *or* **hual·pai** \-l,-\ *n, pl* **walapai** *or* **walapais** *also* **hualapai** *or* **hualapais** *or* **hualpai** *or* **hualpais** *usu cap* [Yuman *Xawálapáiya,* lit., pine tree people] **1 a :** an Indian people of the central Colorado river valley, Arizona **b :** a member of such people **2 :** a Yuman language of the Walapai people

wal·chia \ˈwalkēə, ˈwöl-\ *n, cap* [NL, fr. Johann E. I. *Walch* †1778 Ger. mineralogist + NL *-ia*] **:** a genus of pinaceous fossil trees that resemble araucarias, are characteristic of the Permian but range through the Triassic, and have short triangular spirally arranged falcate leaves and ovate cones with persistent ovate scales

wal·den inversion \ˈwöldən-\ *n, usu cap W* [after Paul *Walden* †1957 Latvian organic chemist] **:** an inversion of configuration of one optically active compound into another that may or may not lead to a change in the direction of optical rotation and that may be of either of two general types: **a :** inversion involving two reactions in which an optically active compound is changed to another by substitution at its asymmetric center and then regenerated (as *dextro*-alanine is changed to *levo*-bromo-propionic acid by nitrosyl bromide and then to *levo*-alanine by ammonia) but as the optical isomer of the original compound **b :** inversion involving one reaction of an optically active compound at its asymmetric center with resulting configurational change from D to L or vice versa regardless of change in optical rotation (as from levorotatory L-bromo-propionic acid to levorotatory D-alanine by ammonia but not from dextrorotatory L-alanine to levorotatory L-bromo-propionic acid because no inversion of configuration occurs although optical inversion does)

wal·den·ses \wälˈden(t)sēz, wöl-\ *or* **val·den·ses** \val-\ *n pl, usu cap* [ME *Waldensis,* fr. ML *Waldenses, Valdenses,* fr. Peter *Waldo* (or *Valdo*) *fl* 12th cent. A.D. Fr. heretic] **:** a body of Christians arising in southern France in the 12th century, adopting Calvinist doctrines in the 16th century, suffering severe persecution until recent times, and now living chiefly in Piedmont — called also *Vaudois*

¹**wal·den·si·an** \(ˈ)=ˈden(t)sēən\ *adj, usu cap* [*Waldenses* + E *-an*] **:** of, relating to, or constituting the Waldenses

²**waldensian** \ˈ"\ *n* -S *usu cap* **:** one of the Waldenses

wal·dey·er's plasma cell \ˈväl,dī(ə)rz-\ *n, usu cap W* [after Heinrich W. G. von *Waldeyer*-Hartz †1921 Ger. anatomist] **:** a coarsely granular connective tissue cell found esp. in the neighborhood of blood vessels

waldeyer's tonsillar ring *n, usu cap W* [after Heinrich von *Waldeyer*-Hartz] **:** a partial ring of tonsillar or adenoid tissue formed by the two palatine tonsils, the pharyngeal tonsil, and the lingual tonsil

waldeyer's vascular layer *n, usu cap W* [after Heinrich von *Waldeyer*-Hartz] **:** the vascular layer of the ovary

waldeyer's zonal layer *n, usu cap W* [after Heinrich von *Waldeyer*-Hartz] **:** LISSAUER'S TRACT

wald·flöte \ˈvält,flœtə\ *n* -S *usu cap* [G, lit., forest flute, fr. *wald* forest (fr. OHG) + *flöte* flute, fr. MF *flaute* — more at WOLD, FLUTE] **:** WALDFLUTE

wald·flute \ˈwöld,flüt, ˈvält,-\ *n* [part trans. of G *waldflöte*] **:** a soft pipe-organ flute stop of 8-foot and 4-foot pitch

wald·hei·mia \wöldˈhīmēə\ *n, cap* [NL, fr. G. F. von *Waldheim* †1853 Ger. paleontologist + NL *-ia*] **:** a genus of brachiopods closely resembling *Terebratula* but having longer brachial loops and including many fossil forms and a few that still exist in the deep sea

wald·horn \ˈwöld,hȯrn, ˈvält,-\ *n* [G, fr. MHG *walthorn,* lit., forest horn, fr. *walt* forest (fr. OHG *wald*) + *horn,* fr. OHG — more at HORN] **1 :** the old valveless hunting horn **:** NATURAL HORN — compare FRENCH HORN **2 :** a pipe-organ reed stop with a tone like that of a natural horn

wald·meister \ˈwöld,mīstə(r), ˈvält-\ *n* -S [G, lit., forest master, forest officer, fr. MHG *waltmeister,* fr. *walt* forest + *meister* master, fr. OHG *meistar,* fr. L *magister* — more at MASTER] **:** SWEET WOODRUFF

wal·dorf salad \ˈwöl,dȯrf-, -d(ə)f-\ *n, usu cap W* [fr. *Waldorf*-Astoria Hotel, N.Y. City] **:** a salad made typically of diced apples, celery, and nuts and dressed with mayonnaise

wald·stein·ia \wöldˈstīnēə\ *n, cap* [NL, fr. Franz A. von *Waldstein* †1823 Austrian botanist + NL *-ia*] **:** a genus of perennial herbs (family Rosaceae) of the north temperate zone resembling strawberries but having yellow flowers that have terminal styles and few carpels and are seated on a short hairy receptacle — see BARREN STRAWBERRY

¹**wale** \ˈwāl, *esp before pause or consonant* -āəl\ *n* -S [ME, fr. OE *walu;* akin to ON *valr* round, L *vola* hollow of the hand or foot, palm, sole, *volvere* to roll — more at VOLUBLE] **1 a :** a streak or ridge made on the skin esp. by the stroke of a whip **:** WEAL, WELT **b :** a narrow raised surface **:** RIDGE ⟨plowing the stubble into ~*s* —John Masefield⟩ **2 a :** one of a number of strakes usu. made of extra thick and strong planks in the sides of a wooden ship **:** ³BEND 2b — usu. used in pl.; see MAIN WALES **b** *obs* **:** GUNWALE **3 a** (1) **:** one of a series of even ribs in the warp or weft of a fabric or sometimes on the diagonal (2) **:** a lengthwise row of loops in a knitted fabric — compare COURSE **b :** the texture esp. of a fabric **4** *or* **whale** \ˈ(h)w-\ **:** a horizontal constructional member made of a strong material (as timber or steel) and used for bracing vertical members (as the sheeting of a trench) **5 :** one of the two ridges on the outside of a horse collar between which the hame lies **6 :** a course of weaving in basketmaking consisting of three or four rods worked alternately one after and over the other to form a binding ⟨a firmly woven ~ round the base is necessary to keep a good shape —Katherine S. Woods⟩ — see BASKET illustration

²**wale** \ˈ"\ *vt* -ED/-ING/-S **1 :** to mark (as the skin) with welts **2 a :** to wattle (as the web of a gabion) esp. with more than two rods at once **b :** to furnish (as a basket) with wales **3 :** to fasten or brace with a constructional wale

³**wale** \ˈ"\ *n* [ME (Sc & northern dial.) *wale, wal,* fr. ON *val* choice; akin to OHG *wala* choice, *wellen* to choose, ON *velja,* Goth *waljan* to choose, *wiljan* to wish — more at WILL] **1** *dial Brit* **:** the act of choosing **:** opportunity for choosing **:** CHOICE **2** *dial Brit* **:** the best one, ones, part, or kind **:** PICK ⟨scones, the ~ o' food —Robert Burns⟩

⁴**wale** \ˈ"\ *vb* -ED/-ING/-S [ME (Sc & northern dial.) *walen,* fr. *wale, wal* choice] *dial Brit* **:** CHOOSE

waled \ˈwā(ə)ld\ *adj, of a fabric* **:** having wales esp. of a specified kind — often used in combination ⟨a blouse of wide-*waled* white piqué —Lois Long⟩

walee *var of* WALI

wale knot *n* [by alter.] **:** WALL KNOT

walepiece \ˈ=,=\ *n* **1 :** ¹WALE 4 **2 :** a horizontal piece esp. of timber attached to a structure (as a pier) to ward off dangerous impact

¹**wal·er** \ˈwālə(r)\ *n* -S *often cap* [New So. *Wal*es, Australia + E *-er*] **:** a horse from New So. Wales **:** a rather large rugged saddle horse of mixed ancestry exported in quantity from Australia to British India for military use during the 19th century

²**waler** \ˈ"\ *or* **whal·er** \ˈ(h)w-\ *n* -S [¹*wale* or *whale* + *-er*] **:** ¹WALE 4

wales \ˈwālz, *esp before pause or consonant* -āəlz\ *adj, usu cap* [fr. *Wales,* peninsula on western part of the island of Great Britain] **:** of or from Wales **:** of the kind or style prevalent in Wales **:** WELSH

walhalla *usu cap, var of* VALHALLA

¹**wa·li** *also* **wa·lee** \ˈwälē\ *n* -S [Ar *walīy* (pl. *wulāt*)] **1 :** an Arab provincial governor **2 :** VALI 1

²**wali** \ˈ"\ *n* -S [Ar *walīy* (pl. *awliyāʼ*), lit., benefactor, guardian] **:** a Muslim saint

wal·ie \ˈwālī\ *var of* WALLY

wal·ing \ˈwāliŋ\ *n* -S [¹*wale* + *-ing*] **1 :** the constructional wales used for bracing vertical members (as the sheeting of a trench) **2 :** ¹WALE 4

wa·lise \wəˈlēs\ *Scot var of* VALISE

¹**walk** \ˈwȯk\ *vb* -ED/-ING/-S [ME *walken* (past *welk,* past part. *walke*), fr. OE *wealcan* to roll, toss (past *weolc,* past part. *wealcen*) and ME *walkien* (past *walkede,* past part. *walked*), fr. OE *wealcian* to roll up, muffle up; akin to MD *walken* to knead, beat, press, full, OHG *walchan,* ON *välka* to roll, L *valgus* bowlegged, Skt *valgati* he hops, jumps] *vi* **1 a** *obs* **:** to move onward or about **:** JOURNEY, ROAM, WANDER **b** (1) *of a spirit* **:** to move about in visible or otherwise perceptible form **:** APPEAR ⟨the time when . . . spirits ~ and ghosts break up their graves —Shak.⟩ (2) **:** to persist or recur hauntingly in the memory ⟨a figure who will ~ in our imagination long after the book has been put down —E.A.Weeks⟩ **c** *obs* **:** CIRCULATE, SPREAD **d** *archaic* **:** to be in motion **e** *obs, of the tongue* **:** to move incessantly **:** WAG **f** *of a ship* **:** to make headway **2 a :** to move along on foot **:** advance by steps ⟨we would ~ on . . . to the next camp —E.E.Shipton⟩ ⟨the millions of cattle that ~*ed* to Kansas —M.C.Boatright⟩ **b** (1) **:** to come or go on foot without hesitation or without ceremony — usu. used with a following adverb or preposition ⟨don't knock; just ~ in⟩ ⟨she'd ~*ed* in on the family —Mary Deasy⟩ ⟨the workmen ~*ed* off their jobs⟩ ⟨the two committee members who felt offended got up and ~*ed* out of the meeting⟩ (2) **:** to come or go as if proceeding on foot promptly or without deliberation — usu. used with a following adverb or preposition ⟨a government so weak as to tempt neighboring countries to ~ in and take over⟩ ⟨not seeing where the attorney's questions were leading, the witness ~*ed* right into his trap⟩ ⟨a figure worthy of the Periclean Age had ~*ed* into our epoch —Lucien Price⟩ **c** (1) **:** to go on foot for exercise or pleasure **:** go for a walk **:** take a walk ⟨made it his habit to ~ around the block ten times before breakfast⟩ ⟨went ~*ing* in the park⟩ (2) *Brit* **:** to engage in courtship esp. by going for walks — used with *out, together, out together,* or a prepositional phrase introduced by *with,* or with *out* followed by a prepositional phrase introduced by *with* ⟨she is ~*ing* out with a garage mechanic⟩ ⟨he is ~*ing* out with our maid⟩ ⟨they start ~*ing* out, they get engaged, and finally they get married —Richard Harrison⟩ ⟨a woman . . . who consents to ~ with you —Thomas Hardy⟩ **d** (1) *of a quadruped* **:** to go on foot at a gait in which there are always at least two feet on the ground — compare ²WALK 9b (2) **:** to ride an animal at such a gait ⟨the horsemen galloped the first half mile and ~*ed* the rest of the way⟩ **e** *of a biped* **:** to go on foot without lifting one foot clear of the ground before the other touches the ground ⟨part of the time we ~*ed* and part of the time we ran⟩ **3 a** *obs* **:** to go away **:** LEAVE **b :** to leave in consequence of being dismissed **4** [trans. of LL *ambulare,* trans. of Heb *hōlēkh*] **a :** to pursue a course of action or way of life **:** conduct oneself **:** BEHAVE ⟨~ warily⟩ ⟨~ in darkness —Jn 8:12(AV)⟩ ⟨everyone who has ~*ed* in sadness because his destiny has not fitted his aspirations —W.H.White⟩ **b :** to be or act in association **:** continue in union **:** ASSOCIATE ⟨~ humbly with thy God —Mic 6:8(AV)⟩ ⟨the British and American peoples will . . . ~ together side by side in majesty, in justice, and in peace —Sir Winston Churchill⟩ ⟨loved to ~ with a minority —W.A.White⟩ **5 :** to move about on foot while sleeping ⟨almost every adult sleepwalker has a history of having ~*ed* as a child —*This Week Mag.*⟩ — usu. used with *in one's sleep* ⟨people who ~ in their sleep⟩ **6 :** to move or progress slowly as if at a walk instead of a run **7 :** to go to first base as the result of a base on balls **8** *of an inanimate object* **a :** to move in a manner that is suggestive of walking ⟨so as not to wobble the ladder and make the poles ~ —*Training Manual for Auxiliary Firemen*⟩ **b :** to stand with an appearance of moving in a particular direction in consequence of having or consisting of similar members repeated at regular intervals suggestive of strides ⟨the long . . . dock that ~*ed* across the mud flats of the bay —F.G.Slaughter⟩ ⟨the transmission towers ~*ed* down a slope —D.S.Boyer⟩ ~ *vt* **1 a :** to pass on foot or as if on foot through, along, over, or upon **:** TRAVERSE, PERAMBULATE ⟨~ the avenue⟩ ⟨~ a tightrope⟩ ⟨had to ~ the floor with the baby almost an hour before he got it to sleep⟩ ⟨evil forces that ~ the world —C.T.Lanham⟩ ⟨the ghost . . . ~*s* the corridors every night —J.P.Marquand⟩ **b :** to perform or accomplish by going on foot ⟨~ guard⟩ **2 a :** to cause (an animal) to go on foot by leading, riding, or driving esp. at a walking pace ⟨a rider ~*ing* his horse⟩ ⟨~*ing* a dog on a leash⟩ ⟨steers that were ~*ed* to market⟩ **b :** to cause to move by walking ⟨formerly when the airship had to be pulled to the ground and ~*ed* into its hangar —*No. Amer. Rev.*⟩ ⟨~*ed* his bicycle up the hill⟩; *specif* **:** to haul (as an anchor) by walking round the capstan **c :** to carry while walking ⟨who had once ~*ed* the mails down the beaches —Marjory S. Douglas⟩ **3 :** to follow on foot as for the purpose of measuring or surveying ⟨~ a boundary⟩ **4 a :** to accompany on foot **:** walk with **:** take for a walk ⟨we'll ~ you to the bus stop⟩ **b :** to compel to walk (as by a command or by support and propulsion) ⟨they ~*ed* you into jail —Karl Shapiro⟩ ⟨it may be necessary to pick the patient up, ~ him about, and stimulate him in other ways in order to keep him awake —Morris Fishbein⟩ **5** *obs* **:** to be present at **:** ATTEND ⟨~ the exchange⟩ **6 :** to bring to a specified condition by walking ⟨~ someone off his feet⟩ ⟨~*ed* the entire afternoon away —Sherwood Anderson⟩ **7 :** to move (an object or objects) in a manner suggestive of walking ⟨she ~*ed* a spinning wheel into the house, making it use first one and then the other of its own spindling legs to achieve progression rather than lifting it by main force —C.E.Craddock⟩ ⟨warships were ~*ing* a barrage up and down the beach —Ira Wolfert⟩ ⟨he ~*ed* his . . . fingers along the couch back —Wallace Stegner⟩ **8 a :** to perform (a dance) at a walking pace ⟨~ a quadrille⟩ **b :** to go through (a play or acting part) perfunctorily as in an early stage of rehearsal **9 a** *chiefly Brit* **:** to put or keep (a young foxhound or other puppy) at walk **b :** to put or keep (a gamecock stag) in a walk **10 :** to pursue as a course of action or way of life ⟨as you ~ your mystic way —W.S.Gilbert⟩ ⟨would have to ~ a careful course —Thomas Sugrue⟩ **11 a :** to give a base on balls to **b :** to cause (a run) to be scored by giving a batter a base on balls with the bases full — sometimes used with *in* ⟨~*ed* in the winning run⟩ — **walk around 1 :** to consider from many different points of view ⟨we *walked around* the problem for two hours —H.J. Laski⟩ **2 :** to treat with caution ⟨critics *walk around* it gently —J.C.Trewin⟩ — **walk away from 1 :** to outrun or get the better of without difficulty **2 :** to survive (an accident) with little or no injury — **walk away with 1 :** to win or take by outdoing one's competitors without difficulty ⟨*walked away with* first prize⟩ ⟨expects to *walk away with* the nomination⟩ **2 :** to take over unexpectedly from someone else **:** ²STEAL 1g ⟨a new actor in a minor role amost *walked away with* the picture⟩ — **walk into 1 a :** ATTACK **b :** to reprimand harshly **:** criticize severely **2 a :** to eat or drink greedily ⟨*walked* right *into* the beer and pretzels⟩ **b :** to use up rapidly — **walk off with 1 a :** to steal and take away ⟨a sneak thief who *walked off with* $35,000 —*N.Y.Times*⟩ **b :** to take over unexpectedly from someone else **:** ²STEAL 1g ⟨a bit player who *walked off with* the show⟩ **2 :** to win or gain esp. by outdoing one's competitors without difficulty ⟨after mortgaging off their costs . . . they were able to *walk off with* $2,084,823 in profits —*Time*⟩ ⟨thirty-four stories which have *walked off with* first prizes —James Kelly⟩ — **walk one's chalks** [prob. fr. the military practice of making a soldier walk along a chalked line to prove that he is sober] *slang* **:** to leave quickly and unceremoniously **:** DECAMP — **walk over** *also* **walk all over :** to disregard the wishes or feelings of **:** treat badly ⟨in those days the histrionic possibilities of young children were unsuspected by the parents and schoolmasters who *walked over* them —H. G.Wells⟩ — **walk over the course 1** *of a racehorse* **:** to go over a course at a walk so as to be judged the winner of a race in which there is no other starter **:** walk over **2 :** to win an easy victory — **walk spanish** *usu cap S* **1 :** to be lifted up by the collar and the seat of the trousers and made to walk on tiptoe **2 :** to leave in consequence of being dismissed, expelled, or discharged ⟨if in his presence we had dared talk Greek we should certainly have *walked Spanish* —Joseph Jefferson⟩ **3 :** to force (a person) to walk Spanish — **walk the chalk line** *or* **walk the chalk mark** *or* **walk chalk** *also* **walk a chalk line :** to behave in a strictly disciplined or obedient way **:** conduct oneself without deviation from propriety — **walk the floor :** to pace back and forth in a room because of pain or esp. worry — **walk the hospitals** *also* **walk the hospital** *or* **walk the wards :** to make the rounds of hospital wards in the study or practice of medicine or surgery — **walk the plank 1 :** to be compelled esp. by pirates to walk along a plank sticking out over the side of a ship until one falls into the sea **2 :** to vacate an office or position under compulsion — **walk the streets :** to walk around on the streets as a prostitute looking for customers — **walk through 1 :** to go through (a play, scene, or acting part) perfunctorily as in an early stage of rehearsal ⟨she merely *walked through* the part, mumbling her lines —*Time*⟩ **2 :** to deal with or carry out perfunctorily ⟨there is a tendency for students to consider such tests a mere matter of routine and to just *walk through* them —*Quarterly Jour. of Speech*⟩

²**walk** \ˈ"\ *n* -S [ME, fr. *walken* to walk] **1 a :** an act or instance of going on foot esp. for exercise or pleasure ⟨go for a ~⟩ ⟨take a ~⟩ ⟨fond of long ~*s*⟩ **b** *obs* **:** PEREGRINATION, TRAVEL **2 a :** accustomed place of walking **:** HAUNT **b** *obs* **:** place or area of movement of an object or objects **:** RANGE, COURSE **3 :** a place designed for walking: **a** (1) **:** a passage (as a portico or aisle) for walking in a church or other public building **:** AMBULATORY (2) **:** a balustraded roof area or a railed platform above the roof of a dwelling house **:** WIDOW'S WALK **b** (1) **:** a path specially arranged or paved for walking ⟨a graveled ~ in a garden⟩ (2) **walks** *pl, obs* **:** PLEASURE GROUNDS ⟨he hath left you all his ~*s,* his private arbors and new-planted orchards —Shak.⟩ (3) **:** SIDEWALK **c** (1) **:** AVENUE 3b (2) **:** a public avenue for promenading **:** PROMENADE **d :** ROPE WALK **4 :** a place or area of land in which animals feed and exercise with minimal restraint: **a** (1) **:** a pen to keep poultry in **:** fowl run (2) **:** a place where a young gamecock is kept for exercise and experience away from other male birds **b :** land serving as pasture esp. for sheep **c** *chiefly Brit* **:** a farm or cottage to which a kennel-bred foxhound or other puppy is sent to develop and to become accustomed to livestock ⟨sending out foxhound puppies to ~ —E.G.W.W.Harrison⟩ ⟨hound puppies are out at ~ —C.E.Hare⟩ **d :** the entire range of a territorial animal **5 :** an area that constitutes a section of a park or esp. forest and is under the charge of a ranger that patrols it **6 :** distance to be walked ⟨living within a short ~ of one's place of employment⟩ ⟨a quarter mile ~ from here⟩; *esp* **:** distance as measured in time required by a walker to cover ⟨within ten minutes' ~⟩ **7** *Brit* **:** a ceremonial procession **8 a :** manner of living **:** CONDUCT, BEHAVIOR **b** *obs* **:** a course of action in a particular set of circumstances **9 a :** the gait of a biped in which the feet are lifted alternately with one foot not being lifted clear of the ground before the other touches the ground ⟨he started at a ~ but soon broke into a run⟩ **b :** the gait of a quadruped in which there are always at least two feet on the ground; *specif* **:** a slow flat-footed four-beat gait of a horse in which the feet strike the ground in the sequence near hind, near fore, off hind, off fore at such a rate that there are always at least two feet on the ground **c :** an extremely low rate of speed ⟨shortage of raw materials slowed production down to a ~⟩ **10 a :** a suitable course or route to walk for exercise or pleasure ⟨there are delightful ~*s* in almost every direction from here⟩ **b :** a route regularly traversed by a person in the performance of a particular activity (as patrolling, begging, or the delivery of mail or commodities) ⟨the postmen's rounds are known as ~*s,* though the postmen may use motor-vans or pedal cycles —W.D.Sharp⟩ **11 :** characteristic manner of walking ⟨his ~ is just like his father's⟩ **12 a :** social or economic status ⟨persons from every ~, including members of various royal families —*N.Y.Times*⟩ — used esp. in the phrase *walk of life* ⟨from all ~*s* of life including even the nobility —Roy Lewis & Angus Maude⟩ **b** (1) **:** range or sphere of action **:** FIELD, PROVINCE ⟨distinguished figures in science, politics, and affairs, . . . and particularly in the ~ of letters —Richard Gottheil⟩ ⟨had a duty to go into the higher ~ of the House of Commons —H.J.Laski⟩ (2) **:** VOCATION — used esp. in the phrase *walk of life* ⟨whatever your ~ of life — actor, journalist, musician, psychiatrist, politician —J.B. Boothroyd⟩ **13 :** ASSOCIATION 1 ⟨a closer ~ with God —William Cowper⟩ **14 :** a West Indian plantation of trees arranged in rows with wide spaces between them ⟨the Spaniards left behind them well-established cacao ~*s* . . . in Jamaica —A.E.Aspinall⟩ **15 :** onward course or journey ⟨a deliberate ~ down the road to moral ruin —M.B.Ridgway⟩ **16 :** DEPARTURE, WALKOUT — used esp. in the phrase *take a walk* **17 :** a trial of speed in walking over a course **:** walking race **18 :** BASE ON BALLS **19 :** an intermittent creeping motion of equipment from a desired fixed position because of vibration or tilting — **in a walk** *adv* **:** with little effort **:** without enough competition or resistance to require much exertion ⟨won *in a walk*⟩

³**walk** \ˈ"\ *vt* -ED/-ING/-S [ME *walken,* fr. MD, to knead, press, full — more at ¹WALK] *Brit* **:** ⁵FULL

walk·able \-kəbəl\ *adj* **1 :** suitable or fit for walking ⟨a ~ path⟩ ⟨~ countryside⟩ ⟨~ shoes⟩ **2 :** capable of being traversed by walking ⟨a ~ distance⟩

walkabout \ˈ==,=\ *n* -S [fr. the phrase *walk about*] *chiefly Austral* **1 a :** a short period of wandering bush life engaged in by an Australian aborigine as an occasional interruption of regular work **b :** a similar period of wandering life engaged in by a nonwhite native of a southwest Pacific island **2 :** a walking tour **:** walking trip

walkabout disease *or* **walking disease** *n* **:** a disease of horses marked by cirrhosis of the liver, severe nervous symptoms, and continuous aimless walking and usu. believed to be caused by eating poisonous vegetation — compare WINTON DISEASE

walk-around \ˈ==,=\ *or* **walk-round** \ˈ=,=\ *n* -S [fr. the phrase *walk around*] **1** *or* **walk-round :** a number in a blackface minstrel show in which all the performers dance around the stage one at a time often with each one doing his specialty on coming to the center of the stage; *broadly* **:** a dance number in which the entire company of performers moves in a circle **b :** the music for such a number ⟨his minstrel leader asked him to compose a new *walk-around* . . . for use the next day —*Time*⟩ **2 :** a circus

act in which a clown or group of clowns walk all the way around the arena performing as they go
walk-around bottle *or* **walk-around oxygen bottle** *also* **walk-around oxygen unit** *or* **walk-around** *n* -s **:** a portable container of oxygen for use in high-altitude flying when moving around in the airplane or as an emergency supply if the airplane's oxygen system fails
walk·a·thon \'wȯkə,thän\ *n* -s [²*walk* + mara*thon*] **1 :** a dance marathon **2 :** a walking marathon
walkaway \'==,=\ *n* -s [fr. *walk away*, v.] **1 :** a race in which the winner finishes at a slow pace because he has outdistanced all other competitors **2 :** an easily won contest **3 :** a thing easily accomplished **4 :** a person that escapes from prison on foot
walk back *vi* **:** to ease back the fall of a hoisting-tackle while keeping it in hand
walk clerk *n, Brit* **:** a bank messenger or clerk that presents bills and checks to other banks for collection
walk down *vt* **1 :** to overcome the effect of (a poison) by walking **2 :** to wear down in walking **:** walk longer or farther than ⟨I could *walk down* most of the boys —Mrs. Humphry Ward⟩ **3** *West* **:** to capture (wild horses) by forcing to keep on the move until exhausted and then maneuvering into an enclosure
walked *past of* WALK
¹**walk·er** \'wȯkə(r)\ *n* -s [ME *walkere*, fr. OE *wealcere*, fr. *wealcan* to roll, toss + *-ere* -er — more at WALK] *dial Brit* **:** ¹FULLER 1
²**walker** \"\ *n* -s [ME, fr. *walken* to walk + *-er* — more at WALK] **1 :** one that walks: as **a** *obs* **:** FORESTER, GAMEKEEPER **b :** one that conducts himself in a specified way ⟨disorderly ~*s*⟩ **c :** a competitor in a walking race **d :** a cursorial insect; *esp* **:** a stick insect or other member of the Phasmatodea **e :** a peddler going on foot **f :** a bird that walks instead of hopping **g :** one that patrols or supervises on foot **h :** a hunter that walks up game **i :** an ambulatory patient **2 :** something used in walking: as **a walkers** *pl, obs* **:** FEET **b :** a framework usu. of metal and cloth mounted on wheels or casters and designed to support a child learning to walk ⟨the baby . . . may be strolling around unassisted or in a ~ —H.R.Litchfield & L.H.Dembo⟩ — called also *go-cart, baby walker* **c :** an apparatus with wheels or gliders, handgrips, and often adjustable crutches that is used by invalids and the handicapped in learning to walk again **d :** a walking shoe

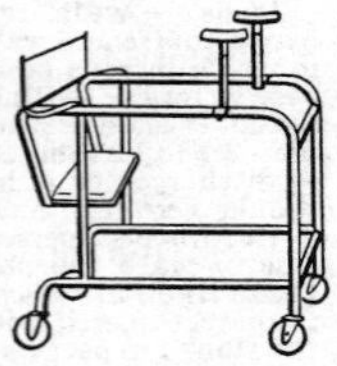
walker 2c

³**walker** \"\ *or* **walker hound** *n* -s *usu cap W* [after John W. *Walker*, 19th cent. Am. sportsman who helped develop the strain] **:** an American foxhound of a strain developed by crossing English foxhounds with several highly regarded American strains
walker-on \'==,=\ *n, pl* **walkers-on :** one that plays a walk-on
walk·ie \'wȯkē\ *n* -s [¹*walk* + *-ie*] **:** a lift truck of platform or forklift type operated by a person on foot
walkie-lookie \'wȯkē'lu̇kē\ *n* -s **:** a complete portable one-man television camera
walkie-talkie *also* **walky-talky** \'wȯkē'tȯkē\ *n, pl* **walkie-talkies** *also* **walky-talkies :** a compact battery-operated radio transmitting and receiving set that is carried on a person's back to provide two-way communication
¹**walk-in** \'=,=\ *adj* [fr. the phrase *walk in*] **1 a :** large enough to be walked into ⟨*walk-in* closet⟩ ⟨*walk-in* refrigerator⟩ **b :** arranged so as to be entered directly rather than through a lobby ⟨*walk-in* apartment⟩ **2 :** being a person that walks in ⟨for treating *walk-in* neurotics rather than locked-in psychotics —*Time*⟩ **:** of or connected with persons that walk in ⟨sales are attributed to *walk-in* trade, rather than to any particular promotion —*Retailing Daily*⟩
²**walk-in** \"\ *n* -s **1 :** a walk-in refrigerator or cold storage room **2 :** an easy election victory
¹**walking** *n* -s [ME, fr. gerund of *walken* to walk — more at WALK] **1 a :** the action of one that walks ⟨does more ~ than he used to⟩ ⟨~ is good exercise⟩ **b :** movement of an inanimate object in a manner suggestive of such action **2 :** kind of behavior ⟨wary ~⟩ **3 :** a journey made on foot **4 :** the condition of a surface (as of a path or walk) for one that is traversing it on foot ⟨the ~ is slippery⟩ **5 :** manner in which one walks
²**walking** *adj* [in sense 1, fr. ME, fr. pres. part. of *walken* to walk; in senses 2 & 3, fr. ME, fr. gerund of *walken* to walk; in other senses, fr. pres. part. of ¹*walk*] **1 :** that walks: as **a :** going around in human form ⟨a ~ encyclopedia⟩ ⟨a ~ advertisement for her boss's fashion departments —Rollie Abrahams⟩ **b :** going around from place to place as a regular practice esp. in carrying out the tasks of an occupation or office **c :** able to walk in spite of a sickness or injury **:** ¹AMBULATORY 4a ⟨inspected troops in their foxholes and talked to ~ wounded —*Springfield (Mass.) Union*⟩ **2 a :** used for or in walking ⟨~ shoes⟩ **:** suitable for walking ⟨London is such a wonderful ~ town —Richard Joseph⟩ **b :** characterized by, connected with, or consisting of the action of walking ⟨a ~ tour⟩ **3 :** of, relating to, or appropriate to a person being dismissed **4 :** that moves or appears to move in a manner suggestive of walking: as **a** *of a plant* **:** propagating itself (as by stolons or rhizomes) in a manner suggestive of strides ⟨~ orchid⟩ **b :** that swings or rocks back and forth ⟨~ beam⟩ **c** *of a livestock brand* **:** having stylized feet — see BRAND illustration **5** *of a disease* **a :** characterized by the affected individual's retention of ability to stay out of bed and walk around ⟨~ pneumonia⟩ **b :** characterized by abnormal or excessive walking **6 :** guided or operated by a man on foot ⟨~ cultivator⟩ ⟨~ plow⟩
walking bass *n* **:** an evenly accented repeated bass figure often in short octaves used esp. in piano blues — compare BOOGIE-WOOGIE
walking beam *n* **:** an oscillating lever that pivots on a central axis and serves for transmitting power in such a way as to produce a reciprocating or reversible motion — called also *working beam*
walking-beam \'==,=\ *vi* -ED/-ING/-S *West, of a horse* **:** to leap in bucking so as to land alternately on front and hind feet
walking boat *or* **walking scow** *n* **:** a scow that is moved by lowering and lifting of spuds and is used esp. for laying pipe in swift rivers
walking boss *n* **:** FOREMAN
walking cast *n* **:** a cast that is worn on a patient's leg and has a stirrup with a heel or other supporting device embedded in the plaster to facilitate walking
walking crane *n* **:** a light crane traveling on an overhead channel iron and a single rail vertically beneath this in the floor
walking delegate *n* **:** a business representative of a labor union appointed to visit members and their places of employment, to secure the enforcement of union rules and agreements, and at times to represent the union in dealing with employers **:** BUSINESS AGENT
walking disease *var of* WALKABOUT DISEASE
walking fern *n* [so called fr. the fact that it seems to move from place to place due to its forming identical new plants from the elongate tips of its fronds] **:** a fern of the genus *Camptosorus* (esp. *C. rhizophyllus*)
walking fish *n* **:** any of various fishes that are able to conserve oxygen so that they can survive for a considerable time out of water: as **a :** SNAKEHEAD 3 **b :** any of several tropical catfishes (as of the genus *Doras* or *Clarias*) **c :** MUDSKIPPER **d :** CLIMBING PERCH
walking gentleman *n* **:** an actor engaged for parts of little importance where impressive appearance is desired
walking heel *n* **1 :** a heel that is somewhat lower and broader than a Cuban heel and is used on women's shoes **2 :** a heel embedded in a walking cast
walking horse *n, sometimes cap W&H* **:** TENNESSEE WALKING HORSE
walking lady *n* **:** the female counterpart of a walking gentleman
walking leaf *n* **1 :** WALKING FERN **2 :** LEAF INSECT
walking leg *also* **walking foot** *n* **:** an appendage of an arthropod adapted for walking
walking line *n* **:** an imaginary line upon which the widths of the treads of a stair are set out generally about 18 inches from the inside of the handrail
walking-out \'==,'=\ *adj* [fr. pres. part. of the phrase *walk out*] *chiefly Brit* **:** prescribed or intended for a soldier on pass ⟨*walking-out* uniform⟩
walking papers *also* **walking orders** *n pl* **:** an order to leave **:** DISMISSAL, DISCHARGE ⟨his boss and his fiancée gave him his *walking papers* on the same day⟩
walking part *n* **:** WALK-ON
walking rapier *or* **walking sword** *n* **:** a very light sword formerly worn as part of a gentleman's civilian costume
walking staff *n* **:** a stick held in the hand and used for support in walking
walking step *n* **:** a simple dance step that when executed with alternate feet results in a rhythmic walk — see ONE-STEP
walking stick *n* **1 :** a stick held in the hand and used for support in walking or esp. as a fashionable and often ornamental accessory for a man taking a walk **2** *usu* **walkingstick** \'==,=\ **:** STICK INSECT; *esp* **:** a phasmid insect (*Diapheromera femorata*) common in parts of the U.S.
walking-stick palm \'==,=-\ *n* **:** a slender Australian pinnate-leaved palm (*Bacularia monostachya*) whose stems are used for walking sticks
walking straw *n* **:** STICK INSECT; *esp* **:** a large Australian phasmid insect (*Palophus titan*) that reaches a length of 10 inches
walking ticket *n* **:** WALKING PAPERS
walking tyrant *n* **:** a stout-legged crested tyrant flycatcher (*Machetornis rixosa*) of So. America
walk-in-walk-out \'='='='=\ *adj, chiefly Austral* **:** characterized by or consisting of the sale of a piece of real property as a completely going concern without removal of any removable property (as furniture or livestock) that is on it at the time
walk·ist \'wȯkəst\ *n* -s [¹*walk* + *-ist*] **:** ²WALKER 1c
¹**walk-mill** \'=,=\ *n* [ME *walkmil*, *walkemilne*, prob. part trans. of MD *walkemole*, fr. *walken* to knead, full + *mole*, *molen* mill; akin to OHG *muli*, *mulin* mill — more at WALK, MILL] *dial Brit* **:** FULLING MILL
²**walk-mill** \"\ *n* [¹*walk*] **:** a mill powered by one or more persons or animals walking
walk off *vt* **:** to rid oneself of by walking ⟨*walking off* a cramp in my leg —Mary R. Rinehart⟩ ⟨started home in a mood of discouragement but soon *walked* it *off*⟩ **:** rid oneself of the effects of by walking ⟨better *walk* some of this food *off* —Evelyn Barkins⟩
walk on *vi* [fr. the phrase *walk on*] **:** to play a walk-on
walk-on \'=,=\ *n* -s **1 :** a small usu. nonspeaking part in a dramatic production — compare ³BIT 3f **2 :** one that plays a walk-on
walk out *vi* **1 :** to go on strike ⟨members of sympathetic . . . unions also *walked out* —*Current Biog.*⟩ **2 :** to walk with long steps **3 :** to take oneself out as an expression of disapproval ⟨at one meeting the United States delegate *walked out* in protest —*Current Biog.*⟩ — often used with *of* ⟨members who *walked out* of the assembly —*New Statesman & Nation*⟩ —
walk out on : to leave abruptly **:** leave before the completion of a performance or process ⟨has even been known to *walk out on* the writhing of some of the screen's most celebrated heavy emoters —*New Republic*⟩ **:** leave in the lurch ⟨*walked out on* his wife and children⟩ **:** ABANDON ⟨thinking of *walking out on* the practice of law and starting a business⟩
walkout \'=,=\ *n* -s [*walk out*] **1 a :** ²STRIKE 7a **b :** an informal or unauthorized strike **2 a :** the action of leaving a meeting or organization as an expression of disapproval ⟨recriminations, ~*s*, border clashes . . . may accompany the United Nations consideration of this question —L.E.Browne⟩ **b :** continued absence from the meetings of an organization as an expression of disapproval ⟨a new effort last week to end Russia's ~ and the U.N. stalemate —*Time*⟩ **3 a :** a prospective customer that leaves a store without making a purchase **b :** the departure of a prospective customer from a store without making a purchase
walk over *vi, of a racehorse* **:** to go over a course at a walk so as to be judged the winner of a race in which there is no other starter
walkover \'=,==\ *n* -s [*walk over*] **1 a** (1) **:** a horse race with only one starter (2) **:** a horse race in which the starters all belong to the same interests or individuals **b :** the action or an instance of walking over on the part of a racehorse ⟨in the case of a purse, the consent of the stewards is necessary to dispense with a ~ —N. Y. State Racing Commission⟩ **2 a :** a one-sided contest **:** easy or uncontested victory **b :** something easily accomplished **3 :** a synchronized swimming stunt which is executed from either a front or back layout position and in which the trunk is brought to a vertical position with the head down and the legs are raised successively in an arc above the water and meet as the body surfaces in the opposite layout position from the start
walk-round *var of* WALK-AROUND
walks *pres 3d sing of* WALK, *pl of* WALK
walks·man \'wȯksmən\ *n, pl* **walksmen** [*walk's* (gen. of ²*walk*) + *man*] *Brit* **:** one that patrols waterworks or waterways on foot for purposes of inspection and maintenance
walk-through \'=,=\ *n* -s [fr. *walk through*, v.] **1 :** a perfunctory performance of a play, scene, or acting part as in an early stage of rehearsal **2 :** a television rehearsal in which the actors go through all stage business without cameras **3 :** a tunnel for pedestrians
walk-trot \'=,=\ *adj, of a horse* **:** THREE-GAITED
walk up *vt* **1 :** to cause (a game bird or mammal) to rise or break cover by approaching on foot ⟨spend a September day *walking up* partridges —J.R.Beddington⟩ — compare DRIVE 8b **2 :** to raise (a stage flat) to a vertical position by lifting and pushing up from beneath starting with the upper edge while someone else holds the lower edge in place with his foot — compare ²FOOT 9 ~ *vi, dial* **:** to walk faster
¹**walk-up** \'=,=\ *adj* [fr. the phrase *walk up*] **1 :** located above the ground floor in a building with no elevator ⟨a *walk-up* apartment⟩ **2 :** consisting of several stories and having no elevator ⟨no *walk-up* tenement, unless fireproof, should exceed six stories in height —J.G.Hill⟩
²**walk-up** \"\ *n* -s **1 :** a building of several stories with no elevator; *esp* **:** a walk-up apartment house ⟨lived on the top floor of a five-flight *walk-up* —Viña Delmar⟩ **2 a :** an apartment located above the ground floor in a building with no elevator ⟨his apartment, a one-room *walk-up* —Truman Capote⟩ **b :** a place of business reached by walking up one or more flights of stairs **3 :** a trapshooting game in which several traps are hidden at intervals on either side of a path along which the shooter is to walk and each trap is sprung without warning as the shooter approaches it
walkway \'=,=\ *n* **:** a passageway used or intended for walking: as **a :** SIDEWALK **b :** a path for pedestrians esp. in a garden or park ⟨box hedges mark the ~*s* —J.B.Cabell⟩ **c :** a passageway in a place of employment (as a factory or restaurant) designed to be walked on by the employees in the performance of their duties ⟨accident prevention by making floors and ~*s* safe —R.H.Lansburgh⟩ **d :** a walk connecting the entrance door of a house with a sidewalk, street, or road ⟨each of the houses had a graveled ~ . . . leading down to the highway —Earl Hamner⟩
walkyrie *usu cap, var of* VALKYRIE
walky-talky *var of* WALKIE-TALKIE
¹**wall** \'wȯl\ *n* -s [ME, fr. OE *weall* rampart, wall; akin to OS *wal* rampart, MHG *wall*; all fr. a prehistoric WGmc word borrowed fr. L *vallum* rampart set with palisades, wall, fr. *vallus* stake, palisade; akin to Skt *vala* beam, pole, Goth *walus* stick, staff, ON *vǫlr* round stick, *valr* round, L *volvere* to roll — more at VOLUBLE] **1 a** (1) **:** a high thick masonry structure forming an enclosure chiefly for defense against invasion ⟨hurled stones and spears at the attackers from the ~⟩ — usu. used in pl. ⟨citizens ran to defend the ~*s* of the city⟩ (2) **:** a masonry fence around a garden, park, or estate ⟨the ~ of the villa follows the road for miles⟩ **b :** a rampart of considerable height and thickness and usu. great length serving as a fortification (as on a border between territories or countries) ⟨the great Chinese ~ extended for more than 1500 miles⟩ **c :** a structure that serves to hold back pressure (as of water or sliding earth) — see RETAINING WALL, SEAWALL **2 :** a vertical architectural member used to define and divide space ⟨a continuously curving ~ gives the building its shape⟩; *esp* **:** one of the sides of a room or building that connects the floor and ceiling or foundation and roof ⟨the inside ~*s* are all movable —*London Calling*⟩ ⟨the house has a glass ~ facing the garden⟩ — see CAVITY WALL, FACED WALL, NONBEARING PARTITION, PARTY WALL, STORAGE WALL **3 :** the side of a footpath next to buildings ⟨the passenger who takes the ~ brushes the dim glass with his sleeve —Charles Dickens⟩ **4 a :** an extreme or desperate position — usu. used in the phrase *to the wall* ⟨schools whose teachers . . . were driven to the ~ financially —Dixon Wecter⟩ ⟨pushing them to the ~ in the competitive struggle —T.W.Arnold⟩ **b :** a state of defeat, failure, or ruin — usu. used in the phrase *to the wall* ⟨let the weakest go to the ~ —*Art & Industry*⟩ ⟨since the war, several . . . magazines have gone to the ~ —P.W.Crowcroft⟩ **5 walls** *pl* **:** a physical, intellectual, or spiritual area of influence ⟨evident to those outside our academic ~*s* —J.B.Conant⟩ **6 a :** the external layer of structural material surrounding an object ⟨surgical instruments for penetrating the ~ of the body⟩ ⟨muscle ~⟩ — often used in pl. ⟨staves form the ~*s* of a barrel⟩ ⟨stomach ~*s*⟩ **b** (1) **:** one of the surfaces of country rock lying adjacent to a vein, ore deposit, or coal seam (2) **:** one of the surfaces of a geological fault zone — see FOOTWALL, HANGING WALL **7 a** (1) **:** something resembling a wall in appearance ⟨a towering mountain ~⟩ ⟨a ~ of water, 75 feet high, . . . rushed upon the city —*Amer. Guide Series: Pa.*⟩ ⟨a stream flowing between the valley ~*s*⟩ (2) **:** something that resembles a wall in functioning esp. by establishing limits or providing defense ⟨a sovereign state would be outside the American tariff ~*s* —S.F.Bemis⟩ ⟨two men hurt on the football team's forward ~⟩ ⟨going through the enemy's ~ in linear formation —Tom Wintringham⟩ **b :** something immaterial or intangible that acts as a barrier to communication, understanding, or accomplishment ⟨the ~ of reserve the old man had built around himself —Ben Riker⟩ ⟨break down the ~ of condescension —Charles Angoff⟩ ⟨unable to break through the ~ of employer resistance —Frank O'Leary⟩ **8 :** the arrangement of tiles previous to the drawing of hands in a Mah-Jongg game
²**wall** \"\ *vt* -ED/-ING/-S [ME *wallen*, fr. *wall*, n.] **1 a :** to provide or cover with a wall ⟨to keep out street noises . . . the house was ~*ed* on that facade —*Current Biog.*⟩ **b :** to surround or confine with or as if with walls **:** hem in — usu. used with *in* ⟨planning to ~ in the garden for privacy⟩ ⟨a lake ~*ed* in by snow-covered peaks⟩ ⟨was ~*ed* in by authority —W.P. Webb⟩ **c :** to separate or shut out by means of or as if by means of a wall **:** PARTITION — usu. used with *off* ⟨~*ed* off half the house to make two apartments⟩ ⟨~*ed* off their world . . . from the rest of human society —H.S.Truman⟩ **d :** to border or form a boundary on in the manner of a wall **:** BOUND ⟨tall chestnut trees ~ the broad avenue⟩ **2 a :** to shut behind a wall **:** seal within or as if within walls **:** IMMURE, INCARCERATE — usu. used with *up* ⟨had ~*ed* the monster up within the tomb —E.A.Poe⟩ ⟨compelled . . . to spend their time ~*ing* up this danger —Lillian Smith⟩ **b :** to seal up (an opening) with or as if with a wall ⟨~*ed* up the crevice —Oliver La Farge⟩ **3 :** to cover the walls of (a room) with something ⟨this study is ~*ed* with books —Lucien Price⟩ **syn** see ENCLOSE
³**wall** \"\ *adj* **:** of or relating to a wall **:** beside, attached to, or growing on a wall ⟨~ cabinets⟩ ⟨a ~ clock⟩ ⟨~ plants⟩
⁴**wall** \"\ *vb* -ED/-ING/-S [ME (Sc) *wawlen*, prob. fr. ME *wawil-* (in *wawil-eghed* walleyed) — more at WALLEYED] *vt* **:** to roll (one's eyes) in or as if in expression of emotion ⟨mooning about, . . . playacting and ~*ing* her eyes —Frances G. Patton⟩ ~ *vi, of the eyes* **:** to roll in a dramatic manner ⟨big eyes would ~ up to the ceiling with a look of fear in them —Carson McCullers⟩
⁵**wall** \"\ *n* -s **:** WALL KNOT
wal·la·ba \'wäləbə *also* 'wȯl-\ *n* -s [Arawak] **:** any of several trees of the genus *Eperua*; *esp* **:** a valuable timber tree (*E. falcata*) of the Guianas and northern Brazil having pinnate leaves, clusters of red flowers, and reddish brown very durable wood that is used for palings and shingles
wal·la·by \'wäləbē, -bi *also* 'wȯl-\ *n, pl* **wallabies** *also* **wallaby** [fr. *wolabā*, native name in New So. Wales, Australia] **1 :** any of various small and medium-sized kangaroos of *Macropus* and several related genera that are more brightly colored and much smaller than the typical kangaroos — see NAIL-TAILED WALLABY, PADEMELON, ROCK WALLABY **2 :** the fur of a wallaby
wallaby acacia *n* **:** a shrubby Australian wattle (*Acacia rigens*) having linear terete phyllodes with short often recurved points
wallaby bush *n* **:** an evergreen shrub (*Beyeria viscosa*) of the family Euphorbiaceae that has small heathlike leaves and chiefly axillary flowers and is found in Australia and Tasmania
wallaby ear *n* **:** a virus disease of Indian corn that is characterized by a dwarfing of the whole plant and an accentuating of its green color and by small swellings on the secondary veins of the underside of top leaves in young plants which enlarge from tip to base of the leaf blade
wallaby grass *n* **:** any of various Australasian grasses of the genus *Danthonia*
wal·lace's line \'wäləsəz-, 'wȯləsəz-\ *also* **wallace line** *n, usu cap W* [after Alfred Russel *Wallace* †1913 Eng. naturalist] **:** a hypothetical boundary separating the characteristic Asiatic fauna and flora from that of Australasia, marking the common boundary of the Oriental and Australian biogeographic regions, and usu. passing between Bali and Lombok, between Celebes and Borneo or to the east of Celebes, and to the east of the Philippines — see WEBER'S LINE
wal·lach *or* **wal·ach** \'wäläk *also* 'wȯl-\ *n* -s *cap* [G *Wallache*, *Walache*, of Slav origin; akin to Czech *Vlach* — more at VLACH] **:** VLACH
¹**wal·la·chi·an** *or* **wa·la·chi·an** \wä'lākēən, wə'- -'lak- *also* wȯ'-\ *n* -s *cap* [*Wallachia*, *Walachia*, former principality now part of Romania + E *-an*] **1 a :** a native or inhabitant of Wallachia **b :** Romanian as spoken in Wallachia **2 :** VLACH
²**wallachian** *or* **walachian** \"\ *adj, usu cap* **1 :** of, relating to, or characteristic of Wallachia **2 :** of, relating to, or characteristic of the Wallachians
wallachian sheep *n, usu cap W* **:** one of a breed of domestic sheep of southeastern Europe and western Asia that have very long upright spirally twisted horns and are used for the production of wool, meat, and milk
wal·la·go \'wälə,gō\ *n* -s [NL, fr. native name in Bengal] **:** a large freshwater catfish (*Wallago attu*) of southeastern Asia
wal·lah *also* **wal·la** \'wälə *also* 'wȯlə\ *n* -s [Hindi *-wālā*, *-wāl* man, one who is in charge, fr. Skt *pāla* protector; akin to Skt *pāti* he protects — more at FUR] **1 :** a person who is associated with a particular type of work or who performs a specific duty or service — usu. used in combination ⟨fancies himself a home workshop ~ —A.C.Spectorsky⟩ ⟨the book ~ was an itinerant peddler —George Orwell⟩ **2 :** a person who holds an important position in an organization or in a particular situation — usu. used in combination ⟨keep . . . these professional staff ~*s* off my neck —William Chamberlain⟩ ⟨appointed head ~ in charge of dinner tonight —Robert Carson⟩
wall anchor *n* **:** BEAM ANCHOR
wall and crown *n* **:** a single wall knot with a crown
wall arcade *n* **:** an ornamental arcade built against or as part of a wall
wal·la·roo \,wälə'rü *also* ,wȯl-\ *n* -s [fr. *wolarū*, native name in New So. Wales, Australia] **:** EURO
wal·la·sey \'wäləsē *also* 'wȯl-\ *adj, usu cap* [fr. *Wallasey*, England] **:** of or from the county borough of Wallasey, England **:** of the kind or style prevalent in Wallasey
wal·la·wal·la \'wälə'wälə *also* 'wȯlə'wȯlə\ *n, pl* **wallawalla** *or* **wallawallas** *usu cap* [Shahaptian, lit., little river, dim. of *wana* river] **1 a :** a Shahaptian people of southeastern Washington and northeastern Oregon **b :** a member of such people **2 :** a Shahaptian language of the Wallawalla people
walla-walla \"\ *n* -s [Hindi *walwalā*, *walwala* tumult, uproar, noise] **:** an unintelligible sound produced by many people talking at once ⟨no noise, no coolies making *walla-walla* —Virginia A. Oakes⟩
wall barley *n* **:** a European annual grass (*Hordeum murinum*) that resembles the related barley but occurs as a weed in waste ground esp. along roadsides and hedgerows
wall bed *n* **:** RECESS BED
wall bee *n* **:** MASON BEE

wallboard \ˈ=,=\ *n* **:** a structural boarding of any of various materials (as wood pulp, gypsum, plastic) made in large rigid sheets and used esp. for sheathing interior walls and ceilings — compare PLASTERBOARD, PLYWOOD

wall box *n* **:** a frame set in a wall to receive a pillow block or bearing for a shaft passing through the wall

wall clamp *n* **:** a clamp for holding walls or parts of a double wall together

wall creeper *n* **:** a small bird (*Tichodroma muraria*) of the family Certhiidae that is mostly gray, black, and white with a crimson wing patch, inhabits cliffs in the mountains of southern Asia, Europe, and northern Africa, and frequents the walls of towns during migration

wall cress *n* **:** any of several low-growing or mat-forming cresses that are often cultivated in rock gardens or allowed to spread over walls: as **a :** a rock cress of the genus *Arabis* **b :** MOUSE-EAR CRESS **c :** AUBRIETIA 2

walled plain *n* **:** a large crater on the surface of the moon having a broad nearly level floor

walled toe *var of* WALL TOE

wall·er \ˈwȯlə(r)\ *n* -s [ME *wallare*, fr. *wallen* to wall + *-are* -er] **:** one that builds or repairs walls

wal·le·ri·an degeneration \wäˈlirēən-, wȯˈlirēən-\ *n, usu cap W* [*wallerian* fr. Augustus V. *Waller* †1870 Eng. physiologist + E *-an*] **:** a degeneration of nerve fibers that follows injury or disease and progresses from the seat of injury along the axon away from the nerve cell body while the part between the seat of injury and the nerve cell body remains intact

wal·let \ˈwälət, ˈwȯl-, *usu* -əd+V\ *n* -s [ME *walet*] **1 :** a bag for carrying miscellaneous articles (as personal belongings) while traveling ⟨without a crust in my ~, as beggars usually have —Harriet Martineau⟩ ⟨grew so weary . . . he drew from his ~ a share of the pearls —J.F.Dobie⟩ — compare KNAPSACK 1 **2 :** any of various folding pocketbooks: as **a :** BILLFOLD 1 **b :** a pocketbook that contains compartments for change, photographs, cards, and keys and often has a snap or zipper fastener **c :** a pocketbook that is large enough to accommodate unfolded foreign currency or personal papers (as a passport or checkbook)

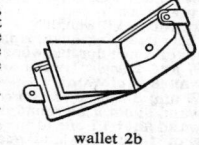

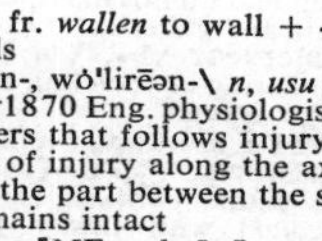
wallet 2b

wall·ette \(ˈ)wȯ¦let\ *n* -s [¹*wall* + *-ette*] **:** a low thin miniature wall (as for ornamental or experimental purposes)

wall·eye \ˈwȯ,lī\ *n* [back-formation fr. *walleyed*] **1 a :** an eye (as of a horse) having a light gray or bluish white iris **b :** an eye having an opaque white cornea **c :** an eye that turns outward showing more than a normal amount of white **2 a :** LEUCOMA **b :** strabismus in which the eye turns outward — called also *exotropia;* compare CROSS-EYE 1 **3 walleyes** *pl* **:** eyes affected with divergent strabismus **4** *or* **walleyed pike** *also* **walleye pike :** a large vigorous American freshwater food and sport fish (*Stizostedion vitreum*) that has large prominent eyes and is related to the perches but more closely resembles the true pike in appearance and behavior

wall-eyed \-īd\ *adj* [by folk etymology (influence of ¹*wall*) fr. ME *wawil-eghed*, part trans. of ON *vagl-eygr* walleyed, fr. *vagl* beam, roost, beam in the eye + *eygr, eygthr* eyed; akin to ON *vega* to move, carry, lift — more at WEIGH] **1 a :** having very light gray or whitish eyes ⟨a ~ horse⟩ **b :** having the eyes directed outward **:** affected with a divergent squint ⟨the operation turned him from cross-eyed to ~⟩ **2 :** affected with leucoma **3 :** marked by a wild irrational staring of the eyes ⟨flailed away in ~ fear —*Time*⟩ ⟨had a ~ fit —Ross Santee⟩ **4 :** having an oblique uncertain appearance or character ⟨~ . . . foreign policy —*New Yorker*⟩

walleye pollack *n* **:** a food fish (*Theragra chalcogramma*) of the northern Pacific related to and closely resembling the pollack

wall fern *n* **:** a low-growing mat-forming fern (*Polypodium vulgare*) that grows esp. in the crevices of walls and is often cultivated as an ornamental

wallflower \ˈ=,=\ *n* **1 :** any of several Old World herbaceous or subshrubby perennial cruciferous plants (genus *Cheiranthus*); *esp* **:** a hardy erect herb (*C. cheiri*) that is widely cultivated for its showy very fragrant usu. yellow or brownish yellow single or double flowers which appear early in the spring **2 :** a plant of the genus *Erysimum* (as the wormseed mustard or prairie rocket) **3 :** a person who from shyness or unpopularity remains on the sidelines of a social activity (as a dance) ⟨a ~ who never wants to meet people⟩ ⟨men were scarce, and ~s wore their peculiar pathetic expression —John Galsworthy⟩ **4** *or* **wallflower brown :** a dark red to moderate reddish brown that is yellower than garnet brown — called also *burnt russet, Cuba, palissandre* **5 :** an Australian desert shrub (*Gastrolobium grandiflorum*)

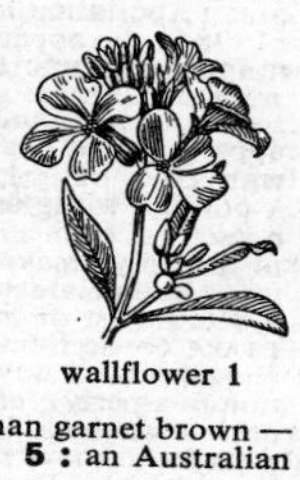
wallflower 1

wall fruit *n* **:** fruit borne by trees trained against a wall

wall garden *n* **:** a garden consisting of plants set in soil in the crevices between the rocks of a wall

wall gecko *n* **:** any of several harmless Old World geckos that feed on insects and have suckers on the feet for clinging to a surface (as a wall)

wall germander *n* **:** an often shrubby European perennial germander (*Teucrium chamaedrys*) that has red-purple or bright rose flowers with red and white spots and is used as a border plant

wall grass *n* **:** a common stonecrop (*Sedum acre*)

wall green *n* **:** a moderate to strong bluish green

wall hanging *n* **:** a drapery or tapestry hung against a wall for decoration

wall hawkweed *n* **:** a European hawkweed (*Hieracium murorum*) with mostly basal leaves and yellow flower heads on glandular stalks that often grows on walls

wall·ing \ˈwȯliŋ\ *n* -s [ME, fr. *wall* + *-ing*] **1 :** WALL ⟨a ~ of stone or sods rises to a height of five or six feet —C.D.Forde⟩ **2 :** material for walls

walling crib *n* **:** a heavy timber or cast-iron ring built into the wall of a mine shaft to support the lining

wall ink *n* **:** a brooklime (*Veronica beccabunga*) that is native to Europe but established in northeastern No. America

wall knot *n* **:** an overhand or double knot that is crowned or double-crowned and made by interweaving the unlaid strands at the end of a rope

wall-less \ˈwȯlləs\ *adj* **:** lacking walls ⟨its *wall-less* ground floor is open to the winds —*Bookman*⟩

wall lettuce *n* **:** a European wild lettuce (*Lactuca muralis*) with coarse foliage and yellow flowers in loose clusters

wall link *n* **:** WALKING FERN

wall lizard *n* **:** a common lizard (*Lacerta muralis*) of southern Europe, Asia Minor, and northern Africa that frequents houses and lives in the chinks and crevices of walls

wall·man \ˈwȯlmən\ *n, pl* **wallmen :** a wrecker who uses a wrecking bar and other hand tools to demolish the roofs and walls of buildings

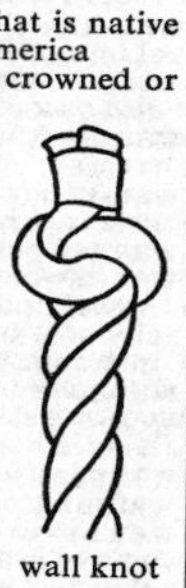
wall knot

wall newspaper *n* **:** an often handwritten or typed newssheet that is usu. posted on a bulletin board or wall ⟨*wall newspapers* found in every shop, office, and farm —Alex Inkeles⟩

wal·lon \wälōⁿ\ *usu cap, archaic var of* WALLOON

¹wal·loon \wäˈlün, wə'- *also* wȯ'-\ *adj, usu cap* [MF *Wallon*, adj. & n., of Gmc origin; prob. akin to OHG *Walah, Walh* Celt, Roman, OE *Wealh* Celt, Welshman — more at WELSH] **1 :** of, relating to, or characteristic of the Walloons **2 :** of, relating to, or written or spoken in the French dialect of the Walloons

²walloon \"\ *n* -s *cap* [MF *Wallon*] **1 :** a member of a chiefly Celtic people of southern Belgium (as Hainaut, Namur, Liége, and Luxembourg), Brabant, and adjacent parts of France — compare FLEMING, BELGIAN **2 :** a French dialect of the Walloons

³walloon \"\ *n* -s [prob. fr. ¹*walloon*] **:** TOBACCO MOSAIC

¹wal·lop \ˈwäləp *also* ˈwȯl-\ *n* -s [ME *wallop, walop*, fr. ONF *walop*, fr. *waloper* to gallop] **1** *obs* **:** GALLOP **2** *obs* **:** a bubbling motion and sound (as of a boiling substance) ⟨let it only boil five or six ~s —George Hartman⟩ **3** *chiefly Brit* **:** a noisy clumsy movement of the body ⟨a sagging sack of flesh . . . he went in with a ~ —Adrian Bell⟩ **4 a :** a powerful blow **:** ²PUNCH 2 ⟨got a hard ~ in the mouth —*Baltimore (Md.) Sun*⟩ ⟨the ~s from the wind made you feel tired —Greville Texidor⟩ **b :** something resembling a wallop esp. in sudden jarring force ⟨the sight of him hit my dried-up soul a ~ —*N. Y. Herald Tribune*⟩ ⟨woodwinds . . . underlined by an explosive percussive ~ —Aaron Copland⟩ **c :** the ability (as of a boxer) to hit hard ⟨has a terrific ~ in his left hand⟩ **5 a :** effective physical, emotional, or psychological force or influence **:** IMPACT ⟨the ~ from an atomic bomb —*N. Y. Times*⟩ ⟨full page advertising . . . carries a tremendous sales ~ —*Playthings*⟩ ⟨a movie with a dramatic ~⟩ ⟨cannot pack the political ~ needed to swing Congress —*New Republic*⟩ **b :** a pleasant or exciting emotional response **:** THRILL, KICK ⟨the kids . . . get a big ~ out of it —Robert Wilder⟩ **6** *Brit* **:** ¹BEER ⟨was a great one for ~ and darts with the villagers in the local —Angus Wilson⟩

²wallop \"\ *vb* -ED/-ING/-S [ME *walopen*, fr. ONF *waloper*] *vi* **1** *obs* **:** GALLOP **2 a :** to move with reckless or disorganized haste **:** advance in a headlong rush ⟨a fat spaniel dog . . . ~*ed* along the deck —D.C.Russell⟩ ⟨ships . . . were ~*ing* across the Atlantic freighted with more cigars —Aldous Huxley⟩ **b** (1) **:** to move violently and often noisily about **:** WALLOW ⟨sea-beasts who roared and rolled and ~*ed* —Rudyard Kipling⟩ ⟨the very cows joined in . . . ~*ing*, tail lashing —Virginia Woolf⟩ (2) **:** to progress in a lurching ungainly manner **:** FLOUNDER ⟨watched the old car ~ down the rutted lane⟩ **3 :** to boil with a loud bubbling noise ⟨an immense pot . . . surging and ~*ing* with some kind of savory stew —Nathaniel Hawthorne⟩ **4** *chiefly Scot* **:** to flap about **:** FLUTTER, FLOP ⟨keep his nether garments from ~*ing* behind him —Peter McNeill⟩ ~ *vt* **1 a :** to thrash soundly (as with the hands or fists) **:** BEAT, POUND, LAMBASTE ⟨always doing the wrong thing and being ~*ed* for it —Ruth Park⟩ ⟨~*ed* the living daylights out of his attacker⟩ **b :** to gain a decisive victory over **:** beat by a wide margin **:** TROUNCE ⟨~*ed* him in the first match they played —Jack Barnaby⟩ ⟨~*ed* the champions 10 to 3 yesterday —*Springfield (Mass.) Republican*⟩ **2 a :** to hit with great force **:** SOCK, SLUG ⟨unfortunately . . . it was a gendarme I had ~*ed* —H.A.Chippendale⟩ **b** (1) **:** to send (as a baseball) a long distance by a solid hit ⟨~*ed* the ball against the facade of the third deck —*N. Y. Times*⟩ (2) **:** to get (as a run in baseball) by batting well ⟨~*ed* 16 home runs last season⟩ **3 :** to scrub (kitchen utensils) clean ⟨by night he ~*ed* pots and pans in a hotel kitchen —R.M. Yoder⟩ **4 :** to move (as material for shipment) by hand ⟨togged like the rest of the gang . . . he ~*s* sacks of sugar, coal, assorted cargo —*Time*⟩

wal·lop·er \-pə(r)\ *n* -s **:** one that wallops

¹walloping *adj* [fr. pres. part. of ²*wallop*] **1 :** outstandingly large in size or degree **:** WHOPPING ⟨accumulate a ~ collection of institutional freaks —*New Yorker*⟩ ⟨able to get a ~ promotion —A.C.Spectorsky⟩ **2 :** exceptionally fine or impressive **:** SMASHING ⟨a ~ new production —Douglas Watt⟩ ⟨the men in the blue-trimmed white . . . won their last race by a ~ twelve lengths —*Newsweek*⟩

²walloping *adv* **:** TERRIFICALLY, SPANKING ⟨going to have a ~ big gas bill —*Lippincott's Mag.*⟩ ⟨a ~ dirty great big umbrella —Richard Llewellyn⟩

¹wal·low \ˈwä¦(,)lō, |lə *also* ˈwȯ|; |lōw *or* |lō+V\ *vb* -ED/-ING/-S [ME *walwen, walowen*, fr. OE *wealwian, wealwian* — more at VOLUBLE] *vi* **1 a :** to roll or move oneself about in an indolent ungainly manner **:** sprawl luxuriously ⟨took films of hippos as they ~*ed* in a mudhole⟩ ⟨too tired to do anything but ~ in a hot tub⟩ **b :** to toss oneself about helplessly or frantically ⟨lay on the ground . . . ~*ing* and pitching and screaming —F.B.Gipson⟩ **c** (1) *of a ship* **:** to pitch and roll in rough water ⟨the boats were ~*ing* in the waves . . . likely to be swamped —J.G.Gilkey⟩ (2) **:** to sail esp. with a heavy rolling motion ⟨~*ed* through a quarter mile of whitecaps —Franc Shor⟩ ⟨fleets . . . that ~ up and down the British coasts —*Lamp*⟩ **d :** to move in an awkward, lurching, and disorganized manner ⟨dawn found the convoy ~*ing* around —Nathaniel Benchley⟩ **e** *of an airplane* **:** to lurch and wobble (as from shifting air currents) ⟨altitudes . . . at which fighters perform sluggishly, ~, lose control —H.W.Baldwin⟩ **2 :** to billow forth **:** SURGE, ROLL ⟨fat polysyllables . . . ~*ed* off his tongue —J.T.Farrell⟩ ⟨the launch heaved on a . . . slowly ~*ing* sea —Aldous Huxley⟩ **3 :** to devote oneself entirely or as if entirely **:** become obsessed (as with a particular mode of behavior or area of interest) — usu. used with *in* ⟨publicly ~*ed* in his infamies —Merle Miller⟩ ⟨the tendency to ~ in national self-absorption —Max Ascoli⟩ ⟨our gripes editor literally ~*s* in gripes —*Jewelers' Circular-Keystone*⟩; *esp* **:** to take unrestrained or excessive pleasure **:** REVEL — usu. used with *in* ⟨enjoy sitting . . . and ~*ing* in the sensual melodies —Osbert Sitwell⟩ **4 a :** to become abundantly supplied **:** LUXURIATE — usu. used with *in* ⟨nauseating baby talk in which some . . . books ~ —Margaret F. Kieran⟩ ⟨a family that ~*s* in money⟩ **b :** to indulge oneself habitually and immoderately — usu. used with *in* ⟨film stars who ~ in luxury⟩ **5 :** to become helpless or ineffectual **:** lose the ability to function naturally or efficiently ⟨the economic catastrophe in which they were . . . ~*ing* —J.P.O'Donnell⟩ ⟨team might be left to ~ in its ignorance —Lennox Robinson⟩ ~ *vt, archaic* **:** to roll (something) about ⟨~*ing* these problems around in his mind —F.B. Gipson⟩

syn WELTER, FLOUNDER, GROVEL: WALLOW implies a movement of rolling to and fro, as of a ship in the trough of a wave or an animal in mire ⟨wind and sea had risen, and the little *Torakina* was rearing, plunging and *wallowing* as she took up the strain of her tow —R.S.Porteous⟩ ⟨a jeep came *wallowing* through the mud —Norman Mailer⟩ ⟨was *wallowing* in self-abasement —*Times Lit. Supp.*⟩ WELTER sometimes implies wallowing but more often implies a rolling or tossing helplessly, as at the mercy of a storm ⟨the lifeboat and its passengers *weltered* in the sea for over a week⟩ ⟨the mass of the people were *weltering* in shocking poverty whilst a handful of owners wallowed in millions —G.B.Shaw⟩ FLOUNDER stresses a helpless stumbling or struggling in an effort to make progress ⟨crews *floundering* through the wet black muck —Marjory S. Douglas⟩ ⟨her feet grew heavier with each step and she *floundered* among the hollows like an odd, awkward fish —Audrey Barker⟩ ⟨many writers have *floundered* in one medium of speech while in another they have moved with ease —H.O.Taylor⟩ GROVEL implies a crawling or wriggling close to the ground, as in abject fear, self-abasement, or complete degradation ⟨fluttered to the ground and *groveled* on the sand in what appeared to be a kind of frenzy —E.A.Armstrong⟩ ⟨one moment he towered in imagination, the next he *groveled* in fear —G.D.Brown⟩ ⟨a mean, timeserving little man, *groveling* odiously before the wealthy people in the district who patronize his shop —Peter Forster⟩

²wallow \"\ *n* -s **1 :** an act or instance of wallowing ⟨the apogee of earthly reward, a luxurious ~ in glamour —R.L. Taylor⟩ **2 a** (1) **:** an area that is wet and muddy or filled with dust and is used by animals for wallowing ⟨elephants using the shallow stream bed for a ~⟩ (2) **:** a depression in the ground formed by the wallowing of animals ⟨great herds left the landscape pitted with ~*s*⟩ — see BEAR WALLOW, BUFFALO WALLOW, HOG WALLOW **b** (1) **:** a declivity or area that is often filled with water or mud and resembles an animal wallow — compare MUDHOLE 1, SWALE 2 ⟨black ~*s* . . . where cars or wagons had been bogged down —L.C.Stevens⟩ ⟨an open field that was often a ~ of mud —Joseph Wechsberg⟩ (2) **:** KOMMETJE **3 :** a state or condition of degradation or degeneracy ⟨the awful ~ that circumstance has plunged him into —John McCarten⟩

³wallow \"\ *vi* [ME *weolewen, wallowen*, fr. OE *wealwian;* akin to MLG *welen* to wither, MD *welken* to welk — more at WELK] *Scot* **:** FADE, WITHER

wal·low·er \|ləwə(r), |lōə(r)\ *n* -s [¹*wallow* + *-er*] **:** one that wallows

wallowish *adj* [obs. E dial. *wallow* tasteless, insipid (fr. ME *walhwe, walh*) + E *-ish* — more at WAUGH] **:** FLAT, INSIPID ⟨give a taste and edge . . . to that dull and ~ flatness —Philemon Holland⟩

wall painting *n* **:** FRESCO 1

¹wallpaper \ˈ=,=\ *n* **:** decorative paper used to cover the walls of a room ⟨hid the plain white walls with hideous flowered ~⟩

²wallpaper \"\ *vt* **:** to provide the walls of (as a room) with wallpaper ~ *vi* **:** to put wallpaper on a wall

wall pellitory *n* **:** a European herb (*Parietaria officinalis*) that has diuretic properties and grows on walls

wall pepper *n* **:** a stonecrop (*Sedum acre*)

wall-piece \ˈ=,=\ *n* **:** a cannon mounted on a wall or a rail of a ship ⟨two large *wall-pieces* . . . loaded . . . with musket balls —*Naval Chronicle*⟩

wall plate *n* [ME *walplate*] **1 :** PLATE 5a(1) — see ROOF illustration **2 :** one of the main side timbers of a mine shaft — compare END PLATE **3 :** SWITCH PLATE

wall plug *n* **:** an electric receptacle having its face flush with or recessed in a wall

wall pressure *n* **:** the pressure exerted on the contents of a plant cell by the cell wall that is equal in force and opposite in direction to the turgor pressure

wall reaction *n* **:** a reaction that is localized on the walls of the containing vessel and is often catalyzed by contact with the walls

wall rock *n* **:** a rock through which a fault or vein runs **:** the country rock next to a fault, vein, or ore deposit

wall rocket *n* **:** any of several plants of the genus *Diplotaxis* found often in quarries and on old walls; *esp* **:** a European weed (*D. tenuifolia*) with rather large yellow flowers that is adventive in No. America

wall rue *or* **wall rue spleenwort** *n* **:** a small delicate spleenwort (*Asplenium rutamuraria*) found on a steep slope (as a wall or cliff) in Eurasia and No. America

walls *pl of* WALL, *pres 3d sing of* WALL

wall speedwell *n* **:** CORN SPEEDWELL

wall street *n, usu cap W&S* [fr. *Wall Street*, street in lower Manhattan, N. Y. City, on and near which are concentrated the Stock Exchange and other exchanges and financial houses] **:** the influential financial interests of the U. S. economy

wall street·er \-,strēd·ə(r)\ *n, usu cap W&S* [*Wall Street*, N. Y. City + E *-er*] **:** a person who is involved in Wall Street ⟨*Wall Streeters* agreed that heavy speculation . . . made the sell-off inevitable —*Newsweek*⟩

wall tent *n* **:** a tent with four perpendicular cloth walls

wall toe *also* **walled toe** *n* **:** a toe of a shoe having the vamp stitched to the top edge of the vertical stiffened sides in the style of a moccasin

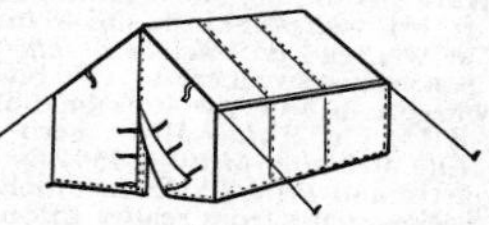
wall tent

wall tree *n* **:** a tree (as a fruit tree) trained against a wall

wall wasp *n* **:** any of several solitary wasps of the genus *Odynerus* that make their nests in the crevices of walls

wallwort \ˈ=,=\ *n* [alter. (influenced by ¹*wall*) of earlier *walwort* danewort, fr. ME *walwort, walwurt*, fr. OE *wealhwyrt*, lit., Welsh herb, foreign herb, fr. *Wealh* Welshman, foreigner + *wyrt* herb, root; prob. fr. the belief that it grew where Welsh blood was spilled — more at WELSH, WORT] **:** any of several plants that grow on or in walls: as **a :** DANEWORT **b :** WALL PELLITORY **c :** a stonecrop (*Sedum acre*) **d :** WALL RUE

wal·ly \ˈwālī\ *adj* [prob. fr. ME (Sc) *wale* choice, pick + *-y* — more at WALE] *Scot* **:** FINE, SPLENDID, STURDY

wal·ly·drai·gle \ˈwālī,drāgəl\ *n* -s [prob. fr. *wally* (prob. contr. of ¹*wellaway*) + *draigle*] *Scot* **:** a feeble, undergrown, or slovenly creature

¹walm *n* -s [ME, bubbling of water, fr. OE *wælm, wielm* action of boiling or bubbling; akin to OHG *walm* action of boiling, OE *weallan, wyllan* to bubble, well — more at WELL] *obs* **:** WALLOP 2

²walm \ˈwäm\ *vi* [ME *walmen*, fr. *walm*, n.] *archaic* **:** to well up (as water) **:** gush forth ⟨waters spring and ~ out of the inner parts of the earth —Stephen Batman⟩

wal·nut \ˈwȯl(,)nət, *usu* -əd+V\ *n* [ME *walnot*, fr. OE *wealhhnutu*, lit., Welsh nut, foreign nut, fr. *Wealh* Welshman, foreigner + *hnutu* nut — more at WELSH, NUT] **1 a :** an edible nut produced by a tree of the genus *Juglans; esp* **:** ENGLISH WALNUT 2 **b** *or* **walnut tree** [ME *walnotetre, walnot tree*] **:** a tree bearing this nut — see TREE illustration **c :** the wood of a walnut tree; *esp* **:** BLACK WALNUT **2 :** any of several trees of genera other than *Juglans:* as **a :** ACAPU **b :** AFRICAN WALNUT **c :** BLACK POISON **3** *chiefly NewEng* **:** HICKORY NUT **4 :** a moderate reddish brown that is the color of the heartwood of the black walnut — distinguished from *walnut brown*

walnut aphid *n* **:** a plant louse (*Chromaphis juglandicola*) that is destructive to walnuts esp. in California

walnut blight *n* **:** a disease of the English walnut caused by a bacterium (*Xanthomonas juglandis*) and characterized by black dead spots on the young fruits, leaves, and shoots

walnut borer *n* **1 :** a blue-winged longicorn beetle (*Gaurotes cyanipennis*) whose larva bores into the wood of the black walnut **2 :** any of several ambrosia beetles (esp. *Anisandrus pyri* or *A. dispar*) that bore under the bark or in the wood of the black walnut

walnut brown *n* **:** a light yellowish brown that is redder, lighter, and stronger than khaki, paler and slightly yellower than cinnamon, slightly redder and lighter than manila, and stronger and slightly redder and lighter than fallow and is the color of the shell of the English walnut — distinguished from *walnut;* called also *taffy*

walnut casebearer *n* **:** a small phycitid moth (*Mineola palliolella*) whose larva lives in a portable case on the walnut

walnut caterpillar *n* **:** the hairy gregarious caterpillar of a walnut moth (*Datana integerrima*)

walnut curculio *n* **:** WALNUT WEEVIL

walnut family *n* **:** JUGLANDACEAE

walnut husk fly *n* **:** any of several trypetid flies (esp. *Rhagoletis completa* and *R. suavis*) whose larvae live in the husks of black and other walnuts

walnut moth *n* **:** any of several moths whose larvae eat the foliage of the walnut: as **a :** REGAL MOTH **b :** IMPERIAL MOTH **c :** LUNA MOTH **d :** any of several red underwings of the genus *Catocala* **e :** a dagger moth (*Acronicta americana*) found also on the maple **f :** any of three arctiid moths of the genus *Halisidota* (*H. caryae, H. tesselaris, H. maculata*) **g :** a moth (*Datana integerrima*) whose larva feeds on and often defoliates walnut, hickory, birch, oak, chestnut, linden, and apple

walnut oil *n* **:** a very pale fatty oil that does not turn yellow, that is obtained from English walnuts, and that is used in foods, artists' colors, paints, and soap

walnut scale *n* **:** a round scale (*Aspidiotus juglans-regiae*) that infests the English walnut

walnut shell *n* **1 :** the shell or half shell of a walnut **2 :** a very light boat ⟨nursed our *walnut shell* tenderly over their crests —Erskine Childers⟩

walnut spanworm *n* **:** a worm that is the larva of a geometrid moth (*Conoides plumogeraria*) and that sometimes defoliates the English walnut in California

walnut sphinx *n* **:** a large brown and gray sphinx (*Cressonia juglandis*) whose larva feeds on the leaves of the black walnut and hickory

walnut weevil *n* **:** any of several weevils (as *Conotrachelus juglandis*) that feed on the foliage and fruit of walnuts

walnut worm *n* **:** the hairy larva of a walnut moth

wal·pi *also* **hual·pi** \ˈwälpē\ *n, pl* **walpi** *or* **walpis** *also* **hualpi** *or* **hualpis** *usu cap* **1 :** a Shoshonean people occupying a pueblo in northeastern Arizona **2 :** a member of the Walpi people

¹wal·pol·ian *also* **wal·pol·ean** \(ˈ)wȯl¦pōlēən *sometimes* (ˈ)wäl¦-\ *adj, usu cap* [Horace *Walpole* †1797 Eng. man of letters + E *-an*] **1 :** of, relating to, or having the characteristics of Horace Walpole or his writings ⟨a *Walpolian* letter writer⟩ **2** [Robert *Walpole* †1745 Eng. statesman + E *-er*] **:** of, relating to, or having the characteristics of Robert

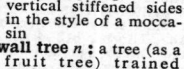

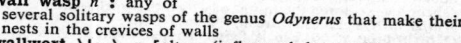

Walpole or his political policies ⟨turned them into sound *Walpolean* Whigs —J.H.Plumb⟩
²**wal·po·lian** \"\ *n -s usu cap* [Horace *Walpole* †1797 + E *-an*, n. suffix] **:** an admirer or student of the writings of Horace Walpole ⟨ardent *Walpolians* and collectors of private press issues —*Saturday Rev.*⟩
wal·pur·gis night \wȧl'pu̇rgəs-, -u̇(ə)gəs-; val'pər|jəs-, wȧl-, wȯl-, -pȧl, -pȧl, |gȧs-/ *or* **wal·pur·gis·nacht** \wȧl'pu̇rgə-, snu̇kt, -u̇(ə)g-\ *n -s usu cap W&N* [*walpurgis night* part trans. of G *walpurgisnacht*, fr. *Walpurgis* St. Walburga †A.D. 777 Eng. saint whose feast day falls on May Day + G *nacht* night, fr. OHG *naht* — more at NIGHT] **1 :** the evening preceding May Day **:** the evening of April 30 believed esp. during medieval and Renaissance times to be an occasion when witches celebrate a sabbat **2 :** something (as an event or situation) having an orgiastic or nightmarish character ⟨the big, wicked party that should be the ... *Walpurgis Night* of his book —*New Republic*⟩ ⟨the relationship ... became a protracted *Walpurgisnacht* —George Stevens⟩
wal·pur·gite \wȧl'pər,jīt, wȯl-, -ġīt\ *n -s* [G *walpurgin* (fr. *Walpurgis*, vein in mine at Schneeberg, central Germany + G *-in* -ine) + E *-ite*] **:** a mineral Bi₄(UO₂)(AsO₄)₂O₄.3H₂O(?) consisting of a hydrous bismuth uranium arsenate and oxide occurring in thin yellow crystals
wal·rus \'wȯlrəs, 'wȧl-\ *n, pl* **walrus** *or* **walruses** [D *walrus, walros,* of Scand origin; akin to Dan & Norw *hvalros* walrus, ON *rosmhvalr* walrus, *hvalr* whale — more at WHALE] **1 :** either of two large marine mammals (family Odobenidae) that may exceed a ton in weight and are hunted for the tough heavy hide, the ivory tusks, the oil yielded by the blubber, and locally for the flesh: **a :** a mammal (*Odobenus rosmarus*) of the northwestern Atlantic and Arctic oceans — called also *Atlantic walrus* **b :** a mammal (*O. divergens*) of the Bering sea and the Arctic coasts of Alaska and Siberia that is sometimes held to be a variety of the Atlantic walrus — called also *Pacific walrus* **2 :** the hide of the walrus used esp. for covering buffing wheels or split and tanned and used for luggage leather
walrus bird *n* [so called fr. its puffing out of its breast like a walrus] **:** PECTORAL SANDPIPER
walrus moustache *n* **:** a heavy often shaggy moustache with drooping ends resembling the moustache of a walrus ⟨an old man with a dirty yellow *walrus moustache* —Anthony West⟩
wal·sall \'wȯl,sȯl\ *adj, usu cap* [fr. *Walsall*, England] **:** of or from the county borough of Walsall, England **:** of the kind or style prevalent in Walsall
walt \'wȯlt\ *adj* [obs. E dial. *walt* to overturn, tumble, totter, fr. ME *walten*; akin to OE *weltan, weltan* to turn, roll — more at WELTER] **1** *archaic, of a ship* **:** tending to list **:** UNSTEADY, ⁹CRANK ⟨a sweet craft, ... a bit ~ perhaps —S.H.Adams⟩
wal·ter mit·ty \'wȯltə(r)'mid-ē\ *n, usu cap* **walter mittys** *usu cap W&M* [fr. *Walter Mitty*, hero of the short story *The Secret Life of Walter Mitty* (1939) by James G. Thurber b1894 Am. artist and writer] **:** a commonplace unadventurous person who seeks escape from reality through daydreaming and typically imagines himself leading a glamorous life and becoming famous ⟨spent his life doing the things of which the world's wistful ... *Walter Mittys* can only dream —James Gray⟩
walter's pine *n, usu cap W* [after Thomas *Walter*, 18th cent. Eng. naturalist] **:** SPRUCE PINE 1a
wal·tham·stow \'wȯlthəm,stō\ *adj, usu cap* [fr. *Walthamstow*, England] **:** of or from the municipal borough of Walthamstow, England **:** of the kind or style prevalent in Walthamstow
wal·ther·ite \'wȯltə,rīt, -rə\ *n -s* [G *waltherit*, fr. *Walther*, a 19th cent. Austrian mining official + G *-it* -ite] **:** a mineral consisting of an ill-defined carbonate of bismuth having green to brownish green doubly terminated prismatic crystals
wal·ther's canal \'vȧltə(r)z-\ *or* **walther's duct** *n, usu cap W* [after Augustin Friedrich *Walther* †1746 Ger. anatomist] **:** any of several small inconstant efferent ducts of the sublingual gland opening into the mouth
¹**wal·to·ni·an** \wȯl'tōnēən\ *n -s usu cap* [Izaak *Walton* †1683 Eng. biographer and author + E *-an*, n. suffix] **:** a follower of Izaak Walton or his writings; *esp* **:** ANGLER ⟨fish that any *Waltonian* might well stare at —John Coulter⟩
²**waltonian** \(')ˌ'···\ *adj, usu cap* [Izaak *Walton* †1683 + E *-an*, adj. suffix] **:** of, relating to, or having the characteristics of Izaak Walton or his writings on angling ⟨sporting facilities include trout fishing in *Waltonian* streams —*London Calling*⟩
walty \'wȯltē\ *adj* [*walt* + *-y*] *of a ship* **:** tending to list **:** ⁹CRANK
¹**waltz** \'wȯlts *also* -ts\ *n -es* [G *walzer*] **1 :** to roll, revolve, dance, fr. OHG *walzan* to turn, roll — more at WELTER] **1 :** a round dance in ¾ time with a strong accent on the first beat of the measure that is characterized by one step to the beat typically executed with a constant gyrating motion at a moderately fast tempo — see ³BOSTON 1 **2 a :** the music for dancing a waltz **b :** an instrumental, orchestral, or vocal composition in ¾ time intended chiefly for concert performance
²**waltz** \"\ *vb* -ED/-ING/-ES [G *walzen*] *vi* **1 a :** to dance a waltz ⟨tried to ~ for the first time in years⟩ **2 a :** to move about in a lively whimsical often aimless manner ⟨think they can just ~ in and out of the house all day⟩ ⟨don't like strangers ~ing around up here —John Hersey⟩ **b :** to move along in an excited, noisy, or attention-seeking manner **:** FLOUNCE ⟨saw the jolly bunch come ~ing in for eats —Sinclair Lewis⟩ ⟨~ed out to the ladies' room to talk and smoke —Catherine Hubbell⟩ **3 a :** to advance easily and successfully **:** proceed without a hitch **:** BREEZE — usu. used with *through* ⟨you'll ~ through most European customs —T.H.Fielding⟩ ⟨~ed through the big games —*Christian Science Monitor*⟩ **b :** to approach boldly — used with *up* ⟨can't just ~ up and introduce ourselves⟩ ~ *vt* **1 :** to lead (a partner) in a waltz **:** dance a waltz with ⟨~ed her around the room at a dizzying clip⟩ **2 a :** to lead (as a person) in a hasty, determined, and unceremonious manner **:** MARCH ⟨grabbed the child's arm and ~ed him upstairs⟩ ⟨~ed him through many phases of religiosity —Clemence Dane⟩ **b :** CARRY, LUG ⟨had to ~ this package all over town⟩ — **waltz matilda** *usu cap M* [*matilda* fr. the feminine name *Matilda*; prob. fr. the manner in which the swagman carried his swag and fr. the fact that he never parted with it and considered himself married to it] *Austral* **:** to travel around on foot esp. carrying a pack or swag — **waltz off** with **:** to win (as a prize) esp. by beating one's opponents easily ⟨*waltzed off with* several honors in this category —Lois Long⟩
³**waltz** \"\ *adj* [¹*waltz*] **:** of, relating to, or having the characteristics of a waltz ⟨~ step⟩ ⟨~ tune⟩
waltz·er \-sə(r)\ *n -s* **:** one that waltzes
waltzing mouse *n* **:** a mouse of a genetic variant or a breed believed to have originated in Japan and characterized by an inability to progress in a straight line and a tendency to whirl about in small circles
waltz jump *n* **:** THREE JUMP
waltz swing *n* **:** a common square-dance swing danced clockwise right side to right side with the gentleman's right hand at the lady's back, his left hand holding her right, and her left hand on his shoulder
waly \'wälı\ *interj* [prob. contr. of ¹*wellaway*] *chiefly Scot* — used to express sorrow
WAM *abbr, often not cap* words a minute
wa·ma·ra \'wȧmərə\ *n -s* [Arawak] **1 :** a tree (*Swartzia tomentosa*) of British Guiana **2 :** the very hard purplish black wood of the wamara that has a straight fine uniform grain and is used for various purposes but sparingly because of the difficulty of working it
wam·ben·ger \'wȧm,bengə(r)\ *n -s* [origin unknown] **:** a widely distributed Australian pouched mouse (*Phascogale penicillata*)
¹**wam·ble** \'wȧmbəl, -wȧm-\ *vb* wambled; wambled; wambling \-b(ə)liŋ\ wambles [ME *wamlen*; akin to Dan *vamle* to become nauseated, L *vomere* to vomit — more at VOMIT] *vi* **1 a :** to feel nausea **b :** *of a stomach* **:** ROLL **2 :** to move unsteadily or with a weaving or rolling motion ⟨a *wambling* conversation⟩ ⟨a story that ~s on and on⟩ ~ *vt* **:** to turn over and over **:** SPIN, REVOLVE
²**wamble** \"\ *n -s* **1 :** a rumbling or disturbance of the stomach **2 :** an irregular gait or movement **:** a reeling or staggering gait
wamble-cropped *also* **wamble-cropt** \'··ˌkrȧpt\ *adj* [²*wam-

¹*ble* + *crop* (stomach) + *-ed*] *dial* **:** having a rumbling stomach; *also* **:** SICKLY
wam·bli·ness \-blēnəs\ *n -ES* **:** the quality or state of being wambly
wambling *adj* [fr. pres. part. of ¹*wamble*] **1 :** REELING, TOTTERING ⟨a ~ gait⟩ **2 :** WEAK, INEFFECTIVE ⟨a ~ teacher⟩ — **wam·bling·ly** *adv*
wam·bly \-blē, -li\ *adj* -ER/-EST [²*wamble* + *-y*] *dial* **:** FAINT, SQUEAMISH; *also* **:** SHAKY
wame \'wȧm\ *n -s* [ME, alter. of *wamb* — more at WOMB] *chiefly Scot* **:** BELLY
wam·pa·no·ag \ˌwȧmpə'nōˌag *also* ˌwȯm-\ *n, pl* **wampanoag** *or* **wampanoags** *usu cap* [Natick *Wampan-ohke*, lit., eastern land, fr. *wampan* white, light, of the dawn + *ohke* land, earth] **1 :** an Indian people of Rhode Island east of Narragansett Bay and neighboring parts of Massachusetts **2 :** a member of the Wampanoag people
¹**wam·pee** \wȧm'pē *also* wȯm-\ *n* [of Algonquian origin; akin to Natick *wampan, wómpi* white, Shawnee *wapa*] **1** *South* **:** ARROW ARUM
²**wampee** *also* **wam·pi** \"\ *n -s* [Chin (Pek) *huang²* -p'i², fr. *huang²* yellow + p'i² skin] **:** an Asiatic tree (*Clausena lansium*) of the family Rutaceae cultivated in Hawaii; *also* **:** its fruit which is about the size of a large grape and which has a hard rind
wam·pish \'wȧmpish\ *vb* -ED/-ING/-ES [origin unknown] *Scot* **:** FLUCTUATE, SWING
wam·pum \'wȧmpəm *also* 'wȯmp-\ *n -s* [short for *wampumpeag*, fr. Narraganset *wampompeag*, fr. *wampan* white + *api* string + *-ag*, pl. suffix] **1 :** beads made of shells polished and strung together in strands, belts, or sashes and used by the No. American Indians as money, ceremonial pledges, and ornaments **2** *slang* **:** MONEY
wampum belt *n* **:** a belt of varicolored wampum arranged in patterns and used as a mnemonic device or ceremonially esp. in the ratification of treaties — compare WAR BELT
wam·pum·peag \-pəm,pēg\ *n -s* [Narraganset *wampompeag* — more at WAMPUM] **:** WAMPUM; *esp* **:** wampum made of the less valuable white rather than dark purple or black shell beads
wampum snake *n* **:** any of several brightly marked American snakes (as the horned viper or hoop snake)
wam·pus \'wȧmpəs *also* 'wȯm-\ *n -ES* [prob. short for *catawampus*] *dial* **:** a strange, objectionable, or monstrous person or thing
wa·mus *or* **wam·mus** \'wȯməs, 'wȧm-\ *or* **war·mus** \'wȯrm-\ *n -ES* [D *wambuis, wammes,* fr. MD *wambeis,* fr. OF *wambeison,* aug. of *wambeis, gambeis* doublet, of Gmc origin; akin to OHG *wamba* belly — more at WOMB] *dial* **:** a warm work jacket made usu. in a belted cardigan style and of sturdy material or woven fabric
¹**wan** \'wȧn *also* 'wȯn\ *adj* **wanner; wannest** [ME, fr. OE *wann, wan* dark, gloomy, livid] **1** *archaic* **:** DARK, DUSKY **:** lead-colored ⟨~ water⟩ **2 a :** suggesting poor health **:** SICKLY, PALLID ⟨a ~ complexion⟩ **b :** lacking human vitality **:** FEEBLE ⟨a ~ personality⟩ **3 a :** DIM, LUSTERLESS ⟨~ stars⟩ **b :** barely perceptible **:** FAINT ⟨a ~ light⟩ **4 :** showing little effort **:** LANGUID ⟨a ~ laugh⟩ **5 :** tending toward or suggestive of failure or incompetence **:** INEFFECTUAL ⟨~ efforts⟩
²**wan** \"\ *vb* **wanned; wanned; wanning; wans** *vi* **:** to grow or become pale or sickly ~ *vt* **:** to make wan **:** cause to appear pale or sickly
³**wan** \"\ *n -s* **:** PALENESS, PALLOR
⁴**wan** \'wȧn *also* 'wȯn\ *dial var of* ONE
wan·chancy \wȧn'chan(t)sē\ *adj* [Sc *wanchance* misfortune (fr. *wan-* deficient, mis- — fr. ME + *chance*) + *-y* — more at WANTON] *chiefly Scot* **:** ILL-FATED, MISCHIEVOUS ⟨the ~ bullet maun have weakened his chest —John Buchan⟩; *also* **:** UNCANNY, WEIRD
wand \'wȧnd *also* 'wȯnd\ *n -s* [ME *wond, wande,* fr. ON *vöndr;* akin to Goth *wandus* rod, OE *windan* to wind, twist — more at WIND] **1** *archaic* **:** a slender often flexible pole used as a pointer, goad, or whip or for fishing or measuring **2 a :** a slender wooden or metal staff carried (as by a verger, beadle, or sheriff) often in advance of a dignitary in a procession **:** VERGE **b** *Scots law* **:** a baton or staff that with the blazon constitutes the insignia of a messenger of a court that must be shown in executing a caption **3 a :** a slender rod often carried by fairies or other beings associated with magic or the supernatural **b :** a slender flexible rod used by conjurers and magicians **4 a :** a peeled stick stuck up as a mark for archers in England **b :** a slat 6 feet by 2 inches used in the U.S. as a target in archery and stood at 100 yards for men and at 60 for women **5 a :** a light rod of wood or metal used in calisthenic exercises or mass gymnastic displays **b :** the rigid tube between the hose and nozzle of a vacuum cleaner
wand bearer *n* **:** a verger in some English cathedrals
¹**wan·der** \'wȧndə(r) *also* 'wȯn-\ *vb* **wandered; wandered; wandering** \-d(ə)riŋ\ **wanders** [ME *wandren, wanderen,* fr. OE *wandrian;* akin to MD & MLG *wanderen* to wander, MHG *wandern,* OE *windan* to turn, wind, twist — more at WIND] *vi* **1 a :** to move about without a fixed course, aim, or goal ⟨~ about the world⟩ **b :** to go idly about for pleasure or relaxation ⟨a crowd ~ing on a village green⟩ **2 a :** to travel esp. slowly by a devious or indirect route **:** take a roundabout or leisurely course ⟨cattle ~ing toward pasture⟩ **b :** to take a slow winding course **:** MEANDER ⟨a ~ing stream⟩ **3 a :** to deviate (as from a path or course) ⟨stray ~ from a trail⟩ **b :** to go astray morally **:** ERR ⟨~ from proper conduct⟩ **4 :** to depart from normal mental status **:** lose touch with everyday rational conduct **:** become harmlessly irrational ⟨old men with ~ing minds⟩ **5 :** to pass esp. without plan from one to another **:** CIRCULATE ⟨a ~ing rumor⟩ ~ *vt* **:** to roam over ⟨~ woodlands⟩
²**wander** \"\ *n -s* **:** the act or action of wandering **:** RAMBLE, STROLL ⟨go for a ~ in the countryside⟩
wan·der·er \-dərə(r)\ *n -s* **:** one that wanders: as **a** *cap* **:** a Scottish Covenanter during the time of persecution **b** (1) **:** a brown and black American butterfly (*Feniseca tarquinius*) of the family Lycaenidae whose larva feeds on woolly aphids of the genus *Schizoneura* esp. on the alder blight; *also* **:** a monarch or other butterfly of the genus *Danaus* (2) **:** WANDERING SPIDER
¹**wandering** *n -s* [ME, fr. gerund of *wanderen* to wander] **1 :** a going or traveling about from place to place esp. pointlessly or leisurely — often used in pl. **2 :** movement away from the proper, normal, or usual course — often used in pl. **3 :** mental deviation usu. of a harmless nature — often used in pl.
²**wandering** *adj* [ME, fr. pres. part. of *wanderen* to wander] **:** characterized by aimless, slow, or pointless movement: as **a :** WINDING, MEANDERING ⟨a ~ course⟩ **b :** not keeping a rational or sensible course ⟨VAGRANT, ERRANT **c :** NOMADIC ⟨~ tribes⟩ **d** *of a plant* **:** having long runners or tendrils **:** TRAILING ⟨~ kidney⟩
wandering albatross *n* [²*wandering*] **:** a large black-winged white albatross (*Diomedea exulans*) widely distributed in southern oceans
wandering ant *n* **:** ARMY ANT
wandering cell *n* **:** an amoeboid phagocyte: as **a :** an actively motile reticuloendothelial cell of the tissues **b :** LEUKOCYTE
wandering dune *n* **:** a dune slowly shifted by the wind because it has not sufficient vegetation to anchor it
wandering jenny *n* **:** MONEYWORT
wandering jew *n, usu cap J* [after the *Wandering Jew*, legendary figure condemned to wander the earth until the second coming of Christ for having mocked at Him on His way to the crucifixion] **1 :** any of several plants of the genera *Zebrina* and *Tradescantia; esp* **:** either of two trailing or creeping cultivated plants (*Zebrina pendula* and *Tradescantia fluminensis*) **2** *dial Brit* **a :** STRAWBERRY GERANIUM **b :** KENILWORTH IVY
wan·der·ing·ly *adv* **:** in a wandering manner
wandering milkweed *n* **:** SPREADING DOGBANE
wan·der·ing·ness *n -ES* **:** the quality or state of being wandering, errant, aimless, or wandering
wandering of the poles [¹*wandering*] **:** the change in position of the terrestrial poles within an area not over 40 feet in diameter caused by slight more or less cyclic shifts of the body of the earth on its rotational axis and resulting in the variation of latitude
wandering rash *n* [²*wandering*] **:** GEOGRAPHIC TONGUE
wandering sailor *also* **wandering sally** *n* **:** MONEYWORT

wandering spider *n* **:** a spider that wanders about in search of its prey rather than trapping it with a fixed web
wandering star *n* **:** any of the seven planets of ancient astronomy
wandering tattler *n* **:** either of two shorebirds (*Heteroscelus incanus* and *H. brevipes*) summering on the coasts and interior of Alaska and Siberia and wintering in many Pacific islands and being similar in form and size to the yellowlegs although the color of their upperparts is a uniform slaty gray
wan·der·lust \'wȧndə(r),lȯst *also* -wȯn-\ *n* [G, fr. *wandern* to wander (fr. MHG) + *lust* desire, pleasure, fr. OHG — more at WANDER, LUST] **:** strong or unconquerable longing for or impulse toward wandering or traveling — **wan·der·lust·er** \-tə(r)\ *n* — **wan·der·lust·ful** \-tfəl\ *adj*
wan·der·oo \ˌwȧndə'rü *also* ˌwȯn-\ *n -s* [Sinhalese *wanduru*, pl. of *vandurā*, fr. Skt *vānara* monkey — more at BANDAR] **1 :** PURPLE-FACED LANGUR **2 :** LION-TAILED MACAQUE
wanders *pres 3d sing of* WANDER, *pl of* WANDER
wander termite *n* **:** any of various termites that forage in the open and do not like the majority remain in the shelter of their nests and galleries
wan·der·year \'···,·\ *n* [trans. of G *wanderjahr*] **:** a year of wandering or traveling esp. before settling down to one's trade or profession
W *and* **F** *abbr* water and feed
wandflower \'·,·\ *n* [*wand* + *flower*] **1 :** a plant or flower of the genus *Sparaxis; esp* **:** a showy often purple-spotted flowers (*S. tricolor*) with tawny yellow often purple-spotted flowers **2 :** GALAX 2
W *and* **I** *abbr* weighing and inspection
wan·dle \'wand²l\ *adj* [prob. irreg. fr. *wand*] *chiefly Scot* **:** SUPPLE, AGILE
wan·doo \(')wȧn'dü\ *n -s* [native name in Australia] **:** a gum tree (*Eucalyptus redunca*) of western Australia yielding a hard tough durable wood and a tanning extract
W *and* **R** *abbr* **1** water and rail **2** welfare and recreation
wands *pl of* WAND
W *and* **S** *abbr, often not cap* whiskey and soda
wand shoot *n* **:** a round of 36 arrows shot at a wand
wand shot *n* **:** one of the shots of a wand shoot
wands·man \'wän(d)zmən *also* 'wȯn-\ *n, pl* **wandsmen** [*wand's* (gen. of *wand*) + *man*] **:** WAND BEARER
wane \'wän\ *vi* -ED/-ING/-S [ME *wanien, wanen,* fr. OE *wanian;* akin to OHG *wanōn* to wane, ON *vana* to lessen; all fr. a prehistoric Gmc adj. represented by OE & OHG *wan* wanting, deficient, absent, ON *vanr,* Goth *wans;* akin to L *vanus* empty, vain, Gk *eunis* bereft, lacking, Skt *ūna* wanting, deficient, and perh. to L *vacare* to be empty, *vacuus* empty] **1 :** to decrease in size or extent **:** DWINDLE: as **a :** to diminish in phase or intensity — used of the moon and other satellites and inferior planets; opposed to *wax;* see MOON illustration **b :** to become less in brilliance or power **:** grow dim — used of light or color **:** to flow out **:** EBB — used of water or the tide **2 :** to fall esp. gradually from power, prosperity, or influence **:** DECAY, DECLINE ⟨a *waning* political party⟩
²**wane** \"\ *n -s* [ME, fr. *wanen* to wane] **1 a :** the act or action of decreasing or diminishing ⟨strength on the ~⟩ **b :** the period or time of decreasing or diminishing ⟨the ~ of colors of a sunset⟩ **2 :** the act, time, or phenomenon of decreasing in phase or intensity; *specif* **:** the period from full phase of the moon to the new moon **3** [ME, defect, shortage, fr. OE *wana;* akin to OE *wan* deficient — more at ¹WANE] **:** an edge or corner defect in lumber characterized by the presence of bark or by lack of wood — compare WANEY 2
waney *or* **wany** \-nē\ *adj* **wanier; waniest** [²*wane* + *-y*] **1 :** waning or diminished in some parts **2** *of sawed timber* **:** cut so near the outside of the log that there is no square edge
wang \'wäŋ\ *n -s* [Chin (Pek) *wang²* king, prince] **:** a Chinese ruler before the 3d century B.C. or a Chinese prince of high rank after the 3d century B.C.
wan·ga *or* **ouan·ga** \'wäŋgə\ *n -s* [Haitian Creole *ouanga,* of Bantu origin; akin to Kimbundu *wanga* witchcraft, Tshiluba *bwanga* charm, fetish] **:** voodoo sorcery; *also* **:** a voodooistic charm or spell
wan·gen·steen apparatus \'wäŋgən,stēn-\ *also* **wangensteen appliance** *n, usu cap W* [after Owen H. *Wangensteen* b1898] **:** the apparatus used in Wangensteen suction
wangensteen suction *n, usu cap W* [after Owen H. *Wangensteen* b1898 Am. surgeon] **:** a method of draining fluid or secretions from body cavities (as the stomach) by means of an apparatus that operates on negative pressure
¹**wan·gle** \'waŋgəl, -aiŋ-\ *vb* **wangled; wangled; wangling** \-g(ə)liŋ\ **wangles** [perh. alter. of ¹*waggle*] *vi* **1 :** to extricate oneself (as from a crowd or difficulty) **:** WIGGLE **2 :** to resort to trickery, makeshift, or devious methods ⟨*wangling* to forestall ultimate payment of a bet⟩ ~ *vt* **1 :** SHAKE, WIGGLE **2 :** to adjust or manipulate for personal or fraudulent ends ⟨FAKE ⟨~ accounts⟩ **3 :** to make or get by or as if by wrangling ⟨~one's way through a crowd⟩ **:** FINAGLE ⟨~ an invitation to a party⟩; *also* **:** to persuade or convince by cunning or devious methods ⟨~ a person into loaning money⟩
²**wangle** \"\ *n -s* **:** the act of wangling; *also* **:** something procured by wangling
wan·gler \-g(ə)lə(r)\ *n -s* **:** one that wangles
wan·hap \'wän,hap\ *n* [Sc *wan-* deficient, mis- (fr. ME) + *hap* — more at WANTON] *Scot* **:** MISFORTUNE, MISHAP
wan·hap·py \(')·'hapi\ *adj* [Sc *wan-* + *happy*] *Scot* **:** UNFORTUNATE
wan·hsi·en \'wänshē'en\ *adj, usu cap* [fr. *Wanhsien,* city of south central China] **:** of or from the city of Wanhsien, China **:** of the kind or style prevalent in Wanhsien
wan·i·gan *or* **wannigan** \'wä|nəgən, |nēg- *also* 'wȯ|\ *or* **wan·gan** *or* **wan·gun** \|ŋg-\ *n -s* [of Algonquian origin; akin to Abnaki *waniigan* trap, lit., that into which something strays] **1 :** a chest for supplies **2 :** a shelter for sleeping, eating, storage, or office space often mounted on wheels or crawler tracks and towed by tractor or mounted on a raft or boat **3 :** debts incurred by lumbermen at a company store
waning *pres part of* WANE
wan·ion \'wänyən\ *n -s* [fr. the obs. phrase *in the waniand* unluckily, lit., in the waning (moon), fr. ME, fr. *waniand,* northern pres. part. of *wanien* to wane] *archaic* **:** PLAGUE, VENGEANCE — used in the phrase *with a wanion*
wan·ka·pin \'wäŋkə,pin\ *n -s* [Ojibwa *wankipin,* lit., crooked root] **:** WATER CHINQUAPIN
wan·kle \'waŋkəl\ *adj* [ME *wankel, wankill,* fr. OE *wancol;* akin to OHG *wanchal* unsteady, *wankōn,* *wanchōn* to stagger, sway — more at WINK] **1** *chiefly dial* **:** UNSTEADY, UNSTABLE; *also* **:** FICKLE, IRRESOLUTE **2** *chiefly dial* **:** SICKLY, FEEBLE
wan·ky \'waŋkē\ *adj* -ER/-EST [alter. of *wankle*] *dial* **:** WEAK, FEEBLE
wan·ly *adv* [ME *wanliche,* fr. ¹*wan* + *-liche* -ly] **:** in a feeble, pale, sickly, or languid manner
wanned *past of* WAN
wan·ne·eick·el \'vänə'īkəl\ *adj, usu cap W&E* [fr. *Wanne-Eickel,* industrial city of western Germany] **:** of or from the city of Wanne-Eickel, Germany **:** of the kind or style prevalent in Wanne-Eickel
wanner *comparative of* WAN
wan·ness \'wännəs *also* 'wȯn-\ *n -ES* [ME *wannesse,* fr. ¹*wan* + *-nesse* -ness] **:** the quality or state of being wan
wannest *superlative of* WAN
wanning *pres part of* WAN
wans *pres 3d sing of* WAN, *pl of* WAN
¹**want** \'wȯnt, 'wänt\ *n -s* [ME *wont, wonte,* fr. OE *wand, wond;* prob. akin to OE *windan* to turn, wind — more at WIND] *dial Brit* **:** a European mole (*Talpa europaeus*)
²**want** \'wȯnt, 'wänt; *want to is often* 'wȯn(t)ə *or* 'wän(t)ə\ *vb* -ED/-ING/-S [ME *wanten,* fr. ON *vanta* to be wanting, deficient — more at WANE] *vt* **1 :** to fail to possess the required or usual amount of **:** LACK ⟨~ strength to walk⟩ **:** be deficient in ⟨~ courtesy⟩ **2 a** (1) **:** to desire without reservation **:** wish earnestly — used with the infinitive ⟨~ing to rise in the world⟩ ⟨~s to be home⟩ (2) **:** to feel a profound yearning for ⟨CRAVE ⟨~ relaxation⟩ **b :** to be inclined to **:** LIKE ⟨call it what you ~, the judge said it was murder⟩ **3** *dial* **:** to dispense with **:** do without **4 :** to have need of ⟨REQUIRE ⟨this motor ~s the attention of a good mechanic⟩ **5 :** to suffer from the lack of ⟨thousands ~ing food and shelter⟩ **6 :** to be under obligation **:** OUGHT, SHOULD — used

with the infinitive ⟨you ~ to act decently in all situations⟩ **7 :** to wish or demand the presence of ⟨the boss ~*s* you in the front office⟩ : wish to speak to or see ⟨the teacher ~*s* you⟩ **8 :** to hunt or seek for apprehension ⟨~*ed* for war crimes⟩ ~ *vi* **1 a** *archaic* : to be lacking or nonexistent : fail to be present, available, or forthcoming **b :** to be deficient or short ⟨it ~*s* three minutes to twelve⟩ **2 :** to be in need (as of food or shelter) : be needy or destitute ⟨the family would never allow their children to ~⟩ **3 :** to have or feel need : LONG — usu. used with *for* and sometimes *of* ⟨never ~*s* for friends⟩ **4 a :** to be necessary or needed ⟨it ~*s* no extended examination . . . to reveal the egregious character of the supposition — C.I.Lewis⟩ **b :** to become required : become morally demanded ⟨it ~*s* all our efforts to succeed⟩ **5 :** to desire earnestly to come or go — used with a directional adverb ⟨the visitor ~*s* in⟩ ⟨the dog ~*s* out⟩ **syn** see DESIRE, LACK

³want \ˈwȯnt, ˈwänt\ *n* -s [ME, fr. *wanten* to want] **1 a :** the quality or state of lacking ⟨~ of common sense⟩ or failing to possess a required or usual amount ⟨a loss incurred by his ~ of two points⟩ **b :** dire need (as of the necessities of life) : DESTITUTION ⟨a nation living in ~⟩ **2 a :** something needed or desired ⟨sufficient means to satisfy his moderate ~*s*⟩ **b :** something wished for or wanted ⟨his ~*s* are rarely satisfied⟩ **3 :** personal defect : FAULT ⟨whatever his ~*s*, he has always been honest⟩ **syn** see ABSENCE

want ad *n* : an advertisement in the classified section of a newspaper stating that something is wanted (as an employee, employment, or a specified article)

want·age \-tij\ *n* -s [²*want* + *-age*] : amount wanting : SHORTAGE

wantage rod *n* : a graduated rod used as a gage of wantage in the contents of a cask or barrel

wanted circular *n* [*wanted* past part. of ²*want;* fr. the use of the word as a heading for the circular] : a circular that bears the picture and description of a person charged with a crime and identifies the police seeking his arrest

want·er \-tə(r)\ *n* -s **1 :** one that wants or is in need **2** *dial* : one wanting a spouse; *esp* : BACHELOR

wanthill \ˈwänt,hil\ *n* [ME *wonthill,* fr. *wont* want, mole + *hill*] *dial Brit* : MOLEHILL

¹wanting *adj* [fr. pres. part. of ²*want*] **1 :** not present : not being in evidence : ABSENT ⟨seed plants are totally ~ there — R.E.Coker⟩ **2 a :** not being up to standards or expectations ⟨I cannot feel that even the programs I find ~ are all of low quality —Gilbert Seldes⟩ **b** (1) : lacking in natural or required ability or capacity : DEFICIENT ⟨a candidate tested and found ~⟩ (2) : inadequately endowed : insufficiently provided : DEFICIENT ⟨~ in common sense⟩ **c** *chiefly dial* : mentally defective ⟨"What does Amen mean?" was always asked of the youngest Todd child, who was, poor boy, ~ —Margaret Deland⟩ **3** *obs* : being in need : DESTITUTE

²wanting *prep* [fr. pres. part. of ²*want*] **1 :** not with : WITHOUT ⟨a book ~ a cover⟩ **2 :** LESS, MINUS ⟨a month ~ two days⟩

want·less \ˈ≈ləs\ *adj* : being without want or desire

want·less·ness *n* -ES [*wantless* + *-ness*] : the quality or state of being without want or desire

want list *n* : a list compiled (as by a hobbyist or the curator of a collection) that indicates specific items lacking and needed and that is circulated among dealers and retailers

¹wan·ton \ˈwȯntᵊn, ˈwän-, -tən\ *adj* [ME, fr. *wan-* deficient, wrong, mis- (fr. OE, fr. *wan* wanting, deficient) + *towen,* past part. of *teen* to draw, train, discipline, fr. OE *tēon* — more at WANE, TOW] **1** *archaic* : lacking discipline : not susceptible to control : UNRULY **2 :** excessively merry or gay : FROLICSOME ⟨a ~ party⟩ ⟨~ holidays⟩ **3 :** UNCHASTE, LEWD, LUSTFUL ⟨~ books⟩; *also* : SENSUAL **4** *obs* : given to self-indulgence and the enjoyment of luxury : VOLUPTUOUS **5 a :** marked by or manifesting heedless disregard of justice or of the rights, safety, and feelings of others : brutally insolent : MERCILESS, INHUMANE ⟨~ victors⟩ ⟨~ cruelty⟩ ⟨~ exercise of power⟩ **b :** having no just foundation or real provocation : willfully malicious ⟨a ~ attack⟩ ⟨~ insults⟩ ⟨~ prejudice⟩ **6 :** being without check or limitation : UNRESTRAINED: as **a :** luxuriantly rank ⟨~ vegetation⟩ **b :** unduly lavish : EXTRAVAGANT, PRODIGAL ⟨~ imagination⟩ ⟨~ speech⟩

²wanton \"\ *n* -s **1 :** a pampered or overindulged individual; *esp* : a spoiled child **2 :** an excessively playful or frolicsome child or animal **3 :** a person given over to luxurious self-enjoyment : TRIFLER ⟨play the ~⟩ **4 :** a lewd or lascivious person

³wanton \"\ *vb* -ED/-ING/-s *vi* **1 :** to engage in amorous play : DALLY **2 :** to indulge in a continuous carefree or voluptuous mode of living : play the voluptuary **3 :** to wallow in unrestrained brutality and cruelty **4 :** to be or become excessively free or extravagant (as in growth, expression, or conduct) : LUXURIATE **5 :** to spend time trifling ~ *vt* : to pass or waste wantonly or in wantonness ⟨~ money away⟩

wan·ton·er \"+ə(r)\ *n* -s [³*wanton* + *-er*] : one that wantons : WANTON

wan·ton·ly *adv* [ME, fr. ¹*wanton* + *-ly*] : in a wanton manner ⟨~ wasting time⟩ ⟨animals ~ killed for sport⟩ ⟨~ disrespectful of personal liberty⟩

wan·ton·ness \-tᵊn(n)əs, -tən(-\ *n* -ES [ME *wantonnes,* fr. ¹*wanton* + *-nes* -ness] **1 :** the quality or state of being wanton ⟨ideas characterized chiefly by their sheer ~⟩ ⟨the ~ of jungle growth⟩ ⟨negligence amounting to ~⟩ **2 :** an instance or example of wanton action

wants *pres 3d sing of* WANT, *pl of* WANT

wantwit \ˈ≈,≈\ *n* [ME, fr. *wanten* to want + *wit*] : a person wanting wit : FOOL

wan·ty \ˈwänti\ *n* -ES [ME *wayntc, wanteye,* prob. fr. *wame, wamb* belly + *tey, tye* tie — more at WAME, WOMB, TIE] *dial Brit* : GIRTH, SURCINGLE; *also* : a leather tie

wany *var of* WANEY

wanze \ˈwänz\ *vb* -ED/-ING/-s [ME *wansen,* fr. OE *wansian,* fr. *wan* wanting, deficient — more at WANE] *archaic* : WANE, DECREASE

¹wap \ˈwap, ˈwäp\ *vi* **wapped; wapped; wapping; waps** [ME *wappen,* prob. of imit. origin] **1** *dial* : to pull or throw roughly : WHOP, STRIKE **2** *dial* : to blow in gusts

²wap \"\ *n* -s [ME, fr. *wappen* to throw, strike, blow in gusts] **1** *dial* : BLOW, KNOCK **2** *Scot* **a :** BLAST, STORM **b :** FIGHT

³wap \"\ *vt* **wapped; wapped; wapping; waps** [ME *wappen,* of unknown origin] *dial* : to fold up : BIND, WRAP

⁴wap \"\ *n* -s **1** *dial* : a wrapping (as a turn of string around a rope or other string) **2** *dial* : a bundle or truss of straw

wap·a·too \ˈwäpə,tü\ *or* **wapata** *or* **wapato** *or* **wappato** *n* -s [Chinook jargon *wapatoo,* fr. Cree *wāpatowa* white mushroom] : either of two plants of the genus *Sagittaria* (*S. latifolia* and *S. cuneata*) having edible tubers

wap·en·take \ˈwäpən,tāk, ˈwap- *also* ˈwȯp-\ *n* -s [ME, fr. OE *wǣpentæc,* fr. ON *vāpnatak* act of grasping weapons, fr. *vāpna* (gen. pl. of *vāpn* weapon) + *tak* act of grasping, fr. *taka* to take; prob. fr. the brandishing of weapons as an expression of approval when the chief of the wapentake entered upon his office — more at WEAPON, TAKE] **1 :** a subdivision of some English shires (as Leicestershire, Lincolnshire, Northampton, Nottinghamshire, and Yorkshire) corresponding to a hundred **2 :** the court or court bailiff of a wapentake

wa·pi·si·a·na \wə,pēsēˈänə\ *or* **wa·pi·sha·na** \,wäpēˈshänə\ *n, pl* **wapisiana** *or* **wapisianas** *or* **wapishana** *or* **wapishanas** *usu cap* **1 a :** an Arawakan people of southern Surinam and adjacent parts of Brazil **b :** a member of such people **2 :** the language of the Wapisiana people

wap·i·ti \ˈwäpəd·ē, -ətē, -i *also* ˈwȯp-\ *n, pl* **wapiti** *or* **wapitis** [of Algonquian origin; akin to Cree *wapitew* white, whitish, Shawnee *wapiti;* fr. its white rump and tail] **1 :** an American elk (*Cervus canadensis* and related forms) that is similar to the European red deer but considerably larger, has antlers with a long heavy beam with brow antler, bay antler, royal antler, surroyal tine, and forked terminal tines but no palmations or cuplike crown, a light reddish buff body becoming dark brown on the head and limbs and blackish on the belly, a short tail and large rump patch of buffy white, and is nearly extinct over most of the U.S. **2 :** an eastern Asiatic red deer (*Cervus elaphus xanthopygus*) related to the wapiti — called also *Altai wapiti*

wap·pen·schaw·ing \ˈwapən,shȯ·iŋ\ *or* **wap·pen·schaw** \-,shȯ\ *n* -s [ME (northern dial.) *wapynschawing,* fr. *wapen* weapon (fr. ON *vāpn*) + *schawing,* gerund of *schawen* to show, fr. OE *scēawian* to look, look at — more at WEAPON, SHOW] : an exhibition of arms according to individual rank formerly made at various seasons in each district of Scotland

wap·per-jawed \ˈwäpə(r)ˌjȯd\ *adj* [origin unknown] : having a crooked, undershot, or wry jaw

wap·pin·ger \ˈwäpinjə(r)\ *n, pl* **wappinger** *or* **wappingers** *usu cap* [of Algonquian origin; akin to Natick *Wampan-ohke,* lit., eastern land — more at WAMPANOAG] **1 :** an Indian people living between the lower Hudson and Connecticut rivers **2 :** a member of the Wappinger people

wap·po \ˈwä(,)pō\ *n, pl* **wappo** *or* **wappos** *usu cap* [AmerSp *guapo* brave, fr. Sp, showy, good-looking] **1 a :** an Indian people of northwestern California **b :** a member of such people **2 :** a Yukian language of the Wappo people

waqf *or* **wakf** \ˈwəkf\ *n* -s [Ar *waqf*] **1 :** an Islamic endowment of property to be held in trust and used for a charitable or religious purpose **2 :** a Muslim religious or charitable foundation created by an endowed trust fund

¹war \ˈwȯ(ə)r, ˈwȯ(ə)\ *n* -s *often attrib* [ME *werre, warre,* fr. ONF *werre,* fr. OHG *werra* confusion, strife, quarrel; akin to OHG *werran* to confuse, L *verrere* to sweep, sweep together, sweep away, and perh. to Gk *errhein* to go, go to ruin, disappear] **1 a** (1) : a state of usu. open and declared armed hostile conflict between political units (as states or nations) ⟨~ cannot exist between two countries unless each of them has its own government —E.D.Dickinson⟩ — see CIVIL WAR, COLD WAR, LIMITED WAR; compare BATTLE, RIOT (2) : a period of armed conflict between political units ⟨fought a ~ over the disputed territory⟩ — sometimes used in pl. ⟨gone off to the ~*s*⟩; *also* : STATE OF WAR 2 (3) : STATE OF WAR 1b ⟨hostilities were officially ended . . . though . . . the ~ was not yet officially over —F.A.Ogg & P.O.Ray⟩ **b** *archaic* : an engagement in a war : BATTLE **c :** the art, activity, profession, or science of military operations : the methods and principle of warfare **d** (1) *obs* : weapons and equipment for war (2) *archaic* : soldiers armed and equipped for war **e :** a conflict carried on by one or a few of the normal means of war or one field of military activity distinguished from other activities in a war ⟨a naval ~ for control of trade routes⟩ ⟨integrating the conduct of the ground and air ~*s*⟩ **2 a :** a state of hostility, conflict, opposition, or antagonism between mental, physical, social, or other forces ⟨these factions were more at ~ than were the two real political parties —Roy Lewis & Angus Maude⟩ ⟨the children would in all probability fare better in peace with one parent than in ~ with two —E.F.Melson⟩ ⟨making ~ on the periodic invasion of insects —Emery Neff⟩ ⟨his innate gentleness at ~ with his fierce sense of power —Robert Payne⟩ **b :** a struggle of any degree of intensity carried on between opposing forces (as desires, social groups, or physical forces) in a particular field or by a particular means or for a particular goal ⟨a ~ against want and destitution and economic demoralization —F.D. Roosevelt⟩ ⟨price ~⟩ ⟨a ~ of scurrilous pamphlets —V.L. Parrington⟩ ⟨a personal ~ against engulfment in the provincial pattern of conformity —Henry Cavendish⟩ ⟨class ~⟩ **3 :** a card game for children in which the cards are turned up one by one, the highest takes the others, and a tie occasions a situation in which the next turn decides; *also* : the situation occasioned by a tie in the game of war

²war \"\ *vi* **warred; warred; warring; wars** [ME *werrien, werren, warren,* fr. *werre* war] **1 :** to make or wage war : carry on armed hostilities ⟨nations . . . *warred* repeatedly against their victims and against one another —H.R.Isaacs⟩ **2 :** to be in active or vigorous conflict or contention esp. during an extended period ⟨the desire for life *warred* with his fear and hate of it —Douglas Stewart⟩ ⟨landowners and squatters *warred* for years over clouded titles —Julian Dana⟩ **syn** see CONTEND

³war \ˈwär\ *adv (or adj)* [ME *werre, war,* fr. ON *verri,* adj., *verr,* adv. — more at WORSE] *chiefly Scot* : WORSE

⁴war \"\ *vt* **warred; warred; warring; wars** [ME *warren,* fr. ³*war*] *Scot* : WORST, OVERCOME

⁵war \ˈwär\ *dial past of* BE

war *abbr* warrant

wa·ra·bi \ˈwȯrəbē, wəˈräbē\ *n* -s [Jap] : a brake (*Pteridium aquilinum*) whose young fronds are eaten in Japan

wa·ral *or* **wor·ral** *or* **wor·rel** \ˈwȯrəl\ *n* -s [Ar *waral*] : an African monitor (*Varanus niloticus*) that is semiaquatic, attains a length of five feet, and lives chiefly on fish and on crocodile eggs

wa·ran·gal \ˈwərəŋgəl\ *adj, usu cap* [*Warangal,* city of south central India] : of or from the city of Warangal, India : of the kind or style prevalent in Warangal

war·a·tah *or* **war·ra·tau** \ˈwȯrə,tȯ, -tä\ *n* -s [native name in Australia] : an Australian plant of the genus *Telopea* (as *T. speciosissima* and *T. oreades*) with heads of showy crimson flowers

war baby *n* [¹*war*] **1 :** a child born or conceived during a war; *esp* : an illegitimate child born in wartime of a serviceman **2 :** an industry or product developed or greatly expanded because of wartime needs ⟨out of the electronic tube . . . has come one particularly tough little . . . *war baby* —*Fortune*⟩ **3 :** a stock or security whose value is greatly enhanced because of a state of war

war bag *or* **war sack** *n* [¹*war;* fr. its being orig. used by soldiers] : a gunny sack, duffle bag, or other container in which a cowboy keeps his personal possessions

war belt *n* : a wampum belt used either to transmit a declaration of war or to summon allies in case of war

warbird \ˈ≈,≈\ *n* **1 :** a military airplane; *also* : a crew member of a military airplane **2** *dial* : SCARLET TANAGER

¹war·ble \ˈwȯrbəl, ˈwȯ(ə)b-, *NewEng & N.Y. City often* ˈwäb-\ *n* -s [in sense 1, fr. ME *werble,* fr. ONF, of Gmc origin; akin to MHG *wirbel* whirl, tuning peg, OHG *wirbil* whirlwind — more at WHIRL; in other senses, fr. ³*warble*] **1 a :** AIR, TUNE, MELODY; *esp* : a joyful song : CAROL **b :** a melodious succession of low and pleasing sounds ⟨a canary's ~⟩ **c :** a musical trill **2 :** the action of warbling **3 :** the art or manner of singing with trills, runs, or quavers **4 :** a tone that is produced electronically usu. by an oscillator and is varied in frequency cyclically over a fixed range

²warble \"\ *vi* [ME *warbellen*] *of a hawk* : to bring together or cross wings upon the back

³warble \"\ *vb* -ED/-ING/-s [ONF *werbler,* fr. *werble* air, modulation, warble] *vi* **1 a :** to sing in a trilling manner or with many turns and variations : sing softly and quaveringly or with rapid modulations in pitch **b** *archaic* : to give forth the low murmuring sound of a running brook : BABBLE **c :** to make or emit sounds with turns, variations, and rapid modulations in pitch ⟨the bluebird *warbled,* the robin called —John Burroughs⟩ **2 :** to become uttered, sounded, or produced with trills, quavers, and rapid modulations in pitch **3 :** SING ~ *vt* **1 :** to sing or utter in a trilling or quavering manner : render with turns, runs, or rapid modulations : TRILL ⟨moan and ~ the latest cowboy songs —D.B.Davis⟩ **2 :** to express by or as if by warbling : utter musically ⟨boys to ~ the praises of God —Norman Douglas⟩

⁴warble \"\ *vi* [origin unknown] *obs* : SHAKE, VIBRATE

⁵warble \"\ *n* -s [perh. of Scan origin; akin to obs. Sw *varbulde* boil, fr. *var* pus + *bulde* swelling; akin to OE *wearr* callosity, *weart* wart and to OE *blāwan* to blow — more at WART, BLOW] **1 :** a swelling under the hide esp. of the back of cattle, horses, and various other mammals caused by the maggot of a botfly or warble fly **2 :** the maggot of a warble fly

war·bled \-bəld\ *adj* [⁵*warble* + *-ed*] : infested with warbles — used of an animal or hide

warble fly *n* [⁵*warble*] : any of various dipterous flies (as an ox warble fly) of the family Oestridae that lay eggs on the feet and legs of cattle and other mammals whence they are licked off and hatch in the mouth or esophagus and burrow through the tissues to the skin and beneath it to the back of the animal where they live until ready to pupate and cause warbles

war·bler \-bl(ə)r\ *n* -s [³*warble* + *-er*] **1 :** one that warbles : SINGER, SONGSTER **2 a :** any of numerous small Old World singing birds of the family Sylviidae many of which are noted songsters and are related more closely to the thrushes with which they are often associated as a subfamily than to the American warblers and are represented in the U.S. only by the kinglets and gnatcatchers — see BLACKCAP, BLUETHROAT, REED WARBLER, SEDGE WARBLER, WHITETHROAT **b :** any of numerous small brightly colored American songbirds that constitute the family Parulidae, are insectivorous, highly migratory, and chiefly arboreal, and have a song which is generally weak and unmusical but very characteristic for each species — called also *wood warbler* — see BLACK-THROATED BLUE WARBLER, CHESTNUT-SIDED WARBLER, WATER THRUSH, YELLOW THROAT, YELLOW WARBLER; compare CHAT, REDSTART **c :** any of numerous small Australasian birds esp. of the genera *Malurus* and *Gerygone* (family Muscicapidae) **3 :** a twirl or flourish to embellish a bagpipe melody

warbler green *n* : a light olive color that is greener and deeper than citrine, redder and deeper than grape green, and redder than old moss green — called also *romantic green*

warbling vireo *n* [*warbling* (pres. part. of ³*warble*) + *vireo*] : a vireo (*Vireo gilvus*) of temperate No. America having a grayish green back and whitish underparts

war·bly \-b(ə)lē\ *adj* -ER/-EST [³*wurble* + *-y*] : marked by warbling : QUAVERY ⟨hoarse tuneless and ~ voices —Peggy Bennett⟩

warbonnet \ˈ≈,≈≈\ *n* [¹*war*] : a ceremonial headdress of some of the Plains Indians that consists of a cap with an extension down the back and is decorated with feathers of the golden eagle

war bride *n* **1 :** a woman who marries a soldier ordered into active service in time of war **2 :** a woman who marries a soldier esp. of a foreign nation met during a time of war

war·burg \ˈwȯr,bərg\ *adj, usu cap* [fr. Otto H. *Warburg* †1938 Ger. physiologist] : of, relating to, or of the kind introduced, described, or devised by the German general physiologist Otto Warburg ⟨*Warburg* flasks⟩ ⟨a *Warburg* respirometer⟩

warburg apparatus *n, usu cap W* : a complex respirometer consisting of a battery of constant-volume manometer-flask units with a mechanically agitated constant-temperature bath and used esp. in the study of cellular respiration and metabolism or fermentation and other enzymatic reactions

warburg's tincture *n, usu cap W* [after Carl *Warburg* 19th cent. Austrian physician] : a liquid preparation containing quinine, aloes, rhubarb, angelica seed, elecampane, saffron, fennel, and other ingredients formerly used as an antiperiodic and invented by Dr. Carl Warburg

warburg's yellow enzyme *n, usu cap W* [after Otto *Warburg* †1938] : YELLOW ENZYME a

war captain *or* **war chief** *n* : an American Indian chief who is the military leader of his group or tribe

war chest *n* : a fund accumulated to finance a war; *broadly* : a fund earmarked for a specific purpose, action, or campaign ⟨a *war chest* with which to finance its drive to unionize the steel industry —*N.Y.Times*⟩

war clause *n* : a clause included in some life insurance policies issued during wartime that limits the insurer's liability to a return of premiums if the insured dies as a result of war or while serving in the military or naval services outside the home area

war cloud *n* : an ominous sign of war : a threat of or a situation that threatens war

war club *n* : a club used by warriors; *esp* : a club-shaped implement used as a weapon by American Indians — compare THROWING-STICK 2

war correspondent *n* : a correspondent employed to report news concerning the conduct of a war and esp. of events at the scene of battle

warcraft \ˈ≈,≈\ *n* **1 :** the art of war : knowledge and skill in the conduct of military operations **2** *pl* **warcraft** : a military or naval ship or plane

war crime *n* : a crime (as genocide, maltreatment of prisoners, or any atrocity) committed during or in connection with war — usu. used in pl.

war cry *n* **1 :** a cry used by a body of fighters in war to encourage each other or to disconcert or terrify the enemy — compare REBEL YELL **2 :** a catchword, phrase, or slogan used to rally people to a group or cause or to emphasize or epitomize a program

¹ward \ˈwȯ(ə)rd, ˈwȯ(ə)d\ *n* -s *often attrib* [ME, fr. OE *weard* (fem.); akin to OHG *warta* act of watching, OE *weard* (masc.) watchman, keeper, guard, OHG *wart,* ON *vörthr,* Goth *daurwards* doorkeeper, OE *warian* to beware, guard — more at WARE] **1 a :** the action or process of guarding : WATCH, GUARD, KEEPING, PROTECTION, CARE — used esp. in the phrase *watch and ward* **b :** WARDSHIP **c :** CASTLE-GUARD **d :** WARDHOLDING **2 a :** a group acting as guards : GUARD, WATCH **b** *obs* : GARRISON **3 :** the state of being under guard or in guardianship; *esp* : confinement under guard : CUSTODY ⟨put them in ~ in the house of the captain of the guard —Gen 40:3 (AV)⟩ **4 :** a place that is guarded or arranged for one in ward: as **a :** the inner court of a castle or fortress **b** (1) *obs* : JAIL, PRISON (2) : a division (as a cell, block, or wing) of a prison **c** *Scot* : an enclosure for cattle **d** (1) : a large room in a hospital where a number of patients are accommodated ⟨a 4-bed ~⟩ ⟨a 12-bed ~⟩ (2) : a division in a hospital for the care of patients suffering the same disease ⟨a diabetic ~⟩ ⟨an isolation ~⟩ **5 :** any of various administrative divisions: as **a :** a division, district, or quarter of a town or esp. a city for representative, executive, or magisterial purposes that is often merely or chiefly a division for election purposes and as such is in the larger cities often subdivided into precincts **b :** a division of the English counties of Cumberland and Northumberland and of some Scottish counties corresponding to a hundred **c :** a small territorial unit or division of a Mormon stake presided over by a bishopric and comprising branches of the church auxiliary organizations and quorums of the Aaronic priesthood **d :** an electoral district in the state of Louisiana **6 :** a projecting ridge of metal in a lock casing or keyhole permitting only the insertion of a key with a corresponding notch; *also* : a corresponding notch in a bit of a key **7 :** a person who is under guard, protection, or surveillance: as **a :** a minor who is subject to wardship **b** *obs* : an orphan who is underage **c** (1) : a person who by reason of minority, lunacy, or other incapacity is under the protection of a court either directly or through a guardian appointed by the court — called also *ward of court;* see WARD IN CHANCERY (2) : the condition or status of a ward **d :** a person or sometimes a state, territory, or body of persons under the protection or tutelage of a person, public agency, or government ⟨the Indians who were ~*s* of the United States⟩ **8 a :** a means of defense : PROTECTION ⟨this staff is ~ against the darts —Henry Treece⟩ **b** *obs* : a guarding or defensive motion or position in fencing

²ward \"\ *vb* -ED/-ING/-s [ME *warden,* fr. OE *weardian;* akin to OHG *wartēn* to observe, watch, take care, ON *vartha* to guard; all fr. a prehistoric WGmc-NGmc verb akin to OE *weard* watchman, guard] *vt* **1 :** to keep watch over : keep in safety or custody : serve as guard, guardian, or protector for ⟨a warden's business is to ~ the people who are put in his charge —Phil Strong⟩ ⟨the bald mountains that ~ the Cap Rock —Margaret Cousins⟩ **2 a :** to fend off (a blow or weapon) : PARRY — usu. used with *off* ⟨shields his face with one arm . . . to ~ off a blow —Inez Karma & Gilbert Millstein⟩ **b :** to turn aside (something threatening or harmful) : DEFLECT — usu. used with *off* ⟨a magic charm to ~ off evil —M.J. Herskovits⟩ ⟨our nation has ~*ed* off all enemies —D.D. Eisenhower⟩ ~ *vi* **1** *archaic* : to fight defensively with a sword, shield, or other weapon : parry blows **2** *obs* : to take care : BEWARE **syn** see PREVENT

¹-ward \wə(r)d\ *also* **-wards** \-dz\ *adj suffix* [*-ward* fr. ME, fr. OE *-weard;* akin to OHG *-wart, -wert* -ward, ON *-verthr,* Goth *-wairths,* L *vertere* to turn — more at WORTH; *-wards* fr. *-wards,* adv.] **1 :** that moves, tends, faces, or is directed toward ⟨migration city*ward* —V.D.Reed⟩ ⟨the door on the river*ward* side —D.C.Peattie⟩ ⟨advances land*wards* from the . . . coast —W.G.East⟩ ⟨hat with the crown up*ward* —William Cowper⟩ **2 :** that occurs or is situated in the direction of ⟨sunrise to right, sunset left*ward* —George Meredith⟩

²-ward \"\ *or* **-wards** \"\ *adv suffix* [*-ward* fr. ME, fr. OE *-weard,* fr. *-weard,* adj. suffix; *-wards* fr. ME, fr. OE *-weardes,* gen. sing. neut. of *-weard,* adj. suffix] **1 :** in a (specified) spatial or temporal direction ⟨signals beamed up*ward* from the ground —F.B.Colton⟩ ⟨the war has gone north*ward* —H.L.Matthews⟩ ⟨after*ward* vigilantism broke loose —V.H.Jensen⟩ ⟨the coastal plain . . . is confined land*wards* by . . . mountains —W.G. East⟩ **2 :** toward a (specified) point, position, or area ⟨bent earth*ward* by a thousand gales —Norman Douglas⟩ ⟨equator*ward* from this latitude —*Science*⟩

ward·able \ˈwȯ(r)dəbəl\ *adj* [¹*ward* + *-able*] : liable to castle-guard

war dance n 1 : a dance usu. representing war in pantomime that is performed by primitive peoples as preparation for battle or in celebration of victory 2 : an American Indian composition consisting of vigorous sideward bouncing steps for a mixed round or toe-heel steps for a male solo that is used as a ceremonial dance or show dance 3 : vigorous jumping about suggestive of an Indian war dance

ward bed n 1 : bed, board, and medical and nursing care in a hospital ward 2 : care of a patient at expense of the hospital in return for providing an opportunity for clinical study (admitted to a *ward bed* because he was of interest to the doctors)

war debt n : a debt contracted by a state in order to carry on and pay for a war

ward·ed \'wȯrdəd, 'wȯ(ə)d-\ adj [¹ward + -ed] : provided with a ward (~ lock) (~ key)

ward eight n [prob. fr. *Ward Eight*, municipal division of Boston, Mass., where it originated] : a mixed drink consisting of whiskey, lemon juice, and grenadine often served with crushed ice and a little soda water in a tall glass and garnished with a maraschino cherry and slice of orange

war democrat n, usu cap W&D : a member of the Democratic party in the border or northern states of the U.S. who favored the prosecution of the Civil War

war·den \'wȯrd°n, 'wȯ(ə)d-\ n -s [ME *wardein*, fr. ONF, fr. *warder* to ward, guard, of Gmc origin; akin to OHG *wartēn* to watch, take care — more at WARD] 1 : one having care or charge of something : GUARDIAN, KEEPER 2 : a person invested with power to govern or control : a chief executive officer: as a : REGENT 2 b : a member of the governing body of a guild and esp. of a livery company of the City of London c : an officer in charge of a port or market d : the governor of a town, district, or fortress e : the chief executive of a borough in Connecticut 1 : the head of a county council in Quebec and the Maritime Provinces 3 a : an official charged with special supervisory duties or with the enforcement of specified laws or regulations (a game ~) (air raid ~) — see FIRE WARDEN b : an official in charge of the operation of a prison c : any of various officials of the British crown or royal household having designated administrative duties (~ of the mint) d (1) : an official in charge of a polling place (2) : an officer who formerly presided at meetings of a ward 4 a : CHURCHWARDEN 2 b : any of various British college officials whose duties range from those of a dean to that of a head of residence c : either of two officials in a symbolic lodge whose duty is to assist the worshipful master — called also respectively *junior warden, senior warden* 5 : GATEKEEPER, PORTER

war·den·ry \-nrē\ n -ES [*warden* + -ry] : WARDENSHIP

warden of the peace [trans. of AF *gardeins de la pees*] : CONSERVATOR OF THE PEACE

war·den·ship \-ⁿ,ship\ n [ME, fr. *wardein* warden + -ship] : the office, jurisdiction, or powers of a warden

¹**ward·er** \'wȯrdər, 'wȯ(ə)də(r)\ n -s [ME, fr. AF *wardere*, fr. *warde* act of guarding (of Gmc origin); akin to OHG *warta* act of watching) + -ere -er — more at WARD] 1 a : one that keeps guard esp. at a tower, gate, or door : WATCHMAN, PORTER b : an officer of a secret society who is stationed near the door inside a lodge room during a meeting — compare SENTINEL 3 2 Brit a : WARDEN; esp : CARETAKER, CUSTODIAN b : a prison guard

²**warder** \"\ n -s [ME, perh. fr. *warden* to ward + -er] : a truncheon or staff used by a king or commander in chief to signal orders

war·der·ship \-,ship\ n [¹warder + -ship] : the office, position, or function of a warder

ward heeler n : HEELER 4

ward hill \'wȯrd-, 'wȯ(ə)d-\ n [alter. of earlier E dial. *wart hill*, fr. *wart* beacon (prob. fr. ON *vartha* beacon) + *hill*; akin to OHG *warta* act of watching — more at WARD] dial Brit : BEACON 1

wardholding \'=,==\ n : tenure by military service orig. at the need of a feudal lord

ward·ian case \'wȯ(r)dēən-\ n, usu cap W [Nathaniel B. *Ward* †1868 Eng. botanist, its inventor + E -*ian*] 1 : a portable case made with glass sides and top and metal, earthen, or wooden base and used in growing or transporting living plants in soil or in pots 2 : GLASS GARDEN

ward in chancery n : a ward under the care of a chancery court

¹**warding** n -s [ME, fr. gerund of ²ward] Scot : confinement in prison

²**warding** n -s [¹ward + -ing] : the making of warded keys

warding file n : a thin file used chiefly for cutting wards in keys

ward·ite \'wȯr,dīt\ n -s [Henry A. *Ward* †1906 Am. naturalist + E -*ite*] : a mineral Na₄CaAl₁₂(PO₄)₈(OH)₁₈·6H₂O consisting of a hydrous basic sodium, calcium, and aluminum phosphate and occurring in green concretionary masses (hardness 5, sp. gr. 2.8)

ward leon·ard system \'wȯrd'lenərd-\ n, usu cap W&L [after Harry *Ward Leonard* †1915 Am. electrical engineer & inventor] : a regenerative electrical system by which variations in motor speeds for all loads carried by a motor are obtained without rheostatic losses in the main circuit

ward·less \'wȯrdləs\ adj : having no ward (a ~ key)

ward meetinghouse n : a Mormon center of worship for a ward that is roughly equivalent to a parish church

ward·mote \'wȯ(ə)d,mōt, -,mōt\ n -s [ME, fr. ¹ward + mot, mote moot] Brit : an assembly of the citizens of a ward; specif : a meeting usu. sitting as a court that is held in each ward of the City of London and has supervision of matters relating to the watch, police, and weights and measures

ward of court : WARD 7c(1)

war dog n 1 : a dog trained to serve on the battlefield 2 a : a thoroughly experienced soldier b : one who demands or threatens war

war·dour street \'wȯ(r)də(r)-\ adj, usu cap W&S [fr. *Wardour Street*, London, England, formerly center of the antique and spurious antique trade] : falsely imitative of archaic forms (*Wardour Street* English)

ward·ress \'wȯrdrəs, -ō(ə)d-\ n -ES [¹warder + -ess] : a female warden in a prison

ward·robe \'wȯr,drōb, -ō(ə)d-\ n [ME *warderobe*, fr. ONF *warderoube*, fr. *warder* to guard (of Gmc origin; akin to OHG *wartēn* to watch, take care) + *roube* booty, robe, of Gmc origin; akin to OHG *roub* booty — more at WARD, ROBE] 1 a : a room or closet where clothes are kept or stored : DRESSING ROOM, CLOTHES CLOSET b : a room in a theater where costumes and properties are kept, repaired, and cared for c : CLOTHESPRESS 1 d (1) : WARDROBE TRUNK 2 : WARDROBE CASE 2 a : the collection of wearing apparel and accessories in the possession of one person, family, or institution or for one season, activity, or occupation (his summer ~) (a new ~ for a trip abroad) b : a number or collection of one article of dress suitable for various occasions (a topper completed his ~ of hats) 3 : the department of a royal or noble household given the care of wearing apparel, jewels, and personal articles

wardrobe bed n : a folding bed serving as a wardrobe when closed

wardrobe case n 1 : a large suitcase having some features (as hangers and compartments) of a wardrobe trunk 2 : WARDROBE TRUNK

wardrobe trunk n : an upright trunk in which garments may be hung and other articles packed in separate compartments

wardroom \'=,==, -'=\ n [¹ward + ¹room] 1 a : the space in a warship allotted for living quarters to the commissioned officers excepting the captain; specif : the messroom assigned to these officers b : the officers dining in a wardroom 2 Brit : GUARDROOM

war drum n : a drum beaten as a summons to war or as an accompaniment to marching or fighting

wards pl of WARD, pres 3d sing of WARD

-wards -es — see -WARD

ward school n : a common school administered by a city ward

ward·ship \'wȯrd,ship, -ō(ə)d-\ n [ME, fr. ¹ward + -ship] 1 a : the office of a guardian or keeper : care and protection of

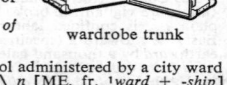
wardrobe trunk

a ward : the right of guardianship : GUARDIANSHIP b : the feudal right to the custody of the body of an infant heir of a knight's service or military sergeanty, by socage, or by copyhold and to the custody of the ward's property orig. with the right of the lord to dispose of the ward in marriage and to retain the rents and profits of his land subject to the ward's right to suitable support and that in guardianship by socage terminated when the ward reached 14 years of age and by military sergeanty at 21; also : a similar right of wardship under Scots feudal law 2 : the state of being under a guardian : the condition of being a ward in a hospital

ward sister n : a British registered nurse who is in charge of a ward in a hospital

wards·man \'wȯ(ə)dzmən\ n, pl wardsmen [wards (gen. of ¹ward) + man] Brit : an inmate or guard in charge of a ward in a prison workhouse

wardwalk n : a periodical round of the wards of a hospital by a member of the medical staff for observation of patients and for clinical instruction — usu. used in pl.

wardwite n [ME, fr. OE *weardwite*, fr. *weard* ward + *wite*] : a fine paid by a tenant to his lord for failure to furnish castle-guard

¹**ware** \'wa(ə)r, 'we, |ə\ n -s [ME, fr. OE *wær*; akin to Fris *wier* seaweed, OE *wīr* wire — more at WIRE] dial Brit : SEAWEED

²**ware** \"\ adj [ME *war, ware*, fr. OE *wær* — more at WARY] 1 : AWARE, COGNIZANT, CONSCIOUS (was ~ of black looks cast at me —Mary Webb) 2 archaic : WARY, VIGILANT, HEEDFUL

³**ware** \"\ vt -ED/-ING/-S [ME *waren*, fr. OE *warian*; akin to OHG *biwarōn* to keep, protect, ON *vara* to be aware; all fr. a WGmc-NGmc verb derived fr. the adjective represented by OE *wær* aware, cautious — more at WARY] 1 : to take heed of : beware of : AVOID, SHUN — used chiefly as a command to hunting animals (~ chase) (~ rabbit) (~ wheat)

⁴**ware** \"\ n -s [ME, fr. OE *waru*; akin to MHG *ware* ware, ON *vara* and prob. to OE *wær* aware, cautious, prudent — more at WARY] 1 a : manufactured articles, products of art or craft, or farm produce offered for sale : articles of merchandise (GOODS, COMMODITIES (the peddler unpacked his ~) b : an item offered for sale : an article of merchandise (a favorite ~ is a Bible —Henry Lee) (buses, trucks, diesel engines and other heavy ~s —Mitchell Gordon) (fruit-vendors who exposed their ~s of brightest hues on the pavement —Norman Douglas) 2 : goods, commodities, manufactures, or produce of a specific class or kind (coopers' ~) (household ~) (mahogany ~) — usu. used in combination (hardware) (silverware) (tinware) (glassware) (tableware): as a : pottery of a particular body size and suitable for table use b : FABRICS, CLOTH c obs : LIVESTOCK d : pottery, dishes, or other items of fired clay (porcelain ~) (earthenware) (chinaware) (a yellow ~ with mottle glaze —Amer. Guide Series: Md.) 3 : an intangible item (as a service or a literary product) that is a marketable commodity (an information officer . . . is under constant pressure to provide more ~s —Herbert Agar) (the ~s of legitimate show business —Amer. Guide Series: N.Y.City) (nothing so quenches the enthusiasm of the teacher as a too-utilitarian view of his ~s —Lyle Owen) 4 : a group of pottery types classified by archaeologists according to characteristics of temper and hardness, type of paste, or similar surface treatment rather than by shape or decoration

⁵**ware** \"\ n -s [ME, fr. ON *vār* — more at VERNAL] Scot : the spring season

⁶**ware** \"\ vt [ME *waren*, fr. ON *verja* to clothe, invest, spend — more at WEAR] Scot 1 : SPEND, EXPEND 2 : SQUANDER, WASTE

war eagle n [so called fr. the use of its feathers in war bonnets by the Plains Indians] : GOLDEN EAGLE

ware goose n [¹ware; fr. its feeding on seaweed] Brit : BRANT

wa·re·hou \,wärə'hō, -hau\ n -s [Maori] : a purple and silver sea bream (*Seriola brama*) widely distributed off southern and eastern Australia and New Zealand and esteemed as food

¹**warehouse** \'=,haus\ n [ME *warehous*, fr. ⁴ware + hous house] 1 : a structure or room for the storage of merchandise or commodities: a : a wholesale establishment of the service type in which large inventories are carried b : a wholesale establishment operated by a chain store organization c : a place for the storing of surplus or reserve stocks of merchandise by a retail store d : a public institution for the storing of goods for others 2 Brit : RETAIL STORE

²**ware·house** \-,auz,-aus\ vt 1 : to deposit, store, or secure in a warehouse; specif, Brit : to allow (imported goods) to be deposited in a public or bonded warehouse or in the government or customhouse stores without duty pending payment of duty and consumption in the home market or reexport free from duty 2 : to put or hold in safekeeping : STORE 3 : to hold a shipment beyond the free time permitted a consignee to obtain or take delivery of his goods

warehouse bond n : a bond for the safe custody and redelivery of stored goods upon surrender of the warehouse receipt

ware·house·man \-,hausmən, -,auzm-, -aû,sman, -,aûz,man, -maa(ə)n\ n, pl warehousemen 1 : one who manages or works in a warehouse; specif : one who acts as a temporary custodian of goods or merchandise stored in his warehouse for a fee 2 Brit a : a wholesale merchant 3 : a pottery worker who inspects, sorts, and stamps bisque

ware·hous·er \-,auzə(r)\ n [¹warehouse + -er] : WAREHOUSEMAN 1

warehouse receipt n : a receipt that constitutes a document of title and is issued by a warehouseman engaged in the business of storage for hire

warehouse-to-warehouse insurance n : marine insurance that covers a cargo through the various stages of transportation, processing, and warehousing from the time it leaves the warehouse of the consignor until it reaches that of the consignee

wareroom \'=,==\ n : a room in which goods are exhibited for sale : SHOP, STORE

wares pl of WARE, pres 3d sing of WARE

war·fa \'wärfə\ n -s [origin unknown] dial : swayback of lambs

war·fare \'wȯr,fa(a)|(ə)r, -fe|, 'wȯ,f. .|ə\ n [ME, military expedition, warfare, fr. *warre*, war + *fare*] 1 : military operations between enemies : armed contest : HOSTILITIES, WAR; broadly : activity undertaken by a political unit (as a state or nation) to weaken or destroy another (diplomatic ~) (economic ~) (psychological ~) 2 : the process of struggle between competing entities : CONFLICT (hills whose owners wage unceasing ~ with drought —Amer. Guide Series: Texas)

war·fa·rin \'wȯ(r)fərən\ n -s [Wisconsin Alumni Research Foundation (its patentee) + *coumarin*] : a crystalline compound C₁₉H₁₆O₄ that is made by condensation of hydroxy-coumarin and benzylidene-acetone, that exerts a biological effect like that of dicoumarol, and that is used as a rodenticide and in medicine as an anticoagulant

war·far·ing \'wȯ(r),fa(a)riŋ, -fer-, -,rēŋ\ n -s [fr. gerund of obs. E *warfare* to wage war, fr. *warfare*, n.] : WARFARE

war feast n : a victory feast esp. of No. American Indians

war footing n : the condition of being prepared to undertake or maintain war

war game n [trans. of G *kriegspiel*] 1 : a simulated battle or campaign designed to test concepts rather than the skill or forces or fitness of troops or equipment and usu. conducted in conferences by officers acting as the opposing staffs — compare COMMAND POST EXERCISE, FIELD EXERCISE, MANEUVER 2 : a two-sided umpired training maneuver with actual elements of the armed forces participating

war gas n : a gas (sense 3) for use in warfare — compare LACRIMATOR, NERVE GAS, STERNUTATOR, VESICANT

war hammer n : a weapon having a heavy head usu. with one blunt and one spiked extremity; esp : one with a long handle for infantry used in medieval warfare esp. for breaking armor

war hatchet n : a hatchet or tomahawk used by American Indians during war or symbolically in declaring war or peace

war hawk n : one who clamors for war; esp : one of a group of American congressmen favoring war with Britain around 1812 primarily in order to annex Canada

warhead \'=,=\ n : the section of a torpedo or other missile containing the explosive, chemical, or incendiary charge and the means of setting it off

war-horse \'=,=\ n 1 : a horse used in war; esp : a powerful horse for military service : CHARGER 2 : a veteran soldier or

public person (as a politician) : an old campaigner, leader, or partisan who has had a stormy but successful career 3 : a work of art (as a musical composition, a ballet, or a play) that because of much repetition as part of the standard repertory has become extremely hackneyed (a symphonic *war-horse*) (a *war-horse* of the concert stage)

wa·ri \'wär,rē, 'wärē\ n -s [fr. native name in western Africa] : MANCALA

warier comparative of WARY

wariest superlative of WARY

war·i·ly \'wa(ə)rəlē, 'wer-,'wār-, -li\ adv [wary + -ly] : in a wary manner : CAUTIOUSLY

war·i·ness \-rēnəs, -rin-\ n -ES : the quality or state of being wary : WATCHFULNESS, CAUTION

waring pres part of WARE

wa·ring·in \,wä'riŋən\ n -s [Jav] : a common fig (*Ficus benjamina*) of India that resembles the banyan, is often cultivated for ornament, and has inedible fruit

war·i·son \'warəsən\ n -s [by misunderstanding by Sir Walter Scott in the *Lay of the Last Minstrel* (1805) of *waryson* in "minstrels, play up for your waryson" in the "Battle of Otterbourne", which is fr. ME *warison* reward, fr. ONF, defense, possessions, fr. *warir* to protect, provide, of Gmc origin; akin to OHG *werien* to defend — more at WEIR] : a bugle call to attack

war kite n : a large kite formerly used to lift a man into the air for military or meteorological observation

wark·loom or **wark·lume** \'wȯrk,klüm\ n [alter. of earlier *workloom*, fr. ME, fr. *work* + *lome*, *loom* loom] Scot : TOOL, IMPLEMENT

war·less \'wȯrləs, -ō(ə)l-\ adj : free from war — **war·less·ly** adv — **war·less·ness** n -ES

war·li \'wȯrlē\ n, pl warli or warlis usu cap 1 : a people of India inhabiting the region north of Bombay 2 : a member of the Warli people

warlike \'=,=\ adj [ME *werlik*, fr. *werre* war + *lik* like] 1 obs : ready for war : equipped to fight 2 : fit for, disposed to, or fond of war : BELLICOSE (~ savages) (a ~ disposition) 3 : of, relating to, concerned with, or useful in war : MILITARY, MARTIAL (accused him of supplying the enemy with ~ stores —Times Lit. Supp.) 4 : befitting or characteristic of war or a soldier (~ fury)

war·ling \'wȯrliŋ, 'wȯr-, -,riŋ\ n [prob. fr. ¹war + -ling: word coined to contrast with *darling*] : a person detested or disliked

war·lock \'wȯr,läk\ n -s [ME *warloghe, warlach*, fr. OE *wærloga* one that breaks faith, scoundrel, the Devil, fr. *wær* faith, troth + -*loga* (fr. *lēogan* to lie, belie, betray) — more at VERY, LIE] 1 : one given to black magic : SORCERER, WIZARD 2 : CONJUROR

war·lock·ry \'wȯrläkrē\ n [warlock + -ry] Scot : SORCERY

warlord \'=,=\ n 1 : a supreme military leader 2 : a military commander exercising civil power seized or maintained by force usu. purely from self-interest and usu. over a limited region with or without recognition of a central government, sometimes having effective control over the central government or administration, and sometimes obtaining de facto or de jure recognition of foreign powers

war·lord·ism \'=,=,lȯ(r),dizəm\ n -s : the policies or practices of a warlord

¹**warm** \'wȯ(ə)rm, 'wȯ(ə)m\ adj -ER/-EST [ME, fr. OE *wearm*; akin to OHG *warm* warm, ON *varmr*, L *formus* warm, Gk *thermos* hot, Skt *gharma* heat, OPruss *gorme*] 1 a (1) : having or manifesting heat esp. to a moderate or pleasurable degree; usu : not quite hot (the ~, almost the hot carriage —William Sansom) (so ~ and balmy that the windows were flung open —W.M.Thackeray) (2) : perceptibly above bodily temperature without being painful or harmful (a ~ bath) (~ soup) b : having the heat naturally appropriate to a living warm-blooded animal (the body was still ~) c : sending or giving out heat usu. to a comfortable or beneficial degree : producing sensations of heat (a ~ radiator) (the sunshine was ~) d : conserving or tending to maintain or preserve heat and a satisfactory degree of heat (~ insulation) (a ~ sweater) e (1) : marked by or conducive to sensations of heat brought about by strenuous exertion when resulting from sport or pleasurable exertion are often accompanied by a glow of well-being (~ after playing tennis) (a ~ climb) (2) : limber and ready for action after preliminary exercise (rewrite the memorized piece until you feel your hand is ~ —C.I.Blanchard & C.E.Zoubek) 2 a : comfortably established or settled : secure and comfortable (a ~ existence in his old age) b Brit : being in comfortable financial circumstances : RICH, WELL-TO-DO 3 a : marked by strong feeling, passion, or enthusiasm : ARDENT, ZEALOUS (being . . . of a ~ and impetuous nature, responded to their affection with quite a tropical ardor —W.M.Thackeray) (expostulated in ~ terms —T.B.Macaulay) b : marked by brisk excitement, lively exchanges, sharp disagreement, hot temper, or anger : not smooth, mild, soothing, or placating (that political campaign, which was a ~ and bitter one —P.B.Kyne) (continual ~ controversy and occasional litigation —R.I.McDavid) 4 a (1) : readily showing or reacting to love, affection, fondness, appreciative pleasure, or gratitude : often demonstratively genial, cordial, sympathetic, or affectionate (his seemingly rough exterior covered a ~ heart —D.E.Smith) (~ with the love of mankind —H.O. Taylor) (a wave of genial friendliness flowed from the ~ silly hearts of Britons —Rose Macaulay) (2) : accompanied by, giving rise to, or giving the impression of a feeling of love, tenderness, gratitude, well-being, or pleasure (his eyes . . . met hers with clear, frank, ~ regard —Zane Grey) (the ~ sense of community life —Andrew Phelan) (a rich ~ voice) (revived ~ memories of pleasant times) b (1) : marked by sexual desire or passion : LEWD, LECHEROUS (another lascivious mother and a ~ daughter —Elizabeth Hardwick) (2) : emphasizing or exploiting sexual imagery or incidents (difficult to see why this book should have been suppressed before the war; there are no ~ passages —Graham Greene) 5 : accompanied or marked by extreme danger, duress, or pain (met with such a ~ reception that he fled —Amer. Guide Series: Md.) 6 a : newly made : still strong : FRESH (a ~ scent) b : near to a goal, object, or solution sought (indicative words . . . show the searcher when he is getting ~ —A.J.Ayer) 7 : having the color or tone of something (as fire or the sun) that imparts heat; specif : of a hue in the range yellow through orange to red syn see TENDER

²**warm** \"\ vb -ED/-ING/-S [ME *warmen* to make warm, become warm; partly fr. OE *wyrman* to make warm; akin to OHG *warmen, wermen* to make warm, ON *verma*, Goth *warmjan*; partly fr. OE *wearmian* to become warm; akin to OHG *warmēn* to become warm; all fr. prehistoric Gmc verbs derived fr. an adjective represented by OE *wearm* warm] vt 1 a : to make warm : communicate a degree of heat to : supply or furnish warmth to (in front of the fireplace ~ing himself —Laura Krey) (the sun ~ing the morning air) (the baby's milk) b : to provide with a means of maintaining heat (of wine red brocade, ~ed with an inner lining of grey squirrel fur —Nora Waln) 2 a : to infuse with or with the appearance of love, friendship, well-being, or pleasure (a fine expression of personal faith ~s the heart of the hearer —William James) (~ed by the sense of renewed solidarity with his group —Thomas Munro) (a voice . . . ~ed . . . by fits of genial, deep chuckling —Osbert Sitwell) (a barrel of home brew . . . ~ed things up —Roderick Finlayson) b : to fill with anger, zeal, hatred, or passion (the sense of urgency increasingly ~s the words of the man —Waldo Frank) c : to impart life, color, or zest to (the blood that ~s an English yeoman —A.E.Housman) (the walls were ~ed and adorned with tapestry —G.M.Trevelyan) (lime juice, which the gentlemen ~ed with a little brandy —Rachel Henning) 3 : to open (a house) by an entertainment : give a housewarming in or for 4 a (1) : to reheat (cooked food) for eating — often used with *over* (bitter coffee ~ed over from the night before —George Bradshaw) (2) : to prepare (a meal) by reheating leftovers — often used with *over* 4 a (1) : to revive or reuse esp. in a situation where vigor, cogency, or significance is no longer present (~ing old feuds for the sake of politics —Dixon Wecter) — usu. used with *over* (his illustrative examples are almost invariably ~ed over from other writings —S.L.A.Marshall) 5 : to make ready for operation or performance by preliminary exercise (sparks shot down toward the water as a turret gunner ~ed his guns

—Howard Hunt) ⟨men ~ing their boat motors —G.S.Perry⟩ — often used with *up* ⟨begin each practice period by ~ing up your hand —C.I.Blanchard & C.E.Zoubek⟩ ~ *vi* **1 :** to become warm or warmer in temperature **:** become moderately heated **:** grow warm ⟨the earth may be gradually ~ing —A.E. Benfield⟩ ⟨June ~ed into July —Josephine Johnson⟩ — sometimes used with *up* ⟨once the milk is in the can it cools down or ~s up very slowly —*Farmer's Weekly (So. Africa)*⟩ **2 a :** to become ardent or interested **:** grow sympathetic, angry, fervent, or impassioned ⟨gaining confidence and ~ing to his task —John Buchan⟩ ⟨many people can only ~ up at a party —Vance Packard⟩ ⟨whose whole face ~ed as she talked —Robert Friedman⟩ ⟨his desire for revenge ~ed easily into madness —John Erskine †1951⟩ **b :** to become filled with affection, love, friendship, or kindliness — used with *to* or *toward* ⟨always ~ed toward anyone who praised his kids —Ross Annett⟩ **3 :** to experience feelings of well-being, success, pleasure, or happiness **:** BASK ⟨we ~ with pleasure at mere mention of their names —Ralph Ellison⟩ **4 :** to become ready for operation or performance by preliminary activity or gradual increase in speed or activity ⟨the radio ~ed and music came on —William George⟩ — usu. used with *up* ⟨planes on deck ready to ~ up and take off —K.M.Dodson⟩ — **warm the bench :** to serve as a substitute on an athletic team **:** be a bench warmer ⟨patiently *warmed the bench* while his teammates played —Margery Miller⟩

³warm \"\ *adv, often* -ER/-EST [ME *warme,* fr. OE *wearme,* fr. *wearm* warm, adj.] **:** WARMLY — usu. used in combination ⟨*warm*-clad⟩ ⟨*warm*-tinted⟩

⁴warm \"\ *n* -s **1 a** [ME, fr. ¹*warm*] *dial* **:** WARMTH, HEAT **b** [²*warm*] *dial* **:** the act of warming or state of being warmed **2** [¹*warm*] **:** BRITISH WARM

war·man \'wȯrmən\ *n, pl* **warmen** [ME *werman,* fr. *werre* war + *man*] **:** WARRIOR, SOLDIER

warm blood *n* **:** a warm-blooded animal (as a bird or mammal)

warm-blooded \'¦-¦--\ *adj* **1 :** having warm blood; *specif* **:** having a relatively high and constant body temperature (as a bird or mammal) usu. considerably above that of the surrounding medium **:** HOMOIOTHERMIC **2 :** fervent or ardent in temper or spirit **:** liable to rapid changes or great extremes in temperament — **warm-blood·ed·ness** *n* -ES

warmed *past of* WARM

warmed-over \'¦-¦--\ *adj* [*warmed* (past part. of ²*warm*) + *over*] **1 :** REHEATED ⟨*warmed-over* cabbage⟩ **2 :** introduced or examined again without new life or interest **:** not fresh **:** STALE ⟨*warmed-over* plays of the commercial theater —Marc Connelly⟩ ⟨most printed lectures are skimpy *warmed-over* tidbits —Carleton Beals⟩

warmed-up \'¦-¦-\ *adj* **1 :** WARMED-OVER 1 **2 :** SHORT-FED

warm·er \'wȯrmər, 'wȯ(ə)mə(r\ *n* -s **1 :** one that warms: as **a :** a workman who heats pipes, rivets, rubber, or other items **b :** a worker who kneads dried devulcanized scrap rubber with pigments between the rolls of a warming mill to form homogeneous lumps for further refining — called also *reclaimer* **c :** a device for warming or keeping warm — usu. used with a qualifying term ⟨foot ~⟩ ⟨vegetable ~⟩ **2 :** FOULING SHOT

warmest *superlative of* WARM

warm front *n* **:** the forward boundary of a warm air mass moving to replace a retreating cold air mass — see FRONT illustration

warm·ful \'-fəl\ *adj* [⁴*warm* + *-ful*] **:** full of or affording warmth

warmhearted \'¦-¦--\ *adj* [¹*warm* + *hearted*] **:** marked by or indicative of ready affection, generosity, cordiality, sympathy, or compassion ⟨a ~ welcome to the stranger⟩ **syn** see TENDER

warm-heart·ed·ness *n* **:** the quality or state of being warmhearted

warm house *n* **:** HOTHOUSE 4

warm-in boy \'-,-\ *n* [²*warm*] **:** one who reheats glassware in a furnace and passes it to the next worker for further processing

warming *n* -s [fr. gerund of ²*warm*] **:** THRASHING, TROUNCING

warming house *n* **:** CALEFACTORY

warming pad *n* **:** a body or bed warmer operated electrically or chemically

warming pan *n* **1 :** a long-handled covered pan filled with live coals used to warm a bed **2 :** one who fills temporarily a position or office intended for another **:** LOCUM TENENS

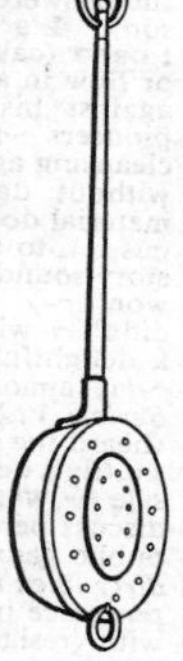

warming pan

warming-up \'-¦-\ *adj* [fr. gerund of *warm up*] **:** of, relating to, consisting of, or used for a warm-up ⟨*warming-up* period⟩ ⟨*warming-up* jacket⟩

war·min·ster broom \'wȯ(r),minz|tə(r)-, -n(t)s|\ *n, usu cap W* [fr. *Warminster,* urban district of Wiltshire, England] **:** a European hybrid broom (*Cytisus praecox*) that has sulphur-yellow flowers densely packed along slender branches and is used as an ornamental

warm·ish \'wȯrmish\ *adj* **:** somewhat warm

warm·ly *adv* [¹*warm* + *-ly*] **1 :** in a manner that causes or maintains warmth ⟨the sun shone ~⟩ ⟨~ wrapped against the cold⟩ **2 :** in a manner characterized or accompanied by warmth of emotion **:** FERVENTLY, ZEALOUSLY, AFFECTIONATELY ⟨audiences received her ~ —Alan Tomkins⟩ ⟨waxed ~ indignant —S.P.B.Mais⟩ **3 :** in a courageous, hostile, aggressive, or violent manner ⟨~ pursued the enemy —Robert Rogers⟩

warm·ness *n* -ES [ME, fr. OE *wearmnes,* fr. *wearm* warm + *-nes* -ness] **:** WARMTH

warmonger \'-,--\ *n* [¹*war* + *monger*] **1** *obs* **:** MERCENARY **2 :** one who stirs up war **:** JINGO

warmongering \'-,-(-)-\ *n* [¹*war* + *mongering*] **:** the acts or practices of a warmonger

war·mouth \'wȯr,mau̇th\ *also* **warmouth bass** *or* **warmouth perch** *n* -s [origin unknown] **:** a freshwater sunfish (*Chaenobryttus coronarius*) of the eastern U. S. chiefly west or south of the Alleghenies

warms *pres 3d sing of* WARM, *pl of* WARM

warm sea *n* **:** WARM WATER

warm sector *n* **:** the region of warm air bounded by the cold front and a warm front of a cyclone

warm sepia *n* **:** COCONUT 4

warm spot *n* **1 :** a cutaneous sensory end organ that is stimulated by an increase of temperature in its immediate environment **2 :** a point or region that is a seat of affection or love ⟨had a *warm spot* in his heart for his childhood sweetheart⟩

warm spring apache *n, usu cap W&S&A* [*warm spring,* trans. of Sp *Ojo Caliente,* name of village in north central New Mexico] **1 :** an American Indian people constituting a subdivision of the Gileños **2 :** a member of the Warm Spring Apache people

warmth \'wȯ(ə)rm(p)th, 'wȯ(ə)m-\ *n* -s [ME *wermth;* akin to MHG *wermede* warmth, OE *wearm* warm — more at WARM] **1 :** the quality or state of being warm in temperature **:** gentle heat ⟨the ~ of the sun⟩ ⟨a snug, cosy ~ enveloped him —O.E. Rölvaag⟩ **2 :** the quality or state of being warm in feeling **:** emotional intensity (as passion, enthusiasm, irritation, anger, or love) ⟨the ~ of his reception⟩ ⟨in the ~ of debate⟩ **3 :** a glowing effect such as is produced by the use of warm colors

warmth·less \-ləs\ *adj* **:** lacking warmth — **warmth·less·ness** *n* -ES

warm up *vi* [²*warm* + *up*] **1 :** to engage in exercise or practice esp. immediately before entering a game or contest in order to limber up the muscles, work up speed, or get in condition ⟨the pitcher was *warming up* with an overhand delivery —Dan Polier⟩ **2 :** to approach a state of or become characterized by violence, conflict, or danger ⟨as the campaign *warmed up* . . . hired assassins had been brought in —H.H.Martin⟩

warm-up \'-,-\ *n* -s [*warm up*] **1 :** a period of practice or a series of exercises designed to loosen the muscles and increase the circulation of an athlete prior to competition **2 :** the running of an engine, radio, or other device prior to operation for the purpose of bringing the working parts and the lubricant to efficient operating temperature **3 :** entertainment provided before a live radio or television audience to make it responsive to the show **4 :** practice or preparation preliminary to an important performance

warm-up suit *n* **:** SWEAT SUIT

warmus *var of* WAMUS

warm water *n* **:** an ocean or sea not in the arctic or antarctic regions

warmwater \'-¦--\ *adj* [*warm water*] **:** of, relating to, or occurring in warm water ⟨a ~ port⟩ ⟨~ fisheries⟩

warn \'wȯ(ə)rn, 'wȯ(ə)n\ *vb* -ED/-ING/-S [ME *warnen,* fr. OE *warnian* to take heed, warn; akin to OHG *warnōn* to take heed, OE *wær* aware, wary — more at WARY] *vt* **1 a :** to put on guard **:** give notice, information, or intimation to beforehand esp. of approaching or probable danger or evil ⟨by . . . the display of a red lamp they managed to ~ the driver —O.S. Nock⟩ ⟨~ed them about the quicksand⟩ — sometimes used with *off* ⟨young folks are ~ed off —Theodore Dreiser⟩ **b :** ADMONISH, REPREHEND, COUNSEL ⟨~ed me not to be too eager —*London Calling*⟩ ⟨against such idiocy we are ~ed by an adage —W.F.Hambly⟩ **c :** to notify or apprise esp. in advance **:** call to one's attention **:** make aware **:** INFORM ⟨must ~ you that they're only my opinions —Richard Joseph⟩ ⟨the mounting heat of June ~ed us that the exposition would close its doors —Agnes Repplier⟩ **2 :** to notify, summon, or dismiss by authority **:** bid to go or leave **:** COMMAND ⟨a corporal called . . . to ~ him for Driving School immediately —Earle Birney⟩ ⟨heroes . . . ~ed so imperiously out of her modern living room —Virginia Woolf⟩ **3 :** to prohibit from advancing, trespassing, or remaining by a warning gesture, notice, order, or device ⟨lighthouses were built to ~ sailors off the rocky . . . coast —*Amer. Guide Series: Oregon*⟩ ⟨~ed away an English vessel —D.E.Clark⟩ ⟨had been in the garden but an armed Partisan appeared and ~ed her inside —Milton Bracker⟩ **4 :** to relate or report as a warning, intimation, caution, or admonishment ⟨the commission could only ~ that chaos and war would result —R.C.Pollock⟩ ~ *vi* **1 :** to give a warning ⟨their titles . . . ~ of a meaning which goes behind story, people, even setting —E.K.Brown⟩ ⟨he ~s against . . . a fatal illusion —A.L.Locke⟩ **2** *dial Brit, of a clock* **:** to strike a specified hour or to make sounds preparatory to striking

syn CAUTION, FOREWARN: WARN is a general term lacking specific connotation and varying in meaning from simple appraisal of something, with or without any possible dangers, to truculent threats of personal violence ⟨the introductory music *warns* us that another enjoyable evening of television is about to commence —*advt*⟩ ⟨I *warn* him that the sword I wear shall pink his lily-scented cassock through and through, next time I catch him underneath your eaves —Robert Browning⟩ CAUTION may suggest a more formal, mild, well-meaning admonition, esp. against imprudence, carelessness, or folly ⟨*cautions* his readers against the common error of looking to antiquity for knowledge —H.T.Buckle⟩ FOREWARN is likely to be used in more specific situations and to imply warning of coming danger given in time to permit prudent defense and safeguarding ⟨very likely the parson had reason for being mad . . . there was a suggestiveness in the names of the acts which would have *forewarned* anybody —Margaret Deland⟩

warn·er \'wȯrnər, 'wȯ(ə)nə(r\ *n* -s **:** one that warns

war neurosis *n* **:** a neurosis (as hysteria or anxiety) occurring in soldiers during war and attributable in large measure to their war experiences — compare COMBAT FATIGUE

¹warning *n* -s [ME, fr. OE *warnung,* fr. *warnian* to warn + *-ung* -ing] **1 a :** the action of one that warns **:** the action or fact of putting one on his guard by intimating danger, evil consequences, or penalties from an act or course of conduct ⟨give ~⟩ ⟨without ~ she began to beat him on the head —Sherwood Anderson⟩ **b :** the fact or state of being warned ⟨he had ~ of his illness⟩ **2 :** something that warns or serves to warn: as **a :** ADMONITION **b :** an example or case having a deterrent effect ⟨his life will be a ~ to others⟩ **c :** CALLING, SUMMONS; *also* **:** a summoning bell or other signal **d :** a notice from one or the other of two parties to a business relation (as of landlord and tenant) that it will be terminated at a certain time **e :** a notice advising a student that his academic or social record is unsatisfactory **f :** a notice, bulletin, or signal that serves to caution of the approach of danger ⟨hurricane ~⟩ ⟨air raid ~⟩; *esp* **:** STORM WARNING **3 :** the partial unlocking of a striking mechanism of a clock accompanied by a sound intimating that the clock is about to strike

²warning \"\ *adj* [partly fr. ¹*warning;* partly fr. pres. part. of *warn*] **:** serving as an alarm, signal, summons, or admonition **:** announcing something imminent or impending or the presence of danger ⟨~ bell⟩ ⟨~ shot⟩ ⟨~ examples of the old vices —J.G.Frazer⟩ — **warn·ing·ly** *adv*

warning coloration *n* **:** an arrangement of colors possessed by an animal otherwise defended that serves to make it conspicuous and thus warn a possible enemy against an attack — compare APOSEMATIC

warning net *n* **:** an integrated system of communications that warns of the approach or movement of hostile or aggressive military forces and esp. of hostile military airplanes

warning piece *n* **:** WARNING; *esp* **:** a deterrent example

warn off *vt, Brit* **:** RULE OFF

war note *n, archaic* **:** an instrumental summons to battle

warns *pres 3d sing of* WARN

warn't \'wȯ(ə)nt, 'wänt *sometimes* 'wənt\ [⁵*war* + *-n't*] **1** *dial* **:** WASN'T **2** *dial* **:** WEREN'T

war of nerves : psychological tactics of assailing the morale of an opponent by broadcasting propaganda, spreading rumors through secret agents or neutral channels, or otherwise creating mental confusion and indecision

wa·ro·pen \wə'rōpən\ *n, pl* **waropen** *or* **waropens** *usu cap* **1 a :** a people inhabiting the coastal area of Geelvink Bay, Netherlands New Guinea **b :** a member of such people **2 :** the Austronesian language of the Waropen people

¹warp \'wȯ(ə)rp, 'wȯ(ə)p\ *n* -s *often attrib* [ME, fr. OE *wearp;* akin to OHG *warf* warp, ON *varp* throw, cast, *verpa* to throw, cast — more at ²WARP] **1 a (1) :** a series or sheet of parallel yarns or threads set up for textile processing; *specif* **:** a series of yarns extended lengthwise in a loom thereby forming the lengthwise threads of a woven fabric and usu. twisted tighter than the filling yarns and sized for protection during the weaving in of the filling threads **(2) :** one of the threads of a warp **(3) :** a fabric classified according to its warp rather than its filling ⟨*warp*-faced⟩ **(4) :** the cords that form the carcass of a pneumatic tire **b :** the basic foundation or material of a structure or entity ⟨the homemade myth that was the ~ of his work —Babette Deutsch⟩ ⟨the ~ of the economic structure is agriculture —*Amer. Guide Series: N. C.*⟩ **2 :** a rope attached at one end to an anchor, post, or other fixed object and used to haul a ship or boat toward the object **3** *dial Brit* **:** a unit of count for fish or oysters equal to 4 or sometimes 3 or 2 ⟨six ~ of herring⟩ **4 a (1) :** sediment deposited by water (as when alluvial soil is formed) **(2) :** sediment developed or disturbed in situ by congeliturbation **(3) :** a bed or layer of deposited sediment **b :** a slight flexure of strata **5** [²*warp*] **a (1) :** the state or fact of being out of true in plane or line; *also* **:** an instance of warping (as a twist, bend, or crook) — used esp. of improperly seasoned wood ⟨a ~ in a door panel⟩ **(2) :** a variation from a true or plane surface; *esp* **:** one caused by warping of lumber **(3) :** the amount a surface warps or an allowance made for warping ⟨the ~ of a board⟩ **b :** a mental twist or aberration **:** a perverse or abnormal way of thinking, judging, or acting ⟨the ~ of the early years will always remain in him a long time —Dixon Wecter⟩

²warp \"\ *vb* -ED/-ING/-S [ME *warpen,* fr. OE *weorpan* to throw, cast; akin to OHG *werfan* to throw, cast, ON *verpa,* Goth *wairpan,* Gk *rhembein* to whirl] *vt* **1 a :** to turn or twist out of shape ⟨trees ~ed by the wind⟩ ⟨the occasional ~ing of logic and possibility —D.R.Weimer⟩; *esp* **:** to twist or bend out of a flat plane by or as if by contraction, curving, drying, dampness, or heat ⟨the hot sun ~ed the cabin's walls⟩ **b :** to give a mental twist to **:** make perverse or biased **:** cause to judge, choose, or act wrongly ⟨their minds are ~ed with suspicion —T.B.Costain⟩ ⟨characters ~ed in infancy and intelligence stunted at school —Bertrand Russell⟩ ⟨a few men at the top, whose thinking is ~ed by dogma —Elmer Davis⟩ **:** cause to turn aside from a chosen or correct ethical, religious, or intellectual choice or path **:** lead astray **:** PERVERT ⟨aroused judgment easily becomes ~ed —Dorothy Sayers⟩ ⟨the social lies that ~ us from the living truth —Alfred Tennyson⟩ **c :** to falsify, misinterpret, or give a false coloring to by wresting or twisting **:** DISTORT ⟨histories . . . are too often ~ed by an unfortunate bias —W.R.Inge⟩ ⟨other forms of political activity, which . . . badly ~ the meaning of elections —Elmo Roper & Louis Harris⟩ **d :** to deflect from a course **:** cause to veer ⟨long-term profit trends of the publicly regulated industries are ~ed from time to time by legislation —Julius Grodinsky⟩ **e :** to change the form of (a wing) by twisting esp. to provide lateral control **f :** to flex slightly (as by differential vertical movements in the earth's crust) **2** [ME *warpen,* fr. ¹*warp*] **a :** to wind (yarns) on a warp beam **:** arrange (yarns) so as to form a warp **b** *obs* **:** FABRICATE, DEVISE **c :** WEAVE, INTERLACE **3** [¹*warp*] **:** to move (as a ship) by hauling on a warp attached to a fixed object (as a buoy or anchor) ⟨as each ship was loaded . . . another vessel would be ~ed into the vacancy at the dock —L.C.Douglas⟩ ⟨with practiced maneuvers the boats were ~ed alongside —Luis Marden⟩ **4** *Brit* **:** to cast (young) prematurely — used of a domestic animal **5** [¹*warp*] **a :** to let the tide or other water in upon (low-lying land) for fertilizing by a deposit of warp **b :** to fill up (as a channel) with warp **:** CHOKE ~ *vi* **1 a :** to become twisted out of shape by or as if by contraction or shrinkage **:** become twisted or bent out of a flat plane ⟨the lock walls of some early canals . . . were of wood, and . . . began to bulge and ~ almost as soon as completed —A.F.Harlow⟩ **b (1) :** to become biased **:** alter a choice, opinion, or liking under influence ⟨he never ~ed from the path of common sense —Timothy Dwight⟩ **(2) :** to have a bias or perverse inclination or attraction **2 a (1)** *of a ship* **:** to become moved by warping ⟨help carriers ~ into dock —*Nat'l Geographic*⟩ **(2) :** to warp a ship **:** move a ship by a warp **b :** to progress slowly or circuitously or with effort as if being warped **c** *archaic* **:** to whirl or glide in the air ⟨a pitchy cloud of locusts, ~ing on the eastern wind —John Milton⟩ **3 :** to wind yarn off bobbins for forming the warp **:** wind a warp on a warp beam **syn** see DEFORM

warp·age \-pij\ *n* -s [²*warp* + *-age*] **:** the action, process, or result of warping

war paint *n* **1 :** paint put on the face and other parts of the body by American Indians as a token of going to war **2 :** full, ceremonial, or official dress **:** REGALIA, FINERY **3 :** MAKEUP 4a

warp and woof *n* **:** WARP 1b ⟨the vigorous Anglo-Saxon base had become the *warp and woof* of English speech —H.R. Warfel⟩

war party *n* **1 :** a group of No. American Indians on the warpath **2 :** a political party advocating or upholding a war **:** a jingoist political group

warpath \'-,-\ *n* [¹*war* + *path*] **1 a :** the route taken by a party of American Indians going on a warlike expedition or to war **b :** the expedition itself or the ensuing state of war **2 :** a hostile course of action or frame of mind

warp beam *n* **:** a double-flanged roll on which warp is wound for a loom

warp·er \'wȯrpər, 'wȯ(ə)pə(r\ *n* -s **:** one that warps: as **a :** a worker who prepares yarn for a warp by winding it in sheet form onto a beam or in rope form into a ball — compare BEAMER 1b **b :** a machine used for this work

warp-face \'-,-\ *adj, of a fabric* **:** having the face formed by warp threads

warping *n* -s [ME, fr. gerund of ²*warp*] **1 :** the preparation of a warp for a loom **2 :** a wound thread attaching a fly to a fishhook

warping bank *n* **:** a bank of earth raised round a field to retain water used in warping

warping board *also* **warping bar** *n* **:** a board with pegs to separate yarn groups used by many hand weavers in preparation of their warps — called also *bartree*

warping bridge *n* **:** DOCKING BRIDGE

warp knit *n* **:** a warp-knitted fabric

warp-knitted \'-¦--\ *adj* **:** produced by warp knitting

warp knitting *n* **:** machine knitting made on a machine that takes yarn from a warp beam and produces fabric with lengthwise threads — compare WEFT KNITTING

warp land *n* **:** land fertilized by warp

warplane \'-,-\ *n* [¹*war* + *plane*] **:** a military airplane; *esp* **:** one designed for combat purposes

war·ple \'wärpəl\ *vb* [perh. freq. of ²*warp*] *Scot* **:** TWIST, INTERTWINE, WRIGGLE

warple way *or* **warple road** \"\ *n* [origin unknown] *dial Eng* **:** BRIDLE PATH

war post *also* **war pole** *n* **:** a post sometimes painted red around which American Indians dance and into which they strike their tomahawks in connection with ceremonies of war

war potential *n* **:** the economic capabilities of a nation to wage war

war power *n* **:** the power to make war; *specif* **:** an extraordinary power exercised usu. by the executive branch of a government in the prosecution of a war and involving an extension (as by legislation or judicial interpretation) of powers constitutionally belonging to the government in peacetime

warp-pile \'-,-\ *adj, of a fabric* **:** having a pile formed by extra warp threads

warp print *n* **:** a fabric with shadowy indistinct patterns produced by printing the warp threads before weaving

warps *pl of* WARP, *pres 3d sing of* WARP

war·ra·gal *or* **war·ri·gal** \'wȯrəgəl\ *n* -s [fr. native name in Australia] **1** *Austral* **:** DINGO **2** *Austral* **:** a wild horse

war·ran·dice \'wärəndəs\ *n* -s [ME, fr. AF *warandise,* alter. of ONF *warantise* guarantee — more at WARRANTISE] **:** an obligation or clause by which a grantor binds himself that the right conveyed will be effectual under Scots law **:** WARRANTY

¹war·rant \'wȯrənt, 'wär-\ *n* -s [ME *warant, warrant* protector, protection, warrant, fr. ONF *warant,* modif. (influenced by *warir* to protect, preserve, of Gmc origin; akin to OHG *werien* to defend) of a Gmc noun represented by OHG *werēnto* guarantor, fr. pres. part. of *werēn* to warrant; akin to OHG *wāra* bond, trust, care — more at WEIR, VERY] **1 a (1) :** sanction furnished by or as if by law or a superior **:** AUTHORIZATION ⟨have the ~ of old friendship —W.B.Yeats⟩; *also* **:** the evidence for or a token of authorization ⟨the prophet may deliver his burden with no ~ but the awful "thus saith the Lord" —M.R.Cohen⟩ **(2) :** something that serves as a pledge, guarantee, or insurance **:** VOUCHER, PLEDGE, SECURITY ⟨his worth is ~ for his welcome hither —Shak.⟩ **b (1) :** something serving as a reason or ground for a belief, opinion, or action **:** JUSTIFICATION, RIGHT, FOUNDATION ⟨these two developments . . . give ~ in saying that the meetings mark the beginning of something new —Dean Acheson⟩ ⟨had heard people speak slightingly — perhaps without ~ — of his business ability —A.W.Long⟩ **(2) :** something serving as confirmation or proof ⟨their obviously increasing sophistication in matters of theory and method is a ~ of prodigious effort —W.W.Taylor⟩ **2 a :** a commission or document giving authority to do something **:** an act, instrument, or obligation by which one person authorizes another to do something which he has not otherwise a right to do and thus secures him from loss or damage; *specif* **:** a writing that authorizes a person to pay or deliver to another and the other to receive money or other consideration ⟨a ~ on a city treasurer⟩ **b (1) :** a precept or writ issued by a competent officer or magistrate authorizing an officer to make an arrest, a seizure, or a search or to do other acts incident to the administration of justice ⟨a ~ of attachment⟩ — see BENCH WARRANT, SEARCH WARRANT **(2) :** a magistrate's summons in a petty or summary proceeding in Virginia; *also* **:** a proceeding so begun **(3) :** a call for a town meeting stating the matters to be acted upon at the meeting **c :** an official certificate of appointment issued to an officer of lower rank than a commissioned officer — see WARRANT OFFICER **d** *Brit* **:** a receipt given to a person who has deposited goods in a warehouse by assignment of which the title to the goods is transferred **e (1) :** a short-term obligation of a municipality or other governmental body issued in anticipation of revenue **(2) :** an instrument issued by a corporation giving to the holder the right to subscribe to the capital stock of the corporation at a fixed price either for a limited period or perpetually **3 :** WARRANT OFFICER **4 :** a declaration of royal or other official determination ⟨precedence is determined by royal ~⟩ — **of warrant** *obs* **:** JUSTIFIED, WARRANTED — **out of warrant** *obs* **:** UNWARRANTED

²warrant \"\ *vt* -ED/-ING/-S [ME *waranten,* fr. ONF *warantir,* fr. *warant* protector, protection, warrant] **1** *obs* **:** PROTECT

2 a : to declare or maintain with little or no fear of being contradicted or belied **:** be sure of **:** be sure that ⟨I ~ he'll be with us when he's wanted —A.B.Paterson⟩ **b :** to assure (a person) of the truth of what is said **:** tell with assurance or positiveness **3 a :** to guarantee to a person good title to and undisturbed possession of (as an estate) **:** secure (an estate granted) to a grantee **:** ASSURE 5c **b :** to provide a guarantee of the security of (as title to property sold) usu. by an express covenant in the deed of conveyance **c :** to guarantee (as a fact or a statement of fact) to be at present or at a future time as represented ⟨the author hereby ~*s* . . . that the said work is an original work —John Gloag⟩ **d :** to guarantee (as goods sold) esp. in respect of the quality or quantity specified ⟨~*ed* against faulty workmanship or material for a period of ninety days after purchase —*advt*⟩ **4 :** to guarantee security or immunity to **:** give assurance against harm, loss, or damage **:** SECURE ⟨I'll ~ him from drowning —Shak.⟩ **5 :** to give authority or power to for doing or forbearing to do something **:** give warrant or sanction to **:** AUTHORIZE ⟨the law ~*s* this procedure⟩ **6 a :** to give proof of the authenticity or truth of **:** ATTEST ⟨his belief that metaphysics gives better ~*ed* knowledge than science —Sidney Hook⟩ **b :** to give assurance of the nature of or for the undertaking of **:** GUARANTEE ⟨a pill ~*ed* to cure measles, toothache, and rupture —C.E.Montague⟩ ⟨the most eloquent preacher, ~*ed* to produce a new religion every Sunday evening —W.L. Alden⟩ **7 :** to serve as or give sufficient ground or reason for **:** require or permit as a consequence **:** JUSTIFY ⟨sufficiently distinct to ~ a name of its own —Jacquetta & Christopher Hawkes⟩ ⟨the deposits contain too high a percentage of sulphur to ~ development —George Wythe⟩ ⟨theologians whose stature ~*ed* inclusion —R.P.Ramsey⟩ **syn** see ASSERT

war·rant·able \-ntəbəl\ *adj* **1 :** capable of being warranted **:** JUSTIFIABLE ⟨a ~ outlay⟩ **2** *of a stag* **:** old enough to be hunted — **war·rant·able·ness** \-bəlnəs\ *n* -ES — **war·rant·ably** \-blē,-bli\ *adv*

war·rant·ee \¦=rən·¦tē\ *n* -S [[2]*warrant* + *-ee*] **:** the person to whom a warranty is made

war·rant·er \'=rəntə(r)\ *n* -S [[2]*warrant* + *-er*] **:** WARRANTOR

war·ran·tise *or* **war·ran·tize** \-n·,tīz\ *n* -S [ME *warantise, warantize*, fr. ONF *warantise*, fr. *warantir* to warrant] **1** *archaic* **:** WARRANT, GUARANTEE **2** *obs* **:** PERMISSION

warrantize *vt* -ED/-ING/-S [ME *warantizen*, fr. *warantise*] *obs* **:** WARRANT, GUARANTEE

war·rant·less \'wȯrəntləs, 'wär-\ *adj* **:** UNWARRANTED ⟨~ accusations⟩

warrant of arrest : a warrant authorizing and commanding the arrest of a specific thing or person designated by name or by description ⟨a John Doe *warrant of arrest*⟩

warrant of attorney : written authority given by a person empowering another to transact business for him; *specif* **:** written authority given by a client to his attorney to appear for him in court and to allow judgment to pass against him esp. in connection with a note or bond accompanied by a defeasance

warrant officer *n* **:** an officer in the army, navy, air force, or marine corps occupying a grade between that of commissioned officer and noncommissioned officer

war·ran·tor \¦=rən·¦tȯ(ə)r, -ȯ(ə), '=rəntə(r)\ *n* -S [[2]*warrant* + *-or*] **:** one that warrants or gives a warranty

warrants *pl of* WARRANT, *pres 3d sing of* WARRANT

war·ran·ty \'wȯrəntē, 'wär-, -ti\ *n* -ES [ME *warantie*, fr. ONF, fr. fem. of *waranti*, past part. of *warantir* to warrant] **1 a** (1) **:** the undertaking or obligation of a feudal lord to defend his vassal tenant in the possession of the land held of him as lord, whether orig. received by the lord by commendation or not or to give the tenant lands of equal value (2) **:** a real covenant binding the grantor of an estate of freehold and his heirs to warrant and defend the title and in case of eviction by title paramount to yield other lands of equal value in recompense — see SPECIAL WARRANTY **b :** a collateral undertaking that a fact regarding the subject of a contract is or will be as it is expressly or impliedly declared or promised to be and although breach of such an undertaking does not void the contract it does make the warrantor liable for damages **c :** a statement expressly or impliedly made in an insurance policy by the insured that a fact relating to the subject of insurance or the risk exists or will exist or that some related act has been done or will be done and that must be literally true or fulfilled if the policy is not to become void — distinguished from *representation* **2 :** something that authorizes, sanctions, supports, or justifies **:** a justificatory mandate or precept **:** substantiating evidence, proof, or assurance **:** WARRANT, AUTHORIZATION ⟨a glib fluency is no ~ of genuine talent —A.T.Weaver⟩ ⟨by what ~ has he assumed such powers⟩ **3 :** a usu. written guarantee of the integrity of a product and the good faith of the maker given to the purchaser and generally specifying that the maker will for a period of time be responsible for the repair or replacement of defective parts and will sometimes also provide periodic servicing ⟨a one-year ~ on a television set⟩

warranty deed *n* **:** a deed containing a covenant of warranty; *esp* **:** one certifying that the covenantor has a good title in fee simple free and clear of all liens and encumbrances and that the covenantor will defend against the claims of all persons

warratau *var of* WARATAH

war·rau \wə'rau̇\ *n, pl* **warrau** *or* **warraus** *usu cap* **1 a :** a people of Venezuela and British Guiana **b :** a member of such people **2 :** the language of the Warrau people

war·rau·an \-au̇ən\ *n* -S *usu cap* [*warrau* + *-an*] **:** the language family of which Warrau is the only member

warred *past of* WAR

war·ree \wä'rē, 'wä(,)rē\ *n* -S [Miskito *ŭári*, prob. fr. Sp *jabalí* wild boar — more at JABALÍ] **:** WHITE-LIPPED PECCARY

war·ren \'wȯrən, 'wär-\ *n* -S [ME *wareine, warenne*, fr. ONF *warenne*, prob. of Gmc origin; akin to OHG *werien* to defend, protect — more at WEIR] **1** *Brit* **a :** a place privileged by prescription or grant from the king for keeping any of various animals (as hares, conies, partridges, or pheasants) **b :** a privilege by royal grant or prescription of hunting in a warren and taking wild animals **2 a :** an area esp. of uncultivated ground for the breeding of rabbits; *also* **:** a place abounding in rabbits **b :** the rabbits inhabiting a warren **3 a :** a tenement or a district as crowded and as full of life as a rabbit warren **:** a densely populated dwelling, slum, or quarter **b :** a maze of narrow winding streets or passages

[1]**war·ren·er** \-nə(r)\ *n* -S [ME *warenner*, fr. ONF *warennier*, fr. *warenne* warren + *-ier* -er] **1 :** a keeper of a warren **:** GAMEKEEPER **2 :** one that maintains a rabbit warren

[2]**war·re·ner** \"\ *n* -S [Tasmanian *warrenah* turbo] **:** any of several small top shells of the southern coast of Australia and Tasmania

war·ren girder *or* **warren truss** \¦wȯ|rən-, ¦wä|\ *n, usu cap W* [after Russell *Warren* †1860 Am. architect] **:** a truss consisting of upper and lower members connected by members arranged in the form of a series of isosceles triangles

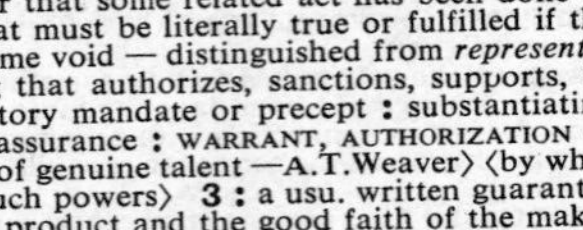
Warren girder

warrigal *var of* WARRAGAL

warring *pres part of* WAR

war·rior \'wȯry|ər, 'wȯ(ə)y|ə(r, 'wȯrē| *also* 'wärē| *sometimes* 'wäry\ *n* -S *often attrib* [ME *werreour, werriour*, fr. ONF *werreieur*, fr. *werreier* to make war (fr. *werre* war) + *-eur* -or — more at WAR] **1 a :** a man engaged or experienced in warfare and esp. in primitive warfare or the close combat typical of ancient or medieval times ⟨the wagon train was attacked by Indian ~*s*⟩; *broadly* **:** a person of demonstrated courage, fortitude, zeal, or pugnacity **b :** an advocate of war **:** JINGO ⟨preventative ~⟩ **2 :** a So. American hummingbird of the genus *Oxypogon* having a helmetlike crest

warrior ant *n* **:** SANGUINARY ANT

warrior bush *n* **:** CURRANT BUSH 2

war·rior·ess \|ərəs\ *n* -ES [*warrior* + *-ess*] **:** a female warrior

war·rior·ship \|ə(r),ship\ *n* [*warrior* + *-ship*] **:** the practices, occupation, or status of a warrior

war risk insurance *n* **1 :** term insurance written by the U.S. government for members of the military and naval forces **2 :** insurance that protects against loss due to acts of war

war road *n* **:** WARPATH 1a

war room *n* **:** a room at a military headquarters where situation maps are maintained

warrtd *abbr* warranted

wars *pl of* WAR, *pres 3d sing of* WAR

war sack *var of* WAR BAG

[1]**war·saw** \'wȯr(,)sȯ, 'wȯ(ə)(,)-\ *adj, usu cap* [fr. *Warsaw*, capital of Poland] **:** of or from Warsaw, the capital of Poland **:** of the kind or style prevalent in Warsaw

[2]**warsaw** \"\ *or* **warsaw grouper** *n* -S [modif. of Sp *guasa*] **:** a large grouper: as **a :** BLACK GROUPER **b :** SPOTTED JEWFISH

war service chevron *n* **:** a small chevron worn on the lower part of the sleeve of a military uniform to indicate that the wearer has seen service in a former war

warship \'=,=\ *n* **:** a government ship employed for war purposes; *esp* **:** one armed for combat — called also WAR VESSEL

[1]**war·sle** *or* **wars·tle** \'wä(r)səl\ *vb* -ED/-ING/-S [ME *werstelen, warstelen*, alter. of *wrestlen, wrastlen* — more at WRESTLE] *Scot* **:** WRESTLE, STRUGGLE, FLOUNDER

[2]**warsle** *or* **warstle** \"\ *n* -S *Scot* **:** a wrestling bout **:** TUSSLE

war song *n* **:** a song relating to war; *esp* **:** a song accompanying an Amerindian war dance that incites military ardor

warst \'wärst\ *dial var of* WORST

wart \'wȯ(ə)r|t, 'wȯ(ə)|, *usu* |d·+V\ *n* -S [ME *werte, wart*, fr. OE *wearte;* akin to OHG *warza* wart, ON *varta*, L *verruca* wart, Skt *varṣman* height, top, surface] **1 a :** a horny projection on the skin usu. of the extremities produced by proliferation of the skin papillae and caused by a virus — called also *verruca vulgaris* **b :** any of numerous verrucous skin lesions **2 :** an excrescence or protuberance more or less resembling a true wart; *specif* **:** a glandular excrescence or hardened protuberance on a plant (as in potato wart) **3 a :** someone or something suggestive of a wart esp. in smallness or obnoxiousness ⟨a misplaced ~ of real estate that nearly everybody wanted cut down —N.M.Clark⟩ **b** *Brit* (1) **:** a junior midshipman (2) **:** a young subaltern

war-tax stamp *also* **war stamp** *n* **:** a postage stamp used to raise war revenue instead of to pay postage

wart cress *n* **:** SWINE CRESS

wart disease *n* **:** POTATO WART

wart·ed \'wȯr|d·əd, 'wȯ(ə)|, |təd\ *adj* [*wart* + *-ed*] **:** having warts **:** VERRUCOSE

wartflower \'=,=\ *n* **:** CELANDINE 1

wart grass *or* **wart spurge** *n* **:** SUN SPURGE

warthog \'=,=\ *n* **:** an African wild hog of the genus *Phacochoerus* (esp. *P. aethiopicus* of southern Africa or *P. africanus* of northeastern Africa) having two pairs of rough warty excrescences on the face and large protruding tusks

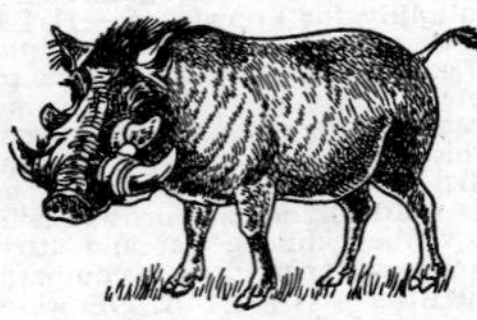
warthog of southern Africa

wartime \'=,=\ *n, often attrib* **:** a period during which a war is in progress ⟨the economies of ~⟩ ⟨~ shortages⟩ ⟨~ rationing⟩

wart·less \'wȯrtləs, 'wȯ(ə)t-\ *adj* **:** having no warts **:** free from warts

wartlike \'=,=\ *adj* **:** resembling a wart

war trail *n* **:** WARPATH 1a

wart snake *n* **:** any of several nonvenomous East Indian snakes constituting the family Acrochordidae, being covered with wartlike tubercles or spinose scales, and usu. lacking cephalic plates and ventral scutes

wartweed \'=,=\ *n, dial Eng* **:** any of several plants thought to cure warts: as **a :** SUN SPURGE **b :** DEVIL'S MILK 1 **c :** CELANDINE 1 **d :** NIPPLEWORT

wartwort \'=,=\ *n* [ME, fr. *wart* + *wort*] **1 :** a lichen of *Verrucaria* or a related genus having a warty thallus **2 :** WARTWEED

warty \'wȯr|d·|ē, 'wȯ(ə)|, |t|, |i\ *adj* -ER/-EST [ME, fr. *wart* + *-y*] **1 :** having warts or wartlike protuberances **:** full of warts **:** covered with warts **:** VERRUCOSE ⟨a ~ leaf⟩ **2 :** of the nature of or resembling a wart **:** WARTLIKE ⟨formation of ~ cutaneous nodules —D.T.Smith⟩

war vessel *n* **:** WARSHIP

war-weariness \'=,===\ *n* **:** a state of disillusion or depression felt toward the end of or immediately after a protracted war

war-weary \'=,==\ *adj* **1 :** affected by war-weariness **:** tired of or depressed by war **2 :** of, relating to, or being a combat plane so worn or damaged as to be beyond repair and consigned to be scrapped, cannibalized, or used for target practice

war whoop *n* **:** a war cry esp. of American Indians

war·wick·ite \'wȯr(w)i,kīt, 'wäri,-\ *n* -S [*Warwick*, village of southeastern N.Y. + E *-ite*] **:** a mineral $(Mg, Fe)_3Ti(BO_4)_3$ consisting of a borate of titanium, iron, and magnesium and occurring in brown to black orthorhombic prisms (hardness 3–4, sp. gr. 3.4)

war·wick·shire *or* **warwick** \'wȯr|ik,shi(ə)r, 'wär|, -|ēk-, -shiə, -‚shə(r), *US also* 'wȯ(r)w|\ *adj, usu cap* [fr. *Warwickshire, Warwick*, county of central England] **:** of or from the county of Warwick, England **:** of the kind or style prevalent in Warwick

[1]**war·wolf** \'wär,=, 'wȯr-\ *archaic var of* WEREWOLF

[2]**war·wolf** \'wȯr,=\ *n, pl* **warwolves** [[1]*war* + *wolf;* trans. of ML *lupus belli*] **:** a medieval siege engine for throwing stones and other missiles

warworn \'=,=\ *adj* [*war* + *worn*] **:** showing the effects of war or military service **:** ruined, ravaged, or laid waste by war

wary \'wa(a)|rē, 'we|, 'wā|, |ri\ *adj* -ER/-EST [[2]*ware* (fr. ME *war, ware*, fr. OE *wær* aware, wary) + *-y;* akin to OHG gi*war* aware, attentive, ON *varr* aware, wary, Goth *wars*, L *verērī* to fear, Gk *horan* to see, *-oros* watcher, *ōra* care] **1 :** marked by keen caution, cunning, and watchful prudence in detecting and escaping danger ⟨these figures were ~ in their movements and perfectly silent of foot —Joseph Conrad⟩ ⟨a subtle diplomacy and ~ tactics —Arnold Bennett⟩ **2 :** PROVIDENT, ECONOMICAL **syn** see CAUTIOUS

war zone *n* **1 :** a zone in which belligerents are conducting hostile operations during a war **2 :** a designated area esp. on the high seas within which rights of neutrals are not respected by a belligerent nation in time of war

[1]**was** [ME (1st & 3d sing. past indic.), fr. OE (1st & 3d sing. past indic. of *wesan* to be); akin to OFris *wesa* to be, *was* was, OHG *wesan* to be, *was* was, ON *vera* to be, *var* was, Goth *wisan* to be, *was* was, Skt *vasati* he lives, dwells, stays, and prob. to L *Vesta* goddess of the hearth, Gk *hestia* hearth, home, goddess of the hearth; basic meaning: to live, stay] *past 1st & 3d sing of* BE, *dial & archaic past 2d sing of* BE, *substand & archaic past pl of* BE, *substand & archaic past subjunctive of* BE

[2]**was** \'wəz, 'wäz *also* 'wȯz\ *n* -ES [ME, fr. [1]*was*] **:** something that was **:** PAST

[3]**was** *pl of* WA

wa·sa·bi \'wäsəbē\ *n* -S [Jap] **1 :** an Asiatic herb (*Eutrema wasabi*) of the family Cruciferae **2 :** the thick greenish root of wasabi that is grated in Japan like horseradish and eaten with fish and other food

was·co \'wä(,)skō\ *n, pl* **wasco** *or* **wascos** *or* **wascoes** *usu cap* [Wasco *wasq'o* cup, small bowl; fr. a cup-shaped rock near their main village always full of water] **1 a :** an Indian people of northern Oregon **b :** a member of such people **2 :** a dialect of Upper Chinook

wase \'wāz\ *n* -S [ME; akin to MLG *wase* bundle of sticks, pad to support a burden on the head, MSw *vasi* bundle of straw] **1** *chiefly dial* **:** a wisp or bundle of hay or straw **2** *chiefly dial* **:** a pad (as of straw) to support a burden on the head

[1]**wash** \'wȯsh, 'wäsh, 'wȯish, *chiefly substand* 'wȯ(ə)rsh *or* 'wärsh\ *vb* **washed** \-sht\ **washed** *or archaic* **wash·en** \-shən\ **washing; washes** [ME *waschen, wasshen, washen*, fr. OE *wascan, wæscan, waxan;* akin to OHG *waskan*, ON *vaska*, OE *wæter* water — more at WATER] *vt* **1 a :** to cleanse by the action of water or other liquid **:** dip, rub, or scrub in or with a liquid for the purpose of cleansing ⟨~ clothes⟩ ⟨~ the hands⟩ ⟨~ the baby⟩ **b :** to remove (as dirt or coloring) by rubbing or drenching with water or other liquid ⟨~ the stain out of the shirt⟩ ⟨~ the mud off the car⟩ **2 a :** to cleanse the body or esp. the hands and face of with water ⟨~*ed* himself thoroughly before sitting down to eat⟩ **b :** to free from ceremonial or moral defilement by cleansing with water or something likened to it in action or effect **:** cleanse or purify spiritually ⟨~ me thoroughly from my iniquity —Ps 51:2 (RSV)⟩ ⟨a quiet that ~*es* your mind clean —Wynford Vaughan-Thomas⟩ **c :** to purge away **:** OBLITERATE — usu. used with *away* ⟨my sins, which were many, are all ~*ed* away —R.H.McDaniel⟩ **d :** to cleanse (as the face or fur) by licking or by rubbing with the paw usu. moistened with saliva — used esp. of cats **3 a :** to bathe or moisten (a bodily part or injury) with a liquid ⟨~ the wound with water⟩ ⟨~ the eyes with a mild antiseptic solution⟩ **b :** to wet with tears ⟨tidings to ~ the eyes of kings —Shak.⟩ **c** (1) **:** to wet thoroughly **:** DRENCH, SATURATE ⟨roses ~*ed* with dew —John Milton⟩ (2) **:** to overspread with light **:** BATHE, SUFFUSE ⟨the sunlight ~*ing* their branches —James Still⟩ ⟨a late moon had come up and the barnyard was ~*ed* with moonlight —Sherwood Anderson⟩ **d** *archaic* **:** to occupy (oneself) in the action or sport of bathing ⟨he went but forth to ~ him in the Hellespont, and being taken with the cramp, was drowned —Shak.⟩ **e :** to pass water over or through esp. so as to carry off material from the surface or interior **4 a :** to touch in flowing **:** flow along the border of **:** dash or overflow against or over **:** LAVE ⟨the countries whose shores are ~*ed* by its waves —*Irish Digest*⟩ **b :** to flow through and supply water to ⟨a fine camping site, ~*ed* by a mountain stream⟩ **5 a :** to move, carry, or deposit by or as if by the force of water in motion ⟨the mill, bridge, dam, and several houses were ~*ed* away in a flood —*Amer. Guide Series: Md.*⟩ ⟨sediment ~*ed* down from the upper lakes —*Amer. Guide Series: Mich.*⟩ ⟨a wave of liberal reform ~*ed* the Indian peones back onto their lands —Green Peyton⟩ **b :** to cause to be in a specified place or condition by or as if by the thrust or sweep of water ⟨sometimes a whole school of pilot whales is trapped in shoal water and ~*ed* ashore —*Amer. Guide Series: N.C.*⟩ ⟨was ~*ed* overboard and drowned —W.A.Ganoe⟩ **6 a :** to wear away by the action of water **:** ERODE ⟨the dirt road had been ~*ed* by heavy rains⟩ **b :** to form (a break or opening) by the action of water ⟨the top speed a boat could make without ~*ing* a break in the berm —Edward Stanley⟩ **7 a :** to subject (as earth, gravel, or crushed ore) to the action of water to separate the valuable material from the worthless or less valuable ⟨the most successful method of ~*ing* sand for gold —Mary S. Broome⟩ — compare [3]LEACH 1a, LIXIVIATE **b :** to separate (particles) from ore or other substance by agitation with or in water **c :** to remove something from as if by the action of water ⟨the words tending to be ~*ed* of all specific meaning —H. P. Van Dusen⟩ **d** (1) **:** to pass through a bath of some liquid to carry off impurities or soluble components (2) **:** to pass (a gas or gaseous mixture) through or over a liquid for the purpose of purifying it esp. by removing soluble components — see [2]SCRUB 2a **e :** to bleach (a carpet or rug) by a chemical process **8 a :** to cover or daub lightly with an application of a liquid (as whitewash or varnish) **b :** to cover with a thin or watery coat of color **:** tint lightly and thinly ⟨the moors are ~*ed* with purple of the wild cranberries —Mary H. Vorse⟩ ⟨an architect's dream in palest grays ~*ed* with mauve —Claudia Cassidy⟩ **c :** to depict or paint by a broad sweep of thin or watery color with a brush — often used with *in* ⟨a few loosely *washed*-in ink blots —W.S. Baldinger⟩ **d :** to overspread (as an animal's throat) with an outer flush or tint of another color **e :** to overlay with a thin coat of metal by deposit from a solution ⟨steel ~*ed* with silver⟩ **9** *dial Eng* **:** to launder clothes for **10 :** to cause to swirl ⟨picked up his glass and ~*ed* the brandy about in its deep base —Helen Howe⟩ **11 :** to shuffle (playing cards) preparatory to dealing; *esp* **:** to shuffle for dealing by another **12 :** to dephosphorize (molten pig iron) by adding substances containing iron oxide and sometimes manganese oxide ~ *vi* **1 :** to cleanse oneself or a part of one's body with water ⟨~*es* before each meal⟩ **2 a :** to become worn away by the action of water **:** become eroded ⟨the harrowed land ~*ed* —Russell Lord⟩ — often used with *away* **b :** to become lost, impaired, or worn away as if by erosion — usu. used with *away* ⟨their social and their cultural identity ~*ed* away after some centuries —A.L.Kroeber⟩ **3 :** to clean something by rubbing or dipping it in water **:** perform the operation of cleansing in water ⟨told . . . she should be at home minding women's work, she answered there were plenty to spin and ~ —R.L.Stevenson⟩ **4 a :** to become carried or floated along on water **:** DRIFT ⟨cakes of ice ~*ing* along the side⟩ **b :** to pour, sweep, or flow in a stream or current ⟨feeling the wind ~ pleasantly against his face —Norman Mailer⟩ ⟨successive waves of pioneers ~*ing* westward —Green Peyton⟩ **5 :** to serve as a cleansing agent ⟨this soap ~*es* thoroughly⟩ **6 a :** to undergo without damage the operation of being laundered ⟨this material doesn't ~ well⟩ **b** (1) **:** to undergo successfully submission to a test or process of proof **:** bear investigation ⟨his story sounds good, but it won't ~⟩ ⟨an interesting theory that won't ~⟩ (2) **:** to inspire belief **:** gain acceptance ⟨that yarn didn't ~ with him —P.E.Lehman⟩ **7 a** *of a wave* **:** BREAK ⟨has a delightful location on the eastern shore, with slow waves ~*ing* almost at the base of its single street —*Amer. Guide Series: Vt.*⟩ **b :** to move with a lapping or splashing sound ⟨heard the ripple ~*ing* in the reeds —Alfred Tennyson⟩ **c :** to shuffle a deck of cards ⟨it's my turn to ~⟩ **8 :** to make a wash sale — **wash one's dirty linen in public :** to carry on or discuss personal, domestic, or private quarrels or scandals in public ⟨advised the members of his party not to *wash their dirty linen in public*⟩ — **wash one's hands of :** to disclaim or renounce interest in, responsibility for, or further connection with ⟨resigned his position and *washed his hands of* the whole mess⟩

[2]**wash** \"\ *n* -ES [ME *wasche*, fr. *waschen* to wash] **1 a** (1) **:** the process or work of washing clothing or household linen ⟨did a full day's ~⟩ **:** the process of being washed ⟨his shirts shrank in the ~⟩ (2) **:** an accumulation of articles (as of clothing) set apart for washing or in process of being washed ⟨a string of ~ hung drying in the hall —Eugene Kinkead⟩ ⟨the family ~⟩ ⟨the week's ~⟩ **b :** the act of washing **:** a cleansing or wetting with water ⟨the car needs a good ~⟩ **c :** a washing of oneself esp. of one's face and hands ⟨recorded all the things which he was supposed to do — the two hot ~*es* and the two cold ~*es* a day —Pierre Burton⟩ ⟨rolled up his sleeves and gave himself a quick ~⟩ **2 a** (1) **:** the surging action or attack of waves ⟨exposed to the ~ of waves at their base —P.E.James⟩ (2) **:** SURGE ⟨her novel comes as a great ~ of fresh air —Sylvia Stallings⟩ **b :** erosion by action of waves **c :** the sound of water breaking against or over a surface ⟨heard the ~ of waves upon rocks —Nevil Shute⟩ **3 a :** a piece of ground washed by the action of a sea or river or sometimes covered and sometimes left dry **:** the shallowest part of a river, estuary, or arm of the sea **b :** BOG, FEN, MARSH **c** (1) **:** a shallow body of water (2) **:** a shallow creek **d** *West* **:** the dry bed of an intermittent stream often at the bottom of a canyon — called also *dry wash* **4 a :** waste liquid (as from a bath) **b** *chiefly dial* **:** stale urine formerly used in washing clothes, soapmaking, and dyeing **c :** SLOP, SWILL **d :** worthless dregs **:** REFUSE **5** *dial chiefly Eng* **:** a dry measure of varying capacity for oysters and whelks **6 a** (1) **:** an insipid or wishy-washy beverage ⟨still felt refreshed and stimulated, after a few swallows of this ~ —Emily Hahn⟩ (2) **:** vapid writing or speech **b** (1) **:** fermented wort from which spirit is distilled — called also *distillers' beer* (2) **:** a mixture of dunder, molasses, water, and scummings used in the West Indies for distillation **7 a :** a wide sweep or splash esp. of color made or as if made by a long stroke with a coarse brush ⟨the leaves had not turned, but there was a gold ~ over everything —Anne G. Winslow⟩ ⟨a magnificent full-grown male with the rich, almost golden-yellow ~ over the belly —Thomas Barbour⟩ **b** (1) **:** a thin coat of paint (as watercolor) ⟨the pencil and ~ studies pinned to the walls —C.D.Lewis⟩ (2) **:** WASH DRAWING (3) **:** a flat tone used for pictorial clarity in architectural drawings **c :** a liquid mixture of slight consistency used for coating a wall or other surface thinly ⟨the cottages are still thatched with straw, and the walls are gay with the old pink ~ —*advt*⟩ **d :** a thin coat of metal laid on something for beauty or preservation or deposited on a metal for counterfeiting a precious metal **8 a :** LOTION 2 ⟨a good ~ for festering or cankered wounds and sores —Emily Holt⟩ **b :** a liquid cosmetic,

dentifrice, or hairdressing ⟨perfumed alcoholic ~*es* have had a vogue —Herman Goodman⟩ **c** : a mixture of ingredients (as beaten egg and water or milk) used by bakers for giving a glaze to baked goods **9 a** : material transported or deposited by water: as (1) : loose or eroded surface material of the earth (as gravel and other rock debris) transported and deposited by running water : ALLUVIUM, SILT; *esp* : coarse alluvium (2) : ALLUVIAL FAN (3) : a mound of detritus spreading in fan-shaped corrugated slopes below a gash in a cliff **b** : the action of run-off water in wearing away soil (as in gullying or sheet erosion) : the eroding of soil by rain wash **10** : an underground den esp. of a bear **11** : soil yielding precious metal or gems under washing **12 a** : the backward current or disturbed water caused by some action or movement (as of oars or a steamer's screw or paddles) : a surge set up by and trailing after some moving object or process (as a ship, storm, or tidal wave) esp. as dissipated in force or transmitted to a distance from the center of the disturbance ⟨was left swaying like a small boat in the ~ of a millionaire's yacht —Maurice Cranston⟩ **b** : a similar disturbance or wavelike agitation in the air set up by the passage of a storm center or rushing object (as an airplane) **c** : a disturbance in the air produced by the passage of an airfoil or propeller ⟨the ~ from the prop tugged at the loose ends of his scarf —Howard Hunt⟩ **d** : the dissipated current or force in the trail of an intellectual or social movement : EDDY ⟨hard to know how much . . . is solid accomplishment that will last, and how much is the ~ of a wave of opinion —A.L.Kroeber⟩ ⟨traveled there in the ~ of the war —J.R.Walsh⟩ **13** : WASH SALE **14 a** : the upper surface of a member or material when given a slope to shed water : WEATHERING **b** : a structure or receptacle shaped so as to receive and carry off water

³wash \"\ *adj* [¹wash] : capable of being washed without injury : WASHABLE ⟨~ fabrics⟩ ⟨a ~ dress⟩ ⟨~ goods⟩

⁴wash *adj* [perh. alter. (influenced by ²*wash*) of *wearish*] *obs* : WASHY, WEAK ⟨their bodies of so weak and ~ a temper —Francis Beaumont & John Fletcher⟩

wa·sha \'wäshə\ *n, pl* **washa** *or* **washas** *usu cap* **1** : a Chitimachan people of southeastern Louisiana **2** : a member of the Washa people

wash·abil·i·ty \ˌwȯshə'bilədē, ˌwäsh-, ˌwȯish-\ *n* : the quality or state of being washable

¹wash·able \'wȯshəbəl, 'wäsh-, 'wȯish-, *chiefly substand* 'wȯrsh- *or* 'wärsh-\ *adj* **1** : capable of being washed without suffering damage or loss of color ⟨a ~ dress⟩ **2** : soluble in water ⟨~ ointment bases —*Amer. Druggist*⟩ ⟨~ ink⟩

²washable \"\ *n* -s : a fabric or garment that may be washed without injury or change

wash and wear *adj* : of, relating to, or constituting a fabric or garment needing little or no ironing to be wearable after washing

washaway \'ˌˌ\ *n* -s [fr. the phrase *wash away*, fr. ¹*wash* + *away*] *Brit* : WASHOUT

wash ball *n* : a ball of toilet soap

wash barrel *n* : a barrel in which split mackerel are washed with salt water to extract the blood before salting

washbasin \'ˌˌ\ *n* : WASHBOWL

washboard \'ˌˌ\ *n, often attrib* **1** : a broad thin plank fixed along a gunwale or set on the sill of a lower deck port to keep out the sea — called also *washstroke, wasteboard* **2** : BASEBOARD **3 a** : a corrugated rectangular surface (as of zinc or glass) in a wooden frame on which clothes are rubbed in washing **b** : a road or pavement so worn by traffic as to be corrugated transversely **c** : a corrugated surface (as of glass or wood)

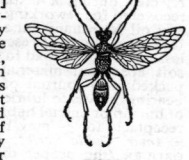

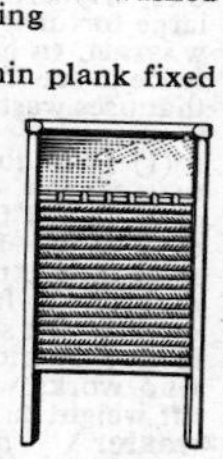
washboard 3a

washboiler \'ˌˌ\ *n* : a large metal vessel used for boiling clothes

wash boring *n* : a boring system by which material loosened by a bit is borne to the surface in the annular space between the bit and casing by water forced down through the pipe bearing the bit

wash bottle *n* : a bottle or flask provided with one bent tube passing through the stopper for directing a stream of water on anything to be washed or rinsed and with means for forcing (as by blowing into a second tube passing through the stopper or by squeezing if the bottle is flexible) the water through the tube

washbowl \'ˌˌ\ *n* : a large bowl for water to wash one's hands and face — called also *washbasin*

wash·brew \'wash,brü, 'wäsh-\ *n, dial Eng* : FLUMMERY 1a

wash brush *n* : a large brush for applying a wash

wash bulkhead *n* : a bulkhead in a ballast tank to prevent excessive movement of liquid in the tank

washcloth \'ˌˌ\ *n* : a cloth used for washing one's face and body

wash–colored \'ˌˌ\ *adj* : colored as if with a wash or water-color

washday \'ˌˌ\ *n* : a day regularly set aside (as once a week) for washing clothes (as of a family or institution) ⟨on the evening of the second ~ —Flora Thompson⟩

wash dirt *n* : earth washed or to be washed for gold : WASHING STUFF

wash·dish \'ˌˌ, *in sense 2* 'wash,- *or* 'wäsh,-\ *n* **1** : WASHBOWL **2** [so called fr. the motion of its tail resembling the motion of one washing dishes] *dial Eng* : PIED WAGTAIL

wash down *vt* **1** : to move or carry downward by action of water or other liquid; *specif* : to facilitate the passage of (food) down the gullet with accompanying swallows of liquid ⟨bolted a hot dog and *washed* it *down* with soda⟩ **2** : to wash the whole length or extent of ⟨*washed down* and scrubbed out with disinfectant, making sure that no corners or grooves . . . are missed out —Henry Wynmalen⟩

washdown \'ˌˌ\ *adj* [*wash down*] : constructed with provision for washing contents downward ⟨a ~ water closet⟩

wash drawing *n* : water-color painting in or chiefly in washes esp. in black, white, and gray tones only

washed *past of* WASH

washed–curd cheese \'ˌˌ-\ *n* [*washed*, past part. of ¹*wash*] : cheddar cheese in which the curd is washed before being pressed into forms to remove a portion of the whey, lactose, and soluble milk salts and produce a soft body with open texture

washed metal *n* : iron treated so as to remove most of the silicon and phosphorus and not too much of the carbon

washed–out \'ˌ'ˌ\ *adj* [fr. past part. of *wash out*] **1 a** : faded in color : lacking in brightness or vividness ⟨a very pale, *washed-out* blue —Eden Phillpotts⟩ **b** *of a photographic print* : lacking detail in highlights **2** : depleted in vigor or animation : played out : EXHAUSTED ⟨worked from seven in the morning until noon, and I was limp, *washed-out* —Richard Wright⟩ **3** : ERODED ⟨coal workings line the route in this hilly, *washed-out* section —*Amer. Guide Series: Pa.*⟩

washed sale *n* : WASH SALE

washed–up \'ˌ'ˌ\ *adj* [fr. past part. of *wash up*] **1** : ready for the discard : done for : played out ⟨as far as he's concerned, you're a *washed-up* nobody —Albert Morgan⟩ **2** *usu* **washed up** : at the end of an association or activity : ready to call it quits : THROUGH ⟨he was completely *washed up* with his wife . . . he never visited her —Morton Faber⟩ ⟨I'm *washed up* with the rackets —Allan Bruce⟩

washen *archaic past part of* WASH

¹wash·er \'wȯshə(r), 'wäsh-, 'wȯish-, *chiefly in substand speech* 'wȯrsh- *or* 'wärsh-\ *n* -s [ME *wassher*, fr. *wasshen* to wash + *-er*] **1 a** : a person who washes; *specif* : a worker who cleans by washing (as clothes, animals, or materials or products in processes of preparation, manufacture, or maintenance) **b** : a machine for washing something: as (1) : a device for removing dirt and soluble impurities from pulp and paper stock (2) : WASHING MACHINE (3) : an apparatus or device for washing photographic materials to remove soluble chemical products (as produced by development or fixing) (4) : an apparatus in which gases are washed : SCRUBBER c ⟨rotary ~*s*⟩ **2** [ME, fr. the motion of its tail resembling the motion of one washing clothes or dishes] *dial Eng* : PIED WAGTAIL **3** : any of various flat thin rings or perforated plates (as of metal or leather) used in joints or assemblies to insure tightness, prevent leakage, or relieve friction — see LOCK WASHER, SPRING WASHER **4** [so called fr. its habit of washing its food before eating] : RACCOON

²washer \"\ *vt* -ED/-ING/-s : to furnish with a washer

wash·er·less \-(r)ləs\ *adj* : not having a washer

wash·er·man \'ˌˌmən\ *n, pl* **washermen 1** : a man who works at washing clothes esp. for hire : LAUNDRYMAN **2** : one who operates a machine that washes: as **a** : a papermaker who washes cooked rags or wood pulp **b** : one who washes devulcanized scrap rubber to remove sodium hydroxide solution

washer–up \'ˌˌ'ˌ\ *n, pl* **washers–up** *Brit* : DISHWASHER ⟨at dinner we applaud the waitresses, cooks, and *washers-up* —Honor Tracy⟩

washerwife \'ˌˌˌ\ *n, Scot* : WASHERWOMAN

washerwoman \'ˌˌˌˌ\ *n, pl* **washerwomen 1** : LAUNDRESS; *esp* : one who takes in washing **2** [so called fr. the resemblance of the up-and-down motion of its tail to the motion of a woman scrubbing clothes] *dial Eng* : PIED WAGTAIL

wash·ery \'wȯshərē, 'wäsh-, 'wȯish-\ *n* -ES [¹*wash* + *-ery*] : a place at which material (as wool, ore, coal, or crushed stone) is freed from impurities or dust by washing

washes *pres 3d sing of* WASH, *pl of* WASH

washfast \'ˌˌ\ *adj* : resistant to fading or discoloration by washing ⟨a ~ blouse⟩ — **wash·fast·ness** *n*

washfountain \'ˌˌˌ\ *n* : a large circular washbowl set in the floor and supplied with running water from a central spray to permit simultaneous use by a number of people

wash gravel *n* : gravel washed to extract gold

washhand \'ˌˌ\ *adj, Brit* : designed for use in washing the hands or for holding utensils for such purpose ⟨a ~ basin⟩ ⟨a ~ stand⟩

washhouse \'ˌˌ\ *n* : a house or building used or equipped for washing; *esp* : one for washing clothes : LAUNDRY

washier *comparative of* WASHY

washiest *superlative of* WASHY

washin \'ˌˌ\ *n* -s [¹*wash* (flow, stream) + *in*] : a permanent twist or warp of an airplane wing such that the tip section has a larger angle of attack than the root section

wash·i·ness \'wȯshēnəs, 'wäsh-, 'wȯish-\ *n* -ES : the quality or state of being washy

washing *n* -s [ME *wasching*, fr. gerund of *waschen* to wash] **1** : the act or action of one that cleanses with water ⟨gave himself a good ~⟩ ⟨gave the clothes a thorough ~⟩ **2 washings** *pl* : liquid that has been used to wash something **b** (1) : metal (as gold dust) obtained by washing (2) : a place or soil yielding metal or gems under washing **c** : material collected by the washing of a bodily cavity ⟨sinus ~*s*⟩ ⟨throat ~*s*⟩ **3 a** : the action of waves or running water : the erosion or removal of material by running water **b washings** *pl* : material abraded or transported by the action of water **4 a** : the operation of bathing, drenching, or coating with a liquid (as in mining ore) **b** : the act or process of applying a thin coat of paint (as water-color) **c** : the dipping of fruits (as apples, pears, or plums) in a dilute solution of hydrochloric acid followed by rinsing in water as a means of removing spray residues that might be toxic to humans **5** : a thin covering or coat ⟨a ~ of silver⟩ **6** : clothes or other articles washed or to be washed esp. at one time : WASH ⟨the ~ was hanging in the back garden —J.I. Jones⟩ **7** : the execution of a wash sale

washing bottle *n* **1** : WASH BOTTLE **2** : a bottle for use in washing gases by passing them through liquid contained in it

washing engine *n* : a device much like a beater in which rags are washed by a stream of water and also reduced to threads and fibers

washing machine *n* : a machine for washing; *specif* : a usu. power-driven machine for washing clothes and household linen

washing powder *n* : a powder for washing (as a soap powder or a powder containing a synthetic detergent and alkaline builder)

washing soda *n* : SODIUM CARBONATE a(3)

washing stuff *n* : an earthy deposit containing gold that may be extracted by washing

wash·ing·ton \'wȯshiŋtən, 'wäsh-, 'wȯish-, -shēŋ- *sometimes* -shənt-, *chiefly in substand speech* 'wȯrsh- *or* 'wärsh-\ *adj, usu cap* **1** [fr. *Washington*, capital city of U.S., after George *Washington* †1799 first president of the U.S.] : of or from the city of Washington, D.C. ⟨a *Washington* legislator⟩ : of the kind or style prevalent in Washington : WASHINGTONIAN **2** *or* **washington state** *usu cap W & often cap S* [fr. *Washington*, northwestern state of U.S., after George *Washington* †1799] : of or from the state of Washington ⟨*Washington* apples⟩ : of the kind or style prevalent in Washington : WASHINGTONIAN

washington clam *n, usu cap W* : a butter clam (*Saxidomus nuttallii*)

washington grass *n, usu cap W & often cap G* : a water shield (*Cabomba caroliniana*)

washington handpress *n, usu cap W* [after George *Washington* †1799] : a hand-operated printing press perfected about 1829

¹wash·ing·to·nia \ˌˌˌ'tōnēə\ *n, cap* [NL, fr. George *Washington* †1799 + NL *-ia*] : a genus of massive fan palms of California and adjacent Mexico having large plicate leaves cut nearly to the middle and often bearing filaments on their margins and a smooth trunk bearing a large shaggy mass of persistent dead leaf remains

²washingtonia \"\ [NL, fr. George *Washington* †1799 + NL *-ia*] *syn of* OSMORHIZA

³washingtonia \"\ [NL, fr. George *Washington* †1799 + NL *-ia*] *syn of* SEQUOIA

¹wash·ing·to·ni·an \ˌˌˌ'tōnēən\ *adj, usu cap* **1** [George *Washington* †1799 first president of the United States + E *-an*] : of, relating to, or characteristic of George Washington **2** [*Washington*, capital city of U.S.A., or northwestern state of U.S.A. + E *-an*] **a** : of, relating to, or characteristic of Washington, D.C., or the state of Washington **b** : of, relating to, or characteristic of the people of Washington, D.C., or the state of Washington

²washingtonian \"\ *n* -s **1** *cap* : a native or resident of Washington, D.C., or the state of Washington **2** *usu cap* [*Washington* Temperance Society, founded 1840 + E *-an*] : a member of the Washington Temperance Society

wash·ing·to·ni·ana \ˌˌˌtōnē'anə, -'änə, -'ānə *also* -'ānə\ *n pl, usu cap* [George *Washington* †1799 + E *-ana*] : material (as papers, books, letters, or relics) relating to George Washington

washington lily *n, usu cap W* : a large white-flowered lily (*Lilium washingtonianum*) of the Pacific coast of the U.S. that is widely cultivated for ornament

washington palm *n, usu cap W* : a large fan palm (*Washingtonia filifera*) with many slender filaments hanging from its leaf margins — called also *California fan palm*

washington pie *n, usu cap W* [after George *Washington* †1799] : cake layers put together with a jam or jelly filling

washington plant *n, usu cap W* : FANWORT

washington post *n, usu cap W&P* : an American ballroom dance of the end of the 19th century

washington's birthday *n, usu cap W&B* [after George *Washington* †1799 first president of the United States] : February 22 observed as a legal holiday in most of the states of the U.S.

washington thorn *n, usu cap W* [fr. *Washington*, D.C., capital city of the U.S.] : a hawthorn (*Crataegus phaenopyrum*) of eastern No. America that is often cultivated for its bright red fruit and showy autumn foliage

wash·i·ta \'wäshəˌtȯ\ *adj, usu cap* [fr. Fort *Washita*, Texas] : of or relating to a subdivision of the Comanchean — see GEOLOGIC TIME table

washita stone *n* [fr. *Washita* (*Ouachita*) river, southwest Arkansas] : a porous variety of novaculite used esp. for sharpening woodworking tools

washland \'ˌˌ\ *n* : land or a stretch of land washed periodically by an overflowing stream

washleather \'ˌˌˌ\ *n* **1** : a soft leather usu. made of split sheepskin dressed with oil in imitation of chamois **2** *chiefly Brit* : a piece of washleather or soft cloth used for dusting or cleaning : CHAMOIS ⟨was flicking over the radiator with a ~ —Nicholas Monsarrat⟩

wash·man \'ˌmən\ *n, pl* **washmen 1 a** : a man who washes clothes : LAUNDRYMAN **b** : a textile worker who scours cloth during manufacturing **2** : a man who applies wash (as in tin-plate making)

wash mill *n* : any of several machines for washing clay, hides, or materials for cement

wash–mouth \'wȯsh,maủth\ *n, dial Eng* : BLABBERMOUTH

washo \'wä(ˌ)shō\ *n, pl* **washo** *or* **washos** *usu cap* **1 a** : an Indian people of the vicinity of Lake Tahoe, California and Nevada **b** : a member of such people **2** : a Washoan language of the Washo people **3** : WASHOAN

wa·sho·an \wä'shōən\ *n* -s *usu cap* [*Washo* + *-an*] : a language family of the Hokan stock comprising the Washo language

wash·oe process \'wä(ˌ)shō-\ *n, usu cap W* [fr. *Washoe* county, northwest Nevada] : a process of treating silver ores by grinding in pans or tubs with the addition of mercury and sometimes of chemicals (as blue vitriol and salt)

wash–off relief \'ˌˌ-\ *n* : an image in relief in color photography produced by hardening the exposed portions of a usu. gelatinous colloid layer and washing off the unhardened portions (as with hot water)

wash oil *n* : oil (as straw oil) used in scrubbing esp. coke-oven gas for absorbing light oil and recovering benzene and other aromatic compounds

wash out *vt* **1** : to wash free of some extraneous substance (as dirt, soap, chemicals) **2 a** : to drain off color in laundering ⟨this fabric is *washed out*⟩ **b** : to deplete of strength or vitality : EXHAUST ⟨after his recent illness, he is *washed out* for the time being⟩ **c** : to cancel out : OFFSET ⟨have *washed out* the effect of government reduction of its debt by the creation of bank deposits —T.O.Waage⟩ **d** : to eliminate as useless or unsatisfactory : DISCARD, REJECT; *specif* : to dismiss (a student or candidate) as failing to qualify **3 a** : to destroy or render useless by the force or action of water ⟨the storm *washed out* the bridge⟩ ⟨the heavy rains *washed out* the road⟩ **b** : to rain out ⟨the second game of the doubleheader was *washed out* by a sudden downpour⟩ ~ *vi* **1** : to become depleted of color or vitality : FADE ⟨technicolor makeup . . . *washes out* on TV —*Newsweek*⟩ **2** : to fail to meet requirements or measure up to a standard; *specif* : to fail in a course of training ⟨*wash out* of flight school⟩ **3** : WASH 2a

washout \'ˌˌ\ *n* -s [*wash out*] **1 a** : a channel cut by erosion in one sedimentary deposit and filled with the material of a younger deposit **b** : the washing out or away of earth esp. in the bed of a road or railroad by rain or a freshet; *also* : a place where the earth is washed away ⟨traffic was delayed by a ~ after the storm⟩ **c** : WASH 3d **2** : the act or process of washing or flushing out a container or pipe; *also* : a plumbing device for such process **3 a** : one that fails to measure up to expectations or requirements : a total loss : FAILURE, FLOP ⟨the first really hopeful idea he had reached had proved a ~ —F.W. Crofts⟩ ⟨the failures, the drunks, the ~*s*, the fellows running away from themselves —Hugh MacLennan⟩ ⟨the day was a ~⟩ **b** : a person (as a flying cadet or college student) who has been failed out of a course of training or study **c** : the act or fact of failing (as in a course of training or study) **4** : a permanent twist or warp of an airplane wing such that the tip section has a smaller angle of attack than the root section **5** : an emergency signal given by hand or lantern to stop a railroad train

wash plain *n* : ALLUVIAL PLAIN

wash plate *n* : any of several plates fitted in a ship's bottom to prevent surging of bilge water when the ship is rolling or pitching : BAFFLE

wash port *n* : FREEING PORT

washpot \'ˌˌ\ *n* : a pot for washing: as **a** : a large metal pot used outdoors for boiling clothes over an open fire ⟨playing out there in the yard . . . around an old fire-blackened ~ —F. B. Gipson⟩ **b** : a pot containing melted tin into which the plates are dipped to be coated in tinplate manufacturing

wash primer *n* : a primer of low nonvolatile content and special adhesive and protective properties for coating metal

washrack \'ˌˌ\ *n* : WASHSTAND 2

washrag \'ˌˌ\ *n* : a piece of cloth used in washing; *specif* : WASHCLOTH

washroom \'ˌˌ\ *n* **1** : a room (as in a restaurant or public building) equipped with washing and toilet facilities : LAVATORY 3a **2** : a room in a dyeing plant in which fabrics are washed

wash sale *n* : a prearranged fictitious sale of securities with no real change of ownership that is made to influence the market or to establish a loss for tax purposes

washstand \'ˌˌ\ *n* **1 a** : a piece of furniture combining features of a table and cupboard and used to hold articles (as a pitcher, basin, or towel) for washing the hands and face **b** : a washbowl (as of porcelain) permanently set in place (as on a wall) and attached to water and drain pipes **2** : a place (as in a garage) having water and drainage facilities for the washing of vehicles

washstrake \'ˌˌ\ *n* -s : WASHBOARD

wash·tail \'wash,-, 'wäsh,-\ *n* [so called fr. the up-and-down motion of its tail] *dial Eng* : PIED WAGTAIL

washtray \'ˌˌ\ *n* : LAUNDRY TRAY

washtrough \'ˌˌ\ *n* : a trough used for washing; *specif* : BUDDLE

washtub \'ˌˌ\ *n* : a tub in which clothes or other items are washed

wash up *vi* **1** : to wash one's face and hands **2** *Brit* : to wash the dishes after a meal ⟨went straight to the sink where his wife was *washing up* —D.H.Lawrence⟩ ~ *vt* **1** : to get rid of by washing ⟨*wash up* the spilled milk⟩ **2** : EXHAUST, FINISH ⟨guess we've *washed up* that subject —Philip Barry⟩ ⟨a setback that *washed* him *up* as a heavyweight contender⟩

washup \'ˌˌ\ *n* -s [*wash up*] **1 a** : the act or process of washing clean ⟨thorough ~*s*, sterilization of cleaned surfaces —*Experiment Station Record*⟩ ⟨presses get frequent ~*s* else their product would be lousy beyond description —P.R.Russell⟩ **b** : the act or process of washing ore **2** : a place for washing

wash·way \'wash,-, 'wäsh,-\ *n, dial Eng* : a place on a roadway covered by running water

washwheel \'ˌˌ\ *n* : a smooth or flanged rotating cylinder in which clothes or other fabrics are washed

washwoman \'ˌˌˌ\ *n, pl* **washwomen** : WASHERWOMAN

washwork \'ˌˌ\ *n* : WASH DRAWING

washy \'wȯshē, 'wäsh-, 'wȯish-, -shi *chiefly in substand speech* 'wȯrsh- *or* 'wärsh-\ *adj* -ER/-EST [²*wash* + *-y*] **1 a** *obs* : full of moisture : WATERY ⟨on the ~ ooze deep channels wore —John Milton⟩ **b** : easily eroding or washing out ⟨a ~ bank⟩ ⟨a ~ hillside⟩ **2 a** : lacking in substance or strength : DILUTED, THIN, WATERY ⟨~ tea⟩ **b** : deficient in brightness or richness of color : PALLID ⟨these strong earth colors attack the frail pink of the cherry blossoms . . . and leave it looking ~ and dirty —Anthony West⟩ ⟨a ~ pink or red with too much blue in it —E.H.M.Cox⟩ **c** : lacking in vigor, individuality, or definiteness ⟨keeping one foot in a sort of ~ respectability —Compton Mackenzie⟩ **3** *obs* : lacking in moral stamina or strength of character : FRIVOLOUS, LOOSE **4 a** *of a domestic animal* : lacking in condition and in firmness of flesh : having a tendency to scour or sweat profusely on slight exertion ⟨a ~ steer⟩ ⟨a ~ horse⟩ **b** : tending to produce flabbiness or scouring in animals ⟨~ grass⟩ ⟨~ feed⟩

was·n't \'wəz°n(t), 'wäz- *also* 'wȯz-; *in rapid speech* 'wəd°n(t); *dial* 'wänt\ [by contr.] : was not

¹wasp \'wäsp, 'wȯsp\ *n* -s [ME *waspe*, fr. OE *wæps, wæfs, wæsp*; akin to OHG *wafsa, wefsa* wasp, Lith *vapsa* gadfly, L *vespa* wasp, OE *wefan* to weave — more at WEAVE] **1 a** : any of numerous winged hymenopterous insects that generally have a slender smooth body with the abdomen attached by a narrow stalk, well-developed wings, biting mouth parts, and in the females and workers a more or less formidable sting, that belong to many different families and include forms of social as well as of solitary habits, and that are largely carnivorous and often provision their nests with caterpillars, insects, or spiders killed or paralyzed by stinging for their larvae to feed on — compare SPHECOIDEA, VESPOIDEA; DIGGER WASP, HORNET, YELLOW JACKET; BEE **b** : any of various hymenopterous insects (as a chalcid fly or ichneumon fly) having larvae that are parasitic esp. on other insect larvae **2 a** : a waspish person **b** : something that stings or infuriates

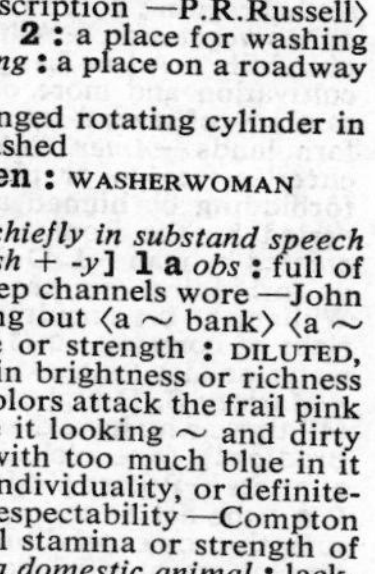
wasp

²wasp \"\ *n* -s *usu cap* [*Women's Air Force Service Pilots*] : a

member of the Women's Air Force Service Pilots of the U. S. Army air forces disbanded in December 1944

wasp ant *n* : VELVET ANT

wasp bee *n* : CUCKOO BEE

wasp beetle *n* : a black-and-yellow longicorn beetle resembling a wasp

wasp fly *n* **1** : any of various syrphus flies that resemble wasps **2** : THICKHEADED FLY

wasp·i·ly \-pəlē\ *adv* [*waspy* + *-ly*] : WASPISHLY

wasp·ish \-pish, -pēsh\ *adj* [¹*wasp* + *-ish*] **1 a** : resembling a wasp in behavior; *esp* : easily irritated : quick to take offence : SNAPPISH, TESTY ⟨witty and ~ and said whatever came into his head about his colleagues —Frank O'Connor⟩ ⟨his answers were crisp, though he could become ~ when annoyed —H.F. & Katharine Pringle⟩ **b** : marked by irritability or petulance ⟨the fourth-raters who use a staff captain's armlet as an excuse for ~ display of minor power —Fred Majdalany⟩ **2** : resembling a wasp in form; *esp* : slightly built ⟨the grim, black spars and ~ hull of a small man-of-war craft —Herman Melville⟩ **syn** see IRRITABLE

wasp·ish·ly *adv* : in a waspish manner

wasp·ish·ness *n* -ES : the quality or state of being waspish

wasp·ling \-pliŋ\ *n* -S [¹*wasp* + *-ling*] : the larva of a social wasp

wasp's nest *n* : HORNET'S NEST

wasp spider *n* : a spider that resembles a wasp in form

wasp waist *n* : a very slender waist; *specif* : a woman's tightly laced waistline

waspy \-pē, -pi\ *adj* -ER/-EST [¹*wasp* + *-y*] **1** : resembling a wasp : WASPISH ⟨a fierce, ~ little animal —F.B.Gipson⟩ **2** : full of wasps

¹**was·sail** \ˈwäsəl, |,säl *also* ˈwō| *sometimes* ˈwal; ˌ-ˈsāl, *esp before pause or consonant* -āəl\ *n* -S [ME *wæs hæil, washail*, fr. ON *ves heill* be in good health, fr. *ves* (imper. sing. of *vera* to be) + *heill* healthy — more at WAS, WHOLE] **1** : an early English toast to someone's health or good luck made when offering him a cup of wine or drinking to him — compare DRINK HAIL **2** : a liquor formerly drunk in England on festive occasions (as at Christmas and Twelfth Night) and made of ale or wine flavored with spices and other ingredients (as sugar, toast, roasted apples) **3** : riotous drinking : REVELRY ⟨became a place of ~ and fellowship —Julian Dana⟩ ⟨a certain seediness in the morning after such ~ —Paul de Kruif⟩ **4** *archaic* **a** : a festive or drinking song or glee **b** : a carol sung by wassailers

²**wassail** \ˈ"\ *vb* -ED/-ING/-S [ME *wesseylen*, fr. *washail* wassail] *vi* **1** : to hold a wassail : CAROUSE **2** *dial Eng* : to sing carols from house to house usu. at Christmas time ~ *vt* : to drink to the health or thriving of ⟨ceremonies of . . . ~*ing* fruit trees, caroling from house to house —Dorothy G. Spicer⟩

wassail bowl *n* **1** : a bowl used for the mixing and serving of wassail **2** : WASSAIL 2

wassail cup *n* : WASSAIL BOWL

was·sail·er \-lə(r)\ *n* -S [²*wassail* + *-er*] **1** : one that carouses : REVELER ⟨some ~s want to linger on until the small hours —John Kobler⟩ **2** *archaic* : one who goes about singing carols

was·sail·ry \-lrī\ *n* -ES [¹*wassail* + *-ry*] : REVELRY

was·ser·mann \ˈwäsə(r)mən, ˈvä-\ *n* -S *usu cap* : WASSERMANN TEST

wassermann reaction *n, usu cap W* [after August von *Wassermann* †1925 Ger. bacteriologist] : a complement-fixing reaction occurring with the serum of syphilitic patients and used as a test for syphilis, being ordinarily made by heating the patient's serum to destroy complement, mixing it with a fortified alcoholic extract of beef heart that is a nonspecific but effective antigen, and adding this mixture to a mixture of washed red blood corpuscles (as of sheep) and a serum (as of rabbit) containing a specific hemolysin for them after which the serum from a syphilitic patient combines with the antigen from the beef heart and absorbs the available complement so that there is no hemolysis while a serum that is not syphilitic causes no reaction in the first mixture and leaves complement free to cause hemolysis when the second mixture is added

wassermann test *n, usu cap W* : a test for the detection of syphilitic infection using the Wassermann reaction

was·sie \ˈwäsē\ *n* -S [origin unknown] : a large cleavage of a crystal (as an octahedron divided in two) split for cutting

wast [alter. (influenced by *was*, 1st & 3d sing. past indic., & *art*, 2d sing. pres. indic.) of ME *were* — more at WERE] *archaic past 2d sing of* BE

wast·able \ˈwāstəbəl\ *adj* [ME, fr. *wasten* to waste + *-able*] : subject to waste

wast·age \-tij, -tēj\ *n* -S [²*waste* + *-age*] **1 a** : loss, decrease, or destruction of something (as by use, decay, erosion, leakage) ⟨the fill is . . . largely the product of mass ~ from nearby hillsides —*Jour. of Geol.*⟩ ⟨the eggs and larvae . . . are subject to tremendous ~ as a result of the activities of carnivores —W.H. Dowdeswell⟩ **b** : losses that occur in a herd of cattle from any cause (as death, disease, or sale) — usu. expressed as a percentage of the number of cattle in the herd **2** *Scot* : a waste or desert place : waste ground **3** : wasteful spending or use of something : loss through wastefulness ⟨man's ~ of the earth's resources —*Brit. Bk. News*⟩ ⟨these delays, these ~s of effort and money —Eric Ambler⟩ **4** : something produced by wastage ⟨chips of flint, chert, and other stone — the ~ of implement making —*Amer. Guide Series: Mich.*⟩

¹**waste** \ˈwāst\ *n* -S [ME *waste, wast*; in sense 1, fr. ONF *wast*, fr. *wast*, adj., wild, desolate, waste, fr. L *vastus* unoccupied, desolate, waste; akin to OE *wēste* desolate, waste, OHG *wuosti*, L *vanus* empty, vain; in other senses, fr. ME *wasten* to waste — more at WANE] **1 a** (1) : an uninhabited or sparsely settled region : WILDERNESS ⟨this ~ of mud; water, and monotonous vegetation —Wilfred Thesiger⟩ ⟨the trackless ~*s* of the pine hills —Adria Langley⟩ (2) : barren land worthless for cultivation and more or less bare of vegetation : DESERT ⟨a sandy ~ of several square miles that was once forest and later farm lands —*Amer. Guide Series: Mich.*⟩ (3) : a desolate and cheerless region or place; *specif* : a place made barren or forbidding by human agency ⟨a quiet countryside was converted by the harvesters into one of the ugliest ~s ever created by man —L.D.Stamp⟩ (4) : something arid, deserted, or forbidding ⟨so was his life become a hopeless ~ —B.A. Williams⟩ **b** : uncultivated land; *specif* : land subject to the right of common **c** (1) : a broad and empty expanse (as of water or air) ⟨outposts staring over the seething Atlantic ~*s* —Marjory S. Douglas⟩ (2) : an endless stretch (as of time) ⟨all those who have died throughout the long ~*s* of time —J.S. Bradford⟩ ⟨one o'clock, and then another long, long ~ of quarters —Rumer Godden⟩ **d** : a disused part of a coal mine **2 a** : the act or action of wasting : useless or profitless consumption or expenditure : loss without equivalent gain ⟨this present era of efficiency ought . . . to avoid the ~ of ability —C.H.Grandgent⟩ ⟨~ of time⟩ ⟨~ of money⟩ **b** : an instance of wasting ⟨thought it was an economic ~ to have a car sitting in the garage all day long —M.M.Musselman⟩ **3 a** : loss through breaking down of bodily tissue **b** : gradual loss or decrease by use, wear, or decay **c** *chiefly dial* : a bodily consumption by disease **4 a** : damaged, defective, or superfluous material produced during or left over from a manufacturing process or industrial operation : material not usable for the ordinary or main purpose of manufacture: as (1) : material rejected during a textile manufacturing process and either recovered for reworking (as yarn) or used usu. for wiping dirt and oil from hands and machinery (2) : SCRAP (3) : fluid (as steam) allowed to escape without being utilized (4) : worthless material removed in mining or digging operations (5) : a soft absorbent material that when saturated with oil and packed in a journal of a railroad car equipped with solid bearings serves to lubricate the journal **b** : refuse from places of human or animal habitation: as (1) : GARBAGE, RUBBISH ⟨no receptacle for ~ may be washed in a pond, lake, or stream —*Amer. Guide Series: N.H.*⟩ (2) **wastes** *pl* : EXCREMENT, ORDURE ⟨the proper disposal, or lack of disposal here, of human ~*s* —*Orient Bk. World*⟩ ⟨barnyard ~*s*⟩ (3) : SEWAGE **c** : material derived by mechanical and chemical weathering and moved down sloping surfaces or carried by streams to the sea ⟨as rock ~ continues to stream away from every part of the area in turn, valleys are widened —Arthur Holmes⟩ **5 a** : destruction or injury done to property (as houses, woods, or land) by a temporary or life tenant to the prejudice of the heir or of him in reversion or remainder — see PERMISSIVE WASTE **b** : destruction, ruin, or devastation caused by some disaster (as war, fire, or flood) ⟨give edge unto the swords that make such ~ —Shak.⟩ **6** *obs* : CONSUMPTION, USE ⟨have the expense and ~ of his revenues —Shak.⟩ **7** : WASTE PIPE **8** *archaic* : OVERABUNDANCE, PROFUSION **syn** see REFUSE — **go to waste** *or* **run to waste** : to flow off as superfluous or waste liquid : become wasted or lost without producing any good or achieving any purpose

²**waste** \ˈ"\ *vb* -ED/-ING/-S [ME *wasten*, fr. ONF *waster*, fr. L *vastare* to lay waste, ravage, fr. *vastus* desolate, waste] *vt* **1** : to lay waste : bring to ruin : DEVASTATE ⟨shown how the Union preserved the States from *wasting* and destroying one another —Van Wyck Brooks⟩ **2** : to cause to shrink in physical bulk or strength : cause to become consumed or weakened : EMACIATE, ENFEEBLE ⟨the emaciated and battered figure of that poet whom desire, disease, and prison *wasted* —F.J. Mather⟩ **3 a** : to wear away or impair gradually : diminish by constant loss : use up : CONSUME ⟨the broad gray summit is barren and desolate-looking . . . *wasted* by ages of gnawing storms —John Muir †1914⟩ ⟨the aboriginal population had been *wasted* by the epidemics of the eighteenth century —W. C.Massey⟩ **b** *archaic* : SPEND, USE ⟨companions that do converse and ~ the time together —Shak.⟩ **c** : to dispose of as waste ⟨the dirty water is drained off from the top and *wasted* into a sewer —V.M.Ehlers & E.W.Steel⟩ **4 a** : to spend or use needlessly, carelessly, or without valuable result : consume or employ to no purpose : SQUANDER ⟨~ money⟩ ⟨~ time⟩ ⟨~ effort⟩ ⟨~ sympathy⟩ **b** : to leave unrecognized or unappreciated ⟨an actor *wasted* on an inattentive audience⟩ ⟨a pun *wasted* on his students⟩ ⟨full many a flower is born to blush unseen and ~ its sweetness on the desert air —Thomas Gray⟩ **c** : to allow to be used inefficiently or become dissipated or lost ⟨heat *wasted* in the process⟩ **d** : to let pass without taking advantage of ⟨~ a golden opportunity⟩ **5** *obs* : IMPOVERISH ⟨have *wasted* myself out of my means —Shak.⟩ ~ *vi* **1 a** : to lose weight, strength, or vitality : become gradually feebler — often used with *away* ⟨women and children . . . *wasting* away in the mills —V.L.Parrington⟩ **b** *of a jockey* : to exercise in order to lose weight ⟨had little difficulty in making eight stone, but . . . took rides at 7 st. 4 lb. and under, and *wasted* hard to make it —Richard Lane⟩ **2 a** : to become diminished in bulk or substance : become worn away by degrees ⟨still remaining, but gradually *wasting* from the surface rock on which they were carved —*Amer. Guide Series: Oregon*⟩ **b** : to become consumed : become used up ⟨allowed our natural riches to ~ with startling rapidity —*U. S. Code*⟩ **3** : ELAPSE, PASS ⟨time ~*s* too fast —Laurence Sterne⟩ **4** : to spend money or consume property extravagantly or improvidently ⟨~ not, want not⟩ **5** : to run off as waste ⟨allowing water to ~ when it reaches a certain elevation —*Water & Sewage Control Engineering*⟩ ⟨~*s* back into the sea through short rivers —Roscoe Fleming⟩

syn SQUANDER, DISSIPATE, FRITTER, CONSUME: WASTE implies ill-considered or thoughtless expenditure, fruitless and sometimes prodigal, without fit return or valuable result ⟨what a tremendous amount of energy is *wasted* in hauling, lifting, and spinning unnecessarily heavy masses of metal —Waldemar Kaempffert⟩ ⟨the windows were thickly frosted over, so that . . . art in dressing them was quite *wasted* —Arnold Bennett⟩ SQUANDER applies to silly, reckless, profuse expenditure likely to impoverish ⟨*squanders* in reckless gambling and debauchery —C.C.Walcutt⟩ ⟨*squandering* your early enthusiasm in futile attempt to excite the world about your ideas and your plans —W.J.Reilly⟩ DISSIPATE may suggest extravagant scattering or dispersion through indulgence or folly to the point of exhaustion ⟨doubtless his great and varied mental powers were *dissipated* by desultory labors, and by his inability to concentrate on a single task —Merle Curti⟩ ⟨unable to weather the storms of Reconstruction, its endowment *dissipated* in worthless securities, the institution was closed —*Amer. Guide Series: N.C.*⟩ FRITTER implies gradual dissipation of resources by piecemeal expenditure by bits, usu. on foolish trifles ⟨*fritter* away a fortune on petty vices⟩ ⟨the cathode was slowly *frittered* away, its substance becoming encrusted on the walls and other parts of the tube —K.K.Darrow⟩ CONSUME may refer to any wasteful devouring or destroying ⟨tuberculosis that *consumed* her at the age of thirty-four —Harry Levin⟩ ⟨for some cities are desolated by ruin, others *consumed* by the sword —G.G. Coulton⟩ **syn** see in addition RAVAGE

— **waste one** : to purposely pitch a bad ball to a batter in a baseball game ⟨was ahead of the hitter and decided to *waste one* in the hope of getting him to swing⟩ — **waste one's breath** : to speak without result : accomplish nothing by speaking

³**waste** \ˈ"\ *adj* [ME *waste, wast*, fr. ONF *wast* — more at ¹WASTE] **1 a** (1) : wild and uninhabited : not supporting or incapable of supporting a living community : BARREN, DESOLATE ⟨~ places⟩ (2) : ARID, DISMAL, EMPTY ⟨the ~ realms of nonexistence —L.P.Smith⟩ **b** : not used for pasture or crops : UNCULTIVATED, UNPRODUCTIVE ⟨a small piece of ~ land which the farmers could readily spare —R.P.T.Coffin⟩ **2** : being in a ruined or uncultivated condition : DEVASTATED ⟨arrives at a large city, burnt and ~ —*Publ's Mod. Lang. Assoc. of Amer.*⟩ ⟨a bombing that laid ~ the city⟩ ⟨for lack of manpower, large areas lie ~⟩ **3** *archaic* : UNOCCUPIED, VACANT ⟨a large ~ barn, which had survived the farmhouse to which it had once belonged —Sir Walter Scott⟩ **4** [¹*waste*] **a** : thrown away or aside as worthless, defective, or of no further use during or at the end of a process : REFUSE ⟨~ water⟩ ⟨~ material⟩ **b** : allowed to escape unused ⟨~ steam⟩ ⟨~ power⟩ **c** : excreted by an animal body ⟨~ matter⟩ **5** [¹*waste*] : serving to conduct or hold refuse material; *specif* : carrying off, providing for, or regulating the outflow of superfluous water ⟨a ~ cock⟩ ⟨a ~ drain⟩ ⟨a ~ spout⟩

waste bank *n* : a bank made of earth excavated during the digging of a ditch and laid parallel to it

¹**wastebasket** \ˈ≈,≈≈\ *n* [³*waste* + *basket*] : a basket for disposing of unwanted odds and ends esp. wastepaper — called also *scrap basket*

²**wastebasket** \ˈ"\ *vt* : to put into a wastebasket

wastebin \ˈ≈,≈\ *n* : TRASH CAN

wasteboard \ˈ≈,≈\ *n* : WASHBOARD

waste bowl *n* : a small bowl forming part of a tea service and used for waste tea or tea leaves

wasted *adj* [ME, fr. past part. of *wasten* to waste] **1** : laid waste : RAVAGED ⟨did fix mine eye upon the ~ building —Shak.⟩ **2** : impaired in strength or health : made weak or thin (as from disease or hunger) : EMACIATED ⟨kept life in his ~ frame not by hope but only by a grim ancient concentration —R.O.Bowen⟩ **3** *obs* : ELAPSED ⟨the chronicle of ~ time —Shak.⟩ **4** : unprofitably used, made, or expended : SQUANDERED ⟨~ effort⟩ ⟨a ~ trip⟩ ⟨~ money⟩

waste·ful \ˈwāstfəl\ *adj* [ME, fr. ¹*waste* + *-ful*] **1** *archaic* : serving to lay waste : causing devastation : DESTRUCTIVE ⟨when ~ war shall statues overturn —Shak.⟩ **2 a** : expending or tending to expend something valuable in a useless or extravagant manner : given to or marked by waste : LAVISH, PRODIGAL ⟨incompetent, ~, and corrupt . . . squandered money in bucketfuls —Allan Nevins & H.S.Commager⟩ ⟨in the same ~ spirit, they had cooked . . . three times more than we could eat —R.L.Stevenson⟩ **b** : causing needless loss or expenditure — used with *of* ⟨a defective boiler that is ~ of fuel⟩ **c** *archaic* : causing loss of bodily strength or weight ⟨lacking the burthen of lean and ~ learnings —Shak.⟩ **3** *archaic* : DESOLATE, UNINHABITED ⟨in wilderness and ~ deserts strayed —Edmund Spenser⟩ — **waste·ful·ly** \-fəlē, -li\ *adv* — **waste·ful·ness** *n* -ES

waste gate *n* **1** : a gate by which superfluous water (as of a reservoir) is discharged **2** : a device for controlling the pressure in the nozzle box of a turbosupercharger by discharging into the free atmosphere a portion of the exhaust gases that would otherwise pass through the turbine wheel : BLAST GATE

waste heat *n* : heat rejected or escaping from furnaces of various types (as coke ovens, cement kilns, or steel furnaces) after it has served its primary purpose

waste-heat boiler *n* : a steam boiler in which waste heat is used to evaporate water into steam

wasteland \ˈ≈,≈\ *n* **1** : barren or uncultivated land : WASTE **2** : a devastated place or area ⟨a ~ of burned houses and barns —A.E.Stevenson b. 1900⟩ ⟨a ~ of ruins and rubble —Robert Shaplen⟩ **3** : something (as an era, a way of life) that is emotionally or spiritually arid, barren, and desolate ⟨a ~ of futility and emptiness —J.W.Aldridge⟩ ⟨a ~ of vulgarity, platitude, and dulled perception —Anthony West⟩

was·tel bread \ˈwästᵊl-\ *or* **wastel cake** *n* [ME *wastel breed*, fr. *wastel* wastel bread (fr. ONF, fr. the Gmc source of OF *gastel* cake) + *breed* bread — more at GATEAU, BREAD] : bread formerly made of very fine flour; *also* : a cake or loaf of such bread

waste leaf *n* **1** : either of two protective extra blank leaves tipped on as the first and last leaves of a book and torn off when endpapers are affixed — called also *smut sheet* **2** : ENDPAPER

waste·less \ˈwāstləs\ *adj* [¹*waste* + *-less*] : incapable of being used up : INEXHAUSTIBLE ⟨a ~ source of energy⟩

waste·man \-tmən\ *n, pl* **wastemen** : a worker who removes waste: as **a** : one who collects and disposes of waste that accumulates during a manufacturing process **b** : a mine worker who keeps working areas and passageways free of refuse and repairs brattices — called also *jerry man*

waste mold *n* : a sculptor's mold that cannot be removed from the cast without being destroyed — compare PIECE MOLD

waste·ness \ˈwās(t)nəs\ *n* -ES [ME *wastnesse*, fr. ³*waste* + *-nesse* -ness] : the quality or state of being waste : a desolate state or condition ⟨a day of trouble and distress, a day of ~ and desolation —Zeph 1:15 (AV)⟩

waste nut *n* : an internally threaded floor flange for a pipe (as for waste)

waste of assets : DEVASTAVIT 1

wastepaper \ˈ≈,≈≈\ *n* **1 a** : paper discarded as superfluous or not fit for a particular use but usu. regarded as valuable raw material in some processes (as the manufacture of paperboard) **b** : worthless paper ⟨invested in fraudulent stocks that are just so much ~⟩ **2** *usu* **waste paper** : ENDPAPER

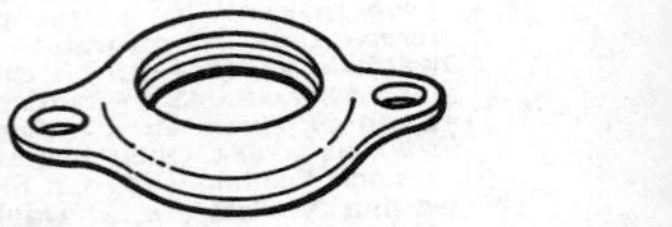

waste nut

wastepile \ˈ≈,≈\ *n* : TALON 3a

waste pipe *n* : a pipe for carrying off superfluous fluid : an escape pipe; *specif* : an outlet pipe for carrying off liquid waste (as from a washbowl, bathtub, or sink)

waste product *n* **1** : debris resulting from a process (as of manufacture) that is of no further use to the system producing it ⟨the *waste products* of one industry may be the raw materials of another⟩ **2** : material (as feces, urine, or desquamated cells) discharged from or stored in an inert form in a living body as a by-product of its vital activities ⟨animal *waste products* fill much of the nitrogen demand of plants⟩

¹**wast·er** \ˈwāstə(r)\ *n* -S [ME, fr. *wasten* to waste + *-er*] **1 a** (1) : one that spends or consumes extravagantly : PRODIGAL, SPENDTHRIFT, SQUANDERER ⟨a ~ who had run through a large fortune⟩ (2) : a dissolute person : GOOD-FOR-NOTHING, WASTREL ⟨a handsome face, though you didn't need to look twice to see that it was the face of a ~ —*Strand Mag.*⟩ **b** : one that uses wastefully or causes or permits waste ⟨a speaker who is a great ~ of words⟩ ⟨a procedure that is a ~ of time⟩ **c** (1) : one that lays waste or ruins : DESOLATER, DESTROYER, DEVASTATOR ⟨the ruin of youth, the ~ of fortunes, the destroyer of families —Lafcadio Hearn⟩ ⟨have created the ~ to destroy —Isa 54:16 (AV)⟩ (2) *archaic* : one of a class of thieves of 14th century England **2 a** : an animal (as a lamb that fails to fatten or a bird rejected for breeding) of inferior quality **b** : something that is useless or defective : an imperfect or inferior manufactured article or object **3** : a jockey who works with specified success or lack of success to take off weight ⟨a bad ~ who can't make the weight⟩

²**waster** \ˈ"\ *n* -S [ME, of unknown origin] *archaic* : a wooden sword or cudgel used in fencing or singlestick

³**waster** \ˈ"\ *n* -S [alter. (influenced by *leister*) of ME *waspere*, fr. *wa-* (of unknown origin) + *spere* spear] *Scot* : LEISTER

wast·er·ful \-(r)fəl\ *adj* [fr. obs. *waster* to be a waster, waste (fr. ¹*waster*) + *-ful*] *Scot* : WASTEFUL

wastery *var of* WASTRY

wastes *pl of* WASTE, *pres 3d sing of* WASTE

wastethrift \ˈ≈,≈\ *n* [²*waste* + *thrift* (savings)] : SPENDTHRIFT

wastetime \ˈ≈,≈\ *n* [²*waste* + *time*] *archaic* : PASTIME

waste-wax process *n* : CIRE PERDUE

wasteway \ˈ≈,≈\ *n* : a channel for carrying off superfluous water

wasteweir \ˈ≈,≈\ *n* : a weir for the escape of superfluous water

wasteyard \ˈ≈,≈\ *n* : a yard for storing refuse

¹**wasting** *adj* [ME, fr. pres. part. of *wasten* to waste] **1** : serving or acting to lay waste : DEVASTATING ⟨see the cities and the towns defaced by ~ ruin —Shak.⟩ **2** : undergoing gradual loss, diminution, or decay ⟨a ~ fortune⟩ ⟨a ~ muscle⟩ ⟨sands and clays brought from the ~ Andes by the great rivers —P.E.James⟩ **3** : causing decay or loss of strength ⟨hectic elements producing ~ fevers in the blood of society —*Times Lit. Supp.*⟩ — **wast·ing·ly** *adv* — **wast·ing·ness** *n* -ES

²**wasting** *n* -S [ME, fr. gerund of *wasten* to waste] **1** *archaic* : the act or action of devastating : DESOLATION ⟨violence shall no more be heard in thy land, ~ nor destruction within thy borders —Isa 60:18 (AV)⟩ **2** : wasteful use or expenditure ⟨the ~ of money⟩ **3 a** : the process or condition of wasting away : gradual loss of strength or substance : ATROPHY ⟨results in sores, ~, and eventually death —J.F.M.Middleton⟩ **b** (1) : gradual consumption or wearing away ⟨mingles Grecian grandeur with the rude ~ of old time —John Keats⟩ (2) : MASS-WASTING **c** : the process of exercising or training to lose weight

wasting asset *n* : property (as mines or lumber tracts) subject to depletion

wasting disease *n* : cobalt deficiency disease of sheep and cattle — compare ¹PINE 3

wasting palsy *or* **wasting paralysis** *n* : CREEPING PARALYSIS

¹**was·trel** \ˈwāstrəl *sometimes* ˈwäs-\ *n* -S [²*waste* + *-rel* (as in *scoundrel*)] **1** *dial Eng* : a piece of waste land beside a road **2 a** : something rejected or discarded as useless or imperfect ⟨~*s* from the workshops of neolithic peoples —A.H.Keane⟩ ⟨in the first thinning only the ~*s* and dead trees are removed —John Simpson⟩ **b** : an emaciated and unhealthy animal **3 a** : GOOD-FOR-NOTHING, PROFLIGATE ⟨was regarded as essentially a ~ and, given the opportunity, a Grade A guttersnipe —Stanley Walker⟩ **b** : VAGABOND, WAIF ⟨the girlish ~ who had drifted into the house —*Harper's*⟩ **4** : one that wastes : SPENDTHRIFT, WASTER ⟨a spendthrift and ~ of the world's stored energy —W.P.Webb⟩

²**wastrel** \ˈ"\ *adj* **1** : rejected as defective : WORTHLESS **2** : wasting or going to waste : SPENDTHRIFT ⟨the end of his now ~ ways —Maristan Chapman⟩

¹**wast·rife** \ˈwā,strīf\ *adj* [¹*waste* + *rife*] *Scot* : WASTEFUL

²**wastrife** \ˈ"\ *n* -S *Scot* : WASTEFULNESS

wast·ry *also* **wast·ery** *or* **wast·rie** \ˈwāstrī\ *n* [²*waste* + *-ry*, *-ery*] *Scot* : PRODIGALITY, WASTE

wasty \ˈwāstē\ *adj* -ER/-EST [¹*waste* + *-y*] **1** *archaic* : WASTEFUL **2** : containing or yielding much waste ⟨~ wool⟩ **3** *of livestock* : excessively fat

¹**wat** \ˈwat\ *Scot var of* WET

²**wat** \ˈwät\ *n* -S *often cap* [ME, prob. fr. *Wat*, nickname for *Walter*] *archaic* : HARE

³**wat** \ˈ"\ *n* -S [Siamese, fr. Skt *vāṭa* enclosed ground] : a Buddhist temple or monastery in Thailand

wa·tap \waˈtäp\ *also* **wa·tape** *or* **wa·ta·pe** \-pē\ *n* -S [CanF *watap*, fr. Algonquin] : a thread made of the stringy roots of any of various coniferous trees and used by American Indians esp. for sewing together strips of birch bark in canoes

¹**watch** \ˈwäch *also* ˈwȯch\ *vb* -ED/-ING/-ES [ME *wacchen*, fr. OE *wæccan*; akin to OE *wacian* to wake — more at WAKE] *vi* **1 a** : to keep vigil as a devotional exercise ⟨taught me how to ~ and pray —Philip Doddridge⟩ **b** : to be awake : to be or continue without sleep : WAKE ⟨could you not ~ one hour —Mk 14:37 (RSV)⟩ **c** : to remain awake during the night in attendance on a sick person ⟨~*ed* by his bedside until morning⟩ **2 a** : to be on one's guard or on the lookout : be attentive or vigilant ⟨~ jealously for any infringements of their rights —W.G.Hardy⟩ **b** : to keep guard : act as guard ⟨told him to ~ outside and see that no one entered⟩ **3 a** : to

keep someone or something under close observation ⟨seemed to feel her eyes on me all the time . . . ~ing, prying, judging —T.B.Costain⟩ **b :** to observe as a spectator **:** look on ⟨the nation ~ed while stocks rose to staggering heights —*Amer. Guide Series: Minn.*⟩ **4** *of an otter* **:** to retire into a lair to rest **5 :** to serve on a ship's watch **6** *of a buoy* **:** to float properly in its place **7 :** to remain unfolded or unclosed — used of a flower **8 :** to look with expectation **:** be expectant **:** WAIT ⟨~ed for the signal⟩ ⟨~ed for the train⟩ **~ vt 1 :** to keep under guard ⟨protected by a pair of high fences ~ed by armed guards —*Lamp*⟩ **2 a :** to observe closely in order to check on action or change **:** keep tabs on ⟨says he's positive they're being ~ed by the police —Mary Deasy⟩ ⟨every eye was fixed aloft, ~ing the masts, which were expected every moment to go over the side —Frederick Marryat⟩ **b :** to look at **:** OBSERVE ⟨~ a bus approaching you —Bertrand Russell⟩ ⟨sat very still and ~ed him —Raymond Chandler⟩ **c :** to be a spectator at **:** look on at ⟨people have a hard time getting to ~ afternoon entertainment in this age —John Lardner⟩ ⟨~ a ball game⟩ **3 a :** to take care of **:** TEND ⟨~ed the baby while her mother shopped⟩ **b :** to attend to **:** OVERSEE ⟨will ~ their plane reservations and their weight, their hotel bookings and their manners —Harry Gordon⟩ **c :** to be careful of ⟨as a performer I'd have to rest, ~ my diet —Barbara B. Jamison⟩ **d :** to make sure ⟨~ that he doesn't fall⟩ **4 :** to keep (a hawk) from sleep for the purpose of tiring and taming ⟨my lord shall never rest, I'll ~ him tame —Shak.⟩ **5 :** to be on the alert for **:** be ready to take advantage of or use **:** wait for **:** BIDE ⟨an adversary of no common prowess was ~ing his time —T.B. Macaulay⟩ ⟨~ed his opportunity⟩ **6 :** to keep in touch with **:** remain aware of or informed about ⟨no one who has ~ed the course of history during the last generation can have felt doubt of its tendency —Henry Adams⟩ **7** *Brit* **:** to provide with watchmen **:** POLICE **syn** see SEE — **watch it :** look out **:** be careful ⟨you got live ammunition there . . . *watch it* —Wirt Williams⟩ — **watch one's step :** to proceed with extreme care **:** act or talk warily ⟨the columnist dealing largely with news always has to *watch his step* if he is to avoid distortion —F.L.Mott⟩ — **watch over :** to have charge of **:** care for **:** SUPERINTEND ⟨*watches over* the safety of perhaps 250 landings and takeoffs a day —Ivor Jones⟩

²watch \"\ *n* -ES [ME *wacche,* fr. OE *wæcce,* fr. *wæccan,* v.] **1 a :** the act of keeping awake for the purpose of guarding, protecting, or attending **:** sleepless vigilance ⟨kept ~ by his bed —Robert Browning⟩ **b** *obs* **:** the state of being awake **:** SLEEPLESSNESS, WAKEFULNESS ⟨fell into a sadness, then into a fast, thence to a ~ —Shak.⟩ **c :** a wake over a dead body **d :** a state of alert and continuous attention to some situation, course of events, or danger ⟨in a position to keep a close ~ over events —R.P.Brooks⟩ ⟨wide open were the gates and no ~ kept —Alfred Tennyson⟩ **e :** close observation over someone **:** SURVEILLANCE ⟨kept a careful ~ over the prisoner⟩ ⟨kept a close ~ over his son⟩ **2 a :** any of the definite divisions of the night made by ancient peoples **b :** one of the indeterminate wakeful intervals marking the passage of night — usu. used in pl. ⟨the silent ~es of the night⟩ **3 a :** one that watches **:** LOOKOUT, WATCHMAN ⟨a yell from the bow ~ —Vincent McHugh⟩ **b** *archaic* **:** the office or function of a sentinel or guard ⟨as I did stand my ~ upon the hill —Shak.⟩ **c** *obs* **:** the cry of a watchman or sentinel ⟨his sentinel, the wolf, whose howl's his ~ —Shak.⟩ **4 :** a person or group of persons charged with the duty or function of protecting life or property or preserving the peace: as **a :** a body of soldiers or sentinels making up the guard of a camp or town ⟨some of the ~ came into the city —Mt 28:11 (AV)⟩ **b :** a watchman or body of watchmen formerly assigned to patrol the streets of a town at night, announce the hours, and act as police ⟨they fight! I will go call the ~ —Shak.⟩ **c** *usu cap* **:** a company of irregular Highland troops ⟨the Black *Watch*⟩ **5 :** a flock of nightingales **6 a** (1) **:** a portion of time during which a part of a ship's company is required to be on deck ready for duty — see AFTERNOON WATCH, DOGWATCH, FIRST WATCH, FORENOON WATCH, MIDWATCH, MORNING WATCH (2) **:** the part of a ship's company required to be on duty during a particular watch ⟨one by one, junior members of the ~ reported that they had been properly relieved —K.M.Dodson⟩ — see PORT WATCH, STARBOARD WATCH (3) **:** a sailor's assigned duty period ⟨everything was peaceful during his ~⟩ **b :** a period of duty **:** SHIFT ⟨was the duty sergeant on the 4 P.M. to midnight ~ for four years —*Springfield (Mass.) Union*⟩ **7 a :** a portable timepiece that has a movement driven in any of several ways (as by a spring or a battery) and is designed to be worn (as on the wrist) or carried in the pocket — compare CLOCK **b** *obs* **:** the dial of a clock **c :** the going train in a striking clock **d :** a ship's chronometer **8 :** a place of observation **:** a lookout station ⟨three of us were catfooting up a shallow draft to our ~es —Ed Shearer⟩ — **on the watch :** on the alert

³watch \"\ *adj* **1 :** used while or for watching **:** qualified to watch **:** used or serving as a lookout ⟨a ~ mastiff⟩ **2 :** of, belonging to, or used by a watchman or watcher ⟨a ~ pole⟩

watch·able \-chəbəl\ *adj* **:** worth watching ⟨her manner . . . totally unselfconscious and yet so ~ for its own sake —Lucien Price⟩

watch and ward *or* **watching and warding** *n* [ME *wacche and warde*] **1 :** the act of keeping guard **:** continuous unbroken vigilance and guard ⟨a handful of men kept *watch and ward* against the Iroquois —Francis Parkman⟩ **2 a :** service as a watchman or sentinel required from a feudal tenant — compare BURGAGE 2 **b :** service as a watchman specified as one of the chief duties of a constable

watch and watch *n* **:** the regular alternation in being on and off watch of the two watches into which a ship's crew is usu. divided

watchband \'=,=\ *n* **:** the bracelet or strap of a wristwatch

watch bell *n* [ME *wacche belle,* fr. *wacche* watch + *belle* bell — more at WATCH, BELL] **:** BELL 3a

watch bill *n* **:** a list of a ship's company divided into watches

watchboat \'=,=\ *n* **:** a boat engaged in patrolling

watch box *n* **1 :** SENTRY BOX **2 :** a shelter for a person (as a watchman or policeman) on watch

watch candle *n* **:** a slow-burning candle used (as by those who watch by the sick or deceased) during night watches or at a shrine

watch cap *n* **:** a knitted close-fitting navy blue cap worn esp. by enlisted men in the U. S. Navy in cold or stormy weather

watchcase \'=,=\ *n* **1** *obs* **:** SENTRY BOX **2 a :** the outside metal covering of the works of a watch **b :** a case for holding a watch

watch chain *n* **:** a usu. precious metal chain fastened to the pendant of a pocket watch — see ALBERT

watch charm *n* **:** a small ornament designed to dangle from a watch chain

watch clock *n* **:** WATCHMAN'S CLOCK

watch coat *also* **watch cloak** *n* **:** a warm overcoat worn esp. by sailors and soldiers on watch in cold or stormy weather

watchcry \'=,=\ *n* **1 :** the cry of a watchman making his rounds **2 :** a word or phrase briefly embodying the guiding principle of a party or movement and used as a slogan **:** WATCHWORD

watch crystal *n* **:** a concavo-convex glass covering the dial of a watch — called also *watch glass*

watch desk *n* **:** a desk in a fire station at which a fireman is on duty at all times

¹watchdog \'=,=\ *n, often attrib* [²*watch* + *dog*] **1 :** a dog kept to guard against trespassers or thieves **2 :** one that guards against loss, waste, theft, or undesirable practices ⟨should deal with its responsibilities in this matter as a ~ on behalf of the nation as a whole —Stephen King-Hall⟩

²watchdog \"\ *vt* **:** to act as a watchdog for ⟨opposed tax funds for television as part of its role of *watchdogging* the public purse —Richard Lewis⟩

watched *past of* WATCH

watch·er \'wächə(r) *also* 'wȯch-\ *n* -S **:** one that watches: as **a :** one that sits up or continues awake at night ⟨get on your nightgown, lest occasion call us, and show us to be ~s —Shak.⟩ **b :** one that keeps awake for the purpose of guarding **:** WATCHMAN ⟨the tapes and the lights instantly alert round-the-clock ~s when a criminal has run afoul of an electric or electronic snare —Alan Hynd⟩ **c :** ANGEL 1b **d** (1) **:** one that keeps watch beside a dead person (2) **:** one that attends a sick person at night **e :** OBSERVER, VIEWER ⟨an intense ~ of the scene —Elizabeth M. Roberts⟩ ⟨the sky ~s tell us of the birth and death of stars —*Scientific American Reader*⟩ **f :** a representative of a party or candidate who is stationed at the polls on an election day to watch the conduct of officials and voters **g :** one that is employed to watch equipment to see that a manufacturing or other process is carried out correctly: as (1) **:** one that runs an embroidering machine (2) **:** a textile worker who watches the fixing of colors on printed cloth **h :** one that tests the gas content of petroleum tanks before cleaners enter them

watches *pres 3d sing of* WATCH, *pl of* WATCH

watch·et \'wächət *also* 'wȯch-\ *n* -S [ME *wachet,* fr. ONF] **1** *or* **watchet blue :** a light blue color ⟨her dressing gown of *watchet blue* —Llewelyn Powys⟩ **2** *archaic* **a :** a light blue cloth **b :** a light blue angler's fly

watcheye \'=,=\ *n* **:** WALLEYE 1; *esp* **:** a walleye of a dog

watch face *n* **:** the dial of a watch

watch fire *n* **:** a fire lighted at night as a signal or for the use of a guard

watch fob *n* **:** ³FOB 2

watch·ful \'wächfəl *also* 'wȯch-\ *adj* **1** *archaic* **a :** not able or accustomed to sleep or rest **:** WAKEFUL ⟨to thee I do commend my ~ soul —Shak.⟩ **b :** causing sleeplessness ⟨~ cares —Shak.⟩ **c :** spent in wakefulness **:** SLEEPLESS ⟨twenty ~, weary, tedious nights —Shak.⟩ **2 :** marked by vigilance ⟨there was a ~ dignity in the room —J.P.Marquand⟩ **3** *archaic* **:** requiring vigilance **4 :** carefully observant or attentive **:** full of vigilance **:** being on the watch ⟨an instructed and ~ physician might well hope to cure you —Nathaniel Hawthorne⟩ ⟨has been equally ~ to assure scope for the states upon which the Union rests —Felix Frankfurter⟩ ⟨~ against attack⟩

syn VIGILANT, WIDE-AWAKE, ALERT: WATCHFUL is a general term indicating being on the lookout, often for danger, adverse developments, or opportunity ⟨glanced aside with a *watchful* air, just as a hound may often be seen to take sidelong note of some suspicious object —Nathaniel Hawthorne⟩ ⟨*watchful* of wind, water, and every movement of his opponents, he lost no chance to gain an inch —G.H.Genzmer⟩ VIGILANT suggests unremitting, keen, often wary watchfulness ⟨the *vigilant* eye of the Town Watch —*Amer. Guide Series: Mass.*⟩ ⟨eternally *vigilant* against attempts to check the expression of opinions that we loathe —O.W.Holmes †1935⟩ WIDE-AWAKE may stress keen awareness of relevant developments and situations ⟨was *wide-awake* now, and practical, ready to cope with the truth, whatever it was —Kathleen Freeman⟩ ALERT suggests careful watchfulness and ready promptness in apprehending danger or coping with difficulty or seizing opportunity ⟨standing silent and *alert,* like a sentinel on duty, in some dark corner —J.G.Frazer⟩ ⟨the auction conducts the sales . . . and is *alert* to expand the market outlet —*Amer. Guide Series: N.H.*⟩

watch·ful·ly \-fəlē, -li\ *adv* **:** in a watchful manner ⟨paused, and the room was ~ silent —J.P.Marquand⟩

watch·ful·ness *n* -ES **:** the quality or state of being watchful

watchful waiting *n* **:** a policy of taking no immediate action with respect to a situation or course of events but of following its development intently

watch glass *n* **1 :** WATCH CRYSTAL **2 a :** a usu. glass dish similar to a watch crystal in shape but made in various sizes **b :** SYRACUSE WATCH GLASS

watch gun *n* **:** a gun sometimes fired on shipboard at 8 p.m. when the first watch begins

watch hand *n* **:** the hour hand or the minute hand of a watch

watchhouse \'=,=\ *n* [ME *wache howsse*] **1 :** a house in which a guard is placed **2 :** a place where persons under temporary arrest are kept **:** POLICE STATION

watching *pres part of* WATCH

watching and warding *var of* WATCH AND WARD

watching brief *n* **1 :** a retainer of a lawyer merely to watch proceedings for one not a party to them **2 :** a commission to observe proceedings (as of a legislative body) for persons who may be concerned in them

watchkeeper \'=,==\ *n* **:** one who serves in a ship's watch; *specif* **:** one (as a quartermaster or radio operator) having special duties requiring a separate routine of watchkeeping from that of the port and starboard watches

watchkeeping \'=,==\ *n* **:** the duty or function of keeping watch

watch key *n* **:** a square-holed key that is used to wind some watches

watch·less \'wächləs *also* 'wȯch-\ *adj* **1 :** not watching **:** lacking in vigilance ⟨a ~ soldier⟩ **2 :** having no watch or watchman **:** UNGUARDED ⟨a ~ fortress⟩ **3 :** not divided into watches **:** not marked by wakefulness ⟨a ~ night⟩ — **watch·less·ness** *n* -ES

watch light *n* **:** a light that is used by watchers or by a watchman

watch line *n* **:** a fire hose left attached to a hydrant for a time as a precautionary measure after fire apparatus has been withdrawn from the scene of a fire

watchmaker \'=,==\ *n* **:** one that makes or repairs watches or clocks

watchmaking \'=,==\ *n* **:** the work or occupation of a watchmaker

watch·man \'=mən\ *n, pl* **watchmen** [ME *waccheman,* fr. *wacche* watch + *man*] **1 :** one who keeps watch **:** GUARD, SENTINEL: as **a :** one formerly assigned to guard the streets of a city by night **b :** one who is employed to stand watch over or to patrol property for the purpose of protecting it against theft, fire, or other damage **c :** one who keeps guard at a particular place to warn persons of imminent danger **d :** a fireman on duty at a watch desk **2 :** ⁵FLAG 3b

watchman beetle *n* **:** a European dorbeetle

watch·man·ly *adj* **:** belonging to or suitable for a watchman

watchman's clock *n* **:** a telltale clock for watchmen; *esp* **:** one in which a single clock contains the apparatus for recording the times of visiting several stations

watchman's rattle *n* **:** ²RATTLE 2b

watch mark *n* **:** a mark formerly worn (as in the U. S. Navy) on the right or the left sleeve to indicate the wearer's watch as the starboard or the port watch

watchmate \'=,=\ *n* **:** a man on duty in the same watch with another

watch meeting *n* **:** a watch-night service

watch night *n* **1 :** a devotional exercise lasting until after midnight and held orig. each month by Wesleyan Methodists and later by them and others on New Year's Eve **2** *usu cap W&N* **:** the last night of the year

watch officer *n* **:** a naval officer or petty officer who stands a watch — compare OFFICER OF THE DECK

watch out *vi* **:** to be vigilant **:** look out — often used with *for* ⟨had better *watch out* for himself, or one day he would be sorry —Robert Westerby⟩

watchout \'=,=\ *n* -S [*watch out*] **:** LOOKOUT 3 ⟨kept an increasing ~ for city and state corruption —*Time*⟩

watch paper *n* **:** an ornamental packing formerly placed inside a watchcase and made of paper fancifully cut or printed and sometimes bearing the maker's or repairer's name

watch pocket *n* **:** ³FOB 1

watch rate *n* **:** a tax rate for meeting the expense of a municipal watch

watch room *n* **1 :** a room for watchmen **2 :** a continuously attended room in a fire station in which alarms are received

watch screw thread *n* **:** a screw thread sometimes used in American watches and having a V profile with a 45-degree included angle for nickel and brass and a 60-degree included angle for steel

watch seal *n* **:** a seal or a trinket in imitation of a seal worn attached to a watch chain

watch spring *n* **:** one of the several springs in a watch; *specif* **:** MAINSPRING

watch stander *n* **:** a member of a ship's company standing watch

watch stuffer *n, slang* **:** one who palms off poor or worthless watches as good ones

watch stuffing *n, slang* **:** the practice of a watch stuffer

watch tackle *n* **:** a light 2-sheave tackle commonly used as a luff upon luff by the watch on shipboard for jobs (as the handling of yardarms) that usu. require all hands — called also *handy-billy, jigger*

watchtower \'=,==\ *n* **1 a :** a tower on which a sentinel is or may be placed **:** LOOKOUT **b :** an observation point ⟨from this somewhat unpromising ~ . . . surveyed English life —*Quarterly Rev.*⟩ **2** *archaic* **:** LIGHTHOUSE **3 :** a turret-shaped projection of the cephalothorax of a spider supporting an eye

watch train *n* **:** the time train of a watch

watchwoman \'=,==\ *n, pl* **watchwomen :** a woman who watches or serves as a guard

watchword \'=,=\ *n* [ME *waccheword,* fr. *wacche* watch + *word*] **1 a** *archaic* **:** a secret word used as a signal permitting a person to pass a guard **:** PASSWORD ⟨stealthy guests have secret ~s, private entrances —Robert Browning⟩ **b :** a word or phrase used as a sign of recognition among members of the same society, class, or group **2** *archaic* **:** a prearranged signal for attack or other action **3** *archaic* **:** a watchman's call **4 a :** a word or motto that embodies a principle or guide to action of an individual or group **:** SLOGAN ⟨the ~ of the conservative is "order" —H.N.Maclean⟩ ⟨"death rather than crime", such is the good man's ~ —W.E.Channing⟩ **b :** a guiding principle ⟨make cost reduction through production efficiency your ~ —*Successful Farming*⟩

watchwork \'=,=\ *n* **:** the wheelwork of a watch; *also* **:** a similar small wheelwork — compare CLOCKWORK

wate \'wāt\ *chiefly Scot var of* ²WOT

¹wa·ter \'wȯd|ə(r), 'wä|, |tə(r)\ *n* -S *often attrib* [ME, fr. OE *wæter;* akin to OHG *wazzar* water, ON *vatn,* Goth *wato* water, L *unda* wave, Gk *hydōr* water, Skt *udan*] **1 a :** the liquid that descends from the clouds as rain, forms streams, lakes, and seas, issues from the ground in springs, and is a major constituent of all living matter and that when pure consists of an oxide of hydrogen H_2O or $(H_2O)_x$ in the proportion of 2 atoms of hydrogen to one atom of oxygen and is an odorless, tasteless, very slightly compressible liquid which appears bluish in thick layers, freezes at 0° C and boils at 100° C, has a maximum density at 4° C and a high specific heat, contains very small equal concentrations of hydrogen ions and hydroxide ions, reacts neutrally, and constitutes a poor conductor of electricity, a good ionizing agent, and a good solvent — compare HEAVY WATER, ICE, STEAM, WATER VAPOR **b** (1) **:** a natural mineral water — usu. used in pl. ⟨drank the ~s for rheumatism⟩ (2) *archaic* **:** a place (as a spa) purveying such waters for remedial purposes **:** WATERING PLACE **2 :** a particular quantity or mass of water: as **a :** a portion of water to drink ⟨brought her ~ in a silver cup⟩ **b** (1) **waters** *pl* **:** the water occupying or flowing in a particular bed ⟨the limpid ~s of a mountain brook⟩ (2) *chiefly Brit* **:** a body of still fresh water **:** LAKE, POND, POOL (3) *chiefly Scot* **:** STREAM, RIVER; *also* **:** land abutting a stream **:** the bank of a stream **c :** a portion of water for a particular use — usu. used in pl. ⟨wash the greens in three ~s⟩ **d :** a quantity or depth of water adequate for some purpose (as navigation) ⟨a boat drawing three feet of ~⟩ ⟨there is ~ for trout⟩ **e waters** *pl* (1) **:** a band of seawater abutting on the land of a particular sovereignty and under the control of that sovereignty **:** the marine territorial waters of a state ⟨an invasion of British ~s⟩ (2) **:** the sea of a particular part of the earth ⟨the fleet was in eastern ~s⟩ **f :** a water supply ⟨threatened to turn off the ~⟩ ⟨our ~ was from springs⟩ **3 :** a means of transport on water or travel or transportation by such ⟨we went by ~⟩ ⟨they came by air but sent their heavy baggage by ~⟩ **4 :** the level of water at a particular state of the tide **:** TIDE ⟨waiting for low ~⟩ ⟨high ~ was at six o'clock⟩ **5 :** any of various liquid preparations containing or resembling water: as **a** (1) **:** a liquid (as a pharmaceutical or cosmetic preparation) prepared (as by solution or infusion) with water — compare FLORIDA WATER, LAVENDER WATER, TOILET WATER (2) **:** a watery solution of a gaseous or readily volatile substance — compare AMMONIA WATER, CAMPHOR WATER **b** *archaic* **:** a distilled fluid (as an essence); *esp* **:** a distilled alcoholic liquor **c** *obs* **:** a strong acid; *esp* **:** NITRIC ACID **6 :** a liquid (as a secretion, effusion, or humor) formed in or circulating in a living body: as **a :** TEARS ⟨a blow that brought the ~ to his eyes⟩ **b :** URINE ⟨passed a bloody ~⟩ **c :** a plant juice or other plant fluid; *esp* **:** COCONUT MILK **d :** SALIVA ⟨the smell of fresh bread brought the ~ to his mouth⟩ **e :** AMNIOTIC FLUID ⟨a dry birth with little ~⟩ — usu. used with *the* and in pl. ⟨after the ~s broke the labor was brief⟩ **7 a :** the limpidity and luster of a precious stone and esp. a diamond ⟨a diamond of the first ~ is perfectly clear and transparent⟩ — compare RIVER 3 **b :** an indicated and usu. exceptional degree of some quality (as excellence or villainy) ⟨a fool of the purest ~⟩ **c :** a wavy lustrous pattern (as of a textile or metal surface) ⟨a shimmering ~ played along the supple blade⟩ **8 :** WATERCOLOR; *esp* **:** a picture done in watercolor **9 a :** capital stock not representing assets of the issuing company and not backed by earning power **b :** fictitious or exaggerated asset entries (as for goodwill or other intangibles or for mining claims or other speculative or undeveloped assets) that give a stock an unrealistic book value — **above water** *adv* **:** out of difficulty or embarrassment — **in deep water :** in serious difficulties **:** beset with trials — **in smooth water :** progressing without impediment — **on the water** *or* **upon the water :** enroute aboard or in a ship at sea ⟨the shipment is still *on the water*⟩

²water \"\ *vb* -ED/-ING/-S [ME *wateren,* fr. OE *wæterian,* fr. *wæter,* n.] *vt* **1 :** to wet or supply with water or watery fluid **:** moisten, sprinkle, or soak with water **:** overflow with water **:** IRRIGATE ⟨~ flowers⟩ ⟨rain ~ing the soil⟩ ⟨with tears ~ing the ground —John Milton⟩ **2 :** to supply (as an army or ship) with water for drink **:** cause or allow to drink **:** give drink to or lead to a stream of water or other drinking place ⟨~ cattle and horses⟩ **3 :** to supply water to (as through the soil) ⟨land or vegetation ~ed by the Missouri⟩ **:** supply (as a boiler or engine) with water **4** *archaic* **:** to embrace within a surrounding or protecting stream, moat, or body of water ⟨a city ~ed about⟩ **5 :** to treat with or as if with water: as **a** *obs* **:** to soak in water (as for softening, macerating, or freshening) **b :** to sprinkle or drench so as to impregnate with water or a solution **c :** to impart a lustrous appearance and wavy pattern to (cloth) by calendering **d :** to spray or sprinkle (as a roadway) with water to lay dust **e :** to flood (as a ship in a lock) with water at the base for lifting **6 a :** to make dilute by or as if by the addition of water ⟨~ing the wine to make it last⟩ — sometimes used with *down* **b :** to reduce by addition or change usu. so as to weaken in force or efficacy **:** temper or soften in pungency, vigor, or positiveness — usu. used with *down* ⟨~ed down his remarks⟩ ⟨took care to ~ his radicalism down in public⟩ **c** (1) **:** to cause (oysters) to swell by soaking in water (2) **:** to cause (livestock) to put on specious weight by salting and watering heavily before marketing **d :** to add to the aggregate par value of (stock or other securities) without a corresponding addition to the assets represented by the security **~ vi 1 :** to form or secrete water or watery matter: as **a :** to produce or shed tears ⟨eyes ~ing from the smoke⟩ **b :** to secrete or become filled with saliva usu. in anticipation of food ⟨mouths ~ed as we waited for dinner⟩ **2 :** to get or take water: as **a :** to take on a supply of water ⟨the boat docked to ~⟩ **b :** to drink water **:** take a drink of water — usu. used of lower animals ⟨lions ~ing at dusk⟩

water adder *n* [ME] **1 :** WATER MOCCASIN **2 :** a common harmless American water snake (*Natrix sipedon*)

wa·ter·age \-ərij\ *n* -S [¹*water* + *-age*] *Brit* **:** transportation (as of goods) by water; *also* **:** money paid for such transportation

water agrimony *n* **1 :** BUR MARIGOLD **2 :** HEMP AGRIMONY

water antelope *n* **:** WATERBUCK

water arum *n* **:** a bog herb (*Calla palustris*) with a long creeping rhizome and reddish berries

water ash *n* **1 :** any of several No. American ashes (as *Fraxinus nigra* and *F. pauciflora*); *specif* **:** a tree (*F. caroliniana*) of river swamps of the southern U. S. **2 :** BOX ELDER

water avens *n* **:** an erect perennial herb (*Geum rivale*) of the north temperate zone with pinnate leaves and few nodding purple flowers

water back *n* **1 :** a cistern used in brewing for storing hot or cold water **2 a :** a reservoir at the back of a wood or coal range for heating and storing water **b :** a system of tubes often enclosed in a solid casting, placed in the firebox of a wood or coal range on the side opposite the oven for heating water, and connected with a storage tank separate from the range

water bag *n* **1 :** a bag for holding water; *esp* **:** one designed to keep water cool for drinking by evaporation through a slightly porous surface **2 a :** the reticulum of a camel or a closely related animal **b :** the fetal membranes enclosing the amniotic fluid — used esp. of domestic animals **c :** a pouch filled with serous fluid; *also* **:** any of several abnormalities of domestic animals characterized by such a pouch

water·bail·age \'==,bālij\ *n* -s **:** a duty imposed on goods transported by water

water bailiff *n* [ME] **1** *obs* **:** an English customs officer required to search ships **2 :** any of various former British officials having specified jurisdiction over the water: as **a :** an official superseded in 1771 having jurisdiction over fishing on the Thames **b :** an official in the Isle of Man having jurisdiction over fishery and some maritime jurisdiction prior to 1885 **c :** a police officer on a river employed esp. for the prevention of poaching

water balance *n* **:** the ratio representing the difference between water assimilated into the body and that lost from the body (as in urine, feces, and sweat) and being under average conditions approximately equal to unity

water ballast *n* **:** water in specially constructed compartments (as of a ship or balloon) to serve as ballast

water ballet *n* **:** a synchronized sequence of evolutions performed by a group of swimmers — compare AQUACADE, SYNCHRONIZED SWIMMING

water bar *n* **1 :** a ridge made across a hill road to divert rain water to one side **2 :** a bar inserted in a joint (as between the wood and stone sills of a window) to prevent passage of water **3 :** a tubular bar built into a fire grate as the heating unit of a system of hot water pipes

water bath *n* **1 :** a bath composed of or using water **2 :** a vessel containing usu. heated water over or in which something (as food) in a separate container is processed — called also *bain-marie*; compare STEAM TABLE

water bear *n* **1 :** POLAR BEAR **2 :** TARDIGRADE

water–bearer \'==,==\ *n* [ME *waterberere*, fr. *water* + *berere* bearer] **:** a carrier of water for drinking or other uses from a well or other source

water–bearing \'==,==\ *adj* **:** yielding or holding water **:** laden with percolating water **:** permeable by water ⟨*water-bearing* strata⟩

water bed *n* **:** a soil or rock layer that is laden with water or through which water percolates; *sometimes* **:** a swampy surface area

water beech *n* **:** AMERICAN HORNBEAM

water beetle *n* **:** any of numerous oval flattened usu. black or dark-colored lustrous aquatic beetles that belong to Dytiscidae and several other families (as Haliplidae, Gyrinidae, and Hydrophilidae) and that swim with great agility by means of their fringed hind legs which act together as oars

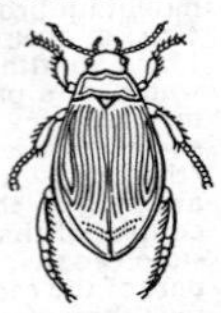
water beetle

water bellows *n pl* **:** TROMPE

water–belly \'==,==\ *n* **:** ascites of domestic mammals or birds

water betony *n* **:** a Eurasian plant (*Scrophularia aquatica*) of moist places with paniculate greenish purple flowers

water bewitched *n, dial Eng* **:** drink (as tea or grog) much diluted; *also* **:** a flat or insipid compound

water–bind \'==,=\ *vt* **:** to consolidate (as road-building material) with water

water birch *n* **:** any of several American birches growing typically in moist places: as **a :** RIVER BIRCH **b :** WESTERN PAPER BIRCH

water bird *n* [ME] **:** an aquatic bird **:** a swimming or wading bird — compare WATERFOWL

water biscuit *n* **1 :** a cracker made of flour and water sometimes with added salt and fat **2 :** any of various hemispherical or discoid masses produced in fresh water both now and in remote geological times by various blue-green algae

water bitternut *n* **:** WATER HICKORY

waterblink \'==,=\ *n* **:** WATER SKY

water blinks *n pl but sing or pl in constr* **:** BLINKS

water blister *n* **1 :** a blister with a clear watery content that is not purulent or sanguineous — compare BLOOD BLISTER **2 a :** a local injury to a plant caused by sunlight converging through a drop of water or a bubble in glass **b :** a disease of pineapples caused by a fungus (*Ceratostomella paradoxa*) and characterized by soft watery lesions on the fruit

water blob *n, dial Eng* **:** any of various aquatic or marsh plants: as **a :** a marsh marigold (*Caltha palustris*) **b :** WHITE WATER LILY

water bloom *n* **1 :** the accumulation of algae and esp. of various blue-green algae at or near the surface of a body of water often occurring suddenly and in large quantities and causing discoloration or forming a definite scum **2 a :** a scum that is formed by water bloom **b :** an algae causing water bloom

water blue *n, often cap W&B* **1 :** SOLUBLE BLUE 1 **2 :** BREMEN BLUE 1

water boa *n* **:** ANACONDA 2

water boat *n* **:** a boat carrying fresh water to ships

water boot *n* **:** a watertight boot for wear in water

waterborne \'==,=\ *adj* **1 :** floated or floating upon the water **:** supported by water so as not to sink or to touch bottom **2 a :** conveyed by water and esp. by boat ⟨~ traffic⟩ **b :** transmitted by water and esp. by drinking water ⟨~ diseases⟩

waterbosh \'==,=\ *n* **:** ¹BOSH 2

water bottle *n* **:** a container (as of leather, rubber, or glass) for carrying or holding water; *specif* **:** a specially constructed vessel that is used for collecting samples of water at any desired depth

water bottom *n* **1 a :** the space between the outer and inner bottom plating in a ship used to carry water ballast **b :** a similar space in a petroleum storage tank **2 :** land underlying water

water bouget *n* **1 :** a leather bag formerly used (as by a soldier) for carrying water and handled suspended one at each end of a pole or yoke **2** *or* **water budget :** a conventionalized representation of a pair of water bougets used as a heraldic charge

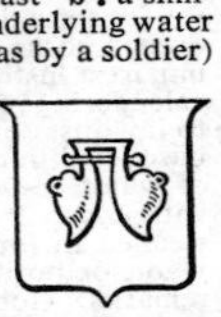
water bouget 2

water bough *n* [ME *water bow*, fr. *water* + *bow*, *bough* bough — more at BOUGH] *dial chiefly Eng* **:** an overshadowed shoot from a tree trunk — compare WATER SPROUT

water–bound \'==,=\ *adj* **1 :** restrained from going by flooding waters **2 :** consolidated or held together by water; *esp* **:** thoroughly soaked at the time of laying so that a natural cement formed from water and stone dust unites the particles — used of a macadam road surface

water bow *n* **:** RAINBOW

water box *n* **1 :** a box-shaped receptacle (as in a steam condenser) for holding water **2 :** WATER GLASS 3

water boy *n* **:** one who keeps a group (as of laborers or football players) supplied with drinking water

waterbrain \'==,=\ *n* **:** GID

water brake *n* **:** a brake working by water pressure; *esp* **:** a locomotive brake that admits water to the locomotive cylinders and offers resistance to movement of the pistons while descending a grade

water brash *n* **:** combined excessive salivation and acid regurgitation

water–break *n* **1 :** a place in a brook where the surface of the water is broken by irregularities on the bottom **2 :** a structure (as a breakwater) for deflecting or breaking the force of moving water

water breaker *n* **:** a cask for holding water used esp. for drinking water aboard ship

water breather *n* **:** an animal that obtains its respiratory oxygen from water usu. by means of gills

water bridge *n* **:** a bridge wall forming a water space at the back of the furnace of a steam boiler system

wa·ter·broo \'wätər,brü, 'wȯt-\ *n, Scot* **:** WATER GRUEL

wa·ter·brose \-,brōz\ *n* **:** a Scots brose of meal and water

water brush *n* **1 :** GROUNDSEL BUSH **2 :** a brush with long soft bristles used esp. for dampening the mane and tail and washing the feet and legs of a horse

water bubbler *n* **:** DRINKING FOUNTAIN

waterbuck \'==,=\ *n* [trans. of Afrik *waterbok*] **:** any of various antelopes that commonly frequent streams or wet lands: as **a :** either of two large coarse-haired reddish brown to grayish brown antelopes (*Kobus ellipsiprymnus* and *K. defassa*) of eastern Africa that are competent swimmers **b :** any of several kobs **c :** REEDBUCK

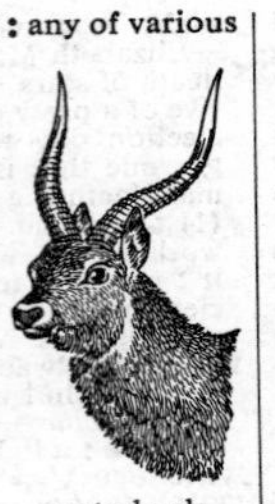
waterbuck

water buffalo *n* **:** an Asiatic buffalo (*Bubalus bubalis* or *Bos bubalis*) that is often domesticated — called also *water ox;* compare ANOA, CARABAO

water bug *n* **:** any of various insects or other small arthropods that frequent water: as **a :** CROTON BUG **b :** any of numerous aquatic bugs esp. of the family Belostomatidae that have long fringed hind legs which act like oars **c** *or* **water boatman :** BOAT BUG **d :** WATER SCORPION

water bugle *n* **:** a bugleweed (*Lycopus virginicus*)

wa·ter·bury \R 'wȯ|d·ə(r),berē, 'wä|, |tə(r)-, -ri *sometimes* -,bər-; –R -ə,ber- *sometimes* -,bər-\ *adj, usu cap* [fr. *Waterbury*, Conn.] **:** of or from the city of Waterbury, Conn. ⟨the *Waterbury* brass industry⟩ **:** of the kind or style prevalent in Waterbury

water–bus \'==,=\ *n* **:** a small boat engaged in the transport of passengers over a regular local route on inland waters in a manner comparable to a bus on land

waterbush \'==,=\ *n* **:** a hardy fast-growing Australian boobyalla (*Myoporum montanum*) that grows esp. along watercourses in dry sandy regions and is often cultivated for shelter belts or hedging

water butt *n* **1 :** a large cask set up on end to contain water and esp. to store rainwater **2 :** a receptacle for water (as for a fountain or lavatory)

water buttercup *n* **1 :** an aquatic plant of the genus *Ranunculus* **2 :** a marsh marigold (*Caltha palustris*)

water cabbage *n* **1 :** a white water lily (*Nymphaea odorata*) **2 :** WATER LETTUCE

water call *n* **:** a trumpet or bugle call summoning mounted troops to water their horses

water caltrop *n* **1 :** WATER CHESTNUT **2 :** either of two pondweeds (*Potamogeton crispus* and *P. densus*)

water carpet *n* **:** GOLDEN SAXIFRAGE

water carriage *n* **1 a :** transportation or conveyance (as of persons or goods) by water **b :** disposal (as of sewage) by means of flowing water **2 :** means or facilities of conveyance by water **3** *dial chiefly Eng* **:** a canal or ditch for draining water

water carrier *n* **1 :** a carrier of goods or people using the sea or waterways in transportation **2 a :** a man or beast that carries or distributes water (as to domestic establishments or troops) **b :** a tank, pipe, or channel for conveying water **c :** a rain cloud

wa·ter·cast·er \'==,kastə(r)\ *n, archaic* **:** a person claiming to diagnose a disease by inspection of a sample of urine

water cat *n* **:** NAIR

water cavy *n* **:** CAPYBARA

water celery *n* **1 :** CURSED CROWFOOT **2 :** TAPE GRASS

water cell *n* **:** a cell containing water; *esp* **:** one of the chambers in which water is stored in a camel's stomach

water–cement ratio *n* **:** the ratio of mixing water to cement in a concrete expressed by volume or by weight or as the number of gallons of water per bag of cement

water centipede *n* **:** HELLGRAMMITE

water channel *n* **:** a channel (as a ditch along a highway) for directing the course of water

waterchat \'==,=\ *n* **1 :** any of numerous So. American tyrant flycatchers of *Fluvicola* and related genera **2 :** a thrush of the genus *Enicurus* (family Turdidae) **:** FORKTAIL

water chestnut *n* **1 a :** a plant of the genus *Trapa* (esp. *T. natans* and *T. bicornis*) **b :** the edible nutlike spiny-angled fruit of a water chestnut **2 a :** a Chinese sedge (*Eleocharis tuberosa*) **b :** the edible tuber of this sedge

water chevrotain *n* **:** a western African chevrotain (*Hyemoschus aquaticus*) that has a larger body and shorter legs than the related kanchils and napus — called also *water deer*

water chicken *n* **:** FLORIDA GALLINULE

water chickweed *n* **1 :** BLINKS **2 :** a water starwort (*Callitriche palustris*)

water chinquapin *n* **:** an American lotus (*Nelumbo lutea*); *also* **:** its edible nutlike seed that has the flavor of a chinquapin

water chute *n* **:** a chute usu. with flowing water that is equipped with boats which slide down into a pool or lake

water civet *n* **:** a tropical African semiaquatic fish-eating civet (*Osbornictis piscivora*) somewhat resembling the otters in habits

water–clear \;==;=\ *adj* **:** perfectly transparent and nearly or wholly colorless ⟨a *water-clear* crystal⟩ ⟨*water-clear* honey⟩

water clock *n* **:** an instrument designed to measure time by the fall or flow of a quantity of water

water closet *n* **1 a :** a closet, compartment, or room for defecation and excretion into a hopper fitted with a device for flushing away with water **:** BATHROOM **b :** the hopper and its accessories **2** *dial* **:** PRIVY

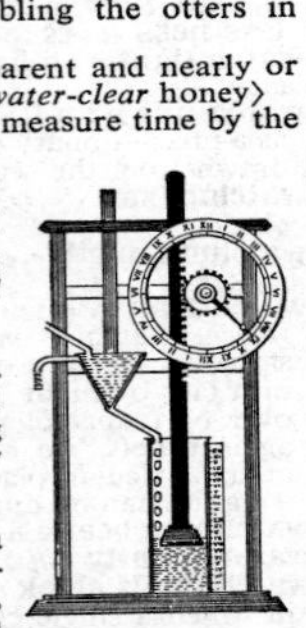
water clock

waterclover \'==,==\ *n* **:** CLOVER FERN

water cock *n* **:** a large gallinule (*Gallicrex cinerea*) of southeastern Asia and the East Indies of which in the breeding season the male is black and has a fleshy red caruncle on the top of its head

water colly *n, dial Brit* **:** WATER OUZEL

watercolor \'==,==\ *n, often attrib* **1 :** a paint of which the liquid is a water dispersion of the binding material (as glue, casein, or a gum) and which is prepared in the form of solid dry cakes or in a semifluid or pasty state in tubes or pans **2 :** the art or method of painting with watercolors **3 :** a picture or design executed in watercolors ⟨an exhibition of ~s⟩

watercolored \'==,==\ *adj* **1 :** of the color of water **:** PELLUCID **2 :** painted in watercolors

watercolorist \'==,===\ *n* **:** one who paints in watercolors

watercolor pencil *n* **:** a pencil with colored lead that when wet flows and blends like watercolor

water column *n* **1 :** WATER GAGE; *also* **:** the column of water in the gage **2 a :** a vertical pipe with valves and spout for delivering water to a locomotive tender **b :** a device that is connected to the back boiler head of a locomotive and bears the water glass, the gauge cocks, and usu. a lighting element

water company *n* **1 :** an organization engaged in the supplying of water for industrial and domestic purposes (as to an urban area) **2 :** a unit of a fire department primarily concerned with and equipped for the purpose of controlling fire by means of water

water–consolidated \'===;===\ *adj* **:** WATER-BOUND 2

water–cool \;=;=\ *vt* **:** to cool by means of water and esp. circulating water (as in a water jacket) ⟨*water-cooling* the engine⟩

water–cooled transformer \'==,=-\ *n* **:** an oil-filled transformer in which the oil is cooled by circulating water

water cooler *n* **1 :** a tank in which water is cooled by circulation round coils containing cold liquid (as brine) **2 :** a tank containing artificially cooled drinking water

water core *n* **1 :** a hollow core through which water circulates in a founding mold and which is used (as in casting a cannon) for cooling the interior of a casting more rapidly than the outside while the metal is solidifying **2 a :** a physiological disease of fruits (as apples) in which parts of the inner tissues esp. close to the core become water-soaked, hard, and glassy **b :** a similar disease of turnips caused by boron deficiency

water couch *n* **1** *chiefly Africa* **:** any of several paspalums: as **a :** JOINT GRASS 1 **b :** DITCH MILLET **2** *Austral* **:** a dropseed (*Sporobolus virginicus*) of New World origin that is a salt-tolerant shore and marsh grass useful as a soil stabilizer and good for grazing

watercourse \'==,=\ *n* **1 :** a channel through which water flows either continuously or intermittently (as seasonally): **a :** a made channel (as a ditch, canal, or aqueduct) for carrying water to or away from a particular place ⟨constructed a ~ to drain the swamp⟩ **b :** a natural channel normally with a definite bed and bounded by banks that is produced wholly or in part by and forms the course of a definite permanent or periodic flow of water **2 :** a stream of water (as a river, brook, or underground stream); *specif* **:** a natural stream arising in a particular watershed and not wholly dependent on surface water in its own immediate vicinity, flowing in a definite course either along a bed between visible banks or through a definite depression (as a ravine or swamp) in surrounding lands, having a definite and permanent or periodic supply of water and a perceptible current in a particular direction, and discharging at a fixed point into a body of still or flowing water (as a lake, a larger stream, or the sea) or disappearing underground **3 a :** a right to make use of the flow of a stream and esp. of one passing through one's land **b :** a right permitting the receipt of water through or its discharge upon land belonging to another and constituting a legal easement **4 :** LIMBER HOLE

water–course \"\ *n* **:** a layer of defective or poor-quality concrete (as in a wall) caused by the accumulation of excess mixing water and fine material at the surface of a pour

water cow *n* **1 :** a female water buffalo **2 :** SEA COW

water crack *n* **1 :** a crack in steel that is larger than a check and that is produced during the process of hardening **2 :** a fine crack in plaster that results from excess water or from the application of the succeeding coats too soon after the first coat

water cracker *n* **:** WATER BISCUIT

watercraft \'==,=\ *n* **1 :** skill in managing boats or in other aquatic activities **2 a :** SHIP, BOAT **b :** equipment for water transport **:** VESSELS

water crake *n* **1 :** WATER OUZEL **2 :** SPOTTED CRAKE **3** *dial Eng* **:** a water rail (*Rallus aquaticus*)

water crane *n* **1 :** a gooseneck apparatus to supply (as to the tender of a locomotive) water from an elevated tank **2 :** a hydraulic crane

water creeper *n* **:** any of numerous widely distributed small but broad flat leathery bugs (family Naucoridae) that are actively predacious in and about freshwater

watercress \'==,=\ *n* [ME *watercresse*, fr. *water* + *cresse* cress — more at CRESS] **1 :** any of several water-loving cresses (family Cruciferae): as **a :** a perennial cress (*Nasturtium officinale*) that grows chiefly in springs or running water and has creeping or floating freely rooting stems and roundish somewhat fleshy pungent leaves which are used in salads and sometimes as a potherb **b :** MARSH CRESS **c :** AMERICAN WATERCRESS **2 :** CRESS GREEN

water crow *n* [ME *water crowe*] **1** *dial Brit* **a :** WATER OUZEL **b :** a European coot (*Fulica atria*) **2 :** SNAKEBIRD 1

water crowfoot *n, pl* **water crowfoots :** an aquatic crowfoot or buttercup: as **a :** a white-flowered herb (*Ranunculus aquatilis*) used in England as food for cattle **b :** YELLOW WATER CROWFOOT

watercup \'==,=\ *n* **1 :** MARSH PENNYWORT **2 :** TRUMPET 3d(2) **3 :** PITCHER PLANT a

water cure *n* **1 :** HYDROPATHY, HYDROTHERAPY **2 :** a torture consisting of forcing a person to drink large quantities of water in a short time

water curtain *n* **:** a sheet of water usu. formed from above (as at the proscenium arch of a theater or in a mine) esp. as a screen to prevent spread of fire

water cut *n* **:** a cut taken by a machine tool when a supply of water is kept on the cutting surface and marked usu. by the production of a bright smooth finish

water cycle *n* [*cycle* fr. *-cycle* (as in *bicycle*)] **:** any of various more or less experimental watercraft propelled by treadles after the manner of a bicycle

water damage insurance *n* **:** insurance against loss that is due to direct damage by rain or leakage of plumbing but not by flood

water deer *n* **1 :** a small Chinese deer (*Hydropotes inermis*) lacking antlers in both sexes and having the upper canines enlarged into tusks in the male **2 :** WATER CHEVROTAIN

water devil *n* **1 :** the rapacious larva of a water beetle of the genus *Dytiscus* — called also *water tiger* **2 :** HELLGRAMMITE

water diviner *n* **:** a dowser for water

water dock *n* [ME *waterdokke*, fr. *water* + *dokke*, dock, *docke* dock — more at DOCK] **1 :** any of several docks growing in wet places: as **a :** a coarse erect European perennial dock herb (*Rumex hydrolapathum*) with a much-branched inflorescence **b :** a very similar dock (*R. orbiculatus*) of eastern No. America **2 :** GOLDEN CLUB

waterdoe \'==,=\ *n* **:** a female waterbuck

water dog *n* [ME *waterdogge*, fr. *water* + *dogge* dog — more at DOG] **1 :** a dog (as a retriever or water spaniel) experienced and strong as a swimmer or trained to retrieve waterfowl **2 a** *dial* **:** OTTER **b :** any of several large salamanders: as (1) **:** MUD PUPPY; *esp* **:** HELLBENDER (2) **:** GIANT NEWT **3 :** a person (as a skilled sailor or swimmer) who is quite at ease on or in the water **4 :** a small cloud that is held to indicate the approach of rain

water dragon *n* **1 :** a large Australian lizard (*Physignathus lesueurii*) that frequents water and is reported to make an uncanny sound by means of inflated cheek pouches **2 a :** a marsh marigold (*Caltha palustris*) **b :** LIZARD'S-TAIL

water–drinking \'==,==\ *adj* **1 :** favoring or habituated to the drinking of water and esp. the waters of mineral springs **2 :** favoring water as a beverage as opposed to alcoholic liquor

waterdrop \'==,=\ *n* **:** a drop or dropping of water; **:** as **a :** RAINDROP **b :** TEARDROP

water dropwort *n* **1 :** a plant of the genus *Oenanthe*; *esp* **:** a European poisonous herb (*O. crocata*) having tuberous roots, a yellow juice that stains the skin, yellow flowers, and foliage resembling that of celery — compare WATER FENNEL **2 :** a leafless herb (*Oxypolis canbyi*) of the southeastern U. S. with hollow leaflike stems and slender compound umbels of tiny white flowers

water drum *n* **:** a drum having the body partly immersed in water or partly filled with water

water dust *n* **:** particles of water composing clouds or fog

water eagle *n* **:** OSPREY

watered *past of* WATER

watered–down \'==;=\ *adj* [fr. past part. of *water down*, v.] **:** made weak as if by the addition of water **:** attenuated or lessened in force or value by watering ⟨turned in a *watered-down* report⟩

watered–silk \'==;=\ *adj* **:** having a pattern like that of silk subjected to watering ⟨the flame grain which gives wood a *watered-silk* appearance⟩

water elephant *n* **:** HIPPOPOTAMUS

water elm *n* **:** any of several trees of the family Ulmaceae that prefer or thrive in a moist environment: as **a :** AMERICAN ELM **b :** WINGED ELM **c :** CEDAR ELM **d :** PLANER TREE **e :** a common Eurasian elm (*Ulmus laevis*) that closely resembles American elm **f :** a tall spreading Japanese tree (*Zelkova serrata*) sometimes cultivated as an ornamental

water engine *n* **1 a :** FIRE ENGINE **b :** an engine used to pump up water (as from a well) **2 :** an engine for applying water power; *also* **:** a hydraulic engine

water equivalent *n* **:** the product of the mass of a body by its specific heat equal numerically to the mass of water that is equivalent in thermal capacity to the body in question

wa·ter·er \'wȯ|d·ərə(r), 'wä|, |tər-\ *n* -s **:** one that waters (as crops, soil, coal, or roadways): as **a :** a person who obtains or supplies drinking water ⟨helping out as a ~ of horses and cleaner of stables⟩ **b :** a device used for supplying water to livestock and esp. poultry and often equipped with an automatic float valve

water eryngo *n* **:** a button snakeroot (*Eryngium aquaticum*)

¹waterfall \'==,=\ *n* [ME, fr. *water* + *fall*] **1 a :** a perpendicular or very steep descent of the water of a stream **:** CASCADE, CATARACT, FALL **b** *obs* **:** a riffle or rapid in a swift stream **2 :** a falling away of the ground such as to cause drainage of water **3 :** something felt to resemble a waterfall: as **a :** a cascade of cloth **b :** a fall of waved hair

²waterfall \"\ *adj* **:** arranged like a waterfall ⟨a ~ arrangement of the drums of a 3-drum hoist in which the axis of the

center drum is higher than that of one end drum and lower than that of the other end drum); *esp* : curving smoothly from horizontal to perpendicular ⟨a ~ edge on a chair seat⟩
water-fast \ˈ=₌,₌\ *adj* **1** *chiefly Scot* : WATERTIGHT **2** : not leachable by water ⟨a *water-fast* dye⟩
water feather *or* **water featherfoil** *n* : a featherfoil (*Hottonia inflata*)
water feeder *or* **water feed** *n* : a device or pipe for supplying water (as in a boiler or tank)
water fence *n* **1** : a stream or ditch that forms a boundary (as of a field) **2** : a fence (as between fields) extending out into a margining body of water so that grazing animals may not pass by water from one plot to another
water fennel *n* **1** : WATER DROPWORT 1; *esp* : a European poisonous herb (*Oenanthe aquatica*) with fibrous roots **2** : WATER STARWORT
water-fennel oil *n* : an essential oil containing phellandrene and phellandral obtained from a water fennel (*Oenanthe aquatica*)
water fern *n* **1** : a fern ally of the families Salviniaceae or Marsileaceae **2** : a fern of the genus *Osmunda* (esp. *O. regalis*) **3** : FLOATING FERN 1
waterfinder \ˈ=₌,₌₌\ *n* : one that is occupied in finding sources of water supply; *esp* : a water dowser
water finish *n* : a very high finish given to paper or board by applying water as it passes the calender stack — compare DRY FINISH — **water-finished** \ˈ=₌\ₑ=₌\ *adj*
water fire *n* : a European acrid aquatic weed (*Bergia ammannioides*) of the family Elatinaceae
wa·ter-fit \ˈwätər,fit\ *or* **wa·ter-foot** \-fu̇t\ *n* [ˡ*water* + *fit* (Sc var of *foot*) or *foot*] *Scot* : a river mouth
water flag *n* **1** : YELLOW IRIS **2** : a common blue flag (*Iris versicolor*)
water flaxseed *n* : GREAT DUCKWEED
water flea *n* : any of various small active dark or brightly colored aquatic entomostracan crustaceans (as of the genera *Cyclops* and *Daphnia*)
waterflood \ˈ=₌,₌\ *n* [ME, fr. OE *wæterflōd* fr. *wæter* + *flōd* flood — more at WATER, FLOOD] **1** : a sweeping flood of water **2** : the act of flooding (as an oilwell) with water
water flow *n* : a flow or flowing of water; *also* : the amount of water flowing (as past a valve) per unit of time
water flower *n* [ME *water flour*, fr. *water* + *flour* flower — more at FLOWER] : WATER BLOOM — usu. used in pl.
water fly *n* **1** : STONE FLY **2** : a fly (as a dragonfly) habitually found over or by the water
water fog *n* : a fine spray or fog formed by sending one high-pressure stream of water against another in the tip of a nozzle and used esp. for checking combustion by its immediate transformation into steam
wa·ter·ford \ˈwȯd|ə(r)fə(r)d, ˈwä|, |tə(r)f-\ *adj, usu cap* [fr. *Waterford*, Ireland] **1** : of or from the county borough of Waterford, Ireland : of the kind or style prevalent in Waterford **2** : of or from County Waterford, Ireland : of the kind or style prevalent in County Waterford
waterfowl \ˈ=₌,₌\ *n* [ME *water foul*, fr. *water* + *foul* fowl — more at FOWL] **1** : a bird that frequents the water or lives about rivers or lakes or on or near the sea; *esp* : a swimming bird **2 waterfowl** *pl* : the swimming game birds as distinguished from upland game birds and shorebirds
water foxtail *n* : MARSH FOXTAIL
water frame *n* : a primitive power spinning machine driven by waterpower
water fringe *n* : FLOATING HEART
waterfront \ˈ=₌,₌\ *n, often attrib* **1** : land, land with buildings, or a section of a town fronting or abutting on a body of water ⟨tenements along the ~⟩ **2** : WATER BACK 2b
water frontage *n* : frontage abutting on water
water funk *n* : a fearful shrinking from water and esp. from entering the water; *also* : a person afflicted with a fear of water
water furrow *n* [ME *water forowe*, fr. OE *wæterfurh*, fr. *wæter* water + *furh* furrow — more at WATER, FURROW] : a furrow for conducting or diverting water
water-furrow \ˈ=₌(,)₌\ *vt* [*water furrow*] : to make water furrows in : drain or irrigate by water furrows
water gage *n* **1** : an instrument for measuring the depth or quantity of water or for indicating the height of its surface esp. in a steam boiler **2** : an instrument for measuring a moderate air pressure hydrostatically (as in a ventilating system) **3** : water pressure expressed in inches of height
water gain *n* : water that bleeds from concrete as it is placed into forms and compacted, accumulates at the surface of the concrete, and usu. increases in amount as the concrete fills more and more of the form
water gall *n* **1** *obs* : a spot of low boggy land **2** *chiefly dial* : a watery or rainy look in the sky usu. accompanying a rainbow; *also* : a secondary or broken rainbow **3** : JELLYFISH
water gang *n* [ME, fr. *water* + *gang*] *chiefly Scot* : a water or stream channel esp. when constructed artificially (as for land drainage or irrigation)
water gap *n* : a pass in a mountain ridge through which a stream runs
water garden *n* **1** : a garden in which aquatic plants predominate **2** : a garden built about a stream or pool as a central feature
water gas *n* : a poisonous flammable gaseous mixture made principally of carbon monoxide and hydrogen with small amounts of methane, carbon dioxide, and nitrogen and usu. by blowing air and then steam over red-hot coke or coal, used esp. formerly as a fuel (as in welding) and after carbureting as an illuminant but chiefly as a source of hydrogen and as a synthesis gas — see BLUE GAS, CARBURETED WATER GAS
water-gas tar *n* : tar formed in making carbureted water gas and used chiefly in tar road materials
ˡ**water gate** *n* [ME *watergate*, fr. *water* + *gate* (way)] *chiefly Scot* : a natural channel for water : WATERCOURSE
²**water gate** *n* [ME *watergate*, fr. *water* + *gat, gate* gate (opening)] **1** : a gate (as of private grounds or a building) giving access to a body of water **2** : a gateway or sluice for the passage of water; *also* : a gate or valve controlling the flow of water : FLOODGATE — compare GATE VALVE **3** : a passageway for passage of traffic by water
water germander *n* : a soft hairy perennial European mint (*Teucrium scordium*) having chiefly axillary rose-pink to purple flowers and found in marshy places
water-gild \ˈ=₌,₌\ *vt* **1** : to gild (a metallic surface) by coating thinly with gold amalgam and then volatilizing the mercury by heat **2** : to electroplate with a thin gold film by simple immersion
water gillyflower *n* : a featherfoil (*Hottonia inflata*) with spongy inflated flower stalks — called also *water violet*
water gladiole *n* : FLOWERING RUSH
water gland *n* : a group of cells situated immediately below a hydathode and serving to regulate the excretion of water
water glass *n* **1** : WATER CLOCK, CLEPSYDRA **2** : a glass vessel for holding water: as **a** : a drinking glass : TUMBLER **b** : a container for growing a flowering bulb (as a hyacinth) in water **c** *archaic* : a finger bowl of glass **3** : an instrument consisting of an open box or tube with a glass bottom used for examining objects in or under the water (as upon the sea bottom in shallow places) **4 a** : a water-soluble substance consisting of sodium silicate $Na_2O.xSiO_2$ of varying composition that is found in commerce as a glassy mass, a stony powder, or a viscous syrupy liquid dissolved in water that is used chiefly as a cement and adhesive, as a builder for soaps and synthetic detergents, as a protective coating and fireproofing agent in papermaking and in the textile industry, in making artificial stone, and in preserving eggs — called also *soluble glass* **b** : a similar substance consisting of potassium silicate — called also *potash water glass* **5** : WATER GAGE 1
water-glass painting *n* : STEREOCHROMY
water gnat *n, Brit* : MARSH TREADER
water goggles *n pl but sing or pl in constr* : a marsh marigold (*Caltha palustris*)
water gold *n* : a liquid amalgam of gold
water grain *n* : a grain imparted to leather by hand-treating it while wet with a cork-covered board
water grampus *n, dial* : HELLGRAMMITE
water grass *n* **1** : any of various grasses or grasslike plants that thrive in wet places: as **a** : DALLIS GRASS **b** *dial Eng* : VELVET GRASS **c** *dial Eng* : HORSETAIL **d** : BARNYARD GRASS **2** *dial Brit* : WATERCRESS
water grate *n* : a furnace grate with hollow water-cooled bars
water green *n* : a pale to grayish yellow green that is yellower and stronger than ingenue
water-ground \ˈ=₌ˈ=\ *adj* : ground between millstones by means of water power ⟨*water-ground* meal⟩
water gruel *n* [ME *water grewel*, fr. *water* + *grewel* gruel — more at GRUEL] : a thin gruel made chiefly with water
water guard *n* : a guard whose duty is to police a harbor or river; *also* : a body of customs officers detailed to watch ships (as to prevent smuggling)
water guinea *or* **water guinea hen** *n* : AMERICAN COOT
water gum *n* **1** : any of several Australian trees that grow near water; *esp* : a small to medium-sized tree (*Tristania laurina*) that yields a tough strong close-grained pinkish wood sometimes used for tool handles and mallets **2** : BLACK GUM 2
water gun *n* : WATER PISTOL
water hair grass *n* : BROOK GRASS
water hammer *n* **1** : a vessel (as a tube) partly filled with water, exhausted of air, and hermetically sealed so that when reversed or shaken the water strikes in solid mass with a sound like that of a hammer **2** : a concussion or sound of concussion of moving water against the sides of a containing pipe or vessel on a sudden stoppage of flow; *esp* : such a concussion or sound made by water in a steam pipe **3** : the act or process of water-hammering
ˡ**water-hammer** \ˈ=₌,₌\ *vi* [*water hammer*] *of water* : to strike with a hammering sound against the walls of a sealed containing vessel from which the air has been removed
²**water-hammer** \ˈ"\ *adj* [*water hammer*] : of or relating to a water hammer; *esp* : characterized by a sharp but quickly fading impact ⟨a *water-hammer* pulse⟩ — compare CORRIGAN PULSE
water hare *n* : SWAMP RABBIT
water haul *n* **1** : a haul of a net that catches no fish **2** : a fruitless effort; *often* : a trip or call wasted because of failure to meet or see a person intended
water hawthorn *n* : CAPE PONDWEED
waterhead \ˈ=₌,₌\ *n* **1** : the source or headwater of a stream **2** : a dammed up body of water (as for supplying a garden or mill); *also* : the height or quantity so retained **3 a** : a large head; *esp* : HYDROCEPHALUS **b** *chiefly dial* : one with an excessively large head and usu. subnormal intelligence
water heater *n* **1** : an apparatus for heating and usu. storing hot water (as for domestic use) **2** : a hot water heating system
water hemisphere *n* : the geographical hemisphere having a maximum surface of water
water hemlock *n* **1 a** : a tall erect Eurasiatic perennial herb (*Cicuta virosa*) that is locally abundant in marshy areas or along streams and is highly poisonous **b** : any of several other plants of the genus *Cicuta* (as the American spotted cowbane) **2** : either of two water dropworts (*Oenanthe crocata* and *O. aquatica*) — compare WATER FENNEL
water hemp *n* **1** : a plant of the genus *Acnida* **2** : HEMP AGRIMONY
water hen *n* : any of various birds of the family Rallidae (as a coot); as **a** : GALLINULE **b** : AMERICAN COOT **c** : any of several Australian birds of the genus *Tribonyx*
water hickory *n* : a hickory (*Carya aquatica*) of the southern U. S. having many narrow leaflets and rather bitter nuts — called also *bitter pecan, water bitternut*
water hog *n* **1** : CAPYBARA **2** : BUSHPIG
water hole *n* **1** : a natural hole or hollow containing water: as **a** : one in the dry bed of an intermittent river **b** : a spring in a desert **c** : a small pool, pond, or lake **2** : a hole in a surface of ice
water holly *n* : an Oregon grape (*Mahonia nervosa*)
water horehound *n* : a mint of the genus *Lycopus*; *esp* : BUGLEWEED
water horizon *n* : a stratum or layer of porous rock that will yield water to a well
water horse *n* [ME, fr. *water* + *hors, horse* horse — more at HORSE] **1** *obs* : HIPPOPOTAMUS **2** : a fabulous water spirit resembling a horse : HIPPOCAMPUS, KELPIE
water horsetail *n* **1** : STONEWORT **2** : an aquatic horsetail (as *Equisetum fleuratile*)
water house *n* : a building in which a head of water forced up (as from a well) is retained in a reservoir for conveyance by pipes
wa·ter·house-frid·er·ich·sen syndrome \ˈwȯd|ə(r),hau̇-ˈsfrid(ə)riksən-, ˈwä|, |tə(r)-\ *n, usu cap W&F* [after Sir Herbert *Waterhouse* †1931 Brit. physician and Carl *Friderichsen* *b*1886 Dan. physician] : acute and severe meningococcemia with hemorrhage into the adrenal glands
waterhouse stop *n, usu cap W* [after Major J. *Waterhouse*, 19th cent. Brit. photochemist] : any one of a set of thin metal plates that each have a round or specially shaped hole corresponding to a particular photographic lens aperture and are inserted as required into a slot in the barrel of a lens esp. for use in photoengraving
water hyacinth *n* : a tropical floating aquatic plant (*Eichhornia crassipes*) having spikes of large blue flowers and roundish leaves and being troublesome in clogging waterways esp. in the southern U. S.
water hyssop *n* : any of several plants of the genus *Bacopa*; *esp* : the small widely distributed creeping herb (*B. monniera*) that is used locally in India as an aperient and diuretic
water ice *n* **1** : a frozen dessert consisting of water, sugar, and flavoring — compare SHERBET 2 **2** : massive ice formed by the downward freezing of water
wa·ter·ie \ˈwȯd|ərē, ˈwä|, |tə-, -ri\ *n* -S [ˡ*water* + *-ie*] : WAGTAIL; *esp* : PIED WAGTAIL
waterier *comparative of* WATERY
wateriest *superlative of* WATERY
wa·ter·i·ly \-rəlē\ *adv* : with watery exudation : in a watery way
water-inch \ˈ=ˈ=\ *n* : the discharge from a circular sharp-edged orifice one inch in diameter with a head of one line above the top edge that is commonly estimated at 14 pints per minute and that constitutes an old unit of hydraulic measure
wa·ter·i·ness \ˈwȯd|ərēnəs, ˈwä|, |tər-, -rin-\ *n* -ES [ME *watrinesse*, fr. *watery, watry* watery + *-nesse* -ness] **1** *obs* **a** : watery matter in a substance **b** : watery secretion **2** : the condition of being watery ⟨the ~ of Venice⟩: as **a** : the condition of being too thin, sodden, or insipid because of the presence of excessive water ⟨a soup tasteless because of ~⟩ ⟨the ~ of blood once supposed to affect malaria victims⟩ **b** : the condition of lacking solid substance as if diluted with water ⟨a flimsy composition with a deadly ~ of style⟩
ˡ**watering** *n* -S [ME, fr. OE *wæterung*, fr. *wæterian* to water + *-ung* -ing — more at WATER] **1** : the act or action of one that waters; *also* : an instance of such **2** *chiefly dial* : a source or supply of water (as for irrigation or cattle) **3** : a ditch for drainage; *also* : marshland with such ditches **4** : a moiré appearance (as of a textile or metal)
²**watering** *adj* [ME, fr. pres. part. of *wateren* to water — more at WATER] : used in watering, serving to water, or providing with or yielding water ⟨a ~ bucket⟩ ⟨~ eyes⟩ ⟨a ~ resort⟩
watering cart *n* : a cart equipped to carry water (as for sprinkling roads or irrigating fields)
wateringhole \ˈ=₌₌,₌\ *n* : WATER HOLE 1
watering house *n, Brit* : a public house providing water for horses and refreshments for coachmen and travelers
watering place *n* [ME] **1** : a place where animals come to drink; *also* : a place (as a pool or container of running water) where livestock may be taken to drink **2** : a place where water supplies (as for a ship or caravan) may be obtained **3** : a health or recreational resort featuring mineral or fresh-water activities
watering pot *n* **1** *or* **watering can** : a vessel usu. in the form of a can with a spout having a perforated nozzle that is used to sprinkle water (as on plants or clothes) **2** : WATERING-POT SHELL
watering-pot shell \ˈ=₌₌,₌-\ *n* : any of several marine bivalve mollusks (genus *Brechites*) having small valves consolidated with a capacious calcareous tube which encloses the entire animal and is closed at the anterior end by a convex disk perforated by many pores like the nozzle of a watering pot; *also* : the shell of such a mollusk
watering slip *n* : an incline built into a river to give firm footing to cattle or horses led there to drink
watering trough *n* **1** : a drinking trough for livestock **2** : TRACK PAN
water injection *n* : introduction of water to an internal-combustion engine to enhance combustion power for quick take-off or bursts in speed
water-in-oil \ˈ=₌=ˈ=\ *adj* : consisting of water dispersed in oil — distinguished from *oil-in-water* ⟨*water-in-oil* emulsions⟩
wa·ter·ish \ˈwȯd|ərish, ˈwä|, |tər-, -rēsh\ *adj* **1 a** : resembling water esp. in appearance or consistency ⟨a ~ discharge⟩ **b** : lacking in intensity : PALE ⟨muddy yellows and ~ blues⟩ ⟨~ moonlight⟩ **2 a** : full of water or watery liquid : DILUTE, THIN, SLOPPY ⟨~ wine⟩ ⟨a ~ gruel⟩ **b** : lacking in substance or savor : FLAT, FLAVORLESS, INSIPID **3 a** : somewhat watery : containing water or water vapor ⟨a ~ sky⟩ ⟨~ land requiring drainage⟩ **b** : marked by considerable wetness ⟨a ~ season⟩ — **wa·ter·ish·ness** *n* -ES
water ivy *n* : a European water crowfoot (*Ranunculus hederaceum*) with white flowers and ivy-shaped leaves that is naturalized in eastern No. America
water jacket *n* : an outer casing which holds water or through which water circulates to cool the interior; *specif* : the enclosed space surrounding the cylinder block of an internal-combustion engine and containing the cooling liquid
water-jacket \ˈ=₌,₌=\ *vt* [*water jacket*] : to provide with a water jacket
water-jet \ˈ=₌,₌\ *adj* : operated or driven by a jet of water
water joint *n* : a joint in a stone pavement that is slightly raised to prevent water from settling therein
water jump *n* : an obstacle (as in a steeplechase) consisting of a pool, stream, or ditch of water
water kelpie *n* : KELPIE
water knot *n* : a knot made with interlocking halfknots and used esp. to join the ends of fishlines
water-laid \ˈ=₌,₌\ *adj* **1** *of cordage* **a** : having a left-hand twist **b** : CABLE-LAID **2** : deposited in or by water : SEDIMENTARY
wa·ter·land·er \ˈwȯd|ə(r),landə(r), ˈwä|, |tə(r),-\ *n* -S *usu cap* [D, lit., inhabitant of Waterland, fr. *Waterland*, district in northern Holland, Netherlands + D *-er*] : one of a liberal body of Dutch Mennonites separated from the conservative Mennonites after 1555 and later reunited with the liberalized older body
wa·ter·land·ian \,₌₌ˈlandēən\ *n, usu cap* [*Waterland* + E *-an*] : WATERLANDER
water lane *n* **1** : a lane with a stream flowing alongside **2 a** : a narrow open passageway through water (as amid weeds, ice, or shipping) **b** : LANE 3a
waterleaf \ˈ=₌,₌\ *n, pl* **waterleafs 1** : a plant of the genus *Hydrophyllum* **2** *pl also* **waterleaves** : a completely unsized paper (as blotting paper)
water leaf *n* : an ornament prob. representing an ivy leaf and found in Greek art
waterleaf family *n* : HYDROPHYLLACEAE
water leg *n* : a downward extension of a steam boiler in the form of a narrow space between vertical plates often nearly surrounding the furnace and ashpit and supporting the boiler
water lemon *n* **1** : JAMAICA HONEYSUCKLE **2** : SWEET CALABASH
water lens *n* : a lens whose refracting medium is water contained in a suitably shaped vessel of transparent material
water lentil *n* : LESSER DUCKWEED — usu. used in pl.
wa·ter·less \ˈwȯd|ə(r)ləs, ˈwä|, |tə(r)-\ *adj* [ME *waterles*, fr. OE *wæterlēas*, fr. *wæter* water + *-lēas* -less] **1** : destitute of or deficient in water : DRY ⟨a ~ well⟩ ⟨had to cross 100 miles of ~ country⟩ **2** : not requiring water (as for cooling or cooking); *often* : AIR-COOLED — **wa·ter·less·ly** *adv* — **wa·ter·less·ness** *n* -ES
waterless cooker *n* **1** : any of various containers usu. with a very thick bottom and a close cover in which food can be cooked without burning in juices released in cooking or in very little water **2** : PRESSURE COOKER
water lettuce *n* : a common tropical floating plant (*Pistia stratiotes*) forming a rosette of spongy wedge-shaped leaves — called also *water cabbage*
water level *n* **1** : an instrument to show the level by means of the surface of water in a trough or in the legs of a U-tube **2** : a slightly inclined level (as in a mine) for draining **3** : the surface of still water: as **a** : the level assumed by the surface of a particular body or column of water **b** : the waterline of a vessel **c** : WATER TABLE 3
water lily *n* **1** : a plant or flower of the family Nymphaeaceae — see LOTUS, SPATTERDOCK **2** : any of various aquatic plants with more or less showy flowers: as **a** : FLOATING HEART **b** : WATER HYACINTH **3** : ZYGADENE

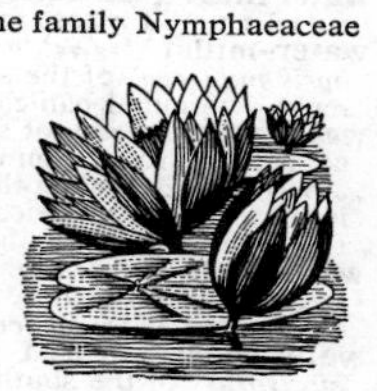
water lily

water-lily family *n* : NYMPHAEACEAE
water-lily tree *n* : a mountain magnolia (*Magnolia fraseri*)
water-lily tulip *n* : a tulip (*Tulipa kaufmanniana*) of Central Asia and Asia Minor having recurved brightly colored petals and being used as an ornamental
water lime *n* **1** : HYDRAULIC LIME **2** : a limestone from which hydraulic lime may be made
waterline \ˈ=₌,₌\ *n* **1 a** : any of several lines that are marked upon the outside of a ship and correspond with the surface of the water when it is afloat on an even keel — see SHIP illustration **b** : any of various lines of a ship, model, or plan parallel with the surface of the water at various heights from the keel **2** : SHORELINE **3 a** : the level represented by the uppermost limit of ground wholly saturated with water : the level of the water in soil : WATER TABLE **b** : the desired or actual level of water (as in a boiler or tank) **4** : a line of stain marking a former passage or upper level of water ⟨the flood left a ~ on housefronts and fences⟩ ⟨~s from old leaks⟩ **5** : a line (as of piping or hose) for carrying water
waterline model *n* : a ship model formed of boards shaped according to the waterlines in the plans and laid upon each other to form a solid model
water lizard *n* **1** : MONITOR LIZARD **2** : any of various mostly large salamanders (as a mud puppy or water dog)
water lobelia *n* : an erect perennial aquatic herb (*Lobelia dortmanna*) of Europe and No. America with submerged spongy leaves and an emersed raceme of blue flowers
waterlocked \ˈ=₌,₌\ *adj* : nearly surrounded by water ⟨a ~ tongue of land⟩
water locust *n* : a honey locust (*Gleditsia aquatica*) growing in swamps and bottomlands of the southern U. S., producing short oval pods, and having dark heavy wood that takes a good polish
wa·ter·log \ˈ=₌,lȯg *also* -,läg\ *vb* [back-formation fr. *waterlogged*] *vt* **1** : to make (as a boat) unmanageable by flooding — used of the sea or a leak **2** : to deprive (as floating timber) of buoyancy by saturation with water **3** : to saturate (as soil) with water; *esp* : to cause the water table of (soil) to rise high enough to expel normal soil gases and interfere with plant growth or cultivation **4** : to cause to deteriorate or to become unmanageable or unserviceable as if by saturation with excess of water ⟨whenever I've got *waterlogged* with study —W.S. Maugham⟩ ⟨an unbalanced capital structure may ~ the strongest company⟩ ~ *vi* : to become sodden, inert, or unmanageable by or as if by excessive saturation with water
wa·ter·logged \-gd\ *adj* [ˡ*water* + *log*, n. + *-ed*] **1** : subjected to waterlogging ⟨a ~ boat⟩ ⟨~ timbers⟩ **2** : EDEMATOUS
wa·ter·loo \ˌwȯd|ə(r)ˌlü, ˌwä|, |tə-\ *n* -S *sometimes cap* [fr. *Waterloo*, Belgium, scene of Napoleon's defeat (1815)] : a decisive or disastrous defeat or reverse
water loop *n* : an unintended uncontrollable violent turn of a seaplane moving on the water at high speed
water louse *n* : an aquatic isopod
water lung *n* : the respiratory tree of a holothurian
water main *n* : a pipe or conduit for conveying water (as from a reservoir)
water mallow *n* : a rose mallow (*Hibiscus moscheutos*)

wa·ter·man \'==mən\ *n, pl* **watermen** [ME, fr. *water* + *man*] **1 :** one that works or lives on or is skilled in the ways of water or watercraft: as **a :** a boatman who plies for hire usu. on inland waters or harbors **b :** a person who makes his living from the water (as by fishing, crabbing, or oystering) **c :** a sprite or demon inhabiting the water **:** MERMAN **d :** a person skilled in boating esp. as a sport; *often* **:** OARSMAN **2 :** one employed in connection with the distributing or supplying of water: as **a :** a worker who releases water through valves or sluices (as in waterworks or for irrigation) **b :** a worker who waters roads (as in a mine) **c** *Brit* **:** an attendant (as on a cabstand) who supplies water to the horses **d :** a worker who quenches coke with water for removal from the oven **e :** a worker who brings billet molds to filling temperature by spraying with hot or cold water **f :** an auto worker who puts water into radiators before cars are driven from the assembly line **3 :** a worker who bales into cars water that has collected in a mine for hauling to the surface or who pumps such water to the surface

wa·ter·man·ship \-n,ship\ *n* **:** the business, skill, or art of a waterman: as **a :** expertness or technique in the handling of a boat and esp. in rowing; *often* **:** skill in managing an oar in the water as distinguished from techniques (as of handling the body) involved in the stroke **b :** expertness or technique in the handling of oneself (as in swimming) in the water **:** personal aquatic skill or understanding

waterman's knot *n* **:** FISHERMAN'S KNOT

water maple *n* **:** any of several maples that prefer or thrive in damp locations: as **a :** RED MAPLE **b :** a silver maple (*Acer saccharinum*)

water marigold *n* **:** a No. American aquatic herb (*Megalodonta beckii*) of the family Compositae having finely dissected leaves and heads of yellow flowers

¹watermark \'==,=\ *n* [¹*water* + *mark*] **1 :** a mark indicating the height to which water has risen or at which it has stood or is expected to stand **:** WATERLINE; *esp* **:** TIDEMARK **2 :** a marking in paper resulting from differences in thickness usu. produced by pressure of a projecting design in the mold or on the dandy roll and visible when the paper is held up to the light; *also* **:** the design or the metal pattern producing the marking — compare IMPRESSED WATERMARK

²watermark \"\ *vt* **1 a :** to mark (paper) with a watermark **b :** to impress (a given design) as a watermark **2 :** to determine the watermark on (a stamp) usu. for philatelic purposes

watermark detector *n* **:** a device for determining the watermark on a stamp

watermark disease *n* **:** a disease of willows and esp. the cricket-bat willow (*Salix alba caerulea*) in England in which a bacterium (*Erwinia salicis*) invades the vessels and causes wilting and browning of the leaves and a brown watery stain of the wood

watermaster \'==,==\ *n* **:** one in charge of the distribution of irrigation water from a main canal

water meadow *n* **:** a meadow or piece of low flat land capable of being kept in fertility by being overflowed from some adjoining stream

watermeal \'==,=\ *n* **:** any of various minute aquatic plants of the genus *Wolffia*

water measure *n* [ME *water mesure,* fr. *water* + *mesure* measure — more at MEASURE] **:** an old English system of capacity measure used for articles shipped by water and based on a bushel defined by statute in 1494 as equal to five pecks Winchester measure and in 1701 as equal to a heaped Winchester bushel

water measurer *n* **:** any of several aquatic insects; *esp* **:** WATER STRIDER

wa·ter·mel·on \'wȯd·ə(r),melən, 'wäl, |tə(r)-, *dial* -,milyən\ *n* **1 a :** a large oblong or roundish fruit having a hard green or white rind that is often striped or variegated and a pink, yellowish, or red pulp that contains a copious sweet watery juice and many seeds **b :** a vine (*Citrullus vulgaris*) that bears watermelons and is native to tropical Africa but widely cultivated **2 :** a deep pink to moderate red that is yellower and stronger than laurel pink and very slightly yellower and stronger than rose dorée **3 :** a skipjack (*Katsuwonus pelamis*)

watermelon begonia *n* **:** a peperomia (*Peperomia sandersi*) used as a greenhouse plant or houseplant and having silvery striped foliage

water meter *n* **:** an instrument for recording the quantity of water passing through a particular outlet

water milfoil *n* **:** an aquatic plant of the genus *Myriophyllum*

water-milfoil family *n* **:** HALORAGACEAE

water mill *n* [ME *water mille,* fr. *water* + *mille* mill — more at MILL] **:** a mill whose machinery is moved by water

water-millet \'==,==\ *n* **:** a tall aquatic perennial grass (*Zizaniopsis mileacea*) of the southern U. S. having long leaves and narrow terminal panicles of flowers

water mint *n* **:** any of several mints that thrive in wet places: as **a :** a European mint (*Mentha aquatica*) sometimes having a perfume resembling that of bergamot and naturalized locally in eastern No. America **b :** a closely related tall hairy mint (*M. longifolia*) of similar distribution

water mite *n* **:** a mite of the group Hydrachnellae; *esp* **:** a free-living freshwater mite of the family Hydrachnidae — called also *water spider, water tick*

water moccasin *n* **1 :** a venomous pit viper (*Agkistrodon piscivorus*) of the southern U. S. that is closely related to the copperhead, is olive or brownish above, paler on the sides, and indistinctly barred with black, has the young much brighter and reddish brown barred with dark brown edged with white, and is semiaquatic and abundant in marshes and abandoned rice ditches where it feeds chiefly on fish and amphibians **2 :** WATER SNAKE a — not used technically

water mold *n* **:** an aquatic fungus; *esp* **:** a mold of the order Saprolegniales

water mole *n* **1 :** DESMAN **2 :** PLATYPUS

water monitor *n* **:** a very large lizard (*Varanus salvator*) of India that frequents the borders of streams, swims actively, and may become five or six feet long; *broadly* **:** any of various aquatic monitors

water monkey *n* **:** a jar or bottle (as of porous earthenware) in which water is cooled by evaporation

water moss *n* **1 :** an aquatic plant (as various algae or liverworts) that suggests a moss in appearance or habit of growth **2 :** a moss of the genus *Fontinalis* (esp. *F. antipyretica*)

water moth *n* **1 :** any of numerous small pyralidid moths (as members of the genera *Nymphula* and *Elophila*) having larvae that live beneath the surface of fresh waters usu. in cases; *esp* **:** a moth of the genus *Acentropus* **2 :** CADDIS FLY

water motor *n* **:** a prime mover driven by water; *specif* **:** a small waterwheel driven by water from a street main

water mouse *n* [ME *watermowse,* fr. *water* + *mous, mowse* mouse — more at MOUSE] **:** any of several relatively small and somewhat aquatic rodents: as **a :** BEAVER RAT **b :** WATER VOLE

water mouth *n, Scot* **:** a river mouth

water navelwort *n* **1 :** a common water milfoil (*Myriophyllum spicatum*) of the north temperate zone **2 :** a marsh pennywort (*Hydrocotyle umbellata*) that is widely distributed in the New World and in Africa

water nerveroot *n* **:** SWAMP MILKWEED

water net *n* **:** a freshwater alga of the genus *Hydrodictyon*

water newt *n* **:** an aquatic salamander **:** TRITON

water nixie *n* **:** a female water sprite

water nut *n* **1 :** WATER CHESTNUT **2 :** WATER CHINQUAPIN

water nymph *n* [ME *water nimphe,* fr. *water* + *nimphe* nymph — more at NYMPH] **1 :** a goddess (as one of the naiads, Nereids, or Oceanids) of classical mythology associated with a body of water **2 a :** a common white water lily (*Nymphaea odorata*); *broadly* **:** a plant or flower of the genus *Nymphaea* **b :** a plant of the genus *Naias* **3 :** DRAGONFLY

water oak *n* **1 :** any of numerous American oaks that thrive in wet soils (as the pin oak, laurel oak, or willow oak) **:** SWAMP OAK; *esp* **:** POSSUM OAK **2** *Austral* **a :** BOTTLEBRUSH 1a(1) **b :** CASUARINA 2

water oat *n* **:** WILD RICE 1a — often used in pl. with sing. or pl. constr.

water of ayr *or* **water-of-ayr stone** *n, usu cap A* [fr. *Water of Ayr* (Ayr), river in Scotland] **:** AYR STONE

water of constitution : water so combined in a molecule that it cannot be removed without disrupting the entire molecule — distinguished from *water of hydration*

water of crystallization : water of hydration that is present in many crystallized substances and that is usu. essential for maintenance of a particular crystal structure (as in Glauber's salt)

water of dehydration : water of hydration set free by chemical changes

water of hydration : water that is chemically combined with a substance to form a hydrate and can be expelled (as by heating) without essentially altering the composition of the substance — distinguished from *water of constitution*

water of life [ME *water of lif,* trans. of LL *aqua vitae* (as in Rev 22:1), trans. of Gk *hydōr zōēs*] **1 :** something that gives spiritual refreshment or eternal life **2** [trans. of ML *aqua vitae*] **:** a strong distilled alcoholic drink (as brandy or whiskey)

water of plasticity : water added to dry clay to make it plastic (as for use by a potter)

water-oleander \'==|==|==\ *n* **:** SWAMP LOOSESTRIFE

wa·ter·ol·o·ger \,wȯ|d·ə'räləjə(r), ,wä|, |tə'-\ *n* -s [¹*water* + -*o-* + -*loger* (fr. -*logy* + -*er*)] *archaic* **:** WATERCASTER

water on the brain : HYDROCEPHALUS

water on the knee : an accumulation of inflammatory exudate in the knee joint often following an injury

water opal *n* **:** HYALITE

water opossum *n* **:** YAPOK

water ordeal *n* **:** an ordeal (as of plunging a bare arm into boiling water) in which water is the testing agent and in which innocence or guilt is held to be proved (as by the condition of the arm) **:** an ordeal of casting an accused person bound hand and foot into a river or pond in which sinking or floating is taken as evidence respectively of innocence or guilt

water organ *n* **:** HYDRAULUS

water ouzel *n* **:** any of several birds of the genus *Cinclus* (esp. *C. cinclus* and *C. mexicanus*) that are related to the thrushes and that are not web-footed but dive into swift mountain streams and walk on the bottom in search of food — called also *dipper*

water over the dam : something that is beyond recall or reconsideration

water ox *n* **:** WATER BUFFALO

water pad·da \-'padə\ *n* [Afrik *waterpadda,* fr. *water* (fr. MD) + *padda* toad, frog, fr. MD *padde* toad; akin to OE *wæter* water and to MLG *padde, pedde* toad — more at WATER, PADDOCK] **:** a southern African burrowing terrestrial toad (*Breviceps gibbosus*)

water paint *n* **:** paint in which water is the volatile portion of the vehicle

water parsley *n* **:** any of several bog or aquatic plants of the family Umbelliferae (as a water parsnip or wild celery)

water parsnip *n* **:** a plant of the genus *Sium*

water parting *n* **:** a summit or boundary line separating the drainage districts of two streams or coasts **:** DIVIDE — compare WATERSHED

water partridge *n* **:** RUDDY DUCK

water pennywort *n* **:** MARSH PENNYWORT

water pepper *n* **:** a widely distributed annual smartweed (*Polygonum hydropiper*) of moist soils having greenish flowers and extremely acrid peppery juice and formerly used in medicine for its irritant and stimulant properties

water persicaria *n* **:** an aquatic herb (*Polygonum amphibium*) of Europe and No. America with floating leaves and emersed dense racemes of pinkish flowers

water pewit *n* **:** PHOEBE

water pheasant *n* **1 :** MERGANSER: **a :** GOOSANDER **b :** HOODED MERGANSER **c :** AMERICAN MERGANSER **2 :** PHEASANT-TAILED JACANA

wa·ter·phone \'==,fōn\ *n* [¹*water* + -*phone*] **:** HYDROPHONE

water pick *n* **:** a small conical metal or plastic water container having a pointed base and a rubber cap with an opening through which the stem of a flower can be inserted and used in making floral designs and arrangements usu. on a foundation of plastic

water pig *n* **1 :** CAPYBARA **2 :** GOURAMI

water pilot *n* **:** a water snake (*Natrix taxispilota*) chiefly of the southeastern U.S.

water pimpernel *n* **1 :** BROOKWEED **2 :** SCARLET PIMPERNEL

water pine *n* **:** a Chinese evergreen tree (*Glyptostrobus pensilis*) that grows in wet places and is commonly planted around the edges of rice fields

water pipe *n* [ME *waterpipe,* fr. *water* + *pipe*] **1 :** a pipe for conveying water **2 :** a smoking device used chiefly in the Orient, made of a bowl mounted on a vessel of water, often provided with a long flexible tube terminating in a mouthpiece, and so arranged that the smoke is drawn from the bowl through the water where it is cooled and up the tube to the mouth — compare HOOKAH, HUBBLE-BUBBLE 1, NARGILEH

water pipit *n* **:** a widely distributed pipit (*Anthus spinoletta*) of the northern hemisphere; *esp* **:** a bird of a common American race (*A. s. rubescens*)

water pistol *n* **:** a toy pistol designed to throw a jet of liquid — called also *water gun*

water plane *n* **1 :** an airplane equipped to land on water **:** SEAPLANE **2 :** the plane of a given waterline of a ship

water plant *n* **:** a plant growing in water **:** AQUATIC, HYDROPHYTE

water plantain *n* **:** a plant of the genus *Alisma*

water-plantain family *n* **:** ALISMATACEAE

water-plantain spearwort *n* **:** a No. American aquatic crowfoot (*Ranunculus ambigens*) that roots freely at the lower nodes and has chiefly narrow acuminate leaves

water platter *n* **:** VICTORIA 2b

water plug *n* **:** FIREPLUG

water pocket *n* **:** a pocket (as in rock) where water may gather; *esp* **:** a water hole in the bed of an intermittent stream occurring typically as a bowl at the foot of a cliff over which the stream leaps when in the flood stage

water point *n* **:** POINT 6f

water polo *n* **:** a goal game played in a swimming pool by teams of seven swimmers with a ball resembling a soccer ball

water poplar *n* **:** any of several poplars that thrive in wet areas: as **a :** a cottonwood (*Populus deltoides*) **b :** BLACK POPLAR

water poppy *n* **:** a Brazilian aquatic herb (*Hydrocleis nymphoides*) cultivated for its yellow flowers that resemble poppies

water pore *n* **1 :** a pore by which the water tubes of various invertebrates open externally **2 :** HYDATHODE

waterpot \'==,=\ *n* [ME *waterpot, waterpott,* fr. *water* + *pot, pott* pot — more at POT] **1 :** a vessel for holding or conveying water **2 :** WATERING POT

waterpower \'==,==\ *n* **1 a :** the power of water employed to move machinery **b :** a fall of water suitable for such use **2 :** a water privilege for a mill

waterpower engineering *n* **:** a branch of civil engineering that deals with the construction of works to develop waterpower

water press *n* **:** HYDRAULIC PRESS

water pressure *n* **:** pressure exerted by water **:** hydraulic pressure **:** HYDROSTATIC PRESSURE

water primrose *n* **:** PRIMROSE WILLOW

water privilege *n* **:** the right to use water esp. as a source of mechanical power; *also* **:** a place (as a mill site) where water is or may be so used

¹waterproof \|==|=\ *adj* [¹*water* + *proof*] **:** impervious to water: as **a :** covered or treated with a material (as a solution of rubber) to prevent permeation by water **b :** relating to or characterizing a machine or structure so constructed that a stream of water may be directed on it under specified conditions without the water entering — **wa·ter·proof·ness** *n* -ES

²waterproof \"\ *n* **1 :** a waterproof fabric **2** *chiefly Brit* **:** RAINCOAT

³waterproof \"\ *vt* **:** to make waterproof

wa·ter·proof·er \"+ə(r)\ *n* **:** one that waterproofs something (as roofs or fabrics): as **a :** a worker who waterproofs something manually or mechanically **b :** a waterproofing material (as for roofs)

waterproofing *n* **1 :** the act or process of making something waterproof **2 :** the condition of being made waterproof **3 :** something (as a treatment or coating) capable of imparting waterproofness

waterproof watch *n* **:** a wristwatch whose movement is enclosed in a case in which the openings for the winding and cover are sealed with gaskets and able to withstand pressures equal to several fathoms of submersion

water pump *n* **:** a pump for raising or circulating water

water puppy *n* **:** MUD PUPPY

water purslane *also* **water puslen** *n* **1 :** MARSH PURSLANE **2 :** a submerged aquatic or mud herb (*Peplis diandra*) of the family Lythraceae that occurs in the central U. S. and Mexico

waterquake \'==,=\ *n* **:** a disturbance of water by seismic action

water rabbit *n* **:** SWAMP RABBIT

water race *n* **:** ¹RACE 2c

water radish *n* **:** YELLOW CRESS b; *esp* **:** a coarse perennial stoloniferous herb (*Rorippa amphibia*) that is widely distributed in the northern hemisphere

water rail *n* **1 :** any of numerous rails of the genus *Rallus* (esp. *R. aquaticus*) **2** *dial Eng* **:** MOORHEN 2

water-rake \'==,=\ *vt* **:** to harvest (cranberries) by flooding the bog and then scooping up the floating berries with a special rake

water ram *n* **:** HYDRAULIC RAM

water rat *n* **1 :** a rodent that frequents water: as **a :** a vole of the genus *Arvicola*; *esp* **:** a common large British vole (*A. amphibius*) **b :** BROWN RAT; *broadly* **:** an amphibious rodent of the genus *Rattus* **c :** MUSKRAT; *esp* **:** ROUND-TAILED MUSKRAT **d :** any of various Australasian rodents of *Hydromys* or a related genus **:** BEAVER RAT **e :** any of several moderate-sized southern African rats (genus *Dasymys*) with long silky fur and scaly tails that commonly inhabit reedbeds **2 :** a waterfront loafer or petty thief

water rate *n* **1** *or* **water rent :** a rate or tax for supply of water **2 :** the amount of water in the form of condensed steam used by a turbine or engine for a given rate of energy output

water rattler *also* **water rattle** *n* **:** DIAMONDBACK RATTLESNAKE

water-repellent \|===|==\ *adj* **:** having a surface that repels water; *esp* **:** treated with a finish that is resistant but not impervious to penetration by water

water requirement *n* **:** the ratio of the weight of water absorbed during the growth of a plant to the dry matter produced often expressed as the number of grams of water taken up per gram of dry weight of plant product

water reserve *n* **:** a tract of land (as in parts of Australia) reserved for feeding streams that are utilized for water supply

water-resistant \|===|==\ *adj* **:** resistant to but not wholly proof against the action or entry of water ⟨a *water-resistant* watchcase⟩

water-ret \'==,=\ *vt* **:** to ret (as flax) with water

water rheostat *n* **:** a rheostat used for dissipating large amounts of electrical energy and made of a vessel (as a tank) that contains water often with added sodium carbonate and usu. has one fixed electrode and one movable electrode

water rice *n* **:** WILD RICE 1a

water right *n* **:** a right to the use of water (as for irrigation) either orig. acquired by appropriation and perfected by beneficial use or derived through ownership of riparian land and in the U.S. if acquired by appropriation resting either in the company making the diversion or in the individual to whose land it is delivered depending upon the statutes and court decisions of the state concerned — compare LITTORAL RIGHT, RIPARIAN RIGHT

water ring *n* **:** a continuous sloping ring or groove cut in the rock around the wall of a mine shaft to catch and divert seepage

water robin *n* **:** a leaden gray Asiatic thrush (*Rhyacornis fuliginosa* or *Phoenicurus fuliginosa*) that frequents running water

water roll *n* **:** a melodious liquid trill in the song of a canary

water-rolled \'==,=\ *adj* **:** worn round or smooth through being rolled by water ⟨*water-rolled* gravel⟩

water rot *n* **1 :** WATER SPOT **2 :** PINK ROT 1

water-rot \'==,=\ *vt* [by folk etymology] **:** WATER-RET

waterrug *n, obs* **:** a shaggy or rough-coated water dog

water rush *n* **:** SOFT RUSH

waters *pl of* WATER, *pres 3d sing of* WATER

water sail *n* **:** a small sail sometimes set under a lower studding sail or under a spanker boom and extended nearly to the water

water sallow *n* **:** GRAY WILLOW 2

water sapphire *n* **:** a deep blue iolite sometimes used as a gem — called also *saphir d'eau*

wa·ter·scape \'==,skāp\ *n* -s [¹*water* + -*scape*] **:** a water or sea view **:** SEASCAPE

water scavenger beetle *n* **:** a water beetle of the family Hydrophilidae

water scorpion *n* **:** any of numerous aquatic bugs constituting the family Nepidae and having the front legs fitted for seizing and holding prey and the end of the abdomen prolonged by a long breathing tube formed of two appressed grooved bristles — called also *water bug*

water seal *n* **:** a seal formed by water to prevent the passage of gas

water set *n* [¹*water* + *set,* past part. of *set*] **:** a trap set under water usu. to avoid human scent on the trap or to drown a trapped animal so that its struggles will not injure the fur or allow escape

water shamrock *n* **:** BUCKBEAN

watershed \'==,=\ *n* [prob. trans. of G *wasserscheide*] **1 :** WATER PARTING **2 :** a region or area bounded peripherally by a water parting and draining ultimately to a particular watercourse or body of water **:** the catchment area or drainage basin from which the waters of a stream or stream system are drawn **3 :** something (as a sloping contour or member) introduced into a structure primarily to shed or throw off water ⟨a narrow ~ over a car window⟩ **4 :** a crucial or dividing point, line, or factor ⟨his achievement would rank as a ~ in recent European history —*Newsweek*⟩ ⟨without crossing the ~ of war —H.L. Stimson⟩ ⟨the ~ moments of history —C.H.Sykes⟩

water shield *n* **1 :** an aquatic plant (*Brasenia schreberi*) with floating leaves olive green above and red below and all underwater parts covered with a thick layer of jellylike slime — called also *water target* **2 :** FANWORT; *esp* **:** a common aquatic plant (*Cabomba caroliniana*) of eastern No. America with oblong to obovate often basally notched floating leaves and white yellow-spotted flowers

water-shield family *n* **:** CABOMBACEAE

watershoot \'==,=\ *n* **1 :** SUCKER, WATER SPROUT **2 a** *obs* **:** water draining off a piece of land **b :** a trough or channel for discharging water (as from a downspout) **c** *also* **watershot** \'==,=\ **:** DRIP 4

water shrew *n* **:** any of numerous semiaquatic shrews usu. living adjacent to swift-flowing streams and having hind feet that are typically fringed with long stiff hairs and are sometimes partially webbed: as **a :** a widely distributed Old World shrew (*Neomys fodiens*) **b :** any of several shrews (genus *Chimarrogale*) of Japan, Borneo, and Sumatra **c :** any of several web-footed shrews (genus *Nectogale*) of Tibetan uplands **d :** a common No. American shrew (*Sorex palustris*)

¹waterside \'==,=\ *n* [ME, fr. *water* + *side*] **:** the land (as the seaside or a riverside) bordering a body of water

²waterside \"\ *adj* **1 :** of, relating to, or located on the waterside ⟨~ trees⟩ **2 :** employed along the waterside ⟨~ workers⟩; *also* **:** of or relating to the workers along the waterside ⟨a ~ strike⟩

wa·ter·sid·er \"+ə(r)\ *n* -s *Austral* **:** LONGSHOREMAN

water silk *n* **:** an alga of the genus *Spirogyra*

water silvering *n* **:** silvering done with silver amalgam

water skegs *n pl but sing or pl in constr* **:** a common yellow iris (*Iris pseudacorus*)

water ski *n* **:** a ski that is broader and shorter than a snow ski and that planes over the water when the skier is towed by a speedboat

water-ski \'==,=\ *vi* [*water ski*] **:** to plane over water on water skis esp. as a sport

waterskin \'==,=\ *n* **:** a container of skin to hold water

water skipper *or* **water skater** *n* **:** WATER STRIDER

water sky *n* **:** dull neutral-colored sky near the horizon caused by the reflection of the color of the sea and so indicating open water when seen over an ice-covered sea — compare BLINK

water slater *n* **:** a freshwater isopod of *Asellus* or related genus

water slide *n* **:** a flume for use esp. in logging

water smartweed *n* **:** any of various mostly perennial smartweeds (*Polygonum punctatum*) having lanceolate to lance-

oblong leaves with a short petiole gradually broadened at the base

watersmeet \'⸗⸗,⸗\ *n* **:** a meeting place of two rivers ⟨each of these torrents ran down a gorge of its own, the one on the east, the other on the west of the ~ —Hilaire Belloc⟩

water smoke *n* **1 :** mist or foggy vapor rising from the surface of a body of water **2 :** the moisture that rises in the firing of clayware in the form of vapor from the green brick as it is undergoing heating

water-smoke \'⸗⸗,⸗\ *vt* **:** to drive off the moisture in (as green brick) in the preliminary stage of burning by means of a slow fire

water snake *n* **:** any of numerous snakes frequenting or inhabiting freshwaters and feeding largely on aquatic animals: as **a :** any of various snakes constituting a cosmopolitan genus (*Natrix*), being common in the eastern U. S. and sometimes a pest in fish hatcheries and rearing pools, and reaching a length of four feet **b :** an eastern Asian or Australian snake of the family Homalopsidae with valvular nostrils and often a compressed tail **c :** WART SNAKE

water snowflake *n* **:** an Asiatic floating plant (*Nymphoides indicum*) often cultivated for its starlike white flowers

water-soak \'⸗⸗,⸗\ *vt* **:** to soak in water **:** fill the interstices of with water ~ *vi* **:** to become soaked with water ⟨a fabric that does not *water-soak* easily⟩

water soldier *n* **1 :** a European aquatic plant (*Stratiotes aloides*) of the family Hydrocharitaceae with bayonet-shaped leaves that are submerged in the vegetative stage and float in the flowering stage **2 :** a water lettuce (*Pistia stratiotes*)

water-soluble \¦⸗⸗¦⸗⸗⸗\ *adj* **:** soluble in water ⟨*water-soluble* vitamin B⟩ — compare SPIRIT-SOLUBLE

water spaniel *n* **:** a rather large spaniel that has a heavy curly coat and is adapted esp. for retrieving waterfowl — see IRISH WATER SPANIEL

water speedwell *n* **:** any of several speedwells; *esp* **:** an aquatic herb (*Veronica anagallis-aquatica*) found in wet places in Eurasia and America

water spider *n* **1 a** *or* **water spinner :** an aquatic European spider (*Argyoneta aquatica*) that constructs beneath the surface of the water a bell-shaped structure of silk which is open beneath and filled with air carried down by the spider in the form of small bubbles **b :** any of various spiders that habitually live on or about the water; *esp* **:** a large American spider (*Dolomedes sexpunctatus*) that runs rapidly on the surface of water **2 :** WATER MITE

water spike *n* **:** any of several plants of the genera *Potamogeton* or *Hydrostachys*

watersplash \'⸗⸗,⸗\ *n* **:** a shallow ford in a stream

water spot *n* **:** any of several diseases of fruits characterized by water-soaked lesions; *esp* **:** a physiological disorder of citrus fruits which occurs during the rainy season and in which the air spaces under the epidermis of the rind become filled with liquid

waterspout \'⸗⸗,⸗\ *n* [ME *water spoute*, fr. *water* + *spoute* spout — more at SPOUT] **1 a :** a pipe, duct, or orifice from which water is spouted or through which it is carried (as from a roof gutter to a cistern) — compare DOWNSPOUT **b :** water spouting out from or as if from a waterspout **2 :** a slender funnel-shaped or tubular column of rapidly rotating cloud-filled wind usu. extending from the underside of a cumulus or cumulonimbus cloud down to a cloud of spray torn up by the whirling winds from the surface of an ocean or lake, being either straight and vertical or inclined and tortuous as it moves along, and consisting largely of water **3 :** a torrential burst of rain **:** rainfall of the nature or intensity of a cloudburst **syn** see WIND

water sprite *n* **1 :** a sprite held to inhabit or haunt the water **:** WATER NYMPH — compare KELPIE, NAIAD, NEREID, NIX **2 :** FLOATING FERN 1

water sprout *n* **1 :** an extremely vigorous but usu. unproductive shoot originating from an adventitious or a latent bud on the trunk or a main limb of a tree (as a fruit tree) — compare WATER SUCKER **2 :** WATER SUCKER

water spruce *n* **:** BLACK SPRUCE 1

water stain *n* **:** a wood stain in which water is the solvent or dispersion medium

water stair *n* **:** a stairway leading to the water (as at a boat landing) — often used in pl. but sing. or pl. in constr.

water star grass *n* **:** a grassy-leaved No. American aquatic herb (*Heteranthera dubia*) with yellow star-shaped blossoms

water starwort *n* **:** a plant of the genus *Callitriche*

wa·ter·stead \'wätə(r),sted, 'wȯtə-\ *n, dial Eng* **:** the bed of a stream

water stoma *n* **:** HYDATHODE

waterstone \'⸗⸗,⸗\ *n* **:** a whetstone or grindstone used with water rather than oil

water stop *n* **1 :** a device or construction designed to bar the passage of water **2 :** a place (as on a stage road) where water is regularly available

water strider *n* **1 :** any of various long-legged bugs that constitute the family Gerridae and move about on the surface of fresh waters or more rarely on the ocean — called also *water skipper* **2 :** a bug of the family Veliidae

water string *n* **:** the final string of casing or pipe set to exclude water from the producing formation of an oil or gas well

water-struck brick \'⸗⸗,⸗-\ *n* **:** brick made by slop-molding — compare SAND-STRUCK BRICK

water sucker *n* **:** a vigorous shoot originating from a bud at the base of or on the root of a plant (as the banana) — compare WATER SPROUT 1

water supply *n* **:** source, means, or process of supplying water (as for a community) usu. including reservoirs, tunnels, and pipelines and often the watershed from which the water is ultimately drawn

water-supply engineering *n* **:** a branch of civil engineering dealing with the development and maintenance of water supplies

water swallow *n* **1 :** WATER WAGTAIL **2** *dial Eng* **:** SINK 5

water system *n* **1 :** a river with its tributaries **2 :** WATER SUPPLY

water tabby *n* **:** a tabby fabric with a watered finish

water table *n* [ME] **1 :** a stringcourse or similar member when projecting so as to throw off water; *esp* **:** the first table above the ground at the top of a foundation and beginning of the upper wall **2 :** a gutter on the side of a road to carry off water **3 :** the upper limit of the portion of the ground wholly saturated with water whether very near the surface or many feet below it — called also *groundwater level*

water tabling *n* **:** architectural water tables (as of a building)

water target *n* **:** WATER SHIELD 1

water taxi *n* **:** a boat functioning (as about a harbor) as a taxi

water telescope *n* **1 :** WATER GLASS 3 **2 :** a telescope devised for looking into a body of water

water tender *n* **1 a :** a workman who attends to the condition of the water in steam boilers **b :** a petty officer (as in the U. S. Navy) in charge in a fireroom and responsible esp. for proper supplying of water to the boilers and adjustment of burners **2 :** a truck equipped with a water tank and used esp. in fire fighting

water thermometer *n* **:** a thermometer filled with water instead of mercury and used esp. for ascertaining the precise temperature at which water is most dense

water thief *n* **1** *obs* **:** PIRATE **2 :** a valve with multiple connections that permits bleeding a large line through several subordinate lines

water thrush *n* **1 :** any of several No. American warblers of the genus *Seiurus* usu. living in the vicinity of streams and having plumage that is olivaceous above and streaked below **2 :** a European water ouzel (*Cinclus cinclus*) **3** *dial Eng* **:** PIED WAGTAIL

water thyme *n* **:** a waterweed (*Elodea canadensis*)

water tick *n* **:** WATER MITE

water tiger *n* **:** WATER DEVIL 1

watertight \¦⸗⸗¦⸗\ *adj* [ME *water thicht*, fr. *water* + *thicht, thight, tight* tight — more at TIGHT] **1 :** of such precision of construction or fit as to be impermeable to water except when under sufficient pressure to produce structural discontinuity by rupture ⟨a ~ flashing⟩ ⟨~ joints⟩ **2 :** so devised (as in planning or phrasing) as to leave no possibility of misconstruction or evasion ⟨a ~ lease⟩ ⟨the precautions taken against cheating were ~ —A.G.N.Flew⟩ ⟨has created a ~ and very real world of his own —C.J.Rolo⟩ — **wa·ter·tight·ness** *n*

watertight compartment *n* **:** a compartment (as in a ship) having watertight doors by which it can be entirely separated from the rest of the structure of which it is a part

water tower *n* **:** a tower or standpipe serving as a reservoir to deliver water at a required head; *specif* **:** a fire apparatus having a vertical pipe that can be extended to various heights and supplied with water under high pressure (as by several motor pumpers) and used to deliver water at heights unattainable by the ordinary apparatus

water treader *n* **:** a bug of the family Mesoveliidae usu. found at the edges of ponds but sometimes on the surface of the water

water tree *n* **:** any of several chiefly tropical plants with fluids that may be used as an emergency source of drinking water: as **a :** a large Ceylonese pitcher plant (*Nepenthes distillatoria*) **b :** an African woody vine (*Tetracera potatoria*) that yields abundant watery sap when a large stem is cut **c :** any of several chiefly arborescent Australian plants (as of the family Proteaceae) that yield a watery sap when the bark or roots are cut; *esp* **:** a needle wood (*Hakea leucoptera*) that stores water in its thickened roots

water trefoil *n* **:** BUCKBEAN

water tube *n* **:** a tube for passing or holding water: as **a :** a tube in some steam boilers in which water circulates and steam is generated **b :** a tube of a system of tubular excretory organs in many invertebrates that have external openings and that are held to be analogous in function to the kidneys of vertebrates

watertube boiler \'⸗⸗,⸗-\ *n* **:** a steam boiler in which water to be heated circulates in tubes exposed to fire and enveloped by hot gases — compare FIRE-TUBE BOILER

water tunnel *n* **:** a device for the study or testing of the flow about bodies in which water is the mobile fluid — compare WIND TUNNEL

water tupelo *n* **:** TUPELO GUM

water turbine *n* **:** a turbine in which the actuating fluid is water

water turkey *n* **:** a New World snakebird (*Anhinga anhinga*)

water tuyere *n* **:** a water-jacketed tuyere

water twist *n* **:** an eddy or whirlpool in a stream

water uintjie *n* **:** CAPE PONDWEED

water vacuole *n* **:** a vacuole containing watery fluid; *esp* **:** CONTRACTILE VACUOLE

water vapor *n* **:** water in a vaporous form esp. when below boiling temperature and diffused (as in the atmosphere) — compare STEAM

water varnish *n* **:** a varnish in which water is the solvent and water-soluble gums are the nonvolatile ingredients

water-vascular \¦⸗⸗¦⸗⸗⸗\ *adj* **:** of, relating to, or made up of vessels that in many invertebrates contain a watery fluid — see WATER-VASCULAR SYSTEM

water-vascular system *n* **:** a system of vessels in echinoderms containing a watery fluid that is analogous to blood, is used for the movement of tentacles and tube feet, and may also function in excretion and respiration

water velvet *n* **:** a plant of the genus *Azolla*

water vine *n* **1 :** any of several Asiatic climbing plants (genus *Phytocrene*) of the family Icacinaceae with stems that yield a copious and refreshing watery sap **2 :** WATER TREE b

water violet *n* **:** WATER GILLYFLOWER

water viper *n* **:** WATER MOCCASIN 1

water vole *n* **:** a vole that frequents water: as **a :** WATER RAT 1a **b :** a western No. American vole (*Microtus richardsoni*)

water wagon *n* **:** a wagon used (as with troops on the march) to carry water — **on the water wagon** *adv* (*or adj*) **:** on the wagon

water wagtail *n* **1 :** WAGTAIL; *esp* **:** PIED WAGTAIL **2 :** WATER THRUSH 1

waterwall \'⸗⸗,⸗\ *n* [ME *waterwal*, fr. *water* + *wal* wall — more at WALL] **1 :** a wall built beside or around a body of water **2 :** an arrangement of pipes carrying water and so grouped as to form a protective wall between a fire (as in a boiler) and the lining of a furnace

water wally *n* **:** a woody herb or low shrub (*Baccharis glutinosa*) ranging from the southwestern U. S. to western So. America and used locally for thatching and in making brooms — called also *batamote*

water wand *n* **:** a device screwed onto the end of a garden hose to reduce the pressure of the water without decreasing the volume

wa·ter·ward \'⸗⸗wə(r)d\ *also* **wa·ter·wards** \-dz\ *adv* **:** toward water or a particular body of water ⟨cattle turning ~⟩

water-washed \'⸗⸗,⸗\ *adj* **:** washed or swept with water; *esp* **:** washed by the waves of the sea

water wave *n* **1 :** a gravity wave on water **2 :** a method or style of setting hair by dampening with water and forming into waves

water-waved \'⸗⸗,⸗\ *adj* **1 :** marked with a pattern or striping suggesting a wave of water **2** *of hair* **:** set in a water wave

waterway \'⸗⸗,⸗\ *n* [ME *waterwey*, fr. OE *wæterweg*, fr. *wæter* water + *weg* way — more at WATER, WAY] **1 :** a way or channel by which water may pass or escape; *often* **:** a made and often grassed channel that is provided to carry storm water away from a point where it is likely to cause erosion **2 a :** the outer planking of a deck of a ship which is much heavier than the rest of the deck and of which the inboard edge is grooved to form a passage for water to the scuppers; *also* **:** the passage so formed — see SHIP illustration **b :** passage in a steel ship formed by angle irons and the deck stringer **3 a :** breadth of water available for passage (as of boats) **:** FAIRWAY 1a ⟨the ~ of a canal⟩ **b :** a way or route for traffic by water **:** a navigable body or course of water ⟨the Great Lakes provide a ~ to the heart of the continent⟩ **4 :** the open passage area in a cock or valve

waterweed \'⸗⸗,⸗\ *n* **:** any of several floating or submerged aquatic plants: as **a :** an American plant (*Elodea canadensis*) that has elongate branching stems and small opposite or verticillate leaves and is naturalized in parts of Europe; *broadly* **:** any plant of the genus *Elodea* **b :** a California primrose willow (*Jussiaea californica*)

water weevil *n* **:** RICE WATER WEEVIL

waterwheel \'⸗⸗,⸗\ *n* [ME *waterwhele*, fr. *water* + *whele* wheel — more at WHEEL] **1 :** a wheel made to rotate by direct action of water: as **a :** a vertical wheel on a horizontal shaft moved at a comparatively low velocity by the action or weight of the water on or in floats or buckets on its rim — see BREAST WHEEL, OVERSHOT WHEEL, PONCELET WHEEL **b :** a turbine operated by water **2 :** a wheel (as a noria) for raising water **3 :** the paddle wheel of a steamship **4 :** a synchronized swimming stunt which is executed with the body lying on the side and in which the knees are drawn toward the chest and the body is propelled in a circle by alternate pedaling movements of the legs and feet

water whip *n* **:** a gun-tackle purchase hooked to a yard (as of a ship) and used in hoisting in moderate weights

water-white \¦⸗⸗¦⸗\ *adj* **:** approaching water in colorlessness and clarity ⟨*water-white* honey from fireweed⟩

water white oak *n* **:** an overcup oak (*Quercus lyrata*)

water willow *n* **1 :** any of several plants that thrive in wet areas and are felt to resemble willows: as **a** (1) **:** PURPLE LOOSESTRIFE (2) **:** SWAMP LOOSESTRIFE **b :** FIREWEED b **c :** a plant of the genus *Justicia; esp* **:** a No. American rhizomatous plant (*J. americana*) that has slender elongated leaves and dense capitate to ellipsoidal inflorescences with pale violet or white flowers **2 :** any of several willows that thrive in wet areas

water wing *n* **1 water wings** *pl* **:** a pneumatic device to give support to the body of a person swimming or learning to swim ⟨disgusted Londoners discovered that their car was as useful to them as *water-wings* in a desert —Mollie Panter-Downes⟩ **2 :** a wall forming a wing to the abutment of a bridge or pier and extending laterally along the shore on either side as a protection from the current

waterwise \'⸗⸗,⸗\ *adv* **:** in the manner of water ⟨flowing ~⟩

water witch *n* **1 :** a witch reputed to live in or haunt a body of water **2 a :** DABCHICK **b** *dial Eng* **:** STORM PETREL **3 a** *or* **water witcher :** a dowser for water **b :** any of various devices for determining usu. electrically the presence of water (as in a tank or underground)

water witching *n* **:** the act of dowsing for water

waterwood \'⸗⸗,⸗\ *n* **1 :** a West Indian tree (*Chimarrhis cymosa*) of the family Rubiaceae with greenish white flowers **2 :** a Central American mangrove (*Cassipourea elliptica*) with hairy white flowers **3 :** a southern African tree (*Syzygium cordatum*) of the family Myrtaceae having light easily worked wood that is used for flooring and joinery

waterwork \'⸗⸗,⸗\ *n* [ME *waterwerk*, fr. *water* + *werk, wurk, work* work — more at WORK] **1 :** something (as a tank, dock, canal lock, levee, or seawall) built in, for, or as a protection against water **2 :** a mechanism, contrivance, or set of equipment for handling water: as **a :** an ornamental or spectacular display of water mechanically produced **:** FOUNTAIN, CASCADE — usu. used in pl. **b** (1) *obs* **:** a mechanical contrivance for raising and distributing water (2) **waterworks** *pl* **:** the whole system of reservoirs, channels, mains, and pumping and purifying equipment by which a water supply is obtained and distributed to consumers; *also* **:** a pumping or purifying station of such a system **c waterworks** *pl* (1) **:** the channels by which sap or other vital fluid is handled in the living body ⟨the complex ~*s* of a tree⟩ (2) *slang* **:** KIDNEYS **3 waterworks** *pl* **:** tears or the shedding of tears

waterworker \'⸗⸗,⸗⸗\ *n* **:** one who works along the waterside, in the waterworks of a city, or in trenching to make drains for carrying water

waterworn \'⸗⸗,⸗\ *adj* **:** worn, smoothed, or polished by the action of water

waterwort \'⸗⸗,⸗\ *n* [ME, fr. OE *wæterwyrt*, fr. *wæter* water + *wyrt* wort — more at WATER, WORT] **1 :** a plant of the family Elatinaceae **2 :** a plant of the family Philydraceae **3 :** MAIDENHAIR SPLEENWORT

waterworthy \'⸗⸗,⸗⸗\ *adj* **:** SEAWORTHY

wa·tery \'wȯ|d·ərē, 'wä|, |tə-, -ri\ *adj, sometimes* -ER/-EST [ME, fr. OE *wæterig*, fr. *wæter* water + *-ig* -y] **1 a :** consisting of or filled with water ⟨fish within their ~ residence —John Milton⟩ ⟨a ~ grave⟩ **b :** containing, sodden with, or yielding water ⟨a ~ stratum⟩ ⟨~ skies⟩ **:** WET, BOGGY ⟨a ~ northland soil⟩ **c :** made of or prepared with water or sometimes with a watery liquid ⟨~ vapors⟩ ⟨a ~ solution⟩ **d :** exuding or infiltrated with a watery liquid ⟨the ~ vesicles of ivy poisoning⟩: as (1) **:** full of lacrimal secretion ⟨with ~ eyes⟩ (2) *obs, of the mouth* **:** WATERING **2 :** felt to resemble water: as **a :** having the fluidity of water **:** lacking or depleted in viscosity **:** THIN ⟨the ~ blood of anemia⟩ ⟨a ~ liquid⟩ **b** (1) **:** deficient in color or intensity as if diluted with water **:** PALE ⟨a ~ blue⟩ ⟨~ sunlight⟩ (2) **:** exhibiting weakness and vapidity **:** PALLID, WISHY-WASHY ⟨a ~ style in writing⟩ **c** (1) **:** lacking in substance and deficient in savor ⟨a ~ soup⟩ (2) **:** having a soft soggy texture ⟨stale ~ vegetables⟩ ⟨a well-flavored fish but inclined to be ~⟩ **3 :** of, relating to, or connected with water ⟨a ~ deity⟩: as **a** *archaic* **:** living or growing in water **:** AQUATIC **b** *of a sign of the zodiac* **:** having a cold and moist complexion

water yarrow *n* **:** a featherfoil (*Hottonia inflata*)

watery hide disease *n* **:** yellow fat disease of mink

watery rot *n* **:** PINK ROT 1

wath \'wath\ *n* -s [ME, of Scand origin; akin to ON *vath* ford; akin to OE *wæd* ford, OHG *wat* ford, OHG *watan* to wade — more at WADE] *chiefly dial* **:** [1]FORD 1

wa·ther \'wäthə(r)\ *chiefly Irish var of* WATER

wats *pl of* WAT

wat·so·nia \wät'sōnēə *also* wȯt-\ *n* [NL, fr. Sir William *Watson* †1787 Eng. botanist + NL *-ia*] **1** *cap* **:** a genus of southern African herbs (family Iridaceae) that resemble gladioli, are often cultivated for ornament, and have showy spikes of nearly regular and mostly red or white flowers and chiefly basal leaves **2** -s **:** any plant or flower of the genus *Watsonia*

wat·so·ni·an \(')⸗¦sōnēən\ *adj, usu cap* [John B. *Watson* †1958 Amer. psychologist + E *-ian*] **:** of or relating to the behavioristic theories of the psychologist Watson

wat·so·ni·us \⸗'sōnēəs\ *n, cap* [NL, after Dr. *Watson*, 20th cent. Nigerian physician] **:** a genus of conical digenetic trematodes (related to *Paramphistomum*) that are parasitic in the intestine of African primates rarely including man

watt \'wä|t *also* 'wȯ|, *usu* |d·+V\ *n* -s [after James *Watt* †1819 Scot. mechanical engineer and inventor] **1 :** the absolute mks unit of power equal to one absolute joule per second and taken as the standard in the U. S. **:** 1/746 horsepower **2 :** a unit of power equal to about 1.00017 watts — called also *international watt*

watt·age \|d·ij, |tij, -ēj\ *n* -s **:** amount of power expressed in watts

wattape *var of* WATAP

watt current *n* **:** the component of the current in an alternating circuit that is in phase with the electromotive force

[1]**wat·teau** \(')wä¦tō, *also* (')wȯ¦-\ *adj, usu cap* [after Jean Antoine *Watteau* †1721 Fr. painter] **1 :** of or relating to the painter Watteau **2** *of women's dress* **:** of the kind or style represented in Watteau's painting: as **a :** having back pleats falling loosely from the neckline to the hem **b** *of a hat* **:** shallow-crowned and having a wide brim turned up at the back to hold flower trimmings

[2]**watteau** \"\ *n, pl* **watteaux** \"\ *often cap* **:** a Watteau hat

watt·er \'wä|d·ə(r), |tə- *also* 'wȯ|\ *n* -s [*watt* + *-er*] **:** one (as a light bulb or a radio station) having a specified wattage — usu. used in combination ⟨you'll need at least a 60 ~ in that lamp⟩ ⟨the station was a 250 ~⟩

watte·ville·ite \'wätvi,līt\ *n* -s *usu cap* [G *wattevillit*, fr. Baron Oscar de *Watteville*, 19th cent. Frenchman + G *-it* -ite] **:** a mineral $Na_2Ca(SO_4)_2.4H_2O$(?) that is a hydrous sulfate of sodium and calcium and occurs as aggregates of minute hairlike crystals

watt-hour \'⸗¦⸗\ *n* **:** a unit of work or energy equivalent to the power of one watt operating for one hour and equal to about 2655 foot-pounds

watt-hour meter *n* **:** a device to record electric energy usu. in kilowatt-hours **:** an integrating wattmeter

[1]**wat·tle** \'wä|d·ᵊl, |tᵊl *also* 'wȯ|\ *n* -s [ME *wattel*, fr. OE *watel, watol, watul;* akin to OE *wætla* & *wethel* bandage, OHG *wadal*] **1 a :** a fabrication of rods or poles interwoven with slender branches, withes, or reeds and used esp. formerly in building construction ⟨the walls were of ~ and covered with moss —R.L. Stevenson⟩ **b :** material (as rods, branches, and reeds) for such construction **c** *dial Eng* **:** STICK, STAVE, WAND **d** *dial Eng* **:** HURDLE 1a **e wattles** *pl* **:** poles laid on a roof to support thatch **2 :** a fleshy dependent process usu. about the head or neck of an animal: as **a :** a naked, fleshy, usu. wrinkled, and highly colored process of the skin hanging from the chin or throat of a bird or reptile — see COCK illustration **b** (1) *dial Eng* **:** a flap of loose hanging flesh on either side of the throat of some swine (2) **:** loose flesh hanging from the human jaw ⟨a ~ of flesh dangled from his jawbone —T.W.Duncan⟩ **c :** a barbel of a fish **d :** a livestock identification mark in which the skin on the dewlap or other part of the body is slit **3** *Austral* **a** (1) *archaic* **:** a tree yielding slender poles suitable for wattle; *esp* **:** a small slender swamp tree (*Callicoma serratifolia*) of the family Cunoniaceae (2) **:** a tree or shrub of the genus *Acacia* — see BLACK WATTLE, GOLDEN WATTLE, SILVER WATTLE **b :** WATTLE BARK

[2]**wattle** \"\ *vt* **wattled; wattled; wattling** \|d·ᵊliŋ, |t(ᵊ)l-\ **wattles** [ME *watlen*, fr. *wattel*, n.] **1 :** to form or build of or with wattle ⟨soon *wattled* the sides and thatched the roof of a snug little camp⟩ **2 a :** to form into wattle **:** interlace (as withes) to form wattle **b :** to unite or make solid and continuous by interweaving light flexible material (as withes or osiers) ⟨*wattling* the stakes into a firm palisade⟩ **3 :** to enclose (as sheep) with or as if with wattle **:** ENFOLD

[3]**wattle** \"\ *n* -s [ME (Sc) *wattell*, of Scand origin; akin to Norw dial. *veitla, veitsla, veitsle* entertainment, party, ON *veizla* gift, entertainment, feast, fr. *veita* to grant, give, give a feast; akin to OHG *weizen* to show, prove, *wizzan* to know — more at WIT] **:** annual entertainment formerly provided the foud in the Orkney and Shetland islands; *also* **:** tax paid in commutation of this service

wattle and daub *n* **:** framework of woven rods and twigs covered and plastered with clay and used in building construction ⟨a rough stable of *wattle and daub*⟩

wattle bark *n* **:** an astringent bark derived from various Australian acacias and used in tanning

wattlebird \'⸗⸗,⸗\ *n* **1 :** any of several Australasian honey eaters of the genus *Anthochaera* having fleshy pendulous ear wattles: as **a :** a common largely grayish brown Australian bird (*A. carunculata*) with white shaft stripes on the feathers of

the upperparts and a white tail tip **b :** a closely related and somewhat similar Tasmanian bird (*A. paradoxa*) **2 :** WATTLE CROW

wattle crow *n* **:** either of two long-tailed slaty gray corvine birds (*Callaeas cinerea* and *C. wilsoni*) of New Zealand having a brightly colored subcircular fleshy wattle on each side of the base of the lower mandible

wattled *adj* **1 a :** furnished with pendent fleshy processes ⟨a ~ goat⟩ **:** having enlarged wattles ⟨a ~ honey eater⟩ **b :** depicted with wattles of a specified color ⟨a cock's head ~ argent⟩ **2 a :** made or strengthened with wattle ⟨a ~ terrace⟩ ⟨~ walls⟩ **b :** formed for temporary use from hurdles of wattle ⟨a ~ sheepfold⟩ **3 :** interlaced into or as if into wattle ⟨~ reeds⟩

wattle day *n, usu cap W&D* **:** August 1 or September 1 according to the forwardness of the flowering of the wattle in each state constituting a general holiday in Australia dedicated to the encouragement of the arts

wattled bird of paradise : a bird of paradise (*Paradigalla carunculata*) having an erect yellowish wattle in front of each eye and a bluish pendent one at each angle of the mouth

wattled crow *n* **1 :** WATTLEBIRD 1 **2 :** WATTLE CROW

wattled honey eater *n* **:** WATTLEBIRD 1

wattled plover *or* **wattled lapwing** *n* **:** any of various plovers of the warmer parts of the Old World that resemble the lapwings but have about the face and esp. between the eye and the bill variously colored fleshy wattles and are usu. placed in a distinct subfamily of Charadriidae

wattled stare *or* **wattled starling** *n* **:** SADDLEBACK 2d

wattle extract *n* **:** a vegetable tanning material made from wattle bark

wattle gum *n* **:** gum arabic obtained from wattles (as *Acacia pycnantha*) in the form of reddish tears or lumps — compare AUSTRALIAN GUM

watt·less component \ˈ=lə̇s-\ *n* [*wattless* fr. *watt* + *-less*] **:** REACTIVE COMPONENT

wattless power *n* **:** REACTIVE VOLT-AMPERES

wattless volt-amperes *n pl* **:** the product of the reactive component of current by voltage or of the reactive component of voltage by current

wattle turkey *n* **:** the Australian brush turkey

wattlework \ˈ==,=\ *n* **:** coarse wickerwork **:** WATTLE 1a

wattling *pres part of* WATTLE

watt·meter \ˈ=,mēd·ə(r), -ētə-\ *n* [ISV *watt* + *-meter*] **1 :** an instrument for measuring electric power in watts **2 :** WATT-HOUR METER

watt-second \ˈ=ˈ=\ *n* **:** JOULE

wa·tu·si *also* **wa·tus·si** \wäˈtüsē, -si\ *or* **wa·tut·si** \-üts-\ *n pl, usu cap* **:** TUSI

wau·co·bi·an \wȯˈkōbēən\ *adj, usu cap* [*Waucoba* mountains, range in eastern Calif. + E *-an*] **:** of or relating to a subdivision of the American Cambrian — see GEOLOGIC TIME table

¹waugh \ˈwȯf\ *adj* [prob. fr. ME *walh, walhwe*, fr. OE *wealg*; akin to OE *wlæc, wlacu* lukewarm — more at WELKIN] **1** *chiefly Scot* **:** INSIPID, NAUSEOUS, STALE **2** *chiefly Scot* **:** FAINT, WEAK

²waugh *also* **wagh** *or* **wah** \ˈwȯ, ˈwä\ *interj* [imit. of a child's cry] — used to express anger, disgust, or grief

¹waught \ˈwäkt\ *vb* -ED/-ING/-S [origin unknown] *chiefly Scot* **:** to drink deep **:** QUAFF

²waught \"\ *n* -S *chiefly Scot* **:** a copious draft

wauk \ˈwȯk\ *Scot var of* WAKE

wau·ke \ˈwau̇kä\ *n* -S [Hawaiian] *Hawaii* **:** PAPER MULBERRY

wau·ke·gan juniper \wȯˈkēgən-\ *n, usu cap W* [fr. *Waukegan*, city in northeastern Illinois] **:** a creeping juniper (*Juniperus horizontalis douglasi*) having long branches and blue-green leaves that turn purplish in winter

wauk·en \ˈwȯkən\ *Scot var of* WAKEN

wauk·rife \ˈwȯ,krīf\ *chiefly Scot var of* WAKERIFE

waul \ˈwȯl\ *var of* WAWL

waulk \ˈwȯk\ *Scot var of* ³WALK

waur \ˈwär\ *Scot var of* ³WAR, ⁴WAR

¹wave \ˈwāv\ *vb* -ED/-ING/-S [ME *waven*, fr. OE *wafian* to wave with the hands; akin to OE *wǣfre* wavering, restless — more at WAVER] *vi* **1 a :** to flutter in a breeze ⟨*waving* battle streamers⟩ **:** float, play, or shake in an air current **:** move up and down or to and fro **:** FLAP **b** *obs* **:** to bob on or as if on the surface of the water **:** toss or fluctuate in water or air **2** *archaic* **:** to waver irresolutely between conflicting courses of action or opinion **:** HESITATE, VACILLATE **3 :** to motion with the hands or with something held in them in signal, greeting, or salute ⟨continued to ~ to him until the train disappeared in the distance⟩ **4 a** *of water* **:** to move in waves, fluctuations, or undulations **:** HEAVE **b** *of a crowd* **:** to move in a restless, irregular, or fluctuating way likened to that of sea waves **5 :** to become moved or brandished to and fro ⟨handkerchiefs *waved* as the president rode by⟩ ⟨his sword *waved* and flashed⟩ **6** *obs* **:** to bend from side to side **:** move sinuously **7 :** to move before the wind with a wavelike motion and appearance ⟨field of *waving* grain⟩ **8 :** to follow a curving line or take a wavy form **:** UNDULATE ⟨seen from a distance, its outline curves and ~*s* in a Romanesque tracery⟩ ~ *vt* **1 :** to swing (something) back and forth; *esp* **:** to lift up (a sacrifice) and move back and forth before the altar in consecration ⟨take the breast of the ram of Aaron's ordination and ~ it for a wave offering before the Lord —Exod 29:26 (RSV)⟩ **2 :** to impart a curving or undulating shape or design to **:** decorate with a wavy surface, edge, or outline ⟨*waved* her hair and manicured her nails⟩ **3 a :** to motion to (someone) to go in an indicated direction or to stop **:** FLAG, SIGNAL ⟨*waved* down an approaching motorist to ask for help⟩ ⟨looked at my identification card and then *waved* me on⟩ **b :** to gesture with (as the arm) in greeting or farewell, in celebration of someone's triumph, or in homage to an honored person **:** make a sweeping, circling, or twirling movement with ⟨*waved* hats and handkerchiefs in welcome to their returning hero⟩ **c :** to indicate by a sweep of hand or arm **:** SIGNIFY ⟨*waved* farewell from the ship's rail⟩ ⟨*waved* dismissal as he turned and left⟩ ⟨the officer *waved* acknowledgement —Wirt Williams⟩ **4 :** to flap (the wings) in or as if in flight **5 :** BRANDISH, FLOURISH, SHAKE ⟨*waved* a loaded pistol menacingly⟩ **6 :** to blow (something) to and fro **:** FLUTTER ⟨the troops plodded by and a desultory breeze *waved* their banners from time to time⟩ **7** *archaic* **:** to move (the head) up and down **:** BOB **8 :** to toss (as a blossom) in the breeze ⟨trees *waved* leafy heads⟩ **syn** see SWING

²wave \"\ *n* -S **1 a :** a ridge or swell on the surface of a liquid (as of the sea) having normally a forward motion distinct from the oscillatory motion of the particles that successively compose it **:** a minute ridge that is largely dependent on surface tension **:** a ridge of larger size that is dependent on the force of gravity **:** an undulation that is dependent on the friction between wind and water — compare BREAKER, RIPPLE **b :** a body of water **2 a :** a shape or outline having successive curves like those of ocean waves **:** one of the crests of such a form or a crest with its adjacent trough **b :** a natural waviness of the hair or a dressing intended to simulate it — compare MARCEL, PERMANENT WAVE **c :** an undulating line or streak (as in glass, steel, or textiles) or a pattern formed by such lines **3 :** something likened to an ocean wave as stormy or unsettling: as **a :** a surge of sensation or emotion ⟨a ~ of nausea⟩ ⟨a ~ of anger⟩ ⟨a ~ of tenderness⟩ **b :** one of the troubles or vicissitudes of life or fortune **c :** a tide of opinion or sentiment carrying many with it **:** a movement sweeping large numbers in a common direction **:** CONTAGION **d :** a peak or climax of intensity **:** the moment of greatest activity or strongest feeling ⟨a ~ of enthusiasm⟩ **4 :** a sweep of hand or arm or of some object held in the hand used as a signal, greeting, or other indication **5 :** a long ridge of ground rounded into the shape of an ocean wave **6 :** a rolling or undulatory movement or one of a series of such movements passing along a surface or through the air **7 :** a movement likened to that of an ocean wave: as **a :** a tide, advance, or surge of settlers **:** one of a succession of influxes of people migrating into a region **b** (1) **:** a large group of animals of one kind ⟨the final ~ of migrating ducks⟩ (2) **:** a sudden rapid increase in an animal population or its effects ⟨a very severe fly-strike ~ followed the moist summer⟩ **c :** a line of attacking or advancing troops, landing craft, combat vehicles, or aircraft ⟨it was D company; our second ~ —H.G.Wells⟩ **8 :** a disturbance or variation that transfers itself and energy progressively from point to point in a medium or in space in such a way that each particle or element influences the adjacent ones and that may be in the form of an elastic deformation or of a variation of level or pressure, of electric or magnetic intensity, of electric potential, or of temperature — see LONGITUDINAL WAVE, TRANSVERSE WAVE **9 :** a change in temperature or a period of hot or cold weather — compare COLD WAVE, HOT WAVE **10 :** EARTH WAVE 1 **11 :** RADIO WAVE **12 :** an undulating or jagged line constituting a graphic representation (as of heart action in an electrocardiogram, brain waves in an electroencephalogram, an earthquake in a seismogram, or a varying electric current in an oscilloscope)

³wave \"\ *archaic var of* WAIVE

⁴wave \"\ *n* -S *usu cap* [*W*omen *A*ccepted for *V*olunteer *E*mergency Service] **1 :** a member of the Women's Reserve of the U. S. Navy formed during World War II **2 :** a woman serving in the U. S. Navy

wave analyzer *n* **:** a harmonic analyzer applied to wave-form-curve analysis

wave antenna *n* **:** a radio antenna of great length with special circuit arrangements permitting utilization of the antenna's directional properties

wave band *n* **1 :** a range of radio-wave frequencies assigned to a particular type of broadcasting (as television or FM) **2 :** ¹CHANNEL 1i

wave base *n* **:** the depth in a body of water (as a lake or sea) at which wave motion becomes inappreciable

wave-built \ˈ=,=\ *adj* **:** built up by the action of lake or sea waves and their concomitant currents ⟨a *wave-built* beach⟩

wave-built terrace *n* **:** a terrace built up of loosened material at the edge of a wave-cut terrace

wave changer *n* **:** a device in a radio transmitting set for effecting a rapid change from one frequency to another

wave-cut \ˈ=,=\ *adj* **:** cut away by the action of waves of a lake or sea and their concomitant currents

wave-cut terrace *n* **:** a shallow-water shelf inclining gently away from the base of an eroded sea cliff

waved *adj* [partly fr. ²*wave* + *-ed*, partly fr. past part. of ¹*wave*] **:** having a wavelike form or outline: as **a :** UNDULATING, INDENTED, CURVING ⟨the ~ cutting edge of a bread knife⟩ **b** *of cloth* **:** having wavelike lines of color **:** WATERED **c :** moved or swung to and fro

wave equation *n* **1 :** a partial differential equation of the second order whose solutions describe wave phenomena (as the transverse vibrations of a stretched string) **2 :** SCHRÖDINGER EQUATION

wave filter *n* **:** ¹FILTER 3

wave form *n* **:** a curve that represents the condition of a wave-propagating medium at a given instant and is usu. a graph in rectangular coordinates whose abscissas represent distances along the direction of propagation and whose ordinates represent the corresponding values of the propagated variation or disturbance — called also *wave shape*

wave front *n* **1 :** a surface composed at any instant of all the points just reached by a vibrational disturbance in its propagation through a medium **2 :** a surface so drawn as to pass through those parts of a wave where the distortion or displacement of the medium through which the wave passes is everywhere the same

wave function *n* **:** a solution of the wave equation

wave guide *n* **:** a metal pipe of circular or rectangular cross section or a dielectric cylinder of such dimensions that it will propagate electromagnetic waves of a given frequency used for channeling ultrahigh-frequency waves in radio and television transmission because of the low loss by attenuation and radiation

wave height *n* **:** the vertical distance between the trough of a wave and the following crest

wavelength \ˈ=,=\ *n* **:** the distance in the line of advance of a wave from any one point to the next point at which at the same instant there is the same phase ⟨if *N* is the frequency of the waves and λ their ~, their velocity of advance is the product *N*λ⟩

wave·less \ˈwāvlə̇s\ *adj* **:** having no waves **:** CALM, SMOOTH, UNRUFFLED

wave·less·ly *adv* **:** in a waveless manner

wave·let \ˈwāvlə̇t\ *n* -S **1 :** a little wave **:** RIPPLE **2 :** one of the elementary waves with a point source of which any advancing wave front is the envelope — see HUYGENS' PRINCIPLE

wavelike \ˈ=,=\ *adj (or adv)* **:** having the form, movement, or other characteristics of a wave **:** resembling a wave in manner of propagation

wave line *n* **:** WAVEMARK

wa·vel·lite \ˈwāvə,līt\ *n* -S [William *Wavell* †1829 Eng. physician + E *-ite*] **:** a mineral $Al_3(PO_4)_2(OH)_3.5H_2O$ consisting of a hydrous basic aluminum phosphate and occurring usu. in hemispherical radiated aggregates varying from white to yellow, green, or black

wavemark \ˈ=,=\ *n* [²*wave* + *mark*] **1 :** a very small ridge of sand made by a wave when it advances upon a low sandy beach and marking the limit of advance **2 :** one of many undulations on the bedding surfaces of a sedimentary rock due to wave action during the period of deposition — compare RIPPLE MARK

wave-mechanical \ˈ==ˈ===\ *adj* **:** of or relating to wave mechanics

wave mechanics *n pl but sing or pl in constr* **:** a theory of matter holding that elementary particles (as electrons, protons, neutrons) have wave properties and seeking a mathematical interpretation of the structure of matter on the basis of these properties

wave·me·ter \ˈwāv,mēd·ə(r)\ *n* [²*wave* + *-meter*] **:** a device to measure the wavelength or the frequency of an electromagnetic or radio signal

wave molding *n* **:** a molding with a profile that suggests one or more breaking waves — compare VITRUVIAN SCROLL

wave moth *n* **:** any of many small geometrid moths of *Sterrha* and related genera having wavy markings on the wings

wave motion *n* **:** the motion of the particles of a medium in mechanically propagated waves (as water waves or sound waves)

wave motor *n* **:** a prime mover engine actuated by waves of water

wave number *n* **:** the number of waves per centimeter of light of a given wavelength **:** the reciprocal of the wavelength ⟨spectroscopists frequently specify a wave by the *wave number* —R.E.Lapp & H.L.Andrews⟩

wave-off \ˈ=,=\ *n* -S [fr. the phrase *wave off*] **:** a visible signal given by an officer on the deck of an aircraft carrier to the pilot of an approaching airplane usu. indicating that his approach is unsatisfactory for a successful landing, and that he must circle the carrier and make a new approach — compare LANDING SIGNAL OFFICER

wave offering *n* **:** a sacrificial offering elevated and swung to and fro in ancient Jewish religious ceremony and afterwards reserved for the personal use of the priestly families

wave of oscillation : a wave in which the particles of water move in closed vertical orbits

wave of the future : a line of historical development prob. sure to shape or dominate the future **:** a movement representing a trend that will inevitably prevail or forces that will certainly triumph

wave of translation : a wave in which the particles of water move forward in the direction of wave propagation

wave packet *n* **:** a pulse (as an electromagnetic pulse) that is the resultant of a number of wave trains of differing wavelengths and speed and has a definite group velocity

wave pattern *n* **:** an undulating line that often appears in primitive ornament (as in the decoration of pottery)

wave plate *n* **1 :** HALF-WAVE PLATE **2 :** QUARTER-WAVE PLATE

¹wa·ver \ˈwāvə(r)\ *vi* **wavered; wavered; wavering** \-v(ə)riŋ\ **wavers** [ME *waveren*; akin to MHG *wabern* to waver, OE *wǣfre* wavering, restless, ON *vafra* to hover about, OE *wefan* to weave — more at WEAVE] **1 a :** to vacillate irresolutely between options or attractions **:** hesitate undecided at a choice **:** fluctuate in opinion, allegiance, or direction **:** act inconstant or uncertain **:** VARY ⟨~*s* between easy tolerance and a bigotry which would have made the Puritans squirm —Green Peyton⟩ ⟨~*ed* between sympathy and superiority —Mary Austin⟩ ⟨~*s* between writing an adult fairy tale, a slick romance, and a social satire —Martin Levin⟩ **b :** to change, alternate, or shift between objects, conditions, uses, or otherwise ⟨a mood that ~*ed* between uncertain cheer and blackest gloom⟩ **2 a :** to weave or sway unsteadily to and fro **:** move back and forth **:** REEL, TOTTER ⟨~*ed* back and forth a little as he spoke —Irwin Shaw⟩ ⟨on this point of view the character stands, ~*s*, or falls —F.J.Hoffman⟩ **b :** to move in an unsteady or uncontrolled manner **:** FLUTTER, QUIVER ⟨the feather ~*ed* to the floor —Elinor Wylie⟩ ⟨a thin grey stinking smoke ~*ed* up —Claud Cockburn⟩ ⟨it ~*ed* as he raised it and fired —Sherwood Anderson⟩ **c :** to approach or withdraw in an undecided or hesitant manner ⟨they both hesitated, and, as it were, ~*ed* uncertainly towards each other —Arnold Bennett⟩ **d :** to follow a changing or random line **:** move in a purposeless way or as if impelled by chance influences ⟨the story ~*s* and loses some of its . . . effectiveness —Edmund Fuller⟩ **3 a :** to move with a shifting or uncertain gaze **:** turn uneasily, timidly, or weakly one way and another ⟨his glance ~*ed* like that of a cornered animal⟩ **b :** to give an unsteady sound **:** QUAVER, SHAKE ⟨her voice ~*ed* with strain⟩ **c :** to evince uncertainty or vagueness of mind (as in great perplexity or shock) **:** WANDER ⟨his wits at last ~*ed* from the prolonged and intense horror⟩ **4 a :** to fluctuate in brightness **:** FLICKER, GLIMMER ⟨the candle flames ~*ed* —Margaret A. Barnes⟩ ⟨the thin blue light ~*ed* and vanished and ~*ed* again —Ellen Glasgow⟩ **b :** to move with the indistinctness or uncertainty of a shadow ⟨the silhouette of a moving cat ~*ed* across the moonlight —Scott Fitzgerald⟩ ⟨before my face ~*ed* an incense cloud the like of which I had never smelt —Elinor Wylie⟩ **5 :** to falter in battle **:** hesitate as if about to give way **:** CHECK ⟨the line ~*ed* and broke —John Buchan⟩ **syn** see HESITATE, SWING

²waver \"\ *n* -S [earlier *waiver*, prob. fr. *waive* + *-er*] *dial Eng* **:** a young tree left uncut during timber clearing

³wav·er \"\ *n* -S [¹*wave* + *-er*] **:** one that waves: as **a :** one that swings something to and fro ⟨they are ~*s* of flags and shouters of slogans⟩ **b :** a vibrating roller that smooths and distributes ink on the inking table of a printing press **c** (1) **:** a hairdresser who does waving (2) **:** a device (as an iron) for waving hair

⁴wa·ver \"\ *n* -S [¹*waver*] **:** an act of wavering, quivering, or fluttering

wa·ver·er \ˈwāvərə(r)\ *n* -S **:** one that wavers; *esp* **:** a vacillating or indecisive person

wa·ver·ing·ly *adv* **:** in a wavering manner

wa·very \-v(ə)rē\ *adj* **:** WAVERING

waves *pres 3d sing of* WAVE, *pl of* WAVE

wave set *n* **:** a somewhat viscous solution with which hair is wet before setting in order to make the waves or curls last

wave shape *n* **:** WAVE FORM

wave·son \ˈwāvsən\ *n* [²*wave* + *-son* (as in AF *floteson* flotsam) — more at FLOTSAM] **:** goods that after shipwreck appear floating on the sea **:** FLOTSAM

wave surface *n* **1 :** WAVE FRONT **2 :** a combination of wave fronts developed simultaneously from a single center (as of light in uniaxial and biaxial crystals) ⟨the *wave surface* for a uniaxial doubly refracting substance consists of a sphere enclosing or enclosed by an ellipsoid of revolution⟩

wave system *n* **:** a system of traffic regulation in which the signals on a street or highway change progressively permitting traffic to proceed at a uniform predetermined speed without stopping

wave theory *n* **1 :** UNDULATORY THEORY **2** [trans. of G *wellentheorie*] **:** a theory in linguistics: branches develop from a parent language (as Indo-European) by waves of linguistic change with the result that adjacent branches have more features in common than those that are widely separated — compare FAMILY-TREE THEORY

wave train *n* **:** a succession of similar waves at equal intervals

wave trap *n* **:** a tuned radio circuit used to improve the selectivity of radio apparatus or to eliminate interference

wave variable *n* **:** a quantity (as the pressure in sound-wave propagation) whose periodic variations are primarily responsible for the propagation of a wave

wave velocity *n* **:** PHASE VELOCITY

wave wheel *n* **1 :** a rope pulley with a groove of wavy outline to increase the grip on the rope **2 :** a wheel with wavy outline used as a cam to give a reciprocating movement

wave winding *n* **:** an armature winding in which the coils are laid in two layers and follow each other on the surface of the armature in the form of waves with the coils being so connected in series that there are only two paths for the flow of current whatever the number of poles in the machine — called also *series winding*; compare LAP WINDING, RING WINDING

wave-worn \ˈ=,=\ *adj* **:** showing attrition from waves

wa·vey *also* **wa·vy** \ˈwāvē\ *n, pl* **waveys** *or* **wavies** [of Algonquian origin; akin to Ojibwa *wêwe* goose, Cree *wehwew*] **:** SNOW GOOSE

wav·i·ly \ˈwāvəlē, -li\ *adv* **:** in a wavy manner

wav·i·ness \-vēnə̇s, -vin-\ *n* -ES **:** the quality or state of being wavy

waving *pres part of* WAVE

wav·ing·ly *adv* **:** in a waving manner

wavy \ˈwāvē, -vi\ *adj* -ER/-EST **1 :** rising or swelling in waves **:** abounding in waves ⟨a ~ lake⟩ **2 :** playing or moving to and fro with an undulating motion **:** FLUCTUATING, WAVERING ⟨a ~ flame⟩ **3 :** having a wavelike form or outline **:** CURVING, ROLLING ⟨~ terrain⟩ **4 :** UNDULATE **5 :** having transverse lines or bars curving in a manner suggesting a succession of waves — compare BARRY-WAVY

¹waw \ˈwȯ\ *n* -S [ME *wawe, waghe*; akin to OE *wagian* to move, swing — more at WAG] *archaic* **:** WAVE

²waw \"\ *vi* -ED/-ING/-S [imit.] *chiefly Scot* **:** to utter the characteristic cry of a cat

³waw \"\ *n* -S *chiefly Scot* **:** the cry of a cat

⁴waw *or* **vav** \ˈväv, ˈvȯv\ *n* -S [Heb *wāw*, lit., hook] **1 :** the sixth letter of the Hebrew alphabet — symbol ו; see ALPHABET table **2 :** the letter corresponding to Hebrew waw in the Phoenician or in any of various other Semitic alphabets

wa·was·keesh \wäˈwä,skēsh\ *n* -ES [prob. fr. Ojibwa *wâwâshkeshi* deer] **:** WAPITI 1

wawl \ˈwȯl\ *vi* -ED/-ING/-S [imit. of an infant's cry] *chiefly Scot* **:** WAIL, HOWL, SQUALL

¹wax \ˈwaks\ *n* -ES *often attrib* [ME *wax, wex*, fr. OE *weax*; akin to OHG *wahs* wax, ON *vax*, Lith *vaškas* wax, and prob. to OHG *wiohha* lint, wick — more at WICK] **1 a :** a substance that is secreted by bees by special glands on the underside of the abdomen, deposited as thin scales, and used after mastication and mixture with the secretion of the salivary glands for constructing the honeycomb, that is then glossy and hard but plastic when warm, insoluble in water but partly soluble in boiling alcohol and in ether, and miscible with oils and fats, and that is a mixture consisting of the palmitate of myricyl alcohol and other higher esters, free cerotic acid, and hydrocarbons — called also *beeswax* **b :** BEESWAX 2 **2 :** any of various natural or synthetic substances resembling beeswax in physical properties or chemical composition or both and used chiefly in candles, in coatings (as for paper), and in polishing materials: as **a :** any of a class of substances (as carnauba wax, spermaceti, Chinese wax) of plant or animal origin that differ from fats in being less greasy, harder, and more brittle and in containing principally esters of higher fatty acids and higher monohydroxy alcohols instead of glycerol, free higher acids and alcohols, and saturated hydrocarbons — see VEGETABLE WAX, WAX INSECT **b :** a solid substance (as ozokerite or paraffin wax) of mineral origin consisting usu. of higher hydrocarbons **:** MINERAL WAX **c :** a pliable or liquid composition that may or may not contain wax and is used esp. in uniting surfaces, excluding air, making patterns or impressions, or producing a waxlike polished surface ⟨etching ~⟩ ⟨dental ~*es*⟩ ⟨floor ~*es*⟩ **d :** a resinous preparation used by shoemakers for rubbing thread **3 :** something likened to wax as soft, impressionable, or readily molded ⟨thy noble shape is but a form of ~, digressing from the valor of a man —Shak.⟩ **4 :** SEALING WAX **5** *or* **wax white :** a pale to grayish greenish yellow **6 :** a waxlike product secreted by plants **7 :** CERUMEN **8 :** a substance secreted by some scales that is similar to beeswax — see WAX INSECT **9 :** a phonograph recording

²wax \"\ *vt* -ED/-ING/-S [ME *waxen, wexen*, fr. *wax, wex* wax] **1 :** to treat, polish, or rub with wax ⟨~ a floor⟩ ⟨~ a thread⟩ **2 :** to stiffen with wax ⟨~ a mustache⟩ **3 :** to record on

phonograph records ⟨a vibrato-cluttered duet . . . ~ed 23 years ago —*Time*⟩

³wax \"\ *vi* **waxed; waxed** \-st\ *or archaic* **wax·en** \-sən\ **waxing; waxes** [ME *waxen, wexen,* fr. OE *weaxan,* akin to OHG *wahsan* to increase, grow, ON *vaxa,* Goth *wahsjan,* Gk *auxanein, auxēre* — more at EKE, v.] **1 a :** to increase in size, numbers, strength, prosperity, or intensity **:** grow larger, fuller, stronger, or more numerous ⟨mankind, let us hope, will dwindle and die more contented than it ever was when it ~ed and struggled —George Santayana⟩ **b :** to grow in volume or duration ⟨as a swelling river or days lengthening in spring⟩ **c :** to grow and develop as an animal or a person does in maturing ⟨ the culmination of the Progressive movement which had been ~ing since before the turn of the century —J.A.Huston⟩ **e :** to grow more active or conspicuous **:** gain in vigor ⟨rancor ~ed among them⟩ **2 :** to increase in phase or intensity — used chiefly of the moon, other satellites, and inferior planets; opposed to *wane;* see MOON illustration **3 :** to assume a specified characteristic, quality, or state **:** BECOME ⟨~ed indignant editorially —America⟩ ⟨ate enormously and ~ed fatter —Edna Ferber⟩

⁴wax \"\ *n* -ES [ME, fr. *waxen* to increase, grow] **1 :** INCREASE, GROWTH ⟨pileated woodpeckers . . . are on the ~ now and are expected to continue so —Christopher Rand⟩ **2 :** the increase in phase or intensity of the moon from new to full or of some other satellite or planet

⁵wax \"\ *n* -ES [perh. fr. ³*wax*] **:** a fit of temper **:** RAGE ⟨had been in a ~ at its loss —John Buchan⟩

⁶wax \"\ *vt* -ED/-ING/-ES [prob. fr. ²*wax*] **:** to get the better of **:** beat soundly or badly ⟨as in a game⟩

wax bean *n* **:** any of various kidney beans that have the pods creamy yellow to bright yellow when suitably matured for use as snap beans — compare GREEN BEAN

wax begonia *n* **:** a cultivated fibrous-rooted begonia derived from the species begonia (*Begonia semperflorens*)

wax·berry \'waks-\ — *see* BERRY **n 1 :** the wax-covered fruit of the wax myrtle; *also* **:** WAX MYRTLE **2 :** SNOWBERRY 1

waxberry cornel *n* **:** RED OSIER 2

waxbill \'ₛ,ₛ\ *n* **:** any of numerous Old World birds of the family Ploceidae having white, pink, or reddish bills of a waxy appearance; *esp* **:** any of various birds of the genus *Estrilda* commonly kept as cage birds

wax-billed \'ₛ;ₛ\ *adj* **:** having a bill suggesting sealing wax in color — used of a bird

waxbird \'ₛ,ₛ\ *n* **:** WAXWING

wax brown *n* **:** BEESWAX 3

waxbush \"\ *n* **:** WAXWEED

wax-chandler \'ₛ,ₛₛ\ *n* [ME *wax chandeler*] **:** a chandler dealing in wax candles

wax cloth *n* **1 :** a fabric waterproofed with wax or paraffin **2 :** OILCLOTH

wax creeper *n, southern Africa* **:** either of two vines of the family Asclepiadaceae: **a :** a plant (*Microloma tenuifolia*) **b :** WAX PLANT 2

wax distillate *n* **:** PARAFFIN DISTILLATE

wax dolls *n pl but sing or pl in constr* **:** a common fumitory (*Fumaria officinalis*)

waxed *past of* WAX

waxed end *or* **wax end** *n* **:** a thread formed of a number of filaments rubbed with shoemaker's wax, usu. pointed with a bristle, and used in sewing leather in which holes have been made ⟨as in shoemaking⟩

waxed paper *or* **wax paper** *n* **:** paper coated or otherwise treated with wax to make it waterproof and greaseproof and used esp. as a wrapping

¹waxen *archaic past part of* ³WAX

²waxen \'waksɔn\ *adj* [ME, fr. ¹*wax* + -*en*] **1 :** made of wax ⟨a ~ record —*Congressional Record*⟩ ⟨~ tapers⟩ **2 :** covered with wax ⟨an ancient ~ writing tablet⟩ **3 :** resembling wax in pliability or impressionability ⟨men have marble, women ~, minds.⟩ —Shak.⟩ **4 a :** having the smooth bloodless appearance of wax **:** seeming to lack vitality or animation **:** PALLID ⟨the poor face with the same awful, ~ pallor —Bram Stoker⟩ **b :** having a lustrous smoothness **5 :** of the color wax

waxen chatterer *n* **:** BOHEMIAN WAXWING

wax engraving *n* **:** a process for preparing letterpress printing surfaces in which the design is cut or formed in a thin wax coating on a metal plate that is then electrotyped or in which hand-cut additions or corrections are made in a regular wax electrotype mold before deposition of the shell

wax·er \'waks(r)\ *n* -s **:** one whose work is applying or polishing with wax: **as a :** one that waxes furniture or automobiles **b :** an operator of a machine for waxing the sprocket holes of motion-picture film to ease passage of the film through the projector **c :** one that puts protective wax on the plain parts of glass articles to protect them while designs are etched **d :** an operator of a machine for waxing yarn to increase its strength

wax·er·man \-(r)mən\ *n, pl* **waxermen :** an operator of a machine for coating paper with a waterproofing wax

waxes *pl of* WAX, *pres 3d sing of* WAX

wax extractor *n* **:** a device or machine for extracting and rendering beeswax from the empty honeycomb by applying heat

waxflower \'ₛ,ₛ\ *n* **1 :** a climbing plant (*Stephanotis floribunda*) of Madagascar often cultivated in the greenhouse for its fragrant white flowers **2 :** an epiphytic tree (*Clusia insignis*) of British Guiana **3 :** INDIAN PIPE **4 :** SPOTTED WINTERGREEN

wax gland *n* **:** a gland ⟨as in the honeybee and some scales⟩ that secretes wax

wax gourd *n* **1 :** a tropical Asiatic twining plant (*Benincasa hispida*) **2 :** the edible fruit of the wax gourd resembling a pumpkin and having a waxy pulverulent coat

wax hair *n* **:** wax secreted by some psyllids or coccids and extruded as a filament through the opening of the wax gland

wax·haw \'waks,hȯ\ *n, pl* **waxhaw** *or* **waxhaws** *usu cap* **1 :** an extinct Siouan people of north central So. Carolina and south central No. Carolina **2 :** a member of the Waxhaw people

waxier *comparative of* WAXY

waxiest *superlative of* WAXY

wax·i·ly \'waksɔlē\ *adv* **:** in a waxy manner

wax·i·ness \'ₛ-sēnós\ *n* -ES **:** the quality or state of being waxy

waxing *n* -s [ME, fr. gerund of *waxen* to treat with wax — more at WAX] **1 :** the act of applying wax ⟨as in polishing⟩ **2 a :** the making of a phonograph record **b :** a phonograph record ⟨orchestral ~s⟩

wax insect *n* **1 :** any of several scales of the family Coccidae that secrete a wax from their bodies; *esp* **:** a Chinese scale (*Ericerus pe-la*) that yields much of the commercial Chinese wax **2 :** any of several homopterous insects of the family Fulgoridae that secrete a wax used by the Chinese ⟨as for candles⟩

wax jack *n* **:** an 18th century silver desk accessory with a central spindle and a very long wax taper coiled about it like a rope with its lighted end held in a socket and used to melt sealing wax

wax light *n* **:** a wax candle **:** TAPER

waxlike \'ₛ,ₛ\ *adj* **:** resembling wax

waxmallow \'ₛ,ₛ(,)ₛ\ *n* [¹*wax* + *mallow*] **:** any of various plants (genus *Malvaviscus*) of the family Malvaceae having drooping flowers like those of the hibiscus

wax·man \'waksmən\ *n, pl* **waxmen :** a worker who removes from the filters wax that accumulates during the pressing of paraffin distillate

wax moth *n* **1 :** BEE MOTH **2 :** a moth (*Achroia grisella*) smaller than the bee moth but similar in appearance and habits — called also *lesser wax moth*

wax myrtle *n* **:** any of several shrubs or trees of the genus *Myrica; esp* **:** a shrub (*M. cerifera*) of eastern No. America having aromatic foliage and small hard berries with a thick coating of white wax that is used for candles — called also *bay myrtle, puckerbush;* see BAYBERRY 2

wax jack

wax painting *n* **:** encaustic painting

wax palm *n* **:** any of several palms that yield wax: as **a :** a pinnate-leaved palm (*Ceroxylon andicolum*) of the Andes on the stem of which is produced a resinous wax which is mixed with tallow to make candles **b :** CARNAUBA 1

wax paper *var of* WAXED PAPER

wax pine *n* **:** a tree of the genus *Agathis*

wax plant *n* **1 :** INDIAN PIPE **2 :** a cultivated twiner (*Hoya carnosa*) of Australia with glossy succulent leaves and umbels of pink and white star-shaped flowers **3 :** any of several begonias with shining foliage **4 :** WAX MYRTLE

wax pocket *n* **:** one of the cavities on the ventral abdominal surface into which wax is secreted by a honeybee

waxpod bean \'ₛ,ₛ-\ *n* **:** WAX BEAN

wax privet *n* **:** JAPANESE PRIVET b

wax process *n* **:** a method of making a foundry pattern in wax and using this pattern either as the master pattern or as a pattern for making the master pattern in white metal

wax red *n* **:** COPPER 5a

wax scale *n* **1 :** a scale that secretes wax — see FLORIDA WAX SCALE **2 :** one of the small flakes of wax secreted in a wax pocket of a honeybee

wax spray *n* **:** a spray or dip of melted paraffin, paraffin emulsion, or a similar material applied to plants in leaf to reduce transpiration after transplanting, to dormant shrubs ⟨as roses⟩ to prevent drying when on display or out of the ground for some other reason, and to cut flowers and root vegetables to prevent wilting

wax stone *n* **:** a lump of mixed earthy matter and mineral boiled in copper vats to separate the wax in the production of ozocerite

wax tablet *n* **:** a writing tablet of wood or bone covered with wax and written on with a style in ancient Roman and medieval times

wax tailings *n pl* **:** a dark-colored residue of former methods of petroleum distillation containing amorphous wax and formerly used in cracking and in waterproofing compositions

wax tree *n* **:** a tree yielding wax: as **a :** JAPANESE WAX TREE **b :** an arborescent evergreen privet (*Ligustrum lucidum*) of eastern Asia that is wholly glabrous, has dark green lustrous leaves and terminal panicles of white flowers, and is sometimes used in mild regions as a street tree **c :** a Chinese ash (*Fraxinus chinensis*) that is commonly encrusted with white wax by a wax insect (*Ericerus pe-la*) and is a major source of Chinese wax **d :** WAX MYRTLE

waxweed \'ₛ,ₛ\ *n* **:** a small purple-flowered herb (*Cuphea petiolata*) of eastern No. America having a viscid pubescence

wax white *n* **:** ¹WAX 5

waxwing \'ₛ,ₛ\ *n* **:** any of several American and Eurasian passerine birds of the genus *Bombycilla* that are chiefly brown with a showy crest and velvety plumage and secondaries that have small red waxlike tips — see BOHEMIAN WAXWING, CEDAR WAXWING; BIRD illustration

waxwork \'ₛ,ₛ\ *n* **1 a :** an effigy in wax usu. representing a person ⟨she sat so still that she might have been a ~ —Agatha Christie⟩ **b waxworks** *pl but sing or pl in constr* **:** an exhibition of wax effigies ⟨visited a ~s⟩ **2 :** BITTERSWEET 2b

wax worm *n* **:** a worm that is the larva of the bee moth

¹waxy \'waksē, -si\ *adj* -ER/-EST **1 a :** made of or resembling wax ⟨round and shiny as a ~ pippin —C.G.Glover⟩ **b :** soft or readily shaped like wax **:** IMPRESSIONABLE **c :** having the smoothness, luster, or whiteness of wax ⟨his thin face had a ~ pallor —Kenneth Roberts⟩ **d :** having a surface covered with wax or having the appearance of such a surface ⟨a ~ leaf⟩ **2 :** affected with amyloid degeneration

²waxy \"\ *adj* -ER/-EST [⁵*wax* + -*y*] **:** ANGRY, VEXED ⟨never does say very much unless he's downright ~ —Samuel Butler †1902⟩ ⟨it's quilts my wife gets ~ about —Bruce Marshall⟩

waxy cast *n* **:** a dense highly refractile urinary cast

waxy corn *n* **:** a Chinese variety of maize whose grains contain only branched-chain starch

waxy corn *or* **waxy maize** *n* **:** an Indian corn with grains that have a waxy appearance when cut, that contain only branched-chain starch, and that are used esp. for desserts and adhesives and as a replacement for tapioca

waxy degeneration *n* **:** AMYLOIDOSIS

waxy flexibility *n* **:** a condition in which a patient's limbs retain any position into which they are manipulated by another person and which occurs esp. in catatonic schizophrenia

¹way \'wā\ *n* -S [ME *way, wey,* fr. OE *weg:* akin to OHG *weg* way, ON *vegr,* Goth *wigs* way, OE *wegan* to move, L *vehere* to carry, Gk *ochein* to carry, *ochos* carriage, Skt *vahati* he carries, pulls] **1 a :** a thoroughfare used or designed for traveling or transportation from place to place **:** PATH, ROAD, STREET ⟨rough uneven ~s —Shak.⟩ ⟨the garagemen across the ~ —William Faulkner⟩ ⟨expressways or limited access ~s of the best modern type —S.J.Williams⟩ ⟨the Appian *Way*⟩ **b :** a band of light in the night sky resembling a road **c :** an opening for passing through ⟨this door is the only ~ into the room⟩ **d :** the roadway of a railroad ⟨permanent ~⟩ **2 :** that along which one passes to reach some place **:** the track traveled by a person or thing in his or its progress or passage **:** the course of travel from one place to another **:** ROUTE ⟨asked the ~ to the museum⟩ ⟨pupils will find their own ~ to school —*Deerfield (Wisc.) Independent*⟩ ⟨the ~ of a ship in the midst of the sea —Prov 30:19 (AV)⟩ ⟨in the streets the unfortunate foot traveler still picked his ~ through the muck —J.W.Krutch⟩ ⟨take a flashlight to light your ~ to the barn⟩ ⟨going your ~ and will be glad to give you a lift⟩ **3 a :** a nonspatial course ⟨as a series of actions or sequence of events⟩ leading in a stated or implied direction or toward a stated or implied objective ⟨cleared the ~ for a more purely rational interpretation of the world —M.F.A.Montagu⟩ ⟨smooth the ~ for statehood —*Current Biog.*⟩ ⟨his entering upon the ~ of salvation —Catherine Rau⟩ ⟨point the ~ to the discovery of new facts —F.A.Geldard⟩ **b (1) :** a course of action ⟨my best ~ is to creep under his gaberdine —Shak.⟩ ⟨take the easy ~ out⟩ **(2)** *obs* **:** the best or most desirable course of action ⟨it is our ~, if we will keep in favor with the King, to be her men and wear her livery —Shak.⟩ **(3) :** the opportunity, capability, or fact of doing as one pleases ⟨had made up his mind, and in the end he had his ~ —Ellen Glasgow⟩ ⟨for any one group to get its ~ —T.V.Smith⟩ ⟨gets the heroine alone in a bedroom and . . . has his ~ with her —*Time*⟩ ⟨time has its ~ with you —Vachel Lindsay⟩ ⟨a possible decision, action, or outcome **:** POSSIBILITY ⟨no ~ but this — killing myself, to die upon a kiss —Shak.⟩ ⟨there were no two ~s about it — this was the rudest, surliest, most ill-mannered town on the face of the earth —Hamilton Basso⟩ **4 a :** the mode in which something is done or happens **:** MANNER, METHOD, STYLE ⟨win him over to our ~ of thinking —A.J.Ayer⟩ ⟨various whose ~ of life seemed so different from that of our own people —Edward Sapir⟩ ⟨manipulate ideas in an original ~ —Vance Packard⟩ ⟨her ~ of doing her hair⟩ ⟨these two books, each admirable in its ~ —*Geog. Jour.*⟩ ⟨one's character is defined by the ~ in which the rules are embodied in one's behavior —Margaret Mead⟩ ⟨often used as the principal word in an adverbial phrase with no preposition ⟨the people who think this ~ —D.W.Brogan⟩ ⟨learn the full meaning of independence the hard ~ —Augusta Baker⟩; often used with and modified by an adjective clause containing no relative pronoun or other introductory word ⟨insight into the ~ the mind actually works —C.I.Glicksberg⟩ ⟨that's the ~ things go⟩ ⟨so that's the ~ you do it⟩ **b :** ASPECT, FEATURE, RESPECT, POINT — used as the principal word in an adverbial phrase with *in* as introductory preposition ⟨people who can in no ~ be classed as criminals —D.W.Maurer & V.H.Jeppel⟩ or sometimes with no preposition ⟨one student who is outstanding in scholarship, another who is outstanding in athletic ability, and a third who is outstanding both ~s⟩ **c :** the condition of being or acting on a specified state — used in phrases with *in* and an adjective ⟨real estate, a field of activity which he had entered in a small ~ —T.H.Jack⟩ ⟨the United States entered the international investment market in a substantial ~ —Frank Parker⟩ **d :** the usual or characteristic state of affairs — used with *with* ⟨he is very censorious, but then that is the ~ with reformed scoundrels ⟨as is the ~ with dreams, I took it to be a sort of personal and private message or communication —Walter de la Mare⟩ **e :** mode of existence as shown esp. by status, occupation, traits, or qualities **:** manner of occurrence — used with *the, this,* or *that* in phrases that contain no preposition

and that stand in predicative or modifying relation to the verb *be* or a few other verbs ⟨so attentive to other women that I have heard his wife ask him a dozen times not to be that ~⟩ ⟨it's too bad we can't offer you a job, but that's just the ~ things are⟩ ⟨what everyone wants to know about the president is how he got this ~ —G.W.Martin⟩ ⟨they themselves are flabby and smug, but they want to stay that ~ —*Time*⟩ ⟨business has been good and we're doing everything we can to keep it that ~ —*Item*⟩ ⟨well, Your Honor, it was this ~⟩ **5 a (1) :** a characteristic or habitual manner of acting ⟨justify the ~s of God to men —John Milton⟩ ⟨ignorant zealot though he was . . . he turned many from evil ~s —H.E.Starr⟩ ⟨it was the white man's ~ to assert himself in any landscape, to change it —Willa Cather⟩ ⟨knew nothing of the ~s of seafaring men —L.C.Douglas⟩ ⟨description of the ~ of nesting gannets —E.A.Armstrong⟩ **(2) :** an individual peculiarity **:** personal trait **:** IDIOSYNCRASY ⟨that's just his ~ and you shouldn't let it bother you⟩ ⟨a good fellow when you get used to his ~s⟩ **(3) :** an ingratiating or otherwise effective mode of behavior ⟨he has such a ~ with him that he makes lots of friends wherever he goes⟩ ⟨keen to show . . . what a ~ he had with him in this matter of tracking down seams —Gwyn Thomas⟩ **(4) :** a recognized practice, tendency, or quality ⟨great actresses have a ~ of scoring some of their most resounding successes in plays which are far from great —Peter Forster⟩ ⟨what seems impossible has a ~ of suddenly coming to you —Denis Johnston⟩ **(5) :** an endaring trick of behavior ⟨greatly captivated by the ~s of his host's children⟩ **(6) :** ability to get along well or to perform well ⟨his ~ with women and his extravagant habits made him many friends and much trouble —W.P.Webb⟩ ⟨had a ~ with animals —Oden Meeker⟩ ⟨has always had a ~ with metals —*Time*⟩ **b :** a regular continued course or mode of life, action, or existence ⟨thanks to their isolation these people go their own ~ in many things —Samuel Van Valkenburg & Ellsworth Huntington⟩ ⟨as the American ~ is made better known to the world —V.G.F. Reynolds⟩ ⟨came up against them in the ~ of business —Stuart Piggott⟩ **c (1) :** a course or mode of life set forth in terms of a standard to be maintained or of gradual difficult progress toward excellence in motivation and action usu. under religious sanctions **:** body of ethical practice esp. as taught by a religion ⟨not in one great Oriental religion only, the *Way* became a symbol of man's onward struggle and upward striving, of a journey towards a state of personal goodness and individual happiness —E.R.Pike⟩ ⟨the ~ to Christ⟩ **(2)** *often cap* **:** the Christian religion ⟨that if he found any belonging to the *Way,* men or women, he might bring them bound to Jerusalem —Acts 9:2 (RSV)⟩ **6 :** the length of a course traversed or to be traversed in space, time, range of possibilities, or progress toward a stated or implied objective **:** DISTANCE ⟨a house a little ~ out of town —Calvin Kentfield⟩ ⟨let me go back a little ~ and give you some background to this basic premise of our foreign policy —Dean Acheson⟩ ⟨transcended but a little ~ the region of commonplace —Thomas Carlyle⟩ ⟨not as capable as his brother by a long ~⟩ ⟨at a cost estimated all the ~ from one to two million dollars⟩ ⟨has come a long ~ in his knowledge of international geography —Gordon Walker⟩ ⟨this proposal should go a long ~ towards meeting another criticism —*Economist*⟩ **7 a :** movement or progress along a spatial or other course ⟨led the ~ into the heart of Chile's southern frontier —P.E.James⟩ ⟨led the ~ to unanimity —Beverly Smith⟩ ⟨held his ~ in spite of all obstacles⟩ ⟨forced his ~ through the crowd⟩ ⟨working his ~ through college⟩; *specif* **:** advancement in one's career ⟨when he had his ~ still to make —Osbert Sitwell⟩ **b :** an advance or progression accompanied by a specified action — used as the object of a verb that serves only to indicate what action accompanies the advance ⟨a white cat purring its ~ gracefully among the wine cups at a feast —Agnes Repplier⟩ ⟨barbarians who cough their ~ through concerts —Justina Hill⟩ **8 :** a method of attaining or accomplishing something **:** MEANS ⟨this delicious easy ~ of getting additional iron and calcium —*advt*⟩ ⟨a ~ to make a living —S.H.Adams⟩ ⟨~s of helping the aged to live out their declining years —A.W.Hummel⟩ ⟨the attack was made, not in the ~ of storm —T.B.Macaulay⟩ — sometimes used as the principal word in an adverbial phrase with no preposition ⟨thought he could win the game that ~⟩ **9 a :** a direction of motion, facing, pointing, or nonspatial advance or tendency — often used as the principal word in an adverbial or adjectival phrase with no preposition ⟨is coming this ~⟩ ⟨turn your head the other ~⟩ ⟨shift his expectation one ~ or another —Margaret Mead⟩ ⟨the money was divided three ~s⟩ ⟨with no glance . . . her ~ —Amy Lowell⟩ ⟨how its decision can go any other ~ —*Commonweal*⟩ ⟨either there is a valid contract or there is not; you cannot have it both ~s⟩ ⟨an honest answer one ~ or the other —M.R.Cohen⟩ ⟨hard to make a very conclusive case either ~ —Bruce Payne⟩ ⟨sometimes a noun is derived from a verb and sometimes it is the other ~ around⟩ **b :** a part of a town, city, country, or the world **:** LOCALITY, DISTRICT, NEIGHBORHOOD, VICINITY — used with a preceding possessive adjective or place-name which in turn is sometimes preceded by a preposition ⟨great explosions coming from Dunkirk ~ —P.W.Thompson⟩ or by no directional word at all ⟨but just rented a tidy-sized farm Shorwell ~ —J.B.Priestley⟩ but most frequently by a directional adverb ⟨the weather has been good out our ~⟩ ⟨that little old college down Cambridge ~ —Jean Stafford⟩ **c (1) :** a direction with reference to the lie of the natural growth ⟨as hair or feathers⟩ ⟨stroking the cat's fur the wrong ~⟩ **(2) :** ¹GRAIN 6d ⟨cut cloth the ~ of the goods instead of on the bias⟩ **d (1) :** one of the lines terminating at a hydraulic or other valve — often used in attributive noun compounds with a numeral as first constituent ⟨a four-*way* valve⟩ **(2) :** one of the operating positions of an electric switch — used in attributive noun compounds with a numeral as first constituent ⟨a three-*way* switch⟩ **e :** participating party **:** PARTICIPANT — used in attributive noun compounds with a numeral as first constituent ⟨a three-*way* discussion⟩ **10 a :** condition esp. with regard to health, prosperity, or future prospects ⟨if the people cannot depend upon the promises of their president they are in a bad ~ —J.P.Warburg⟩ ⟨been very ill this week . . . and though now in a ~ to be well, am like to be confined some days longer —Thomas Gray⟩ ⟨the state was in a fair ~ to get a new instrument of government —*Nation*⟩ ⟨would have put himself in a fair ~ of getting shot —Charles Dickens⟩ ⟨put him in the ~ of another chance —Hamilton Basso⟩ ⟨if anyone were in the ~ of getting information —F.Tennyson Jesse⟩ **b** *Brit* **:** a state of mind; *esp* **:** a condition of abnormal nervous tension or excitement ⟨she was quite in a ~ —Arnold Bennett⟩ **11 a :** room to advance, pass, or progress **:** opportunity to proceed ⟨give ~⟩ ⟨make ~⟩ **b :** freedom of action or opportunity ⟨let me have ~ . . . to find this practice out —Shak.⟩ **c :** a place or position to be occupied by someone else or something else — used as object of *make* ⟨several one-family houses torn down to make ~ for an apartment house⟩ **12 :** scope or range of observation, experience, or possible acquisition ⟨intrigues with low women that fell in my ~ —Benjamin Franklin⟩ **13 a ways** *pl but sometimes sing in constr* **:** an inclined structure usu. of timber upon which a ship is built or upon which a ship is supported in launching ⟨the ~s are either of yellow or pitch pine —A.C.Holms⟩ ⟨owned three steamboats, . . . a marine ~s, and several landing fleets —Frederick Way⟩ ⟨all American flag shipping, afloat or on the ~s —*N. Y. Herald Tribune*⟩ — compare BILGE WAYS, DOGSHORE, GROUND WAYS, SLIDING WAYS **b ways** *pl* **:** the longitudinal guides or guiding surfaces on the bed of a machine ⟨as a planer or lathe⟩ along which a table or carriage moves **c :** a structure or member of a set of structures designed to guide the movement of an object along a strictly determined path ⟨stainless steel weatherstripping . . . serves as sash ~ for both upper and lower sash —*Sweet's Catalog Service*⟩ **14 :** a group with common features **:** CATEGORY, KIND, DESCRIPTION — usu. used in a prepositional phrase introduced by *in* ⟨has little in the ~ of financial resources —L.M. Chamberlain⟩ ⟨everything you need in the ~ of vitamins —Gregor Felsen⟩ ⟨have picked up one or two gems in the antique ~ —H.J.Laski⟩ ⟨in the ~ of compensation, he was allowed a pension —James Mill⟩ **15 a :** the motion or speed of a ship or boat through the water ⟨a ship on starting gathers ~⟩ ⟨when actually moving through the water, a vessel has ~ on her; if moving too fast she is said to have too much ~ on

—*Manual of Seamanship*⟩ **b :** the motion or speed of something or someone traveling otherwise than through water ⟨the pavement was on a slight incline, the perambulator had a little ~ on it, and the whole force of the wind behind —J.D. Beresford⟩ **16 :** a line of business or of professional activity **17 :** RIGHT-OF-WAY 1,2 **18** *dial Brit* **:** REASON, CAUSE **19** *usu cap* **:** a Navaho ceremonial rite that consists largely of chants and dances and is performed for protection against various ill effects and assurance of general well-being and good fortune ⟨Red Ant *Way*⟩ ⟨Mountain Top *Way*⟩

syn WAY, ROUTE, COURSE, PASSAGE, PASS, ARTERY mean, in common, a track or path traversed in going from one place to another. WAY is general and inclusive of any track or path, often figurative, specif. signifying a road in combinations or special phrases ⟨rail*way*⟩ ⟨high*way*⟩ ⟨the only other village was one day's mule trip farther into the interior, but the *way* was so steep and slippery in places that we walked almost as much as we rode —C.B.Hitchcock⟩ ⟨the water continues its *way* down the valley for 5 kilometers —N.R.Heiden⟩ ⟨the *way* was now open for the final act —W.C.Ford⟩ ROUTE signifies a way, often circuitous, followed with regularity by a person or animal or laid out to be followed as by a tourist or army ⟨a paper *route*⟩ ⟨a milk truck following a morning delivery *route*⟩ ⟨the dog team trails and canoe *routes* of trader, trapper and missionary in the bush country —W.J.Granberg⟩ ⟨a much traveled main *route* from Boston to Albany⟩ COURSE is often interchangeable with ROUTE but more often implies a path followed by or as if by a stream, star, or other moving natural object impelled by or in a path determined by natural forces ⟨the *course* of a river⟩ ⟨a meteor's *course*⟩ ⟨a ship's *course*⟩ ⟨the *course* of the seasons⟩ or a predetermined or more or less compulsory way or route followed in human activities or enterprises ⟨a *course* of study for an academic degree⟩ ⟨a golf *course*⟩ ⟨a race*course*⟩ PASSAGE stresses a crossing over or a passing through, often designating the thing passed through, usu. something narrow where transit might be restricted ⟨a rough *passage* to America by boat⟩ ⟨a narrow *passage* from kitchen to basement⟩ ⟨restrict the *passage* into the stomach⟩ PASS usu. designates a passage through or over something that presents an obstacle (as a mountain or river) ⟨a narrow *pass* over the Alps⟩ ⟨a shallow ford constituted the only *pass* across the river⟩ ARTERY is applied to one of the great continuous traffic channels (as a great central rail route, river, or highway) from which branch off smaller or shorter channels ⟨the Congo river would remain the main traffic *artery* —G.G.Weigend⟩ ⟨the main *artery* between Buffalo and Niagara Falls —*Retailing Daily*⟩ ⟨the need for improvement of main *arteries* interconnecting cities and for express highways in cities —*Britannica Bk. of the Yr.*⟩ **syn** see in addition METHOD

— all the way *also* **the whole way** *adv* **1 :** as far as possible ⟨a resolute attempt to go *the whole way* in the direction of complete analysis —A.N.Whitehead⟩ **2 :** from the beginning to the end or to this point ⟨it has been New Hampshire, New Hampshire with me *all the way* —Robert Frost⟩ ⟨stays in the game *all the way* —J.W.Rouse⟩ **3 :** so far as complete agreement or compliance ⟨can't go *the whole way* with the book —Louis Kronenberger⟩ ⟨went *all the way* for Moscow —*Time*⟩ **4 :** so far as not to stop short of sexual intercourse ⟨she went *all the way* with him⟩ **— by way of** *prep* **1 :** by the agency of **:** through the medium of ⟨master workmen may receive instructions *by way of* drafts, models, frames —B.G.Gerbier⟩ **2 :** as an instance or example of **:** for the purpose of ⟨*by way of* illustration⟩ **3 :** by the route that passes through **:** VIA ⟨drove home *by way of* the mountains⟩ **4 a :** in the habit of — used with a following gerund ⟨was *by way of* being particular about his appearance —Cicely F. Smith⟩ **b :** in the state of — used with a following gerund ⟨is *by way of* doing better work now than formerly⟩ **— each way** *Brit, of a bet on a racehorse* **:** to win or to place **— go out of one's way :** to take special pains **:** act with or as if with a deliberate purpose ⟨*went out of his way* to stimulate consumption while retaining strict curbs on investment —*New Statesman & Nation*⟩ ⟨could have deceived only those who *went out of their way* to be deceived —R.D.Altick⟩ **— go the way of :** to pass out of existence or into a declining state like ⟨is Christian civilization *going the way of* the Roman Empire —*Time*⟩ **— have everything one's own way** *or* **have it all one's own way :** to carry out one's plans without effective opposition ⟨the victorious invaders *had everything their own way*⟩ **— hold way** *or* **keep way** *obs* **:** to keep pace **— in a big way :** emphatically so **:** THOROUGHLY, ENTHUSIASTICALLY **— in a way** *adv* **1** *also* **in a kind of way** *or* **in a sort of way :** within limits **:** with reservations ⟨I like the new arrangement, *in a way*⟩ **2 :** from one point of view ⟨*in a way*, elementary schooling is more important than secondary schooling⟩ **— in one's way** *also* **in the way 1 :** on or along one's path, road, or course **:** in a position to be encountered by one ⟨an opportunity had been put *in my way* —Ellen Glasgow⟩ **2** *obs* **:** while traveling or proceeding **:** in the course of one's journey **3 :** in such a position as to obstruct or hinder **:** constituting an obstruction, obstacle, or encumbrance ⟨trees were unhesitatingly cut down if they were *in the way* —David Fairchild⟩ ⟨knowledge unused is like dead lumber, constantly *in our way* —T.V.Smith⟩ ⟨let a mere fact stand *in the way* of a good idea —Arthur Knight⟩ **4** *in the way, Brit* **:** at hand **:** within reach **:** PRESENT ⟨I was not *in the way* at first, and knew nothing of it —Jane Austen⟩ **5** *obs* **:** constituting or involving a gain on one's part ⟨it might have been thousands *in my way* had I continued my business —Mathew Bishop⟩ **— make the best of one's way** *Brit* **:** to go as quickly as possible **— one's way around** *also* **one's way about 1 :** the details and procedures with which familiarity is needed ⟨soon learned *his way around*⟩ ⟨knows *his way about*⟩ **2 :** the modes of behavior needed for successful functioning in ⟨knew *his way around* Washington⟩ **— on the way** *or* **on one's way :** moving along one's course **:** in progress **:** COMING, GOING, ADVANCING **— out of the way** *or* **out of one's way 1 a :** out of or outside of the proper course of action **:** in the wrong **:** out of place **b :** WRONG, AMISS, IMPROPER ⟨oblivious of having said anything *out of the way* —Gilbert Parker⟩ **2 a :** off the beaten track **:** hard to reach or find **:** in or to a secluded place **:** some distance away **b :** UNUSUAL, REMARKABLE ⟨met nothing more *out of the way* than a cow eating and an old man walking —Virginia Woolf⟩ **3 :** off the course one is following or intends to follow ⟨this town is fifty miles *out of his way*⟩ ⟨such a digression would take us too far *out of our way*⟩ **4 a :** in or into such a position as not to obstruct ⟨I'll move my car *out of your way* so that you can pull out of the driveway⟩ **:** in or into a condition of having been already dealt with or accomplished ⟨after the months of preparatory work are *out of the way* —*Amer. Fabrics*⟩ **b :** in or into such a position as not to be run over or collided with ⟨before your father backs the car out of the garage, get your doll *out of the way*⟩ **:** out of the path of a dangerous advance ⟨get *out of the way* of the train⟩ ⟨*out of* harm's *way*⟩ **5** *out of one's way, Brit* **:** outside one's field of activity or interest **:** not in one's line **6** *obs* **:** not in the usual or proper place **:** LOST, MISLAID **7** *out of one's way, obs* **:** constituting or involving a loss on one's part ⟨it may be ten pounds *out of my way* to be turned out of my work —John Nelson⟩ **— the way 1** *Irish* **:** in such a way that ⟨they soldered the bottom of a tin dish to the top of his skull *the way* you could hear his brains ticking inside —James Stephens⟩ **2** *Irish* **:** in order that ⟨it's only letting on you are to be lonesome, *the way* you'd get around me now —J.M. Synge⟩ **3 :** in view of the manner in which ⟨you'd think we were millionaires, *the way* we have to finance this department —Dorothy Sayers⟩ **— the way of all flesh 1** *also* **the way of all the earth :** the course or passage from life to death ⟨the days of David drew nigh that he should die, and he charged his son Solomon, saying: I am going *the way of all flesh* —3 Kings 2:1–2 (DV)⟩ ⟨this day I am going *the way of all the earth* —Jos 23:14 (AV)⟩ **2 :** the common experience of all mankind **— under way** *adv* **1** *of a ship or boat* **a :** in motion through the water **b :** not at anchor **:** not made fast to the shore **:** not aground **2 :** in motion along a course **:** in progress **:** on the way

²way *vt* -ED/-ING/-S *obs* **:** to break or train (a horse) to the road

³way \ˈwā\ *adj* **:** of, connected with, or constituting an intermediate point on the route from one place to another

⁴way \"\ *adv* [ME, short for *away, on way* — more at AWAY] **1** *chiefly dial* **:** ¹AWAY 2 ⟨go ~⟩ **2 a :** ¹AWAY 7 ⟨sleeves that dangle ~ below the tips of the fingers —Lois Long⟩ ⟨forging ~ ahead in education —J.T.Farrell⟩ **b** *chiefly dial* **:** all the way **:** ²CLEAR c ⟨pull the switch ~ back⟩ **c** *dial* **:** EXTREMELY ⟨till ~ late in the morning —Mary S. Watts⟩ **— from way back 1 :** from an out-of-the-way rural locality **2 :** from a time far in the past **:** of long standing ⟨friends *from way back*⟩ **3 :** of the most thoroughgoing or expert kind ⟨a deadbeat *from way back*⟩ ⟨an artist *from way back* —Mark Twain⟩

⁵way \"\ *v imper* [prob. alter. of *whoa*] *dial Brit* — used as a command to a team or draft animal to stop

-way \ˌwā\ *adv suffix* [ME, fr. ¹*way*] **:** in (such) a way, course, direction, or manner ⟨broad*way*⟩ ⟨lyra*way*⟩

way and structures *n pl* **:** the fixed facilities of a railroad including the track and structures needed for its operation

wa·yang *also* **wa·jang** \ˈwä,yäŋ\ *n* -S [Jav *wayang*, lit., shadow] **:** an Indonesian and esp. Javanese dramatic representation of mythological events in a puppet shadow play or by human dancers

¹wayback \ˈ⸗,⸗\ *adj* [fr. the phrase (*from*) *way back*] **:** of, relating to, or situated in the backcountry

²wayback \"\ *n, dial* **:** RUSTIC, YOKEL

waybeam \ˈ⸗,⸗\ *n* **:** a beam supporting a way; *specif* **:** either of two longitudinal beams resting on transverse girders and supporting the rails of a road crossing a bridge

way bennet *or* **way bent** *n* **:** WALL BARLEY

¹waybill \ˈ⸗,⸗\ *n* [¹*way* + *bill*] **1 :** a list of passengers in a public vehicle **2 :** an itinerary prepared for a traveler **3 :** a document that is prepared by the carrier (as a railroad company) transporting a shipment of goods, that contains such information as the nature of the shipment, the name of its consignor and consignee, its origin, route, destination, and the charges paid, and that serves as a means of identification, a guide for routing, and a basis for freight accounting and almost all other carrier records and statistics

²waybill \"\ *vt* -ED/-ING/-S **:** to enter in a waybill **:** send accompanied by a waybill

way-bit *n* [alter. (influenced by ¹*way*) of northern dial. phrase *wee bit* little] *obs* **:** a little distance

way·bread \ˈwā,bred\ *n* [ME *weybrede*, fr. OE *wegbrǣde*; akin to MD *wegebrede* broad-leaved plantain, OHG *wegabreita*; all fr. a prehistoric WGmc compound whose first constituent is represented by OE *weg* way and whose second constituent is akin to OE *brād* broad; fr. its broad leaves and the fact that it frequently grows by the wayside — more at WAY, BROAD] *Brit* **:** BROAD-LEAVED PLANTAIN 1

way car *n* **1 :** ¹CABOOSE 3 **2 :** a freight car used to transport less-than-carload shipments to way stations

way chain *n, Brit* **:** a clog or brake for the wheel of a vehicle

¹wayed \ˈwād\ *adj* [ME, fr. ¹*way* + *-ed*] **:** having such a way or such or so many ways — used in combination ⟨wide-*wayed*⟩

²wayed *past of* WAY

¹way·fare \ˈwā,fa(a)(ə)r, -,fe(, |ə\ *n* [ME, fr. ¹*way* + *fare*, n.] **1** *archaic* **:** an act or course of journeying **2** *obs* **:** money or provisions for a journey

²wayfare \"\ *vi* -ED/-ING/-S **:** JOURNEY, TRAVEL

way·far·er \-,fa(a)rə(r), -,fer-\ *n* -S [ME *weyfarere*, fr. *wey* way + *-farere* traveler, fr. *faren* to go, travel + *-ere* -er — more at FARE] **1 :** a traveler esp. on foot **2 :** a transient patron of an inn or hotel

way·far·ing \-riŋ, -rēŋ\ *adj* [ME *wayfaringe*, alter. (influenced by *-inge* ³-ing) of *wayfarende*, fr. OE *wegfarende*, fr. *weg* way + *farende*, pres. part. of *faran* to go — more at WAY, FARE] **:** traveling esp. on foot **:** being on a journey **:** PASSING

wayfaring tree *n* **1 :** a Eurasian shrub (*Viburnum lantana*) that has large ovate leaves and dense cymes of small white flowers and is common along waysides **2 :** HOBBLEBUSH

way freight *n* **1 :** freight for a way station **2 :** a freight train stopping to put off goods at way stations

waygang \ˈ⸗,⸗\ *n* [⁴*way* + *gang*, n.] *Scot* **:** the act of leaving **:** DEPARTURE

¹waygate *n* [⁴*way* + *gate* (journey, way)] *obs* **:** the act of leaving **:** DEPARTURE

²waygate \ˈ⸗,⸗\ *n* [¹*way* + *gate* (journey, way)] *Brit* **:** PATH, PASSAGEWAY

¹waygoing \ˈ⸗,⸗⸗\ *n* [⁴*way* + *going*] *chiefly Scot* **:** the act of leaving **:** DEPARTURE

²waygoing \"\ *adj* **1** *chiefly Scot* **:** going away **:** DEPARTING **2** *Brit* **:** of or relating to one that goes away

waygoing crop *n* **:** AWAY-GOING CROP

way·goose \ˈwā,güs\ *n, pl* **waygooses** [origin unknown] *dial Eng* **:** WAYZGOOSE

waying *pres part of* WAY

waylay \(ˈ)⸗;⸗\ *vt* **waylaid; waylaid; waylaying; waylays** [¹*way* + *lay*] **1 a :** to lie in wait for **:** attack from ambush ⟨another band . . . waiting there to ~ him —S.H.Adams⟩ ⟨many a family coach was *waylaid* and its occupants robbed —F.W.Burgess⟩ **b :** to take possession of (something in transit) from or as if from ambush **:** INTERCEPT **c :** to stop (someone) for the purpose of conversation ⟨on the way out a group of seniors *waylaid* the president and asked if something couldn't be done about one of the boys who could not graduate —Josephine Y. Case⟩ **d :** to defeat or overwhelm as if by a surprise attack ⟨the 1930's, when social need once more *waylaid* the masses of Americans —Louis Filler⟩ ⟨I am *waylaid* by beauty —Edna S. V. Millay⟩ **2 :** to beset (as a passageway) with a force capable of attacking whoever approaches **3** *obs* **:** to check the course of **:** OBSTRUCT, BLOCK

wayleave \ˈ⸗,⸗\ *n* [ME *wayleve*, fr. ¹*way* + *leve* leave] **1 :** an easement consisting of permission to cross land or of a right-of-way across land **2** *or* **wayleave rent :** the rent paid for a wayleave

way·less \ˈwāləs\ *adj* [ME *wayles, weyles*, fr. OE *weglēas*, fr. *weg* way + *-lēas* -less] **:** having no road or path

way mail *n* **1 :** mail picked up or left off at a way station **2 :** mail given to a mail carrier en route from one post office to another

waymaker \ˈ⸗,⸗⸗\ *n* [ME *way maker*] **1 :** one that makes a road; *specif* **:** an English royal official of the 16th and early 17th centuries with the duty of keeping the highways in good repair **2** *obs* **:** PRECURSOR

way·man \ˈwāmən\ *n, pl* **waymen 1 :** a railroad laborer employed in laying or keeping in repair the tracks **2 :** a shipwright that prepares and lays launching ways

waymark \ˈ⸗,⸗\ *n* **:** an object serving as a guide to someone traveling

way·ment \ˈwāmənt\ *vi* -ED/-ING/-S [ME *waymenten*, fr. ONF *waimenter*, fr. *wai*, interj., woe (of Gmc origin; akin to Goth *wai*, interj., woe) + OF *menter* (as in *lamenter* to lament) — more at WOE, LAMENT] *archaic* **:** LAMENT, GRIEVE

way-off \ˈ⸗;⸗\ *adj* [fr. the adverbial phrase *way off*] *dial* **:** FAR-OFF 1

way of necessity : a right-of-way that arises from necessity (as when one buys land accessible only over other lands of the vendor) and terminates when the necessity ceases

way of the cross *usu cap W&C* **1 :** STATIONS OF THE CROSS **2 :** the course taken in visiting in succession the stations of the cross

way of the wine : the left-to-right direction in which wine is passed at table

way passenger *n* **:** a passenger getting on or off at a way station or other intermediate point on a line of travel

way point *n* **:** an intermediate point on a route or line of travel; *esp* **:** WAY STATION

waypost \ˈ⸗,⸗\ *n* **:** GUIDEPOST 1

wayrod \ˈ⸗,⸗\ *n* [¹*way* + *rod*] **:** the carriage rod of a typewriter

¹ways *pl of* WAY, *pres 3d sing of* WAY

²ways \ˈwāz\ *n pl but sing in constr* [ME *wayes*, fr. *wayes*, gen. of ¹*way*] **1 :** WAY 9a ⟨come a little nearer this ~ —Shak.⟩ **2 :** WAY 6 ⟨a long ~ from home⟩ ⟨went a good ~⟩

-ways \ˌwāz\ *adv suffix* [ME *-ways, -weys*, fr. *wayes, weyes*, gen. of *way, wey* way — more at WAY] **:** in (such) a way, course, direction, or manner ⟨side*ways*⟩ ⟨bar*ways*⟩

ways and means *n pl* [ME *weys and menes, weyes and meanes*] **1 :** methods and resources for accomplishing something and esp. for defraying expenses **2 a** *often cap W&M* **:** methods and resources for raising the necessary revenues for the expenses of a political unit (as a nation or state) **b** *often cap W&M* **:** a legislative committee concerned with this function ⟨the chairman of *Ways and Means* was formerly appointed at the beginning of a new Parliament —T.E.May⟩ ⟨the *Ways and Means* made its first formal proposals on tax legislation for the current session of Congress —*N.Y.Times*⟩

¹way shaft *n, Brit* **:** ¹WINZE

²way shaft *n* [alter. of *weighshaft*] **:** ¹ROCKSHAFT

¹wayside \ˈ⸗,⸗\ *n* [ME] **:** the side of a road or path **:** land adjacent to a road or path ⟨cornfields along the ~⟩ ⟨many former advocates of this policy have fallen by the ~⟩

²wayside \"\ *adj* **:** of, connected with, or situated at the side of a road or path ⟨~ flowers⟩; *specif* **:** situated adjacent to a highway so as to be accessible to motorists ⟨~ restaurants⟩

wayside cross *n* **:** a cross set up along a road or path as a place for the devotions of passersby

wayside pulpit *n* **:** an outdoor bulletin board used by a church for posting pointed and provocative messages before passersby

way station *n* **:** an intermediate station between principal stations on a line of travel esp. on a railroad **:** local station

way-stop \ˈ⸗,⸗\ *n* **:** an intermediate stop on a line of travel

waythorn \ˈ⸗,⸗\ *n* **:** a common buckthorn (*Rhamnus cathartica*) of Eurasia

way traffic *n* **:** traffic involving way stations **:** local traffic

way train *n* **:** a train that stops at way stations **:** accommodation train for passengers

way·ward \ˈwāwə(r)d\ *adj* [ME *wayward, weyward*, short for *awayward, aweyward* turned away, fr. *away, awey*, adv., away + *-ward* — more at AWAY] **1 :** characterized by extreme willfulness and by determination to follow one's own capricious, wanton, or depraved inclinations to the point of being ungovernable ⟨the ~ child who persists in wandering away —A.R.Mead⟩ ⟨the glamorous sin . . . associated with what is known as ~ passion —*Tomorrow*⟩ ⟨the ~ power of the emotionally excited masses —Vernon Mallinson⟩ **2 :** following no clear principle or law **:** UNPREDICTABLE, ERRATIC ⟨there was no room in that precision for the eccentricity, the ~ act —Graham Greene⟩ **3 :** opposite to what is desired or expected **:** UNTOWARD, VEXING ⟨~ fate⟩ **syn** see CONTRARY

wayward child *or* **wayward minor** *n* **:** a child having a status arbitrarily defined by statute in some states, usu. being under a stated age, habitually associating with vicious or immoral persons, or growing up in circumstances likely to cause him to commit crimes or be willfully disobedient of parental or other lawful authority and therefore become subject to custodial care and protection for his own welfare — compare JUVENILE DELINQUENT, STUBBORN CHILD

waywarden \ˈ⸗,⸗⸗\ *n* [¹*way* + *warden*] **1 :** a supervisor of highways esp. as an elected member of a board **2** *Brit* **:** one that maintains the trenches of a sewage disposal plant

way·ward·ly *adv* [ME *weywardly*, fr. *weyward* wayward + *-ly*] **:** in a wayward manner

way·ward·ness *n* -ES [ME *weywardnesse*, fr. *weyward* wayward + *-nesse* -ness] **:** the quality or state of being wayward

way-wise \ˈ⸗,⸗\ *adj* **1** *of a horse* **:** well broken esp. for use on the road or on a racetrack **2** *dial* **:** EXPERIENCED

way·wis·er \ˈwā,wīzə(r)\ *n* -S [part trans. of D *wegwijzer* guide, signpost, waywiser, lit., one that shows the way, fr. *weg* way + *wijzer* one that shows, fr. MD *wiser*, fr. *wisen* to show; akin to MD *wijs* wise, OE *wīs* — more at WISE] **:** an instrument (as an odometer or pedometer) for measuring the distance traversed by a walker, vehicle, or ship

way·wode \ˈwā,wōd\ *n* -S [by alter.] **:** VAIVODE

wayworn \ˈ⸗,⸗\ *adj* **:** wearied by traveling

waywort \ˈ⸗,⸗\ *n* [ME *waywurt*, fr. ¹*way* + *wurt* wort; fr. its prevalence along roads] **:** ¹SCARLET PIMPERNEL

wayz·goose \ˈwāz,güs\ *n, pl* **wayzgooses** [alter. of *waygoose*] **:** a printers' annual outing or entertainment

¹wa·zir \wəˈzi(ə)r\ *n* -S [Ar *wazīr* — more at VIZIER] **:** VIZIER

²wazir \"\ *or* **wa·ziri** \-irē\ *n, pl* **wazir** *or* **wazirs** *or* **waziri** *or* **waziris** *usu cap* **:** a member of a Pathan people inhabiting Waziristan in northwestern West Pakistan

wb *abbr* weber

WB *abbr* **1** wallboard **2** warehouse book **3** *often not cap* water ballast **4** water board **5** waybill **6** weather bureau **7** westbound **8** wet bulb **9** wheelbase

WBC *abbr* white blood cells; white blood count

WBS *abbr, often not cap* without benefit of salvage

WC *abbr* **1** water closet **2** west central **3** will call **4** without charge **5** wood casing **6** working capital

w chromosome *n, usu cap W* **:** a sex chromosome of the kind distinctively characteristic of the female in organisms (as moths) in which the female has two kinds of sex chromosomes — compare Z CHROMOSOME

wd *abbr* **1** weed **2** wind **3** window **4** wood **5** word **6** would **7** wound

WD *abbr* **1** war damage **2** war department **3** works department

wdg *abbr* **1** winding **2** wording

wdr *abbr* wider

wdt *abbr* width

¹we \(ˈ)wē, ˌwi, *before* "re" *or* "are" *usu* (ˌ)wi\ *pron, pl in constr* [ME, fr. OE *wē*; akin to OHG *wir* we, ON *vēr*, Goth *weis*, Skt *vayam*] **1 a :** I and the rest of a group that includes me **:** you and I **:** you and I and another or others **:** I and another or others not including you — used as a nominative pronoun of the first person plural as the subject of a verb ⟨~ live here⟩ ⟨~ the people of the United States . . . do ordain and establish this constitution —*U.S.Constitution*⟩ or in the predicate after a copulative verb ⟨it is ~ who are the virtuous ones —Vance Packard⟩ or in comparisons after *than* or *as* when the first term in the comparison is a subject ⟨you know as much about it as ~⟩ or in some absolute constructions ⟨ignorant, you say? ~?⟩ or after *but* in a compound subject ⟨none but ~ may say this⟩; used archaically as subject of an immediately preceding verb to introduce a request or proposal made by the speaker or writer to the group that includes himself where the current construction in ordinary present-day English consists of *let us* or *let's* followed by the verb ⟨prepare ~ for our marriage —Shak.⟩; see OUR, US; compare I, OURS **b :** people in general including the speaker or writer ⟨when ~ mind labor, then only, we're too old —Robert Browning⟩ **2 :** ²I 1 — used by kings and other sovereigns ⟨our sometime sister, now our queen, . . . have ~ . . . taken to wife —Shak.⟩; used by editors and other writers to keep an impersonal character or to avoid the egotistical sound of a repeated *I* **3 a** *dial chiefly Eng* **:** US — used emphatically as object of a verb or preposition ⟨to poor ~ thine enmity's most capital —Shak.⟩ ⟨the likes of ~⟩ **b** *chiefly substand* **:** US — used in a compound object or in apposition with a following noun ⟨he disturbed those in the dining room, those in the hall, and even ~ who had retired upstairs⟩ ⟨as to ~ men —Fanny Burney⟩ **4 :** YOU — used coaxingly (as to a child) ⟨~ don't want to wake Daddy, do ~⟩ or encouragingly (as to a patient) ⟨how are ~ feeling this morning⟩ or in sarcasm ⟨aren't ~ getting a little impudent⟩

²we \ˈwē\ *n* -S **:** a group that is consciously felt as such by its members ⟨the crowd is like a community in that it can be any size, the difference being that the *We* precedes the I —Howard Griffin⟩

¹wea \ˈweə\ *dial var of* WOE

²wea \ˈwäə\ *n, pl* **wea** *or* **weas** *usu cap* **1 a :** an Indian people of Indiana associated with the Miami **b :** a member of such people **2 :** the language of the Wea people

wea *abbr* weather

we-adar *usu cap W&A, var of* VEADAR

¹weak \ˈwēk\ *adj* -ER/-EST [ME *waike, weike, weke*, fr. ON *veikr*; akin to OE *wāc* pliant, soft, weak, OHG *weih* yielding, soft, OE *wīcan* to yield, give way, OHG *wīhhan*, ON *vīkja* to move, turn, recede — more at WEEK] **1 :** lacking strength **:** not strong: as **a :** deficient in strength of body ⟨~ with hunger⟩ ⟨sick man welcomed him as eagerly as his ~ state permitted —Charles Reade⟩ **b :** not able to sustain or exert much weight, pressure, or strain **:** having small capability of exerting or resisting force ⟨~ rope⟩ ⟨~ joint in a chair⟩ ⟨red planet possesses only a ~ gravity —J.G.Vaeth⟩ ⟨~ ignition spark⟩ **c :** not able to resist external force or withstand attack **:** easily subdued or overcome ⟨even if the ~ witness tells the truth he is a slender reed —L.P.Stryker⟩ **d :** readily subject to failure, collapse, or breakdown ⟨~ heart⟩ ⟨~ nerves⟩ **2 a :** mentally or intellectually deficient **:** lacking judgment or discernment ⟨a superstition imposing only on ~ intellects⟩ **b :** not having full conviction **:** not firmly decided **:** WAVERING, VACILLATING ⟨realize how ~ the love of truth is in the majority —W.R.

Inge⟩ **c** : resulting from or indicating lack of judgment, discernment, or firmness : UNWISE, FOOLISH ⟨not generosity but mere ~ indulgence⟩ **d** : not able to withstand temptation or persuasion : easily impressed or swayed ⟨~ virtue⟩ ⟨~ determination⟩ ⟨men are so ~ and women so unscrupulous —W.S.Maugham⟩ **3** : not having power to convince : not supported by force of truth or logic ⟨~ argument⟩ ⟨~ case at law⟩ **4 a** : lacking in power to perform properly a function or office ⟨~ eyes⟩ ⟨~ sense of direction⟩ **b** : lacking skill or proficiency ⟨a good fielder but a ~ batter⟩ ⟨special tutoring for the ~*er* students⟩ **c** : showing or indicating a lack of skill or aptitude ⟨mathematics was his ~*est* subject⟩ ⟨his penetration of human psychology and his creation of character is ~ —R.A.Hall b. 1911⟩ **d** : wanting in vigor of expression or artistic effect ⟨~ line⟩ ⟨~ retort⟩ ⟨a painfully ~ story apparently meant to be fantasy —Raymond Walters b. 1912⟩ **5** : lacking force of utterance or sound : not sonorous : FAINT ⟨sick man spoke in a ~ voice⟩ ⟨~ protest⟩ **6 a** : not thoroughly or abundantly impregnated with the usual or required ingredients : DILUTE ⟨~ coffee⟩ ⟨~ acid solution⟩ **b** : lacking normal intensity or potency ⟨~ colors⟩ ⟨~ strain of virus⟩ ⟨~ winter sunlight⟩ **c** : lacking contrast : THIN ⟨~ photographic negative⟩ **d** *of flour* : made from a soft wheat and containing a relatively low percentage of gluten and lacking cohesiveness — opposed to *strong* **7 a** : not having or exerting authority or political power ⟨~ king⟩ ⟨~ government⟩ **b** : not equal to the need or emergency : INEFFECTIVE, IMPOTENT ⟨~ attempts at resistance⟩ ⟨~ measures to control crime⟩ **8 a** *of a verb* : belonging to a conjugation that forms the past tense and past participle by adding the suffix *-ed* or *-d* or *-t* (as *dash, dashed; grate, grated; deal, dealt*) : REGULAR — opposed to *strong* **b** *of a noun or adjective declension* : having the less full case inflection characteristic of Proto-Germanic stems in *-n* (as Old English *oxa, oxan;* German *ochs, ochsen*) — opposed to *strong* **c** : of or relating to a class of Hebrew or Syriac consonants or to a verb having one or more such consonants in the root **9 a** : bearing the minimal degree of stress occurring in the language : LIGHT ⟨~ syllable⟩ ⟨~ stress⟩ **b** : having little or no stress and obscured vowel sound : UNEMPHATIC — used of monosyllabic pronouns, prepositions, auxiliaries ⟨*would* is often heard in its ~ form *'d*⟩ **10** : tending toward a lower price ⟨wheat is ~⟩ ⟨a ~ market⟩ **11** : having only a slight degree of ionization in solution — used of acids and bases; opposed to *strong*

syn WEAK, FEEBLE, FRAIL, FRAGILE, INFIRM, and DECREPIT mean, in common, not strong enough to bear strain or pressure or stand up under difficulty or effort. WEAK, of wider application than all the rest and interchangeable with any of them, implies deficiency, inferiority, or impairment of strength, power, skill, control, or influence ⟨a sick and *weak* old man⟩ ⟨a *weak* rung of a ladder⟩ ⟨Antonius was *weak* and vicious, and Catiline could mould him as he pleased —J.A.Froude⟩ ⟨a *weak*, timid face —Sherwood Anderson⟩ ⟨to say that one part of a painting, drama, or novel is too *weak*, means that some related part is too strong —John Dewey⟩ ⟨a *weak* excuse⟩ ⟨a *weak* police department⟩ FEEBLE suggests extreme pitiable weakness, usu. of persons or their acts or utterances ⟨a *feeble* old man⟩ ⟨a *feeble* attempt to resist oppression⟩ ⟨a *feeble* cough⟩ ⟨a *feeble* excuse⟩ ⟨a *feeble* imagination⟩ FRAIL, implying physical weakness, suggests rather a natural delicacy or slightness of constitution than an impairment of strength ⟨seemed rather *frail*, for there was a delicate pallor on his high, intelligent forehead and there was an invalid's languor in his whole attitude —Jean Stafford⟩ ⟨begins to lose the rather *frail* grasp she has on reality — *New Yorker*⟩ ⟨beauty, that *frailest* and most elusive of concepts —W.H.Auden⟩ FRAGILE, frequently interchangeable with FRAIL, stresses the idea of extremely easy destructibility ⟨a tall *fragile* vase⟩ ⟨the spirit of a little boy is a *fragile* thing and not to be pushed around beyond endurance —Christine Govan⟩ ⟨a wild deer, *fragile* and untamed —Elinor Wylie⟩ INFIRM implies loss especially of physical strength, and a consequent instability or unsoundness, often implying illness or old age ⟨the present king, *infirm* both in body and mind —A.T.Mahan⟩ ⟨mighty in reasoning but *infirm* in moral feeling —W.L.Sullivan⟩ ⟨an old man too *infirm* to go out in wet weather⟩ ⟨lack of direction in the main plan, *infirm* judgments, and cowardly estimates — Maurice Bowra⟩ DECREPIT applies to things or persons worn out or broken down by use or age ⟨grown so *decrepit* and feeble with old age as to threaten demise altogether —W.M. Thackeray⟩ ⟨a *decrepit* ramshackle building⟩ ⟨our own civilization appears to be growing *decrepit* and ready to fall — Bertrand Russell⟩ ⟨government that replaced the *decrepit* monarchy and corrupt dictatorship —Oscar Handlin⟩

²**weak** \"\ *n* -s : the thinnest most flexible portion of a foil blade : the foremost one third of the blade

³**weak** \"\ *vb* -ED/-ING/-s [ME *waiken, weiken,* fr. *waike, weike* weak] *archaic* : WEAKEN

weak·en \'wēkən\ *vb* **weakened; weakened; weakening** \-k(ə)niŋ\ **weakens** [¹*weak* + *-en*] *vt* **1** : to make weak : lessen the strength of : ENFEEBLE ⟨disease ~*s* the body⟩ ⟨fatigue ~*ed* his grip⟩ ⟨wetting ~*s* paper⟩ ⟨floodwaters ~*ed* the foundations of the bridge⟩ ⟨doubts ~*ed* his resolve⟩ ⟨hypotheses which . . . ~ rather than affirm purely mechanistic interpretations of nature —J.W.Krutch⟩ **2** : to reduce in intensity or effectiveness ⟨milk ~*ed* one half to two thirds with plain boiled water —Morris Fishbein⟩ ~ *vi* **1** : to become weak ⟨steadily ~*ing* storm⟩ : lose strength or spirit or determination : become less firm or resolute ⟨the Middle West was ~*ing* in its allegiance to the Democratic party —*Amer. Guide Series: Ind.*⟩ **2** : to change from a complex to a simple sound (as from a diphthong to a long vowel) : change from a strong to a weak sound : change from an open to a close vowel

syn WEAKEN, ENFEEBLE, DEBILITATE, UNDERMINE, SAP, CRIPPLE, DISABLE can mean, in common, to lose or cause to lose strength, vigor, or energy. WEAKEN, the most general of the group, signifies the loss of physical strength, soundness, or stability, or, in extension, of quality, intensity, or effective power ⟨*weakened* by failing health —C.H.Lincoln⟩ ⟨the days and nights of dissipation had *weakened* and depressed him — Louis Bromfield⟩ ⟨has left rural churches *weakened* in numbers and financial resources —*Amer. Guide Series: N.Y.*⟩ ⟨the spirit of adventure is not stimulated but *weakened* by poverty —M.R.Cohen⟩ ENFEEBLE implies a more obvious condition, usu. suggesting a helplessness or feebleness or forcelessness ⟨despite an *enfeebled* body, the mental faculties . . . can remain intact to the very end of life —*Current Biog.*⟩ ⟨can excessive reading actually *enfeeble* one's thinking apparatus —A.N. Whitehead⟩ ⟨the years had not *enfeebled* his acting —E.H. Collis⟩ DEBILITATE suggests a less marked, usu. more temporary, impairment of strength or vitality ⟨ivy *debilitates* trees, disintegrates mortar in walls and dislodges roof tiles —F.D. Smith & Barbara Wilcox⟩ ⟨avoid embroilments which *debilitate* our strength —*Current Biog.*⟩ ⟨the fears and the rages that *debilitate* —H.A.Overstreet⟩ UNDERMINE and SAP suggest a weakening by the effects of some surreptitious or insidious force, often carrying the idea of a draining of strength or a slow caving in or breaking down ⟨the members of his family *undermined* by dissipation, crime and madness —*Times Lit. Supp.*⟩ ⟨the emotions which would have *undermined* and demoralized him had he not sworn beforehand to abjure that —Marcia Davenport⟩ ⟨a gradual oxidation of the rubber thread which *undermines* the quality of the rubber —Albert Thompson & Sigfrid Bick⟩ CRIPPLE, meaning basically to maim or mutilate, suggests a serious impairment of force or effect similar to if not greater than that caused by a loss of a limb to a person ⟨the brain-injury victims, *i.e.*, those who have been *crippled* by such things as blows, encephalitis, or a sustained high fever in infancy —*Time*⟩ ⟨a heavy winter snowfall *cripples* transportation —Corey Ford⟩ DISABLE implies any force that makes unfit or which incapacitates, especially suddenly ⟨*disabled* for field work by an accident which resulted in the loss of his right leg —C.W.Mitman⟩ ⟨*disabled* the car so it wouldn't run —W.W.Haines⟩ ⟨an indifferent memory *disabled* him from mastering the Indian languages —Francis Parkman⟩

weak·en·er \-k(ə)nə(r)\ *n* -s : one that weakens

weaker *comparative of* WEAK

weaker sex *n* : WOMANKIND

weaker vessel *n* [so called fr. the metaphor in 1 Pet 3:7 (AV)] : WOMAN

weakest *superlative of* WEAK

weak feints *or* **weak faints** *n pl* : the last runnings in the distillation of alcoholic liquor (as whiskey)

weakfish \'ˌ=ˌ=\ *n* [obs. D *weekvis*, fr. *week* soft, tender, weak (fr. MD *weec*) + *vis* fish (fr. MD *visch, vis*); fr. its tender flesh; akin to OE *wāc* soft and to OE *fisc* fish — more at WEAK, FISH] **1** : any of several marine food fishes (genus *Cynoscion*); *esp* : a common sport and market fish (*C. regalis*) of the eastern coast of the U. S. from Cape Cod to Florida — see SPOTTED WEAKFISH **2** : ²MAIGRE 1

weak grade *n* : a member of an ablaut series (as a low or a neutral vowel) occurring in a syllable bearing reduced stress

weakhanded \'ˌ=ˌ=\ *adj* **1 a** : having weak hands **b** : DISPIRITED **2** : having an insufficient number of employees : SHORTHANDED

weak–headed \'ˌ=ˌ=\ *adj* : having a weak head: as **a** : liable to dizziness : easily affected by drinking **b** : wanting in strength of mind or purpose : WEAK-MINDED **c** : having a feeble intellect — **weak-head·ed·ly** *adv* — **weak-head·ed·ness** *n* -ES

weakhearted \'ˌ=ˌ=\ *adj* [¹*weak* + *hearted*] : of little courage : FAINTHEARTED ⟨the ~ liberals have left us and we are ready to build —Henry Wallace⟩ — **weak·heart·ed·ly** *adv* — **weak·heart·ed·ness** *n*

weaking *pres part of* WEAK

weak·ish \'wēkish\ *adj* : somewhat weak ⟨~ tea⟩ ⟨~ market⟩ — **weak·ish·ly** *adv* — **weak·ish·ness** *n* -ES

weak–kneed \'ˌ=ˌ=\ *adj* : easily yielding : lacking will power or resolution : IRRESOLUTE ⟨role of the dissenter is not for the *weak-kneed* —B.F.Wright⟩ — **weak-kneed·ly** *adv* — **weak-kneed·ness** *n* -ES

weak·li·ness \'wēklēnəs\ *n* -ES : the quality or state of being weakly : PUNINESS

¹**weak·ling** \'wēkliŋ, -lēŋ\ *n* -s [¹*weak* + *-ling*] : one that is weak in body or character or mind ⟨football, of course . . . the dream of every male ~ —Dorothy Witton⟩ ⟨greedy and often half-witted and half-alive ~*s* who will do anything for cigars, champagne, motorcars —G.B.Shaw⟩

²**weakling** \"\ *adj* : lacking strength or fortitude ⟨~ government that permits such a mess to fester —Don Porter⟩

¹**weak·ly** *adv* -ER/-EST [ME *weikly, wekely*, fr. *weike, weke* weak + *-ly*, adv. suffix] : in a weak manner ⟨~ agreed to a compromise⟩ : to a weak degree : FEEBLY, SLIGHTLY ⟨painting and drawing were ~ developed —Clark Wissler⟩

²**weak·ly** *adj* -ER/-EST [¹*weak* + *-ly*, adj. suffix] : not strong or robust : FEEBLE, WEAK ⟨~ infant⟩ : SICKLY, PUNY ⟨~ plant⟩

weak mayor *n* : a mayor in a mayor-council method of municipal government whose powers of policy-making and administration are by charter in large degree subordinate to the council — compare COUNCIL-MANAGER PLAN, STRONG MAYOR

weak–minded \'ˌ=ˌ=\ *adj* : having or indicating a weak mind : FOOLISH ⟨thinks I'm *weak-minded* because I play golf —W.H. Wright⟩; *sometimes* : FEEBLEMINDED — **weak-mind·ed·ly** *adv* — **weak-mind·ed·ness** *n*

weak neck *n* : a physiological disease of sorghum characterized by breaking of the stalk below the head

weak·ness *n* -ES [ME *waikenes, weikenes*, fr. *waike, weike* weak + *-nes* -ness] **1** : the quality or state of being weak : want of strength : lack of vigor ⟨it was a month after his illness before he recovered from his ~⟩; *also* : an instance or a period of feebleness or vacillation ⟨agreed in a moment of ~ to become chairman⟩ **2** : something that is a mark of lack of strength or resolution : FAULT, DEFECT ⟨admitting frankly the possession of vices and ~*es* that all of us have and few of us care to acknowledge —H.L.Mencken⟩ **3** : an object of special desire, concern, or fondness ⟨~ for salted peanuts⟩ ⟨the thirteenth century had a ~ for the word *speculum* —H.O.Taylor⟩

weaks *pl of* WEAK, *pres 3d sing of* WEAK

weak side *n* **1** : the side or aspect of a person's character or disposition through which he is most easily influenced esp. for the worse **2** : the side of a football formation having the smaller number of players

weak sister *n* : a member of a group who needs aid : an element or factor that is weak and ineffective as compared with others in the group ⟨weed out the *weak sisters* among the salesmen⟩ ⟨a subject introduced into the curriculum for the benefit of the *weaker sisters* —Kemp Malone⟩

weaky \'wēki\ *adj* [¹*weak* + *-y*] *dial Eng* : WET, DAMP

¹**weal** \'wēl, *esp before pause or consonant* 'wēəl\ *n* -s [ME *wele, weale*, fr. OE *wela*, akin to OS *welo* weal, OE *wel* well — more at WELL, adv.] **1** *obs* : WEALTH, RICHES **2** : a sound, healthy, or prosperous state : WELL-BEING, PROSPERITY, HAPPINESS, WELFARE — used chiefly in the phrase *weal or woe* ⟨power of determining the ~ or woe of the people —J.G. Frazer⟩ **3** *obs* : BODY POLITIC, COMMONWEAL ⟨the special weltherwe of our English ~ —Shak.⟩

²**weal** \"\ *vt* -ED/-ING/-s [alter. (influenced by *wheal*) of *wale*] : to raise weals on (as with a whip) : WALE

³**weal** \"\ *n* -s [alter. (influenced by *wheal*) of *wale*] : a stripe or raised line made by a stroke (as of a whip) on the skin : WALE

weald \'wēld, *esp before pause or consonant* 'wēəld\ *n* -s [fr. the *Weald*, wooded district in Kent, Surrey, & Sussex counties, southeast England, alter. (influenced by OE *weald*) of ME *Weeld* the Weald, fr. OE *weald* wood, forest — more at WOLD] **1** : a heavily wooded area : FOREST ⟨*Weald* of Kent⟩ **2** : a wild or uncultivated usu. upland region : WOLD ⟨by glimmering waste and ~ —Alfred Tennyson⟩

wealpublic *n* [ME *weale publique*, fr. *weale* weal + *publique* public, adj.; trans. of L *bonum publicum*] **1** *obs* : the public good **2** *obs* : COMMONWEALTH

wealth \'welth *also* -ltth\ *n* -s [ME *welthe*, fr. *wele* weal] **1** *obs* : WEAL, WELFARE, GOOD, HAPPINESS ⟨let no man seek his own, but every man another's ~ —1 Cor 10:24 (AV)⟩ **2** : large possessions : abundance of things that are objects of human desire : abundance of worldly estate : AFFLUENCE, RICHES **3** : abundant supply : large accumulation ⟨piles up a great ~ of detail to show —Ruth Moore⟩ ⟨~ of original documents⟩ : PROFUSION ⟨~ of curly black hair⟩ ⟨described with a ~ of examples⟩ **4 a** : all property that has a money value or an exchangeable value ⟨money, ~, possessions, and particularly the accumulation, retention, and use of them, are the distinguishing mark of the middle classes —Ray Lewis & Angus Maude⟩ ⟨slaves . . . were a ~ to be squandered without limit to make more ~ —Marjory S. Douglas⟩ **b** : all material objects that have economic utility; *esp* : the stock of useful goods having economic value in existence at any one time ⟨national ~⟩

wealth·i·ly \-thəlē, -li\ *adv* [*wealthy* + *-ly*] : with riches : with material success : in a wealthy manner

wealth·i·ness \-thēnəs, -thin-\ *n* -ES : the quality or state of being wealthy : RICHNESS, OPULENCE

wealth·less \-thləs\ *adj* [*wealth* + *-less*] : having no money or property

wealthy \-thē, -thi\ *adj* -ER/-EST [ME *welthy*, fr. *welthe* wealth + *-y*] **1** *obs* : enjoying a condition of well-being : physically well cared for **2** : having wealth : having large possessions of lands, goods, money, or securities : OPULENT, AFFLUENT ⟨school for the sons of ~ families⟩ **3** : characterized by abundance : AMPLE, FULL, ABUNDANT ⟨fishes of fruits of a land ~ in both —Douglas Carruthers⟩ **syn** see RICH

¹**wean** \'wēn\ *vt* -ED/-ING/-s [ME *wenen*, fr. OE *wenian* to accustom, wean; akin to OHG *giwennen* to accustom, ON *venja*, OE *wunian* to dwell, be used to — more at WONT] **1** : to accustom (a child or other young animal) to loss of mother's milk : cause to cease to depend on the mother for nourishment; *also* : to accustom (young animals) to get along without some special comfort ⟨~ chicks from the hover⟩ **2** : to detach or alienate the affections of from some object of desire : reconcile to the deprivation or loss of something ⟨the troubles of age were intended . . . to ~ us gradually from our fondness of life —Jonathan Swift⟩ ⟨low prices of movies may have ~*ed* large sections of the public away from the legitimate theater —Donald Messenger⟩ ⟨~*ed* my young soul from yearning after thine —Emily Brontë⟩ **syn** see ESTRANGE

²**wean** \"\ *n* -s [contr. of *wee ane* wee one, fr. *wee* + *ane*] *dial Brit* : INFANT, CHILD

weaned·ness \'wēnədnəs, -ēn(d)nəs\ *n* -ES [*weaned* (past part. of ¹*wean*) + *-ness*] : the quality or state of being weaned; *esp* : detachment from worldly things

wean·el \'wēnᵊl\ *n* -s [ME *weynelle*, fr. *wenen, weynen* to wean] *dial Eng* : WEANLING

wean·er \'wēnə(r)\ *n* -s **1** : one that weans; *specif* : a device for preventing animals that are being weaned from suckling **2** : a young animal weaned from its mother: as **a** *chiefly Austral* : a lamb between weaning and its first shearing or up to the appearance of the first two permanent teeth **b** : a weaned calf **c** : a weaned pig

wean·ie \'wēni\ *n* -s [¹*wean* + *-ie*] *Scot* : BABY

¹**wean·ling** \'wēnliŋ, -lēŋ\ *n* -s [¹*wean* + *-ling*] : a child or animal newly weaned

²**weanling** \"\ *adj* : recently weaned; *also* : of or relating to a weanling

wean·ly \'wēnli\ *adj* [²*wean* + *-ly*] : CHILDISH, FEEBLE

wean·yer \'wēnyə(r)\ *n* -s [irreg. fr. ¹*wean* + *-er*] *dial Eng* : WEANLING

¹**weap·on** \'wepən, *dial* 'wēp-\ *n* -s [ME *wepen, wepne*, fr. OE *wǣpen*; akin to OHG *wāffan* weapon, ON *vāpn*, Goth *wepna* (pl.) weapons] **1** : an instrument of offensive or defensive combat : something to fight with : something (as a club, sword, gun, or grenade) used in destroying, defeating, or physically injuring an enemy ⟨the rifle is the basic infantry ~ —M.M.Johnson⟩ **2** : an animal's claw, teeth, talon, spur, or beak used as a means of attack; *esp* : the spur of a gamecock **3** : a means of contending against another ⟨has codes of honor, rules, beliefs, and other ~*s* to protect him on the trail —Donn Byrne⟩ ⟨a politician who uses character assassination as a political ~ —Croswell Bowen⟩ ⟨sarcasm was his favorite ~⟩

syn WEAPON and ARM indicate something used in combat as an instrument or means of attack or defense. WEAPON applies to anything used or usable in injuring, destroying, or defeating an enemy or opponent. ARM, usu. in the plural, signifies an instrument or object designed for or used in fighting ⟨a large yearly appropriation for *arms*⟩ but is often restricted to the class of weapons wielded by the hand and arm (as swords, pistols, or rifles)

²**weapon** \"\ *vt* -ED/-ING/-s [ME *wepnen*, fr. OE *wǣpnian*, fr. *wǣpen* weapon] : ARM ⟨a folk in a cold climate . . . crudely ~*ed* —*Time*⟩

¹**weap·on·eer** \ˌwepəˈni(ə)r\ *n* -s [¹*weapon* + *-eer*] : one who activates an atomic bomb into readiness for release upon a target

²**weaponeer** \"\ *vi* -ED/-ING/-s : to engage in developing and perfecting military weapons ⟨caught up with or surpassed us in the matter of atomic ~*ing* —Philip Wylie⟩

weap·on·less \'wepənləs\ *adj* [ME *wepneles*, fr. OE *wǣpenlēas*, fr. *wǣpen* weapon + *-lēas* -less] : lacking weapons : UNARMED

weap·on·ry \-nrē\ *n* -ES [¹*weapon* + *-ry*] **1** : aggregate of weapons ⟨jellyfish . . . are equipped with ingenious ~ —*Newsweek*⟩ **2** : the science of designing and making weapons ⟨approaching era of nuclear ~ —Russell Baker⟩

weapon salve *n* : a salve believed to cure a wound by being applied to the weapon that made the wound

weapons carrier *n* : a light truck designed to carry machine guns or mortars and their crews

weap·on·shaw·ing \'wepən,shȯ-iŋ\ *or* **weap·on·shaw** \-,shȯ\ *or* **weap·on·show·ing** \-,shōiŋ\ *or* **weap·on·show** \-,shō\ *dial var of* WAPPENSCHAWING

weaponsmith \'ˌ=ˌ=\ *n* : a maker of weapons

¹**wear** \'wa(ə)(ə)r, 'we|, |ə\ *vb* **wore** \'wō(ə)r, 'wȯ(ə)r, -ōə, -ō(ə)\ **worn** \'wō(ə)rn, 'wȯ(ə)rn, -ōən, -ō(ə)n\ *or substand* **wore; wearing; wears** [ME *weren*, fr. OE *werian* to clothe, put on, wear; akin to OHG *werien* to clothe, ON *verja* to clothe, invest, spend, Goth *wasjan* to clothe, L *vestis* clothing, garment, Gk *hennynai* to clothe, *esthēs* clothing, Skt *vaste* he puts on, wears] *vt* **1** : to bear or have upon the person ⟨*wore* a coat⟩ ⟨~ a riding habit⟩ : to have attached to the body or part of it or to the clothing ⟨*wore* a ring on her left hand⟩ ⟨~ a necklace⟩ ⟨*wore* a badge on his lapel⟩ ⟨*wore* a red ribbon in her hair⟩ **2 a** : to use habitually for clothing or adornment ⟨~*s* a toupee⟩ ⟨~*s* size eleven shoes⟩ ⟨still ~*ing* black for her husband⟩ **b** : to carry on or as if on the person ⟨~ a sword⟩ ⟨~ a cane⟩ ⟨~*s* the stamp of suffering on his face⟩ ⟨these sixty years he ~*s* lightly —I.A.Gordon⟩ **3 a** : to hold the rank or dignity or position signified by (an ornament) ⟨~ the royal crown⟩ ⟨~ the palm⟩ ⟨born to ~ the purple⟩ **b** : to have or show an appearance of ⟨*wore* a happy smile⟩ ⟨his face *wore* its usual solemn expression⟩ ⟨if malice and vanity ~ the coat of philanthropy —R.W.Emerson⟩ **c** : to show or fly (a flag or colors) on a ship **4 a** : to cause to deteriorate by use ⟨gave away suits she had scarcely *worn*⟩ **b** : to impair or diminish by use or attrition : consume or waste gradually ⟨age had *worn* and sharpened the fine features —Virginia Woolf⟩ — used often with *away* ⟨letters on the stone had been *worn* away by weathering⟩ or *down* ⟨mountains *worn* down to low hills⟩ or *off* ⟨silver plating *worn off* here and there⟩ or *through* ⟨coat *worn* through at the elbows⟩ **5** : to cause or produce gradually by friction or attrition ⟨~ a channel in the rock⟩ ⟨~ a hole in the rug⟩ **6** : to exhaust or lessen the strength of : WEARY, FATIGUE ⟨the strain of the war had been ~*ing* them —Lucien Price⟩ **7** *archaic* : to let (time) go by : PASS, SPEND **8** : to cause (a ship) to go about by putting the helm up instead of down as in tacking so that the vessel's stern is presented to the wind ~ *vi* **1 a** : to endure use : last under use or the passage of time ⟨this coat material should ~ for years⟩ **b** : to retain quality or vitality ⟨attempt to find out how certain orchestral works are . . . ~*ing* —Deems Taylor⟩ **2** : to diminish or decay through use ⟨heels of his boots were ~*ing* unevenly⟩ : suffer damage or extinction by use or by passage of time : PASS — used usu. with *away, off, on, out* ⟨his patience began to ~ away⟩ ⟨waiting for the effect of the drug to ~ off⟩ ⟨it grew colder as the day *wore* on⟩ **3** : to grow or become by or as if by attrition or use — used with some adjectives ⟨his stock of money began to ~ very low —Sir Walter Scott⟩ ⟨felt his temper ~*ing* thin and ready to snap⟩ ⟨hair ~*ing* thin on top⟩ **4** *Scot* : PROCEED, PROGRESS **5** *of a ship* : to go about by turning the stern to the wind — compare TACK 1b — **wear blue** *of a car or train* : to display a blue flag or blue light to indicate the undergoing of inspection or repair : be delayed by car trouble — **wear green** *of a train* : to display green flags to indicate that another section of the same train follows — **wear on** : IRRITATE, RUB, FRAY ⟨silence and darkness of the grove were ~*ing on* him, eroding his courage —Norman Mailer⟩ — **wear stripes** [fr. the traditional striped uniform worn by prisoners] : to serve in prison — **wear the trousers** *or* **wear the pants** : to have the controlling authority in a household — **wear the willow** : to be in mourning

²**wear** \"\ *n* -s [ME *were*, fr. *weren* to wear] **1** : the act of wearing or state of being worn : USE ⟨clothes for everyday ~⟩ ⟨a 5-year-old ox will have all his teeth in *wear* —*Animal Management*⟩ ⟨discarded after years of hard ~⟩ **2 a** : clothing or an article of clothing usu. of a particular kind or fashionable style; *esp* : clothing worn for a special occasion or popular during a specific period ⟨examples of beautiful 16th century glove ~⟩ ⟨motley's the only ~ —Shak.⟩ — often used in combination ⟨fashions in neck*wear*⟩ ⟨fabric expressly for travel*wear* —*Women's Wear Daily*⟩ **b** : FASHION, VOGUE ⟨realizes that the flowers from his garden may not always be the ~ —H.S.Canby⟩ **3** : wearing quality : durability under use ⟨shown 2 to 2½ times the ~ life of comparable gauges . . . of all silk hose —W.E.Shinn⟩ **4** : the result of wearing or use : diminution or impairment due to use ⟨better cornering and reduced tire ~ on turns —*Annual Report General Motors Corp.*⟩ ⟨*wear*-resistant surface⟩

³**wear** \'wi(ə)r\ *vt* -ED/-ING/-s [ME *weren* to defend, protect, fr. OE *werian* — more at WEIR] *Scot & dial Eng* : to collect and drive (as sheep) into an enclosure

wear·abil·i·ty \,wa(ə)rəˈbiləd-ē, ,wer-\ *n* [¹*wearable* + *-ity*] : capacity or suitability for being worn; *esp* : durability under wear

¹**wear·able** \'wa(ə)rəbəl, 'wer-\ *adj* [¹*wear* + *-able*] : capable of being worn : suitable to be worn ⟨~ hearing aid⟩

²**wearable** \"\ *n* -s : GARMENT — used usu. in pl. ⟨soft dressmaker lines are found in all feminine ~*s* these days —*Westinghouse Mag.*⟩ ⟨summer ~*s*⟩

wear and tear *n* : the loss or injury to which something is subjected by or in the course of use; *esp* : normal depreciation

wear down *vt* : to weary and overcome by persistent resistance

or pressure ⟨monitoring ten panels of instruments . . . for hours at a stretch can *wear* a man *down* —Richard Thruelsen⟩
wear·er \-rə(r)\ *n* -s [ME *werer*, fr. *weren* to wear + *-er*] **:** one that wears or carries something as a covering or accessory of the body ⟨~ of a cloak⟩ ⟨the crown and its ~⟩
wea·ri·able \ˈwirēəbəl, ˈwēr-\ *adj* **:** capable of being wearied **:** easily wearied — **wea·ri·a·ble·ness** *n* -ES
wearied *adj* [fr. past part. of ³*weary*] **:** FATIGUED, EXHAUSTED ⟨ills of mind . . . which oppress the ~ brain of the thinker —J.W.Krutch⟩ — **wea·ried·ly** *adv* — **wea·ried·ness** *n* -ES
wearier *comparative of* WEARY
wearies *pres 3d sing of* WEARY, *pl of* WEARY
weariest *superlative of* WEARY
wea·ri·ful \ˈwirēfəl, ˈwēr-, -rif-\ *adj* [ME *weriful*, fr. *werien* to weary + *-ful*] **1 :** causing weariness **:** wearying to the patience or endurance **:** TEDIOUS, VEXATIOUS ⟨~ delay —John Buchan⟩ **2 :** full of weariness **:** WEARIED — **wea·ri·ful·ly** \-f(ə)lē\ *adv* — **wea·ri·ful·ness** *n* -ES
wea·ri·less \-rēləs, -ril-\ *adj* [ME *weriles*, fr. *werien* to weary + *-les* -less] **:** TIRELESS, UNWEARIABLE — **wea·ri·less·ly** *adv*
wea·ri·ly \-rəlē, -li\ *adv* **:** in a weary manner ⟨~ threw myself on the bed in my clothes —Mary W. Shelley⟩
wear-in \ˈ=,=\ *n* -s **:** BREAK-IN 1, 3
wea·ri·ness \ˈwirēnəs, ˈwēr-, -rin-\ *n* -ES [ME *werinesse*, fr. OE *wērignes*, fr. *wērig* weary + *-nes* -ness] **1 :** the quality or state of being weary **:** FATIGUE, TIREDNESS ⟨ready to drop from ~⟩ **2 :** tedium or ennui resulting from monotony or satiation ⟨when she turned into the house, she knew to ~ what she should find awaiting her —Ellen Glasgow⟩
¹**wearing** *n* -s [ME *wering*, fr. gerund of *weren* to wear] *obs* **:** CLOTHES, GARMENTS ⟨give me my nightly ~, and adieu —Shak.⟩
²**wearing** *adj* [ME *wering*, fr. gerund of *weren* to wear] **:** intended for wearing on the person ⟨~ apparel⟩
³**wearing** *adj* [fr. pres. part. of ¹*wear*] **1 :** causing or inflicting wear **:** FATIGUING, EXHAUSTING ⟨~ journey⟩ **2 :** subjected to wear ⟨~ surface of a tooth⟩
wearing course *n* **:** the surface layer of a pavement that takes the wear of traffic
wear·ing·ly *adv* **:** in a wearing manner **:** FATIGUINGLY
wear iron *or* **wear plate** *n* [²*wear*] **:** an iron plate to take the wear: as **a :** CRAMP IRON **b** *Brit* **:** TIE PLATE 3
wear·ish \ˈwirish\ *adj* [ME *werische*] **1** *dial* **a :** TASTELESS, INSIPID **b :** SICKLY, WITHERED **c :** SQUEAMISH **2** *dial* **:** being raw and cold ⟨~ mist⟩
wea·ri·some \ˈwirēsəm, ˈwēr-, -ris-\ *adj* [ME *werisom*, fr. *werien* to weary + *-som* -some] **:** causing weariness **:** TIRESOME, TEDIOUS ⟨other people's dreams are so dreadfully ~ —Walter de la Mare⟩ ⟨ski tows . . . eliminating ~ climbing to the top of the trails —*Amer. Guide Series: N.H.*⟩ — **wea·ri·some·ly** *adv* — **wea·ri·some·ness** *n* -ES
wear off *vi* **:** to diminish gradually in effect **:** pass away ⟨it's late and the liquor begins to *wear off* —John Steinbeck⟩ ⟨they must be unhappy when the novelty *wears off* —Glenway Wescott⟩
wear out *vb* [ME *weren out*, fr. *weren* to wear + *out*] *vt* **1 :** to make useless esp. by long or hard usage ⟨*wore out* four pairs of gloves shaking 6000 hands —Jane Muskie⟩ **2 :** HARASS, TIRE, EXHAUST ⟨economic sections are so detailed . . . that they *wear out* the reader —R.V.Harlow⟩ ⟨hope you're not going to *wear* yourself *out* waiting on him —Ellen Glasgow⟩ **3 :** ERASE, EFFACE **4 :** to endure through **:** OUTLAST ⟨*wear out* a storm⟩ **5 :** to consume (as time) tediously ⟨*wear out* idle days⟩ **6** *dial* **:** BEAT, WHIP ⟨things mama used to say she'd *wear* us *out* for saying —Lillian Smith⟩ ~ *vi* **:** to become useless from long or excessive wear or use ⟨when a field is *wearing out*, the corn growing shorter and bearing fewer ears —Merran McCulloch⟩
wear-out \ˈ=,=\ *n* -s [*wear out*] **:** depreciation through wear ⟨the rapidity of *wear-out* of a piece of machinery⟩
wearproof \ˈ=,=\ *adj* [²*wear* + *proof*] **:** resistant to wear ⟨~ tool⟩
wears *pl of* WEAR, *pres 3d sing of* WEAR
¹**wea·ry** \ˈwirē, ˈwēr-, -ri\ *adj* -ER/-EST [ME *wery*, fr. OE *wērig*; akin to OS *wōrig* weary, OHG *wuorag* intoxicated, OE *wōrian* to wander, totter, ON *ōrar* (pl.) fits of madness, Gk *hōrakian* to faint] **1 a :** having the strength much impaired by toil or exertion **:** worn out in respect to strength, endurance, vigor ⟨followed by troops of ~, dirty children —Irving Bacheller⟩ ⟨~ wings that rise and fall all day long —Edna S. V. Millay⟩ **b :** having lost freshness or virtue or usefulness ⟨if another leftover is some ~ noodles —R.P.Smith⟩ ⟨programs on television have degenerated into ~, predictable repetitions of each other —Edwin O'Connor⟩ **2 :** expressing or characteristic of weariness ⟨~, disillusioned note of futility in our life —J.C. Powys⟩ ⟨a ~ sound that was not a sigh nor a groan —Charles Dickens⟩ **3 :** having one's patience, tolerance, or pleasure exhausted **:** impatient of the continuance or recurrence of something — used with *of* ⟨councils grew ~ of reiterating a demand which could not be enforced —R.W.Southern⟩ ⟨~ to death of this eight years profitless war —Harold Nicolson⟩ **4 :** exhausted by suffering or sorrow **:** mentally or spiritually fatigued **:** SAD ⟨effete, ~, burnt-out revolutionists —H.F. Mooney⟩ ⟨a world grown ~ with fear —Robert Payne⟩ **5 :** causing weariness of body or spirit ⟨ahead of them lay many ~ miles of desert sand —G.F.Hudson⟩ **:** TIRESOME, TEDIOUS ⟨bacon, beans, and bread make a ~ meal three times a day —Allan Seager⟩ **6** *Scot & dial Eng* **a :** SICKLY, PUNY, WEAK **b :** WRETCHED, GRIEVOUS, UNFORTUNATE, DISASTROUS
²**weary** \"\ *adv* -ER/-EST **:** WEARILY, WEARYINGLY
³**weary** \"\ *vb* -ED/-ING/-ES [ME *werien*, fr. OE *wērigian*, *wērgian*, fr. *wērig* weary] *vi* **1 :** to become weary **:** TIRE ⟨tendency to ~ of burdens —Dean Acheson⟩ **2 :** to become exhausted in patience, tolerance, or liking ⟨telling stories when they *wearied* of cards and games —A.B.Paterson⟩ ⟨people ~ of old lies —Stuart Chase⟩ **3 :** to wait wearily **:** long or pine in expectation ⟨paced up and down . . . ~*ing* for the boat to get around —William Black⟩ ⟨~*ing* in spiritual wastes of sand and thorns —C.E.Montague⟩ **4 :** to bring on weariness **:** become monotonous or boring **:** PALL ~ *vt* **1 :** to reduce or exhaust the physical strength or endurance of **:** FATIGUE ⟨think out a solution without ~*ing* the body by needless movement —James Hewitt⟩ **2 :** to make mentally or spiritually weary **:** exhaust the patience or tolerance of ⟨exceeds and *wearies* credibility —John Mason Brown⟩ ⟨anxieties that lined his forehead and *wearied* his mind —Lennox Robinson⟩ — often used with *out* ⟨paternal affection was not yet *wearied* out —T.B.Macaulay⟩
syn see TIRE
⁴**weary** \ˈwiri\ *n* -ES [prob. fr. ¹*wary*] *Scot* **:** CURSE, PLAGUE — used in mild imprecation ⟨oh, ~ on the wars —Sir Walter Scott⟩
wearying *adj* [fr. pres. part. of ³*weary*] **:** that wearies ⟨find the life of the cafes more congenial than the ~ tensions of the casino —A.G.N.Flew⟩ — **wea·ry·ing·ly** *adv*
weary out *vt* **:** to pass or spend (time) in monotony, tedium, or longing ⟨*wearied out* the lonely days⟩
weary willie *n, usu cap both Ws* [¹*weary* + *Willie*, nickname for *William*] **:** one who avoids or dislikes work ⟨a general truancy by the *Weary Willies*, leaving the work-gluttons to do their share and do it better —*Manchester Guardian Weekly*⟩; *specif* **:** TRAMP ⟨the railroad had helped to create the *Weary Willie* —S.H.Holbrook⟩
weas *pl of* WEA
wea·sand *or* **wea·zand** *also* **we·sand** \ˈwēzᵊnd\ *n* -s [ME *wesand*, fr. (assumed) OE *wǣsend* gullet; akin to OE *wāsend* gullet, OFris *wāsande* windpipe, OHG *weisunt* windpipe, gullet] **1 a** *archaic* **:** GULLET, ESOPHAGUS **b :** the musculature associated with the gullet and the windpipe **:** THROAT ⟨cut his ~ with thy knife —Shak.⟩ **2** *archaic* **:** WINDPIPE, TRACHEA
wease-allan \wēˈzalən\ *dial var of* WEESE-ALLAN
¹**wea·sel** \ˈwēzəl\ *n, pl* **weasels** *also* **weasel** [ME *wesele*, fr. OE *weosule*, *wesle*; akin to OHG *wisula* weasel, OSw *visla*, L *virus* slimy liquid, poison, stench, and prob. to Skt *visra* musty, smelling of raw meat — more at VIRUS] **1 a :** any of various small slender-bodied carnivorous mammals (genus *Mustela*) that are related to the minks and polecats, are very active, bold, and bloodthirsty, kill many small birds and mammals and esp. great numbers of mice, rats, and other vermin, and have a mostly reddish brown coat with white or yellowish underparts which in the northern forms turns white in winter and a black-tipped tail — see BONAPARTE'S WEASEL, ERMINE, LEAST WEASEL, LONG-TAILED WEASEL, YELLOW WEASEL **b :** any of various mammals felt to resemble the true weasels in appearance or habits — usu. used in combination **c :** the fur or pelt of any of these animals **2** *usu cap* **:** a South Carolinian — used as a nickname **3 :** a person like a weasel in furtiveness, elusiveness, cunning, treachery **:** SNEAK **4 :** WEASEL WORD **5 :** a light personnel and cargo carrier self-propelled on wide rubber-padded semiflexible tracks and built either as a land vehicle capable of traveling over snow or ice or sand or as an amphibious vehicle with baffle plates on the tracks capable also of traversing swamps and rivers
²**weasel** \"\ *vi* **weaseled; weaseled; weaseling** \-z(ə)liŋ\ **weasels** [*weasel word*] **1 :** to use weasel words **:** EQUIVOCATE ⟨uneasy and evasive liar who ~*ed* and retreated when his credibility was questioned —*New Republic*⟩ **2 :** to escape from or evade a situation or obligation — often used with *out* ⟨the way men will ~ out of their missteps —Jean Stafford⟩
weasel cat *n* **:** LINSANG
weasel coot *or* **weasel duck** *n* **:** a female or young male of the smew
weasel-faced \ˈ==,=\ *adj* **:** having a thin sharp face like that of a weasel
weasel family *n* **:** MUSTELIDAE
weaselfish \ˈ==,=\ *n* **:** ROCKLING 1
weasel-headed armadillo \ˈ==,==-\ *n* **:** PELUDO
weasel lemur *n* **:** a small active lemur (*Lepilemur mustelinus*) that is reddish brown above, grayish brown below, and white on the throat — called also *mattock*
weasellike \ˈ==,=\ *adj* **:** resembling a weasel in form or behavior ⟨~ head⟩ ⟨~ agility⟩
wea·sel·ly \ˈwēz(ə)lē\ *adj* [¹*weasel* + *-ly*] **:** resembling or suggesting a weasel esp. in appearance ⟨weak-chinned ~ face⟩
weaselsnout \ˈ==,=\ *n* [¹*weasel* + *snout*] **:** a yellow-flowered European dead nettle (*Lamium luteum*)
weasel spider *n* **:** an arachnid of the order Solpugida
weasel word *n* [¹*weasel* + *word*; fr. the weasel's habit of sucking the contents out of an egg while leaving the shell superficially intact] **:** a word that destroys the force of a statement by equivocal qualification ⟨though I have couched my comments . . . in the most innocuous of *weasel words* —Richard Joseph⟩ **:** a word used in order to evade or retreat from a direct or forthright statement or position ⟨*weasel words* are the adman's way of crossing his finger behind his back when he makes a somewhat elastic statement —Robert Littell⟩
weasel-worded \ˈ==ˈwərdəd\ *adj* [*weasel word* + *-ed*] **:** containing weasel words **:** phrased with deliberate ambiguity **:** lacking forthrightness
wea·ser \ˈwēzə(r)\ *also* **weaser sheldrake** *n* -s [origin unknown] **:** the American merganser
wea·son \ˈwēzᵊn\ *Scot var of* WEASAND
¹**weath·er** \ˈwet͟hə(r)\ *n* -s [ME *weder*, fr. OE; akin to OHG *wetar* weather, ON *vethr*, OSlav *vetrŭ* wind, and perh. to Skt *vāta* wind — more at WIND] **1 :** state of the atmosphere at a definite time and place with respect to heat or cold, wetness or dryness, calm or storm, clearness or cloudiness **:** meteorological condition **2 a :** a particular kind of atmospheric state **:** one of the possible or known states of the atmosphere — used chiefly in pl. ⟨good hat for all ~*s*⟩ ⟨in most ~*s* the sheep and cattle . . . could be driven to the capital —G.M.Trevelyan⟩ **b :** a condition or vicissitude of life or fortune ⟨changes in our own country's moral ~ —E.R.May⟩ ⟨dark ~ of fatality and grim resolution —Thomas Wolfe⟩ **3 :** disagreeable atmospheric conditions: as **a :** RAIN, STORM ⟨we are expecting some ~⟩ ⟨because of tide and brewing ~ —P.A.Zahl⟩ **b** *obs* **:** a shower of rain or snow **c** *obs* **:** SKY **d :** cold air and dampness ⟨clothing to keep out the ~⟩ **4 a :** the direction from which the wind is blowing **:** WINDWARD **b :** the windward side **5 :** the angle that the sail of a windmill makes with its plane of revolution **6** [³*weather*] **:** WEATHERING **7** [²*weather*] **:** the portion of siding or shingles that is exposed rather than hidden by overlap ⟨a ~ of four inches⟩ — **under the weather 1 :** somewhat ill **2 :** somewhat drunk
²**weather** \"\ *adj* **:** being toward the direction from which the wind blows **:** WINDWARD ⟨~ beam⟩ ⟨~ braces⟩ — opposed to *lee*
³**weather** \"\ *vb* **weathered; weathered; weathering** \-t͟h(ə)riŋ\ **weathers** [ME *wederen*, *wetheren*, fr. *weder* weather] *vt* **1 :** to expose to the open air **:** subject to the action of the elements **2 a :** to sail or pass to the windward of ⟨~ a cape⟩ **b :** to make headway against (a storm or hard blow) **3 :** to bear up against and come safely through (a storm or a threatening or dangerous time) ⟨now we have ~*ed* another war —*Lancet*⟩ **4 a :** to slope (as a roof) so as to shed water **b :** to set (the sails of a windmill) so they will be adjusted to the wind **5 :** to tether (a hawk) unhooded in the open air **6 :** to make unable to move because of bad weather — used usu. with *in* ⟨wouldn't want to get ~*ed* in among those high passes —F.V.W.Mason⟩ ~ *vi* **1 :** to undergo or endure the action of the elements **:** wear away, disintegrate, discolor, or deteriorate under atmospheric influences ⟨shingles had ~*ed* to a silvery gray⟩ — often used with *away* ⟨where the softer rock has ~*ed* away into soil⟩ **2 :** to last under use or exposure or passage of time ⟨some paints ~ better than others⟩ **3** *dial* **:** STORM — **weather along :** to make headway in adverse weather — **weather on** *or* **weather upon :** to gain the advantage of by sailing to windward of
weath·er·abil·i·ty \,wet͟hərəˈbiləd-ē\ *n* [³*weather* + *-ability*] **:** capability of withstanding weather ⟨~ of a plastic⟩
weather-beaten \ˈ=,==\ *also* **weather-beat** \ˈ=,=\ *adj* [¹*weather*] **1 :** beaten by severe weather **:** worn or damaged by exposure to the weather **2 :** toughened, tanned, or bronzed by the weather ⟨*weather-beaten* face⟩
¹**weatherboard** \ˈ==,=\ *n* **1 :** CLAPBOARD, SIDING **2 :** the weather side of a ship
²**weatherboard** \"\ *vt* **:** to nail boards upon (a roof or wall) so as to lap one over another to exclude and shed rain
weatherboard·ing \" +iŋ\ *n* [*weatherboard* + *-ing*] **:** CLAPBOARDS, SIDING
weather-bound \ˈ==,=\ *adj* **:** kept in port or at anchor or from travel or sport by bad weather — called also *weather-fast*
weather bow *n* [²*weather*] **:** the side of the bow toward the wind
weather box *n* [¹*weather*] **:** WEATHER HOUSE
weather breeder *n* **:** a fine day often of unusual calmness and clearness that precedes stormy weather
weather bureau *n* **:** an organization engaged in the collection of weather reports as a basis for weather predictions, storm warnings, and the compiling of statistical records
weather-burned \ˈ==,=\ *adj* [¹*weather* + *burned*, past part. of *burn*] **:** browned by sun and wind
weather cast *n* **:** a weather forecast
weather caster *n* [*weather cast* + *-er*] **:** a weather forecaster
weather chart *n* **:** WEATHER MAP
weather cloth *n* **:** a tarpaulin used to shield men on watch on the deck or bridge of a ship from rain or wind
¹**weathercock** \ˈ==,=\ *n* [ME *wedercoc*, fr. *weder* weather + *cok*, *coc* cock] **1 a :** a vane often in the figure of a cock mounted so as to turn freely with the wind and show its direction **b :** a person or thing that changes readily or often **:** one who veers with every change of current opinion ⟨~*s* before the prevailing winds of doctrine —*Scribner's*⟩ **2 :** JEWELWEED **a**
²**weathercock** \"\ *vt* **1 :** to supply with a weathercock ⟨~ a steeple⟩ **2 :** to serve as a weathercock for ⟨~ the forces of revolution⟩ ~ *vi* **:** to behave like a weathercock; *specif*, *of an airplane* **:** to turn into the wind

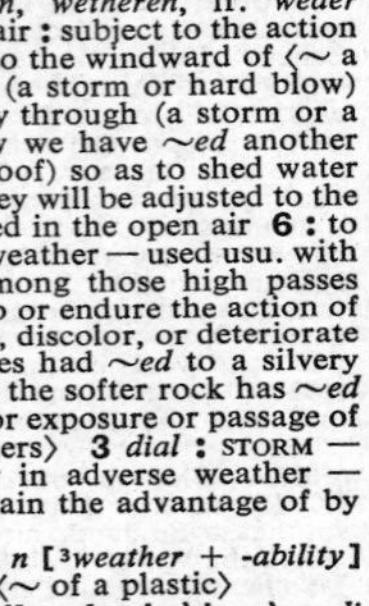

weathercock 1a

weather contact *n* **:** an electrical contact due to poor insulation during wet weather
weather cross *n* **:** a leakage between wires due to wet weather
weather cycle *n* **:** periodic recurrence of some feature of the weather
weather deck *n* **:** a deck having no overhead protection from the weather — see DECK illustration
weather door *n* **1 :** an opening in a louver **2 :** TRAPDOOR 2 **3 :** STORM DOOR
weathered *adj* [fr. past part. of ³*weather*] **1 :** seasoned by exposure to the weather **2 a :** altered in color, texture, composition, or form by exposure to the weather ⟨~ ice⟩ **b** *of woodwork* **:** artificially given the appearance caused by weathering **3 :** made sloping so as to throw off water ⟨~ windowsill⟩ — see JOINT illustration
weathered oak *n* **1 :** FUMED OAK **2 :** LEAFMOLD
weath·er·er \ˈwet͟h(ə)rə(r)\ *n* -s **:** one that weathers
weather eye *n* **1 :** an eye quick to observe coming changes in the weather ⟨the old-timer with his *weather eye* proves to be nearer the mark than we are with all our paraphernalia —G.H. T. Kimble⟩ **2 :** constant and shrewd watchfulness and alertness ⟨the chief in order to preserve his dynasty had always to keep a *weather eye* on these rising families —Ralph Linton⟩
weather-fast \ˈ==,=\ *adj* **:** WEATHER-BOUND
weatherfish \ˈ==,=\ *n* **:** any of several European and Asiatic loaches (genus *Misgurnus*) that burrow in mud at the bottom of streams and ponds but are supposed to become restless and swim about during thunderstorms — compare DOJO
weather flag *n* **:** a flag used to indicate the weather expected in from 12 to 36 hours
weather gall *n* **:** SUN DOG
weather gauge *n* [²*weather*] **1 :** the position of a sailing ship to the windward of another that gives an advantage in maneuvering **2 : a** superior position **:** ADVANTAGE ⟨got the *weather gauge* on him now⟩
weather-gauge \ˈ==,=\ *vt* [*weather gauge*] **:** to keep the weather gauge of
weathergaw \ˈ==,=\ *Scot var of* WEATHER GALL
weatherglass \ˈ==,=\ *n* [¹*weather*] **1** *obs* **:** THERMOMETER **2 :** a simple instrument for showing changes in atmospheric pressure by the changing level of liquid in a spout connected with a closed reservoir; *broadly* **:** BAROMETER
weathergleam \ˈ==,=\ *n*, *chiefly Scot* **:** clear or light sky near the horizon
weather-going tide \ˈ==,==-\ *n* [²*weather*] **:** a tide running against the wind
weatherhead \ˈ==,=\ *n* [¹*weather*] *dial Eng* **:** SECONDARY RAINBOW
weath·er·headed \ˈwet͟hə(r),-\ *adj* [*weather-* (prob. alter. of ¹*wether*) + *headed*] *archaic* **:** FOOLISH
weather helm *n* [²*weather*] **1 :** a tendency of a sailing vessel to come up into the wind ⟨catboats . . . generally carry very heavy *weather helms* —H.A.Calahan⟩ **2 :** the condition of the helm when put or held slightly toward the weather side

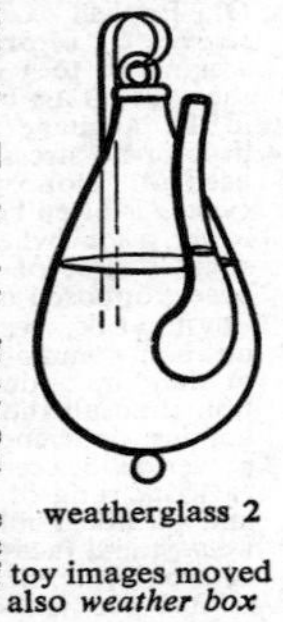
weatherglass 2

weather house *n* [¹*weather*] **:** a toy house that indicates changes in atmospheric humidity by the appearance or retirement of toy images moved by varying tension of a gut string — called also *weather box*
weatherier *comparative of* WEATHERY
weatheriest *superlative of* WEATHERY
weathering *n* -s [fr. gerund of ³*weather*] **1 :** exposure of a hawk to the weather **2 :** the action of the elements in altering the color, texture, composition, or form of exposed objects; *specif* **:** the physical disintegration and chemical decomposition of earth materials at or near the earth's surface **3 :** slope given to a surface (as of a sill) to throw off water
weather joint *n* **:** a masonry joint in which the mortar is recessed at the top with the trowel while the mortar is still green
weath·er·li·ness \ˈwet͟hə(r)lēnəs, -lin-\ *n* -ES **:** the quality of being weatherly
weath·er·ly *adj* [¹*weather* + *-ly*] **:** able to sail close to the wind with little leeway ⟨do not know how ~ the ship will be . . . how well she will go to windward —Alan Villiers⟩
weathermaker \ˈ==,==\ *n* **:** a weather prophet
weatherman \ˈ==,=\ *n*, *pl* **weathermen :** one who gives out reports and forecasts of the weather **:** METEOROLOGIST
weather map *n* **:** a synoptic chart showing the principal meteorological elements (as temperature, pressure, precipitation, wind direction and speed, air masses, fronts) at a given hour and over an extended region — called also *weather chart*
weather molding *n* **1 :** DRIP 4 **2 :** ASTRAGAL 1a
weath·er·most \ˈwet͟hə(r),mōst\ *adj* [²*weather* + *-most*] **:** farthest to windward
weather observer *n* [¹*weather*] **:** one whose duty is the systematic observation, measurement, and reporting of meteorological conditions
weath·er·ol·o·gy \,wet͟həˈräləjē\ *n* -ES [¹*weather* + *-o-* + *-logy*] **:** METEOROLOGY
Weath·er-Om·e·ter \-ˈämədə(r)\ *trademark* — used for a machine for testing the ability of paints and coatings to withstand weather
weather out *vi* [³*weather*] **:** to become exposed as surrounding softer rock disintegrates ⟨strata were pushed into folds that have now *weathered out* into long east-west ridges —*Amer. Guide Series: Ark.*⟩
weather plant *n* [¹*weather*] **:** a plant whose leaves are sensitive to atmospheric influences and are thus supposed to indicate weather changes; *specif* **:** INDIAN LICORICE
¹**weatherproof** \ˈ==,=\ *adj* **:** able to withstand exposure to weather without damage or loss of function ⟨~ cost⟩ ⟨~ electric wiring⟩ — **weath·er·proof·ness** *n*
²**weatherproof** \"\ *vt* **:** to make weatherproof ⟨~ a cabin⟩
weather report *n* **:** a systematic statement of the existing and usu. the predicted meteorological conditions over a particular area
weathers *pl of* WEATHER, *pres 3d sing of* WEATHER
weather sheet *n* [²*weather*] **:** a rope that extends the windward corner of a square sail
weather ship *n* [¹*weather*] **:** a ship that goes to sea specifically to obtain weather observations for use by meteorologists
weather shore *n* [²*weather*] **:** a shore lying to the windward ⟨ships hug a *weather shore* to get a lee, but they give a lee shore a wide berth —Gavin Douglas⟩
weather side *n* **:** the side (as of a ship) to windward **:** the side exposed to weather
weather signal *n* [¹*weather*] **:** a visual signal (as a flag or lights) giving information about predicted temperature, rain or snow, or wind direction — compare STORM SIGNAL
weather slating *n* **:** slate used on side walls of a building
weather stain *n* **:** discoloration caused by exposure to the weather ⟨walls with the *weather stains* of centuries⟩
weather-stained \ˈ==,=\ *adj* [¹*weather* + *stained*] **:** discolored by exposure to the weather ⟨*weather-stained* statue⟩
weather station *n* **:** a station for taking, recording, and reporting meteorological observations
weather strip *also* **weather stripping** *n* **:** a strip of material to cover the joint of a door or window and the sill, casing, or threshold so as to exclude rain, snow, and cold air
weather-strip \ˈ==,=\ *vt* [*weather strip*] **:** to apply weather strip to
weather table *n* **:** WATER TABLE 1
weather tide *n* [²*weather*] **:** a tide setting against the wind
weathertight \ˈ==,=\ *adj* [¹*weather* + *tight*] **:** proof against wind and rain ⟨~ storage bin⟩ — **weath·er·tight·ness** *n*
weather tile *n* **:** any of a series of tiles covering a wall and overlapped like shingles
weather vane *n* **:** VANE 1a
weath·er·ward \ˈwet͟hə(r)wə(r)d\ *adv* [¹*weather* + *-ward*] **:** toward the wind or the weather side ⟨the ~ wall of every building —Tom Hopkinson⟩
weather wheel *n* [²*weather*] **:** the position of responsibility at the weather side of the helm of a ship when two or more helmsmen are stationed at the wheel — compare LEE WHEEL
weather-wise \ˈ==,=\ *adj* [ME *wederwise*, fr. *weder* weather + *wise*] **1 :** skillful in forecasting the changes of the weather **2 :** skillful in forecasting changes in opinion or feeling ⟨a *weather-wise* politician⟩
weatherworn \ˈ==,=\ *adj* **:** worn by exposure to the weather ⟨white slab, on which the letters were faint —Ruth Suckow⟩
weath·ery \ˈwet͟h(ə)rē\ *adj* -ER/-EST [¹*weather* + *-y*] **1 :** changeable like the weather **2 :** impaired in quality by unseasonable rains ⟨~ tea⟩

weat·ings \'wētiŋz\ *n pl* [prob. fr. *wheat* + *-ing*] *Brit* : MIDDLINGS 1b

¹weave \'wēv\ *vb* **wove** \'wōv\ *or* **weaved; wo·ven** \'wōvən\ *or* **weaved; weaving; weaves** [ME *weven*, fr. OE *wefan*; akin to OHG *weban* to weave, ON *vefa*, Gk *hyphos* web, *hyphainein* to weave, Skt *ubhnāti* he laces up, covers over, *ūrṇavābhi* spider] *vt* **1 a :** to form (cloth) by interlacing strands (as of yarn); *specif* **:** to make (cloth) on a loom by interlacing warp and filling threads **b :** to interlace (as threads) into a cloth ⟨~ wool into tweeds⟩ **c :** to join, mend, or embroider (woven or knitted fabric) with stitches that match or imitate those of the article **d :** to make (as a basket or wreath) by intertwining rushes, twigs, or flowers ⟨~ a chair seat⟩ ⟨~ a garland⟩ ⟨the girls . . . ~ crowns of snowdrops, violets, and other flowers —J.G.Frazer⟩ **2 :** SPIN — used chiefly of spiders and some insects **3 :** to twist together or interlace esp. to form a texture, fabric, or design **:** ENTWINE ⟨~ osiers into baskets⟩ ⟨~ the holly round the Christmas hearth —Alfred Tennyson⟩ **4 a :** to produce by elaborately combining available materials or elements **:** CONTRIVE ⟨~ a plot⟩ ⟨enchantments that you *wove* —G.B.Shaw⟩ — often used with *about* or *around* ⟨~ a new romance about the fallen hopes —V.L.Parrington⟩ ⟨~ around it a story of violence and intrigue —John Brooks⟩ **b :** to bring together and interrelate so as to form a coherent whole **:** JOIN, UNITE — usu. used with *into* or *together* ⟨had *woven* episodes from many sources into a single narrative⟩ ⟨richly ~*s* together varied aspects of experience —*New Republic*⟩ **c :** to introduce as an appropriate element **:** work in — usu. used with *in* or *into* ⟨*weaving* in an exciting subplot —Chad Walsh⟩ ⟨*wove* into their songs the theme of jubilee —W.F.Hambly⟩ **5** *Scot* **:** KNIT **6 :** to direct (as the body) in a winding or zigzag course esp. to avoid obstacles ⟨going about the crowd and *weaving* her person in and out —Thomas DeQuincey⟩ ~ *vi* **1 :** to work at weaving **:** make cloth **2** *of an insect* **:** to spin a web or cocoon **3 :** to move in a devious, winding, or zigzag course turning or twisting in and out esp. to avoid obstacles ⟨~*s* down the ice with the puck⟩ ⟨*weaved* in and out through the traffic⟩ ⟨*weaving* through opposing tacklers for a 20-yard gain⟩ ⟨among them ran the children, playing, *weaving* in and out —Irwin Shaw⟩ **4 a :** to move across and back repeatedly **:** SHUTTLE ⟨can ~ back and forth between periods of time at his will —Bernard DeVoto⟩ **b :** to spread a weld by moving the electrode back and forth across the line of travel in arc welding

²weave \"\ *n* -s **1 :** something woven; *esp* **:** woven cloth **:** FABRIC **2 :** any of the patterns or methods for interlacing the threads of woven fabrics — see PLAIN WEAVE, SATIN WEAVE, TWILL WEAVE **3 :** a slow lateral motion of the projected image on a motion-picture screen

³weave \"\ *vb* -ED/-ING/-S [ME *weven* to move to and fro, wave, signal; akin to ON *veifa* to wave — more at WIFE] *vt*, *obs* **:** to signal to (a ship or its passengers) by waving ~ *vi* **1 a :** to move unsteadily or waveringly from side to side **:** SWAY ⟨a tree *weaving* before it falls⟩ ⟨his knees buckle slightly as he ~*s* on his feet —Wayne Hughes⟩ ⟨was *weaving* and had trouble finding the keyhole —Polly Adler⟩ ⟨his eyes close, his head ~*s*, and the music . . . starts —*Time*⟩ **b** (1) **:** to move from side to side incessantly and restlessly **:** ROCK, OSCILLATE ⟨the preacher . . . *weaving* first to one side of the platform and then the other —Mark Twain⟩ (2) *of a horse* **:** to sway and shift weight nervously — compare WEAVING ⟨the horse that bucks . . . ~*s* —*Amer. Guide Series: Nev.*⟩ **c :** to lurch or stagger from side to side while moving forward **:** REEL, CAREEN ⟨*weaving* down the sidewalk was a trio of drunken sailors —*Boston Herald*⟩ **2 :** to work one's way toward or away from a boxing opponent while eluding his blows with swaying, turning, and slipping movements of the body ⟨a middleweight . . . fast, shifty, hard-hitting, *weaving* in with short, savage punches —Gene Tunney⟩

¹weav·er \-və(r)\ *n* -s [ME *wever*, fr. *weven* to weave + *-er*] **1 :** one that works at weaving: as **a :** one that weaves textiles on hand or automatic looms **b :** one that mends garments by reweaving **c :** one that weaves baskets (as of rattan or cane) **d :** INTERLACER 2 **2 :** a reed or splint that is woven (as in basketry) over and under the staves **3 :** WEAVERBIRD

²weaver *var of* WEEVER

weaverbird \'==,=\ *n* **:** any of numerous Asiatic, East Indian, and African birds of the family Ploceidae that resemble finches in general appearance but have ten instead of nine primaries and that vary widely in habits and coloration but are mostly characterized by their construction of elaborate nests of interlaced grass and other vegetation which are chiefly either pensile with an entrance at the bottom or on the side or large, dome-shaped, and inhabited by many pairs of birds — see AVADAVAT, JAVA SPARROW, SOCIABLE WEAVERBIRD, WHYDAH

weaver finch *n* **:** WEAVERBIRD

weavers broom *n* [*weaver's* (gen. of ¹*weaver*) + *broom*; fr. its use in weaving baskets] **:** SPANISH BROOM 1

weaver shell *n* **:** SHUTTLE SHELL

weaver's knot *or* **weaver's hitch** *n* **:** SHEET BEND

weavers'-shuttle \'==,=\ *n* **:** EGG COWRY

weaves *pres 3d sing of* WEAVE, *pl of* WEAVE

weave shed *n* **:** a room or building housing looms

weaving *n* -s [ME *weving*, fr. gerund of *weven* to weave] **1 a :** the process of forming cloth usu. on a loom by the interlacing of threads, yarns, or other strands **b :** the business of making cloth **2 :** a debilitating vice of nervous stabled horses consisting of rhythmic swaying back and forth while shifting the weight from one side to the other **3 :** the action of a vehicle that alternately diverges from and merges into traffic flows moving in the same direction, shifting from one lane to another, and repeatedly crossing the paths of other vehicles

weazand *var of* WEASAND

wea·zen \'wēzᵊn\ *vb* -ED/-ING/-S [alter. of *wizen*] **:** SHRINK

wea·zened \-ᵊnd\ *also* **wea·zen** \-ᵊn\ *adj* [alter. of *wizened*, *wizen*] **:** WIZENED

weazen-faced \'==,=\ *adj* **:** having a wizened face

¹web \'web\ *n* -s *often attrib* [ME, fr. OE; akin to OHG *weppi* web, ON *vefr*, OE *wefan* to weave — more at WEAVE] **1 a :** a fabric as it is being woven on a loom or as it appears when removed from a loom ⟨a ~ of lace⟩ **b** *archaic* **:** a garment made of such a fabric **c :** the filmlike sheet of fibers delivered by various textile machines esp. on a card ⟨~*s* of fibers are produced in a wide sheet⟩ ⟨carded ~*s* of nylon⟩ **d :** WARP ⟨~ and woof⟩ **2 a :** COBWEB 1 ⟨the spider spins its ~⟩ ⟨the ~*s* of the silkworm⟩ ⟨the crossed ~*s* are attached to the frame of the surveyor's telescope⟩ **b :** SNARE, ENTANGLEMENT ⟨enmeshed in the ~ of conflict and fear —William Peden⟩ ⟨the most intricate ~ of espionage and intrigue that any modern state has endured —R.H.Jackson⟩ **3 :** a tissue or membrane of an animal or plant: as **a :** the membrane uniting fingers or toes either at their bases (as in man) or for a greater part of their length (as in many water birds and amphibians) — see GOOSE illustration **b :** the tissue between the larger veins of a leaf esp. of tobacco **4 :** WEBBING 2 **5** *archaic* **:** a thin film growing over or covering the eye **6 a :** a thin metal sheet, plate, or strip **b :** the vertical plate or portion connecting the upper and lower flanges or parts of a girder or rail — see T RAIL illustration **c :** the arm of a crank **7 a :** an intricate structure resembling or suggestive of something woven **:** MAZE ⟨the ~ of little wrinkles that radiated from the corners of her eyes —Hamilton Basso⟩ ⟨silvery birches spread a fragile ~ of loveliness over the highway —*Amer. Guide Series: Maine*⟩ ⟨a ~ of railroad tracks —*Amer. Guide Series: Fla.*⟩ **b :** a complex arrangement, pattern, or development ⟨the stuff of our lives is . . . a tangled ~ —Havelock Ellis⟩ ⟨this intricate ~ of social relations —Ralph Pieris⟩ ⟨the economy . . . has become a closely woven ~ —Roger Burlingame⟩ ⟨the close ~ of history —Herbert Agar⟩ **8 :** the series of barbs implanted on each side of the shaft of a feather **:** VANE, VEXILLUM **9 a :** a continuous sheet of paper manufactured or undergoing the process of manufacture on a paper machine **b :** a reel of such paper for use in a rotary printing press **10 :** a thin portion of material or a partition molded into hollow tile or other earthenware product to strengthen it **11 :** the portion of a ribbed vault between the ribs **12 :** SNOWSHOE ⟨would . . . get out their ~*s* and snowshoe down —Helen Rich⟩ **13 :** a radio or television network ⟨news analysts are . . . covered by the ~'*s* contract restricting private comment —Saul Carson⟩ ⟨the ~ was made up of member stations of the . . . Intercollegiate Broadcasting System —*Newsweek*⟩

²web \"\ *vb* **webbed; webbed; webbing; webs** [in sense 1, fr. ME *webben*, fr. OE *webbian* to weave, devise; akin to ON *vefja* to wind, wrap, MHG *weben* to weave, OE ¹*web*; in other senses, fr. ¹*web*] *vt* **1** *archaic* **:** to weave (a cloth or fabric) with a loom **2 a :** to weave a web upon ⟨spiders ~ the grasses⟩ **b :** to cover with a web or network ⟨roads *webbed* the forest land, connecting outlying farms . . . with the towns —*Amer. Guide Series: Tenn.*⟩ **3 :** ENTANGLE, ENSNARE ⟨the spider ~*s* a fly⟩ ~ *vi* **:** to construct or form a web ⟨the electrical cables which *webbed* everywhere —Fred Bradna & Hartzell Spence⟩ ⟨the mist *webbed* in her hair —Grace H. Flandrau⟩ ⟨it was so cold . . . the hairs in his nostrils *webbed* into instant ice —Wallace Stegner⟩

webbed \'webd\ *adj* [¹*web* + *-ed*] **:** provided with a web: as **a :** having the toes or fingers united by a web ⟨the ~ feet of aquatic fowls⟩ **b :** COBWEBBED

web·bing \'webiŋ, -bēŋ\ *n* -s [¹*web* + *-ing*] **1 a :** a narrow woven or braided fabric of textile fibers with or without rubber or other elastomer **b :** a strong narrow fabric closely woven of plied yarns that is designed for bearing weight and is used esp. for straps, harness, or upholstery **c :** a strap or girth of a hand printing press **2 :** a webbed state (as of the toes of a bird); *also* **:** the membranous web involved **3 :** a finish defect consisting of intersecting cracks and ridges formed usu. when a varnish or other coating expands on the surface it covers **:** ALLIGATORING

webbing clothes moth *also* **webbing moth** *n* **:** a clothes moth (*Tineola bisselliella*) whose larva attacks carpets, tapestry, and other woolen goods and forms a web in which it lives

web blight *n* **:** a disease of beans and other crop plants caused by a fungus (*Pellicularia filomentosa*) and characterized by a mycelial growth on or around water-soaked spots on stems, leaves, and pods

web·by \'webē\ *adj* -ER/-EST [¹*web* + *-y*] **:** of, relating to, or consisting of a web ⟨long ~ hair hung down over their emaciated faces —Jack Belden⟩

we·be·los \'wēbə,lōz\ *n*, *pl* **webelos** [fr. the phrase *we'll be loyal scouts*] **:** a cub scout of the fifth rank who is at least 10½ years old and is preparing for entrance into boy scouting

weber \'webə(r), 'vāb-,'wēb-\ *n* -s [after Wilhelm E. *Weber* †1891 Ger. physicist] **:** the practical mks unit of magnetic flux equal to that flux which in linking a circuit of one turn produces in it an electromotive force of one volt as the flux is reduced to zero at a uniform rate of one ampere per second **:** 10^8 maxwells

weber-fechner law \-'fek\|nə(r)-, -k\|\ *n*, *usu cap W&F* [after Ernst H. *Weber* †1878 Ger. physiologist & anatomist, & Gustav T. *Fechner* †1887 Ger. psychologist] **:** an approximately accurate generalization in neurophysiology that attempts to relate the intensity of a sensation to the intensity of a stimulus by ascribing to the JND a constant proportionality to the original stimulus

we·be·ri·an \we'birēən, vā'-,wē'-\ *adj*, *usu cap* [Max *Weber* †1920 Ger. sociologist and political economist + E *-ian*] **:** of or relating to the socioeconomic theories of Max Weber

weberian apparatus *n*, *usu cap W* [Ernst H. *Weber* †1878 + E *-an*] **:** the entire set of structures including the Weberian ossicles and their ligaments by which the air bladder of some fishes is connected to the ear

weberian ossicle *n*, *usu cap W* **:** one of the series of small bones that extends from the dorsal wall of the air bladder to the region of the ear in fishes (order Ostariophysi)

weber·ite \'webə,rīt, 'vāb-,'wēb-\ *n* -s [Dan *weberit*, fr. Theobald *Weber*, 19th cent. Dan. industrialist + Dan *-it* -ite] **:** a mineral Na_2MgAlF_7 consisting of a fluoride of sodium, magnesium, and aluminum

weber's corpuscle *or* **weber's pouch** *n*, *usu cap W* [after Moritz I. *Weber* †1875 Ger. anatomist] **:** PROSTATIC UTRICLE

weber's law *n*, *usu cap W* [after Ernst H. *Weber* †1878] **:** WEBER-FECHNER LAW

weber's line *n*, *usu cap W* [after Max *Weber* †1937 Ger. zoologist] **:** a hypothetical boundary lying approximately along the Australo-Papuan Shelf and being sometimes preferred to Wallace's line as the common boundary of the Oriental and Australian biogeographic regions

web-fed \'=;=\ *adj* **:** designed to print a continuous roll of paper ⟨*web-fed* rotary newspaper press⟩ — compare SHEET-FED

webfoot *in sense 1* '=,=, *in senses 2 & 3* '=,=\ *n*, *pl* **webfeet** [¹*web* + *foot*] **1 :** a foot having webbed toes **2 :** a bird or other animal having webbed feet **3** *also* **web·foot·er** \-;füdə(r)\ *usu cap* **:** OREGONIAN — used as a nickname

web-footed \'=;==\ *adj* [¹*web* + *footed*] **:** having webbed feet

web-footed shrew *n* **:** WATER SHREW

web frame *n* **:** a frame of heavy scantling used in ship construction and made by riveting a wide plate to a frame and stiffening the plate by riveting two reverse frames to its inner edge

web-glazed \'=;=\ *adj* **:** glazed in a calender having alternate rolls of polished iron and compressed cotton or paper

web glazing *n* **:** the glazing or finishing of paper in web form

web lead *n* **:** sheet lead

web·less \'webləs\ *adj* **:** having no webs

weblike \'=,=\ *adj* **:** similar to or suggestive of a web

web member *n* **:** one of the several members joining the top and bottom chords of a truss or lattice girder

web plate *n* **:** a plate connecting the flanges of a plate girder or a built-up steel column

web press *n* **:** a press that prints a web or continuous roll or reel of paper

web printing *n* **:** the action or the process of printing on a web press

web rot *n* **:** a rot of the tobacco leaf affecting chiefly the tissue between the main veins

webs *pl of* WEB, *pres 3d sing of* WEB

web saw *n* **:** a saw stretched in a frame

web spinner *n* **:** an insect that spins a web: as **a :** any of various small slender campodeiform insects with biting mouthparts that constitute the order Embiodea and live in silken tunnels that they spin **b :** WEBWORM

web·ster \'webztə(r), -bst-\ *n* -s [ME, fr. OE *webbestre* female weaver, fr. *webbian* to weave, devise + *-estre* -ster — more at WEB, v.] *archaic* **:** WEAVER

web·ste·ri·an \(')webz¦tirēən, -b¦st-, -tēr-\ *adj*, *usu cap* **1** [Daniel *Webster* †1852 Am. lawyer & statesman + E *-ian*] **:** of, relating to, or characteristic of the statesman Daniel Webster **2** [Noah *Webster* †1843 Am. lexicographer & author + E *-ian*] **:** of, relating to, or characteristic of the lexicographer Noah Webster or his dictionary

web-winged \'=;wiŋd\ *adj* [¹*web* + *winged*] **:** having wings formed by membranes extended between digits

webworm \'=,=\ *n* **:** any of various caterpillars that are more or less gregarious and spin large webs in which they live

wechs·ler-belle·vue test \,wekslə(r)'bel,vyü-\ *n*, *usu cap W&B* [after David *Wechsler* b1896 Am. psychologist and *Bellevue* Psychiatric Hospital] **:** a test of general intelligence and coordination involving both verbal and performance tests

¹wed \'wed\ *n* -s [ME, fr. OE *wedd* pledge, agreement, security; akin to OHG *wetti* pledge, ON *veth*, Goth *wadi*, L *vad-*, *vas* bail, security] **1** *dial Brit* **:** a person or thing given or deposited as a pledge **2** *dial Brit* **:** STAKE, WAGER

²wed \"\ *vb* **wedded** *also* **wed; wedded** *also* **wed; wedding; weds** [ME *wedden* to engage, pledge, marry, fr. OE *weddian*; akin to MHG *wetten* to pledge, ON *vethja* to wager, Goth *gawadjon* to espouse, marry, OE *wedd* pledge] *vt* **1 :** to take for wife or husband by a formal ceremony **:** MARRY ⟨bring me to your mother's house and there I will ~ you —Padraic Colum⟩ ⟨with this ring I thee ~ —*Bk. of Com. Prayer*⟩ **2 :** to join or bind in marriage ⟨he was *wedded* on July 12 —Francis Hackett⟩ ⟨the book gives the name of the minister who ~ them⟩ **3** *dial Brit* **:** ENGAGE, PLEDGE, WAGER **4 a :** to unite or join firmly as if by the affections or bond of marriage ⟨has ~ himself to the traditions of his people⟩ ⟨soon she too was . . . *wedded* to the place —S.T.Williamson⟩ ⟨was ~ to misfortune at birth⟩ **b :** to place in close or intimate association ⟨the far distant day when coal was *wedded* to iron —G.M. Trevelyan⟩ ⟨has invested millions of dollars to ~ farm and factory in continuous cycles of production —*Current Biog.*⟩ ⟨the English pantomime . . . ~*s* music hall and the fairy tale —Henry Hewes⟩ **5** *archaic* **:** to lend support to (as a cause) **:** ESPOUSE ~ *vi* **:** to enter into matrimony ⟨she ~ while still very young⟩

wedded *also* **wed** *adj* [*wedded* fr. ME, fr. OE *geweddod*, fr. past part. of *weddian* to wed; *wed* fr. ME *wedde*, fr. past part. of *wedden* to wed] **1 :** joined in marriage **:** MARRIED ⟨wilt thou have this woman to thy ~ wife —*Bk. of Com. Prayer*⟩ ⟨the ~ pair leave the church⟩ **2 :** of or relating to marriage or persons married ⟨no greater blessing . . . than pure ~ love —M.J.Huber⟩ ⟨forsaking his sole existence for the ~ life⟩ ⟨~ bliss⟩ **3 a :** devotedly or firmly attached or joined as if by marriage ⟨that kind of mellow wisdom . . . not ~ to private dogmas —H.J.Laski⟩ ⟨attract voters not ~ to either of the two major parties —*Times Lit. Supp.*⟩ ⟨a good boy, *wed* to peace and study —Carl Sandburg⟩ ⟨gaiety . . . ~ to melancholy —John Mason Brown⟩ **b :** existing in close or intimate association ⟨form and subject matter are ~ from the beginning —Edward Sapir⟩ ⟨austerity and discipline ~ to labor and endurance —W.C.Dickinson⟩ ⟨the gramophone ~ to the thin sweet singing of the olive leaves in the evening wind —John Galsworthy⟩

wed·dell·ite \wə'de,līt, 'wedᵊl,īt\ *n* -s [*Weddell* sea, arm of southern Atlantic ocean in Antarctica + E *-ite*] **:** a mineral $CaC_2O_4.2H_2O$ consisting of hydrous oxalate of calcium that is polymorphous with whewellite and is found as tiny isolated crystals in mud at the bottom of the Weddell sea, Antarctica

wed·dell seal \wə'del-, ¦wedᵊl-\ *n*, *usu cap W* [after James *Weddell* †1834 Eng. navigator] **:** a large brown antarctic seal (*Leptonychotes weddelli*) valued for its flesh and blubber

wed·der \'wedə(r)\ *n* -s [ME *weder* — more at WETHER] *Brit* **:** WETHER 2

wed·ding \'wediŋ, -dēŋ\ *n* -s [ME, fr. OE *weddung*, fr. *weddian* to wed + *-ung* -ing] **1 a :** the marriage ceremony usu. with its accompanying festivities **:** NUPTIALS, ESPOUSAL ⟨sending out invitations to the ~⟩ **b :** a wedding anniversary or its celebration — usu. used in combination ⟨golden ~⟩ **2 :** an act, process, or instance of joining or uniting in close association often of opposed or disparate elements ⟨the result was a ~ of the delicate and the rough —D.S.Stewart⟩ ⟨has not yet achieved the ~ of the serious and the popular —Harold Rogers⟩ ⟨this production is a happy ~ of taste, talent, and technique —Lila Glaser⟩ **3 :** a strong fine-textured smooth dull writing paper suitable for engraved wedding invitations

wedding cake *n* **:** a cake made for a wedding: as **a :** a dark unleavened fruited cake usu. elaborately decorated **b :** a light fruited cake or a white butter cake usu. heavily frosted and decorated

wedding day *n* **1 :** the day of a wedding **2 :** the anniversary of a wedding day

wed·ding·er \'wediŋə(r)\ *n* -s [*wedding* + *-er*] *dial Brit* **:** one present at a wedding esp. as a guest

wedding flight *n* **:** NUPTIAL FLIGHT

wedding march *n* **:** a march of slow tempo and stately character composed or played to accompany the bridal procession

wedding ring *n* [ME, fr. *wedding* + *ring*] **:** a ring often consisting of a plain gold or platinum band given by the groom to the bride during the wedding service; *also* **:** a similar ring given by the bride to the groom in a double-ring service

¹wedge \'wej\ *n* -s [ME *wegge*, fr. OE *wecg*; akin to OHG *weggi*, *wecki* wedge, ON *veggr*, Lith *vagis* wedge, peg, and prob. to L *vomis*, *vomer* plowshare, Gk *ophnis*] **1 :** a piece of material (as wood or metal) tapering to a thin edge used for splitting wood or rocks, for raising heavy bodies, and by being driven into a space between objects for tightening ⟨drove the ~ into the log with a maul⟩ **2 a :** a lump or mass of something solid ⟨ate ~*s* of brown bread dipped in coffee —Kay Boyle⟩ ⟨fine, well-aged Herkimer county cheddar . . . is sold in ~*s* —*New Yorker*⟩ ⟨a thick ~ of estuarine clay was laid down over the earlier valley peats —J.N.Jennings & Joyce Lambert⟩ **b** *obs* **:** a gold or silver ingot **3 a :** something (as a device, policy, or action) causing a breach or separation ⟨time . . . to unite this country instead of attempting to drive a ~ between any segments of our population —Earl Bunting⟩ ⟨slavery . . . had driven a ~ between the North and the South —Oscar Handlin⟩ ⟨driving a ~ of sardonic laughter and comment into the wall of prejudice —V.P.Hass⟩ **b :** something used to initiate an extended action or development ⟨looked upon the union . . . as a growing ~ in the fight to end discrimination —*Current Biog.*⟩ ⟨bill is merely another ~ to pry billions out of the American exchequer —J.S.Lawrence⟩ ⟨the officers' fraternity . . . was taken as the entering ~ of military despotism —Dixon Wecter⟩ ⟨the thin end of the improving ~ has come in —John Russell b. 1872⟩ **4 :** something shaped like or suggestive of a wedge: as **a :** an array of troops or tanks drawn up or moving in the form of a wedge ⟨the armored ~ drove forward to make openings in the enemy line⟩ **b :** a formation of flying wild fowl ⟨the high ~ and honk of birds flying south —Meridel LeSueur⟩ **c :** a section of land narrowing to a point ⟨a small ~ of an island —Iain Hamilton⟩ ⟨a ~ of green forest juts out into the field⟩ **d :** VOUSSOIR **e** (1) **:** the wedge-shaped stroke in cuneiform characters ⟨cuneiform . . . is at first sight only a meaningless jumble of ~*s* —S.L.Caiger⟩ (2) **:** HAČEK **f :** a wedge-shaped region of high barometric pressure **g** (1) **:** WEDGE HEEL (2) **:** a shoe that has a wedge heel **h :** an iron golf club that has a broad low-angled face for giving maximum loft from sand traps and from deep rough **:** a heavy niblick **i :** a piece of optical glass or crystal (as in a compensator or a photometer) having a progressive variation in thickness or absorption density from one side to the other **5 :** the type of cutting and piercing machinery formerly classed as a mechanical power **6 :** a piece of bone removed (as from a foot) to correct deformity or malposition (a ~ resection)

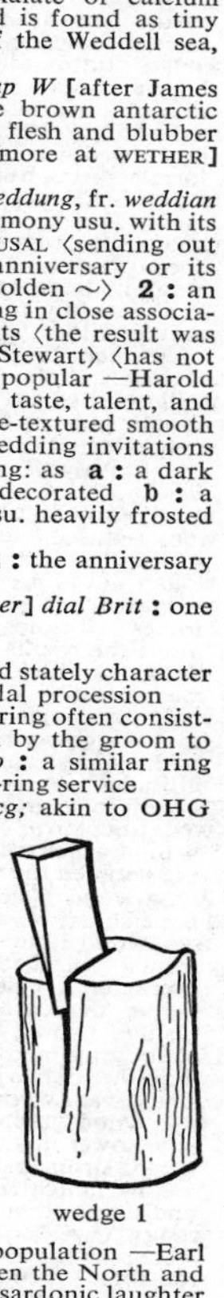

wedge 1

²wedge \"\ *vb* -ED/-ING/-S [ME *weggen*, fr. *wegge* wedge] *vt* **1 :** to fasten or tighten by driving or forcing in a wedge ⟨~*s* the pegs in tightly⟩ ⟨the carpenter ~*s* up the post under the beam⟩ ⟨the builder ~*s* the wooden partition to the overhead construction⟩ **2 :** to force or drive (an object) into something where it is tightly held **:** SQUEEZE ⟨the flood ~*s* debris into the crotches of the trees⟩ ⟨was *wedged* in between his two bedfellows, both of whom were aggressively large —T.B.Costain⟩ ⟨the houses . . . appear to be *wedged* in the rocky hillside —*Amer. Guide Series: Md.*⟩ ⟨seeking to ~ an advancing force between the enemy's strongpoints⟩ **3 :** to separate or force apart with or as if with a wedge ⟨the axman ~*s* open the log for finer splitting⟩ ⟨seeks to ~ apart his enemies, to divide and conquer⟩ **4 :** to cram or pack into a small or restricted space **:** CROWD ⟨thousands of homes had been *wedged* into the tiny valley⟩ ⟨Sunday driving ~*s* the cars together on miles of congested highways⟩ **5 :** to overthrow or direct the fall of (a tree) by driving wedges into the kerf made by the sawyer **6 :** to cut (clay) into wedge-shaped masses and work by dashing together to expel air bubbles ~ *vi* **:** to become tight or fixed by or as if by being wedged ⟨hold the wood properly so the saw will not ~⟩ — **wedge one's way :** to push or move in or forward in the manner of a wedge ⟨~*s* his way into the crowd⟩ ⟨*wedged* its way into the national market —*Advertising Age*⟩

wedgebill \'=,=\ *n* [¹*wedge* + *bill*] **1 :** an Australian crested bird (*Sphenostoma cristatum*) that has a wedge-shaped bill and is related to the bellbird (*Oreoica gutturalis*) **2 :** a So. American hummingbird (*Schistes geoffroyi*) having a very thick tapered bill

wedge bone *n* **:** a small unpaired bone or nodule that often occurs between the centra of the cervical vertebrae of lizards

wedge clamp *n* **:** a clamp with one end contacting the work below its surface and the other end butting against a crosspiece so that the tightening of a bolt passing through its center causes the clamp to wedge the work in position

wedge coupling *n* **:** a shaft coupling that grips with an action similar to that of a wedge

wedged \'wejd\ *adj* [¹*wedge* + *-ed*] **:** shaped like a wedge ⟨~ cuneiform characters⟩ ⟨the ~ formation of flying geese⟩

wedge disks *n pl* **:** disks usu. rotating and arranged in sets of two wedging a member between their surfaces
wedge furnace \'wej-\ *n, usu cap W* [after Utley *Wedge*, its inventor] **:** a mechanical shaft furnace for roasting ore that has several hearths one above the other and rabbles attached to a central revolving shaft
wedge gage *n* **:** a wedge with a graduated edge to measure the width of a space into which it is thrust
wedge gear *n* **:** a friction gear wheel with wedge-shaped circumferential grooves
wedge graft *n* **:** CLEFT GRAFT
wedge heel *n* **:** a heel extending from the back of the shoe to the front of the shank and having a tread formed by an extension of the sole — called also *wedge*

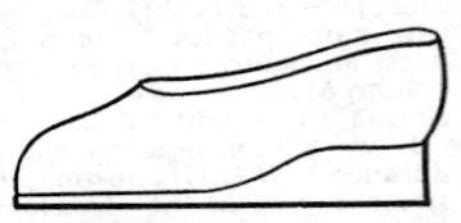
wedge heel

wedge micrometer *n* **:** a sensitive wedge gage
wedge of emersion *or* **wedge of immersion :** the wedge-shaped volume of a ship that emerges from the water or is immerged when the ship is inclined or heeled
wedge out *vi* **:** to become progressively thinner or narrower to the point of disappearance ⟨the reservoir bed *wedges out* toward the east⟩
wedge photometer *n* **:** an instrument for comparing stellar brightnesses on the basis of the calibrated progressive absorption of a neutral-density optical wedge or wedge of glass
wedg·er \'wejə(r)\ *n* -s [²*wedge* + *-er*] **:** a shoe worker who sets a wedge between the outsole and upper at the shank to form a spring heel — called also *springer*
wedge shell *n* [¹*wedge*] **:** a marine bivalve mollusk of the family Donacidae; *also* **:** its wedge-shaped shell
wedge spectrogram *n* **:** a photograph obtained with a wedge spectrograph
wedge spectrograph *n* **:** a spectrograph in which the light is modulated by an optical wedge
wedge–tailed \'=;=\ *adj* **:** having a tail that has the middle pair of feathers longest with the rest successively and decidedly shorter and all more or less attenuate
wedge–tailed dove *or* **wedge–tailed pigeon** *n* **:** any of various Asiatic pigeons of the genus *Treron*
wedge–tailed eagle *n* **:** an Australian eagle (*Uroaëtus audax*) that destroys lambs and young kangaroo — called also *eagle-hawk*
wedge–tailed gull *n* **:** ROSS'S GULL
wedge–tailed shearwater *n* **:** a shearwater (*Puffinus pacificus*) of the Pacific and Indian oceans
wedge verse *n* **:** rhopalic verse
wedgework \'=,=\ *n* **:** the action of frost, roots, and other forces in disintegrating rocks as if by the insertion of a wedge; *also* **:** the results of such action
Wedg·ies \'wejēz, -jiz\ *trademark* — used for shoes having a wedge heel
wedging *n* -s [fr. gerund of ²*wedge*] **:** the act or process of one that wedges; *specif* **:** the springing out or dislodging of ice or rock by frost acting as a wedge ⟨frost ~ . . . is common at high altitudes wherever suitably jointed rocks and water are exposed to a great daily range of temperatures —R.F.Flint⟩
wedging crib *or* **wedging curb** *n* **:** a curb of close-fitting planks behind which wedges are driven in to make a watertight packing between the tubbing in a shaft and the rock walls
Wedg·wood \'wej,wu̇d\ *trademark* — used for a pottery (as bone china, jasperware, or queensware)
wedgwood blue *n, often cap W* [fr. *Wedgwood*, a trademark; from a typical color of Wedgwood ware] **1 :** a variable color averaging a pale blue that is redder, stronger, and slightly lighter than average powder blue, redder and lighter than Sistine, lighter, stronger, and slightly redder than average cadet gray, and redder, lighter, and stronger than old blue **2 :** either of two colors averaging a grayish purplish blue — see DARK WEDGWOOD
wedgwood green *n, often cap W* **:** a grayish yellow green that is yellower, lighter, and slightly less strong than average sage green, stronger, slightly yellower, and lighter than mermaid, yellower, lighter, and stronger than palmetto, and yellower and deeper than celadon
wedgy \'wejē, -ji\ *adj* -ER/-EST [¹*wedge* + *-y*] **:** resembling a wedge in shape
wed·lock \'wed,läk\ *n* -s [ME *wedlac, wedlok*, fr. OE *wedlāc*, fr. *wedd* pledge + *-lāc*, suffix denoting activity, prob. fr. *lāc* warlike activity, play — more at WED, LAKE (amusement)] **1** *obs* **:** the marriage bond or contract **2 a :** the state of being married **:** MARRIAGE, MATRIMONY ⟨where love cannot be, there can be left of ~ nothing but the empty husk —John Milton⟩ **b** *archaic* **:** a marital union **:** a wedded life **3** *obs* **:** WIFE — **out of wedlock** *adv* **:** with the natural parents not legally married to each other
wednes·day \'wenzdē, -di *also* -(,)dā\ *n* -s *usu cap* [ME *wodnesday, wednesday*, fr. OE *wōdnesdæg;* akin to OFris *wōnsdei* Wednesday, ON *ōthinsdagr;* all fr. a prehistoric WGmc-NGmc compound formed from components represented by OE *Wōden*, the chief god of the Germanic peoples, identified with the Roman Mercury, and OE *dæg* day; trans. of L *Mercurii dies*, lit., day of Mercury (the Roman god of commerce and the planet Mercury) — more at DAY] **:** the fourth day of the week **:** the day following Tuesday
wednes·days \-ēz,-iz,-āz\ *adv, usu cap* **:** on Wednesday repeatedly **:** on any Wednesday
weds *pl of* WED, *pres 3d sing of* WED
¹**wee** \'wē\ *n* -s [ME *wei, we*, fr. OE *wǣge* weight, wey — more at WEIGH, n.] *chiefly Scot* **:** a little bit **:** short time ⟨bide a ~⟩
²**wee** \"\ *adj, sometimes* **we·er** \'wē(ə)r, 'wi(ə)r\ *sometimes* **we·est** \'wēəst\ [ME *we*, fr. *we*, n., wee] **1 :** very small **:** LITTLE, YOUNG ⟨a ~ tot of about five⟩ **2 :** very early ⟨awakened in the ~ hours of the morning⟩ **syn** see SMALL
³**wee** \"\ *interj* [imit.] — used to simulate the squeal of a pig
¹**weed** \'wēd\ *n* -s [ME *wed, weed*, fr. OE *wēod* herb, grass, weed; akin to OS *wiod* weed, MD *wiet*, OHG *wiota* fern] **1 a** (1) **:** an introduced plant growing in ground that is or has been in cultivation usu. to the detriment of the crop or to the disfigurement of the place **:** an economically useless plant **:** a plant of unsightly appearance; *esp* **:** one of wild or rank growth (2) **:** a tree or shrub of low economic value that tends to grow freely and by its presence to exclude or retard more valuable plants ⟨gray birch is a common ~ species in much of New England⟩ (3) **:** a form of vegetable life of exuberant growth and injurious effect (as various molds or bacteria frequently contaminating cultures) (4) **:** a forb in rangeland **b :** wild growth usu. in the nature of rank grass or undergrowth ⟨the land must be cleared of ~ —Emil Lengyel⟩ **2 :** a marine or freshwater plant **:** SEAWEED **3 :** an obnoxious growth, thing, or person ⟨militarism is a tough ~ to kill —F.S. Oliver⟩ **4 a :** TOBACCO; *esp* **:** tobacco prepared for use (as a cigar or cigarette) ⟨making the students promise to shun both ~ and wine —*Time*⟩ **b** *slang* **:** MARIJUANA **5 a :** something of little value; *specif* **:** an animal of poor conformation, lacking in stamina, and unfit to breed from **b :** an animal that is detrimental esp. in preoccupying habitats that might otherwise harbor more desirable forms ⟨carp forms one of the worst ~ species in some areas⟩ or in damaging the habitat value of the land on which they live ⟨uncontrolled deer herds may become serious ~*s*⟩
²**weed** \"\ *vb* -ED/-ING/-S [ME *weden*, fr. OE *wēodian;* akin to OS *wiodōn* to weed, MD *wieden*, OE *wēod* weed] *vi* **:** to remove weeds or something harmful ~ *vt* **1 a :** to free from noxious plants **:** clear of weeds ⟨~ a garden⟩ **b** (1) **:** to free from something that is hurtful or offensive (2) **:** to diminish by removing the less desirable portions of **:** CULL ⟨before beginning to classify and catalog an old library, ~ the collection —Susan Akers⟩ ⟨~ a stable of horses⟩ **2 a :** to remove on account of being a weed ⟨~ crabgrass from the lawn⟩ **b :** to remove on account of being harmful or superfluous **:** get rid of — often used with *out* ⟨~ out impractical schemes not worth further appraisal —R.P.Cooke⟩
³**weed** \"\ *n* -s [ME *wede*, fr. OE *wǣd, gewǣde;* akin to OS *wād, giwādi* clothing, OHG *wāt, giwāti*, ON *vāth* cloth, clothing, Lith *austi* to weave] **1 a :** an article of clothing **:** GARMENT; *esp* **:** one that is indicative of a person's occupation, situation, or position — often used in pl. **b :** something that resembles an outer garment **:** FLESH **2 :** an article or style of dress usu. black worn as a sign of mourning: as **a :** a widow's black veils — usu. used in pl. ⟨she had abandoned the cocoon of crape but still wore ~*s* —Arnold Bennett⟩ **b :** a band of crape or heavy black cloth worn on a man's hat as a sign of mourning — usu. used in pl. ⟨a coachman and a footman both with ~*s* on their hats —Kate D. Wiggin⟩
⁴**weed** \"\ *n* -s [by shortening fr. obs. Sc *wedenonfa'* ague, lit., attack of madness, fr. OE *wēde, wēden-* mad, frenzied + Sc *onfa'* attack, fr. ME *onfall*, fr. OE *onfeall*, fr. *on* + *feall* fall; akin to OE *wōd* mad — more at WOOD, ON, FALL] **1 :** a sudden illness or relapse often attended with fever **2 a :** lymphangitis in the horse accompanied by fever and marked by swelling of the legs **b :** mastitis esp. of sheep
weed·age \-dij\ *n* -s [¹*weed* + *-age*] **:** WEEDS
weed burner *n* **:** a device for burning or flaming weeds esp. along railroad tracks usu. consisting of large torches fired by petroleum fuels
weed·ed \'wēdəd\ *adj* [in sense 1, fr. past part. of ²*weed;* in sense 2, fr. ¹*weed* + *-ed*] **1 :** cleared of weeds **2 :** having many weeds **:** WEEDY
weed·er \'wēdə(r)\ *n* -s **:** one that weeds: as **a :** one of various devices for freeing an area (as a garden) from weeds **b :** one whose work is weeding (as farm or garden crops, lawns, flower beds)

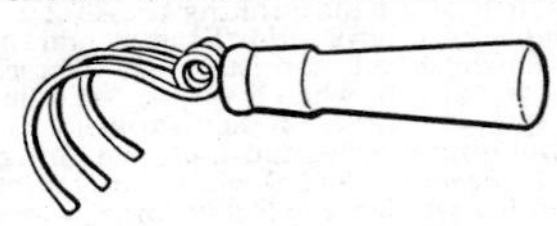
weeder a

weed·ery \-dərē\ *n* -ES [¹*weed* + *-ery*] **:** WEEDS; *also* **:** a place full of weeds
weed fallow *n* **:** fallow land where weeds are permitted to grow
weedhook \'=,=\ *n* [ME *wedehoke*, fr. OE *wēodhōc*, fr. *wēod* weed + *hōc* hook] **:** a hook to cut weeds; *specif* **:** a curved steel rod attached by one end to a plow beam and extending to the front and side of the plow bottom for bending over weeds so that they are completely buried in a furrow bottom by the furrow slice
weed·i·cide \'wēdə,sīd\ *n* -s [¹*weed* + *-i-* + *-cide*] **:** HERBICIDE
weed killer *n* **:** HERBICIDE
weed·less \'wēdləs\ *adj* **1 :** free from weeds ⟨a ~ garden⟩ **2 :** made in such a manner as not to catch in or become clogged by weeds
weed species *n* **:** a species having the potentiality for overpopulating an area and upsetting its normal biological balance
weed tree *n* **:** a tree of a kind having little or no commercial value ⟨the poplar is a *weed tree* in some coniferous forests⟩
¹**weedy** \'wēdē, -di\ *adj* -ER/-EST [ME, fr. ¹*weed* + *-y*] **1 :** abounding with weeds ⟨a ~ garden⟩ **2 a :** of, relating to, or consisting of weeds **b :** resembling a weed esp. in respect to rank growth or ready propagation in cultivated places ⟨a plant of ~ habit⟩ **3 :** noticeably lean and scrawny **:** LANKY ⟨light carriage with its pair of ~, young horses —Joseph Hergesheimer⟩ ⟨he was ~; on his pale thin face was the look of delicate health —Oliver LaFarge⟩
²**weedy** \"\ *adj* [³*weed* + *-y*] **:** dressed in mourning ⟨she was as ~ as in the early days of her mourning —Charles Dickens⟩
wee folk *n pl* **:** FAIRIES
wee frees \-'frēz\ *n pl, usu cap W&F* [fr. *Wee Free* (*Kirk*), nickname applied to minority of the Free Church of Scotland] **:** members of the Free Church of Scotland formed of a minority of the original Free Church of Scotland who refused to enter into a merger in 1900 with the United Presbyterian Church to form the United Free Church of Scotland
week \'wēk\ *n* -s [ME *weke, wike, wolk*, fr. OE *wice, wicu, wucu;* akin to OHG *wehha, wohha* week, *wehsal* change, turn, ON *vika* week, Goth *wiko* order, turn, L *vicis* change, turn, ON *vikja* to move, turn, OE *wīr* wire — more at WIRE] **1 a :** one of a series of seven-day cycles used in various calendars but esp. in the Jewish and Gregorian calendars and in the old Julian calendar from the time of Constantine **b** (1) **:** a week beginning with a specified day or containing a specified holiday ⟨the ~ of the 18th⟩ ⟨Easter ~⟩ ⟨Christmas ~⟩ (2) **:** a week appointed for public recognition of some cause ⟨Better Speech *Week*⟩ ⟨Fire Prevention *Week*⟩ **2 a :** any seven consecutive days **b :** a series of regular working, business, or school days during each seven-day period **c :** one of the four periods into which in accounting a month is often divided in reporting gross earnings with the first three containing seven days each and the fourth including the rest of the month **d :** a regularly recurring calendrical cycle of days unrelated to astronomical phenomena usu. smaller than a month ⟨spends a native ~ of four days —M.J.Herskovits⟩ **3 a :** a week ago from a specified day ⟨it was Sunday ~ when he came⟩ ⟨she was here this day ~⟩ ⟨last Sunday ~⟩ **b :** a week from a specified day ⟨the game will be played on Saturday ~⟩ ⟨next Sunday ~⟩ ⟨school begins a ~ today⟩
week·day \'=,dā\ *n, often attrib* [ME *wolkday*, fr. OE *wicdæg* day of the week, fr. *wice, wicu* week + *dæg* day] **:** a day of the week except Sunday or sometimes except Saturday and Sunday **:** WORKING DAY
week·days \-āz\ *adv* **:** on weekdays repeatedly **:** on any weekday ⟨gets up early ~⟩
¹**week·end** \'wē,kend\ *n* **:** the end of the week **:** the period between the close of one working or business or school week and the beginning of the next (as from Friday evening to Monday morning or from Saturday evening to Tuesday morning)
²**weekend** \"\ *vi* **:** to spend the weekend ⟨~*ed* with friends⟩
weekend bag *or* **weekend case** *or* **week·end·er** \'wē-,kendə(r)\ *n* **:** a traveling bag of a size to carry clothing and personal articles for a weekend trip
week·end·er \'wē,kendə(r)\ *n* -s [²*weekend* + *-er*] **1 :** one that vacations for a weekend ⟨~*s* in the country . . . who prefer nature to neon —*New Yorker*⟩ **2 :** one that comes to visit for a weekend
week·ends \-n(d)z\ *adv* **:** on weekends repeatedly **:** on any weekend ⟨sleeps late ~⟩
¹**week·ly** \'wēklē, -li\ *adv* [ME *wikely*, fr. *wike* week + *-ly*] **:** every week **:** once a week **:** by the week
²**weekly** \"\ *adj* [*week* + *-ly*] **1 :** occurring, appearing, or being made, done, or acted upon every week or once a week **2 :** reckoned by the week ⟨a ~ rate of pay⟩ ⟨a ~ rental⟩
³**weekly** \"\ *n* -ES **:** a weekly newspaper or periodical
week·night \'=,=\ *n* **:** a weekday night
week·nights \'=,nīts\ *adv* **:** on weeknights repeatedly **:** on any weeknight ⟨gets six hours' sleep ~⟩
week of prayer : a week beginning with the first Sunday in January each year instituted in 1846 by the Evangelical Alliance and observed by various Protestants throughout the world
week work *n* **1 :** the weekly service of labor due from a villein or unfree tenant to his feudal lord usu. amounting to 2 or 3 days but 4 or 5 in summer **2 :** work for which one is employed by the week
¹**weel** \'wē(ə)l\ *n* -s [ME *wel, wele*, fr. OE *wǣl* eddy, pool; akin to MD *wael* pool, OLF *wāl* abyss, OHG *wuolen* to stir up, rumple, Skt *valati* he turns — more at VOLUBLE] *dial Eng & Scot* **:** a deep still pool; *also* **:** WHIRLPOOL
²**weel** \"\ *n* -s [ME *wyle, wele*, fr. OE *wile-* (fr. *wilige* basket) — more at WILLY] **1 a :** a wickerwork or slotted trap for fish, esp. eels **b :** a conventionalized heraldic representation of such a trap **2 :** a basket esp. for fish
³**weel** \"\ *dial Eng & Scot var of* ⁴WELL
weem \'wēm\ *n* -s [ScGael *uaim, uaimh*] *Scot* **:** a natural or artificial cavern or pit; *esp* **:** one used as a place of habitation
ween \'wēn\ *vt* -ED/-ING/-S [ME *wenen*, fr. OE *wēnan;* akin to OHG *wānen* to ween, ON *væna* to hope, Goth *wenjan*, Skt *vanati* he wishes — more at WISH] **1** *archaic* **:** BELIEVE, CONCEIVE, IMAGINE, SUPPOSE **2** *archaic* **:** EXPECT, PURPOSE
weenie *var of* WIENIE
wee·ny \'wēnē\ *also* **ween·sy** \-n(t)sē\ *adj, sometimes* -ER/-EST [²*wee* + *tiny*] **:** exceptionally tiny **syn** see SMALL
¹**weep** \'wēp\ *vb* **wept** \'wept\ **wept; weeping; weeps** [ME *wepen*, fr. OE *wēpan;* akin to OHG *wuoffan* to weep, ON *œpa* to cry, scream, Goth *wopjan* to cry out, OSlav *vabiti* to call to, summon] *vt* **1 :** to express deep sorrow for usu. by shedding tears **:** BEWAIL, LAMENT ⟨the poet stayed to ~ the rose's fading —Katherine Hoskins⟩ **2 a :** to pour forth (tears) from the eyes ⟨*wept* tears of joy⟩ **b** *obs* **:** to shed drop by drop ⟨my heart ~*s* blood in anguish —Ben Jonson⟩ **3 a :** to spend in weeping — used with *away* ⟨into some low cave to crawl and there . . . ~ my life away —Alfred Tennyson⟩ **b :** to bring (oneself) to a specified condition by shedding tears ⟨finally *wept* herself to sleep⟩ **4 :** to utter or express while shedding tears ⟨~*ing* his welcomes forth —Shak.⟩ **5 :** to exude (as sap or serous fluid) slowly **:** OOZE ~ *vi* **1 :** to reveal an extreme inner emotion by a visual display esp. of lamentation and crying **:** express grief or other passion by shedding tears ⟨they *wept* together in silence —H.W.Longfellow⟩ **2 a :** to drop water **:** DRIP ⟨a sadder day had not been seen; even the clouds *wept*⟩ **b :** to flow or run in drops ⟨the blood ~*s* from my heart —Shak.⟩ **c :** to leak in trickles ⟨the bulkhead's buckling . . . and she's beginning to ~ down the joints —F.W.Crofts⟩ **3 :** to droop over **:** BEND ⟨the willow ~*s*⟩ **4 a :** to discharge a serous fluid ⟨~*ing* burned areas⟩ **b** *of the stem of a plant* **:** to exude water under pressure **:** BLEED **5 :** to form beads of liquid on the surface ⟨baked meringue is sometimes seen to ~⟩ — **weep one's heart out :** to cry long and exhaustingly
²**weep** \"\ *n* -s **1 :** weeping or a fit of weeping ⟨there was a scene — a ~ or two —Rudyard Kipling⟩ — often used in pl. **2 :** an exudation of moisture **:** LEAK
³**weep** \"\ *n* -s [imit.] **:** LAPWING
weep·er \'wēpə(r)\ *n* -s [ME *weper*, fr. *wepen* to weep + *-er*] **1 a :** one that weeps **:** one that sheds tears **b :** a professional mourner **2 :** a small statue of a figure in mourning frequently found in medieval tomb sculpture **3 :** a badge of mourning in the 18th and 19th centuries: as **a :** a white band worn as a cuff or on a cuff **b :** a man's long black hatband **c :** a widow's black veil — usu. used in pl. **4 :** CAPUCHIN 3 **5 :** a penitent who in the early church stood in the atrium begging the prayers of those who entered **6 :** a streamer of moss hanging from a tree **7 a :** WEEP HOLE **b :** SPARGE PIPE **8 :** long and flowing side-whiskers
weep hole *n* **:** a hole in a retaining wall, canal paving, or other structure to drain off accumulated water which might otherwise induce inordinate pressure back of or under the structure
weeping *adj* [ME *weping*, fr. pres. part. of *wepen* to weep] **1 :** accompanied by tears **:** TEARFUL ⟨~ gratitude⟩ **2 :** expressing or showing emotion by shedding tears ⟨held the ~ girl in his arms⟩ **3 :** exuding liquid in drops or very slowly **:** surcharged with moisture **:** OOZING ⟨pustular ~ folliculitis⟩ **4 :** RAINY, DRIPPING ⟨a ~ day⟩ **5 :** having slender pendent branches — used esp. of a tree
weeping cross *n* [trans. of ML *crux lacrimans*] **:** a cross erected on or by the highway esp. for the devotions of penitents
weeping cypress *n* **:** a tree (*Cupressus penebris*) with graceful drooping branches used as an ornamental in cemeteries and conservatories
weeping golden bell *or* **weeping forsythia** *n* **:** a Chinese shrub (*Forsythia suspensa*) with pendulous branches and yellow flowers
weeping honey locust *n* **:** a tree that is a variety (*Gleditsia triacanthos bujoti*) of the common honey locust characterized by pendulous branchlets
weeping lantana *n* **:** TRAILING LANTANA
weeping love grass *n* **:** a perennial southern African grass (*Eragrostis curvula*) introduced into the U.S. esp. for erosion control
weep·ing·ly *adv* [ME *wepingly*, fr. *weping* weeping + *-ly*] **:** in a weeping manner
weeping monkey *n* **:** CAPUCHIN 3
weeping mountain ash *n* **:** a variety (*Sorbus aucuparia pendula*) of the mountain ash of Eurasia with long pendulous branches
weeping myall *n* **:** an Australian acacia (*Acacia pendula*) with pendulous branches and very hard heavy durable dark brown or purplish wood
weeping oak *n* **1 :** CALIFORNIA WHITE OAK **2 :** an oak that is a variety (*Quercus robur pendula*) of the English oak characterized by pendulous branches
weeping pea tree *n* **:** a tree that is a horticultural variety (*Caragana arborescens pendula*) of a common Asiatic pea tree and has showy yellow flowers and pendulous branches
weeping red cedar *n* **:** a juniper that is a variety (*Juniperus virginiana pendula*) of the common red cedar characterized by pendulous branchlets
weeping rock *n* **:** a porous rock from which water oozes
weeping spring *n* **:** a spring that discharges water slowly
weeping spruce *n* **:** a tall spruce (*Picea breweriana*) of California and Oregon with slender pendulous branches and soft, heavy, and close-grained wood — called also *Brewer's spruce*
weeping willow *n* **:** an Asiatic willow (*Salix babylonica*) that is familiar in general cultivation from which it often escapes, has branches that droop perpendicularly, and occurs in several varieties
weeps *pres 3d sing of* WEEP, *pl of* WEEP
weepy \'wēpē, -pi\ *adj* -ER/-EST [¹*weep* + *-y*] **1 :** oozing moisture **:** SEEPY **2 :** tending to be tearful **:** verging on tears ⟨a ~ old lady —S.V.Benét⟩
weer *comparative of* WEE
weese–allan *or* **weese–allen** \wē'zalən\ *n* [origin unknown] *Scot* **:** PARASITIC JAEGER
wee·shy *also* **wee·shie** \'wēshē\ *adj* [prob. fr. ²*wee*] *Irish* **:** TINY, WEENY
weest *superlative of* WEE
¹**weet** \'wēt\ *vb* -ED/-ING/-S [ME *weten*, alter. of *witen* — more at WIT] *archaic* **:** KNOW ⟨I bind on pain of punishment the world to ~ we stand up peerless —Shak.⟩
²**weet** \"\ *Scot var of* WET
weet·less \-ləs\ *adj* [¹*weet* + *-less*] **:** UNWITTING
weet–weet \'wēt-,wēt\ *n* -s [imit.] **1** *dial Eng* **:** the common European sandpiper **2** *dial* **:** SPOTTED SANDPIPER
weety \'wētē\ *adj* [²*weet* + *-y*] *Scot* **:** RAINY
wee·ver \'wēvə(r)\ *also* **weever fish** *or* **weaver** *n* -s [ONF *wivre* viper — more at WYVERN] **:** any of several edible marine fishes of the family Trachinidae that have a broad spinose head with the eyes looking upward and a long dorsal fin supported by many strong sharp venomous spines that cause painful wounds: as **a :** a British weever (*Trachinus draco*) that becomes a foot long — called also *greater weever* **b :** a British weever (*T. vipera*) that is about half as large — called also *lesser weever*
wee·vil \'wēvəl *sometimes* -(,)vil\ *n* -s [ME *wivil, wevel*, fr. OE *wifel;* akin to OHG *wibil* beetle, ON *tordyfill* dung beetle, Lith *vabalas* beetle, OE *wafian* to wave — more at WAVE] **:** any of numerous snout beetles (group Rhynchophora) in which the head is elongated and usu. curved downward to form a snout bearing the jaws at the tip, the antennae are usu. geniculate, and the covering of the body is rough and hard and which although of small size may be very injurious as the larvae of some live in nuts, fruit, and grain and eat out the interior while the larvae of others bore under the bark and into the pith of trees and other plants — see BOLL WEEVIL, PEA WEEVIL, SEED WEEVIL, STRAWBERRY CROWN BORER

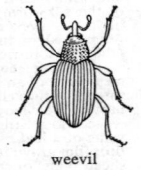

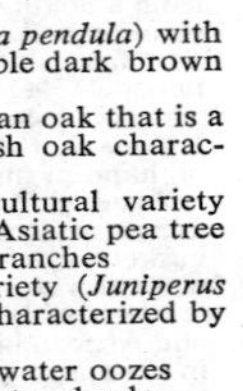
weevil

wee·viled *or* **wee·villed** \-ld\ *adj* [*weevil* + *-ed*] **:** WEEVILY
wee·vily *or* **wee·vil·ly** \-v(ə)lē, -li\ *adj* **:** infested with weevils
wee–wee \'wē,wē\ *vi* **wee-weed; wee-weed; wee-weeing; wee-wees** [baby talk] **:** URINATE — not often in polite use
²**wee–wee** \"\ *n* -s **:** URINE — not often in polite use
weeze \'wēz\ *vi* -ED/-ING/-S [ME *wesen*, fr. OE *wēsan*, fr. *wōs* juice, sap — more at SHUTUR SOWAR] *Scot & dial Eng* **:** OOZE
WEF *abbr, often not cap* with effect from
¹**weft** \'weft\ *n* -s [ME, fr. OE; akin to ON *veptr* weft, OE *wefan* to weave — more at WEAVE] **1 a :** the thread or yarn that crosses the warp and extends from selvage to selvage of a cloth **:** the thread carried by the shuttle **:** a filling thread **:** WOOF, PICK **b :** yarn used for this purpose **2 :** WEB, FABRIC; *also* **:** an article of woven fabric ⟨let thy ~ be of one woof and warp —Elizabeth B. Browning⟩ **3 :** a thin layer esp. of cloud, mist, or smoke **4 :** filling for baskets or mats; *also* **:** the fabric made with them **5 :** a thin feltlike layer of interlacing hyphae **6 :** a switch used by beginners for practice training in hairdressing techniques
²**weft** \"\ *vi* -ED/-ING/-S **:** to form or weave a weft

³weft \"\ *n* -s [by alter.] *archaic* : WAIF
⁴weft *var of* WAFT
weft fork *n* [¹*weft*] : FILLING FORK
weft-knit \'ˌ=ˌ=\ *or* **weft-knitted** \'=ˌ==\ *adj* : made by weft knitting ⟨most sweaters, bathing suits . . . are made of *weft-knit* fabrics —G.A.Urlaub⟩
weft knitting *n* : knitting in which each row of loops is formed by a crosswise thread made chiefly on circular or flat machines — compare WARP KNITTING
weftwise \'=ˌ=\ *adj* [¹*weft* + *-wise*] : of or relating to the weft : running across the warp : CROSSWISE ⟨a ~ design⟩
we·ge·ner hypothesis \'vāgənə(r)-\ *n, usu cap W* [after Alfred L. *Wegener* †1930 Ger. geophysicist] : a hypothesis in geology: the existing continents were orig. one land area of which portions have separated and since Carboniferous time have slowly drifted apart moving on a plastic substratum
we-group \'wē,=\ *n* [*we* + *group*] : INGROUP
wehr·lite \'wər,līt, 'wer-\ *n* -s [F, fr. A. *Wehrle* †1835 Austrian mining commissioner + F *-ite*] : a mineral approximately Bi_2Te_3 consisting of a native alloy of bismuth and tellurium
wehr·macht \'ver,mä|kt, 'veə,m-, -mȧl, |k̟t\ *n* -s *usu cap* [G, fr. *wehr* defense (fr. OHG *werī*) + *macht* force, might, fr. OHG *maht* — more at WEIR, MIGHT] : the armed forces esp. of Germany from 1935 to 1945
wei·bull·ite \'wī,bu̇,līt\ *n* -s [Sw *weibullit*, fr. Kristian Oskar M. *Weibull* †1923 Swed. mineralogist + Sw *-it* -ite] : a mineral PbBi(S,Se) consisting of seleniferous sulfide of lead and bismuth and occurring usu. in massive prismatic to fibrous aggregates
weid \'wēd\ *Scot & Irish var of* ⁴WEED
wei·ge·la \wī'jēlə, -'gē-, 'wījələ, 'wīgələ\ *n* [NL, fr. Christian E. *Weigel* †1831 Ger. physician] **1** *cap* : a genus of showy shrubs (family Caprifoliaceae) sometimes esp. formerly included in the genus *Diervilla* but distinguished by having the corolla not 2-lipped **2** -s : any shrub of the genus *Weigela* (esp. *W. florida*)
wei·ge·lia \wī'jēlēə, -'gēl-\ *n* -s [NL, fr. Christian E. *Weigel* †1831 + NL *-ia*] **1** : WEIGELA 2 **2** : a moderate red that is yellower and paler than cerise, claret (sense 3a), or average strawberry (sense 2a) and paler than Turkey red
wei·gert's method \'vīgə(r)ts-\ *n, usu cap W* [after Karl *Weigert* †1905 Ger. pathologist] : a method of tracing the course of medullated nerve fibers by hardening the tissues in a solution of potassium dichromate and staining the sections for myelin sheaths
¹weigh \'wā\ *vb* -ED/-ING/-S [ME *weyen, weghen*, fr. OE *wegan* to move, carry, weigh; akin to OHG *wegan* to move, carry, weigh, ON *vega* to move, carry, weigh, Goth *gawigan* to move, shake, L *vehere* to carry — more at WAY] *vt* **1** : to examine by a balance : ascertain the heaviness of ⟨~ myself on a bathroom scales⟩ ⟨a thinking brain capable of ~*ing* stars or atoms —L.C.Eiseley⟩ — often used with *up* ⟨when cotton was picked and ~*ed up* —Lillian Smith⟩ **2** *obs* : ESTEEM, REGARD **3 a** : OUTWEIGH ⟨a clean windscreen . . . could ~ the balance between life or death on the roads —Priscilla Hughes⟩ — often used with *down* **b** : COUNTERBALANCE ⟨better placed than some to ~ the particular criticisms against the general indictment —Barbara Ward⟩ — sometimes used with *off* ⟨the two commands must be ~*ed* off the one against the other —J.C.Swaim⟩ **c** : to make heavy : WEIGHT ⟨sewing silk, ~*ed* with fillers to lend luster —A.A. Stonehill⟩ ⟨sack of meal slung over his shoulder and ~*ing* him forward —E.L.Thomas⟩ — often used with *down* ⟨his style is ~*ed* down with localisms —*Americas*⟩ ⟨she ~*ed* down her repertory with these plays —Frances Frenaye⟩ **4** : to consider or examine for the purpose of forming an opinion or coming to a conclusion : consider carefully esp. by balancing one quality, aspect, or thing against another in order to make a choice, decision, or judgment : EVALUATE, PONDER ⟨in philosophy, the fact, the theory, the alternatives, and the ideal are ~*ed* together —A.N.Whitehead⟩ ⟨grand jury is currently ~*ing* indictments —*Newsweek*⟩ ⟨no tedious ~*ing* of pros and cons —*Irish Digest*⟩ ⟨experts are already ~*ing* the significance of the move —*Nation*⟩ — often used with *up* ⟨~*ing* up several propositions —*Farmer's Weekly (So. Africa)*⟩ ⟨accustomed to ~ up situations and make decisions quickly —*Times Rev. of Industry*⟩ **5 a** : to heave up (an anchor) preparatory to sailing **b** *archaic* : HEAVE, HOIST, RAISE **6** : to measure or portion out (a definite quantity of a commodity or substance) on or as if on a scales — often used with *out* or *up* ⟨~ out equal portions⟩ **7** : to hold or balance in the hand for or as if estimating the weight ⟨~*ed* a stone, then threw it⟩ **8** : to determine the force in pounds that will draw (a bow) the length of the appropriate arrow **9** : to determine the pressure required to pull (the trigger of a firearm) ~ *vi* **1 a** : to have weight : be heavy : have a specified weight ⟨he ~*s* 200 pounds⟩ ⟨a sirloin steak ~*ing* six pounds —Jane Nickerson⟩ **b** : to register a weight (as on a scales) — used with *in* or *out* and *at* ⟨a largemouth bass that ~*ed* in at better than fourteen pounds —Horace Sutton⟩ ⟨the hog ~*ed* out at 225 pounds after butchering⟩ — compare WEIGH IN, WEIGH OUT **2** : to be considered as important : have weight in the intellectual balance : carry weight : COUNT, MILITATE, TELL ⟨such recommendations will ~ in the candidate's favor⟩ ⟨those pieces of evidence will ~ heavily against him⟩ ⟨for the purposes of an editor of poetry stylistic evidence is evidence that must ~ —*Times Lit. Supp.*⟩ ⟨arguments which . . . would be likely to ~ with other conscientious parents —Bertrand Russell⟩ **3 a** : to press down with or as if with a heavy weight ⟨have one's gun ~*ing* on one's arm —T.H.White b. 1906⟩ ⟨extension of his erudition (which never ~*s*) to other literatures —A.T.MacAllister⟩ ⟨taxes ~ heavily on the incentive to save —A.E.Buck⟩ **b** : to be a source of doubt, indecision, worry, or regret : have a saddening or disheartening effect ⟨shook their heads sadly . . . as though the recollection of the interview ~*ed* heavily —R.H. Davis⟩ — usu. used with *on* or *upon* ⟨the responsibility for her decision ~*ed* on her —Laura Krey⟩ ⟨their insecurity ~*s* upon them and causes much bitterness —L.S.B.Leakey⟩ **4** : to weigh anchor ⟨the fleet ~*ed* and proceeded to the anchorage —S.E.Morison⟩ **5 a** : to weigh in ⟨finished third in a 2500-meter hurdle race . . . and went in to ~ —Ernest Hemingway⟩ **b** : to weigh out ⟨the jockeys ~*ed* before the race⟩ **syn** see BURDEN, CONSIDER, DEPRESS — **weigh anchor 1** : to hoist a boat's anchor **2** : to make ready to start — **weigh one's words** : to choose or use one's words deliberately
²weigh \"\ *n* -s [ME *weye, weighe*, fr. OE *wǣge* weight, wey; akin to OHG *wāga* weight, scale, ON *vāg* weight, scale, OE *wegan* to move, carry, weigh] **1** *dial Eng* : WEY **2** : WEIGHING ⟨cheating the miners on the ~ —James Higgins⟩ ⟨recommendations as to ~*s*, qualities, and grades —*Jour. of Home Economics*⟩
³weigh \"\ *n* -s [alter. of *way*] : WAY — used in the phrase *under weigh* as a variant of *under way* ⟨the ship's captain . . . immediately got under ~ —Deneys Reitz⟩ ⟨studies under ~ will show . . . the meaning of different scores —*Science*⟩ ⟨the political reaction which was already under ~ —George Orwell⟩
weigh·able \'wāəbəl\ *adj* [ME *weiable*, fr. *weien, weyen* to weigh + *-able*] : capable of being weighed
weigh·age \'wāij\ *n* -s [¹*weigh* + *-age*] *Brit* : a duty or toll paid for weighing merchandise
weighbar \'=ˌ=\ *or* **weighbar shaft** *n* [¹*weigh* + *bar*] *Brit* : ROCKSHAFT; *esp* : one in a radial gear
weighbeam \'=ˌ=\ *n* [¹*weigh* + *beam*] : a large steelyard
weighbridge \'=ˌ=\ *n* [¹*weigh* + *bridge*] : a platform scale flush with the roadway (as for weighing vehicles, cattle, or coal)
weigh down *vt* [ME *weghen down*] **1** : to cause to bend down or sink : OVERBURDEN ⟨branches *weighed down* with fruit⟩ ⟨faculty members . . . already *weighed down* with heavy teaching loads —*Educational & Psychological Measurement*⟩ ⟨the term, being so *weighed down* with false meaning —M.F.A. Montagu⟩ **2** : OPPRESS, DEPRESS ⟨a melancholy damp . . . to *weigh* thy spirits *down* —John Milton⟩ ⟨a black depression *weighed* me *down* —Kenneth Roberts⟩
weighed *adj* [fr. past part. of ¹*weigh*] : TESTED, TRIED, EXPERIENCED, BALANCED ⟨~ judgments⟩
weigh·er \'wāə(r), 'we(ə)r, 'weə\ *n* -s [ME *weyer*, fr. *weyen* to weigh + *-er* — more at WEIGH] : one that weighs: as **a** : one that weighs materials or products for purposes of verification, adjustment, or record **b** : a customs inspector who determines and records the weight of merchandise **c** : a worker who weighs out ingredients for a given product
weighhouse \'=ˌ=\ *n* [ME *weyhous*, fr. *weyen* to weigh + *hous* house] : a building at or within which goods are weighed
weigh in *vi* **1 a** : to have oneself or one's possessions (as baggage) weighed (as before an airplane flight) **b** *of a boxer or wrestler* : to have oneself weighed by a medical examiner on the day of a fight **c** *of a jockey* : to have oneself weighed with saddle and weights at the finish of a race — compare WEIGH OUT **2** : to enter as a participant, contributor, or mediator ⟨a bystander *weighed in* to stop the fight⟩ ⟨with a battle of quick wits to be fought in front of 500 people nature *weighs in* with an increased dose of adrenalin —D.E.Morris⟩ ~ *vt* **1** : to take the weight of esp. before an airplane flight or as a test of qualification before a contest (as a boxing match) **2** : to take the weight of (a jockey) after a race — compare WEIGH OUT
weigh-in \'=ˌ=\ *n* -s [*weigh in*] : an instance of weighing in a contestant : the act of weighing in contestants ⟨the official *weigh-in* usually takes place about noon —Nat Fleischer⟩
weighing *n* -s [ME *weying*, fr. gerund of *weyen* to weigh] **1 a** : the act of one that weighs ⟨weights for the more precise ~*s* in physical and chemical laboratories —T.W.Lashof & L.B.Macurdy⟩ **b** : a quantity weighed as one lot **2** *Brit* : the settling or subsiding of a mine roof
weighing machine *n* : ¹SCALE 2c
weigh larry *n* : ⁴LARRY 2
weighlock \'=ˌ=\ *n* [¹*weigh* + *lock*] : a lock (as on a canal) in which boats are weighed and their tonnage is settled
weigh·man \'wāmən\ *n, pl* **weighmen** [¹*weigh* + *man*] : a man whose work is weighing articles or goods : WEIGHER
weighmaster \'=ˌ==\ *n* [¹*weigh* + *master*] : a company employee or licensed public official who verifies the weight of loads (as of coal, ore, or grain)
weigh·ment \'wāmənt\ *n* -s : an act of weighing ⟨sensitivity permits ~*s* to fractions of a gram —*advt*⟩
weigh out *vi, of a jockey* : to have oneself weighed with saddle and weights before the start of a race — compare WEIGH IN 1c ~ *vt* : to take the weight of (a jockey) before the start of a race as a test of qualification — compare WEIGH IN 2
weigh-out \'=ˌ=\ *n* -s [*weigh out*] : the weighing out of a jockey
weighs *pres 3d sing of* WEIGH, *pl of* WEIGH
weigh scale *n* [ME *weyscale*, fr. *weyen* to weigh + *scale*] **1** : SCALEPAN **2 weigh scales** *pl* : a pair of scales
weighshaft \'=ˌ=\ *n* [¹*weigh* + *shaft*] : ROCKSHAFT
¹weight \'wāt, *usu* -ād·+V\ *n* -s [ME *weght, wight*, fr. OE *wiht*; akin to MHG *gewiht* weight, ON *vætt* weight, OE *wegan* to weigh — more at WEIGH] **1 a** : the often specified amount that a thing weighs : quantity of heaviness ⟨a basketball player with a playing ~ of 215 pounds⟩ ⟨two hundred and fifty pounds is considered the most desirable ~ for butchering . . . hogs —F.J.Haskin⟩ ⟨a diamond of five carats ~⟩ ⟨gross ~⟩ ⟨net ~⟩ — see LEGAL WEIGHT **b** (1) : the standard or established amount that a given thing should weigh — see SHORT WEIGHT (2) : one of the classes into which contestants in a sports event (as a boxing or wrestling match) or other contest are divided according to their body weight ⟨preliminary bouts in several ~*s*⟩ ⟨learnt when to stand and fight at his own ~ —H.A.Sinclair⟩ — see FEATHERWEIGHT; compare CATCHWEIGHT (3) : the poundage including that of the jockey, equipment, and any added lead that is necessary to make up the total required to be carried by a horse in a handicap race according to its rated ability (4) : BASIS WEIGHT **2 a** : a quantity or thing weighing a fixed and usu. specified amount ⟨equal ~ of water and air⟩ ⟨the necessary ~ of cold water is placed in a large steam-jacketed cooking kettle —*Bindery Glues*⟩ **b** : a heavy object (as a ball of metal) that is thrown, put, or lifted as an athletic game or exercise — compare HAMMER 4, SHOT 2b **c** : one of the iron disks used in playing the game of shuffleboard **3 a** : a unit of weight or mass ⟨table of ~*s*⟩ — see MEASURE table, METRIC SYSTEM table **b** : a piece of metal, glass, wood, or other material having an exact specified weight for use in weighing other articles (as in a scale) **c** *dial* : a customary local unit for a particular commodity **d** : a system of related units of weight ⟨avoirdupois ~⟩ ⟨troy ~⟩ **e** *Austral* : PENNYWEIGHT **4 a** : a ponderous mass : something heavy : LOAD ⟨a heavy ~ to carry so far⟩ **b** : a heavy contrivance or object to hold or press something down or to counterbalance: as (1) : a piece of lead or other relatively heavy material attached to a fishing line to cause it to sink (2) : PAPERWEIGHT ⟨a collection of very good-looking ~*s* —*New Yorker*⟩ (3) : a piece of lead sewed into a hem (as of a coat or curtain) to keep it hanging straight ⟨drapery ~⟩ (4) : a heavy metal object used to drive a clock **c** : the heaviness of overlying material (as rock over a mine shaft) **d** : CORPULENCE ⟨had grown portly with the years, but carried his ~ well —F.J.Mather⟩ **5 a** : BURDEN, PRESSURE ⟨could force a rescue by sheer ~ of numbers —T.B.Costain⟩ ⟨hangs like some guilty ~ of dark, unfathomed remembrances upon my energies —Thomas De Quincey⟩ ⟨never thought her poor brain could stand the ~ of such a secret —Kathleen Freeman⟩ ⟨the ~ of sky and stone seemed to slow the pace of the Sunday walkers —Kay Boyle⟩ **b** : PONDEROUSNESS ⟨empire fell to pieces of its own ~, largely because it had never been able to build any system of government except a simple tyranny —C.S. Forester⟩ **6 a** : relative heaviness : ponderability regarded as a property of matter ⟨~ is a quality of material substances⟩ **b** : the force with which a body is attracted toward the earth or a celestial body by gravitation and which is a quantity dependent on the place where it is determined : the product of the mass of a body by the local gravitational acceleration expressed in any of the units (as pound, ounce, newton, or dyne) by which force is measured **7 a** : the relatively great importance or authority accorded something ⟨had a great reputation in the parish for sober living and ~ in business —Mary Deasy⟩ ⟨discussion of the merits and demerits of toll roads produced a debate of considerable ~ —*N.Y. Times*⟩ **b** : measurable influence esp. in determining the acts of others ⟨throw one's ~ behind a candidate⟩ ⟨the professor had a lot of ~ to throw around the campus —Bennett Cerf⟩ **c** : power to influence the judgment ⟨their opinions always carried ~ —A.W.Long⟩ ⟨gives some ~ to his assertion that the act was sudden and unpremeditated —E.L.Pearson⟩ ⟨these replies lend ~ to the generally-expressed view —*Wall Street Jour.*⟩ **8** : something acting with heavy or overpowering force ⟨principles and rules . . . have petrified with the accumulated ~ of precedent on precedent —B.N.Cardozo⟩ ⟨futile to think of escape from the ~ of global responsibilities —Oscar Handlin⟩ ⟨having first justified with a ~ of scholarship my unscholarly assumption —F.R.Leavis⟩ **9** : the pull required to draw a bow to the full extent and measured in pounds **10** : the quality (as lightness or heaviness) that makes a fabric or garment suitable or adaptable for a particular use or season — often used in combination ⟨dress-*weight*⟩ **11** : ATOMIC WEIGHT **12** : the degree of thickness of the strokes of a type character **13** : stress value, quantity, or general sonority in individual sounds, syllables, and units of rhythmic structure in verse **14 a** : a relative value assigned to an item in a group or series under consideration ⟨the use of some system of ~*s* for differences in skills is difficult —W.E.Moore⟩ ⟨few data are available on the relative ~ of various emotions —J.E.Anderson⟩ ⟨if you have five problems . . . allot your time proportionately unless a ~ is given —W.F.Crum⟩ ⟨the most useful direct source was given a ~ of ten, the second most useful, a ~ of nine —Saul Herner⟩ **b** (1) : the frequency of an item in a frequency distribution (2) : a number assigned to express the relative importance of such an item (3) : the factor by which the value of such an item is multiplied in forming the weighted average of the values of the various items **syn** see IMPORTANCE, INFLUENCE
²weight \"\ *vt* -ED/-ING/-S **1 a** : to load or make heavy with or as if with a weight ⟨~ the head of a golf club with lead⟩ ⟨sat next to a dame who was ~*ed* with jewels —H.J.Laski⟩ ⟨never had he dreamed that words could be so ~*ed* with unfamiliar meaning —Christine Weston⟩ — often used with *down* ⟨a coarse net is thrown over the roof and ~*ed* down —L.D.Stamp⟩ **b** : to increase in heaviness by adding an inferior ingredient ⟨tea that has been ~*ed*⟩ **c** : to make (yarn or cloth) heavier by adding any of various substances (as sizing, clay, or flock); *esp* : to pass (silk) through baths of tin salts **d** : to make thicker ⟨with the camera lens, type can be reduced, enlarged, ~*ed*, slanted —*Book Production*⟩ **2** : to oppress with a burden (as sorrow, dejection, or discouragement) — often used with *down* ⟨was ~*ed* down with many cares⟩ **3 a** : WEIGH 1 ⟨test tubes and crucibles . . . and scales that ~*ed* your signature —Thomas Wood †1950⟩ **b** : to feel the weight of : HEFT ⟨~ a stone⟩ **4 a** : to assign a value expressing the relative importance of (a thing) as the result of a measurement or judgment **b** : to attach factors indicative of their relative frequency or importance to the various items of a frequency distribution ⟨the prices thus obtained were ~*ed* according to the net sales of each type of store —*Experiment Station Record*⟩ **5** : to arrange, bias, or incline in a particular direction by manipulation ⟨the tax structure . . . which was ~*ed* so heavily in favor of the upper classes —A.S.Link⟩ ⟨legislatures create vested and sentimental interests which ~ national policy in the direction of patchwork rather than mosaic —H.D.Lasswell⟩ **6** : to assign a handicap weight to (a racehorse) **7** : to shift the burden of weight upon ⟨~ the inside ski⟩ **syn** see BURDEN
³weight \"\ *n* -s [ME *wheit, wehit, weght*, akin to OE *wiht* weight — more at ¹WEIGHT] : a leather-covered hoop like a sieve but without holes used for winnowing grain
weight·age \'wād·ij\ *n* -s [²*weight* + *-age*] : the assignment of a quota (as of members of a legislature) to a particular segment of the population as a special favor or concession in a proportion above that allowable on a strictly numerical basis
weight agreement *n* : an arrangement between shippers and carriers that allows the use of estimated weight of shipment components in obtaining freight charges and total weight
weight box *or* **weight pocket** *n* : a channel in a window frame in which the sash weights move up and down
weight boy *n* : a textile worker who weighs yarn and distributes it to winders
weight cloth *n* : a saddlecloth into which flat lead pieces are fitted when a jockey's weight is less than the amount his horse must carry
weighted *adj* [fr. past part. of ²*weight*] **1** : made heavy or weighty : LOADED ⟨~ silk⟩ **2 a** : relatively evaluated or adjusted ⟨a system of ~, proportionate voting —*Current Biog.*⟩ **b** : having a statistical weight attached ⟨construct a ~ aggregative index number —F.E.Croxton & D.J.Cowden⟩ — **weight·ed·ly** *adv* — **weight·ed·ness** *n* -ES
weighted average *or* **weighted mean** *n* : an average of the values of a set of items to each of which is accorded a weight indicative of its frequency or relative importance
weighted value *n* : the product of the value of an item of a frequency distribution by its weight
weight·er \'wād·ə(r)\ *n* -s : one that weights; *specif* : a textile worker who increases the weight of yarns or fabrics by adding substances by chemical or mechanical methods
weight font *n* : type packaged in an assortment and quantity sufficient to fill a job case and sold by weight
weight for age : a weight apportioned to a racehorse according to its age irrespective of any other penalties or allowances
weight·i·ly \'wād·ᵊl|ē, -ātl, |əl|, |i\ *adv* : in a weighty manner ⟨the speech was weighty in substance and ~ delivered —J.A. Froude⟩ ⟨moved slowly and ~ —Mary R. Rinehart⟩
weight·i·ness \|ēnəs, |in-\ *n* -ES : the quality or state of being weighty
¹weighting *n* -s [fr. gerund of ²*weight*] **1 a** : the act of one who weights ⟨some of the author's ~*s* might be disputed —Walter Millis⟩ **b** : something used as a weight **2** *or* **weighting allowance** *Brit* : a salary differential to compensate for a difference in living costs ⟨given a London ~⟩
²weighting *Brit var of* WEIGHING 2
weight in hand : the actual weight of an archery bow
weight·less \'wātləs\ *adj* : having no weight : having little weight : being without perceptible weight : lacking apparent gravitational pull ⟨how ~ her coat had seemed —John Updike⟩ ⟨a ~ opportunist —*Time*⟩ ⟨a baby bat . . . fluffy and ~ as a moth —Frederic Prokosch⟩ ⟨a ~ environment⟩ — **weight·less·ly** *adv* — **weight·less·ness** *n* -ES
weight lifter *n* : one that competes in or exercises by means of weight lifting
weight lifting *n* : a sport in which barbells are lifted competitively or as an exercise — compare CLEAN AND JERK, PRESS 9a, SNATCH
weight man *n* : an athlete who competes in one or more field events (as the hammer throw, shot put, discus throw, or javelin throw)
weight of metal : the total weight of the projectiles that can be fired from a single gun in a given time or of those that can be fired simultaneously from an assemblage of guns
weight of wind : the wind pressure measured in inches of water that is supplied to a pipe-organ stop or group of stops
Weight·om·e·ter \wād·'äməd·ə(r)\ *trademark* — used for an automatic weighing device
weights *pl of* WEIGHT, *pres 3d sing of* WEIGHT
weighty \'wād·ē, -āt|, |i\ *adj* -ER/-EST [ME, fr. ¹*weight* + *-y*] **1 a** : having much importance or consequence : MOMENTOUS ⟨let me have your advice in a ~ affair —Jonathan Swift⟩ ⟨a ~ problem⟩ **b** : expressing or characterized by seriousness or gravity : EARNEST, SOLEMN ⟨a ~ plea⟩ ⟨looked upon me with a ~ countenance —William Penn⟩ ⟨a rather ~ pause —Louis Auchincloss⟩ ⟨a ~, consequential, humorless manner —Kingsley Amis⟩ **2 a** : weighing a considerable amount ⟨a ~ load⟩ ⟨several loads of extremely ~ cattle —*Chicago Daily Drovers Jour.*⟩ ⟨put the ~ parcel back into the woman's arms —G.G. Carter⟩ **b** : of large size : CORPULENT ⟨a ~ man⟩ **c** : falling or pressing heavily ⟨a ~ blow⟩ **d** : heavy in proportion to its bulk : of high specific gravity ⟨a ~ metal⟩ **3** : hard to be borne : BURDENSOME, GRIEVOUS, ONEROUS ⟨a ~ evil⟩ **4** *obs* : of standard weight ⟨contract to be paid in ~ money —John Locke⟩ **5** : having much force, influence, or authority : POWERFUL, TELLING ⟨is pretty clear that no book in the 18th century made quite so ~ or so wide an impact —H.J.Laski⟩ **syn** see HEAVY
wei·hai·wei \'wā'hī'wī\ *adj, usu cap* [fr. *Weihaiwei*, China] : of or from the city of Weihaiwei, China : of the kind or style prevalent in Weihaiwei
weil-fe·lix reaction \'vī(ə)l'fāliks-\ *or* **weil-felix test** *n, usu cap W&F* [after Edmund *Weil* †1922 and Arthur *Felix* b1887 Austrian physicians] : an agglutination test for various rickettsial infections (as typhus fever and scrub typhus) using particular strains of bacteria of the genus *Proteus* that have antigens in common with the rickettsias to be identified
weil's disease \'vī(ə)lz-, 'wī(ə)lz-\ *n, usu cap W* [after Adolf *Weil* †1916 Ger. physician] : a leptospirosis that is characterized by chills, fever, muscle pain, and hepatitis manifested by more or less severe jaundice and that is caused by a spirochete (*Leptospira icterohaemorrhagiae*)
wei·mar·an·er \'vīmə,ränə(r)\, 'wī-, -,rän-, -,ran-, ,==ˌ=\ *n* [G, fr. *Weimar*, city in central Germany where the breed was developed] **1** *usu cap* : a German breed of large gray, short-haired sporting dogs with pendulous ears and cropped tail **2** -s *often cap* : a dog of the Weimaraner breed
¹wei·mar·i·an \vī'ma(a)rēən, wī-\ *adj, usu cap* [*Weimar*, Germany + E *-an*] **1** : of, relating to, or characteristic of Weimar, Germany **2** : of, relating to, or characteristic of the residents of Weimar, Germany
²weimarian \"\ *n* -s *cap* : a native or resident of Weimar, Germany
weiner *var of* WIENER
wein·man·nia \wīn'manēə\ *n, cap* [NL, fr. J. W. *Weinmann*, 18th cent. Ger. apothecary + NL *-ia*] : a large genus of shrubs and trees (family Cunoniaceae) that are found chiefly in the southern hemisphere and have opposite mostly simple leaves, racemose flowers, a free ovary, and 2-celled 2-valved capsules — see TENIO
wein·schenk·ite \'vīn,sheŋ,kīt\ *n* -s [G *weinschenkit*, fr. Ernst H. O. K. *Weinschenk* †1921 Ger. petrographer + G *-it* -ite] : a mineral $(Er,Y)PO_4.2H_2O$ consisting of a hydrous phosphate of rare earths and occurring in white rounded aggregates and radiating masses
¹weir \'wi|(ə)r, 'we(a)|, 'we|, |(ə)\ *n* -s [ME *were*, fr. OE *wer*; akin to OHG *werī* defense, ON *ver* fishing-place, OE *werian* to defend, protect, hinder, OHG *werien, werren* to defend, ON

verja, Goth *warjan* to defend, L *aperire* to open, *operire* to close, cover, Gk *erysthai* to protect, guard, Skt *vṛṇoti* he covers, envelops, holds back, surrounds] **1 :** a fence or enclosure (as of stakes, brushwood, or netting) set in a stream, tideway, or inlet of the sea for taking fish **:** FISHGARTH ⟨eel ~⟩ ⟨herring ~⟩ **2 a :** a dam in a stream to raise the water level or divert its flow — see LEAPING WEIR **b :** a notch in a levee or other barrier across or bordering a stream to regulate the flow of water (as in time of flood) — see WASTEWEIR **3** *dial Eng* **:** a bank or levee built to hold a river in its bed or to direct it into a new bed **4 :** a device (as a notch in a dam) for determining the quantity of water flowing over it from measurements of the depth of water over the crest or sill and known dimensions of the device — see CIPOLLETTI WEIR

²weir \"\ *vt* -ED/-ING/-S **:** to put a weir in or on ⟨~ a river⟩

³weir \'wi(ə)r\ *Scot var of* WAR

weir basin *n* **:** a wide approach to the upstream side of an irrigation weir constructed so as to reduce to a minimum the effect of the momentum of the approaching water on the flow over the weir

weir box *n* **:** a wooden or concrete box oblong in shape and open at both ends which is set lengthwise in a canal and in which a weir for the measurement of irrigation water is set crosswise

¹weird \'wi(ə)rd, -i(ə)d\ *n* -S [ME *wierd, werd, wird*, fr. OE *wyrd*; akin to OHG *wurt* fate, ON *urthr* weird, fate, OE *weorthan* to become — more at WORTH] **1 a :** FATE, DESTINY, LOT, FORTUNE; *esp* **:** ill fortune **:** a disastrous destiny **b** *usu cap* **:** ¹FATE 3, NORN **2 a :** SOOTHSAYER **b :** SPELL, CHARM **c :** a supernatural tale **3 :** PROPHECY, PREDICTION

²weird \"\ *vt* -ED/-ING/-S [ME (Sc) *weirden, werden*, fr. *wierd, werd* fate] **1** *Scot* **:** to assign to a certain fate **:** DESTINE **2** *Scot* **:** to foretell or assign as a fate **:** PREDICT

³weird \"\ *adj* -ER/-EST [ME (Sc) *werd*, fr. *werd*, n., fate] **1** *archaic* **:** of, relating to, or dealing with fate or the Fates **2 a :** of or relating to witchcraft or to the supernatural **:** caused by or suggesting magical influence ⟨Spanish horses, which appeared as ~ centaurs to the amazed Indians —R.W. Murray⟩ ⟨~ stories of the supernatural, rousing terror and pity —Frank Monaghan⟩ **b :** UNEARTHLY, MYSTERIOUS ⟨a ~ desert of congealed lava —Tom Marvel⟩ ⟨around the sun appears the ~, pearly corona seen on earth only during total eclipses —Waldemar Kaempffert⟩ ⟨the ~, ringing voices of veeries —W.P.Smith⟩ **3 :** curious in nature or appearance **:** of strange or extraordinary character **:** ODD, UNUSUAL, FANTASTIC ⟨some trick of the moonlight, some ~ effect of shadow —Bram Stoker⟩ ⟨in this section grow many ~ varieties of cactus —*Amer. Guide Series: Texas*⟩ ⟨~ prophets popped up everywhere —G.W.Johnson⟩ ⟨some of his statements on local and state politics are a bit ~ —G.E.Mowry⟩

syn WEIRD, EERIE, and UNCANNY agree in the sense of fearfully or mysteriously strange or fantastic. WEIRD applies in one sense to something unearthly or preternaturally mysterious; in another sense, to something strangely or absurdly queer ⟨something a trifle *weird* about leaving the little man alone among those dead servants —G.K.Chesterton⟩ ⟨a touch of the *weird* or ghostly —P.E.More⟩ ⟨a procession of *weird* characters: sorcerers, syndics, half-wits, adolescent girls in pregnancy, hermaphrodites —Richard Plant⟩ ⟨preaching a *weird* interpretation of the Scriptures —*Amer. Guide Series: Ind.*⟩ EERIE suggests an uneasy, often fearful premonition that malign powers or influences are at work ⟨some *eerie* moments among the corpses —*Times Lit. Supp.*⟩ ⟨the flutes keep up an *eerie* wail —Horace Sutton⟩ ⟨the poem has an *eerie* quality, like that of dream or of neurosis —Yvor Winters⟩ ⟨the spruce trees and rocks loomed out of the fog in *eerie*, blurred shapes —Jean Potter⟩ UNCANNY suggests in one sense uncomfortable strangeness or mysteriousness; in another more common sense, merely beyond ordinary powers to comprehend or as though supernatural ⟨some *uncanny* apparition in a graveyard⟩ ⟨the machines operate with *uncanny* precision at high speeds —*Envelope*⟩ ⟨the natives display *uncanny* proficiency in detecting the whereabouts of fish —Bill Beatty⟩

weird·ie *or* **weirdy** \-dē\ *n, pl* **weirdies** *slang* **:** one that is extraordinarily strange, eccentric, or unnatural ⟨filmland's horrific *weirdies* —*Newsweek*⟩

weird·less \-dləs\ *adj, chiefly Scot* **1 :** ILL-FATED **2 :** IMPROVIDENT — **weird·less·ness** *n* -ES *chiefly Scot*

weirdlike \'ˌ=ˌ=\ *adj* **:** WEIRD

weird·li·ness \-dlēnəs\ *n* -ES *chiefly Scot* **:** the quality or state of being weirdly

¹weird·ly *adj* -ER/-EST [¹*weird* + -*ly*] **1** *Scot* **:** PROSPEROUS, FORTUNATE **2** *chiefly Scot* **:** of or relating to the supernatural **:** GHOSTLY

²weirdly *adv* [³*weird* + -*ly*] **:** in a weird manner ⟨the ~ beautiful moonlight —Joseph Furphy⟩

weird·ness *n* -ES **:** the quality or state of being weird

weird sister *n, usu cap W&S* [ME *werd sister*] **:** ¹FATE 3, NORN

weiring *n* -S [fr. gerund of ²*weir*] **1 :** the building of a weir (as in a stream for catching fish) **2 :** material for building a weir

weir·less \'=ləs\ *adj* **:** lacking a weir **:** not provided with weirs

weirs *pl of* WEIR, *pres 3d sing of* WEIR

weir vine *n* [¹*weir*] **:** a tuberous-rooted morning glory (*Ipomoea calobra*) that is an aggressive weed and reputed to be responsible for livestock poisoning in parts of Australia

weis·bach·ite \'wīs,ba,kīt\ *n* -S [G *weisbachit*, fr. Julius A. *Weisbach* †1901 Ger. mineralogist + G -*it* -ite] **:** a variety of anglesite containing barium

weisenheimer *var of* WISENHEIMER

¹weis·man·ni·an \vī'smänēən, wī'sman-\ *adj, usu cap* [August *Weismann* †1914 Ger. biologist + E -*an*, adj. suffix] **:** of or relating to the theories or teachings of Weismann

²weismannian \"\ *n* -S *usu cap* [August *Weismann* + E -*an*, n. suffix] **:** an adherent of Weismann

weis·mann·ism \'vī,smä,nizəm, 'wīsmə,n-\ *n* -S *usu cap* [August *Weismann* †1914 + E -*ism*] **:** the theories of heredity and development proposed by August Weismann; *esp* **:** the concepts of continuity of the germ plasm and dichotomy of germ and soma with their correlates of germinal transmission of hereditary qualities and absence of inheritance of acquired characters

weiss beer \'wīs-, 'vīs-\ *n* [G *weissbier*, lit., white beer] **:** a light-colored highly effervescent beer made from unboiled wheat-malt worts with top-fermentation yeast

weiss·ite \'wī,sīt\ *n* -S [Louis *Weiss*, 20th cent. Am. mine owner + E -*ite*] **:** a mineral Cu_5Te_3 consisting of a massive bluish black copper telluride

weiss·nicht·wo \'vī,snik(t)'vō\ *n* -S *usu cap* [fr. *Weissnichtwo*, imaginary city in the satirical work *Sartor Resartus* (1833–34) by Thomas Carlyle †1881 Scot. essayist and historian, fr. G *weiss nicht wo* (I) know not where] **:** an indefinite, unknown, or imaginary place

weit·spek·an \'wit,spekən\ *n* -S *usu cap* [Yurok *Weitspekw*, a Yurok village + E -*an*] **:** a language family of the Ritwan stock comprising only Yurok

we·jack \'wē,jak\ *n* -S [of Algonquian origin; akin to Ojibwa *otchig* fisher, Cree *otchek*; perh. influenced by Ojibwa *wajashk* muskrat] **1 :** FISHER 2 **2 :** WOODCHUCK

we·ka \'wekə\ *n* -S [Maori] **:** any of several flightless New Zealand rails (genus *Gallirallus*, syn. *Ocydromus*) of thievish disposition having short wings each with a spur used in fighting — called also *Maori hen, wood hen*

welch *var of* WELSH

welch bacillus \'welch-, -lsh-\ *n, usu cap W* [after William Henry *Welch* †1934 Am. pathologist] **:** a clostridium (*Clostridium perfringens*) that causes gas gangrene

welchman *var of* WELSHMAN

welch plug *n* [prob. fr. the name *Welch*] **:** a plug for sealing an unused end of an oil passage drilled through a hollow crankshaft, crank arm, or crankpin

¹wel·come \'welkəm, 'weuk-\ *interj* [ME, alter. (influenced by *wel* well) of *wilcume*, fr. OE *wilcume, wilcume*, fr. *wilcuma* desirable guest; akin to OHG *willicomo* desirable guest; prob. both fr. a prehistoric WGmc compound whose constituents are represented by OE *will, willa* will, wish and OE *cuma* guest; akin to OE *cuman* to come — more at WELL, WILL, COME] — used to express a greeting of pleasure or goodwill or a cordial salutation to a guest or newcomer upon his arrival

²welcome \"\ *vt* -ED/-ING/-S [ME *welcomen*, alter. (influenced by *wel* well) of *wilcumen*, fr. OE *wilcumian*, fr. *wilcuma*, interj., welcome & *wilcuma*, n., desirable guest] **1 :** to greet (as a visitor) with courtesy or cordiality **:** receive hospitably and gladly **:** give a friendly reception to **:** make welcome ⟨ran . . . to ~ them at the door —J.C.Powys⟩ ⟨they *welcomed* the travelers home⟩ **2 :** to greet or receive with something esp. of an unpleasant nature ⟨they *welcomed* the intruder with a hail of bullets⟩ **3 a :** to greet heartily or joyfully ⟨*welcomed* his arrival from abroad⟩ **b :** to greet with pleasure the coming or occurrence of **:** accept with an expression of pleasure ⟨no mariner . . . ~s rough water —S.E.Morison⟩ ⟨those who deplore and those who ~ the change —John Strachey⟩ ⟨the society ~*s* applications from interested persons⟩

³welcome \"\ *adj* [ME, alter. (influenced by *wel* well) of *wilcume* desirable guest, fr. OE *wilcuma*] **1 :** received gladly into one's presence or companionship **:** admitted willingly to the company, house, or entertainment **:** highly acceptable as a visitor or companion ⟨a ~ guest⟩ ⟨visitors are always ~ here⟩ **2 :** giving pleasure **:** highly acceptable, agreeable, or pleasing **:** received with gladness or delight esp. in response to a need or desire ⟨revivals offered ~ interludes in pioneer life —*Amer. Guide Series: Minn.*⟩ ⟨the sight of the island was right ~ —Herman Melville⟩ ⟨providing an easy and ~ solution of an . . . awkward problem —W.L.Sperry⟩ **3 :** freely or willingly permitted **:** cordially invited ⟨he was ~ to come and go —W.M. Thackeray⟩ ⟨if anybody happened to be able to toss off a better one he was ~ to —R.G.G.Price⟩ **syn** see PLEASANT

⁴welcome \"\ *n* -S **1 a :** a cordial, kindly, pleasant, or hearty greeting or reception given to one (as a guest, newcomer, or stranger) usu. upon arrival ⟨to thee and thy company I bid a hearty ~ —Shak.⟩ ⟨a packed house . . . roared a three-minute ~ —*Current Biog.*⟩ ⟨the ~ he received justified his visit —A.R.Forde⟩ **b :** a greeting or reception resembling such an act of welcoming but having a different nature usu. of a specified kind ⟨our men gave the enemy a hot ~ —Bill Alcine⟩ ⟨the delegation received a rather cool ~⟩ **2 :** the action of welcoming or of saluting or treating as welcome **:** hearty or hospitable reception (as of a stranger or guest) ⟨bore the means of goodly ~, flesh and wine —Alfred Tennyson⟩

welcome home *n* [fr. the phrase *welcome home*] **1 :** a reception usu. of a cordial nature provided to celebrate the return home of a person ⟨invited me to a supper for my *welcome home* —Philemon Holland⟩ **2 :** an expression of welcome made at a person's homecoming ⟨the *welcome home* which rang from every spire and steeple —*London Daily Telegraph*⟩

wel·come·ly *adv* **1 :** with a feeling or expression of welcome **:** with joy, pleasure, or hospitality **:** GLADLY ⟨I have been very kindly and ~ entertained —Thomas Chalmers⟩ **2 :** in a manner so as to produce welcome, gratification, or pleasure ⟨the conductor's ~ brisk tempo —Robert Lawrence⟩ ⟨the picture is ~ modest in all that it attempts —Brendan Gill⟩

welcome mat *n* **:** something held to resemble a mat placed before a door as a symbol of hospitality and pleasant reception ⟨rolled out the *welcome mat* for the visiting dignitaries⟩

wel·come·ness *n* -ES *archaic* **:** the quality or state of being welcome

wel·com·er \-mə(r)\ *n* -S **:** one that welcomes ⟨a crowd of ~*s* awaited the incoming train⟩ ⟨the traditional ~ of the outcast, America —J.R.Krueger⟩

¹weld \'weld\ *also* **woald** *or* **wold** *or* **would** \'wōld\ *n* -S [ME *welde, wold*; akin to MLG *wolde* weld, MD *woude*] **1 :** DYER'S ROCKET **2 :** a yellow dye that is obtained from weld and contains luteolin as its chief coloring **3 :** ACACIA 5

²weld \'weld\ *vb* -ED/-ING/-S [alter. (influenced by *welled*, past part. of *well* to boil, rise, well) of obs. E *well* to weld, fr. ME *wellen* to boil, well, weld — more at WELL] *vi* **:** to become or be capable of being welded **:** undergo junction by welding ⟨iron ~*s* easily⟩ ⟨the parts ~*ed* together perfectly⟩ ~ *vt* **1 a :** to unite or consolidate (as metallic parts) by heating to a plastic or fluid state the surfaces of the parts to be joined and then allowing the metals to flow together with or without the addition of other molten metal or by hammering or compressing with or without previous softening by heat — compare GAS WELDING **b :** to unite (plastics) in a similar manner by heating **c :** to produce or repair (as an article) by this method ⟨~*ed* pipe⟩ ⟨~*ed* the crack in the tube⟩ **d :** to produce or create as if by such a process ⟨~ a political party out of . . . divisive elements —Gladwin Hill⟩ ⟨solidarity ~*ed* out of emergency —Amy Loveman⟩ ⟨West ~*s* reply to Soviet —Carlyle Morgan⟩ **2 :** to unite closely or intimately **:** join closely or inseparably **:** form into or as if into a single unit ⟨her gratitude ~*ed* her to him forever —Harrison Smith⟩ ⟨~ the warring Gaelic and English elements into a Norman-Irish nation —Brian Fitzgerald⟩ **3 :** to cause (tissues) to form a seal by adhesion

³weld \"\ *n* -S **1 :** a welded joint **:** the junction of a welded piece — see ARC WELD, BUTT WELD, CAULK WELD, CLEFT WELD, MASH WELD, PLUG WELD, RIPPLE WELD, RIVET WELD, SCARF-WELD, SEAM WELD **2 :** the union of metals by welding **:** the state or condition of being welded **3 :** the adhesion of tissues to form a seal ⟨a natural ~ formed by the healing together of artery and vein⟩

⁴weld \"\ *adj* [³*weld*] **:** WELDABLE; *specif* **:** made without complete fusion ⟨~ iron⟩ ⟨~ steel⟩

weld·abil·i·ty \,weldə'bilədē\ *n* **:** the quality, state, or property of being weldable **:** the capacity to undergo welding ⟨the chief factors governing ~ of aluminum —E.G.West⟩ ⟨tables on ~ of materials —W.A.Stanley⟩

weld·able \'weldəbəl\ *adj* **:** capable of being welded

welded tuff *n* **:** a tuff deposit sufficiently thick and hot at the time of emplacement that the fragments soften and coalesce to form a rock which simulates rhyolite or obsidian

weld·er \'weldə(r)\ *n* -S **:** one that welds: as **a :** one whose work is welding **b :** a machine used in welding

welder's helmet *n* **:** a helmet used in arc welding that shields the front of the head, has a protective lens for the eyes, and is fitted with a headgear on which it can usu. be tilted up out of the way

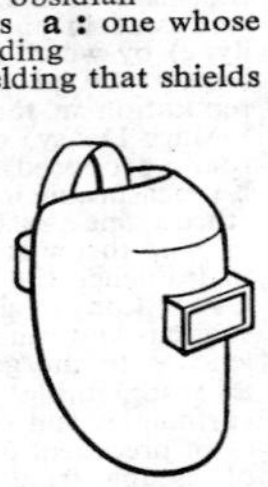

welder's helmet

welding *n* -S [fr. gerund of ²*weld*] **:** the action or process of making or joining with a weld

welding blowpipe *or* **welding torch** *n* **:** a blowpipe used in fusion welding

welding powder *n* **:** a powder used as a flux in welding

welding rod *n* **:** a rod or heavy wire that melts and thus supplies metal in fusion welding

weld·less \'weldləs\ *adj* **:** having no welds **:** made without a weld ⟨~ chain⟩ ⟨~ steel tubes⟩

weld·ment \-dmənt\ *n* -S **:** a unit formed by welding together an assembly of pieces ⟨the gear housings . . . are made of steel castings and ~*s* —Carl Himmelright⟩

weld metal *n* **:** the part of the metal of a welded joint that has been fused in its formation

wel·don process \'weldən-\ *n, usu cap W* [after Walter *Weldon* †1885 Eng. chemist] **:** a process used formerly for the recovery of manganese dioxide in making chlorine from hydrochloric acid in a stoneware still by adding lime to the still liquor and oxidizing with air to precipitate a mud containing calcium manganite and yielding chlorine when recirculated and treated with hydrochloric acid

wel·dor \'weldə(r)\ *n* -S [²*weld* + -*or*] **:** one whose work is welding **:** one skilled in welding **:** WELDER a

weld screw *n* **:** a screw that has a flat offset head and can be made captive by spot welding

¹wel·fare \'wel,fa(a)(ə)r, -,fe(, |ə\ *n* -S [ME, fr. the phrase *wel faren* to fare well, fr. OE *wel faran*, fr. *wel* well + *faran* to fare — more at WELL, FARE] **1 a :** the state of faring or doing well **:** thriving or successful progress in life **:** a state characterized esp. by good fortune, happiness, well-being, or prosperity ⟨we can use the knowledge . . . for the future ~ of humanity —H.S.Truman⟩ ⟨a generous mother who sincerely seeks her child's ~ —H.M.Parshley⟩ ⟨increasing production has made ~ for all seem . . . possible —A.J.Toynbee⟩ — opposed to *illfare* **b :** the state or condition (as of a person or enterprise) in regard to well-being; *esp* **:** one's condition in regard to health, happiness, or prosperity ⟨the effects of climate upon the ~ . . . of man —D.H.K.Lee⟩ ⟨guilty of gross negligence of the ~ of his workers —T.P.Whitney⟩ **c :** the sum of individual utilities **:** a social optimum **2 :** WELFARE WORK ⟨helped to make music a recognized part of industrial ~ —Kenneth Baynes⟩ **3 :** RELIEF 2a

²welfare \"\ *adj* **:** of, relating to, or concerned with welfare and esp. with improvement of the welfare of social groups (as children, workers, or underprivileged or disabled persons) ⟨~ agencies⟩ ⟨~ services⟩ ⟨private ~ foundations⟩

welfare capitalism *n* **:** capitalism characterized by a concern for the welfare of various social groupings (as workers) expressed usu. through social-security programs, collective-bargaining agreements, state industrial codes, and other guarantees against insecurity

welfare economics *n* **:** a branch of economics dealing with human welfare, the defining of wealth, and the establishment of guides for social policy aiming at the maximization of total individual utilities

welfare factor *n* **:** any factor (as availability of food or shelter) that tends to stimulate population growth — compare DECIMATING FACTOR

welfare fund *n* **:** a fund usu. established by an employer from which benefits are paid to employees in time of sickness or other specified occasion and commonly set up in response to union pressure and as a contractual obligation

welfare state *n* **1 :** a social system based upon the assumption by a political state of primary responsibility for the individual and social welfare of its citizens usu. by the enactment of specific public policies (as health and unemployment insurance, minimum wages and prices, and subsidies to agriculture, housing, and other segments of the economy) and their implementation directly by governmental agencies **2 :** a political unit (as a nation or state) characterized by the operation of the system of the welfare state

welfare stat·er \-'stād·ə(r)\ *n* **:** one that believes in or advocates a welfare state

welfare statism *n* **:** a belief in or the advocacy or practice of policies associated with or designed to bring about a welfare state

welfare work *n* **1 :** organized efforts by a community, organization, or individual for the social betterment and general improvement in the welfare of a group in society (as underprivileged or disabled persons) **2 :** the provision of fringe benefits (as group insurance and pension plans, medical services, and educational and recreational activities) by a corporation as a labor policy esp. during the first quarter of the 20th century

wel·far·ism \'wel,fa(a),rizəm, -,fe(,r-\ *n* -S **:** the complex of policies, attitudes, and beliefs associated with welfare statism ⟨the bias of the Administration toward ~ —Jules Abels⟩ ⟨part of the same structure of ~ is government support of farm products prices —*Wall Street Jour.*⟩

welk \'welk\ *vi* -ED/-ING/-S [ME *welken*, prob. fr. MD; akin to OHG *irwelkēn* to welk, *irwelhēn* to become soft, *wolkan* cloud] **1** *dial chiefly Eng* **:** to lose freshness or greenness **:** dry up **:** FADE, WILT, WITHER **2** *obs* **:** to become less (as in power or brightness) **:** WANE

wel·kin \'welkən\ *n* -S [ME *welkin, welkne, wolkne* cloud, welkin, fr. OE *wolcen*; akin to OS & OHG *wolkan* cloud, *welk* moist, gentle, faded, OE *wlæc, wlacu* lukewarm, OIr *folc* flood of water, OSlav *vlaga* moisture] **1 :** the vault of heaven **:** FIRMAMENT, SKY ⟨fearsome storm-god . . . with his great ~ shuddering voice —Weston La Barre⟩ ⟨a chorus . . . that made the very ~ ring —Thomas Barbour⟩ **2 :** the celestial regions as the abode of God or the gods **:** the heavens **3 :** the upper atmosphere **:** the air in which clouds float ⟨the Air Force, as the custodian of our ~ —*New Yorker*⟩ ⟨scattered songsters probe the ~ —Jack Lusby⟩

¹well \'wel\ *n* -S [ME *welle*, fr. OE (northern & Midland dial.) *welle*; akin to OHG *wella* wave, ON *vella* boiling heat, OE *weallan* to bubble, boil — more at ³WELL] **1 a :** an issue of water from the earth **:** a spring rising to the surface of the earth and forming a pool or rivulet **:** a pool fed by a spring ⟨the ~ flows in a pure and abundant stream from the granite rock —J.M.Jephson & L.A.Reeve⟩ **b :** a spring of water traditionally held to be of miraculous origin or to have supernatural healing or magical powers and often associated with a particular saint ⟨St. Gulval's *Well* . . . was famous for its prophetic properties —W.C.Meller⟩ **c** (1) **:** MINERAL SPRING (2) **wells** *pl* **:** a place where mineral springs are located and where invalids often resort **:** WATERING PLACE 3, SPA — used chiefly in place names ⟨Tunbridge *Wells*⟩ **d** *chiefly Scot* **:** a fountain fed by a spring **e** (1) **:** something resembling a spring (as in flowing or being used for drinking) ⟨start the ~*s* of plenty bubbling . . . with British gold —J.P.Fitzpatrick⟩ (2) **:** an origin from which something springs or arises **:** a source of supply **:** FOUNTAIN, WELLSPRING ⟨the ~*s* of his loquacity were dried up —C.S.Forester⟩ ⟨the native ~ of English in our young —J.M.Barzun⟩ (3) **:** a dangerous eddy **:** WHIRLPOOL — used esp. of eddies near the northern coast of Scotland **2 :** a pit or hole sunk (as by digging, boring, or drilling) into the earth to such a depth as to reach a supply of water, generally having a cylindrical form, and often walled with stone, bricks, or tubbing to prevent the earth from caving in **3 :** a part of a boat or other craft resembling a well: as **a :** a vertical enclosure in the middle of a ship's hold that reaches from the bottom to the lower deck and that contains and is designed to protect from damage and facilitate the inspection of the pumps — called also *pump well* **b :** a compartment in the hold of a fishing boat that is level at the sides but has holes in the bottom to let in water to keep fish alive **c** (1) **:** a vertical passage into which a propeller may be drawn up or from which a periscope may be raised (2) **:** a hollow compartment recessed in an airplane wing or fuselage into which a unit (as a wing flap or landing gear wheel) retracts **d :** an enclosure in a ship's bottom into which water drains and is then pumped out; *esp* **:** the space between two tanks or sections of the double bottom or between either and a bulkhead **e :** a vertical passage in the bow of some old-style monitors in which the anchor is stowed **f :** the part of the main deck between the raised forecastle and the poop of a well-decked ship **4 :** a shaft or pit dug or bored in the earth: as **a :** one used for the storage of ice **b :** a shaft or excavation in the earth made in military mining from which run branches or galleries **c :** a shaft or hole sunk to obtain oil, brine, or gas ⟨an oil ~⟩ ⟨salt ~*s*⟩ **d :** RELIEF WELL **e** (1) **:** a pit or hole in the ground reaching to hardpan or bedrock (2) **:** a hollow cylinder of reinforced concrete, steel, timber, or masonry built in such a hole as a support for a bridge or building **f :** a tile stack for drainage **5 :** a part of a building or similar structure resembling a well: as **a :** an open space extending vertically through floors of a structure (as a stairwell or elevator shaft) ⟨a spiral stairway with an open ~ extending through three stories —*Amer. Guide Series: Md.*⟩ **b :** the space in an English law court set off immediately in front of the judge's bench and usu. occupied by solicitors **c :** an open shaft formed by surrounding walls and extending vertically through the floors of a structure to provide light and air to interior areas **d :** the place in a lecture hall, legislative chamber, or similar large assembly room where the speaker is located and around which the seats rise in tiers or on a slope **:** the area between the rostrum or stage and the first row of seats **:** PIT **6 :** a heraldic bearing representing the part of the wall of a well aboveground **7 :** a vessel or space having a construction or shape that suggests a well for water: as **a :** a space or receptacle resembling a box located in the body of a vehicle and used for luggage **b :** a deep drawer or hollow interior area used as a receptacle in a piece of furniture (as a desk or bureau) ⟨pine cupboard . . . having hinged cover over a ~ —*Parke-Bernet Galleries Cat.*⟩ ⟨a ~ with a compartmented interior⟩ **c :** the lower part of a furnace into which the molten metal runs **d :** a small receptacle in a larger vessel or unit ⟨the ~ in a jar of paste⟩ ⟨the ~ of a fountain pen⟩ ⟨this bent pipe had a bowl which retained the objectionable moisture in its ~ —*Irish Digest*⟩ ⟨lubricating oil ~*s* located in a planer bed⟩ — see INKWELL **e** (1) **:** an indentation or cavity in a surface ⟨tree ~*s*⟩ ⟨cellar window ~*s*⟩ (2) **:** one of the tiny depressed spots incised or etched in a gravure plate and holding the ink when the surface of the plate is wiped clean before a sheet is printed (3) **:** the

dark center of a diamond cut too thick **8 a :** something resembling a well in being damp, cool, deep, or dark ⟨a great ~ of a cupboard⟩ ⟨make your room a cool ~ of dusk —Claudia Cassidy⟩ **b :** something resembling a well in constituting a deep vertical hole ⟨the ~ in a glacier⟩ ⟨poked ~s in the biscuit to hold the molasses —Eudora Welty⟩ ⟨a stove ~⟩ **c :** something held to resemble a well in constituting a deep reservoir from which one may draw ⟨a great ~ of friendship and respect for . . . the United States —R.M.Nixon⟩ ⟨the inner ~ of strength into which the peasant woman . . . must repeatedly dip —Lucy Crockett⟩ **9 a :** a pronounced minimum of a variable in physics ⟨energy ~⟩ ⟨potential ~⟩ **b :** a region in which such minimum occurs **10 :** STILLING BASIN **11 :** [1]FOUNTAIN 4 **12 :** a small leather cup fixed to or suspended from an archer's belt to hold the tips of arrows thrust thereunder

[2]**well** \"\ *adj* [ME *welle*, fr. *welle*, n.] **1 :** of, relating to, or having the characteristics of a well ⟨utilized the ~ principle in construction⟩ ⟨a ~ cover⟩ ⟨~ rope⟩ ⟨~ shape⟩ **2 :** used in connection with a well ⟨a ~ sweep⟩ ⟨~ drill⟩ **3 :** designed so as to have a part that is held to resemble a well ⟨the ~ railroad cars⟩ ⟨the ~ type of saddle⟩ ⟨~ slides⟩ **4 :** having a wellhole ⟨a ~ staircase⟩ ⟨~ stairs⟩

[3]**well** \"\ *vb* -ED/-ING/-S [ME *wellen*, fr. OE (northern & Midland dial.) *wellan* to cause to well; akin to MHG *wellen* to cause to well, ON *vella*; causative fr. the root of OE *weallan* to bubble, boil, OHG *wallan*, ON *vella* to well over, boil, L *volvere* to roll — more at VOLUBLE] *vi* **1 :** to rise to the surface in a copious stream and then usu. flow forth ⟨a clear small stream . . . ~*ed* from a rock hard by —G.P.R.James⟩ ⟨tears ~*ed up* in her eyes⟩ ⟨a spring . . . ~*ed* out of the rock into a stone basin —Willa Cather⟩ **2 :** to rise to the surface like a flood of liquid : spring up and often pour forth ⟨anger ~*ed* in his stomach like bile —Hugh MacLennan⟩ — often used with *up* ⟨great pity ~*ed up* from his generous heart —Rafael Sabatini⟩ ⟨an immense yearning for security ~*ed* up through the land —Oscar Handlin⟩ ~ *vt* **:** to pour forth from the depths ⟨some classic fountain . . . ~*ed* its pure waters in a sacred shade —Washington Irving⟩

[4]**well** \"\ *adv* **bet·ter** \'bedə(r), -etə-\ **best** \'best\ [ME *wel*, fr. OE; akin to OHG *wela, wola* well, ON *vel*, Goth *waila* well, OE *wyllan* to wish — more at WILL] **1 a :** in a good or proper manner : in accordance with a high standard of morality : in a way that is morally good : JUSTLY, RIGHTLY ⟨it is . . . doing ~ that entitles us to heaven —William Burkitt⟩ **b :** satisfactorily with respect to conduct or action ⟨worked ~ under difficult conditions⟩ ⟨the inability . . . of these children to do ~ in advanced academic areas —J.B.Conant⟩ **2 a :** in a manner that constitutes good treatment or confers a benefit : CONSIDERATELY, GENEROUSLY, KINDLY ⟨wished them ~⟩ ⟨spoke ~ of your idea⟩ **b :** in a kindly or friendly manner : with friendly words : with favor or welcome ⟨was ~ received at court⟩ ⟨her first novel was ~ received by the critics⟩ **3 a :** with skill or aptitude : in a skillful or expert manner : EXCELLENTLY, EXPERTLY ⟨sing ~⟩ ⟨paints ~⟩ ⟨a wonderful story, ~ written and sensitive —Peter Blake⟩ **b :** SATISFACTORILY ⟨plan has worked ~⟩ **c :** with good appearance or effect : ELEGANTLY ⟨carried himself ~⟩ **4 :** with careful or close attention : ATTENTIVELY ⟨watch ~ what I do⟩ **5 :** to a high point or degree ⟨they got on ~ together⟩ ⟨~ deserved the honor⟩ ⟨she did not seem so ~ pleased⟩ ⟨the legendary lore which I love so ~ —Sir Walter Scott⟩ ⟨you will be ~ rewarded by a visit —Dana Burnet⟩ — often used in combination ⟨a *well*-equipped kitchen⟩ ⟨*well*-populated areas⟩ **6 :** to the full degree or extent : FULLY, QUITE ⟨~ aware of the difficulties⟩ ⟨~ worth the price⟩ ⟨~ out of sight⟩ ⟨~ past the appropriate age⟩ ⟨arrived before dinner had ~ begun⟩ ⟨~ able to take care of himself⟩ **7 a :** in a way appropriate to the facts or circumstances : FITTINGLY, PROPERLY, RIGHTLY ⟨as the author ~ says⟩ ⟨a large box will answer the need almost equally ~⟩ **b :** in a prudent manner : SENSIBLY — used with *do* ⟨reasonable people . . . will do ~ to demand better evidence —M.R.Cohen⟩ ⟨do ~ to examine the grounds for this adverse opinion —I.A.Richards⟩ **8 :** in accordance with the occasion or circumstances : as a natural result or consequence : with propriety or good reason : NATURALLY, PROPERLY ⟨I cannot ~ refuse⟩ ⟨this decision may ~ be questioned⟩ ⟨took pride, as ~ she might, in her hair —Samuel Richardson⟩ ⟨old residents . . . speak of it with considerable affection, as ~ they might —John De Meyer⟩ **9 a :** in such manner as is desirable or pleasing : as one could wish : without harm or accident : FAVORABLY, FORTUNATELY, HAPPILY, PROSPEROUSLY, SUCCESSFULLY ⟨everything went ~ that morning⟩ ⟨piano and violin do not mix too ~ even in chamber music —P.H.Lang⟩ **b :** with success from a material point of view : ADVANTAGEOUSLY, PROPERLY ⟨he married ~⟩ ⟨he hadn't made a fortune . . . but he'd done fairly ~ —Frank Sargeson⟩ **10 a :** without trouble or difficulty : EASILY, READILY ⟨nor were the refugees such as a country can ~ spare —T.B.Macaulay⟩ ⟨appearing to know more of that abode of evil than she ~ could —H.S.Scott⟩ ⟨no transcript can ~ be found which does not differ from its prototype in some small points —F.H.A.Scrivener⟩ **b :** in all likelihood : INDEED ⟨a basic conflict that may ~ last for the balance of this century —J.B.Conant⟩ ⟨maintenance of the high level of expenditures . . . might ~ have a disastrous effect —D.W.Mitchell⟩ **11 :** in a state of prosperity, plenty, or comfort : in a prosperous or affluent manner ⟨he lives ~⟩ **12 :** in a thorough manner : to an extent approaching completeness ⟨after being ~ dried with a sponge⟩ **13 a :** without doubt, uncertainty, or question : CLEARLY, DEFINITELY ⟨~ remembered the stirring appeal⟩ ⟨~ knew the penalty⟩ **b :** CLOSELY, FAMILIARLY, INTIMATELY ⟨must know their own country ~ —*London Calling*⟩ **c :** in exact outlines : CLEARLY, DEFINITELY ⟨the tree stood out ~ against the horizon⟩ ⟨remembered ~ the incident he mentioned⟩ **14 :** with spirit and courage : BRAVELY, GALLANTLY ⟨fought ~ against overwhelming odds⟩ **15 :** with equanimity or good nature : without resentment ⟨reported that he took the disappointment ~⟩ **16 :** to a considerable extent : more than a little : CONSIDERABLY, FAR ⟨grows in hot, moist regions ~ into the temperate zone —G.S.Brady⟩ ⟨a population of ~ over a million people —L.D.Stamp⟩ ⟨~ north of the island —George Bradshaw⟩ **17 :** ENOUGH, SUFFICIENTLY — used in giving nautical commands (as concerning hoisting or lowering or bracing yards) — **as well** *adv* [ME *as wel*] **1 :** in addition : ALSO, TOO ⟨resists not only DDT but other well-known insecticides *as well* —H.J.Clausen⟩ ⟨worked as a shipwright in . . . Singapore, where he was an armament officer *as well* —*Current Biog.*⟩ **2 :** to the same extent or degree : as much ⟨the court . . . is open *as well* to the humblest as to the mightiest —*Adoptive Rite Ritual*⟩ ⟨our churchmen have become wealthy *as well* by the gifts of pious persons as by . . . bribes —Sir Walter Scott⟩ **3 a :** with equivalent or comparable effect ⟨my devotion might *as well* have been offered to . . . a statue in a museum —W.B.Yeats⟩ **b :** to a slight or possible advantage ⟨might just *as well* become reconciled to the fact that you're going to have trouble —Richard Joseph⟩ — **as well as** *adv* [ME *as wel as*] **:** and not only : and in addition ⟨is skillful *as well as* strong⟩ ⟨introduced the use of the gnomon . . . *as well as* made the first map —Benjamin Farrington⟩

[5]**well** \", *dial* 'wal\ *interj* [ME *wel*, fr. OE, fr. *wel*, adv.] **1** — used to express satisfaction with what has been said or done **2 a** — used to express assent or resignation **b** — used to express surprise and expostulation and often reduplicated **3** — used to indicate resumption of a thread of discourse or to introduce a remark

[6]**well** \'wel\ *adj* [ME *wel*, fr. *wel*, adv.] **1 a :** being in good standing or estimation : being on good terms : being in favor ⟨of great importance to us . . . to be ~ with the French government —H.J.Temple⟩ **b** *archaic* **:** being on terms of intimacy or familiarity ⟨all our set were ~ with some fine woman or other —B.H.Malkin⟩ **c :** pleased or satisfied with oneself ⟨being extremely ~ with himself —Agnes Bennett⟩ **2 :** being a cause for satisfaction or approval : SATISFACTORY, PLEASING ⟨saw . . . that all was not ~ with him —Washington Irving⟩ ⟨all's ~ that ends well⟩ **3 a :** being in a state of affluence or prosperity : WELL-OFF ⟨he must be very ~ in the world —B.H.Malkin⟩ — see WELL-TO-DO **b :** being in satisfactory condition or circumstances ⟨he will not change while he is as ~ where he is⟩ **4 :** being in accordance with advantage : deserving to be recommended : ADVISABLE, DESIRABLE ⟨it is not ~ to anger him⟩ ⟨it might be ~ for you to review the four basic steps —W.J.Reilly⟩ — sometimes used with *as* ⟨if you stay . . . it is as *well* to bring plenty of provisions —G.W.Murray⟩ **5 a :** being in health : sound in body and mind : free of or recovered from sickness, infirmity, disease, or ailment : HEALTHY ⟨a ~ man⟩ ⟨he looks ~⟩ **b (1) :** CURED ⟨the rheumatism . . . is now near quite ~ —Jonathan Swift⟩ **(2) :** being in a good or sound condition ⟨his health . . . is still pretty ~ —Oliver Goldsmith⟩ **6 :** pleasing or satisfactory in appearance ⟨looked very ~ when he was dressed —Ellery Queen⟩ ⟨the polished floor looks ~ —Herbert Spencer⟩ **7** *archaic* **:** good in quality or character ⟨it is really very ~ for a novel —Jane Austen⟩ **8 :** being a cause for thankfulness : lucky and gratifying : FORTUNATE ⟨it is ~ that this has happened⟩ — **all very well :** proper under the circumstances ⟨it is *all very well* . . . to advise the French in the columns of the *New York Times* —Frank Gorrell⟩ — **very well** — used to signify agreement, approval, or understanding of instructions — **well and good** — used to signify acceptance (as of a situation or decision) ⟨if that's the case, *well and good* — we can proceed accordingly⟩

syn see HEALTHY

[7]**well** \'wel\ *n, pl* **well :** a well person : one sound in health — usu. used collectively ⟨prevent the ~ from becoming ill⟩

[8]**well** \"\ *n* -S [ME *wel*, fr. *wel*, adv., well] *obs* **:** WELL-BEING ⟨restore you to your wonted ~ —Edmund Spenser⟩

[9]**well** \"\ *n* -S [[4]*well*] *chiefly Brit* **:** WELL ENOUGH ⟨when best to operate and when to leave ~ alone —Harvey Graham⟩ ⟨content to let ~ alone and to maintain . . . a defensive policy —C.E.Robinson⟩

well·a·day \'welə¦dā\ *n or interj* [by alter.] **:** WELLAWAY

well-advised \¦=¦==\ *adj* [ME *wel avised*, fr. *wel* well + *avised* advised] **1 :** acting with wisdom, wise counsel, or proper deliberation : PRUDENT ⟨he would be *well-advised* to heed this advice⟩ **2 :** resulting from, based upon, or showing careful deliberation or wise counsel ⟨a *well-advised* silence⟩ ⟨*well-advised* plans⟩

well-affected \¦==¦==\ *adj* **:** favorably disposed or inclined (as toward a person or a political authority)

well-and-tree platter \'==¦=-\ *n* **:** a platter having a depressed design of a trunk and branches through which meat juices flow into a large depression at one end

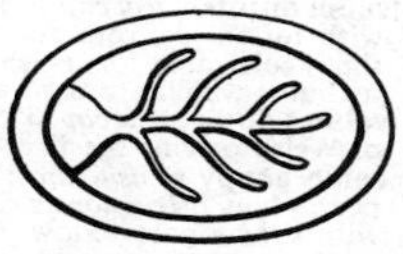
well-and-tree platter

well-appointed \¦=¦==\ *adj* **:** having good and complete equipment : properly fitted out ⟨a most comfortable and *well-appointed* residence —O.F.Morshead⟩

[1]**well·a·way** \'welə¦wā\ *interj* [ME *welaway, weleaway*, alter. (influenced by *wel* well and *away*) of *weilawei*, fr. OE *weilāwei*, lit., woe! lo! woe!, alter. (influenced by ON *vei* woe) of *wālāwā*, fr. *wā* woe + *lā* lo + *wā* woe — more at WELL, WOE] — used to express sorrow or lamentation

[2]**wellaway** \"\ *n* -S [ME *welaway*, fr. *welaway*, interj.] **:** LAMENT ⟨whispering her sad ~ —Thomas Woolner⟩

well-a-wins \-winz\ *Scot var of* WELLAWAY

well-being \'=¦==\ *n* **:** the state or condition of being well : a condition characterized by happiness, health, or prosperity : moral or physical welfare ⟨the elders were responsible . . . for the spiritual *well-being* of the people —V.L.Parrington⟩ ⟨achieved a degree of economic *well-being* —*Amer. Guide Series: N.Y.*⟩ ⟨a threat to the *well-being* of the republic —Lewis Nordyke⟩ ⟨an increased sense of *well-being*⟩ — opposed to *ill-being*

[1]**well-beloved** \¦==¦=(ə)\ *adj* [ME *welbeloved*, fr. *wel* well + *beloved*] **1 :** sincerely and deeply loved ⟨my *well-beloved* wife⟩ **2 :** sincerely respected — used in various ceremonial forms of address

[2]**well-beloved** \"\ *n* [ME *welbeloved*, fr. *welbeloved*, adj.] **:** a well-beloved person : a dearly loved one

well-beseen *adj* [ME *wel besein*, fr. *wel* well + *besein, beseen*, past part. of *beseen* to see, regard, favor — more at BESEE] *obs* **:** having or making a good appearance

well boat *n* **:** a boat having a well in which fish or lobsters can be kept alive

wellborn \'=¦=\ *adj* [ME *wel born*, fr. OE *wel-boren*, fr. *wel* well + *boren* born] **1 a :** born of a family of good, noble, or high standing ⟨a rich and ~ husband —Clement Greenberg⟩ **b :** having the characteristics of an offspring of such birth; *esp* **:** gentle and courteous in manner **2 :** born of parents genetically fitted for the production of sound offspring

well-breathed \'=¦=\ *adj* [ME *wel brethed*, fr. *wel* well + *brethed* breathed] **:** having good breathing capacity : strong or sound of wind ⟨on thy *well-breath'd* horse keep with thy hounds —Shak.⟩

well-bred \'=¦=\ *adj* **1 a :** belonging to a good family and properly brought up : having good breeding ⟨a gentleman *well-bred* and of good name —Shak.⟩ **b :** displaying good breeding : refined in manners : courteous in speech and behavior : CULTIVATED, REFINED ⟨a young man too *well-bred* to admit how bored he was —Mary Austin⟩ ⟨a happy and *well-bred* community —T.C.Roughley⟩ **2 :** of good breed : having a good pedigree ⟨*well-bred* swine⟩ ⟨*well-bred* horses⟩

well car *n* **:** a railroad flatcar having a depression or opening in the center of the deck for handling oversize loads that would not on regular flat cars come within overhead clearance limitations — called also *well-hole car*

well casing *n* **1 :** the tubular boring or drilling apparatus used in sinking a well and esp. an oil well **2 :** the tubular lining of a bored or drilled well

well-child clinic *n* **:** a clinic devoted to the proper care of and the prevention of diseases in small children (as by instructions and inoculations)

well-closed \'=¦=\ *adj* **:** of uniform formation — used of paper; contrasted with *wild*

well-conditioned \¦=¦==\ *adj* [ME *wele condicionde*, fr. *wele, wel* well + *condicionde, condiciouned* conditioned] **1 :** characterized by proper disposition, morals, or behavior : RIGHT-MINDED **2 :** having a good physical condition : HEALTHY, SOUND ⟨a *well-conditioned* animal⟩

well cress *n* [ME *welle-carse*, fr. OE *wyllecærse*, fr. *wylle, welle* well + *cærse* cress — more at WELL (spring), CRESS] **:** WATERCRESS 1a

well-day \'=¦=\ *n* **:** a day characterized by one's freedom from sickness ⟨the victim of a slight, ramshackly physique . . . never knowing a *well-day* —V.L.Parrington⟩; *specif* **:** one free from attacks of a recurrent disorder ⟨repeated cold and hot fits . . . with one or more *well-days* between them —Michael Underwood⟩

well deck *n* [[1]*well*] **:** a space on the weather deck of a ship lying at a lower level between a raised forecastle or poop and the bridge superstructure

well-decked \'=,dekt\ *adj* **:** having a well deck ⟨a *well-decked* ship⟩

well decker *n* **:** a well-decked ship

well-disposed \¦=¦==\ *adj* [ME *weldisposed*, fr. *wel* well + *disposed*] **:** having a good disposition; *esp* **:** disposed to be friendly, favorable, or sympathetic

well-done \'=¦=\ *adj* [ME] **1 :** rightly or properly performed : skillfully executed ⟨a *well-done* job⟩ **2 :** cooked thoroughly : cooked until the center is brownish-gray ⟨a *well-done* roast⟩ ⟨ordered a steak *well-done*⟩

well drain *n* **1 :** a well or pit for draining wet land **2 :** a drain discharging into a well

well-drain \'=,=\ *vt* [*well drain*] **:** to drain (land) by well drains from which the water is pumped out

well-dressing \'=¦==\ *n* **:** an ancient custom in rural areas in England of adorning local wells with floral decorations usu. as part of a religious service in thanksgiving for an abundant supply of pure water

welled \'weld\ *adj* [[1]*well* + *-ed*] **:** having or constructed with a well ⟨a ~ fishing boat⟩ ⟨a plate with a ~ center⟩

well enough *n* [fr. the phrase *well enough*] **:** an existing fairly satisfactory condition ⟨I should have let *well enough* alone —Louis Auchincloss⟩ ⟨unable to leave *well enough* alone⟩

wel·ler·ism \'welə,rizəm\ *n* -S *usu cap* [Sam *Weller*, witty servant of Mr. Pickwick in the story *Pickwick Papers* (1836–37) by Charles Dickens †1870 Eng. novelist] **:** an expression of comparison comprising a usu. well-known quotation followed by a facetious sequel (as "every one to his own taste," said the old woman as she kissed the cow)

well-favored \'=¦==\ *adj* [ME *wel favoured*, fr. *wel* well + *favoured*, past part. of *favouren* to favor — more at FAVOR] **:** having a fine or attractive appearance : pleasing to the eye : GOOD-LOOKING, HANDSOME ⟨Rachel was beautiful and *well-favored* —Gen 29:17 (AV)⟩ our Southern women are *well-favored* —Lillian Hellman⟩ — **well-fa·vored·ness** *n* -ES

well-fixed \'=¦=\ *adj* **:** having plenty of money or property : WELL-TO-DO, PROSPEROUS ⟨being a *well-fixed* boy in a poor neighborhood had its disadvantages —*Time*⟩

well-found \'=¦=\ *adj* **1** *archaic* **:** tried and found to be well or good : COMMENDABLE **2 :** fully furnished : properly equipped ⟨a *well-found* ship⟩

well-founded \'=¦==\ *adj* **1 :** constructed on a solid or firm foundation ⟨a *well-founded* building⟩ **2 :** having a firm foundation in fact : based on excellent reasoning, information, judgment, or grounds ⟨hope your fears are not *well-founded* —Allen Upward⟩ ⟨a doctrine . . . *well-founded* in principle —Richard Olney⟩

well grass *n, Scot* **:** WATERCRESS

well-groomed \'=¦=\ *adj* **1 :** well dressed and scrupulously neat ⟨*well-groomed* men⟩ **2** *of a horse* **:** carefully tended and curried **3 :** well cared for : made neat, tidy, and attractive down to the smallest details ⟨a *well-groomed* lawn⟩

well-grounded \'=¦==\ *adj* **:** WELL-FOUNDED

well-grown \'=¦=\ *adj* **:** having attained a satisfactory growth or development; *esp* **:** having almost reached maximum physical growth

well-hained \'=¦hānd\ *adj, chiefly Scot* **:** well or carefully preserved ⟨some buxom widow or *well-hained* spinster —John Galt⟩

well-handled \'=¦==\ *adj* [ME *wel handeled*, fr. *wel* well + *handeled*, past part. of *handelen* to handle — more at HANDLE] **1 :** being or having been managed or administered efficiently ⟨a *well-handled* fund⟩ **2 :** having been handled a great deal ⟨*well-handled* goods on a store counter⟩

wellhead \'=,=\ *n* [ME *wellehevd*, fr. *welle* well + *heved* head — more at WELL (spring), HEAD] **1 :** the place where a spring emerges from the ground : the source from which a stream flows ⟨traveled . . . among the ~s of wild rivers —R.L. Stevenson⟩ **2 :** the principal source : FOUNTAINHEAD ⟨from the ~ of pure science flow fertilizing streams which serve industry —Benjamin Farrington⟩ **3 a :** the top of a well ⟨Federal price control of natural gas at the ~ —Gene Smith⟩ **b :** a structure built over the top of a well ⟨an authentic Roman ~⟩

well-heeled \'=¦=\ *adj* **:** having plenty of money : WELL-FIXED ⟨well-dressed, *well-heeled* and well-mannered clientele —Richard Thruelsen⟩ ⟨an expert lobby every whit as influential and *well-heeled* as the China lobby —*Atlantic*⟩

wellhole \'=,=\ *n* **1 :** the hole, pit, or shaft of a well **2 a :** the open space in a floor or through a series of floors for the accommodation of a staircase **b :** the open space about which the stairs of a winding or circular staircase turn **3 :** a cavity for movement of a counterbalance or similar mechanical device

well-hole car *n* **:** WELL CAR

well house *n* [ME *welhous*, fr. *welle* well + *hous* house] **:** a covered structure (as a house or room) built around the top of a well

well-hung \'=¦=\ *adj* **1 :** hung skillfully and therefore working readily and freely : fluent in speech : GLIB ⟨a *well-hung* tongue⟩ **2 :** attached or suspended so as to hang well ⟨a *well-hung* skirt⟩ **3 :** hung long enough to acquire the proper flavor — used chiefly of game

welling *pres part of* WELL

[1]**wel·ling·ton** \'weliŋtən\ *or* **wellington boot** *n* -S *usu cap W* [after Arthur Wellesley, 1st Duke of *Wellington* †1852 Brit. general and statesman] **1 :** a leather boot having a loose top with the front usu. coming above the knee **2 :** HALF WELLINGTON **3 :** a high rubber boot often reaching to the knee

[2]**wellington** \"\ *adj, usu cap* [fr. *Wellington*, New Zealand] **1 :** of or from Wellington, the capital of New Zealand : of the kind or style prevalent in Wellington **2 :** of or from the provincial district of Wellington, New Zealand : of the kind or style prevalent in Wellington provincial district

wel·ling·to·nia \,weliŋ'tōnēə\ [NL, fr. 1st Duke of *Wellington* †1852 + NL *-ia*] *syn of* SEQUOIA

wel·ling·to·ni·an \¦==¦tōnēən\ *adj, usu cap* [1st Duke of *Wellington* †1852 + E *-an*] **:** of, relating to, or having the characteristics of the Duke of Wellington

well-knit \'=¦=\ *adj* [ME *wele knitte*, fr. *wele, wel* well + *knitte* knit, past part. of *knitten* to knit — more at KNIT] **:** firmly knit; *esp* **:** firmly and strongly constructed, compacted, or framed ⟨a *well-knit* athlete⟩ ⟨a *well-knit* argument⟩ ⟨a *well-knit* composition⟩ ⟨*well-knit* communities⟩

well-known \'=¦=\ *adj* [ME *wel knowen*, fr. [4]*well* + *knowen* known] **:** fully known: as **a :** widely known : generally acknowledged : known to many ⟨one of their most *well-known* physical peculiarities —C.D.Forde⟩ ⟨a *well-known* drama critic⟩ ⟨dined at a *well-known* restaurant⟩ **b :** closely, intimately, or thoroughly known ⟨a *well-known* voice reached her ears —Fanny Burney⟩

well-liking \'=¦==\ *adj* [ME *wel liking*, fr. *wel* well + *liking*, pres. part. of *liken* to like — more at LIKE] **:** being in good condition : having a good appearance : HEALTHY, THRIVING ⟨the righteous . . . shall be fat and *well-liking* —*Bk. of Com. Prayer*⟩

well log *n* **:** [1]LOG 3b(3)

well-looked \'=¦=\ *adj, chiefly Scot* **:** GOOD-LOOKING ⟨she must have been beautiful and still *well-looked* —J.G. Lockhart⟩

well-made play \'=¦=-\ *n* **:** a play constructed according to a predetermined pattern and aiming at neatness of plot and theatrical effectiveness but often being mechanical and stereotyped

well-mannered \'=¦==\ *adj* **:** having or displaying good manners : showing good taste : properly behaved : COURTEOUS, POLITE, WELL-BRED 1b ⟨*well-mannered* folk of comfortable means —Robert Shaplen⟩ ⟨a soundly constructed cabinet of *well-mannered* contemporary design —*advt*⟩ ⟨a *well-mannered* colt⟩

well-mean·er \'='mēnə(r)\ *n* **:** a well-meaning person : one whose intentions are good ⟨*well-meaners* think no harm —John Dryden⟩

well-meaning \'=¦==\ *adj* [ME *wel-mening*, fr. *wel* well + *mening*, pres. part. of *menen* to intend — more at MEAN] **:** having or motivated by good intentions but often producing unwelcome results through inefficiency or lack of wisdom ⟨the son's *well-meaning* efforts threw a singular chill upon the father's admirers —W.S.Maugham⟩ ⟨a rather stupid, *well-meaning* mother —*N. Y. Herald Tribune Bk. Rev.*⟩

well·ness *n* -ES **:** the quality or state of being in good health

well-nigh \'=¦=\ *adv* [ME *welneih, wel-neh*, fr. *wel* well + *neih, neh* nigh] **:** very nearly : ALMOST ⟨the resulting recording is *well-nigh* perfect —Thomas Heinitz⟩ ⟨the right of any senator to speak out at *well-nigh* any time —Lindsay Rogers⟩ ⟨for *well-nigh* a quarter of a century —*Blackwood's*⟩

well-off \'=¦=\ *adj* **1 :** being in good condition : situated in favorable circumstances : fortunately situated ⟨he doesn't know when he's *well-off* —H.A.Smith⟩ **2 :** well provided : having no lack — used esp. with *for* ⟨we are very *well-off* now for outdoor labor —Rachel Henning⟩ **3 :** WELL-TO-DO ⟨died so *well-off* that he was able to leave each of his eight children one million dollars —Green Peyton⟩

well over *vi* **:** OVERFLOW ⟨his heart *welled over* with joy —D.C. Murray⟩

well point *n* **:** a hollow pointed rod with a perforated intake driven into an excavation to lower the water table by pumping and thus minimize flooding during construction

well-read \'=¦=\ *adj* **:** characterized by extensive reading : well informed or deeply versed through reading ⟨our high respect for a *well-read* man —R.W.Emerson⟩ — often used with *in* ⟨a person *well-read* in medieval history⟩

well-ribbed-up \'=¦=\ *adj* **:** WELL-SPRUNG

well rig *also* **well rigging** *n* **:** the apparatus used in boring and finishing a well

wells *pl of* WELL, *pres 3d sing of* WELL

well-set \'ˌ=ˈ=\ *adj* [ME *wel sett*, fr. *wel* well + *sett* set]
1 : properly or skillfully set : well or firmly established
2 : strongly built : firmly knit ⟨the sailor short but *well-set* —Alexander Hamilton †1732⟩

well-set-up \'ˌ=ˌ=ˈ=\ *adj* : well formed, framed, or fashioned ⟨a handsome *well-set-up* blond young man —Dorothy C. Fisher⟩

well shrimp *n* : any of various usu. blind and white crustaceans living in subterranean waters and wells

wells·ian \'welzēən\ *adj, usu cap* [Herbert G. *Wells* †1946 Eng. novelist, sociological writer and historian + E -*an*] : of, relating to, or characteristic of H. G. Wells or his writings ⟨a pseudo-mystical . . . utopia in the *Wellsian* plan —Allen Tate⟩

wells·ite \'wel.zīt\ *n -s* [Horace L. *Wells* †1924 Am. chemist + E -*ite*] : a mineral (Ba,Ca,K₂)Al₂Si₃O₁₀.3H₂O of the phillipsite group consisting of a silicate of aluminum, calcium, barium, and potassium

well smack *n* : ⁶SMACK b

well-spoken \'ˌ=ˈ=\ *adj* [ME *wel spoken*, fr. *wel* well + *spoken*]
1 : speaking well, kindly, or fittingly : courteous and refined in speech ⟨found these people gentle, pious, and *well-spoken* —Willa Cather⟩ ⟨a knight *well-spoken* —Shak.⟩ **2** : spoken with propriety ⟨*well-spoken* words⟩

wellspring \'ˌ=ˌ=\ *n* [ME *wel spring*, fr. OE *wyllspring*, *welspring*, fr. *wylle*, *welle* well + *spring*] **1** : a source of continual supply or emanation ⟨our colleges . . . are ~s of humanistic and scientific learning —A.W.Griswold⟩ ⟨understanding is a ~ of life unto him that hath it; but the instruction of fools is folly —Prov 16:22 (AV)⟩ **2** : FOUNTAINHEAD 1 ⟨water . . . drawn recently from a ~ —J.D.Chambers⟩

well-sprung \'ˌ=ˈ=\ *adj* : rounded rather than lank or flattened — used of the rib cage or body contour of a domestic animal or bird

wellstrand \'ˌ=ˌ=\ *n -s* [ME *welle strond*, fr. *welle* well + *strond* strand] *Scot* : a stream flowing from a spring

well sweep *n* : SWEEP 1a

well-tempered \'ˌ=ˈ=\ *adj* [ME *wel temperit*, fr. *wel* well + *temperit* tempered] **1 a** *obs* : properly constituted physically ⟨a strong *well-tempered* stomach —Algernon Sydney⟩ **b** : having a good or equable disposition; *esp* : GOOD-NATURED ⟨a discreet and *well-tempered* officer —George Grote⟩ **2** : treated so as to develop the desired degree of hardness and elasticity ⟨*well-tempered* steel⟩ ⟨a *well-tempered* sword blade⟩ **3** : mixed to the proper consistency — used esp. of mortar and clay

well-thought-of \'ˌ=ˈ=ˌ=\ *adj* : being of good repute : REPUTABLE ⟨a *well-thought-of* young man⟩

well-thought-out \'ˌ=ˈ=ˈ=\ *adj* : logically considered : well and carefully reasoned ⟨moved according to a *well-thought-out* plan —Edita Morris⟩ ⟨another *well-thought-out* bit of wisdom —S.H.Adams⟩

well-timbered \'ˌ=ˈ=\ *adj* **1 a** : well braced or strengthened by timbers ⟨a *well-timbered* house⟩ ⟨a *well-timbered* mine⟩ **b** : strongly made or put together : having a good structure or constitution ⟨a *well-timbered* horse⟩ **2** : having a good quantity of growing timber ⟨a *well-timbered* tract of land⟩

well-timed \'ˌ=ˈ=\ *adj* **1 a** : happening or coming at an opportune moment : done at a suitable, convenient, or good time : TIMELY ⟨*well-timed* political reforms⟩ **b** : actuated at the proper moment or in regular time ⟨*well-timed* oars⟩ **2** : trained or adjusted to keep proper time ⟨a *well-timed* crew⟩ ⟨a *well-timed* chronometer⟩ **syn** see SEASONABLE

¹well-to-do \'ˌ=ˌ=ˈ=\ *adj* [fr. the phrase *to do well*] **1** : having more than adequate material and esp. financial resources : having plenty of money or a comfortable income : being in easy or affluent circumstances : PROSPEROUS, WELL-OFF ⟨a fashionable and *well-to-do* family —*Hearst's*⟩ ⟨*well-to-do* but not with one of the great fortunes —John Buchan⟩ **2** : indicating or having the characteristics of prosperity ⟨the house had a *well-to-do* look⟩ ⟨a *well-to-do* suburb with pronounced intellectual interests —Jane Cobb⟩

²well-to-do \'ˌ=ˌ=ˌ=\ *n pl* : well-to-do persons — usu. used with *the* ⟨only the *well-to-do* could afford to patronize them —Foster Hailey⟩ ⟨favored as a resort by the *well-to-do* —*Amer. Guide Series: Mich.*⟩

well-to-live \'ˌ=ˌ=ˈ=\ *adj* [fr. the phrase *to live well*] *chiefly dial* : WELL-TO-DO

well tomb *n* : a tomb having a well or shaft for an entrance

well-to-pass \'ˌ=ˌ=ˈ=\ *adj* [fr. the phrase *to pass well*] *Scot* : WELL-TO-DO

well trap *n* : a trap (as in a sewer or drainpipe) holding water and checking the escape of foul air and odors

well-turned \'ˌ=ˈ=\ *adj* **1** : symmetrically shaped or rounded : well formed : SHAPELY ⟨her *well-turned* form⟩ ⟨a *well-turned* ankle⟩ **2** : concisely and appropriately expressed ⟨a *well-turned* phrase⟩ ⟨a *well-turned* compliment⟩ **3** : expertly rounded or turned ⟨a *well-turned* arch⟩ ⟨*well-turned* columns⟩

well-willed \'ˌ=ˈ=\ *adj* [ME] *chiefly Scot* : favorably, kindly, or generously disposed

well-willer \'ˌ=ˌ=\ *n* [ME] **1** : one bearing goodwill : one disposed to be kind or friendly : WELL-WISHER **2** *obs* : AMATEUR ⟨so much a *well-willer* to the satire that he spares no man —John Dryden⟩

well-willing \'ˌ=ˈ=\ *adj* [ME] *archaic* : favorably or kindly disposed : BENEVOLENT, LOYAL ⟨ruggedly faithful and *well-willing* to their friends —R.L.Stevenson⟩

well-wish \'ˌ=ˌ=\ *n* : a good or kindly wish ⟨tendered hurried *well-wishes* —Linton Wells⟩

well-wisher \'ˌ=ˌ=\ *n* : one that wishes well to another ⟨*well-wishers* made contributions toward her musical education —*Current Biog.*⟩ ⟨he knows the park service has many *well-wishers* —R.M.Yoder⟩

well-wishing \'ˌ=ˌ=\ *n* : the act of one who wishes well to another ⟨much hand-shaking and *well-wishing* —J.R.Harris⟩

well-worn \'ˌ=ˈ=\ *adj* **1 a** : having been much used or worn ⟨*well-worn* shoes⟩ **b** : made stale or threadbare by use : TRITE, COMMONPLACE ⟨a *well-worn* quotation⟩ ⟨a *well-worn* theme⟩ **2** : worn well or properly ⟨*well-worn* honors⟩

welly \'weli\ *adv* [by contr.] *dial Eng* : WELL-NIGH ⟨~ thirty miles off —George Eliot⟩

wels \'welz\ *n -ES* [G, fr. MHG; akin to OPruss *kalis* sheatfish] : SHEATFISH

Wels·bach \'welz.bak, -.bäk\ *trademark* — used for a burner for producing gaslight by the combustion of a mixture of air and gas or vapor to heat to incandescence a gas mantle or for the mantle used with such a burner

¹welsh or **welch** \'welsh, -lch\ *adj, usu cap* [ME *walisch*, *welisch*, fr. OE (northern & Midland dial.) *wælisc*, *welisc* Celtic, Welsh, foreign, fr. OE *Walh*, *Wealh* Celt, Welshman, foreigner (of Celtic origin; akin to the source of L *Volcae*, a Celtic people of southeastern Gaul) + -*isc* -ish] **1 a** : of, relating to, or characteristic of Wales **b** : of, relating to, or characteristic of the Welsh people **2** : of, relating to, or characteristic of the Welsh language

²welsh or **welch** \'�"\ *n* [ME *Walsche*, *Welsse*, fr. *walisch*, *welisch*, adj.] **1** *pl in constr, cap* : the natives or inhabitants of Wales descended from romanized Britons **2** -ES *cap* : a Celtic language of the Welsh people possessing an extensive and actively growing literature and used as the language of education in some communities in Wales — see INDO-EUROPEAN LANGUAGES table **3** -ES *usu cap* : WELSH PONY **4** or **welsh black** *a usu cap W&B* : a Welsh breed of large black dual-purpose cattle **b** -ES *usu cap W & often cap B* : an animal of this breed **5 a** *usu cap* : a Welsh breed of long-bodied lop-eared swine of good bacon type **b** -ES or **welsh pig** *usu cap W & often cap P* : an animal of this breed

³welsh or **welch** \'�"\ *vi* -ED/-ING/-ES [prob. fr. ¹*welsh*] **1** : to cheat by avoiding payment of bets ⟨~ed on a daily-double payoff⟩ **2** : to avoid dishonorably the fulfillment of an obligation ⟨~ on its contract with the government for slum clearance —*New Republic*⟩

welsh cob *n* **1** *usu cap W&C* : a breed of medium-sized cobby horses with a high stylish action developed by interbreeding Welsh ponies with larger horses (as hackneys or thoroughbreds) **2** *usu cap W & often cap C* : a horse of the Welsh Cob breed

welsh cor·gi \-'kȯrgē\ *n, pl* **welsh corgis** *usu cap W* : a short-legged long-backed dog with foxy head belonging to either of two Welsh varieties — see CARDIGAN, PEMBROKE

welsh drake *n, usu cap W* : GADWALL

welsh dresser also **welsh cupboard** *n, usu cap W* : a cabinet (as for a dining room) with open shelves above a table surface and drawers and often closed cupboards below

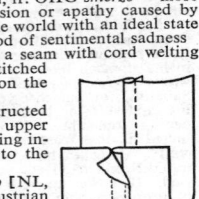

Welsh dresser

welsh·er or **welch·er** \'welshə(r), -lch-\ *n -s* : one that welshes

welsh groin *n, usu cap W* : an underpitch groin

welsh harp *n, usu cap W* : a large triple harp with two rows of strings tuned diatonically in unison and the third row supplying the chromatic sharps and flats

welsh main *n, usu cap W* : a cockfight in which a number of cocks are paired, the winners again paired, and so on until there is but a single survivor

welsh·man or **welch·man** \'˛=mən\ *n, pl* welshmen or welchmen [ME *Walsheman*, *wellisseman*, fr. OE *Wilisc man*, fr. *wilisc*, *wielisc* Welsh + *man*] **1** *cap* : a native or inhabitant of Wales : one of the Welsh **2** *South* : BLACK BASS; *esp* : SMALLMOUTH BLACK BASS

welsh mortgage *n, usu cap W* : an obsolete mortgage in which the mortgagee may keep the rents and profits of the estate in satisfaction of interest but cannot enforce payment of the principal and the mortgagor can redeem at any time by payment of the principal — compare LIVING PLEDGE

welsh mountain *n, usu cap W&M* : a breed of small white horned upland sheep of good mutton conformation native to Wales

welsh mountain pony *n, usu cap W&M* : a small sturdy pony native to the mountains of Wales and seldom exceeding 12 hands in height

welsh mountain sheep *n, usu cap W&M* : a sheep of the Welsh Mountain breed

welsh·ness *n -ES usu cap* : the quality or state of being Welsh : Welsh character

welsh onion *n, usu cap W* : an Asiatic onion (*Allium fistulosum*) with tufted glabrous foliage and slender bulbs that is sometimes cultivated for its leaves which are used in seasoning and its bulbs which are used as early green onions

welsh pony *n, usu cap W* : any of several stocky sturdy ponies of Welsh origin; *specif* : WELSH MOUNTAIN PONY

welsh poppy *n, usu cap W* : a widely cultivated western European plant (*Meconopsis cambrica*) of the family Papaveraceae with showy pale-yellow pedunculate flowers

welsh process *n, usu cap W* : a process in which ore (as copper ore) is smelted to matte that is then changed to metallic copper by alternate roasting and smelting in reverberatories and which is mostly superseded by Bessemer converting

welsh rabbit *n, usu cap W* [¹*rabbit* 1] : melted and often seasoned cheese sometimes mixed with ale or beer and poured over toasted bread or crackers

welsh rarebit *n, usu cap W* [by alter.] : WELSH RABBIT

welsh runt *n, usu cap W* : one of the Welsh breed of cattle

welsh·ry or **welsh·ery** \'welsh(ə)rē, -lch-\ *n -ES usu cap* : a district or quarter (as of a town or city) populated by the Welsh

welsh springer spaniel *n* **1** *usu cap W & both Ss* : a Welsh breed of red and white or orange and white small-eared springer spaniels somewhat smaller and more active than the English springer **2** *usu cap W & often cap both Ss* : a dog of the Welsh Springer Spaniel breed

welsh terrier *n, usu cap W&T* **1** : a breed of wiry-coated terriers resembling airedales but smaller and developed in Wales for hunting otter, fox, and badger **2** *usu cap W & often cap T* : a dog of the Welsh Terrier breed

welsh vault *n, usu cap W* : an underpitch vault — see VAULT illustration

welshwoman \'˛=ˌ=\ *n, pl* **welshwomen** *cap* [ME *Walssh-woman*, fr. *walssh*, *welisch* Welsh + *woman*] : a woman native or inhabitant of Wales

¹welt \'welt\ *vb* -ED/-ING/-S [ME *welten*, of Scand origin; akin to ON *velta* to roll, turn over — more at WELTER] *chiefly dial* : OVERTURN

²welt \'�"\ *n -S* [ME *welte*, *walte*; perh. akin to ME *welten* to overturn] **1 a** : a strip of leather or other material inserted in a shoe between the edges of the sole and upper through which the sole and upper are stitched or stapled together — see GOODYEAR WELT, STORM WELT **b** : a strip of material (as leather) used to ornament the upper of a shoe **2 a** : a doubled edge, strip, insert, or seam sewn (as on a garment) for ornament or reinforcement: as **(1)** : a folded-back edge of a straw or felt hat brim **(2)** : an applied edge along the front of a vest or the top of a pocket **(3)** : WELTING 1b **b** : the top strip or hem of heavier yarn in machine-knit stockings **3 a** : an elongated raised area on a surface : a raised stripe or band : RIDGE **b** : a raised area, ridge, or seam on the body surface (as from scarring or a blow) **c** *dial* : a heavy or damaging blow ⟨hit him a ~ with a club⟩ **4 a** : a strip of wood fastened over a flush seam or joint or an angle to strengthen it **b** : a strip riveted or otherwise fastened upon the edges of plates that form a butt joint in steam boilers and sheet-steel work

³welt \'�"\ *vb* -ED/-ING/-S [ME *welten*, fr. ²*welt*] **1** : to furnish with a welt; *specif* : to stitch a welt on (a shoe) **2 a** : to raise a welt on the skin of **b** : to hit hard **3** *Brit* : to join (two pipes) by lapping the metal at the ends one over the other and pressing the lapped portion together ~ *vi* : to become marked with welts

⁴welt \'�"\ *var of* ²WILT

welt·an·schau·ung \'velt.än.shaúəⁿ, -aú-(ˌ)uⁿ\ *n, pl* **weltanschauungs** \-ⁿz\ *or* **welt·an·schau·en** \-ⁿən\ *often cap* [G, lit., world view, fr. MHG, fr. OE *weltan*, *wæltan*, OHG *walzan*, ON *velta* to roll, turn over, Goth *waltjan* to roll, L *volvere* — more at VOLUBLE] **1** : a conception of the course of events in and of the purpose of the world as a whole forming a philosophical view or apprehension of the universe : the idea embodied in a cosmology : outlook on the world — called also *world view* **2** : philosophy of life : IDEOLOGY **3** : the cosmologic conception of society and its institutions held by its members

welted thistle *n* : a European biennial thistle (*Carduus crispus*) that is introduced in No. America and has the flower heads in crowded clusters at the ends of spiny-winged branches

¹welter \'weltə(r)\ *vb* **weltered**; **weltered**; **weltering** \-t(ə)riŋ\ **welters** [ME *welteren*; akin to MD *welteren* to roll, wrap, MHG *welzeren* to turn, roll, OE *weltan*, *wæltan*, OHG *walzan*, ON *velta* to roll, turn over, Goth *waltjan* to roll, L *volvere* — more at VOLUBLE] *vi* **1 a** : to twist or roll one's body (as of a hog in mire) : WRITHE, TOSS, TUMBLE **b** : to rise and fall or toss about in or with waves ⟨survivors . . . ~ed in the sea for four days —*Time*⟩ **2** : to become deeply sunk, soaked, or involved ⟨score technical successes, even if their backers ~ in red ink —Gilbert Gabriel⟩ **3** *dial* : to move unsteadily : REEL, STAGGER **4** : to be in a state of turmoil ⟨cabs, carriages and crosstown cars all ~ing together —Brander Matthews⟩ ~ *vt*, *obs* : to cause to roll or overturn **syn** see WALLOW

²welter \'�"\ *n* : a state of wild disorder : TURMOIL ⟨the long rollers . . . crash in a ~ of foam —*Amer. Guide Series: Calif.*⟩ ⟨the ~ of anarchy, murder, civil war, bankruptcy, pestilence, and famine —*London Times*⟩ **2** : RIOT ⟨with a ~ of color in its own formal flower beds —Alan Edwards⟩ **2** : a chaotic mass or jumble ⟨a ~ of flailing hoofs and sods of turf —James Reynolds⟩ ⟨an atrocious road . . . that was a ~ of mud in the winter —Walter Macken⟩ ⟨this section is . . . a bewildering ~ of classical, Arabian, scholastic, and magical ideas —Harvey Graham⟩

³welter \'�"\ *vt* -ED/-ING/-S [prob. fr. *welt*] : WITHER, WILT ⟨as in *wither*⟩

⁴welter \'�"\ *n -S cap* [prob. fr. ²*welt* + -*er*] : WELTERWEIGHT 1,3 ⟨boxed with top-line pro ~s and soon they were paying him for working out —Lester Bromberg⟩

⁵welter \'�"\ *adj* : of, relating to, or being a race in which welterweights are carried

⁶welt·er \'�"\ *n -S* [³*welt* + -*er*] : one that welts; *specif* : a worker who forms or fastens welts on shoes, hosiery, leather goods, or straw-hat brims

welter-out \'˛=ˌ=\ *n* : a rander who trims shoe welts

welterweight \'˛=ˌ=\ *n* [⁴*welter* + *weight*] **1** : a heavyweight horseman **2** : a weight of 28 pounds sometimes imposed in a horse race (as a steeplechase or hurdle race) in addition to weight for age **3** : a boxer or wrestler of a weight class heavier than a lightweight and lighter than a middleweight: as **a** : a professional boxer weighing more than 135 but not over 147 pounds **b** : an intercollegiate boxer weighing more than 135 but not over 145 pounds

welting *n -S* [fr. gerund of ³*welt*] **1 a** : the welts sewed or otherwise attached (as to a garment) for strengthening or decoration **b** : trimming made of a cotton cord covered with a bias strip of fabric and used in seams or along edges of slipcovers, bedspreads, or upholstery **c** : material for welts **2** : a beating such as might raise welts

welt·po·li·tik \'velt.pōlə'tēk\ *n -s* [G, fr. *welt* world (alter. of OHG *weralt*, *worold*) + *politik* politics, fr. F *politique* — more at WORLD, POLITIC] : participation in the discussion and decision of international problems : international politics

welts *pres 3d sing of* WELT, *pl of* WELT

welt·schmerz \'velt.shmerts\ *n -ES often cap* [G, lit., world pain, fr. *welt* world + *schmerz* pain, fr. OHG *smerzo* — more at SMART (n.)] **1** : mental depression or apathy caused by comparison of the actual state of the world with an ideal state : sentimental pessimism **2** : a mood of sentimental sadness

welt seam *or* **welted seam** *n* **1** : a seam with cord welting inserted **2** : a flat thickened seam stitched first on the wrong side and then on the right side

welt shoe *n* : a shoe or boot constructed with a welt that is united to the upper lining and insole lip without stitching inside the shoe and then attached to the outsole

wel·witsch·ia \wel'wichēə\ *n, cap* [NL, fr. Friedrich *Welwitsch* †1872 Austrian botanist + NL -*ia*] : a monotypic genus of desert plants (family Gnetaceae) of southwestern Africa characterized by a trunk less than a foot high but often six feet in circumference, two persistent leaves that grow at the base and die at the apex, and cone-shaped inflorescences

welt seam 2

wem \'wem\ *n -S* [ME, alter. (influenced by *wemmen* to stain, fr. OE *wemman*, fr. *wamm* spot, stain) of OE *wamm* spot, stain; akin to OS *wam* evil, crime, ON *vamm* blemish, Goth *wamm* spot and perh. to ON *vāma* sickness, nausea — more at VOMIT] **1** *archaic* : a moral stain **2** *chiefly dial* : a flaw or stain in something material **3** *archaic* : a bodily spot or scar

wem·bley \'wemblē, -li\ *adj, usu cap* [fr. *Wembley*, England] : of or from the municipal borough of Wembley, England : of the kind or style prevalent in Wembley

¹wen \'wen\ *n -S* [ME, *wen*, *wenne*, fr. OE *wenn*; akin to MLG *wene* wen, Dan dial. *vann* and prob. to OE *wund* wound — more at WOUND] **1** : a cyst formed by obstruction to the excretion of material from a sebaceous gland and filled with sebaceous material : SEBACEOUS CYST **2** : an abnormal growth protruding from a surface : EXCRESCENCE

²wen \'�"\ *n -S* [OE] : a rune adopted into the Old English alphabet having the value of Modern English *w* and after the 13th century being entirely replaced by that letter

we·natch·ee or **we·natchi** \wə'nachē\ *n, pl* wenatchee or wenatchees or wenatchi or wenatchis *usu cap* **1 a** : an Indian people of north central Washington **b** : a member of such people **2** : a dialect of the Salishan language of Columbia

¹wench \'wench\ *n -ES* [ME *wenche*, short for *wenchel* child, fr. OE *wencel*; akin to OHG *wanchal* unsteady, *wankōn* to stagger, totter, flicker — more at WINK] **1 a** : a young woman : GIRL ⟨good girl . . . you were the best-dressed ~ in the room —Sinclair Lewis⟩ **b** *chiefly dial* : a female child **c** : a female servant : MAID **2** : a lewd woman **3** : a girl or woman of a socially low class ⟨known as a female impersonator, and introduced the Negro ~ characterization to minstrelsy —C.F. Wittke⟩

²wench \'�"\ *vi* -ED/-ING/-ES : to consort with lewd women; *esp* : to practice fornication

wench·er \-ch(ə)r\ *n -S* : one that wenches

wen·chow \'wən.jō\ *adj, usu cap* [fr. *Wenchow*, China] : of or from the city of Wenchow, China : of the kind or style prevalent in Wenchow

¹wend \'wend\ *vb* -ED/-ING/-S [ME *wenden*, fr. OE *wendan*; akin to OHG *wenten* to turn, wend, ON *venda*, Goth *wandjan*; causative fr. the root of E *wind* (to turn)] *vi* **1** *obs* : to occur in the course of events : come about **2** *obs* : to turn from one direction, position, condition, or form to another **3** *obs* : to go or pass away : DEPART, END **4** : to direct one's course : go one's way : PROCEED, TRAVEL ⟨through the fields and the woods and over the walls I have ~ed — Robert Frost⟩ ~ *vt* **1** *obs* : to change the direction, position, or character of **2** *archaic* : to turn (a ship's head) in tacking **3** *obs* : to cause (oneself) to go : BETAKE **4** : to proceed on (one's way) : go on : DIRECT ⟨leisurely the governor and his associates ~ed their way . . . up the valley —J.E.Winston⟩

²wend \'�"\ *n -S cap* [G *Wende*, fr. OHG *Winida*; akin to OE *Winedas*, fr. L, fr. *Vindelici* people], pl. Wends, ON *Vindir*] **1** : a member of a Slavic people occupying eastern Germany to the Baltic sea during the early medieval period and now surviving along the middle and upper Spree river **2** : WENDISH

wendigo *var of* WINDIGO

¹wend·ish \'wendish, -dēsh\ *adj, usu cap* [fr. *Wende* Wend + -*isch* -ish] : of or relating to the Wends or their language

²wendish \'˛\ *n -ES cap* : the West Slavic language of the Wends

w-engine *n, cap W* : an internal-combustion engine in which three sets of cylinders are arranged side by side in three planes making angles so that a cross section perpendicular to the shaft would have the general shape of the letter W

wen-li \'wən'lē\ *n -S* [Chin (Pek) *wên²-li³*, fr. *wên²* literature + *li³* style] : the archaic style of classical Chinese literary composition having many complex rules and prevailing until the literary revolution of 1917 : a literary style of Chinese as distinguished from colloquial style — compare PAI-HUA

wen·lock \'wen.läk\ *n, usu cap* [fr. *Wenlock*, borough of Shropshire, England] : a subdivision of the Upper Silurian in Great Britain

wen·lock·i·an \(')wen'läkēən\ *adj, usu cap* [*Wenlock*, England + E -*an*] : of or relating to a subdivision of the European Silurian — see GEOLOGIC TIME table

wen·nel \'wenᵊl\ *dial var of* WEANEL

wen·ny \'wenē, -ni\ *adj* -ER/-EST [¹*wen* + -*y*] **1** : having the character of a wen : resembling a wen **2** : afflicted with wens

wen·ro \'wen.rō\ *or* **wen·roh·ro·non** \ˌ˛=ˈrō.nän\ *n -s usu cap* : ERIE

wens *pl of* WEN

wens·ley·dale \'wenzlē.dāl\ *n -s usu cap* [fr. *Wensleydale*, locality in Yorkshire, England] **1 a** : a white cheese eaten fresh before curing **b** : a pale soft cheese blue-veined after curing **2** : a hornless long-wooled mutton type sheep of an English breed developed by intercrossing Leicesters and native Yorkshire sheep

¹went \'went\ [ME, past & past part. of *wenden* to turn, go — more at WEND] *past or substand past part of* GO

²went \'˛\ *n -S* [ME, fr. *wenden*; influenced by ME *went*, past of *wenden* & by OE *wend* course, fr. *wendan* to wend — more at WEND] **1** *Brit* : a traveled way : ROAD, LANE, ALLEY, PASSAGE; *specif* : CROSSROAD ⟨the finger post at the centre of a four ~ way —*Architect & Building News*⟩ **2** *obs* : a turn of events

wen·tle·trap \'wentᵊl.trap\ *n* [D *wenteltrap* winding stair, fr. MD *wendeltrappe*, fr. *wendel* turning, winding (fr. *wenden* to turn) + *trappe* step, stairs; akin to OE *wendan* to turn, wend — more at WEND, TRAP] **1** : any of numerous graceful usu. white spirally coiled and tapering gastropod mollusk shells that have longitudinal ridges surrounding the whorls, are favorites with collectors, and include one form formerly commanding very high prices — called also *staircase shell* **2** : any

of various mollusks (family Epitoniidae) of which the shell is a wentletrap

wen-yen \ˈwən'yen\ *n* -s [Chin (Pek) *wên²-yen²*, fr. *wên²* literature + *yen²* language] : written Chinese of or conforming to the complex style used in classical literature : classical Chinese — compare PAI-HUA

wen·zel \ˈven(t)səl\ *n* -s [G, lit., servant, knave, fr. *Wenzel* Czech, fr. *Wenzeslaus* Wenceslas, after *Wenzeslaus* St. Wenceslas †A.D.935 Duke of Bohemia and patron saint of Czechoslovakia] : JACK 1c(1)

wept *past of* WEEP

wer *also* **were** \ˈwər, ˈwe(ə)r, ˈwi(ə)r\ *n* -s [OE *wer* man, husband, wergild — more at VIRILE] : WERGILD

were [ME *were* (2d sing. past indic. and 1st, 2d, & 3d sing. past subj.), *weren* (past pl. indic. & subj.), fr. OE *wǣre* (2d sing. past indic. and 1st, 2d, & 3d sing. past subj. of *wesan* to be), *wǣron* (past pl. indic. of *wesan*), *wǣren* (past pl. subj. of *wesan*); akin to OFris *wēre* were (2d sing. past indic. of *wesa* to be), OHG *wāri* (2d sing. past indic. of *wesan* to be) — more at WAS] *past 2d sing & pl, past subjunctive, dial past 1st & 3d sing of* BE

weren't \R ˌwər(-ə)nt, -R ˌwənt *or* ˌwərənt *sometimes* ˌwənt; *archaic or Brit* ˌwa(ə)(ə)rnt *or* ˌwe| *or* |rənt *or* |ənt\ [by contr.] : were not

were·wolf *also* **wer·wolf** \ˈwi(ə)r,wu̇lf, ˈwər-, ˈwe(ə)r-, ˈwiə,w-, ˈwə,w-, ˈweə,w-\ *n, pl* **were·wolves** \-lvz\ [ME, fr. OE *werewulf, werwulf;* akin to MD *weerwolf,* OHG *werwolf;* all fr. a prehistoric WGmc compound whose constituents are represented by OE *wer* man and OE *wulf* wolf — more at WOLF] **1** : a person transformed temporarily or permanently into a wolf or capable of assuming a wolf's form : LYCANTHROPE **2** : a person whose cunning savagery suggests that of a werewolf

werf \ˈverf\ *n* -s [Afrik, lit., shipyard, fr. MD — more at WHARF] *southern Africa* : the space around homestead and outbuildings : FARMYARD

wer·gild *or* **wer·geld** *also* **were·gild** \ˈwər,gild, ˈwe(ə)r-, ˈwi(ə)r-\ *n* -s [ME, fr. OE; akin to MD *weergelt,* OHG *wergelt* wergild; all fr. a prehistoric WGmc compound whose constituents are represented by OE *wer* man and OE *gild, geld* payment — more at VIRILE, GELD (tax)] : the value set in Anglo-Saxon and Germanic law upon the life of a man in accordance with a fixed scale increasing from the churl to the king and paid as compensation to the kindred or lord of a slain person or as a fine for some serious crime — compare BLOOD FEUD, BLOODWITE, ERIC

we·ri \ˈwārē\ *n* -s [Maori] : AWETO

werl·hof's disease \ˈver(ə)l,hōfs-\ *n, usu cap W* [after Paul G. *Werlhof* †1767 Ger. physician] : PURPURA HEMORRHAGICA

¹wer·ne·ri·an \wər'nirēən, (ˈ)ver-\ *adj, usu cap* [Abraham G. *Werner* †1817 Ger. geologist and mineralogist + E *-an*] **1** : of or relating to A.G.Werner who classified minerals according to their external characters and advocated the theory that the strata of the earth's crust were formed by depositions from water **2** : of or according to the Wernerian system or theory : NEPTUNIAN

²wernerian \"\ *n* -s *usu cap* : a supporter of the Wernerian theory : NEPTUNIST

wer·ner·ite \ˈwərnə,rīt\ *n* -s [F, fr. A.G.*Werner* †1817 + F *-ite*] : SCAPOLITE

wer·nick·e's area \ˈvernəkəz-, -kēz-\ *n, usu cap W* : the part of the superior temporal convolution that houses Wernicke's center

wernicke's center *n, usu cap W* [after Karl *Wernicke* †1905 Ger. neurologist] : the auditory word center located in the posterior part of the superior temporal convolution

wernicke's convolution *or* **wernicke's gyrus** *n, usu cap W* [after Karl *Wernicke* †1905] : the superior temporal convolution

wernicke's prism *n* [prob. after F. Alexander *Wernicke* †1915 Ger. mathematician and physicist] : a direct prism for projection

wer·o·wance \ˈwerə,wan(t)s\ *n* -s [Delaware (Virginia dial.) *wirowántēsu,* lit., he is rich, fr. *wiro* to be rich] : an Indian chief of Virginia or Maryland; *broadly* : a No. American Indian chief

wersh \ˈwersh\ *Scot var of* WEARISH

werst *var of* VERST

wert [alter. (influenced by *art,* 2d sing. pres. indic.) of ME *were* — more at WERE] *archaic past 2d sing & archaic past subjunctive 2d sing of* BE

wer·the·ri·an *also* **wer·te·ri·an** \(ˈ)ver'tirēən\ *adj, usu cap* [*Werther,* romantic hero of the love story *Die Leiden des Jungen Werthers* The Sorrows of Werther (1774) by Johann Wolfgang von Goethe †1832 Ger. poet + E *-an*] : resembling or characteristic of Werther; *esp* : morbidly sentimental

wer·ther·ism \ˈverd·ə,rizəm\ *n* -s *usu cap* [*Werther* + E *-ism*] : the quality or state of being Wertherian

wes *pl of* WE

we·sak \ˈwe,säk\ *n* -s *usu cap* [Sinhalese, Baisakh (month of the Hindu year), fr. Skt *Vaiśākha*] : the Buddhist New Year festival celebrating the birthday of the Buddha at the May full moon

wesand *var of* WEASAND

we'se \ˈwēz\ [by contr. & alter. fr. *we is*] *dial* : we are

wes·kit \ˈweskət\ *n* -s [alter. of *waistcoat*] : VEST 2a, 2b

¹wes·ley·an \ˈweslēən, ˈwez-\ *adj, usu cap* [John *Wesley* †1791 and his brother Charles *Wesley* †1788 Eng. theologians + E *-an*] : of, relating to, or characteristic of John or Charles Wesley or Wesleyanism

²wesleyan \"\ *n* -s *usu cap* : METHODIST; *esp* : an adherent of Wesleyanism

wes·ley·an·ism \-ēə,nizəm\ *also* **wes·ley·ism** \-ē,izəm\ *n* -s *cap* [*wesleyanism* fr. ¹*wesleyan* + *-ism, wesleyism* fr. John *Wesley* †1791 + E *-ism*] : METHODISM 1; *specif* : the system of Arminian Methodism taught by John Wesley — compare CALVINISM

wesleyan methodist *n, usu cap W&M* : a Protestant Christian dedicated to the principles of evangelical Christianity taught by John Wesley; *specif* : a member of any of various bodies of Methodists (as the Wesleyan Methodists of Great Britain, the Wesleyan Methodist Church of America, the Irish Wesleyan Methodist Church, the Wesleyan Methodist Connection, the Wesleyan Methodist Church in Canada, or the Wesleyan Methodist Association)

we·sort \ˈwē,sȯrt\ *n, usu cap* [prob. fr. *we sort* (i.e., our sort)] : one of a group of people of mixed white, Indian, and Negro ancestry living in southern Maryland

wes·sel \ˈwesəl\ *adv* [irreg. fr. *west*] *Scot* : WESTWARD

wes·sel·ton \-tən, -tᵊn\ *n* -s [fr. *Wesselton,* one of the Kimberley mines, Kimberley, So. Africa] : a high-grade diamond ranking below a river

wes·sex·man \ˈwesəksmən\ *n, pl* **wessexmen** *cap* [*Wessex,* section of southern England + E *-man*] : a native or inhabitant of Wessex

wessex saddleback *n* [fr. *Wessex,* England, where it was orig. bred] **1** *usu cap W&S* : an old British breed of medium-sized black white-belted swine perhaps not distinct from the American Hampshire **2** *-s usu cap W & often cap S* : an animal of the Wessex saddleback breed

¹west \ˈwest\ *adv* [ME, fr. OE; akin to OHG *westar* to the west, ON *vestr* and prob. to L *vesper, vespera* evening, Gk *hesperos*] **1** : to, toward, or in the west : WESTWARD **2** : to the realm of the departed beyond the sunset — used in the phrase *to go west* ⟨realized what awaited her if I 'went ~' —*Time*⟩ ⟨what had seemed a promising line of research had gone ~ —F.W.Crofts⟩

²west \"\ *adj* [ME, fr. OE *west-,* fr. *west,* adv.] **1 a** : situated toward or at the west ⟨the ~ meadow⟩ ⟨the ~ side of the house **b** [ME, fr. OE *westan-,* fr. *westan,* adv.; akin to OHG *westana* from the west, ON *vestan;* derivative fr. the root of E ¹*west*] : coming from the west ⟨a ~ wind⟩ **2** : situated in the opposite direction from the altar of a church : lying in that part of the church directly opposite the chancel

³west \"\ *n* -s [ME, fr. *west,* adv.] **1 a** : the general direction of sunset : the direction toward the left of one facing north **b** : the part of the sky in which celestial bodies set; *specif* : the place on the horizon where the sun sets when it is near one of the equinoxes **c** : the cardinal point directly opposite to east — abbr. *W;* see COMPASS CARD **d** : the point of the horizon having an azimuth or bearing of 270° and marking one intersection of the horizon and the celestial equator : the direction of the sky's daily apparent rotation : the direction opposite to that of the earth's rotation and its revolution around the sun **2** *usu cap* **a** : regions or countries lying to the west of a specified or implied point of orientation (as in the U. S. the states lying in general west of the Mississippi river); *specif* : the noncommunist countries of Europe and America ⟨held discussions on disarmament proposals put forward by the *West*⟩ **b** : something (as people, culture, or institutions) characteristic of the West ⟨a book such as this makes for closer understanding between the East and the *West* for the insight it gives into the Chinese mind —*Times Lit. Supp.*⟩ ⟨accused the *West* of plotting a new war —*Sat. Eve. Post*⟩ ⟨the old *West* of gun-toting marshals and Pony Express⟩ **3** : the west wind **4** *often cap* **a** : the one of four positions at 90-degree intervals that lies toward the west **b** : a person (as a bridge player) occupying such a position in the course of a specific activity

⁴west \"\ *vi* -ED/-ING/-S [ME *westen,* fr. *west,* adv.] : to move or veer toward the west

⁵west \"\ *n* -s [origin unknown] *dial Eng* : ⁴STY

westabout \ˈ==,=\ *adv (or adj)* [²*west* + *about*] : about in tacking so as to head west; *broadly* : toward the west : WESTWARD

¹west african *adj, usu cap W&A* [*West Africa* + E *-an*] **1** : of, relating to, or characteristic of West Africa — usu. used specif. of the part of Africa lying to the north of the Gulf of Guinea and often excluding Morocco, northern Algeria, and Tunisia **2** : of, relating to, or characteristic of the West Africans

²west african *n, cap W&A* : a native or inhabitant of West Africa — usu. used specif. of the Negro peoples of the part of Africa lying to the north of the Gulf of Guinea

west african oil palm *n, usu cap W&A* : AFRICAN OIL PALM

west african pidgin *n, usu cap W&A* : an English-based pidgin language in use in various areas in West Africa, particularly the Cameroons

west aramaic *n, cap W&A* : WESTERN ARAMAIC

west-atlantic \ˌ==ˈ==\ *n, cap W&A* : a branch of the Niger-Congo family of languages including Wolof, Serer, Balante, Limba, Temne, Kissi, and Gola which are spoken in West Africa from Senegal to Liberia and Fulani which has spread eastward from Senegal to the Cameroons

westbound \ˈ=,=\ *adj* [¹*west* + *bound*] : traveling or headed in a westerly direction; *broadly* : headed west or south — used of freight cars in railroad accounting

¹west by north : a compass point that is one point north of due west : N 78° 45′ W — abbr. *WbN, W by N;* see COMPASS CARD

²west by north *adv (or adj)* **1** : toward west by north **2** : from west by north

¹west by south : a compass point that is one point south of due west : S 78° 45′ W — abbr. *WbS, W by S;* see COMPASS CARD

²west by south *adv (or adj)* **1** : toward west by south **2** : from west by south

west coast hemlock *n* : WESTERN HEMLOCK

¹west·er \ˈwestə(r)\ *vi* [ME *westren,* fr. ¹*west* + *-ren* (as in *clatren* to clatter)] **1** : to move westward ⟨began his ~*ing* in 1678 —Bernard De Voto⟩ — used esp. of a celestial body in its course ⟨a ~*ing* sun shone through the rose window —*N.Y. Times*⟩ **2** : to turn, veer, or shift to the west

²wester \"\ *n* -s [²*west* + *-er*] **1** : a strong west wind ⟨the ~ came as steady as the trades —John Masefield⟩ **2** : a storm with west winds

wes·ter·li·ness \-lēnəs, -lin-\ *n* -ES : the situation of being westerly

wes·ter·ling \ˈwestərliŋ, -təl-, -tᵊl-\ *n* -s [obs. E *wester* western + E *-ling*] *archaic* : WESTERNER

¹wes·ter·ly \ˈwestə(r)lē, -li; -R -təl- *sometimes* -tᵊl-\ *adj* [obs. E *wester* western (fr. ME, fr. OE *westra* more towards the west, fr. *west,* adv. + *-ra* -er) + E *-ly*] **1** : situated or directed toward the west : WESTERN ⟨a ~ suburb⟩ ⟨wended their way in a ~ direction up the valley —J.E.Winston⟩ **2** : blowing from the west ⟨a ~ breeze⟩

²westerly \"\ *adv* **1** : from the west ⟨the wind blew ~⟩ **2** : toward the west ⟨we began to steer away ~ —Daniel Defoe⟩

³westerly \"\ *n* -ES : a wind blowing from the west ⟨the prevailing *westerlies* of the temperate zones⟩

west·er·most \ˈwestə(r),mōst, *esp Brit also* -,məst\ *adj* [obs. E *wester* western + E *most*] : WESTERNMOST

¹west·ern \ˈwestə(r)n, -R *also* -tᵊn\ *adj* [ME *westeren, westerne,* fr. OE *westerne;* akin to OHG *westrōni* western, ON *vestrænn,* derivative fr. the root of E ¹*west*] **1** *often cap* : of, relating to, originating or dwelling in, or characteristic of a region conventionally designated West: as **a** : steeped in or stemming from the Greco-Roman traditions of the Occident rather than those of Islam, India, or the Far East ⟨the *Western* tradition began to take distinctive shape with the mingling of Greco-Roman and Hebraic-Christian elements in the later days of the Roman Empire —J.A.Corry⟩ ⟨in the nineteenth century, the adoption of . . . superior *Western* technology appeared to Far Eastern statesmen to be a legitimate risk as well as an imperative necessity —A.J.Toynbee⟩ ⟨barriers, between a ~ eye and the beauty of a Chinese vase —J.A.Macy⟩ **b** : European rather than Slavic in character ⟨never ceased to compare Russia with Europe . . . to estimate Russian possibilities in terms of the preliminary conditions that had made *Western* institutions possible —Edmund Wilson⟩ **c** : of or relating to the noncommunist countries of Europe and America ⟨~ emphasis on individualism⟩ ⟨American tendency to consult with the *Western* powers on what is good for Asia, instead of first consulting with the Asian nations themselves —Mochtar Lubis⟩ **d** (1) : of or relating to the American West ⟨~ settlers⟩ ⟨~ plains⟩ ⟨~ cattle ranches⟩ ⟨the ~ grosbeak closely resembles the rose-breasted grosbeak except in plumage⟩ (2) : of or relating to folk music characteristic of the American West ⟨favorite hillbilly — or, if you prefer, ~ — crooner —*Ochiltree (Texas) County Herald*⟩ (3) : of or relating to a literary western ⟨resorts to every typical *Western* element: the fugitive bandit, the sheriff in pursuit, the girl, the gun play, and the great outdoors —Delmore Schwartz⟩ **2 a** : situated in or lying toward the west ⟨around the ~ and southern sides of the track are grandstands —*Amer. Guide Series: Ind.*⟩ ⟨islands in the ~ half of the archipelago⟩ **b** : coming from the west — used chiefly of the wind ⟨a ~ gale⟩ **c** (1) : going toward or facing the west ⟨the ~ voyage of Columbus⟩ ⟨a room with a ~ exposure⟩ (2) : corresponding to the westering course of the sun : DECLINING ⟨we . . . on the ~ side of life —H.W.Longfellow⟩ **3** *usu cap* : of or relating to the Roman Catholic and Protestant segment of Christianity ⟨*Western* liturgies⟩ — compare EASTERN ORTHODOX

²western \"\ *n* -s **1** *often cap* : WESTERNER **2 a** : one that is produced in or characteristic of a western region and esp. the western U. S. ⟨ewes in this experiment were two-year-old ~*s* —W.C.Coffey⟩ ⟨in felt hats ranchers prefer broad-brimmed ~*s*⟩ **b** : GENERAL AMERICAN **c** : WESTERN SANDWICH **3** *often cap* : a story of frontier life ⟨historical novels also rank high, and so do murder mysteries and *Westerns* —Bruce Bliven b. 1889⟩ ⟨a traditional *Western* in a novel Australian setting —*Films in Review*⟩; *specif* : a play (as a moving picture or a radio or television play) dealing usu. with life in the western U.S. during the latter half of the 19th century ⟨rattling good ~ about the first cattle drive over the Chisholm Trail —*Time*⟩ ⟨~*s,* those simple . . . sagas of manly men and womanly women —Virginia Graham⟩

western aramaic *n, cap W&A* : the subgroup of Aramaic languages used in Syria and Palestine and by people from this area including the language of the Aramaic portions of the Bible and of the Targums

western arborvitae *n* : CANOE CEDAR

western australia *adj, usu cap W&A* [fr. *Western Australia,* state in Australia] : of or from the state of Western Australia : of the kind or style prevalent in Western Australia : WESTERN AUSTRALIAN

¹western australian *adj, usu cap W&A* **1** : of, relating to, or characteristic of Western Australia : WESTRALIAN **2** : of, relating to, or characteristic of the Western Australians : WESTRALIAN

²western australian *n, cap W&A* : a native or inhabitant of Western Australia : WESTRALIAN

western azalea *n* : a deciduous shrub (*Rhododendron occidentale*) of the Coast range of No. America having usu. white flowers

western baboon *n* : a common baboon (*Papio papio*) of the Guinea coast of Africa

western balsam *n* : LOWLAND FIR

western bezoar *n, usu cap W* : a bezoar consisting chiefly of calcium phosphate found in the Peruvian llama

western birch *n* : WESTERN PAPER BIRCH

western black pine *n* **1** : JEFFREY PINE **2** : the wood of the Jeffrey pine

western blight *n* : WESTERN TOMATO BLIGHT

western bluebird *n* : a bluebird (*Sialia mexicana occidentalis*) of western No. America that is typically more purplish than the eastern form and has a patch of chestnut on the back

western brome grass *n* : a perennial grass (*Bromus marginatus*) of western No. America valued as a range grass

western buckeye *n* : a shrub (*Aesculus arguta*) of the central U. S. sometimes cultivated for its palmately compound leaves and dense racemes of yellow flowers

western catalpa *n* : a large often cultivated tree (*Catalpa speciosa*) having purple-streaked paniculate flowers and long thick podlike fruits — called also *cigar tree, hardy catalpa;* compare INDIAN BEAN 1

western cedar *n* **1** *or* **western juniper a** : a timber tree (*Juniperus occidentalis*) of the Pacific coast of the U. S. often of shrubby growth in the mountains **b** : the wood of the western cedar tree **2** : CANOE CEDAR

western chicken flea *n* : a rather large flea (*Ceratophyllus niger*) that breeds in hen droppings and feeds as an adult on various birds and mammals including man

western chimpanzee *n* : a chimpanzee of Sierra Leone that is sometimes considered a separate race (*Pan troglodytes verus*)

western chokecherry *n* : a chokecherry (*Padus demissa*) of the western U. S.

western church *n, usu cap W & often cap C* **1** : the churches of the West and esp. of western Europe and the Americas : Western Christianity **2** : one of the churches of Western Christianity (as the church of the Latin Patriarchate)

western coffee *n* : CASCARA BUCKTHORN

western crab apple *n* : IOWA CRAB

western daisy *n* : an herb (*Astranthium integrifolia*) of the central U. S. that has violet flowers and a branched stem, resembles and is closely related to the common English daisy, and is often included in the genus *Bellis*

western diamond rattlesnake *or* **western diamondback** *n* : a large and notably venomous rattlesnake (*Crotalus atrox*) of dry areas of the southwestern U. S. and adjacent Mexico with a predominantly grayish to buffy ground, large light-margined rhomboid to diamond-shaped blotches on the back, and a black and white ringed tail

western dogwood *n* : PACIFIC DOGWOOD

western dropwort *n* : a medicinal herb (*Gillenia trifoliata*) used by American Indians

western duck sickness *n* : DUCK SICKNESS

west·ern·er \R ˈwestə(r)nər, -R -tənə(r *also* -tᵊnə(r\ *n* -s *usu cap* **1 a** : a native or inhabitant of a western region ⟨*Westerners* from French West and Equatorial Africa —Michael Barbour⟩; *esp* : a native or inhabitant of the western U. S. ⟨the nasal twang of a *Westerner*⟩ **b** : a native or inhabitant of an occidental country ⟨*Westerners* do not understand Asiatics —H.B.Acton⟩ **c** : a supporter of the ideals and policies of the noncommunist countries of Europe and America ⟨many ~*s* mistakenly supposed that because the Soviet mind was politically mutilated it could not achieve much in science and technology —E.K.Lindley⟩ **2 a** : an adherent or advocate of western beliefs and practices ⟨a *Westerner* who wants to grapple with this subject, must try, for a few minutes, to slip out of his native Western skin and look . . . through the eyes of the great non-Western majority of mankind —A.J.Toynbee⟩ **b** : a member of the 19th-century Russian intelligentsia advocating the adoption of western European institutions or culture — compare SLAVOPHILISM

western fir *n* **1 a** : DOUGLAS FIR **b** : any of several western No. American trees of the genus *Abies* **2** : the wood of a western fir

western frame *n* : PLATFORM FRAME

western framing *n* [so called fr. its use in the western U. S.] : a method of building construction in which the supporting studs extend from the top of each tier of joists to the underside of the tier next above so that each floor is independently framed

western grape rootworm *n* : a grape rootworm (*Adoxus obscurus*)

western grape skeletonizer *n* : a small zygaenid moth (*Harrisina brillians*) whose larva is an important pest of grape in California

western grebe *n* : a large grebe (*Aechmophorus occidentalis*) of western No. America

western hemisphere *n* : the vertical half of the earth that lies chiefly to the west of the Atlantic ocean and includes No. and So. America and minor land masses

western hemlock *n* : a commercially important timber tree (*Tsuga heterophylla*) ranging from Alaska to California and having leaves that are of uniform width throughout and lack prominent pale stomatic lines beneath — called also *Pacific hemlock, west coast hemlock;* compare EASTERN HEMLOCK

western hindi *n, cap W&H* : a group of Indic dialects of northern India

west·ern·ism \-,nizəm\ *n* -s *often cap* **1 a** : a locution or pronunciation characteristic of a western region and esp. of the western U. S. **b** : an attitude or trait characteristic of a westerner **2 a** : a western institution or concept ⟨the Japanese took over the forms of ~, including a constitution and a parliament —Nathaniel Peffer⟩ **b** : adherence to or advocacy of western traditions and techniques

west·ern·iza·tion \ˌ==nəˈzāshən, -,nīˈz-\ *n* -s *often cap* : conversion to or adoption of western traditions or techniques

west·ern·ize \ˈ==,nīz\ *vb* -ED/-ING/-s *see -ize in Explan Notes* *vt* **1** : to imbue with qualities native to or associated with a western region and esp. the western U. S. **2** : OCCIDENTALIZE ~ *vi* : to become occidentalized

western kingbird *n* : ARKANSAS KINGBIRD

western larch *n* **1** *or* **western tamarack** : an important timber tree (*Larix occidentalis*) of western No. America with pale green sharply pointed leaves and oblong cones — called also *Oregon larch* **2** : the wood of the western larch

west·ern·ly *adj* : WESTERLY

western meadowlark *n* : a meadowlark (*Sturnella neglecta*) of western No. America

west·ern·most \ˈ==,mōst, *esp Brit also* -,məst\ *adj* : farthest to the west : most western

western mountain ash *n* : an ash (*Sorbus sitchensis*) of the Pacific coast of No. America — called also *mountain ash*

western mugwort *n* : PRAIRIE SAGE

western palm warbler *n* : a warbler (*Dendroica palmarum*) of central Canada and the Mississippi valley having yellowish underparts and a chestnut crown when adult

western paper birch *n* : a birch (*Betula fontinalis*) of western No. America resembling the paper birch of the northeastern U. S. but with brownish bark — called also *mountain birch, swamp birch, western birch*

western paradise *n, usu cap W&P* : PURE LAND

western peach borer *n* : a borer that attacks peach and other stone fruit trees in western No. America and is considered a variety (*graefi*) of the eastern peach tree borer

western peony *n* : an herbaceous perennial (*Paeonia brownii*) native to western U. S., but cultivated elsewhere for its brownish red flowers

western pine *n* : PONDEROSA PINE

western pine beetle *n* : a destructive bark beetle (*Dendroctonus brevicomis*) attacking various pines in the western U. S.

western pitch pine *n* : PONDEROSA PINE

western plum *n* : SIERRA PLUM

western poppy *n* : a showy Californian annual herb (*Papaver californicum*) with flowers having striking red petals that are green at the base

western ragweed *n* : a coarse perennial ragweed (*Ambrosia psilostachya*) that resembles common ragweed but has perennial creeping roots — called also *perennial ragweed*

western red cedar *n* **1 a** : ROCKY MOUNTAIN JUNIPER **b** : the

wood of Rocky Mountain juniper **2 a :** CANOE CEDAR **b :** the wood of the canoe cedar **3 :** WESTERN CEDAR 1

western red lily *n* **:** a slender erect herb (*Lilium umbellatum*) of the prairies of central No. America having narrow mostly alternate leaves and erect orange-red flowers spotted toward the base

western redtail *n* **:** a red-tailed hawk (*Buteo borealis calurus*) of western No. America

western ring-necked snake *n* **:** a small innocuous No. American snake (*Storeria occipitomaculata*) that is dark gray or brown above and on the undersurface white anteriorly and reddish posteriorly — called also *red-bellied snake*

western roll *n, usu cap W* **:** a technique of high jumping in which the leg farthest from the bar lifts first, the jumper's side is to the bar as the body passes over it, and a three-point landing is made on the take-off leg and both hands — compare EASTERN ROLL, SCISSORS

western rust *n* **:** a rust of the raspberry caused by a fungus (*Phragmidium imitans*)

western rye *or* **western rye grass** *n, usu cap W* **:** SLENDER WHEAT GRASS

western saddle *n, often cap W* **:** STOCK SADDLE

western sage *n* **:** either of two plants of the western U. S.: **a :** PRAIRIE SAGE **b :** an herb (*Artemisia ludoviciana*) that resembles prairie sage

western sa·moa \-sə'mōə\ *adj, usu cap W&S* [fr. *Western Samoa,* country in South Pacific ocean] **:** of or from the country of Western Samoa **:** of the kind or style prevalent in Western Samoa

western sand cherry *n* **:** a dwarf ornamental shrub (*Prunus besseyi*) of the western U. S. with elliptic leaves and large sweet edible fruit

western sandpiper *n* **:** a small sandpiper (*Ereunetes mauri*) very closely related to the semipalmated sandpiper which it chiefly replaces in western No. America but frequently occurring also along the Atlantic coast

western sandwich *n* **:** a sandwich of which the filling usu. is a beaten egg cooked with minced ham and onion — called also *Denver sandwich, western*

western sneezeweed *n* **:** a rather rank perennial herb (*Helenium hoopesii*) of the western U. S. having yellow flowers, being poisonous to stock, and causing spewing sickness in sheep

western spruce *n* **:** SITKA SPRUCE

western sudanic *n, usu cap W&S* **:** a language family of West Africa to which were added the Bantu and Adamawa-Eastern languages to form the Niger-Congo family

western sugar maple *n* **:** a forest tree (*Acer grandidentatum*) of western No. America having the leaves hairy underneath and the lobes usu. toothed — called also *bigtooth maple*

western tanager *n* **:** a tanager (*Piranga ludoviciana*) of western No. America the male of which is black, yellow, and orange-red

western tent caterpillar *n* **:** a caterpillar that is the larva of a lasiocampid moth (*Malacosoma pluviale*) and that feeds on cherry, apple, and other trees in western U. S. and Canada

western tomato blight *or* **western yellow blight** *n* **:** a disease of the tomato that is common west of the Rocky mountains and is caused by the curly top virus of sugar beets and transmitted by the beet leafhopper but produces entirely different effects from typical curly top (as yellowing of foliage sometimes with some purple coloration, premature ripening of the fruit, or rigidity of the foliage)

western wallflower *n* **1 :** a prairie rocket (*Erysimum asperum*) chiefly of the western U. S. having orange-yellow flowers **2 :** SPREADING DOGBANE

western wheatgrass *n* **1 :** a valuable forage grass (*Agropyron smithii*) of the western U. S. **2 :** BLUESTEM 1a

western white fir *n* **:** LOWLAND FIR

western white pine *n* **1 :** a white pine (*Pinus monticola*) with stout blue-green leaves 2 to 4 inches long and long-stalked cones 5 to 12 inches long **2 :** PONDEROSA PINE 1 **3 :** LIMBER PINE

western X-disease *n* **:** a disease of peaches and cherries caused by a form or strain of the X-disease virus found in northwestern U. S. and adjacent Canada

western yellow pine *n* **:** PONDEROSA PINE

western yew *n* **:** PACIFIC YEW

westers *pres 3d sing of* WESTER, *pl of* WESTER

west germanic *n, usu cap W&G* **:** a subdivision of the Germanic languages including English, Frisian, Dutch, and German

west goth *n, cap W&G* **:** VISIGOTH

west ham *adj, usu cap W&H* [fr. *West Ham,* southeastern England] **:** of or from the county borough of West Ham, England **:** of the kind or style prevalent in West Ham

west highland *n, usu cap W&H* [fr. *West Highlands,* western part of the Highlands of Scotland] **:** a breed of small very hardy beef cattle from the Highlands of Scotland having thick shaggy hair varying from dun to brindle or black and long curved horns set widely apart

west highland white terrier *n, usu cap 1st W&H* **:** a small white dog of a breed developed in Scotland to dig out small quarry that has a hard uncurled outer coat about 2½ inches long, a soft undercoat, a medium-width head with powerful jaws and sharp-pointed small ears, a compact body, short and muscular forelegs and hind legs, and a tail about five or six inches long

west indiaman *n, usu cap W&I* [*West India* + E *man*] **:** a sailing ship formerly running to the West Indies and the east coast of America and usu. much smaller than East Indiamen

¹west indian *adj, usu cap W&I* [*West India* (former name of the *West Indies,* group of islands enclosing the Caribbean sea) + E *-an,* adj. suffix] **:** of, relating to, or characteristic of the West Indies or its people

²west indian *n, cap W&I* [*West India* + E *-an,* n. suffix] **:** a native or inhabitant of the West Indies

west indian arrowroot *n, usu cap W&I* **:** INDIAN ARROWROOT 1b

west indian birch *n, usu cap W&I* **:** GUMBO LIMBO 1

west indian boxwood *n, usu cap W&I* **:** ZAPATERO 2b

west indian cane weevil *n, usu cap 1st W&I* **:** a tropical American snout beetle (*Metamasius hemipterus*) that is destructive to sugarcane esp. in the West Indies

west indian cherry *n, usu cap W&I* **:** BARBADOS CHERRY 1

west indian ebony *n, usu cap W&I* **:** COCUSWOOD

west indian fruit fly *n, usu cap W&I* **:** a small fly (*Anastrepha mombinpraeoptans*) of the family Trypetidae whose larvae develop in citrus and other fruits in tropical America

west indian gherkin *n, usu cap W&I* **:** GHERKIN 1

west indian ivy *n, usu cap W & 1st I* **:** a climbing plant of the genus *Marcgravia*

west-indian-ivy family *n, usu cap W & 1st I* **:** MARCGRAVIACEAE

west indian locust *n, usu cap W&I* **:** a tropical American tree (*Hymenaea courbaril*) yielding hard brown wood used for building and having bijugate leaves, white flowers, and woody pods containing an edible pulp

west indian mahogany *n, usu cap W&I* **:** a mahogany (*Swietenia mahogani*); *also* **:** MAHOGANY 1a(1)

west indian peach scale *n, usu cap W&I* **:** a widely distributed polyphagous scale insect (*Aulacaspis pentagona*) that is esp. destructive to peach and mulberry and occurs generally in tropical and subtropical regions

west indian sandalwood *n, usu cap W&I* **:** a Jamaica rosewood (*Amyris balsamifera*)

west indian satinwood *n, usu cap W&I* **:** SATINWOOD 2a(1)

west indian tea *n, usu cap W&I* **:** a goatweed (*Capraria biflora*) the leaves of which are sometimes used in the West Indies for tea

west indian yellowwood *n, usu cap W&I* **:** HERCULES'-CLUB 1a

west india seal *n, usu cap W&I* **:** a large earless seal (*Monachus tropicalis*) of the West Indies that is nearly extinct

west indies *adj, usu cap W&I* [fr. *West Indies,* group of islands between North and South America enclosing the Caribbean sea; fr. the belief of Columbus that it was a new route to India] **:** of or from the West Indies group of islands **:** of the kind or style prevalent in the West Indies **:** WEST INDIAN

west·ing \'westiŋ\ *n* -s [in sense 1, fr. ¹*west* + *-ing;* in sense 2, fr. gerund of ⁴*west*] **1 :** difference in longitude to the west from the last preceding point of reckoning **2 :** westerly progress **:** a going westward ⟨trade winds . . . would blow me across on my ~ as they had blown Columbus —Alan Villiers⟩

west·land \'westlənd\ *adj, usu cap* [fr. *Westland,* New Zealand] **:** of or from the provincial district of Westland, New Zealand **:** of the kind or style prevalent in Westland provincial district

westland pine *n, usu cap W* [fr. *Westland,* New Zealand] **:** SILVER PINE 4

west·lin \'westlən\ *or* **west·ling** \", -liŋ\ *adj* [*westlin* alter. of *westland,* fr. ²*west* + *land; westling* alter. (influenced by *-ing*) of *westlin*] *Scot* **:** WESTERLY ⟨when the fringe was red on the ~ hill —James Hogg⟩

west·lins \-nz\ *or* **west·lings** \-nz, -ŋz\ *adv* [³*west* + *-lins* (alter. of *-lings*) or *-lings*] *Scot* **:** to the west

west lo·thi·an \-'lōthēən, -thyən\ *adj, usu cap W&L* [fr. *West Lothian,* Scotland] **:** of or from the county of West Lothian, Scotland **:** of the kind or style prevalent in West Lothian

west·meath \(')wes(t)¦mēth\ *adj, usu cap* [fr. *Westmeath,* Ireland] **:** of or from county Westmeath, Ireland **:** of the kind or style prevalent in county Westmeath

west·min·ster chimes \'wes(t),minztə(r)-, -n(t)stə(r)-, *substand* (')=¦minəstə(r)-\ *n, usu cap W* [fr. *Westminster,* section of London in which the House of Parliament is located] **:** clock chimes on four bells or gongs fashioned after the tune of the chimes on the House of Parliament clock in London

west·mor·land \'wes(t)mə(r)lənd, *U S also* (')=¦mōrl- *or* (')=¦mȯrl- *or* (')=¦mōəl- *or* (')=¦mȯ(ə)l-\ *adj, usu cap* [fr. *Westmorland,* England] **:** of or from the county of Westmorland, England **:** of the kind or style prevalent in Westmorland

west·most \'wes(t)mōst, *esp Brit also* -,məst\ *adj* [alter. (influenced by ¹*most*) of ME *westmest,* fr. OE, superl. of *west,* adv.] **:** WESTERNMOST ⟨the appeal of our ~ land is in its . . . terrain, climate —Aubrey Drury⟩

west·ness \'wes(t)nəs\ *n* -ES **:** the quality or state of being west

¹west-northwest \(¦)=¦=¦=\ *adv (or adj)* [ME *west-north-west*] **1 :** toward west-northwest **2 :** from west-northwest

²west-northwest \"\ *n* **:** a compass point that is two points north of due west **:** N 67°30′ W — abbr. *WNW;* see COMPASS CARD

Wes·ton \'westən\ *trademark* — used for a voltaic cell used as a standard of electromotive force

west·phal balance \'wes(t),fōl-\ *n, usu cap W* [prob. after Wilhelm H. *Westphal,* 20th cent. Ger. physicist] **:** a balance having the buoyancy of a float balanced by sliding weights that is used for determining specific gravity (as of liquids or mineral fragments) — called also *Mohr balance*

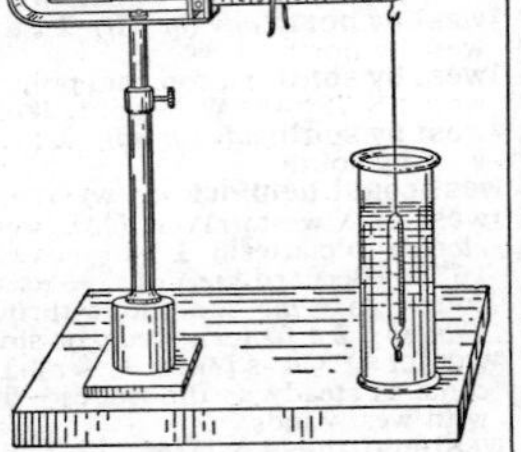

Westphal balance

¹west·pha·lian \(')wes(t)¦fālyən, -lēən\ *adj, usu cap* [*Westphalia,* former province of Prussia + E *-an*] **1 a :** of, relating to, or characteristic of Westphalia or Westphalians **b :** of, relating to, or characteristic of the Westphalian dialect **2 :** of or relating to a subdivision of the Upper Carboniferous — see GEOLOGIC TIME table

²westphalian \"\ *n* -s *cap* **:** a native or inhabitant of Westphalia

westphalian ham *n, usu cap W* **:** a ham of distinctive flavor produced by smoking with juniper brush

west point *n, often cap W&P* [fr. *West Point,* U. S. military academy at West Point, N. Y.] **:** a grayish blue that is redder and paler than electric, duller and very slightly redder than copenhagen, and duller and very slightly greener than Gobelin

¹wes·tra·lian \(')we¦strālyən *sometimes* -lēən\ *adj, usu cap* [*Westralia* (contr. of *Western Australia*) + E *-an*] **:** of, relating to, or characteristic of Western Australia or its inhabitants

²westralian \"\ *n* -s *cap* **:** a native or inhabitant of Western Australia

westralian jewfish *n, usu cap W* **:** JEWFISH 2a

wests *pl of* WEST, *pres 3d sing of* WEST

west saxon *n, cap W&S* [ME] **1 :** a native or inhabitant of the West Saxon kingdom **2 :** a dialect of Old English **:** the chief literary dialect in pre-Conquest England

west semitic *n, cap W&S* **:** the Semitic languages other than Akkadian

¹west-southwest \(¦)=¦=¦=\ *adv (or adj)* [ME *west southwest*] **1 :** toward west-southwest **2 :** from west-southwest

²west-southwest \"\ *n* **:** a compass point that is two points south of due west **:** S 67°30′ W — abbr. *WSW;* see COMPASS CARD

west virginia *adj, usu cap W&V* [fr. *West Virginia,* state in the east central U. S., fr. ²*west* + *Virginia,* eastern state of which West Virginia was a part until the American Civil War] **:** of or from the state of West Virginia ⟨*West Virginia* coal⟩ **:** of the kind or style prevalent in West Virginia **:** WEST VIRGINIAN

¹west virginian *adj, usu cap W&V* [*West Virginia* + E *-an*] **:** of, relating to, or characteristic of West Virginia or West Virginians

²west virginian *n, cap W&V* **:** a native or resident of West Virginia

¹west·ward \'westwə(r)d\ *adv (or adj)* [ME, fr. OE *westweard,* fr. ¹*west* + *-weard* -ward] **:** toward the west ⟨the pioneers trekked ~⟩

²westward \"\ *n* **:** westward direction or part ⟨the Rockies lie to the ~⟩

west·ward·ly *adv (or adj)* **:** in a westward direction

west·wards \-dz\ *adv* [³*west* + *-wards*] **:** WESTWARD ⟨walked swiftly ~ through the twilight —Michael Arlen⟩

¹wet \'wet, *usu* -ed·+V\ *vb* **wet** *or* **wetted; wet** *or* **wetted; wetting; wets** [ME *weten,* fr. OE *wǣtan,* fr. *wǣt,* adj., wet] *vt* **1 :** to make wet **:** soak or moisten with water or other liquid **:** dip in a liquid ⟨sand *wetted* by the waves —G.W.Murray⟩ ⟨~ his pencil and got ready to write —Josephine Pinckney⟩ **2 :** to suffuse (the eyes) with tears **:** dampen (something) with tears **:** fall on and moisten (something) **3 :** to take a drink or treat to a drink in celebration or honor of ⟨~ a bargain⟩ ⟨~ a commission in the army⟩ **4 :** to soak (grain) in malting **5 :** to urinate in or on ⟨~ the bed⟩ **6 :** to make (tea) by pouring boiling water on the leaves ⟨I ~ a cup of tea —Bryan MacMahon⟩ **~** *vi* **1 :** to become wet **2 :** URINATE — **wet one's whistle :** to take a drink ⟨'tis a hot day and I think our friends will need to *wet their whistles* before long —*Boys' Life*⟩ — **wet the other eye :** to take another drink of liquor ⟨moisten your clay, *wet the other eye* —Charles Dickens⟩

²wet \"\ *adj* **wetter; wettest** [ME *wet, wete, wette,* partly fr. past part. of *weten* to wet & partly fr. OE *wǣt;* akin to OFris *wēt* wet, ON *vātr* wet, *vatn* water — more at WATER] **1 a :** consisting of, containing, covered with, or soaked with water or some other liquid **:** having water or other liquid on the surface or penetrating beyond it **:** MOIST ⟨~ tears⟩ ⟨the ~ sea⟩ ⟨a ~ floor⟩ ⟨~ fields⟩ ⟨got his clothes ~ when he fell in the water⟩ ⟨a rag ~ with oil⟩ ⟨cheeks ~ with happy tears⟩ **b :** moistened by dipping in or sprinkling with water or other liquid ⟨it had been raining and the newspaper at the door was ~⟩ ⟨grass ~ with dew⟩ **c** *of natural gas* **:** containing appreciable quantities of gasoline or other readily condensable hydrocarbons **2 :** RAINY; as **a :** having frequent rains ⟨the ~ season⟩ **b :** promising rain ⟨a ~ sky⟩ **c :** laden with or bearing moisture or vapor **:** HUMID ⟨a ~ wind⟩ **d :** accompanied by rain ⟨the city gave us a ~ welcome⟩ **3 :** still moist enough to smudge or smear ⟨the signature was still ~⟩ ⟨~ paint⟩ **4 :** not processed, dried, or reduced **:** remaining in or near the natural state of a freshly caught fish **5 a :** devoted to, associated with, or used for drinking or conviviality ⟨have a ~ night —W.M.Thackeray⟩ **b :** addicted to drink **c :** showing some degree of intoxication **:** DRUNK, SLOPPED **d :** consisting of alcoholic liquor ⟨~ cargo⟩ **e :** trading in alcoholic liquor ⟨a ~ canteen⟩ **f :** permitting the manufacture and sale of alcoholic liquor **:** not prohibiting traffic in intoxicants ⟨a ~ county⟩ **g :** committed to or advocating a policy of permitting such traffic or opposed to its prohibition ⟨a ~ candidate⟩ ⟨a ~ platform⟩ **6 :** preserved, bottled, or put up in liquid (as fruit in syrup or a zoological specimen in alcohol) **7 :** lax in the observances of one's sect — used chiefly of a Friend **8 :** employing or done by means of or in the presence of water or other liquid ⟨~ extraction of copper⟩ ⟨a ~ process⟩ — compare DRY 3b **9** *of a boat* **:** tending to take water or spray over the bows or sides **10 :** perversely wrong **:** away off **:** wide of the mark **:** MISGUIDED ⟨he's all ~⟩ **11 a :** designed to contain liquids **:** TIGHT ⟨a ~ cask⟩ ⟨~ barrel⟩ **b :** of or having reference to such containers ⟨~ coopering⟩ ⟨a ~ cooper⟩ **12 :** giving milk **:** LACTATING ⟨a ~ cow⟩ **13 :** SLOW 5e **14 :** grown in wet or damp soil ⟨a ~ crop⟩ **15** *of stolen livestock* **:** smuggled across a river by fording **16 :** soiled with one's own urine — used chiefly of a baby **17 :** not accepted as a good fellow or a regular guy **18 :** sloppily sentimental ⟨touches of silliness which might so easily have been merely ~ —Kingsley Amis⟩

syn DAMP, DANK, MOIST, HUMID: WET is a general term describing either something with an outer layer covered with water or other liquid or something soaked throughout more or less thoroughly ⟨a *wet* sidewalk⟩ ⟨drying her *wet* hands⟩ ⟨*wet* clothes⟩ ⟨a *wet* sponge⟩ DAMP may suggest slight or moderate wetness, sometimes unpleasant, permeating, or dispiriting, sometimes useful ⟨the chill and the vapor taken together told a poor tale of the island. It was plainly a *damp,* feverish, unhealthy spot —R.L.Stevenson⟩ ⟨the rain poured down with quiet persistency. Everything in the boat was *damp* and clammy —J.K.Jerome⟩ ⟨sheets should be *damp* when ironed⟩ DANK is almost never without the notion of sickly, disagreeable, or penetrating dampness ⟨*dank* with the marshy moisture of many low grounds —Charles Dickens⟩ ⟨passed his hand across his forehead. It was *dank* with clammy sweat —Oscar Wilde⟩ ⟨from the jungle a *dank* sulphurous breeze exuded —Norman Mailer⟩ MOIST suggests a moderate or slight wetness, enough to keep a thing from being described as dry ⟨the *moist* forehead of a sick man⟩ ⟨the depths of the valley, where the air was *moist* and cool —C.B.Nordhoff & J.N.Hall⟩ HUMID usu. applies to moisture in the air ⟨the *humid* prairie heat, so nourishing to wheat and corn, so exhausting to human beings —Willa Cather⟩

³wet \"\ *n* -s [ME *wet, wete,* fr. OE *wǣt, wǣta,* fr. *wǣt,* adj., wet] **1 :** WATER, WETNESS, MOISTURE ⟨gleaming and trembling drops of ~ —Marjory S. Douglas⟩ ⟨carefully wringing the ~ out —W.H.Hudson †1922⟩ **2 a :** rainy weather **:** RAIN, RAINSTORM ⟨stay out all night in the ~ —H.L.Davis⟩ **b** *chiefly Austral* **:** the rainy season ⟨had begun shearing, but were sorely hindered by the ~ —Rachel Henning⟩ **3 a** *chiefly Brit* **:** a drink of alcoholic liquor ⟨cross over to the ale tent for your ~ —A.J.Liebling⟩ **b :** an advocate of a policy of permitting the sale of intoxicating liquors — opposed to *dry* ⟨the drys lied to make prohibition look good; the ~*s* lied to make it look bad —G.W.Johnson⟩

we·ta \'wād·ə\ *n* -s [Maori] **:** any of various large wingless long-horned insects (family Stenopelmatidae) of New Zealand; *esp* **:** a large clumsy insect (*Deinacrida heteracantha*) measuring four inches in length

wet-and-dry-bulb thermometer \¦=¦=¦=-\ *n* **:** PSYCHROMETER

wetback \'=,=\ *n* [²*wet* + *back*] **:** a Mexican who enters the U.S. illegally (as by wading or swimming the Rio Grande) ⟨~*s* . . . willing to work for nothing if a rancher would conceal them —Irving Shulman⟩ — compare BRACERO

wet bargain *n* **:** DUTCH BARGAIN

wetbird \'=,=\ *n* [so called fr. the belief that its cry foretells rain] *dial Eng* **:** CHAFFINCH

wet blanket *n* **1 :** a blanket soaked in water (as for quenching a fire) **2 :** someone or something that quenches or dampens enthusiasm or pleasure ⟨a woman who cannot laugh is a *wet blanket* —W.M.Thackeray⟩

wet-blanket \'=¦==\ *vt* [*wet blanket*] **:** to quench or dampen with or as if with a wet blanket **:** DISCOURAGE, DEPRESS

wet-bulb temperature \'=¦=-\ *n* **:** temperature indicated by a wet-bulb thermometer that is lower than the actual temperature of the air — compare PSYCHROMETER

wet-bulb thermometer *n* **:** the thermometer with moistened bulb in a psychrometer

wet butt *n* **:** a softening and discoloration of tobacco caused by freezing before curing is complete

wet cell *n* **:** a voltaic cell in which the electrolyte is a liquid

wet-clean \'=¦=\ *vt* **:** to clean by means of water

wet cleaning *n* **:** cleaning in which water is used

wet dock *n* **:** a dock where the water is shut in and kept at a given level to facilitate the loading and unloading of ships

wet dog *n* **:** a tobacco leaf with undesirable odor and color

wet down *vt* **:** to dampen by sprinkling with water

wet dream *n* **:** an erotic dream culminating in orgasm and in the male accompanied by nocturnal emission

wet end *n* **:** the part of a paper machine between the point where the stock is fed in and the driers

wet-fast·ness \'=¦=s(t)nəs\ *n* **:** resistance to change on wetting — used esp. of a dye

wet feet *n* **:** the condition of plants growing with excessive water at their roots

wet fly *n* **:** any of various artificial flies intended to be presented to fish below the surface of the water

wet fog *n* **:** fog that wets objects exposed to it

wet goods *n pl* **:** liquid goods in casks or bottles (as paints, oils, beer, or spirits); *esp* **:** intoxicating liquors

wet-grind \'=¦=\ *vt* **:** to grind under a coolant liquid

weth·er \'wethə(r)\ *n* -s [ME *wether, weder,* fr. OE *wether;* akin to OHG *widar* ram, ON *vethr* ram, Goth *withrus* lamb, L *vitulus* calf, *vetus* old, Gk *etos* year, Skt *vatsa* calf, *vatsara* year; basic meaning: yearling] **1** *obs* **:** a male sheep **:** RAM **2 :** a male sheep castrated before sexual maturity usu. when only a few weeks old and before the development of secondary sex characters — compare BELLWETHER **3 :** a male goat castrated when young

wetherhog \'==,=\ *n* [*wether* + *hog*] *dial Brit* **:** a wether of the second season

¹wetland \'=,=\ *n* [²*wet* + *land*] **:** land containing much soil moisture (as swamp or bog) — usu. used in pl. ⟨discussed the effect of dwindling ~*s* on ducks and geese —R.R.Camp⟩

²wetland \"\ *adj, of a plant* **:** growing or thriving in wetlands

wet lap *n* **:** a sheet of pulp removed from a wet machine

wet·ly *adv* **:** in a wet manner

wet machine *or* **wet press** *n* **:** a papermaking machine that forms slush pulp into heavy sheets by pressing out enough water so that the sheet may be cut from the roll and folded into laps — called also *decker*

wet milking *n* **:** the milking of a cow or other animal with the hands and teats wet (as with milk) often resulting in udder infections in cattle

wet mill *n* **:** a sawmill at which logs are sorted in water

wet milling *n* **:** a process of milling (as of corn) involving preliminary soaking in water or other liquid

wet mix *n* **:** the mixture obtained when water is added to cement, sand, and coarse aggregate

wet mop *n* **:** a mop for swabbing floors with water

wet-my-lip \'=(,)=,=\ *n* [imit. of its note] *dial Eng* **:** QUAIL 1a(1)

wet·ness *n* -ES [ME *wetnes,* fr. OE *wǣtnes,* fr. *wǣt* wet + *-nes* -ness — more at WET] **1 a :** the quality or state of being wet **b :** something wet (as a wet spot) **2 :** WETNESS FRACTION

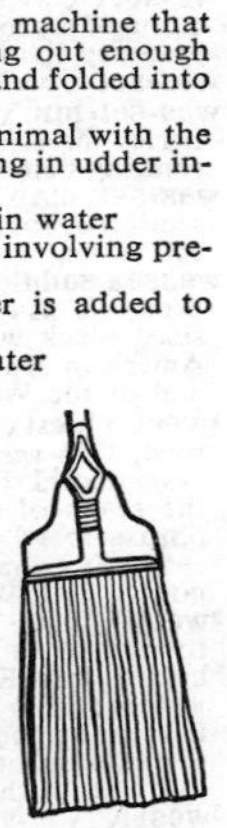

wet mop

wetness fraction *n* **:** a fraction expressing the ratio of the weight of free water particles to that of the whole in a quantity of wet steam

wet nurse *n* **:** one that cares for and suckles young not her own

wet-nurse \'=¦=\ *vt* [*wet nurse*] **1 :** to care for and suckle as a wet nurse **2 :** to devote unremitting or excessive care to **:** tend sedulously ⟨not up to the court to *wet-nurse* the schools —J.J.Parker⟩

wet off *vt* **:** to detach (blown glass) from a blowpipe or prepare for fracture at some other point by touching with a tool often wet with water

wet out *vt* **:** to wet thoroughly; *specif* **:** to make (textiles) more

absorbent by treating with a wetting agent prior to dyeing or bleaching
wet pan *n* **:** a machine used for grinding and blending clays and consisting of a circular iron pan in which heavy wheels or rollers revolve
wet–pipe system \'=¦=-\ *n* **:** a sprinkler system in which the pipes contain water under pressure even when not in use
wet plate *n* **:** an iodized collodion-coated photographic glass plate exposed while wet after sensitizing in a silver nitrate solution — compare COLLODION PROCESS
wet–plate process \'=¦=-\ *n* **:** an early collodion process
wet pleurisy *n* **:** pleurisy with effusion of exudate into the pleural cavity
wet pox *n* **:** FOWL POX b
wet–process machine \'=¦=-\ *n* **:** a machine for cleaning apples and pears of spray residues by means of washes, sprays, and dips of either acid or alkaline solutions
wetproof \'=¦=\ *adj* **:** WATERPROOF
wet pulp *n* **:** paper pulp from a wet machine usu. containing 50 to 65 percent of water
wet return *n* **:** a pipeline in a steam heating system for returning water of condensation to the boiler that being located below the waterline of the boiler can contain only water rather than the steam mixed with water which a return pipe located above the waterline may contain
wet rot *n* **1 :** a soft rot in which the decayed tissues are markedly watery **2 :** decay of timber by fungi that attack wood having high moisture content
wets *pres 3d sing of* WET, *pl of* WET
wet–salt \'=¦=\ *vt* **:** to treat (hides) with wet salt — compare DRY-SALT
wet–shod \'=¦=\ *adj* [ME] *dial* **:** having one's shoes or feet wet
wet smack *n, slang* **:** a social misfit **:** a dull or obnoxious person
wet steam *n* **:** steam composed of water vapor mixed with droplets of liquid water — compare DRY STEAM
wet strength *n* **:** the tensile strength of paper when wet
wet suit *n* **:** a close-fitting suit made of material (as sponge rubber) that water will go through but that retains body heat and worn (as by a water skier or skin diver) esp. in cold water
wet·ta·bil·i·ty \,wed·ə'biləd·ē, ,wetə'bilətē, -i\ *n* **:** the quality or state of being wettable or the degree to which something can be wet
wet·ta·ble \'wed·əbəl, -etə-\ *adj* **:** capable of being wetted; *specif* **:** having the ability (as after the addition of a wetting agent) of being wetted by or readily mixing with water or other liquid — used of insoluble substances ⟨DDT supplied as a ~ powder may be suspended in water —*Introduction to Agric. Biochem.*⟩
wettable sulfur *n* **:** finely divided sulfur to which a wetting agent has been added for use in agricultural sprays
wetted *past of* WET
wetted surface *n* **:** the surface of a ship's hull in contact with the water under specified conditions
wet·ter \'wed·ə(r), -etə-\ *n* -S **:** one that wets: as **a :** a workman who wets the work in various manufacturing processes **b :** WETTING AGENT
wetter–off \'==¦=\ *n, pl* **wetters–off** [fr. *wet off,* v.] *Brit* **:** CRACKER-OFF
wetter–out \'==¦=\ *n, pl* **wetters–out :** a worker who wets out textiles
wettest *superlative of* WET
wetting *pres part of* WET
wetting agent *or* **wetting–out agent** \¦==¦=-\ *n* **:** any of numerous water-soluble or liquid usu. synthetic organic substances that promote spreading of a liquid on a surface or penetration into a material esp. by their oriented adsorption on the surfaces in such a way that the wetting liquid is no longer repelled and that are used in mixing solids with liquids, in spreading liquids on surfaces, and as penetrants (as in the textile industry or in spraying with insecticides or fungicides) **:** a surface-active agent having higher wetting power than detergent or other powers
wet·tish \'wed·|ish, -et|, |ēsh\ *adj* **:** somewhat wet **:** MOIST
wet wash *n* **:** laundry returned damp and unironed
wet–waxed \'=¦=\ *adj, of waxed paper* **:** so made that much of the wax remains on the surface as a nearly continuous film — compare DRY-WAXED
wet well *n* **:** FISH WELL
wet wind *n* **:** any one of the winds at any given place that are most frequently followed by rain or snow
wetwood \'=,=\ *n* **:** wood having a water-soaked or translucent appearance because of abnormally high water content sometimes due to bacteria and sometimes to physiological factors
wex·ford \'weksfə(r)d\ *adj, usu cap* [fr. *Wexford,* Ireland] **:** of or from County Wexford, Ireland **:** of the kind or style prevalent in County Wexford
wey \'wā\ *n* -S [ME, fr. OE *wǣge* weight, wey — more at WEIGH (n.)] **:** any of various old units of weight used locally in the British Isles esp. for cheese, wool, and salt; *also* **:** a Scotch and Irish unit of capacity (as for coal or grain) equal to 41.28 bushels
wey·mouth pine \'wāməth-\ *n, usu cap W* [after Thomas Thynne †1714 first Viscount of *Weymouth*] **:** WHITE PINE 1a
WF *abbr* **1** water finish **2** wing forward **3** wrong font
wg *abbr* wing
WG *abbr* **1** weight guaranteed **2** wire gauge
wgt *abbr* weight
wh *abbr* **1** which **2** white
WH *abbr* **1** water heater **2** *often not cap* watt-hour
wha \(¦)(h)wȧ, -wa\ *Scot & dial Eng var of* WHO
whaap *var of* WHAUP
whabby *var of* WABBY
¹whack \'hwak *also* 'wak\ *vb* -ED/-ING/-S [prob. of imit. origin] *vt* **1 a :** to strike with a smart or resounding blow ⟨~ his desk with a schoolmaster's ruler that serves him as a gavel —Janet Flanner⟩ ⟨~ the ball into left field⟩ ⟨~ the little boy for talking back⟩ **b :** to cut with or as if with a whack **:** CHOP ⟨ran down and captured turkey gobblers and ~*ed* off their heads —C.T.Jackson⟩ ⟨the house ~*ed* $63.8 million from the proposed . . . budget —*New Republic*⟩ **c :** to take vigorous action against ⟨the French police . . . have ~*ed* some of the smartest bars in town with gigantic fines —Janet Flanner⟩ **2 :** to put, get, or make by vigorous or hurried action — often used with *up* or *out* ⟨before their homes were finished, the busy colonists had ~*ed up* . . . a sort of meeting place and school —S.H.Holbrook⟩ ⟨~*ed up* half a million signatures to its petition against the bill —Mollie Panter-Downes⟩ **3 a :** to work as a driver of (oxen or mules) **:** DRIVE **b :** to drive to greater speed or activity — usu. used with *up* **4** *chiefly Brit* **:** to get the better of **:** DEFEAT ⟨if you are ~*ed* today, you may win tomorrow —Winnie Barber⟩ **~** *vi* **:** to strike something with a smart or resounding blow ⟨wanted to dawdle . . . and ~ at things with a switch —Marcia Davenport⟩
²whack \"\ *n* -S **1 a :** a smart or resounding blow ⟨gave the rioter a ~ on the head with his nightstick⟩; *also* **:** the sound of or as if of such a blow ⟨heard the ~ of the speedboat on the waves⟩ **b :** a vigorous attack ⟨takes a good ~ at false living and false gods —Virgilia Peterson⟩ **2 a :** PORTION, SHARE, ALLOWANCE ⟨a European calamity fund . . . into which every country would pay its ~ —Mollie Panter-Downes⟩ **b** *chiefly Brit* **:** the statutory daily minimum ration of food and drink allowed a merchant seaman ⟨we lived on our bare ~ —Albert Sonnichsen⟩ **3** *Midland* **:** AGREEMENT, BARGAIN, DEAL **4 :** CONDITION, STATE ⟨the tycoon is in fine ~ —John Hay †1905⟩ **5 a :** an opportunity or attempt to do something **:** CHANCE ⟨having first ~ at original-cast album privileges —J.M.Conly⟩ **:** TRY ⟨some horsebreaker had already taken a ~ at these ponies and hadn't done a very cute job —F.B.Gipson⟩ **b :** a single action or occasion **:** STROKE, TIME ⟨made several style changes with one ~⟩ ⟨borrow fifty dollars all at one ~ —G.S.Perry⟩ — **out of whack 1 :** out of order or shape ⟨threw his back *out of whack* doing a tango —*Time*⟩ ⟨everything was completely *out of whack,* none of the joints fitted —Norman Mailer⟩ ⟨repairing everything that got *out of whack* —Joseph Mitchell⟩ **2 :** out of accord ⟨parts washing is *out of whack* with their other production methods —*Automotive Industries*⟩
³whack *var of* WACK
whacked *adj* [fr. past part. of ¹*whack*] *Brit* **:** EXHAUSTED
whack·er \-kə(r)\ *n* -S **1 :** one that whacks: as **a :** the driver of a team of oxen or mules **:** DROVER **b :** CAR KNOCKER **2 :** something uncommonly large; *specif* **:** a great lie
¹whack·ing \-kiŋ, -kēŋ\ *adj* [fr. pres. part. of ¹*whack*] **:** very large **:** WHOPPING ⟨swept . . . into power with a ~ parliamentary majority —J.W.Vandercook⟩
²whacking \"\ *adv* **:** VERY, EXTREMELY ⟨a ~ big diamond⟩ ⟨a ~ good story⟩
whack up *vt* [²*whack*] **:** to divide into shares ⟨a tidy $3,000,000 profit which they *whacked up* among themselves —*Time*⟩
whack–up \'=¦=\ *n* -S [*whack up*] **:** the act of whacking up; *specif* **:** the division of the loot of a robbery
whacky *var of* WACKY
whae \(¦)(h)wā\ *Scot & dial Eng var of* WHO
whahoo *var of* WAHOO
whai·sle *or* **whai·zle** \'(h)wāzəl\ *Scot var of* WHEEZLE
wha·ka·pa·pa \¦(h)wäkə¦päpə, 'fäk-\ *n* -S [Maori] **:** a Maori genealogy
¹whale \'hwāl, *esp before pause or consonant* -āəl; *also* 'wā-\ *n, pl* **whale** *or* **whales** *often attrib* [ME, fr. OE *hwæl;* akin to OHG *hwal* whale, ON *hvalr,* and prob. to L *squalus,* a sea fish] **1 :** an aquatic mammal of the order Cetacea that superficially resembles a large fish and is valued commercially for whale oil, for the flesh which is used as human food and in animal feeds and fertilizers, and formerly for baleen; *esp* **:** one of the larger members of this group — compare DOLPHIN, PORPOISE; see TOOTHED WHALE, WHALEBONE WHALE, ZEUGLODON **2 a :** a person or thing with an extraordinary appetite or keenness ⟨a ~ for work⟩ ⟨a whale of the great ship — an insatiable ~ that ate men and gold —James Dugan⟩ **b :** a person or thing impressive in size or qualities or superlatively good of kind ⟨not impressed by the pronouncements of the scientific ~*s*⟩ ⟨a ~ of a difference⟩ ⟨a ~ of a story⟩ — often used intensively in the phrase *a whale of a* ⟨borrowed a ~ of a lot of money⟩ ⟨a ~ of a good time⟩

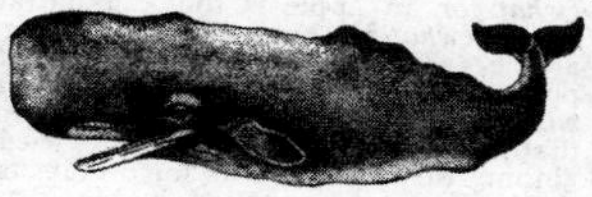

sperm whale

²whale \"\ *vi* -ED/-ING/-S **:** to engage in whale fishing
³whale \"\ *vb* -ED/-ING/-S [origin unknown] *vt* **1 :** LASH, THRASH ⟨~ a boy for lying⟩ **2 :** to strike or hit vigorously ⟨~ the ball for a home run⟩ **3 :** to bring by thrashing or striking ⟨~ the dust out of the carpets⟩ **4 :** to defeat soundly ⟨*whaled* their rivals 20 to 0⟩ **~** *vi* **:** to perform an action with great vigor; *esp* **:** to make a vigorous attack on a person or thing — often used with *away* ⟨uses his daily column to ~ away at his pet peeves⟩
⁴whale *var of* WALE
whaleback \'=,=\ *n* [¹*whale* + *back*] **1 :** something (as a hill or wave) shaped like the back of a whale **2 a :** TURTLEBACK c **b :** a steamship having sides curving in towards the ends, a spoon bow, and a very convex upper deck formerly used (as for carrying grain or ore) on the Great Lakes
whale–backed \'=¦=\ *also* **whaleback** \'=¦=\ *adj* **:** shaped like or resembling a whale's back
whaleback roof *n* **:** RAINBOW ROOF
whale barnacle *n* **:** any of several barnacles of *Coronula* and related genera that are parasitic on whales
whalebird \'=,=\ *n* **:** any of several gregarious seabirds that follow whaling ships to feed on oil and offal; *esp* **:** a petrel of the genus *Prion* of southern oceans having a peculiar broad lamellate bill
whaleboat \'=,=\ *n* **1 :** a long narrow rowboat made with a bold sheer, both ends sharp and raking, a lean afterbody, and no deadwood, often steered with an oar, and formerly used by whalemen for hunting whales **2 :** a long narrow flat-floored rowboat or motorboat that is sharp and rounded at both ends in the manner of the original whaleboats, that is fitted with buoyancy tanks, and that is often carried by warships and merchant ships
whalebone \'=,=\ *n* -S *often attrib* [¹*whale* + *bone*] **1 :** BALEEN **2 :** an article made of baleen (as a strip used to stiffen a corset or dress)
whalebone tree *n* **:** a medium-sized tree (*Pseudomorus brunoniana*) of the family Moraceae of Norfolk island and Australia having yellow close-grained hard wood
whalebone whale *n* **:** any of various usu. large whales having in the adult plates of baleen dependent from the upper jaw instead of teeth, frequenting chiefly colder regions, and constituting the suborder Mysticeti — see FINBACK, GRAY WHALE, HUMPBACK, RIGHT WHALE, RORQUAL; compare TOOTHED WHALE
whale catcher *also* **whale chaser** *n* **:** a sturdy fast quick-turning steel ship about 135 feet in length equipped with a harpoon gun in the bow and used for hunting whales as one of a fleet attached to a factory ship
whale factory ship *n* **:** a large ship designed to take aboard and obtain oil and other products from whales
whale feed *or* **whale food** *n* **:** BRIT 2
whale fin *n* **:** BALEEN
whale finger *n* **:** ERYSIPELOID
whale fisher *or* **whale fisherman** *n* **:** WHALER 1
whale fishery *n* **1** *or* **whale fishing :** the occupation of taking whales **2 :** a region where whales are pursued
whalehead \'=,=\ *or* **whale–headed stork** \'=¦==-\ *n* **:** SHOEBILL
whalehide \'=,=\ *n* **:** a parchmentized wet strength kraft paper
whale iron *n* **:** HARPOON
whalelike \'=,=\ *adj* **:** resembling a whale or that of a whale
whale line *also* **whale rope** *n* **1 :** a strong solidly made 3-strand manila rope about six inches in diameter used in whaling as a harpoon line or towline **2** *slang* **:** a cowboy's manila lariat
whale louse *n* **1 :** any of several degenerate amphipod crustaceans (genus *Cyamus*) parasitic on cetaceans **2 :** WHALE BARNACLE
whale·man \'=mən\ *n, pl* **whalemen 1 :** a man employed on a whaling ship **2 :** a whaling ship
whale oil *n* **:** a water-white to brown oil obtained from the blubber of whales and used in tempering steel, in dressing leather, after hydrogenation in making margarine and soap, as a lubricant, and formerly as an illuminant — called also *train oil*
¹whal·er \'hwālə(r) *also* 'wāl-\ *n* -S [¹*whale* + *-er*] **1 :** a person or ship employed in the whale fishery **:** WHALEMAN **2 :** WHALEBOAT 2 **3** *also* **whaler shark :** any of several moderate to large size sharks (genus *Carcharhinus*) common along shore and in estuaries about Australia, New Guinea, and New Zealand **4** *Austral* **:** a strolling bushman **:** SWAGMAN, SUNDOWNER; *esp* **:** a swagman who keeps near some large river ascending on one bank and descending on the other
²whaler \"\ *n* -S [³*whale* + *-er*] **1 :** one that whales **2 :** something extraordinary (as in size) **:** WHOPPER
³whaler *var of* WALER
whal·ery \'hwālərē *also* 'wāl-\ *n* -ES [¹*whale* + *-ery*] **1 :** WHALE FISHERY 1 **2 :** a shore station or factory ship where whales are taken for the extraction of oil and other products
whales *pl of* WHALE, *pres 3d sing of* WHALE
whale shark *n* **:** a harmless shark (*Rhincodon typus*) found in all tropical waters, reaching a length of 45 feet, having very small teeth, and feeding on small fish and other animals strained out of the water by its fine-set gill rakers
whaleship \'=,=\ *n* **:** a ship used in whaling **:** WHALER
whale's–tongue \'=,=\ *n, pl* **whale's–tongues :** a marine worm of the genus *Balanoglossus*
whale sucker *n* **:** a remora (*Remilegia australis*) of the Pacific ocean
¹whaling *n* -S [fr. gerund of ²*whale*] **:** the occupation of catching and rendering whales
²whaling *n* -S [fr. gerund of ³*whale*] **:** THRASHING, BEATING
³whaling *adj* [fr. pres. part. of ³*whale*] **:** WHACKING ⟨a ~ price to pay⟩
⁴whaling *adv* **:** VERY, EXTREMELY ⟨a ~ big family⟩
whaling gun *n* [¹*whaling*] **:** a gun or other device for discharging a projectile (as a harpoon or bomb) at a whale
whaling master *n* **1 :** a captain of a whaling vessel **2 :** a man in charge of a whaling station
whaling port *n* **:** a port where many whalers are owned or registered
whally \'(h)wȯlē\ *adj* [prob. alter. of *walleyed*] **:** having the iris of light color **:** WALLEYED
whalp \'(h)walp\ *Scot & dial var of* WHELP
¹wham \'hwam, -aa(ə)m *also* 'wa-\ *n* -S [imit.] **1 :** the loud sound of a hard impact or explosion ⟨startled by the harsh ~ of a gun going off —R.M.Randall⟩ **2 :** a solid blow ⟨shook the table with an emphatic ~ of his fist⟩
²wham \"\ *vb* **whammed; whammed; whamming; whams** *vt* **:** to propel, strike, or beat forcibly or so as to produce a loud impact ⟨~ two shots into the man —Charles Askins b. 1907⟩ ⟨~ the culprit with her broom⟩ ⟨~ a bass drum⟩ **~** *vi* **:** to make a wham **:** hit or explode with a loud or heavy impact ⟨shells from the battleships were *whamming* over our heads —Ernie Pyle⟩ ⟨skids and ~*s* against a stone wall⟩
³wham \"\ *or* **wham·mo** \-,mō\ *adv* [*wham* fr. ¹*wham; whammo* fr. ¹*wham* + *-o*] **:** with violent abruptness ⟨quietly fishing when ~ — I got a strike⟩ ⟨you're sitting around talking and ~ something starts —Norman Mailer⟩
whame \'(h)wām\ *n* -S [origin unknown] **:** GADFLY
wham·mel *or* **wham·mle** \'(h)waməl\ *dial var of* WHEMMEL
wham·my \'hwamē *also* 'wamē *or* -mi\ *n* -ES [prob. fr. ¹*wham* + *-y*] **1 :** something used to bring good or bad luck **:** a magical practice, gesture, or object **2 :** a supernatural power bringing bad luck to a person **:** a magical curse or spell **:** JINX, HEX ⟨put the ~ on a player by talking about his success⟩ **3 :** a potent force or attack; *specif* **:** a paralyzing or lethal blow
whamp \'(h)wȧmp\ *n* -S [origin unknown] *dial Eng* **:** WASP
wham·ple \'(h)wampəl\ *n* -S [origin unknown] *Scot* **:** BLOW, STROKE
whan \(¦)(h)wän, (¦)(h)wan\ *dial var of* WHEN
¹whang \'hwaŋ, 'hwaiŋ *also* 'wa-\ *n* -S [alter. of ME *thwang* thong — more at THONG] **1** *dial* **a :** THONG **b** *or* **whang leather :** RAWHIDE **2 :** an act or instance of whanging: **a :** BLOW, WHACK **b** *Brit* **:** a large piece or slice **:** CHUNK **3 :** PENIS — often considered vulgar
²whang \"\ *vb* -ED/-ING/-S *vt* **1 a** *dial* **:** FLOG, BEAT, THRASH **b :** to propel or strike with force ⟨~ the ball up against the left-field fence —*Springfield (Mass.) Republican*⟩ ⟨stopped so suddenly his head ~*ed* the dashboard⟩ **2** *chiefly Scot* **:** to chop off or up **~** *vi* **1 :** to strike or beat with force or violence ⟨riveters were still ~*ing* away at the bulkheads —James Dugan⟩ **2 :** to attack vigorously ⟨~*ed* away in the Gazette — . . . clamoring for a primary system —W.A.White⟩ ⟨~ away at arithmetic and spelling until . . . I could quit school —C.T.Jackson⟩
³whang \"\ *n* -S [imit.] **:** a loud sharp vibrant or resonant sound ⟨the ~ of hammers⟩
⁴whang \"\ *vb* -ED/-ING/-S *vi* **:** to make a whang ⟨the cymbals ~ —Vachel Lindsay⟩ ⟨the racket smacked, the sheep gut ~*ed* and the white ball came steaming across —R.P.Warren⟩ **~** *vt* **:** to strike with a whang **:** make a whang with ⟨~ a guitar⟩
whang·doo·dle \(')(h)waŋ¦düd°l, -waiŋ-\ *n* [origin unknown] **1 a :** an imaginary creature of undefined character **b :** one that whangs; *esp* **:** a person that vigorously assails objects of his dislike **2 :** stuff and nonsense **:** POPPYCOCK, FRIPPERY **3 whangdoodles** *pl* **:** ROODLES
whang·ee *also* **whang·hee** \(')(h)waŋ¦gē\ *n* -S [prob. fr. Chin (Pek) *huang² -li²* fr. *huang²* yellow + *li²* bamboo cane] **1 :** any of several Chinese bamboos of the genus *Phyllostachys* **2 :** a walking stick or riding cane of whangee
whang up *vt* **:** to make in a hasty manner
whap *var of* WHOP
wha·pu·ku \'h(w)ä,pükə, 'wä-\ *n* -S [Maori] **:** a large edible marine fish (*Polyprion oxygeneios*) of New Zealand waters that is closely related to or perhaps identical with the stonebass
whar \(¦)(h)wär, (¦)(h)wȧ(r\ *dial var of* WHERE
wha·re \'(h)wärā, 'fä-\ *n* -S [Maori] **1 :** a Maori hut or house **2** *NewZeal* **:** a temporary or roughly built hut in the bush
¹wharf \'(h)wȯ(ə)r|f, -ō(ə)|\ *n, pl* **wharves** \|vz\ *also* **wharfs** *often attrib* [ME *wherf, wharf,* fr. OE *hwearf* turn, exchange, crowd, bank, wharf; akin to MD *werf* shipyard, OHG *hwarb* turn, ON *hvarf* circle, crowd, OE *hweorfan* to turn, move around, OHG *hwerban,* ON *hverfa,* Goth *hwairban,* Gk *karpos* wrist; basic meaning: turn] **1 :** a structure of timber, masonry, cement, earth, or other material built along or at an angle from the shore of navigable waters (as a harbor or river) and made with a sometimes partially covered platform so that vessels may lie close alongside to receive and discharge cargo and passengers; *specif* **:** a structure of open rather than filled construction extending parallel to the shoreline **2** *obs* **:** the bank of a river or the shore of the sea
syn WHARF, DOCK, PIER, QUAY, SLIP, BERTH, JETTY, and LEVEE signify a structure used by boats and ships for taking on or landing cargo or passengers. WHARF, prob. the oldest of the terms applies to any structure projecting from the shore that permits boats or ships to lie alongside for loading or unloading ⟨a ship maneuvering slowly up to the *wharf*⟩ ⟨the townsfolk rush to the *wharves* to welcome with cheers and banners the precious cargo of food —*Life*⟩ ⟨at the foot of this street . . . a rude *wharf* of logs was chained together and moored —*Amer. Guide Series: Vt.*⟩ ⟨a boy sitting on the edge of the *wharf,* his feet dangling in the water⟩ DOCK is usu. interchangeable with WHARF but can be restricted to signify an enclosed basin which permits the entrance of a vessel for loading or unloading or which, with floodgates and a method of exhausting water, can be used for building or repairing ships ⟨a summer lake cottage with a short *dock* for canoes and rowboats⟩ ⟨a *dock* on Occoquan Creek —*Amer. Guide Series: Va.*⟩ ⟨the New York *docks*⟩ ⟨bring a ship into *dock* for repairs⟩ PIER is interchangeable with DOCK or WHARF esp. a large or long one shooting out quite a distance into a body of water ⟨a sloping earthen *pier* for the launching of boats —G.S.Perry⟩ ⟨a fishing dragger unloading its catch at a *pier* —Don Smith⟩ ⟨pulled the canoe up on the *pier* to empty it⟩ ⟨the New York harbor *piers*⟩ QUAY usu. refers to an artificial embankment lying along or projecting from a shore and mainly used for loading or unloading; the term normally applies to wharves or piers characteristic of small places ⟨so she, also, got into the small boat; and together they went in to the *quay,* and got ashore —William Black⟩ ⟨a *quay* is a docking facility at which ships lie parallel to the shoreline —*N.Y. Times*⟩ SLIP applies to a sloping ramp usu. constructed or used where the shore is high and shore water shallow ⟨on the *slip* a thick water hose was connected from a hydrant to the ship —Vernon Pizer⟩ ⟨rolling barrels down a *slip* into the ship's hold⟩ BERTH and less commonly SLIP (in a second sense) apply to the space between two piers or wharves which gives room for a ship when anchored or not in use, although SLIP is more common for such a space construed for ferryboat landings or boardings ⟨about to sail from her *berth* at the foot of Fifth Street —*Ships and the Sea*⟩ ⟨a deep-chested liner rears through the thin haze, easing her way to a Hudson river *berth* —*Amer. Guide Series: N.Y. City*⟩ ⟨transatlantic liners in adjoining *slips* down at the docks⟩ ⟨a series of steamship piers and ferry *slips*⟩ JETTY although commonly applied to a structure serving as a breakwater for a harbor applies also to a small pier of timbers, usu. not very substantial ⟨the harbor, from 30 to 60 feet deep, is protected by white marble *jetties* —*Amer. Guide Series: Fla.*⟩ ⟨fishermen . . . take their accustomed places on the wharves and *jetties* for the summer sport of gawking —Anthony Anable⟩ ⟨a *jetty* is usu. built so that it lies parallel with the direction of the tidal stream, and at such *jetties* ships should always berth against the stream —*Manual of Seamanship*⟩ LEVEE applies to an embankment for confining or restricting floodwaters but in the South and West, where a levee is often used for landing, the term is often the equivalent of QUAY ⟨build emergency *levees* to control a dangerously rising river⟩ ⟨down by the river's borders the new *levees* proclaim the grandsons' plans for a resurrected river traffic —*Amer. Guide Series: Minn.*⟩
²wharf \"\ *vb* -ED/-ING/-S *vt* **1** *obs* **:** to guard or secure by a firm wall of timber or stone constructed like a wharf **2 :** to furnish with a wharf **3 :** to place upon a wharf **:** bring to a wharf **~** *vi* **:** DOCK
wharf·age \-fij\ *n* -S [ME, fr. ¹*wharf* + *-age*] **1 a :** the provision or the use of a wharf **b :** the handling or stowing of goods on a wharf **2 a :** the charge for the use of a wharf for freight handling or ship dockage **b :** a charge assessed for

handling incoming or outgoing cargo on a wharf **3 :** the wharf accommodations of a place **:** WHARVES

wharf boat *n* **:** a boat moored and used for a wharf at a bank of a river or in a like situation where the height of the water is so variable that a fixed wharf is impracticable

wharf borer *n* **:** a small wood boring beetle (*Nacerda melanura*) of the family Oedemeridae that is destructive to piling and wood under wharves, buildings near the water, and sometimes telegraph poles

wharf crab *n* **:** a small pink crab (*Pachygrapsus gracilis*) common on piles along the tropical American Atlantic coast

wharfe·dale \'(h)wȯ(r)f,dāl\ *n* -s *usu cap* [fr. *Wharfedale*, district of western Yorkshire, England; fr. the manufacture of such presses in the district] *Brit* **:** STOP-CYLINDER PRESS

wharf fish *n* **:** CUNNER b

wharf·ie \'(h)wȯ(r)fē\ *n* -s [¹*wharf* + -*ie*] *Austral* **:** STEVEDORE, LONGSHOREMAN

wharf·ing \'(h)wȯ(r)fiŋ, -fēŋ\ *n* -s [¹*wharf* + -*ing*] **1 a :** something serving as a wharf **b :** the materials of a wharf **c :** the wharves of a harbor **2 :** the facing of seawalls and embankments with sheet piling secured by ties

wharf·in·ger \-fənjə(r)\ *n* -s [irreg. fr. *wharfage* + -*er*] **1 :** a person or company operating a marine terminal with facilities for the berthing of ships and the loading, unloading, and storage of goods **:** the operator or manager of a commercial wharf; *specif* **:** one in charge of the handling of freight at a wharf who assigns the workers and facilities needed for the loading and unloading, storage, or removal of goods **2** *Brit* **:** the representative of a shipowner or charterer who receives goods at a wharf and checks the amount and condition of goods received, loaded, and unloaded

wharf·less \'=ləs\ *adj* **:** having no wharf

wharf·man \-mən\ *n, pl* **wharfmen :** DOCKMAN

wharfmaster \'=,==\ *n* **:** the manager of a wharf (as of a municipality) **:** WHARFINGER

wharf monkey *n* **:** a terrestrial isopod of the genus *Ligia* common about wharves along the coasts of most warm countries

wharf rat *n* **1 :** BROWN RAT **2 :** a person who loafs or sometimes lives around wharves sometimes with intent to steal from ships or warehouses

wharfs *pres 3d sing of* WHARF, *pl of* WHARF

wharf spike *n* **:** DOCK SPIKE

¹**wharl** \'(h)wärl, -wȧl\ *n* -s [imit.] **:** a guttural pronunciation of the letter *r* **:** BURR

²**wharl** *var of* WHORL

wharn·cliffe meeting \ˈ(h)wȯ(r)n,klif-\ *n, usu cap W* [after Edward Mackenzie, 1st Earl of *Wharncliffe* †1899 Brit. railway chairman] **:** a meeting of the proprietors or members of a British company convened as required by a standing order of parliament to approve a bill to be presented to parliament conferring powers on the company

whar·ton's duct \'(h)wȯ(r)tᵊnz-\ *n, usu cap W* [after Thomas *Wharton* †1673 Eng. physician and anatomist] **:** the duct of the submaxillary gland that opens into the mouth on a papilla at the side of the frenum of the tongue

wharton's jelly *n, usu cap W* **:** a soft connective tissue that occurs in the umbilical cord and consists of large stellate fibroblasts and a few wandering cells and macrophages embedded in a homogeneous jellylike intercellular substance

wharve \'(h)wȯ(ə)rv, -ō(ə)v\ *n* -s [ME *wherve*, fr. OE *hweorfa*; akin to OHG *hwerbo* turn, whirl, hinge, OE *hweorfan* to turn — more at WHARF] **:** WHORL 1

wharves *pl of* WHARF

whase \(ˌ)(h)wäz, -wōz, -wāz\ *chiefly Scot var of* WHOSE

¹**what** \(ˌ)(h)wä|t, (ˌ)(h)wə| *also* (ˌ)(h)wō|; *usu* |d·+V\ *pron* [ME, fr. OE *hwæt*, neut. of *hwā* who; akin to OHG *hwaz*, neut. interr. pron., ON *hvat*, Goth *hwa* — more at WHO] **1 a** (1) — used in direct or indirect questions as an interrogative pronoun expressing inquiry about the identity of an object or matter ⟨~ is this⟩ ⟨~ did you say⟩ ⟨~ are those things on the table⟩ ⟨~ happened after that⟩ ⟨tell me ~ you are looking for⟩ ⟨I wonder ~ his motives were⟩ ⟨he knows ~ he should do⟩ ⟨he knows ~ to do⟩ ⟨he's looking for something, but I don't know ~⟩ ⟨the controversy . . . centers largely on . . . who advocated ~ —*Christian Science Monitor*⟩; often used by itself esp. to ask for repetition of an utterance not properly heard or understood or to indicate that the speaker has heard someone addressing him and is ready to listen to whatever the one addressing him wishes to say; often used in connection with another word or words to ask for repetition of the particular part of an utterance that has not been properly heard or understood ⟨found ~⟩ (2) **:** a person or thing of how much value or consequence — used in rhetorical questions ⟨~ is man, that thou art mindful of him —Ps 8:4 (AV)⟩ ⟨~'s Hecuba to him, . . . that he should weep for her —Shak.⟩ ⟨~ is home without a mother —Septimus Winner⟩ **b** (1) *archaic* **:** ¹WHO 1 — used predicatively in direct or indirect questions as an interrogative pronoun expressing inquiry about the identity of a person ⟨~ is it but thought so? ~ are they that think it —Shak.⟩ ⟨lo ~ is he . . . is it not Lancelot —Alfred Tennyson⟩ (2) — used predicatively in direct or indirect questions as an interrogative pronoun expressing inquiry about the character, occupation, position, or role of a person ⟨~ do you think I am, a fool⟩ ⟨ask him ~ he wants to be when he grows up⟩ ⟨you are the villain and she is the heroine, but ~ is he⟩ **c :** how much ⟨~ do people generally tip —Richard Joseph⟩ ⟨to know ~ of any great man survives —Irwin Edman⟩ **d** (1) — used as an exclamation expressing surprise or excitement and frequently introducing a question ⟨~, no breakfast⟩ (2) *chiefly dial* — used to call someone or to engage someone's attention in order to say something to him ⟨~, Diggory? You are having a lonely walk —Thomas Hardy⟩; often followed by *ho* ⟨~, ho! slave —Shak.⟩ **e :** one or ones of what sort — used predicatively ⟨~ is she, that all our swains commend her —Shak.⟩ ⟨you know ~ he is about anything disagreeable — how he simply ignores its existence —Richard Bagot⟩ ⟨you know not ~ temptation is —Robert Browning⟩ **f :** how noteworthy a thing — used interjectionally ⟨~ has God wrought —Num 23:23 (RSV)⟩ **g :** SOMETHING — used in a few more or less fixed expressions directing attention to a suggestion or statement that the speaker is about to make ⟨I'll tell you ~⟩ ⟨tell you ~⟩ ⟨do you know ~⟩ ⟨know ~⟩ **h** — used after *or* at the end of a question to express inquiry about the possibilities not included in the immediately preceding word or series of words ⟨is it a freak, or ~⟩ ⟨is it a reptile, an amphibian, or ~⟩ ⟨is it raining, or snowing, or ~⟩ **i** *chiefly Brit* — used esp. at the end of an utterance as a tag that is essentially meaningless but has the appearance of inviting agreement or disagreement with the statement just made ⟨a clever play, ~⟩ **2** *chiefly substand* — used as a function word to introduce a restrictive or nonrestrictive relative clause and to serve as a substitute within that clause for the substantive modified by that clause ⟨the guy ~ says 'taint so —*Amer. Songbag*⟩ ⟨the newspaper placard, ~ had kicked itself loose from one corner —Richard Llewellyn⟩; compare ⁴THAT 1, ²WHICH 3, ¹WHO 3 **3 a :** that which **:** those which **:** those things that **:** those who or whom **:** the one or ones that ⟨the wind was . . . blowing in a direction opposite to ~ would carry the sparks to the lumber —W.L. Moore †1927⟩ ⟨any imposts or duties on imports or exports, except ~ may be absolutely necessary for executing its inspection laws —*U. S. Constitution*⟩ ⟨attributed it to the folly of ~ he conceived to be irresponsible demagogues —Robert White⟩ ⟨has no income but ~ he gets from his writings⟩ ⟨have no children but ~ you see here⟩ — sometimes used parenthetically or at the beginning of a sentence in reference to a clause or phrase that is yet to come or is not yet complete ⟨but, ~ more amazed him, his wife had willingly accompanied their flight —John Dryden⟩ ⟨the number of summonses jumped . . . at a rate of close to 200,000 a year. *What*'s more, the magistrates . . . give stiffened fines —G.S.Perry⟩ ⟨he brought also, ~ is rarer than depth of moralism, an art finely rounded —Carl Van Doren⟩; compare ²WHICH 3 **b :** as much as **:** as many as ⟨the individual soul . . . must struggle alone, with ~ of courage it can command —Bertrand Russell⟩ ⟨there are 34 candidates on the squad, nearly triple ~ reported for competition three years ago —*Springfield (Mass.) Union*⟩ **c :** the kind that **:** the same as ⟨the speech was very much ~ everyone expected⟩ ⟨a sleepy little town that is just ~ it was forty years ago⟩ **:** equal to that which ⟨countries whose economic strength is not ~ it was⟩ **4 a :** ¹WHATEVER 1a ⟨come ~ may⟩ ⟨say ~ you will⟩ **b** *obs* **:** WHOEVER 1 ⟨~ in the world he is that names me traitor, villain-like he lies —Shak.⟩ — **no matter what :** regardless of anything else ⟨wait there till I come back, *no matter what*⟩ — **what about 1 :** what is to be said about **:** what is the situation with respect to ⟨*what about* a house, and schools for the children —J.G.Gilkey⟩ **2 :** how about ⟨*what about* coming with us⟩ ⟨*what about* doing it yourself⟩ — **what an if** *or* **what and if** *archaic* **:** what if — **what else 1 :** anything else **:** unspecified other things ⟨with promise of his sister, and *what else* —Shak.⟩ **2 :** CERTAINLY **:** yes indeed — used after a statement to emphasize it or by itself as an emphatic affirmative reply to a question — **what for 1** *chiefly dial* **:** what kind of — used either inseparably or with a verb and its subject between *what* and *for* ⟨*what* is he *for* a fool —Shak.⟩; used with an immediately following object of *for* usu. consisting of a singular count noun with indefinite article ⟨*what for* an apple is that⟩, a plural count noun with no article ⟨*what for* horses are those⟩, or a mass noun with no article ⟨*what for* tobacco are you smoking⟩ **2 :** for what purpose **:** for what reason **:** WHY — usu. used with the other words of a question between *what* and *for* ⟨*what* did you do that *for*⟩ except when used alone; used inseparably at the beginning of a question in some dialects ⟨*what for* did you do that⟩ **3 :** punishment esp. by blows or by a sharp reprimand ⟨puts his little boy across his knee and gives him *what for* —Rebecca West⟩ ⟨gave him *what for* in violent Spanish —*New Yorker*⟩ ⟨Mama certainly gave Papa the *what for* —Marquis James⟩ **:** rough treatment inflicted esp. on an offender ⟨went away to give the . . . generals *what for* —J.T. Winterich⟩ **:** severe pain ⟨my corn's a-giving me *what for* —A.E.Coppard⟩ — **what have you :** what not ⟨novels, plays, short stories, travelogues, and *what have you* —Haldeen Braddy⟩ ⟨sell it, broadcast it, set it to music, or *what have you* —Margaret Nicholson⟩ ⟨barbarous or medieval or *what have you* —S.M.Kuhn⟩ — **what if :** what will or would be the result if ⟨*what if* it be a poison —Shak.⟩ **:** what does it matter if ⟨he won't object, and anyway, *what if* he does⟩ — **what it takes :** the ability, qualities, or resources needed for success or for the attainment of a particular goal ⟨he certainly has more of *what it takes* than anybody else of his generation —Edmund Wilson⟩ ⟨those who have *what it takes* to solve the problems in an environment —W.J.Reilly⟩ — **what of 1 :** what is to be said about **:** what is the situation with respect to ⟨watchman, *what of* the night —Isa 21:11 (RSV)⟩ **2 :** what importance can be assigned to ⟨all this is so; but *what of* this, my lord —Shak.⟩ — **what's o'clock** *Brit* **:** what time is it **:** what time it is — **what's what** *or* **what is what** *or* **what was what :** the true state of things ⟨exploration of *what's what* with the American businessman —*advt*⟩ ⟨all the . . . millionaire paper-mill women knew *what was what* when it came to fashion —Edna Ferber⟩ — **what's with** *slang* **:** what is the reason for **:** what is wrong with — **what though 1** *obs* **:** what does that matter ⟨I keep but three men and a boy . . . but *what though?* yet I live like a poor gentleman born —Shak.⟩ **2 :** what does or would it matter if **:** even granting or supposing that ⟨*what though* the rose have prickles, yet 'tis plucked —Shak.⟩ ⟨*what though* the field be lost? all is not lost —John Milton⟩

²**what** \"\ *adv* [ME, fr. OE *hwæt*, fr. *hwæt*, neut. interr. pron.] **1** *obs* **:** WHY ⟨~ should I stay —Shak.⟩ **2 :** HOW **:** in what respect **:** how much ⟨~ does it matter⟩ **3 a :** PARTLY — used two or more times in the same sentence to introduce a pair or series of prepositional phrases in parallel construction ⟨~ with the war, ~ with the sweat, ~ with the gallows, and ~ with poverty, I am custom-shrunk —Shak.⟩ ⟨~ through banks, and ~ through policemen, the concern has dwindled to nothing —Thomas DeQuincey⟩ **b** — used to introduce a prepositional phrase that expresses cause and has more than one object ⟨~ for poisons, conspiracies, and assassinations . . . there was no going there by day —Laurence Sterne⟩; used principally before phrases beginning with *with* ⟨~ with the drought and a strike in the mine, life is hard —*Time*⟩

³**what** \"\ *adj* [ME, fr. ¹*what*] **1 a** (1) — used in direct or indirect questions as an interrogative adjective expressing inquiry about the identity or nature of a person, object, or matter ⟨~ minerals do we export⟩ ⟨~ news have you had from him⟩ ⟨~ arrangements have been made⟩ ⟨declaring ~ officer shall then act as president —*U.S. Constitution*⟩ ⟨the debate . . . as to who made ~ blunder —C.B.Randall b. 1891⟩ (2) **:** how much ⟨finally got it written — with ~ effort, and ~ joy, only the amateur writer knows —Elmer Davis⟩ **b** (1) **:** how remarkable for good or bad qualities **:** how surprising **:** how great **:** how small — used esp. in exclamatory utterances and in dependent clauses of like nature ⟨~ a county for marine wonders —R.M.Lockley⟩ ⟨~ a suggestion⟩ ⟨with ~ relief this priggish load of nonsense falls from our shoulders —Sean O'Faolain⟩ ⟨you can imagine ~ a struggle we had⟩ ⟨~ a chance⟩ ⟨~ fools these mortals be —Shak.⟩; usu. followed by *a* or *an* when the following noun is a singular count noun (2) — used esp. in exclamatory utterances and in dependent clauses of like nature before a combination of a descriptive adjective and its noun and serving to intensify the meaning of the adjective ⟨~ a charming girl⟩ ⟨remembering ~ great disappointment he had felt⟩ ⟨~ partial judges are our love and hate —John Dryden⟩; usu. followed by *a* or *an* when the noun is a singular count noun **2 a** (1) **:** ¹WHATEVER 1a ⟨serve ~ master you like⟩ ⟨invent ~ excuses you please⟩ (2) **:** ANY ⟨she wore not upon her person any female ornament of ~ kind soever —Sir Walter Scott⟩ **b :** the . . . that **:** such . . . as **:** as much . . . as **:** as many . . . as ⟨the rescue ship came back with ~ survivors had been found⟩ ⟨to restrain ~ power either the devil or any earthly enemy hath to work us woe —John Milton⟩ ⟨~ time we had left was spent on fruitless errands —Bruce Mason⟩ — **what countryman :** a native or inhabitant of what country — used in direct or indirect questions — **what price 1 :** what is the value of ⟨*what price* glory —Laurence Stallings & Maxwell Anderson⟩ **2 :** what is the situation with respect to **:** what do you think of **:** how about — **what time 1 :** at the time that **:** WHEN, WHILE ⟨*what time* I am afraid, I will put my trust in thee —Ps 56:3 (AV)⟩ ⟨they kept their powerful jaws wide open, *what time* a bird hopped about . . . picking food from between the teeth —*Times Lit. Supp.*⟩ — **what way 1** *dial chiefly Brit* **:** HOW ⟨*what way* was he drowned —J.M. Synge⟩ **2** *Scot* **:** WHY

⁴**what** \'=\ *n* -s [ME, fr. ¹*what*] **1 a** *obs* **:** STUFF, MATTER, SUBSTANCE ⟨such homely ~ as serves the simple clown —Edmund Spenser⟩ **b :** THING, OBJECT **2 a :** the thing or things involved or meant or referred to **:** the identity or nature of something ⟨the ~ and how of jazz —P.V.R.Key⟩ **b :** all that may be known or stated about an individual thing **:** the complex of qualities that constitute the character of a thing — compare ⁶THAT 2

⁵**what** \(ˌ)=\ *conj* [¹*what*] *substand* — used esp. after *than* as a function word introducing a clause ⟨she can run better than ~ I can —W.S.Maugham⟩

whatabouts \'==,=\ *also* **whatabout** \'==,=\ *n, pl* **whatabouts** [¹*what* + *about, abouts* (as in *whereabouts*)] **:** the things with which one is busied

what-do-you-call-it *or* **what-do-you-call-them** *also* **what-do-you-call-her** *or* **what-do-you-call-him** \'(h)wä|d·ə,==, -wə-,-wō-, |tdə-\ *n* -s **:** a thing or person that the speaker cannot (as from not knowing or from forgetting) or does not wish to name ⟨hand me one of those little *what-do-you-call-thems*⟩

what-e'er \=ˈ=\ *pron* [by contr.] **:** WHATEVER

¹**whatever** \(ˈ)=ˈ==\ *pron* [ME, fr. ¹*what* + *ever*] **1 a :** anything that **:** everything that ⟨take ~ you want⟩ ⟨~ Earth, all-bearing mother, yields —John Milton⟩ **b :** no matter what ⟨seeing only his faults, and seeing them as unforgivable in his case ~ they may be elsewhere —C.H.Sykes⟩ ⟨~ the cause, this animosity grew deeper and deeper —E.V.Burkholder⟩ **c :** anything at all **:** any of various other things that might also be mentioned **:** what not ⟨any appliance — stove, lantern, or ~ — that is fueled by gasoline —*New Yorker*⟩ ⟨until you find your buffalo or rhinoceros or ~ —Alan Moorehead⟩ ⟨a marriage contract — whether it is monogamous or polygamous or ~ —Weston La Barre⟩ ⟨workers constantly walk in . . . arguing, complaining, or ~ —*Time*⟩ **d :** something similar but hard to identify or classify with certainty ⟨had lain abed some days with the measles or ~ —Mary Austin⟩ ⟨wouldn't have had a moustache when a small boy or ~ —Henry James †1916⟩ **2 :** ¹WHAT 1a(1) — used in questions expressing astonishment or perplexity ⟨~ do you mean by that⟩

²**whatever** \"\ *adj* [ME, fr. ³*what* + *ever*] **1 a :** any . . . that **:** all . . . that ⟨and buy peace . . . on ~ terms could be obtained —C.S.Forester⟩ ⟨have provided most of the backbone for ~ musical tradition we have —Virgil Thomson⟩ **b :** no matter what ⟨by ~ circumstances he had been led to a hatred of the slave power and a heightened devotion to the Union, the change was one which in a measure transformed him —W.J. Ghent⟩ **2 a :** any . . . at all ⟨men and women of ~ scholastic training or none at all —Alvin Johnson⟩ **b :** being in existence **:** of any kind at all — used for emphasis after the substantive it modifies ⟨any language ~ —W.D.Preston⟩ ⟨no damage ~ —A.T.Weaver⟩ ⟨the most entrancing young girl ~ —Carl Van Doren⟩

³**whatever** \"\ *adv* [²*what* + *ever*] **:** in any case ⟨but how far could I trust them, and in what way were they different from the trustees? *Whatever*, I was committed; I'd learn in the process of working with them, I thought —Ralph Ellison⟩

what-is-it \=ˈ==\ *or* **what·sis** \'(h)wätsəs, -wət-,-wōt-\ *or* **what·sit** \-tsət\ *n* [*what-is-it* fr. the expression *what is it*; *whatsis* perh. alter. of the expression *what's this*; *whatsit* perh. fr. the expression *what's it*] **:** a thing of unspecified, nondescript, or mysterious character

whatlike \'=,=\ *adj* [¹*what* + *like*] *dial* **:** of what sort or kind — used as an indefinite relative

what·man \'(h)wätmən, -wōt-\ *n* -s [after James *Whatman*, 18th cent. Eng. paper manufacturer] **:** a drawing paper or board of high quality

what·ness *n* -ES [¹*what* + -*ness*] **:** the what of a thing; *esp* **:** QUIDDITY

whatnot \'=,=\ *n* -s [fr. the query *what not?*, fr. ¹*what* + *not*] **1 a :** any of various other things that might also be mentioned ⟨electric refrigerators, washing machines, radios, television sets, or ~ —F.L. Allen⟩ ⟨stockbrokers, solicitors, auctioneers, ~ —John Galsworthy⟩ ⟨every aspect — historical, geographical, and ~ — of tea —Mollie Panter-Downes⟩ ⟨some other thing (intuitionism or ~) —J.H.Muirhead⟩ ⟨beaches, parks . . . harbors, and a lot of less worthy government ~s may benefit —Hale Champion⟩ **b :** a nondescript person or thing ⟨the biggest souvenir of all the gimmicks and ~s . . . a huge globe —*Springfield (Mass.) Republican*⟩ **c :** MISCELLANY ⟨a straggling army of human ~ (adventurers, scientists, convict laborers) —*Time*⟩ **2 :** a light open set of shelves for bric-a-brac

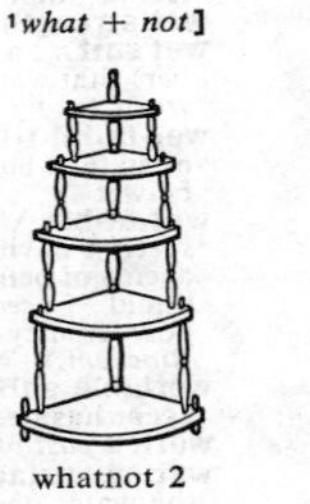

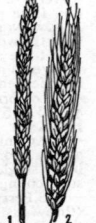

whatnot 2

whatreck \(ˈ)=ˈ=\ *adv* [fr. the query *what reck?*, fr. ³*what* + obs. *reck* care, heed, fr. *reck*, vb.] *Scot* **:** NOTWITHSTANDING

whats *pl of* WHAT

what's \(ˌ)(h)wäts, (ˌ)(h)wəts *also* (ˌ)(h)wōts\ [¹*what* + '*s*] **1 :** what is ⟨*what's* his name⟩ **2 :** what has ⟨*what's* he done⟩ **3 :** what does ⟨*what's* he want⟩

what's its name *or* **what's their name** *or* **what's her name** *or* **what's his name** *n* **:** WHAT-DO-YOU-CALL-IT

whatso \(ˈ)=ˈ=\ *pron or adj* [ME, fr. ¹*what* + *so*] **:** WHATEVER

what·so·e'er \ˌ=sōˈwe(ə)r, ˌ=sōˈe(ə)r, -a(a)(ə)r, -eə, -a(a)ə\ *pron* [by contr.] **:** WHATSOEVER

¹**what·so·ev·er** \ˌ=sōˈwevə(r), -sōˈev-\ *pron* [ME, fr. *whatso* + *ever*] **:** ¹WHATEVER 1a, 1b ⟨wife that ailed, do ~ he would —Robert Browning⟩

²**whatsoever** \"\ *adj* **:** ²WHATEVER ⟨~ things are true . . . think on these things —Phil 4:8 (AV)⟩; *esp* **:** of any kind soever ⟨exercise exclusive legislation in all cases ~ over such district —*U. S. Constitution*⟩

what·som·ever \ˌ=səmˈevə(r)\ *also* **what·som·dev·er** \-səmˈde-\ *adj or pron* [ME *whatsomever*, fr. *what sum* whatever (fr. ¹*what* + ME — northern dial. — *sum*, rel. adv., as, of Scand origin; akin to ON *sem* as, OE *same* — in *swā same* so as, likewise) + *ever* — more at SAME] *dial* **:** WHATSOEVER

what·ten *or* **whatn** *also* **what·en** \'(h)wätᵊn, -wə- also -wō-\ *or* **what·na** \-tnə\ *adj* [ME (northern dial.) *whatkin*, fr. ³*what* + *kin* kindred, kind of — more at KIN] **1** *dial* **:** what kind of **2** *dial* **:** WHAT

what with *prep* [²*what*] **:** on account of ⟨*what with* summertime it was still broad daylight when, around half past eight, I entered the big living room —Valentine Williams⟩

what-you-call-it *or* **what-you-call-them** *also* **what-you-call-her** *or* **what-you-call-him** \'(h)wächə,==, -wəch-, -wōch-, -chē,==\ *n* -s **:** WHAT-DO-YOU-CALL-IT ⟨supposed to go to church on *what-you-call-it* Sunday⟩

what-you-may-call-it *or* **what-you-may-call-them** *also* **what-you-may-call-her** *or* **what-you-may-call-him** \-chəmə,==, -chem-\ *n* -s **:** WHAT-DO-YOU-CALL-IT ⟨decided that the *what-you-may-call-it* was a boat rather than a car⟩ ⟨went to *what-you-may-call-her's* house⟩

what-you-may·jig·ger \-məˌjigə(r)\ *n* [*what-you-may-call-it* + E dial. thingumajigger, alter. of *thingumajig*] **:** THINGUMBOB, WHAT-DO-YOU-CALL-IT

whau \'(h)waù, ˈfaù\ *n* -s [Maori] **1 :** a New Zealand tree (*Entelea arborescens*) of the family Tiliaceae **2 :** the very light wood of the whau used esp. for making floats for native fishing nets

¹**whaup** \'(h)wäp, -wȧp\ *n, pl* **whaup** *also* **whaups** [imit.] *Scot & dial Eng* **:** a European curlew (*Numenius arquata*) — called also *great whaup*

²**whaup** \"\ *n* -s [alter. of ²*whoop*] *Scot & dial Eng* **:** OUTCRY, FUSS

whaur \(ˌ)hwȯr, (ˌ)hwär\ *Scot & Irish var of* WHERE

¹**wheal** \'hwēl, *esp before pause or consonant* -ēəl; *also* 'wē-\ *vt* -ED/-ING/-S [alter. (influenced by obs. E *wheal* to suppurate, come to a head, fr. ME *whelen*, fr. OE *hwelian*; perh. akin to Latvian *kvēle* inflammation) of *wale*] **:** to make or cause wheals upon ⟨now am ~*ed*, one wide wound all of me —Robert Browning⟩

²**wheal** \"\ *n* -s [alter. (influenced by obs. E *wheal* pustule, fr. ME *whele*; akin to OE *hwelian* to suppurate) of *wale*] **:** a sudden elevation on the skin surface: **a :** a ridge or mark raised on the skin by or as if by a stroke of a whip **:** WALE, WEAL, WELT ⟨his back covered with ~s from the lashing⟩ **b :** the transient lump occurring at the site of injection of a solution before the solution is normally dispersed **c :** a steep-sided elevation with a rounded or flat top that is often accompanied by itching or burning and forms the characteristic lesion of urticaria

whealing *n* -s **:** the act or process of developing or being marked by wheals

whealworm \'=,=\ *n* [obs. E *wheal* pustule + *worm*] **:** CHIGGER 2

wheat \'hwēt *also* 'wēt, *usu* -ēd·+V\ *n* -s *often attrib* [ME *whete*, fr. OE *hwǣte*; akin to OHG *weizzi* wheat, ON *hveiti*, Goth *hwaiteis* wheat, OE *hwīt* white — more at WHITE] **1 :** a cereal grain that yields a fine white flour, is the chief breadstuff of temperate climates, is used also in alimentary pastes, and is important in animal feeds esp. as bran or middlings — see WHOLE WHEAT FLOUR **2 :** any of various grasses that constitute the genus *Triticum*, are characterized by wide climatic adaptability, and are cultivated in most temperate areas for the wheat they yield and on a major commercial scale esp. in Europe, No. America, and Australia; *esp* **:** an annual cereal grass (*T. aestivum* syn. *T. vulgare*) that is known only as a cultigen and has a long dense 4-sided spike of which each spikelet contains two, three, or sometimes more white to dark-red kernels that separate readily from the chaff in threshing — called also *common wheat*; see CLUB WHEAT, DURUM WHEAT, EINKORN, EMMER, POLISH WHEAT, SPELT **3 a wheats** *pl, Brit* **:** wheat plants ⟨the ~s are not doing well⟩ **b :** a crop or kind of wheat ⟨tried a new Canadian ~ this year⟩ ⟨the ~ in the northern states⟩ **4 :** a variable color averaging a light yellow that is less strong and very slightly lighter than average maize, redder

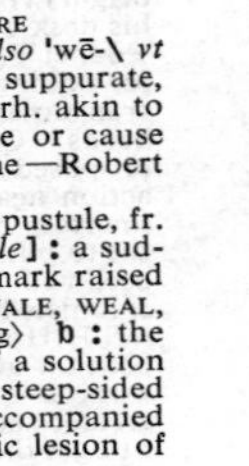

1 2

wheat: *1* beardless, *2* bearded

and less strong than popcorn, and redder and duller than jasmine
wheat and rye nematode *n* : WHEATWORM
wheat aphid *or* **wheat aphis** *n* : any of several plant lice of the family Aphididae (as the grain aphid *Macrosiphum granarium* and *Rhopalosiphum prunifoliae*) that suck the sap of growing wheat — called also *wheat louse, wheat plant louse*
wheat beetle *n* **a** : SAW-TOOTHED GRAIN BEETLE **b** : DRUGSTORE BEETLE
wheat belt *n* : an agricultural region in which more land is devoted to the production of wheat than to any other one crop ⟨off with his plane and his combines on his annual swing northward through the *wheat belt* —E.L.Howe⟩
wheatbird \ˈ=,=\ *n* : HORNED LARK
wheat bread *n* : a bread made of a combination of white and whole wheat flours as distinguished from bread made entirely of whole wheat flour or white flour
wheat bug *n* : a true bug (as *Miris tritici* or a related species) that damages wheat
wheat bulb fly *n* : the adult of the wheat bulb worm
wheat bulb worm *n* : the larva of a small fly (as *Meromyza americana* in No. America or *Hylemyia coarctata* in Europe) that infests the stalk of wheat
wheat cake *n* : a griddle cake made of wheat flour
wheat chafer *n* : a beetle (as *Anisoplia austriaca* in parts of Europe) that feeds on growing wheat
wheat cutworm *n* : a lepidopterous larva (as the fall army worm and several true cutworms) that cuts off the stalk of wheat at the base
wheat duck *n* : BALDPATE 2
[1]**wheatear** \ˈ=,=\ *n* [ME *whete ere*, fr. *whete* wheat + *ere* ear (of grain) — more at EAR] : an ear or spike of wheat
[2]**wheatear** \"\ *n* [back-formation fr. *wheatears*, prob. by folk etymology or euphemism fr. *white arse*] : a small bird (*Oenanthe oenanthe*) of northern Europe, Asia, and Alaska that is related to the stonechat and whinchat, that in the male has a bluish gray back, buffy breast, white rump and belly, blackish wings, and a black line through the eye, and that inhabits chiefly rocky places
wheatear cockle *n* [[1]*wheatear*] : WHEATWORM
wheat eel *or* **wheat eelworm** *n* : WHEATWORM
[1]**wheat·en** \ˈhwēt³n *also* ˈwē-\ *adj* [ME *wheten*, fr. OE *hwǣten*, fr. *hwǣte* wheat + *-en* — more at WHEAT] : of, relating to, or made of wheat ⟨~ bread⟩ ⟨~ straw⟩
[2]**wheaten** \"\ *n* -s : the color of wheat; *specif* : a pale yellow or fawn characteristic of certain breeds of dogs
wheat fly *n* **1** : WHEAT MIDGE **2** : WHEAT GALLFLY **3** : HESSIAN FLY **4** : any of several flies of the genus *Oscinis* (as *O. soror*) whose larvae live in the stems of wheat
wheat gallfly *n* : the imago of the jointworm
wheat germ *n* : the embryo or germ of the wheat kernel separated in milling flour and used in food products as a source of vitamins
wheat–germ oil *n* : a yellow unsaturated fatty oil obtained from wheat germ and containing vitamin E
wheatgrass \ˈ=,=\ *n* : a grass of the genus *Agropyron*: as **a** : BEARDED WHEATGRASS **b** : WESTERN WHEATGRASS **c** : COUCH GRASS
wheathead armyworm *n* : a worm that is the larva of a noctuid moth (*Faronta diffusa*) and is destructive to the heads of timothy, wheat, and other grasses
wheat jointworm *n* : a jointworm (*Harmolita tritici*) that attacks wheat and sometimes other cereal grasses
wheatland \ˈ=,=\ *n* : land sown or suitable for sowing with wheat
wheatland plow *n* : ONE-WAY
wheat·less \ˈ=ˌləs\ *adj* : having no wheat
wheat louse *n* : WHEAT APHID
wheat maggot *n* : a maggot that is the larva of a wheat fly and esp. of a wheat midge
wheatmeal \ˈ=,=\ *n* [ME *whetemele*, fr. OE *hwǣtemelu*, fr. *hwǣte* wheat + *melu* meal — more at MEAL (flour)] *chiefly Brit* : a pure unbleached meal obtained by grinding the entire unadulterated wheat berries
wheat midge *n* **1** : a small two-winged fly (*Sitodiplosis mosellana*) that is destructive to growing wheat both in Europe and America **2** : HESSIAN FLY
wheat mite *n* : FLOUR MITE
wheat mosaic *or* **wheat rosette** *n* : a virus disease of wheat characterized by either a light yellowish green or a dark bluish green mottling and streaking
wheat moth *n* : a moth (as a grain moth, Mediterranean flour moth, or meal moth) whose larvae devour the grains of wheat chiefly after it is harvested — compare ANGOUMOIS GRAIN MOTH
wheat pest *n* : a small midge (*Oscinis frit*) that does great damage to wheat in Europe
wheat pit *n* : a market or exchange where wheat stocks are bought and sold
wheat plant louse *n* : WHEAT APHID
wheat poisoning *n* : grass tetany affecting cattle grazing on wheat
wheat rust *n* **1** : any of three destructive diseases of wheat caused by rust fungi: as **a** : stem rust of wheat that may attack leaf sheathes, leaves, and spike, as well as the culm of the plant **b** : orange leaf rust of wheat **c** : stripe rust of wheat **2** : a rust fungus (as *Puccinia graminis*) that attacks wheat
wheats *pl of* WHEAT
wheat sawfly *n* **1** : WHEAT STEM SAWFLY **2** : any of several small American sawflies of the genus *Dolerus* (as *D. collaris* and *D. arvensis*) whose larvae injure the stems or heads of wheat **3** : a sawfly (*Pachynematus extensicornis*) whose larvae feed on the blades of wheat and other grasses
wheat scab *n* : a destructive disease of wheat caused by fungi of the genera *Fusarium* and *Gibberella* and characterized by bleached blighted heads and kernels with a scabby appearance from the tufted mycelia outgrowths — compare HEAD BLIGHT
wheat smut *n* : a smut of wheat (as bunt)
wheat stem maggot *n* : a maggot that is the larva of a small pale yellow black-striped fly (*Meromyza americana*) of the family Chloropidae and that bores in the stems of wheat and other cereals
wheat stem rust *n* : WHEAT RUST 1a
wheat stem sawfly *n* **1** : a No. American sawfly (*Cephus cinctus*) having larvae that bore in the stems of wheat and other small grains causing great loss of crop **2** : EUROPEAN WHEAT STEM SAWFLY
wheat·stone bridge \ˈ(h)wēt,stōn-, *chiefly Brit* -,stən-\ *n, usu cap W* [after Sir Charles *Wheatstone* †1875 Eng. physicist] : a bridge for measuring electrical resistances consisting of a conductor joining two branches of a circuit
wheatstone cipher *n, usu cap W* [after Sir Charles *Wheatstone*] : a progressive-alphabet cipher in which the next alphabet is used whenever the plaintext letter does not stand later in the plain component than the preceding plaintext letter
wheatstone transmitter *n, usu cap W* [after Sir Charles *Wheatstone*] : an automatic telegraph transmitter using a perforated tape engaging with one end of a marking rod or lever the other end of which opens and closes the circuit
wheat strawworm *n* : a worm that is the larva of a small chalcid wasp (*Harmolita grandis*) and that is highly destructive to wheat and other grasses
wheat take-all *n* : TAKE-ALL
wheat thief *n* **1** : GROMWELL **2** : [3]CHESS
wheat thrips *n* : any of numerous thrips that infest wheat and damage the grain: as **a** : FLOWER THRIPS **b** : GRAIN THRIPS **c** : GRASS THRIPS
wheat weevil *n* **1** : GRAIN WEEVIL **2** : the rice weevil when found in wheat **3** : WHEAT THRIPS
wheatworm \ˈ=,=\ *n* : a small nematode worm (*Anguina tritici*) that is parasitic on wheat, oats, and other grasses, that invades the plant at the leaf axil as a larva where it induces stunting and distortion of leaves, and that subsequently passes to the inflorescence and causes the seeds to be replaced by galls in which the larva matures and produces a new generation of larvae to be distributed in the soil when the gall is shed and decays — called also *wheat eel*
whee \ˈhwē *also* ˈwē\ *interj* [origin unknown] — used to express delight or general exuberance
[1]**whee·dle** \ˈhwēdᵊl *also* ˈwē-\ *vb* **wheedled; wheedled; wheedling** \-d(ᵊ)liŋ\ **wheedles** [origin unknown] *vt* **1 a** : to influence or inveigle by soft words or flattery : COAX, CAJOLE ⟨how she *wheedled* him —W.S.Gilbert⟩ ⟨many of whom had to be *wheedled* . . . and coddled for weeks before they could be persuaded —*N.Y.Times*⟩ **b** : to allure, draw, or induce by wheedling — usu. used with *into* ⟨~s me into feeling fond of her in spite of myself —G.B.Shaw⟩ ⟨no hucksters to ~ you into buying souvenirs —Frederick Nebel⟩ ⟨had threatened and *wheedled* hundreds of heathens into Christianity —Vicki Baum⟩ **2 a** : to gain or get away by wheedling ⟨the first move of any politician . . . was to ~ the editorial backing of some newspaper —W.A.Swanberg⟩ — usu. used with *from* or *out of* ⟨~s a couple of dollars house money from him —H.H.Reichard⟩ ⟨*wheedled* consent from them —C.V.Little⟩ ⟨have scrounged and begged . . . in an effort to ~ money out of the American public —A.J.Daley⟩ ⟨young herons . . . ~ a meal out of mother after fledging —*Nat'l Geographic*⟩ **b** : to get or take something from by wheedling — usu. used with *out of* ⟨had *wheedled* the . . . woman out of her geraniums —Mary Austin⟩ ⟨~ you out of a horse —J.B.Cabell⟩ ~ *vi* : to use soft words or flattery ⟨when he chose to ~, was hard to resist — John Buchan⟩ — **wheedle one's way** : to move or advance toward an objective by wheedling ⟨*wheedle their way* into a soft berth where 50 men do the work of 10 —Frank O'Leary⟩ ⟨*wheedled his way* onto the stage —*Time*⟩ ⟨responsible officials have often been able to circumvent extremist popular opinions and to *wheedle their way* towards moderation and good sense —Walter Lippmann⟩
[2]**wheedle** \"\ *n* -s : an act or instance of wheedling
whee·dling·ly *adv* : in a wheedling manner : with wheedling
[1]**wheel** \ˈhwēl, *esp before pause or consonant* -ēəl; *also* ˈwē-\ *n* -s *often attrib* [ME *whel, wheel, whele*, fr. OE *hweogol, hweohl, hweol*; akin to OFris *hwēl* wheel, MD *wiel*, MLG *wēl*, ON *hvēl, hjōl* wheel, L *colere* to cultivate, inhabit, Gk *kyklos* ring, circle, cycle, wheel, *pelesthai* to be, become, *telos* end, OSlav *kolo* wheel, Skt *cakra* wheel, *carati* he moves, goes; basic meaning: to bend, turn] **1 a** : a circular frame of hard material that may be solid, partly solid, or spoked and that has a hub at the center for attachment to or suspension from an axle on which it may revolve and bear a load esp. along the ground **b** : such a circular framework often with cogs or teeth on the rim used to transmit or modify force and motion in machinery or a mechanical contrivance **2** : a wheel designed for a specific purpose, a structure resembling a wheel, or a contrivance or apparatus having a wheel as its principal part: as **a** : a chiefly medieval instrument of torture resembling a cartwheel and designed for stretching, disjointing, or otherwise mutilating a victim **b** : POTTER'S WHEEL **c** : SPINNING WHEEL **d** : STEERING WHEEL **e** : a screw propeller on a boat **f** : BICYCLE 1 **g** : any of many revolving disks or drums (as a wheel of fortune, lottery wheel, or a roulette wheel) used as gambling paraphernalia **3 a** : the imaginary wheel symbolizing fate or chance that personified fortune is said to turn ⟨so much often depends on the turn of fortune's ~⟩ **b** : a recurring course, development, or action : ROUND, CYCLE ⟨reach back through all those turns of the ~ of time — Marcia Davenport⟩ ⟨the ~ of events is brought full circle in four farm seasons —Robert Hazel⟩ ⟨by . . . World War II the ~ of history had made a full turn —R.M.Upton⟩ **4** : something resembling a wheel in shape or motion: as **a** : a usu. symbolic circular design in ancient art having radii suggesting spokes **b** : CARTWHEEL 1a **c** : a round flat cheese ⟨a ~ of mild cheddar —Leslie Waller⟩ **d** : a circular design in needlework with radiating bars resembling a cartwheel or a spider's web **e** : one of the revolving concentric spheres to which the planets and fixed stars are attached in the Ptolemaic astronomical system **f** : a firework that rotates while burning — compare PINWHEEL **5** : a movement similar to that of a wheel: as **a** : a curving or circular movement ⟨the dizzying ~ of the dance⟩ ⟨the graceful ~ of the gulls over the harbor⟩ **b** : a rotation or turn usu. about an axis or center; *specif* : a turning movement of troops or ships in line in which the units preserve alignment and relative positions as they change direction by pivoting on a unit at the end of the line or upon an imaginary point beyond it ⟨eventually the great movement out of the beachhead would be by an enormous left ~, bringing our front onto the line of the Seine —D.D.Eisenhower⟩ **6 a** : a moving or essential part of something resembling a machine ⟨the ~s of social progress have turned but slowly —Gilbert Parker⟩ ⟨the ~s of government⟩ ⟨making sure that the library ~s turn easily —H.M.Lydenberg⟩ **b** (1) : a directing or controlling force or person ⟨in this complex world there are ~s within driving forces without⟩ ⟨a big financial ~ in her company . . . is serving as a dollar-a-year man in Washington —John McCarten⟩ (2) : a political leader usu. in a party organization ⟨got a firm promise of financial help from several Tammany ~s —W.A.Swanberg⟩ **7** : the refrain or burden of a song — compare [4]BOB 4 **8 a** : a string or circuit of theaters or places of entertainment ⟨lifted her from a burlesque ~ and made her a star —William Du Bois⟩ ⟨Oklahoma City and Tulsa are on wrestling ~s and boxing circuits —*Amer. Guide Series: Okla.*⟩ **b** : a sports league ⟨treasurer of her league and tops the ~ in averages —*Woman Bowler*⟩

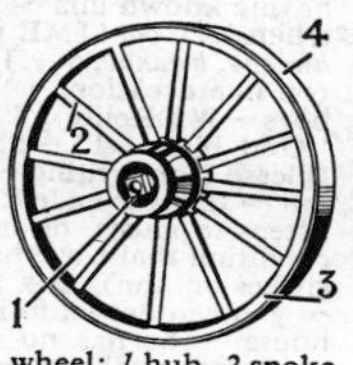

wheel: *1* hub, *2* spoke, *3* felly, *4* tire

[2]**wheel** \"\ *vb* -ED/-ING/-S [ME *whelen*, fr. *whel, wheel, whele* wheel, n.] *vi* **1 a** : to move or turn like a wheel on or as if on an axis : REVOLVE ⟨always showing the same face to the earth, the moon does not ~ on its own center⟩ **b** (1) : to become giddy ⟨the head ~s in the sudden fast turns⟩ (2) : SWAY, REEL ⟨an inebriate ~s down the street⟩ **2** : to turn about a pivot (as in marching) while maintaining a straight or unbroken front ⟨the soldiers ~*ed* in platoons —Van Wyck Brooks⟩ ⟨the battalion would have ~*ed* to the flank and cut off the Germans from . . . escape —Walter Bernstein⟩ **3 a** : to turn and face toward a different direction often in sudden fashion ⟨~*ed* and entered the monastery —Gilbert Parker⟩ ⟨~*ed* round in his chair with his eyes wide upon her —E.T.Thurston⟩ ⟨the commander ~*ed* about and walked briskly aft —L.C.Douglas⟩ **b** : to alter or reverse one's opinion or course of action ⟨her mind will ~ around to the other extreme —Liam O'Flaherty⟩ **4** : to move or go in a circuit or spiral : CIRCLE ⟨a flock of . . . pigeons ~s over the curving roofs —James Cameron⟩ ⟨the sun ~*ed* over the sky — John Steinbeck⟩ ⟨the earth will ~ around its orbit —Waldemar Kaempffert⟩ ⟨the plane ~s off to the west⟩ **5** : to extend in a circle or curve ⟨across valleys where young cotton ~*ed* slowly in fanlike rows —William Faulkner⟩ ⟨the shadows ~ across the snow⟩ **6** : to drive or go on or as if on wheels or in a vehicle with wheels ⟨she ~*ed* to the door —Nelson Algren⟩ ⟨the hack ~*ed* more slowly as the driver puzzled out addresses —T.W.Duncan⟩ ⟨climbs on his bicycle and ~s down the road⟩ **7** : to make with a wheel a series of small indentations along the upper edge of the heel of a shoe ~ *vt* **1** : to cause to turn or revolve on or as if on an axis : ROTATE ⟨reloaded and ~*ed* the cylinders to make certain they were turning free and fast — S.H.Holbrook⟩ **2 a** : to convey or move on or as if on wheels or in a wheeled vehicle ⟨she is carried down and ~*ed* everywhere —Arnold Bennett⟩ ⟨an authentic hospital patient was ~*ed* in —R.M.Yoder⟩ ⟨so much American writing on education is ~*ed* remorselessly out again and even embellished — Brand Blanshard⟩ **b** : to draw or push on wheels ⟨~*ed* his big guns into action —*Current Biog.*⟩ ⟨he was ~*ing* the bicycle which Dougal had ridden —John Buchan⟩ **c** : to drive or operate (a vehicle) often at high speed ⟨~*ing* trucks along cement highways with sleepy eyes —Julian Dana⟩ ⟨taxicab drivers ~ their vehicles through the streets with gay abandon —*Geog. School Bull.*⟩ ⟨was ~*ing* a passenger train towards Knoxville —H.G.Monroe⟩ **3** : to cause (a rank or body of troops) to turn on a pivot in uniform alignment ⟨the officer ~s the company around the flank⟩ **4** : to make or perform in a circle, spiral, or curve ⟨where the beetle ~s his droning flight —Thomas Gray⟩ **5** : to turn (a person or animal) in or toward a different direction ⟨bewilderment ~*ed* her round —Michael Arlen⟩ ⟨~*ed* my horse and cantered off —Eve Langley⟩ ⟨~*ed* her horse about —Clara Morris⟩ **6 a** : to dress (a skin) on a wheel : FLUFF **b** : PINWHEEL **7** : to indent (the upper edge of the heel of a shoe) with a corrugated wheel **8** : to convey or transmit (electric power) through or over transmission lines ⟨the refusal of the . . . company, which owns the power lines that run from the dam to their farms, to ~ government power —*New Republic*⟩ **syn** see TURN — **wheel and deal** : to take the part of a leader or wheel and to take charge of affairs or arrangements ⟨showed the town how an absolute dictator *wheels and deals* —*Newsweek*⟩
wheel·age \-lij\ *n* -s [[1]*wheel* + *-age*] : a tax or toll on the passage of wheeled vehicles
wheel alignment *n* : the alignment or adjustment of the front wheel suspension and steering mechanism of an automotive vehicle
wheel and axle *n* : a mechanical device consisting of a grooved wheel turned by a cord or chain with a rigidly attached axle (as for winding up a weight) together with the supporting standards — see SIMPLE MACHINE
wheel animal *or* **wheel animalcule** *also* **wheel bearer** *n* : ROTIFER
wheel-back \ˈ=,=\ *n* : a chair back having a splat or spindles cut out, carved, or arranged so as to represent a wheel
wheel barometer *n* : a siphon barometer that is equipped with a float from which a cord passes over a pulley and moves an index
[1]**wheelbarrow** \ˈ=,(,)=\ *n* [ME *whelbarewe*, fr. *whel* wheel + *barewe* barrow — more at BARROW (cart)] **1** : a small vehicle with handles and one or more wheels for carrying small loads; *esp* : a vehicle with a single wheel suspended between the ends of two shafts that support a boxlike body and serve as handles at the rear — compare BARROW, HANDBARROW **2** : an exercise in which a person walks on his hands with his body supported in an inclined position by another who holds his legs in the manner of the handles of a wheelbarrow ⟨the children play ~ at the party⟩
[2]**wheelbarrow** \"\ *vt* -ED/-ING/-S : to convey or transport in a wheelbarrow
wheel·bar·row·er \-rəwə(r)\ *n* : one that conveys loads in a wheelbarrow
wheelbarrow sprayer *n* : a small sprayer consisting usu. of a pressure tank, a spray receptacle, and a hose and nozzle suspended and moved on the frame of a wheelbarrow
wheelbase \ˈ=,=\ *n* **1** : the figure enclosed by lines through the points of contact of the wheels of a vehicle with the surface or rails on which they run; *esp* : the length of this figure measured in the direction of motion of the vehicle **2** : the distance in inches between the front and rear axles of an automotive vehicle or between the centers of the points of contact of the front and rear wheels with the ground
wheelbox \ˈ=,=\ *n* : a box or casing containing the steering gear of a ship and supporting the wheel
wheel bug *n* : a large No. American reduviid bug (*Arilus cristatus*) with a high serrated crest on its prothorax that sucks the blood of other insects
wheel chain *n* : a chain used as a wheel rope on a ship
wheelchair \ˈ=,=\ *n* : a chair mounted on wheels and usu. propelled by the occupant by means of hand rims attached to the two large side wheels — compare BATH CHAIR

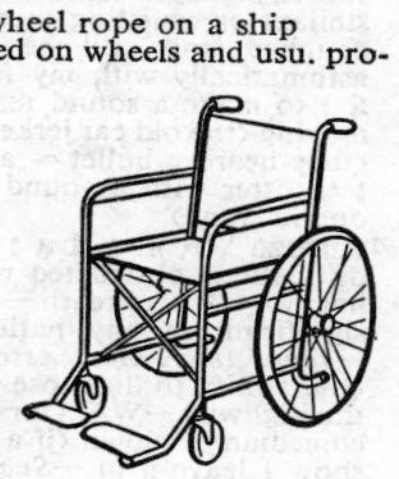
wheelchair

wheel chock *n* : a wedge-shaped wooden block or metal structure placed in front of the wheels of an airplane to prevent its motion on the ground
wheel control *n* : the control of an airplane by the wheel of the control column; *also* : CONTROL COLUMN
wheel cross *n* : an ancient 4-spoked wheel design used esp. by the Celts in the Bronze Age to represent the chariot of the sun
wheel cultivator *n* **1** : a cultivator with blades on the periphery of a wheel **2** *or* **wheel hoe** : a cultivating machine mounted on and supported by wheels and often pushed by hand
wheeled \ˈhwē(ə)ld *also* ˈwē-\ *adj* [[1]*wheel* + *-ed*] **1** : furnished or equipped with wheels ⟨~ vehicles⟩ ⟨a ~ plough⟩ **2** : moving or functioning by means of wheels ⟨~ traffic⟩
wheel·er \-ēlə(r)\ *n* -s [ME *wheler*, fr. *whel* wheel + *-er*] **1** : a maker of wheels **2** : one that wheels: as **a** : a worker who trucks loads of materials or products by hand (as at a factory, construction project, or mine) : PUSHER **b** : one that turns so as to face in a different direction; *specif* : a fighting cock that maneuvers by pretending to run away and then suddenly turning to attack his pursuing opponent **c** : WHEEL SCRAPER **3** : a horse or other draft animal pulling in the position nearest the front wheels of a wagon ⟨with our big team as ~s —Emma Yates⟩ **4** : a vehicle (as a truck or locomotive) having wheels ⟨a big eight ~ of a mighty fame —Carl Sandburg⟩ **5** : one of the granite paving blocks laid contiguous to the curb esp. on grades to carry heavy wheel loads **6** : one that indents shoes with a wheel ⟨welt ~⟩
wheel excavator *n* : a power-driven wheel-supported machine used for excavating trenches for tile drains — compare BACKHOE
wheel governor *n* : a common type of shaft governor arranged inside the rim of a wheel
wheelhorse \ˈ=,=\ *n* **1 a** : a horse that in a hitch of four or more horses pulls a vehicle in a position nearest the front wheels **b** : a horse that is a strong and willing worker **2** : a steady and effective worker or adherent esp. in a political party or body ⟨had been a useful ~ pushing through legislation desired by the administration —R.D.Leigh⟩ ⟨the day-to-day work of the union is carried on by a few ~s who are willing to put in the necessary time —L.G.Reynolds⟩
wheelhouse \ˈ=,=\ *n* : a structure housing a wheel: as **a** : PILOTHOUSE **b** : PADDLE BOX
wheeling *n* -s [ME *wheling*, fr. gerund of *whelen* to wheel — more at WHEEL] **1** : the act or process of one that wheels **2** : the condition of a road relative to passage on wheels ⟨reports good ~ over the new turnpike⟩ **3** : an ornamental line made on the sole or heel of a shoe by means of a corrugated wheel
wheel lathe *n* : a lathe designed esp. for turning locomotive and railroad car wheels
wheel·less \ˈ(h)wē(ə)lləs\ *adj* **1** : having no wheels ⟨dragging a ~ stoneboat⟩ **2** : lacking wheeled vehicles ⟨criminals, degenerates, the genuinely low types . . . are entirely missing in ~ societies —J.W.Vandercook⟩
wheel load *n* : the part of the load of a vehicle that is carried by a single wheel and transmitted by it to a road surface or a track
wheel lock *n* : an obsolete gunlock in which sparks are struck from a flint or a piece of iron pyrites by a revolving wheel; *also* : a gun equipped with such a gunlock
wheel·man \ˈ=mən\ *n, pl* **wheelmen** **1** : one who tends or manages a wheel: as **a** : HELMSMAN **b** : the driver of an automobile ⟨you had to have a ~ to drive the getaway car and . . . an extra gunman —*Police Gazette*⟩ **2** : CYCLIST
wheel map *n* : a medieval map made in the shape of a disk with Jerusalem usu. at the center
wheel money *n* : a wheel-shaped metal object of the Bronze Age regarded by some as money and by others as a symbol of the sun
wheel of fortune **1** : WHEEL 3a **2** : a gambling device consisting of a revolving wheel with sections indicating chances taken or bets placed
wheel of life : the endless series of transmigratory cycles of birth, death, and rebirth esp. in Buddhism : the process of samsara resembling a wheel
wheel ore *n* : the mineral bournonite esp. when occurring in wheel-shaped twin crystals
wheel organ *n* : the corona of a rotifer
wheel plate *n* : QUADRANT PLATE
wheel plow *n* : a plow mounted on wheels
wheelrace \ˈ=,=\ *n* : the place in which a waterwheel is set
wheel report *n* : a listing of cars comprising a train as it enters or leaves a yard on which the conductor records all setoffs and pickups en route
wheel rod *n* : a length of metal rod taking the place of a portion of a wheel chain or wheel rope

wheel rope *n* **:** a rope on a ship leading from the axis or barrel of a steering wheel or from a steering engine to the tiller for moving the rudder

wheels *pl of* WHEEL, *pres 3d sing of* WHEEL

wheel scraper *n* **:** a road or earth scraper mounted on wheels

wheels·man \'(h)wē(ə)lzmən\ *n, pl* **wheelsmen :** one who handles or steers with a wheel; *esp* **:** HELMSMAN

wheelspin \'=,=\ *n* **:** the rotation of the wheels of a wheeled vehicle with little or no traction

wheel tracery *n* **:** tracery (as in a wheel window) radiating from a center like the spokes of a wheel

wheel trap *n* **:** a fish trap used esp. in Alaska consisting of a wheel revolved by the current and provided with scoops for taking fish and a receptacle in which the scoops deposit them

wheel tree *n* **1 :** PADDLEWOOD **2 :** an Australian tree (*Stenocarpus sinuatus*) of the family Proteaceae that is widely cultivated as a shade tree and for its circular clusters of showy bright red to orange scarlet flowers

wheel trolley *n* **:** a grooved rotating wheel attached to the end of the trolley pole of an electric railway car or bus for making constant rolling contact with the trolley wire

wheel watch *n* **:** a watch or tour of duty at the wheel of a ship ⟨standing a long *wheel watch* in the slow hours of the night⟩

wheel well *n* **:** a recessed compartment on the underside of an airplane for the reception of a wheel of a retractable landing gear

wheel window *n* **:** a circular window having radiating mullions like the spokes of a wheel — compare ROSE WINDOW, WHEEL TRACERY

wheelwork \'=,=\ *n* **:** wheels in gear and their connected parts in a mechanism

wheelwright \'=,=\ *n* [ME *whelwright*, fr. *whel* wheel + *wright*] **:** a man whose occupation is to make or repair wheels and wheeled vehicles; *specif* **:** an automobile serviceman who repairs or adjusts wheels

wheely \'hwēlē *also* 'wē- *or* -li\ *adj* **:** of or relating to a wheel or a circular form or movement

[1]**wheen** \'(h)wēn\ *adj* [ME (Sc) *quheyne*, fr. OE *hwǣne*, *hwēne*, adv., somewhat, a little, instr. of *hwōn* little] *dial Brit* **:** not many **:** FEW ⟨get a ~ biscuits for the beasts —J.J.Bell⟩

[2]**wheen** \"\ *n* -S [ME (Sc) *quheyne*, fr. OE *hwǣne*, *hwēne*, adv., somewhat, a little] *dial Brit* **:** a considerable number **:** a fair amount ⟨for quite a ~ of years —*Irish Digest*⟩ ⟨mix in a ~ of common life for novelty and variation —Joseph Macleod⟩

whee·ple \'(h)wēpəl\ *vb* -ED/-ING/-S [imit.] *vi, dial Brit* **:** to utter a prolonged whistle or shrill cry ⟨a curlew ~*s*⟩ ~ *vt, dial Brit* **:** to give forth (a shrill cry or whistle) **:** WHISTLE ⟨he sometimes *wheepled* a tune of his own making —G.D.Brown⟩

[1]**wheeze** \'hwēz *also* 'wēz\ *vb* -ED/-ING/-S [ME *whesen*, prob. of Scand origin; akin to ON *hvǣsa* to hiss; akin to OE *hwǣst* action of blowing, L *queri* to complain, Skt *śvasiti* he breathes, snorts, sighs] *vi* **1 :** to breathe with difficulty with a usu. audible sibilant or whistling sound ⟨went to every doctor and still he coughed and still he *wheezed* —N.R.Nash⟩ ⟨I *wheezed* asthmatically with my face in the ground —A.R.Matthews⟩ **2 :** to make a sound resembling that of wheezing esp. while moving ⟨the old car jerked and *wheezed* over the country road⟩ ⟨they heard a bullet ~ about their heads —J.H.Stuart⟩ ~ *vt* **:** to utter with a sound of wheezing ⟨the ancient organ ~*s* out its tune⟩

[2]**wheeze** \"\ *n* -S **1 a :** a sibilant whistling sound caused by difficult or obstructed respiration ⟨unmoving except for the heavy ~ of his breath —Herbert Gold⟩ ⟨a history of ~ is . . . significant in any patient presenting a mass in the chest —*Jour. Amer. Med. Assoc.*⟩ **b :** a sound similar to a wheeze ⟨the ability to diagnose accurately a ~ under a hood . . . on the highway —W.C.Oursler⟩ **2 a** (1) **:** a stage joke told by a comedian or clown ⟨if a ~ clicks at a matinee and an evening show I leave it in —*Success Mag.*⟩ (2) **:** such a joke oft repeated and widely known ⟨few plays have ever succeeded in gathering . . . so many of the old familiar ~*s* —*Nation*⟩ (3) **:** a practical joke **:** TRICK ⟨thought it was just a ~ of the purser to turn us all out bright and early —Thomas Wood †1950⟩ **b :** a trite saying or proverb ⟨the ancient ~ that Hollywood buys good stories about bad girls and makes them into bad stories about good girls —R.L.Blakesley⟩ ⟨the ~ that in life you get exactly what you give —T.H.Fielding⟩

wheez·i·ly \-zəlē, -li\ *adv* **:** in a wheezy manner

wheez·i·ness \-zēnəs, -zin-\ *n* -ES **:** the quality or state of being wheezy

wheez·ing·ly *adv* **:** with a wheeze ⟨the asthmatic speaks ~⟩

whee·zle \'hwēzəl *also* 'wē-\ *vi* -ED/-ING/-S [freq. of [1]*wheeze*] *dial Brit* **:** WHEEZE

wheezy \-zē, -zi\ *adj* -ER/-EST **1 :** inclined to wheeze **:** affected with wheezing ⟨fat, stiff-jointed, ~ veterans —Robert Graves⟩ **2 :** making or having a wheezing sound ⟨the ~ music of a Gramophone —W.S.Maugham⟩ ⟨owns a ~ old car —F.L.Allen⟩

whe·kau \'(h)we,kau̇, 'fe-\ *n* -S [Maori] **:** LAUGHING OWL

[1]**whelk** \'hw|elk, |eu̇k *also* 'w|\ *n* -S [ME *wilke*, *welke*, *whelke*, fr. OE *weoloc*, *wioloc*; akin to MD *willoc*, *wilc*, *welc* whelk, ON *vīl* intestines, L *volvere* to turn — more at VOLUBLE] **1 :** any of numerous large marine gastropod mollusks of the family Buccinidae: as **a :** a snail of the genus *Buccinum*; *esp* **:** a large elongated snail (*B. undatum*) of both coasts of the Atlantic that is much used as food in Europe **b :** any of various No. American mollusks of the genus *Busycon* **:** WINKLE 2 — see RED WHELK **2 :** any of various mollusks of families other than Buccinidae that resemble whelks — usu. used with a qualifying term; compare DOG WHELK

[2]**whelk** \"\ *vi* -ED/-ING/-S **:** to obtain or gather whelks

[3]**whelk** \"\ *n* -S [ME *whelke*, fr. OE *hwylca*, fr. *hwelian* to suppurate, come to a head — more at WHEAL] **1 :** PAPULE, PUSTULE **2 :** WELT, WALE, WHEAL

[1]**whelked** \-kt\ *adj* [[1]*whelk* + *-ed*] **:** formed like a whelk shell **:** TWISTED, CONVOLUTED ⟨~ horns⟩

[2]**whelked** \"\ *adj* [[3]*whelk* + *-ed*] *archaic* **:** having whelks or ridges on the flesh

whelk tingle *n* [[1]*whelk*] **:** DOG WHELK

whelm \'hw|elm, |eu̇m *also* 'w|\ *vb* -ED/-ING/-S [ME *whelmen*, perh. alter. (influenced by *helmen* to helm) of *whelven* to turn upside down — more at HELM, WHELVE] *vt* **1 a** *dial Eng* **:** to turn (as a dish or vessel) upside down usu. to cover something **b :** to throw or place (an object) upon something so as to engulf or crush it ⟨~*s* his hat down over his eyes⟩ **2 a :** to cover or engulf completely usu. so as to wreck or destroy **:** BURY, SUBMERGE ⟨sand all around them, about to creep up on them and ~ them —Mary H. Vorse⟩ ⟨the avalanche ~*s* the mountain village in tons of snow⟩ **b :** to engulf or overcome in the manner of a storm or flood with usu. disastrous effect ⟨winter darkness ~*s* the woods⟩ ⟨long afterwards ~*ed* in some European convulsion —G.M.Trevelyan⟩ ⟨booming money . . . so fast that the problem was how to get rid of it before it ~*ed* you into suffocation —William Faulkner⟩ **c :** to overcome in thought or feeling **:** OVERWHELM ⟨had been so ~*ed* in astonishment that they had not lifted a finger to aid their chief —C.E.Craddock⟩ ⟨drawn into overmastering passion, ~*ed* with a rush of joy and triumph —G.A.Wagner⟩ ⟨gathering around to ~ him with arguments⟩ ~ *vi* **:** to pass or go over something so as to bury or submerge ⟨the river ~*ed* —Kenneth Rexroth⟩ ⟨the battle lines ~*ed* and divided —C.P.Aiken⟩ **syn** see OVERPOWER

[1]**whelp** \'hw|elp, |eu̇p *also* 'w|\ *n* -S [ME, fr. OE *hwelp*; akin to OS *hwelp* whelp, OHG *hwelf*, *welf*, ON *hvelpr* whelp, and perh. to OE *hwelan* to war, rage, *hlōwan* to low — more at LOW] **1 a :** one of the young of various carnivorous mammals (as the wolf, otter, or fox) ⟨the tracks of the mother wolverine and three full-size ~*s* —*Fur-Fish-Game*⟩; *specif* **:** one of the young of a dog **b :** a young boy or girl ⟨the older folk would be huddled together . . . praying for their wayward ~*s* —L.C. Douglas⟩ **2 a :** an ill-considered or despised person ⟨that awkward ~ with his money bags —Joseph Addison⟩ **b** *obs* **:** the offspring of such a person or being ⟨the devil's ~*s*⟩ **c :** PUP 2 ⟨the young ~ had learned his lesson —Edna Ferber⟩ **3 a :** any of the longitudinal ribs or ridges on the barrel of a capstan or windlass — usu. used in pl. ⟨the ~*s* of a windlass⟩ **b :** SPROCKET 2a **4** *Brit* **:** a medium-sized auxiliary warship first constructed in the early 17th century **5** *usu cap* **:** TENNESSEAN — used as a nickname

[2]**whelp** \"\ *vb* -ED/-ING/-S [ME *whelpen*, fr. *whelp*, n.] *vt* **1 :** to bring forth **:** give birth to — used esp. of the female dog ⟨the bitch ~*s* her young⟩ **2** *archaic* **:** to bring forth as if by giving birth ⟨~*s* a pack of lies⟩ ~ *vi* **:** to bring forth young ⟨where they crawl out on the ice to ~ —O.F.Backer⟩

[3]**whelp** \"\ *n* -S [alter. of *welt*] *dial* **:** WELT, WALE ⟨rubbed the mare and showed me a ~ on her left flank —T.H.Phillips⟩

whelp·less \'=,ləs\ *adj* **:** having no whelps; *esp* **:** bereft of whelps

whelve \'(h)welv, -weu̇v\ *vt* -ED/-ING/-S [ME *whelven*, fr. OE *gehwielfan*, *gehwelfan* to arch, bend over; akin to OHG *welben* to vault, arch — more at GULF] *dial Eng* **:** to turn (as a dish or vessel) upside down usu. to cover something

[1]**whem·mel** *or* **whem·mle** \'(h)weməl\ *vb* -ED/-ING/-S [alter. of *whelm*] *vt, Scot* **:** OVERTURN, UPSET ~ *vi, Scot* **:** to stumble or become overturned

[2]**whemmel** *or* **whemmle** \"\ *n* -S *Scot* **:** CONFUSION, OVERTHROW

[1]**when** \(ˌ)hwen, (ˌ)wen, ˌ(h)wən\ *adv* [ME *when*, *whan*, fr. OE *hwenne*, *hwanne*; akin to OFris *hwenne* when, OHG *hwenne*, *hwanne*, Goth *hwan* when, how, OE *hwā* who — more at WHO] **1 a :** at what time **:** in what period ⟨how long ago ⟨asked him ~ it happened⟩ **:** how soon **:** after how long a lapse of time ⟨~ will he return⟩ **b :** in what circumstances ⟨~ shall we three meet again —Shak.⟩ **2 :** at which time **:** and then **:** WHEREUPON ⟨the tree will eventually die of old age and fall down ~ the problem solves itself —F.D.Smith & Barbara Wilcox⟩ **3 :** at, in, or during which ⟨a generation ~ medical science has . . . prolonged the span of life —*N.Y. Times*⟩ **4 :** ENOUGH ⟨say ~⟩ **5 :** at a former time; *esp* **:** at a less prosperous time ⟨his old associates . . . brag fondly of having known him ~ —Vance Packard⟩

[2]**when** \"\ *conj* [ME *when*, *whan*, fr. OE *hwenne*, *hwanne*, fr. *hwenne*, *hwanne*, adv.] **1 a :** at or during the time that **:** WHILE ⟨on one occasion, ~ a boy, I went fishing with three other boys —W.J.Reilly⟩ ⟨I could not say "Amen!" ~ they did say "God bless us!" —Shak.⟩ **b :** just after the moment that ⟨please stop writing ~ the bell rings⟩ ⟨went back to his old job ~ the war ended⟩ **c :** at any and every time that ⟨~ he listens to music, he falls asleep⟩ **2 :** in the event that **:** on condition that **:** IF ⟨the batter is out ~ he bunts foul with two strikes on him⟩ **3 a :** considering that ⟨why use water at all ~ you can drown in it —Stuart Chase⟩ ⟨how can he buy the house ~ he has no money⟩ **b :** in spite of the fact that **:** ALTHOUGH ⟨he gave up politics ~ he might have made a great career in it⟩

[3]**when** \"\ *pron* [[1]*when*] **:** what or which time ⟨in 1934, since ~ he has been working at landscapes and portraits —*Horizon*⟩

[4]**when** \'hwen *also* 'wen\ *n* -S [[1]*when*] **:** the time in which something is done or comes about ⟨piecing together the story of my visit there — the ~ and the why of it —W.B.Mowery⟩ ⟨remembering exactly the who, ~, what and how of any occasion —J.M.Barzun⟩

when·as \(')(h)we'naz, ˌ(h)wə'-\ *conj* [ME (Sc) *when as*, fr. ME [1]*when* + *as*] **1** *archaic* **:** at the or any time when **:** WHILE ⟨~ in silks my Julia goes —Robert Herrick †1674⟩ **2** *archaic* **:** for the reason that **:** AS **3** *obs* **:** ALTHOUGH, WHEREAS ⟨cried "All hail!" ~ he meant all harm —Shak.⟩

[1]**whence** \'hwen(t)s *also* 'we-\ *adv* [ME *whennes*, *whannes*, fr. *whenne*, *whanne* whence (fr. OE *hwanon*, *hwanone*) + *-s*, gen. sing. noun ending functioning adverbially; akin to OS *hwanan* whence, OHG *hwanān*, *hwanana* whence, OE *hwā* who — more at WHO, -S] **1 a :** from what place ⟨are the pigments imported and, if so, ~ —*Notes & Queries on Anthropology*⟩ — often used with *from* ⟨asks from ~ these lines come —*N.Y. Times Bk. Rev.*⟩ **b :** from what source, origin, antecedent, or cause ⟨~ do these questionings well up —S.C.Pepper⟩ — often used with *from* ⟨from ~ could this possibility issue —F.S.Haserot⟩ **2 :** from or out of which place, source, or cause ⟨a native of Europe, ~ it was introduced into many parts of the world —Jane Nickerson⟩ ⟨sketches the lawless society ~ the ballads sprang —DeLancey Ferguson⟩ — often used with *from* **3 :** upon which ground **:** by reason of or in consequence of which fact or circumstance **:** WHEREFORE ⟨came a whacking header onto my arms and nose and nothing broke — ~ I infer that my bones are not yet chalky —O.W. Holmes †1935⟩

[2]**whence** \"\ *n* -S **:** a place or source from which someone or something springs **:** ANTECEDENT ⟨deals only with the momentary what, neglecting the ~ —J.P.M.Somerville⟩

whenceforth \'(')=,=\ *adv, archaic* **:** WHENCE ⟨another house, ~ his flame . . . shines stark —A.D.Ficke⟩

whenceforward \'=,=\ *adv* **:** from which time or place onward

[1]**whencesoever** \',==,==\ *conj* **:** from any or every place from which **:** no matter from what place

[2]**whencesoever** \"\ *adv* **:** from what place soever **:** from what cause or source soever

whencever \'(')=,=\ *conj* [[1]*whence* + *ever*] **:** WHENCESOEVER

[1]**when·ev·er** \(h)we'nevə(r), (h)wə'-\ *conj* [ME *when ever*, fr. [2]*when* + *ever*] **1 :** at any or all times that **:** in any or every instance in which ⟨~ he leaves the house, he always takes his umbrella⟩ **2** *chiefly Scot* **:** as soon as ⟨~ he entered my room, he rushed at me . . . and shed tears of delight over our romantic meeting after twenty years —Harry Lauder⟩

[2]**whenever** \"\ *adv* **1 :** at whatever time **:** no matter when ⟨welcomes originality ~ shown⟩ **2** *usu* **when ever :** WHEN — used in questions expressing surprise or bewilderment ⟨*when ever* did I make such a promise⟩

when–issued \'=(,)=\ *adj* [fr. the phrase *when issued*] **:** of, relating to, or constituting a securities contract on which settlement is not required until the securities are ready for delivery

when·ness \'hwennəs *also* 'we-\ *n* -ES **:** position or relation in time

whenso \'hwen(,)sō\ *conj* [ME *when so*, fr. [1]*when* + *so*] *archaic* **:** WHENSOEVER

[1]**when·so·ev·er** \ˌhwensə'wevə(r), -sō'e- *also* ¦wen-\ *conj* [ME, fr. *when so* + *ever*] **:** at what time soever **:** at whatever time **:** WHENEVER ⟨ye have the poor with you always, and ~ ye will ye may do them good —Mk 14:7 (AV)⟩

[2]**whensoever** *adv, obs* **:** at any time whatever ⟨if his fitness speaks, mine is ready; now or ~ —Shak.⟩

when·som·ev·er \-sə,me-\ *adv or conj* [ME, alter. (influenced by *-som-* as in *whatsomever*) of *whensoever*] *chiefly dial* **:** WHENSOEVER

[1]**where** \(ˌ)hw|e(ə)r, (ˌ)w|, |eə *sometimes* |a(ə)(ə)r *or* |a(ə)ə; *when completely unstressed often* (h)wə(r); *more often under secondary than primary stress* (h)wər(·) *or* (h)wə̄\ *adv* [ME *where*, *wher*, fr. OE *hwǣr*; akin to OHG *hwār* where, ON *hvar*, Goth *hwar* where, Skt *karhi* when, OE *hwā* who — more at WHO] **1 a** (1) **:** at or in what place ⟨~ do you think you are⟩ ⟨asked him ~ he lived⟩ ⟨~'*s* the fire⟩ (2) **:** in what situation, position, or circumstances **:** at what point ⟨~, precisely, should a man's crusading zeal abate —Lucien Price⟩ ⟨~ else numerically are you going to draw the line —Weston La Barre⟩ (3) **:** in what respect or particular ⟨does not hesitate, as he looks back, to admit ~ he was wrong —*Times Lit. Supp.*⟩ **b :** to what or which place **:** in what or which direction **:** to what goal or result **:** WHITHER ⟨~ are you rushing⟩ ⟨doesn't know ~ he is heading⟩ **c :** from what place or source ⟨~ did he get such an absurd idea⟩ **2** *archaic* **:** HERE, THERE — used to call attention to something or indicate direction of movement ⟨but soft, behold! lo, ~ it comes again —Shak.⟩ **3 :** at which part, stage, or passage ⟨I forget ~ we were reading⟩

[2]**where** \"\ *conj* [ME *where*, *wher*, fr. OE *hwǣr*, fr. *hwǣr*, adv.] **1 a :** at or in the place in which ⟨~ you lodge I will lodge —Ruth 1:16 (RSV)⟩ **b :** to the place at, in, or to which ⟨~ you go I will go —Ruth 1:16 (RSV)⟩ **:** a place at, in, or to which ⟨couldn't see well from ~ he was sitting⟩ **c :** at the part, stage, or passage at which ⟨toward the end of the book, ~ the author tells of the heroine's return home⟩ **2 :** WHEREVER ⟨removed all restrictions on his movements and permitted him to go ~ he wished⟩ **3 :** at or in which place ⟨the room ~ he was working⟩ ⟨the store ~ she bought her clothes⟩ **4 :** WHEREAS ⟨~ she was fascinated by people he shows here only a laboriously sophisticated amusement —Anthony Quinton⟩ **5 a :** under conditions in which **:** in circumstances in which ⟨it is unfortunately necessary to determine this ~ the custody of the children is involved —Louis Auchincloss⟩ **b :** in the respect in which ⟨~ others are weak, he is strong⟩ **c :** so far as **:** to the extent that ⟨the prospects . . . were truly and literally hopeless, ~ England was concerned —Sacheverell Sitwell⟩ **d :** of such a sort that ⟨limited definition to such explanations of the meaning of a symbol as asserted the equivalence of two expressions; ~ the defining expression had to contain more symbols than the defined expression —R.G.F.Robinson⟩

[3]**where** \"\ *n* -S [ME *where*, *wher*, fr. *where*, *wher*, adv.] **:** LOCATION, PLACE; *esp* **:** the place in which something mentioned is or occurs ⟨discussed the ~ and how of the accident⟩

[4]**where** \"\ *pron* [[1]*where*] **:** what or which place ⟨~ did you come from⟩

[1]**where·abouts** \'=ə,bau̇ts, ,==¦=\ *also* **where·about** \-t\ *adv* [*whereabouts* fr. ME *wheraboutes*, fr. ME *wher aboute* + *-s*, gen. sing. noun ending functioning adverbially; *whereabout* fr. ME *wher aboute*, fr. *wher* where + *aboute*, *about* about — more at -S] **1 :** about where **:** near what place ⟨to know at the outset ~ the line will be drawn —F.W.Maitland⟩ **2** *obs* **:** at what work **:** on what business or errand ⟨I must not have you henceforth question me whither I go, nor reason *whereabout* —Shak.⟩

[2]**whereabouts** \"\ *n pl but sing or pl in constr, also* **whereabout :** the place or general locality where a person or thing is ⟨had for long been determined to discover the *whereabout* of the gold country —*Times Lit. Supp.*⟩ ⟨his ~ was known only to his personal staff —*Fortune*⟩ ⟨his ~ are kept secret —*Manchester Guardian Weekly*⟩

whereafter \(')=¦==\ *adv* [ME *wherafter*, fr. *wher* where + *after*] **:** after which ⟨dissolve the starch glaze, ~ the chintzes become dull fuzzy cotton —*For Instance*⟩

whereanent \'=¦=,=\ *adv* [[1]*where* + *anent*] *chiefly Scot* **:** concerning which

[1]**whereas** \(')=¦=\ *conj* [ME *where as*, fr. [1]*where* + *as*] **1** *archaic* **:** WHERE ⟨home she came, ~ her mother blind sat in eternal night —Edmund Spenser⟩ **2 :** considering that **:** in view of the fact that **:** SINCE — usu. used to introduce a preamble (as to a law or contract) that is the basis of a following declaration, affirmation, command, or request **3 a :** when in fact **:** while on the contrary **:** the case being in truth that — used to introduce a statement in opposition or contrast to a preceding or sometimes following statement ⟨was spending practically all of his time on the inside dealing with things, ~ his yearnings were to deal more with people —W.J.Reilly⟩ **b :** ALTHOUGH ⟨seeing I have once begun, I will speak to my Lord, ~ I am dust and ashes —Gen 18:27 (NCE)⟩ ⟨~ it is quite dangerous to draw conclusions . . . one cannot avoid being struck with some gross changes —Abram Kardiner⟩ **c :** at the same time that **:** WHILE ⟨its isolation favored the development of a unified and distinctive culture, ~ its nearness to the European continent was a guarantee against a too sharp differentiation from western civilization —Kemp Malone⟩

[2]**whereas** \"\ *n* -ES **1 :** an introductory statement of a formal or legal document **:** PREAMBLE ⟨learned his way through ~*es* at . . . law school —Roland Gelatt⟩ **2 :** a conditional or qualifying statement ⟨dilutes it with various discreet ~*es* —H.L.Mencken⟩

whereat \(')=¦=\ *adv* [ME *whare at*, fr. *whare*, *where*, *wher* where + *at*] **1 :** at or toward which ⟨an icy tea party, ~ the girl was present, unexplained, unaccounted for, and ignored —Maurice Hewlett⟩ **2 :** in consequence of which **:** on which account **:** WHEREUPON ⟨~ the seeker after precision may wax angry or sarcastic —H.A.Overstreet⟩

where away *adv* **1 :** in what direction — usu. used aboard ship as a question in response to a call from a lookout that something (as land) has been sighted **2** *usu* **whereaway** \'==,=\ *chiefly dial* **:** WHEREABOUTS

whereby \(')=¦=\ *adv* [ME *wherby*, fr. *where*, *wher* where + *by*] **1 a :** by or through which **:** by the help of which **:** in accordance with which ⟨the means ~ such an end is effected —Norman Friedman⟩ ⟨the old logic of judgment, ~ discipline meant salvation —D.R.Meyer⟩ **b** *archaic* **:** near or along which ⟨the throne ~ she fell —Alfred Tennyson⟩ **2** *obs* **:** by what **:** HOW ⟨~ shall I know this —Lk 1:18 (AV)⟩ **3 a :** as a result of which **:** in consequence of which ⟨a respite, four days' grace, ~ she told her story to the world —Robert Browning⟩ **b** *chiefly dial* **:** WHEREUPON ⟨~ thou didst desire to eat some, ~ I told thee they were ill for a green wound —Shak.⟩

wherefor \(')=¦=\ *adv* [ME *wherfor*, *wherfore* for which, for what reason, fr. *where*, *wher* where + *for*, *fore* for] **:** for which ⟨a mistake the responsibility ~ is his alone⟩

[1]**where·fore** *R* 'hwe|r,fō(ə)r, -fȯ(ə)r *also* 'w| *sometimes* |a(ə)r,- *or* -fər; -*R* |eə,fōə, -fȯ(ə) *sometimes* |a(ə)ə,- *or* -,fə, +V " *or* -fō(ə)r *or* -fȯ(ə)r *or* -,fər\ *adv* [ME *wherfor*, *wherfore* for which, for what reason] **1 :** for what reason **:** for what end or object ⟨~ do I assume these royalties —John Milton⟩ **2** *archaic* **:** in consequence of which **:** WHY

[2]**wherefore** *also* **where·for** \"\ *conj* [ME *wherfor*, *wherfore*, fr. *wherfor*, *wherfore*, adv.] **:** for that reason **:** and in consequence of that fact or consideration **:** so ⟨the Lord . . . rested the seventh day; ~ the Lord blessed the sabbath day —Exod 20:11 (AV)⟩

[3]**wherefore** \"\ *n* -S [[1]*wherefore*] **:** an answer or statement giving an explanation **:** CAUSE, REASON ⟨they say every why hath a ~ —Shak.⟩ ⟨totally in the dark as to the whys and ~*s* of her sister's moods —Mrs. Humphry Ward⟩

wherefrom \(')=¦=\ *adv* **:** from which ⟨exhibitions of materials in use ~ one could obtain objective information —*Internat'l Council for Building Documentation*⟩

wherein \(')=¦=\ *adv* [ME *wherin*, fr. *where*, *wher* where + *in*] **1 :** in what **:** in what particular or regard ⟨~ consists the peculiarity in the connotation of a relative name —J.S.Mill⟩ **2 a :** in which **:** WHERE ⟨citizens of the United States and of the State ~ they reside —*U.S. Constitution*⟩ **b :** in the course of or during which ⟨a period ~ he took no active part in politics⟩ **3 :** in regard to which ⟨a controversy ~ he took a prominent part⟩ **4** *obs* **:** in whatever regard ⟨~ our entertainment shall shame us we will be justified in our loves —Shak.⟩

whereinsoever \¦=¦=,==¦==\ *adv* **:** in whatever matter, respect, or action

where·into \(ˌ)=¦=+\ *adv* **:** into which ⟨the brook ~ he loved to look —R.W.Emerson⟩

where·ness *n* -ES **:** the quality or state of being in a particular place **:** position or presence in a definable place ⟨where was the ~ of a dreamer —Ross Lockridge⟩

whereof \(')=¦= *sometimes* -¦äf\ *adv* [ME *wherof*, fr. *where*, *wher* where + *of*] **1 :** of what ⟨knows ~ he speaks —H.U. Ribalow⟩ ⟨~ are you made, that millions of strange shadows on you tend —Shak.⟩ **2 a :** of which ⟨modernized old houses, ~ even the new ones are often as classically beautiful as ever —*Yankee*⟩ ⟨punishment for crime ~ the party shall have been duly convicted —*U.S. Constitution*⟩ **:** of whom ⟨the very earliest poets ~ there is record —J.C.Powys⟩ **b** *archaic* **:** with or by which ⟨wine ~ his sire . . . was poisoned —Christopher Marlowe⟩

whereon \(')=¦=\ *adv* [ME *wheron*, fr. *where*, *wher* where + *on*] **1** *archaic* **:** on what ⟨~ do you look —Shak.⟩ **2 a :** on which ⟨conducted ranches ~ to grow supplies for sale —P.A. Rollins⟩ ⟨that day . . . ~ he says I shall yield up my crown —Shak.⟩ **b :** to, toward, or upon which ⟨the things ~ he cast his eyes —R.W.Emerson⟩ **c :** in the course of which **:** in connection with which ⟨installed a service between New York and San Francisco, ~ the planes flew only by daylight —A.F. Harlow⟩ **d :** following which **:** WHEREUPON ⟨~ the people answered with a shout —Robert Browning⟩

whereout \(')=¦=\ *adv* [ME *wherout*, fr. *where*, *wher* where + *out*] *archaic* **:** out of which **:** WHENCE

whereover \(')=¦==\ *adv* [ME *wherover*, fr. *where*, *wher* where + *over*] **:** over which ⟨~ richest leaves have lain —Mark Van Doren⟩

wheres *pl of* WHERE

whereso \'=(,)=\ *conj* [ME *wher so*, fr. *where*, *wher*, adv., where + *so*] *archaic* **:** WHERESOEVER

[1]**where·so·ev·er** \ˌhwersə'wevə(r), -sō'e- *also* ¦wer-\ *conj* [ME *wheresoever*, fr. *wher so* + *ever*] *archaic* **:** in, to, or from whatever place

[2]**wheresoever** *adv, obs* **:** in any place whatever

where·som·ev·er \-sə,me-\ *conj* [ME *whersomever*, *whersumever*, fr. ME (northern dial.) *wher sum* wherever (fr. ME

where, wher where + ME — northern dial. — *sum,* rel. adv., as) + ME *ever* — more at WHATSOEVER] *chiefly dial* : WHERESOEVER

wherethrough \(')=¦=\ *conj* [ME *wherthrough,* fr. *where, wher* where + *through*] **1 a** : through which : from one side to another of which ⟨foliage ~ the sun shot sudden showers of light —Robert Nichols⟩ **b** : during which ⟨seven long years of lack ~ he hath not ceased to seek for thee —Edwin Arnold⟩ **2** : because of which : on account of which ⟨is in control of clocks, ~ it calls the tune —David Morton⟩

whereto \(')=¦=\ *adv* [ME *wherto,* fr. *where, wher* where + *to*] **1** : to what : to what place, purpose, or end ⟨~ tends all this —Shak.⟩ **2** : to which ⟨the present species, ~ the latter term would perhaps be more appropriate —James Stevenson-Hamilton⟩

whereunder \(')=¦==\ *conj* [ME *wherunder,* fr. *where, wher* where + *under*] : under which ⟨trees ~ the animals may find shelter —Henry Wynmalen⟩

where·until \(¦)=+\ *adv, chiefly dial* : WHERETO

where·unto \"+\ *adv* [ME *wherunto,* fr. *where, wher* where + *unto*] : WHERETO

whereup \(')=¦=\ *conj* : up which

whereupon \'==,=, ,==¦=\ *adv* [ME *wherupon,* fr. *where, wher* where + *upon*] **1 a** *obs* : for what reason : WHEREFORE ⟨hath sent to know . . . ~ you conjure from the breast of civil peace such bold hostility —Shak.⟩ **b** *archaic* : upon what ⟨~ are the foundations thereof fastened —Job 38:6 (AV)⟩ **2** : upon which : on the top or surface of which ⟨a point of rock ~ a pale-colored village balanced itself —Elizabeth Bowen⟩ **3 a** *obs* : by reason of which ⟨~ I command thee to open thy affair —Shak.⟩ **b** *archaic* : upon which as ground or support ⟨~ Saint Ambrose makes a comment with much fruit —Robert Browning⟩ **4** : closely following and in consequence of which ⟨has to banish his wicked foster brothers . . . ~ they become pirates —G.B.Saul⟩ **5** *obs* : concerning which ⟨this remedy, ~ we are now present here together —Shak.⟩ **6** *archaic* : to, toward, or on which ⟨that ~ they set their minds —Ezek 24:25 (AV)⟩

[1]**wher·ev·er** \(h)we'revə(r), (h)wə'-\ *adv* [ME *wher ever,* fr. *where, wher,* adv., where + *ever*] **1** : where in the world — used in questions expressing astonishment or bewilderment ⟨~ did you get that hat⟩ **2** : at, in, or to any or every place in or to which ⟨he goes ~ needed⟩ : in every instance or circumstance in which ⟨help is given ~ needed⟩ **3** : anywhere at all ⟨explore northward or ~ by sea —Bernard De Voto⟩

[2]**wherever** \"\ *conj* [ME *wher ever,* fr. *where, wher,* adv., where + *ever*] : at, in, or to any or all places that : in any circumstance in which ⟨~ he goes, he is welcomed with open arms⟩ ⟨~ it is possible, he tries to help out⟩

[1]**wherewith** \(')=¦=\ *adv* [ME *wherwith,* fr. *where, wher* where + *with*] **1** *archaic* : with what ⟨if the salt have lost his savor, ~ shall it be salted —Mt 5:13 (AV)⟩ **2 a** : with which : by means of which ⟨no metal tools ~ to break ground —Russell Lord⟩ ⟨the pleasant rites ~ the pagan Teutons had celebrated the victory of the sun —Will Durant⟩ **b** *archaic* : by reason of which : on account of which ⟨dreamed dreams, ~ his spirit was troubled —Dan 2:1 (AV)⟩ **3** *archaic* : WHEREAT, WHEREUPON ⟨close to her ear touching the melody; ~ disturbed, she uttered a soft moan —John Keats⟩

[2]**wherewith** \"\ *pron* [ME *wherwith,* fr. *wherwith,* adv.] : that with or by which — used with an infinitive ⟨had not ~ to feed himself⟩

[3]**wherewith** \"\ *n* -S : WHEREWITHAL

[1]**where·with·al** \'=wə,thȯl, -,thȯl, ,=='=\ *adv* [[1]*where* + *withal*] **1** *archaic* : WHEREWITH **1** ⟨take no thought, saying . . . ~ shall we be clothed —Mt 6:31 (AV)⟩ **2** : out of or by means of which ⟨the material ~ to have evolved this elegant creature, man —Weston La Barre⟩

[2]**wherewithal** \"\ *pron* : WHEREWITH ⟨buying lots of old iron at sales, in the hope of finding therein ~ to patch up his dilapidated machines —Adrian Bell⟩

[3]**wherewithal** \'==,=\ *n* -S [[2]*wherewithal*] : means or resources for purchasing or doing something ⟨must present to the courts the ~ to create a framework of liberty under law —Herbert Feinstein⟩; *specif* : financial resources : MONEY ⟨had to keep raising his budget and rushing out to find more ~ —*New Yorker*⟩

[1]**wher·ret** \'(h)wərət\ *n* -S [imit.] *chiefly dial* : a cuff on the face or ear : BOX, SLAP

[2]**wherret** \"\ *vt* -ED/-ING/-S *chiefly dial* : to give a cuff or blow to

[3]**wherret** *or* **wherrit** \"\ *vt* -ED/-ING/-S [perh. alter. of *worrit*] *dial* : TEASE, WORRY

wher·ry \'hwerē, -ri *also* 'we-\ *n* -ES [ME *whery*] **1** : any of various light boats: as **a** : a long light rowboat made sharp at both ends and used to transport passengers on rivers and about harbors **b** : a narrow open racing or exercise boat rowed by one person with sculls **c** : a small square-sterned rowboat pulled by a single pair of oars **2** : a large light barge, lighter, or fishing boat varying in type in different parts of Great Britain; *specif* : a broad-beamed light-draft cargo or passenger boat with sharp stem and stern, little freeboard, and usu. a single gaff sail without a boom — called also *Norfolk wherry*

wher·ry·ite \-rē,īt\ *n* -S [Edgar T. *Wherry b*1885 Am. mineralogist + E *-ite*] : a mineral $Pb_4Cu(CO_3)$ $(SO_4)_2$-$(OH,Cl)_2O$(?) consisting of a basic carbonate and sulfate of lead and copper and sometimes containing chlorine

wher·ry·man \'==mən\ *n, pl* **wherrymen 1** *chiefly Brit* : one who works on a wherry or who rows passengers in a wherry for hire **2** : WATER STRIDER

[1]**whet** \'hwet *also* 'wet; *usu* -ed·+V\ *vt* **whetted; whetted; whetting; whets** [ME *whetten,* fr. OE *hwettan;* akin to OHG *wezzen* to whet, ON *hvetja* to whet, incite, Goth *gahwatjan* to incite; causative fr. the adj. represented by OE *hwæt* bold, vigorous, OHG *waz* sharp, ON *hvatr* bold, vigorous; prob. akin to L *triquetrus* three-cornered] **1 a** : to sharpen (as a tool edge) by rubbing on or with something (as a stone) : HONE ⟨~ a scythe⟩ ⟨~ a knife⟩ ⟨an axe *whetted* to a razor edge⟩ **b** : to rub vigorously together as if sharpening ⟨*whetted* his hands . . . to get them warm —J.H.Stuart⟩ **2** *archaic* : urge on : INCITE, AROUSE ⟨I will ~ on the king —Shak.⟩ **3** : to make keen or more acute (as a faculty or desire) : STIMULATE, EXCITE ⟨~ the appetite⟩ ⟨curiosity . . . *whetted* rather than satisfied —G.N.Ray⟩ ⟨~*s* the emotions to bullfight sharpness —H.W.Young⟩ — **whet one's whistle** *archaic* : WET ONE'S WHISTLE

[2]**whet** \"\ *n* -S **1** *dial* **a** : a spell of work between two whettings of the scythe : TURN **b** : TIME, WHILE ⟨I'll bear it this ~ —Charlotte Brontë⟩ ⟨stood talking a long ~⟩ **2** : something that sharpens or makes keen (as desire or appetite): **a** : GOAD, INCITEMENT ⟨gave a ~ to his revenge⟩ **b** : APPETIZER ⟨gives our wish for blue a ~ —Robert Frost⟩; *esp* : a drink of liquor : APERITIF ⟨the beery breath of a ~ . . . taken as he came along —Charles Dickens⟩

[1]**wheth·er** \(¦)(h)weth̲ə(r) *also* (¦)(h)wəth̲-\ *pron* [ME, fr. OE *hwæther, hwether;* akin to OHG *hwedar* which of two, ON *hvārr,* Goth *hwathar,* L *uter,* Gk *poteros,* Skt *katara;* all fr. a prehistoric IE compound pronoun formed from the root of the pronoun represented by Skt *ka* who by the addition of a comparative suffix *-ter-* — more at WHO] **1** *archaic* : which one of the two : [2]WHICH 1a ⟨~ of them twain did the will of his father —Mt 21:31 (AV)⟩ ⟨might get a great deal or a little, we did not know ~ —Daniel Defoe⟩ **2** *archaic* : whichever one of the two : [1]WHICHEVER ⟨put it into . . . glasses or pots, ~ you have —Eliza Moxon⟩

[2]**whether** \"\ *adj* [ME, fr. OE *hwæther, hwether,* fr. *hwæther, hwether,* pron.] **1** *obs* : being which one of the two : [1]WHICH 1a ⟨the dispute ~ life is to be preferred, the active or the contemplative —Henry Dodwell⟩ **2** *obs* : being whichever one of the two : [2]WHICHEVER

[3]**whether** \"\ *conj* [ME, fr. OE *hwæther, hwether,* fr. *hwæther, hwether,* pron.] **1** — used as a function word followed usu. by correlative *or* or by *or whether* to indicate (1) until the early 19th century a direct question involving alternatives ⟨~ does doubting consist in embracing the affirmative or negative side of a question —George Berkeley⟩; (2) an indirect question involving alternatives ⟨hard to decide ~ he should agree or ~ he should raise certain objections⟩ ⟨the question as to ~ a man is really the best judge of his own life work or not —T.H. Savory⟩ ⟨compelled to doubt ~ universal schooling will suffice to curb our evil instincts —A.L.Guérard⟩; (3) alternative conditions or possibilities ⟨a material form, ~ animate or inanimate —J.G.Frazer⟩ ⟨I was of two minds ~ to go or stay —Helen Eustis⟩ ⟨passing judgment on ~ or not a given school was performing satisfactorily —J.B.Conant⟩ ⟨see me no more, ~ he be dead or no —Shak.⟩ ⟨the undergraduate, ~ he be a concentrator in the sciences, the humanities, or the social sciences —*General Education in a Free Society*⟩ **2** : EITHER — used with correlative *or* ⟨aimed to win ~ by hook or crook⟩ ⟨seated him next to her ~ by accident or design⟩ **3** *obs* : WHEREVER, IF ⟨charity never faileth: but ~ there be prophecies, they shall fail —1 Cor 13:8 (AV)⟩

[4]**wheth·er** \'hw¦eth̲ə(r) *also* 'w¦ *or* ¦əth̲-\ *n* -S : a choice between alternatives ⟨considering all the whys and ~*s* of the matter⟩

whether or no *also* **whether or not** *adv* : in any case : WILLY-NILLY ⟨I will go *whether or no*⟩ ⟨obliged to take the stranger by the hand *whether or not* and show him civilities —Mark Twain⟩

whetrock \'=,=\ *n, South* : WHETSTONE

whet slate *n* : a variety of slate used for sharpening cutting instruments

whetstone \'=,=\ *n* [ME *whetston,* fr. OE *hwetstān,* fr. *hwettan* to whet + *stān* stone] **1** : a natural or artificial stone for whetting edge tools ⟨a blade sharpened on a well-oiled ~⟩ **2** : something that sharpens, makes keen, or stimulates (as the wit or the appetite) ⟨the dullness of the fool is the ~ of the wits —Shak.⟩

whetted *past of* WHET

whet·ten \-et°n\ *vt* -ED/-ING/-S [irreg. fr. [1]*whet* + *-en,* v. suffix] : WHET

whet·ter \-ed·ə(r)\ *n* -S : one that whets ⟨a ~ of scythes⟩ ⟨a ~ of the appetite⟩

whetting *pres part of* WHET

[1]**whew** \'(h)wü, 'hyü\ *vi* -ED/-ING/-S [ME *whewen,* of imit. origin] **1** : to make a whistling noise : WHISTLE ⟨the soft ~*ing* of the cranes flying overhead —Lawrence Durrell⟩ **2** : to utter an exclamatory whew ⟨he ~*ed* with relief when they all got safely over —J.T.Farrell⟩ **3** *dial* : to move quickly : bustle about

[2]**whew** \", *as an exclamation a whistling sound consisting typically of* k̲ *followed by voiceless* ü *or of voiceless* ue̲ *preceded by a rounding of the lips & followed by voiceless* ü\ *n* -S **1** : a whistling sound ⟨the ~ of the plover⟩ ⟨the ~ of lead still singing in their ears —Thomas Carlyle⟩ **2** : a sound like a half-formed whistle uttered as an exclamation ⟨gave a long ~ when he realized the size of the job⟩ — used interjectionally chiefly to express amazement, discomfort, or relief ⟨~! never have I seen such flying feet —Arnold Bennett⟩ ⟨~, it's hot here⟩ ⟨~, that was a close call⟩

whew duck *n, dial Brit* : WIDGEON 1a(1)

whew·ell·ite \'hyüə,līt\ *n* -S [William *Whewell* †1866 Eng. philosopher + E *-ite*] : a mineral $CaC_2O_4.H_2O$ consisting of calcium oxalate occurring in colorless or white monoclinic crystals polymorphous with weddellite

whew·er \'(h)wüə(r), 'hyü-\ *n* -S [[2]*whew* + *-er*] *dial Eng* : WIDGEON 1a

whewl \'(h)wül\ *vi* -ED/-ING/-S [imit.] *dial Eng* : to cry complainingly : WHINE, HOWL

[1]**whey** \'hwā *also* 'wā\ *n* -S [ME, fr. OE *hwæg;* akin to MD *wey* whey, *hoy* whey, MLG *hoie,* and perh. to L *caseus* cheese — more at CHEESE] : the serum or watery part of milk containing sugar, minerals, and lactalbumin that is separated from the thicker or more coagulable part or curd esp. in the process of making cheese

[2]**whey** \"\ *vb* -ED/-ING/-S *vt* : to cause whey to separate from (milk or buttermilk) ~ *vi* : to separate in the form of whey

[3]**whey** \"\ *adj* **1** : of or relating to whey ⟨~ powder⟩ ⟨~ butter⟩ **2** : resembling whey (as in consistency or color) : WATERY, PALE ⟨a sprig . . . with a ~ face and a satchel —Sir Walter Scott⟩

whey·ey \-āē\ *adj* [[1]*whey* + *-y*] : consisting of, containing, or resembling whey : WHEYISH

whey-face \'=,=\ *n* : a person having a pale face (as from fear) : WEAKLING ⟨thou lily-liver'd boy . . . *whey-face* —Shak.⟩

whey-faced \'=,=\ *adj* : having a face suggestive of whey : PALE, PALLID ⟨straggled . . . in little processions, *whey-faced,* thin, ragged —Jan Struther⟩

whey·ish \-āish\ *adj* : somewhat like whey — **whey·ish·ness** *n* -ES

whf *abbr* wharf

whfg *abbr* wharfage

whge *abbr* wharfage

[1]**which** \(¦)hwich, (¦)wich\ *adj* [ME, which, of what kind, fr. OE *hwilc;* akin to OHG *wilīh* which, of what kind, OSw *hvilkin* of what kind, Goth *hwileiks;* all fr. a prehistoric Gmc compound whose first constituent is akin to OE *hwā* who and whose second constituent is represented by OE *gelīc* like — more at WHO, LIKE] **1 a** : being what one or ones out of a group — used as an interrogative adjective in direct or indirect questions ⟨~ tie should I wear with this shirt⟩ ⟨deciding ~ candidate he is going to vote for⟩ ⟨kept a record of ~ employees took their vacations in July and ~ ones in August⟩ **b** *obs* : [3]WHAT 1 a (1) ⟨from ~ lord to ~ lady —Shak.⟩ **2** : WHICHEVER ⟨it will not fit, turn it ~ way you like⟩ **3** — used as a function word to introduce a nonrestrictive relative clause and to modify a noun in that clause and to refer together with that noun to a word or word group in a preceding clause or to an entire preceding clause or sentence or longer unit of discourse ⟨that a new currency should be made ready for any possible emergency, ~ currency would . . . be available for immediate use —Jack Bennett⟩ ⟨the word occurs as a Yiddish loan in German, ~ language might thus have been the medium of transmission —Thomas Pyles⟩ ⟨a licensed practitioner of medicine of the state of Tennessee, ~ practitioner must also sign the prescription —*Bull. of Meharry Med. Coll.*⟩ ⟨that this city is a rebellious city . . . : for ~ cause was this city destroyed —Ezra 4:15 (AV)⟩ ⟨Abraham had two sons, the one by a bondmaid, the other by a free woman. But he who was of the bondwoman was born after the flesh; but he of the free woman was by promise. *Which* things are an allegory —Gal 4:22–4 (AV)⟩; sometimes used archaically with preceding *the* ⟨I am appointed a preacher, and an apostle, and a teacher of the Gentiles. For the ~ cause I also suffer these things —2 Tim 1:11–12 (AV)⟩

[2]**which** \"\ *pron* [ME, fr. OE *hwilc,* fr. *hwilc,* adj., which, of what kind] **1 a** : what one or ones out of a group — used as an interrogative pronoun in direct or indirect questions ⟨~ of those houses do you live in⟩ ⟨~ of you want tea and ~ want lemonade⟩ ⟨he asked ~ he should take⟩ ⟨he is down at the lake swimming or canoeing, I don't know ~⟩ **b** : [1]WHAT 1a(1) — used as recently as the 17th century in questions of regular syntactical form containing a verb with a subject that may or may not be *which* itself ⟨I have many ill qualities. *Which* is one —Shak.⟩; used dialectally by itself to ask for repetition of an utterance not properly heard or understood; sometimes used in informal speech in connection with other words to ask for repetition or explanation of the particular part of an utterance that has not been properly heard or understood ⟨he said he wanted a ~⟩ **2** : [1]WHICHEVER ⟨take ~ you like⟩ **3** — used as a function word to introduce a restrictive or nonrestrictive relative clause and to serve as a substitute within that clause for the substantive modified by that clause; used in any grammatical relation within the relative clause except that of a possessive; used esp. in reference to animals, inanimate objects, groups, or ideas ⟨fish ~ are dangerous at some particular time of the year —Margaret Mead⟩ ⟨grapefruit juice . . . sweetened to improve its palatability for the rats, ~ would not otherwise drink it —Henry Hicks⟩ ⟨the bonds ~ represent the debt —G.B.Robinson⟩ ⟨the kind of . . . church ~ you would expect a decent body of merchants to erect —Douglas Goldring⟩ ⟨a generation ~ had been taught . . . to appreciate the beauty of simplicity —Bernard Groom⟩ ⟨they form the Samnite tribes, ~ settled south and southeast of Rome —Ernst Pulgram⟩ ⟨some of the difficulties ~ must be guarded against —*Eastman Kodak Monthly Abstract Bull.*⟩ ⟨new problems arose, the investigation of ~ would necessitate additional material —Robert Balk⟩; used freely in reference to persons as recently as the 17th century ⟨our Father ~ art in heaven —Mt 6:9 (AV)⟩, and still occas. so used ⟨a human ~ . . . would unhesitatingly sacrifice a score of opossums for a real scientific need —William Beebe⟩ ⟨which of the children ~ are threatened —H.R.Hays⟩ but usu. with some implication of emphasis on the function or role of the person rather than on the person himself ⟨the Republican presidential electors ~ we had chosen at the state convention —W.A.White⟩ ⟨chiefly they wanted husbands, ~ they got easily —Lynn White⟩; used by speakers on all educational levels and by many reputable writers, though disapproved by some grammarians, in reference to an idea expressed by a word or group of words that is not necessarily a noun or noun phrase ⟨the attitude is . . . that failure to publish is tantamount to suppression, ~ of course it isn't —R.H.Rovere⟩ or in reference to a clause or sentence ⟨in August of that year he resigned that post, after ~ he engaged in ranching —*Current Biog.*⟩ ⟨I have forgotten them now. *Which* makes no difference —W.A.White⟩; sometimes used parenthetically in reference to a clause that is yet to come or is not yet complete ⟨yours is the earth and everything that's in it, and — ~ is more — you'll be a man —Rudyard Kipling⟩ ⟨he demonstrated — ~ was indeed the truth — that the days of capitalism were numbered —Christopher Hollis⟩; used regularly to introduce a restrictive relative clause having as its antecedent the demonstrative pronoun *that* ⟨ultimate truth still remains in that outside world of that ~ is —Weston La Barre⟩; sometimes used archaically with preceding *the* ⟨this time of long silence, of reverie, in the ~ . . . his eyes were placidly shut —Maurice Hewlett⟩; sometimes used after *so* or *such* with the implication that the action or state expressed in the clause introduced by *which* is a real or appropriate consequence of what is expressed by the phrase containing *so* or *such* ⟨there is not any argument so absurd, ~ is not daily received —Jeremy Bentham⟩ ⟨there rooted betwixt them then such an affection ~ cannot choose but branch now —Shak.⟩; sometimes used dialectally with a following personal pronoun or possessive adjective referring to the same antecedent ⟨she had a big something under her arm ~ I couldn't make out what it was —Helen Eustis⟩ ⟨the man ~ his head was cut off —*Western Folklore*⟩; occasionally used dialectally as a word that merely introduces a clause or sentence and has no reference to any expressed or implied antecedent ⟨~ we had a small game —Bret Harte⟩; compare [4]THAT 1, WHO, WHOSE, [1]WHAT 3a — **which is which** *or* **which was which** : what is or was the distinct and esp. nameable identity of each member of a group — used as a direct or indirect question ⟨those two fellows are the Jones brothers, John and William, but *which is which*⟩ ⟨so many kings of France named Louis that I can hardly remember *which was which*⟩

whichaway \'==,=\ *dial var of* WHICHWAY

[1]**which·ev·er** \(h)wi'chevə(r)\ *pron* [ME *which ever,* fr. [2]*which* + *ever*] : whatever one or ones out of a group : no matter which one or ones ⟨would like to speak to your father or your mother, ~ is at home⟩ ⟨take two of the four elective subjects, ~ you prefer⟩ ⟨enter law or some other profession, but ~ you choose, put your whole heart into it⟩

[2]**whichever** \"\ *adj* : being whatever one or ones out of a group : no matter which ⟨walk . . . back to ~ chair he happened to be using at the time —Grace Metalious⟩ ⟨a general reserve fund out of which additional advertising money could be drawn to back ~ books need it —*Publishers' Weekly*⟩ ⟨its soothing . . . effect will be the same ~ way you take it —*Punch*⟩

[1]**which·so·ev·er** \¦hwichsō¦wevə(r), -sō¦e- *also* ¦wi-\ *pron* [ME, fr. *which so* whichever (fr. [2]*which* + *so*) + *ever*] : WHICHEVER

[2]**whichsoever** \"\ *adj* : WHICHEVER

whichway *also* **whichways** \'=,=\ *adv* **1** *dial* : WHERE ⟨~ is he⟩ **2** : EVERY WHICH WAY ⟨leaving her towel and brush and comb lying ~ —W.D.Edmonds⟩

[1]**whick·er** \'hwikə(r) *also* 'wi-\ *also* **wick·er** \'wi-\ *vi* -ED/-ING/-S [imit.] : NEIGH, WHINNY ⟨horses . . . pawed, and ~*ed* —John Masefield⟩

[2]**whicker** \"\ *n* -S : NEIGH, WHINNY

[1]**whid** \'(h)wid\ *n* -S [origin unknown] **1** *Brit* : WORD **2** *Scot* : LIE

[2]**whid** \"\ *n* -S [perh. of Scand origin; akin to ON *hvitha* squall of wind — more at WHITHER] *Scot* : a silent rapid motion

[3]**whid** \"\ *vi, Scot* : to move nimbly and silently

whidah *var of* WHYDAH

whiel·don ware \'(h)wēldən-\ *n, usu cap 1st W* [after Thomas *Whieldon* †1795 Eng. potter] : a fine English ceramic ware produced by Thomas Whieldon (1719–95) at his Staffordshire pottery and often characterized by marbleized and tortoise-shell effects

[1]**whiff** \'hwif *also* 'wif\ *n* -S [imit.] **1 a** (1) : a quick puff or slight gust of air ⟨the wind came in ~*s* —Wallace Stegner⟩ (2) : a puff, gust, or wave of odor ⟨wafted a feline ~ —David Walker⟩ (3) : a puff or gust of vapor, gas, or liquid in the air ⟨a ~ of smoke hangs over a sleeping volcano —Richard Church⟩ ⟨~*s* of spray from the fountain —Lawrence Durrell⟩ **b** (1) : an inhalation of odor, smoke, gas, or vapor ⟨she went off at the first ~ of ether —O.S.J.Gogarty⟩ (2) *obs* : a drink or sip of liquor **c** : a slight puffing or whistling sound ⟨the almost inaudible ~ of his spread wings —Saul Bellow⟩ **2** : a slight trace or sample : INTIMATION, HINT ⟨his unerring detection of the faintest ~ of sentiment —H.J.Muller⟩ ⟨there is more than a ~ of propaganda —Richard Mallett⟩

[2]**whiff** \"\ *vb* -ED/-ING/-S *vi* **1** : to move with or as if with a puff of air; *also* : to make or produce a puffing or whistling sound **2** : to emit whiffs **3** : to inhale an odor : engage in sniffing **4** : FAN 4 ~ *vt* **1 a** : to carry or convey by or as if by a whiff : BLOW ⟨the storm . . . ~*ed* smoke and ashes into their faces —Isak Dinesen⟩ **b** : to expel or puff out in a whiff : EXHALE **c** : SMOKE 3a **2** : to cause (a batter) to fan in baseball or softball : strike out

[3]**whiff** \"\ *n* -S [origin unknown] : any of several flatfishes related to the turbot; *esp* : a small European fish (*Lepidorhombus megastoma*)

whif·fet \'hwifət *also* 'wi-\ *n* -S [prob. alter. of *whippet*] **1** : a very small dog **2** : a small, young, or unimportant person : WHIPPERSNAPPER

[1]**whif·fle** \'hwifəl *also* 'wi-\ *vb* **whiffled; whiffled; whiffling** \-f(ə)liŋ\ **whiffles** [prob. fr. [2]*whiff* + *-le*] *vi* **1 a** *of the wind* : to blow unsteadily or in gusts **b** (1) : FLICKER, FLUTTER (2) : to change from one course or opinion to another as if blown by the wind : be fickle : VACILLATE **2 a** : to emit or produce a light whistling or puffing sound **b** : to flourish a sword in sword dancing so as to produce a whistling sound ~ *vt* **1** : to blow, disperse, emit, or expel with or as if with a whiff **2** : to flourish (a sword) in sword dancing so as to produce a whiffling sound

[2]**whiffle** \"\ *n* -S : the action, motion, or sound of whiffling

[1]**whif·fler** \'(h)wiflə(r)\ *n* -S [alter. of earlier *wifler,* fr. obs. E *wifle* battle-ax (fr. ME, fr. OE *wifel* dart, javelin) + E *-er;* akin to ON *veifa* to wave — more at WIFE] *Brit* : one that clears the way for a procession

[2]**whif·fler** \'hwif(ə)lə(r) *also* 'wi-\ *n* -S [[1]*whiffle* + *-er*] **1** : one that frequently changes his opinion or course **2** : one that uses shifts and evasions in argument

whif·fle·tree \'hwifəl(,)trē, -,tri *also* 'wi-\ *or* **whip·ple·tree** \-ipəl-\ *n* [*whiffletree* alter. of *whippletree,* fr. *whipple-* (perh. irreg. fr. *whip*) + *tree*] : the pivoted swinging bar to which the traces of a harness are fastened and by which a vehicle or implement is drawn — called also *singletree, swingletree;* compare DOUBLETREE

[1]**whig** \'(h)wig\ *n* -S [origin unknown] *Scot* : any of various elements or products of milk; *esp* : WHEY

[2]**whig** \'hwig *also* 'wig\ *n* -S *usu cap* [short for *whiggamore*] **1** : a Presbyterian or Covenanter in Scotland in the 17th century — compare TRUE BLUE **2** : one favoring the exclusion in 1679–80 of the Duke of York from the line of succession to the British throne principally because of his Roman Catholicism — usu. used disparagingly; opposed to *Tory* **3** : a member or supporter of the Whig party in British politics **4** : an American favoring colonial interests and esp. independence from Great Britain during the American Revolution — opposed to *Tory* **5** : a member or supporter of the Whig party in American politics

[3]**whig** \"\ *adj, usu cap* **1** : of, relating to, or characterized by Whiggery: as **a** : of, relating to, or constituting one of the two major British political groups of the 18th and early 19th cen-

turies arising from the Roundheads and associated chiefly at first with support of the Hanoverians but later with efforts to limit the royal authority and increase parliamentary power and with preference for Dissenters rather than the established Anglican church — compare CONSERVATIVE 2b(1), KING'S FRIENDS, LIBERAL 5d(1), RADICAL 3c(1), TORY a **b :** of, relating to, or constituting a major 19th century American political party arising about 1834 from the National Republicans and other groups opposed to the Jacksonian Democrats and associated chiefly with manufacturing, commercial, and financial interests, a protective tariff, a national government public works program, and opposition to a strong presidency until succeeded about 1854 by the Republican party **2 :** favoring, belonging to, or composed of members of a Whig party or group ⟨*Whig* candidates⟩ ⟨*Whig* platform⟩

⁴whig \'(h)wig\ *vi* **whigged; whigged; whigging; whigs** [perh. fr. ²*whig*] *Scot* **:** to move steadily on **:** jog along

whig·ga·more \'(h)wigə,mō(ə)r\ *n* -s *usu cap* [perh. irreg. fr. obs. E dial. *whig* yokel, rustic, perh. fr. E ¹*whig*] **1 :** a member of a band composed largely of inhabitants of the southwestern part of Scotland that in 1648 marched to Edinburgh to oppose the king, Duke of Hamilton, and court party **2 :** ³WHIG 1

whig·gery \'hwigərē, -ri *also* 'wi-\ *n* -ES *usu cap* **1 :** the principles, policies, and practices of or associated with Whigs ⟨American Liberalism . . . smacks more of eighteenth-century *Whiggery* —*Manchester Guardian Weekly*⟩ **2 :** a Whig party or its members ⟨sympathize with the low-churchmen of *Whiggery* —D.P.French⟩

whig·gi·fy \-gə,fī\ *vt* -ED/-ING/-ES *sometimes cap* **:** to make Whig **:** influence by Whig principles or policies

whig·gish \-gish, -gēsh\ *adj, sometimes cap* **:** of, relating to, or having the characteristics of a Whig **:** inclined toward Whiggery ⟨~ principles⟩

whig·gish·ly *adv, often cap* **:** in a whiggish manner ⟨persons . . . ~ inclined —Narcissus Luttrell⟩

whig·gism *or* **whig·ism** \'hwi,gizəm *also* 'wi,-\ *n* -s *usu cap* **:** WHIGGERY 1

whig·ling \-gliŋ\ *n* -s *usu cap* **:** a petty Whig

whig·ma·lee·rie *also* **whig·ma·lee·ry** \,hwigmə'lirē, -ri *also* ,wig-\ *n, pl* **whigmaleeries** [origin unknown] **1 :** WHIM, VAGARY, FANCY ⟨shy fellow full of caprice and ~ —*Life*⟩ **2 :** an odd or fanciful contrivance **:** GIMCRACK, NOTION ⟨producing gadgets, gimmicks, fizgigs, and ~s for Latin-American consumption —Alva Johnston⟩

¹while \'hwīl, *esp before pause or consonant* -īəl; *also* 'wī-\ *n* -s [ME *whil, while,* fr. OE *hwīl;* akin to OHG *hwīla* time, while, ON *hvīla* bed, Goth *hweila* time, while, L *quies* rest, quiet, OSlav *pokojĭ* rest] **1 a :** a period of time **:** TIME ⟨any critic may after a ~ exhaust his interest in a subject —C.W.Shumaker⟩ ⟨takes us quite a ~ to find out —Sean O'Faolain⟩ **b :** the time during which an action takes place or a condition exists ⟨looking here and there and calling his name, though I knew all the ~ it was too late —Mary Webb⟩ ⟨went to her herb garden for her seasonings . . . and thus preserved the health of her family, the ~ she saved her purse —Van Wyck Brooks⟩ **c :** the time at which an event takes place **:** a time marked by the occurrence of an action or a condition **:** OCCASION ⟨one ~, it seems, he trapped in the . . . mountains —J.F.Dobie⟩ ⟨were ~s when I was terrible bored —John Buchan⟩ **d :** a relatively short period of time **:** a brief time ⟨if you've been reading this book for over an hour, you'd better put it aside for a ~ —W.J.Reilly⟩ ⟨went away and came back again in a ~ —Pearl Buck⟩ **e :** the period of time needed (as for the performance of an action) ⟨a breathing ~ —Shak.⟩ **f** *archaic* **:** a time marked by bad conditions ⟨God help the ~ —Shak.⟩ **2 :** the time and effort used (as in the performance of an action) **:** TROUBLE, EXERTION ⟨aesthetic matters are important, and . . . it is worth the ~ of a healthy male to take them seriously —H.L.Mencken⟩ ⟨knew all the right people too because it was worth their ~ to know him —J.P.Marquand⟩

²while \"\ *conj* [ME *whil, while,* fr. *whil, while,* n.] **1 a :** during the time that ⟨instructed and encouraged the boy ~ he made an almost incredible . . . record of precocity —Alexander Cowie⟩ ⟨were killed ~ attempting a burglary —A.F.Harlow⟩ **b :** until the end of the time that **:** as long as ⟨~ there's life there's hope⟩ **c :** during which time **:** and during the same time **:** and meanwhile ⟨hurried to get ready ~ the others just sat⟩ **2** *archaic* **:** UNTIL ⟨~ hunger make you eat —Christopher Marlowe⟩ **3 a :** at the same time that on the contrary **:** when on the other hand **:** WHEREAS ⟨for many people a line of ten words requires perhaps eight fixations, ~ a good reader can grasp half a line as a unit —Russell Cosper & Barriss Mills⟩ ⟨~ her book shows the uneven hand of a novice at writing, it frequently stops the reader by its poetic simplicity —Rose Feld⟩ **b :** in spite of the fact that **:** ALTHOUGH ⟨~ the evidence he has obtained may be said to fit the theory, the importance of some of it is questionable —*Notes & Queries*⟩ ⟨~ a magnificent organizer of espionage, he was a poor observer himself —Allen Upward⟩ **4 :** at the same time that in a similar manner **:** when correspondingly **:** and also ⟨~ the book will be welcomed by scholars, it will make an immediate appeal to the general reader —*Brit. Bk. News*⟩ ⟨wild grapes grow in profusion along the sides of back roads, ~ blackberries and wild raspberries are common —*Amer. Guide Series: N.H.*⟩

³while \"\ *prep* [ME *whil,* fr. *whil, while,* n.] *archaic* **:** UNTIL ⟨~ then, God be with you —Shak.⟩

⁴while \"\ *vb* -ED/-ING/-S [¹*while*] *vt* **:** to cause to pass esp. without boredom or in a pleasant manner — usu. used with *away* ⟨*whiled* away the tedium of debate by drawing caricatures —Dumas Malone⟩ ⟨may ~ away the time tootling on his recorder —*Newsweek*⟩ ~ *vi, archaic* **:** to pass tediously —

whil·er \-lə(r)\ *n* -s

whileas \(')=,=\ *conj, archaic* **:** WHILE

whilere \(')=,=\ *adv* [ME *whileer,* fr. OE *hwīle ǣr,* fr. *hwīle* formerly, once (fr. *hwīle,* accus. of *hwīl* time, while) + *ǣr* early, earlier — more at ERE] *archaic* **:** a while ago **:** some time before

¹whiles \'hwī(ə)lz *also* 'wī-\ *conj* [ME, fr. *whil, while,* conj., while + -*es,* gen. sing. ending of nouns (functioning adverbially) — more at -S] **1** *archaic* **:** WHILE 1 **2** *obs* **:** UNTIL ⟨he shall conceal it ~ you are willing it shall come to note —Shak.⟩ **3** *obs* **:** WHILE 3a

²whiles \"\ *n* [ME, fr. -*whiles* (as in *otherwhiles*) — more at OTHERWHILE] *archaic* **:** WHILE 1a, 1b, 1c, 1d

³whiles \"\ *adv* [ME(Sc) *quhilis* at times, formerly, fr. ME(Sc) *quhile,* ME *while* at times, formerly (fr. OE *hwīle* formerly, once) + ME(Sc) -*is,* ME -*es,* gen. sing. ending of nouns (functioning adverbially)] *chiefly Scot* **:** at times **:** from time to time **:** SOMETIMES ⟨we read your things in the paper, and we ~ read about you —John Buchan⟩

whil·ie *also* **whiley** \'(h)wīli\ *n* [¹*while* + -*ie*] *Scot* **:** a little while

¹whilk \'(h)wilk\ *chiefly Scot var of* WHICH

²whilk \"\ *archaic var of* WHELK

whil·kut \'hwil,küt *also* 'wī-\ *n, pl* **whilkut** *or* **whilkuts** *usu cap* **1 :** an Athapaskan people of the Mad river valley in northwestern California **2 :** a member of the Whilkut people

whil·la·bal·loo \'(h)wiləbə,lü\ *Scot & Irish var of* HULLABALOO

whil·la·loo *also* **whil·la·luh** *or* **whil·li·lew** \'(h)wilə,lü\ *n* [IrGael *uile liūgh*] *dial Brit* **:** HULLABALOO

whil·li·kers \'(h)wilə̇kə(r)z, -lēk-\ *or* **whil·li·kins** \-kə̇nz\ *interj* [origin unknown] **:** ⁶GEE

whil·ly \'(h)wili\ *vt* [prob. irreg. fr. ¹*whillywha*] *Scot* **:** CAJOLE, WHEEDLE, GULL

¹whil·ly·wha *also* **whil·ly·whaw** \'(h)wili,(h)wȯ\ *n* -s [origin unknown] **1** *Scot* **:** a deceitful flatterer **2** *chiefly Scot* **:** a coaxing deceitful speech — usu. used in pl.

²whillywha \"\ *vt, Scot* **:** to dupe by flattering **:** WHEEDLE, CAJOLE ~ *vi, Scot* **:** to talk in a coaxing manner

¹whi·lom \'hwīləm *also* 'wī-\ *adv* [ME, formerly, at times, fr. OE *hwīlum* at times, dat. pl. of *hwīl* time, while — more at WHILE] *archaic* **:** at a time in the past **:** FORMERLY, ONCE

²whilom \"\ *adj* [ME, fr. *whilom,* adv.] **:** having been at an earlier time **:** FORMER ⟨the poor gentleman had grievous treatment at the hands of ~ friends —Agnes Repplier⟩

¹whilst \'hwī(ə)lst *also* 'wī-\ *conj* [ME *whilest,* alter. of ¹*whiles*] **1** *chiefly Brit* **:** WHILE 1, 3, 4 **2** *archaic* **:** UNTIL

²whilst \"\ *n* [ME (northern dial.) *quilest,* fr. ME (northern dial.) *quilest,* ME *whilest,* conj.] *archaic* **:** WHILE

¹whim \'hwim *also* 'wim\ *n* -s [short for *whim-wham*] **1** *archaic* **:** a fanciful or fantastic device, object, or creation **2 :** a capricious or eccentric idea, notion, or vagary usu. occurring suddenly or spontaneously **:** CAPRICE, FANCY ⟨every royal master had ~s of his own — antiquated prejudices, family ties, fragments of knowledge to which he attached exaggerated importance —A.J.P.Taylor⟩ ⟨the ~ struck him to become an army flier —Green Peyton⟩ ⟨a defense of reason against unreason, conviction against ~, knowledge against mere shifting mood-of-the-moment —Alan Devoe⟩ ⟨~s of nature⟩ ⟨~s of fate⟩ **3 a** *or* **whim gin** *also* **whin** \-in\ **:** a hoisting device esp. for raising ore or water from mines consisting of a large vertical drum on which a rope is wound with one or more radiating arms or beams to which a horse may be yoked — called also *whimsy* **b** *Austral* **:** a large jinker

²whim \"\ *vt* **whimmed; whimmed; whimming; whims :** to desire fancifully or capriciously

whim·brel *or* **wimbrel** \'(h)wimbrəl\ *n* -s [perh. imit.] **:** a European curlew (*Numenius phaeopus*) related and similar to the Hudsonian curlew of America

whim gin *n* **:** WHIM 3a

¹whim·per \'hwimpə(r) *also* 'wi-\ *vb* **whimpered; whimpered; whimpering** \-p(ə)riŋ\ **whimpers** [imit.] *vi* **1 a :** to make a low whining plaintive or broken sound ⟨had seen the old general ~ like a whipped dog —F.M.Ford⟩ **b :** to complain or protest with or in the manner of a whimper **:** WAIL, WHINE ⟨always coming around to ~ over his troubles⟩ ⟨knocking on the door to ~ for admission⟩ **2 :** to make a low plaintive murmuring sound ⟨the wind ~s in the aspens⟩ ⟨the tiny brook ~s softly through the stones and mosses⟩ ~ *vt* **:** to utter with or in a whimper ⟨they neither bray nor ~ nihilism; they prefer to fight —Charles Lee⟩ ⟨were forever ~*ing* that God had hidden his face from them —L.C.Douglas⟩

²whimper \"\ *n* -s **1 :** a low whining broken cry **:** a low peevish sound expressive of complaint or grief ⟨the baby continued to cry, but its cries . . . were little more than troubled ~s —Roark Bradford⟩ ⟨when the pack had been taken over half a dozen fields, there came a ~ and then a lifting chorus —E.J. Oates⟩ ⟨the moaning ~ of the tenor saxophone⟩ **2 :** a petulant or puling complaint or protest ⟨without even a ~ of protest from party headquarters —*Time*⟩ ⟨the old ~ of sterility that comes up in every decade —*New Statesman & Nation*⟩

whim·per·ing·ly *adv* [*whimpering* (pres. part. of ¹*whimper*) + -*ly*] **:** in a whimpering manner **:** with whimpering

whim·si·cal \'hwimzə̇kəl, -zēk- *also* 'wi-\ *adj* [¹*whimsy* + -*ical*] **1 :** full of, actuated by, or exhibiting whims **:** CAPRICIOUS, NOTIONAL, FANCIFUL ⟨although so sedate, she was also ~ and freakish —Virginia Woolf⟩ ⟨hard to tell when he was really peevish or merely ~ —W.L.Howard⟩ **2 a :** resulting from or determined or characterized by whim or caprice ⟨a glint of provocative, ~ fun in his blue eyes —Monica Pearson⟩ ⟨~ notions which indicate that reason is out of touch with the real —Marjorie Harris⟩ ⟨~, precarious, unlikely ventures —Audrey Barker⟩ ⟨~ evaluations of justice and equity . . . based on a purely social concept —*Current Biog.*⟩ ⟨many of these ~ creations seem to suffer from too much striving to be different —Betty Pepis⟩ **b :** subject to erratic behavior or unpredictable change **:** UNCERTAIN ⟨one cotton mill and a ~ power plant —Virginia A. Oakes⟩ ⟨a ~ market fluctuating according to world conditions⟩ ⟨the ~ moods of the Alpine sun —Claudia Cassidy⟩ — **whim·si·cal·ly** \-zə̇k(ə)lē, -zēk-, -li\ *adv* — **whim·si·cal·ness** *n* -ES

whim·si·cal·i·ty \,hwimzə'kalədē, -lətē, -i *also* ,wi-\ *n* -ES **:** the quality or state of being whimsical **:** WHIMSICALNESS ⟨to liberate a small nation simply because one approves of it is mere ~ —Robert Lynd⟩

whim·sied \'hwimzēd, -zid *also* 'wim-\ *adj* **:** filled with whimsies **:** WHIMSICAL

¹whim·sy *or* **whim·sey** \-zē, -zi\ *n, pl* **whimsies** *or* **whimseys** [irreg. fr. *whim-wham*] **1 :** WHIM, CAPRICE, VAGARY ⟨applies the results of scientific knowledge . . . to satisfy material human needs and *whimsies* —I.I.Rabi⟩ ⟨our peculiar *whimseys,* prejudices, or intellectual limitations —M.R.Cohen⟩ ⟨carved by the ~ of ancient glaciers —*Christian Science Monitor*⟩ **2 :** a fanciful or fantastic device, object, or creation esp. in writing, art, or decoration ⟨can mix realism with an agreeable touch of poetry and fantasy that never degenerates into ~ —*Times Lit. Supp.*⟩ ⟨tells himself that myth is mere ~ having no relevance to human life —Richard Chase⟩ ⟨Victorian ~ returned . . . and glitter and embroidery replaced the lack of fabric trimming —*Fashion Digest*⟩ **3 :** WHIM 3a

²whimsy *or* **whimsey** \"\ *adj* **:** WHIMSICAL

whim·sy-wham·sy \-'(h)wamzē\ *n* -ES [redupl. of ¹*whimsy*] **:** WHIM-WHAM ⟨gremlins are . . . supposed to cause trouble such as engine failure in airplanes, a curious piece of *whimsy-whamsy* —Henry Alexander⟩ ⟨the theme of displaced war orphans . . . becomes here, in spite of shrewd descriptive touches, plain *whimsy-whamsy* —Sarah Campion⟩

whim-wham \'hwim,(h)wam, -aam *also* 'wi-\ *n* [origin unknown] **1 :** a whimsical object or device esp. of ornament or dress **:** TRIFLE, TRINKET ⟨a beret and a raffish tweed *whim-wham* —S.J.Perelman⟩ ⟨among the 16 *whim-whams* missing: . . . a pair of earrings —*Time*⟩ **2 :** NOTION, FANCY, WHIM ⟨these papers on society and its *whim-whams* or fads —E.W. Morse⟩ ⟨relish for personalities, gossips, *whim-whams* —S.T. Williams⟩ **3 whim-whams** *also* **wim-wams** *pl* **:** JIMJAMS, JITTERS ⟨took barbiturates to kill the *whim-whams* —G.V. Jones⟩ ⟨that job would have given me the *whim-whams* for a month —Howard Greig⟩

¹whin \'hwin *also* 'win\ *n* -s [ME (northern dial.) *quin,* of unknown origin] **:** a particularly hard rock; *esp* **:** one that on weathering cumbers the ground with large fragments **:** WHINSTONE

²whin \"\ *n* -s [ME *whynne,* of Scand origin; akin to Sw *ven* bent grass, Norw *kvein* bent grass, Sw dial. *hven* swamp — more at OBSCENE] **1 :** FURZE **2 :** WOODWAXEN

³whin *var of* WHIM

whin·berry \'=,=— *see* BERRY\ *n* [alter. (influenced by ²*whin*) of earlier *winberry,* fr. ME *wynneberie,* fr. OE *wīnberige* whortleberry, grape — more at WINEBERRY] *dial Eng* **:** WHORTLEBERRY 1

whinchat \'=,=\ *n* [²*whin* + *chat*] **:** a small European saxicoline bird (*Saxicola rubetra*) that is mottled brown and buff above and buff below with white markings on the wings and above and below the eyes and that is usu. found in grassy meadows

whin·dle \'(h)windᵊl\ *vi* [freq. of ¹*whine*] *dial chiefly Eng* **:** WHINE, WHIMPER

¹whine \'hwīn *also* 'wīn\ *vb* -ED/-ING/-S [ME *whinen,* fr. OE *hwīnan* to whiz; akin to ON *hvīna* to whiz and perh. to OSlav *svistati* to hiss] *vi* **1 a :** to utter a high-pitched plaintive or distressed cry ⟨hearing the dog ~ at the door⟩ ⟨tossing and turning, the child ~s in its sleep⟩ **b :** to make a sound similar to such a cry ⟨the saws buzz and ~ —*Amer. Guide Series: Maine*⟩ ⟨sirens *whined* loud and clear —*Springfield (Mass.) Union*⟩ ⟨car starters ~ and trucks . . . rattle out —Marjory S. Douglas⟩ **c :** to move or proceed with the sound of a whine ⟨mosquitoes *whined* through the dark —Josephine Johnson⟩ ⟨the bullet *whined* over the heads of the boys —S.H.Holbrook⟩ ⟨a taxi *whined* through the streets —Walter Sorell & Denver Lindley⟩ ⟨the wind . . . *whined* and moaned through the rigging —Kenneth Roberts⟩ **2 :** to utter a complaint or lament with or as if with a whine ⟨is not a man to ~ and complain; he has too much spirit —Jane Austen⟩ ⟨~ about . . . her troubles —E.A.Weeks⟩ ⟨the counteraction of the doctrine of love when that pules and ~s —R.W.Emerson⟩ ~ *vt* **:** to utter or express with or as if with a whine ⟨the prisoner ~s his innocence⟩ ⟨~ the song in nasal tones⟩ ⟨~ their troubles to the world⟩

²whine \"\ *n* -s **1 a :** a prolonged high-pitched cry usu. expressive of distress or pain ⟨weak, premature babies will cry with a low feeble ~ . . . like the mewing of a cat —Morris Fishbein⟩ ⟨the strange uncontrollable ~ of a man weeping —Graham Greene⟩ — compare WHIMPER **b :** a sound resembling such a cry ⟨the ~ of the wind and the hiss of the sleety snow —F.V.W. Mason⟩ ⟨the ~ of the saw biting into a log —*Amer. Guide Series: Ark.*⟩ ⟨the ~ and whistle of bombs —Peter Ustinov⟩ ⟨the high-pitched ~ of the engines —*London Calling*⟩ ⟨the ~ of the Hawaiian boy's guitar —Frances McFadden⟩ **2 :** a complaint or lament uttered with or as if with a whine ⟨wearied by the unremitting ~ of her special pleading —Dwight MacDonald⟩ ⟨if your letter is a gripe or ~, it will be brushed off —H.D.Scott⟩ ⟨the self-pitying ~ of most contemporary fiction —Selden Rodman⟩

whin·er \-nə(r)\ *n* -s **:** one that whines

whing \'(h)wiŋ *also* 'wiŋ\ *n* -s [imit.] **:** a sharp high-pitched ringing sound ⟨came the sustained ~ of a bullet that ricocheted somewhere near —Donald Stokes⟩ — sometimes used interjectionally

whing–ding \'(h)wiŋ,diŋ\ *var of* WINGDING

whinge \'(h)winj\ *vi* **whinged; whinged; whingeing** *also* **whinging; whinges** [fr. (assumed) ME (northern dial.) *whingen,* fr. OE *hwinsian;* akin to OHG *winsōn* to moan; derivative fr. the root of E ¹*whine*] *dial Brit* **:** WHINE, WHIMPER

whing·er \'(h)wiŋ(g)ə(r), -injə-\ *n* -s [by alter.] *chiefly Scot* **:** WHINYARD

whin·i·ness \'hwīnēnə̇s, -nin- *also* 'wī-\ *n* -ES **:** the quality or state of being whiny **:** QUERULOUSNESS

whin·ing·ly *adv* [*whining* (pres. part. of ¹*whine*) + -*ly*] **:** in a whining tone or manner ⟨the boards creaked ~ beneath their feet —Donn Byrne⟩

whin·ner \'hwinə(r) *also* 'wi-\ *vi* [freq. of ¹*whine*] **1** *dial* **:** to whine feebly **2** *dial* **:** WHINNY, WHICKER

whin·nock \'(h)winək\ *vi* [prob. irreg. fr. ¹*whine*] *dial Eng* **:** WHIMPER

¹whin·ny \'hwinē, -ni *also* 'wi-\ *adj* [ME *whynny,* fr. *whynne* whin + -*y*] *archaic* **:** abounding in gorse or furze

²whinny \"\ *vb* -ED/-ING/-ES [perh. irreg. fr. ¹*whine*] *vi* **:** to neigh esp. in a low or gentle fashion **:** WHICKER ⟨the white mares . . . *whinnied* and shook their bells —William Saroyan⟩ ⟨she was stepping high and *whinnied* to her old teammates of the wagon —Hervey Allen⟩ ~ *vt* **:** to utter with or as if with a whinny ⟨the horses ~ their greeting from the stalls⟩

³whinny \"\ *n* -ES **1 :** NEIGH, WHICKER ⟨a low ~ told her in what stall her horse would be —Elizabeth M. Roberts⟩ **2 :** a sound resembling a whinny **:** WHINE ⟨gave a kind of ~ between hysteria and indignation —Katherine A. Porter⟩ ⟨a clatter of machinery and the piercing ~ of old valves —John Cheever⟩

whins *pl of* WHIN

whinstone \'=,=\ *n* [¹*whin* + *stone*] **:** basaltic rock **:** TRAP; *also* **:** any of various other dark resistant rocks (as chert)

whiny *or* **whiney** \'hwīnē, -ni *also* 'wī-\ *adj* **whinier; whiniest :** WHINING, QUERULOUS ⟨people get rude and ~ and exacting when they are exhausted —Peggy Durdin⟩

whin·yard \'hwinyə(r)d *also* 'wi-\ *n* [ME *whyneherd, whyneard*] **:** a short sword

¹whip \'hw|ip *also* 'w|; *dial* |ùp *or* |əp\ *vb* **whipped; whipped; whipping; whips** [ME *wippen, whippen;* akin to MLG & MD *wippen* to move up and down, sway, swing, MHG *wipfen* to jump, leap, OE *wipian* to wipe — more at WIPE] *vt* **1 a :** to take, pull, snatch, jerk or otherwise move very quickly and forcefully — usu. used with *out* ⟨*whipped* out his gun —Green Peyton⟩ ⟨*whipped* out an old tattered leather wallet —Irwin Shaw⟩ **b :** to throw or project with great speed ⟨*whipped* a fast ball across⟩ ⟨saw a rocket *whipped* into space —John Lardner⟩ **2 a :** to strike with a lash, rod, whip, or other slender lithe implement ⟨*whipped* Macleod across the face with his cane —Ian Finlay⟩ **:** to punish by beating **:** FLOG ⟨*whipped* for witchcraft —*Amer. Guide Series: Conn.*⟩; *broadly* **:** SPANK ⟨a tired child should never be *whipped*⟩ **b :** to drive with a whip **:** make go by or as if by using a whip **:** force or urge on ⟨*whipped* up the old mare —E.T.Thurston⟩ ⟨have to ~ themselves to their work —Ira Wolfert⟩ **c :** to make or bring out by or as if by striking with a whip ⟨the wind *whipped* tears in her eyes⟩ **d :** to strike as a lash does ⟨a brisk breeze *whipped* the surface of the river —C.S.Forester⟩ **3 a :** to bind or wrap (as a fishing rod) with twine or other small cord in order to protect and strengthen ⟨~ a rope⟩ **b :** to bind (a rope end) with sail twine or other small stuff in order to prevent fraying or unlaying **4 a :** to punish esp. with stinging words **:** make suffer **:** ABUSE ⟨they would ~ me with their fine wits —Shak.⟩ **b :** CONFOUND ⟨~ me such honest knaves —Shak.⟩ **5 :** to seam or hem with shallow overcasting stitches (as on gloves, napkins, lace) **6 :** to thoroughly overcome **:** DEFEAT ⟨they never knew when they were *whipped* —L.C.Douglas⟩ ⟨the crew is not out to ~ a rival boat —Frederick Way⟩ **7 :** to stir up **:** AROUSE, INCITE — usu. used with *up* ⟨deliberately trying to ~ up a new emotion —Ellen Glasgow⟩ ⟨*whipped* up his interest in radical causes —Ishbel Ross⟩ **8 :** to make or compose in or as if in an extemporaneous manner **:** produce in a hurry — usu. used with *up* ⟨a sketch . . . an artist might ~ up but not the actual blueprint —*N.Y.Times*⟩ **9 :** to fish (water) with rod, line, and artificial lure with a motion like that employed in using a whip **10 :** to beat (as eggs) usu. with a whisk, fork, or other instrument to increase volume by incorporation of air into the material ⟨*whipping* plastic⟩ **11 :** to gather together or hold together for united action in the manner of a party whip ~ *vi* **1 :** to move nimbly **:** start, turn, go or pass quickly or suddenly **:** WHISK ⟨*whipped* around the corner⟩ ⟨*whipping* through the supper dishes —C.B.Davis⟩ **2 :** to thrash about flexibly in the manner of a whiplash **:** SWISH ⟨a flag on shore is *whipping* out from its staff —H.A.Calahan⟩ **3 :** to fish by whipping the water — **whip into shape :** to bring forcefully to a desired state or condition ⟨could have been *whipped into shape* at a fraction of the cost of government study —C.B. Rawson⟩ — **whip the devil around the stump :** to effect by indirect means or by subterfuge what cannot be accomplished directly ⟨it was characteristic . . . that he could *whip the devil around the stump* yet really give him a whipping —G.W.Johnson⟩

²whip \"\ *n* -s [ME *wippe, whippe,* fr. *wippen, whippen,* v.] **1 a :** an instrument consisting usu. of a handle and lash forming a flexible rod that is used for whipping — see HORSEWHIP, RIDING WHIP

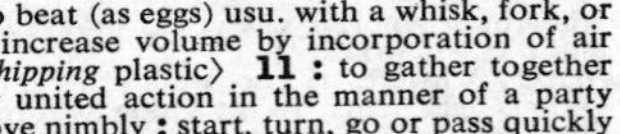

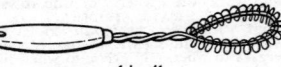

whip 4b

b : something that resembles or acts as a whip ⟨the wind had a ~ in it —J.B.Clayton⟩ ⟨more violent in their wielding of the ~ of scorn —F.B.Millett⟩ ⟨he will never be a ~ for any cause —Jean Burden⟩ **2 :** a stroke or cut with or as if with a whip ⟨a quick ~ of the eyes and he passed —D.M.Davin⟩ **3 a :** a plant (as a fruit tree) having one season's growth from the time of budding or grafting and usu. forming a simple unbranched shoot **b :** a tall slender tree unlikely to develop into a desirable crop tree and harmful to its neighbors by its swaying **4 a :** a dessert made by whipping a portion of the ingredients (as cream, whites of eggs, ice cream, or gelatine) **b :** a kitchen utensil made of braided or coiled wire or perforated metal with a handle and used in whipping cream, whites of eggs, or other materials **5 :** one of the arms of a windmill on which the sails are spread **6 a :** SINGLE WHIP **b :** DOUBLE WHIP **7 :** one that handles a whip: as **a :** a driver of horses **:** COACHMAN ⟨a noted ~ in those days of the stagecoach —H.C.Barnabee⟩ **b :** WHIPPER-IN 1 **8 :** an extra yarn in figure weaving not belonging to either warp or filling **9 a :** a member of a legislative body appointed by his political party to act as a liaison between the leaders and the other members of the party primarily to enforce party discipline and to secure the attendance of party members at important sessions esp. for voting **b** *sometimes cap* **:** a document received by a member of the British House of Commons from his political party ⟨the ~ recites the business to be taken in the following week —Herbert Morrison⟩ **10 :** WHIP-ROUND **11 a :** a whipping motion **:** a thrashing about ⟨the ~ of a snapped cable⟩ **b :** the transverse vibration of the muzzle end of long guns **c :** an unstable motion back and forth in a mechanical part (as a loose bearing) **12 :** the quality of being flexible **:** FLEXIBILITY, GIVE ⟨knobby canes with the ~ of whalebone and the toughness of steel —*Irish Digest*⟩ ⟨a racket frame that has too much ~ —Jack Kramer⟩ **13 :** any of various pieces that operate with a quick vibratory motion (as a spring in an electrical device for making a circuit or a rocking lever actuated by the prolong in a piano action) **14 :** an amusement device of cars which circle with sudden jerks **15 :** a short vertical antenna usu. used in mobile radio equipment consisting of a rod or streamlined stub similar in general appearance to a horsewhip

whipbird \'=,=\ *n* **:** COACHWHIP BIRD

whipcord \'=,=\ *n, often attrib* [ME *wippecord, whippecord,* fr. *wippe, whippe* whip + *cord*] **1 a :** a thin tough cord made of

braided or twisted hemp or catgut often used for whips and whiplashes **b :** a twilled cloth made usu. of hard-twisted cotton or worsted yarns with fine diagonal cords or ribs on the face and used chiefly for sportswear, uniforms, and upholstery **2 :** either of two marine brown algae having very long slender flexible fronds: **a :** a seaweed (*Chorda filum*) of the order Laminariales **b :** a smaller seaweed (*Chordaria flagelliformis*) of the order Chordariales

whipcrack \ˈ⸗,⸗\ *n* **:** the cracking of a whip; *also* **:** a sound resembling the crack of a whip ⟨the hollow rising hum of skis . . . ended in the tiny furious ~*s* of flapping pants as the jumper became airborne —*Newsweek*⟩

whip–cracker \ˈ⸗,⸗⸗\ *n* **:** one that cracks a whip **:** one whose position enables him to exact authority

whip crane *n* **:** a simple form of crane on the principle of the wheel and axle

whip eel *n* **:** an eel of the family Moringuidae

whip–ended \ˈ⸗,⸗⸗\ *adj, of an archery bow* **:** bending too much near the ends

whip graft *n* **1** *or* **whip and tongue graft :** a plant graft made by interlocking a small tongue and notch in the obliquely cut base of the scion with corresponding cuts in the stock — called also *tongue graft;* see GRAFT illustration **2 :** SPLICE GRAFT

whip grass *n* **:** an American nut rush (*Scleria triglomerata*) with stout angled stems and flat leaves

whip hand *n* **1 :** the hand holding the whip in driving **2 :** positive control **:** ADVANTAGE ⟨have been negotiating as if they had the *whip hand* —*N.Y.Times*⟩

whip hoist *n* **:** SINGLE WHIP

whip kick *n* **:** BREASTSTROKE KICK

¹**whiplash** \ˈ⸗,⸗\ *n* [²*whip* + *lash*] **1 a :** the lash of a whip ⟨the lion trainer's ~ —E.B.White⟩ **b :** something resembling or thought to resemble a blow from a whip ⟨the ~ of fear or panic —R.S.Banay⟩ ⟨the ~ of inflation —E.O.Hauser⟩ **2 :** a flagellum having a long rigid basal portion and a short thin lash — compare FLIMMER, TINSEL

²**whiplash** \"\ *vt* **:** to flay with or as if with a whip ⟨~*ed* by that determination that distinguished him —B.P.Thomas⟩

whiplash injury *n* **:** injury of the cervical spine and cerebral concussion occurring in an automobile collision which causes forceful flexion or extension of the neck and violent oscillation of the head forward and backward or backward and forward

whiplike \ˈ⸗,⸗\ *adj* **:** resembling a whip ⟨the ~ tail of the stingray⟩

whipmaster \ˈ⸗,⸗⸗\ *n* **:** one that uses a whip **:** one that exerts power and control

whip·pa·ree *also* **whip·pe·ree** \ˌhwipəˈrē *also* ˌwi-\ *n* -S [alter. of *whip ray*] **:** STINGRAY

whipped *adj* [fr. past part. of ¹*whip*] **1 :** subjected to whipping **2 :** beaten until light and frothy ⟨~ cream⟩ **3 :** beaten with or as if with a whip **:** BROKEN, DEFEATED ⟨the men . . . had the ~ look of vagabonds —Kenneth Roberts⟩

whip·per \ˈhwipə(r) *also* ˈwi-\ *n* -S **:** one that whips

whipper–in \ˈ⸗⸗ˈ⸗\ *n, pl* **whippers–in** [*whip in,* v. + *-er*] **1 a :** a huntsman's assistant who whips in the hounds **b :** one whose position is analogous to a huntsman's assistant **2 :** WHIP 9 **3 :** the last horse in a race

whip·per·snap·per \ˈhwipə(r),snapə(r) *also* ˈwi-\ *n* [alter. (influenced by *whip*) of *snippersnapper*] **:** a diminutive, insignificant, or presumptuous person

whippertail \ˈ⸗⸗,⸗\ *n, NewEng* **:** a common smooth dogfish (*Mustelus canis*) of the western Atlantic

whip·pet \ˈhwipət *also* ˈwi-; *usu* -əd·+V\ *n* -S [prob. fr. ¹*whip* (to move nimbly) + *-et*] **1 a** *obs* **:** a small dog **b :** a small swift slender dog of greyhound type developed in the north of England from a cross between the Italian greyhound and a terrier **2** *also* **whippet tank :** a small tank used in World War I by the Allied armies

whip·pi·ness \ˈhwipēnəs *also* ˈwi-\ *n* -ES **:** the quality or state of being whippy

whipping *n* -S [fr. gerund of ¹*whip*] **1 :** the act of one that whips: as **a :** a severe beating or chastisement ⟨took the ~ without a murmur⟩ **b :** stitching with small overcasting stitches **c :** fishing in water with rod, line, and artificial lures **2 :** material used to whip or bind: as **a :** small stuff with which a rope end is whipped; *also* **:** the finished lashing or binding as opposed to the material it is made of **b :** pitched twine that binds together the head and shaft of a golf club **c :** SERVING 3

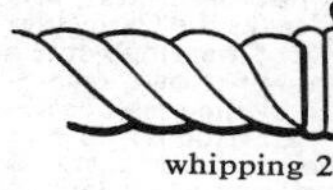
whipping 2a

whipping boy *n* **1 :** a boy formerly educated with a prince and punished in his stead **2 :** SCAPEGOAT ⟨the favorite *whipping boy* of French letters, the French middle class —*Time*⟩

whipping cream *n* **:** cream suitable for whipping containing not less than 30 percent and as much as 36 percent of butterfat — compare COFFEE CREAM

whipping post *n* **:** a post formerly usu. in public to which offenders are tied to be legally whipped

whipping tom *n, usu cap T* [*Tom* fr. *Tom,* nickname for *Thomas*] **:** one conspicuous for whipping others

whipping top *or* **whip top** *n* **:** a top that is spun by whipping

whippletree *var of* WHIFFLETREE

whip·poor·will \ˌ(h)wipə(r)ˌwil *also* -i(p)(ˌ)pu̇rˌw- *or* -u̇əˌw-\ *n* -S [imit.] **1 :** a nocturnal goatsucker (*Caprimulgus vociferus*) of the eastern U.S. and Canada that is related to the European nightjar, that is seldom seen although its call is often heard at nightfall or just before dawn, that is spotted, barred, and vermiculated with black, brown, and buffy, and that has the terminal half of the outer tail feathers white and a crescent in the throat which is white in the male and buffy in the female **2** *NewEng* **:** a moccasin flower (*Cypripedium acaule*)

whippoorwill's–shoe \ˈ⸗⸗,⸗ˈ⸗\ *n, pl* **whippoorwill's–shoes 1 :** an American plant of the genus *Cypripedium* **2** *also* **whippoorwill's–boot** \ˈ⸗⸗,⸗ˈ⸗\ *pl* **whippoorwill's–boots :** a pitcher plant (*Sarracenia purpurea*)

whip purchase *n* **:** WHIP CRANE

whip·py \ˈhwipē *also* ˈwi-\ *adj* -ER/-EST [²*whip* + *-y*] **1 :** of, relating to, or resembling a whip **2 :** unusually resilient **:** SPRINGY ⟨a very ~ fly rod —J.D.Bates⟩

whip ray *n* **:** STINGRAY

whip roll *n* **:** a roll or bar above the warp beam and behind the reed over which the warp threads pass in the process of weaving

whip–round \ˈ⸗,⸗\ *n* -S [fr. the phrase *whip round*] *chiefly Brit* **:** a collection of money made usu. for a benevolent purpose ⟨we'll have a *whip-round* and . . . make up for what was in your purse —*Strand Mag.*⟩

whips *pres 3d sing of* WHIP, *pl of* WHIP

¹**whipsaw** \ˈ⸗,⸗\ *n* [²*whip* + *saw*] **1 :** a narrow pit saw tapering from butt to point, having hook teeth, and averaging from 5 to 7½ feet in length for use by one or two men **2 :** a two-man crosscut saw

²**whipsaw** \"\ *vt* **1 :** to saw with a whipsaw **:** cut as if with a whipsaw **2 :** to cheat or victimize (an opponent) esp. at poker by collusion of two players only one of whom can win but both of whom raise so as to increase the size of the pot **3 :** to use more favorable terms gained (as in one company) as the precedent or leverage to win equal or greater concessions from (as a related company)

whip scorpion *n* **:** an arachnid of the order Pedipalpida

whip shot *n* **:** a method of throwing dice so that one or both dice will not change vertical position while in the air or spinning along a surface but will come to rest with the same number topmost as when they left the shooter's hand

whip snake *n* **:** any of various slender snakes: as **a :** a long bright-green harmless tree snake (*Philodryas viridissimus*) of So. America — called also *emerald whip snake* **b :** COACHWHIP SNAKE **c :** a snake of a boigid genus (*Dryophis*) of Asia having a long leaflike head **d :** any of several small Australian snakes (genera *Demansia* and *Denisonia*) that are venomous but not deadly

whipsocket \ˈ⸗,⸗\ *n* **1 :** the whipstock into which a lash is fitted **2 :** a socket into which the butt end of a whip is inserted when the whip is not in use

whip stall *n* **:** a maneuver in which an airplane is put into a steeper climbing attitude than it is able to maintain and is held in this attitude until the speed is reduced to the stalling speed causing it to whip sharply into a steep nose down attitude that is maintained until flying speed is regained

whip·ster \ˈhwipstə(r) *also* ˈwi-\ *n* -S [¹*whip* + *-ster*] **1 :** WHIPPERSNAPPER **2 :** one that uses a whip

¹**whipstitch** \ˈ⸗,⸗\ *vt* [¹*whip* + *stitch,* n.] **1 :** WHIP 5 **2 :** OVERCAST 3a

²**whipstitch** \"\ *n* **1 :** a shallow overcasting stitch **2 :** a small interval of time **:** INSTANT, MINUTE

whipstock \ˈ⸗,⸗\ *n* **1 :** the handle of a whip **2 :** a long wedge dropped into or placed in a petroleum well to deflect the drill to one side of some obstruction

whiptail \ˈ⸗,⸗\ *n* **1 :** a whip-tailed animal: as **a :** WHIP SCORPION **b :** a long-tailed skua **c :** a lizard of the genus *Cnemidophorus* **d** *or* **whip–tailed shark :** THRESHER 2 **e :** a relatively large bluish-gray wallaby (*Macropus parryi*) with a long slender tail that occurs in mountain forests of Queensland and New South Wales and is readily tamed **f :** GRENADIER **2 :** a disease of cauliflower that is very prevalent on acid soils, is caused by malnutrition and in some cases by molybdenum deficiency, and is characterized by narrowed ruffled leaves with irregular edges sometimes reduced nearly to the midrib **3** *usu* **whip tail :** a slender tail tapering from the base towards the tip

whip–tailed *also* **whiptail** \ˈ⸗,⸗\ *adj* **:** having a tail like a whiplash

whip–tailed lizard *n* **:** WHIPTAIL 1c

whip–tailed ray *n* **:** STINGRAY

whip–tailed scorpion *n* **:** WHIP SCORPION

whip thread *or* **whip yarn** *n* **:** a secondary warp thread twisted around another warp thread to make the fabric firmer and used esp. in lappet weaving

whip–tom–kelly \ˈ⸗,⸗ˈ⸗⸗\ *n* [imit.] **:** any of various vireos (as the black-whiskered vireo)

whip–tongue \ˈ⸗,⸗\ *n* **:** a wild madder (*Galium mollugo*)

whip top *var of* WHIPPING TOP

whipworm \ˈ⸗,⸗\ *n* [so called fr. its shape] **:** a parasitic nematode worm (as the human whipworm [*Trichuris trichiura*]) of the family Trichuridae characterized by a body that is thickened posteriorly and is very long and slender anteriorly

¹**whir** *also* **whirr** \R ˈwh|ər *also* ˈw|, + *vowel* |ər·; |ə̄, + *suffixal vowel* |ər· *also* |ər, + *vowel in a following word* |ər· *or* |ə̄ *also* |ər\ *vb* **whirred; whirred; whirring; whirs** [ME (Sc) *quirren,* prob. of Scand origin; akin to Dan *hvirre* to whirl, whir, ON *hverfa* to turn around — more at WHARF] *vi* **:** to fly, revolve, or move rapidly with the sound of a whir ⟨grouse and ptarmigan *whirred* across the uplands —*Amer. Guide Series: Wash.*⟩ ⟨the small electric fan . . . *whirred* with a monotonous drone —Erskine Caldwell⟩ ⟨the breezes ~ through the trees —Gladwin Hill⟩ ⟨telephone *whirred* —Claud Cockburn⟩ ~ *vt* **:** to move or carry rapidly with the sound of whirring ⟨had been *whirring* the dial of the telephone —Erle Stanley Gardner⟩ ⟨the car ~*s* him away into the night⟩

²**whir** *also* **whirr** \"\ *n* -S [ME (Sc) *quirre,* fr. *quirren,* v.] **:** a continuous fluttering or generally vibratory sound made by something in rapid motion ⟨the hunter may delight in the ~ of the ruffed grouse —*Amer. Guide Series: N.H.*⟩ ⟨the strident ~ of the big locusts —Willa Cather⟩ ⟨the ~ of wheels and spinning tops —K.K.Darrow⟩ ⟨the ~ of spinning propellers —*Amer. Guide Series: Conn.*⟩

¹**whirl** \ˈhw|ərl *also* ˈw|, *esp before pause or consonant* |ər·əl; |ə̄l, |əil\ *vb* -ED/-ING/-S [ME *whirlen,* prob. of Scand origin; akin to ON *hvirfla* to whirl; akin to MD *wirvel, wervel, warvel* bolt for closing a door, hinge, whirlwind, *wervelen* to turn, OHG *wirbil* whirlwind, ON *hvirfill* circle, ring, crown of the head, *hverfa* to turn around — more at WHARF] *vi* **1 a :** to move or turn in a circle or similar curve **:** CIRCLE ⟨his sister ~*s* round and round on the carousel —H.N.Maclean⟩ ⟨our sun and the stars near it are ~*ing* in roughly circular orbits —B.J.Bok⟩ **b :** to move circularly in various or random directions esp. with force or speed ⟨the wind . . . ~*ed* round her in eddies and spirals —J.C.Powys⟩ ⟨the dancers ~ about the room⟩ ⟨his thoughts were ~*ing* wildly —Morley Callaghan⟩ ⟨separated by a wide gulf in which ~*ed* the nothingnesses of training and temperament —S.E.White⟩ **2 a :** to turn on or around an axis like a wheel **:** SPIN, REVOLVE, ROTATE ⟨the potter's wheel ~*s* at its work⟩ ⟨the eddies of the flooding river ~ menacingly⟩ **b :** to turn abruptly around or aside **:** WHEEL ⟨~*ed* about to the door —Liam O'Flaherty⟩ ⟨the tiger saw the movement and ~*ed* to face me —Edison Marshall⟩ ⟨strode away 20 paces, ~*ed* suddenly, and blazed away —C.B.Davis⟩ **c :** to turn around while bent considerably out of true through the effect of centrifugal force **3 :** to pass, move, or go quickly **:** SPEED, RUSH ⟨the landlady ~*ed* down the hallway —J.B.Clayton⟩ ⟨the carriages used to ~ by the house⟩ ⟨the General Court ~*ed* into special session —J.R.Aswell & E.J.Michelson⟩ **4 :** to become giddy or dizzy **:** REEL ⟨all of a sudden my head ~*ed,* and the lights went out and I fell —Dorothy Baker⟩ ~ *vt* **1 :** to drive, impel, or convey with or as if with a rotary motion ⟨cottonwoods . . . snapped off and were ~*ed* away —*Amer. Guide Series: Tenn.*⟩ ⟨the pair jumped into a car and were ~*ed* away —S.H.Adams⟩ ⟨has been ~*ed* . . . to the height of fame —T.H.White b.1915⟩ **2 a :** to cause to turn usu. rapidly on or around an axis **:** ROTATE ⟨the catapult officer ~*ed* one finger above his head —J.A.Michener⟩ ⟨subjects will be ~*ed* at speed approaching 1000 miles an hour —*All Hands*⟩ ⟨~*ed* the helpless characters around while war or peace was being decided —Henri Peyre⟩ **b :** to cause to turn abruptly around or aside ⟨caught a swift purple gaze of eyes as she ~*ed* her head —Zane Grey⟩ **3** *obs* **:** to throw or hurl violently with a revolving motion ⟨a sling to ~ stones⟩ **4** *archaic* **:** to cause to become giddy ⟨the sight of the vast canyon ~*s* his brain⟩ **5 :** TWIST 5 **syn** see TURN

²**whirl** \"\ *n* -S [ME *whirle,* fr. *whirlen,* v.] **1 :** WHORL 1 **2 a :** a rapid rotating or circling movement **:** SPIN, GYRATION ⟨the ~ of the buzz saw —*Amer. Guide Series: La.*⟩ ⟨gave the crank a ~ —John Hermann⟩ ⟨snatched up a black net scarf . . . and with a sudden ~ draped herself —Winifred Bambrick⟩ ⟨guide vanes add ~ to the working fluid —E.L.Hunsaker & W.A.Stoner⟩ **b :** something undergoing such a movement **:** VORTEX, EDDY ⟨the ~*s* of the pool⟩ ⟨tropical cyclones are small cyclonic ~*s* —Sverre Petterssen⟩ **3 a :** a confused tumult **:** COMMOTION, BUSTLE ⟨had plunged into a ~ of work —Will Irwin⟩ ⟨a ~ of people riding or walking to the market place —*Lamp*⟩ ⟨we avoided the gay social ~ . . . because we wanted something more solid from life —Gráinne Andrews⟩ **b :** a confused or disturbed mental state **:** TURMOIL ⟨passed his days in a ~ of febrile excitement —Emily Skeel⟩ ⟨that these distinguished men were calling upon me quite set me in a ~ —David Fairchild⟩ ⟨my mind is in a ~ all the time —Arnold Bennett⟩ **4 :** rapid, intense, or impelled movement **:** RUSH ⟨the ~ of vehicles fills the streets⟩ ⟨a ten-day ~ through allied capitals —*N.Y.Times*⟩ ⟨had forgotten his lunch and returned in a ~ to get it —Agnes S. Turnbull⟩ **5 :** a whorl of parts on a plant or animal **:** VERTICIL **6 :** a hook or reel of a rope winch by which the strands of a rope are twisted; *also* **:** the winch to which the hook or reel is attached **7 :** an experimental or brief attempt **:** TRY ⟨there had been her own veto of a career as a fashion designer after a trial ~ —*Current Biog.*⟩ ⟨took a ~ at the intellectual life —Kay Rogers⟩ ⟨pleaded with us to give whale steak a ~ —*New Yorker*⟩

whirlabout \ˈ⸗⸗,⸗\ *n* -S [fr. *whirl about,* v.] **:** the act or process of whirling about ⟨amid a ~ of colored carnival lights —Samuel Yellen⟩

whirlbat *n* [alter. (influenced by ¹*whirl*) of *hurlbat*] *obs* **:** ³CESTUS

whirlblast \ˈ⸗,⸗\ *n* **:** WHIRLWIND, HURRICANE

whirlbone \ˈ⸗,⸗\ *n* [ME *whirlebon,* fr. *whirlen* to whirl + *bon* bone — more at BONE] **1** *dial Eng* **:** HUCKLEBONE 1 **2** *dial Eng* **:** PATELLA

whirl drill *n* **:** a hand drill consisting of a spindle with a small heavy flywheel near the drill end turned by two twisted strings attached to the other end of the spindle and to the ends of a transverse piece that slides on the spindle

whirl·er \-lə(r)\ *n* -S **:** one that whirls: as **a :** DERVISH 2 **b :** a circular appliance capable of being rotated by hand used by potters for finishing wares **c :** a whirling table for coating photographic plates **d :** a machine for putting a sensitized coating on the printing plate in offset lithography **e :** a hook for twisting hemp into rope yarn

whirl·ey crane \-lē-\ *or* **whirley** *n* -S [*whirley* alter. of ¹*whirly*] **:** a crane free to rotate 360 degrees in picking up and depositing its load

whirl·i·cote \ˈhwərlə,kōt *also* ˈwər-\ *n* -S [prob. alter. of ME *whirlecole,* fr. *whirlen* to whirl + *-cole* (origin unknown)] **:** a heavy and luxurious carriage **:** COACH

whirlier *comparative of* WHIRLY

whirlies *pl of* WHIRLY

whirliest *superlative of* WHIRLY

¹**whirl·i·gig** \ˈhwərlə,gig, |ə̄l-, |əil- *also* ˈw|\ *n* [ME *whirlegigge,* fr. *whirlen* to whirl + *gigge* top — more at GIG] **1 :** a child's toy having a whirling or spinning motion **2 :** a mechanical apparatus having a whirling or rotary movement: as **a :** a medieval instrument for punishing petty offenders consisting of a wooden cage for whirling around an offender at high speed **b :** MERRY-GO-ROUND **3 :** something that continuously whirls, moves, or changes: as **a** *obs* **:** a fanciful trifle or notion **b :** a circling or repetition of time or events **:** WHEEL ⟨their best work outlines the ~ of taste —Douglas Bush⟩ ⟨the ~ of fortune —J.D.Hart⟩ **c** *archaic* **:** a flighty inconstant person **4 :** WHIRLIGIG BEETLE

²**whirligig** \"\ *vi* **:** to whirl like a whirligig **:** SPIN, TURN

whirligig beetle *n* **:** any of numerous beetles of the family Gyrinidae that have a firm oval usu. dark body with a bronzy luster and that live mostly on the surface of water where they move swiftly about in curves

whirling *pres part of* WHIRL

whirling dervish *n* **:** DERVISH 1

whirl·ing·ly *adv* **:** with a whirling movement

whirling table *n* **:** any of various apparatus for producing rapid rotary and usu. horizontal motion (as to demonstrate a law in physics or to coat plates evenly in photography)

whirl plate *n* **:** a disk inserted in a sprayer nozzle with holes designed to impart a whirling action to the spray

¹**whirlpool** \ˈ⸗,⸗\ *n* [²*whirl* + *pool*] **1 a :** water moving rapidly in a circle so as to produce a depression or cavity in the center into which floating objects may be drawn **:** EDDY, VORTEX — compare MAELSTROM **b :** a body of water having a more or less circular motion caused by its flowing in an irregular channel or by the meeting of opposing currents **c :** WHIRLPOOL BATH **2 a :** a confused tumult and bustle **:** WHIRL ⟨walking down the gangway into a furious human ~ of customs, passport regulations, and bellowing loudspeakers —Wynford Vaughan-Thomas⟩ ⟨the turbulent ~ of pioneer politics —*Amer. Guide Series: Minn.*⟩ **b :** a magnetic or impelling force by which something is or may be pulled under or engulfed ⟨refusing to be drawn into this ~ of intrigue —A.D.White⟩ ⟨under their stagnant respectability are ~*s* of evil and passion —Laurent LeSage⟩ ⟨a seething ~ of competition and intrigue in which everyone is . . . unscrupulous —David Cecil⟩ **3 :** GURGES

²**whirlpool** \"\ *vi* **:** to eddy or spin around like a whirlpool ⟨the feather . . . ~*ed* down —Gerald Durrell⟩

whirlpool bath *n* **:** a therapeutic bath in which a whirling churning stream of hot water is forcibly directed against a part of the body

whirlpuff \ˈ⸗,⸗\ *n* [ME *whirle puff,* fr. *whirlen* to whirl + *puff, puf, puffe* puff — more at PUFF] *dial Eng* **:** a whirling gust or blast of wind

whirls *pres 3d sing of* WHIRL, *pl of* WHIRL

whirl·wig \ˈhwərl,wig *also* ˈwə-\ *n* [blend of *whirligig* and *earwig*] **:** WHIRLIGIG BEETLE

¹**whirlwind** \ˈ⸗,⸗\ *n, often attrib* [ME *whirlwind, whirlewind,* fr. *whirlen* to whirl + *wind*] **1 a :** a small rotating windstorm of limited or localized extent marked by an inward and upward spiral motion of the lower air that is followed by an outward and upward spiral motion and usu. a progressive motion at all levels **:** a vortex of air — see DUST DEVIL ⟨little ~*s* twisted and died across the prairie —Edwin Granberry⟩ ⟨a small ~ knocked two men off their feet and whisked away paper cartons and other debris —*Springfield* (*Mass.*) *Daily News*⟩ **b :** TORNADO 2a **2 a :** a confused rush or tumultuous procession of events or developments **:** WHIRL ⟨lived in a ~ of examiner's meetings, visits on business . . . innumerable callers, some political jobs —H.J.Laski⟩ ⟨~ of our departure —David Fairchild⟩ ⟨the ~ of child stardom —Joanna Spencer⟩ **b :** a destructive force or agency ⟨the storm has been sown, and the ~ must be reaped —Gilbert Parker⟩ ⟨farmers are reaping another golden crop of corn, and Republicans are reaping a political ~ —W.M.Blair⟩ **syn** see WIND

²**whirlwind** \"\ *vi* **:** to move like a whirlwind ⟨is ~*ing* through the states on his campaign⟩

¹**whirly** \ˈhwərlē, |ə̄l-, |əil-, -li *also* ˈw|\ *adj* -ER/-EST [¹*whirl* + *-y*] **:** marked by or exhibiting a rotary or whirling motion

²**whirly** \"\ *n* -ES **:** a small whirlwind

whirlybird \ˈ⸗⸗,⸗\ *n* **:** HELICOPTER

whirr *var of* WHIR

whir·ra \ˈ(h)wirə\ *var of* WIRRA

whirred *past of* WHIR

whirring *pres part of* WHIR

whir·ry \ˈ(h)wəri\ *vb* **whirried; whirried; whirrying; whirries** [perh. blend of ¹*whir* and *hurry*] *vt, Scot* **:** to convey quickly ~ *vi, Scot* **:** HURRY

whirs *pres 3d sing of* WHIR, *pl of* WHIR

whir·tle \ˈhwərd·ᵊl *also* ˈwə-\ *n* -S [ME *wirtil*] **:** a perforated steel die through which wires or tubes are drawn

¹**whish** \ˈhwish *also* ˈwi-\ *vb* -ED/-ING/-ES [imit.] *vt* **:** to urge on or cause to move with a whish ⟨heard them ~*ing* up the sheep —Joseph Hocking⟩ ⟨heard him ~ the match across his pants —Helen Rich⟩ ~ *vi* **1 :** to make a sibilant sound **:** move with a whish ⟨a starter ~*ed,* and an engine took hold —G.R. Stewart⟩ ⟨water ~*es* past the prow⟩ **2 :** to move fast **:** WHIZ ⟨trees ~ past the train windows⟩ ⟨~*es* in with a roar and bursts in the street —Ernest Hemingway⟩

²**whish** \"\ *n* -ES **:** a rushing sound **:** SWISH — used interjectionally to convey an impression of rapid movement ⟨touched a match to the skyrocket and ~ it was off⟩

³**whish** \ˈ(h)wish\ *vb* -ED/-ING/-ES [imit.] *dial Brit* **:** SHUSH — often used in the imperative to enjoin silence

¹**whisht** \ˈ(h)wisht\ *n* -S [imit.] *chiefly Scot & Irish* **:** HUSH, SILENCE ⟨the ~ of death upon his face —Louise Garnett⟩ — often used interjectionally to enjoin silence ⟨~ now . . . I hear people again coming by the stream —J.M.Synge⟩

²**whisht** \"\ *chiefly Scot & Irish var of* ³WHISH

¹**whisk** \ˈhwisk *also* ˈwi-\ *n* -S [ME *wisk,* prob. of Scand origin; akin to ON *visk* wisp; akin to OE *wiscian* to plait, gran*wisc* awn, OHG *wisc* wisp, L *viscus* entrails, *virga* branch, twig, rod, Skt *veṣka* noose, *vēṣa* costume; basic meaning: to turn] **1 a :** a quick light brushing or whipping motion **:** FLICK, SWISH ⟨as the tear dripped slowly down . . . caught it with a neat little ~ of her tongue —Katherine Mansfield⟩ ⟨could . . . hear the ~ and slither of tails —James Schuyler⟩ **b :** a swift passage ⟨the line's four-times-a-week ~ from London to home (two hours) —Horace Sutton⟩ **2 :** something used as or resembling a whip or brush: as **a :** a hairlike insect appendage — used esp. of the setae of the Plectoptera **b :** a small usu. wire kitchen implement used for hand beating of food (as eggs, cream, or potatoes) — compare WHIP 4b **c** (1) **:** a flexible bunch (as of twigs, feathers, or straw) attached to a handle for use as a brush — compare FEATHER DUSTER, FLY WHISK (2) **:** WHISK BROOM **d :** TUFT, WISP ⟨wind . . . skiffing the ~ of her frock —Bruce Marshall⟩ **e :** the tail of an angler's fly **3 :** a wide ornamental collar of fine fabric and lace usu. supported at the back and worn in the early 17th century **4 :** a plant part (as a panicle of broomcorn) used in making brushes

²**whisk** \"\ *vb* -ED/-ING/-S [ME (Sc) *quhisken,* of Scand origin; akin to ON *viska* to wipe, whish; akin to OE *wiscian* to plait — more at ¹WHISK] *vi* **1 :** to move nimbly and quickly **:** FRISK, POP ⟨gray bodies ~ up and down the hickory trunks —Marjorie K. Rawlings⟩ ⟨porters . . . bowed and ~*ed* about him —Frederick Way⟩ **2 :** to travel swiftly **:** ZIP ⟨the Broadway Limited . . . ~*ed* through like a comet —*True*⟩ ~ *vt* **1 a :** to impart brisk or rapid motion to **:** FLICK, WHIP ⟨seeing him ~ his eloquent tail —E.S.McCartney⟩ ⟨showed both sides, draped it over her left hand, ~*ed* away the cloth —Martin Gardner⟩ ⟨machine picks up threads . . . and ~*s* them into a detachable aluminum hopper for ready disposal —*Steel*⟩ **b :** to transport swiftly **:** HURRY, SPEED ⟨dreams of rocket ships that will ~ him across the Atlantic between breakfast and luncheon —Waldemar Kaempffert⟩ ⟨too soon . . . their mother would ~ them off to bed —Flora Thompson⟩ ⟨an endless belt ~*s* the shopper's

groceries . . . out to pickup stations —J.N.Wallace⟩ **2 :** to mix or fluff up by or as if by beating with a whisk ⟨~*ing* a mixture in a yellow bowl —Kathryn Grondahl⟩ ⟨wind . . . ~*ed* and matted the flakes into huge grey discs —O.E.Rölvaag⟩ **3 :** to brush or wipe off lightly ⟨~ crumbs from the table⟩ ⟨can be ~*ed* clean with a damp cloth —*advt*⟩

3whisk \"\ *interj* — used to convey an impression of sudden swift motion ⟨he's going to taste it, when ~! it's gone —Hugh Walpole⟩

4whisk \"\ *n* -s [perh. fr. 1*whisk*] *dial* **:** WHIST

whisk broom *n* **:** a small broom with a short handle used esp. as a clothes brush or for light cleaning chores

1whisk·er \'hwiskə(r) *also* 'wi-\ *n* -s [2*whisk* + *-er*] **1 a :** a hair of the beard — usu. used in pl. ⟨had a two days' growth of thick, grizzled ~*s* —Danforth Ross⟩ **b whiskers** *pl* (1) *archaic* **:** MOUSTACHE (2) **:** the part of the beard growing on the sides of the face or on the chin; *esp* **:** SIDE-WHISKERS **c :** HAIRBREADTH ⟨temperatures hovered a ~ below freezing —*Springfield* (*Mass.*) *Daily News*⟩ **2 a :** one of the long projecting hairs or bristles growing near the mouth of an animal (as a cat or bird) **b :** an antenna or feeler esp. of an insect **c whiskers** *pl* **:** an abundant grayish white growth of a mold (genus *Mucor* and related fungi) on food (as bread or meat) consisting of superficial hyphae **3** *or* **whisker boom :** an outrigger extending on each side of the bowsprit to spread the jib and flying jib guys — usu. used in pl.; see SHIP illustration **4 :** a hairy shred or filament likened to a whisker: as **a :** CAT WHISKER **b :** HAIRLINE 2c(4) — usu. used in pl.

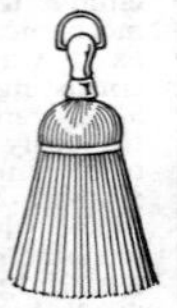

whisk broom

2whisker \"\ *vt* -ED/-ING/-S **1 :** to furnish with whiskers ⟨a ~*ed* jersey with rabbit's hair content —*Women's Wear Daily*⟩ **2 :** to remove the splinters from (a gun stock)

whisk·er·age \-kərij\ *n* -s [1*whisker* + *-age*] **:** style of wearing the whiskers ⟨changes had come about in . . . facial ~ —Thomas Wolfe⟩

whisk·ered \-kə(r)d\ *adj* [1*whisker* + *-ed*] **:** having or wearing whiskers

whiskered auklet *n* **:** an auklet (*Aethia pygmaea*) having filamentous white feathers on the sides of the head

whiskered bat *n* **:** a small bat (*Myotis mystacinus*) of Europe and Asia having a fringe of long hairs on its upper lip

whiskered tern *n* **:** a common tern (*Chlidonias hybrida*) of the warmer parts of the Old World having a broad white stripe at the corner of the mouth

whisker jumper *n* **:** a stay leading from the end of a whisker boom to secure it to the cutwater — usu. used in pl.; see SHIP illustration

whisker pole *n* **:** a light boom with jaws at one end that fit around the mast and a point at the other end that goes through the clew of the jib to wing it out when running before the wind

whisk·ery \-kərē\ *adj* **:** having or resembling whiskers ⟨a ~ chin⟩ ⟨this yarn has ~ roots —Colin Simpson⟩

1whis·key *or* **whis·ky** \'hwiskē, -ki *also* 'wi-\ *n, pl* **whiskeys** *or* **whiskies** *often attrib* [IrGael *uisce beathadh* & ScGael *uisge beatha*, lit., water of life, fr. OIr *uisce* water + *bethad*, gen. of *bethu* life; akin to Gk *hydōr* water and to Gk *bios* life, mode of life — more at WATER, QUICK] **1 :** a distilled alcoholic liquor that is made from fermented mash of grain (as rye, corn, barley, or wheat) or potatoes and usu. contains from 40 percent to 50 percent of alcohol — compare BLENDED WHISKEY, BOURBON 4, SCOTCH WHISKY **2 :** a drink of whiskey ⟨takes an occasional ~⟩

2whiskey *or* **whisky** \"\ *n, pl* **whiskeys** *or* **whiskies** [2*whisk* + *-y*] **:** a gig with a small body that resembles a chair and is suspended on leather braces attached to springs — compare DENNET

3whiskey \"\ *usu cap* — a communications code word for the letter *w*

whiskey poker *n* [1*whiskey*] **:** draw poker in which an extra hand is dealt facedown and may be taken entire by the first player who then if he has not passed discards his original hand faceup for exchange individually or entire by each following player until one of the players knocks, the drawing ends, and the hands are shown to determine the winner

whiskey sour *n* **1 :** a cocktail usu. made of whiskey, bitters, sugar, and varying proportions of lemon juice shaken up in cracked ice and served with a fruit garnish (as orange or maraschino cherry) **2 :** a slender usu. footed glass for serving a whiskey sour

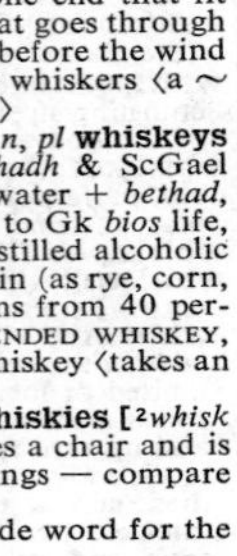

whiskey sour 2

whis·kin \'hwiskən\ *n* -s [origin unknown] *archaic* **:** a shallow drinking bowl

whisking *pres part of* WHISK

whisks *pl of* WHISK, *pres 3d sing of* WHISK

whisky cherry *n* **:** BLACK CHERRY 2

whisky jack *n* [alter. of obs. *whisky john*, fr. Cree *wiskatjân*] **:** CANADA JAY

whisp *var of* WISP

1whis·per \'hwispə(r) *also* 'wi-\ *vb* **whispered; whispered; whispering** \-p(ə)riŋ\ **whispers** [ME *whisperen*, fr. OE *hwisprian*; akin to OHG *hwispalōn* to whisper, ON *hvīskra* to whisper, *hvīna* to whiz — more at WHINE] *vi* **1 :** to speak softly with little or no vibration of the vocal cords esp. with the aim of preserving secrecy ⟨everybody ~*ing* and then stopping when he came in —Mary Barrett⟩ **2 :** to make a sibilant sound that resembles whispering ⟨the ~*ed*; the kettle hummed —Ellen Glasgow⟩ ⟨a breeze ~*s* through the pines⟩ ~ *vt* **1 a :** to address in a whisper ⟨I'd ~ her, and take her for a midnight stroll —Padraic Colum⟩ **b :** to influence or impel by whispering ⟨a voice . . . ~*s* me on —E.R.B.Lytton⟩ **2 a :** to report or suggest confidentially ⟨the ~*ed* reason behind much of the opposition —*Newsweek*⟩ ⟨no evil lurked in . . . their hearts to ~ doubts concerning the goodness of life —V.L.Parrington⟩ **b :** to utter or communicate in or as if in a whisper ⟨they sat closely together as she ~*ed* some of her pleasantest memories —T.B.Costain⟩ ⟨he ~*ed* . . . "the coast is clear" —Archie Binns⟩

2whisper \"\ *n* -s **1 a :** an act or instance of whispering ⟨~*s* so fierce they could be heard all over the house —Peggy Bennett⟩; *specif* **:** speech in which vibration of the vocal cords is replaced by a fricative sound made by the breath in the whisper glottis while the cord glottis is closed **b :** a sibilant sound that resembles whispered speech **:** SUSURRUS ⟨a smoldering log settled with a ~ on the hearth —Ngaio Marsh⟩ **2 a :** a whispered rumor or suggestion ⟨never been a ~ of anything crooked about them —F.W.Crofts⟩ **b :** a confidential report or communication **3 :** a barely discernible quantity **:** HINT, TRACE ⟨hardly a ~ of concern has been voiced —Eric Sevareid⟩ ⟨a ~ of the perfume she used —C.O.Gorham⟩

whis·per·er \-pərə(r)\ *n* -s **1 :** one that whispers; *specif* **:** RUMORMONGER **2 :** a horse trainer who soothes unmanageable mounts by whispering to them

whisper glottis *n* [fr. its use in the production of whisper] **:** the opening between the arytenoid cartilages as distinguished from that between the vocal cords proper — compare CORD GLOTTIS

1whispering *n* -s [ME, fr. OE *hwisprung*, fr. *hwisprian* to whisper + *-ung* -ing] **1 a :** whispered speech ⟨~ caused by laryngitis⟩ **b :** GOSSIP, RUMOR ⟨foul ~*s* are abroad —Shak.⟩ **2 :** a sibilant sound **:** WHISPER ⟨flitting shapes and tiny ~*s* —Marjory S. Douglas⟩

2whispering *adj* [fr. pres. part. of 1*whisper*] **1 :** making a sibilant sound **:** SUSURRANT ⟨music in a quick and ~ rhythm —Archibald MacLeish⟩ **2 a :** told in or confined to a whisper ⟨a ~ tale⟩ ⟨a ~ voice⟩ **b :** communicating in whispers ⟨~ lovers⟩ **c :** spreading confidential and esp. derogatory reports ⟨~ tongues can poison truth —S.T.Coleridge⟩ — **whis·per·ing·ly** *adv*

whispering bells *n pl but sing or pl in constr* [2*whispering*] **:** CALIFORNIA YELLOW BELLS

whispering campaign *n* [1*whispering*] **:** the systematic dissemination by word of mouth of derogatory rumors or charges esp. against a candidate for public office ⟨his opponents had ruined his career by a *whispering campaign* —Willa Cather⟩

whispering gallery *or* **whispering dome** *n* **:** a gallery or dome so constructed that sounds produced in the area are concentrated in another by reflection from the walls so that feeble sounds are audible at an extraordinary distance

whis·per·ous \'hwisp(ə)rəs *also* 'wi-\ *adj* [2*whisper* + *-ous*] **:** WHISPERY — **whis·per·ous·ly** *adv*

whis·pery \-rē, -ri\ *adj* [2*whisper* + *-y*] **1 :** resembling a whisper ⟨stopped his breathing . . . to be able to hear any sound, however small and ~ —W.V.T.Clark⟩ **2 :** full of whispers ⟨a swamp is a ~ place —Edward Kimbrough⟩

1whist \'(h)wist\ *dial Brit var of* 3WHISH

2whist \'hwist *also* 'wi-\ *adj* [ME, fr. 1*whist*] **:** QUIET, SILENT ⟨the winds are ~ —J.R.Drake⟩

3whist \"\ *n* -s [alter. (perh. influenced by 1*whist* — fr. the silence observed during play) of earlier *whisk*, prob. fr. 2*whisk*; fr. whisking up the tricks] **:** a card game for four players in two partnerships that is played with a pack of 52 cards dealt one at a time of which the last card belongs to the dealer and is turned to determine trump for the hand and that scores one point for each trick in excess of six and sometimes additional points for the ace, king, queen, and jack of trumps — see LONG WHIST, SHORT WHIST; compare 4BRIDGE

whist drive *n, Brit* **:** a progressive whist party

whist family *n* **:** a group of card games including whist and games from which it developed or which are based on it — compare BRIDGE

1whis·tle \'hwisəl *also* 'wi-\ *n* -s *often attrib* [in sense 1, fr. ME, fr. OE *hwistle*; akin to OE *hwistlian* to whistle; in other senses, fr. ME, fr. *whistlen* to whistle] **1 a :** a small wind instrument in which sound is produced by the forcible passage of breath through a slit in a short tube (as of wood or metal) ⟨willow ~⟩ ⟨police ~⟩ — compare FIPPLE FLUTE **b :** a device through which air or steam is forced into a cavity or against a thin edge to produce a shrill whistling sound ⟨boat ~⟩ ⟨factory ~⟩ **2 a :** a shrill clear sound produced by forcing breath out or air in through the puckered lips ⟨her figure . . . inspires admiring ~*s* —*Time*⟩ **b :** the sound produced by a whistle ⟨the ~ of a distant train⟩ **c :** a signal (as a warning or summons) given by or as if by whistling ⟨all his followers . . . were ready at his ~ —T.B.Macaulay⟩ **3 :** a sound that resembles a whistle ⟨a ~ of wings —William Beebe⟩ ⟨the whine and ~ of bombs —Peter Ustinov⟩; *specif* **:** the shrill clear note of a bird or other animal ⟨the ~ of a cardinal⟩ ⟨the ~ of a marmot⟩

2whistle \"\ *vb* **whistled; whistled; whistling** \-s(ə)liŋ\ **whistles** [ME *whistlen*, fr. OE *hwistlian*; akin to ON *hvīsla* to whisper, *hvīna* to whiz — more at WHINE] *vi* **1 a :** to utter a shrill clear sound by blowing or drawing air through the pursed lips ⟨sat up and *whistled* with surprise —T.B.Costain⟩ **b :** to utter a shrill note or call resembling a whistle ⟨the dove ~*s* and the pigeons coo —Louise Bogan⟩ **c :** to make a shrill clear sound esp. due to rapid movement ⟨wind *whistled* among the cornices —Louis Bromfield⟩ ⟨bullets began to ~ among the branches —Stephen Crane⟩ **d :** to blow or sound a whistle **2 a :** to signal by or as if by whistling ⟨the referee ~*s* and play is resumed⟩ **b :** to issue an order or summons by or as if by whistling ⟨~ to a dog⟩ ⟨~ for a taxi⟩; *specif* **:** to demand without result ⟨never returned the book he borrowed so next time he wants one he can just ~⟩ ⟨did a sloppy job so he can ~ for his money⟩ **3 :** SQUEAL 2a ~ *vt* **1 a :** to signal or summon by or as if by whistling ⟨*whistled* the chief engineer to give her all he could —H.A.Chippendale⟩ — often used with *up* ⟨persuaded . . . to put off *whistling* up the law —William Brandon⟩ ⟨~ up hypothetical vectors . . . to explain the facts for them —*Amer. Naturalist*⟩ **b :** to dismiss by or as if by whistling ⟨told him he might . . . ~ me off, save himself, and I would say no word of blame —Mary Johnston⟩ ⟨that . . . historical happening cannot be *whistled* away —*Times Lit. Supp.*⟩ **c :** to impel or influence by whistling ⟨*whistled* himself out of the scrub and back onto the road —Stetson Kennedy⟩ **2 a :** to utter or express in a whistle ⟨~ a tune⟩ ⟨a group of reclining soldiery *whistled* appreciation each time they passed —Margery Sharp⟩ ⟨quail ~ about us their spontaneous cries —Wallace Stevens⟩ **b :** to send or drive with a whistle ⟨~ a shot or two over his head —Alan Le May⟩ ⟨broke off a switch and *whistled* it angrily through the air —D.C.Peattie⟩ **3** *obs* **:** to disclose confidentially **:** WHISPER ⟨they dare speak felony, ~ treason —John Taylor⟩ — **whistle in the dark :** to keep up one's courage by or as if by whistling ⟨a series of optimistic statements and much *whistling in the dark* —Rupert Emerson⟩

whis·tle·able \-ləbəl\ *adj* **:** capable of being whistled ⟨a ~ tune⟩

whistle duck *n* **:** AMERICAN GOLDENEYE

whistle–pig \'⸗⸗,⸗\ *n, chiefly Midland* **:** WOODCHUCK

whistle post *n* **:** a marker alongside a railroad track designating a point at which trains are to whistle (as for a station or crossing)

whistle punk *n* **:** a lumberjack who operates the signal wire running to a donkey engine whistle

whis·tler \'hwis(ə)lə(r) *also* 'wi-\ *n* -s [ME, fr. OE *hwistlere*, fr. *hwistlian* to whistle + *-ere* -er] **1 :** one that whistles: as **a :** a player on the fife, flute, or pipe **b** (1) **:** any of various Australian and Polynesian birds (as of the genus *Pachycephala*) that are related to the shrikes and have a whistling call — called also *thickhead* (2) **:** AMERICAN GOLDENEYE **c :** a large mountain marmot (*Marmota caligata*) of northwestern No. America of a hoary color with blackish head and feet **d :** a broken-winded horse **e :** a rising and falling noise heard on radio resulting from an electrical disturbance caused by a lightning discharge **2 :** one that evokes whistles of admiration ⟨it was a ~ of a story . . . while it lasted —*Newsweek*⟩

whis·tle·ri·an \(')(h)wi¦slirēən\ *adj, usu cap* [James A. M. *Whistler* †1903 Am. painter and etcher + E *-ian*] **:** of, relating to, or having the characteristics of the painter Whistler or his work

1whistle–stop \'⸗⸗,⸗\ *n* **1 a :** a small station at which trains stop only on signal **:** FLAG STOP **b :** a small community **:** TANK TOWN ⟨posters that brought in the yokels from fifty miles around every *whistle-stop* we played —Bennett Cerf⟩ **2 :** a brief personal appearance esp. by a political candidate usu. on the rear platform of a train during the course of a tour ⟨allowing people to savor his personality (which is the real purpose of a *whistle-stop*) while thawing them out with an anecdote —John Mason Brown⟩ **3 :** an insignificant or routine way station ⟨Gander, that global *whistle-stop* in the midst of Newfoundland's immense forests —*Friends Intelligencer*⟩ ⟨life is a *whistle-stop* between eternities —Rosa Marinoni⟩

2whistle–stop \"\ *vi* **1 :** to make a tour (as a campaign swing) pausing at all way stations ⟨*whistle-stop* across the country⟩ **2 :** to make personal appearances or speeches at whistle-stops ⟨*whistle-stopping* eastward through Utah in behalf of the . . . Democratic ticket —I.W.Russell⟩

whistlewing \'⸗⸗,⸗\ *n* **:** AMERICAN GOLDENEYE

whistlewood \'⸗⸗,⸗\ *n* **:** a tree with an easily separable bark used for making whistles: as **a :** STRIPED MAPLE **b :** BASSWOOD 1 **c :** WILLOW **d :** ALDER **e :** SYCAMORE 2 **f :** ROWAN TREE

1whistling *n* -s [ME, fr. OE *hwistlung*, fr. *hwistlian* to whistle + *-ung* -ing] **1 a :** an act or instance of emitting whistles ⟨by repeated ~ and the display of a red lamp they managed to warn the driver —O.S.Nock⟩ ⟨myna birds kept up an impudent cackling and ~ —John Dos Passos⟩ **b :** WHISTLE ⟨the ~ of the wind⟩ **2 :** ROARING 2

2whistling *adj* [ME, fr. pres. part. of *whistlen* to whistle] **:** equipped with or making the sound of a whistle ⟨~ teakettle⟩ ⟨came in to land in a ~ sideslip —*Sydney* (*Australia*) *Bull.*⟩ — **whis·tling·ly** *adv*

whistling arrow *n* [2*whistling*] **:** an arrow with a perforated head that whistles in flight

whistling buoy *n* **:** a buoy that makes a whistling sound due to the action of waves and usu. marks a shoal or channel entrance — see BUOY illustration

whistling dick *n* **:** an Australian shrike thrush (*Colluricincla harmonica*)

whistling duck *n* **1 :** GOLDENEYE **2 :** TREE DUCK **3 :** AMERICAN SCOTER

whistling eagle *or* **whistling kite** *n* **:** a small Australian fishing kite (*Haliastur sphenurus*) related to the Brahminy kite — called also *whistling hawk*

whistling frog *n* **:** a small So. American terrestrial frog (*Leptodactylus ocellatus*) whose call is a clear whistle

whistling hawk *n* **1 :** WHISTLING EAGLE **2 :** CHANTING FALCON

whistling jar *n* **:** an ancient Peruvian clay bottle often in the form of a bird or animal with two apertures so arranged that when a liquid is poured from one the inrushing air produces a whistling sound in the other

whistling marmot *n* **:** WHISTLER 1c

whistling moth *n* **:** an Australian moth (*Hecatesia fenestrata*) of the family Agaristidae that in the male has a ribbed membranous area on the fore wing which produces whistling noise in flight

whistling plover *n* **1 :** GOLDEN PLOVER **2 :** BLACK-BELLIED PLOVER

whistling snipe *n* **:** WOODCOCK 1a(2)

whistling swan *n* **1 :** a wild swan (*Olor columbianus*) with a soft musical note formerly widely distributed in No. America and still breeding in some numbers in Alaska and northwestern Canada and migrating to and wintering in the U.S. chiefly in the southern Atlantic states **2 :** WHOOPER SWAN

whistling teal *n* **:** TREE DUCK

whistling thrush *n* **:** any of several thrushes of the genus *Myophonus* of Asia and the East Indies that are generally black glossed with blue, have a patch of bright blue on each shoulder, and have a loud clear whistle

whis·tly \'hwis(ə)lē *also* 'wi-\ *adj* [1*whistle* + *-y*] **:** resembling a whistle

1whit \'hwit *also* 'wi-; *usu* -id·+V\ *chiefly dial var of* WHITE

2whit \"\ *n* -s [alter. of ME *wight, wiht* creature, thing, bit — more at WIGHT] **:** the smallest part or particle imaginable **:** BIT, JOT, IOTA ⟨cared not a ~⟩ ⟨so shall I no ~ be behind in duty —Shak.⟩

3whit \"\ *adj, usu cap* [*Whit*sunday] **:** WHITSUN

4whit \"\ *interj* [imit.] — used to simulate the chirp of a bird or a quick dull sound (as of a bullet striking)

1white \'hwīt *also* 'wī-; *usu* -īd·+V\ *adj* -ER/-EST [ME *white, whit*, fr. OE *hwīt*; akin to OHG *hwīz, wīz* white, ON *hvītr*, Goth *hweits*, Skt *śiśvinde* it has become white, *śveta* white] **1 a :** free from color **:** quite colorless and transparent **b** (1) **:** of a color like that of new snow or clean milk **:** having the color of good bond paper or the traditional lily; *specif* **:** of the color white ⟨well-bleached linen is perfectly ~⟩ ⟨~ roses⟩ (2) *of light* **:** having some energy in nearly every part of the visible spectrum **c :** light or pallid in color: as (1) **:** having the natural color largely abstracted through use or age **:** WHITENED, GRAYED ⟨the ~ hairs of old age⟩ ⟨a dress ~ from many washings⟩; *often* **:** shown to be aged by whitened hair ⟨this ~ old man⟩ (2) **:** light yellow or amber in color ⟨a ~ table wine⟩ (3) **:** deficient in color **:** ASHEN, WAN ⟨lips ~ with fear⟩ (4) **:** lustrous pale gray **:** SILVERY ⟨cheap tableware of some ~ alloy⟩; *also* **:** made of silver (5) *of cordage* **:** not darkened by an impregnation of tar (6) *of an organism or one of its parts* **:** deficient in pigmentation **:** ALBINO, ALBINOTIC **2 a** *of a human being* (1) *archaic* **:** having lightly pigmented skin, hair, and eyes **:** fair-complexioned **:** BLONDE (2) *sometimes cap* **:** belonging to a racial group or subdivision of a racial group characterized by reduced skin pigmentation, typically represented by the European Caucasoids, and usu. specif. distinguished from persons belonging to groups marked by black, brown, yellow, or red skin coloration (3) **:** being of white ancestry either wholly unmixed with Negro blood or having an admixture of Negro blood less than that specified in various statutes of some states of the U.S. **b :** of, relating to, or consisting of white and esp. Caucasoid people ⟨~ races⟩ ⟨~ Australia⟩ ⟨~ schools⟩ **c :** marked by upright fairness **:** straightforward and kindly **:** square-dealing ⟨a ~ man if ever there was one⟩ **3 :** free from spot or blemish: as **a :** free from moral stain or impurity **:** outstandingly righteous **:** INNOCENT ⟨a ~ spirit⟩ ⟨seeing everything as spiritually black or ~⟩ **b :** unmarked by writing or printing ⟨balancing the ~ spaces on the sheet⟩ **c :** not marked by or connected with malignant influences or intent **:** not intended to cause harm ⟨a ~ lie⟩ ⟨~ magic⟩ **d :** burnished or polished until shining bright and free from spot or mar ⟨clad in ~ armor⟩ **e :** notably pleasing or auspicious **:** FAVORABLE, FORTUNATE **4 :** clothed or covered with something white: as **a** (1) **:** wearing or habited in white ⟨~ friars⟩; *also* **:** of, relating to, or being a religious order (as the Carmelite) of which the garb is white ⟨a ~ abbey⟩ (2) **:** wearing white armor ⟨a ~ knight⟩ **b :** covered with snow **:** SNOWY ⟨the ~ hills of a northern winter⟩; *also* **:** marked by the presence of snow ⟨a long ~ winter⟩ ⟨hoping for a ~ Christmas⟩ **c :** made white by some covering deposit ⟨floors ~ with dust⟩ **5** *obs* **a :** designed to make a good impression **:** superficially pleasing or plausible **:** SPECIOUS **b :** regarded with especial favor **:** FAVORITE **6 a** *archaic* (1) *of a grain crop* **:** becoming lighter colored in ripening (2) *of soil* **:** suited to the growing of white crops **b :** that is whitened in the course of processing or purifying ⟨~ soap⟩ ⟨a fine ~ flour⟩ **7 a** (1) **:** heated to the point of whiteness — see WHITE HEAT (2) **:** characteristic of a white heat ⟨metal heated to a ~ glow⟩ **b :** notably ardent **:** violently heated **:** PASSIONATE ⟨a ~ fury⟩ **8** [so used fr. the white flag of the Bourbons] **a :** being or acting in opposition to a radical or revolutionary policy or doctrine **:** ultraconservative or reactionary in outlook and action ⟨a ~ faction in French politics⟩ — compare RED 7a **b :** instigated or carried out by reactionary forces usu. as a counterrevolutionary measure ⟨a ~ terror⟩ ⟨a ~ purge⟩ **9 :** not featuring open warfare and the shedding of blood but involving oblique methods ⟨a ~ war of propaganda and bribery⟩ **10 :** of, relating to, or constituting a musical tone quality characterized by a controlled pure sound, a lack of warmth and color, and a lack of resonance

2white \"\ *adv* -ER/-EST **:** in a fair upright manner **:** DECENTLY, WHITELY ⟨treated us ~⟩

3white \"\ *n* -s [ME *white, whit*, fr. OE *hwīt*, fr. *hwīt*, adj.] **1 a :** the neutral or achromatic object color of greatest lightness **:** the lightest gray **:** the achromatic color bearing the least resemblance to black **b :** the one of the six psychologically primary colors that is characteristically perceived to belong to objects which reflect diffusely nearly all incident energy throughout the visible spectrum **c :** any of several object colors of very low or zero saturation and high or very high lightness; *esp* **:** a very light gray **2 a :** a white-colored part of something (as meat or wood): as (1) **:** a clear semifluid mass of albuminous material surrounding the yolk of an egg — see EGG illustration (2) **:** the white part of the ball of the eye surrounding the transparent cornea (3) **whites** *pl* **:** blank spaces in a printed picture or design; *also* **:** the corresponding parts of a plate or mold (4) **:** the light-colored pieces in a two-handed board game; *also* **:** the player by whom or the side of the board from which these are played (5) **whites** *pl* **:** wing feathers of the male ostrich **b :** a white spot: as (1) *archaic* **:** a white target (2) **:** the fifth or outermost circle of an archery target; *also* **:** a shot that hits it (3) **:** a light-colored mark shot at in rovers (4) **:** a mark pinned on a butt **3 :** one that is or approaches the color white: as **a** (1) **:** white clothing ⟨the bride was dressed in ~⟩ (2) **whites** *pl* **:** a white costume of a usu. specified kind ⟨naval personnel in summer ~*s*⟩ ⟨tennis ~*s*⟩ **b :** white cloth **c :** WHITE WINE **d** (1) **:** a white mammal (as a horse or a hog) — compare CHESTER WHITE, YORKSHIRE (2) **:** any of numerous butterflies of *Pieris* and related genera in which the color is usu. white ⟨the cabbage butterfly is often known as the cabbage ~⟩ **e :** a white pigment (as zinc oxide) **f :** a white-colored product (as white flour, pins, or sugar) — usu. used in pl. **4** *archaic* **:** SILVER; *esp* **:** a silver coin **5 whites** *pl* **:** LEUKORRHEA **6** *often cap* **:** a person with a white skin **:** a member of the Caucasoid division of mankind **7** *often cap* **a :** a member of a white party esp. in European politics; *esp* **:** one of the Bianchi **b :** a person of ultraconservative political outlook **:** REACTIONARY — **in the white 1** *of a skin* **:** limed but not yet tanned **2** *of woodwork* **:** dressed and smoothed but not yet painted or varnished

4white \"\ *vt* -ED/-ING/-S [ME *whiten*, fr. 1*white*] **:** WHITEN

5white \"\ *vb* -ED/-ING/-S [alter. of obs. *thwite*, fr. ME *thwiten* — more at WHITTLE] *Brit* **:** CUT, WHITTLE

whiteacre \'⸗,⸗⸗\ *n* **:** a particular piece of land esp. in distinction from blackacre — used as an arbitrary name

white adder's–mouth \-'⸗⸗,⸗\ *n* **:** a small No. American terrestrial orchid (*Malaxis brachypoda*) with a single leaf and a spike of greenish white flowers

white adder's–tongue *n* **:** a white-flowered dogtooth violet (*Erythronium albidum*) found in mountainous woods of eastern No. America — called also *white clintonia*

white admiral *n* **:** any of several butterflies of the genus

Limenitis having white bands on the wings; *esp* : BANDED PURPLE — compare RED ADMIRAL

white agaric *n* : PURGING AGARIC

white alder *n* **1 a** : any of several native alders (as *Alnus rhombifolia*) of western No. America **b** : GRAY ALDER **2** : any shrub or tree of the genus *Clethra* **3** : a southern African tree (*Platylophus trifoliatus*) of the family Cunoniaceae **4** : PRIVET ANDROMEDA **5** : a winterberry (*Ilex verticillata*)

white-alder family *n* : CLETHRACEAE

white alert *n* : the all-clear signal after an alert; *also* : the period of return to normalcy following an alert — compare BLUE ALERT, RED ALERT, YELLOW ALERT

white alkali *n* **1** : a mixture of salts (as sodium sulfate, magnesium sulfate, and sodium chloride) forming a white crust on some alkali soils **2** : refined soda ash

white ant *n* : TERMITE

white-ant \'⸗¦⸗\ *vt* -ED/-ING/-S [*white ant*] : to wreck or take over surreptitiously as if by the boring of termites : undermine by underhanded means ⟨the popular front was *white-anted* by a Communist minority⟩

white antimony *n* : VALENTINITE

white apple *n* : GROUNDNUT 2a

white apple leafhopper *n* : a cicadellid insect (*Typhlocyba pomaria*) that infests apples in parts of the U.S. and Canada

white arsenic *n* : ARSENIC TRIOXIDE

white ash *n* **1 a** (1) : an American ash (*Fraxinus americana*) having leaves pale green or silvery white below — see TREE illustration (2) : the hard brownish wood of white ash used for tools, furniture, and interior finishings **b** : GREEN ASH **c** : FRINGE TREE **d** : any of several Australian eucalypts (esp. *Eucalyptus coriacea*, *E. fraxinoides*, or *E. globulus*) **e** : WHITE ALDER 2 **2** : OAR 1a

white-ash \'⸗¦⸗\ *adj* [*white ash*] : made of the wood of white ash

white ash herb *n* : GOUTWEED

white asp *or* **white aspen** *n* : WHITE POPLAR 1a

white avens *n* : a bennet (*Geum virginianum*)

white bachelor's-button *n* : WHITE CAMPION a

whiteback \'⸗,⸗\ *n* : CANVASBACK

white-backed skunk \'⸗,⸗-\ *n* : HOG-NOSED SKUNK

white bacon *n, South & Midland* : BACON 3

whitebait \'⸗,⸗\ *n* [¹*white* + *bait*] **1** : the young of several European herrings and esp. of the common herring (*Clupea harengus*) or of the sprat (*C. sprattus*) **2** : any of various small fishes likened to the European whitebait and used as food: as **a** : ICEFISH a **b** : the young of various fishes of the genus *Galaxias* and of several salmonid fishes (genus *Retropinna*) that appear in large schools in New Zealand rivers and lakes **c** : any of various smelts (family Osmeridae) of the coast of California **d** : any of numerous silversides (family Atherinidae) **e** : any of various anchovies of both fresh and salt water in the U.S.

white baker *n, Brit* : SPOTTED FLYCATCHER

white ball *n* : CUE BALL 2

white ballet *n* [trans. of F *ballet blanc*] : BALLET BLANC

white balsam *n* **1** : either of two firs of western America: **a** : WHITE FIR 1a(1) **b** : ALPINE FIR **2** : BALSAM OF PERU **3** : a balsamweed (*Gnaphalium obtusifolium*)

white baneberry *also* **white bead** *n* : a white-fruited baneberry (as *Actaea alba* of No. America) — called also *white cohosh*

whitebark \'⸗,⸗\ *n* **1** : any of several American trees (as the white poplar or whitebark pine) with pale or whitish bark **2** *Austral* : a blueberry ash (*Elaeocarpus cyaneus*)

whitebark pine *also* **whitebarked pine** \'⸗,⸗-\ *n* : a pine (*Pinus albicaulis*) of the western U.S. having thin pale brown or creamy white bark and soft brittle wood

white bass *n* **1** : a No. American freshwater food fish (*Lepibema chrysops*) that is abundant in the region of the Great Lakes and upper Mississippi and very similar to the yellow bass but shorter and more compressed **2** : WHITE PERCH 1

white basswood *n* : an American basswood (*Tilia heterophylla*) of the Allegheny region

white bay *n* **1** : RED BAY **2** : SWEET BAY 2

white·beam \'⸗,bēm\ *n* [¹*white* + *-beam* (as in *quickbeam*] : a European ornamental tree (*Sorbus aria* or *Pyrus aria*) having leaves with a white-tomentose undersurface, corymbose white flowers, and red fruits

white bean *n* : an Australian tree (*Ailanthus imberbiflora*) with up to 50 leaflets in each pinnate leaf and a thin fruit in the form of a pod

white bear *n* **1** : GRIZZLY BEAR **2** : POLAR BEAR

whitebeard \'⸗,⸗\ *n* [ME *whiteberd*, fr. ¹*white* + *berd* beard] : an old man : GRAYBEARD

white bedstraw *n* : WILD MADDER 2a

white beech *n* **1** : AMERICAN BEECH **2** *dial Eng* : HOP HORNBEAM **3** : QUEENSLAND BEECH

white beet *n* : CHARD

white-bellied nuthatch \'⸗,⸗⸗-\ *n* : WHITE-BREASTED NUTHATCH

white-bellied seal *n* : MONK SEAL

white-bellied swallow *n* : a widely distributed No. American swallow (*Iridoprocne bicolor*) that nests in holes in trees and is iridescent greenish blue above and pure white below

whitebelly \'⸗,⸗⸗\ *n* : any of several birds with wholly or partly white underparts: as **a** : BALDPATE 2 **b** : PRAIRIE CHICKEN 1 **c** : SHARP-TAILED GROUSE **d** : a pigeon (*Leptotila jamaicensis*) common in Jamaica

white ben *n* [¹*white* + obs. *behen*, *ben* bladder campion, fr. NL *behen*] : BLADDER CAMPION 1

white bent *also* **white bent grass** *n* **1** : a redtop (*Agrostis alba*) **2** : MATGRASS 1b

white·berry \'⸗- — *see* BERRY\ *n* : WHITE BANEBERRY

whitebill \'⸗,⸗\ *n* **1 a** : AMERICAN COOT **b** : SLATE-COLORED JUNCO **2** : a West Indian sardine (*Harengula macrophthalmus*)

white birch *n* **1** : either of two European birches with white or ash-colored bark: **a** : a birch (*Betula pendula*) with smooth twigs and markedly drooping branches **b** : a birch (*B. pubescens*) with pubescent twigs and somewhat drooping branches **2** : either of two No. American birches with predominantly white bark: **a** : PAPER BIRCH **b** : AMERICAN GRAY BIRCH

whitebird \'⸗,⸗\ *n, Brit* : SPOTTED FLYCATCHER

white bird's-eye *n* : either of two common stitchworts (*Stellaria media* and *S. holostea*)

white biskop *n* : a biskop (*Sparodon durbanensis* or *Sparus durbanensis*) that is usu. somewhat smaller than the black biskop, is silvery with grayish fins and somewhat bluish above, and has the two middle upper teeth large and protruding

white blast *n* : injury to plants caused by the feeding of insects (as the onion thrips) and characterized by a fading and shriveling of the tissues

white blister *n* : WHITE RUST

white blood cell *n* : a blood cell that does not contain hemoglobin : LEUKOCYTE

white-blooded \'⸗¦⸗⸗\ *adj* : having blood that is not reddened by hemoglobin; *often* : ANEMIC

white·blow \'hwīt,blō *also* 'wī-\ *n* [fr. earlier *whiteblowe grass*, fr. obs. *whiteblowe* whitlow (alter. of ME *whitflowe*) + *grass* — more at WHITLOW] : WHITLOW GRASS a

white bomb·way *also* **white bomb·we** \-'bäm(,)(b)wā\ *or* **white bom·be** \-m(,)bā\ *n* [origin unknown] : an Indian timber tree (*Terminalia procera*) having lustrous light brown wood with slight dark streaks

white bone *n, often cap W&B* **1** : a lower class Lolo; *esp* : a free descendant of Chinese captives — distinguished from *black bone* **2** : a Kazak noble descended from a medieval Khan — distinguished from *black bone*

white book *n* [ME *whit boke*, fr. *whit* white + *boke*, *book* book] : an official report of government affairs bound in white — compare WHITE PAPER

whitebottle \'⸗,⸗⸗\ *n* **1** : BLADDER CAMPION 1 **2** : DAISY 1b

white box *n* : any of several Australian eucalypts having white or light-colored bark

white·boy \'⸗,bȯi\ *n* **1** *archaic* : a favored person : PET **2** *usu cap* [so called fr. their wearing white shirts outside their other clothes as a means of recognition on their night raids] : one of an agrarian association formed among the Irish peasants in 1761 esp. to redress their grievances against their landlords and to resist collection of tithes

white·boy·ism \-ȯi,izəm\ *n* -s *usu cap* : the principles or conduct of the Whiteboys

white brant *n* : LESSER SNOW GOOSE

white brass *n* : an inferior brass containing more than 49 percent zinc

white bread *n* [ME *whitbred*, fr. *whit* white + *breed* bread] : bread made from white and esp. bleached flour — compare WHOLE WHEAT FLOUR

white break *n* : a virus disease of the gladiolus characterized by gray or yellowish specking or streaking resembling thrips injury and by striking white blotchery of colored flowers

white-breasted nuthatch \'⸗,⸗⸗-\ *n* : a common nuthatch (*Sitta carolinensis carolinensis*) of America east of the Rocky mountains that has a black head, largely bluish gray upper parts, and the underbody mostly white

white bronze *n* : a very light colored bronze having large proportion of tin in its composition

white broom *n* : a low European shrub (*Cytisus albus*) with trifoliolate leaves and yellowish white flowers

white brush *n* : a low shrub (*Lippia ligustrina*) of the southwestern U.S. and adjacent Mexico having fragrant white racemose flowers that yield much honey

white bryony *n* : either of two European bryonies (*Bryonia alba* and *B. dioica*)

white bud *n* : a zinc deficiency disease of Indian corn characterized by light yellow streaking and white necrotic spotting in the young emerging leaves

white buffalo *n* **1** : MOUNTAIN GOAT 1 **2** *or* **white buffalo fish** : SMALLMOUTH BUFFALO

white bur-sage *n* : a low whitish brittle-twigged somewhat spiny shrub (*Franseria dumosa*) of the southwestern U.S. that is a locally important browse plant esp. for sheep and goats

white bush *n* **1** *Brit* : a white-flowered hawthorn **2** : a sweet pepperbush (*Clethra alnifolia*) **3** : PRIVET ANDROMEDA

white buttercup *n* : GRASS-OF-PARNASSUS

white butterfly *n, chiefly Brit* : WHITE 3d(2)

white buttonwood *n* **1** : WHITE MANGROVE 1 **2** : a plane (*Platanus occidentalis*) of eastern No. America having the lobes of the leaves shallow and broader than long

white cake *n* : a butter cake in which the whites but not the yolks of eggs are used

white camas *n* : a camas (*Zigadenus glaucus*) chiefly of eastern U.S. having a creamy white perianth that is suffused with green, bronze, or purple

white campion *n* : any of several white-flowered herbs: as **a** : a viscid-pubescent European herb (*Lychnis alba*) with fragrant flowers — called also *white cockle* **b** : STARRY CAMPION **c** : SNOWY CAMPION

white cankerroot *or* **white cankerweed** *n* : a rattlesnake root (*Prenanthes alba*)

white·cap \'⸗,kap\ *n* **1 a** : the male of the European redstart **b** *Brit* : WHITETHROAT 1 **c** : TREE SPARROW 1 **2** : a wave crest breaking into white foam **3 a** : HORSE MUSHROOM **b** : HARDHACK 1 **4 a** : one who wears a white cap **b** *also* **white·cap·per** *usu cap* \-pə(r)\ : a member of a group using a white cap as an identifying badge; *esp* : one of a self-appointed vigilance committee attempting by lynch-law methods to drive away or coerce persons obnoxious to it

white carp *n* : CARPSUCKER

white cast iron *n* : WHITE IRON 2

white cat *or* **white catfish** *n* : any of several No. American freshwater catfishes (genus *Ictalurus*); *esp* : a catfish (*I. catus*) that is native to coastal streams of the eastern and southern U.S. and introduced in California and Nevada, is pale olive to bluish above and silvery below, and reaches a length of two feet

white cedar *n* **1** : any of various No. American trees: as **a** (1) : SOUTHERN WHITE CEDAR (2) : the soft wood of the southern white cedar largely used for shingles, boats, woodenware, and posts **b** : PORT ORFORD CEDAR **c** : MACNAB CYPRESS **d** : CALIFORNIA JUNIPER **e** : CANOE CEDAR **f** : INCENSE CEDAR **g** : a common arborvitae (*Thuja occidentalis*) — see TREE illustration **2 a** : a timber tree (*Protium altissimum*) of Guiana **b** : its fragrant wood used esp. for cabinetwork and canoes **3** *Austral* : CHINABERRY 2; *also* : its wood **4** : any of several So. American trees of the genus *Tabebuia*

white cell *n* : WHITE BLOOD CELL

white cement *n* : a portland cement made from raw materials very low in the iron compounds that give the gray color to the usual portland cement

white chamomile *n* : a common chamomile (*Anthemis nobilis*)

white·chap·el cart \'hwīt,chapəl- *also* 'wī-\ *or* **whitechapel** *n* -s *usu cap W* [fr. *Whitechapel*, district of eastern London, England] : a light 2-wheeled spring cart used esp. for family or light delivery service

white charlock *n* : JOINTED CHARLOCK

white-cheeked goose \'⸗,⸗-\ *n* : a goose that constitutes a variety (*Branta canadensis occidentalis*) of the Canada goose and has the white head patch divided by a black band under the throat so as to form two cheek patches

white-cheeked pintail *n* : BAHAMA DUCK

white cherry *n* : COACHWOOD 1b

white chestnut oak *n* : CHESTNUT OAK

white-chinned petrel \'⸗,⸗-\ *n* : a large petrel (*Procellaria aequinoctialis*) of southern oceans that is all black except for a white mark on the chin and often extended on to the face

white chip *n* **1** : a white-colored poker chip that is usu. the least valuable chip **2** : a token or sum of insignificant worth — compare BLUE CHIP

white chub *n* : SPOTTAIL SHINER

white cinnamon *n* **1** : WINTER'S BARK **2** : CANELLA 3

white clematis *n* : any of several clematises; *esp* : a white-flowered clematis (*Clematis ligusticifolium*) of western No. America

white clergy *n* : the Russian Orthodox secular clergy — distinguished from *black clergy*

white clintonia *n* : WHITE ADDER'S-TONGUE

white cloud mountain fish *also* **white cloud** *n* : a very small Chinese freshwater fish (*Tanichthys albonubes*) that is brilliantly striped in gold and blue with the caudal fin red and tipped with white in the male and is often kept in the tropical aquarium

white clover *n* : a clover with white flowers: as **a** : WHITE DUTCH CLOVER **b** : WHITE SWEET CLOVER

white coal *n* **1 a** : WATERPOWER **b** : ELECTRICITY **2** : TASMANITE

whitecoat \'⸗,⸗\ *n* **1** : a very young hair seal and esp. a harp seal **2** : the soft pliable white woolly skin of the whitecoat

white coat *n* : the finishing coat in plastering

white cockle *n* : WHITE CAMPION a

white cohosh *n* : WHITE BANEBERRY

white-collar \'⸗¦⸗⸗\ *adj* **1** : belonging or relating to a population segment or class made up of salaried employees (as teachers, sales persons, office workers, civil servants) whose duties permit the wearing of street clothes and call for well-groomed appearance — compare BLUE-COLLAR **2** : of, relating to, characteristic of, or restricted to individuals of the white-collar segment or of a corresponding socioeconomic level ⟨*white-collar* housing⟩ ⟨*white-collar* crime⟩

whitecomb \'⸗,⸗\ *n* : favus of fowls that is marked by proliferation of grayish white crumbly crusts about the comb, earlobes, and wattles and sometimes progresses to the feathered surfaces where loss of feathers and cuplike encrusted lesions may follow

white commissure *n* : the ventral commissure of the spinal cord

white coolwort *n* : FALSE MITERWORT

white copperas *n* **1** : GOSLARITE **2** : COQUIMBITE

white coral *n* : a graceful branched coral (*Amphihelia oculata*) native to the Mediterranean

whitecorn \'⸗,⸗\ *n, dial Brit* : a small grain (as wheat, barley, or oats) that becomes light-colored as it ripens

white cornel *n* : FLOWERING DOGWOOD

white corpuscle *n* : LEUKOCYTE

white count *n* [*white* (*corpuscle*) + *count*] : the count or the total number of the leukocytes in blood usu. stated as the number in one cubic millimeter

white crab *n* **1** : GHOST CRAB **2** : GREAT LAND CRAB

white crappie *n* : a crappie (*Pomoxis annularis*) that is typically smaller and more silvery than the black crappie, highly esteemed as a panfish, and often used for stocking small ponds — called also *white perch*

white-crested touraco \'⸗,⸗⸗-\ *n* : a southern African touraco (*Tauraco corythaix*)

white cricket *n* : TREE CRICKET

white croaker *n* : either of two fishes found along the California coast: **a** : KINGFISH 1a(2) **b** : QUEENFISH a

white crop *n* : a crop of grain (as wheat, rye, barley, or oats) that loses its green color or becomes white in ripening as distinguished from a green crop or a root crop

white-cross diatom *n* : a diatom of a genus (*Stauroneis*) related to *Navicula* with longitudinal and transverse bands that form a cross

white crow *n, Africa* : an Old World vulture (*Neophron percnopterus*)

white-crowned pigeon \'⸗,⸗-\ *n* : a large chiefly slate-colored pigeon (*Columba leucocephala*) of Florida and the West Indies having the head white above

white-crowned sparrow *n* : a sparrow (*Zonotrichia leucophrys*) of northern and western No. America that is related to the white-throated sparrow and has the head striped with white and black

whitecup \'⸗,⸗\ *n* : a prostrate woody Argentine herb (*Nierembergia rivularis*) with white or rarely blue-tinged or rose-tinged tubular flowers

white curlew *n* : WHITE IBIS

white currant *n* : any of various white-fruited garden currants derived from a natural species (*Ribes sativum*)

white cutch *n* : GAMBIER

white cypress *n* **1** : a bald cypress (*Taxodium distichum*) **2** : WHITE CYPRESS PINE

white cypress pine *n* : an Australian evergreen timber tree (*Callitris glauca*) yielding a pale fragrant insect-resistant timber

whited *adj* [ME, fr. past part. of *whiten* to white] **1** : covered with white or whiting; *esp* : WHITEWASHED **2** : made white : WHITENED, BLEACHED

white daisy *n* : DAISY 1b

white dammar *n* : PINEY DAMMAR

white damp *n* : a poisonous gas encountered in coal mines and made up chiefly of carbon monoxide

white dead nettle *n* : a European dead nettle (*Lamium album*) with white flowers

white deal *n, Brit* : NORWAY SPRUCE; *also* : its wood

white death shark *n* : GREAT WHITE SHARK

white diarrhea *n* : any of several diseases of birds or mammals marked by passage of pale or whitish diarrheic stools: as **a** : pullorum disease esp. in young birds **b** : WHITE SCOURS **c** : coccidiosis of chickens

white dock *n* : a perennial No. American dock (*Rumex mexicanus*) with pale-green leaves like those of a willow

white dogwood *n* **1** : any of several white-flowered shrubs or trees of the genus *Cornus* (as flowering dogwood) **2** *Brit* : GUELDER ROSE

whited sepulcher *n* [so called fr. the simile applied by Jesus to the scribes and Pharisees, Mt 23:27 (AV)] : a person inwardly corrupt or wicked but outwardly or professedly virtuous or holy : HYPOCRITE

white dutch clover *also* **white dutch** *n, usu cap D* : a Eurasian clover (*Trifolium repens*) that has long stalked leaves and round heads of white or pink-tinged flowers and is a common ingredient of lawn and pasture grass-seed mixtures and an important honey plant — compare WHITE SWEET CLOVER, SHAMROCK

white dwarf *n* : a whitish star of high surface temperature and very low intrinsic brightness usu. with a mass about comparable to that of the sun but of such small dimensions that its average density is enormous

white-ear \'⸗,⸗\ *n* [alter. of (assumed) ME *whit-ers*, fr. *whit* white + *ers* rump — more at ASS] : ²WHEATEAR

white eardrops *n pl but sing or pl in constr* : DUTCHMAN'S-BREECHES

white-eared hummingbird \'⸗,⸗-\ *n* : a hummingbird of the genus *Hylocharis* (as *H. leucotis* of Central America or *H. xantusii* of Lower California)

white earth *n* **1** : a siliceous earth from eastern Bavaria used as a substrate for organic pigments for paints **2** : an impure silica

white elephant *n* **1** : an albinic Indian elephant of which more or less of the usual dark pigment is absent from the skin giving it a pale color and which is rare and sometimes venerated in India, Ceylon, Siam, and Burma **2 a** : a property requiring much care and expense and yielding little profit **b** : an object (as a gadget or trinket) that is no longer esteemed by its owner though not without value to others ⟨conducted a *white elephant* sale to help the church⟩ **3** : a badge or emblem showing the figure of a white elephant

white elm *n* **1** : AMERICAN ELM **2** : ROCK ELM 1

white ensign *n* : the British naval ensign

white-eye \'⸗,⸗\ *n* **1 a** : SILVEREYE **b** : WHITE-EYED VIREO **c** : WHITE-EYED DUCK a **2 a** : HADDOCK **b** : WALLEYE 4

white-eyed coot \'⸗,⸗-\ *n* : WHITE-WINGED SCOTER

white-eyed duck *also* **white-eyed pochard** *n* : either of two pochards having males with the irises of the eyes white: **a** : a widely distributed Old World duck (*Aythya nyroca*) **b** : an Australian duck (*Aythya australis*) — called also *hardhead*

white-eyed tit *n* : SILVEREYE

white-eyed towhee *n* : a towhee (*Pipilo erythrophthalmus alleni*) of Florida

white-eyed vireo *n* : a vireo (*Vireo griseus*) of the eastern U.S. with a greenish olive back, white underparts, and a yellow ring around the white eye

white-eyelid monkey *n* : MANGABEY

whiteface \'⸗,⸗\ *n* **1** : a white-faced animal; *specif* : HEREFORD **2 a** : BALDPATE 2; *also* : BLUE-WINGED TEAL **b** : any of several Australian passerine birds of the genus *Aphelocephala* that resemble tits **3 a** : dead-white facial makeup **b** : a performer (as a clown) wearing whiteface

white-faced \'⸗¦⸗\ *adj* **1 a** : having a wan pale face **b** : having the face white in whole or in part — used esp. of animals in which other parts of the body, hair, or plumage are dark **2** : having a white facing : white-fronted ⟨a *white-faced* storefront⟩ ⟨a *white-faced* hem⟩

white-faced duck *or* **white-faced teal** *n* : BLUE-WINGED TEAL

white-faced glossy ibis *n* : a glossy ibis (*Plegadis guarauna*) occurring from the southwestern U.S. southward through much of So. America and having reddish lores and usu. white feathers about the base of the bill

white-faced hornet *n* : a large American hornet (*Vespula maculata*) predominantly dull black with striking white markings on head, thorax, and abdomen — called also *bald-faced hornet*

white father *n, usu cap W&F* [so called fr. his customarily dressing in white] : a member of the Society of African Missioners founded about 1868 by the Abbé Lavigerie

white feather *n* [so called fr. the superstition that a white feather in the plumage of a gamecock is an indication that he is a poor fighter] : a mark or symbol of cowardice — used chiefly in the phrase *show the white feather*

white fiber *n* **1** : a medullated nerve fiber **2** : one of the inelastic fibers of typical connective tissue

white fibrous tissue *n* : typical connective tissue in which white fibers predominate as distinguished from elastic tissue

white·field·ian \(')hw|it¦fēldēən, |īt *also* (')w|\ *also* **white·field·ite** \'⸗,fēl,dīt\ *n* -s *usu cap* [George *Whitefield* †1770 Eng. evangelist and founder of Calvinistic Methodists + E *-ian*, *-ite*] : an adherent or follower of the evangelist George Whitefield

white fig *n* : PURPLE FIG

white finch *n, dial Eng* : CHAFFINCH

white fir *n* **1 a** : any of several firs of western America: as (1) : a tree (*Abies concolor*) with a narrow erect crown, pale foliage, and soft wood that is used for lumber — called also *California white fir*, *Colorado fir* (2) : LOWLAND FIR (3) : AMABILIS FIR (4) : ALPINE FIR **b** : the wood of a white fir **2** *Brit* : NORWAY SPRUCE; *also* : its wood **3** : a Chinese evergreen tree (*Cupressus funebris*) with gracefully drooping branches

¹whitefish \'ˌ=,=\ *n, pl* **whitefish** *or* **whitefishes** [ME *whitfish*, fr. *whit* white + *fish*] **1 a :** any of various food fishes (family Salmonidae) esp. of the genus *Coregonus* that resemble the salmon and trout in having an adipose dorsal fin but have a smaller and nearly or quite toothless mouth and that inhabit clear lakes and streams of No. America, Europe, and Asia — see LAKE WHITEFISH, MENOMINEE WHITEFISH, ROCKY MOUNTAIN WHITEFISH; compare CISCO, HOUTING, LAKE HERRING **b :** any of various fishes (as a menhaden, a young bluefish, or a whiting) in some respect felt to resemble the true whitefishes **c** *Brit* **:** any of various market fishes (as cod, sole, halibut) with white flesh that is not oily **d :** BELUGA **2 :** the flesh of a whitefish esp. as an article of food

²whitefish \"\ *vi* **:** to fish for whitefish — **whitefisher** \'=,==\ *n* — **whitefishery** \'=,=(=)=\ *n*

white flag *n* **1 :** a flag or something used as a flag of plain white that in all civilized armies is recognized as a flag of truce and as a token of surrender when displayed over a place, position, or body of men **2 :** a token of weakness or yielding

white flesh·er \-'fleshə(r)\ *n* [*white flesh* (fr. ¹*white* + *flesh*) + *-er*] *dial* **:** RUFFED GROUSE

white flux *n* **:** a flux consisting chiefly of potassium carbonate and obtained as a white or grayish mass by the deflagration of tartar with an equal or larger amount of saltpeter

whitefly *n* **:** any of numerous small injurious homopterous insects constituting the family Aleyrodidae, being related to the scales, and being usu. covered with a white or gray powder — see CITRUS WHITEFLY, GREENHOUSE WHITEFLY

whitefoot \'=,=\ *n, pl* **whitefeet** *see sense 3* **1 :** a white mark on a horse's foot between the fetlock and the coffin; *also* **:** a horse having such a mark **2** *usu cap* **:** one of a secret society replacing the Whiteboys in Ireland about 1832 **3** *pl* **white-foots :** WHITE-FOOTED MOUSE

white-footed mouse \'=,==-\ *n* **:** any of numerous No. American mice of the genus *Peromyscus; esp* **:** a common woodland mouse (*P. leucopus*) of the eastern U.S.

white fox *n* **:** ARCTIC FOX

white friar *n, often cap W&F* [ME *white frere*, fr. ¹*white* + *frere* friar; fr. his white habit] **:** a Carmelite monk

white fringe *n* **:** FRINGE TREE

white-fringed beetle *also* **white-fringed weevil** \'=,=-\ *n* **:** a flightless beetle (*Pantomorus leucoloma* or *Graphognathus leucoloma*) native to So. America but recently introduced into Australia and the southeastern U.S. where it is a pest of cultivated plants

white fringed orchid *or* **white fringed orchis** *n* **:** a bog orchid (*Habenaria albiflora*) of eastern No. America with sheathing leaves and a spike of pure-white fringed flowers

white fringe fungus *n* **:** a fungous parasite (*Fusarium aleyrodis*) of the white fly

white fritillary *n* **:** a California bulbous herb (*Fritillaria liliacea*) with white and sometimes green-veined flowers

whitefront \'=,=\ *n* **:** WHITE-FRONTED GOOSE

white-fronted capuchin \'=,==-\ *n* **:** a So. American monkey (*Cebus albifrons*) of a reddish brown color with white face, forehead, shoulders, and breast

white-fronted goose *n* **:** a large widely distributed grayish brown goose (*Anser albifrons*) of northern Europe and No. America with a white forehead and black, white, and gray underparts — see TULE GOOSE

white-fronted lemur *n* **:** a lemur (*Lemur albifrons*) of Madagascar having a white forehead

white-fronted owl *n* **:** SAW-WHET OWL

white frost *n* **:** FROST 1c(1)

white fungus *or* **white fungus disease** *n* **1 :** a disease of fishes caused by a fungus (*Saprolegnia ferox*) and characterized by a white coating of hyphae esp. on peripheral parts (as fins) **2 :** a disease of insects caused by a fungus of the genus *Beauveria* — compare CALCINO

white gall *n* **:** an oak apple collected after the escape of its gall wasp and lighter in color and poorer in tannin than a green gall

white game *n* **:** ptarmigan in winter plumage

white gasoline *or* **white gas** *n* **:** gasoline containing no tetraethyl lead

white gentian *n* **:** FEVERROOT

white ginger *n* **1 :** the rootstock of ginger dried and scraped — called also *African ginger, cochin ginger;* distinguished from *black ginger* **2 :** a large Indian herb (*Hedychium coronarium*) that is widely cultivated in warm regions for its showy white fragrant flowers

white goat *n* **:** MOUNTAIN GOAT 1

white gold *n* **1 :** a pale alloy of gold that somewhat resembles silver or platinum and usu. contains nickel with or without other alloying metals (as tin, zinc, or copper) **2 :** a natural resource (as sugar or cotton) that is white or becomes white in processing

white goldenrod *n* **:** SILVERROD 2

white goods *n pl* **1 a :** white fabrics esp. of cotton or linen **b :** articles (as sheets, towels, tablecloths, or curtains) orig. or typically made of white cloth **2 :** major household and esp. electric appliances (as washers, stoves, or refrigerators) that are typically finished in white enamel

white goose *n* **:** SNOW GOOSE

white goosefoot *n* **:** LAMB'S-QUARTERS 1

white gourd melon *also* **white gourd** *n* **:** WAX GOURD 2

white grama *n* **:** a grass (*Leersia virginica*) found in moist places in the eastern U.S.

white granite *n* **:** a ceramic ware like or identical with ironstone china

white grass *n* **1 :** VELVET GRASS **2 :** WHITE GRAMA

white grease *n* **:** lard considered unfit for human consumption and used industrially — compare YELLOW GREASE

white grouse *n* **1 :** PTARMIGAN **2 :** SHARP-TAILED GROUSE

white grub *n* **:** a grub that is the larva of a June beetle or other related beetle and that feeds on the roots of grasses and other plants

white grunt *n* **:** a common grunt (*Haemulon plumieri*) of Florida and the West Indies that is typically striped with blue and a brassy yellow

white guard *n, sometimes cap W&G* [from the *White Guard*, anti-Communist force organized in Finland in 1918] **:** a reactionary or counterrevolutionary force or party

white guillemot *n* **:** BLACK GUILLEMOT — used esp. when it is in winter plumage

white gum *n* **:** any of numerous Australian eucalypts (as *Eucalyptus viminalis, E. haemastoma, E. gunnii, E. coriacea*) having notably pale bark

white gyrfalcon *n* **:** a gyrfalcon (*Falco rusticolus candicans*) of northern No. America that is predominantly white with slaty or brownish gray barring or spotting on the upper parts

white-haired \'=¦=\ *adj* [ME *white-harid*, fr. ¹*white* + *hered, harid* haired] **1 :** having white hair or covered with white hairs ⟨a *white-haired* plant⟩ **2 :** FAIR-HAIRED 2

white hake *n* **:** a hake (*Urophycis tenuis*) that is a leading food fish along the New England coast and southward

white·hall \'hwīt¦hȯl *also* 'wī-\ *adj, usu cap* [fr. *Whitehall*, thoroughfare of Westminster metropolitan borough, London, England, lined with chief offices of the British government] **:** of or relating to Whitehall esp. as symbolizing the British government or its policies ⟨a *Whitehall* statement⟩

whitehanded \'=¦==\ *adj* **1 a :** having white hands **b :** having white paws **2 :** having or keeping the hands free from evil acts; *broadly* **:** PURE, UNSTAINED, UNSULLIED

whitehanded gibbon *n* **:** LAR

white-hard \'=¦=\ *adj* **:** quite dry but unfired — used of clay or clay ware

white harvest *n* **:** a harvest when the ground is white from hoarfrost **:** a late harvest

white hat *n, slang* **:** an enlisted man in the U.S. Navy

white hawk *n, Irish* **:** a male hen harrier

whitehead \'=,=\ *n* **1 :** any of various birds with more or less white about the head: as **a :** BLUE GOOSE **b :** SURF SCOTER **c :** a small New Zealand bird (*Mohoua ochrocephala albicilla*) that resembles a warbler **d :** a domestic pigeon of a breed distinguished by a white head **2 :** MILIUM 3 **3 :** any of several diseases of grasses characterized by bleaching of the heads: as **a :** such a condition in oats due to stem injury by maggots or thrips **b whiteheads** *pl but sing or pl in constr* **:** TAKE-ALL

white-headed \'=¦==\ *adj* **1 a :** having the head white **b** (1) **:** having white hair (2) **:** having very light hair **2 :** highly favored **:** FORTUNATE ⟨the *white-headed* boy . . . of the new generation —Van Wyck Brooks⟩

white-headed eagle *n* **:** BALD EAGLE

white-headed fungus *or* **white-headed scale fungus** *n* **:** a fungus (*Podonectria coccicola*) that is parasitic on scales and esp. the purple scale and the Glover scale

white-headed goose *n* **:** BLUE GOOSE

white-headed gull *n* **:** HEERMANN'S GULL

white-headed harpy *n, Brit* **:** MARSH HARRIER

white-headed stilt *n* **:** a stilt (*Himantopus leucocephalus* or *H. himantopus leucocephalus*) that is predominantly white with black wings and markings on nape and mantle and that is widely distributed in the southwestern Pacific including Australia and New Zealand — see KAKI

white-headed tern *n* **:** a So. American tern (*Sterna trudeaui*) that has the top of the head white and without a black crest

white-headed woodpecker *n* **:** a woodpecker (*Dendrocopos albolarvatus*) of the Sierra Nevada and Cascade ranges that is predominantly black with a white wing patch, white head and neck, and a red patch just above the nape

¹white·head·ian \(')hwīt¦hedēən *also* (')wī-\ *adj, usu cap* [Alfred North *Whitehead* †1947 Eng. mathematician and philosopher + E *-ian*] **:** of, relating to, or typical of Alfred North Whitehead or his organismic or process philosophy

²whiteheadian \"\ *n* **-s** *usu cap* **:** a follower of A. N. Whitehead

white heart *n* **1 white hearts** *pl but sing or pl in constr* **:** DUTCHMAN'S-BREECHES **2 :** SQUIRREL CORN

white-heart hickory *n* **:** MOCKERNUT

white heat *n* **1 :** a temperature (as for copper and iron from 1500° to 1600° C) higher than red heat at which a body becomes brightly incandescent so as to appear white **2 :** a state of intense mental or physical strain, emotion, or activity ⟨his anger was at *white heat*⟩ ⟨the campaign was at a *white heat*⟩

white heath aster *n* **:** HEATH ASTER

white heel splitter *n* **:** a large No. American freshwater mussel (*Lasmigona complanata*) with a sharp alate process behind the umbones

white heifer disease *n* **:** a congenital abnormality of the reproductive organs of heifers resulting in sterility and occurring chiefly in white or nearly white animals of the Shorthorn breed

white hellebore *n* **1 :** an herb of the genus *Veratrum* (as the European *V. album* or the American *V. viride*) — called also *false hellebore* **2 :** the roots or rhizomes of a white hellebore

white heron *n* **1 :** GREAT WHITE HERON **2 :** SNOWY EGRET

white hickory *n* **1 :** any of several hickories (as the shagbark or mockernut) **2 :** the firm whitish sapwood of a hickory

white holland *n, usu cap W&H* **:** a medium-sized pure-white domestic turkey of a variety possibly derived as a sport from the Bronze

white holly *n* **:** a common American holly (*Ilex opaca*)

white honeyflower *n* **:** LOCUST 3a(2)

white honeysuckle *n* **1 :** SWAMP AZALEA **2** *dial Eng* **:** WHITE CLOVER **3 :** HONEYSUCKLE 2b

white hoolet *n, dial Eng* **:** BARN OWL

white hope *n* **1** *slang* **:** a white contender for a pugilistic championship held by a colored person **2 :** one of which much is expected; *esp* **:** a person undertaking a difficult task

white horde *n, usu cap W&H* **:** a Mongolian people powerful in Russia in the 14th century — compare GOLDEN HORDE

white horehound *n* **:** HOREHOUND 1a

white horse *n* **1 :** WHITECAP 2 **2 :** a large mass of tough sinewy oilless substance lying in the head of a sperm whale just above the upper jaw and extending in streaks into the junk above it **3 :** any of several suckers; *esp* **:** a common sucker (*Catostomus commersoni*)

white·horse \'hwīt,hō(ə)rs *also* 'wī-\ *adj, usu cap* [fr. *Whitehorse*, town of southern Yukon, Canada] **:** of or from Whitehorse, the capital of Yukon Territory, Canada **:** of the kind or style prevalent in Whitehorse

white horse nettle *n* **:** TROMPILLO

white-hot \'=¦=\ *adj* **:** being at or radiating white heat; *esp* **:** ardently zealous or fervid

white house *adj, usu cap W&H* [fr. the *White House*, mansion in Washington, D.C. assigned to the use of the president of the United States] **:** of or relating to the White House esp. as symbolizing the presidency or its policies ⟨the *White House* staff⟩

white hun *n, usu cap W&H* **:** EPHTHALITE

white hunter *n* **:** a white man who is expert in jungle lore and usu. serves as guide and professional hunter to an African safari

white ibis *n* **1 :** an ibis (*Eudocimus albus*) of tropical America and the southern U.S. having white plumage with the wings tipped with black **2 :** an Asiatic ibis (*Threskiornis melanocephala*) having the plumage chiefly white and the bare skin of head and neck blue-black

white ice *n* **:** coarsely granular porous ice (as of a glacier) that is usu. formed by compaction of snow and appears white to the eye **:** NÉVÉ — compare BLACK ICE, BLUE ICE

white indian *n, usu cap W&I* **:** an American Indian of light or partially albino complexion: as **a :** a Cuna of Panama **b :** MENOMINI

white indian hemp *n, usu cap I* **:** SWAMP MILKWEED

white ipecac *or* **white ipecacuanha** *n* **1 :** IPECAC SPURGE **2 a :** a Brazilian plant (*Ionidium ipecacuanha*) of the family Violaceae **b :** the root of this plant which has the properties of ipecac

white iron *n* **1 :** iron in thin sheets coated with tin **:** TINPLATE **2 :** a hard silvery-white pig iron or cast iron having its carbon content almost entirely in combined form

white ironbark *n* **:** any of several Australian eucalypts (esp. *Eucalyptus paniculata* and *E. leucoxylon*) with pale bark and light-colored very hard wood used esp. in bridges and buildings and for railroad ties

white iron pyrites *n pl but sing or pl in constr* **:** MARCASITE 1b

white ironwood *n* **1 a :** a timber tree (*Hypelate trifoliata*) of the family Sapindaceae that occurs in Florida and the West Indies and has edible berries **b :** the hard wood of this tree that is used in shipbuilding and for wheel spokes, tool handles, and similar items and that resembles mahogany — called also *Madeira wood* **2 a :** a southern African timber tree (*Toddalia lanceolata*) of the family Rutaceae **b :** the dark tough elastic hard wood of this tree

white jade *n* **:** ALABASTER 2

white kalmuck *n, usu cap W&K* **:** an Altaic Tartar

white kite *n, Irish* **:** a male hen harrier

white label *n* [so called fr. its bearing a hand-written or typed white label in contrast to the printed label used on trade records] **:** one of the first group of phonograph records pressed from a recording usu. for executive, artist, and reviewer opinion

white lady *n* **:** a cocktail consisting of gin, Cointreau liqueur, lemon juice, and often white of egg shaken with cracked ice and strained before serving

white lady's-slipper *or* **white lady-slipper** *n* **:** a No. American lady's slipper (*Cypripedium candidum*) having greenish white flowers striped purplish within

white lake bass *n* **:** WHITE BASS

white land crab *n* **:** GREAT LAND CRAB

white lark *n, dial Eng* **:** SNOW BUNTING

white latten *n* **:** TINPLATE

white lauan *n* **:** a light-colored lauan; *esp* **:** a grayish red wood obtained from a Philippine tree (*Pentacme contorta*) of the family Dipterocarpaceae and often used as a substitute for mahogany

white laurel *n* **1 :** SWEET BAY 2 **2 :** a shrub (*Rhododendron occidentalis*) of the Pacific coast of the U.S. with yellow-blotched flowers

white lead *n* [ME *white led*, fr. ¹*white* + *leed, led* lead] **:** any of several poisonous white pigments containing lead: as **a :** a pigment consisting of basic lead carbonate of variable composition and physical properties that is usu. produced from metallic lead or litharge, acetic acid, moisture, and carbon dioxide by various processes (as the Dutch process, Carter process, or chamber process) and marketed as a heavy powder or as a paste in linseed oil, that has good hiding power esp. in the case of the finer particle sizes and forms tough flexible films tending to chalk and darkening by reaction with hydrogen sulfide in industrial atmospheres, and that is now used chiefly in exterior paints often in mixtures with other white pigments — called also *basic carbonate white lead, ceruse;* see FLAKE WHITE, KREMNITZ WHITE **b :** a pigment that consists essentially of a mixture of equimolar ratios of normal lead sulfate and monobasic lead sulfate and is used in mixtures with other pigments in exterior paints — called also *basic sulfate white lead;* compare SUBLIMED WHITE LEAD **c :** a pigment consisting either of a basic lead silicate approximately $Pb_3(OH)_2SiO_3$ or of a surface layer of monobasic lead silicate and monobasic lead sulfate on a core of silica — called also *basic silicate white lead*

white lead ore *n* **:** CERUSSITE

white leaf *n* **1 :** WHITE POPLAR 1a **2 :** tragacanth consisting of thin translucent pieces of horny texture

white leather *n* **1 :** leather prepared with alum and salt **:** tawed leather **2 :** the ligamentum nuchae of a quadruped

white-leaved sage \'=,=-\ *n* **:** PURPLE SAGE 1

white leg *n* **:** MILK LEG 1

white leghorn *n, often cap W&L* **:** a pure white domestic fowl of outstanding egg-producing ability constituting a variety of the Leghorn breed

white lettuce *n* **:** RATTLESNAKE ROOT a

white light *n* **1 :** light that has the same spectral energy distribution as unobstructed noon sunlight and is approximately the same as that of a blackbody radiator at 6000° C **2 :** light that to the normal eye matches the color of noon sunlight although it may have a different spectral energy distribution

white lightning *n* **:** MOONSHINE 3

¹white lime *n* **:** pure lime

²white lime *or* **white linden** *n* **:** any of several lindens or basswoods with leaves white or whitish beneath

white line *n* [trans. of NL *linea alba*] **:** a band or edge of something white: as **a** (1) **:** LINEA ALBA (2) **:** the tendinous arch of the pelvic fascia (3) **:** the cross section of the leafy layer of a horse's hoof where the periphery of the sole unites with the lower border of the wall and bars of the hoof **b :** a blank line in a printed text **c :** untarred rope or other cordage **d :** a line or part of a metal cut or engraving that prints white by reason of having the design cut away and the background left high; *also* **:** the technique of producing such effects **e :** a stripe painted on a road and used to guide traffic

white-line \'=,=\ *vt* [*white line*] **:** to mark with a white line

white-lined sphinx \'=,=-\ *n* **:** an American sphinx moth (*Celerio lineata*) whose larvae eat the leaves of cotton, apple, grape, currant, and many other plants, whose fore wings are olive brown with a longitudinal buff stripe and with most of the veins lined with white, and whose hind wings are black with a central reddish band

white linn *n* **:** WHITE LIME

white-lipped \'=¦=\ *adj* **:** having white lips

white-lipped peccary \'=,=-\ *n* **:** a peccary (*Tayassu pecari*) that is larger than the collared peccary and predominantly blackish with whitish cheeks

white-lipped snake *n* **:** an Australian elapid snake (*Denisonia coronoides*) that is related to the copperhead but not esp. dangerous, is brown to olive above shading to creamy white or salmon pink ventrally, and has the upper lip usu. white and bounded by a black streak and sometimes a yellow collar about the neck

white liquor *n* **:** the cooking liquor prepared from recovered alkali in the sulfate and soda processes

white list *n* **:** a list of approved or favored items: as **a :** a list of business concerns that are worthy of patronage by reason of compliance with usu. specified conditions (as in regard to treatment of employees) **b :** a list of cultural or amusement items (as plays or books) approved (as in respect to moral worth or orthodoxy) **c :** a list of actual or potential employees who are desirable for employment — compare BLACKLIST

white-list \'=,=\ *vt* [*white list*] **:** to include on a white list

white-livered \'=¦==\ *adj* [¹*white* + *livered;* fr. the former belief that the choleric temperament depends on the body's producing large quantities of yellow bile] **:** deficient in vigor and courage **:** COWARDLY, PUSILLANIMOUS ⟨a *white-livered* backslider⟩ ⟨born *white-livered*⟩

white liverwort *n* **:** GRASS-OF-PARNASSUS

white locoweed *also* **white loco** *n* **:** a perennial herb (*Oxytropis lambertii*) of the western U.S. that is very poisonous to stock and has linear to elliptic or oblong leaves and elongate flower clusters

white locust *n* **:** LOCUST 3a

white lotion *n* **1 :** a fluid astringent preparation made of lead acetate, zinc sulfate, and water and used largely in veterinary practice for wounds, scratches, or suppurations **2 :** a preparation made of sulfurated potash instead of lead acetate and used in dermatologic practice for various skin diseases

white louse *or* **white louse scale** *n* **:** a scale (*Unaspis citri*) that is esp. destructive to citrus in Australia

white lupine *n* **:** a Eurasian white-flowered lupine (*Lupinus albus*) widely cultivated for forage and erosion control

¹white·ly *adv* [ME *whitly*, fr. *whit* white + *-ly*, adv. suffix] **:** so as to show or appear white **:** with an effect of whiteness ⟨reflect light ~ like clouds or snow —*Time*⟩

²white·ly *adj* [ME *whitly*, fr. *whit* white + *-ly*, adj. suffix] *chiefly Scot* **:** light in color **:** WHITISH, PALE

white mahogany *n* **1 a :** a pale or light-colored mahogany **b :** PRIMAVERA 2 **2 a :** an Australian eucalypt (*Eucalyptus triantha* or *E. acmenoides*) that yields a pale strong straight-grained wood used esp. for railway ties and posts **b :** the wood of this tree

white maire *n* **:** a small New Zealand tree (*Olea lanceolata*) with slender opposite leaves and small apetalous flowers followed by red pulpy drupes

white mallow *n* **1 :** MARSHMALLOW 1 **2 :** ALKALI MALLOW

white mangrove *n* **1 :** a small shrub to moderately large tree (*Laguncularia racemosa*) of the family Combretaceae that grows in brackish waters along the seacoasts of western Africa and tropical America, has flowers with fine small petals and a persistent top-shaped calyx, and is locally important as a source of tannins **2 :** a small or medium-sized tree (*Avicennia officinalis*) growing in brackish water esp. along the shores of the southwestern Pacific, having leaves white beneath, and yielding hard pale lumber and usable quantities of tannin; *broadly* **:** any of several mangroves of the genus *Avicennia*

white man's burden *n* [fr. "The White Man's Burden" (1899), poem by Rudyard Kipling †1936 Eng. writer] **:** the supposed duty of the white peoples to manage the affairs of the undeveloped colored races

white·man's foot \'=,manz-\ *n* **:** BROAD-LEAVED PLANTAIN

white mapau *n* **:** either of two New Zealand trees: **a :** a small often shrubby tree (*Carpodetus serratus*) with panicles of small white flowers followed by shining black capsules **b :** TARATA

white maple *n* **1 a :** any of several maples having pale bark: as (1) **:** SILVER MAPLE (2) **:** OREGON MAPLE (3) **:** RED MAPLE **b :** WHITE MAPAU **2 :** the clear pale sapwood of a sugar maple (*Acer saccharum*)

white mariposa *n* **:** a California perennial herb (*Calochortus venustus*) with typically white red-blotched flowers

white-marked tussock moth \'=,=-\ *n* **:** a tussock moth (*Hemerocampa leucostigma*) having larvae that sometimes defoliate various shade and fruit trees

white marlin *n* **:** a sport fish (*Makaira albida*) of the Atlantic ocean that is blue above and silvery below and seldom attains a weight of 100 pounds — compare BLUE MARLIN

white matter *n* **:** neural tissue esp. of the brain and spinal cord that consists largely of medullated nerve fibers, has a whitish color, and typically underlies the cortical gray matter or is gathered into central tracts and peripheral nerves

white meat *n* [ME *whit-mete*, fr. *whit* white + *mete* meat] **1** *archaic* **:** food (as butter or cheese) derived from milk **:** dairy products **2 a** (1) **:** a meat (as veal or pork) that is light in color esp. when cooked — compare RED MEAT (2) **:** meat of those portions (as breast and wings) of a table fowl that are nearly white when cooked — compare DARK MEAT **b** *South* **:** fat salt pork **:** FATBACK **3** *slang* **:** ACTRESS

white-meat tuna *n* [*white meat*] **:** ALBACORE; *also* **:** the canned flesh of this fish

white melilot *n* **:** WHITE SWEET CLOVER

white merganser *n, dial Eng* **:** a smew (*Mergus albellus*)

white metal *n* **1 :** any of several lead-base or tin-base bearing

metals **2 :** any of several white alloys (as pewter or britannia) **3 :** copper matte having virtually all the iron removed and containing therefore about 80 percent copper and 20 percent sulfur

white mica *n* **:** MUSCOVITE

white miller *n* **1 a :** CASEMAKING CLOTHES MOTH **b :** a common American arctiid moth (*Diacrisia virginica*) that is pure white with a few small black spots — compare WOOLLY BEAR **2 :** an artificial angling fly with white wings and hackle, white silk body, and silver ribbing and tag

white mineral oil *n* **:** LIQUID PETROLATUM

white mineral primer *n* **:** a white pigment consisting of calcium carbonate

white mint *n* **:** a peppermint with light-green stems and foliage that is cultivated chiefly in Europe — compare BLACK MINT

white mold *n* **1 :** COTTONY ROT **2 :** any of several diseases of plants that resemble cottony rot and are caused by fungi esp. of the genus *Ramularia* or *Erostrotheca*

white monk *n, often cap W&M* [ME, fr. *white* + *monk;* fr. the color of his habit] **:** a Cistercian monk

white moss *n* **:** a pale grayish or whitish moss (genus *Leucobryum*) growing chiefly in open damp woodlands and forming rounded masses like large pincushions; *esp* **:** a common moss (*L. glaucum*) of eastern No. America

white mountain apache *n, usu cap W&M&A* [fr. *White Mountain* (Sierra Blanca Peak) in southern New Mexico] **:** a division of the San Carlos Apache

white mountain ash *n* [[1]*white* + *mountain ash*] **:** an Australian mountain ash (*Eucalyptus fraxinoides*) that has rough bark on the lower trunk and yields a lumber very similar to that of the European or American ashes

white mountain butterfly *n, usu cap W&M* [fr. *White Mountains,* mountains of the Appalachian range in northern New Hampshire] **:** a delicate brownish butterfly (*Oeneis melissa semidea*) of the family Satyridae found near the peaks of the White mountains

white mouse *n* **:** an albino house mouse

white mulberry *n* **:** an Asiatic mulberry tree (*Morus alba*) with white to light or dull red fruits that is the favored tree for feeding silkworms and is widespread in cultivation and as an escape — compare BLACK MULBERRY

white mule *n* [so called fr. its lack of color and fr. its powerful kick] **:** MOONSHINE 3

white mullein *n* **:** a densely hairy Eurasian herb (*Verbascum lychnitis*) with racemose white flowers that is naturalized in No. America

white mullet *n* **1 :** a silvery mullet (*Mugil curema*) of the Atlantic and Pacific coasts **2 :** any of several silvery suckers of the genus *Moxostoma* (family Catostomidae); *esp* **:** a fish (*M. papillosum*) of the coastal streams from the Dismal swamp southward

white mundic *n* **:** ARSENOPYRITE

white muscle disease *n* **1 :** STIFF-LAMB DISEASE **2 :** a disease of calves similar to or identical with stiff-lamb disease

white mustard *n* **:** a Eurasian mustard (*Brassica hirta*) with rough-hairy foliage, a long-beaked hispid pod, and pale yellow seeds that yield mustard and mustard oil — compare BLACK MUSTARD

whit·en \'hwīt°n *also* 'wī-\ *vb* **whitened; whitened; whiten·ing** \-t(°)niŋ\ **whitens** [ME *whitenen,* fr. [1]*white* + *-nen* -en] *vt* **1 :** to make white or whiter in any way (as by bleaching or blanching or by whitewashing) ⟨~ cloth⟩ **2 :** to give an often specious appearance of purity, guiltlessness, or propriety to **3 :** to deposit a white film of silver on (a metal) by simple immersion **~** *vi* **:** to grow white **:** turn or become white ⟨the hair ~s with age⟩ ⟨the sea ~s with foam⟩ **syn** see PALLIATE

white-necked raven \'ˌ=ˌ=-\ *n* **:** a raven (*Corvus cryptoleucus*) of the southwestern U.S. having the neck feathers white at the base but black at the tips

whitened *adj* [fr. past part. of *whiten*] **:** made white; *esp* **:** given an artificial or specious whiteness (as by bleaching or glossing over)

white negro *n, usu cap N* **1 :** a light-complexioned Negro (as a mulatto) **2 :** an albinotic Negro

whit·en·er \-t(°)nə(r)\ *n* -S **:** one that whitens: as **a :** an agent (as a bleach) used to impart whiteness to something **b :** a worker whose occupation involves whitening something or applying a whitener to something **c :** a worker who removes a thin layer from hides to remove imperfections or to expose superior leather

white·ness *n* -ES [ME *whitnes,* fr. OE *hwītnes,* fr. *hwīt* white + *-nes* -ness — more at WHITE] **1 :** the quality or state of being white: as **a** (1) **:** white color (2) **:** degree of resemblance to white color **b :** lack of ruddy warmth in the complexion **:** dull pallor (as from terror, grief, or illness) **:** PALENESS **c :** freedom from stain or blemish **:** PURITY, CLEANNESS **2 :** white substance

white night *n* [trans. of F *nuit blanche*] **:** a sleepless night

[1]**whitening** *n* -S [fr. gerund of *whiten*] **1 :** the act or process of making or becoming white **2 :** something that is used to make white **:** WHITING **3 :** the operation of shaving leather on the flesh side to even its thickness

[2]**whitening** *adj* [fr. pres. part. of *whiten*] **1 :** serving to whiten or active in whitening ⟨a ~ compound⟩ ⟨the ~ action of a bleach⟩ **2 :** tending to whiten **:** gradually becoming white ⟨these ~ bones⟩

whitening stone *n* **:** a sharpening and polishing stone used esp. by cutlers; *also* **:** a finishing grindstone of fine texture

white noise *n* [so called fr. the analogy of its composition to that of white light] **:** a heterogeneous mixture of sound waves (as thermal noise) extending over a wide frequency range

white-nosed guenon *or* **white-nosed monkey** \'ˌ=ˌ=-\ *n* **:** a monkey (*Cercopithecus nictitans*) of western central Africa marked with a white blotch on the muzzle

white note *n* **:** an open-faced musical note (as a 𝅗𝅥 or 𝅝)

white nun *n* **:** SMEW

white nun orchid *or* **white nun** *n* **:** a very showy tropical American orchid (*Lycaste skinneri*) bearing solitary predominantly white flowers that are often suffused with rose or marked with rosy crimson

white oak *n* **1 :** any of numerous Old World and American oaks having 6 to 8 stamens in each floret, acorns that mature in one year and have the inner surface of the shell smooth, the acorn cup covered with woody scales, and leaf veins that never extend beyond the margin of the leaf: as **a** (1) **:** DURMAST (2) **:** ENGLISH OAK **b :** a large slow-growing long-lived oak (*Quercus alba*) of the eastern U.S. having leaves with usu. 7 deep rounded entire lobes, moderately large acorns, and stout spreading branches that form a broad open head and yielding a moderately heavy wood that is very hard and strong and esp. durable when exposed (as by contact with soil) to damp — see TREE illustration **c :** any of various other American oaks (as the bur oak or the basket oak) felt to resemble the eastern white oak **2 :** wood or lumber obtained from white oak trees

white oakum *n* **:** oakum from untarred rope

white of egg *n, pl* **whites of egg** *or* **whites of eggs :** WHITE 2a(1)

white of the eye : WHITE 2a(2)

white oil *n* **:** any of various colorless odorless tasteless mineral oils prepared from a high-boiling petroleum distillate (as by treating with sulfuric acid, neutralizing, washing, and filtering hot through activated carbon or clay) and used as lubricants for textile and food machinery and in medicine and pharmaceutical preparations

white opal *n* **:** an opal with a predominantly light-colored body

white out *vt* [[4]*white* + *out*] **:** to widen the spacing and esp. the interlinear spacing in (printed matter) by or as if by inserting leads

whiteout \'ˌ=ˌ=\ *n* -S [[4]*white* + *out*] **:** a surface weather condition in an arctic area in which no object casts a shadow, the horizon cannot be seen, and only dark objects are discernible and which is caused by heavy cloud cover over a snow surface so that light coming through the clouds is essentially equal to the light reflected off the snow

white owl *n* **1 a :** SNOWY OWL **b :** BARN OWL **2** *dial* **:** a chamber pot

white paper *n* **1 :** a government report on any subject; *esp* **:** an English publication that is usu. less extensive than a blue book **2 :** a detailed or authoritative report ⟨the network prepared a *white paper* on farm problems⟩ — compare WHITE BOOK

white pareira *also* **white pareira brava** *n* **:** a white or yellowish starchy root that is obtained from a tropical American woody vine (*Abuta rufescens*) and has properties similar to true pareira — compare YELLOW PAREIRA

white partridge *n* **:** PTARMIGAN

white pear *n* **:** either of two southern African timber trees: **a :** a tree (*Pterocelastrus rostratus*) of the family Celastraceae yielding a hardwood used esp. in wagons **b :** a tree (*Apodytes dimidiata*) of the family Icacinaceae yielding a good construction timber

white pelican *n* **:** a very large American pelican (*Pelecanus erythrorhynchos*) that is predominantly white with black wing feathers; *also* **:** any of several similar Old World pelicans (esp. *P. onocrotalus*)

white pepper *n* **:** pepper ground after the outer husk has been removed

white peppermint *n* **1 :** an Australian eucalypt (*Eucalyptus stuartiana*) with a spreading crown and pendulous branches **2 :** WHITE MINT

white perch *n* **1 :** a small anadromous sea bass (*Morone americana*) that is dark green above and silvery below, is found along the coast and in coastal streams of the eastern U.S., and is closely related to the yellow bass **2 :** FRESHWATER DRUM **3 :** a pile perch or related fish of California **4 :** WHITE CRAPPIE

white petroleum jelly *or* **white petrolatum** *n* **:** PETROLATUM b

white phosphorus *n* **:** the element phosphorus in its white or yellowish allotropic form — called also *yellow phosphorus*

white pickle *or* **white-pickle mosaic** *n* **:** a cucumber mosaic in which the fruit becomes pale-colored

white pigweed *n* **:** LAMB'S-QUARTERS 1

white pine *n* **1 a :** a tall-growing pine (*Pinus strobus*) of eastern No. America having smooth bark, long-stalked green cones, leaves in clusters of five, and young shoots with tufts of hair below the insertion of the leaf bundles — called also *American white pine, eastern white pine;* see TREE illustration **b :** any of several other evergreen trees felt to resemble the white pine esp. in having leaves in bundles of five: as (1) **:** SUGAR PINE (2) **:** WESTERN WHITE PINE (3) **:** LIMBER PINE (4) **:** LODGEPOLE PINE (5) **:** WHITEBARK PINE (6) **:** ENGLEMANN SPRUCE **c :** the wood of a white pine and esp. of the eastern white pine which is much used in building construction **2 a** *Austral* (1) **:** any of several camphorwoods (esp. *Callitris robusta*) (2) **:** SHE-PINE (3) **:** COLONIAL PINE **b** *NewZeal* **:** KAHIKATEA

white pine aphid *n* [*white pine*] **:** a plant louse (*Cinara strobi*) that feeds on twigs and branches of white pine in the eastern U.S.

white pine blister rust *also* **white-pine rust** *n* **:** a disease of 5-leaved pine (as Swiss pine or various No. American white pines) that is prob. of Asiatic origin but widely established in Europe and No. America, is caused by a rust fungus (*Cronartium ribicola*) with a complex life cycle requiring a plant of the genus *Ribes* (as a currant or gooseberry) as alternate host, and is marked by destructive invasion of the bark and underlying tissues with swelling and girdling of the infected branch or tree leading to death of the parts above the lesion — compare FELT RUST

white pine resin *n* **:** SANDARAC 3b

white pine weevil *n* **:** a small elongated brownish weevil (*Pissodes strobi*) that feeds in and destroys the new shoots of white pine and Norway spruce and sometimes of other pines and spruces

white pitch *n* **:** a turpentine oleoresin obtained in Europe chiefly from the Scotch pine or the cluster pine, purified by melting with water and straining, and frequently substituted for Burgundy pitch — compare GALIPOT

white plague *n* **:** tuberculosis of the lungs

white plantain *n* **1 :** a pussytoes (*Antennaria plantaginifolia*) **2 :** a rattlesnake plantain (*Goodyera repens*)

white pointer *n, Austral* **:** GREAT WHITE SHARK

white pond lily *n* **:** any of several white-flowered water lilies; *esp* **:** a common No. American water lily (*Nymphaea odorata*) with very fragrant white flowers and rhizomes sometimes used as an astringent

white popinac *n* **:** a small evergreen tropical American leguminous tree (*Leucaena glauca*) that is sometimes cultivated in warm regions for its showy globose heads of white flowers and is widely naturalized in tropical regions

white poplar *n* **1 a :** a Eurasian poplar (*Populus alba*) that is widely cultivated and naturalized in the U.S. and has whitish bark and leaves with a white-tomentose lower surface **b :** an aspen (*Populus tremuloides*) of the U.S. with small leaves and long petioles **2 :** the wood of a tulip tree (*Liriodendron tulipifera*)

white port *n* **:** a heavy-bodied straw-colored dessert wine

white potato *n* **:** POTATO 2a(2)

white prairie clover *n* **:** a prairie clover (*Petalostemon candidum*) of central No. America with terminal spikes of white-petaled flowers

white precipitate *n* **:** either of two mercury-ammonia compounds: **a :** AMMONIATED MERCURY **b :** a crystalline compound $Hg(NH_3)_2Cl_2$ usu. obtained by adding a solution of mercuric chloride to a hot solution of ammonia and ammonium chloride — called also *fusible white precipitate*

white primary *n* **:** a party primary in a southern state open to white voters only ⟨Supreme Court . . . decisions which outlawed the *white primary* —*New Republic*⟩

whiteprint \'ˌ=ˌ=\ *n* **:** a diazotype in which the graphic image appears in black or a color on a white background; *also* **:** a process used for making such prints

white puccoon *n* **:** BLOODROOT 1

white pudding *n* **:** any of several light-colored sausages: as **a :** a mixture of meat (as heart, lungs, liver, or muscle) ground with beef suet or pork fat, mixed with bread crumbs, herbs, onion, and spices, stuffed into sausage casings, and fried or broiled fresh **b :** a mixture of chopped pork fat and oatmeal seasoned with onion, salt, and pepper, stuffed into sausage casings, and cooked fresh

white purslane *n* **:** FLOWERING SPURGE

white pyrite *n* **:** MARCASITE

white quebracho *n* **:** QUEBRACHO 1a

whiter *comparative of* WHITE

white rainbow *n* **:** a bow or arc of light formed by refraction and reflection from drops of water (as of a cloud of fog) too minute to give distinctly the concentric bands of color of the typical rainbow

white rat *n* **:** a rat of an albino strain f the Norway rat that is used extensively as a laboratory animal in biological experimentation

white ratany *n* **:** CHACATE

white rattlesnake *n* **:** a rattlesnake (*Crotalus mitchellii*) of the desert regions of the southwestern U.S. that is light yellowish gray with small brown spots

white rent *n* [ME *white rente,* fr. [1]*white* + *rente* rent] **:** rent reserved or payable in silver — opposed to *black rent;* compare ALBA FIRMA

white rhinoceros *n* **:** a large African rhinoceros (*Ceratotherium simus*) that is a light slaty gray and rare over most of its former range

white ribbon *n* **:** the distinctive badge of various organizations for the promotion of sexual purity or temperance

white robin *n* **:** WHITE CAMPION a

white robin snipe *n* **:** a knot when in fall plumage

white rock *n, usu cap W&R* [[1]*white* + (*Plymouth*) *rock*] **1 :** a white domestic fowl of the Plymouth Rock breed **2 :** any heavy-bodied white domestic fowl as distinguished from a white leghorn or a colored fowl — used esp. in the live poultry market

whiteroot \'ˌ=ˌ=\ *n* **:** BUTTERFLY WEED 1

white rot *n* **1 :** any of several plants (as marsh pennywort and butterwort) formerly held to produce rot in sheep **2 a :** a disease of grapes caused by an imperfect fungus (*Coniothyrium diplodiella*) that produces white or grayish brown-bordered spots on young shoots and fruit **b :** any of several wood rots of various trees caused chiefly by fungi of the genus *Fomes* **c :** a fungous rot of onions, garlic, shallots, and related plants caused by a fungus (*Sclerotinia cepivorum*) and characterized by production of abundant white mycelium **3 :** a watery spoiled condition of eggs in which the white is mixed with the yolk; *also* **:** an egg so spoiled

whiterump \'ˌ=ˌ=\ *n* [[1]*white* + *rump*] **1 :** HUDSONIAN GODWIT **2** *Brit* **:** WHEATEAR

white-rumped sandpiper \'ˌ=ˌ=-\ *n* **:** a common small migratory sandpiper (*Erolia fuscicollis*) of eastern No. America that breeds in the arctic and winters in southern So. America and that is streaked buff and grayish brown with a conspicuous white rump

white-rumped shrike *n* **:** a western No. American shrike (*Lanius ludovicianus excubitorides*) that is largely gray above and plain white on the underparts

white russian *n, usu cap W&R* [*White Russia,* region of western U.S.S.R. + E *-an*] **:** BELORUSSIAN

white rust *n* **1 :** any of various fungous diseases of plants caused by fungi of the genus *Albugo* and characterized by a white powdery mass of conidia exposed by the rupture at maturity of sori produced just beneath the epidermis of the host **2 :** a fungus of the genus *Albugo*

whites *pl of* WHITE, *pres 3d sing of* WHITE

white sage *n* **:** any of several shrubs of western America having canescent or hoary foliage: as **a :** a low shrub (*Ramona polystachya*) of the western U.S. and adjacent Mexico **b :** a common sagebrush (*Artemisia ludoviciana*) **c :** WINTER FAT **d :** CHAMISO **e :** a California aromatic shrubby herb (*Salvia apiana*) that is a good source of honey

white sale *n* **:** a sale of white goods

white salmon *n* **1 :** SILVER SALMON **2 :** a large squawfish (*Ptychocheilus lucius*) of the Colorado river basin that reaches a length of five feet **3 :** YELLOWTAIL a **4 :** INCONNU

white sandbox *n* **:** a young or second-growth sandbox tree with white wood — compare YELLOW SANDBOX

white sanicle *n* **:** WHITE SNAKEROOT

white sapota *also* **white sapote** *n* **:** a Mexican and Central American tree (*Casimiroa edulis*) cultivated for its round pulpy edible fruit, styptic leaves, and narcotic seeds

white sapphire *n* **:** clear or colorless corundum

white sauce *n* **:** a sauce in which the thickening agent (as flour) has not been browned, which consists essentially of milk, cream, or stock with flour and seasoning, and which forms the basis for various sauces ⟨mushroom sauce made with a basic *white sauce*⟩ — see VELOUTÉ

white scale *n* **:** any of various white or pale scales: as **a :** an oleander scale (*Aspidiotus hederae*) **b :** COTTONY-CUSHION SCALE **c :** ROSE SCALE

white scour *n* **:** an infectious diarrhea of calves and sometimes lambs found shortly after birth, marked by profuse yellowish-white discharges, with great dullness, prostration, sunken eyes, retracted belly, hurried breathing, and a subnormal temperature, and caused usu. by coliform bacteria — usu. used in pl.

white sea bass *n* **:** a large croaker (*Cynoscion nobilis*) of the Pacific coast of No. America that is bluish gray above and silvery below, is closely related to the Atlantic weakfishes, and is an important sport and food fish

white senega *n* **1 :** SENEGA ROOT **2 :** SENEGA 2b

white shad *n* **:** a shad (*Alosa sapidissima*)

white shark *n* **:** GREAT WHITE SHARK

white sheep *n* **1 :** DALL SHEEP **2 :** a normal well-behaved individual among a group of discreditable individuals — compare BLACK SHEEP

white shellac *n* **:** a shellac prepared by bleaching orange shellac

white shirt *n, South* **:** REDHEADED WOODPECKER

white shrimp *n* **:** LAKE SHRIMP

whiteside \'ˌ=ˌ=\ *n, dial Eng* **:** GOLDENEYE

white-sided dolphin \'ˌ=ˌ=-\ *n* **:** a spectacled dolphin (*Lagenorhynchus acutus*) of the northern Atlantic

white-sided duck *n* **:** TUFTED DUCK 1

white silk-cotton tree *n* **:** an East Indian tree (*Cochlospermum religiosum*) that yields a gum and has seed pods which yield a fiber — compare BASSORA GUM, KUMBI

white siris *n* **1 a :** a tree (*Albizzia procera*) of India and eastward to the Philippines having a bark used locally as a source of fish poisons and yielding a wood somewhat resembling walnut and resistant to termite attack **b :** a rather large chiefly tropical Australian tree (*Ailanthus imberbiflora*) having a very light soft straight-grained wood often used for toys and boxes **2 :** the wood of a white siris

white sister *n, usu cap W&S* **:** a member of a religious congregation founded by the Abbé Lavigerie as an auxiliary to the White Fathers

white slave *n* **1 :** a woman or girl held unwillingly for purposes of commercial prostitution **2 :** a woman or girl who is transported knowingly in interstate or foreign commerce or in territory subject to federal jurisdiction for purposes of prostitution or debauchery or for other immoral purpose or practice with the intention of inducing, enticing, or compelling her to such purpose or practice and without regard to whether her consent is given

white slaver *n* **:** one engaged in white slave traffic **:** a procurer of white slaves

white slavery *n* **:** enforced prostitution

[1]**whitesmith** \'ˌ=ˌ=\ *n* [[1]*white* + *smith*] **1 :** one who works in tinned or galvanized iron or white iron **:** TINSMITH **2 :** a worker in iron who finishes or polishes the work — sometimes distinguished from *blacksmith*

[2]**whitesmith** \"\ *vi* **:** to work as a whitesmith

white smut *n* **1 :** a plant disease caused by a fungus of the genus *Entyloma* and characterized by light-colored leaf spots formed by the sori and covered with aerial conidia that give them a white powdery appearance **2 :** a fungus of the genus *Entyloma*

white snail *n* **1 :** ROMAN SNAIL **2 :** a European snail (*Helix pisana*) introduced into California where it is a serious pest of citrus plants

white snakeroot *n* **:** a No. American herb (*Eupatorium rugosum*) bearing flat-topped clusters of small white flower heads and being a cause of trembles and milksickness — called also *white sanicle*

white snipe *n* **1** *chiefly Midland* **:** SANDERLING **2** *West* **:** AVOCET

white snowbird *n* **:** SNOW BUNTING

white soapwort *n* **:** RED CAMPION

white sock *n, pl* **white sox :** BLACKFLY — usu. used in pl.

white soft paraffin *n* **:** PETROLATUM b

white sour *n* **1 :** a treatment (as of cotton) with dilute hydrochloric or sulfuric acid to complete the bleaching process and cleanse the fabric **2 :** the bath or solution used in the white sour

white speck *n* **:** FROGEYE a(1)

white spine *or* **white-spine cucumber** *n* **:** any of various cucumbers that bear rather large fruits with pointed white tubercles and are esp. suitable for forcing and slicing

white spirit *n* **:** PETROLEUM SPIRIT — often used in pl.

white spot *n* **1 :** any of several diseases of plants marked by light-colored lesions: as **a :** a disease of alfalfa characterized by spotting and yellowing of the foliage and caused by an unbalanced water supply (as from heavy rainfall following a drought) **b :** HEAT CANKER **c :** a disease of turnips caused by a fungus (*Cercosporella brassicae*) **2 :** ICH — usu. used in pl.

white spruce *n* **1 :** any of several spruces: as **a :** a No. American spruce (*Picea glauca*) with short blue-green leaves and slender cones **b :** ENGELMANN SPRUCE **2 :** the wood of a white spruce; *esp* **:** the light pale tough straight-grained wood of the common white spruce (*Picea glauca*) which is used for construction and as a source of paper pulp

white squall *n* **:** a sudden gust of wind or furious blow that is reputed to come up without being marked in its approach otherwise than by whitecaps or white broken water on the surface of the sea — compare BLACK SQUALL

white squill *n* **:** a commercial squill in which the bulb scales are white or yellowish and which is obtained esp. in Malta — compare RED SQUILL

whitest *superlative of* WHITE

white staff *n* **1 a :** a white wand or staff that is a symbol of office of several officials (as of the British government or royal household) **b :** an office of which a white staff is a symbol **2** *also* **white staff officer :** an official who carries a white staff

white star *n* **1 :** a star of spectral type *A* or *F* having a moderate surface temperature and a white or yellowish color

2 a : an annual morning glory (*Ipomoea lacunosa*) of the southern U. S. with star-shaped leaves and small white or purplish flowers **b :** a bellflower (*Campanula carpatica alba*) with white flowers
white steenbras *n* **:** a southern African sea bream (*Pagellus lithognathus*) — compare RED STEENBRAS
white-stem filaree *n* **:** MUSK CLOVER
white stem pine *n* **:** WHITEBARK PINE
white's thrush *n, usu cap W* [after Gilbert *White* †1793 Eng. clergyman and naturalist] **:** a ground thrush (*Zoothera dauma aurea*) of eastern Asia that rarely straggles to Europe
white stock *n* **:** soup stock made from veal or chicken without colored seasonings and often used in white sauce
white stone *n* **:** a clear colorless imitation gem (as a rhinestone) that simulates the diamond
white stopper *n* **:** any of several trees of the genus *Calyptranthes; esp* **:** a common West Indian tree (*C. pallens*) with light gray bark, shining leaves, and small paniculate flowers
white stork *n* **:** a large white stork (*Ciconia ciconia*) with red bill and legs and black flight feathers that is the common stork of Europe
white streak *n* **:** a virus disease of narcissus characterized by dark green narrow streaks on leaves and flower stems that after flowering turn whitish gray or yellowish
white stringybark *n* **:** an Australian stringybark (*Eucalyptus eugenioides*) with white wood
white stuff *n* **1 :** a composition of whiting and glue used by gilders to cover frames before gilding **2** *slang* **:** any of several addictive drugs usu. taken by injection
white stumpnose *n* **:** a southern African sea bream (*Rhabdosargus tricuspidens*) that closely resembles the common silver bream but is usu. much smaller and is an important sport and market fish — compare RED STUMPNOSE
white sturgeon *n* **:** a sturgeon (*Acipenser transmontanus*) of the Pacific coast of No. America that is the largest freshwater fish of No. America, may become 11 feet long and weigh over half a ton, and is marketed in large numbers
white substance of schwann *usu cap 2d S* [after Theodor *Schwann* †1882 Ger. naturalist, anatomist, & physiologist] **:** MYELIN
white sucker *n* **1 :** a common sucker (*Catostomus commersonii*) **2 :** any of various redhorses **3 :** CARPSUCKER
white sugar *n* [ME *white sugre*, fr. ¹*white* + *sugre* sugar] **:** sugar that in bulk appears white; *esp* **:** GRANULATED SUGAR
white sunday *n, usu cap W&S* [by alter. (influenced by the etymology of *Whitsunday*)] **:** WHITSUNDAY
white supremacist *n* [*white supremacy* + *-ist*] **:** an advocate of or believer in white supremacy ⟨*white supremacists* . . . devise new methods to disenfranchise Negroes —*New Republic*⟩
white supremacy *n* **1 :** the supremacy of white persons over all other racial groups **2 :** a doctrine based on a belief in the inherent superiority of the white race over the Negro race and the correlative necessity for the subordination of Negroes to whites in all relationships; *esp* **:** one that seeks to perpetuate such alleged superiority by restricting political, economic, and social powers and opportunities to white persons ⟨resentment among the colored peoples of the world against the arrogance of *white supremacy* —Frances Witherspoon⟩
white surf fish *n* **:** any of several surf fishes of the California coast that are white or dull silvery in color
white swallowwort *n* **:** a European twining vine (*Cynanchum vincetoxicum*) whose root has been used as an emetic, cathartic, and diuretic
white swamp gum *n* **:** CIDER GUM
white swamp honeysuckle *n* **:** SWAMP AZALEA
white sweet clover *n* **:** a white-flowered usu. tall-growing and biennial sweet clover (*Melilotus alba*) that is a valuable honey plant — called also *white melilot; compare* HUBAM CLOVER
white sycamore *n* **1 :** a bushy-headed Australian tree (*Cryptocarya obovata*) with the leaves pale on the undersurface **2 :** a showy tree (*Polyscias elegans*) of the family Araliaceae that is sometimes cultivated for ornament
whitetail \ˈ⸗,⸗\ *n* **:** any of various animals with white about the tail: as **a :** WHITE-TAILED DEER **b** *dial Eng* **:** WHEATEAR **c :** an Ecuadorian hummingbird (*Urochroa bougueri*) with a partially white tail
white-tailed deer \ˈ⸗,⸗-\ *n* **:** any of various widely distributed No. American deers usu. held to constitute races of a single species (*Odocoileus virginianus*) and characterized by a rather long tail white on the undersurface and graceful forward-arching antlers with upright basal snags
white-tailed eagle *n* **1 :** BALD EAGLE **2** *Brit* **:** WHITE-TAILED SEA EAGLE
white-tailed emerald *n* **:** either of two greenish Central American hummingbirds of the genus *Elvira*
white-tailed gnu *n* **:** a very dark gnu (*Connochaetes gnu*) having a partially white tail and being formerly abundant in southern Africa but nearly or wholly extinct
white-tailed hawk *n* **:** a large hawk (*Buteo albicaudatus*) ranging from Texas to So. America and having the underparts, rump, and tail predominantly white
white-tailed jackrabbit *n* **:** a jackrabbit (*Lepus townsendi*) of the northern great plains that has a white tail and commonly becomes wholly white in winter
white-tailed kite *n* **:** a kite (*Elanus leucurus majusculus*) of warm and tropical America that is largely gray above with black wing coverts and white head, breast, tail, and underparts
white-tailed mongoose *n* **:** a mongoose of the genus *Ichneumia* distinguished by its white tail
white-tailed ptarmigan *n* **:** a rather small ptarmigan (*Lagopus leucurus*) of mountainous regions from Alaska to New Mexico that becomes pure white in winter
white-tailed sea eagle *n* **:** a bulky long-winged sea eagle (*Haliaeetus albicilla*) that is distinguished by a short white wedge-shaped tail
white-tailed tropic bird *n* **:** a tropic bird (*Phaëthon lepturus*) that has a yellow bill and white tail
white tamarind *n* **1 :** a timber tree (*Acacia glomerosa*) of Mexico and Central America **2 :** the hard heavy tough elastic straight-grained nearly white wood of the white tamarind that is used esp. for floors, joinery, and tool handles
white tassel flower *n* **:** a prairie clover (*Petalostemon candidus*) with silky spikes of white flowers — called also *white tassels*
white tassels *n pl but sing or pl in constr* **:** WHITE TASSEL FLOWER
white tea tree *n* **1 :** an Australian tea tree (*Melaleuca leucadendron*) with white bark **2 :** a New Zealand tea tree (*Leptospermum ericoides*) with heathlike foliage
white tern *n* **:** a Pacific tern of the genus *Gygis*
white thistle *n* **:** PRICKLY POPPY
whitethorn \ˈ⸗,⸗\ *n* [ME *white thorn*, fr. *white* + *thorn*] **1 a :** a hawthorn (*Crataegus oxycantha*) **b :** SCARLET HAW **2 :** any of several acacias that have peeling bark which gives the trunk a whitish appearance **3 :** a whitish-barked shrub (*Ceanothus incana*) of the coastal mountains of the western U. S. that has often spinose branchlets, leaves whitish beneath, and small white flowers in panicles
white thread *n* **:** a bark disease of rubber trees (genus *Hevea*) and cacao caused by a basidiomycete (*Cyphella heveae*) and characterized by the appearance of white strands of mycelium on the tapped surfaces of the trees
whitethroat \ˈ⸗,⸗\ *n* **1 :** an Old World warbler (*Sylvia communis*) with a white throat, pale gray cap, rusty upperparts, and pale pinkish buff underparts — called also *greater whitethroat* **2 :** WHITE-THROATED SPARROW
white-throated sparrow \ˈ⸗,⸗⸗-\ *n* **:** a common brown sparrow (*Zonotrichia albicollis*) of eastern No. America having a striped crown and a large white patch on the throat
white-throated thickhead *n* **:** THUNDERBIRD 1
white tie *n* **1 :** the white bow tie worn with men's formal evening dress — compare BLACK TIE **2 :** formal evening dress for men ⟨an affair requiring *white tie*⟩
whitetip \ˈ⸗,⸗\ *n* **:** a hummingbird of the genus *Urosticte* with white-tipped tail feathers
white tip *n* **1 :** a disease of leeks esp. in Britain caused by a fungus (*Phytophthora porri*) and characterized by yellowing and dieback of the leaf tips which finally turn white **2 :** any of several diseases of cereal grasses (as maize) and other crop plants caused by mineral deficiencies and resembling fungous white tip in symptoms **3 :** a disease of rice caused by a nematode (*Aphelenchoides oryzae*) and characterized by whitening of the leaf tips
whitetip clover *n* **:** a clover (*Trifolium variegatum*) having flowers purple but often with a white tip
white titi *n* **:** TITI 1b
white-toothed shrew \ˈ⸗,⸗-\ *n* **:** any of various shrews of *Crocidura* or related genera having white teeth — compare RED-TOOTHED SHREW
whitetop \ˈ⸗,⸗\ *n* **1 a** (1) **:** a redtop (*Agrostis alba*) (2) **:** a grass (*Fluminea festucacea*) of northwestern No. America that is an important source of food for wild birds (3) *also* **white topped grass :** any of several grasses of the genus *Danthonia* (esp. *D. pilosa*) **b :** FLEABANE **c :** WHITE SNAKEROOT **d :** any of several Australian eucalypts; *esp* **:** a widely distributed blackbutt (*Eucalyptus pilularis*) **e :** HOARY CRESS **2 :** a covered wagon with a white top
white-topped aster \ˈ⸗,⸗-\ *n* **:** a plant of the genus *Sericocarpus*
white trash *n* **:** POOR WHITES
white trefoil *n* **:** WHITE DUTCH CLOVER
white trout *n* **1 :** SAND SQUETEAGUE **2 a** *dial Eng* **:** a young sea trout **b :** SUNAPEE TROUT
white trumpet lily *n* **:** a lily (*Lilium longiflorum*) with very fragrant long funnel-formed pure white flowers borne singly or in pairs
whitevein \ˈ⸗,⸗\ *n* **:** a disease of tobacco manifesting itself in the veins of the leaves which become white during curing — often used in pl. but sing. in constr.
white vervain *also* **white verbena** *n* **:** a common American vervain (*Verbena urticaefolia*) with narrow spikes of white flowers
white vitriol *n* **:** zinc sulfate heptahydrate
white wagtail *n, chiefly Brit* **:** PIED WAGTAIL
¹**whitewall** \ˈ⸗,⸗\ *n* [¹*white* + *wall;* fr. its white underparts] *dial Eng* **:** SPOTTED FLYCATCHER
²**whitewall** \"\ *or* **whitewall tire** *n* [¹*white* + *wall*] **:** an automobile tire having a white sidewall
white walnut *n* **1 a** (1) **:** BUTTERNUT 1b (2) **:** an American hickory; *esp* **:** SHAGBARK HICKORY 1 **b :** the light-colored wood of one of these trees often as specif. distinguished from black walnut **2** *Austral* **:** WHITE SYCAMORE 1
whiteware \ˈ⸗,⸗\ *n* [¹*white* + *ware*] **:** a class of ceramic products that include porcelain, china, pottery, earthenware, stoneware, and vitreous tile, are usu. but not necessarily white, and consist typically of clays, feldspar, potter's flint, and whiting
¹**whitewash** \ˈ⸗,⸗\ *vb* [³*white* + *wash*, v.] *vt* **1 :** to wash, treat, or cover with white liquid composition; *esp* **:** to whiten with whitewash **2 :** to give a speciously pure or fair appearance to: as **a :** to gloss over or cover up (as vices or crimes) **b :** to exonerate or clear (as a person) of charges by means of a superficial or perfunctory investigation or examination or through artful or biased presentation of data **c** *Brit* (1) **:** to legally clear (a bankrupt) of liabilities (2) **:** to free a bankrupt from (debt) by a legal process **3 :** to hold (an opponent) scoreless in a game or contest **:** shut out **4 :** to cause a permanent efflorescent scum to form on (brick) usu. by careless drying, too rapid an application of heat in a kiln, or the use of a clay containing soluble sulfates ~ *vi* **1 :** to whitewash something or someone **2 :** to become whitewashed **:** take whitewash ⟨the wall ~*es* very easily⟩ **syn** see PALLIATE
²**whitewash** \"\ *n* **1 :** a liquid composition that imparts a white coating to a surface: as **a :** a liquid (as a skin bleach) for whitening the skin **b :** a composition (as of lime and water or whiting, size, and water) for whitening structural surfaces (as of plaster, masonry, or wood) **c :** bird excrement esp. when appearing as a chalky coating on or about a nest or perching site **2 a :** an act or instance of glossing over (as a vice or a reputation) or of clearing a bankrupt; *often* **:** a production or activity (as a book, an article, a verdict, a report, or an investigation) that whitewashes somebody or something **b :** a defeat in a contest in which the loser fails to score **3 :** an efflorescence on the surface of a brick
whitewasher \ˈ⸗,⸗⸗\ *n* **:** one that whitewashes; *esp* **:** one who puts on whitewash
white water *n* **1 a :** frothy water (as in breakers, rapids, or waterfalls) **:** QUICKWATER **b :** sea water appearing light in color over a sandy bottom **2 :** water that has been separated in a paper mill from pulp or paper stock and carries short fibers, fillers, and soluble materials — compare SAVE-ALL
white-water \ˈ⸗,⸗⸗\ *vi, of a whale* **:** to beat the water with the flukes
white water crowfoot *n* [¹*white* + *water crowfoot*] **:** a white-flowered water crowfoot
white water lily *n* [¹*white* + *water lily*] **:** a white-flowered water lily of the genus *Nymphaea* (esp. *N. odorata*) as distinguished from the yellow water lilies of the genus *Nymphaea*
white wavey *n* **:** LESSER SNOW GOOSE
white wax *n* **:** any of various waxes that are naturally white or are rendered so by bleaching: as **a :** BEESWAX 2b — used esp. in pharmacy **b :** CHINESE WAX
white wax scale *n* **:** a scale (*Ceroplastes destructor*) that is a pest on citrus in parts of Australia
white way *n* [*great white way*] **:** a brilliantly lighted street or avenue esp. in a city's business or theater district
white weasel *n* **:** ERMINE 1
whiteweed \ˈ⸗,⸗\ *n* **:** any of various weeds with a white or whitish flower: as **a :** DAISY 1b **b :** HOARY CRESS **c :** DAISY FLEABANE
white whale *n* **:** BELUGA 2
white wheat *n* **:** a wheat with white or pale yellow kernels that are usu. soft and suitable for pastry flour — compare SOFT WHEAT
white widgeon *n, dial Eng* **:** SMEW
white wild indigo *n* **:** a white-flowered plant of the genus *Baptisia*
white willow *n* **1 :** a large willow (*Salix alba*) of Eurasia and northern Africa that is often cultivated and has silky pubescent leaves, gray bark, and light soft tough wood — called also *Huntingdon willow* **2 :** any of several American willows having canescent leaves
white wine *n* [ME *white win*, fr. ¹*white* + *win* wine] **:** a wine ranging in color from faintly yellow (as champagne) to amber (as sherry) that is produced from light-colored grapes or from dark grapes fermented without the pulp, skins, and seeds — compare RED WINE, ROSÉ
whitewing \ˈ⸗,⸗\ *n* **1 a** *Brit* **:** CHAFFINCH **b :** WHITE-WINGED SCOTER **c :** a white-winged dove (*Zenaida asiatica*) found in Jamaica **2 :** a person and esp. a street sweeper wearing a white uniform
white-winged \ˈ⸗ˈ⸗\ *adj* **:** having wings that are white or marked with white
white-winged blackbird *n* **:** LARK BUNTING
white-winged black tern *n* **:** a widely distributed but predominantly Eurasian black tern (*Chlidonias leucopterus*) with conspicuous white shoulder patches and tail
white-winged chough *n* **:** a black Australian corvine bird (*Corcorax melanorhamphus*) that is black with white wing patches
white-winged crossbill *n* **:** a crossbill (*Loxia leucoptera*) of northern No. America with two white wing bars in both sexes
white-winged dove *n* **:** a wild pigeon (*Zenaida asiatica*) of the southern U. S. and southward
white-winged junco *n* **:** a rather large western junco (*Junco aikeni*) that is light gray above and has two white bars on each wing
white-winged scoter *also* **white-winged coot** *n* **:** a large and very common American scoter (*Melanitta deglandi*) that is closely related to the velvet scoter of Europe and has a white speculum of the wing and in the adult male a white spot under the eye
white witch *n* **:** a witch who practices white magic **:** a beneficent witch
white wolf *n* **:** a large wolf (*Canis lupus tundrarum*) of arctic No. America
whitewood \ˈ⸗,⸗\ *n* **1 :** any of various trees that have light-colored or almost white wood: as **a :** BASSWOOD 1a **b :** COTTONWOOD 1 **c :** TULIP TREE **d** (1) **:** either of two trees (*Tabebuia leucoxylon* and *T. pentaphylla*) that are found in the West Indies (2) **:** either of two lauraceous trees (*Ocotea leucoxylon* and *Nectandra antillana*) of the same region **e :** CANELLA 3 **f** (1) **:** a tree (*Atalaya hemiglauca*) of the family Sapindaceae that is found in Australia (2) **:** a cheesewood (*Pittosporum bicolor*) of the same region **g** *Brit* (1) **:** LINDEN (2) **:** WAYFARING TREE (3) **:** NORWAY SPRUCE **2 a :** the wood of a whitewood; *esp* **:** the pale yellowish or brownish soft wood of the tulip tree that is used chiefly for woodenware and interior finishings and in boatbuilding **b :** SAPWOOD **3 :** a rather small tropical American tree (*Drypetes diversifolia*) of the family Euphorbiaceae with milky white bark and ivory white fruits
whitewood bark *n* **:** CANELLA ALBA
white wood sorrel *n* [¹*white* + *wood sorrel*] **:** a white-flowered wood sorrel (as *Oxalis acetosella*)
white work *n* **:** needlework done in white on a white fabric
whiteworm \ˈ⸗,⸗\ *n* **:** WHITE GRUB
white worm *n* **:** an enchytraeid worm used as food for aquarium fish — compare ENCHYTRAE
white wreath aster *n* **:** a No. American herb (*Aster multiflorus*) with a profusion of small white flower heads
whitey *var of* WHITY
white yam *n* **:** a yam (*Dioscorea alata*) that is widely cultivated throughout Australasia and Polynesia for its large roots which have a fine white flesh and are eaten baked or boiled or cooked with coconut milk
white yolk *n* **:** a light yellow yolk that forms thin layers and alternates with yellow yolk in the yolk mass of a bird's egg
whitey wood *n* **:** MAHOE 3
whit·field's ointment \ˈhwit,fēldz- *also* ˈwi-\ *also* **whitfield ointment** \-d-\ *n, usu cap W* [after Arthur *Whitfield* †1947 Eng. dermatologist] **:** an ointment that contains benzoic acid and salicylic acid and is used for its keratolytic effect in treating ringworm and other fungal skin diseases
¹**whith·er** \ˈhwithə(r) *also* ˈwi-\ *adv* [ME *whither, whider*, fr. OE *hwider*, fr. *hwi-* (akin to L *quis* who) + *-der* (as in *hider* hither) — more at WHO, HITHER] **1 :** to what place — used interrogatively ⟨~ went the whistling winds⟩ **2 :** to what or which place — used relatively ⟨we came unto the land ~ thou sentest us —Num 13:27 (AV)⟩ **3 :** to what point, degree, end, conclusion, or design **:** WHEREUNTO, WHERETO — used interrogatively or relatively in a sense not physical ⟨~ will this abuse drive him⟩ ⟨nor have I . . . ~ to appeal —John Milton⟩
²**whither** \"\ *conj* [ME *whither, whider*, fr. OE *hwider*, fr. *hwider*, adv.] **:** to the place at, in, or to which **:** WHERE ⟨whence I departed, ~ I return —Robert Browning⟩
³**whither** \"\ *vb* -ED/-ING/-S [ME (Sc) *quhediren, quhethiren, quhidderen*, of Scand origin; akin to Norw dial. *kvidra* to move rapidly to and fro, ON *hvitha* squall of wind, OE *hwitha, hwithu* air, breeze, *hwīnan* to make a whizzing sound — more at WHINE] *vi, chiefly Scot* **:** HURRY, RUSH, WHIZ, BLUSTER ~ *vt, chiefly Scot* **:** to throw violently **:** HURL, SHAKE
⁴**whither** \"\ *n* -S [ME (Sc) *quhidder*, fr. *quhidderen* to *witinc*, fr. *wit* white + *-inc* -ing; akin to OE *hwīt* white and to blow] **:** HURRY, RUSH, FLURRY, GUST
whitherso \ˈ⸗⸗,⸗\ *adv* [ME, fr. ¹*whither* + *so*] *archaic* **:** WHITHERSOEVER
whithersoever \ˈ⸗⸗(,)⸗ˈ⸗⸗\ *adv* [ME, fr. ¹*whither* + *so* + *ever*] **:** to whatever place **:** to what place soever **:** WHERESOEVER ⟨I will go ~ you lead⟩
whitherto *adv* [¹*whither* + *to*] *obs* **:** WHITHER
whith·er·ward \-(r)wə(r)d\ *also* **whith·er·wards** \-dz\ *adv* [ME *whitherward, whiderwardes*, fr. *whither, whider* whither + *-ward, -wardes, -ward, -wards*] **:** in what direction **:** toward what or which place **:** toward the place that ⟨knowing not ~ to turn for aid⟩
¹**whit·ing** \ˈhwīd·|iŋ, -īt|, |ēn *also* ˈwī-\ *n* -S [ME, fr. MD *witinc*, fr. *wīt* white + *-inc* -ing; akin to OE *hwīt* white and to OE *-ing* — more at WHITE, -ING] **:** any of various marine food fishes: as **a** (1) **:** a common European fish (*Merlangus merlangus*) of the family Gadidae (2) **:** SILVER HAKE; *broadly* **:** a fish of the genus *Merluccius* **b :** any of several No. American sciaenid fishes (genus *Menticirrhus*) — see CORBINA 1, KING WHITING, NORTHERN WHITING, SILVER WHITING **c** *Austral* (1) **:** a fish of the genus *Sillago* (2) **:** a kelpfish of the genus *Odax*
²**whiting** \"\ *n* -S [ME, fr. gerund of *whiten* to white] **1** *archaic* **:** the act or process of making white (as by whitewashing or bleaching) **2 :** calcium carbonate prepared as powder by grinding chalk, limestone, or a synthetic product (as precipitated calcium carbonate) and used as a pigment and extender, in putty, and in rubber compounding and paper coating
whiting time *n* [²*whiting*] *obs* **:** the time for bleaching clothes
¹**whit·ish** \ˈhwīd·|ish, -īt|, |ēsh *also* ˈwī-\ *adj* [ME, fr. ¹*white* + *-ish*] **1 :** somewhat white **:** approaching white **2** *of a color* **:** of a light tint **:** PALE, DILUTE
²**whitish** \"\ *n* -ES **:** a whitish color
whit·ish·ness *n* -ES **:** the quality or state of being whitish
whit·leather \ˈhwit,- *also* ˈwi-\ *n* [ME *whitlether*, fr. *whit* white + *lether* leather] **:** WHITE LEATHER
whit·ley council \ˈhwitlē- *also* ˈwi-\ *n, usu cap W&C* [after John H. *Whitley* †1935 Eng. labor expert] **:** one of the permanent voluntary boards in various English industries that are representative of both capital and labor and are organized to settle wages, hours, and other matters of dispute
whit·ling \ˈhwitliŋ *also* ˈwit-\ *n* -S [¹*whit* + *-ling*] **:** SEA TROUT; *esp* **:** a large sea trout
whit·lock·ite \ˈhwit,lä,kīt *also* ˈwi-\ *n* -S [Herbert P. *Whitlock* †1948 Am. mineralogist + E *-ite*] **:** a rare mineral $Ca_3(PO_4)_2$ consisting of calcium phosphate in hexagonal crystals
whit·low \ˈhwit(,)lō *also* ˈwi-\ *n* -S [ME *whitflawe, whitflowe, whitlowe*, prob. fr. *whit* white + *flawe* flaw] **:** ³FELON 1
whitlow grass *n* **:** any of several inconspicuous herbs formerly thought to cure whitlow: as **a :** an annual weed (*Draba verna*) of Europe and No. America with a rosette of basal leaves and tiny flowers succeeded by oblong pods — called also *shadflower* **b :** a small Old World saxifrage (*Saxifraga tridactylites*) **c :** WHITLOWWORT
whitlowwort \ˈ⸗⸗,⸗\ *n* [*whitlow* + *wort;* fr. its being supposed to cure whitlow] **:** a plant of the genus *Paronychia*
whit·man·ese \ˈhwitmə¦nēz, -ēs *also* ¦wi-\ *n* -S *usu cap* [Walt *Whitman* †1892 Am. poet + E *-ese*] **:** language or expression of the kind characteristic of the poet Walt Whitman
whit·man·esque \-¦nesk\ *or* **whit·ma·ni·an** \hwitˈmānēən *also* wi-\ *adj, usu cap* [Walt *Whitman* †1892 + E *-esque* or *-ian*] **:** of, relating to, or resembling Whitman or his literary style
whit·ma·ni·ac \⸗ˈmānē,ak\ *n, usu cap* [blend of *Whitman* and *maniac*] **:** an enthusiast about the poet Whitman
whit·mon·day \ˈ⸗ˈ⸗(,)⸗\ *n, usu cap* [³*whit* + *monday*] **:** the day after Whitsunday observed as a legal holiday in England, Wales, and Ireland
whitney *var of* WITNEY
whit·rack \ˈ(h)wit,rak\ *or* **whit·rick** \-,rik\ *var of* WHITTRET
whit·ster \ˈhwitstə(r) *also* ˈwi-\ *n* -S [ME, fr. *whiten* to white + *-ster*] **:** a linen bleacher
¹**whit·sun** \ˈhwitsən *also* ˈwi-\ *adj, usu cap* [ME *whitson*, fr. *whitsonday* Whitsunday] **:** of, relating to, or observed on Whitsunday or at Whitsuntide ⟨*Whitsun* eve⟩ ⟨*Whitsun* plays⟩
²**whitsun** \"\ *n* -S *usu cap* [by shortening] **:** WHITSUNTIDE
whitsun ale *n, usu cap W* **:** a church-ale formerly held at Whitsuntide
whit·sun·day \ˈhwitˈsəndē, -di, -tsən,dā\ *n, usu cap* [ME *whitesunnedei, witsonday*, fr. OE *hwīta sunnandæg*, lit., white Sunday, fr. *hwīt* white + *sunnandæg* Sunday; prob. fr. the custom of wearing white robes by the newly-baptized, who were numerous at this season] **1 :** PENTECOST 2 **2 :** the 15th day of May that is under Scots law the usual day for the removal of tenants of both burgh and rural tenements
whitsun farthings *n pl, usu cap W* **:** offerings formerly made to the parish priest or to the mother church at Pentecost
whitsun monday *n, usu cap W&M* **:** WHITMONDAY
whitsun term *n, usu cap W* **:** the third term of the academic year at a Scottish university beginning in mid-April and lasting for 9 or 10 weeks
whit·sun·tide \ˈ⸗⸗,tīd\ *n, usu cap* [ME *whitsontide*, fr. *whitson* whitsun + *tide*] **:** the week beginning with Whitsunday and esp. the first three days of this week **:** the season of Pentecost
whitsun tuesday *n, usu cap W&T* [¹*whitsun* + *tuesday*] **:** WHIT-TUESDAY
whit·taw·er \ˈhwi,tȯ(ə)r *also* ˈwi-\ *also* **whit·taw** \-ȯ\ *n* -S

[ME *whittawer*, fr. *whit*lether whiteleather + *tawer*] **1** *archaic* **:** one who processes skins by tawing (as to form rawhide) **2** *chiefly dial* **:** a harness maker **:** SADDLER

whit·ten \'(h)wit³n\ *or* **whitten tree** *n* -s [fr. (assumed) ME *whitten tree*, fr. OE *hwītingtrēow*, fr. *hwīt* white + *-ing* + *trēow* tree] *dial Eng* **:** any of several trees or shrubs: as **a :** GUELDER-ROSE **b :** WAYFARING TREE **c :** ROWAN TREE

whit·ter·ick \'(h)witərik\ *n* -s [prob. imit.] *dial Brit* **:** a European curlew (*Numenius arquata*)

whit·tie-what·tie \'(h)witi,(h)wäti\ *n* -s [prob. redupl. of ¹*what*] *Scot* **:** vague or frivolous talk **:** indecisive or evasive conduct **:** PRETEXT

¹**whit·tle** \'hwid³l, -it³l *also* 'wi-\ *n* -s [ME *whitel*, fr. OE *hwītel;* akin to ON *hvītill* white bed cover, OE *hwīt* white] **1** *archaic* **:** a covering (as a cloak, shawl, or blanket) of heavy fabric **2** *chiefly dial* **:** a flannel (as a petticoat or band) for a baby

²**whittle** \"\ *n* -s [ME *whittel*, alter. of *thwitel*, fr. *thwiten* to cut down, whittle, fr. OE *thwītan;* akin to ON *thveita* to hew, hurl, and perh. to Lith *tvyskinti* to strike sharply] **1 :** KNIFE; *esp* **:** a large strong sheath or clasp knife **2** *dial Brit* **:** WHETSTONE, STEEL

³**whittle** \"\ *vb* **whittled; whittled; whittling** \-d-³liŋ, -t(³)liŋ\ **whittles** *vt* **1 a :** to pare or cut off chips from the surface of (wood) with a knife **:** cut or shape (as a piece of wood) by so paring or cutting ⟨~ a stick⟩ **b :** to form by whittling ⟨*whittled* a whip from limber ash⟩ — often used with *out* ⟨*whittling* out clothespins while he talked⟩ **2 :** to reduce, diminish, remove, or destroy gradually as if by cutting off bits with a knife **:** PARE ⟨a new line designed to ~ the waist⟩ — usu. used with an adverb (as *away, down, off, up*) ⟨~ down expenses⟩ ⟨~ away a fortune⟩ **3** *obs* **:** to whet the spirits of by drink **:** ply with liquor **:** make inebriated **~** *vi* **1 :** to cut or shape a piece of wood by slowly paring it with a knife **2 :** to wear oneself or another out with worrying or fretting

⁴**whit·tle** \'(h)wit³l\ *n* -s [by alter.] *chiefly Scot* **:** WHITLOW

whit·tler \'hwid-lə(r), -it(³)l- *also* 'wi-\ *n* -s **:** one that whittles

whittling *n* -s [fr. gerund of ³*whittle*] **:** a piece cut away in whittling **:** CHIP, SHAVING

whit·tret \'(h)witrət\ *n* -s [ME *whitrat*, fr. *whit* white + *rat*] *chiefly Scot* **:** WEASEL

whit-tuesday \'⸗'⸗(,)⸗\ *n, usu cap W&T* [³*whit* + *tuesday*] **:** the day after Whitmonday

whit week *n, usu cap 1st W & sometimes cap 2d W* [³*whit*] **:** WHITSUNTIDE

whit·worth's quick return \'hwit,wərths- *also* 'wi-\ *n, usu cap W* [after Sir Joseph *Whitworth* †1887 Eng. mechanical engineer and inventor] **:** a quick return in which the follower is a bar rotating or oscillating about one end and carrying a sliding driving sleeve or block rotated uniformly in a circle eccentric to the bar's motion

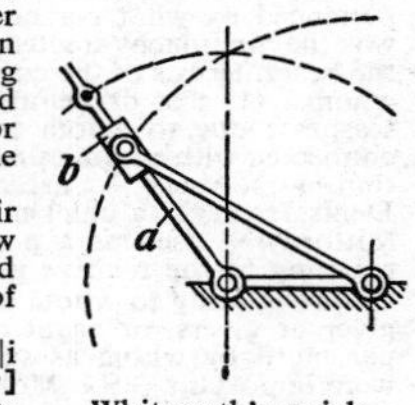

Whitworth's quick return: *a* follower, *b* sleeve

whitworth thread *n* [after Sir Joseph *Whitworth* †1887] **:** a screw thread with V-shaped cut used chiefly in Britain for screws of larger sizes

whity *or* **whitey** \'hwīd-|ē, -īt|, |i *also* 'wī-\ *adj* [¹*white* + *-y*] **:** WHITISH — usu. used in combination ⟨a dull ~ gray⟩ ⟨~ yellow hair⟩

¹**whiz** *or* **whizz** \'hwiz *also* 'wiz\ *vb* **whizzed; whizzed; whizzing; whizzes** [imit.] *vi* **:** to hum, whir, or hiss like a speeding object (as an arrow or ball) passing through air **:** fly or move swiftly with a hissing or buzzing sound **~** *vt* **:** to cause to whiz: as **a :** to project with sufficient speed to produce a whiz **b :** to rotate very rapidly; *specif* **:** to treat (as grain or sugar) in a whizzer

²**whiz** *or* **whizz** \"\ *n, pl* **whizzes 1 a :** a hissing, buzzing, or whirring sound ⟨the air filled with a ~ from passing traffic⟩ **b :** a movement or passage of something accompanied by such a sound ⟨following the ~ of the bee with her eye⟩; *sometimes* **:** a fast trip ⟨took a ~ to the shore⟩ **2 :** an arrangement or agreement felt to be satisfactory **:** BARGAIN, DEAL

³**whiz** *or* **whizz** \"\ *adv* [²*whiz*] **:** with a whiz

⁴**whiz** \"\ *n, pl* **whizzes** [prob. alter. (influenced by ¹*whiz*) of *wiz*] **:** a person notably qualified or able usu. in a specified field of interest **:** WIZARD 3 ⟨a ~ at mathematics⟩

whizbang *or* **whizzbang** \'⸗,⸗\ *n* [²*whiz* + *bang*] **1 a :** a whizzing ending in a bang **b :** one that speeds usu. noisily to a climax **:** WHIZ **2 a :** a small shell of such high velocity that the sound it makes in passing through the air is almost simultaneous with its explosion **b :** a firecracker or similar firework resembling such a shell **c :** a robot bomb

whiz-bang \'⸗'⸗\ *adj* **:** EXCELLENT, EXPERT, NOTABLE ⟨a *whiz-bang* technician⟩

whizgig \'⸗,⸗\ *n* [¹*whiz* + *gig*] **:** something (as a toy) that whirls with a whizzing sound

whiz·zer \'hwizə(r) *also* 'wi-\ *n* -s **1 :** one that whizzes: as **a :** BULL-ROARER **b :** a centrifugal machine for drying something (as grain, sugar, nitrated cotton) **:** HYDROEXTRACTOR; *also* **:** its attendant **2 :** something notable of its kind: as **a :** an outstandingly attractive or able person **:** WHIZ; *esp* **:** a showily beautiful person **b :** a shrewd, slick, or mischievous trick ⟨the ~ they pulled on us⟩

whizzing *adj* [fr. pres. part. of ¹*whiz*] **:** that whizzes — **whizzing·ly** *adv*

whizzing stick *n* **:** BULL-ROARER

whiz·zle \'hwizəl *also* 'wi-\ *vb* -ED/-ING/-s [¹*whiz* + *-le*] *vi* **:** WHIZ; *esp* **:** make a whizzing sound **~** *vt* **:** to get by stealth or cunning

whl *abbr* wheel

whm *abbr* weighmaster

¹**who** \(')hü, ,ü\ *pron* [ME, fr. OE *hwā;* akin to OHG *hwer*, interrog. pron., who, OSw *hvar*, Goth *hwas*, L *quis*, interrog. pron., who, *qui*, rel. pron., who, Gk *tis*, interrog. pron., who, Skt *ka*] **1 :** what person or persons **:** which person or persons — used as an interrogative pronoun in direct or indirect questions and serving to ask for specification ⟨~ were appointed to serve on the committee⟩ ⟨tell me ~ was elected president⟩ or to ask for identification ⟨~ is that at the door⟩ ⟨find out ~ they are⟩ or to question someone's character, status, authority, or antecedents ⟨~ are you to give orders to us⟩ or to represent a personal name not properly heard or understood ⟨Mrs. ~⟩ or to introduce a rhetorical question implying the answer *no one* or *nobody* ⟨~ cares⟩ ⟨~ wouldn't⟩ ⟨by the cut of my clothes, the pattern of my shoes and ~ knows what unconscious attributes, he recognized me as an American —Saul Bellow⟩; used by speakers on all educational levels and by many reputable writers, though disapproved by some grammarians, as the object of a verb or a following preposition ⟨~ did I see but a Spanish lady —Padraic Colum⟩ ⟨~ do you think I got a letter from —Walt Whitman⟩ ⟨do not know ~ the message is from —G.K.Chesterton⟩ or less frequently as the object of a preceding preposition ⟨between ~ —Shak.⟩ ⟨stolen from ~ —Ruth Park⟩; compare WHAT, WHOM, WHOSE **2 a :** any person or persons that **:** WHOEVER — used with or without a correlative substantive in a following main clause ⟨~ tells me true, though in his tale lie death —Shak.⟩ ⟨~ seeks, and will not take when once 'tis offered, shall never find it more —Shak.⟩ ⟨his almost obsessional anxiety for personal sincerity, suffer ~ may —Sean O'Faolain⟩; used without criticism as the subject of the clause that it introduces; used by speakers on all educational levels and by reputable writers, though disapproved by some grammarians, as the object of a verb in the clause that it introduces ⟨I serve ~ I like —*Irish Digest*⟩; compare WHAT, WHOM **b** *archaic* (1) **:** the particular person or persons that **:** he, she, or those that ⟨a fair wrought car . . . ~ stood therein did seem of great renown —John Keats⟩ (2) *pl in constr* **:** some persons that — used after *there* ⟨if there be ~ convulsively insist upon it —Walt Whitman⟩ **3** — used as a function word to introduce a restrictive or nonrestrictive relative clause and to serve as a substitute within that clause for the substantive modified by that clause; used esp. in reference to persons ⟨any reader ~ wishes to join with me in this argument —J.E.Baker⟩ ⟨novelists ~ write . . . as they must —Malcolm Cowley⟩ ⟨my father, ~ was a lawyer⟩ but also in reference to groups ⟨Congress, ~ can always speak more precisely —C.P.Curtis⟩ ⟨a generation ~ had known nothing but war —R.B.West⟩ ⟨the English firms ~ opened branches in New York —Hellmut Lehmann-Haupt⟩ or in reference to animals ⟨these were a pair of owls, ~ . . . showed little sign of alarm —Nathaniel Hawthorne⟩ ⟨one of those dogs ~ . . . fawn all over tramps —Nigel Balchin⟩ or in reference to inanimate objects esp. with the implication that the object is felt to have personality ⟨dolls of an older age bracket, ~ are supposed to provide a little girl with a feeling of having a younger sister —*New Yorker*⟩ or with the implication that the reference is really to a person or persons possessing or producing or operating the object ⟨a number of deep southern accents ~ assert that they have been immensely impressed —Blake Clark⟩ ⟨a late legendary accretion, contradicted by earlier sources ~ maintain a Davidic ancestry —F.M.Cross⟩ ⟨the plaintive woodwinds ~ opened the passage —Marcia Davenport⟩; sometimes used after *such* with the implication that the action or state expressed in the clause introduced by *who* is a real or appropriate consequence of what is expressed by *such* or by the phrase containing *such* ⟨such ~ . . . no beauty lack —Shak.⟩; used universally and without criticism as the subject of the clause that it introduces; used by speakers on all educational levels and by many reputable writers, though disapproved by some grammarians, as the object of a verb in the clause that it introduces ⟨old peasants . . . ~, if isolated from their surroundings, one would expect to see in a village church —John Berger⟩ or less frequently as the object of a preceding or following preposition in the clause that it introduces ⟨of ~ I know nothing —Raymond Paton⟩; compare ⁴THAT 1, WHICH, WHOM, WHOSE — **as who** *archaic* **:** as one that **:** as if someone ⟨he nods at us, *as who* should say, "I'll be even with you" —Shak.⟩ ⟨she recoiled — *as who* finds thorns where she sought flowers —Robert Browning⟩ ⟨such speech . . . was probably . . . a mere freak of the tongue . . . *as who* should go to a masked ball in guise of Mephistopheles —John Morley⟩ — **as who should say** *archaic* **:** so to speak ⟨I would build large — in fine embossed vaults and painted arches, *as who should say* —Henry James †1916⟩ — **who is who** *or* **who's who** *or* **who was who :** the identity of or the noteworthy facts about each of a number of persons ⟨lived in this town long enough to know *who's who*⟩ ⟨before I had learned *who was who*⟩

²**who** \'hü\ *n* -s **:** the person or persons involved or meant or referred to ⟨I shall ask the next banana peddler the ~ and the why of it —Carl Sandburg⟩

whoa \'(h)wō, 'hō *also* **wo** *or* **woa** \'wō\ *v imper* [ME *whoo, who*] — a command to a draft animal to stand still — compare GIDDAP

who·dunit \(')hü'dənət, *usu* -əd-+V\ *n* -s [fr. the substandard expression *who done it*] **:** a detective story or a mystery story presented as a novel, a play, or a motion picture ⟨the tautness of a fine ~ —*Newsweek*⟩

who·ev·er \hü'evə(r)\ *pron* [ME *who ever*, fr. ¹*who* + *ever*] **1 :** whatever person **:** any person at all that **:** no matter who — used in any grammatical relation except that of a possessive ⟨sells . . . eggs to ~ has the money to buy —J.R.Chamberlain⟩ ⟨~ he picks has to have the stature of a collaborator, not a subordinate —*Time*⟩ ⟨~ she weds, she never descends below the rank to which she was born —Agnes M. Miall⟩ ⟨he is a good man himself, ~ his friends are⟩ ⟨that is not true, ~ you heard it from⟩ **2 :** ¹WHO 1 — used in questions expressing astonishment or perplexity ⟨~ can that be⟩

¹**whole** \'hōl, *dial* 'həl *or with a vowel approaching* ə\ *adj* [ME *hool* healthy, unhurt, entire, fr. OE *hāl;* akin to OHG *heil* healthy, unhurt, ON *heill*, Goth *hails* healthy, well, W *coel* omen, OSlav *cělŭ* healthy, unhurt] **1 a** (1) **:** free of wound or injury **:** UNHURT ⟨thousands . . . who have been killed or wounded . . . might still be alive and ~ —Patrick McMahon⟩ (2) **:** recovered from a wound or injury **:** RESTORED (3) **:** HEALED ⟨here, with one balm for many fevers found, ~ of an ancient evil, I sleep sound —A.E.Housman⟩ **b :** free of defect, damage, or impairment **:** INTACT, UNBROKEN, UNMARRED ⟨anxious lest they were broken and thus make an evil omen, but they were ~ —Pearl Buck⟩ **c :** physically sound and healthy **:** free of disease or deformity ⟨they that are ~ need not a physician —Lk 5:31 (AV)⟩ **2 a :** having all its proper parts or components **:** lacking nothing that belongs to it **:** diminished or reduced in no way **:** ENTIRE ⟨have given a ~ philosophy of history interpreted through these factors —P.A.Sorokin⟩ ⟨brings on a ~ symphony of hammerings and hissings —R.M. Hodesh⟩ ⟨a quorum for the purpose shall consist of two thirds of the ~ number of senators —*U.S.Constitution*⟩ **b :** containing all its natural constituents, components, or elements **:** deprived of nothing by refining, processing, or separation **:** UNMODIFIED ⟨~ blood⟩ ⟨~ milk⟩ **3 a :** constituting the total sum or undiminished entirety of **:** INTEGRAL ⟨engineering feats . . . that have severed ~ continental land masses —M.J. Herskovits⟩ ⟨give their ~ time to the study of patients —*Official Register of Harvard Univ.*⟩ ⟨a ~ two miles of the riverbank had been acquired by the city —Leslie Charteris⟩ **b :** each of or all of the ⟨lost money the ~ 10 days⟩ ⟨took part in the ~ series of battles⟩ **c** *chiefly Scot* **:** constituting the entire number or the totality of — usu. used with *the* or a possessive pronoun **4 a :** constituting an undivided unit **:** UNBROKEN, UNCUT ⟨~ nuts⟩ ⟨a ~ roast suckling pig⟩ **b :** directed to one end **:** completely focused or channeled **:** not scattered or dispersed **:** CONCENTRATED, UNDISTRACTED ⟨gave it his ~ attention⟩ ⟨put his ~ soul into the performance⟩ **5 :** seemingly complete or total ⟨the ~ aim of present strategy is to deter aggression —Denis Healey⟩ **:** very great ⟨felt a ~ lot better for the news⟩ ⟨very many **:** EXTENSIVE ⟨~ farms were overrun⟩ **:** LARGE, TREMENDOUS **6 :** constituting a person in his full nature, development, or relations: as **a :** involving mind, body, and emotions ⟨the ~ child — physical, emotional, social — is now considered in planning his remedial work —*College English*⟩ ⟨the spiritual life is or should be a harmonious development of the ~ man —W.R.Inge⟩ **b :** involving moral, social, economic and all other activities and relationships ⟨the central focus of education is the student . . . this is the ~ student in all his relationships and adjustments —D.D.Feder⟩

syn ENTIRE, TOTAL, ALL, GROSS: WHOLE may imply that nothing, or nothing salient, has been left out, omitted, ignored, depreciated, alloyed, or taken away ⟨devoting his *whole* energy to the task⟩ ⟨he of the *whole* party might be supposed untouched by the passion of death —Thomas De Quincey⟩ ⟨throughout his *whole* career he was keenly alive to the course of political events —W.C.Ford⟩ ENTIRE may suggest a being completed, finished, or perfected ⟨my strength is unimpaired, my mind is *entire* —O.S.J.Gogarty⟩ ⟨always the *entire* person, never the mere teacher, who spoke —C.N. Greenough⟩ TOTAL may imply that all possible items or constituents have been counted, weighed, reckoned, or considered ⟨the Soviet threat is *total;* it affects every form of human endeavor —H.S.Truman⟩ ⟨open our homes and our community life to these visitors from abroad so that they can see how we live in our *total* social environment —D.J.Shank⟩ ALL, followed by *the* or by a possessive or demonstrative pronoun sometimes equals WHOLE ⟨*all* the city was in an uproar⟩ ⟨*all* the cake was eaten⟩ or sometimes ENTIRE ⟨*all* their development⟩ ⟨*all* their attention focused on the scene⟩ or sometimes TOTAL ⟨*all* his savings⟩ GROSS adds the indication that no deductions, as for costs, taxes, and replacement funds, have been made ⟨his *gross* salary was a thousand a month, but various taxes made large inroads in this⟩ ⟨the foregoing figures are *gross*, rather than net dividends —*Yrbk. of Railroad Information*⟩ — **out of whole cloth :** out of pure fabrication **:** without basis ⟨a tissue of lies made up *out of whole cloth* —*Current History*⟩

²**whole** \"\ *adv* [ME *hoole*, fr. *hool*, adj., healthy, unhurt, entire — more at ¹WHOLE] **:** ENTIRELY, ALTOGETHER — used in combination chiefly in contrast to *half* ⟨laying a half-dirty cloth upon a *whole*-dirty deal table —Sir Walter Scott⟩

³**whole** \"\ *n* -s [ME *hool*, fr. *hool*, adj.] **1 :** a complete amount or sum **:** a number, aggregate, or totality lacking no part, member, or element **:** an unreduced or unimpaired entirety ⟨the ~ of our creative literature . . . has this law of nature behind it —Herbert Agar⟩ ⟨the ~ of their relationship passed before him —Hamilton Basso⟩ **2 :** something constituting a complex unity **:** a coherent system or organization of parts fitting or working together as one ⟨built its "A" mill, incorporating parts of earlier buildings, and unifying the ~ by a new facade —*Amer. Guide Series: Minn.*⟩ ⟨a musical design can be discovered in particular scenes, and in his more perfect plays as ~*s* —T.S.Eliot⟩ **syn** see SUM — **on the whole** *adv* **1 :** in view of all the circumstances or conditions **:** all things considered ⟨*on the whole* it seemed best to cut the visit short⟩ **2** *archaic* **:** at the end **:** in conclusion **:** FINALLY **3 :** in general **:** in most instances **:** despite some exceptions **:** TYPICALLY ⟨fathers *on the whole* listed three times as many favorable as unfavorable reactions to having children —C.B.Palmer b. 1910⟩

whole binding *n* **:** FULL BINDING

whole blood *n* [ME *hole blode*, fr. *hole, hool* entire, whole + *blode, blood* blood] **1 :** descent from the same two parents rather than only one — used esp. in the phrase *brothers (or sisters) of the whole blood;* compare HALF BLOOD **2 :** FULL BLOOD

whole-bound \'⸗'⸗\ *adj* **:** FULL-BOUND

whole cannon *n* **:** a 16th and 17th century cannon throwing a projectile weighing from 70 to 120 pounds — compare DEMICANNON

whole-colored \'⸗,⸗⸗\ *adj, chiefly Brit* **:** being all of one color **:** CONCOLOROUS

whole culverin *n* **:** a 16th and 17th century culverin throwing a ball of from 40 to 60 pounds — compare DEMICULVERIN

whole deal *n* **:** a deal board 1¼ inches thick — compare SLIT DEAL

whole-footed *adj* [ME *hole-foted*, fr. *hole, hool* entire, whole + *foted* footed] *obs* **:** having the feet whole (as a solid-hoofed animal or a web-footed bird)

whole gale *n* **:** wind having a speed of 55 to 63 miles per hour — see BEAUFORT SCALE table

wholehearted \'⸗'⸗⸗\ *adj* **:** undivided in purpose, enthusiasm, or will **:** HEARTY, ZESTFUL ⟨~ cooperation⟩ ⟨~ effort⟩ **syn** see SINCERE

whole·heart·ed·ly *adv* **:** in a wholehearted manner

whole·heart·ed·ness *n* **:** the quality or state of being wholehearted

whole hog *n* **:** the whole way or farthest limit **:** ALL ⟨they are the "*whole hog* or none" variety —H.L.Ickes⟩ — used esp. in the phrase *go the whole hog* ⟨went the *whole hog* and named a name —*Time*⟩ ⟨go *whole hog* for knitwear —*New Yorker*⟩ ⟨you might as well go the *whole hog* and line all the dales and lakes with factories —S.P.B.Mais⟩

whole-hog·ger \-'hògə(r), -'häg-\ *n* **:** one that supports or promotes something without reservation, qualification, or hesitation **:** one that goes the limit or the whole hog ⟨a *whole-hogger* for economy in every constituency except his own —*Irish Statesman*⟩

¹**whole-length** \'⸗'⸗\ *adj* **1 :** carried to the full or natural extent **:** not curtailed or abbreviated **:** UNABRIDGED ⟨a *whole-length* analysis⟩ **2 :** having, accommodating, or representing the full height of the human figure **:** not proportionately reduced or foreshortened ⟨a *whole-length* mirror⟩ ⟨a *whole-length* portrait⟩ ⟨a *whole-length* statue⟩

²**whole-length** \'⸗,⸗\ *n* **:** a whole-length picture or statue ⟨on the walls were framed *whole-lengths* of a number of 19th century authors⟩ — compare HALF-LENGTH

whole life insurance *n* [*whole life* (fr. ¹*whole* + *life*) + *insurance*] **:** ORDINARY LIFE INSURANCE

wholely *var of* WHOLLY

whole meal *n* **1 :** WHOLE-WHEAT FLOUR **2** *Brit* **:** WHEATMEAL

whole·ness *n* -ES [ME *hoolnesse*, fr. *hool* entire, whole + *-nesse* -ness] **:** the quality or state of being whole **:** an unreduced or unbroken completeness or totality **:** a hale vigor or soundness **:** INTEGRITY

whole note *n* **:** a musical note equal in value to four quarter notes or two half notes — called also *semibreve;* see NOTE illustration

whole number *n* **:** INTEGER

whole plate *n, chiefly Brit* **:** a photographic plate or film 6½x8½ inches in size

whole rest *n* **:** a musical rest corresponding in value to a whole note

wholes *pl of* WHOLE

whole-sail \'⸗,⸗\ *adj* **:** being a breeze or wind that permits use of full sail or of nearly full sail **:** not requiring taking in of light sails

¹**whole·sale** \'hōl,sāl\ *n* [ME *holesale*, fr. *hole, hool* entire, whole + *sale*] **1 :** the sale of goods or commodities in quantity usu. for resale (as by a retail merchant) **2 :** a large scale or indiscriminate transaction or maneuver — used esp. in the phrase *by wholesale* ⟨killed off the pests by ~⟩

²**wholesale** \"\ *adj* **1 :** of, relating to, or engaged in the sale of goods or commodities in quantity for resale ⟨a ~ grocer⟩ ⟨a ~ lot of store fixtures⟩ ⟨~ failures increased by 36 percent —Eric Sevareid⟩ **2 :** performed on a large scale **:** handling or affecting large numbers or quantities **:** EXTENSIVE, MASSIVE ⟨~ blackmail and extortion amounting to millions —A.L. Vogelback⟩ ⟨~ character assassination —R.L.Roy⟩ ⟨the ~ intrusion of the neon-lit world of mass entertainment — film, radio, jazz — has also left its mark —M.J.Lasky⟩ ⟨a ~ attack upon those who teach English in our colleges —J.D.Adams⟩ **3 :** marked by failure of discrimination, selection, or discretion **:** made, applied, or carried out so as to affect large numbers in the same way without regard to the merits of individual instances ⟨the ~ character of this answer prevents critical examination and discrimination of the particular facts involved in the actual problem —John Dewey⟩

³**wholesale** \"\ *adv* [²*wholesale*] **:** in a wholesale manner ⟨although wartime experience yielded valuable lessons, it cannot be applied ~ to peace —*Economist*⟩

⁴**wholesale** \"\ *vb* -ED/-ING/-S [¹*wholesale*] *vi* **:** to sell at wholesale ⟨averaged a straight $50 markup when he *wholesaled* to the bootlegger —*Motor Trend*⟩ ⟨small plastic novelties that ~ at $2 a hundred⟩ **~** *vt* **:** to sell (something) at wholesale ⟨it was *wholesaling* education in diluted form —Dwayne Orton⟩

wholesale life insurance *n* [²*wholesale* + *life insurance*] **:** life insurance covering a smaller group of employees than the minimum required for a group life insurance policy

whole·sal·er \-ālə(r)\ *n* -s [¹*wholesale* + *-er*] **:** a merchant middleman who sells chiefly to retailers, other merchants, or industrial, institutional, and commercial users mainly for resale or business use — called also *jobber*

whole snipe *n* **:** a common snipe (*Capella gallinago*) of Europe and parts of Asia and Africa — compare GREAT SNIPE, JACKSNIPE

whole·some \'hōlsəm *also* -lts-\ *adj, often* -ER/-EST [ME *holsom, hoolsom*, fr. *hol, hool* healthy, entire, whole + *-som* -some] **1 :** promoting health or well-being of mind or spirit **:** tending to moral soundness or vigor **:** corrective or sanative in effect **:** BENEFICIAL, SALUTARY ⟨passes through the ~ ordeal of the royal presence, and issues from it free from all taint —W.M.Thackeray⟩ ⟨brought these difficult situations into the ~ light of world public opinion —Huntington Gilchrist⟩ **2 a :** promoting health of body **:** health-giving **:** SALUBRIOUS ⟨perhaps because our sedative airs are more ~ for those who suffer from high blood pressure —Rebecca West⟩ **b :** tending to restore health **:** CURATIVE, REMEDIAL ⟨prescribe a ~ regimen for the convalescents⟩ **3 a :** sound in body, mind, or morals **:** not sickly, morbid, or diseased **:** HEALTHY ⟨the ~ gush of natural feeling —Nathaniel Hawthorne⟩ ⟨she may be described as plain in appearance, but with a ~ air —C.G.Bowers⟩ **b :** having the simple health or vigor of normal domesticity ⟨~ as the smell of homemade bread just out of the oven —Pamela Taylor⟩ ⟨~ family life⟩ **4 a** *obs* **:** SEAWORTHY **b** *archaic* **:** safely navigable — used of the sea **5 a :** having the value of a needed warning **:** based on well-grounded fear **:** CAUTIONARY, PRUDENT ⟨lived in a ~ dread of her tempers —T.B. Costain⟩ ⟨had too ~ an awareness of the logical difficulties —Benjamin Farrington⟩ **b :** SAFE ⟨it wouldn't be ~ for you to go down there —Mark Twain⟩ **syn** see HEALTHFUL, HEALTHY

whole·some·ly *adv* [ME *holsomliche*, fr. *holsom* wholesome + *-liche* -ly] **:** in a wholesome manner

whole·some·ness *n* -ES [ME *holsomnesse*, fr. *holsom* wholesome + *-nesse* -ness] **:** the quality or state of being wholesome

whole-souled \'⸗'⸗\ *adj* **:** moved by ardent enthusiasm or single-minded devotion or attachment **:** WHOLEHEARTED ⟨has demonstrated a *whole-souled* allegiance to the democratic world —B.C.Limb⟩ ⟨men whose dedication to their country was *whole-souled* —Eric Sevareid⟩ **syn** see SINCERE

whole step *or* **whole tone** *n* **:** a musical interval comprising two half steps (as C–D or F♯–G♯)
whole stuff *n* **:** STUFF 2c
whole–time \ˈ⸗;⸗\ *adj* **:** FULL-TIME ⟨never possible to maintain a *whole-time* company —Gabriel Fallon⟩
whole–tone scale *n* **:** a musical scale progressing by whole steps
whole vamp *n* **:** a one-piece shoe upper seamed at the back above the heel
whole wheat *adj* **:** made of ground entire wheat berries
whole wheat flour *n* **:** flour that is ground from the whole grain and contains all the constituents of the wheat kernels
who·lism \ˈhō,lizəm\ *n* -S [by alter. (influenced by ³*whole*)] **:** HOLISM
who·lis·tic \(ˈ)hō¦listik\ *adj* [by alter. (influenced by ³*whole*)] **:** HOLISTIC
whol·ly *also* **whole·ly** \ˈhōl(l)ē, \|i, *when emphatic also* ˈhōll\|\ *adv* [ME *hoolly,* fr. *hool* entire, whole + *-ly*] **1 :** to the full or entire extent **:** without diminution or reduction **:** ALTOGETHER, COMPLETELY, TOTALLY ⟨the land is used ~ for crops —P.E. James⟩ **2 :** to the exclusion of other things **:** SOLELY ⟨in order to devote himself ~ to this work he resigned —G.F.Smythe⟩ ⟨much prefer to be ~ agriculturalists —L.S.B.Leakey⟩
whom \(ˌ)hüm, ˌüm\ *pron, objective case of* WHO [ME, fr. OE *hwām,* dat. of *hwā* who — more at WHO] **1 :** ¹WHO 1 — sometimes used as object of a verb or a following preposition ⟨~ shall I send —Isa 6:8 (AV)⟩ ⟨my question was ~ were all the Christmas signals for —W.T.Scott⟩ or more frequently as the object of a preceding preposition ⟨never send to know for ~ the bell tolls —John Donne⟩ though now often considered stilted esp. in oral use; occas. used as predicate nominative with a copulative verb esp. in the vicinity of a preposition or a verb of which it might mistakenly be considered the object ⟨~ say ye that I am —Mt 16:15 (AV)⟩ ⟨regardless of ~ his friends may be⟩ **2 a :** ¹WHO 2a — used as object of a verb or preposition ⟨~ he strikes his crooked tushes slay —Shak.⟩ ⟨I will . . . be gracious to ~ I will be gracious —Exod 33:19 (AV)⟩ ⟨ask ~ you will⟩ **b** *archaic* **:** ¹WHO 2b — used as object of a verb or preposition ⟨how can I curse ~ God has not cursed —Num 23:8 (RSV)⟩ ⟨there are to ~ my satire seems too bold —Alexander Pope⟩ **3 :** ¹WHO 3 — used as the object of a verb or a preceding preposition ⟨those ~ oppression had goaded to rebellion —T.B.Macaulay⟩ ⟨the universities, by ~ he was abundantly honored —J.A.Pollard⟩ ⟨his pet toad ~ he fed regularly —Osbert Sitwell⟩ ⟨these moral types, ~ all recognize —V.S.Pritchett⟩ or less frequently as the object of a following preposition ⟨the man ~ you addressed the letter to⟩; sometimes used as the subject of the clause that it introduces esp. in the vicinity of a verb of which it might mistakenly be considered the object ⟨a . . . recruit ~ he hoped would prove to be a crack salesman —Bennett Cerf⟩ ⟨people . . . ~ you never thought would sympathize —Shea Murphy⟩
whom·ev·er \hüˈmevə(r)\ *pron, objective case of* WHOEVER [ME *whom ever,* fr. *whom* + *ever*] **:** WHOEVER 1 — used as object of a verb or preposition ⟨so that she could help ~ she married —Lillian Ross⟩ ⟨~ this alleged autobiography . . . is about, it is a real life —*Springfield (Mass.) City Library Bull.*⟩; sometimes used as the subject of a verb or as predicate nominative with a copulative verb esp. after a preposition or a verb of which it might mistakenly be considered the object ⟨simple possession of the note would be enough to insure the future of ~ held it —Arthur Knight⟩ ⟨I go out to talk to ~ it is —*Guatemala News*⟩ ⟨he attacked ~ disagreed with him⟩
¹**whomp** \ˈhw\|ämp *also* ˈw\| *or* \|ōmp\ *or* **whoomp** \\|ümp\ *n* -S [imit.] **:** a loud slap, crash, or crunch ⟨an alert beaver slaps his heavy flat tail with a tremendous ~ on the surface of the water —Alan Devoe⟩ ⟨could hear the occasional ~ of their guns echoing across the hills —William English⟩
²**whomp** \ˈ"\ *vb* -ED/-ING/-S *vi* **:** BANG, SLAP ⟨bombs ~*ed* down —*advt*⟩ ~ *vt* **1 :** BANG, SLAP **2 :** to defeat overwhelmingly **:** TROUNCE ⟨~*ed* their arch-rival in the season's climactic football game⟩
whomp up *vt* **1 :** to stir up **:** AROUSE ⟨*whomp up* interest in the unveiling of new models —*Time*⟩ **2 :** to knock together **:** cook up ⟨have a syndicate call you up and ask you to *whomp up* something special for them —Mel Lazarus⟩ ⟨*whomped up* a story, mailed it, and sat back to await a check —*New Orleans (La.) Times-Picayune*⟩
whom·so \ˈhüm,sō\ [ME *whom so,* fr. *whom* + *so*] *objective case of* WHOSO
whom·so·ev·er \ˌhümsōˈevə(r), -sōˈe-\ [ME, fr. *whom so* + *ever*] *objective case of* WHOSOEVER
¹**whoo** \ˈhwü *also* ˈwü\ *interj* [origin unknown] — used to express sudden excitement, astonishment, or relief
²**whoo** \ˈhü\ *n* -S [imit.] **:** the cry of an owl
¹**whoof** \ˈhwu̇f *also* ˈwu̇f\ *n* -S [imit.] **:** a deep snorting sound (as made by a four-footed animal)
²**whoof** \ˈ"\ *vb* -ED/-ING/-S *vi* **:** to utter a whoof **:** SNORT ~ *vt* **:** SNORT, BLOW
¹**whoop** \ˈhüp, ˈhw\| *also* ˈw\| *or* \|üp; *with reference to coughing* ˈh\|üp, \|üp *also* ˈhw\| *sometimes* ˈw\|\ *vb* -ED/-ING/-S [ME *whopen,* alter. of *hopen, houpen,* fr. MF *houpper,* of imit. origin] *vi* **1 :** to utter a whoop in expression of eagerness, enthusiasm, or enjoyment **:** SHOUT, HALLOO ⟨made a man want to cry and ~ all at the same time —Laura Krey⟩ **2 :** to utter the cry of an owl **:** HOOT **3 :** to give the spasmodic cough of whooping cough **4 :** to roar support **:** express vociferous endorsement ⟨was ~*ing* for leftist candidates⟩ **5 a :** to go with a roar **:** move with a loud noise of the vehicle or with a shouting of the occupants ⟨a noisy gang, squashed into five cars and a taxi, were ~*ing* through the quieter squares —Dorothy Sayers⟩ ⟨the Western express . . . ~*s* out through the suburbs —Lawrence Constable⟩ **b :** to be rushed through by acclamation or with noisy support ⟨the bill ~*ed* through both houses⟩ **c :** to blow loudly ⟨a stiff west wind was ~*ing* in off the prairies —F.B.Gipson⟩ ~ *vt* **1 a :** to utter, cheer on, or express with a whoop **:** urge or press clamorously ⟨~*ed* us in to wash for lunch —William DuBois⟩ ⟨machine men crowded on his bandwagon, ~*ed* him into office —William Manchester⟩ ⟨~*ed* a welcome⟩ **b :** to rush through or adopt with noisy enthusiasm ⟨it ~*ed* through on a voice vote a stopgap foreign aid appropriation bill —*Current Biog.*⟩ **2 a :** to arouse sentiment for **:** agitate in behalf of **:** BOOM ⟨the literary reviews for five or six years past have been ~*ing* up all sorts of palpable quacks —H.L.Mencken⟩ **b :** to stir up **:** EXCITE ⟨~*s* up a selling boom —Wallace Stegner⟩ **3 :** BOOST, RAISE ⟨the tip ~*ed* the price up to 80 times the prewar quotation —Sylvia F. Porter⟩ ⟨so if I was fool enough to never ~ the ante I'd get the credit for lying anyway —Sinclair Lewis⟩ — **whoop it up 1 :** to celebrate riotously or noisily **:** CAROUSE ⟨a bunch of the boys were *whooping it up* in the Malamute saloon —R.W.Service⟩ ⟨mobs of drunken men were *whooping it up* —S.H.Holbrook⟩ **2 :** to stir up enthusiasm **:** beat the drum ⟨tried to *whoop it up* again afterwards in the Senate —*New Republic*⟩ ⟨*whooping it up* for tribal self-government —Oliver La Farge⟩
²**whoop** \ˈ"\ *n* -S [ME *whope* (used interjectionally), alter. of *houp,* fr. *hopen, houpen,* v.] **1 a :** a sound expressive of eagerness, exuberance, or jubilation ⟨goes out on the town with a ~ and a holler —John McCarten⟩ — often used interjectionally **b :** the shout of men in battle or pursuit **:** WAR CRY ⟨with ~ and halloo, like a troop of Don Cossacks —Washington Irving⟩ **c :** a shout of hunters (as at the kill) **2 :** the cry of an owl **:** HOOT **3 :** the crowing intake of breath following a paroxysm in whooping cough **4 :** a variation of hide-and-seek **5 :** the smallest bit **:** HOOT, DAMN ⟨didn't give a ~⟩ ⟨not worth a ~⟩
³**whoop** \ˈhüp\ *n* -S [alter. of ⁴*hoop*] **:** HOOPOE
whoop-de-do *or* **whoop-de-doo** \ˈh\|üpdē¦dü, ˈhw\| *also* ˈw\| *or* \|üp-\ *n* -S [prob. irreg. fr. ²*whoop*] **1 :** hilarious partying **:** roistering conviviality **:** HIGH JINKS ⟨there is dancing in the streets, music, singing and general *whoop-de-do* —Al Colby⟩ **2 :** an organized public affair or activity of any of various kinds: as **a :** a lively social function or party **b :** the spectacle of political contest, oratory, and maneuver ⟨political *whoop-de-do*⟩ **c :** the doings contrived to attract attention to a commercial promotion **:** a publicity stunt or campaign ⟨enlisted every means of publicity in the *whoop-de-do* of launching a new car⟩ **3 :** agitated public discussion or debate **:** a stir of opinion ⟨a lot of foolish *whoop-de-do* in England when it was announced that an American was going to portray royalty in this film —John McCarten⟩
¹**whoop·ee** \ˈhw\|u̇(,)pē, \|ü(- ˈ⸗ *also* ˈw\| *sometimes* ˈh\|\ *or* **hoop·ee** \ˈh\|\ *interj* [irreg. fr. ²*whoop*] — used to express exuberant delight
²**whoopee** *or* **hoopee** \ˈ⸗(,)⸗\ *n* -S **1 :** the feverish alcohol-and-sex partying first widely conspicuous during the U.S. prohibition era — often used in the phrase *make whoopee* ⟨accused her of making ~ while he was locked up, and of being unfaithful to him —Edmund Wilson⟩ **2 :** any boisterous convivial fun ⟨college-boy ~ —*Amer. Guide Series: Md.*⟩
whoop·er \ˈh\|üpə(r), ˈhw\| *also* ˈw\| *or* \|üp\ *n* -S **1 :** one that whoops **2 :** WHOOPING CRANE
whooper swan \ˈ⸗⸗-\ *also* **hoop·er** \ˈh\|\ *or* **hooper swan** *n* -S **:** a common Old World swan (*Olor cygnus*)
whooping cough *n* **:** an infectious inflammation of the air passages with a convulsive spasmodic cough sometimes followed by a crowing intake of breath — called also *pertussis*
whooping crane *n* **:** a large white nearly extinct No. American crane (*Grus americana*) noted for its loud whoop
whooping swan *n* **:** WHOOPER SWAN
whoop·la \ˈh\|ü,plä, ˈhw\| *also* ˈw\| *or* \|u̇,-\ *n* -S [alter. (influenced by ²*whoop*) of *hoopla*] **1 :** a noisy commotion **:** TO-DO ⟨newspaper ~ about the new champion⟩ ⟨the whole ~ is making readers expect too much —Theodore Pratt⟩ **2 :** boisterous merrymaking **:** SHINDIG, WHOOPEE ⟨throw ~ or stay out all night —Calder Willingham⟩
whoops *like* OOPS\ *interj* [irreg. fr. ²*whoop*] — used to express mild apology, surprise, or dismay
whoop–up \ˈ⸗,⸗\ *n* -S [fr. the verb phrase *whoop up*] **:** a rousing affair **:** WHOOP-DE-DO
whoos *pl of* WHOO
¹**whoosh** \ˈhw\|ush *also* ˈw\| *or* -üsh\ *or* **woosh** \ˈw\|\ *vb* -ED/-ING/-ES [imit.] *vi* **:** to rush past or gush out **:** move explosively **:** HISS ⟨an occasional car ~*ed* by on the road —Hollis Alpert⟩ ⟨black oil ~*ed* up as the drill broke through⟩ ~ *vt* **:** to move (someone or something) with an explosive or sibilant rush or gush **:** operate or carry on a current of air or other fluid ⟨~*ed* the doors open —Raymond Chandler⟩ ⟨its rotors ~ the dust or chemicals or seed exactly where the farmer wants them —F.J.Taylor⟩
²**whoosh** \ˈ"\ *n* -ES **:** a swift or explosive rush **:** GUSH, HISS ⟨a branch load of snow slipped to the ground with a faint ~ —Oliver La Farge⟩ ⟨a ~ of air so powerful that roofs were lifted from their homes —Dean Jennings⟩ ⟨with a ~ the fire took hold —John Onslow⟩
whoo·sis \ˈhüzəs\ *or* **whoo·sy** \-zē\ *n, pl* **whoosises** *or* **whoosies** [*whoosis* perh. alter. of the expression *who's this; whoosy* perh. alter. of the expression *who's he*] **:** someone or something whose name one does not know or cannot recall **:** an indefinite or unspecified person or thing or one that is representative or typical ⟨don't print Senator *Whoosis'* blowoff yesterday —F.L.Mott⟩ ⟨the choke will be a ~ on the dash —F.C.Othman⟩
¹**whop** *also* **whap** \ˈhw\|äp *also* ˈw\| *or* \|ȯp\ *or* **wop** \ˈw\|\ *vt* **whopped; whopped; whopping; whops** [ME *whappen,* alter. of *wappen* to throw, strike, blow in gusts — more at WAP] **1 :** to pull or whip out **2 a :** to belabor heavily **:** BEAT, STRIKE, THRASH ⟨feel like somebody just *whopped* me in the belly with a sledgehammer —Budd Schulberg⟩ **b :** to defeat totally **:** OVERCOME, VANQUISH ⟨*whopped* a highly touted football eleven⟩
²**whop** \ˈ"\ *or* **wop** \ˈ"\ *n* -S [ME *whapp,* alter. of *wap* — more at WAP] **:** a heavy blow **:** THUD, THUMP — often used interjectionally
whop·per \-pə(r)\ *n* -S [¹*whop* + *-er*] **1 :** something unusually large or otherwise extreme or extravagant of its kind ⟨returned with an armful of harmonicas, ranging in length from one inch to a ~ of over two feet —*New Yorker*⟩ ⟨spent a thousand dollars on a ~ of a black velvet backdrop —R.L. Taylor⟩ **2 :** an extravagant or monstrous lie ⟨droning ~*s* into the telephone and unloading misrepresented stocks —A.W. Baum⟩
¹**whopping** *adj* [fr. pres. part. of ¹*whop*] **:** extremely large **:** EXTRAORDINARY, EXTRAVAGANT, OUTRAGEOUS ⟨netted a ~ buffalo —G.S.Perry⟩ ⟨distills a good deal of sardonic fun from the ~ errors of the nation's oracles —C.J.Rolo⟩
²**whopping** *adv* **:** EXTREMELY, IMMENSELY, VERY ⟨they all got ~ drunk —Jim Rearden⟩ ⟨a ~ big cruise ship —*New Yorker*⟩
³**whopping** *n* -S [fr. gerund of ¹*whop*] **:** a heavy pounding or beating
whor·age \ˈhōrij, ˈhȯr-\ *n* -S **:** WHORE
¹**whore** \ˈhō(ə)r, ˈhȯ(ə)r, -ōə, -ō(ə), *chiefly euphemistic* ˈhu̇(ə)r *or* -ūə\ *n* -S [ME *hore, hoore,* fr. OE *hōre;* akin to OHG *huora* whore, ON *hōra* whore, *hōrr* adulterer, Goth *hors* adulterer, L *carus* dear — more at CHARITY] **1 :** a woman who practices unlawful sexual commerce; *esp* **:** one who prostitutes her body for hire **:** HARLOT, PROSTITUTE **2 :** one regarded as actuated by corrupt, unworthy, or idolatrous motives ⟨our own 20th-century species of literary ~ —H.J.Kaplan⟩
²**whore** \ˈ"\ *vb* -ED/-ING/-S *vi* **1 a :** to have unlawful sexual intercourse with a whore **b :** to play the whore **:** act as a prostitute **2 :** to pursue a faithless, unworthy, or idolatrous desire ⟨go a *whoring* after their gods —Exod 34:15 (AV)⟩ ⟨the great depression has not sent them *whoring* after planned economy —E.A.Mowrer⟩ ~ *vt, obs* **:** to corrupt by lewd intercourse **:** DEBAUCH ⟨he that hath kill'd my king, and *whored* my mother —Shak.⟩
whore·dom \-dəm\ *n* -S [ME *hordom,* fr. ON *hōrdōmr* adultery, fr. *hōrr* adulterer + *-dōmr* -dom] **1 a :** the conduct or practices of a whore **:** bawdy behavior **:** HARLOTRY, PROSTITUTION **b :** the practice of consorting with whores **:** illicit intercourse with whores **c :** unlawful sexual indulgence **:** FORNICATION, LEWDNESS, UNCHASTITY **2 :** faithless, unworthy, or idolatrous practices or pursuits **:** DISLOYALTY ⟨philosophers and pupils alike were pulled along in the stream of ~ and sin —Maurice Samuel⟩
whorehouse \ˈ⸗,⸗\ *n* [ME *horehous,* fr. *hore* whore + *hous* house] **:** BROTHEL
whoremaster \ˈ⸗,⸗⸗\ *n* **:** a man consorting with whores or given to lechery **:** FORNICATOR
whoremonger \ˈ⸗,⸗⸗\ *n, archaic* **:** WHOREMASTER
whorer *n* -S *obs* **:** WHOREMASTER
whore's bird *n* **:** BASTARD
whore·son \ˈhōrsᵊn, ˈhȯr- -ōəs-, -ō(ə)s-\ *n, often attrib* [ME *horesone,* fr. *hore* whore + *sone* son] **1 :** BASTARD **2 :** a coarse fellow — used as a generalized term of abuse
whor·ish \ˈhōrish, ˈhȯr-, -rēsh\ *adj* **1 :** of or resembling a whore **:** LEWD **2** *obs* **:** DISLOYAL, IDOLATROUS, UNFAITHFUL
¹**whorl** \ˈhw\|ō(ə)rl, \|ərl, *esp before pause or consonant* -rəl; \|ō(ə)l, \|əl, \|əil *also* ˈw\| *also* **wharl** \\|är(ə)l\ *n* -S [ME *whorle, wharle, whorwhil, wharwyl,* prob. alter. of *whirle, wherle, wherwill* whorl of a spindle, whirl — more at WHIRL] **1 :** a drumlike section on the lower part of a spindle in spinning or like section on the spindle of a spinning machine serving as a pulley for the tape drive that rotates the spindle **2 :** an arrangement of two or more anatomical parts or organs of one kind in a circle around the same point on an axis ⟨a ~ of leaves⟩ ⟨a ~ of flowers⟩ **3 a :** something that whirls, coils, or spirals or whose form suggests such movement ⟨~*s* of rising chimney smoke⟩ ⟨a first grade school paper of Spencerian push-ups and ~*s* —William Humphrey⟩ **b :** a circular or spiral shape; *esp* **:** one used as a design motive (as in furniture) **4 :** one of the turns of a univalve shell **5 :** a terra-cotta disk that suggests a whorl, is found in ruins of ancient cities in Asia Minor, Africa, Italy, and India, and is supposed by some to have been used on spindles **6 :** a fingerprint in which the central papillary ridges turn through at least one complete circle — see FINGERPRINT illustration
²**whorl** \ˈ"\ *vb* -ED/-ING/-S *vt* **:** to arrange or form in coiled or spiral shapes ⟨the ~*ed* grain of his hair —Crary Moore⟩ **:** arrange in a whorl ~ *vi* **:** to turn with a spinning or spiral motion **:** SWIRL, WHIRL ⟨watching the . . . billowing snow as it ~*ed* down —Jean Stafford⟩ ⟨hung over the banister until the blood ~*ed* in her eyes —Nancy Cardozo⟩
whorled \-ld\ *adj* [¹*whorl* + *-ed*] **:** having or arranged in whorls; *esp* **:** VERTICILLATE ⟨~ leaves⟩
whorled aster *n* **:** a No. American perennial herb (*Aster acuminatus*) with apparently whorled leaves and showy white flowers
whorled loosestrife *n* **:** a common No. American yellow-flowered herb (*Lysimachia quadrifolia*) with whorls of four or five leaves
whorled mallow *n* **:** CURLED MALLOW
whorled milkweed *n* **:** either of two No. American milkweeds with narrow leaves and greenish white flowers: **a :** an herb (*Asclepias verticillata*) mostly of the eastern states **b :** an herb (*A. galioides*) of the Great Plains region
whorled pogonia *or* **whorled snakemouth** *n* **:** a No. American green-flowered terrestrial orchid (*Isotria verticillata*) with a whorl of five leaves
whorled rosinweed *n* **:** a tall perennial herb (*Silphium trifoliatum*) of the eastern U.S. with yellow flowers and leaves in whorls of three
whorlflower \ˈ⸗,⸗\ *n* **:** a Eurasian herb of the genus *Morina* (family Dipsacaceae) with flowers in dense whorls
whorl foot *n* **:** SCROLL FOOT
whorl grass *n* **:** BROOK GRASS
whorly \-lē\ *adj* [¹*whorl* + *-y*] **:** WHORLED
whorlywort \ˈ⸗⸗,⸗\ *n* **:** CULVER'S ROOT
whort \ˈhw\|ərt, \|ōl, \|əil *also* ˈw\|; *usu* \|d·+V\ *or* **whor·tle** \\|d·ᵊl, \|tᵊl\ *or* **wort** \ˈw\|\ *n* -S [*whort* alter. of E dial. *hurt,* short for E *hurtleberry; whortle* short for *whortleberry; wort* alter. of *whort*] **1 :** WHORTLEBERRY 1a **2 :** BEARBERRY 1
whor·tle·berry \ˈ⸗⸗- — *see* BERRY\ *n* [alter. of *hurtleberry*] **1 a :** a sweet edible European blueberry that is purplish black with a glaucous bloom **b :** a low-growing erect rhizomatous shrub (*Vaccinium myrtillus*) whose fruit is a whortleberry **2 a :** HUCKLEBERRY 1a **b :** BLUEBERRY 1
whos *pl of* WHO
¹**whose** [ME *whos* (gen. of ¹*who,* ¹*what*), alter. (influenced by ¹*who*) of *whas, whes,* fr. OE *hwæs,* gen. of *hwā* who, *hwæt* what — more at WHO, WHAT] *obs possessive of* ¹WHO *and* ¹WHAT
²**whose** \(ˌ)hüz *sometimes* ˌüz\ *adj* [ME *whos,* gen. of ¹*who,* ¹*what*] **1 :** of what person or persons: **a :** of or belonging to what person or persons as possessor or possessors **:** due to what person or persons **:** inherent in what person or persons **:** associated or connected with what person or persons ⟨~ gorgeous vesture heaps the ground —Robert Browning⟩ ⟨inquire ~ son the stripling is —1 Sam 17:56 (RSV)⟩ — compare ¹WHO 1 **b :** of or relating to what person or persons as author or authors, doer or doers, giver or givers, or agent or agents **:** effected by what person or persons **:** experienced by what person or persons as subject ⟨~ plays are greater than Shakespeare's⟩ ⟨so many people have helped me that I don't know ~ help has been most valuable⟩ — compare ¹WHO 1 **c :** of or relating to what person or persons as object of an action **:** experienced by what person or persons as object ⟨in ~ honor was the monument erected⟩ ⟨asking ~ promotion would be in the best interests of the company⟩ — compare ¹WHO 1 **2 a :** of whom: (1) **:** of or belonging to whom as possessor or possessors **:** due to whom **:** inherent in whom **:** associated or connected with whom ⟨a man ~ shoes do not fit⟩ ⟨an organization ~ members . . . exercise influence in every continent —Denis Healey⟩ ⟨a chicken ~ head has been cut off —Nancy Mitford⟩ — used as a possessive adjective corresponding in meaning to the relative pronoun *who;* compare ¹WHO 3 (2) **:** of or relating to whom as author or authors, doer or doers, giver or givers, or agent or agents **:** effected by whom **:** experienced by whom as subject ⟨the law courts, ~ decisions were important —F.L.Mott⟩ — used as a possessive adjective corresponding in meaning to the relative pronoun *who;* compare ¹WHO 3 (3) **:** of or relating to whom as object of an action **:** experienced by whom as object ⟨that maid ~ sudden sight hath thralled my wounded eye —Shak.⟩ ⟨these puissant legions, ~ exile hath emptied heaven —John Milton⟩ — used as a possessive adjective corresponding in meaning to the relative pronoun *who;* compare ¹WHO 3 **b :** of which: (1) **:** of or belonging to which as possessor or possessors **:** inherent in which **:** associated or connected with which ⟨inventor of simple clothes ~ elegance derives from her hand-finished detail —Lois Long⟩ ⟨a sentence ~ grammatical subject is a demonstrative pronoun —R.E.Gahringer⟩ — used as a possessive adjective corresponding in meaning to the relative pronoun *which;* compare ²WHICH 3 (2) **:** of or relating to which as agent or agents **:** effected by which **:** resulting from which ⟨the current thought . . . to ~ influences he was subject —L.P.Smith⟩ ⟨a simple legal monopoly ~ reward to the inventor would be primarily in royalties —Robert Reuben⟩ — used as a possessive adjective corresponding in meaning to the relative pronoun *which;* compare ²WHICH 3 (3) **:** of or relating to which as object of an action **:** undergone by which as object ⟨the first poem ~ publication he ever sanctioned —J.W.Krutch⟩ ⟨logical techniques ~ extravagant use is known to give rise to . . . paradoxes —C.G.Hempel⟩ — used as a possessive adjective corresponding in meaning to the relative pronoun *which;* compare ²WHICH 3 **3 a :** of any person or persons that **:** of whomever ⟨~ hatred is covered by deceit, his wickedness shall be showed before the whole congregation —Prov 26:26 (AV)⟩ ⟨ask ~ advice you please⟩ — compare ¹WHO 2a **b** *archaic* **:** the particular person or persons of whom **:** he, she, or those of whom ⟨"Happy," I said, "~ home is here" —R.W.Emerson⟩ — compare ¹WHO 2b(1)
³**whose** \ˈ"\ *pron, sing or pl in constr* [ME *whos,* gen. of ¹*who,* ¹*what*] **:** whose one or whose ones — used without a following noun as a pronoun equivalent in meaning to the adjective *whose* ⟨~ shall those things be, which thou hast provided —Lk 12:20 (AV)⟩ ⟨tell me ~ it was —Shak.⟩ ⟨God, ~ I am, and whom I serve —Acts 27:23 (AV)⟩
¹**whosesoever** \ˈ⸗;⸗;⸗⸗\ *adj* [²*whose* + *soever*] **:** ¹WHOSEVER ⟨~ sins ye remit —Jn 20:23 (AV)⟩
²**whosesoever** \ˈ"\ *pron* **:** ²WHOSEVER
¹**whos·ever** \(ˈ)hü¦zevə(r)\ *adj* [²*whose* + *ever*] **:** of, belonging to, or relating to whomever ⟨~ hat this is, I wish he would come and claim it⟩
²**whosever** \ˈ"\ *pron* **:** whosever one or whosever ones — used without a following noun as a pronoun equivalent in meaning to the adjective *whosever* ⟨~ these gloves are, I wish he would come and claim them⟩
who·so \ˈhü(,)sō\ *pron* [ME *who so,* fr. *who* + *so*] **:** WHOEVER
who·so·ev·er \ˌhüsōˈwevə(r), -sōˈe-\ *pron* [ME, fr. *who so* + *ever*] **:** whatever person **:** any person whatever that **:** WHOEVER
whosomever *pron* [ME *whosumever, whasumever,* fr. ME (northern dial.) *wha sum* whoever (fr. ME — northern dial. — *wha* who — fr. OE *hwā* + ME — northern dial. — *sum,* rel. adv., as) + ME *ever* — more at WHATSOMEVER] *obs* **:** WHOEVER
who's who \ˈhüz-\ *n, often cap both Ws* [fr. the expression *who is who, who's who*] **1 :** any of various compilations containing brief biographical sketches of distinguished or prominent persons in a geographical area or a professional or other group ⟨a list of officers and members . . . and a *who's who* of cartographers —*Geog. Rev.*⟩ **2 :** the leaders of a community or group **:** those exercising influence or power **:** ELITE ⟨the event will draw . . . the *who's who* of the film capital —*Los Angeles (Calif.) Examiner*⟩
WHP *abbr, often not cap* water horsepower
whr *abbr* whether
whs *abbr* warehouse
whse *abbr* warehouse
whsle *abbr* wholesale
whsmn *abbr* warehouseman
whsng *abbr* warehousing
wht *abbr* white
whuff \ˈhwəf *also* ˈwəf\ *or* **whuf·fle** \-fəl\ *vb* -ED/-ING/-S [imit.] **:** to blow noisily
whump \ˈhwəmp *also* ˈwə-\ *vi* -ED/-ING/-S [imit.] **:** BANG, THUMP
whurl \ˈhwərl\ *vi* -ED/-ING/-S [imit.] *archaic* **:** to make any of various throaty sounds (as a roar, snarl, or purr)
whvs *abbr* wharves
¹**why** \(ˌ)(h)wī\ *adv* [ME, fr. OE *hwȳ, hwī;* akin to ON *hvī* why; both fr. a prehistoric NGmc-WGmc instrumental case form of the pronoun represented by OE *hwæt* what — more at WHAT] **1 :** for what cause, reason, or purpose **:** on what account **:** to what end **:** WHEREFORE — used to introduce a question in direct or indirect discourse ⟨~ must you make difficulties⟩ ⟨asked ~ the work had been stopped⟩ **2 a :** for which **:** on account of which — used chiefly with *reason* to introduce a relative clause ⟨the reason ~ his conclusion seemed plausible —R.J. Butler⟩ **b :** for what reason or cause **:** on account of what —

used without an expressed antecedent to introduce a relative clause ⟨I don't know ~ he left town⟩ — **for why** *dial* : BECAUSE, WHY

²why \'hwī *also* 'wī\ *n* -S [ME, fr. *why*, adv.] **1** : the reason or cause of something ⟨a surging symphonic commentary on the ~ of man's being —William Peden⟩ ⟨statistical studies solve the problems of where and when; for the hows and ~s we must generally use other techniques —G.W.Brainerd⟩ ⟨a baffling problem : ENIGMA ⟨all the great ~s of life —H.G. Wells⟩

³why \'hwī *also* 'hwī\ *interj* [¹*why*] — used to indicate a pause or the resumption after a pause in expression ⟨if America splits the infinitive, ~, the infinitive is split, and no rule will mend it —A.L.Guérard⟩

whyd·ah *or* **whid·ah** \'hwidə *also* 'wi-\ *n* -S [alter. (influenced by *Whydah*, *Ouidah*, town in southern Dahomey where such birds are found) of *widow* (in *widow bird*)] : any of various African weaverbirds which are mostly black with white or buffy markings, which are often kept as cage birds, and of which the males although no larger than a canary have drooping tail feathers often a foot in length during the breeding season — compare PARADISE WEAVER

why·ev·er \hwī'evə(r) *also* wī-\ *adv* : for whatever reason : WHY

why·for \'hwī,-, *or* wī-\ *n* -S [E dial. *whyfor*, adv., why, fr. E ¹*why* + *for*] : REASON, WHEREFORE ⟨provided the ~s of the programs themselves —Arthur Krock⟩

why-not *n* [fr. the expression *why not*] *obs* : a return challenge demanding what bars an action or negates an assertion — **at a why-not** *obs* : at a disadvantage

whyo \'hwī,ō *also* 'wī-\ *n* -S [fr. *oh-why-oh-why-oh*, signal cry of a former New York City gang] : a member of a gang of holdup men

WI *abbr* **1** *often not cap* when issued **2** wrought iron

wi' \(')wi\ *Scot & dial var of* WITH

WIA *abbr* wounded in action

wibbly-wobbly \'wib(ə)lē,=(=)-\ *adj* [by redupl.] : WOBBLY

wich *or* **wych** \'wich, 'wīch\ *n* -ES [ME *wiche*, *wyche*, fr. -*wich*, -*wīc* -wich (suffix of place-names, as in *Northwich*, *Middlewich*, districts of England associated with salt manufacturing), fr. *wīc* dwelling place, village, town — more at WICK (farm)] *dial Eng* : SALT PIT

¹wich·i·ta \'wichə,tò\ *n*, *pl* **wichita** *or* **wichitas** *usu cap* **1 a** : a Caddo people or confederacy of peoples ranging between the Arkansas river in Kansas and central Texas **b** : a member of such people **2** : the language of the Wichita people

²wichita \"\ *adj*, *usu cap* [fr. *Wichita*, Kansas] : of or from the city of Wichita, Kansas : of the kind or style prevalent in Wichita

wich·i·tan \-ə̇(ə)n\ *n* -*s* *cap* [*Wichita*, city in south central Kansas *or* Wichita Falls, city in northern Texas + E -*an*] : a native or resident of Wichita, Kansas, or Wichita Falls, Texas

wi·chu·rai·ana \,wəˌchůrē'anə, -rə'yə-, -änə\ *also* **wi·chu·ra** \wəˈchůrə\ *or* **wichura rose** *n*-*s* [*wichuraiana* fr. NL (specific epithet of *Rosa wichuraiana*), fr. M. E. *Wichura* †1866 Ger. lawyer and botanist + NL -*iana*, -*ana*, fr. L, fem. of -*ianus*, -*anus* -an; *wichura* fr. M. E. *Wichura*] : an Asiatic rose (*Rosa wichuraiana*) which has prostrate creeping stems and from which several rambler roses have been developed

¹wick \'wik\ *n* -S [ME *wicke*, *wike*, *weke*, fr. OE *wēoce*; akin to OHG *wiohha* lint, wick, OIr *figim* I weave, OE *wōcie* noose, Skt *vagurā* net, noose; basic meaning : to weave, web] **1 a** : a bundle of fibers or a loosely twisted, braided, or woven cord, tape, or tube usu. of soft spun cotton threads that by capillary attraction draws up to be burned a steady supply of the oil in lamps or the melted tallow or wax in candles **b** : a strip of material (as gauze or strands of catgut) placed in a wound to serve as a drain **2** : WICKING

²wick \"\ *n* -S [ME *wike*, dwelling place, village, town, farm, fr. OE *wīc*; akin to OFris *wīk* dwelling place, town, OHG *wīch*; all fr. a prehistoric WGmc word borrowed fr. L *vicus* village — more at VICINITY] *dial Eng* : FARMSTEAD; *specif* : a dairy farm or house

³wick \"\ *n* -S [ME *wik*, fr. ON *vik*; akin to ON *vīkja* to move, turn] *archaic* : CORNER, ANGLE; *esp* : a corner of the eye or mouth

⁴wick \'wik, 'wīk\ *n* -S [ON *vik*; akin to OE *wīc* bay, creek, MLG *wīk* bay, creek, ON *vīkja* to move, turn — more at WEEK] *chiefly Scot* : a small inlet : CREEK

⁵wick \"\ *vb* -ED/-ING/-S [origin unknown] *vt* : to make an inwick upon (another stone) in curling — *vi* **1** : INWICK — **wick a bore** : to make a shot through a wick or narrow port in curling

⁶wick \"\ *n* -S **1** : a narrow port or passageway in the course in curling that is flanked by the stones of previous players **2** : INWICK

⁷wick \"\ *dial Eng var of* ¹QUICK

⁸wick \"\ *dial Eng var of* WEEK

wickape *var of* WICOPY

wick·a·wee \'wikə,wē\ *n*-S [perh. of Algonquian origin; akin to Natick *wequai* light] : an Indian paintbrush (*Castilleja coccinea*)

¹wick·ed \'wikə̇d\ *adj* -ER/-EST [ME, alter. (influenced by -*ed*) of *wicke* wicked] **1** : evil in character, behavior, tendency, or influence : being or acting contrary to moral or divine law : SINFUL, BAD ⟨a ~ ruler⟩ ⟨the ~ stepmother⟩ ⟨a ~ deed⟩ ⟨a ~ intent⟩ ⟨a ~ book⟩ ⟨a ~ law⟩ ⟨so simple and trustful . . . it would be ~ to hurt her —Mary Webb⟩ **2 a** : having a bad disposition : INTRACTABLE, VICIOUS — used esp. of an animal ⟨a ~ horse⟩ **b** : inclined to mischief; *esp* : playfully or engagingly mischievous : ROGUISH ⟨smiling . . . at the ~, witty little girl —Jean Stafford⟩ **c** : open to censure : WRONG, REPREHENSIBLE ⟨however ~ it may be to try to shock the public —Clive Bell⟩ **d** : verging on the indecent : IMPROPER, RISQUÉ ⟨sing ~ lyrics in the corners of the bar —Horace Sutton⟩ **e** : showing or expressing ill will : MALEVOLENT, MALICIOUS ⟨a ~ look⟩ ⟨a woman with a ~ tongue in her head⟩ ⟨a ~ anecdote⟩ ⟨a cauldron of ~ gossip —L.P.Smith⟩ **3 a** (1) : disgustingly unpleasant; *esp* : offensive to the smell or taste : VILE ⟨a gas with a ~ odor⟩ (2) *archaic* : poor in quality ⟨they talk ~ French —Horace Walpole⟩ **b** *archaic* : POISONOUS, NOXIOUS ⟨~ dew . . . from unwholesome fen —Shak.⟩ **c** : causing or likely to cause harm : DANGEROUS ⟨a ~ storm⟩ ⟨the ~ horns of a bull⟩ **d** : difficult to pass through or over : almost impassable or impenetrable ⟨find their way over the ~ roads —C.G.Bowers⟩ ⟨the ~ sort of scrub jungle —Edison Marshall⟩ **e** : causing discomfort or distress : SEVERE ⟨suffering through ~ winter weather⟩ ⟨a ~ headache⟩ **f** : causing annoyance : TROUBLESOME, VEXATIOUS ⟨a ~ growth of weeds⟩ **4 a** : going beyond reasonable limits : OUTRAGEOUS, TERRIBLE ⟨had a ~ fire loss⟩ ⟨a ~ shame⟩ ⟨charged ~ prices⟩ ⟨a ~ examination⟩ ⟨was game to take a ~ amount of punishment —Althea Gibon⟩ **b** (1) : showing impressive or formidable skill : EXCELLENT ⟨plays a ~ game of bridge⟩ ⟨dances a ~ Charleston —*Bookman*⟩ **2** : difficult to cope with or to compete against ⟨a ~ drive⟩ **syn** see BAD

²wicked \"\ *n*, *pl* **wicked** [ME, fr. ¹*wicked*] : a wicked person — usu. used in pl. with *the* ⟨the ~ are made to suffer —*Publishers' Weekly*⟩

³wicked \"\ *adv* [ME, fr. ¹*wicked*] *chiefly dial* : WICKEDLY

⁴wicked \'wikt\ *adj* [¹*wick* + -*ed*] : having a wick — used chiefly in combination ⟨a two-wicked lamp⟩

wick·ed·ly *adv* [ME, fr. ¹*wicked* + -*ly*] : in a wicked manner: as **a** : EVILLY, INIQUITOUSLY ⟨~ ruined a trusting partner⟩ **b** : OFFENSIVELY, HORRIBLY ⟨this book is ~ superficial —*Times Lit. Supp.*⟩ **c** : VICIOUSLY, FIERCELY ⟨~ repressive of important civil liberties —*New Statesman & Nation*⟩ **d** : MALICIOUSLY ⟨this gay little book . . . is ~ witty —Regina J. Woody⟩ ⟨the most ~ amusing epigrams ever coined —Stephen Williams⟩

wick·ed·ness *n* -ES [ME, fr. ¹*wicked* + -*ness*] **1 a** : the quality or state of being wicked : EVIL, SINFULNESS ⟨policies of almost unmitigated ~ —Alfred Cobban⟩ **b** : wicked character or conduct : VICE ⟨though the bars are closed . . . ~ goes on —Green Peyton⟩ **2** : something wicked : a wicked action ⟨rushed off to some of her ~es —Joseph Conrad⟩

wick·en \"\ *dial Eng var of* WIGGEN

¹wick·er \'wikə(r)\ *n* -S [ME *wiker* of Scand origin; akin to Sw dial. *vikker* willow, Sw *vika* to bend, ON *vīkja* to move, turn — more at WEEK] : a small pliant twig or osier : a rod

for plaiting basketwork : WITHE **2 a** : WICKERWORK **b** : something made of wicker (as a basket)

²wicker \"\ *adj* : made or consisting of wicker : incased in wickerwork ⟨a ~ basket⟩ ⟨a ~ chair⟩ ⟨a ~ flask⟩

³wicker \"\ *vt* -ED/-ING/-S : to incase or cover (as a bottle or chair) with wickerwork

⁴wicker *var of* WHICKER

wickerwork \'==,=\ *n*, *often attrib* : work consisting of a texture of osiers, twigs, or rods : BASKETRY ⟨a huge figure of ~ cages⟩

wick·et \'wikə̇t, *usu* -ə̇d-+V\ *n* -S [ME *wiket*, fr. ONF, of Gmc origin; akin to MD *wiket*, *winket* wicket, *wiken* to yield, give way, OE *wīcan* — more at WEAK] **1** : a small gate or door; *esp* : one forming part of or placed near a larger gate or door **2** : an opening that resembles a window; *esp* : a grilled or grated window (as at a ticket office, cashier's or teller's desk) **3 a** : a small gate for emptying the chamber of a canal lock or regulating the amount of water passing through a channel (as to a waterwheel) **b** : the entrance door to a kiln : any gate of a shutter dam **2** : a very wide stall or heading used with very wide pillars in the wicketwork system of coal mining in North Wales **4 a** : either of the two frameworks at which the ball is bowled in cricket consisting of three stumps stuck close together in the ground and surmounted with two bails placed end to end in grooves on the top **b** : STUMP 7a **c** : a rectangular area of a cricket field with a long dimension of 22 yards bounded by the two bowling creases and a width of 10 feet — called also *pitch* ⟨a fast ~⟩ ⟨a bowler's ~⟩ **d** (1) : the period of play from the commencement of a batsman's innings to his dismissal ⟨the fifth ~ added only 17 runs⟩ (2) : the part of this period when two batsmen are together ⟨a profitable first-wicket partnership⟩ **e** : one innings by a batsman that is not completed or not begun ⟨a team wins by 4 ~s when with two not-out players batting and 3 men yet to go in it surpasses the opposing team's total score⟩ **f** : dismissal of a batsman ⟨the bowler worked hard for his ~s⟩ ⟨the bowler captured 7 ~s in one innings⟩ **5** : an arch or hoop in croquet — **on a bad wicket** : in a weak or unfavorable position ⟨forced to fight a by-election *on a bad wicket* —Sir Winston Churchill⟩ — **on a good wicket** : in a strong or favorable position ⟨the organized interests are *on a fairly good wicket* as regards their share in the national income —A.J. Bruwer⟩

wicket dam *n* : SHUTTER DAM

wicket door *or* **wicket gate** *n* : WICKET 1

wicketkeep \'==,=\ *n* [by shortening] : WICKETKEEPER

wicketkeeper \'==,=\ *n* : a fieldsman in cricket wearing gloves and pads who stands behind the striker's wicket and whose chief duties are to catch, stump, or run out the batsman and to prevent byes — see CRICKET illustration

wicketwork \'==,=\ *n* : a bord-and-pillar system of coal mining in which the very wide pillars left to support the roof are not recovered

wick·ing \'wikiŋ, -kēŋ\ *n* -S [¹*wick* + -*ing*] : material used for wicks

wick·i·up \'wikē,əp\ *n* -S [Sac, Fox & Kickapoo *wikiyap* house, dwelling, hut] **1** : a hut used by the nomadic Indians of the arid regions of the western and southwestern U.S. that is typically elliptical in form and has a rough frame covered with reed mats or grass or brushwood — compare LODGE 8a **2** : any rude temporary shelter or hut

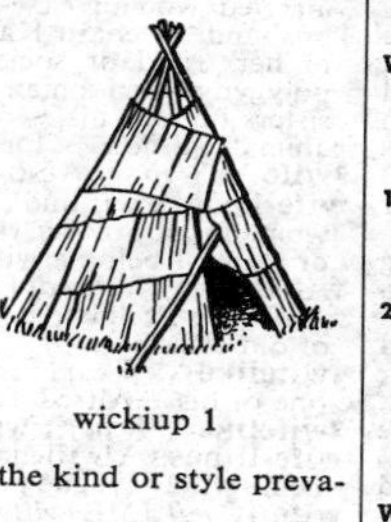

wickiup 1

wick·liff·ian \(')wiˈkliəfē·ən\ *or* **wick·liff·ite** \'wiklə,fīt\ *n* -S [John *Wickliffe* (Wycliffe) †1384 Eng. religious reformer and theologian + E -*an* *or* -*ite*] *usu cap* : LOLLARD 2

wick·low \'wi,klō\ *adj*, *usu cap* [fr. County *Wicklow*, Ireland] : of or from County Wicklow, Ireland : of the kind or style prevalent in County Wicklow

wicks *pl of* WICK, *pres 3d sing of* WICK

wick·up \'wi,kəp\ *n*-S [Cree *wikupiy*] : WICOPY

wicky \'wikē, -ki\ *n* -ES [prob. alter. (influenced by -*y*) of ²*quicken*] **1** *chiefly South* : any of various low-growing laurels (genus *Kalmia*); *esp* : SHEEP LAUREL **2** *dial Eng* : ROWAN TREE 1

wic·o·py *or* **wick·a·pe** \'wikəpē\ *n*, *pl* **wicopies** *or* **wickapes** [Cree *wikupiy* inner bark of basswood] **1** : LEATHERWOOD 1a **2** : a basswood (*Tilia glabra*) **3** : WILLOW HERB 1

¹wid \'wid\ *Scot var of* WOOD

²wid \(')wid\ *dial var of* WITH

wid *abbr* widow; widower

wi·dal's reaction *or* **wi·dal reaction** \wē'dal(z)-, v\, -däl(z)-\ *n*, *usu cap* W [after Fernand *Widal* †1929 Fr. physician] : a specific reaction consisting in agglutination of typhoid bacilli or other salmonellas when mixed with serum from a patient having typhoid fever or other salmonella infection and constituting a test for the disease

widal's test *or* **widal test** *n*, *usu cap* W [after F. *Widal*] : a test for detecting typhoid fever and other salmonella infections using the Widal reaction

wid·der \'widə(r)\ *dial var of* WIDOW

wid·der·shins \'widə(r),shinz\ *or* **with·er·shins** \'withə(-\ *adv* [MLG *weddersinnes*, fr. MHG *widersinnes*, fr. *widersinnen* to go back, go against, fr. *wider* back, against, again (fr. OHG *widar*) + *sinnen* to travel, go, fr. OHG *sinnan* (akin to OHG *sind* journey, road); *withershins* alter. (influenced by obs. E *wither*-, prefix, fr. OE, against, counter, fr. *wither*, adv.) of *widdershins* — more at WITH, SEND] : in a left-handed or contrary direction : CONTRARILY, COUNTERCLOCKWISE — used esp. of ritual circumambulation; compare DEASIL ⟨turned to his right, knowing that it is unlucky to walk about a church ~ —Dorothy Sayers⟩

¹wid·di·fow *also* **wid·di·fu'** \'widi,fü\ *adj* [¹*widdy* + *fow*, *fu*'] *Scot* : fit for the gallows : RASCALLY

²widdifow *also* **widdifu'** \"\ *n*-*S Scot* : GALLOWS BIRD, RASCAL

wid·dle \'widɔl\ *vi* -ED/-ING/-S [short for earlier *widdle-waddle*, redupl. of *waddle*] **1** *chiefly dial* : WRIGGLE **2** *chiefly dial* : WADDLE

wid·dle \"\ *n* -S **1** *chiefly dial* : STRUGGLE **2** *chiefly dial* : WRIGGLE

wid·drim \'widrəm\ *also* **wid·den·dream** \'widən,drēm\ *n* -S [OE *wōddrēam*, fr. *wōd* mad + *drēam* joy, noise — more at VATIC, DREAM] *chiefly Scot* : mental excitement or confusion : a mad fit : FURY

¹wid·dy \'widi\ *n* -ES [ME (Sc) *widdy*, *wedde*, *wethy*, fr. *wethy*, *withie* withy, fr. OE *wīthig* willow, withy — more at WITHY] **1** *Scot & dial Eng* : a rope made of osiers or similar twigs : WITHY **2** *Scot & dial Eng* : a hangman's noose : HALTER

²wid·dy \-dē, -di\ *dial var of* WIDOW

¹wide \'wīd\ *adj* -ER/-EST [ME *wid*, *wide*, fr. OE *wīd*; akin to OHG *wīt* wide, large, ON *vithr*; prob. all fr. a prehistoric WGmc-NGmc compound formed from components represented by OE *with* against, towards, opposite and Goth *iddja* he went — more at WITH, ISSUE] **1 a** : having or covering great extent : SPACIOUS, VAST ⟨the whole ~ world⟩ ⟨~ seas⟩ ⟨~ cottonfields⟩ ⟨a ~ agricultural and dairying area —*Amer. Guide Series: Mich.*⟩ **b** : extending over, reaching, or affecting a vast area : far-spreading : EXTENSIVE ⟨large windows . . . commanded a ~ sweep of the far ravine slopes —Victor Canning⟩ ⟨a painter of ~ reputation⟩ **c** : extending throughout or covering a specified area or scope — often used in combination ⟨city-*wide*⟩ ⟨nation*wide*⟩ ⟨a world*wide* problem⟩ ⟨industry-*wide* bargaining⟩ **d** : having a large scope or range : covering, including, or allowing great variety or breadth : not limited : COMPREHENSIVE, ALL-INCLUSIVE ⟨a ~ assortment⟩ ⟨~ experience⟩ ⟨insurance with ~ coverage⟩ ⟨historical works addressed to a very ~ public —G.M.Trevelyan⟩ ⟨far too ~ a query to be dealt with —Guy Eden⟩ **e** : marked by breadth and tolerance : not limited or constrained by parochialism or prejudice : LIBERAL, BROAD ⟨the utmost desire to be ~ and impartial —John Galsworthy⟩ ⟨a statesman of ~ views⟩ **f** : AMPLE, ROOMY ⟨a national taste for ~ trousers⟩ **2 a** : having extension from side to side of a specified dimension ⟨3 feet ~⟩ ⟨a mile-*wide* lake⟩ ⟨a trail one man ~⟩ ⟨piled in tiers 4 cans ~⟩ **b** : having much distance or extent between

the sides : large in breadth relative to its length or to others of its kind : not narrow : BROAD ⟨a ~ road⟩ ⟨a ~ arch⟩ ⟨the *widest* part of a river⟩ ⟨a horse with a ~ muzzle⟩ ⟨brawny girls, ~ as they were tall —Truman Capote⟩ **c** : opened, expanded, or stretched apart to the fullest extent ⟨~ nostrils⟩ ⟨stared with ~ eyes⟩ — often used postpositively ⟨greeted him with arms ~⟩ **3** \'=\ ³LAX 2 **3** : extending over a considerable distance between limits ⟨~ variations in ability among students⟩ ⟨the ~ difference in their stations in life —T.B.Costain⟩ **b** : having or showing a great difference or fluctuation between the highest and lowest levels ⟨as of prices quoted or bid and asked on an exchange⟩ ⟨a ~ drop in hog prices⟩ ⟨a need to provide for *wider* operating margins in a business⟩ **c** (1) : distant from a specified place — used with *of* ⟨thirty miles ~ of the place appointed —Jonathan Swift⟩ (2) : *archaic* : different or divergent from something specified — used with *of* ⟨examine whose notions are *widest* of the common road —George Berkeley⟩ (3) : straying or deviating from something specified — used with *of* ⟨far ~ of reality —Lucien Price⟩ (4) *obs* : missing the truth : WRONG, INCORRECT ⟨he was a little ~ there —Elkanah Settle⟩ (5) *obs* : mentally unsound : DELIRIOUS ⟨still, still far ~ —Shak.⟩ (6) : far off the intended course : away from the point aimed at ⟨a ~ arrow⟩ ⟨pitched four ~ balls⟩ ⟨a ~ shot⟩ — used often in the expression *wide of the mark* ⟨nothing could be more ludicrously ~ of the mark —F.R.Leavis⟩ **4** *of an animal ration* : relatively rich in carbohydrate as compared with protein — compare NARROW **5** *slang Brit* : WIDE-AWAKE, SOPHISTICATED **b** : characterized by clever but ethically questionable behavior : SHARP ⟨a good fellow so long as you watched out for yourself . . . a ~ man —Robert Westerby⟩ **syn** see BROAD

²wide \"\ *adv* -ER/-EST [ME, fr. OE *wide*, fr. *wīd*, adj., wide] **1 a** : over a great distance or extent : FAR, WIDELY ⟨wandered ~ through many lands⟩ — used often in the phrase *far and wide* ⟨searched far and ~⟩ **b** : over a specified distance, area, or extent ⟨expanded the business country-*wide* within a few years⟩ **2 a** : so as to leave much space or distance between ⟨told to stand with legs *wider* apart⟩ **b** : so as to move apart or away ⟨shaking ~ thy yellow hair —P.B.Shelley⟩ **c** : so as to pass at or clear by a considerable distance ⟨ran ~ around left end for a 10-yard gain⟩ **3** : to the fullest extent : COMPLETELY ⟨opened her eyes ~⟩ ⟨spread the map ~⟩ — often used as an intensive with *open* ⟨a *wide*-open window⟩ ⟨the *wide*-open spaces⟩ ⟨a locomotive running with the throttle ~ open⟩ ⟨left himself ~ open to criticism⟩ **4 a** : so as to pass to the side of or away from the intended course or miss the aim or objective : ASTRAY ⟨the bullet went ~⟩ ⟨drove ~ of the green on the short sixth hole⟩ **b** *chiefly dial* : at a considerable distance : FAR — often used with *of* ⟨lying . . . ~ of all other forts —George Washington⟩

³wide \"\ *or* **wide ball** *n* -S : a bowled ball in cricket that is delivered so high or wide of the wicket as to be out of the striker's reach, that does not count in the over unless hit, and that counts one run unless otherwise scored from — compare EXTRA 1c

wide-angle \'=,==\ *adj* **1** : having or covering an angle of view wider than the ordinary — used esp. of lenses of shorter than normal focal length **2** : having, involving the use of, or relating to a wide-angle lens ⟨*wide*-angle camera⟩ ⟨*wide*-angle photography⟩

¹wide-awake \,===\ *adj* **1** : fully awake : not drowsy or dull : KNOWING, KEEN, ALERT ⟨he was tired, exhausted, and yet *wide*-awake —Vicky Baum⟩ ⟨listened with *wide*-awake interest —A.C.Whitehead⟩ **2** : KNOWING, SHARP ⟨a *wide*-awake town⟩ **syn** see WATCHFUL

²wide-awake \'===\ *n* -S **1** : **wide-awake hat** : a low-crowned and wide-brimmed soft felt hat worn chiefly by men **2** *usu cap* : a member of any of the companies of young men in the presidential campaign of 1860 favoring the Republican candidate and wearing uniforms including a wide-awake hat **3** [prob. imit. of its cry] **a** : SOOTY TERN **b** : any of several terns resembling the sooty tern

wide-awake·ness \,=====\ *n* -ES : the quality or state of being wide-awake : ALERTNESS, LIVELINESS ⟨saw signs of a new *wide*-awakeness in the company personnel⟩

wide-eyed \',==\ *adj* **1** : having the eyes widely open ⟨lay *wide*-eyed, staring . . . at the flickering lights —Zane Grey⟩ **2** : struck with wonder or astonishment : AMAZED ⟨watched *wide*-eyed as the handlers drew the reptiles from their containers —*Amer. Guide Series: Texas*⟩ **3** : marked by unsophisticated or uncritical acceptance or admiration : NAÏVE ⟨*wide*-eyed idol-worshiping theatergoers —Leslie Rees⟩ ⟨*wide*-eyed innocence⟩ ⟨a *wide*-eyed belief in the goodness of everybody⟩

wide-flung \',=,=\ *adj* : FAR-FLUNG

wide gage *n* : BROAD GAGE

wide·ly *adv* : in a wide manner: as **a** : over a wide space or extent : EXTENSIVELY ⟨traveled ~⟩ **b** : over a wide range : BROADLY ⟨a ~ representative selection of recent books⟩ **c** : with a great distance between : FAR, GREATLY ⟨~ separated outposts⟩ ⟨~ varying concepts⟩ **d** : to a great extent or degree ⟨departed ~ from his prepared address⟩

wide·mouthed \',=\ *adj* **1** : having a wide mouth ⟨a ~ person⟩ ⟨a ~ bottle⟩ **2 a** : uttered with wide open mouth : LOUD, RESOUNDING ⟨~ blasphemy⟩ **b** : DEVOURING, GREEDY ⟨~ time⟩

wid·en \'wīd'n\ *vb* **widened**; **widened**; **widening** \-d(ə)niŋ\ **widens** [¹*wide* + -*en*] *vt* **1** : to increase the width of : BROADEN ⟨~ a road⟩ ⟨~ the breach between the former friends⟩ **2** : to enlarge the scope or extend the range of : EXPAND ⟨~ing . . . the domain of freedom —Stephen Duggan⟩ — *vi* **1** : to grow or become wide or wider ⟨a river ~ing at a bend⟩ ⟨my nostrils ~ to the smell —Amy Lowell⟩ **2** : to increase in extent or scope ⟨his interests ~ed in college⟩ ⟨a vocabulary that ~ed from use —W.A.White⟩

wid·en·er \-d(ə)nə(r)\ *n* -S : one that widens: as **a** : BROACH 5 **b** : REAMER a(1)

wide·ness *n* -ES [ME *widnesse*, fr. OE *wīdnes*, fr. *wīd* wide + -*nes* -ness — more at WIDE] : the quality or state of being wide : BREADTH, WIDTH

wider *comparative of* WIDE

wide-ranging \'=,==\ *adj* : covering a wide range : extensive in scope : COMPREHENSIVE ⟨a list of *wide*-ranging topics⟩ ⟨*wide*-ranging studies⟩

wide-screen \'=,=\ *adj* : of or relating to a projected picture whose aspect ratio is substantially greater than 1.33:1 ⟨*wide*-screen presentation⟩ ⟨the *wide*-screen process⟩

wide-spectrum \'=,==\ *adj*, *of a medicinal substance* : BROAD-SPECTRUM

widespread \'=,=\ *adj* **1** : widely extended or spread out ⟨~ wings⟩ ⟨~ horns⟩ ⟨a ~ layer of yellow gravel —*Amer. Guide Series: Tenn.*⟩ **2** : widely circulated or diffused : generally prevalent ⟨a ~ doctrine⟩ ⟨~ dissatisfaction⟩

wide-spreading \'=,==\ *adj* **1** : stretching or extending far ⟨*wide*-spreading plains⟩ ⟨*wide*-spreading shade⟩ **2** : spreading over or affecting a wide area : FAR-REACHING ⟨*wide*-spreading disease⟩

widest *superlative of* WIDE

wide-watered \'=,==\ *adj* **1** : having a wide expanse of water: as **a** : bordering the sea ⟨some *wide*-watered shore —John Milton⟩ **b** : traversed by wide streams ⟨the *wide*-watered fen —Alexander Pope⟩

widework \'=,=\ *n* : a bord-and-pillar system of coal mining in which the very narrow pillars left to support the roof are not recovered

wid·geon *also* **wi·geon** \'wijən\ *n*, *pl* **widgeon** *or* **widgeons** [origin unknown] **1 a** : any of several freshwater ducks of the genus *Mareca* that are between the teal and the mallard in size: as (1) : an Old World duck (*M. penelope*) that has in the male a pale buff crown, chestnut head and neck, grayish lavender breast, and white belly (2) : BALDPATE **2** (3) : a duck (*M. sibilatrix*) of southern So. America that has the entire head nearly white **b** *chiefly dial* : any of various ducks of other genera: as (1) : SAND WIDGEON (2) : SEA WIDGEON **2** *obs* : a foolish fellow : SIMPLETON, GOOSE

widgeon coot *n* : RUDDY DUCK

widgeon grass *n* **1** : EELGRASS 1 **2** : TASSEL GRASS

wid·get \'wijə̇t, *usu* -ə̇d-+V\ *n* -S [alter. of *gadget*] **1** : a usu. small device, contrivance, or mechanical part (as a fitting or attachment) : GADGET ⟨the manufacture of anything from four-motor bombers to . . . ~s —R.T.Frankensteen⟩; *specif* : a small cylindrical container for carrying messages (as of stock

exchange transactions) through pneumatic tubes **2 :** an unnamed article considered for purposes of hypothetical example as the typical product of a company ⟨allowing the manufacturer to deduct the fair market value of the ~*s* —*Harvard Law Rev.*⟩

wid·ish \ˈwīdish, -dēsh\ *adj* [¹*wide* + *-ish*] **:** somewhat wide ⟨~ shoulders⟩ ⟨a ~ collection⟩

wid·man·staet·ten figures \ˈwidmən,s|tetᵊn-, ˈvitmən,s(h)|\ *also* **wid·man·staet·ti·an figures** \¦==¦s(h)ted·ēən-\ *n pl, usu cap W* [*widmanstaetten* after Aloys B. *Widmannstätten* †1849 Austrian mineralogist; *widmanstaettian* fr. Aloys B. *Widmannstätten* + E *-an*] **:** figures that appear on etched meteoric iron and exhibit its crystalline structure

¹**wid·ow** \ˈwi(,)dō, -də; -dəw, -dō+V\ *n* -s [ME *widewe, widwe,* fr. OE *widewe, wuduwe;* akin to OHG *wituwa, witawa* widow, Goth *widuwo,* L *vidua* widow, *-videre* to separate, Gk *ēitheos* unmarried youth, Skt *vidhavā* widow, *vidhura* separated from, *vindhate* he lacks] **1 a :** a woman who has lost her husband by death and has not since remarried — often used as if a title before a woman's marriage name ⟨the ~ Jones⟩ ⟨a tavern kept by ~ Smith⟩ **b :** a particular woman identified as having survived her husband and often as having thereby acquired legal rights that are not lost by subsequent remarriage by her though they may sometimes be lost by decree, statute, or construction (as on account of the survivor's desertion or adultery) **c** *dial Brit* **:** WIDOWER **d :** a woman whose husband deserts her or spends much time (as in a sports activity) away from her **:** GRASS WIDOW 2 — usu. used with a qualifying word ⟨poker ~⟩ ⟨fishing ~⟩ ⟨club ~⟩; compare GOLF WIDOW **2 :** one of a special class of women in the early Christian church serving as deaconesses in the performance of works of charity and in some liturgical offices (as the baptism of women) **3 :** an extra hand or part of a hand of cards that is dealt face down and usu. placed at the disposal of the highest bidder — see KITTY, SKAT **4 a :** a short line ending a paragraph and appearing at the top of a printed page or column **b :** a short line at the foot of a page or column

²**widow** \"\ *vt* -ED/-ING/-S **1 :** to cause to become a widow **:** bereave (a person) of a spouse ⟨women ~*ed* by the war⟩ ⟨he hath ~*ed* and unchilded many a one —Shak.⟩ **2 :** to survive as the widow of ⟨let me be married to three kings . . . and ~ them all —Shak.⟩ **3 :** to deprive of something greatly loved or needed **:** make desolate — usu. used with *of* ⟨the ~*ed* isle —John Dryden⟩ ⟨tank supporters . . . ~*ed* of tanks —A.J. Liebling⟩

widow-bench \ˈ=(,)=,=\ *n* **:** the portion besides her jointure allowed to a widow from her deceased husband's estate in English law — compare FREE BENCH

widow bewitched *n, chiefly dial* **:** a woman separated from her husband **:** GRASS WIDOW 2

widow bird *or* **widow finch** *n* [so called fr. its dark plumage and long black tail feathers like a widow's veil] **:** WHYDAH

widow duck *n* **:** a West Indian tree duck (*Dendrocygna viduata*)

wid·ow·er \ˈwidəwə(r), -dōə-\ *n* -s [ME *widewer,* fr. *widewe* widow + *-er*] **1 :** a man who has lost his wife by death and has not married again **2 :** a particular man identified as having survived his wife and often as having thereby acquired legal rights that are not lost by subsequent remarriage by him though they may sometimes be lost by decree, statute, or construction (as on account of the survivor's desertion or adultery)

wid·ow·ered \-ə(r)d\ *adj* **:** made a widower ⟨his ~ father —William Humphrey⟩

wid·ow·er·hood \-ə(r),hu̇d\ *n* **1 :** the quality or state of being a widower **2 :** the period during which a man remains a widower

widowhead *n* [ME *widewehed,* fr. *widewe* widow + *-hed* -hood (akin to ME *-hod, -had* -hood)] *obs* **:** WIDOWHOOD

wid·ow·hood \ˈ=(,)=,hu̇d\ *n* [ME *widewehod, widewehad,* fr. *widewe* widow + *-hod, -had* -hood — more at WIDOW] **1 :** the quality or state of being a widow ⟨destined to an early ~⟩ **2 :** the period during which a person remains a widow ⟨married again after a brief ~⟩

widow lady *n, chiefly dial* **:** WIDOW

wid·ow·ly *adj* **:** of, relating to, or befitting a widow ⟨~ grief⟩

widow-maker \ˈ=(,)=,==\ *n* **:** something dangerous to a worker's life or health; *specif* **:** a loose limb hanging in or falling from a tree in logging

wid·ow·man \-,mən\ *n, pl* **widowmen** *chiefly dial* **:** WIDOWER

widow monkey *n* **:** a So. American titi (*Callicebus torquatus*) that is black except for dull whitish arms, neck, and face and a ring of pure white around the face

widow right *n* **:** a widow's right (as dower, quarantine, or statutory share) in her deceased husband's estate

widows *pl of* WIDOW, *pres 3d sing of* WIDOW

widow's chamber *n* **:** the bedchamber apparel and furniture passing to the widow of a freeman of London by a custom formerly recognized in English law

widow's-cross \ˈ=(,)=ˈ=\ *n, pl* **widow's-crosses :** an evergreen fleshy-leaved herb (*Sedum pulchellum*) of the eastern U.S. often cultivated for its rosy purple showy flowers

widow's frill *n* **:** STARRY CAMPION

widow's mite *n* [so called fr. the widow who cast two mites (a farthing) into the Temple treasury (Mark 12:42)] **:** a small contribution that is willingly given and is all one can afford ⟨gave his *widow's mite* to the cause⟩

widow's peak *n* [so called fr. the former belief that it is an omen of early widowhood] **:** PEAK 8

widow's quarantine *n* **:** QUARANTINE 1

widow's-tears \ˈ=(,)=ˈ=\ *n pl but sing or pl in constr* **:** SPIDERWORT 1a

widow's walk *n* [so called fr. its use by the wives of seamen] **1 :** a railed observation platform built above the roof of a coastal dwelling for an unobstructed outlook to sea — called also *captain's walk* **2 :** a balustraded roof area

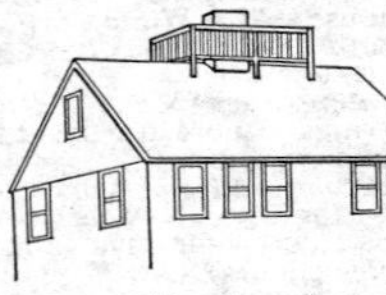

widow's walk

widow woman *n, chiefly dial* **:** WIDOW

width \ˈwidth, -itth, *chiefly substand* -ith\ *n, pl* **widths** \"s, -idts, -it(t)s\ [¹*wide* + *-th*] **1 :** a distance from side to side **:** measure taken at right angles to length **:** BREADTH ⟨the ~ of a ribbon⟩ ⟨the ~ of a printed letter⟩ ⟨carpeting available in several ~*s*⟩ ⟨traveled across the ~ of the country⟩ **2 a :** largeness or greatness in extent **:** SPACIOUSNESS, SCOPE, RANGE ⟨gives you no idea of the ~ and the depth of his knowledge —K.C.Wheare⟩ ⟨the ~ of his invective —H.J.Laski⟩ **b :** FULLNESS, AMPLITUDE ⟨give ~ to a sleeve⟩ **c :** freedom from narrowness, constraint, or limitation **:** COMPREHENSIVENESS, LIBERALITY ⟨a ~ of view⟩ ⟨concerned to give medical education a greater cultural ~ —Walter Moberly⟩ **3 :** a measured and cut piece of material ⟨a ~ of calico⟩ ⟨a ~ of board⟩ **4 :** girth at the widest part — used of a shoe last and usu. given by a letter designating a standard size ⟨wears an E ~ shoe⟩

widthways \ˈ=,=\ *adv* **:** WIDTHWISE

widthwise \ˈ=,=\ *adv* **:** in the direction of the width **:** LATITUDINALLY ⟨trimmings placed ~ —*Women's Wear Daily*⟩

wie·de·mann effect \ˈvēdə,män-, ˈwēdəmən-\ *n, usu cap W* [after Gustav H. *Wiedemann* †1899 Ger. physicist] **:** twisting of a ferromagnetic rod due to the joint action of a longitudinal current in the rod and a longitudinal magnetic field — compare MAGNETOSTRICTION

wiedemann-franz law \-ˈfrän(t)s-, -ˈfran(t)s-\ *n, usu cap W&F* [after Gustav H. *Wiedemann* †1899 and Rudolph *Franz* †1902 Ger. physicists] **:** a statement in physics: at a given temperature the ratio of the thermal to the electrical conductivity has nearly the same value for most metals and approximately is proportional to the absolute temperature of the metal

wiegela *syn of* WEIGELA

wield \ˈwēld, *esp before pause or consonant* -ēəld\ *vt* -ED/-ING/-S [ME *welden* to have power over, control, fr. OE *wieldan;* akin to OHG *waltan* to rule, ON *valda* to rule, wield, Goth *waldan* to rule, dominate, OIr *flaith* power, rule, L *valēre* to be strong, be well, be worth, Lith *veldėti* to rule, Toch B *walo* king] **1** *chiefly dial* **:** to deal successfully with **:** MANAGE ⟨weighty work, which he cannot ~ by himself —Thomas Fuller⟩ **2 :** to use (as a tool or instrument) esp. with full command or power **:** HANDLE, MANIPULATE, CONTROL ⟨~ a broom⟩ ⟨~ a paintbrush⟩ ⟨~*ed* a pen with clerkly precision —T.B.Costain⟩ ⟨~*ed* the two languages with facility⟩ **3 a :** to show or exert one's power or authority by means of **:** GOVERN, RUN ⟨those who ~*ed* the bureaucratic machine —Hugh Seton-Watson⟩ **b :** to exercise (as power, authority, sovereignty) **:** EMPLOY ⟨~ influence⟩ ⟨a highly centralized executive ~*ing* absolute power —Aldous Huxley⟩ **4** *obs* **:** EXPRESS ⟨I love you more than word can ~ the matter —Shak.⟩ **syn** see HANDLE

wield·er \-də(r)\ *n* -s **:** one that wields (as a weapon or implement)

wieldy \-dē, -di\ *adj* **1 :** capable of wielding **:** STRONG ⟨entrusted to ~ hands —Anthony Harris⟩ **2 :** capable of being wielded **:** MANAGEABLE ⟨is a large but ~ book —*New Republic*⟩

wien bridge \ˈvēn-, ˈwēn-\ *n, usu cap W* [after Max *Wien* †1938 Ger. physicist] **:** a bridge for measuring or comparing capacitances — compare BRIDGE 6

wie·ner *or* **wei·ner** \ˈwēnə(r)\ *n* -s [*wiener* short for *wienerwurst; weiner* alter. of *wiener*] **:** FRANKFURTER

wie·ner schnit·zel \ˈvēnə(r),shnitsəl, ˈwēnə(r),sn-\ *n, usu cap W* [G, lit., Vienna cutlet] **:** a thin breaded veal cutlet served with a garnish (as lemon wedges, capers, or a fried egg)

wie·ner·wurst \ˈwēnə(r),= — *last syllable as at* LIVERWURST\ *n* [G, fr. *Wiener* of Vienna (fr. *Wien* Vienna) + *wurst* sausage, fr. OHG — more at WURST] **1 :** VIENNA SAUSAGE **2 :** FRANKFURTER

wie·nie *or* **wee·nie** \ˈwēnē, ˈwinē, -ni\ *n* -s [*wienie* fr. *wiener* + *-ie; weenie* alter. of *wienie*] *slang* **:** WIENER

wien's displacement law \ˈvēnz-, ˈwēnz-\ *n, usu cap W* [after Wilhelm *Wien* †1928 Ger. physicist] **:** a statement in physics: the wavelength of thermal radiation most copiously emitted by a blackbody is inversely proportional to the absolute temperature of the body

wies·ba·den \ˈvēs,bädᵊn, ˈvis-\ *adj, usu cap* [fr. *Wiesbaden,* Germany] **:** of or from the city of Wiesbaden, Germany **:** of the kind or style prevalent in Wiesbaden

wie·sen·bo·den \ˈvēzᵊn,bōdᵊn\ *n* -s [G, meadow soil, fr. *wiesen* (pl. of *wiese* meadow, fr. OHG *wisa*) + *boden* ground, soil, fr. OHG *bodam* bottom; akin to OE *wāse* mud, mire — more at OOZE, BOTTOM] **:** any of an intrazonal group of dark brown to black meadow soils rich in organic matter with gray underlayers developed through poor drainage in humid or subhumid grassy or sedgy regions

¹**wife** \ˈwīf\ *n, pl* **wives** \-īvz\ [ME *wif,* fr. OE *wīf;* akin to OHG *wīb* woman, wife, ON *vīf* woman; perh. akin to ON *veipr* head covering — more at WIPE] **1 a** *dial* **:** WOMAN — compare OLD WIFE **b :** a woman acting in a specified capacity — used in combination: as (1) **:** one who sells something **:** VENDER ⟨a fish*wife*⟩ ⟨an oyster*wife*⟩ (2) **:** one who has charge of something **:** KEEPER ⟨hen*wife*⟩ (3) **:** a woman worker ⟨washer*wife*⟩ ⟨hostler*wife*⟩ **2 a :** a married woman ⟨a ~ can take credit for the good in her husband —Lenard Kaufman⟩ **b :** a woman who on the basis of her tribal or societal institutions is married ⟨in sororal polygyny when a man married the eldest daughter each of her sisters became his ~ also⟩ **3 :** the female of a pair of mated animals ⟨a new ~ for the gander is introduced into the pen⟩

²**wife** \"\ *vb* -ED/-ING/-S [ME *wifen,* fr. *wif* wife] **:** WIVE

wife·hood \ˈwīf,hu̇d\ *n* [ME *wifhod, wifhode,* fr. OE *wīfhād* womanhood, fr. *wīf* woman, wife + *-hād* -hood] **:** the quality or state of being a wife ⟨achieved the status of ~⟩

wife·less \-ləs\ *adj* [ME *wifles,* fr. OE *wīflēas,* fr. *wīf* wife + *-lēas* -less] **:** having no wife ⟨the only ~ man in the group of old classmates⟩

¹**wifelike** \ˈ=,=\ *adv* **:** in a wifely manner ⟨laid, ~, her hand in one of his —Alfred Tennyson⟩

²**wifelike** \"\ *adj* **:** WIFELY

wife·li·ness \ˈwīflēnəs, -lin-\ *n* -ES **:** the quality or state of being wifely ⟨vague piecemeal efforts at ~ —Martha Gellhorn⟩

wife·ly *adj* [ME *wifly,* fr. OE *wīflic,* fr. *wīf* wife + *-līc* -ly] **1 :** of, relating to, or befitting a wife ⟨~ virtues⟩ ⟨~ duty⟩ ⟨a ~ act⟩ **2 :** having the character or look of a wife ⟨stout and ~, in her chaste cambric nightgown —Ellen Glasgow⟩

wife's equity \ˈwīfs- *sometimes* -īvz-\ *n* **:** the equitable right or claim of a married woman prior to the married women's separate property acts as against her husband or his assignees or creditors to a reasonable provision (as by way of settlement) out of her choses in action or out of any property of hers under the jurisdiction of the court of chancery for the support of herself and her children

wif·ey *or* **wif·ie** \ˈwīfē, -fi\ *n* -s **:** WIFE — not often in formal use

wif·ish \-fish, -fēsh\ *adj* **:** WIFELY

¹**wig** \ˈwig\ *n* -s [ME *wigge,* fr. MLG, wedge, wedge-shaped cake; akin to MD *wegge* wedge, OHG *weggi, wecki* — more at WEDGE] *Brit* **:** a bun flavored with spices and caraway seeds

²**wig** \"\ *n* -s [short for ¹*periwig*] **1 a :** a manufactured covering of hair for the head usu. made of human hair that is woven or attached to a piece of net or a skullcap and worn as a cover for baldness or thin hair or as part of theatrical costume, official or professional dress, or fashionable attire ⟨London barristers wearing ~*s*⟩ ⟨the elaborately curled and powdered ~*s* of the 18th century⟩ — see PERUKE **b :** TOUPEE 2 **2 a :** a person wearing a wig (as a judge or lawyer) **b :** DIGNITARY, BIGWIG **3 :** an act of wigging **:** REBUKE **4 a :** the coarse fur on the shoulders of a large male hooded seal **b :** a male fur seal — **wigs on the green :** a bitter dispute **:** FUSS, CLASH ⟨feared . . . *wigs on the green* at the annual stockholders' meeting —*Time*⟩

³**wig** \"\ *vt* **wigged; wigged; wigging; wigs 1 :** to supply with a wig **2 :** to scold severely **:** CENSURE, REBUKE ⟨*wigged* me for being there the other night —*Delineator*⟩ **syn** see SCOLD

wig·an \ˈwigən\ *n* -s [fr. *Wigan,* Lancashire, England, where it was orig. manufactured] **:** a plain-weave cotton fabric with a stiff finish used for interlining (as in tailored coats or jackets)

wig block *n* **:** a round-topped block for making, dressing, or holding a wig

wigeon *var of* WIDGEON

wigged \ˈwigd\ *adj* **:** wearing a wig ⟨the judge, all ~ and robed⟩

wig·gen *or* **wig·gin** \ˈwigən\ *n* -s [alter. of ²*quicken*] *dial* **:** ROWAN TREE 1

wig·ger \-gə(r)\ *n* -s **:** WIGMAKER

wig·gery \-gərē, -ri\ *n* -ES **1 :** the use of wigs ⟨preferred ~ to baldness —Anthony Trollope⟩ **2 :** a business dealing in wigs ⟨a visit to a nearby theatrical ~ —P.G.Wodehouse⟩

wig·ging \-giŋ, -gēŋ\ *n* -s [²*wig* + *-ing*] **1 :** severe censure from one in authority **:** DRESSING DOWN, SCOLDING ⟨the ~ I received from my editor —C.A.Lejeune⟩ **2** *Austral* **a :** the removal of wool from around the eyes of sheep to prevent obstruction of vision **b :** wool so removed — usu. used in pl. ⟨~*s* . . . mixed with good-quality lambs' wool —R.G. Montgomery⟩

¹**wig·gle** \ˈwigəl\ *vb* **wiggled; wiggled; wiggling** \-g(ə)liŋ\ **wiggles** [ME *wiglen, wigelen,* of LG or D origin; akin to MLG *wiggelen* to totter, reel, MFlem *wigelen* to totter, reel, rock, MD *wiege* cradle; akin to OHG *wiga* cradle, OE *wegan* to move — more at WAY] *vi* **1 :** to move back and forth or up and down with quick jerky or shaking motions **:** JIGGLE, OSCILLATE ⟨a compass needle *wiggling* crazily⟩ ⟨the screen . . . image ~*s* —M.C.Faught⟩ ⟨high heels that make a woman ~ . . . when she walks —Wolcott Gibbs⟩ **2 :** to proceed with twisting and turning movements **:** WRIGGLE, WORM ⟨~ through a crowd⟩ ⟨has an unimaginable gift of *wiggling* in wherever he wants to —O.W.Holmes †1935⟩ ~ *vt* **:** to cause to wiggle ⟨*wiggled* his eyebrows —John Fountain⟩ ⟨found his toe and *wiggled* it —Winifred Bambrick⟩

²**wiggle** \"\ *n* -s **1 :** the motion of one that wiggles ⟨she was all smiles . . . and ~*s* coming down the broad stairs —Calvin Kentfield⟩ **2 :** shellfish or fish in cream sauce with peas ⟨shrimp ~⟩ — **get a wiggle on** *slang* **:** hurry up **:** HUSTLE ⟨better *get a wiggle on* or we'll be late⟩

wiggle nail *n* **:** CORRUGATED FASTENER

wig·gler \-g(ə)lə(r)\ *n* -s [¹*wiggle* + *-er*] **1 :** one that wiggles **2 :** the larva or pupa of the mosquito — called also *wriggler* **3 :** a tool for positioning work centers accurately by exaggerating deviations

wiggle-tail \ˈ==,=\ *n* **1 :** WIGGLER **2** *dial* **:** TADPOLE

wiggle-tail cultivator *n* **:** a riding row-crop cultivator designed to permit easy control of the cultivator gangs in the cultivation of crooked rows

¹**wiggle-waggle** \¦==¦==\ *adj* [redupl. of ¹*wiggle*] **:** INDECISIVE, VACILLATING ⟨has gone *wiggle-waggle* and cannot be persuaded to be categorical —Lionel Hale⟩

²**wiggle-waggle** \"\ *vi* [redupl. of ¹*wiggle*] **:** to move jerkily back and forth **:** wiggle and waggle from one thing to another **:** VACILLATE ⟨*wiggle-waggles* between appeals for charity and responsible state action —*Nation*⟩

³**wiggle-waggle** \"\ *or* **wiggle-woggle** \¦==¦==\ *n* **:** something (as an amusement park contrivance) that wiggle-waggles ⟨flip-flaps, switchbacks, *wiggle-waggles* —Rose Macaulay⟩

wig·gly \ˈwig(ə)lē, -li\ *also* **wiggly-waggly** \¦=(=)¦=(=)=\ *adj* **:** tending to wiggle **:** WIGGLING, WRIGGLY ⟨follow a ~ course⟩ ⟨~ lines⟩ ⟨~ worms⟩

wig·gy \ˈwigē\ *adj* -ER/-EST [¹*wig* + *-y*] **1 :** marked by excessive gravity and formality **:** POMPOUS ⟨a dried up, ~ . . . little scandalmonger —Richard Dehan⟩ **2 :** BEWIGGED

¹**wight** \ˈwīt, *usu* -īd.+V\ *n* -s [ME *wight, wiht* creature, thing, fr. OE *wiht;* akin to OHG *wiht* creature, thing, ON *vættr* creature, being, Goth *waihts* thing, OSlav *veštĭ*] **1 :** a living being **:** CREATURE, MAN ⟨no patriarch he . . . but a withered, anxious, crabbed ~ —Compton Mackenzie⟩ ⟨yonder a maid and her ~ —Thomas Hardy⟩ ⟨one of those benighted ~*s* —Norman Cousins⟩ ⟨any luckless ~ . . . who gets his wife in bad with her boss —G.W.Johnson⟩ **2** *archaic* **:** a preternatural being (as a fairy or witch) ⟨protection against uncouth ~*s* —William Morris⟩

²**wight** \"\ *adj* [ME *wight, wiht,* of Scand origin; akin to ON *vīgr* skilled in fighting, in fighting condition (neut. *vīgt*), *vīg* fight — more at VICTOR] **1** *archaic* **:** VALIANT, STALWART **2** *dial* **a :** STRONG **b :** SWIFT

³**wight** \"\ *or* **wight·ly** *adv* [*wight* fr. ME, fr. *wight, wiht* strong, swift; *wightly* fr. ME, fr. *wight, wiht* strong, swift + *-ly*] *dial* **1 :** STRONGLY **2 :** SWIFTLY

wig·less \ˈwigləs\ *adj* **:** having or wearing no wig ⟨tumbles headlong and ~ to the floor —Agnes Repplier⟩

wigmaker \ˈ=,==\ *n* **:** one that makes or deals in wigs

wigs *pl of* WIG, *pres 3d sing of* WIG

wig·town·shire \ˈwigtən,shi(ə)r, -,tau̇n-\ *or* **wigtown** *adj, usu cap* [fr. *Wigtownshire* or *Wigtown,* Scotland] **:** of or from the county of Wigtown, Scotland **:** of the kind or style prevalent in Wigtown

¹**wig·wag** \ˈwi,gwag, -aa(ə)g, -aig\ *vb* [E dial. *wig* to move, shake (prob. back-formation fr. E ¹*wiggle*) + E ¹*wag*] *vi* **1 :** to signal by waving a flag or portable light according to a code in which movements to the right and left are the elements of the code alphabet and a movement to the front indicates the end (as of a word or message) **2 :** to make a signal (as with the hand or arm) ⟨~*s* through the window of his office —*advt*⟩ ~ *vt* **1 :** to signal (as a message) by wigwagging ⟨the mariner *wigwagged* the necessary directions —*Amer. Guide Series: Conn.*⟩ **2 :** to cause to wigwag ⟨*wigwagged* the white flags —*Blue Bk.*⟩

²**wigwag** \"\ *n, often attrib* **1 a :** the art or practice of wigwagging ⟨no wireless reports . . . and the papers got their news by ~ —Harland Manchester⟩ ⟨~ system⟩ **b :** a wigwagged message **2 :** a polishing device used by watchmakers and clockmakers in which the polisher has a back-and-forth motion

wigwag signal *n* **:** a signal at a railway grade crossing that indicates the approach of a train by the horizontal swinging of a disk

wig·wam \ˈwi,gwäm *also* -gwȯm\ *n* -s [Abnaki & Massachuset *wīkwām,* lit., their dwelling] **1 a :** a hut of the Indians of the region of the Great Lakes and eastward having typically an arched top and consisting of a framework of poles overlaid with bark, rush mats, or hides — compare LODGE 8a **b :** a roughly similar hut ⟨a rough ~ fashioned of fir boughs —F.V. W.Mason⟩ **2 :** a large building serving as the headquarters or meeting place (as convention hall) of a U.S. political organization (as the convention hall of the Republican Party in 1860 or any of the successive buildings housing the Tammany Society of New York) **3 :** a moderate brown that is yellower, lighter, and stronger than chestnut brown, auburn, bay, or tobacco and redder, lighter, and stronger than coffee

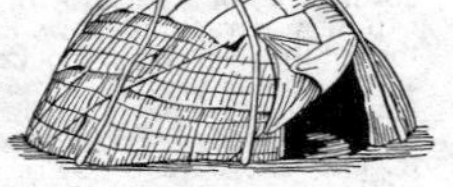

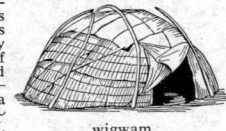

wigwam

wiik·ite \ˈvē,kīt\ *n* -s [Sw *wiikit,* fr. F. J. *Wiik* †1909 Finnish mineralogist + Sw *-it* -ite] **:** a mineral consisting probably of a mixture of samarskite, betafite, and perhaps allanite and occurring in pegmatite in Impilakhti parish on Lake Ladoga, Finland

wijs method \ˈvīs-\ *n, usu cap W* [after Jacob J. Alexander *Wijs* †1942 Dutch analytical chemist] **:** a method for determining the iodine number (as of an oil or fat) that consists in adding a solution of iodine monochloride in glacial acetic acid and estimating the excess of unused halogen by titration with sodium thiosulfate

wi·ke·no \wəˈkā(,)nō\ *n, pl* **wikeno** *or* **wikenos** *usu cap* **1 :** a Bellabella people of British Columbia **2 :** a member of the Wikeno people

wi·ki·wi·ki \ˈwēkē,wēkē\ *adv* [Hawaiian] *Hawaii* **:** QUICKLY, FAST

wik·stroe·mia \wikˈstrōmēə, -rēm-\ *n, cap* [NL, fr. J. E. *Wikström* †1856 Swed. botanist + NL *-ia*] **:** a genus of chiefly Asiatic shrubs (family Thymelaeaceae) including some (as *W. canescens*) with bark that yields a fiber used in making paper and cloth

wil·bur·ite \ˈwilbə,rīt\ *n* -s *usu cap* [John *Wilbur* †1856 Am. Quaker preacher + E *-ite*] **:** a member of the Religious Society of Friends (Conservative) formed in the U. S. in 1845 as a protest on behalf of Inner Light against the doctrine of the Gurneyites

wil·co \ˈwil(,)kō\ *interj* [short for the phrase *will comply*] — used esp. in radio and signaling to indicate that a message received will be complied with

¹**wild** \ˈwīld, *esp before pause or consonant* ˈwīəld\ *adj* -ER/-EST [ME *wilde,* fr. OE; akin to OHG *wildi* wild, ON *villr* wild, gone astray, bewildered, Goth *wiltheis* wild, W *gwyllt,* Corn *guyls*] **1 a** (1) **:** living in a state of nature **:** inhabiting natural haunts (as the forest or open field) **:** not tamed or domesticated ⟨a ~ ox⟩ ⟨~ duck⟩ (2) **:** being one of a kind not ordinarily subjected to domestication ⟨the tame ~ goose finally flew away⟩ — compare FERAL (3) **:** SHY 1a **b** (1) **:** growing or produced without the aid and care of man **:** not cultivated **:** brought forth by unassisted nature or by animals not domesticated **:** NATIVE ⟨~ furs⟩ ⟨the closest ~ relative of cultivated corn —P.C.Mangelsdorf⟩ ⟨~ honey⟩ (2) **:** related to or resembling a corresponding cultivated or domesticated organism — used in vernacular names of plants and animals; see WILD OAT, WILD ONION **c :** not living near or associated with man — used esp. of a mosquito that does not breed near human habitations in distinction from one that habitually does so **d :** of or belonging to organisms in a state of nature **:** typical of undomesticated animals or uncultivated plants ⟨the ~ state⟩ ⟨~ nature⟩ **2 a :** not inhabited or cultivated ⟨the only profit in ~ land was to clear and plant it with one's own hands or to sell it —*Amer. Guide Series: N.Y.*⟩ **b :** not being or appearing amenable to human habitation or cultivation **:** ROUGH, WASTE, DESOLATE ⟨becomes much ~*er* as the trees give place to bare granite crags —S.P.B.Mais⟩ **3 a** (1) **:** not subjected to restraint or regulation **:** UNCONTROLLED, INORDINATE, UNGOVERNED ⟨mobs are ~, unpredictable, vicious, and insanely cruel when aroused —P.I.Wellman⟩ ⟨the ~ frenzy of religious camp meetings —J.T.Adams⟩ ⟨a piano played with a ~ exuberance —Louis Bromfield⟩ (2) **:** abandoned to or overcome by passion, desire, or emotion ⟨the frenzied old man, ~ with hatred and insane with baffled desire —W.M. Thackeray⟩ ⟨~ with grief⟩; *also* **:** passionately eager, enthusiastic, desirous, or angry ⟨he was ~ to own a toy train —J.C.Furnas⟩ ⟨his sponsors . . . are ~ about him as a salesman —Howard Taubman⟩ ⟨boys ~ for the venture —Marjory S. Douglas⟩ ⟨straining and ~ to take to the air —Kay Boyle⟩ ⟨was ~ at people talking, and upsetting him —Sheila Kaye-Smith⟩ (3) **:** not amenable to control, restraint, or domestication **:** UNRULY, UNGOVERNABLE, RECKLESS ⟨bars and bowling alleys full of ~ youths breezily and brutally telling each other off —Robert Lowry⟩ ⟨a rabble of ~ country lads —W.B.

Yeats⟩ ⟨the zebra is too ~ to be used as a draft animal⟩ ⟨a ~ mop of hair —Irwin Shaw⟩ (4) *of a ship* : hard to steer or tending to yaw from the course (5) : not capped : not brought into controlled or regulated production — used of an oil or gas well **b** : marked by turbulent violent agitation : ROUGH, TEMPESTUOUS, STORMY ⟨the sea against the west coast was ~ with storm —Ernesta D. Barlow⟩ ⟨it's a ~ night . . . to be out in the rain —J.M.Synge⟩ **c** : LICENTIOUS, DISSOLUTE **d** : exceeding normal or conventional bounds in thought, design, conception, execution, or nature : EXTRAVAGANT, FANTASTIC, VISIONARY ⟨overmatched in lush, easy wealth the ~*est* dreams of fantasy —T.H.White b. 1915⟩ ⟨remonstrating against the ~ project —H.E.Scudder⟩ ⟨~ beliefs about the origin of these fishes —J.L.B.Smith⟩ ⟨the ~*est* complexity ever added to the steam engine —George Zabriskie⟩ ⟨a ~ array of bathhouses, dance halls, freak shows, fun houses —*Amer. Guide Series: N.Y. City*⟩ ⟨a necktie of ~ colors and pattern⟩ **e** (1) : become destructive or ferocious through escape from normal restraints ⟨~ cells forming a tumor⟩ ⟨a dog gone ~⟩ (2) : escaped from or beyond human control ⟨the brakes gave out and . . . not even a fool would ride a ~ truck . . . with an overload of logs —Hugh Fosburgh⟩ — compare WILDFIRE **f** (1) : characteristic or indicative of strong or overwhelming passion, desire, or emotion ⟨looked at me with a ~ stare of agony —Walter O'Meara⟩ ⟨a ~ gleam of delight in his eyes —*Irish Digest*⟩ ⟨taken his ~ words in earnest —George Meredith⟩ (2) : characterized or marked by the presence or activity of unruly, intemperate, abandoned, or impassioned persons ⟨a ~ 5-hour street battle —*Current History*⟩ ⟨a ~, frontier town —*Amer. Guide Series: Texas*⟩ ⟨found dead on a beach, apparently following a ~ party —M.S.Forbes⟩ **4 a** : not acculturated to an advanced civilization : RUDE, UNCIVILIZED, BARBARIC ⟨~ natives⟩ ⟨~ practices⟩ **b** : not yielding to a governmental authority : SAVAGE, INTRACTABLE, REBELLIOUS ⟨~ border tribes⟩ **c** : resembling a barbarian or a wild animal : BRUTALIZED ⟨dirty, ~, and degraded as only the worst slaves of antiquity had been —Lewis Mumford⟩ **5** : characteristic of, appropriate to, or expressive of wilderness, wildlife, or people in a simple or uncivilized society or environment ⟨~ and rugged grandeur —Elinor Wylie⟩ ⟨~ love of freedom —Meridel Le Sueur⟩ ⟨in the brush a soft persuasive cooing . . . subtle and ~ and unobtrusive —John Burroughs⟩ **6 a** : deviating from a natural or expected course, goal, or practice : acting, appearing, or being manifested in an unexpected, undesired, or unpredictable manner : RANDOM, ERRATIC ⟨impulsive grammar and ~ spelling —C. W. Cunnington⟩ ⟨giving a ~ guess, I suggested that the model was one twelfth the size of the ordinary chair —S.P.B. Mais⟩ ⟨~ price fluctuations —W.R.Langdon⟩ ⟨swing across traffic in a ~ circle —Green Peyton⟩ **b** : not accounted for by known theories ⟨afterimages . . . although perhaps not strictly hallucinations might be alleged as ~ sense-data —R.J. Hirst⟩ **7** : great in extent, size, quantity, or intensity : EXTREME, PRODIGIOUS ⟨~ and precarious leaps —D.L.Busk⟩ ⟨a ~ headache that did not leave her for days —Louis Bromfield⟩ ⟨the world's ~*est* religious fanatics —Isaac Deutscher⟩ **8** *of a playing card* : having a denomination determined by the will of the holder — compare DEUCES WILD, JOKER **9** *of paper* : loose and irregular in formation so as to appear mottled when looked through — contrasted with *well-closed*

[2]wild \"\ *n* -s **1** : a region or tract that is sparsely inhabited or uncultivated : WILDERNESS ⟨the ruthless life of the ~ —James Stevenson-Hamilton⟩ ⟨settlers had to cross this Indian-infested ~ —*Amer. Guide Series: Texas*⟩ ⟨living in the ~*s* of Africa hunting crocodiles —*Publishers' Weekly*⟩ **2** : a wild, free, or natural life or existence ⟨corn in the ~ may well have been a plant with low survival value —P.C.Mangelsdorf⟩

[3]wild \"\ *adv* **1** : WILDLY ⟨~ shy about seeing any of her own people —Mary Deasy⟩ **2** : without regulation or control : UNCONTROLLEDLY ⟨given over to violence, society is an engine running ~ —F.H.Giddings⟩

wild alder *n* : GOUTWEED

wild alfalfa *n* **1** : SWEET CLOVER **2** : a yellow-flowered Eurasian medic (*Medicago falcata*) **3** : a scurfy pea (*Psoralea tenuiflora floribunda*) **4** : DEERWEED

wild allspice *n* : SPICEBUSH

wild almond *n* **1** : a southern African tree (*Brabejum stellatifolium*) of the family Proteaceae; *also* : its edible seed sometimes used in place of coffee **2** : JAVA ALMOND **3** : any of various trees of the genus *Prunus* (esp. *P. fasciculata*)

wild and woolly *adj* : marked by boisterous and untamed ways of living and by lack of polish and refinement ⟨the *wild and woolly* West of the American plains and mesas —B.S.Mason⟩

wild angelica *n* : a European herb (*Angelica sylvestris*) with compound leaves and white flowers that is adventive on Cape Breton island

wild apple *n* **1** : an apple that grows wild: as **a** : OREGON CRAB APPLE **b** : SIBERIAN CRAB **2** : the fruit of the native cranberry

wild arum *n* : CUCKOOPINT

wild ash *n* : AMERICAN MOUNTAIN ASH

wild ass *n* : any of several plain-colored or nearly plain-colored equine mammals (as the kiang or onager) of Asia and northeast Africa that are related to and resemble the domesticated ass

wild balsam *n* : JEWELWEED b

wild balsam apple *n* : WILD CUCUMBER c

wild banana *n* : a banana (as *Musa glauca* or *M. davyae*) that grows wild

wild barley *n* : any of various grasses of the genus *Hordeum* that are not commonly cultivated for grain: as **a** : WALL BARLEY **b** : a biennial or perennial No. American weedy grass (*H. jubatum*) with bristly awns and glumes that may injure the mouths of grazing animals

wild basil *n* : an aromatic herb (*Satureia vulgaris*) that is widely distributed in the U. S., Europe, and Asia and that has capitate clusters of small pink-and-white flowers

wild bean *n* : any of various wild plants of the family Leguminosae; *esp* : any of various plants of the genera *Phaseolus*, *Apios*, and *Strophostyles*

wild bee *n* : any of numerous undomesticated social bees; *also* : the honeybee when escaped from domestication

wild beet *n* **1** : PIGWEED a **2** : a perennial evening primrose (*Oenothera fruticosa*) of the eastern and central U.S. that is sometimes used as a potherb

wild begonia *n* : a dock (*Rumex venosus*) with broad rose-colored veiny wings on the fruit — called also *wild hydrangea*

wild bergamot *n* : MONARDA 2; *esp* : a fragrant No. American herb (*Monarda fistulosa*) having a terminal capitate cluster of rather large pink or purple flowers

wild black cherry *n* : BLACK CHERRY 2

wild black currant *n* : any of several uncultivated black-fruited currants; esp. : an unarmed No. American shrub (*Ribes americanum*) with racemose greenish yellow flowers and black smooth fruit — called also *flowering currant*

wild bleeding heart *n* : a weak glaucous herb (*Dicentra eximia*) of the eastern U.S. that has finely divided leaves and is often cultivated for its rose-pink short-spurred showy flowers

wild bluegrass *n* : any of several forage grasses of the genus *Poa* (esp. *P. sandbergii*) found in prairie regions of No. America

wild blue phlox *n* : a showy No. American herb (*Phlox divaricata*) often cultivated for its profusion of tubular blue faintly fragrant flowers — called also *wild sweet William*

wild boar *n* : a wild hog (*Sus scrofa*) of continental Europe, southwestern Asia, and northern Africa from which most domestic swine have been derived and which has coarse and grizzled hair and the tusks or canines of both jaws often much enlarged; *broadly* : any of various related wild hogs of southeastern Asia

wild·bore \'wī(ə)ld,bō(ə)r\ *n* -s [origin unknown] : a formerly popular durable woolen dress fabric

wild brier *n* : an uncultivated species of brier: as **a** : DOG ROSE **b** : SWEETBRIER

wild buckwheat *n* **1** : BLACK BINDWEED 1 **2** : a low-growing shrub of the genus *Eriogonum* (esp. *E. fasciculatum*)

wild bugloss *n* : BUGLOSS 4

wild burnet *n* : a burnet (*Sanguisorba canadensis*) of No. America

wild cabbage *n* **1** : a plant that is the wild original of the cultivated cabbage and is common near the seacoast in various parts of Europe **2** : a succulent herb (*Caulanthus crassicaulis*) of the family Cruciferae that is native to the western U.S. and has edible foliage

wild calla *n* **1** : an arrow arum (*Peltandra sagittaefolia*) of the southern U. S. **2** : WATER ARUM

wild canary *n* **1** : GOLDFINCH 3 **2** : YELLOW WARBLER 1a

wild caraway *n* **1** : either of two Indian plantains (*Cacalia suaveolens* and *C. atriplicifolia*) **2** : YAMP

wild carrot *n* : a Eurasian weed (*Daucus carota*) that is prob. the original of the cultivated carrot, is widely naturalized as a weed, and has an acrid and unpleasantly flavored root — called also *lace flower, Queen Anne's lace*

[1]wildcat \'=,=\ *n* -s *see sense 1b* [ME *wilde cat*, fr. *wilde* wild + *cat*] **1 a** : either of two cats that somewhat resemble the domestic tabby cat in color and pattern but are usu. somewhat heavier in build and that are usu. held to be among the ancestors of the domestic cat: (1) : EUROPEAN WILDCAT (2) : KAFFIR CAT **b** *or pl* **wildcat** : any of various small or medium-sized cats (as the jungle cat, the lynx, or the ocelot) **c** : a feral domestic cat **2** : a savage quick-tempered hard-fighting person **3 a** : wildcat currency **b** : a wildcat oil or gas well **c** : a wildcat strike **4** : a drum or wheel on a windlass having in its circumference a deep groove with projections that engage the links of a chain cable as it passes and thus regulate the speed of the cable : CABLE WHEEL — called also *cable holder*

[2]wildcat \"\ *adj* **1 a** (1) : financially irresponsible or unreliable ⟨~ banks⟩ ⟨worthless stock in a ~ mine⟩ (2) : issued by a financially irresponsible banking establishment ⟨~ currency⟩ **b** : operating or being produced or carried on outside the bounds of standard, recognized, or legitimate business practices ⟨~ breweries⟩ ⟨~ stock speculation⟩ ⟨~ promoters⟩ ⟨a ~ airline⟩ **c** : of, relating to, concerned with, or being an oil or gas well drilled in territory not known to be productive ⟨there may be oil but drilling for it would be strictly a ~ operation —*Newsweek*⟩ ⟨~ wells⟩ ⟨~ drilling⟩ **d** : initiated by a group of workers without formal union approval or in violation of a contract ⟨~ strike⟩ ⟨~ work stoppage⟩ **2 a** : *of a cartridge* : having a bullet of a standard commercial caliber but using an expanded case or a case designed for a bullet of a greater caliber but necked down for the smaller bullet **b** *of a rifle* : using wildcat cartridges

[3]wildcat \"\ *vi* **wildcatted; wildcatted; wildcatting; wildcats** **1** : to prospect and drill an experimental oil or gas well or sometimes a mine shaft in territory not known to be productive **2** : to engage in wildcat speculations, operations, or enterprises **3** : to run a railroad locomotive and tender

wild·cat·ter \"+ə(r)\ *n* -s [[3]*wildcat* + *-er*] **1** : one that drills wells in the hope of finding oil in territory not known to be an oil field **2** : one that promotes unsafe and unreliable enterprises; *esp* : one that sells stock in enterprises of this kind **3** [*wildcat (cartridge)* + *-er*] : one that designs, builds, or fires wildcat cartridges and rifles as a hobby

wild celandine *n* : JEWELWEED

wild celery *n* : TAPE GRASS

wild cherry *n* **1** : an uncultivated cherry tree or its fruit: as **a** : BIRD CHERRY **b** : PIN CHERRY **c** : BLACK CHERRY 2 **2** : a tropical American shrub (*Rhacoma crossopetalum*) of the family Celastraceae; *also* : the edible red fruit of this shrub **3** : a dark red to purplish red that is stronger and slightly lighter than plum violet, stronger and slightly darker than neutral red, and much stronger than sultana — called also *vin rosé*

wild chervil *n* **1** : a coarse erect biennial herb (*Anthriscus sylvestris*) of the family Umbelliferae that is widely distributed in the Old World and an introduced weed in eastern No. America **2** : HONEWORT b

wild chestnut *n* **1 a** : a proteaceous shrub (*Brabejum stellatifolia*) of southern Africa **b** : the nut of this plant containing a kernel that is edible when roasted **2** : a southern African tree (*Calodendron capense*) of the family Rutaceae with panicles of handsome white flowers for which it is sometimes cultivated; *also* : its edible black seed **3** : a Philippine tree (*Castanopsis philippinensis*) related to the true chestnut; *also* : the seed of this tree

wild cinnamon *n* **1** : a tree (*Canella winterana*) of Florida and the West Indies with white bark and small flowers in terminal cymes **2** *or* **wild clove** : BAYBERRY 1a

wild clary *n* : WILD SAGE 1

wild coffee *n* **1** : FEVERROOT **2** : CASCARA BUCKTHORN **3** : a plant of the genus *Psychotria*

wild columbine *n* : COLUMBINE 1a

wild comfrey *n* : either of two perennial herbs (*Cynoglossum virginianum* and *C. boreale*) of the eastern U. S. having large bristly leaves and small blue flowers

wild corn *n* : a clintonia (*Clintonia umbellulata*)

wild cotton *n* **1** : COTTON GRASS **2 a** : a shrubby herb (*Gossypium thurberi*) of southern Arizona and Mexico **b** : any of various cultivated cottons that have escaped and established themselves in subtropical or tropical areas **3** : any of several plants of the genera *Abutilon* and *Hibiscus* (esp. *H. moscheutos*) **4** *Austral* : any of various milkweeds; *esp* : either of two milkweeds (*Asclepias fruticosa* and *A. physocarpa*) that have been introduced into Australia from So. Africa and are poisonous to cattle

wild cranesbill *n* : any of several wild geraniums (esp. *Geranium maculatum* and *G. dissectum*)

wild crocus *n* : PASQUEFLOWER

wild cucumber *n* : any of various vines related to or felt to resemble the cucumber: as **a** : SQUIRTING CUCUMBER **b** : STAR CUCUMBER **c** : a No. American vine (*Echinocystis lobata*) with greenish spiny fruit — called also *wild balsam apple*

wild currant *n* : any of several plants of the genus *Ribes* that produce fruit resembling cultivated currants

wild date *n* **1** : a Spanish bayonet (*Yucca mohavensis*) of southern California with edible fruit used by the Indians **2** : an Indian date (*Phoenix sylvestris*) that is grown for ornament and has gray-green leaves

wild dilly *n* : [4]DILLY 2

wild dog *n* : any of various undomesticated mammals of the family Canidae (as the dingo, the African hunting dog, or the dhole) that are felt to resemble domestic dogs esp. as distinguished from jackals or wolves

wild dove *n* : MOURNING DOVE

wild duck *n* : an undomesticated duck; *esp* : MALLARD

wil·de·beest \'wildə,bēst *sometimes* 'vi-\ *n, pl* **wildebeests** \-ts\ *also* **wildebeest** \-t\ *or* **wildebees·te** \-tə\ [Afrik *wildebees* (pl. *wildebeeste*), fr. *wild, wilde* wild (fr. MD *wilt, wilde*; akin to OE *wilde* wild) + *bees* beast, ox, fr. MD *beeste* beast, animal, fr. OF *beste* — more at WILD, BEAST] : GNU

wil·de dagga \'wildə-\ *n* [Afrik, fr. *wild, wilde* wild + *dagga*] : DAGGA 2

wild elder *n* : BRISTLY SARSAPARILLA

wild emmer *n* : WILD WHEAT 1

[1]wilder *comparative of* WILD

[2]wil·der \'wildə(r)\ *vb* -ED/-ING/-S [prob. irreg. fr. *wilderness*] *vt* **1** *archaic* : to lead astray **2** *archaic* : BEWILDER, PERPLEX ~ *vi, archaic* : STRAY, WANDER

wil·der·ment \-(r)mənt\ *n* [*wilder* + *-ment*] *archaic* : BEWILDERMENT

wil·der·muth's auricle \'wildə(r),müts-\ *or* **wildermuth's ear** *n, usu cap W* [after Hermann A. *Wildermuth* †1907 Ger. neurologist] : an ear in which the antihelix is large and the helix bent downward

wil·der·ness \'wildə(r)nəs\ *n* -ES [ME *wildernesse*, fr. *wildern*, *wildren* wild (fr. OE *wilddēoren* of or like wild beasts, fr. *wilddēor, wildēor*, alter. — influenced by *dēor* beast — of assumed OE *wildor* wild beast — whence OE *wildru*, pl., wild beasts; akin to OE *wilde* untamed, wild) + *-nesse* -ness — more at WILD, DEER] **1 a** (1) : a tract of land or a region (as a forest or a wide barren plain) uncultivated and uninhabited by human beings : WILD, WASTE (2) : an empty or pathless area or region ⟨in remote ~*es* of space groups of nebulae are found —G.W.Gray b. 1886⟩ (3) : a part of a garden devoted to wild growth **b** : something likened to a wilderness in barrenness, confusion, or dangerousness ⟨the ~ in the mind, the desert wastes in the heart —Anne M. Lindbergh⟩ ⟨a ~ of tumbledown shacks and gasworks —T.D.Durrance⟩ ⟨a ~ of sociological theory —H.J.Muller⟩ ⟨such a ~ of black hair that he appeared to be wearing a shako —*New Yorker*⟩ **2** *obs* : WILDNESS **3** : a confusing multitude or mass : a great number or quantity ⟨I would not have given it for a ~ of monkeys —Shak.⟩

wilderness area *n* : an area (as of national forest land) set aside by government for preservation of natural conditions for scientific or recreational purposes

wildest *superlative of* WILD

wild-eyed \'=,=\ *adj* **1** : appearing or being furious or raving ⟨a *wild-eyed* and frantic young man, pale, dishevelled, and palpitating, burst into the room —A. Conan Doyle⟩ **2** : consisting of or favoring extreme political or social measures : RADICAL, VISIONARY ⟨a *wild-eyed* internationalist dream of a world state —A.H.Vandenberg †1951⟩ ⟨*wild-eyed* reformers and rubble theorists —Gordon Merrick⟩

wild fig *n* **1** : CAPRIFIG **2** : any of several wild plants of the genus *Ficus* native to Florida (as *F. aurea*) **3** : a West Indies tree (*Clusia flava*) or its fig-shaped fruit

wildfire \'=,=\ *n* [ME *wilde fire*, fr. *wilde* wild + *fire*] **1** : a sweeping and destructive conflagration **2 a** : a flammable composition very hard to quench when kindled : GREEK FIRE **b** : something resembling or suggesting wildfire in unquenchable intensity or inclusiveness in action ⟨spread through the crowd like ~⟩ **3** : the ignis fatuus or a similar phosphorescent appearance **4** : HEAT LIGHTNING **5** : a destructive disease of tobacco caused by a bacterium (*Pseudomonas tabaci*) and characterized by small brown spots usu. surrounded with broad yellowish halos that enlarge quickly, turn tan or dark brown, dry or rot, and fall out — compare BLACKFIRE

wild flag *n* **1** : an Australian plant of the genus *Patersonia* (family Iridaceae); *also* : its showy blue or purple flower **2** : SWEET FLAG

wild flax *n* **1** : GOLD OF PLEASURE **2** : any of several wild plants of the genus *Linum* (esp. *L. lewissi*)

wild flower *n* : the flower of a wild or uncultivated plant; *also* : the plant bearing such a flower

wild forget-me-not *n* : any of several wild flowers (as a bluet) with blossoms suggestive of forget-me-nots

wild four-o'clock *n* : a common umbrellawort (*Mirabilis nyctaginea*) of the central and southern U. S.

wildfowl \'=,=\ *n* [ME *wilde foul*, fr. *wilde* wild + *foul* fowl] : GAME BIRD; *esp* : a game waterfowl (as a wild duck or Canada goose)

wildfowl·er \"+ə(r)\ *n* [*wildfowl* + *-er*] : one that engages in wildfowling

wildfowl·ing \"+iŋ\ *n* -s [*wildfowl* + *-ing*] : the hunting of wildfowl as a sport or occupation

wild foxglove *n* **1** : DOWNY FALSE FOXGLOVE **2** : a plant of the genus *Pentstemon*

wild fuchsia *n* : a California perennial (*Zauschneria californica*) that is related to the fuchsias and sometimes cultivated for its showy scarlet flowers

wild garden *n* : a garden in which colonies of hardy wild and garden plants are naturalized in positions where they will appear to be growing naturally

wild garlic *n* : any of several usu. pungent weedy plants of the genus *Allium*; *esp* : CROW GARLIC

wild gasoline *or* **wild gas** *n* : gasoline that is too volatile for commercial use; *esp* : natural gasoline that has not been stabilized

wild geranium *n* : any of several plants of the family Geraniaceae: as **a** : CRANESBILL; *esp* : SPOTTED CRANESBILL **b** : STORKSBILL 1

wild ginger *n* **1** : a tropical Old World aromatic plant (*Zingiber zerumbet*) related to and resembling common ginger **2 a** : a No. American perennial herb (*Asarum canadense*) with kidney-shaped to cordate leaves, purplish brown flowers, and a pungent creeping rhizome — called also *black snakeroot, Canada ginger* **b** : any of various other plants of the genus *Asarum* — see HEARTLEAF **3** : an Australian perennial plant (*Alpinia coerulea*) related to the common ginger

wild goose *n, pl* **wild geese** [ME *wilde gos*, fr. OE *wilde gōs*, fr. *wilde* wild + *gōs* goose] **1** : an undomesticated goose: as **a** *Eng* : GREYLAG **b** : CANADA GOOSE **2** : an Irish Jacobite who left Ireland after the abdication of James II and served in the French army; *broadly* : an expatriate Irishman

wild gooseberry *n* **1** : any of several plants of the genus *Ribes*; *esp* : a common No. American spiny shrub (*R. cynosbati*) with racemose green flowers and bitter bristly green fruit **2** : the fruit of a wild gooseberry

wild-goose chase *n* [so called fr. the characteristic flight of wild geese in a group spaced at intervals behind a leader that sets the course] **1** *obs* : a cross-country ride in which the leading horseman can set the course for all contestants so long as he can hold the lead **2** : a pursuit after something unattainable : a futile pursuit or chase

wild-goose plum *n* **1** : either of two wild plums (*Prunus hortulana* and *P. munsoniana*) of the central and south central U.S. that have reddish to yellow fruits and have given rise to several cultivated plums **2** : any of various cultivated plums that are or are thought to be derived from the native wild-goose plums

wild gourd *n* : PRAIRIE GOURD

wild grape *n* **1** : a grape growing in nature; *often* : a species grape (as a fox grape) **2** : a southern African vine (*Rhoicissus capensis*) of the family Vitaceae with kidney-shaped leaves and yellow green to black fruit in loose bunches

wild guelder rose *n* : CRANBERRY BUSH 2

wild hazel *n* **1** : an American hazel (*Corylus americana*) **2** : JOJOBA

wild hedgebur *n* : CLEAVERS

wild heliotrope *n* : any of various plants of the genus *Phacelia* having blue or purple flowers

wild hemp *n* **1** : HEMP AGRIMONY **2** : GREAT RAGWEED **3** : a hemp nettle (*Galeopsis tetrahit*)

wild hip·po \-'hi(,)pō\ *n* -s [[1]*wild* + *hippo*, alter. of *ipecac*] **1** : IPECAC SPURGE **2** : FLOWERING SPURGE

wild hoarhound *n* : any of several bonesets (as *Eupatorium rotundifolium* or *E. verbenaefolium*)

wild holly *n* : MOUNTAIN HOLLY 1

wild hollyhock *n* : any of several mallows (esp. of the genera *Callirhoë*, *Sidalcea*, and *Sphaeralcea*) resembling the common hollyhock

wild honeysuckle *n* **1** : PINXTER FLOWER **2** : SCARLET GAURA **3** : any of several shrubs of the genus *Lonicera* (esp. *L. dioica*) that grow wild

wild hop *n* : VIRGIN'S BOWER b

wild horse *n* [ME *wilde hors*, fr. OE, fr. *wilde* wild + *hors* horse] **1** : an undomesticated horse (as Przhevalski's horse) **2** : a feral domestic horse

wild hyacinth *n* **1** : a No. American bulbous plant (*Camassia scilloides*) with linear basal leaves and white racemose flowers **2** : WOOD HYACINTH **3** : BRODIAEA 2

wild hydrangea *n* **1** : a No. American shrub (*Hydrangea arborescens*) having white flowers and being cultivated for ornament **2** : WILD BEGONIA

wild hyssop *n* : BLUE VERVAIN

wild indigo *n* **1** : a plant of the genus *Baptisia*: as **a** : INDIGO BROOM **b** : BLUE FALSE INDIGO **2** : BASTARD INDIGO 2

[1]wild·ing \'wīldiŋ, -dēŋ\ *n* -s [[1]*wild* + *-ing*] **1 a** (1) : a wild or uncultivated plant of natural origin and growth; *usu* : a wild apple or crab apple (2) : the fruit of a wilding **b** : a cultivated plant sprung up spontaneously : ESCAPE **2** : a wild animal

[2]wilding \"\ *adj* : not tame : not domesticated or cultivated : WILD ⟨~ bee —W.C.Bryant⟩

wild ipecac *n* **1** : IPECAC SPURGE **2** : FEVERROOT

wild iris *n* : BLUE FLAG

wild irishman *n, usu cap I, NewZeal* : TUMATAKURU

wild·ish \'wīldish, -dēsh\ *adj* : somewhat wild — **wild·ishness** *n* -ES

wild ivy *n* : an Australian woody vine (*Platylobium triangulare*) of the family Leguminosae having leaves suggesting those of English ivy, yellow flowers, and broad flat pods and being often cultivated

wild jalap *n* **1** : MAYAPPLE 1 **2** : MAN-OF-THE-EARTH

wild job's tears *n pl but sing or pl in constr, usu cap J* : VIRGINIA FALSE GROMWELL

wild kale *n* **1** : CHARLOCK **2** : WILD RADISH

wild land *n* **:** land that is uncultivated or unfit for cultivation **:** WASTELAND, DESERT

wild leek *n* **:** either of two perennial herbs of the genus *Allium:* **a :** a coarse Old World herb (*A. ampeloprasum*) that is widely naturalized, has a large bulb with papery outer coats, and bears a tall stalk of whitish or greenish purple-tinged flowers **b :** a No. American herb (*A. tricoccum*) with a slender bulb, fleshy leaves, and whitish flowers

wild lemon *n* **1 :** MAYAPPLE 1 **2 a :** any of several Australian shrubs (as *P. oleifolia*) of the genus *Plectronia* (family Rubiaceae) **b :** a caper (*Capparis nobilis*) **3** *NewZeal* **:** TARATA

wild lettuce *n* **1 a :** a weedy lettuce that is an escape from a cultivated strain **b :** any of several native wild plants of the genus *Lactuca:* as (1) **:** PRICKLY LETTUCE (2) **:** a blue lettuce (*L. pulchella*) (3) **:** a tall No. American herb (*L. canadensis*) that resembles prickly lettuce but lacks spines **2 :** FALSE WINTERGREEN

wild licorice *also* **wild liquorice** *n* **1 :** a No. American herb (*Glycyrrhiza lepidota*) that is closely related to the true licorice and has a root with similar properties — called also *American licorice* **2 :** INDIAN LICORICE **3 :** any of several plants with sweetish roots: as **a :** either of two bedstraws (*Galium circaezans* and *G. lanceolatum*) **b :** an Australian germander (*Teucrium corymbosum*) **4 :** BUTTONBUSH

wildlife \ˈ≈,≈\ *n, often attrib* [¹*wild* + *life*] **:** living things that are neither human nor domesticated; *esp* **:** the mammals, birds, and fishes that are hunted by man for sport or food — compare GAME

wild lilac *n* **:** a shrub of the genus *Ceanothus*

wild lily of the valley 1 : FALSE LILY OF THE VALLEY **2 :** WHITE ADDER'S-TONGUE **3 :** either of two wintergreens of the genus *Pyrola:* **a :** a plant (*P. elliptica*) with oblong leaves and white to pinkish flowers that is prob. native to Japan but widely distributed in No. America **b :** a plant (*P. rotundifolia*) with rounded leaves and very fragrant creamy white flowers that is widely distributed in northerly parts of both Old and New Worlds; *esp* **:** FALSE WINTERGREEN

wild lime *n* **1 :** MOUNTAIN PLUM **2 :** COLIMA **3 :** OGEECHEE LIME

wild·ling \ˈwī(ə)l(d)liŋ, -(d)lēŋ\ *n* -s [¹*wild* + *-ling*] **1 :** a wild flower, plant, or seedling **2 :** a wild animal

wild lupine *n* **:** an erect herb (*Lupinus perennis*) of eastern and central No. America with palmately compound leaves and showy racemose blue flowers — called also *Indian beet, old-maid's-bonnet*

wild·ly \ˈwī(ə)l(d)lē, -(d)li\ *adv* [ME *wildely*, fr. *wilde* wild + *-ly*] **:** in a wild manner

wild madder *n* **1 :** MADDER 1, 2 **2 :** either of two bedstraws: **a :** a Eurasiatic herb (*Galium mollugo*) that has ample panicles of small white flowers and is naturalized in eastern No. America — called also *infant's-breath, white bedstraw* **b :** an American herb (*G. tinctorium*) with terminal flowers in clusters of two or three

wild man *n* **1 a :** an uncivilized man **:** SAVAGE **b :** a man of fierce and ungovernable character **c :** a man holding radical political views **2** *also* **wild man of the woods :** ORANGUTAN

wild mandrake *n* **1 :** an enchanter's nightshade (*Circaea lutetiana*) **2 :** MAYAPPLE 1

wild mango *n* **:** an African tree (*Irvingia gabonensis*) of the family Simaroubaceae with an edible yellow fruit that somewhat resembles the mango but is valued esp. for its oil-rich seed and a hard heavy greenish wood that is exceptionally resistant to termite attack — see DIKA 2a, DIKA BREAD

wild mangosteen *n* **1 :** SANTOL **2 :** the fruit of the santol

wild marigold *n* **1 :** POT MARIGOLD **2 :** PINEAPPLE WEED

wild marjoram *n* **:** a Eurasian perennial herb (*Origanum vulgare*) with the spikes of flowers clustered in panicles — compare SWEET MARJORAM

wild masterwort *n* **:** GOUTWEED

wild millet *n* **:** any of various grasses related to or felt to resemble millet: as **a :** a foxtail of the genus *Setaria* **b :** BARNYARD GRASS; *broadly* **:** any of several grasses (as shama millet) of the genus *Echinochloa*

wild mint *n* **:** a wild plant of the family Labiatae; *specif* **:** PENNYROYAL

wild monkshood *n* **:** a perennial No. American herb (*Aconitum uncinatum*) having leaves divided only to the base and the inflorescence being a loose panicle and flowers with a hooded erect sepal

wild morning glory *n* **1 :** HEDGE BINDWEED **2 :** FIELD BINDWEED

wild musk *n* **:** ALFILARIA

wild mustard *n* **:** any of several plants of the family Cruciferae; *esp* **:** CHARLOCK

wild·ness \ˈwī(ə)l(d)nəs\ *n* -ES [ME *wildenesse*, fr. *wilde* wild + *-nesse* -ness] **1 :** WILDERNESS **2 :** the quality or state of being wild

wild nutmeg *n* **:** MACASSAR NUTMEG

wild oat *n* **1 a :** a wild grass of the genus *Avena:* as (1) **:** a European annual weed (*A. fatua*) that is common in meadows and pastures (2) **:** WILD RED OAT **b :** TALL OAT GRASS **c :** a plant of the genus *Uvularia* **2 wild oats** *pl* **a :** offenses and indiscretions ascribed to youthful exuberance **b :** male premarital promiscuity — usu. used in the phrase *sow one's wild oats*

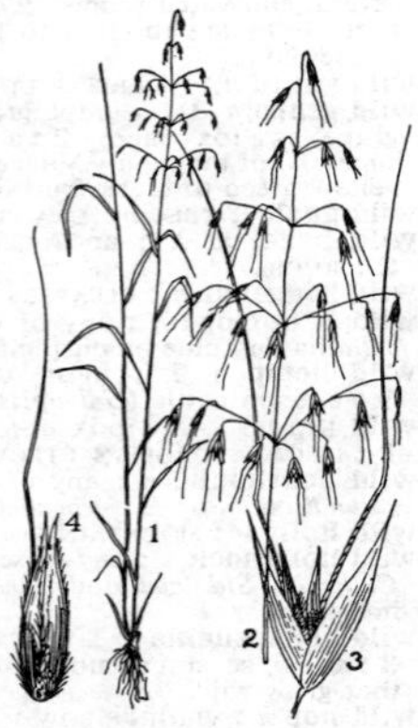

wild oat 1a (1): *1* whole plant, *2* panicle, *3* single spikelet, *4* lemma

wild oat grass *n* **1 :** WILD OAT 1 **2 :** YELLOW OAT GRASS **3 :** a grass of the genus *Danthonia*

wild-oat kicker *n* **:** a grain cleaner in which the sieve is so constructed that the kernels come to an angle in the throat which they cannot pass through and are kicked backward in the direction of the throw of the sieve and eventually discharged from the machine

wild oleander *n* **:** SWAMP LOOSESTRIFE

wild olive *n* **1 :** OLEASTER 2 **2 :** any of various trees that resemble the olive or have fruits resembling its fruit: as **a :** TUPELO 1 **b :** SILVER BELL **c :** DEVILWOOD **d :** MASTIC BULLY **e :** OLEASTER 1; *also* **:** any of several related shrubs and trees **f :** JAVA ALMOND **g :** MOUNTAIN PLUM **h** (1) **:** an Indian tree (*Elaeocarpus serratus*) with a lightweight streaked grayish wood (2) **:** a tree (*Putranjiva roxburghii*) of the family Euphorbiaceae of southeastern Asia with leaves and fruits used in folk medicine

wild onion *n* **1 :** any of several plants of the genus *Allium:* as **a :** NODDING ONION **b :** CROW GARLIC **2** *West* **:** DEATH CAMAS **3 :** a bulbless fleshy-leaved Australian plant (*Breebine semibarbata*) of the family Liliaceae

wild opium *n* **1 :** WILD LETTUCE 1c **2 :** PRICKLY LETTUCE

wild orange *n* **1 :** TRIFOLIATE ORANGE **2 :** *South* **:** CHERRY LAUREL 1 **3** *Austral* **:** WILD LEMON 2a **4 :** a West Indian tree (*Drypetes glauca*) of the family Euphorbiaceae **5 :** HERCULES'-CLUB 1a

wild orange lily *n* **:** WOOD LILY 1b

wild pansy *n* **:** a common and long-cultivated European herb (*Viola tricolor*) which has rounded basal leaves and pinnately parted stem leaves and short-spurred flowers that are prevailingly blue or purple mixed with white and yellow and from which most of the common garden pansies are derived — called also *heartsease, johnny-jump-up*

wild parsley *n* **:** any of numerous wild plants of the family Umbelliferae with finely divided foliage resembling that of parsley; *esp* **:** CORN PARSLEY

wild parsnip *n* **:** the wild original form of the cultivated parsnip growing as a weed in both Europe and America and having an acrid and bitter root

wild passionflower *n* **:** MAYPOP

wild pea *n* **:** any of several usu. vining plants of the family Leguminosae and esp. of the genera *Lathyrus, Vicia,* or *Strophostyles*

wild peach *n* **1 :** any of various trees or shrubs of the genus *Prunus* (esp. *P. andersonii*) **2** *South* **:** CHERRY LAUREL 1 **3 :** an African tree of the genus *Kiggelaria* (family Flacourteaceae)

wild peanut *n* **:** HOG PEANUT

wild pear *n* **1 :** an uncultivated shrub or tree of the genus *Pyrus* **2 :** a So. American timber tree (*Clethra tinifolia*) that resembles the pear tree in habit and foliage

wild pennyroyal *n* **:** any of several low-growing aromatic herbs of the family Labiatae (esp. of the genera *Mentha* and *Satureia*)

wild pepper *n* **1 :** a tropical Old World shrub (*Vitex trifolia*) with pleasantly aromatic foliage and seeds that are used in folk medicine **2** *dial Eng* **:** YARROW **3 :** JACK-IN-THE-PULPIT **4 :** PAINTED TRILLIUM

wild peppergrass *n* **:** PEPPERGRASS 1

wild petunia *n* **:** a plant of the genus *Ruellia*

wild pig *n* **:** PECCARY

wild pigeon *n* **:** an undomesticated pigeon: as **a :** ROCK PIGEON **b :** PASSENGER PIGEON

wild pine *n* **1 :** SCOTCH PINE **2 :** any of various West Indian plants of the family Bromeliaceae; *esp* **:** PINGUIN

wild pineapple *n* **1 :** PINGUIN **2 :** either of two plants of the genus *Ananas* (*A. bracteata* and *A. magdalenae*)

wild pink *n* **1 a :** an American catchfly of the genus *Silene; esp* **:** a catchfly (*S. caroliniana*) of the eastern U. S. having pale-pink or whitish flowers **b :** any of several pinks (as the Deptford pink) growing wild **2 :** an orchid (*Arethusa bulbosa*) with sepals and petals arching over the column and typically magenta pink

wild pitch *n* **:** a baseball pitch that cannot be caught or controlled by the catcher with ordinary effort and that enables a base runner to advance

wild plantain *n* **:** a tropical American plant (*Heliconia caribaea*) resembling the banana but having brilliant orange flowers with scarlet sheaths and leaves that are used in the West Indies as coverings for packages

wild plum *n* **1 :** an uncultivated plum; *esp* **:** one of a species (as *Prunus domestica* or *P. americana*) that is closely related to or a source of the cultivated plums **2 :** WILD PRUNE **3 :** BLACK APPLE

wild portulaca *n* **:** a purslane (*Portulaca oleracea*)

wild potato *n* **1 :** MAN-OF-THE-EARTH 1 **2 :** a tropical American plant (*Ipomoea fastigiata*) sometimes held to be the source of the sweet potato **3 :** WAPATOO **4 :** a spring beauty (*Claytonia virginica*)

wild prune *n* **:** a southern African tree (*Pappea capensis*) having hard wood used for furniture; *also* **:** the edible red fruit of the wild prune resembling that of the cherry

wild pumpkin *n* **:** PRAIRIE GOURD

wild quinine *n* **:** AMERICAN FEVERFEW

wild radish *or* **wild rape** *n* **:** any of several plants of the genus *Raphanus; esp* **:** JOINTED CHARLOCK

wild raisin *n* **1 :** SHEEPBERRY 1 **2 :** WITHE ROD

wild red cherry *n* **:** PIN CHERRY

wild red currant *n* **1 :** a straggling or reclining shrub (*Ribes triste*) with branches often rooting and purplish to smoke-colored flowers **2 :** a red-fruited southern African shrub or tree of the genus *Rhus* (esp. *R. laevegata*)

wild red oat *n* **:** an oat (*Avena sterilis*) of the Mediterranean region sometimes held to be the progenitor of the modern cultivated oat

wild red raspberry *n* **:** RED RASPBERRY 1a, 1b **:** RED RASPBERRY

wild rhubarb *n* **:** CANAIGRE

wild rice *n* **1 a :** a tall aquatic No. American perennial grass (*Zizania aquatica*) with panicles bearing pistillate flowers above and staminate below and grain that is used for food formerly esp. by the Indians and now also gathered and marketed **b :** an Asiatic grass (*Z. latifolia*) resembling No. American wild rice **2 :** SHAMA MILLET

wild rocket *n* **1 :** a spider flower (*Cleome serrulata*) **2 :** HEDGE MUSTARD

wild rose *n* **1 :** any of various roses growing wild: as **a :** SWEETBRIER **b :** SWAMP ROSE **2 :** a dark pink that is bluer and deeper than dusty coral and stronger and slightly lighter than colonial rose

wild rosemary *n* **1 :** BOG ROSEMARY **2 :** MARSH TEA **3 :** a small Australian shrub (*Cassinia laevis*) of the family Compositae

wild rubber *n* **:** rubber derived from uncultivated trees and esp. from a Brazilian tree (*Hevea brasiliensis*) as distinguished from that derived from plantation trees — compare PARA RUBBER

wild rye *n* **:** any of several grasses of the genus *Elymus*

wild sage *n* **1 :** a Eurasian sage (*Salvia verbenaca*) that is naturalized in No. America and has blue flowers and foliage resembling that of the verbena — called also *vervain sage, wild clary* **2 :** SAGEBRUSH **3 :** RED SAGE

wild sago *n* **:** COONTIE

wild sapodilla *n* **:** ⁴DILLY 2

wild sarsaparilla *n* **1 :** a common No. American perennial herb (*Aralia nudicaulis*) having long-stalked basal ternate leaves with pinnately 3- to 5-foliolate divisions, greenish flowers borne usu. in three simple umbels, and aromatic roots used as a substitute for sarsaparilla **2 :** a catbrier (*Smilax glauca*)

wild senna *n* **:** any of various plants of the genus *Cassia; esp* **:** a No. American perennial herb (*C. marilandica*) the leaves of which are used medicinally in the same manner as the officinal senna

wild sensitive plant *n* **:** any of several herbs of the genus *Cassia* **:** SENSITIVE PEA

wild service tree *also* **wild service** *n* **:** SERVICE TREE 1b

wild sheep *n* **:** an undomesticated sheep (as the argali, the mouflon, or the bighorn)

wild silk *n* **:** silk furnished by wild silkworms — compare TUSSAH

wild silkworm *n* **:** any of various chiefly Asiatic silkworms which have not been domesticated (as the tussah, yamamai, pernyi, and ailanthus silkworms) and whose silk is commercially valuable

wild snakeroot *n* **:** GROUND IVY 1

wild snapdragon *n* **:** a toadflax (*Linaria vulgaris*)

wild snowball *n* **:** NEW JERSEY TEA

wild spikenard *n* **1 :** FALSE SPIKENARD **2 :** WILD SARSAPARILLA 1

wild spinach *n* **:** any of several plants of the genus *Chenopodium* (as *C. album* and *C. bonus-henricus*) sometimes used as substitutes for spinach

wild stonecrop *n* **:** a succulent herb (*Sedum ternatum*) of rocky woods in the eastern U.S. that is often cultivated for its cymose white flowers

wild strawberry *n* **1 :** an uncultivated plant of the genus *Fragaria:* as **a :** a European plant (*F. vesca*) naturalized or native in No. America having luscious red or rarely white fruit and being one of the species used in breeding the common garden strawberry **b :** VIRGINIA STRAWBERRY **c :** CHILEAN STRAWBERRY **2 :** the fruit of a wild strawberry plant

wild succory *n* **:** CHICORY

wild sunflower *n* **1 :** any of several uncultivated plants of the genus *Helianthus* **2 :** ELECAMPANE

wild swan *n* **:** any swan except the tamed mute swan; *esp* **:** WHOOPER SWAN

wild sweet pea *n* **:** CATGUT 3a

wild sweet potato *n* **1 :** MAN-OF-THE-EARTH 1 **2 :** SAND VINE

wild sweet william *n, often cap 2d W* **1 :** a phlox (*Phlox maculata*) of the eastern U.S. often cultivated for its blue or purple flowers **2 :** WILD BLUE PHLOX **3 :** a soapwort (*Saponaria officinalis*)

wild tamarind *n* **:** any of several West Indian trees (as *Lysiloma bahamensis* and species of *Pithecolobium*) that resemble the tamarind

wild tansy *n* **1 :** RAGWEED 2a **2 :** YARROW

wild tare *n* **:** any of several vetches; *esp* **:** NARROW-LEAVED VETCH

wild teasel *n* **:** a Eurasian herb (*Dipsacus sylvestris*) that resembles fuller's teasel and is naturalized in the U.S.

wild thyme *n* **:** a perennial thyme (*Thymus serpyllum*) that is common on banks and hillsides in Europe and naturalized in the U.S. and spreads by creeping stems — called also *creeping thyme*

wild tobacco *n* **1 :** any of several plants of the genus *Nicotiana:* as **a :** a shrubby poisonous So. American herb (*N. glauca*) widely naturalized — called also *marihuana, tree tobacco* **b :** an herb (*N. rustica*) of eastern No. America formerly cultivated by the Indians **2 :** a tropical shrub (*Solanum verbascifolium*) with white flowers and yellow fruit **3 :** a tropical American herb (*Pluchea odorata*) with aromatic foliage and pink flowers **4 :** INDIAN TOBACCO 1

wild tomato *n* **1 :** BLOODBERRY **2 :** HORSENETTLE; *also* **:** a related weed (*Solanum triflorum*) with deeply pinnatifid leaves and green berries

wild tonguegrass *n* **:** PEPPERGRASS 1

wild tulip *n* **1 a :** a native European tulip (*Tulipa sylvestris*) **b** *dial Eng* **:** GUINEA-HEN FLOWER **2 :** MARIPOSA LILY

wild turnip *n* **1 a :** any of several plants of the genus *Brassica; esp* **:** RUTABAGA **b :** WILD RADISH **2 :** JACK-IN-THE-PULPIT **3 :** BREADROOT 1

wild type *n* **:** the typical form of an organism as ordinarily encountered in nature in contrast to atypical mutant individuals whether naturally occurring or induced in the laboratory

wild valerian *n* **:** GARDEN HELIOTROPE 1

wild vanilla *n* **:** a perennial herb (*Trilisa odoratissima*) of the southeastern U.S. with leaves having the fragrance of vanilla and being sometimes mixed with tobacco to give aroma

wild vetch *n* **1 :** PRAIRIE TREFOIL **2 :** any of various vetches (esp. *Vicia cracca*)

wild vine *n* **:** a vine that grows wild: as **a :** BRYONY **b :** BLACK BRYONY **c :** FOX GRAPE

wild wall *n* **:** a flat on a motion picture or television set that can be quickly and silently removed during shooting

wild west *also* **wild western** *adj, often cap 1st W & usu cap 2d W* [fr. *Wild West*, name applied to the western U.S. in its frontier period] **:** of, relating to, or concerned with the western U.S. in its frontier and lawless period ⟨*wild West* magazine⟩ ⟨*wild West* show⟩

wild wheat *n* **:** a wheat (*Triticum dicoccum dicoccoides*) that occurs wild in Palestine, is sometimes held to be the prototype of cultivated wheat, and has a brittle rachis with the joints separating at maturity and stiff glumes holding the kernels very tightly — called also *wild emmer*

wildwind \ˈ≈,≈\ *n* **:** HURRICANE

wild winterpea *n* **:** SINGLETARY PEA

wild wisteria *n* **:** GROUNDNUT 2a

wildwood \ˈ≈,≈\ *n* **:** a wood unaltered or unfrequented by man

wild woodbine *n* **1 :** VIRGINIA CREEPER **2 :** YELLOW JESSAMINE 2

wild yam *n* **1 :** any of various uncultivated plants of the genus *Dioscorea* (as *D. paniculata* of eastern No. America) **2 :** NATIVE POTATO 1

wild yeast *n* **:** any of various yeasts occurring naturally in the air or on surfaces esp. of fruits as distinguished from those selected and artificially cultivated (as for use in brewing or baking)

wild yellow lily *n* **:** MEADOW LILY

¹wile \ˈwīl, *esp before pause or consonant* ˈwīəl\ *n* -s [ME *wil*, fr. (assumed) ONF, prob. of Gmc origin; akin to OE *wigle* divination, sorcery — more at WITCH] **1 :** a trick or stratagem intended to ensnare or deceive **:** a sly artifice; *also* **:** a beguiling or playful trick **2 :** TRICKERY, DECEITFULNESS, GUILE **syn** see TRICK

²wile \"\ *vt* -ED/-ING/-S [ME *wilen*, fr. *wil* wile] **1 :** to lure by or as if by a magic spell **:** ENTICE, BEGUILE, ALLURE ⟨his sermons would ~ the birds from the trees —John Buchan⟩ **2** [perh. alter. (influenced in meaning by L *decipere diem*, lit., to cheat the time, F *tromper le temps*) of *while*] **:** to pass or spend pleasurably **:** WHILE — often used with *away* ⟨~ away the long days —Virginia Woolf⟩

wile·ly \ˈwī(ə)llē\ *adj* [¹*wile* + *-ly*] **:** WILY

wil·fley table \ˈwilflē-\ *n, usu cap W* [after *Wilfley*, its inventor] **:** a sand table that separates heavy mineral particles from lighter gangue by means of longitudinal riffles impeding the downward flow and a horizontal reciprocating motion carrying the heavy particles off the end of the table — compare SHAKING TABLE

wilful *var of* WILLFUL

wil·ga \ˈwilgə\ *n* -s [fr. native name in New South Wales] **:** an Australian plant of the genus *Geijera* (family Rutaceae); *esp* **:** a tree (*G. parviflora*) with aromatic hard wood and foliage resembling that of a willow

wil·ger \ˈwilgə(r)\ *n* -s [ME *wilghe* willow — more at WILLOW] **:** OSIER 1a

wil·helms·ha·ven \ˈvil,helmz,hävən\ *adj, usu cap* [fr. *Wilhelmshaven*, seaport of northwest Germany] **:** of or from the city of Wilhelmshaven, Germany **:** of the kind or style prevalent in Wilhelmshaven

wilier *comparative of* WILY

wiliest *superlative of* WILY

wil·i·ly \ˈwīlə̇lē, -əli\ *adv* **:** in a wily manner **:** SLYLY

wil·i·ness \-ilēnə̇s, -lin-\ *n* -ES **:** the quality or state of being wily

wi·li·wi·li \ˈwēlēˈwēlē\ *n* -s [Hawaiian] **:** any of several coral trees of the islands of the Pacific ocean having light soft wood which is often used for the outriggers of canoes; *esp* **:** a Hawaiian tree (*Erythrina sandwicensis*) with brilliant orange-red or sometimes yellow flowers

wilk \ˈwilk\ *archaic var of* WHELK

wil·ke·ite \ˈwilkē,īt\ *n* -s [R. M. *Wilke*, 20th cent. Am. mineral collector + E *-ite*] **:** a mineral consisting of an hydroxyl-apatite in which phosphorous is partly replaced by carbon, sulfur, silicon, or a combination thereof — compare APATITE

¹will \wəl, (ə)l, (ˌ)wil\ *vb, past* **would** \wəd, ˌ(ə)d, (ˌ)wu̇d\ *or archaic 2d sing* **wouldst** \ˌwə(d)zt, (ˌ)wu̇(d)zt, -dst, -tst\ *or* **would·est** \ˈwu̇də̇st\ *pres sing & pl* **will** *or archaic 2d sing* **wilt** \ˌwəlt, (ˌ)wilt\ [ME *wille, will, wil* wish, wishes, desire, desires, intend, intends (1st & 3d sing. pres. indic., past *wolde, wold*, infin. *willen*), fr. OE *will, wylle* (past *wolde*, infin. *wyllan*); akin to OHG *willu* wish, will, *wili* wishes, will (infin. *wellen, wollen*), ON *vilja* wish, will, *vill* wishes, will (infin. *vilja*), *velja* to choose, Goth *wiljau* wish, will, *wili* wishes, will (infin. *wiljan*), *waljan* to choose, L *velle* to wish, Gk (Doric) *lēn*, Skt *vr̥ṇoti* he chooses, likes] *vt* **:** DESIRE, WISH ⟨call it what you ~⟩ — often used in the form *would* with an object clause ⟨*would* that I were young again⟩ ⟨I *would* to heaven I had never seen him⟩ ~ *verbal auxiliary* **1** — used to express desire, choice, willingness, consent, or in negative constructions refusal ⟨apparently the immortal gods ~ have no part in this affair —John Buchan⟩ ⟨perverse set of facial muscles that ~ not, like those of other people, interpret the language of his soul —Emily Brontë⟩ ⟨how long ~ we put up with the . . . refusal of refrigerators to fit —*Pencil Points*⟩ ⟨could find no one who *would* take the job⟩ ⟨if we ~ all do our best, we shall succeed⟩ ⟨~ you please stop that racket⟩ **2** — used to express frequent, customary, or habitual action or natural tendency or disposition ⟨has a quick temper and ~ get angry over nothing⟩ ⟨*would* fall asleep reading his newspaper⟩ ⟨~ sit for hours watching the sea⟩ ⟨~ work one day and loaf the next⟩ **3 a** — used to express simple futurity ⟨much like a delayed action bomb that ~ not explode for half a generation —C.P.Taft⟩ ⟨cherish the belief that some day a perfect society ~ banish evil —Crane Brinton⟩ ⟨tomorrow morning I ~ wake up in this first-class hotel suite —Tennessee Williams⟩ ⟨have not employed it and probably never ~ —R.W.Bliss⟩ ⟨some other time we ~ say what it was —*Notes & Queries*⟩ ⟨list . . . ~ be sent as usual for a stamped and addressed envelope —May L. Becker⟩ ⟨cannot foresee what ~ happen, but a study of past changes may give us an idea as to what may happen —C.E.P. Brooks⟩ ⟨problem of corruption and morality ~ remain very real and earnest —Estes Kefauver⟩ **b** — used to express simple action or intention without conscious reference to future time ⟨quite a famous view . . . good many people ~ stop and take pictures of it —G.W.Brace⟩ ⟨we ~ now illustrate the procedure in detail —Z.S.Harris⟩ ⟨I ~ give you two propositions for the year 1778: a little learning was a dangerous thing, and so was being an American —A.W.Griswold⟩ **4** — used to express capability or sufficiency ⟨square pegs ~ not fit in round holes⟩ ⟨this ~ do if there is nothing better⟩ ⟨back seat ~ hold three passengers⟩ ⟨might go for a tramp somewhere. My finances ~ just run to it —John Buchan⟩ ⟨this ~ serve to illustrate the kind of problem —F.N.Robinson⟩ ⟨found that his old rubbers

would not go over his new shoes⟩ ⟨three yards of cloth ~ make a skirt and jacket⟩ **5** — used to express probability or recognition and often equivalent to the simple verb ⟨that ~ be the milkman at the back door⟩ ⟨this house with the green shutters ~ be theirs⟩ ⟨she *would* have been about twenty when she married⟩ ⟨discover a plant growing and clinging close to the rocks. This ~ be the walking fern or walking leaf —Anne Dorrance⟩ ⟨glass that hides the pendulum ~ often display a fine example of primitive painting —Ellwood Kirby⟩ **6 a** — used to express determination, insistence, persistence, or willfulness ⟨I have made up my mind to go and go I ~⟩ ⟨for some perverse reason he ~ put his worst foot forward⟩ ⟨had what the doctors ~ call influenza, as though there were only one form of it —Lord Dunsany⟩ ⟨police are excellent fellows, but . . . they ~ hare off after motive, which is a matter for psychologists —Dorothy Sayers⟩ **b** — used to express inevitability ⟨accidents ~ happen⟩ ⟨what ~ be, ~ be⟩ ⟨murder ~ out⟩ **7** — used to express a command, exhortation, or injunction ⟨you ~ do as I say, at once⟩ ⟨color arrangements ~ be as prescribed in instructions issued by the Commanding General —*Army Regulations & Ordinances*⟩ ⟨proposing . . . that all disputes . . . ~ be referred to an impartial tribunal —T.F. Reynolds⟩ ⟨with his petition the applicant ~ produce the evidence on which he relies—F.J.Grant⟩ ~ *vi* **1 :** to have a wish or desire **:** be inclined or disposed **:** be pleased ⟨Lord, if thou *wilt*, thou canst make me clean —Mt 8:2 (AV)⟩ ⟨for better, for worse, and whether we ~ or no —*advt*⟩ ⟨factors for which man is responsible and which he can control or change if he ~ —L.A.White⟩ **2** *archaic* **:** will go ⟨thither ~ I then —Sir Walter Scott⟩ — **if you will :** if you wish to call it that ⟨a kind of preoccupation, or obsession *if you will* —Louis Auchincloss⟩ — **will I, nill I** *or* **will he, nill he** *or* **will ye, nill ye :** whether I, he, or you will it or not **:** WILLY-NILLY

²will \ˈwil\ *n* -s [ME *wille, will, wile, wil*, fr. OE *willa, will*; akin to OHG *willo, willio* will, ON *vili, vil*, Goth *wilja* will, *wiljan* to wish — more at ¹WILL] **1 :** DESIRE, WISH; *esp* **:** a desire to act in a particular way: **a :** DISPOSITION, INCLINATION, LIKING ⟨my poverty, but not my ~, consents —Shak.⟩ ⟨not, sir, from want of ~, for she is docile and obedient —W.H. Hudson †1922⟩ ⟨primary determinant is the claims of the parties, their desires and ~*s* —Samuel Alexander⟩ ⟨responsible artist has no ~ to confuse emotion and thinking —René Wellek & Austin Warren⟩; *often* **:** desire or inclination to act in a particular way in contrast to means or ability ⟨had a strong ~ to succeed but little capacity⟩ ⟨where there's a ~ there's a way⟩ ⟨perceived that granted the ~ they could link their abilities to the new world —*Times Lit. Supp.*⟩ ⟨with the best ~ in the world . . . could not live forever —Max Peacock⟩ ⟨proof of their capacity and ~ to watch and warn and purge — B.N.Cardozo⟩ **b :** fleshly or carnal desire **:** APPETITE, PASSION ⟨a fear of hunger and death, and a ~ for food and springtime and life —Emma Hawkridge⟩ ⟨his own ~ stirred to the woman —Dan Jacobson⟩ **c :** CHOICE, DETERMINATION, INTENTION ⟨a universe as devoid of ~ and purpose as man, deterministically viewed, appears to be —F.B.Millett⟩ ⟨too much disposed to make the empire a thing of plan and ~ —H.G. Wells⟩ ⟨impels you to do things against your reasoned ~ and intentions —Rose Macaulay⟩ **2 a :** something wished for or desired; *esp* **:** a choice or determination of one having authority, discretion, or power ⟨thy ~ be done —Mt 6:10 (AV)⟩ ⟨he holds him with his glittering eye . . . the mariner hath his ~ —S.T.Coleridge⟩ ⟨failed to accomplish his ~⟩ ⟨determined to have his ~ of them⟩ ⟨will do it . . . if it is God's ~ that it should be done —Gilbert Parker⟩ ⟨the means at his disposal for making his ~ known by the written word —R.W.Southern⟩ ⟨let him be apprehended and learn our awful ~ —W.S.Gilbert⟩ ⟨man's attempt to impose his own ~ on things —Norman Goodall⟩ **b** (1) *archaic* **:** an expression of a desire or a determination **:** REQUEST, COMMAND, DECREE (2) [fr. the phrase *our will is* which introduces it] **:** the part of a summons or other signet letter that expresses its will or command **3 :** the act or process or the felt or known experience of willing: **a :** the act of choosing or determining **:** settlement of mental uncertainty or indecision **:** choice or decision of a mental issue **:** VOLITION 2 **b :** the total conscious process involved in effecting a decision **c :** action directed esp. toward a goal clearly known in advance and requiring effort to overcome obstacles or contrary desires — compare CONATION **4 a :** a mental power or a disposition or the sum of mental powers or dispositions manifested in such operations and functions as wishing, choosing, desiring, intending ⟨the precise relation between the activities of human ~*s* and other forms of activity in the natural world is a highly speculative problem —H.H.Williams⟩: as (1) *Scholasticism* **:** the faculty of the soul coordinate with the intellect that determines rational choices in accordance with what the intellect has determined as good or bad; *also* **:** a choice determined by the will esp. as distinguished from instinctive or purely natural desires (2) **:** a faculty of the mind that is usu. contrasted with thought and feeling and determines action and esp. moral action in accordance with ideals, principles, and facts ⟨the moral ~, controlled by consciousness of duty that transcends sense and experience —John Dewey⟩ (3) **:** the combined rational and irrational, conscious and unconscious forces within a person that determine his choices and actions ⟨the ~ . . . is a collective term for all the impulses to motion or action —G.S.Morris⟩; *also* **:** the rational conscious forces or the irrational unconscious forces separately ⟨what people want when they talk about freedom . . . is the idea that the conscious ~ is the master of their destiny —John Hospers⟩ (4) **:** a disposition to act according to particular principles or to conform in conduct and thought to particular or ideal ends ⟨the ~ to believe⟩ ⟨the ~ to agree⟩ ⟨pathetically preserve the ~ to conquer, even when life no longer presents them with anything worth winning —Lawrence Binyon⟩ ⟨like all the young ladies of fiction in her period, she had cultivated the ~ to faint —S.M.Crothers⟩ — compare GOOD WILL, ILL WILL **b :** the collective desire, intention, or determination of a group or of mankind either when all are agreed or as determined by an interplay and elimination of divergent and conflicting wishes ⟨the ~ of the people⟩ ⟨give expression to a national ~ —W.J.Shepard⟩ ⟨the law cannot be more important than the local ~ to have this law —Spencer Parratt⟩ ⟨yielded to what was clearly the popular ~ —Lindsay Rogers⟩ **c** *often cap* **:** a transcendent reality of which individual wills are particular and partial manifestations **5 :** power coupled with desire or intention: **a :** power to control, determine, or dispose **:** arbitrary disposal ⟨deliver me not over unto the ~ of mine enemies —Ps 27:12 (AV)⟩ ⟨victims of a despot's ~⟩ ⟨the nameless chief whose ~ raised this stupendous fortress — Jacquetta & Christopher Hawkes⟩ ⟨the serf did not know today what he would have to do tomorrow — he was at the ~ of another —R.W.Southern⟩ **b :** power of controlling one's own actions or emotions **:** SELF-CONTROL, SELF-DIRECTION ⟨a man of iron ~⟩ ⟨faltering man . . . advanced a step or two by his own ~ —Thomas Hardy⟩ ⟨wife who was just my shadow without any character or ~ of her own —Havelock Ellis⟩ ⟨his ~, so long lying fallow, was overborne by her determination — Joseph Conrad⟩ ⟨the sudden collapse of her ~ when the strangers enter her house —Bernard De Voto⟩ **c :** the power of choosing and of acting in accordance with choice ⟨an indomitable ~ that knew but one course — to break as much new land as possible each day —O.E.Rölvaag⟩ ⟨science, which gave us this dread power . . . does not show us how to prevent its baleful use. Only in the ~ of universal disarmament lies the answer —B.M.Baruch⟩ **6 :** a legal declaration of a person's mind as to the manner in which he would have his property or estate disposed of after his death; *esp* **:** a written instrument legally executed by which a man makes disposition of his estate to take effect after his death — see NUNCUPATIVE WILL; compare DEED, TESTAMENT — **against one's will :** in opposition to one's own inclination or to another's wish or intention ⟨was practicing the violin, as usual *against his will*⟩ ⟨father disowned her for marrying *against his will*⟩ — **at will** *adv* **:** as one wishes **:** as or when it pleases or suits oneself ⟨dreamer apparently moves about *at will* in the past, as well as in the present —Weston La Barre⟩ ⟨blues sweep up from below, driving the school to the surface, there feeding upon them *at will* —L.K.Parritt⟩ ⟨mounted . . . on bases that could be rotated *at will* —*Military Rev.*⟩ **:** subject to one's discretion or pleasure **:** at one's disposal ⟨where person enters land by permission of owner for an indefinite period, and without reservation of rent, he is tenant *at will* by implication —*North Eastern Reporter*⟩ — **of one's own will** *or* **of one's own free will :** of one's own accord **:** VOLUNTARILY — **one's own sweet will :** one's own wish or intention ⟨disposing of it in the fullness of time at *his own sweet will* —Edward Sapir⟩ — **with a will** *adv* **:** with willingness and zeal **:** EARNESTLY, ENERGETICALLY, HEARTILY ⟨went to work *with a will* to qualify himself —H.E. Scudder⟩

³will \"\ *vb* -ED/-ING/-S [ME *willen*, fr. OE *willian*, fr. *willa* will] *vt* **1** *archaic* **:** to long for **:** DESIRE, WISH **2 a :** to order or direct by a will or testament ⟨~*ed* that his property be divided equally among his children⟩ **b** (1) **:** to dispose of or give by a will **:** BEQUEATH, DEVISE ⟨~*ed* his entire estate to his wife⟩ ⟨~*ed* his property away from his own family⟩ (2) **:** to hand down or transmit as if by a will or testament ⟨the abundant beauty he ~*ed* to the world —*Time*⟩ ⟨these things are literally in our blood and in our bones . . . ~*ed* to us genetically — Weston La Barre⟩ **3 :** to determine by the will (as to do something or that something shall be done or shall come about): as **a** (1) **:** to decide or decide upon by an act of choice or volition ⟨fully aware that he lives in an age of conformity, he is proud that his conformity is ~*ed* —Leo Marx⟩ ⟨the assumption . . . that institutions are rational and ~*ed* —H.J.Muller⟩ ⟨American people . . . have ~*ed* that all of their sons and daughters shall be educated to the limit of their capacity —*English Language Arts*⟩ ⟨efforts of the business man can never be successful unless the community ~*s* it so —Roy Lewis & Angus Maude⟩ (2) **:** DECREE, ORDAIN ⟨if Providence so ~*s* it⟩ (3) **:** INTEND, PURPOSE ⟨~*ed* more mischief than they durst — A.E.Housman⟩ ⟨can adjust a few screws, then go away entirely, knowing that his precise work will be finished for him exactly as he ~*ed* it —Roger Burlingame⟩ ⟨believe that whatever is ~*ed* can be achieved if only you invent the right machines —Norman Podhoretz⟩ **b** (1) **:** to attempt to cause or bring about by exercise of the will ⟨haunted by the thought that he had ~*ed* her death⟩ ⟨all humans desire objects and ~ their attainment —Samuel Alexander⟩ ⟨a positive nihilist, an intellectual force ~*ing* destruction —T.S.Eliot⟩ ⟨author ~*s* a meaning into a passage that cannot sustain it —Charles Jackson⟩ (2) **:** to bring about by power of the will ⟨the more accurate understanding of disease . . . that some of it is psychological, even to the extent that it is ~*ed* by the patient — H.A.Overstreet⟩ ⟨a last despairing attempt to ~ the kind of life he wanted into existence —D.H.Lawrence⟩ ⟨entranced, he tried . . . to ~ the vision to remain —Olive Johnson⟩ ⟨~*ed* his countenance back to composure —J.H.Wheelwright⟩ **c :** to influence or control (as another person) by exercise of one's will (as through hypnotism) **4** *archaic* **:** COMMAND, ENJOIN, ORDER ~ *vi* **1 :** to exercise the will ⟨striving might be bearable were there a highest good, to which, by ~*ing*, I could attain — Josiah Royce⟩ ⟨would no longer have to go on ~*ing* against her —F.M.Ford⟩ **2 :** DESIRE, WISH: as **a :** DECIDE, DETERMINE, DECREE ⟨king nominated as he ~*ed* to bishopric and abbacy — Hilaire Belloc⟩ ⟨the right . . . to dispose of his labor and capital as he ~*ed* —C.A.Cooke⟩ **b :** CHOOSE, ELECT, PREFER ⟨watching the . . . donkeys and mules which wandered as they ~*ed* —Nicholas Monsarrat⟩ ⟨trees that have grown where they ~*ed* out of the jumble —Martin Flavin⟩

syn WILL, BEQUEATH, DEVISE, LEAVE, and LEGATE can mean to give a part or the whole of one's possessions to another by a last will and testament. WILL implies the provision or the existence of a last will and testament ⟨*will* your property to your children⟩ ⟨*will* a sum of money to a charitable institution⟩ BEQUEATH is much used in wills by the testator and in legal, historical, and literary use, often implying no more than a proved intention ⟨*bequeath* to each of my sons an equal division of all I own⟩ ⟨*bequeathed* to the organization his personal fortune and the entire income from his real estate⟩ BEQUEATH in legal use is commonly distinguished from DEVISE by implying a gift of personalty rather than a gift of realty ⟨*devised* his library, his public and private papers and letters, as well as the stately "Mount Vernon" with its surrounding 4,000 acres —G.W.Goble⟩ LEAVE is the usual unspecific term for any of the preceding terms ⟨at his death the man *left* his small independent income to his brother⟩ ⟨*leave* a legacy to the town⟩ LEGATE is the same as BEQUEATH except in always implying a formal will ⟨my library of manuscripts I *legate* to my alma mater⟩

⁴will \"\ *adv* (*or adj*) [ME, fr. ON *villr* wild, gone astray — more at WILD] **1** *dial* **:** out of the way **:** ASTRAY **2** *dial* **:** at a loss

⁵will \"\ *vi* [ME *willen*, fr. ON *villask*, reflex. of *villa* to bewilder, fr. *villr* wild, bewildered, gone astray] *dial* **:** to become lost **:** go astray **:** WANDER

will·able \-ləbəl\ *adj* [³*will* + *-able*] **:** capable of being willed or wished **:** that may be determined by will

wil·lam·ette mite \wəˈlamət\ *n, usu cap W* [fr. *Willamette* river valley, northwest Oregon] **:** a plant-feeding mite (*Tetranychus willamettei*) that is a serious pest on raspberries in parts of the U.S. and Canada

will-call \ˈ=ˌ=\ *n* [fr. the phrase (*the purchaser*) *will call*] **1 :** a retail sale in which something is reserved by a deposit with full payment to be made when the merchandise is called for at a later date **2 :** LAYAWAY 2

willed \ˈwild\ *adj* [ME, fr. ²*will* + *-ed*] **1 :** having a will esp. of a specified kind — used chiefly in combination ⟨strong-*willed*⟩ ⟨weak-*willed*⟩ **2** *archaic* **:** DISPOSED, INCLINED — **willed·ness** \ˈwil(d)nəs\ *n* -ES

wil·lem·ite \ˈwiləˌmīt\ *n* -S [G *willemit*, fr. *Willem* (William) I †1843 king of the Netherlands + G *-it* -ite] **:** a mineral Zn_2SiO_4 consisting of zinc silicate, occurring in hexagonal prisms and in massive or granular forms, and varying in color from white or greenish yellow to green, reddish, and brown

will·er \ˈwilə(r)\ *n* -S [³*will* + *-er*] **:** one that wills; *esp* **:** one that wields an influence (as in hypnotism) by means of the will

willes·den \ˈwilzdən\ *adj, usu cap* [fr. *Willesden*, municipal borough of southeast England] **:** of or from the municipal borough of Willesden, England **:** of the kind or style prevalent in Willesden

willesden paper *n, usu cap W* **:** paper waterproofed by the Willesden process

willesden process *n, usu cap W* [so called fr. its original use in paper manufacturing at Willesden, England] **:** a process for waterproofing cellulose material (as paper, canvas, or rope) by passing it through Schweizer's reagent and drying to give a green varnished surface

wil·let \ˈwilət, *usu* -əd.+V\ *n, pl* **willet** [imit.] **:** a large shore bird (*Catoptrophorus semipalmatus*) of the eastern and Gulf coasts and the central parts of No. America having summer plumage barred and mottled with blackish patches and in winter the upperparts plain brownish gray, the breast pale gray, and the belly white

¹wil·ley \ˈwilē\ *n* -S [alter. of ¹*willy*] **:** WILLOW 3a

²willey \"\ *vt* **willeyed; willeyed; willeying; willeys :** to process (as cotton) with a willey **:** WILLOW

wil·ley·er \-ēə(r)\ *n* -S [²*willey* + *-er*] **1 :** WILLOWER 1 **2 :** WILLOW 3a

will·ful *or* **wil·ful** \ˈwilfəl\ *adj* [ME *wilful*, fr. (assumed) OE *wilful* willing (whence OE *wilfullice* willfully), fr. OE *wil* will + *-ful*] **1 :** governed by will without yielding to reason or without regard to reason **:** obstinately or perversely self-willed ⟨devil took possession . . . I became obstinate and ~ —L.N. Chambers⟩ ⟨seemed ~ as children, believing that the wish justified the act —C.B.Nordhoff & J.N.Hall⟩ ⟨the moral passions are even more ~ and imperious and impatient than the self-seeking passions —Lionel Trilling⟩ **:** STUBBORN ⟨possibly a few ~ people might deny that Vermont is the most beautiful state —Bernard DeVoto⟩ **2 :** done deliberately **:** not accidental or without purpose **:** INTENTIONAL, SELF-DETERMINED ⟨a ~ injury⟩ ⟨~ murder⟩ ⟨~ distortion of the facts⟩ ⟨alleged ~ failure to register —*Current Biog.*⟩ **3** *obs* **:** ready or disposed to comply **:** WILLING **4** *obs* **:** done of one's own free will **:** not compulsory **syn** see UNRULY, VOLUNTARY

will·ful·ly *or* **wil·ful·ly** \-fəlē, -li\ *adv* [ME *wilfully*, fr. OE *wilfullice*, fr. (assumed) OE *wilful* + OE *-lice* -ly] **:** in a willful manner

will·ful·ness *or* **wil·ful·ness** *n* -ES [ME *wilfulnesse*, fr. *wilful* + *-nesse* -ness] **:** the quality or state of being willful

will·ge·rodt-kin·dler reaction \ˈvilgəˌrōtˈkindlə(r)-\ *n, usu cap W&K* [after Conrad *Willgerodt*, 19th cent. Ger. chemist, and K. H. J. *Kindler* b1891 Ger. chemist] **:** a modified Willgerodt reaction in which the ketone is heated with sulfur and a dry amine in an open apparatus provided the amine (as morpholine) is sufficiently high boiling

willgerodt reaction *n, usu cap W* **:** a reaction usu. of an aryl alkyl ketone $ArCO(CH_2)_nH$ (as acetophenone) with an aqueous solution of yellow ammonium polysulfide in a heated sealed tube to yield an amide $Ar(CH_2)_{n-1}CONH_2$ (as alpha-phenyl-acetamide) substituted terminally by aryl

¹wil·liam \ˈwilyəm\ *n* -S *often cap* [fr. *bill*, after *Bill* (nickname for *William*): *William*, given name] **:** a piece of paper money **:** BILL ⟨a ten-dollar ~⟩

²william \"\ *usu cap* — a communications code word for the letter *w*

william and mary *n, usu cap W&M* [after *William* III †1702 and *Mary* II †1694 joint sovereigns of England] **:** a style of English furniture popular from about 1689 to the early 18th century that shows Dutch influence and is characterized by the use of walnut, grained veneers, trumpet legs, needlepoint upholstery, and teardrop brasses

wil·liam·ite \-yəˌmīt\ *n* -S *usu cap* [*William* III †1702 prince of Orange & King of England + E *-ite*] **:** a partisan of William of Orange

wil·liams·ite \ˈwilyəmˌzīt\ *n* -S [L. W. *Williams*, 19th cent. Am. mineral collector + E *-ite*] **:** a mineral consisting of a green variety of serpentine used for decorative purposes

wil·liam·so·nia \ˌwilyəmˈsōnēə\ *n, cap* [NL, fr. William C. *Williamson* †1895 Eng. naturalist + NL *-ia*] **:** a genus (the type of the family Williamsoniaceae) of fossil cycads having slender more or less branched stems and conspicuous bracts or scales associated with the fructification and occurring in rocks from the Upper Triassic to Middle Cretaceous in both the New and Old Worlds

wil·liam·son's blue \ˈwilyəmsənz-\ *or* **williamson's violet** *n, usu cap W* [after Alexander W. *Williamson* †1904 Eng. chemist] **:** any of several iron blue pigments

williamson synthesis *n, usu cap W* [after Alexander W. *Williamson* †1904] **:** a method of synthesizing ethers by reaction of a sodium alkoxide with a halogen derivative of a hydrocarbon (as an alkyl halide) ⟨ethyl cellulose is made by the *Williamson synthesis*⟩

wil·lie \ˈwilē\ *n* -S [prob. fr. waybill, after *Bill* (nickname for *William*); *Willie*, nickname for *William*] **:** a waybill for a loaded railroad car

willie-boy \ˈ=ˌ=\ *n, often cap W* [*Willie* (nickname for *William*) + E *boy*] *slang* **:** a dandified or effeminate young fellow

willied *past of* WILLY

wil·lie gow \ˈwiliˈgü\ *n* [*Willie* (nickname for *William*) + Sc *gow*, alter. of *gull*] *dial chiefly Scot* **:** HERRING GULL

willie haw·kie \-ˈhȯki\ *n* [*Willie* (nickname for *William*) + E dial. (Ir) *hawkie* grebe, of unknown origin] *Irish* **:** LITTLE GREBE

¹willies *pl of* WILLY, *pres 3d sing of* WILLY

²wil·lies \ˈwilēz, -liz\ *n pl* [origin unknown] **:** a fit of nervousness or of acute mental uneasiness or discomfort **:** CREEPS, HEEBIE-JEEBIES — used with *the* ⟨gives his mother the ~ by walking across on the handrails —John Sack⟩ ⟨always get the ~ when I see them sparks flying around —Maxwell Griffith⟩ ⟨keeping people fresh after they're dead. Give you the ~ —Ngaio Marsh⟩

willie wagtail *n* [*Willie* (nickname for *William*) + *wagtail*] **1** *Scot* **:** PIED WAGTAIL **2 :** a common, conspicuous, and very tame black-and-white wagtail (*Rhipidura leucophrys*) of Australia, New Guinea, and the Solomon islands

wil·lie-waught \ˈwiliˌwäkt\ *n* -S [by incorrect division fr. *guidwillie waught* in *Auld Lang Syne* by Robert Burns †1796 Scot. poet] **:** a deep draft (as of ale)

¹will·ing \ˈwiliŋ, -lēŋ\ *n* -S [ME, fr. OE *willung*, fr. *willian* to will + *-ung* -ing] *archaic* **:** DESIRE, LONGING

²willing \"\ *adj, sometimes* -ER/-EST [ME, fr. pres. part. of *willen* to be willing — more at ¹WILL] **1 :** inclined or favorably disposed in mind **:** READY ⟨felt ~ rather to starve at sea than to confront such perils —R.L.Stevenson⟩ **:** are ~ to prefer the better when the best is unattainable —M.R.Cohen⟩ ⟨must be ~ to be educated —Vera M. Dean⟩ ⟨~ and eager to help⟩ ⟨mothers are now ~, even anxious, to take their children to the nurses —Margaret Biddle⟩ **2 :** ready or prompt to act or to respond **:** not slow, lazy, or reluctant ⟨that instinct which makes each sex . . . the ~ slave of the other —Richard Jefferies⟩ ⟨~ workers⟩ ⟨a ~ horse⟩ ⟨turn a ~ ear to popular protests —V.L.Parrington⟩ ⟨where ears are ~, talk tends to be loud and long —Aldous Huxley⟩ ⟨a ~ source of information —Paul Moor⟩ ⟨wind . . . increased in strength, urging on the too ~ waves —*Harper's*⟩ **3** *archaic* **:** DESIROUS, WISHFUL **4** *obs* **:** DELIBERATE, INTENTIONAL **5 :** done or borne or given or accepted of choice or without reluctance **:** VOLUNTARY ⟨a ~ sacrifice⟩ ⟨~ obedience⟩ **6** [fr. pres. part. of ³*will*] **:** of or relating to the will or power of choosing **:** VOLITIONAL ⟨the ~ faculty⟩ **7** *Austral* **:** STRENUOUS ⟨a bit ~, but not too bad — G.H.Johnston⟩ **syn** see VOLUNTARY

³willing \"\ *adv, archaic* **:** WILLINGLY

willinghearted \ˈ=ˌ=ˈ=\ *adj* [²*willing* + *hearted*] **:** heartily willing or disposed

will·ing·hood \ˈwiliŋˌhu̇d\ *n* [²*willing* + *-hood*] **:** WILLINGNESS

will·ing·ly *adv* [ME, fr. ²*willing* + *-ly*] **:** in a willing manner

will·ing·ness *n* -ES **:** the quality or state of being willing

will-in-the-wisp *obs var of* WILL-O'-THE-WISP

wil·lis's artery \ˈwiləsəz-\ *n, usu cap W* [after Thomas *Willis* †1675 Eng. anatomist and physician] **:** COMMUNICATING ARTERY

willis's circle *n, usu cap W* [after Thomas *Willis* †1675] **:** CIRCLE OF WILLIS

willis's cords *or* **willis's trabeculae** *n pl, usu cap W* [after Thomas *Willis* †1675] **:** slender fibers crossing the venous sinuses of the dura mater esp. at the lower extremity of the superior sagittal sinus

willis system *n, usu cap W* [after Robert *Willis* †1875 Eng. mechanician] **:** a system of using for the generating circle of cycloidal teeth a circle equal in radius to a pinion having twelve teeth of the given pitch

wil·li·waw *or* **wil·ly·waw** \ˈwilēˌwȯ\ *or* **wul·li·wa** \ˈwəl-\ *n* -S [origin unknown] **1 a :** a sudden violent gust of cold land air common along mountainous coasts of high latitudes **b :** any sudden violent wind **2 :** a violent commotion or agitation **:** STORM, TEMPEST ⟨kicking up a great ~ of dust —*Time*⟩

will-less \ˈwilləs\ *adj* [²*will* + *-less*] **:** involving no exercise of the will **:** INVOLUNTARY ⟨blind *will-less* obedience⟩ **:** having no will **:** not exercising the will ⟨how circumstances . . . ensnared him and would have made *will-less* a far more intransigent character —Harvey Breit⟩ ⟨thinks human beings are as *will-less* as rats in a trap —J.T.Farrell⟩ ⟨baffled, unknowingly powerful, utterly *will-less* —*New Republic*⟩ — **will-less·ly** *adv* — **will-less·ness** *n* -ES

wil·lock \ˈwilək\ *n* -S [*Will* (nickname for *William*) + *-ock*] *chiefly Brit* **:** any of several birds of the family Alcidae: **a :** GUILLEMOT **b :** PUFFIN **c :** RAZORBILL 1

will-o'-the-wisp \ˌwiləthəˈwisp\ *also* **will-of-the-wisp** \-ləfth-\ *n* [*Will* (nickname for *William*) + *of* + *the* + *wisp*] **1 :** IGNIS FATUUS **2 :** a delusive goal ⟨followed the *will-o'-the-wisp* of universal disarmament —G.F.Eliot⟩ — **will-o'-the-wisp·ish** \-pish\ *adj*

¹wil·low \ˈwi(ˌ)lō, -lə; -ˌləw *or* -ˌlō+V\ *n* -S *often attrib* [ME *wilghe, welew, wilowe*, fr. OE *welig*; akin to MD, MLG, & MHG *wilge* willow, Gk *helikē*, and perh. to Gk *helissein* to wind — more at HELENIUM] **1 a :** a tree or shrub of the genus *Salix* many of which are of economic importance as sources of wood, osiers, or bark useful for tanning and a few of which (as the white willow and weeping willow) are ornamental shade trees **b :** any of several other plants more or less like a willow — compare DESERT WILLOW, WILGA, WILLOW HERB **2 :** something derived from a willow tree: as **a :** OSIER 2 **b :** a sprig or garland of willow (as of weeping willow) worn as a symbol of lost love ⟨twenty years time, when you're wearing the ~, you'll be sorry you went about outgrowing everybody in such a hurry —Margaret Kennedy⟩ **c :** an object made of willow wood; *esp* **:** CRICKET BAT **3** [alter. of ¹*willy*] **a :** a textile machine in which cotton or wool is opened and cleaned by a

spiked drum revolving in a box studded internally with spikes — called also *willower, willy* **b :** DUSTER 1b

2willow \"\ *vt* -ED/-ING/-S **1 :** to open and clean (textile fibers) with a willow **2 :** to put (raw material for making paper pulp) through a duster

willow acacia *n* **:** either of two Australian shrubby acacias (*Acacia saligna* and *A. salicina*) having showy yellow flower heads and phyllodia that resemble willow leaves

willow aphid *n* **:** any of several plant lice that feed on willows; *esp* **:** an aphid (*Pterochlorus salignus*) occurring in Africa, Asia, Europe, and No. America

willow beauty *n* **:** a European geometrid moth (*Selidosema gemmaria*)

willow beetle *n* **:** any of several leaf beetles that feed on the leaves of willows; *also* **:** any beetle that bores in the wood

willowbiter \'⸗⸗,⸗⸗\ *n, Brit* **:** either of two titmice: **a :** BLUE TIT **b :** MARSH TIT

willow blight *n* **:** either of two fungous diseases of willow: **a :** WILLOW SCAB **b :** BLACK CANKER 1b

willow borer *n* **1 :** any of several small bronzy longicorn beetles of the genus *Agrilus* that bore in the sapwood of the willow tree and often kill it: as **a :** a beetle (*A. politus*) **b :** a beetle (*A. anxius*) that infests also poplars and birches **2 :** POPLAR BORER **3 :** a European weevil (*Cryptorhynchus lapathi*) introduced and destructive to willows in the eastern U.S.

willow cat *or* **willow catfish** *n* **:** a large yellowish unspotted catfish (*Ictalurus anguilla*) of the lower Mississippi valley — called also *Fulton cat*

willow chafer *n* **1 :** GOLDSMITH BEETLE b **2 :** any of several beetles related to the goldsmith beetle

willow cottonwood *n* **:** a narrow-leaved cottonwood (*Populus angustifolia*) of western No. America

wil·lowed \'wilōd\ *adj* [1*willow* + *-ed*] **:** edged with or abounding in willows ⟨elm-lined roads and ~ backwaters —Elizabeth Pennell⟩

wil·low·er \'wilōwə(r), -lōə(r)\ *n* -S [2*willow* + *-er*] **1 :** a textile worker who operates a willow **2 :** WILLOW 3a

willow family *n* **:** SALICACEAE

willow fly *n* **:** any of various greenish European stone flies of the genus *Chloroperla*

willow gall *also* **willow apple** *n* **:** any of various galls on willow leaves or shoots; *esp* **:** PINECONE WILLOW GALL

willow goldfinch *n* **:** a goldfinch (*Spinus tristis salicamans*) of the Pacific coast

willow grain *n* **:** a surface finish produced on leather by boarding

willow green *n* **:** a variable color averaging a light olive that is greener, lighter, and stronger than citrine, greener and deeper than grape green, and greener, lighter, and stronger than old moss green

willow herb *n* **1 :** a plant of the genus *Epilobium; esp* **:** FIREWEED b — see HAIRY WILLOW HERB **2 a :** PURPLE LOOSESTRIFE **b :** SWAMP LOOSESTRIFE

willow lark *n, dial Eng* **:** SEDGE WARBLER

willow leaf beetle *n* **:** any of various often destructive cerambycoid beetles that feed esp. on the leaves of willows: as **a** (1) **:** a beetle (*Lina scripta*) that often defoliates and kills willows and poplars (2) **:** a beetle (*Pyrrhalta decora*) of similar habits **b :** a beetle (*Phyllodecta vitellinae*)

willow-leaved jasmine \'⸗⸗,⸗-\ *n* **:** a So. American shrub (*Cestrum parqui*) often cultivated for its greenish yellow fragrant flowers

willowlike \'⸗⸗,⸗\ *adj* [1*willow* + *like*] **:** resembling or characteristic of a willow **:** WILLOWY

willow louse *n* **:** a plant louse that infests the willow; *esp* **:** an aphid (*Clavigerus salicis*) common in the U.S.

willow moth *n* **:** any of numerous moths whose larvae infest the willow tree; *esp* **:** either of two dagger moths (*Acronicta oblinita* and *A. americana*)

willow myrtle *n* **:** an Australian shrub or tree (*Agonis flexuosa*) of the family Myrtaceae with willowlike leaves and showy white flowers in axillary heads

willow oak *n* **:** any of several oaks with lanceolate leaves: as **a** (1) **:** an oak (*Quercus phellos*) of the eastern U.S. with linear entire leaves (2) **:** the soft but strong and heavy light-brown wood of this tree that is sometimes used in construction **b :** LAUREL OAK 1a

willow pattern *n* **:** a design used in decorating willowware

willow poplar *n* **:** BLACK POPLAR 1

willow ptarmigan *or* **willow grouse** *n* **:** a ptarmigan (*Lagopus lagopus*) that is circumpolar in distribution

willows *pl of* WILLOW, *pres 3d sing of* WILLOW

willow sawfly *n* **:** any of numerous sawflies that infest the willow: as **a :** a large American sawfly (*Cimbex americana*) whose larva is pale greenish with a black dorsal stripe **b :** a steel-blue sawfly (*Dolerus arvensis*) or a related smaller brownish fly (*D. bicolor*) **c :** a black sawfly (*Nematus ventralis*) whose yellow-spotted blackish larva infests also the wild cherry

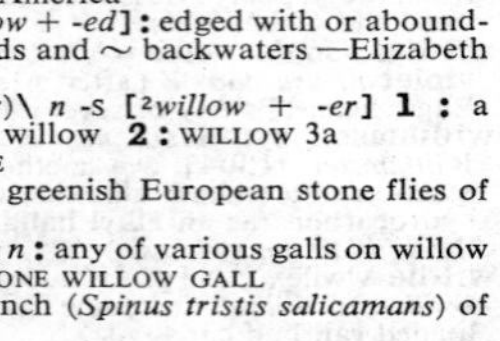

willow sawfly a

willow scab *n* **:** a disease of willow trees caused by a fungus (*Fusicladium saliciperdum*) and characterized by rapid killing of leaves and canker and dieback of young shoots — called also *willow blight*

willow shoot *n* **1 :** a shoot or branch of a willow **2 :** one of the abnormal slender willowlike shoots produced by peach trees affected with yellows — compare PEACH YELLOWS

willow slug *n* **:** a slug that is the larva of a willow sawfly

willow slug caterpillar *n* **:** a caterpillar that is the spinose larva of a moth (*Euclea delphinii*) and that feeds on willow, oak, pear, and other deciduous trees

willow thrush *n* **:** a thrush (*Hylocichla fuscescens salicicola*) closely related to the veery

willow tit *n* **:** BLACK-CAPPED CHICKADEE

willow tree *n* [ME *wilowe tree*, fr. *wilowe* willow + *tree*] **1 :** a tree of the genus *Salix* **2 :** an Australian tree or shrub of the genus *Pittosporum*

willow warbler *also* **willow sparrow** *n* **:** any of several Old World warblers of the genus *Phylloscopus; esp* **:** a small songbird (*P. trochilus*) common in Europe that is delicate greenish above and white below — compare KENNICOTT'S WILLOW WARBLER

willowware \'⸗⸗,⸗\ *n* **:** blue-and-white dinnerware decorated with a story-telling design featuring a large willow tree by a little bridge introduced into England from China in the late 18th century and widely copied in Europe and America usu. in blue but sometimes also in red

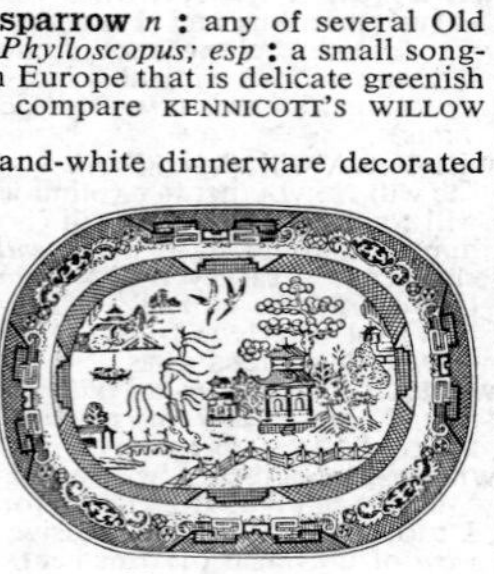

willowware platter

willowweed \'⸗⸗,⸗\ *n* **1 :** a European loosestrife (*Lysimachia vulgaris*) — called also *willowwort* **2** *dial Eng* **:** any of various narrow-leaved plants of the genus *Polygonum* **3 :** WILLOW HERB

willow-wielder \'⸗⸗,⸗⸗\ *n* **:** one that wields a willow; *esp* **:** a cricket batsman

willowworm \'⸗⸗,⸗\ *n* **:** a worm that is the larva of a willow moth or willow sawfly

willow wren *n* **1 :** WILLOW WARBLER **2 :** CHIFFCHAFF

wil·lowy \'wilōwē, -lō̇, |i\ *adj* [*willow* + *-y*] **1 :** WILLOWED **2 :** resembling a willow **:** gracefully tall and slender **:** DELICATE, SUPPLE ⟨a sheath that belongs only on ~ women —*New Yorker*⟩

willpower \'⸗,⸗\ *n* **:** WILL 5b

wills *pl of* WILL, *pres 3d sing of* WILL

will·some \'wilsəm\ *adj* [ME *wilsom*, fr. 2*will* + *-som* -some] *archaic* **:** WILLFUL

will to power [trans. of G *wille zur macht*] **1 :** the drive of the Nietzschean superman to perfect and transcend the self through the possession and exercise of creative power ⟨the *will to power* . . . is as far from a lust for domination as it is from the pursuit of pleasure for its own sake —*Times Lit. Supp.*⟩ **2 :** a conscious or unconscious desire to exercise authority over others ⟨populations enslaved by a dictator's *will to power*⟩

wil·lugh·beia \,wilə'bēə\ *n, cap* [NL, after Francis *Willughby* †1672 Eng. naturalist] **:** a genus of often climbing shrubs (family Apocynaceae) having small flowers with a one-celled ovary and a pulpy indehiscent fruit

will-wil·let \'wil'wilət\ *n* [imit.] *chiefly South* **:** WILLET

will-with-the-wisp \'wilwithə'wisp\ *n* [*Will* (nickname for *William*) + *with* + *the* + *wisp*] *archaic* **:** WILL-O'-THE-WISP

1wil·ly \'wilē, -li\ *n* -ES [fr. (assumed) ME, fr. OE *wiliga, wilige;* akin to OE *welig* willow — more at WILLOW] **1** *dial Eng* **a :** a large wicker basket **b :** a wicker fish trap **2 :** WILLOW 3a

2willy \"\ *vt* **willied; willied; willying; willies :** WILLOW 1

wil·ly-muf·ty \'wili,məfti\ *n* [*willy* (alter. of 1*willow*) + E dial. *mufty*, a kind of warbler, irreg. fr. *muff*] *dial Eng* **:** WILLOW WARBLER

wil·ly-nil·ly \'wilē'nilē, -li. . .li\ *adv* (*or adj*) [alter. of *will I nill I* or *will he nill he* or *will ye nill ye*] **:** by compulsion **:** without regard to individual inclination **:** HELPLESSLY, INEVITABLY ⟨let the world drift *willy-nilly* towards disaster —C.P.Romulo⟩ ⟨animals . . . forced together *willy-nilly* by the action of wind, tidal currents, or waves —W.C.Allee⟩ ⟨*willy-nilly*, the situations in which we use words —I.A.Richards⟩

willy-wagtail \'⸗⸗'⸗,⸗\ *n* [*Willy* (nickname for *William*) + *wagtail*] **:** WILLIE WAGTAIL

willywaw *var of* WILLIWAW

wil·ly-wick·et \'wili,wikət\ *n* [imit.] *dial Brit* **:** a common Eurasian sandpiper (*Tringa hypoleucos*) that is dark olive brown above and has largely white underparts

wil·ly-wil·ly \'wilē,wilē\ *n, pl* **willy-willies** [prob. fr. native name in Australia] *Austral* **:** TROPICAL CYCLONE

wil·ming·ton \'wilmiŋtən\ *adj, usu cap* [fr. *Wilmington*, commercial and industrial city of northern Delaware] **:** of or from the city of Wilmington, Del. ⟨*Wilmington* schools⟩ **:** of the kind or style prevalent in Wilmington

wil·ming·to·ni·an \,wilmiŋ'tōnēən\ *n* -S *cap* [*Wilmington*, Del. + E *-ian*] **:** a native or resident of Wilmington, Delaware

wilms's tumor \'vilmzə̇z-\ *n, usu cap W* [after Max *Wilms* †1918 Ger. surgeon] **:** a sarcoma of rapid development affecting the kidney chiefly of children and made up of embryonal elements

wil·na \'vilnə\ *or* **wil·no** \-l(,)nō\ *adj, usu cap* [*Wilna* fr. G, Vilnyus, capital of Lithuania; *Wilno* fr. Pol, Vilnyus] **:** VILNYUS

wil·son chamber \'wilsən-\ *n, usu cap W* [after C. T. R. *Wilson* †1959 Scot. physicist] **:** CLOUD CHAMBER

wil·so·ni·an \wil'sōnēən\ *adj, usu cap* [Woodrow *Wilson* †1924 28th president of the U.S. + E *-an*] **:** of, relating to, or characteristic of Woodrow Wilson ⟨affirm the *Wilsonian* principle of the right of national self-determination for all peoples —E.E.Schaftschneider⟩

wil·son·ism \'wilsə,nizəm\ *also* **wil·so·ni·an·ism** \wil'sōnēə,n-\ *n, -s usu cap* [*wilsonism* fr. Woodrow *Wilson* †1924 + E *-ism; wilsonianism* fr. *wilsonian* + *-ism*] **:** principles or practices advocated by Woodrow Wilson

wilson's petrel *n, usu cap W* [after Alexander *Wilson* †1813 Am. ornithologist] **:** a petrel (*Oceanites oceanicus*) that breeds in the southern hemisphere but is common in the north Atlantic in summer

wilson's phalarope *n, usu cap W* [after Alexander *Wilson*] **:** a phalarope (*Steganopus tricolor*) breeding on the northern Great Plains in Canada

wilson's plover *n, usu cap W* **:** a ring plover (*Charadrius wilsonia*) of the coast of the U.S., Central America, and So. America

wilson's snipe *n, usu cap W* **:** an American snipe (*Capella gallinago delicata*)

wilson's tern *n, usu cap W* **:** a widely-distributed medium-sized tern (*Sterna hirundo*) with a white deeply forked tail, red black-tipped bill, and orange red feet

wilson's thrush *n, usu cap W* **:** VEERY

wilson's warbler *or* **wilson's blackcap** *n, usu cap W* **:** a small fly-catching warbler (*Wilsonia pusilla*) of eastern and northern No. America that is bright yellow with a black crown — called also *blackcap*

1wilt *archaic pres 2d sing of* WILL

2wilt \'wilt\ *vb* -ED/-ING/-S [alter. of *welk*] *vi* **1 a :** to lose turgor as a result of water loss ⟨the plants ~*ed* under the hot sun⟩ **b :** to become limp **:** SAG, COLLAPSE ⟨the parachute . . . starting to ~ as its great circumference swayed over and touched the paving —J.G.Cozzens⟩ **2 a :** to break down or give way **:** become dispirited **:** FLAG, SUCCUMB ⟨~*ed* before his opponent's barrage of hard drives —John Rendel⟩ ⟨nor did I ever see the nation droop and ~ as we saw it wither under the panic of 1907 —W.A.White⟩ **b :** to lose vitality **:** EBB, FADE ⟨almost laughable the way the bluster ~*ed* out of him —Ross Annett⟩ ⟨the romance . . . blossomed for six or seven months and then ~*ed* —Saxe Commins⟩ **~** *vt* **:** to cause to wilt; *esp* **:** to make (salad greens) limp by marinating in hot grease **syn** see DROOP

3wilt \"\ *n* -S **1 :** an act or instance of wilting or the state of being wilted ⟨feels a distinct ~ of enthusiasm —*Time*⟩ ⟨the train ride . . . brought him to his painting in an advanced state of August ~ —Lucien Price⟩ **2** *also* **wilt disease a :** a disease of plants characterized by loss of turgidity esp. in leaf tissues, by subsequent drooping, and often by shriveling and caused by the activities of insects, viruses, fungi, and bacteria (as by actually obstructing the water-carrying vessels or by producing substances toxic to them) and by abnormal physiological or soil conditions — see FUSARIUM WILT, VERTICILLIOSIS **b :** a highly infectious often fatal disease of various caterpillars caused by a filterable virus which develops mainly in the nuclei of the cells in the insect's body, causes the viscera to liquefy, and aids greatly in reducing the abundance of many noxious insects (as the gypsy moth)

wilting *n* -S [fr. gerund of 2*wilt*] **:** a condition of decreased turgidity in the cells of a plant — see INCIPIENT WILTING, PERMANENT WILTING, TEMPORARY WILTING

wilting coefficient *also* **wilting point** *n* **:** the level of soil moisture at which water becomes unavailable to plants and permanent wilting ensues **:** ECHARD

wilting range *n* **:** the range of soil-moisture percentages throughout which permanent wilting occurs **:** the range between the wilting coefficient and ultimate complete permanent wilting or even death of the plant

1wil·ton \'wilt°n *also* -tən\ *n* -S *usu cap* [fr. *Wilton*, municipal borough of southern England] **:** a carpet woven with loops like the Brussels carpet but differing from it in being heavier, having a velvet cut pile, being generally of better materials, and having designs adapted from Oriental patterns

2wilton \"\ *adj, usu cap* [fr. *Wilton* farm, near Grahamstown, southern Union of South Africa] **:** of, relating to, or constituting a Mesolithic culture of southern Africa characterized by cave dwellings, rock shelters, and rock paintings

1wilt·shire \'wilt,shi(ə)r, -,shiə, -,shə(r)\ *adj, usu cap* [fr. *Wiltshire*, county of southern England] **:** of or from Wiltshire, England **:** of the kind or style prevalent in Wiltshire

2wiltshire \"\ *or* **wiltshire horn** *n, usu cap W&H* **:** an old English breed of pure-white sheep with long spirally curved horns and a long arched head

3wiltshire \"\ *or* **wiltshire cheese** *n, usu cap W* **:** an English cheese similar to derby

wiltshire bacon *n, usu cap W* **:** bacon from a Wiltshire side

wiltshire side *n, usu cap W* **:** half of a lean hog carcass with foreleg cut off at or above the knee joint and hind leg cut off at or above the hock joint used fresh or after removal of large bones cured and smoked in one piece

wily \'wīlē, -li\ *adj* -ER/-EST [ME, fr. *wil* wile + *-y*] **1 :** full of guile **:** CRAFTY ⟨too ~ a villain to remain in a place where he knows he will be searched for —C.B.Nordhoff & J.N.Hall⟩ ⟨led us by devious routes along precipitous trails . . . to film the ~ sheep —A.M.Bailey⟩ **2 :** showing artful cunning **:** CLEVER, SUBTLE ⟨it was ~ of her to wear a green stone . . . that intensified the green of her eyes —Frances Towers⟩ **syn** see SLY

wim·ber·ry \'wim— *see* BERRY\ *var of* WHINBERRY

1wim·ble \'wimbəl\ *n* -S [ME, fr. AF, fr. MD *wimmel* auger; akin to MLG *wimmel* auger] **1 :** any of various instruments for boring holes: as **a :** GIMLET **b :** a brace whose head and handle both are used in turning **c** (1) **:** an auger for boring in earth (2) **:** a scoop for clearing out boreholes in mines **2 :** an instrument for twisting ropes

2wimble \"\ *vb* **wimbled; wimbled; wimbling** \-b(ə)liŋ\ **wimbles** [ME *wimblen*, fr. *wimble*, n.] *vt* **1** *archaic* **:** to bore with or as if with a wimble **2 :** to twist (as rope) with a wimble **~** *vi, archaic* **:** BORE, PENETRATE

3wimble \"\ *adj* [origin unknown] *archaic* **:** ACTIVE, SPRIGHTLY

wimbrel *var of* WHIMBREL

WIMC *abbr, often not cap* whom it may concern

wim·ick *or* **wim·mick** \'wimik\ *vi* -ED/-ING/-S [imit.] *dial Eng* **:** CRY, WHIMPER

wim·mera rye grass \'wimərə-\ *n, usu cap W* [fr. *Wimmera*, Australia] *Austral* **:** a Mediterranean grass (*Lolium subulatum*) grown in Australia for forage

1wim·ple \'wimpəl\ *n* -S [ME *wimpel*, fr. OE; akin to OS *wimpal* veil, banner, MD *wimpel* veil, banner, wimple, OE *wīpian* to wipe — more at WIPE] **1 :** a cloth covering for the neck and the sides of the face that is pinned to the hair, a band, or a hat and worn esp. by women in the late medieval period and by nuns **2** *Scot* **a :** a crafty turn **:** TWIST **b :** CURVE, BEND **3** *Brit* **:** RIPPLE

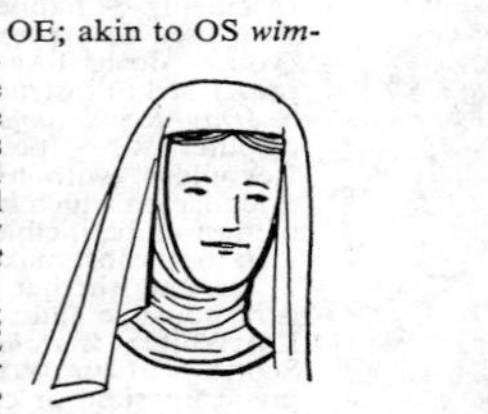

wimple 1

2wimple \"\ *vb* **wimpled; wimpled; wimpling** \-p(ə)liŋ\ **wimples** [ME *wimplen*, fr. *wimpel*, n.] *vt* **1 :** to cover with or as if with a wimple **:** VEIL, WRAP **2 :** to cause to ripple ⟨a warm south wind *wimpled* her fields of golden grain —Cy Warman⟩ **~** *vi* **1 :** to fall or lie in folds **2** *chiefly Scot* **:** to follow a curving course (as of a stream) **:** MEANDER, TWIST, WIND **3 :** RIPPLE ⟨over the little brook which *wimpled* along below towered an arch —J.R.Lowell⟩ ⟨a third voice came *wimpling* and warbling —Virginia Woolf⟩

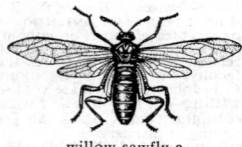

wimpled *adj, obs* **:** BLINDFOLDED ⟨this ~, whining, purblind, wayward boy —Shak.⟩

wims·hurst machine \'wimz,hərst-\ *n, usu cap W* [after James *Wimshurst* †1903 Eng. engineer] **:** an electric machine of the induction type having two closely parallel glass plates revolving in opposite directions and bearing a set of metal carriers corresponding pairs of which on the two plates act momentarily as small electrophorus elements and usu. being provided with Leyden jars for storing the accumulated charges

wim-wams *var of* WHIM-WHAMS

1win \'win\ *vb* **won** \'wən\ **won; winning; wins** [ME *winnen*, fr. OE *winnan* to struggle, fight, toil; akin to OHG *winnan* to struggle, fight, ON *vinna* to work, avail, conquer, win, Goth *winnan* to suffer, L *vener-, venus* love, sexual desire, *venerari* to venerate, Skt *vanati, vanoti* he desires, loves, Hitt *uen-, uent-* to copulate; basic meaning: to strive] *vi* **1 :** to gain the victory in a contest **:** overcome an opponent **:** PREVAIL, SUCCEED ⟨struck for higher wages and *won* —*Amer. Guide Series: N.Y.*⟩ — often used with *out* as an intensive ⟨in most mature adults these counterforces of course ~ out —Fredric Wertham⟩ **2 a :** to succeed esp. by effort in arriving at a place or a state **:** succeed in getting **:** GET ⟨beasts that had *won* to the high ground —J.R. Fethney⟩ ⟨making a great effort . . . he might ~ back to cool sanity —*Hearst's*⟩ ⟨the production *won* through finally owing to the sincerity of the two leading actors —T.C.Worsley⟩ **b** *chiefly Scot* **:** to work up the ability **:** MANAGE, CONTRIVE **3 a** *archaic* **:** to obtain an advantage **:** be in a superior position **:** be master or conqueror — used with *upon, on,* or *of* ⟨have seen . . . the firm soil ~ of the watery main —Shak.⟩ **b :** to gain favor or influence — used with *upon* or *on* ⟨~*s* upon me hourly —S.T.Coleridge⟩ **~** *vt* **1 :** to get possession of by or as if by effort **:** GAIN, OBTAIN, SECURE ⟨made as many as 300 tenement-house calls a week and *won* an intimate knowledge of the poor man —Jerome Ellison⟩ ⟨*won* master's degrees in education and philosophy —*Newsweek*⟩ ⟨*winning* his way up —Charles Dickens⟩ ⟨regiments which *won* fame —H.L.Merillat⟩ ⟨*won* the support of influential friends —C.G.Woodson⟩ **2 a :** to conquer in or as if in battle and take into possession ⟨the individual foot soldier who alone is able to ~ and hold ground —D.W.Mitchell⟩ ⟨the refinery goes up on land *won* from the desert and the sea —Geoffrey Godsell⟩ **b** *obs* **:** to defeat (a person) in a fight **:** BEAT **c :** to be the victor in ⟨just as we *won* the war, so we can ~ the peace —Helen Douglas⟩ ⟨sought means to ~ the election —W.C.Ford⟩ **3 :** to obtain in return for work **:** EARN ⟨the several ways in which men have *won* their livelihood —W.G.V.Balchin & Norman Pye⟩ **4 a :** to gain in or as if in competition ⟨~*s* a prize⟩ ⟨*won* a senate seat —Carol L. Thompson⟩ ⟨*won* several battle stars . . . and a commendation ribbon —*Current Biog.*⟩ ⟨*won* his point easily⟩ **b** *obs* **:** to gain (as time or space) so as to have an advantage ⟨your way is shorter . . . you'll ~ two days upon me —Shak.⟩ **c :** to take (a trick) in a card game **5 a :** to influence so as to gain the favor of **:** make friendly or favorable to oneself or to one's cause ⟨a mellow charm that ~*s* the listener in unassuming ways —Harold Rogers⟩ ⟨*won* the hearts of his military staff —F.L. Paxson⟩ ⟨makes the neutral reader wonder whether it is aimed to ~ him for the communist or the fascist state —C.D.Lewis⟩ ⟨~ back to active church membership many who had lost contact —E.C.Helmreich⟩ — often used with *over* ⟨resort to argument in order to ~ him over to our way of thinking —A.J. Ayer⟩; *specif* **:** to induce (another) to accept oneself in marriage ⟨his deformity prevents him from *winning* the woman he loves —F.E.Coenen⟩ **b** *archaic* **:** PERSUADE, ENTICE ⟨the man whom music ~*s* to stay nigh —Alexander Pope⟩ **6 a** *chiefly dial* **:** HARVEST, GATHER **b** (1) **:** to obtain (as ore, coal, clay) from a mine or pit (2) **:** to prepare (as a vein or bed) for regular mining esp. by making shafts, gangways, and levels (3) **:** to recover (as metal) from ore **7 :** to reach esp. by effort ⟨were worsted in the field, but many lived to ~ the great cave —H.R.Haggard⟩ **syn** see GET

2win \"\ *n* -S **1 :** an act or instance of winning esp. in a game or contest **:** VICTORY ⟨had all their ~*s* in cycling and swimming —*News from New Zealand*⟩; *specif* **:** first place at the finish of a horse race — compare PLACE, SHOW **2 :** something that is won (as in a game or contest) **:** GAIN, PROFIT, TAKE, WINNING

3win \"\ *vi* **winned; winned; winning; wins** [ME *winen;* akin to OE *wunian* to reside, live — more at WONT] *dial Brit* **:** RESIDE, LIVE

4win \"\ *vt* [prob. fr. 1*win*] *dial Brit* **:** to dry (as hay) by exposure to the air or heat

1wince \'win(t)s\ *vi* -ED/-ING/-S [ME *wenchen, winchen, winsen*, fr. (assumed) ONF *wencier, wenchier*, of Gmc origin like OF *guenchier* to turn aside, swerve; akin to OHG *wankōn* to totter, waver, ON *vakka* to stray, wander about, OE *wancol* unsteady, *wincian* to blink, close one's eyes — more at WINK] **1** *archaic* **:** to kick restively from pain or impatience ⟨a fly . . . may sting a stately horse and make him ~ —Samuel Johnson⟩ **2 :** to shrink back involuntarily (as from pain) **:** draw back or contract in an attempt to avoid pain **:** FLINCH ⟨sharp stinging flurries of snow that made you ~ and gasp —John Connell⟩ ⟨her eyes *winced* with the glare of the sun —Waldo Frank⟩ ⟨took a pleasure in saying things that made his wife ~ —Rudyard Kipling⟩ **syn** see RECOIL

2wince \"\ *n* -S **1** *archaic* **:** KICK **2 :** an act or instance of involuntarily drawing back or contracting esp. in reaction to pain ⟨took the cruel blow without ~ or cry —A. Conan Doyle⟩ ⟨thought with an unpleasant ~ of the money that he had already spent —Gabrielle Long⟩

3wince \"\ *Brit var of* 1WINCH 1b, 3

1winc·er \-sə(r)\ *n* -S [ME *wynsare*, fr. *winsen* to wince + *-are* -er] **:** one that winces; *specif, archaic* **:** KICKER

2wincer \"\ *Brit var of* WINCHER

win·cey \'win(t)sē\ *or* **win·sey** \-nzē\ *n* -S [alter. (influenced by the *w* of *linsey-woolsey*) of *linsey*] **:** a plain or twilled fabric with wool weft and cotton or linen warp that is used esp. for warm shirts, skirts, and pajamas

win·cey·ette \',win(t)sē¦et\ *n* -S **:** a British flannelette of cotton napped on both sides and used esp. for underwear, pajamas, and house dresses

1winch \'winch\ *n* -ES [ME *winche*, fr. OE *wince;* akin to OE *wincian* to close one's eyes, blink — more at WINK] **1 a** *obs* **:** ROLLER, REEL **b :** a roller placed between two dyeing vats in

such a way that the fabric placed over the roller can be shifted from one vat to the other **2 :** any of various machines or instruments for hauling or pulling: as **a :** a powerful machine having one or more barrels or drums on which to coil a rope, cable, or chain for hauling or hoisting **:** WINDLASS **b** *Brit* **:** a reel for a fishing rod **c :** any of various textile machines having a roller for moving fabric through a vat during finishing and dyeing processes **3 :** a crank with a handle for giving motion to a revolving part of a machine

²**winch** \"\ *vt* -ED/-ING/-ES **1 :** to hoist or haul with or as if with a winch **2 :** to put into a dyeing vat by means of a winch

³**winch** \"\ *archaic var of* ¹WINCE

winch·er \-chə(r)\ *n* -S **:** one who operates a winch **:** WINCHMAN

win·ches·ter bushel \ˈwin,chestə(r)-, -nchə̇s-\ *n, usu cap W* [after *Winchester*, England] **:** a unit of dry capacity equal to 2150.42 cubic inches or the volume of a cylinder 18½ inches in internal diameter and 8 inches deep

winchester goose *n, usu cap W* [fr. *Winchester*, England; fr. the fact that in the 16th cent. the brothels of Southwark were under the jurisdiction of the bishop of Winchester] **1** *obs* **:** a venereal disease causing a swelling in the groin **2** *obs* **:** a person infected with a venereal disease: *specif* **:** PROSTITUTE

winchester measure *n, usu cap W* [fr. *Winchester*, England] **:** an old English series of measures orig. made standard at Winchester, England

winch·man \ˈwinchmən\ *n, pl* **winchmen :** one who runs a winch; *specif* **:** a worker who moves heavy objects (as machinery, ship's cargo, fishing nets, or logs) by means of a winch

winc·ing·ly *adv* **:** in a wincing manner

¹**wind** \ˈwind, *chiefly poetic* ˈwīnd\ *n* -S *often attrib* [ME *wind, winde*, fr. OE *wind*; akin to OHG *wint* wind, ON *vindr*, Goth *winds*, L *ventus*; all fr. a prehistoric IE participial stem fr. the root represented by OE *wāwan* to blow, OHG *wāen*, Goth *waian*, Gk *aēnai*, Skt *vāti* it blows, *vāta* wind] **1 a :** a natural movement of air of any velocity; *esp* **:** air in natural motion parallel to the surface of the earth ⟨a light ~ had come up⟩ ⟨the ~s devastated the city⟩ — compare CURRENT **b :** an artificially produced movement of air ⟨felt the ~ of a bullet as it passed his temple —C.B.Kelland⟩ **2 a :** a destructive force or influence ⟨the ~ of war had swept his home away —Stuart Cloete⟩ ⟨sow the ~ and reap the whirlwind⟩ **b :** a force or agency that carries along or influences ⟨withstood the ~s of popular opinion —Felix Frankfurter⟩ ⟨the bracing ~s of human sympathy and understanding —J.D.Adams⟩ **c :** TENDENCY, TREND ⟨quick perception of the way campus ~s were blowing —Arnold Nicholson⟩ ⟨too much impressed by current theological ~s —I.G.Whitchurch⟩ **3 a** (1) **:** the air that is inhaled and exhaled by the lungs **:** BREATH ⟨leaned there on the cable, catching his ~ —Wright Morris⟩ ⟨smote him with brutal violence in the stomach, knocking the ~ out of him —Dorothy Sayers⟩ (2) **:** power of respiration **:** ability to breathe properly ⟨established his own studio for the businessman anxious about his weight and his ~ —D.G. Villard⟩ ⟨~ and leg muscles —*Athletic Jour.*⟩ (3) **:** the pit of the stomach where a blow may paralyze the diaphragm and cause temporary loss of breath **:** SOLAR PLEXUS ⟨hit a small boy in the ~ to see him double up —W.B.Yeats⟩ **b :** breath used in speaking ⟨wrote . . . in sonorous and rolling sentences in which one can still hear the ~ of his oratory —Marjory S. Douglas⟩ **4 :** gas generated in the stomach or the intestines **5 a :** compressed air or gas ⟨was considered a little balmy when he seriously proposed stopping a train with ~ —W.J. Reilly⟩ **b** *archaic* **:** AIR ⟨the sword itself must be wrapped up close . . . that it taketh no ~ —Francis Bacon⟩ **6 :** something that is insubstantial: as **a :** mere talk **:** idle words ⟨talks about erasing the border by a march on the North. This is mere ~. There will be no march —J.V.Kelleher⟩ **b :** NOTHING, NOTHINGNESS ⟨theories based on ~⟩ **c :** vain self-satisfaction ⟨all puffed up with ~⟩ **7 a :** air carrying a scent (as of a hunter or game) ⟨a great number of deer . . . entirely ignorant of anything amiss till after they passed me and received my ~ —Ed Shearer⟩ **b** *archaic* **:** exposure to the public **:** CURRENCY — used with *get* or *take* ⟨the project had taken ~ and created a general sensation —W.H.Prescott⟩ **c :** slight information esp. about something intended to be kept secret **:** INTIMATION ⟨the unhappy reporters who by this time had got ~ of something and turned up in battalions —Dorothy Sayers⟩ ⟨caught ~ of this situation —Richard Hellman⟩ **8 a :** air used for producing musical tone: as (1) **:** breath passed through the vocal organs in singing (2) **:** breath used to blow a wind instrument (3) **:** the compressed air used to produce sound on an organ **b** (1) **:** musical wind instruments esp. as distinguished from strings and percussion ⟨music for strings and for ~ —D.W.Stevens⟩ ⟨the triplets played by the ~s —Max Rudolf⟩ ⟨a good deal of ~ detail is lost —Edward Sackville-West & Desmond Shawe-Taylor⟩ (2) **winds** *pl* **:** the players of wind instruments esp. in an orchestra **9 a :** a direction from which the wind may blow **:** a point of the compass; *esp* **:** one of the cardinal points ⟨come from the four ~s, O breath, and breathe upon these slain —Ezek 37:9 (RSV)⟩ **b :** the direction from which the wind is blowing — used esp. with regard to a sailing ship's course **10 :** a condition of oblivion, ineffectualness, or waste — usu. used in pl. ⟨cast the facts of royal history to the ~s and invented his own essential drama —Leslie Rees⟩ ⟨went through deep snow, all anxiety thrown to the four ~s —D.B.MacMillan⟩ **11 :** MONEY ⟨came to me this morning to raise the ~ —Anthony Trollope⟩ **12 :** a state of intoxication ⟨I'm not in the ~ at all events, for you see I'm perfectly sober —Frederick Marryat⟩ — compare SHEET IN THE WIND **13 :** a big fuss **:** DISTURBANCE ⟨raised the ~ over the inferior merchandise⟩ **14 a :** a state of fear — used with *up* ⟨deathtraps, hard to fly, easy to crash . . . good pilots had their ~ up about the planes —H.H.Arnold & I.C. Eaker⟩ ⟨you put the ~ up me —Richard Llewellyn⟩ **b :** a state of nervous irritable excitement — used with *up* ⟨got their ~ up about the neighbors' new fence⟩

syn BREEZE, GALE, HURRICANE, GUST, BLAST, SQUALL, ZEPHYR, WHIRLWIND, CYCLONE, TYPHOON, TORNADO, WATERSPOUT, TWISTER: WIND is a general term applicable to air in any sort of natural motion ⟨light western *winds*⟩ ⟨*winds* of gale force⟩ BREEZE is applicable to a relatively light but fresh wind with moderate velocity, often to a pleasing wind ⟨not a steady, strong *breeze* like the trade winds of the low latitudes, but a boisterous stormy wind —P.E.James⟩ ⟨enjoying the brisk *breeze* that blew about his yellow hair —William Black⟩ GALE indicates a high wind, one between a breeze and a hurricane, sometimes of destructive force ⟨not an inch of shelter anywhere in a *gale*, and the salt rain driven by the wind penetrates the thickest coat —Richard Jefferies⟩ HURRICANE indicates a wind of maximum velocity and consequent destructive violence ⟨towns and villages wrecked by the *hurricane*⟩ GUST indicates a sudden short wind, usu. more severe than a puff, often accompanied by rain ⟨a great *gust* of wind shook the windows of the house —J.C.Powys⟩ BLAST may indicate a sudden wind with severe driving force ⟨a copse of dark firs swayed uneasily under the heavy *blasts* of the gathering storm —F.V.W.Mason⟩ SQUALL refers to any sudden violent gust, esp. to a sea gust with driving force ⟨continuous and violent *squalls* nearly wrecked the craft —Alexander Klemin⟩ ZEPHYR indicates a light gentle delicate wind, one that would not disturb halcyon weather ⟨soft the *zephyr* blows —Thomas Gray⟩ WHIRLWIND may apply to any swirling wind; technically it indicates a rotating windstorm with the lower air spiraling inward and upward ⟨the *whirlwind* came fast. I could see the tops of the trees writhing and twisting —John Onslow⟩ CYCLONE often indicates a rotating system of very high destructive winds about a moving center of low pressure ⟨*cyclones* like those that lift roofs off houses in Kansas —Waldemar Kaempffert⟩ TYPHOON is used in reference to cyclones in Asian Pacific waters ⟨*typhoons* in Joseph Conrad's novels⟩ TORNADO refers to a swirling wind accompanied by a funnel-shaped cloud moving with a force so violent that it cannot be measured accurately ⟨Kansas takes to the cyclone cellar when a *tornado* sweeps by and sucks wells dry —Waldemar Kaempffert⟩ WATERSPOUT indicates a funnel-shaped or tubular column of wind enclosing a quantity of water. TWISTER is a general informal term for any swirling wind like a tornado or waterspout ⟨the first *twisters* hit in the early evening —*Time*⟩ ⟨when a *twister* had come at home, all the windows in Mr. Dannenbaum's house had been blown out —Jean Stafford⟩

—between wind and water 1 : near the waterline of a ship **:** in the part of a side of a ship that rises above and falls below the surface of the water esp. with reference to damage **2 :** at a serious or dangerous point **— by the wind** *or* **on a wind** *or* **on the wind :** close to the wind **— down the wind** *archaic* **:** toward, to, or in a state of decay **— have in the wind :** to be on the scent of **— have the wind of 1 :** to be on the side from which the wind is blowing with respect to **:** be to windward of **2 :** to be on the scent of **3 :** to have a superior position to **:** have at a disadvantage **— in the wind** *adv* (*or adj*) **:** about to happen **:** ASTIR, AFOOT, UP ⟨something was *in the wind*⟩ ⟨other projects than a new building were *in the wind* —Ben Riker⟩ **— near the wind 1 :** close to the wind **:** CLOSE-HAULED **2 :** close to a point of danger **:** near the permissible limit ⟨one of his racy tales, heavily spiced with native argot and sailing perilously *near the wind* —Edward Lockspeiser⟩ **— off the wind :** away from the direction from which the wind is blowing **:** sailing free **— under the wind 1 :** on the side away from the direction from which the wind is blowing **:** to leeward **2 :** in a place that is protected from the wind **:** under the lee

²**wind** \ˈwind\ *vb* -ED/-ING/-S [ME *winden*, fr. ¹*wind*] *vt* **1 :** to smell the scent of **:** follow by the scent ⟨an otter could ~ a fish at 40 furlongs —C.E.Hare⟩ **2 :** to expose to the air or wind **:** dry by exposing to air **3** *dial chiefly Brit* **:** WINNOW **4 :** to take the breath away from **:** make short of breath ⟨her hoof hit my side and ~*ed* me —Adrian Bell⟩ ⟨until acclimated, a person becomes ~*ed* from exertion —Bob Koonce⟩ **5 :** to regulate the wind supply of (an organ pipe) **6 :** to rest (as a horse) in order to allow the breath to be recovered **~** *vi* **1 :** to scent game **:** sniff in the air as if catching the scent of game — used of an animal and esp. of a dog **2** *dial* **:** to pause for breath

³**wind** \ˈwīnd, ˈwind\ *vb* **winded** \-də̇d\ *or* **wound** \ˈwaůnd\ **winded** *or* **wound; winding; winds** [¹*wind* (but often altered in pronunciation & conjugation by influence of ⁴*wind*)] *vt* **1 :** to cause (as a horn) to sound by blowing esp. with the breath **:** BLOW ⟨little fishing boats ~ their conchs —Mary H. Vorse⟩ **2 :** to sound (as a call or note) on or as if on a horn ⟨*wound* a rousing call —R.L.Stevenson⟩ **~** *vi* **:** to produce a sound on or as if on a horn

⁴**wind** \ˈwīnd\ *vb* **wound** \ˈwaůnd\ *also* **winded; wound** *also* **winded; winding; winds** [ME *winden*, fr. OE *windan* to turn, twist, move with speed or force, brandish; akin to OHG *wintan* to wind, ON *vinda*, Goth *biwindan* to wind around, wrap, us*windan* to plait, Umbrian *ohavendu* let him turn aside, Arm *gind* ring; basic meaning: twist] *vi* **1 a** *obs* **a** (1) **:** to move with speed or force **:** RUSH, SPRING (2) **:** PASS **b :** GO, PROCEED ⟨~ away, be gone I say —Shak.⟩ **2** *archaic* **:** WRIGGLE, SQUIRM, WRITHE **3 :** to bend out of a flat plane **:** WARP **4 a** *obs* **:** to move in a curve ⟨a creature that I teach to fight, to ~, to stop, to run directly on —Shak.⟩ **b :** to have a curving course or shape **:** extend in curves ⟨a small road that *wound* up through pines —G.W.Brace⟩ ⟨the staircase *wound* round this hall —Margaret Deland⟩ ⟨a cave which ~s far into the cliff —A.A.Grace⟩ **c :** to move on a curving esp. sinuous course ⟨the river ~s down through rugged terrain⟩ ⟨a long caravan of cars *wound* through the streets —*Phoenix Flame*⟩ ⟨within the lines of these universal qualities ~ the divergencies of medieval thought —H.O.Taylor⟩ **5 a :** to move so as to encircle ⟨loose tapes which ~ around the baby's limbs —Morris Fishbein⟩ **b :** to exhibit the defective gait of winding **6 a :** to change the direction toward which the prow is headed **:** turn when lying at anchor **b :** to lie with the prow headed toward a designated point of the compass **7** *of a horse* **:** to turn or veer to the left **:** HAW **~** *vt* **1 a** *obs* **:** to make by or as if by twisting, plaiting, or weaving **:** WEAVE **b :** to bring into a close relationship as if by weaving or wrapping **:** ENTANGLE, INVOLVE, ENMESH ⟨the greatest crises of life steal on us imperceptibly and have sometimes . . . *wound* us in their consequences before we know —William Black⟩ — often used with *up* ⟨compassion . . . is intricately *wound* up with the doctrine of right living —Edmond Taylor⟩ **c :** to introduce sinuously or stealthily **:** INSINUATE ⟨the impulse to know . . . ~s itself into every action —H.O.Taylor⟩ **d** *obs* **:** to put (as money) into circulation **:** CIRCULATE **2** *archaic* **:** to hold in the hand and use **:** WIELD, HANDLE **3 a :** to encircle or cover with something pliable **:** bind with or as if with loops of string or layers of cloth ⟨*wound* the top with a new piece of string⟩ ⟨the women were *wound* up in fishtailed skirts —G.H.Reed b. 1887⟩ ⟨sleep thou, and I will ~ thee in my arms —Shak.⟩ **b** (1) **:** to turn completely or repeatedly esp. about an object with which contact is made **:** COIL, TWINE, WRAP ⟨*wound* a heavy scarf around his neck⟩ ⟨devised a way of ~*ing* silk on a spool —*Amer. Guide Series: N.J.*⟩ (2) **:** to remove by unwinding **:** UNWIND — used with *off* or *from* ⟨*wound* all the thread off the bobbin⟩ **c** (1) **:** to hoist or haul (as coal from a pit) by means of a rope, cable, or chain that is pulled by machinery — often used with *up* ⟨~ up a bucket from a well —Adrian Bell⟩ (2) **:** to move (a ship) by hauling (as on a capstan) **d** (1) **:** to tighten the spring of in order to start or keep running ⟨four hours of moderate light ~ the clock completely —*Jewelers' Circular-Keystone*⟩ — often used with *up* ⟨*wound* up the toy soldiers⟩ (2) *obs* **:** to make tighter (as the strings of a musical instrument) **:** TIGHTEN, TUNE — often used with *up* (3) **:** to move with a crank **:** CRANK ⟨*wound* down the window on the right hand side of the car —J.M.Cain⟩ **e :** to raise to a high level (as of excitement, tension, or preparedness) — usu. used with *up* ⟨get so easily *wound up* . . . about these things that we could go on and on —W.F.Hambly⟩ **4 a :** to cause to move in a curving line **:** cause to follow a curving course or path ⟨processions . . . *wound* themselves about the town in circles —Julian Dana⟩ **b** (1) *archaic* **:** to turn the course or direction of; *esp* **:** to turn or lead (a person) as one wishes ⟨can ~ the proud earl to his will —Sir Walter Scott⟩ (2) *obs* **:** ATTRACT, LURE, ENTICE **c** (1) **:** to cause (as a ship) to change direction **:** TURN (2) **:** to turn (as a ship) end for end **d :** to traverse on a curving course ⟨~s the wood —John Dryden⟩ **e** (1) **:** to effect by or as if by curving ⟨*wound* his way up the tree —Willa Cather⟩ ⟨the forest through which the river ~s its course —Alexander MacDonald⟩ (2) **:** to follow the curving course of ⟨enabled travelers to reach the Mississippi without ~*ing* the endless curves of the Arkansas —*Amer. Guide Series: Ark.*⟩ **f :** to turn (a horse) to the left

syn TWIST, TWINE, ENTWINE, COIL, CURL, WREATHE agree with WIND in referring either to a circular, spiral, or writhing motion or to a curved and bent outline or shape; WIND esp. emphasizes action or motion, orig. an even-paced, repeated turning about a fixed point, now frequently a rambling or climbing in serpentine curves over an extended area ⟨*wind* thread or tape on a reel⟩ ⟨the road *winds* along the river⟩ TWIST orig. and basically is to turn two threads about each other; it retains the suggestion of revolving within a narrow compass or of an outline having many small kinks rather than describing large loops or curves ⟨the train *wound* around the mountain⟩ ⟨the dancer *twisted* slowly about herself⟩ ⟨a *winding* river⟩ ⟨a *winding* staircase⟩ TWINE orig. is close to TWIST but does not have the connotation of tortuousness; it suggests something long and supple draped in spirals or loops about a solid body ⟨the symbol of a serpent *twined* round a staff⟩ ⟨vines *twining* about a tree may kill it⟩ ENTWINE is orig. an intensive form of TWINE; it may suggest merely a complete twining about or an inextricable entanglement. COIL, CURL, and WREATHE place less emphasis on the action or motion of bending than on the resulting shape; COIL means to roll, wind, or spin in rings or spirals ⟨she wore her hair *coiled* on top of her head⟩ ⟨the waters in the maelstrom *coiled* and hissed⟩ CURL refers to the appearance made by a body of greater length than thickness in bending from its full extension into a shape suggesting a coil of hair, or by a flat surface in rippling and creasing ⟨smoke *curling* in the blue air⟩ ⟨*curling* waves tossed against the shore⟩ ⟨lips *curled* in derision⟩ WREATHE may suggest creasing or crinkling ⟨*wreathed* in smiles⟩ or the assumption of a wreathy appearance ⟨mists of night *wreathe* up from meadows —Walter de la Mare⟩

⁵**wind** \ˈwīnd\ *n* -S **1 :** a mechanism (as a winch) for winding **2 :** an act or instance of winding: as **a** (1) **:** the condition of being warped or twisted ⟨took the board out of ~⟩ (2) **:** the amount of warp **b :** an act or instance of hoisting or pulling by a mechanism that winds (as a winch) **c :** an act or instance of tightening the spring of a mechanism (as a watch or clock) **d :** COIL, TWIST, TURN **e :** a particular method of winding ⟨a very open ~ is used on the size tube . . . to minimize thread to thread adhesion —V.A.Schiffer⟩

wind·age \ˈwindij, -dēj\ *n* -S [¹*wind* + *-age*] **1 a :** the space between the projectile of a smoothbore gun and the surface of the bore **b :** the difference between the diameter of the bore of a muzzle-loading rifled cannon and that of the projectile cylinder **2 a :** the amount of sight deflection necessary to compensate for wind displacement so as to aim a gun accurately **b** (1) **:** the influence of the wind in deflecting the course of a projectile (2) **:** the amount of deflection due to the wind **3 a :** the disturbance of the air caused by a passing object (as a projectile) **b :** air friction against a rapidly moving rotating object (as a flywheel or the armature of a dynamo) **4 :** the surface exposed (as by a ship) to the wind

wind angle *n* **:** the angle between the true course of an airplane and the direction of the wind

windbag \ˈ=,=\ *n* [ME *wind bagge*, fr. ¹*wind* + *bagge* bag] **1 :** a bag of wind or air; *specif* **:** the bag of a bagpipe **2 :** a loquacious usu. pompous person who has little to say **:** one who talks volubly to little effect

wind·bag·gery \"+ərē\ *n* -ES [*windbag* + *-ery*] **:** pompous meaningless talk

wind band *n* **1 :** a band of wind instruments; *esp* **:** a military band **2 :** the wind instruments of an orchestra **:** WINDS

wind beam *n* [ME *windbeme*, fr. ¹*wind* + *beem, beme* beam; fr. its function as a wind-brace] **:** COLLAR BEAM

windbeaten \ˈ=,==\ *adj* [¹*wind* + *beaten*, past part. of *beat*] **:** beaten by or as if by the wind

wind-bell \ˈ=,=\ *n* **1 :** a cluster of small pieces of glass or metal tied loosely together in such a way that they tinkle when blown by the wind ⟨the bell-like tinkle of glass *wind-bells* suspended along the corridor —Herman Smith⟩ **2 :** a bell that is light enough to be moved and sounded by the wind

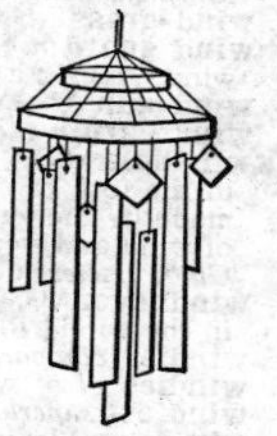

wind-bell 1

wind belt *n* **:** a belt or row of trees planted to serve as a windbreak **:** SHELTERBELT

wind·berry \ˈwin(d)- — *see* BERRY\ *n* **:** MOUNTAIN CRANBERRY

wind bill *n, Scot* **:** ACCOMMODATION BILL

windblow \ˈ=,=\ *n* [prob. back-formation fr. *windblown*] **:** a deposit of windblown sand

windblown \ˈ=,=\ *adj* **1 :** blown by the wind ⟨the summits . . . are so ~ that they can scarcely be called skiable —C.M.Dudley⟩ ⟨masses of sandstone and ~ sands —*Jour. of Geol.*⟩; *specif* **:** having a permanent set or character of growth determined by the prevailing winds ⟨the ~ trees along the coast⟩ **2 :** cut so that the ends turn outward and to the front as if blown by a wind from behind ⟨the ~ bob of the flapper —Lois Long⟩

wind-borne \ˈ=,=\ *adj* **:** carried by the wind ⟨*wind-borne* sand —*Plane Talk*⟩ ⟨*wind-borne* soil deposits —*Amer. Guide Series: Wash.*⟩

windbound \ˈ=,=\ *adj* **1 :** prevented from sailing by a contrary or a high wind ⟨the crews of schooners ~ under the lee of the island —*Amer. Guide Series: Mich.*⟩ **2 :** held back as if by an unfavorable wind

wind box *n* **1 :** a receptacle from which a blast of air is supplied (as to the tuyeres of a cupola, blast furnace, or forge) **2 :** WIND-CHEST

wind-brace \ˈ=,=\ *n* **:** a brace (as a strut) to strengthen a frame or structure against the wind

wind bracing *n* **1 :** the act or process of bracing a frame against winds **2 :** WIND-BRACES

windbreak \ˈ=,=\ *n* **1 :** something that breaks the force of the wind: as **a :** rowed or clumped trees or shrubs that give protection against the wind esp. to buildings and nearby gardens and orchards — compare SHELTERBELT **b :** a rough temporary wall for protection against the wind **2 :** the breaking of trees by the wind

windbreaker \ˈ=,==\ *n* [¹*wind* + *breaker*] **:** something that breaks the wind **:** WINDBREAK

Windbreaker \"\ *trademark* — used for an outer jacket made of wind-resistant material

wind-broken \ˈ=,==\ *adj, of a horse* **:** having the power of breathing impaired by the rupture, dilatation, or running together of air cells of the lungs so that while the inspiration is by one effort, the expiration is by two **:** affected with pulmonary emphysema or with heaves

windburn *n* **1 :** injury caused by excessive wind on foliage or thin bark **2 :** an irritated condition of the skin that is analogous to sunburn and caused by exposure to the wind

windburned \ˈ=,=\ *adj* [¹*wind* + *burned*, past part. of *burn*] **:** burned by the wind **:** showing the effects of windburn ⟨~ arms⟩

wind catcher *n* **:** WIND SCOOP

windcharger \ˈ=,==\ *n* **:** a generator driven by a windmill and used to charge storage batteries

windcheater \ˈ=,==\ *n, chiefly Brit* **:** an outer jacket of wind-resistant material

wind-chest \ˈ=,=\ *n* **:** a reservoir for supplying air under pressure to the pipes or reeds of an organ

wind chill *n* **:** the cooling effect of moving air on a body expressed as the amount of heat lost per unit area per unit of time and taking into account both temperature and wind speed

wind cloud *n* **:** a cloud accompanied or followed by considerable wind

wind colic *n* **1** *archaic* **:** intestinal colic **2 :** BLOAT 2b **:** BLOAT COLIC ⟨a horse with *wind colic*⟩

wind cone *n* **:** WIND SOCK

wind conveyor *n* **:** CONVEYER 2a(9)

wind cripple *n* **:** a tree stunted or injured by the wind

wind direction *n* **:** the direction from which the wind blows

winddog \ˈ=,=\ *n* **:** SUN DOG

wind drift *n* **:** the drift of the wind; *specif* **:** the average direction of the wind over a period of time

¹**winded** \ˈwində̇d\ *adj* [ME, fr. ¹*wind* + *-ed*] **:** having wind or breath of a designated kind — usu. used in combination ⟨long-*winded*⟩

²**winded** *adj* [fr. past part. of ²*wind*] **:** having lost one's breath esp. from exertion **:** short of breath ⟨both boys were thoroughly ~ at the end of the race⟩

wind egg *n* [¹*wind*; fr. the former belief that such eggs were the result of conception by the wind] **:** an unimpregnated, addled, or imperfect egg; *esp* **:** an egg with a soft noncalcareous shell

wind engine *n* **:** an engine that gets its motive power from the wind (as a windmill or the rotor of a rotor ship)

¹**wind·er** \ˈwīndə(r)\ *n* -S [⁴*wind* + *-er*] **:** one that winds: as **a** (1) **:** a worker who winds yarn or thread (2) **:** a textile worker who operates a machine for winding yarn from one package to another — called also *redrawer, swifter* (3) **:** ²TUBER d (4) **:** an operator of a machine for forming strips of paper into spiral tubing for use in making containers or covers **b** *obs* (1) **:** TENDRIL (2) **:** a twining plant **c** (1) **:** WINCH (2) **:** REEL, SPOOL (3) **:** any of various textile machines for winding thread and yarn on or off bobbins, reels, spools, or cones (4) **:** a machine used in papermaking that winds into rolls the slit and trimmed paper coming from the reels **d :** a key for winding a mechanism (as a clock) **e :** a step that is wider at one end than at the other (as in a spiral staircase) — compare FLIER

²**wind·er** \ˈwīndə(r), ˈwin-\ *n* -S [³*wind* + *-er*] **:** one that winds a horn or other wind instrument

³**wind·er** \ˈwində(r)\ *n* -S [²*wind* + *-er*] **:** something that takes the breath away: as **a :** a hard blow with the fist **b :** a fast run

wind erosion *n* **:** the erosion and dispersal of topsoil by the wind esp. in dust storms

windfall \ˈ=,=\ *n, often attrib* [ME, fr. ¹*wind* + *fall*] **1 a :** something that is blown down by the wind: as (1) **:** a tree knocked down by the wind (2) **:** fruit blown off a tree **b :** an area of being blown down by the wind ⟨excessive ~ in the residual stands —W.N.Sparhawk⟩ **c :** a tract where the trees have been blown down by the wind **2 :** an unexpected or sudden

gain or advantage 〈the decline in Atlantic fares may enable me to steal over one day if I get a ~ —H.J.Laski〉 〈detectives questioning neighbors . . . soon found themselves with a ~ of leads —E.D.Radin〉 〈all the ~ money received by housing promoters —Alvin Shuster〉

windfallen \ ˈ �ˌ⸱\ *adj* [¹*wind* + *fallen*] : blown down by the wind

wind-fertilization \ ˌ ⸱ˌ⸱⸱⸱\ *n* : ANEMOPHILY

wind-fertilized \ ˈ ⸱ˌ⸱⸱\ *adj* [¹*wind* + *fertilized*, past part. of *fertilize*] : ANEMOPHILOUS

windfirm \ ˈ ⸱ˌ⸱\ *adj* : firm enough to withstand strong wind 〈one of the most ~ of trees —*Scientific American*〉

windfish \ ˈ ⸱ˌ⸱\ *n* 1 : a fallfish (*Semotilus corporalis*) of northeastern No. America 2 : GOLDEN SHINER

windflaw \ ˈ ⸱ˌ⸱\ *n* : a gust of wind : FLAW

windflower \ ˈ ⸱ˌ⸱⸱\ *n* 1 : ANEMONE 1 2 : RUE ANEMONE

wind-force \ ˈ ⸱ˌ⸱\ *n* 1 : a definite number (as 5 or 7) on an arbitrary wind scale — compare BEAUFORT SCALE 2 : the pressure exerted by a wind

wind furnace *n* : a natural-draft furnace

windgall \ ˈ ⸱ˌ⸱\ *n* 1 : a soft tumor or synovial swelling on a horse's leg in the region of the fetlock joint 2 : SUN DOG

wind-galled \ ˈ ⸱+d\ *adj* [*windgall* + *-ed*] : affected with windgall

wind gap *n* : a notch in the crest of a mountain ridge : a pass that is not occupied by a stream — called also *air gap, wind valley*

wind gauge *n* 1 : an instrument used (as in target firing) to determine and sometimes record the force and direction of the wind : ANEMOMETER 2 : a graduated scale on the rear sight of a small-arms rifle by which the sight can be adjusted to correct the deviation of the bullet due to a wind component perpendicular to the line of fire 3 : a device on a pipe organ for measuring and indicating the amount of wind pressure

wind-grass \ ˈ ⸱ˌ⸱\ *n* 1 : SILKY BENT GRASS 2 : ROUGH BENT

wind guard *n* : something that gives protection against the wind; *specif* : a chimney cowl

wind-gun \ ˈ ⸱ˌ⸱\ *n, archaic* : AIR RIFLE 1

wind harp *n* : AEOLIAN HARP

windhole \ ˈ ⸱ˌ⸱\ *n* 1 : a ventilating shaft in a mine 2 : a hole in the foot of an organ pipe for admitting wind 3 : a hole made by the action of the wind 〈sandstone formations tooled by centuries of wind and weather, pockmarked with ~s and caves —*Amer. Guide Series: Calif.*〉

windhover \ ˈ ⸱ˌ⸱\ *n* [¹*wind* + *hover*, v.; fr. its habit of hovering in the wind] *Brit* : KESTREL

windier comparative of WINDY

windies *pl of* WINDY

windiest superlative of WINDY

win-di-go \ ˈwindəˌgō\ *also* **wen-di-go** \ ˈwen-\ *n* -s [Ojibwa] : a cannibalistic creature of Algonquian mythology believed to have been a lost hunter forced by hunger to eat human flesh and thereafter to have become a crazed man-eating ogre roaming the forest

wind-i-ly \ ˈwindəlē, -li\ *adv* : in a windy manner

wind indicator *n* : a large weathercock mounted on the ground at airports to indicate the direction of the wind

wind-i-ness \ -dēnəs, -din-\ *n* -ES [ME *windinesse*, fr. ¹*windy* + *-nesse* -ness] : the quality or state of being windy: as **a** : FLATULENCE **b** : lack of substance : VERBOSITY, POMPOSITY 〈showed up the ~ of their arguments, the sublime folly of their attempts —Virginia Woolf〉 **c** : the presence of wind in the atmosphere 〈average hourly velocity is considered a good index of ~ —*New Yorker*〉 **d** : BREATHINESS

¹wind-ing \ ˈwīndiŋ, -dēŋ\ *n* -s [ME, fr. OE *windung*, something twined or plaited, a hurdle, fr. *windan* to wind + *-ung* -ing] **1 a** (1) : the material (as wire or rope) that is wound or coiled about an object (as an armature) (2) : a single turn of the wound material **b** *chiefly dial* : a pliable rod : WITHY **2 a** : the action of coiling, twining, or twisting a pliable material about an object or about itself 〈the ~ of thread on a spool〉 〈silk ~〉 **b** : the manner of winding pliable material about an object — see SERIES WINDING, SHUNT WINDING **3 a** : a curved or sinuous course, passage, or line 〈knows all the ~s of the cave —A.A.Grace〉 **b** (1) : movement or progress in a curve or a series of curves 〈following the ~s of the creek until it led us far back into the hills —Mary S. Broome〉 (2) : a sinuous movement in conduct or thought : a devious or tortuous way or method — usu. used in pl. 〈all the ~s of this sordid intrigue —J.W.Beach〉 **4 a** : the act or action of hoisting or pulling by means of a mechanism that winds (as a winch) **b** : the act or action of tightening a spring or other mechanism (as in a clock or watch) by turning a key, stem, or screw **5** : the state, quality, or fact of being twisted or warped out of a plane 〈drove wooden piles that would stay out of ~〉 **6** : a defective gait of a horse in which one foreleg is twisted in front of and around the other

²winding \ ˈ ⸱\ *adj* [fr. present participle of ⁴*wind*] **1** : marked by winding: as **a** : having a pronounced curve 〈the rough ~ stairs of the medieval fortress —Claudia Cassidy〉; *esp* : SPIRAL **b** : having a course that winds 〈a ~ road〉 **c** : DIGRESSIVE, RAMBLING 〈the conclusion of the long and ~ stories —Sir Walter Scott〉 **2** *obs* : TRICKY, DECEITFUL, WILY **3** : STAGGERING, REELING 〈a kick that sent him ~ —G.S.Perry〉 — **wind-ing-ly** *adv* — **wind-ing-ness** *n* -ES

winding engine *n* : a hoisting engine : HOIST

winding frame *n* : WINDER c(3)

winding pendant *n* : a pendant secured around a masthead into an eye at the lower end of which a winding tackle hooks

winding pinion *n* : a small steel wheel in the winding mechanism of a watch with both radial and perpendicular teeth through which the winding stem fits

winding rack *n* : a toothed sector or bar activated by a plunger in the case that winds up the repeating mechanism in a repeating watch

winding-sheet \ ˈ ⸱ˌ⸱\ *n* [ME *winding shete*, fr. ¹*winding* + *shete* sheet] **1** : a sheet in which a corpse is wrapped : SHROUD **2** : a sheetlike formation of tallow or wax around a guttered candle that is an omen of death or calamity

winding strips or **winding sticks** *n pl* : two equal short straightedges with parallel edges placed transversely on a surface to test its trueness

winding tackle *n* : a tackle consisting of a fixed triple block and a double or triple movable block hooked to a winding pendant for hoisting heavy articles in or out of a ship

wind instrument *n* [¹*wind*] : a musical instrument sounded by wind esp. by the breath

wind-jam \ ˈwin(d)ˌjam, -aam\ *vi* [back-formation fr. *windjammer*] *slang* : to talk excessively : talk a great deal without saying anything of substance

wind-jam-mer \ -mə(r)\ *n* -s [¹*wind* + *jam*, v. + *-er*] *slang* : a wind instrument player: as **a** : a brass player in a circus band **b** : an army bugler or trumpeter **2** *slang* : a very talkative person : WINDBAG **3 a** : SAILING SHIP **b** : a member of the crew of a sailing ship

wind-lace \ ˈwindləs\ *archaic var of* WINDLASS

¹wind-lass \ ˈwindləs\ *n* -ES [ME *wynlase, wyndelas, wyndlas*, alter. (prob. influenced by ME *windlen*, freq. of *windan* to wind) of *wyndas*, fr. ON *vindāss*, fr. *vinda* to wind + *āss* pole, beam] **1** : any of various machines for hoisting or hauling: as **a** : a horizontal barrel supported in vertical standards and turned by a crank with a handle so that the hoisting rope is wound around the barrel — see DIFFERENTIAL WINDLASS **b** : a horizontal barrel with whelps turned by handspikes inserted in radial holes near each end and formerly used to raise the anchor — compare CAPSTAN **c** : a powerful steam or electric winch having a horizontal or a vertical shaft and two drums that is used to raise the anchor and is mounted on the forecastlehead **d** : a winch used in agriculture that has a vertical drum and is operated by a tractor **2** : a small winch formerly used to bend a crossbow

²windlass \ ˈ ⸱\ *vt* -ED/-ING/-ES : to hoist or haul with or by a windlass

³windlass *n* -ES [alter. (influenced by ⁴*wind*) of ME *wanlas*] **1** *obs* : a roundabout way taken to intercept game in hunting

windlass

2 *obs* : a circuitous method : ARTIFICE, MANEUVER

wind-lass-er \ -sə(r)\ *n* -s [¹*windlass* + *-er*] : an operator of a windlass

¹win-dle \ ˈwin(d)ᵊl\ *n* -s [ME, fr. OE *windel* basket, fr. *windan* to wind, twist, plait — more at WIND] : a locally varying measure (as for wheat) used in northern England and Scotland

²windle \ ˈ ⸱\ *n* [perh. fr. ¹*wind*] *dial Eng* : REDWING 1

win-dles \ ˈwin(d)ᵊlz\ *n pl but sing or pl in constr* [E dial. *windle*, short for *windlestraw*] : a ribgrass (*Plantago lanceolata*)

wind-less \ ˈwindləs\ *adj* [ME *windles*, fr. ¹*wind* + *-les* -less] : marked by absence of wind 〈a ~ day〉 — **wind-less-ly** *adv* — **wind-less-ness** *n* -ES

win-dle-straw \ ˈwin(d)ᵊlˌstrȯ\ *also* **win-dle-strae** \ -rāˌ\ *n* -s [fr. (assumed) ME *windlestraw, windlestree*, fr. OE *windelstrēaw*, fr. *windel* basket + *strēaw* straw — more at WINDLE, STRAW] **1** *Brit* : a dry thin stalk of grass **2** *Brit* : any of various grasses with an elongated stalk **3** *chiefly Scot* : something that is weak, light, or insubstantial; *specif* : a thin or weak person **4** : WHITETHROAT 1

win-dlin \ ˈwindlən\ *or* **win-dling** \ -lən, -liŋ\ *n* -s [perh. fr. gerund of obs. *windle* to wind, fr. ME *windlen* — more at WINDLASS] *chiefly Scot* : a bundle of hay or straw

wind load *n* [¹*wind*] : the load on a structure due to the action of the wind

wind machine *n* **1** : a machine for creating an artificial wind: as **a** : a machine for creating a blast of air on a theatrical stage **b** : a large fan used to circulate air in an orchard to prevent frost damage **2** : a device used for imitating the sound of the wind (as in a theater)

wind mantle *n* : WINDBREAK 1a — used chiefly in forestry

¹windmill \ ˈ ⸱ˌ⸱\ *n* [ME *windmulle*, fr. ¹*wind* + *mille, mulle* mill] **1 a** : a mill operated by the wind usu. acting on oblique vanes or sails which radiate from a horizontal shaft — compare SMOCK MILL **b** : any of various similar mechanisms: (1) : a wind-driven water pump (2) : a wind-driven electric generator **c** : the wind-driven wheel of a mill operated by the wind or of a similar mechanism **2** : something that resembles or suggests a windmill: as **a** : PINWHEEL 2a **b** *slang* : HELICOPTER **c** : a prostrate annual plant (*Allionia incarnata*) of the Colorado and Mohave deserts that has viscid stems and white to rose flowers in groups of three **3 a** *obs* : a fanciful scheme or plan [so called fr. the episode in *Don Quixote* by Miguel de Cervantes Saavedra †1616 Span. writer, in which the hero attacks windmills under the illusion that they are giants] : an imaginary wrong, evil, or opponent — used esp. in the phrase *to tilt at windmills*

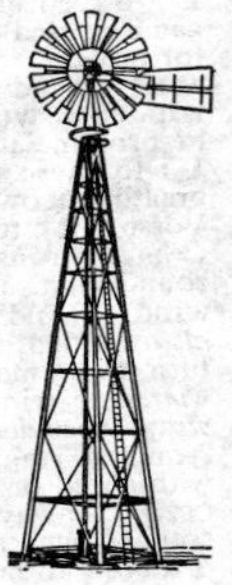

²windmill \ ˈ ⸱\ *vt* : to cause to move like a windmill 〈~ed his arms —John & Ward Hawkins〉 ~ *vi* : to move like a windmill 〈the other soldier hit him . . . they were ~ing into each other without doing any damage —Thomas Williams〉; *specif* : to rotate from the force of the air when the engine is not operating 〈the propeller . . . will ~ and crank the engine —F.H.Colvin〉

windmill-er \ ˈ ⸱+ə(r)\ *n* [¹*windmill* + *-er*] : the operator of a windmill

windmill grass *n* : any of various grasses of the genus *Chloris*; *esp* : an Australian grass (*C. truncata*) having numerous long spikes disposed like the vanes of a windmill

windmill palm *n* : a hemp palm (*Trachycarpus excelsa*)

windmill pink *n* : a European catchfly (*Silene gallica*) with hairy foliage and small white racemose flowers that is widely naturalized in No. America

wind motor *n* : WINDMILL 1b

wind music *n* : music written for or produced by wind instruments

win-dore \ ˈwinˌdō(ə)r\ *n* -s [alter. (influenced by *door*) of ¹*window*] *archaic* : WINDOW

¹win-dow \ ˈwinˌdō, -ˌdȯ; -dəw\ *or* -ˌdō + V; *dial* ˈwindər *or* -dē *or* -di\ *n* -s *often attrib* [ME *windowe*, fr. ON *vindauga*, fr. *vindr* wind, air + *auga* eye — more at WIND, EYE] **1 a** (1) : an opening in a wall of a building or a side of a vehicle to admit light usu. through a transparent or translucent material (as glass), usu. to permit vision through the wall or side, and often to admit air (2) : an opening in a partition or a wall through which business is carried on (as by a bank teller or a ticket agent) **b** : a space behind a window; *esp* : a space behind a glass window that is used for display esp. of merchandise **c** (1) : the casement, sash with its fittings, or other framework that closes a window opening (2) : WINDOWPANE 〈the ball broke a ~〉 **2** : a means of entrance (as to the mind); *esp* : a means of obtaining information or maintaining contact 〈dedicated himself to the task of keeping his society a ~ on the West —Charles Hodges〉 **3 a** : any of various openings resembling or suggestive of a window: as (1) : a small opening through which it is possible to see: SLOT (2) : FENSTER (3) : FENESTRA (4) : a transparent panel (as in an envelope, paper bag, or carton) (5) : a transparent plate (as in the front of a diving helmet) **b** : EYE 〈a pair of indigo ~s —*N.Y.Sun*〉 **c** : a small polished facet on the surface of a rough gemstone that permits inspection of the interior **4** : strips of foil or metal-coated paper dropped from airplanes to interfere with an enemy's radar detection by creating spurious images — called also *chaff* **5** : a hairless patch on a pelt or fur

²window \ ˈ ⸱\ *vt* -ED/-ING/-S **1** *obs* : to place in a window **2** : to provide with or as if with windows

window back *n* : the inside face of the piece of wall between the windowsill and the floor esp. when ceiled

window band *n* : RIBBON WINDOWS

window bar *n* **1** : a wood or metal division between the panes of a window **2** : a bar for fastening a window or a shutter **3** : a bar for preventing passage through a window

window bay *n* : BAY WINDOW

window board *n* : a board used in a window as a part of the ledge or frame or as a shutter

window bole *n, chiefly Scot* : a small opening in a wall to let in light and air usu. closed with a wooden shutter

window box *n* **1** : one of the hollows in the sides of a window frame for the weights that counterbalance a lifting sash **2** : a box designed to hold soil for growing plants on a windowsill or at the level of the sill

window card *n* : a descriptive advertising card used in a retail store window

window decoration *n* : a decoration for a window; *esp* : material used to trim a retail store window

window display *n* : a display of goods in a window designed to attract customers

window-dress \ ˈ ⸱ˌdres\ *vt* [back-formation fr. *window dresser*] : to make appear more attractive or more favorable 〈may be necessary to *window-dress* . . . an offering of bonds —*Scientific American*〉

window dresser *n* [¹*window* + *dresser*] **1** : one that arranges merchandise and decorations in a show window — called also *window trimmer* **2** : one that distorts facts or puts up a front in order to make a favorable impression 〈value him as one of the greatest *window dressers* of their party and defenders of its misdeeds —*Nation*〉

window dressing *n* [¹*window* + *dressing*] **1** *Brit* : the wooden or stone trim of a window **2** : the arrangement of merchandise and decorations in a show window esp. of a retail store **3 a** (1) : the act or practice of making a false or misleading statement of facts (as of financial condition or a political situation) or of putting up a front in order to make a better impression 〈too much *window dressing* by companies which hire . . . half-dozen Negroes just to prove for the record that they do not discriminate —Elmo Roper〉 (2) : the making of adjustments (as in bank statements) that are within the limits of acceptable practice to improve the appearance of a financial position **b** : something that improves the external appearance (as of an organization or an action) and helps to make a better impression : FRONT, FACADE, COVER-UP 〈letting big business run the show with labor representation on his staff only as *window dressing* —*Wall Street Jour.*〉 〈the sententious piety is

merely *window dressing*, a means of passing off spicy stories —A.E.Rodway〉

windowed *adj* [¹*window* + *-ed*] **1** : having windows **2** : having ornamental openings **3** : filled with holes : RAGGED

windowed plant *also* **window plant** *n* : any of several plants esp. of *Mesembryanthemum* or the related genus *Fenestraria* having transparent triangular areas in their leaves

window-efficiency ratio *n* : DAYLIGHT FACTOR

window envelope *n* : an envelope having a transparent panel through which the address on the enclosure is visible

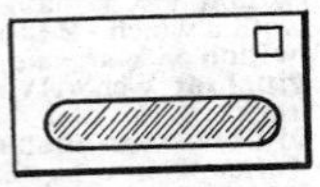

window fixture *n* : a piece of furniture or a form used in dressing a store window

window envelope

window fly *n* : any of several small black flies of the family Scenopinidae that are often found on windows; *esp* : a fly (*Scenopinus fenestralis*) whose larvae feed on the larvae of the clothes moth

window frame *n* : the frame of a window that receives and holds the sashes or casements

win-dow-ful \ ˈ ⸱ˌfu̇l\ *n, pl* **windowfuls** *also* **windowsful** [¹*window* + *-ful*] : as much or as many as a window will hold or allow to pass through or be visible 〈let in a whole ~ of light —*Commonweal*〉 〈a full train . . . piled with ~s of faces —Bruce Marshall〉

window gardening *n* : the growing of ornamentals in receptacles placed in the windows of the home

window glass *n* : sheet glass made in shapes suitable for windows

window head *n* : the upper transverse member of a window

win-dow-less \ ˈ ⸱ˌləs\ *adj* : having no window — **win-dow-less-ness** *n* -ES

windowlight \ ˈ ⸱ˌ⸱\ *n* : WINDOWPANE 1

win-dow-man \ ˈ ⸱ˌmən\ *n, pl* **windowmen** : a man in charge of a window (as in a ticket office or a bank)

window martin *or* **window swallow** *n* : MARTIN 1

window mirror *n* : a small mirror placed outside a window (as of an automobile) and adjusted to reflect objects within a desired area

window-money \ ˈ ⸱ˌ⸱⸱\ *n, archaic* : WINDOW-TAX

window oyster *or* **window shell** *n* : WINDOWPANE OYSTER

windowpane \ ˈ ⸱ˌ⸱\ *n* **1** : a pane in a window **2** : a thin spotted American flounder (*Lophopsetta maculata*) remarkable for its translucency

windowpane oyster *or* **windowpane shell** *n* : a mollusk of the genus *Placuna* that is esp. common in the Philippines and has a large flat somewhat pearly paper-thin shell used for thousands of years esp. by the Chinese as a substitute for glass

windows *pl of* WINDOW, *pres 3d sing of* WINDOW

window screen *n* **1** : a screen usu. of wire mesh designed to fit into a window frame and keep out insects when the window is open **2** : an ornament (as a grille, lattice, or piece of stained glass) used to fill a window opening

window seat *n* : a seat at a window: as **a** : a seat built into a window recess **b** : an upholstered stool with arms designed to fit into a window recess

window shade *n* : SHADE 7g

window-shop \ ˈ ⸱ˌ⸱\ *vi* : to look at the displays in store windows without going inside the stores to make purchases

window-shopper \ ˈ ⸱ˌ⸱⸱\ *n* : one that window-shops

windowshut \ ˈ ⸱ˌ⸱\ *n, archaic* : WINDOW SHUTTER

window shutter *n* : a shutter for a window

windowsill \ ˈ ⸱ˌ⸱\ *n* : the sill of a window; *specif* : the horizontal member at the bottom of a window opening

window stop *n* : a narrow strip that holds a window sash in position in a window frame

window-tax \ ˈ ⸱ˌ⸱\ *n* : a tax formerly levied in England on all windows and openings for light in houses in cities and towns

window trim *n* **1** : WINDOW DECORATION **2** : the moldings covering the jambs and head of a window

window trimmer *n* : WINDOW DRESSER 1

win-dowy \ ˈwindəwē\ *adj* [¹*window* + *-y*] : having many windows or openings

windpipe \ ˈ ⸱ˌ⸱\ *n* : the passage for the breath from the larynx to the lungs : TRACHEA

wind-pollinated \ ˈ ⸱ˌ⸱⸱⸱⸱\ *adj* [¹*wind* + *pollinated*, past part. of *pollinate*] : pollinated by wind-borne pollen

wind poppy *n* : a California wild poppy (*Papaver heterophyllum or Meconopsis heterophylla*) with variable pinnate or pinnately divided leaves and bright brick-red flowers with a dark blotch at the base of each petal

wind power *n* : mechanical power derived from winds

windproof \ ˈ ⸱ˌ⸱\ *adj* : proof against the wind 〈a ~ jacket〉

wind-puff \ ˈ ⸱ˌ⸱\ *n* **1** : puffing of the skin about a wound caused by air that has entered (as after the caponizing of a cockerel) **2** : WINDGALL 1

wind pump *n* : a pump moved by a windmill

wind resistance *n* : the resistance that still air offers to movement esp. of a vehicle

wind ripple *n* : one of many wavelike undulations produced on the surface of sand by wind and occas. found in rocks of aeolian origin

windroad \ ˈ ⸱ˌ⸱\ *n* : AIRWAY 1

wind-rode \ ˈ ⸱ˌ⸱\ *adj* [¹*wind* + *rode*, chiefly dial. past part. of *ride*] : caused to ride with head to the wind practically unaffected by tide or current — used of a ship at anchor with wind and tide approximately opposed; opposed to *tide-rode*

windroot \ ˈ ⸱ˌ⸱\ *n* **1** : BUTTERFLY WEED 1

wind rose *n* **1 a** : a European poppy (*Papaver argemone*) adventive in No. America having red dark-eyed flowers **b** : a purple-flowered perennial southern European herb (*Roemeria hybrida*) of the family Papaveraceae **c** : PRICKLY POPPY **d** : CORN POPPY **2** [G *windrose* compass card, lit., rose of winds, fr. *wind* (fr. OHG *wint*) + *rose* (fr. L *rosa*) — more at WIND, ROSE] **a** : a diagram showing for one place the relative frequency or frequency and strength of winds from different directions **b** : a diagram showing the average occurrence of other meteorological phenomena (as rain and sunshine) with winds from different directions

¹wind-row \ ˈwin(d)ˌrō\ *also* **win-row** \ ˈwin.rō\ *n* [¹*wind* + *row*] **1 a** (1) : a row of hay raked up to dry before being rolled or pitched into cocks (2) : a similar row (as of grain) for drying **b** : a row heaped up by or as if by the wind 〈powdery new snow . . . cut sharp in ~s —Brooks Atkinson〉 〈the tides heap the western beaches with ~s of shells —Marjory S. Douglas〉 **c** (1) : a long low ridge of road-making material that has been scraped to the side of a road (2) : BANK, RIDGE, HEAP 〈these rock ~s, piled up as fields are cleared of stones, hold water on the land —Quentin Keynes〉 〈beneath the wagons lay ~s of slumbering men —T.W.Duncan〉 **2** : a furrow in which sugarcane stalks are laid in order to obtain a new crop of cane from the eyes of the stalks or to protect the stalks from frost

²windrow \ ˈ ⸱\ *also* **winrow** \ ˈ ⸱\ *vt* -ED/-ING/-S : to put into windrows

wind-row-er \ -ōə(r)\ *n* -s [²*windrow* + *-er*] **1** : a curved finger device attached to the rear of the cutter bar of a mowing machine to windrow the swath **2** : SIDE-DELIVERY RAKE **3** : SWATHER **4** : a sugarcane cutter that drops the cut cane into large rows

winds *pl of* WIND, *pres 3d sing of* WIND

windsail \ ˈ ⸱ˌ⸱\ *n* **1** : the sail of a windmill **2** : a wide tube or funnel of canvas used to carry air for ventilation into the lower compartments of a ship

wind scale *n* : a series of numbers or words corresponding to various ranges of wind speeds for indicating the force of the wind — see BEAUFORT SCALE

wind scoop *n* : a scoop-shaped device attached to an air port of a ship to direct outside air inside the ship — called also *wind catcher*

wind scorpion *n* [trans. of Ar *ʿaqrab al-rīḥ*; fr. its extreme agility] : an arachnid of the order Solpugida

windscreen \ ˈ ⸱ˌ⸱\ *n* **1** : a screen that protects against the wind **2** *Brit* : an automobile windshield

wind shake *n* **1** : a shake in timber attributed to high winds 〈pine free from knots, *wind shakes*, and other defects —*U.S. Daily*〉 **2** : a defective condition marked by wind shakes

wind-shaken \ ˈ ⸱ˌ⸱⸱\ *adj* **1** : shaken by the wind **2** : affected by wind shake

wind sheet *n* **:** the current of air that strikes the upper lip of a flue pipe in an organ
wind shelf *n* **:** SMOKE SHELF
windshield \'=,=\ *n* **1 :** a shield that protects against the wind: as **a** (1) **:** a transparent screen (as of glass) that protects the occupants of a vehicle from the wind; *esp* **:** a transparent glass screen that forms the upper front of the passenger compartment of an automobile (2) **:** a metal screen to prevent the wind from blowing on a flame **b :** a tight cuff inside the sleeve of a coat or jacket to keep the wind out **2 :** a cap of light metal placed over the head of a projectile to streamline it
windshield wing *n* **:** an adjustable glass piece attached to the side of the windshield of an automotive vehicle
windshield wiper *n* **:** a device usu. in the form of a rubber squeegee attached to an oscillating arm for wiping the windshield of an automobile or other vehicle
wind–shift line *n* **:** SQUALL LINE
windship \'=,=\ *n* **:** SAILING SHIP
wind–shock \'=,=\ *n, archaic* **:** WIND SHAKE 1
windslab \'=,=\ *n* **:** a crust or mass of snow packed tightly by the wind
wind slash *n* **:** WINDFALL 1c
wind sock *also* **wind sleeve** *n* **:** a truncated cloth cone that is open at both ends and mounted in an elevated position with the large end held open by a rigid ring in a vertical plane so that the cone is free to rotate about a vertical axis to indicate the direction of the wind — called also *wind cone*
[1]**wind·sor** \'winzə(r)\ *adj, usu cap* [fr. *Windsor,* municipal borough of southern England and seat of Windsor Castle, principal residence of England's sovereigns] **1 :** of or from the town of Windsor, England **2 :** of or originating with the household of Windsor Castle
[2]**windsor** \"\ *or* **windsor soap** *n* -s *usu cap W* **:** a scented usu. brown soap
[3]**windsor** \"\ *adj, usu cap* [fr. *Windsor,* city of southeast Ontario, Canada] **:** of or from the city of Windsor, Ont. **:** of the kind or style prevalent in Windsor
[4]**windsor** \"\ *adj, usu cap* [*Windsor chair*] **:** made in the style of a Windsor chair ⟨a *Windsor* settee⟩
windsor bean *also* **windsor** *n* -s *usu cap W* [[1]*windsor*] **:** BROAD BEAN
windsor blue *n, often cap W* **:** a grayish purplish blue that is redder and paler than average delft and redder, lighter, and stronger than average navy blue
windsor chair *also* **windsor** *n* -s *usu cap W* [[1]*windsor*] **:** a wooden chair of stick construction having a spindle back, turned raking legs, and usu. a saddle seat

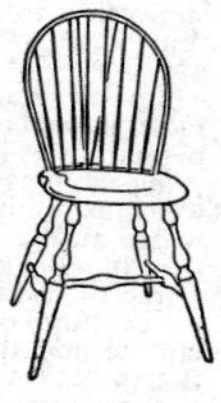
Windsor side chair

windsor green *n, often cap W* **:** LIGHT CHROME GREEN
windsor knot *n, usu cap W* **:** a knot used for tying four-in-hand ties that is wider than the usual four-in-hand knot
windsor tan *n, often cap W* **:** a brownish orange that is redder and duller than leather, less strong, slightly yellower, and lighter than spice, slightly yellower and lighter than prairie brown, and slightly redder and darker than Titian, amber brown, or gold pheasant
windsor tie *n, usu cap W* **:** a broad necktie usu. tied in a loose bow
wind–splitter \'=,==\ *n* **:** a streamlined train of the early 20th century
wind sprint *n* **:** a sprint performed as a training exercise to develop the wind
wind stack *n* **:** a stack of straw made by a wind stacker
wind stacker *n* **:** an apparatus using an air current generated by a fan to stack straw from a threshing machine
wind·ster \'wīn(d)ztə(r), -n(t)st-\ *n* -s [[4]*wind* + *-ster*] *archaic* **:** a person who winds thread or yarn
wind stop *n* [[1]*wind*] **1 :** the part of a window frame that covers the joint between the movable sash or casement and the hanging stile **2 :** WEATHER STRIP
windstorm \'=,=\ *n* **:** a storm characterized by high wind with little or no precipitation
windsucker \'=,==\ *n* [[1]*wind* + *sucker*] **:** a horse that has the habit of wind sucking
wind sucking *n* [[1]*wind* + *sucking,* gerund of *suck*] **:** a bad habit of horses which is related to, often associated with, and similar in effect to crib-biting and in which an affected animal presses the mouth against or grasps with the teeth the manger or other object, arches the neck, and swallows or goes through the motions of swallowing quantities of air
windswept \'=,=\ *adj* [[1]*wind* + *swept,* past part. of *sweep*] **:** swept by or as if by wind
wind–swift \'=,=\ *adj* **:** swift as the wind
wind tee *n* **:** a large weather vane shaped like an airplane or a horizontal letter T located on or near a landing field to indicate wind direction to airplane pilots — called also *landing T*
windthrow \'=,=\ *n* **:** the uprooting and overthrowing of trees by the wind
wind–throw \"\ *vt* [*windthrow*] **:** to uproot and overthrow (a tree) in the wind ⟨a celebrated walnut which was *wind-thrown* . . . some years back —Colin Gibson⟩
wind thrush *n, dial Eng* **:** REDWING 1
windtight \'=,=\ *adj* **:** AIRTIGHT 1
wind–trunk \'=,=\ *n* **:** the duct by which compressed air passes from the bellows to the wind-chest of a pipe organ
wind tunnel *n* **:** a tunnellike passage through which air is blown at a known velocity to determine the effects of wind pressure on an object (as an airplane part or model or a guided missile) placed in the passage — compare WATER TUNNEL
wind up *vb* [[4]*wind* + *up*] *vt* **1** *archaic* **:** to bring together (as a speech) in a final summarizing statement **:** sum up **2 :** to bring to a conclusion **:** END ⟨*wound up* their 27th annual convention here with high praise for the . . . hospitality and cooperation —Benjamin Welles⟩ ⟨a final chapter for the woman golfer *winds up* an unusually helpful manual —*Times Lit. Supp.*⟩ **3 a :** to put in order for the purpose of bringing to an end ⟨the companies are *winding up* their business affairs by retiring their capital stock and paying dividends —*Monsanto Mag.*⟩ ⟨top strategists wished they could *wind up* this session of Congress —*Newsweek*⟩ **b :** to put in order for the purpose of disposal and transferring title **:** SETTLE ⟨an estate is to be *wound up* —*Farmer's Weekly (So. Africa)*⟩ **~** *vi* **1 a :** to come to a conclusion **:** END ⟨*wound up* with a glorification of the resistance movement —A.H.Vandenberg †1951⟩ **b :** to arrive in a place, situation, or condition at the end or as a result (as of a course of action) **:** end up ⟨almost all check crooks *wind up* in jail —Joseph Nolan⟩ ⟨though they started as simple farmers they *wound up* as millionaires —W.P.Webb⟩ **2 a :** to give a preliminary swing to the arm (as before pitching a baseball) **b :** to make preparations **:** work up preliminary momentum **:** get ready ⟨disc jockey . . . *winding up* for an affirmation about snow tires —C.W.Morton⟩
[1]**windup** \'=,=\ *n* -s [*wind up*] **1 a :** the act of bringing to an end ⟨the ~ of certain paper formalities next month —*Wall Street Jour.*⟩ ⟨no ~ report but an introduction —Meyer Levin⟩ **b :** a concluding act or part **:** END, FINISH, SETTLEMENT ⟨a very good ~ to a successful evening —Agnes M. Miall⟩ **2 :** a preliminary swing of the arm (as before pitching a baseball)
[2]**windup** \"\ *adj* [[4]*wind* + *up*] **:** having a part designed for winding up; *esp* **:** having a spring that is wound up by hand for operation ⟨~ toys⟩
wind valley *n* [[1]*wind*] **:** WIND GAP
wind vane *n* **1 :** the sail of a windmill **2 :** VANE 1a
[1]**wind·ward** \'win(d)wə(r)d, *esp nautical* -ndə(r)d\ *adj* [[1]*wind* + *-ward*] **1 a :** moving toward the direction from which the wind is blowing **:** sailing against the wind ⟨a ~ tide⟩ **b :** situated toward the direction from which the wind is blowing ⟨the side the wind reaches first is the ~ . . . side —Gavin Douglas⟩ — opposed to *leeward* **2 :** WEATHERLY — **wind·ward·ness** *n* -ES
[2]**windward** \"\ *n* -s **:** the side or direction from which the wind is blowing ⟨to sail to ~ . . . sail about 45° away from the direction of the wind, then change the direction —H.A.Calahan⟩ — opposed to *leeward* — **to windward** *adv* **:** into or in an advantageous position
wind·ward·ly *adj* [[2]*windward* + *-ly*] **:** WINDWARD 1b, 2

wind·ward·most \-d,mōst\ *adj* [[1]*windward* + *-most* (as in *foremost*)] *archaic* **:** most windward
windway \'=,=\ *n* **:** a passage for air: as **a :** an airway (as for ventilation) in a mine **b :** the narrow slit between the languet and lower lip of an organ flue pipe through which the air current is directed against the upper lip
windwheel \'=,=\ *n* **:** a wheel rotated by the wind to drive a mechanism (as a windmill)
wind–wing \'=,=\ *n* **1 :** WINDSHIELD WING **2 :** a small panel in an automobile window that can be turned outward for ventilation
[1]**windy** \'windē, -di\ *adj* -ER/-EST [ME, fr. OE *windig,* fr. [1]*wind* + *-ig* -y] **1 a :** marked by considerable movement of air: as (1) **:** regularly blown on or through by the wind ⟨a ~ headland running out to the gray northern sea —Andrew Lang⟩ ⟨a tottering structure with vast ~ rooms —Sally Carrighar⟩ (2) **:** marked by strong wind ⟨~ gusts of hail —Mary Austin⟩ ⟨got soaked in a ~ downpour⟩ (3) **:** marked by the presence of more wind than usual ⟨a ~ day⟩ (4) **:** swayed by the wind **:** moving to and fro in the wind ⟨the rank ~ grass of this prairie —Sinclair Lewis⟩ **b** (1) **:** resembling or suggestive of the wind in or as if in physical quality **:** VIOLENT, STORMY (2) *obs* **:** CHANGEABLE, INCONSTANT **c :** producing or controlling wind **2 a :** FLATULENT 2 ⟨an empty ~ stomach —J.M. Synge⟩ **b :** FLATULENT 3 ⟨~ buns —Edith C. Rivett⟩ **3 a :** marked by inflated often pretentious verbosity **:** characterized by long-windedness and lack of substance **:** VERBOSE, BOMBASTIC ⟨~ after-dinner eulogies —J.D.Hart⟩ ⟨a ~ politician⟩ **b :** lacking content or substance **:** EMPTY, INSUBSTANTIAL, FLIMSY ⟨this ~ study promoted the increasing emptiness of philosophy —H.O.Taylor⟩ **4 a** *archaic* **:** productive of pride or conceit **b** *chiefly Scot* **:** PROUD, CONCEITED **5 :** played by means of wind; *esp* **:** played on a wind instrument ⟨a larghetto non troppo with responses by the oboes, clarinets, flutes, and bassoons that was a ~ delight —Janet Flanner⟩ **6 :** BREATHY **7** *chiefly Brit* **:** FRIGHTENED, FEARFUL, NERVOUS — **on the windy side :** out of reach **:** SAFE, CLEAR ⟨still you keep o' th' *windy side* of the law —Shak.⟩
[2]**windy** \"\ *n* -ES **1** *slang* **:** an exaggerated story **:** a tall tale **2** *slang* **:** BLUFF, HOAX
windy city *adj, usu cap W&C* [fr. *the Windy City,* nickname for Chicago] *slang* **:** of or relating to the city of Chicago, Ill. ⟨*Windy City* politicos⟩
[1]**wine** \'wīn\ *n* -s *often attrib* [ME *win,* fr. OE *wīn;* akin to OHG *wīn* wine, ON *vīn,* Goth *wein;* all fr. a prehistoric Gmc word borrowed fr. L *vinum* wine, of non-IE origin; akin to the source of Gk *oinos* wine, Arm *gini*] **1 a :** the fermented juice of the grape containing varying percentages of alcohol and having a composition and character that depends chiefly upon the grapes used and the climate and soil of the area in which they are grown — see APPETIZER WINE, DESSERT WINE, FORTIFIED WINE, SPARKLING WINE, TABLE WINE; RED WINE, ROSÉ, WHITE WINE; GENERIC WINE, VARIETAL WINE; HIGH WINE, LOW WINE **b :** a wine, mixture of water and wine, or wine substitute (as grape juice) used in Christian communion services **:** SACRAMENTAL WINE **c :** a pharmaceutical preparation using fined wine as a vehicle ⟨~ of iron⟩ **2 :** the usu. fermented juice of various agricultural products (as peaches, oranges, blackberries) used as a beverage **3 :** something resembling wine esp. in an ability to invigorate, intoxicate, or spread a feeling of well-being ⟨his was the sparkling ~ of speech —*Manchester Guardian Weekly*⟩ ⟨tasted the ~ of audience approbation —*Western Speech*⟩ ⟨could catch . . . the ~ of a high, clean air —Emerson Hough⟩ **4 :** WINEGLASS 1 ⟨shearing off . . . ~s to their proper height —Percival Marson⟩ **5** *Brit* **:** a social gathering in an English university at which wine is served ⟨when I go out to a ~ I always bring my own straws —W.W.Reade⟩ **6 :** a variable color averaging a dark red that is yellower and duller than cranberry, yellower, less strong, and very slightly lighter than average garnet, and bluer and duller than pomegranate
[2]**wine** \"\ *vb* -ED/-ING/-S *vt* **:** to treat to wine **:** provide with wine esp. at a dinner ⟨would ~ and dine the . . . members of Congress —*American*⟩ **~** *vi* **:** to drink wine esp. with a dinner ⟨*wined* and dined with the leading citizens of each country during his tour of Europe⟩
wineberry \'=- — *see* BERRY\ *n* [ME *winberi, winberie* grape, wineberry, fr. OE *wīnberige* grape, fr. *wīn* wine + *berige, berie* berry — more at BERRY] **1 :** a raspberry (*Rubus phoenicolasius*) of China and Japan grown for ornament and for the small red acid fruits half enclosed in the hairy calyx **2 :** MAKOMAKO 1
wine–cask borer \'=,=-\ *n* **:** any of several ambrosia beetles that make burrows in the wood of wine casks
wine cellar *n* **:** a room used for storing wines
wine cooler *n* **:** a vessel or container in which wine is cooled or kept cool; *specif* **:** a metal-lined wooden container on castered legs often with a lid used esp. in the 18th and early 19th centuries for cooling wine ⟨a Baltimore Hepplewhite mahogany inlaid *wine cooler* —*advt*⟩

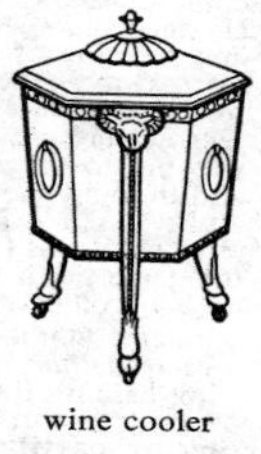
wine cooler

wine–cup \'=,=\ *n* **:** FRINGED POPPY MALLOW
wine dregs *n pl* **:** DREGS OF WINE
wine ferment *n* **:** WINE YEAST
wine fly *n* **:** a fly (as the vinegar fly) found about wine vats
wine gallon *n* **:** an old English unit of capacity for wine equal to the volume of a cylinder seven inches in diameter and six inches high and equivalent to the standard U.S. gallon
[1]**wineglass** \'=,=\ *n* **1 :** a drinking glass that is used for serving wine and has a foot and stem and a variously shaped cup holding from four to six ounces **2 :** a unit of measure that is used in mixing drinks and is equal to four ounces
[2]**wineglass** \"\ *adj* **:** having the shape of a wineglass ⟨lawns . . . covered with ~ elms and willows —Van Wyck Brooks⟩
wine grape *n* **:** a grape used in making wine; *esp* **:** a European grape (*Vitis vinifera*)
winegrower \'=,==\ *n* **:** one that cultivates a vineyard and makes wine from the grapes
wine growing *n* **:** the occupation or industry of cultivating vineyards and producing wine
winehouse \'=,=\ *n* **:** WINESHOP ⟨each political party . . . has its own hotel and ~ in town —Joseph Wechsberg⟩
wine jar *n* **:** TUN SHELL 2
wine lees *n pl* [ME *win lies,* fr. *win* wine + *lies,* pl. of *lie* lee — more at LEE] **:** DREGS OF WINE
wine·less \'=ləs\ *adj* **:** lacking wine ⟨a ~ banquet⟩
wine of ipecac *n* **:** a solution of an alcoholic extract of ipecac in sherry wine or diluted alcohol
wine of opium *n* **:** a solution of opium in aromatized sherry or diluted alcohol having the strength of ordinary laudanum
wine palm *n* **:** any of several palms (as the coquito and the macaw palm) whose sap is used to make palm wine — compare TODDY PALM
wine plant *n* **:** a common garden rhubarb (*Rheum rhaponticum*)
winepress \'=,=\ *n* **:** a vat in which juice is expressed from grapes by treading or by means of a plunger
wine purple *n* **:** a moderate purplish red that is bluer and deeper than average rose or violine pink and bluer than magenta rose
wine red *n* **:** the variable color of red wine averaging a dark red that is stronger and slightly yellower and lighter than average wine, yellower and duller than cranberry, and yellower, lighter, and stronger than average garnet
win·ery \'win(ə)rē, -ri\ *n* -ES **:** a building or plant where wine is made
wines *pl of* WINE, *pres 3d sing of* WINE
wineshop \'=,=\ *n* **:** a café or tavern that specializes in serving wine
wineskin \'=,=\ *n* **:** a bag made from almost the entire skin of an animal and used for holding wine — compare BOTTLE 1b
wine stone *n* **:** [1]ARGOL
wine taster *n* **1 :** one that tests wine by tasting **2 :** a small flat bowl used to hold a sample of wine being tested
wine thrush *n* [so called fr. its color] *dial Eng* **:** REDWING 1
winey *var of* WINY
wine yeast *n* **:** a yeast (esp. *Saccharomyces cerevisiae*) that induces alcoholic fermentation in grape juice — called also *wine ferment*
wine yellow *n* **:** a pale to grayish yellow that is greener and less strong than Naples yellow or cream buff
[1]**wing** \'wiŋ\ *n* -s *often attrib* [ME *winge, wenge,* of Scand origin; akin to Dan & Sw *vinge* wing, ON *vængr;* akin to OE *wāwan* to blow, OHG *wāhen, wāen,* OSw *vīa,* Goth *waian* to blow, Skt *vāti* it blows — more at WIND] **1 a :** an organ of aerial flight **:** one of the movable feathered or membranous paired appendages by means of which an animal (as a bird, bat, or insect) is able to fly; *also* **:** such an appendage even though rudimentary if possessed by an animal belonging to a group characterized by the power of flight — see [3]BAT, BIRD 2a, PTERODACTYL **b :** any of various organic structures (as of the flying fish, flying frog, or flying lemur) providing means of limited flight **c :** one of the broad thin anterior lobes of the foot of a pteropod **d :** the shoulder of a hare or rabbit **2 :** an appendage or part likened to a wing in shape, appearance, or position: as **a :** a device (as for swimming) attached to the shoulders **b :** a shoulder ornament or knot; *esp* **:** a projecting piece attached at the shoulder edge of a 17th century gown or doublet **c** (1) **:** a vane of an arrow (2) **:** the part of a footing forming a side of the splice on an arrow **d :** ALA ⟨the ~ of the nose⟩; *esp* **:** any of the four winglike processes of the sphenoid **e :** a curving lock of hair ⟨has two ~s of pure white in her black hair —Frances Crane⟩ **f :** the arc-shaped piece on a pair of wing compasses or dividers that permits the legs to be fixed at a desired angle **g :** the outside corner of the share of a moldboard plow **h :** a turned-back or extended edge on an article of clothing — see WING COLLAR **i :** a sidepiece at the top of an armchair **j :** a projecting part on one side of a fishnet or at the entry of a trap or corral **k :** either of the parts of a double door or screen **l** (1) **:** a foliaceous, membranous, or woody expansion on a plant (as along the sides of various stems and petioles, of samaras, or of some capsules) (2) **:** either of the two lateral petals of a papilionaceous flower **m :** WING RAIL **n** *Brit* **:** a curved fender for a vehicle; *also* **:** a projecting sidepiece of a dashboard or carriage top **o :** either or any of two or more projections serving as guides (as on a check valve) or as stops (as on a gudgeon) to prevent turning in the socket **3 a :** one of the vanes of a windmill **b :** one of the floats of a waterwheel **c :** SAIL **d :** one of the airfoils that develop a major part of the lift which supports a heavier-than-air airplane **4 a :** a means of flight or rapid progress ⟨fear lent ~s to inspiration —*Time*⟩ **b :** the special attribute of a divine messenger ⟨know that ~s have brushed us⟩ or an angelic nature ⟨seems almost to have sprouted ~s lately⟩ **5 a :** the act or manner of flying **:** FLIGHT ⟨dog required to . . . exhibit steadiness to ~ and shot —W.F.Brown b. 1903⟩ ⟨crow makes ~ to the rooky wood —Shak.⟩ **b :** strength of flight **:** ability to fly **6 a :** ARM; *esp* **:** a throwing or pitching arm **b :** throwing ability **7 a :** the part of the hold or orlop deck of a ship that is nearest the sides **b :** the outboard ends of a ship's bridge **c :** a platform or an overhanging portion of the deck of a ship projecting forward and abaft the paddle box of a side-wheel steamer and supporting the box and protecting the wheel **d :** an addition at the end of a dam but not necessarily in line with it **:** WING WALL **e :** WING JAM **8 :** a side or outlying region or district ⟨no stone in the whole of that ~ of Pakistan suitable for . . . road metalling —D.G.Bridson⟩ **9 :** a part or feature of a building projecting from and subordinate to the main or central part; *broadly* **:** any section of a building ⟨surgical ~ of a hospital⟩ **10 a :** one of the pieces of scenery at the side of the stage **b wings** *pl* **:** the area at the side of the stage out of sight ⟨performers waiting in the ~s for their cues⟩ **11 a :** a division of an army or fleet on either side of a main central body **b :** either member of a body of troops that is divided into two parts **c :** either side or outer extremity of a chess board **d :** one of the positions or players on either side of a center position or of the central lengthwise line of the field, court, or rink in a team sport; *esp* **:** such a position or player on the forward line of a team **12 a :** either of two opposing groups within an organization or society **:** FACTION **b :** a section of an organized body (as a political party or legislative chamber) representing a group or faction holding distinct opinions or policies — compare LEFT WING, RIGHT WING **13 :** a unit of military airplanes: **a :** a unit of an echelon of the U.S. Air Force higher than a group and lower than an air division composed of a headquarters and usu. four groups **b :** two or more squadrons of naval airplanes not carrier based ⟨heavy attack ~⟩ ⟨patrol ~⟩ **14 :** a tap dance step characterized by a sideward slide and retrieve of one foot; *also* **:** a waltz step similarly executed — **on the wing 1 :** in flight **:** FLYING **2 :** in motion **:** TRAVELING ⟨*on the wing* gathering material for his novels —James Reynolds⟩ — **on wings** *adv* **:** as if flying **:** LIGHTHEARTEDLY — **take wing :** to begin flight **:** depart swiftly **:** fly away — **under one's wing :** under one's protection **:** in one's charge or care
[2]**wing** \"\ *vb* -ED/-ING/-S *vt* **1** *obs* **a :** to carve (a bird) for serving **b :** to pluck the wings from (as an insect) **2 a :** to fit with wings ⟨sailcloth that ~*ed* the clipper ships —*Women's Wear Daily*⟩ **b :** to attach feathers to (an arrow) **:** FLETCH ⟨he himself who had ~*ed* the arrow of his fate —C.S.Forester⟩ **3 :** to enable to fly or move swiftly **:** give speed to ⟨fear ~*ed* his feet⟩ **4** *archaic* **:** to supply with pieces or divisions at the side **:** FLANK **5 a :** to wound in the wing **:** disable the wing of ⟨~ a flying duck⟩ **:** bring down by shooting **b :** to hit or wound (as with a bullet) without killing ⟨~*ed* by a sniper⟩ **6 :** to pass through in flight **:** traverse with or as if with wings ⟨the blue deep thou *wingest* —P.B.Shelley⟩ **7 :** to effect or achieve by flying ⟨~*ing* our way out to India —Dillon Sipley⟩ **8 :** to send off swiftly **:** let fly **:** DISPATCH ⟨would start to ~ punches —A.J.Liebling⟩ **9 :** to shift (weights) in a ship to near the sides in order to lengthen the period of roll — used usu. with *out* ⟨~ out ballast⟩ **10 :** to set (a sail) to catch a following wind — used with *out* ⟨jibs are ~*ed out* by means of a whisker pole —G.W.Elder & Ernest Ratsey⟩ **11** *dial* **:** to brush or sweep with or as if with a wing **~** *vi* **1 :** to go with or as if with wings **:** FLY, SAIL ⟨swallows ~*ing* southward⟩ ⟨watch the racing fleets ~ up to the start —E.A.Weeks⟩ **2** *of a horse* **:** to swing one or more of the legs out from the body
wing and wing *adv* **:** with sails boomed out on both sides ⟨running *wing and wing* before the wind⟩
wingback \'=,=\ *n* **:** a football back whose position on offense is outside of the offensive end; *also* **:** the position of a player so stationed
wing back formation *n* **:** an offensive formation in football in which a back is placed just behind or slightly beyond and to the rear of an end
[1]**wing band** *n* **1 :** WING BAR 1 **2 :** a metal clip placed in the wing of a domestic fowl for purposes of identification
[2]**wing band** *vt* **:** to mark (a bird) with a wing band
wing bar *n* **1 :** a line of contrasting color across the middle of a bird's wing made by markings on the wing coverts — see COCK illustration **2 :** a sandbar which partially crosses the entrance to a bay or mouth of a river
wing bay *n* **:** SPECULUM 5
wingbeat \'=,=\ *n* **:** a stroke of a bird's wings in flying
wing bolt *n* **:** a bolt having a head like a wing nut
wing bow *n* **:** the lesser coverts of the shoulder or bend of a bird's wing when distinctively colored — used esp. of poultry; see GOOSE illustration
wing car *n* **:** a car suspended off the center line of an airship — called also *sidecar*
wing case *n* **:** ELYTRON 1
wing cell *n* **1 :** one of the areas bounded by veins in an insect's wing **2 :** CELL 3c
wing chair *or* **winged chair** *n* **:** an upholstered armchair with high solid back and sides turned at such an angle that they provide a rest for the head and protection from drafts — called also *draft chair, lug chair*

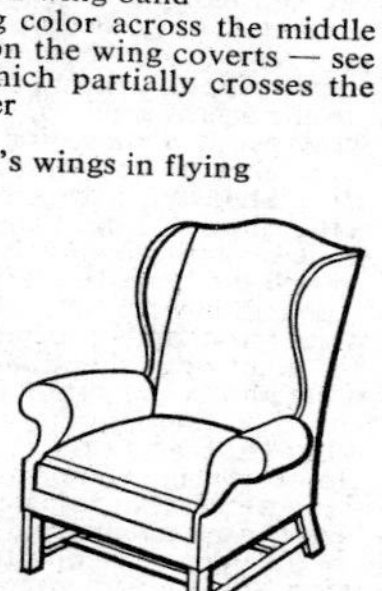
wing chair

wing collar *n* **1 :** a man's stand-up collar having the upper

corners turned down to form wings and worn esp. for formal dress **2 :** a woman's folding or spreading collar with pointed corners
wing commander *n* **:** an officer (as in the British Royal Air Force) equivalent in rank to a lieutenant-colonel in the army
wing compass *n* **:** a carpenter's compass having a metal arc and binding screw for setting at the desired degree of opening
wing cover *n* **:** ELYTRON 1
wing covert *n* **:** one of the coverts of the wing quills — see BIRD illustration
wing dam *n* **:** PIER DAM
wing–dam \'ˌ=\ *vt* [*wing dam*] **:** to provide (as a river) with a wing dam
wing deck *n* **:** WING 7c
wing·ding \'wiŋ,diŋ\ *n* -s [origin unknown] **1** *slang* **a :** a nervous seizure or attack induced by narcotics **b :** a pretended fainting fit or illness **c :** a fit of rage **:** TANTRUM **d :** SPREE **2 a :** a wild or lively or lavish party **b** *slang* **:** a social affair ⟨a series of proms and ~*s* his frat was giving —Frank Sullivan⟩
wing dividers *n pl* **:** a pair of dividers that resemble a wing compass
winged \ˈwiŋd *or except in sense 1a(2)* ˈwiŋəd\ *adj* [ME, fr. *winge* wing + *-ed*] **1 a** (1) **:** having wings ⟨~ seed⟩ ⟨~ mirror⟩ ⟨~ statue of Mercury⟩ (2) **:** having wings of a specified character — usu. used in combination ⟨strong-*winged*⟩ ⟨white-*winged*⟩ ⟨double-*winged* hospital building⟩ **b :** using wings in flight **:** capable of flight ⟨~ insect⟩ ⟨all ~ creatures⟩ **2 a :** soaring with or as if with wings **:** LOFTY, ELEVATED ⟨free, passionate, ~ love — Sinclair Lewis⟩ **b :** SWIFT, RAPID ⟨the ~ days flew on —Winston Churchill⟩ ⟨~ gossip of the town —A.W.Long⟩
winged disk *n* **:** SUN DISK
winged elm *or* **wing elm** *n* **:** a No. American elm (*Ulmus alata*) having twigs and young branches with prominent corky projections
winged everlasting *n* **:** an Australian herb (*Ammobium alatum*) with white woolly foliage and winged stems
wing·ed·ly \'wiŋədlē\ *adv* **:** on or as if on the wing **:** LIGHTLY, SWIFTLY, EXALTEDLY
wing·ed·ness *n* -ES **:** the quality or state of having wings
winged pea *n* **:** a European annual herb (*Lotus tetragonolobus*) having a 4-winged edible pod
winged pigweed *n* **:** a bushy annual weed (*Cycloloma atriplicifolium*) of the family Chenopodiaceae of central No. America having the flowers greenish and the fruiting calyx horizontally winged
winged spindle tree *or* **winged euonymus** *n* **:** a shrub or small tree (*Euonymus alatus*) of China and Japan that has winged branches and is used as an ornamental
winged thistle *n* **:** an annual thistle (*Carduus tenuiflorus*) of New Zealand where it has become a troublesome weed because of its prolific seeding
winged yam *n* **:** WHITE YAM
wing·er \'wiŋə(r)\ *n* -s [¹*wing* + *-er*] **1 :** a cask stowed in the wing of a ship **2 :** a player in a wing position in football, soccer, rugby, hockey; *esp* **:** BREAKAWAY 6
wing feather *n* **:** one of the feathers of a bird's wing; *esp* **:** one of the flight feathers
wingfish \'ˌ=\ *n* **:** a sea robin having large pectoral fins like wings
wing flap *n* **:** a hinged or pivoted and sometimes extensible portion of an airplane wing used to increase the lift and drag for making landings at reduced speeds
wing–footed \'ˌ==\ *adj* **1 :** having winged feet **:** SWIFT, FLEET ⟨*wing-footed* messenger⟩ **2 :** having the anterior lobes of the foot so modified as to form a pair of winglike swimming organs — used of the pteropod mollusks
wing forward *n* **:** a position or player on the wing of a forward line in a team game (as soccer, rugby, or hockey); *esp* **:** BREAKAWAY 6
wing game *n, Brit* **:** GAME BIRDS — distinguished from *ground game*
wing gap *n* **:** GAP 4a(1)
wing half *or* **wing halfback** *n* **:** the right or left halfback in hockey or soccer or rugby
wingier *comparative of* WINGY
wingiest *superlative of* WINGY
winging *pres part of* WING
wing jam *n* **:** a jam of logs that slants upstream until the upper end rests against the shore
wing key *n* **:** BIT KEY
wing·less \'ˌləs\ *adj* **1 :** having no wings ⟨~ insect⟩ **2 a :** incapable of flight ⟨~ bird⟩ **b :** slow-moving **:** PEDESTRIAN ⟨~ verse⟩ — **wing·less·ness** *n* -ES
wing·let \-lət\ *n* -s **1 :** a very small wing **2 :** BASTARD WING
winglike \'ˌ=\ *adj* **:** resembling a wing in form or lateral position
wing loading *or* **wing load** *n* **:** the gross weight of an airplane fully loaded divided by the area of the supporting surface
wing louse *n* **:** a biting louse (*Lipeurus caponis*) that occurs on the wing feathers of poultry
wing·man \'ˌmən\ *n, pl* **wingmen :** a pilot that flies behind and outside the leader of a flying formation so as to furnish support or protection; *also* **:** the plane flown in this position
wing mite *n* **:** a feather mite (*Pterolichus obtusus*) that is parasitic on poultry
wing net *n* **:** a fishing stake net with side extensions
wing nut *n* **1 :** a nut with wings affording a grip for the thumb and finger **2 :** a tree of the genus *Pterocarya*

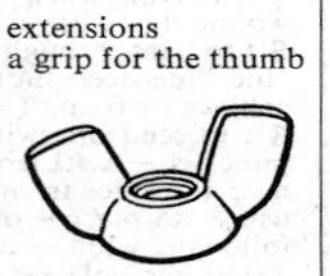

wing nut 1

wingover \'ˌ==\ *n* -s [fr. the phrase *wing over*] **:** a flight maneuver in which a plane is put into a climbing turn until nearly stalled after which the nose is allowed to fall while the turn is continued until normal flight is attained in a direction opposite to that in which the maneuver was entered
wing pad *n* **:** the undeveloped wings of the active pupa of an insect
wing passage *n* **:** a passageway in a ship below the main deck next to a side
wing petal *n* **:** WING 2 1 (2)
wingpiece \'ˌ=\ *n* **:** a piece of scenery slid in from the wings
wing plow *n* **:** a snowplow with side extensions
wing quill *n* **:** one of the flight feathers of a bird's wing
wing rail *n* **:** either of the two outside rails of a railroad frog of which both are rigid in a rigid frog and one is hinged in a spring rail frog
wing roll *n* **:** rotation of an airplane on its longitudinal axis
wings \'wiŋz\ *n pl* **:** insignia consisting of an outspread pair of stylized bird's wings which with various superimposed devices are awarded usu. on completion of prescribed training (as to a qualified pilot, bombardier, gunner, navigator, observer, flight surgeon, or other crew member or a balloon pilot in the armed services) — called also *aviation badge*
wing scout *n* **:** a senior girl scout who is a member of a troop specializing in aviation
wing sheath *n* **:** ELYTRON
wing shell *n* **1** *obs* **:** ELYTRON **2 a :** any of various marine bivalves of the family Pteriidae and esp. the genus *Pteria* in which the hinge border projects like a wing **b :** a shell of the genus *Strombus* **c :** a pteropod shell **d :** a piddock shell
wing shooting *n* **:** the act or practice of shooting at game birds in flight or at flying targets
wing shot *n* **1 :** a shot at a flying bird or target **2 :** one skilled in wing shooting
wing skid *n* **:** a skid attached to an airplane wing near the tip to protect the wing from contact with the ground
wing slot *n* **:** an adjustable opening between either the leading edge of an aileron and the rest of a wing or the leading edge of a wing and a cap fitting over it
wing snail *n* **:** PTEROPOD
wingspan \'ˌ=\ *n* [¹*wing* + *span*] **:** the length of an airplane wing measured between outermost tips regardless of intervening elements
wingspread \'ˌ=\ *n* **:** the spread of the wings **:** WINGSPAN; *specif* **:** the extreme measurement between the tips or outer margins of the wings (as of a bird or insect) when fully extended or expanded
wingstem \'ˌ=\ *n* [¹*wing* + *stem*] **1 :** GOLDEN IRONWEED **2 :** CROWNBEARD
wing three-quarter *n* **:** a rugby player positioned at either end of the three-quarter line; *also* **:** the position of such a player
wing tie *n* **:** a bow tie with flaring ends
wing tip *n* **1 :** a toecap having a point extending back toward the throat of the shoe and curving sides extending toward the shank **2 :** a shoe having a wing tip
wing-tip flare \'ˌ=-\ *n* **:** an electrically operated light attached to the tips of airplane wings
wing-tip float *n* **:** a small float on the underside of a tip of the lower wing of a seaplane
wing top *n* **:** a wing-shaped metal top that fits on a Bunsen burner and gives a broad flat flame
wing tract *n* **:** the tract bearing the wing feathers including the primaries, secondaries, and wing coverts — compare PTERYLOSIS
wing transom *n* **:** the upper and outer transom of the stern frame of a ship
wing truss *n* **:** the structural frame comprising struts, wires or tie rods, and spars by which the wing loads of an airplane are transmitted to the fuselage
wing valve *n* **:** a check valve provided with wings to guide the valve to its seat
wing wale *n* **:** WING 7c
wing wall *n* **:** a subordinate lateral wall (as an abutment) or an oblique retaining wall (as of a bridge approach)
wingy \'wiŋē, -iŋi\ *adj* -ER/-EST **1 :** having wings **:** RAPID, SWIFT **2 :** soaring with or as if with wings **:** LOFTY **3 :** resembling or suggesting a wing in shape or position **:** WINGLIKE ⟨~ sleeves⟩
winier *comparative of* WINY
winiest *superlative of* WINY
wining *pres part of* WINE
win·ish \'wīnish\ *adj* [¹*wine* + *-ish*] **:** of, relating to, characteristic of, or resembling wine
¹wink \'wiŋk\ *vb* -ED/-ING/-S [ME *winken*, fr. OE *wincian;* akin to MD *winken* to stagger, wink, OHG *winchan* to stagger, wink, *wankōn* to stagger, totter, flicker, ON *vakka* to stray, hover, Lith *vengti* to avoid, Skt *vañgati* he limps — more at PREVARICATE] *vi* **1 a :** to close one's eyes ⟨kept my eyes shut . . . I ~*ed* as close as ever I could —Sir Walter Scott⟩ **b** *obs* **:** to take a nap **:** SLEEP **2 a :** to give a glance or sign with the eyes ⟨saw her mother ~ at her across the room and knew she would have to leave⟩ **b :** to shut one eye briefly in a teasing or jocular manner ⟨never did any harm to ~ at a pretty girl⟩ ⟨grinned and ~*ed* knowingly⟩ **3 :** to close and open the eyelids quickly and involuntarily ⟨staring at each other as if a bet were depending on the first man who ~*ed* —George Eliot⟩ **4 :** to avoid seeing or noting something as if by closing the eyes **:** CONNIVE — usu. used with *at* ⟨have ~*ed* at his frequent absences from school —George Sampson⟩ ⟨stubbornly refused to ~ at a violation of the law —Oscar Handlin⟩ **5 :** to gleam or flash fitfully or intermittently **:** FLICKER, TWINKLE ⟨at twilight, when the little fires ~ in the mountain dusk —E.W. Smith⟩ ⟨the house windows are ~*ing* with yellow lamplight —Phil Stong⟩ ⟨copper pans ~ on the walls —Katherine Mansfield⟩ **6 a :** to terminate suddenly **:** come to an end — usu. used with *out* ⟨when his employment . . . ~*ed* out he had bought a one-way ticket —Ellery Sedgwick⟩ ⟨the spark of enterprise has by no means ~*ed* out in this young generation —Dixon Wecter⟩ **b :** to stop shining — usu. used with *out* ⟨the lights ~*ed* out along the bridge —Elizabeth Enright⟩ **7 :** to signal a message with a light ⟨the destroyer was ~*ing* urgently —Vincent McHugh⟩ **~ *vt* 1 :** to cause to open and shut ⟨~*ed* his eyelids once or twice and squared his jaw —Donn Byrne⟩ **2 :** to affect or influence by or as if by blinking the eyes ⟨replied, shaking her head, ~*ing* back the tears —Frank Norris⟩ **3 :** to signal with (a light) esp. by blinking ⟨~*ing* their flashlights hopefully —M.W.Childs⟩ **4 :** to disregard or ignore intentionally ⟨there was no ~*ing* the matter: these two were enemies —Georgiana Pentlarge⟩
²wink \"\ *n* -s [ME, fr. *winken* to wink] **1 a :** a closing of the eyelids in or as if in sleep **:** a brief period of sleep **:** NAP ⟨sleep was one ~ —George Meredith⟩ ⟨I didn't get a ~ on the night —Hall Caine⟩ **b** *obs* **:** DEATH ⟨give mine enemy a lasting ~ —Shak.⟩ **2 a :** a glance or sign with or as if with the eyes usu. of admonition, command, direction, or invitation ⟨the bloke . . . tipped him the ~ —Richard Llewellyn⟩ ⟨had the ~ from Moscow —*New Republic*⟩ **b :** an act of winking; *esp* **:** the brief shutting of one eye ⟨a ~ of his eye and a twist of his head soon gave me to know I had nothing to dread —Clement Moore⟩ **3 a :** the time required to close and open an eye **:** an exceedingly brief period **:** INSTANT ⟨quick as a ~⟩ ⟨he was gone in a ~⟩ **b :** the smallest possible amount ⟨so dark, we couldn't see a ~⟩ ⟨an average of a ~ over 10 p.c. for the eighteen years —*Sydney (Australia) Bull.*⟩ **4 :** a quick closing and opening of the eyelids **:** BLINK ⟨several ~*s* brushed the tears away⟩ ⟨the eyelid . . . is likely to give a small reflex ~ to any sudden stimulus —R.S.Woodworth⟩ **5 :** an intermittent gleam **:** FLASH, SPARKLE ⟨the planes were little silver ~*s* way out to the west —Joseph Dever⟩ ⟨saw the ~ at her bow and thought she was signaling —Vincent McHugh⟩
³wink \"\ *n* -s [by shortening] *Brit* **:** ²PERIWINKLE
⁴wink \"\ *n* -s [short for *tiddledywink*] **:** a small disk used in the game tiddledywinks — called also *tiddledywink*
wink·er \-kə(r)\ *n* -s **:** one that winks: as **a :** a horse's blinder **:** BLINKER **b :** EYE ⟨just keep your ~*s* glued to me —*Metropolitan Mag.*⟩; *also* **:** EYELASH ⟨rolled his left eyelid up with careful fingers and . . . found the ~ —P.D.Boles⟩ **c :** CONCUSSION BELLOWS
winking cartilage *n* **:** the nictitating membrane when cartilaginous (as in a horse and various other mammals)
wink·ing·ly *adv* **:** in a winking manner
winking muscle *n* **:** the orbicularis of the eye that by its contraction draws the eyelids together
¹win·kle \'wiŋkəl\ *n* -s [short for *periwinkle*] **1 :** ²PERIWINKLE **2 :** any of various whelks esp. of the genus *Busycon* that destroy large numbers of oysters and clams by drilling their shells and rasping away their flesh
²winkle \"\ *vt* -ED/-ING/-S **:** to displace, extract, or evict from a position — usu. used with *out* ⟨failed to ~ out those two or three machine guns which were firing through some concealed opening —Peter Rainier⟩ ⟨the first year of nursing training ~*s* out most of the unsuitable subjects —Cormac Swan⟩
³winkle \"\ *vi* -ED/-ING/-S [¹*wink* + *-le*] **:** TWINKLE
winn \'win\ *chiefly Scot var of* ²WIND 3
win·na \ˈwinə\ [alter. (influenced by ¹*na*) of ME *winnot*, contr. of *will not*] *Scot* **:** will not
win·nable \'winəbəl\ *adj* **:** able to be won ⟨the war is not militarily ~ —Thomas Griffith⟩
win·nard \'winə(r)d\ *n* -s [prob. by shortening & alter. fr. G dial. *weingartdrossel* winnard, lit., vineyard thrush, fr. G *weingarten* vineyard (fr. MHG *wîngarte*, fr. *wîn* wine — fr. OHG — + *garte* garden, fr. OHG *garto*) + *drossel* thrush, fr. OHG *droscala* — more at WINE, YARD, THRUSH] *dial Eng* **:** the European redwing
win·ne·ba·go \ˌwinə'bā,gō\ *n, pl* **winnebago** *or* **winnebagos** *or* **winnebagoes** *usu cap* **1 a :** a Siouan people in eastern Wisconsin south of Green Bay **b :** a member of such people **2 :** the language of the Winnebago people
winned *past of* WIN
win·ner \'winə(r)\ *n* -s [ME, fr. *winnen* to win + *-er* — more at WIN] **:** one that wins: as **a :** one that is or will become successful esp. through praiseworthy ability and hard work **b :** a victor esp. in games and sports **c :** one that brings victory **d :** one that wins admiration ⟨a real ~ is her day costume —Lois Long⟩ **e :** FACEMAN **f :** a card that wins a trick or may be expected to win a trick **:** PLAYING TRICK
winner's circle *n* **:** an enclosure near a racetrack where the winning horse and jockey are brought for photographs and awards
win·nie \'winē, -ni\ *n* -s *usu cap* [*winner* + *-ie*] **:** any of several bronze statuettes awarded annually by a professional group for fashion design
¹win·ning \'winiŋ, -nēŋ\ *n* -s [ME, fr. gerund of *winnen* to win] **1 :** the act of one that wins **:** ACQUISITION, VICTORY ⟨the ~ of the peace —Norman Foerster⟩ **2 :** a captured territory **:** CONQUEST ⟨the Antonine ~*s* . . . rose in revolt against the overstretched-out garrison —Jacquetta & Christopher Hawkes⟩ **3 :** the gaining esp. of a follower or of another's allegiance or trust ⟨the ~ of the people to his political beliefs⟩ **4 :** something one wins; *esp* **:** the money won by success in a competition **:** GAIN, PROFIT — usu. used in pl. ⟨gave . . . total ~*s* as $6119 —*Current Biog.*⟩ **5 a :** a shaft or pit opening made to win coal **b** (1) **:** a portion of a coal bed ready for mining (2) **:** a more or less isolated section of a mine
²winning \"\ *adj* [fr. pres. part. of ¹*win*] **1 a :** of, relating to, or used for or in the act of winning ⟨before a country is ready to relinquish any ~ weapons it must have more than words to reassure it —B.M.Baruch⟩ **b :** successful in competition ⟨a ~ team⟩ **2 :** adapted to win favor **:** ATTRACTIVE, CAPTIVATING, CHARMING ⟨an engaging modesty and a ~ sense of humor —R.M.Lovett⟩ ⟨a ~ rather than forceful personality —F.H.Ristine⟩ **syn** see SWEET
winning gallery *n* **:** a netted opening which is below the side penthouse, which is farthest from the dedans, and into which a played ball is counted as winning in court tennis
winning hazard *n* **:** a hazard in pool that pockets the object ball
win·ning·ly *adv* **:** in a winning manner ⟨smiled ~ —S.E. White⟩ ⟨the familiar theme is ~ presented —Caroline Tunstall⟩
win·ning·ness *n* -ES **:** the quality or state of being winning ⟨conscious of his charm, of the ~ of his personal style —Lionel Trilling⟩
winning opening *n* **:** the dedans, grille, or winning gallery of a court-tennis court
win·ni·nish *also* **win·no·nish** *n, pl* **win·ni·nish** *also* **win·no·nish** \ˌwinə'nish\ [Montagnais *wananish*, dim. of *wanans* salmon] **:** OUANANICHE
win·ni·peg \'winə,peg\ *adj, usu cap* [fr. *Winnipeg*, Manitoba] **:** of or from Winnipeg, the capital of Manitoba **:** of the kind or style prevalent in Winnipeg
win·ni·peg·ger \-gə(r)\ *n* -s *cap* [*Winnipeg* + E *-er*] **:** a native or resident of Winnipeg, Manitoba
¹win·nock \'winək\ *n* -s [ME (Sc) *windok, windowe* — more at WINDOW] *Scot* **:** WINDOW ⟨the doors and ~*s* rattle —Robert Burns⟩
²winnock \"\ *var of* WHINNOCK
¹win·now \'wi(,)nō, -nə, *often* -əw+V\ *vb* -ED/-ING/-S [ME *winewen, windewen*, fr. OE *windwian* to fan, winnow; akin to OHG *wintōn* to fan, winnow, Goth *diswinthjan*, L *ventilare* to fan, winnow, *vannus* winnowing fan, *ventus* wind — more at WIND] *vt* **1 a** (1) **:** to separate and drive off (as chaff) by subjection to wind or a current of air (2) **:** to get rid of (as that which is undesirable or unwanted) **:** take out **:** DELETE, REMOVE — often used with *out* ⟨~ out certain inaccuracies —Stanley Walker⟩ **b :** to analyze and assort to obtain the most desirable **:** SELECT, SEPARATE, SIFT ⟨~*ed* out facts and probabilities from prejudices —William Vogt⟩ ⟨an old hand at ~*ing* what is true and significant —Oscar Lewis⟩ **2 a :** to treat (as grain) by exposure to wind or a current of air so that waste matter is eliminated ⟨when the grain was flailed they ~*ed* it —Pearl Buck⟩ **b :** to treat in a manner resembling this **:** free of useless, unwanted, or baser components ⟨~ the immense number of applications —W.H.Hale⟩ ⟨the lack of discipline and the failure to ~ her material —Dachine Rainer⟩ **3 :** to beat with or as if with wings **:** make a way through by flying ⟨geese ~*ing* the purple dusk⟩ **4 :** to blow on **:** FAN ⟨the wind ~*ing* his thin white hair —*Time*⟩ **~ *vi* 1 a :** to separate chaff from grain by fanning **b :** to separate the desirable from the undesirable by careful perusing ⟨appointed an editor to ~ through the day's diplomatic dispatches and produce a daily news file —W.M.Healy⟩ **2 :** to move or pass on a course with or as if with wings ⟨the petrel . . . came ~*ing* in from afar on the sea —D.L.Sharp⟩ **3 :** to blow in gusts
²winnow \"\ *n* -s **1 :** a device for winnowing **2 :** the act of winnowing **:** a motion resembling that of winnowing
win·now·er \-nəwə(r)\ *n* -s [ME *winewer*, fr. *winewen* to winnow + *-er*] **:** one that winnows; *esp* **:** a winnowing machine
winnowing basket *or* **winnowing–fan** \'ˌ==ˌ=\ *n* **1 :** a device for winnowing grain **2 :** a representation of a winnowing basket used as a heraldic design
wi·no \'wī,nō\ *n* -s [¹*wine* + *-o*] **:** one who is chronically addicted to drinking wine
winrace \'ˌ=\ *n* [fr. the phrase *win* (the) *race*] **:** the fastest time made by the winning horse in a public trotting race
winrow *var of* WINDROW
wins *pres 3d sing of* WIN, *pl of* WIN
winsey *var of* WINCEY
wins·low's foramen \'winz,lōz-\ *n, usu cap W* [after Jacques B. *Winslow* †1760 Fr. anatomist] **:** EPIPLOIC FORAMEN
wins·low system \'winz,lō-\ *n, usu cap W* [after Thomas Newby *Winslow* †1942 Am. lawyer, mathematician, and bridge expert] **:** a method of bidding at contract bridge based upon valuation of an ace as 1½ probable tricks, king 1, queen ½, and jack ¼ and on the principle that the lowest-ranking four-card suit regardless of its high-card content should be bid first
win·some \'win(t)səm\ *adj, sometimes* -ER/-EST [ME *wonsom, wonsum*, fr. OE *wynsum*, fr. *wynn* joy, pleasure (akin to OS *wunnia* joy, pleasure, OHG *wunna, wunnī*) + *-sum* -some; akin to L *venus* love — more at WIN] **1 :** causing joy or pleasure **:** AGREEABLE, PLEASANT, WINNING ⟨~ tableaux of old-fashioned literary days —J.D.Hart⟩ ⟨the wide-eyed and ~ lass —*Current Biog.*⟩ **2 :** very lighthearted **:** CHEERFUL, GAY ⟨misled by ill example and a ~ nature —Francis Jeffrey⟩ **syn** see SWEET
win·some·ly *adv* **:** in a winsome manner
win·some·ness *n* -ES **:** the quality or state of being winsome ⟨the calculating ~ of a man who is spoiled by the ladies —Kenneth Roberts⟩
¹win·ter \'wintə(r)\ *n* -s *often attrib* [ME, fr. OE; akin to OHG *wintar*, ON *vetr*, Goth *wintrus*, and prob. to OE *wæter* water — more at WATER] **1 a :** the season between autumn and spring reckoned astronomically as extending from the December solstice to the March equinox **b :** the season comprising the months of December, January, and February **c** *Brit* **:** the season comprising the months of November, December, and January **d :** the colder half of the year — contrasted with *summer* **e :** the rainy season in the tropics **f :** the season reckoned astronomically in the southern hemisphere as extending from the June solstice to the September equinox **2 :** YEAR ⟨happened many ~*s* ago⟩; *esp* **:** one of the years of one's life ⟨a man of 70 ~*s*⟩ **3 :** a period felt to resemble winter esp. in being marked by dreariness, lack of activity, adversity, or decay **4** [*winter yellowlegs*] *chiefly NewEng* **:** GREATER YELLOWLEGS
²winter \"\ *vb* **wintered; wintered; wintering** \-ntəriŋ, -n·triŋ\ **winters** [ME *wintren*, fr. ¹*winter*] *vi* **1 :** to pass the winter ⟨~ in the city⟩ ⟨bears ~*ing* in a rocky den⟩ **2 :** to feed or find food during the winter — used with *on* ⟨small birds ~*ing* on the seeds of weeds and grasses⟩ **~ *vt* 1 :** to keep, feed, or manage during the winter ⟨~ young cattle on straw⟩ **2 :** to affect like winter **:** give a wintery aspect to **3 :** WINTERIZE
win·tera \'wintərə\ *n, cap* [NL, after John *Wynter* (or *Winter*), 16th cent. Brit. naval officer] **:** the type genus of the family Winteraceae
win·ter·a·ce·ae \ˌ==ˈrāsē,ē\ *n pl, cap* [NL, fr. *Wintera*, type genus + *-aceae*] **:** a small family of chiefly tropical shrubs and trees (order Ranales) characterized by alternate aromatic pellucid-dotted leaves without stipules and rather small usu. cymose or fasciculate flowers with a single whorl of carpels and sometimes included in Magnoliaceae
winter aconite *n* **:** a small Old World perennial herb (*Eranthis hyemalis*) often cultivated for its bright yellow flowers which often are produced before the snow is off the ground
winter annual *n* **:** a plant that germinates in autumn, lives through the winter, and produces seed and dies in the following growing season
winter apple *n* **:** a late-ripening apple that keeps well in winter
winter band *n* **:** the annulus of a fish scale
winter barley *n* **:** barley that is sown in the fall and ripens during the following spring or summer
winter beer *n* **:** SCHENK BEER
winterberry \'ˌ=— *see* BERRY\ *n* **:** any of various American plants of the genus *Ilex* having bright red berries persistent through the winter: as **a :** BLACK ALDER 1 **b :** SMOOTH WINTERBERRY

winter bird *n* : any of several birds seen chiefly in winter; *esp* : ATLANTIC KITTIWAKE

winterbloom \'==,=\ *n* **1** : WITCH HAZEL 2a **2** : AZALEA

winter bonnet *n, dial Brit* : a European gull (*Larus canus*)

winterbound \'==,=\ *adj* : restrained (as from a favored sport or other outdoor activity) by winter

winterbourne \'==,=\ *n* : a stream that flows only or chiefly in winter

winter bud *n* **1** : STATOBLAST **2** : the dormant much condensed shoot of a woody plant enclosed in protective scales or covering that enable it to survive the winter

winter bunting *n* : SNOW BUNTING

winter cabbage *n* : any of various cabbages that will survive the winter in the open in mild regions (as the southern U.S.); *esp* : SAVOY 1

winter cauliflower *n* : BROCCOLI 1

winter cherry *n* **1 a** : CHINESE LANTERN PLANT **b** : the fruit of this plant **2** : BALLOON VINE **3** : JERUSALEM CHERRY

winter chip bird *n* : TREE SPARROW 2

winter-clad \'=¦=\ *adj* : clothed suitably for winter

winter count *n* : a calendar or year record of the No. American Indians involving pictographic accounts of events and serving as tribal chronicles

winter crane fly *n* : a fly of the family Trichoceratidae often appearing in swarms during fall, winter, and spring

wintercreeper \'==,==\ *n* : an evergreen shrubby, trailing, or climbing euonymus (*Euonymus fortunei*) that is widely cultivated as an ornamental in several horticultural varieties differing chiefly in habit or in form or color of leaves

winter cress *n* [prob. trans. of D *winterkers*] : any of several Eurasian yellow-flowered cresses constituting the genus *Barbarea* and sometimes cultivated for winter salad

winter crookneck *n* : any of several crooknecks that are winter squashes of the pumpkin group, are noted for their keeping qualities, and usu. have smooth variously striped rinds — compare SUMMER CROOKNECK

winter crop *n* : a crop (as of oats) fall-sown for growth during the winter and maturing in the spring

winter daffodil *n* : an autumn-blooming perennial herb (*Sternbergia lutea*) of the Mediterranean region having solitary yellow flowers and being often grown as an ornamental

winter duck *n* **1** *Brit* : PINTAIL 1a **2** : OLD SQUAW

wintered *adj* [fr. past part. of ²*winter*] : subjected to the action of wintery conditions : chilled or altered by exposure to winter

winter egg *n* : a thick-shelled usu. sexually produced egg of many and esp. freshwater invertebrates that lives through the winter and hatches in the spring — compare SUMMER EGG

win·ter·er \'wintərə(r), -n·trə(r)\ *n* -s : one that winters: as **a** : a winter resident or visitor ⟨the southern ~s⟩ ⟨some birds are coastal ~s⟩ **b** *archaic* : an animal taken in charge through a winter **c** : a fur trader's employee formerly remaining in Indian country throughout the winter

winter-fallow \'=¦==\ *vt* [¹*winter* + *fallow*, v.] : to fallow in the winter

winter fallow *n* [¹*winter* + *fallow*, n.] : ground fallowed in winter

winter fat *n* : a tomentose shrub (*Eurotia lanata*) of the family Chenopodiaceae that is common in parts of the southwestern U.S. and yields valuable forage to stock — called also *white sage, winter sage*

¹winterfeed \'=¦=\ *vb* [¹*winter* + *feed*, v.] *vt* **1** : to provide (as cattle) with feed to supplement or replace pasturage during the winter **2** : to feed out (as grain) to livestock during the winter ~ *vi* : to winterfeed grain or livestock ⟨had to ~ because of the heavy storms⟩

²winterfeed \"\ *n* [¹*winter* + *feed*, n.] : livestock feed for winter use ⟨~ for 50 head⟩

winter flounder *n* : a rusty brown often red-spotted flounder (*Pseudopleuronectes americanus*) of northeastern No. America that is an important market fish esp. in winter

winter garden *n* : a garden maintained in winter whether outdoors or in a conservatory

winter golf *n* : golf played under special rules that permit a player to improve the lie of his ball when on the fairway

winter grape *n* : CHICKEN GRAPE

winter grass *n* : any of several grasses that provide winter grazing or forage

win·ter·green \'wintə(r),grēn\ *n* [trans. of D *wintergroen*] **1** : a plant of the genus *Pyrola*; *esp* : a plant (*P. minor*) of northern latitudes that has small round basal evergreen leaves — see SHINLEAF **2 a** : any of various plants of the genus *Gaultheria*; *esp* : a low evergreen No. American herb (*G. procumbens*) with white bell-shaped flowers followed by spicy red berries and shining aromatic leaves that yield a useful oil — see CHECKERBERRY, WINTERGREEN OIL **b** : the flavor of wintergreen oil; *also* : something (as a lozenge) flavored with this oil **3** : PIPSISSEWA **4** : a dark yellowish green that is duller and slightly greener than holly green (sense 1), greener, lighter, and stronger than deep chrome green, greener and duller than golf green, and greener and slightly lighter than average hunter green — compare WINTER GREEN

winter green *n* [¹*winter* + *green*] : a moderate yellowish green that is deeper than tarragon, yellower and duller than malachite green, and yellower and deeper than verdigris — compare WINTERGREEN

wintergreen barberry *n* : a Chinese evergreen shrub (*Berberis julianae*) that is used as an ornamental and has glabrous branchlets, 3-parted spines, acute spiny-toothed leaves, and black fruit

wintergreen family *n* : PYROLACEAE

wintergreen oil *n* **1** : a colorless, yellowish, or reddish aromatic essential oil obtained from macerated leaves of wintergreen, composed principally of methyl salicylate, and used similarly — called also *gaultheria oil*; compare BIRCH OIL 2 **2** : METHYL SALICYLATE

winter gull *n, Brit* : a common European gull (*Larus canus*) — called also *winter mew*

winter-habited \'=¦habəd·əd\ *adj* : having growth of such a character as to require a period of cold weather to mature and produce seed — used esp. of a winter wheat; compare SPRING-HABITED

winter hail *n* : hail consisting of small pellets of ice that are frozen raindrops from nimbus clouds — compare SUMMER HAIL

winterhain \'=¦=\ *vi* -ED/-ING/-S *dial Brit* : to let pasture lie without cattle in winter esp. in order to take off a crop of hay in the spring

winterhardiness \'=¦=¦==\ *n* : the quality or state of being winter-hardy

winter-hardy \'=¦=¦=\ *adj* : hardy in respect to winter conditions; *esp* : able to withstand much cold ⟨*winter-hardy* chrysanthemums⟩

winter hawk *n* : RED-SHOULDERED HAWK

winter hazel *n* : any of several Asiatic deciduous shrubs or small trees (genus *Corylopsis*) that are closely related to the witch hazels and are sometimes cultivated for their yellow flowers which appear in nodding racemes subtended by large bracts before the unfolding of the leaves — called also *flowering hazel*

winter heath *or* **winter heather** *n* : SPRING HEATH

winter heliotrope *n* : a European sweet coltsfoot (*Petasites fragrans*) with lilac flower heads

winter honeysuckle *n* : a widely cultivated half-evergreen Chinese shrub (*Lonicera fragrantissima*) with stiff leathery leaves and very fragrant creamy-white flowers borne in winter or early spring and followed by red fruits

winter huckleberry *n* : FARKLEBERRY

winterier *comparative of* WINTERY

winteriest *superlative of* WINTERY

wintering *pres part of* WINTER

winter injury *n* : injury to plants (as woody plants) occurring in winter and caused usu. directly by low temperatures, by lack of water, or by the effect of these on immature wood

win·ter·ish \'wintərish, -n·trish\ *adj* [¹*winter* + *-ish*] : suitable to winter : suggestive of winter : somewhat wintry — **win·ter·ish·ly** *adv*

winter itch *n* : an itching disorder affecting some persons in winter esp. in a dry climate

win·ter·iza·tion \,wintərə'zāshən, -a,rī'z-\ *n* -s **1** : the quality or state of being winterized **2** : the act or process of winterizing

win·ter·ize \'==,rīz\ *vt* -ED/-ING/-S [¹*winter* + *-ize*] : to make ready for winter or winter use and esp. resistant or proof against the freezing temperature, wind, and snow of winter: as **a** : to treat (a fatty oil) by cooling so that a solid portion is precipitated and then filtering : DESTEARINATE **b** : to make (as an automobile) ready or safe for use in freezing weather with deicers, special lubricants, antifreeze, and similar equipment **c** : to outfit (as a weapon) with protective coverings or equipment against freezing weather

winter jasmine *n* : a trailing Chinese shrub (*Jasminum nudiflorum*) that is often used as an ornamental and has green stems and bright yellow flowers

winter-kill \'=¦=\ *vt* : to cause the death of (as plants) by exposure to winter conditions ~ *vi* : to die as a result of exposure to winter conditions and esp. to conditions of unusual severity ⟨the wheat *winter-killed* badly during the dry open winter⟩

winterkill \"\ *n* [*winter-kill*] : mortality resulting from severe winter conditions (as of fish by smothering in an ice-covered shallow lake)

winter leaf *n* : SEDGE 3

win·ter·less \'==ləs\ *adj* : free from winter : not characterized by wintery conditions (as of weather)

winter lettuce *n* : ENDIVE

winterlong \'=¦=\ *adj* [ME, fr. ¹*winter* + *long*] : excessively or tiresomely long

win·ter·ly *adj* [¹*winter* + *-ly*] : of or resembling winter : occurring in winter : suitable to winter : WINTRY, CHEERLESS

winter melon *n* : a muskmelon (*Cucumis melo inodorus*) having a smooth rind and a sweet white or greenish flesh that lacks a musky aroma

winter mew *n, Brit* : WINTER GULL

winter midge *n* : any of various flies that sometimes appear in numbers or in swarms in winter; *esp* : WINTER CRANE FLY

winter moth *n* : any of several geometrid moths (as *Operophtera brumata* or *Erannis tiliaria*) in which the females are often wingless

winter oats *n pl but sing or pl in constr* : any of various oats that are sown in the fall and harvested early the following summer

winter oil *n* : oil prepared so as not to solidify or become cloudy in moderately cold weather: as **a** : cottonseed oil deprived of the stearin **b** : a relatively thin lubricating oil

winter onion *n* : any of several garden onions that persist from year to year, usu. form small bulbs, and are used chiefly for early salad onions

winter pause *n* : a more or less prolonged period occurring in winter between successive cycles of the egg-laying of a domestic fowl

winterpea \'==,=\ *n* : a peavine (*Lathyrus hirsutus*) with densely silky pods that is native to the Mediterranean region but introduced into the U.S. as a green manure or winter forage crop

winter pear *n* : a late-ripening pear that keeps well in winter

winter plum *n* : PERSIMMON 1a; *also* : the fruit of this tree

winter-proud \'=¦=\ *adj, chiefly Brit* : prematurely grown or luxuriant — used of a fall-sown crop

winter purslane *n* **1** : an Indian lettuce (*Montia perfoliata*) **2** : PURSLANE SPEEDWELL

winter quarters *n pl but sing or pl in constr* : a winter residence or station (as of a military unit or a circus)

winter radish *n* : any of various cultivated radishes (as the daikons) mostly of oriental origin that have large compact firm-fleshed roots which may be kept through much of the winter

winter rape *n* : ²RAPE 2

winter rose *n* **1** : CHRISTMAS ROSE **2** : any of various late-blooming roses of the hybrid perpetual type

winter rye *n* : any of various ryes that are sown in the fall and harvested early in the following summer

winters *pl of* WINTER, *pres 3d sing of* WINTER

winter sage *n* : WINTER FAT

winter savory *n* : a perennial savory (*Satureia montana*) that is an erect subshrub with coriaceous lanceolate-linear leaves and pink or white flowers and that has been cultivated for its foliage which has a flavor of thyme

winter's bark *n, often cap W* [after John Wynter (or Winter), 16th cent. Brit. naval officer] **1** : an aromatic bark with tonic and stimulant properties **2** : an evergreen tree (*Drimys winteri*) found from Mexico southward throughout So. America and yielding winter's bark and a light soft straight-grained brown wood that somewhat resembles and is used similarly to basswood

winter sheldrake *n* : GOOSANDER

winter skate *n* : a skate (*Raja diaphanes*) of the Atlantic coast of the U.S. closely resembling the little skate but of a lighter color and somewhat larger size

winter sleep *n* : HIBERNATION

winter snipe *n* : an American red-backed sandpiper (*Erolia alpina pacifica*)

winter solstice *n* **1** : the point in the sky occupied by the sun on or about December 22d when winter begins in the northern hemisphere; the December solstice **2** : the time at which the sun reaches the December solstice for dwellers in the northern hemisphere or the June solstice for those in the southern hemisphere

winter spore *n* : a resting spore that serves to carry a plant over the winter — compare SUMMER SPORE

winter squash *n* : any of various squashes derived from a natural species (*Cucurbita maxima*) or pumpkins from a species (*C. moschata*) that are used chiefly as table vegetables when fully mature and are capable of withstanding storage for several months — compare SUMMER SQUASH

winter sucker *n* : SPOTTED SUCKER 1

winter sunscald *n* : sunscald of woody plants occurring in winter and caused by freezing of areas of bark and the underlying tissues esp. on the sun-exposed side which is exposed to wide daily temperature variation

winter sweet *n* **1 a** : WILD MARJORAM **b** : CRETAN DITTANY **2** : JAPAN ALLSPICE **3** : an ornamental African shrub or small tree (*Acocanthera spectabilis*) of the family Apocynaceae growing in warm countries and having thick leathery leaves, white or pink flowers, and globose purplish black fruit

winter sweet pea *n* : DARLING PEA

winter teal *n* : GREENWING

winter tick *n* : an ixodid tick (*Dermacentor albipictus*) that is actively parasitic during the winter months on domestic and big-game animals in parts of western U.S. and Canada

wintertide \'==,=\ *n* [ME, fr. OE *wintertīd*, fr. ¹*winter* + *tīd* time — more at TIDE] : the season of winter : WINTERTIME

wintertime \'==,=\ *n* [ME, fr. ¹*winter* + *time*] : the period when wintry weather prevails : WINTER

winter vetch *n* : HAIRY VETCH

winter wagtail *n* : GRAY WAGTAIL

win·ter·ward \'==wə(r)d\ *also* **win·ter·wards** \-dz\ *adv* [¹*winter* + *-ward, -wards*] : in the direction of winter

winterweed \'==,=\ *n* : a weedy plant that remains green during winter: as **a** : a common chickweed (*Stellaria media*) **b** : IVY-LEAVED SPEEDWELL

winter wheat *n* : a wheat that is sown in autumn and ripens the following spring or summer

winter wren *n* : a very small wren (*Troglodytes troglodytes hiemalis*) of the coniferous forests of the northern U.S. and Canada that migrates southward in winter, is dark cinnamon brown barred with black, and is the American representative of the common European wren

winter yellowlegs *n pl but sing or pl in constr* : GREATER YELLOWLEGS

win through *vi* : to survive difficulties and reach a desired or satisfactory end ⟨his strong constitution *won through* to recovery⟩ ⟨only the greatest efforts would allow them to *win through* to the headwaters of the river⟩

win·tle \'wint³l\ *vi* [prob. fr. Flem *windtelen* to roll, reel; akin to MD *wentelen* to roll] *Scot* : STAGGER, REEL, WRIGGLE, ROLL

win to *vi, chiefly Scot* : to begin to eat : fall to

win·ton disease \'wint³n, -tən-\ *n, usu cap W* [prob. fr. *Winton*, town in southern South Island, New Zealand] : cirrhosis of the liver in horses and cattle resulting from the chronic poisoning by toxic constituents of ragworts and other noxious plants eaten in the pasturage — compare WALKABOUT DISEASE

win·tri·ly \'win·trəlē, -li\ *adv* : in a wintry manner : so as to be wintry

win·tri·ness \-trēnəs, -trin-\ *n* -ES : the quality or state of being wintry

win·try \-trē, -ri\ *or* **win·tery** \-ntərē, -n·trē, -ri\ *adj* -ER/-EST [*winter* + *-y*] **1** *archaic* : of, relating to, occurring in, or suitable to winter **2** : resembling or characteristic of winter : HIEMAL, COLD, STORMY ⟨was subjected to severe ~ weather⟩ **3 a** : subjected to the action of winter : weathered by winter ⟨brown ~ grasses⟩ **b** : seeming as if affected by winter : AGED, WHITE, CHILLING, CHEERLESS ⟨a ~ smile⟩

win·tun \(')win·¦tün\ *or* **win·tu** \-ü\ *n, pl* **wintun** *or* **wintuns** *or* **wintu** *or* **wintus** *usu cap* [Wintun, people] **1 a** : an Indian people of the Sacramento valley, California **b** : a member of such people **2** : a Copehan language of the Wintun people **3** : COPEHAN 1

winy *or* **winey** \'wīnē, -ni\ *adj* **winier**; **winiest** [ME *wyny*, fr. *win, wyn* wine + *-y*] **1 a** : having the taste or qualities of wine : resembling wine : VINOUS ⟨grapes of a ~ taste⟩ ⟨a ~ color⟩ **b** *of the air* : crisply fresh and fragrant ⟨~ autumn skies⟩ **2** : influenced or affected by wine or spirits : DRUNKEN

¹winze \'winz\ *n* -s [alter. of earlier *winds*, prob. fr. *winds*, pl. of ⁵*wind*] : a vertical or steeply inclined opening or passageway driven to connect one mine working place with another at a lower level

²winze \"\ *n* [Flem or D *wensch* wish, fr. MD, fr. *wenschen* to wish; akin to OHG *wunsken* to wish — more at WISH] *Scot* : CURSE

¹wipe \'wīp\ *vb* -ED/-ING/-S [ME *wipen*, fr. OE *wīpian*; akin to OHG *wīfan* to swing, wind around, *weif* bandage, ON *veipr* head covering, Goth *weipan* to crown, *wipja* crown, L *vibrare* to vibrate, Skt *vepate* he trembles, it vibrates] *vt* **1 a** : to rub with or as if with something soft for cleaning or drying ⟨*wiped* his nose with his handkerchief⟩ ⟨~ the enamel with a damp cloth⟩ **b** : to clean or dry by rubbing ⟨~ your shoes before going in⟩ — usu. used with *on* ⟨*wiped* his hands on the grass⟩ **c** : to draw, pass, or move for or as if for rubbing or cleaning ⟨*wiped* his hand across his forehead⟩ ⟨*wiping* a soft cloth back and forth over the waxed surface⟩ **2 a** : to remove by or as if by rubbing ⟨~ the tears off⟩ ⟨*wiping* off the spilled oil⟩ ⟨*wiped* the smudge away with his hand⟩ ⟨~ out what you have written⟩ **b** : to completely expunge : OBLITERATE, ABOLISH, CANCEL ⟨his heroic end *wiped* his foolish life from human memory⟩: as (1) : to cause to cease to exist : ANNIHILATE — usu. used with *out* ⟨the enemy *wiped* out the defending force⟩ (2) : to terminate by or as if by payment — usu. used with *off* or *out* ⟨received money to ~ off most of his debts⟩ ⟨past dishonor *wiped* out by valiant deeds⟩ (3) : to exhaust (a margin) on an exchange — used with *out* ⟨the fall in prices *wiped* out his margin⟩ **3 a** *chiefly dial* : to punish either with physical violence or stern censure; *usu* : STRIKE, BEAT, DRUB **b** *obs* : CHEAT, DEFRAUD, TRICK **4 a** : to spread in a thin and rather uniform layer by or as if by wiping ⟨~ a coating of heavy grease over all exposed surfaces⟩ **b** : to form (a joint between lead pipes) by applying solder in repeated increments that are individually spread and shaped with greased cloth pads ~ *vi* : to make a motion of or like that of wiping something ⟨she *wiped* vigorously but the stain remained⟩ **syn** see EXTERMINATE — **wipe one's boots on** : to treat with indignity : withhold respect from — **wipe one's eye 1** : to get in ahead of one; *esp* : to shoot game another has aimed at **2** : to take the conceit out of one — **wipe the floor with** *or* **wipe the ground with** : to defeat decisively

²wipe \"\ *n* -s **1 a** (1) : BLOW, STRIKE, SWIPE (2) *obs* : a mark from or as if from a blow **b** : a harsh sarcastic remark : GIBE, JEER **2** : an act or instance of wiping ⟨give the table a ~ with your cloth⟩ **3 a** *slang* : HANDKERCHIEF **b** : WIPER a(3) **c** : a small surgical sponge (as of gauze or cellulose) **4** *or* **wipe off** : a transitional effect during a projected picture whereby one scene progressively replaces another as a boundary line moves across vertically, horizontally, or in some special pattern

wipe break *or* **wipe breaker** *n* : an electrical interrupter consisting essentially of one or more wipers revolving against contact pieces

wipe joint *n* : a wiped plumbing joint

wip·er \'wīpə(r)\ *n* -s : one that wipes: **a** (1) : something (as a towel or sponge) used for wiping (2) *slang* : HANDKERCHIEF (3) : a projecting tooth, tumbler, eccentric, tappet, or cam on a rotating or oscillating piece used esp. for raising a stamper, the helve of a power hammer, or other part intended to fall by its own weight (4) *or* **wiper ring** : RING OILER (5) : a rod or an attachment to hold a rag for wiping out the bore of the barrel of a firearm (6) : a moving contact for making connections with the terminals of an electrical device (as a rheostat) — compare ³BRUSH 3a **b** (1) : a roundhouse employee who cleans locomotives (2) : a worker who removes dirt and grease from machinery (as in a shop or engine room) (3) : a worker who with an asbestos pad wipes surplus aluminum from the sealed joints of glass bricks

wiper shaft *n* : a shaft carrying a wiper or a wiper wheel on machinery

wiper wheel *n* : a wheel (as in a trip hammer) with wipers on its rim

wipe up *vt* : to make clean by or as if by wiping : MOP UP, DEFEAT, DESTROY

wiping contact *n* [*wiping* (gerund of ¹*wipe*) + *contact*] : an electric contact made by wiping or rubbing one surface on another

wiping rod *n* : WIPER a(5)

wir \(')wir\ *adj* [by alter.] *Scot & dial Eng* : OUR

wir·able \'wīrəbəl\ *adj* : capable of being wired

¹wire \'wī(ə)r, -īə\ *n* -s *often attrib* [ME, fr. OE *wīr*; akin to ON *vīravirki* wirework, filigree, OHG *wiara* fine gold, L *viēre* to twist together, plait, Gk *iris* rainbow; basic meaning: bend, turn] **1 a** : metal in the form of a usu. very flexible thread or slender rod **b** : a thread or rod of such material — compare CORD 3b **2** : the strings of a musical instrument; *broadly* : STRINGED INSTRUMENT **3 a** : WIREWORK; *esp* : WOVEN WIRE ⟨screen ~⟩ **b** : the meshwork of parallel or woven wire on which the wet web of paper forms and is drained **4** : a wire-like thing (as a thin plant stem or a hair); *specif* : BINE, STOLON 1a ⟨hop ~s⟩ ⟨strawberry ~s⟩ **5** *usu* **wires** *pl* **a** : a system of wires used to operate the puppets in a puppet show **b** : the network of hidden influences controlling the action of a person or organization ⟨pull the ~s for office⟩ **6 a** : a line of wire for conducting electrical current — compare CORD 3b **b** (1) : a telegraph wire or cable (2) : a telegraph system ⟨send a message by ~⟩ ⟨the ~s of Europe were hot with telegrams —C.E. Black & E.C.Helmreich⟩ (3) : TELEGRAM, CABLEGRAM ⟨send a ~⟩ ⟨~ news⟩ **c** : a telephone wire or system ⟨heard a familiar voice over the ~⟩ ⟨as soon as she could get that man off the ~ —F.M.Ford⟩ **7** : a metal snare (as for rabbits) **8** *Scot* : KNITTING NEEDLE **9** *slang* : PICKPOCKET; *esp* : the member of a pickpocket team who picks the victim's pocket **10** : fencing or a fence of barbed wire ⟨a horse cut by ~⟩ ⟨behind the ~ of a prison stockade⟩; *also* : a barbed wire entanglement (as on a battlefield) **11** : WIRE ROPE **12** : a wire-haired dog **13** : a wire strung high between the winning posts between which the horses pass at the finish of a race ⟨finished a dismal last at the ~ —F.M.Blunk⟩; *broadly* : the finish line of a race ⟨as the campaign goes down to the ~ —Elmo Roper & Louis Harris⟩ **14** : a wire on which acrobats perform ⟨~ act⟩ ⟨~ walker⟩ — see HIGH WIRE, SLACK WIRE, TIGHTWIRE **15 a** : a long rod or strip of metal with a smooth or cutting edge used in the formation of looped or cut pile in carpet weaving **b** : the fineness of carpets measured by the number of rows of tufts per inch **16** : metal thread or rod used in surgery to suture soft tissue or transfix fractured bone — compare TANTALUM GAUZE **17** : information surreptitiously or privately exchanged between gamblers (as by a signal) **18** : magnetic recording wire — **under the wire** *adv (or adj)* **1** : at the finish line ⟨the third horse *under the wire*⟩ **2** : before a deadline : at the last moment ⟨pay one's taxes just *under the wire*⟩ — **under wire** : fenced with barbed wire ⟨six sections *under wire*⟩

²wire \"\ *vb* -ED/-ING/-S [ME *wiren*, fr. ¹*wire*] *vt* **1** : to provide with wire : use wire on for any purpose : string, stiffen, or connect with wire ⟨~ cords⟩ ⟨~ beads⟩ ⟨~ a skeleton⟩ ⟨~ a fence⟩ ⟨~ a hat⟩ ⟨~ a house for electricity⟩ ⟨~ electric lights together⟩ **2** : to snare by means of a wire ⟨~ a rabbit⟩ **3** : to send or send word to by telegraph ⟨~ me the

news⟩ **4 :** to place (a croquet ball) behind the wire of an arch thus preventing a successful shot ~ *vi* **:** to send a telegraphic message ⟨~ home for money⟩
wire agency *n* **:** WIRE SERVICE
wirebar \ˈ=,=\ *n* **:** a cast bar of metal ready for making into wire
wirebird \ˈ=,=\ *n* [so called fr. the wire grass in which it lives] **:** a plover (*Charadrius sanctaehelenae*) of the island of St. Helena
wire bridge *n* **:** a bridge suspended from wire cables
wire brush *n* **:** ³BRUSH 1b
wire cloth *n* **:** a fabric of woven metallic wire (as for strainers)
wire coat *n* **:** a coat (as of various dogs) of extremely wiry and dense outer hair
wire copy *n* **:** copy sent to a newspaper, periodical, or news broadcast by a wire service
wire–cut \ˈ=ˌ=\ *adj* **:** cut or shaped by or as if by a taut wire ⟨*wire-cut* brick⟩ ⟨*wire-cut* tile⟩ — compare MOLDED BRICK 1
wire cutter *n* **:** a worker or appliance employed in cutting wire
wired *adj* [ME, fr. past part. of *wiren* to wire] **1 :** reinforced by wire (as for strength or stiffness) **2 :** furnished with wires (as for electricity or telephone connections) **3 :** bound with wire ⟨a ~ container⟩ **4 :** having a wirework netting or fence ⟨a ~ enclosure for chickens⟩ **5 :** back to back (sense 2)
wired music *n* **:** a sound reproducing system using a central disc reproducing system and telephone-line connections to many loudspeakers located in customers' factories, shops, and offices
wired radio *or* **wired wireless** *also* **wire radio** *n* **:** a system for distributing radio programs over wire lines or by means other than the usual method of transmitting the signals through space
wire drag *n* **:** a wire usu. several thousand feet in length, maintained horizontally at any desired depth by means of attached weights, buoyed at intervals, towed by a power boat at each end, and used to locate submerged obstructions projecting above the depth at which it is set
wiredraw \ˈ=,=\ *vt* [back-formation fr. *wiredrawer*] **1 a :** to draw or stretch forcibly **:** ELONGATE, DISTORT, WREST ⟨my sense has been *wiredrawn* into blasphemy —John Dryden⟩ **b :** to draw or spin out to great length, tenuity, or overrefinement **:** ATTENUATE **2 :** to draw (metal) into wire
wiredrawer \ˈ=,=(=)\ *n* [ME, fr. ¹*wire* + *drawer*] **:** one that draws metal into wire
wiredrawing *n* [fr. gerund of *wiredraw*] **:** the act, process, or occupation of drawing metal into wire
wiredrawn \ˈ=ˌ=\ *adj* [fr. past part. of *wiredraw*] **:** drawn out long and fine like wire **:** excessively minute and fine ⟨~ comparisons —Virginia Woolf⟩ ⟨~ theories⟩
wire edge *n* **1 :** the thin wirelike thread of metal sometimes formed on the edge of a tool (as a chisel or razor) in attempting to sharpen it **2 :** an edge on a coin forming a high thin border around the design
wire–feed \ˈ=ˌ=\ *adj* [¹*wire* + *feed*, n.] *of a machine tool* **:** having apparatus for maintaining a feed of wire
wire gauge *n* **1 :** a gauge esp. for measuring the diameter of wire or the thickness of sheet metal often consisting of a metal plate with a series of notches of various widths in its edge **2 :** any of various systems consisting of a series of standard sizes used in describing the diameter of wire or the thickness of sheet metal **3 :** any of the designated sizes in a wire gauge system

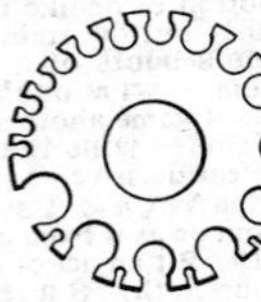
wire gauge

wire gauze *n* **:** a gauzelike weave of fine wires **:** an esp. fine wire cloth — compare TANTALUM GAUZE
wire glass *also* **wired glass** *n* **:** glass with wire netting embedded in it during manufacture to reduce the probability of its shattering when cracked by shock or by heat — called also *safety glass*
wire grass *n* **:** any of various grasses having wiry culms or leaves: as **a :** a European slender-stemmed meadow grass (*Poa compressa*) widely naturalized in the U.S. and Canada — called also *Canada bluegrass* **b :** YARD GRASS **c :** BERMUDA GRASS **d :** any of several grasses of the genus *Aristida* **e :** any of several grasses of the genus *Sporobolus* **f :** NIMBLE WILL **g :** LITTLE BLUESTEM **h :** RANGE GRASS **i :** BROOMROOT
wire grub *n* **:** WIREWORM
wire gun *n* **:** WIRE-WOUND GUN
wirehair \ˈ=,=\ *n* **:** a wirehaired fox terrier
wirehaired \ˈ=ˌ=\ *adj* **:** having a stiff wiry outer coat of hair — used esp. of a dog
wirehaired pointing griffon *n* **:** a large bird dog originating in Europe and having a harsh wiry coat, a long skull, a square muzzle, and a definite moustache and eyebrows
wirehaired terrier *n* **:** a wirehaired fox terrier
wire house *n* **:** a brokerage firm connected with its branch offices and correspondents by private leased telephone or telegraph wires
wire lath *n* **:** a plaster base consisting of wire netting
¹**wire·less** \ˈwī(ə)rlə̇s\ *adj* **1 :** having no wire or wires **2** *chiefly Brit* **:** of or relating to radiotelegraphy, radiotelephony, or radio
²**wireless** \"\ *n* -ES **1 a :** RADIOTELEGRAPH ⟨~ message⟩ **b** *or* **wireless telephony :** RADIOTELEPHONY ⟨~ operator⟩ **c** *chiefly Brit* **:** RADIO ⟨turn on the ~⟩ ⟨heard on the ~⟩ ⟨~ set⟩ ⟨state-controlled ~⟩ **2 :** a moderate blue that is greener and duller than average copen or Dresden blue and paler and slightly redder than azurite blue
³**wireless** \"\ *vb* -ED/-ING/-ES [²*wireless*] **:** RADIO ⟨the lightship ~*ed* a warning to vessels in the vicinity —*Amer. Guide Series: N.C.*⟩
wireless compass *n, chiefly Brit* **:** RADIO COMPASS, DIRECTION FINDER
wire·less·ly *adv* [¹*wireless* + -*ly*] **:** by a means not employing wires **:** by means of radio
wire·less·ness *n* -ES **:** the quality or state of being wireless
wireless telegraphy *also* **wireless telegraph** *n* **:** RADIOTELEGRAPH
wireless telephone *n* **:** RADIOPHONE 2
wirelike \ˈ=,=\ *adj* **:** resembling a wire esp. in thinness and flexibility **:** WIRY ⟨~ plant stems⟩
wire line *n* **1 :** a line using wire; *esp* **:** a telegraph or telephone line **2 :** CHAIN LINE
wire·man \ˈ=mən\ *n, pl* **wiremen** [¹*wire* + *man*] **1 a :** LINEMAN 2 **b :** one who installs and repairs electric wiring (as in buildings, mines, automobiles, railroad cars, or telegraphic apparatus) **c :** a maintenance electrician who keeps electrical equipment (as motors, switches, or switchboards) in running condition **2 :** an operator of a machine for bending sheet-metal stamping over a wire to form a finished edge
wire mark *n* **:** the impression made on the bottom side of a paper web by the surface contour of the wire — compare WATERMARK 2
wire micrometer *n* **:** FILAR MICROMETER
wire money *n* **:** money consisting of larins
wire nail *n* **:** a nail made of wire; *specif* **:** any one of several nails made of wire and designed for special uses — see BOX NAIL, FINISHING NAIL; compare CUT NAIL
wire netting *n* **:** a texture of woven wire coarser than wire gauze
wirephoto \ˈ=ˌ=(,)=\ *vt* [*Wirephoto*] **:** to transmit (a picture) by electrical signals over wire lines
Wirephoto \"\ *trademark* — used for a photograph transmitted by electrical signals over telephone wires
wire plant *n* **:** a woody almost leafless New Zealand vine (*Muehlenbeckia complexa*) rampant in California as an introduced plant — called also *maidenhair-vine, wire vine*
wire–pull \ˈ=ˌ=\ *vi* [back-formation fr. *wire-puller*] **:** to pull wires ⟨working to *wire-pull* and intrigue —P.L.Ford⟩
wire–puller \ˈ=ˌ==\ *n* [¹*wire* + *puller*] **:** one that uses secret or underhand means to influence the acts of a person or organization ⟨a hardheaded practical *wire-puller*, unyieldingly jealous of his career —John Gunther⟩
wire–pulling *n* -S [¹*wire* + *pulling*, gerund of *pull*] **:** the use of means to influence secretly the acts of a person or organization ⟨economic power or political *wire-pulling* —S.E.Morison⟩ ⟨can be done but it needs a week of *wire-pulling* and persuasion —Enid Bagnold⟩
wir·er \ˈwīrə(r)\ *n* -S **:** one that wires or uses wire **:** WIREMAN; *esp* **:** a trapper who uses a wire trap
wire radio *var of* WIRED RADIO
wire–record \ˈ=ˌ=ˌ=\ *vt* [back-formation fr. *wire recorder*] **:** to make a wire recording of ⟨*wire-record* an interview⟩
wire recorder *n* [¹*wire* + *recorder*] **:** a magnetic recorder using magnetic wire
wire recording *n* [¹*wire* + *recording*] **:** magnetic recording on magnetic wire; *also* **:** the recording made by this process
wire reducer *n* **:** a heavy curved wire used in the seed cups of grain drills to cut down the rate of planting of small seeds
wire rod *n* **:** a metal rod from which wire is drawn
wire room *n* [so called fr. its being provided with apparatus for the receipt of race results by wire] **:** a room or establishment where bookmaking is carried on under cover of legitimate business
wire rope *n* **:** a rope formed wholly or chiefly of wires — compare CABLE, FLAT ROPE, FLATTENED STRAND ROPE, HAND ROPE 2, STEEL-CLAD ROPE, TRANSMISSION ROPE
wire ropeway *or* **wire tramway** *n* **:** a ropeway using a wire cable
wire rush *n* **:** any of various plants with wiry stems; *esp* **:** a slender rushlike New Zealand herb (*Hypolaena lateriflora*) of the family Restionaceae that has scaly leaves and often grows in dense mats
wires *pl of* WIRE, *pres 3d sing of* WIRE
wire saw *n* **:** HELICOIDAL SAW
wire service *n* **:** a news agency that sends out syndicated news copy by wire to subscribing newspapers, periodicals, or news broadcasters
wire–shafted \ˈ=ˌ==\ *adj* **1 :** having all or part of the shaft without webs ⟨*wire-shafted* feather⟩ **2** *of a bird* **:** having wire-shafted feathers
wire side *n* **1** *of handmade paper* **:** the side of the sheet in contact with the mold during manufacture — called also *right side* **2** *of machine-made paper* **:** the side of the sheet in contact with the wire during manufacture — called also *wrong side;* compare FELT SIDE
wire silver *n* **:** native silver in the form of wires or threads
wiresmith \ˈ=,=\ *n* **:** one who makes wire esp. by the old method of hammering up strips of metal
wire solder *n* **:** solder in the form of wire
wire stem *n* **:** a disease of cabbage, cauliflower, and related plants that is caused by a fungus (*Pellicularia filamentosa*) and is similar to damping-off but attacks older seedlings and produces a constricted wiry stem
wire stitch *n* **1 :** SADDLE STITCH **2 :** SIDE STITCH
wire–strain gauge \ˈ=ˌ=-\ *n* **:** a device that consists of a fine wire firmly bonded to thin paper and that when attached to an object subjected to stress indicates minute changes in strain by corresponding changes in electrical resistance of the wire as it is likewise elongated
wire stretcher *n* **:** a device used (as in fencing) to pull wire taut
wire tack *n* **:** a tack machine-fabricated from wire stock
wiretail \ˈ=,=\ *n, West* **:** RUDDY DUCK
wire–tailed \ˈ=ˌ=\ *adj* **:** having wire-shafted tail quills
wire–tailed bird of paradise **:** TWELVE-WIRED BIRD OF PARADISE
¹**wiretap** \ˈ=ˌ=\ *vb* [back-formation fr. *wiretapper*] *vi* **:** to tap a telephone or telegraph wire to get messages, information, or evidence ~ *vt* **:** to obtain (information) by tapping a wire
²**wiretap** \"\ *n* **1 :** the act or an instance of wiretapping ⟨transcripts of ~*s* made by the police department —*N.Y. Times*⟩ **2 :** a device for wiretapping ⟨had used a ~ in this detection —*Current Biog.*⟩
³**wiretap** \"\ *adj* **:** obtained by or involving wiretapping ⟨~ evidence⟩ ⟨a ~ scandal⟩
wiretapper \ˈ=ˌ==\ *n* [¹*wire* + *tapper*] **1 :** one that taps telephone or telegraph wires to get messages, information, or evidence **2 :** a swindler who professes to have information obtained by tapping wires
wire–toothed leather \ˈ=ˌ=-\ *n* **:** leather set or studded with wire teeth and used esp. for covering the cylinders of carding machines
wire twist *n* **:** a combination of welded and twisted wires used in making the barrels of some shotguns
wire vine *n* **:** WIRE PLANT
wireway \ˈ=,=\ *n* **1 :** a conduit for wires; *esp* **:** one to conceal electric wires in a building while rendering them permanently accessible **2 :** a cash or parcel railway having wire tracks **3 :** WIRE ROPEWAY
wireweed \ˈ=,=\ *n* **:** KNOTGRASS 1
wire wheel *n* **1 :** a rotary wire brush (as for cleaning metalwork) **2 :** a wheel (as for motorcars) with spokes of wire

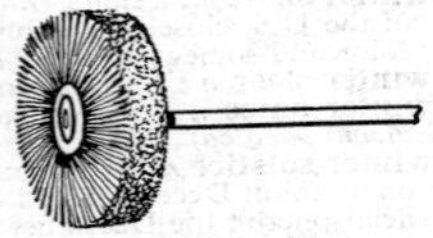
wire wheel

wirework \ˈ=,=\ *n* **1 :** work of wires; *esp* **:** openwork made of wire **:** WIRE NETTING **2 :** walking on wires esp. by acrobats
wireworker \ˈ=ˌ==\ *n* [¹*wire* + *worker*] **:** one that makes things (as cables) from wire
wireworm \ˈ=,=\ *n* **1 :** a worm that is the slender hard-coated larva of various click beetles and is very destructive to the roots of plants **2 :** MILLIPEDE; *esp* **:** one of the genus *Julus* that is often a pest in English gardens **3 :** a common stomach worm (*Haemonchus contortus*) of ruminants — called also *twisted wireworm*
wire–wound gun \ˈ=ˌ=-\ *n* **:** a gun in the construction of which an inner tube either entire or in segments is wound with wire under tension to insure greater soundness and uniformity of resistance and in which hoops and jackets are sometimes shrunk on the tube over the wire — compare DAMASCUS BARREL
wir·i·ly \ˈwīrəlē, -li\ *adv* **:** in a wiry manner
wir·i·ness \-rēnə̇s, -rin-\ *n* -ES **:** the quality or state of being wiry
wiring *n* -S [fr. gerund of ²*wire*] **1 :** the act, practice, or an instance of providing or using wire **2 a :** a system of wires **:** WIREWORK; *esp* **:** an arrangement of wires used for electric distribution (as in a building) **3 :** the process of mounting with wire in taxidermy
wiring diagram *n* **:** a line drawing showing how the electrical connections of a device are made
wiring die *n* **:** one of a set of shaping dies consisting of a matrix and a punch for curling sheet metal around a wire to form a rim (as of a tinware utensil) or for making a similar rim without the wire
wiring press *n* **:** a shaping press for curling sheet metal around a wire to form a rim (as of a tinware utensil) or for making a similar rim without the wire — see WIRING DIE
wirk \ˈwərk\ *Scot var of* WORK
wirl \ˈwərl\ *or* **wirl·ing** \-lən, -liŋ\ *n* -S [origin unknown] *Scot & dial Eng* **:** a stunted or puny creature
wirr \ˈwər\ *n or vb* [imit.] *Scot* **:** GROWL
wir·ra \ˈwirə\ *interj* [*oh wirra*, fr. IrGael *a Muire*, lit., O Mary] *Irish* — usu. used to express lament, grief, or concern
wir·rah \ˈwirə\ *n* -S [fr. native name in Australia] **:** an Australian spotted food fish (*Acanthistius serratus*) of the family Serranidae
wir·ri·cow \ˈwərə,kü\ *var of* WORRICOW
wiry *also* **wirey** \ˈwīrē, -ri\ *adj* **wirier**; **wiriest** [¹*wire* + -*y*] **1 a :** made or consisting of wire ⟨a ~ cage⟩ **b :** resembling wire in form and flexibility ⟨crown of ~ gray curls —Anne Parrish⟩ ⟨~ grass⟩ **c (1)** *of sound* **:** produced by or suggestive of the vibration of wire ⟨her ~, plaintive voice —Marcia Davenport⟩ ⟨beyond a ~ cheeping, has no song —D.C. Peattie⟩ **(2)** *in sound reproduction* **:** characterized by excessive accentuation of higher-pitched tones **2** *of the pulse* **:** small but tense **3 :** characterized by a lean supple vigorous physique **:** SINEWY ⟨the ~ figure of a long-distance runner —*Phoenix Flame*⟩ ⟨chariots drawn by the ~ little British ponies —A.C.Whitehead⟩
wis \ˈwis\ *vb* [by incorrect division fr. *iwis* (understood as *I wis*, with *wis* incorrectly supposed to be an archaic pres. indic. of ¹*wit*] *archaic* **:** KNOW
wis·con·sin \wə̇ˈskän(t)sən\ *adj, usu cap* [fr. *Wisconsin*, northern state of U. S., of Algonquian origin; prob. akin to Ojibwa *wishkonsing* place of the beaver] **1 :** of or from the state of Wisconsin ⟨*Wisconsin* dairy products⟩ **:** of the kind or style prevalent in Wisconsin **2 :** belonging to the fourth glacial stage during the glacial epoch in No. America
wis·con·sin·ite \-sə,nīt\ *n* -S *cap* [*Wisconsin*, state of U.S. + E -*ite*] **:** a native or resident of the state of Wisconsin
wisconsin weeping willow *n, usu cap 1st W* **:** a hybrid willow (*Salix blanda*) derived from a cross between the weeping willow and the crack willow
wisconsin white pine *n, usu cap 1st W* **1 :** a common white pine (*Pinus strobus*) **2 :** the wood of the Wisconsin white pine tree
wis·dom \ˈwizdəm\ *n* -S [ME, fr. OE *wīsdōm*, fr. *wīs* wise + -*dōm* -dom] **1** *usu cap* **:** the effectual mediating principle or personification of God's will in the creation of the world **:** LOGOS **2 a (1) :** accumulated information **:** philosophic or scientific learning **:** KNOWLEDGE ⟨all the ~ of the ages . . . available at negligible cost to all of us within the covers of books —Bennett Cerf⟩ **(2) :** accumulated lore or instinctive adaptation ⟨a heritage of animal ~ built up through many generations of . . . fighting for existence —J.T.McNish⟩ **b :** the intelligent application of learning **:** ability to discern inner qualities and essential relationships **:** INSIGHT, SAGACITY ⟨a long book, illuminated not only with learning but with ~ —Gerald Bullett⟩ ⟨~ grows out of the temper and heart of a man as well as out of his intellect —James Bryce⟩ — compare VIRTUE **c :** good sense **:** JUDGMENT, PRUDENCE ⟨faced with a vote of no confidence . . . had the ~ to resign —B.K.Sandwell⟩ **d** *obs* **:** SANITY ⟨pray heaven his ~ be not tainted —Shak.⟩ **3 a** *archaic* **:** an embodiment of wisdom **:** APHORISM **b :** a wise attitude or course of action ⟨the English aristocracy showed a statesmanlike readiness to admit newcomers . . . a ~ which marked them off from the pedigree-ridden and politically frivolous aristocracies of Europe —D.W.Brogan⟩ **c** *archaic, often cap* **:** a person of superior intellectual attainments ⟨many of the best ~*s* of our nation —Gervase Markham⟩ — often used as a title or mode of address ⟨can your ~ possibly entertain a wish to converse with me —Sir Walter Scott⟩ **4 :** the teachings of the ancient wise men (as of Babylon, Egypt, or Palestine) relating to the art of living and sometimes to philosophical problems concerning the universe, man, or God and forming a class of literature represented in the Hebrew books of Job, Proverbs, Ecclesiastes, Ecclesiasticus, and the Wisdom of Solomon **syn** see SENSE
wisdom tooth *n* [trans. of NL *dentes sapientiae* (pl.), lit. teeth of wisdom; fr. their not usually being cut until the late teens] **:** the last tooth of the full set on each half of each jaw in man
¹**wise** \ˈwīz\ *n* -S [ME, fr. OE *wīse* manner, melody; akin to OHG *wīsa* manner, style, tune, ON *vīsa* stanza, ōthruvīs otherwise, Gk *eidos* appearance, form, kind, *idein* to see — more at WIT] **:** MANNER, WAY ⟨the house differed in no ~ from its neighbors —Maurice Samuel⟩ — often used in combination ⟨like*wise*⟩ ⟨other*wise*⟩
²**wise** \"\ *adj* -ER/-EST [ME *wise, wis, wys*, fr. OE *wīs* wise, knowing; akin to OHG *wīs* wise, ON *viss*, Goth unweis unknowing, OE *witan* to know — more at WIT] **1 a (1) :** characterized by wisdom **:** SAGE, SAGACIOUS ⟨the ~ man and teacher of the tribe —Nancy K. Hosking⟩ ⟨men may be ~ . . . though their fund of knowledge is small —S.H.Slichter⟩ **(2) :** all-wise ⟨which the ~ powers deny us for our good —Shak.⟩ **b (1) :** well informed or instructed **:** KNOWLEDGEABLE ⟨a portion of reading quite indispensable to a ~ man —R.W.Emerson⟩ ⟨grew up . . . ~ in plants, wild animals, and the habits of their own goats and sheep —T.E.Lawrence⟩ **(2) :** showing instinctive wisdom ⟨these dogs are bred . . . as rugged individuals each ~ in his own nose —D.C.Peattie⟩ **c :** exercising sound judgment **:** JUDICIOUS, PRUDENT ⟨conservation and ~ use of resources can make a wealthy people in a lonely land —H.W.Odum⟩ ⟨~ handling of a situation⟩ ⟨a ~ investment⟩ **2** *archaic* **:** mentally sound **:** SANE **3 a :** evidencing or hinting at the possession of inside information **:** KNOWING ⟨when questioned about the incident he looked ~ but refused to talk⟩ ⟨the ~ money was ten to one⟩ **b :** possessed of inside information **:** ALERT ⟨unless they're ~ to the slow, steady creep of the tide, they'll be in up to their hub caps before they realize it —J.W.Noble⟩ ⟨able to sneak it in without the MPs getting ~ —James Jones⟩ ⟨old timers put him ~ to the tricks of cardsharpers⟩ **c :** shrewdly resourceful **:** CRAFTY, SMART **4** *archaic* **:** skilled in magic or divination **5 :** INSOLENT, SMART-ALECKY, FRESH ⟨a bunch of ~ kids throwing snowballs at buses⟩
syn SAGE, SAPIENT, JUDICIOUS, PRUDENT, SENSIBLE, SANE: WISE indicates discernment based not only on factual knowledge but on judgment and insight ⟨*wise* men . . . anticipate possible difficulties, and decide beforehand what they will do if occasions arise —J.A.Froude⟩ ⟨she was also *wise* beyond her years, and she knew that when he no longer needed her advice he would dispense with her —Harrison Smith⟩ SAGE is used interchangeably with WISE but may also suggest venerability ⟨the *sage* enchanter Merlin's subtle schemes —William Wordsworth⟩ ⟨her *sage* plan to make the family feel her worth, and to conquer the members of it one by one —George Meredith⟩ SAPIENT may imply a canny shrewdness rather than profound wisdom ⟨the *sapient* leader who shall bring order out of the wild misrule —V.L.Parrington⟩ ⟨a *sapient*, instructed, shrewdly ascertaining ignorance —Walter Pater⟩ JUDICIOUS suggests judgment that is fair, level-headed, sound, and wise ⟨it is not *judicious*, unbiased, academic; it is passionate, biased and provocative —H.L.Matthews⟩ ⟨with *judicious* officers the most unruly seamen can at sea be kept in some sort of subjection —Herman Melville⟩ PRUDENT suggests exercise of the restraint of sound practical wisdom and discretion to avoid anything rash or ill-advised ⟨too *prudent* to say or hint anything which could create a suspicion in her colleague's breast —Anthony Trollope⟩ ⟨in the pursuit of pleasure, as in the purchase of securities, the *prudent* Southern gentleman has always preferred safety to hazard —Ellen Glasgow⟩ SENSIBLE describes action according to good sense and accustomed rationality ⟨let us, like *sensible* men, choose the lesser evil —John Strachey⟩ ⟨any *sensible* doctor when stricken by disease distrusts his own introspective diagnosis and calls in a colleague —C.K.Ogden & I.A.Richards⟩ SANE, usu. contrasted with *insane*, indicates mental soundness, rationality, and level-headedness without wild quirks or deep derangements ⟨I am no lunatic in a mad fit, but a *sane* man fighting for his soul —Bram Stoker⟩ ⟨praise all their wares in terms so extravagant that a *sane* buyer is instantly steeled against believing even that percentage of these praises which may perhaps be true —C.E.Montague⟩
³**wise** \"\ *n, pl* **wise** [ME, fr. OE *wīsa*, fr. *wīs* wise] **:** WISE MAN, SAGE — usu. used in pl. ⟨a word to the ~ is sufficient⟩ ⟨books . . . by the ~ of other days —V.L.Parrington⟩
⁴**wise** \"\ *adv* [ME, fr. ²*wise*] *archaic* **:** WISELY
⁵**wise** \"\ *vb* -ED/-ING/-S [²*wise*] *vt* **:** to supply with information **:** make wise ⟨I'll ~ you. You've been bilked —*McClure's*⟩ — usu. used with *up* ⟨think their talent will flower magically if they are *wised up* to a few tricks of the trade —Jan Peerce⟩ ~ *vi* **:** to become informed or knowledgeable **:** get hep **:** LEARN — used with *up* ⟨you can ~ up on details . . . by reading a booklet —*Kiplinger Washington Letter*⟩ ⟨people are *wising up* . . . to the fact that they have been deprived of a lot of good music —*Wall Street Jour.*⟩
⁶**wise** \"\ *vt* -ED/-ING/-S [ME *wisen*, fr. OE *wīsian*; akin to OHG *wīsen* to show the way, ON *vīsa*, Goth fullaweisjan to persuade; all fr. a prehistoric Gmc adj. represented by OE *wīs* wise, knowing] **1** *chiefly Scot* **a :** to show (a person) the way **:** DIRECT, GUIDE **b :** ADVISE, PERSUADE ⟨took me by the hand, and *wised* me to go back —John Galt⟩ **2** *chiefly Scot* **:** to divert or impel in a given direction **:** SEND, TURN ⟨fish rushed . . . before him, as he quietly *wised* them shoreward —J.K.Hunter⟩
-wise \ˌwīz\ *adv comb form* [ME, fr. OE -*wīsan*, fr. *wīse* manner — more at ¹WISE] **1 a :** in the manner of ⟨crab*wise*⟩ ⟨fan*wise*⟩ **b :** in the position or direction of ⟨end*wise*⟩ ⟨slant*wise*⟩ ⟨clock*wise*⟩ **2 :** with regard to **:** in respect of ⟨style*wise*⟩
wise·acre \ˈwī,zākə(r)\ *n* -S [MD *wijssegger* soothsayer, modif. (influenced by MD *segger* sayer, fr. *seggen* to say + -*er*; akin to OE *secgan* to say) of OHG *wīzzago* prophet; akin to OE *wītega* wise man, prophet, *witan* to observe, see to, re-

proach — more at SAY, WITE] **1 :** one who represents himself as well-informed or clever **:** KNOW-IT-ALL, SMART ALECK ⟨has now demonstrated that this subterranean reservoir, which ~s contended was fed by a flowing underground stream, can be emptied and caused to remain empty —D.D.Martin⟩ **2 :** WISE MAN, SAGE — usu. used disparagingly ⟨some of the saws of the old rural ~s —A.O.D.Claxton⟩

[1]wisecrack \'=,=\ *n* [[2]*wise* + *crack*] **:** a clever remark or rejoinder **:** QUIP, WITTICISM ⟨always trying to banish tension and worry with a quip or a ~ —C.W.M.Hart⟩ ⟨essays . . . interspersed with sardonic ~s in which supposedly lofty ideals are mercilessly derided —*Times Lit. Supp.*⟩ **syn** see JOKE

[2]wisecrack \"\ *vi* **:** to make a wisecrack ⟨is humorous and can ~ on occasions —Walter Pach⟩ ~ *vt* **:** to say by way of a wisecrack **:** QUIP

wise·crack·er \-kə(r)\ *n* [[2]*wisecrack* + *-er*] **:** one that makes wisecracks **:** SMART ALECK

wise guy *n* **:** a cocky conceited fellow **:** KNOW-IT-ALL, WISEACRE ⟨the *wise guy* who was going to show . . . headquarters how to run a battle —R.M.Ingersoll⟩ ⟨talks like a *wise guy* —Delmore Schwartz⟩

wisehead \'=,=\ *n* **:** WISEACRE

wisehearted \'=¦==\ *adj* [[2]*wise* + *hearted*] **:** of an understanding disposition **:** DISCERNING ⟨a ~ observer would have guessed at once the reason for her tears⟩

wiselike \'=,=\ *adj* [[2]*wise* + *like*] *chiefly Scot* **:** of a rational or suitable nature **:** SENSIBLE, BECOMING

wise·ling \'wīzliŋ, -lēŋ\ *n* -s [[2]*wise* + *-ling*] *archaic* **:** WISEACRE, WITLING

wise·ly *adv, sometimes* -ER/-EST [ME, fr. OE *wīslice*, fr. *wīs* wise + *-līce* -ly] **:** in a wise manner **:** DISCERNINGLY, PRUDENTLY

wise man *n* [ME, fr. OE *wīs man*, fr. *wīs* wise + *man*] **:** a man of unusual learning, judgment, or insight often serving as a counselor **:** SAGE; *specif* **:** a member of a scholarly class esp. in Palestine during the biblical period distinguished from both priest and prophet as a thinker versed in general ethical and religious questions and fostering instruction of religious truths with a practical import and a distinctive emphasis on the role of wisdom in the conduct of daily life — compare WISDOM 4

wise·ness *n* -ES [ME *wisnesse*, fr. *wis, wise* + *-nesse* -ness] **:** the quality or state of being wise **:** WISDOM

wis·en·heim·er *or* **weis·en·heim·er** \'wīzᵊn,hīmə(r)\ *n* -s [[2]*wise* + G *-enheimer* (as in G family names such as *Guggenheimer, Oppenheimer*)] **:** one who has the air of knowing all about something or everything **:** WISEACRE ⟨emerges from comparative obscurity to national prominence — much to the . . . chagrin of the ~s —Arthur Godfrey⟩

wi·sent \'vē,zent\ *n* -s [G, fr. OHG *wisunt* — more at BISON] **:** a European bison (*Bison bonasus*) — called also *aurochs*

wiser *comparative of* WISE

wises *pl of* WISE, *pres 3d sing of* WISE

wisest *superlative of* WISE

wisewoman \'=,==\ *n, pl* **wisewomen** [ME, fr. [2]*wise* + *woman*] **1 :** a woman versed in charms, conjuring, or fortune-telling **:** SEERESS, WITCH **2 :** MIDWIFE

[1]wish \'wi|sh, *dial* 'wu̇| *or* |sht\ *vb* -ED/-ING/-ES [ME *wisshen*, fr. OE *wȳscan*; akin to OHG *wunsken* to wish, ON *œskja*, Skt *vāñchati* he wishes, *vanati, vanoti* he loves, desires — more at WIN] *vt* **1 a :** to have a desire for **:** WANT, CRAVE ⟨the best friend a man could ~⟩ ⟨they want to be led, and they ~ to remain free —Alexis de Tocqueville⟩ **b :** to yearn for (something unattainable) ⟨I ~ I were young again⟩ ⟨about this time of year I begin to ~ that some one would invent a bathing suit that could be worn to work —*Nation's Business*⟩ **c** *archaic* **:** to hope against hope ⟨I ~ I suffer no prejudice by it —Philip Henry⟩ **2 a :** to invoke upon ⟨~ the team success⟩ — often used in formulas of greeting ⟨~ him good night⟩ **b :** to harbor a specified feeling for ⟨very sincerely ~ him happy —Jane Austen⟩ ⟨embarrassed by her parents' solicitude and ~*ed* them miles away⟩ **c** *dial* **:** to invoke evil on by witchcraft **:** CONJURE ⟨when he hears that he has been ~*ed*, he . . . takes to his bed at once —E.B.Tylor⟩ **3 a :** to give form to (a wish) ⟨~ a wish⟩ **b :** to express a wish for ⟨the Persians did not ~ a strong ruler —William Clark⟩ ⟨students who ~ help in planning their courses⟩ **c :** to request in the form of a wish **:** ORDER ⟨my mother ~*es* you to get the car ready⟩ ⟨when a visitor . . . ~*es* a license to operate a rented car —Bert Pierce⟩ ⟨do you ~ cream or lemon in your tea⟩ **4 a :** to have the intention of **:** PROPOSE ⟨the point I ~ to make⟩ ⟨if men really ~ to be good, they will become good —J.B. Mozley⟩ **b :** to look forward to **:** ANTICIPATE ⟨at length the day so long ~*ed* and expected came —Clara Reeve⟩ **c** *archaic* **:** to speak favorably of **:** RECOMMEND ⟨I was ~*ed* to your worship, by a gentleman —Ben Jonson⟩ ⟨an acquaintance . . . had ~*ed* her to that place —Sir Walter Scott⟩ **d :** to confer (something unwanted) upon someone **:** FOIST ⟨at the annual meeting the job of secretary was ~*ed* on me —F.S.Blanchard⟩ ⟨a friend ~*ed* a small blue mule on me —E.A.Mills⟩ ~ *vi* **1 :** to have a desire **:** WANT, LONG ⟨~ for a puppy⟩ ⟨~ for the courage to stand up to a bully⟩ ⟨as enthralling a pastime as anybody . . . could ~ for —*New Yorker*⟩ **2 :** to make a wish ⟨~ on a falling star⟩ **syn** see DESIRE

[2]wish \"\ *n* -ES [ME *wisshe*, fr. *wisshen* to wish] **1 a :** an act or instance of wishing **:** unfulfilled desire **:** LONGING, WANT ⟨if ~*es* were horses, beggars would ride⟩ ⟨religion is built not on ~*es* but of will —W.L.Sullivan⟩ **b :** an object of desire **:** GOAL ⟨our only ~ was to reach some inhabited place and get something to eat —Heinrich Harrer⟩ **2 a :** an expressed desire **:** indirect mandate **:** WILL ⟨discharge their functions . . . in full accord with the popular ~ —*London Calling*⟩ **b :** a request couched in terms of wishing ⟨cross your fingers and make a ~⟩ ⟨out of deference to his parents' ~*es* —E.S.Bates⟩ **3 a :** an expression of good will ⟨take from my mouth, the ~ of happy years —Shak.⟩ ⟨when you see him, give him my best ~*es*⟩ **b** *archaic* **:** an invocation of evil **:** MALEDICTION ⟨this was my ~: be thou (quoth I) accurst —Shak.⟩

wisha \'wishə\ *interj* [IrGael *ō* oh + *muise* indeed] *chiefly Irish* — used as an intensive or to express surprise

wishbone \'=,=\ *n* [so called fr. the superstition that when two persons pull it apart the one getting the longer fragment will have his wish granted] **1** *or* **wishing bone :** a furcula in front of the breastbone in a bird consisting chiefly of the two clavicles ankylosed at their median or lower end and usu. movably articulated with both the scapula and coracoid at the other end and often having at the median point of union a process that is large and flattened in the domestic fowl **2 :** something that resembles the wishbone of a bird: as **a :** an automobile suspension **b :** a crossarm for electric wires on poles

wishbone bush *n* **:** any of various plants of the genus *Mirabilis; esp* **:** a California four-o'clock (*Mirabilis laevis*) with red flowers

wishbone flower *n* **:** TORENIA 2

wish·er \-shə(r)\ *n* -s **:** one that wishes ⟨~s were ever fools —Shak.⟩

wish·ful \'=fəl\ *adj* [[2]*wish* + *-ful*] **1** *obs* **:** fulfilling a wish **:** ATTRACTIVE, DESIRABLE ⟨having so ~ an opportunity . . . I could not but send you this friendly salute —James Howell⟩ **2 a :** expressive of a wish **:** HOPEFUL, LONGING ⟨looked at the toys with ~ eyes⟩ ⟨the performance of ~ magical exercises —Frederica de Laguna⟩ **b :** having a wish **:** EAGER, DESIROUS ⟨~ to have your cake and eat it —P.B.Kyne⟩ **3 :** based on wishes rather than reality ⟨the ~, ideal America of the American myth —Joseph Frank⟩ ⟨indulged . . . in ~ dreams of an easy peace —Hans Kohn⟩ — **wish·ful·ly** \-fəlē, -li\ *adv*

wish fulfillment *n* **:** the gratification of a desire esp. as gained symbolically (as in dreams, daydreams, symptomatic acts, or neurotic symptoms)

wish·ful·ness *n* -ES **:** the quality or state of being wishful

wishful thinker *n* **:** one that indulges in wishful thinking

wishful thinking *n* **1 :** illusory attribution of actuality to what one wishes to be or become true and discovery of justifications for what one wants to believe through unconscious motivation in order to avoid facing painful or unpleasant facts **2 :** AUTISM, WISH FULFILLMENT

[1]wishing *n* -s [ME *wisshing*, fr. gerund of *wisshen* to wish] **:** an act or instance of wishing ⟨~ won't pay the rent⟩

[2]wishing *adj* [fr. pres. part. of [1]*wish*] **1** *archaic* **:** WISHFUL ⟨returned to cheer his ~ tenant's sight —Allan Ramsay †1758⟩ **2** [[1]*wishing*] **:** regarded as having the power to grant wishes ⟨~ cap⟩ ⟨~ well⟩

wish·ly *adv* [prob. alter. (influenced by [1]*wish*) of *wistly*] *archaic* **:** INTENTLY, WISHFULLY

wish·osk·an \wə'shäskən\ *n* -s *usu cap* **:** a language family of the Ritwan stock comprising only Wiyot

wish·ram \'wi,shram\ *n, pl* **wishram** *or* **wishrams** *usu cap* **1 a :** an Indian people of Klickitat county in the southern part of the state of Washington **b :** a member of such people **2 :** a dialect of Upper Chinook

wisht \'wisht\ *adj* [prob. fr. past part. of E dial. *wish* to invoke evil upon, bewitch] *dial Brit* **:** DISMAL, EERIE

wish-wash \'wish,wȯsh, -,wäsh, -,wōish, *chiefly in substand speech* -,wȯrsh *or* -,wärsh\ *n* [redupl. of [2]*wash*] **1 :** a weak thin drink **2 :** insipid talk or writing **:** CLAPTRAP, TWADDLE ⟨forget all the *wish-wash* about neoromanticism —Louis MacNeice⟩

wishy-washily \¦wishē¦wȯshəlē, -ishi¦, ¦wäsh-, ¦wōish-, -li, *chiefly in substand speech* ¦wȯrsh- *or* ¦wärsh-\ *adv* **:** in a wishy-washy manner **:** INSIPIDLY

wishy-washiness \-shēnəs, -shin-\ *n* **:** the quality or state of being wishy-washy **:** INSIPIDITY

wishy-washy \-shē, -shi\ *adj* [redupl. of *washy*] **1 :** lacking in strength or flavor **:** WEAK, INSIPID ⟨their *wishy-washy*, watery wine —Andrew Balfour⟩ **2 :** lacking in character or determination **:** VAPID, NAMBY-PAMBY ⟨pale, *wishy-washy* eyes —Jack London⟩ ⟨dim, *wishy-washy* pseudo-Impressionism —R.M.Coates⟩ ⟨a *wishy-washy* neutralist platform —*Time*⟩ **syn** see INSIPID

wising *pres part of* WISE

wis·ket \'wiskət, *usu* -əd·+V\ *n* -s [E dial., small twig, basket, prob. of Scand origin; akin to ON *visk* wisp — more at WHISK] *dial Eng* **:** BASKET; *esp* **:** a straw provender basket

wis·li·ze·nus's cottonwood \¦vislət¦sānəsəz-\ *n, usu cap W* [after Frederick A. *Wislizenus* †1889 Am. physician and explorer born in Germany] **:** a poplar (*Populus wislizenii*) of the southwestern U.S. that is often planted as a shade tree in arid regions and has large yellowish green leaves — called also *Wiz·le·zen's poplar* \'vislə,zānz-\

wislizenus oak *n, usu cap W* [after Frederick A. *Wislizenus* †1889] **:** a live oak (*Quercus wislizenii*)

[1]wisp \'wisp\ *also* **whisp** \'hwisp *also* 'wisp\ *n* -s [ME *wisp, wips*; perh. akin to OE *wīpian* to wipe — more at WIPE] **1 a :** a small handful (as of hay or straw) **b :** something that resembles a wisp: as (1) **:** a tenuous strip or fragment ⟨a ~ of chiffon⟩ ⟨roughly-chinked log-cabins . . . stood in a ~ of open —S.V.Benét⟩ ⟨strange ~s of psychological jargon —*Times Lit. Supp.*⟩ (2) **:** a filamentous streak ⟨a ~ of smoke or cloud⟩ ⟨~s of mist floated like trails of luminous dust —Joseph Conrad⟩ (3) **:** something frail or fleeting ⟨a delicate little ~ of an old lady —*Century Mag.*⟩ ⟨a mere ~ of a smile —L.C.Douglas⟩ (4) **:** WILL-O'-THE-WISP **c :** a flock of birds (as snipe) **2** *chiefly Brit* **a :** a pad of twisted or plaited hay or straw for grooming the coat of an animal **b :** a twisted wreath or wad (as of straw or hemp) used as a buffer **c :** a thick twist of hay or straw used as a torch

[2]wisp \"\ *vb* -ED/-ING/-S *vt* **1** *chiefly Brit* **a :** to rub down or massage (as a horse) with a wisp **b :** CRUMPLE, TWIST **2 :** to make or cover with wisps ⟨a cigarette ~*ing* smoke at the corner of his mouth —Raymond Chandler⟩ ⟨the sky all ~*ed* with mist —W.F.Wray⟩ ~ *vi* **:** to emerge or drift in wisps ⟨a thread of smoke ~*ing* out of the funnel —William Wertenbaker⟩ ⟨her hair began to ~ into her eyes —Mary Manning⟩

wisp·i·ly \-pəlē, -li\ *adv* **:** in a wispy manner

wisp·i·ness \-pēnəs, -pin-\ *n* -ES **:** the quality or state of being wispy

wisp·ish \-pish, -pēsh\ *adj* [[1]*wisp* + *-ish*] **:** resembling a wisp **:** INSUBSTANTIAL, WISPY

wispy \-pē, -pi\ *adj* -ER/-EST [[1]*wisp* + *-y*] **:** consisting of, resembling, or characterized by wisps **:** FRAIL, NEBULOUS ⟨hair . . . drawn carelessly at the back into a ~ bun —Fred Majdalany⟩ ⟨a ~ little fellow with small hands and feet —Edmund Wilson⟩ ⟨have only a few, ~ memories of my existence prior to our moving there —Marc Connelly⟩

wis·sel \'wisəl\ *n* -s [ME, exchange, fr. MD; akin to OHG *wehsal* change, turn, ON *gjafavīxl* exchange of gifts — more at WEEK] **1** *chiefly Scot* **:** CHANGE 6b **2** *chiefly Scot* **:** RETRIBUTION — used esp. in the phrase *get the wissel of one's groat*

[1]wist *past of* WIT

[2]wist \'wist\ *n* -s [ML *wista*, prob. fr. OE *wist* food, sustenance; akin to OHG *wist* food, sustenance, ON *vist*] **:** an old Sussex unit of land area estimated as equal to 16 or 18 acres or in Anglo-Saxon times to 60 acres

[3]wist \"\ *vt* -ED/-ING/-S [alter. (influenced by [1]*wist*) of *wis*] *archaic* **:** KNOW ⟨it . . . took at last a certain shape I ~ —S.T. Coleridge⟩

wis·tar·berg glass \'wistər,bərg-\ *n, usu cap W* [fr. *Wistarberg*, name of the glassworks where it was produced, fr. Caspar *Wistar* †1752 + G *berg* mountain, fr. OHG — more at BARROW] **:** glass made in southern New Jersey in the 18th century

wis·tar glass \'wistə(r)-\ *n, use cap W* [after Caspar *Wistar* †1752 Am. glass manufacturer] **:** WISTARBERG GLASS

wis·tar·ia \wə'stirēə, -tēr- *also* -ter- *or* -ta(a)r- *or* -tār-\ *n* -s [NL, alter. (influenced by the name *Wistar*) of *Wisteria*] **1 :** WISTERIA 2 **2 a :** a pale purple that is redder and paler than average lavender, bluer and lighter than phlox pink, and bluer, lighter, and stronger than flossflower blue **b :** a light violet that is redder, less strong, and slightly darker than average bright periwinkle — called also *wistaria violet*

wistaria blue *n* **:** a light purplish blue that is redder and deeper than lupine and darker and slightly redder than average periwinkle

wistaria violet *n* **:** WISTARIA 2b

wis·te·ria \-tirēə, -tēr-\ *n* [NL, fr. Caspar *Wistar* †1818 Am. physician + NL *-ia*] **1** *cap* **:** a genus of chiefly Asiatic mostly woody vines (family Leguminosae) several members of which are grown for ornament and which have pinnately-compound leaves and showy blue, white, purple, or rose pealike flowers in long drooping racemes that are succeeded by long flattened pods **2** -s **:** any plant or flower of the genus *Wisteria*: as **a :** CHINESE WISTARIA **b :** JAPANESE WISTARIA

wist·ful \'wistfəl\ *adj* [*wistly* + *-ful*; in senses 2 & 3 influenced in meaning by [2]*wish*] **1** *obs* **:** INTENT **2 a :** full of timorous longing or unfulfilled desire **:** MELANCHOLY, YEARNING ⟨those ~ little ads which the lovelorn . . . place in the classified columns —E.B.White⟩ ⟨the ~ gaze of the explorer has turned upward to the clouds —Waldemar Kaempffert⟩ **b :** inspiring wistfulness **:** reminiscently evocative ⟨the ~ fragility of all new feeling —Marcia Davenport⟩ ⟨deserted buildings above which ~ flags fly bravely —George Haines⟩ **3 :** musingly sad **:** PENSIVE, MOURNFUL ⟨the sensitive and ~ response of a poet to the gentler phase of beauty —*Amer. Guide Series: Minn.*⟩ ⟨would fix her eyes on the distance in dreary contemplation, and her mind would follow her eyes, in a vacant and ~ regard —G.D.Brown⟩ — **wist·ful·ly** \-fəlē, -li\ *adv*

wist·ful·ness *n* -ES **:** the quality or state of being wistful ⟨his eyes already had the exile's ~ —Mollie Panter-Downes⟩

wis·ti·ti \'wistətē\ *also* **wis·tit** \-tət\ *or* **ouis·ti·ti** \'wistətē\ *n* -s [F *ouistiti*, of imit. origin] **:** MARMOSET; *esp* **:** a marmoset (*Callithrix jacchus*)

wist·less \'wistləs\ *adj* [fr. *wistful*, after such pairs as *heedful: heedless*] *archaic* **:** HEEDLESS

wistly *adv* [prob. fr. [1]*whist* + *-ly*] *obs* **:** INTENTLY, WISTFULLY

[1]wit \'wit, *usu* -id·+V\ *vb, past* **wist** \'wist\ *past part* **wist**; *pres part* **witting**; *pres 1st & 3d sing* **wot** \'wät, *usu* -äd·+V\ [ME *witen* (1st & 3d sing. pres. *wot, wat*, pres. pl. *witen*, past *wiste*, past part. *witen, wist*), fr. OE *witan* (1st & 3d sing. pres. *wāt*, pres. pl. *witon*, past *wiste, wisse*, past part. *witen*); akin to OHG *wizzan* to know (1st & 3d sing. pres. *weiz*, past *westa, wessa*, past part. *giwizzan*), ON *vita* (1st & 3d sing. pres. *veit*, past *vissa*, past part. *vitathr*), Goth *witan* to know (1st sing. pres. *wait*, past *wissa*), L *vidēre* to see, Gk *eidenai* to know, *oida* I know, *idein* to see, Skt *veda* I know, he knows, *vidyā* knowledge; basic meaning: to see] *vt* **1 a** *archaic* **:** to be aware of **:** KNOW ⟨little *witting* that so soon shadows would close in upon them —J.M.Barrie⟩ — used in imperative to convey positive assurance ⟨please you ~: the epitaph is . . . writ —Shak.⟩ **b** *chiefly Midland* **:** THINK, SUPPOSE ⟨they are too bold and crafty, I ~ —Horace Kephart⟩ **2** *obs* **:** to find out **:** DISCOVER, LEARN ⟨stood afar off, to ~ what would be done to him —Exod 2:4 (AV)⟩ ~ *vi* **1** *archaic* **:** to be aware **:** KNOW ⟨we ~ well of many things that we would never prove —Adeline Whitney⟩ **2** *archaic* **:** to become informed

[2]wit \"\ *n* -s [ME, fr. OE; akin to OHG *wizzi* knowledge, understanding, wit, ON *vit*, Goth *-witi* knowledge, OE *witan* to know — more at [1]WIT] **1 a :** MIND, MEMORY ⟨cannot put himself inside the ~ of the slow Neanderthal —Emma Hawkridge⟩ **b :** reasoning power **:** INTELLIGENCE ⟨the moron who hasn't the ~ to hold a job —F.L.Allen⟩ **c** *obs* **:** mechanical skill **:** INVENTIVENESS ⟨the enemy was oftener overcome . . . by the architect's ~ —James Leoni⟩ **2 a :** SENSE 2a — often used in pl. ⟨thou hast more of the wild goose in one of thy ~s, than I am sure I have in my whole five —Shak.⟩ **b** (1) **:** mental soundness **:** SANITY ⟨you have lost your ~, or you would never say such a thing —Humayun Kabir⟩ — often used in pl. ⟨scared me out of my ~s —A.J.Russell⟩ (2) **:** mental capability **:** pragmatic resourcefulness **:** INGENUITY ⟨has enough shrewd ~ to handle any situation —John Erskine †1951⟩ — often used in pl. ⟨wrested submission from nature by their determination and ~s —John DeMeyer⟩ ⟨was at her ~s' end —Edith Sitwell⟩ **3 a :** astuteness of perception or judgment **:** ACUMEN, WISDOM ⟨the ~ that gives sharp decisions on matters of high policy —Constance Foley⟩ ⟨if love is a thorn, they show no ~ who foolishly hug and foster it —W.S.Gilbert⟩ **b :** creative imagination **:** intellectual brilliance or subtlety ⟨skill in improvising fugues is a matter of ~ and inclination rather than an exhibition of facility in execution —A.E.Wier⟩ ⟨poems . . . where an atmosphere of ~ and elegance assures poignancy of meaning —R.P.Blackmur⟩; *specif* **:** the ability to discover amusing analogies between apparently unrelated things and to express them cleverly ⟨follow the metaphysical school of writers of ~ —Stephen Spender⟩ **c** (1) **:** a talent for banter or persiflage (2) **:** REPARTEE, SATIRE ⟨brevity is the soul of ~⟩ ⟨~ has been made a weapon of political dispute —G.F. Sensabaugh⟩ **4 a :** a man of superior intellectual attainments **:** THINKER, BRAIN ⟨nimble and versatile Athenian ~s trained to preternatural acuteness by the debates of the law courts and the Assembly —G.L.Dickinson⟩ **b :** an imaginatively perceptive and articulate individual esp. skilled in banter or persiflage

syn HUMOR, IRONY, SARCASM, SATIRE, REPARTEE: WIT implies intellectual brilliance and quickness in perception combined with a gift for expressing ideas in an entertaining, often laughter provoking, pointed way, usu. connoting the unexpected or apt turn of phrase or idea and often suggesting a certain brittle unfeelingness ⟨portrayed feminine character with an extraordinary *wit* and insight —John Erskine †1951⟩ ⟨a speech as full of *wit* and brilliance as any he had ever made —Stewart Cockburn⟩ ⟨had a playful *wit* which was sometimes very biting —Gertrude Stein⟩ HUMOR in this comparison can signify a disposition to see the ludicrous, comical, ridiculous, or absurd or to give it expression or can apply to the expression itself, often suggesting a generalness or a greater kindliness or sympathy with human failings than does WIT ⟨a man of great *humor*, full of jokes and laughter⟩ ⟨was always saved by her crisp sense of *humor*, her shrewd and mischievous wit —Havelock Ellis⟩ ⟨parliamentary *humor* is not remarkable for its subtlety. It is broad rather than deep. It is *humor*, not wit —E.H.Collis⟩ ⟨the modern sense of *humor* is the quiet enjoyment and implicit expression of the fun of things —Louis Cazamian⟩ ⟨a *humor* that grows from a deep understanding of human foibles and fortitudes, a humor of compassionate knowledge as well as of situation —Katherine G. Jackson⟩ IRONY applies chiefly to a way of speaking or writing in which the meaning intended is contrary to that expressed on the surface ⟨beset with confusion and humiliation he said in blunt *irony*, "I am certainly enjoying myself"⟩ but in a more literary or dramatic sense it implies a deeper perception of the discrepancies implicit in life and character or applies to the actual discrepancies (as between appearance and reality, what is promised and what fulfilled, what is intended and what achieved, what seemingly should be and what actually is), applying frequently to a situation in which what results is the direct, often tragic, opposite of what was desired, intended, or worked for ⟨the dramatic *irony* of the play in which the hero intent upon the greatest good he knows achieves by his very pursuit of it destruction and death⟩ ⟨the patient had sought violent death, but, with the usual *irony* of life, it was the doctor whom sudden death overcame —Havelock Ellis⟩ ⟨the *irony* of Fielding's life that at the moment of his success he lost his happiness —*Time*⟩ ⟨an *irony* of nature that our teeth, which decay so painfully while we live, stop decaying at our death, and outlast all the rest of us —Leonard Woolley⟩ SARCASM applies chiefly to a type of humor intended to cut or wound, often employing ridicule or bitter irony ⟨the satire has become in some instances *sarcasm* — and heavy sarcasm at that —John Woodburn⟩ SATIRE can apply to any criticism or censure relying on exposure, often by irony and often subtle, of the ridiculous or absurd qualities of something ⟨Jonson's drama is only incidentally *satire*, because it is only incidentally a criticism upon the actual world —T.S.Eliot⟩ ⟨*satire*, which holds up to ridicule conduct, beliefs, or institutions disapproved of by the author, may be seriously corrective in purpose, and in such case is intermediate between pure comedy and social drama —K.T.Rowe⟩ ⟨one whose conversation dealt a good deal in *satire* and jokes at someone else's expense⟩ REPARTEE, sometimes still applied to a witty or clever retort, applies chiefly to the power or the art of replying quickly and with wit, humor, or, infrequently, sarcasm ⟨half a dozen smart *repartees* were possible —Aldous Huxley⟩ ⟨she has a clever, coherent way of making her points, and is concise in reply if questioned, quick at *repartee* if heckled —Rose Macaulay⟩ **syn** see in addition MIND

wi·tan \'wi,tän\ *n pl* [OE, pl. of *wita* sage, advisor; akin to OHG *wizzo* sage, Goth *-wita* one who knows, *witan* to know — more at [1]WIT] **1 :** members of the king's advisory council in Anglo-Saxon England **2 :** WITENAGEMOT

[1]witch \'wich\ *n* -ES [ME *wyche*, fr. OE *wice, wic*; prob. akin to OE *wīcan* to yield, give way — more at WEAK] **:** any of several trees having pliant branches

[2]witch \"\ *n* -ES [ME *wicche*, fr. OE *wicca*, masc., wizard & *wicce*, fem., witch; akin to OE *wiccian* to practice witchcraft, MHG *wicken* to bewitch, to divine, OE *wigle* divination, *wiglian* to divine, *wig* idol, image, ON *vē* temple — more at VICTIM] **1 a** *dial Brit* **:** WIZARD, SORCERER **b** (1) **:** a woman practicing the black arts **:** SORCERESS ⟨Halloween ~ on a broomstick⟩ ⟨heard of one old ~ changing herself into a pigeon —John Rhys⟩ (2) **:** an ugly old woman **:** CRONE, HAG ⟨a skinny old ~ with a face like a meat ax and a voice like a buzz saw —Helen Eustis⟩ **c** (1) **:** one supposed to possess supernatural powers esp. by compact with the devil or a familiar (2) **:** a magic spell **:** HEX ⟨it's my idea . . . he put the ~*es* on it —Helen Rich⟩ **d** *or* **witch·er** \-chə(r)\ -s **:** DOWSER **2 :** one that bewitches ⟨the quaint ~ memory —P.B.Shelley⟩; *specif* **:** a particularly charming or alluring woman **3 a** (1) **:** STORM PETREL (2) **:** GREBE (3) *or* **witch bird :** ANI **b** *also* **witch flounder :** a small-mouth blackish or brownish deepwater flounder (*Glyptocephalus cynoglossus*) of the North Atlantic that is of some importance as a food fish **c :** WITCH MOTH

[3]witch \"\ *adj* **:** of, relating to, or used against witches ⟨~ cult⟩ ⟨~ doors used to ward off evil spirits⟩

[4]witch \"\ *vb* -ED/-ING/-ES [ME *wicchen*, fr. OE *wiccian* to practice witchcraft] **1 :** BEWITCH **2 :** DOWSE

witch alder *n* [[1]*witch*] **:** FOTHERGILLA 2

witch ball *n* **:** a hollow sphere of plain or striated glass hung in cottage windows in the 18th century to ward off evil spirits but later often posed on top of a vase or suspended by a cord (as from the mantelpiece or rafters) for decorative effect

witch cake *n* **:** a cake made by a witch for working magic or for use in testing one accused of witchcraft

witchcraft \'=,=\ *n* [ME *wicchecraft*, fr. OE *wiccecræft*, fr. *wicca, wicce* wizard, witch + *cræft* craft] **1 a :** an act or instance of employing sorcery esp. with malevolent intent **:** a magical rite or technique ⟨in practicing ~, the witch . . . secured an article of the proposed victim's clothing —J.J. Honigmann⟩ **b :** the exercise of supernatural powers **:** alleged intercourse with the devil or with a familiar **2 :** an irresistible influence or fascination **:** CHARM, ENCHANTMENT ⟨he hath a ~ over the king in's tongue —Shak.⟩ ⟨the ~ of harmonic sound —R.W.Emerson⟩ **syn** see MAGIC

witch doctor *n* **1** : a professional worker of magic in a primitive society occupying a tribal position similar to that of a shaman or medicine man who by the use of spells, charms, herbal remedies, and incantations seeks to cure illness, detect witches, and counteract malevolent magical influences — called also **witchman** **2** : one employing techniques or mumbo jumbo like those of a witch doctor ⟨a clairvoyant or *witch doctor* of some kind —Osbert Sitwell⟩ ⟨political *witch doctors*⟩ ⟨*witch doctors* of modern business . . . exorcising the demon of pessimism —C.W.Ferguson⟩

witch doctress *n* : a female witch doctor

witch elm *var of* WYCH ELM

witch·en \'wichən\ *n* -s [short for *witchen* elm, fr. *witchen,* adj. (fr. ¹*witch* + *-en*) + *elm*] **1** *archaic* : WYCH ELM **2** : a rowan tree (*Sorbus aucuparia*)

witch·ery \-ch(ə)rē, -ri\ *n* -ES **1 a** : the practice of witchcraft : SORCERY ⟨an old crone accused of ~⟩ **b** : an act or instance of witching — usu. used in pl. ⟨a woman infamous for sortileges and *witcheries* —Sir Walter Scott⟩ **2** : an irresistible fascination : CHARM, SPELL ⟨lovingly . . . dallies with the ~ of the old learning —P.E.More⟩ **syn** see MAGIC

witch·es' brew *or* **witch·es' broth** *also* **witch's brew** \'wichəz-\ *n* : a fearsome mixture : a confused condition ⟨a fantastic *witches' brew* of contradictions —*Newsweek*⟩

witches'-broom \��"�\ *n* *or* **witch broom** *n* : an abnormal tufted growth of small branches on a tree or shrub caused by fungi, viruses, mistletoes, insect injury, or physiological disturbances — called also **hexenbesen, staghead**

witches'-butter \��344\ *n* **1** : any of various gelatinous bluegreen algae esp. of the genus *Nostoc* **2** : a yellow jelly fungus (*Tremella lutescens*)

witches' cauldron *n* : an unholy combination or set of circumstances : a turbid or menacing situation ⟨let us look into this *witches' cauldron* — the battle of Germany —J.F.C. Fuller⟩

witches'-horse \��344\ *n* : STICK INSECT

witches' milk \��344\ *n* : MARE'S TAIL 2a **2** *or* **witch's milk** : secretion from the mammary glands of the newborn of both sexes presumably due to placental permeability to the lactation-producing hormones of the mother

witches' money-bags *n* : an orpine (*Sedum telephium*)

witches' sabbath *n, often cap* W&S : SABBAT

witches' stirrup *or* **witches' bridle** *n* : a tangle in a horse's mane

witches'-thimble \��344\ *n, dial Eng* : any of several European plants: as **a** : a harebell (*Campanula rotundifolia*) **b** : SEA CAMPION **c** : a foxglove (*Digitalis purpurea*) **d** : a bluebottle (*Centaurea cyanus*)

witch·et·ty grub \'wichəd-ē, -chətē, -i\ *or* **witchetty** *n* -ES [*witchetty* native name in Australia] : any of various large white grubs that are larvae esp. of moths of the genus *Cossus,* frequent the roots of Australian acacia, are relished by the aborigines, and form the chief food of the marsupial mole

witchfinder \'��344\ *n* : a detector of witches; *specif* : a 17th century investigator charged with hunting down and obtaining evidence against supposed witches

witch fire *n* : SAINT ELMO'S FIRE

witch flounder *n* : WITCH 3b

witchgrass \'��344\ *n* [²*witch* + *grass*] **1** : COUCH GRASS 1a **2** : any of several grasses of the genus *Panicum; esp* : a No. American panic grass (*P. capillare*) with slender brushy panicles that is often a weed on cultivated land — called also **tumble grass**

witch hazel \'wich·hāzəl, 'wi,chā-, -ə'�\ *n* [¹*witch*] **1 a** : WYCH ELM **b** : HORNBEAM 1a **c** : ROWAN TREE 1 **2 a** : a tree or shrub of the genus *Hamamelis; as* **a** : a common shrub (*Hamamelis virginiana*) of eastern No. America having leaves like those of the hazel and small yellow flowers that appear after the leaves have fallen **(2)** : VERNAL WITCH HAZEL **b** : an alcoholic solution of a distillate of the bark of a witch hazel (*H. virginiana*) widely used as a remedy for bruises and sprains and as a mildly astringent lotion

witch-hazel family *n* : HAMAMELIDACEAE

witch hob·ble \-'häbəl\ *or* **witch hop·ple** \-'häpəl\ *n* [¹*witch*] **1** : HOBBLEBUSH **2** : CRANBERRY BUSH 2

witch·hood \'�,hůd\ *n* : the state of being a witch

witch-hunt \'�\ *n* **1** : a searching out and persecution of persons accused of witchcraft **2** : an investigation of or campaign against dissenters (as political opponents) conducted on the pretext of protecting the public welfare and resulting in public persecution and defamation of character ⟨*witch-hunts* for reds in faculties —Laird Bell⟩ ⟨a fascist *witch-hunt* against all those who dare to question Russian policies —Alexander Baird⟩ — **witch-hunter** \'�\ *n*

witch-hunting \'�\ *n* : the act or process of carrying on a witch-hunt ⟨various forms of hysteria such as *witch-hunting* and a search for scapegoats —N.J.Padelford⟩ — compare RED-BAITING

¹witch·ing \'wiching, -chēŋ\ *n* -s [ME *wicching,* fr. OE *wiccung,* fr. *wiccian* to practice witchcraft + *-ung* -ing — more at WITCH] : the practice of witchcraft : SORCERY

²witching \'�\ *adj* [fr. pres. part. of obs. E *witch* to practice witchcraft, fr. ME *wicchen,* fr. OE *wiccian*] **1** : of, relating to, or suitable for sorcery or supernatural occurrences ⟨'tis now the very ~ time of night, when churchyards yawn —Shak.⟩ ⟨the ~ light of a fen fire —O.E.Rölvaag⟩ **2** [fr. pres. part. of ⁴*witch*] : BEWITCHING, FASCINATING ⟨a terrain which nature has adorned with ~ beauty —Raymond Moley⟩ — **witch·ing·ly** *adv*

witching stick *n* : DOWSING ROD

witch light *n* : SAINT ELMO'S FIRE

witchlike \'�\ *adj* : having the gnarled appearance or evil character associated with witches ⟨elderbushes and hawthorns, all old, crabbed and ~ —H.E.Bates⟩

witch·man \'�342mən\ *n, pl* **witchmen** \'�\ : WITCH DOCTOR

witch-mark \'�\ *n* : a mark on the body supposedly identifying or caused by a witch

witch moth *n* : any of various noctuid moths some of which are large and which belong to *Erebus* and related genera; *specif* : BLACK WITCH

witch's brew *var of* WITCHES' BREW

witch's pouch *n* : SHEPHERD'S PURSE

witch stick *n* : DOWSING ROD

witchweed \'�\ *n* [²*witch* + *weed*] : any of several hemiparasitic herbs of the genus *Striga* (family Scrophulariaceae) with yellow irregular flowers

witchwoman \'�\ *n, pl* **witchwomen** : a female witch doctor

witchwood \'�\ *n* [¹*witch* + *wood*] *dial Eng* **a** : WYCH ELM **b** : ROWAN TREE 1 **c** : a spindle tree (*Euonymus europaeus*) **2** : AMERICAN MOUNTAIN ASH **3** : MARRON GLACÉ

witchy \'wichē, -chi\ *adj* -ER/-EST **1** : resembling or characteristic of a witch : MALEVOLENT, WITCHLIKE ⟨a terrible little woman, a little ~ moron —Peggy Bennett⟩ **2** : produced by or suggestive of witchcraft ⟨~ little houses . . . straight from a child's book of fairy tales —William Sansom⟩ ⟨there was a round moon . . . and the yard was full of a white ~ radiance —C.G.D.Roberts⟩

wit-cracker *n, obs* : one who makes wisecracks

¹wite \'wīt, *usu* -īd-\ *n* V\ *n* -s [ME, fr. OE *wite;* akin to OHG *wizi* fine, punishment, ON *viti* fine, punishment, OE *witan* to look after, blame] **1 a** : a penal fine for serious crimes payable under early English law to the king or other authority having jurisdiction — see BLOODWITE **b** : an exemption from payment of such a fine **2** *chiefly Scot* : responsibility for a fault or misfortune ⟨now it's done . . . and who's to bear the ~ of it —R.L.Stevenson⟩

²wite \"\ *vt* [ME *witen,* fr. OE *wītan* to see to, look after, reproach, blame; akin to OS *wītan* to blame, OHG *wizan* to blame, punish, ON *víta* fine, OE *witan* to be aware, know — more at WIT, v.] *chiefly Scot* : to impute blame to : CENSURE, REPROACH

wi·te·na·ge·mot *or* **wi·te·na·ge·mote** \'wit'nəgə̇,mōt, ·wit'n-'ägə,mo-\ *n* [OE *witena gemōt,* fr. *witena* (gen. pl. of *wita* sage, advisor) + *gemōt* gemot — more at WITAN, GEMOT] : an Anglo-Saxon council of perhaps 100 nobles, prelates, and influential officials convened from time to time to advise the king on administrative and judicial matters — called also *witan;* compare GEMOT, MOOT 1a

wit-gat \'wit,gat\ *or* **wit·gat·boom** \-,bům\ *n* -s [*witgat* fr. Afrik., short for *witgatboom,* lit., white hole tree, fr. MD *wit*

---

white + *gat* hole, opening + *boom* tree; akin to OE *hwīt* white, *gæt* opening, *bēam* tree — more at WHITE, GATE, BEAM] : a So. African shrub or tree (*Boscia albitrunca*) of the family Capparidaceae having white hard close-grained wood and roots that are roasted as a coffee substitute

¹with \(')with̸, ̸th, ̷wə\ *prep* [ME, fr. OE, prep. & adv., against, opposite, toward, with; akin to OE *wither* against, OS *with, withar* against, with, OHG *widar* against, back, again, ON *vith, withr* against, with, Goth *withra* against, OSlav *vŭtorŭ* other, second, Skt *vi* apart, asunder, *vitaram* farther and perh. to L *vitium* fault, vice; basic meaning: apart, divided] **1 a** : in opposition to : AGAINST ⟨fought bitterly ~ his partner⟩ ⟨had had a constant tussle ~ insomnia —Lucien Price⟩ **b** : away from : so as to be separated or detached from ⟨broke ~ his family and left home⟩ ⟨severed diplomatic relations ~ its neighbor⟩ ⟨parted ~ him at the door⟩ **2 a** : alongside of : near to ⟨the boat was running close in ~ the land⟩ **b** : in a line or on a course paralleling the direction or movement of ⟨~ the grain⟩ ⟨~ the wind⟩ **c** : in the same direction as the course or motion of : favorable to ⟨the wind was ~ the boat⟩ ⟨the tide is ~ us⟩ **3 a** — used as a function word to indicate the one to whom a communication or statement is made ⟨a grave mistake to go into long explanations . . . such a person —W.J.Reilly⟩ **b** *archaic* : in the mind or will of : WITHIN ⟨consider ~ yourselves, to bring in . . . a lion among ladies is a most dreadful thing —Shak.⟩ **4 a** — used as a function word to indicate one that shares in an action, transaction, or arrangement ⟨we who have worked ~ them day and night —J.K. Blake⟩ ⟨three quarters of its annual business . . . is now done ~ Americans —E.O.Hauser⟩ ⟨a salon . . . brought off in an academic town ~ young men and women on cookies and hot chocolate —Lucien Price⟩ **b** — used as a function word to indicate the object of attention, notice, or feeling ⟨their satisfaction ~ the institution —E.P.Vonderhaar⟩ ⟨get tough ~ him⟩ ⟨angry ~ her⟩ ⟨in love ~ her⟩ **c** : in respect to : so far as concerns ⟨on friendly terms ~ all nations⟩ ⟨expressed agreement ~ his views⟩ ⟨seemed to be all right ~ her whether we bought or not —G.P.Musselman⟩ **d** — used to indicate the object of an adverbial expression of imperative force ⟨off ~ his head⟩ ⟨away ~ him⟩ **e** : as the doer, giver, or victim of ⟨charged ~ murder⟩ ⟨threatened ~ tuberculosis⟩ **f** : OVER, UPON ⟨no longer has any influence ~ him⟩ **g** : in the performance, operation, or use of ⟨prospering ~ their dairy industry —C.B.Hitchcock⟩ ⟨the trouble ~ this machine⟩ ⟨something went wrong ~ the radio⟩ **5 a** — used as a function word to indicate the object of a statement of comparison, equality, or sameness ⟨this house is identical ~ the one you have just seen⟩ ⟨on equal terms ~ the other applicants⟩ **b** — used as a function word to express agreement or concurrence ⟨if we accept this evidence we must conclude, ~ him, that the painting is a forgery⟩ ⟨oar flashing ~ oar⟩ **c** : on the side of : willing to give aid or support to : FOR ⟨if he's trying to cut down accidents, I'm ~ him⟩ ⟨the election will show whether the people are ~ him in this new policy⟩ **d** : as well as : not inferior to ⟨can pitch ~ the best of them⟩ **6 a** : in the judgment or estimation of ⟨he stood well ~ his fellow classmates⟩ **b** : in or according to the experience or practice of ⟨~ many of us, our ideas seem to fall by the wayside —W.J.Reilly⟩ ⟨the surrealists . . . the ideal is nothing else than the material world reflected by the human mind —Herbert Read⟩ ⟨an accustomed action ~ her, to seem thus washing her hands —Shak.⟩ **c** : after the manner, judgment, or practice of : LIKE ⟨suffer ~ Job⟩ **7 a** *archaic* : by the direct act of ⟨here is himself, married, as you see, ~ traitors —Shak.⟩ **(2)** *obs* : born of or procreated by ⟨she speaks, and 'tis such sense that my sense breeds ~ it —Shak.⟩ **b** : by means of : by the use or agency of : THROUGH ⟨the plot is unfolded almost entirely ~ the camera rather than ~ words —*Time*⟩ ⟨one of the nicest ways to say "Merry Christmas" is ~ a gift you've created yourself —*Item*⟩ ⟨just got in ~ the bus —Alasdair Carmichael⟩ **c** : by the presence, addition, or contiguity of ⟨bordered front and back ~ boxwood hedges —*Amer. Guide Series: Pa.*⟩ ⟨an attic filled ~ junk⟩ ⟨an atmosphere permeated ~ suspicion⟩ **8 a** : as a result of : in consequence of : because of ⟨pale ~ anger⟩ ⟨had woken up, about 1 o'clock, ~ a fellow blowing his horn —Dorothy Sayers⟩ ⟨was rosy ~ breasting the hill —Maurice Hewlett⟩ **8 b** — used as a function word to indicate manner of action ⟨ran ~ effort⟩ ⟨spoke ~ ease⟩ **b** — used as a function word to indicate a related or supplementary fact or circumstance ⟨stark silence ~ no recognition whatsoever is the common reception ~ W.J.Reilly⟩ ⟨morning sessions are largely case problems, ~ guest speakers in the afternoon —C.F.Craig⟩ ⟨remains essentially unchanged, ~ many old houses now largely owned by summer residents —*Amer. Guide Series: N.H.*⟩ **c** — used as a function word to indicate an emotional or mental state accompanying a specified action ⟨~ purity and holiness will I pass my life and practice my art —Hippocratic Oath⟩ ⟨looked on ~ horror⟩ **d** — used as a function word to indicate a circumstance accompanying or a result attendant on a specified action ⟨looking out over the water ~ his chin supported on his hands —E.G.O'Neill⟩ ⟨told us about it ~ detail —W.A.White⟩ ⟨escaped ~ a brief imprisonment when less affluent agitators were hanged —*Amer. Guide Series: N.C.*⟩ ⟨attacked ~ great loss of life⟩ **e** — used as a function word to indicate connection or relationship in idea, state, or action ⟨taking one day ~ another⟩ ⟨~ such speed, caution was impossible⟩ **9 a** : immediately consequent upon — used before a demonstrative pronoun ⟨~ this she seizeth on his sweating palm —Shak.⟩ **b** : at the moment or time of ⟨is up ~ the dawn⟩ : on the occurrence of or as a result of the occurrence of ⟨~ whose death the scepter passed into other hands —Kemp Malone⟩ ⟨~ the outbreak of the Civil War he returned North —T.S.Palmer⟩ **c** — used as a function word to indicate a person or thing that serves as a point of departure or conclusion ⟨we will begin ~ you⟩ ⟨ended the lecture ~ this quotation⟩ **d** : at the same time as : at the time a specified action or event is performed or experienced by ⟨men who were born just before or ~ the century —Manès Sperber⟩ ⟨the captain went down ~ his ship⟩ **e** : in the course of ⟨~ time the amount of fossil fuels remaining approaches zero —W.P.Webb⟩ **f** : in proportion to ⟨the pressure varies ~ the depth⟩ **10 a** — used as a function word to indicate addition or supplement ⟨his own funds, ~ the money he borrowed, enabled him to gain control of the business⟩ **b** : inclusive of ⟨it costs five dollars, ~ the tax⟩ **c** *archaic* — used as a function word to invoke evil or misfortune ⟨show your knave's visage, ~ a pox to you —Shak.⟩ **d** — used as a function word to indicate something given, received, or taken for granted ⟨~ your leave⟩ ⟨~ your permission⟩ **e** — used as a function word to introduce a refrain (as of a poem or song) ⟨~ hey, ho, the wind and the rain —Shak.⟩ **f** — used as a function word to indicate combination or mixture of ingredients ⟨blend melted chocolate ~ the batter⟩ ⟨heat milk ~ honey⟩ **g** : joined to : placed, arranged, or grouped in the same space, combination, package, or getup as ⟨put the bill away ~ the others⟩ ⟨ordered onion ~ his hamburger⟩ ⟨wore a cloth cap ~ his sport shirt⟩ **h** — used as a function word to introduce an expression of gratitude, regard, or affection esp. in a message or letter ⟨we return your contribution ~ thanks⟩ ⟨~ the compliments of the author⟩ **11 a** — used as a function word to indicate accompaniment or companionship ⟨a man of sorrows and acquainted ~ grief —Isa 53:3 (AV)⟩ **b** : at the time of : VISITING ⟨her mother is ~ her for the summer⟩ : in attendance on : SEEING ⟨the doctor is ~ him now⟩ **c** : in the company of : as companion of ⟨went to the theater ~ his wife⟩ ⟨his long friendship ~ his rival for the week⟩ **d** : present to ⟨this hot spell has been ~ us for a week⟩ ⟨peace be ~ you⟩ **e** : as part of : having membership or participation in ⟨seven hundred and one men who graduated from Harvard ~ the class of 1904 —F.D. Roosevelt⟩ ⟨goes along ~ the crowd⟩ ⟨has been ~ the firm for twenty years⟩ **12 a** : in the care, guidance, or possession of ⟨left the money ~ his mother⟩ ⟨carried his prejudices abroad ~ him⟩ ⟨the children went to the fair ~ their teacher⟩ **b** : having the possession, keeping, or guidance of : having, holding, or wearing ⟨came ~ good news⟩ ⟨a bride ~ a large dowry⟩ ⟨a diplomat ~ important missions —G.C. Sellery⟩ ⟨marched in ~ their uniforms of scarlet and gold —P.D.Whitney⟩ **c** : characterized or distinguished by ⟨a man ~ a hot temper⟩ ⟨a woman ~ a sharp tongue⟩ ⟨a knife ~ a dull

---

blade⟩ **d** : by reason of having, containing, or giving forth ⟨it was pouring ~ rain —Archibald Marshall⟩ ⟨the air is sharp ~ frost —Corey Ford⟩ **e** — used as a function word to indicate one that possesses a specified attribute ⟨has a pleasing way ~ her⟩ **f** — used as a function word to indicate an object or source of concern or puzzlement ⟨what's ~ him⟩ ⟨what's ~ liberalism today —Eric Goldman & Mary Paull⟩ **13 a** : allowing for : in spite of : NOTWITHSTANDING ⟨a really tip-top man, ~ all his wrongheadedness —H.J.Laski⟩ **b** : except at the cost or loss of ⟨cannot do this ~ impunity⟩ ⟨cannot attain this ~ honor⟩ **c** — used as a function word to indicate a qualification or proviso ⟨accepted the offer ~ certain conditions⟩ **d** : except for ⟨finds that, ~ one group of omissions and one important addition, they reflect that curriculum —Gilbert Highet⟩ — **with it** — see ¹IT — used as the hand ⟨wake up and get with it⟩ — **with the sun** *adv* : in the direction of the sun's motion as it appears to one facing south in the northern hemisphere : CLOCKWISE — opposed to *against the sun*

²with \'with, -th\ *adv* : so as to have something present or added ⟨I'll have my hamburger ~⟩

³with *also* **withe** \'with\ *n, pl* **withes** [alter. of *width*] : one of the partitions between the flues in a chimney

¹with·al \wə̇'thȯl, -'thȯl\ *adv* [ME *withal, withall,* fr. *with,* prep., + *al, all* all — more at WITH, ALL] **1** : together with this : in addition : BESIDES ⟨he was a supporter of all constructive work and ~ an excellent business man —A.W.Long⟩ **2** *archaic* : THEREWITH ⟨if he do bleed, I'll gild the faces of the grooms ~ —Shak.⟩ **3** : on the other hand : for all that : NEVERTHELESS ⟨incessantly badgering, cajoling and driving, but a gentleman ~ —Anthony Leviero⟩ ⟨her voice was hoarse and rough but had an appealing warmth ~ —Peter Abrahams⟩

²withal \"\ *prep* [ME *withall,* fr. *withall,* adv.] *archaic* : WITH — used postpositively with a relative or interrogative pronoun as object ⟨tell you who time ambles ~ —Shak.⟩

wi·tha·nia \wə̇'thänēə\ *n, cap* [NL, fr. unknown origin) + NL *-ia*] : a small genus of Old World tropical shrubs (family Solanaceae) having woolly leaves and clustered bell-shaped flowers with an enlarged fruiting calyx and including one plant (*W. coagulans*) used in the East Indies as a substitute for rennet in making cheese

with·draw \wə̇th'drȯ, with-\ *vb* [ME *withdrawen,* fr. ¹*with* + *drawen* to pull, draw — more at DRAW] *vt* **1 a** : to take back or away (something bestowed or possessed) ⟨*withdrew* her acceptance of the invitation —*Current Biog.*⟩ ⟨~s her awareness and love from the one person . . . who most deserves her awareness and love —Lionel Trilling⟩ ⟨~s her hand from his⟩ **b** : to remove from use or cultivation ⟨lands *withdrawn* from commercial use —*Amer. Guide Series: Wash.*⟩ **2 a** : to remove or draw out from a place or position ⟨~ strip slowly from water —*Monsanto Mag.*⟩ ⟨from his dispatch case . . . *withdrew* a document —*Time*⟩ **b** : to turn away (as the eyes) from an object of attention ⟨*withdrew* his eyes from the scene⟩ ⟨*withdrew* his glance⟩ **c** : to remove (money) from a place of deposit or investment ⟨~ to draw back or aside (as a curtain or veil) **(2)** : to draw back (as a bolt) from a fastening **3 a** *archaic* : to disengage or remove (oneself) from a place, position, office, or situation ⟨~ yourselves and leave us here alone —Shak.⟩ **b** : to draw away or turn aside from some activity or interest : DISTRACT, DIVERT ⟨even so grave an undertaking could not wholly ~ her from more congenial pursuits —Walter Bagehot⟩ **c** : to cause to return or retire from a place or activity ⟨*withdrew* his son from the school⟩ ⟨*withdrew* the troops from the attack⟩ **d** : to dismiss (a jury) from a jury **4 a** : to eliminate from consideration or set outside of a category or group ⟨*withdrew* his name from the list of nominees⟩ ⟨had *withdrawn* one dogma after another from the domain of pure reason —G.G.Coulton⟩ **b** **(1)** : to abandon the prosecution of : cease to proceed with ⟨~ its objections to the . . . agreements —*Current Biog.*⟩ **(2)** : ANNUL ⟨~ his order⟩ **(3)** : RELINQUISH ⟨~ his support of the group⟩ **c (1)** : to make a retraction of (an assertion or expression) : take back : RECALL, UNSAY ⟨demanded that the speaker ~ the word *fraudulent*⟩ **(2)** : to recall or remove (a motion) from consideration under parliamentary procedure ~ *vi* **1 a** : to move back or away from a place, position, group, or person : RETIRE ⟨the dancers ~ to a clear space at the farther end of the banqueting-hall —Lafcadio Hearn⟩ ⟨was forced more and more to ~ from the gaieties of the capital —Martha T. Stephenson⟩ **b** : to draw back from a battlefield or area of conflict : RETREAT ⟨must either maintain ourselves there in force or ~ —*Atlantic*⟩ **2 a** : to remove oneself from participation or activity in something ⟨*withdrew* from the church of her family —*Amer. Guide Series: Tenn.*⟩ ⟨*withdrew* from newspaper work to devote his full time to writing —*Atlantic Bull.*⟩ **b** : to resign from or cease attendance at a school or course of study ⟨*withdrew* after a year or so without taking a degree —*Current Biog.*⟩ **c** : to become socially or emotionally detached ⟨her mother . . . had *withdrawn* farther and farther into herself —Ethel Wilson⟩ **3** : to recall a motion from consideration under parliamentary procedure **syn** see GO

with·draw·able \-'ȯdəbəl\ *adj* : capable of being withdrawn

with·draw·al \-ȯ(ə)l\ *n* -s **1 a** : retreat or retirement esp. into a more secluded or less exposed place or position ⟨sought national security in ~ from areas of conflict —A.O.Wolfers⟩ ⟨their furtive glances, odd silences, and sudden ~s into family jocularity and isolation —Virginia Woolf⟩ **b** : an operation by which a military force disengages from the enemy **c** : DETACHMENT ⟨this immense power of ~, this concentration upon the things of the spirit —Agnes Repplier⟩ **2** : RETRACTION, REVOCATION ⟨insisted upon a ~ of the statement and a public apology⟩ **3** : the act of drawing someone or something back from or out of a place or position ⟨the commission of the League of Nations which supervised the ~ of foreigners —*Times Lit. Supp.*⟩ **4 a** : the act of taking back or away something that has been granted or possessed ⟨the ~ of storage privileges —*Amer. Guide Series: Minn.*⟩ ⟨the ~ of esteem or love —Abram Kardiner⟩ **b** : removal from a place of deposit or investment ⟨made several large ~s from the bank within the space of a week⟩ **c** : the discontinuance of administration or use of a drug ⟨discomfort resulting from ~ of the opiate⟩ ⟨the ~ effects of barbiturates⟩

withdrawal symptom *n* : one of a group of symptoms (as nausea, sweating, or depression) produced in a person by deprivation of an addicting drug

with·draw·er \-ȯ(ə)r, -ȯə\ *n* [ME, fr. *withdrawen* to withdraw + *-er*] : one that withdraws

withdrawing *adj* [fr. pres. part. of *withdraw*]; *specif* : RECEDING, RETIRING ⟨a sharp face that was sour and ~ —J.A.Michener⟩ — **with·draw·ing·ness** *n* -ES

withdrawing room *n* [*withdraw* fr. gerund of *withdraw*] : a room for retirement from another room (as a dining room) : DRAWING ROOM

with·draw·ment \-mənt\ *n* -s : WITHDRAWAL

with·drawn \-ȯn\ *adj* [fr. past part. of *withdraw*] **1** : removed from immediate contact or easy approach : ISOLATED, SECLUDED ⟨during the long windswept winters is a lonely, ~ community —*Amer. Guide Series: Mich.*⟩ ⟨led cramped, ~ lives —Gordon Merrick⟩ **2** : socially detached and unresponsive : INTROVERTED ⟨there is nothing ~ or coldly impersonal about him —Nancy Ross⟩ — **with·drawn·ness** \-ȯnnə̇s\ *n* -ES

¹withe \'with *also* -ith *or* -īth, *dial* 'hwith\ *n* -s [ME, fr. OE *withthe* — more at WITHY] **1 a** : a band consisting of a twig twisted **b** : a slender flexible branch or twig (as of osier) used as a band or rope : WITHY **c** : a slender twig ⟨the young man imagines that he can fight his way through the world with a ~ of sorrel wood —Donn Byrne⟩ ⟨a small ~ of a man —Peter De Vries⟩ **2** : a tropical American weedy herb (*Heliotropium fruticosum*) whose stems are used in Jamaica for making baskets **b** : WITHE ROD **3** *also* **wythe** \"\ : **a** : a boom iron; *specif* : the boom iron that secures the flying jib boom **b** : a metal ring or band on a mast or other spar **4** *or* **wythe** \"\ : TIER 2d

²withe \"\ *vt* -ED/-ING/-S [ME *withen,* fr. ¹*withe*] **1** *archaic* : to wind or twist like a withe **2 a** : to bind or fasten with a withe **b** : to snare (deer) with a noose of withes

³withe *var of* WITH

with·en \'withən, 'wǐth-\ *n* -s [ME, prob. short for *withen-tre* willow tree, fr. *withen,* adj. (prob. fr. *withy* + *-en*) + *tre* tree] *archaic* : WILLOW

¹with·er \'withə(r)\ *vb* **withered; withered; withering**

\-th(ə)riŋ\ **withers** [ME *widderen, widren;* prob. akin to ME *wederen* to weather — more at WEATHER] *vi* **1 :** to become dry and sapless **:** shrivel up ⟨crops ~*ed* and crumbled to dust —*Amer. Guide Series: Texas*⟩ **2 :** to lose bodily moisture **:** become dried up **:** waste away in body ⟨seeming to contract, to ~ before their shocked eyes, with his cheeks and the hollows behind his ears all sunken in —Angus Mowat⟩ **3 :** to lose vitality, force, or freshness **:** DECAY, DECLINE, FADE ⟨the tariffs and prohibitions which caused industries to flourish or ~ —*Times Lit. Supp.*⟩ — often used with *away* **~** *vt* **1 a :** to cause (as a plant) to dry up **:** SHRIVEL ⟨the cold winds blew from the east, ~*ing* grass and plants and trees —Kathleen Freeman⟩ **b :** to subject (tea leaves) to a drying process **c :** to check the growth of (germinating barley) on the malting floor in brewing **2 :** to cause to shrink, wrinkle, or decay ⟨age cannot ~ her —Shak.⟩ **3 a :** to cause to lose freshness, vitality, or force ⟨control will ~ science by destroying its precious essence of originality and spontaneity —R.P.Patterson⟩ **b :** to make speechless or incapable of action **:** PARALYZE, STUN ⟨~*ed* him with a look —Dorothy Sayers⟩ ⟨before she could ~ him for his impertinence, he swept her on to the floor in a waltz —Anthony Glyn⟩

²wither \"\ *n* -s **:** the process of withering tea leaves ⟨black, well twisted leaf denotes a good ~ —W.A.Ukers⟩

withered *adj* [fr. past part. of ¹*wither*] **:** shriveled and shrunken from drying **:** WIZENED ⟨a lanky scarecrow of a man with ~ face and lantern jaws —W.F.Starkie⟩ ⟨leaning heavily on ~ phrases —Kevin Desmond⟩ — **with·ered·ness** *n* -ES

withered leaf *n* **:** FEUILLE MORTE

withered rose *n* **:** a grayish red to moderate reddish brown

with·er·er \-th(ə)rə(r)\ *n* -s **:** one that withers

withering *adj* **1 :** acting or serving to cut down or destroy **:** ANNIHILATING, DEVASTATING ⟨guns mounted on railway cars opened a ~ fire —Alexander Forbes⟩ ⟨to compliments inflated I've a ~ reply —W.S.Gilbert⟩ **2 :** used for drying or curing ⟨~ floor⟩ — **with·er·ing·ly** *adv*

with·er·ite \ˈwithə,rīt\ *n* -s [G *witherit*, irreg. fr. William *Withering* †1799 Eng. physician + G *-it* -ite] **:** a mineral $BaCO_3$ consisting of a native barium carbonate isostructural with aragonite and occurring as orthorhombic white or gray six-sided twin crystals and also in columnar or granular masses (hardness 3–3.75, sp. gr. 4.27–4.35)

with·er·nam \ˈwithə(r),näm\ *n* -s [ME, fr. AF, fr. OE *wither* against + *nām* seizure, fr. *niman* to take — more at WITH, NIMBLE] **1 :** the action of taking by way of reprisal **:** a second or reciprocal distress of other goods in lieu of goods taken by a first distress and eloigned **2 :** a writ used in connection with the action of replevin that issues to a defendant in replevin when he has obtained judgment for a return of the chattels replevied and fails to obtain them on the writ of return and that authorizes the taking of other goods of the same value — called also *capias in withernam, writ of reprisal*

withe rod *n* [¹*withe*] **:** either of two No. American viburnums (*Viburnum cassinoides* and *V. nudum*) with tough slender shoots like those of an osier and flat heads of white or creamy flowers

with·ers \ˈwithə(r)z\ *n pl* [prob. fr. obs. E *wither-* (prefix), against, in resistance of, counter (fr. OE, fr. *wither*, adv., against) + E *-s*, n. pl. suffix; fr. the withers being the parts which resist the pull in drawing a load] **1** *also* **wither a :** the ridge between the shoulder bones of a horse — see HORSE illustration **b :** the part between the shoulder bones at the base of the neck in various animals (as the deer, ox, or sheep) **2 :** FEELINGS, SENSIBILITIES ⟨our ~ are unwrung —Shak.⟩ ⟨try to wring your ~ with a story of attempted suicide —Richard Blaker⟩

withershins *var of* WIDDERSHINS

withertip \ˈ=₌,=\ *n* [¹*wither* + *tip*] **:** a blighting of terminal shoots or of the tips of leaves esp. characteristic of various anthracnoses of citrus plants — compare CITRUS ANTHRACNOSE, LIME ANTHRACNOSE

withertop \ˈ=₌,=\ *n* [¹*wither* + *top*] **:** a calcium deficiency disease of flax characterized by loss of turgidity of the stem near its apex and subsequent death of the tip

withes *pl of* WITHE, *pres 3d sing of* WITHE

withewood \ˈ=,=\ *n* [¹*withe* + *wood*] **:** WITHE ROD

with·hold \wəthˈhōld, withˈh-\ *vb* **with·held** \-ˈheld\ **with·held** *or archaic* **with·hold·en** \-ˈhōldən\ **with·hold·ing; withholds** [ME *withholden*, fr. ¹*with* + *holden* to hold — more at HOLD] *vt* **1 :** to hold back **:** keep from action **:** CHECK, RESTRAIN ⟨frequent bursts of grief . . . obliged her, at intervals, to ~ her pen —Jane Austen⟩ **2 :** to desist or refrain from granting, giving, or allowing **:** keep in one's possession or control **:** keep back ⟨distribute among the youngsters all blankets and provisions and gear, ~*ing* for myself only a canteen —Hodding Carter⟩ ⟨~ permission⟩ **3** *obs* **:** to keep prisoner **:** DETAIN ⟨she perforce ~*s* the loved boy —Shak.⟩ **~** *vi* **:** FORBEAR, REFRAIN ⟨a police traffic commission *withheld* from banning them —John Robbins⟩ **syn** see KEEP

with·hold·er \-də(r)\ *n* **:** one that withholds

with·hold·ing \-diŋ, -dēŋ\ *n* [ME *withholding*, fr. gerund of *withholden* to withhold] **:** the act or procedure of deducting a tax payment from income at the source

withholding tax *n* **:** a deduction levied as a tax upon income (as salaries, wages, fees, or dividends) at the source

withier *comparative of* WITHY

withiest *superlative of* WITHY

¹with·in \wəˈthin, -thin\ *adv* [ME *withinne, withinnen*, fr. OE *withinnan*, fr. *with*, prep. + *innan*, adv. & prep., in, inwardly, within, fr. *in*, prep. — more at WITH, IN] **1 a :** on the inside or on the inner side **:** INTERNALLY, INSIDE ⟨had plastered the walls and whitewashed them ~ and without —Ellen Glasgow⟩ **b :** inside the body **:** underneath the skin ⟨a man whose blood is warm ~ —Shak.⟩ **c :** HEREIN ⟨the person ~ named⟩ **2 :** inside the bounds of a place or region ⟨but whom they fear'd without, they found ~ —John Dryden⟩ ⟨traitors ~, as well as exiles without —George Grote⟩ **3 a :** in or into a building **:** INDOORS ⟨rooms for rent, inquire ~⟩ **b :** in an inner room or enclosure ⟨presenting action which must be shown ~ (as in a curtained study or bedroom) —Leslie Hotson⟩ **c :** behind the scenes — used in stage directions ⟨one calls ~ —Shak.⟩ **d :** at home ⟨not being ~ when he called —Jane Austen⟩ **4 :** in one's inner thought, disposition, or character **:** INWARDLY ⟨an air of aloofness about him . . . he lived ~ —H.A. McHugh⟩ ⟨outwardly calm but raging ~⟩

²within \"\ *prep* [ME *withinne, withinnen*, fr. OE *withinnan*, fr. *with*, prep., + *innan*, adv. & prep.] **1** — used as a function word to indicate enclosure or containment: as **a :** in the inner being of ⟨build up a state of tension ~ themselves —Vance Packard⟩ ⟨his heart sank ~ him⟩ **b** (1) **:** in the inner or interior part of **:** INSIDE OF ⟨the water is stored ~ the soil —W.P.Webb⟩ ⟨the spirit of adventure being strong ~ me —H.A.Chippendale⟩ (2) **:** in the limits or compass of **:** not beyond ⟨research conducted ~ university grounds —J.B. Conant⟩ ⟨~ the country⟩ ⟨~ the company⟩ **c :** enclosed or confined by ⟨~ the walls⟩ ⟨~ the doors⟩ **d :** forming a section of **:** included in ⟨a continent ~ a continent —Allan Murray⟩ ⟨a musical ~ a musical —*Time*⟩ **e** *archaic* **:** on the further side of **:** approached by means of **2 a** (1) **:** not longer in time than **:** before the end or since the beginning of ⟨~ four years he had become superintendent —*Current Biog.*⟩ ⟨troops would be withdrawn . . . ~ two years after the end of the war —F.W.D.Deakin⟩ (2) *obs* **:** during the course of **:** at any time during ⟨died ~ the year of our redemption four hundred twenty-six —Shak.⟩ **b** (1) **:** not exceeding in quantity or degree ⟨lived ~ his income⟩ (2) — used as a function word to indicate a specified difference or margin of error ⟨came ~ two percentage points of a perfect mark⟩ ⟨guessed her weight to ~ two pounds⟩ **c :** not farther in length or distance than **:** nearer than ⟨took pictures ~ feet of stampeding elephants, ~ inches of the fangs of deadly snakes —H.C.Adamson⟩ ⟨~ one short flight of a cuckoo from this home —John Galsworthy⟩ **d** (1) **:** not going outside the scope or influence of **:** subject to ⟨societies have to operate ~ the possibilities and limitations of their particular historical situation —Erich Fromm⟩ ⟨the producer must indeed work ~ conditions set by consumers' demand —G.D.H.Cole⟩ (2) — used as a function word to indicate accessibility to some action, effort, or means of perception ⟨~ reach⟩ ⟨~ sight⟩ ⟨~ hearing⟩ (3) **:** not beyond the capacity or power of ⟨indulge in indoor and outdoor sports ~ their physical capabilities —J.A.Brussel⟩ ⟨the hunter will usually gallop well ~ himself —Henry Wynmalen⟩ **3 a :** to the inside of **:** INTO ⟨sunk the sea ~ the earth —Shak.⟩ ⟨escaped, however, and fled ~ the British lines —*Amer. Guide Series: N. H.*⟩ **b** *archaic* **:** in or into the midst or keeping of ⟨take every object by the hand, and lead it ~ me —Walt Whitman⟩ **c** (1) — used as a function word to indicate self-containment or independence ⟨the world to which they belonged . . . was strictly circumscribed and complete ~ itself —Laurence Binyon⟩ (2) **:** with respect to **:** so far as concerns ⟨things good ~ themselves but beyond the possibility of accomplishment —W.J.Humphreys⟩ **d** *obs* **:** in the control of ⟨good madam, keep yourself ~ yourself —Shak.⟩

³within \"\ *adj* **:** lying or to be found inside **:** ENCLOSED, INCLUDED ⟨the ~ complaint⟩ ⟨the ~ indictment⟩

⁴within \"\ *n* -s **:** an inner or enclosed place or space ⟨the ~ of the stand always has an air of coziness —John McNulty⟩

withindoors \=ˈ=:=\ *adv* [fr. the phrase *within doors*] **:** INDOORS

withing *pres part of* WITHE

¹with·in·side \wəˈthinˈsīd, -th-\ *also* **with·in·sides** \-dz\ *adv* [*withinside* fr. *within* + *side* (as in *inside*); *withinsides* fr. *withinside* + *-s*] **1** *archaic* **:** on the inner side **2 a :** on the inside ⟨perceived almost immediately ~ the missing turbot —Hugh McCrae⟩ **b :** INDOORS ⟨sat ~ tailor-wise and busily stitching —R.L.Stevenson⟩

²withinside \"\ *prep, archaic* **:** INSIDE ⟨has put certain whim-whams ~ the glass —Thomas Gray⟩

with·ness *n* -ES [¹*with* + *-ness*] **:** the state or fact of being close to or connected with someone or something **:** close association or proximity ⟨two people with each other in ~ —Truman Capote⟩

¹with·out \wəˈthaủt, -thaủt, *usu* -d.+V\ *prep* [ME *withoute, withouten*, fr. OE *withūtan*, fr. *with*, prep. + *ūtan*, adv., outside, fr. *ūt* out — more at WITH, OUT] **1 a :** at, to, or on the outside of **:** exterior to ⟨had to stand ~ the door —F.L.Packard⟩ ⟨had placed themselves ~ the church —Valentine Ughet & Eleanor Davis⟩ ⟨solidarity and goodwill within and ~ the clan —W.W. Howells⟩ **b :** out of the range of ⟨today, it is a goal, not ~ our immediate grasp, but attainable —S.J.Holbel⟩ **c :** BEYOND, PAST ⟨just ~ the trees —William Bartram⟩ **2 :** not derived from or connected with **:** external to ⟨light in me, light ~ me, everywhere change —Robert Browning⟩ **3 a :** not using or being subjected to ⟨spent the evening ~ conversation⟩ ⟨worked ~ coercion⟩ **b :** exempt or free from ⟨~ end⟩ ⟨~ fail⟩ ⟨~ fear⟩ **4 a :** not accompanied by or associated with **:** separated from ⟨smoke ~ fire⟩ ⟨taste ~ extravagance⟩ ⟨music ~ tears⟩ **b :** suffering the deprivation or absence of **:** not having **:** LACKING ⟨~ money or resources⟩ ⟨~ a roof over his head⟩ **c :** lacking the company or companionship of ⟨could not live ~ her⟩ **5 a :** not securing or receiving ⟨was fired ~ explanation⟩ ⟨was welcomed back ~ reproaches⟩ **b :** not admitting of ⟨a condition ~ remedy⟩ **c** — used as a function word to indicate the absence or neglect of an action ⟨people who look ~ seeing, listen ~ hearing, read ~ understanding, and act ~ thinking —*Phoenix Flame*⟩

²without \"\ *adv* [ME *withoute, withouten*, fr. OE *withūtan*, fr. *with*, prep. + *ūtan*, adv.] **1 :** on the outside **:** EXTERNALLY ⟨the church, a decent enough fourteenth-century . . . structure ~ —Osbert Lancaster⟩ **2 a :** outside of a particular place; *specif* **:** outside of the house **:** OUTDOORS ⟨an afternoon which was dismal ~ and within —Lucien Price⟩ **b :** outside of a class, community, or membership **3 :** in outward action, circumstance, or being **:** OUTWARDLY ⟨whether ~ or within, never . . . flagging in energy or zest —Emily Skeel⟩ ⟨within be fed, ~ be rich no more —Shak.⟩ **4 :** with a lack of something **:** so as to be deprived ⟨his parents were poor, and he learned to do ~⟩ ⟨go ~⟩

³without \"\ *n* -s **:** an outer place or region ⟨from the far ~ to the deep within —James Stephens⟩ ⟨a disintegration from within, aided no doubt by the allied victory, but not imposed from ~ —C.E.Black & E.C.Helmreich⟩

⁴without \"\ *conj* [ME *withoute*, fr. *withoute*, prep.] *chiefly dial* **:** EXCEPT, UNLESS ⟨not ~ the prince be willing —Shak.⟩ ⟨you don't know about me ~ you have read a book —Mark Twain⟩

withoutdoor *adj* [fr. *withoutdoor*, adv.] *obs* **:** OUTDOOR, EXTERIOR ⟨praise her but for this, her ~ form —Shak.⟩

withoutdoors *also* **withoutdoor** \=ˈ=:=\ *adv* [fr. the phrase *without doors, without door*] **1 :** OUTDOORS ⟨the candles alight in the room . . . made all things ~ loom strange —Thomas Hardy⟩ **2** *usu* **without doors :** outside of a group, community, or deliberative body ⟨in arguing the case before the generality of voters *without doors* a more cautious approach was necessary —V.L.Parrington⟩

with·out·en \wəˈthaủtᵊn, -thaủ-\ *prep* [alter. (influenced by ¹*outen*) of *without*] *chiefly dial* **:** WITHOUT ⟨come to this country ~ a cent —Elizabeth M. Roberts⟩

without prejudice *adv (or adj)* **:** without injury to or detraction from one's own rights or claims or any cause of action or defense asserted

¹with·out·side \wəˈthaủtˈsīd, -th-\ *adv* [*without* + *side* (as in *outside*)] **1** *archaic* **:** on the outer part or surface **2** *archaic* **:** OUTDOORS

²withoutside \"\ *prep, archaic* **:** OUTSIDE

with prejudice *adv (or adj)* **:** final and binding with the effect of res judicata

with·stand \wəthˈstand, with-, -aa(ə)nd\ *vt* [ME *withstanden, withstonden*, fr. OE *withstandan*, fr. ¹*with* + *standan* to stand — more at STAND] **1 a :** to stand up against **:** offer opposition to **:** RESIST; *esp* **:** to make a successful stand against ⟨the first vertebrate I have ever known to ~ the army ants —William Beebe⟩ ⟨capable of ~*ing* a prolonged infantry siege —*Amer. Guide Series: Pa.*⟩ ⟨having *withstood* the pressure of her parents —Rose Macaulay⟩ **b :** to be proof against the pressure, impact, or effect of **:** be unaffected by ⟨looks well built to ~ work and worry —R.M.Yoder⟩ ⟨~ the drying up during the summer of the shallow ponds where it frequently lives —W.H.Dowdeswell⟩ **c :** to resist yielding to the attraction or influence of **:** FORBEAR ⟨the questionable capacity of most men, including himself, to ~ temptation —Laura Krey⟩ **2** *archaic* **:** to stop or obstruct the course of **:** stand in the way of **~** *vi* **:** to make resistance **:** OPPOSE, RESIST ⟨was firm, *withstood*, refused —Robert Browning⟩ **syn** see CONTEST

with·stand·er \-də(r)\ *n* [ME *withstonder*, fr. *withstonden* to withstand + *-er*] **:** one that withstands

with·stand·ing·ness *n* -ES **:** power or inclination to withstand

with·stay \wəthˈstā, with-\ *vt* [¹*with* + *stay*] **:** to delay or hinder the course or coming of **:** WITHSTAND

with·wind \ˈwi,thwīnd\ *n* [ME *withewinde*, fr. OE *withewinde, withowinde*, fr. *withe-, witho-* (prob. akin to *withthe* withe) + *winde*, prob. fr. *windan* to turn — more at WIND] **:** BINDWEED

¹withy \ˈwithē\ *n* -ES [ME, fr. OE *withig*; akin to OE *withthe* withe, OHG *wīda* willow, ON *vīthr* willow, *vith* withy, Goth *kunawida* chain, L *vitis* vine, *vitex* chaste tree, Gk *oisos* chaste tree, *itea* willow, *in-*, *is* tendon, sinew, muscle, OSlav *viti* to turn, wind, L *viēre* to twist together, plait — more at WIRE] **1 :** WILLOW; *esp* **:** OSIER 1 **2 a :** a flexible slender twig or branch (as of osier); *esp* **:** one used for binding **b :** a loop or hoop formed with a withy

²withy \ˈwithē *also* -ithē *or* -īthē, *dial* ˈhwithē\ *adj* -ER/-EST [¹*withe* + *-y*] **:** like a withy **:** flexible and tough; *specif* **:** AGILE, WIRY ⟨as ~ as a rattlesnake —W.R.Waterman⟩

withywind \ˈ=₌,=\ *n* [alter. (influenced by ¹*withy*) of *withwind*] **:** BINDWEED

wit·less \ˈwitləs\ *adj* [ME *witles*, fr. OE *witlēas*, fr. ²*wit* + *-lēas* -less] **1 :** destitute of understanding **:** wanting intelligence, wisdom, or good sense **:** lacking or not guided by judgment **:** FOOLISH, HEEDLESS, ILL-JUDGED ⟨interrupted by some ~ coxcombs⟩ ⟨~ obstinacy⟩ **2 :** mentally deranged **:** out of one's wits **:** INSANE, MAD **3 a :** deficient in mental capacity **:** having undeveloped or impaired intellectual power **:** lacking in intelligence **:** dull-witted **:** STUPID **b :** incapable of understanding or apprehending something ⟨~ to discern true values⟩ **4 :** lacking knowledge, awareness, or consciousness of something ⟨~ of the storm his words excite —Peter Crook⟩ **5 :** destitute of wit ⟨a matter-of-fact speech entirely ~⟩

wit·less·ly *adv* **:** in a witless manner **:** FOOLISHLY, STUPIDLY

wit·less·ness *n* -ES **:** the quality or state of being witless **:** FOLLY, SENSELESSNESS, STUPIDITY ⟨the oratory . . . broke new ground in oppressiveness and ~ —R.H.Rovere⟩

wit·ling \ˈwitliŋ\ *n* -s [²*wit* + *-ling*] **:** a person of little wit or understanding **:** a pretender to wit **:** one given to smart sayings inferior in wit ⟨ye newspaper ~*s!* ye pert scribbling folks! —Oliver Goldsmith⟩

wit·loof \ˈwit,lōf\ *or* **witloof chicory** *n* -s [D dial. *witloof* chicory, lit., white foliage, fr. D *wit* white (fr. MD) + *loof* foliage, fr. MD, leaf; akin to OE *hwīt* white and *lēaf* leaf — more at WHITE, LEAF] **:** CHICORY 1; *also* **:** its crown of foliage as a salad green **:** ENDIVE 2

¹wit·ness \ˈwitnəs\ *n* -ES [ME *witnesse*, fr. OE *witnes* knowledge, testimony, witness, fr. *wit*, n. + *-nes* -ness — more at WIT] **1 a** (1) **:** attestation of a fact or an event **:** EVIDENCE, TESTIMONY (2) *obs* **:** attestation or evidence provided by a person in court **b :** such testimony by signature or oath **2 :** one that gives evidence regarding matters of fact under inquiry; *specif* **:** one who testifies or is legally qualified to testify in a cause or to give evidence before a judicial tribunal or similar inquiry ⟨no person . . . shall be compelled in any criminal case to be a ~ against himself —*U.S.Constitution*⟩ ⟨one of the oil industry's most persuasive ~*es* before congressional committees —*Current Biog.*⟩ **3 a :** one who is called on to be present at a transaction so as to be able to testify to its having taken place (as one who witnesses a will, deed, or marriage); *specif* **:** one who sees the execution of an instrument and subscribes it to confirm its authenticity by his testimony ⟨no ~ . . . can take any benefit under any testamentary document which is witnessed by him —Edward Jenks⟩ **b** *obs* **:** a sponsor or godparent at baptism **4 a :** one that is cognizant of something by direct experience **:** one who beholds or otherwise has personal knowledge of something ⟨a ~, though hardly . . . an actor, in these scenes —J.H.Newman⟩ ⟨standing there, I was ~ of a little incident —A.T.Quiller-Couch⟩ ⟨the clock also was a ~ to the success of the evening —Viola Meynell⟩ — see EARWITNESS, EYEWITNESS **b :** one, often God, who is invoked as cognizant of a fact and offered as one's surety — usu. used in asseverations ⟨though, God's my ~, there's no spite in me —Charles Kingsley⟩ **c :** one who by action or word gives testimony of fidelity to Christ and the Christian faith ⟨you may feel the call to be a ~ for Jesus —Rex Ingamells⟩ **5 a :** something that serves as or furnishes evidence or proof **:** an evidential mark, sign, or token ⟨prehistoric peoples left behind material ~*es* to their cultures —Brewton Berry⟩ ⟨the party's press . . . is likewise ~ to its weakened state —J.G.Colton⟩ **b :** something that serves as an evidential example offered in substantiation of a statement — used to introduce a name or instance ⟨the universities are showing the way, ~ their contribution to winning the war —Walter Moberly⟩ ⟨our grammar — ~ our verb system — is a marvel of flexibility —Charlton Laird⟩ — sometimes used with *as* ⟨outlaws have always been romanticized . . . as ~ Jesse James —*Ballad Book*⟩ **c :** a manuscript or an early version of a manuscript that in textual criticism constitutes evidence of authority for a text — usu. used in pl. ⟨few of these ~*es* contain the complete New Testament —I.M. Price⟩ **d :** public testimony by word or deed to one's religious faith ⟨live a life of Christian ~ alongside Communism —F.T. Cartwright⟩ ⟨the church . . . is not to abdicate its Christian ~ to government and secular society —K.D.Miller⟩ **6 :** PROOF 5b **7** *usu cap* **:** a member of Jehovah's Witnesses — **bear one witness :** to give evidence in corroboration of one's action or assertion **:** serve as a witness of one's action — **bear witness :** to furnish or constitute proof esp. by oral or written testimony ⟨great structures which *bear witness* to the prestige of the leaders —*Irish Digest*⟩ ⟨you will *bear witness* that I have done so⟩ — **with a witness** *archaic* **:** with clear evidence **:** without a doubt **:** to a great degree **:** with a vengeance **:** EFFECTUALLY, UNMISTAKABLY ⟨this, I confess, is haste *with a witness* —Robert South⟩

²witness \"\ *vb* -ED/-ING/-ES [ME *witnessen*, fr. *witnesse* witness] *vt* **1 :** to furnish evidence or proof such as to establish **:** give testimony to **:** provide oral or written evidence of **:** bear witness to **:** testify to **:** ATTEST ⟨early writers ~ the antiquity of the custom⟩ ⟨ready to ~ that the handwriting is that of the defendant⟩ **2 :** to act as legal witness of: as **a** *obs* **:** to give formal or sworn evidence of (as in court) ⟨you said you saw one here in court could ~ it —Shak.⟩ **b :** to see the execution of (as of an instrument) and subscribe for the purpose of establishing authenticity **:** attest formally by signature **:** sign as a witness of the execution of (as a signature or writing) ⟨~ a will⟩ **c :** to be formally present as a witness of (as a transaction or the execution of a convict) **3 :** to give or constitute evidence of **:** furnish proof of **:** serve as a token or sign showing **:** BETOKEN, EVINCE ⟨your actions ~ your guilt⟩ ⟨our wounds ~ the ferocity of the attack made upon us⟩ **4 :** to establish by sworn or attested evidence contained therein **:** furnish formally attested evidence of — used of a document ⟨this indenture further ~*es* that injury to stock amounts to two hundred dollars⟩ **5 a** *obs* **:** to show or evidence by one's behavior ⟨he roll'd his eyes that ~*ed* huge dismay —Alexander Pope⟩ **b :** to bear witness to (as an object of allegiance or devotion) by speech or conduct **:** show evidence of by one's behavior ⟨more effectively to ~ Christ in our daily lives⟩ **6 :** to see or know by reason of personal presence **:** have direct cognizance of **:** observe with one's own eyes or ears **:** be present as an observer at **:** experience by personal observation — used esp. of something of a formal nature or of more than ordinary significance ⟨the inauguration . . . is said to have been ~*ed* by ten million persons —F.L.Mott⟩ ⟨the accident was ~*ed* by many fishermen —Norman Douglas⟩ **7 :** to constitute the scene of **:** form part of the setting of **:** be associated with ⟨this village ~*ed* . . . the last stand of the mule-drawn streetcar —*Amer. Guide Series: La.*⟩ ⟨the French Revolution ~*ed* some . . . bloody massacres —Alfred Cobban⟩ ⟨the postwar period has ~*ed* a number of developments in exchange rate practices —R.F.Mikesell⟩ **~** *vi* **1 :** to bear witness **:** give evidence **:** TESTIFY — usu. used with *to* or *against* ⟨hoping that they might ~ to the truth of his doctrine —J.L.Teller⟩ ⟨in these ways we ~ against our professed faiths —J.F.Dulles⟩ **2 :** to make known to others (as by speech or conduct) the religious experience one has undergone or the religious truths in which one believes **:** bear witness to one's religious convictions

³witness \"\ *adj* [ME *witnesse*, fr. *witnesse*, n., witness] **1 :** of, relating to, or used by a witness ⟨~ room⟩ ⟨~ fee⟩ **2 :** serving as a landmark or survey reference point ⟨~ tree⟩ ⟨~ stake⟩ — compare WITNESS CORNER

wit·ness·able \-səbəl\ *adj* **:** capable of being witnessed ⟨the workings of one mind are not ~ by other observers —Gilbert Ryle⟩

witness-box \ˈ=₌,=\ *n, chiefly Brit* **:** an enclosure in which a witness sits or stands while testifying in court ⟨entered the *witness-box* —*Contemporary Rev.*⟩

witness corner *n* **:** a post or monument used esp. by surveyors as a reference point for the location of an inaccessible corner

witnessed *adj* [fr. past part. of ²*witness*] **:** attested by a witness; *specif* **:** attested by a disinterested broker — used of a securities transaction for the account of a broker who is in default on a contract made on the floor to deliver or accept delivery of such securities ⟨a ~ purchase⟩ ⟨a ~ sale⟩

wit·ness·er \-sə(r)\ *n* -s [ME, fr. *witnessen* to witness + *-er*] *archaic* **:** one that witnesses **:** WITNESS

witnesses *pl of* WITNESS, *pres 3d sing of* WITNESS

witness stand *n* **:** a usu. raised platform where a witness sits or stands while testifying in court or before an investigating committee ⟨chose to take the *witness stand* in her own defense —W.C.Mathes⟩ ⟨put upon the *witness stand* at a congressional hearing —Upton Sinclair⟩

wit·ney *or* **whit·ney** \ˈ(h)witnē, -ni\ *n* -s [*Witney*, town in Oxfordshire, England where it was orig. manufactured] **1 :** a heavy woolen cloth used esp. for blankets **2 :** a soft woolen overcoating with a napped surface similar to chinchilla

wi·to·to *also* **ui·to·to** \wēˈtōd·(,)ō\ *n, pl* **witoto** *or* **witotos** *also* **uitoto** *or* **uitotos** *usu cap* **1 a :** a people of southeastern Colombia **b :** a member of such people **2 :** the language of the Witotoan people of uncertain relationship — **wi·to·to·an** *or* **ui·to·to·an** \-ōd·əwən\ *adj, usu cap*

wits *pl of* WIT

wit·te·boom \ˈvid·ə,būm\ *n, pl* **witteboom** [Afrik, prob. fr. MD *witboom* white poplar, lit., white tree, fr. *wit* white + *boom* tree; akin to OE *hwīt* white and *bēam* tree — more at WHITE, BEAM] *southern Africa* **:** SILVER TREE 1

wit·ted \ˈwid·əd, -itəd\ *adj* [ME, fr. ²*wit* + *-ed*] **:** having wit

or understanding — usu. used in combination ⟨a dull-*witted* adaptation of the . . . classic —Philip Hamburger⟩ ⟨make the keenest-*witted* man . . . little better than a blunderer —Allen Upward⟩ — **wit·ted·ness** *n* -ES

1wit·ter \ˈwid·ə(r), -itə-\ *n* -S [obs. E *witter* sign, mark, token, prob. back-formation fr. E *wittering*] : the tee aimed at in curling

2witter \"\ *n* -S [origin unknown] *chiefly Scot* : BARB

wit·ter·ing \ˈwitərən, -riŋ\ *n* -S [ME (Sc) *wittering, witering,* fr. gerund of *witteren, witeren* to clarify, inform, teach, of Scand origin; akin to ON *vitra* to manifest, reveal, *vitr* wise, *vita* to know — more at WIT] *chiefly Scot* : a piece of information (as a sign, token, or hint)

1witt·gen·stein·ian \ˌvitgənˌs(h)tīnēən\ *adj, usu cap* [Ludwig *Wittgenstein* †1951 Austrian philosopher + E *-an*] : of, relating to, or having the characteristics of the philosopher Ludwig Wittgenstein or his methods of linguistic analysis

2wittgensteinian \"\ *n* -S *usu cap* : a follower of Wittgenstein or an advocate of his analytical methods in philosophy

wit·ti·chen·ite \ˈwid·əkə,nīt\ *n* -S [G *wittichenit,* fr. *Wittichen,* Baden, Germany, its locality + G *-it* -ite] : a mineral Cu_3BiS_3 consisting of a tin-white to steel-gray copper bismuth sulfide and usu. occurring massive

wit·ti·cism \ˈwid·ə,sizəm, -itə,-\ *n* -S [*witty* + *-cism* (as in *criticism*)] **1** *archaic* : a mean, sarcastic, or contemptible gibe : JEER **2** : a witty saying, sentence, or phrase : a clever or amusing expression : a piece of wit **syn** see JOKE

wit·ti·cize \-,sīz\ *vi* -ED/-ING/-S [fr. *witticism,* after E *criticism: criticize*] : to express oneself wittily or indulge in witticisms

wit·ti·ly \ˈwid·ᵊlē, -itᵊl-, |ᵊli, |əl-\ *adv* [ME *wittiliche,* fr. *witty* + *-liche* -ly] : in a witty manner ⟨the doctor reasons very ~ but not convincingly —James Boswell⟩ ⟨so ~ satirical that the House rocked with laughter —*Amer. Guide Series: Minn.*⟩

wit·ti·ness \|ēnəs, |in-\ *n* -ES : the quality or state of being witty ⟨the ~ of his remarks⟩

1wit·ting \ˈwid·iŋ, -itiŋ, -ēŋ\ *n* -S [ME, fr. gerund of *witen* to know — more at WIT] **1** *chiefly dial* : knowledge or awareness of something : COGNIZANCE **2** *chiefly dial* : information obtained or communicated : INTELLIGENCE, NEWS, TIDINGS

2witting \"\ *adj* [fr. pres. part. of *1wit*] **1 a** : cognizant or aware of something : CONSCIOUS ⟨came to make you ~ of the same —F.S.Ellis⟩ **b** : consciously being or doing something specified ⟨a ~ tool of the Communists⟩ **2** : done with the knowledge of the doer : performed or acted consciously, deliberately, or knowingly : INTENTIONAL ⟨~ lies and all sorts of hypocrisy —H.B.Alexander⟩ ⟨this process of ~ repression —W.H.R.Rivers⟩

wit·ting·ly *adv* : with knowledge or awareness of what one is doing : by design : CONSCIOUSLY, DELIBERATELY, INTENTIONALLY, KNOWINGLY ⟨never ~ wishing to do hurt to anyone —Bruce Marshall⟩ ⟨had ~ exceeded his authority —R.G. Usher⟩

witt·ite \ˈwi,tīt\ *n* -S [Sw *wittit,* fr. T. *Witt,* 20th cent. mining engineer + Sw *-it* -ite] : a mineral $Pb_5Bi_6(S,Se)_{14}$ consisting of a sulfide and selenide of lead and bismuth

1wit·tol \ˈwid·ᵊl, -itᵊl\ *n* -S [earlier *wit-wal,* fr. ME *wetewold,* fr. *weten, witen* to be aware, know + *-wold* (as in *cakewold* cuckold) — more at WIT] **1** *archaic* : a man who is aware of and submits to his wife's infidelity : a tame or contented cuckold **2** : a half-witted person : one having little sense or perception : FOOL

2wittol \"\ *n* -S [perh. alter. of *whitetail*] *dial Eng* : WHEATEAR

wit·ty \ˈwid·ē, -it|, |i\ *adj, usu* -ER/-EST [ME, fr. OE *wittig,* fr. *2wit* + *-ig* -y] **1 a** *chiefly dial* : having good mental capacity : CLEVER, INTELLIGENT **b** *obs* : possessed of cunning or craftiness esp. in intrigue : WILY **2 a** : evincing or requiring good mental capacity : clever in conception : ingenious or subtle in expression ⟨fallacies . . . concealed in florid, ~ or involved discourses —John Locke⟩ ⟨architecture as elaborate and costly as it was ingenious and ~ —John Summerson⟩ ⟨the costumes are sumptuous and ~ —Virgil Thomson⟩ **b** *obs* : skillfully contrived for an evil purpose : ingeniously and cunningly devised ⟨the most ~ and exquisite torments —John Scott †1695⟩ **3** : marked by or full of wit : amusingly or cleverly novel (as in expression or point of view) : smartly facetious or jocular ⟨one of the *wittiest* books in English —Irving Howe⟩ ⟨makes a number of wise and ~ comments —S.K.Padover⟩ **4 a** : possessing wit : quick or ready in the perception or expression of amusing points of view and of intellectually entertaining congruities and incongruities : brightly or cleverly facetious ⟨unpredictably ~, eloquent, and satirical in his sermons —G. H. Genzmer⟩ ⟨seeks to establish the picture of ~ and adroit parliamentarian —*N.Y.Times*⟩ **b** *obs* : sharply critical : SARCASTIC ⟨so unmercifully ~ upon the women —Joseph Addison⟩

syn HUMOROUS, FACETIOUS, JOCULAR, JOCOSE: WITTY suggests cleverness, quickness, and sparkle of mind esp. in repartee, sometimes caustic ⟨the *witty* treatment of beauty as a coin that shines by being kept current —Cleanth Brooks⟩ ⟨she was clever, *witty,* brilliant, and sparkling beyond most of her kind —Rudyard Kipling⟩ ⟨everybody was being exquisitely *witty* at their expense —Roy Lewis & Angus Maude⟩ HUMOROUS is generic, applying to anything that provokes laughter, usu. genial ⟨broad smiles broke out on the faces of the friends. Sometimes, they thought, life was very, very *humorous* —John Steinbeck⟩ ⟨physicists have a little *humorous* puzzle which asks: How can you prove that the temperature of Hell is uniform —Warren Weaver⟩ ⟨wizened *humorous* physiognomy long ago earned him the nickname of Prune-face —J.A. Coleman⟩ FACETIOUS usu. applies to clumsy or inappropriate jesting or somewhat derogatorily to attempts at wittiness or humorousness that please their maker more than others ⟨scowl at all *facetious* remarks at his expense⟩ ⟨used to be merely *facetious* as often as he was funny —*N.Y. Herald Tribune Bk. Rev.*⟩ JOCULAR can mean playfully humorous but usu. implies a fondness for joking, suggesting strongly a temperamental desire to keep others amused ⟨in these careless days he was always gleeful and *jocular,* even as afterwards his entire saintly life was glad with an invincible gaiety of spirit —H.O. Taylor⟩ ⟨the watercolor lesson enlivened by the *jocular* conversation of the kindly, humorous old man was always great fun —Joseph Conrad⟩ JOCOSE is close to FACETIOUS though less derogatory, suggesting a habitual waggishness or sportiveness ⟨sometimes composed something gay and even *jocose* —J.N. Forkel⟩ ⟨considered it a laughable affair, and was continually bobbing his head out the galley door to make *jocose* remarks —Jack London⟩ ⟨colonies of tiny shingled shacks, each labeled clearly with its sentimental or *jocose* name —F.L.Allen⟩

wit·wall \ˈwi,twȯl\ *n* -S [obs. E, golden oriole, fr. obs. G *witwal, wittewal* (now *widewal, wiedewal*), fr. MHG *witewal, wittewal,* fr. *wite* wood (fr. OHG *witu*) + *-wal* (of unknown origin) — more at WOOD] *dial Brit* : the European great spotted woodpecker

wive \ˈwīv\ *vb* -ED/-ING/-S [ME *wiven,* fr. OE *wīfian,* fr. *wīf* woman, wife — more at WIFE] *vi* : to marry a woman : take a wife : get married ~ *vt* **1** : to marry to a wife : provide with a wife : obtain a wife for **2** : to take for a wife : take to wife : make one's wife **3** : to become the wife of ⟨any drab would suffice to ~ such pitiful adventurers —J.R.Lowell⟩

wivern *or* **wiver** *var of* WYVERN

wives *pl of* WIFE

wi·yot \ˈwī,yät\ *n, pl* **wiyot** *or* **wiyots** *usu cap* **1 a** : a Ritwan people of the coast of northern California **b** : a member of such people **2** : the language of the Wiyot people

wiz \ˈwiz\ *n* -ES [by shortening] : WIZARD 3

1wiz·ard \ˈwizə(r)d\ *n* -S [ME *wysard,* fr. *wys* wise + *-ard* — more at WISE] **1** *archaic* : a man of wisdom and knowledge : SAGE, WISE MAN **2** : one devoted to the black art : one skilled in the knowledge and practice of the occult arts : a man who practices witchcraft : MAGICIAN, SORCERER **3** : one endowed with exceptional skill or able to achieve something held to be impossible : a genius or prodigy esp. in a particular field of endeavor ⟨one of the early production ~*s* of Hollywood —*New Yorker*⟩ ⟨he is the math ~ of the class —F.G.Jennings⟩ ⟨a financial ~⟩ **4** : WITCH DOCTOR, MEDICINE MAN **syn** see EXPERT

2wizard \"\ *adj* **1** : possessed of the powers or characteristics of a wizard : being a wizard : having magical influence or power ⟨the ~ eye of the fire —P.E.More⟩ **2** : of, relating to, or associated with wizardry : MAGICAL, BEWITCHED, CHARMED, ENCHANTED ⟨~ wands⟩ **3** *chiefly Brit* : superlative in design, appearance, or performance : worthy of the highest praise : EXCELLENT, EXTRAORDINARY ⟨she was a ~ dancer —Paul Gallico⟩ ⟨this cake is ~ —Elizabeth Goudge⟩

3wizard \"\ *vb* -ED/-ING/-S *vi* : to practice wizardry or magic art ~ *vt* : to transport by or as if by wizardry ⟨we were ~*ed* . . . to what looked like rangeland —A.H.Brown⟩

wiz·ard·ly *adj* : of or relating to a wizard : resembling, befitting, or having the characteristics of a wizard : WEIRD ⟨a ~ creature⟩ ⟨~ powers⟩

wiz·ard·ry \ˈwizə(r)drē, -ri\ *n* -ES **1** : the art or practices of a wizard : magic skill : SORCERY, WITCHCRAFT **2** : something held to resemble the art of a wizard : a seemingly magical transforming power or influence ⟨proved his ~ as a vote-getter —Beverly Smith⟩ ⟨employs electronic ~ to track down stray communications signals —W.E.Laidlaw⟩ ⟨the ~ of science⟩ **syn** see MAGIC

1wizen \ˈwiz'n, ˈwēz-\ *vb* **wizened; wizened; wizening** \-z(ᵊ)niŋ\ **wizens** [ME *wisenen,* fr. OE *wisnian, weosnian;* akin to OHG *wesanēn* to wither, ON *visna* to wither, L *viescere* to shrivel, wither, Lith *vysti* to wither, L *viēre* to twist together — more at WIRE] : to dry up : WITHER, SHRIVEL

2wizen \"\ *adj* [back-formation fr. *wizened*] : WIZENED ⟨his face would be wrinkled and ~ —Oscar Wilde⟩ ⟨growing thin and ~ in a solitary prison —W.S.Gilbert⟩

wiz·ened \-nd\ *adj* [fr. past part. of *1wizen*] : dried up and shrunken : thin and shrivelled : WEAZEN, WITHERED ⟨~ trees at timberline —Alicita & Warren Hamilton⟩ ⟨~ apples⟩ ⟨the scars gave him a ~ and drawn appearance —F.L.Paxson⟩

wiz·zled \ˈwizəld\ *adj* [*1wizen* + *-led* (as in *shrivelled, wrinkled*)] : wizened and shrivelled — usu. used with *up* ⟨a little old woman with a ~ up face —*Knickerbocker*⟩

wk *abbr* **1** weak **2** week **3** *sometimes cap* well-known **4** work **5** wreck

wkg *abbr* working

wkly *abbr* weekly

wkr *abbr* **1** worker **2** wrecker

WL *abbr* **1** waterline **2** wavelength

wldr *abbr* welder

wm *abbr, sometimes cap* wattmeter

WM *abbr* **1** watermark **2** white metal

wmk *abbr* watermark

wmkd *abbr* watermarked

wn *abbr* winch

wnd *abbr* wind

wng *abbr* warning

WNP *abbr* wire nonpayment

WNW *abbr* west-northwest

1wo \ˈwō\ *archaic var of* WOE

2wo *or* **woa** *var of* WHOA

WO *abbr* **1** wait order **2** walkover **3** war office **4** warrant officer **5** water-in-oil **6** wireless operator **7** *often not cap* without

1woad \ˈwōd\ *n* -S [ME *wod, wood,* fr. OE *wād;* akin to MD *wede* woad, OHG *weit* woad, L *vitrum* woad, glass (fr. its color), Gk *isatis* woad] **1** : a plant of the genus *Isatis; esp* : a European biennial herb (*I. tinctoria*) formerly grown for the blue coloring matter yielded by its leaves **2** : a blue dye prepared esp. formerly from the leaves of woad and containing indigo (sense 1b) as its essential constituent **3** : a dark blue that is slightly paler than the color marine corps, paler than Japan blue, and redder and duller than Peking blue

2woad \"\ *vt* -ED/-ING/-S [ME *wooden,* fr. *wood, wod* woad] : to dye or treat with woad

woad·er \-də(r)\ *n* -S [ME *woder,* fr. *wod* woad + *-er*] : WOADMAN

woad·man \-dmən\ *n, pl* **woadmen** : one who dyes with woad

woad vat *n* : a vat containing woad for reducing natural indigo by fermentation

woad·wax·en \ˈwōd,waksən\ *also* **woad·wax** \-,waks\ *n, pl* **woadwaxens** *also* **woadwaxes** [*woadwaxen* alter. (influenced by *1woad*) of *woodwaxen; woadwax* alter. (influenced by *1woad*) of *woodwax*] : WOODWAXEN

woald *var of* WELD

wob \ˈwäb\ *Scot & dial Eng var of* WEB

WOB *abbr, often not cap* washed overboard

wob·be·gong \ˈwäbē,gäŋ\ *n* -S [native name in New So. Wales] *Austral* : CARPET SHARK

1wob·ble *also* **wab·ble** \ˈwäbəl *also* ˈwȯb-\ *vb* **wobbled; wobbled; wobbling** \-b(ə)liŋ\ **wobbles** [prob. fr. LG *wabbeln* to wobble; akin to MHG *wabelen* to waver, ON *vafla* to hover about, OE *wǣfre* wavering, restless — more at WAVER] *vi* **1 a** : to move or move along with an irregular rocking or staggering motion : move or swing unsteadily and clumsily backward and forward or from side to side : vary from a true course by tilting unsteadily from side to side ⟨ducks go *wobbling* by in two straight lines —Norman MacCaig⟩ ⟨the baby's head *wobbled* safely to rest on her shoulder —Margaret A. Barnes⟩ ⟨saw an open car ahead of her ~ to the side of the road, one of its tires flat —*New Yorker*⟩ **b** : to shake unsteadily : TREMBLE, QUAVER ⟨a *wobbling* chin⟩ ⟨his voice *wobbled*⟩ **2** *dial Eng* : to boil vigorously **3** : to waver or vacillate between different courses of action, policies, or parties : show indecision ⟨his first play . . . *wobbled* between melodrama and passionate tragedy —Sheldon Cheney⟩ ~ *vt* : to cause to move with an unsteady wobbling or lurching motion from one side to the other ⟨most airplanes plunge straight, others ~ their wings as they dive —Wolfgang Langewiesche⟩

2wobble *also* **wabble** \"\ *n* -S **1 a** : a hobbling or rocking unequal motion (as of a wheel unevenly hung) : a staggering to and fro : a wobbling gait ⟨a rotational ~ of the earth's axis in space —S.F.Mason⟩ **b** : an erratic unsteadily directed movement : FLUCTUATION ⟨a faint ~ of doubt —Robert Lynd⟩ ⟨the sort of serious ~ that accompanies maladjustments between political and economic development —Colin Legum⟩ **c** : an intermittent variation (as in volume of sound) : QUAVER ⟨a ~ in the sound of a phonograph record⟩ ⟨a vocal ~⟩ **2 wobbles** *pl but usu sing in constr* : a disease of horses that is marked by degenerative changes in the spinal cord and nerves resulting in ataxia chiefly of the hind legs and that in Australia has been reported to result from feeding on various palms but in the U.S. is held to be a recessive hereditary trait

wobble plate *n* : SWASH PLATE

wobble pump *n* : an auxiliary hand pump used to supply fuel to the carburetor of an airplane engine when the power-driven pump fails or for forcing fuel from an extra tank

wob·bler *also* **wab·bler** \-b(ə)lə(r)\ *n* -S : one that wobbles: as **a** : an elliptic cutterhead placed on a shaft at such an angle as to correspond with an oblique section of a right circular cylinder **b** : either of the grooved ends more or less resembling either a 3-lobed or 4-lobed gear wheel in cross section that project beyond the housings in a rolling mill and transmit power to a roll from the junction boxes **c** : a fishing lure of the spoon type that wobbles when drawn through the water

wobble saw *n* : DRUNKEN SAW

wob·bli·ness *also* **wab·bli·ness** \-b(ə)lēnəs\ *n* -ES : the state of being wobbly

wobbling *also* **wabbling** *adj* : that wobbles, permits a vacillating motion, or operates with such motion — **wob·bling·ly** *also* **wab·bling·ly** *adv*

wobbling disk *n* : SWASH PLATE

wobbling of the pole **1** : the slow gyration of the earth's axis in space as a result of lunisolar precession **2** : NUTATION 2 **3** : the wandering of the poles

1wob·bly *also* **wab·bly** \-b(ə)lē, -li, *or* **wob·ble·dy** \-bəldē, -di\ *adj* -ER/-EST [*wobbledy* fr. *wobbled* (past part. of *wobble*) + *-y*] **1** : inclined to shake, sway, or quaver unsteadily : wavering or trembling uncertainly (as from wear or fatigue) : SHAKY ⟨a ~ chair⟩ ⟨a ~ government⟩ ⟨felt a little ~ when he saw all the people —R.C.Wood⟩ ⟨~ handwriting⟩ **2** : given to vacillation or inclined to vacillate : FLUCTUATING, IRRESOLUTE, UNCERTAIN, DOUBTFUL ⟨after a very ~ introduction, he writes with vigor and clarity —*New Statesman & Nation*⟩ ⟨sound way of bolstering ~ foreign economies —*Time*⟩ ⟨the statistics were a bit ~ — good round figures not exempt from the suspicion of exaggeration —G.B.Munson⟩

2wobbly \"\ *n* -ES *usu cap* [origin unknown] : a member of the Industrial Workers of the World ⟨life was real and . . . earnest for the *Wobblies* of yesteryear —John Cournos⟩

wob·bu·la·tor \ˈwäbyə,lād·ə(r)\ *n* -S [*1wobble* + *-ulator* (as in *modulator*)] : a testing device for radio sets in which the frequency is varied periodically and automatically over a predetermined range

WOC \ˌdəbəl(ˌ)yü,ō'sē, -lyə,ō-\ *n* -S [*WOC, abbr.*] : one serving as a dollar-a-year man esp. in the U.S. government

WOC *abbr, often not cap* : without compensation

wod *dial var of* WOULD

wodge \ˈwäj\ *n* -S [prob. alter. of *wedge*] *Brit* : a bulky bulging object : MASS, LUMP ⟨mopped up the mess with a special ~ of blotting paper —Margery Allingham⟩ ⟨an enormous ~ of English press cuttings —Richard Aldington⟩

1woe \ˈwō\ *interj* [ME *wo, wa,* fr. OE *wā;* akin to OHG *wē* interj. used to express grief, ON *vei,* Goth *wai,* L *vae*] — used to express grief, regret, or distress

2woe \"\ *adj* [ME *wo, wa,* fr. *wo, wa,* interj.] *dial* : WOEFUL, SORROWFUL, GRIEVED, MISERABLE, MELANCHOLY ⟨he waxed wondrous ~ —Edmund Spenser⟩

3woe \"\ *n* -S [ME *wo, wa,* fr. *wo, wa,* interj.] **1 a** : a miserable or sorrowful state : a condition of deep suffering from misfortune, affliction, or grief : DISTRESS ⟨a scene of ~⟩ ⟨a tale of ~⟩ ⟨for weal or ~⟩ ⟨want and ~⟩ — often used in denunciation or in exclamations of sorrow ⟨~ to me! For I am lost —Isa 6:5 (RSV)⟩ **b** : CALAMITY, MISFORTUNE, TROUBLE — usu. used in pl. ⟨economic ~*s*⟩ ⟨papers and magazines are always full of their gripes, squawks, and ~*s* —E.L.Jones⟩ **2** : CURSE, ANATHEMA ⟨this ~ came out of Christ's mouth —Samuel Rutherford⟩ **syn** see SORROW

woe·be·gone \ˈwōbē,gȯn, -bə,- *also* -,gän\ *adj* [ME *wo begon,* fr. *wo,* n., woe + *begon,* past part. of *begon* to go about, beset, fr. OE *begān,* fr. *be-* + *gān* to go — more at GO] **1** *archaic* : beset or overwhelmed with woe : immersed in grief or sorrow : WOEFUL ⟨so ~ was he with pains of love —Edward Fairfax⟩ **2 a** : exhibiting a condition of suffering, great woe, sorrow, or misery ⟨their ~ faces⟩ ⟨a grimy ~ expression —Israel Zangwill⟩ **b** : dismal-looking : DESOLATE, DILAPIDATED ⟨a ~ village⟩ **syn** see DOWNCAST

woe·be·gone·ness \-nnəs\ *n* : the quality or state of being woebegone

woe·ful *also* **wo·ful** \ˈwōfəl\ *adj, sometimes* **woefuller;** *sometimes* **woefullest** [ME *woful, waful,* fr. *wo, wa,* n., woe + *-ful*] **1** : full of woe : distressed with grief or calamity : SAD, SORROWFUL, AFFLICTED, WRETCHED ⟨two ~ young people —Walter de la Mare⟩ ⟨a ~ sight⟩ ⟨bade us farewell with ~ prophecies —*Springfield (Mass.) Union*⟩ **2** : involving, bringing, or relating to woe ⟨a ~ want⟩ ⟨O ~ day! O day of woe! —Ambrose Philips⟩ **3** : PALTRY, CALAMITOUS, LAMENTABLE, DEPLORABLE ⟨the notes . . . are in part ~ nonsense —Herbert Weinstock⟩ ⟨a ~ lack of balance —A.L.Scott⟩ ⟨~ shortage of commodities —J.F.Scott⟩

woe·ful·ly *also* **wo·ful·ly** \-f(ə)lē, -li\ *adv* [ME *wofully,* fr. *woful* + *-ly*] : in a woeful manner : MOURNFULLY, WRETCHEDLY, DEPLORABLY ⟨these reports were ~ inadequate —Vera M. Dean⟩ ⟨fine performances lavished on ~ thin material —Arthur Knight⟩

woe·ful·ness *also* **wo·ful·ness** *n* -ES : the quality or state of being woeful

woeh·ler·ite *or* **wöh·ler·ite** \ˈvōlə,rīt\ *n* -S [G *wöhlerit,* fr. Friedrich *Wöhler* †1882 Ger. chemist + G *-it* -ite] : a mineral $NaCa_2(Zn,Cb)Si_2O_8(O,OH,F)$ consisting of a basic silicate of zirconium, calcium, sodium, niobium, and other minerals in yellow or brown prismatic crystals

woevine \ˈ=,=\ *n* [*3woe* + *vine*] : DODDER LAUREL

wof·fler \ˈwäflə(r)\ *n* -S [prob. fr. E dial. *woffle* to glide along quickly (prob. freq. of *woft* to waft, alter. of E *waft*) + E *-er*] *Brit* : REPAIRER

woft \ˈwäft\ *Scot var of* WEFT

1wog \ˈwäg\ *Scot var of* WAG

2wog \"\ *n* -S *sometimes cap* [prob. short for *golliwog*] : a native of a Middle Eastern country — usu. used disparagingly

3wog \"\ *n* -S [prob. short for *polliwog*] *chiefly Austral* : a pathogenic microorganism ⟨the oxygen in the air immediately kills the ~*s* that have caused the trouble —*Sydney (Australia) Bull.*⟩; *broadly* : an injurious or repugnant organism ⟨spiders, centipedes, beetles, and innumerable other ~*s* —I.L.Idriess⟩

WOG *abbr, often not cap* with other goods

wog·gle \ˈwägəl *also* ˈwȯg-\ *vb* **woggled; woggled; woggling** \-g(ə)liŋ\ **woggles** [alter. (influenced by *1wobble*) of *1waggle*] : WAGGLE

wohl degradation *or* **wohl reaction** \ˈvōl-\ *n, usu cap W* [after Alfred *Wohl* fl 1920 Ger. chemist] : a sequence of reactions for converting an aldose sugar to one containing one carbon atom less (as galactose to lyxose) by forming the oxime of the original aldose and next the corresponding acetylated nitrile and finally removing hydrogen and cyanogen in the form of hydrogen cyanide by means of ammoniacal silver hydroxide

wöh·ler's law \ˈvōlə(r)z-\ *n, usu cap W* [after Friedrich *Wöhler* †1882 Ger. chemist] : a law of strength of materials: the breaking strength of a material decreases with repetition of the strain and with the range of the strain variations

wohl·fahr·tia \vōlˈfärd·ēə\ *n* [NL, perh. modif. (influenced by G *wohlfahrt* welfare) of Peter *Wolfart* †1726 Ger. medical writer + NL *-ia*] **1** *cap* : a genus of larviparous sarcophagid flies that commonly deposit their larvae in wounds or on the intact skin of man and domestic animals causing severe cutaneous myiasis **2** -S : any fly of the genus *Wohlfahrtia*

wohl·will process \ˈvōl,vil-\ *n, usu cap W* [after Emil *Wohlwill* †1912 Ger. inventor] : an electrolytic process for refining gold using a hydrochloric-acid electrolyte

woi·lie \ˈwȯilē\ *n* -S [native name in Western Australia] : a rat kangaroo (*Bettongia penicillata*) of temperate Australia

woi·wode \ˈwȯi,wōd\ *n* [alter. of *voivode,* fr. Russ *voevoda* — more at VAIVODE] : VAIVODE

WOJG *abbr* warrant officer junior grade

wo·kas \ˈwōkəs\ *n* -ES [Klamath *wókas* seed of the wokas] **1** : a western American spatterdock (*Nuphar polysepalum*) **2** : the dried and roasted seeds of the wokas used as food among the Klamath Indians

woke *past of* WAKE

woken *past part of* WAKE

wo·kowi \wōˈkōwē\ *n* -S [Comanche] : MESCAL 1

WOL *abbr* wharf owner's liability

1wold \ˈwōld\ *n* -S [ME *wald, wold,* fr. OE *weald, wald* wood, forest; akin to OHG *wald* forest, ON *vǫllr* field, meadow and perh. to OE *wilde* untamed, wild — more at WILD] **1** : an upland plain : a region without woods ⟨between the forests were open ~*s* —Charles Kingsley⟩ ⟨deeds of hill and ~ —Robert Browning⟩ ⟨midday hush in many wilds and ~*s* —Norman Douglas⟩ **2** : an open hilly or rolling region ⟨the Yorkshire ~*s*⟩

2wold *var of* WELD

wold mouse *n, Brit* : VOLE

wolds·man \ˈwōldzmən\ *n, pl* **woldsmen** : one who dwells on a wold or in a region of wolds

1wolf \ˈwu̇lf\ *n, pl* **wolves** *see sense 1* \-lvz\ *often attrib* [ME, fr. OE *wulf;* akin to OHG *wolf,* ON *ūlfr,* Goth *wulfs,* L *lupus,* Gk *lykos,* Skt *vṛka*] **1** *pl also* **wolf** **a** : any of various large dog-like mammals of the genus *Canis* that are crafty, rapacious, and very destructive to game, sheep, and cattle and will sometimes attack man esp. when several animals have gathered in a pack; *esp* : any of various forms of a species (*C. lupus*) which was once almost universally present in the

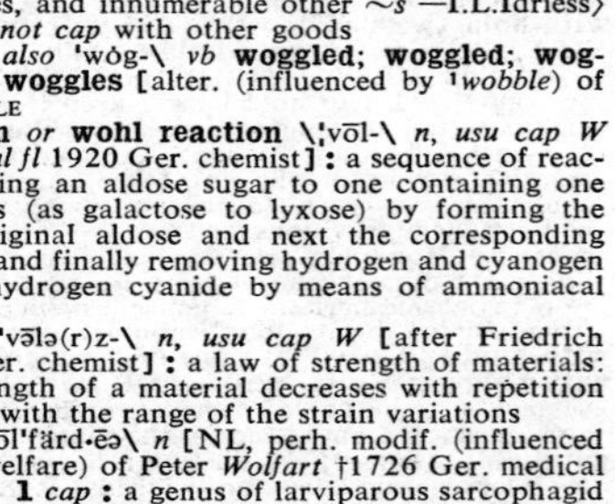

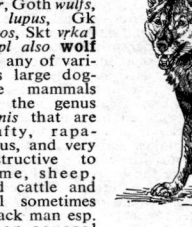

wolf

northern hemisphere and of which the common European form (*C. l. lupus*) is yellowish or brownish gray with rather coarse fur, erect pointed ears, and a bushy tail — see COYOTE, DIRE WOLF, GRAY WOLF, JAPANESE WOLF, RED WOLF **b** : the fur of a wolf **c** : TASMANIAN WOLF **d** : EGYPTIAN JACKAL **2 a** (1) : a fierce, rapacious, or destructive person (2) : a relentless crafty person (3) : a clever experienced trader (as in securities) — compare LAMB 3c (4) : a man forward, direct, and zealous in amatory attentions to women : MASHER (5) *slang* : an active homosexual **b** (1) : a corrupting or destructive agency ⟨boys and girls now being thrown to the *wolves* of paternal ignorance, social neglect, and youthful impulses —P.L.Boynton⟩ (2) : dire poverty : FAMINE, STARVATION — used with *door* ⟨keep the ~ from the door⟩ ⟨the ~ is at the door⟩ (3) : a voracious appetite ⟨deaden the gnawing ~ within —Elizabeth C. Gaskell⟩ **c** [trans. of ML *lupus*] *archaic* : an eating ulcer or cancer **d** (1) : a grub that is the larva of various small beetles or moths and that infests granaries (2) : the maggot of a warble fly **3** [G; fr. the howling sound] **a** (1) : dissonance in some chords on organs, pianos, or other instruments with fixed tones tuned by unequal temperament (2) : an instance of such dissonance **b** : a harshness due to faulty vibration in various tones in a bowed instrument **4** : a cub scout of the second rank who is at least eight years old — **wolf in sheep's clothing** : one who cloaks a hostile intention with a friendly manner

²wolf \"\ *vb* -ED/-ING/-S *vt* : to eat greedily : devour ravenously ⟨~*ed* two large plates of the stew —D.G.Gerahty⟩ ⟨~*ing* every volume on social and economic matters he could lay his hands on —*Time*⟩ ⟨sustained high-speed driving ~*s* up a lot more gas than ordinary commuter travel —P.W. Kearney⟩ ~ *vi* **1** : to hunt for wolves **2** : to philander aggressively

wol·fach·ite \'vōl,fäk,īt\ *n* -S [G *wolfachit*, fr. *Wolfach*, Baden, Germany + G *-it* -ite] : a silver-white or tin-white mineral Ni(As,Sb)S consisting of nickel sulfide, arsenide, and antimonide

wolf·berry \'wu̇lf- — *see* BERRY\ *n* [*wolf* + *berry*] **1** : a western American shrub (*Symphoricarpos occidentalis*) sometimes cultivated for its white berries **2** : MOUNTAIN CRANBERRY **3** : BITTERSWEET 2a **4** : any of various plants of the genus *Lycium*; *esp* : MATRIMONY VINE

wolf call *n* : a whistle, howl, or other sound by a male expressing approval or admiration of a girl's or woman's appearance

wolf·camp \'wu̇lf,kamp\ *adj, usu cap* [fr. *Wolfcamp*, locality near Leonard Mountain, western Texas] : of or relating to a subdivision of the American Permian — see GEOLOGIC TIME table

wolf child *n* : a child popularly believed to have been suckled and reared by wolves or other wild animals

wolf cub *n, Brit* : a boy who is a member of a division of the Boy Scouts for boys from 8 to 11 years old — compare CUB SCOUT

wolf dog *n* **1** : any of various large dogs (as the Irish wolfhound) formerly kept for hunting wolves **2** : the offspring of a cross between a wolf and a domestic dog **3** : a dog resembling or thought to resemble a wolf irrespective of its actual breeding

wolf eel *n* : a long slender wolffish (*Anarhichthys ocellatus*) occurring along the coast from Alaska to southern California

wolfe·ite \'wu̇l,fīt\ *n* -S [Caleb Wroe *Wolfe* b1908 Am. crystallographer + E *-ite*] : a mineral $(Fe,Mn)_2(PO_4)(OH)$ that consists of basic iron phosphate and is isomorphous with triploidite and isostructural with sarkinite

wolf·er \'wu̇lfə(r)\ *n* -S [²*wolf* + *-er*] **1** : one that hunts wolves usu. for their pelts **2** : one that wolfs food or drink

wolf·fia \'wu̇lfēə, 'vōl-\ *n, cap* [NL, fr. Johann F. *Wolff* †1806 Ger. physician and botanist + NL *-ia*] : a genus of widely distributed floating aquatic plants (family Lemnaceae) that are the smallest flowering plants known, consist merely of a minute ovoid or globose leafless thallus producing the flowers from clefts or grooves, and are distinguished from members of the genus *Lemna* by the one-celled anthers and by the absence of roots

¹wolff·ian *also* **wolf·ian** \-ēən\ *adj, usu cap* [Christian von *Wolff* (*Wolf*) †1754 Ger. philosopher + E *-an*] : of or relating to Christian Wolff or his rationalistic philosophy

²wolffian \"\ *adj, often cap* [Kaspar Friedrich *Wolff* †1794 Ger. anatomist and embryologist + E *-an*] : discovered or first described by Kaspar Friedrich Wolff

wolffian body *n, often cap W* [²*wolffian*] : MESONEPHROS

wolffian duct *n, often cap W* [²*wolffian*] : MESONEPHRIC DUCT

wolffian ridge *n, often cap W* [²*wolffian*] **1** : a longitudinal ridge on either side of the trunk in some vertebrate embryos (as of the chick) from which the limb buds arise **2** : a slight ridge on either side of the midline in vertebrate embryos giving rise to the mesonephros

wolffian tubule *n, often cap W* [²*wolffian*] : a mesonephric tubule

wolffish \'ˌˌ\ *n* [¹*wolf* + *fish*] : any of several large marine blennies notable for their strong teeth and ferocity: as **a** : a blenny (*Anarhichas lupus*) of the north Atlantic that is brownish or bluish gray with from 9 to 12 dark crossbars, has a tough scaleless skin from which fine leather is made, and reaches a length of 4 to 6 feet **b** : a similar fish (*A. orientalis*) of the north Pacific that is plain brown in color — see WOLF EEL

wolff–kish·ner reaction \'wu̇lf'kishnə(r)-\ *n, usu cap W&K* [after Ludwig *Wolff* fl1914 and N. *Kishner* fl1914 Ger. chemists] : an indirect reduction of an aldehyde or ketone to the corresponding hydrocarbon by heating the hydrazone or semicarbazone derivative with an alcoholic solution of sodium ethoxide or with solid potassium hydroxide

wolf grape *n* **1** : BITTERSWEET 2a **2** : CHICKEN GRAPE

wolf herring *n* : a large greatly elongated voracious clupeoid fish (*Chirocentrus dorab* or possibly related species) that has long powerful fangs, is widely distributed along tropical Indo-Pacific shores, and is in some areas esteemed as food though fierce and dangerous to handle

wolf·hound \'wu̇lf,hau̇nd, -l,fau̇-\ *n* : any of several large dogs used now or orig. in hunting the wolf and other large animals — compare BORZOI, IRISH WOLFHOUND

wolf·ian \'wu̇lfēən, 'vōl-\ *adj, often cap* [Friedrich August *Wolf* †1824 Ger. classical philologist and Homeric critic] : of or relating to Friedrich August Wolf

wolfier *comparative of* WOLFY

wolfiest *superlative of* WOLFY

wolfing *pres part of* WOLF

wolf–in–the–tail \'ˌˌˌ\ *n* : nonspecific debility of cattle — compare HOLLOW HORN

wolf·ish \'wu̇lfish, -fēsh\ *adj* [¹*wolf* + *-ish*] : of or characteristic of a wolf : having the qualities or form of a wolf : WOLFLIKE; *esp* : FEROCIOUS, RAVENOUS ⟨the smell of such fare would prove no irresistible temptation to ~ nostrils —C.G.D.Roberts⟩ ⟨a ~ wind had begun to clamor at the doors —Archibald Rutledge⟩ ⟨a ~ pursuit of pleasure —G.K.Chesterton⟩

wolf·ish·ly *adv* : in a wolfish manner : RAVENOUSLY ⟨eyed our food ~ —Virginia D. Dawson & Betty D. Wilson⟩

wolf·ish·ness *n* -ES : the quality or state of being wolfish

wolflike \'ˌˌ\ *adj* : resembling, suggestive of, or having the characteristics of a wolf

wolf·ling \'wu̇lflin\ *n* -S [ME *wulfling*, fr. *wulf*, *wolf* wolf + *-ling*] : a little or young wolf

wolf note *n* : WOLF 3

wolf number \'wu̇lf-, 'vōlf-\ *n, usu cap W* [after Rudolf *Wolf* †1893 Swiss astronomer] : SUNSPOT NUMBER

wolf pack *n* [intended as trans. of G *rudel* flock, herd, pack (in *rudeltaktik* wolf-pack tactics, *rudelsystem* wolf-pack system)] **1 a** : a tactical unit of two or more submarines that make a coordinated attack on shipping **b** : a group of two or more fighter planes making a coordinated attack **2** : a roving gang of roughneck teen-agers

wolf·ram \'wu̇lfrəm, 'vōl-\ *n* -S [G, alter. (influenced by *wolf* wolf) of *wolffram*, *wolform*, *volfram*, of unknown origin] **1** : TUNGSTEN — symbol *W*; see ELEMENT table **2** : WOLFRAMITE

wolfram– *or* **wolframo–** *comb form* [ISV *wolfram*] : TUNGST- ⟨*wolframic*⟩ ⟨*wolframo*phosphate⟩

wolf·ram·ate \-rə,māt\ *n* -S [ISV *wolfram-* + *-ate*] : TUNGSTATE

wolf·ram·ic \wu̇l'framik\ *adj* [*wolfram-* + *-ic*] : TUNGSTIC

wolframic acid *n* : TUNGSTIC ACID

wolf·ra·mine \'wu̇lfrə,mēn, -,mən\ *n* -S [*wolfram-* + *-ine*] : TUNGSTITE

wolf·ra·min·i·um \,wu̇lfrə'minēəm\ *n* -S [NL, fr. *wolfram-* + *-inium* (as in *aluminium*)] : a light aluminum alloy similar to romanium

wolf·ram·ite \-rə,mīt, *usu* -īd.+V\ *n* -S [G *wolframit*, fr. *wolfram-* + *-it* -ite] : a mineral $(Fe,Mn)WO_4$ that consists of an iron manganese tungstate of a usu. brownish or grayish black color and submetallic luster, is isomorphous with and intermediate between huebnerite and ferberite, occurs in monoclinic crystals commonly twinned so as to imitate orthorhombic tabular forms and in granular or columnar masses, shows a highly perfect cleavage, and is used as a source of tungsten and tungsten compounds (hardness 5–5.5, sp. gr. 7.1–7.5) — called also *wolfram*

wolfram lamp *n* : TUNGSTEN LAMP

wolfram ocher *n* : TUNGSTITE

wolfs *pres 3d sing of* WOLF

wolfs·bane \'wu̇lfs,bān\ *n* [*wolfs* (gen. of *wolf*) + *bane*; trans. of NL *lycoctonum*, lit., wolf-killing] **1** : ACONITE 1; *esp* : a highly variable yellow-flowered Eurasian herb (*Aconitum lycoctonum*) with a somewhat fibrous rootstock and broadly lobed leaves — compare MONKSHOOD **2** : WINTER ACONITE

wolf's–head \'ˌˌ\ *n* [ME *wolfeshevede*, fr. OE *wulfesheāfod*, interj. used in wolf-hunting and in pursuing an outlaw, lit., head of a wolf, fr. *wulfes* (gen. of *wulf* wolf) + *heāfod* head — more at WOLF, HEAD] **1** *archaic* : OUTLAW **2** *archaic* : OUTLAWRY

wolfskin \'ˌˌ\ *n, often attrib* **1** : the skin of a wolf **2** : a garment or blanket made of this skin

wolf's–milk \'ˌˌ\ *n, pl* **wolf's–milks** [so called fr. its acrid milky juice] : SPURGE: as **a** : LEAFY SPURGE **b** : SUN SPURGE

wolf's moss *n* [prob. so called fr. its having been used to poison wolves] : a yellow lichen (*Letharia vulpina*) of arctic and alpine regions sometimes used for a dye

wolf snake *n* : any of various harmless colubrid snakes having elongated teeth: as **a** : CAPE WOLF SNAKE **b** : any of a genus (*Lycodon*) of active arboreal nocturnal snakes widespread in southeastern Asia

wolf's peach *n, archaic* : TOMATO

wolf spider *n* : any of various active wandering ground spiders belonging to the family Lycosidae — see TARANTULA

wolf teeth *n pl* : the ratchet and crown wheels that mesh on curved tooth flanks and similarly relieved tooth backs in a fine pocket watch

wolf tone *n* : WOLF 3

wolf tooth *also* **wolf's tooth** *n* **1** : a small vestigial first premolar that is sometimes present in a horse on each side in front of the normal grinders and that is regularly found in some fossil members of the family Equidae **2** : NEEDLE TOOTH **3** : a protruding incisor (as in a guinea pig or rabbit)

wolf tree *n* : a forest tree whose size and position cause it to prevent the growth of many small and potentially more valuable trees around it by usurping their space, light, and nourishment

wolf vault *n* : a vault in gymnastics in which one leg is in squat position and the other is extended to its own side as the body passes over the apparatus

wolf whistle *n* : a wolf call consisting of a 2-toned whistle

wolf willow *n* : BUFFALO BERRY

wolfy \'wu̇lfē\ *adj* -ER/-EST : resembling a wolf (as in fierceness)

wol·las·ton doublet \'wu̇ləstən-\ *n, usu cap W* [after William H. *Wollaston* †1828] : a magnifying glass made of two planoconvex lenses and designed to correct spherical and chromatic aberration

wol·las·ton·ite \-tə,nīt\ *n* -S [William H. *Wollaston* †1828 Eng. chemist and physicist + E *-ite*] : a triclinic mineral $CaSiO_3$ of a white to gray, red, yellow, or brown color consisting of native calcium metasilicate occurring usu. in cleavable masses and sometimes in tabular twinned crystals (hardness 4.5–5, sp. gr. 2.8–2.9) — called also *tabular spar*

wollaston prism *n, usu cap W* [after William H. *Wollaston* †1828] : a double-image compound prism producing two divergent beams of light plane-polarized at right angles to each other and consisting of two equal right-angled prisms of Iceland spar or quartz cemented along their long faces and so cut that in the one light passes along the optic axis and in the other at right angles to that axis

wollaston wire *n, usu cap W* [after William H. *Wollaston* †1828] : a very fine usu. platinum wire used for cross hairs in telescope eyepieces

wol·lo·mai \'wälə,mī\ *n* -S [native name in New So. Wales] : SNAPPER 3c

wo·lof \'wō,läf\ *also* **jo·lof** \'yō-\ *or* **vo·lof** \'vō-\ *n* -S *usu cap* **1 a** : a people of the western Sudan near the mouth of the Senegal and Gambia rivers who are among the most deeply pigmented of Africans **b** : a member of such people **2 a** : a West-Atlantic language of the Wolof people **b** : a trade language in Senegal

wolve \'wu̇lv\ *vi* -ED/-ING/-S [fr. ¹*wolf*, after such pairs as E ¹*half*: *halve*, v.] **1** : WOLF **2** *of a pipe organ* : to produce a sound like the howl of a wolf (as from failure of air supply)

wol·ve·boon \'vōlvə,bün\ *n* -S [Afrik, lit., wolf bean, irreg. fr. MD *wolf* + *boon*, *bone* bean; akin to OE *wulf* wolf and OHG *bōna* bean — more at WOLF, BEAN] : a small southern African tree or shrub (*Toxicodendrum capensis*) of the family Euphorbiaceae with very poisonous foliage

wolv·er \'wu̇lvə(r)\ *n* -S [*wolve* + *-er*] **1** : one that behaves like a wolf **2** : one that hunts wolves

wol·ver·hamp·ton \'wu̇lvə(r),ham(p)tən\ *adj, usu cap* [fr. *Wolverhampton*, England] : of or from the county borough of Wolverhampton, England : of the kind or style prevalent in Wolverhampton

wol·ver·ine *also* **wol·ver·ene** \,wu̇lvə'rēn\ *n* -S *see sense 1* [alter. of earlier *wolvering*, prob. irreg. fr. *wolv-* (as in *wolves*, *wolvish*) + *-ing*, n. suffix] **1** *pl also* **wolverine** : a northern No. American carnivorous mammal (*Gulo luscus*) of the family Mustelidae that resembles and is often considered conspecific with the glutton of Europe, is blackish with a pale forehead and a light band on each side of the body, and is noted for its thievishness, strength, and cunning — called also *carcajou* **b** : the fur of the wolverine **2** *usu cap* : MICHIGANDER — used as a nickname

wolves *pl of* WOLF

wolv·ish \'wu̇lvish\ *adj* [ME, fr. *wolves* + *-ish*] *archaic* : WOLFISH

¹wom·an \'wu̇mən *sometimes esp in the South* 'wōm- *or* 'wəm-\ *n, pl* **wom·en** \'wimən\ [ME *woman*, *wumman*, *wimman*, *wimmon*, *wifmon*, fr. OE *wifmon*, *wifman*, fr. *wif* woman, wife + *mon*, *man* man — more at WIFE, MAN] **1 a** (1) : a female human being — distinguished from *man* ⟨the *women* gardened and cooked while the men hunted and fished⟩ (2) : an adult female human being — distinguished from *girl* ⟨the *women* and girls formed a glee club⟩ (3) : a female human being as such and without regard to any special status (as of birth, position, or office) ⟨she is a queen but she is also a ~⟩ (4) : a female human being of a class or character lower than that normally considered a lady **b** : a female human being belonging to a particular and usu. specified category (as by birth, residence, or membership) ⟨a ~ of affairs⟩ ⟨several Christian *women*⟩ — usu. used in combination ⟨char*woman*⟩ ⟨washer*women*⟩; compare MAN 2b **c** (1) *chiefly dial* : WIFE (2) : MISTRESS 6a (3) *women*, *pl* : human females as partners in sexual intercourse or irregularities ⟨refrained from *women* during Lent⟩ **d** (1) : one possessing in high degree the qualities considered distinctive of womanhood (as gentleness, affection, and domesticity or on the other hand fickleness, superficiality, and folly) (2) : womanly character or quality : WOMANLINESS **2** : the female part of the human race : female human beings esp. when viewed as a natural kind or personified as an individual : WOMANKIND ⟨~ is the glory of all created existence —Samuel Richardson⟩ **3** : a human female that serves or is subordinate to another ⟨expect the ~ to come in to clean the rugs⟩; *esp* : one that is the personal maid of another

²woman \"\ *adj* [ME, fr. *woman*, n.] **1** : of, belonging to, or characteristic of a woman : WOMANLY ⟨~ talk⟩ ⟨~ clothes⟩ **2** : FEMALE ⟨a ~ doctor⟩ ⟨~ students⟩ ⟨memorable ~ characters of world literature —*Tomorrow*⟩

³woman \"\ *vt* -ED/-ING/-S [¹*woman*] **1** : to make into a woman or the likeness of a woman **2** *obs* : to make effeminate **3** *obs* : to associate (one) with a woman ⟨to have him see me ~*ed* —Shak.⟩ **4** : to furnish or staff with women

woman chaser *n* : PHILANDERER

woman–child \'ˌˌ\ *n, archaic* : a female infant

womanfolk \'ˌˌ\ *n, pl* **womenfolk** *also* **womanfolk** *or* **womenfolks** [²*woman* + *folk*] **1** *chiefly dial* : WOMAN **2** *womenfolk also womanfolk or womenfolks pl* : the women of a group (as a family or community) ⟨get the *womenfolk* off to the hills —E.M.Forster⟩

wom·an·ful·ly \-nfəlē\ *adv* [¹*woman* + *-fully* (as in *manfully*)] : with womanly constancy or spirit

woman–grown \'ˌˌ\ *adj* : grown to womanhood

woman hater *n* : MISOGYNIST

wom·an·head \-n,hed\ *n* [ME *womanhede*, fr. ¹*woman* + *-hede* -hood (akin to ME *-hod*, *-had* -hood)] *archaic* : WOMANHOOD

wom·an·hood \-n,hu̇d\ *n* [ME *womanhod*, fr. ¹*woman* + *-hod* -hood] **1** : the state of being a woman : the distinguishing character or qualities of a woman or of womankind **2** : WOMEN, WOMANKIND ⟨the ~ of a nation⟩

wom·an·house \'wu̇mən,hüs\ *n* [²*woman* + *house*] *Scot* : LAUNDRY

wom·an·ish \'wu̇mənish *sometimes esp in the South* 'wōm- *or* 'wəm-\ *adj* [ME, fr. ¹*woman* + *-ish*] **1** *archaic* : of or belonging to women : done by women ⟨~ work⟩ **2** : characteristic of a woman : suitable to or resembling a woman : FEMININE ⟨love her for the sake of her gentle and ~ ways —A.W.Kinglake⟩ ⟨nothing ~ in the room except a full-length mirror —Raymond Chandler⟩ **3** : unsuitable to a man or to a strong character of either sex : not strong or virile ⟨hence, ~ fears, traitors to love and duty —S.T.Coleridge⟩ ⟨disdaining all the ~ peace talk about them —James Cameron⟩ ⟨womanly, yet quite unlike the ~ women —George Meredith⟩ **syn** see FEMALE

wom·an·ish·ly *adv* : in a womanish manner

wom·an·ish·ness *n* -ES : the quality or state of being womanish

wom·an·i·ty \wu̇'manəd-ē\ *n* -ES : the nature of women : normal womanhood : WOMANLINESS

wom·an·ize \'wu̇mə,nīz *sometimes esp South* 'wōm- *or* 'wəm-\ *vb* -ED/-ING/-S *vt* : to make effeminate ~ *vi* **1** *archaic* : to become effeminate **2** : to pursue or associate illicitly with women

wom·an·iz·er \-zə(r)\ *n* -S : a man who pursues or associates illicitly with women ⟨men who had been terrific ~*s* —Polly Adler⟩

womankind \'ˌˌ\ *n* [ME *woman kinde*, fr. ¹*woman* + *kinde* kind] **1** : the females of the human race : WOMEN ⟨~ with her tools of magic, the broom and mop —Nathaniel Hawthorne⟩ **2** : the women members of a family, household, or community ⟨businessmen and their ~ —S.P.Sherman⟩ **3** *archaic* : a female person

wom·an·less \-nləs\ *adj* : without a woman : having no women ⟨~ men⟩

¹womanlike \'ˌˌ\ *adj* [ME, fr. ¹*woman* + *like*, adj.] : resembling or characteristic of a woman : having qualities natural to or peculiar to women: as **a** *of a woman* : manifesting characteristic feminine foibles ⟨a ~ lack of promptness⟩ **b** *of a man* : WOMANISH ⟨ashamed at being surprised in a ~ expression of sorrow —Sir Walter Scott⟩ **syn** see FEMALE

²womanlike \"\ *adv* [ME, fr. ¹*woman* + *like*, adv.] : WOMANLY

wom·an·li·ness \-nlēnəs, -lin-\ *n* -ES : the quality of being womanly

¹wom·an·ly *adj, often* -ER/-EST [ME *wommanlich*, fr. *womman* woman + *-lich* -ly, adj. suffix] **1** : marked by qualities characteristic of a woman; *esp* : marked by qualities becoming a well-balanced adult woman ⟨~ manners⟩ ⟨~ advice⟩ **2** : possessed of the character or behavior befitting a grown woman : no longer childish or girlish : becoming to a grown woman ⟨little girl . . . wearing a ~ sort of bonnet much too large for her —Charles Dickens⟩ **3** : characteristic of, belonging to, or suitable to women : conforming to or motivated by a woman's nature and attitudes rather than a man's ⟨convinced that drawing was a waste of time, if not downright ~, like painting on China —Kenneth Roberts⟩ ⟨her usual ~ volubility —Anthony Trollope⟩ **syn** see FEMALE

²wom·an·ly *adv* [ME *wommanliche*, fr. *womman* woman + *-liche* -ly, adv. suffix] : in a womanly or distinctively feminine manner

wom·an·ness \-mən(n)əs\ *n* -ES : WOMANLINESS

woman of letters **1** : a learned woman **2** : a literary woman

woman of the bedchamber : one of a group of ladies of noble family attendant on a British queen or princess and ranking below those bearing the title *lady of the bedchamber* but having similar duties — called also *bedchamber woman*

woman of the house : LADY OF THE HOUSE

woman of the street *or* **woman of the streets** : PROSTITUTE, STREETWALKER

woman of the town : PROSTITUTE, WHORE

woman of the world **1** : a sophisticated or worldly woman **2** : a woman of the world of fashion or high life

woman–post \'ˌˌ\ *n, archaic* : a female messenger

womanpower \'ˌˌ\ *n* : power available from or supplied by the effort of women ⟨mobilization of ~ reserves —Fritz Sternberg⟩ ⟨the Navy called for ~ to take over administrative and desk work —Walter Karig⟩

womans *pres 3d sing of* WOMAN

woman's man *n* : LADIES' MAN

woman's rights *n pl* : the legal, political, and social rights of women : FEMINISM 2

woman's–tongue tree \'ˌˌ-\ *or* **woman's tongue** *n* [so called fr. the clatter of its dry pods when ripe] : LEBBEK

woman suffrage *n* : the suffrage possessed and exercised by women — compare MANHOOD SUFFRAGE, UNIVERSAL SUFFRAGE

woman–suffragist \'ˌˌˌˌ\ *n, pl* **woman–suffragists** *or* **women–suffragists** : an advocate of woman suffrage

¹womb \'wüm\ *n* -S [ME *wombe*, *wambe*, *wamb*, fr. OE *wamb*, *womb*; akin to OHG *wamba* belly, ON *vömb* belly, womb, Goth *wamba* belly] **1** *obs* : BELLY **2 a** : UTERUS ⟨transgressors from the ~ —William Cowper⟩ ⟨the lamb . . . leaves the ~ —*New Zealand Jour. of Agric.*⟩ ⟨each adult female fly carries over 50 living larvae in her ~ —*Farm Management*⟩ **b** : CRADLE 1b ⟨from the ~ to the tomb⟩ **3 a** : a cavity or space like a womb in containing and enveloping ⟨the soul remembers the primal silence, the ~ of Night —C.I.Glicksberg⟩ **b** : a place or space where something is generated or produced ⟨the snow . . . would have been shed off around the sides, and piled down into the glacier ~*s* —John Muir †1914⟩ **c** : a period of gestation : circumstances providing the protection and nurture necessary for birth or early development ⟨the Church, a survival from the dying society, became the ~ from which in due course the new one was born —A.J.Toynbee⟩ ⟨prepared themselves to leave the ~ of government protection —S.T. Kimball⟩ ⟨the embryonic State would strangle in its ~ —Tom Marvel⟩

²womb \"\ *vt* -ED/-ING/-S : to enclose in or as if in a womb ⟨a new era was born . . . ~*ed* in war's destruction —*Time*⟩

wom·bat \'wäm,bat *also* 'wȯm-, *usu* -ad.+V\ *n* -S [native name in New So. Wales] **1 a** : any of several sturdily built Australian marsupials (family Vombatidae) having stocky bodies, short legs, and rudimentary tails, and in general resembling small bears — see HAIRY-NOSED WOMBAT **b** : the fur of the wombat **2** : KOALA 2

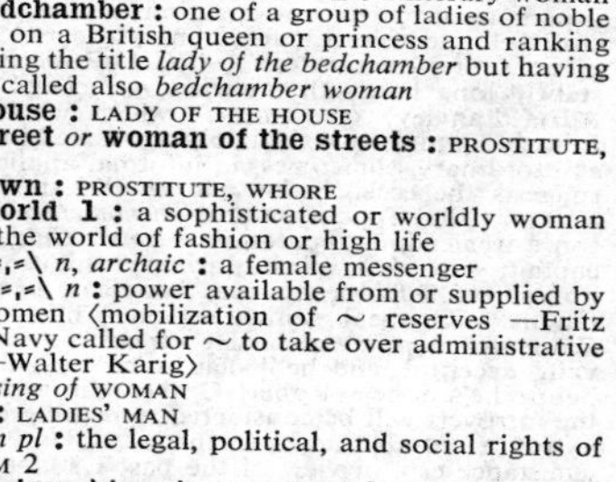

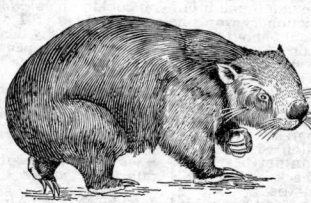

wombat

wombed \'wümd\ *adj* [ME, fr. *wombe* womb + *-ed*] : having a womb

wom·ble \'wäməl\ *dial var of* WAMBLE

womby \'wümē\ *adj* -ER/-EST [¹*womb* + *-y*] *archaic* : HOLLOW

women *pl of* WOMAN

womenfolk *or* **womenfolks** *pl of* **womanfolk**

womenkind \'==,=\ *n* [ME *womenkinde*, fr. *women* + *kinde* kind] : WOMANKIND 1, 2 ⟨a special place was set apart for the ~ to come and pray —Elizabeth Montizambert⟩ ⟨the tasks ~ had to perform —*New Zealand Home Jour.*⟩

women's room *n* : LADIES' ROOM

womens·wear *or* **women's wear** \'==,=\ *n* **1** *usu* *women's wear* : clothing for women **2** : a fabric (as worsted) suitable for women's clothing

wom·mera *also* **wom·era** *or* **wom·er·ah** \'wämərə *also* 'wōm-\ *or* **woom·era** *or* **woom·er·ah** \'wům-\ *n* -s [native name in New So. Wales] : THROWING-STICK; *specif* : one used by Australian aborigines

womp \'wämp\ *n* -s [imit. of the sound of a small explosion (as of an electric bulb)] : an abrupt increase in the illumination of a television screen resulting from an abrupt increase in signal strength

¹won \'wən\ *vi* **wonned; wonned; wonning; wons** [ME *wonen, wunen*, fr. OE *wunian* — more at WONT] *archaic* : DWELL, ABIDE ⟨the wild beast, where he ~s in forest wild —John Milton⟩

²won [ME *wan, won* (past) & *wonnen* (past part.), fr. OE *wann, wonn* (past) & *gewunnen* (past part.)] *past of* WIN

³won \'wən\ *dial var of* ONE

¹won·der \'wəndə(r)\ *n* -s [ME *wonder, wunder*, fr. OE *wundor;* akin to OHG *wuntar* wonder, ON *undr*] **1** : a cause of astonishment or surprise : something that excites wonder : MARVEL ⟨fingers and toes are apparent ~s to the little baby —C.S.Kilby⟩: as **a** : a fact or circumstance giving occasion to be surprised ⟨it's a ~ he wasn't killed⟩ ⟨no ~ he left after being insulted so⟩ ⟨the ~ is that he was nominated at all —J.A. Huston⟩ ⟨small ~ that all this extraordinary activity . . . would have exhausted his vitality —H.W.Wiley⟩ **b** : an extraordinary deed or occurrence attributed to supernatural agency : MIRACLE ⟨performed among you . . . with signs and ~s and mighty works —2 Cor 12:12 (RSV)⟩ **c** : something extraordinarily effective : a marvelous result or achievement ⟨a new hairdo that did ~s for her looks⟩ ⟨free individuals working together . . . can accomplish ~s —J.C.Penney⟩ **d** : a person or thing that excites amazed admiration ⟨a secretary who is a ~ of efficiency⟩ ⟨the pyramids and other ~s of the ancient world⟩ **2** : the quality of exciting amazed admiration ⟨the beauty and ~ of some of these lovely melodies —Warwick Braithwaite⟩ ⟨the glories of His righteousness and ~s of His love —Isaac Watts⟩ **3 a** : a state of fascinated or questioning attention before what strikes one as strange beyond understanding : an attitude or feeling of amazed admiration or nascent, perplexed, or bewildered curiosity aroused by the extraordinary and unaccountable : a sense of mystery : MARVELING ⟨stood struck with wide-eyed ~ before the colossal statue⟩ ⟨two impulses in man: one is to accept and take for granted; the other is to look with inquiry and ~ —J.E.Park⟩ ⟨looked at each other in silent ~ —G.D.Brown⟩ **b** : a feeling of doubt or uncertainty : a curious concern ⟨your ~ as to what will become of your shares when the banks are nationalized —G.B.Shaw⟩ **4** *obs* : great esteem : ADMIRATION **5** : a twisted cruller

syn MARVEL, PRODIGY, MIRACLE, PHENOMENON: WONDER usu. designates what excites surprise, astonishment, or amazement typically by its perfection, greatness, or inexplicableness ⟨the *wonders* of Creation —L.P.Smith⟩ ⟨she is a *wonder* at her job —R.E.Roberts⟩ ⟨a *wonder* how many wild animals survive⟩ MARVEL usu. designates what excites surprise or astonishment by its extraordinariness, strangeness, or curiousness ⟨the endurance of the inequalities of life by the poor is the *marvel* of human society —J.A.Froude⟩ ⟨their hypocrisy is a perpetual *marvel* to me —W.M.Thackeray⟩ ⟨the *marvel* of the play is the bewildering rapid chaotic action —T.S.Eliot⟩ ⟨a *marvel* on the flying trapeze⟩ PRODIGY designates what makes one marvel because of its oddness or unusualness, esp. in degree of skill, endurance, size, or accomplishment ⟨a *prodigy* of wastefulness, corruption, ignorance, and indolence —T.B.Macaulay⟩ ⟨performed *prodigies* in transporting to France a gigantic army —G.W.Johnson⟩ ⟨women performing *prodigies* of endurance, bravery, and hope —*Newsweek*⟩ ⟨the Shoshones feared . . . this *prodigy*, the first white man they had ever seen —A.J. Toynbee⟩ ⟨a land of *prodigies*: mountains, precipices, cataracts, dead craters, snowy ascents, vertiginous cliffs —*Amer. Guide Series: Calif.*⟩ MIRACLE applies to something very unusual, esp. so contrary to normal expectations that it seems to surpass human comprehension and often approaches the supernatural ⟨their conversations are *miracles* of studied, stilted eloquence —B.R.Redman⟩ ⟨the ears of an owl are a very *miracle* of sensitiveness —C.G.D.Roberts⟩ ⟨studied constantly long hours that were a *miracle* of concentration —Adria Langley⟩ ⟨the *miracle* which we call genius —J.L. Lowes⟩ PHENOMENON, implying something exceptional or extraordinary, sometimes, in informal application to persons, suggests the eccentric or odd ⟨it did snow considerably in Vermont that July, a natural *phenomenon* that gave Thompson a tremendous reputation —*Amer. Guide Series: Vt.*⟩ ⟨the captain — a *phenomenon* during prohibition because he was honest —J.F.Dinneen⟩ ⟨an American *phenomenon*, a self-taught mechanical genius —Don Wharton⟩ ⟨your nephew Caligula is a *phenomenon*. He's treacherous, cowardly, lustful, vain, deceitful, and he'll play some very dirty tricks on you before he's done —Robert Graves⟩ ⟨in a group of extroverts the introvert will be considered something of a *phenomenon*⟩ — **for a wonder** *adv* : in the way of an extraordinary circumstance esp. in view of the past : SURPRISINGLY ⟨the children, *for a wonder*, kept still long enough for her to hear⟩ — **to a wonder** *archaic* : to an astonishing extent ⟨she was ugly *to a wonder* —William Cowper⟩

²wonder \"\ *adj* **1** : of an extraordinary character : being such as excites amazed admiration : WONDERFUL, MARVELOUS ⟨a family of chemicals . . . of such exciting potency that the popular name for them is "~ hormones" —D.C.Cooley⟩ ⟨~ fibers and miracle finishes⟩ **2** : of or relating to things that excite amazed admiration ⟨a ~ city⟩ ⟨a ~ book⟩ ⟨the Elizabethan ~ age of adventure —*Spectator*⟩ **3** : having or manifesting magical power ⟨wore a ~ bag around his neck⟩

³wonder \"\ *adv, archaic* : WONDERFULLY, AMAZINGLY, EXCEEDINGLY, VERY ⟨delicate ~ white crystals —*Westminster Gazette*⟩

⁴wonder \"\ *vb* **wondered; wondered; wondering** \-d(ə)riŋ\ **wonders** [ME *wondren, wundren*, fr. OE *wundrian;* akin to OHG *wuntarōn* to wonder, ON *undra* to wonder, OE *wundor* wonder] *vi* **1 a** : to be in a state of rapt or questioning attention toward the extraordinary or mysterious : feel or become struck with wonder : MARVEL ⟨~*ed* at the delicacy of form and color —W.B.Yeats⟩ ⟨though no . . . rapturous insight troubled her childlike soul, yet she could ~ and gaze —A.J.Munby⟩ **b** : to feel or become struck with surprise ⟨couldn't help ~*ing* at the size of the servings⟩ ⟨~*ed* to see them all standing there waiting⟩ ⟨shouldn't ~ if he came after all⟩ ⟨I ~ . . . that he keeps that reminder of his sufferings by him —Charles Dickens⟩ **2** : to wish to know something : feel curiosity or doubt : query in the mind ⟨~*ed* as to the feasibility of the plan⟩ ⟨said he had found it but you couldn't help ~*ing*⟩ ⟨looks up in the dictionary words he ~s about⟩ ~ *vt* **1** : to be curious or in doubt about : wish to know ⟨~*ed* why they came⟩ ⟨~ if it will rain⟩ ⟨on whom, one ~s, do these expensive weeklies live —Aldous Huxley⟩ : ask or puzzle in one's mind about ⟨~*ed* what he should do⟩ **2** *archaic* : to look upon with often admiring wonder ⟨I felt all, loved all, ~*ed* all —Charles Lamb⟩ **3** *dial* : to cause to wonder — usu. used in the phrase *it wonders me* **4** : to make an occasion for wonder — usu. used in the phrase *to be wondered* ⟨it is little to be ~*ed* that her students idolized her⟩

won·der·berry \'==- — *see* BERRY\ *n* **1** : the edible fruit of the black nightshade — called also *sunberry* **2** : BLACK NIGHTSHADE

won·der·boom \'vändə(r),büm\ *n* -s [Afrik, lit., wonder tree, fr. MD, fr. *wonder* + *boom* tree; akin to OE *wundor* wonder and OHG *boum* tree — more at WONDER, BEAM] : a fig (*Ficus pretoriae*) with fruits borne in the leaf axils of the terminal branchlets that is widely distributed in tropical and subtropical Africa

wonder boy *n* : a very popular or successful person

wonder child *n* : a child prodigy

wonder drug *n* : MIRACLE DRUG

won·der·er \'wəndərə(r)\ *n* -s : one that wonders

¹won·der·ful \-də(r)fəl\ *adj, sometimes* **wonderfuller;** *sometimes* **wonderfullest** [ME, fr. OE *wundorful*, fr. *wundor* wonder + *-ful* -ful] **1 a** : exciting wonder : MARVELOUS, SURPRISING, STRANGE, ASTONISHING ⟨a feast ~ to behold⟩ **b** *obs* : MIRACULOUS **2** : unusually good, interesting, amusing, lovely : ADMIRABLE — used as a generalized term of approval ⟨in love with a ~ girl⟩ ⟨having a ~ time⟩ — **won·der·ful·ness** *n* -ES

²wonderful \"\ *adv* [ME, fr. ¹*wonderful*] *dial* : WONDERFULLY ⟨gets ~ excited —Adrian Bell⟩

won·der·ful·ly \-f(ə)lē, -li\ *adv* [ME *wonderfulliche*, fr. ¹*wonderful* + *-liche* -ly] **1** : in such a way or to such an extent as to excite wonder : MARVELOUSLY, AMAZINGLY ⟨a ~ beautiful sunset⟩ ⟨had worked ~ for years⟩ **2** : EXCEEDINGLY, VERY ⟨not very imaginative but ~ pleasing —George Saintsbury⟩

won·der·ing·ly *adv* : in a wondering manner ⟨looked ~ at the skyscrapers⟩

won·der·land \'wəndə(r),land, -laa(ə)nd, -,lənd\ *n* **1** : a fairylike imaginary realm **2** : a place (as one containing extraordinary natural features) that excites admiration or wonder ⟨a scenic ~⟩

won·der·less \-(r)ləs\ *adj* : having no wonder

won·der·ment \-(r)mənt\ *n* -s **1** : a state or feeling of wonder : ASTONISHMENT, SURPRISE ⟨saw with ~ that her fingers were trembling —Walter Macken⟩ **2** : something exciting wonder : a cause of or occasion for wonder; *also* : something that evokes admiring wonder **3** : the quality of being wonderful or marvelous **4** : an exclamation or other utterance expressive of wonder **5** : curiosity about something : WONDERING ⟨their ~ about the outcome⟩

wondermonger \'==,=\ *n* [¹*wonder* + *monger*] : a person who tells of or exploits strange or freakish things

won·der·some \-(r)səm\ *adj, dial Brit* : WONDERFUL

wonderwork \'=,=\ *n* **1** : WONDER 1b **2** : something that excites amazed admiration

wonder-worker \'=,==\ *n* : one that performs wonders

wonderworld \'==,=\ *n* : WONDERLAND

¹won·drous \'wəndrəs\ *adj* [alter. (influenced by *-ous*) of ME *wonders*, adj., wondrous, fr. *wonders*, gen. of ¹*wonder*] : exciting wonder or surprise : WONDERFUL, ASTONISHING, MARVELOUS ⟨a ~ fairy tale⟩ ⟨colors and shades changed in slow, ~ transformation —Zane Grey⟩ ⟨~ new ways to kill bacteria —Vance Packard⟩ — **won·drous·ly** *adv* — **won·drous·ness** *n* -ES

²wondrous \"\ *adv, archaic* : WONDERFULLY ⟨grew ~ cold —S.T.Coleridge⟩

wone *archaic var of* WON

wong *n* -s [ME, fr. OE *wong, wang;* akin to OHG *-wang* field, ON *vangr* garden, field, Goth *wangs*] *obs* : FIELD, MEADOW

wonga-wonga \'wäŋə'wäŋə\ *or* **wonga** \'wäŋə\ *n* -s [native names in New So. Wales] **1 a** : an Australian woody vine (*Pandorea pandorana*) with loose panicles of yellowish white flowers **b** *Austral* : a narrow-leaved cattail (*Typha angustifolia*) **2** : a very large Australian pigeon (*Leucosarcia melanoleuca*) with very white flesh

wong·shy \'wäŋ'shē\ *n* -ES [Chin (Pek) *huang²-chih¹* yellow gardenia] **1** : an Asiatic tree (*Gardenia grandiflora*) **2** : a yellow dye containing crocin derived from the pods of the wongshy

wo-ni \'wō'nē\ *n, pl* **wo-ni** *or* **wo-nis** *usu cap* **1** : a Nosu people of southern Yunnan province of China subject to the Chinese **2** : a member of the Wo-ni people

won·ing *or* **won·ning** \'wəniŋ\ *n* -s [ME, fr. OE *wunung*, fr. *wunian* to dwell + *-ung* -ing — more at WONT] *dial* : DWELLING

won·ky \'wäŋkē\ *adj* [alter. of *wanky*] **1** *Brit* : UNSTEADY, SHAKY ⟨the bridge stands . . . though one of the arches is ~ —*Manchester Guardian Weekly*⟩ **2** *Brit* : AWRY, WRONG ⟨hoped that nothing had gone ~ with the dinner —P.G. Wodehouse⟩

won·na \'wənə\ [by contr.] *dial Brit* : will not

wonne *var of* ²WON

wonned *past of* WON

wonning *pres part of* WON

wons *pres 3d sing of* WON, *pl of* WON

¹wont \'wȯnt, 'wōnt *sometimes* 'wänt *or* 'wənt\ *adj* [ME *wont, woned*, fr. past part. of *wonen, wunen* to dwell, be used to, fr. OE *wunian;* akin to OHG *wonēn* to dwell, remain, be used to, ON *una* to dwell, be content, Goth *-wunan* to be content, Skt *vanati* he loves — more at WIN] : ACCUSTOMED, USED — used predicatively ⟨slept longer than he was ~⟩ and usu. followed by *to* and an infinitive ⟨assumed an air of great gravity, as he was ~ to do when about to perpetrate a joke —O.S.J. Gogarty⟩; *also* : INCLINED, APT ⟨fresh, intimate, and revealing as letters are ~ to be —Gladys Wrigley⟩

²wont \"\ *n* -s [ME, fr. past part. of *wonen* to be used to] : CUSTOM, HABIT, USE, USAGE ⟨life is an affair of use and ~ and persists substantially unchanged —Walter Moberly⟩ ⟨far more serious and thoughtful than was her ~ —William Black⟩
syn see HABIT

³wont \"\ *vb* **wont; wont** *or* **wonted; wonting; wonts** [ME *wunten*, prob. fr. *wunt, wont*, past part. of *wunien, wonen* to be used to] *vt* : ACCUSTOM, HABITUATE ⟨~ ourselves with their strange aspect —R.W.Emerson⟩ ~ *vi* : to have the habit or custom of doing something — usu. followed by *to* and an infinitive ⟨the merry pipe, that ~ to cheer the harvesting —Robert Bridges †1930⟩

won't \'wōnt *also* 'wənt *sometimes* 'wünt\ [by contr.] : will not

wont·ed \'wȯntəd, 'wōn- *sometimes* 'wän- *or* 'wən-\ *adj* [ME, prob. fr. ²*wont* + *-ed*] : ACCUSTOMED, CUSTOMARY, ⟨maintained his ~ courtesy⟩ **syn** see USUAL

wont·ed·ly *adv* : CUSTOMARILY, USUALLY

wont·ed·ness *n* -ES : the condition of being habituated to a thing, person, or practice

wont·less \-tləs\ *adj, archaic* : UNACCUSTOMED, UNWONTED

won ton \'wän·'tän\ *n, pl* **won tons** [Chin (Cant) *wan t'an*] : filled pockets of noodle dough boiled in and eaten with soup

¹woo \'wü\ *vb* -ED/-ING/-S [ME *wowen*, fr. OE *wōgian;* perh. akin to L *vovēre* to vow — more at VOW] *vt* **1** : to solicit in love : sue for the affection of and usu. marriage with : COURT ⟨could ~ her and win her —Theodor Reik⟩ **2** : to solicit or entreat esp. with ingratiating importunity : beseech solicitously ⟨the young author trying to ~ his reader, via heavy humor —Frances Keene⟩ **3** : to seek to gain or bring about : act in such a way as to tend to bring about ⟨feels entitled to all the dollars it can ~ from the public —Jerome Ellison⟩ **4** : to tend to bring about unintentionally ⟨~*ing* defeat —Florence Converse⟩ ~ *vi* **1** : to court a woman : make love **2** : to make pleading solicitation or invitation

²woo \"\ *n* -s : LOVE — used esp. in the phrase *pitch woo*

³woo \"\ *vi* -ED/-ING/-S [origin unknown] : MAH-JONGG

¹wood \'wůd, 'wōd, 'wüd\ *adj* [ME *wod*, fr. OE *wōd* mad — more at VATIC] **1** *archaic* : INSANE, MAD **2** *archaic* : ENRAGED, VIOLENT

²wood \'wůd\ *n* -s [ME *wode, wude*, fr. OE *wudu, widu;* akin to OHG *witu* wood, ON *vithr* tree, wood, OIr *fid* tree] **1 a** (1) : a dense growth of trees usu. greater in extent than a grove and smaller than a forest ⟨out in the ~ —J. G.Frazer⟩ — often used in pl. but sing. or pl. in constr. ⟨would take our children into a nearby ~s —Herbert Gold⟩ (2) : growing trees found in natural groves ⟨gentle risings covered with ~ —Thomas Gray⟩ **b** : a tract of land on which stand growing trees : WOODLAND **c** *archaic* : FOREST 6a **2** : the hard fibrous substance that makes up the greater part of the stems and branches of trees or shrubs beneath the bark, is found to a limited extent in herbaceous plants, and consists technically of the aggregated xylem elements intersected in many plants with the rays **3 a** : the trunks or large branches of trees sawed or otherwise prepared for commercial use : TIMBER, LUMBER — see HARDWOOD, SOFTWOOD **b** : trees or branches cut or sawed for use in a fire : FIREWOOD **4** : a form or condition of wood substance or timber; *esp* : the wood of a particular kind of tree ⟨some ~s warp easily⟩ **5** : something made of wood: as **a** : a part (as a handle or shaft) made of wood **b** : a wooden cask or keg ⟨draft beer from the ~ —B.M.Brown⟩ **c** : BOWL 1b **d** : a golf club (as a driver, brassie, or spoon) having a wooden head — compare IRON **e** : pins in a bowling alley; *esp* : pins that have been knocked down **6** : the fundamental substance of a person's character ⟨of what ~ a minister is made —Benjamin Disraeli⟩ **7** : ALMOND BROWN **8** : a wood shot in golf — **out of the wood** *Brit* : out of the woods — **out of the woods** : escaped from a situation of perplexity, anxiety, peril, or difficulty : safe after hazard ⟨after rallying from the . . . attack, the patient believed he was *out of the woods* —S.H. Adams⟩

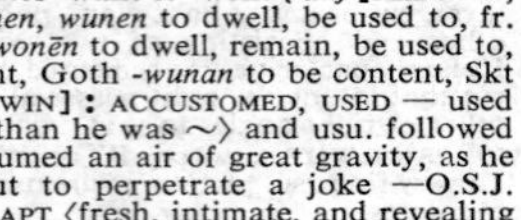

1 2 3 4

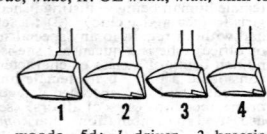

woods, 5d: *1* driver, *2* brassie, *3* spoon, 4 cleek

³wood \"\ *adj* **1** : made of wood : WOODEN **2** : suitable or used for or engaged in or in cutting or otherwise working with wood **3** *or* **woods** \-dz\ : living or growing in woods

⁴wood \"\ *vb* -ED/-ING/-S *vt* **1** : to supply or load with wood esp. for fuel ⟨~*ing* the stove —Jan Burroway⟩ **2** : to cover with a growth of trees : plant with trees **3** : to surround (the jack) with bowls in the game of bowls ~ *vi* : to gather or take on wood — often used with *up*

wood agate *n* : agate formed by petrifaction of wood

wood alcohol *n* : METHANOL — distinguished from *grain alcohol*

wood alloy *n* : a mixture of wood and other substances (as urea or resin) often in layers that have been subjected to heat and pressure producing density, hardness, and stability in excess of the wood itself — compare COMPREG

wood almond *n* : the oily edible seed of a West Indian woody vine (*Hippocratea comosa*); *also* : the plant itself

wood anemone *n* : any of several spring-flowering plants of the genus *Anemone* with tuberous roots, a single whorl of leaves, and solitary white flowers: as **a** : a common anemone (*A. quinquefolia*) of eastern No. America with solitary often pink-tinged white flowers **b** : a European anemone (*A. nemorosa*) that is common in deciduous woodlands

wood ant *n* **1 a** : a large widely distributed ant (*Formica rufa*) or a related American ant (*F. exsectoides*) that lives in woods and builds large nests **b** : CARPENTER ANT **2** : TERMITE

wood apple *n* **1** : a small tree (*Limoina acidissima* or *Feronia elephantum*) of the family Rutaceae of southeastern Asia that yields a hard heavy durable yellowish wood and is often cultivated for its acid hard-rinded fruit which is used as a food and together with the leaves in folk medicine **2** : the fruit of the wood apple

wood-apple *n* : a gum obtained from the wood apple and used like gum arabic

wood aster *n* : any of several asters of eastern No. America usu. growing in woods (esp. *Aster cordifolius, A. macrophyllus*, and *A. divaricatus*)

wood avens *n* : a European avens (*Geum urbanum*) with bright yellow flowers that is adventive in the northeastern U.S.

wood baboon *n* : ⁶DRILL

woodbark \'=,=\ *n* : a grayish yellowish brown that is stronger than deer, lighter and stronger than acorn, and lighter, stronger, and slightly yellower than olive wood — called also *blondine, sable*

wood bass *n* : GREEN SUNFISH

wood bedstraw *n* : a European perennial herb (*Galium sylvaticum*) with narrow leaves in groups of six or eight and open panicles of tiny white flowers that is naturalized in the eastern U. S. — called also *Scotch mist*

wood betony *n* **1** : a common betony (*Stachys betonica*) **2** : a lousewort (*Pedicularis canadensis*) of eastern No. America with pinnately parted leaves and irregular red or yellowish flowers in bracted spikes

woodbin \'=,=\ *n* : a bin for holding firewood

woodbine \'=,=\ *also* **woodbind** \'=,=\ *n* [ME *wodebinde*, fr. OE *wudubinde*, fr. *wudu* wood + *-binde* (fr. *bindan* to tie, bind); fr. its winding about trees — more at WOOD, BIND] **1** : any of several honeysuckles; *esp* : a European twining shrub (*Lonicera periclymenum*) **2** : VIRGINIA CREEPER **3** : YELLOW JESSAMINE **2** **4** : HEDGE BINDWEED 1

woodbine green *n* : a moderate yellow green to olive green that is yellower and stronger than art green — called also *peridot*

wood bison *n* **1** *also* **wood buffalo** : a bison that is a variety (*Bison bison athabascae*) of the American bison and is restricted to wooded regions of northern Alberta, Canada **2** : WOODLAND BISON

wood block *n* **1** : a solid block of wood usu. with plane faces **2** : WOODCUT **3** : BLOCK 1g

wood-block \'=,=\ *adj* [*wood block*] : made of, done with, or printed from wood blocks ⟨*wood-block* printing⟩ ⟨*wood-block* prints⟩

wood borer *n* **1** : a grub that is the wood-boring larva of any of numerous beetles (as a click beetle, longicorn beetle, buprestid, or weevil) — compare APPLE TREE BORER **2** : a borer (as the peach tree borer) that is the larva of any of various lepidopterous insects and esp. of a clearwing moth or a goat moth **3** : a borer that is the larva of a horntail (family Siricidae) **4** : any of several bivalve mollusks (as the teredos and members of the genus *Xylophaga*) that bore in wood **5** : any of several small crustaceans (as the gribble) that bore in wood

wood-boring \'=¦==\ *adj* : excavating galleries in wood in feeding or in constructing a nest ⟨*wood-boring* worms had eaten many of . . . the boxes —David Masters⟩

woodbound \'=¦=\ *adj* **1** : bound with wood **2 a** : having trees or hedges as obstructions to agriculture **b** : surrounded by woodland

woodbox \'=,=\ *n* : WOODBIN

wood brick *n* : wood of the size and shape of a brick inserted in brickwork to supply a hold for the attachment of finishings

wood brown *n* : ALMOND BROWN

wood bud *n* : a plant bud that produces a shoot or branch — compare FLOWER BUD

woodburning \'=,==\ *n* : the art or process of burning a design upon a usu. wood or leather surface esp. with an electrically heated tool

wood·bury·type \'wůd,berē,tīp, -,bər-\ *n* [Walter Bentley *Woodbury* †1885 Eng. photographer and inventor + E *type*] : a process in which a gelatin relief produced by photographic methods and hardened is powerfully pressed on a plate of soft metal to produce an intaglio impression that upon inking may be used to print pictures directly; *also* : a print thus made

wood-carver \'=,==\ *n* : a person whose occupation is wood carving

wood carving *n* : the art of fashioning or ornamenting objects of wood by cutting with a sharp implement held in the hand; *also* : an object of wood so fashioned or ornamented

wood charcoal *n* : charcoal prepared from wood : CARBO LIGNI

woodchat \'=,=\ *n* **1** : any of several Asiatic birds of the family Turdidae and the genus *Erithacus* the males of which are mostly bright blue marked with red or rufous beneath **2** *or* **woodchat shrike** : a European shrike (*Lanius senator*) whose males have the head and nape rufous red and the back, wings, and tail black varied with white

woodchopper \'=,==\ *n* : one engaged in chopping wood and esp. chopping down trees

¹wood·chuck \'wůd,chək\ *n* -s [by folk etymology fr. Ojibwa *otchig* fisher, marten, or Cree *otcheck*] **1** : a thickset marmot (*Marmota monax*) of the northeastern U.S. and Canada with a chiefly grizzled reddish brown color — called also *groundhog* **2** : any of various marmots of mountainous parts of western No. America that are related to the eastern woodchuck

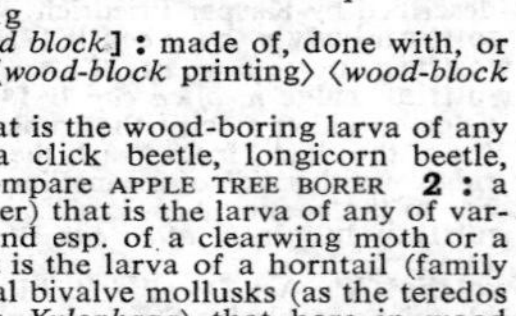

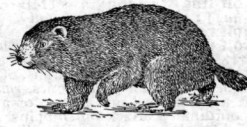

woodchuck 1

²woodchuck \"\ *n* -s [¹*wood* + *chuck* (to pat, jerk)] : RED-HEADED WOODPECKER

wood coal *n* **1** : CHARCOAL **2** : LIGNITE

woodcock \'=,=\ *n, pl* **woodcocks** *or* **woodcock** [ME *wodecok*, fr. OE *wuducocc*, fr. *wudu* wood + *cocc* cock — more at WOOD, COCK] **1 a** (1) : an Old World limicoline bird (*Scolopax rusticola*) that ranges from the British Isles to Japan, migrates south-

ward, and has large eyes, a long bill very sensitive at the tip used in probing the ground for earthworms, and a variously mottled black, chestnut, gray, and buff color (2) : a smaller related American bird (*Philohela minor*) that is distinguished by having the three outer primaries shortened and conspicuously narrowed instead of the first only as in the European woodcock, that frequents woodlands, and that is prized as a game bird **b :** PILEATED WOODPECKER **2** [so called fr. the ease with which the woodcock is taken in a snare] *archaic* **:** a gullible person **:** SIMPLETON **3** *or* **woodcock soil :** a soil consisting of clay and gravel **4** *or* **woodcock shell :** the shell of any of various mollusks of the genus *Murex* having a very long canal

woodcock snipe *n* **1** *Brit* **:** GREAT SNIPE **2 :** WOODCOCK 1a(2)

wood cooker *n* **:** VATMAN b

wood copper *n* **:** a fibrous olivenite

wood crab *n* **:** an amphibious crab (*Sesarma cinereum*) that resembles the related fiddler crabs and lives on or about wharves or sometimes in mangrove swamps along the Atlantic coast of tropical America

woodcraft \'⸗,⸗\ *n* **1 :** skill and practice in anything relating to the woods and esp. in maintaining oneself and making one's way, in hunting or trapping, or in tracking and studying wildlife **2 :** skill in shaping or constructing articles from wood

wood cree *n, usu cap W&C* [trans. of Cree *Sakawithiniwuk*, lit., people of the woods] **1 :** an Algonquian people formerly inhabiting the northeastern portion of the Cree territory — compare PLAINS CREE **2 :** a member of the Wood Cree people

woodcreeper \'⸗,⸗⸗\ *n* **:** WOODHEWER 1

woodcut \'⸗,⸗\ *n* **1 a :** the process or technique of cutting a design on wood usu. with the grain or sometimes on metal for use as a letterpress printing surface — compare WOOD ENGRAVING **b :** a print so produced **2 :** a letterpress printing surface consisting of a wooden block with a usu. pictorial design cut with the grain

woodcutter \'⸗,⸗⸗\ *n* **1 :** a person who cuts wood **2 :** one that produces woodcuts

[1]**woodcutting** \'⸗,⸗⸗\ *n* **1 :** WOODCUT **2 :** the action or occupation of cutting wood or timber

[2]**woodcutting** \'⸗¦⸗⸗\ *adj* **1 :** of or relating to woodcuts or making woodcuts **2 :** engaged in or designed or used for cutting wood ⟨a ~ circular saw⟩

wood dove *n* [ME *wode dowe*] **:** WOOD PIGEON; *esp* **:** STOCK DOVE

wood drake *n* **:** the male of the wood duck

wood duck *n* **1 :** a showy American duck (*Aix sponsa*) which nests in hollow trees and the male of which has a large crest and plumage varied with green, purple, black, white, and chestnut — called also *summer duck, wood widgeon* **2 :** HOODED MERGANSER **3 :** an Australian goose (*Chenonetta jubata*) having elongated deep brown feathers on the rear part of the neck

[1]**wooded** *past of* WOOD

[2]**wood·ed** \'wu̇dəd\ *adj* **:** covered with growing trees

wood·en \'wu̇dᵊn\ *adj, sometimes* -ER/-EST **1 a :** made or consisting wholly or sometimes partly of wood ⟨~ houses⟩ ⟨~ box⟩ **b** *obs* **:** engaged in or concerned with the preparation of wood **c :** resembling or producing a sound characteristic of a struck hollow wooden object ⟨the ~ sound of numskulls being soundly hit —Edith Sitwell⟩ **2 a :** resembling wood in stiffness and lack of resilience ⟨the hands are also . . . ~, not only hard, but lifeless —C.W.H.Johnson⟩ ⟨wooden-faced country people —William Faulkner⟩ ⟨a ~ military posture⟩ ⟨a ~ and inflexible policy —W.M.Dacey⟩ **b :** lacking in ease, grace, charm, liveliness, lifelikeness, interest, or zest **:** AWKWARD, CLUMSY, DRY, LIFELESS, DULL ⟨hear the ~ dialogue —Shak.⟩ ⟨cooperation . . . has frequently been reluctant and ~ —Woodrow Wyatt⟩ ⟨party debates are ~ and tedious formalities —Christopher Hollis⟩ ⟨a ~ and perfunctory pedagogue —John Dewey⟩ ⟨book is ~ and insensitive —George Nobbe⟩ **3 :** WOODED **syn** see STIFF

wooden brick *n* **:** WOOD BRICK

wood engraver *n* **1 :** an engraver on wood; *esp* **:** one that makes wood engravings **2 :** ENGRAVER BEETLE

wood engraving *n* **1 a :** the art or process of cutting a design upon wood and esp. upon the end grain of wood for use as a letterpress printing surface — compare WOODCUT 1a **b :** a wooden letterpress printing surface bearing a usu. pictorial design produced by wood engraving **2 :** a design printed from a wood engraving

woodenhead \'⸗⸗,⸗\ *n* **:** BLOCKHEAD

wooden–headed \¦⸗⸗¦⸗⸗\ *adj* **:** STUPID, DULL, UNINTELLIGENT

wooden horse *n* **1** *archaic* **:** SHIP **2 :** a ridged or studded wooden device which soldiers formerly were condemned to sit astride as a military punishment

wooden indian *n, usu cap I* **:** a standing wooden image of an American Indian brave used esp. formerly for advertising before a cigar store

wood·en·ly *adv* **:** in a wooden manner

wood·en·ness \-ᵊn(n)əs\ *n* -ES **:** the quality or state of being wooden

wooden nickel *n* **1 :** a wooden commemorative or souvenir token having the value of a five-cent piece **2** *or* **wooden nutmeg :** something utterly worthless accepted as a gift or purchased by a gullible person

wooden pear *n* **:** NATIVE PEAR

wooden shoe *n* **:** SABOT 1a

wooden spoon *n* **:** a spoon made of wood presented orig. at Cambridge University to the man ranking lowest among those taking honors in the mathematical tripos and at other colleges and universities to other selected recipients **2 :** the recipient of a wooden spoon

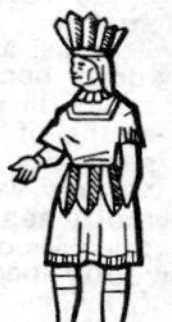

wooden Indian

wooden tongue *n* **:** actinobacillosis or actinomycosis of cattle esp. when chiefly affecting the tongue

wooden walls *n pl* [trans. of Gk *xylinon teichos*, sing.] **:** warships used as coastal defense

woodenware \'⸗⸗,⸗\ *n* **:** articles made of wood for table, kitchen, and other domestic use ⟨salad bowls and other ~⟩

wood·eny \'wu̇dᵊnē, -ᵊni\ *adj* [*wooden* + *-y*] **:** WOODEN

wood·er \'wu̇də(r)\ *n* -S **:** a person that cuts or gathers wood esp. for fuel

wood fern *n* **:** any of various ferns of the genus *Dryopteris*

wood fiber *n* **1 :** XYLEM FIBER **2 :** wood reduced to fine shreds

wood–fibered plaster \'⸗¦⸗⸗-\ *n* **:** a gypsum plaster containing shredded wood fiber to reduce the weight and to improve its sound-absorbing properties

wood filler *n* **:** a composition of silica and oil or varnish to fill the pores of open-grained wood (as oak) before varnishing

woodfish \'⸗,⸗\ *n* **:** SILVERFISH 2

wood float *n* **:** FLOAT 5a

wood flour *n* **:** finely powdered wood or sawdust used chiefly as an adsorbent in dynamite and as a filler in plastics and linoleum — called also *wood meal*

wood flower *n* **:** WOOD ROSE 1

wood fretter *n* **:** an animal that in the adult or larval stage bores in the wood or beneath the bark of trees **:** WOOD BORER

wood fringe *n* **:** CLIMBING FUMITORY

wood frog *n* **1 :** a common eastern No. American frog (*Rana sylvatica*) that lives chiefly in moist woods and woodland pools and is drab or yellowish brown with a black stripe on each side of the head **2 :** a brightly colored western No. American frog (*Rana aurora*) of similar habitats to the eastern wood frog

wood gas *n* **:** gas obtained by the destructive distillation of wood, composed chiefly of hydrogen, carbon monoxide, carbon dioxide, and methane, and used as a fuel and illuminant

wood·gate rust \'wu̇d,gāt-\ *n* [fr. *Woodgate*, Oneida County, N.Y.] **:** a disease of the Scotch pine caused by a rust fungus of the genus *Cronartium* that forms galls upon twigs and branches

wood gatherer *n, usu cap W&G* **:** the second of four ranks attained by camp fire girls — compare FIRE MAKER, TORCH BEARER, TRAIL SEEKER

woodgeld \'⸗,⸗\ *n* [ME *wodegeld*, fr. *wode* wood + *geld* tax, fr. OE *gield, geld* — more at GELD] **:** money paid in feudal times for the privilege of gathering or cutting wood in a forest; *also* **:** immunity from this payment granted by the king

wood grass *n* **1 :** an American perennial grass (*Sorghastrum nutans*) that is valued for hay and has long flat leaves and large plumelike panicles **2 :** KNOTROOT GRASS

wood groundsel *n* **:** a European annual herb (*Senecio sylvaticus*) that is widely naturalized as a weed in No. America and has pinnatifid leaves and small yellow flower heads in corymbs

wood grouse *n* **1** *Brit* **:** CAPERCAILLIE **2 :** SPRUCE GROUSE

woodgrub \'⸗,⸗\ *n* **:** a grub that is the larva of any of numerous wood-boring insects

wood gum *n* **:** XYLAN

wood hen *n* [ME *wodehen*, fr. *wode* wood + *hen*] **1 :** WOODCOCK 1a(2) **2 :** WEKA

woodhewer \'⸗,⸗⸗\ *n* **1 :** any of numerous So. and Central American birds (family Dendrocolaptidae) that have a curved bill and stiffened tail feathers and climb and feed like woodpeckers — called also *tree creeper* **2 :** WOODPECKER

wood hoopoe *n* **:** a bird of the genus *Phoeniculus*

woodhorse \'⸗,⸗\ *n* **:** WALKING STICK 2

wood horsetail *n* **:** a common herb (*Equisetum sylvaticum*) of the north temperate zone with drooping whorls of usu. forked branches

wood·house·ite \'wu̇d,hau̇,sīt\ *n* -S [Charles D. *Woodhouse* b1888 Am. mineralogist + E *-ite*] **:** a mineral $CaAl_3(PO_4)(SO_4)(OH)_6$ of the beudantite group consisting of a basic sulfate and phosphate of aluminum and calcium isomorphous with svanbergite, hinsdalite, corkite, and beudantite

wood hyacinth *n* **:** a European squill (*Scilla nonscripta*) having a scape bearing a raceme of drooping blue, purple, white, or sometimes pink bell-shaped flowers — called also *harebell*

wood ibis *n* **1 :** a large wading bird (*Mycteria americana*) of the family Ciconiidae that frequents wooded swamps of So. and Central America and the southern U. S., has the bill heavy at the base and the head and upper neck naked in the adult, and is white with tail and primaries black **2 :** any of various Old World birds of the genus *Ibis* — called also *wood stork*

woodier *comparative of* WOODY

woodies *pl of* WOODY

woodiest *superlative of* WOODY

wood·i·ness \'wu̇dēnəs, -din-\ *n* -ES **1 :** the quality, state, or condition of being woody **2 :** a virus disease of passion fruit esp. troublesome in Australia and characterized by woody tissue in the fruit and gradual decline of the vines

[1]**wooding** *pres part of* WOOD

[2]**wood·ing** \'wu̇diŋ, -dən\ *n* [[1]*wood* + *-ing*] *Scot* **:** GROVE, WOOD

wood jack *n* **:** a pucellas having prongs tipped with wood

woodkern \'⸗,⸗\ *n* [[1]*wood* + *kern* (soldier)] **:** an Irish robber or outlaw frequenting a forest

woodknife \'⸗,⸗\ *n* [ME *wodeknif*, fr. *wode* wood + *knif* knife] *archaic* **:** DIRK, DAGGER

[1]**wood·land** \'⸗lənd, -,land, -,laa(ə)nd\ *n* [ME *wodeland*, fr. OE *wudulond*, fr. *wudu* wood + *lond* land — more at WOOD, LAND] **1 a :** land covered with woody vegetation **:** TIMBERLAND, FOREST **b :** a plot of wooded land managed or used in conjunction with a farm **:** WOODLOT **2** *or* **woodland green :** a moderate olive green that is greener and darker than holly green (sense 2) and greener and slightly deeper than Lincoln green

[2]**woodland** \"\ *adj* [ME *wodeland*, fr. *wodeland*, n.] **1 a :** of, relating to, or occurring in woodland ⟨a shady ~ path⟩ ⟨~ streams⟩ **b :** growing or living in woodland ⟨~ herbs⟩ ⟨~ birds⟩ **c :** constituting or made up of woodland ⟨large ~ areas⟩ **2** *usu cap* **:** of or belonging to a cultural pattern extending over midwestern, eastern, and northeastern U. S. and Canada beginning about 500 B.C. and in some areas extending into historic times characterized by flexed burials, side-notched and stemmed projectile points made from cores, grooved axes, and a usu. grit-tempered pottery in globular forms with conical or truncated base and no handles

woodland bison *n* **:** a bison that is an eastern variety (*Bison bison pennsylvanicus*) of the American bison and is prob. extinct as a pure race

woodland brown *n* **:** a dark grayish brown that is slightly yellower than average chocolate brown and slightly yellower and less strong than African brown

woodland caribou *n* **:** any of several rather large caribou of wooded regions including one formerly abundant in much of the northern U. S. but now nearly exterminated

wood·land·er \'wu̇dləndə(r)\ *n* -S **:** an inhabitant of woodland

woodland rose *n* **:** MUSCADE

woodland star *n* **:** a plant of the genus *Lithophragma* of the family Saxifragaceae; *esp* **:** a California perennial herb (*L. affinis*) cultivated for its racemose white flowers

wood lark *n* [ME *wodelarke*, fr. *wode* wood + *larke* lark] **:** a small European lark (*Lullula arborea*) that utters its notes while on the wing

wood laurel *n* **1 :** SPURGE LAUREL 1 **2 :** MOUNTAIN LAUREL 1

wood·less \'wu̇dləs\ *adj* **:** having no wood; *esp* **:** TREELESS

wood lily *n* [ME *wode lilie*] **1 a :** LILY OF THE VALLEY **b :** a red-flowered lily (*Lilium philadelphicum*) of the eastern U. S. — called also *red lily* **c :** a plant of the genus *Trillium* **2 :** a wintergreen (*Pyrola minor*) **3 :** an Australian orchid (*Dendrobium speciosum*) with creamy fragrant flowers

wood lock *n* **:** a piece of wood fitted between a gudgeon and a pintle to keep a rudder from rising

woodlot \'⸗,⸗\ *n* **:** a relatively restricted area devoted to the growing of forest trees ⟨a farm ~⟩

wood louse *n* **1 :** a terrestrial isopod crustacean (suborder Oniscoidea) that has a flattened elliptical body often capable of being rolled into a ball and seven pairs of walking legs, is commonly dull brown or gray, usu. lives under stones or bark, and may damage the roots of young trees — called also *pill bug, slater, sow bug;* compare SEA LOUSE **2 :** any of several small wingless insects of the order Corrodentia that live under bark, in the crevices of walls, and among old books and papers — compare BOOK LOUSE, DEATHWATCH **3 :** TERMITE

wood·man \'wu̇dmən\ *n, pl* **woodmen** [ME *wodeman*, fr. *wode* wood + *man*] **1 a :** WOODSMAN **b :** one who cuts wood esp. for fuel **2** [fr. Modern *Woodmen* of America, society founded at Lyons, Iowa in 1883 and *Woodmen* of the World, society founded at Omaha, Nebraska in 1890] **:** a member of either of two independent fraternal and beneficiary societies

wood meadow grass *n* **:** a slender European grass of shady places (*Poa nemoralis*) of some agricultural value

wood meal *n* **:** WOOD FLOUR

wood mint *n* **:** either of two No. American herbs of the genus *Blephilia* (*B. hirsuta* and *B. celiata*)

wood mite *n* **:** any of numerous mites (family Oribatidae) that are free-living usu. in moss or under stones in wooded or shady areas

woodmonger \'⸗,⸗⸗\ *n* [ME *wodemonger*, fr. *wode* wood + *monger*] **:** a dealer in wood

wood·mote \'wu̇d,mōt\ *n* -S [[1]*wood* + *-mote* (as in *gemote*)] **:** a former minor English forest court with cognizance of trespasses in a forest

wood moth *n* **:** a moth with a larva that bores in wood: as **a :** any of various moths of the family Cossidae **b :** any of various dull heavy-bodied moths of the family Zeuzeridae; *esp* **:** an Australian moth (*Xyleutes boisduvali*) with narrow brownish wings heavily covered with gray scales and having a span of up to 10 inches in the larger female, a large cylindrical abdomen, and a 6 to 7 inch larva that bores in various eucalypts and is considered a delicacy by the aborigines

wood mouse *n* **:** a mouse inhabiting wooded regions: as **a :** a European mouse (*Apodemus sylvaticus*) **b :** any of various American white-footed mice (*Peromyscus*) **c :** RED-BACKED MOUSE

wood·ness *n* -ES [ME *wodnesse, wodnes*, fr. OE *wōdnes*, fr. *wōd* mad + *-nes* -ness — more at VATIC] **1** *archaic* **:** INSANITY, MADNESS **2** *archaic* **:** RAGE, FURY

wood nettle *n* **:** an American perennial herb (*Laportea canadensis*) found in rich woods and provided with stinging hairs

woodnote \'⸗,⸗\ *n* **:** a sound or call (as of a bird) natural in a wood

wood nymph *n* **1 :** a nymph living in woods — called also *dryad* **2 a :** any of several showy moths of the genus *Euthisanotia* with bright-colored larvae some of which (as *E. grata* and *E. unio*) feed on leaves of the grapevine **b :** GRAYLING **c :** any of several So. American hummingbirds of the genus *Thalurania* the males of which are bright blue or green and blue **d :** SATYR 3

wood oil *n* **1 :** any of various oils derived from wood: as **a :** GURJUN BALSAM **b :** an oil (as pine oil) obtained by the destructive distillation of wood **2 :** TUNG OIL

wood–oil tree *n* **:** TUNG TREE

wood–oil–tree family *n* **:** DIPTEROCARPACEAE

wood opal *n* **:** wood petrified with opal

wood owl *n* **1 :** an owl living in trees; *esp* **:** an owl of the genus *Strix* (as the European tawny owl and American barred owl) **2** *Brit* **:** LONG-EARED OWL

wood paper *n* **:** paper made from wood pulp

wood parenchyma *n* **:** the vertical and usu. axially arranged parenchyma of the xylem that is believed to function chiefly in carbohydrate storage — compare PHLOEM PARENCHYMA, RAY PARENCHYMA

wood partridge *n* **1 :** any of several small partridges of Java, Sumatra, Borneo, and neighboring regions belonging to the genera *Caloperdix, Rollulus*, and *Melanoperdix* **2 :** SPRUCE GROUSE

wood pea *n* **:** FLAT PEA 1

woodpecker \'⸗,⸗⸗\ *n* **:** any of numerous birds of the family Picidae that have zygodactyl feet, stiff spiny tail feathers used in climbing or resting on tree trunks, a usu. extensile tongue, a very hard bill used to drill the bark or wood of trees for insect food or to excavate nesting cavities, and generally parti-colored usu. strongly contrasted black, white, brown, green, yellow, orange, and red plumage in varying proportions — see CALIFORNIA WOODPECKER, DOWNY WOODPECKER, FLICKER, GREAT SPOTTED WOODPECKER, GREEN WOODPECKER, HAIRY WOODPECKER, IMPERIAL WOODPECKER, IVORY-BILLED WOODPECKER, PICULET, PILEATED WOODPECKER, REDHEADED WOODPECKER SAPSUCKER, THREE-TOED WOODPECKER, WRYNECK

wood pewee *n* **:** a small tyrant flycatcher (*Contopus virens*) of eastern No. America that is dark olive-gray on the back, grayish olive on the breast and sides, and yellowish white on the belly and that has a very plaintive note resembling the syllables *pee-a-wee; also* **:** a related bird (*C. sordidulus*) that inhabits western No. America

wood pigeon *n* **1 :** RINGDOVE 1; *also* **:** any of various related Asiatic pigeons **2 :** BAND-TAILED PIGEON **3 :** a large purple and white pigeon (*Hemiphaga novaeseelandiae*) of New Zealand **4 :** STOCK DOVE

woodpile \'⸗,⸗\ *n* **:** a pile of wood (as firewood)

wood pimpernel *n* **:** a European loosestrife (*Lysimachia nemorum*) with nearly prostrate stems and yellow flowers

wood pink *n* **:** a caespitose European herb (*Dianthus sylvestris*) that is used as an ornamental and has odorless purple flowers

wood pocket *n* **:** a virus disease of citrus and esp. lemons characterized by breaks or defects on the bark beneath which the wood is discolored

wood poppy *n* **:** CELANDINE POPPY

woodprint \'⸗,⸗\ *n* **:** WOODCUT

wood pulp *n* **:** pulp from softwood or hardwood that is made either mechanically or by a chemical process and that is used in making paper, rayon, and other cellulose derivatives — compare GROUNDWOOD, SODA PULP, SULFATE PROCESS, SULFITE PULP

wood pussy *n* **:** SKUNK

wood quail *n* **1 :** WOOD PARTRIDGE 1 **2 :** any of numerous heavy-billed forest-dwelling tropical American birds of the genus *Odontophorus* resembling partridges

wood–queest \'⸗,⸗\ *or* **wood–quest** \'⸗,kwest\ *n, dial Eng* **:** RINGDOVE

wood rabbit *n* **:** COTTONTAIL

woodrack car \'⸗,⸗-\ *n* **:** a flat car with attached ends and sometimes sides for hauling wood and usu. pulpwood loaded transversely

wood rail *n* **:** a forest-dwelling rail; *esp* **:** a member of the tropical American genus *Aramides*

woodranger \'⸗,⸗⸗\ *n* **:** RANGER 4a

wood rat *n* **:** any of numerous native voles of *Neotoma* and related genera (family Cricetidae) of the southern U. S. and western No. America having soft fur light gray to ocherous above and white below, well-furred tails, and large ears — compare PACK RAT

wood ray *n* **:** XYLEM RAY

woodreed \'⸗,⸗\ *n* **1 :** any of several tall perennial grasses (genus *Cinna*) chiefly of moist woodlands — compare INDIAN REED **2 :** BUSHGRASS

woodreeve \'⸗,⸗\ *n, Brit* **:** an overseer of a forest

wood robin *n* **1 :** any of several muscicapine New Zealand birds of the genus *Petroica* that are grayish black and white or pure white and are good songsters **2 :** WOOD THRUSH 1

wood rose *n* **1 a :** the corrugated often flowerlike woody scar left upon the host when a mistletoe is wrenched from its support — called also *wood flower* **b :** a shrub rose (*Rosa gymnocarpa*) of the California coastal area having long straight prickles, red flowers, and pear-shaped or globose fruit with deciduous calyx lobes **2 :** a light grayish brown to reddish brown that is darker and slightly less strong than sandstone — called also *sorghum brown*

wood rosin *n* **:** rosin obtained from the stumps or other dead wood of pine trees (as longleaf pine) by solvent extraction along with the volatile turpentine or after removal of the turpentine by steam distillation

wood·ruff \'wu̇(,)drəf\ *n* -S [ME *woderofe, woderove*, fr. OE *wudurofe*, fr. *wudu* wood + *-rofe* (perh. akin to ON *rōfa* hard part of a tail, MLG *röve* turnip) — more at WOOD, RAPE (herb)] **:** a plant of the genus *Asperula*: as **a :** SWEET WOODRUFF **b :** DYER'S WOODRUFF

woodruff key *n, usu cap W* [prob. fr. the name *Woodruff*] **:** a shaft key made in the form of a segment of a disk and used with shafts not more than 2½ inches in diameter

wood rush *n* **:** a plant of the genus *Luzula* (as *L. campestris*) growing chiefly in woodlands and having the leaf sheaths open and the capsule few-seeded

[1]**woods** *pl of* WOOD, *pres 3d sing of* WOOD

[2]**woods** *var of* WOOD

wood sage *n* **1 :** a European germander (*Teucrium scorodonia*) with one-sided racemes of yellow flowers that is naturalized in No. America **2 :** AMERICAN GERMANDER

wood's alloy *or* **wood's metal** *n, usu cap W* [after B. *Wood*, 20th cent. Am. metallurgist] **:** a fusible alloy containing about 50 percent bismuth with lead, tin, and cadmium that melts at about 160° F

wood sandpiper *n* **:** an Old World shorebird (*Tringa glareola*) related to the green sandpiper and the American solitary sandpiper

woods colt *n* **1 :** a horse that is the offspring of a chance mating **2 :** BASTARD

wood screw *n* **:** a pointed metal screw formed with a sharp thread of comparatively coarse pitch for insertion in wood

woodsere \'⸗,⸗\ *n* -S [[1]*wood* + *sere*, adj.] **:** CUCKOO SPIT 1

wood shamrock *n* **:** a wood sorrel (*Oxalis montana*)

[1]**woodshed** \'⸗,⸗\ *n* **:** a shed for storing wood and esp. firewood

[2]**woodshed** \"\ *vi* **woodshedded; woodshedded; woodshedding; woodsheds** [fr. E slang *woodshed*, n., an arduous rehearsal esp. for a radio program, fr. E [1]*woodshed;* fr. woodsheds being formerly used in administering sound parental thrashings] **:** to practice on a musical instrument

wood sheldrake *n* **:** HOODED MERGANSER

woodshop \'⸗,⸗\ *n* **:** a shop in which woodworking is carried on

wood shot *n* **1 :** a golf shot played with a wood **2 :** a shot in a racket game in which the ball or shuttlecock is stroked with any of the wooden parts of the racket rather than the strings

wood shrike *n* **:** either of two tropical Asiatic birds (genus *Tephrodornis*) related to the minivets but superficially resembling shrikes in the shape of the bill and their gray, black, and white plumage

wood·sia \'wu̇dzēə\ *n, cap* [NL, fr. Joseph Woods †1864 Eng. botanist + NL *-ia*] **:** a genus of small or medium-sized rock-inhabiting ferns (family Polypodiaceae) of temperate or cold regions having pinnate or bipinnate fronds, round sori, and wholly inferior roundish or stellate indusia

woodside \'⸗,⸗\ *n* [ME *wod side, wode side*] **:** the margin of or country bordering on a wood

woodskin \'⸗,⸗\ *n* [*wood* + *skin*] **:** bark from which canoes are made; *also* **:** a canoe made of bark ⟨~s of the Indians had passed up and down and left no trace —William Beebe⟩

wood slave *n* **:** a small gecko (*Sphaerodactylus argus* or a related species) of Jamaica

wood's light \'wu̇dz-\ *n, usu cap W* [after Robert W. *Wood*

†1955 Am. physicist] **:** ultraviolet obtained from a suitable source (as an arc) by means of a special filter and used to reveal the presence of fluorescent minerals, to detect counterfeit currency and forgeries of documents or paintings, and in the diagnosis of various forms of tinea

woods·man \ˈwu̇dzmən\ *n, pl* **woodsmen** [*woods* (gen. of *wood*) + *man*] **1 :** one who lives in or frequents a forest **:** an expert in the arts and skills of living or travelling in the woods **2 :** one who works in the woods; *specif* **:** a foreman in charge of the felling of trees and removal of logs

woodsmoke \ˈ=,=\ *n* **:** smoke produced by burning wood

wood snail *n* **:** a European edible snail (*Helix nemoralis*)

wood snipe *n* **:** WOODCOCK 1a(2)

wood sorrel *n* **1 a :** a plant of the genus *Oxalis; esp* **:** a white-flowered to reddish flowered stemless herb (*O. montana*) with trifoliate leaves that is sometimes considered to be the original shamrock **b :** any of several yellow-flowered plants of the related genus *Xanthoxalis* **2 :** SHEEP SORREL 1 **3 :** a West Indian begonia (*Begonia acutifolia*)

wood-sorrel family *n* **:** OXALIDACEAE

woods phlox *n* **:** SOAPWORT 1

wood spirit *n* **:** METHANOL; *esp* **:** crude methanol obtained as a distillate from wood — sometimes used in pl.

wood·spite \ˈ=,spīt\ *n* -s [alter. of earlier *wood-speight, woodspecht,* fr. ¹*wood* + *speight, specht* green woodpecker, fr. ME *specht,* prob. fr. MD, woodpecker; akin to OHG *speh, speht* woodpecker — more at PIE] **:** GREEN WOODPECKER

wood spurge *n* **1 :** a European spurge (*Euphorbia amygdaloides*) with greenish yellow terminal flower clusters **2 :** a No. American spurge (*Euphorbia commutata*) resembling the European wood spurge

woods run *n* **:** the average run of logs of all sizes and grades as they come from the forest

wood star *n* **:** any of several small chiefly So. American hummingbirds (as of the genera *Chaetocercus* and *Acestrura*)

woodstone \ˈ=,=\ *n* **:** petrified wood

wood stork *n* **:** WOOD IBIS; *esp* **:** an Old World wood ibis

wood strawberry *n* **:** any of several wild strawberries; *esp* **:** a European herb (*Fragaria vesca*)

wood sugar *n* **1 :** xylose obtained from plant sources **2 :** a mixture of pentose and hexose sugars obtained by the hydrolysis of pentosans and cellulose of wood

wood swallow *n* **:** any of several Australasian and Asiatic passerine birds (as of the genus *Artamus*) related to the shrikes but resembling swallows — called also *swallow shrike*

¹**woodsy** \ˈwu̇dzē, -zi\ *adj* -ER/-EST [*woods* + *-y,* adj. suffix] **:** of, relating to, characteristic of, suggestive of, or of the nature of woods ⟨look for trillium and violets in ~, shady spots —*Girl Scout Handbk.*⟩ ⟨pine walled and smelling fresh and ~ —Adria Langley⟩

²**woodsy** \"\ *n* -ES [*woods* + *-y,* n. suffix] **:** BACKWOODSMAN 1

wood tar *n* **:** tar obtained by the destructive distillation of wood either as a deposit from pyroligneous acid or as a residue from the distillation of the acid or of wood turpentine and used in the crude state as fuel or for preserving rope and wood and for caulking or fractionated to yield creosote, oils, and pitch — compare PINE TAR

wood-tar creosote *n* **:** CREOSOTE 1

wood-tar pitch *n* **:** PITCH 1b

wood thrush *n* **1 :** a large thrush (*Hylocichla mustelina*) of eastern No. America that is rusty brown on the head and back becoming olivaceous on the rump and tail, has the under parts white marked with large tear-shaped spots, frequents woods and thickets, and is noted for its loud clear song **2 :** MISTLE THRUSH **3 :** SONG THRUSH 1

wood tick *n* **:** any of several ixodid ticks whose young cling to bushes but fasten on the body of an animal touching them often producing troublesome sores; *esp* **:** AMERICAN DOG TICK

wood tin *n* **:** cassiterite occurring in fibrous form

wood tortoise *or* **wood terrapin** *or* **wood turtle** *n* **:** a common No. American tortoise (*Clemmys insculpta*) the shell of which is marked with strong grooves and ridges like sculptured figures

woodturner \ˈ=,==\ *n* **:** one whose occupation is wood turning

wood turning *n* **:** the art or process of fashioning wooden pieces or blocks into various forms and shapes by means of a lathe

wood turpentine *n* **:** turpentine oil obtained from pine and other resinous woods by steam distillation, destructive distillation, or extraction with solvents; *esp* **:** TURPENTINE 2b

wood-vamp \ˈ=,=\ *n* **:** DECUMARY

wood vetch *also* **wood vetchling** *n* **1 :** a European vetch (*Vicia sylvatica*) sometimes planted for forage **2 :** a slender perennial vetch (*Vicia caroliniana*) growing chiefly in rich open woodland in eastern and central No. America

wood vinegar *n* **1 :** PYROLIGNEOUS ACID **2 :** imitation vinegar consisting essentially of dilute acetic acid colored with caramel

wood violet *n* **1 a :** HEDGE VIOLET **b :** BIRD'S-FOOT VIOLET **2 :** a deep purple that is bluer and stronger than hyacinth violet, bluer and deeper than petunia violet, and bluer, lighter, and stronger than imperial purple (sense 2)

wood·wall *or* **wood·wale** \ˈwu̇,d(w)ȯl, -,dwal, -,dᵊl\ *n* -s [ME *wodewale* golden oriole, fr. or akin to MD *wedewale;* akin to MHG *witewal* golden oriole — more at WITWALL] *Brit* **:** GREEN WOODPECKER

wood want *n* **:** a thinness or wane on the edge of a barrel stave

wood warbler *n* **1 :** an American warbler esp. of the genus *Dendroica* — compare BAY-BREASTED WARBLER, BLACK-POLL WARBLER, BLACK-THROATED GREEN WARBLER, CAPE MAY WARBLER, CHESTNUT-SIDED WARBLER, MYRTLE WARBLER, PINE WARBLER, PRAIRIE WARBLER, YELLOW WARBLER **2 :** a European warbler (*Phylloscopus sibilatrix*)

¹**wood·ward** \ˈwu̇,dwȯrd\ *n* -s [ME *wodeward,* fr. OE *wuduweard,* fr. *wudu* wood + *weard* ward] **:** an English forest officer charged with guarding a wood

²**wood·ward** \-dwə(r)d\ *adv* [¹*wood* + *-ward*] **:** toward a wood

wood·war·dia \wu̇ˈdwärdēə\ *n, cap* [NL, fr. Thomas J. *Woodward* †1820 Eng. botanist + NL *-ia*] **:** a genus of chain ferns (family Polypodiaceae) having linear lanceolate pinnae and sori in rows

wood·ward·ite \ˈwu̇dwə(r),dīt\ *n* [Samuel P. *Woodward* †1865 Eng. naturalist + E *-ite*] **:** a mineral $Cu_4Al_2(SO_4)(OH)_{12}.2\text{–}4H_2O$ consisting of a hydrous basic sulfate of copper and aluminum found in greenish blue to turquoise-blue botryoidal concretions orig. in Cornwall

woodware \ˈ=,=\ *n* **:** WOODENWARE

wood wasp *n* **1 :** HORNTAIL **2 :** a European wasp (*Vespa sylvestris*) that builds its nest in trees **3 :** any of various solitary wasps that excavate galleries in decaying wood

wood·wax·en \ˈwu̇,dwaksən\ *also* **woodwax** \ˈ=,=\ *n, pl* **woodwaxens** *also* **woodwaxes** [ME *wodewexen,* alter. of OE *wuduweaxe,* fr. *wudu* wood + *-weaxe* (prob. fr. *weaxan* to grow) — more at WOOD, WAX] **:** a yellow-flowered Eurasian shrub (*Genista tinctoria*) common as a weed in England, adventive in No. America, and sometimes cultivated for ornament — called also *dyer's-broom, dyeweed, greenweed, greenwood, whin, woadwaxen*

wood widgeon *n* **:** WOOD DUCK 1

¹**wood·wind** \ˈwu̇,dwind\ *or* **woodwind instrument** *n* **1 :** one of a group of orchestral or band wind instruments comprised of flutes, clarinets, oboes, bassoons, and sometimes saxophones **2 :** the woodwind section of a band or orchestra

²**woodwind** \"\ *adj* **:** of, relating to, or resembling a woodwind instrument, a performer on a woodwind instrument, or the music performed on woodwinds ⟨~ quintet⟩

wood-wool \ˈ=,=\ *n* **:** fine wood shavings or prepared wood fibers used for surgical dressings, as a substitute for hair and plaster, and as a packing and insulating material

woodwork \ˈ=,=\ *n* **1 :** work made of wood ⟨war called for an immense production of all kinds of ~ — furniture for barracks and huts, ammunition cases, vehicles, rifle-stocks —Gordon Russell⟩; *esp* **:** interior fittings (as moldings or stairways) of wood ⟨richly carved ~ with fruits and garlands frames the fireplace —H.S.Morrison⟩ — compare MILLWORK **2 :** work (as carpentry or joinery) done in or with wood

woodworker \ˈ=,==\ *n* **1 a :** a person who works in wood (as a carpenter, joiner, or cabinetmaker) **b :** MILLMAN 2 **c :** a worker who makes wooden tools, forms, templates, dies, and other items used in the construction of aircraft parts **2 :** a woodworking machine for various kinds of work consisting of a planer and circular saw and having attachments for dadoing, routing, boring, mortising, and other operations

¹**woodworking** \ˈ=,==\ *adj* **:** of, relating to, engaged in, or used for working or shaping things of wood

²**woodworking** \"\ *n* **:** the act, process, or occupation of working with wood **:** CARPENTRY, JOINERY, TURNERY

woodworm \ˈ=,=\ *n* **:** a worm that is the larva of a wood borer

wood wren *n* **1 :** WOOD WARBLER **2 :** WILLOW WARBLER

woodwright \ˈ=,=\ *n* **:** WOODWORKER

¹**woody** \ˈwu̇dē, -di\ *adj* -ER/-EST [ME *woddy, wody,* fr. *wode* wood + *-y*] **1 a :** abounding or overgrown with woods ⟨~ land⟩ **b** *obs* **:** of or relating to woods **:** SYLVAN **2 a :** of or containing wood or wood fibers **:** consisting mainly of hard lignified tissues ⟨a perennial herb with a ~ crown⟩ **b :** having woody parts ⟨a ~ perennial⟩ **3 :** characteristic of or resembling wood ⟨a ~ taste⟩

²**woody** \ˈwədi, ˈwüdi\ *n* -ES *Scot* **:** WITHY 2

woodyard \ˈ=,=\ *n* **:** a yard for storing or sawing wood

woody aster *n* **:** a woody herb (*Aster xylorrhiza*) of the western U.S. that is very poisonous to sheep

woody fiber *n* **1 :** XYLEM **2 :** a wood fiber

woody nightshade *n* **:** BITTERSWEET 2a

woody pear *n* **:** NATIVE PEAR

woody tongue *n* **:** WOODEN TONGUE

wooed *past of* WOO

woo·er \ˈwüə(r), ˈwu̇(ə)r, ˈwu̇ə\ *n* -s [ME *wowere,* fr. OE *wōgere,* fr. *wōgian* to woo + *-ere* -er — more at WOO] **:** one that woos **:** SUITOR, COURTER, LOVER

¹**woof** \ˈwu̇f, ˈwüf\ *n* -s [alter. (influenced by *weave* and *warp*) of earlier *ofe,* fr. ME *oof,* fr. OE *ōwef,* fr. *ō-* (fr. *on*) + *wefan* to weave — more at WEAVE] **1 a :** a filling thread or yarn in weaving **:** WEFT **b :** thread for or as if for the woof **c :** woven fabric; *also* **:** the texture of such a fabric **2 :** a basic or essential element or material ⟨the ~ of his chorus . . . is an infectious Negro song —Lazare Saminsky⟩ ⟨the warp is twelve fugues and the ~ twelve interludes —*Saturday Rev.*⟩

²**woof** \"\ *vt* -ED/-ING/-S **:** to weave in the manner of a woof crossing a warp

³**woof** \ˈwu̇f\ *n* -s [imit.] **1 :** a low gruff sound typically produced by a dog as a suppressed bark **2 :** a low note emitted by sound reproducing equipment — contrasted with *tweet*

⁴**woof** \"\ *vi* -ED/-ING/-S **:** to make the sound of a woof ⟨the bull . . . ~*ed* through wide nostrils —Ernest Hemingway⟩

woof·er \ˈwu̇fə(r)\ *n* -s **:** a loudspeaker that is usu. larger than a tweeter, is responsive only to the lower acoustic frequencies, and is used for reproducing sounds of low pitch

wooing *pres part of* WOO

woo·ing·ly *adv* **:** ATTRACTIVELY, ALLURINGLY

¹**wool** \ˈwu̇l\ *n* -s *often attrib* [ME *wolle, wulle,* fr. OE *wull;* akin to OHG *wolla* wool, ON *ull,* Goth *wulla* wool, L *vellus* fleece, *lana* wool, *lanugo* down, Gk *lēnos* wool, Skt *ūrṇā*] **1 :** the soft wavy or curly hypertrophied undercoat of various hairy mammals made up of fibers consisting of linear aggregates of keratin molecules within a matrix that are distinguished from typical hairs by their covering of minute projecting scales to which the felting property of the fiber is due, saturated in its natural state with fatty and other materials (as suint, yolk), and esp. developed by selective breeding in the domesticated sheep where it more or less completely replaces the primitive double coat — see BLOOD 7, FLEECE 1a, 1b, SPINNING COUNT **2 a** (1) **:** a textile fiber produced from raw wool that is characterized by absorbency, insulation, resiliency, a tendency to shrink in hot water, and ability to take and hold dyes well and that may be spun into woolen or worsted yarn or used for felt, flock, or stuffing (2) **:** textile fiber from the fleece of the sheep or lamb or from the hair of the Angora or Kashmir goat, camel, alpaca, llama, or vicuna used for the first time in the making of a finished product — used as a label on products; called also *virgin wool;* compare REPROCESSED, REUSED **b :** a yarn spun from such wool for weaving, knitting, or crocheting **c :** a product of wool; *esp* **:** a woven fabric or garment of such fabric **3 :** something resembling or suggesting wool in texture or appearance **:** a flocculent substance or mass: as **a :** a dense felted pubescence on the surface of plants **:** TOMENTUM **b :** a material formed (as by shredding or melting and blowing) into a filamentous mass — usu. used in combination; see LEAD WOOL, MINERAL WOOL, STEEL WOOL **c :** short thick often crisp curly hair on a human head **d :** the thick furry or hairy coat of some insects (as hairy caterpillars) **e :** the flocculent waxy secretion of some scales **4 :** something that conceals the truth or impedes understanding ⟨the cozy generalizations . . . were part of the same ~ of self-deception —Norman Cousins⟩ — usu. used in the phrase *pull the wool over one's eyes* ⟨taken for several hundred dollars by a sharper who pulled the ~ over his eyes⟩ **5 :** WOOL SPONGE — **all wool and a yard wide :** marked by superior quality, genuineness, or ingenuousness — **in one's wool :** persistently annoying **:** in one's hair — **in the wool** *Austral, of a sheep* **:** ready for shearing

²**wool** \"\ *vt* -ED/-ING/-S **1 :** to pull or tousle the hair of **2 :** to treat roughly **:** rough up **:** tussle with **:** BEAT

woolball \ˈ=,=\ *n* **:** a hairball of a sheep

wool-blind \ˈ=,=\ *adj, of a sheep* **:** having wool that is grown over the eyes and interferes with vision

wool blindness *n* **:** impaired vision in woolly-faced sheep due to wool covering the eyes

wool card *n* **:** a machine with bent wire teeth for carding wool — **wool carder** *n* — **wool carding** *n*

wool classer *n, Austral* **:** WOOL GRADER

wool classing *n, Austral* **:** WOOL GRADING

wool clip *n* **:** the annual crop of wool ⟨the Australian *wool clip*⟩

wool comb *n* **:** a machine for laying wool fibers in parallel relationship and dropping out fibers shorter than a predetermined length

wool comber *n* **:** one that combs wool

woold \ˈwüld\ *vt* -ED/-ING/-S [obs. D *woelde,* past part. (taken as verb) of *woelen* to woold, fr. MD, to toss, twist, woold; akin to OHG *wuolen* to stir up, rumple — more at WEEL] **:** to wind or wrap a rope or chain round (as a mast or yard sprung or made of two or more pieces) at a fish or scarf for strengthening

woold·er \-də(r)\ *n* -s [alter. (influenced by *woold*) of earlier *woller,* prob. fr. obs. D *woelen* to woold + E *-er*] **1 :** a stick used (as in woolding) to tighten a rope at a knot **2** *or* **woolder stick :** one of the handles of the ropemaking top formed by a wooden pin passing through it

woolding *n* -s [alter. (influenced by *woold*) of earlier *wooling,* fr. ME *wolinge, woling,* prob. fr. MD, action of binding, wolding, fr. *woelen, wolen* to twist, woold] **:** a rope or chain used in woolding

wool-dyed \ˈ=,=\ *adj* **:** DYED-IN-THE-WOOL

wool eating *n* **:** a gnawing of wool esp. where stained with urine or feces that occurs esp. in stabled sheep and is prob. a form of pica

wooled \ˈwu̇ld\ *adj* **1 :** having wool of a specified quality — often used in combination ⟨a long-*wooled* sheep⟩ **2 :** bearing wool **:** UNSHORN ⟨the price advantage of ~ lambs⟩

¹**wool·en** *or* **wool·len** \ˈwu̇lən\ *adj* [ME *wollen,* fr. OE *wullen,* fr. *wull* wool + *-en*] **1 :** made of wool ⟨~ goods⟩; *specif* **:** of, being, or made from a soft fuzzy loosely twisted yarn that is spun from short wool fibers separated by carding and is used esp. for knitting and for napped and bulky fabrics — compare WORSTED **2** *obs* **:** wearing coarse woolen due to poverty or penance **3 :** of or concerned with the manufacture, commercial handling, or sale of woolen products ⟨a ~ mill⟩ ⟨~ workers⟩

²**woolen** *or* **woollen** \"\ *n* -s [ME *wollen,* fr. *wollen,* adj.] **1 :** a fabric made of wool; *specif* **:** any of various loosely woven fabrics made of woolen yarns usu. having a fuzzy or napped face and used esp. for clothing and blankets ⟨tweed is a popular ~⟩ **2 :** garments of woolen fabric — usu. used in pl. **3 :** woolen yarn

wool·er \-lə(r)\ *n* -s [¹*wool* + *-er*] **:** an animal (as an Angora rabbit) bred or kept for its wool

woo·lert \ˈwülə(r)t\ *n* -s [prob. alter. of E dial. *owlard* barn owl, fr. E *owl* + *-ard*] *dial Eng* **:** BARN OWL

wool extract *n* **:** EXTRACT WOOL

wool fast blue *n, often cap W&F&B* **:** any of several acid dyes — see DYE table I (under *Acid Blue 59* and *102*)

wool fat *n* **:** wool grease esp. after refining **:** LANOLIN

woolfell \ˈ=,=\ *n* [ME *wolle felle,* fr. *wolle* wool + *felle, fel* fell] *Brit* **:** a skin from which the wool has not been sheared or pulled

woolf engine \ˈwu̇lf-\ *n, usu cap W* [after Arthur *Woolf* †1837 Eng. mining engineer] **1 :** the first practical compound engine **2 :** a compound engine having no receiver

wool-gather \ˈ=,==\ *vi* [back-formation fr. *woolgathering*] **:** to indulge in woolgathering — **woolgatherer** \ˈ=,===\ *n*

woolgathering \ˈ=,=(=)=\ *n* **1 :** the act of gathering wool shed from the sheep in tufts and found caught on bushes **2 :** the act of indulging in vagrant fancies **:** foolish or purposeless thinking or imagining

wool grade *n* **:** one of the recognized standard categories into which wool is divided, based chiefly on fineness of fiber — compare BLOOD 7, SPINNING COUNT

wool grader *n* **:** one that grades or classes fleeces

wool grading *n* **:** the separation of whole fleeces according to quality, condition, soundness, and color into lots similar in character and value

wool grass *n* **1 :** an American sedge (*Scirpus cyperinus*) with numerous clustered woolly spikelets **2 :** RAVENNA GRASS

wool grease *n* **:** a fatlike slightly sticky substance coating the surface of the fibers of sheep's wool that is extracted by organic solvents or now usu. by scouring with soap or synthetic detergents, that is classed chemically as a wax rather than a fat because it contains chiefly esters of cholesterol, lanosterol, and other higher alcohols with various fatty acids, and that is used esp. in dressing leather and furs, in lubricating greases, in slushing compounds, in printing inks, and as a source of lanolin — called also *degras, wool fat, wool wax*

wool green S *n, usu cap W&G* **:** an acid dye — see DYE table I (under *Acid Green 50*)

woolgrower \ˈ=,==\ *n, chiefly Brit* **:** one that raises sheep for the production of wool

wool-hat \ˈ=,=\ *n* **1 :** a broad-brimmed hat of coarse wool felt **2** *also* **woolhatter** \ˈ=,==\ [*woolhatter* fr. *wool-hat* + *-er*] **:** a small farmer in the South (as in Georgia)

woolhead \ˈ=,=\ *n* **:** BUFFLEHEAD

woolier *comparative of* WOOLY

woolies *pl of* WOOLY

wooliest *superlative of* WOOLY

wooling *pres part of* WOOL

woolled \ˈwu̇ld\ *chiefly Brit var of* WOOLED

woollen *var of* WOOLEN

wool·len·ize \ˈwu̇lə,nīz\ *vt* -ED/-ING/-S **:** to give (vegetable fiber) the appearance of wool by chemical treatment

woollike \ˈ=,=\ *adj* **:** resembling wool in texture or appearance

wool·li·ness \ˈwu̇lēnəs, -lin-\ *n* -ES **:** the quality or state of being woolly

¹**wool·ly** *also* **wooly** \ˈwu̇lē, -li\ *adj* **woollier** *also* **woolier; woolliest** *also* **wooliest** [¹*wool* + *-y,* adj. suffix] **1 a :** of, relating to, or bearing wool ⟨a besmocked yokel . . . with his ~ flock —*N.Y. Herald Tribune Bk. Rev.*⟩ **:** having the character of wool ⟨although these animals are true sheep, their coat is hairy and not ~ —*Natural History*⟩ **b :** characteristic of wool ⟨the ~ smell of wet mittens —Merle Crowell⟩ **2 :** resembling wool or that of wool ⟨a ~ fog⟩ ⟨a ~ beard⟩ **3 a :** thickly covered with long hair or fuzz ⟨~ cloth coats⟩ ⟨a child's ~ bunny⟩; *specif* **:** LANATE **b** *of lumber* **:** that dresses with a stringy or fuzzy surface ⟨alder is inclined to be ~ and should be sanded —Andrew Wood & Thomas Linn⟩ **4 :** wanting in clearness, definiteness, or sharpness of outline **:** CONFUSED, BLURRY ⟨substitute clear and distinct ideas for vague and ~ ones —F.R.Cowell⟩ ⟨~ thinking⟩ ⟨the guides confessed that they were somewhat ~ on dates —*Time*⟩ **:** INDISTINCT ⟨the ~ sound of a worn record⟩ ⟨~ lithographs from old plates⟩ **5 :** marked by a sometimes violent lack of order or restraint; *typically* **:** having the rough virility of the West in frontier times

²**wool·ly** *also* **wool·ie** *or* **wooly** \ˈwu̇lē, -li\ *n, pl* **woollies** *or* **woolies** [¹*wool* + *-y* or *-ie,* n. suffix] **1 :** a garment made from wool: as **a** *chiefly Brit* **:** a woolen sweater **b :** underclothing of knitted wool — usu. used in pl. **2** *West & Austral* **:** SHEEP

³**wool·ly** *or* **wooly** \ˈwu̇lē, -li\ *n, pl* **woollies** *or* **woolies** [by shortening & alter.] **:** WILLIWAW

woolly alder aphid *n* **:** a plant louse (*Prociphilus tessellatus*) that feeds on the alder and secretes a white woolly substance

woolly ant *n* **:** VELVET ANT

woolly aphid *n* **:** any of several plant lice of the genus *Eriosoma* that are covered with a dense coat of white filaments somewhat resembling fine wool or cotton; *esp* **:** WOOLLY APPLE APHID — called also *woolly plant louse*

woolly apple aphid *n* **:** a cosmopolitan dull reddish woolly aphid (*Eriosoma lanigerum*) that is primarily a bark feeder attacking both aerial parts and roots of apple and other trees — called also *American blight*

woolly bear *also* **woolly bear caterpillar** *n* **:** any of various rather large very hairy caterpillars that are usu. larvae of moths of the family Arctiidae, feed on plants and include some destructive pests (as the salt-marsh caterpillar) — see YELLOW WOOLLY BEAR

woolly beard grass *n* [so called fr. the silky hairs on the spikes] **:** a grass of the genus *Erianthus*

woolly beech aphid *n* **:** a widely distributed plant louse (*Phyllaphis fagi*) that feeds on various beeches

woolly buckeye *n* **:** a small tree or shrub (*Aesculus discolor*) of the southern U.S. often cultivated for its red and yellow flowers and its tomentose leaves

woolly buckthorn *n* **:** FALSE BUCKTHORN

woolly butt *n* **1 :** any of several eucalypts having woolly trunks: as **a :** an Australian eucalypt (*Eucalyptus longifolia*) having hard wood used for many purposes and bark that is fibrous on old trees **b :** WOOLLY GUM **2 :** BASTARD MAHOGANY 1a(1)

woolly croton *n* **:** HOGWORT

woolly finger *n* **:** any of several grasses of the genus *Digitaria; esp* **:** a southern African grass (*D. pentzii*) introduced into the U.S. (as for pasture)

woolly fleece *n* **:** CIRROCUMULUS

woolly foot *or* **woolly foot grama** *n* [so called fr. its woolly base] **:** a valuable grazing grass (*Bouteloua eriopoda*) found in arid regions of the U.S. and adjacent Mexico

woolly gum *n* **:** a blackbutt (*Eucalyptus pilularis*)

woolly head *n, South* **:** an impenetrable thicket of rhododendron or mountain laurel

woolly-headed \ˈ==ˈ==\ *adj* **1 :** having hair resembling wool **2 :** marked by vague or confused perception or thinking

woolly hedge nettle *n* **:** LAMB'S EARS

woolly knot *n* **:** a crown-gall tumor from which many fine roots are formed — compare HAIRY ROOT

woolly lemur *or* **woolly avahi** *n* **:** a small long-tailed woolly-haired lemur (*Lichanotus laniger* or *Avahi laniger*) of Madagascar closely related to the larger indri

woolly lip fern *n* **:** a small No. American fern (*Cheilanthes lanosa*) having stipes and lower frond surfaces densely woolly

woolly locoweed *also* **woolly loco** *n* **:** a perennial herb (*Astragalus mollissimus*) of the western U.S. having compound leaves and dense spikes of violet-purple flowers and foliage that is poisonous to cattle

woolly mammoth *n* **:** a heavy-coated mammoth (*Mammuthus primigenius*) common in the colder portions of the northern hemisphere and known not only from fossil remains but also from the drawings of palaeolithic man and from entire cadavers unearthed from frozen Siberian tundras — called also *northern mammoth*

woolly manzanita *n* **:** a tomentose California shrub (*Arctostaphylos tomentosus*) that is common in the chaparral and has white or pink flowers and brownish red fruit

woolly monkey *n* **1 :** any of several large prehensile-tailed monkeys (genus *Lagothrix*) of the Amazon basin **2 :** WOOLLY SPIDER MONKEY

woolly opossum *n* **:** an opossum of the genus *Philander* having no well-developed pouch and carrying the young on the mother's back

woolly painted cup *n* **:** a white woolly somewhat shrubby California herb (*Castilleja foliolosa*) with greenish yellow flowers

woolly pink *n* **:** CORN COCKLE

woolly plant louse *n* **:** WOOLLY APHID

woolly-pod \'==,=\ *n* **:** any of several plants of the genus *Astragalus* that have pubescent seed pods
woollypod vetch \'==,=-\ *n* **:** a European vetch (*Vicia dasycarpa*) naturalized in the U. S. and used for forage
woolly py·rol \-'pī,rōl, -rōl\ *n* [*pyrol* fr. NL *Pyrola*] **:** URD
woolly rhinoceros *n* **:** an extinct 2-horned rhinoceros (*Opsiceros antiquitatis* or *Rhinoceros antiquitatis*) inhabiting the arctic regions during the Pleistocene, having a dense coat of woolly hair, and being found frozen in the ice of Siberia with the flesh and hair well preserved
woolly root *n* **:** HAIRY ROOT
woolly spider monkey *n* **:** any of several Brazilian spider monkeys (genus *Brachyteles*) characterized by stocky build, rounded head, and finely woolly fur
woolly thistle *n* **1 :** COTTON THISTLE **2 :** a thistle (*Cirsium flodmanii*) of western No. America with white woolly leaves
woolly whitefly *n* **:** a whitefly (*Aleurothrixus floccosus*) widespread in the warmer countries of the New World and injurious to citrus fruits, guavas and other trees
woolly wolf *n* **:** CHANCO
woolly worm *n* **1 :** a sawfly larva that covers itself with a white woolly secretion **2 :** WOOLLY BEAR 1
wool maggot *n* **:** the larva of a blowfly (as *Phormia regina*) that causes strike in sheep
wool·man \'wu̇lmən\ *n, pl* **woolmen** [ME *wolleman,* fr. *wolle* wool + *man*] **:** a dealer in wool
wool moth *n* **:** CLOTHES MOTH
wool·ner's tubercle \'wu̇lnə(r)z-\ *or* **woolner's point** *or* **woolner's tip** *n, usu cap W* [after Thomas *Woolner* †1892 Eng. sculptor and poet] **:** DARWIN'S TUBERCLE
wool oil *n* **1 :** any oil used for oiling wool before spinning **2 a :** an oily substance in wool fiber that makes the fiber soft and pliable **b :** an oil obtained (as by distillation with steam) from wool grease
woolpack \'=,=\ *n* [ME *wolpak, wullepak,* fr. *wolle, wulle* wool + *pak* pack] **1 a :** a wrapper of canvas or other strong fabric into which fleeces are packed for shipment **b :** the complete package of wool and wrapper **2 :** something resembling or suggesting a woolpack; *esp* **:** a rounded cumulus cloud springing from a horizontal base
woolrock \'=,=\ *n* **:** a finely fibrous woollike rock material manufactured from limestone and other rocks
wool rot *n* **:** RAIN ROT
wools *pl of* WOOL, *pres 3d sing of* WOOL
woolsack \'=,=\ *n* [ME *wollesak,* fr. *wolle* wool + *sak* sack] **1 :** a sack for wool **2** [so called fr. its being made of a large square bag of wool without back or arms and covered with cloth] **a :** a rectangular divan that is the official seat of the Lord Chancellor in the House of Lords **b :** the office of Lord Chancellor **3 :** an official seat in the House of Lords for one of the judges of the High Court of Justice **4 :** the office of a judge
wool scour *n, Austral* **:** a place for scouring wool
wool scourer *n* **:** an operator of a machine for scouring raw wool
wool·sey \'wu̇lzē, -zi\ *n* -s [by shortening] **:** LINSEY-WOOLSEY
woolshed \'=,=\ *n* **:** a building or range of buildings (as on an Australian sheep station) in which sheep are sheared and wool is prepared for market
woolskin \'=,=\ *n* [ME *wolle skin*] **:** a sheepskin having the wool still on it
woolsorter \'=,==\ *n* **:** one that sorts wool according to grade specifications
woolsorter's disease *n* **:** pulmonary anthrax that is an occupational hazard due to inhalation of bacterial spores (*Bacillus anthracis*) from contaminated wool or other hair
woolsower \'=,==\ *n* **:** a multicellular gall on the white oak made by a gallfly (*Andricus seminator*) in which each cell is covered by a coating of woolly filaments
wool sponge *n* **:** a soft-fibered durable commercial sponge; *esp* **:** a sponge (*Hippiospongia lachne*) occurring in the Gulf of Mexico, the Caribbean sea, and off the southeastern coast of Florida
wool stapler *n* **:** one that deals in wool; *esp* **:** one that buys raw wool and sorts it before selling to a manufacturer
wool table *n* **:** a strong table with various devices for collecting and bundling loose wool for marketing
wool·ton pie \'wu̇ltən-\ *n, usu cap W* [after Frederick James Marquis, 1st Baron *Woolton* †1964 Eng. businessman] **:** a vegetable pie
wool top *n* [ME *wolletoppe,* fr. *wolle* wool + *toppe* top] **:** TOP 2c(1)
wool tree *n* **:** a tree of the genus *Ceiba*; *esp* **:** CEIBA 2a
wool twine *n* **:** a twine (as of paper, jute) for bundling wool
wool·ward \'wu̇lwə(r)d\ *adv* [ME *wolleward, welleward,* prob. fr. (assumed) OE *wullwerd,* fr. OE *wull* wool + *-werd* wearing, fr. stem of *werian* to wear — more at WOOL, WEAR] *archaic* **:** with woolen next to the skin (as in penance)
wool waste *n* **:** WASTE 4a(1)
wool wax *n* **:** WOOL GREASE
woolweed \'=,=\ *n* **:** PIPEWORT
woolwheel \'=,=\ *n* **:** a hand and foot operated spinning wheel for spinning wool
woolwork \'=,=\ *n* **:** needlework (as embroidery on canvas or knitting) made with wool
wooly *var of* WOOLLY
woomera *or* **woomerah** *var of* WOMMERA
woon *also* **wun** \'wün\ *n* -s [Burmese *wun*] **:** a governor or other administrative officer in Burma
woops *like* OOPS\ *interj* [by alter.] **:** OOPS
woos *pres 3d sing of* WOO, *pl of* WOO
woosh *var of* WHOOSH
wootz \'wüts\ *or* **wootz steel** *n* -ES [prob. alter. of *wook,* fr. Kanarese *ukku* steel] **:** a steel made anciently in India by crude methods in small crucibles according to the oldest known process for making fused steel
wooz·i·ly \'wüzəlē, 'wüz-, -li\ *adv* **:** in a woozy manner
wooz·i·ness \-zēnəs, -zin-\ *n* -ES **:** the quality or state of being woozy
woozy \-zē, -zi\ *adj* [prob. alter. of *oozy*] **1 :** BEFUDDLED ⟨still ~ from the narcotics which eased the pain —*Time*⟩ ⟨pseudo-mystical doctrine which he finds impracticable and ~ —A.J. Nock⟩ **2 :** affected with dizziness, mild nausea, or weakness **:** SICK ⟨she came out nicely, but I felt ~ in the stomach —B.T. Guyton⟩ **3 :** resembling an alcoholic hallucination or euphoria or something experienced in one ⟨a woozy way of making life look delightfully ~ —*Time*⟩ **4 :** VAGUE, BLURRY, WOOLLY ⟨~ sentimentality⟩
[1]**wop** *var of* WHOP
[2]**wop** \'wäp\ *n* -s *sometimes cap* [It (Sicilian & Neapolitan dial.) *guappo* bold, handsome, bully, dandy, fr. Sp *guapo*] **:** ITALIAN — usu. used disparagingly
[1]**wopse** \'wäps\ *dial var of* WASP
[2]**wopse** \"\ *vt* -ED/-ING/-S [origin unknown] *dial* **:** to heap, wrap, or tangle in a disorderly way
[3]**wopse** \"\ *n* -s *dial* **:** a disorderly mass **:** HEAP, MESS, TANGLE
wopsy \-sē\ *adj* **:** marked by disorder **:** IRREGULAR ⟨if your top-knot is very indifferent and ~, take intensive hair treatments —*Delineator*⟩
wor *abbr, often cap* worshipful
[1]**worces·ter** \'wu̇stə(r)\ *adj, usu cap* [*Worcester,* city in west central England] **1 :** of or from the city of Worcester, England **:** of the kind or style prevalent in Worcester **2** [*Worcestershire, Worcester,* county in west central England] **:** WORCESTERSHIRE **3** [*Worcester,* city in central Massachusetts] **:** of or from the city of Worcester, Mass. ⟨*Worcester* factories⟩ **:** of the kind or style prevalent in Worcester
[2]**worcester** \"\ *n* -s *usu cap* **:** WORCESTER CHINA
worcester china *or* **worcester porcelain** *n, usu cap W* **:** a soft paste porcelain made at Worcester, England, since 1751
[1]**worces·ter·shire** \-,shi(ə)r, -shiə, -shə(r)\ *adj, usu cap* [*Worcestershire,* county in west central England] **:** of or from Worcestershire, England **:** of the kind or style prevalent in Worcestershire
[2]**worcestershire** \"\ *n* -s *usu cap* **:** WORCESTERSHIRE SAUCE
worcestershire sauce *or* **worcester sauce** *n, usu cap W* **:** a pungent sauce of soy, vinegar, and many other ingredients orig. made in Worcester, England
[1]**word** \'wərd, 'wəd, 'wəid\ *n* -s *often attrib* [ME, fr. OE; akin to OHG *wort* word, ON *orth,* Goth *waurd,* L *verbum* word, Gk *eirein* to say, *rhēma* word, *rhētōr* orator, Lith *vardas* name] **1 a :** something that is said **:** UTTERANCE, STATEMENT ⟨my father loved you; he said he did, and with his deed did crown his ~ —Shak.⟩ ⟨not a ~ about his plans⟩ ⟨said a ~ to his employer on behalf of a friend who was looking for work⟩ **b words** *pl* (1) **:** TALK, DISCOURSE, SPEECH, LANGUAGE ⟨putting one's feelings into ~*s*⟩ ⟨wonderful beyond ~*s*⟩ (2) **:** the text of a vocal musical composition ⟨trivial ~*s* set to splendid music⟩ **c** (1) **:** a short conversation ⟨would like to have a ~ with you⟩ (2) **:** a short remark ⟨a ~ of advice⟩ **2 a** (1) **:** a speech sound or series of speech sounds that symbolizes and communicates a meaning without being divisible into smaller units capable of independent use **:** linguistic form that is a minimum free form ⟨the order of the ~*s* in a phrase⟩ ⟨the meaning of a ~⟩ (2) **:** the entire set of linguistic forms produced by combining a single base with various inflectional elements (as affixes) without change in the part of speech ⟨*man, man's, men,* and *men's* are different forms of one ~⟩ — see PARADIGM **b :** a written or printed character or combination of characters representing a spoken word; *esp* **:** any segment of written or printed discourse ordinarily appearing between spaces or between a space and a punctuation mark ⟨average number of ~*s* to a line⟩ **c :** CODE GROUP **d :** a combination of electrical or magnetic impulses conveying a quantum of information in communication and computer work **3 :** ORDER, COMMAND, INSTRUCTION ⟨don't move till I give the ~⟩ ⟨his ~ is law⟩ **4** *or* **word of god** *usu cap W & cap G* **a :** the divine Wisdom esp. as finding manifestation in the world and man and above all in Jesus Christ **:** LOGOS; *specif* **:** the second person of the Trinity ⟨the Logos is both the reason and the *Word of God* —W.F.Howard⟩ ⟨Christ is the *Word* become flesh —J.A.Mackay⟩ **b :** the gospel message **:** [1]GOSPEL 1; *also* **:** the content, communication, and effectual implementation of the gospel in the lives of men ⟨the Bible contains the *Word of God* to man —L.A.Weigle⟩ ⟨preach the *Word* in the mountains of eastern Tennessee —H.L.Mencken⟩ **c :** a self-revelation from God to men **:** God's disclosure of himself to men; *also* **:** the expressed or manifested mind and will of God ⟨God's *Word* was one of the most general terms used by Israel for revelation —G.E.Wright⟩ **d :** God's creative and redemptive activity esp. as manifested in the creation and preservation of the world and in acts of salvation in the lives of men ⟨by the *Word of God* heavens existed long ago —2 Pet 3:5 (RSV)⟩ ⟨upholding the universe by his *Word* of power —Heb 1:3 (RSV)⟩ ⟨for the *Word of God* is living and active, sharper than any two-edged sword —Heb 4:12 (RSV)⟩ **e :** a holy book **:** canon or collection of sacred scriptures divinely inspired by God ⟨will be readings from the *Words of God* — the Torah, the Bible, the Koran —Edris Rice-Wray⟩ **5 a :** NEWS, REPORT, ACCOUNT, MESSAGE, INFORMATION — used in the singular and often with no article ⟨brought ~ that a financial backer of the expedition . . . had died —*Amer. Guide Series: Maine*⟩ ⟨sent ~ . . . that he planned to attend —*N.Y. Times*⟩ ⟨in Washington when the ~ came of a great defeat at Bull Run⟩ **b :** common talk or report **:** RUMOR — used in the singular and often with no article ⟨~ of the prowess of the twelve-year-old got about —*Current Biog.*⟩ ⟨the ~ has gone about that there will be no prosecution —Tom Fitzsimmons⟩ **6 :** the act of speaking or of making verbal communication of any kind ⟨loyal in ~ and deed⟩ **:** product of such an act ⟨what people learn from the written ~⟩ **7 a :** SAYING, PROVERB, MAXIM **b :** a motto esp. in heraldry **8 a** (1) **:** PROMISE ⟨I give you my ~⟩ ⟨kept her ~⟩ ⟨as good as his ~⟩ (2) **:** the honor involved in the keeping of a promise ⟨pledged himself on his ~ to be present⟩ **b :** an assertion implying the authority or truthfulness of the person making it ⟨not that I doubt your ~⟩ ⟨take my ~ for it⟩ ⟨has the doctor's ~ for it that no operation is needed⟩ **9 :** a quarrelsome utterance or conversation ⟨one ~ led to another⟩ — usu. used in pl. ⟨some ~*s* between him and his father⟩ ⟨he and his friend had ~*s* and parted⟩ and sometimes with an adjective modifier ⟨some hard ~*s* passed between them⟩ **10 a :** a verbal signal **:** PASSWORD, WATCHWORD **b :** the most appropriate term to indicate what kind of action is required or prevalent — used in the predicate after *the* ⟨in dealing with difficult children, patience is the ~⟩ **c :** the most appropriate term to express the idea intended — used in the predicate after *the* ⟨mediocre is not the ~ for his performance; it was incredibly bad⟩
syn WORD, VOCABLE, and TERM can mean any letter or combination of letters or any sound or combination of sounds capable of being pronounced and expressing an idea that is by tradition or common consent associated with the letters or the sounds. WORD applies to a letter or combination of letters or a sound or a combination of sounds that forms an indivisible whole constituting one of the ultimate units of a language; VOCABLE throws emphasis upon a word as pronounced or spelled rather than as a unit of meaning ⟨a flat denial of poetic possibilities, in the case of any *vocable,* is liable to disastrous refutation —J.L.Lowes⟩ ⟨accustomed to songs in which the words are often merely convenient *vocables* with the melody usually more important than the text —Evelyn H. Scholl⟩ TERM applies both to words and to phrases that express a whole idea and form one of the units of expression in a language, applying esp. to units with a more or less precise technical use or meaning ⟨the *term* communism is used today to describe both a political philosophy and its translation into reality —H.W.Gatzke⟩ ⟨"the most important woman in Finland" is a *term* which has been applied —*Current Biog.*⟩ ⟨all professions are likely to develop innumerable *terms* that constitute an almost private jargon
— **at a word** *adv* **1 :** at a single word of command, request, or suggestion **2 :** in short **:** to sum up **:** CONCISELY — **good word 1 :** a favorable statement ⟨say a *good word* for him⟩ **2 :** good news ⟨spreading the *good word*⟩ ⟨hello, there; what's the *good word*⟩ — **in a word** *also* **in one word :** in short **:** to sum up — **in so many words :** in exactly those terms ⟨implied that such actions were criminal but did not say so *in so many words*⟩ **2 :** in plain forthright language ⟨*in so many words,* she wasn't fit to be seen —Jean Stafford⟩ — **my word** — used to express surprise ⟨*my word,* what a nasty look she gave you⟩ — **of few words :** not inclined to say more than necessary **:** LACONIC ⟨a man *of few words*⟩ — **of many words :** TALKATIVE, VERBOSE — **of one's word :** that can be relied on to keep a promise — used only after *man* or *woman* ⟨a man *of his word*⟩ ⟨a woman *of her word*⟩ — **upon my word** *also* **on my word :** with my assurance **:** ASSUREDLY, INDEED ⟨*upon my word,* I never heard of such a thing⟩ — **words of one syllable :** plain forthright language ⟨he has had a bit too much; in *words of one syllable,* he is drunk⟩
[2]**word** \"\ *vb* -ED/-ING/-S [ME *worden,* fr. *word,* n. — more at [1]WORD] *vi, archaic* **:** to use words **:** SPEAK ~ *vt* **1 :** to utter or recite as spoken words **2** *obs* **:** to ply with words **3 :** to express in words **:** PHRASE ⟨a strongly ~*ed* message⟩ **4** *obs* **:** to bring into some condition by talking ⟨be ~*ed* to death —James Howell⟩ — **word it** *obs* **:** to bandy words **:** DISPUTE
word accent *var of* WORD STRESS
word·age \-dij, -dēj\ *n* -s **1 a :** WORDS ⟨keeps the music programs tied together with ~ —Saul Carson⟩ **b :** VERBIAGE 1 ⟨all the lobby and meeting-room ~ produced only these skimpy results —*Newsweek*⟩ **2 :** the number or quantity of words ⟨six long stories, ranging in ~ from 17,000 to 35,000 —Anthony Boucher⟩ **3 :** the use or choice of words **:** WORDING 2 ⟨signs of youth and inexperience in the ~, some of which is at random —*N. Y. Herald Tribune Bk. Rev.*⟩
word association *n* **:** free association in which a word serves as the stimulus object
word association test *n* **:** a method for exploring the content of the mind wherein the subject is required to respond to a stimulus word with the first word he thinks of or with one of a specified class of words
word-blind \'=,=\ *adj* **:** afflicted with word blindness
word blindness *n* **:** a condition in which a person is no longer able to recognize the words that he sees **:** ALEXIA
wordbook \'=,=\ *n* **1 :** a book containing a collection of words **:** VOCABULARY, DICTIONARY, LEXICON **2 :** LIBRETTO
word-bound \'=,=\ *adj* **:** lacking in fluency **:** taciturn because of limited vocabulary or unwillingness to talk
word-building \'=,==\ *n* **:** the act or process of forming words: **a :** WORD-FORMATION **b :** the act or process of spelling out words (as in a contest) with the use of only those letters found in a particular word or phrase
word-catcher \'=,==\ *n* **1 :** one that cavils at words **2 :** one that collects words and their different senses **:** LEXICOGRAPHER — used disparagingly
word-catching \'=,==\ *n* -s **:** concern with minute points of wording
word class *n* **:** a linguistic form class whose members are words; *esp* **:** PART OF SPEECH 1
word-deaf \'=,=\ *adj* **:** afflicted with word deafness
word deafness *n* **:** loss or lack of the ability to recognize words that are heard
word·er \'wərdər\ *n* -s **1** *obs* **:** a verbose person **2 :** one that puts something into words
word family *n* **:** a group of cognate words esp. within a single language ⟨the *word family* to which English *write, rewrite writer,* and *writ* belong⟩
word field *n* **:** FIELD 8c
word-formation \'==',==\ *n* **:** the formation of words in a language by the processes of derivation and composition
word for word *adv* [ME] **:** in the exact words **:** VERBATIM, LITERALLY, EXACTLY ⟨repeated the message *word for word*⟩
word-for-word \'==',=\ *adj* [*word for word*] **:** being in or following the exact words ⟨a *word-for-word* translation⟩ **:** VERBATIM ⟨the *word-for-word* transmission of legends —George Grey⟩
word game *n* **:** a game in which players compete in forming, thinking of, or guessing words according to a set of rules
word-hoard \'=,=\ *n* [trans. of OE *wordhord*] **:** a supply of words **:** VOCABULARY ⟨given to much free and easy unlocking of his *word-hoard* —G.K.Anderson⟩
word·ie \'wərdi\ *n* -s [[1]*word* + *-ie*] *Scot* **:** a mere word **:** WORD
wordier *comparative of* WORDY
wordiest *superlative of* WORDY
word·i·ly \'wərd[ə]lē, 'wəd|, 'wəid|, |əl|, |i\ *adv* **:** in a wordy manner
word·i·ness \-dēnəs, -din-\ *n* -ES **:** the quality or state of being wordy
wording *n* -s [fr. gerund of [2]*word*] **1 :** the act of talking or of uttering as words **2 :** the act or manner of expressing in words **:** PHRASING, PHRASEOLOGY ⟨mystical writing where the ~ takes on poetic quality —Thomas Munro⟩
word·ish \-dish\ *adj* **1** *obs* **:** made up of or having to do with words **:** VERBAL **2** *obs* **:** containing more words than necessary **:** VERBOSE, WORDY — **wordishly** *adv, obs* — **wordishness** *n* -ES *obs*
wor·dle \'wərd[ə]l\ *n* -s [alter. of ME *wirtil* whirtle] **:** any of several pivoted pieces forming the throat of an adjustable die used in drawing wire or lead pipe
word·less \'wərdləs, 'wəd-, 'wəid-\ *adj* [ME *wordles,* fr. [1]*word* + *-les* -less] **1 :** not expressed or not expressible in words ⟨choking exasperation and ~ shame —Thomas Wolfe⟩ **:** involving no use of words ⟨~ intercourse with rude nature —John Burroughs⟩ **2 a :** saying nothing **:** SILENT, SPEECHLESS ⟨he stood helpless — ~ even —Lew Wallace⟩ **b :** lacking ability or inclination to express oneself freely in words **:** INARTICULATE, TACITURN ⟨a calm, ~ man —W.A.White⟩ **3 :** not consisting of or accompanied by words ⟨with a ~ squeak —P.G.Wodehouse⟩ ⟨the ~ language of architecture —E.M. Bridge⟩ ⟨~ music⟩ — **word·less·ly** *adv* — **word·less·ness** *n* -ES
word-lore \'=,=\ *n* **:** study of or information about words ⟨a modest book on *word-lore* —Ernest Weekley⟩
word-magic \'=,==\ *n* **:** magic involving the use of words in a manner determined by a belief that the very act of uttering a word summons or directly affects the person or thing that the word refers to
word-man \'=,=\ *n, pl* **word-men :** one that is skilled in the use of words
wordmonger \'=,==\ *n* **:** a dealer in words: as **a :** one that uses words for show or without enough regard for meaning **b :** a writer by profession
word-mongering \'=,=(=)=\ *n* **:** the use of empty or bombastic words ⟨mere *word-mongering* divorced from actual life —Forrest Morgan⟩
word-mongery \'=,məŋg(ə)rē, -mäŋ-\ *n* -ES [[1]*word* + *-mongery* (as in *ironmongery*)] **:** WORD-MONGERING
word-music \'=,==\ *n* **:** the musical quality of spoken language or of written language designed to be spoken (as in a play)
word of god *usu cap W & cap G* **:** WORD 4
word of honor : a promise or engagement made with or confirmed by a pledge of one's honor for its fulfillment
word of mouth : oral communication ⟨news spread by *word of mouth*⟩
word-of-mouth \'==',=\ *adj* [*word of mouth*] **:** orally communicated **:** involving or consisting of oral communication ⟨*word-of-mouth* advertising⟩
word order *n* **:** the order or arrangement of words in a phrase, clause, or sentence
word-paint \'=,=\ *vt* [back-formation fr. *word-painter* & *word-painting*] **:** to depict graphically in words
word-painter \'=,==\ *n* **:** a writer of vivid or graphic descriptive power
word-painting \'=,==\ *n* **1 :** WORD PICTURE **2 :** the action of depicting something graphically in words
word-perfect \'=,==\ *adj* **:** being in the state of having completely and accurately memorized something consisting of words ⟨an actor may become *word-perfect* in his part —C.S. Myers⟩
word picture *n* **:** a graphic or vivid description in words
wordplay \'=,=\ *n* **1 :** verbal wit based on the peculiarities of words and esp. on the various meanings expressed by a single word or by two or more words of like sound ⟨a pun is a form of ~⟩ **2 :** an instance of wordplay
words *pl of* WORD, *pres 3d sing of* WORD
word salad *n* **:** a jumble of extremely incoherent speech as sometimes observed in schizophrenia
word-sign \'=,=\ *n* **:** a visual or tactile symbol or group of symbols representing a word: as **a :** a single character used to represent a word in a regular system of writing **:** LOGOGRAM ⟨the *word-signs* used in Egyptian hieroglyphic writing⟩ **b :** a stroke or simple character used in shorthand as a brief way of representing a word of frequent occurrence or a derivative of such a word **c :** a braille character of one cell or two cells that can stand for a whole word
word-slinger \'=,==\ *n* **:** a professional writer; *esp* **:** a hack writer
wordsmith \'=,=\ *n* **:** a craftsman or artist whose medium is words
words of administration : the words spoken by the officiating clergyman in administering the Communion elements to the people
words of institution : the portion of a Christian Communion service based on the words of Mk 14:22–24 and used as the warrant from Jesus Christ for the continued celebration of the Eucharist
words of limitation : the words in a deed or will that describe the nature and extent of the estate granted or devised
words of procreation : the words necessary in conveying a fee in tail to indicate to whose children the conveyed estate is to be entailed
word-spinning \'=,==\ *n* **:** the action or process of expressing oneself in words in a showy or esp. verbose manner
word square *n* **1 :** ACROSTIC 3 **2 word squares** *pl but sing in constr* **:** a game in which each player tries to fill letters as they are called one at a time into a block of squares to form words horizontally and vertically
word·ster \'wərdztə(r), -dst-\ *n* -s **:** one that is adept in the use of words esp. in an empty or bombastic manner
word-stock \'=,=\ *n* **:** the vocabulary of a language, dialect, or idiolect
word stress *or* **word accent** *n* **:** the manner in which stresses are distributed on the syllables of a word — compare SENTENCE STRESS
[1]**words·worth·ian** \,wərdz'wərthēən\ *n* -s *usu cap* [William *Wordsworth* †1850 Eng. poet + E *-an,* n. suffix] **1 :** a follower, imitator, or admirer of the poet Wordsworth **2 :** a student of or authority on Wordsworth or his works
[2]**wordsworthian** \¦=¦===\ *adj, usu cap* [William *Wordsworth* + E *-an,* adj. suffix] **:** of, resembling, belonging to, or charac-

teristic of the poet Wordsworth or his poetry — **words·worth·ian·ism** \ˌ=ˈ==ə,nizəm\ *n* -s *usu cap*
word value *n* : the effectiveness of a word to express the exact shade of meaning desired and to fit into the rhythmical structure of a phrase or sentence
¹wordy \ˈwərdē, ˈwȯd-, ˈwəid-, -di\ *adj* -ER/-EST [ME, fr. OE *wordig*, fr. ¹*word* + *-ig* -y] **1** : using or containing many words : VERBOSE ⟨a ~ and insolent braggart —Sir Walter Scott⟩ ⟨finding ~ fault with the conditions under which he lives —Agnes Repplier⟩ **2** : of, belonging to, or consisting of words : VERBAL ⟨~ war⟩
syn WORDY, VERBOSE, PROLIX, DIFFUSE, and REDUNDANT can all mean using or marked by the use of more, usu. far more, words than are necessary to express the thought. WORDY suggests garrulousness when applied to what is spoken ⟨the newspapers of the day . . . printed long *wordy* editorials —Marjory S. Douglas⟩ ⟨proceedings, which were long and disorderly, were delayed by *wordy* disputes —F.H.Underhill⟩ ⟨a senile and *wordy* character⟩ VERBOSE suggests overabundance of words as a literary or rhetorical fault ⟨slow, *verbose*, and ineffective instructional methods —R. E. De Kieffer⟩ ⟨not diffuse, but they are *verbose* in the exact sense of that term; they are too luxurious in words —H.S.Canby⟩ PROLIX implies so much attention to minute detail as to extend the matter beyond all due bounds, strongly implying tediousness ⟨his style is . . . excessively long-winded and *prolix* —R.A.Hall b. 1911⟩ ⟨the style is forceful, repetitive and *prolix* —Cyril Connolly⟩ DIFFUSE implies lack of compactness and sense of point, suggesting a wordy ranging over a subject ⟨this is a sprawling, formless, *diffuse*, and unselective book —Orville Prescott⟩ ⟨fear . . . that I was getting too *diffuse*; but now I am glad that I went into detail from the first —Bram Stoker⟩ REDUNDANT applies to something superfluous, to repetitious and unnecessary words or phrases, or to a speaker or writer whose style is marked by them, usu. habitually ⟨she had been, like nearly all very young writers, superfluous of phrase, *redundant* —Rose Macaulay⟩ ⟨a wordy, *redundant*, cliché-ridden style⟩ ⟨a most *redundant* after-dinner speaker⟩
²wordy \ˈwərdi\ *chiefly Scot var of* WORTHY
wore [ME (Sc) *wour* (past)] *past or substand past part of* WEAR
wore-out \ˈ=ˌ=\ *substand var of* WORN-OUT
¹work \ˈwərk, ˈwə̄k, ˈwəik\ *n* -s [ME *werk, work*, fr. OE *werc, weorc, worc*; akin to OHG *werc, werah* work, ON *verk*, Gk *ergon* work, *erdein, rhezein* to do, make sacrifice, Av *varəzyeiti* he works] **1** : activity in which one exerts strength or faculties to do or perform: **a** : sustained physical or mental effort valued as it overcomes obstacles and achieves an objective or result ⟨the hours of busiest ~ and closest application —W.C. Brownell⟩ — contrasted with *play* **b** : the labor, task, or duty that affords one his accustomed means of livelihood ⟨six days shalt thou labor and do all thy ~ —Exod 20:9 (AV)⟩ ⟨the ~ of a permanent secretary is worth £3,000 a year —Virginia Woolf⟩ **c** : strenuous activity marked by the presence of difficulty and exertion and absence of pleasure ⟨sculling against a swift current is ~ —Richard Jefferies⟩ **d** : occasional or temporary activity toward a desired end : CHORE ⟨the ~ of putting up storm windows⟩ **e** : a specific task, duty, function, or assignment often being a part or phase of some larger activity ⟨the handler's ~ is to put the goods on the siding but not to load the car⟩ **2 a** : energy expended by natural phenomena ⟨these boulder deposits are the ~ of glaciers⟩ **b** : the result of such energy ⟨sand dunes are the ~ of sea and wind⟩ **c** : the transference of energy that is produced by the motion of the point of application of a force (as when a compressed spring in a toy gun by its expansion and loss of potential energy gives kinetic energy to a bullet or when the falling weight of a pile driver drives in a pile) and is measured by multiplying the force and the displacement of its point of application in the line of action — see ERG, JOULE, KILOGRAM-METER **3 a** : something that results from a particular manner or method of working, operating, or devising ⟨tracked down by careful police ~⟩ ⟨sonata with intricate passage ~ for the right hand⟩ ⟨telecast was notable for the flexibility of the camera ~ —Irene Kuhn⟩ **b** : something that results from the use or fashioning of a particular material ⟨silver ~ of earlier artists⟩ ⟨fine porcelain ~ in many styles⟩ or employment of a particular technique ⟨boxes adorned with elaborate filigree ~⟩ **c** : NEEDLEWORK, FANCYWORK **4 a** : a fortified structure (as a fort, earthen barricade, trench) **b works** *pl* : structures in engineering (as docks, bridges, or embankments) or mining (as shafts or tunnels) **5 works** *pl but sing or pl in constr* : a place where industrial labor is carried on : PLANT, FACTORY ⟨cement ~*s*⟩ ⟨chemical ~*s*⟩ ⟨start in the office rather than in the ~*s* —Roy Lewis & Angus Maude⟩ **6 works** *pl* : the working or moving parts of a mechanism ⟨cleaning the ~*s* of a clock⟩ **7 a** *dial Eng* : DISTURBANCE, BOTHER, TO-DO, TROUBLE **b** : froth or foam caused by fermentation **8 a** : something produced or accomplished by effort, exertion, or exercise of skill ⟨this book is the ~ of many hands⟩ **b** : something produced by the exercise of creative talent or expenditure of creative effort : artistic production ⟨literary, scientific, and artistic ~*s*, including writings, musical, dramatic, and cinematographic works, and paintings, engravings, and sculpture —*Universal Copyright Convention*⟩ **c** : the act or process of working a degree — used in Masonic and some other ritualistic orders ⟨made the ~ up-to-date, brisk, with only one 45-minute degree —C.W. Ferguson⟩ **9 works** *pl* : performance of moral or religious acts ⟨faith by itself if it has no ~*s*, is dead —Jas 2:17 (RSV)⟩ ⟨salvation by ~*s*⟩ ⟨performance of all the ~*s* prescribed by the law —E.F.Scott⟩ **10 a** : effective operation : EFFECT, RESULT ⟨wait for time to do its healing ~⟩ ⟨loathed war and all its ~*s* —V.L.Parrington⟩ **b** : manner of working : WORKMANSHIP, MANAGEMENT, EXECUTION ⟨better tools make for better ~⟩ **11 a** : the material or piece of material that is operated upon at any stage in the process of manufacture ⟨the ~ was put under the drop hammer and quickly pounded into shape for the next operation⟩ **b** : ore before it is dressed **12** : BREAK 4c(6) **13 works** *pl* **a** : everything possessed or available ⟨I had the ~*s*, the bottom half of the menu, from grapefruit to rice pudding —Saul Bellow⟩ ⟨builders are including complete kitchens . . . and buyers want the ~*s* —*Kiplinger Washington Letter*⟩ ⟨the whole ~*s*, rod, reel, tackle box, went overboard⟩ **b** : subjection to drastic treatment : unsparing or ruthless handling : all possible abuse including murder — usu. used with *get* ⟨get the ~*s*⟩ or *give* ⟨gave him the ~*s*⟩ **14** *slang* : dice designed for cheating
syn OCCUPATION, EMPLOYMENT, BUSINESS, PURSUIT, CALLING: WORK is the general term with less specific connotation and wider application than others in this series; it may or may not suggest laborious, burdensome, onerous expenditure of energy ⟨the *work* of a ditchdigger⟩ ⟨a miner's *work* is difficult⟩ OCCUPATION may indicate the trade, craft, vocation, or profession which one has chosen and prepared himself for and which one is apt usu. to follow ⟨allowed to choose his *occupation* —W.R.Inge⟩ or whatever occupies one's time and energies, quite purposefully as a means of livelihood or less so as an avocation or interest ⟨a generation still in the process of discovering its own identity and desperately engaged in that *occupation* —R.B.West⟩ EMPLOYMENT is likely to center attention on an employer-employee relationship and imply an agreement or contract about wages or working conditions ⟨resumed his *employment* with the Smith Plumbing Company, plumbing being his occupation⟩ or may indicate merely that at which one employs himself, without suggestions of work ⟨their chief *employment* is to talk of what they once were and of what they may yet be —T.B.Macaulay⟩ BUSINESS suggests work of a commercial or mercantile nature and is likely to be limited to situations of authority unless the question of a rightful or suitable assumption of a role or function is concerned ⟨his *business* is selling insurance and my work as clerk in his office is not very hard⟩ BUSINESS in situations not involving means of livelihood may be used in reference to financial transactions or to necessary and burdensome tasks but hardly to avocations ⟨the messy *business* of infant feeding —*New Yorker*⟩ PURSUIT may suggest either a vocation or an avocation followed with zeal or resolution ⟨lost all soul or sensation, but for this one *pursuit* —Mary W. Shelley⟩ ⟨the law, being a profession, was accounted a more gentlemanly *pursuit* than business —Edith Wharton⟩ CALLING may indicate a profession or vocation to which one has been called by some inspiration or intuition ⟨that luckiest of fairy-gifts, a *calling*, an industry, something that she loved to do —L.P.Smith⟩ or may indicate the simplest craft or trade ⟨in his shepherd's *calling* he was prompt —William Wordsworth⟩
syn LABOR, TOIL, TRAVAIL, GRIND, DRUDGERY: WORK is a very general word usable in a variety of contexts; LABOR differs from WORK in often being limited to purposive, necessary expenditure of effort, usu. of a fatiguing or onerous nature ⟨*labor* is doing what we must; leisure is doing what we like —G.B. Shaw⟩ ⟨any activity becomes *work* when it is directed by accomplishment of a definite material result, and it is *labor* only as the activities are onerous, undergone as mere means by which to secure a result —John Dewey⟩ TOIL indicates fatiguing prolonged work ⟨the labor of sifting, combining, constructing, expunging, correcting, testing: this frightful *toil* is as much critical as creative —T.S.Eliot⟩ TRAVAIL is likely to stress painfulness, difficulty, or struggle in work ⟨the sentimentalist escapes the stern *travail* of thought —J.L.Lowes⟩ ⟨I must admit the doubt in view of the *travail* that I suffered —B.N.Cardozo⟩ GRIND suggests dreary monotonous repetition of burdensome or taxing work ⟨nothing left for my mother to do but to take in student boarders. This she did until every child was out of college — a long hard *grind* —A.W.Long⟩ DRUDGERY applies to continuing dull, menial, irksome work ⟨*drudgery* can be cut down. Most men have had to dig for their lives since Adam, but this is now avoidable —Francis Hackett⟩ ⟨the act of scrupulous revision (endless pruning and trimming for the sake of a sound and flexible prose style) that provides the writer's best solace even while it makes *drudgery* —Ellen Glasgow⟩
— **at work 1** : engaged in working (as at one's occupation) **2** : OPERATING, FUNCTIONING ⟨stronger pressures that have been *at work* on the national character —W.C.Dickinson⟩ ⟨evidence of a fine culture *at work* even in the lowliest carpenter —*Amer. Guide Series: N.H.*⟩ — **in the works** : in process of preparation or development or completion ⟨a plan of reorganization is reported to be now *in the works*⟩ — **in work 1** : in process of being done ⟨company . . . has three films *in work* right now —Kirk Douglas⟩ **2** *of a horse* : in training — **make short work of** : to deal with or dispose of quickly or summarily — **out of work** : without regular employment : JOBLESS
²work \"\ *adj* **1** : suitable or styled for wear while working ⟨~ clothes⟩ ⟨~ shoes⟩ **2** : used for work ⟨~ elephant⟩
³work \"\ *vb* **worked** \-kt\ *or* **wrought** \ˈrȯt, *usu* -ȯd·+V\ **worked** *or* **wrought; working; works** [ME *worchen, worken, werken* (past *wroughte, wroghte*, past part. *wrought, wroght*), fr. OE *wyrcan, wircan* (past *worhte*, past part. *geworht*); akin to OHG *wurchen, wirchen* to work (past *worhta*, past part. *giworht*), ON *yrkja* (past *orti*, past part. *yrt, ort*), Goth *waurkjan* (past *waurhta*), OE *weorc* work — more at ¹WORK] *vt* **1** : to bring to pass : EFFECT ⟨~ havoc⟩ ⟨~ miracles⟩ ⟨had meant to ~ her own will on the interior of the house —Arnold Bennett⟩ **2 a** : to fashion or create by expending labor or exertion upon : FORGE, SHAPE ⟨~ flint into tools⟩ **b** : to make or decorate with needlework; *esp* : EMBROIDER ⟨the buttonholes of the dress were ~*ed* in a contrasting color⟩ ⟨~*ed* a floral design in wool and silk on the shawl⟩ **3 a** : to prepare for use by stirring or kneading ⟨~ the putty into the right consistency⟩ **b** : to bring into a desired form by a gradual process of cutting, hammering, scraping, pressing, stretching ⟨~ cold steel⟩ **4** : to set or keep in motion, operation, or activity ⟨~ cattle in a roundup⟩ : cause to operate or produce ⟨a pump ~*ed* by hand⟩ ⟨~ a quarry⟩ ⟨~ farmland⟩ **5** : to work out (a problem) : SOLVE ⟨~ difficult calculations in his head⟩ **6 a** : to cause to toil or labor ⟨~*ed* his horses nearly to death⟩ : get work out of : cause to perform ⟨~ dogs in a circus act⟩ **b** : to make use of ⟨~*ed* her charm and looks to get her way⟩ : EXPLOIT **c** : to control or guide the operation of ⟨all the yard switches are ~*ed* from a central tower⟩ **7** : to carry on an operation through or in or along ⟨the salesman ~*ed* both sides of the street⟩ ⟨fisherman ~*ed* the stream from the bridge down to the pool⟩ **8** : to pay for with labor or service ⟨~ out a fine⟩ ⟨~ off a debt⟩ ⟨~*ed* his way through college⟩ **9 a** : to get (oneself or an object) into or out of a condition or position by gradual stages ⟨~*ed* himself out of his bonds and called the police⟩ ⟨~*ed* himself into a position of leadership⟩ ⟨patiently ~*ing* the boulder out of the hole⟩ ⟨swinging his arms to ~ the stiffness out of his shoulders⟩ **b** : CONTRIVE, ARRANGE — used chiefly with *it* ⟨we can ~ it so that you can take your vacation⟩ **10 a** *archaic* : to influence by acting upon : LEAD, INDUCE ⟨I have been ~*ing* him to abandon her —Sir Walter Scott⟩ **b** : to practice trickery or cozenage or some devious procedure on for some end ⟨~*ed* the management for a free ticket⟩ **c** : EXCITE, PROVOKE ⟨~*ed* himself into a rage⟩ **11** : to work off (sense 2) **12** : to bud or graft (plants) — usu. used with *on* ⟨apples ~*ed* on seedling stocks are often esp. vigorous⟩ **13** : to sort (mail) by place of destination **14** : to manipulate (a bait or lure) for fish with maximum effectiveness in a natural manner **15** : to go through the ceremonies of (a degree) — used in Masonic and some other ritualistic orders ~ *vi* **1 a** : to exert oneself physically or mentally esp. in sustained effort for a purpose or under compulsion or necessity — contrasted with *play* **b** : to perform or carry through a task requiring sustained effort or continuous repeated operations ⟨~*ed* for hours clearing up the yard⟩ ⟨~*ing* away at his algebra⟩ ⟨~*ing* all day over a hot stove⟩ ⟨~*ing* on his book for years⟩ **c** : to perform work or fulfill duties regularly for wages or salary ⟨he ~*s* at plumbing⟩ ⟨~*s* in an insurance office⟩ ⟨~*s* for an oil company⟩ ⟨obliged to ~ for a living⟩ **2 a** *archaic* : ACT, BEHAVE **b** *obs* : CONTRIVE, ARRANGE **3** : to function or operate according to plan or design ⟨the mechanism was heavy and awkward but it ~*ed*⟩ ⟨hinges ~ better with oil⟩ **4** : to exert an influence or tendency ⟨developments which ~ for increasing the significance of the net income figure —*Jour. of Accountancy*⟩ **5** : to produce a desired effect or result : SUCCEED ⟨all things ~ together for good to them that love God —Rom 8:28 (AV)⟩ — often used with *out* ⟨hoped the plan would ~ out⟩ **6 a** : to make way slowly and with difficulty : move or progress laboriously or with sustained effort ⟨~*ed* up from office boy to president⟩ **b** : to sail to windward **7** : to permit of being worked : react in a specified way to being worked ⟨this wood ~*s* easily⟩ **8 a** : to be in agitation or restless motion ⟨the sea ~*s* high —Shak.⟩ **b** : FERMENT 1 — used esp. of a liquid or yeast **c** : to move slightly in relation to another part — used of parts (as of a ship's frame or plates) normally rigidly connected ⟨~*ed* in a seaway . . . and leaked —Alan Villiers⟩ **d** : to move in an undesigned direction due to imperfect fitting ⟨the shaft ~*s* in its bearing⟩ **e** *of rock* : to undergo slow moving, heaving, sinking, or sliding **f** : to get into a specified condition by slow or imperceptible movements ⟨the knot ~*ed* loose⟩ ⟨plug ~*ed* out of the pipe⟩ ⟨his jacket had ~*ed* up at the back of his neck⟩ **9** : to work a degree — used in Masonic and some other ritualistic orders
syn see ACT — **work at** : to be engaged or employed in : PRACTICE ⟨trained as a carpenter but seldom *works at* it⟩ ⟨less attractive girls must *work* harder *at* being popular —Lester David⟩ — **work double tides** : to perform the labor of two days in one — **work even** : to continue a knitting pattern without any alteration — **work into** : to force, urge, or insinuate into ⟨*worked* his foot *into* the boot⟩ ⟨*work* new courses *into* the curriculum⟩ — **work on 1** : AFFECT ⟨poetry *works on* the mind of the reader — not directly but by indirection —C.I.Glicksberg⟩ ⟨*worked on* his sympathies to get a loan⟩ **2** : to strive to influence or persuade ⟨noble hero . . . is *worked on* and betrayed by devilish Italian cunning —F.R. Leavis⟩ ⟨sent a high-priced lobby to *work on* the legislature —Beverly Smith⟩ — **work one's way** : to advance slowly against resistance or obstruction ⟨*worked his way* to the center of the jostling crowd⟩ ⟨*worked his way* cautiously down the cliff⟩ — **work the oracle** *Brit* : to gain something or succeed by scheming or wire pulling; *specif* : to raise money by doubtful ways — **work upon** : to have effect upon : operate on : PERSUADE, INFLUENCE ⟨so *worked upon* her adopted father with his threats —Max Peacock⟩ — **work water** *of a boiler* : FOAM, PRIME
work·abil·i·ty \ˌwərkəˈbilәd-ē, ˌwə̄k-, ˌwəik-, -lətē, -i\ *n* : the quality or state of being workable
work·able \ˈwərkəbəl, ˈwə̄k-, ˈwəik-\ *adj* **1** : capable of being worked ⟨~ plastic⟩ ⟨~ vein of coal⟩ ⟨~ lumber⟩ **2** : capable of being put into successful operation : PRACTICABLE, FEASIBLE ⟨finding a ~ program for disarmament —C.E.Egan⟩ — **work·able·ness** *n* -ES
work·a·day \-kə,dā\ *adj* [alter. of earlier *workyday*, fr. obs. *workyday* workday (n.), fr. ME *werkeday*, irreg. fr. *werk* work + *day*] **1** : relating to or suited for working days ⟨~ clothes⟩ **2** : EVERYDAY, PROSAIC, ORDINARY ⟨invested ~ things and people with romance and fantasy —Margaret Rutherford⟩
work and back *n* : SHEETWORK 1
work-and-back \ˈ==ˈ=\ *adv (or adj)* [*work and back*] : SHEETWISE
work and tumble *or* **work and flop** *vb* : to print by the work-and-tumble method
work-and-tumble \ˈ==ˈ==\ *or* **work-and-flop** \ˈ==ˈ=\ *adv (or adj)* : with all the pages of a signature imposed in one form so that when the sheet is printed, turned over side for side, backed, and cut two complete copies result
work and turn *vb* : to print by the work-and-turn method
work-and-turn \ˈ==ˈ=\ *adv (or adj)* : with all the pages of a signature imposed in one form so that when the sheet is printed, turned over end for end, backed, and cut two complete copies result
work and twist *or* **work and whirl** *vb* : to print by the work-and-twist method
work-and-twist *or* **work-and-whirl** \ˈ==ˈ=\ *adj* : involving a method whereby a sheet is printed twice on the same side from a two-up form by reversing the sheet when feeding the second time so that the part already printed by the first section of the form will be printed by the second section and vice versa
work-away \ˈ=ə,wā\ *n* [³*work* + *a* + *way*] : a person who works his passage on a ship
workbag \ˈ=,=\ *n* : a bag for holding implements or materials for work; *esp* : a bag for holding needlework
workbank \ˈ=,=\ *n* : ³BANK 3b
workbasket \ˈ=,==\ *n* : a basket for needlework
workbench \ˈ=,=\ *n* : a strong heavy waist-high table on which the work esp. of mechanics, machinists, and carpenters is performed
workboard \ˈ=,=\ *n* : a board providing support and surface for manual work
workboat \ˈ=,=\ *n* : a boat used for work purposes (as commercial fishing, harbor and waterway maintenance, ferrying supplies and machinery) rather than for sport or for passenger or naval service
workbook \ˈ=,=\ *n* **1** : a book outlining a suggested course of study in some subject or field **2** : a book or pamphlet setting forth rules governing the manner or method of work **3** : a book in which is recorded work done or planned **4** : a student's individual exercise or practice book consisting of a progressive series of problems to be solved directly on the pages and often supplementing the use of a textbook
workbox \ˈ=,=\ *n* : a box for holding instruments and materials esp. for needlework
work-brittle \ˈ=,==\ *adj* [¹*work* + *brittle*] *dial* : INDUSTRIOUS
work camp *n* : a camp for workers: as **a** : PRISON CAMP 1 **b** : a short-term group project in which individuals from one or more religious organizations volunteer their labor for the purpose of helping others in need; *also* : the group of workers of such a project
work car *n* : a railroad car used in the construction and maintenance of track
work curve *n* : a graphic record of the amount done in each successive part of a prolonged period of work — compare FATIGUE CURVE
¹workday \ˈ=,=\ *n* [ME *werkday*, fr. *werk* work + *day*] **1** : a day on which work is performed as distinguished from Sunday or a holiday : WORKING DAY **2 a** : the period of time in a day during which work is performed **b** : the number of hours determined by law, custom, or agreement during which a workman hired at a stated wage must work to be entitled to a day's pay
²workday \"\ *adj* : WORKADAY
work-dog \ˈ=,=\ *n* : WORKING DOG
worked *adj* [fr. past part. of ³*work*] : that has been subjected to some process of development, treatment, or manufacture ⟨cottons that have a ~ look and discourage need for any elaboration —*Women's Wear Daily*⟩ ⟨newly ~ field⟩ ⟨wall of ~ stone⟩
worked lumber *n* : lumber that has been matched or lapped or patterned or molded
worked up *adj* [fr. past part. of *work up*] : emotionally aroused : EXCITED, ANGRY ⟨was quite *worked up* and said they had been very anxious for our safety —A.F.Ellis⟩
work·er \ˈwərkər; ˈwə̄kə(r, ˈwəik-\ *n* -s [ME *worcher, werker*, fr. *worchen, werken* to work + *-er*] **1** : DOER, CREATOR ⟨~ of miracles⟩ ⟨~ of magic spells⟩ **2 a** : LABORER, TOILER ⟨~*s* in the Lord's vineyard⟩ ⟨migratory ~*s* in the orchards⟩ **b** : one who is employed esp. at manual or industrial labor for a wage ⟨rate increases for all the ~*s* in the steel industry⟩ **c** : one who works in a particular field ⟨~*s* in cancer research⟩ or industry or with a particular material — often used in combination **d** : a member of the working class ⟨party of ~*s* and small farmers⟩ **3** : one of the neuter usu. sterile individuals of the social ants, bees, and termites — see ANT illustration, HONEYBEE illustration **4 a** : a 2-handled scraping knife used in dressing leather **b** : a bobbin that moves across the pillow forming the pattern in bobbin lace — compare HANGER 5 **c** : any of various small rollers or cylinders in a textile machine (as a fearnought or carder) that has wire teeth set at such an angle as to draw the fiber bodily away from the large cylinder — compare STRIPPER 5 **5** *or* **worker plate** : a usu. electrotype plate from which printing is done — compare CASTER 1b **6 a** : one who works for a political party or party machine esp. to get out the vote **b** : SOCIAL WORKER **7** : WORKING FIRE
worker cell *n* : any of the smaller cells of a honeycomb in which larvae of worker bees are reared
worker comb *n* : the portion of honeycomb composed of worker cells
worker major *n* [*worker* + *major*, adj.] : MAXIM 4
worker minor *n* [*worker* + *minor*, adj.] : MINIM 6
worker-priest \ˈ==ˈ=\ *n* : a French Roman Catholic priest who for missionary purposes spends part of each weekday as a worker in a secular job
work farm *n* : a farm on which minor offenders are confined and put to work
workfellow \ˈ=,=(,)=\ *n* [¹*work* + *fellow*] : one engaged in the same work with another : companion in work
workfolk *or* **workfolks** \ˈ=,=\ *n pl* : working people; *esp* : farm workers
work force *n* **1** : the workers engaged in a specific activity ⟨the factory's *work force*⟩ **2** : the number of workers potentially assignable for any purpose ⟨yearly additions to the nation's *work force*⟩
work·ful \ˈwərkfəl\ *adj, archaic* : DILIGENT, INDUSTRIOUS
work function *n* : the energy that is needed for a particle to come from the interior of a medium and break through the surface — used esp. of the photoelectric and thermionic emission of electrons from metals
workgirl \ˈ=,=\ *n* : a girl employed for wages in manual labor esp. in industry
workhand \ˈ=,=\ *n* : a person employed (as on a farm or in a factory or shop) by someone else
work harden *vt* [¹*work*] : to harden and strengthen (metal) by cold-working
work hardness *n* : hardness of a metal induced by cold-working
workhead \ˈ=,=\ *n* : a head (as of a lath) that holds the work
workhorse \ˈ=,=\ *n* **1** : a horse used chiefly for labor as distinguished from driving, riding, or racing **2 a** : a person who undertakes arduous labor **b** : a markedly useful or durable vehicle, craft, or machine ⟨helicopter today . . . is the ~ of the air —W.O.Murphy⟩ **3** : SAWHORSE, TRESTLE 1a
workhouse \ˈ=,=\ *n* [ME *werkhous*, fr. OE *weorchūs*, fr. *weorc* work + *hūs* house] **1** *obs* : WORKSHOP, FACTORY **2** *Brit* : a house in which able-bodied poor are maintained at public expense and compelled to labor **3** : a house of correction in which minor offenders are confined and put to work
work in *vt* [³*work*] **1** : to insert or cause to penetrate by repeated or continued effort ⟨spread on the ointment and *work it in* thoroughly with the fingers⟩ **2** : to interpose or insinuate gradually or unobtrusively ⟨*work in* a few topical jokes⟩ : add

as an ingredient or so as to be an integral part : INTERWEAVE, INTERMINGLE

1working *adj* [fr. gerund of *3work*] **1 :** adequate to permit work to be done : sufficient in strength or numbers to accomplish results ⟨the party has a ~ majority in the senate⟩ ⟨~ knowledge of at least one other modern language —B.B.Thomas⟩ **2 :** assumed or adopted to permit or facilitate further work or activity ⟨a ~ draft of a peace treaty was submitted for discussion⟩ ⟨necessity for ~ agreements with her neighboring states on interstate construction projects —*Amer. Guide Series: N.J.*⟩

2working *n* -s [fr. gerund of *3work*] : an excavation or group of excavations made in mining, quarrying, or tunneling — used chiefly in pl. ⟨the ~s extended for miles underground⟩

working asset *n* [*1working*] : an asset other than a capital asset

working ball *n* [*working* (pres. part. of *3work*) + *ball*] : a bowling ball having sufficient spin to scatter the pins upon impact

working barrel *n* : the cylinder of a deep-well or mine pump

working beam *n* : WALKING BEAM

working capital *n* [*1working*] **1 :** capital currently used in business operations; *specif* : the excess of current assets over current liabilities **2 :** all capital of a business except that invested in capital assets

working card *n* [*working*, gerund of *3work*] : UNION CARD 1

working circle *n* : an area of forest from which a sustained yield of timber and by-products is planned

working class *n* [*working*, pres. part. of *3work*] : the class of people who are employed for wages usu. in manual labor; *also* : the social class, grade, or stratum made up of these workers

working-class \ˈ==ˌ=\ *adj* [*working class*] : relating to, deriving from, or suitable to the class of wage workers ⟨*working-class* attitude⟩ ⟨*working-class* virtues⟩ ⟨*working-class* solidarity⟩

working day *n* [*working*, gerund of *3work*] **1 :** a day when work is normally done as distinguished from Sundays and legal holidays **2 :** WORKDAY 2

working-day \ˈ==ˌ=\ *adj* [*working day*] : relating to or characteristic of working days : WORKADAY ⟨how full of briers is this *working-day* world —Shak.⟩

working dog *n* : a dog suited by size, breeding, or training for useful labor (as draft, sled, or herding work) as distinguished from one suited primarily for pet, show, or sporting use

working drawing *n* : a scale drawing of an object to be made or structure to be built intended for direct use by the workman — compare DETAIL DRAWING

working face *n* **1 :** FACE 10a **2 :** the surface (as of a block of stone or wood) to be operated upon or measured from ⟨measure the desired thickness from the *working face*⟩

working fire *n* : a fire requiring considerable work to extinguish : a bad fire

working fit *n* [*1working*] : SNUG FIT

working fluid *n* [*working*, pres. part. of *3work*] : a fluid working substance

working gauge *n* [*working*, gerund of *3work*] : a gauge used in testing work in the process of manufacture

working hole *n* : a hole in the side of a glass furnace through which molten glass is drawn off

working hunter *n* : a horse in a competitive event judged according to the pace, manners, way of going, and jumping style without regard to conformation

working hypothesis *n* [*1working*] : a hypothesis adopted as a guide to experiment or investigation or as a basis of action

working load *n* [*working*, gerund of *3work*] : the maximum load that a rope or structural member or machine is designed to bear

work·ing·man \ˈ==ˌman, -ˌmaa(ə)n\ *n, pl* **workingmen** [*working* (pres. part. of *3work*) + *man*] : one who works for wages usu. at manual labor : one of the working class as distinguished from the professional and business classes

working model *n* : a model of an actual or proposed machine that can do on a small scale the work which the machine itself does or is expected to do ⟨a *working model* of a freight locomotive⟩

working order *n* : a condition of a machine in which it functions according to its nature and purpose ⟨put a watch in good *working order*⟩

working paper *n* [*working*, gerund of *3work*] **1 a :** a paper on which tentative figures, memoranda, data, or analyses of accounts are set down during the conduct of a survey (as an audit) of a business **b :** a tentative statement prepared to serve as a basis for discussion or negotiation **2 working papers** *pl* : official documents legalizing the employment of a minor ⟨before being employed the boy had to produce his *working papers*⟩

working party *n* **1 :** a body of servicemen detailed to perform an assigned task beyond their ordinary duties **2** *Brit* : a committee created to investigate a problem ⟨report of the *working party* on the employment of blind persons —*Brit. Information Services*⟩

working pattern *n* : a pattern made from a master pattern and used in the making of the mold in which the required part is cast

working pit *n* : a mine shaft in which ore is hoisted and workmen are carried

working rod *n* : PUNTY

workings *pl of* WORKING

working sail *n* [*working*, pres. part. of *3work*] : one of the sails normally used in all weathers as distinguished from light sails added for light winds

working stress *n* [*working*, gerund of *3work*] : the stress to which material may be safely subjected in the course of ordinary use

working substance *n* [*working*, pres. part. of *3work*] : a usu. fluid substance that through changes of temperature, volume, and pressure is the means of carrying out thermodynamic processes or cycles (as in a heat engine or a refrigerating machine)

workingwoman \ˈ==ˌ==\ *n, pl* **workingwomen 1 :** a woman who is gainfully employed **2 :** the wife of a workingman

work in process : work in any of the stages through which it passes in being made into a finished product out of raw material

work in progress : work with which an artist or writer is engaged but which is not completed or approaching completion

work lead *n* : LEAD BULLION

work·less \ˈ=ləs\ *adj* [*1work* + *-less*] **1** *obs* : not accomplishing any work or effect : not functioning **2** *obs* : not carried out in practice **3 :** being without work or out of work : UNEMPLOYED, JOBLESS — **work·less·ness** *n* -ES

work load *n* **1 :** the amount of work or of working time expected from or assigned to an employee **2 :** the total amount of work to be performed by a department or other group of workers in a period of time ⟨weekly *work load*⟩

work·man \ˈ=mən\ *n, pl* **workmen** [ME *werkman*, fr. OE *weorcman*, fr. *weorc* work + *man*] **1 :** WORKINGMAN **2 :** a skilled laborer : ARTISAN, CRAFTSMAN ⟨certain more or less educated *workmen* rough of speech and manner —W.B.Yeats⟩ **3 :** one who creates or fashions esp. with skill and expertness ⟨untiring *workmen*, they have spared no pains to produce a poetry finer than that of any other country —Amy Lowell⟩

workmanlike \ˈ==ˌ=\ *adj* [ME *werkmanlike*, fr. *werkman* workman + *like*] : worthy of a good workman : well performed : SKILLFUL ⟨the book is a ~ job, with chronology, bibliography, and index —Louise S. Bechtel⟩ ⟨~ vocalization of a difficult part —Irving Kolodin⟩

1work·man·ly *adv* [ME *warkmanly*, fr. *werkman*, *warkman* workman + *-ly*, adv. suffix] *archaic* : in a skillful manner ⟨so ~ the blood and tears are drawn —Shak.⟩

2workmanly *adj* [*workman* + *-ly*, adj. suffix] : WORKMANLIKE

work·man·ship \ˈ==ˌship\ *n* [ME *werkmanschipe*, fr. *werkman* workman + *-schipe* -ship] **1 :** the art or skill of a workman : the execution or manner of making or doing something : CRAFTSMANSHIP; *also* : the quality imparted to a thing in the process of making : the character given to a work by the art or skill of the workman ⟨a vase of exquisite ~⟩ **2 :** something that is effected, made, or produced : MANUFACTURE, WORK; *esp* : something made by manual labor ⟨such roofs . . . are splendid pieces of ~ —Richard Jefferies⟩

workmaster \ˈ=ˌ==\ *n* : a master workman

workmate \ˈ=ˌ=\ *n, chiefly Brit* : a fellow worker

workmen's compensation insurance *n* : insurance against statutory damages (as provided by a workmen's compensation act) arising from injury to employees while in the employ of the insured employer

work of art 1 : a product of one of the fine arts; *esp* : a painting or sculpture of high artistic quality **2 :** an act or thing giving high aesthetic satisfaction to the beholder or auditor : something that has value or gives pleasure apart from its practical effect or usefulness ⟨take a detached view of their own lives and look upon them rather as *works of art* —André Maurois⟩

work off *vt* [*3work*] **1 :** to dispose of or get rid of by work or activity ⟨*work off* a debt⟩ ⟨pick a fight to *work off* a grudge⟩ : finish up ⟨when current defense contracts are *worked off* —*Time*⟩ **2 :** to print in final form for delivery or further processing : run off ⟨*work off* a poster⟩ ⟨*work off* a job⟩ **3 :** to palm off : pass off ⟨tried to *work off* the poem as his own⟩

work out *vt* **1 :** to effect by labor and exertion ⟨*work out* your own salvation —Phil 2:12 (AV)⟩ ⟨each novel's leading character *works out* his destiny —Otis Fellows⟩ **2 a :** to solve (as a problem) by a process of reasoning or calculation **b :** to devise, arrange, or achieve esp. by resolving difficulties or conflicts ⟨a better route was *worked out* —G.R.Stewart⟩ ⟨*work out* a plan of complete reconstruction —S.P.B.Mais⟩ ⟨*worked out* a compromise agreement that ended the dispute⟩ **c :** DEVELOP, ELABORATE ⟨whole sonata . . . was deeply felt and finely *worked out* —*N.Y. Times*⟩ ⟨though the final situation is not *worked out* with psychological profundity —Leslie Rees⟩ **3 :** to discharge fully (as a debt) by labor instead of money payment ⟨servants who had *worked out* their terms of servitude —R.A.Billington⟩ **4 :** to exhaust (as a mine or vein) by working **~** *vi* **1 a :** to prove effective or practicable or suitable ⟨if the plan *works out* satisfactorily⟩ **b :** to amount to a total or calculated figure : come to a figure — used with *at* ⟨this rate *works out* at an increase of 88°F for every mile . . . towards the center of the earth —W.E.Swinton⟩ **2 :** to go through a training or practice session esp. in an athletic specialty ⟨*works out* daily with sparring partners⟩ **3 :** to work outside the home as hired help : hire out

workout \ˈ=ˌ=\ *n* -s [*work out*] **1 :** a practice game, bout, or run : an exercise designed to test one's fitness or to increase one's fitness esp. for athletic competition ⟨daily ~s with barbells⟩ **2 :** a test or trial for determining ability or capacity or suitability ⟨in the production of dangerous war materials . . . automation has had its most complete ~ —Robert Bendiner⟩

work-out \ˈ=ˌ=\ *adj* [*work out*] *of a market* : not characterized by firm bids and offers

work over *vt* [*3work*] **1 :** to subject to thorough examination or study or treatment ⟨shelf stock would get thoroughly *worked over* as shoppers sought out packages with the latest dates —*Modern Packaging*⟩ ⟨spent some time in *working over* the available books —A.T.Weaver⟩ ⟨*working over* not only the edge and point but the entire surface of their artifacts —A.L.Kroeber⟩ **2 a :** to do over : REWORK ⟨saved the play by *working* the first act *over*⟩ ⟨*worked over* the old furniture⟩ **b :** to revise or alter radically or systematically ⟨the frontier . . . had *worked* them *over* inside —W.P.Webb⟩ **3 a :** to beat up or manhandle esp. with deliberate thoroughness ⟨none of them hesitated to *work* a man *over* for shifting a little out of line or talking —R.O.Bowen⟩ ⟨*working* them *over* with sabers, billies, and gun butts —*Time*⟩ **b :** to pick the pockets of **c :** to subject to thorough or systematic artillery fire, bombing, or strafing ⟨destroyers had *worked over* the point with their five-inch guns —Bill Alcine⟩

workpeople \ˈ=ˌ==\ *n pl* [*1work* + *people*] *chiefly Brit* : WORKERS, EMPLOYEES

work permit *n* : an authorization to work on a given job issued by a union to a nonmember

workpiece \ˈ=ˌ=\ *n* : a piece of work in process of manufacture

workplace \ˈ=ˌ=\ *n* : a place (as a shop or factory) where work is done

work print *n* : a completely edited motion-picture print used as a guide in cutting the original negative from which the final production prints will be made

work relief *n* : relief of the unemployed through wages paid for jobs provided by the government on public works

workroom \ˈ=ˌ=\ *n* : a room used esp. for manual work

works *pl of* WORK, *pres 3d sing of* WORK

works council *n* : a body or committee formed by an employer among workers within his organization for the discussion of problems of industrial relations

work sheet *n* **1 a :** a sheet that is used in making preliminary plans, auxiliary computations, notes, or comments as a guide in doing some piece of work **b :** a specially prepared sheet, pamphlet, or booklet containing data of assistance in planning and accomplishing some piece of work **c :** a working paper used by an accountant to assemble figures for financial statements of a business; *specif* : a sheet with a sufficient number of columns to provide for entering the trial balance, adjusting entries, profit and loss, and balance sheet items **2 a :** a sheet of paper on which are printed exercises and problems to be solved by a student **b :** a leaf or page in a workbook **3 :** JOB TICKET 1

workshop \ˈ=ˌ=\ *n* **1 a :** a small establishment where manufacturing or craftwork is carried on by a proprietor with or without helpers and often without power machinery — compare FACTORY, MACHINE SHOP **b :** a place or a method of literary or artistic creation ⟨not what the composer tells us about his ~ but what he is able to convey . . . through his finished work alone —Eric Blom⟩ **2 a :** a course or seminar emphasizing free discussion, exchange of ideas, demonstration of methods, and practical application of skills and principles given mainly for adults already employed in the field esp. of the social sciences and the practical and fine arts ⟨summer ~ in short-story writing⟩ ⟨choreographers' ~⟩ **b :** LABORATORY 1b

work-shy \ˈ=ˌ=\ *adj* [*1work* + *shy*] : disinclined or unwilling to work : LAZY

works manager *n* : an official in a manufacturing company who is usu. the head of the production departments

work song *n* : a song sung in rhythm with work — compare CHANTEY

work spreading *n* [*1work* + *spreading*, gerund of *spread*] : a method of reducing unemployment by the arrangement of work and working hours of employees so as to spread the available work among the largest practicable number of workers

workstand \ˈ=ˌ=\ *n* [*2work* + *stand*] : WORKTABLE

workstock \ˈ=ˌ=\ *n* : farm livestock (as horses and mules) kept for labor rather than for production of a marketable product

work stone *n* : an inclined grooved stone or iron plate to conduct molten lead from the hearth in a lead smelting furnace to the metal pot

work stoppage *n* : concerted cessation of work by a group of employees usu. more spontaneous and less serious than a predetermined and organized strike

work-stopper \ˈ=ˌ==\ *n, chiefly Austral* : a labor organizer who induces workmen to strike in order to obtain their objectives

work-study program *n* : a high school or college student's program so planned as to allow for work experience

worktable \ˈ=ˌ==\ *n* : a table for holding working materials and implements; *esp* : a small table with drawers and other conveniences for needlework

work ticket *n* **1 :** JOB TICKET 1 **2 :** JOB ORDER

work train *n* : a train for transporting men and materials for construction, repairs, or maintenance of a railroad

work up *vb* [*3work*] *vt* **1 :** to stir up : ROUSE, EXCITE ⟨*work up* indignation against the murderers —C.H.Sykes⟩ : summon up ⟨the novelist can *work up* sufficient interest in them to record their minor and pathetic self-deceptions —Dachine Rainer⟩ ⟨*work up* a sweat in a gymnasium⟩ **2 :** DEVELOP, ELABORATE ⟨to have *worked up* a scheme to the point where it is necessary to have outside capital —Mary Austin⟩ ⟨*work up* some strong emotional scenes —Henry Hewes⟩ ⟨*work up* a comedy act⟩ **3 :** to keep (a crew) at work upon needless jobs for punishment **~** *vi* **1 :** to rise gradually and steadily in intensity or emotional tone ⟨story develops . . . and *works up* to a brilliant conclusion —*Sydney (Australia) Bull.*⟩ ⟨afternoon thunderstorm beginning to *work up* —G.R.Stewart⟩ **2 :** to improve in efficiency ⟨the fleet . . . has been gradually *working up* as it steams eastward —H.W.Baldwin⟩ **3 :** to rise to the printing surface — used of a space, lead, or other part of a form not intended to print

work-up \ˈ=ˌ=\ *n* -s [*work up*] **1 :** an unintended mark upon a printed sheet caused by the rising in the chase of a space, lead, or piece of furniture while the job is on the press or the form is being molded for plating **2 :** the laboratory, X-ray, and other procedures involved in the diagnostic study of a patient with regard to his symptoms or complaints ⟨cardiac *work-up*⟩ ⟨entered the hospital for a gastric *work-up*⟩

workweek \ˈ=ˌ=\ *n* [*1work* + *week*] : the hours or days of work in a calendar week ⟨40-hour ~⟩ ⟨a 5-day ~⟩

workwoman \ˈ=ˌ==\ *n, pl* **workwomen** : a woman who works : a female worker

1world \ˈwərld, *esp before pause or consonant* -rəl; ˈwə̄ld\ *n* -s [ME *weorold, world*, fr. OE *weorold, woruld, worold* human existence, this world, age; akin to OHG *weralt, worolt* age, world, ON *verǫld*; all fr. a prehistoric WGmc-NGmc compound whose first constituent is represented by OE *wer* man and whose second constituent is akin to OE *yldo* age, *ald* old — more at VIRILE, OLD] **1 a :** the earthly state of human existence : this present life **b :** a future state of existence : the life after death — usu. used with a qualifier ⟨a better ~ where he expected to meet all . . . who had gone before him —Van Wyck Brooks⟩ ⟨the next ~⟩ **2 a :** the earth with all its inhabitants and all things upon it ⟨a Great Spirit who rules the ~ —F.J.Haskin⟩ ⟨a voyage around the ~⟩ **b :** something (as a sphere or whole) held to resemble or suggest the world **3 :** individual experience of or concern with life on earth : the sum of the affairs which affect the individual : course of life : CAREER ⟨I hope the ~ goes well with you⟩ **4 :** all the inhabitants of the earth : the whole of mankind : the human race : human society ⟨the whole ~ was redeemed by Christ —H.P. Liddon⟩ **5 :** the concerns of the earth and its affairs as distinguished from heaven : the pursuits and interests of this life as distinguished from the life to come : the present existence and its interests : temporal or mundane affairs ⟨I too love the earth and hate the ~ —George Santayana⟩ **6 :** secular affairs or interests as distinguished from religious or clerical **7 :** the earth and the heavens : the entire universe as an orderly system : the system of created things **8 :** a part of the universe constituting a distinct entity and usu. possessing one or more peculiar and identifying characteristics ⟨the lower ~⟩ — see NETHERWORLD, UNDERWORLD **9 :** the section of mankind engrossed in the concerns or pleasures of this present life and as a result often held to constitute the ungodly part of mankind : worldly persons **10 a :** a particular division, section, or generation of the inhabitants of the earth distinguished by living together at the same place or at the same time **b (1) :** a more or less definite class or division of persons distinguished by some usu. specified characteristic (as interests or occupation) ⟨insistence upon a more complete devotion from the performing and listening ~s —J.N.Burk⟩ **(2) :** the sphere, domain, region, or realm of the interests of a particular group of persons ⟨my experiences in the academic ~ —Hans Meyerhoff⟩ ⟨the ~ of American history⟩ **11 :** human society : the scene of the customs, practices, and interests of men as social beings : public or social affairs and occupations : social or business life, manners, and usages ⟨voices which we hear in solitude . . . grow faint and inaudible as we enter into the ~ —R.W.Emerson⟩ **12 :** a period or age of human history having certain peculiar and identifying characteristics ⟨the ~ of the 19th century⟩ **13 :** a part, division, or section of the earth together with its inhabitants and concerns that is a separate independent unit : a division of the globe with its inhabitants : a part of the globe as known or contemplated at a particular period or by a particular people — see NEW WORLD, OLD WORLD **14 :** the sphere or scene of one's life and action : the area of one's interests and activities : the realm in which one moves or lives ⟨among the friends of his three ~s, the intellectuals, the . . . family circle, and the farmers —H.S. Canby⟩ **15 :** an indefinitely great multitude or quantity : a large number : an infinite or vast amount ⟨there were ~s of cattle in Texas —E.C.Abbott & Helena Smith⟩ ⟨you will find a ~ of delight in some of the lovely pieces —*Irish Digest*⟩ — sometimes used adverbially with *a* or in pl. ⟨a ~ too wide⟩ ⟨his vernacular was ~s away from her formal art —Carl Van Doren⟩ **16 a :** the whole body of living persons : people in general : society at large : PUBLIC **b :** the people of a particular district or area in general : local society **17 :** WORLD'S PEOPLE **18 :** a group of beings or things having certain characteristics in common and held to constitute a whole **19 :** one of the grand divisions or primary groups of natural objects : KINGDOM 6 ⟨animal ~⟩ ⟨inorganic ~⟩ **20 :** a planet or other celestial body; *esp* : one that is inhabited and the scene of interests analogous to those of earth dwellers **21 :** an area of the hand or fingers held by palmists to represent mind in the case of the upper division or material matters in the case of the middle division or sensual or base qualities in the case of the lower division: **a :** an area of a finger constituted by a phalanx or of the thumb constituted by a phalanx or the Mount of Venus ⟨the three ~s of palmistry apply just as much to the thumb as to any of the fingers —W.G.Benham⟩ **b :** a division of the hand constituted by the fingers or by the area between the base of the fingers and the middle of the palm or by the area between the middle of the palm and the wrist — **against the world :** against all opposition : in the face of all mankind — **for worlds :** for all the wealth in the world : on any account — usu. used in the negative ⟨I wouldn't stand in his way *for worlds* —W.S.Gilbert⟩ — **in the world :** among innumerable possibilities : EVER — used as an intensive ⟨where *in the world* did you go⟩ ⟨what *in the world* is it⟩ — **out of this world :** of the highest quality : remarkably fine : of extraordinary excellence : MAGNIFICENT, SUPERB ⟨her voice is simply *out of this world*⟩ ⟨genuine Belgian cooking that is *out of this world* —T.H. Fielding⟩

2world \"\ *adj* **1 :** of or relating to the world ⟨a ~ hypothesis⟩ ⟨a ~ championship⟩ **2 a :** extending or found throughout the world : UNIVERSAL, WORLDWIDE ⟨~ affairs⟩ ⟨~ problems⟩ ⟨a ~ language⟩ ⟨~ culture⟩ **b :** involving or applying to the whole world ⟨~ government⟩ ⟨a ~ state⟩ ⟨~ politics⟩ **c :** known and usu. renowned throughout the world ⟨~ figures⟩ ⟨a ~ artist⟩

world-beater \ˈ=ˌ==\ *n* : one that does or is able to excel all others of its kind (as in quality or performance) : CHAMPION ⟨a very good artist without being a *world-beater* —*Sydney (Australia) Bull.*⟩ ⟨a story . . . that is a *world-beater*, bar none —*Blue Bk.*⟩

world communion sunday *n, usu cap W&C&S* : the first Sunday in October on which ecumenical Christians around the world celebrate Holy Communion as an expression of their Christian unity

world day of prayer *usu cap W&D&P* : the first Friday in Lent observed by ecumenical Christians around the world as a day of worship and prayer for missions

world federalism *n* **1 :** federalism on a worldwide basis **2** *usu cap* **a :** the principles and policies of the World Federalists **b :** the body or movement composed of World Federalists

1world federalist *adj, usu cap W&F* : of, relating to, or associated with World Federalism ⟨*World Federalist* principles⟩

2world federalist *n* **1 :** an adherent or advocate of world federalism **2** *usu cap* : a member of a movement arising after World War II advocating the formation of a federal union of the nations of the world with limited but positive governmental powers

world·ful \-dˌfu̇l\ *n, pl* **worldfuls** [*1world* + *-ful*] : as much or as many as would fill a world ⟨a whole ~ of light and joy —William Black⟩

world ground *n* : the underlying basis of reality

world·ing \-diŋ\ *n* -s [alter. (influenced by *2-ing*) of *worldling*] : WORLDLING

world island *n, usu cap W & I* : the landmass consisting of Europe, Asia, and Africa ⟨who rules the *World Island* commands the world —H.J.Mackinder⟩ — used chiefly in geopolitics; compare HEARTLAND

world·let \-dlət\ *n* -s [*1world* + *-let*] : a little world

world·li·ness \-dlēnəs, -lin-\ *n* -ES [ME *worldlynesse*, fr. *worldly* + *-nesse* -ness] : the quality or state of being worldly : a disposition or tendency to emphasize the things of the

world rather than those of the spirit **:** devotion to or love of worldly affairs usu. accompanied by neglect of religious duties or spiritual needs

world·ling \-dliŋ, -lēŋ\ *n* -s [¹*world* + *-ling*] **1 :** a person engrossed in the concerns of this present world **:** one devoted to this world and its interests, pleasures, and enjoyments **:** a worldly or worldly-minded person ⟨among ~*s* unlikely to be offended by a whiff of the smoking room —J.B.Boothroyd⟩ **2 :** a citizen or inhabitant of the world **:** EARTHLING 1 ⟨the new element where . . . the pressure would kill a ~ in a few seconds —J.E.Belliveau⟩

world·ly \ˈwər(ə)l(d)lē, ˈwōl(d)-, -(d)li\ *adj, sometimes* -ER/-EST [ME, fr. OE *woruldlic*, fr. *woruld* world + *-lic* -ly] **1 :** of or relating to this world **:** associated with the earthly existence of man **:** earthly rather than heavenly or spiritual ⟨concentration upon ~ goods and ~ advancement —Lewis Mumford⟩ ⟨the ~ kind of charm one associates with cabaret singers —Henry Hewes⟩ ⟨~ fame⟩ **2** *archaic* **:** of, relating to, or associated with the earth or its inhabitants **:** EARTHLY 1a ⟨~ creatures⟩ **3 :** interested in or concerned with the enjoyments of this present existence **:** devoted to the world and its pursuits **:** characterized by interest in and concentration on practical and immediate affairs and concerns (as success, gain, pleasure, or self-esteem) and indifference to matters spiritual ⟨the most ~ of the eighteenth-century ecclesiastics —Hilaire Belloc⟩ ⟨the fashionable talk of her ~ rival —W.M.Thackeray⟩ **4 :** WORLDLY-WISE **syn** see EARTHLY

worldly-minded \ˈ==ˈ==\ *adj* **:** devoted to or engrossed in worldly interests **:** having one's thoughts or interests set upon things of this world ⟨one society is genuinely pious, another *worldly-minded* —H.L.Kroeber⟩ — **worldly-mind·ed·ness** *n*

worldly-wise \ˈ==ˈ=\ *adj* [ME, fr. *worldly* in a worldly manner (fr. *worldly*, adj.) + *wise*] **:** wise as to things and ways of this world

worldly wise·man \-ˈwīz,man, -ˌmən\ *n, often cap both Ws* [*worldly-wise* + *man*] **:** one wise in the ways of the world ⟨a *worldly wiseman* among idealists —R.M.Lovett⟩

world power *n* [trans. of G *weltmacht*] **:** a political unit (as a nation or state) powerful enough to affect the entire world by its influence or actions — compare GREAT POWER

world premiere *n* **:** the first regular performance (as of a theatrical production) anywhere

worlds *pl of* WORLD

world's end *n* **:** the end or most distant part of the world **:** the remotest regions of the earth — compare THULE

world series *n* **1 :** a series of baseball games played in the fall of each year between the pennant winners of the major leagues to decide the professional championship of the U.S. **2 :** a championship contest resembling the world series ⟨the *world series* of dogdom⟩

world's fair *n* **:** an international exposition usu. featuring exhibits and participants from all over the world ⟨the sort of temporary structure you see at a *world's fair* —E.B.White⟩

world's fair plant *n, usu cap W&F* [so called fr. its use as a garden decoration at the Chicago World's Fair of 1893] **:** SUMMER CYPRESS

world-shaking \ˈ=ˌ==\ *adj* **:** sufficiently important to affect decisively the entire world **:** EARTHSHAKING ⟨the contest . . . was no *world-shaking* affair —G.C.Sellery⟩

world soul *n* **:** a spiritual being having the same relation to the world as a whole that the soul has to the individual being **:** an animating spirit or creative principle of the universe related to the world as the human soul is to the body **:** an intelligent animating, indwelling principle of the cosmos held to be its organizing or integrating cause or its source of motion — compare ABSOLUTE 2a(1), ATMAN, NOUS 1a

world's people *n pl* **:** persons who are not members of one's own religious group — used chiefly by the Friends and the Shakers

world spirit *n* **1 :** the animating spirit of the universe **:** WORLD SOUL **2 :** ²GOD b(1), b(2), b(3)

world's record *n* **:** a record officially recognized as the best established anywhere in the world ⟨set a new *world's record* for the 100-yard dash⟩

world's wonder *n* **:** SOAPWORT 1

world view *n* [trans. of G *weltanschauung*] **:** WELTANSCHAUUNG ⟨the ceremonial cycle . . . reflects and reaffirms the Hopi *world view* —Laura Thompson⟩ ⟨each individual has his own experiences and out of them forms his *world view* —J.L. Myres⟩

world war *n* **:** a war involving most of the nations or a preponderant portion of the territory of the earth

¹world·ward \ˈwər(ə)ldwərd\ *adv* [¹*world* + *-ward*] **:** in the direction of or toward the world ⟨went ~ from the island —Bayard Taylor⟩

²worldward \ˈ"\ *adj* **:** directed toward or facing the world ⟨~ conduct⟩

world-weariness \ˈ=ˌ===\ *n* **:** the quality or state of being world-weary

world-weary \ˈ=ˌ=\ *adj* **:** weary of the world or wearied by the life of the world; *esp* **:** bored by overindulgence in material pleasures ⟨a *world-weary* young man⟩ ⟨our *world-weary* generation⟩

worldwide \ˈ=ˈ=\ *adj* **:** extended or extending throughout the entire world ⟨movement toward ~ unity in the churches —Liston Pope⟩ ⟨a ~ empire⟩ ⟨~ disarmament⟩

world-wise \ˈ=ˌ=\ *adj* **:** WORLDLY-WISE ⟨a statesman . . . experienced and *world-wise* —*Fortnightly Rev.*⟩

world without end *adv* [ME *world withouten end*, fr. *world* + *withouten* without + *end*] **:** as if in a state of existence having no end **:** ETERNALLY, FOREVER ⟨as it was in the beginning, is now, and ever shall be, *world without end* —*Bk. of Com. Prayer*⟩

¹world-without-end \ˈ==ˌ=ˈ=\ *adj* **:** lasting for all time **:** EVERLASTING, ETERNAL, PERPETUAL ⟨a time . . . too short to make a *world-without-end* bargain in —Shak.⟩

²world-without-end \ˈ"\ *n* **:** a state of existence having no end **:** ETERNITY, PERPETUITY

¹worm \ˈwərm, ˈwōm, ˈwəim\ *n* -s *often attrib* [ME, fr. OE *wyrm* serpent, dragon, worm; akin to OHG *wurm* serpent, dragon, worm, ON *ormr*, Goth *waurms* serpent, L *vermis* worm, Gk *rhomos* woodworm] **1 a :** EARTHWORM; *broadly* **:** an annelid worm **b :** any of numerous relatively small more or less elongated usu. naked and soft-bodied animals resembling an earthworm: as (1) **:** a member of the old group Vermes (2) **:** an insect larva; *esp* **:** one that is a destructive grub, caterpillar, or maggot (3) **:** SHIPWORM (4) **:** BLINDWORM **2 a :** a human being resembling a worm or reptile as an object of contempt, loathing, or pity **:** WRETCH ⟨made me feel a ~ for my ignorance —H.J.Laski⟩ ⟨who, like the ~*s* they are, hide under the rock of the Fifth Amendment —*Phoenix Flame*⟩ **b :** something that inwardly torments or devours in a manner suggestive of the gnawing, boring, or working of a worm ⟨the ~ of care . . . gives her no rest —Padraic Fallon⟩ ⟨the ~ of conscience gnaws incessantly⟩ **c** *obs* **:** an impulse, perversity, or marked irrationality of mind **3** *archaic* **:** SNAKE, SERPENT, DRAGON **4 a :** a disorder caused by the presence of parasitic worms in the body and esp. in the intestines **:** HELMINTHIASIS — usu. used in pl. **b** *Scot* **:** TOOTHACHE **5 a :** LYTTA **b :** VERMIS **6 :** something (as a mechanical device) spiral or vermiculate in form or appearance: as **a :** a double corkscrew on the end of a rammer for extracting a wad or ball from a muzzle-loading gun **b :** the thread of a screw **c :** a short revolving screw whose threads gear with the teeth of a worm wheel or a rack — compare WORM THREAD **d** (1) **:** a tube or pipe twisted into coils; *also* **:** a system of such coiled tube or pipe (2) **:** a spiral condensing tube used in distilling **e** (1) **:** ARCHIMEDES' SCREW (2) **:** a conveyor working on the principle of such a screw **7 :** something resembling or suggestive of an earthworm ⟨far away . . . a miniature ~ of train rolled tinily along the embankment —Bruce Marshall⟩ ⟨in some line regiments a black ~ in the gold lace . . . denotes a perpetual mourning for some famous general —*N.Y.Times*⟩

²worm \ˈ"\ *vb* -ED/-ING/-S *vi* **1 :** to hunt or dig for worms ⟨birds and children are ~*ing* on the lawn after the rain⟩ **2 a :** to move, go, or proceed sinuously in or as if in the manner of a worm ⟨~*ed* through the snow and peered over a snow-covered rock beside the roadway —F.V.W.Mason⟩ ⟨we ~*ed* into the . . . office —Vincent McHugh⟩ ⟨the preposterous irrelevancy which ~*ed* through his mind —Marcia Davenport⟩ **b** (1) **:** to proceed or make one's way insidiously or deviously often with harmful intent or effect — usu. used with *into* ⟨spies ~ into important positions⟩ ⟨plans to ~ into his teacher's favor⟩ ⟨they have ~*ed* into the government and the labor movement —*Newsweek*⟩ (2) **:** to evade or escape in indirect or subtle fashion **:** WRIGGLE — usu. used with *out of* ⟨hopes to ~ out of his difficulties⟩ ⟨will do wrong and then try to ~ out of his punishment if he can⟩ **3 :** to lay a small line or yarn in the interstices between the strands of a larger rope in order to make an even surface before parceling and serving **4 :** to fish with worm as bait ~ *vt* **1 :** to cut the lytta from under the tongue of (a dog) to prevent madness **2 :** to make a screw thread on ⟨a machine that ~*s* screws⟩ **3 :** to cause to be eaten by worms ⟨a ~*ed* tree stump⟩ ⟨finds that his winter suit has been badly ~*ed*⟩ ⟨the old beams are firm and have not been ~*ed*⟩ **4 :** to remove or clear out worms from ⟨the dog has been ~*ed*⟩ **5 a :** to cause to move or proceed in or as if in the manner of a worm ⟨solid rock into which the drill had ~*ed* its long tongue —Thomas Wood †1950⟩ ⟨~ his big brown hand into his trousers pocket —J.N.Hall⟩ ⟨the queue ~*ed* itself on a little —Jan Struther⟩ ⟨~*ed* the strip deep into the American public consciousness —Coulton Waugh⟩ **b :** to insinuate or introduce (oneself) by devious or subtle means — usu. used with *into* ⟨seeks to ~ himself into a commanding position⟩ ⟨the group is ~*ing* itself into public favor⟩ **6 :** to wind rope or yarn spirally round and between the strands of (as a cable) before serving ⟨~ rope⟩ **7 a :** to obtain or extract by artful or insidious questioning ⟨determined not to let them ~ the secret from him⟩ — usu. used with *out of* ⟨~*ed* this information out of the prisoner —Shipley Thomas⟩ ⟨had ~*ed* out of them what they had been doing —Oscar Wilde⟩ **b :** to procure or acquire by pleading, asking, or persuading ⟨is trying to ~ a pension from the government⟩ — usu. used with *out of* ⟨is expected in time to ~ all the money out of him⟩ ⟨is ~*ing* permission out of his parent⟩ **8 :** to clean or draw a wad or cartridge from (a muzzle-loading firearm) with a wormer

worm bark *n* **1 :** the bark of the cabbage bark sometimes used in medicine as a vermifuge — compare SURINAM CABBAGE TREE **2 :** CABBAGE BARK

wormcast \ˈ=ˌ=\ *n* **1 :** a cylindrical mass of earth voided by an earthworm **2 :** the fossil trail of a worm

worm conveyor *n* **:** CONVEYER 2a(8)

worm drive *n* **:** a drive or propulsion gear comprising a worm engaged with a driver gear usu. at right angles

worm-eaten \ˈ=ˌ==\ *adj* [ME *worm-eten*, fr. ¹*worm* + *eten*, past part. of *eten* to eat] **1 a :** eaten or burrowed by worms ⟨*worm-eaten* timber⟩ **b :** resembling something filled with wormholes **:** PITTED ⟨the material has a *worm-eaten* appearance⟩ **2 :** WORN-OUT, ANTIQUATED, DECAYED ⟨attempting new projects with *worm-eaten* methods⟩ ⟨wanted to update the *worm-eaten* regulations⟩

worm-eating warbler \ˈ=ˌ==-\ *n* [¹*worm* + *eating*, pres. part. of *eat*] **:** a warbler (*Helmitheros vermivorus*) of the eastern U.S. of chiefly terrestrial habits that is olivaceous above and creamy below with black and buffy stripes on the crown

worm eel *n* **:** any of numerous small wormlike burrowing tropical eels (family Echelidae) in some respects resembling the large conger eels

worm·er \ˈwərmər\ *n* -s **1 :** one that worms; *specif* **:** a drug or medicine used to remove or clear out worms (as from dogs or poultry) **2 a :** a double corkscrew on the end of a rammer for extracting a wad or cartridge from a muzzle-loading gun **b :** a rammer with such a screw

worm fence *n* **:** a zigzag fence with each section consisting of usu. six to eight rails that interlock with the rails of adjacent sections and are supported by crossed poles — called also *snake fence*, *Virginia fence*

worm gear *n* **1 :** WORM WHEEL **2 :** a gear of a worm and a worm wheel working together

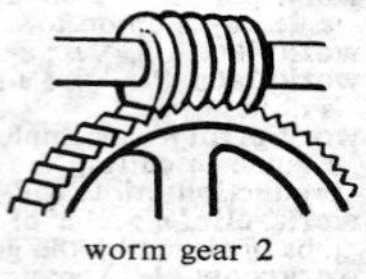

worm gear 2

worm grass *n* **1 :** PINKROOT **2 :** a European white-flowered stonecrop (*Sedum album*)

wormhole \ˈ=ˌ=\ *n* **:** the burrow of a worm; *esp* **:** a minute hole in wood, cloth, or paper made by a worm or larva

wor·mi·an bone \ˈwō(r)mēən-\ *n, usu cap W* [NL *wormianus* of Worm, fr. Ole *Worm* †1654 Dan. physician + L *-ianus* -ian] **:** a small irregular plate of bone interposed in a suture between large cranial bones

wormier *comparative of* WORMY

wormiest *superlative of* WORMY

worming *n* -s [fr. gerund of ²*worm*] **1 :** the action of one that worms **2 :** small stuff used to worm a rope or cable

worm·ish \ˈwərmish\ *adj* [¹*worm* + *-ish*] **:** WORMLIKE

worm·less \-mləs\ *adj* **:** free from or lacking worms

wormlike \ˈ=ˌ=\ *adj* **:** resembling or suggestive of a worm **:** VERMIFORM

worm·ling \-mliŋ\ *n* -s [¹*worm* + *-ling*] **1 :** a small worm **2 :** WRETCH ⟨the poor ~*s* of the earth⟩

worm lion *n* **:** any of various flies (genus *Vermileo*) of the family Rhagionidae having larvae that excavate pits in the sand like those of the ant lion

worm lizard *n* **:** a wormlike limbless lizard of the genus *Amphisbaena*

worm moss *n* **:** CORSICAN MOSS

worm-nest \ˈ=ˌ=\ *n* **:** a swelling or nodule in the brisket or flank of cattle containing worms of the genus *Onchocerca*

worm out *vt* [²*worm* + *out*] **1 :** to push or force out by subtle pressure or undermining ⟨is trying to *worm* his partner *out* of the business⟩ **2 :** to dispossess or take from by subtle or deceptive means ⟨his associates hope to *worm* him *out* of his inheritance⟩

worm powder *n* [¹*worm*] **:** an anthelmintic powder

wormroot \ˈ=ˌ=\ *n* **:** PINKROOT

worms *pl of* WORM, *pres 3d sing of* WORM

wormseed \ˈ=ˌ=\ *n* [ME *wyrmsed*, fr. *wyrm*, *worm* worm + *sed* seed] **1 :** any of various plants whose seeds possess anthelmintic properties: as **a :** any of several ragweeds (as *Artemisia santonica* and *A. pauciflora*) **b :** MEXICAN TEA **2 a :** the fruit of the Mexican tea **b :** SANTONICA 2; *also* **:** LEVANT WORMSEED 1

wormseed mustard *n* **:** a slender yellow-flowered mustard (*Erysimum cheiranthoides*) that is often troublesome as a weed and has seed formerly reputed to be anthelmintic

wormseed oil *n* **:** either of two essential oils: **a :** LEVANT WORMSEED OIL **b :** CHENOPODIUM OIL

worm's-eye view \ˈ=ˌ=-\ *n* **:** a view as if by a worm from below or the underside ⟨from both the bird's-eye view of the executive and the *worm's-eye view* of the employee, she has been familiar with industrial problems —*Current Biog.*⟩

worm shell *n* **:** a shell of *Vermetus* or a related genus

worm snake *n* **:** any of various small harmless burrowing snakes of wormlike appearance: as **a :** THUNDER SNAKE 2 **b :** BLIND SNAKE

worm thread *n* **:** a form of screw thread suitable for the worms of worm gearing

worm trail *n* **:** any of various markings in fossiliferous rocks made by the passage of extinct worms

worm tube *n* **1 :** the membranous shell-like tube made by many marine worms; *also* **:** such a tube when fossilized **2 :** WORM 6d(2)

wormweed \ˈ=ˌ=\ *n* **:** PINKROOT

worm wheel *n* **:** a toothed wheel gearing with the threads of a worm

worm-wheel hob thread *n* **:** the thread form on hobs used for cutting worm-wheel teeth or worm threads

worm wire *n* **:** FISH TAPE

wormwood \ˈ=ˌ=\ *n* [ME *wormwode*, alter. (influenced by ¹*worm* & *wode* wood) of *wermode*, fr. OE *wermōd* wormwood, absinthe; akin to OHG *wermuota* wormwood] **1 :** a plant of the genus *Artemisia*; *esp* **:** a European woody herb (*A. absinthium*) of a bitter slightly aromatic taste used chiefly in making absinthe **2 :** something bitter, galling, or grievous **:** BITTERNESS ⟨the gall and ~ of being a cripple —Dixon Wecter⟩ ⟨it was ~ for him to accept charity⟩

wormwood oil *n* **:** a dark green to brown bitter narcotic essential oil obtained from the leaves and tops of a wormwood (*Artemisia absinthium*) and used as a flavoring agent in liqueurs and esp. formerly in medicine as a tonic and anthelmintic — called also *absinthe oil*

wormwood sage *n* **:** a perennial white or tawny tomentose sagebrush (*Artemisia frigida*) with a stout woody crown, small leaves twice or thrice ternately divided, and flower heads with many long hairs between the flowers

wormy \ˈwərmē, ˈwōm-, ˈwəim-, -mi\ *adj* -ER/-EST [ME, fr. ¹*worm* + *-y*] **1 :** attacked or burrowed by worms ⟨~ wood⟩ ⟨a ~ apple⟩ **2 :** infested or afflicted with worms ⟨~ fish⟩ ⟨a ~ dog⟩ **3 :** full of or abounding in worms ⟨the ~ soil⟩ ⟨a ~ grave⟩ **4 :** resembling or suggestive of the appearance, habits, or condition of a worm ⟨~ lengths of licorice candy⟩ ⟨all the ~ expressions indicative of bad conscience, false modesty, and genteelism —J.M.Barzun⟩

wormy halibut *n* **:** Pacific halibut infected with a myxosporidian protozoan (*Unicapsula muscularis*) that invades the muscle fibers and forms long swollen cysts which make the flesh unsuitable for table use

worn [ME] *past part of* WEAR

worn-down \ˈ=ˈ=\ *adj* **1 :** showing the effect of wear ⟨a *worn-down* pair of shoes⟩ ⟨the worn-down riverbed⟩ ⟨a *worn-down* estate⟩ **2 :** nervously exhausted or fatigued ⟨a *worn-down* woman weary of eternal housework⟩ ⟨a *worn-down* and enfeebled old man⟩

worn·ness \ˈwōrnnəs, ˈwȯr-\ *n* -ES **:** the quality or state of being worn ⟨overhead rehearsal lights . . . drained the color from the scenery and accentuated its wrinkled ~ —Truman Capote⟩

worn-out \ˈ=ˈ=\ *adj* [fr. past part. of *wear out*] **1 :** used, damaged, or worn to the extent of being nearly or completely useless or unserviceable **:** DILAPIDATED ⟨an old *worn-out* suit⟩ ⟨a *worn-out* automobile⟩ **2 :** entirely spent or exhausted in strength, energy, or vitality **:** DISSIPATED, DEPLETED ⟨fertilizer was applied to *worn-out* soils —P.E.James⟩ ⟨buying *worn-out* horses and cattle⟩ **3 :** being out of fashion or use **:** STALE, TRITE, HACKNEYED ⟨a recurrence of *worn-out* adjectives makes much of his work monotonous —Roland Mathias⟩ ⟨the poet is betrayed by clichés and *worn-out* figures of speech —Burges Johnson⟩ — **worn-out·ness** *n* -ES

wo·ro·ni·na·ce·ae \wə,rōnəˈnāsē,ē\ *n pl, cap* [NL, fr. *Woronina*, genus of fungi (fr. Michael S. *Woronin* †1903 Russ. mycologist) + *-aceae*] *in some classifications* **:** a family of simple fungi (order Chytridiales) distinguished from others of the order by biflagellate zoospores

worral *or* **worrel** *var of* WARAL

wor·ri·cow \ˈwəri,kü\ *n* [¹*worry* + *cow* (goblin)] *Scot* **:** BUGABOO, HOBGOBLIN; *specif* **:** DEVIL

worried *adj* [fr. past part. of ¹*worry*] **1 :** mentally troubled or concerned **:** DISTRESSED ⟨they were perplexed, vexed and ~ —Ernie Pyle⟩ **2 :** marked or accompanied by worry ⟨a ~ frown⟩ ⟨made one last ~ check of their patients —J.P.O'Neill⟩ ⟨gave one of his ~ mornings to a . . . scouting of proposed contracts —J.G.Cozzens⟩ — **wor·ried·ly** \ˈwər·|ədlē, ˈwə·r|, |ēd-, -li\ *adv*

wor·ri·er \|ēə(r)\ *n* -s **:** one that worries

wor·ri·less \|ələs\ *adj* [²*worry* + *-less*] **:** free from care or worries

wor·ri·ment \|ēmənt, |im-\ *n* -s [¹*worry* + *-ment*] **:** an act or instance of worrying; *also* **:** TROUBLE, WORRY ⟨when the news spread . . . there was ~, fear, anger —A.S.Romer⟩ ⟨my lameness . . . was another ~ —Hamlin Garland⟩

wor·ri·some \|ēsəm, |is-\ *adj* [*worry* + *-some*] **1 :** causing distress or worry ⟨there arises . . . a particularly ~ predicament —P.B.Rice⟩ ⟨the most ~ job on the flight deck —Richard Thruelson⟩ ⟨nothing more ~ than strong enemy probing patrols —E.J.Kahn⟩ **2 :** inclined to worry or fret ⟨she will be efficiently ~ about his sore throats, headaches —H.A. Overstreet⟩ ⟨the conviction of my more ~ friends that the two extremes . . . will join forces to destroy the democratic system —T.N.Stern⟩ — **wor·ri·some·ly** *adv*

¹wor·rit \ˈwərət\ *vb* -ED/-ING/-S [alter. of ¹*worry*] *vt, dial Eng* **:** VEX, DISTRESS, WORRY ~ *vi, dial Eng* **:** to become worried or show anxiety or concern

²worrit \ˈ"\ *n* -s *dial Eng* **:** a worried condition; *also* **:** WORRY, TROUBLE

¹wor·ry \ˈwər·|ē, ˈwə·r|, |i\ *vb* -ED/-ING/-ES [ME *wirien, werien, worien* to strangle, worry with the teeth, fr. OE *wyrgan* to strangle; akin to OHG *wurgen* to strangle, ON *virgill* halter, Lith *veržti* to constrict, press, OE *wringan* to wring] *vt* **1** *dial Brit* **:** CHOKE, STRANGLE **2 a :** to harass by tearing, biting, or snapping esp. at the throat ⟨wolves ~ the sheep⟩ ⟨the dog is ~*ing* a bone⟩ **b :** to bite at or upon ⟨*worried* his lower lip with his teeth —Jack Dillon⟩ ⟨pounced on a hangnail and *worried* it with her teeth —Edna Ferber⟩ **c :** to touch, poke, or disturb (something) repeatedly ⟨*worried* his breakfast rather than ate it —Charles Dickens⟩ ⟨snores that seemed to ~ the back of her nose —Richard Llewellyn⟩ ⟨was ~*ing* the pattern of the carpet with his toes⟩ ⟨is learning to ~ the sword of his opponent⟩ **d :** to change the position of, convey, or adjust usu. in a specified place by repeated pushing, hauling, or moving back and forth ⟨Lucas *worried* off the cap —John Updike⟩ — often used with *into* ⟨we inched a log to the bank . . . and *worried* it into the stream —Kenneth Roberts⟩ ⟨the heavy implement had to be lifted . . ., *worried* into position, bolted into place —*Time*⟩ **3 a :** to assail with rough or aggressive attack or treatment **:** HARASS, TORMENT ⟨it was unseemly to the last degree that the disciples . . . should ~ and vex each other with injurious treatment —William Cowper⟩ ⟨the artillery *worries* the enemy with intermittent shelling⟩ ⟨a ghost will ~ him to the grave —Ernest Beaglehole⟩ **b :** to subject to persistent or nagging attention or effort ⟨France's government amended and *worried* the agreement right up to the last moment —*Time*⟩ ⟨no other play in which Shakespeare *worries* a word like that —William Empson⟩ ⟨opinions long since discussed and *worried* to the bone —*Current History*⟩ — often used with *out* ⟨will ~ out the meaning of a pamphlet . . . beyond his capacity —J.A.R.Pimlott⟩ ⟨professors . . . are apt to ~ all the light and joy out of knowledge —M.B.Smith⟩ ⟨hotels were ~*ing* out ways to increase services —P.J.C.Friedlander⟩ **c :** to plague or beset with requests or demands **:** IMPORTUNE ⟨needled and nudged and *worried* him till . . . he consented —Ellery Sedgwick⟩ ⟨the child *worries* its parents with questions⟩ — often used with *out* ⟨teacher . . . began to ~ the life out of me to complete it —David Fairchild⟩ **4 :** to afflict with mental distress or agitation **:** make anxious **:** FRET, TROUBLE ⟨a routine task which permits their minds to wander and . . . doesn't ~ them at night —W.J.Reilly⟩ ⟨his careful repetitions, his imaginative shortcuts . . . ~ the academic mind —Margery Bailey⟩ ⟨what's ~*ing* you —Robert Keable⟩ ~ *vi* **1** *dial Brit* **:** to become choked or strangled **:** CHOKE **2 :** to move, proceed, or progress by unceasing or difficult effort **:** STRUGGLE ⟨the ancient car *worries* up the hill⟩ — usu. used with *along* or *through* ⟨*worried* along six months trying to support a large . . . family —Scott Fitzgerald⟩ ⟨one must ~ through the work of the week⟩ **3 :** to feel or experience concern, disquietude, or anxiety **:** FRET ⟨if her uncle had been troubled . . . a few years more served only to show how uselessly he had *worried* —Stark Young⟩ ⟨although sheep and goats do not ~ as we do, they can . . . be brought into states of chronic unrelieved tension —H.S.Liddell⟩ — often used with *about* or *over* ⟨began to ~ about venturing so far from home in the new car —M.M.Musselman⟩ ⟨pay . . . a good travel agent and let him ~ about this sort of detail —Richard Joseph⟩ ⟨*worried* over her husband's health —Ruth P. Randall⟩

syn ANNOY, FRET, HARASS, HARRY, NAG, PLAGUE, PESTER, BOTHER, TEASE, TANTALIZE: WORRY suggests continued menacing, attacking, or disturbing to drive a quarry or enemy to despair, rashness, submission, or defeat ⟨a policy of *worrying* the enemy⟩ ⟨took on the mighty galleons like terriers *worrying* bulls —Nora Stirling & Ruth Knight⟩ ⟨*worried* into his grave by the leaden-faced likeness of a British spy whom he had hanged —*Amer. Guide Series: N.Y.*⟩ ANNOY may refer to continued molesting, intruding, interfering with, hectoring, or otherwise bedeviling until the victim is angered or discomposed ⟨one or more dogs that will locate the lion . . . and are almost certain to *annoy* the wounded beast into disclosing himself sooner or later —James Stevenson-Hamilton⟩ FRET may suggest a rancorous eating or gnawing at or a continuing vexing that leaves one no peace ⟨that hidden bond which at

other moments galled and *fretted* him so as to mingle irritation with the very sunshine —George Eliot⟩ ⟨*fretting* their team into skittishness and then pretending to be terror-stricken —H.L.Davis⟩ HARASS may apply to continual attacks, persecutions, or exactions that fray, exhaust, or distract ⟨*harassed* by the depredations of British raiders —*Amer. Guide Series: Conn.*⟩ ⟨the new government was *harassed* by internal controversies and by assassinations, disorders, and insurrections —J.F.Bell⟩ HARRY may suggest more directly oppressive persecution than HARASS ⟨had been *harrying* the main pirate fleets about the coast of Cuba —Marjory S. Douglas⟩ ⟨*harrying* Southern sympathizers by arbitrary arrests —*Encyc. Americana*⟩ NAG indicates an annoying or discomposing by persistent rebuke or reminder about shortcomings ⟨the only one who *nagged* him and tried to get him to behave himself —Delmore Schwartz⟩ ⟨let her children's minds alone. She did not pry into their thoughts or *nag* them —Willa Cather⟩ PLAGUE applies to tormenting affliction of painful disease or something likened to it ⟨the gastric disturbance which has been *plaguing* him for years —*Newsweek*⟩ ⟨the civil war which has *plagued* the republic since its inception —*Americana Annual*⟩ ⟨horse thieves were the worst nuisance, next to Indians; and they would go on *plaguing* Texas for thirty years —Green Peyton⟩ PESTER may suggest constant annoyance by or like that by vermin or children ⟨*pestered* with incredible swarms of flies, fleas, and bugs —Tobias Smollett⟩ ⟨*pester* the president with urgencies which perhaps no other man in Washington would have ventured —S.H.Adams⟩ BOTHER indicates vexatious troubling, often continued, that interferes with composure, serenity, or concentration ⟨*bothered* by incompetence in many places, ignorance in others and downright double-dealing in still others —F.V.W.Mason⟩ ⟨*bothered* with a lot of phone calls asking you to this luncheon and that meeting —W.H.Whyte⟩ TEASE applies to the annoyance of either repeated importunities or vexing railleries ⟨I say you cannot go and I will not be *teased* about it —Pearl Buck⟩ TANTALIZE suggests awakening expectation and withholding or frustrating satisfaction ⟨a young dancer, holding aloft in one arm an infant whom she *tantalizes* with a bunch of grapes held high in the other hand —*Amer. Guide Series: Mass.*⟩ ⟨low islands swung over the horizon and *tantalized* us with the belief that they were mainland —Farley Mowat⟩ **syn** see in addition ANNOY

2worry \"\ *n* -ES **1 a :** mental distress or agitation resulting from concern usu. for something impending or anticipated **:** ANXIETY ⟨got on better with my work, being free of ~ —Mary Webb⟩ ⟨hours of . . . careful thought, new administrative problems, ~ —Bruce Payne⟩ ⟨was in a state of ~ because of fear for the loss of her commercial eminence —A.F.Harlow⟩ **b :** an instance or occurrence of such distress or agitation ⟨after a while . . . my mind comes out of the ~ and I start thinking straight —Bant Singer⟩ ⟨is in a great ~ about her school grades⟩ **c :** a cause of worry **:** TROUBLE, DIFFICULTY, COMPLICATION ⟨has another serious ~ about the boys, their tendency to steal⟩ ⟨a bother and a ~ . . . is the London traffic —Richard Joseph⟩ ⟨his biggest ~ is transportation⟩ — often used in pl. ⟨was also in better health and spirits . . . fairly free from *worries* —Havelock Ellis⟩ ⟨wearied him . . . with household *worries* —Haldane Macfall⟩ ⟨few are without financial *worries*⟩ **d :** a state of unease and irritability in quadruped mammals resulting from exposure to biting arthropods (as flies or ticks); *also* **:** an organism causing such worry **2 :** the act or process of seizing an animal with the teeth and shaking it so as to kill or injure it ⟨the corpse of the otter was thrown to the hounds . . . in the ~ —Eric Bennett⟩ **syn** see CARE

wor·ry·ing·ly *adv* [*worrying* (pres. part. of 1*worry*) + *-ly*] **:** in a worrying manner **:** with worry

worry line *n, usu cap W* **:** a line on the palm that intersects the Lifeline or a fine line rising from the Lifeline and is usu. held by palmists to indicate an impediment to a person's career

worrywart \'==,=\ *n* **:** one who is inclined to expect the worst or worry unduly **:** PESSIMIST, FUSSBUDGET ⟨you're a ~ and . . . get yourself into a sweat about things that can't be helped or haven't happened and probably never shall happen —*Chatelaine*⟩

1worse \'wərs, 'wə̄s, 'wəis\ *adj, comparative of* BAD *or of* ILL [ME *werse, wurse, worse*, fr. OE *wiersa, wyrsa;* akin to OHG *wirsiro* worse, ON *verri*, Goth *wairsiza;* comparative (with the suffix represented by OE *-ra*) of a root perh. represented by OHG *werran* to confuse — more at WAR, -ER] **1 :** of inferior or deteriorated quality, value, or material condition ⟨the swampy land he bought appears ~ than the rocky land he sold⟩ ⟨his shoes are rather the ~ for wear⟩ ⟨the monuments were . . . in a state the ~ for an earthquake —Douglas Carruthers⟩ ⟨his house . . . was the ~ for the weather —H.M. Tomlinson⟩ **2 a :** more unfavorable, unpleasant, or unlucky **:** more painful or grievous **:** less agreeable or desirable ⟨the consequences of the second attempt are ~⟩ ⟨was not the artistic type . . . ~ luck —James Jones⟩ ⟨are questions of degree and . . . are none the ~ for it —E.N.Griswold⟩ ⟨if the facts indicate that the hero is inadequate, so much the ~ for the facts —G.W.Johnson⟩ **b :** more faulty, unsuitable, or incorrect **:** ill-conceived **:** UNATTRACTIVE, INAPPROPRIATE ⟨displays manners ~ than those of a boor⟩ ⟨the food is bad, the service ~⟩ ⟨would not convey the thought that an opinion is the ~ for being lightened by a smile —B.N.Cardozo⟩ **c :** less skillful or efficient **:** doing work more poorly ⟨~ than any carpenter I know⟩ **3 a :** bad, evil, ill, or corrupt in a greater degree **:** more reprehensible ⟨it may be no ~ to cheat than to steal⟩ ⟨breed ~ criminals out of men —Hodding Carter⟩ **b :** poorer in health or physical condition **:** more sick or infirm ⟨appears ~ since his accident⟩ ⟨decided to let the tooth get ~ —W.J. Reilly⟩ ⟨people have been kept awake for five or six days . . . without being any the ~ for it physically —Geoffrey Jefferson⟩

2worse \"\ *n* -S [ME, fr. OE *wyrse*, fr. neut. of *wyrsa*, adj.] **1 a :** something that is worse ⟨if he were not dead, ~ must have happened to him —Vicki Baum⟩ ⟨living in an atmosphere . . . full of boredom and sometimes of ~ —Louis Bromfield⟩ ⟨threatened excommunication and ~ —G.C.Sellery⟩ ⟨thought he was an atheist and ~ —Van Wyck Brooks⟩ **b :** a greater degree of ill or badness **:** the quality or state of being worse ⟨if ~ comes to worst⟩ ⟨had taken a turn for the ~ —Greer Williams⟩ ⟨whether the change was for the better or for the ~ —*Times Lit. Supp.*⟩ **2 :** a person of inferior or less virtuous character ⟨fear there will be a ~ come in his place —Shak.⟩ ⟨tossing the rascals out only to see their places taken by ~⟩

3worse \"\ *adv, comparative of* BAD *or of* ILL [ME *werse, wurse, worse*, fr. OE *wiers, wyrs;* akin to OHG *wirs* worse, ON *verr*, Goth *wairs;* all fr. the root represented by OE *wiersa*, adj., worse] **:** in a worse manner **:** to a worse extent or degree ⟨we sleep ~ in very hot weather —Geoffrey Jefferson⟩ ⟨this week the confusion . . . has become ~ confounded —*Economist*⟩ ⟨it is possible for a society to attain new peaks in its culture while many of its members are ~ off than before —A.L.Kroeber⟩ ⟨I write the better when laurel-crowned and the ~ for criticism —W.T.Scott⟩

4worse \"\ *vb* -ED/-ING/-S [1*worse*] *vt, archaic* **:** to make worse ~ *vi, archaic* **:** to become worse **:** WORSEN

worse·ment \-smənt\ *n* -S [4*worse* + *-ment*] **:** deterioration in the value or usefulness of a piece of real property caused by action taken by outside persons or interests without the consent of the owner of the property — compare BETTERMENT

wors·en \'wərsᵊn, 'wə̄s-, 'wəis-\ *vb* **worsened; worsened; worsening** \-s(ᵊ)niŋ\ **worsens** [ME *worsenen*, fr. 1*worse* + *-nen -en*] *vt* **:** to make worse **:** cause to deteriorate **:** IMPAIR ⟨the unfortunate disputes . . . still further ~*ed* relations —Sir Winston Churchill⟩ ⟨revolution . . . actually ~*ed* their economic status —*New Republic*⟩ ⟨heavy storms ~*ed* the fuel shortage⟩ ~ *vi* **:** to become worse **:** DETERIORATE ⟨the lot of the slaves ~*ed* —W.L.Sperry⟩ ⟨international relations may suddenly ~⟩ ⟨the seas . . . were distinctly higher and the weather was obviously ~*ing* —Bill Redgrave⟩

worse·ness *n* -ES **:** the quality or state of being worse

worser *substand comparative of* BAD *or of* ILL

1wor·ship \'wərshəp, 'wə̄sh-, 'wəish-\ *n* [ME *worschipe, worshipe*, fr. OE *weorthscipe*, fr. *weorth* worthy + *-scipe* -ship — more at WORTH] **1 a** *archaic* **:** HONOR, REPUTE, CREDIT **b** *archaic* **:** DIGNITY, IMPORTANCE, RANK **c** *sometimes cap, chiefly Brit* **:** a person of standing or importance — used as a title or mode of address esp. for holders of various high offices ⟨his *Worship* the Sheriff —Max Peacock⟩ **2 :** the reverence or veneration tendered a divine being or supernatural power; *also* **:** an act, process, or instance of expressing such veneration by performing or taking part in religious exercises or ritual ⟨all ~ is an effort of the individual to realize . . . the real presence of the Divine —W.W.Comfort⟩ **3 :** a form or type of worship or religious practice with its creed and ritual ⟨foreigners had been thronging to Rome, bringing with them their foreign cults, and she had permitted these ~*s* —John Buchan⟩ ⟨members of the Handsome Lake ~ may greet each as brother and sister —F.W. Voget⟩ **4 :** respect, admiration, or devotion for an object of esteem ⟨it cannot be called love that a lad of twelve . . . felt for an exalted lady, his mistress: but it was ~ —W.M.Thackeray⟩ ⟨the ~ of the movie hero —J.M.Barzun⟩ ⟨the ~ of the machine —C.I.Glicksberg⟩ ⟨the materialism of America, its new sense of power, its old ~ of success —Irwin Edman⟩

2worship \"\ *vb* **worshiped** *or* **worshipped; worshiped** *or* **worshipped; worshiping** *or* **worshipping; worships** [ME *worschipen, worshipen*, fr. *worschipe* worship] *vt* **1 :** to honor or reverence as a divine being or supernatural power **:** VENERATE ⟨the Father, the Son, and Holy Spirit are uncreated and are to be ~*ed* together as one God —K.S.Latourette⟩ ⟨the emperor, . . . ~*ed* as a god, is to serve as an instrument —Vera M. Dean⟩ **2 :** to regard with respect, honor, or devotion **:** ADORE ⟨in the Renaissance men ~*ed* antiquity —Stephen Spender⟩ ⟨admire the poetry and ~ the memory of the poet —William Du Bois⟩ ⟨whom I . . . ~*ed* as only a young lover can —J.A.Rice⟩ ⟨in his calm, unexcited way, he ~*s* success —Rose Macaulay⟩ ⟨he had the wildness we all ~*ed* —Eudora Welty⟩ ~ *vi* **:** to perform or take part in worship or the act of worship ⟨asks why people ~ and gives three reasons —E.E.Aubrey⟩ ⟨the old wooden meeting house where he had ~*ed* for so long —Catherine D. Bowen⟩ ⟨content to ~ at the shrine of the respectable and the traditional —C.I.Glicksberg⟩ **syn** see REVERE

wor·ship·able \-pəbəl\ *adj* [2*worship* + *-able*] **:** WORSHIPFUL 3

wor·ship·er *or* **wor·ship·per** \-pə(r)\ *n* -S [ME *worschiper*, fr. *worschipen* to worship + *-er*] **:** one that worships

wor·ship·ful \-pfəl\ *adj* [ME *worschipful*, fr. *worschip* worship + *-ful*] **1 a** *archaic* **:** marked by a good quality or property **:** NOTABLE, DISTINGUISHED **b** *usu cap, chiefly Brit* — used as a formal title for various persons or groups of rank or distinction ⟨the *Worshipful* Company of Carpenters —E.E.Reynolds⟩ ⟨*Worshipful* Grand Masters and Wardens —C.W.Ferguson⟩; compare RIGHT WORSHIPFUL **2 :** rendering adoration or reverence **:** VENERATING, WORSHIPING ⟨litanies may express all kinds of ~ attitudes —M.H.Shepherd⟩ ⟨the feeling . . . was more than warm; it was ~ —M.M.Hunt⟩ ⟨a vast audience . . . attentive, but not ~ —Corra Harris⟩ **3 :** warranting worship or capable of being worshiped ⟨the giant ~ effigies . . . commanding the conquered palace squares —Alfred Frankfurter⟩ ⟨any disrespect shown to the ~ animal . . . had to be atoned for —J.G.Frazer⟩ — **wor·ship·ful·ly** \-fəlē, -li\ *adv* — **wor·ship·ful·ness** *n* -ES

wor·ship·ing·ly *or* **wor·ship·ping·ly** *adv* [*worshiping, worshipping* (pres. part. of 2*worship*) + *-ly*] **:** in a worshiping or adoring manner ⟨regarding her ~⟩

wor·ship·less \-pləs\ *adj* **:** lacking worship or worshipers **:** UNWORSHIPED

1worst \'wərst, 'wə̄st, 'wəist\ *adj, superlative of* BAD *or of* ILL [ME *worste, werste*, fr. OE *wyrresta, wyrsta, wierresta, wersta;* akin to OHG *wirsisto* worst, ON *versta;* superlative (with the suffix represented by OE *-st, -est*) of the root found in OE *wiersa* worse — more at WORSE, -EST] **1 :** most bad, evil, ill, or corrupt **:** most reprehensible ⟨his ~ fault⟩ ⟨man's ~ sin⟩ ⟨the ~ villain⟩ ⟨cottages of the ~ landlords had at least fresher air than the overcrowded slums —G.B.Shaw⟩ **2 a :** most unfavorable, unpleasant, or unlucky **:** most painful or grievous **:** least agreeable or desirable ⟨the ~ fate that can befall any nation —Kemp Malone⟩ ⟨the periodic famines . . . lost their ~ terrors —G.M.Trevelyan⟩ ⟨this is their ~ problem —Darcy Ribeiro⟩ ⟨his ~ enemies . . . admitted that he had thrown out the grafters —R.E.Merriam⟩ ⟨the ~ part of the arctic winter —Brigitte Gerland⟩ ⟨the ~ kind of indigestion —C.S.Forester⟩ **b :** most unsuitable, faulty, unattractive, or ill-conceived ⟨has the ~ manners she ever saw⟩ ⟨usually chooses the ~ time to visit⟩ ⟨their latest decision is probably the ~ step they can take⟩ **c :** least skillful or efficient **:** doing work most poorly ⟨the ~ plumber you can hire⟩ ⟨the ~ sort of equipment for the job at hand⟩ **3 :** most wanting in quality, value, or material condition ⟨unaccountably choosing the ~ land of the tract⟩ ⟨his house is not the ~ for being built of secondhand lumber⟩ ⟨poor planning and equipment may well bring about the ~ results⟩ — **the worst way** *adv* **:** very much **:** as much as possible ⟨such men certainly did seem to need indoctrination *the worst way* —J.G.Cozzens⟩ ⟨wanted to be an opera singer *the worst way*⟩

2worst \"\ *n* -S [ME *worste, werste*, fr. *worste, werste*, adj.] **1 :** something that is worst: as **a :** something that is most reprehensible or morally objectionable ⟨can usually be expected to do and say the ~⟩ ⟨so pure of heart that his ~ is another man's good⟩ **b :** something that is most unfavorable, unpleasant, or unlucky **:** a state most painful or grievous or least desirable or agreeable ⟨may as well learn the ~⟩ ⟨prepare for the ~⟩ ⟨the great storm doing its ~⟩ ⟨in his sulk he can be seen at his ~⟩ ⟨the ~ is yet to come⟩ **c :** something that is most wanting in quality, value, or material condition ⟨can be counted on to choose the ~⟩ ⟨examples of the ~ and the best of the period's architecture —*Amer. Guide Series: Minn.*⟩ ⟨of all the faulty pieces of work he selected only a few of the ~⟩ **d :** the greatest degree of ill or badness ⟨if worse comes to ~⟩ **2 :** one who is most reprehensible or deficient in moral character or being ⟨the ~ of a vicious lot⟩ ⟨of all the dishonest politicians, he is the ~⟩

3worst \"\ *adv, superlative of* BAD *or of* ILL [ME *worst, werst*, fr. OE *wyrst, wyrrest, wierst*, superlative of *wyrs, wiers* worse] **:** to the most extreme degree of badness or inferiority **:** in a manner most bad, unpleasant, unfortunate, harmful ⟨the mining centers suffered ~ —George Farwell⟩ ⟨groups who need the subsidies ~ lose out —T.W.Arnold⟩ ⟨the ~ dressed person present⟩

4worst \"\ *vt* -ED/-ING/-S [1*worst*] **1** *chiefly archaic* **:** WORSEN **2 a :** to get the better of in a fight, conflict, or contest **:** DEFEAT, OVERTHROW ⟨one who had been personally ~*ed* in combat —A.C.Whitehead⟩ ⟨had been ~*ed* in his first encounter with partisan government —Tremaine McDowell⟩ ⟨the champion ~*s* all his opponents⟩ **b :** to defeat in a debate, argument, or suit **:** OUTDO, BEST ⟨could so easily ~ . . . his mother in the medium of words —E.K.Brown⟩ ⟨seeking to ~ his detractor in a court of law⟩

1wor·sted \'wu̇stəd, 'wərs-, 'wə̄s-, 'wəis-\ *n* -S [ME *worstede, worsted*, fr. *Worthstede, Worsted* (now *Worstead*), parish & village of Norfolk, England] **1** *or* **worsted yarn :** a smooth compact yarn spun with average to hard twist from long wool fibers that have been carded and combed and used esp. for firm napless fabrics, carpeting, or knitting wools **2 :** any of various closely woven fabrics (as gabardine and serge) made from worsted yarns usu. with a smooth napless face and used esp. for suitings and tailored garments

2worsted \"\ *adj* [ME, fr. 1*worsted*] **1 :** made of worsted or worsted yarn ⟨~ suiting⟩ ⟨~ suit⟩ **2 :** of, relating to, or concerned with worsted or worsted products esp. in manufacture and commercial handling ⟨~ mill⟩

worsted card *n* **:** a wool card that produces lap for combing as distinguished from the woolen card that produces sliver for spinning

1wort \'wər|t, 'wȯ(ə)r|, 'wə̄|, 'wəi|, -ȯ(ə)|, *usu* |d·+V\ *n* -S [ME *wurt, wort, wert*, fr. OE *wyrt* herb, plant, root; akin to OHG *wurz* herb, plant, ON *urt* herb, Goth *waurts* root, L *radix*, Gk *rhiza* — more at ROOT] **1 a :** PLANT; *esp* **:** an herbaceous plant — usu. used in combination **b** *archaic* **:** POTHERB **2 worts** *pl, obs* **:** CABBAGES

2wort \"\ *n* -S [ME, fr. OE *wyrt;* akin to OS *wurtia* spice, MHG *würze* spice, brewer's wort, OE *wyrt* herb, plant, root — more at 1WORT] **:** an infusion of malt consisting of a dilute solution of sugars that is fermented to form beer

3wort *var of* WHORT

1worth \'wərth, 'wə̄th, 'wəith\ *vi* -ED/-ING/-S [ME *worthen*, fr. OE *weorthan, wurthan;* akin to OHG *werdan* to become, ON *vertha*, Goth *wairthan*, L *vertere* to turn, Skt *vartate* it is turned, happens, Lith *versti* to turn, *virsti* to fall, become] *archaic* **:** to come to be **:** BECOME — usu. used in the phrase *woe worth* with a following noun or pronoun

2worth \"\ *adj* [ME, fr. OE *weorth* of (a specified) value, worthy; akin to OHG *werd* worth, worthy, ON *verthr*, Goth *wairths*, OE *wierthe* worth, worthy] **1** *archaic* **:** having monetary or material value ⟨my time or labor was little ~ —Daniel Defoe⟩ **2** *archaic* **:** exhibiting or marked by desirable or useful qualities **:** ESTIMABLE ⟨she is a woman more ~ than any man —Shak.⟩ ⟨whose life, whose thoughts were little ~ —Alfred Tennyson⟩

3worth \"\ *prep* [ME, fr. OE *weorth*, adj.] **1 a :** having the value of **:** equal in value to ⟨the horse is ~ $300⟩ ⟨grants in . . . the state were to be ~ millions in timber and iron —*Amer. Guide Series: Minn.*⟩ ⟨decide whether they are ~ the price asked —S.H.Adams⟩ ⟨the matter is not ~ a straw⟩ ⟨what's it ~⟩ **b :** having possessions or income equal to **:** equal in worth to **:** possessed of ⟨he is ~ at least $500,000⟩ ⟨was ~ a small fortune —Angus Macleod⟩ **2 :** furnishing an equivalent for **:** justifying the expenditure or exchange of ⟨are incentives ~ the effort —Bruce Payne⟩ ⟨doesn't think he's ~ a damn —Hamilton Basso⟩ **3 :** deserving of ⟨such books are ~ deliberate and thoughtful perusal —L.R.McColvin⟩ ⟨the scene is well ~ a visit —Ted Sumner⟩ ⟨ideals ~ fighting for⟩ ⟨the question of what emotions are ~ expressing —C.W.H.Johnson⟩ ⟨hardly ~ our attention⟩ **4 :** capable of ⟨ran for all he was ~⟩ — **worth one's salt :** worth one's salary or keep ⟨is so useless as to be hardly *worth his salt*⟩; *also* **:** having substantial or significant value or merit ⟨it isn't long before an author *worth his salt* can emerge with material for a best seller —Phyllis McGinley⟩

4worth \"\ *n* -S [ME, fr. OE *weorth;* akin to OHG *wert* value, price, worth, ON *verth*, Goth *wairth;* all fr. a prehistoric substantive use of the adjective represented by Goth *wairths* worth, worthy] **1 a :** monetary value ⟨mining operations of tremendous ~ —R.L.Taylor⟩ ⟨farmhouse and lands of little ~⟩ **b :** the equivalent of a specified amount or figure ⟨a penny's ~ of wine —E.O.Hauser⟩ ⟨$130 ~ of corn and alfalfa —Clyde Hostetter⟩ ⟨insuring that the government gets its money's ~ —T.W.Arnold⟩ ⟨an hour's ~ of hard labor⟩ **2 :** the usu. relative value of something measured or judged by its qualities or by the esteem with which it is regarded ⟨device that proved its ~ —C.L.Boltz⟩ ⟨collections of independent essays or chapters of varying ~ —F.N.Robinson⟩ ⟨the ultimate ~ of elaborate techniques —Howard M. Jones⟩ ⟨the ultimate test of true ~ is pleasure —G.L.Dickinson⟩ **3 a :** moral, intellectual, or personal value ⟨inspired by a sense of individual human ~ —George Woodcock⟩ ⟨the child . . . whose dignity and ~ are respected —Dorothy Barclay⟩ ⟨problem of aging is to retain a sense of ~ —George Lawton⟩ **b :** MERIT, EXCELLENCE ⟨most colleges offer scholarships on the basis of need and ~⟩ ⟨work at which they have proved their ~ and their competence —F.J.R.Rodd⟩ ⟨propensity is to build up reputations beyond their intrinsic ~ —*Atlantic*⟩ **4 :** the value of one's material possessions **:** WEALTH, RICHES ⟨his personal ~ is estimated at five million⟩ **syn** see VALUE

worth·ful \-thfəl\ *adj* [4*worth* + *-ful*] **1 :** full of worth or merit **:** HONORABLE, WORTHY ⟨a good and ~ man⟩ ⟨something which is superhuman . . . and supremely ~ —H.C.Smith⟩ **2 :** having value or worth **:** ESTEEMED, VALUABLE ⟨transmitting to the young that which they regard as ~ in their culture —J.L.Childs⟩ — **worth·ful·ness** *n* -ES

worthiest of blood *Brit* **:** most worthy of those of the same blood to succeed or inherit — usu. used with reference to males as opposed to females

wor·thi·ly \'wərt͟hə̇lē\ *adv* [ME, fr. 1*worthy* + *-ly*] **:** in a worthy manner **:** with worthiness

wor·thi·ness \-t͟hēnə̇s\ *n* -ES [ME *worthinesse*, fr. 1*worthy* + *-nesse* -ness] **:** the quality or state of being worthy

worth·less \'wərthlə̇s, 'wə̄th-, 'wəith-\ *adj* [4*worth* + *-less*] **1 a :** lacking value or material worth **:** VALUELESS ⟨finding the country flooded with ~ currency and black markets —*Current Biog.*⟩ ⟨insisted that the Sudan was a ~ desert —Herman Ausubel⟩ **b :** of no value, use, or profit **:** USELESS ⟨the stream took a bend back toward the ocean, and it would be ~ to follow it any longer —Norman Mailer⟩ ⟨their estimated costs of clothing may well be ~ unless the girls . . . pin them down to accuracy —J.A.Leavitt & C.O.Hanson⟩ ⟨such statistical knowledge may be ~ to many people⟩ **2 a :** lacking moral character **:** LOW, DESPICABLE ⟨deceived by a ~ woman⟩ ⟨ran off with a ~ laughing fellow who lived by gambling —Sinclair Lewis⟩ **b :** lacking merit or worth **:** UNPRODUCTIVE, INCOMPETENT ⟨its vast possessions . . . had been squandered by ~ abbots —H.O.Taylor⟩ ⟨so ~ that they had to plunder friends as well as foes —Charles Kingsley⟩ — **worth·less·ly** *adv* — **worth·less·ness** *n* -ES

worthwhile \'=¦=\ *adj* [2*worth* + *while*, n.] **:** being worth the time spent **:** of sufficient value to repay the effort ⟨if any ~ results were to be achieved —H.L.Ickes⟩ ⟨a ~ trip for sightseers —Lucy Burnham⟩ ⟨make life a ~ experience —Y.H. Krikorian⟩ — **worth·while·ness** *n* -ES

1wor·thy \'wərt͟hē, 'wə̄t͟h-, 'wəit͟h-, -t͟hi\ *adj, usu* -ER/-EST [ME, fr. 4*worth* + *-y*] **1 a :** having worth, value, or importance **:** GOOD, ESTIMABLE ⟨has become the ~ custom to hold a benefit performance —R.P.Cooke⟩ ⟨the results of moral rules are not always as ~ as the motives for adopting them —W.L.Miller⟩ ⟨great and ~ things —H.D.Thoreau⟩ ⟨became identified with many ~ causes —A.E.Wier⟩ **b :** marked by personal qualities warranting honor, respect, or esteem **:** HONORABLE, MERITORIOUS ⟨the tribunal was composed of ~ men . . . of eminent respectability and talents —J.L.Motley⟩ ⟨the father was a ~ burgher, innkeeper, and brewer —Dora Clark⟩ ⟨announcing . . . that his former wife was not a ~ woman —H.F.Coleru⟩ **2 a :** having sufficient worth, value, or importance **:** sufficiently good or estimable ⟨performing deeds ~ to be handed down in . . . legends —C.B.Nordhoff & J.N.Hall⟩ ⟨think of something ~ to say —William Saroyan⟩ — often used with *of* ⟨mere resort to defensive measures is not ~ of the American spirit —*New Republic*⟩ ⟨brings to basketball an intensity ~ of a loftier pursuit —Stanley Frank⟩ ⟨a cause ~ of the best endeavors —W.H.Allison⟩ **b :** possessing personal qualities of sufficient worth, respect, or esteem **:** sufficiently honorable or meritorious ⟨no student deemed ~, and chosen for admission, would be kept out by lack of funds —N.M.Pusey⟩ ⟨a ~ successor⟩ ⟨a ~ antagonist⟩ ⟨every man ~ to be called a man —Thomas De Quincey⟩ — often used with *of* ⟨~ of his hire⟩ ⟨are ~ of the great faith, the high hopes, we have placed in them —F.D.Roosevelt⟩ ⟨you might be . . . *worthier* of yourself —Charles Dickens⟩

2worthy \"\ *n* -ES [ME, fr. 1*worthy*] **:** a person of eminence, distinction, or renown ⟨a great New England ~ —Van Wyck Brooks⟩ ⟨keep alive the memory of many *worthies* —Perry Miller⟩

3worthy \"\ *adv* [ME, fr. 1*worthy*] **:** WORTHILY

4worthy *vt* -ED/-ING/-ES [ME *worthyen*, fr. 1*worthy*] *obs* **:** to make worthy **:** EXALT, HONOR

worts *pl of* WORT

1wot *pres 1st & 3d sing of* WIT

2wot \'wät\ *vb* **wotted; wotted; wotting; wots** [ME *woten*, alter. (influenced by *wot*, 1st & 3d sing. of *witen*) of *witen* to know — more at WIT] *vt, dial chiefly Brit* **:** to have knowledge of **:** KNOW ~ *vi, dial chiefly Brit* **:** to have knowledge — often used with *of* ⟨perhaps other kingdoms that we ~ not of —D.C. Peattie⟩

3wot \"\ *substand var of* WHAT

wou·bit \'wü,bit\ *n* -S [ME *wolbode*, fr. *woll* wool + *-bode* (perh. akin to OE *budda* beetle)] *dial Brit* **:** a hairy caterpillar; *esp* **:** WOOLLY BEAR

wough \'wō, 'wȯ\ *n* -S [ME *wogh*, fr. OE *wōg, wāh;* akin to OFris *wāch* wall, OS *wēg*, L *vincire* to bind, lace — more at VETCH] **1** *dial Brit* **:** the wall or partition of a house **2** *Scot* **:** the wall rock beside a vein of lead

1would \ˌwəd, ˌ(ə)d, (ˈ)wu̇d\ [ME *wolde, wulde, wold*, fr. OE *wolde;* akin to OHG *wolta* wished, desired, ON *vilda*, Goth *wilda* — more at WILL] *past of* WILL **1 a** *archaic* **:** WISHED, DESIRED, INTENDED ⟨he ~ that they should go⟩ **b** *archaic* **:** wish for **:** WANT ⟨what ~ these people⟩ ⟨they ~ a word with us⟩ **c** (1) **:** strongly desire **:** WISH ⟨I ~ I had brought better news

—W.S.Gilbert⟩ ⟨we ~ all were perfect —Edward Sapir⟩ (2) — used in auxiliary function with *rather* or *sooner* to express preference between alternatives ⟨his flock ~ rather let him starve than increase the living by one penny —Emily Brontë⟩ ⟨he ~ sooner die than face them⟩ **2 a** — used in auxiliary function to express wish, desire, or intent ⟨the problem of him who ~ determine the . . . pattern of a language —*Internat'l Jour. of Amer. Linguistics*⟩ ⟨~ unite the nations of America into a real system —C.R.Fish⟩ **b** — used in auxiliary function to express willingness or preference ⟨as ye ~ that men should do to you, do ye also to them likewise —Lk 6:31 (AV)⟩ ⟨parents ~ have their children do well⟩ **c** — used in auxiliary function to express plan or intention ⟨promised that we ~ correct . . . mistakes —Virginia Prewett⟩ ⟨deciding that they ~ visit as many friends as possible⟩ **d** — used in auxiliary function in the negative to express refusal ⟨contrary to advice he ~ not have an auxiliary engine in his boat⟩ ⟨despite a good offer, he ~ have none of it⟩ **e** — used in auxiliary function to express disposition or inclination ⟨~ express the opinion that the . . . question has been practically settled —Norman Douglas⟩ ⟨~ propose that all candidates be accepted⟩ ⟨~ like to recommend a series of articles —R.C.Pooley⟩ **f** — used in auxiliary function to express insistence or determination ⟨regardless of warnings he ~ play with fire⟩ ⟨the child ~ have its way⟩ ⟨he ~ not be crossed⟩ ⟨you might expect that he ~ not be deterred⟩ **3** — used in auxiliary function to express custom or habitual action ⟨we ~ meet every morning —O.S.J.Gogarty⟩ ⟨the swagman ~ for long periods be without . . . female company —William Power⟩ ⟨he ~ stand . . . blows without winking or shedding a tear —Emily Brontë⟩ **4** — used in auxiliary function to express consent or choice ⟨could be helped if he ~ only do his part⟩ ⟨~ put it off indefinitely if he could⟩ **5 a** — used in auxiliary function in the conclusion of a conditional sentence to express a contingency or possibility ⟨if he were coming, he ~ be here now⟩ ⟨had all the possibilities been ruled out, we ~ have had to accept all three —Z.S.Harris⟩ ⟨~ have done it myself but for my temporary incapacitation —Sir Winston Churchill⟩ **b** (1) — used in auxiliary function in the conclusion of a conditional sentence to express volition or intention ⟨if I were a librarian, I ~ put this book in . . . my display —Pearl Buck⟩ ⟨if we had thought that the institute was a school, we ~ never have come —*Time*⟩ (2) — used in auxiliary function in a statement of advice or recommendation based on the implied condition *if I were you* ⟨I ~ go today while the weather is pleasant⟩ ⟨telling them he *wouldn't* take any such risk, he ordered them to go home⟩ **c** — used in auxiliary function in a noun clause completing a statement of desire, request, or advice ⟨we wish that he ~ go⟩ ⟨the express desire of his parents was that he ~ finish school⟩ ⟨prefer that she ~ not go again⟩ **6 a** — used in auxiliary function to express futurity from a point of view in the past ⟨kept on looking for . . . the money that ~ solve his problems —E.L.Acken⟩ ⟨the lowness of his funds ~ presently compel his return —John Buchan⟩ ⟨proposed a council . . . whereby peace ~ be preserved —F.L.Schuman⟩ **b** — used in auxiliary function to express probability or presumption in past or present time ⟨the hands of the watch show that it ~ be about five o'clock that it was submerged⟩ ⟨no one, for example, could have predicted . . . whether or not his pistol ~ have missed fire —L.A.White⟩ ⟨at this time of day the fire ~ have burned low —P.H.Newby⟩ ⟨from his appearance he ~ be the one we are looking for⟩ **7** : COULD ⟨no stone ~ shatter that glass⟩ ⟨the barrel ~ hold 20 gallons⟩ **8** — used in auxiliary function to express a request with which voluntary compliance is expected ⟨~ you please help us⟩ **9** *obs* : ought to ⟨that ~ be scanned —Shak.⟩ **10** — used in auxiliary function to express doubt or uncertainty ⟨the explanation . . . ~ seem to go deeper —F.H.Hartmann⟩ ⟨for the survival of our society it ~ appear essential —Dorothy Barclay⟩ ⟨the mechanics of transmitting the sound were perfect, I ~ say —Philip Hamburger⟩ **11** : SHOULD ⟨knew I ~ enjoy the trip⟩ ⟨~ be glad to know the answer⟩ ⟨feel that we ~ recognize them easily⟩ ⟨if you ~ be interested, I could arrange an interview⟩ ⟨it was ordered that he ~ go⟩

²would \'wu̇d\ *n* -s : a conditional or undecided wish or intention ⟨a life of inaction cluttered with ~s⟩

³would *var of* WELD

¹would-be \'=,=\ *adj* [fr. the phrase *would be*] : desiring or professing to be : wishing to be reputed ⟨good musicianship will enable a *would-be* conductor . . . to improve himself —Warwick Braithwaite⟩ ⟨retaliatory power is one strong deterrent to a *would-be* aggressor —D.D.Eisenhower⟩ — often used disparagingly ⟨looked like what he was, a *would-be* fighter who . . . had nowhere to go —Hamilton Basso⟩ ⟨turn lesson notes into *would-be* textbooks and go in vain the round of the publishers —James Britton⟩

²would-be \"\ *n* -s : one who wishes to be or to be reputed something one is not — usu. used disparagingly ⟨compelled to listen to has-beens and *would-bes* trying to put over bad plays —A.L.Burt⟩ ⟨nothing but these *would-bes* in New York getups, drinking tea —Sinclair Lewis⟩

would·ing \'wu̇diŋ\ *n* -s [fr. ¹*would*, after such pairs as ¹*will*: ¹*willing*] *archaic* : emotion of desire : INCLINATION

wouldn't \'wu̇d°nt\ [by contr.] : would not

wouldst *or* **wouldest** *archaic past 2d sing of* WILL

woulff bottle \'wu̇lf-\ *n, usu cap W* [alter. of *Woulfe bottle*, after Peter *Woulfe* †1803 Eng. chemist] : a bottle or jar with two or three necks used in washing or absorbing gases

¹wound \'wünd, *chiefly dial* 'wau̇nd\ *n* -s [ME *wunde, wound*, fr. OE *wund*; akin to OHG *wunta* wound, ON *und*] **1 a** : an injury to the body consisting of a laceration or breaking of the skin or mucous membrane usu. by a hard or sharp instrument forcefully driven or applied ⟨has a deep festering knife ~ across the palm⟩ ⟨the hollow-nosed bullet leaves a jagged ~⟩ **b** (1) : an opening made in the skin or a membrane of the body incidental to a surgical operation or procedure (2) : a cut or slash made on a tree or plant ⟨a metal receptacle to catch the sap that dripped from the ~ —Hamilton Basso⟩ **2 a** : a mental or emotional hurt or blow to the pride, sensitivity, or reputation ⟨lived . . . under the uneasy strain of avoiding ~s to their self-esteem —Oscar Handlin⟩ ⟨inflicts ~s upon the human spirit which no surgery can heal —Virginia Woolf⟩ ⟨in the hospital wards he was confronted with every type of psychiatric ~ —Don Wharton⟩ **b** : a similar hurt or blow affecting a political body or a social group and usu. giving rise to resentments or animosities ⟨wish that the bitter strike would leave no deep ~s —Mary K. Hammond⟩ ⟨reopens the party's ~s by attacking the past leadership —R.L.Strout⟩ ⟨the perfect way to heal many of the world's worst ~s —P.M.Mazur⟩

syn TRAUMA, TRAUMATISM, LESION, BRUISE, CONTUSION: WOUND generally implies a significant injury inflicted by an outside agent (as a gun, knife, or fist) that breaks the skin and usu. the tissues beneath ⟨a gunshot *wound*⟩ ⟨the *wound* made by the surgeon's knife⟩ TRAUMA designates physical injury or mental or emotional shock that leaves a lasting morbid or abnormal impression on the mind ⟨a birth *trauma*⟩ ⟨the *traumata* of war⟩ ⟨discomfort, pain, and *trauma* to the middle ear —H.G.Armstrong⟩ ⟨great social *traumas* like the French Revolution and the American Civil War —Alexander Heard⟩ although sometimes it extends in meaning to designate the effects of a traumatic injury or a TRAUMATISM ⟨the multiple symptoms of a *traumatism* — a fear of dirt or scum, a constant washing of the hands, much talk about impurity⟩ LESION designates the effect on the tissues caused by a wound, trauma, or injury resulting from disease or degeneration, implying a pathological alteration in tissue or loss of function ⟨tubercular *lesions* in the lungs⟩ ⟨occasionally the so-called rheumatic *lesions* affect the joints, giving symptoms like those of growing pains —Morris Fishbein⟩ ⟨some obscure sort of psychological *lesion* —Nathaniel Burt⟩ BRUISE is the standard and CONTUSION the medical term for an injury ordinarily the result of impact that results in the disorganization of subcutaneous tissues with usu. no break in the skin but with black and blue discoloring ⟨a *bruise* on the arm from a flying stone⟩ ⟨a *contusion* on the hip from a fall on the ice⟩

²wound \"\ *vb* -ED/-ING/-S [ME *wunden, wounden*, fr. OE *wundian*; akin to OHG *wuntōn* to wound, ON *undathr* wounded (part.), Goth *gawundondans* wounding (part. pl.); all fr. a prehistoric Gmc verb derived fr. the root of OE *wund* wound] *vt* **1 a** : to inflict a wound upon : CUT, STAB, PIERCE, LACERATE ⟨using his knife to ~ and maim his opponent⟩ ⟨flying shrapnel had ~*ed* several others⟩ ⟨the bullet ~*ed* him in the shoulder⟩ ⟨had been ~*ed* in the battle —E.K.Alden⟩ **b** : to make a tear, breach, or opening in (something) in the manner of a wound ⟨was sure he had mortally ~*ed* the submarine —Walter Karig⟩ ⟨the trees are ~*ed* and the sap allowed to run out —G.S.Brady⟩ ⟨the volcanic crust is ~*ed* by the upheaval⟩ **2** : to hurt or damage as if by a wound : INJURE ⟨had tried to ~ him by some cheap irony, sarcasm, or just plain rudeness —Bruce Mason⟩ ⟨the ability to ~ the enemy through trade . . . by applications of the rule of contraband —F.L.Paxson⟩ ⟨the 18th century . . . was so ~*ed* by the memories of the religious wars —Herbert Agar⟩ **~** *vi* : to inflict a wound ⟨intending only to ~, not to kill⟩ ⟨critical remarks often ~ deeply⟩

³wound [ME *wounden* (past pl. & past part.), fr. OE *wundon* (past pl.) & *gewunden* (past part.)] *past of* WIND

wound chevron *or* **wound stripe** *n* : a small gold chevron formerly worn on the lower part of the right sleeve of the U. S. army uniform to indicate that the wearer had been wounded in action

wound cork *n* : cork formed over the wounded surface of a tree or plant — compare PERIDERM

¹wounded *adj* [ME, fr. past part. of *wounden* to wound] : injured, hurt by, or suffering from a wound ⟨nursing his ~ arm⟩ ⟨does not wish to leave a ~ name behind him —E.C. Wagenknecht⟩ ⟨seeking to salve her ~ feelings⟩ ⟨the underbrush had to be cut away and ~ fields reopened —Russell Lord⟩ ⟨had gone up with the 8th Army . . . working on ~ tanks —Irwin Shaw⟩ — **wound·ed·ly** *adv*

²wounded *n, pl* **wounded** : one that is wounded — usu. used collectively ⟨treatment of the ~⟩

wound fungus *n* : a fungus that is a wound parasite

wound gall *n* : an elongated swollen or tuberous gall on the branches of the grapevine caused by a vine borer (*Ampeloglypter sesostris*) whose larvae inhabit the galls

wound hormone *n* : a substance (as traumatic acid) that promotes the healing of wounds in plants

wound·i·ly \'wündəlē, 'wau̇n-\ *adv* [²*woundy* + *-ly*] *chiefly archaic* : EXCESSIVELY, EXTREMELY ⟨that gauntlet of yours is ~ heavy —J.H.Wheelwright⟩

wound·ing·ly *adv* : in a wounding manner : HURTFULLY

wound·less \'wündləs\ *adj* **1** *obs* : INVULNERABLE ⟨the ~ air —Shak.⟩ **2** : free from wounds : UNWOUNDED

wound parasite *n* : a usu. weakly parasitic fungus that becomes established in a plant following damage by other agencies

wound rocket *n* [so called fr. its use in healing wounds] : YELLOW ROCKET

wound root *n* : a root originating in callus tissue near a cut or damaged surface as distinguished from a root arising from a normal meristematic region or from a primary root

wound–rotor motor \'=,==-\ *n* [*wound*, past part. of *wind*] : an induction motor with a rotor having a polyphase winding to permit secondary circuit adjustment not possible in the case of a squirrel-cage induction motor

¹wounds *pl of* WOUND, *pres 3d sing of* WOUND

²wounds \'wau̇ndz\ *interj* [fr. the oath *by God's wounds*] *archaic* — used as an oath or strong affirmation

woundwort \'=,=\ *n* : any of various plants whose soft downy leaves have been used in the dressing of wounds: as **a** : KIDNEY VETCH **b** : a mint of the genus *Stachys* **c** : a comfrey (*Symphytum officinale*) **d** : HERCULES, ALLHEAL

¹woundy \'wündē, 'wau̇n-\ *adv* [²*wounds* + *-y*] *dial chiefly Eng* : EXTREMELY, EXCESSIVELY

²woundy \"\ *adj* [²*wounds* + *-y*] *dial chiefly Eng* : very great : EXTREME

wou·ra·li \wü'rälē\ *or* **wou·ra·ri** \-ärē\ *n* -s [Macushi] : CURARE

wou-wou \'wau̇,wau̇\ *or* **wah-wah** \'wä,wä\ *n* -s [Sundanese *owa*] **1** : SILVER GIBBON **2** : AGILE GIBBON

¹wove [ME *wof, woof*, alter. of *waf*, fr. OE *wæf*] *past of* WEAVE

²wove \'wōv\ *adj* [*wove*, archaic past part. of ¹*weave*] *of paper* : made with a dandy roll covered with woven wire and therefore showing no laid lines

woven [ME, alter. of *weven, iweven*, fr. OE *wefen, gewefen*] *past part of* WEAVE

woven wire *n* : wire crossed and interlaced to form a network

¹wow \'wau̇\ *interj* — used as an exclamation of pleasure, surprise, or strong feeling

²wow \"\ *n* -s [¹*wow*] : a sensational hit : a striking success ⟨a lively and entertaining story . . . should be a ~ on the screen —E.E.Calkins⟩ ⟨was a ~ in the campus frolic —Robertson Davies⟩ ⟨as a radio sportscaster . . . was called a ~ from the start —*Current Biog.*⟩ ⟨a correct translation of these documents would be a ~ —*Nation*⟩

³wow \"\ *vt* -ED/-ING/-S : to excite to enthusiastic admiration ⟨~*ed* their audience with a knowing parody —Bennett Cerf⟩ ⟨was ~*ing* the voters everywhere with his . . . political minstrelsy —*Time*⟩ ⟨will borrow almost any idea which is currently ~*ing* the customers —Martin Mayer⟩

⁴wow \"\ *vi* -ED/-ING/-S [imit.] *dial Brit* : HOWL, WAIL, MEW

⁵wow \"\ *n* -s [imit.] **1** *dial chiefly Brit* : BARK, WHINE, WAIL **2** : a distortion in reproduced sound consisting of a relatively slow rise and fall of pitch caused by variation of speed in the sound reproducing system (as in the record, film, tape, or motor); *also* : the variation in speed causing such a distortion — compare FLUTTER 4a

wowf \'wau̇f\ *adj* [origin unknown] *Scot* : WILD, CRAZED

wowser \'wau̇zə(r)\ *n* -s [origin unknown] *chiefly Austral* : one who is censoriously hostile to minor vices or disapproves of various forms of popular amusement (as Sunday sports) — used disparagingly of an obtrusively puritanical person ⟨responsible for closed restaurants, limited movies . . . and a sanctimonious appearance of the streets are the ~s —J.M. Raleigh⟩ ⟨both were denounced as equally obscene by the . . . ~s —H.L.Mencken⟩

woyawai *or* **woyaway** *usu cap, var of* WAIWAI

WP *abbr* **1** wastepaper **2** water packed **3** *often not cap* waterproof; waterproofing **4** weather permitting **5** weatherproof **6** white phosphorus **7** wild pitch **8** wire payment **9** without prejudice **10** working point **11** working pressure

WPA *abbr* with particular average

WPC *abbr, often not cap* watts per candle

wpfl *abbr* worshipful

wpm *abbr* words per minute

wpn *abbr* weapon

WPP *abbr, often not cap* waterproof paper packing

wr *abbr* writing paper

WR *abbr* **1** wardroom **2** warehouse receipt **3** war risk **4** washroom **5** with rights

¹wrack *also* **rack** \'rak\ *n* -s [ME, fr. OE *wræc*; akin to OE *wrecan* to drive, drive out, punish — more at WREAK] **1** *archaic* **a** : PUNISHMENT; *also* : VENGEANCE **b** : vengeful or hostile attack or persecution **2 a** : disastrous and violent damage, defeat, or dislocation : RUIN, DOWNFALL, DESTRUCTION ⟨times of ~ and misery —A.L.Kroeber⟩ ⟨his few acres, heavily mortgaged and gone to ~ —Dixon Wecter⟩ **b** *obs* : a cause of ruin **c** *dial* : something that has suffered wrack : something shattered or destroyed **d** : a vestigial remain of something destroyed ⟨of the original simple scheme hardly a ~ remains —Nathan Isaacs⟩

²wrack \"\ *n* -s [ME *wrak*, fr. MD; akin to OE *wræc* punishment, something driven by the sea] **1 a** : a wrecked ship **b** : a piece of wreckage ⟨nosing his boat among ~ heaps to salvage piling that has come loose —R.J.Smith⟩ **c** (1) : SHIPWRECK 2 (2) : SHIPWRECK 3 **d** *dial* : the violent destruction of a structure, machine, or vehicle **2 a** : marine vegetation (as eelgrass or various seaweeds); *esp* : KELP — compare SEA WRACK **b** : any of various dried seaweeds used for coarse cordage, stuffing, or other purposes **c** : vegetable rubbish collected on water, cast on the shore, or piled in a field : WEEDS

³wrack \"\ *vb* -ED/-ING/-S [ME *wracken*, fr. *wrak* shipwreck, wreckage] *vi, obs* : to become wrecked or ruined : undergo destruction **~** *vt* : to wreck beyond repair : utterly ruin : cause the destruction of ⟨the wind may ~ a house that isn't adequately nailed —*Design for Homes*⟩ **syn** see DESTROY

⁴wrack \"\ *vb* -ED/-ING/-S [by alter.] : ⁴RACK ⟨a land ~*ed* by domestic fears and uncertainty —Mark Gayn⟩ ⟨tend to ~ or distort the car frame —*Power*⟩ ⟨~*ed* with scurvy —Stuart Keate⟩ ⟨depth charges ~*ed* aft of them —R.O.Bowen⟩

⁵wrack \"\ *n* -s [by alter.] : ³RACK

⁶wrack \"\ *n* -s [by alter.] : ¹RACK 2a

wrack·ful \-fəl\ *adj* : causing wrecks or wreckage : DESTRUCTIVE, INJURIOUS

wrack grass *n* [²*wrack*] : EELGRASS 1

wraith \'rāth\ *n, pl* **wraiths** \-ths *sometimes* -t͟hz\ [origin unknown] **1 a** : an apparition of a living person in his exact likeness seen usu. just before his death — compare DOPPELGÄNGER **b** : a visible apparition of a dead person : GHOST, SPECTER **2** : WATER SPRITE **3** : an insubstantial copy, remainder, or appearance of something : SHADOW ⟨pale ~s of their formidable namesakes —*Times Lit. Supp.*⟩ ⟨hits not the ~ of socialism but the flesh and blood of the farmers —M.W. Straight⟩ **4** : a barely visible gaseous or vaporous column resembling a wraith ⟨thin ~s of smoke curled up and lost themselves in the sky —E.A.McCourt⟩

wrake *obs var of* ³WRACK *vt*

wran \'ran\ *dial Brit var of* WREN

wrang \"\ *dial var of* WRONG

¹wran·gle \'raŋgəl, -aiŋ-\ *vb* **wrangled; wrangled; wrangling** \-g(ə)liŋ\ **wrangles** [ME *wranglen*; akin to LG *wrangeln* to wrangle, *wrangen* to struggle, wrestle, ME *wringen* to wring, twist, wrest — more at WRING] *vi* **1** : to dispute angrily : quarrel peevishly and noisily : BRAWL, ALTERCATE, BICKER **2** : to engage in argument, dispute, or controversy ⟨solemn conclaves dignifiedly *wrangled* over proper compounding of herbs or incense —L.C.Douglas⟩ **~** *vt* **1 a** : to obtain by wrangling ⟨started to ~ one or two scholarships . . . for gifted children —Gertrude Samuels⟩ **b** : to influence or persuade by wrangling **c** : to waste or expend in wrangling ⟨had been *wrangling* away their reserves —Bruce Marshall⟩ **2 a** : to round up, corral, herd, and care for (as horses) : take charge of (a remuda) ⟨*wrangling* cattle for a living⟩ **b** : direct and oversee the activities of (guests at a dude ranch) ⟨on the lookout for some handsome, easy-talking gent to ~ tenderfeet —F.B.Gipson⟩

²wrangle \"\ *n* -s **1** : an angry, bitter, noisy, or prolonged dispute or quarrel ⟨emerged victorious in nasty ~s with old guardists —*Newsweek*⟩ **2** : the action or process of wrangling : angry disputation : CONTROVERSY ⟨after an hour's ~, both of these disputes to go over until tomorrow —A.H.Vandenberg †1951⟩ **syn** see QUARREL

wran·gler \-ŋg(ə)lə(r)\ *n* -s **1** : one that wrangles: **a** : an angry or bickering disputant **b** : a participant in an argument, debate, or controversy **c** *obs* : OPPONENT, ANTAGONIST **2** : one who obtains first class honors in the mathematical tripos at Cambridge University — see SENIOR WRANGLER **3** : HORSE WRANGLER; *broadly* : COWBOY

¹wrap \'rap, *dial* 'räp\ *vb* **wrapped** *also* **wrapt** \-pt\ **wrapped** *also* **wrapt; wrapping; wraps** [ME *wrappen*; prob. akin to Dan dial. *vravle* to twist together, wind, Gk *rhaptein* to sew, stitch together — more at RHAPSODY] *vt* **1 a** : to cover, envelop, or enclose esp. entirely or to a great extent within a covering (as a garment or cloth) esp. by winding or folding ⟨let him ~ her shoulders in the white shawl —Marcia Davenport⟩ — often used with *about, around*, or *up* ⟨he was *wrapped* up in a blanket —Georg Meyers⟩ **b** : to envelop (as with paper) and usu. secure (as with string) for protection or convenience in transportation or storage : enclose in a package, parcel, or bundle : do up — usu. used with *up* ⟨the waitress ~s up your table-scraps in a napkin —Corey Ford⟩ ⟨*wrapped* up in Christmas wrapping paper —*Crompton & Royton Chronicle*⟩ **c** : to enclose wholly or partially by coiling, looping, grasping, or embracing ⟨a store-bought watermelon *wrapped* in her arms —Eudora Welty⟩ ⟨*wrapped* in chains —H.E.Rieseberg⟩ **d** : to coil, fold, draw, or twine (as a string or cloth) esp. so as to envelop or encompass — usu. used with *about, around*, or *round* ⟨~ a rubber band around the thread tight up against the nut —*Gadgets Annual*⟩ ⟨~ a car around a pole —Mel Heimer⟩ ⟨the cold rain *wrapped* his thin shirt and trousers round his body and legs —Marcia Davenport⟩ ⟨lay down, *wrapping* the cloak about her —Louis Bromfield⟩ **e** : to serve as a surrounding cover, envelope, wrapping, coil, loop, or band for ⟨a white mink stole will ~ her —*Springfield (Mass.) Union*⟩ **2** *obs* : to double or gather up in pliant folds so as to be more compact : FOLD ⟨the napkin . . . *wrapped* together in a place by itself —Jn 20:7 (AV)⟩ **3 a** : to envelop or enclose completely ⟨the bluffs . . . *wrapped* in mist —*Amer. Guide Series: Tenn.*⟩ ⟨dusk had *wrapped* the city —T.B.Costain⟩ ⟨store was *wrapped* in flames —*N. Y. Herald Tribune*⟩ **b** : to involve, encompass, suffuse, or surround with or in an aura, viewpoint, condition, feeling, or state ⟨the sense of fate that *wrapped* his folktales —Van Wyck Brooks⟩ ⟨the whole thing was *wrapped* in disgrace —Robert Reid⟩ **c** : to engross the attention or interest of to the exclusion of anything else : completely involve mentally or emotionally ⟨a boy and girl *wrapped* in a world of each other —Harold Griffin⟩ ⟨walked along *wrapped* in my own thoughts —Carolyn Hannay⟩ — usu. used with *up* ⟨*wrapped* up in a ceremonial veneration of the past —Oscar Handlin⟩ ⟨he was all *wrapped* up in his daughter —Erle Stanley Gardner⟩ **4 a** : to conceal or obscure the nature as if by enveloping or enfolding : hide by enveloping in something extraneous, irrelevant, vague, or verbose ⟨its origin is *wrapped* in multiplied legends —*Amer. Guide Series: Ark.*⟩ — often used with *up* ⟨the book is overwritten and *wrapped* up in needless jargon —Sidney Hook⟩ ⟨agriculturists and private utilities equally ~ up their selfish interests in states' rights language —C.H.Pritchett⟩ **b** : VEIL, CONCEAL ⟨clouds *wrapped* the peak from view⟩ **5** : to enclose as if with a protective covering ⟨*wrapped* in the authority of his office —*Newsweek*⟩ ⟨have become impatient with those . . . who ~ themselves in the Constitution —*Episcopal Churchnews*⟩ **6** : to add as a wrap — used with *round* or *around* ⟨as inserts in the printed book, halftone illustrations may be . . . *wrapped* around a certain number of text pages —*Publisher to Author*⟩ **7** : to enclose within a small compass — usu. used with *up* ⟨a little brochure was designed to ~ up a selling message along with some more information —*Printers' Ink*⟩ ⟨~s up two important driving conveniences . . . into one handy accessory —*Buick Mag.*⟩ **~** *vi* **1 a** : to wind, coil, or twine so as to partially or completely encircle something ⟨windshields have compound curves that ~ around —*Christian Science Monitor*⟩ ⟨a vine ~s round the pillar⟩ **b** : to become spread over a person or object as a covering ⟨coats that ~ around —*advt*⟩ **2** : to put on clothing : DRESS — usu. used with *up* ⟨~ up warm, and we'll go —W. F. De Morgan⟩ **3** : to be subject to covering, enclosing, or packaging — usu. used with *up* ⟨the hydrogen bomb ~s up into a fairly small package —R.H.Rovere⟩

²wrap \"\ *archaic var of* ³RAP

³wrap \", *dial* 'räp\ *n* -s [ME *wrappe*, fr. *wrappen* to cover, wrap] **1 a** (1) : a covering that encompasses something : WRAPPER, WRAPPING ⟨put . . . into gaily drawn paper ~s —*Newsweek*⟩ (2) : material for wraps ⟨use of transparent film as a ~ for bundling packages —*Modern Packaging*⟩ (3) : the process or product or a manner of wrapping ⟨supervising the ~ of a great sheaf of tiger lilies —Christopher Morley⟩ ⟨produces uniformly neat, tight ~s —*Fishing Gazette*⟩ **b** : an article of clothing that may be wrapped round a person; *esp* : a garment (as a coat, jacket, or shawl) for outdoor wear as part of a costume or in cold or stormy weather **c** : a warm covering (as a blanket or shawl) used while traveling or sleeping **d** : a 4-page insert folded around text leaves of a book and sewed in — called also *wraparound* **2 a** : a single turn or convolution of something wound round an object ⟨at the end of each strip I would make a couple of ~s with wire to hold the bark in place —W.D.Wallace⟩ **b** : a unit of length in warping equivalent to 3000 yards **c** : a surface pattern or clock on men's hose made by knitting in extra yarns **3 wraps** *pl* **a** : RESTRAINT ⟨was under ~s from the higher command —G.S.Patton⟩ ⟨is unequivocal when she takes off the ~s —Edmund Fuller⟩ **b** : SECRECY, CENSORSHIP ⟨the plan was kept carefully under ~s until after the election —Don Pryor⟩ ⟨airplane makers took the ~s off a brand-new jet engine —*New Orleans (La.) Times-Picayune*⟩

wraparound \'==,=\ *n* -s [fr. *wrap around*, v.] **1** : a garment (as a dress, robe, skirt, or coat) made with a full-length opening and adjusted to the figure by wrapping around **2** : WRAP 1d **3** : an object that encircles or esp. curves and laps over another ⟨~ windshield⟩

wrap·page \'rapij, -pēj, *dial* 'räp-\ *n* -s **1** : something that

wraps : an outer covering (as of a package); *also* : wrapping material **2** : WRAPPER 3

wrappedwork \ˈ=,=\ *n* [*wrapped* (past part. of ¹*wrap*) + *work*] : basketwork in which the weft is wrapped once around each warp in turn

¹**wrap·per** \ˈrapə(r), *dial* ˈräp-\ *n* -s [ME *wrappere*, fr. *wrappen* to wrap + *-ere* -er] **1** : that in which something is wrapped : a piece of material formed into a wrapping for a parcel, package, or article ⟨candy ~⟩ ⟨coin ~⟩ : as **a** : a tobacco leaf used for the outside covering of plugs, twists, and esp. cigars — compare BINDER, FILLER **b** (1) : JACKET 3f(1) (2) : the paper cover of a pamphlet or booklet or of a book not bound in boards — often used in pl. (3) : a paper wrapping around a finished book covering it entirely and usu. having sealed ends **c** : a sheet of paper for wrapping around but not completely enclosing a newspaper or magazine in the mail; *also* : such a sheet bearing an imprinted stamp esp. for mailing newspapers **d** : a sheet spread over unused furniture or merchandise in a store or warehouse as a protection against dust or fading **2** : one that wraps; *esp* : one whose work is wrapping articles usu. to protect, decorate, or facilitate handling or storing them **3** : an article of clothing designed to be worn wrapped around the body: as **a** : DRESSING GOWN ⟨in her ~ and nightgown —Louis Auchincloss⟩ ⟨a baby's ~ of pink flannel —Ellen Glasgow⟩ **b** : MOTHER HUBBARD **c** : SHAWL ⟨she had thrown a loose white ~ round her shoulders —Mabel Collins⟩ **d** *dial Eng* : a workman's apron, overall, or smock

²**wrapper** \"\ *vt* -ED/-ING/-S : to envelop in or provide with a wrapper — often used with *up*

wrap·per·ing \-pəriŋ, -rēŋ\ *n* -s [¹*wrapper* + *-ing*] **1** : coarse material used for wrapping **2** : a loose outer garment for outdoor wear

wrapping *n* -s [ME, fr. gerund of *wrappen* to wrap] **1 a** : something used to wrap an object : WRAPPER, COVERING, WRAP ⟨tear the ~s from a parcel⟩ ⟨the natural man beneath the theological ~s —V.L.Parrington⟩ **b** : clothing or an article of clothing that swathes or envelops ⟨the little children help to take away the baby's ~s —Nora Waln⟩ **2** : the act or process in basketwork of passing the weft completely around each warp in turn

wrapping-gown \ˈ==,=\ *n* : NIGHTGOWN

wraprascal \ˈ=,==\ *n* [¹*wrap* + *rascal*] : a long loose overcoat worn esp. in the 18th century

wraps *pres 3d sing of* WRAP, *pl of* WRAP

wrapt *past of* WRAP

wrap up *vt* **1 a** : to bring to an esp. successful conclusion : END, FINISH, CONCLUDE ⟨*wrapped up* the case to their own satisfaction —John Lardner⟩ ⟨ready to *wrap up* the truce —*N.Y. Times*⟩ **b** : to confirm or assure the success of (as something practically won, reached, or assured) ⟨*wrapped up* the fight in the seventh round —*Globe & Mail*⟩ **2** : to involve deeply ⟨indeed, the whole policy of a cabinet may be *wrapped up* in the tax proposals —F.A.Ogg & Harold Zink⟩ ⟨the success of America is all *wrapped up* in and almost completely dependent on the efforts of 160 million people —G.M.Humphrey⟩ **3** : to make a single comprehensive report from ⟨the stories of newsmen on the scene were . . . *wrapped up* under a Tokyo dateline —Bruce Westley⟩

wrap-up \ˈ=,=\ *n* -s [*wrap up*] : a summarizing news report ⟨in just a moment we'll give you the *wrap-up* —Harry Wismer⟩

wrasse \ˈras, -aa(ə)s, -ais\ *n* -s [Corn *wragh, gwragh*] : any of numerous elongate compressed but heavy-bodied usu. brilliantly colored marine fishes of the family Labridae that are related to the parrot fishes but have separate teeth in their jaws and conspicuous thick lips, that are common along rocky shores, and that include various important food fishes esp. of warm seas as well as some that are reputed poisonous — see BALLAN, DONCELLA, GREEN WRASSE, HOGFISH 1a

¹**wrath** \ˈrath, ˈräth, ˈräth, *chiefly Brit* ˈrȯth\ *n* -s [ME *wrath*, *wrathe, wraththe*, fr. OE *wrǣththu, wrǣththo*, fr. *wrāth* angry, wroth — more at WROTH] **1** : a strong enraged feeling expressed vehemently and accompanied by bitterness, malignancy, or condemnation ⟨the ~ of the workers and peasants was being roused to liquidate the national capitalists —Raja Hutheesing⟩ **2** : righteous indignation and condemnation esp. of a deity or sovereign; *also* : retribution inspired by righteous indignation : justified punishment ⟨threats of the ~ to come —Max Peacock⟩ **3 a** *archaic* : a fit of anger : a moment or period of malignant or indignant feeling **b** : an act inspired by wrath **4** : intense force or raging violence usu. joined with a seeming malevolence ⟨the great ~ of summer's heat has enveloped the state —Rufus Jarman⟩ **syn** see ANGER

²**wrath** \"\ *adj* : WRATHFUL

wrath·ful \-fəl\ *adj* [ME, fr. ¹*wrath* + *-ful*] **1** : feeling wrath : vehemently incensed and condemnatory, bitter, or vindictive **2** : arising from, marked by, or indicative of wrath **3** : having a threatening, ominous, or violent appearance ⟨~ skies⟩ **syn** see ANGRY

wrath·ful·ly \-fəlē, -li\ *adv* [ME *wrathfulliche*, fr. *wrathful* + *-liche* -ly] : in a wrathful manner

wrath·ful·ness *n* -ES [ME *wrathefulnesse*, fr. *wratheful, wrathful* + *-nesse* -ness] : the quality or state of being wrathful

wrath·i·ly \-thəlē, -li\ *adv* : in a wrathy manner

wrathy \-thē, -thi\ *adj* -ER/-EST [¹*wrath* + *-y*] : WRATHFUL

wrawl \ˈrȯl\ *vi* -ED/-ING/-S [ME *wrawlen*, of imit. origin] *dial Brit* : CRY, HOWL, MEWL

wrax·le \ˈraksəl\ *vi* **wraxled; wraxled; wraxling** \-s(ə)liŋ\ **wraxles** [ME *wraxlen*, fr. OE *wraxlian, wræxlian;* akin to OE *wrǣstlian* to wrestle — more at WRESTLE] *dial* : WRESTLE

¹**wreak** \ˈrēk\ *vt* -ED/-ING/-S [ME *wreken*, fr. OE *wrecan* to drive, drive out, punish, avenge; akin to MD *wreken* to punish, avenge, OHG *rehhan* to avenge, ON *reka* to drive, push, avenge, Goth *wrikan* to persecute, L *urgēre* to press, drive, urge, Lith *vargti* to suffer distress and perh. to Skt *vrajati* he goes, proceeds; basic meaning: push, drive] **1 a** (1) *archaic* : to take vengeance for : inflict punishment in retribution for : AVENGE ⟨~ thy wrongs in battle line —Sir Walter Scott⟩ (2) *archaic* : to avenge an injury done to ⟨grant me some knight to . . . ~ me for my son —Alfred Tennyson⟩ **b** : to act so as to exact or inflict (vengeance or punishment) ⟨the woeful retribution Nature ~*ed* upon a life of indulgence —George Meredith⟩ ⟨~ vengeance on the disturbers of their rights —R.W.Southern⟩ **2 a** : to give free play or course to (a drive or an esp. malevolent feeling) : find outlet for in action or expression : INDULGE, GRATIFY ⟨must ~ my anger somewhere —H.J.Laski⟩ ⟨during one of these explosions he ~*s* the fullness of his fury upon his wife —Michele Cantarella⟩ ⟨could ~ his hungry curiosity upon her —Arnold Bennett⟩ **b** : to express or release completely : EXPEND ⟨an agony quickly ~*ed* and exhausted —F.J.Mather⟩ ⟨~*ing* our energies upon reforms —B.N.Cardozo⟩ **3** : to bring about (harm) : CAUSE, INFLICT ⟨employed to ~ evil on personal enemies —*Notes & Queries on Anthropology*⟩ ⟨the terribly severe winter . . . ~*ed* havoc among the animals —Alexander Tewnion⟩

²**wreak** \"\ *n* -s [ME *wreke*, fr. *wreken* to punish, avenge, wreak] *archaic* : REVENGE, VENGEANCE

wreak·ful \-fəl\ *adj, archaic* : REVENGEFUL

¹**wreath** \ˈrēth\ *n, pl* **wreaths** \-t͟hz, -ths\ [ME *wrethe*, fr. OE *writha;* akin to OE *wrīthan* to twist — more at WRITHE] **1** : something twisted or intertwined into an approximately circular or spiral shape ⟨the tight plaited ~ of hair above her shrunken face —Helen Shaw⟩: as **a** (1) : a coronet, band, or fillet of intertwined flowers or leaves worn or bestowed as a mark of honor or victory or symbol of esteem : GARLAND, CHAPLET ⟨laurel ~⟩ (2) : a representation of such a garland made in metal or stone as a decoration (3) : an arrangement of foliage or flowers with or without decorative accessories on a circular base (as of wire) ⟨Christmas ~⟩ ⟨funeral ~⟩ **b** : an heraldic representation of a band or roll encircling a helmet, supporting a crest, and usu. representing a twist of two cords of silk one of which is tinctured like the principal metal and the other like the principal color in the arms; *also* : CHAPLET 1b **c** : the tail of a boar **d** *archaic* : a winding motion or the product of a winding motion : a partial or complete twist or twisting about a circle **e** : a cluster of spiraling or intertwining tendrils **f** : one of the turns of a spiral or ringed structure : WHORL **g** : a rising and coiling stream of smoke or vapor **h** : the part of the string or handrail in a geometrical stair that twists around a curve **2** *obs* : CREASE, WRINKLE **3** : a drift or bank of snow

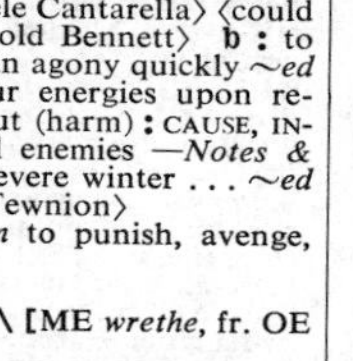

wreath 1a(3)

²**wreath** \"\ *vb* -ED/-ING/-S : WREATHE

wreathe \ˈrēth\ *vb* -ED/-ING/-S [partly fr. ME *wrethen, writhen*, past part. of *writhen* to writhe and partly fr. ¹*wreath* — more at WRITHE] *vt* **1 a** : to cause to writhe : TWIST, CONTORT ⟨*wreathing* his hands —C.S.Forester⟩ **b** : to alter the configurations of (the face) so as to smile ⟨their faces *wreathed* with pleasant social smiles —Margaret A. Barnes⟩ **2 a** : to shape into a wreath or something resembling a wreath ⟨daisies and buttercups *wreathed* into a garland⟩ **b** : INTERWEAVE ⟨muted violins ~ a delicate countermelody —E.J.Stringham⟩ **c** : to coil so as to encircle something ⟨*wreathed* his legs about his stool⟩ **3** : to encircle, adorn, or crown with or as if with a wreath ⟨a poet's brow *wreathed* with laurel⟩ ⟨a high-waisted skirt . . . is *wreathed* with a black suede belt —*New Yorker*⟩ ⟨clouds *wreathed* the tallest pinnacles —G.W.Long⟩ **4** *obs* : to cause to rotate by force : twist about : wrench or turn forcibly **5** *Scot* : to surround or burden with (a yoke) ~ *vi* **1** : to twist in coils : WRITHE ⟨like the cobras they travel with head raised, and the body sways with a . . . *wreathing* movement —C.H.Curran & Carl Kauffeld⟩ ⟨smoke *wreathing* slowly from his short pipe —E.L.Thomas⟩ **2** : to take on the shape of a wreath : to move or extend in circles or spirals **syn** see WIND

wreath·en \ˈrēthən\ *adj* [ME *wrethen*, fr. past part. of *writhen* to writhe] **1** *archaic* : made into a wreath : WREATHED **2** *archaic* : formed, united, or disposed by or as if by twining or interweaving : INTERLACED, INTERTWINED

wreath·er \-thə(r)\ *n* -s : one that wreathes

wreath goldenrod *n* : a No. American perennial herb (*Solidago caesia*) with alternate lanceolate leaves and interrupted axillary clusters of yellow flower heads

wreath·ing·ly *adv* : in a wreathing manner : SPIRALLY

wreath·less \ˈrēthləs\ *adj* : having no wreath

wreath·let \-lət\ *n* -s : a small wreath

wreath shell *n* : TURBAN SHELL

wreathy \ˈrēthē, ˈre̅t͟hē, -i\ *adj* **1** : having the form of a wreath : WREATHED, TWISTED, CURLED, SPIRAL **2** : constituting a wreath

¹**wreck** \ˈrek\ *n* -s [ME *wrek*, fr. AF *wrek, wrec, warec*, of Scand origin; akin to ON *rek* wreck, *reka* to drive, push — more at WREAK] **1** : something that is cast up on the land by the sea; *specif* : goods and other material cast upon the land by the sea after a shipwreck ⟨when flotsam, jetsam and lagan are thrown by the waves on land, they become ~ —F.D.Smith & Barbara Wilcox⟩ **2** *dial Brit* : WRACK 2 **3 a** : the destruction or injury of a vessel by being cast on shore or on rocks or by being disabled or sunk by the force of winds or waves or by other accident : SHIPWRECK; *also* : an instance of such destruction or foundering **b** : the action of wrecking or the fact or state of being wrecked : destruction, disorganization, or serious injury of something esp. by violence : the process of bringing or being brought to disaster ⟨tempted motorists to such high speeds that ~*s* were frequent —*Amer. Guide Series: Ark.*⟩ ⟨two points of view are left, after the ~ of the naïve progress-myth —Herbert Agar⟩ **4 a** : a hulk or the ruins of a wrecked or stranded ship : a ship dashed against rocks or land and broken or otherwise made useless; *also* : a dilapidated old ship beyond or near the end of service **b** : the disordered or broken remains of something that has been wrecked, demolished, or otherwise ruined ⟨saw the ~ of a great civilization . . . and nothing left except some ruins and rocks —F.D.Roosevelt⟩ ⟨are these rings, perhaps, the ~*s* of ancient novae —Waldemar Kaempffert⟩ ⟨in the ~ of the ancient literature it is not easy to illustrate as abundantly —Benjamin Farrington⟩; *also* : the physically or spiritually broken or decayed remains of a person ⟨seeing the ~ of the flamboyant figure, to offer him food and drink —E.V.Lucas⟩ ⟨a ~ of former talent —H.J.Laski⟩ **c** : something that has been wrecked or disabled : something shattered or in a state of ruin or dilapidation ⟨an equally prominent location to deposit the ~ of a car —G.R.Stewart⟩; *also* : a person or animal of broken constitution, health, or spirits ⟨such work killed many of them, or deformed them, or left them tubercular ~*s* —Stringfellow Barr⟩ ⟨this poor ~ of a gutless coward —Barnaby Conrad⟩

²**wreck** \"\ *vb* -ED/-ING/-S [ME *wrekken*, fr. *wrek* wreck] *vt* **1** : to cast ashore **2 a** : to reduce to a ruinous state by violence : overthrow, shatter, or destroy by force : cause to crash or suffer ruin ⟨~ a train⟩ ⟨the cashier's errors ~*ed* the bank⟩ : break up completely : FRUSTRATE ⟨~ a political program⟩ ⟨ambition ~*ed* his marriage⟩ **b** : to destroy, disable, or seriously damage (as a ship) by driving against the shore or on rocks or by causing to become unseaworthy or to founder : SHIPWRECK **c** : to involve in a wreck : cause to suffer or to be lost by shipwreck : ruin, damage, or imperil by wreck ⟨~*ed* freight⟩ ⟨passengers ~*ed* on the coast⟩ **d** : to involve in irreparable disaster or ruin ⟨~ himself with dissipation⟩ ⟨~ their future happiness⟩ **e** : to bring to a condition of complete physical impairment or to an unsound condition ⟨~ his constitution⟩ **3 a** *obs* : WREAK 1b **b** : WREAK 3 ⟨they ~ havoc with hives, smashing commercial hives into splinters —*Wildlife in North Carolina*⟩ **4** : to free (tar) of liquid accumulated on the surface ~ *vi* **1** : to suffer wreck : become wrecked ⟨when the car ~*ed* at 3:30 a.m. —*Springfield (Mass.) Daily News*⟩ **2** : to search out, remove, rob, salvage, or repair wreckage or a wreck **syn** see DESTROY

wreck·age \-kij, -kēj\ *n* -s [²*wreck* + *-age*] **1** : the act or process of wrecking or the state of being wrecked ⟨its mutilated statues surviving the ~ of centuries —Agnes Repplier⟩ ⟨tried for alleged espionage, ~, counterrevolution —N.S. Timasheff⟩ **2 a** : something that has been wrecked : the remains of a wreck **b** : fragments of wreck or of a wreck **c** : broken, disrupted, and disordered parts or material from a wrecked building or structure **3** : wretched or degraded beings cast off by society

wreck·er \ˈrekə(r)\ *n* -s **1** : one that wrecks: as **a** : one that wrecks ships (as by false signals) esp. for plunder **b** : one whose work is the demolition and removal of buildings or structures and usu. the salvage of material **c** : one that disrupts or frustrates plans, processes, or progress ⟨counterrevolutionary ~*s* had wormed their way into the census bureau and doctored the figures —Edmund Stevens⟩ **2 a** : one that searches for or works upon the wrecks of ships: as (1) : one that appropriates wreck washed ashore or visits a wreck for plunder (2) : one that is employed in saving a wrecked or abandoned ship or property or lives from a wrecked ship **b** (1) : a ship employed in searching for or salvaging wrecked ships (2) : a railroad train or car equipped to clear wreckage from tracks, repair damaged roadbed and trackage, set upright usable rolling stock, and remove damaged rolling stock (3) : an automotive vehicle with hoisting apparatus and mechanical equipment for towing wrecked or disabled automobiles, freeing automobiles stalled in snow or mud, or making minor repairs or adjustments at the roadside — called also *tow car* **c** : one that purchases or acquires junked automobiles and salvages parts and material **d** : an operator of a railroad or automotive wrecker

wreckfish \ˈ=,=\ *n* [¹*wreck* + *fish;* fr. its being often found with wreckage] : STONEBASS

wreck·ful \ˈ=fəl\ *adj, archaic* : causing wreck : involving ruin : DESTRUCTIVE

¹**wrecking** *n* -s [fr. gerund of ²*wreck*] **1 a** : the action of causing a shipwreck esp. to obtain plunder **b** : the action or process or an instance of causing ruin, destruction, or the complete frustration of an enterprise **2** [¹*wreck* + *-ing*] : the action or occupation of saving or salvaging wrecked ships, vehicles, structures, or cargoes

²**wrecking** *adj* : engaged, used, or adapted or equipped for use in wrecking or demolishing something or in salvaging shipwrecks or otherwise removing wrecks or recovering ships, railroad rolling stock, or automobiles from a wrecked or disabled condition ⟨~ crew⟩ ⟨~ car⟩

wrecking ball *n* : SKULL CRACKER

wrecking bar *n* : an iron bar with one end bent and split to form a claw for pulling nails and the other end slightly bent and chisel-shaped for prying

wrecking frog *n* : RERAILER

wreckling *obs var of* RECKLING

wrecks *pl of* WRECK, *pres 3d sing of* WRECK

wreck train *n* : a train equipped to clear tracks of debris or damaged equipment following a wreck or destruction by other means

¹**wren** \ˈren\ *n* -s [ME *wrenne*, fr. OE *wrenna, wrænna;* prob. akin to OHG *rentilo* wren, Icel *rindill*] **1** : any of numerous small more or less brown singing birds constituting the family Troglodytidae; *esp* : a very small European wren (*Troglodytes troglodytes*) of a dark brown color barred and mottled with black that has a short erect tail and is a good singer — see CACTUS WREN, CANYON WREN, CAROLINA WREN, HOUSE WREN, MARSH WREN, ROCK WREN, WINTER WREN **2** : any of numerous small singing birds more or less like the true wrens in size and habits; *esp* : any of various European warblers (as the reed wren, sedge warbler, willow wren, golden-crested kinglet, or ruby-crowned kinglet) **3** *slang* : a young woman : GIRL

²**wren** \"\ *n* -s *usu cap* [*W*omen's *R*oyal *N*aval Service] : a member of the Women's Royal Naval Service established as an auxiliary of the British Navy during World War I, reorganized during World War II, and subsequently incorporated into the regular navy

wren babbler *n* : any of numerous small timaliine birds of *Napothera* and several related genera common in southern Asia and the East Indies

wren-boy \ˈ=,=\ *n, Brit* : one of a party of masked or costumed male singers that goes from house to house on Boxing Day carrying a holly bush with a wren or bright bits of cloth attached and begging gifts

¹**wrench** \ˈrench\ *vb* -ED/-ING/-ES [ME *wrenchen*, fr. OE *wrencan* to twist, wrench; akin to OHG *renken* to twist, wrench, Lith *rengtis* to bend over heavily, twist oneself, L *vergere* to bend, incline, Skt *varjati* he bends, turns; basic meaning: turning, bending, twisting] *vi* **1 a** : to make or seem to make a sudden, sharp, or violent turning or twisting motion ⟨of a sudden her heart ~*ed* —Scott Fitzgerald⟩ ⟨the trail teetered down into a gulch and ~*ed* up the other side —A.B.Guthrie⟩; *also* : to undergo a turning or twisting by an outer force **b** *of a hare* : to veer so as to approach at less than a right angle **2** : to perform the action of pulling or straining at something with an esp. violent twisting ⟨tighten the nuts by light ~*ing* —B.G.A. Skrotzki & W.A.Vopat⟩ ⟨suspense ~*ing* at the pit of his stomach —Marcia Davenport⟩ ~ *vt* **1** : to twist violently to one side or out of line, shape, or position ⟨the wind ~*ed* the stems double —Pearl Buck⟩ ⟨~*ed* his head around —F.V.W. Mason⟩ **2** : to injure or disable by a violent twisting or straining : SPRAIN ⟨every joint and every muscle was ~*ed* —R.O.Bowen⟩ **3** : to alter from an original, normal, or true significance, intention, situation, or function ⟨a readiness to ~ language in order to gain nervous immediacy —Irving Howe⟩ ⟨these, then, are the highlights of the essay ~*ed* from their context —L.W.Elder⟩; *esp* : DISTORT, PERVERT ⟨a distributive language . . . has been ~*ed* . . . to make it fit an alien grammar —Charlton Laird⟩ ⟨each object is ~*ed* from its original purpose and changed into a work of art —G.H. Hamilton⟩ **4 a** : to pull, jerk, or tighten by a twisting motion or with violence ⟨~*ed* open the back door —Patrick Campbell⟩ **b** : to wrest or force by or as if by a violent wrench or sudden twist : snatch forcibly ⟨by a terrible effort ~*ed* the tightening fingers away —Oscar Wilde⟩ ⟨~*ed* the jacket from him with unnecessary violence —G.B.Shaw⟩ ⟨~*ing* every penny from the poor —Michael McLaverty⟩ ⟨custom ~*ed* from her a small, stiff bow —Elizabeth Bowen⟩ **c** : to violently alter the situations, surroundings, or characteristics of ⟨had to ~ themselves back to the dull reality of the apartment —Bernard Frizell⟩ ⟨~*ed* from their older tribal society and thrust into new ways of life —H.R.Isaacs⟩ **5** : to cause (a hare) to swerve in a wrench **6** : to cause to suffer emotional distress or mental anguish : RACK ⟨a kaleidoscope of heart-*wrenching* incidents —*Newsweek*⟩ **7** *NewZeal* : ROOT-PRUNE

syn WREST, WRING: WRENCH indicates a twisting or turning with considerable force, often with an abrupt tug or yank, so that the thing affected is twisted, distorted, or forced out of position; it may stress the violence of exertion in pulling or yanking ⟨carelessly *wrenching* the pipe until it bent⟩ ⟨a *wrenching* effect on the basic structural line —Sidney Hyman⟩ ⟨jerked and *wrenched* savagely at his bridle, stopping the hard-breathing animal with a furious pull near the colonel —Stephen Crane⟩ WREST commonly indicates a twisting or wrenching, sometimes with crude violence, sometimes with continuing deftness and dexterity, from another's possession into one's own ⟨through the efforts of bold and ambitious men who *wrest* the power from the lords —Frank Thilly⟩ ⟨while one group of Mississippi valley pioneers advanced into the Southwest to *wrest* Texas from its Mexican owners —R.A.Billington⟩ ⟨when we could *wrest* the initiative from our enemies —F.D. Roosevelt⟩ WRING indicates a compressive twisting together, often to express or extract ⟨*wring* out wet clothes⟩ ⟨more farm output, both of foodstuffs and raw materials, must be *wrung* from the hard-pressed peasants —H.R.Lieberman⟩ ⟨*wringing* more blackmail from this unwarlike nation —C.S.Forester⟩

²**wrench** \"\ *n* -ES **1** : an act of wrenching or an instance of being wrenched: as **a** : a violent twisting to one side or out of shape or a pull with or as if with twisting ⟨with an immense ~ . . . he shook the men from off his back —Liam O'Flaherty⟩ **b** (1) : a sharp twist or sudden jerk straining muscles or ligaments : SPRAIN (2) : an injury by twisting (as in a joint) **c** : an often distorting or perverting alteration from a normal pattern or original signification ⟨in . . . the famous speech . . . a curious ~ and change of tone occurs shortly before the ending —Margery Bailey⟩ **d** : a separation or other change in circumstances causing acute emotional distress ⟨the ~ it must have been for my wife to leave her infant son at home —O.S.J. Gogarty⟩ ⟨it would be more of a ~ . . . to change . . . than to continue in the old cumbersome habits —A.L.Kroeber⟩; *also* : a painful twinge of feeling or sometimes a temporary or permanent psychological alteration caused by separation, loss, or other emotionally or psychologically disturbing events ⟨does not require too much of a psychological ~ for a hardened soldier to get rid of one, two, or three, if he is not in a mood to take prisoners —Theodore Draper⟩ ⟨the ~ from my childish faith in my father as perfect and omniscient —G.B.Shaw⟩ **2** : a turn at an acute angle made by a coursed hare **3** : a hand tool that usu. consists of a bar or lever with adapted or adjustable jaws, lugs, or sockets either at the ends or between the ends and is used for holding, twisting, or turning a bolt, nut, screwhead, pipe or other object; *also* : a power tool for similar purposes **4** : a physical system consisting of a force and a couple in a plane perpendicular to the force **5** : something causing a total upset or breakdown — used in such phrases as *throw a wrench into* ⟨before he could land another job, hard luck threw a ~ into his plans —F.B.Gipson⟩

³**wrench** \"\ *dial var of* RINSE

wrenched \-cht\ *adj* [fr. past part. of ¹*wrench*] : of, relating to, or being an accent that for the sake of metrical conformity is forced from a normally stressed syllable to one that is normally unstressed ⟨the accent on *land* in "and whén he cáme to fár Scotlánd" is ~⟩ — compare HOVERING ACCENT

wrench·er \-chə(r)\ *n* -s : one that wrenches or works with a wrench

wrenches *pres 3d sing of* WRENCH, *pl of* WRENCH

wrench head *n* : a head for a bolt or screw shaped (as square or hexagonal) so as to be readily gripped between the jaws of a wrench

wrench·ing·ly *adv* : to a wrenching degree ⟨can pose for the wife a ~ tough dilemma —W.H.Whyte⟩

wren·let \ˈrenlət\ *n* -s : a little wren

wren·ne·an *or* **wren·ni·an** \ˈrenēən\ *adj, usu cap* [Christopher *Wren* †1723 Eng. architect + E *-an*] : of, relating to, or having the characteristics of the architect Wren or his works

wrens *pl of* WREN

wren's flower *n* [prob. after Christopher *Wren* †1723] : HERB ROBERT

wren-tit \ˈ=,=\ *n* : a small brown California bird (*Chamaea fasciata*) resembling a wren and having soft plumage and a long tail and short rounded wings — see PALLID WREN-TIT

wren warbler *n* : any of several small Asiatic and African sylviid birds of the genus *Prinia* some of which construct nests similar to those of tailorbirds

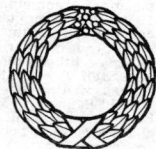

[1]**wrest** \ˈrest\ *vb* -ED/-ING/-S [ME *wresten, wrasten,* fr. OE *wrǣstan* to turn, twist, wrest; akin to ON *reista* to wrest, wring, bend, OE *wrīthan* to twist — more at WRITHE] *vt* **1 a :** to pull, force, or move by violent wringing or twisting movements ⟨the rumble of freight being ~*ed* ashore —Archie Binns⟩ **b** *obs* **:** to insert by forcible twisting or wrenching **2 :** to gain with difficulty by or as if by coercive force, violent action, or steady determined labor ⟨they ~ a narrow survival from their extreme environment —A.L.Kroeber⟩ ⟨a tragedy that ~*s* poetry from what is sordid and properly colloquial —John Gassner⟩ ⟨~ control of the government from the military —W.J.Coughlin⟩ **3 a :** to divert to an unintended, unnatural, or esp. improper use ⟨wrong of her to take life in her hands and try to ~ it to her own purpose —Agnes S. Turnbull⟩ ⟨the evidence . . . was violently ~*ed* to fit the narrowness of the theory —F.A. Pottle⟩ **b** (1) **:** to misinterpret or misapply (a law) intentionally ⟨~ the laws so as to make officers appear guilty of offenses —*Salvation Army Orders*⟩ (2) *obs* **:** to divert or prevent (as a legal proceeding) from a just action or decision ⟨thou shalt not ~ judgment —Deut 16:19 (AV)⟩ **c :** to deflect or change from a true or normal bearing, significance, or interpretation **:** DISTORT ⟨every day they ~ my words —Ps 56:5 (AV)⟩ ~ *vi, obs* **:** to force one's way with violent effort **syn** see WRENCH

[2]**wrest** \ˈ"\ *n* -s [ME *wrest, wrast,* fr. *wresten, wrasten* to wrest] **1 :** the action of wresting **:** WRENCH, TWIST **2 :** a key or wrench formerly used for turning wrest pins in a harp, piano, or other stringed musical instrument

[3]**wrest** \ˈ"\ *n* -s [alter. (influenced by [2]*wrest*) of obs. E dial. *rest, reest,* fr. ME *rest,* fr. OE *rēost*] **:** the curved surface of a plow moldboard

wrest block *n* **:** PIN BLOCK

wrest·er \ˈrestə(r)\ *n* -s **:** one that wrests meanings **:** PERVERTER

[1]**wres·tle** \ˈresəl, ÷ ˈras-\ *vb* **wrestled; wrestled; wrestling** \-s(ə)liŋ\ **wrestles** [ME *wrestlen, wrastlen,* fr. OE *wrǣstlian,* freq. of *wrǣstan* to turn, twist, wrest — more at WREST] *vi* **1 a :** to contend by grappling with and striving to trip or throw down an opponent — see WRESTLING **b :** to combat or overcome an opposing tendency or force, an unworthy psychic drive, or an antagonistic person or group ⟨he *wrestled* with his soul for a long time —Nicolas Slonimsky⟩ ⟨*wrestling* all his life with a feeling that he must be two different people at the same time —Eleanor Harris⟩ ⟨the devilish and the divine ~ for this boy's soul —Lee Rogow⟩ ⟨had to ~ desperately for a living in a . . . more competitive economy —C.J.Rolo⟩ **c :** to engage in deep or serious thought, consideration, or debate ⟨the engineer who must ~ with mining, water-supply, or transportation problems —P.E.James⟩ ⟨brooding over and *wrestling* with ideas —M.R.Cohen⟩ ⟨*wrestling* with the difficulties of transforming the reality of experience into the autonomous reality of fiction —Carlos Lynes⟩ **d :** to engage in or as if in a violent or determined purposive struggle ⟨stevedores *wrestled* with their loads —Joseph Wechsberg⟩ ⟨a nest of ants *wrestling* and tugging at a handful of bread crumbs —Norman Mailer⟩ ⟨less painful to slip a check into an envelope than ~ with the Christmas crowds —*New Yorker*⟩ **e :** to pray earnestly ⟨God's Son was *wrestling* in an agony of prayer —W.F. Hambly⟩ **2 a :** to twist about **:** WRITHE, SQUIRM **b :** to proceed or attempt to proceed with labored or strenuous effort ⟨the icebreaker . . . could smash, slash, and ~ almost indefinitely through solid pack ice —R.E.Byrd⟩ ~ *vt* **1 a :** to engage in (a match, bout, or fall) in wrestling **b :** to wrestle with **:** seek to throw down in or as if in wrestling ⟨~ an alligator⟩ **2 :** to thrust or carry with an action or an effort like wrestling **:** move or force by or as if by wrestling ⟨*wrestled* cotton bales on the levee —H.A.Sinclair⟩ ⟨*wrestled* a kind of manhole from the top of one tank —*New Yorker*⟩ ⟨~ the car along gravelly roads —R.M.Hodesh⟩

syn TUSSLE, GRAPPLE, SCUFFLE: WRESTLE applies to a struggling for mastery by the use, mainly or solely, of dexterous holds with the hands, arms, or legs; figuratively, it may designate a laborious striving at close quarters for mastery ⟨the perfectionist's instinct for *wrestling* with a problem until he had shaped it to his mental image —Irving Kolodin⟩ ⟨the senate was *wrestling* with the definition of unfair practices —F.L.Paxson⟩ TUSSLE may suggest a lighter, less arduous contesting or coping with at close quarters ⟨in bed screaming, determined to run away, *tussling* with my mother and father —Richard Wright⟩ ⟨all major presidents have *tussled* with the Supreme Court —R.A.Billington⟩ GRAPPLE may center attention on coming to grips with and striving for a vantage hold calculated to gain one mastery ⟨*grappled* and fell with his man, and shot him with a pistol —C.S.Forester⟩ ⟨a serious intelligence that must *grapple* with realities and shape them to its will —V.L.Parrington⟩ SCUFFLE may apply to a short, haphazard, and not very serious contest involving confusion, scrambling, and noise ⟨*scuffled* together, their laughter hooting down the street —Gordon Webber⟩

[2]**wrestle** \ˈ"\ *n* -s **:** the action or an instance of wrestling ⟨after a lengthy ~, he succeeded in extracting a tooth —R.L.Taylor⟩ ⟨the metaphysical ~ with the question of what is reality —Robert Richman⟩; *specif* **:** a struggle between two persons to see which will throw the other down **:** a wrestling bout

wres·tler \-s(ə)lə(r)\ *n* -s [ME *wrestlere, wrastlere,* fr. OE *wrǣstlere,* fr. *wrǣstlian* to wrestle + *-ere* -er] **:** one that wrestles; *specif* **:** one that engages in the sport of wrestling

wrestling *n* -s [ME *wresteling, wrasteling,* fr. OE *wrǣstlung,* fr. *wrǣstlian* to wrestle + *-ung* -ing] **:** the act of one who wrestles; *specif* **:** the sport consisting of the hand-to-hand combat between two unarmed contestants who seek to throw each other — compare CATCH-AS-CATCH-CAN, GRECO-ROMAN WRESTLING, JUJITSU

wrest pin *n* **:** a pin in a stringed musical instrument (as a harp, piano) around which the ends of the strings are coiled and by which the instrument is tuned

wrest plank *n* **:** PIN BLOCK

wrests *pres 3d sing of* WREST, *pl of* WREST

wretch \ˈrech\ *n* -ES [ME *wrecche,* fr. OE *wrecca, wræcca* outcast, exile, stranger; akin to OS *wrekkio* outcast, stranger, OHG *reccho, reckio* banished man, outcast, OE *wrecan* to drive out, punish — more at WREAK] **1 a :** a miserable person **:** one profoundly unhappy or in great misfortune, poverty, or distress ⟨starving, spiritless ~*es* —F.V.W.Mason⟩ **b :** something (as a child or pet) in slight misfortune ⟨the poor darling ~ —P.L.Fermor⟩ **2 :** one sunk in vice or degradation **:** a base, despicable, or vile person **:** one who is wicked, cruel, or contemptible ⟨a malignant ~ will cut his own throat because he sees you give alms to the deserving —Edmund Burke⟩

wretch·ed \ˈrechəd\ *adj, usu* -ER/-EST [ME *wrecched,* fr. *wrecche* wretch + *-ed*] **1 :** deeply afflicted, dejected, or distressed from want, disease, or mental anguish **:** extremely unhappy or unfortunate ⟨the ~ wife of the innocent man thus doomed to die —Charles Dickens⟩ ⟨the most ~ of all the sufferers from medieval lack of cleanliness —Edwin Benson⟩ **2 a :** characterized by or tending to produce misery **:** SQUALID, DISMAL, FOUL ⟨living conditions are ~ because the soil is so poor and dry —Juan Comas⟩ ⟨~ houses along the tracks . . . so old that some of them had earthen floors —Morley Callaghan⟩ **b :** producing or being marked by discomfort or distress ⟨spend a ~ night on the floor —Archie Binns⟩ ⟨a ~ journey by stage —Elinor Wylie⟩ ⟨~ health⟩ **3 :** having a mean or contemptible nature or appearance: as **a :** BASE, VILE **b :** MEAGER, PALTRY, INSUFFICIENT ⟨his ~ store of a few dried beans —Pearl Buck⟩ **c :** marked by mistreatment, undernourishment, or overuse **:** SHABBY, OUTWORN, GAUNT ⟨the scrawniest, ~*est* horse I had ever seen —Peter Kalischer⟩ ⟨a ~ purple and black costume that was frayed and stained —Barnaby Conrad⟩ ⟨the most ~ set of animals that he could buy . . . mangy lions and panthers and sick bears —Robert Graves⟩ **d :** exhibiting very poor quality or ability **:** inexpert, crude, or scanting in execution ⟨the latter poem being so ~ by the standard of the former —Robert Fitzgerald⟩ ⟨the army's ~ supply system had blundered again —F.V.W.Mason⟩ ⟨coinage of this period is noted for its ~ workmanship —J.F.Lhotka⟩ **syn** see MISERABLE

wretch·ed·ly *adv* [ME *wrecchedliche,* fr. *wrecched* wretched + *-liche* -ly] **1 :** in a wretched manner **2 :** to a deplorable or distressing degree **:** LAMENTABLY

wretch·ed·ness *n* -ES [ME *wrecchednesse,* fr. *wrecched* wretched + *-nesse* -ness] **:** the quality or state of being wretched **:** distress or hardship that is caused esp. by deprivation or affliction

wretch·less \ˈ≈ləs\ *adj* [by alter.] *obs* **:** RECKLESS

wretch·less·ness *n* -ES [by alter.] **1** *obs* **:** RECKLESSNESS **2 :** callous disregard

wrfg *abbr* wharfage

WRI *abbr* war risk insurance

wried *past of* WRY

wrier *comparative of* WRY

wriest *superlative of* WRY

[1]**wrig·gle** \ˈrigəl\ *vb* **wriggled; wriggled; wriggling** \-g(ə)liŋ\ **wriggles** [ME *wrigglen,* fr. or akin to MLG *wriggeln* to wriggle; akin to D *wriggelen* to jerk, squirm, Norw dial. *rigla* to totter, OE *wrigian* to turn, go — more at WRY] *vi* **1 :** to move the body or a bodily part to and fro with short writhing motions like a worm **:** SQUIRM, WRITHE ⟨*wriggled* uncomfortably in his chair —Israel Zangwill⟩ **2 :** to move or advance with short quick contortions or by twisting and turning **:** go sinuously **:** MEANDER ⟨*wriggled* up the narrow gap between the cliff and the ice —*Sydney (Australia) Bull.*⟩ ⟨the narrowest apertures were wide enough for him to ~ through —R.M. Lovett⟩ ⟨an alluvial river *wriggling* downhill —A.W.Baum⟩ **3 :** to extricate or insinuate oneself or reach a goal by subtle maneuvering, equivocation, or ingratiation ⟨careful to ~ out of final opinions stated in quotable form —John Mason Brown⟩ ⟨attempts to ~ free from the moral obligation —John Burke⟩ ~ *vt* **1 :** to cause to move in short quick contortions **:** bring or set in motion by twisting or turning ⟨dancing girls . . . *wriggled* their hips in sensuous contortions —Harrison Forman⟩ **2 :** to introduce, insinuate, or bring into a state or place by or as if by wriggling ⟨*wriggled* her little person out over their backs —F. Tennyson Jesse⟩ ⟨languages can ~ themselves . . . into another compartment in a fairly short span —A.L.Kroeber⟩ **3 :** to proceed upon (one's way) by wriggling ⟨using every handhold on the rock in front I *wriggled* . . . my way up —John Hunt & Edmund Hillary⟩

[2]**wriggle** \ˈ"\ *n* -s **1 :** the action of wriggling **:** a short or quick writhing motion or contortion **:** a flection of the body **2 :** a formation or marking of sinuous design **:** something having a sinuous course or appearance caused or as if caused by wriggling ⟨the wavy ledges that once served as handles . . . degenerated to mere decorative ~*s* —V.G.Childe⟩ ⟨a ~ of barbed wire . . . marks the line of schism —A.J.Liebling⟩ **3 :** EYEBROW 3

wrig·gler \-g(ə)lə(r)\ *n* -s **:** one that wriggles; *specif* **:** WIGGLER 2

wrig·gling·ly *adv* **:** in a wriggling manner

wrig·gly \-g(ə)lē, -li\ *adj* -ER/-EST [[1]*wriggle* + *-y*] **:** wriggling or tending to wriggle **:** SQUIRMING

wright \ˈrīt, *usu* -īd.+V\ *n* -s [ME *wright, wrighte,* fr. OE *wyrhta, wryhta* worker, maker, wright; akin to OFris *wrichta* worker, OHG *wurhto* worker, OE *weorc, worc* work — more at WORK] **:** a workman in wood **:** CARPENTER — usu. used in combination ⟨mill*wright*⟩ ⟨ship*wright*⟩

wright buckwheat \ˈrīt-\ *n, usu cap W* [after Charles *Wright* †1885 Am. botanical explorer] **:** a woody-stemmed perennial (*Eriogonum wrightii*) of the desert regions of southwestern No. America

wright lippia *n, usu cap W* [after Charles *Wright* †1885] **:** a spreading aromatic shrub (*Lippia wrightii*) of the deserts of California

wright's stain \ˈrīts-\ *n, usu cap W* [after James Homer *Wright* †1928 Am. pathologist] **:** a stain that is a modification of the Romanowsky stain and is much used in staining blood and blood-living parasites

[1]**wring** \ˈriŋ\ *vb* **wrung** \ˈrəŋ\ **wrung; wringing; wrings** [ME *wringen,* fr. OE *wringan;* akin to MD *wringen* to wring, OHG *ringan* to strain, wrestle, struggle — more at WORRY] *vt* **1 a :** to compress by squeezing or twisting esp. so as to make dry or to extract moisture or liquid ⟨~ the laundry dry⟩ ⟨~ berries for wine⟩ **b** *obs* **:** to subject to extortion or coercion **:** SQUEEZE, OPPRESS **2 a :** to extract or obtain by or as if by twisting and compressing ⟨humidity . . . is *wrung* out by the gallon —Jim Riggs⟩ **b :** to exact or acquire by violence or coercion, against resistance, or with difficulty ⟨had to ~ whatever we've had out of barren ground —Ellen Glasgow⟩ ⟨wealth . . . *wrung* from the work of others —Bruce Marshall⟩ ⟨~ trade concessions from local rulers —Stringfellow Barr⟩ ⟨a confession was *wrung* from him —Harry Silver⟩ **c :** to bring to a specified state by or as if by compressing and squeezing **:** DRAIN ⟨never one to let an issue pass until it has been *wrung* dry —Cabell Phillips⟩ ⟨her voice was *wrung* of its . . . richness —Virginia Woolf⟩ **3 a :** to twist with a forcible or violent wrenching motion **:** twist so as to strain or sprain ⟨~ his neck⟩ **:** to twist (as a face) into a distorted shape **:** CONTORT, SCREW ⟨a smile *wrung* his lips —Ellen Glasgow⟩ **b :** to twist together (clasped hands) as a sign of anguish, despair, or disapproval ⟨she *wrung* her hands in mock despair —Oscar Wilde⟩ ⟨~*ing* your hands and complaining about the poor preparation of the students —J.B.Conant⟩ **c :** to bend or twist out of position or course ⟨a gust of wind *wrung* the sailboat to the side⟩ **4 :** to place, position, or insert by a twisting or writhing movement ⟨two blocks are *wrung* side by side on an optical flat —C.E.Haven & A.G.Strang⟩ ⟨~ or tap them into the holes —H.D.Burghardt & Aaron Axelrod⟩ **5 :** to affect painfully by or as if by a pinching, squeezing, twisting, or contorting action **:** cause distress or anguish to **:** RACK, TORMENT, TORTURE ⟨bumping over the rutted roads *wrung* her stomach muscles —Adria Langley⟩ ⟨where the shoe ~*s* him⟩ ⟨the plight of these people is a human tragedy which ~*s* the heart —H.G.Rickover⟩ **6 :** to shake (a hand) vigorously, tightly, or heartily as a greeting or a sign of affection ⟨*wrung* his hand like a pump handle —*English Digest*⟩; *also* **:** to press the hand of **7 :** WREATHE, COIL ~ *vi* **1 :** to twist and turn esp. in pain, discomfort, or anguish **:** SQUIRM, WRITHE ⟨~*s* at some distress —Shak.⟩ **2 :** to undergo pain or anguish **syn** see WRENCH

[2]**wring** \ˈ"\ *n* -s [ME, fr. *wringen* to wring] **:** the act or process of wringing

wringbolt \ˈ≈,≈\ *n* [alter. of *ringbolt*] **:** an eyebolt with the end cut in a wood screw used in shipbuilding as a temporary plate while the permanent fastenings are being driven

wring·er \ˈriŋə(r)\ *n* -s [[1]*wring* + *-er*] **1 :** a worker who removes excess moisture from articles (as textiles, clothing, tobacco leaves, or leather) by wringing between rollers or in a centrifugal extractor **2 :** a machine or device for pressing out liquid or moisture ⟨clothes ~⟩ ⟨mop ~⟩ **3 :** an event, experience, or process that causes pain, hardship, or exhaustion — used in the phrase *through the wringer* ⟨workers, who have already undergone two loyalty or security investigations . . . must go through the ~ a third time —Elmer Davis⟩

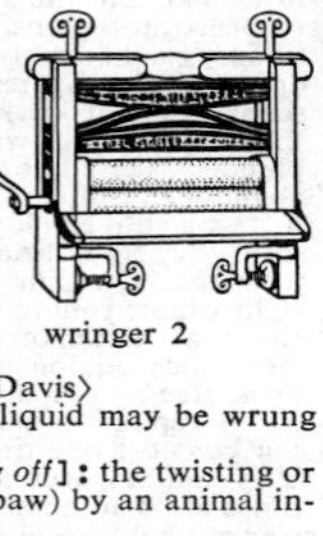

wringer 2

wringing-wet \ˈ≈≈ˈ≈\ *adj* **:** so wet that liquid may be wrung out

wring-off \ˈ≈,≈\ *n* -s [fr. the phrase *wring off*] **:** the twisting or gnawing off of a caught body part (as a paw) by an animal intent on escaping a trap

wringstaff \ˈ≈,≈\ *n, pl* **wringstaves** [*wring* (as in *wringbolt*) + *staff*] **:** a strong piece of wood used in the ring of a wringbolt

[1]**wrin·kle** \ˈriŋkəl\ *n* -s [ME, back-formation from *wrinkled* twisted, winding, prob. fr. OE *gewrinclod,* past part. of *gewrinclian* to wind, fr. *ge-* (perfective and collective prefix) + *-wrinclian* to wind; akin to OE *wrencan* to twist — more at CO-, WRENCH] **1 :** a small ridge, prominence, or furrow esp. when formed on a surface by the shrinking or contraction of a smooth substance **:** a slight fold **:** CORRUGATION, CREASE ⟨~*s* in cloth⟩: as **a :** a small crease or ridge in the skin esp. when due to age, care, or fatigue ⟨a withered face, with the shiny skin all drawn into ~*s* —Arnold Bennett⟩; *also* **:** loose pendulous folds of skin on the forehead and cheeks of some dogs ⟨a bloodhound with excellent ~⟩ **b :** a ripple on the surface of a liquid **c :** a ridge or fold as a topographical configuration ⟨a slight ~ on the surface of the ice cap —P.E. Victor⟩ **2 a :** METHOD, TECHNIQUE, *also* **:** information about a method **:** SUGGESTION, HINT ⟨welcomed the ~ about ruling a fine line with a knife edge through carbon paper —*Publishers' Weekly*⟩ ⟨learning countless little ~*s* on how to care for clothes in winter —Theodora Stanwell-Fletcher⟩ **b :** an innovation in method, technique, or equipment **:** a change in customary procedure or attitude ⟨the sit-down strike, an obstructionist ~ imported from abroad —*Current History*⟩ ⟨a new ~ whereby the exhaust gases are used to spin small turbines geared direct to the propeller shaft —P.J.C. Friedlander⟩ **3 :** FAULT, BLEMISH ⟨undertook to defend the Church with all her ~*s* —V.G.Kiernan⟩

[2]**wrinkle** \ˈ"\ *vb* **wrinkled; wrinkled; wrinkling** \-k(ə)liŋ\ **wrinkles** *vi* **1 :** to be or become marked with or contracted into wrinkles **:** become puckered or shrink into furrows and ridges ⟨the corners of her eyes *wrinkling* with amusement —Morley Callaghan⟩ ⟨his stomach *wrinkled* up like an unpropped wall collapsing on its own foundations —Liam O'Flaherty⟩ **2 :** to move or become moved in slight furrows, waves, or coils ⟨his pajama jacket had *wrinkled* up to his chin —Alan Moorehead⟩ ⟨a single wave starts lightly and easily shoreward, *wrinkling* between reeds —Theodore Roethke⟩ ~ *vt* **1 :** to contract into furrows and prominences **:** make wrinkles in **:** CORRUGATE, CREASE, PUCKER ⟨a homemade pink voile dress . . . *wrinkled* as tissue paper —Eudora Welty⟩ ⟨young mountain belts, where . . . the earth has recently been *wrinkled* and cracked —Howel Williams⟩ **2 :** to form wrinkles in the integument of or surrounding ⟨~ her nose appreciatively —Elizabeth Goudge⟩ ⟨*wrinkling* up his face as though he had already forgotten —P.H.Newby⟩

[3]**wrinkle** \ˈ"\ *n* -s [by alter.] *dial* **:** WINKLE

wrin·kled·ness *n* -ES **:** the quality or state of being wrinkled

wrin·kle·less \ˈ≈≈ləs\ *adj* **:** having no wrinkles **:** SMOOTH

wrinkle-lipped bat \ˈ≈≈ˈ≈-\ *n* **:** any of various widely distributed chiefly tropical free-tailed bats (family Molossidae)

wrin·kly \ˈriŋk(ə)lē, -li\ *adj* -ER/-EST **:** having wrinkles **:** CORRUGATED, CREASED

wrisberg's cartilage *n, usu cap W* [after Heinrich A. *Wrisberg* †1808 Ger. anatomist] **:** CARTILAGE OF WRISBERG

wrisberg's ganglion *n, usu cap W* [after Heinrich A. *Wrisberg* †1808] **1 :** a small ganglion in the superficial cardiac plexus **2 :** GASSERIAN GANGLION

wrisberg's nerve *n, usu cap W* [after Heinrich A. *Wrisberg* †1808] **1 :** GLOSSOPALATINE NERVE **2 :** the medial brachial cutaneous nerve

wrist \ˈrist\ *n* -s *often attrib* [ME, fr. OE; akin to OFris *wrist, wirst* wrist, MHG *rist* wrist, ankle, ON *rist* instep, OE *wrǣstan* to turn, twist — more at WREST] **1 :** the joint or the region of the joint between the human hand and the arm or a corresponding part on a lower animal **:** CARPUS ⟨~ strap⟩ ⟨~ stroke⟩ **2 :** the part of a garment or glove covering the wrist

wrist·band \ˈris(t),≈ *archaic chiefly Brit* ˈriz,≈ *or* -,bənd\ *n* **1 :** the lower part of a sleeve covering the wrist and usu. being a cuff, ruffle, or band **2 :** something in the shape of a band encircling the wrist

wrist·bone \ˈris(t)ˈ≈\ *n* **1 :** a carpal bone **2 :** the styloid process of the radius in man that forms a prominence on the outer side of the wrist above the thumb

wrist-drop \ˈris(t),≈\ *n* **:** paralysis of the extensor muscles of the hand causing the hand to hang down at the wrist

wrist·er \ˈristə(r)\ *n* -s **1 :** a warm knitted covering for the wrist **2 :** a machine operator who stitches the wristbands to gloves and mittens

wrist joint *n* **:** the articulation at the wrist

wrist·let \ˈris(t)lət\ *n* -s **:** a band or strap encircling the wrist; *specif* **:** a close-fitting knitted band worn for warmth and attached to a sleeve, glove, or mitten

wristlet watch *n, Brit* **:** WRISTWATCH

wrist·lock \ˈrist,≈\ *n* **:** a wrestling hold in which one contestant is thrown or made helpless by a twisting grip on the wrist

wrist pin *n* **:** a stud or pin that forms a journal (as in a crosshead or trunk piston) for a connecting rod — see CROSSHEAD illustration

wrist play *n* **:** batting in cricket characterized by free movement of the wrists

wrist shot *n* **:** a short golf stroke played chiefly from the wrists and usu. with an iron

wrist·watch \ˈris,twäch\ *n* **:** a small watch attached to a bracelet or strap to fasten about the wrist

wrist·work \ˈris,twərk\ *n* **:** flexion of the wrist (as in stroking a ball); *esp* **:** WRIST PLAY

wristy \ˈristē, -ti\ *adj* -ER/-EST **:** using wrist play

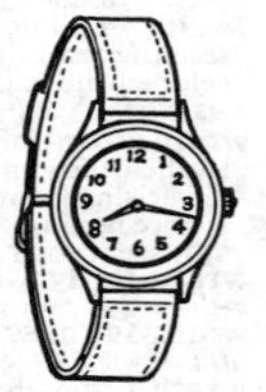

wristwatch

writ \ˈrit, *usu* -id.+V\ *n* -s [ME, fr. OE; akin to ON *rit* writing, writ, Goth *writs* stroke, letter — more at WRITE] **1 :** something that is written **:** writing or a written document — used esp. in the phrases *holy writ* and *sacred writ* **2 a :** a formal written document; *specif* **:** a legal instrument in epistolary form issued under seal in the name of the English monarch from Anglo-Saxon times to declare his grants, wishes, and commands — see ORIGINAL WRIT **b :** an order or mandatory process in writing issued under seal in the name of the sovereign or of a court or judicial officer from the proper authority commanding the person to whom it is directed to perform or refrain from performing an act specified therein: as (1) **:** one used in a particular legal action ⟨~ of account⟩ ⟨~ of aiel⟩ ⟨~ of covenant⟩ ⟨~ of detinue⟩ (2) **:** one used to enforce a right ⟨~ of dower⟩ ⟨~ of entry⟩ ⟨~ of possession⟩ (3) **:** one used to convey a command or put something (as a court decision) in force ⟨~ of execution⟩ — see WRIT OF PROHIBITION (4) **:** one used to redress a wrong ⟨~ of spoliation⟩ **c :** such a written order held to constitute a symbol of the power and authority of the issuer ⟨the mountain ranges . . . halted the reach of the royal ~ and the king's command —W.C.Dickinson⟩ — usu. used with *run* ⟨northern Zululand was a sort of Alsatia where the Queen's ~ did not run —Deneys Reitz⟩ ⟨peoples outside the United States where our laws do not govern and our ~ does not run —Dean Acheson⟩ **d :** a document issued usu. by the clerk of the crown in chancery directing the returning officer of a British parliamentary constituency to hold an election for a member of the House of Commons

writ·able \ˈrīd.əbəl, -ītə-\ *adj* [[1]*write* + *-able*] **:** capable of being put in writing **:** reducible to written form

writ·a·tive \ˈrīd.əd.iv\ *adj* [[1]*write* + *-ative*] **:** addicted to writing

[1]**write** \ˈrīt, *usu* -īd.+V\ *vb* **wrote** \ˈrōt, *usu* -ōd.+V\ *also dial* **writ** \ˈrit, *usu* -id.+V\ *or South* **writ·ten** \ˈritᵊn\ **written** *also* **writ** *or dial* **wrote; writing; writes** [ME *writen,* fr. OE *wrītan* to scratch, draw, engrave, write; akin to OS *wrītan* to tear, wound, scratch, write, OHG *rīzan* to tear, ON *rīta* to write on parchment, Goth *writs* stroke, letter, Gk *rhinē* file, rasp, Skt *vrana* wound, tear, *vrhati* he tears, plucks; basic meaning: incision, tearing] *vt* **1 a** (1) **:** to draw or form by or as if by scoring or incising a surface ⟨creases . . . *written* by laughter —Monica Pearson⟩ (2) **:** to trace (a symbol or a meaningful combination of symbols) by carving or scoring **:** INSCRIBE ⟨a psalter *written* on wax —Eleanor Hull⟩ ⟨the engraver *wrote* the inscription composed for the trophy⟩ **b** (1) **:** to form or trace (a character or series of characters) on paper or other suitable material with a pen or pencil ⟨~ 7 instead of 9⟩ (2) **:** to form or record (a meaningful sign) by a series of written characters ⟨*wrote* 1000 words this afternoon —Arnold Bennett⟩ (3) **:** to spell in writing ⟨words *written* alike but pronounced differently⟩ **c :** to write significant or legible characters upon **:** cover, fill, or fill in by writing ⟨~ a check⟩ ⟨~ ten pages a day⟩ ⟨~ a postcard⟩ **d :** to form or produce (a legible character) in, upon, or by means of a suitable medium ⟨his name *written* in lights on the marquee⟩ ⟨an advertisement *written* by skywriting⟩ ⟨*wrote* the letter *A* on the frosted windowpane⟩ **e :** to produce (symbols or words) by machine ⟨by hitting combinations of keys, a child can ~ the letters he wants —Lois Henderson⟩ **f :** DICTATE 1 ⟨*wrote* the speech twice; the first time he forgot to put a disc in his dictation machine —Leonard Lyons⟩ **2 :** to put down esp. on paper in order to record, relate, or explain **:** set down in writing ⟨whose life has lately been *written* —Norman Douglas⟩ ⟨may have *written* these notes about that date —R.S.Whipple⟩ ⟨when a

man ~s his wrongs —W.L.Sullivan⟩: as **a :** to draw up **:** DRAFT ⟨get a lawyer to ~ your will⟩ ⟨~ a more liberal program which might run into a presidential veto —John Bird⟩ **b** (1) **:** to compose in a literary form **:** be the author of **:** construct according to literary precepts ⟨more concerned to ~ an adventure story than to compile a careful geographical work —*Geog. Jour.*⟩ ⟨this middle eighteenth century *wrote* little literature —V.L.Parrington⟩ ⟨all the poetry that has ever been *written* —T.S.Eliot⟩ ⟨~ the libretto for an opera⟩ ⟨*wrote* a suitable epitaph —J.G.Colton⟩ (2) **:** to compose in musical form **:** be the composer of ⟨a commission to ~ an opera —H.T. & D.A.Schnittkind⟩ ⟨~ a string quartet⟩; *also* **:** to produce musical notation for ⟨the guitar is sounded an octave lower than *written*⟩ **c :** to set forth in written language **:** express in literary form **:** reveal, describe, treat of, or depict by means of words ⟨the great poet, in *writing* himself, writes his time —T.S.Eliot⟩ ⟨could not ~ a claim —John McNulty⟩ ⟨if I could ~ the beauty of your eyes —Shak.⟩ **d** (1) **:** to communicate a message by ⟨judged that at least one of every fifty residents . . . had *written* me a letter —Jane Woodfin⟩ (2) **:** to make known in writing ⟨*wrote* that he was leaving⟩ **e :** to use or exhibit (a specific script, language, or literary form or style) in writing ⟨blind people who ~ Braille —Lois Henderson⟩ ⟨~*s* French with ease⟩ ⟨~*s* a free and easy vernacular⟩ ⟨~ poetry⟩; *esp* **:** to make use of (an easy flowing script) ⟨taught to ~ cursive rather than to print⟩ **f :** to write contracts or orders for ⟨dealers began to get traffic and ~ business —William McNeill⟩ ⟨~ options on securities⟩; *esp* **:** UNDERWRITE ⟨~ life insurance⟩ **3 :** to make a permanent impression of **:** mark indelibly ⟨a law of right conduct, *written* in our hearts —Herbert Agar⟩ ⟨history, adventure, and romance are *written* in the doorways and roof lines —*Amer. Guide Series: Del.*⟩ **4 :** to communicate with in writing **:** write a message to ⟨he *wrote* them upon his arrival⟩ **5 :** to style, call, sign, or exhibit in writing **:** set down **:** record to be something ⟨his desire to ~ himself M.A. on the title page —J.H.Sledd & G.J.Kolb⟩ **6 :** to make necessary **:** ORDAIN, FATE ⟨so be it, it is *written* —D.C.Peattie⟩ **7 :** to cause to appear evident or obvious **:** impress the stamp of ⟨the happiness and peace *written* on the faces of these people —G.P.Musselman⟩ ⟨his crafty caution *written* all over him —H.J.Laski⟩ **8 :** to bring, force, effect, or cause the introduction or removal of by writing ⟨major achievements of the U. S. labor movements are *written* into collective bargaining contracts —V.G.Reuther⟩ ⟨has *written* the forlorn little working girl . . . into American fiction —Harry Hansen⟩ ⟨his love was *written* into his affectionate letters —Ruth P. Randall⟩ ⟨~ oneself into fame and fortune —Charles Lee⟩ **9 :** to take part in or bring about (something worthy of recording) ⟨medical research in America today is *writing* one of the most heartwarming chapters in the story of mankind —*advt.*⟩ ⟨the Colorado river has been *writing* a record of history in the earth's crust —*Hot-Metal Magic*⟩ **10** READ 1i **~** *vi* **1 a :** to make significant characters or inscriptions by or as if by incising, scratching, engraving, or esp. penning ⟨*wrote* on stone tablets⟩; *also* **:** to permit or be adapted to writing ⟨this pen ~*s* well⟩ **b :** to form or produce letters, words, or sentences with a pen, pencil, or machine ⟨on the typewriter, having taught herself to ~ by position and touch —S.H.Adams⟩ **2 :** to compose, communicate by, or send a letter ⟨*wrote* home in glowing terms of the land of their adoption —*Lutheran Quarterly*⟩ ⟨had *written* to some missionary society —W.B.Yeats⟩ **3 a :** to produce or be engaged in producing a poem, book, play, story, or article **:** give literary or journalistic form to a conception, plot, or happening ⟨*writing* on a second novel —J.K.Hutchens⟩ ⟨*wrote* to a simple and direct theme — human endurance —Leslie Rees⟩ ⟨*writing* despairingly of her husband's being drafted —Margaret Redfield⟩ **b :** to compose music ⟨~ in the sonata form⟩ ⟨~ for four voices⟩ **c :** to become regularly employed or occupied in writing: as (1) **:** to become engaged in journalism **:** do editorial work or reporting ⟨~*s* for the press⟩ (2) **:** to follow the profession of author or composer — **write home about :** to comment on at length and esp. in a favorable manner ⟨as a forest, it was nothing to *write home about* —Gerard Newton⟩ ⟨the entertainment at the embassy was something to *write home about*⟩ — **write one's own ticket :** to select a course of action or a position or salary entirely according to one's own wishes or desires ⟨allowed the scientists to *write their own tickets* for the kind of research setup they want —E.P.Snow⟩ — **writ large** *also* **written large :** written or manifested on an expanded scale or in a clearer or more prominent manner ⟨the results are *writ large* in the story of the war —J.P.Baxter b.1893⟩ ⟨the problems of modern totalitarianism are only our own problems *writ large* —*Times Lit. Supp.*⟩ — **writ small :** on a diminished scale ⟨personality is culture *writ small* —C.K.Kluckholn⟩

[2]write \"\ *n* -s **:** sharp clear typewritten lettering or impression ⟨clearness of ~⟩

write down *vt* **1 :** to commit to writing **:** record in written form ⟨*write down* each letter as you receive it —*Boy Scout Handbk.*⟩ ⟨instruments . . . which automatically *write down* their impressions of temperature —Waldemar Kaempffert⟩ ⟨*writes* herself *down* as a United States citizen —*Current Biog.*⟩ **2 :** to record, regard, or reveal as being ⟨not to be somewhat hilarious would be to *write* oneself *down* a bore —H.A. Overstreet⟩ **3 a :** to depreciate, disparage, or injure by writing ⟨has very properly *written down* his value as a straight novelist —*Times Lit. Supp.*⟩ **b :** to reduce in status, rank, or value ⟨the legal position of the service secretaries was therefore *written down* —T.K.Finletter⟩; *specif* **:** to reduce the book value of ⟨*write down* an asset⟩ **c :** to play down in writing ⟨each of the men's parts is deliberately *written down* to leave her role supreme —*Times Lit. Supp.*⟩ **~** *vi* **:** to write so as to appeal to a lower level of taste, comprehension, or intelligence **:** popularize or simplify unduly ⟨unnecessary *writing down* to the juvenile audience —Anthony Boucher⟩

write-down \'=,=\ *n* -s [*write down*] **:** a deliberate reduction in the book value of an asset **:** the process of purposively reducing value

write in *vt* [ME *writen in*] **1 a :** to insert in a document, text, or other writing ⟨*write in* an amendment to a law⟩ **b** (1) **:** to insert (a name not listed on a ballot or voting machine) in an appropriate space by writing or use of a printed sticker (2) **:** to cast (a vote) in this manner **2 :** to write to a center of activity or source of supply ⟨teachers are encouraged to *write in* their requests —James Britton⟩

write-in campaign \'=;=-\ *n* **:** a political campaign carried on to encourage writing in a candidate's name

write-in vote *or* **write-in** *n* -s **:** a vote cast by writing in the name of a candidate ⟨received 10,000 *write-in votes* for governor⟩ ⟨a heavy *write-in vote* for his opponent⟩

write off *vt* **1 a** (1) **:** to reduce the estimated value of **:** DEPRECIATE ⟨the $50,000,000 item of "Good Will" . . . had been *written off* to a nominal $1 —*Woolworth's First 75 Years*⟩ (2) **:** to take off the books **:** CANCEL ⟨*write off* uncollectibles⟩ **b :** to derogate or deny the worth of **:** regard or concede to be lost, outmoded, exhausted, outworn, destroyed, or useless ⟨the lighter, translucent style was more or less *written off* —Israel Citkowitz⟩ ⟨*writing* its mission *off* as a complete failure —*Current History*⟩ **c :** DESTROY, KILL, END ⟨*written off* a pretty shabby kind of life by getting himself killed —Angus Mowat⟩ **2 :** to write fluently, rapidly, or without hesitation ⟨set to work to learn what he had *written off* by heart —Nevil Shute⟩

write-off \'=,=\ *n* -s **1 a :** an elimination from the books **:** CANCELLATION **b :** the act of eliminating from the books ⟨the *write-off* of uncollectibles⟩ **2 a :** a reduction in book value **:** DEPRECIATION ⟨a *write-off* for amortization⟩ **b :** the act of reducing book value

write out *vt* **1 :** to put in writing ⟨*wrote out* the Greek alphabet —Joseph Gaer⟩; *esp* **:** to put into a full and complete written form **:** make a full record or statement of in writing ⟨the book in which he *wrote out* his plots —Peter Forster⟩ **2 :** to exhaust the literary ability or resources of (oneself) by writing too much ⟨an American who had *written* himself *out* —Perry Miller⟩

writ·er \'rīd·ə(r), -ītə-\ *n* -s [ME *writere*, fr. OE *wrītere*, fr. *wrītan* to write + *-ere* -er — more at WRITE] **1 :** one that practices writing as an occupation: as **a** (1) **:** one that writes books, articles, or other material for publication (2) **:** one that writes stories, scenarios, or advertising for motion pictures (3) **:** a composer of music **b** (1) **:** SCRIVENER, SCRIBE (2) **:** a clerk of the East India Company (3) **:** YEOMAN 1f **c** (1) **:** WRITER TO THE SIGNET (2) *Scot* **:** LAWYER, SOLICITOR; *also* **:** a lawyer's chief clerk **d** (1) **:** one that writes insurance (2) **:** one that accepts, records, and issues receipts for bets as agent of a numbers game **e :** one that transcribes or paints lettering for signs or ornaments **2 a :** one that writes or is able to write **:** PENMAN **b :** BRAILLEWRITER **3 :** a person engaged in writing ⟨a number of agricultural economists, the ~ included —C.C.Mitchell⟩ ⟨eludes this ~'*s* memory —E.A. Lahey⟩

writer's cramp *also* **writer's palsy** *or* **writer's spasm** *n* **:** a painful spasmodic cramp of muscles of the hand or fingers brought on by excessive use in writing

writ·er·ship \'==,ship\ *n* **:** the position or function of a writer in the East India Company

writer to the signet [ME] **:** a Scotch judicial officer responsible for preparing warrants, writs, and other documents and being orig. a clerk in the office of the secretary of state

writes *pres 3d sing of* WRITE, *pl of* WRITE

write up *vt* [ME (Sc) *writen up*] **1 a :** to write an account of **:** describe fully ⟨stuff on the early history of toleration . . . which, when *written up*, will . . . be quite new —H.J.Laski⟩ ⟨*wrote* him *up* on the front page —Irwin Deutscher⟩ **b :** to put into finished written form (as the raw material of a report or a piece of fiction) ⟨*write up* a story idea in the form of a one-act play⟩ ⟨*wrote up* his notes on the train⟩ **c :** to increase the interest or significance of (a piece of writing) by attractive language or presentation **2 :** to bring up to date the writing of **3 :** to set down an unduly high value for **:** increase the book value of ⟨*write up* an asset⟩ **4 :** to write a summons for **:** prefer charges against ⟨cars found parked in the streets . . . will be *written up* —*Springfield (Mass.) Union*⟩

write-up \'=,=\ *n* -s [*write up*] **1 a :** an esp. flattering written or printed official, literary, or journalistic account **b :** a written or printed account designed to emphasize or overstress the interest or significance of a topic **2 a :** an increase in the book value or alleged assets of a corporation **b :** the act of setting down an unduly high value

[1]writhe \'rīth\ *vb* -ED/-ING/-S [ME *writhen*, fr. OE *wrīthan* to twist; akin to OHG *rīdan* to turn, twist, ON *rītha* to twist, writhe, OSw *vrītha* to twist, Lith *riesti* to wind, roll, OE *wrigian* to turn, go — more at WRY] *vt* **1 a :** to twist into coils or folds **b :** to twist so as to distort, strain, break off, or cause pain **:** WRENCH, WRING **c :** to twist (the body or a bodily part) in pain **2 :** INTERTWINE ⟨so *writhed* together that you can liken them only to a forest of snakes —Thomas Wood †1950⟩ **~** *vi* **1 a :** to move or proceed with twists and turns **:** wind in a sinuous fashion ⟨wreaths of windblown smoke . . . ~ in long spirals —Alice Duncan-Kemp⟩ ⟨the line *writhed* across the canvas —F.J.Mather⟩ ⟨a six-foot boa constrictor . . . *writhed* up a high-tension tower —*Time*⟩ **b :** to exhibit writhing markings **:** become covered with twists and contortions ⟨the canvas ~*s* with curves —F.J. Mather⟩ ⟨a black tonneau *writhing* with carvings —Earle Birney⟩ **2 :** to become twisted, contorted, or wrested about in or as if in pain or struggling ⟨*writhed* and thrashed . . . in a sort of convulsion —C.G.D.Roberts⟩ ⟨the victim ~*s* and curls amid the stench of burning flesh —H.G.Armstrong⟩ ⟨dancing girls leaped and *writhed* and wriggled their hips —Harrison Forman⟩ **3 :** to suffer keenly from something tormenting ⟨touched some hidden nerve of pride, and made her ~ in agony —G.D.Brown⟩ ⟨corrupt men in the machines ~ in the presence of his obvious integrity —Helen Fuller⟩

syn AGONIZE, SQUIRM, WRITHE mean to twist or turn, usu. continually, in physical or mental distress. WRITHE always suggests nervous or convulsive contortions; in application to physical distress it implies great pain; in application to mental distress, it implies a torturing sense of embarrassment, shame, bafflement, or frustration ⟨saw an owl rise with the tiny rabbit *writhing* in its claws —Willard Robertson⟩ ⟨a great human hulk *writhing* under the unutterable torments of mastery he cannot contend with —George Meredith⟩ ⟨the rest of one's being *writhes* helplessly under a double shame —J.C. Powys⟩ AGONIZE can suggest either severe pangs (as of torture or anguish) or the struggles of one straining violently for a particular end (as victory) ⟨finally recognizes the hopelessness of his marriage and clears out, upset and *agonized* over events —Chad Walsh⟩ ⟨the gray-minded people who cannot rejoice just as they cannot *agonize* —Edith Hamilton⟩ ⟨her tender, innocent *agonizings* for . . . the children's happiness —Agnes S. Turnbull⟩ SQUIRM implies wriggling or turning on a less dignified scale, suggesting great uneasiness rather than profound distress, as from shrinking or wincing under sarcasm or embarrassment ⟨*squirmed* like a little boy called on to explain himself before the principal —Dorothy Baker⟩ ⟨felt so embarrassed that I *squirmed* —Edita Morris⟩

[2]writhe \"\ *n* -s **:** an act or instance of writhing **:** CONTORTION, TWIST ⟨a more than ordinary ~ of the body —Aldous Huxley⟩

writh·en \'rithən\ *adj* [ME, fr. OE, fr. *gewrithen*, past part. of *wrīthan* to twist] **1 :** INTERTWINED; *also* **:** COILED, LOOPED **2 :** subjected to writhing **:** WRITHED, TWISTED, CONTORTED ⟨~ thorns and strange wild flowers —S.P.B.Mais⟩ ⟨lay ~ and gasping on the pavement —Arthur Morison⟩

writh·ing·ly \'rīthiŋlī\ *adv* **:** in a writhing manner **:** with or by twisting

wri·thled \'rithəld\ *adj* [[1]*writhe* + *-led* (as in *wrinkled*)] *archaic* **:** WRINKLED, SHRIVELED

[1]writing *n* -s [ME, fr. gerund of *writen* to write — more at WRITE] **1 :** the act or process of one who writes ⟨with one ~, copies may be made —E.M.Robinson⟩: as **a :** the act or art of forming letters on stone, paper, wood, or other suitable medium to record the ideas which characters and words express or to communicate the ideas by visible signs **:** the use of characters to record in visible form words or sounds ⟨if ~ were not to be done on stone with a chisel but on wood or papyrus —Georg Steindorff & K.C.Seele⟩ ⟨~ on the air with the index finger . . . took the place of pad and pencil —Caroline Yale⟩; *specif* **:** HANDWRITING 1 **b :** the act or practice of literary, journalistic, or other composition in words ⟨engaged in the ~ of a novel⟩; *also* **:** the act or practice of musical composition ⟨his adroit ~ for the keyboard —Arthur Berger⟩ **2 :** something written: as **a :** letters or characters formed on a surface that serve as visible signs of ideas, words, or symbols ⟨alphabetic ~⟩ ⟨cuneiform ~⟩ ⟨syllabic ~⟩ ⟨do you recognize the ~⟩ **b :** a letter, note, or notice used to communicate or record information **c** (1) **:** a written composition **:** a book, pamphlet, poem, article, or other literary production **:** PUBLICATION ⟨his biographies and ~*s* on medical subjects —*Current Biog.*⟩ ⟨a wide variety of ~*s* about literature —C.W. Shumaker⟩ ⟨his collected ~*s* in 10 volumes⟩ (2) **:** a musical composition (3) **:** a literary, artistic, or musical composition (as a novel or sculpture) that can be copyrighted **d :** INSCRIPTION **e** (1) **:** a written or printed paper or document (as a deed, contract, pleading in court) (2) **:** an impression of characters on paper or other substance by printing, photography, pencil, pen and ink, or other means **3 :** a style or form of composition **:** a manner of literary or musical expression ⟨straightforward narrative interspersed with passages in baroque ~⟩ **4 :** the occupation of a writer; *esp* **:** the profession of authorship — **writing on the wall :** HANDWRITING ON THE WALL

[2]writing *adj* **1** [[1]*writing*] **:** of, relating to, or used in or for writing ⟨~ table⟩ ⟨~ pad⟩ **2** [fr. pres. part. of [1]*write*] **:** engaged in writing

writing arm *n* **:** the wooden arm of a tablet-arm chair widened to form a writing surface

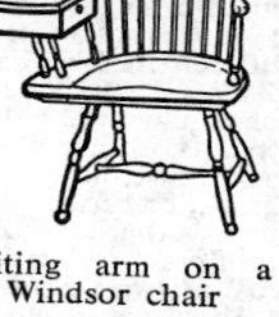
writing arm on a Windsor chair

writing bureau *n, Brit* **:** BUREAU 1a

writing chair *n* [ME *writing chare*] **1 :** CORNER CHAIR **2 :** TABLET-ARM CHAIR

writing desk *n* **:** a desk often with a sloping top for writing upon; *also* **:** a portable case containing writing materials for and having a surface for writing

writing ink *n* **:** ink that is to be used with a pen and that may be permanent (as a blue-black ink) consisting essentially of a dispersion of gallic acid or tannin, ferrous sulfate, and often a blue dye in water or nonpermanent containing soluble dyes and including washable inks — compare INDIA INK 2

writing master *n* **:** an instructor in penmanship

writing paper *n* **:** paper intended for writing upon with ink that is usu. finished with a smooth surface and sized

writing school *n* **:** a school teaching mainly writing common till the end of the 18th century and found in frontier regions still later

writ of assistance **1 :** a writ issued by a court of equity to a sheriff, marshal, or other law officer for the enforcement of an order or decree of the court; *esp* **:** one used to enforce an order for the possession of lands **2 :** a writ issued to a sheriff or other officer to aid in the search for smuggled or otherwise uncustomed goods

writ of certiorari : CERTIORARI

writ of cla·re con·stat \-,kla(a)rē'känz,tat\ [*clare constat* fr. L, it is clearly established] **:** a writ in Scots law by which a superior confirms the heirship of a person claiming to be the next heir of the last tenant deceased — compare PRECEPT OF CLARE CONSTAT

writ of consultation : a writ by which a cause improperly removed by prohibition from one court to another is returned to the court from which it came — compare PROCEDENDO

writ of cosinage : a writ formerly used to recover possession of an estate in lands when a stranger has entered after the death of a lineal kinsman

writ of election : a writ to order the holding of an election; *specif* **:** one used to call a special election to fill a vacancy in an elective office ⟨when vacancies happen in the representation of any state . . . the executive authority of such state shall issue *writs of election* to fill such vacancies —*U.S.Constitution*⟩

writ of error : a writ that lies in a competent court after judgment in an action at law in a court of record directing the latter to examine the record or more commonly to remit the record to an appellate court in order that some alleged error in the proceedings or in the judgment of the court may be corrected if it exists ⟨appeal has now generally superseded the proceeding by *writ of error*⟩ — compare CORAM NOBIS

writ of extent : a writ formerly used to recover debts of record to the British crown and under which the lands, goods, and person of the debtor might all be seized to secure payment

writ of extent in aid : a writ of extent issued at the suit of a crown debtor against his debtor

writ of extent in chief : a writ of extent issued at the suit of the crown

writ of inquiry : a writ issued in an action at law where the defendant has suffered judgment to pass against him by default in order to ascertain and assess the plaintiff's damages where they cannot readily be ascertained by mere calculation

writ of privilege : a writ to deliver a privileged person from custody when arrested in a civil suit

writ of prohibition : a writ issued by a superior tribunal and directed to an inferior court commanding the latter to cease from the prosecution of a suit depending before it

writ of protection **1 :** a writ issued out of the chancery to free an English subject absent overseas on royal service from most legal suits but usu. not charges of felony and in disuse since the 17th century **2 :** a judicial writ issued to a person required to attend court (as party or juror) and intended to secure him from arrest in coming, staying, and returning

writ of recaption : a rarely used writ by which pending an action of replevin damages may be recovered for one whose goods being distrained for rent or service are distrained again for the same cause

writ of reprisal : WITHERNAM 2

writ of right **1 :** an original writ used to protect a feudal tenant in the enjoyment of his freehold property by trial of the rights of the parties in the court of the manor **2 :** a common law writ for restoring to its owner freehold property unjustly withheld

writ of right close : a writ of right used for tenants of the ancient demesne and directed to the bailiff of the manor commanding the lord to do right in his court

writ of right patent : a writ of right directed to the sheriff and used in behalf of a person claiming to hold land by free tenure of a mesne lord

writ of summons : a writ issued by the clerk of the crown on behalf of the British monarch summoning a lord spiritual or a lord temporal to attend parliament

writs *pl of* WRIT

written [ME *writen, written* (past part.), fr. OE *gewriten*] *past part & South past of* WRITE

wrizzled *adj* [alter. of *writhled*] *obs* **:** WRINKLED, SHRIVELED

wrm *abbr* wardroom

wrnt *abbr* warrant

WRO *abbr, often not cap* war risks only

wrocht \'räkt\ *Scot var of* WROUGHT

wro·claw \'vrȯt,släf\ *adj, usu cap* [fr. *Wroclaw*, Poland] **:** of or from the city of Wroclaw, Poland **:** of the kind or style prevalent in Wroclaw

[1]wrong \'rȯŋ *also* 'räŋ\ *n* -s [ME *wrong, wrang*, fr. OE *wrang*, fr. (assumed) OE *wrang, adj.* — more at [2]WRONG] **1 :** an injurious, unfair, or unjust act **:** violation of the right ⟨set forth once again . . . so many were the ~*s* that were to be righted, the grievances to be redressed —Malcolm Muggeridge⟩ ⟨two ~*s* don't make a right⟩ **2 :** something that is wrong, immoral, or unethical; *esp* **:** principles, practices, or conduct contrary to justice, goodness, or equity or to laws accepted as having divine or human sanction ⟨not to know right from ~⟩ ⟨the ~ is not all on one side⟩ **3 :** action or conduct inflicting harm without due provocation or just cause **:** serious injury wantonly inflicted or undeservedly sustained **:** unjust or unmerited treatment ⟨have done so with a sense of ~ toward her —Gretchen Finletter⟩ ⟨see ~*s* on all sides⟩ ⟨roused by a sense of ~ to herself or others —Gilbert Parker⟩ **4 :** the state, position, or fact of being or doing wrong ⟨was all-powerful and never in the ~ —F.M.Ford⟩: as **a :** the state of being mistaken or incorrect ⟨the election showed clearly how far in the ~ his predictions had been⟩ **b :** the state of being guilty of an unpardonable offense or of indefensible conduct or procedure ⟨thorough investigation proved him irreparably in the ~⟩ **5** *archaic* **:** physical harm or damage ⟨newts and blindworms do no ~, come not near our Fairy Queen —Shak.⟩ **6 :** a violation of the legal rights of another **:** an invasion of right to the damage of the party who suffers it **:** TORT — see PRIVATE WRONG; compare PUBLIC WRONG

[2]wrong \"\ *adj, sometimes* **wrong·er** \-ŋə(r)\ *sometimes* **wrong·est** \-ŋəst\ [ME *wrong, wrang*, fr. (assumed) OE *wrang*, of Scand origin; akin to ON *rangr* awry, wrong, Dan & Norw *vrang;* akin to MD *wranc* sour, bitter, MHG *ranc* action of twisting, OE *wringan* to wring — more at WORRY] **1 :** deviating from what is just and good **:** lacking in moral rectitude and integrity ⟨parsons . . . thought it would be ~ for them . . . to undertake combatant service —Rose Macaulay⟩ **2 :** not according to the moral standard **:** not ethically right or just **:** SINFUL, IMMORAL ⟨~ principles of conduct⟩ ⟨some habits are not ~ but are unsocial⟩ ⟨those who hold that a lie is always ~ —Bertrand Russell⟩ **3 :** not right or proper according to a specified or implied code, standard, or convention **:** at variance with what is generally acceptable or preferable ⟨packing off those who talked to the ~ people —R.S.Brown⟩ ⟨unfortunately was seen in all the ~ places⟩ **4 :** not fitted or qualified for a particular intention or purpose **:** lacking suitability **:** INAPPROPRIATE ⟨the person in the ~ job who fails —W.J.Reilly⟩ ⟨it seemed that he had said the ~ thing —Max Peacock⟩ **5 :** not agreeing with or conforming to facts **:** ERRONEOUS, INCORRECT ⟨gives his book a ~ date —DeLancey Ferguson⟩ ⟨the figures are correct but the sum is ~⟩ **6 :** not up to the mark **:** not quite right **:** AMISS, UNSATISFACTORY ⟨there is something ~ about the way the story ends⟩ ⟨what's ~ with tea —Herbert Passin⟩ ⟨don't see anything ~ with it⟩ **7 :** not in accordance with one's intent, end, needs, or expectations ⟨went up the ~ valley and lost several precious days —Heinrich Harrer⟩ ⟨took the ~ size container and ran out of water⟩ **8 :** of, relating to, or constituting the side of something that is usu. held to be opposite to the principal one, that is the one naturaliy or by design turned down, inward, or away from one,

and that is the least finished or polished ⟨the ~ side of the fabric⟩ ⟨pulled her pocket ~ side out —Margaret Deland⟩ ⟨using the ~ end of the brush —David Sylvester⟩ **9** : of, relating to, or being the side that one disagrees with or disapproves of ⟨the intellectual exercise of arguing on the ~ side of a question⟩ **10 a** : least favorable, convenient, or safe : DISADVANTAGEOUS ⟨the ~ side of the railroad tracks —J.A. Morris b. 1904⟩ ⟨the tide was ~ for a landing —Carl Markwith⟩ **b** : contrary or opposite to that which is desirable, customary, or legitimate ⟨a broken-down old soldier on the ~ side of seventy —D.G.Gerahty⟩ ⟨got started on the ~ foot —Lee Greene⟩ ⟨driving on the ~ side of the white line —*Phoenix Flame*⟩ ⟨born on the ~ side of the blanket⟩ ⟨swallowed something the ~ way and almost choked⟩ **11 a** : acting, thinking, or judging in a manner at variance with truth or the facts : incorrect in opinion, judgment, or procedure : MISTAKEN ⟨the book . . . is often amusing, always arch and clever, and usually ~ —John Farrelly⟩ **b** : mentally unstable : INSANE ⟨he is ~ in the head⟩ **12 a** : betting that a dice shooter's next roll or series of rolls will lose **b** : due to lose on the next roll or series of rolls — used of a dice shooter ⟨ten bucks he's ~⟩

³wrong \"\ *adv* [ME *wrong, wrang,* fr. *wrong, wrang,* adj.] **1** : in a way inconsistent with fact or truth : in a mistaken or erroneous manner : without accuracy : INCORRECTLY ⟨guessed ~⟩ ⟨did his homework all ~⟩ **2** : without regard for what is proper or fitting : without propriety ⟨embarrassment made him act ~⟩ **3** : in a manner not regarded as just or upright ⟨should be made to put right what he has done ~⟩ **4 a** : in a wrong direction : AMISS, ASTRAY ⟨the package sent ~ by the post office⟩ ⟨got lost because he turned ~ at the junction⟩ **b** : without regard for moral laws : on an evil or unvirtuous course ⟨a slum environment may cause a child to go ~⟩ **5** : in an unsuccessful or unfortunate way ⟨what has gone ~ and what has led to the government's failure —J.G.Palfrey⟩ **6** : out of working or proper functional order or condition ⟨the lock of one of them goes ~ —Charles Dickens⟩ ⟨his kidneys may go ~ —H.A.Overstreet⟩ **7** : in a wrong position or relationship : in a false light ⟨don't get me ~ —T.V.Smith⟩

⁴wrong \"\ *vt* -ED/-ING/-S [ME *wrongen, wrangen,* fr. *wrong, wrang,* adj.] **1 a** : to do wrong to : treat with injustice : deprive of some right or withhold some act of justice from ⟨where we have ~*ed* the public trust, let there be no excuses —A.E.Stevenson b.1900⟩ **b** : to treat disrespectfully or dishonorably : VIOLATE ⟨the girl he had loved and married and ~*ed* —Zane Grey⟩ **2** : to deprive wrongfully : DEFRAUD, DISPOSSESS — usu. used with *of* ⟨it would ~ the Indians out of their land —William Bartram⟩ **3** *archaic* : to mar the appearance or effect of : IMPAIR, SPOIL ⟨an indifferent good play but ~*ed* by the women . . . in their parts —Samuel Pepys⟩ **4** : to impute a base motive to : dishonor or discredit esp. by false statement : MALIGN ⟨you ~ him; his interests are wider than that —Israel Zangwill⟩ **5** : to harm physically : INJURE **6** : BLANKET 3d

syn OPPRESS, PERSECUTE, AGGRIEVE: WRONG suggests injuring someone in some unjust way; for example, by depriving him of rightful property or by violating something he holds sacred ⟨he had *wronged* her; he had betrayed her; he had trampled her pride in the dust —Ellen Glasgow⟩ OPPRESS suggests causing someone to suffer by inhumanely laying a too heavy burden upon him ⟨no matter how high it raises prices, how much it controls supply or to what extent it *oppresses* the general consumer —C.A.Cooke⟩ ⟨*oppress* with excessive taxation⟩ PERSECUTE suggests relentlessly or unremittingly subjecting someone to annoyance or suffering ⟨*persecute* a child by constant criticism⟩ ⟨when true science was *persecuted* under the Roman tyrants, superstition and false philosophy flourished the more —*Encyc. Americana*⟩ AGGRIEVE suggests giving someone by an injustice (as a wrong or oppression) reason for protest ⟨the too familiar story of a sensitive child *aggrieved* by devilish adults —Elizabeth Janeway⟩ ⟨provisions should be made for recourse to the courts by parties who may be *aggrieved* by such orders —S.T.Powell⟩

wrongdoer \'═¦══\ *n* [ME *wrong doer*] **1** : one that does wrong; *esp* : a transgressor of moral laws **2** : one who violates the legal right of another to his damage for which a legal remedy is available : one who commits a tort or trespass : one guilty of malfeasance : TORT-FEASOR, TRESPASSER

wrongdoing \'═¦══\ *n* [ME *wrongedoeing,* fr. ¹*wrong* + *doing,* n.] **1** : evil behavior or action : transgression of moral or civil law **2** : an instance of doing wrong

wronged *adj* [fr. past part. of ⁴*wrong*] : being injured unjustly : suffering a wrong : HARMED, VIOLATED

wrong·er \'rȯŋə(r) *also* 'räŋ-\ *n* -S [ME, fr. *wrongen* to wrong + *-er*] **1** : one that wrongs or does wrong **2** *obs* : one that misuses : ABUSER

wrongest *superlative of* WRONG

wrong font *n* : a character in a piece of printing that is not of the same font as the other characters or does not match them in style or size or that is contrary to specification — abbr. *wf*

wrong·ful \'═fəl\ *adj* [ME, fr. ¹*wrong* + *-ful*] **1** : full of wrong : INJURIOUS, UNJUST, UNFAIR ⟨a ~ act⟩ **2** : not rightful esp. in law : having no legal sanction : UNLAWFUL, ILLEGITIMATE ⟨the ~ heir to a throne⟩ ⟨~ occupation of an estate⟩ — **wrong·ful·ly** \-f(ə)lē, -li\ *adv* — **wrong·ful·ness** \-fəlnəs\ *n* -ES

wrongful abstraction *n* : the unauthorized taking and removal by an employee of his employer's property in violation of instructions or the employer's legal rights resulting in loss or damage to the employer regardless of who may benefit therefrom

wrongful death *n* : the unjustified killing of another

wronghead \'═,═\ *n* [²*wrong* + *head*] : one that is wrongheaded

wrongheaded \'═¦══\ *adj* **1** : stubborn in adherence to wrong opinion or principles : obstinately wrong : PERVERSE ⟨too ~ to . . . abandon his original objective —Robert Graves⟩ **2** : marked by perversity ⟨politics seem so complicated and so ~ —Felix Walter⟩ ⟨a quite ~ view of the poet —Douglas Bush⟩ — **wrong·head·ed·ly** *adv* — **wrong·head·ed·ness** *n* -ES

wronghearted \'═¦══\ *adj* [²*wrong* + *hearted*] : wrong or perverse in feeling : UNJUST — **wrong·heart·ed·ness** *n*

wronging *pres part of* WRONG

wrong·ly *adv* [ME *wrongly, wrongliche,* fr. ²*wrong* + *-ly, -liche* -ly] **1** : in an improper or inappropriate fashion or way ⟨the sort of story that ~ handled would make the most dreadful melodrama —*Sydney (Australia) Bull.*⟩ **2** : without justice or fairness ⟨wouldst not play false and yet wouldst ~ win —Shak.⟩ **3** : without accuracy : INCORRECTLY ⟨the police pass was ~ filled up —Arnold Bennett⟩ **4** : in error : by mistake ⟨rightly or ~ these men had a different philosophy of education —C.S. Stine⟩

wrong·ness *n* -ES : the quality or state of being wrong: as **a** : the lack of correctness or suitability ⟨a fisherman can explain . . . the ~ of the weather or the bad water —*Wall Street Jour.*⟩ **b** : the lack of moral uprightness or justice ⟨those which judge the rightness or ~ of acts by their consequences —Lucius Garvin⟩

wrong·ous \'rȯŋəs *also* 'räŋ-\ *adj* [alter. (influenced by *-ous*) of earlier *wrongus, wrangus,* fr. ME *wrongwise, wrongwis wrangwis,* fr. *wrong, wrang,* adj., wrong + *wise, wis* wise — more at WRONG, WISE] **1** : characterized by unfairness : INIQUITOUS, WRONGFUL **2** : lacking propriety : UNFITTING **3** : ILLEGAL, UNLAWFUL ⟨~ imprisonment⟩ — **wrong·ous·ly** *adv*

wrongs *pl of* WRONG, *pres 3d sing of* WRONG

wrong side *n* **1** *of handmade paper* : the side opposite the wire side **2** *of machine-made paper* : WIRE SIDE

wrong'un \'═ən\ *n* -S [contr. of *wrong one*] : GOOGLY

wron·ski·an \'(v)rä¦nzkēən, -rō¦, ¦nskēən\ *or* **wronskian determinant** *n* -S *usu cap W* [Józef Maria *Wroński* (Hoene-*Wroński*) †1853 Pol. mathematician and philosopher + E *-an*] : a mathematical determinant whose first row consists of *n* functions of *x* and whose following rows consist of the successive derivatives of these same functions with respect to *x*

wrop \'räp\ *dial var of* WRAP

wros·tle \'räs³l\ *dial Eng var of* WRESTLE

wrote [ME *wroot* (past), fr. OE *wrāt*] *past or dial past part of* WRITE

wroth \'rȯth *also* 'rōth *or* 'räth\ *adj* [ME *wroth, wrath,* fr. OE *wrāth;* akin to OS *wrēth* angry, OHG *reid* twisted, ON *reithr* angry, wroth, OE *wrīthan* to twist — more at WRITHE] **1** : moved to intense anger : highly incensed : WRATHFUL ⟨but ~ as he was on his return, a short struggle . . . ended in a reconciliation —J.R.Green⟩ **2** : being in wild commotion : TURBULENT ⟨the ~ sea's waves are edged with foam —Robert Browning⟩ **syn** see ANGRY

wroth·ful \'═fəl\ *adj* [obs. E *wroth* anger, wrath (fr. ME, fr. *wroth,* adj.) + E *-ful*] : filled with anger

wrothy \-thē\ *adj* -ER/-EST [*wroth* + *-y*] : WRATHFUL

wrought \'rȯt, *usu* -ȯd.+V\ *adj* [ME *wrought, wroght,* fr. *wrought, wroght* (past part. of *worchen, worken* to work), fr. OE *geworht* (past part. of *wyrcan* to work) — more at WORK] **1** : CREATED, SHAPED ⟨and a young lad whose freckled face bore as . . . finely ~ features as one could wish to see —Sidney Lovett⟩ **2 a** : worked into shape by artistry or effort : FASHIONED, FORMED ⟨beautifully ~ garland of spring flowers⟩ **b** : fashioned with particular adherence to form or style ⟨this highly ~, artificial conversation, with its . . . high-piled metaphors —Virginia Woolf⟩ ⟨the most highly ~ and finished of English elegies —Marion Tucker⟩ **3** : finished in an elaborate decorative style : EMBELLISHED, EMBROIDERED, ORNAMENTED ⟨the slippers were . . . curiously ~ with colored beads —William Black⟩ ⟨the screen was . . . ~ with a rather florid Louis Quatorze pattern —Oscar Wilde⟩ **4** : processed for use : MANUFACTURED ⟨a gown of ~ silk⟩ **5 a** : beaten into shape by tools : shaped by a mechanical action (as rolling, forging, extrusion, or drawing) : HAMMERED — used of metals ⟨a bracelet of ~ silver⟩ ⟨a tray of ~ copper⟩ ⟨~ brass and ~ bronze are less expensive than some other metals —A.H. Brownell⟩ **b** : produced by one of these methods ⟨searched the shops for ~ work⟩ **6** : not crude or plain : FINISHED ⟨the ~ oaken beams —John Keats⟩ **7** : deeply stirred : possessed of an excited state of mind : unduly stimulated ⟨when I am highly ~, I faint —W.S.Gilbert⟩ — often used with *up* ⟨let myself get ~ up over nothing —Ellen Glasgow⟩

wrought iron *n* : a commercial form of iron containing less than 0.3 percent and usu. less than 0.1 percent carbon and carrying also 1 or 2 percent of slag mechanically mixed with it and orig. made directly from ore (as in the Catalan forge) but subsequently by puddling — compare INGOT IRON

wrps *abbr* wrappings

wrt *abbr* wrought

wrung \'rəŋ\ *adj* [ME *wrungen,* fr. *wrungen* (past part. of *wringen* to wring), fr. OE *gewrungen* (past part. of *wringan* to wring) — more at WRING] **1** : subjected to wringing : SQUEEZED **2** : marked by suffering, grief, or pain : thoroughly distressed ⟨looked so ~ and shaken —H.L.Davis⟩

¹wry \'rī\ *vb* **wried; wried; wrying; wrys** [ME *wrien,* fr. OE *wrigian* to turn, incline, go; akin to OFris *wrīgia* to bow, bend, MHG *rigel* kerchief wound around the head, OE *wrigels* covering, veil, L *ricula* small veil, *rica* headkerchief, veil, MLG *wrīch* twisted, cranky, Gk *rhoikos* crooked, Lith *rišti* to bind, tie, Av *urvisyeiti* he turns, revolves; basic meaning: turning, winding] *vi* **1** : to make contortions : TWIST, WRITHE ~ *vt* **1** *obs* : to turn aside, away, or around : AVERT, DEFLECT **2 a** : to twist around : WRING **b** : to pull out of or as if out of proper shape : make awry **3** : to contort in order to express emotion ⟨knows he is goin to die and ~*s* up his face —R.P. Warren⟩

²wry \"\ *adj* -ER/-EST **1 a** : turned abnormally to one side ⟨~ neck⟩ ⟨~ mouth⟩ **b** : having a bent or twisted shape or condition : CONTORTED ⟨the tangle of ~ shadows thrown about the hut by a small flame —C.E.Montague⟩ **2 a** : twisted to express an emotion usu. of disgust or displeasure ⟨took another drink . . . making a ~ face —Erskine Caldwell⟩ **b** : made by a deliberate distortion of the facial muscles often to express irony or mockery ⟨at the door he turned with a ~ smile —Agnes S. Turnbull⟩ **3** : marked by perversity : contrary to what is considered right : WRONGHEADED ⟨wondered how he had come to make such a ~ thing of his life —Elizabeth Taylor⟩ **4 a** : marked by a clever twist often with a hint of irony ⟨the ~ humor of the poem —W.L.Sperry⟩ ⟨with a ~ Scottish wit —*Time*⟩ **b** : grimly humorous often with a hint of bitterness ⟨a ~ pleasure to be . . . reminded of all that one is missing —Irwin Edman⟩ ⟨many seem to incline to the ~ view that taxes are here to stay —C.H.Greenewalt⟩ ⟨a chorus of ~ laughs —Lou Stoumen⟩

³wry \"\ *adv* [²*wry*] : AWRY

wrybill \'═,═\ *or* **wry-billed plover** *n* : a peculiar shorebird (*Anarhynchus frontalis*) of New Zealand that is related to the plovers and unique in having its bill sharply deflected to the right

wry-billed \'═¦═\ *adj* : having the bill bent to one side

wry·ly *adv* : in a wry manner : with a caustic twist : DRYLY ⟨smiled rather ~ to himself —Louis Auchincloss⟩ ⟨a ~ humorous study of lower-middle-class life in a London suburb —*Time*⟩

wrymouth \'═,═\ *n* [²*wry* + *mouth*] : a large eellike blenny (*Cryptacanthodes maculatus*) of the northern Atlantic coast of No. America

wry-mouthed \'═¦═\ *adj* **1** : having a crooked or distorted mouth **2** : twisted as if coming from a wry mouth : having a caustically bitter or humorous turn or twist ⟨plenty of thrilling incident and . . . *wry-mouthed* satire —R.E.Roberts⟩

wryneck \'═,═\ *n* [²*wry* + *neck*] **1** : any of various woodpeckers (genus *Jynx*) that differ from the typical woodpeckers in having soft tail feathers and a peculiar manner of writhing the neck: as **a** : a common bird (*J. torquilla*) of Europe and Asia that is intimately variegated in black, brown, and buff **b** : a similar bird (*J. pectoralis*) of central and southern Africa **2** : one that has a wry neck **3** : TORTICOLLIS

wry·ness *n* -ES : the quality or state of being wry ⟨big in the way it treats human beings with a ~ born of compassion —Eric Goldman⟩

wrytail \'═,═\ *n* [²*wry* + *tail*] : a tail twisted to one side; *specif* : a genetic variation in domestic cattle in which the base of the tail is distorted and the tail partially turned to right or left

WS *abbr* **1** water-soluble **2** water supply **3** weather station **4** weather stripping **5** wetted surface **6** wingspread **7** writer to the signet

w's *or* **ws** *pl of* W

w-shaped \'══(,)═¦═\ *adj, cap W* : having the shape of a capital W

WSW *abbr* west-southwest

wt *abbr* **1** warrant **2** weight **3** without

WT *abbr* **1** war tax **2** wartime **3** water tank **4** water tender **5** watertight **6** wireless telegraphy **7** wireless telephone; wireless telephony **8** *often not cap* with title

wth *abbr* width

wthr *abbr* weather

wtr *abbr* **1** waiter **2** winter **3** writer

wu \'wü\ *n* -S *usu cap* [Chin (Pek) *wu²*] : a group of Chinese dialects spoken in the lower Yangtze valley

wu·chang \'wü¦chäŋ\ *adj, usu cap* [fr. *Wuchang,* China] : of or from the city of Wuchang, China : of the kind or style prevalent in Wuchang

wuch·er·e·ria \,wükə'rirēə\ *n, cap* [NL, fr. O. *Wucherer,* 19th cent. Ger. physician + NL *-ia*] : a genus of filarial worms (family Dipetalonematidae) including the parasite (*W. bancrofti*) of tropical elephantiasis and a related worm (*W. malayi*)

wud \'wüd\ *adj* [alter. of ¹*wood*] *chiefly Scot* : INSANE, MAD

wud·dy \'wüdi\ *var of* WIDDY

wu·han \'wü¦hän\ *adj, usu cap* [fr. *Wuhan,* China] : of or from the city of Wuhan, China : of the kind or style prevalent in Wuhan

wu·hu \'wü¦hü\ *adj, usu cap* [fr. *Wuhu,* China] : of or from the city of Wuhu, China : of the kind or style prevalent in Wuhu

wu·lam·ba \wü'lämbə\ *n, pl* **wulamba** *or* **wulambas** *usu cap* : an Australian people of Arnhemland

wul·fen·ite \'wülfə,nīt\ *n* -S [G *wulfenit,* fr. Franz Xaver von *Wulfen* †1805 Austrian mineralogist + G *-it* -ite] : a tetragonal mineral $PbMoO_4$ consisting of native lead molybdate that is isomorphous with stolzite and prob. with scheelite and powellite and that is bright orange-yellow to red, gray, green, or brown usu. in tabular crystals and also in granular masses (hardness 2.75–3, sp. gr. 6.7–7.0) — called also *yellow lead ore*

wull \(¦)wəl\ *Scot var of* WILL

wulliwa *var of* WILLIWAW

wump \'wəmp\ *or* **wumph** \-m(p)f\ *n* -S [imit.] : a heavy sound caused esp. by a falling object ⟨with a dull *wumph* ice bridges we had used during the day would collapse overnight —John Hunt⟩

wun *var of* WOON

wun·der·kind \'vündə(r),kint, 'wən-\ *n, pl* **wunderkin·der** \-ində(r)\ *or* **wunderkinds** [G, fr. *wunder* wonder (fr. OHG *wuntar*) + *kind* child, fr. OHG — more at WONDER, KIN] : a child prodigy : one that succeeds in a competitive or highly difficult field or profession at an early age ⟨naturally he is spoiled, being such a ~ —Eleanor Clark⟩ ⟨violinist who was . . . at one time a ~ —Christina Stead⟩ ⟨the ~ of advertising at 31⟩

wundt·i·an \'vüntēən\ *adj, usu cap* [Wilhelm *Wundt* †1920 Ger. physiologist and psychologist + E *-an*] : of or relating to Wilhelm Wundt or his theories or investigations

wung-out \'wəŋ¦═\ *adj* [fr. the verbal phrase *wing out,* after such pairs of phrases as E *wring out: wrung out*] : having sails set wing and wing

wup *Scot var of* ²OOP

wup·per·tal \'vüpər,täl\ *adj, usu cap* [fr. *Wuppertal,* Germany] : of or from the city of Wuppertal, Germany : of the kind or style prevalent in Wuppertal

wur·ley \'wərlē\ *n, pl* **wurleys** *or* **wurlies** [native name in So. Australia] **1** : a native Australian hut **2** : the nest of the house-building rat of Australia

würm \'vü(ə)rm, 'wü(ə)rm, 'wərm, *Ger* 'vœrm\ *n* -S *usu cap* [fr. *Würm,* lake in southern Germany] : the fourth and last stage of glaciation in Europe

würm·ian \-ürmēən, -ərm-,-œrm-\ *adj, usu cap* : of or relating to the Würm

wur·rung \'wərəŋ\ *n* -S [native name in Australia] : a nail-tailed wallaby (*Onychogalea lunata*) of southwestern and central Australia

wur·rup \-rəp\ *n* -S [native name in Australia] : a hare wallaby (*Lagorchestes hirsutus*) of the central and western parts of Australia

wurst *R* 'wərst, 'wü(ə)rst, –*R* 'wəst, 'wüəst, *R* + –*R* 'wüst *sometimes* 'wüsht\ *n* -S [G, fr. OHG; akin to MLG & MD *worst* — more at BRATWURST] : SAUSAGE 1a

wur·ster's salt \'wər¦stərz-, 'wü(r)¦, 'vür¦\ *n, usu cap W* [after C. *Wurster fl* 1805 Ger. chemist] : any of several deeply colored semiquinones formed by partial oxidation (as with bromine) of the conjugate acid of *para*-phenylenediamine or its *N*-alkyl derivatives: as **a** *or* **wurster's red** *or* **wurster's red salt** : a red product made fom N,N-dimethyl-*para*-phenylenediamine **b** *or* **wurster's blue** *or* **wurster's blue salt** : a blue product made from tetramethyl-*para*-phenylenediamine

wurtz column \'wə¦rts-, 'wü¦\ *or* **wurtz tube** *n, usu cap W* [after Charles A. *Wurtz* †1884 Fr. chemist] : a bulbed fractionating column for laboratory distillations

wurtz-fittig reaction *or* **wurtz-fittig synthesis** \'═'fid·ig-\ *n, usu cap W&F* [after Charles A. *Wurtz* †1884 Fr. chemist and Rudolf *Fittig* †1910 Ger. chemist] : a synthesis of aliphatic or usu. alkyl-substituted aromatic hydrocarbons (as toluene) from two molecules of organic halogen compound (as one molecule each of methyl bromide and bromo-benzene) and two atoms of sodium — compare FITTIG REACTION, WURTZ REACTION

wurtz·i·lite \'wərtsə,līt\ *n* -S [Henry *Wurtz* †1910 Am. mineralogist and chemist + connective *-i-* + *-lite*] : an asphalt similar to uintaite in composition

wurtz·ite \'wərt,sīt\ *n* -S [F, fr. Charles A. *Wurtz* †1884 Fr. chemist + F *-ite*] : a brownish black mineral ZnS that consists of zinc sulfide in hemimorphic hexagonal crystals or a fibrous state and that is polymorphous with sphalerite — **wurtz·it·ic** \(')wərt¦sid·ik\ *adj*

wurtz reaction *n, usu cap W* [after Charles A. *Wurtz* †1884] : a synthesis of aliphatic hydrocarbons (as butane) from two molecules of an alkyl halide (as ethyl iodide) and two atoms of sodium

wurzel *n* -S [by shortening] : MANGEL-WURZEL

wu·sih \'wü¦shē\ *adj, usu cap* [fr. *Wusih,* China] : of or from the city of Wusih, China : of the kind or style prevalent in Wusih

wüst·ite *also* **wust·ite** \'wü,stīt, 'vœ,-\ *n* -S [G *wüstit,* fr. Ewald *Wüst fl* 1907 Ger. geologist + G *-it* -ite] : an artificial mineral FeO consisting of ferrous oxide

wusun *usu cap, var of* USUN

wuth·er \'wəthə(r)\ *vi* -ED/-ING/-S [alter. of ³*whither*] *dial Eng* : to blow with a dull roaring sound ⟨from time to time the wind ~*ed* in the chimney at his back —R.L.Stevenson & Lloyd Osbourne⟩

wu wei \'wü'wā\ *n* [Chin (Pek) *wu² wei²,* lit., not to act] : the practice advocated by Taoism of letting one's action follow the simple and spontaneous course of nature (as by keeping to a minimum governmental organization and regulation) rather than interfering with the harmonious working of universal law by imposing arbitrary and artificial forms : doing or making nothing except in conformity to the Tao

wu·wei \'wü¦wā\ *adj, usu cap* [fr. *Wuwei,* China] : of or from the city of Wuwei, China : of the kind or style prevalent in Wuwei

WVTR *abbr* water vapor transmission rate

WW *abbr* **1** warehouse warrant **2** water-white **3** waterworks **4** *often not cap* with warrants **5** world war

WWA *abbr* with the will annexed

wy·an·dot *also* **wy·an·dotte** \'wīən,dät\ *n, pl* **wyandot** *or* **wyandots** *also* **wyandotte** *or* **wyandottes** *usu cap* **1 a** : a subgroup of the Hurons **b** : a member of such people **2** : the language of the Wyandot people

wy·an·dotte \-,dät\ *n* [prob. fr. *Wyandotte* Wyandot] **1** *usu cap* : an American breed of medium-sized domestic fowls that are derived largely from dark Brahmas and spangled Hamburgs, are in the typical variety white laced with black, and are bred in several color varieties **2** -S *often cap* : a bird of the Wyandotte breed

wych *var of* WICH

wych elm *or* **witch elm** \'wi,chelm, -eům, ═'═ *also* **wych hazel** \'wich,hāzəl, 'wi,chā-, ═'══\ *n* [*wych* fr. ME *wyche* — more at WITCH (tree)] **1** : a Eurasian elm (*Ulmus glabra*) that is common in England, Scotland, and Ireland and has shorter leafstalks but larger fruit than English elm **2** : the wood of the wych elm

wyc·liff·ian *or* **wyc·lif·ian** \(')wi¦klifēən\ *adj, usu cap* [John *Wycliffe* (*Wyclif*) †1384 + E *-an*] : WYCLIFFITE

wyc·liff·ism *or* **wyc·lif·ism** \'wiklə,fizəm\ *n* -S *usu cap* [John *Wycliffe* (*Wyclif*) + E *-ism*] : the teachings or principles of John Wycliffe

wyc·liff·ist *or* **wyc·lif·ist** \-,fəst\ *n* -S *usu cap* [ME *Wiclifist,* fr. John *Wiclif* (Wycliffe, Wyclif) + E *-ist*] : LOLLARD 2

¹wyc·liff·ite *also* **wyc·lif·ite** \-,fīt\ *n* -S *usu cap* [John *Wycliffe* (*Wyclif*) †1384 Eng. religious reformer and theologian + E *-ite*] : LOLLARD 2

²wycliffite *also* **wyclifite** \"\ *adj, usu cap* : of or relating to John Wycliffe or his doctrines teaching that all secular and ecclesiastical authority is derived from God and is forfeited by one who is in mortal sin, that the doctrine of transubstantiation is false, and that monasticism is to be condemned

wyc·ombe chair \'wickəm-\ *n, usu cap W* [fr. High *Wycombe,* locality in Buckinghamshire, England, where it was extensively manufactured in the 19th century] : WINDSOR CHAIR

wyde \'wīd\ *Scot var of* WADE

wye *also* **wy** \'wī\ *n* -S **1** : the letter Y **2** : something resembling the letter Y in shape

wye level *n* : Y LEVEL

wy·e·thia \wī'ēthēə\ *n, cap* [NL, fr. Nathaniel J. *Wyeth* †1856 Am. explorer + NL *-ia*] : a genus of plants (family Compositae) that resemble sunflowers, are found esp. in the western U.S., and have pistillate fertile ray flowers

¹wyke·ham·ist \'wikəməst\ *n* -S *usu cap* [NL *Wykehamista,* fr. William of *Wykeham* (Wickham) †1404 Eng. prelate and statesman who founded Winchester College + L *-ista* -ist] : a student or graduate of Winchester College

²wykehamist \"\ *adj, usu cap* : of or belonging to Winchester College

wylie·coat \'wīli,kōt, 'wil-\ *n* [ME (Sc) *wyle cot,* fr. *wyle* (of unknown origin) + *cot, cote* coat — more at COAT] **1** *chiefly Scot* : a warm undergarment **2** *chiefly Scot* : PETTICOAT **3** *chiefly Scot* : a nightgown for a woman or child

¹wynd \'wīnd\ *n* -S [ME (Sc) *wynde,* prob. fr. *wynden* to

proceed, go, turn, wind, fr. OE *windan* — more at WIND, v.] *chiefly Scot* : a very narrow street : ALLEY, CLOSE

²**wynd** \ˈwin(d)\ *or* **wyne** \ˈwīn\ *v imper* [ME (Sc) *wynden* to proceed, go, turn] *chiefly Scot* : HAW

wyn·ker·nel \ˈwiŋkə(r),nel\ *n* [perh. alter. of ¹*win* + *kernel*] *dial Eng* : MOORHEN 1

wyn·yar·dia \wənˈyärdēə\ *n, cap* [NL, fr. *Wynyard*, town on northwestern coast of Tasmania + NL *-ia*] : a genus of Tasmanian Pliocene or Miocene primitive fossil phalangers sometimes regarded as ancestral to the modern Australian opossums

wy·o·ming \(ˈ)wīˈōmiŋ, -mēŋ\ *adj, usu cap* [fr. *Wyoming*, state in the western U.S., fr. *Wyoming* valley, eastern Pennsylvania, fr. Lenape *M'cheuwómink*, site prob. located in the Wyoming valley, lit., on the great plain] : of or from the state of Wyoming ⟨a *Wyoming* ranch⟩ : of the kind or style prevalent in Wyoming

wy·o·ming·ite \-ˌīt\ *n* -s *cap* [*Wyoming* state + E *-ite*] : a native or resident of the state of Wyoming

wyte *chiefly Scot var of* WITE

wythe *var of* WITHE

wy·vern *also* **wi·vern** \ˈwīvə(r)n\ *or* **wi·ver** \-və(r)\ *n* -s [ME *wyvere, guivere* viper, fr. ONF *wivre* & OF *guivre* viper, wyvern, modif. (influenced by OHG *wipera* adder, snake, fr. L *vipera*) of L *vipera* — more at VIPER] **1 a** : a fabulous animal usu. represented as a 2-legged winged creature resembling a dragon — compare COCKATRICE **b** : the heraldic representation of such a monster **2** : an image or figure made in the likeness of a wyvern

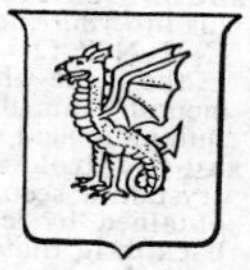

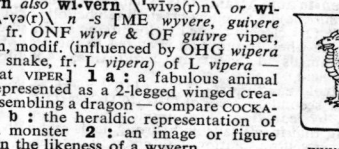

wyvern 1b

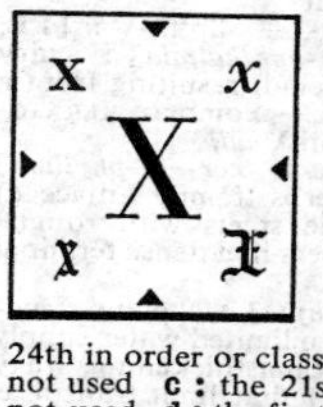

¹**x** \ˈeks\ *n, pl* **x's** *or* **xs** *or* **x'es** *or* **xes** \ˈeksəz\ *often cap, often attrib* **1 a** : the 24th letter of the English alphabet **b** : an instance of this letter printed, written, or otherwise represented **c** : a speech counterpart of orthographic *x* (as *x* in *xylophone, extra, next,* or *ox*) **2** : ten — see NUMBER table **3** : a printer's type, a stamp, or some other instrument for reproducing the letter *x* **4** : someone or something arbitrarily or conveniently designated *x*: as **a** : the 24th in order or class **b** : the 23d in order or class when j is not used **c** : the 21st in order or class when j, v, and w are not used **d** : the first in an order or class including x, y, and sometimes z **5 a** : UNKNOWN QUANTITY 1 ⟨find the value of *x* in the equation *x*−4=3⟩ **b** : an arbitrarily chosen value from the domain of a variable ⟨in the equation *y*=*x*², let *x*=4⟩ **c** : X-COORDINATE **6 a** : something (as a cross) having the shape of the letter X **b** : something (as a $10 bill) marked with an X **7** [so called fr. the use of the letter in crossing out mistakes in writing] : something (as a statement, answer, or result) that is wrong : MISTAKE, ERROR **8** *x's pl, often cap* : ATMOSPHERICS 1 **9** : the basic or monoploid number of chromosomes of a polyploid series : the number contained in a single genome — compare N

²**x** \ˈ"\ *vt* **x-ed** *also* **x'd** *or* **xed**; **x-ed** *also* **x'd** *or* **xed** \ˈekst\ **x-ing** *or* **x'ing** \ˈeksiŋ\ **x'es** *or* **xes** \ˈeksəz\ **1** : to mark with an *x* ⟨*x-ed* his ballot clearly⟩ **2** : to cancel or obliterate with or as if with a series of *x's* — usu. used with *out* ⟨*x-ing* out most of what he had written⟩

³**x** *abbr, often cap* **1** cross **2** ex **3** experimental **4** extra **5** xenon

⁴**x** *symbol* **1** unknown quantity **2 a** times : by **b** hybrid ⟨the license reads Dachshund *x*⟩ ⟨a tall willow (*Salix x blanda*) developed in cultivation⟩ : hybridity **c** out of ⟨a litter by a grade sire *x* a scrub dam⟩ **3** *cap* [fr. the Greek letter X] Christ : Christian **4** power of magnification **5** *cap* reactance **6** abscissa **7** crossed with **8** kiss **9** a playing card of low rank **10** *cap* chemical group — used esp. of a univalent anion or typically univalent negative radical (as halogen) in general formulas **11** the person in question — used esp. by an illiterate in place of a signature **12** the place in question — used on a map or picture **13** — used to indicate choice or approval (as on a ballot)

xan·ci·dae \ˈzaŋkəˌdē, ˈzansə-\ *n pl, cap* [NL, fr. *Xancus*, type genus + *-idae*] : a family of gastropod mollusks (suborder Rachiglossa) comprising the oriental chank and related forms

xan·cus \ˈzaŋkəs\ *n, cap* [NL, perh. modif. of Skt *śaṅkha* conch — more at CONCH] : the type genus of the family Xancidae — compare CHANK SHELL

xanth- *or* **xantho-** *comb form* [NL, fr. Gk, fr. *xanthos*; perh. akin to OHG *hasan* gray — more at HARE] **1** : yellow ⟨*xanthoma*⟩ ⟨*xanth*elasma⟩ ⟨*xantho*derma⟩ **2** : xanthic acid ⟨*xanth*ate⟩ **3** : yellow or yellowish and ammoniacal — in names of salts of cobalt ⟨*xantho*cobaltic chloride⟩

xan·tha·mide \ˈzan(t)thəˌmīd, zanˈtha,m-, -məd\ *n* [*xanth-* + *amide*] : an amide ROCSNH$_2$ of a xanthic acid

¹**xan·thate** \ˈzanˌthāt\ *n* -s [*xanth-* + *-ate*] : a compound that is a salt or ester of a xanthic acid and that is usu. colorless and soluble in the case of the alkali metal salts but yellow and insoluble in the case of the copper salts ⟨sodium ~⟩ ⟨potassium butyl ~ C_4H_9OCSSK⟩ — compare VISCOSE

²**xanthate** \ˈ"\ *vt* -ED/-ING/-S : to convert (as alkali cellulose) into a xanthate by reaction with carbon disulfide — compare SULFIDE

xan·tha·tion \zanˈthāshən\ *n* -s [*xanthate* + *-ion*] : the process of xanthating ⟨~ is a step in the manufacture of viscose⟩

xan·the·las·ma \ˌzan(t)thəˈlazmə\ *n* -s [NL, fr. *xanth-* + Gk *elasma* metal plate] : xanthoma of the eyelid

xan·thene \ˈzanˌthēn\ *n* -s [*xanth-* + *-ene*] **1 a** : a white

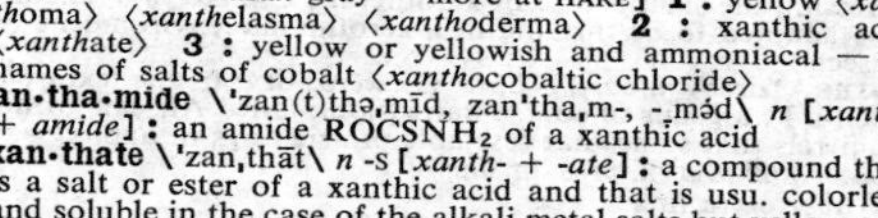

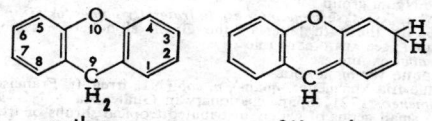

xanthene *3H-xanthene*

xanthene

crystalline heterocyclic compound $C_{13}H_{10}O$ obtained by reduction of xanthone — called also *9H-xanthene*; compare STRUCTURAL FORMULA **b** : an isomeric compound $C_{13}H_{10}O$ that is the parent of the colored forms of the xanthene dyes — called also *3H-xanthene* **2** : any of various derivatives of the two xanthenes; *esp* : XANTHENE DYE

xanthene dye *n* : any of a group of brilliant fluorescent yellow to pink to bluish red dyes characterized by the presence of the xanthene nucleus, known sometimes in colorless as well as colored forms, and used chiefly in dyeing textile fibers, in coloring paper, in producing fluorescent effects, and as organic pigments — see PHTHALEIN, RHODAMINE; compare TRIPHENYLMETHANE DYE

xan·the·nyl \ˈzan(t)thəˌnil\ *or* **xan·thyl** \-thəl\ *n* -s [*xanthene* or ISV *xanth-* + *-yl*] : a univalent radical $C_{13}H_9O$ derived from xanthene

xan·thi·an \ˈzan(t)thēən\ *adj, usu cap* [*Xanthus* + E *-an*] : of or relating to the ancient town of Xanthus in Lycia in Asia Minor ⟨the *Xanthian* marbles⟩

xan·thic \ˈzan(t)thik\ *adj* [F *xanthique*, fr. *xanth-* + *-ique* -ic] **1 a** : of, relating to, or tending toward a yellow color **b** *of a flower* : colored with some tint of yellow — compare CYANIC 2 **2** : of or relating to xanthin or xanthine

xanthic acid *n* **1 a** : a colorless unstable oily thio acid C_2H_5OCSSH obtained in the form of its potassium salt by reaction of potassium ethoxide with carbon disulfide; *O*-ethyl dithiocarbonate **b** : any of a series of analogous unstable thio acids ROCSSH obtained in the form of their salts by reaction of alkoxides with carbon disulfide : an *O*-ester of dithio-carbonic acid ⟨methyl *xanthic acid* CH_3OCSSH⟩ **2** : a hypothetical thio acid HOCSSH whose *O*-esters are the xanthic acids : dithio-carbonic acid

xan·thi·dae \ˈzan(t)thəˌdē\ *n pl, cap* [NL, fr. *Xanthus*, type genus (fr. Gk *xanthos* yellow) + *-idae*] : the largest family of crabs (superfamily Brachyrhyncha) comprising chiefly small littoral or shallow water marine crabs with oval carapaces armed with spines or lobes along the anterolateral margin and including the edible stone and coral crabs

xan·thid·i·um \zanˈthidēəm\ *n, cap* [NL, fr. *xanth-* + *-idium*] : a genus of deeply constricted spiny desmids (family Desmidiaceae) including some that are common plankton forms

xan·thin \ˈzan(t)thən\ *n* -s [ISV *xanth-* + *-in*] : a carotenoid pigment (as cryptoxanthin or zeaxanthin) soluble in alcohol

xan·thine \ˈzanˌthēn, ˈzan(t)thən\ *n* -s [ISV *xanth-* + *-ine*; fr. its yellow residue when evaporated with nitric acid] **1** : a feebly basic crystalline nitrogenous compound $C_5H_4N_4O_2$ that is found esp. in animal tissue and in various plants, forms by hydrolysis of guanine, and yields uric acid on oxidation; 2,6-dihydroxypurine — compare HYPOXANTHINE **2** : any of various derivatives of xanthine — compare CAFFEINE, THEOBROMINE, THEOPHYLLINE

xanthine oxidase *n* : a crystallizable flavoprotein enzyme containing iron and molybdenum that promotes the oxidation esp. of hypoxanthine and xanthine to uric acid and of many aldehydes to acids and that is obtained usu. from milk or liver

xan·thip·pe \zanˈt(h)ipē\ *or* **xan·tip·pe** \-ˈti-\ *n* -s *usu cap* [after *Xanthippe*, wife of Socrates †399 B.C. Greek philosopher] : an ill-tempered woman : SHREW

xan·thism \ˈzanˌthizəm\ *n* -s [*xanth-* + *-ism*] : coloring (as of the skin or pelt) marked by a predominance of yellow pigments

xan·thi·um \ˈzan(t)thēəm\ *n, cap* [NL, fr. Gk *xanthion*, a plant used to dye the hair yellow, fr. *xanthos* yellow] : a genus of coarse and rough or spiny herbs (family Compositae) having small heads of greenish flowers of which the pistillate enclosed in an involucre becomes a burr covered with hooked bristles — see COCKLEBUR

xantho- — see XANTH-

xan·tho·ceph·a·lus \ˌzan(t)thōˈsefələs\ *n, cap* [NL, fr. *xanth-* + *-cephalus*] : a genus of blackbirds comprising only the yellow-headed blackbird of western No. America

xan·thoc·er·as \zanˈthäsərəs\ *n, cap* [NL, fr. *xanth-* + *-ceras*] : a monotypic genus of Chinese shrubs (family Sapindaceae) that have pinnately compound leaves, racemose rather showy white flowers with red or yellow spots, and a fruit resembling the horse chestnut but without prickles

xan·thoch·roi \zanˈthäkrəˌwī\ *n pl, sometimes cap* [NL, fr. *xanth-* + Gk *ōchroi*, nom. pl. masc. of *ōchros* pale, yellow] : caucasoids having light hair and fair skin — compare MELANOCHROI

xan·tho·chro·ic \ˌzan(t)thəˈkrōik\ *adj* [NL *xanthochroi* + E *-ic*] **1** : relating to or belonging to the xanthochroi **2** [NL *xanthochroia* + E *-ic*] : relating to or marked by xanthochroism

xan·thochroid \ˈzan(t)thəˌkrōid, zanˈthäˌk-\ *adj* [NL *xanthochroi* + E *-oid*] : XANTHOCHROIC 1

xan·thoch·ro·ism \zanˈthäkrəˌwizəm\ *n* -s [NL *xanthochroia* yellow skin discoloration (fr. Gk *xanthochroos* xanthochroous + NL *-ia*) + E *-ism*] **1** : abnormal coloration of feathers (as in some parrots) in which yellow replaces the normal color **2** : a genetic variation in various vertebrates characterized by local or general absence of black and brown pigment with normal development of the red and golden pigments (as of skin or feathers) resulting in a yellow to reddish coloration

xan·tho·chro·mia \ˌzan(t)thəˈkrōmēə\ *n* -s [NL, fr. *xanth-* + *-chromia*] : yellowish discoloration (as of the skin or cerebrospinal fluid) — **xan·tho·chro·mic** \ˌ==ˈ=mik\ *adj*

xan·thoch·ro·ous \(ˈ)zanˈthäkrəwəs\ *adj* [Gk *xanthochroos*, fr. *xanth-* + *-chroos* -chroous] : having a yellowish skin and fair hair

xan·thoc·o·nite \zanˈthäkəˌnīt\ *n* -s [G *xanthokon* xanthoconite (fr. *xanth-* + Gk *konis* dust) + E *-ite*; fr. the color of its streak powder — more at INCINERATE] : a cochineal-red to orange-yellow to brown mineral Ag_3AsS_3 consisting of a silver arsenic sulfide and occurring in tabular crystals and often flat rhombohedrons — compare PROUSTITE

xan·tho·derm \ˈzan(t)thəˌdərm\ *n* -s [ISV *xanth-* + *-derm*] : a person with a yellow skin; *esp* : one belonging to a race characterized by yellow skin

xan·tho·der·ma \ˌ==ˈdərmə\ *n* -s [NL, fr. *xanth-* + *-derma*] : yellow color of the skin

xan·tho·gen \ˈzan(t)thəjən, -ˌjen\ *n* -s [ISV *xanth-* + *-gen*] : either of two univalent radicals: **a** : the radical C_2H_5OCSS— derived from xanthic acid (sense 1a) **b** : the radical HOCSS— derived from xanthic acid (sense 2)

xan·tho·gen·ate \ˈzan(t)thəjəˌnāt, zanˈthäjə,n-\ *n* -s [ISV *xanthogen* + *-ate*] : XANTHATE

xan·tho·gen·ic acid \ˌ==ˈ=jenik-\ *n* [ISV *xanthogen* + *-ic*] : XANTHIC ACID 1

xan·tho·leucophore \ˌzan(t)(ˌ)thō+\ *n* [*xanth-* + *leucophore*] : a leucophore (as of a frog) containing yellow pigment as well as guanine — compare XANTHOPHORE

xan·tho·ma \zanˈthōmə\ *n, pl* **xanthomas** \-məz\ *or* **xan·thoma·ta** \-məd·ə\ [NL, fr. *xanth-* + *-oma*] : a condition that is marked by the development (as on the eyelids, neck, or back) of irregular yellow patches or nodules on the skin and is seen in disturbances of cholesterol metabolism

xan·tho·ma·to·sis \(ˌ)zanˌthōməˈtōsəs\ *n, pl* **xanthomatoses** \-ōˌsēz\ [NL, fr. *xanthomat-, xanthoma* + *-osis*] : a disturbance of cholesterol metabolism marked by an increase of cholesterol in the body with deposit of xanthomatous matter in the skin and other tissues sometimes in tumorous masses

xan·thoma·tous \(ˈ)zanˈthäməd·əs, -thōm-\ *adj* [NL *xanthomat-, xanthoma* + E *-ous*] : of, relating to, marked by, or characteristic of xanthoma or xanthomatosis

xan·tho·mel·a·noi \ˌzan(t)thōˈmeləˌnōi\ *n pl, sometimes cap* [NL, fr. *xanth-* + Gk *melanoi*, nom. pl. masc. of *melanos* black; akin to Gk *melas* black — more at MULLET] : xanthomelanous peoples

xan·tho·mel·a·nous \ˌ==ˈmelənəs\ *adj* [*xanth-* + *melanous*] : having olive or yellow skin and black hair

xan·thom·e·ter \zanˈthäməd·ə(r)\ *n* [*xanth-* + *-meter*] : a chromometer for use with sea or lake water

xan·thom·o·nad \zanˈthäməˌnad\ *n* -s [NL *Xanthomonad-, Xanthomonas*] : a bacterium of the genus *Xanthomonas*

xan·thom·o·nas \-ˌnəs, -ˌnas\ *n, cap* [NL, fr. *xanth-* + *-monas*] : a large genus of bacteria (family Pseudomonadaceae) that are distinguished from members of the closely related *Pseudomonas* by production of yellow pigments insoluble in water and that include numerous plant pathogens some of which cause necrotic conditions

xan·thone \ˈzanˌthōn\ *n* -s [ISV *xanth-* + *-one*] : a crystalline ketone $C_6H_4(CO)(O)C_6H_4$ that is the parent of several natural yellow pigments (as gentisin), that is usu. obtained by distilling phenyl salicylate, and that gives a yellow solution with pale blue fluorescence in sulfuric acid; xanthen-9-one

xan·tho·phore \ˈzan(t)thəˌfō(ə)r\ *n* -s [*xanth-* + *-phore*] : a chromatophore containing a yellow pigment that is typically a carotinoid and occurring esp. in fishes and crustaceans

xan·tho·phy·ce·ae \ˌ==ˈfīsēˌē\ *n pl, cap* [NL, fr. *xanth-* + *-phyceae*] : a class of algae (division Chrysophyta) in which the green pigments of the chromatophores are partially masked by xanthophyll and reserves are commonly stored in the form of oil and which comprise the yellow-green algae

xan·tho·phyll \ˈ==ˌfil\ *n* -s [F *xanthophylle*, fr. *xanth-* + *-phylle* -phyll] **1** : LUTEIN 1 **2** : any of several neutral yellow carotenoid pigments that are found esp. in the flowers, fruits, or leaves of plants and that are oxygen derivatives (as carotenols or ketones) of the carotenes but differ from the carotenes by their preferential solubility in alcohol and by their insolubility in petroleum ether ⟨~ esters⟩ — **xan·tho·phyl·lic** \ˌ==ˈfilik\ *adj* — **xan·tho·phyl·lous** \-ləs\ *adj*

xan·tho·phyl·lite \ˌ==ˈfiˌlīt\ *n* [G *xanthophyllit*, fr. *xanth-* + *-phyll* + *-it* -ite; fr. its color and foliated structure] : SEYBERTITE

xan·tho·proteic reaction *or* **xanthoproteic test** \ˈzan(t)thə + ...-\ *n* [ISV *xanth-* + *proteic*] : the reaction of warm concentrated nitric acid with tyrosine or tyrosine-containing proteins (as in human skin) to form a yellow color that is intensified to orange-yellow by the addition of alkali

xan·thop·ter·in \zanˈthäptərən\ *n* -s [*xanth-* + *pter-* + *-in*] : a yellow crystalline amphoteric high-melting pigment $H_2NC_6HN_4(OH)_2$ that occurs esp. in the wings of yellow butterflies and also in the urine of mammals and that is convertible into leucopterin by oxidation and into folic acid by the action of various microorganisms; 2-amino-4,6-dihydroxy-pteridine

xan·tho·purpurin \ˌzan(t)(ˌ)thō+\ *n* [ISV *xanth-* + *purpurin*] : PURPUROXANTHIN

xan·tho·rham·nin \ˌzan(t)thəˈramnən\ *n*-s [ISV *xanth-* + *rhamn-* + *-in*] : a yellow crystalline glycoside $C_{34}H_{42}O_{20}$ that occurs in Persian berries and yields rhamnetin and rhamninose on enzymatic hydrolysis

xan·tho·rhi·za *or* **xan·thor·rhi·za** \ˌzan(t)thəˈrīzə\ *n* -s [NL, fr. *xanth-* + *-rhiza*] : a plant of the genus *Zanthorhiza* : YELLOWROOT

xan·tho·ria \zanˈthōrēə\ *n, cap* [NL, irreg. fr. Gk *xanthos* yellow — more at XANTH-] : a genus of yellow or orange and foliaceous or arborescent lichens

xan·thor·rhoea \ˌzan(t)thəˈrēə\ *n* [NL, fr. *xanth-* + *-rrhea*; fr. the yellow gum it exudes] **1** *cap* : a genus of Australian plants (family Liliaceae) having a thick woody trunk or caudex that bears a cluster of stiff linear leaves and a dense terminal spike of small flowers — see GRASS TREE **2** -s : any plant of the genus *Xanthorrhoea*

xan·tho·siderite \ˌzan(t)(ˌ)thō+\ *n* [G *xanthosiderit*, fr. *xanth-* + *siderit* siderite] : GOETHITE

xan·tho·sine \ˈzan(t)thəˌsēn, -sən\ *n* -s [*xanth-* + *-sine* (as in *guanosine*)] : a crystalline nucleoside $C_{10}H_{12}N_4O_6$ that is formed by deamination of guanosine and yields xanthine and ribose on hydrolysis

xan·tho·sis \zanˈthōsəs\ *n, pl* **xantho·ses** \-ōˌsēz\ [NL, fr. *xanth-* + *-osis*] **1** : yellow discoloration of the skin from abnormal causes **2** : a virus disease of the strawberry plant characterized by crinkling and curling, yellowing and dwarfing of the leaves, and stunting of the entire plant

xan·tho·so·ma \ˌzan(t)thəˈsōmə\ *n, cap* [NL, fr. *xanth-* + *-soma*] : a genus of tropical American aroids having hastate leaves, a shield-shaped style projecting beyond the ovary, and thick tubers — see YAUTIA

xan·tho·toxin \ˌzan(t)thə+\ *n* [ISV *xanth-* + *toxin*] : a crystalline lactone $C_{12}H_8O_4$ obtained esp. from the fruits of an African tree (*Zanthoxylum senegalense*) and used in conjunction with ultraviolet light in the treatment of vitiligo

xan·thot·ri·chous \(ˈ)zanˈthä·trəkəs\ *adj* [*xanth-* + *-trichous*] : having blonde or yellow hair

xan·thou·ra \zanˈthürə\ [NL, fr. *xanth-* + *-ura*] *syn of* CYANOCORAX

xan·thous \ˈzan(t)thəs\ *adj* [*xanth-* + *-ous*] **1** : having yellowish, red, auburn, or brown hair **2** : marked by yellow coloration ⟨a ~ tumor⟩

xan·thox·e·nite \zanˈthäksəˌnīt\ *n* -s [*xanth-* + *xen-* + *-ite*] : a mineral $2Ca_2Fe(PO_4)_2(OH).3H_2O$ consisting of a basic hydrous calcium ferric phosphate and occurring in thin yellow monoclinic plates

xan·thox·y·la·ce·ae \(ˌ)zanˌthäksəˈlāsēˌē\ [NL, fr. *Xanthoxylum* + *-aceae*] *syn of* ZANTHOXYLACEAE

xan·thox·y·le·tin \-ˈlētᵊn\ *n* -s [*xanthoxyl-* (fr. NL *Xanthoxylum*) + *-et-* + *-in*] : a crystalline compound $C_{15}H_{14}O_4$ obtained from the bark of a prickly ash (*Zanthoxylum americanum*) — called also *xanthoxylin-N*

xan·thox·y·lin \zanˈthäksələn\ *n* -s [ISV *xanthoxyl-* (fr. NL *Xanthoxylum*) + *-in*] **1 a** : a crystalline phenolic ketone $C_{10}H_{12}O_4$ obtained from seeds of a shrubby Chinese tree (*Zanthoxylum piperitum*) **b** : any of several crystalline compounds obtained from the bark of other trees of the genus *Zanthoxylum*; *esp* : XANTHOXYLETIN **2** *or* **xanthoxylin extract** : a purified alcoholic extract of prickly-ash bark

¹**xan·thox·y·lum** \-ləm\ [NL, fr. *xanth-* + *-xylum*] *syn of* ZANTHOXYLUM

²**xanthoxylum** \ˈ"\ *var of* ZANTHOXYLUM

xanth·uren·ic acid \ˌzan(t)th(y)əˈrenik-\ *n* [*xanth-* + *-urenic* (as in *kynurenic*)] **:** a yellow crystalline phenolic acid $(HO)_2$-C_9H_4NCOOH closely related to kynurenic acid and excreted in the urine when tryptophan is added to the diet of experimental animals deficient in pyridoxine; 4,8-dihydroxy-quinaldic acid

xan·thy·drol \zanˈthīˌdrōl, -rōl\ *n* [ISV *xanth-* + *hydrol*] **:** a crystalline secondary alcohol $C_6H_4(CHOH)(O)C_6H_4$ that is obtained by reduction of xanthone and is readily oxidized back to it, that forms salts with strong acids and with sulfuric acid gives a yellow solution with green fluorescence, and that is used esp. to characterize and determine urea by the formation of an insoluble product; xanthen-9-ol

xan·thyl \ˈzan(t)thəl\ *var of* XANTHENYL

xan·tu·si·idae \ˌzantəˈsīəˌdē\ *n pl, cap* [NL, fr. *Xantusia*, type genus (fr. János *Xántus* †1894 Hung. ornithologist + NL *-ia*) + *-idae*] **:** a small family of nocturnal carnivorous ovoviviparous terrestrial lizards of arid southwestern No. America

xan·tus's murrelet \ˈ(k)s|ăn.tüshəz-, ˈsh|\ *n, usu cap X* [after János *Xántus* †1894] **:** a murrelet (*Endomychura hypoleucus*) of the California and Mexican coast that is slaty gray above and has white underparts and wing lining

xar·que \ˈshärkē, -kə\ *n* -s [Pg, fr. Sp *charque, charqui*] **:** CHARQUI

xat \ˈkät\ *n* -s [Haida] **:** a carved pole erected as a memorial to the dead by some Indians of western No. America

xa·ve·ri·an \zāˈvirēən, zaˈv-\ *adj, usu cap* [irreg. fr. St. Francis *Xavier* †1552 Span. Jesuit missionary + E *-an*] **:** of, relating to, or named after St. Francis Xavier

xaverian brother *n, usu cap X&B* **:** a member of a teaching congregation of lay brothers in the Roman Catholic Church founded in 1839 in Bruges

x–axis \ˈ=,==\ *n* **1 :** the axis of abscissas in a plane Cartesian coordinate system **2 :** one of the three axes in a three-dimensional rectangular coordinate system

x–body \ˈ=,==\ *n, usu cap X* **:** an amoeboid or amorphous inclusion body typical of some virus diseases of plants

XC *abbr* ex coupon

x–chair \ˈ=,=\ *n, usu cap X* **:** a usu. folding chair of ancient origin in which the legs cross to support the seat and are continuous with the arms

x chromosome *n, usu cap X* **:** a sex chromosome that carries factors for femaleness and usu. occurs paired in each female zygote and cell and single in each male zygote and cell — compare Y CHROMOSOME, Z CHROMOSOME

x–coordinate \ˈ==,=(=)=\ *n* **1 :** ABSCISSA **2 :** one of the three coordinates in a three-dimensional rectangular coordinate system

XD *abbr, often not cap* ex dividend

x'd *past of* X

x–disease \ˈ==,=\ *n, usu cap X* **:** any of various usu. virus diseases of obscure etiology and relationships: as **a :** a viral encephalitis of man first detected in Australia — called also *Australian X-disease* **b :** BLUE COMB **c :** HYPERKERATOSIS 2b **d :** a serious and widespread virus disease of peaches and related stone fruits characterized by yellowing and shot-holing of the leaves, early defoliation, and loss or mummification of the fruit — called also *yellow-red virosis*

Xe *symbol* xenon

xe·bec \ˈzēˌbek, zəˈbek\ *n* -s [prob. modif. (influenced by obs. Sp *xabeque* xebec — now *jabeque* — or Catal *xabec*, both fr. Ar *shabbāk*) of F *chebec*, fr. Ar *shabbāk*] **:** a Mediterranean sailing ship that has a long overhanging bow and stern, is usu. three-masted with a lateen rig, but often carries square sails on the foremast

x–ed *also* **xed** *past of* X

xe·ma \ˈzēmə\ *n, cap* [NL] **:** a monotypic genus of small black-headed gulls of arctic America having a slightly forked tail

xen- *or* **xeno-** *comb form* [LL, fr. Gk, fr. *xenos*] **1 :** guest **:** foreigner ⟨*xeno*mania⟩ **2 a :** strange **:** foreign ⟨*Xen*urus⟩ **b :** intrusive ⟨*xeno*lith⟩ **c :** HETER- ⟨*xeno*genesis⟩

xen·acan·thi \ˌzenəˈkanˌthī\ *n pl, cap* [NL, irreg. fr. *xen-* + Gk *akantha* spine — more at ACANTH-] *syn of* XENACANTHINI

¹xen·acan·thine \ˌzenəˈkan(t)thən, -anˌthīn\ *adj* [NL *Xenacanthini*] **:** of or relating to the Xenacanthini

²xenacanthine \ˈ"\ *n* -s [NL *Xenacanthini*] **:** a fish or fossil of the division Xenacanthini

xen·acan·thi·ni \ˌzenəˌkanˈthīˌnī, -ˈkan(t)thəˌnī\ *n pl, cap* [NL, fr. *xen-* + *acanth-* + *-ini*] *in some classifications* **:** a division of fossil elasmobranchs that is nearly equivalent to Ichthyotomi

xe·nar·chi \zəˈnärˌkī\ *n pl, cap* [NL, fr. *xen-* + Gk *archos* rectum, anus; akin to Gk *archein* to begin — more at ARCHI-] *in some classifications* **:** an order of fishes that comprises only the pirate perches and is usu. included in the order Salmopercae

xe·nar·thra \zəˈnärthrə\ *n pl, cap* [NL, fr. *xen-* + *arthra*, pl. of *arthron*] **:** a suborder or other division of Edentata comprising the American anteaters, armadillos, sloths, and usu. the extinct ground sloths — **xe·nar·thral** \-thrəl\ *or* **xe·nar·throus** \-thrəs\ *adj* — **xe·nar·thran** \-thrən\ *adj or n*

-x·ene \kˌsēn\ *n comb form* -s [F *-xène*, fr. Gk *-xenos* stranger, fr. *xenos*] **1 :** substance rarely associated with (such) a mineral ⟨anthraco*xene*⟩ **2 :** intrusive mineral of (such) a character ⟨leuco*xene*⟩ ⟨caco*xene*⟩

xe·nia \ˈzēnēə, -nyə\ *n* -s [NL, fr. Gk, hospitality, fr. *xenos* guest + *-ia* -y] **:** the effect of genes introduced by a male nucleus on structures (as endosperm or the fruit of a seed plant) other than the embryo; *also* **:** the effect of a gene capable of manifesting its dominant influence in the presence of two allelic genes — compare DOUBLE FERTILIZATION, METAXENIA

xe·nial \-nēəl, -nyəl\ *adj* [Gk *xenios* xenial (fr. *xenos* guest) + E *-al*] **:** of, relating to, or constituting hospitality or relations between host and guest and esp. among the ancient Greeks between persons of different cities ⟨~ relationship⟩ ⟨~ customs⟩

xe·nic·i·dae \zəˈnisəˌdē\ *n pl, cap* [NL, fr. *Xenicus*, genus of passerine birds (fr. Gk *xenikos* of a stranger or foreigner, fr. *xenos* guest, stranger + *-ikos* -ic) + *-idae*] *syn of* ACANTHISITTIDAE

xe·ni·um \ˈzēnēəm\ *n, pl* **xe·nia** \-nēə\ [L, fr. Gk *xenion*, fr. neut. of *xenios* of hospitality, xenial] **1 :** a present given among the ancient Greeks and Romans to a guest or stranger and esp. to a foreign ambassador **2** *xenia pl* **:** gifts sometimes given compulsorily to medieval rulers and churches

xeno·ber·y·ces \ˌzenōˈberəˌsēz\ *n pl, cap* [NL, fr. *xen-* + *Beryces*, pl. of *Beryx*, genus of fishes] *in some classifications* **:** a small order of fishes related to and commonly included in Berycomorphi

xeno·biosis \ˌzenəˌbīˈōsəs\ *n, pl* **xenobio·ses** \-ōˌsēz\ [NL, fr. *xen-* + *-biosis*] **:** symbiosis in which members of two species of ants live together in the same nest but do not rear their young in common

xen·o·blast \ˈzenəˌblast\ *n* [*xen-* + *-blast*] **:** a crystal in metamorphic rock that is not bounded by its own faces but has its outlines impressed upon it by neighboring crystals — contrasted with *idioblast* — **xen·o·blas·tic** \ˌ==ˈblastik\ *adj*

xeno·cen·tric \ˌzenəˈsentrik\ *adj* [*xen-* + *-centric*] **:** oriented toward or preferring a culture other than one's own

xe·noc·ra·te·an \zeˌnäkrəˈtēən, zəˈn-\ *adj, usu cap* [*Xenocrates* †314 B.C. Greek Platonic philosopher + E *-an*] **:** XENOCRATIC

xen·o·crat·ic \ˌzenəˈkrad·ik\ *adj, usu cap* [*Xenocrates* †314 B.C. Greek Platonic philosopher + E *-ic*] **:** of or relating to the philosopher Xenocrates or to his doctrines in which he combined Pythagorean conceptions with Platonism

xeno·cryst \ˈzenəˌkrist\ *n* -s [*xen-* + *-cryst*] **:** a crystal foreign to the rock in which it occurs — **xeno·crys·tic** \ˌ==ˈkristik\ *adj*

xeno·diagnosis \ˌzenō+\ *n* [NL, fr. *xen-* + *diagnosis*] **:** the detection of a parasite (as a blood parasite of man) by allowing a suitable intermediate host (as an insect) to consume supposedly infected material (as blood) and after an incubation period examining the intermediate host for the parasite ⟨doubtful cases of Chagas' disease confirmed by ~⟩

xeno·diagnostic \ˈ"+\ *adj* [ISV *xen-* + *diagnostic*] **:** of, relating to, or involving xenodiagnosis

xen·o·do·chei·on·ol·o·gy \ˌzenədəˌkīəˈnäləjē\ *n* -ES [Gk *xenodocheion* inn + E *-o-* + *-logy*] **:** the lore of hotels and inns

xen·o·do·che·um \ˌzenədəˈkēəm\ *n* -s [LL, fr. Gk *xenodocheion*, fr. *xenodochein* to entertain guests, fr. *xen-* + *dechesthai* to take, receive; akin to Gk *dokein* to seem good — more at DECENT] **:** an ancient Greek inn or hostel

xen·o·do·chi·um \-ˈkīəm\ *n, pl* **xenodo·chia** \-ēə\ [LL, fr. Gk *xenodocheion* inn] **:** a medieval house for the care of the poor, strangers, pilgrims, or the sick

xe·nog·a·my \zəˈnägəmē\ *n* -ES [ISV *xen-* + *-gamy*] **:** fertilization by cross-pollination; *esp* **:** cross-pollination between flowers on different plants — compare GEITONOGAMY

xeno·genesis \ˌzenə+\ *n* [NL, fr. *xen-* + L *genesis*] **:** the fancied production of an organism altogether and permanently unlike the parent

xeno·glos·sy \ˈzenəˌgläsē, -lȯsē\ *n* -ES [ISV *xen-* + *gloss-* + *-y*] **:** purported use (as by a medium) while in a trance state of a language unknown to the individual under normal conditions

xeno·lith \ˈzenəˌlith\ *n* -s [*xen-* + *-lith*] **:** a fragment of a rock included in another rock — **xeno·lith·ic** \ˌ==ˈlithik\ *adj*

xeno·mania \ˌzenə+\ *n* [NL, fr. *xen-* + *mania*] **:** an inordinate attachment to foreign things (as customs, institutions, manners, fashions)

xe·no·mi \zəˈnōˌmī\ *n pl, cap* [NL, fr. *xen-* + Gk *ōmos* shoulder; fr. the distinct character of the pectoral arch — more at HUMERUS] *in some classifications* **:** an order of soft-rayed freshwater teleost fishes comprising the blackfish (*Dallia pectoralis*) and being commonly included usu. in the order Haplomi or among the Isospondyli

xeno·mor·pha \ˌzenəˈmȯrfə\ [NL, fr. *xen-* + *-morpha*] *syn of* TARDIGRADA 2

xeno·mor·phic \ˌ==ˈmȯrfik\ *adj* [*xen-* + *-morphic*] **:** ALLOTRIOMORPHIC

xenon \ˈzeˌnän, ˈzeˌnän\ *n* -s [Gk, neut. of *xenos* strange] **:** a heavy colorless inert gaseous element that occurs in air to the extent of about one part in 20 million by volume and in gases from hot springs, that is obtained along with krypton from liquid air, and that is used in thyratrons and specialized electric lamps — symbol *Xe*; see ELEMENT table

xen·o·pel·ti·dae \ˌzenəˈpeltəˌdē\ *n pl, cap* [NL, fr. *Xenopeltis*, type genus (fr. *xen-* + Gk *peltē* small shield) + *-idae* — more at PELTA] **:** a family of harmless terrestrial or burrowing snakes that is intermediate in many respects between the Boidae and Colubridae and includes solely the sunbeam snake

xe·noph·a·ne·an \zəˌnäfəˈnēən\ *adj, usu cap* [*Xenophanes*, 6th cent. B.C. Greek philosopher + E *-an*] **:** of or relating to the Eleatic philosopher Xenophanes or his doctrines noteworthy for their emphatic but perhaps pantheistic monotheism

xeno·phile \ˈzenəˌfīl\ *n* -s [ISV *xen-* + *-phile*] **:** one attracted to foreign things (as manners, styles, people) — **xe·noph·i·lous** \zeˈnäfələs, zəˈn-\ *adj*

xeno·phobe \ˈzenəˌfōb\ *n* -s [ISV *xen-* + *-phobe*] **:** one unduly fearful of what is foreign and esp. of people of foreign origin **:** a xenophobic person

xeno·pho·bia \ˌ==ˈfōbēə\ *n* [NL, fr. *xen-* + *phobia*] **:** fear and hatred of strangers or foreigners or of anything that is strange or foreign

xeno·phobic \ˌ==ˈfōbik *also* -ˈfäb-\ *adj* [NL *xenophobia* + E *-ic*] **:** of, relating to, or characterized by xenophobia ⟨~ responses⟩ ⟨a ~ person⟩

xen·o·phon·te·an \ˌzenəˈfäntēən, -ˌfänˈ.tē-\ *or* **xen·o·phon·ti·an** \-ˈfäntēən\ *or* **xen·o·phon·tine** \-ˈfänˌtīn, -äntᵊn\ *adj, usu cap* [Gk *Xenophōnt-*, *Xenophōn* Xenophon †355 B.C.? Greek historian and essayist + E *-an* or *-ine*] **:** of or relating to Xenophon

xe·noph·o·ra \zəˈnäfərə\ *n* [NL, fr. *xen-* + *-phora*] **1** *cap* **:** a genus of gastropod mollusks comprising the carrier snails (coextensive with the family Xenophoridae of the suborder Taenioglossa) **2** -s **:** any mollusk of the genus *Xenophora* — **xe·noph·o·ran** \-rən\ *adj*

xeno·pithe·cus \ˌzenəpəˈthēkəs, -ˈpithək-\ *n, cap* [NL, fr. *xen-* + *-pithecus*] **:** a genus of eastern African Lower Miocene apes known from imperfect fossil remains and possibly on the ancestral line of the orangutan

xeno·plas·tic \ˌzenəˈplastik\ *adj* [*xen-* + *-plastic*] **:** involving or occurring between distantly related individuals ⟨a successful ~ graft between plants of different genera is rare⟩ — **xeno·plas·ti·cal·ly** \-tək(ə)lē\ *adv*

xeno·pod·i·dae \ˌzenəˈpädəˌdē\ *n pl, cap* [NL, fr. *Xenopod-*, *Xenopus* + *-idae*] **:** a family of amphibians comprising *Xenopus* and a few related genera that are often included in the family Pipidae

xenopsyl·la \ˌzeˌnäpˈsilə, ˌzenōˌsilə\ *n, cap* [NL, fr. *xen-* + Gk *psylla* flea — more at PSYLLA] **:** a genus of fleas (family Pulicidae) including several (as the oriental rat flea) that are important as vectors of plague

xe·nop·te·ri \zəˈnäptəˌrī\ [NL, fr. *xen-* + Gk *pteron* wing — more at FEATHER] *syn of* XENOPTERYGII

xe·nop·te·ryg·ii \zəˌnäptəˈrijēˌī, (ˌ)zeˌn-\ *n pl, cap* [NL, fr. *xen-* + *-pterygii*] **:** an order of bony fishes that is coextensive with the family Gobiesocidae

xen·o·pus \ˈzenəpəs\ *n, cap* [NL, fr. *xen-* + *-pus*] **:** a genus that comprises African aquatic frogs having broad triangular heads, weak forelimbs, powerful, clawed hindlimbs, and no tongue or teeth and is sometimes made the type of a separate family but more often included among the Pipidae

xeno·rhyn·chus \ˌzenəˈriŋkəs\ *n, cap* [NL, fr. *xen-* + *-rhynchus*] **:** a genus of East Indian and Australian storks

xe·nos \ˈzēˌnäs\ *n, cap* [NL, fr. Gk *xenos* stranger, strange] **:** a genus of strepsipterons that are parasites of various wasps

xeno·sau·ri·dae \ˌzenəˈsȯrəˌdē\ *n pl, cap* [NL, fr. *Xenosaurus*, type genus (fr. *xen-* + *-saurus*) + *-idae*] **:** a monotypic family of slender-bodied Mexican lizards that is held to be intermediate between Iguanidae and Anguidae and comprises forms with the upper surface covered with minute granules and tubercles

xen·o·time \ˈzenəˌtīm\ *n* -s [F *xénotime*, irreg. (influence of *xén-* xen-) fr. Gk *kenos* empty, vain + *timē* honor; fr. the fact that it was wrongly thought at first to contain a new metal] **:** a mineral YPO_4 that is a phosphate of yttrium occurring in usu. brown or yellow tetragonal crystals and rolled grains and that often also contains thorium, erbium, cerium, or other elements (hardness 4–5, sp. gr. 4.45–4.56)

-x·e·nous \ksənəs\ *adj comb form* [Gk *-xenos* stranger, fr. *xenos*] **:** host ⟨lipo*xenous*⟩

xe·nu·rus \zəˈn(y)ürəs\ [NL, fr. *xen-* + *-urus*] *syn of* CABASSOUS

-x·e·ny \ˌksənē, -ni\ *n comb form* -ES [Gk *-xenos* + E *-y*] **:** (such) a host relationship ⟨lipo*xeny*⟩

xenyl \ˈzenᵊl, ˈzēn-\ *n* -s [ISV *xen-* + *-yl*] **:** a univalent radical $C_6H_5C_6H_4$- derived from biphenyl; biphenyl-yl

xer- *or* **xero-** *comb form* [LL, fr. Gk *xēr-*, *xēro-*, fr. *xēros* — more at SERENE] **1 a :** dry **:** arid ⟨*xer*ic⟩ **b :** dry place ⟨*xero*philous⟩ **2 :** using a dry process in the making of (such) a product ⟨*xero*graphy⟩ ⟨*xero*printing⟩

xe·ra·fin \ˈsherəˌfēⁿ, -ēn\ *also* **xe·ra·fim** *or* **xe·ra·phim** \-ēⁿ, -ēm\ *n* -s [Pg *xerafim*, fr. Ar *sharīfī*, fr. *sharīf* noble] **:** a silver coin current in Portuguese India before the 19th century and worth 300 to 360 reis

xe·ran·the·mum \zəˈran(t)thəməm\ *n* [NL, fr. *xer-* + *-anthemum*] **1** *cap* **:** a genus of annual densely tomentose herbs (family Compositae) native to southern Europe, containing one of the most widely cultivated everlastings (*X. annuum*), and having solitary chaffy or silvery flower heads with purplish tubular flowers **2** -s **:** any plant or flower of the genus *Xeranthemum*

xe·rarch \ˈziˌrärk, ˈzēˌr-\ *adj* [*xer-* + *-arch*] *of an ecological succession* **:** developing in a dry place — compare HYDRARCH, MESARCH

xe·ric \ˈsirik, ˈzēr-\ *adj* [*xer-* + *-ic*] **1** *of an environment* **:** low or deficient in moisture that is available for the support of plant life — compare HYDRIC, MESIC **2 :** of, relating to, or suited to a xeric environment **:** XEROPHYTIC — **xe·ri·cal·ly** \-k(ə)lē\ *adv*

xe·ro·cole \ˈzirəˌkōl\ *or* **xe·roc·o·lous** \zəˈräkələs\ *adj* [*xer-* + *-cole* or *-colous*] **:** XEROPHILOUS

xe·ro·der·ma \ˌzirəˈdərmə\ *n* -s [NL, fr. *xer-* + *-derma*] **:** a disease of the skin characterized by dryness and roughness and a fine scaly desquamation

xe·ro·gel \ˈzirəˌjel\ *n* [G, fr. *xer-* + *gel*] **:** a solid formed from a gel by drying with unhindered shrinkage — compare AEROGEL

xero·graph·ic \ˌzirəˈgrafik\ *adj* [ISV *xerography* + *-ic*] **:** of, relating to, used in, or prepared by xerography ⟨~ techniques⟩ ⟨a ~ print⟩

xe·rog·ra·phy \zəˈrägrəfē\ *n* -ES [ISV *xer-* + *-graphy*] **:** the formation of pictures or copies of graphic matter by the action of light on an electrically charged photoconductive insulating surface in which the latent image usu. is developed with powders that adhere only to the areas that remain electrically charged and in which the image formed by the powders sometimes is transferred to a sheet of paper

xe·ro·morph \ˈzirəˌmȯrf\ *n* [ISV *xer-* + *-morph*] **:** a plant with typical xerophytic morphology; *esp* **:** XEROPHYTE — **xe·ro·mor·phism** \-rˌbizəm\ *n* — **xe·ro·mor·phy** \-rfē\ *n* -ES

xe·ro·mor·phic \ˌ==ˈmȯrfik\ *also* **xe·ro·mor·phal** \-fəl\ *or* **xe·ro·mor·phous** \-fəs\ *adj* [*xeromorph* + *-ic* or *-al* or *-ous*] **1 :** of, relating to, or being a xeromorph **2** [*xer-* + *-morphic* or *morph-* + *-al* or *-morphous*] **:** of, relating to, or constituting climatic conditions favorable for the development of xerophilous vegetation

xe·roph·a·gy \zəˈräfəjē\ *also* **xe·ro·pha·gia** \ˌzirəˈfāj(ē)ə\ *n, pl* **xerophagies** *also* **xerophagias** [LL *xerophagia*, fr. Gk *xērophagia* eating of dry food, fr. *xērophagein* to eat dry food (fr. *xēros* dry + *phagein* to eat) + *-ia* -y — more at SERENE, BAKSHEESH] **:** the strictest Christian fast which is observed chiefly in the Eastern churches during Lent or esp. Holy Week and in which only bread, salt, water, and vegetables may be eaten and meat, fish, milk, cheese, butter, oil, wine, and all seasonings or spices are excluded

xe·ro·phile \ˈzirəˌfīl\ *or* **xe·ro·phil** \-ˌfil\ *n* -s [ISV *xer-* + *-phil*, n. comb form] **:** XEROPHYTE

xe·roph·i·lous \zəˈräfələs\ *or* **xe·ro·phile** \ˈzirəˌfīl\ *also* **xe·ro·phil·ic** \ˌzirəˈfilik\ *or* **xe·ro·phil** \ˈ==ˌfil\ *adj* [*xerophilous*, *xerophilic* fr. *xer-* + *-philous* or *-philic*; *xerophile*, *xerophil* ISV *xer-* + *-phil*, adj. comb form] **:** thriving in or tolerant or characteristic of an environment that is poor in available moisture ⟨a *xerophile* vegetation⟩ ⟨several ~ snails⟩ **:** adapted to life in the presence of minimal amounts of water ⟨*xerophilic* leaves⟩ — **xe·roph·i·ly** \zəˈräfəlē\ *n* -ES

xe·roph·o·bous \zəˈräfəbəs\ *adj* [*xer-* + *-phobous*] *of a plant* **:** having little capacity to resist drought

xe·roph·thal·mia \ˌziˌräfˈthalmēə, ˌzēˌr-, ÷ -äpˈth-\ *n* [NL, fr. Gk *xērophthalmia*, fr. *xēr-* xer- + *-ophthalmia*] **:** a dry thickened lusterless condition of the eyeball resulting from a severe systemic deficiency of vitamin A — compare KERATOMALACIA — **xe·roph·thal·mic** \ˌ=ˌ=ˈ=mik\ *adj*

xe·ro·phyl·lum \ˌzirəˈfiləm\ *n, cap* [NL, fr. *xer-* + *-phyllum*] **:** a small genus of tall No. American herbs (family Liliaceae) having thick woody rootstocks, simple stems with rough-edged linear leaves, and small white flowers in a dense terminal raceme — see SOUR GRASS, SQUAW GRASS

xe·ro·phyte \ˈzirəˌfīt\ *n* -s [ISV *xer-* + *-phyte*] **:** a plant structurally adapted for life and growth with a limited water supply esp. by means of mechanisms (as epidermal thickening, waxy or resinous coats, or dense pubescence) that limit transpiration or that provide for the storage of water — used both of desert plants and of those occupying environments (as salt marshes or acid bogs) where water absorption is impeded by excess salts or acids in solution; compare HYDROPHYTE, MESOPHYTE

xe·ro·phyt·ic \ˌ==ˈfid·ik\ *adj* **:** of, relating to, typical of, or being a xerophyte **:** showing xeric adaptations ⟨~ vegetation⟩ ⟨~ structural adaptations⟩ ⟨a ~ life⟩ — **xe·ro·phyt·i·cal·ly** \-d·ək(ə)lē\ *adv*

xe·ro·phyt·ism \ˈ==ˌfīd·ˌizəm\ *n* -s **:** the quality or state of being xerophytic

xe·ro·phyt·iza·tion \ˌ==ˌfīd·əˈzāshən, -d·ˌīˈz-\ *n* -s [*xer-* + *phyt-* + *-ization*] **:** adaptation to more xeric conditions esp. as a factor in speciation

xe·ro·plas·tic \ˌzirōˈplastik\ *adj* [*xer-* + *-plastic*] **:** induced by or developing under the influence of a xeric environment

xe·ro·printing \ˈzirə, ˈzērō+,-\ *n* [*xer-* + *printing*] **:** an application of xerography to the mass production of graphic images in which the image plate is fixed to a cylinder and automatically charged and powdered for repeated electrostatic transfer of an image to machine-fed paper

xe·ro·radiograph \ˌzi(ˌ)rō, ˌzē(ˌ)rō+\ *n* [*xer-* + *radiograph*] **:** a radiograph made with the use of xerographic techniques to record the image — **xe·ro·radiographic** \ˈ"+\ *adj*

xe·ro·radiography \ˈ"+\ *n* [*xer-* + *radiography*] **:** radiography using xerographic techniques to record the image

xe·ro·sere \ˈzirəˌsi(ə)r\ *n* [*xer-* + *sere*] **:** the seral stages of a xerarch succession **:** a dry-land sere

xe·ro·sis \zəˈrōsəs\ *n, pl* **xero·ses** \-ōˌsēz\ [NL, fr. Gk *xērōsis*, fr. *xēr-* xer- + *-ōsis* -osis] **:** abnormal dryness of a body part or tissue (as the skin or conjunctiva)

xe·ro·sto·mia \ˌzirəˈstōmēə\ *n* -s [NL, fr. *xer-* + *-stomia*] **:** abnormal dryness of the mouth due to insufficient secretions

xe·ro·therm \ˈzirəˌthərm\ *n* [ISV *xer-* + *-therm*] **:** a plant that thrives in a hot dry environment

xe·ro·ther·mic \ˌ==ˈthərmik\ *adj* [*xer-* + *thermic*] **1 a :** being hot and dry **:** characterized by heat and dryness ⟨a ~ climate⟩ ⟨a prolonged postglacial ~ period⟩ **b :** concerned with or stressing the significance of xerothermic climate ⟨a ~ theory⟩ **2 :** adapted to or thriving in a xerothermic environment ⟨~ insects⟩

xe·rus \ˈzirəs\ *n, cap* [NL, fr. Gk *xēros* dry; fr. the texture of the fur] **:** a genus of coarse-haired long-tailed African ground squirrels that somewhat resemble prairie dogs in habits

x'es *or* **xes** *pl of* X, *pres 3d sing of* X

XF *abbr* extra fine

x factor *n* **:** a relevant but unidentified factor

xg *abbr* crossing

x height *n* **:** the distance between the top and bottom of a printed letter (as x, a, r, w) without an ascender or descender; *also* **:** the corresponding dimension in the type from which such letters are printed

xho·sa *also* **xo·sa** \ˈkōsə, ˈkō|, |zə\ *n, pl* **xhosa** \-ə\ *or* **xhosas** \-əz\ *or* **ama·xho·sa** \ˌämə+\ *or* **ama·xo·sa** *or* **ama·ko·sa** *also* **xosa** *or* **xosas** *usu cap* **1 a :** a Ngoni Bantu-speaking people of eastern Cape Province related to the Zulu **b :** a member of such people **2 :** a Bantu language of the Xhosa people closely related to Zulu and Swazi with which it forms the Ngoni group

xi \ˈzī, ˈksī, ˈksē *sometimes esp in fraternity names* ˈekˌsī\ *n* -s [Gk] **:** the 14th letter of the Greek alphabet — symbol Ξ or ξ; see ALPHABET table

XI *abbr* ex interest

xicaque *var of* JICAQUE

xi·me·nia \hīˈmēnēə, -mān-\ *n, cap* [NL, irreg. fr. Francisco *Ximénez* †1721? Span. missionary in Guatemala + NL *-ia*] **:** a small genus of widely distributed tropical shrubs or trees (family Olacaceae) having alternate leaves, a persistent calyx, bearded petals, and drupaceous fruit — see FALSE SANDALWOOD, SOUR PLUM 2

xin·ca \ˈshiŋkə\ *n* -s *usu cap* **1 a :** an Indian people of southeastern Guatemala **b :** a member of such people **2 :** a Xincan language of the Xinca people

xin·can \-kən\ *n* -s *usu cap* [*Xinca* + E *-an*] **:** a language family of uncertain relationships comprising the Xinca language

x–ing *or* **x'ing** *pres part of* X

x–intercept \ˈ=,==,=\ *n* **:** the x-coordinate of the point where a line, curve, or surface intersects the x-axis

xiph- *or* **xiphi-** *or* **xipho-** *comb form* [NL, fr. Gk, fr. *xiphos*] **1 :** swordlike **:** sword-shaped ⟨*xipho*phyllous⟩ ⟨*xiphi*plastron⟩ **2 :** xiphoid and ⟨*xipho*costal⟩

xiph·i·as \ˈzifēəs\ *n* [NL, fr. L, swordfish, fr. Gk, *xiphos* sword] **1** *cap* **:** a genus (the type of the family Xiphiidae) of large scombroid fishes comprising the common swordfish **2** *pl* **xiphias :** SWORDFISH

xi·phid·io·cercaria \zəˌfidē(ˌ)ō+\ *n* [NL, fr. Gk *xiphidion* (dim. of *xiphos* sword) + NL *cercaria*] **:** a cercaria having a stylet in the oral sucker with which it actively penetrates the definitive host

xiphi·hu·mer·alis \ˌzifēˌhyüməˈralәs, -rāl-, -räl-\ *n* [NL, fr. *xiph-* + *humeralis* humeral, fr. *humerus* + L *-alis* -al] **:** a muscle in some mammals that extends from the xiphoid cartilage to the proximal end of the humerus

xiph·i·oid \ˈzifēˌȯid\ *adj* [NL *Xiphias* + E *-oid*] **:** resembling or related to the genus *Xiphias*

xiphi·plastral \ˌzifə+\ *adj* [NL *xiphiplastron* + E *-al*] **:** of or relating to the xiphiplastron

xiphi·plastron \"+\ n, pl **xiphiplastra** [NL, fr. xiph- + plastron] : the posterior and fourth lateral plate in the plastron of a turtle

xiphi·sternal \"+\ adj [NL xiphisternum + E -al] : of or relating to the xiphisternum

xiphi·sternum \"+\ n, pl **xiphisterna** [NL, fr. xiph- + sternum] **1** : the posterior segment of the sternum : XIPHOID PROCESS **2** : XIPHIPLASTRON

xiph·is·ura \ˌzifəˈsürə\ or **xiphi·ura** \-fēˈ(y)u̇-\ or **xiph·ura** \ˈzīˈf(y)u̇-\ [xiphisura fr. NL, alter. of Xiphosura; xiphiura, xiphura fr. NL, fr. + -ura] syn of XIPHOSURA

xiph·i·um iris \ˌzifēəm-\ n, sometimes cap X [xiphium fr. NL, fr. Gk xiphion corn flag, fr. xiphos sword] : SPANISH IRIS

xipho·costal \ˈzifə-\ adj [xiph- + costal] : of, relating to, or connecting the xiphoid process and the ribs

xiph·odon \ˈzifəˌdän\ n, cap [NL, fr. xiph- + -odon] : a genus of small two-toed artiodactyls (suborder Tylopoda) from the Eocene of Europe (the type of the family Xiphodontidae)

¹xiph·oid \ˈzīˌfȯid, ˈzī-\ also **xi·phoi·dal** \zīˈfȯidᵊl, zəˈf-\ adj [xiphoid fr. NL xiphoides, fr. Gk xiphoeidēs, fr. xiphos sword + -oeidēs -oid; xiphoidal fr. NL xiphoides + -al] **1** : shaped like a sword : ENSIFORM **2** : of, relating to, or constituting the xiphisternum

²xiphoid \"\ n -s : XIPHISTERNUM, XIPHOID PROCESS

xiphoid bone n : a slender ossification in the nuchal ligament of some birds (as the cormorant)

xiphoid cartilage n : XIPHOID PROCESS 1

xiphoid process n **1** : the posterior and lowest division of the sternum in man that is usu. more or less cartilaginous throughout life; broadly : XIPHISTERNUM **2** : the tail of a king crab

xi·phop·a·gus \zəˈfäpəgəs\ n -ES [NL, fr. xiph- + -pagus] : an abnormality of animal twinning in which the twins are joined at the xiphoid process — compare SIAMESE TWIN

xi·phoph·o·rus \zəˈfäfərəs\ n, cap [NL, fr. xiph- + -phorus] : a genus of topminnows (family Poeciliidae) comprising the swordtails

xipho·phyl·lous \ˌzifəˈfiləs\ adj [xiph- + -phyllous] : having sword-shaped leaves

xiph·os·ura \ˌzifəˈsürə\ n pl, cap [NL, fr. Gk xiphos sword + NL -ura] : an order of arthropods comprising the king crabs and extinct related forms and usu. including only the two recent genera Limulus (syn. Xiphosurus) and Tachypleus with species along the American coast of the Atlantic and Tachypleus with species along the Asiatic coast of the Pacific — **xiph·os·uran** \ˌˌˈsürən\ adj or n — **xiph·os·ure** \ˌsü(ə)r\ n — **xiph·os·urous** \ˌˌˈsürəs\ adj

xiph·y·dri·idae \ˌzifəˈdrīəˌdē\ n pl, cap [NL, fr. Xiphydria, type genus (fr. Gk xiphydrion, a shell fish, fr. xiphos sword) + -idae] : a small family of horntails comprising the wood wasps and characterized by a thorax humped in front resembling a neck

x-irradiate \ˌˌˈ⸱⸱ˌ⸱⸱\ vt, usu cap X : to irradiate with X rays — **x-irradiation** \ˌˌˌ⸱⸱ˌ⸱⸱\ n, usu cap X

xis pl of XI

xl abbr **1** crystal **2** extra large

x line n : a horizontal line bounding the upper limit of the x height of a letter

x-man \ˈeksˌman\ n, pl **x-men** : a postal service employee who checks a railway car in mail service for possible lost or mislaid mail

xmas \ˈkrisməs sometimes ˈeksm-\ n -ES usu cap [x (symbol for Christ) + -mas (in christmas)] : CHRISTMAS

xn abbr ex new

XN abbr, often cap Christian

xnty abbr, often cap Christianity

XO abbr executive officer

xo·a·non \ˈzōəˌnän\ n, pl **xoa·na** \-ənə\ [Gk] : a primitive image of wood sometimes recalling in shape the block or tree-trunk from which it was cut

xo·no·tlite \ˈzōnəˌtlīt\ n -s [G xonotlit, fr. Tetala de Xonotla, village in Pueblo, Mexico, its locality + G -it -ite] : a mineral 5CaSiO₃·H₂O that is a hydrous calcium silicate

xosa usu cap, var of XHOSA

XP \ˈkīˈrō\ symbol [fr. the Greek letters XP] — used as a Christian symbol and monogram for Christ

x-protein \ˈ(ˌ)⸱+\ n, often cap X : a fraction of plasma protein held to be distinct from globulin, albumin, or fibrinogen or to be a complex of these possessing special properties by reason of its physical state — see CONGLUTININ

XQ abbr cross question

XR abbr, often not cap ex rights

x-radiate \ˈ⸱ˌ⸱⸱ˌ\ vt, often cap X : to expose (as a body part) to X-radiation

x-radiation \ˈ⸱ˌ⸱⸱ˌ⸱⸱\ n, usu cap X **1** : exposure to X rays (as for therapeutic purposes) : IRRADIATION **2** : radiation composed of X rays

x ray \ˈeksˌrā also ˈ⸱ˌ⸱\ n, usu cap X [¹x; trans. of G x-strahl] **1** : any of the electromagnetic radiations having the nature of visible light but a wavelength approximately between 0.1 and 100 angstroms that is usu. produced by bombarding a metallic target with fast electrons in vacuum so that the spectrum of the radiation emitted consists of lines characteristic of the target material and that has the properties of ionizing a gas upon passage through it, of penetrating through various thicknesses of all solids, of producing secondary radiations by impinging on material bodies, and of acting on photographic films and plates and on fluorescent screens : a photon or a stream of photons produced by excitation of an atom by impact of a fast moving electron **2** : a photograph obtained by the use of X rays

x-ray \"\ vb, often cap X, vt : to expose to the action of X rays : examine, treat, or photograph with X rays : IRRADIATE ~ vi : to employ X rays

xray \"\ usu cap — a communications code word for the letter x

x-ray absorbing glass n : glass that resists the penetration of X rays and gamma rays and ordinarily contains a high content of lead oxide

x-ray fish n : GLASSFISH

x-ray microscope n, usu cap X : an instrument in which X-ray diffraction patterns of crystals are translated into pictures showing the relative positions of the atoms in a crystal as if in a photomicrograph of very high magnification

x-ray photograph or **x-ray picture** n, usu cap X : a shadow picture made with X rays; esp : one revealing the internal structure of objects opaque to ordinary light — **x-ray photography** n, usu cap X

x-ray spectrograph n, usu cap X : a spectrograph for dispersing X rays and measuring their wavelengths

x-ray spectrometer n, usu cap X : a spectrometer for measuring the angles of diffraction of X rays produced by reflection from a crystal or for measuring X-ray spectra

x-ray spectrum n, usu cap X : the spectrum of an emission of X rays that is obtained by dispersion with either a crystal grating or a ruled grating

x-ray therapy n, usu cap X : ROENTGENOTHERAPY

x-ray tube n, usu cap X : a high-vacuum tube in which a concentrated stream of electrons from a thermionic cathode strikes a metal target and produces X rays from the side of the tube at right angles in a quantity and intensity that is controlled by the cathode temperature, with a wavelength and hardness that depends upon the voltage applied to the tube terminals, and with a spectral character determined by the material of the target

x's or xs pl of x

x-stool \ˈ⸱ˌ⸱\ n, cap X : the simplest and most ancient of stools supported on an X-shaped frame and often designed to fold — compare X-CHAIR

x-stretcher \ˈ⸱ˌ⸱⸱\ n, cap X : a crossed stretcher for furniture

xt abbr, often cap Christian

xtal abbr crystal

xtian abbr, often cap Christian

xtra \ˈekstrə\ usu cap — a communications code word for the letter x

xtry abbr extraordinary

xty abbr, often cap Christianity

XU abbr, often not cap x unit

x unit n, usu cap X : a unit of wavelength that is used for X rays and gamma rays and that is equal to approximately 10⁻¹¹ centimeters

---

xu·rel \like JUREL\ n -s [modif. of Sp jurel — more at JUREL] **1** : BIG-EYED SCAD **2** : SAUREL

x virus n, usu cap X **1** : a latent virus **2** : a latent virus disease in which symptoms are absent

XW abbr, often not cap ex warrant

xx-disease \ˈ⸱ekˌseks-\ n, usu cap both Xs [so called fr. being of obscure etiology] : HYPERKERATOSIS 2b

xy·el·i·dae \zīˈeləˌdē\ n pl, cap [NL, fr. Xyela, type genus (fr. Gk xyēlē curved knife, fr. xyein to scratch, scrape) + -idae] : a small family of primitive sawflies having larvae that feed on the foliage of trees

xyl- or **xylo-** comb form [L, fr. Gk, fr. xylon; perh. akin to Lith šulas pillar, post, OE syl — more at SILE] **1 a** : wood : woody ⟨xylophagous⟩ ⟨xyloma⟩ **b** : xylem **2 a** : xylene ⟨xylic⟩ ⟨xyloquinone⟩ **b** : xylose ⟨xylonic acid⟩ ⟨xyloketose⟩ **3** xylo-, usu ital : having the stereochemical arrangement of atoms or groups found in xylose ⟨L-xylo-ascorbic acid⟩

xy·lan \ˈzīˌlan\ n [ISV xyl- + -an] : a pentosan that yields xylose on hydrolysis, that occurs in the cell walls of land plants, and that comprises up to one third of straw, corncobs, oat hulls, and cottonseed hulls and up to one quarter of wood

xy·lar·ia \zīˈla(ə)rēə\ n, cap [NL, fr. xyl- + -aria] : the type genus of Xylariaceae comprising fungi with perithecia borne in the upper part of erect black corky or woody stromata — see BLACK ROOT ROT

xy·lar·i·a·ce·ae \(ˌ)zīˌla(ə)rēˈāsēˌē\ n pl, cap [NL, fr. Xylaria, type genus + -aceae] : a family of ascomycetous fungi (order Sphaeriales) characterized by dark brown to black usu. nonseptate ascospores and conidia borne superficially on the stroma

xy·la·ry \ˈzīˌlərē\ adj [xyl- + -ary] : of, relating to, associated with, or constituting wood and esp. xylem ⟨wax does not seem to be secreted ... in the ~ tissues of plants — Economic Geology⟩

xy·leb·o·rus \zīˈlebərəs\ n, cap [NL, fr. Gk xylēboros eating wood, fr. xylē- (fr. xylon wood) + boros gluttonous, fr. bora food, meat — more at VORACIOUS] : a large genus of small ambrosia beetles

xy·lem \ˈzīˌlem, -ˌlem\ n -s [G, fr. Gk xylon wood] : a complex tissue in the vascular system of higher plants consisting of vessels, tracheids, or both usu. together with wood fibers and parenchyma cells, functioning chiefly in conduction but also in support and storage, and typically constituting the woody element (as of a plant stem) — compare PHLOEM

xylem fiber n : any of various fibers located in or associated with xylem and typically having an angular cross-section and heavily lignified walls with prominent bordered pits — compare PHLOEM FIBER

xylem parenchyma n : WOOD PARENCHYMA

xylem ray or **xylary ray** n : a vascular ray or portion of a vascular ray that is located in xylem — called also wood ray; compare PHLOEM RAY

xy·lene \ˈzīˌlēn\ n -s [ISV xyl- + -ene] **1** : any of three toxic flammable oily isomeric aromatic hydrocarbons $C_6H_4(CH_3)_2$ that are dimethyl homologues of benzene and are obtained from wood tar or commercially in mixtures of the three with ethylbenzene from light oils from coal tar or coke-oven gas or from petroleum distillates by processes for producing toluene: **a** : the ortho isomer used chiefly in making phthalic anhydride — called also ortho-xylene, o-xylene **b** : the para isomer used chiefly in making terephthalic acid — called also para-xylene, p-xylene **c** : the meta isomer occurring in the mixtures in larger amounts than the other components and used chiefly in making isophthalic acid and xylidines — called also meta-xylene, m-xylene **2** : a commercial mixture containing xylenes and ethylbenzene used chiefly as a solvent, as a blending agent esp. in aviation gasoline, or in making various organic compounds

xylene light yellow n, often cap X&L&Y : an acid dye — see DYE TABLE I (under Acid Yellow 17)

xylene musk n : MUSK XYLENE

xy·lene·sul·fonic acid \ˌzīˌlēn-..-\ n [xylene + sulfonic] : any of six crystalline isomeric acids $(CH_3)_2C_6H_3SO_3H$ obtained by sulfonation of the xylenes but most readily of ortho- and meta-xylenes, which can thus be separated from para-xylene in the commercial mixture

xy·le·nol \ˈzīləˌnȯl, -ˌnōl\ n -s [ISV xylene + -ol] : any of six crystalline isomeric phenols $(CH_3)_2C_6H_3OH$ or a mixture of them derived from the xylenes, found in coal tar, and used chiefly as disinfectants and in making phenolic resins; dimethyl-phenol; esp : the meta or 3,5-isomer constituting the most abundant xylenol in coal tar — compare CHLOROXYLENOL

xy·le·nyl \ˌ⸱ˌ⸱nil, ˌ⸱⸱ -yl\ [xylene + -yl] : XYLYL

xy·leu·tes \zīˈlüdēˌ(ˌ)ēz\ n, cap [NL, fr. Gk xyleus woodcutter, fr. xyleuein to cut wood, fr. xylon wood] : a genus of moths (family Zeuzeridae) comprising the wood moths of Australia and southeast Asia

xylia \ˈzīlēə, ˈzil-\ n, cap [NL, fr. xyl- + -ia; fr. the woody pod] : a genus of Asiatic trees (family Leguminosae) having globose heads of small greenish flowers succeeded by falcate compressed pods — see ACLE, PYINKADO

xy·lic acid \ˈzīˌlik-, ˈzil\ n [ISV xyl- + -ic] : any of six isomeric crystalline carboxylic acids $(CH_3)_2C_6H_3COOH$ derived from xylene; dimethyl-benzoic acid

xyli·dine \ˈzīləˌdēn, ˈzil-, -ˌdᵊn\ n -s [ISV xyl- + -idine] **1** : any of six toxic liquid or low-melting crystalline compounds $(CH_3)_2C_6H_3NH_2$ that are amino derivatives of the xylenes and are made from them by nitration and subsequent reduction and that are used chiefly as intermediates for azo dyes and in organic synthesis: as **a** : the asymmetric meta isomer constituting the major part of mixed xylidines; 2,4-dimethyl-aniline — called also 2,4-xylidine, meta-4-xylidine **b** : the pale yellow crystalline para isomer; 2,5-dimethyl-aniline — called also 2,5-xylidine **c** : the crystalline asymmetric ortho isomer used in synthesizing riboflavin; 3,4-dimethyl-aniline — called also 3,4-xylidine, ortho-4-xylidine **2** : a commercial mixture of xylidines produced from commercial xylene

xy·lin·de·in \zīˈlindēən\ n -s [F xylindéine, fr. xyl- + inde indigo + -ine — more at INDE BLUE] : a yellow to brown crystalline compound $C_{34}H_{26}O_{11}$ produced by a fungus (Peziza aeruginosa) in green-rotted wood that dyes wool and cotton green

xy·li·tol \ˈzīləˌtȯl, -ˌtōl\ n -s [xyl- + -itol] : a sweet crystalline pentahydroxy alcohol $C_5H_7(OH)_5$ obtained by reduction of xylose

xylo- — see XYL-

xylo·ascorbic acid \ˌzīˌ(ˌ)lō-...-\ n : ASCORBIC ACID 1

xy·lo·bal·sa·mum \ˌzīlōˈbȯlsəməm\ n [L, fr. Gk xylobalsamon, fr. xyl- + balsamon balsam tree, balsam — more at BALM] : the dried twigs or fragrant wood of a balm of Gilead (Commiphora meccanensis)

xy·loc·o·pa \zīˈläkəpə\ n, cap [NL, fr. Gk xylokopos wood-cutter, fr. xyl- + -kopos (fr. koptein to cut off) — more at CAPON] : a genus of carpenter bees that is the type of the family Xylocopidae

xy·lo·cop·i·dae \ˌzīlōˈkäpəˌdē\ n pl, cap [NL, fr. Xylocopa, type genus + -idae] : a family that comprises hairy stout usu. large chiefly tropical bees which excavate nest galleries in dry wood or pithy stems and that is sometimes made a subfamily of Apidae

xy·lo·gly·phy \zīˈlägləfē, ˈzīlōˌglifē\ n -ES [xyl- + Gk glyphē carving, fr. glyphein to carve + E -y — more at GLYPH] : artistic wood carving

xy·lo·graph \ˈzīləˌgraf, -ˌrȧf\ n [back-formation fr. xylography] : an engraving on wood; also : an impression from such an engraving : a print made by xylography

xy·log·ra·pher \zīˈlägrəfə(r)\ n -s [xylography + -er] : one that practices or is skilled in xylography

xy·lo·graph·ic \ˌzīləˈgrafik\ also **xy·lo·graph·i·cal** \-fəkəl\ adj [xylographic fr. F xylographique, fr. xylographie + -ique -ic; xylographical fr. xylographie + -ical] : of, relating to, or expressed in xylography — **xy·lo·graph·i·cal·ly** \-f(ə)k(ə)lē\ adv

xy·lo·graph·i·ca \ˌˌˈ⸱⸱⸱fəkə\ n pl [NL, fr. neut. pl. of (assumed) NL xylographicus xylographic, fr. L xyl- + graphicus graphic] : BLOCK BOOKS

xy·log·ra·phy \zīˈlägrəfē\ n -ES [F xylographie, fr. xyl- + -graphie -graphy] **1 a** : WOOD ENGRAVING **b** : WOODCUT **2** : the art of making prints from the natural wood grain **3** : a method of printing in colors upon wood

xy·loid \ˈzīˌlȯid\ adj [ISV xyl- + -oid] : resembling wood

: having the qualities or nature of wood : WOODY, LIGNEOUS

xy·lo·ketose \ˌzīˌ(ˌ)lō-\ n [ISV xyl- + ketose] : XYLULOSE

xy·lol \ˈzīˌlȯl, -ˌlōl\ n -s [ISV xyl- + -ol] : XYLENE — used esp. of the commercial mixture

xy·lol·o·gy \zīˈläləjē\ n -ES [ISV xyl- + -logy] : a branch of dendrology dealing with the gross and the minute structure of wood

xy·lo·man·cy \ˈzīləˌman(t)sē\ n -ES [ISV xyl- + -mancy] : divination by means of pieces of wood

xy·lom·e·ter \zīˈlämətə(r)\ n [ISV xyl- + -meter] : an instrument used to determine specific gravity of wood

-x·y·lon \ˌksəˌlän\ n comb form [NL, fr. Gk xylon — more at XYL-] **1** : one having (such) wood — in generic names ⟨Haematoxylon⟩ **2** : one living in (such) a relation to wood ⟨Hypoxylon⟩ **3** : wood ⟨laurinoxylon⟩

xy·lon·ic acid \(ˌ)zīˈlänik-\ n [ISV xyl- + -onic] : an acid $C_4H_5(OH)_4COOH$ obtained as a syrup by oxidizing xylose

Xy·lo·nite \ˈzīləˌnīt\ trademark — used for a plastic

¹xy·loph·a·ga \zīˈläfəgə\ n, cap [NL, fr. xyl- + -phaga] : a genus of marine bivalve mollusks (family Pholadidae) that bore holes in wood

²xylophaga \"\ n pl, cap [NL, fr. xyl- + -phaga] : a group of insects that feed on or in wood; esp : a division of beetles

xy·lo·phag·i·dae \ˌzīləˈfajəˌdē\ n pl, cap [NL, fr. Xylophagus, type genus (fr. Gk xylophagos xylophagous) + -idae] : a family of dipterous flies whose predaceous larvae frequently live in decayed wood

xy·loph·a·gous \(ˈ)zīˈläfəgəs\ adj [Gk xylophagos wood-eating, fr. xyl- + -phagos -phagous] : feeding on or in wood — used esp. of insect larvae, crustaceans, and mollusks

xy·loph·i·lous \(ˈ)zīˈläfələs\ adj [xyl- + -philous] : attracted to wood : growing or living in or on wood ⟨~ fungi⟩ ⟨a ~ beetle⟩

xylo·phone \ˈzīləˌfōn also ˈzil-\ n [xyl- + -phone] **1 a** : a percussion musical instrument consisting of a series of wooden bars graduated in length to sound the musical scale, supported on belts of straw or felt, and sounded by striking with two small wooden hammers and comprising from 30 to 55 bars arranged in two rows

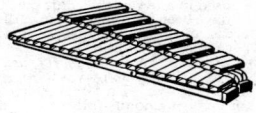

xylophone 1a

and tuned chromatically with or without carefully tuned resonators **b** : an organ percussion stop of similar tone quality **2** : an instrument to determine the elastic properties of woods

xy·lo·phon·ic \ˌ⸱ˈfänik\ adj : relating to or sounding like a xylophone

xy·lo·phon·ist \ˈzīləˌfōnəst also ˈzilə₊fōn- sometimes zīˈläfən- or zəˈläfən-\ n -s : a performer on the xylophone

xy·lo·pia \zīˈlōpēə\ n, cap [NL, prob. fr. xyl- + -opia] : a large genus of chiefly tropical American trees or shrubs (family Annonaceae) with coriaceous often distichous leaves, rather large flowers, aromatic berries, and usu. bitter wood — see EMBIRA, GUINEA PEPPER

xy·lo·porosis \ˌzīlə+\ n [NL, fr. xyl- + porosis] : a disease of citrus trees associated with lack of compatability between scion and stock and characterized by pits in the xylem

xy·lo·pyrography \"+\ n [xyl- + pyrography] : pyrography upon wood

xy·lo·quinone \"+\ n [ISV xyl- + quinone] : any of several yellow crystalline compounds $(CH_3)_2C_6H_2O_2$ obtained in general by oxidation of xylidines or xylenols; dimethyl-benzoquinone

xy·lose \ˈzīˌlōs also -ōz\ n -s [ISV xyl- + -ose] : a crystalline aldose sugar of the pentose class $C_5H_{10}O_5$ that is not fermentable with ordinary yeasts and that is found esp. in the D-form as a constituent of xylans and obtained therefrom by hydrolysis with acids — compare WOOD SUGAR

xy·lo·side \ˈzīləˌsīd-ˌsȧd\ n -s [xylose + -ide] : a glycoside that yields xylose on hydrolysis

xy·los·ma \zīˈläzmə\ n, cap [NL, fr. xyl- + -osma] : a genus of American and Asiatic usu. evergreen trees and shrubs (family Flacourtiaceae) with axillary thorns and fine-textured woods

xy·lo·stro·ma \ˌzīləˈstrōmə\ n, pl **xylostroma·ta** \-məd-ə\ also **xylostromas** [NL, fr. xyl- + stroma] : the closely felted sterile mycelium of various wood-destroying fungi formerly believed to represent a distinct genus — **xy·lo·stro·ma·toid** \-mə₊tȯid\ adj

xy·lo·tile \ˈzīlə₊tīl\ n -s [G xylotil, fr. xyl- + Gk tilos something plucked, fr. tillein to pluck] : a mineral approximately $(Mg,Fe)_3Fe_2Si_2O_{20}\cdot11H_2O$ that is a hydrous iron magnesium silicate, occurs in delicately fibrous forms, and is derived from alteration of asbestos or chrysolite

xy·lo·tom·ic \ˌzīlə₊tämik\ also **xy·lo·tom·i·cal** \-mȯkəl\ adj : of or relating to xylotomy

xy·lot·o·mist \-məst\ n -s : one skilled in xylotomy

xy·lot·o·mous \(ˈ)zīˌläd₊əməs\ adj [xyl- + -tomous] : capable of boring or cutting wood — used of an insect

xy·lot·o·my \-mē\ n -ES [xyl- + -tomy] : the art of preparing sections of wood (as by means of a microtome) for microscopic examination

xy·lo·trya \ˌzīlə₊trīə\ n, cap [NL, fr. xyl- + Gk tryein to rub, wear out; akin to Gk tribein to rub, grind — more at THROW] : a genus of marine bivalves that is closely related to and often included in Teredo and comprises forms as destructive to timber

xy·lo·typographic \ˌzīlə+\ adj [xyl- + typographic] : of or relating to wooden type : printed from wooden type or from wood blocks — **xy·lo·typography** \"+\ n

xy·lu·lose \ˈzī(y)ə₊lōs also ˈzil-\ n -s [xyl- + -ulose (as in cellulose)] : a ketose sugar $C_5H_{10}O_5$ of the pentose class that is formed from xylose by epimerization and from D-arabitol by bacterial oxidation, that like ribulose plays a role in carbohydrate metabolism, and that is found in the urine in cases of pentosuria; threo-pentulose

-x·y·lum \ˌksəˌləm\ n comb form [NL, fr. Gk xylon — more at XYL-] : one having (such) wood — in generic names ⟨Erythroxylum⟩ ⟨Zanthoxylum⟩

xy·lyl \ˈzīˌlil\ n -s [ISV xyl- + -yl] : any of several isomeric univalent radicals C_8H_9 derived from the three xylenes by removal of a hydrogen atom; esp : a radical of the formula $(CH_3)_2C_6H_3-$; dimethyl-phenyl — compare TOLYL

xy·lyl·ene \ˈzīlə₊lēn\ n -s [ISV xylyl + -ene] **1** : any of several isomeric bivalent radicals C_8H_8 derived from the three xylenes by removal of one hydrogen atom from each of two carbon atoms; esp : any of the three radicals having the formula $-CH_2C_6H_4CH_2-$; phenylene-di-methylene **2** : a reactive hydrocarbon $CH_2=C_6H_4=CH_2$ that is formed by pyrolysis of para-xylene under low pressure followed by quick chilling in a solvent at $-80°$ C and that polymerizes to an insoluble white mass at room temperature — called also para-xylylene, p-xylylene

xyr·phoid \ˈzīˌfȯid, ˈzi-\ adj or n [by alter.] : XIPHOID

xyr·i·da·ce·ae \ˌzirəˈdāsēˌē\ n pl, cap [NL, fr. Xyrid-, Xyris, type genus + -aceae] : a family of herbs (order Xyridales) with basal equitant usu. distichous leaves and leafless scapes bearing flowers in dense heads in the axils of imbricated scales — see XYRIS — **xyr·i·da·ceous** \-ᵊsˈdāˌshəs\ adj

xyr·i·da·les \ˌzirəˈdā(ˌ)lēz\ n pl, cap [NL, fr. Xyrid-, Xyris + -ales] : an order of monocotyledonous herbs having flowers mostly with regular corolla and compound superior ovary — see BROMELIACEAE, COMMELINACEAE, XYRIDACEAE

xy·ris \ˈzī(ə)rəs\ n, cap [NL, fr. L, an iris, fr. Gk] : a large genus (the type of the family Xyridaceae) of chiefly American marsh herbs having mostly yellow flowers with three sepals of which the two lateral are small, keeled, and persistent and the other is membranous and spreading — see YELLOW-EYED GRASS

xyst \ˈzist\ n -s [L xystus] : XYSTUS

xys·tum \ˈzistəm\ n, pl **xys·ta** \tə\ [Gk xyston, fr. neut. of xystos scraped, polished, fr. xyein to scrape, polish] : XYSTUS

xys·tus \ˈzistəs\ n, pl **xys·ti** \ˌstī, -ˌstē\ [L, fr. Gk xystos, fr. xystos, adj., scraped, polished, fr. its smooth floor] : a long and open portico used esp. by ancient Greeks or Romans for athletic exercises in wintry or stormy weather; sometimes : a walk lined with trees

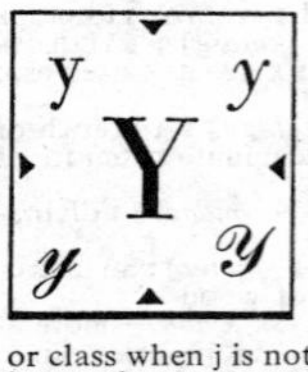

¹y \'wī\ *n, pl* **y's** *or* **ys** \'wīz\ *often cap, often attrib* **1 a :** the 25th letter of the English alphabet **b :** an instance of this letter printed, written, or otherwise represented **c :** a speech counterpart of orthographic *y* (as *y* in *yard, my, city,* or Swedish *fyr*) **2 :** a printer's type, a stamp, or some other instrument for reproducing the letter *y* **3 :** someone or something arbitrarily or conveniently designated *y:* as **a :** the 25th in order or class **b :** the 24th in order or class when j is not used **c :** the 22d in order or class when j, v, and w are not used **d :** the second in order or class when x is made the first **4 :** something having the shape of the letter Y: as **a :** a forked holder to support the telescope of a leveling instrument or the axis of a theodolite **:** WYE **b :** a principal railroad track and two diverging branches arranged like the letter Y that with a cross track connecting the diverging branches are used in reversing engines or trains **c :** SIAMESE 4 **5 a :** UNKNOWN QUANTITY 1 **b :** Y-COORDINATE

²y \"\ *adj, cap* [abbr. of *Young* (as in *Young Men's Christian Association, Young Women's Christian Association, Young Men's and Young Women's Hebrew Association*)] **:** of or relating to the Young Men's Christian Association, the Young Women's Christian Association, or the Young Men's and Young Women's Hebrew Association

³y *abbr, often cap* **1** yard **2** year **3** yellow **4** yen **5** yeoman; yeomanry **6** younger; youngest **7** your

⁴y *symbol* **1** unknown quantity **2** an ordinate **3** *cap* admittance **4** *cap* yttrium

y- *prefix* [ME *y-, i-,* fr. OE *ge-,* perfective, associative, and collective prefix (often used to form perfective verbs whose past participles were subsequently made to function as the past participles of the corresponding simple verbs) — more at CO-] — used in a few esp. archaic past participles that have survived or have been revived from an earlier period of the language and occas. in other verb forms coined by analogy with such past participles ⟨*y*pointing⟩

¹**-y** *also* **-ey** \ē, i\ *adj suffix, usu* **-ier;** *usu* **-iest** [ME, fr. OE *-ig;* akin to OHG *-ig* -y, ON *-igr,* Goth *-eigs, -igs,* L *-icus,* Gk *-ikos,* Skt *-ika*] **1 a :** characterized by **:** full of — in adjectives formed from nouns ⟨blossom*y*⟩ ⟨dirt*y*⟩; in many words formed from a base word having final postconsonantal mute *e* and with omission of the *e* ⟨mir*y*⟩ ⟨mir*ey*⟩ ⟨spin*y*⟩ ⟨spin*ey*⟩; accompanied by doubling of the final consonant of the base word immediately after a short stressed vowel ⟨legg*y*⟩ ⟨mudd*y*⟩; in the form *-ey* regularly after a final *y* ⟨clay*ey*⟩ or vowel other than postconsonantal mute *e* ⟨mosquito*ey*⟩ ⟨glu*ey*⟩ sometimes with a change of *y* to *i* ⟨ski*ey*⟩ or where *-y* would duplicate another word ⟨hol*ey*⟩ **b :** having the character of **:** composed of — in adjectives formed from nouns ⟨ic*y*⟩ ⟨water*y*⟩ ⟨lac*y*⟩ ⟨wax*y*⟩ ⟨rant*y*⟩ **c :** characteristic of, resembling, or suggesting someone or something indicated **:** having some of the qualities of **:** that is like or like that of — in adjectives formed from nouns ⟨home*y*⟩ ⟨wintr*y*⟩ ⟨folks*y*⟩ ⟨garbag*y*⟩ ⟨win*y*⟩ often with a disparaging connotation ⟨gadget*y*⟩ ⟨milquetoast*y*⟩ ⟨schoolteacher*y*⟩ ⟨rabbit*y*⟩ ⟨Hollywood*y*⟩ ⟨bedroom*y*⟩ ⟨barn*y*⟩ ⟨stag*y*⟩ **d :** devoted to **:** addicted to **:** enthusiastic over — in adjectives formed from nouns ⟨hors*y*⟩ ⟨outdoors*y*⟩ ⟨ism*y*⟩ **2 a :** tending or inclined to — in adjectives formed from verbs ⟨cling*y*⟩ ⟨sleep*y*⟩ ⟨chatt*y*⟩ ⟨cri*ey*⟩ **b :** giving occasion for (specified) action ⟨tear*y*⟩ ⟨yumm*y*⟩ — usu. in adjectives formed from verbs ⟨munch*y*⟩ ⟨picnick*y*⟩ **c :** performing (specified) action or being in a (specified) mode of existence **:** -ING — in adjectives formed from verbs ⟨twinkl*y*⟩ ⟨curl*y*⟩ **3 a :** somewhat **:** rather **:** -ISH — in adjectives formed from adjectives ⟨purpl*y*⟩ ⟨sued*y*⟩ ⟨wooden*y*⟩ **b :** having (such) characteristics to a marked degree ⟨Scotch*y*⟩ ⟨Dutch*y*⟩ or in an affected or superficial way ⟨French*y*⟩ — in adjectives formed from adjectives

²**-y** \"\ *n suffix, pl* **-ies** [ME *-ie,* fr. OF, fr. L *-ia,* fr. Gk *-ia, -eia*] **1 :** state **:** condition **:** quality — chiefly in combining forms derived from French, Latin, or Greek ⟨-alg*y*⟩ ⟨-andr*y*⟩ ⟨-crac*y*⟩ ⟨-soph*y*⟩ ⟨-tom*y*⟩ **2 :** activity, place of business, or goods dealt with ⟨chandler*y*⟩ ⟨cooper*y*⟩ ⟨laundr*y*⟩ ⟨executr*y*⟩ **3 :** whole body or group ⟨soldier*y*⟩

³**-y** \"\ *n suffix, pl* **-ies** [ME *-ie,* fr. AF, fr. L *-ium*] **:** instance of a (specified) action ⟨expir*y*⟩ ⟨entreat*y*⟩ ⟨inquir*y*⟩

⁴**-y** — see -IE

y' \y(ə)\ *pron* [by contr.] **:** YOU ⟨*y'*know⟩ ⟨*y'*all⟩

ya *var of* YAH

ya·ba bark \'yäbə-\ *n* [*yaba* fr. AmerSp, prob. fr. Taino] **:** ANGELIM

¹**yab·ber** \'yabə(r)\ *also* **yabber-yabber** \ˌ==ˌ==\ *n* -s [prob. modif. (influenced by *jabber*) of *yabba,* native name in Australia] *Austral* **:** TALK, JABBER, LANGUAGE, CONVERSATION ⟨all ~ and chatter ceased around the campfires —Francis Birtles⟩

²**yabber** \"\ *vi* -ED/-ING/-s *Austral* **:** to indulge in yabber

³**yabber** \"\ *n* -s [by alter.] **:** YABBY

yab·bi \'yabē\ *n, pl* **yabbies** [native name in Tasmania] **:** TASMANIAN WOLF

yab·by *or* **yab·bie** \'yabē\ *n, pl* **yabbies** [native name in Gippsland] **:** a small burrowing crayfish (*Parachaeraps bicarinatus*) that is found in most creeks and water holes in Australia

ya·bim *or* **ja·bim** \'yäbəm\ *n, pl* **yabim** *or* **yabims** *or* **jabim** *or* **jabims** *usu cap* **1 a :** a Melanesian people of Morobe, Territory of New Guinea **b :** a member of such people **2 :** the language of the Yabim people

ya·cal \'yäkəl\ *n* -s [Tag *yakál*] **1 :** any of several hard heavy durable yellowish brown woods obtained from trees of the family Dipterocarpaceae chiefly in the Philippines — compare LAUAN **2 :** a tree whose wood is a yacal

yac·a·re \'yakəˌrā, ˌ==ˈ=\ *var of* JACARE

ya·ca·ta \'yäkəd·ə\ *n* -s [MexSp *yácata*] **:** a mound of earth in Mexico faced with stone without mortar and probably a habitation site

yac·ca \'yakə\ *n* -s [AmerSp *yaca,* fr. Taino] **1 :** any of several West Indian podocarps (as *Podocarpus coriacea* and *P. purdieana*), **2 :** the wood of a yacca

yacca gum *n* **:** ACAROID RESIN

¹**yacht** \'yät, *usu* -äd·+V\ *n* -s *often attrib* [earlier *yaught,* fr. obs. D *jaght* (now *jacht*), fr. MLG *jacht,* short for *jachtschiff, jageschiff* light sailing vessel, fast pirate ship, lit., hunting ship, fr. *jacht-, jage* hunt (fr. *jagen* to hunt, fr. OHG *jagōn*) + *schiff* ship, fr. OHG *skif;* akin to OFris *jagia* to hunt and perh. to Skt *yahu* restless, swift, strong — more at SHIP] **1 :** a sailing or power boat used for pleasure (as racing or cruising) and characteristically built for speed with a sharp prow and graceful lines: as **a :** any of various large racing and cruising sailboats (as of the international class) **b :** a steam-driven or motor-driven ship or large powerboat equipped often elegantly for pleasure cruising or private travel (as by a head of state) **2 :** a dice game played in numerous forms and under various names with 5 or 10 dice in which the object is to make certain combinations in a prescribed number of casts

²**yacht** \"\ *vi* -ED/-ING/-s **:** to race or cruise in a yacht ⟨the Spanish pretender now ~s, plays golf —*Current Biog.*⟩

yacht chair *n* **:** a light nonadjustable folding armchair for outdoor use

yacht club *n* **:** an association of yachtsmen organized to promote, organize, and regulate yachting (as racing)

yacht ensign *n* **:** a U. S. ensign resembling the national ensign but having the stars on the union replaced by a white foul anchor surrounded by 13 white stars in a circle and authorized by law to be flown on licensed yachts owned by citizens

yachting *n* -s [fr. gerund of ²*yacht*] **:** the action, fact, or pastime of racing or cruising in a yacht

yacht rope *n* **:** rope of the best quality usu. made from fine soft white Manila fibers

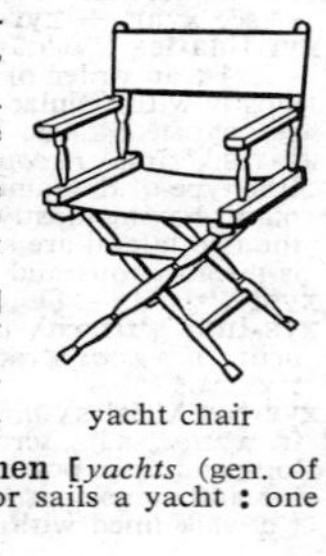

yacht chair

yachts·man \'yätsmən\ *n, pl* **yachtsmen** [*yachts* (gen. of ¹*yacht*) + *man*] **:** a person who owns or sails a yacht **:** one devoted to yachting

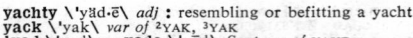

yachty \'yäd·ē\ *adj* **:** resembling or befitting a yacht

yack \'yak\ *var of* ²YAK, ³YAK

¹**yad** \'yad\ *or* **yade** \'yād\ *Scot var of* YAUD

²**yad** \'yäd\ *n, pl* **ya·da·yim** \yä'däyəm\ [Heb *yadh* hand] **:** a pointer tapering into the shape of a closed hand with extended index finger used as a guide for the reader of the scrolls of the Law in a synagogue

yae \'yā\ *adj* [alter. of *ae*] *chiefly Scot* **:** ONE

yaff \'yaf\ *vi* -ED/-ING/-s [imit.] *Scot* **:** BARK, YELP, YAP

yaf·fil \'yafəl\ *dial Eng var of* ¹YAFFLE

yaf·fin·gale \'yafənˌgāl *sometimes* -fiŋˌg- *or* -fēnˌg-\ *n* -s [¹*yaffle* + *-ingale* (as in *nightingale*)] *dial Eng* **:** GREEN WOODPECKER

¹**yaf·fle** \'yafəl\ *or* **yaf·fler** \-f(ə)lə(r)\ *n* -s [*yaffle* imit. of the bird's laughing sound; *yaffler* fr. *yaffle* + *-er*] *dial* **:** GREEN WOODPECKER

²**yaffle** \"\ *vi* -ED/-ING/-s [*yaff* + *-le*] *dial Eng* **:** YAFF

³**yaffle** \"\ *n* -s [origin unknown] *dial* **:** ARMFUL

ya·ger \'yägə(r)\ *n* -s [modif. of G *jäger* — more at JAEGER] **1 :** JAEGER 1 **2 :** a rifle having a short barrel and large bore formerly used in the U. S.

yagi \'yägē, 'yagē\ *n* -s [after Hidetsugu *Yagi* b1886 Jap. electrical engineer who developed it] **:** a highly directional and selective shortwave antenna consisting of a horizontal conductor of one or two dipoles connected with the receiver or transmitter and of a set of nearly equal insulated dipoles parallel to and on a level with the horizontal conductor

ya·gua \'yägwə\ *n* -s [AmerSp, fr. Taino] **1 :** a Puerto Rican palm (*Roystonea borinqueana*) that resembles the royal palm **2 :** the thick woody sheathing leaf base of the yagua palm

ya·gua·za \yə'gwäsə,-äzə\ *n* -s [AmerSp *yaguasa,* prob. fr. Taino] **:** a tree duck (*Dendrocygna arborea*) of the West Indies

¹**yah** *also* **ya** \'yä, 'yȧ\ *interj* [prob. imit. of the sound of retching] — used to express disgust, contempt, defiance, or derision

²**yah** *or* **jah** \'yä\ *n, cap* [Heb *Yāh*] **:** YAHWEH

yah·gan \'yägən\ *n, pl* **yahgan** *or* **yahgans** *usu cap* [*Yahga,* locality in Tierra del Fuego frequented by the Yahgans + E *-an*] **1 a :** a nomadic hunting and fishing people of Tierra del Fuego **b :** a member of such people **2 :** the language of the Yahgan people

ya·hi \'yähē\ *n, pl* **yahi** *or* **yahis** *usu cap* [Yahi, person] **1 a :** an extinct Indian people of the Pitt river valley in northern California **b :** a member of such people **2 :** a Yanan language of the Yahi people

ya·hoo \'yäˌhü, yä'hü, 'yāˌhü, yə'hü\ *n* -s *often cap* [fr. *Yahoo,* one of an imaginary race of brutes having the form of men in *Gulliver's Travels* (1726) by Jonathan Swift †1745 Brit. satirist] **:** an uncouth or rowdy person

ya·hoo·ism \-üˌizəm\ *n* -s *often cap* **:** behavior characteristic of a yahoo **:** ROWDYISM

yahr·zeit *also* **jahr·zeit** \'yärˌtsīt, 'yȯrˌ-\ *n* -s *often cap* [Yiddish *yartsayt, yortsayt,* fr. MHG *jārzīt* anniversary, lit., year's time, fr. *jār* year (fr. OHG) + *zīt* time, fr. OHG — more at YEAR, TIDE] **:** the anniversary of the death of a parent or near relative observed annually among Jews by the recital of the Kaddish and the lighting of a memorial candle or lamp

ya·hu \'yäˌhü\ *n, cap* [NL, transliteration of the Hebrew tetragrammaton *Yhwh* as some modern scholars believe it was pronounced before the Jews ceased to pronounce it about three centuries B.C.] **:** YAHWEH

yah·weh *also* **jah·veh** *or* **jah·weh** *or* **yah·veh** *or* **jah·ve** *or* **jah·we** *or* **yah·vè** *or* **yah·we** *or* **ja·vé** \'yä(ˌ)w|ā, 'yä(-, -)v|, |e\ *n* -s *cap* [NL, fr. Heb *Yhwh*] **:** ²GOD — used as a scholarly transliteration of the Hebrew tetragrammaton; compare JEHOVAH, YAH, YHWH

yah·wism *also* **jah·vism** *or* **jah·wism** *or* **yah·vism** \-ˌwizəm, -ˌvi-\ *n* -s *cap* **1 :** the religion and worship of Yahweh — compare ELOHISM **2 a :** the religion of the Israelites **b :** the early preexilic phase of the Judaic religion

¹**yah·wist** *also* **jah·vist** *or* **jah·wist** *or* **yah·vist** \-ˌwəst, -ˌvə-\ *n* -s *usu cap* **1 :** the author of the Yahwistic or J passages of the Old Testament which refer to God as *Yahweh* and which are believed to have emanated from Judah, the southern kingdom of the ancient Israelites — called also *Jehovist;* compare JEHOVAH **2 :** a worshiper of Yahweh

²**yahwist** \"\ *adj, usu cap* **:** YAHWISTIC

yah·wis·tic *also* **jah·wis·tic** *or* **yah·vis·tic** \(')yä¦wistik, (')yä¦-, -¦vi-, -tēk\ *adj, usu cap* **1 :** characterized by the use of *Yahweh* as the name of God **:** written by the Yahwist — used of some parts of the Old Testament; **2 :** of, belonging to, or characteristic of the religion and worship of Yahweh ⟨the *Yahwistic* faith⟩ ⟨a *Yahwistic* rite⟩

yair \'ya(a)|(ə)r, 'ye|, |ə, *Scot* 'yār\ *n* -s [ME (Sc & northern dial.) *yare,* fr. OE *-gear* enclosure (as in *mylengear* mill enclosure); prob. akin to OE *geard* enclosure — more at YARD] *chiefly Scot* **:** an enclosure for catching salmon as the tide ebbs

ya·jé \yä'hā\ *n* -s [AmerSp *yajé, yagé*] **:** a Brazilian plant (*Prestonia amazonica*) of the family Apocynaceae

¹**yak** \'yak\ *n, pl* **yaks** *also* **yak** [Tibetan *gyak*] **:** a large wild or domesticated ox (*Bos grunniens* syn. *Poephagus grunniens*) of Tibet and adjacent elevated parts of central Asia having short smooth hair on the back and long wavy hair on the breast, sides, legs, and tail, being in the wild blackish brown and up to about six feet high at the shoulder and 1200 pounds in weight but smaller and varying in color under domestication, and living as a beast of burden and source of flesh, milk, hide, and hair

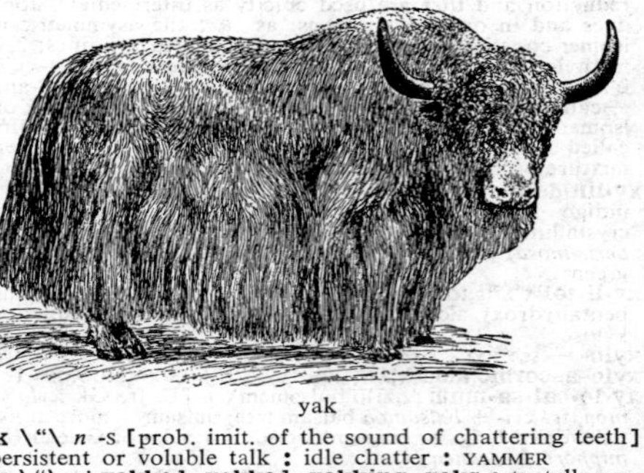

yak

²**yak** \"\ *n* -s [prob. imit. of the sound of chattering teeth] **:** persistent or voluble talk **:** idle chatter **:** YAMMER

³**yak** \"\ *vi* **yakked; yakked; yakking; yaks :** to talk persistently **:** CHATTER, YAMMER ⟨*yakked* on endlessly about her operation⟩ ⟨the old man would ~ at us for not showing proper respect —Edward Newhouse⟩

⁴**yak** \", 'yäk\ *n* -s [imit.] **1** *slang* **:** LAUGH ⟨the jokes that used to get snickers now get ~s —Douglas Anderson⟩ **2** *slang* **:** JOKE, GAG ⟨grinding out ~s for radio comedians —Robert Fontaine⟩

ya·ka \'yäkə\ *n, pl* **yaka** *or* **yakas** *usu cap* **:** a member of a Bantu people near the mouth of the Congo river widely known for their carved masks

yak·a·mik \'yakəmik\ *n* -s [modif. of Pg *jacami,* fr. Tupi] **:** TRUMPETER 3a

ya·kan \'yäkən\ *n* -s *usu cap* **:** a member of a Moro people inhabiting the interior of Basilan Island, Philippines

¹**yak·e·ty-yak** *or* **yak·i·ty-yak** *also* **yack·e·ty-yak** \'yakəd·ē-'yak\ *n* -s [by redupl.] **:** ²YAK

²**yakety-yak** *or* **yakity-yak** *also* **yackety-yak** \"\ *vi* **:** ³YAK

yak·i·ma \'yakəˌmȯ, -ˌmä\ *n, pl* **yakima** *or* **yakimas** *usu cap* **1 a :** a Shahaptian people or group of peoples of the lower Yakima river valley, south central Washington **b :** a member of such people **2 :** the language of the Yakima people

ya·kin \'yäˌkēn, 'yäˌk-\ *n* -s [native name in Assam] **:** TAKIN

yak·ka \'yakə\ *or* **yak·ker** \-kə(r)\ *n* -s [native name in Queensland] *Austral* **:** WORK, LABOR

yak·o·nan \'yakənən\ *n* -s *usu cap* **:** a language family of the Penutian stock in Oregon consisting of Alsea, Siuslaw, and Yaquina

yak·sha *also* **yak·sa** \'yakshə\ *n* -s *often cap* [Skt *yakṣa*] **:** a local tutelary spirit or earth jinn of India regarded as a patron of wealth and fertility

ya·kut \yə'küt\ *n, pl* **yakut** *or* **yakuts** *usu cap* **1 a :** a Turkic people of northeastern Siberia living mainly in the Lena river basin and practicing herding, crafts, and trading and in the south some agriculture **b :** a member of such people **2 :** the Turkic language of the Yakut people

yak·u·tat \'yakəˌtat\ *n, pl* **yakutat** *or* **yakutats** *usu cap* **1 :** a Tlingit people occupying the area about Yakutat Bay, Alaska **2 :** a member of the Yakutat people

yakutat bear *n, usu cap Y* [from *Yakutat* Bay, Alaska] **:** a large brown bear (*Ursus dalli*) of the vicinity of Yakutat Bay related to the Kodiak bear

yakutat hut *n, usu cap Y* [fr. *Yakutat* Bay, Alaska] **:** a square demountable temporary structure built of prefabricated wood panels

¹**yak-yak** \(')ya¦kyak\ *n* [by redupl.] **:** ²YAK

²**yak-yak** \"\ *vi* [by redupl.] **:** ³YAK

yale \'yāl, *esp before pause or consonant* -āəl\ *n* -s [ME *eale,* fr. L, an animal of Ethiopia] **:** a mythical beast resembling an antelope, having large erect tusks and long horns pointing in any direction at will, and sometimes being represented as a supporter for heraldic arms

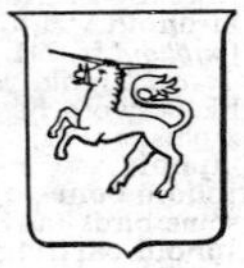

yale

yale blue *n, often cap Y* [fr. *Yale* University, New Haven, Connecticut] **:** a deep blue that is lighter and stronger than royal (sense 8b), redder and paler than imperial blue, and redder and very slightly paler than Napoleon blue

yam \'yam, -aa(ə)m\ *n* -s [earlier *inany, iname, nname,* fr. Pg *inhame* & Sp *ñame,* of West African origin; prob. akin to Fulani *nyami* to eat] **1 a :** the edible starchy tuberous root of various plants of the genus *Dioscorea* (as *D. sativa* or *D. alata*) that largely replaces the potato as a staple food in tropical climates and is cooked in the same way but has coarser flesh **b :** a plant of the genus *Dioscorea* (as *D. paniculata*) **c :** any of several similar plants — usu. used in combination ⟨round ~⟩ ⟨native ~⟩ **2 a** *Scot* **:** POTATO **b :** SWEET POTATO; *esp* **:** one with deep orange flesh that remains moist when baked

yama·craw \'yäməˌkrȯ, 'yam-\ *n* -s *usu cap* **:** YAMASEE

yam·a·mai \ˌyamə'mī\ *n* -s [Jap] **1 :** a large Japanese silkworm (*Antheraea yamamai*) whose larva feeds on the oak and furnishes excellent silk **2 :** silk produced by the yamamai

yam·a·nai \-'nī\ *n* -s [Burmese *yamanē*] **:** a Burmese tree (*Gmelina arborea*) the hard wood of which is used for making clogs

ya·ma·see *or* **ya·mas·see** \'yäməsē\ *or* **yem·as·see** \'yem-\ *n, pl* **yamasee** *or* **yamasees** *or* **yamassee** *or* **yamassees** *or* **yemassee** *or* **yemassees** *usu cap* **:** an Indian of a Muskogean people of the lower Savannah and the coast of Georgia driven to Florida after defeat by the whites in 1716 and finally incorporated with the Creeks and Seminoles

ya·ma·to \yä'mä(ˌ)tō\ *n, pl* **yamato** *cap* [Jap] **:** a Japanese of the principal racial stock of Japan that is of ancient origin, has possibly Alpine characteristics, and is supposed to have entered Japan from the mainland in the protohistoric period — compare AINU

yam bean *n* **:** a tropical twining plant (*Pachyrhizus erosus*) with tuberous roots resembling turnips which are eaten raw as a salad or cooked and edible pods and seeds which yield rotenone and oils

yamel \'yäməl,'yam-\ *also* **yam·hill** \'yamˌhil\ *n, pl* **yamel** *or* **yamels** *also* **yamhill** *or* **yamhills** *usu cap* **1 :** a Kalapooian people of the Yamhill river valley, northwestern Oregon **2 :** a member of the Yamel people

ya·men \'yämən\ *n* -s [Chin (Pek) *ya²-men²*] **:** an establishment used by a Chinese government official or department for official business and often as a residence **:** HEADQUARTERS, OFFICE, COURT

yam family *n* **:** DIOSCOREACEAE

ya·mi \'yämē\ *n, pl* **yami** *or* **yamis** *usu cap* **1 a :** a Malaysian people inhabiting Botel Tobago Island, near southern Formosa **b :** a member of such people **2 :** an Austronesian language of the Yami people

¹**yam·mer** \'yamə(r)\ *vb* **yammered; yammered; yammering; yammers** [alter. (influenced by G *jammern*) of ME *yomeren* to murmur, complain, be sad, fr. OE *gēomrian;* akin to OHG *jāmarōn* to complain, be sad, *jāmar* distress, misery — more at KATZENJAMMER] *vi* **1 a :** to utter repeated cries of distress or sorrow **:** WAIL, WHIMPER ⟨a child that kept ~*ing* till its mother came⟩ **b :** to utter persistent complaints **:** WHINE, GRUMBLE, SCOLD ⟨~*ed* at an umpire loudly enough to get himself tossed out of a game —*Time*⟩ **2 :** to talk persistently or volubly and often loudly ⟨~*ing* and gesticulating to each other about their . . . adventures —Frederick Mears⟩ ⟨caused the purists to ~ for censorship —D.W.Maurer⟩ ⟨~*s* away about the brotherhood of man —P.B.Kyne⟩ **3 :** to make a loud repetitive noise ⟨heard the diesels ~*ing* monotonously belowdecks⟩ ~ *vt* **:** to utter complainingly, insistently, or volubly

²**yammer** \"\ *n* -s **:** a yammering utterance or noise ⟨set up a petulant ~⟩ ⟨the ~ of a machine gun⟩

yamp \'yamp\ *or* **yam·pa** *also* **yam·pah** \-mpə\ *n* -s [of Shoshonean origin; akin to Shoshoni *yampa* yamp, Ute *yampä*] **:** either of two western No. American plants of the genus *Carum* (*C. gairdneri* and *C. kelloggii*) with fleshy edible roots — called also *squawroot;* see INDIAN POTATO; compare CARAWAY

yam·pee \'yampē\ *n* -s [perh. fr. *yampee* yamp] **:** CUSH-CUSH

yams *pl of* YAM

yam stick *n* **:** a hardwood stick three or four feet in length with edged or pointed ends used by the aboriginal women of Australia for digging (as roots or bulbs)

yam tree *n* **:** either of two black kurrajongs (*Sterculia diversifolia* and *S. quadrifida*)

¹**yan** \'yan\ *Scot & dial Eng var of* ONE

²**yan** \'yän\ *dial var of* YON

ya·na \'yänə\ *n, pl* **yana** *or* **yanas** *usu cap* [Yana, person] **1 a :** an extinct Indian people of the Pitt river valley of northern California **b :** a member of such people **2 :** a Yanan language of the Yana people

ya·na·co·na \ˌyänə'kōnə\ *n* -s [AmerSp, fr. Quechua *yanacuna,* pl. of *yana* servant, slave] **:** a Peruvian or Bolivian Indian serf or servant on an estate

ya·nan \'yänən\ *n* -s *usu cap* [*Yana* + E *-an*] **:** a language family of the Hokan stock comprising Yahi and Yana

yan·der \'yandə(r)\ *dial var of* YONDER

¹**yang** \'yäŋ\ *n* -s [Chin (Pek) *yang²* bright, masculine principle] **:** the masculine and positive principle (as of activity, height, light, heat, or dryness) in nature that according to traditional Chinese cosmology combines and interacts with its opposite yin to produce all that comes to be

²**yang** \'yaŋ, -aiŋ\ *n* -s [imit.] **:** the cry of the wild goose **:** HONK

³**yang** \"\ *vi* -ED/-ING/-s **:** to make the natural honking cry of the wild goose

⁴**yang** \'yäŋ\ *n* -s [Thai *yāng*] **:** a Siamese gurjun (*Dipterocarpus tuberculatus*)

yang·chow \'yäŋ¦jō\ *adj, usu cap* [fr. *Yangchow,* China] **:** of or from the city of Yangchow, China **:** of the kind or style prevalent in Yangchow

yang·go·na \yäŋ'gōnə\ *or* **ya·qo·na** \yə'kōnə\ *n* -s [Fijian *yanggona*] **:** KAVA

yang-kin \'yäŋ'kin\ *n* -s [Chin *yang²-k'in²,* prob. fr. *yang²* foreign + *ch'in²* lute, guitar] **:** a Chinese dulcimer

yang ko \'yäŋ'kō\ *n* [Chin (Pek) *yang¹-ko¹,* lit., rice song] **:** a Chinese dance and song of transplanting rice

yang shao \'=¦shau̇\ *adj, usu cap Y&S* [Chin (Pek) *yang³-shao²*] **:** of or relating to a late Neolithic and Bronze Age culture of north China characterized by small settlements of circular pit houses, irrigation, loom weaving, and a fine painted pottery and in its late stage by metallurgy

yang·tao \'=¦tau̇\ *n* -s [Chin (Pek) *yang²-t'ao²*] **:** a Chinese woody vine (*Actinidia chinensis*) often cultivated for its nearly orbicular leaves which are white-woolly beneath and for its yellowish white flowers followed by edible fruits like large gooseberries

¹**yank** \'yaŋk, -aiŋk\ *n* -s *usu cap* [by shortening] **:** YANKEE

²**yank** \"\ *n* -s [origin unknown] **1** *Scot* **:** a sudden hard blow **2 :** a strong sudden pull **:** JERK

³yank \"\ *vb* -ED/-ING/-S *vt* **1 :** to pull with a quick vigorous movement ⟨angrily ~*ed* the weed out by the roots⟩ **2 :** to cause to go in a rude or abrupt manner ⟨the offending copies were ~*ed* out of the school libraries —*Time*⟩ ⟨~*ed* before the school board to explain his statement⟩ **3 :** to take out or away in a quick vigorous or rudely abrupt manner ⟨have his tonsils ~*ed*⟩ ⟨he was ~*ed* in the sixth when he issued three walks —*N.Y. Times*⟩ **~** *vi* **:** to pull on something with a quick vigorous movement ⟨~*ed* at the door trying to open it⟩ ⟨the other man ~*ed* down on the halyard and the flags fell —Wirt Williams⟩ **syn** see JERK

yankapin *var of* YONCOPIN

¹yan·kee \ˈyaŋkē, -aiŋ-\ *n* -S *usu cap* [origin unknown] **1 a :** a native or inhabitant of New England **b :** a New Englander descended from old New England stock; *specif* **:** one having qualities of character (as conservatism, thrift, pertinacity, or shrewdness) and often also of speech traditionally associated with inhabitants of New England **c :** a native or inhabitant of the northern States as distinguished from a Southerner **d :** a native or citizen of the U.S. **2 :** the English language as spoken or pronounced by Yankees; *esp* **:** New England dialect

²yankee \"\ *adj, usu cap* **1 :** of, relating to, or characteristic of the Yankees **2 :** having qualities (as shrewdness, reserve, or mechanical ingenuity) traditionally ascribed to New England Yankees

³yankee \"\ *usu cap* — a communications code word for the letter *y*

yankee corn *n, usu cap Y* **:** FLINT CORN

yan·kee·dom \ˈ==,dəm\ *also* **yankee–doodle·dom** \,==-ˈdüdᵊldəm\ *n* -S *usu cap Y & D* **1 :** the realm of the Yankees **2 :** YANKEES

yankee–doodle \,==ˈdüdᵊl\ *n* -S *usu cap Y&D* [fr. *Yankee Doodle*, popular song during the American Revolutionary War] **:** YANKEE

yan·kee·fy \ˈ==,fī\ *vt* -ED/-ING/-ES *usu cap* [¹*yankee* + *-fy*] **:** to cause to become like a Yankee ⟨regarded by the natives as *Yankeefied* and foreign —Nell Lewis⟩

yan·kee·ism \-ē,izəm\ *n* -S *usu cap* **1 :** a Yankee idiom, word, or custom **2 :** Yankee characteristics or customs

yan·kee·ize \-,īz\ *vt* -ED/-ING/-S *usu cap* **:** YANKEEFY

yankeeland \ˈ==,=\ *n, usu cap* **:** the region inhabited by Yankees ⟨youth of twenty years . . . with an air about him suspiciously redolent of *Yankeeland* —*Encore*⟩

yankee machine *n, usu cap Y* **:** a paper machine in which the web of paper is dried completely on a single large polished steam-heated cylinder

yank·ton \ˈyaŋktən, -aiŋ-\ *n, pl* **yankton** *or* **yanktons** *usu cap* [Dakota *ihanketonwan* end village] **1 :** one of the western prairie subdivisions of the Dakota people **2 :** a dialect of Dakota

yank·to·nai \,=təˈnā\ *n, pl* **yanktonai** *or* **yanktonais** *usu cap* [Dakota *ihanketonwanna* little end village] **:** one of the western prairie subdivisions of the Dakota people

yan·ni·gan \ˈyanəgən, -aneg-\ *n* -S [perh. alter. of *young one*] **:** a member of a scrub team in baseball

yan·qui \ˈyäŋkē\ *n* -S *often cap* [Sp, fr. E ¹*yankee*] **:** a citizen of the U.S. as distinguished from a Latin American

yan·tra \ˈyəntrə\ *n* -S [Skt] **:** a geometrical diagram used like an icon in meditation upon or worship of a deity chiefly in tantric worship

¹yao \ˈyau̇\ *n, pl* **yao** *or* **yaos** *usu cap* **1 a :** an aboriginal people inhabiting chiefly mountainous parts of southwestern China, northern Thailand, Laos, and Tonkin **b :** a member of such people **2 :** the language of the Yao people — see MIAO-YAO

²yao \"\ *n, pl* **yao** *or* **yaos** *usu cap* **1 a :** an African people living in the vicinity of Lake Nyasa, Central Africa **b :** a member of such people **2 :** a Bantu language of the Yao people

¹yap \ˈyap\ *vb* **yapped; yapped; yapping; yaps** [imit.] *vi* **1 :** to bark snappishly **:** YELP ⟨followed by four little dogs who *yapped* at his heels⟩ **2 :** to talk in a shrill insistent often idle manner **:** CHATTER, SCOLD ⟨the local paper . . . had been *yapping* for years about the need for a swimming pool —G.S. Perry⟩ ⟨~ at him for staying away so long —Walter Karig⟩ **~** *vt* **:** to utter in a yappy manner **:** BARK

²yap \"\ *n* -S **1 a :** a snappish bark **:** YIP, YELP **b :** shrill insistent often idle talk **:** CHATTER, COMPLAINT **2 a :** an unsophisticated, ignorant, or uncouth person **:** BUMPKIN, GREENHORN **b :** a contemptible person **3** *slang* **:** MOUTH ⟨told him to shut his ~⟩ ⟨always shooting off his ~⟩

yap·ese \(ˈ)yaˈpēz, (ˈ)yä-, -pēs\ *n, pl* **yapese** *cap* [*Yap* island + E *-ese*] **:** a Micronesian native or inhabitant of Yap island in the Caroline Islands

yap·man \ˈyapmən, ˈyäp-\ *n, pl* **yapmen** *cap* [*Yap* island + *man*] **:** YAPESE

ya·pock *or* **ya·pok** \yəˈpäk, ˈyapək\ *n* -S [fr. *Oyapock* (*Oyapok*), river in northern So. America; fr. its presence in large numbers on the river's banks] **:** an aquatic opossum (*Chironectes minimus*) of So. America

yapon *or* **yapa** *var of* YAUPON

yapp binding \ˈyap-\ *also* **yapp** *n* -S [after *Yapp*, a 19th cent. Eng. bookseller] *Brit* **:** DIVINITY CIRCUIT BINDING

yap·per \ˈyapə(r)\ *n* -S [¹*yap* + *-er*] **:** one that yaps ⟨a nation of ~*s* and listeners and movie watchers —H.A.Lincoln⟩

yap·ping·ly *adv* **:** in a yapping manner

yap·py \ˈyapē\ *adj* -ER/-EST [¹*yap* + *-y*] **1 :** given to yapping ⟨affections were expended on ~ little beasts —*New Yorker*⟩ **2 :** resembling or characteristic of a yap

yaqona *var of* YANGGONA

ya·qui \ˈyäkē\ *n, pl* **yaqui** *or* **yaquis** *usu cap* **1 a :** a Taracahitian people of Sonora, Mexico **b :** a member of such people **2 :** the language of the Yaqui people

ya·quina \yəˈkwēnə, -kwinə\ *n, pl* **yaquina** *or* **yaquinas** *usu cap* **1 a :** an Indian people of the Pacific coast of Oregon **b :** a member of such people **2 :** a Yakonan language of the Yaquina people

yar *var of* YARE

yar·age \ˈyarij, -rēj\ *n* -S [¹*yare* + *-age*] *chiefly Brit* **:** HANDINESS, MANEUVERABILITY — used of a ship

yar·ak \ˈyarak\ *n* -S [Per *yārakī* power, strength] **:** good flying condition **:** FETTLE — used of a hawk or other bird used in hunting ⟨eagles . . . are difficult to get into ~ —Douglas Carruthers⟩

ya·ray \yəˈrī\ *n* -S [AmerSp] **:** any of several slender Puerto Rican fan palms (esp. *Sabal causiarum*) the leaves of which are widely used in making hats

yarb \ˈyärb, ˈyȧb\ *dial var of* HERB

yar·bor·ough \ˈyär(,)bərə, -,brə\ *n* -S *usu cap* [after Charles Anderson Worsley, 2d Earl of *Yarborough* †1897 Eng. nobleman who was said to have bet a thousand to one against the dealing of such a hand] **:** a hand in bridge or whist containing no card higher than a nine

¹yard \ˈyärd, ˈyȧd\ *n* -S [ME *yarde, yerde*, fr. OE *gierd, geard* rod, twig, measure, yard; akin to OHG *gart* stick, goad, ON *gaddr* goad, spike, Goth *gazds* goad, MIr *gat* willow twig, L *hasta* spear] **1 :** any of various units of measure: as **a** *dial Eng* **:** ROD, POLE, PERCH **b** *obs* **:** YARD OF LAND **c :** a unit of length equal in the U.S. to 0.9144 meter and in Great Britain to the distance at 62°F between two transverse marks on two gold plugs in a bronze bar kept at the Standards Office of the Board of Trade at Westminster — abbr *yd.*; see MEASURE table **d :** a unit of volume (as for sand or gravel) equal to a cubic yard **2** *archaic* **:** PENIS **3 a :** a great length or quantity ⟨his photographic memory enabled him to tuck away ~*s* of facts and quotations —R.B.Nye⟩ **b** *slang* **:** one hundred dollars **4 :** a long spar tapered toward the ends and set athwart a mast to support and spread the head of a square sail, lateen, or lugsail or to hoist signal flags **:** GAFF — compare ²BOOM 1; see SHIP illustration

²yard \"\ *n* -S [ME *yard, yerd, yerde*, fr. OE *geard* enclosure, court, yard; akin to OHG *gart* enclosure, *garto* garden, ON *garthr* yard, Goth *gards* house, L *hortus* garden, Gk *chortos* farmyard, Skt *gṛha* house, *harati* he takes; basic meaning: to gird, enclose] **1 a :** a small usu. walled and often paved vacant area open to the sky and adjacent to a building **:** COURT **b :** the grounds of a public building or group of buildings ⟨inn ~⟩; *specif* **:** CAMPUS 1 ⟨college ~⟩ **c :** a usu. high-walled open-air exercise area for prisoners ⟨prison ~⟩ **2 a :** the grounds immediately surrounding a house and usu. comprising lawn, shrubbery and other plantings, recreation and service areas ⟨front ~⟩ **b :** an area devoted to the cultivation of crops **:** GARDEN, FIELD **3 a** (1) **:** an enclosure for poultry or livestock ⟨chicken ~⟩ (2) **:** a group of beehives kept together and managed as a unit **b** (1) **:** an area set aside for a particular business or activity (2) **:** an assembly or storage area ⟨rows of snowplows in the city ~*s*⟩; *specif* **:** LANDING 2b **c :** a system of tracks and sidings usu. at a railroad terminal used for storage and maintenance of cars and making up trains **4 :** a locality in a forest where moose or deer herd in winter for feeding and protection ⟨moose ~⟩

³yard \"\ *adj* [ME, fr. ²*yard*] **1 a :** of, relating to, or employed in the yard or garden surrounding a house ⟨~ light⟩ ⟨~ boy⟩ **b :** belonging to or stationed in a courtyard ⟨~ gate⟩ ⟨~ dog⟩ **2 :** of or from a run or enclosure for animals ⟨~ dung⟩ **3 :** attached to or employed by an establishment operating a yard ⟨~ patrol⟩ ⟨~ craft⟩ **4 :** of, relating to, or employed in a railroad yard ⟨~ clerk⟩ ⟨~ engine⟩ ⟨~ service⟩

⁴yard \"\ *vb* -ED/-ING/-S [²*yard*] *vt* **1 a :** to drive into or confine in a restricted area **:** HERD, PEN ⟨the sheep were ~*ed* at night —Rex Ingamells⟩ **b :** to confine to winter quarters ⟨when the deer are ~*ed* in deep snow —Hugh Fosburgh⟩ **2 :** to deliver to or store in a yard ⟨~ a freight car⟩; *esp* **:** to pile (logs) temporarily at a central point (as on a landing) **~** *vi* **:** to congregate in winter quarters ⟨mild winters, allowing deer to roam rather than ~ —*Wildlife Rev.*⟩ — often used with *up* ⟨show a tendency to ~ up near favorite feeding areas —Frank Dufresne⟩

¹yard·age \-dij, -dēj\ *n* -S [²*yard* + *-age*] **1 :** the use of a livestock enclosure for animals in transit provided by a railroad at a station **2 :** a charge made by a railroad for the use of a livestock enclosure

²yardage \"\ *n* -S [¹*yard* + *-age*] **1 :** the linear yards of advance made or cubic yards mined used as a basis for determining wages of coal miners **2 a :** an aggregate number of yards ⟨a large ~ of work-shirt chambrays —John Hoye⟩ ⟨the par and ~ of each of the ten golf courses — *N.Y.Herald Tribune*⟩ **b :** an amount expressed in yards: as (1) **:** an extent (as of cloth) measured in linear yards ⟨the dress floats out to an extravagant drift of ~ at the hem —*N.Y. Times*⟩ (2) **:** a distance covered in linear yards ⟨running plays that piled up ~ —*Time*⟩ (3) **:** an area covered in square yards ⟨increase plaster ~ by sizing dry walls⟩ (4) **:** a volume of material in cubic yards ⟨every great dam requires the moving of immense ~ —*Newsweek*⟩ **3 :** YARD GOODS ⟨they've been buying satin ~ . . . for a month now —Ray Bradbury⟩

yar·dang \ˈyär,däŋ\ *n* -S [Turk, abl. of *yar* steep bank, precipice] **:** a sharp-crested ridge carved by wind erosion from soft but coherent deposits (as clayey sand)

yardarm \ˈ=,=\ *n* [¹*yard* + *arm*] **:** either end of the yard of a square-rigged ship usu. including the outer quarter — see SHIP illustration

yardbird \ˈ=,=\ *n* **1 :** a soldier assigned to a menial task (as policing an area) or restricted to a limited area as a disciplinary measure **2 :** an untrained or inept enlisted man ⟨the rank of ~ — one level below private — has never been officially recognized —*N.Y.Times*⟩ ⟨everyone from the company commander to the sorriest ~ —Burtt Evans⟩

yard boss *n* **1 :** a foreman who directs laborers in the yard of an industrial plant **2** *also* **yarder boss :** a logger who directs and assists chokermen, riggers, and other workmen in a yard where logs are stored

yard conductor *n* **:** a railroad employee who directs a switch engine crew in accordance with the yardmaster's instructions

yard donkey *n* **:** YARDER

yard·er \ˈyärdər, ˈyȧdə(r\ *n* -S [²*yard* + *-er*] **:** a donkey engine that is used to haul logs from the stump to the skid road or to a landing

yard goods *n pl* **:** fabrics sold by the yard **:** PIECE GOODS

yard grass *n* **:** a coarse annual grass (*Eleusine indica*) that has flowers in fingerlike spikes and is widely distributed as a weed esp. in lawns

yarding *n* -S [fr. gerund of ⁴*yard*] **1 :** the act or process of conveying something (as logs) to an enclosure, assembly point, or loading point **2** *chiefly Austral* **:** delivery or arrival of livestock at the market ⟨a heavy ~ of lambs⟩

yardland \ˈ=,=\ *n* [ME *yerdlond*, fr. *yerde* yard (measure) + *lond* land] **:** VIRGATE

yard limit *n* **:** the point at which a line of track enters or leaves a railroad yard

yard–long bean \ˈ=,=-\ *n* **:** ASPARAGUS BEAN

yard lumber *n* **:** lumber intended for general building purposes that is of various shapes and sizes and is less than 5 inches thick

¹yard·man \ˈyärdmən, ˈyȧd-\ *n, pl* **yardmen** [²*yard* + *man*] **1 :** a man employed by the day to do such outdoor work as mowing lawns, shoveling snow, and washing automobiles **2 :** one who works in the yard of a commercial establishment; *esp* **:** one who supervises the handling of building materials in a lumberyard **3 :** a railroad man employed in yard service

²yardman \"\ *n, pl* **yardmen** [¹*yard* + *man*] **:** a sailor assigned to the yards

yardmaster \ˈ=,==\ *n* **:** the man in charge of operations in a railroad yard

yard of ale 1 : a slender horn-shaped glass about three feet tall usu. holding two or three pints **2 :** the amount contained in a yard of ale

yard of land [ME *yerde of londe*] **1 :** VIRGATE **2 :** a strip of land a rod wide; *esp* **:** one having an area of ¼ acre

yard rope *n* **:** a rope kept rove off at a masthead for sending the yard up or down

yards *pl of* YARD, *pres 3d sing of* YARD

yardstick \ˈ=,=\ *n* **1 a :** a measuring stick three feet long usu. marked off in feet, inches, and fractions of inches **b :** a standard basis of calculation ⟨these distances were the ~*s* for measuring . . . extragalactic distances —Adolph Knopf⟩ **2 :** a test or standard applied in making a critical judgment **:** CRITERION, TOUCHSTONE ⟨development of atomic power by the Government as a ~ for measuring the costs of private producers —Don Pryor⟩ ⟨let the general good be our ~ on every great issue —D.D.Eisenhower⟩ ⟨the level of excellence achieved in the novel . . . provides an imposing ~ against which the film repeatedly will be measured —Arthur Knight⟩ **syn** see STANDARD

yard tackle *n* **:** a tackle used on the lower yard of a ship; *esp* **:** a heavy double or treble purchase for hoisting

yardwand \ˈ=,=\ *n* [ME *yerde wande*] *archaic* **:** YARDSTICK

¹yare \ˈya(a)ǝr, ˈye|, |ǝ; ˈyär, ˈyȧ(r\ *adj* -ER/-EST [ME, fr. OE *gearu, gearo*; akin to OHG *garo* ready, complete, ON *gerr* ready, perfect, skilled, OHG *garawen* to prepare, OE *gierwan* to prepare, cook and prob. to OE *wearm* warm — more at WARM] **1** *archaic* **:** set for prompt action **:** READY **2** *or* **yar** \ˈyär, ˈyȧ(r\ **a :** characterized by speed and agility **:** NIMBLE, LIVELY **b** *of a ship* **:** easily handled **:** MANEUVERABLE — **yare·ly** *adv, archaic*

²yare \"\ *adv* [ME, fr. OE *gearo, gearwe*; akin to OE *gearo, gearu* ready] *archaic* **:** QUICKLY

ya·re·ta \yəˈräd·ə\ *n* -S [AmerSp, fr. Quechua] **:** any of several densely cushioned resinous Andean herbs of the genera *Azorella* and *Laretia* (family Umbelliferae) commonly used as fuel — called also *llareta*

ya·ri·ya·ri \,yärēˈyärē\ *n* -S [native name in Guiana] **:** any of various lancewoods of the genus *Dugetia* (family Annonaceae)

yark \ˈyärk\ *var of* YERK

yar·kan·di \yärˈkändē, -kan-\ *n, pl* **yarkandi** *or* **yarkandis** *cap* **:** a native or inhabitant of Yarkand, an oasis city in the west end of the Tarim Basin of Chinese Turkistan — compare UIGHUR

yar·ke *or* **yar·kee** \ˈyärkē\ *n* -S [F *yarqué*, of Cariban origin; akin to Galibi *yaracaro* monkey, Macusi *youareka*] **:** SAKI

yarm \ˈyärm, ˈyȧm\ *vi* -ED/-ING/-S [ME *yarmen*, fr. OE *gyrman, grymman*] *dial Brit* **:** to utter a discordant cry **:** SHRIEK, WAIL — used esp. of the cry of an animal

yar·mouth \ˈyärməth, ˈyȧm-\ *adj, usu cap* [fr. *Yarmouth*, locality in Des Moines County, Iowa] **:** belonging to the second interglacial interval during the glacial epoch in No. America

yar·mul·ke *or* **yar·mel·ke** \ˈyärməlkə, -ȧm-\ *n* -S [Yiddish, fr. Ukrainian & Pol *jarmułka* small hat, skullcap, prob. fr. Turk *yağmurluk* raincoat, fr. *yağmur* rain] **:** a skullcap worn esp. by Orthodox and Conservative Jewish males in the synagogue, the house, and study halls

¹yarn \ˈyärn, ˈyȧn\ *n* -S *often attrib* [ME *yarn, yern*, fr. OE *gearn*; akin to OHG *garn* yarn, ON *görn* gut, Gk *chordē* string, L *haru*spex soothsayer, diviner basing his predictions on inspection of animal entrails, *hernia* rupture, Lith *žarna* intestine, Skt *hirā* vein] **1 a :** a continuous strand often of two or more plies that is composed of carded or combed fibers twisted together by spinning, filaments laid parallel or twisted together, or a single filament, is made from natural or synthetic fibers and filaments or blends of these, and is used for the warp and weft in weaving and for knitting or other interlacings that form cloth **b :** a similar strand of metal, glass, asbestos, paper, or plastic used separately or in blends **c :** THREAD; *esp* **:** a component of a plied thread **d :** ROPE YARN 1 **2 a :** an entertaining narrative of real or fictitious adventures **:** ANECDOTE, STORY ⟨the whodunit, the western, and the space ~ continue to find readers —J.D.Adams⟩; *esp* **:** a tall tale ⟨spun into the narrative a little ~ which he had fabricated last night in bed —O.E.Rölvaag⟩ **b :** CONVERSATION, CHAT ⟨a ~ with the boys on the dock —Anthony Anable⟩ ⟨stopped to have a ~ with me —Eve Langley⟩

²yarn \"\ *vb* -ED/-ING/-S *vi* **1 :** to tell a yarn ⟨men ~ of the harbor's famous pilots —George Farwell⟩ ⟨all the personal zest of a man ~*ing* about his past —J.D.Hart⟩ **2 :** to have a conversation **:** CHAT, GOSSIP ⟨whistling about the place, ~*ing* with the fishermen at the breakwater —Vance Palmer⟩ **~** *vt* **:** to envelop or pack (as a pipe joint) with yarn

yarn–dye \ˈ=,=\ *vt* **:** to dye before weaving or knitting — distinguished from *piece-dye*

yarn·er \ˈyärnər, ˈyȧnə(r\ *n* -S **1 :** a teller of yarns or tall tales **2 :** a pipelayer who caulks joints (as with oakum or yarn)

yarning iron *n* **:** a blunt caulking iron usu. with an offset blade

yarning iron

yarn man *or* **yarn boy** *n* **:** a stock clerk for textile yarns

yarn number *n* **:** COUNT 8a

yarn over *vi* **:** to make an additional stitch in knitting or crocheting by bringing the yarn forward over the needle or hook

ya·ro·slavl \,yärəˈslävəl\ *adj, usu cap* [fr. *Yaroslavl*, U.S.S.R.] **:** of or from the city of Yaroslavl, U.S.S.R. **:** of the kind or style prevalent in Yaroslavl

yarovize *var of* JAROVIZE

yar·pha \ˈyärfə\ *n* -S [of Scand origin; akin to ON *jörfi* gravel, *jörth* earth — more at EARTH] *Scot* **:** PEAT BOG

yarr \ˈyär\ *n* -S [prob. fr. Fris *jīr*] **:** CORN SPURREY

yar·ran \ˈyarən\ *n* -S [native name in New So. Wales] **1 :** a rather small Australian acacia (*Acacia homalophylla*) that is a minor fodder tree and an important source of firewood and fence posts **2 :** a showy chiefly coastal bastard myall (*Acacia glaucescens*) with somewhat silvery foliage and fluffy spikes of flowers

yar·row \ˈya(,)rō, -rə; -rəw, -rō+V\ *n* -S [ME *yarowe, yarwe*, fr. OE *gearwe*; akin to MD *gerwe, garwe* yarrow, OHG *garwa, garawa*] **:** a plant of the genus *Achillea*; *esp* **:** a strong-scented Eurasian herb (*A. millefolium*) widely naturalized in No. America with finely dissected leaves and small white or rarely pink corymbose flowers

ya·ru·ro \yəˈrü(,)rō\ *or* **ya·ru·ra** \-rə\ *n, pl* **yaruro** *or* **yaruros** *or* **yarura** *or* **yaruras** *usu cap* **1 :** an Indian people of the state of Apure in Venezuela **2 :** a member of the Yaruro people

ya·ru·ru \-,rü\ *n* -S [native name in Guiana] **:** the wood of any of various trees of the genus *Aspidosperma* (esp. *A. excelsa*)

yash·mak *also* **yas·mak** \yäshˈmäk, ˈyash,mak\ *n* -S [Turk *yaşmak*] **:** a veil worn by Muslim women wrapped around the upper and lower parts of their faces so that only the eyes remain exposed to public view

yasht \ˈyasht, ˈyəsht\ *n* -S [Av *yashtay* adoration] **:** one of the hymns to angels or lesser divinities forming part of the Avesta

yat·a·ghan \ˈyad·ə,gan, -,gən\ *also* **at·a·ghan** \ˈad·ə-\ *n* -S [Turk *yatağan*] **:** a long knife or short saber common among Muslims made without a cross guard and usu. with a double curve to the edge and a nearly straight back

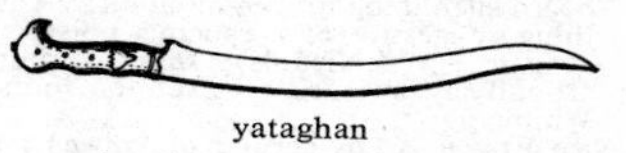

yataghan

yat·a·lite \ˈyad·ə,līt\ *n* -S [*Yatala*, Queensland, Australia + E *-ite*] **:** a pegmatoid rock composed of amphibole which is poikilitic with magnetite and sphene and may also contain minor amounts of apatite, microcline, and albite

yatch \ˈyach\ *n* -ES [by alter.] **:** YACHT

¹yate \ˈyāt\ *Scot var of* GATE

²yate \"\ *n* -S [native name in western Australia] **1 :** any of various eucalypts (as *Eucalyptus cornuta* and *E. occidentalis*) **2 :** the wood of a yate tree

Yat·ren \ˈyaˌtrən\ *trademark* — used for chiniofon

¹yat·ter \ˈyad·ə(r)\ *n* -S [prob. fr. ¹*yap* + *-ter* (as in *chatter*)] **:** idle talk **:** CHATTER ⟨among the ~ there are these sentences of sudden wisdom —*Times Lit. Supp.*⟩

²yatter \"\ *vi* -ED/-ING/-S **:** to make idle chatter **:** PRATTLE ⟨the ladies can go right on ~*ing* about . . . the lovely doilies —Relman Morin⟩

yaud \ˈyȯd, ˈyäd\ *n* -S [earlier *yald*, fr. ON *jalda* mare, of Finno-Ugric origin; akin to Mordvin *elde, äldä* mare] *chiefly Scot* **:** MARE

yauld \ˈyȯl(d), ˈyal(d)\ *adj* [origin unknown] *chiefly Scot* **:** being in vigorous health **:** ENERGETIC ⟨if I was young and ~ —John Buchan⟩

yaum·er \ˈyämər\ *Scot var of* YAMMER

yaup *var of* YAWP

yau·pon *also* **ya·pon** \ˈyü,pän, ˈyȯ,p-\ *or* **ya·pa** \-,pä,-pȧ\ *or* **you·pon** \ˈyü,pän\ *n* -S [Catawba *yopún*, dim. of *yop* tree, shrub] **:** any of several shrubs or trees of the genus *Ilex*; *esp* **:** a holly (*I. vomitoria*) of the southern U.S. with smooth elliptical leaves used as a substitute for tea and esp. formerly in the black drink of the Indians

yau·tia \yau̇ˈtēə\ *n* -S [AmerSp *yautia*, fr. Taino] **:** any of several aroids chiefly of tropical America or their starchy edible tubers that are cooked and eaten like yams or potatoes: as **a :** a plant of the genus *Xanthosoma* (esp. *X. sagittifolium*) — called also *spoonflower* **b :** TARO

ya·va·pai \,yävəˈpī\ *n, pl* **yavapai** *or* **yavapais** *usu cap* **1 a :** an Indian people of central Arizona **b :** a member of such people **2 :** a Yuman language of the Yavapai people

¹yaw \ˈyȯ\ *n* -S [origin unknown] **1 :** an angular displacement from a straight line or course **:** DEVIATION: as **a :** a movement of a ship by which it temporarily swerves off course **:** SHEER **b :** angular motion about the normal axis of an airplane ⟨checking the plane's characteristics in roll, pitch and ~ —*Boeing Mag.*⟩ **c** (1) **:** the angle formed by the longitudinal axis of a bullet or missile and the tangent to its trajectory (2) **:** the wobble of a bullet or missile rotating in flight **2 :** an erratic sideward motion **:** LURCH ⟨gave a beery ~ in the saddle —R.L.Stevenson⟩

²yaw \"\ *vb* -ED/-ING/-S *vi* **1 a :** to deviate erratically from a course ⟨vessels ~ in following seas when . . . more or less out of steering control —W.P.Moore⟩ ⟨suddenly the rocket ship ~*s* hard left —Arthur Murray⟩ ⟨fighting the wheel as the jeep ~*ed* from side to side —Frank Schreider⟩ **b :** to veer away from the normal axis ⟨for an instant the muzzle ~*ed* up at the moon —Vincent McHugh⟩ **2 :** to become deflected **:** SWERVE ⟨his mind kept ~*ing* drunkenly —Norman Mailer⟩ **~** *vt* **:** to cause to yaw ⟨twisted us, and ~*ed* us until the helmsman's life was a burden to him —*Outing*⟩

³yaw \"\ *vb* -ED/-ING/-S [prob. alter. of ¹*yawn*] **:** GAPE, YAWN

⁴yaw \"\ *n* -S [back-formation fr. *yaws*] **:** one of the lesions characteristic of yaws — see MOTHER YAW

ya·wa·ta \yəˈwäd·ə\ *adj, usu cap* [fr. *Yawata*, Japan] **:** of or from the city of Yawata, Japan **:** of the kind or style prevalent in Yawata

yawing moment *n* [*yawing* fr. pres. part. of ²*yaw*] **:** a moment that tends to rotate an airplane about its vertical axis ⟨*yawing moment* is positive when its tends to turn the plane to the right and negative when it turns the plane to the left⟩

¹yawl \ˈyȯl\ *vb* -ED/-ING/-S [ME *yaulen, yallen*, prob. of imit. origin] *dial Brit* **:** HOWL, SCREAM

²yawl \"\ *n* -s [LG *jolle, jölle, jelle*] **1 a :** a ship's small boat usu. rowed by four or six oars and often schooner-rigged : JOLLY BOAT **b :** a light fishing boat with stem and stern alike usu. carrying one, two, or three lugsails **2 :** a fore-and-aft rigged sailboat with a mainmast stepped a little farther forward than in a sloop and carrying a mainsail and one or more jibs and with a small mizzenmast far aft usu. placed abaft the rudderpost — compare KETCH

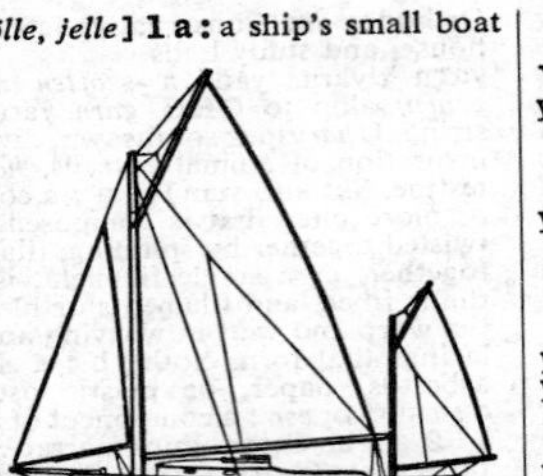
yawl 2

yawmeter \'ˌ=,==\ *n* [¹*yaw* + *-meter*] **:** an instrument for measuring the angle of yaw of an airplane **:** a sideslip indicator

¹yawn \'yȯn, 'yän\ *vb* -ED/-ING/-S [ME *yanen, yanien,* alter. (influenced by *ganen* to gape, yawn, fr. OE *gānian*) of *yenen,* *yonen, yeonien,* fr. OE *ginian, geonian;* akin to OE *gīnan* to yawn, OHG *ginēn, geinōn,* ON *gīna,* L *hiare,* Gk *chainein,* OSlav *zijati*] *vi* **1 a :** to gape cavernously **:** present a wide gulf or breach ⟨this ~*ing* fissure may plunge 50 feet or more —G.W.Long⟩ ⟨the vast gap that ~*ed* between the gentleman officer and the common seaman —Mary A. Hamilton⟩ **b :** to open up ⟨stood staring at the floor, as if gazing into a pit which had ~*ed* suddenly before his eyes —Marcia Davenport⟩ **2 a :** to take a deep breath with the jaws widespread usu. as an involuntary reaction to fatigue or boredom ⟨close the book, ~, and go to bed⟩ ⟨both hens and turkeys ~, especially at roosting time —W.P.Blount⟩ **b** *archaic* **:** to stare openmouthed (as in awe or terror) ⟨methinks it should be now a great eclipse . . . and that the affrighted globe should ~ at alteration —Shak.⟩ ~ *vt* **1** *archaic* **a :** to cause to open ⟨stood beside the murderer's bed, and ~*ed* her ghastly wound —Robert Southey⟩ **b :** to make or proffer by opening **2 a :** to utter with a yawn ⟨~ a reply⟩ **b :** to accomplish with or impel by yawns ⟨~*ed* my way through . . . French —Malcolm Cowley⟩ ⟨have long been laughed or ~*ed* out of court —A.L.Guérard⟩

²yawn \"\ *n* -s **1 :** an unfilled opening **:** GAP, CAVITY ⟨struck lightly and . . . lay still, staring up at an oblong ~ that closed with a clattering vibration of loose planks —William Faulkner⟩ ⟨leaning . . . over the ~ of a grave to scatter his handful of earth —Elizabeth Bowen⟩ **2 a :** a deep usu. involuntary intake of breath through the wide open mouth ⟨a dull speech greeted with ~*s*⟩ ⟨the telltale ~ of the addict who needs a shot —*Time*⟩ **b :** DULLNESS, TEDIUM ⟨their zeal was quickly blunted by the ~ of habit around them —Bruce Marshall⟩

yawn·er \-nə(r)\ *n* -s **:** one that yawns

yawn·ful \'ˌ=fəl\ *adj* **:** inspiring yawns ⟨a ~ book⟩ — **yawn·ful·ly** \-fəlē\ *adv*

yawning *adj* [ME *yaning,* fr. pres. part. of *yanen* to yawn] **1 :** wide open **:** CAVERNOUS, GAPING ⟨a ~ hole⟩ **2 :** showing fatigue or boredom by yawns ⟨a ~ congregation⟩ — **yawn·ing·ly** *adv*

yawny \-nē\ *adj* -ER/-EST **:** full of or inspiring yawns **:** SOPORIFIC ⟨a ~ audience⟩ ⟨a ~ lecture⟩

¹yawp *or* **yaup** \'yȯp\ *vi* -ED/-ING/-S [ME *yolpen,* prob. fr. past part. of *yelpen* to boast, call out, yelp — more at YELP] **1 a :** to make a raucous noise **:** BAWL, SQUAWK ⟨~*ed* at the top of her lungs —Maritta Wolff⟩ ⟨a foghorn howled once, twice, and ~*ed* into silence again —Leslie Waller⟩ **b :** to raise a clamor **:** COMPLAIN, YAMMER ⟨a man must have . . . the right to quit his job, and the right to ~ —J.R.Chamberlain⟩ ⟨the doctor ~*ed* about economics —Idwal Jones⟩ **2** [alter. of *gaup*] *dial* **:** GAPE, STARE — **yawp·er** \-pə(r)\ *n* -s

²yawp *also* **yaup** \"\ *n* -s **1 :** a raucous noise **:** SQUAWK, YELL ⟨broke into barbaric ~*s* suggesting colicky infants —*Duncan Aikman*⟩ **2 :** TALK; *esp* **:** foolish complaining talk ⟨never heard such dang-fool ~ in my life —C.T.Jackson⟩ **3 :** something suggestive of a raucous noise ⟨the existentialist ~ of despair —W.I.Nichols⟩; *specif* **:** rough vigorous language ⟨sound my barbaric ~ over the roofs of the world —Walt Whitman⟩

yawping *n* -s [fr. gerund of ¹*yawp*] **:** a strident or prattling utterance ⟨some of his ~*s* are directed against his employees —Charles Lee⟩ ⟨moldy characters and philosophical ~*s* about life —*Time*⟩

yawroot \'ˌ=,=\ *n* [⁴*yaw* + *root;* prob. fr. the belief that it cures yaws] **:** QUEEN'S-DELIGHT

¹yaws *pl of* YAW, *pres 3d sing of* YAW

²yaws \'yȯz\ *n pl but sing or pl in constr* [of Cariban origin; akin to Calinogo *Yáya* the disease] **:** an infectious contagious but not venereal tropical disease that is caused by a spirochete (*Treponema pertenue*) which cannot be distinguished morphologically from the syphilis spirochete (*T. pallidum*) and that is characterized by a primary ulcerating lesion on the skin followed by a secondary stage in which ulcers develop all over the body and by a third stage in which the bones are involved — called also *frambesia;* compare BEJEL

yaws fly *n* **:** a chloropid fly that transmits yaws

yawshrub \'ˌ=,=\ *n* [⁴*yaw* + *shrub*] **:** QUEEN'S-DELIGHT

yawweed \'ˌ=,=\ *n* [⁴*yaw* + *weed*] **:** a tropical American shrub (*Morinda royoc*) formerly considered a remedy for yaws with small white odorous flowers

yaw yin \'yȯ'yin\ *also* **yeh jen** \'ye'yən\ *n, pl* **yaw yin** *or* **yaw yins** *usu cap both Ys&J* [Chin (Pek) *yeh³-jen²,* lit., savage people] **:** CHINGPAW

yax·che \(')yäsh¦chä\ *n* -s [AmerSp *yaxché,* fr. Maya *yaxche, yaaxche,* lit., green tree] **:** SILK-COTTON TREE

y-axis \'ˌ=,==\ *n* **1 :** the axis of ordinates in a plane Cartesian coordinate system **2 :** one of the three axes in a three-dimensional rectangular coordinate system

ya·ya \yä'yä\ *n* -s [AmerSp, of Cariban origin] **:** any of several tropical American trees: as **a :** a gum-yielding tree (*Protium panamense*) of Panama — called also *copa* **b :** LANCEWOOD 2 **c :** CHAPARRO 3

yazidi *usu cap, var of* YEZIDI

yazoo \'ya,zü, 'yä,-\ *n, pl* **yazoo** *or* **yazoos** *usu cap* **1 :** a Tunican people of the lower Yazoo river valley, west central Mississippi **2 :** a member of the Yazoo people

YB *abbr* yearbook

Yb *symbol* ytterbium

y box *n, cap Y* **:** a box containing three wires of equal resistance joined to a common point and used in connection with a three-phase electrical system to furnish the central point

YC *abbr* yacht club

y chromosome *n, usu cap Y* **:** a sex chromosome ordinarily occurring only in the male zygote and cells and formerly supposed to carry factors for maleness that are now usu. thought to exist in autosomes — compare X CHROMOSOME

yclept *or* **ycleped** [ME (past part. of *yclepen* to call, name), fr. OE *geclipod,* past part. of *geclipian* to call, name, fr. *ge-,* perfective, associative, and collective prefix (akin to OHG *gi-,* perfective, associative, and collective prefix) + *clipian* to speak, cry out, call — more at CO-, CLEPE] *past part of* CLEPE

y connection *n, cap Y* **1 :** STAR CONNECTION **2 :** SIAMESE 4

y-coordinate \'=ˌ=(=)=\ *n* **1 :** the ordinate in a plane Cartesian coordinate system **2 :** one of the three coordinates in a three-dimensional rectangular coordinate system

y current *n, usu cap Y* **:** the current through one branch of the star arrangement of a three-phase circuit

yd *abbr* yard

yday *abbr* yesterday

ydg *abbr* yarding

¹ye \(')yē, -yi, *in a few phrases in which it is preserved* ̱ē *or* i\ *pron* [ME *ye, yhe,* fr. OE *gē* (suppletive 2d pers. nom. pl. of *thū, thu* thou) — more at YOU, THOU] **:** ¹YOU 1a — used from the earliest times to the late 13th century only as a plural pronoun of the second person in the nominative case including direct address and still surviving archaically and in many dialects in this use alongside of other more recently originated uses ⟨that ~ may be the children of your Father which is in heaven —Mt 5:45 (AV)⟩ ⟨waft, ~ winds, His story —Reginald Heber⟩ ⟨avast, ~ rogues —Frank Yerby⟩; sometimes used without archaic or dialectal flavor in mock invocations ⟨~ gods and little fishes⟩; used from the late 13th century also as a singular pronoun of the second person in the nominative case including direct address, at first only as the appropriate form of address to a person of high social status or to a person not well known to the speaker but later without this limitation except in a few English dialects, and still surviving archaically and in many dialects in this use ⟨My Lord of Gloucester, now ~ grow too hot —Shak.⟩ ⟨sweet mother, do ~ love the child —Alfred Tennyson⟩ ⟨d' ye stand there, knave, and see your master robbed —Charles Reade⟩; used from the late 14th century also as a singular or plural pronoun of the second person in contexts where the objective case form of an inflected pronoun is the one to be expected and still surviving archaically and in many dialects in this use ⟨vain pomp and glory of this world, I hate ~ —Shak.⟩ ⟨I come, . . ., strange news to tell ~ —John Dryden⟩; compare ¹THEE, ¹THOU

²ye \ ̱yē, yi, *or like* ¹THE\ *definite article* [alter. of OE *þē* the; fr. the fact that in some medieval manuscripts the runic letter *þ* (*th*) became indistinguishable from the Roman letter *y* and as the runic letter grew obsolete printers often used the *y* to replace it] *archaic* **:** THE — often used in business names to suggest an earlier time ⟨*Ye Olde Gifte Shoppe*⟩

YE *abbr, often not cap* yellow edges

¹yea \'yā\ *adv* [ME *ye, ya,* fr. OE *gēa, gē;* akin to OHG & ON *jā* yes, Goth *ja, jai*] **1 :** YES — formerly used in answer to a question not involving a negative but now superseded by *yes* except in oral voting **2 :** more than this **:** not only so but — used to mark addition or substitution of a more explicit or emphatic phrase and thus interchangeable with *nay* ⟨I therein do rejoice, ~, and will rejoice —Phil 1:18 (AV)⟩

²yea \"\ *n* -s [ME *ye, ya,* fr. *ye, ya,* adv.] **1 a :** AFFIRMATION, ASSENT ⟨his ~ meant more than the oath of most men⟩ **b —** used interjectionally (as in a college cheer) to express encouragement or gratification ⟨~, team⟩ **2 a :** an affirmative vote **b :** a person casting a yea vote ⟨stood regularly with the ~*s* in promoting the welfare state⟩

yeah *any of the vowel-final pronunciations at* ¹YES\ *adv* [by alter.] **:** YES

yean \'yēn\ *vb* -ED/-ING/-S [ME *yenen,* fr. (assumed) OE *geēanian,* fr. OE *ge-* (perfective & collective prefix) + *ēanian* to yean; akin to L *agnus* lamb, Gk *amnos,* OIr *ūan,* OSlav *agne*] **:** to bring forth young (as a sheep or a goat) **:** LAMB

yean·ling \-liŋ, -lēŋ\ *n* -s *often attrib* [*yean* + *-ling*] **1 :** LAMB ⟨a ~ lamb⟩ **2 :** KID

year \'yi(ə)r, 'yiə\ *n* -s [ME *yeer, yere,* fr. OE *gēar;* akin to OHG *jār* year, ON *ār,* Goth *jer,* Gk *hōros* year, *hōra* season of the year, time of day, hour, Av *yārə* year, L *ire* to go — more at ISSUE] **1 a :** the period of about 365¼ solar days required for one revolution of the earth around the sun and generally indicated by the return of the sun to the same part of the sky or by the recurrence of the seasons **b :** the time required for the apparent sun to return to an arbitrary fixed or moving reference point in the sky (as the March equinox for the tropical year or a point among the stars for the sidereal year) **c :** the time in which any planet completes a revolution about the sun ⟨the ~ of Jupiter⟩ ⟨the ~ of Saturn⟩ **2 a :** a cycle in the Gregorian calendar having 365 or 366 days divided into 12 months beginning with January and ending with December — compare LEAP YEAR **b :** a major cycle of days in a calendar usu. having some correspondence with the solar or the lunar year or with both **c :** a period of time equal to one year of the Gregorian calendar but beginning at a different time ⟨within a ~⟩ ⟨a ~ from today⟩ — see FISCAL YEAR **3 :** ACADEMIC YEAR **4 a :** a calendar year that belongs to a particular era or system of reckoning or bears a specified number in the sequence of the years of such an era ⟨died in the ~ of Our Lord 1900⟩ ⟨the time was the ~ of the hegira 300⟩ — compare ANNO DOMINI, ANNO LUCIS **b :** a numbered calendar year ⟨omitted to add the ~ when he dated the letter⟩ **5 a :** 12 months of punishment or imprisonment ⟨the judge gave him 15 ~*s*⟩ **b :** a remission of temporal or purgatorial punishment for sin to an extent equivalent to one year of canonical penance in the Roman Catholic Church — compare INDULGENCE 1 **6 years** *pl* **:** a time or era marked in some special way **:** a period taken as a unit notable for a particular characteristic ⟨~*s* of plenty⟩ **7 a :** 12 months that constitute a measure of age or duration ⟨her 21st ~⟩ ⟨a man of 80 ~*s*⟩ — often used in combination ⟨a *year*-old child⟩ ⟨a 50-*year* record⟩ **b years** *pl* **:** AGE ⟨a man in ~*s* but a child in understanding⟩ **c years** *pl* **:** OLD AGE ⟨he was slipping into ~*s* apace —Robert Browning⟩ **8 :** the annual cycle of the seasons in which there is a recurrent period of the growth, ripening, and decay of vegetation **9 :** any of various sometimes vaguely delimited periods of time longer than a calendar year ⟨the international geophysical ~ was fixed at 18 months⟩ — see GREAT YEAR **10 :** CLASS 2e ⟨he was in my ~ at college⟩

ye·a·ra \yä'ärə\ *n* -s [origin unknown] **:** POISON OAK b

year and a day *n* [ME *yere and a day*] **:** the time allowed in various legal limitations of time for an act or an event to take place so that there shall certainly be an interim of a full year from and including the day an event happens when this period is computed after an event

year-around *var of* YEAR-ROUND

year-bearer \'ˌ=,==\ *n* **1 :** one of four day names in the Maya and Aztec calendars that name a year **2 :** one of the 52 names of days that designate a year in a Maya and Aztec calendar round

yearbook \'ˌ=,=\ *n* **:** a book published yearly as a report or summary of the statistics or facts of a year and intended as a reference book **:** a school or college class album **:** ANNUAL ⟨~*s* giving . . . information about learned societies —H.B. Van Hoesen & F.K.Walter⟩ ⟨the most common publications in the secondary school are . . . the newspaper, the magazine, and the ~ —W.T.Gruhn⟩ ⟨fine pictorial ~*s* on furniture and design —Martin James⟩

year class *n* **:** the group of young of one kind of animal produced during one year — used chiefly of fishes

year clock *n* **:** a clock running for a year on a single winding; *esp* **:** ANNIVERSARY CLOCK

¹year-end \'ˌ=ˌ=\ *n* **:** the end of the calendar year

²year-end \"\ *adj* **:** made at the year-end ⟨*year-end* report⟩ **:** occurring or existing at the year-end ⟨*year-end* upsurge of prices⟩ ⟨*year-end* inventory⟩

¹year·ling \'yi(ə)rliŋ, 'yiəl-,'yərl-,'yōl-, -lēŋ, -lən\ *n* -s [ME *yerling,* fr. *yere* year + *-ling*] **1 a :** one (as a child or plant) that is a year old; *esp* **:** an animal one year old or in the second year of its age — used chiefly of livestock **b :** a racehorse between January 1st of the year after the year in which it was foaled and the next January 1st ranging in actual age from nearly newborn to nearly two years of age **2 :** a member of the next to the lowest class in a military academy (as West Point)

²yearling \"\ *adj* **:** a year old **:** having passed a first anniversary but not a second

yearlong \'ˌ=ˌ=\ *adj (or adv)* **:** lasting through a year

¹year·ly \'yi(ə)rlē, -iəlē, -li\ *adj* [ME *yeerly, yerely,* fr. OE *gēarlic,* fr. *gēar* year + *-lic* -ly] **:** reckoned by the year **:** occurring, appearing, or being made, done, or acted upon every year or once a year **:** ANNUAL

²yearly \"\ *adv* [ME *yerly, yerely,* fr. OE *gēarlice,* fr. *gēar* year + *-lice* -ly (adv. suffix)] **:** every year **:** once a year **:** from year to year **:** ANNUALLY ⟨blessings ~ bestowed⟩ ⟨~ will I do this rite —Shak.⟩

yearly meeting *n, usu cap Y&M* **1 :** an organizational unit of the Society of Friends composed of many Quarterly Meetings that is the most comprehensive Quaker administrative group **2 :** a session of a Yearly Meeting

¹yearn \'yərn, 'yən, 'yəin\ *vb* -ED/-ING/-S [ME *yernen,* fr. OE *giernan, geornan;* akin to OE *georn* desirous, eager, OHG *gern* eager, willing, *gerōn* to desire, ON *gjarn* eager, willing, *girna* to desire, Goth *-gairns* desirous, *gairnei* wish, L *horiri, hortari* to urge, incite, encourage, cheer, Gk *chairein* to rejoice, enjoy, Skt *haryati* he likes, yearns for] *vi* **1 :** to experience a strong desire or craving ⟨her heart ~*ed* for one of the beautifully designed timepieces —David Walden⟩ ⟨young men who ~*ed* to succeed at letters —John Mason Brown⟩ ⟨~*ed* after the social and economic setup of the 19th century —R.G. Woolbert⟩ **2 :** to feel tenderness, compassion, or love **:** become moved or drawn emotionally ⟨~*ed* over her with a father's tenderness and a mother's infinite self-giving⟩ **3 :** to express longing by tone of voice or by that of a musical instrument ⟨his talk ~*ed* after something elusive⟩ ⟨the organ ~*ed* in the half light⟩ ~ *vt* **1** *obs* **:** to move to pity, mourning, or compassion **:** GRIEVE **2 :** to voice in a longing manner **:** speak or utter so as to express craving or desire ⟨~*ed* out the tender, vivid lyric of an ageless desire⟩ **syn** see LONG

²yearn \"\ *n* -s **:** an eager desire **:** LONGING, YEARNING

³yearn \"\ *vb* -ED/-ING/-S [ME *yernen,* prob. fr. OE *iernan* to run, flow, coagulate — more at RUN] *chiefly Scot* **:** COAGULATE, CURDLE

yearn·er \'yərnər; 'yənə(r, 'yəin-\ *n* -s **:** one that yearns ⟨~*s* for an absolute government —Russell Lord⟩

yearn·ful \-fəl\ *adj* [ME *yeornful* eager, anxious, fr. OE *geornful,* fr. *georn* desirous, eager + *-ful*] **:** full of yearning **:** MOURNFUL

¹yearning *n* -s [ME *yerning,* fr. OE *geornung,* fr. *geornan* to yearn + *-ung* -ing] **:** the act of one that yearns **:** eager or anxious longing **:** tender compassion ⟨man's infinite ~ to know the truth about himself —L.C.Eiseley⟩ ⟨the amorous ~*s* of lovers for the unattainable —Harrison Smith⟩

²yearn·ing \'yērniŋ, -nən\ *n* -s [ME *yerning,* fr. gerund of *yernen* to curdle] *chiefly Scot* **:** RENNET

yearn·ing·ly *adv* **:** in a yearning manner

year of confusion : the year 46 B.C. when the Julian calendar was introduced 708 years from the founding of Rome

year of grace : a year of the Christian era ⟨down to the present *year of grace*⟩ ⟨the *year of grace* 1955⟩

year-round \'ˌ=ˌ=\ *or* **year-around** \'ˌ=ˌ==\ *adj* **:** effective, employed, or operating for the full year **:** not seasonal ⟨a *year-round* children's theater —*Newsweek*⟩ ⟨surf-bathing, boating, golf, and tennis are *year-around* enjoyments —*Fortune*⟩

year-round·er \'ˌ=ˌ=də(r)\ *n* **:** someone or something whose residence, occupation, or use is the same at all seasons

years *pl of* YEAR

year's mind *n* [ME *yeris minde,* fr. OE *gēargemynd,* fr. *gēar* year + *gemynd* memory, commemoration, mind — more at YEAR, MIND] **:** a Roman Catholic requiem mass for a deceased person held on or near the anniversary of death or burial — compare MONTH'S MIND

year's purchase *n* **:** ²PURCHASE 2b(1)

yeas *pl of* YEA

yea-sayer \'ˌ=ˌ=(=)\ *n* **1 :** one whose attitude is that of confident affirmation ⟨he is a *yea-sayer* who sees all of life's evil, but declares that man is worthy of his name only when he joyously accepts all of life's risks —B.R.Redman⟩ **2 :** YES-MAN

yea-saying \'ˌ=ˌ==\ *adj* **:** AFFIRMATIVE, POSITIVE ⟨a *yea-saying* culture, noble, proud, and free —*Saturday Rev.*⟩

¹yeast \'yēst, *chiefly dial* 'ēst\ *n* -s [ME *yest,* fr. OE *gist, giest;* akin to ON *jastr* yeast, MHG *jest* foam, OHG *jesan* to ferment, Gk *zestos* boiled, *zein* to boil, seethe, Skt *yasyati* it seethes] **1 a :** a usu. creamy or yellowish surface froth or sediment that occurs esp. in saccharine liquids (as fruit juices or malt worts) in which it promotes alcoholic fermentation, that consists of a suspension of cells of a fungus of the family Saccharomycetaceae, and that is used esp. in the making of alcoholic liquors and as a leaven in baking — see BOTTOM YEAST, TOP YEAST, ZYMASE **b :** a commercial product containing yeast plants packaged either as moist cakes or dry cakes or granules and used esp. as a leaven in baking **c** (1) **:** a minute fungus (esp. *Saccharomyces cerevisiae*) that is present and functionally active in yeast and usu. has little or no mycelium but reproduces by budding (2) **:** any of various similar fungi esp. of the orders Endomycetales and Moniliales **2 :** something resembling the froth of yeast fermentation (as the foam or spume of waves) ⟨they melt into thy ~ of waves —Lord Byron⟩ **3 :** something that causes ferment or activity, creates a lift or drive, or adds vitality ⟨education is . . . the great expression of democratic ~ at work —B.G.Gallagher⟩ ⟨were all seething with the ~ of revolt —J.F.Dobie⟩ ⟨the living ~ of conscience —H.M.Robinson⟩ ⟨had taken the ~ out of me —Hugo Johanson⟩

²yeast \"\ *vb* -ED/-ING/-S *vi* **:** FERMENT, FROTH ~ *vt* **:** to impregnate with yeast

yeast cake *n* **:** a cake of compressed yeast

yeast·i·ly \-tələ̄, -li\ *adv* **:** in a yeasty manner

yeast·i·ness \-tēnəs, -tin-\ *n* -ES **:** the quality or state of being yeasty

yeastlike \'ˌ=,=\ *adj* **:** resembling yeast

yeast nucleic acid *n* **:** RIBONUCLEIC ACID

yeast plant *or* **yeast cell** *n* **:** an individual plant of a yeast typically consisting of a primary cell bearing one or more buds

yeast spot *n* **:** a disease of lima bean, cowpea, and related plants caused by a yeast (*Nematospora phaseoli*) that attacks the seeds within the pods

yeasty \-tē, -ti\ *adj* -ER/-EST **1 :** of, consisting of, or resembling yeast **:** having the froth of yeast or one suggesting it ⟨a ~

YEARS OF THREE OF THE PRINCIPAL CALENDARS

CALENDAR	YEAR CHRONOLOGY	YEAR BEGINS	NUMBER OF DAYS common years	NUMBER OF DAYS leap years	LEAP YEARS
GREGORIAN	From Roman year 754, the year immediately following the birth of Christ as placed by Dionysus Exiguus in the 753d year of Rome	Ten days after the winter solstice	365	366	Every fourth year but only those centesimal years divisible by 400
JEWISH	From the Creation as fixed at 3761 B.C.	First new moon after the autumnal equinox. The postexilic year began in the spring with the month Nisan, this now being sometimes called the ecclesiastical year	353 defective 354 regular 355 perfect *or* abundant (There is no regular pattern for defective, regular, and perfect years; adjustments are made so that certain holidays will fall on proper days of the week)	383 384 385	The 3d, 6th, 8th, 11th, 14th, 17th, and 19th years of each 19-year cycle
MUSLIM	From the year of the Hegira, A.D. 622	Retrogresses through the seasons; the year 1 began on Friday, July 16	354	355	The 2d, 5th, 7th, 10th, 13th, 16th, 18th, 21st, 24th, 26th, 29th year of each 30-year cycle

froth covered the mash —C.B.Nordhoff & J.N.Hall› ‹the puddles . . . foamed with a ~ scum —Ellen Glasgow› **2 a :** turbulent with immaturity, incompleteness, or youth **:** not yet settled or formed ‹those ~ years between childhood and maturity —P.E.More› ‹when our American world was young and ~ —Catherine D. Bowen› **b** (1) **:** pregnant with future developments **:** full of the signs of things to come **:** churning with growth ‹the journalism of that ~ decade furnished the springs of modern news techniques —F.L.Mott› (2) **:** marked by deep or massive ferment **:** alive with the processes of change ‹this is a ~ field in which circumstances keep altering cases —R.M. Yoder› ‹the ~ darkness at the mind's base —Bernard DeVoto› **c :** full of vitality, initiative, or resource **:** EBULLIENT, EXUBERANT ‹the reporters were ~ Bohemians —Bruce Catton› ‹the ~ ardor of the famous old Odessa merchants —Esther & Joseph Riwkin› ‹~ and mercurial liberals —*Reporter*› **d :** marked by frothiness or triviality **:** FRIVOLOUS ‹~ chatter›

yeat·man·ite \'yātmə,nīt\ *n* -s [Pope *Yeatman* †1953 Am. mining engineer + E *-ite*] **:** a rare mineral $(Mn,Zn)_{16}Sb_2Si_4O_{29}$ consisting of a pseudo-orthorhombic oxide and silicate of manganese, zinc, and antimony

yeats·ian \'yātsēən\ *adj, usu cap* [William Butler *Yeats* †1939 Irish poet and dramatist + E *-an*] **:** of or relating to W. B. Yeats or his poetic style or influence ‹*Yeatsian* pentameters —*Times Lit. Supp.*›

yed·da \'yedə\ *or* **yed·do** \-e(,)dō\ *n* -s [origin unknown] **:** a natural unsplit straw for hats

yed·do spruce \'ye(,)dō-\ *n, usu cap Y* [fr. *Yeddo* (*Yedo*), now Tokyo, Japan] **:** an evergreen tree (*Picea jezoensis*) of eastern Asia often cultivated as an ornamental and having dark green leaves that have white bands above and are silvery white beneath — called also *Japanese spruce*

yede *vi* -ED/-ING/-S [obs. E *yede* (past & past part. of E *go*), fr. ME *yede, yeode* (past of *gon, gan* to go), fr. OE *ēode*, 3d pers. past of *gān* to go — more at ISSUE, GO] *obs* **:** GO, PROCEED

yee·la·man \'yēləmən\ *n* -s [by alter.] **:** HIELEMAN

yegg \'yeg\ *or* **yegg·man** \-mən\ *n, pl* **yeggs** *or* **yeggmen** [origin unknown] **:** SAFECRACKER, ROBBER

yeh \'ye\ *adv* [by alter.] **:** YES

yeh jen *usu cap Y&J, var of* YAW YIN

yei·bi·chai \'yābə,chī\ *n* -s *usu cap* [Navaho *ye'ibeshichai*] **1 :** a Navaho supernatural represented by a masked dancer in an initiation or curative ceremony **2 :** the ceremony performed by Yeibichai dancers

yel *abbr* yellow

yeld \'yeld\ *var of* [2]EILD

[1]**yell** \'yel\ *vb* -ED/-ING/-S [ME *yellen*, fr. OE *giellan*; akin to OHG *gellan* to yell, ON *gjalla*, OE *galan* to sing, scream] *vi* **1 a :** to utter a loud cry, scream, or shout usu. expressive of intense emotion (as of excitement, pain or fear, pleasure or joy) ‹the two boys *~ed* with fear —Pearl Buck› ‹the crowd *~ed* and shouted with delight —Sherwood Anderson› ‹the hyenas were *~ing* like demons› **b :** to make an articulate utterance with a scream or shout ‹hearing him ~ for help with what words he could muster› ‹is *~ing* across the water to ask who we are› **c :** to give a cheer usu. in unison (as at an athletic contest) ‹we *~ed* together for the teams —*Duke Univ. Alumni Register*› **2 :** to make a loud strident noise resembling or suggestive of a yell ‹the wind shouts in the sails and *~s* through the rigging› ‹the brook crashes and *~s* down the rocky pitch› ‹the locomotive *~s* in warning and thunders over the crossing› **3 :** to complain or protest with or as if with a yell ‹gives the extremists a chance to ~ —O.W.Holmes †1935› ‹let the opposition ~, we have the vote› **~** *vt* **1 :** to utter or declare with or as if with a yell **:** SHOUT ‹as the students leave they ~ "Merry Christmas" back and forth› ‹able to ~ a warning just in time› ‹the other boys ~ names at him› **2 :** to affect or bring to a specified state or condition by yelling ‹*~ed* up the dogs —Hugh Fosburgh› ‹~ the team to victory› ‹the crows are *~ing* their heads off›

[2]**yell** \"\ *n* -s [ME, fr. *yellen* to yell] **:** an act or instance of yelling: as **a :** an often involuntary scream or shout resulting from intense excitement or strong emotion ‹with *~s* of fiendish delight the savages greeted their enemy —Francis Birtles› ‹a waiting crowd . . . let out a tumultuous ~ of greeting —Carl Sandburg› ‹heard the lacerating ~ of a scared bird shrill in his ear —W.W.Gibson› **b :** a shout consisting of an articulated phrase or statement **c :** a characteristic shout or cry (as in battle) ‹the Apache ~› ‹the rebel ~› **d :** a usu. rhythmic shout or cheer consisting of a specified set of syllables or words used esp. in schools or colleges to encourage or support athletic teams **e :** a noise suggestive of or resembling a yell ‹the hoarse, strident ~ of the siren —Donn Byrne›

yell leader *n* **:** CHEERLEADER

[1]**yel·low** \'yel(,)lō, |lō\; |ləw *or* |lō + V; *dial or NewEng & Brit* + V |lər; *dial* 'yal\ (*but* 'yalə(r) *often occurs in standard speech when "high" precedes*\ *adj* -ER/-EST [ME *yelwe, yellow, yalow*, fr. OE *geolu*; akin to OHG *gelo* yellow, ON *gulr* yellow, OIr *gel* white, L *helvus* light bay, Gk *chlōros* greenish yellow, Skt *hari* yellowish, greenish; basic meaning: shimmer, glow] **1 a :** of the color yellow **:** of a color of the hue of sulfur or of a hue somewhat less red than that of gold **b :** changed to a yellow hue through age, disease (as jaundice), or discoloration **:** YELLOWED, SALLOW ‹~ parchment› ‹~ skin› **c :** having a yellow or mulatto complexion or skin ‹immigration of Orientals raised a false specter of the peril of the ~ races› ‹having had a white father, he is known as a ~ Negro› ‹the ~ girl stopped —R.P.Warren› **2** *archaic* **:** affected with envy **:** JAUNDICED, JEALOUS **3 a :** gaining or holding interest by printing or headlining sensational or scandalous items or ordinary news sensationally distorted ‹tempers might have subsided altogether had not a ~ newspaper . . . exhorted the soldiers to stand for their rights —Dixon Wecter› ‹the same technique of sensationalism that had lured new readers to the ~ journals —H.L.Smith b. 1906› ‹set his newspaper off sharply from the ~ journalism of morbid sensationalism which flowered . . . at the turn of the century —F.L.Mott› **b :** MEAN, DISHONORABLE, COWARDLY ‹the little ~ stain of treason —M.W.Straight› ‹is too ~ to stand up and fight› ‹has a pronounced ~ streak›

[2]**yellow** \"\ *vb* -ED/-ING/-S *vt* **:** to make or turn yellow **:** cause to have a yellow tinge or color ‹old clothes and papers that time and neglect have *~ed*› ‹wild daffodils were *~ing* the grassy slopes —Victoria Sackville-West› ‹the sun *~s* the meadow› **~** *vi* **:** to become or turn yellow ‹I let my tobacco ~ for about a week —Caroline Gordon› ‹the leaves ~ in the fall›

[3]**yellow** \"\ *n* -s [ME *yelow, yalow*, fr. *yelow, yalow* yellow (adj.)] **1 a :** a color whose hue resembles that of ripe lemons or sunflowers or is that of the portion of the spectrum lying between green and orange **b :** the one of the four psychologically primary hues that is evoked in the normal observer under normal conditions by radiant energy of the wavelength 580 millimicrons **c :** one of the six psychologically primary object colors — compare PRIMARY 4a **d :** one of the subtractive primaries **e :** a pigment or dye that colors yellow **2 :** something that is yellow or is chiefly distinguished by a yellow color: as **a :** a person having yellow skin ‹had engaged blacks, browns, *~s* about equally —Frances Gaither› **b :** [2]SULPHUR **c :** the yolk of an egg **d :** YELLOW SPONGE **3 yellows** *pl* **:** JAUNDICE, WEIL'S DISEASE **4 yellows** *pl* **:** any of several plants: as **a :** YELLOW LADY'S-SLIPPER **b :** CRAMBLING ROCKET **5 yellows** *pl* **:** any of several plant diseases (as of aster, celery, or peach) caused by fungi, bacteria, malnutrition, or esp. by viruses and characterized by yellowing of the foliage and stunting

yellow adder's-tongue *n* **:** DOGTOOTH VIOLET b(1)

yellow alder *n* **:** a tropical American shrubby herb (*Turnera ulmifolia*) with lanceolate oblong leaves and axillary solitary yellow flowers

yellow alert *n* **:** the preliminary stage of alert (as when hostile or unidentified aircraft are nearing a defended area); *also* **:** the signal for this — compare BLUE ALERT, RED ALERT, WHITE ALERT

yellow angelfish *or* **yellow angel** *n* **:** ANGELFISH 2

yellow ant *n* **:** an ant (as some members of the genus *Lasius*) predominantly yellow in color; *esp* **:** the widely distributed ant (*Acanthomyops flavus*) that nests chiefly in open grassland

yellow ash *n* **:** YELLOWWOOD 1a

yellow asphodel *n* **:** an asphodel (*Asphodeline lutea*) with usu. yellow flowers

yellow atrophy *n* **:** ACUTE YELLOW ATROPHY

yellow avens *n* **:** either of two herbs of the genus *Geum* (*G. strictum* and *G. macrophyllum*)

yellow azalea *n* **:** FLAME AZALEA

yellow baboon *n* **:** a long-tailed yellowish African baboon (*Papio cynocephalus*)

yellow bachelor's-button *n* **:** ORANGE MILKWORT

yellowback \'==,=\ *n* [[1]*yellow* + *back*] **1 :** GOLD CERTIFICATE **2 :** a cheap and usu. sensational novel; *esp* **:** one sold in yellow board or paper covers in the late 19th and early 20th centuries **3 :** a freshwater mussel (*Lampsilis anodontoides*) of the Mississippi valley and southeastern U. S. having a heavy shell covered with yellow periostracum and highly valued for mother-of-pearl

yellow balm *n* **:** WHORLED LOOSESTRIFE

yellow balsam *n* **1 :** JEWELWEED b **2 :** a strong-scented West Indian shrub (*Croton flavens*)

yellow-banded hussar \'==,==-\ *n* **:** an Australian snapper (*Lutjanus amabilis*) that is largely pink with a broad yellow band along each side and is an excellent table fish taken chiefly with hook and line

yellow bark *n* **1 :** CALISAYA BARK **2 :** YELLOW-BARK OAK; *also* **:** the bark of this oak

yellow-bark oak *also* **yellow-barked oak** \'==,=-\ *n* **:** a black oak (*Quercus velutina*)

yellow bartonia *n* **:** a yellow-flowered screwstem (*Bartonia virginica*) common in eastern No. America

yellow bass *n* **:** a yellow No. American freshwater bass (*Morone interrupta*) with several more or less broken black stripes or bars that is related to and resembles the much larger marine striped bass and is native to the Mississippi drainage from southern Minnesota and Wisconsin to Texas and Louisiana

yellow basswood *n* **:** a common linden (*Tilia glabra*) of No. America

yellow bat *n* **:** a showy southern African insectivorous bat (*Scotophilus nigrita*) with black wings and canary yellow underparts

yellow bear *n* **:** YELLOW WOOLLY BEAR

yellow beardtongue *n* **:** a perennial herb (*Penstemon confertus*) of the Rocky mountain region having showy yellow flowers

yellow bear's-foot *n* **:** a leafcup (*Polymnia uvedalia*)

yellow bedstraw *n* **:** a common yellow-flowered bedstraw (*Galium verum*) — called also *yellow cleavers*

yellow-bellied flycatcher \'==,=-\ *n* **:** a small flycatcher (*Empidonax flaviventris*) of eastern No. America

yellow-bellied racer *n* **:** BLUE RACER

yellow-bellied sapsucker *or* **yellow-bellied woodpecker** *n* **:** a small woodpecker (*Sphyrapicus varius*) of the eastern U.S. that feeds partly on the sap of trees

yellow-bellied terrapin *n* **:** a terrapin (*Pseudemys scripta*) of the southeastern U.S. having the carapace marked with yellow lines and the plastron yellow or brownish

yellow bells *n pl but sing or pl in constr* **:** any of several plants with bell-shaped yellow flowers: as **a :** DOGTOOTH VIOLET b(1) **b :** CALIFORNIA YELLOW BELLS **c :** YELLOW ELDER

yellowbelly \'==,==\ *n* [[1]*yellow* + *belly*] **1 a :** PUMPKINSEED 1 **b :** SQUAWFISH 1 **c :** CALLOP **d** *NewZeal* **:** any of several flatfishes (as *Ammotretis guntheri*) that are important market fish **e** *southern Africa* **:** a guasa (*Epinephelus guaza*) **2 :** YELLOW BERRY 2 **3 :** one who is yellow **:** COWARD ‹was called a ~ when he would not enlist at the beginning of the war› **4 a :** a person having a yellow skin **b** *Southwest* **:** MEXICAN — usu. used disparagingly ‹two kinds of ethics, one for us and one for the *yellowbellies* across the line —E.L.Jones›

yellow berry *n* **1 yellow berries** *pl* **:** BUCKTHORN BERRIES **2 :** a condition of mature grains of hard wheat resulting from nitrogen deficiency and marked by the occurrence of light yellow opaque soft and starchy kernels among the normally hard dark translucent red amber grains; *also* **:** one of these kernels **3** *usu* **yel·low·berry** \'==-—*see* BERRY\ **:** PERSIAN BERRY

yellow bile *n* [trans. of Gk *xanthē cholē*] **:** a humor of medieval physiology believed to be secreted by the liver and to cause irascibility — compare BLACK BILE

yellowbill \'==,=\ *n* [[1]*yellow* + *bill*] **:** SCOTER

yellow-billed cuckoo \'==,=-\ *n* **:** a common No. American cuckoo (*Coccyzus americanus*)

yellow-billed loon *n* **:** a loon (*Gavia adamsi*) found in the northern part of the northern hemisphere

yellow-billed magpie *n* **:** a magpie (*Pica nutalli*) found in California

yellow-billed tropic bird *n* **:** a tropic bird (*Phaëthon lepturus*)

yellow birch *n* **1 :** a No. American birch (*Betula lutea*) with lustrous gray or yellow thin bark **2 :** the hard strong light brown wood of the yellow birch tree used esp. for furniture and buttons

yellowbird \'==,=\ *n* **1 :** any of various American goldfinches **2 :** YELLOW WARBLER 1a

yellow blight *n* **1 :** a wilt of potatoes caused by a fungus (*Sclerotinia sclerotiorum*) **2 :** WESTERN TOMATO BLIGHT

yellow bluestem *n* **:** a tropical beardgrass (*Andropogon ischaemum*) that is adventive in parts of the U.S. and used as a pasture grass in the dry southern regions

yellow body *n* [trans. of NL *corpus luteum*] **:** CORPUS LUTEUM

yellow book *n, usu cap Y&B* [trans. of F *livre jaune*] **:** an official report of government affairs bound in yellow ‹the Hungarian government issues a *Yellow Book* in which it details its charges of treason —*Current History*›

yellow box *n* **:** a gum tree (*Eucalyptus melliodora*) of southern Australia having yellow inner bark and hard yellowish wood somewhat resembling boxwood — called also *yellow jacket*

yellow boy *n, Brit* **:** a gold coin

yellow-breasted bunting \'==,==-\ *n* **:** a bunting (*Emberiza aureola*) that is common in northern Russia and Siberia, winters in tropical Asia, and in the adult male is chestnut above with a buff stripe over the eye and a yellow breast crossed by a narrow chestnut band

yellow-breasted chat *n* **:** a large American chat (*Icteria virens*) that is greenish brown above with a bright yellow throat and breast and a white abdomen, that breeds chiefly in the eastern half of the U.S., that winters in Mexico and Central America, and that is noted for its expert mimicking of other birds

yellow bronze *n* **:** BRONZE YELLOW

yellow broom *n* **:** INDIGO BROOM

yellowbrush \'==,=\ *n* **:** a bright green shrubby plant (*Chrysothamnus viscidiflorus*) of western No. America that bears bright yellow flowers in midsummer

yellow buckeye *n* **:** SWEET BUCKEYE

yellow buckthorn *n* **:** a No. American shrub (*Rhamnus caroliniana*) having leaves yellowish on the lower surface — called also *Indian cherry*

yellow bullhead *n* **:** a yellowish dark-mottled bullhead (*Ameiurus natalis*) widely distributed in central No. America and represented by subspecies in eastern coastal streams

yellow bunting *n* **:** YELLOWHAMMER 1

yellow calla *n* **:** a golden calla (*Zantedeschia elliottiana*) that resembles the common calla and is widely cultivated for its yellow spathes

yellow cancerroot *n* **:** a leafless scaly parasitic herb (*Orobanche fasciculata*) of western No. America having solitary purplish yellow irregular flowers

yellow carabeen *n* **:** CARABEEN

yellow carmine *n* **:** DUTCH ORANGE

yellow cartilage *n* **:** ELASTIC CARTILAGE

yellow cat *or* **yellow catfish** *n* **:** any of several more or less yellow No. American catfishes; *esp* **:** FLATHEAD CATFISH

yellow catechu *or* **yellow cutch** *n* **:** GAMBIER

yellow cedar *n* **1 a :** an evergreen tree (*Chamaecyparis nootkatensis*) of the Pacific coast of No. America often cultivated for ornament; *also* **:** the hard yellow wood of this tree — called also *Alaska cedar* **b :** WESTERN CEDAR 1a **c :** ARBORVITAE 1 **2** *Austral* **:** a sumac (*Rhus rhodanthema*) that yields tannin

yellow cell *n* **:** ZOOXANTHELLA

yellow centaury *n* **1 :** YELLOWWORT **2 :** a Barnaby's thistle (*Centaurea solstitialis*)

yellow chamomile *n* **:** a Eurasian perennial herb (*Anthemis tinctoria*) naturalized in No. America with hairy divided leaves and yellow heads — called also *golden marguerite*

yellow charlock *n* **:** CHARLOCK

yellow chestnut oak *n* **:** CHINQUAPIN OAK b

yellow cinchona *n* **:** CALISAYA BARK

yellow cleavers *n pl but sing or pl in constr* **:** YELLOW BEDSTRAW

yellow clintonia *n* **:** a common woodland herb (*Clintonia borealis*) of temperate regions of No. America with yellow nodding flowers and small round blue fruit

yellow clover *n* **:** either of two hop clovers (*Trifolium aureum* and *T. procumbens*)

yellow clover aphid *n* **:** a plant louse (*Therioaphis trifolii*) that occurs in many parts of the U.S. and is esp. destructive to alfalfa in the southwestern states

yellow cobra *n* **:** CAPE COBRA

yellow cockscomb *n* **:** a rattle (*Rhinanthus crista-galli*)

yellow copperas *n* **:** COPIAPITE

yellow copper ore *n* **:** CHALCOPYRITE

yellow corydalis *n* **:** YELLOW HARLEQUIN

yellow cottonwood *n* **:** a common cottonwood (*Populus deltoides*)

yellow cress *n* **:** a cress with yellow flowers: as **a :** WINTER CRESS **b :** any of several plants (as marsh cress) of the genus *Rorippa*

yellow cross *also* **yellow cross liquid** *n* [so called fr. the symbol used by the Germans in World War I to mark the shells containing it] **:** MUSTARD GAS

yellowcrown \'==,=\ *n* [[1]*yellow* + *crown*] **:** MYRTLE WARBLER

yellow-crowned night heron \'==,=-\ *n* **:** a night heron (*Nyctanassa violacea*) that has a buffy white crown and is found in the southern U.S. and in So. America

yellow cypress *n* **1 :** YELLOW CEDAR 1a **2 :** a bald cypress (*Taxodium distichum*)

yellow daisy *n* **1 :** BLACK-EYED SUSAN **2 :** ORPIMENT 2

yellow day lily *n* **:** DAY LILY 1

yellow deal *n* **1** *Brit* **:** the wood of the Scotch pine and of a red pine (*Pinus resinosa*) **2 :** the wood of a yellow pine (*Pinus echinata*)

yellow devil *n* **:** any of several yellow-flowered hawkweeds (as *Hieracium pratense* and *H. floribundum*)

yellow dip *n* **:** the oleoresin obtained after the first year trees have been tapped for turpentine

yellow dock *n* **1 :** BITTER DOCK **2 :** CURLED DOCK

yellow dog *n* **1 :** MONGREL, CUR **2 :** a contemptible, worthless, or yellow person ‹any man who didn't stand by his friends . . . was a *yellow dog* —S.H.Adams›

yellow-dog \'==,=\ *adj* [*yellow dog*] **1 :** of or relating to a yellow dog or characteristics associated with a yellow dog ‹pursues *yellow-dog* tactics to gain his ends› **2 :** of or relating to opposition to trade unionism or a labor union ‹the Administration's *yellow-dog* injunction has reached the Supreme Court —J.L.Lewis›

yellow-dog contract *n* **:** a contract of employment in which a worker disavows membership in and agrees not to join a labor union during the period of his employment

yellow dwarf *n* **:** any of several plant diseases (as yellow dwarf of potato and onion yellow dwarf) characterized by yellowing of the foliage and stunting

yellow earth *n* **:** impure yellow ocher

yellowed *past of* YELLOW

yellow edge *n* **:** a virus disease of the strawberry characterized chiefly by a marginal chlorosis of the leaf, shortening of the leaf stalk, leaf curling, and dwarfing

yellow eel *n* **:** an eel during the period of growth which varies from about 5 to about 20 years and before it matures as a silver eel — compare ELVER

yellow elder *n* **:** a tropical American shrub or small tree (*Stenolobium stans*) of the family Bignoniaceae that has compound leaves and profuse clusters of yellow funnel-shaped flowers and in the tropics is widely planted for ornament — called also *shower of gold, yellow trumpet flower*

yellow enzyme *n* **:** any of several yellow flavoprotein respiratory enzymes widely distributed in nature: as **a :** a crystallizable enzyme obtained from yeast and constituted of a complex of riboflavin phosphate and a protein — called also *old yellow enzyme, Warburg's yellow enzyme* **b :** an enzyme obtained from yeast and constituted of a complex of flavin adenine dinucleotide and a protein — called also *new yellow enzyme*

yellower *comparative of* YELLOW

yellowest *superlative of* YELLOW

yellow-eye \'==,=\ *n* [[1]*yellow* + *eye*] **:** GOLDENSEAL

yellow-eyed grass \'==,=-\ *n* **:** a plant of the genus *Xyris*; *esp* **:** any of several such plants of the pine barrens of the southern U.S.

yellow-eyed-grass family *n* **:** XYRIDACEAE

yellow-eyed hawk *n* **:** IGNOBLE HAWK

yellow fat *or* **yellow fat disease** *n* **:** a disease of young ranched mink prob. associated with faulty diet and marked by inflammation of the fatty tissues, subcutaneous edema, and varied visceral lesions — called also *watery hide disease*

yellow fever *n* **:** an acute infectious disease that is characterized by sudden onset, prostration, fever, relatively slow pulse, albuminuria, jaundice, and tendency to hemorrhage esp. from the stomach, that is caused by a virus transmitted by a mosquito, and that occurs esp. in tropical and semitropical areas — called also *yellow jack*

yellow-fever fly *n* **:** a small fly of the genus *Sciara*

yellow-fever mosquito *n* **:** a small dark-colored mosquito (*Aëdes aegypti*) of the warmer parts of the world that is the usual agent in the transmission of yellow fever — compare ANOPHELES, CULEX

yellow fiber *n* **:** ELASTIC FIBER

yellowfin \'==,=\ *n* [[1]*yellow* + *fin*] **1 a** *Scot* **:** TROUT **b** *Brit* **:** a sea trout smolt **2 a :** YELLOWFIN TUNA **b :** YELLOWFIN CROAKER

yellowfin croaker *n* **:** a common croaker (*Umbrina roncador*) of the southern California coast that is grayish or greenish with a metallic brassy luster and is a highly esteemed shallow-water sport fish

yellowfin grouper *n* **:** a medium-sized grouper (*Mycteroperca venenosa*) of the tropical western Atlantic that is olive to grayish or sometimes bright scarlet above, mottled or spotted with red or black along the sides, and yellow or orange at the tips of the pectoral fins

yellow-finned roncador *or* **yellow-fin roncador** \'==,=-\ *n* **:** YELLOWFIN CROAKER

yellow-fin trout *or* **yellow-finned trout** *n* **:** a large and showy cutthroat trout (*Salmo macdonaldi*) that has yellow fins and is native to Twin Lakes, Colorado

yellowfin tuna *n* **:** either of two tunas (*Neothunnus argentivittatus* and *N. macropterus*) of the Atlantic and of the Pacific respectively that are smaller and finer fleshed than the bluefin

yellow fir *n* **1 :** SCOTCH PINE **2 :** DOUGLAS FIR **3 :** LOWLAND FIR

yellowfish \'==,=\ *n* **1 :** ATKA MACKEREL **2 :** CONEY 5a **3 :** YELLOWFIN GROUPER

[1]**yellow flag** *n* [[1]*yellow* + *flag* (plant)] **:** YELLOW IRIS

[2]**yellow flag** *n* [[1]*yellow* + *flag* (banner)] **:** QUARANTINE FLAG

yellow flax *n* **:** a yellow-flowered flax or similar plant; *esp* **:** an Indian shrub (*Reinwardtia indica*) having flowers usu. in axillary or terminal clusters

yellow flower *n* **:** CHARLOCK

yellow-flowered watercup \'==,==-\ *n* **:** HUNTSMAN'S-HORN

yellow foxglove *n* **1** *or* **yellow gerardia :** FALSE FOXGLOVE **2 :** a European yellow-flowered herb (*Digitalis lutea*)

yellow foxtail *n* **:** a common weedy and bristly grass (*Setaria glauca*) found in nearly all temperate countries

yellow fringed orchid *or* **yellow fringed orchis** *n* **:** a terrestrial orchid (*Habenaria ciliaris*) of eastern No. America having lanceolate leaves and showy spikes of yellow or orange fringed flowers

yellow gentian *n* **1 :** a bitterwort (*Gentiana lutea*) of southern Europe having yellow flowers — see GENTIAN 2 **2 :** a gentian (*Dasystephana flavida*) of eastern No. America with yellowish flowers **3 :** AMERICAN COLUMBO

yellow ginger *n* **:** a large yellow-flowered herb (*Hedychium flavum*) that is similar to the white ginger and occurs both wild and cultivated in Hawaii

yellow ginseng *n* **:** BLUE COHOSH

yellow goatfish *n* **:** a goatfish (*Upeneus martinicus*) — compare [2]MULLET 2

yellow goatsbeard *n* **:** a European herb (*Tragopogon pratensis*) that is naturalized as a weed in No. America and that

has keeled leaves and yellow heads of flowers that close by noon — called also *meadow salsify*
yellow gowan *n, dial Brit* **:** any of several yellow-flowered plants: as **a :** CROWFOOT 1 **b :** a marsh marigold (*Caltha palustris*) **c :** DANDELION 1
yellow granadilla *n* **:** JAMAICA HONEYSUCKLE
yellow grease *n* **:** an inedible fat obtained esp. from the parts of hogs not used in making lard, from condemned animals, or from refuse fat and used as a lubricant — compare WHITE GREASE
yellow-green alga *n* **:** an alga of the division Chrysophyta with the chlorophyll masked by brown or yellow pigment
yellow ground *n* [trans. of Afrik *geelgrond*] **:** kimberlite found in the upper portion of a pipe
yellow grouper *n* **1 :** a grouper (*Mycteroperca olfax*) of the Pacific coast of Central and So. America **2 :** YELLOWFIN GROUPER
yellow grub *n* **:** a larval trematode worm (genus *Clinostomum*) that encysts in the flesh of fishes
yellow grunt *n* **:** a yellow black-banded grunt (*Haemulon sciurus*) used as a food fish and found from Florida to the West Indies and south to Brazil
yellow guayacan *n* **:** BETHABARA
yellow gularis *n* **:** GULARIS a
yellow gum *n* **1 :** any of several Australian eucalypts (as *Eucalyptus gunnii*) **2 :** BLACK GUM 1a
yellow-haired porcupine \'⸗⸗,⸗-\ *n* **:** a somewhat yellowish American porcupine (*Erethizon epixanthum*)
yel·low·ham·mer \'⸗⸗,hamə(r)\ *n* [alter. of earlier *yelambre*, fr. (assumed) ME *yelwambre*, fr. *yelwe* yellow + (assumed) *ambre* yellowhammer, fr. OE *amore*; akin to OS *amer* yellowhammer, OHG *amaro* yellowhammer, *amaro, amari* spelt, emmer] **1 :** a common European finch (*Emberiza citrinella*) that in the male is bright yellow on the breast, neck, and sides of the head with the back yellow and brown and the top of the head and the tail quills blackish — called also *yellow bunting* **2 :** YELLOW-SHAFTED FLICKER
yellow harlequin *n* **:** a slender low-branching No. American herb (*Corydalis flavula*) with conspicuously bracted and spurred pale yellow flowers — usu. used in pl.; called also *yellow corydalis*
yellowhead \'⸗⸗,⸗\ *n* [¹*yellow* + *head*] **1 :** BUSH CANARY **2 :** YELLOW-HEADED BLACKBIRD
yellow-headed blackbird \'⸗⸗,⸗⸗-\ *n* **:** a large blackbird (*Xanthocephalus xanthocephalus*) of central western No. America that in the male is black with the head and neck orange or yellow
yellow-headed spruce sawfly *n* **:** a No. American sawfly (*Pikonema alaskensis*) that often defoliates spruce in eastern Canada and the northeastern U.S.
yellow-headed tit *n* **:** VERDIN
yellow henbane *n* **:** a ground-cherry (*Physalis viscosa*) found on seabeaches from Virginia to So. America with greenish yellow dark-centered flowers and orange or yellow fruit
yellow hercules *n, usu cap H* **:** HERCULES'-CLUB 1a
yellow honeysuckle *n* **1 :** either of two honeysuckles: **a :** a woody vine (*Lonicera dioica*) of eastern No. America with yellowish green flowers **b :** a twining or loosely climbing shrub (*L. flava*) of the southern U.S. with orange-yellow flowers **2 :** FLAME AZALEA
yellow indian grass *n, usu cap I* **:** WOOD GRASS 1
yellow indian paint *n, usu cap I* **:** GOLDENSEAL 1
yellow indian shoe *n, usu cap I* **:** a yellow lady's-slipper (*Cypripedium parviflorum*)
yellow indigo *n* **:** INDIGO BROOM
yellowing *n* -s [fr. gerund of ²*yellow*] **:** the process or result of becoming yellow; *specif* **:** a symptom of disease caused by a lack of or a reduced amount of chlorophyll in the foliage of a plant or tree
yellow iris *n* [¹*yellow*] **:** a common yellow-flowered iris (*Iris pseudacorus*) of Europe and northern Africa that is naturalized in the U.S. and often cultivated — called also *yellow flag, yellow water flag*
yel·low·ish \'yelə̇wish, -lō̇|, \|ēsh\ *adj* [ME *yelowissche*, fr. *yelow* yellow + *-issche*, *-ish* -ish] **:** somewhat yellow **:** having a tinge of yellow ⟨a ~ green⟩
yellow jack *n* **1 :** YELLOW FEVER **2 :** QUARANTINE FLAG **3 a :** a silvery and golden food fish (*Caranx bartholomaei*) of Florida and the West Indies **b :** the related blue runner
yellow jacket *n* [¹*yellow* + *jacket*] **1** *or* **yellow hornet :** any of various small yellow-marked social wasps of the family Vespidae that commonly nest in the ground — compare HORNET **2 :** any of several Australian eucalypts with yellowish bark: as **a :** YELLOW BOX **b :** a red gum (*Eucalyptus rostrata*) **3** [so called fr. the color of the capsules] *slang* **:** BARBITURATE 2

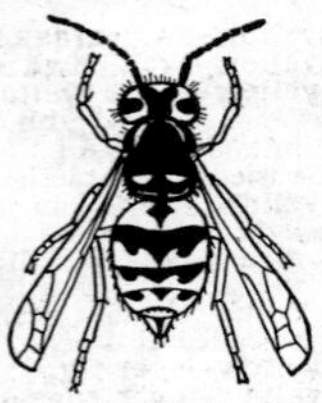

yellow jacket

yellow jessamine *also* **yellow jasmine** *n* **1 :** JASMINE 1a(2) **2 :** a twining shrub (*Gelsemium sempervirens*) having evergreen leaves and fragrant yellow flowers with a funnelform corolla — called also *Carolina jessamine*
yellowknife \'⸗⸗,⸗\ *n, pl* **yellowknife** *or* **yellowknives** *usu cap* [¹*yellow* + *knife*; fr. their use of copper implements] **1 :** an Algonquian people living east of Great Slave Lake, Canada, being closely related to the Chipewyan, and speaking the same language **2 :** a member of such people
yellow lady's-slipper *also* **yellow lady-slipper** *n* **:** a yellow-flowered orchid of the genus *Cypripedium* (as *C. calceolus*, *C. parviflorum*)
yellow lantern *n* **:** SPATTERDOCK 1
yellow late rust *n* **:** a rust of the blackberry caused by a rust fungus (*Kuehneola albida*)
yellow lead ore *n* **:** WULFENITE
yellow leaf *n* **1 :** any of several diseases of plants characterized by chlorosis of the foliage (as cherry leaf spot) **2 :** the latter years of life **:** OLD AGE ⟨my way of life is fall'n into the sere, the *yellow leaf* —Shak.⟩ ⟨fifty-three . . . the *yellow leaf* is upon me —Christopher Isherwood⟩
yellow leaf blight *n* **:** a mosaic disease of cotton
yellow leaf blotch *n* **:** a disease of alfalfa caused by a fungus (*Pyrenopeziza medicaginis*) and characterized by bright yellow or orange spots with small black dots chiefly on the undersides of the leaves
yellow leafcup *n* **:** a roughish hairy leafcup (*Polymnia uvedalia*) with yellow flowers
yellow leaf roll *n* **:** a virus disease of peaches esp. in California characterized by yellowing and upward rolling of the leaf, some scorching on the leaf margins and necrotic spotting, and early dropping of the leaves
yellow-legged goose \'⸗⸗,⸗(⸗)-\ *n* **:** WHITE-FRONTED GOOSE
yellow-legged plover *n* **:** YELLOWLEGS
yellow-leg·ger \'⸗⸗,legə(r)\ *n* [¹*yellow* + *leg* + *-er*] **:** YELLOWLEGS
yellowlegs \'⸗⸗,⸗\ *n pl but sing or pl in constr* [¹*yellow* + *legs*, pl. of *leg*] **:** either of two American shore birds that are related to the greenshank and have long yellow legs: **a :** GREATER YELLOWLEGS **b :** LESSER YELLOWLEGS
yellow lemur *n* **:** KINKAJOU
yellow lily *n* **:** MEADOW LILY
yellow linn *n* **:** a cucumber tree (*Magnolia acuminata*)
yellow locust *n* **1 :** LOCUST 3a(2) **2 :** YELLOWWOOD 1a
yellow lotus *or* **yellow nelumbo** *n* **:** AMERICAN LOTUS
yellow lupine *n* **1 :** a European yellow-flowered lupine (*Lupinus luteus*) cultivated as a forage plant **2 :** an annual herb (*Crotalaria retusa*) of tropical Asia that has yellow flowers and is cultivated as a forage crop in the tropics
yel·low·ly *adv* [¹*yellow* + *-ly*] **:** with a yellow light or color ⟨the brand-new ropes . . . glistened ~ —Adria Langley⟩
yellow mackerel *n* **:** BLUE RUNNER
yellow madder *n* **:** DUTCH PINK 2
yellow mahogany *n* **:** BRAZILIAN MAHOGANY 1
yellow mandarin *n* **:** a low pubescent No. American herb (*Disporum lanuginosum*) found in rich woods and having greenish flowers with narrow segments
yellow maple *n* **:** a variable color averaging a moderate yellowish brown that is lighter, stronger, and slightly redder than Bismarck brown and lighter, stronger, and very slightly yellower than cinnamon brown
yellow-mar·gined leaf-beetle \'⸗⸗,märjənd-\ *n* [¹*yellow* + *margin* + *-ed*] **:** a chrysomelid beetle (*Microtheca ochroloma*) that is destructive to crucifers esp. in the southeastern U.S.
yellow marsh saxifrage *n* **:** a slender perennial bog herb (*Saxifraga hirculus*) of the family Saxifragaceae that is found in alpine regions of the northern hemisphere and has a terminal solitary bright yellow red-spotted flower
yellow mealworm *n* **:** a mealworm that is the larva of a beetle (*Tenebrio molitor*)
yellow melilot *n* **:** YELLOW SWEET CLOVER 1
yellow metal *n* **:** MUNTZ METAL
yellow milkweed *n* **:** BUTTERFLY WEED 1
yellow milkwort *n* **:** ORANGE MILKWORT
yellow moccasin flower *or* **yellow noah's-ark** *n, usu cap N* **:** a yellow lady's-slipper (*Cypripedium parviflorum*)
yellow mombin *n* **:** a hog plum (*Spondias mombin*) with yellowish white flowers and yellow fruit
yellow mountain saxifrage *n* **:** a tufted perennial herb (*Saxifraga aizoides*) of alpine regions of the northern hemisphere having ciliate leaves and yellow sometimes orange-spotted corymbose flowers
yellow mustard *n* **:** CHARLOCK
yellow myrtle *n* **1 :** CALIFORNIA LAUREL **2 :** MONEYWORT
yellow-necked caterpillar \'⸗⸗,⸗-\ *n* **:** a predominantly black gregarious caterpillar with a yellow thorax, yellow longitudinal stripes, and a covering of white hairs down each side that is the larva of a handmaid moth (*Datana ministra*) and that is often a destructive defoliator of fruit and other deciduous trees and shrubs
yel·low·ness *n* -ES [ME *yelownes*, fr. *yelow* yellow + *-nes* -ness] **:** the quality or state of being yellow
yellow nightshade *n* **:** BUFFALO BUR
yellow-nosed albatross \'⸗⸗,⸗-\ *n* **:** an albatross (*Diomedea chlororhynchos*) of southern seas that is distinguished by the narrower black edging of the underwings and by a bright yellow ridge on the upper beak
yellow nut grass *n* **:** CHUFA
yellow oak *n* **1 :** a black oak (*Quercus velutina*) **2 :** CHINQUAPIN OAK a
yellow oat grass *also* **yellow oats** *n* **:** a Eurasian grass (*Trisetum flavescens*) with yellow panicles that is sometimes cultivated
yellow ocher *n* [ME *yelu okyr*, fr. *yelow, yelu* yellow + *oker, okyr* ocher] **1 :** a mixture of limonite usu. with clay and silica used as a pigment **2 :** a moderate orange yellow that is yellower and darker than deep chrome yellow — called also *Chinese yellow, English ocher, French ocher, imperial yellow, Italian lake, mineral yellow, ocher yellow, Oxford chrome, Oxford ocher, oxide yellow, permanent yellow, quercitron lake, yellow sienna*
yellow oleander *n* **:** a West Indian shrub or small tree (*Thevetia nereifolia*) with showy clusters of yellow flowers and leaves resembling those of the oleander
yellow owl *n* **:** BARN OWL
yellow oxeye *n* **1 :** CORN MARIGOLD **2 :** BLACK-EYED SUSAN
yellow oxide *also* **yellow oxide of iron** *n* **:** a synthetic pigment consisting essentially of hydrated ferric oxide and similar in color to yellow ocher but more intense
yellow palm warbler *n* **:** a chiefly terrestrial warbler (*Dendroica palmarum hypochrysea*) of eastern No. America that is largely grayish brown above with bright yellow underparts
yellow pareira *also* **yellow pareira brava** *n* **:** a pareira that is the root of a tropical American woody vine (*Abuta amara*), is bright yellow in color and extremely bitter in flavor, and contains some of the same alkaloids as the true pareira — compare WHITE PAREIRA
yellow pa·ril·la \-pə'rilə\ *n* [¹*yellow* + sarsa*parilla*] **:** CANADA MOONSEED
yellow pea *n* **:** FALSE LUPINE
yellow perch *n* **:** a common No. American perch (*Perca flavescens*) that is yellowish with dark green bands and is an excellent food and sport fish
yellow peril *n, often cap Y&P* **1 :** a danger to Western civilization held to arise from expansion of the power and influence of Oriental peoples (as the Chinese and Japanese) **2 :** a threat to Western living standards developed through the incursion into Western countries of Oriental laborers willing to work for very low wages and under inferior working conditions
yellow phlox *n* **:** WESTERN WALLFLOWER 1
yellow phosphorus *n* **:** WHITE PHOSPHORUS
yellow pickerel *or* **yellow pike** *or* **yellow pikeperch** *n* **:** WALLEYE 4
yellow pickle *n* **:** a nutritional disturbance of cucumbers causing premature ripening
yellow pimpernel *n* **1 :** a perennial herb (*Taenidia integerrima*) of the family Umbelliferae of eastern No. America with ternate leaves and compound umbels of yellow flowers **2 :** WOOD PIMPERNEL
yellow pine *n* **1 :** any of various No. American pines: as **a :** a shortleaf pine (*Pinus echinata*) **b :** LONGLEAF PINE **c :** TABLE-MOUNTAIN PINE **d :** a pitch pine (*Pinus rigida*) **e :** LOBLOLLY PINE 1 **f :** PONDEROSA PINE **g :** ARIZONA PINE **2 :** the wood of a yellow pine
yellow plover *n* **:** GOLDEN PLOVER
yellow plum *n* **:** an often shrubby and somewhat spiny wild plum (*Prunus americana*) with red to yellow fruit — compare AMERICAN PLUM
yellow podzolic soil *or* **yellow soil** *n* **:** any of a group of zonal soils developed under coniferous or mixed forests in warm-temperate moist climates and composed of thin organic and organic-mineral layers resting on a grayish yellow leached layer that in turn rests on a yellow layer
yellow poinciana *n* **:** PRIDE OF BARBADOS
yellow poll *n* **1 :** WIDGEON 1a(1) **2 :** YELLOW WARBLER 1
yellow pond lily *n* **:** SPATTERDOCK
yellow poplar *n* **1 a :** TULIP TREE **b :** TULIPWOOD 1 **2 :** the soft and light but durable wood of the common cucumber tree (*Magnolia acuminata*) of the southeastern U.S.
yellow poppy *n* **1 :** a prickly poppy (*Argemone mexicana*) **2 :** CELANDINE POPPY
yellow precipitate *n* **:** yellow mercuric oxide esp. for use in ophthalmic ointments
yellow prickly ash *n* **:** HERCULES'-CLUB 1a
yellow prussiate of potash *n* **:** POTASSIUM FERROCYANIDE
yellow prussiate of soda *n* **:** SODIUM FERROCYANIDE
yellow puccoon *n* **:** GOLDENSEAL 1
yellow pyrites *n* **:** CHALCOPYRITE
yellow rail *n* **:** a very small American rail (*Coturnicops noveboracensis*) of which the lower parts are dull yellow and darkest on the breast and the back is streaked with brownish, yellow, and black color and spotted with white
yellow rain lily *n* **1 :** a bulbous herb (*Zephyranthes texana*) of the prairies of Texas with basal linear leaves and showy yellow or copper-colored purple-striped flowers **2 :** an herb (*Zephyranthes longifolia*) with clear-yellow flowers that is closely related to the Texas plant
yellow rattle *n* **:** RATTLE 3a
yellow redpoll *n* **:** YELLOW PALM WARBLER
yellow-red virosis *n* **:** X-DISEASE d
yellow rocket *n* **:** a winter cress (esp. *Barbarea vulgaris*)
yellow rockrose *also* **yellow rose** *n* **:** SHRUBBY CINQUEFOIL
yellowroot \'⸗⸗,⸗\ *n* [¹*yellow* + *root*] **:** any of several plants with yellow roots: as **a :** SHRUB YELLOWROOT **b :** GOLDENSEAL 1 **c :** a goldthread (*Coptis groenlandica*) **d :** TWINLEAF
yellow root rot *n* [¹*yellow* + *root rot*] **:** a root rot of fir, spruce, pine, and larch caused by a club fungus (*Sparassis radicata*)
yellow-rumped warbler \'⸗⸗,⸗-\ *or* **yellowrump** \'⸗⸗,⸗\ *n* **:** MYRTLE WARBLER
yellow rust *n* **:** STRIPE RUST
yellows *pres 3d sing of* YELLOW, *pl of* YELLOW
yellow sage *n* **:** RED SAGE 1
yellow sally *n, usu cap S* **:** a greenish or yellowish European stone fly (genus *Chloroperla*)
yellow sandbox *n* **:** a mature sandbox tree with yellowish wood — compare WHITE SANDBOX
yellow sanders *n* **1 :** any of several tropical American trees or shrubs: as **a :** MOUNTAIN PLUM **b :** a West Indian tree (*Zanthoxylum flavum*) **2 a :** the wood of a yellow sanders **b :** GRANADILLA WOOD 3
yellow sarsaparilla *n* **:** CANADA MOONSEED
yellow scale *n* **:** a scale (*Aonidiella citrina*) that is closely related to the California red scale and attacks citrus in the southwestern U. S., India, and Japan
yellow sedge *n* **1 :** a common sedge (*Carex flava*) with yellowish green culms that is found in No. America and Europe **2 :** YELLOW IRIS
yellowseed \'⸗⸗,⸗\ *n* [¹*yellow* + *seed*] **:** FIELD CRESS
yellow-shafted flicker \'⸗⸗,⸗⸗-\ *n* **:** a common woodpecker (*Colaptes auratus*) of eastern No. America conspicuous from its large size and bright symmetrical markings among which are a black crescent on the breast, red nape, white rump, and yellow shafts to the tail and wing feathers — called also *yellowhammer*
yellowshank \'⸗⸗,⸗\ *n* [¹*yellow* + *shank*] **:** YELLOWLEGS
yellowshanks *or* **yellowshins** \'⸗⸗,⸗\ *n pl but sing or pl in constr* [¹*yellow* + *shanks* (pl. of *shank*) or *shins*, pl. of *shin*] **:** YELLOWLEGS
yellow shore crab *n* **:** a shore crab (*Hemigrapsus oregonensis*) of the Pacific coast that generally resembles the purple shore crab but is yellow or gray often with purplish brown or black spots, lacks red on the chelae, and has notably hairy legs
yellow sienna *n* **:** YELLOW OCHER
yel·low·sis \'yelōsə̇s\ *n, pl* **yellow·ses** \-ō,sēz\ [NL, fr. E ¹*yellow* + NL *-sis*] **:** a photodynamic disease of Scottish sheep marked by dermatitis esp. of the head and face with accumulation of cells and fluid in the subcutaneous spaces and by jaundice — compare GEELDIKKOP
yellow skegs \-'skegz\ *n pl but sing or pl in constr* [¹*yellow* + E dial. *skegs*, pl. of *skeg* yellow iris, of unknown origin] **:** YELLOW IRIS
yellow snake *n* **:** a West Indian boa (*Epicrates inornatus*) that is common in Jamaica, becomes from 8 to 10 feet long, and has a body that is yellowish or yellowish green mixed with black and anteriorly with black lines
yellow snakeleaf *or* **yellow snowdrop** *n* **:** DOGTOOTH VIOLET
yellow soap *n* **:** a yellow to brown soap used chiefly in laundering; *esp* **:** ROSIN SOAP 1
yellow soft paraffin *n* **:** PETROLATUM a
yellow soil *var of* YELLOW PODZOLIC SOIL
yellow sponge *n* **:** a yellow or brownish short-fibered commercial sponge (*Spongia barbara* or *S. officinalis barbara*) occurring in the Gulf of Mexico and in the Atlantic ocean off the West Indies
¹yellow spot *n* [trans. of NL *macula lutea*] **:** MACULA LUTEA
²yellow spot *n* [¹*yellow* + *spot*] **1 :** a small American skipper (*Polites peckius*) of the family Hesperiidae having brownish wings with a large irregular bright-yellow spot on each of the hind wings that is most conspicuous beneath **2 :** TOMATO HORNWORM **3 :** any of several plant diseases characterized by yellow spotting on the foliage: as **a :** TOMATO STREAK **b :** a sugarcane disease that is serious in Australia and is caused by a fungus (*Cercospora kopkei*) **c :** a disease of wheat caused by a fungus (*Helminthosporium tritici-vulgaris*) **d :** a virus disease of pineapple
yellow spruce *n* **1 :** RED SPRUCE **2 :** SITKA SPRUCE **3 :** DOUGLAS FIR
yellow star *n* **1 :** SNEEZEWEED 1a **2 :** SOLAR STAR
yellow star grass *n* **:** a perennial grasslike herb (*Hypoxis hirsuta*) of eastern No. America with loose umbels of yellow star-shaped flowers
yellow star thistle *n* **:** a Barnaby's thistle (*Centaurea solstitialis*)
yellow starwort *n* **:** ELECAMPANE
yellow stone *n* **:** a grayish greenish yellow that is slightly paler than the color hay, paler than absinthe yellow, and greener and duller than dusty yellow — compare YELLOWSTONE
yellowstone \'⸗⸗,⸗\ *n* **:** a dark grayish yellow that is redder, stronger, and slightly lighter than California green or olive-sheen and very slightly greener than honey — compare YELLOW STONE
yellow stonecrop *n* **1 :** DWARF HOUSELEEK **2 :** a stonecrop (*Sedum acre*)
yellowstone trout *n, usu cap Y* [fr. *Yellowstone* river & *Yellowstone* Lake, northwest Wyoming] **:** a cutthroat trout of the northern Rocky mountain area that is sometimes distinguished as a separate species (*Salmo lewisi*)
yellow strawberry *n* **:** INDIAN STRAWBERRY 1
yellow stringybark *or* **yellow stringy** *n* **:** any of various stringybarks (esp. *Eucalyptus muelleriana*)
yellow stripe *n* **:** a virus disease of sugarcane characterized by a mottling and striping of the foliage
yellow-striped armyworm \'⸗⸗,⸗(⸗)-\ *n* **:** a caterpillar that is the larva of a noctuid moth (*Prodenia ornithogalli*) and that is a general plant feeder in the western U. S. and a serious pest on cotton in the southern states
yellow stripe rust *n* **:** STRIPE RUST
yellow suckling *or* **yellow suckling clover** *n* **:** a rather small annual hop clover of European origin but widely naturalized and sometimes sown for cover crop or pasture
yellow sugarcane aphid *n* **:** a plant louse (*Sipha flava*) that feeds on sugarcane, grain, and orchard grass in the southern U. S.
yellow swallowtail *n* **:** TIGER SWALLOWTAIL
yellow sweet clover *n* **1 :** a biennial yellow-flowered Eurasian sweet clover (*Melilotus officinalis*) that has aromatic leaves sometimes used as a carminative or flavoring agent, is widely cultivated esp. as a green manure and cover crop, and is naturalized in many parts of the world **2 :** BITTER CLOVER
yellow tacamahac *n* **:** an East Indian tree (*Calophyllum inophyllum*); *also* **:** an oleoresin obtained from this tree
yellowtail \'⸗⸗,⸗\ *n, pl* **yellowtail** *or* **yellowtails** [¹*yellow* + *tail*] **:** any of various fishes having a yellow or yellowish tail: as **a :** an amberfish of the genus *Seriola* — see CALIFORNIA YELLOWTAIL **b :** a mademoiselle (*Bairdiella chrysura*) **c :** RAINBOW RUNNER **d :** PINFISH a **e** *or* **yellowtail snapper :** a common snapper (*Ocyurus chrysurus*) of the tropical western Atlantic and West Indies that is olive above and broadly striped with yellow along the sides and on the tail and highly esteemed for sport and food **f :** SPOT 7 **g** *Austral* **:** a small yellowish green carangid food fish (*Trachurus declivis*) **h :** RUSTY DAB **i :** ¹BUMPER 3
yellowtail rockcod *or* **yellowtail rockfish** *n* **:** a commercially important rockfish (*Sebastodes flavidus*) of the Pacific coast of No. America that is grayish brown above shading to white below and spotted with yellow on the sides and has a yellow tail fin
yellow tang *n* **:** a rockweed (*Ascophyllum nodosum*)
yellow tarweed *n* **:** a sticky annual California herb (*Hemizonia virgata*) of the family Compositae with crowded small leaves and axillary yellow flower heads
yellow teat disease *n* **:** ANAPLASMOSIS
yellow thick head *n* [trans. of Afrik *geeldikkop*] **:** GEELDIKKOP
yellow thistle *n* **:** a thistle (*Cirsium horridulum*) of eastern No. America having yellow heads
yellowthroat \'⸗⸗,⸗\ *n* [¹*yellow* + *throat*] **:** any of several American ground warblers of the genus *Geothlypis*; *esp* **:** MARYLAND YELLOWTHROAT
yellow-throated marten \'⸗⸗,⸗⸗-\ *n* **:** a large strikingly marked yellow and black mustelid mammal (*Charronia flavigula*) of mountainous southern China and Burma
yellow-throated vireo *n* **:** a vireo (*Vireo flavifrons*) of eastern No. America with bright yellow throat and breast
yellow-throated warbler *n* **:** a wood warbler (*Dendroica dominica*) of the southern U. S.
yellow tip *n* [¹*yellow* + *tip*] **:** a copper deficiency disease of cereals characterized by chlorotic leaf tips and failure of the plants to set seed
yellow tit *n* **:** any of several crested titmice of the genus *Parus* that are natives of southern Asia and have chiefly yellow and green plumage
yellow toadflax *n* **:** a toadflax (*Linaria vulgaris*)
yellowtop \'⸗⸗,⸗\ *n* [¹*yellow* + *top*] **1 a :** any of several goldenrods; *esp* **:** EARLY GOLDENROD — sometimes pl. but sing. in constr. **b :** BITTER CLOVER **c :** GOLDEN CROWNBEARD **2 :** any of several plant diseases characterized by yellowing of the upper foliage: as **a :** a disease of alfalfa of undetermined

cause characterized by a pronounced yellowing of the upper portions of affected plants **b** : a yellowing of alfalfa tops caused by the punctures of the potato leafhopper

yellow trefoil *n* : BLACK MEDIC

yellow trumpet *n* : HUNTSMAN'S-HORN

yellow trumpet flower *n* : YELLOW ELDER

yellow ultramarine *n* : any of various yellow pigments (as barium yellow)

yellow umbil *n* : a yellow lady's-slipper (*Cypripedium parviflorum*)

yellow vetchling *n* : MEADOW PEA

yellow violet *n* : any of several violets with yellow flowers; *esp* : SWEET VIOLET

yellow viper *n* : FER-DE-LANCE

yellow vole *n* : a buff-colored Asiatic vole (*Microtus brandtii*)

yellow wagtail *n* : a wagtail of the genus *Motacilla*; esp : a common Eurasian wagtail (*M. flava*) of which a race (*M. j. tschutschensis*) reaches the coast of northwestern Alaska

yellow warbler *n* **1 a** : a small No. American warbler (*Dendroica petechia*) very common throughout the U. S. and frequently breeding in shade trees in cities and villages and having the male bright yellow with brown streaks on the underparts **b** : any of various related warblers of Central America and the West Indies **2** *dial Eng* : WILLOW WARBLER

yellowware *n* : pottery made from buff clay and covered with a yellowish transparent glaze

yellow wart *n* : POTATO WART

yellow wash *n* : a suspension of yellow mercuric oxide in water prepared by adding a solution of mercuric chloride to limewater and used as an antiseptic application to syphilitic sores and in eczema

yellow watercress *n* : a plant of the genus *Rorippa*: as **a** : a Eurasian perennial weedy herb (*R. sylvestris*) naturalized in No. America in wet places and having divided leaves and yellow flowers in loose racemes **b** : MARSH CRESS

yellow water crowfoot *n* : an aquatic buttercup (*Ranunculus flabellaris*) of northern No. America with finely divided leaves and rather showy yellow flowers

yellow water flag *n* : YELLOW IRIS

yellow water lily *n* : a yellow-flowered water lily; esp : SPATTERDOCK

yellow wax *n* : any of various yellow waxy substances: as **a** : BEESWAX 2a **b** : a semisolid portion of wax tailings obtained in petroleum distillation

yellow weasel *n* : a large orange-brown kolinsky (*Mustela siberica*)

yellowweed \ˈ⸳⸳⸳\ *n* **1** : SNEEZEWEED 1 **2** : any of several goldenrods **3** : ²RAPE **2 4** : TANSY RAGWORT **5** : DYER'S ROCKET **6** : WINTER CRESS **7** : BALL MUSTARD

yellow willow *n* **1** : GOLDEN WILLOW **2** : a No. American shrub or small tree (*Salix lutea*) having branches and branchlets that are yellow and then become gray and leaves that are yellow-green above

yellow willow herb *n* : a common loosestrife (*Lysimachia vulgaris*)

yellow-winged bat \ˈ⸳⸳,⸳-\ *n* : a tropical African insectivorous bat (genus *Lavia*) having more or less clear yellow wings

yellow-winged sparrow *n* : a grasshopper sparrow (*Ammodramus savannarum pratensis*)

yellowwood \ˈ⸳⸳\ *n* \¹yellow + wood\ **1** : any of various trees having wood that is yellowish or yielding a yellow extract: as **a** : a tree (*Cladrastis lutea*) of the southern U. S. that has odd-pinnate leaves and showy white fragrant flowers in terminal clusters and heavy hardwood which yields a yellow dye — called also *gopherwood* **b** : OSAGE ORANGE **c** : SWEETLEAF **d** : BUCKTHORN **e** : SMOKE TREE 1 **f** : FLORIDA BOXWOOD **g** : SHRUB YELLOWROOT **h** : any of various West Indian trees or shrubs of the genus *Zanthoxylum*; esp : SATINWOOD 2a(1) **i** : FUSTIC 1a **j** (1) : an Australian tree (*Achronychia laevis*) of the family Rutaceae (2) : SASSAFRAS 3a(2) (3) : an Australian sumac (*Rhus rhodanthema*) that yields a dark yellow wood (4)¹: LONG JACK **k** : SOUTH AFRICAN YELLOWWOOD; *broadly* : an African tree of the genus *Podocarpus* **1** : any of several trees of the genus *Terminalia* **2** : the wood of a yellowwood tree

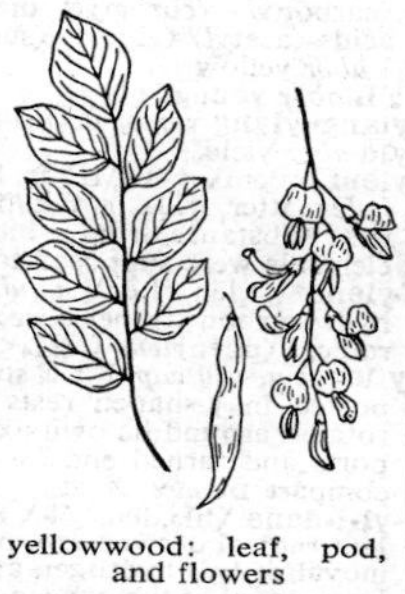

yellow wood sorrel *n* : a yellow-flowered plant of the genus *Oxalis*

yellow woolly bear *n* : a woolly bear that is the larva of an ermine moth (*Diacrisia virginica*) and is predominantly yellow in color — called also *yellow bear*

yellowwort \ˈ⸳⸳\ *n* : a European yellow-flowered bitter herb (*Chlora perfoliata*) of the family Gentianaceae that is sometimes used as a tonic

yellow wove *n* : a cheap blue wove paper

yellow wren *n* **1** : a willow warbler (*Phylloscopus trochilus*) **2** *dial Eng* : WOOD WARBLER 2

yel·lowy \ˈ⸳⸳⸳\ *adj* [¹yellow + -y] : YELLOWISH

yellow yam *n, South* : SWEET POTATO

yellow yel·drock \-ˈyeldrək\ *n* [¹yellow + E dial. *yeldrock, yeldrick, yeldring* yellowhammer, fr. ¹yellow] *dial Brit* : YELLOWHAMMER

yellow yolk *n* : darker yolk that alternates with white yolk and forms the thicker layers of the central yolk mass (as of a bird's egg)

¹yelm \ˈyelm\ *n* -s [ME, fr. OE *gelm, gilm* sheaf] *dial Eng* : a bundle of combed straw for thatching

²yelm \ˈ⸳\ *vi* -ED/-ING/-s *dial Eng* : to prepare bundles of straw for thatching

¹yelp \ˈyelp, ˈyelp\ *vb* -ED/-ING/-s [ME *yelpen* to boast, call out, fr. OE *gielpan* to boast, exult; akin to OE *gielp* pride, arrogance, praise, OHG *gelph* outcry, revelry, ON *gjalp* boasting, Lith *gulbinti* to praise, and prob. to OE *giellan* to yell — more at YELL] *vi* **1** : to utter a sharp quick cry (as of a hound or turkey) : bark shrilly **2** : to squeal, cry out, or call in shrill sharp manner (ladies and gentlemen who ~ at one another with unmistakable breeding —Wolcott Gibbs) (woodwind cascades that veritably ~ with exuberance —Winthrop Sargeant) ~ *vt* : to utter with a yelp (~ing a few phrases in his surprisingly shrill falsetto voice —James Cameron)

²yelp \ˈ⸳\ *n* -s **1** : the sharp shrill bark of a dog or other animal **2** : a sharp cry or call : SQUEAL (the audience let out a ~ of welcome —*New Yorker*)

yelp·er \-pə(r)\ *n* -s **1** : one that yelps: as **a** : a yelping dog **b** *dial Eng* : AVOCET **c** *dial Eng* : GREATER YELLOWLEGS **d** *dial Eng* : REDSHANK 1 **2** : an instrument used by hunters to produce a call or whistle imitating the yelp of the wild turkey hen **3** : one whose utterance is a sound without sense or resembles a dog's bark (that species of orators called the ~s —Sir Walter Scott)

yemassee *usu cap*, var of YAMASEE

yem·en \ˈyemən, ˈyām-\ *adj*, *usu cap* [fr. *Yemen*, kingdom of southwest Arabia] : of or from Yemen or the kind or style prevalent in Yemen : YEMENI

¹yem·e·ni \-nē\ *n -s usu cap* [Ar *yamaniy*, fr. *Yaman* Yemen] : YEMENITE

²yemeni \ˈ⸳⸳\ *adj*, *usu cap* : YEMENITE

¹yem·en·ite \-mə,nīt\ *n -s usu cap* [*Yemen* + E *-ite*] : a native or inhabitant of the sultanate of Yemen in southern Arabia

²yemenite \ˈ⸳⸳⸳\ *adj*, *usu cap* : of or relating to Yemen or its inhabitants

¹yen \ˈyen\ *n* -s usu cap [Jap *en* circle, yen, fr. Chin (Pek) *yüan²* round, circle, dollar] **1** : the basic monetary unit of Japan — see MONEY TABLE **2** : a coin or note representing one yen

²yen \ˈ⸳\ *n* -s [Chin (Cant) *yân²* craving as for opium or drink] **1** : an impelling craving for opium or some other narcotic (wanted a fix to get his ~ off) **2** : a strong desire or propensity : LONGING (a ~ to see the world) : URGE (whatever you have a ~ to do — ride, swim, or fish —*Saturday Night*)

³yen \ˈ⸳\ *vi* yenned; yenned; yenning; yens : to desire intensely : LONG, YEARN

---

yen·der \ˈyendə(r)\ *dial var of* YONDER

yen·hok \ˈyen'häk\ *n* [Chin (Cant) *yin-hŏk*, fr. *in*, *yin* opium + *hŏk* dipper, ladle] : a needlelike instrument used in the preparation of opium pills

yeni \ˈyenē\ *n -s* [NL (specific epithet of *Calospiza yeni*), of AmerInd origin] : a showy tanager (*Calospiza chilensis* syn. *C. yeni*) of eastern Ecuador, Bolivia, and Peru

yen·i·sei \ˈyenə'sā\ *n -s cap* [fr. *Yenisei* river, western Siberia] : the Uralic language of the Yeniseian people — see URALIC LANGUAGES table

yen·i·sei·an \ˈ⸳⸳⸳-ēən\ *n -s usu cap* [*Yenisei* river, western Siberia + E *-an*] **1** : a member of one of a group of peoples in the Yenisei river country including the Sagai — called also *Yenisei-Ostyak* **2** : a language family spoken in the valley of the Middle Yenisei river in Siberia of which Ket is the only member still spoken

yenisei-ostyak \ˈ⸳⸳⸳'⸳⸳⸳\ *n -s usu cap* Y&O [*Yenisei* river + E *ostyak*] **1** : YENISEIAN 1 **2** : KET

yen-shee \ˈyen'shē\ *n* [Chin (Cant) *yin-shi*, fr. *in*, *yin* opium + *shi* filth, excrement] : the residue formed in the bowl of an opium pipe by smoking

yen·tai \ˈyen⸳'tī\ *adj*, *usu cap* [fr. *Yentai* (Chefoo), commercial city of northeast China] : CHEFOO

¹yeo \ˈyō\ *dial Brit var of* EWE

²yeo *var of* YO

yeo *or* **yeom** *dial Brit var of* yeomanry

yeo·man \ˈyōmən\ *n, pl* yeomen [ME *yoman, yeman*, perh. contr. of *yong man, yeng man* young man, attendant, fr. *yong, yeng* young + *man*] **1 a** : an attendant or officer in a royal or noble household performing menial services (~ of the wardrobe); *esp* : one ranking between a sergeant and a groom or between a squire and a page **b** : a person attending or assisting another (as an official) : RETAINER **c** : YEOMAN OF THE GUARD **d** : a seaman, petty officer, or warrant officer (as in the Royal Navy) who assists (as in having charge of stores or signaling procedure) the officer of a particular department **e** : a petty officer (as in the U.S. Navy) who performs clerical duties and is responsible for keeping records and reports and providing information (as on insurance, transportation, or promotions) relating to his department **f** : a clerk who keeps records on board a ship — called also *writer* **2 a** : a small farmer who cultivates his own land; *specif* : one belonging to a class of English freeholders ranking below the gentry and formerly qualified by owning property worth 40 shillings a year to enjoy certain legal privileges (as jury duty) **b** : any person of the social rank of yeoman or of similar rank : a member of the first or most respected class of common people : one of the highest class not entitled to heraldic arms **c** : a member of the British military yeomanry **3** : one that performs great and laborious services (the biscuit pans . . . were the *yeomen* of our kitchen —Alberta Constant)

²yeoman \ˈ⸳⸳\ *adj* [ME *yoman, yeman*, fr. *yoman yeman*, n.] **1** : of, relating to, or being a yeoman (of ~ rank) (a ~ farmer) **2** : consisting of yeomen (the ~ class) **3** : characteristic of or befitting a yeoman (a man of big build, of ~ appearance, countrified by nature and wish —*Current Biog.*) **4** : characterized by laborious effort and great usefulness (did ~ service) (performed ~ work) (gave ~ help)

yeo·man·ette \ˈyōmə'net\ *n -s* [¹yeoman + -ette] : a woman serving as a yeoman in the U.S. naval reserve force during and immediately after World War I

¹yeo·man·ly \ˈyōmənlē\ *adj* [¹yeoman + -ly] **1** : of, relating to, or having the rank of a yeoman **2** : becoming or suitable to a yeoman : STURDY, LOYAL

²yeo·man·ly \ˈ⸳⸳⸳\ *adv* : in a manner befitting a yeoman : BRAVELY

yeoman of the guard : a member of a military corps attached to the British royal household since the 15th century to guard the sovereign, appointed from retired enlisted men and non-commissioned officers, and divided into two groups serving as ceremonial attendants of the sovereign and as warders of the Tower of London — compare GENTLEMAN-AT-ARMS

yeo·man·ry \ˈyōmənrē\ *n -es* [ME *yomanry, yemanry*, fr. *yoman, yeman* yeoman + *-ry*] **1** *obs* : the position or rank of a yeoman **2** : the whole body of yeomen; *specif* : the body of small landed proprietors of the middle class **3** : a British volunteer cavalry force created in 1761 as a home defense force from yeomen and officered by country gentlemen and reorganized in 1907 into part of the territorial force

yeoman usher *n* : the deputy of the black rod

yep \ˈyep\ *or* **yup** \ˈyəp\ *adv* [by alter.] : YES — not often in formal use; compare NOPE

yer \ˈyə(r)\ *or* **yere** \(ˈ)yi(ə)r\ *dial var of* YOUR

-yer — see ²-ER

ye·ra·va \ˈyā'rävə\ *also* era·va \ə'-\, *n, pl* yerava *or* yeravas *usu cap* : one of a very dark-skinned people in Coorg prob. of Dravidian origin and formerly subjects of the Kodagu

yerb \ˈyərb\ *dial var of* HERB

yer·ba bue·na \ˈyerbə'bwānə, ⸳⸳⸳'⸳⸳⸳\ *n* [Sp, lit., good herb] : a trailing perennial evergreen herb (*Satureia douglasii*) of British Columbia, Idaho, and California that has small white flowers and has been used as an anthelmintic and emmenagogue

yer·bal \ˈyər'bäl\ *n, pl* yerba·les \-⸳'läs\ [AmerSp, fr. *yerba*] : a plantation of maté or a district in which it abounds

yerba man·sa \-'män(t)sə; -'man-\ *n* [modif. of MexSp *yerba del manso*, lit., farmhouse herb] : a stoloniferous herb (*Anemiopsis californica*) of the family Saururaceae of the western U.S. and Mexico with a pungent rootstock and small spicate flowers subtended by a white involucre suggesting an anemone

yerba ma·té \-'mä(,)tā\ *n* [AmerSp *yerba maté*; fr. *yerba* herb, plant (fr. L *herba* grass, herb) + *mate* maté] : MATÉ

yerba reu·ma \-'rümə\ *n* [modif. of MexSp *yerbarreuma*, fr. *yerba* herb + *reuma* cold, catarrh, fr. L *rheuma* — more at *rheum*] **1** : a low Californian undershrub (*Frankenia palmeri*) densely covered with small leaves and tiny white flowers **2** : ALKALI HEATH

yerba san·ta \-'säntə, -'san-\ *n* [MexSp, lit., holy herb] : any of several shrubs of the genus *Eriodictyon*; esp : an evergreen shrub (*E. californicum*) of California whose aromatic leaves are used as an expectorant and to mask the bitter taste of various drugs

yer·cum \ˈyərkəm\ *n -s* [Tamil *yerkum*] : MUDAR

¹yerd \ˈyərd\ *dial var of* YARD

²yerd \ˈ⸳\ *chiefly Scot var of* EARTH

yere \ˈyi(ə)r\ *dial var of* HERE

yer·e·van \ˈyerə'vän\ *or* **er·e·van** *or* **er·i·van** \ˈe-\ *adj*, *usu cap* [*Yerevan or Erevan or Erivan*, capital of Armenian S.S.R.] : of or from the city of Yerevan, U.S.S.R. or of the kind or style prevalent in Yerevan

¹yerk \ˈyərk\ *vb* -ED/-ING/-s [ME *yerken*] *vt* **1 a** *archaic* : to pull (a stitch) tight in making a shoe **b** : to bind tightly **2** *dial* **a** : to beat (as with a rod or whip) : THRASH **b** : to attack (as with harsh words) or excite vigorously : stir up : GOAD **3** *dial* **a** : to cause to move abruptly : JERK, HURL, KICK **b** : to strike up (as a song) **4** *dial* : to begin with zest ~ *vi* **1** *obs* : to lash out with the heels **2** *dial* : to move hastily or suddenly

²yerk \ˈ⸳\ *n -s* **1** *Scot* : THUMP, LASHING, KICK, STAB **2** *dial* : a quick movement : JERK

yer·ra *or* **yer·rah** \ˈyerə\ *interj* [IrGael *a* O + *Dia* God (fr. OIr) + *ara* arrah; akin to L *deus* god — more at DEITY] — used as a mild oath

yert·chuk \ˈyər,chək\ *n -s* [native name in Australia] : a medium sized Australian eucalypt (*Eucalyptus consideniana*) with rough flaky bark and pale gummy inner bark

yes \ˈyes\ *adv* [(ˈ)yes, ˈyeʊ, ˈyeə & a multiplicity of other variants, among them ˈye, (ˈ)yas, (ˈ)yēs, ˈyə, (ˈ)yās, ˈyi, ˈya(ə), ˈya(ə), (ˈ)yiə, ˈ(ˈ)yeə, ˈyə, ˈā(y)ə, ˈe(y)ə, ˈa(y)ə; to the variants transcribed as vowel-final, p or glottal stop may be added\ *adv* [ME *yes, yis*, fr. OE *gēse, gīse*, prob. fr. *gēa* yea + *sī*, 3d sing. imper. of *bēon* to be (suppletive infinitive) — more at YEA, BE] **1** — used as a function word to express assent or agreement in answer to a question, command, or request (are you ready to leave? *Yes*, I am ready) (~, I will be glad to have lunch with you) (~ I said I will — James Joyce) **2** — used as a function word formerly to constitute and now usu. to introduce correction or contradiction of a negative assertion, direction, or request (you couldn't have meant that. *Yes*, I did mean it) (don't say that! *Yes*, I will) **3 a** — used as a function word to express agreement with the content or implications of a preceding statement (~, I see your point) (~, such a policy would be

---

fatal) **b** — used as a function word to express conditional assent to a statement or proposal subject to or limited by a following objection (this is a good meal. *Yes*, but I prefer my wife's cooking) **4** — used as a function word to emphasize a following affirmative or to introduce a more emphatic, specific, or comprehensive statement (this is a possible, ~, a probable explanation) (a source of inspiration to himself and to his people, ~, to humanity —Ernst Feise) **5** — used as a function word to indicate uncertainty or polite interest or attentiveness ("*Yes?*" he said as he saw the stranger waiting to speak to him)

²yes \ˈ⸳\ *n, pl* yeses *also* yesses **1** : an act or instance of agreeing or assenting by the use of the word *yes* : AFFIRMATION (overcome them with ~es, undermine them with grins . . . agree them to death and destruction —Ralph Ellison) **2 a** : an affirmative vote, decision, or opinion (the proposal was carried by a margin of ten ~es) **b** *yeses pl* : persons voting in the affirmative (when it was announced that the motion had been defeated, there was a shout of protest from the ~es)

³yes \ˈ⸳\ *vb* yessed *also* yesed; yessed *also* yesed; yessing *also* yesing; yesses *also* yeses *vi* : to express agreement or assent (was better at *yessing* than at developing original ideas) ~ *vt* : to give assent to : agree with (all she had to do was ~ him when he was talkin' —Norman Mailer)

ye·shi·va *or* **ye·shi·vah** *or* **ye·shi·bah** \yə'shēvə\ *n, pl* **yeshivas** *or* **yeshivahs** *or* **yeshibahs** \-vəz\ *or* **yeshi·vot** *or* **yeshi·voth** *or* **yeshi·both** *or* **yeshi·bot** \yashē'vōt, -ōth\ [LHeb *yĕshībhāh*, fr. Heb, sitting, seat] **1** : a school for advanced Talmudic study : a Talmudic academy **2** : an orthodox Jewish rabbinical seminary or college **3** : a Hebrew-English day school providing both secular and religious instruction

yeshiva bocher *n* [Yiddish *yeshive bokher*, lit., yeshiva youth] : BAHUR

yes-man \ˈ⸳⸳⸳\ *n, pl* yes-men [¹yes + man] : a person who agrees with everything that is said to him; *esp* : a self-seeker who endorses or supports without criticism every opinion or proposal of an associate or superior : SYCOPHANT, TOADY (depriving himself of the advice of all but timid souls and *yesmen* —*Harper's*) — compare NO-MAN

ye·so \ˈyā(,)sō\ *n -s* [Sp, fr. L *gypsum*] : GYPSUM

yest \ˈyest\ *archaic var of* YEAST

yest *abbr* yesterday

¹yes·ter \ˈyestə(r)\ *adj* [yesterday] *archaic* : of or relating to yesterday

²yester \ˈ⸳\ *n -s* [by shortening] *chiefly dial* : YESTERDAY

¹yes·ter·day \ˈyestə(r)dē, -di, -(r)(,)dā\ *adv* [ME *yesterday, yesterday*, fr. OE *giestran dæg, geostran dæg, gystran dæg*, n. & adv., fr. *giestran* yesterday + *dæg* day; akin to OHG *gestaron* yesterday, ON *i gær* yesterday, tomorrow, Goth *gistradagis* tomorrow, L *heri* yesterday, Gk *chthes*, Skt *hyas*] **1** : on the last day past : on the day preceding today (the affair took place ~) **2** : at a time not long past : only a short time ago (I was not born ~)

²yesterday \ˈ⸳⸳⸳\ *n* [ME *yisterday, yesterday*, fr. OE *geostran dæg*] **1** : the day last past : the day next before the present (had come up into the bows to resume his ~'s toil —C.S. Forester) **2** : recent time : time not long past (nobody comprehended the footwork of a running animal until the ~ of instantaneous photography —R.C.Murphy) (late in the earth's history, a mere geologic ~ —Marjory S. Douglas) **3** : past time — usu. used in pl. (all our ~s have lighted fools the way to dusty death —Shak.) (far back in the dim ~s —Stanley Walker) (the beauty they love is all in their tremendous ~ —Mollie Panter-Downes)

³yesterday \ˈ⸳⸳⸳\ *adj* : of or relating to yesterday or to a very recent time or period

yes·ter·day·ness *n -es* : the quality of being yesterday

yes·ter·eve \ˈyestə'rēv\ *or* **yes·ter·e·ven** \-'vin\ *adv* [yester- (as in *yesterday*) + *eve* or *even* or *evening*] *archaic* : on the evening of yesterday

²yestereve \ˈ⸳⸳⸳\ *or* **yestereven** \ˈ⸳⸳⸳\ *or* **yesterevening** \ˈ⸳⸳⸳\ *n, archaic* : the evening of yesterday : the evening last past

¹yes·ter·morn \ˈyestər'mȯ(ə)rn\ *or* **yes·ter·morn·ing** \-'ȯrniŋ\ *adv* [yester- (as in *yesterday*) + *morn* or *morning*] *archaic* : on the morning of yesterday

²yestermorn \ˈ⸳⸳⸳\ *or* **yestermorning** \ˈ⸳⸳⸳\ *n, archaic* : the morning of yesterday : the morning of the day last past

yes·tern \ˈyestə(r)n\ *adj* [by alter.] *archaic* : YESTER

yes·ter·night \ˈyestə(r)'nīt\ *adv* [ME *yisternight, yesternight*, fr. OE *gystran niht*, fr. *giestron* yesterday + *niht* night] *archaic* : on the night last past

²yesternight \ˈ⸳⸳⸳\ *n, archaic* : the night last past

¹yes·ter·year \ˈyestə(r)'yi(ə)r, -tə,yi(ə)r\ *n* [yester- (as in *yesterday*) + *year*] **1** : last year (where are the snows of ~ —D.G. Rossetti) **2** : a period not long past : the recent past (perhaps some of the quiet matrons in the queue were the phrenetic bobby-soxers of ~ —*New Yorker*)

²yesteryear \ˈ⸳⸳⸳\ *adv* : in the recent past (library problems . . . are the same today as ~ —H.C.Saucer)

yes·treen \ye'strēn\ *adv* [ME(Sc) *yistrevin*, fr. *yisterday* yesterday + *evin* evening, alter. of ME *even*] *chiefly Scot* : on yesterday evening (left here ~ —John Buchan)

²yestreen \ˈ⸳⸳\ *n -s chiefly Scot* : last evening or night

yesty *abbr* yesterday

¹yet \(ˈ)yet, *usu* -ed·+V\ *adv* [ME *yet, yit, yut*, fr. OE *gīet, gīeta, gȳt*; akin to OFris *ieta, eta, ita* yet] **1 a** : besides what has been considered or mentioned already : in addition : as well : ALSO (had ~ another side to his character —R.A.Hall b.1911) (by ordinary post, as I could furnish ~ another . . . if that went wrong —O.W.Holmes †1935) **b** : EVEN — used as an intensive with comparatives (at a ~ faster speed) (came nearer and ~ nearer) or after *nor* (have never voted for him, nor ~ intend to) **c** *substand* : on top of everything else : no less (today you can buy one off a showroom floor — and with a discount, ~ —I.T.Galanoy) (writes a whole book about them. With pictures, ~ —J.N.Leonard) **2 a** : continuously up to or as late as the present or some specified time : as previously : STILL (animals ~ thrive at the bottom —R.E.Coker) (riches were still respectable, the rise of a millionaire was ~ a romance —Osbert Sitwell) (had developed a great civilization while ~ pagans —Kemp Malone) **b** : up to now : so far : HITHERTO (linguistic evidence has ~ yielded but a scanty return to the historian of culture —Edward Sapir) (there is ~ to be any scientist of any repute who encourages . . . the saucer-prophets —*Saturday Rev.*) **c** : at this or that time : as soon as now (is it time to go ~) (has the mail arrived ~) **d** *archaic* : at length : FINALLY (ere ~ the bees hum about globes of clover —John Keats) (could feel in the soft air the flowers that were ~ to show themselves —J.B.Benefield) **3 a** : at some future time : before all is done : EVENTUALLY (wish to get to him the two blue woolen shirts . . . and will try to do it ~ —Walt Whitman) **b** *archaic* : during the continuance of the present into the future; from now on : HENCEFORTH (~ a little while and the world seeth me no more. But ~, because I live, ye shall live also, and ~ the world seeth me not; but ye see me . . . and, because I live, and, then I go unto him that sent me —Jn 7:33 (AV)) **4** : HOWEVER, NEVERTHELESS, NOTWITHSTANDING (the verse, which nowhere bursts into a flame of poetry, is ~ economical and tidy —T.S.Eliot) (a life that was austere and which was happy because of its purpose —R.M.Hodesh)

²yet *conj* [ME *yut, yit, yut, yit yet*, adv.] **1** : BUT (a few pretty rivers that look like prime trout water, ~ they are not —Pete Barrett) **2** : THOUGH (my soul, ~ I know not why, hates nothing more than he —Shak.)

³yet \ˈ⸳\ *adj* [¹yet] : existing or lasting up to the present or a specified time : still continuing (the ~ ruler, but not for long)

yet·a·pa \ˈyetə,pä\ *n -s* [prob. of AmerInd origin] : a fork-tailed flycatcher (genus *Gubernetes*) of southern Brazil and Argentina

ye·ti \ˈyetē\ *n -s* [Tibetan] : ABOMINABLE SNOWMAN

¹yet·ling \ˈyetliŋ\ *also* **yet·lin** \-lin\ *n* [ME *yetling*, fr. *yeten, yetten* to pour, found, cast (fr. OE *gēotan*) + *-ling* — more at FOUND] **1** *chiefly Scot* : a usu. cast-iron pot **2** *chiefly Scot* : something made of cast iron **3** : CAST IRON

²yetling \ˈ⸳⸳\ *n -s* [ME, fr. OE *geat* — more at GATE] *chiefly Scot* : GATE

yet·zer \ˈyātsə(r)\ *n, pl* yet·za·rim \ˌyätsä'rēm\ *or* yetzers [LHeb *yēṣer*, fr. Heb, form, frame, purpose] : the impulse or inclination with which man is endowed according to Jewish traditional belief

yetzer ha·ra \-'härə\ *n* [LHeb *yēṣer hār'ā* evil inclination] : man's inclination or impulse to evil considered as an essential part of human nature in Jewish traditional belief

¹yeuk \ˈyük\ *vi* -ED/-ING/-S [ME (northern) *yykyn, yukyn,* fr. OE *giccan* — more at ITCH] *chiefly Scot* : ITCH
²yeuk \"\ *n* -S *chiefly Scot* : ITCHING
yeuky \-ki\ *adj* [¹*yeuk* + *-y*] *chiefly Scot* : ITCHY
yew \ˈyü\ *n* -S [ME *ew,* fr. OE *ēow, īw;* akin to OHG *īwa* yew, ON *ȳr,* OIr *ēo,* W *ywen,* OSlav *iva* willow] **1 a** : any of numerous shrubs or trees of the genus *Taxus* many of which yield valuable timbers and some of which are widely cultivated for their rich evergreen foliage; *esp* : ENGLISH YEW **b** : the wood of a yew; *esp* : the heavy fine-grained light brown or red wood of English yew that is valued esp. for cabinetwork, bows, and hoops **2** *archaic* : twigs or branches of the yew tree used as symbols of grief **3** *archaic* : an archery bow made of yew

twig of yew with ripe fruit

yew·berry \ˈyü- — *see* BERRY\ *n* : the fruit of the yew
yew·en \ˈyüən\ *adj* [*yew* + *-en*] *archaic* : made of yew
yew family *n* : TAXACEAE
yew green *n* : a moderate olive green that is yellower, stronger, and slightly lighter than cypress green, greener and darker than holly green (sense 2), and greener, darker, and slightly stronger than Lincoln green
yew pine *n* : BLACK SPRUCE 1
yew podocarpus *n* : a tree (*Podocarpus macrophyllus* and esp. the variety *P. m. maki*) of China and Japan that is used as an ornamental hedge plant and has lanceolate leaves and gray fissured bark
yew tree *n* [ME *ew tree,* fr. *ew* yew + *tree*] : YEW 1a
yez \ˈyēz\ *pron, pl in constr* [¹*ye* + *-s,* n. pl. suffix] *Irish* : YOU
yez·i·di \ˈyezədē\ *or* **ya·zi·di** \ˈyäzədē\ *n* -S *usu cap* [prob. of Iranian origin] : a member of a syncretistic religious sect inhabiting a small area in Iraq, Syria, and Soviet Armenia, comprising several Kurdish-speaking peoples, and worshiping an angel believed to have been formerly the author of evil but to be now actively good and chief among seven angels to whom the supreme but transcendent God has left the government of the world
yfere *adv* [ME *ifere, yfere, in fere,* prob. fr. *in* + *fere* company, fr. OE *gefēre,* fr. *ge-* associative prefix + derivative of root of *faran* to travel — more at CO-, FARE] *obs* : TOGETHER
y-gun \ˈ=,=\ *n, cap Y* [¹*y* + *gun;* fr. its forked shape] : an antisubmarine gun having two barrels that form a fork to permit the simultaneous firing of depth charges on each side of the ship on which the gun is mounted
YH *abbr* youth hostel
YHS *var of* IHS
YHWH *also* **YHVH** *or* **JHVH** *or* **JHWH** *or* **IHVH** *n* [Heb *YHWH*] : YAHWEH — a transliteration of the tetragrammaton
yid \ˈyid\ *n* -S *usu cap* [Yiddish, fr. MHG *Jude, Jüde,* fr. OHG *Judo, Judeo,* fr. L *Judaeus* — more at JEW] : JEW — usu. taken to be offensive
¹yid·dish \ˈyidish, -dēsh\ *n* -ES *cap* [Yiddish *yidish,* short for *yidish daytsh,* lit., Jewish German, fr. MHG *jüdisch diutsch,* fr. *jüdisch* Jewish (fr. *Jüde* Jew + *-isch* -ish) + *diutsch* German, fr. OHG *diutisc* — more at DUTCH] : a High German language spoken by Jews chiefly in eastern Europe and areas to which Jews from eastern Europe have migrated and commonly written in Hebrew characters — called also *Judeo-German;* see INDO-EUROPEAN LANGUAGES table
²yiddish \"\ *adj, usu cap* **1** : of, relating to, or characteristic of Yiddish ⟨a *Yiddish* word⟩ **2** : consisting of or written in Yiddish ⟨*Yiddish* newspapers⟩ ⟨*Yiddish* literature⟩
yid·dish·ism \-di,shizəm\ *n* -S *usu cap* [¹*yiddish* + *-ism*] **1** : a movement characterized by advocacy of the Yiddish language and culture **2** : a usage, word, phrase, or idiom peculiar to Yiddish
¹yid·dish·ist \-shəst\ *n* -S *usu cap* [¹*yiddish* + *-ist*] : an adherent of Yiddishism
²yiddishist \"\ *adj, usu cap* : of, relating to, or advocating yiddishism ⟨*Yiddishist* schools⟩ ⟨a *Yiddishist* movement⟩
yid·dish·keit \-sh,kīt\ *n* -S *usu cap* [Yiddish *yidishkeyt,* fr. *yidish,* adj., Jewish (fr. MHG *jüdisch*) + *-keyt* -hood, fr. MHG *-keit,* alter. of *-heit,* fr. OHG — more at -HOOD] : Jewish character or quality : Jewish way of life : JEWISHNESS
¹yield \ˈyēld, *esp before pause or consonant* ˈyēəld\ *vb* -ED/-ING/-S [ME *yielden, yelden,* for OE *gieldan, geldan;* akin to OHG *geltan* to pay, render, requite, ON *gjalda,* Goth *fargildan,* and perh. to OSlav *žlěsti* to pay] *vt* **1** *archaic* : to give a reward to : RECOMPENSE, REQUITE, REWARD — used chiefly as an expression of gratitude or good will ⟨tend me tonight two hours . . . and the gods ~ you for't —Shak.⟩ **2** : to give or render as fitting, rightfully owed, or required ⟨~ him obedience in lawful things —G.P.R.James⟩ **3** *archaic* : RETURN 5b ⟨he ~*ed* to this suggestion a ready and rapturous assent —Charles Dickens⟩ **4 a** *archaic* : to hand over : DELIVER, OFFER, PRESENT ⟨our soul cannot but ~ you forth to public thanks —Shak.⟩ **b** : to grant as an act of grace or as a concession : give or bestow as a favor ⟨the king ~*ed* the citizens the right of justice —J.R.Green⟩ ⟨refused to ~ passage⟩ **5** : to give up possession of upon claim or demand: as **a** : to give up (as one's breath, life, or spirit) and so die or expire ⟨~*ed* up the ghost and was gathered unto his people —Gen 49:33 (AV)⟩ **b** : to surrender or relinquish to the physical control of another : hand over possession of ⟨refused to ~ the fortress to the enemy⟩ — sometimes used with *up* ⟨the Indians agreed . . . to ~ up their British flags —Grace L. Nute⟩ **c** : to surrender or submit (oneself) to another ⟨each Babylonian woman was in duty bound . . . to ~ herself to a stranger —H.M.Parshley⟩ ⟨emotions do not ~ themselves readily to a verbal pin —Ernest & Pearl Beaglehole⟩ **d** : to give (oneself) up to an inclination, temptation, or habit : submit, give over, or incline (oneself) to some influence : dedicate or devote (oneself) to something ⟨a temptation to which he ~*ed* himself —H.O.Taylor⟩ ⟨she ~*ed* herself up . . . to the rhythm of a waltz —Victoria Sackville-West⟩ **e** (1) : to relinquish one's possession of (as a position of advantage or point of superiority) ⟨~ precedence⟩ ⟨traffic required to ~ right of way⟩ ⟨~*ed* the premiership to his rival⟩ (2) : to relinquish (as the floor or a period of allotted speaking time) to another member of a legislative assembly ⟨~ the floor to the senator from Nebraska⟩ **f** : to hand over or resign to the moral control of another : give to another the political, economic, or social direction of : RELINQUISH ⟨~ sovereignty to an international organization⟩ ⟨~*ed* her heart to another⟩ **6 a** *obs* : to acknowledge as being correctly specified : ALLOW, CONCEDE ⟨I ~ it just . . . and submit —John Milton⟩ **b** (1) : to admit the validity or cogency of ⟨~*ed* the point⟩ ⟨unwilling to ~ the argument⟩ (2) *archaic* : CONSENT, AGREE ⟨~*ed* to ask for mercy —Jane West⟩ **c** *obs* : to admit to be true : concede to be so ⟨hard . . . to ~ they have done amiss —Nicholas Rowe⟩ **7 a** : to bear or bring or put forth as a natural product esp. as a result of cultivation ⟨clover seed . . . ~*s* from 6 to 10 bushels on the cutover lands —*Amer. Guide Series: Minn.*⟩ **b** : to furnish as output or as return or result of expended effort ⟨their soil ~*s* treasures of every kind —H.T.Buckle⟩ **c** : to produce as a result : give as a product ⟨this prediction is susceptible of a test which ~*s* a yes or no answer —J.B.Conant⟩ **d** : to give up in response to one's efforts : render as the result of the application of skill, persistence, or hard work ⟨words, under the analyses now indicated, ~ the history of their origin —Edward Clodd⟩ — often used with *up* ⟨caves . . . which have not yet ~*ed* up their secrets to the eyes of man —Bill Beatty⟩ **8** : to give forth : DISCHARGE, EMIT ⟨air-swept lindens ~ their scent —Matthew Arnold⟩ **9 a** : to produce or furnish to supply a need : provide for use or to serve a purpose : AFFORD ⟨cotton can be treated to ~ a series of products —*Industrial & Engineering Chemistry*⟩ ⟨several makes of engine ~ considerably more power —Grenville Manton⟩ ⟨the language too condensed to ~ quotable lines —J.D.Hart⟩ **b** : to give rise to : CAUSE, OCCASION ⟨the election ~*ed* only one surprise⟩ **c** (1) : to produce as return from an expenditure or investment : furnish as profit or interest : PAY, RETURN ⟨an investment that now ~*s* him 6 percent⟩ ⟨first steam whaler afloat . . . ~*ed* $151,000 net —*Amer. Guide Series: Conn.*⟩ ⟨it will prosper and ~ a fair return on the . . . investment —Leo Wolman⟩ (2) : to produce as revenue : bring in ⟨a levy . . . was proposed in order to ~ £4 million —Alzada Comstock⟩ ⟨gasoline tax ~*s* $10,108,965 in first eight months —*Car Life*⟩ **d** *obs* : to present to view : EXHIBIT ~ *vi* **1** : to make or give a return : be fruitful or productive : BEAR, PRODUCE ⟨the impoverished soil would not ~ without application of fertilizers —*Amer. Guide Series: Md.*⟩ ⟨the apple trees did not ~ well this year⟩ **2** : to give up and cease resistance or contention: as **a** : to surrender and concede being defeated, vanquished, or worsted ⟨the enemy suddenly ~*ed* —M.R.Cohen⟩ **b** : to cease opposition : give up the contest : SUBMIT, SUCCUMB ⟨after several hours of debate, the opposition ~*ed*⟩ **c** : to cease to withstand the effect of some action ⟨short words which nowhere ~ to analysis —Edward Sapir⟩ ⟨whole passages ~ neatly when translated by shorthand —Fletcher Pratt⟩ **d** : to agree to accept or comply with something : exhibit willingness rather than opposition : DEFER ⟨~*ed* to the secondary role for which his talent equipped him —Van Wyck Brooks⟩ **3** : to give way to pressure or influence exerted upon one : submit to urging, persuasion, or entreaty : consent or agree to something : cease opposition or objection to something : comply with something ⟨if you ~ to that impulse —T.B.Costain⟩ ⟨~ to the urgent invitation —D.S.Muzzey⟩ ⟨refused to ~ to their demands⟩ ⟨~*s* to her seducer with hardly a struggle —T.S. Eliot⟩ **4 a** : to give way under physical force so as to bend, stretch, or break ⟨the dirt road was so soft it ~*ed* to the foot like a feather bed —*Amer. Guide Series: N.Y. City*⟩ ⟨nylon does not ~ to stretch as readily as rubber yarns —W. E.Shinn⟩ **b** : to lose power of resistance to some physical action or agent (as pressure, friction, or heat) so as to be affected by it ⟨ores that ~ readily to reduction processes —*Amer. Guide Series: Wash.*⟩ ⟨the door suddenly ~*ed* to her hand —Jane Austen⟩ **c** : to permit oneself to be deflected : change one's course in deference : turn aside ⟨refused to ~ a particle from his resolution⟩ **5 a** : to give place or precedence (as to one having superior right or claim) : acknowledge the superiority of someone else ⟨I ~ to no one in my respect for his creative program —R.N.Denney⟩ ⟨the way of life of these peoples must ~ to the culture of the white man —*Current Biog.*⟩ ⟨the acts of New York must ~ to the law of Congress —John Marshall⟩ **b** : to be inferior in some often specified respect ⟨their mutton ~*s* to ours but their beef is excellent —Jonathan Swift⟩ **c** : to give way to or be succeeded by someone or something else ⟨pavements . . . ~*ed* to dirt roads —Giorgio de Santillana⟩ ⟨the cold thin air of the mountains ~*ed* to sweltering heat as they descended —Bernard De Voto⟩ ⟨hard conditions of life . . . ~*ed* to more propitious circumstances —Van Wyck Brooks⟩ **6** : to relinquish the floor of a legislative assembly (as for a period of time or a question) ⟨~ to the senator from Connecticut⟩

syn SUBMIT, CAPITULATE, SUCCUMB, BOW, DEFER, RELENT: YIELD is a general term referring to any sort of giving in before force, domination, argument, entreaty, appeal ⟨after some further argument I *yielded* the point —W.H.Hudson †1922⟩ ⟨went into the Peace Conference willing to *yield* everything to English interests —H.L.Mencken⟩ ⟨not a man to *yield* weakly —Havelock Ellis⟩ SUBMIT more strongly indicates giving up after conflict, contention, or resistance to the will, control, or disposition of another ⟨not only has faith in divine Providence but *submits* to it humbly —Herbert Agar⟩ ⟨must *submit* ourselves to the will of God —Mary Austin⟩ ⟨tamely *submitted* to the rebuffs —A.T.Quiller-Couch⟩ CAPITULATE centers attention on a definite act of surrendering or giving up to a stronger force or power ⟨how easily we *capitulate* to badges and names, to large societies and dead institutions —R.W. Emerson⟩ ⟨the universities would *capitulate* to a young, vigorous and revolutionary creed, in tune with the Zeitgeist —Walter Moberly⟩ SUCCUMB is likely to indicate utter yielding through weakness or exhaustion ⟨*succumbing* before the barbarian invasions —H.O.Taylor⟩ ⟨presidents who have attempted independent action have soon *succumbed* to the power of the government —Ernest Barker⟩ BOW may be used in reference to situations in which a party that has not been vanquished gives in or yields for politic or courteous reasons ⟨their habit of *bowing* to public opinion —Bertrand Russell⟩ ⟨*bowed* to political expediency and requested Blair's resignation —W.E.Smith⟩ ⟨soon learned to *bow* before his wife's more stormy moods —Samuel Butler †1902⟩ DEFER strongly connotes yielding brought about by respect for another or for his position or authority ⟨everybody must *defer.* A nation must wait upon her decision, a dean and chapter truckle to her wishes —Victoria Sackville-West⟩ ⟨the banker who was a free man, who ran his own bank in his own way, *deferring* only slightly to the nonsense of the federal bank inspectors —W.A. White⟩ RELENT is used in situations in which a dominant party abates his rigor or mollifies his wrath because of entreaty, consideration, or resurgence of easier nature ⟨might have *relented* and repented having wrung a promise from her —Margaret Deland⟩ **syn** see in addition BEAR, RELINQUISH

²yield \"\ *n* -S *often attrib* [ME *yelde,* fr. *yelden* to yield] **1** : something (as the amount, quantity, or product) yielded: as **a** (1) : the aggregate of products resulting from growth or cultivation ⟨a goodly ~ of fruit —Francis Bacon⟩ ⟨an increased ~ per acre⟩ ⟨~*s* average over twenty pounds of fruit per plant —*Irish Independent*⟩ (2) : the aggregate of products resulting from a chemical reaction and usu. expressed as the percentage actually obtained of the amount theoretically possible (3) : the amount of explosive energy expended by a nuclear explosion usu. expressed in kilotons of TNT that would produce an explosion resulting in the expending of the same amount of energy **b** : the quantity of a product resulting from exploitation of natural resources ⟨the ~ of a well in barrels of oil⟩ ⟨fishermen . . . are finding that the ~ per hour of trawling is dropping —*Irish Digest*⟩ **c** : the revenue obtained from a tax or levy **d** : the return upon a financial investment usu. expressed as a percentage of cost ⟨the ~ on a bond⟩ ⟨a 4% ~⟩ **e** : the actual or the normal product of a stand of timber **f** : the number of proof gallons of spirit obtained from a bushel of grain in distilling **2 a** : the capacity of yielding produce or other product ⟨a fruit belt owes its abundant ~ to climatic conditions —*Amer. Guide Series: Mich.*⟩ **b** : the capacity to yield under pressure or tension ⟨a material with high ~⟩
yield·able \-dəbəl\ *adj* : capable of yielding : disposed to yield
yield·ance \-dən(t)s\ *n* -S [¹*yield* + *-ance*] *archaic* : the action of yielding : COMPLIANCE, CONCESSION, SUBMISSION, SURRENDER ⟨blissful ~ to her sweet allure —Thomas Hardy⟩
yielded *past of* YIELD
yield·er \-də(r)\ *n* -S [ME *yeldere,* fr. *yelden* to yield + *-ere* -er] : one that yields: as **a** : one that surrenders, concedes, or gives in ⟨I was not born a ~ —Shak.⟩ **b** : something that yields produce or products : something that produces or furnishes — usu. used with qualifier ⟨direct taxes . . . proved poor ~*s* —C.L.Jones⟩ ⟨a variety of corn that is established as a good ~⟩
yield gene *n* [²*yield* + *gene*] : any of a group of complementary genes no one of which has apparent individual effect; *esp* : one that directly or indirectly affects (as by increasing resistance to disease or to drouth) the yield of various field crops
yielding *adj* [fr. pres. part. of ¹*yield*] **1** : PRODUCTIVE ⟨a new type of wheat — claimed to be extra high ~ —*Wall Street Jour.*⟩ **2** : inclined to give way (as to pressure) : lacking rigidity or stiffness : FLEXIBLE ⟨made of a ~ rubber or similar springing material —T.C.J.O'Connell⟩ ⟨a deep ~ mass of leaf mold —*Geog. Jour.*⟩ **3** : disposed to submit or comply : having a tendency to give in, surrender, or agree : COMPLIANT, SUBMISSIVE, TRACTABLE ⟨too ~ to make a stand against any encroachment —V.L.Parrington⟩ ⟨too ~ and indecisive a character —Jane Austen⟩
yield·ing·ly *adv* : in a yielding manner
yield·ing·ness *n* -ES : the quality or state of being yielding ⟨the ~ of the cartilaginous substance —William Paley⟩
yield insurance *n* [²*yield*] : insurance that guarantees investors a stated yield on their investment in approved residential housing
yield point *n* : a stress sufficiently beyond the elastic limit that the material begins to exhibit plastic properties and continues to deform without further increase of load — used esp. of tension; compare YIELD VALUE
yields *pres 3d sing of* YIELD, *pl of* YIELD
yield strength *n* : the stress at which a piece under strain is deformed some definite amount (as 0.1 or 0.2 percent)
yield table *n* : a tabulation indicating the volume of wood per unit area of forest to be expected at different ages of the trees
yield value *n* : the minimum shearing or normal stress required to produce continuous deformation in a solid
yill \ˈyil\ *chiefly Scot var of* ALE
yill-caup \ˈ=,=\ *n* [*yill* + *caup*] *Scot* : a vessel from which ale is drunk
yilt *var of* GILT
¹yin \ˈyin\ *chiefly Scot var of* ONE
²yin \"\ *n* -S [Chin (Pek) *yin*¹ dark, feminine principle] : the feminine and negative principle (as of passivity, depth, darkness, cold, wetness) in nature that according to traditional Chinese cosmology combines with its opposite yang to produce all that comes to be
yince \ˈyin(t)s\ *chiefly Scot var of* ONCE
ying·kow \ˈyiŋ¦kau̇, -kō\ *adj, usu cap* [fr. *Yingkow,* city and port of southern Manchuria] : of or from the city of Yingkow, Manchuria : of the kind or style prevalent in Yingkow
y-intercept \ˈ=ˈ=,=\ *n* : the y-coordinate of the point where a line, curve, or surface intersects the y-axis
¹yip \ˈyip\ *vb* **yipped; yipped; yipping; yips** [imit.] *vi* **1 a** : to bark or cry sharply, quickly, and often continuously esp. from eagerness — used chiefly of a dog **b** : to make a sound resembling the yip of a dog : utter a short sharp cry **2** : to complain sharply and loudly : SQUEAL ~ *vt* : to utter or emit by or as if by yipping
²yip \"\ *n* -S : a noise made by or as if by yipping ⟨barked again . . . then tapered off in a long dimenuendo of ~*s* —B.V. Dryer⟩ ⟨let out a ~ of discovery —Emily Hahn⟩ ⟨not another ~ from either complainant —C.W.Morton⟩
¹yipe \ˈyīp\ *vi* -ED/-ING/-S [imit.] : to cry out sharply esp. from surprise or pain ⟨*yiped* when he touched the hot stove⟩
²yipe \"\ *n* -S : a noise made by or as if by yiping ⟨the sudden ~ of a mongrel hurt —Wallace Stegner⟩ — used interjectionally in both sing. and pl.
yip·pee \ˈyipē\ *interj* — used to express exuberant delight or triumph
yird \ˈyərd\ *chiefly Scot var of* EARTH
yirk \ˈyərk\ *Scot var of* YERK
¹yirr \ˈyər\ *vi* -ED/-ING/-S [imit.] *Scot* : to growl or snarl in the manner of a dog
²yirr \"\ *n* -S *Scot* : a sound made by or as if by yirring : GROWL, SNARL
yirth \ˈyərth\ *chiefly Scot var of* EARTH
yite \ˈyīt\ *n* -S [origin unknown] *dial Brit* : EUROPEAN YELLOWHAMMER
yiz·kor \ˈyizkə(r)\ *n* -S *often cap* [Heb *yizkōr* remember; fr. the first word of the prayer] : a Jewish memorial service or prayer for the dead recited usu. in the synagogue on Yom Kippur, on the last day of Passover, on Shemini Atzereth, and on the second day of Shabuoth
-yl \ˌəl, ˌil, -ˌēl, (*when t, d, or n precedes*) ᵊl; *chiefly Brit* ˌīl\ *n comb form* -S [Gk *hylē* wood, matter; first used in G *benzoyl,* lit., fundamental material of benzoic acid, fr. *benz-* + Gk *hylē* — more at HYLE] : chemical radical: as **a** : univalent radical ⟨eth*yl*⟩ ⟨pyrid*yl*⟩ ⟨hydrox*yl*⟩ **b** : radical containing oxygen ⟨carbon*yl*⟩ ⟨chrom*yl*⟩ including a few radicals of organic acids ⟨acet*yl*⟩ ⟨glyc*yl*⟩ ⟨succin*yl*⟩; compare -OYL
yl *abbr* yellow
YL *abbr* young lady
ylang-ylang *var of* ILANG-ILANG
yld *abbr* yield
ylem \ˈīləm\ *n* -S [ME, fr. MF *ilem,* prob. fr. ML *hylem,* acc. of *hyle* matter, fr. L, fr. Gk *hylē* — more at HYLE] : the primordial first substance from which according to some theories the elements were supposed to be formed — compare HYLE
-ylene \ˌəˌlēn, ᵊlˌēn\ *n suffix* -S [*-yl* + *-ene*] **1** : unsaturated hydrocarbon ⟨piper*ylene*⟩ — compare -ENE **2** : bivalent radical ⟨phen*ylene* C_6H_4<⟩
y level *n, usu cap Y* : a surveyor's level with a telescope supported in y-shaped rests and as a result capable of being rotated around its own axis or of being taken out of the supports and turned end for end for purposes of adjustment — compare DUMPY LEVEL
-yl·i·dene \ˈiləˌdēn, ˌəl-\ *n suffix* -S [ISV *-yl* + *-idene*] : bivalent radical derived esp. from a saturated hydrocarbon by removal of two hydrogen atoms from the same carbon atom or by removal of the oxygen atom of an aldehyde ⟨citr*ylidene*⟩ — in the system adopted by the International Union of Pure and Applied Chemistry; compare -IDENE
-yl·i·dyne \ˈiləˌdīn, ˌəl-\ *n suffix* -S [ISV *-yl* + *-idyne*] : trivalent radical derived esp. from a saturated hydrocarbon by removal of three hydrogen atoms from the same carbon atom ⟨eth*ylidyne* $CH_3C{\equiv}$⟩ — in the system adopted by the International Union of Pure and Applied Chemistry
y ligament *n, usu cap Y* [¹*y* + *ligament;* fr. its branching] : ILIOFEMORAL LIGAMENT
y moth *n, usu cap Y* [so called fr. its y-shaped marking] : SILVER Y MOTH
yn *abbr* yen
ynam·bu \ˌēnämˈbü\ *n* -S [Pg *inambu, inhambu,* fr. Tupi *inambú*] : a very large tinamou (*Rhynchotus rufescens*) of southern Brazil and Argentina
-yne \ˌīn\ *n suffix* -S [ISV alter. of *-ine*] : unsaturated straight-chain hydrocarbon characterized by the presence of one triple bond — in the system adopted by the International Union of Pure and Applied Chemistry to replace the ending *-ine* in this sense ⟨hex*yne*⟩; distinguished from *-ane* and *-ene*
yo *also* **yeo** \ˈyō\ *interj* [ME *yo, io,* interj.] — used esp. by sailors as a signal to commence hauling on a rope
YO *abbr* **1** yarn over **2** year-old
yob \ˈyäb\ *n* -S [back slang for *boy*] *Brit* : FELLOW, YOKEL
yock \ˈyäk\ *slang var of* ⁴YAK
yock·er·nut \ˈyäkə(r),nət\ *or* **yock·ey·nut** \-kē,n-\ *n* [*yocker-, yockey-* (prob. irreg. fr. *wankapin*) + *nut*] : WATER CHINQUAPIN
yod \ˈyōd, ˈyȯd, ˈyäd\ *n* [prob. fr. *yodh*] : the voiced glide or spirant sound \y\ that is the first sound of the English word *yes*
¹yo·del *or* **jo·del** \ˈyōdᵊl\ *vb* **yodeled** *or* **yodelled; yodeled; yodelled; yodeling** *or* **yodelling** \-d(ᵊ)liŋ\ **yodels** [G *jodeln,* fr. G (southern dial.), fr. G (southern dial.) *jo,* interj.] *vi* : to sing in a manner common among the Swiss and Tyrolean mountaineers by suddenly changing from chest voice to head voice or falsetto and the reverse; *also* : to shout or call in a similar manner ~ *vt* : to sing (a tune) by yodeling
²yodel *or* **jodel** \"\ *n* -S : a song or refrain sung by yodeling; *also* : a yodeled shout or cry
yo·del·er \-d(ᵊ)lə(r)\ *n* -S : one that yodels
yodh *also* **yod** *or* **jod** *or* **iod** \ˈyōd, ˈyu̇d\ *n* -S [Heb *yōdh,* lit., hand] **1** : the 10th letter of the Hebrew alphabet — symbol ׳; see ALPHABET table **2** : the letter of the Phoenician or of any of various other Semitic alphabets corresponding to Hebrew yodh
yo·ga \ˈyōgə\ *n* -S [Skt, lit., yoking, union, disciplined activity, fr. *yunakti* he yokes — more at YOKE] **1** : union of the individual self with the universal spirit (as in samadhi) **2** *usu cap* : a major orthodox system of Hindu philosophy based on Sankhya but differing from it in being theistic and characterized by the teaching of raja-yoga as a practical method of liberating the self **3 a** : the suppression through progressive discipline (as raja-yoga) of all activity of body, mind, and individual will in order that the self may realize its distinction from them and attain liberation from all pain and suffering **b** : a system of exercises for attaining bodily or mental control and well-being **4** : a discipline by which the individual prepares himself for liberation of the self and union with the universal spirit — see RAJA-YOGA
yo·ga·ca·ra \ˌyōgəˈkärə\ *n* -S *usu cap* [Skt *yogācāra,* fr. *yoga* + *ācāra* custom, rule of conduct — more at ACHARYA] **1** : one of the two major philosophical systems of Mahayana Buddhism agreeing with Madhyamika that external objects are unreal but holding that mind is real and that objects which appear to be external and material are in fact ideas or states of consciousness — compare VIJNANAVADA **2** *or* **yo·ga·ca·rin**

\-rȯn\ [Skt *yogācāra, yogācārin*, fr. *yogācāra* (philosophical system)] **:** an adherent of Yogacara

yogh \ˈyōk, ˈyäk, ˈyōg, ˈk, ˈg\ *n* -S [ME *yogh, ʒogh, ʒok, yoʒ*] **:** a letter ʒ used in Middle English to represent a voiced velar fricative, a voiced palatal fricative, or sometimes a voiceless velar or palatal fricative

yo·gi \ˈyōgē\ *n* -S [Skt *yogin*, fr. *yoga*] **1** *also* **yo·gin** \-gin\ *also* **jo·gi** \ˈyōgē\ **:** a person who practices yoga; *esp* **:** a Hindu ascetic seeking self liberation through bodily and mental disciplines (as of posture, breathing, or concentration) and sometimes credited with supernormal powers **2** *or* **yogin** *usu cap* **:** an adherent of Yoga philosophy **3 :** a markedly reflective or mystical person

yo·gic \-gik\ *adj* [*yoga* + *-ic*] **1 :** of or relating to the practice of yoga **2 :** of or relating to philosophic Yoga

yo·gism \-ˌgizəm\ *n* -S [*yoga* + *-ism*] **1** *usu cap* **:** the teachings of Yoga **2 :** the practice of Yoga

yo·gurt *or* **yo·ghurt** *also* **yo·ghourt** \ˈyōgə(r)t\ *n* -S [Turk *yoğurt*] **:** a fermented slightly acid semifluid milk food made of skimmed cow's milk and milk solids to which cultures of two bacteria (*Lactobacillus acidophilus* and *Streptococcus thermophilus*) have been added

yo·him·bé \yəˈhimbā, -bē\ *also* **yo·him·bi** \-bē\ *or* **yo·him·bi·hi** \-bəˌhē\ *n* -S [of Bantu origin; akin to Duala *djombé* yohimbé] **:** a tropical African tree (*Corynanthe yohimbe*) of the family Rubiaceae the bark of which yields yohimbine

yo·him·bine \-mˌbēn, -bən\ *n* -S [ISV *yohimbé* + *-ine*] **1 :** a crystalline alkaloid $C_{21}H_{26}N_2O_3$ that is the principal alkaloid of yohimbé bark and that has sympathomimetic and hypotensive effects and has been used in the form of its hydrochloride as an aphrodisiac — called also *quebrachine* **2 :** any of several alkaloids isomeric with yohimbine and occurring with it ⟨alpha-*yohimbine*⟩

yo–ho \yōˈhō\ *interj* — used as a signal for effort or to attract attention

yoicks \ˈyȯiks\ *interj* [alter. of *hoicks*] **1** *archaic* — used as a cry of encouragement to foxhounds **2** *archaic* — used to express excitement or exultation

yo·jan \ˈyōjən\ *or* **yo·ja·na** \-jənə\ *n* -S [Hindi & Skt; Hindi *yojan*, fr. Skt *yojana* yoking, distance traversed in one yoking, fr. *yunakti* he yokes — more at YOKE] **:** any of various Hindu units of distance varying from 4 to 10 miles; *esp* **:** a unit equal to about 5 miles

yok \ˈyäk\ *slang var of* ⁴YAK

¹**yoke** \ˈyōk\ *n* -S *see sense 2* [ME *yok*, fr. OE *geoc*; akin to OHG *joh* yoke, ON *ok* yoke, Goth *juk* yoke (of oxen), L *jugum* yoke, *jungere* to join, Gk *zygon* yoke, *zeugnynai* to yoke, join, Skt *yuga* yoke, *yunakti* he yokes, joins] **1 a (1) :** a bar or frame of wood by which two draft animals (as oxen) are joined at the heads or necks for working together and esp. for drawing a plow or a load that is usu. a piece of timber hollowed or made curving near each end and laid on the necks of the oxen, secured in place by a bow passing under and enclosing each neck, and fastened through the timber **(2) :** an arched or curved device formerly laid upon the neck of a defeated person; *also* **:** an arch consisting of a spear resting horizontally upon two upright spears under which a captured foe is compelled to pass as a symbol of submission **(3) :** a frame worn on the neck of an animal (as a cow, pig, or goose) to prevent passage through a fence or hedge **(4) :** a usu. wooden frame fitted to a person's shoulders to carry a load suspended in two equal portions on opposite sides of the body **(5) :** a bar by which the end of the tongue of a wagon or carriage is suspended from the collars of a harness **b :** a tie securing two architectural members together; *specif* **:** the horizontal piece forming the head of a window frame **c (1) :** a crosspiece on the head of a boat's rudder to whose ends are attached lines leading forward either to the hands of a steersman or to the drum of a steering wheel so that the boat can be steered farther forward **(2) :** CONTROL COLUMN **d :** a frame or convex piece from which a bell is hung **e :** a clamp or similar piece that embraces two other parts to hold or unite them in their respective or relative positions: as **(1) :** a strap connecting a slide valve to the valve stem **(2) :** the soft iron block or bar (as in a dynamo) permanently connecting the pole pieces of an electromagnet **(3) :** a slotted crosshead used in some steam engines in place of a connecting rod **(4) :** the lower cap on the masthead of a yacht **f :** FIELD FRAME **g :** an assembly that fits around the neck of a cathode ray or picture tube and that contains coils used to control the position of the electron beam in the tube **2** *pl usu* **yoke a :** two animals yoked together ⟨ordinarily drawn by five or six ~ of oxen —W.F.Harris⟩; *also* **:** a pair of animals that work normally together ⟨kept eight ~ of oxen hauling supplies —Marjory S. Douglas⟩ **b** *obs* **:** PAIR, COUPLE **3 a :** an old Kentish unit of land area equal to ¼ sulung **b :** an Austrian cadastral unit equal to 1.42 acres **4 a (1) :** an oppressive agency reducing to subjection, submission, humiliation, or servitude ⟨thrown off the ~ of the mother country —C.G.Fenwick⟩ ⟨the young girl would rid herself of her mother's ~ —H.M.Parshley⟩ **(2) :** SERVITUDE, SLAVERY, BONDAGE, SERVICE ⟨my ~ is easy, and my burden is light —Mt 11:30 (RSV)⟩ **b (1) :** something that connects or binds **:** RELATIONSHIP, TIE, LINK, BOND ⟨since it recognizes no other truth . . . than its own, it needs must . . . bring everything under one ~ —M.R.Cohen⟩ **(2) :** the matrimonial bond; *esp* **:** one in which the partners are unequal **5 :** a fitted or shaped section of a garment to which a gathered, pleated, or flared section is attached used as the top of a skirt or the shoulder section of any of various garments and esp. of a shirt, blouse, or coat

²**yoke** \"\ *vb* -ED/-ING/-S [ME *yoken*, fr. OE *geocian*, fr. *geoc*, n., yoke — more at ¹YOKE] *vt* **1 a (1) :** to put a yoke on **:** join in or with a yoke ⟨continued stolidly *yoking* his oxen —A.C. Whitehead⟩ ⟨an ox . . . had been *yoked* together with a skinny poll-cow —O.E.Rölvaag⟩ **(2) :** to fit a yoke about the neck of (an animal) to prevent passage **b :** to attach a draft animal (as an ox) to ⟨~ a cart⟩ *also* **:** to attach (a draft animal) to something ⟨~ a horse to a cart⟩ **2 :** to couple, join, link, or associate as if by a yoke ⟨*yoked* two goals together in the title of his book —J.D.Hart⟩ ⟨*yoked* to a life and a companionship unvarying —James Boyd⟩ **3** *archaic* **:** to bring into bondage **:** hold in subjection **:** OPPRESS **4 :** to set to a task or operation **:** put to work ⟨*yoked* his great imagination to constant labor —W.R.Nicoll⟩ **~** *vi* **1 :** to be in intimate association **:** become joined or linked esp. in marriage or companionship **:** CONSORT ⟨we'll ~ together, like a double shadow —Shak.⟩ **2** *Scot* **:** to apply oneself vigorously **:** set to work — usu. used with *to*

³**yoke** *var of* YOLK

⁴**yoke** \ˈyōk\ *usu cap* — a communications code word for the letter *y*

yoke bone *n* **:** ZYGOMATIC BONE

yoke elm *n* **1 :** HORNBEAM 1a **2 :** a Himalayan tree (*Carpinus viminea*); *also* **:** its heavy hard wood

yokefellow \ˈ=ˌ=(ˌ)=\ *n* [trans. of Gk *syzygos*] **:** a close associate or companion **:** MATE, FELLOW, PARTNER; *esp* **:** a partner in marriage

yoke–footed \ˈ=ˌ==\ *adj* **:** YOKE-TOED

yo·kel \ˈyōkəl\ *n* -S [perh. fr. E dial. *yokel* green woodpecker, of imit. origin] **:** an unpolished, naive, or gullible inhabitant of a rural area or of a small town ⟨the legendary ~ who rushed onto the stage to rescue the heroine —Hunter Mead⟩ ⟨evidently peasants, some of them young ~s from the plow, no doubt ignorant and stupid —George Santayana⟩ **syn** see BOOR

yo·kel·ish \-k(ə)lish\ *adj* **:** characteristic of or resembling a yokel **:** RUDE, UNCOUTH

yo·kel·ry \-kəlrē, -ri\ *n* -ES **:** gullible unsophisticated country-folk **:** YOKELS

yokemate \ˈ=ˌ=\ *n* **:** YOKEFELLOW

yoke riveter *n* **:** a pneumatic riveter connected by a yoke with a dolly so that the center lines of the two coincide

yokes *pl of* YOKE, *pres 3d sing of* YOKE

yoke–toed \ˈ=ˌ=\ *adj* **:** having two toes in front and two behind ⟨most woodpeckers are *yoke-toed*⟩ **:** ZYGODACTYL

yoking *n* -S [fr. gerund of ²*yoke*] **1** *Scot* **:** CONTEST, BOUT **2** *dial Brit* **:** a period of steady work esp. by a plowman and team **3** *slang* **:** a street assault **:** MUGGING

yok·kai·chi \yōˈkīchē\ *adj, usu cap* [*Yokkaichi*, city in southern Honshu, Japan] **:** of or from the city of Yokkaichi, Japan **:** of the kind or style prevalent in Yokkaichi

yo·ko·ha·ma \ˌyōkəˈhämə\ *adj, usu cap* [*Yokohama*, city in southeast Honshu, Japan] **:** of or from the city of Yokohama, Japan **:** of the kind or style prevalent in Yokohama

yokohama bean *n, usu cap Y* **:** the ash-colored plump seed resembling the Lima bean of a Japanese vine (*Mucuna hasjoo*) or the white pod containing it; *also* **:** the vine itself that bears dark-purple showy racemes

yokohama fowl *n, usu cap Y* **:** JAPANESE FOWL

yo·ko·su·ka \ˌyōkəˈsükə *also* yəˈkäskə\ *adj, usu cap* [*Yokosuka*, city in southeast Honshu, Japan] **:** of or from the city of Yokosuka, Japan **:** of the kind or style prevalent in Yokosuka

yo·kuts \ˈyō(ˌ)kəts\ *n, pl* **yokuts** [Yokuts, people] **1 a :** an Indian people of the San Joaquin Valley and adjacent Sierra Nevada slopes, California **b :** a member of such people **2 :** a Mariposan language of the Yokuts people **3 :** MARIPOSAN

yol·dia \ˈyōldēə\ *n, cap* [NL, fr. Count *Yoldi* †1852 Span. nobleman in charge of the royal naturalistic collection of Denmark + NL *-ia*] **:** a large genus of small primitive bivalve mollusks (family Nuculamidae) widely distributed in temperate and Arctic seas

yole \ˈyōl\ *n* -S [alter. of *yawl*] **:** a usu. open sailing boat of the Shetland and Orkney islands smaller than a fifie and with usu. one raked mast

yolk \ˈyōk *also* ˈyōlk *dial* ˈyelk *or* ˈyəlk\ *or* **yoke** \ˈyōk\ *n* -S [ME *yolke, yelke*, fr. OE *geolca, geoloca*, fr. *geolu* yellow — more at YELLOW] **1 a :** the yellow spheroidal mass of stored food that forms the inner portion of the egg of a bird or reptile and is surrounded by the white — see WHITE YOLK, YELLOW YOLK; EGG illustration **b** *archaic* **:** the whole contents of an ovum which may be distinguished into a protoplasmic formative portion and an ergastric nutritive portion **c :** the material stored in an ovum that supplies food material to the developing embryo, consists chiefly of vitellin, nucleoprotein and other proteins, lecithin, and cholesterol, may be sparse and diffuse (as in a placental mammal) or copious and specif. arranged (as at the center or at one pole of the ovum), and when copious exerts a profound influence on the course of segmentation **2** [prob. alter. of (assumed) ME *yoke*, fr. (assumed) OE *ēowoca*; akin to MD *ieke* yolk (of wool); derivative fr. the root of E *¹ewe*] **:** oily material permeating wool in the natural state and consisting of wool fat, suint, and debris of various sorts **3** *obs* **:** the best or most important part **:** CENTER, ESSENCE

yolk cell *n* **:** a nucleated cytoplasmic mass that is derived from the egg nucleus of an arthropod and provides nutriment for the developing embryo

yolk cord *n* **:** a slender protoplasmic cord that connects the yolk glands with the egg chambers in an insect (as an aphid)

yolk duct *n* **:** VITELLINE DUCT

yolked \-kt, *often* ˌ= *in combination*\ *adj* **:** having a yolk — usu. used in combination

yolk fry *n* **:** fry of fish between hatching and complete absorption of the yolk sac

yolk gland *n* **:** VITELLARIUM

yolk nucleus *n* **1 :** a formed body possibly associated with yolk formation present in the cytoplasm of many developing oocytes **2 :** a nucleus in yolk **:** VITELLOPHAG

yolk plate *n* **:** one of the lamellae into which the yolk of the egg of amphibians and various fishes splits

yolk plug *n* **:** a pluglike mass of yolk cells found in the blastopore of the embryos of some vertebrates

yolk sac *n* **:** a membranous sac that is attached to an embryo and encloses food yolk (as in most vertebrates and cephalopods), that is continuous through the vitelline duct with the intestinal cavity of the embryo, that being abundantly supplied with blood vessels is throughout embryonic life and in some forms later the chief organ of nutrition, and that in placental mammals is nearly vestigial and functions chiefly prior to the elaboration of the placenta

yolk–sac placenta *n* **:** a structure in some sharks resembling a placenta, consisting of the vascular embryonic yolk sac wall intimately associated with the vascular maternal uterine or oviducal wall, and serving to nourish the embryo

yolk stalk *n* **:** the narrow tubular stalk connecting the yolk sac with the embryo

yolky \-kē, -ki, *stressed* ˈ==\ *adj* -ER/-EST [*yolk* + *-y*] **1 :** relating to, resembling, or containing yolk **2** [prob. alter. of (assumed) ME *yoky*, fr. OE *ēowocig*, fr. (assumed) OE *ēowoca* yolk (of wool) + OE *-ig* -y — more at YOLK] **:** full of yolk **:** GREASY — used of unwashed wool

yolk yellow *n* **:** a strong yellow that is greener and stronger than gamboge and slightly stronger than light chrome yellow — called also *primuline yellow*

yo·ma·wood \ˈyōməˌ-\ *n* [perh. fr. Burmese *youma* mountain range + E *wood*] **:** the wood of an Asiatic padauk esp. Andaman padauk

yom kip·pur \(ˈ)yōmˈkipər, ˌyəm-, (ˈ)yōm-, (ˈ)yäm-; ˈ=ki-ˈpù(ə)r\ *n, cap Y&K* [Heb *yōm kippūr*, fr. *yōm* day + *kippūr* atonement] **:** a solemn Jewish fast day falling on the 10th day of Tishri and marked by continuous prayer and repentance according to the rites described in Leviticus 16 — called also *Day of Atonement*

yom tob *or* **yom tov** \ˈyō(m(ˌ)tәv, ˈyəl *sometimes* |n(ˌ)t-; ˈyōmˈtōv\ *n, pl* **yo·mim to·bim** *or* **yo·mim to·vim** \ˌyōməm-ˈtōvəm, yōˌmēmtōˈvēm\ [Heb *yōm ṭōbh*, fr. *yōm* day + *ṭōbh* good] **:** a Jewish holiday or festival

yo·mud \ˈyōməd\ *n, pl* **yomud** *or* **yomuds** *usu cap* **1 :** a Turkoman people inhabiting the Khorezm oasis of Soviet Turkestan **2 :** a member of the Yomud people

¹**yon** \ˈyän, ˈyōn, ˈyən\ *adj* [ME, fr. OE *geon*; akin to OHG *ienēr, enēr*, adj., that, ON *inn* the, Goth *jains*, adj., that, L *enim*, conj., for, Gk *enē* day after tomorrow, OSlav *onŭ* he, that] **1** *chiefly dial* **:** that or lies some distance away in the indicated place or direction **:** YONDER **2** ⟨the nighest is four miles off, over ~ snowy hills —Herman Melville⟩ **2** *dial* **:** YONDER 1 ⟨friends on the ~ side of the Potomac —Hervey Allen⟩

²**yon** \"\ *pron* [ME, fr. *yon*, adj.] *dial* **:** that or those yonder ⟨marryin' a man like ~ —Neil Munro⟩

³**yon** \"\ *adv* [ME (Sc), fr. ME *yon*, adj.] **1 :** YONDER 1 ⟨~ the gallows used to clank —A.E.Housman⟩ ⟨palaces here and pleasure domes ~ —John Beaufort⟩ **2 :** THITHER, BACKWARD ⟨scattered here and ~ —Calder Willingham⟩

⁴**yon** \ˈyän\ *n* -S [origin unknown] **:** an Indian tree (*Anogeissus acuminata*) of the family Combretaceae with hard heavy yellowish wood that is esp. strong and useful for handles and shafts

yon·cal·la *also* **yon·kal·la** *or* **yon·ka·la** \yäŋˈkälə\ *n, pl* **yoncalla** *or* **yoncallas** *also* **yonkalla** *or* **yonkallas** *or* **yonkala** *or* **yonkalas** *usu cap* **1 :** a Kalapooian people of southwestern Oregon **2 :** a member of the Yoncalla people

yon·co·pin *also* **yon·ka·pin** *or* **yan·ka·pin** \ˈyäŋkəˌpin\ *n* -S [modif. of Ojibwa *wankipin*, lit., crooked root] **:** WATER CHINQUAPIN

¹**yond** \ˈyänd, ˈyōnd, ˈyənd\ *adv* [ME, fr. OE *geond*; akin to Goth *jaind* to that place, OE *geon*, adj., yonder — more at YON] *archaic* **:** YONDER

²**yond** \"\ *adj* [ME, fr. *yond*, adv.] *dial Brit* **:** YON

³**yond** \"\ *pron* [ME, fr. *yond*, adj.] *Brit* **:** that or those yonder

⁴**yond** \"\ *prep* [short for ²*beyond*] *archaic* **:** BEYOND, PAST

⁵**yond** *adj* [derived fr. ¹*yond* (through misunderstanding of the words *a tygre yond in Ynde*, actually meaning "a tiger yonder in India", in line E1199 of Chaucer's *Canterbury Tales*)] *obs* **:** RAGING

¹**yon·der** \ˈyändə(r) *sometimes* ˈyōn- *or* ˈyən-\ *adv* [ME, fr. *yond* + *-er* (as in *hider* hither)] **:** at or in that indicated somewhat distant place usu. within sight ⟨off ~ on a high rise —F.B.Gipson⟩ ⟨look way back ~ down the hill —Eudora Welty⟩

²**yonder** \"\ *adj* [ME, fr. *yonder*, adv.] **1 :** farther removed **:** more distant **:** THITHER ⟨a pleasant hay meadow . . . bordered it on the ~ side —Agnes S. Turnbull⟩ **2 :** being at a distance within view or at a place or in a direction known or indicated ⟨could not see any trees save one, way ~ in the stubble field —Jean Stafford⟩ ⟨down at the bottom of that road ~ —Dorothy G. Spicer⟩

³**yonder** \"\ *pron* [¹*yonder*] **:** something that is or is in an indicated somewhat distant place ⟨sending chips from here to ~ —Maristan Chapman⟩

yo·ni \ˈyōnē\ *n* -S [Skt, vulva] **:** a figure representing the female genitals serving as the formal symbol under which Shakti is worshiped — compare LINGAM — **yo·nic** \-nik\ *adj*

yonker *var of* YOUNKER

yon·kers \ˈyäŋkə(r)z\ *adj, usu cap* [*Yonkers*, city in southeast New York] **:** of or from the city of Yonkers, N.Y. ⟨a *Yonkers* resident⟩ **:** of the kind or style prevalent in Yonkers

yon·kers·ite \-ˌzīt\ *n* -S *cap* **:** a native or resident of Yonkers, New York

yons *pl of* YON

yont \ˈyänt\ *Scot var of* YOND

¹**yoo–hoo** \ˈyüˌhü\ *interj* [origin unknown] — used to attract attention or as a call to persons

²**yoo–hoo** \"\ *vi* -ED/-ING/-S **:** to attract attention or call by or as if by shouting *yoo-hoo* ⟨arrived and *yoo-hooed* at the door —John Selby⟩

yore \ˈyō(ə)r, -ȯ(ə)r, -ōə, -ȯ(ə)\ *n* -S [ME, fr. *yore*, adv., long ago, fr. OE *geāra*, fr. *gēar* year — more at YEAR] **:** time past and esp. long since past — usu. used in the phrase *of yore* ⟨prize the region less highly than of ~ —R.A.Billington⟩ ⟨the finishing school of ~ is just about finished —H.R.Allen⟩

¹**york** \ˈyȯ(ə)rk, -ō(ə)k\ *adj, usu cap* [*York*, city in northern England] **1 :** of or from the city of York, England **:** of the kind or style prevalent in York **2** [*Yorkshire, York*, county in northern England] **:** YORKSHIRE

²**york** \"\ *vt* -ED/-ING/-S [back-formation fr. ²*yorker*] **:** to bowl out (a batsman) in cricket with a yorker

york boat *n, usu cap Y* [*York* Factory, trading post in northeast Manitoba, Canada] **:** a large rowboat used for hauling freight on inland waterways in the Canadian Northwest

¹**york·er** \ˈyȯrkər, -ō(ə)k-\ *n* -S *cap* [New *York*, state in the eastern U.S. + E *-er*] **1 :** a native or resident of New York esp. in colonial times **2** [*York*, city and county in southern Pennsylvania + E *-er*] **:** a native or resident of York, Pennsylvania or of York county, Pennsylvania

²**yorker** \"\ *n* -S [*York*, county in northern England + E *-er*] **:** a bowled ball in cricket that pitches in or close to the blockhole

³**yorker** \"\ *n* -S [New *York*, city in southeast New York (state) + E *-er*; fr. the popularity of such hogs with butchers in New York City] **:** a light but high-quality well-finished market hog suitable for fresh pork production

yorker brethren *n pl, usu cap Y&B* [¹*yorker* + *brethren*; fr. their origin mainly in York county, Pennsylvania] **:** members of a small body of River Brethren in the U.S. — called also *Old Order Brethren*

york gum *n, usu cap Y* [*York*, town in southwest Western Australia] **:** any of various eucalypts (esp. *Eucalyptus loxophleba* and *E. foecunda*) of Australia having pale brown wood with white markings

york·ish \-kish\ *adj, usu cap* [*York*, English royal house with reigning monarchs 1461–70 and 1471–85 (fr. *York*, city and county in northern England) + E *-ish*] **:** YORKIST

¹**york·ist** \-kəst\ *n* -S *cap* [*York*, English royal house + E *-ist*] **:** a member or supporter of the English royal house of York founded by Richard, Duke of York, in the time of Henry VI and continued by Edward IV, Edward V, and Richard III — compare LANCASTRIAN

²**yorkist** \"\ *adj, usu cap* **:** of or relating to the royal house of York

york rite *n, usu cap Y & often cap R* [*York*, city and county in northern England] **1 :** a ceremonial observed by one of the Masonic systems **2 :** a system or organization that observes the York rite and confers in the U.S. 13 degrees of which the last three are in commanderies of Knights Templar and in England four degrees — compare SCOTTISH RITE

york round *n, usu cap Y* **:** a men's round in archery consisting of 72 arrows fired at 100 yards, 48 at 80 yards, and 24 at 60 yards

york shilling *n, usu cap Y* [New *York*, state in the eastern U.S.] **:** a New York shilling worth about 12½ cents

¹**york·shire** \ˈyȯ(r)kˌshi(ə)r, -iə, -shə(r)\ *adj, usu cap* [*Yorkshire, York*, county in northern England] **:** of or from the county of York, England **:** of the kind or style prevalent in York

²**yorkshire** \"\ *n* -S *usu cap* **1 :** any of several breeds or strains of white swine originated in Yorkshire, England; *esp* **:** LARGE WHITE **2** -S **:** a swine of a Yorkshire breed or strain — compare MIDDLE WHITE

yorkshire bond *n, usu cap Y* **:** FLYING BOND

yorkshire canary *n, usu cap Y* **:** a canary of a variety distinguished by long slim erect build

yorkshire chair *n, usu cap Y* **:** a small chair with knobbed turned legs, straight uprights ending at the top with scrolls, and a broad carved top rail and a wide splat arched above and crescent-cut below made esp. in England in the 17th and 18th centuries

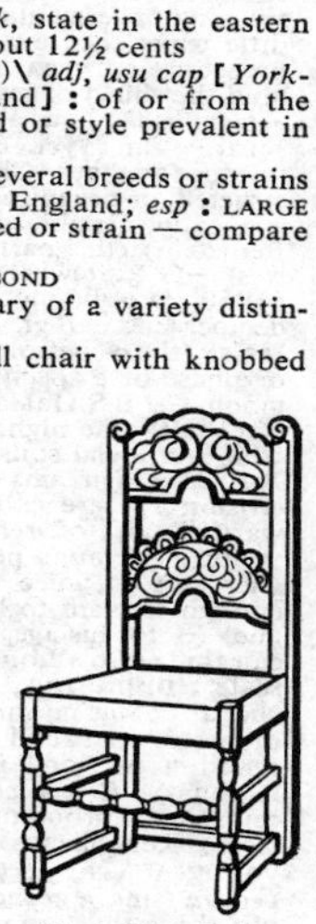
Yorkshire chair

yorkshire coach horse *n, usu cap Y* **:** a large strong bay or brown horse with dark legs, mane, and tail belonging to an English breed derived largely from the Cleveland bay

yorkshire fog *n, usu cap Y* **:** VELVET GRASS

yorkshire grease *n, usu cap Y* **:** wool grease recovered by scouring

yorkshire light *n, usu cap Y* **:** a window made with sashes sliding in one plane as distinguished from hinged casements and with a usu. horizontal movement to avoid the necessity of a weighted sash

york·shire·man \-ˌmən, -ˌman, -ˌmaa(ə)n\ *n, pl* **yorkshiremen** *cap* **:** a native or inhabitant of Yorkshire, England

yorkshire pudding *n, usu cap Y* **:** a batter of eggs, flour, and milk baked in meat drippings

yorkshire sanicle *n, usu cap Y* **:** a butterwort (*Pinguicula vulgaris*)

yorkshire terrier *n, usu cap Y* **:** a toy terrier having a compact body and straight silky hair that often trails on the ground and is colored a dark steel blue from the occiput to the root of the tail, a rich golden tan on the head, and a bright tan on the chest

yorkshire tyke *n, usu cap Y* **:** YORKSHIREMAN

york spot *n, usu cap Y* [*York* Imperial, variety of apple developed in York county, Pennsylvania (fr. *York*, county in southern Pennsylvania) + E *spot*] **:** a cork disease of apples

york state *adj, usu cap Y* [New *York*, state in the eastern U.S.] **:** NEW YORK 2

yo·ru·ba \ˈyȯrəbə, ˈyōr-\ *n, pl* **yoruba** *or* **yorubas** *usu cap* **1 a :** a Negro people of the eastern Guinea coast mainly between Dahomey and the lower Niger **b :** a member of such people **2 :** a Kwa language of the Yoruba people

yo·ru·ban \-bən\ *adj, usu cap* **:** of or relating to the Yoruba

yo·shi·no paper \yəˈshē(ˌ)nō-\ *n, usu cap Y* [perh. fr. *Yoshino*, town in central Honshu, Japan] **:** a Japanese tissue made from the fibers of the paper mulberry

¹**you** \(ˈ)yü, yə, -yē, *in "you're" usu & in "you'll" often* (ˌ)yù; *dial* (ˈ)yō; *the* y *& a preceding* t *are usu* ch (=t+sh) *as in "not you," the* y *& a preceding* d *are usu* j (=d+zh) *as in "did you"*\ *pron* [ME *you, yow*, fr. OE *ēow*, used as dat. & accus. of *gē* you; akin to MD *u* you (used as dat. & accus. of *gi, ge* you), OHG *iu* (used as dat. of *ir* you), ON *ythr* (used as dat. & accus. of *ēr* you), Goth *izwis* (used as dat. & accus. of *jus* you), and prob. to L *vos* you — more at RENDEZVOUS] **1 a :** the one or ones being addressed — used currently and freely as the pronoun of the second person singular or plural in any grammatical relation except that of a possessive; used from Old English times to the 13th or 14th century only as a plural pronoun of the second person in the dative or accusative case as direct or indirect object of a verb or as object of a preposition and still current in this use alongside of other more recently originated uses ⟨I'll meet ~ there, fellows⟩ ⟨we will give ~ ten minutes to disperse⟩ ⟨presents for ~ two⟩; used since the 13th or 14th century also as a singular pronoun of

the second person as direct or indirect object of a verb or as object of a preposition, at first only as the appropriate form of address to a person of high social status or to a person not well known to the speaker but later without this limitation ⟨I shall . . . obey ~, madam —Shak.⟩ ⟨can I pour ~ a cup of tea⟩ ⟨a suit tailored just for ~⟩; used since the 14th century also as a plural pronoun of the second person in the nominative case and at any rate since the 16th century also in direct address ⟨~ have among you killed a sweet and innocent lady —Shak.⟩ ⟨stand still, ~ ever-moving spheres of heaven —Christopher Marlowe⟩; used since the 15th century also as a singular pronoun of the second person in the nominative case and at any rate since the early 16th century also in direct address, at first only as the appropriate form of address to a person of high social status or to a person not well known to the speaker but later without this limitation ⟨~ shall not go, my lord —Shak.⟩ ⟨stop that, ~ little pest⟩; sometimes used as a vague indirect object simply to suggest the concern or involvement of the one or ones being addressed or even with little or no meaning ⟨a civil modest wife, and one . . . that will not miss ~ morning nor evening prayer —Shak.⟩ ⟨he could knock ~ off forty Latin verses in an hour —W.M.Thackeray⟩; used like the adjective *your* with a gerund by speakers and writers on all educational levels though disapproved by some grammarians ⟨there is no point in ~ waiting any longer⟩; see YE, YOUR, YOURS; compare THEE, THOU **b** (1) **:** YOURSELVES — used reflexively as indirect object of a verb ⟨build ~ cities —Num 32:24 (AV)⟩ or object of a preposition ⟨divide it between ~⟩ or direct object of a verb ⟨prepare ~, lords —Shak.⟩ (2) **:** YOURSELF — used reflexively as indirect object of a verb ⟨you'd better find ~ another place to hang your hat —T.H. Phillips⟩ or object of a preposition ⟨bring your wife with ~⟩ or direct object of a verb ⟨Your Highness shall repose ~ at the Tower —Shak.⟩ **2 :** ²ONE 1b(1) ⟨when ~ have summed up all the factors of a man that can be measured ~ have still not described or understood him —A.L.Nickerson⟩ — **for you :** displayed in his, her, its, or their characteristic nature or behavior ⟨he's already forgotten he was hurt — that's a child *for you*⟩ — often used disparagingly ⟨that's a woman driver *for you*⟩ — **to you 1 :** according to the form of a name or title that is proper for you to use ⟨not John, if you don't mind — Mr. Doe *to you*⟩ **2 :** in easily understandable nontechnical language ⟨trinitrotoluene (TNT *to you*)⟩

²**you** \ˈyü\ *n* -s **1 :** a person indistinguishable from the one being addressed ⟨in everything but outward appearance he is another ~⟩ **2 :** the personality of the person being addressed ⟨the real ~⟩

you–all \(ˈ)yüˌȯl, ˈyȯl\ *pron* **:** YOU — usu. used in addressing two or more persons or sometimes one person as representing also another or others ⟨down here we can always spot Yankees by the way they use *you-all* in the singular —Arthur Gordon⟩ ⟨*you-all* should stop arguing among yourselves⟩

¹**young** \ˈyəŋ\ *adj* **youn·ger** \-ŋgə(r)\ **youn·gest** \-ŋgəst\ [ME *yong*, fr. OE *geong*; akin to OHG *jung* young, ON *ungr* young, Goth *jungs* youthful, new, L *juvenis* young, Skt *yuvan*] **1 :** being in the first or relatively early stage of life, growth, or development: as **a :** not long born **:** being in the first part of life **:** not yet arrived at adolescence, maturity, or age ⟨mothers with very ~ children⟩ ⟨a strapping ~*er* brother —R.T.Bird⟩ ⟨~ people⟩ ⟨a ~ family⟩ ⟨a ~ man⟩ ⟨you have but a very few years to be ~ and handsome —Jonathan Swift⟩ ⟨forgot that he was once ~ and passionate —Carl Van Doren⟩ ⟨~ puppies⟩ ⟨a spirited ~ colt⟩; *specif* **:** JUNIOR 1a ⟨the ~ Mr. Smith⟩ ⟨it was ~ Alex who . . . informed his father —Glenway Wescott⟩ **b :** of an early, tender, or desirable age esp. for use as food ⟨fresh ~ lamb⟩ ⟨~ pork⟩ ⟨~ corn on the cob⟩ **c :** being in an early or immature state of development or cultivation ⟨in place of the old will come new ~ scarlet oaks and beech, 10 feet high when planted —P.L.Ritzema⟩ ⟨apple sawfly caterpillars attack the ~ fruit in early summer⟩ ⟨~ shoots of the new grass⟩; *specif* **:** being in an early stage of ripening or fermentation ⟨a ~ cheese⟩ ⟨~ wine⟩ **2 :** having little experience esp. in a newly begun course of action or procedure **:** UNPRACTICED ⟨liked to hide my blunders . . . behind the shield of pretence that I was ~, naive, inexperienced —*Omnibook*⟩ ⟨was always ~ for liberty . . . of the intellect and spirit —Van Wyck Brooks⟩ ⟨the world was as yet too ~ in science for that —Charlton Laird⟩ **3 a :** newly formed, constructed, or organized **:** recently come into being **:** NEW ⟨she is a ~ ship, capable of outrunning most submarines —Walter Bernstein⟩ ⟨this part of the road is ~*er* than the part farther west —G.R.Stewart⟩ ⟨when the war was ~ —Thomas Wood †1950⟩ ⟨a ~ boom town —*Current Biog.*⟩ ⟨a model for the ~ democracies —*Brit. Bk. News*⟩ ⟨the ~*er* universities —S.P.B. Mais⟩ ⟨the ~ petroleum industry⟩ **b :** being in the early part or phase of a specified development or period of time ⟨a ~ moon —J.B.S.Haldane⟩ ⟨the day was still ~ —Agnes S. Turnbull⟩ ⟨the night is yet ~ —R.H.Croll⟩ **c :** YOUTHFUL 5 ⟨the ~ alluvial soils . . . have not yet developed a profile — R.E.Crist⟩ ⟨streams that have just entered upon their work of erosion . . . are called ~ streams —V.C.Finch & G.T.Trewartha⟩ **4 :** of, relating to, or having the characteristics of youth or a young person ⟨trying to stay ~ as he grows old⟩ ⟨her soft ~ voice —Walter O'Meara⟩ ⟨loves the language enough to want to keep it always ~ and racy —C.E.Montague⟩ ⟨~ for his age⟩ ⟨wearing the ~*est* and giddiest hats they can find —Lois Long⟩ **5 :** simulative of something in its full scale **:** DIMINUTIVE, MINIATURE ⟨under her hands the harpsichord . . . was no small and ancient instrument, but a whole ~ orchestra in sound —Osbert Sitwell⟩ ⟨the heavy rain produced a ~ flood in the street⟩ ⟨his souvenirs form a ~ museum⟩ **6** *usu cap* **:** forming or representing a new or rejuvenated group or movement esp. of a political nature ⟨the *Young* Republicans⟩ ⟨*Young* Germany⟩ ⟨*Young* Italy⟩

²**young** \"\ *n, pl* **young** *also* **youngs** [ME *yonge*, fr. OE *geonga* (sing.), *geonge*, *geongan* (pl.), fr. *geong*, adj.] **1** *young*, *pl* **:** those that are young: as **a :** young persons **:** YOUTH ⟨a story for ~ and old⟩ ⟨impart to the ~ the cultural heritage —Thomas Munro⟩ ⟨the ~ have a harder time of it than any previous generation —Hans Weigel⟩ **b :** the offspring of human beings or of animals before or for a short time after birth ⟨parents must think out . . . what this means to their own ~ —Dorothy Barclay⟩ ⟨talking to him as all women talk to their ~ —Farley Mowat⟩ ⟨watching animals . . . with ~ — C.K.Ogden⟩ ⟨bringing forth their ~⟩ **2 :** a single recently born or hatched animal **:** OFFSPRING ⟨producing one ~ each year⟩ — **with young :** PREGNANT — used of a female animal

youngberry \ˈ≈,–\ — *see* BERRY\ *n* [after B. M. *Young fl* 1900 Am. fruit grower who developed it] **:** the large sweet reddish black fruit of a hybrid between a trailing blackberry and a southern dewberry grown in western and southern U.S.; *also* **:** the trailing hybrid bramble

youn·ger \ˈyəŋgə(r)\ *n* -s [ME *yonger*, fr. OE *geongra* disciple, servant, alter. (influenced by *geong*) of *gyngra*, fr. *gyngra*, compar. of *geong* young] **1 :** an inferior in age **:** JUNIOR — usu. used with a possessive pronoun ⟨his sister is several years his ~⟩ **2 :** a young person **:** OFFSPRING — usu. used in pl. ⟨all the ~*s* are going to the circus with their families⟩ **3 a :** the dealer in a two-handed card game **b :** the partner of the eldest hand in a four-handed partnership game

youn·gest \-gəst\ *n, pl* **youngest** [ME *yongest*, *yongeste*, alter. (influenced by *yong* young) of *yingest*, *yingeste*, fr. OE *gyngesta*, *gyngsta*, fr. *gyngst*, superl. of *geong* young] **:** one that is least old; *esp* **:** the youngest child or member of a family ⟨you can go back to your law office after our ~ grows up — Evelyn Barkins⟩

young fustic *n* **1 :** FUSTET 2 **2 :** the coloring matter that is extracted from fustet dyewood — see DYE table I (under *Natural Brown 1*)

young–helmholtz theory \ˈyəŋˈhel|m,hōlts, -ˈheu̇l|-\ *n, usu cap Y&H* [Thomas *Young* †1829 Eng. physician and physicist and Hermann L. F. von *Helmholtz* †1894 Ger. physicist] **:** a theory in color vision: the eye has three separate elements each of which is stimulated by a different primary color

young hyson *n* **:** a hyson tea made from young leaves

young·ish \ˈyəŋish, -ēsh\ *adj* **:** somewhat young **:** more nearly resembling or characteristic of a young person than one of maturity or middle age ⟨a ~ but not adolescent audience — Virgil Thomson⟩ ⟨~ spinsters —*New Yorker*⟩ ⟨prematurely bald, ~ —T.M.Johnson⟩

young lady *n* [ME *yong lady*, fr. *yong* young + *lady*] **:** a usu. unmarried young woman of grace, manners, or distinction ⟨is becoming quite a *young lady*⟩

¹**young·ling** \ˈyəŋliŋ, -lēŋ\ *n* -s [ME *yongling*, fr. OE *geongling*, fr. *geong* young + *-ling*] **:** one that is young: as **a :** a young person **:** YOUTH ⟨a thin blond ~ —D.C.Peattie⟩ ⟨an automobile . . . is no treat to quite a large proportion of our ~*s* —F.A.Swinnerton⟩ **b :** a young animal or offspring of an animal ⟨the ~ rejoined its mother who . . . led her darling away into the tall grass —Roy Bedichek⟩ ⟨nerves . . . so placed in the ~ as to provide for the migration —*Book of Fishes*⟩

²**youngling** \"\ *adj* **:** YOUNG, YOUTHFUL

young·ly *adv* **1 :** in a young or youthful manner ⟨her . . . dark hair was ~ dressed —Margaret Sloper⟩ **2 :** early in life **:** in youth ⟨had been a passionate and ~ matured girl —Philip Wylie⟩

young man *n* [ME *yong man*, fr. *yong* young + *man*] **1 :** a male youth; *esp* **:** one in early manhood **2 :** a youth employed as a helper **3 :** male sweetheart **:** BEAU ⟨she is entertaining her *young man* this evening⟩

young·ness *n* -ES **:** YOUTHFULNESS

young–old \ˈ≈ˈ≈\ *adj* **:** old in years but having the characteristics of youth

young one \ˈyəŋ(w)ən, *dial* -ŋəm *or* ˈyōŋə-\ *n* [ME *yong oon* young person, fr. *yong* young + *oon* one] **1 :** a young human being **:** CHILD, YOUNGSTER ⟨they've got eleven *young ones*, eleven brats now —Elizabeth M. Roberts⟩ **2 :** a young animal

young people *n* **:** the youth usu. between the ages of 12 and 24 ministered to by a Protestant Christian church or denomination; *esp* **:** the organized youth group of a church ⟨the *young people*'s meeting⟩ ⟨*young people*'s service⟩ ⟨the *young people* have invited the Connecticut valley youth to be their guests —*Springfield (Mass.) Unity News*⟩

youngs *pl of* YOUNG

young's experiment \ˈyəŋz-\ *n, usu cap Y* [after Thomas *Young* †1829 Eng. physician and physicist] **:** an experiment in which light diverging from one slit passes through two narrow slits very close together and then falls on a screen so that a series of parallel bands are observed on the screen because of interference of light from the two slits

young's modulus *n, usu cap Y* **:** the ratio of the tensile stress in a material to the corresponding tensile strain — see MODULUS OF ELASTICITY

young·ster \ˈyəŋztə(r), -ŋ(k)st-\ *n* -s **1 a :** a usu. vigorous or lively young person **:** YOUTH ⟨communities which do not have adequate facilities for the ~ in trouble —J.B.Costello⟩ ⟨tells us . . . of the adolescence of this ~ —H.G.Wells⟩ ⟨a bumper crop of teen-age ~*s* fast ripening into . . . soldiers —*U.S.News & World Report*⟩ **b :** CHILD ⟨the mother with her ~*s* tumbling about her feet⟩ **c :** a person in the relatively early years of manhood or of a career ⟨it is among the ~*s*, aged from 20 to 40, that the flame of confidence burns brightest —Drew Middleton⟩ ⟨only a handful . . . left, most of them ~*s* in their twenties and thirties —*Saturday Rev.*⟩ **d :** an older or aged person retaining the vitality or vigor of youth ⟨a sprightly ~ of eighty, he's still going strong doing six shows a day —*Irish Digest*⟩ **2 a :** a midshipman who has served less than four years — compare OLDSTER 1 **b :** a sophomore at a military academy (as the U.S. Naval Academy) **3 a :** a young mammal, bird, or plant esp. of a domesticated or cultivated breed or type ⟨owners can try out their ~*s* for the first time on a racecourse —Dennis Craig⟩ ⟨one ~ . . . old enough to fly —T.M.Downs⟩ ⟨no trees except for a few hardy ~*s* —Nathaniel Burt⟩ **b youngsters** *pl, dial* **:** the young leaves of the common wintergreen (*Gaultheria procumbens*) **4 :** something newly formed, instituted, or established ⟨ballet . . . was just about a hundred years old, practically a ~ as art forms go —Anatole Chujoy⟩ ⟨joined hands with another promising ~, a journalistic fraternity —*Quill*⟩

youngs·town \ˈyəŋz,tau̇n\ *adj, usu cap* [*Youngstown*, city in northeast Ohio] **:** of or from the city of Youngstown, Ohio ⟨*Youngstown* steel mills⟩ **:** of the kind or style prevalent in Youngstown

young thing *n* [ME *yong thing* young person, fr. *yong* young + *thing* person, living being, thing] **1 :** a young person; *esp* **:** a young woman ⟨sweet *young thing*⟩ **2 :** a young animal; *specif* **:** a horse not yet old enough to be completely trained and ready for use

young turk *n, usu cap Y&T* [*Young Turk*, member of a revolutionary party in Turkey in the early years of the 20th cent.] **:** an insurgent or a member of an insurgent group in a political party **:** LIBERAL, RADICAL ⟨are the *Young Turks* . . . opposed to the ossified conservatism of the older so-called statesmen — John Gunther⟩ ⟨the truculence of the *Young Turks* colliding with the standpat South —Alistair Cooke⟩

youn·ker *or* **yon·ker** \ˈyəŋkə(r)\ *n* -s [D *jonker* young nobleman, young man of high rank, fr. MD *jonchere*, fr. *jonc* young (akin to OE *geong* young) + *here* lord, master (akin to OHG *hērro*, *hēriro* lord, master, fr. *hēriro*, compar. of *hēr* old) — more at YOUNG, HOAR] **1 a :** a young man **:** YOUNGSTER **b :** CHILD **2** *archaic* **:** a junior seaman on board ship

youpon *var of* YAUPON

¹**your** [ME, fr. OE *ēower* (used as gen. of *gē* you); akin to OHG *iuwēr* of you, ON *ythar*, Goth *izwara* of you, OE *ēow* (used as dat. & accus. of *gē* you) — more at YOU] *obs possessive of* YE

²**your** \ˌyə(r), (ˌ)yü(ə)r, (ˌ)yō(ə)r, (ˌ)yȯ(ə)r, -üə, -ōə, -ȯ(ə), *South chiefly substand* (ˌ)yō; *for* t & d + y *see* ¹YOU\ *adj* [ME, fr. OE *ēower*; akin to OHG *iuwēr* your, ON *ytharr*, *ythvarr*, Goth *izwar*; derivative fr. the root of E ¹*you*] **1 a :** of or belonging to you or yourself or yourselves as possessor or possessors **:** due to you **:** inherent in you **:** associated or connected with you ⟨~ heart⟩ ⟨~ talents⟩ ⟨~ bodies⟩ **b :** of or relating to you or yourself or yourselves as author or authors, doer or doers, giver or givers, or agent or agents **:** effected by you **:** experienced by you as subject **:** that you are capable of ⟨~ contributions⟩ ⟨with ~ permission⟩ ⟨by ~ assembling here⟩ ⟨working ~ hardest⟩ **c :** of or relating to you or yourself or yourselves as object of an action **:** experienced by you as object ⟨~ discharge from the army⟩ ⟨~ election as the officers for the coming year⟩ **d :** that you have to do with or are supposed to possess or to have knowledge or a share of or some special interest in ⟨you students know ~ geography⟩ — sometimes used with little or no meaning almost as an equivalent to the definite article *the* ⟨~ worm is ~ only emperor for diet —Shak.⟩ ⟨if ~ pragmatist-instrumentalist is asked for an opinion —M.B.Smith⟩ **e :** that is esp. significant for you **:** that brings you good fortune or prominence — used with *day* or sometimes with other words indicating a division of time ⟨congratulations on the prizes; this is really ~ day⟩ **2 :** of, belonging to, or relating to one or oneself ⟨when you face the north, east is at ~ right⟩ — compare ¹YOU 2

yourn \(ˈ)yō(ə)rn, (ˈ)yü(ə)rn, (ˈ)yȯ(ə)rn, -üən, -ōən, -ȯ(ə)n, *for* t & d + y *see* ¹YOU\ *pron* [ME *youren*, fr. *youre*, *your* your + *-n* (as in *min* mine)] *chiefly dial* **:** YOURS

¹**yours** *pronunciations at* ²YOUR (*except first*) + z\ *pron* [ME *yours*, *youres*, fr. *your* + *-s*, *-es* -ˈs] **1 a :** your one **:** your ones — used without a following noun as a pronoun equivalent in meaning to the adjective *your* ⟨either my fault or ~⟩ ⟨these tomatoes are ~⟩; often used esp. with an adverbial modifier in the complimentary close of a letter to express the polite fiction that the sender puts himself entirely at the receiver's disposal ⟨~ truly⟩ ⟨~ faithfully⟩ ⟨sincerely ~⟩; often used after *of* to single out one or more members of a class belonging to or connected with the one or ones being addressed ⟨a neighbor of ~⟩ ⟨some favorite records of ~⟩ or merely to identify something or someone as belonging to or connected with the one or ones being addressed without any implication of membership in a more extensive class ⟨that arthritis of ~⟩ ⟨all those cats of ~⟩ ⟨that wry humor of ~⟩ **b :** your family ⟨sending best wishes to you and ~⟩ **c :** your letter ⟨this is in reply to ~ of the 24th⟩ — usu. considered stylistically undesirable **2 :** something belonging to you **:** what belongs to you ⟨all that is mine is ~ —Lk 15:31 (RSV)⟩ **3 :** something belonging to one **:** what belongs to one ⟨when you have worked hard, you naturally want to get the reward that is rightfully ~⟩ — compare ¹YOU 2 — **yours truly :** I, ME, MYSELF ⟨I can take care of *yours truly*⟩ ⟨if it suits you, it's all right with *yours truly*⟩

²**yours** *adj, obs* **:** ²YOUR 1 — used as the first of two modifiers of the same noun

yourself \ˈ≈ˈ≈\ *pron* [ME, fr. ²*your* + *self*, n.] **1 a :** that identical one that is you **:** the self that belongs to you **:** the self that is yours — used at first only in reference to a person of high social status or a person not well known to the speaker ⟨as many, worthy lady, to ~ —Shak.⟩ but later without this limitation; used reflexively as object of a preposition or direct or indirect object of a verb ⟨why should you be so cruel to ~ —John Milton⟩ ⟨be careful or you might hurt ~⟩ ⟨how much time do you allow ~ for a shave⟩ or for emphasis in apposition esp. with *you* or *ye* or after an imperative verb ⟨an ice pick which you ~ had bought —Erle Stanley Gardner⟩ ⟨you said the same thing ~⟩ ⟨I'd like to see you do any better ~⟩ ⟨carry the packages ~⟩ or for emphasis instead of nonreflexive *you* as object of a preposition or direct or indirect object of a verb ⟨a method developed . . . by men like ~ —Bernard Bloch⟩ ⟨asked me to give your wife and ~ his best wishes⟩ or for emphasis instead of *you* or instead of *you yourself* as predicate nominative ⟨the only one I am worried about is ~⟩ or in comparisons after *than* or *as* ⟨nobody is better qualified for the job than ~⟩ or as part of a compound subject ⟨we hope your husband and ~ can be there⟩ or in archaic or substandard use as only subject of a verb either in the third person singular form or in the same form that would agree with *you* as subject ⟨I'm all right; how's ~⟩ ⟨~ are tall —Robert Browning⟩ or in absolute constructions ⟨~ a cautious man, you expect caution in others⟩ **b :** your normal, healthy, or sane condition ⟨when you came to ~ again after the accident⟩ **:** your normal, healthy, or sane self ⟨you are not ~ today⟩ **2 :** ONESELF ⟨it is more restful to ride in a car that someone else is driving than to drive a car ~⟩ ⟨the registrant testified that, in his belief, the Bible does believe in defending ~ but not with weapons —J.J.Smith⟩ ⟨the process of coming to ~ after being under an anesthetic⟩

yourselves \ˈ≈ˈ≈\ *pron pl* [fr. *yourself*, after E *self*: *selves*] **1 :** those identical ones that are you **:** the selves that belong to you **:** the selves that are yours — used reflexively as object of a preposition or direct or indirect object of a verb ⟨you have a right to be proud of ~⟩ ⟨you need not trouble ~ about that⟩ ⟨so that you children can get ~ a treat⟩ or for emphasis in apposition esp. with *you* or *ye* or after an imperative verb ⟨that ye will not fall upon me ~ —Judg 15:12 (AV)⟩ ⟨do your homework ~⟩ or for emphasis instead of nonreflexive *you* as object of a preposition or direct or indirect object of a verb ⟨here are some presents for your children and also some for ~⟩ or for emphasis instead of *you* or instead of *you yourselves* as predicate nominative ⟨it was ~ broke compact and played false —Robert Browning⟩ or in comparisons after *than* or *as* ⟨by my birth I am held no less than ~ to know the limits of honor —P.B.Shelley⟩ or as part of a compound subject ⟨what do your neighbors and ~ think of the new highway⟩ or archaically as only subject of a verb ⟨now ~ have heard these things —Robert Browning⟩ or in absolute constructions ⟨envy me not the chance, ~ more fortunate —Robert Browning⟩ **2 :** the normal, healthy, or sane condition of you persons **:** your normal, healthy, or sane selves ⟨you will feel more like ~ after a good rest⟩

yous *pl of* YOU

youse *or* **yous** \(ˌ)yüz, ˌyəz, ˌyəs, (ˌ)yüs\ *pron* [¹*you* + ¹*-s*] *substand* **:** YOU — usu. used in addressing two or more persons or sometimes one person as representing also another or others ⟨the two of ~ —J.M.Synge⟩ ⟨the rest of ~ —J.A. Hetherington⟩

youth \ˈyüth\ *n, pl* **youths** \-t͟hz,-ths\ *often attrib* [ME *youthe*, fr. OE *geoguth*; akin to MD *joget* youth, OHG *jugund*, Goth *junda* youth, OE *geong* young — more at YOUNG] **1 a :** the time of life when one is young; *esp* **:** the period between childhood and maturity ⟨left two little girls who . . . spent their motherless ~ with their widowed father —Havelock Ellis⟩ ⟨in his ~ . . . combined cotton and dairy farming with acquiring an education —*Current Biog.*⟩ ⟨incongruities of ~ and age —John Galsworthy⟩ **b :** the early period of existence, growth, or development ⟨following its lively ~ the community lapsed into quietude —*Amer. Guide Series: Texas*⟩ ⟨dinosaurian knowledge was still in its ~ —W.E.Swinton⟩ ⟨many potentially sound animals are ruined . . . especially in ~ —*Farming*⟩ **2 a :** a young person; *esp* **:** a young male between the ages of adolescence and maturity ⟨at the age of fourteen the ~ entered . . . the office —A.L.Churchill⟩ ⟨a ~ aged 17 years —*Jour. Amer. Med. Assoc.*⟩ ⟨~*s* with something better than a secondary education —Roy Lewis & Angus Maude⟩ ⟨sold . . . to men, women, ~*s* of both sexes, and even to children —*Amer. Bk. Publishers Council*⟩ **b :** young persons or creatures — usu. pl. in constr. ⟨a future for the ~ who enter the teaching profession —*Education Digest*⟩ ⟨only seven out of ten ~ of high school age are now enrolled —B.H.Alberty⟩ ⟨that American ~ on the nation's campuses is not given . . . disappointment —B.G.Gallagher⟩ **c** *sometimes cap* **:** youth personified or youth in general ⟨~ in its search for life's permanent values —*Brit. Bk. News*⟩ ⟨~ will be served⟩ ⟨for ~ nothing is insurmountable⟩ **3 :** the fresh or vigorous condition or appearance of body, mind, or spirit characteristic of the period between childhood and maturity **:** YOUTHFULNESS ⟨restore an old man to ~ —Sara Jordan⟩ ⟨an inevitable symptom of the city's ~ and vigor —*Amer. Guide Series: Minn.*⟩ ⟨these ancient stories have the perennial ~ of human charm —H.O.Taylor⟩ **4 :** the quality or state of being young ⟨succeeded admirably in spite of his extreme ~ —F.T.Persons⟩ **5 :** the first stage into which a cycle of erosion is commonly divided ⟨all the erosional stages from the features of ~ to those of old age —V.C.Finch & G.T.Trewartha⟩

syn ADOLESCENCE, PUBERTY, PUBESCENCE, YOUTH are frequently used interchangeably to refer to the period between childhood and maturity. YOUTH, the most inclusive of these terms, applies sometimes to the entire period from childhood to maturity, sometimes to the period only between the maturing of the sexual organs and attaining to other types of maturity; more than the other terms YOUTH suggests the vigor, innocence, and ingratiating attributes generally associated with this early period of life and so has come to suggest vigor or fullness of life generally. ADOLESCENCE designates the same period as YOUTH in its most restricted sense, but carries a stronger implication of immaturity, suggesting the inexperience or awkwardness or mental or emotional instability often characteristic of that period of life; in legal use it designates the period from puberty to full legal age or majority. Strictly, PUBERTY designates the age at which the symptoms of sexual maturing appear, as the growth of beard and alteration of voice range in boys or breast development in girls; legally this age is fixed at fourteen for boys and twelve for girls. More broadly, PUBERTY covers the earlier period of adolescence. PUBESCENCE is sometimes used as the equivalent of PUBERTY or more specif. signifies the early years of sexual maturing.

youth–and–old–age \ˈ≈≈,≈ˈ≈\ *n* **:** ZINNIA 2

youth·en \ˈyüthən\ *vb* -ED/-ING/-S *vt* **:** to make youthful in appearance, behavior, or qualities of mind or feeling **~** *vi* **:** to become youthful in appearance or characteristics

youth fellowship *n, often cap Y&F* **:** the organized youth group of a Protestant Christian church or denomination

youth·ful \ˈyüthfəl\ *adj* **1 :** of, relating to, or appropriate for youth or the period of youth ⟨could remember from his ~ enlisted days —J.G.Cozzens⟩ ⟨his ~ optimism and his cheerful trust in men —Katherine McNamara⟩ **2 :** not yet advanced beyond the early stage of growth or development ⟨in the ~ shell the dorsal valve develops a nearly straight posterior . . . margin —J.A.Thomson b. 1881⟩ ⟨a hotbed of ~ plants⟩ ⟨a ~ culture —Stringfellow Barr⟩ **3 :** possessing or characterized by youth **:** not old or mature ⟨~ dancers crowd the floor⟩ ⟨the ~ pitcher handles himself like a veteran⟩ **4 :** having the vitality or freshness of youth **:** FRESH, VIGOROUS ⟨seems a bit dated now . . . but it is skillful, fluent, and ~ —Arthur Berger⟩ ⟨a ~ octogenarian —W.J.Ghent⟩ ⟨of the most brilliant colors and ~ cut —W.M.Thackeray⟩ **5 :** having accomplished or undergone little erosion ⟨high mountain chains of ~ topography —L.C.Reed⟩ ⟨valleys . . . carved by vigorous ~ streams —*Science*⟩ ⟨the ~ volcanic islands —*Jour. of Geol.*⟩ — compare CYCLE OF EROSION

syn JUVENILE, PUERILE, BOYISH, VIRGIN, VIRGINAL, MAIDEN: YOUTHFUL indicates simply a pertinence or appropriateness to youth; it is likely to be benign or appreciative, noncommittal, or extenuating in its suggestion ⟨in old age when the circula-

tion to the skin is lessened, the skin loses its *youthful* appearance —Morris Fishbein⟩ ⟨with bare shoulders and a little necklace, and a light blue sash, she looked the image of *youthful* innocence and girlish happiness —W.M.Thackeray⟩ ⟨*youthful* indiscretions⟩ JUVENILE often stresses the fact of youth and immaturity or of suitability to it; it may be used to stigmatize lack of adult judgment ⟨*juvenile* activities⟩ ⟨*juvenile* fiction⟩ ⟨the majority of the Irish people were only mildly sympathetic with the rebels, and regarded their desperate rebellion as *juvenile* melodrama —Paul Blanshard⟩ ⟨whereas adolescents looked upon this intense absorption as *juvenile* and had much more sophisticated attitudes —J.E.Anderson⟩ PUERILE may factually describe the acts or utterances of a boy or girl, esp. one quite young; it often stigmatizes childish immaturity in situations in which adult maturity can be expected or hoped for ⟨*puerile* digestive upsets⟩ ⟨it was dishonest, it was absurd, and it was *puerile* —Bernard De Voto⟩ ⟨badly constructed, incoherent, *puerile* in conception and presentation, and written in shoddy journalese —D.S.Savage⟩ BOYISH is often used in reference to the attractive or engaging qualities of normal, vigorous, unsophisticated boys ⟨*boyish* ardor⟩ ⟨*boyish* frankness⟩ ⟨had always, in a shy, *boyish* fashion, worshipped his big brother —B.A.Williams⟩ ⟨her features were clear-cut, her neck long and slender, her figure slim and *boyish* —Elizabeth Goudge⟩ VIRGIN stresses inexperience, esp. sexual inexperience, often with accompanying ingenuousness ⟨he was married, and the secret could be given only to a *virgin* youth —W.T.Corlett⟩ ⟨the picture of youth, unprotected innocence, and humble *virgin* simplicity —W.M. Thackeray⟩ VIRGINAL may be closely synonymous with VIRGIN; it is more likely to connote chastened or pure suggestions of virgin inexperience ⟨though she had lost long ago her *virginal* loveliness, she had ripened at middle age into a handsome and fruitful-looking woman —Ellen Glasgow⟩ MAIDEN may be a less frank synonym for VIRGIN ⟨a *maiden* aunt⟩ or it may apply to a first effort ⟨a *maiden* speech⟩ or suggest youthful chaste inexperience ⟨the *maiden* chastity and simplicity of these furnishings⟩ ⟨the young ladies on board, whom . . . the Cambridge lads and their pale-faced tutor avoided with *maiden* coyness —W.M.Thackeray⟩

youth·ful·ly \-fəlē, -li\ *adv* : in a youthful manner ⟨he is still ~ erratic⟩

youth·ful·ness *n* -ES : the quality or state of being youthful

youthful offender *or* **youth offender** *n* : a young lawbreaker usu. between the ages of 16 and 22 who has not committed a crime punishable by death or life imprisonment and toward whom a criminal court may use juvenile court procedures to attempt rehabilitation without imprisonment or other usual penalties

youth group *n* : a group of youths or young persons forming a part or a unit of an organized social, political, or religious institution ⟨the church sponsors a *youth group*⟩ ⟨the *youth groups* held another congress —E.A.Peers⟩

youth·head \'yüth,hed, -ū,thed\ *n* [ME *youthede, youthhede,* fr. *youthe, youth* youth + *-hede* -hood (akin to ME *-hod, -had* -hood)] *chiefly Scot* : the state or time of youth

youth·hood \-th,hùd\ *n* : the fact, condition, state, or time of being young

youth hostel *n* : HOSTEL 2b

youth hosteler *or* **youth hosteller** *n* **1** : one that stays at a youth hostel while traveling **2** : one that supervises a youth hostel

youth·ly *adj, archaic* : YOUTHFUL

youth movement *n* : a political, religious, or social movement or agitation led by or consisting chiefly of youth or young people and usu. aiming at reform or revolution ⟨ready . . . to join the Nazi *youth movements* —Brit. Bk. News⟩ ⟨the liberal section of younger Americans, the type out of whom *youth movements* are made —Nation⟩ ⟨basic to all *youth movements* are a deep dissatisfaction with the existing . . . order, a desire to change this order —Hans Kohn⟩ — compare YOUTH GROUP

youth-on-age \'⸗,⸗'⸗\ *n* : PICKABACK PLANT

youths *pl of* YOUTH

youthy \'yüthē, -thi\ *adj* -ER/-EST **1** *chiefly Scot* : YOUTHFUL **2** : affecting youthful habits or dress ⟨a ~ lady in her middle sixties⟩

¹yow \'yaù\ *dial Brit var of* YOU

²yow \"\ *interj* [ME *yowe*] — used to express excitement, joy, or surprise

³yow \'yō, 'yaù\ *dial Brit var of* EWE

¹yowl \'yaùl, *esp before pause or consonant* -aùəl\ *vb* -ED/-ING/-S [ME *yowlen, youlen,* prob. of imit. origin] *vi* **1** : to utter a loud cry of grief, pain, or distress usu. in a long and mournful fashion : WAIL, HOWL ⟨the dog pacing the fence ~s at every step⟩ ⟨the boy caught his finger in an office door and ~ed —Daniel Lang⟩ **2** : to complain or protest with or as if with yowls ⟨the children are ~ing over who is going first⟩ ⟨the Congressman ~s at his party for weak support⟩ ⟨those conditions that guarantee . . . the right to ~ —Fortune⟩ ~ *vt* : to utter or express with or as if with yowls ⟨the dog ~s his pain to the world⟩

²yowl \"\ *n* -S [ME (Sc) *yowle,* fr. ME *yowlen, youlen,* v.] : a loud long mournful wail or howl ⟨as of a dog or cat⟩ ⟨the familiar ~ that, taken up by the pack, is such melodious music —F.G.Turnbull⟩ ⟨giving an occasional ~ of excitement —R.A.W.Hughes⟩ ⟨wild, discordant yells and ~s —Broadway Mag.⟩ ⟨the raucous ~ of a motorcar's horn —Hearst's⟩

¹yowt \'yaùt\ *vi* -ED/-ING/-S [ME (Sc) *yowten,* of imit. origin] *dial Brit* : HOWL, YELP, YELL

²yowt \"\ *n* -S *dial Brit* : HOWL, YELL

yo-yo \'yō(,)yō\ *n, pl* **yo-yos** *also* **yo-yoes** [native name in the Philippines] : a thick deeply grooved double disk with a string attached to its center that is made to fall and rise to the hand by unwinding and rewinding on the string

YP *abbr* **1** yard patrol **2** yellow pine **3** yield point **4** young people

yper·ite \'ēpə,rīt\ *n* -S [F *ypérite,* fr. *ypér-* (fr. *Ypres, Ieper,* commune in northwest Belgium where it was used in World War I) + *-ite*] : MUSTARD GAS

y point *n, usu cap Y* : the neutral point for a three-phase electrical circuit

ypointing \'i⸗⸗, ē'-\ *adj* [y- + *pointing*] *archaic* : pointing or reaching toward a specified thing — usu. used in the phrase *star-ypointing* ⟨or that his hallowed reliques should be hid under a *star-ypointing* pyramid —John Milton⟩

ypon·o·meu·ta \(,)ē,pänə'myüd-ə\ *n, cap* [NL, prob. irreg. fr. Gk *hyponomeutēs* miner, fr. *hyponomeuein* to undermine, fr. *hyponomos* underground passage, fr. *hypo-* + *-nomein* to eat away beneath, fr. *nemein* to pasture — more at NIMBLE] : a genus of black-spotted white moths that is the type of the family Yponomeutidae and that comprises the ermine moths

¹ypon·o·meu·tid \(,)'⸗;⸗⸗'myüd-əd\ *adj* [NL *Yponomeutidae*] : of or relating to the Yponomeutidae

²yponomeutid \"\ *n* -S [NL *Yponomeutidae*] : a moth of the family Yponomeutidae

ypon·o·meu·ti·dae \-id-ə,dē\ *n pl, cap* [NL, fr. *Yponomeuta* type genus + *-idae*] : a family of tineoid moths including ermine moths and various brightly colored moths some of which have larvae that are injurious to fruits

y potential *n, usu cap Y* : the potential difference between a terminal and the neutral point of a three-phase armature

yr *abbr* **1** year **2** younger **3** your

yrly *abbr* yearly

yrs *abbr* years

YS *abbr* **1** yellow spot **2** yield strength **3** young soldier

y's or **ys** *pl of* Y

y-shaped \'⸗,⸗\ *adj, cap Y* : having the shape of a capital Y

yst *abbr* youngest

Yt *symbol* yttrium

y theodolite *n, cap Y* : a theodolite with the telescope supported in y's

yt·ter·bic \i'tərbik\ *adj* [ytterbium + *-ic*] : of, relating to, or containing ytterbium — used esp. of compounds in which this element is trivalent

yt·ter·bi·um \-bēəm\ *n* -S [NL, fr. *Ytterby,* Sweden, where gadolinite is found + NL *-ium*] : a metallic element of the rare-earth group that closely resembles yttrium and occurs with it and other related elements in several minerals (as xenotime and gadolinite) and that forms green salts in which it is bivalent and colorless salts in which it is trivalent — symbol *Yb;* see ELEMENT table

ytterbium metal *n* : YTTRIUM METAL

yt·ter·bous \-bəs\ *adj* [ytterbium + *-ous*] : of, relating to, or containing ytterbium — used esp. of compounds in which this element is bivalent

yt·tria \'i-trēə\ *n* -S [NL, fr. *yttri-* (irreg. fr. *Ytterby,* Sweden, where gadolinite is found) + *-a*] : yttrium oxide Y_2O_3 obtained as a heavy white powder and used esp. formerly in incandescent gas mantles

yt·tri·a·lite \-ə,līt\ *n* -S [*yttria* + *-lite*] : an olive-green massive mineral $(Y,Gd,Th)_2Si_2O_7$ consisting of a silicate chiefly of thorium, yttrium, and gadolinium

yt·tric \'i-trik\ *adj* [ISV *yttri-* + *-ic*] : of, relating to, or containing yttrium

yt·trif·er·ous \i'trifərəs\ *adj* [ISV *yttri-* + *-ferous*] : bearing or containing yttrium or related elements

yt·tri·um \'i-trēəm\ *n* -S [NL, *yttria,* after such pairs as NL *lithia: lithium*] : a trivalent metallic element that is usu. included among the rare-earth metals because it resembles them chemically and occurs with them in several minerals (as gadolinite, xenotime, yttrotantalite, euxenite) — symbol *Y;* see ELEMENT table

yttrium metal *n* : any of a group of metals separable as a group from other metals occurring with them and in addition to yttrium including the rare-earth metals holmium, erbium, thulium, ytterbium, and lutetium and sometimes gadolinium, terbium, and dysprosium — compare TERBIUM METAL

yt·tro·co·lum·bite \,i-trō+\ *n* [*yttria* + *-o-* + *columbite*] : YTTROTANTALITE

yt·tro·cra·site \-⸗⸗'krā,sīt\ *n* -S [*yttrium* + *-o-* + *cras-* (fr. Gk *krasis* mixing, combination) + *-ite* — more at CRASIS] : a mineral approximately $(Y,Th,U,Ca)_2(Ti,Fe,W)_4O_{11}$ or $(Y,Th,-U,Ca)(Ti,Fe,W)_2O_5(OH)$ consisting of an oxide or basic oxide of the yttrium metals, thorium, uranium, titanium, iron, and tungsten and occurring in pitchy-black orthorhombic crystals (hardness 5.5–6, sp. gr. 4.8)

yt·tro·fluor·ite \-⸗⸗+\ *n* [G *yttrofluorit,* fr. *yttr-* (fr. NL *yttrium*) + *-o-* + *fluorit* fluorite, fr. It *fluorite*] : a fluorite containing yttrium earths

yt·tro·tan·ta·lite \"+\ *n* [Sw *yttrotantal* yttrotantalite (fr. *yttr-,* fr. NL *yttria* + *-o-* + *tantal* tantalum, fr. NL *tantalum*) + E *-ite*] : a mineral $(Fe,Y,U,Ca,etc.)(Cb,Ta,Zr,-Sn)O_4$ consisting of a metamict oxide of iron, yttrium, uranium, calcium, columbium, tantalum, zirconium, tin, and other minerals and probably related to samarskite — called also *yttrocolumbite*

¹yu·an \'yüən, yü'än\ *also* **yuan dollar** *n, pl* **yuan** *also* **yuan dollars** [Chin (Pek) *yüan²,* lit., round, circular] **1** : the basic monetary unit of China established in 1914 — see MONEY table **2** : a coin or note representing one yuan

²yuan \"\ *n, pl* **yuan** *or* **yuans** *usu cap* [Chin (Pek) *yüan⁴,* lit., hall, courtyard] : a department of government in the Nationalist government of China ⟨executive *Yuan*⟩ ⟨legislative *Yuan*⟩ ⟨judicial *Yuan*⟩ ⟨control *Yuan*⟩ ⟨examination *Yuan*⟩

yu·ba \'yübə\ *n* -S [perh. native name in Australia] : a messmate *(Eucalyptus obliqua)*

yuca \'yükə, 'yəkə⟩ *also* **yuc·ca** \'yəkə *sometimes* 'yüka *or* 'yükə⟩ *also* **juca** \'yükə, 'yəkə, 'yükə⟩ *n* -S [NL *jucca,* fr. 15th cent. Taino *yuca*] : CASSAVA

yu·ca·tan \,yükə'tan, -tän⟩ *n* -S [*Yucatán,* peninsula in southeast Mexico] : FRENCH YELLOW

yu·ca·tec \-⸗⸗,tek⟩ *also* **yu·ca·te·co** \,⸗⸗'tā(,)kō⟩ *n, pl* **yucatec** *or* **yucatecs** *usu cap* [Sp *Yucatán, Yucatec,* peninsula in southeast Mexico] **1 a** : an Indian people of the Yucatán peninsula, Mexico **b** : a member of such people **2** : a Mayan language of the Yucatec people **3** *pl* **yucatecs** [Sp *yucateco,* fr. *Yucatán,* peninsula in southeast Mexico, fr. *Yucatán,* state in the northern part of Yucatán peninsula] : a native or inhabitant of Yucatán state or of the Yucatán peninsula, Mexico

yu·ca·tec·an \,⸗⸗'tekən⟩ *adj, usu cap* [Sp *yucateco* + E *-an*] **1** : of or relating to the Yucatec Indians or their language **2** : of or relating to the Yucatecs of Yucatán state or of the Yucatán peninsula, Mexico

yuc·ca \'yəkə *sometimes* 'yüka *or* 'yükə⟩ *n* [NL, fr. Sp *yuca,* of unknown origin] **1** *cap* : a genus of American sometimes arborescent plants (family Liliaceae) having long pointed often rigid fibrous-margined leaves on a woody caudex and bearing a large panicle of white blossoms — see ADAM'S NEEDLE, BEAR GRASS 1a, JOSHUA TREE, SOAP PLANT c, SPANISH DAGGER **2** *also* **yuca** \'yükə, 'yəkə, 'yükə⟩ -s **a** : any plant of the genus *Yucca* **b** : a flower cluster of one of these plants

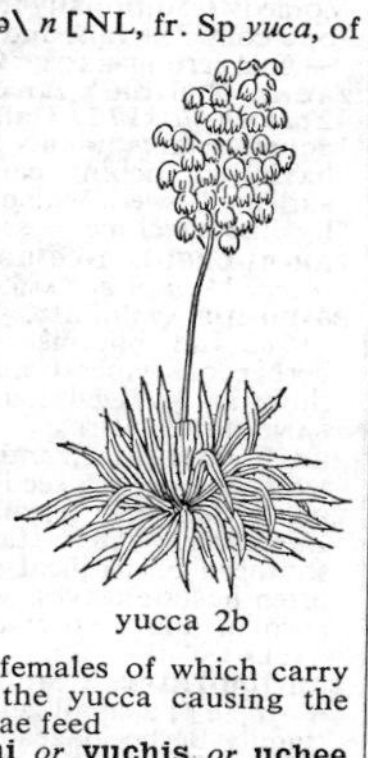

yucca 2b

yucca borer *n* **1** : a California boring weevil *(Scyphophorus yuccae)* **2** : a large butterfly *(Megathymus yuccae)* of the family Hesperiidae whose larva bores in yucca roots

yucca cactus *or* **yucca palm** *n* : an arborescent yucca; *esp* : JOSHUA TREE

yucca fertilizer *or* **yucca pollenizer** *n* : YUCCA MOTH

yucca moth *n* : any of several silvery tineoid moths (genus *Tegeticula*) the females of which carry pollen that fertilizes the flowers of the yucca causing the growth of a seed pod in which the larvae feed

yu·chi *or* **uchee** \'yüchē⟩ *n, pl* **yuchi** *or* **yuchis** *or* **uchee** *or* **uchees** *usu cap* **1 a** : an Indian people of southeastern U.S. **b** : a member of such people **2 a** : a Uchean language of the Yuchi people **3** : UCHEAN

yuchian *var of* UCHEAN

yueh \'yü'ä⟩ *n, pl* **yueh** *or* **yuehs** *usu cap* [Chin (Pek) *Yüeh⁴*] : one of a group of south China people formerly occupying the coastal provinces from Chekiang southward, having affinities with the early Yao and early Vietnamese, and founding an empire reaching its greatest height at Canton in Kwangtung Province

yueh-chi *or* **yueh-chi-tocharian** *n, pl* **yueh-chi** *or* **yueh-chi-tocharians** *usu cap Y & cap T* : TOCHARIAN

yueh-p'an \-'pän⟩ *n, pl* **yueh-p'an** *usu cap Y* : a division of the Hsiung-Nu held to be ancestors of the Avars

yuft \'yüft⟩ *n* -S [Russ *yuft',* *yukht',* perh. fr. Per *juft* pair; fr. the practice of tanning hides in pairs; akin to Av *yuxta-* pair, yoke (of oxen), Skt *yukta* yoke (of oxen), *yunakti* he yokes — more at YOKE] : RUSSIA LEATHER

yu·ga \'yügə⟩ *n* -S [Skt, yoke, pair, race of men, age of the world — more at YOKE] : one of the four ages of a Hindu world cycle each shorter and less righteous than the one preceding — see DVAPARA YUGA, KALI YUGA, KRITA YUGA, TRETA YUGA; compare KALPA, PRALAYA

¹yu·go·slav \'yü(,)gō,släv, -läv, -läv⟩ *or* **yu·go·slav·ian** \,⸗⸗'⸗⸗⸗⸗⸗⸗, -vēən, -vyən⟩ *also* **ju·go·slav** \'yü(,)gō-\ *or* **ju·go·slav·ian** \,yü(,)gō-\ *n* -s *cap* [Yugoslav fr. F *Yougoslave,* fr. Serb *jugo-* (fr. *jug* south, fr. OSlav *jugŭ*) + G *Slawe* Slav, fr. ML *Sclavus;* Yugoslavian, Jugoslavian fr. *Yugoslavia, Jugo-*

slavia + *-an,* n. suffix; Jugoslav fr. G *Jugoslawe* — more at AUGELITE, SLAVE] : a native or inhabitant of Yugoslavia — compare CROATIAN, SOUTH SLAV

²yugoslav \"\ *or* **yugoslavian** \"\ *also* **jugoslav** \"\ *or* **jugoslavian** \"\ *adj, usu cap* [Yugoslav, Jugoslav fr. Yugoslav, Jugoslav; Yugoslavian, Jugoslavian, Jugoslavian fr. Yugoslavia, Jugoslavia + E *-an,* adj. suffix] **1** : of, relating to, or characteristic of the people of Yugoslavia **2** : of, relating to, or characteristic of the kind or style prevalent in Yugoslavia

yu·go·slav·ia *also* **ju·go·slav·ia** \,⸗-(,)⸗'⸗vēə⟩ *adj, usu cap* [Yugoslavia, Jugoslavia, country in southeast Europe] : of or from Yugoslavia : of the kind or style prevalent in Yugoslavia : YUGOSLAV, YUGOSLAVIAN

yu·go·slav·ic *also* **ju·go·slav·ic** \,⸗⸗'⸗slavik, -läv-, -läv-, -vēk⟩ *adj, usu cap* [¹Yugoslav, Jugoslav + *-ic*] : YUGOSLAV

yu·gur \'yü(,)gə(r)⟩ *n, pl* **yugur** *or* **yugurs** *usu cap* **1** : a nomadic pastoral people of northeast Asia — compare YUGUR **2** : a member of the Yugur people

yu·it \'yüət⟩ *n, pl* **yuit** *or* **yuits** *usu cap* [Esk, men, people] **1** : the Eskimos of Siberia and St. Lawrence Island, Alaska — compare INNUIT **2** : a member of the Yuit people

¹yuk \'yok⟩ *slang var of* ⁴YAK

²yuk \"\ *interj* [imit. (of a sardonic laugh)] — used reduplicatively to express amusement or derision

yu·ka·ghir *or* **yu·ka·gir** \,yü(,)kə'gi(ə)r⟩ *n, pl* **yukaghir** *or* **yukaghirs** *or* **yukagir** *or* **yukagirs** *usu cap* **1 a** : a group of formerly strong mongoloid peoples of northeastern Siberia surviving along the southern tributaries of the Kolyma river above Verkhne Kolymsk and having a culture of the Tungus type **b** : a member of any of such peoples **2 a** : the language of the Yukaghir people **b** : a family of languages of which only Yukaghir is still extant or well-known — see PALEO-SIBERIAN

yuke \'yük⟩ *var of* YEUK

yu·ki \'yükē⟩ *n, pl* **yuki** *or* **yukis** *usu cap* [Wintun, lit., stranger, enemy] **1 a** : an Indian people of the Eel river valley and adjacent Pacific coast, northwestern California **b** : a member of such people **2 a** : a Yukian language of the Yuki and Huchnom peoples **b** : YUKIAN

yu·ki·an \'yükēən⟩ *n* -S *usu cap* : a language family of northwestern California comprising Yuki and Wappo perhaps related to Hokan

yu·kon \'yü,kän⟩ *adj, usu cap* [Yukon, territory in northwest Canada] : of or from Yukon Territory, Canada : of the kind or style prevalent in Yukon Territory

yu·kon·er \-nə(r)⟩ *n* -S *cap* : a native or inhabitant of the Yukon Territory, Canada

yu·kon·ite \-,nīt⟩ *n* -S *cap* : ARSENIOSIDERITE

yukon time *or* **yukon standard time** *n, cap Y* : the time of the 9th time zone west of Greenwich that includes the Yukon Territory and part of southern Alaska and is four hours slower than eastern time

yu·lan \'yü,län, -lan⟩ *n* -S [Chin (Pek) *yü⁴-lan²,* fr. *yü⁴* jade + *lan²* orchid] : a Chinese magnolia *(Magnolia denudata)* with large white very fragrant flowers that appear before the leaves

yule \'yül⟩ *n* -S *often cap, often attrib* [ME *yol, yole,* fr. OE *gēol;* akin to OE *gēola* December or January, ON *jōl* heathen winter feast, yule, Christmas, *ȳlir* month ending near the winter solstice, Goth *jiuleis* (in *fruma jiuleis* November)] : the feast of the nativity of Jesus Christ : CHRISTMAS, CHRISTMASTIDE

yule clog *n, archaic* : YULE LOG

yule log *n, usu cap Y* : a large log formerly brought in with much ceremony and put on the hearth on Christmas Eve as the foundation of the fire ⟨the burning of the *Yule log* and the drinking of wassail —R.E.Meyer⟩

yuletide \'⸗,⸗⟩ *n, often cap* : the Christmas season; *esp* : CHRISTMASTIDE

yu·loh \'yü,lō⟩ *n* -S [prob. fr. Chin (Cant) *iü-lŏ* to scull a boat from the stern, fr. *iü* to agitate, shake + *lŏ* oar] : a Chinese sculling oar with a fixed fulcrum

yu·ma \'yümə⟩ *n, pl* **yuma** *or* **yumas** *usu cap* **1 a** : an Indian people of southwestern Arizona and the adjacent parts of Mexico and California **b** : a member of such people **2** : the Yuman language of the Yuma people

¹yu·man \-mən⟩ *n* -S *usu cap* : a language family of the Hokan stock in Arizona, California, and Mexico comprising Akwa'ala, Cochimi, Cocopa, Diegueño, Havasupai, Kamia, Kiliwa, Maricopa, Mohave, Walapai, Yavapai, and Yuma

²yuman \"\ *adj, usu cap* **1** : of or relating to Yuman **2** *also* **yu·ma** \-mə⟩ : PATAYAN

yuma point *n, usu cap Y* [*Yuma* county, northeastern Colorado] : a stone projectile point first found in northeastern Colorado that is not fluted and is longer, narrower, and more painstakingly flaked than the Folsom point

yum-my \'yəmē, -mi⟩ *adj* -ER/-EST [*yum-* (as in *yum-yum*) + *-y*] : highly attractive or pleasing : DELECTABLE ⟨~ flavors like . . . munchy coconut —*advt*⟩ ⟨~ pastel shades —*advt*⟩

yum-yum \'yəm,yəm⟩ *interj* [imit.] — used to express pleasurable satisfaction esp. in the taste of food

yun \'yün⟩ *n, pl* **yun** *usu cap* : a Laotian of the right bank of the Mekong distinguished by tattooing on the body rather than the legs and thighs

yun·ca \'yünkə⟩ *or* **yun·ga** \-ṇgə⟩ *also* **yun·ka** \-ṇkə⟩ *n, pl* **yunca** *or* **yuncas** *or* **yunga** *or* **yungas** *usu cap* [AmerSp *Yunca, Yunga,* fr. *yunga, yunca* yunga] **1 a** : a group of Indian peoples of the coast of Peru **b** : a member of any of the peoples of this group **2** : the language of the Yunca people now superseded by Quechua and Spanish

yun·can *or* **yun·kan** \-kən⟩ *adj, usu cap* : relating to or designating the language of the Yunca

yun·ga \'yüṇgə⟩ *n* -S [AmerSp *yunga, yunca,* fr. Quechua] : a densely wooded valley or slope in So. America

yun·gan \'yüṇgən⟩ *n* -S [native name in Queensland, Australia] : DUGONG 2

yun·gas \'yüṇgəs⟩ *n* -S [origin unknown] : a Peruvian rice rat *(Oryzomys mamorae* or *Oecomys mamorae)*

¹yun·nan·ese \,yünə'nēz, -nēs⟩ *also* **yun·nan** \yü'nan, -nän⟩ *adj, usu cap* [*yunnanese* fr. *Yunnan,* province in south China + E *-ese; yunnan* fr. *Yunnan,* province in south China] : of or relating to the province of Yunnan, China, or its inhabitants

²yunnanese \"\ *n, pl* **yunnanese** *cap* : a native or inhabitant of the Chinese province of Yunnan

yup *var of* YEP

yu·pik \'yüpik⟩ *n* -S *usu cap* : an Eskimo-Aleut language spoken across arctic America from western Alaska to Greenland

yu·rak \yə'rak⟩ *n* -S *usu cap* **1** : one of the Samoyeds of the arctic coast region from the Yenisei to the White sea **2** : the Uralic language of the Yurak people — see URALIC LANGUAGES table

yu·rok \'yü,räk, -'rək⟩ *n, pl* **yurok** *also* **yuroks** *usu cap* **1 a** : a Ritwan people of northern California **b** : a member of such people **2** : the language of the Yurok people

yurt \'yürt⟩ *also* **yur·ta** \-tə⟩ *n* -S [Russ *yurta,* of Turkic origin; akin to Turk *yurt* home, dwelling] : a circular domed tent consisting of skins or felt stretched over a collapsible lattice framework and used by the Kirghiz and other Mongol nomads of Siberia

yu·ruk *or* **ju·ruk** \yə'rùk⟩ *n* -S [Turk *yürük*] **1** *usu cap* : one of a nomadic shepherd people of the mountains of southeastern Anatolia **2** : a Turkish rug from the Konya and Karaman regions, southeastern Anatolia, characterized by bold geometric designs and vivid colors

yu·ru·na \,yürə'nä⟩ *n, pl* **yuruna** *or* **yurunas** *usu cap* [Tupi, fr. *yurú* mouth + *una* black] **1 a** : a group of Tupian peoples of the Xingú river valley, northern Brazil **b** : a member of any of the peoples of this group **2** : the language of the Yuruna people

y-worm \'⸗,⸗⟩ *n, cap Y* [so called fr. the appearance of the large female and small male permanently associated in copulation] : GAPEWORM

¹z \'zē, *chiefly Brit* 'zed, *archaic or dial* 'izə(r)d\ *n, pl* **z's** *or* **zs** \-ēz, -dz\ *often cap, often attrib* **1 a :** the 26th and last letter of the English alphabet **b :** an instance of this letter printed, written, or otherwise represented **c :** a speech counterpart of orthographic *z* (as *z* in *zone, haze* or French *zone, seize*) **2 a :** a printer's type, a stamp, or some other instrument for reproducing the letter *z* **3 :** someone or something arbitrarily or conveniently designated *z:* as **a :** the 26th in order or class **b :** the 25th in order or class when j is not used **c :** the 23d in order or class when j, v, and w are not used **d :** the third in order or class when x is made the first **4 :** something having the shape of the letter z ⟨a Z bar⟩ **5 a :** UNKNOWN QUANTITY 1 **b :** Z-COORDINATE **6 :** a buzzing sound (as of snoring) — usu. used in multiples (as *z-z* or *zzz*)

²z *abbr, often cap* **1** zero **2** zinc **3** zloty **4** zone

³z *symbol, cap* **1** atomic number **2** impedance **3** zenith distance

'z *like* ⁴'s\ *n* [by alter.] **:** ⁴'s

za·ba·glio·ne \,(d)zäbəl'yōnē\ *also* **za·ba·io·ne** *or* **za·ba·jo·ne** \-bə'y-\ *n* -s [It *zabaglione, zabaione* — more at SABAYON] **:** a mixture of eggs, sugar, and wine or fruit juice beaten over hot water until thick and light and served in a glass

za·bra \'zäbrə, 'sä-\ *n* -s [Sp, fr. Catal *atzaura*, fr. Ar *zawraq* small boat] **:** a sailing vessel resembling a small frigate and used chiefly by the Spanish in the 16th and 17th centuries

zab·rze \'zäb,zhä\ *adj, usu cap* [*Zabrze*, city in southwest Poland] **:** of or from the city of Zabrze, Poland **:** of the kind or style prevalent in Zabrze

za·ca·te \zə'käd·ē, sə-\ *n* -s [AmerSp, coarse grass, zacate, fr. Nahuatl *zacatl*] **1 :** forage of grassy plants **:** HERBAGE **2** [PhilSp, fr. AmerSp] *Philippines* **:** RICEGRASS 1

za·ca·teco \,zäkə'tā(,)kō, -te(,)kō, ,sä-\ *also* **za·ca·tec** \,≈≈-'tek\ *n, pl* **zacateco** *or* **zacatecos** *also* **zacatec** *or* **zacatecs** *usu cap* **1 :** a Nahuatlan people of the states of Zacatecas and Durango, Mexico **2 :** a member of the Zacateco people

zac·a·ton \'zakə,tōn, 'sa-\ *n* -s [AmerSp *zacatón* — more at SACATON] **:** any of several grasses with tough wiry stems native to or cultivated in arid or dry regions of the U.S. and adjacent Mexico: as **a :** BROOMROOT **b :** GUINEA GRASS 1 **c :** either of two Mexican grasses (*Epicampes stricta* and *Festuca amplissima*) **d :** SACATON

zacco *var of* ZOCCO

zad \'zad\ *chiefly dial var of* ZED

zad·dik *or* **tzad·dik** *or* **tsad·dik** *also* **za·dik** *or* **tza·dik** *or* **tsa·dik** \'tsädik\ *n, pl* **zad·dik·im** *or* **tzad·dik·im** *or* **tsad·dik·im** *also* **za·dik·im** *or* **tza·dik·im** *or* **tsa·dik·im** \tsä'dikəm, tsä,dē'kēm\ [Heb *ṣaddīq* just, righteous] **1 :** a righteous and saintly person **2 :** the spiritual leader of a modern Hasidic community — compare REBBE

¹za·dok·ite \'zādə,kīt\ *n* -s *usu cap* [*Zadok*, high priest of Israel during the reign of King David + E *-ite*] **1 :** a Zadokite priest **2 :** a member of the Zadokite sect

²zadokite \"\ *adj, usu cap* **1 :** of or relating to Zadok or a line of priests of the highest rank descended from him ⟨the *Zadokite* priesthood⟩ **2 :** of, relating to, or constituting a Jewish rigorist sect seceding from orthodox Judaism and settling in Damascus in the second century B.C.

zaf·fer *or* **zaf·fre** \'zafə(r)\ *also* **zaf·free** \-frē\ *or* **zaf·far** *or* **zaf·fir** \-fə(r)\ *n* -s [It *zaffera*, prob. fr. L *sapphirus* sapphire — more at SAPPHIRE] **1 a :** an impure cobalt oxide obtained as a dark earthy powder usu. by roasting cobaltite or smaltite and used in the manufacture of smalt and as a blue ceramic color **b :** SMALT **2 :** any of various mixtures of zaffer (as with silica or iron oxide)

¹zag \'zag, -aa(ə)g, -aig\ *n* -s [*-zag* (in *zigzag*)] **1 a :** one of the sharp turns, angles, or alterations in a zigzag course **b :** one of the short straight lines or sections of a zigzag course at an angle to a zig **c :** a movement or direction at an angle to a zig **2 :** ZIG 2

²zag \"\ *vi* **zagged; zagged; zagging; zags** [*-zag* (in *zigzag*)] **:** ZIG

za·glos·sus \zə'gläsəs, -glȯs-\ *n, cap* [NL, fr. *za-*, intensive prefix (fr. Gk *za* through, fr. *dia*) + *-glossus* (fr. Gk *glōssa* tongue) — more at DIA-, GLOSS] **:** a genus of spiny anteaters of New Guinea — see ECHIDNA 1b

za·greb \'zä,greb\ *adj, usu cap* [*Zagreb*, city in northwest Yugoslavia] **:** of or from the city of Zagreb, Yugoslavia **:** of the kind or style prevalent in Zagreb

za·guan \zə'gwän, sə-\ *n* -s [Sp *zaguán* vestibule, entry, fr. Ar *usṭuwān* porch, vestibule, prob. fr. Gk *stoa* portico; akin to Gk *stylos* pillar — more at STEER] **:** a passageway leading from the entrance door to the central patio in houses commonly found in the southwestern U.S. and Mexico

zaidi \'zīdē\ *also* **zaid·ite** \-,dīt\ *n* -s *usu cap* [after *Zaid*, 8th cent. A.D. Muslim leader descended from Muhammad] **:** a member of a Muslim sect of Yemen that constitutes one of the three major branches of Shi'a, recognizes a continuing line of imams descended through Zaid who is the fifth imam, and is closest to Sunna in its doctrine

zain *var of* ZAYIN

za·kat \zə'kät\ *also* **za·kah** \-kä\ *n* -s [Ar *zakāt*] **:** an annual alms tax or poor rate that each Muslim is expected to pay as a religious duty and that is used for charitable and religious purposes

za·kus·ka *also* **za·koos·ka** \zə'kuskə\ *n, pl* **zakus·ki** \-skē\ *or* **zakuska** [Russ *zakuska*, fr. *zakusit'* to have a snack, fr. *za* for, behind + *-kusit'* (fr. *kus* morsel); akin to Lith dial. *ažu, až* for, behind, Arm *z* with regard to, and to Gk *knōdōn* sword, Lith *kąsti* to bite, L *cinis* ashes — more at INCINERATE] **:** HORS D'OEUVRE

¹za·lamb·do·dont \zə'lamdə,dänt\ *adj* [NL *Zalambdodonta*] **:** of or relating to the Zalambdodonta

²zalambdodont \"\ *n* -s [NL *Zalambdodonta*] **:** a mammal of the division Zalambdodonta

za·lamb·do·don·ta \,≈≈'däntə\ *n pl, cap* [NL, fr. *za-*, intensive prefix + Gk *lambda* (Λ) + NL *-odonta*] *in former classifications* **:** an artificial division of Insectivora comprising the tenrecs and the golden moles which have narrow molars with V-shaped transverse crowns

zal·o·phus \'zaləfəs\ *n, cap* [NL, fr. *za-*, intensive prefix + *-lophus* (fr. Gk *lophos* crest)] **:** a genus of rather small eared seals including the California sea dog

za·ma·cue·ca \,zämə'kwākə, ,sä-\ *n* -s [AmerSp] **:** CUECA

za·man \zə'män, sə-\ *or* **za·mang** \-äŋ\ *n* -s [Sp & Carib; Sp *samán*, fr. Carib *zamang*] **:** RAIN TREE

za·man·do·que \,zämən'dōkē, ,sä-\ *or* **za·man·do·gue** \-ōgē\ *n* -s [MexSp *samandoque*] **:** a Mexican plant (*Hesperaloe funifera*) of the family Liliaceae with long slender leaves that yield a long soft flexible istle fiber

za·mar·ra \zə'märə, sə-\ *n* -s [Sp — more at SAMARRA] **:** a sheepskin coat worn chiefly by Spanish shepherds

zambal *usu cap, var of* SAMBAL

Zam·be·si \zam'bēzē\ *trademark* — used for a direct azo dye; see DYE table I (under *Direct Black 17* and *78*)

zam·be·zian *or* **zam·be·sian** \(')zam¦bēzhən\ *adj, usu cap* [*Zambezi, Zambesi*, river in south central and southeast Africa + E *-an*] **:** of or relating to the Zambezi river

zam·bia \'zambēə\ *adj, usu cap* [fr. *Zambia*, country in southern Africa] **:** of or from the country of Zambia **:** of the kind or style prevalent in Zambia

zam·bi·an \-bēən\ *n* -s *cap* [*Zambia*, Africa + E *-an*] **:** a native or inhabitant of Zambia — **zambian** *adj, usu cap*

zam·bo \'z¦äm(,)bō, 's¦, |am-\ *n* -s [AmerSp, Negro, mulatto — more at SAMBO] **:** a Latin-American of mixed Indian and Negro ancestry

zam·bo·an·ga \,zämbə'wäŋgə, ,sä-\ *adj, usu cap* [*Zamboanga*, city in western Mindanao, Philippines] **:** of or from the city of Zamboanga, Philippines **:** of the kind or style prevalent in Zamboanga

zam·e·nis \'zamənəs\ *n, cap* [NL, modif. of Gk *zamenēs* mighty, raging, fr. *za-*, intensive prefix + *-menēs* (fr. *menos* strength, fierceness, spirit) — more at ZAGLOSSUS, MIND] **:** a large genus of European and Asiatic colubrid snakes closely resembling and in some classifications including a black snake (*Coluber constrictor*) of the U.S.

za·mia \'zāmēə\ *n* [NL, fr. L (in fem. pl. form *zamiae*), MS. var. of *azaniae*, fem. pl. of (assumed) L *azanius*, adj., opening while still on the tree (said of a pinecone), prob. fr. Gk *azainein* to dry up; akin to Gk *azein* to parch — more at ARDOR] **1** *cap* **:** a genus of tropical and subtropical American cycads having a short thick sometimes subterranean caudex, a crown of palmlike leaves, and oblong cones — see COONTIE **2** -s **:** any plant of the genus *Zamia*

za·mi·a·ce·ae \,≈≈'āsē,ē\ *n pl, cap* [NL, fr. *Zamia* + *-aceae*] *in some classifications* **:** a family of cycads that includes the genus *Zamia* and is commonly itself included in Cycadaceae

zam·i·crus \'zaməkrəs\ *n, cap* [NL, fr. *za-*, intensive prefix (fr. Gk) + *-micrus* (fr. Gk *mikros* small); fr. the size of the molars — more at MICR-] **:** a genus of edentates from the Miocene of Argentina related to *Megatherium* but no larger than sloths

zamin·dar *or* **zemin·dar** \zə¦mēn¦där, ¦zamən-, ¦zemən-, ¦zämən-\ *n* -s [Hindi *zamīndār*, fr. Per, fr. *zamīn* land + *-dār* holder; akin to Skt *kṣam* earth, ground — more at HUMBLE, BHUMIDAR] **1 :** a collector of revenues from the cultivators of the land of a specified district for the government of India during the period of Muslim rule **2 :** a feudatory under the British government of India having rights of private property in a large amount of land by paying to the government a fixed substantial revenue raised from the cultivators **3 :** an absentee landlord usu. acting as an intermediary between the cultivators and the government in the period after Indian independence

zamin·da·ri *or* **zamin·da·ry** *or* **zemin·da·ri** *or* **zemin·da·ry** \≈,≈'därē, ≈≈'d-\ *n, pl* **zamindaris** *or* **zamindaries** *or* **zemindaris** *or* **zemindaries** [Hindi *zamīndārī*, fr. Per, fr. *zamīndār*] **1 :** the system of landholding and revenue collection by zamindars **2 :** the jurisdiction or office of a zamindar **3 :** the land held or administered by a zamindar — compare AMANI

zam·o·rin *also* **zam·o·rine** \¦zamə¦rēn\ *n* -s [Pg *samorim*, fr. Malayalam *sāmūri*, fr. *sāmudri* lord of the sea, fr. Skt *samudra* ocean, fr. *sam* together + *-udra* (akin to Skt *udan* water) — more at SAME, WATER] **:** the Hindu sovereign of Calicut and surrounding territory

za·mouse \zə'müs\ *also* **ga·moos** *or* **ga·mouse** \gə-\ *n, pl* **zamouses** *also* **gamooses** *or* **gamouses** [Ar *jāmūs*] **:** BUSH COW 1

zam·po·gna *or* **zam·po·ña** *also* **sam·po·gna** \(t)säm'pōnyə, zam-\ *n* -s [*zampogna, sampogna* fr. It *zampogna*, modif. of LL *symphonia*, a musical instrument, perh. the panpipe, fr. L, harmony of sounds; *zampoña* fr. Sp, modif. of LL *symphonia* — more at SYMPHONY] **1 :** PANPIPE **2 :** BAGPIPE

za·mu·co \zə'mü(,)kō, sə-\ *or* **za·mu·cu** \-kü\ *n, pl* **zamuco** *or* **zamucos** *or* **zamucu** *or* **zamucus** *usu cap* **1 a :** a group of peoples of the northern Chaco **b :** a member of any of such peoples **2 :** the language of the Zamuco peoples

zam·zum·mim \zam'zəməm\ *or* **zam·zum·mims** \-əmz\ *n pl, usu cap* [Heb *zamzummīm*] **:** aboriginal giants reported in the Old Testament to have inhabited the region of Ammon prior to the coming of the Ammonites — compare ANAKIM, EMIM, REPHAIM

zan·cli·dae \'zaŋklə,dē\ *n pl, cap* [NL, fr. *Zanclus*, type genus + *-idae*] **:** a family of marine fishes consisting of the Moorish idols and resembling in many respects the related surgeonfishes but lacking the distinguishing spines of the latter and having above the eyes bony outgrowths resembling horns — compare TEUTHIDIDAE

zan·clus \-ləs\ *n, cap* [NL, fr. Gk *zanklon* sickle] **:** a genus coextensive with the family Zanclidae

zan·de \'zandē\ *or* **zan·deh** \-də\ *n, pl* **zande** *or* **zandes** *or* **zandeh** *or* **zandehs** *usu cap* **1 a :** an African people of considerable prominence in the history and development of the region of the Congo-Sudan frontier esp. over the past century **b :** a member of such people **2 :** an Adamawa-Eastern language of the Zande people spoken in the northern Congo and southwestern Sudan

zan·der \'zandə(r), 'zaan-\ *n, pl* **zander** *or* **zanders** [G *zander*, perh. of Slav origin; akin to Pol *sandacz* zander] **:** a pike perch (*Lucioperca sandra* or *L. lucioperca*) of central Europe related to the walleyed pike

za·ni·ly \'zān³lē\ *adv* **:** in a zany manner

za·ni·ness \-nēnəs, -nin-\ *n* -ES **:** the quality or state of being zany ⟨fleeting moments of impulsive ~ —Walter Terry⟩

zan·ja \'zäŋhə, 'sä-\ *n* -s [AmerSp, fr. Sp, ditch, trench] **:** an irrigating canal **:** an irrigation ditch

zan·je·ro \zän'he(,)rō, sä-\ *n* -s [AmerSp, fr. *zanja*] **:** one in charge of water distribution from zanjas

zan·ni \'(d)zänē\ *n, pl* **zanni** *or* **zannis** *usu cap* [It, fr. It dial. (Lombardy) *Zanni*, nickname fr. the name It *Giovanni* John, fr. LL *Joannes* — more at JOHN] **1 :** a madcap clown in masked comedy traditionally from Bergamo, Italy usu. playing the part of a comic servant and indulging in acrobatic antics and tricks — compare PIERROT **2 :** a clown resembling Harlequin

zan·ni·chel·lia \,zanə'kelēə\ *n, cap* [NL, fr. Gian Girolamo *Zannichelli* †1729 Ital. botanist + NL *-ia*] **:** a small genus of aquatic plants (family Potamogetonaceae) of wide distribution having branching capillary stems, small acute leaves, and axillary flowers which with the leaves are orig. enclosed in a hyaline envelope — see HORNED PONDWEED

zan·ni·chel·li·a·ce·ae \,≈,≈,lē'āsē,ē\ [NL, fr. *Zannichellia* + *-aceae*] *syn of* POTAMOGETONACEAE

za·no·nia \zə'nōnēə, -ōnyə\ *n, cap* [NL, fr. Giacomo *Zanoni* †1682 Ital. botanist + NL *-ia*] **:** a genus of Indo-Malayan herbaceous vines (family Cucurbitaceae) with small panicled flowers, 3-valved fruits, and broadly winged seeds — see BANDOLEER FRUIT

zan·te currant \¦zantē-\ *n, usu cap Z* [*Zante*, island in southwest Greece] **:** a seedless grape or raisin

zan·te·des·chia \,zantə'deskēə\ *n, cap* [NL, fr. Giovanni *Zantedeschi* †1846 Ital. botanist + NL *-ia*] **:** a small genus of southern or tropical African aroids with basal long-stalked often hastate leaves, very showy spathes usu. mistaken for a corolla, and a stout central spadix — see CALLA 2, YELLOW CALLA

zan·tho·rhi·za \,zan(t)thə'rīzə\ *n, cap* [NL, irreg. fr. *xanth-* + *-rhiza*] **:** a small genus of No. American low shrubby plants (family Berberidaceae) with purplish brown flowers and very bitter yellow roots

zan·thox·y·la·ce·ae \(,)zan,thäksə'lāsē,ē\ *n pl, cap* [NL, fr. *Zanthoxylum* + *-aceae*] *in some classifications* **:** a family of dicotyledonous plants comprising solely the genus *Zanthoxylum* and being usu. included in Rutaceae

zan·thox·y·lum \≈'≈sələm\ *n* [NL, irreg. fr. *xanth-* + *-xylum*] **1 a** *cap* **:** a genus of widely distributed shrubs or trees (family Rutaceae) having odd-pinnate leaves, small greenish flowers with 2 to 5 pistils, and 2-valved fleshy capsules **b** -s **:** any plant of the genus *Zanthoxylum* **2** -s *also* **xanthoxylum :** the dried bark of prickly ash or hercules'-club formerly used as a diaphoretic and stimulant

zan·ti·ot \'zantēət, -ē,ät\ *or* **zan·ti·ote** \-ē,ōt\ *n* -s *cap* [*Zante*, island in southwest Greece + E *-iot, -iote* (as in *cypriot, cypriote*)] **:** a native or resident of Zante

¹za·ny \'zānē, -ni\ *n* -ES [It *zanni* — more at ZANNI] **1 a :** a subordinate fool, clown, acrobat, or mountebank who mimics ludicrously the tricks of his principal **:** an assistant to a mountebank (as in old comedies) **:** MERRY-ANDREW **b :** a usu. professional clown or buffoon **2 :** an assistant or lieutenant attendant upon another; *specif* **:** a slavish follower **:** TOADY — usu. used contemptuously **3** *obs* **:** a wretched or ridiculous imitator **:** a feeble mimic **4 :** one who makes a buffoon or laughingstock of himself to amuse others **5 :** SIMPLETON

²zany \"\ *vt* -ED/-ING/-ES *archaic* **:** to play the zany to **:** imitate in the manner of a zany

³zany \"\ *adj* -ER/-EST **:** being or having the characteristics of a zany **:** fantastically or irrationally ludicrous **:** mildly insane **:** CRAZY ⟨a ~ sense of humor —*N.Y. Herald Tribune Bk. Rev.*⟩

za·ny·ism \-nē,izəm\ *n* -s **:** a characteristic or practice of a zany **:** BUFFOONERY

zan·za \'zanzə\ *or* **san·sa** \'san(t)sə\ *also* **zan·ze** \'zanzə\ *n* -s [Ar *sanj* castanets, cymbals, fr. Per *sanj*] **:** an African musical instrument consisting of graduated sets of tongues of wood or metal inserted into and resonated by a wooden box and sounded by plucking with the fingers or thumbs

zan·zi·bar copal \¦zanzə¦bär, -bà(r-\ *n, usu cap Z* [*Zanzibar*, island off the northeast coast of Tanganyika, Tanzania, eastern Africa] **:** a hard copal derived from a tree (*Trachylobium verrucosum*) of the family Leguminosae — called also *animé*

zan·zi·ba·ri \¦≈≈¦bärē\ *n* -s *cap* [Ar *zanjibārīy* of or relating to Zanzibar, fr. *Zanjibār* Zanzibar] **1 :** the Arabic dialect spoken in Zanzibar **2 :** a native or resident of Zanzibar

za·pa·ran \'zäpərən, 'sä-\ *adj, usu cap* **:** of, relating to, or constituting the Zaparo

za·pa·ro \'zäpərō, 'sä-\ *n, pl* **zaparo** *or* **zaparos** *usu cap* **1 a :** a group of peoples of eastern Ecuador and northern Peru **b :** a member of any of such peoples **2 :** the language of the Zaparo people

za·pa·ro·an \,≈≈'rōən\ *n* -s *usu cap* **:** a language family of eastern Ecuador and northern Peru that includes Coronado and Zaparo

za·pa·te·a·do \,zäpətē'ä(,)dō, ,sä-, -ē'aů\ *n* -s [Sp, fr. *zapatear* to strike with the shoe, tap with the feet, fr. *zapato* shoe — more at SABOT] **1 :** a rhythmic stamping or tapping step characteristic of Spanish dancing **2 :** a Spanish or Latin-American dance marked by the zapateado

za·pa·teo \,≈≈'tā(,)ō\ *n* -s [Sp, fr. *zapatear*] **:** ZAPATEADO 2

za·pa·te·ro \,≈≈'te(,)rō\ *n* -s [Sp, lit., shoemaker, fr. *zapato* shoe] **1 :** a leatherjacket (*Oligoplites saurus*) **2** [AmerSp, fr. Sp] **a :** a tropical American timber tree (*Casearia praecox*) **b :** the wood of this tree — called also *West Indian boxwood*

zap flap \'zap-\ *n* [prob. after Edward F. *Zap*, 20th cent. Am. aeronautical engineer] **:** a split flap in which the hinge axis moves aft as the flap is deflected, thus increasing the area of the wing as well as its camber

¹za·phren·tid \zə'frentəd\ *adj* [NL *Zaphrentidae*, family of tetracorals in some classifications, fr. *Zaphrentis* + *-idae*] **:** of or relating to the genus *Zaphrentis* or family Zaphrentidae

²zaphrentid \"\ *n* -s [NL *Zaphrentidae*] **:** a zaphrentid tetracoral

za·phren·tis \-ntəs\ *n, cap* [NL] **:** a genus (sometimes made the type of the family Zaphrentidae) of solitary cup-shaped tetracorals that are common in Paleozoic formations and have numerous septa radiating from a deep pit in one side of the cup

za·phren·toid \-n-,tȯid\ *adj* [NL *Zaphrentis* + E *-oid*] **:** resembling or related to the genus *Zaphrentis* or family Zaphrentidae

¹zap·o·did \'zapədəd\ *adj* [NL *Zapodidae*] **:** of or relating to the Zapodidae

²zapodid \"\ *n* -s [NL *Zapodidae*] **:** a zapodid rodent

za·pod·i·dae \zə'pädə,dē\ *n pl, cap* [NL, fr. *Zapod-, Zapus*, type genus + *-idae*] **:** a widely distributed family of myomorph rodents that includes the jumping mice of No. America and related Old World mice

za·pon fast dye \'zä,pän-\ *n, usu cap Z&F* [*Zapon*, trade name for a lacquer, fr. G *zaponlack*] **:** any of several solvent dyes — see DYE table I (under *Solvent Orange 5, Solvent Red 8* and *35*, and *Solvent Yellow 19*)

za·po·ro·zhe \,zäpə'rȯzhə\ *adj, usu cap* [*Zaporozhe*, city in southeast Ukraine, U.S.S.R.] **:** of or from the city of Zaporozhe, U.S.S.R. **:** of the kind or style prevalent in Zaporozhe

za·po·ta gum \zə'pōd·ə-\ *n* [NL *zapota* (specific epithet of the sapodilla *Achras zapota*), fr. Sp *zapote* sapodilla — more at SAPOTA] **:** CHICLE

zapote *var of* SAPOTE

za·po·tec \'zäpə,tek, 'sä-\ *n, pl* **zapotec** *or* **zapotecs** *usu cap* [Sp *Zapoteca*, fr. Nahuatl *Tzapoteca*, lit., people of the land of the sapodillas, fr. *tzapotlan* place of the sapodillas (fr. *tzapotl* sapodilla) + *-teca* (pl. of *-tecatl*, suffix denoting origin)] **1 a :** an Indian people of the state of Oaxaca, Mexico **b :** a member of such people **2 :** a Zapotecan language of the Zapotec people

za·po·tecan \,≈≈'tekən, -tek-\ *n* -s *usu cap* **1 :** a language stock of southern Mexico comprising Chatino and the several languages all known as Zapotec **2 :** the peoples speaking Zapotecan languages

za·pu·pe \zə'pü(,)pē, pə-\ *n* -s [AmerSp] **1 :** any of various Mexican agaves (as *Agave zapupe* and *A. deweyana*) that yield fiber somewhat similar to henequen **2 :** the fiber of a zapupe

za·pus \'zäpəs\ *n, cap* [NL *Zapod-, Zapus*, fr. *za-*, intensive prefix + *-pod-, -pus* -pus — more at ZAGLOSSUS] **:** the type genus of Zapodidae

za·ra·go·za \¦sàrà¦gō(,)sà, ¦thàrà¦gō(,)thà\ *adj, usu cap* [*Zaragoza, Saragossa*, city in northeastern Spain] **:** SARAGOSSA

za·rah \zə'rä\ *n* -s [origin unknown] **:** KAZOO

zar·a·thus·trian \¦zarə¦thüstrēən\ *also* **zar·a·thus·tric** \-strik\ *adj, usu cap* [*Zarathustra* (Zoroaster) *fl ab* 6th cent. B.C. founder of Zoroastrianism (fr. Av *Zarāthushtra-*) + E *-an* or *-ic*] **:** ZOROASTRIAN

zara·tite \'zärə,tīt, 'zar-\ *n* -s [Sp *zaratita*, fr. Señor *Zarate*, 19th cent. Spaniard + Sp *-ita* -ite] **:** a hydrous basic nickel carbonate $Ni_3(CO_3)(OH)_4.4H_2O$ occurring in emerald-green incrustations or compact masses

za·re·ba *or* **za·ri·ba** *also* **ze·ri·ba** \zə'rēbə\ *n* -s [Ar *zarībah* enclosure, pen] **:** an improvised stockade constructed esp. of thornbushes and used for defense in parts of Africa

zar·e·ma \'zärəmə\ *or* **zar·ma** \-rmə\ *n, usu cap* **:** DYERMA

zarvanism *usu cap, var of* ZERVANISM

zar·zue·la \zärz'wälə, ,zärzə'w-, sär'sw-, ,särsə'w-\ *n* -s [Sp, prob. fr. *La Zarzuela*, royal residence near Madrid where it was first performed] **:** a Spanish opera having spoken dialogue and usu. a comic subject

zastruga *var of* SASTRUGA

zau·ber·flö·te \'tsaůbə(r),flād·ə, -lǣd·ə, *G* -lœtə\ *n* -s [fr. *Die Zauberflöte* (English title *The Magic Flute*), opera first presented in 1791 with music by Wolfgang Amadeus Mozart †1791 Austrian composer and libretto by Emanuel Schikaneder †1812 Ger. theater manager and librettist] **:** a stopped flute pipe-organ stop of harmonic length

zausch·ne·ria \zȯsh'nirēə\ *n* [NL, fr. Johann B. J. *Zauschner* †1799 Bohemian naturalist + NL *-ia*] **1** *cap* **:** a small genus of California perennial herbs (family Onagraceae) with scarlet racemose flowers like those of fuchsia and comose seeds **2** -s **:** any plant of the genus *Zauschneria*

zax \'zaks\ *n* -ES [E dial., alter. of ¹*sax*] **:** a tool for trimming and puncturing roofing slates

z–axis \'≈,≈≈\ *n* **:** one of the axes in a three-dimensional rectangular coordinate system **:** a line perpendicular to the plane of a polar coordinate system at the pole — compare CYLINDRICAL COORDINATE

za·yin *or* **za·in** \'zäyən, 'zī(y)ən\ *n* -s [Heb *zayin*] **:** the seventh letter of the Hebrew alphabet — symbol ז; see ALPHABET table

z chromosome *n, usu cap Z* **:** a sex chromosome of the kind occurring doubled in the male and singly either with or without a W chromosome in organisms (as moths) in which the female is heterogametic — compare X CHROMOSOME

z–coordinate \'≈≈≈(≈)≈\ *n* **1 :** one of the three coordinates in a three-dimensional rectangular coordinate system **2 :** the third coordinate in a cylindrical coordinate system

ZD *abbr* zenith distance

zdar·sky tent \'st¦ärskē-, 'zd|, zə'd|\ *n, usu cap Z* [after Mathias *Zdarsky* †1940 Austrian skiing expert] **:** an esp. prepared light sheet of cloth that is used for shelter instead of a tent — called also *bivouac sheet*

zdra·vets oil \'zdrävəts-\ *n* [prob. fr. *Zdravets*, town in Bulgaria] **:** geranium oil obtained esp. from a woody-stemmed geranium (*Geranium macrorrhizum*) in Bulgaria and Cyprus

zea \'zēə\ *n* [NL, fr. Gk *zea, zeia* single-grained wheat; akin to Skt *yava* barley] **1** *cap* **:** a genus of large grasses having broad ribbon-shaped leaves and monoecious flowers of which the staminate forms an ample terminal panicle and the pistillate is in a sessile axillary spike enveloped by numerous bracts — see INDIAN CORN **2** -s **:** the fresh styles and stigmas of Indian corn formerly used as a diuretic

zeal \'zēl, *esp before pause or consonant* -ēəl\ *n* -s [ME *zele*, fr. LL *zelus*, fr. Gk *zēlos* zeal, emulation, jealousy; akin to Gk (Dor dial.) *zamia* loss and perh. to OIr *āilid* he desires ardently, Russ *yaryĭ* furious, Skt *yāvan* aggressor] **1** *archaic* **:** ardor of feeling taking the form usu. of jealousy or indignation ⟨I the Lord have spoken it in my ~ —Ezek 5:13 (AV)⟩ **2** *obs* **:** ardent desire esp. to do or have something ⟨this doth infer the ~ I had to see him —Shak.⟩ **3 :** impassioned eagerness esp. in favor of a person or a cause **:** active enthusiastic interest mounting to fervor ⟨entered with ~ upon this task —C.S.Sydnor⟩ ⟨a fearless tenacity equivalent to religious ~ —Russell Kirk⟩ **4** *obs* **:** ZEALOT **syn** see PASSION

zea·land·er \'zēləndə(r)\ *n* -s *usu cap* [*Zealand, Sjælland*, island in eastern Denmark + E *-er*] **1 :** a native or inhabitant

of Zealand in Denmark 2 [*Zealand, Zeeland,* province of southwest Netherlands + E *-er*] : ZEELANDER
zeal·less \ˈzēlləs\ *adj* : lacking zeal
¹**zeal·ot** \ˈzelət, *usu* -əd·+V\ *n* -s [LL *zelotes,* fr. Gk *zēlōtēs,* fr. *zēlos*] **1** *usu cap* : one of a fanatical sect bitterly opposing the Roman domination of Palestine during the great rebellion and the siege of Jerusalem and opposing not only the Romans but other Jewish factions — see SICARIUS **2 a** : one who is zealous : one who embraces a cause and supports it with vigor and enthusiasm **b** : one who is carried away by his zeal : a fanatical partisan **syn** see ENTHUSIAST
²**zealot** \"\ *adj* : being or characteristic of a zealot
zea·lot·ic \zəˈläd·ik, zēˈ-\ *adj* : of, resembling, or suitable to a zealot : ardently zealous
zeal·ot·ism \ˈzeləd·,izəm\ *n* -s : ZEALOTRY
zeal·ot·ry \-ə·trē, -ri\ *n* -ES : the character and behavior of a zealot : an excess of zeal : fanatical devotion; *also* : an instance of such behavior or disposition
zeal·ous \ˈzeləs\ *adj* [ML *zelosus,* fr. LL *zelus* zeal + L *-osus* -ose] : filled with or characterized by zeal : warmly engaged or ardent esp. in behalf of something : marked by a fervent partisanship for a person, a cause, or an ideal ⟨a ~ supporter of the Confederacy —D.Y.Thomas⟩ ⟨impetuous in his enthusiasm, ~ for liberty —G.H.Genzmer⟩
zeal·ous·ly *adv* : in a zealous manner ⟨worked ~ to raise funds⟩
zeal·ous·ness *n* -ES : the quality or state of being zealous
zealous witness *n* : a witness showing partiality for the side that first calls him to the stand in a trial and eagerness to volunteer what he thinks will be advantageous to that side
ze·a·xan·thin \,zēə+\ *n* -s [ISV *zea-* (fr. NL *Zea,* genus name of Indian corn) + *xanthin*] : a yellow crystalline carotenoid alcohol $C_{40}H_{54}(OH)_2$ that is isomeric with lutein and occurs widely with it and that is the chief pigment of yellow Indian corn : a dihydroxy β-carotene — compare VIOLAXANTHIN
¹**zebra** \ˈzēbrə, *Brit also* ˈzeb-\ *n, pl* **zebras** *also* **zebra** [It, fr. Sp *cebra, zebra,* fr. OSp *zebra, zebro, enzebro* wild ass, perh. fr. (assumed) VL *eciferus* wild horse, alter. of L *equiferus,* fr. *equus* horse + *ferus* wild — more at EQUINE, FIERCE] **1** : any of several fleet African equine mammals related to the horse and the ass but distinctively and conspicuously patterned in stripes of black or dark brown and white or buff — see BURCHELL'S ZEBRA, GRÉVY'S ZEBRA, MOUNTAIN ZEBRA **2** *or* **zebra butterfly** : a black yellow-striped butterfly (*Heliconius charitonius*) of the family Heliconiidae found in southern Florida and the West Indies **3** : any of various objects bearing stripes like those of the zebra **4 a** : ZEBRA FISH **b** : a small southern African sargo (*Diplodus trifasciatus*) highly esteemed for sport and food

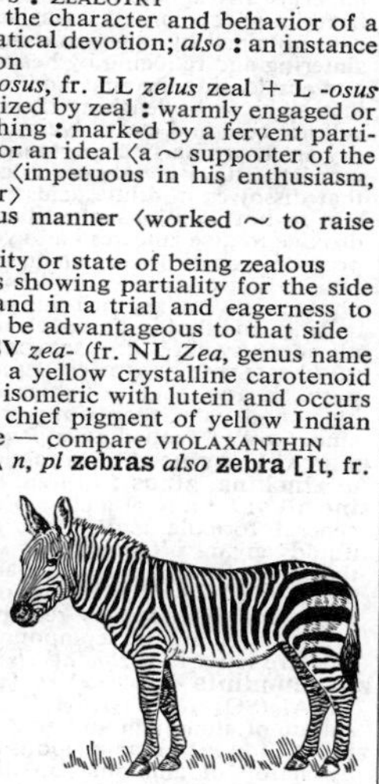
zebra

²**zebra** \"\ *usu cap* — a communications code word for the letter z
zebra antelope *n* : a small bush antelope (*Cephalophus doriae*) of Liberia that is brown with black cross stripes
zebra–back \ˈ==,=\ *also* **zebra bird** *n* : RED-BELLIED WOODPECKER
zebra caterpillar *n* : a caterpillar that is the larva of an American noctuid moth (*Ceramica picta*), that is light yellow with a broad black stripe on the back and lateral stripes crossed with white, and that feeds on cultivated plants (as cabbages, beets)
zebra civet cat *n* : a banded palm civet (*Hemigalus hardwickii*)
zebra finch *n* : a small Australian weaverbird (*Poephila castanotis* or *Taeniopygia castanotis*) whose plumage is mainly light gray and white but with the upper tail coverts broadly barred black and white and the sides of the head orange-rufous and which is commonly kept in captivity
zebra fish *n* : any of various barred fishes: as **a** : a small Australian sea fish (*Melambaphes zebra*) of the family Girellidae that is olive above and pinkish below with nine dark crossbars **b** : a small dark-barred Canadian variety of the log perch **c** *also* **zebra danio** : a very small blue-and-silver-striped Indian danio (*Brachydanio rerio*) often kept in the tropical aquarium; *also* : any closely related and similarly marked danio
zebra grass *n* : a grass (*Miscanthus sinensis zebrinus*) that has leaves with yellow or white longitudinal stripes
ze·bra·ic \zəˈbrāik, zeˈ-, -āek\ *adj* : of the nature of or characteristic of the zebra : ZEBRALIKE
zebralike \ˈ==,=\ *adj* : resembling or suggesting a zebra esp. in color or marking : ZEBRAIC
ze·brano \zəˈbrä(,)nō\ *or* **ze·brana** \-,nə\ *n* -s [ISV, irreg. fr. ¹*zebra*] : ZEBRAWOOD
zebra parrakeet *n* : BUDGERIGAR
zebra plant *n* : a Brazilian herb (*Calathea zebrina*) with leaves striped green and yellowish white that is widely cultivated as a foliage plant
zebra shark *n* : LEOPARD SHARK c
zebra spider *n* : a European hunting spider (*Salticus scenicus*)
ze·brass \ˈzē,bras, -aa(ə)s, -ais\ *n* -ES [¹*zebra* + *ass*] : a hybrid produced by breeding a zebra with an ass
zebra swallowtail *n* : a very large swallowtail butterfly (*Papilio marcellus*) of eastern No. America which has greenish white or yellowish white wings barred with black and whose larva feeds on the papaw
zebra–tailed lizard \ˈ==,=-\ *n* : GRIDIRON-TAILED LIZARD
zebra wolf *also* **zebra opossum** *n* : TASMANIAN WOLF
zebrawood \ˈ==,=\ *n* **1** : any of several trees or shrubs having mottled or striped wood: as **a** : a tropical American and East African tree (*Connarus guianensis*) with strikingly marked hard wood used in cabinetwork **b** : a tropical Asiatic and African shrub (*Guettarda speciosa*) of the family Rubiaceae from the flowers of which a perfume is extracted in India **c** : NAKEDWOOD 2 **d** : MARBLEWOOD 1a **e** : an arariba (*Centrolobium robustum*) **f** : any of various African timber trees (genus *Brachystegia*) with pale golden heartwood uniformly striped with dark brown or black — called also *zingana* **2 a** : the wood of the zebrawood **b** : GONCALO ALVES 2
zebrawood family *n* : CONNARACEAE
ze·bri·na \zəˈbrīnə\ *n, cap* [NL, fr. G *zebra* (fr. Pg *zêbra,* fr. OPg *zevra, zevro* wild ass, perh. fr. assumed VL *eciferus* wild horse) + NL *-ina;* fr. the striped leaves — more at ZEBRA] : a small genus of trailing herbs (family Commelinaceae) of New Mexico and Mexico having ovate or oblong leaves and flowers with sepals and petals united into a tube — see WANDERING JEW 1
ze·brine \ˈzē,brīn, -,brən\ *adj* [¹*zebra* + *-ine*] : relating to or resembling a zebra : characteristic of a zebra : suggesting a zebra esp. in marking
¹**ze·broid** \-,brȯid\ *adj* [¹*zebra* + *-oid*] : related to or resembling a zebra
²**zebroid** \"\ *n* -s : a hybrid between a male zebra and a female horse used as a work animal in some tropical areas because of its docility and its resistance to disease and heat injury
zebru·la \ˈzebrələ, ˈzeb-\ *or* **ze·brule** \ˈzē,brül\ *n* -s [*zebrula* alter. (influenced by *-ula*) of *zebrule,* fr. *zebra* + *mule*] : ZEBROID
ze·bu \ˈzē,byü, -bü\ *n* -s [F *zébu,* perh. modif. of Tibetan *mdzopho* male of a hybrid of the yak bull and the zebu] : an Asiatic ox (*Bos indicus*) domesticated and differentiated into many breeds in India, China, the East Indies, and parts of Africa, used chiefly for draft, for riding, or for milk or flesh, and distinguished from European cattle with which it crosses freely by the presence of a large fleshy hump over the shoulders, a loose skin prolonged into dewlap and folds under the belly, pendulous ears, and marked resistance to the injurious effects of heat and insect attack — compare BRAHMAN

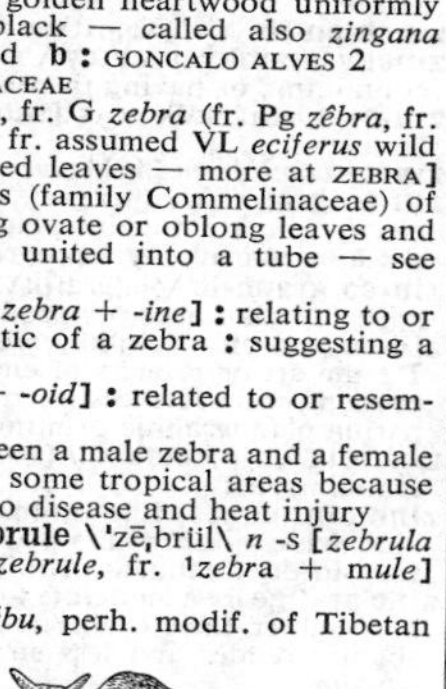
zebu

ze·bub \ˈzē,bəb\ *n* -s [Ar *dhubāb*] : ZIMB
zebu cattle *n pl* : ZEBUS
zeb·u·lun·ite \ˈzebyələ,nīt\ *n* -s *usu cap* [*Zebulun,* tenth son of Jacob (Gen 30:20) and ancestor of the tribe (fr. LL *Zabulon,* fr. Heb *Zĕbhūlūn*) + E *-ite*] : a member of the Hebrew tribe of Zebulun
zec·chi·no \zeˈkē(,)nō, tse-\ *n, pl* **zecchi·ni** \-nē\ *or* **zecchinos** [It — more at SEQUIN] : SEQUIN 1
zech·in *or* **zec·chin** *or* **zec·chine** \ˈzekən\ *n* -s [It *zecchino*] : SEQUIN 1
zech·stein \ˈzek,stīn\ *adj, usu cap* [G, lit., mine stone, fr. *zeche* mine (fr. MHG, company, society) + *stein* stone, fr. OHG; akin to OE *teohh* company, society, *teohhian* to determine, propose, OHG *zehōn* to order, arrange, and prob. to Goth *gateihan* to tell — more at DICTION, STONE] : of or relating to a subdivision of the European Permian — see GEOLOGIC TIME table
zed \ˈzed\ *n* -s [ME, fr. MF *zede,* fr. LL *zeta* zeta, fr. Gk *zēta*] *chiefly Brit* : the letter *z*
zedakah *n, pl* **zedakoth** *or* **zedakot** *var of* TZEDAKAH
zed·o·ar·ia \,zedəˈwa(a)rēə\ *n* -s [ML] : ZEDOARY
zed·o·ary \ˈ==,werē\ *n* -ES [ML *zedoaria, zedoariu n,* fr. Ar or Per; Ar *zadwār,* fr. Per] : a fragrant East Indian drug of a warm bitter aromatic taste formerly used in medicine as a stimulant and still used in India and derived from the rhizome of various plants of the genus *Curcuma* (esp. *C. zedoaria*)
zee \ˈzē\ *n* -s : the letter *z*
zee·land·er \ˈzēləndə(r)\ *n* -s *cap* [*Zeeland,* province of southwest Netherlands + E *-er*] : a native or inhabitant of Zeeland in the Netherlands
zee·man effect \ˈzā,män, ˈzēmən-\ *n, usu cap Z* [after Pieter *Zeeman* †1943 Dutch physicist] : a phenomenon that is observed in the emission spectrum when a source of radiation is placed in a magnetic field or observed in the absorption spectrum when an absorbing medium is placed in a magnetic field and that consists of the breaking of single spectral lines into three or more components which are polarized
ze·i·dae \ˈzēə,dē\ *n pl, cap* [NL *Zeus,* type genus + *-idae*] : a family of marine fishes (order Zeomorphi) comprising the John Dorys
ze·i·form \-ə,fȯrm\ *adj* [NL *Zeus* + E *-iform*] : resembling the Zeidae
zei·gar·nik effect \z|īˈgärnik-, ts|\ *n, usu cap Z* [after Bluma *Zeigarnik,* 20th cent. Ger. psychologist] : the psychological tendency to remember an uncompleted task rather than a completed one
ze·in \ˈzēən\ *n* -s [NL *Zea* + E *-in*] : a prolamin constituting the principal protein in corn that is usu. obtained as a yellowish powder by extracting corn gluten with aqueous isopropyl alcohol and that is used chiefly in making textile fibers, plastics, printing inks, varnishes and other coatings, and adhesives and sizes
zeit·geist \ˈtsīt,gīst\ *n* -s *often cap* [G, fr. *zeit* time (fr. OHG *zīt*) + *geist* spirit, fr. OHG — more at TIDE, GHOST] : the spirit of the time : the general intellectual and moral state or the trend of culture and taste characteristic of an era ⟨the ~ of these centuries . . . operated against the development of a pure science —J.K.Robertson⟩ ⟨speed is a part of our ~; it is basic . . . to our ability to produce —V.E.Leichty⟩
zel·koua \zelkəwə\ [NL, fr. Georgian *tselkva*] *syn of* ZELKOVA
zel·ko·va \-kəvə\ *n, cap* [NL, fr. Georgian *tselkva*] : a small genus of shrubs and trees (family Ulmaceae) occurring in temperate regions of the Old World and having simple leaves, small apetalous polygamous flowers, and small oblique drupes
¹**ze·mi** \zəˈmē, sə-\ *n, pl* **zemi** *or* **zemis** [Sp *zemi,* fr. Taino *cemi, zemi, zeme*] **1** : a spirit or supernatural being of the aboriginal Tainos of the West Indies **2** : an object believed to be the dwelling of a spirit and to possess magic potency; *esp* : FETISH, IDOL
²**ze·mi** \ˈzāmē\ *n, pl* **zemi** *or* **zemis** *usu cap* **1** : a Naga people found chiefly in the Barail area of the Assam-Burma frontier region **2** : a member of the Zemi people
ze·mi·ism \zəˈmē,izəm, sə-\ *n* -s [¹*zemi* + *-ism*] : the body of Taino beliefs and practices regarding zemis
zemindar *var of* ZAMINDAR
zemindari *var of* ZAMINDARI
ze·mi·roth *or* **ze·mi·rot** \zəˈmē,rōt(h), -ōs\ *n pl* [Heb *zĕmīrōth* (pl.), fr. *zamēr* to sing] : religious songs sung usu. in Hebrew typically around the table at the Sabbath meal
zem·mi \ˈzemē\ *or* **zem·ni** \-mnē\ *n* -s [Russ dial. (*shchenyuk*) *zemny,* lit., earth puppy, fr. *shchenyuk* puppy + *zemny* of earth, fr. *zemlya* earth; akin to L *humus* earth — more at HUMBLE] : a large eastern European mole rat (*Spalax typhlus*)
zen \ˈzen\ *n* -s *usu cap* [Jap, religious meditation, fr. Chin (Pek) *ch'an²,* fr. Pali *jhāna,* fr. Skt *dhyāna* — more at DHYANA] **1** *or* **zen buddhism** *usu cap Z&B* : a Japanese school of Mahayana Buddhism that teaches self-discipline, deep meditation, and the attainment of enlightenment by direct intuitive insight into a self-validating transcendent truth beyond all intellectual conceptions and characteristically expresses its teachings in paradoxical and nonlogical forms — see KOAN, MONDO, SATORI **2** *or* **zen buddhist** *usu cap Z&B* : an adherent of Zen
ze·na·ga \zəˈnägə\ *n, pl* **zenaga** *or* **zenagas** *usu cap* **1 a** : a Berber people of southern Morocco with other peoples under the general designation of Moors dominating western Africa in the 11th century and producing the Almoravid Caliphate **b** : a member of such people **2** : the Berber language of the Zenaga people
ze·na·i·da \zəˈnāədə\ *n* [NL, fr. *Zénaïde* †1854 cousin and wife of Prince Charles Lucien Bonaparte †1857] **1** *cap* : a genus of tropical American pigeons that has one species (*Zenaida aurita*) reaching the West Indies and formerly the Florida coast and one (*Zenaida asiatica*) occurring in the southwestern United States **2** *or* **zenaida dove** -s : any bird of the genus *Zenaida*
ze·na·i·du·ra \zə,nāəˈd(y)ürə\ *n, cap* [NL, fr. *Zenaida* + *-ura*] : a genus of pigeons that includes the common American mourning dove
¹**ze·na·na** \zəˈnänə\ *n* -s [Hindi *zanāna,* fr. Per, fr. *zan* woman; akin to Skt *jani* — more at QUEEN] : the part of a dwelling in which the women of a family are secluded in India and Persia : HAREM, SERAGLIO
²**zenana** \"\ *adj* : of or relating to zenanas : relating to the women of the zenanas
ze·ner cards \ˈzēnə(r)-\ *n pl, usu cap Z* [after Karl E. *Zener* †1964 Am. psychologist] : a set of 25 cards that consists of 5 cards of each of 5 kinds bearing a circle, a rectangle, a cross, wavy lines, or a star and that is used in research in extrasensory perception

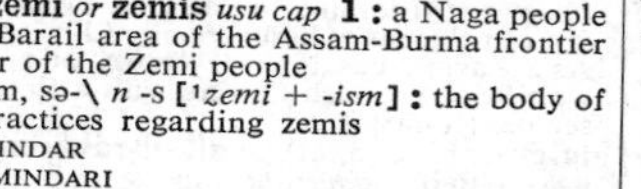
Zener cards

¹**ze·nith** \ˈzēnəth, *chiefly Brit* ˈzen-\ *n* -s [ME *cenit, senyth,* fr. MF *cenith,* fr. ML, fr. OSp *zenit,* modif. (prob. due to scribal error) of Ar *samt (ar-ra's)* way (of the head)] **1** : the point of the celestial sphere that is vertically above the observer and directly opposite the nadir or that is vertically above any given point on the earth's surface **2 a** : the vault of the sky : the upper region of the heavens **b** : the highest point reached in the heavens by a celestial body **3** : the point of culmination : the greatest height : ACME, PEAK, SUMMIT ⟨classical studies reached their ~ in the twelfth century —H. O.Taylor⟩ ⟨at the ~ of his fame —Alvin Redman⟩ ⟨in his early fifties, at the ~ of his powers —John Buchan⟩ **4** *or* **zenith blue** : a light purplish blue that is redder than lupine and bluer and paler than average periwinkle
²**zenith** \"\ *adj* : located at or relating to the zenith
ze·nith·al \-thəl\ *adj* **1** : of or relating to the zenith : located at or near the zenith **2** : drawn to show correct directions from the center ⟨a ~ map⟩ : of or relating to zenithal equidistant projection
zenithal equidistant projection *n* : AZIMUTHAL EQUIDISTANT PROJECTION
zenith distance *or* **zenith angle** *n* : the angular distance of a celestial object from the zenith measured by the arc of a vertical circle intercepted between the object and the zenith : the complement of the altitude
zenith eyepiece *n* : an eyepiece or adapter containing a right-angle prism or a plane mirror to reflect the rays from an object near the zenith to the side of a refracting telescope for more convenient observation — called also *diagonal eyepiece*
zenith star *n* : a star that culminates near the zenith
zenith telescope *or* **zenith tube** *n* : a telescope that is installed in a fixed vertical position so that it can be used only to observe stars crossing the meridian near the zenith which is at the center of its field of view and that is used for precise time and latitude determinations
ze·nith·ward \ˈ==,wə(r)d\ *or* **ze·nith·wards** \-dz\ *adv* [¹*zenith* + *-ward* or *-wards*] : toward the zenith ⟨a ray of everlasting light . . . that had shot itself ~ —Thomas Carlyle⟩
zen·ker's degeneration \ˈtseŋkə(r)z-, ˈze|\ *n, usu cap Z* [after Friedrich Albert von *Zenker* †1898 Ger. pathologist] : AMYLOIDOSIS
zenker's fluid *n, usu cap Z* [after Konrad *Zenker* †1894 Ger. histologist] : a fixing fluid much used in histological technique and composed of potassium dichromate, mercuric chloride, sodium sulfate, glacial acetic acid, and water
zen·nist \ˈzenəst\ *n* -s *usu cap* [*zen* + *-ist*] : ZEN 2
ze·no·ni·an \zəˈnōnēən\ *adj, usu cap* **1** [L *Zenon-, Zeno* Zeno, 5th cent. B.C. Greek Eleatic philosopher (fr. Gk *Zēnōn*) + E *-ian*] : of or relating to the Eleatic philosopher Zeno, his doctrines, or his paradoxes **2** [L *Zenon-, Zeno* Zeno, 4th & 3d cent. B.C. Greek philosopher and founder of Stoicism, (fr. Gk *Zēnōn*) + E *-ian*] : of or relating to Zeno, the founder of Stoicism
zeno·pho·bia \,zenəˈfōbēə\ *n* [by alter.] : XENOPHOBIA
zens *pl of* ZEN
ze·oid \ˈzē,ȯid\ *adj or n* [NL *Zeoidei*] : ZEOMORPH
ze·oi·dei \zēˈȯidē,ī\ *n pl* [NL, fr. *Zeus* + *-oidei*] *syn of* ZEOMORPHI
ze·o·lite \ˈzēə,līt\ *n* -s [Sw *zeolit,* fr. Gk *zein* to boil + *-o-* + Sw *-lit* -lite, fr. F *-lite;* fr. their intumescence under the blowpipe — more at YEAST] **1** : any of a family of hydrous silicates that include several groups (as the monoclinic phillipsite group, the rhombohedral chabazite group, the monoclinic natrolite group, and the monoclinic heulandite group) as well as minerals not yet classified, that are analogous in composition to the feldspars with aluminum, sodium, potassium, and calcium as their chief metals, that occur as secondary minerals in cavities of lavas (as amygdaloidal basalt) and less frequently in granite and gneiss, and that have the capacity to act as cation exchangers or as molecular sieves (hardness usu. 3.5–5.5, sp.gr. 2.0–2.4) **2** : any of various silicates that are processed natural materials (as glauconite or greensand) or synthetic granular sodium aluminum silicates used in water softening and as adsorbents — **ze·o·lit·ic** \ˈ==ˈlid·ik\ *adj*
ze·ol·i·ti·za·tion \zē,äləd·əˈzāshən, -əd·,īˈz-\ *n* -s : the act or process of zeolitizing
ze·ol·i·tize \zēˈälə,tīz\ *vt* -ED/-ING/-S **1** : to convert into a zeolite **2** : to fill (as the openings in a rock) with zeolites **3** : to treat in a process using zeolite
¹**zeo·morph** \ˈzēə,mȯrf\ *adj* [NL *Zeomorphi*] : of or relating to the Zeomorphi
²**zeomorph** \"\ *n* : a fish of the order Zeomorphi
zeo·mor·phi \ˈ==ˈmȯr,fī\ *n pl, cap* [NL, fr. *zeo-* (fr. *Zeus*) + *-morphi*] : a small order of marine bony fishes that in many respects are intermediate between the Berycomorphi and Percomorphi and that include the John Dorys and a few related forms
ze·oph·yl·lite \zēˈäfə,līt\ *n* -s [G *zeophyllit,* fr. *zeolit* zeolite + *phyll-* + *-it* -ite; fr. its occurrence in small plates] : a mineral $Ca_4Si_3O_7(OH)_4F_2$ consisting of a basic calcium silicate and fluoride of calcium often containing iron
zep \ˈzep\ *n* -s *often cap* [by shortening] : ZEPPELIN
Zeph·i·ran \ˈzefə,ran\ *trademark* — used for benzalkonium chloride
¹**zeph·yr** \ˈzefə(r)\ *n* -s [earlier *Zephyrus,* west wind (personified), fr. ME *Zephirus,* fr. L *Zephyrus,* god of the west wind, & *zephyrus* west wind, zephyr, fr. Gk *Zephyros,* god of the west wind, & *zephyros* west wind; prob. akin to Gk *zophos* darkness, west] **1 a** : a soft warm breeze from the west **b** : any gentle breeze **2** : any of various lightweight fabrics and articles of clothing (as a small shawl, a duster, or a hat) **3** : a pinkish gray to pale yellowish pink **syn** see WIND
²**zephyr** \"\ *adj, of a yarn or fabric* : very lightweight, soft, and fine
zeph·yr·an·thes \,zefəˈran,thēz\ *n, cap* [NL, fr. Gk *zephyros* zephyr + NL *-anthes*] : a genus of American bulbous plants (family Amaryllidaceae) having solitary pink, white, or yellowish solitary flowers with broad segments and stamens of different lengths
zeph·yr·e·an \,zefəˈrēən\ *or* **ze·phyr·ian** \zəˈfirēən\ *or* **zeph·yr·ous** \ˈzefərəs\ *adj* [¹*zephyr* + *-ean* or *-ian* or *-ous*] : of the character of, resembling, or suggesting a light breeze
zephyr lily *n* : a plant of the genus *Zephyranthes; esp* : a tropical American plant (*Z. carinata*) often cultivated for its rose-red flowers
zep·pe·lin \ˈzep(ə)lən\ *n* -s *often cap* [after Count Ferdinand von *Zeppelin* †1917 Ger. aeronaut and airship manufacturer] : a rigid airship consisting of a cylindrical trussed and covered frame supported by internal gas cells; *broadly* : AIRSHIP
ze·quin *or* **ze·quine** \zəˈkēn, ˈzekən, ˈzekwən\ *n* -s [alter. (influenced by It *zecchino* sequin) of *sequin*] : SEQUIN 1
zer·da \ˈzərdə\ *n* -s [Ar *zerdawā,* prob. of Per origin] : FENNEC
zeriba *var of* ZAREBA
¹**ze·ro** \ˈzē(,)rō, ˈzi(-\ *n, pl* **zeros** *also* **zeroes** [F or It; F *zéro,* fr. It *zero,* fr. ML *zephirum,* fr. Ar *ṣifr* empty, cipher, zero] **1 a** : the numerical symbol 0 denoting the absence of all magnitude or quantity : CIPHER, NAUGHT **b** : the number represented by the symbol 0 : a number or element that leaves unchanged any number or element to which it is added — see NUMBER table **c** : a mathematical value intermediate between positive and negative quantities **2 a** (1) : the point of departure in reckoning; *specif* : the point from which the graduation of a scale (as of a thermometer) commences (2) : the temperature represented by the zero mark on a thermometer **b** : ZERO HOUR 1 **c** (1) : the basic setting of the rear sight of a firearm that compensates for inaccuracies of weapon and of firing habits and for elevation required at a given range and that causes the firearm to hit where aimed under normal conditions (2) : the adjustment (as for elevation, windage) required for a gun or other device to achieve accuracy under specific operating conditions **3** : a person or thing that has no importance, influence, or independent existence : NONENTITY, NOBODY, NOTHING, CIPHER **4 a** (1) : a state or condition of total absence or of neutrality between opposites : NOTHING, NAUGHT ⟨a face that registered ~ no matter what happened⟩ ⟨the two eyewitnesses for the State added up to ~, for the defense made mincemeat of their testimony —Ross Colin⟩ ⟨reduce the mortality rate to ~⟩ ⟨hold the reversible reaction of the chemical to ~⟩ (2) : absence of an overt linguistic feature when this absence is itself significant because of the presence of such a feature at corresponding points in the language ⟨some vowel which earlier followed the final consonant but which was later reduced to ~ —R.A.Hall b. 1911⟩ **b** : the lowest point ⟨his spirits fell to ~ —Margaret Kennedy⟩ **5** : something arbitrarily or conveniently designated zero: as **a** : the lowest in order or class ⟨a speech so bad it rated a ~⟩ **b** : the space numbered 0 on a roulette wheel
²**zero** \"\ *adj* **1** : of, relating to, or being a zero: as **a** : forming a fixed point of departure in reckoning ⟨set the gauge back to the ~ mark⟩ ⟨time zones extending from the ~ meridian⟩ ⟨used the founding date as the ~ year of its era⟩ **b** : having no magnitude or quantity or being intermediate between positive and negative magnitudes or quantities : not any ⟨~ velocity⟩ ⟨~ gravity⟩ ⟨~ angle⟩ ⟨~ lift⟩ ⟨~ toe-in⟩ ⟨~ inches⟩ ⟨~ mass⟩ : NIL ⟨chances of making up the lost time were ~⟩ **c** (1) : ABSENT, LACKING ⟨the ~ modification in the past of *cut* in comparison with *loved, sang*⟩ (2) : having no modified inflectional form : UNMODIFIED ⟨the noun *fish* has a ~ plural *fish* as well as a regular plural *fishes*⟩ **d** (1) : belonging to or being a group or class arbitrarily or conveniently designated *zero* (2) : of, relating to, or being a logical class having no members : NULL, EMPTY ⟨the ~ denotation of the term *unicorn*⟩ ⟨~ class⟩ **2 a** *of an atmospheric ceiling* : limiting vision to 50

feet or less **b** *of horizontal visibility* **:** limited to 165 feet or less

³zero \"\ *vb* -ED/-ING/-ES *vt* **1 :** to adjust (as by firing under test conditions) the zero of — often used with *in* ⟨~*ed* in his rifle at 100 yards⟩ **2 :** to adjust (an instrument or device) to zero value or into synchronism **3 a :** to concentrate firepower (as of mortar or artillery) on the exact range of — usu. used with *in* ⟨it must operate from fixed bases which can be ~*ed* in by the enemy —Carl Spaatz⟩ **b :** to bring to bear on the exact range of a target **:** TRAIN — usu. used with *in* ⟨artillery and mortars were ~*ed* in on all crossroads and avenues of approach —S.J.Tobin⟩ **4 :** to reduce to zero ~ *vi* **1 :** to adjust fire (as of mortars or artillery) on a specific target — usu. used with *in* ⟨an enemy battery that ~*ed* in on the crossroad⟩ **2 :** to move near to or focus attention on a person or thing as if on a target **:** CLOSE — usu. used with *in* ⟨bird-dogs ~*ing* in on coveys of hidden quail —J.N.Leonard⟩ ⟨congressional opponents who ~*ed* in on the bill⟩

¹zero beat *n* [²*zero*] **:** a condition in which two radio frequencies are adjusted to equality by first producing beats between them and then reducing the beat frequency to zero — compare HETERODYNE

²zero beat *vb* **:** to adjust to zero beat

zero-beat reception *n* [¹*zero beat*] **:** a method of reception with an electron tube in generating condition in exact synchronism with the received wave as determined by zero beat — compare HOMODYNE

zero drift *n* **:** a gradual change in the scale zero of a measuring instrument (as a thermometer or a galvanometer)

zeroes *pl of* ZERO, *pres 3d sing of* ZERO

zero grade *n* **:** the most reduced form of the weak ablaut grade in which the vowel disappears entirely

zero group *n* **:** the group of inert gases having a valence of zero in the periodic table

zero hour *n* **1 a :** the hour at which a previously planned attack or other military operation is started — compare H HOUR **b :** the scheduled time for an action or operation (as the firing of a rocket) to occur or begin — compare COUNTDOWN **2 :** a time when a vital decision or decisive change in the course of events is impending **:** CRISIS **3 :** the time set as a basis for reckoning the time of day

ze·ro·ize \ˈzērō,īz, ˈzir-\ *vt* -ED/-ING/-S [¹*zero* + *-ize*] **:** to return (as a calculating machine) to zero

zero-lift angle \ˈ≈(,)≈-≈-\ *n* **:** the angle of attack of an airfoil when the lift is zero

zero oil *n* **:** an oil (as a lubricating oil) that becomes too viscous to flow or begins to deposit solid material at a temperature of 0° F by the cold test

zero-order reaction \ˈ≈(,)≈-≈≈-\ *n* **:** a chemical reaction in which the rate of reaction is constant and independent of the concentration of the reacting substances — compare ORDER OF A REACTION

zero-point energy \ˈ≈(,)≈-≈-\ *n* **:** energy remaining in a substance at the absolute zero of temperature

zero potential *n* **1 :** the ideal potential of a point infinitely distant from all electrification **2 :** the actual potential of the surface of the earth taken as a point of reference — compare GROUND 7b

zeros *pl of* ZERO

zero-sum game \ˈ≈(,)≈-≈-\ *n* **:** a game in which the cumulative winnings equal the cumulative losses

ze·roth \ˈzē,rōth, ˈzi,-\ *adj* [¹*zero* + *-th*] **:** having serial number zero **:** ZERO ⟨a grating spectrum of ~ order⟩ ⟨the ~ power of a number⟩

zerovalent \ˈ≈(,)≈ˈ≈≈\ *adj* [¹*zero* + *valent*] **:** having a valence of zero

zero-zero \ˈ≈(,)≈ˈ≈(,)≈\ *adj* **1 :** characterized by or being atmospheric conditions reducing ceiling and visibility to zero ⟨a *zero-zero* fog⟩ ⟨*zero-zero* weather⟩ **2 :** limited to zero by atmospheric conditions ⟨ceiling and visibility may be unlimited one moment, and *zero-zero* seven minutes later —*All Hands*⟩

zer·van·ism \ˈzərvə,nizəm\ *also* **zar·van·ism** \ˈzär-\ *n* -S *usu cap* [*Zervan, Zarvan*, an ancient Iranian god + E *-ian*] **:** an ancient Iranian religion or Zoroastrian heretical sect teaching that infinite time is the originating principle of existence and prior to the dual principles of good and evil held ultimate by orthodox Zoroastrianism and influencing Mithraism

zer·van·ite \-ə,nīt\ *also* **zar·van·ite** \-ə,nīt\ *n* -S *usu cap* [*Zervan, Zarvan* + E *-ite*] **:** an adherent of Zervanism

¹zest \ˈzest\ *n* -S [obs. F *zest* (now *zeste*) orange or lemon peel] **1 :** a piece of the peel or of the thin oily outer skin of an orange or lemon used as flavoring (as for liquor) **2 :** a quality of enhancing enjoyment **:** PIQUANCY ⟨younger children added a ~ and life to the . . . fair —*Springfield (Mass.) Union*⟩ ⟨hot tamales also added ~ to the diet —R.W.Murray⟩ **3 :** keen enjoyment **:** RELISH, GUSTO ⟨years of grinding work . . . had failed to kill her ~ for living —Edna Ferber⟩ ⟨enjoying the meal with full youthful ~ —J.C.Powys⟩ ⟨people who are losing their ~, imagination, joy, and awe, and are filled with boredom —J.B.Priestley⟩

²zest \"\ *vt* -ED/-ING/-S **:** to give a relish or flavor to **:** heighten the taste or relish of

zest·ful \ˈzestfəl\ *adj* [¹*zest* + *-ful*] **:** full of zest **:** marked by keen enjoyment ⟨housecleaning time — that ~ desire to banish clutter —Bernice Caswell⟩ — **zest·ful·ly** \-fəlē, -li\ *adv* — **zest·ful·ness** *n* -ES

zesty \ˈzestē, -ti\ *adj* [¹*zest* + *-y*] **:** having or characterized by zest **:** PIQUANT

ze·ta \ˈzād·ə, -ātə *also* ˈzē-\ *n* -S [Gk *zēta*, of Sem origin; prob. akin to Heb *ṣādhē* sadhe] **:** the sixth letter of the Greek alphabet — symbol Z or ζ; see ALPHABET table

zeta potential *n* **:** the potential difference across an electric double layer usu. between a solid surface and a liquid — called also *electrokinetic potential;* compare STREAMING POTENTIAL

¹ze·tet·ic \zəˈted·ik\ *adj* [Gk *zētētikos*, fr. *zētētos* (verbal of *zētein* to seek for, inquire) + *-ikos* -ic; prob. akin to Skt *diyati* he flies, soars — more at DINO-] **:** proceeding by inquiry

²zetetic \"\ *n* -S [Gk *zētētikos*, fr. *zētētikos*, adj.] **:** SKEPTIC, SEEKER; *specif* **:** one of a group of Pyrrhonist philosophers

zet·land \ˈzetlənd\ *adj, usu cap* [fr. *Zetland*, Scottish county comprising the Shetland islands] **:** of or relating to the county of Zetland, Scotland **:** SHETLAND

zeug·ite \ˈzü,gīt\ *n* -S [ISV *zeug-* (fr. Gk *zeugnynai* to yoke, join) + *-ite* — more at YOKE] **:** a structure (as a basidium or promycelium) within which the dikaryotic phase of a fungus ends and nuclear fusion occurs

¹zeu·glo·don \ˈzüglə,dän\ [NL *Zeuglodont-, Zeuglodon*, fr. Gk *zeuglē* loop or strap of a yoke (fr. *zeugnynai* to yoke) + NL *-odont-, -odon*] *syn of* BASILOSAURUS

²zeuglodon \"\ *or* **zeu·glodont** \-nt\ *n* -S **:** any of the extinct slender toothed whales constituting the genus *Basilosaurus*

³zeuglodon \"\ *adj* **:** of or relating to the zeuglodons

zeu·glo·don·tia \,≈≈ˈdänch(ē)ə\ *n pl, cap* [NL, fr. *Zeuglodont-, Zeuglodon* + *-ia*] **:** a suborder of Cetacea comprising extinct Eocene and Miocene toothed whales of *Basilosaurus* and related genera — **zeu·glo·don·tian** \;≈≈ˈdänch(ē)ən\ *adj or n*

zeu·glo·don·toid \;≈≈ˈdän,tȯid\ *adj* [NL *Zeuglodont-, Zeuglodon* + E *-oid*] **:** ZEUGLODONTIAN

zeu·glop·tera \≈ˈgläptərə\ *n pl, cap* [NL, fr. Gk *zeugle-* loop or strap of a yoke + NL *-ptera*] *in some classifications* **:** an order coextensive with the family Micropterygidae

zeug·ma \ˈzügmə\ *n* -S [L *zeugmat-, zeugma*, fr. Gk, lit., juncture, joining, fr. *zeugnynai* to yoke, join — more at YOKE] **1 :** the use of a word (as an adjective or verb) to modify or govern two or more words usu. in such a manner that it applies to each in a different sense or makes sense with only one ⟨*opened the door and her heart to the homeless boy* is an example of ~⟩ — compare SYLLEPSIS **2 :** connection of syllables not permitting diaeresis or caesura in classical prosody **:** CLOSE JUNCTURE — **zeug·mat·ic** \(ˈ)zügˈmad·ik, -atˌ, |ēk\ *adj* — **zeug·mat·i·cal·ly** \|ək(ə)lē, |ēk-, -li\ *adv*

zeu·ner·ite \ˈzȯinə,rīt\ *n* -S [G *zeunerit*, fr. Gustav *Zeuner* †1907 Ger. physicist and engineer + G *-it* -ite] **:** a mineral $Cu(UO_2)_2(AsO_4)_2.10\text{-}16H_2O$ consisting of a hypothetical hydrous copper uranium arsenate analogous to torbernite, autunite, uranocircite, saléeite, and uranospinite and found in natural specimens that generally prove to be metazeunerite

ze·us \ˈzüs\ *n, cap* [NL, fr. L, a kind of fish, fr. Gk *zaios*] **:** the type genus of the family Zeidae

zeu·ze·ra \züˈzirə\ *n, cap* [NL] **:** a genus (the type of the family Zeuzeridae) of moths including the leopard moth and some related moths

zeu·zer·i·dae \züˈzerə,dē\ *n pl, cap* [NL, fr. *Zeuzera*, type genus + *-idae*] **:** a family of moths that is often considered a subfamily of Cossidae and that comprises the leopard moth and other large dull mottled grayish or brownish moths — see XYLEUTES

ZF *abbr* **1** zero frequency **2** zone of fire

ZG *abbr* zoological garden

zhda·nov \ˈzhdänəf\ *adj, usu cap* [fr. *Zhdanov*, U.S.S.R.] **:** of or from the city of Zhdanov, U.S.S.R. **:** of the kind or style prevalent in Zhdanov

zho *var of* DZO

ZI *abbr* zone of interior

zia *usu cap, var of* SIA

zi·a·met \zēˈä,met\ *n* -S [Turk *ziamat*, fr. Ar *zaʿāmah*] **:** a fief larger than a timar formerly granted for service in the Turkish army

zi·a·rat \zēˈä,rät\ *or* **zi·a·ra** \-ˈärə\ *n* -S [Hindi *ziyārat* visiting a shrine, pilgrimage, fr. Per, fr. Ar] **:** a tomb of a Muslim saint **:** SHRINE

zib·el·ine *also* **zib·el·line** \ˈzibə,lēn, -līn\ *n* -S [MF, fr. OIt *zibellino*, of Slav origin; akin to Russ *sobol'* sable — more at SABLE] **1 :** SABLE 2b **2 :** a soft lustrous fabric of wool that is mixed with mohair, alpaca, or camel's hair to form a long silky nap which is pressed down and that is made in various weights for coats, suits, and dresses

zib·et *or* **zib·eth** \ˈzibət\ *n* -S [It *zibetto* & ML *zibethum*, fr. Ar *zabād* civet perfume] **:** a common Asiatic civet cat (*Viverra zibetha*)

zi·do·ni·an \zīˈdōnēən\ *n* -S *cap* [*Zidon* Sidon (fr. Heb *Ṣīdōn*) + E *-an*] **:** SIDONIAN

zie·ger *also* **zi·ger** \ˈzēgə(r)\ *n* -S [G *zieger*, fr. MHG *ziger* whey, whey cheese — more at SAPSAGO] **:** a cheese made from whey consisting principally of albumin

zie·gler catalyst \ˈzēglə(r)-\ *n, usu cap Z* [after Karl *Ziegler* b1898 Ger. chemistry institute director] **:** a catalyst (as triethyl-aluminum or a complex of a trialkyl-aluminum with titanium tetrachloride) that promotes an ionic type of polymerization of ethylene, propylene, or related olefins at atmospheric pressure with the resultant formation of a relatively high-melting polyethylene, a stereoregular polypropylene, or similar product

zier·vo·gel process \ˈtsir,fōgəl-\ *n, usu cap Z* [prob. after *Ziervogel*, 19th cent. Ger. metallurgist] **:** a process of extracting silver from its ores by roasting them so as to convert it into sulfate, leaching with water to dissolve the sulfate, and precipitating the silver by means of scrap iron or other reagent

zie·tri·si·kite \,zē·trəˈsē,kīt\ *n* -S [*Zietrisika*, Moldavia + E *-ite*] **:** a mineral wax resembling ozokerite

zif *also* **ziw** \ˈzif\ *n* -S *usu cap* [Heb *ziw*] **:** the 2d month of the ancient Hebrew calendar corresponding to Iyar

¹zig \ˈzig\ *n* -S [*zig-* (in *zigzag*)] **1 a :** one of the sharp turns, angles, or alterations in a zigzag course ⟨a zigzag pattern with . . . diamonds planted at each ~ and zag —*New Yorker*⟩ **b :** one of the short straight lines or sections of a zigzag course at an angle to a zag ⟨the stripes making first a ~, then a zag —Lois Long⟩ **c :** a movement or direction at an angle to a zag ⟨~ to the right . . . followed by a zag to the left —*N.Y.Times*⟩ **2 :** a sharp alteration or change of direction (as in a process or policy) ⟨evolutionary ~s and zags to adjust to the harshest conditions of nature —Gladwin Hill⟩ ⟨every ~ and zag of the official line —Roy Essoyan⟩

²zig \"\ *vi* **zigged; zigged; zigging; zigs** [*zig-* (in *zigzag*)] **:** to execute one of the turns or to follow one of the sections of a zigzag course ⟨*zigged* to the right and zagged back on course —*Monsanto Mag.*⟩ ⟨our policies have *zigged* and zagged too much —H.W.Baldwin⟩

zig·a·de·nus \,zigəˈdēnəs\ *n, cap* [NL, alter. of *Zygadenus*, fr. Gk *zygadēn* jointly, in pairs, fr. *zygon* yoke, pair — more at YOKE] **:** a genus of herbs (family Liliaceae) of No. America and Asia having basal linear leaves and a terminal panicle of whitish or greenish flowers with a flat spreading perianth — see DEATH CAMAS

zig·gu·rat \ˈzigə,rat\ *or* **zik·u·rat** *or* **zik·ku·rat** \ˈzikə-\ *n* -S [Assyr-Bab *ziqqurratu* pinnacle, mountain top] **:** an ancient Babylonian temple tower consisting of a lofty pyramidal structure built in successive stepped-back stages with outside staircases and a shrine at the top

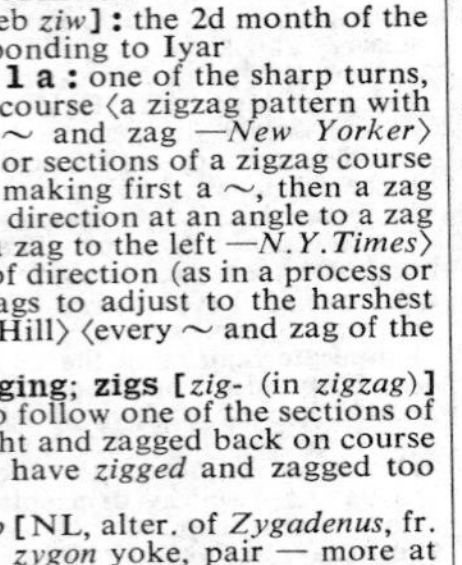
ziggurat

¹zig·zag \ˈzig,zag, -aa(ə)g, -aig\ *n* -S [F, prob. fr. G *zickzack*] **1 :** one of a series of short sharp turns, angles, or alterations in a course ⟨the ~s of the mountain roads —Vincent Starrett⟩ ⟨the party line has been a series of violent ~s —*Nation*⟩ **2 :** something having the form or character of a series of short sharp turns, angles, or alterations ⟨draw a ~ in the air —Annette Dinsmore⟩ ⟨a blue necktie with cherry red ~s —Lawrence Williams⟩: as **a :** a zigzag road or fence ⟨a split-rail ~⟩ **b :** a zigzag approach in siege operations to avoid enfilade fire **c :** a molding running in a zigzag line **:** a chevron or series of chevrons

²zigzag \"\ *adv* **:** in or by a zigzag path or course ⟨birds . . . flew ~ with a shrill cry —Elizabeth Bowen⟩

³zigzag \"\ *also* **zig·zag·gy** \-gē\ *adj* **:** having short sharp turns or angles **:** running this way and that in an onward course ⟨a ~ path⟩ ⟨~ stitching⟩

⁴zigzag \"\ *vb* **zigzagged; zigzagged; zigzagging; zigzags** *vt* **1 :** to trace a zigzag upon **2 :** to form into a zigzag ⟨office buildings . . . slightly *zigzagged* to fit available ground space —*Amer. Guide Series: Ark.*⟩ ~ *vi* **:** to lie in, proceed along, or consist of a zigzag course ⟨lightning *zigzagging* through the pungent air —William Beebe⟩ ⟨a faint little path that *zigzagged* through ferny undergrowth —G.C.Bestor⟩ ⟨his line of thought suddenly *zigzagged* into the . . . practical —Helen Howe⟩

zigzag clover *n* **:** a European red-flowered clover (*Trifolium medium*) — called also *cow clover*

zigzag endpaper *n* **:** an endpaper made with an accordion fold

zig·zag·ged·ly \(ˈ)zigˈzagədlē\ *adv* [*zigzagged* (past part. of ⁴*zigzag*) + *-ly*] **:** in a zigzag manner ⟨skimmed ~ a scant inch from the ground —Lloyd Zimpel⟩

zig·zag·ged·ness \-dnəs\ *n* -ES **:** the quality or state of being zigzag

zig·zag·ger \ˈzig,zagə(r)\ *n* -S **1 :** one that zigzags **2 :** a sewing machine attachment for appliquéing, joining, or seaming with a zigzag line of stitching

zig·zag·gery \-agərē\ *n* -ES **:** a zigzag method or course

zigzag rule *n* **:** a measuring rule made in sections that fold together

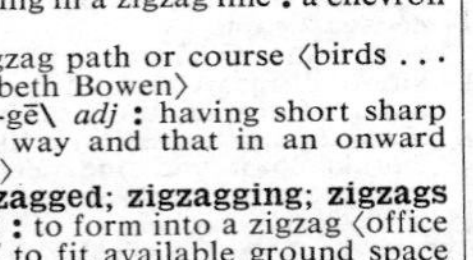
zigzag rule

zikr \ˈzikər\ *var of* DHIKR

zil·lah \ˈzilə\ *n* -S [Hindi *zila'*, *zil'*, fr. Ar *ḍil'* rib, part] **:** an administrative district or division in India

zil·lion \ˈzilyən\ *n* -S *often attrib* [¹*z* + *-illion* (as in *million*) — more at MILLION] **:** a large indeterminate number ⟨a ~ mosquitoes⟩

zi·mar·ra \zəˈmärə\ *n* -S [It — more at SIMAR] **:** a black cassock with attached cape and purple sash, buttons, and piping worn esp. in the house by Roman Catholic prelates — called also *simar*

zimb \ˈzim(b)\ *n* -S [Amharic *zemb, zimb, zenb*] **:** a large two-winged fly native to Abyssinia and prob. of the family Tabanidae

zim·ba·lon \ˈtsimbə,län\ *or* **zim·ba·loon** \-lün\ *n* -S [G *zimbalon*, fr. Hung *cimbalom* — more at CIMBALOM] **:** CIMBALOM

zim·bel \ˈtsimbəl\ *n* -S [G, fr. OHG *zymbal*, fr. L *cymbalum* — more at CYMBAL] **:** CYMBAL 1b

zim·mer·mann reaction *or* **zim·mer·mann test** \ˈzimə(r)mən-\ *n, usu cap Z* [after Wilhelm *Zimmermann* b1910 Ger. physiological chemist] **:** the formation of a colored mixture on mixing of a ketone, alkali, and *meta*-dinitrobenzene

zim·mi \ˈzimē\ *var of* DHIMMI

zi·moc·ca \zəˈmäkə\ *also* **zimocca sponge** *n* -S [NL] **:** a rather harsh commercial sponge (*Spongia zimocca* or *S. officinalis zimocca*) of a massive more or less conical form occurring in the Mediterranean Sea

¹zinc \ˈziŋk\ *n* -S *often attrib* [G *zink*, perh. fr. *zinke* point, barb, prong, fr. OHG *zinko;* akin to OHG *zint* point, spike, tine; fr. its forming jags under certain temperatures — more at TINE] **1 :** a bluish white crystalline bivalent metallic element of low to intermediate hardness that is ductile when pure but in the commercial form is brittle at ordinary temperatures and becomes ductile on slight heating, that occurs abundantly in minerals (as sphalerite, zincite, smithsonite, willemite, and franklinite) commonly associated with lead minerals, that is usu. obtained by concentrating the ores, roasting, and either sintering and reducing by heating with coal or coke, distilling and condensing the zinc, and casting the resulting liquid metal into slabs or by leaching the roasted concentrate with dilute sulfuric acid and electrolyzing, that corrodes in moist but not dry air at ordinary temperature and in contact with most common structural metals corrodes sufficiently to protect them, that dissolves in dilute acids to give zinc salts and hydrogen and in hot solutions of sodium hydroxide or potassium hydroxide to give zincates and hydrogen, that is used chiefly as a protective coating for iron and steel, as rolled sheets and strips for roofing and other building purposes, dry batteries, and photoengravers' and printing plates, and in alloys esp. for die-casting, and that is a trace element in plant and animal metabolism — symbol *Zn;* see BRASS, GALVANIZED IRON, MOSSY ZINC, SPELTER, ZINC DUST, ZINC OXIDE; ELEMENT table **2 :** a purplish gray that is lighter and slightly bluer than crane, bluer and paler than dove gray or granite, and bluer than cinder gray — called also *cloud gray, gray dawn*

²zinc \"\ *vt* **zinced** *or* **zincked; zinced** *or* **zincked; zincing** *or* **zincking; zincs :** to treat or coat with zinc **:** GALVANIZE

zinc alkyl *n* **:** any of a class of organic zinc compounds of the general formula ZnR_2 that are typically colorless mobile liquids giving off poisonous vapors with disagreeable odors that ignite readily in air, that are made usu. by the action of an alkyl iodide (as ethyl iodide) on a zinc-sodium or zinc-copper alloy, and that are very reactive and hence much used in the synthesis of organic compounds ⟨dimethyl-zinc and diethyl-zinc are important *zinc alkyls*⟩

zincaluminite \;≈≈+\ *n* [*zinc* + *aluminite*] **:** a mineral $Zn_6Al_6(SO_4)_2(OH)_{26}.5H_2O$ consisting of a hydrous basic sulfate of aluminum and zinc

zinc amide *n* **:** an amorphous compound $Zn(NH_2)_2$ obtained by action of ammonia on diethyl-zinc — compare SODIUM AMIDE

zinc ammonium chloride *n* **:** a crystalline salt $ZnCl_2.2NH_4Cl$ or $(NH_4)_2ZnCl_4$ used as a welding, soldering, and galvanizing flux **:** ammonium tetrachloro-zincate

zinc·ate \ˈziŋ,kāt\ *n* -S [*zinc* + *-ate*] **:** any of various compounds (as the sodium hydroxo-zincates $Na[Zn(OH)_3].3H_2O$ and $Na_2[Zn(OH)_4].2H_2O$) formed by reaction of zinc oxide or zinc with solutions of alkalies

zinc blende *n* **:** SPHALERITE

zinc bloom *n* [trans. of G *zinkblüte*] **:** HYDROZINCITE

zinc carbonate *n* **:** a crystalline salt $ZnCO_3$ occurring in nature as smithsonite; *also* **:** any of several basic carbonates of zinc occurring as hydrozincite or synthetically prepared and used chiefly as pigments

zinc chloride *n* **:** a poisonous caustic deliquescent readily soluble salt $ZnCl_2$ usu. in the form of granules or fused sticks that is made synthetically (as by reaction of zinc or zinc oxide with hydrochloric acid) and that is used chiefly in preserving and fireproofing wood, in parchmentizing paper and treating textile fibers and fabrics, as a catalyst in organic synthesis, and as a disinfectant and astringent

zinc chromate *n* **1 a :** a yellow crystalline normal salt $ZnCrO_4$ **b :** any of various basic salts; *esp* **:** a golden yellow pigment $4Zn(OH)_2.ZnCrO_4$ used in corrosion-inhibiting priming coats **2 :** ZINC YELLOW — not used systematically

zinc chrome *n* **:** ZINC YELLOW

zinc dust *n* **:** powdery metallic zinc usu. containing zinc oxide in varying amounts that collects as a bluish gray powder during distillation of zinc and that is used chiefly as a reducing agent, as a pigment in corrosion-resistant coatings for iron and steel, and in sherardizing

zinc engraving *n* **1 :** the art or process of photoengraving in zinc **2 :** a zinc linecut or halftone

zinc etching *n* **1 :** the process of making linecuts on zinc **2 :** a zinc linecut

zinc finish *n* **:** the finish obtained when paper is plated between sheets of zinc

zinc flowers *n pl* **:** FLOWERS OF ZINC

zinc gray *n* **:** any of various zinc pigments: as **a :** ZINC DUST **b :** ground sphalerite **c :** a mixture of zinc white with finely divided charcoal or with lithopone, chalk, or other pigments

zinc green *n* **1 :** COBALT GREEN **2 :** any of various green pigments consisting essentially of mixtures of zinc yellow and Prussian blue **3 :** DEEP CHROME GREEN

zinc hydrosulfite *n* **:** a crystallizable salt ZnS_2O_4 made by addition of sulfur dioxide to a warm aqueous slurry of zinc dust (as in the manufacture of sodium hydrosulfite) and used as a bleach; zinc dithionite — not used systematically

zinc·ic \ˈziŋkik\ *adj* [ISV *zinc* + *-ic*] **:** relating to, containing, or resembling zinc

zinc·if·er·ous \(ˈ)ziŋˈkif(ə)rəs, (ˈ)zinˈsi-\ *adj* [ISV *zinc* + *-iferous*] **:** containing or yielding zinc

zinc·i·fi·ca·tion \,ziŋkəfəˈkāshən\ *n* -S [fr. *zincify*, after such pairs as E *purify: purification*] **:** the act or process of zincifying

zinc·i·fy \ˈziŋkə,fī\ *vt* -ED/-ING/-ES [*zinc* + *-ify*] **:** to coat or impregnate with zinc **:** ZINC, GALVANIZE

zinc·ite \ˈziŋ,kīt\ *n* -S [G *zinkit*, fr. *zink* + *-it* -ite] **1 :** a brittle deep-red to orange-yellow hexagonal mineral ZnO consisting of zinc oxide that occurs in massive or granular form (hardness 4–4.5, sp. gr. 5.43–5.7) — called also *red oxide of zinc, red zinc ore* **2 :** an ore of zinc that occurs in New Jersey

zinck·en·ite \ˈziŋkə,nīt\ *n* -S [by alter.] **:** ZINKENITE

zincky *or* **zinky** *or* **zincy** \ˈziŋkē\ *adj* [*zinc* + *-y*] **:** relating to, containing, or having the appearance of zinc

zin·co \ˈziŋ(,)kō\ *n* -S [short for *zincograph*] *Brit* **:** a zinc linecut

zinco- *comb form* [ISV *zinc* + *-o-*] **:** zinc ⟨*zincolysis*⟩

zin·co·graph \ˈziŋkə,graf, -räf\ *n* -S [back-formation fr. *zincography*] **1 :** a zinc plate prepared for use in zincography **2 :** a print made by zincography

zin·co·graph·ic \;≈≈ˈgrafik\ *also* **zin·co·graph·i·cal** \-fəkəl\ *adj* **:** of, relating to, or produced by zincography

zin·cog·ra·phy \ziŋˈkägrəfē\ *n* -ES [ISV *zinco-* + *-graphy*] **1 :** the art or process of engraving or photoengraving letterpress printing surfaces on zinc **2 :** the art or process of preparing planographic printing surfaces on zinc

zinc·oid \ˈziŋ,kȯid\ *adj* [*zinc* + *-oid*] **:** of, relating to, or resembling zinc

zinc ointment *n* **:** an ointment that consists of 20 percent of zinc oxide mixed with a petrolatum and white wax base and is used in the treatment of skin diseases

zinc orange *n* **:** a moderate to strong orange that is yellower and lighter than carrot red, lighter than Mars yellow, and slightly redder and less strong than sunburst — called also *cowslip*

zin·co·type \ˈziŋkə,tīp\ *n* [*zinco-* + *type*] **:** ZINCOGRAPH

zinc·ous \ˈziŋkəs\ *adj* [*zinc* + *-ous*] **:** ZINCIC

zinc oxide *n* **:** an infusible water-insoluble white solid ZnO that turns yellow when heated, that occurs in nature as zincite, that is obtained as a light white powder when zinc is burned, that is produced commercially usu. either by the direct American process of oxidizing zinc vapors during distillation before they have condensed or by the indirect French process of oxidizing the vapors of boiling zinc metal after condensation, and that is used chiefly as a pigment, in compounding rubber, and in pharmaceutical and cosmetic preparations (as ointments and powders) — see FLOWERS OF ZINC, ZINC WHITE

zinc peroxide *n* **:** any of various white to yellowish white powders regarded as mixtures of the peroxide ZnO_2 of zinc,

zinc hydroxide, and zinc carbonate or zinc oxide and used chiefly as disinfectants, astringents, and deodorants because of their ability to release oxygen in contact with moist organic matter

zinc phosphide *n* **:** a dark gray powdery compound Zn_3P_2 having an odor resembling that of garlic and used as a rodenticide

zincs *pl of* ZINC, *pres 3d sing of* ZINC

zinc silicate *n* **:** a silicate of zinc; *esp* **:** the fluorescent crystalline orthosilicate that occurs in nature as willemite, that is made synthetically from zinc oxide and silica or a silicate solution, and that is used in activated form in phosphors

zinc spar *n* **:** SMITHSONITE

zinc spinel *n* [approximate trans. of F *spinelle zincifère*, lit., zinciferous spinel] **:** GAHNITE

zinc standard cell *n* **:** CLARK CELL

zinc stearate *n* **:** an insoluble salt usu. of commercial stearic acid and usu. containing some zinc oxide that is prepared as a fine bulky powder and is used in ointments and toilet powders, in compounding rubber, and as a drier and flatting agent for paints

zinc sulfate *n* **:** a crystalline salt $ZnSO_4$ that is usu. obtained by reaction of sulfuric acid with zinc, zinc oxide, or a roasted zinc ore, that normally crystallizes from solutions as the efflorescent heptahydrate occurring also as the mineral goslarite, and that is used chiefly in coagulating baths for viscose rayon, in fertilizers and sprays, in making lithopone and other zinc chemicals, in dyeing and printing, in flotation, and in medicine as an astringent and emetic

zinc sulfide *n* **:** a fluorescent compound ZnS that occurs in nature as sphalerite and wurtzite, that is obtained synthetically as a white to yellowish powder (as by precipitation with hydrogen sulfide from a solution as a zinc salt), and that is used as a white pigment esp. in the form of lithopone and as a luminous pigment in crystallized activated form — see LUMINOUS PAINT, PHOSPHOR

zinc te·troxy·chromate \-te¦träksō+\ *n* [*tetroxychromate* fr. *tetra-* + *oxy-* + *chromate*] **:** the basic zinc chromate $4Zn(OH)_2.ZnCrO_4$ — not used systematically

zin·cum \ˈziŋkəm\ *n* -s [NL, fr. G *zink*] **:** ZINC

zinc vitriol *n* [trans. of NL *vitriolum zinci*] **:** zinc sulfate heptahydrate

zinc white *n* **:** zinc oxide that is used as a white pigment (as in house paints, antifouling paints, water colors, enamels, and glazes), that is the whitest of all pigments, and that is permanent and not poisonous but lacks the opacity and covering power of white lead or titanium dioxide

zinc yellow *n* **1 :** a greenish yellow pigment that is usu. made by reaction of zinc oxide, potassium dichromate, and sulfuric acid and then has the approximate composition $4ZnO.K_2O.4CrO_3.3H_2O$ of a complex salt and that is used chiefly in corrosion-inhibiting priming coats and in printing inks — called also *zinc chrome* **2 :** LIGHT CHROME YELLOW

zin·diq \zin'dēk\ *n* -s [Ar *zindīq*] **:** a heretic characterized by an extreme religious infidelity to Islam

zin·eb \ˈzi,neb\ *n* -s [*zinc ethylene-bis-dithiocarbamate*] **:** an agricultural fungicide $(-CH_2NHCSS)_2Zn$ obtained as a white powder or crystals **:** zinc ethylene-bis-dithiocarbamate

zin·fan·del \ˈzinfən,del\ *n* -s *often cap* [perh. fr. a European place name] **:** a red table wine of claret type made from a small black vinifera grape that is grown chiefly in California

¹zing \ˈziŋ\ *n* -s [imit.] **1 :** a shrill humming noise ⟨the ~ of machine-gun bullets —F.J.Bell⟩ **2 :** LIVELINESS, ENTHUSIASM, VIM ⟨lost its youthful frontier ~ —Joseph Stocker⟩; *also* **:** a quality that arouses enthusiasm, interest, or vitality ⟨a subtropical ~ to the air —M.F.K.Fisher⟩

²zing \"\ *vi* -ED/-ING/-S **:** to give forth or to travel with a humming sound ⟨the sound of tires ~*ing* away into the night —Dorothea & S.E.Jones⟩ ⟨played his own twelve-string guitar, and its . . . strings ~*ed* at breakneck time —Frederic Ramsey⟩

zin·ga·na \ˈziŋgənə\ *n* -s [It, fem. of *zingano, zingaro* gypsy; fr. its brown color] **:** ZEBRAWOOD 1f

zing·el \ˈtsiŋəl\ *n* -s [G, fr. MHG, girth, fr. L *cingulum, cingula* girdle — more at CINGLE] **:** a small brownish green edible freshwater European perch (*Zingel zingel*) having a round elongated body and a prominent snout

zin·ger·one \ˈzinjə,rōn\ *n* -s [ISV *zinger-* (irreg. fr. NL *Zingiber*) + *-one*] **:** a pungent crystalline phenolic ketone $C_{11}H_{14}O_3$ present in traces in ginger oil but made synthetically from vanillin and acetone; 4-(3-oxo-butyl)-guaiacol — see SHOGAOL

zin·gi·ber \ˈzinjəbə(r)\ *n* [NL, fr. L, ginger — more at GINGER] **1** *cap* **:** a genus of tropical Asiatic and Polynesian plants (family Zingiberaceae) having tuberous rootstocks, leafy stems, and a coned cluster of imbricated bracts of which each bract encloses from one to three flowers — see GINGER **2** -s **:** any plant of the genus *Zingiber*

zin·gi·ber·a·ce·ae \,zinjəbəˈrāsē,ē\ *n pl, cap* [NL, fr. *Zingiber*, type genus + *-aceae*] **:** a family of tropical monocotyledonous plants (order Musales) consisting of leafy perennial herbs with aromatic rootstocks and very irregular flowers having a single perfect stamen — **zin·gi·ber·a·ceous** \¦≈≈≈¦rāshəs\ *adj*

zin·gi·ber·a·les \,≈≈≈ˈrā(,)lēz\ [NL, fr. *Zingiber* + *-ales*] *syn of* MUSALES

zin·gi·ber·ene \ˈ≈≈≈,rēn\ *n* -s [ISV *zingiber-* (fr. NL *Zingiber*) + *-ene*] **:** a liquid sesquiterpene hydrocarbon $C_{15}H_{24}$ constituting with bisabolene the chief component of ginger oil

zin·gi·ber·ol \-,rōl, -,rȯl\ *n* -s [ISV *zingiber-* (fr. NL *Zingiber*) + *-ol*] **:** a fragrant liquid sesquiterpenoid alcohol $C_{15}H_{25}OH$ obtained from ginger oil

zinj·an·thro·pus \zinˈjan(t)thrəpəs\ *n* [NL, fr. Ar *Zinj* eastern Africa + NL *-anthropus*] **1** *cap* **:** a genus of fossil hominids based on a skull found in eastern Africa, characterized by very low brow and large molars, and tentatively assigned to the Lower Pleistocene **2** *pl* **zinjanthro·pi** \-rə,pī\ *or* **zinjanthropuses :** an individual or fossil of the genus *Zinjanthropus*

zin·ke \ˈziŋkə\ *also* **zink** \-k\ *n* -s [G *zinke* point, prong, cornet — more at ZINC] **:** CORNET 1a

zin·ken·ite \ˈziŋkə,nīt\ *n* -s [G *zinkenit*, fr. J. K. L. *Zinken* †1862 Ger. mineralogist + G *-it* -ite] **:** a steel-gray mineral $Pb_6Sb_{14}S_{27}$ of metallic luster consisting of a lead antimony sulfide and occurring in orthorhombic crystals and in masses (hardness 3–3.5, sp. gr. 5.30–5.35)

zinky *var of* ZINCKY

zin·nia \ˈzinēə, -nyə *also* ˈzēn-\ *n* [NL, fr. Johann G. *Zinn* †1759 Ger. physician and botanist + NL *-ia*] **1** *cap* **:** a small genus of tropical American herbs (family Compositae) having showy flower heads with long-lasting ray flowers and floral bracts imbricated in several series **2** -s **:** any flower or plant of the genus *Zinnia*

zinn·wald·ite \ˈtsin,väl,tīt\ *n* -s [G *zinnwaldit*, fr. *Zinnwald*, Bohemia, its locality + G *-it* -ite] **:** a pale violet, yellow, brown, or dark gray mineral $K_2(Li,Fe,Al)_6(Si,Al)_8O_{20}(OH,F)_4$ that consists of mica containing iron and lithium

zin·zi·ber \ˈzinzəbə(r)\ [NL, alter. of L *zingiber* ginger] *syn of* ZINGIBER

zin·zi·ber·a·ce·ae \,zinzəbəˈrāsē,ē\ [NL, fr. *Zinziber* + *-aceae*] *syn of* ZINGIBERACEAE

zi·on \ˈzīən\ *n* -s *usu cap* [fr. *Zion*, height in the northeastern part of Jerusalem, Palestine, that was once the site of Solomon's Temple and the seat of government of the kingdom of Judah and that was later identified with Jerusalem and Palestine as the birthplace and spiritual center of Judeo-Christianity and the earthly abode of God, fr. ME *Sion*, fr. OE, fr. LL, fr. Heb *Ṣiyyōn*] **1 a :** the Jewish people **:** ISRAEL **b :** the Jewish homeland that is symbolic of Judaism or of Jewish national aspiration **2** *also* **si·on** \ˈsīən\ **:** CITY OF GOD **3 :** UTOPIA ⟨sought to set up perpetual *Zions* in the backcountry —W.H.Hale⟩

zioncheck \ˈ≈≈,≈\ *n, usu cap* [prob. fr. *Zion* (sense 3) + *check*] **:** a card game of the contract rummy group

zi·on·ism \ˈzīə,nizəm\ *n* -s *usu cap* [*Zion* (Palestine) + E *-ism*] **:** a theory, plan, or movement for setting up a Jewish national or religious community in Palestine

¹zi·on·ist \-nəst\ *also* **zi·on·is·tic** \¦zīə¦nistik, -tēk\ *adj, usu cap* [*Zion* + E *-ist* or *-istic*] **1 :** of or relating to Zionism **2 :** adhering to or advocating Zionism

²zionist \"\ *n* -s *usu cap* **:** an adherent or supporter of Zionism

¹zi·on·ite \ˈzīə,nīt\ *n* -s *usu cap* [*Zion* (city of God) + E *-ite*] **1 :** a citizen of Zion **:** one of the chosen people of God **2 :** RONSDORFER

²zionite \"\ *n* -s *usu cap* [*Zion* (Palestine) + E *-ite*] **:** a person who favors Zionism **:** ZIONIST

³zionite \"\ *n* -s *usu cap* [*Zion* City (now Zion, Illinois), religious community of the Christian Catholic Church + E *-ite*] **:** a follower of John Alexander Dowie (1848–1907) founder of Zion City, Illinois and of the Christian Catholic Church

zi·on·ward \ˈzīənwə(r)d\ *adv, usu cap* **:** toward Zion **:** HEAVENWARD

¹zip \ˈzip\ *vb* **zipped; zipped; zipping; zips** [imit. of the sound of an object flying past the hearer] *vi* **1 :** to move or act with speed and usu. with force, vigor, or enthusiasm ⟨particles which ~ through outer space with the speed of light —*Newsweek*⟩ ⟨bright-faced waitresses were *zipping* by in trim white-collared uniforms —P.E.Deutschman⟩ **2 :** to travel with a sharp hissing or humming sound ⟨rifle fire *zipped* over them —Nevil Shute⟩ ~ *vt* **1 :** to impart speed or force to ⟨tunnel which ~*s* traffic under the . . . mountain —Richard Thruelsen⟩ **2 :** to add zest, interest, or life to — often used with *up* ⟨~ up an old folk tune with a little dash of swing —T.D.Clark⟩

²zip \"\ *n* -s **1 :** a sudden sharp hissing or sibilant sound (as made by a flying bullet) **2 :** ENERGY, VIM, SNAP, FORCE, DASH ⟨~ in his stride and a gleam in his eye —*Phoenix Flame*⟩

³zip \"\ *n* -s *often attrib* [by shortening] **1** *also* **zipp** \"\ *chiefly Brit* **:** ZIPPER **2 :** the act or process of opening or closing a zipper

⁴zip \"\ *vb* **zipped; zipped; zipping; zips** [back-formation fr. ¹*zipper*] *vt* **1 a :** to close or open with a zipper **:** to fasten or unfasten (an article equipped with a zipper) ⟨my rubber suit *zipped* up to my chin —F.S.Herman⟩ ⟨*zipping* the brief case closed —J.A.Phillips⟩ ⟨*zipped* up my jacket —J.J.Custer⟩ **b :** to cause (a zipper) to open or shut ⟨the top of the zipper still to be *zipped* —*New Yorker*⟩ **2 :** to enclose or wrap by fastening a zipper ⟨a dozen children in all, *zipped* and buttoned into their snowsuits —E.J.Kahn⟩ ⟨possessions are securely *zipped* inside —*Harper's Bazaar*⟩ **3 :** BUTTON 3 ⟨kept his mouth *zipped* tight for weeks —Carl Sifakis⟩ ~ *vi* **1 :** to close or open a zipper ⟨fingers ~ and hook and fasten —Agnes de Mille⟩ **2 :** to become or be designed to become open, closed, or attached by means of a zipper ⟨the lining ~*s* in easily⟩

⁵zip \"\ *n* -s [Maya] **:** any of a number of small gods known to the ancient Mayas as the supernatural protectors of the deer

zip–fastener \ˈ≈,≈(≈)≈\ *n, chiefly Brit* **:** ZIPPER

zip fuel *n* **:** a jet or rocket fuel that has a higher heat content than a hydrocarbon fuel

zip gun *n* **:** a homemade gun that is constructed from a toy pistol or length of pipe, has a firing pin usu. powered by a rubber band, and fires a .22 caliber bullet ⟨teen-age gangs with *zip guns*⟩

¹ziph·i·id \ˈzifēəd\ *adj* [NL *Ziphiidae*] **:** ZIPHIOID

²ziphiid \"\ *n* -s [NL *Ziphiidae*] **:** ZIPHIOID

zi·phi·idae \zəˈfīə,dē\ *n pl, cap* [NL, fr. *Ziphius*, type genus + *-idae*] **:** a family of toothed whales that are 12 to 30 feet long, have the front of the head drawn out so as to suggest a beak and the teeth wanting or reduced to one or two on each side of the lower jaw, and are related to the sperm whales and sometimes esp. formerly included with them in the family Physeteridae

¹ziph·i·oid \ˈzifē,ȯid\ *adj* [NL *Ziphius* + E *-oid*] **:** of or relating to the Ziphiidae

²ziphioid \"\ *n* -s **:** a whale of the family Ziphiidae

ziphi·sternum \¦zifə+\ *n* [NL, by alter.] **:** XIPHISTERNUM

ziph·i·us \ˈzifēəs\ *n, cap* [NL, modif. of Gk *xiphios* swordfish, fr. *xiphos* sword] **:** a genus (the type of the family Ziphiidae) of nearly cosmopolitan beaked whales

zipped *adj* [fr. past part. of ⁴*zip*] **:** ZIPPERED

zip·pe·ite \ˈtsipə,īt\ *n* -s [G *zippeit*, fr. Franz X. M. *Zippe* †1863 Austrian mineralogist + G *-it* -ite] **:** a mineral approximately $(UO_2)_2(SO_4)(OH)_2.4H_2O$ consisting of a hydrous basic sulfate of uranium

¹zip·per \ˈzipə(r)\ *n* -s *often attrib* [fr. *Zipper*, a trademark] **:** a fastener consisting of two rows of metal or plastic teeth on strips of tape for binding to the edges of an opening (as of a garment or bag) and having a sliding piece that closes the opening by drawing the teeth into interlocking position

²zipper \"\ *vt* -ED/-ING/-S **:** ⁴ZIP

zippered *adj* **:** equipped with a zipper

zip·py \ˈzipē, -pi\ *adj* -ER/-EST [²*zip* + *-y*] **:** full of zip **:** BRISK, SNAPPY

zi·ram \ˈzī,ram\ *n* -s [*zinc* + *-ram* (as in *thiram*)] **:** a zinc salt $[(CH_3)_2NCSS]_2Zn$ obtained as a white powder or crystals and used as a rubber accelerator and agricultural fungicide; zinc dimethyl-dithiocarbamate — used esp. of the fungicide

zir·con \ˈzər,kän, ˈzə̄-, ˈzəi-, *sometimes* -,kən\ *n* -s [G *zirkon* (now usu. *zirkon*), modif. of F *jargon* jargoon, zircon, fr. It *giargone*] **:** a tetragonal mineral $ZrSiO_4$ consisting of a zirconium silicate and occurring usu. in square prisms of adamantine luster and brown or grayish color (hardness 7.5, sp. gr. usu. about 4.7) — see HYACINTH, STARLITE

zircon- *comb form* [ISV, fr. NL *zirconia*] **:** zirconium ⟨*zirconsyenite*⟩

zir·con·ate \ˈzərkə,nāt\ *n* -s [ISV *zircon-* + *-ate*] **:** any of various compounds (as sodium zirconate Na_2ZrO_3) obtained usu. by heating zirconium oxide and a metal oxide or carbonate

zir·co·nia \(,)zərˈkōnēə, zə-, zə̄-, zəi-\ *n* -s [NL, fr. ISV *zircon* + NL *-ia*, fem. n. suffix] **:** ZIRCONIUM OXIDE ⟨~ refractories⟩

zir·con·ic \-ˈkänik\ *adj* [ISV *zircon-* + *-ic*] **:** of, relating to, or containing zirconium

zir·con·if·er·ous \¦zərkə¦nif(ə)rəs\ *adj* [*zircon* + *-iferous*] **1 :** containing or yielding zircon **2** [*zircon-* + *-iferous*] **:** containing or yielding zirconium

zir·co·ni·um \(,)zərˈkōnēəm, zə-, zə̄-, zəi-\ *n* -s [NL, fr. ISV *zircon* + NL *-ium*] **:** a steel-gray strong ductile high-melting chiefly tetravalent metallic element that occurs widely in combined form esp. in zircon and baddeleyite, that is now obtained usu. from sands containing zircon by heating with carbon and chlorine and passing the volatile zirconium tetrachloride formed into hot molten magnesium or sodium to yield a spongy form of the free metal containing up to three percent of hafnium, that resembles titanium and hafnium chemically and in massive form has good corrosion resistance at ordinary or moderately elevated temperatures, and that is used in spinnerets for viscose rayon, in getters for vacuum tubes, in steel making, and when freed from hafnium in nuclear reactors as a structural material and as a cladding material for uranium because of its ability to allow the passage of low-speed neutrons — symbol *Zr*; see ELEMENT table

zirconium hydride *n* **:** a gray to black brittle powder ZrH_2 used as a getter in vacuum tubes, as a bonding agent for abrasives and ceramics, in powder metallurgy, and in delay-fuse mixtures in flare shells

zirconium oxide *or* **zirconium dioxide** *n* **:** a refractory crystalline compound ZrO_2 that occurs in nature as baddeleyite, that is usu. obtained as a heavy hard white insoluble powder by heating zircon with carbon in an arc furnace and burning the product in air, and that is used chiefly in refractories (as crucibles and cements), in thermal and electric insulation, in abrasives, in enamels and glazes as an opacifying pigment, and esp. formerly in incandescent lamps because of its brilliant luminosity when heated — called also *zirconia*

zirconium silicate *n* **:** a fluorescent crystalline insoluble salt $ZrSiO_4$ that occurs in nature as zircon and can be obtained synthetically by mixing solutions of sodium silicate and a soluble zirconium salt (as zirconium oxychloride), that is decomposed into zirconium oxide at high temperatures, and that is used in refractories, in electric insulation, in abrasives, and in enamels and porcelains

zir·con·oid \ˈzərkə,nȯid\ *n* -s [*zircon* + *-oid*] **:** a ditetragonal dipyramid

zir·co·nyl \-kənᵊl\ *n* -s [ISV *zircon-* + *-yl*] **:** the bivalent radical ZrO consisting of zirconium and oxygen ⟨~ chloride is the oxychloride $ZrOCl_2$⟩

zi·ri·co·te \,zirəˈkōtā\ *n* -s [AmerSp] **:** a tree (*Cordia dodecandra*) of Mexico and Central America having brown wood streaked with dark almost black lines

zir·kel·er·ite \ˈzərklə,rīt\ *n* -s [G *zirklerit*, fr. *Zirkler*, 20th cent. Ger. director of mines + G *-it* -ite] **:** a mineral $(Fe,Mg,Ca)_9Al_4Cl_{18}(OH)_{12}.14H_2O$ consisting of a basic hydrous chloride of iron, magnesium, calcium, and aluminum

zir·phaea \zə(r)ˈfēə\ *n, cap* [NL] **:** a genus of rock-boring marine bivalve mollusks related to *Pholas*

ziryen *cap, var of* ZYRIAN

¹zith·er \ˈzithə(r), ˈzithə(r)\ *also* **zit·tern** \ˈzid·ə(r)n\ *n* -s [*zither* fr. G, fr. OHG *zitera, cithara* cittern, fr. L *cithara*, fr. Gk *kithara*; *zittern* alter. (influenced by *cittern*) of *zither*] **:** a musical instrument consisting of a shallow sound-board set horizontally before the performer and overlaid with 30 to 40 strings some of which pass over a fretted fingerboard, are stopped with the left hand, and are played by a plectrum on the right thumb to produce the melody and the remainder of which are tuned in fourths and plucked by the fingers of the right hand — compare CITTERN

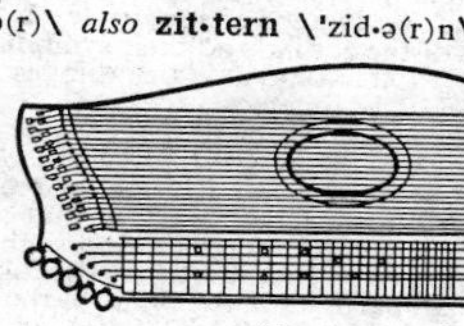

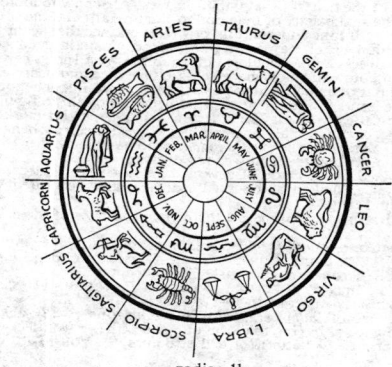

zither

²zither \"\ *vi* -ED/-ING/-S **:** to play on the zither

zith·er·ist \-ərəst\ *n* -s **:** a player on the zither

ziw *usu cap, var of* ZIF

zi·za·nia \zəˈzānēə\ *n, cap* [NL, fr. LL *zizanium* darnel, cockle, fr. Gk *zizanion*] **:** a genus of tall monoecious grasses having long flat leaves and ample panicles of one-flowered spikelets — see WILD RICE

ziz·ia \ˈzizēə\ *n, cap* [NL, fr. I. B. *Ziz*, 19th cent. Ger. botanist + NL *-ia*] **:** a small genus of No. American herbs (family Umbelliferae) with ternately compound leaves, yellow flowers in compound umbels, and flat wingless fruit — see GOLDEN ALEXANDER, GOLDEN MEADOW PARSNIP

ziz·i·phus \ˈzizəfəs\ *n* [NL, fr. L *zizyphus* jujube tree, fr. *zizyphum* jujube — more at JUJUBE] **1** *cap* **:** a large genus of spiny chiefly tropical American and Asiatic shrubs (family Rhamnaceae) having triple-veined leaves and small cymose flowers with a 2-celled ovary — see CHRIST'S-THORN, JUJUBE, LOTUS TREE **2** -ES **:** any plant of the genus *Ziziphus*

zi·zith *or* **zi·zit** *or* **tsi·tsith** *or* **tzi·tzith** *also* **si·sith** *or* **tzi·tzis** \ˈtsitsəs, tsēˈtsēt\ *n pl* [Heb *ṣīṣith*] **:** the fringes or tassels of entwined cords or threads worn by Jewish males at the 4 corners of the outer garment or on the tallith and the arba kanfoth as reminders of God's commandments in accordance with the scriptural passages Deut 22:12 and Num 15:37–41

zl *abbr* zloty

zlo·ty \ˈzlȯtē, -ti\ *n, pl* **zlotys** *also* **zloty** [Pol *złoty*, lit., golden, fr. *złoto* gold; akin to Russ *zoloto* gold, OHG *gold* — more at GOLD] **1 :** the basic monetary unit of Poland — see MONEY table **2 :** a coin representing one zloty

Zn *symbol* **1** azimuth **2** zinc

zo- *or* **zoo-** *comb form* [Gk *zōi-, zōio-*, fr. *zōion*; akin to Gk *zōē* life — more at QUICK] **1 :** animal **:** animal kingdom or kind ⟨*zoology*⟩ ⟨*zoophile*⟩ ⟨*zooid*⟩ ⟨*zoanthropy*⟩ **2** [Gk *zō-, zōo-* alive, fr. *zōos*; akin to Gk *zōē* life] **:** motile ⟨*zoogonidium*⟩

zoa *pl of* ZOON

-zoa \ˈzōə\ *n pl comb form* [NL, fr. Gk *zōia*, pl. of *zōion*] **:** animals — in the names of taxa ⟨*Bryozoa*⟩ ⟨*Echinozoa*⟩

zoaea *var of* ZOEA

zo·an·thar·ia \,zōənˈtha(a)rēə\ *n pl, cap* [NL, fr. *Zoanthus* + *-aria*] **:** a subclass of Anthozoa that comprises forms with a hexamerous arrangement of the usu. simple tentacles or septa or both and that includes most of the recent corals and sea anemones

¹zo·an·thar·i·an \¦≈≈¦tha(a)rēən\ *adj* [NL *Zoantharia* + E *-an*] **:** of or relating to the Zoantharia

²zoantharian \"\ *n* -s **:** a coelenterate of the subclass Zoantharia

zo·an·the·ae \zōˈan(t)thē,ē\ [NL] *syn of* ZOANTHIDEA

zo·an·thid \zōˈan(t)thəd\ *also* **zo·an·thoid** \-n,thȯid\ *n* -s [*zoanthid* fr. NL *Zoanthidea*; *zoanthoid* fr. NL *Zoanthus* + E *-oid*] **:** a coelenterate of the order Zoanthidea

zo·an·thid·ea \,zōənˈthidēə\ *n pl, cap* [NL, fr. *Zoanthus* + *-idea*] **:** a small order of Zoantharia comprising solitary or colonial and mostly epizoic coelenterates resembling small sea anemones but distinguished by absence of a pedal disk and by an arrangement of mesenteries suggesting that of the fossil tetracorals

zo·an·thid·e·an \¦≈≈¦thidēən\ *also* **zo·an·thid** \zōˈan(t)thəd\ *adj* [*zoanthidean* fr. NL *Zoanthidea* + E *-an*; *zoanthid* fr. NL *Zoanthidea*] **:** of or relating to the Zoanthidea

zo·an·tho·deme \zōˈan(t)thə,dēm\ *n* [ISV *zoantho-* (fr. NL *Zoanthus*) + *deme*] **:** the aggregate of zooids in a compound anthozoan

zo·an·thro·py \zōˈan(t)thrəpē\ *n* -ES [*zo-* + *-anthropy* (as in *lycanthropy*)] **:** a monomania in which a person believes himself changed into an animal and acts like one

zo·an·thus \zōˈan(t)thəs\ *n, cap* [NL, fr. *zo-* + Gk *anthos* flower — more at ANTHOLOGY] **:** a large genus (the type of the family Zoanthidae) of zoanthidean colonial polyps that are widely distributed in tropical seas, are united at their bases by stolons, resemble groups of small anemones, and have short, brightly colored tentacles

zo·ar·ces \zōˈär,sēz\ *n, cap* [NL, fr. Gk *zōarkēs* life-supporting, fr. *zōē* life + *-arkēs* supporting (fr. *arkein* to defend, support) — more at QUICK, ARK] **:** the type genus of the family Zoarcidae

zo·ar·ci·dae \-rsə,dē\ *n pl, cap* [NL, fr. *Zoarces*, type genus + *-idae*] **:** a family of chiefly arctic and antarctic blennies comprising the eelpouts

zo·ar·i·al \zōˈa(a)rēəl\ *adj* [NL *zoarium* + E *-al*] **:** of or relating to a zoarium

zo·ar·ite \ˈzōə,rīt, ˈzōr,īt, ˈzȯ,rīt\ *n* -s *usu cap* [*Zoar*, Ohio + E *-ite*] **:** a member of a 19th century communal sect of German Protestant separatists and founders of the Zoar Community at Zoar, Ohio in 1817 — called also *Bimelerite, Bimmeler*

zo·ar·i·um \zōˈa(a)rēəm\ *also* **zo·o·ar·i·um** \,zōə'-\ *n, pl* **zoar·ia** \-ēə\ [NL, fr. *zo-* + *-arium*] **:** a colony of colonial bryozoans

zo·ca·lo \ˈzōkə,lō\ *n* -s [MexSp *zócalo*, fr. Sp, socle, fr. It *zoccolo*] **:** the public square of a Mexican city or town **:** PLAZA

zoc·co \ˈzä(,)kō\ *or* **zoc·co·lo** \ˈzäkə,lō\ *or* **zac·co** \ˈzä(,)kō\ *n* -s [*zocco* fr. It, sock, socle, fr. L *soccus* sock; *zoccolo* fr. It, sock, wooden shoe, socle, dim. of *zocco*; *zacco* modif. of It *zocco* — more at SOCLE] **:** SOCLE

zo·di·ac \ˈzōdē,ak\ *n* -s [ME, fr. MF *zodiaque*, fr. L *zodiacus*, fr. Gk *zōidiakos*, fr. *zōidiakos*, adj., of carved or painted figures,

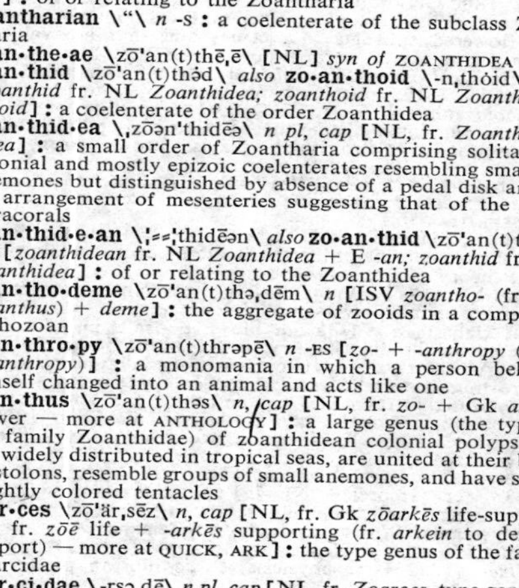

zodiac 1b

of the zodiac, fr. *zōidion* carved or painted figure, sign of the zodiac, dim. of *zōion* living being, animal, figure, image; akin to Gk *zōē* life — more at QUICK] **1 a :** an imaginary belt in the heavens usu. 18 degrees wide that encompasses the apparent paths of all the principal planets except Pluto, that has the ecliptic as its central line, and that is divided into 12 constellations or signs each taken for astrological purposes to extend 30 degrees of longitude **b :** a figure representing the signs of the zodiac and their symbols **2 :** a cyclic course (as of time) **:** CALENDAR, CIRCUIT ⟨moves through a ~ of feasts and fasts —R.W.Emerson⟩

zo·di·a·cal \zō'dīəkəl\ *adj* [*zodiac* + *-al*] **:** of, relating to, or within the zodiac ⟨~ figure⟩ ⟨~ symbols⟩ ⟨~ constellations⟩

zodiacal light *n* **:** a diffuse glow seen in the west after twilight and in the east before dawn that appears wedge-shaped and lies along the ecliptic, is widest in the parts near the sun, and is believed to be caused by the reflection of sunlight from myriads of small particles in the plane of the solar system

zo·di·oph·i·lous \ˌzōdē¦äfələs\ *adj* [Gk *zōidion* (dim. of *zōion* animal) + E *-philous*] **:** ZOOPHILIC a

zo·ea *also* **zo·aea** \zō'ēə\ *n, pl* **zoe·ae** \-ē,ē\ *or* **zoeas** [NL, fr. Gk *zōē* life] **:** an early larval form of decapod crustaceans and esp. of crabs and anomurans that commonly precedes the megalops and that is distinguished by the relatively large cephalothorax commonly bearing three or four long spines, the conspicuous eyes, the relatively large and fringed antennae and mouthparts used for swimming, the rudimentary thoracic appendages, and the long slender abdomen having small or no swimmerets

zo·e·a·form \-'ēə,fȯrm\ *adj* **:** having the form or appearance of a zoea

zo·e·al \-'ēəl\ *adj* **:** of, relating to, or being a zoea ⟨~ forms⟩ ⟨~ stages⟩

zoecial *var of* ZOOECIAL

zoecium *var of* ZOOECIUM

zoell·ner illusion \'tsəlnə(r)-\ *n, usu cap Z* **:** ZÖLLNER ILLUSION

zoellner's lines *n pl, usu cap Z* **:** ZÖLLNER'S LINES

zo·et·ic \zō'ed·ik\ *adj* [Gk *zōē* life + E *-etic*] **:** of or relating to life **:** LIVING, VITAL

zo·e·trope \'zōē,trōp\ *also* **zo·o·trope** \'zōə-\ *n* -s [*zoetrope* fr. *Zoetrope*, a trademark; *zootrope* alter. (influenced by *zo-*) of *zoetrope*] **:** an optical toy in which figures on the inside of a revolving cylinder are viewed through slits in its circumference and appear like a single animated figure

zo·go \'zō(,)gō\ *n* -s [Papuan] **:** something that is sacred or holy to the people of the Torres strait; *esp* **:** a charm or sacred object held to have wonder-working power

zo·ic \'zōik\ *adj* [Gk *zōikos*] **:** of or relating to animals or animal life and action

¹-zo·ic \¦zōik, -ōēk\ *adj comb form* [Gk *zōikos* of or pertaining to animals, fr. *zōi-* zo- + *-ikos* -ic] **:** animal **:** having a (specified) animal mode of existence **:** animallike ⟨holozoic⟩ ⟨phanerozoic⟩ ⟨coprozoic⟩ ⟨cytozoic⟩

²-zoic \"\ *adj comb form* [Gk *zōē* life + E *-ic* — more at QUICK] **:** of or relating to a (specified) geological era ⟨Archeozoic⟩ ⟨Mesozoic⟩

zo·id \'zōəd\ *n* -s [*zo-* + *-id*] **:** ZOOID

zo·id·i·oph·i·lous \ˌzō¦idē¦äfələs\ *adj* [Gk *zōidion* (dim. of *zōion* animal) + E *-philous* — more at ZODIAC] **:** ZOOPHILIC a

zo·i·dog·a·mous \ˌzōə¦dägəməs\ *adj* [*zoid* + *-o-* + *-gamous*] **:** fertilizing by a spermatozoid or motile cell

zo·i·lus \'zōiləs\ *n, pl* **zoiluses** \-səz\ *also* **zoi·li** \-,lī\ *usu cap* [after, *Zoilus* 4th cent. B.C. Greek rhetorician and critic who was notable for the severity of his criticisms of Homer's poems] **:** a bitter and usu. enviously carping critic **:** one given to unjust quibbling and faultfinding **:** BELITTLER, CAVILER — compare ARISTARCH, MOMUS

zoi·sia \'zȯisēə, 'zȯizēə, 'zȯishə\ *n, cap* [NL, fr. Karl von *Zois* †1800 Ger. botanist + NL *-ia*] **:** a small genus of Asiatic grasses that have creeping rhizomes, short pointed leaves, and one-flowered spikelets in racemes and that are valued as lawn grasses esp. in warm regions — see ZOYSIA

zois·ite \'zȯi,sīt\ *n* -s [G *zoisit*, fr. Baron Sigismund *Zois* von Edelstein †1819 Slovenian nobleman + G *-it* -ite] **:** an orthorhombic mineral $Ca_2Al_3Si_3O_{12}OH$ consisting of a basic calcium aluminum silicate that is related to epidote and that occurs massive or in prismatic grayish, brown, green, or rose crystals

zois·it·iza·tion \ˌzȯisəd·ə'zāshən\ *n* -s [*zoisite* + *-ization*] **:** the process of converting feldspar into zoisite — compare SAUSSURITIZATION

¹zo·ism \'zō,izəm\ *n* -s [Gk *zōē* life + E *-ism*] **:** a doctrine that the phenomena of life are due to a peculiar vital principle **:** the theory of élan vital

²zoism \"\ *n* -s [ISV *zo-* + *-ism*] **:** reverence for animal life **:** belief in animal powers and influences

zo·ist \'zōəst\ *n* -s [Gk *zōē* life + E *-ist*] **:** an advocate or adherent of the doctrine of zoism — **zo·is·tic** \zō'istik\ *adj*

zo·kor \'zō,kȯr\ *n* -s [native name in the Altai mountains] **:** a burrowing rodent (*Myotalpa aspalax*) native to the Altai mountains that resembles a mole rat

zo·la·esque \¦zōlə¦esk\ *adj, usu cap* [Émile *Zola* †1902 Fr. novelist + E *-esque*] **:** of, relating to, or suggestive of Zola or his writings

zol·ler·nia \zə'lərnēə\ *n, cap* [NL, irreg. fr. Hugo *Zöller* †1933 Ger. explorer + NL *-ia*] **:** a small genus of Brazilian timber trees (family Leguminosae) with simply pinnate leaves, nearly regular flowers, and a woody legume

zöll·ner illusion \'tsəlnə(r)-\ *n, usu cap Z* [after Johann K. F. *Zöllner* †1882 Ger. physicist] **:** the illusion produced by Zöllner's lines

zöllner's lines *n pl, usu cap Z* [after Johann K. F. *Zöllner* †1882] **:** parallel lines made to appear to converge or diverge by oblique intersections

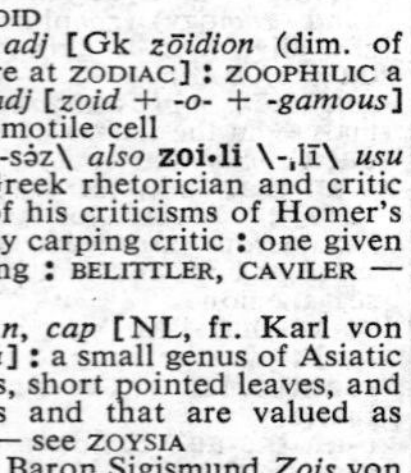
Zöllner's lines

zoll·ver·ein \'tsȯlfə,rīn\ *n* -s *usu cap* [G, fr. *zoll* toll, duty (fr. OHG *zol*) + *verein* union, society — more at TOLL, VEREIN] **:** CUSTOMS UNION

zo·lot·nik \¦zȯlət¦nēk, -nik\ *n* -s [Russ, fr. *zoloto* gold + *-nik*, n. suffix denoting a thing connected with something specified — more at ZLOTY] **:** a Russian unit of weight equal to 4.266 grams or a small fraction of an ounce

zom·bi *or* **zom·bie** \'zämbē\ *n* -s [of Niger-Congo origin; akin to Kongo & Kimbundu & Tshiluba *nzambi* god, Kongo *zumbi* good-luck fetish, image] **1 a** (1) **:** the deity of the python in West African voodoo cults (2) **:** the snake deity of the voodoo rite in Haiti and the southern U.S. **b :** the supernatural power or essence that according to voodoo belief may enter into and reanimate a dead body **c :** a will-less and speechless human in the West Indies capable only of automatic movement held to have died and been reanimated but often believed to have been drugged into a catalepsy for the hours of interment **2 a :** a person thought to resemble the so-called walking dead **:** DOPE **b :** a person markedly strange or abnormal in mentality, appearance, or behavior **:** CHARACTER, QUEER **c** *Canada* **:** a home-defense army conscript unwilling to volunteer for overseas service **3 :** a very tall mixed drink made of several kinds of rum, liqueur, and fruit juice, shaken and served with ice, and decorated with mint and fruit

zom·bi·ism \-ē,izəm\ *n* -s **:** the beliefs and rites of the cult of the zombi

zon- *or* **zono-** *comb form* [Gk *zōn-*, *zōno-*, fr. *zōnē* — more at ZONE] **1 :** girdle **:** belt **:** band ⟨*Zonites*⟩ ⟨*Zonochlorite*⟩ **2 :** zone **:** zonal ⟨*zoniferous*⟩ ⟨*zonoplacental*⟩

zo·na \'zōnə\ *n, pl* **zo·nae** \-,nē, -,nī\ *or* **zonas** [L, girdle, zone, herpes zoster] **:** HERPES ZOSTER

zon·al \'zōnᵊl\ *adj* [LL *zonalis*, fr. L *zona* zone + *-alis* -al] **:** of, relating to, or having the form of a zone ⟨the ~ frontier⟩ ⟨a ~ division⟩ ⟨a ~ pattern of cell structure⟩ — **zon·al·ly** \-ᵊlē, -ᵊli\ *adv*

zonal equation *n* **:** the mathematical relation that belongs to all the planes of a zone of a crystal and expresses their common position with reference to the axes

zonal geranium *n* **:** FISH GERANIUM

zonal rotation *n* **:** the rotation at unequal rates of the visible surfaces of various astronomical bodies (as the sun, Jupiter, or Saturn)

zonal soil *n* **1 :** a major soil group often classified as a category of the highest rank and generally covering a wide geographic region or zone and embracing soils that are well-developed from the parent material by the normal soil-forming action of climate and living organisms — compare AZONAL SOIL, INTRAZONAL SOIL **2 :** a soil (as many grassland and desert soils) belonging to a major soil group or category

zonal structure *n* **:** a structure characterized by the arrangements (as of color or inclusions) of a crystal in parallel or concentric layers that usu. follow the outline of the crystal and mark the changes that have taken place during its growth

zona pel·lu·ci·da \-pə'lüsədə, -pel'yü-\ *n, pl* **zonae pellucidae** \-ə,dē, -,dī\ [NL, transparent zone] **:** the transparent more or less elastic outer layer or envelope of an ovum often traversed by numerous radiating striae

zona ra·di·a·ta \-,rādē'äd·ə, -'ad·ə\ *n, pl* **zonae radiatae** \-'äd·,ē, -'ad·,ē, -d·,ī\ [NL, radiate zone] **:** ZONA PELLUCIDA; *esp* **:** one having unusually distinct striations

zo·nar·ia \zō'na(a)rēə\ *n pl, cap* [NL, fr. neut. pl. of L *zonarius* of a belt, zonal] *in former classifications* **:** a division of Mammalia comprising forms (as the carnivores and some ungulates) having a zonary placenta

zo·na·ry \'zōnərē, -ri\ *adj* [L *zonarius*, fr. *zona* + *-arius* -ary] **1 :** ZONAL **2** *of a placenta* **:** having villi arranged in a band (as in carnivores and elephants)

zon·ate \'zō,nāt, *usu* -ād·+V\ *also* **zon·at·ed** \-ād·əd\ *adj* [*zonate* fr. NL *zonatus*, fr. L *zona* + *-atus* -ate; *zonated* fr. NL *zonatus* + E *-ed*] **:** marked with zones **:** RINGED, BELTED

zo·na·tion \zō'nāshən\ *n* -s [¹*zone* + *-ation*] **1 :** formation in zones, bands, or concentric layers **:** zonate structure ⟨~ of a growing plant cell⟩ **2 :** arrangement or distribution of kinds of organisms in biogeographic zones ⟨altitudinal ~ of coniferous trees⟩

zon·da \'z|ōndə, 's|, |sn-\ *n* -s [AmerSp] **:** a hot enervating north wind that sweeps down from the Andes over the Argentine pampas

¹zone \'zōn\ *n* -s [L *zona* girdle, belt, zone, fr. Gk *zōnē*; akin to Gk *zōma* girdle, *zōnnynai* to gird, Lith *juosti* to gird, Av *yasta* encircled, girt] **1 a :** any of five great divisions of the earth's surface with respect to latitude and temperature — see FRIGID ZONE, TEMPERATE ZONE, TORRID ZONE **b :** any division of a planetary surface bounded by two encircling parallels ⟨~*s* of the sun's surface⟩ **c :** a belt around the heavens bounded usu. by small circles parallel to the equator of the system of coordinates involved ⟨~*s* of declination in the equatorial system⟩ **d** *obs* **:** the course or range of a celestial body (as the sun) ⟨the sun . . . in the great ~ of heaven —John Milton⟩ **e :** the portion of the surface of a sphere included between two parallel planes **:** the part of a surface of revolution between two planes perpendicular to the axis **f :** a series of faces of a crystal whose intersection lines with each other are all parallel **2** *archaic* **:** GIRDLE, BELT, BAND ⟨how to loose the ~ of virgins —Robert Herrick †1674⟩ **3 :** something that forms a concentric band ⟨surrounding the hub lies the middle ~ . . . largely residential —J.E.Pate⟩**:** as **a :** any encircling anatomical area or structure; *specif* **:** one of the three regions in the retina of the eye differing in color sensitivity ⟨all hues can be seen with the inner or central ~, blue and yellow with the middle, and only colorless light with the outer⟩ **b** (1) **:** a typically band-formed part of a biogeographic region that usu. has a distinct slope and a markedly uniform climate and supports a similar fauna and flora throughout its extent **:** LIFE ZONE ⟨a marine littoral ~⟩ ⟨the Austral ~⟩ (2) **:** such a zone characterized by the dominance of some life form ⟨the laminarian ~ below low tide⟩ ⟨a broad ~ of elfin woodland⟩ **c :** a belt, layer, or series of layers of earth materials (as rock) characterized by some particular property, action, or content ⟨the ~ of saturation⟩ ⟨the eohippus ~⟩ **4 :** a region or area set off or characterized as distinct from surrounding or adjoining parts ⟨the danger ~⟩ ⟨a ~ of influence⟩ ⟨erogenous ~⟩ ⟨the movement of individuals . . . into and out of the survey ~ —J.M.Mogey⟩ ⟨a ~ of uncertainty and hesitation in . . . foreign policy —*Atlantic*⟩ **5 :** one of the sections or divisions of an area or territory created for a particular purpose ⟨a ~ of military occupation⟩ ⟨divided the country into 10 sales ~*s*⟩**:** as **a :** a section of a city that has been zoned **b :** any one of the eight concentric bands of territory centered on any given postal shipment point that is arbitrarily designated as a distance bracket for U.S. parcel post mail so that shipments to all points within it may be charged at a single rate — called also *parcel post zone* **c :** one of the numbered sections into which a large city or metropolitan area is divided in the U.S. postal system so that placing the appropriate number after the name of the post office in the address on postal matter facilitates sorting and delivery of the mail — called also *postal delivery zone* **d :** the aggregate of stations in a direction or on a line of railroad situated between various maximum and minimum limits from a point at which a shipment of traffic originates **e :** any distance (as within a circular area or on a single line) within which the same fare is charged by a common carrier ⟨the 20-cent fare ~⟩ **f :** an area on a field of play ⟨the end ~*s* of a football field⟩ **g :** a stretch of roadway, section of a thoroughfare, or part of a street system in which certain traffic regulations are in force ⟨school ~⟩ ⟨no-parking ~⟩ ⟨no-passing ~⟩ — compare SAFETY ZONE **h :** a space at the curb reserved for the loading and unloading of materials and people ⟨a commercial loading ~⟩ ⟨bus loading ~⟩ **6 :** a row of positions on a punched card of a computer

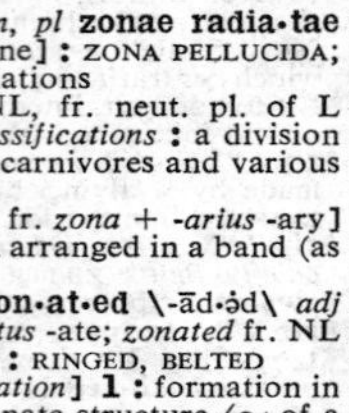

zones 1a

²zone \"\ *vt* -ED/-ING/-S **1 :** to surround with or include within a zone or band **:** ENCIRCLE ⟨waist and . . . bosom agreeably *zoned* —Arnold Bennett⟩ ⟨the . . . horizon is *zoned* with a mellow uniform band of light —E.K.Kane⟩ **2 :** to arrange in or mark off into zones ⟨~*s* the world into climatic provinces⟩ ⟨*zoned* the house into sleeping, service, and living areas⟩; *specif* **:** to partition (a city, borough, or township) by ordinance into zones or sections reserved for different purposes (as residence, business, or manufacturing or combinations of these) and governed by appropriate building regulations (as of the height and area of all structures) ⟨*zoned* the neighborhood as residential⟩

zone axis *n* **:** a straight line to which all faces of a given zone of a crystal are parallel

zoned \'zōnd\ *adj* [¹*zone* + *-ed*] **:** wearing the zone that is symbolic of virginity **:** VIRGIN, CHASTE ⟨fair ~ damsels —Alexander Pope⟩

zone defense *n* **:** a system of defense in various sports (as basketball and football) in which each defensive player guards an assigned zone or section of the court or field — compare MAN-TO-MAN DEFENSE

zone fire *n* **:** fire (as of artillery) delivered at successive ranges and sometimes with varying deflections to cover surely the area in which the target lies

zone·less \'zōnləs\ *adj* **:** wearing no zone or girdle **:** UNGIRT ⟨reeling goddess with the ~ waist —William Cowper⟩

zone line *n* **:** a line marking the limit or boundary of a zone; *specif* **:** BLUE LINE 2

zone of action : an area of responsibility that is defined by boundaries and assigned to a military unit in any situation involving action (as advance, attack, or retrograde movement) — compare SECTOR

zone of clouds : a belt of clouds prevailing over the ocean near the equator

zone of combined fracture and flow : the part of the earth between the zone of fracture and the zone of flow where the rocks may break or flow according to conditions (as of deformation or strength of the materials)

zone of fire : the area within which a particular military unit is prepared to deliver fire

zone of flow *or* **zone of flowage :** the subsurface part of the earth underlying the zone of fracture and including the larger part of the earth in which the fracturing of rocks is prevented by pressure and all deformation is by a sort of flow

zone of fracture : the part of the earth's crust in which deformation may result in and be accompanied by fracture

zone of interior : the part of the theater of war that is not included within the theater of operations

zone of mobility *or* **zone of weakness :** ASTHENOSPHERE

zone of ro·lan·do \-rō'län(,)dō, -län-\ *usu cap R* [after Luigi *Rolando* †1831 Ital. anatomist] **:** MOTOR AREA

zone of silence : a region surrounding a source of sound in which because of interference or refraction the sound is inaudible though it can be heard in more distant regions

zone phenomenon *n* **:** the occurrence of prozones in antibody-antigen mixtures

zone plate *n* **:** an optical device that consists of a series of concentric opaque rings of such width that rays from alternate half-period elements are cut off and that has some properties of a converging lens

zone servant *n* **:** a leader of the Jehovah's Witnesses responsible for a particular area within the charge of a regional servant

zone time *n* **:** standard time applied at sea in which the surface of the globe is divided into 24 zones of 15° or one hour each, the 0 zone extends 7½° east and west of the meridian of Greenwich, and the zones are designated by the number of hours that must be applied to the local time to obtain Greenwich time

zo·nif·er·ous \(')zō¦nif(ə)rəs\ *adj* [*zon-* + *-iferous*] **:** having a zone **:** ZONED

zoning *n* -s [fr. gerund of ²*zone*] **:** the act or process of zoning (as in city planning) ⟨~ ordinances⟩ ⟨~ commission⟩

zo·nite \'zō,nīt\ *n* -s [ISV *zon-* + *-ite*] **:** a body segment of a diplopod

zo·ni·tes \zō'nīd·(,)ēz\ *n, cap* [NL, fr. *zon-* + *-ites*] **:** the type genus of the family Zonitidae

¹zo·ni·tid \'zōnəd·əd\ *adj* [NL *Zonitidae*] **:** of or relating to the Zonitidae

²zonitid \"\ *n* -s **:** a snail of the family Zonitidae

zo·nit·i·dae \zō'nid·ə,dē\ *n pl, cap* [NL, fr. *Zonites*, type genus + *-idae*] **:** a family of small terrestrial snails (suborder Stylommatophora) having a thin depressed shell with sharp peristome

zo·ni·toi·des \,zōnə'tȯi(,)dēz\ *n, cap* [NL, fr. *Zonites* + L *-oides* -oid] **:** a genus of usu. small rather flat amber-colored land snails (family Zonitidae) that have a simple lip not turned back

zono- — see ZON-

zo·no·chlo·rite \,zō(,)nō'klōr,īt, -ō,rīt\ *n* -s [*zon-* + *chlor-* + *-ite*] **:** an impure prehnite occurring in green pebbles of banded structure

zo·no·ciliate \¦=(,)=+\ *adj* [*zon-* + *ciliate*] **:** having a band of cilia — used esp. of annelid larvae

zo·no·limnetic \"+\ *adj* [ISV *zon-* + *limnetic*; orig. formed as G *zonolimnetisch*] **:** of or relating to a definite zone in depth — used esp. of freshwater planktonic animals

zo·no·placental \"+\ *adj* [*zon-* + *placental*] **1 :** having a zonary placenta **2 :** of or relating to the Zonaria

zo·no·plac·en·ta·lia \,zō(,)nō,plasᵊn·'tālēə\ [NL, fr. *zon-* + *Placentalia*] *syn of* ZONARIA

zo·no·trich·ia \,zōnə'trikēə\ *n, cap* [NL, fr. *zon-* + *trich-* + *-ia*] **:** a genus of rather large New World sparrows (family Fringillidae) occurring chiefly in western No. America and having the upperparts largely brown and the underparts unmarked grayish white — see GAMBEL SPARROW, GOLDEN-CROWNED SPARROW, WHITE-CROWNED SPARROW, WHITE-THROATED SPARROW

zon·ta \'zäntə\ *n* -s *usu cap* [Sioux *zon'-ta* honest, trustworthy] **:** one of an organization of service clubs made up of executive women each of whom is a sole representative of one business or profession in a community

zonu·la \'zōnyələ, 'zän-\ *n, pl* **zonu·lae** \-ə,lē, -,lī\ *or* **zonulas** [L] **:** ZONULE; *specif* **:** ZONULE OF ZINN

zo·nu·lar \'zōnyələ(r)\ *adj* **:** of or relating to a zonule

zon·ule \'zōn,yül\ *n* -s [L *zonula*, dim. of *zona* girdle, belt, zone — more at ZONE] **1 :** a little zone, belt, or girdle **2 :** the suspensory ligament of the eye

zonule of zinn \-'tsin\ *usu cap 2d Z* [after Johann G. *Zinn* †1759 Ger. physician and botanist] **:** the suspensory ligament of the crystalline lens of the eye

zo·nure \'zōnyə(r)\ *n* -s [NL *Zonurus*] **:** GIRDLE-TAILED LIZARD

zo·nu·ri·dae \zōn'yürə,dē\ *n pl, cap* [NL, fr. *Zonurus*, type genus (fr. *zon-* + *-urus*) + *-idae*] *syn of* CORDYLIDAE

zoo \'zü\ *n* -s [short for *zoological garden*] **1 :** a zoological garden or collection of living animals usu. for public display **2** *slang* **:** a place (as a prison, shop cafeteria, or railway caboose) in which people are crowded together haphazardly

zoo- — see ZO-

zooarium *var of* ZOARIUM

zoo·benthos \¦zōə+\ *n* [NL, fr. *zo-* + *benthos*] **:** animal life of the benthos

zoo·cecidium \"+\ *n, pl* **zoocecidia** [NL, fr. *zo-* + *cecidium*] **:** a plant gall caused by an animal (as an insect, mite, or nematode worm)

zoo·chlorella \¦zōə+\ *n, pl* **zoochlorellae** [NL, fr. *zo-* + *Chlorella*] **:** any of various minute green algae (genus *Chlorella*) that habitually live symbiotically within the cytoplasm of some protozoans and other invertebrates

zo·o·chore \'zōə,kō(ə)r\ *n* -s [*zo-* + *-chore*] **:** a plant distributed by living animals

zoo·cultural \¦zōə+\ *adj* [*zo-* + *cultural*] **:** ZOOTECHNICAL

zoo·culture \'zōə+,-\ *n* [*zo-* + *culture*] **:** ZOOTECHNY

zo·oe·cial *also* **zo·e·cial** \zō'ēshəl\ *adj* [NL *zooecium*, *zoecium* + E *-al*] **:** of, relating to, or constituting a zooecium

zo·oe·ci·um *also* **zo·e·ci·um** \-shēəm\ *n, pl* **zooe·cia** *also* **zoe·cia** \-ēə\ [NL, fr. *zo-* + Gk *oikos* house + NL *-ium* — more at VICINITY] **:** one of the cells or tubes that enclose the feeding zooids of a bryozoan

zoo-ecology \¦zōə+\ *n* **:** a branch of ecology dealing with the relation of animals to their environment and to other animals

zoo·eras·tia \,zōōē'rastēə\ *n* -s [NL *zooerastia*, fr. *zo-* + *-erastia* (as in *paederastia* pederasty)] **:** BESTIALITY 3

zoo·eras·ty \'zōōē,rastē\ *n* -ES [NL *zooerastia*] **:** ZOOERASTIA

zoo·flagellate \¦zōə+\ *n* [*zo-* + *flagellate*] **:** a member of the Zoomastigina **:** a flagellate protozoan lacking photosynthesis and other plantlike characteristics — compare PLANTLIKE FLAGELLATE

zoo·ful \'zü,fu̇l\ *n* -s **:** enough to fill a zoo

zoo·gamete \¦zōə+\ *n* [ISV *zo-* + *gamete*] **:** a motile gamete esp. of a plant (as an alga)

zo·o·gen·ic \¦zōə¦jenik\ *adj* [ISV *zo-* + *-genic*] **:** caused by or associated with animals or their activities ⟨a ~ virus⟩ ⟨~ fossiliferous rocks⟩

zo·og·e·nous \zō'äjənəs\ *also* **zo·o·ge·ne·ous** \¦zōə¦jēnēəs\ *adj* [*zo-* + *-genous*] **:** ZOOGENIC

zoo·geographer \¦zōə+\ *n* [*zoogeography* + *-er*] **:** a specialist in zoogeography **:** a student of animal distribution

zoo·geographic *also* **zoo·geographical** \"+\ *adj* [*zoogeographic* ISV *zoogeography* + *-ic*; *zoogeographical* fr. *zoogeography* + *-ical*] **:** of or relating to zoogeography or to the natural distribution of animals — **zoo·geographically** \"+\ *adv*

zoo·geography \"+\ *n* [ISV *zo-* + *geography*] **:** a branch of biogeography concerned with the geographical distribution of animals and esp. with the determination of the land and marine areas characterized by special groups of animals and the study of the causes and significance of such groups — compare PHYTOGEOGRAPHY

zo·o·glea *also* **zo·o·gloea** \,zōə'glēə\ *n, pl* **zoogleas** \-ēəz\ *or* **zoogle·ae** \-ē,ē\ [NL, fr. *zo-* + MGk *gloia*, *glia* glue — more at CLAY] **:** a gelatinous or mucilaginous mass that is characteristic of the growth of various bacteria when growing in fluid media rich in organic material and is made up of the bodies of the bacteria embedded in a matrix of swollen confluent capsule substance — **zo·o·gle·al** \¦==¦glēəl\ *adj*

zoog·ler \'züglə(r)\ *n* -s [origin unknown] **:** FROGGER 1

zoo·gonidium \¦zōə+\ *n, pl* **zoogonidia** [NL, fr. *zo-* + *gonidium*] **:** an active or motile gonidium **:** SWARM SPORE, ZOOSPORE

zoo·grafting \'zōə+,-\ *n* [*zo-* + *grafting*] **:** the use of animal tissue in surgical grafting

zo·og·ra·pher \zō'ägrəfə(r)\ *n* -s [*zo-* + *-grapher*] *archaic*

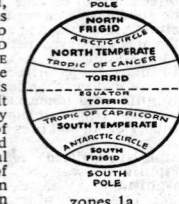

: one who describes or depicts animals and their forms and habits

zo·o·graph·ic \ˌzōəˈgrafik\ *or* **zo·o·graph·i·cal** \-fəkəl\ *adj* [zoography + -ic or -ical] **1** : of, relating to, or consisting of graphic or verbal description of animals **2** : ZOOGEOGRAPHIC

zo·og·ra·phy \zōˈägrəfē\ *n* -ES [Gk zōio- (fr. zōion animal) + E -graphy — more at ZOON] **1** : descriptive zoology **2** : ZOO-GEOGRAPHY

zo·oid \ˈzōˌoid\ *n* -s [zo- + -oid] : an entity that resembles but is not wholly the same as a separate individual organism: as **a** : an organized body (as a phagocyte or a sperm cell) having locomotion **b** : a more or less independent animal produced (as by fission, proliferation, or strobilation) by other than direct sexual methods and so having an equivocal individuality — used esp. of a single person of a compound organism (as a hydroid, coral, or bryozoan colony) — **zo·oi·dal** \(ˈ)zōˌoid'l\ *adj*

zo·oi·di·oph·i·lous \zōˌoidēˈäfələs\ *adj* [prob. alter. of zoidiophilous] : ZOOPHILIC a

zooks \ˈzúks, ˈzüks\ *interj* [origin unknown] — used as a mild oath

zo·ol·a·ter \zōˈälədə(r)\ *n* -s [zo- + -later] : one that practices zoolatry

zo·ol·a·trous \-ətrəs\ *adj* [zoolatry + -ous] : of, relating to, or constituting zoolatry

zo·ol·a·try \-rē\ *n* -ES [NL zoolatria, fr. zo- + LL -latria -latry] **1** : worship directed toward particular kinds of animals often as representative of a natural force, as incarnation of some deity, or as symbolic of some power or protector (as a tribal ancestor) **2** : excessive preoccupation with or devotion to animals and esp. to a domestic pet

zo·ol·o·ger \zōˈäləjə(r)\ *n* -s [NL zoologia zoology + E -er] *archaic* : ZOOLOGIST

zo·o·log·i·cal \ˌzōəˈläjəkəl, -jēk-, ÷ˌzüˈ-\ *also* **zo·o·log·ic** \-jik, -jēk\ *adj* [zoology + -ical or -ic] **1** : of, relating to, or occupied with zoology **2** : of, relating to, or affecting lower animals often as distinguished from man ⟨~ infections⟩ — **zo·o·log·i·cal·ly** \-jək(ə)lē, -jēk-, -li\ *adv*

zoological garden *n* : a garden or park where wild animals are kept for exhibition

zo·ol·o·gist \zōˈäləjəst, ÷ zü-\ *n* -s : a specialist in zoology

zo·ol·o·gize \-ˌjīz\ *vb* -ED/-ING/-S *vi* **1** : to study zoology **2** : to collect animals for study ~ *vt* : to subject to zoological investigation

zo·ol·o·gy \-ləjē, -ji\ *n* -ES [NL zoologia, fr. zo- + -logia zoology] **1** : a science that deals with animals : a branch of biology concerned with the animal kingdom and its members as individuals and classes and with animal life and animal morphology together with anatomy, histology, and cytology, physiology, embryology, genetics, taxonomy, paleontology, ecology, and various other sciences in whole or in part **2** : a treatise on zoology **3 a** : animal life (of a region) : FAUNA ⟨the ~ of Australia⟩ **b** : the properties and vital phenomena exhibited by an animal, animal type, or group : animal physiology ⟨the ~ of a crustacean⟩

¹zoom \ˈzüm\ *vb* -ED/-ING/-S [imit.] *vi* **1** : to move with or make a loud but low hum or buzz **2** *of an airplane* : to climb for a short time at an angle greater than that which can be maintained in steady flight so that the machine is carried upward at the expense of its stored kinetic energy **3 a** *of a motion-picture or television camera* : to move toward or away from an object rapidly while keeping the object in focus **b** *of a motion-picture or television image* : to appear to come closer to or to move away from the observer as the result of varying the focal length of the camera lens ~ *vt* : to cause (as a motion-picture or television image) to zoom

²zoom \"\ *n* -s **1 a** : an act or process of zooming: as (1) : a sudden increase in the upward slope of the flight path of an airplane; *broadly* : a sharp upward movement (as of a business cycle) (2) : a process by which an image is made to grow or to shrink rapidly in the field of view of a motion-picture or television camera **b** : a zooming sound **2** : a cocktail consisting of brandy, honey, and cream shaken in ice and served in a wine glass

zo·o·mas·ti·gi·na \ˌzōəˌmastəˈjīdə\ *or* **zo·o·mas·ti·go·da** \-ˈgōdə\ *or* **zo·o·mas·ti·go·ta** \-ˈgōd-\ *or* syn of ZOOMASTIGINA

zo·o·mas·ti·gi·na \-ˈjīnə\ *n pl, cap* [NL, fr. zo- + mastig- + -ina] : a subclass of Mastigophora that comprises holozoic or saprozoic flagellates lacking chromatophores and stigma and that includes the orders Hypermastigina, Polymastigina, Protomonadina, and Rhizomastigina — compare PHYTO-MASTIGINA

zo·om·e·ter \zōˈämədə(r)\ *n* [zo- + -meter] : an animal that because of regularly recurrent parallel fluctuations in population can be used to predict the scarcity or abundance of another animal

zo·o·met·ric \ˌzōəˈmetrik\ *or* **zo·o·met·ri·cal** \-rəkəl\ *adj* [zo- + -metric or metrical] : designed for the measurement of animals and esp. for the estimation of a measure of bulk (as weight) through determination of some linear measurement (as girth) ⟨a ~ tape⟩

zoo-mim·ic \ˈzōəˌmimik\ *adj* [zo- + mimic] *of a primitive culture* : imitative of animal behavior esp. in the use of animal parts (as teeth and horns) in making tools and weapons

zoom lens *n* : a camera lens in which the focal length and the image size can be varied continuously so that the image remains in focus at all times — called also *varifocal lens*

zo·o·morph \ˈzōəˌmorf\ *n* [ISV zo- + -morph] : something in the form of an animal; *esp* : a conventional image or symbol of a zoomorphized deity or supernatural being

zo·o·mor·phic \ˌzōəˈmorfik\ *adj* [ISV zo- + -morphic] **1** : having the form of often stylized animals ⟨~ writing⟩ **2 a** : of, relating to, or constituting a zoomorphized deity or supernatural being **b** : of, relating to, or like a zoomorph **3** : of or relating to zoomorphism

zo·o·mor·phism \-ˌmorˌfizəm\ *n* -s [ISV zo- + -morphism] **1** : the representation of deity in the form or with the attributes of the lower animals **2** : the use of animal forms in art or symbolism

zo·o·mor·phize \-ˌfīz\ *vt* -ED/-ING/-S [zoomorphic + -ize] : to conceive of or symbolize or represent (a deity or supernatural being) as an animal ⟨zoomorphizing their clan founder so a spirit bear so that this animal became the totem of and taboo to members of the clan⟩

zo·on \ˈzōˌän\ *n, pl* **zoa** \ˈzōə\ [NL, fr. Gk zōion animal; akin to Gk zōē life — more at QUICK] **1** : the whole product of one fertilized egg whether consisting of a single individual (as a dog), a colony of associated persons (as many hydroids), or an asexually-produced progeny of a sexually-produced individual (as some aphids) — often distinguished from *zooid* **2** : ZOOID — often distinguished from *zooid*

-zoon \"\ *n comb form, pl* **-zoa** \"\ [NL, fr. Gk zōion animal] : living being : animal : zooid ⟨anthozoon⟩ ⟨hematozoon⟩ ⟨spermatozoon⟩

zo·o·no·my \zōˈänəmē\ *n* -ES [NL zoonomia, fr. zo- + L -nomia -nomy] : PHYSIOLOGY

zo·o·no·sis \zōˈänəsəs, ÷zü-, *n, pl* **zoo·no·ses** \-ˌsēz\ [NL, fr. zo- + -nosis (fr. Gk nosos disease)] : a disease communicable from animals to man under natural conditions — compare ZOOZOOTIC

zo·o·not·ic \ˌzōəˈnädik\ *adj* [fr. NL zoonosis, after such pairs as NL neurosis; E neurotic] : of, relating to, or constituting a zoonosis

zoo-pa·le·on·tol·o·gy \ˌzōə+\ *n* [zo- + paleontology] : PALEOZO-OLOGY

zoo-par·a·site \"+\ *n* [zo- + parasite] : a parasitic animal — **zoo-par·a·sit·ic** \"+\ *adj*

zoo-path·o·log·i·cal \"+\ *adj* [in sense 1, fr. zoopathology + -ical; in sense 2, fr. zoo- + pathological] **1** : of or relating to zoopathology **2** : pathological to lower animals

zoo-pa·thol·o·gy \ˌzōə+\ *n* [zo- + pathology] : a branch of pathology dealing with the diseases of the lower animals

zooph *abbr* zoophytological; zoophytology

zo·oph·a·ga \zōˈäfəgə\ *n pl, cap* [NL, fr. zo- + -phaga] *in former classifications* : a major division of Mammalia comprising the flesh-eating mammals — **zo·oph·a·gan** \-gən\ *n -s*

zo·o·pha·gin·e·ae \ˌzōəfəˈjinēˌē\ *n pl, cap* [NL, fr. zo- + phag- + -ineae] *in some classifications* : a suborder of Virales comprising animal viruses

zo·oph·a·gous \zōˈäfəgəs\ *adj* [ISV zo- + -phagous] **1** : feeding on animals : CARNIVOROUS **2** [NL Zoophaga + E -ous] : of or relating to the Zoophaga

zoo-pharmacological \ˌzōə+\ *adj* [zo- + pharmacological] : of or relating to the pharmacology of animal organs or tissues

zoo-pharmacy \"+\ *n* [zo- + pharmacy] : veterinary pharmacy

zoo-phile \ˈzōəˌfīl\ *n* -s [zo- + -phile] : a zoophilic individual

zo·oph·il·ia \ˌzōəˈfilēə\ *also* **zo·oph·i·lism** \zōˈäfəˌlizəm\ *n* -s [zoophilia fr. NL, fr. zo- + -philia; zoophilism fr. zo- + phil- + -ism] : the quality or state of being zoophilic; *esp* : an erotic fixation on animals that may result in sexual excitement through real or fancied contact — compare ZOOERASTIA

zo·o·phil·ic \ˌzōəˈfilik\ *or* **zo·oph·i·lous** \zōˈäfələs\ *adj* [zo- + -philic or -philous] : having an attraction to or preference for animals: as **a** *usu* zoophilous : adapted to pollination by animals other than insects — compare ENTOMOPHILOUS **b** : afflicted with sexual zoophilia **c** *of an insect* : preferring lower animals than man as a source of food — compare AN-DROPHILIC

zo·oph·i·list \zōˈäfələst\ *n* -s [zo- + phil- + -ist] : a lover of animals: **a** : a person concerned with the rights of lower animals and their protection from abuse **b** : one afflicted with zoophilia

zo·oph·i·lite \-fəˌlīt\ *n* -s [zo- + phil- + -ite] : ZOOPHILIST

zo·oph·i·ly \zōˈäfəlē\ *n* -ES [NL zoophilia] : ZOOPHILIA

zoo-pho·bia \ˈzōə+\ *n* [NL, fr. zo- + -phobia] **1** : morbid fear of animals **2** : the fear of animal spirits or of zoomorphized entities — **zoo-pho·bous** \zōˈäfəbəs\ *adj*

zo·o·phor·ic \ˌzōəˈforik\ *adj* [L zoophorus + E -ic] : of, relating to, or employing a zoophorus

zo·oph·o·rus \zōˈäfərəs\ *n, pl* **zoopho·ri** \-fəˌrī\ [L, fr. Gk zōiophoros, fr. zōi- zo- + -phoros -phore] : a frieze having continuous relief sculptures of men or animals or both

zoo-phys·ics \ˈzōə+\ *n pl but sing or pl in constr* [zo- + physics] : the scientific study of the physical principles underlying the structure and uses of the organs of animals

zo·oph·y·ta \zōˈäfədˌə\ *n pl, cap* [NL, fr. Gk zōophyta, pl. of zōophyton] *in former classifications* : an extensive artificial and heterogeneous group of invertebrates mostly incapable of locomotion that commonly includes all or many of the forms distinguished as coelenterates, sponges, bryozoans, echinoderms, protozoans, and worms but is sometimes restricted to coelenterates and sponges or to anthozoans alone

zo·o·phyte \ˈzōəˌfīt\ *n* -s [Gk zōophyton, fr. zō- zo- + phyton plant — more at PHYT-] **1** *obs* : a plant resembling an animal **2** : any of numerous invertebrate animals (as a coral, gorgonian, sea anemone, hydroid, bryozoan, or sponge) more or less resembling plants in appearance or mode of growth; *esp* : one (as many corals and hydroids) that forms a branching arborescent or massive colony attached to a substrate — **zo·o·phyt·ic** \ˌzōəˈfidˌik\ *adj*

zoo-plankter \ˈzōə+\ *n* [zo- + plankter] : a planktonic animal ⟨copepods and other ~s⟩

zoo-plankton \ˈzōə+\ *n* [zo- + plankton] : animal life of the plankton — **zoo-planktonic** \"+\ *adj*

zo·o·prax·i·scope \ˌzōəˈpraksəˌskōp\ *n* [zo- + praxis + -scope] : the fact that it usu. showed pictures of a moving animal] : a motion-picture projector invented about 1882

zoos *pl of* ZOO

zoo-sperm \ˈzōə+, -ˌ\ *n* [ISV zo- + sperm] **1** : SPERMATOZOID 2; SPERMATOZOON 2 : ZOOSPORE

zo·o·sporangiophore \ˈzōə+\ *n* [zo- + sporangiophore] : a sporangiophore that bears zoosporangia

zo·o·sporangium \"+\ *n, pl* **zoosporangia** [NL, fr. zo- + sporangium] : a spore case or sporangium bearing zoospores

zo·o·spore \ˈzōə+, -ˌ\ *n* [ISV zo- + spore] : an independently motile spore: as **a** (1) : a motile usu. naked and flagellated asexual spore (as of an alga or lower fungus) — called also *swarm spore* (2) : ZOOGONIDIUM **b** : PLANOGAMETE 1 : a flagellated gamete of a foraminiferan (2) : a minute amoeboid or flagellated product of protozoan sporocyst division whether sexual or asexual — **zo·o·spor·ic** \ˌzōəˈspōrik, -por-, -pär-\ *or* **zo·os·po·rous** \zōˈäspərəs, "zōəˈspōrəs, -spor-\ *adj*

zo·o·sporif·er·ous \ˌzōəspəˈrifərəs, -spōr'if-, -spor-\ *adj* [zoospore + -iferous] : producing zoospores

zo·o·sporocyst \ˈzōə+\ *n* [zoospore + cyst] : a unicellular zoosporangium — compare SPOROCYST

zo·os·ter·ol \zōˈästəˌrol, -ˌrōl\ *n* [zo- + sterol] : any of a group of sterols (as cholesterol or coprostanol) of animal origin — compare PHYTOSTEROL

zo·o·taxy \ˈzōəˌtaksē\ *n* -ES [ISV zo- + -taxy] : zoological taxonomy

zo·o·tech·ni·cal \ˌzōəˈteknəkəl\ *also* **zo·o·tech·nic** \-nik\ *adj* [zootechnical fr. zootechny + -ical; zootechnic ISV zootechny + -ic] : of or relating to zootechny

zo·o·tech·ni·cian \ˌzōəˌtekˈnishən\ *n* [ISV zootechnic] : a specialist in zootechny

zo·o·tech·nics \ˌzōəˈtekniks\ *n pl but sing or pl in constr* [zootechnic + -s] : ZOOTECHNY 1

zo·o·tech·ny \ˈzōəˌteknē\ *n* -ES [ISV zo- + -techny; prob. orig. formed as F zootechnie] **1** : the scientific art of maintaining and improving animals under domestication including breeding, genetics, nutrition, and housing : the technology of animal husbandry **2** : methods and devices for capturing and utilizing animals esp. as employed by nonliterate people

zo·o·the·ism \ˈzōəˌthēˌizəm, ˌzōəˈth-\ *n* [zo- + -theism] : belief in animal gods — compare ZOOLATRY

zoo-therapy \ˈzōə+\ *n* [ISV zo- + therapy] : veterinary therapeutics

zo·ot·o·my \zōˈädəmē\ *n* -ES [zo- + -tomy] **1** : the dissection of animals **2** : animal anatomy esp. as studied on a comparative basis : comparative anatomy

zoo-totemism \ˈzōə+\ *n* [zo- + totemism] : belief in or use of animals as totems

zootrope *var of* ZOETROPE

zo·o·troph·ic \ˌzōəˈträfik\ *adj* [zo- + -trophic] : HETERO-TROPHIC — used esp. by protozoologists

zoot suit \ˈzüt-\ *n* [origin unknown] : a flashy suit of extreme cut typically consisting of a thigh-length jacket with wide padded shoulders and peg-top trousers tapering to zoomorphized cuffs — **zoot-suiter** \ˌ=ˌ=ˌ\ *n -s*

zooty \ˈzüd-ē\ *adj* [zoot suit + -y] : typical of a zoot-suiter : extreme or flashy in manner or style ⟨a ~ haircut⟩

zo·o·type \ˈzōəˌtīp\ *n* [zo- + type] : an animal serving as a type; *also* : the type so represented — **zo·o·typ·ic** \ˌ=ˌ=ˈtipik\ *adj*

zo·o·xan·thel·la \ˌzōəzanˈthelə\ *n, pl* **zooxanthel·lae** \-ˌē, -ˌī\ [NL, fr. zo- + xanth- + -ella] : one of the minute pigmentary bodies occurring in various radiolarians and a few marine invertebrates (as some flatworms and polyps) commonly held to be symbiotic unicellular yellow-green algae

zoo-zoo \ˈzü, zü\ *n* -s [imit. of its sound] *dial Eng* : RINGDOVE

zop·pa \ˈtsäpə, ˈtsä-\ *or* **zop·po** \-pō\ *adj* [It, lit., limping] : SYNCOPATED — used as a direction in music ⟨alla zoppa⟩

zo·que \ˈsōkā\ *n, pl* **zoque** \-\ *or* **zo·ques** \-ˈās\ *usu cap* **1 a** : a Zoquean people of Oaxaca, Chiapas, and Tabasco Mexico **b** : a member of the Zoque people **2** : the language of the Zoque people

zo·que·an \ˈsōkēən\ *or* **zoquean** *n, pl* **zoquean** *or* **zoqueans** *usu cap* [Zoque + E -an] **1 a** : a Mexican Indian people of eastern Tabasco and the adjacent districts of Chiapas and Oaxaca **b** : a member of such people **2** : a language stock of southern Mexico that includes Zoque, Mixe, and Popoluca

zo·ril \ˈzōrəl, ˈzär-\ *or* **zo·rille** \zəˈril\ *also* **zo·ril·la** \-lə\ *or* **zoril·lo** \-i(ˌ)lō\ *n* -s [F zorille, fr. Sp zorrilla, zorrillo, dim. of zorra, zorro fox, fr. OSp zorrar to drag, of imit. origin] **1** : a North African muishond (*Ictonyx frenata*) related to the striped muishond **2** : a North African muishond — compare MUISHOND

zo·ril·la \zəˈrilə\ *n* -s *cap* [NL, fr. Sp zorrilla] var of ICTONYX

zo·ril·lo \zəˈri(ˌ)lō\ *n* -s [Sp, lit., little fox, skunk, dim. of zorro fox] : a tropical American shrub or small tree (*Roupala darienensis*) of the family Proteaceae that has an offensive skunklike odor and is used as a remedy for headache

¹zo·ro·as·tri·an \ˌzōrōˈwastrēən, ˌzōˈrō-, -rōˈä-, -aas-\ *adj, usu cap* [Zoroaster fl ab 6th cent. B.C. founder of Zoroastrianism (fr. L Zoroastres, fr. Gk Zōroastrēs, fr. Av Zarathushtra-) + E -an] : of or relating to Zoroaster or Zoroastrianism

²zoroastrian \"\ *n, usu cap* : an adherent of Zoroastrianism — compare GABAR, PARSI

zo·ro·as·tri·an·ism \"-ˌnizəm\ *n* -s *cap* : a religion founded in Persia by the prophet Zoroaster teaching the worship of Ahura Mazda as the source of all good and requiring the practice of good thoughts, words, and deeds and the renunciation of evil — compare PARSISM

zo·ro·ty·pus \ˌzōrəˈtīpəs\ *n, cap* [NL, fr. Gk zōros pure, sheer + L typus type] : the sole genus of the order Zoraptera

zor·ra \ˈzórə\ *n* -s [AmerSp zorra, sorra] : any of several coarse tropical grasses

zor·tzi·co \zó(r)ˈsē(ˌ)kō\ *n* -s [Basque, fr. zortzi eight; fr. its time] : a Basque song or dance in ⁵⁄₈ time and dotted rhythm

zos·ter \ˈzostə(r)\ *n* -s [L, fr. Gk zōstēr girdle — more at HERPES ZOSTER] : HERPES ZOSTER

zos·te·ra \ˈzästərə\ *n* -s *cap* [NL, fr. Gk zōstēr girdle, a seaweed] : a small genus of widely distributed marine plants (family Potamogetonaceae) with branching stems, distichous leaves, and monoecious flowers that are borne in a spadix — see EELGRASS

zos·te·ra·ce·ae \ˌzästəˈrāsēˌē\ *n pl, cap* [NL, fr. Zostera + -aceae] *in some classifications* : a family of widely distributed marine or aquatic herbs (order Naiadales) that is nearly or exactly equivalent to Potamogetonaceae

zos·te·rop·i·dae \ˌzästəˈräpəˌdē\ *n pl, cap* [NL, fr. Zosterop-, Zosterops, type genus + -idae] : a family of passerine birds consisting of the silvereyes

zos·te·rops \ˈzästəˌräps\ *n, cap* [NL, fr. Gk zōstēr girdle + ōp-, ōps eye — more at OPTIC] : the type genus of the family Zosteropidae

zotzil *usu cap, var of* TZOTZIL

zou·ave \zuˈäv, -ˌäv, ˌzü, ˈzwäv, ˈzwäv\ *n* -s *usu cap* [F, fr. Zwawa, tribe of Kabyles in the Djurdjura mountains, Algeria] **1** : one of a body of French infantry orig. composed of Algerians that is characterized by a colorful uniform of gaiters, baggy trousers, short and open-fronted jacket, and usu. tasseled cap or turban and by very quick and spirited drill **2** : a member of one of the bodies of soldiers (as a number of volunteer regiments in the army of the U.S. in the Civil War) adopting the dress and drill of the Zouaves

zounds \ˈz(w)aun(d)z, ˈz(w)ün(d)z\ *interj* [euphemism for *God's wounds*] — used as a mild oath

zou-zou *var of* ZU-ZU

zow·ie \ˈzauē, -aúi\ *interj* [imit. of the sound of a speeding vehicle] — used to express astonishment and admiration over something sudden or speedy; used also to express enthusiasm or delight

Zouave 1

¹zoy·sia \ˈzoisēə, ˈzoizēə, ˈzoishə\ [NL] *syn of* ZOISIA

²zoysia \"\ *n* -s : a grass of the genus *Zoisia*: as **a** : MANILA GRASS **b** : KOREAN LAWN GRASS

Zr *symbol* zirconium

ZS *abbr* zoological society

z's *or* **zs** *pl of* Z

ZT *abbr* zone time

z-twist \ˈ=ˌ=\ *n, cap Z* : an openband twist

zu·brow·ka \zübˈrovkə\ *n* -s [Pol żubrówka, fr. Russ zubrovka sweet grass, zubrowka] : a dry straw-colored chiefly Russian liqueur of vodka flavored with herbs

zuc·chet·to \züˈkedˌō, ˌzú-\ *n* -s [It, fr. zucca gourd, head, fr. LL cucutia, a gourd; perh. akin to L cucurbita gourd — more at GOURD] : a small round skullcap worn by Roman Catholic ecclesiastics in colors that vary according to the rank of the wearer — compare BIRETTA

zuc·chi·ni \züˈkēnē, -ni *also* -ˈchē-\ *n, pl* **zucchini** *or* **zucchinis** [It, pl. of zucchino, dim. of zucca gourd] : a summer squash that is characterized by bushy growth and smooth slender cylindrical straight to slightly curved fruits with very dark green or blackish green skin and thick greenish white or creamy white flesh and is usu. preferred for table use when from five inches to a foot long — compare COCOZELLE

zu·fo·lo *or* **zuf·fo·lo** \ˈtsüfəˌlō, *or* pl **zufo·li** *or* **zuffo·li** \-ˌlē\ [It, fr. OIt, whistle, whistling, hiss, fr. (assumed) VL sufilus, sifilus, fr. L sibilare to hiss, whistle — more at SIBILANT] : a little flute or flageolet; *esp* : one used to teach birds

zug·zwang \ˈtsükˌtsfäŋ\ *n* -s [G, fr. zug pull, tug + zwang force, coercion; akin to OHG ziohan to pull and dwingan to press, oppress, compel — more at TOW, THONG] : the necessity of moving in chess when it is to one's disadvantage

zui·sin \ˈzoizn\ *n* -s [perh. of Algonquian origin; akin to Ojibwa jishib duck, Pequot m'shizzeege sheldrake] : BALD-PATE 2

zu'l-hij·ja \zülˈhijə\ *n usu cap Z&H, usu cap* var of DHU'L-HIJJA

zu'l-ka·dah \zülˈkä(ˌ)dä\ *n usu cap Z&K, var of* DHU'L-QADAH

¹zu·lu \ˈzü(ˌ)lü\ *n, pl* **zulu** *or* **zulus** *usu cap* **1 a** : a Bantu-speaking Ngoni people of Natal related to the Xhosa and other peoples of southern Africa **b** : a member of the Zulu people **2** : a Bantu language of the Zulu people closely related to Xhosa and Swazi with which it forms the Ngoni group and of considerable literary importance as one of the leading Bantu languages of southern Africa

²zulu \"\ *n* [prob. fr. ¹zulu] **1** : a 2-masted Scotch lugger with straight stem, raking and narrow stern, and very lofty fore lug **2 a** : a 19th century U.S. or Canadian railroad car or train carrying immigrants and their possessions **b** : a person or group traveling in a zulu

³zulu \"\ *n usu cap* — a communications code word for the letter z

zum·boo·ruk \zəmˈbüˌrək\ *n* -s [Ar zanbūrak, fr. Per zanbūrah, fr. zanbūr hornet] : a small cannon that is mounted on a swivel; *esp* : one that is fired from a rest on the back of a camel

zu·ñi \ˈzün(y)ē\ *n, pl* **zuñi** *or* **zuñis** *usu cap* [Sp, fr. Keresan sini middle] **1 a** : a people occupying a pueblo in western New Mexico **b** : a member of the Zuñi people **2** : the language of the Zuñi people

zu·ñi·an \ˈzünēən\ *n, pl* **zuñian** *usu cap* [Zuñi + E -an] : a language family consisting of Zuñi only

zuñi brown *n, cap Z* : AUBURN

zun·yite \ˈzünˌyīt\ *n* -s [Zuñi Mine, near Silverton, Colo. + E -ite] : a mineral $Al_{13}Si_5O_{20}(OH,F)_{18}Cl$ consisting of a basic silicate, chloride, and fluoride of aluminum and occurring in minute transparent tetrahedrons

zu·rich \ˈzürik, -ˌrik\ *adj, usu cap* [fr. Zurich *or* Zürich, Switzerland] : of or from the city of Zurich, Switzerland : of the kind or style prevalent in Zurich

zutuhil *or* **zutugil** *usu cap, var of* TZUTUHIL

zuur·veldt \ˈzür, velt\ *n* [Afrik zuurveld, fr. MD zuur, suur sour + veld, veld field; akin to OE & OHG sūr sour — more at SOUR, VELD] : SOURVELD

zu·zim \ˈzüˌzim\ *or* **zu·zims** \-mz\ *n, pl, usu cap* [Heb zūzim] : ZAMZUMMIM

zu-zu *also* **zou-zou** \ˈzüˌzü\ *n, pl* **zuzu** *or* **zouzou** [F, fr. zouave] : a member of a Zouave regiment in the Civil War

zwan·zi·ger \ˈtsfän(t)sigə(r), tsvänt-\ *n* -s [G, fr. zwanzig twenty, fr. OHG zweinzug, fr. zwein- (akin to OE tẁēgen, twā, tū two) + -zug group of 10 — more at TWO, EIGHTY] : a former Austrian and German billon coin of 20 kreutzers

zwet·schen·was·ser \ˈtsfechənˌväsər\ *n, -s* [G, lit., plum water, fr. zwetschen (pl. of zwetsche plum) + wasser water, fr. OHG wazzar — more at WATER] : a colorless plum brandy with a bitter almond taste

zwick·au \ˈtsfiˌkau, ˈtsvi-\ *adj, usu cap* [fr. Zwickau, Germany] : of or from the city of Zwickau, Germany : of the kind or style prevalent in Zwickau

zwickau prophet *n, usu cap Z* **:** a member of a 16th century Anabaptist sect centered in Zwickau whose leaders (as Storch and Münzer) claimed prophetic powers

zwie·back \ˈswē,bak, ˈzw-, -wī,- *also* -bäk\ *n, pl* **zwieback** *or* **zwiebacks** [G, lit., twice baked, fr. *zwie-* (fr. OHG *zwi-* twice) + *backen* to bake, fr. OHG *bahhan;* trans. of It *biscotto* biscuit — more at TWI-, BAKE] **:** a usu. sweetened bread enriched with eggs that is first prepared and baked and then sliced and toasted until dry and crisp

zwing·er \ˈtsfiŋə(r), ˈtsvi-\ *n* -s [G, fr. MHG *twinger, zwinger* one that forces or constrains, narrow space between the wall of a castle and the outer walls, fr. *twingen, dwingen* to press, oppress, fr. OHG *dwingan* — more at THONG] **:** a fortress protecting a city

[1]**zwing·li·an** \ˈzwiŋ(g)lēən\ *also* **zwing·li·an·ist** \-nəst\ *n* -s *usu cap* [*zwinglian* fr. Ulrich *Zwingli* †1531 Swiss religious reformer + E *-an*, n. suffix; *zwinglianist* fr. [2]*zwinglian* + *-ist*] **:** a follower or adherent of Zwingli or Zwinglianism

[2]**zwinglian** \"\ *adj, usu cap* [Ulrich *Zwingli* †1531 + E *-an*, adj. suffix] **:** of or relating to Zwingli or Zwinglianism

zwing·li·an·ism \-ēə,nizəm\ *n* -s *usu cap* **:** the teachings of Zwingli; *specif* **:** the doctrine that in the Lord's Supper there is an influence of Christ upon the soul but that the true body of Christ is present by the contemplation of faith and not in essence or reality

zwisch·en·spiel \ˈtsfishən,shpēl, ˈtsvi-\ *n* [G, fr. *zwischen* between (fr. MHG, fr. OHG *zwiskēn*, dat. pl., both, fr. *zwisk*, adj., twofold, fr. an old distributive numeral akin to Goth *tweihnai* two each) + *spiel* play, fr. OHG *spil* — more at BETWIXT, SPIEL] **:** a musical interlude **:** INTERMEZZO

zwit·ter·ion \ˈtsvid·əˌrīən\ *n* [G, fr. *zwitter* hybrid (fr. OHG *zwitaran*, fr. *zwi-* double, twice) + ISV *ion* — more at TWI-] **:** DIPOLAR ION — **zwit·ter·ion·ic** \ˌ==ˌrīˈänik\ *adj*

zyg- *or* **zygo-** *comb form* [NL, fr. Gk, fr. *zygon* — more at YOKE] **1 a :** yoke **:** connecting in the manner of a yoke **:** joining ⟨*zygo*sphene⟩ ⟨*zyg*antrum⟩ ⟨*zygo*neure⟩ **b :** zygomatic ⟨*zyg*ion⟩ **2 :** yoked state or part **:** pair ⟨*zygo*dactyl⟩ ⟨*zygo*dont⟩ **3 :** union **:** fusion **:** zygosis ⟨*zygo*spore⟩ ⟨*zygo*genesis⟩

zyg·a·dene \ˈzigə,dēn, ˈzīg-\ *n* -s [NL *Zygadenus*] **:** a plant of the genus *Zigadenus*

zyg·a·de·nine \,==ˈdē,nēn, -ˌnən\ *n* -s [ISV *zygaden-* (fr. NL *Zygadenus*) + *-ine*] **:** a crystalline alkaloid $C_{27}H_{43}NO_7$ that is obtained from plants of the genera *Zigadenus* and *Veratrum*

zyg·a·de·nus \-ˈdēnəs\ [NL] *syn of* ZIGADENUS

zy·gae·nid \zīˈjēnəd\ *adj* [NL *Zygaenidae*] **:** of or relating to the Zygaenidae

[1]**zy·gae·ni·dae** \-nə,dē\ [NL, fr. *Zygaena* (fr. Gk *zygaina* hammerheaded shark) + *-idae*] *syn of* SPHYRNIDAE

[2]**zygaenidae** \"\ *n pl, cap* [NL, fr. *Zygaena*, type genus (fr. Gk *zygaina*) + *-idae*] **:** a family of moths including the foresters, burnet moths, and related moths most of which are bright-colored and day-flying

zy·gan·trum \zīˈgan·trəm, zəˈ-\ *n, pl* **zygan·tra** \-rə\ *also* **zygantrums** [NL, fr. *zyg-* + LL *antrum* cavity of the body — more at ANTRUM] **:** a fossa on the posterior median part of the neural arch of a vertebra (as of a snake) that accommodates the zygosphene of the next vertebra

zyg·apophysis \ˈzig, ˈzīg+\ *n, pl* **zygapophyses** [NL, fr. *zyg-* + *apophysis*] **:** one of the articular processes of the neural arch of a vertebra of which there are usu. two anterior and two posterior

zyg·i·on \ˈzigē,än, ˈzij-\ *n, pl* **zygia** \-ēə\ *also* **zygions** [NL, fr. *zyg-* + *-ion* (as in *gonion*)] **:** a craniometric point at either end of the bizygomatic diameter

zy·gite \ˈzī,jīt\ *n* -s [Gk *zygitēs*, fr. *zygon* yoke, thwart + *itēs* -ite — more at YOKE] **:** a rower of the middle tier in an ancient trireme or in the upper tier of a bireme

zyg·nema \zigˈnēmə\ *n, cap* [NL, fr. *zyg-* + *-nema*] **:** a genus of common filamentous algae (family Zygnemataceae) having two stellate chromatophores in each cell

zyg·ne·ma·les \,zignəˈmā(,)lēz\ [NL, fr. *Zygnema* + *-ales*] *syn of* ZYGNEMATALES

zyg·ne·ma·ta·ce·ae \zig,nēməˈtāsē,ē\ *n pl, cap* [NL, fr. *Zygnemat-, Zygnema*, type genus + *-aceae*] **:** a family of common freshwater algae (order Zygnematales) often forming bright green slimy masses in stagnant or running water and consisting of unbranched cylindrical filaments with green chromatophores arranged in spiral bands, stars, or rarely straight bands — see SPIROGYRA, ZYGNEMA — **zyg·ne·ma·ta·ceous** \=ˌ==ˈtāshəs\ *adj*

zyg·ne·ma·ta·les \-ˈtā(,)lēz\ *n pl, cap* [NL, fr. *Zygnemat-, Zygnema* + *-ales*] **:** an order of green algae (class Chlorophyceae) that include the pond scums and desmids, are distinguished by the absence of asexual reproduction and lack of flagellated reproductive structure, and reproduce sexually by fusion of amoeboid gametes — compare AKONTAE

zygo- — see ZYG-

zy·go·cactus \ˈzīgō, ˈzigō+\ *n, cap* [NL, fr. *zyg-* + *Cactus*] **:** a small genus of Brazilian cacti having flat fleshy usu. branched joints, showy red or pink flowers, and red fleshy fruits and including the widely cultivated crab cactus

zy·goc·i·ty \zīˈgäsəd·ē, zəˈ-\ *n* -ES [*zygo*tic + *-city* (as in *velocity*)] **:** zygotic condition ⟨rules for the diagnosis of ~ in cattle twins —John Hancock⟩

[1]**zy·go·dac·tyl** \ˈzīgōˈdaktəl, ˈzig-\ *or* **zy·go·dac·ty·lous** \-tələs\ *also* **zy·go·dac·tyle** \-təl\ *adj* [*zygodactyl, zygodactyle* ISV *zyg-* + *dactyl; zygodactylous* fr. *zyg-* + *-dactylous*] **1 :** having the toes arranged two in front and two behind — used of a bird **2 :** SYNDACTYL ⟨familial occurrence of ~ hands⟩

[2]**zygodactyl** \"\ *also* **zygodactyle** \"\ *n* -s **:** a zygodactyl bird (as a woodpecker or parrot)

zy·go·dac·ty·lae \,==ˈdaktə,lē\ *or* **zy·go·dac·ty·li** \-,lī\ *n pl, cap* [NL, fr. *zyg-* + *-dactylae, -dactyli* (fr. *dactylus* dactyl)] *in former classifications* **:** a group of nonpasserine birds consisting of those having zygodactyl feet

zy·go·dac·tyl·ism \-,lizəm\ *n* -s [*zyg-* + *-dactylism*] **:** the condition of being zygodactyl or of having zygodactyl feet

zy·go·dont \ˈzīgə,dänt, ˈzig-\ *adj* [ISV *zyg-* + *-odont*] **:** having or being molar teeth with four tubercles in which the tubercles are united in pairs by crests

zy·go·genesis \ˈzīgō, ˈzigō+\ *n* [NL, fr. *zyg-* + *genesis*] **:** reproduction by means of specialized germ cells or gametes **:** sexual and biparental reproduction

zy·goid \ˈzī,gȯid, ˈzi,-\ *adj* [*zyg-* + *-oid*] **:** of or relating to a zygote **:** ZYGOTIC

zy·golo·bous \ˈzīgə,lōbəs, (ˈ)zīˈgäləbəs\ *adj* [*zyg-* + *lob-* + *-ous*] *of the prostomium of an annelid worm* **:** not set off by a groove from the first true segment

zy·go·ma \zīˈgōmə, zəˈ-\ *n, pl* **zygoma·ta** \-məd·ə\ *also* **zygomas** [NL, fr. Gk *zygōma*, fr. *zygoun* to yoke, join together, fr. *zygon* yoke — more at YOKE] **1 :** ZYGOMATIC ARCH **2 :** ZYGOMATIC PROCESS a **3 :** ZYGOMATIC BONE

[1]**zy·go·mat·ic** \ˈzīgəˈmad·ǀik, ˈzig-, -atǀ, ǀēk\ *adj* [NL *zygomaticus*, fr. *zygomat-, zygoma* + L *-icus* -ic] **:** of, relating to, constituting, or situated in the region of the zygoma and esp. the zygomatic arch as a whole

[2]**zygomatic** \"\ *n* -s **:** ZYGOMATIC BONE

zygomatic arch *n* **:** the arch of bone that extends along the front or side of the skull beneath the orbit, is formed in most mammals by the union of the zygomatic bone with the maxillary bone in front and the zygomatic process of the temporal bone behind, and in lower vertebrates may be modified by the addition of other bones or may be duplicated (as in some reptiles) — compare DIAPSIDA

zygomatic bone *n* **:** a bone of the side of the face below the eye that in mammals forms part of the zygomatic arch and part of the orbit and articulates with the temporal, sphenoid, frontal, and maxillary bones and in birds is slender and rodlike and joins the maxilla and quadratojugal **:** a malar bone — called also *cheekbone*

zygomatic muscle *n* **:** a slender band of muscle on either side of the face arising from the zygomatic bone and inserting into the orbicularis oris and skin at the corner of the mouth

zygomatic nerve *n* **:** a branch of the maxillary nerve that divides into a facial branch supplying the skin of the prominent part of the cheek and a temporal branch supplying the skin of the anterior temporal region — called also respectively *zygomaticofacial nerve, zygomaticotemporal nerve*

zygomatico- *comb form* [NL, fr. *zygomaticus* zygomatic] **:** zygomatic and ⟨*zygomatico*maxillary⟩

zy·go·mat·i·co·auricularis \ˈzīgəˈmad·əkō, ˈzig-+\ *n* [NL, fr. *zygomatico-* + *auricularis*] **:** the anterior auricularis muscle

zy·go·mat·i·co·temporal \"+\ *adj* [*zygomatico-* + *temporal*] **1 :** of, relating to, or uniting the zygomatic arch and the temporal bone ⟨the ~ suture⟩ **2 :** of, relating to, or constituting a foramen in the zygomatic bone that gives passage to the temporal branch of the zygomatic nerve

zygomatic process *n* **:** any of several bony processes that enter into or strengthen the zygomatic arch: as **a :** a long slender process of the temporal or squamosal bone helping to form the zygomatic arch **b :** a process of the zygomatic bone articulating with the temporal bone **c :** a narrow process of the frontal bone articulating with the zygomatic bone **d :** a broad rough process of the maxilla articulating with the zygomatic bone

zygomatic suture *n* **:** the zygomaticotemporal suture

zy·go·mat·i·cus \,zīgəˈmad·əkəs, ,zig-\ *n* -ES [NL, fr. *zygomaticus* zygomatic] **:** ZYGOMATIC MUSCLE

zy·go·max·il·la·re \,zīgə,maksəˈla(a)rē, ,zig-\ *n* -s [NL, fr. *zyg-* + *maxillare*, fr. neut. sing. of L *maxillaris* maxillar] **:** ZYGOMAXILLARY POINT

zy·go·maxillary \ˈzīgō, ˈzigō+\ *adj* [ISV *zyg-* + *maxillary*] **:** of, relating to, or joining the maxilla and zygoma

zygomaxillary point *n* **:** a craniometric point at the lower end of the zygomaticotemporal suture

zy·go·mor·phic \ˈzīgəˈmȯrfik, ˈzig-, -ȯ(ə)f-, -fēk\ *also* **zy·go·mor·phous** \-fəs\ *adj* [*zyg-* + *-morphic*] **:** bilaterally symmetrical; *specif* **:** capable of division into essentially symmetrical halves by only one longitudinal plane passing through the axis ⟨the ~ pea flower⟩ — compare ACTINOMORPHIC — **zy·go·mor·phism** \,==ˈmȯ(r),fizəm\ *n* -s — **zy·go·mor·phy** \ˈ==,mȯrfē\ *n* -ES

zy·go·my·cete \ˈzīgōˈmī,sēt, ˈzig-, -ō,mīˈsēt\ *n* -s [NL *Zygomycetes*] **:** a fungus of the subclass Zygomycetes

zy·go·my·ce·tes \,==,mīˈsēd·ēz\ *n pl, cap* [NL, fr. *zyg-* + *-mycetes*] **:** a subclass of fungi (class Phycomycetes) distinguished from the Oomycetes by gametangia that are morphologically alike and by sexually produced zygospores — see ENTOMOPHTHORALES, MUCORALES — **zy·go·my·ce·tous** \ˈ==,=ˈsēd·əs\ *adj*

zy·go·my·cet·i·dae \,==,=ˈsed·ə,dē\ [NL, fr. *Zygomycetes* + *-idae*] *syn of* ZYGOMYCETES

zy·go·neure \ˈzīgə,n(y)u̇r, ˈzig-\ *n* -s [*zyg-* + NL *neuron*] **:** a connecting neuron

zy·go·phore \ˈzīgə,fō(ə)r, ˈzig-\ *n* -s [*zyg-* + *-phore*] **:** a specialized hyphal branch giving rise to another that forms the gamete in some molds (family Mucoraceae) — **zy·go·phor·ic** \ˈ==ˈfȯrik\ *adj*

zy·go·phy·ce·ae \,zīgəˈfīsē,ē, ,zig-, -ˈfis-\ *n pl, cap* [NL, fr. *zyg-* + *-phyceae*] *in some esp former classifications* **:** a class that comprises greenish unicellular or filamentous algae having conspicuous chromatophores and multiplying by simple division and by conjugation and that includes the desmids and pond scums and usu. also the diatoms — compare ZYGNEMATALES — **zy·go·phy·ceous** \ˈ==ˈfishəs\ *adj*

zy·go·phyl·la·ce·ae \,zīgōfəˈlāsē,ē, ,zig-\ *n pl, cap* [NL, fr. *Zygophyllum*, type genus + *-aceae*] **:** a family of herbs, shrubs, or trees (order Geraniales) distinguished by pinnate or bifoliolate stipulate leaves and axillary pentamerous flowers — see GUAIACUM 1, TRIBULUS — **zy·go·phyl·la·ceous** \ˈ===ˈlāshəs\ *adj*

zy·go·phyl·lum \,zīgəˈfiləm, ,zig-\ *n, cap* [NL, fr. *zyg-* + *-phyllum*] **:** a genus of Old World shrubs (family Zygophyllaceae) that are distinguished mainly by the opposite bifoliate leaves — see BEAN CAPER

zy·gop·tera \zīˈgäptərə\ *n pl, cap* [NL, fr. *zyg-* + *-ptera*] **:** a suborder of Odonata comprising forms that are distinguished from the typical dragonflies by a slenderer elongated body, by narrow equal wings held upright in repose, and by aquatic larvae that have a pair of paddle-shaped tracheal gills at the apex of the abdomen — see DAMSELFLY; compare ANISOPTERA — **zy·gop·ter·an** \-rən\ *adj or n* — **zy·gop·ter·ous** \-rəs\ *adj*

zy·gop·ter·a·ce·ae \zī,gäptəˈrāsē,ē\ *n pl, cap* [NL, fr. *Zygopteris*, type genus + *-aceae*] **:** a family of primitive Paleozoic ferns of Europe and the U.S. having pinnae in two or four series at an angle to the plane of the leaf blade

zy·gop·ter·i·da·ce·ae \-tərəˈdāsē,ē\ [NL, fr. *Zygopterid-, Zygopteris* + *-aceae*] *syn of* ZYGOPTERACEAE

zy·gop·ter·i·des \,zīgäpˈterə,dēz\ [NL] *syn of* ZYGOPTERA

zy·gop·ter·is \zīˈgäptərəs\ *n, cap* [NL, fr. *zyg-* + *-pteris*] **:** the type genus of Zygopteraceae

zy·go·saccharomyces \ˈzīgō, ˈzigō+\ *n, cap* [NL, fr. *zyg-* + *Saccharomyces*] **:** a genus of yeasts (family Saccharomycetaceae) in which ascospore formation is preceded by conjugation and which is often included in *Saccharomyces*

zy·gose \ˈzī,gōs, ˈzi,-\ *adj* [back-formation fr. *zygosis*] **:** of or relating to zygosis

zy·go·sis \zīˈgōsəs, zəˈ-\ *n, pl* **zygo·ses** \-ō,sēz\ [NL, fr. *zyg-* + *-osis*] **:** zygote formation **:** union of gametes **:** CONJUGATION — used esp. in combination; see HETEROZYGOSIS

zy·gos·i·ty \-ˈgäsəd·ē\ *n* -ES [NL *zygosis* + E *-ity*] **:** zygotic quality or characteristics **:** specific inheritance

zy·go·sperm \ˈzīgə, ˈzigə+,-\ *n* [*zyg-* + *sperm*] **:** ZYGOSPORE

zy·go·sphe·nal \ˈzīgəˈsfēnᵊl, ˈzig-\ *adj* **:** of, relating to, or constituting a zygosphene

zy·go·sphene \ˈ==,sfēn\ *n* -s [*zyg-* + Gk *sphēn* wedge — more at SPOON] **:** a median process on the front part of the neural arch of the vertebrae of most snakes and some lizards — see ZYGANTRUM

zy·go·sphere \ˈzīgə, ˈzigə+,-\ *n* [*zyg-* + *sphere*] **:** a plant gamete capable of uniting with a similar one to form a zygospore

zy·go·sporangium *also* **zy·go·sporange** \ˈ==+\ *n, pl* **zygosporangia** *also* **zygosporanges** [NL *zygosporangium*, fr. *zyg-* + *sporangium*] **:** a sporangium in which zygospores are produced

zy·go·spore \ˈ==+,-\ *n* [ISV *zyg-* + *spore*] **:** a plant spore (as in a conjugate alga) that is formed by conjugation of two similar sexual cells, usu. has a thickened and ornamented wall and serves as a resting spore, and ultimately produces the sporophytic phase of the plant — compare OOSPORE — **zy·go·spor·ic** \ˈ==+ˈspȯrik\ *adj*

zy·go·style \ˈzīgə,stīl, ˈzig-\ *n* [*zyg-* + *-style*] **:** the terminal caudal vertebra

zy·go·tax·is \,zīgəˈtaksəs, ,zig-\ *n* [NL, fr. *zyg-* + *-taxis*] **:** the attraction between two zygophores or suspensors that is immediately responsible for conjugation

zy·gote \ˈzī,gōt, ˈzi,-, *usu* -ōd·+V\ *n* -s [Gk *zygōtos* yoked, fr. *zygoun* to yoke, join together, fr. *zygon* yoke — more at YOKE] **:** a cell formed by the union of two gametes **:** a fertilized egg **:** ZYGOSPORE; *broadly* **:** the developing individual produced from such a cell

zy·go·tene \ˈzīgə,tēn, ˈzig-\ *n* [ISV *zyg-* + *-tene;* orig. formed as F *zygotène*] **:** the synaptic stage in meiosis in which homologous chromosomes pair intimately

zy·got·ic \(ˈ)zīˈgäd·ik, zəˈg-\ *adj* **:** of, relating to, or existing as a zygote — often used in combination — **zy·got·i·cal·ly** \-d·ək(ə)lē\ *adv*

zy·go·toid \ˈzīgə,tȯid, ˈzig-\ *n* -s [*zygote* + *-oid*] **:** a multinucleate zygospore

-zy·gous \ˈzīgəs, ˌzəgəs, ˌzēgəs\ *adj comb form* [Gk *-zygos*, fr. *zygon* yoke] **1 :** yoked **:** zygomatic ⟨crypto*zygous*⟩ **2 :** having (such) a zygotic constitution ⟨hetero*zygous*⟩

zy·go·zoospore \ˈzīgō, ˈzigō+\ *n* [*zyg-* + *zoospore*] **:** a motile zygospore

zym- *or* **zymo-** *comb form* [NL, fr. Gk, fr. *zymē* — more at ENZYME] **1 :** leaven **:** concerned with fermentation ⟨*zymo*lysis⟩ ⟨*zymo*phosphate⟩ **2 :** ferment **:** enzyme ⟨*zymo*genesis⟩ ⟨*zymo*sthenic⟩

zy·mase \ˈzī,mās\ *n* -s [ISV *zym-* + *-ase*] **:** a complex of enzymes that brings about glycolysis, that was orig. found in yeasts and bacteria and is also present in higher plants and animals, and that may be separated by filtration or dialysis into the apozymase and the coenzyme diphosphopyridine nucleotide

zyme \ˈzīm\ *n* -s [Gk *zymē* leaven, ferment] **:** FERMENT, ENZYME

-zyme \,zīm\ *n* -s *comb form* [Gk *zymē* leaven] **:** enzyme ⟨histo*zyme*⟩ ⟨lyso*zymes*⟩

zy·min \ˈzīmən\ *n* -s [*zym-* + *-in*] **1 :** ZYME **2 :** pancreatin prepared as a powder

zy·mo·gen \ˈzīməjən, -,jen\ *n* -s [ISV *zym-* + *-gen*] **:** an inactive protein precursor (as trypsinogen or pepsinogen) of an enzyme esp. a proteolytic enzyme that is secreted in living cells and can be activated by catalysis (as by a kinase or an acid) ⟨~ granules⟩ — called also *proenzyme*

zy·mo·gen·ic \ˈ==ˈjenik\ *adj* [in sense 1, fr. *zym-* + *-genic;* in sense 2, fr. *zymogen* + *-ic*] **1 :** producing fermentation **:** AMYLOLYTIC; *broadly* **:** obtaining energy by amylolytic processes **2 :** of or relating to a zymogen

zy·mog·e·nous \(ˈ)zīˈmäjənəs\ *adj* [*zym-* + *-genous*] **:** ZYMOGENIC

zy·mol·o·gy \zīˈmäləjē, -ji\ *n* -ES [NL *zymologia*, fr. Gk *zym-* (fr. *zymē* leaven) + L *-logia* -logy] **:** a science that deals with fermentation

zy·mo·plas·tic \ˈzīmōˈplastik\ *adj* [*zym-* + *-plastic*] **:** participating in the formation of enzymes — compare THROMBOPLASTIC

zy·mo·san \ˈzīmə,san\ *n* -s [*zymosis* + *-an*] **:** a largely carbohydrate fraction of the yeast cell that is used in the assay of properdin

zy·mo·scope \ˈzīmə,skōp\ *n* [ISV *zym-* + *-scope*] **:** an apparatus for determining the fermenting power of yeast by measuring the amount of carbon dioxide evolved from a given quantity of sugar

zy·mo·sis \zīˈmōsəs\ *n, pl* **zymo·ses** \-ō,sēz\ [NL, fr. Gk *zymōsis*, fr. *zymoun* to ferment + *-sis*] **:** FERMENTATION

zy·mos·ter·ol \zīˈmästə,rȯl, -rōl\ *n* [*zym-* + *sterol*] **:** a crystalline unsaturated sterol $C_{27}H_{43}OH$ occurring with ergosterol in yeast fat, resembling ergosterol chemically, and yielding cholestanol on hydrogenation

zy·mos·then·ic \ˈzīməsˈthenik\ *adj* [*zym-* + *sthenic*] **:** strengthening the activity of an enzyme

zy·mot·ic \(ˈ)zīˈmäd·ǀik, -ätǀ, ǀēk\ *adj* [Gk *zymōtikos* causing fermentation, fr. *zymōtos* fermented (verbal of *zymoun* to ferment, fr. *zymē* leaven) + *-ikos* -ic — more at ENZYME] **1 :** of, relating to, causing, or caused by fermentation **2 :** of, relating to, constituting, or causing an infectious or contagious disease — **zy·mot·i·cal·ly** \ǀək(ə)lē, ǀēk-, -li\ *adv*

zy·mur·gy \ˈzī,mərjē\ *n* -ES [*zym-* + *-urgy*] **:** a branch of applied chemistry that deals with fermentation processes (as in wine making or brewing)

zyr·i·an \ˈzirēən\ *n, pl* **zyrian** *or* **zyrians** *cap* [fr. *Zyrian* Autonomous Area (Komi Republic), U.S.S.R.] **1 :** KOMI 1 **2** *also* **zir·yen** \ˈzir,yen, zərˈy-\ [*ziryen* fr. F *zyriène*] **:** the Finno-Ugric language of the Komi people — called also *Komi;* see URALIC LANGUAGES table

zyth·ia \ˈzithēə\ *n, cap* [NL, fr. Gk *zythos* beer, ale (perh. akin to Gk *zymē* leaven) + NL *-ia*] **:** a genus (the type of the family Zythiaceae) of imperfect fungi characterized by white or bright-colored fleshy or waxy pycnidia and hyaline nonseptate spores

zyth·i·a·ce·ae \,zithēˈāsē,ē\ *n pl, cap* [NL, fr. *Zythia*, type genus + *-aceae*] **:** a family of imperfect fungi (order Sphaeropsidales) — see ZYTHIA

zy·thum \ˈzīthəm\ *n* -s [L, fr. Gk *zythos*] **:** beer of ancient times: as **a :** beer of ancient Egypt **b :** beer of the northern peoples

zy·zo·mys \ˈzīzə,mis\ *n, cap* [NL, alter. of *Zygomys*, fr. *zyg-* + *-mys*] **:** a genus of small Australian murid rodents characterized externally by short rounded ears and long slightly tufted tail which is usu. all white and by upper molar teeth in which the outermost of the usual three tubercles constituting the cross crests is practically absent

zyz·zo·ge·ton \,zizəˈjē,tän\ *n, cap* [NL, fr. *Zyzza*, genus of leafhoppers in former classifications (prob. of imit. origin) + Gk *geitōn* neighbor] **:** a genus of large So. American leafhoppers (family Cicadellidae) having the pronotum tuberculate and the front tibiae grooved

Britannica
World Language
Dictionary

17·68

Compiled

under the Direction of the Editorial Staff of

ENCYCLOPÆDIA BRITANNICA, INC.

Chicago · London · Toronto · Geneva · Sydney · Tokyo · Manila

THE UNIVERSITY OF CHICAGO

BRITANNICA WORLD LANGUAGE DICTIONARY
IS PUBLISHED WITH THE ADVICE
AND CONSULTATION OF THE
FACULTIES OF THE UNIVERSITY OF CHICAGO

Britannica
World Language Dictionary

BRITANNICA WORLD LANGUAGE DICTIONARY

IS COMPILED UNDER THE DIRECTION OF THE

EDITORIAL STAFF OF ENCYCLOPÆDIA BRITANNICA

Warren E. Preece
THE GENERAL EDITOR

English List Adviser

Mitford M. Mathews, Ph.D.
Former Editor, Dictionary Department
University Press
University of Chicago

Editor of Commercial and Banking
Terms in All Seven Languages

Frank Gaynor

French Editor

Norman B. Spector, Ph.D.
Assistant Professor, Department of
Romance Languages
University of Chicago

German and Yiddish Editor

Uriel Weinreich, Ph.D.
Former Professor of Linguistics and
Yiddish Studies
on the Atran Chair
Columbia University
New York, New York

German Editor (in part)

J. Collins Orr, M.A.
Associate Professor, Department of
Modern Languages
Purdue University
Lafayette, Indiana

Italian Editor

Louis R. Rossi, Ph.D.
Assistant Professor, Department of
Romance Languages
Northwestern University
Evanston, Illinois

Spanish Editor

Harry Edward Hausser, Ph.D.

Swedish Editor

Karin Franzen, Fil. Kand.
Lecturer in Swedish
University of Chicago

General Adviser

David G. Speer, D. ès L.
Associate Professor, Department of
Modern Languages
Purdue University
Lafayette, Indiana

Coordinators

Pauline Thorson Johnsen
AND
Ruth Soffer Marquis

Editorial Advisers and Consultants

Grateful acknowledgment is made to the following faculty members
of universities and colleges whose detailed suggestions represented an important contribution
to the original edition of the Britannica World Language Dictionary.

Aldrich, Clide E.
(*Consultant in* FRENCH)
Head, Department of Modern Foreign Languages
Butler University
Indianapolis, Indiana

Anderson, Vernon L.
(*Consultant in* GERMAN)
Associate Professor, Department of Languages
Brigham Young University
Provo, Utah

Atkins, Stuart
(*Consultant in* GERMAN)
Department of Foreign Languages
University of California
Santa Barbara, California

Bailey, Richard E.
(*Consultant in* FRENCH)
Professor of Foreign Languages and Chairman of
Humanities
Oklahoma State University
Stillwater, Oklahoma

Banner, James Worth
(*Consultant in* SPANISH)
Former Director, Foreign Language Studies
Rollins College
Winter Park, Florida

Bates, Arthur Seymour
(*Consultant in* FRENCH)
Professor of Modern Languages
Sweet Briar College
Sweet Briar, Virginia

Bieghler, Edward Wilson
(*Consultant in* SPANISH, FRENCH)
Head, Department of Foreign Languages
State College
Indiana, Pennsylvania

Bieter, Reverend Frederic A.
(*Consultant in* FRENCH, GERMAN)
Chairman, Department of Foreign Languages
College of St. Thomas
St. Paul, Minnesota

Bigge, Adolph E.
(*Consultant in* GERMAN)
Former Head, Department of Modern Foreign
Languages
University of Kentucky
Lexington, Kentucky

Bolelli, Tristano

(*Consultant in* ITALIAN)
Professor, Department of Linguistics
University of Pisa
Pisa, Italy

Bolinger, Dwight L.

(*Consultant in* SPANISH)
Professor of Spanish
University of Colorado
Boulder, Colorado

Bonno, Gabriel

(*Consultant in* FRENCH)
Professor of French
University of California at Los Angeles
Los Angeles, California

Braasch, Theodor William

(*Consultant in* GERMAN)
Professor Emeritus and Former Head of Department of German
Western Reserve University
Cleveland, Ohio

Brandt, Thomas O.

(*Consultant in* GERMAN)
Professor and Chairman of Department of German
Colorado College
Colorado Springs, Colorado

Brenninger, Ralph A.

(*Consultant in* FRENCH, GERMAN)
Professor of Foreign Languages
Fresno State College
Fresno, California

Brett, Lewis Edward

(*Consultant in* SPANISH)
Professor and Chairman of Department of Romance Languages
Queens College
Flushing, New York

Bricca, John Francis

(*Consultant in* ITALIAN, SPANISH)
Former Professor of Spanish and Chairman of Foreign Language Department
Loyola University
Los Angeles, California

Brunell, Robert H.

(*Consultant in* FRENCH, SPANISH, GERMAN, ITALIAN)
Professor of Romance Languages and English
Auburn Community College
Auburn, New York

Buchanan, Charles D.

(*Consultant in* GERMAN)
Professor of German
Alfred University
Alfred, New York

Burgess, Robert M.

(*Consultant in* FRENCH)
Professor of French and Chairman of the Department of Foreign Languages
Montana State University
Missoula, Montana

Cannon, Harry S.

(*Consultant in* GERMAN)
Former Head, Modern Languages
Montana State College
Bozeman, Montana

Causey, James Young

(*Consultant in* SPANISH)
Professor of Spanish and Chairman of the Department of Spanish
Davidson College
Davidson, North Carolina

Chisholm, Hulda Hepperle

(*Consultant in* GERMAN)
Chairman of the Language Arts Division
Ventura College
Ventura, California

Clagett, Marjorie E.

(*Consultant in* FRENCH)
Teacher of French
Western State College
Bowling Green, Kentucky

Colombo, Primitivo

(*Consultant in* FRENCH, ITALIAN)
Professor of Modern Languages
Duquesne University
Pittsburgh, Pennsylvania

Condoyannis, George E.

(*Consultant in* GERMAN, FRENCH, SPANISH, ITALIAN)
Associate Professor of Modern Languages
Saint Peter's College
Jersey City, New Jersey

Corbière, Anthony Sylvain

(*Consultant in* FRENCH, SPANISH, ITALIAN)
Professor and Head of Department of Romance Languages
Muhlenberg College
Allentown, Pennsylvania

Cornell, Kenneth Hall

(*Consultant in* SPANISH)
Professor, Modern Language Department
St. Bonaventure University
St. Bonaventure, New York

Cress, Allan M.

(*Consultant in* GERMAN)
Associate Professor and Head of Department
University of Wichita
Wichita, Kansas

Crow, John A.

(*Consultant in* SPANISH)
Department of Spanish and Portuguese
University of California at Los Angeles
Los Angeles, California

Dahl, Leif Christopher

(*Consultant in* FRENCH)
Dean of Westminster College and Chairman of Department of Romance Languages
Westminster College
Fulton, Missouri

Daus, Federico A.

(*Consultant in* SPANISH, FRENCH)
Department of Philosophy and Letters, Institute of Geography
University of Salvador
Buenos Aires, Argentina

Dawes, Melissa Martin

(*Consultant in* SPANISH)
Professor and Head of Department of Modern Languages
Oregon State College
Corvallis, Oregon

Dickman, Adolphe Jacques

(*Consultant in* FRENCH)
Professor and Head, Department of Modern and Classical Languages
University of Wyoming
Laramie, Wyoming

Diez de Medina, Eduardo

(*Consultant in* SPANISH)
Director de la Academia Boliviana de la Lengua
La Paz, Bolivia

Dowling, John Clarkson

(*Consultant in* SPANISH)
Professor and Chairman of the Department of Spanish and Portuguese
Indiana University
Bloomington, Indiana

Downs, Lynwood G.

(*Consultant in* GERMAN)
Former Professor Emeritus of German
University of Minnesota
Minneapolis, Minnesota

Duncan, Robert Manly

(*Consultant in* SPANISH)
Chairman, Department of Modern and Classical Languages
University of New Mexico
Albuquerque, New Mexico

Dunnington, G. Waldo

(*Consultant in* GERMAN)
Professor of German
Northwestern State College
Natchitoches, Louisiana

Ehrlich, Gerd W.

(*Consultant in* GERMAN, FRENCH)
Social Science and Language Teacher
Essex Community College
Baltimore, Maryland

Elkins, Eugene

(*Consultant in* FRENCH)
Associate Professor and Head of Department of French
Cornell College
Mt. Vernon, Iowa

Ellert, Frederick C.

(*Consultant in* GERMAN)
Chairman, Department of German-Russian
University of Massachusetts
Amherst, Massachusetts

Elliott, Robert W.

(*Consultant in* FRENCH)
Former Professor of French and Chairman
Division of Languages
Bates College
Lewiston, Maine

Fabien, René

(*Consultant in* GERMAN)
Professor of German and Director of the Department
John Carroll University
Cleveland, Ohio

Fitch, Girdler B.

(*Consultant in* FRENCH, SPANISH)
Professor and Head of Department of Modern Languages
The Citadel
Charleston, South Carolina

Forkey, Leo O.

(*Consultant in* FRENCH, SPANISH)
Chairman, Department of Foreign Languages
Drake University
Des Moines, Iowa

Frank, Julius

(*Consultant in* GERMAN)
Assistant Professor of German
Fairleigh Dickinson University,
Teaneck Campus
Teaneck, New Jersey

French, Howard P.

(*Consultant in* GERMAN)
Department of Foreign Languages
Southern Illinois University
Carbondale, Illinois

Funke, Erich

(*Consultant in* GERMAN)
Professor and Head, Department of German
State University of Iowa
Iowa City, Iowa

Gauthier, Reverend Joseph D., S.J.

(*Consultant in* FRENCH, SPANISH, ITALIAN, GERMAN)
Chairman, Modern Language Department
Boston College
Chestnut Hill, Massachusetts

Gilbert, Donald M.

(*Consultant in* FRENCH, SPANISH)
Former Professor of Modern Languages
Albion College
Albion, Michigan

Gilbert, Russell Wieder

(Consultant in GERMAN)
Professor of German
Susquehanna University
Selinsgrove, Pennsylvania

Gowa, Ferdinand H.

(Consultant in GERMAN)
Professor of German and Chairman of the Department of Modern Foreign Languages
Fisk University
Nashville, Tennessee

Greene, Edward J. H.

(Consultant in FRENCH)
Head, Department of Modern Languages
University of Alberta
Edmonton, Alberta, Canada

Grimm, John C. M.

(Consultant in FRENCH, SPANISH)
Former Chairman, Department of Modern Languages
Dickinson College
Carlisle, Pennsylvania

Guinagh, Kevin

(Consultant in SPANISH)
Head, Foreign Language Department
Eastern Illinois University
Charleston, Illinois

Hale, Clarence B.

(Consultant in FRENCH)
Professor of Greek and Chairman of Foreign Language Department
Wheaton College
Wheaton, Illinois

Harrison, Benjamin I.

(Consultant in FRENCH)
Professor and Chairman of Department of Modern Languages
University of Mississippi
University, Mississippi

Hartman, Alexander P.

(Consultant in GERMAN)
Professor of French and German and Head, Department of Modern Foreign Languages
State University of South Dakota
Vermillion, South Dakota

Haugen, Einar I.

(Consultant in SWEDISH)
Thompson Professor of Scandinavian Languages
University of Wisconsin
Madison, Wisconsin

Haydon, Charles E.

(General Consultant)
Department of Foreign Languages
Pacific Lutheran College
Tacoma, Washington

Hilborn, Harry Warren

(Consultant in SPANISH)
Professor and Head of Department of Spanish
Queen's University
Kingston, Ontario, Canada

Hinkle, Lawrence Earl

(Consultant in FRENCH, GERMAN, SPANISH)
Former Professor and Head of Department of Modern Languages
North Carolina State College
Raleigh, North Carolina

Holzmann, Albert W.

(Consultant in GERMAN)
Professor of German Language and Literature and Chairman, Department of German
Rutgers University
New Brunswick, New Jersey

Hughes, John P.

(Consultant in GERMAN, FRENCH, SPANISH)
Professor of Modern Languages
St. Peter's College
Jersey City, New Jersey

Indovina, Josephine Lucille

(Consultant in ITALIAN)
Instructor of Italian and Chairman of Foreign Language Department
Los Angeles City College
Los Angeles, California

Inserni, Frank M.

(Consultant in SPANISH)
Assistant Professor, Department of Romance Languages
Clark University
Worcester, Mass.

Irvin, Leon P.

(Consultant in FRENCH)
Chairman, Department of Romance Languages
Miami University
Oxford, Ohio

Janisse, Denis Raymond

(Consultant in FRENCH)
Professor of French and Chairman of the Department of Modern Languages
University of Detroit
Detroit, Michigan

Johnson, Harvey Leroy

(Consultant in SPANISH)
Professor and Chairman of Department of Spanish and Portuguese
Indiana University
Bloomington, Indiana

Johnson, William Devers

(Consultant in SPANISH)
Professor and Chairman, Department of Languages
Texas College of Arts and Industries
Kingsville, Texas

Johnson, William E.

(Consultant in SPANISH, FRENCH)
Professor of Languages
Central Missouri State College
Warrensburg, Missouri

Jordan, Gilbert J.

(Consultant in GERMAN)
Professor and Chairman of Department of German
Southern Methodist University
Dallas, Texas

Kalbfleisch, Herbert K.

(Consultant in GERMAN)
Professor of German
University of Western Ontario
London, Ontario, Canada

Keating, L. Clark

(Consultant in FRENCH, SPANISH)
Chairman, College of Arts and Sciences, Department of Modern Foreign Languages
University of Kentucky
Lexington, Kentucky

Kehlenbeck, Alfred P.

(Consultant in GERMAN)
Professor and Head of Department of Modern Languages
Iowa State University
Ames, Iowa

Kestenberg, Louis

(Consultant in GERMAN)
Professor of History
University of Houston
Houston, Texas

Kloeckner, Emil Paul

(Consultant in GERMAN, FRENCH)
Former Chairman of the Department of German
St. Johns University
Brooklyn, New York

Krauss, Paul Gerhardt

(Consultant in GERMAN)
Department of German
Ohio University
Athens, Ohio

Lafeuille, Germaine

(Consultant in FRENCH)
Professor of French
Wellesley College
Wellesley, Massachusetts

Langford, Walter M.

(Consultant in SPANISH)
Department of Modern Languages
University of Notre Dame
Notre Dame, Indiana

Leliepvre, Madeleine

(Consultant in FRENCH)
Former Professor of French and Head of Modern Language Department
St. Lawrence University
Canton, New York

Lemke, Victor J.

(Consultant in GERMAN)
Professor and Chairman of German Department
West Virginia University
Morgantown, West Virginia

Lieberman, Julius

(Consultant in GERMAN)
Associate Professor and Head of German Department
Marshall College
Huntington, West Virginia

Liptzin, Sol

(Consultant in YIDDISH)
Professor, Department of Germanic and Slavic Languages
City College
New York, New York

Loughridge, Rachel

(Consultant in FRENCH, SPANISH)
Professor, Department of Foreign Languages
Central Michigan University
Mount Pleasant, Michigan

Ludlum, Charlotte Perry

(Consultant in SPANISH)
Professor and Chairman, Department of Ancient Languages, and Chairman, Department of Romance Languages
Berea College
Berea, Kentucky

McCluney, Daniel C., Jr.

(Consultant in GERMAN)
Head of Department of German
University of Illinois
Chicago, Illinois

McGee, Sidney L.

(Consultant in FRENCH)
Chairman, Department of Foreign Languages
Tennessee Polytechnic Institute
Cookeville, Tennessee

McKinney, Mary Emma

(Consultant in GERMAN)
Professor of Classics Emeritus
Albion College
Albion, Michigan

McLean, Malcolm D.

(Consultant in SPANISH)
Former Assistant Professor of Romance Languages and Chairman, Division of Foreign Languages and Literatures
University of Arkansas
Fayetteville, Arkansas

McMahon, John Frederick

(Consultant in GERMAN)
Professor of German
Lawrence College
Appleton, Wisconsin

McNamee, Lawrence F.

(Consultant in GERMAN)
Professor of English and German
East Texas State College
Commerce, Texas

Magoon, Wallace H.

(Consultant in GERMAN, FRENCH)
Professor and Head of Foreign Language Department
Ball State Teachers College
Muncie, Indiana

Manchester, Paul T.

(Consultant in SPANISH)
Chairman, Department of Romance Languages
Vanderbilt University
Nashville, Tennessee

Matenko, Percy
(*Consultant in* GERMAN, YIDDISH)
Professor of German
Brooklyn College
Brooklyn, New York

Melz, Christian F.
(*Consultant in* GERMAN, SPANISH)
Professor of Foreign Languages
University of Nevada
Reno, Nevada

Mezzacappa, Antonio Libero
(*Consultant in* FRENCH, ITALIAN, SPANISH)
Professor and Chairman, Department of Modern
Languages
Northeastern University
Boston, Massachusetts

Minn, Jay Paul
(*Consultant in* FRENCH)
Assistant Professor, Department of Modern
Languages
Purdue University
West Lafayette, Indiana

Moehlenbrock, Arthur H.
(*Consultant in* GERMAN)
Professor of German
Furman University
Greenville, South Carolina

Moraud, Marcel Ian
(*Consultant in* FRENCH)
Burgess Professor of Romance Languages
Hamilton College
Clinton, New York

Morgan, William I.
(*Consultant in* GERMAN)
Associate Professor of German
University of North Dakota
Grand Forks, North Dakota

Muehsam, Gerd
(*Consultant in* GERMAN)
Associate Librarian
Cooper Union
New York, New York

Muller, Siegfried H.
(*Consultant in* GERMAN)
Professor and Chairman, Department of German
Adelphi College
Garden City, New York

Neuse, Werner
(*Consultant in* GERMAN)
Professor and Director of the German School
Middlebury College
Middlebury, Vermont

Newby, Lee Clinton
(*Consultant in* FRENCH, GERMAN, SPANISH)
Professor and Head of Modern Language Depart-
ment
State College
San José, California

Nylander, Ivan
(*Consultant in* SWEDISH)
Assistant Professor
University of Minnesota, Duluth
Duluth, Minnesota

Oelschläger, Victor R. B.
(*Consultant in* SPANISH, FRENCH, GERMAN,
ITALIAN)
Professor of Spanish and Head, Department of
Modern Languages
Florida State University
Tallahassee, Florida

Owens, J. Henry
(*Consultant in* FRENCH)
Head of the Department of Foreign Languages
Eastern Michigan University
Ypsilanti, Michigan

Pauck, Charles E.
(*Consultant in* GERMAN)
Professor of German
Berea College
Berea, Kentucky

Peacock, Vera L.
(*Consultant in* FRENCH, SPANISH)
Chairman, Department of Foreign Languages
Southern Illinois University
Carbondale, Illinois

Pelmont, Raoul A.
(*Consultant in* FRENCH)
Cultural Attaché
French Embassy
New York, New York

Price, Erwin Hugh
(*Consultant in* FRENCH)
Former Chairman, Modern Languages Department
Mississippi State University
State College, Mississippi

Pucci, Dominic Louis
(*Consultant in* SPANISH, ITALIAN)
Professor and Head of Department of Spanish and
Italian Languages and Literatures
Wayne State University
Detroit, Michigan

Richardson, Leonard T.
(*Consultant in* FRENCH, SPANISH, ITALIAN)
Head of Departments of Ancient Languages and
Modern Languages
Youngstown University
Youngstown, Ohio

Richardson, Ruth
(*Consultant in* SPANISH)
Head of Spanish Department
Adelphi College
Garden City, New York

Richter, Fritz K.
(*Consultant in* GERMAN, FRENCH)
Professor of Language and Literature
Illinois Institute of Technology
Chicago, Illinois

Rickey, Harry Wynn
(*Consultant in* FRENCH)
Chairman, Department of French
Southern Methodist University
Dallas, Texas

Robinson, Henry L.
(*Consultant in* FRENCH)
Professor and Chairman of Department of French
Baylor University
Waco, Texas

Root, Winthrop H.
(*Consultant in* GERMAN)
Professor of German
Williams College
Williamstown, Massachusetts

Sandri, Luigi D.
(*Consultant in* ITALIAN)
Chairman, Modern Language Department
University of San Francisco
San Francisco, California

Saxe, Nathaniel Edgar
(*Consultant in* FRENCH, GERMAN)
Head, Department of Modern Languages
Washburn University
Topeka, Kansas

Scaglione, Aldo D.
(*Consultant in* ITALIAN)
Associate Professor of Italian
University of California
Berkeley, California

Schirokauer, Arno C.
(*Consultant in* GERMAN)
Professor of German
The Johns Hopkins University
Baltimore, Maryland

Schneider, Henry III
(*Consultant in* GERMAN)
Professor of German Language and Literature,
and Chairman of German Department
Ripon College
Ripon, Wisconsin

Schuster, Christian
(*Consultant in* GERMAN)
Associate Professor of German
Temple University
Philadelphia, Pennsylvania

Sharton, Felix Edward
(*Consultant in* GERMAN)
Former Head, Department of Germanic Languages
and Literature
Westminster College
Fulton, Missouri

Shiver, Sam M.
(*Consultant in* GERMAN)
Professor and Chairman of Department of
German
Emory University
Atlanta, Georgia

Shurter, Robert L.
(*Consultant in* GERMAN)
Director of the Division of Humanities and Social
Studies
Case Institute of Technology
Cleveland, Ohio

Sideleau, Reverend Canon Arthur
(*Consultant in* FRENCH)
Former Dean of the Faculty of Letters
University of Montreal
Montreal, Quebec, Canada

Sinnema, John R.
(*Consultant in* GERMAN)
Professor of German
Baldwin-Wallace College
Berea, Ohio

Smith, W. Vernon
(*Consultant in* SPANISH)
Former Professor of Spanish
Sacramento Junior College
Sacramento, California

Spagnoli, John J.
(*Consultant in* FRENCH)
Professor and Chairman of Department of Mod-
ern Languages
Brooklyn College
Brooklyn, New York

Speroni, Charles
(*Consultant in* ITALIAN)
Professor of Italian
University of California
Los Angeles, California

Spiker, Claude C.
(*Consultant in* FRENCH)
Emeritus Professor of Romance Languages
West Virginia University
Morgantown, West Virginia

Steel, Eric M.
(*Consultant in* FRENCH)
Professor of French
State University of New York
Brockport, New York

Steinhauer, Harry
(*Consultant in* GERMAN)
Professor of German
University of California
Santa Barbara, California

Stephens, Stephen De Witt
(*General Consultant*)
Former Professor of English and Director of the
Division of Humanities
Newark College of Rutgers University
Newark, New Jersey

Stine, Dorothy Pearce
(*Consultant in* FRENCH, SPANISH)
Head, Department of Modern Languages
Lamar State College of Technology
Beaumont, Texas

Stonecipher, Sibyl
(*Consultant in* GERMAN)
Associate Professor, Department of Foreign
Languages
Western Kentucky State College
Bowling Green, Kentucky

Stoudemire, Sterling A.

(*Consultant in* SPANISH)
Professor of Spanish and Chairman of the Department of Romance Languages
University of North Carolina
Chapel Hill, North Carolina

Strem, George G.

(*Consultant in* FRENCH, GERMAN)
Professor Emeritus and Former Coordinator of Foreign Language Programs
Chico State College
Chico, California

Swain, James O.

(*Consultant in* SPANISH, FRENCH)
Former Chairman, Department of Romance Languages
University of Tennessee
Knoxville, Tennessee

Taras, Anthony F.

(*Consultant in* FRENCH, SPANISH)
Associate Professor and Chairman, Department of Modern Languages
Ithaca College
Ithaca, New York

Vail, Curtis C. D.

(*Consultant in* GERMAN)
Former Professor and Executive Officer of Germanic Languages and Literature
University of Washington
Seattle, Washington

Virtanen, Reino

(*Consultant in* FRENCH, GERMAN)
Professor of Romance Languages
University of Nebraska
Lincoln, Nebraska

Vollmer, Clement

(*Consultant in* GERMAN)
Emeritus Professor and Chairman, Department of Germanic Languages and Literature
Duke University
Durham, North Carolina

Waldinger, Ernst

(*Consultant in* GERMAN)
Professor of German
Skidmore College
Saratoga Springs, New York

Wann, Harry Vincent

(*Consultant in* FRENCH, SPANISH, GERMAN)
Former Head of Foreign Language Department
Indiana State Teachers College
Terre Haute, Indiana

Weinstein, Leo

(*Consultant in* FRENCH, YIDDISH)
Associate Professor of French
Stanford University
Stanford, California

Wicks, Charles Beaumont

(*Consultant in* FRENCH)
Professor and Head of Department of Romance Languages
University of Alabama
University, Alabama

Wiese, Herbert Frank

(*Consultant in* GERMAN)
Chairman, Department of Foreign Languages
Coe College
Cedar Rapids, Iowa

Will, Samuel F.

(*Consultant in* FRENCH)
Chairman, French and Italian Department
Indiana University
Bloomington, Indiana

Williamson, Edward

(*Consultant in* ITALIAN)
Chairman, Department of Romance Languages
Wesleyan University
Middletown, Connecticut

Winchell, Homer Best

(*Consultant in* SPANISH, FRENCH)
Professor, Department of Foreign Languages
United States Naval Academy
Annapolis, Maryland

Wolfe, Warren J.

(*Consultant in* FRENCH, SPANISH)
Former Professor and Chairman of Languages
University of Idaho
Moscow, Idaho

Woolket, Joseph J.

(*Consultant in* SPANISH)
Professor and Head of Department of Modern Languages
A. and M. College of Texas
College Station, Texas

Woolsey, Arthur Wallace

(*Consultant in* SPANISH)
Professor and Director, Department of Foreign Languages
Texas Woman's University
Denton, Texas

Wormhoudt, Arthur

(*Consultant in* FRENCH, GERMAN)
Professor of Language and Literature
William Penn College
Oskaloosa, Iowa

Zeydel, Edwin H.

(*Consultant in* GERMAN)
Former Professor and Head of Department of Germanic and Slavic Languages and Literature; Fellow of the Graduate School
University of Cincinnati, Cincinnati, Ohio

Zollinger, (Mrs.) Anna R.

(*Consultant in* GERMAN, FRENCH)
Associate Professor of German
Brooklyn College
Brooklyn, New York

Contents

Plan of the
Britannica World Language Dictionary

This work brings together the leading languages of the Western world for the purpose of quick translation and reference. English and six other modern languages now appear side by side in one convenient place.

The *Britannica World Language Dictionary* has two principal parts. Part I, beginning on page 2681 of this volume, is a list of common English words, with their translations into the six other languages—French, German, Italian, Spanish, Swedish and Yiddish. Besides the word list proper, the following special material is in Part I: letters of the alphabet, cardinal numbers, ordinal numbers, days of the week, months of the year and common first names.

Part II, beginning on page 2777 of this volume, is an almost exact reverse of Part I. It consists of six separate sections—an alphabetical word list for each of the six other languages, with the pronunciation of each word and the English translation of each. The same special lists that appear in Part I (alphabets, numbers, days of the week, etc.) also appear in Part II, but realphabetized according to the particular language. Each of the six language sections also contains a list of useful expressions, an explanation of general grammar and a key to pronunciation.

Objectives of the Dictionary

This Dictionary was conceived by Robert C. Preble, former president of Encyclopædia Britannica, Inc., to achieve the following editorial objectives:

1. To stimulate a more active interest in modern languages, particularly among the young.

2. To encourage the casual reader to look up common words in other languages that he sees in print.

3. To enable the reader to pronounce such words, understandably at least.

4. To provide an elementary understanding of grammatical variations and basic sentence construction.

5. Generally, to provide an acceptable multilanguage dictionary for home and office use of those persons, young and old, who have had little or no formal instruction in languages other than English.

The Seven Languages

It is estimated that the seven languages of the *Britannica World Language Dictionary* are spoken by about 700,000,000 persons—roughly a fifth of the total world population. Considering only the Western world, however, these 700,000,000 comprise three-quarters of the population. Thus the Dictionary may prove to be an instrument of communication between the various parts of the Western world—a major section of today's free world. Since it was necessary to limit the Dictionary to English and six other languages, those selected were representative of the largest population groups. An arbitrary selection of languages in widest international usage and restricted to the Western world obviously omitted Chinese, Japanese and Russian (including languages of the satellite countries).

A word about the inclusion of Yiddish: to our knowledge, this is the first time Yiddish words have appeared in dictionary form in Roman characters so that they are understandable to all who read English.

Selection of the Word List

The English word list in this Dictionary is the product of detailed studies of word frequency to determine the most commonly used words of the language. The initial lists were amplified by the English consultants and by each of the editors for the six other languages. Special lists—dealing with common business terms, common household and personal use words such as "air conditioning" and "ball-point pen"—were also incorporated into the main list, which after many more testings became the basic list of the Dictionary—the most frequently used words of the English language.

The selection did not end here, however. Next it was necessary to determine the commonest meanings of the words selected (there are more than 100 separate meanings in English for the verb "to run," for example). One of the sources used for this purpose was the monumental *Semantic Count of English Words* by Edward L. Thorndike and Irving Lorge. Selection of the commonest meanings of each word in the English list thus permitted parallel translations in Part I into each of the six other languages. For each of the latter languages, too, detailed semantic studies were made to determine the commonest word equivalent. In this work the editors also acknowledge their debt to Miss Helen S. Eaton, whose semantic frequency lists for French, German and Spanish were pioneers in the field.

Finally, the first edition was placed in the hands of 155 prominent language educators of the United States and other countries (see pp. 2666–2670 for their names). Their many helpful suggestions were incorporated into the final work.

Pronunciation

Instead of a formal system of phonetics, the editors of this Dictionary adopted one of simplicity and usefulness for a beginning or casual reader. Where possible, pronunciation is indicated by English words or syllables that can be pronounced in only one way. Thus the French *précis* is rendered "*pray*-SEE," which no English-speaking person can possibly mispronounce. The editors purposely avoided the adoption of strict rules in this connection, however, and did not hesitate to violate consistency whenever that seemed best to serve their purposes of simplicity.

Syllables are divided by hyphens, and the accented syllable is always in small capital letters; the others are in lower-case italic letters. Only one diacritical mark, the umlaut, is used: *ü* in French, German and Swedish to indicate a sound for which there is no written English equivalent—the *ee* pronounced with round lips; *ö* is also used in German and Swedish to indicate the *i* sound as in "fir." A ligature, ‿, is used to bind into one syllable sounds whose separate values might otherwise be lost. The German word *Knie*, for instance, is rendered "K‿NEE," to call attention to the fact that the K is pronounced, not silent as in the English word "knee."

That, in brief, is the complete system of "phonetics" used in this Dictionary.

No attempt was made to give the finer shades of pronunciation. The objective was simply this: to give the pronunciation of each word in such a way that *a person totally unfamiliar with the language can be understood by one who speaks the language fluently.* Whenever the consultants were in doubt, they tested alternate pronunciations on groups of persons to find which specific one seemed best.

Obviously, the simplified system used in this Dictionary cannot be used by readers to attain any degree of perfection in pronouncing an unfamiliar language. Even the most complex system of phonetics cannot lead to really adequate pronunciation. The finer tones and overtones of another language can be mastered only after years of aural contact with it.

In the case of varying pronunciations of the languages represented in this Dictionary, the editors have used the form which those of the western world are most likely to meet. Thus, the Castilian pronunciation of Spanish (*th* sound for *z* and *c*, etc.) was discarded in favor of the pronunciation of Latin America. Standard German is used throughout, as is the "Parisian"

French. The Yiddish pronunciation is "American," stemming directly from the northeast European area (White Russia, Lithuania and northeastern Poland).

The Grammar Sections

A unique feature of this Dictionary is the inclusion of grammar sections with each of the six lists of Part II. Many dictionaries of modern languages have only brief explanations of grammatical principles, or none at all. This definitely limits the usefulness of such dictionaries. They give verbs, for example, only in the infinitive form and do not take the trouble to point out any of the numerous inflections that occur in any language. They tell one how to say "to eat," but not "I ate" or "I ate the apples."

The *Britannica World Language Dictionary* treats the grammars of the six languages of Part II in fairly extended form and in parallel arrangement so that comparison is made as easy as possible. Starting with the simplest aspects of grammar—the articles and nouns—each of the grammar sections progresses to the more difficult parts of speech—pronouns, adjectives and verbs. The verb section tells how to conjugate all the regular verbs of each language in the principal moods and tenses, then how to conjugate the irregular verbs.

The editors hope that by presenting these grammar sections with the word lists they may encourage readers to attempt simple translations from one language to another and to form short sentences in one or more of the languages.

In this connection readers are referred to the special section "Helpful Hints in Use of the Britannica World Language Dictionary," beginning on the following page.

Credits

In addition to the staff members named on the editors' page of this Dictionary (p. 2666), the editors wish to express their appreciation of the contributions of Newton R. Calhoun of the Winnetka, Ill., public schools, who did extensive work in directing use of the excellent U.S. Army manuals on language during World War II. These manuals pioneered in the use of simplified pronunciation and discarded all but a few phonetic symbols. The editors are likewise indebted to William Nicoll, who designed the typography; also to Mrs. Gertrude Anderson, Mrs. Ruth D. Asch, Marie F. Chiaro, Mrs. Mae H. MacKay, Mrs. Harriet Milburn, Mrs. Kathleen Ray and the many other regular staff members of the editorial department of *Encyclopædia Britannica* who helped prepare the final manuscript of this Dictionary for the printer.

LIST OF ABBREVIATIONS

acc.	accusative	dat.	dative	indic.	indicative	perf.	perfect
acctg.	accounting	def.	definite	inf.	infinitive	photog.	photography
adj.	adjective	dem.	demonstrative	intens.	intensive	physiol.	physiology
adv.	adverb	econ.	economics	interj.	interjection	pl.	plural
agric.	agriculture	educ.	education	interrog.	interrogative	pol.	political
anat.	anatomy	elec.	electricity	irr.	irregular	poss.	possessive
anthrop.	anthropology	equiv.	equivalent	Jud.	Judaism	prep.	preposition
arith.	arithmetic	f., fem.	feminine	m., masc.	masculine	pres.	present
art.	article	ff.	following	math.	mathematics	print.	printing
astron.	astronomy	fin.	finance	mech.	mechanical	pron.	pronoun
auto.	automotive	gen.	genitive	med.	medicine	punct.	punctuation
biol.	biology	geog.	geography	mil.	military	rad.	radio
bot.	botany	geom.	geometry	min.	mineral	rel.	relative, religion
bus.	business	govt.	government	mus.	music	sing.	singular
cf.	compare	gram.	grammar	n.	neuter, noun	subj.	subjunctive
chem.	chemistry	imp.	impersonal	nom.	nominative	transp.	transportation
cond.	conditional	imperf.	imperfect	nn.	nonneuter	v.	verb
conj.	conjunction	indef.	indefinite	obj.	object	zool.	zoology

Helpful Hints on Use of the Britannica World Language Dictionary

The dictionary is a tool. Like any tool, the *Britannica World Language Dictionary* has its capabilities and its limitations. It must be handled correctly in order to produce satisfactory results. Let us see what this Dictionary is capable of doing for you.

Finding Translations

First of all, the Dictionary can provide you with the equivalents of the commonest words in English and six important languages.

Let us suppose that you want to know what the word for "table" is in another language. Look for the word "table" in the list of words of Part I (*English to Other Languages* section, beginning on page 2681). There you will find that "table" is most commonly *table* in French, *Tisch* in German, *tavola* in Italian, *mesa* in Spanish, *bord* in Swedish and *tish* in Yiddish.

Building Sentences

But suppose you are not satisfied merely with knowing the equivalents of English words and wish to say something with those words. The problem becomes more involved. Translation of ideas from one language into another is not merely a question of taking words and setting them into the other tongue. Word order and grammatical rules differ from one language to another. For this reason a grammar section has been included for each of the languages. In order to express an idea in a given language we must consult the grammar section for that language. Let us take an example:

We have already looked up the words for "table." We have *table*, *Tisch*, *tavola*, *mesa*, *bord* and *tish*. But we cannot do anything with these words. How do we say "the table"? The grammar sections will help here. We see in the word lists that in French *table* is feminine, in German *Tisch* is masculine, in Italian *tavola* is feminine, in Spanish *mesa* is feminine, in Swedish *bord* is neuter and in Yiddish *tish* is masculine. Reference to the grammar pages will show us that in French "the," feminine, is *la*, that in German "the," masculine, is *der, des, dem, den*, according to the case of the noun it modifies. Let us choose *der*, the subject form. In Italian and Spanish, feminine "the" is again *la*. In Swedish "the," neuter, is *-et* attached to the end of the noun. In Yiddish "the" as a masculine subject form is *der*. Thus we have found that we can say "the table" in six languages:

French	*la table*	Spanish	*la mesa*
German	*der Tisch*	Swedish	*bordet*
Italian	*la tavola*	Yiddish	*der tish*

By a similar process we find that "a table" is expressed in the six languages as:

French	*une table*	Spanish	*una mesa*
German	*ein Tisch*	Swedish	*ett bord*
Italian	*una tavola*	Yiddish	*a tish*

(For the sake of simplicity hereafter in this section we shall confine the examples to three languages only—French, German and Spanish.)

But let us try to say more about the table. How shall we say "the long table"? "Long" is an adjective, and we shall refer to our grammar sections, under the heading "Adjectives," before trying to use the words *long, lang* and *largo* which we have found in the word lists. From the grammar section we find that the expression will be:

French	*la table longue*
German	*der lange Tisch*
Spanish	*la mesa larga*

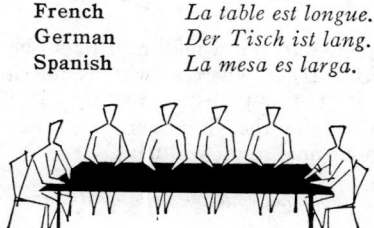

In each language the adjectives, as also the other parts of speech, follow somewhat different patterns. We see that most French adjectives follow the words they modify, rather than come before, as in English. The same is true for Spanish. In German the adjectives precede their nouns. Unlike English in another way, French, German and Spanish adjectives have endings which vary according to the noun or pronoun they modify. Only by reference to the grammar section can we tell what ending to add to each adjective. In French *la table* is feminine, and any adjective modifying it must also be feminine. The feminine form of the word *long* is *longue* in French. If we were to talk about more than one table, we should have to say *les tables longues* in French. Similarly the expression would also change for the other languages.

Let us now try to say something more about the table. What would be the equivalent, in French, of "The table is long"? We are changing our expression by the addition of the verb "is." Consulting the verb list of our grammar section we find that the appropriate form (a part of "to be") is *est*. In the same way we can find the desired forms in German and Spanish, and we can now say:

French	*La table est longue.*
German	*Der Tisch ist lang.*
Spanish	*La mesa es larga.*

The procedure would be the same for the other languages. Notice that in German the adjective ending disappears when the adjective follows the noun, but that it is retained in French and Spanish.

We can say more. Suppose we try to express: "The table which you see is long." We have our basic sentence to which has been added the expression "which you see." We could just as well have said "that you see." In both cases the meaning is

the same. Our first problem will be to discover the equivalents for "which (that)," "you" and "see." If we are planning to translate this into French we shall discover that we have a list something like this:

qui, que	which or that
vous	you
voir	to see

Let us first establish which form of *voir* goes with *vous* as the subject. If we refer to the verb list in the French grammar section, we find that the correct form (present) is *voyez*. We have, then, *vous voyez*. Should we use *qui* or *que*? Our grammar section again helps us. Under "Pronouns" we learn that *qui* is the subject of a verb, while *que* is the object. Since *vous* is the subject, we know that *que* must be the word we want. Our complete sentence will read:

La table que vous voyez est longue.

In like manner we can express the same sentence in German and Spanish:

German	*Der Tisch, den Sie sehen, ist lang.*
Spanish	*La mesa que usted ve es larga.*

Of course we must remember in each case to check the appropriate grammar sections for information as to the proper forms to use.

From these few examples it is at once apparent how very many ideas can be expressed through the proper use of the Dictionary. Most sentences follow this basic pattern: Subject—Verb—Predicate (objects of the verb, or modifiers). The possibilities for variation are almost endless.

Changing Tenses of Verbs

So far our expression has been entirely in the present tense. (Beginners who must learn to speak a foreign language within a short period of time can usually get along by using the present tense only.) Other tenses, such as the past and the future, sometimes involve other problems. Let us try to put our basic sentence into the past tense: "The table which you saw was long." There are two verbs, two past tenses. Putting it into French, we see that the two past tenses are not considered to be the same. Reference to our grammar section will show us that

"saw," a completed action, would most likely be expressed in the present perfect tense, whereas "was" is descriptive and will be expressed in the imperfect. (See pp. 2830–31, French grammar.) Except for the verbs our basic sentence remains the same, and our final result will be:

La table que vous avez vue était longue.

Note here that the past participle *vu* has an added *-e* to make it agree in gender and number with its object, *que*, which precedes it. *Que* stands for *table* and is therefore feminine (see explanation of this rule on p. 2828). Of course if we had said: "You saw the table," the object follows the verb, and there is then no agreement: *Vous avez vu la table.*

We can construct similar sentences in German and Spanish:

German	*Der Tisch, den Sie sahen, war lang.*
Spanish	*La mesa que usted vió era larga.*

The other tenses, too, can be substituted for the past. It must be remembered however that in German particularly the question of word order plays an important role. It is a simple operation to put our original sentence into the future in French:

La table que vous verrez sera longue.

The same simplicity also applies to Spanish:

La mesa que usted verá será larga.

In each of these cases the future tense is one word. But in German, as in English, the future consists of two words. Unlike English, however, one of those words must come in a special place—at the end of the clause. Reference to the future tense section of the German grammar section will show us that our sentence in German will be:

Der Tisch, den Sie sehen werden, wird lang sein.

The other tenses can be handled in much the same way, remembering in this respect that the grammar section is a useful guide.

Negative Expressions

Occasionally you may wish to make a statement negative. The sentence "The table is long" would then become "The table is not long," "not" being the word for expressing negation in English. If we consult the French grammar, we see that for that language there are two words which make up a negative: *ne* (or *n'* before a vowel) and *pas*. The first one is placed before the verb, and the second one comes after the verb. Thus our sentence in the negative would read:

La table n'est pas longue.

But in German and in Spanish, where only one word is used, the sentence would read:

German	*Der Tisch ist nicht lang.*
Spanish	*La mesa no es larga.*

Here again the question of word order for each language must be remembered.

Making Questions

In English we have two simple devices for making a question out of a statement. We may simply invert the word order of the subject and the verb, in the case of the verb "to be." Our sentence "The table is long" then becomes "Is the table long?" In the case of other verbs, we simply put "do" or "does" ("did" for the past or "will" for the future) before the statement. Thus, "You see the table" might become, according to the circumstances, "Did you see the table?" "Do you see the table?" or "Will you see the table?" For a past tense using an auxiliary we merely invert the word order, as with "is": "Have you seen the table?"

For the other languages it is not always so simple, and you will have to consult the grammar section again for specific directions about formulating a question. For instance you will note that in French practically any statement can be made into a question, simply by putting *Est-ce que...* before it. This really amounts to saying, "Is it that..." It is the simplest way of forming a question. There are other means, and they are slightly more complicated. Many of them are indicated in the grammar section.

General Suggestions

With the foregoing, we have now built up possibilities for saying a large number of things in any of the six other languages. Yet before you attempt any amount of serious translation from

English, you are reminded that the Dictionary, like any tool, has its limitations, and that to produce good results it must be used properly. You should bear in mind the following essential points:

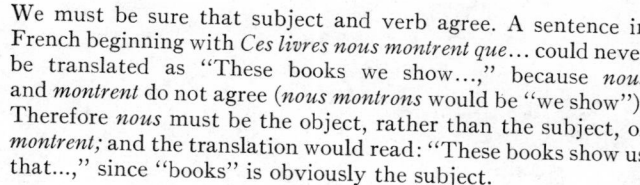

1. The word lists are necessarily limited. Therefore this Dictionary contains only words of a broad, general nature. Do not expect it to be capable of translating special uses for each word (for example, end-table, work-table), or highly technical, scientific or medical material.

2. Before attempting a translation, reduce your expression to its simplest form. Weed out slang, complicated phrases, long literary expressions and unusual words. The more involved your expression, the more chances for going astray. Your chances of expressing your idea correctly are better if you adhere as much as possible to the basic structure of Subject—Verb—Predicate, illustrated by our original sentence.

3. You may find that the word you are looking for is not in our list. If this occurs, try to find a synonym for it. There is almost always another word, or perhaps even several, with essentially the same meaning. For instance, the word "inasmuch" is not to be found in the English list. But if you think a moment, you will find that you can say about the same thing by using the word "since," which is found in the word list.

4. Rely on the grammar section for much useful advice on such questions as verb forms, word order, pronouns, agreement of adjectives and the like. If you intend to try some translation into a given language, it is well to read through the grammar section, so as to be familiar, in advance, with some of the problems which may arise, and with some of the important points wherein that language may differ from English usage.

Translation into English

Up to this point we have considered only the problem of translating from English into another language. In translating from the other language into English the problem becomes slightly different, because we cannot control the simplicity of the sentence.

In general, therefore, it is advisable at first not to attempt translating material which seems too involved.

Nevertheless, and within certain limits, it is possible to translate from other languages into English with the aid of this dictionary. We should first set up a list of basic steps to carry out the translation.

1. Our first step, when dealing with any sentence, must be to discover the verb, or all the verbs, in the sentence. The verb is the key word of every expression. Around it the entire sentence is built. Discovering the verb includes establishing its person, number, tense and mood.

2. Having discovered the verb, we must next ascertain its subject. Usually, except in questions, this is the word immediately preceding the verb. But it is not necessarily so.

We must be sure that subject and verb agree. A sentence in French beginning with *Ces livres nous montrent que...* could never be translated as "These books we show...," because *nous* and *montrent* do not agree (*nous montrons* would be "we show"). Therefore *nous* must be the object, rather than the subject, of *montrent;* and the translation would read: "These books show us that...," since "books" is obviously the subject.

3. Our next step should be to discover, somewhat as we have done in step 2, what are the objects of the verb, if the verb has any objects. That is, having ascertained the action (verb) and the source of the action (subject), we must find the object of that action, if such object exists. Our grammar sections must help us here. We note, for example, that the direct object of a German verb is in the accusative case and that the indirect object (i.e., "to him," "to me," etc.) is dative. If we are dealing with a German sentence we seek words in these cases, near our verbs, in order to fit them into their role in the sentence. In French, however, word order is highly important. The noun objects follow the verb, whereas pronoun objects usually precede the verb, except in the imperative. There are also special rules for the relative position when there is more than one pronoun object.

4. Our fourth step will be to decide what are the modifiers and which words they modify. Remember that in French most adjectives follow the words they modify, whereas in German they precede. Adverbs in French may precede or follow, but are always in close association with the words they modify. We can know these facts only by becoming familiar with the respective grammar section.

5. We now have our verbs, subjects, objects and modifiers. We should next try to see the over-all structure of the sentence by separating it into its various clauses and phrases. In other words, we try to isolate the different thought groups and see them in their relationships to each other. Each clause will center about a separate verb-subject-object combination, and each phrase will generally begin with a preposition.

6. Our sixth and last step will be to assemble our sentence into a logical whole, putting verbs, subjects, objects, modifiers and phrases in their natural places in the English word order.

Remember, in looking up the English equivalent of a foreign word you may run across in your reading or elsewhere, you can find its pronunciation at the same time. Learning to pronounce the word will help you to fix it permanently in your memory.

When Words Fail

Normally, the careful following of the above six steps will give us a satisfactory sentence. From time to time, however, since we cannot simplify our original text as we did with the English, we may find that a given word is not in our word list. Remember, the lists are necessarily limited.

In such cases the best thing to do is to leave a blank space in your translation, going on to the rest of the sentence. Once the rest of the thought is completed, the meaning of the missing word may often be suggested by the entire sentence. In some cases, too, the missing word is so similar to a corresponding English word that the meaning is at once clear.

The reader will find notes of explanation at the beginning of each of the Other-Language-to-English word lists—notes that will help him use the lists most effectively.

Britannica
World Language Dictionary

Part I

English
to
Other Languages

French · German · Italian · Spanish · Swedish · Yiddish

English

to other languages

English	French	German	Italian	Spanish	Swedish	Yiddish
a (an)	un, une	ein, eine	un, uno, una, un'	un, una	en, ett	a, an
abandon (give up), to	abandonner	aufgeben	abbandonare	abandonar	uppge	avekvarfn
abbreviation	abréviation,f.	Abkürzung,f.	abbreviazione,f.	abreviatura,f.	förkortning,nn.	kirtsung,f.
abdomen	abdomen,m.	Bauch,m.	addome,m.	abdomen,m.	buk,nn.	boykh,m.
abide (stay), to	rester	bleiben	dimorare	permanecer	stanna	blaybn
ability	capacité,f.	Fähigkeit,f.	capacità,f.	habilidad,f.	förmåga,nn.	feikayt,f.
able (capable)	capable	fähig	capace	capaz	duglig	feik
aboard	à bord	an Bord	a bordo	a bordo	ombord	oyf der shif
abolish, to	abolir	abschaffen	abolire	abolir	avskaffa	opshafn
about (approximately)	environ	ungefähr	circa	cerca de	avskaffa	opshafn
about (concerning)	de	über	circa	sobre	ungefär	beerakh
above (higher than, *prep.*)	au-dessus de	über	al di sopra di	sobre	om	vegn
above (overhead, *adv.*)	en haut	oben	in alto	arriba	över	iber
abroad (in foreign land)	à l'étranger	im Ausland	all'estero	en el extranjero	däruppe	oybn
absence	absence,f.	Abwesenheit,f.	assenza	utomlands	utomlands	in oysland
absent	absent	abwesend	assente	ausencia,f.	frånvaro,nn.	feln,n.
absolute (complete)	absolu	vollkommen	assoluto	absoluto	frånvarande	felndik
absorb (suck up), to	absorber	aufnehmen	assorbire	absorber	fullständig	absolut
abundance	abondance,f.	Fülle,f.	abbondanza,f.	abundancia,f.	absorbera	aynzapn
abundant	abondant	reichlich	abbondante	abundante	överflöd,n.	shefe,f.
abuse (misuse), to	abuser de	missbrauchen	abusare di	abusar de	riklig	shefedik
accent (speech)	accent,m.	Aussprache,f.	accento,m.	acento,m.	skymfa	shlekht bahandlen
accent (stress)	accent,m.	Betonung,f.	accento,m.	acento,m.	brytning,nn.	aktsent,m.
accept, to	accepter	annehmen	accettare	aceptar	accent,nn.	trop,m.
acceptance (approval)	agrément,m.	Bejahung,f.	approvazione,f.	aprobación,f.	anta(ga)	onnemen
acceptance (receipt)	acceptation,f.	Annahme,f.	accettazione,f.	aceptación,f.	gillande,n.	onnemen,n.
accident (chance)	hasard,m.	Zufall,m.	caso,m.	casualidad,f.	mottagande,n.	onnemen,n.
accident (mishap)	accident,m.	Unfall,m.	accidente,m.	accidente,m.	slump,nn.	tsufal,m.
accommodate (have room for), to	loger	unterbringen	accomodare	hospedar	olyckshändelse, nn.	umglik,n.
accompany (go along with), to	accompagner	begleiten	accompagnare	acompañar	härbärgera	aynordenen
accomplish, to	accomplir	vollbringen	compiere	cumplir	följa med	bagleytn
accord (agreement)	accord,m.	Übereinstim-mung,f.	accordo,m.	acuerdo,m.	utföra	oyfton
according to (in accordance with)	selon	nach	secondo	según	överensstäm-melse,nn.	heskem,m.
accordion	accordéon,m.	Ziehharmonika,f.	fisarmonica,f.	acordeón,m.	enligt	loyt
account (bank account)	compte,m.	Konto,n.	conto,f.	cuenta,f.	dragspel,n.	harmonye,f.
account (calculation)	calcul,m.	Rechnung,f.	conto,m.	cuenta,f.	konto,n.	konte,n.
account (report)	rapport,m.	Mitteilung,f.	rapporto,m.	relato,m.	beräkning,nn.	khezhbn,m.
accountant	comptable,m.	Buchführer,m.	contabile,m.	contador,m.	redogörelse,nn.	barikht,m.
account for (explain), to	expliquer	Rechenschaft geben über	render conto di	explicar	kamrer,nn.	khezhbn-firer,m.
accumulate (amass), to	accumuler	anhäufen	accumulare	acumular	redogöra för	farentfern
accurate	exact	genau	accurato	exacto	hopa	onklaybn
accusation	accusation,f.	Anklage,f.	accusa,f.	acusación,f.	noggrann	pinktlekh
accuse, to	accuser	anklagen	accusare	acusar	anklagelse,nn.	bashuldikung,f
accustom oneself, to	habituer, s'	gewöhnen, sich	abituarsi	acostumbrarse	anklaga	bashuldikn
ache	mal,m.	Schmerz;m.	dolore,m.	dolor,m.	vänja sig	tsugevoynen zikh
ache, to	avoir mal	schmerzen	dolere	doler	värk,nn.	veytik,m.
achieve (attain), to	atteindre	erzielen	realizzare	lograr	värka	vey ton
acid (*n.*)	acide,m.	Säure,f.	acido,m.	ácido,m.	uppnå	dergeyn
acknowledge (admit), to	reconnaître	anerkennen	riconoscere	reconocer	syra,nn.	zayers,n.
acknowledge (note receipt of), to	accuser réception (de)	bestätigen	accusare ricevuta (di)	acusar recibo	erkänna	moyde zayn
acorn	gland,m.	Eichel,f.	ghianda,f.	bellota,f.	erkänna motta-gandet av	bashtetikn
acquaint (inform), to	informer	bekannt machen	informare	enterar	ekollon,n.	khazerish nisl,n.
acquaintance (knowledge)	connaissance,f.	Kenntnis,f.	conoscenza,f.	conocimiento,m.	underrätta	bakenen
acquaintance (person known)	connaissance,f.	Bekannte,m.,f.	conoscenza,f.	conocido,m.	kännedom,nn.	kantshaft,f.
acquire, to	acquérir	erwerben	acquistare	adquirir	bekant,nn. (pl. bekanta)	bakanter,m.
across (beyond)	au-delà de	jenseits	al di là di	al otro lado de	förvärva	krign
across (from side to side)	sur	über	sopra	de un lado a otro	på andra sidan	oyf yener zayt
across (to the other side)	à travers	über	attraverso	a través de	tvärs över	ariber
act (deed)	acte,m.	Tat,f.	atto,m.	acto,m.	över	ariber
act (dramatic unit)	acte,m.	Auftritt,m.	atto,m.	acto,m.	handling,nn.	tuung,f.
act (behave), to	conduire, se	verhalten, sich	comportarsi	portarse	akt,nn.	akt,m.
act (do), to	agir	handeln	agire	obrar	bete sig	firn zikh
action (deed)	action,f.	Handlung,f.	azione,f.	acción,f.	handla	handlen
active (energetic)	actif, -tive	tätig	attivo	activo	handling,nn.	aktsie,f.
active (in force)	en vigueur	gültig	rigore in	vigente	aktiv	aktiv
activity (exertion of energy)	activité,f.	Tätigkeit,f.	attività,f.	actividad,f.	verksamhet,nn.	aktivitet,f.

English	French	German	Italian	Spanish	Swedish	Yiddish
actor (player)	acteur,*m.*	Schauspieler,*m.*	attore,*m.*	actor,*m.*	skådespelare,*m.*	aktyor,*m.*
actress	actrice,*f.*	Schauspielerin,*f.*	attrice,*f.*	actriz,*f.*	skådespelerska,*f.*	aktrise,*f.*
actual (real)	réel, -le	wirklich	vero	verdadero	verklig	faktish
adapt, to	adapter	anpassen	adattare	adaptar	lämpa	tsupasn
add (find sum of), to	additionner	addieren	addizionare	sumar	addera	tsugebn
add (include), to	ajouter	hinzufügen	aggiungere	añadir	medräkna	tsugebn
adding machine	additionneuse,*f.*	Rechenmaschine,*f.*	macchina calcolatrice,*f.*	máquina de sumar,*f.*	räknemaskin,*nn.*	rekhn-mashin,*f.*
addition (process of adding)	addition,*f.*	Addition,*f.*	addizione,*f.*	suma,*f.*	addition,*nn.*	tsugebn,*n.*
addition (supplement)	supplément,*m.*	Zusatz,*m.*	aggiunta,*f.*	adición,*f.*	tillägg,*n.*	tsugob,*m.*
additional	additionnel, -le	zusätzlich	supplementare	adicional	ytterligare	tsugob-...
address (postal directions)	adresse,*f.*	Anschrift,*f.*	indirizzo,*m.*	dirección,*f.*	adress,*nn.*	adres,*m.*
address (speech)	discours,*m.*	Rede,*f.*	discorso,*m.*	discurso,*m.*	anförande,*n.*	rede,*f.*
addressee	destinataire,*m.,f.*	Adressat,*m.*	destinatario,*m.*	destinatario,*m.*	adressat,*nn.*	adresat,*m.*
adequate (sufficient)	suffisant	genügend	adeguato	adecuado	tillräcklig	genugik
adjective	adjectif,*m.*	Beiwort,*n.*	aggettivo,*m.*	adjetivo,*m.*	adjektiv,*n.*	adyektiv,*m.*
adjust (regulate), to	ajuster	einstellen	aggiustare	ajustar	justera	regulirn
administration (bus.)	administration,*f.*	Verwaltung,*f.*	amministrazione,*f.*	administración,*f.*	förvaltning,*nn.*	administratsye,*f.*
admiral	amiral,*m.*	Admiral,*m.*	ammiraglio,*m.*	almirante,*m.*	amiral,*nn.*	admiral,*m.*
admiration	admiration,*f.*	Bewunderung,*f.*	ammirazio,*f.*	admiración,*f.*	beundran,*nn.*	bavunderung,*f.*
admire, to	admirer	bewundern	ammirare	admirar	beundra	bavundern
admission (right to enter)	entrée,*f.*	Zutritt,*m.*	ammissione,*f.*	entrada,*f.*	tillträde,*n.*	arayntrit,*m.*
admit (concede), to	reconnaître	zugeben	ammettere	conceder	medge	moyde zayn
admit (permit to enter), to	laisser passer	her-, hin-ein-lassen	ammettere	dar entrada	lämna tillträde	araynlozn
adopt (embrace), to	adopter	annehmen	adottare	adoptar	anta(ga)	onnemen
adorable	adorable	lieblich	adorabile	adorable	förtjusande	tayer
adore, to	adorer	anbeten	adorare	adorar	tillbe	fargetern
adorn (beautify), to	orner	verzieren	ornare	adornar	pryda	batsirn
advance (progress)	progrès,*m.*	Fortschritt,*m.*	progresso,*m.*	adelanto,*m.*	framsteg,*n.*	gang foroys,*m.*
advance (go forward), to	avancer	vorrücken	avanzare	avanzar	gå framåt	geyn foroys
advantage	avantage,*m.*	Vorteil,*m.*	vantaggio,*m.*	ventaja,*f.*	fördel,*nn.*	mayle,*f.*
adventure	aventure,*f.*	Abenteuer,*n.*	avventura,*f.*	aventura,*f.*	äventyr,*n.*	avanture,*f.*
adverb	adverbe,*m.*	Umstandswort,*n.*	avverbio,*m.*	adverbio,*m.*	adverb,*n.*	adverb,*m.*
advertise (give notice of), to	(faire) annoncer	annoncieren	annunziare	anunciar	tillkännage	anonsirn
advertise (sponsor advertising), to	faire de la publicité	Reklame... machen	fare della pubblicità	poner anuncios	annonsera	reklamirn
advertisement	annonce,*f.*	Anzeige,*f.*	annunzio,*m.*	anuncio,*m.*	annons,*nn.*	anons,*m.*
advice	conseil,*m.*	Rat,*m.*	consiglio,*m.*	consejo,*m.*	råd,*n.*	eytse,*f.*
advise (counsel), to	conseiller	raten	consigliare	aconsejar	råda	eytsen
advocate, to	recommander	befürworten	raccomandare	abogar por	förfäkta	haltn fun
aerial (antenna)	antenne,*f.*	Antenne,*f.*	antenna,*f.*	antena,*f.*	antenn,*nn.*	antene,*f.*
affair (matter)	affaire,*f.*	Sache,*f.*	affare,*m.*	asunto,*m.*	angelägenhet,*nn.*	inyen,*m.*
affect (influence), to	influer sur	betreffen	influenzare	influir en	påverka	virkn oyf
affect (pretend), to	affecter	heucheln	affettare	afectar	låtsa	makhn dem onshtel fun
affection (love)	affection,*f.*	Zuneigung,*f.*	affetto,*m.*	cariño,*m.*	tilligivenhet,*nn.*	libshaft,*f.*
affectionate (loving)	affectueux, -tueuse	zärtlich	affettuoso	cariñoso	tilligiven	varem
afford (have the means), to	permettre, se	leisten, sich	permettersi	permitirse	ha råd	farginen zikh
afraid	pris de peur	ängstlich	impaurito	temeroso	rädd	dershrokn
Africa	Afrique,*f.*	Afrika,*n.*	Africa,*f.*	Africa	Afrika,*n.*	Afrike,*n.*
African (*adj.*)	africain	afrikanisch	africano	africano	afrikansk	afrikanish
after (*conj.*)	après que	nachdem	dopo che	después (de) que	sedan	nokh dem vi
after (*prep.*)	après	nach	dopo	después de	efter	nokh
afternoon	après-midi,*m.*	Nachmittag,*m.*	pomeriggio,*m.*	tarde,*f.*	eftermiddag,*nn.*	nokhmitik,*m.*
afterward (later)	ensuite	nachher	dopo	después	efteråt	dernokhdem
again	encore	wieder	di nuovo	otra vez	igen	vider
against	contre	gegen	contro	contra	emot	kegn
age (accumulated years)	âge,*m.*	Alter,*n.*	età,*f.*	edad,*f.*	ålder,*nn.*	elter,*m.*
agency (business firm)	agence,*f.*	Vertretung,*f.*	agenzia,*f.*	agencia,*f.*	agentur,*nn.*	agentur,*f.*
agency (instrumentality)	action,*f.*	Mittel,*n.*	intervento,*m.*	medio,*m.*	förmedling,*nn.*	mitl,*n.*
agent (representative)	agent,*m.*	Vertreter,*m.*	rappresentante,*m.,f.*	agente,*m.*	agent,*nn.*	agent,*m.*
ago (past, *adj.*)	il y a...	vor	fa	hace..., hacía... (*see p. 3019*)	för...sedan	mit...tsurik
agony (mental pain)	angoisse,*f.*	Qual,*f.*	angoscia,*f.*	agonía,*f.*	själskval,*n.*	yesurim, *pl.*
agree (assent), to	consentir	beistimmen	acconsentire	asentir	samtycka	maskim zayn
agree (concur), to	convenir	übereinstimmen	essere d'accordo	estar de acuerdo	överensstämma	maskim zayn
agreeable (pleasing)	agréable	angenehm	gradevole	agradable	angenäm	ongenem
agreement (mutual understanding)	accord,*m.*	Übereinkunft,*f.*	accordo,*m.*	acuerdo,*m.*	enighet,*nn.*	heskem,*m.*
agree with, to	être d'accord avec	einverstanden sein...mit	essere d'accordo con	estar de acuerdo con	vara ense med	maskim zayn mit
agriculture	agriculture,*f.*	Landwirtschaft,*f.*	agricoltura,*f.*	agricultura,*f.*	jordbruk,*n.*	agrikultur,*f.*
ahead (forward)	en avant	vorwärts	avanti	adelante	framåt	foroys
ahead (in front)	devant	voraus	davanti	delante	före	fornt
aid	aide,*f.*	Hilfe,*f.*	aiuto,*m.*	ayuda,*f.*	hjälp,*nn.*	hilf,*f.*
aid, to	aider	helfen	aiutare	ayudar	hjälpa	helfn

English	French	German	Italian	Spanish	Swedish	Yiddish
aim (purpose)	but,*m.*	Zweck,*m.*	scopo,*m.*	propósito,*m.*	mål,*n.*	tsil,*m.*
aim (direct), to	viser	zielen	puntare	apuntar	sikta	tsiln
air (atmosphere)	air,*m.*	Luft,*f.*	aria,*f.*	aire,*m.*	luft,*nn.*	luft,*f.*
air conditioning	climatisation,*f.*	Klimaanlage,*f.*	aria condizionata,*f.*	acondicionamiento del aire,*m.*	luftkonditionering,*nn.*	luft-regulirung,*f.*
aircraft carrier	porte-avions,*m.*	Flugzeugträger,*m.*	nave portaerei,*f.*	portaaviones,*m.*	hangarfartyg,*n.*	mutershif,*f.*
air mail	poste aérienne,*f.*	Luftpost,*f.*	Posta Aerea,*f.*	correo aéreo,*m.*	flygpost,*nn.*	luftpost,*f.*
airplane	avion,*m.*	Flugzeug,*n.*	aeroplano,*m.*	aeroplano,*m.*	flygmaskin,*nn.*	aeroplan,*m.*
airport	aéroport,*m.*	Flughafen,*m.*	aeroporto,*m.*	aeropuerto,*m.*	flygfält,*n.*	fliplats,*m.*
air raid	raid aérien,*m.*	Luftangriff,*m.*	incursione aerea,*f.*	incursión aérea,*f.*	flyganfall,*n.*	onfli,*m.*
aisle (passageway)	passage,*m.*	Gang,*m.*	passaggio,*m.*	pasillo,*m.*	gång,*nn.*	durkhgang,*m.*
alarm (fear)	alarme,*f.*	Furcht,*f.*	allarme,*m.*	alarma,*f.*	oro,*nn.*	shrek,*m.*
Alaska	Alaska,*f.*	Alaska,*n.*	Alaska,*m.*	Alaska	Alaska,*n.*	Alaske,*f.*
Albania	Albanie,*f.*	Albanien,*n.*	Albania,*f.*	Albania	Albanien,*n.*	Albanye,*f.*
alcohol	alcool,*m.*	Alkohol,*m.*	alcool,*m.*	alcohol,*m.*	alkohol,*nn.*	alkohol,*m.*
alike (similar)	pareil, -le	gleich	simile	semejante	lika	enlekh
alike (similarly)	pareillement	gleich	similmente	del mismo modo	likaledes	enlekh
alive	vivant	lebendig	vivo	vivo	levande	lebedik
all (entirely, *adv.*)	tout	ganz	tutto	enteramente	alldeles	in gantsn
all (every, *adj.*)	tout	jeder	ogni	todo	alla	ale
all (everything, *n.*)	tout,*m.*	alles	tutto,*m.*	todo,*m.*	allt	alts
all (whole of, *adj.*)	tout	ganz	tutto	todo	hel	gants
allegiance	fidélité,*f.*	Treue,*f.*	fedeltà,*f.*	lealtad,*f.*	tro och lydnad	getrayshaft,*f.*
allergy (*med.*)	allergie,*f.*	Allergie,*f.*	allergia,*f.*	alergia,*f.*	allergi,*nn.*	alergye,*f.*
alliance	alliance,*f.*	Bündnis,*n.*	alleanza,*f.*	alianza,*f.*	förbund,*n.*	alyants,*f.*
allow (permit), to	permettre	erlauben	permettere	permitir	tillåta	derloybn
alloy (metal)	alliage,*m.*	Legierung,*f.*	lega,*f.*	aleación,*f.*	legering,*nn.*	geshmelts,*n.*
ally	allié,*m.*	Verbündete,*m.,f.*	alleato,*m.*	aliado,*m.*	bundsförvant,*nn.*	aliirter,*m.*
almond	amande,*f.*	Mandel,*f.*	mandorla,*f.*	almendra,*f.* (*fruit*)	mandel,*nn.*	mandl,*m.*
almost	presque	fast	quasi	casi	nästan	kimat
alone	seul	allein	solo	solo	ensam	aleyn
along (lengthwise of)	le long de	entlang	lungo	a lo largo de	längs	lengoys
aloud	à haute voix	laut	ad alta voce	en voz alta	högt	hoykh
alphabet	alphabet,*m.*	Alphabet,*n.*	alfabeto,*m.*	alfabeto,*m.*	alfabet,*n.*	alef-beys,*m.*
already	déjà	schon	già	ya	redan	shoyn
also	aussi	auch	anche	también	också	oykh
altar	autel,*m.*	Altar,*m.*	altare,*m.*	altar,*m.*	altare,*n.*	altar,*m.*
alter (make different), to	changer	(ver)ändern	alterare	alterar	ändra	baytn
although	bien que	obgleich	benchè	aunque	ehuru	khotsh
altogether (entirely)	complètement	ganz	interamente	enteramente	alldeles	in gantsn
aluminum	aluminium,*m.*	Aluminium,*n.*	alluminio,*m.*	aluminio,*m.*	aluminium,*n.*	aluminyum,*n.*
always	toujours	immer	sempre	siempre	alltid	shtendik
amaze, to	étonner	erstaunen	stupire	asombrar	förvåna	fargafn
amazement	étonnement,*m.*	Erstaunen,*n.*	stupore,*m.*	asombro,*m.*	häpnad,*nn.*	fargafung,*f.*
ambassador	ambassadeur,*m.*	Botschafter,*m.*	ambasciatore,*m.*	embajador,*m.*	ambassadör,*nn.*	ambasador,*m.*
amber (*adj.*)	ambré	bernsteinfarbig	del colore dell'ambra	color de ámbar	bärnstensgul	burshtinen
ambition	ambition,*f.*	Ehrgeiz,*m.*	ambizione,*f.*	ambición,*f.*	ärelystnad,*nn.*	ambitsye,*f.*
ambitious (aspiring)	ambitieux, -tieuse	ehrgeizig	ambizioso	ambicioso	ärelysten	ambitsyez
ambulance	ambulance,*f.*	Krankenwagen,*m.*	autoambulanza,*f.*	ambulancia,*f.*	ambulans,*nn.*	ambulans,*m.*
amendment (enacted change)	amendement,*m.*	Zusatzartikel,*m.*	emendamento,*f.*	enmienda,*f.*	tillägg,*n.*	farbeserung,*f.*
America	Amérique,*f.*	Amerika,*n.*	America,*f.*	América	Amerika,*n.*	Amerike,*f.*
American (*adj.*)	américain	amerikanisch	americano	norteamericano	amerikansk	amerikanish
amid	au milieu de	mitten in	in mezzo di	en medio de	mitt ibland	in mitn
among	parmi	unter	fra	entre	mitt ibland	in mitn
amortization (*bus.*)	amortissement,*m.*	Tilgung,*f.*	ammortizzazione,*f.*	amortización,*f.*	amortering,*nn.*	amortizatsye,*f.*
amortize, to	amortir	amortisieren	ammortizzare	amortizar	amortera	amortizirn
amount	somme,*f.*	Betrag,*m.*	somma,*f.*	cantidad,*f.*	summa,*nn.*	skhum,*m.*
amount to, to	monter à, se	betragen	ammontare	montar a	belöpa sig till	batrefn
ample	ample	reichlich	sufficiente	suficiente	riklig	beshefe
Amsterdam	Amsterdam,*m.*	Amsterdam,*n.*	Amsterdam,*f.*	Amsterdam	Amsterdam,*n.*	Amsterdam,*n.*
amuse, to	amuser	unterhalten	divertire	divertir	roa	farvayln
amusement	amusement,*m.*	Vergnügung,*f.*	divertimento,*m.*	diversión,*f.*	nöje,*n.*	farvaylung,*f.*
ancestor	ancêtre,*m.,f.*	Vorfahr,*m.*	antenato,*m.*	ascendiente,*m.*	förfader,*nn.* (*pl.* -fäder)	oves,*pl.*
anchor	ancre,*f.*	Anker,*m.*	ancora,*f.*	ancla,*f.*	ankare,*n.*	anker,*m.*
ancient	ancien, -ne	uralt	antico	antiguo	forntida	fartsaytik
and	et	und	e, ed	y, e	och	un
angel	ange,*m.*	Engel,*m.*	angelo,*m.*	ángel,*m.*	ängel,*nn.*	malakh,*m.*
anger	colère,*f.*	Zorn,*m.*	collera,*f.*	enojo,*m.*	vrede,*nn.*	kaas,*m.*
angle (*geom.*)	angle,*m.*	Winkel,*m.*	angolo,*m.*	ángulo,*m.*	vinkel,*nn.*	vinkl,*m.*
angry	en colère	zornig	adirato	enojado	arg	broygez
anguish	angoisse,*f.*	Qual,*f.*	angoscia,*f.*	angustia,*f.*	vånda,*nn.*	payn,*f.*
animal	animal,*m.*	Tier,*n.*	animale,*m.*	animal,*m.*	djur,*n.*	khaye,*f.*
ankle	cheville,*f.*	Knöchel,*m.*	caviglia,*f.*	tobillo,*m.*	fotled,*nn.*	knekhl,*n.*
anniversary	anniversaire,*m.*	Jahrestag,*m.*	anniversario,*m.*	aniversario,*m.*	årsdag,*nn.*	yortog,*m.*
announce, to	annoncer	melden	annunziare	anunciar	tillkännage	moydie zayn

English	French	German	Italian	Spanish	Swedish	Yiddish
announcement	déclaration,*f.*	Meldung,*f.*	annunzio,*m.*	anuncio,*m.*	tillkännagivande,*n.*	moydoe,*f.*
annoy (irk), to	ennuyer	ärgern	annoiare	fastidiar	förarga	tshepen
annual	annuel, -le	jährlich	annuale	anual	årlig	yerlekh
annuity	rente,*f.*	Jahresrente,*f.*	rendita,*f.*	vitalicio,*m.*	årsränta,*nn.*	yorgelt,*n.*
annul, to	annuler	aufheben	annullare	anular	upphäva	mevatl zayn
another (different, *adj.*)	un autre	ein anderer	un altro	otro	en annan	an ander
another (different one, *pron.*)	un autre	ein anderer	un altro	otro	en annan	an anderer, an andere
another (one more, *adj.*)	encore un	noch ein	un altro	otro	ännu en	nokh a
another (one more, *pron.*)	encore un	noch ein	un altro	otro	en till	nokh eyner, nokh eyne
answer	réponse,*f.*	Antwort,*f.*	risposta,*f.*	respuesta,*f.*	svar,*n.*	entfer,*m.*
answer (address reply to), to	répondre à	antworten	rispondere a	responder a	svara	entfern
answer (give answer to), to	répondre à	beantworten	rispondere	contestar	besvara	entfern oyf
ant	fourmi,*f.*	Ameise,*f.*	formica,*f.*	hormiga,*f.*	myra,*nn.*	murashke,*f.*
anthology	anthologie,*f.*	Anthologie,*f.*	antologia,*f.*	antología,*f.*	antologi,*nn.*	antologye,*f.*
anthropology	anthropologie,*f.*	Anthropologie,*f.*	antropologia,*f.*	antropología,*f.*	antropologi,*nn.*	antropologye,*f.*
antibiotic	antibiotique,*m.*	Antibiotikum,*n.*	antibiotico,*m.*	antibiótico,*m.*	antibioticum,*n.* (*pl.* -tica)	antibiotik,*m.*
anticipate (expect), to	attendre à, s'	erwarten	aspettarsi	anticipar(se)	förutse	rikhtn zikh oyf
antiquity (ancientness)	antiquité,*f.*	Altertümlichkeit, *f.*	antichità,*f.*	antigüedad,*f.*	ålderdomlighet, *nn.*	fartsaytikayt,*f.*
anxiety	inquiétude,*f.*	Angst,*f.*	ansia,*f.*	ansiedad,*f.*	ängslan,*nn.*	umru,*f.*
anxious (uneasy)	inquiet, -quiète	beunruhigt	ansioso	inquieto	orolig	umruik
anxious (wanting very much)	désireux, -reuse	eifrig	molto desideroso	deseoso	ivrig	zhedne
any (any at all, *adj.*)	n'importe quel	irgendwelche	qualsiasi	cual(es)quier(a)	någon alls	abi velkher
any (any one, *adj.*)	n'importe quel	irgend ein	qualsiasi	cualquier(a)	någon	abi velkher
any (a quantity of, *adj.*)	de (d'); du, de la (de l'); des	irgendwelche	del (*see p.* 2946)	algo de	någon	velkhe(r) es iz
any (every, *adj.*)	tout	jeder	ogni	todo	varje	yeder
any (*pron.*)	en	welche	ne	alguno	någon	keyne
anybody (anybody whosoever)	n'importe qui	wer immer	chiunque	cualquier persona	någon alls	abi ver
anybody (not...anybody)	personne	niemand	nessuno	nadie	någon	keyner nit
anybody (somebody)	quelqu'un	irgend jemand	qualcuno	cualquiera	någon	ver es iz
anyhow (in any case)	de toute façon	jedenfalls	in ogni caso	de todos modos	i varje fall	say vi say
anyone (anyone whosoever)	n'importe qui	wer immer	chiunque	cualquier persona	någon alls	abi ver
anyone (not...anyone)	personne	keiner	nessuno	ninguno	någon	keyner nit
anyone (someone)	quelqu'un	irgendeiner	qualcuno	alguno	någon	ver es iz
anything (anything whatever)	n'importe quoi	was immer	qualunque cosa	cualquier cosa	något alls	abi vos
anything (not...anything)	rien	nichts	niente	nada	något	keyn zakh nit
anything (something)	quelque chose	irgendetwas	qualche cosa	algo	något	vos es iz
anyway (in any case)	en tout cas	jedenfalls	comunque	de cualquier modo	i varje fall	say vi say
anywhere (not...anywhere)	nulle part	nirgends	in nessuna parte	en ninguna parte	någonstans	in ergets nit
anywhere (wheresoever)	n'importe où	wo immer	in qualunque luogo	dondequiera	var som helst	vu es iz
apart	à part	für sich allein	a parte	aparte	för sig själv	bazunder
apartment	appartement,*m.*	Wohnung,*f.*	appartamento,*m.*	departamento,*m.*	lägenhet,*nn.*	dire,*f.*
apologize, to	excuser, s'	entschuldigen, sich	scusarsi	disculparse	be om ursäkt	betn mekhile
apostle	apôtre,*m.*	Apostel,*m.*	apostolo,*m.*	apóstol,*m.*	apostel,*nn.*	apostol,*m.*
apparent (obvious)	évident	offenbar	evidente	aparente	tydlig	bashaymperlekh
appeal (entreaty)	appel,*m.*	Bitte,*f.*	appello,*m.*	súplica,*f.*	vädjan,*nn.*	bakoshe,*f.*
appeal (ask reconsideration of), to	appeler de	appellieren	appellare contro	apelar	överklaga	apelirn
appeal to (entreat), to	supplier	ersuchen	supplicare	suplicar	vädja till	betn zikh bay
appear (come in sight), to	apparaître	erscheinen	apparire	aparecer	bli synlig	bavayzn zikh
appear (seem), to	paraître	scheinen	sembrare	parecer	synas	oyszen
appearance (aspect)	aspect,*m.*	Aussehen,*n.*	apparenza,*f.*	apariencia,*f.*	utseende,*n.*	oysze,*m.*
appease (calm), to	apaiser	beschwichtigen	placare	aplacar	lugna	aynshtiln
appendicitis	appendicite,*f.*	Blinddarmentzündung,*f.*	appendicite,*f.*	apendicitis,*f.*	blindtarmsinflammation,*nn.*	apenditsit,*m.*
appetite	appétit,*m.*	Appetit,*m.*	appetito,*m.*	apetito,*m.*	aptit,*nn.*	apetit,*m.*
applause	applaudissements,*m.pl.*	Beifall,*m.*	applauso,*m.*	aplauso,*m.*	applåd,*nn.*	aplodisment,*m.*
apple	pomme,*f.*	Apfel,*m.*	mela,*f.*	manzana,*f.*	äpple,*n.*	epl,*m.*
application (request)	demande,*f.*	Gesuch,*n.*	domanda,*f.*	solicitud,*f.*	ansökan,*nn.*	aplikatsye,*f.*
application (use)	application,*f.*	Anwendung,*f.*	applicazione,*f.*	aplicación,*f.*	användning,*nn.*	onvendung,*f.*
apply (be fitting), to	convenir	zutreffen	convenire	aplicarse	passa	pasn
apply (put to use), to	appliquer	anwenden	applicare	aplicar	tillämpa	onvendn
appoint, to	nommer	ernennen	nominare	nombrar	utnämna	bashtimen
appointment (meeting)	rendez-vous,*m.*	Verabredung,*f.*	appuntamento, *m.*	cita,*f.*	avtal,*n.*	bashtelung,*f.*
appointment (nomination)	nomination,*f.*	Ernennung,*f.*	nomina,*f.*	nombramiento, *m.*	utnämning,*nn.*	bashtimung,*f.*
appraisal (*bus.*)	expertise,*f.*	Wertschätzung,*f.*	valutazione,*f.*	valoración,*f.*	värdering,*nn.*	shatsung,*f.*
appreciate (be grateful for), to	reconnaître	schätzen	gradire	agradecer	uppskatta	opshatsn
appreciate (perceive fully), to	apprécier	schätzen	apprezzare	apreciar	inse	dershatsn

English	French	German	Italian	Spanish	Swedish	Yiddish
apprentice (trade student)	apprenti,*m.*	Lehrling,*m.*	apprendista,*m.,f.*	aprendiz,*m.*	lärling,*nn.*	lernyingl,*m.*
approach (come near to), to	approcher de, s'	nähern, sich	avvicinarsi a	acercarse (a)	nalkas	derneentern zikh tsu
approval	approbation,*f.*	Billigung,*f.*	approvazione,*f.*	aprobación,*f.*	gillande,*n.*	haskome,*f.*
approve (sanction), to	approuver	genehmigen	approvare	aprobar	godkänna	bashtetikn
approve (think well of), to	approuver	billigen	approvare	aprobar	gilla	haltn fun
apricot	abricot,*m.*	Aprikose,*f.*	albicocca,*f.*	albaricoque,*m.*	aprikos,*nn.*	aprikos,*m.*
apron (garment)	tablier,*m.*	Schürze,*f.*	grembiale,*m.*	delantal,*m.*	förkläde,*n.*	fartekh,*m.*
apt to (prone to)	enclin à	geneigt	propenso a	dispuesto a	benägen att	olel tsu
arch (curved structure)	voûte,*f.*	Bogen,*m.*	arco,*m.*	arco,*m.*	valv,*n.*	boygn,*m.*
architect	architecte,*m.*	Baukünstler,*m.*	architetto,*m.*	arquitecto,*m.*	arkitekt,*nn.*	arkhitekt,*m.*
area (extent)	étendue,*f.*	Grundfläche,*f.*	area,*f.*	área,*f.*	yta,*nn.*	shetakh,*m.*
area (region)	région,*f.*	Gebiet,*n.*	regione,*f.*	región,*f.*	trakt,*nn.*	gegnt,*f.*
Argentina	Argentine,*f.*	Argentinien,*n.*	Argentina,*f.*	la Argentina	Argentina,*n.*	Argentine,*f.*
Argentinian (*adj.*)	argentin	argentinisch	argentino	argentino	argentinsk	argentinish
argue (maintain), to	maintenir	behaupten	sostenere	sostener	påstå	taynen
argument (dispute)	dispute,*f.*	Auseinandersetzung,*f.*	disputa,*f.*	disputa,*f.*	dispyt,*nn.*	vikuakh,*m.*
arise (come about), to	élever, s'	entstehen	nascere	surgir	uppstå	oyfkumen
arithmetic	arithmétique,*f.*	Arithmetik,*f.*	aritmetica,*m.*	aritmética,*f.*	räkning,*nn.*	aritmetik,*f.*
arm (*anat.*)	bras,*m.*	Arm,*m.*	braccio,*m.*	brazo,*m.*	arm,*nn.*	orem,*m.*
arm, to	armer	bewaffnen	armare	armar	beväpna	bavofenen
armor	armure,*f.*	Panzer,*m.*	armatura,*f.*	armadura,*f.*	rustning,*nn.*	pantser,*m.*
army	armée,*f.*	Heer,*n.*	esercito,*m.*	ejército,*m.*	armé,*nn.*	armey,*f.*
around (*prep.*)	autour de	um	intorno a	alrededor de	omkring	arum
arouse (excite), to	exciter	aufregen	destare	excitar	uppväcka	oyfrudern
arrange (place), to	arranger	einordnen	disporre	colocar	ordna	oysseydern
arrange (plan), to	arranger	einrichten	ordinare	hacer arreglos (para)	arrangera	aynordenen
arrangement (order)	arrangement,*m.*	Einordnung,*f.*	disposizione,*f.*	colocación,*f.*	ordning,*nn.*	seyder,*m.*
arrangement (preparation)	disposition,*f.*	Vorbereitung,*f.*	preparativo,*m.*	preparativo,*m.*	arrangemang,*n.*	tsugreytung,*f.*
arrest (halt), to	arrêter	aufhalten	arrestare	detener	hejda	opshteln
arrest (take into custody), to	arrêter	verhaften	arrestare	arrestar	häkta	arestirn
arrival	arrivée,*f.*	Ankunft,*f.*	arrivo,*m.*	llegada,*f.*	ankomst,*nn.*	onkum,*m.*
arrive, to	arriver	ankommen	arrivare	llegar	ankomma	onkumen
arrow	flèche,*f.*	Pfeil,*m.*	freccia,*f.*	flecha,*f.*	pil,*nn.*	fayl,*m.*
art	art,*m.*	Kunst,*f.*	arte,*f.*	arte,*m.,f.*	konst,*nn.*	kunst,*f.*
artery (*anat.*)	artère,*f.*	Schlagader,*f.*	arteria,*f.*	arteria,*f.*	pulsåder,*nn.*	arterye,*f.*
arthritis	arthrite,*f.*	Arthritis,*f.*	artrite,*f.*	artritis,*f.*	ledgångsreumatism,*nn.*	artrit,*m.*
article (literary composition)	article,*m.*	Artikel,*m.*	articolo,*m.*	artículo,*m.*	artikel,*nn.*	artikl,*m.*
article (thing)	article,*m.*	Sache,*f.*	oggetto,*m.*	cosa,*f.*	sak,*nn.*	kheyfets,*m.*
artificial (synthetic)	artificiel, -le	künstlich	artificiale	artificial	konst-	kinstlekh
artist	artiste,*m.,f.*	Künstler,*m.*	artista,*m.,f.*	artista,*m.,f.*	konstnär,*m.*	kinstler,*m.*
artistic (tasteful)	artistique	künstlerisch	elegante	artístico	artistisk	kinstlerish
as (equally, *adv.*)	aussi	wie	così	tan	lika	azoy vi
as (in the role of, *prep.*)	en	als	come	como	som	vi
as (in the same way, *conj.*)	comme	wie	come	como	som	azoy vi
as (while, *conj.*)	pendant que	während	mentre	mientras	medan	beshas
ascend (go upward along), to	monter	besteigen	ascendere	ascender	gå uppför	aroyfkrikhn
ashamed (mortified)	honteux, -teuse	beschämt	vergognoso	avergonzado	skamsen	farshemt
ashes	cendres,*f.pl.*	Asche,*f.*	cenere,*f.*	cenizas,*f.pl.*	aska,*nn.*	ash,*n.*
ash tray	cendrier,*m.*	Aschenbecher,*m.*	portacenere,*m.*	cenicero,*m.*	askkopp,*nn.*	ashtetsl,*n.*
Ash Wednesday	mercredi des Cendres,*m.*	Aschermittwoch, *m.*	giorno delle Ceneri,*m.*	miércoles de ceniza,*m.*	askonsdag,*nn.*	ashmitvokh,*m.*
Asia	Asie,*f.*	Asien,*n.*	Asia,*f.*	Asia	Asien,*n.*	Azye,*f.*
Asiatic (*adj.*)	asiatique	asiatisch	asiatico	asiático	asiatisk	azyatish
aside (away)	à part	beiseite	da parte	aparte	åt sidan	in a zayt
ask (put question to), to	demander (à)	fragen	domandare	preguntar	fråga	fregn
ask (request), to	demander à	bitten um	chiedere	pedir	be	betn
ask about, to	informer sur, s'	fragen über	interrogare circa	preguntar por	fråga om	fregn vegn
asleep (sleeping)	endormi	eingeschlafen	addormentato	dormido	sovande	ayngeshlofn
asparagus	asperges,*f.pl.*	Spargel,*m.*	asparago,*m.*	espárrago,*m.*	sparris,*nn.*	sparzhe,*f.*
aspect (phase)	aspect,*m.*	Hinsicht,*f.*	aspetto,*m.*	aspecto,*m.*	synvinkel,*nn.*	aspekt,*m.*
aspirin	aspirine,*f.*	Aspirin,*n.*	aspirina,*f.*	aspirina,*f.*	aspirin,*nn.* or *n.*	aspirin,*m.*
assault, to	attaquer	angreifen	assalire	asaltar	överfalla	bafaln
assemble (bring together), to	assembler	zusammenbringen	riunire	reunir	samla	tsunoyfklaybn
assemble (meet), to	assembler, s'	versammeln, sich	adunarsi	reunirse	samlas	tsunoyfklaybn zikh
assembly (meeting)	réunion,*f.*	Versammlung,*f.*	adunanza,*f.*	reunión,*f.*	sammankomst, *nn.*	farzamlung,*f.*
assent, to	approuver	beistimmen	assentire	asentir	samtycka	maskim zayn
assert (declare), to	maintenir	behaupten	affermare	afirmar	försäkra	derklern
assertion (declaration)	assertion,*f.*	Behauptung,*f.*	asserzione,*f.*	afirmación,*f.*	försäkran,*nn.*	derklerung,*f.*
assess (impose tax), to	imposer	besteuern	fissare le tasse	gravar	taxera	bashtayern
asset (*bus.*)	valeur,*f.*	Aktivposten,*m.*	bene,*m.*	partida del activo,*f.*	tillgångar,*nn. pl.*	aktivn,*pl.*
assign (prescribe lesson), to	assigner	aufgeben	assegnare	asignar	ge i uppgift	fargebn
assignment (*educ.*)	devoir,*m.*	Aufgabe,*f.*	compito,*m.*	tarea escolar,*f.*	läxa,*nn.*	fargebung,*f.*

English	French	German	Italian	Spanish	Swedish	Yiddish
assignment (legal transfer)	cession, *f.*	Abtretung, *f.*	cessione, *f.*	cesión, *f.*	överlåtelse, *nn.*	ibershraybn, *n.*
assist, to	aider	beistehen	assistere	ayudar	bistå	tsuhelfn
assistance	aide, *f.*	Beistand, *m.*	assistenza, *f.*	ayuda, *f.*	bistånd, *n.*	hilf, *f.*
assistant	aide, *m.*,*f.*	Gehilfe, *m.*	assistente, *m.*,*f.*	ayudante, *m.*	assistent, *nn.*	asistent, *m.*
associate (relate), to	associer	verbinden	mettere in relazione	asociar	associera	farbindn
association (body of persons)	société, *f.*	Verein, *m.*	associazione, *f.*	asociación, *f.*	förening, *nn.*	farband, *m.*
assume (take for granted), to	considérer comme admis	annehmen	assumere	dar por sentado	förutsätta	meshaer zayn
assure, to	assurer	versichern	assicurare	asegurar	försäkra	farzikhern
astonish, to	étonner	erstaunen	stupire	asombrar	förvåna	farkhideshn
astonishment	étonnement, *m.*	Erstaunen, *n.*	stupore, *m.*	asombro, *m.*	förvåning, *nn.*	khidesh, *m.*
asylum (institution)	asile, *m.*	Anstalt, *f.*	casa di salute, *f.*	asilo, *m.*	anstalt, *nn.*	anshtalt, *f.*
at (by)	à	bei; an	a	a	vid, på	bay
at (for the price of)	à	um	a	a	för	tsu
at (in)	à	bei; in	in	en	i	bay; in
at (near)	près de	neben	presso	a	vid	lebn
at (on)	sur	auf	su	en	på	oyf
at (to, toward)	à	um, gegen	verso	a	till	oyf
Athens	Athènes, *f.*	Athen, *n.*	Atene, *f.*	Atenas	Aten, *n.*	Aten, *n.*
athlete	athlète, *m.*,*f.*	Athlet, *m.*	atleta, *m.*,*f.*	atleta, *m.*	idrottsman, *nn.* (*pl.* -män)	atlet, *m.*
athletic	athlétique	athletisch	atletico	atlético	idrotts-...	atletish
Atlantic (*n.*)	Atlantique, *m.*	Atlantische Ozean, *m.*	Atlantico, *m.*	Atlántico, *m.*	Atlanten, *nn.*	Atlantik, *m.*
atlas	atlas, *m.*	Atlas, *m.*	atlante, *m.*	atlas, *m.*	kartbok, *nn.* (*pl.* -böcker)	atlas, *m.*
atmosphere (air)	atmosphère, *f.*	Luft, *f.*	atmosfera, *f.*	atmósfera, *f.*	atmosfär, *nn.*	atmosfer, *f.*
atmosphere (environment)	atmosphère, *f.*	Atmosphäre, *f.*	atmosfera, *f.*	ambiente, *m.*	atmosfär, *nn.*	atmosfer, *f.*
atom	atome, *m.*	Atom, *n.*	atomo, *m.*	átomo, *m.*	atom, *nn.*	atom, *m.*
atomic bomb	bombe atomique, *f.*	atomische Bombe, *f.*	bomba atomica, *f.*	bomba atómica, *f.*	atombomb, *nn.*	atomishe bombe, *f.*
attach (join), to	attacher	anhängen	attaccare	acompañar	fästa	tsutshepen
attachment (legal seizure)	saisie, *f.*	Beschlagnahme, *f.*	sequestro, *m.*	embargo, *m.*	konfiskation, *nn.*	konfiskatsye, *f.*
attack (personal assault)	attaque, *f.*	Angriff, *m.*	aggressione, *f.*	agresión, *f.*	överfall, *n.*	onfal, *m.*
attack (assault physically), to	attaquer	angreifen	aggredire	agredir	överfalla	bafaln
attain (arrive at), to	atteindre	erreichen	raggiungere	alcanzar	uppnå	dergeyn biz
attempt	tentative, *f.*	Versuch, *m.*	tentativo, *m.*	tentativa, *f.*	försök, *n.*	pruv, *m.*
attempt, to	tenter	versuchen	tentare	procurar	försöka	pruvn
attend (be present at), to	assister à	beiwohnen	assistere a	asistir	bevista	bayzayn
attendance (presence)	présence, *f.*	Anwesenheit, *f.*	assistenza, *f.*	asistencia, *f.*	närvaro, *nn.*	bazukh, *m.*
attention (heed)	attention, *f.*	Aufmerksamkeit, *f.*	attenzione, *f.*	atención, *f.*	uppmärksamhet, *nn.*	akht, *f.*
attentive (heedful)	attentif, -tive	aufmerksam	attento	atento	uppmärksam	oyfmerkzam
attic	mansarde, *f.*	Dachboden, *m.*	soffitta, *f.*	desván, *n.*	vind, *nn.*	boydem, *m.*
attire (apparel)	vêtements, *m.pl.*	Kleidung, *f.*	abbigliamento, *m.*	atavío, *m.*	klädsel, *nn.*	halboshe, *f.*
attitude (manner)	attitude, *f.*	Haltung, *f.*	atteggiamento, *m.*	actitud, *f.*	hållning, *nn.*	haltung, *f.*
attorney	avocat, *m.*	(Rechts)Anwalt, *m.*	avvocato, *m.*	abogado, *m.*	advokat, *nn.*	advokat, *m.*
attract, to	attirer	anziehen	attrarre	atraer	tilldra(ga)	tsutsien
attraction	attraction, *f.*	Anziehung, *f.*	attrattiva, *f.*	atracción, *f.*	attraktion, *nn.*	atraktsye, *f.*
attractive (pleasing)	attrayant	anziehend	attraente	atractivo	tilldragande	tsutsiendik
attribute (characteristic)	attribut, *m.*	Eigenschaft, *f.*	attributo, *m.*	atributo, *m.*	egenskap, *nn.*	eygnshaft, *f.*
auction (sale)	vente à l'enchère, *f.*	Versteigerung, *f.*	vendita all'asta, *f.*	subasta, *f.*	auktion, *nn.*	litsitatsye, *f.*
audience	auditoire, *m.*	Publikum, *n.*	uditorio, *m.*	auditorio, *m.*	publik, *nn.*	oylem, *m.*
audit (*n.*)	vérification de comptes, *f.*	Bücherrevision, *f.*	appuramento, *m.*	intervención, *f.*	revision, *nn.*	bikher-revizye, *f.*
auditor	vérificateur des comptes, *m.*	Revisor, *m.*	sindaco, *m.*	interventor, *m.*	revisor, *nn.*	roye-khezbn, *m.*
auditorium	salle, *f.*	Hörsaal, *m.*	auditorio, *m.*	salón de actos, *m.*	mötessal, *nn.*	zal, *m.*
aunt	tante, *f.*	Tante, *f.*	zia, *f.*	tía, *f.*	faster; moster, *nn.*	mume, *f.*
Australia	Australie, *f.*	Australien, *n.*	Australia, *f.*	Australia	Australien, *n.*	Oystralye, *n.*
Australian (*adj.*)	australien, -ne	australisch	australiano	australiano	australisk	oystralish
Austria	Autriche, *f.*	Österreich, *n.*	Austria, *f.*	Austria	Österrike, *n.*	Estraykh, *n.*
Austrian (*adj.*)	autrichien, -ne	österreichisch	austriaco	austríaco	österrikisk	estraykhish
author	auteur, *m.*	Verfasser, *m.*	autore, *m.*	autor, *m.*	författare, *nn.*	mekhaber, *m.*
authority (person with power)	autorité, *f.*	Bevollmächtigte, *m.*,*f.*	autorità, *f.*	autoridad, *m.*,*f.*	auktoritet, *nn.*	oytoritet, *m.*
authority (power)	autorité, *f.*	Vollmacht, *f.*	autorità, *f.*	autoridad, *f.*	myndighet, *nn.*	makht, *f.*
authorization	autorisation, *f.*	Bevollmächtigung, *f.*	autorizzazione, *f.*	autorización, *f.*	bemyndigande, *n.*	oytorizirung, *f.*
autobiography	autobiographie, *f.*	Selbstbiographie, *f.*	autobiografia, *f.*	autobiografía, *f.*	självbiografi, *nn.*	oytobiografye, *f.*
automobile	automobile, *f.*	(Kraft)Wagen, *m.*	automobile, *f.*	automóvil, *m.*	automobil, *nn.*	oytomobil, *m.*
autumn	automne, *m.*	Herbst, *m.*	autunno, *m.*	otoño, *m.*	höst, *nn.*	harbst, *m.*
available	disponible	zur Verfügung stehen	disponibile	disponible	tillgänglig	tsu krign
avenue (street)	avenue, *f.*	Allee, *f.*	corso, *m.*	avenida, *f.*	gata, *nn.*	evenyu, *f.*
average (mean, *n.*)	moyenne, *f.*	Durchschnitt, *m.*	media, *f.*	término medio, *m.*	medeltal, *n.*	durkhshnit, *m.*
average (ordinary, *adj.*)	moyen, -ne	durchschnittlich	mediocre	mediano	genomsnittlig	durkhshnitlekh
avert (prevent), to	détourner	abwenden	impedire	impedir	avvärja	farhitn

English	French	German	Italian	Spanish	Swedish	Yiddish
aviator	aviateur,*m.*	Flieger,*m.*	aviatore,*m.*	aviador,*m.*	flygare,*nn.*	flier,*m.*
avoid, to	éviter	vermeiden	evitare	evitar	undvika	oysmaydn
await, to	attendre	erwarten	attendere	esperar	invänta	vartn oyf
awake	éveillé	wach	sveglio	despierto	vaken	vakh
awaken (make awaken), to	réveiller	aufwecken	svegliare	despertar	väcka	vakh
awaken (rouse oneself), to	réveiller, se	aufwachen	svegliarsi	despertarse	vakna	oyfvekn
aware	averti	bewusst	conscio	enterado	medveten	oyfvekn zikh
away (absent, *adj.*)	absent	weg	assente	ausente	borta	visndik
away (from a place, *adv.*)	loin	entfernt	via	lejos	bort	nito
awe	crainte (respectu-euse),*f.*	Ehrfurcht,*f.*	timore,*m.*	pavor,*m.*	vördnad,*nn.*	avek
						yiras-hakoved, *m.*
awful	terrible	furchtbar	terribile	terrible	förskräcklig	shreklekh
awhile (*adv.*)	un moment	eine Weile	per qualche tempo	por un rato	en stund	a vayle
awkward	maladroit	ungeschickt	goffo	torpe	tafatt	umgelumpert
axe	hache,*f.*	Axt,*f.*	ascia,*f.*	hacha,*f.*	yxa.*nn.*	hak,*f.*
baby	bébé,*m.*	Kindlein,*n.*	bambino,*m.*	criatura,*f.*	spädbarn,*n.*	oyfele,*n.*
bachelor (unmarried man)	célibataire,*m.*	Junggeselle,*m.*	scapolo,*m.*	soltero,*m.*	ungkarl,*nn.*	bokher,*m.*
back (*anat.*)	dos,*m.*	Rücken,*m.*	dorso,*m.*	espalda,*f.*	rygg,*nn.*	rukn,*m.*
back (rearward, *adv.*)	en arrière	zurück	indietro	atrás	bakåt	tsurik
back (reverse side)	revers,*m.*	Rückseite,*f.*	dorso,*m.*	dorso,*m.*	baksida,*nn.*	hintershte zayt,*f.*
backward (in reverse, *adv.*)	(à) reculons	umgekehrt	a ritroso	hacia atrás	baklänges	farkert
backward (rearward, *adv.*)	en arrière	rückwärts	indietro	hacia atrás	bakåt	hintervaylekhts
bacon	lard,*m.*	Speck,*m.*	carnesecca,*f.*	tocino,*m.*	rökt fläsk,*n.*	beykon,*m.*
bad, worse, worst	mauvais, pire, (le) pire	schlimm, schlimmer, (der) schlimmst(e)	cattivo, peggiore, (il) peggiore	malo, peor, (el) peor	dålig, sämre, sämst	shlekht, erger, ergst
badger (animal)	blaireau,*m.*	Dachs,*m.*	tasso,*m.*	tejón,*m.*	grävling,*nn.*	taks,*m.*
bag (purse)	sac à main,*m.*	Handtasche,*f.*	borsa,*f.*	bolsa,*f.*	handväska,*nn.*	tash,*f.*
bag (sack)	sac,*m.*	Sack,*m.*	sacco,*m.*	saco,*m.*	påse,*nn.*	zekl,*n.*
baggage (luggage)	bagages,*m.pl.*	Gepäck,*n.*	bagaglio,*m.*	equipaje,*m.*	bagage,*n.*	bagazh,*m.*
bait (for animals)	appât,*m.*	Köder,*m.*	esca,*f.*	cebo,*m.*	bete,*n.*	farnarekhts,*n.*
bake (be cooking), to	cuire (au four)	backen	cuocere al forno	cocer en horno	(*no equiv.*)	bakn zikh
baker	boulanger,*m.*	Bäcker,*m.*	panettiere,*m.*	panadero,*m.*	bagare,*nn.*	beker,*m.*
balance (equilibrium)	équilibre,*m.*	Gleichgewicht,*n.*	equilibrio,*m.*	equilibrio,*m.*	balans,*nn.*	glaykhvog,*f.*
bald (hairless)	chauve	kahl	calvo	calvo	skallig	lise
ball (sphere)	balle,*f.*	Ball,*m.*	palla,*f.*	pelota,*f.*	boll,*nn.*	pilke,*f.*
balloon	ballon,*m.*	Ballon,*m.*	pallone,*m.*	globo,*m.*	ballong,*nn.*	balon,*m.*
ballot	scrutin,*m.*	Wahlzettel,*m.*	scheda di votazione,*f.*	papeleta,*f.*	valsedel,*nn.*	shtimtsetl,*n.*
ball-point pen	stylo à bille,*m.*	Kugelschreiber,*m.*	penna a sfera,*f.*	pluma fuente de punto de bolo, *f.*	kulpenna,*nn.*	bolpoynt-feder, *f.*
banana	banane,*f.*	Banane,*f.*	banana,*f.*	plátano,*m.*	banan,*nn.*	banane,*f.*
band (gang)	bande,*f.*	Bande,*f.*	banda,*f.*	cuadrilla,*f.*	gäng,*n.*	bande,*f.*
band (instrumental group)	musique,*f.*	Kapelle,*f.*	banda musicale, *f.*	banda,*f.*	orkester,*nn.*	kapelye,*f.*
band (ribbon)	ruban,*m.*	Band,*n.* (*pl.* Bänder)	nastro,*m.*	cinta,*f.*	band,*n.*	stenge,*f.*
bandage	bandage,*m.*	Verband,*m.*	benda,*f.*	venda,*f.*	bandage,*n.*	bandazh,*m.*
bandit	bandit,*m.*	Bandit,*m.*	bandito,*m.*	bandido,*m.*	bandit,*nn.*	bandit,*m.*
banish (exile), to	exiler	verbannen	bandire	desterrar	landsförvisa	farshikn
banjo	banjo,*m.*	Banjo,*m.*	banjo,*m.*	banjo,*m.*	banjo,*nn.*	bandzho,*m.*
bank (shore)	rive,*f.*	Ufer,*n.*	riva,*f.*	ribera,*f.*	strand,*nn.* (*pl.* stränder)	breg,*m.*
bank (treasury)	banque,*f.*	Bank,*f.*	banca,*f.*	banco,*m.*	bank,*nn.*	bank,*m.*
banker	banquier,*m.*	Bankier,*m.*	banchiere,*m.*	banquero,*m.*	bankir,*nn.*	bankir,*m.*
banking	opérations de banque,*f.pl.*	Bankwesen,*n.*	commercio bancario,*m.*	banca,*f.*	bankrörelse,*nn.*	bankireray,*f.*
bankruptcy	faillite,*f.*	Bankrott,*m.*	fallimento,*m.*	quiebra,*f.*	konkurs,*nn.*	bankrot,*m.*
banner	bannière,*f.*	Banner,*n.*	bandiera,*f.*	pendón,*m.*	fana,*nn.*	fon,*f.*
banquet	banquet,*m.*	Festmahl,*n.*	banchetto,*m.*	banquete,*m.*	bankett,*nn.*	banket,*m.*
baptism	baptême,*m.*	Taufe,*f.*	battesimo,*m.*	bautismo,*m.*	dop,*n.*	kristikung,*f.*
bar (barroom)	bar,*m.*	Bar,*f.*	bar,*m.*	cantina,*f.*	bar,*nn.*	bar,*m.*
bar (pole)	barre,*f.*	Stange,*f.*	barra,*f.*	palanca,*f.*	stång,*nn.* (*pl.* stänger)	shtang,*m.*
bar (block), to	barrer	(ver)sperren	sbarrare	impedir	spärra	farshteln
barber	coiffeur,*m.*	Frisör,*m.*	barbiere,*m.*	barbero,*m.*	barberare,*nn.*	sherer,*m.*
bare (nude)	nu	nackt	nudo	desnudo	bar	naket
bargain (advantageous purchase)	occasion,*f.*	Gelegenheitskauf,*m.*	occasione,*f.*	ganga,*f.*	gott köp,*n.*	metsie,*f.*
bargain (agreement)	marché,*m.*	Abmachung,*f.*	patto,*m.*	trato,*m.*	överenskommelse,*nn.*	gesheft,*n.*
bargain (negotiate), to	négocier	verhandeln über	contrattare	negociar	köpslå	dingen zikh
bark (of tree)	écorce,*f.*	(Baum)Rinde,*f.*	corteccia,*f.*	corteza,*f.*	bark,*nn.*	kore,*f.*
bark (bay), to	aboyer	bellen	abbaiare	ladrar	skälla	biln
barley	orge,*f.*	Gerste,*f.*	orzo,*m.*	cebada,*f.*	korn,*n.*	gershtn,*pl.*
barn	étable,*f.*	Scheune,*f.*	stalla,*f.*	establo,*m.*	ladugård,*nn.*	shtal,*m.*
barometer	baromètre,*m.*	Luftdruckmesser,*m.*	barometro,*m.*	barómetro,*m.*	barometer,*nn.*	barometer,*m.*
barrel (cask)	tonneau,*m.*	Fass,*n.*	barile,*m.*	barril,*m.*	fat,*n.*	fas,*f.*
barren	stérile	unfruchtbar	sterile	estéril	ofruktbar	umfrukhperdik
barrier	barrière,*f.*	Schranke,*f.*	barriera,*f.*	barrera,*f.*	skrank,*n.*	shterung,*f.*
base (foundation)	base,*f.*	Sockel,*m.*	base,*f.*	base,*f.*	sockel,*nn.*	baze,*f.*
base (found), to	fonder	begründen	basare	basar	grunda	bazirn
baseball	base-ball,*m.*	Baseball,*m.*	giuoco a palla,*m.*	béisbol,*m.*	baseboll,*nn.*	beysbol,*m.*

English	French	German	Italian	Spanish	Swedish	Yiddish
basement	sous-sol,*m.*	Keller,*m.*	sottosuolo	sótano,*m.*	källarvåning,*nn.*	keler,*m.*
bashful	timide	schüchtern	ritroso	vergonzoso	blyg	shemevdik
basis	base,*f.*	Grundlage,*f.*	base,*f.*	base,*f.*	grundval,*nn.*	yesod,*m.*
basket	panier,*m.*	Korb,*m.*	paniere,*m.*	cesta,*f.*	korg,*nn.*	korb,*m.*
basketball	basket-ball,*m.*	Korbball,*m.*	pallacanestro,*m.*	baloncesto,*m.*	korgboll,*nn.*	koyshbol,*m.*
Basle	Bâle,*f.*	Basel,*n.*	Basilea,*f*	Basilea	Basel,*n.*	Bazl,*n.*
bat (animal)	chauve-souris,*f.*	Fledermaus,*f.*	pipistrello,*m.*	murciélago,*m.*	fladdermus,*nn.* (*pl.* -möss)	fledermoyz,*f.*
bat (club)	batte,*f.*	Schläger,*m.*	bastone,*m.*	bate,*m.*	slagträ,*n.*	beysbol-bet,*m.*
bath	bain,*m.*	Bad,*n.*	bagno,*m.*	baño,*m.*	bad,*n.*	vane,*f.*
bathe (take a bath), to	prendre un bain	baden	prendere un bagno	bañarse	bada	bodn zikh
bathing suit	maillot de bain, *m.*	Badeanzug,*m.*	costume da bagno,*m.*	traje de baño,*m.*	baddräkt,*nn.*	bodkostyum,*m.*
bathroom	salle de bain,*f.*	Badezimmer,*n.*	stanza da bagno, *f.*	(cuarto de) baño, *m.*	badrum,*n.*	bodtsimer,*m.*
bathtub	baignoire,*f.*	Badewanne,*f.*	vasca da bagno,*f.*	bañera,*f.*	badkar,*n.*	vane,*f.*
batter (flour mixture)	pâte,*f.*	Teig,*m.*	pasta,*f.*	batido,*m.*	smet,*nn.*	teyg,*n.*
battery (artillery)	batterie,*f.*	Batterie,*f.*	batteria,*f.*	batería,*f.*	batteri,*n.*	baterye,*f.*
battery (primary cell)	pile,*f.*	Batterie,*f.*	pila elettrica,*f.*	pila seca,*f.*	batteri,*n.*	baterye,*f.*
battery (storage)	accumulateur,*m.*	Akkumulator,*m.*	accumulatore,*m.*	acumulador (eléctrico),*m.*	batteri,*n.*	akumulator,*m.*
battle	bataille,*f.*	Schlacht,*f.*	battaglia,*f*	batalla,*f.*	strid,*nn.*	shlakht,*f.*
battleship	cuirassé (de ligne),*m.*	Linienschiff,*n.*	corazzata,*f.*	acorazado,*m.*	slagskepp,*n.*	pantsershif,*f.*
Bavaria	Bavière,*f.*	Bayern,*n.*	Baviera,*f.*	Baviera	Bajern,*n.*	Bayern,*n.*
bay (inlet)	baie,*f.*	Bucht,*f.*	baia,*f.*	bahía,*f.*	vik,*nn.*	ayngos,*m.*
be, to	être	sein	essere	ser; estar (*see* p. 3019)	vara	zayn
beach (strand)	plage,*f.*	Strand,*m.*	spiaggia,*f.*	playa,*f.*	(sand)strand,*nn.* (*pl.* stränder)	plazh,*m.*
bead (jewelry)	perle (de collier), *f.*	Perle,*f.*	perla,*f.*	cuenta,*f.*	pärla,*nn.*	krel,*f.*
beam (radio signal)	axe radiobalisé, *m.*	Richtstrahl,*m.*	segnale,*m.*	eje radiodirector, *m.*	radiosignal,*nn.*	radyoshtral,*m.*
beam (rafter)	poutre,*f.*	Balken,*m.*	trave,*f.*	viga,*f.*	bjälke,*nn.*	balkn,*m.*
beam (ray)	rayon,*m.*	Strahl,*m.*	raggio,*m.*	rayo,*m.*	stråle,*nn.*	snop likht,*m.*
beam (direct, *rad.*), to	diriger	senden	trasmettere	dirigir (una radiodifusión)	rikta	shtraln
beam (shine), to	rayonner	strahlen	brillare	estar radiante	stråla	onshteln
bean (string bean)	haricot vert,*m.*	(grüne) Bohne, *f.*	fagiolino,*m.*	haba,*f.*	böna,*nn.*	fasolye,*f.*
bear (animal)	ours,*m.*	Bär,*m.*	orso,*m.*	oso,*m.*	björn,*nn.*	ber,*m.*
bear (carry), to	porter	tragen	portare	llevar	bära	trogn
bear (endure), to	supporter	ertragen	sopportare	soportar	uthärda	fartrogn
bear (give birth to), to	enfanter	gebären	partorire	parir	föda	gevinen
beard	barbe,*f.*	Bart,*m.*	barba,*f.*	barba,*f.*	skägg,*n.*	bord,*f.*
bearer (*banking*)	porteur,*m.*	Überbringer,*m.*	portatore,*m.*	portador,*m.*	innehavare,*nn.*	brenger,*m.*
beast (animal)	bête,*f.*	Tier,*n.*	bestia,*f.*	bestia,*f.*	djur (fyrfota),*n.*	khaye,*f.*
beat (defeat), to	battre	besiegen	vincere	vencer	besegra	goyver zayn
beat (thrash), to	battre	schlagen	battere	pegar	slå	shlogn
beautiful	beau, belle	schön	bello	bello	vacker	sheyn
beauty	beauté,*f.*	Schönheit,*f.*	bellezza,*f.*	belleza,*f.*	skönhet,*nn.*	sheynkayt,*f.*
beaver (animal)	castor,*m.*	Biber,*m.*	castoro,*m.*	castor,*m.*	bäver,*nn.*	biber,*m.*
because (*conj.*)	parce que	weil	perchè	porque	emedan	vayl
because of (*adv.*)	à cause de	wegen	a causa di	a causa de	på grund av	makhmes
become, to	devenir	werden	diventare	hacerse	bli(va)	vern
become of (happen to), to	devenir	werden aus	avvenire	ser de	bli(va) av	vern fun
bed	lit,*m.*	Bett,*n.*	letto,*m.*	cama,*f.*	säng,*nn.*	bet,*f.*
bedroom	chambre à coucher,*f.*	Schlafzimmer,*n.*	camera,*f.*	alcoba,*f.*	sovrum,*n.*	shloftsimer,*m.*
bee	abeille,*f.*	Biene,*f.*	ape,*f.*	abeja,*f.*	bi,*n.*	bin,*f.*
beech (tree)	hêtre,*m.*	Buche,*f.*	faggio,*m.*	haya,*f.*	bok,*nn.*	buk,*m.*
beef	boeuf,*m.*	Rindfleisch,*n.*	manzo,*m.*	carne de vaca,*f.*	nötkött,*n.*	rinderns,*n.*
beer	bière,*f.*	Bier,*n.*	birra,*f.*	cerveza,*f.*	öl,*n.*	bir,*n.*
beet (red root)	betterave,*f.*	rote Rübe,*f.*	barbabietola rossa,*f.*	remolacha,*f.*	rödbeta,*nn.*	burik,*m.*
beetle	scarabée,*m.*	Käfer,*m.*	scarafaggio,*m.*	escarabajo,*m.*	skalbagge,*nn.*	zhuk,*m.*
before (ahead, *adv.*)	avant	vorn(e)	davanti	adelante	före	fun fornt
before (earlier, *adv.*)	plus tôt	früher	prima	antes	förut	frier
before (earlier than, *prep.*)	avant (de)	vor	prima di	antes de	före	far
before (in front of, *prep.*)	devant	vor	davanti a	delante de	framför	far
before (in the past, *adv.*)	auparavant	vorher	un tempo	antes	förut	frier
before (prior to the time when, *conj.*)	avant que	bevor	prima che	antes (de) que	innan	eyder
beforehand (*adv.*)	par avance	(im) voraus	in anticipo	antes	i förväg	frier
beg (entreat), to	supplier	bitten	supplicare	rogar	bönfalla	betn zikh bay
beg (solicit alms), to	mendier	betteln	mendicare	mendigar	tigga	betlen
beggar	mendiant,*m.*	Bettler,*m.*	mendicante,*m.*	mendigo,*m.*	tiggare,*nn.*	betler,*m.*
begin (come into being), to	commencer	beginnen	cominciare	empezar	börja	onheybn zikh
begin (start to do), to	commencer	anfangen	cominciare	comenzar	börja	onheybn
beginning	commencement, *m.*	Anfang,*m.*	principio,*m.*	principio,*m.*	början,*nn.*	onheyb,*m.*
behave (conduct oneself), to	conduire, se	benehmen, sich	comportarsi	conducirse	uppföra sig	oyffirn zikh

English	French	German	Italian	Spanish	Swedish	Yiddish
behavior	conduite,*f.*	Benehmen,*n.*	comportamento, *m.*	conducta,*f.*	uppförande,*n.*	oyffir,*m.*
behind (in the rear, *adv.*)	en arrière	hinten	di dietro	detrás	bakom	hintn
behind (late, *adv.*)	en retard	hinterher	in ritardo	con retraso	efter	hintershtelik
behind (*prep.*)	derrière	hinter	dietro a	detrás de	bakom	hinter
behold, to	voir	ansehen	mirare	mirar	skåda	derzen
Belgian (*adj.*)	belge	belgisch	belga	belga	belgisk	belgish
Belgium	Belgique,*f.*	Belgien,*n.*	Belgio,*m.*	Bélgica	Belgien,*n.*	Belgye,*f.*
belief (opinion)	opinion,*f.*	Glaube,*m.*	opinione,*f.*	opinión,*f.*	tro,*nn.*	meynung,*f.*
believe (accept), to	croire	glauben	credere	creer	tro	gleybn
bell	cloche,*f.*	Glocke,*f.*	campanello,*m.*	campana,*f.*	klocka,*nn.*	glok,*m.*
bellow (roar), to	mugir	brüllen	muggire	bramar	ryta	ritshen
belly (abdomen)	ventre,*m.*	Bauch,*m.*	pancia,*f.*	vientre,*m.*	buk,*nn.*	boykh,*m.*
belong (be a part of), to	faire partie de	gehören	appartenere	pertenecer	tillhöra	gehern
belong to (be the property of), to	appartenir à	gehören	appartenere a	pertenecer	tillhöra	gehern tsu
beloved (*adj.*)	bien-aimé	geliebt	amato	querido	älskad	balibt
below (lower down, *adv.*)	en bas	unten	di sotto	abajo	nedanför	untn
below (lower than, *prep.*)	au-dessous de	unter(halb)	sotto (a)	debajo de	under	unter
belt (article of clothing)	ceinture,*f.*	Gürtel,*m.*	cintura,*f.*	cinto,*m.*	bälte,*n.*	gartl,*m.*
bench (long seat)	banc,*m.*	Bank,*f.*	banco,*m.*	banco,*m.*	bänk,*nn.*	bank,*f.*
bend (be bent), to	courber, (se)	beugen, sich	piegarsi	encorvarse	böja sig	beygn zikh
bend (make bend), to	plier	biegen	piegare	doblar	böja	beygn
beneath (below, *adv.*)	au-dessous	unten	di sotto	abajo	nedanför	untn
beneath (below, *prep.*)	au-dessous de	unter	sotto	bajo	under	unter
benefit (advantage)	profit,*m.*	Vorteil,*m.*	profitto,*m.*	ventaja,*f.*	fördel,*nn.*	toyve,*f.*
bent (curved)	courbé	gebogen	curvo	encorvado	krokig	oysgeboygn
bent (penchant)	penchant,*m.*	Neigung,*f.*	disposizione,*f.*	propensión,*f.*	böjelse,*nn.*	netie,*f.*
Berlin	Berlin,*m.*	Berlin,*n.*	Berlino,*m.*	Berlín	Berlin,*n.*	Berlin,*n.*
Berne	Berne,*f.*	Bern,*n.*	Berna. *f.*	Berna	Bern,*n.*	Bern,*n.*
berry (fruit)	baie,*f.*	Beere,*f.*	bacca,*f.*	baya,*f.*	bär,*n.*	yagde,*f.*
berth (train bunk)	couchette,*f.*	(Schlafwagen) Bett,*n.*	cucetta,*f.*	litera,*f.*	bädd,*nn.*	betl,*n.*
beside (next to, *prep.*)	à côté de	neben	accanto a	al lado de	bredvid	lebn
beside (other than, *prep.*)	à part	ausser	oltre a	además de	utom	khuts
besides (moreover, *adv.*)	en outre	ausserdem	inoltre	además	dessutom	khuts dem
best (*adj.*)	(le) meilleur	best	(il) migliore	(el) mejor	bäst	best
bestow, to	accorder	verleihen	conferire	otorgar	skänka	bashenken
bet	pari,*m.*	Wette,*f.*	scomessa,*f.*	apuesta,*f.*	vad,*n.*	gevet,*n.*
bet, to	parier	wetten	scommettere	apostar	slå vad om	vetn zikh
betray (deceive), to	trahir	verraten	tradire	traicionar	slå vad	vetn zikh
betray (reveal), *to*	trahir	verraten	tradire	descubrir	röja	aroysgebn
better (*adj.*)	meilleur	besser	migliore	mejor	bättre	beser
better (*adv.*)	mieux	besser	meglio	mejor	bättre	beser
between (*prep.*)	entre	zwischen	fra	entre	mellan	tsvishn
beware of, to	prendre garde à	hüten vor, sich	guardarsi da	guardarse de	akta sig för	hitn zikh far
bewilder, to	ahurir	verwirren	confondere	aturdir	förvirra	tsetumlen
beyond (farther on than, *prep.*)	au-delà de	über...hinaus	oltre	más allá de	bortom	vayter fun
beyond (out of reach of, *prep.*)	au-dessus de	jenseits	al di sopra di	más allá de	bortom	vayter fun
Bible	Bible,*f.*	Bibel,*f.*	Bibbia,*f.*	Biblia,*f.*	bibel,*nn.*	bibl,*f.*
bibliography	bibliographie,*f.*	Schrifttum,*n.*	bibliografia,*f.*	bibliografía,*f.*	bibliografi,*nn.*	bibliografye,*f.*
bicycle	bicyclette,*f.*	(Fahr)Rad, *n.*	bicicletta,*f.*	bicicleta,*f.*	cykel,*nn.*	velosiped,*m.*
bid (amount offered)	offre,*f.*	Angebot,*n.*	offerta,*f.*	postura,*f.*	anbud,*n.*	onbot,*m.*
bidder (*bus.*)	enchérisseur,*m.*	Bieter,*m.*	offerente,*m.,f.*	postor,*m.*	spekulant,*nn.*	onboter,*m.*
big	grand	gross	grande	grande	stor	groys
bill (beak)	bec,*m.*	Schnabel,*m.*	becco,*m.*	pico,*m.*	näbb,*nn.*	shnobl,*m.*
bill (currency)	billet,*m.*	Geldschein,*m.*	biglietto (di banca),*m.*	billete,*m.*	sedel,*nn.*	banknot,*m.*
bill (invoice)	facture,*f.*	Rechnung,*f.*	fattura,*f.*	factura,*f.*	räkning,*nn.*	khezhbn,*m.*
bill of exchange	traite,*f.*	Wechsel,*m.*	cambiale,*f.*	letra de cambio,*f.*	växel,*nn.*	veksl,*m.*
bill of lading	connaissement,*m.*	Frachtbrief,*m.*	polizza di carico, *f.*	conocimiento de embarque,*m.*	fraktsedel,*nn.*	frakhttsetl,*n.*
bill of sale	contrat de vente, *m.*	Verkaufschein, *m.*	atto di vendita, *m.*	carta de venta,*f.*	köpebrev,*n.*	farkoyf-tsetl,*n.*
billiards	billard,*m.*	Billard,*n.*	giuoco del bigliardo,*m.*	billar,*m.*	biljard,*nn.*	bilyard,*m.*
bind (tie), to	lier	binden	legare	atar	binda	bindn
biography	biographie,*f.*	Lebensgeschichte,*f.*	biografia,*f.*	biografía,*f.*	biografi,*nn.*	biografye,*f.*
biology	biologie,*f.*	Biologie,*f.*	biologia,*f.*	biología,*f.*	biologi,*nn.*	biologye,*f.*
birch (tree)	bouleau,*m.*	Birke,*f.*	betulla,*f.*	abedul,*m.*	björk,*nn.*	beryoze,*f.*
bird	oiseau,*m.*	Vogel,*m.*	uccello,*m.*	ave,*f.*	fågel,*nn.*	foygl,*m.*
birth	naissance,*f.*	Geburt,*f.*	nascita,*f.*	nacimiento,*m.*	födelse,*nn.*	geboyrn,*n.*
birthday	anniversaire,*m.*	Geburtstag,*m.*	compleanno,*m.*	cumpleaños,*m.*	födelsedag,*nn.*	geboyrn-tog,*m.*
bishop	évêque,*m.*	Bischof,*m.*	vescovo,*m.*	obispo,*m.*	biskop,*nn.*	biskup,*m.*
bit (small part)	morceau,*m.*	Bisschen,*n.*	pezzetto,*m.*	poquito,*m.*	smula,*nn.*	bisl,*n.*
bite	coup de dents,*m.*	Biss,*m.*	morso,*m.*	mordedura,*f.*	bett,*n.*	bis,*m.*

English	French	German	Italian	Spanish	Swedish	Yiddish
bite, to	mordre	beissen	mordere	morder	bita	baysn
bitter	amer, -mère	bitter	amaro	amargo	bitter	biter
black	noir	schwarz	nero	negro	svart	shvarts
blackberry	mûre sauvage,*f.*	Brombeere,*f.*	mora di rovo,*f.*	mora,*f.*	björnbär,*n.*	shvartse maline, *f.*
blackbird	merle,*m.*	Star,*m.*	merlo,*m.*	mirlo,*m.*	koltrast,*nn.*	amstl,*m.*
blackboard	tableau noir,*m.*	Wandtafel,*f.*	lavagna,*f.*	pizarra,*f.*	svart tavla,*nn.*	tovl,*m.*
blacksmith	forgeron,*m.*	Schmied,*m.*	fabbro ferraio, *m.*	herrero,*m.*	smed,*nn.*	shmid,*m.*
bladder (*anat.*)	vessie,*f.*	Harnblase,*f.*	vescica,*f.*	vejiga,*f.*	blåsa,*nn.*	penkher,*m.*
blade (cutting tool)	lame,*f.*	Klinge,*f.*	lama,*f.*	hoja,*f.*	blad,*n.*	kling,*f.*
blame	faute,*f.*	Schuld,*f.*	colpa,*m.*	culpa,*f.*	skuld,*nn.*	shuld,*f.*
blame, to	blâmer	tadeln	biasimare	culpar	klandra	bashuldikn
blank (unmarked)	blanc, -he	leer	in bianco	en blanco	blank	pust
blanket	couverture,*f.*	Decke,*f.*	coperta,*f.*	manta,*f.*	filt,*nn.*	koldre,*f.*
blast (explode), to	faire sauter	sprengen	far saltare	volar	spränga	oyfraysn
blaze (burn brightly), to	flamber	lodern	fiammeggiare	arder	flamma	flamen
bleach (make white), to	blanchir	bleichen	imbiancare	blanquear	bleka	bleykhn
bleat, to	bêler	blöken	belare	balar	bräka	meken
bleed (lose blood), to	saigner	bluten	sanguinare	sangrar	blöda	blutikn
blend (mixture)	mélange,*m.*	Mischung,*f.*	miscela,*f.*	mezcla,*f.*	blandning,*nn.*	gemish,*m.*
blend (mix), to	mélanger	mischen	mescolare	mezclar	blanda	mishn
bless, to	bénir	segnen	benedire	bendecir	välsigna	bentshn
blessing (boon)	bienfait,*m.*	Segen,*m.*	grazia,*f.*	bendición,*f.*	välsignelse,*nn.*	brokhe,*f.*
blind (lacking sight)	aveugle	blind	cieco	ciego	blind	blind
blind, to	aveugler	blenden	accecare	cegar	blända	blind makhn
bliss	félicité,*f.*	Wonne,*f.*	felicità,*f.*	felicidad,*f.*	sällhet,*nn.*	glikzelikayt,*f.*
blister	ampoule,*f.*	Blase,*f.*	vescichetta,*f.*	ampolla,*f.*	blåsa,*nn.*	penkher,*m.*
blizzard	tempête de neige,*f.*	Schneesturm,*m.*	tempesta di neve,*f.*	ventisca,*f.*	snöstorm,*nn.*	zaverukhe,*f.*
block (solid piece)	bloc,*m.*	Block,*m.*	blocco,*m.*	bloque,*m.*	block,*n.*	blok,*m.*
block (obstruct), to	bloquer	(ver)sperren	ingombrare	obstruir	spärra	farshparn
blond	blond	blond	biondo	rubio	blond	blond
blood	sang,*m.*	Blut,*n.*	sangue,*m.*	sangre,*f.*	blod,*n.*	blut,*n.*
bloom, to	fleurir	blühen	fiorire	florecer	blomma	blien
blossom	fleur,*f.*	Blüte,*f.*	fiore,*m.*	flor,*f.*	blom,*nn.*	kveyt,*f.*
blot (stain)	tache,*f.*	Klecks,*m.*	macchia,*f.*	mancha,*f.*	fläck,*nn.*	flek,*m.*
blot (stain), to	tacher	beflecken	macchiare	manchar	fläcka ner	klekn
blot out (efface), to	effacer	austilgen	cancellare	tachar	utplåna	oysmekn
blouse (shirtwaist)	blouse,*f.*	Bluse,*f.*	blusa,*f.*	blusa,*f.*	blus,*nn.*	bluze,*f.*
blow (stroke)	coup,*m.*	Schlag,*m.*	colpo,*m.*	golpe,*m.*	slag,*n.*	klap,*m.*
blow (breathe out), to	souffler	blasen	esalare	soplar	blåsa	blozn
blow (make move), to	pousser	blasen	fare volare	soplar	blåsa	blozn
blue	bleu	blau	azzurro	azul	blå	bloy
blueberry	myrtille,*f.*	Heidelbeere,*f.*	bacca di mirtillo,*f.*	arándano,*m.*	blåbär,*n.*	shvartse yagde, *f.*
blueprint	photocalque,*m.*	Blaupause,*f.*	cianografia,*f.*	heliograbado,*m.*	blåkopia,*nn.*	plan,*m.*
blunder	bévue,*f.*	Fehler,*m.*	balordaggine, *f.*	disparate,*m.*	blunder,*nn.*	grober feler,*m.*
blunt (dull)	émoussé	stumpf	smussato	embotado	slö	temp
blush, to	rougir	erröten	arrossire	ruborizarse	rodna	reytlen zikh
board (council)	conseil,*m.*	Ausschuss,*m.*	consiglio,*m.*	junta,*f.*	styrelse,*nn.*	rot,*m.*
board (plank)	planche,*f.*	Brett,*n.*	tavola,*f.*	tabla,*f.*	bräde,*n.*	bret,*f.*
boarding house	pension (de famille),*f.*	Pension,*f.*	pensione,*f.*	pensión,*f.*	pensionat,*n.*	pansyon,*m.*
boast, to	vanter, se	prahlen	vantarsi	jactarse	skryta	barimen zikh
boat	bateau,*m.*	Boot,*n.*	battello,*m.*	barco,*m.*	båt,*nn.*	shifl,*n.*
body (*anat.*)	corps,*m.*	Körper,*m.*	corpo,*m.*	cuerpo,*m.*	kropp,*nn.*	guf,*m.*
boil (bubble up), to	bouillir	kochen	bollire	hervir	koka	kokhn
bold (courageous)	hardi	kühn	ardito	atrevido	djärv	drayst
Bolivia	Bolivie,*f.*	Bolivien,*n.*	Bolivia,*m.*	Bolivia	Bolivia,*n.*	Bolivye,*f.*
bolt (lock)	verrou,*m.*	Riegel,*m.*	stanghetta,*f.*	cerrojo,*m.*	regel,*nn.*	rigl,*m.*
bolt (long metal fastener)	boulon,*m.*	Bolzen,*m.*	bollone,*m.*	perno,*m.*	bult,*nn.*	shroyf,*m.*
bomb (projectile)	bombe,*f.*	Bombe,*f.*	bomba,*f.*	bomba,*f.*	bomb,*nn.*	bombe,*f.*
bond (debenture)	obligation,*f.*	Schuldschein,*m.*	obbligazione,*f.*	bono,*m.*	obligation,*nn.*	obligatsye,*f.*
bond (emotional tie)	lien,*m.*	Band,*n.* (*pl.* Bande)	legame,*m.*	lazo,*m.*	band,*n.*	band,*m.*
bone	os,*m.*	Knochen,*m.*	osso,*m.*	hueso,*m.*	ben,*n.*	beyn,*m.*
bonus (extra wages)	surpaye,*f.*	Sondervergü- tung,*f.*	premio,*m.*	prima,*f.*	bonus,*nn.*	premye,*f.*
book	livre,*m.*	Buch,*n.*	libro,*m.*	libro,*m.*	bok,*nn.* (*pl.* böcker)	bukh,*n.*
book (engage space), to	retenir	bestellen	prenotare	reservar	beställa biljett	bashteln
bookkeeper (*bus.*)	teneur de livres, *m.*	Buchhalter,*m.*	contabile,*m.,f.*	tenedor de libros,*m.*	bokhållare,*nn.*	bukhhalter,*m.*
bookkeeping (*bus.*)	tenue des livres,*f.*	Buchhaltung,*f.*	contabilità,*f.*	contabilidad,*f.*	bokföring,*nn.*	bukhhalterye,*f.*
booklet	livret,*m.*	Broschüre,*f.*	libretto,*m.*	folleto,*m.*	broschyr,*nn.*	broshur,*f.*
boom (*bus.*)	boom,*m.*	Konjunktur,*f.*	prosperità,*f.*	prosperidad,*f.*	högkonjunktur, *nn.*	oyfbli,*m.*
boot (footgear)	botte,*f.*	Stiefel,*m.*	stivale,*m.*	bota,*f.*	stövel,*nn.*	shtivl,*m.*

English	French	German	Italian	Spanish	Swedish	Yiddish
border (edge)	bord,*m.*	Rand,*m.*	bordo,*m.*	borde,*m.*	kant,*nn.*	breg,*m.*
border (frontier)	frontière,*f.*	Grenze,*f.*	confine,*m.*	frontera,*f.*	gräns,*nn.*	grenets,*m.*
boredom	ennui,*m.*	Lang(e)weile,*f.*	noia,*f.*	aburrimiento,*m.*	tråkighet,*nn.*	langvayl,*f.*
born, to be	naître	geboren sein (werden)	nascere	nacer	född	geboyrn vern
borrow, to	emprunter	borgen	prendere a prestito	tomar (pedir) prestado	låna	antlayen
borrower (*bus.*)	emprunteur,*m.*	Borger,*m.*	mutuatario,*m.*	prestatario,*m.*	låntagare,*nn.*	antlayer,*m.*
bosom	sein,*m.*	Busen,*m.*	seno,*m.*	seno,*m.*	barm,*nn.*	buzem,*m.*
boss (master)	patron,*m.*	Chef,*m.*	padrone,*m.*	patrón,*m.*	chef,*nn.*	shef,*m.*
botany	botanique,*f.*	Botanik,*f.*	botanica,*f.*	botánica,*f.*	botanik,*nn.*	botanik,*f.*
both (*adj.*)	les deux	beide	tutti e due	los dos	båda	beyde
both (*pron.*)	tous (les) deux	beide	entrambi	los dos	båda	beyde
bother (annoy), to	ennuyer	stören	infastidire	molestar	besvära	shtern
bottle	bouteille,*f.*	Flasche,*f.*	bottiglia,*f.*	botella,*f.*	flaska,*nn.*	flash,*f.*
bottom	fond,*m.*	Boden,*m.*	fondo,*m.*	fondo,*m.*	botten,*nn.*	dek,*f.*
bough	rameau,*m.*	Ast,*m.*	ramo,*m.*	rama,*f.*	gren,*nn.*	tsvayg,*m.*
bounce, to	bondir	springen	balzare	rebotar	studsa	opshpringen
bound (leap)	bond,*m.*	Sprung,*m.*	balzo,*m.*	salto,*m.*	hopp,*n.*	shprung,*m.*
boundary (limit line)	limite,*f.*	Grenze,*f.*	limite,*m.*	límite,*m.*	gräns,*nn.*	grenets,*m.*
bow (nod)	salut,*m.*	Verbeugung,*f.*	inchino,*m.*	inclinación,*f.*	bugning,*nn.*	farneyg,*m.*
bow (of ship)	avant,*m.*	Bug,*m.*	prora,*f.*	proa,*f.*	för,*nn.*	fornt,*m.*
bow (in greeting), to	incliner, s'	verbeugen, sich	fare un inchino	hacer reverencia	buga (sig)	farneygn zikh
bowels (*anat.*)	intestins,*m.pl.*	Eingeweide,*n.*	viscere,*f.pl.*	intestinos,*m.pl.*	inälvor,*nn.pl.*	gederem,*pl.*
bowl (dish)	bol,*m.*	Schüssel,*f.*	scodella,*f.*	cuenco,*m.*	skål,*nn.*	shisl,*f.*
box (container)	boîte,*f.*	Schachtel,*f.*	scatola,*f.*	caja,*f.*	ask,*nn.*	kestl,*n.*
box (fight), to	boxer	boxen	fare il pugilato	boxear	boxas	boksn zikh
boy (lad)	garçon,*m.*	Junge,*m.*	ragazzo,*m.*	muchacho,*m.*	pojke,*nn.*	yingl,*m.*
Boy Scout	boy-scout,*m.*	Pfadfinder,*m.*	Boy Scout,*m.*	Niño Explorador,*m.*	boyscout,*nn.*	skoyt,*m.*
bracelet	bracelet,*m.*	Armband,*n.*	braccialetto,*m.*	pulsera,*f.*	armband,*n.*	braslet,*m.*
braid (plait), to	tresser	flechten	intrecciare	hacer trenzas	fläta	farflekhtn
brain (*anat.*)	cerveau,*m.*	Gehirn,*n.*	cervello,*m.*	cerebro,*m.*	hjärna,*nn.*	markh,*m.*
brake	frein,*m.*	Bremse,*f.*	freno,*m.*	freno,*m.*	broms,*nn.*	tormoz,*m.*
branch (bough)	branche,*f.*	Zweig,*m.*	ramo,*m.*	rama,*f.*	gren,*nn.*	tsvayg,*m.*
brand (trade mark)	marque,*f.*	Marke,*f.*	marca,*f.*	marca (de fábrica),*f.*	(varu)märke,*n.*	marke,*f.*
brandy	eau-de-vie,*f.*	Kognak,*m.*	acquavite,*f.*	aguardiente,*m.*	konjak,*nn.*	konyak,*m.*
brass (metal, *n.*)	laiton,*m.*	Messing,*n.*	ottone,*m.*	latón,*m.*	mässing,*nn.*	mesh,*m.*
brassiere	soutien-gorge,*m.*	Büstenhalter,*m.*	reggipetto,*m.*	sostén,*m.*	brösthållare,*nn.*	stanik,*m.*
brave	brave	tapfer	coraggioso	valiente	modig	heldish
Brazil	Brésil,*m.*	Brasilien,*n.*	Brasile,*m.*	(el) Brasil	Brasilien,*n.*	Brazil,*n.*
Brazilian (*adj.*)	brésilien, -ne	brasilianisch	brasiliano	brasileño	brasiliansk	brazilish
breach of contract (*bus.*)	rupture de contrat,*f.*	Vertragsbruch, *m.*	rottura di contratto,*f.*	contravención del contrato,*f.*	kontraktsbrott, *n.*	kontrakt-brekhung,*f.*
bread	pain,*m.*	Brot,*n.*	pane,*m.*	pan,*m.*	bröd,*n.*	broyt,*n.*
breadth (width)	largeur,*f.*	Breite,*f.*	larghezza,*f.*	anchura,*f.*	bredd,*nn.*	breyt,*f.*
break (come apart), to	casser, se	brechen	rompersi	romperse	gå sönder	brekhn zikh
break (make divide), to	rompre	abbrechen	rompere	romper	bryta	brekhn
break (make smash), to	casser	zerbrechen	rompere	romper	slå sönder	tsebrekhn
breakfast	petit déjeuner,*m.*	Frühstück,*n.*	(prima) colazione,*f.*	desayuno,*m.*	frukost,*nn.*	iberbaysn,*m.*
breast	sein,*m.*	Brust,*f.*	petto,*m.*	pecho,*m.*	bröst,*n.*	brust,*f.*
breath	haleine,*f.*	Atem,*m.*	fiato,*m.*	aliento,*m.*	andedräkt,*nn.*	otem,*m.*
breathe (draw breath), to	respirer	atmen	respirare	respirar	andas	otemen
breed (stock)	race,*f.*	Rasse,*f.*	razza,*f.*	raza,*f.*	ras,*nn.*	rase,*f.*
breeze	brise,*f.*	Lüftchen,*n.*	brezza,*f.*	brisa,*f.*	bris,*nn.*	vintl,*n.*
bribe, to	suborner	bestechen	corrompere	sobornar	muta	unterkoyfn
brick (building material)	brique,*f.*	Ziegel,*m.*	mattone,*m.*	ladrillo,*m.*	tegel,*n.*	tsigl,*m.*
bride	mariée,*f.*	Braut,*f.*	sposa,*f.*	novia,*f.*	brud,*nn.*	kale,*f.*
bridge (span)	pont,*m.*	Brücke,*f.*	ponte,*m.*	puente,*m.*	bro,*nn.*	brik,*f.*
bridge, contract	bridge au plafond,*m.*	Bridge,*n.*	bridge a contratto,*m.*	juego de naipes,*m.*	kontrakt-bridge,*nn.*	bridzh,*m.*
bridle (harness)	bride,*f.*	Zaum,*m.*	briglia,*f.*	brida,*f.*	betsel,*n.*	tsayml,*n.*
brief (fleeting)	bref, brève	kurz	breve	breve	kort	kurts
briefcase	serviette,*f.*	Aktenmappe,*f.*	portafoglio,*m.*	cartera,*f.*	portfölj,*nn.*	teke,*f.*
bright (shining)	brillant	hell	brillante	brillante	ljus	glantsik
brilliant (remarkable)	brillant	glänzend	brillante	brillante	briljant	glentsndik
bring, to	apporter	bringen	portare	traer	ta(ga) med	brengen
brink (verge)	bord,*m.*	Rand,*m.*	orlo,*m.*	borde,*m.*	rand,*nn.*	rand,*m.*
British (*adj.*)	britannique	britisch	britannico	británico	brittisk	british
brittle	fragile	spröde	fragile	quebradizo	skör	brekhik
broad (wide)	large	breit	largo	ancho	bred	breyt
broadcasting (*rad.*)	radio-diffusion,*f.*	Rundfunkübertragung,*f.*	radio diffusione, *f.*	radiofusión,*f.*	radioutsändning, *nn.*	radyo-transmitirung,*f.*
broker (*bus.*)	courtier,*m.*	Makler,*m.*	sensale,*m.*	corredor,*m.*	mäklare,*nn.*	mekler,*m.*
brokerage (fee)	frais de courtage,*m.pl.*	Maklergebühr,*f.*	provvigione (di sensale),*f.*	corretaje,*m.*	mäklararvode, *n.*	meklergelt,*n.*
bronchitis	bronchite,*f.*	Bronchitis,*f.*	bronchite,*f.*	bronquitis,*f.*	bronkit,*nn.*	bronkhit,*m.*
bronze (*n.*)	bronze,*m.*	Bronze,*f.*	bronzo,*m.*	bronce,*m.*	brons,*nn.*	brondz,*n.*

English	French	German	Italian	Spanish	Swedish	Yiddish
brooch	broche,*f.*	Brosche,*f.*	spillone,*m.*	broche,*m.*	brosch,*nn.*	brosh,*f.*
brood over, to	remâcher	brüten über	ruminare tristamente	cavilar	grubbla över	klern vegn
brook	ruisseau,*m.*	Bach,*m.*	ruscello,*m.*	arroyo,*m.*	bäck,*nn.*	ritshke,*f.*
broom	balai,*m.*	Besen,*m.*	scopa,*f.*	escoba,*f.*	kvast,*nn.*	bezem,*m.*
brother	frère,*m.*	Bruder,*m.*	fratello,*m.*	hermano,*m.*	bro(de)r, *nn.* (*pl.* bröder)	bruder,*m.*
brother-in-law	beau-frère,*m.*	Schwager,*m.*	cognato,*m.*	cuñado,*m.*	svåger,*nn.*	shvoger,*m.*
brown	brun	braun	marrone	pardo (castaño)	brun	broyn
bruise	meurtrissure,*f.*	Quetschung,*f.*	ammaccatura,*f.*	cardenal,*m.*	blåmärke,*n.*	sinyak,*m.*
brunette (*adj.*)	brune	brünett	bruna	moreno	brunett	brunet
brush (scrubbing utensil)	brosse,*f.*	Bürste,*f.*	spazzola,*f.*	cepillo,*m.*	borste,*nn.*	barsht,*f.*
Brussels	Bruxelles,*f.*	Brüssel,*n.*	Bruxelles,*f.*	Bruselas	Bryssel,*n.*	Brisl,*n.*
brute (animal, *n.*)	brute,*f.*	Tier,*n.*	bestia,*f.*	bruto,*m.*	best,*nn.*	bestye,*f.*
bubble, to	bouillonner	sprudeln	formare bolle	burbujear,*f.*	bubbla	blezlen
buck (male deer)	daim,*m.*	Bock,*m.*	daino,*m.*	macho del ciervo,*m.*	bock,*nn.*	hirsh,*m.*
bucket	seau,*m.*	Eimer,*m.*	secchia,*f.*	cubeta,*f.*	hink,*nn.*	emer,*m.*
bud (*bot.*)	bourgeon,*m.*	Knospe,*f.*	germoglio,*m.*	botón,*m.*	knopp,*nn.*	knosp,*m.*
budget (*n.*)	budget,*m.*	Budget,*n.*	bilancio,*m.*	presupuesto,*m.*	budget,*nn.*	budzhet,*m.*
Buenos Aires	Buenos-Aires,*m.*	Buenos Aires,*n.*	Buenos Aires,*f.*	Buenos Aires	Buenos Aires,*n.*	Buenos Aires,*n.*
buffalo	buffle,*m.*	Büffel,*m.*	bufalo,*m.*	bisonte,*m.*	buffel,*nn.*	bufloks,*m.*
bug (insect)	insecte,*m.*	Kerbtier,*m.*	insetto,*m.*	bicho,*m.*	insekt,*nn.*	zhuk,*m.*
bugle	clairon,*m.*	Signalhorn,*n.*	tromba,*f.*	corneta,*f.*	horn,*n.*	trumeyt,*m.*
build, to	bâtir	bauen	fabbricare	edificar	bygga	boyen
building	bâtiment,*m.*	Gebäude,*n.*	fabbricato,*m.*	edificio,*m.*	byggnad,*nn.*	binyen,*m.*
bulb (light bulb)	ampoule,*f.*	Glühbirne,*f.*	lampada (incandescente),*f.*	bombilla,*f.*	glödlampa,*nn.*	lempl,*n.*
Bulgaria	Bulgarie,*f.*	Bulgarien,*n.*	Bulgaria,*f.*	Bulgaria	Bulgarien,*n.*	Bulgarye,*n.*
bulk (largest part)	gros,*m.*	Hauptteil,*m.*	grosso,*m.*	mayor parte,*f.*	huvuddel,*nn.*	rov,*n.*
bull (male bovine)	taureau,*m.*	Stier,*m.*	toro,*m.*	toro,*m.*	tjur,*nn.*	oks,*m.*
bullet	balle,*f.*	Kugel,*f.*	pallottola,*f.*	bala,*f.*	kula,*nn.*	koyl,*f.*
bundle (parcel)	paquet,*m.*	Paket,*n.*	pacco,*m.*	paquete,*m.*	packe,*nn.*	pekl,*n.*
burden (load)	fardeau,*m.*	Last,*f.*	carico,*m.*	carga,*f.*	börda,*nn.*	mase,*f.*
bureau (chest)	commode,*f.*	Kommode,*f.*	cassettone,*m.*	cómoda,*f.*	byrå,*nn.*	komod,*m.*
bureau (office)	bureau,*m.*	Büro,*n.*	ufficio,*m.*	oficina,*f.*	byrå,*nn.*	byuro,*m.*
burglar	cambrioleur,*m.*	Einbrecher,*m.*	ladro,*m.*	ladrón,*m.*	inbrottstjuv, *nn.*	aynbrekher,*m.*
burial	enterrement,*m.*	Begräbnis,*n.*	sepoltura,*f.*	entierro,*m.*	begravning,*nn.*	kvure,*f.*
burn (be on fire), to	brûler	brennen	bruciare	arder	brinna	brenen
burn (set fire to), to	brûler	verbrennen	bruciare	quemar	bränna	farbrenen
burst, to	éclater	bersten	scoppiare	estallar	brista	platsn
bury (entomb), to	ensevelir	begraben	seppellire	enterrar	begrava	bagrobn
bus	autobus,*m.*	Omnibus,*m.*	autobus,*m.*	ómnibus,*m.*	buss,*nn.*	oytobus,*m.*
bush (plant)	buisson,*m.*	Busch,*m.*	cespuglio,*m.*	arbusto,*m.*	buske,*nn.*	kust,*m.*
business (commerce)	affaires,*f.pl.*	Geschäft,*n.*	affari,*m.pl.*	negocio,*m.*	affärer,*nn. pl.*	gesheft,*n.*
businessman	homme d'affaires,*m.*	Geschäftsmann, *m.*	uomo d'affari, *m.*	hombre de negocios,*m.*	affärsman,*nn.* (*pl.* -män)	gesheftsman,*m.*
bust (statue)	buste,*m.*	Büste,*f.*	busto,*m.*	busto,*m.*	byst,*nn.*	byust,*m.*
busy (occupied)	occupé	beschäftigt	occupato	ocupado	upptagen	farnumen
but (if not, *conj.*)	sinon	ausser dass	se non	a menos que	om inte	saydn
but (yet, *conj.*)	mais	aber	ma	pero	men	ober
butcher	boucher,*m.*	Fleischer,*m.*	macellaio,*m.*	carnicero,*m.*	slaktare,*nn.*	katsev,*m.*
butter	beurre,*m.*	Butter,*f.*	burro,*m.*	mantequilla (-teca),*f.*	smör,*n.*	puter,*f.*
butterfly	papillon,*m.*	Schmetterling,*m.*	farfalla,*f.*	mariposa,*f.*	fjäril,*nn.*	flaterl,*n.*
button	bouton,*m.*	Knopf,*m.*	bottone,*m.*	botón,*m.*	knapp,*nn.*	knepl,*n.*
buy, to	acheter	kaufen	comprare	comprar	köpa	koyfn
buyer	acheteur,*m.*	Käufer,*m.*	cliente,*m.,f.*	parroquiano,*m.*	köpare,*nn.*	koyfer,*m.*
by (prep., *math.*)	par	mal	per	por	gånger	oyf
by (near, *prep.*)	près (de)	bei	presso	junto a	vid	bay
by (prior to, *prep.*)	avant	vor	prima di	antes de	före	biz
by (via, *prep.*)	par	über	per	por	via	durkh
by-law	statut,*m.*	Statut,*n.*	statuto,*m.*	estatuto,*m.*	stadga,*nn.*	statut,*m.*
by-product	sous-produit,*m.*	Nebenprodukt,*n.*	sottoprodotto,*m.*	derivado,*m.*	biprodukt,*nn.*	bayprodukt,*m.*
cab (taxi)	taxi,*m.*	Taxe,*f.*	tassì,*m.*	taxi,*m.*	taxi,*nn.*	taksi,*m.*
cabbage	chou,*m.*	Kohl,*m.*	cavolo,*m.*	col,*f.*	kål,*nn.*	kroyt,*n.*
cabin (of ship)	cabine,*f.*	Kabine,*f.*	cabina,*f.*	camarote,*m.*	hytt,*nn.*	kayute,*f.*
cabinet (*govt.*)	cabinet,*m.*	Kabinett,*n.*	gabinetto,*m.*	gabinete,*m.*	ministär,*nn.*	kabinet,*m.*
cable (rope)	câble,*m.*	Kabel,*n.*	gomena,*f.*	cable,*m.*	kabel,*nn.*	kabl,*m.*
cable, to	câbler	kabeln	cablografare	cablegrafiar	telegrafera	kablen
cablegram	câblogramme,*m.*	Kabelgramm,*n.*	cablogramma,*m.*	cablegrama,*m.*	kabeltelegram,*n.*	kablgram,*f.*
cage	cage,*f.*	Käfig,*m.*	gabbia,*f.*	jaula,*f.*	bur,*nn.*	shtayg,*f.*
Cairo	Le Caire,*m.*	Kairo,*n.*	Il Cairo	Cairo	Kairo,*n.*	Kairo,*n.*
cake (dessert)	gâteau,*m.*	Kuchen,*m.*	torta,*f.*	torta,*f.*	tårta,*nn.*	kukhn,*m.*
calculate (compute), to	calculer	berechnen	calcolare	calcular	beräkna	oysrekhenen
calendar	calendrier,*m.*	Kalender,*m.*	calendario,*m.*	calendario,*m.*	almanacka,*nn.*	kalendar,*m.*
calf (*anat.*)	mollet,*m.*	Wade,*f.*	polpaccio,*m.*	pantorrilla,*f.*	vad,*nn.*	lidke,*f.*
calf (animal)	veau,*m.*	Kalb,*n.*	vitello,*m.*	ternero,*m.*	kalv,*nn.*	kalb,*n.*

English	French	German	Italian	Spanish	Swedish	Yiddish
call (shout)	cri,*m.*	Ruf,*m.*	chiamata,*f.*	grito,*m.*	rop,*n.*	ruf,*m.*
call (shout), to	crier	rufen	chiamare	gritar	ropa	rufn
call (summon), to	appeler	rufen lassen	chiamare	llamar	tillkalla	rufn
calm (*adj.*)	calme	ruhig	calmo	tranquilo	lugn	ruik
calorie	calorie,*f.*	Kalorie,*f.*	caloria,*f.*	caloría,*f.*	kalori,*nn.*	kalorye,*f.*
camel	chameau,*m.*	Kamel,*n.*	cammello,*m.*	camello,*m.*	kamel,*nn.*	keml,*m.*
camera	appareil photographique,*f.*	Kamera,*f.*	apparecchio fotografico,*m.*	cámara,*f.*	kamera,*nn.*	aparat,*m.*
camp (encampment, *mil.*)	camp,*m.*	Lager,*n.*	accampamento, *m.*	campamento,*m.*	läger,*n.*	lager,*m.*
campaign (*mil.*)	campagne,*f.*	Feldzug,*m.*	campagna,*f.*	campaña,*f.*	fälttåg,*n.*	kampanye,*f.*
can (tin)	boîte,*f.*	(Konserven)-Büchse,*f.*	latta,*f.*	lata,*f.*	(konserv)burk, *nn.*	pushke,*f.*
can (*v.*)	(*see* pouvoir, *p.* 2835)	(*see* können, *p.* 2892 ff.)	(*see* potere, *p.* 2958)	(*see* poder, *p.* 3023)	(*see* kunna, *p.* 3078)	(*see* kenen, *p p.* 3133–34)
Canada	Canada,*m.*	Kanada,*n.*	Canadà, *m.*	(el) Canadá	Kanada,*n.*	Kanade,*f.*
Canadian (*adj.*)	canadien, -ne	kanadisch	canadese	canadiense	kanadensisk	kanadish
canal	canal,*m.*	Kanal,*m.*	canale,*m.*	canal,*m.*	kanal,*nn.*	kanal,*m.*
canary	serin,*m.*	Kanarienvogel, *m.*	canarino,*m.*	canario,*m.*	kanariefågel, *nn.*	kanarik,*m.*
cancel (revoke), to	annuler	aufheben	annullare	cancelar	annulera	anulirn
cancer	cancer,*m.*	Krebs, *m.*	cancro,*m.*	cáncer,*m.*	kräfta,*nn.*	rak,*m.*
candidate	candidat,*m.*	Kandidat,*m.*	candidato,*m.*	candidato,*m.*	kandidat,*nn.*	kandidat,*m.*
candle	bougie,*f.*	Kerze,*f.*	candela,*f.*	vela,*f.*	(stearin)ljus,*n.*	likht,*f.*
candy	bonbons,*m.pl.*	Süssigkeit,*f.*	dolci,*m.pl.*	dulce,*m.*	sötsaker,*nn.pl.*	tsukerl,*n.*
cane (walking stick)	canne,*f.*	Spazierstock,*m.*	bastone,*m.*	bastón,*m.*	käpp,*nn.*	shtekn,*m.*
cannon	canon,*m.*	Kanone,*f.*	cannone,*m.*	cañón,*m.*	kanon,*nn.*	harmat,*m.*
canoe	canoë,*m.*	Kanu,*n.*	canoa,*f.*	canoa,*f.*	kanot,*nn.*	kanu,*m.*
canvas (cloth)	toile,*f.*	Leinwand,*f.*	tela di canapa,*f.*	lona,*f.*	kanfas,*nn.*	layvnt,*m.*
canvasser (*bus.*)	placier,*m.*	Hausierer,*m.*	venditore ambulante,*m.*	solicitador,*m.*	subskribentsamlare,*nn.*	verbirer,*m.*
cap (hat)	casquette,*f.*	Mütze,*f.*	berretto,*m.*	gorra,*f.*	mössa,*nn.*	hitl,*n.*
capable (competent)	capable	tüchtig	capace	capaz	duglig	feik
capacity (volume)	capacité,*f.*	Inhalt,*m.*	capacità,*f.*	capacidad,*f.*	kubikinnehåll,*n.*	araynnem,*m.*
cape (headland)	cap,*m.*	Kap,*n.*	capo,*m.*	cabo,*m.*	udde,*nn.*	kap,*m.*
capital (city)	capitale,*f.*	Hauptstadt,*f.*	capitale,*f.*	capital,*f.*	huvudstad,*nn.* (*pl.* -städer)	hoyptshtot,*f.*
capital (wealth)	capital,*m.*	Grundkapital, *n.*	capitale,*m.*	capital,*m.*	kapital,*n.*	kapital,*m.*
captain (officer)	capitaine,*m.*	Kapitän,*m.*	capitano,*m.*	capitán,*m.*	kapten,*nn.*	kapitan,*m.*
captive (prisoner)	captif,*m.*	Gefangene,*m.,f.*	prigioniero,*m.*	cautivo,*m.*	fånge,*nn.*	gefangener,*m.*
capture (seize), to	capturer	festnehmen	catturare	prender	gripa	khapn
car (auto)	voiture,*f.*	Auto,*n.*	auto,*f.*	coche,*m.*	bil,*nn.*	oyto,*m.*
car, railroad	wagon,*m.*	(Eisenbahn)-Wagen,*m.*	vagone,*m.*	vagón,*m.*	vagn,*nn.*	vagon,*m.*
carbon (*chem.*)	carbone,*m.*	Kohlenstoff,*m.*	carbonio,*m.*	carbono,*m.*	kol,*n.*	koylnshtof,*m.*
carbon copy	copie au carbone,*f.*	Durchschlag,*m.*	copia (a carta carbone),*f.*	copia (en papel carbón),*f.*	genomslagskopia,*nn.*	kopye,*f.*
card, calling	carte (de visite), *f.*	Visitenkarte,*f.*	carta (da visita), *f.*	tarjeta de visita, *f.*	visitkort,*n.*	kartl,*n.*
card, playing	carte (à jouer), *f.*	Spielkarte,*f.*	carta (da giuoco),*f.*	naipe,*m.*	spelkort,*n.*	kort,*f.*
card, postal	carte postale,*f.*	Postkarte,*f.*	cartolina,*f.*	tarjeta,*f.*	brevkort,*n.*	kartl,*n.*
cardboard	carton,*m.*	Pappe,*f.*	cartone,*m.*	cartón,*m.*	papp,*nn.*	karton,*m.*
care (concern)	souci,*m.*	Sorge,*f.*	cura,*f.*	cuidado,*m.*	bekymmer,*n.*	zorg,*f.*
care (custody)	charge,*f.*	Fürsorge,*f.*	custodia,*f.*	custodia,*f.*	vård,*nn.*	hazhgokhe,*f.*
care (heed)	attention,*f.*	Acht,*f.*	attenzione,*f.*	atención,*f.*	omsorg,*nn.*	akhtleygung, *f.*
care (be concerned), to	soucier, se	kümmern, sich	preoccuparsi (di)	interesarse en	bry sig om	arn
career	carrière,*f.*	Laufbahn,*f.*	carriera,*f.*	carrera,*f.*	karriär,*nn.*	karyere,*f.*
careful (cautious)	prudent	vorsichtig	cauto	cuidadoso	försiktig	opgehit
careless (negligent)	négligent	nachlässig	trascurato	descuidado	vårdslös	opgelozn
cargo	cargaison,*f.*	Ladung,*f.*	carico,*m.*	cargamento,*m.*	last,*nn.*	frakht,*f.*
carload (*bus.*)	voiturée,*f.*	Wagenladung,*f.*	carrata,*f.*	carretada,*f.*	vagnslast,*nn.*	vagon,*m.*
carnation	oeillet,*m.*	Nelke,*f.*	garofano,*m.*	clavel,*m.*	nejlika,*nn.*	negele,*n.*
carnival	carnaval,*m.*	Karneval,*m.*	carnevale,*m.*	carnaval,*m.*	karneval,*nn.*	karnaval,*m.*
carpenter	charpentier,*m.*	Zimmermann,*m.*	falegname,*m.*	carpintero,*m.*	snickare,*nn.*	stoler,*m.*
carpet	tapis,*m.*	Teppich,*m.*	tappeto,*m.*	alfombra,*f.*	matta,*nn.*	tepekh,*m.*
carriage (baby buggy)	voiture d'enfant, *f.*	Kinderwagen,*m.*	carrozzina,*f.*	coche (para niños),*m.*	barnvagn,*nn.*	vegele,*n.*
carriage (horse-drawn vehicle)	voiture,*f.*	Wagen,*m.*	carrozza,*f.*	coche,*m.*	vagn,*nn.*	karete,*f.*
carriage (posture)	port,*m.*	(Körper)-Haltung,*f.*	portamento,*m.*	porte,*m.*	hållning,*nn.*	haltung,*f.*
carrier (*bus.*)	transporteur,*m.*	Spediteur,*m.*	portatore,*m.*	portador,*m.*	transportör, *nn.*	ariberfirer,*m.*
carrot	carotte,*f.*	Mohrrübe,*f.*	carota,*f.*	zanahoria,*f.*	morot,*nn.* (*pl.* -rötter)	mer,*f.*
carry (bear), to	porter	tragen	portare	llevar	bära	trogn
cart	charrette,*f.*	Karren,*m.*	carretta,*f.*	carro,*m.*	kärra,*nn.*	vogn,*m.*
cartoon (caricature)	caricature,*f.*	Karikatur,*f.*	caricatura,*f.*	caricatura,*f.*	karikatyrteckning,*nn.*	karikatur,*f.*
carve (cut designs), to	graver	schnitzen	intagliare	tallar	snida	shnitsn
case (instance)	cas,*m.*	Fall,*m.*	caso,*m.*	caso,*m.*	fall,*n.*	fal,*m.*
cash (money)	(argent) comptant,*m.*	Bargeld,*n.*	contanti,*m.pl.*	efectivo,*m.*	kontanter,*nn.* *pl.*	mezumen,*n.*

English	French	German	Italian	Spanish	Swedish	Yiddish
cash (receive cash for), to	toucher	einlösen	incassare	hacer efectivo	inkassera	aynkasirn
cashier	caissier,*m.*	Kassierer,*m.*	cassiere,*m.,f.*	cajero,*m.*	kassör,*nn.*	kasirer,*m.*
cast (throw), to	lancer	werfen	gettare	arrojar	kasta	varfn
castle	château,*m.*	Schloss,*n.*	castello,*m.*	castillo,*m.*	slott,*n.*	shlos,*m.*
casual (offhand)	détaché	beiläufig	disinvolto	casual	i förbigående	kilakharyad
cat	chat,*m.*	Katze,*f.*	gatto,*m.*	gato,*m.*	katt,*nn.*	kats,*f.*
catalogue	catalogue,*m.*	Katalog,*m.*	catalogo,*m.*	catálogo,*m.*	katalog,*nn.*	katalog,*m.*
catch (nab), to	attraper	fangen	acchiappare	coger	fånga	khapn
caterpillar	chenille,*f.*	Raupe,*f.*	bruco,*m.*	oruga,*f.*	kålmask,*nn.*	shleyerl,*m.*
cathedral	cathédrale,*f.*	Dom,*m.*	cattedrale,*f.*	catedral,*f.*	domkyrka,*nn.*	katedral,*m.*
Catholic (*adj.*)	catholique	katholisch	cattolico	católico	katolsk	katoylish
cattle	bétail,*m.*	Rindvieh,*n.*	bestiame,*m.*	ganado vacuno, *m.*	boskap,*nn.*	fikh,*n.*
cauliflower	chou-fleur,*m.*	Blumenkohl,*m.*	cavolfiore,*m.*	coliflor,*f.*	blomkål,*nn.*	kalifyor,*m.*
cause	cause,*f.*	Ursache,*f.*	causa,*f.*	causa,*f.*	grund,*nn.*	sibe,*f.*
cause, to	causer	verursachen	causare	causar	förorsaka	goyrem zayn
caution (heed)	prudence,*f.*	Vorsicht,*f.*	cautela,*f.*	precaución,*f.*	försiktighet,*nn.*	opgehitkayt,*f.*
caution (warn), to	avertir	warnen	avvertire	advertir	varna	vorenen
cave	caverne,*f.*	Höhle,*f.*	caverna,*f.*	cueva,*f.*	grotta,*nn.*	heyl,*f.*
cease (be at an end), to	cesser	aufhören	cessare	cesar	sluta	oyfhern
cease (desist), to	cesser	aufhören	cessare	dejar de	upphöra	oyfhern
cedar (tree)	cèdre,*m.*	Zeder,*f.*	cedro,*m.*	cedro,*m.*	ceder,*nn.*	tsederboym,*m.*
cede, to	céder	übergeben	cedere	ceder	avstå	optretn
ceiling (of room)	plafond,*m.*	Decke,*f.*	soffitto,*m.*	cielo raso,*m.*	tak,*n.*	stele,*f.*
celebrate, to	célébrer	feiern	celebrare	celebrar	fira	oprikhtn
celery	céleri,*m.*	Sellerie,*m.*	sedano,*m.*	apio,*m.*	selleri,*nn.,n.*	selerye,*f.*
cell (*biol.*)	cellule,*f.*	Zelle,*f.*	cellula,*f.*	célula,*f.*	cell,*nn.*	kemerl,*n.*
cellar	cave,*f.*	Keller,*m.*	cantina,*f.*	bodega,*f.*	källare,*nn.*	keler,*m.*
cello	violoncelle,*m.*	Cello,*n.*	violoncello,*m.*	violoncelo,*m.*	cello,*nn.* (*pl.* celli)	violontshel,*m.*
cement	ciment,*m.*	Zement,*m.*	cemento,*m.*	cemento,*m.*	cement,*nn.*	tsement,*m.*
cemetery	cimetière,*m.*	Friedhof,*m.*	cimitero,*m.*	cementerio,*m.*	kyrkogård,*nn.*	beys-oylem,*m.*
census	recensement,*m.*	Volkszählung,*f.*	censimento,*m.*	censo,*m.*	folkräkning,*nn.*	folkstseylung,*f.*
center	centre,*m.*	Mittelpunkt,*m.*	centro,*m.*	centro,*m.*	centrum,*n.* (*pl.* -tra)	tsenter,*m.*
central	central	zentral	centrale	central	central	tsentral
century	siècle,*m.*	Jahrhundert,*n.*	secolo,*m.*	siglo,*m.*	århundrade,*n.*	yorhundert,*m.*
cereal (grain)	céréale,*f.*	Getreide,*n.*	cereale,*m.*	cereal,*m.*	sädesslag,*n.*	tvue,*f.*
cereal (prepared food)	céréale,*f.*	(*no equiv.*)	cereale confezio-nato,*m.*	cereal,*m.*	(*no equiv.*)	kashe,*f.*
ceremony	cérémonie,*f.*	Zeremonie,*f.*	cerimonia,*f.*	ceremonia,*f.*	ceremoni,*nn.*	tseremonye,*f.*
certain (particular)	certain	gewiss	certo	cierto	viss	gevis
certain (sure)	certain	sicher	sicuro	cierto	säker	zikher
certainly (of course!, *interj.*)	certainement	selbstverständ-lich	certamente	por cierto	javisst	avade
certainly (surely, *adv.*)	sûrement	sicher	certamente	ciertamente	säkert	zikher
certificate	certificat,*m.*	Bescheinigung, *f.*	certificato,*m.*	certificado,*m.*	intyg,*n.*	bashtetikung,*f.*
certify, to	certifier	beglaubigen	certificare	certificar	intyga	bashtetikn
chain	chaîne,*f.*	Kette,*f.*	catena,*f.*	cadena,*f.*	kedja,*nn.*	keyt,*f.*
chair	chaise,*f.*	Stuhl,*m.*	sedia,*f.*	silla,*f.*	stol,*nn.*	shtul,*m.*
chairman	président,*m.*	Vorsitzende,*m.,f.*	presidente,*m.,f.*	presidente,*m.*	ordförande,*nn.*	forzitser,*m.*
chalk	craie,*f.*	Kreide,*f.*	gesso,*m.*	tiza,*f.*	krita,*nn.*	krayd,*f.*
challenge	défi,*m.*	Herausforde-rung,*f.*	sfida,*f.*	desafío,*m.*	utmaning,*nn.*	aroysruf,*m.*
chamber of commerce	chambre de commerce,*f.*	Handelskammer, *f.*	camera di com-mercio,*f.*	cámara de comercio,*f.*	handelskam-mare,*nn.*	handls-kamer,*f.*
champion	champion,*m.*	Meister,*m.*	campione,*m.*	campeón,*m.*	mästare,*nn.*	tshempyon,*m.*
chance (fate)	hasard,*m.*	Zufall,*m.*	caso,*m.*	casualidad,*f.*	tillfällighet,*nn.*	tsufal,*m.*
chance (opportunity)	occasion,*f.*	Gelegenheit,*f.*	occasione,*f.*	ocasión,*f.*	tillfälle,*n.*	gelegnhayt,*f.*
chance (possibility)	chance,*f.*	Aussicht,*f.*	possibilità,*f.*	posibilidad,*f.*	möjlighet,*nn.*	shans,*m.*
change (alteration)	changement,*m.*	(Ver)Änderung, *f.*	cambiamento,*m.*	cambio,*m.*	ändring,*nn.*	bayt,*m.*
change (become different), to	changer	ändern, sich	cambiare	alterarse	ändras	baytn zikh
change (make different), to	changer	verändern	cambiare	cambiar	ändra	baytn
channel (strait)	canal,*m.*	Kanal,*m.*	stretto,*m.*	canal,*m.*	sund,*n.*	kanal,*m.*
chap (fellow)	type,*m.*	Kerl,*m.*	Tizio,*m.*	chico,*m.*	grabb,*nn.*	bokher,*m.*
chapel	chapelle,*f.*	Kapelle,*f.*	cappella,*f.*	capilla,*f.*	kapell,*n.*	kapelye,*f.*
chapter (of book)	chapitre,*m.*	Kapitel,*n.*	capitolo,*m.*	capítulo,*m.*	kapitel,*n.*	kapitl,*m.*
character (nature)	caractère,*m.*	Charakter,*m.*	carattere,*m.*	carácter,*m.*	karaktär,*nn.*	kharakter,*m.*
character (person portrayed)	personnage,*m.*	Person,*f.*	personaggio,*m.*	personaje,*m.*	person,*nn.*	parshoyn,*m.*
characteristic (typical)	caractéristique	bezeichnend	caratteristico	característico	karaktäristisk	kharakteristish
charge (accusation)	accusation,*f.*	Anklage,*f.*	accusa,*f.*	acusación,*f.*	anklagelse,*nn.*	bashuldikung,*f.*
charge (price)	prix,*m.*	Preis,*m.*	prezzo,*m.*	precio,*m.*	pris,*n.*	optsol,*m.*
charge (responsibility)	charge,*f.*	Aufsicht,*f.*	incarico,*m.*	cargo,*m.*	ansvar,*n.*	akhrayes,*f.*
charge, to (*elec.*)	charger	laden	caricare	cargar	ladda	onlodn
charge (accuse), to	charger	anklagen	incolpare	acusar	anklaga	bashuldikn
charge (debit), to	imputer	anschreiben	addebitare	cargar	debitera	farrekhenen
charge account	compte courant, *m.*	laufende Rechnung,*f.*	conto corrente, *m.*	cuenta cor-riente,*f.*	konto,*n.*	farrekhn-konte, *f.*
charity (philanthropy)	bienfaisance,*f.*	Wohltätigkeit,*f.*	beneficenza,*f.*	caridad,*f.*	välgörenhet,*nn.*	tsdoke,*f.*

English	French	German	Italian	Spanish	Swedish	Yiddish
charm (attraction)	charme,*m.*	Reiz,*m.*	attrattiva,*f.*	encanto,*m.*	charm,*nn.*	kheyn,*m.*
charm (delight), to	charmer	bezaubern	incantare	encantar	förtrolla	farkishefn
charming	charmant	reizend	incantevole	encantador	förtjusande	kheynevdik
chart (graph)	graphique,*m.*	Diagramm,*n.*	diagramma,*m.*	cuadro,*m.*	tabell,*nn.*	diagram,*f.*
charter (act of incorporation)	charte,*f.*	Urkunde,*f.*	statuto,*m.*	escritura de constitución,*f.*	urkund,*nn.*	tsharter,*m.*
chase, to	poursuivre	jagen	inseguire	perseguir	jaga	
chaste	chaste	keusch	casto	casto	kysk	nokhyogn
chat, to	causer	plaudern	conversare	charlar	prata	tsniesdik
chatter, to	bavarder	plappern	chiacchierare	parlotear	pladdra	shmuesn
cheap (inexpensive)	(à) bon marché	billig	a buon mercato	barato	billig	plaplen
cheat (defraud), to	frauder	betrügen	truffare	engañar	lura	volvl
						opnarn
check (bank check)	chèque,*m.*	Scheck,*m.*	assegno,*m.*	cheque,*m.*	check,*nn.*	tshek,*m.*
check (examination)	vérification,*f.*	Kontrolle,*f.*	controllo,*m.*	inspección,*f.*	kontroll,*nn.*	kontrol,*f.*
check (restraint)	frein,*m.*	Hemmung,*f.*	freno,*m.*	represión,*f.*	hejdande,*n.*	ophalt,*m.*
check (stop), to	arrêter	aufhalten	frenare	impedir	hejda	ophaltn
check (test), to	vérifier	prüfen	controllare	comprobar	kontrollera	kontrolirn
cheek	joue,*f.*	Backe,*f.*	guancia,*f.*	mejilla,*f.*	kind,*nn.*	bak,*f.*
cheer (applaud), to	acclamer	Beifall rufen	acclamare	aplaudir	ropa bifall	aplodirn
cheer (gladden), to	égayer	aufheitern	rallegrare	alegrar	uppmuntra	derfreyen
cheerful (joyful)	gai	heiter	gaio	jovial	glad	freylekh
cheese	fromage,*m.*	Käse,*m.*	formaggio,*m.*	queso,*m.*	ost,*nn.*	kez,*m.*
chemistry	chimie,*f.*	Chemie,*f.*	chimica,*f.*	química,*f.*	kemi,*nn.*	khemye,*f.*
cherish, to	chérir	hegen	nutrire	abrigar	omhulda	tayer haltn
cherry (fruit)	cerise,*f.*	Kirsche,*f.*	ciliegia,*f.*	cereza,*f.*	körsbär,*n.*	karsh,*f.*
chess	échecs,*m.pl.*	Schach,*n.*	giuoco degli scacchi,*m.pl.*	ajedrez,*m.*	schack,*nn.*	shokh,*m.*
chest (*anat.*)	poitrine,*f.*	Brust,*f.*	petto,*m.*	pecho,*m.*	bröstkorg,*nn.*	brust,*f.*
chest (box)	coffre,*m.*	Kiste,*f.*	cassa,*f.*	arca,*f.*	kista,*nn.*	kastn,*m.*
chestnut (tree)	châtaignier,*m.*	Kastanie,*f.*	castagno,*m.*	castaño,*m.*	kastanj,*nn.*	kestnboym,*m.*
chew, to	mâcher	kauen	masticare	mascar	tugga	kayen
chicken	poulet,*m.*	Huhn,*n.*	pollo,*m.*	pollo,*m.*	kyckling,*nn.*	hun,*f.*
chicken pox	varicelle,*f.*	Windpocken,*f. pl.*	varicella,*f.*	varicela,*f.*	vattenkoppor, *nn.pl.*	vintpokn,*pl.*
chief (leading)	principal	Haupt-...	primo	principal	förnämst	hoypt-...
chiefly (mainly)	surtout	hauptsächlich	principalmente	principalmente	huvudsakligen	der iker
child	enfant,*m.,f.*	Kind,*n.*	bambino,*m.*	niño,*m.*	barn,*n.*	kind,*n.*
childhood	enfance,*f.*	Kindheit,*f.*	infanzia,*f.*	niñez,*f.*	barndom,*nn.*	kindhayt,*f.*
Chile	Chili,*m.*	Chile,*n.*	Cile,*m.*	Chile	Chile,*n.*	Tshile,*n.*
Chilean (*adj.*)	chilien, -ne	chilenisch	cileno	chileno	chilensk	tshilenish
chill (coldness)	froideur,*f.*	Kälte,*f.*	freddezza,*f.*	frío,*m.*	kyla,*nn.*	tshilenish
chill (shivering sensation)	frisson,*m.*	Frösteln,*n.*	brividi,*m.pl.*	escalofrío,*m.*	rysning,*nn.*	frestl,*n.*
chilly	frais, fraîche	kühl	freddo	fresco	kylig	tsiter,*m.*
chimney	cheminée,*f.*	Schornstein,*m.*	camino,*m.*	chimenea,*f.*	skorsten,*nn.*	kil
						koymen,*m.*
chin	menton,*m.*	Kinn,*n.*	mento,*m.*	barba,*f.*	haka,*nn.*	gombe,*f.*
China	Chine,*f.*	China,*n.*	Cina,*f.*	China	Kina,*n.*	Khine,*f.*
Chinese (*adj.*)	chinois	chinesisch	cinese	chino	kinesisk	khinezish
chisel (tool)	ciseau,*m.*	Meissel,*f.*	cesello,*m.*	cincel,*m.*	stämjärn,*n.*	dlot,*m.*
chocolate	chocolat,*m.*	Schokolade,*f.*	cioccolata,*f.*	chocolate,*m.*	choklad,*nn.*	shokolad,*m.*
choice (act of choosing)	choix,*m.*	Wahl,*f.*	scelta,*f.*	selección,*f.*	val,*n.*	oysklayb,*m.*
choir	choeur,*m.*	Chor,*m.*	coro,*m.*	coro,*m.*	kör,*nn.*	khor,*m.*
choke, to	étouffer	(er)würgen	soffocare	ahogar	kväva	shtikn
cholera	choléra,*m.*	Cholera,*f*	colera,*f.*	cólera (asiático), *m.*	kolera,*nn.*	kholere,*f.*
choose (select), to	choisir	wählen	scegliere	escoger	välja	oysklaybn
chosen	choisi	auserwählt	scelto	escogido	vald	oysderveylt
Christ	Christ,*m.*	Christus,*m.*	Cristo,*m.*	Cristo,*m.*	Kristus,*m.*	Kristus,*m.*
Christian (*n.*)	chrétien,*m.*	Christ,*m.*	cristiano,*m.*	cristiano,*m.*	kristen,*nn.* (*pl.* kristna)	Krist,*m.*
Christmas	Noël,*m.*	Weihnachten,*f. pl.*	Natale,*m.*	Navidad,*f.*	jul,*nn.*	nitl,*m.*
chromium	chrome,*m.*	Chrom,*m.*	cromo,*m.*	cromo,*m.*	krom,*nn.*	khrom,*m.*
chronicle	chronique,*f.*	Chronik,*f.*	cronaca,*f.*	crónica,*f.*	krönika,*nn.*	khronik,*f.*
church	église,*f.*	Kirche,*f.*	chiesa,*f.*	iglesia,*f.*	kyrka,*nn.*	kloyster,*m.*
cigar	cigare,*m.*	Zigarre,*f.*	sigaro,*m.*	cigarro,*m.*	cigarr,*nn.*	tsigar,*m.*
cigarette	cigarette,*f.*	Zigarette,*f.*	sigaretta,*f.*	cigarrillo,*m.*	cigarett,*nn.*	papiros,*m.*
cinnamon	cannelle,*f.*	Zimt,*m.*	cannella,*f.*	canela,*f.*	kanel,*nn.*	tsimering,*m.*
circle (*geom.*)	cercle,*m.*	Kreis,*m.*	circolo,*m.*	círculo,*m.*	cirkel,*nn.*	tsirkl,*m.*
circular (*adj.*)	circulaire	kreisförmig	circolare	circular	cirkelrund	krayz,*m.*
circular (letter or brochure, *bus.*)	circulaire,*f.*	Rundschreiben, *n.*	circolare,*f.*	circular,*f.*	cirkulär,*n.*	kaylekhdik tsirkular,*m.*
circulation (dissemination)	circulation,*f.*	Umlauf,*m.*	diffusione,*f.*	circulación,*f.*	spridning,*nn.*	farshpreytung,*f.*
circumference	circonférence,*f.*	(Kreis)Umfang, *m.*	circonferenza,*f.*	circunferencia,*f.*	omkrets,*nn.*	arumnem,*m.*
circumstance (external condition)	circonstance,*f.*	Umstand,*m.*	circonstanza,*f.*	circunstancia,*f.*	omständighet, *nn.*	umshtand,*m.*
circus	cirque,*m.*	Zirkus,*m.*	circo,*m.*	circo,*m.*	cirkus,*nn.*	tsirk,*m.*
citizen	citoyen,*m.*	(Staats)Bürger,*m.*	cittadino,*m.*	ciudadano,*m.*	medborgare,*nn.*	birger,*m.*
city	ville,*f.*	Stadt,*f.*	città,*f.*	ciudad,*f.*	stad,*nn.* (*pl.* städer)	shtot,*f.*
civil (polite)	poli	höflich	civile	civil	artig	eydl
civil (secular)	civil	bürgerlich	civile	civil	borgerlig	tsivil
civilization (civilized condition)	civilisation,*f.*	Zivilisation,*f.*	civilizzazione,*f.*	civilización,*f.*	civilisation,*nn.*	tsivilizatsye,*f.*

English	French	German	Italian	Spanish	Swedish	Yiddish
civilization (culture)	civilisation, f.	Kultur, f.	civiltà, f.	civilización, f.	kultur, nn.	tsivilizatsye, f.
claim	revendication, f.	Anspruch, m.	reclamo, m.	reclamación, f.	anspråk, n.	pretenzye, f.
claim, to	revendiquer	beanspruchen	reclamare	reclamar	fordra	pretendirn
clam	palourde, f.	Venusmuschel, f.	vongola, f.	almeja, f.	mussla, nn.	klem, m.
clang, to	résonner	klirren	risuonare	resonar	klinga	brazgen
clap (applaud), to	applaudir	klatśchen	applaudire	aplaudir	klappa händerna	aplodirn
clarinet	clarinette, f.	Klarinette, f.	clarinetto, m.	clarinete, m.	klarinett, nn.	klarnet, m.
clasp (embrace), to	serrer	umarmen	abbracciare	abrazar	omfamma	arumnemen
class (kind)	classe, f.	Klasse, f.	genere, m.	clase, f.	klass, nn.	klas, m.
classic (first-class, adj.)	classique	klassisch	classico	clásico	klassisk	klasish
classic (first-class work)	classique, m.	Meisterwerk, n.	classico, m.	obra clásica, f.	klassiskt verk, n.	klasish verk, n.
classroom	salle de classe, f.	Klassenzimmer, n.	aula, f.	aula, f.	klassrum, n.	klastsimer, m.
clause (stipulation)	clause, f.	Klausel, f.	clausola, f.	cláusula, f.	klausul, nn.	paragraf, m.
claw (of animal)	griffe, f.	Klaue, f.	artiglio, m.	uña, f.	klo, nn.	nogl, m.
claw (of bird)	serre, f.	Kralle, f.	artiglio, m.	garra, f.	klo, nn.	nogl, m.
clay	argile, f.	Ton, m.	argilla, f.	arcilla, f.	lera, nn.	leym, f.
clean	propre	rein	pulito	limpio	ren	reyn
clean, to	nettoyer	reinigen	pulire	limpiar	rengöra	reynikn
clear	clair	klar	chiaro	claro	klar	klor
clearance (customs clearance)	dédouanement, m.	Zollabfertigung, f.	sdoganamento, m.	despacho de aduana, m.	tullklarering, nn.	tsol-silek, m.
clearance sale	vente de soldes, f.	Ausverkauf, m.	vendita di liquidazione, f.	(venta de) liquidación, f.	slutrealisation, nn.	oysfarkoyf, m.
clerk (salesperson)	vendeur, m.	Verkäufer, m.	commesso, m.	dependiente, m.	affärsbiträde, n.	farkoyfer, m.
clever	habile	klug	accorto	hábil	skicklig	klug
cliff	falaise, f.	Klippe, f.	precipizio, m.	risco, m.	klippa, nn.	feldz, m.
climate (weather)	climat, m.	Klima, n.	clima, m.	clima, m.	klimat, n.	klimat, m.
climb (rise), to	monter	steigen	salire	subir	stiga	heybn zikh
climb (scale), to	gravir	steigen	salire	escalar	klättra uppför	krikhn oyf
cloak (apparel)	manteau, m.	Umhang, m.	mantello, m	capa, f.	kappa, nn.	mantl, m.
clock	horloge, f.	Uhr, f.	orologio, m.	reloj, m.	klocka, nn.	zeyger, m.
close (intimate)	intime	nah	intimo	íntimo	nära	noent
close (near, adv.)	près (de)	nah	vicino (a)	cerca	nära	noent
close (finish), to	terminer	schliessen	terminare	concluir	sluta	shlisn
close (shut), to	fermer	schliessen	chiudere	cerrar	stänga	farmakhn
cloth	étoffe, f.	Stoff, m.	stoffa, f.	tela, f.	tyg, n.	shtof, m.
clothe, to	habiller	ankleiden	abbigliare	vestir	klä(da)	onton
clothing	vêtements, m. pl.	Kleidung, f.	vestiario, m.	ropa, f.	kläder, nn. pl.	halboshe, f.
cloud	nuage, m.	Wolke, f.	nuvola, f.	nube, f.	moln, n.	volkn, m.
cloudy (overcast)	nuageux, -geuse	wolkig	nuvoloso	nublado	mulen	volkndik
clove	clou de girofle, m.	(Gewürz)Nelke, f.	garofano, m.	clavo, m.	kryddnejlika, nn.	negele, n.
clover	trèfle, m.	Klee, m.	trifoglio, m.	trébol, m.	klöver, nn.	konishine, f.
club (association)	cercle, m.	Verein, m.	circolo, m.	club, m.	klubb, nn.	klub, m.
club (cudgel)	massue, f.	Keule, f.	bastone, m.	palo, m.	klubba, nn.	flokn, m.
clutch (automotive device)	embrayage, m.	Kupplung, f.	frizione, f.	embrague, m.	koppling, nn.	kuplung, f.
coach, railroad	voiture, f.	Personenwagen, m.	carrozza, f.	vagón, m.	personvagn, nn.	zitsvagon, n
coach (train), to	instruire	trainieren	insegnare	entrenar	träna	aynkneln
coal	charbon, m.	Kohle, f.	carbone (fossile), n.	carbón, m.	kol, n.	koyln, pl.
coarse	grossier, -sière	grob	grossolano	tosco	grov	grob
coast (seaboard)	côte, f.	Küste, f.	costa, f.	costa, f.	kust, nn.	yam-breg, m.
coat (man's overcoat)	pardessus, m.	Mantel, m.	soprabito, m.	gabán, m.	överrock, nn.	mantl, m.
coat (woman's overcoat)	manteau, m.	Mantel, m.	paltò, m.	abrigo de mujer, m.	kappa, nn.	mantl, m.
cock (rooster)	coq, m.	Hahn, m.	gallo, m.	gallo, m.	tupp, nn.	hon, m.
cocktail	cocktail, m.	Cocktail, m.	cocktail, m.	coctel, m.	cocktail, nn.	kokteyl, m.
cocoa	cacao, m.	Kakao, m.	cacao, m.	cacao, m.	kakao, nn.	kakao, m.
coconut	(noix de) coco, m.	Kokosnuss, m.	cocco, m.	coco, m.	kokosnöt, nn. (pl. -nötter)	kokosnus, m.
code (law)	code, m.	Gesetzbuch, n.	codice, m.	código, m.	lagbok, nn. (pl. -böcker)	kodeks, m.
coffee	café, m.	Kaffee, m.	caffè, m.	café, m.	kaffe, n.	kave, f.
coffee pot	cafetière, f.	Kaffeekanne, f.	caffetiera, f.	cafetera, f.	kaffepanna, nn.	kavenik, m.
coffin	cercueil, m.	Sarg, m.	bara, f.	ataúd, m.	likkista, nn.	orn, m. (Jew.)
coil (elec.)	bobine, f.	Spule, f.	bobina, f.	carrete, m.	spole, nn.	shpul, f.
coin	pièce (de monnaie), f.	Münze, f.	moneta, f.	moneda, f.	mynt, n.	matbeye, f.
coke	coke, m.	Koks, m.	coke, m.	coque, m.	koks, nn.	koks, m.
cold (adj.)	froid	kalt	freddo	frío	kall	kalt
cold (disease)	rhume, m.	Erkältung, f.	raffreddore, m.	resfriado, m.	förkylning, nn.	farkilung, f.
cold (low temperature)	froid, m.	Kälte, f.	freddo, m.	frío, m.	kyla, nn.	kelt, f.
collapse (cave in), to	effondrer, s'	einstürzen	crollare	caerse	störta in	aynfaln
collar	col, m.	Kragen, m.	colletto, m.	cuello, m.	krage, nn.	kolner, m.
collect (bring together), to	assembler	sammeln	raccogliere	reunir	samla	klaybn
collect, to (bus.)	encaisser	einziehen	riscuotere	cobrar	inkassera	aynmonen
collection	collection, f.	Sammlung, f.	raccolta, f.	colección, f.	samling, nn.	zamlung, f.
Colombia	Colombie, f.	Kolumbien, n.	Colombia, f.	Colombia	Columbia, n.	Kolombye, f.
colon (punct.)	deux-points, m. pl.	Doppelpunkt, m.	due punti, m. pl.	dos puntos, m. pl.	kolon, n.	toplpunkt, m.

English	French	German	Italian	Spanish	Swedish	Yiddish
colonel	colonel, *m.*	Oberst, *m.*	colonnello, *m.*	coronel, *m.*	överste, *nn.*	kolonel, *m.*
colonial	colonial	kolonial	coloniale	colonial	kolonial	kolonyal
colonist	colon, *m.*	(An)Siedler, *m.*	colono, *m.*	colono, *m.*	nybyggare, *nn.*	kolonist, *m.*
colony	colonie, *f.*	Kolonie, *f.*	colonia, *f.*	colonia, *f.*	koloni, *nn.*	kolonye, *f.*
color	couleur, *f.*	Farbe, *f.*	colore, *m.*	color, *m.*	färg, *nn.*	kolir, *m.*
colt	poulain, *m.*	Füllen, *n.*	puledro, *m.*	potro, *m.*	föl, *n.*	zhrebtshik, *m.*
column (pillar)	colonne, *f.*	Säule, *f.*	colonna, *f.*	columna, *f.*	kolonn, *nn.*	zayl, *m.*
column (*print.*)	colonne, *f.*	Spalte, *f.*	colonna, *f.*	columna, *f.*	spalt, *nn.*	omed, *m.*
comb (for hair)	peigne, *m.*	Kamm, *m.*	pettine, *m.*	peine, *m.*	kam, *nn.*	kam, *m.*
combat	combat, *m.*	Kampf, *m.*	combattimento, *m.*	combate, *m.*	kamp, *nn.*	kamf, *m.*
combination	combinaison, *f.*	Verbindung, *f.*	combinazione, *f.*	combinación, *f.*	kombination, *nn.*	kombinatsye, *f*
combine (coalesce), to	combiner, se	vereinigen, sich	combinarsi	combinarse	förena sig	fareynikn zikh
combine (make join), to	combiner	verbinden	combinare	combinar	kombinera	kombinirn
come, to	venir	kommen	venire	venir	komma	kumen
comedy (comic play)	comédie, *f.*	Komödie, *f.*	commedia, *f.*	comedia, *f.*	komedi, *nn.*	komedye, *f.*
comfort (ease)	confort, *m.*	Bequemlichkeit, *f.*	comodità, *f.*	comodidad, *f.*	bekvämlighet, *nn.*	bakvemkayt, *f.*
comfort (solace)	consolation, *f.*	Trost, *m.*	conforto, *m.*	consuelo, *m.*	tröst, *nn.*	treyst, *f.*
comfort (console), to	consoler	trösten	confortare	consolar	trösta	treystn
comfortable (affording comfort)	confortable	behaglich	comodo	cómodo	bekväm	bakvem
comic strip	série de dessins humoristiques, *f.*	Bilderserie, *f.*	disegni a fumetti, *m.pl.*	historieta cómica, *f.*	skämtserie, *nn.*	bildershtreyf, *m.*
comma	virgule, *f.*	Komma, *n.*	virgola, *f.*	coma, *f.*	komma, *n.*	kome, *f.*
command (authority)	commandement, *m.*	Befehl, *m.*	comando, *m.*	mando, *m.*	kommando, *n.*	komande, *f.*
command (order)	ordre, *m.*	Befehl, *m.*	comando, *m.*	orden, *f.*	order, *nn.*	bafel, *m.*
command (order), to	ordonner	befehlen	comandare	mandar	kommendera	bafeln
commander (officer)	commandant, *m.*	Befehlshaber, *m.*	comandante, *m.*	comandante, *m.*	befälhavare, *nn.*	komandir, *m.*
commence (make a start), to	commencer	anfangen	principiare	comenzar	börja	onheybn zikh
comment (remark)	observation, *f.*	Bemerkung, *f.*	osservazione, *f.*	observación, *f.*	anmärkning, *nn.*	bamerkung, *f.*
comment, to	commenter	Bemerkungen machen	commentare	comentar	anmärka	komentirn
commerce (trade)	commerce, *m.*	Handel, *m.*	commercio, *m.*	comercio, *m.*	handel, *nn.*	miskher, *m.*
commercial	commercial	kommerziell	commerciale	comercial	kommersiell	komertsyel
commission (fee)	commission, *f.*	Provision, *f.*	commissione, *f.*	comisión, *f.*	provision, *nn.*	komisye, *f.*
commission (group)	commission, *f.*	Ausschuss, *m.*	commissione, *f.*	comisión, *f.*	kommission, *nn.*	komisye, *f.*
commissioner (deputized person)	commissaire, *m.*	Kommissar, *m.*	commissario, *m.*	comisario, *m.*	ombud, *n.*	komisyoner, *m.*
commit (perpetrate), to	commettre	begehen	commettere	cometer	begå	bageyn
commitment (*bus.*)	engagement, *m.*	Verpflichtung, *f.*	impegno, *m.*	compromiso, *m.*	förpliktelse, *nn.*	hiskhayves, *f.*
committee	comité, *m.*	Ausschuss, *m.*	comitato, *m.*	comité, *m.*	kommitté, *nn.*	komitet, *m.*
commodity	marchandise, *f.*	Ware, *f.*	derrata, *f.*	mercancía, *f.*	vara, *nn.*	skhoyre, *f.*
common (usual)	ordinaire	gewöhnlich	comune	ordinario	vanlig	geveyntlekh
common (vulgar)	vulgaire	gemein	volgare	vulgar	simpel	prost
commonwealth	république, *f.*	Staatenbund, *m.*	repubblica, *f.*	estado, *m.*	statsförbund, *n.*	komonvelt, *m.*
communication (intercourse)	communication, *f.*	Verbindung, *f.*	comunicazioni, *f.pl.*	comunicación, *f.*	förbindelse, *nn.*	komunikatsye, *f.*
communication (message)	communication, *f.*	Mitteilung, *f.*	comunicazione, *f.*	comunicación, *f.*	meddelande, *n.*	yedie, *f.*
communism	communisme, *m.*	Kommunismus, *m.*	comunismo, *m.*	comunismo, *m.*	kommunism, *nn.*	komunizm, *m.*
community (neighborhood	quartier, *m.*	Gemeinde, *f.*	vicinanza, *f.*	vecindad, *f.*	(*no equiv.*)	kibets, *m.*
community (the public)	public, *m.*	Gemeinschaft, *f.*	società, *f.*	público, *m.*	samhälle, *n.*	klal, *m.*
compact (brief)	concis	kurz	conciso	conciso, *m.*	kortfattad	kompakt
compact (packed firmly)	compact	gedrungen	compatto	compacto	kompakt	kompakt
companion	compagnon, *m.*	Gefährte, *m.*	compagno, *m.*	compañero, *m.*	kamrat, *nn.*	khaver, *m.*
company (*bus.*)	compagnie, *f.*	Gesellschaft, *f.*	ditta, *f.*	compañía, *f.*	bolag, *n.*	firme, *f.*
company (guests)	invités, *m.pl.*	Gesellschaft, *f.*	ospiti, *m.pl.*	visita, *f.*	gäster, *nn.pl.*	gest, *m.pl.*
company (*mil.*)	compagnie, *f.*	Kompanie, *f.*	compagnia, *f.*	compañía, *f.*	kompani, *n.*	kompanye, *f.*
comparative	relatif, -tive	verhältnismässig	relativo	relativo	relativ	farglaykhik
compare (consider relatively), to	comparer	vergleichen	confrontare	comparar	jämföra	farglaykhn
comparison	comparaison, *f.*	Vergleich, *m.*	confronto, *m.*	comparación, *f.*	jämförelse, *nn.*	farglaykh, *m.*
compartment (of train)	compartiment, *m.*	Abteil, *n.*	compartimento, *m.*	compartimiento, *m.*	kupé, *nn.*	kupe, *m.*
compass (drawing instrument)	compas, *m.*	Zirkel, *m.*	compassi, *m.pl.*	compás, *m.*	passare, *nn.*	tsirkl, *m.*
compass (magnetic instrument)	boussole, *f.*	Kompass, *m.*	bussola, *f.*	brújula, *f.*	kompass, *nn.*	kompas, *m.*
compel, to	forcer	zwingen	costringere	obligar	tvinga	neytn
compensation (*bus.*)	compensation, *f.*	Vergütung, *f.*	risarcimento, *m.*	remuneración, *f.*	ersättning, *nn.*	kompensatsye, *f.*
competent (able)	compétent	leistungsfähig	competente	competente	duglig	kompetent
competition (*bus.*)	concurrence, *f.*	Konkurrenz, *f.*	concorrenza, *f.*	competencia, *f.*	konkurrens, *nn.*	konkurents, *f.*
competitor (*bus.*)	concurrent, *m.*	Konkurrent, *m.*	concorrente, *m.,f.*	rival, *m.*	konkurrent, *nn.*	konkurent, *m.*
complain, to	plaindre, se	klagen	lagnarsi	quejarse	klaga	baklogn zikh
complaint	plainte, *f.*	Klage, *f.*	lagnanza, *f.*	queja, *f.*	klagomål, *n.*	tayne, *f.*
complete (entire)	complet, -plète	vollständig	completo	completo	fullständig	fulshtendik
complete (finish), to	achever	vollenden	completare	completar	avsluta	derendikn
complex (complicated)	complexe	verwickelt	complicato	complejo	invecklad	komplitsirt

English	French	German	Italian	Spanish	Swedish	Yiddish
compliment	compliment,*m.*	Kompliment,*n.*	complimento,*m.*	cumplimiento,*m.*	komplimang,*nn.*	kompliment,*m.*
comply (acquiesce), to	soumettre, se	fügen, sich	consentire (a)	cumplir	samtycka	nokhkumen
compose, to (*mus.*)	composer	komponieren	comporre	componer	komponera	komponirn
composition (make-up)	composition,*f.*	Zusammensetzung,*f.*	composizione,*f.*	composición,*f.*	sammansättning, *nn.*	tsunoyfshtel,*m.*
compound (mixture)	composé,*m.*	Verbindung,*f.*	composto,*m.*	compuesto,*m.*	sammansättning, *nn.*	gemish,*m.*
compound interest	intérêts composés,*m.pl.*	Zinseszinsen,*pl.*	interesse composto,*m.*	interés compuesto,*m.*	ränta på ränta, *nn.*	protsent oyf protsent,*m.*
comprehend (understand), to	comprendre	begreifen	comprendere	comprender	förstå	bagrayfn
compromise (mutual concessions)	compromis,*m.*	Kompromiss,*m.*	compromissione, *f.*	transacción,*f.*	kompromiss,*nn.*	pshore,*f.*
comrade	camarade,*m.,f.*	Kamerad,*m.*	compagno,*m.*	camarada,*m.,f.*	kamrat,*nn.*	khaver,*m.*
conceal, to	cacher	verbergen	celare	ocultar	dölja	farborgn
conceive (imagine), to	concevoir	vorstellen, sich	concepire	concebir	tänka sig	masig zayn
concentrate (make converge), to	concentrer	konzentrieren	concentrare	reconcentrar	koncentrera	kontsentrirn
conception (notion)	idée,*f.*	Begriff,*m.*	concetto,*m.*	concepto,*m.*	föreställning,*nn.*	hasoge,*f.*
conception (*physiol.*)	conception,*f.*	Empfängnis,*f.*	concezione,*f.*	concepción,*f.*	befruktning,*nn.*	fargeyn in trogn, *n.*
concern (business firm)	maison,*f.*	Unternehmen,*n.*	ditta,*f.*	casa,*f.*	affärsföretag, *n.*	firme,*f.*
concern (affect), to	concerner	angehen	riguardare	concernir	angå	ongeyn
concerning (regarding)	concernant	betreffend	riguardo a	respecto a	angående	benoygeye
concert (musical performance)	concert,*m.*	Konzert,*n.*	concerto,*m.*	concierto,*m.*	konsert,*nn.*	kontsert,*m.*
conclude (make end), to	conclure	schliessen	concludere	concluir	avsluta	farendikn
conclusion (decision)	conclusion,*f.*	Schluss,*m.*	conclusione,*f.*	conclusión,*f.*	beslut,*n.*	oysfir,*m.*
conclusion (end)	conclusion,*f.*	Schluss,*m.*	conclusione,*f.*	conclusión,*f.*	slut,*n.*	oysloz,*m.*
concrete (artificial stone)	béton,*m.*	Beton,*m.*	calcestruzzo,*m.*	hormigón,*m.*	betong,*nn.*	beton,*m.*
concrete (real)	concret, -crète	konkret	concreto	concreto	konkret	konkret
condemn (censure), to	condamner	verurteilen	condannare	condenar	fördöma	fardamen
condense (compress), to	condenser	verdichten	condensare	condensar	kondensera	kondensirn
condition (state)	état,*m.*	Zustand,*m.*	condizione,*f.*	condición,*f.*	tillstånd,*n.*	matsev,*m.*
condition (stipulation)	condition,*f.*	Bedingung,*f.*	condizione,*f.*	condición,*f.*	villkor,*n.*	tnay,*m.*
conduct (manage), to	conduire	leiten	condurre	conducir	leda	onfirn mit
conductor (*mus.*)	directeur,*m.*	Dirigent,*m.*	direttore,*m.*	director,*m.*	dirigent,*nn.*	dirigent,*m.*
conductor (ticket collector)	chef de train,*m.*	Schaffner,*m.*	controllore,*m.*	revisor,*m.*	konduktör,*nn.*	kondukter,*m.*
confer (bestow), to	conférer	verleihen	conferire	conferir	tilldela	oysteyln
conference (meeting)	conférence,*f.*	Konferenz,*f.*	conferenza,*f.*	conferencia,*f.*	konferens,*nn.*	zitsung,*f.*
confess (admit), to	avouer	gestehen	confessare	confesar	erkänna	moyde zayn zikl
confidence (trust)	confiance,*f.*	Vertrauen,*n.*	confidenza,*f.*	confianza,*f.*	förtroende,*n.*	tsutroy,*m.*
confident (self-assured)	assuré	selbstbewusst	confidente	confiado en sí mismo	självsäker	zikher bay zikh
confidential (private)	confidentiel, -le	vertraulich	confidenziale	confidencial	konfidentiell	konfidentsyel
confine (limit), to	limiter	beschränken, auf...	limitare	limitar	begränsa	bagrenetsn
confirm (corroborate), to	corroborer	bestätigen	confermare	confirmar	bekräfta	bashtetikn
confirmation (corroboration)	corroboration,*f.*	Bestätigung,*f.*	confermazione,*f.*	confirmación,*f.*	bekräftelse,*nn.*	bashtetikung,*f.*
conflict (opposition)	conflit,*m.*	Gegensatz,*m.*	conflitto,*m.*	conflicto,*m.*	konflikt,*nn.*	konflikt,*m.*
conflict (struggle)	conflit,*m.*	Streit,*m.*	conflitto,*m.*	conflicto,*m.*	strid,*nn.*	sikhsekh,*m.*
confuse (mix up), to	embrouiller	verwirren	confondere	confundir	förvirra	tsemishn
confusion (disorder)	confusion,*f.*	Verwirrung,*f.*	confusione,*f.*	confusión,*f.*	förvirring,*nn.*	behole,*f.*
congratulate, to	féliciter	gratulieren	congratulare con	felicitar	gratulera	gratulirn
congregation (religious community)	congrégation,*f.*	Gemeinde,*f.*	parrocchiani,*m.* *pl.*	feligreses,*m.pl.*	församling,*nn.*	kongregatsye,*f.*
congress (legislature)	congrès,*m.*	Kongress,*m.*	legislatura,*f.*	legislatura,*f.*	kongress,*nn.*	kongres,*m.*
conjunction (*gram.*)	conjonction,*f.*	Bindewort,*n.*	congiunzione,*f.*	conjunción,*f.*	konjunktion,*nn.*	konyunktsye,*f.*
connect (link), to	joindre	verbinden	connettere	conectar	förbinda	tsunoyfbindn
connection (relationship)	rapport,*m.*	Zusammenhang, *m.*	rapporto,*m.*	relación,*f.*	samband,*n.*	shaykhes,*f.*
conquer, to	vaincre	erobern	vincere	conquistar	besegra	aynnemen
conquest	conquête,*f.*	Eroberung,*f.*	conquista,*f.*	conquista,*f.*	besegrande,*n.*	aynnemen,*n.*
conscience	conscience,*f.*	Gewissen,*n.*	coscienza,*f.*	conciencia,*f.*	samvete,*n.*	gevisn,*n.*
conscious (aware)	conscient	bewusst	conscio	consciente	medveten	visik
consent, to	consentir	zustimmen	consentire	consentir	samtycka	maskim zayn
consequence	conséquence,*f.*	Folge,*f.*	conseguenza,*f.*	consecuencia,*f.*	följd,*nn.*	konsekvents,*f.*
consequently	par conséquent	infolgedessen	in conseguenza	por consiguiente	följaktligen	bekheyn
conservative (cautious)	prudent	konservativ	prudente	conservador	försiktig	konservativ
consider (reflect on), to	considérer	überlegen, sich	considerare	considerar	överväga	batrakhtn
considerable (*adj.*)	considérable	beträchtlich	considerevole	bastante	betydlig	nishkoshedik
consideration (regard)	considération,*f.*	Rücksicht,*f.*	riguardo,*m.*	consideración,*f.*	hänsyn,*nn.*	aynzeenish,*n.*
consideration (thought)	considération,*f.*	Überlegung,*f.*	considerazione,*f.*	consideración,*f.*	betraktande,*n.*	batrakhtung,*f.*
consignee (*bus.*)	consignataire, *m.,f.*	Empfänger,*m.*	consegnatario,*m.*	consignatario,*m.*	mottagare,*nn.*	opnemer,*n.*
consignment (*bus.*)	envoi,*m.*	Sendung,*f.*	consegna,*f.*	remesa,*f.*	sändning,*nn.*	shikung,*f.*
consist of (comprise), to	consister en (dans)	bestehen aus	consistere in	consistir en	bestå av	bashteyn fun
consolation (comfort)	consolation,*f.*	Trost,*m.*	consolazione,*f.*	consuelo,*m.*	tröst,*nn.*	nekhome,*f.*
constant (continual)	continuel, -le	dauernd	continuo	constante	ständig	keseyderdik
constitute (make up), to	constituer	bilden	costituire	constituir	inrätta	tsunoyfshteln
constitution (law)	constitution,*f.*	Verfassung,*f.*	costituzione,*f.*	constitución,*f.*	författning,*nn.*	konstitutsye,*f.*
constitution (nature)	constitution,*f.*	Konstitution,*f.*	costituzione,*f.*	constitución,*f.*	konstitution,*nn.*	tsunoyfshtel,*m.*

English	French	German	Italian	Spanish	Swedish	Yiddish
construct, to	construire	(er)bauen	costruire	construir	bygga	boyen
construction (fabrication)	construction,*f.*	Bau,*m.*	costruzione,*f.*	construcción,*f.*	konstruktion,*nn.*	konstruktsye,*f.*
consul	consul,*m.*	Konsul,*m.*	console,*m.*	cónsul,*m.*	konsul,*nn.*	konsul,*m.*
consult (seek professional advice of), to	consulter	zu Rate ziehen	consultare	consultar	rådfråga	meyashev zayn zikh mit
consume, to	consommer	verbrauchen	consumare	consumir	förbruka	farnitsn
consumption (using up)	consommation,*f.*	Verbrauch,*m.*	consumo,*m.*	consumo,*m.*	förbrukning,*nn.*	farnits,*m.*
contact (meeting)	contact,*m.*	Berührung,*f.*	contatto,*m.*	contacto,*m.*	kontakt,*nn.*	kontakt,*m.*
contain, to	contenir	enthalten	contenere	contener	innehålla	araynnemen
contemporary (modern)	contemporain	heutig	contemporaneo	contemporáneo	modern	haynttsaytik
contempt (scorn)	mépris,*m.*	Verachtung,*f.*	disprezzo,*m.*	desprecio,*m.*	förakt,*n.*	bitl,*m.*
contend (maintain), to	soutenir	behaupten	pretendere	sostener	vidhålla	haltn
content (satisfied)	content	zufrieden	contento	contento	nöjd	bafridikt
contents	contenu,*m.*	Inhalt,*m.*	contenuto,*m.*	contenido,*m.*	innehåll,*n.*	inhalt,*m.*
contest	concours,*m.*	(Wett)Kampf, *m.*	concorso,*m.*	concurso,*m.*	tävlan,*nn.*	konkurs,*m.*
contest (dispute), to	contester	bestreiten	contestare	disputar	bestrida	bakemfn
continent (*geog.*)	continent,*m.*	Weltteil,*m.*	continente,*m.*	continente,*m.*	kontinent,*nn.*	kontinent,*m.*
continual	continuel, -le	dauernd	continuo	continuo	ständig	keseyderdik
continuation	suite,*f.*	Fortsetzung,*f.*	continuazione,*f.*	continuación,*f.*	fortsättning,*nn.*	hemshekh,*m.*
continue, to	continuer	fortsetzen	continuare	continuar	forsätta	mamshikh zayn
continuous	continu	dauernd	continuo	continuo	oavbruten	keseyderdik
contraband	contrebande,*f.*	Konterbande,*f.*	contrabbando,*m.*	contrabando,*m.*	kontraband,*n.*	kontrabande,*f.*
contract	contrat,*m.*	Vertrag,*m.*	contratto,*m.*	contrato,*m.*	kontrakt,*n.*	opmakh,*m.*
contract (make shrink), to	contracter	zusammenziehen	contrarre	contraer	sammandra(ga)	ayntsien
contradict (deny), to	démentir	widersprechen	contraddire	contradecir	bestrida	soyser zayn
contrary (opposite)	contraire	entgegengesetzt	contrario	contrario	motsatt	farkert
contrast	contraste,*m.*	Gegensatz,*m.*	contrasto,*m.*	contraste,*m.*	kontrast,*nn.*	kontrast,*m.*
contribute, to	contribuer	beitragen	contribuire	contribuir	bidra(ga)	gebn tsu shtayer
contribution	contribution,*f.*	Beitrag,*m.*	contribuzione,*f.*	contribución,*f.*	bidrag,*n.*	tsushtayer,*m.*
control (direct), to	diriger	steuern	dirigere	dirigir	styra	bahershn
convenience	commodité,*f.*	Bequemlichkeit, *f.*	comodità,*f.*	comodidad,*f.*	bekvämlighet,*nn.*	bakvemkayt,*f.*
convenient	commode	bequem	comodo	cómodo	bekväm	bakvem
convention (meeting)	assemblée,*f.*	Tagung,*f.*	congresso,*m.*	congreso,*m.*	sammankomst, *nn.*	tsuzamenfor,*m.*
conversation	conversation,*f.*	Unterhaltung,*f.*	conversazione,*f.*	conversación,*f.*	samtal,*n.*	shmues,*m.*
conversion rate (*bus.*)	conversion,*f.*	Kurs,*m.*	conversione,*f.*	conversión,*f.*	konverterings-värde,*n.*	kurs,*m.*
convert (proselyte)	converti,*m.*	Bekehrte,*m.,f.*	convertito,*m.*	prosélito,*m.*	omvänd,*nn.*(*pl.* -a)	ger,*m.*(*Jud.*)
convert (transform), to	convertir	umwandeln	convertire	convertir	förvandla	farvandlen
convey (communicate), to	communiquer	mitteilen	comunicare	comunicar	meddela	ibergebn
convey (transport), to	transporter	befördern	trasportare	transportar	befordra	ariberfirn
conviction (belief)	conviction,*f.*	Überzeugung,*f.*	convinzione,*f.*	convicción,*f.*	övertygelse,*nn.*	ibertsaygung,*f.*
convince, to	convaincre	überzeugen	convincere	convencer	övertyga	poyeln
convoy (*mil.*)	convoi,*m.*	(Schutz)Geleit,*n.*	convoglio,*m.*	convoy,*m.*	konvoj,*nn.*	konvoy,*m.*
cook	cuisinier,*m.*	Koch,*m.*	cuoco,*m.*	cocinero,*m.*	kock,*m.*	kukher,*m.*
cook (heat food), to	(faire) cuire	kochen	cuocere	cocer	koka	kokhn
cook (prepare meals), to	faire la cuisine	kochen	cucinare	cocinar	laga mat	kokhn
cool (having low temperature)	frais, fraîche	kühl	fresco	fresco	sval	kil
cool (make less hot), to	rafraîchir	kühlen	rinfrescare	enfriar	avkyla	kiln
cooperation	coopération,*f.*	Mitwirkung,*f.*	cooperazione,*f.*	cooperación,*f.*	samarbete,*n.*	kooperatsye,*f.*
cooperative (*n.*)	coopérative,*f.*	Genossenschaft, *f.*	società coopera-tiva,*f.*	asociación coope-rativa,*f.*	kooperativ före-ning,*nn.*	kooperativ,*m.*
co-owner (*bus.*)	copropriétaire, *m.,f.*	Miteigentümer, *m.*	comproprietario, *m.*	copropietario,*m.*	delägare,*nn.*	mitbazitser,*m.*
copartnership (*bus.*)	coassociation,*f.*	offene Handels-gesellschaft,*f.*	comproprietà,*f.*	sociedad regular colectiva,*f.*	delägarskap,*n.*	shutfeshaft glaykh oyf glaykh,*f.*
Copenhagen	Copenhague,*f.*	Kopenhagen,*n.*	Copenaghen,*f.*	Copenhague	Köpenhamn,*n.*	Kopnhavn,*n.*
copper	cuivre,*m.*	Kupfer,*n.*	rame,*m.*	cobre,*m.*	koppar,*nn.*	kuper,*n.*
copy (duplicate)	copie,*f.*	Kopie,*f.*	copia,*f.*	copia,*f.*	kopia,*nn.*	kopye,*f.*
copy (of a publication)	exemplaire,*m*	Exemplar,*n.*	esemplare,*m.*	ejemplar,*m.*	exemplar,*n.*	ekzemplar,*m.*
copy (imitate), to	copier	nachahmen	copiare	copiar	kopiera	nokhmakhn
copyright (*n.*)	copyright,*m.*	Urheberrecht,*n.*	proprietà lette-raria,*f.*	propiedad,*f.*	förlagsrätt,*nn.*	drukrekht,*n.*
cord (rope)	corde,*f.*	Strick,*m.*	corda,*f.*	cuerda,*f.*	rep,*n.*	shpagat,*m.*
cordial (*adj.*)	cordial	herzlich	cordiale	cordial	hjärtlig	hartsik
cork (stopper)	bouchon,*m.*	Kork,*m.*	tappo,*m.*	corcho,*m.*	kork,*nn.*	korek,*m.*
corn (maize)	maïs,*m.*	Mais,*m.*	granturco,*m.*	maíz,*m.*	majs,*nn.*	kukuruze,*f.*
corner (angle)	coin,*m.*	Ecke,*f.*	angolo,*m.*	rincón,*m.*	hörn,*n.*	vinkl,*m.*
corner (street intersection)	coin,*m.*	Ecke,*f.*	angolo,*m.*	esquina,*f.*	hörn,*n.*	rog,*m.*
corporal (*mil.*)	caporal,*m.*	Korporal,*m.*	caporale,*m.*	cabo,*m.*	korpral,*nn.*	kapral,*m.*
corporation	société (enregi-strée),*f.*	A.G. (Aktien-gesellschaft),*f.*	società anonima, *f.*	sociedad anó-nima,*f.*	bolag,*n.*	korporatsye,*f.*
corpse	cadavre,*m.*	Leiche,*f.*	cadavere,*m.*	cadáver,*m.*	lik,*n.*	barminen,*m.*
correct	exact	richtig	corretto	correcto	riktig	rikhtik
correspond (agree), to	correspondre	entsprechen	corrispondere	corresponder	överensstämma	shtimen
correspondence (letters)	correspondance,*f.*	Briefwechsel,*m.*	corrispondenza,*f.*	correspondencia, *f.*	brevväxling,*nn.*	korespondents,*f.*
correspondence school	école par corre-spondance,*f.*	Fernunterrichts-schule,*f.*	scuola per corri-spondenza,*f.*	escuela por corre-spondencia,*f.*	korrespondens-institut,*n.*	korespondents-shul,*f.*

English	French	German	Italian	Spanish	Swedish	Yiddish
correspondent (letter writer)	correspondant, *m.*	Korrespondent, *m.*	corrispondente, *m.,f.*	correspondiente, *m.*	korrespondent, *nn.*	korespondent, *m.*
correspond with (write to), to	correspondre avec	korrespondieren	corrispondere con	corresponderse con	brevväxla med	korespondirn
cosmetic (*n.*)	cosmétique,*m.*	Schönheitsmittel, *n.*	cosmetico,*m.* (*pl.* -ci)	cosmético,*m.*	skönhetsmedel,*n.*	kosmetik,*f.*
cost (price)	prix,*m.*	Preis,*m.* (*pl.* Kosten)	costo,*m.*	costa,*f.*	kostnad,*nn.*	prayz,*m.*
cost, to	coûter	kosten	costare	costar	kosta	kostn
Costa Rica	Costa-Rica,*f.*	Kostarika,*n.*	Costa Rica,*f.*	Costa Rica	Costa Rica,*n.*	Kostarike,*f.*
costly	coûteux, -teuse	kostbar	costoso	costoso	dyrbar	tayer
costume	costume,*m.*	Kostüm,*n.*	costume,*m.*	traje regional,*m.*	kostym,*nn.*	kostyum,*m.*
cot (bed)	lit de camp,*m.*	Feldbett,*n.*	lettino,*m.*	catre,*m.*	turistsäng,*nn.*	betl,*n.*
cotton (boll)	coton,*m.*	Baumwolle,*f.*	cotone,*m.*	algodón,*m.*	bomull,*nn.*	bavl,*m.*
cotton (fabric)	cotonnade,*f.*	Baumwolle,*f.*	tela di cotone,*f.*	(tela de) algodón, (*f.*)*m.*	bomullstyg,*n.*	bavl,*m.*
couch	canapé,*m.*	Couch,*f.*	sofà,*m.* (*pl.* sofà)	sofá,*m.*	soffa,*nn.*	kanape,*f.*
cough	toux,*f.*	Husten,*m.*	tosse,*f.*	toz,*f.*	hosta,*nn.*	hust,*m.*
could (*v.*)	(*see* pouvoir, p. 2835)	(*see* konnte, p. 2892 ff.)	(*see* potere, p. 2958)	(*see* poder, p. 3023)	(*see* kunna, p. 3078)	(*see* volt gekent, p. 3134)
council	conseil,*m.*	Rat,*m.*	consiglio,*m.*	consejo,*m.*	råd,*n.*	rot,*m.*
counsel (advice)	conseil,*m.*	Rat(schlag),*m.*	consiglio,*m.*	consejo,*m.*	råd,*n.*	eytse,*f.*
counsel (lawyer)	avocat,*m.*	Anwalt,*m.*	avvocato,*m.*	abogado,*m.*	advokat,*nn.*	advokat,*m.*
counsel, to	conseiller	beraten	consigliare	aconsejar	råda	eytsen
count (enumerate), to	compter	zählen	contare	contar	räkna	tseyln
countenance (face)	visage,*m.*	Antlitz,*n.*	viso,*m.*	semblante,*m.*	ansikte,*n.*	ponim,*n.*
counter (table)	comptoir,*m.*	Ladentisch,*m.*	banco,*m.*	mostrador,*m.*	disk,*nn.*	tombank,*m.*
counterfeit (*adj.*)	faux, fausse	gefälscht	contraffatto	falso	falsk	falsh
countersignature (*bus.*)	contreseing,*m.*	Gegenzeichnung, *f.*	controfirma,*f.*	contrafirma,*f.*	kontrasignering, *nn.*	kegn-unter-shrift,*f.*
count (rely) on, to	compter sur	verlassen, sich auf…	contare su	contar con	räkna på	rekhenen oyf
country (countryside)	campagne,*f.*	Land,*n.*	campagna,*f.*	campo,*m.*	landsbygd,*nn.*	land,*n.*
country (nation)	pays,*m.*	Land,*n.*	paese,*m.*	país,*m.*	land,*n.* (*pl.* länder)	land,*n.*
couple (pair, *n.*)	couple,*m.*	Paar,*n.*	coppia,*f.*	pareja,*f.*	par,*n.*	por,*f.*
coupon (detachable certificate)	coupon,*m.*	Abschnitt,*m.*	cupone,*m.*	cupón,*m.*	kupong,*nn.*	kupon,*m.*
courage	courage,*m.*	Mut,*m.*	coraggio,*m.*	valor,*m.*	mod,*n.*	mut,*m.*
course, of	bien sûr	selbstverständ-lich	naturalmente	por supuesto	naturligtvis	avade
court (of law)	tribunal,*m.*	Gericht,*n.*	tribunale,*m.*	tribunal,*m.*	domstol,*nn.*	gerikht,*n.*
court (of ruler)	cour,*f.*	Hof,*m.*	corte,*f.*	corte,*f.*	hov,*n.*	hoyf,*m.*
courteous (polite)	courtois	höflich	cortese	cortés	artig	eydl
courtesy	courtoisie,*f.*	Höflichkeit,*f.*	cortesia,*f.*	cortesía,*f.*	artighet,*nn.*	eydlkayt,*f.*
cousin	cousin,*m.*	Vetter,*m.*	cugino,*m.*	primo,*m.*	kusin,*nn.*	shvesterkind,*n.*
cover (lid)	couvercle,*m.*	Deckel,*m.*	coperchio,*m.*	tapa,*f.*	lock,*n.*	dekl,*n.*
cover, to	couvrir	(be)decken	coprire	tapar	täcka	tsudekn
cow	vache,*f.*	Kuh,*f.*	vacca,*f.*	vaca,*f.*	ko,*nn.*	ku,*f.*
coward	lâche,*m.,f.*	Feigling,*m.*	codardo,*m.*	cobarde,*m.*	feg stackare,*nn.*	pakhdn,*m.*
crab (shellfish)	crabe,*m.*	Krebs,*m.*	granchio,*m.*	cangrejo,*m.*	krabba,*nn.*	krab,*m.*
crack (fissure)	fente,*f.*	Riss,*m.*	fessura,*f.*	grieta,*f.*	spricka,*nn.*	shpalt,*m.*
crack (make split), to	fendre	spalten	fendere	hender	spräcka	shpaltn
cradle	berceau,*m.*	Wiege,*f.*	culla,*f.*	cuna,*f.*	vagga,*nn.*	vig,*f.*
craft (trade)	métier,*m.*	Handwerk,*n.*	mestiere,*m.*	oficio,*m.*	hantverk,*n.*	melokhe,*f.*
craft (vessel)	embarcation,*f.*	Schiff,*m.*	barca,*f.*	embarcación,*f.*	fartyg,*n.*	shif,*f.*
cramp (*med.*)	crampe,*f.*	Krampf,*m.*	crampo,*m.*	calambre,*m.*	kramp,*nn.*	kurtsh,*m.*
crash (loud noise)	fracas,*m.*	Krach,*m.*	fracasso,*m.*	estruendo,*m.*	brak,*n.*	krakh,*m.*
crash (be smashed), to	écraser, s'	abstürzen	fracassarsi	estrellarse	haverera	krakhn
crave (desire), to	être affamé (de)	verlangen, nach…	desiderare arden-temente	anhelar	längta efter	garn
crawl (creep), to	ramper	kriechen	strisciare	arrastrarse	krypa	poyzen
crayon	crayon de cou-leur,*m.*	Buntstift,*m.*	pastello,*m.*	lápiz,*m.*	färgkrita,*nn.*	tseykhnshtift,*m.*
craze (fad)	manie,*f.*	Verrücktheit, *f.*	andazzo,*m.*	manía,*f.*	mani,*nn.*	shigoen,*m.*
crazy	fou, folle	verrückt	pazzo	loco	tokig	meshuge
cream	crème,*f.*	Sahne,*f.*	panna,*f.*	nata,*f.*	grädde,*nn.*	shmant,*m.*
create, to	créer	(er)schaffen	creare	crear	skapa	bashafn
creation	création,*f.*	Schöpfung,*f.*	creazione,*f.*	creación,*f.*	skapande,*n.*	bashafung,*f.*
creature (living being)	créature,*f.*	(Lebe)Wesen,*n.*	creatura,*f.*	criatura,*f.*	varelse,*nn.*	bashefenish,*n.*
credit (*bus.*)	crédit,*m.*	Kredit,*m.*	credito,*m.*	crédito,*m.*	kredit,*nn.*	kredit,*m.*
credit (commendation)	mérite,*m.*	Ehre,*f.*	merito,*m.*	crédito,*m.*	ära,*nn.*	onerkenung,*f.*
credit, to (*bus.*)	créditer	gutschreiben	accreditare	abonar en cuenta	kreditera	kreditirn
creditor (*bus.*)	créancier,*m.*	Gläubiger,*m.*	creditore,*m.*	acreedor,*m.*	fordringsägare, *nn.*	kreditor,*m.*
creek (stream)	ruisseau,*m.*	Bach,*m.*	ruscello,*m.*	arroyo,*m.*	bäck,*nn.*	taykhl,*n.*
creep, to	ramper	schleichen	strisciare	arrastrarse	krypa	krikhn
crest (summit)	crête,*f.*	Gipfel,*m.*	vetta,*f.*	cumbre,*f.*	krön,*n.*	kam,*m.*
crew	équipage,*m.*	Mannschaft,*f.*	equipaggio,*m.*	tripulación,*f.*	besättning,*nn.*	manshaft,*f.*
cricket (insect)	grillon,*m.*	Grille,*f.*	grillo,*m.*	grillo,*m.*	syrsa,*nn.*	gril,*f.*
crime	crime,*m.*	Verbrechen,*n.*	delitto,*m.*	crimen,*m.*	brott,*n.*	farbrekh,*m.*

English	French	German	Italian	Spanish	Swedish	Yiddish
criminal (*adj.*)	criminel, -le	kriminal-...	criminale	criminal	brottslig	farbrekherish
criminal (*n.*)	criminel,*m.*	Verbrecher,*m.*	delinquente,*m.,f.*	criminal,*m.*	brottsling,*nn.*	farbrekher,*m.*
crimson	cramoisi	karmesinrot	cremisino	carmesí	högröd	purpl
cripple	estropié,*m.*	Krüppel,*m.*	storpio,*m.*	cojo,*m.*	krympling,*nn.*	kalike,*m.,f.*
crisis	crise,*f.*	Krise,*f.*	crisi,*f.* (*pl.* crisi)	crisis,*f.*	kris,*nn.*	krizis,*m.*
crisp (brittle)	croquant	knusperig	croccante	crujiente	skör	krukhle
critic	critique,*m.*	Kritiker,*m.*	critico,*m.*	crítico,*m.*	kritiker,*nn.*	kritiker,*m.*
criticism (censure)	critique,*f.*	Tadel,*m.*	critica,*f.*	crítica,*f.*	kritik,*nn.*	kritik,*f.*
criticism (judgment)	critique,*f.*	Kritik,*f.*	critica,*f.*	crítica,*f.*	kritik,*nn.*	kritik,*f.*
crooked	tortu	krumm	torto	torcido	krokig	krum
crop (produce)	récolte,*f.*	Ernte,*f.*	raccolto,*m.*	cosecha,*f.*	skörd,*nn.*	produkt,*m.*
cross (crucifix)	croix,*f.*	Kreuz,*n.*	croce,*f.*	cruz,*f.*	kors,*n.*	tseylem,*m.*
cross (crossbreed), to	croiser	kreuzen	incrociare	cruzar	korsa	kreytsn
cross (traverse), to	traverser	überschreiten	traversare	atravesar	färdas över	aribergeyn
crossing (intersection)	croisement,*m.*	Kreuzung,*f.*	incrocio,*m.*	encrucijada,*f.*	korsning,*nn.*	kreytsung,*f.*
crossing (ocean voyage)	traversée,*f.*	Überfahrt,*f.*	traversata,*f.*	travesía,*f.*	överresa,*nn.*	ariberforn,*n.*
crossroads	carrefour,*m.*	Strassenkreu-zung,*f.*	incrocio,*m.*	encrucijada,*f.*	korsväg,*nn.*	sheydveg,*m.*
crow (bird)	corbeau,*m.*	Krähe,*f.*	corvo,*m.*	cuervo,*m.*	kråka,*nn.*	kro,*f.*
crowd	foule,*f.*	Menge,*f.*	folla,*f.*	muchedumbre,*f.*	mängd,*nn.*	oylem,*m.*
crown (headdress)	couronne,*f.*	Krone,*f.*	corona,*f.*	corona,*f.*	krona,*nn.*	kroyn,*f.*
crown, to	couronner	krönen	coronare	coronar	kröna	kreynen
crude	brut	roh	grezzo	tosco	rå	grob
cruel	cruel, -le	grausam	crudele	cruel	grym	akhzoryesdik
cruise (voyage)	croisière,*f.*	Vernügungs-reise,*f.*	crociera,*f.*	viaje por mar,*m.*	kryssning,*nn.*	hanoe-nesie,*f.*
cruiser (ship)	croiseur,*m.*	Kreuzer,*m.*	incrociatore,*m.*	crucero,*m.*	kryssare,*nn.*	kreytser,*m.*
crumb	miette,*f.*	Krume,*f.*	briciola,*f.*	migaja,*f.*	smula,*nn.*	brekl,*n.*
crumble, to	effriter	zerkrümeln	polverizzare	desmenuzar	söndersmula	tsebreklen
crush, to	écraser	zerquetschen	schiacciare	machacar	krossa	tseshmetern
crust	croûte,*f.*	Kruste,*f.*	crosta,*f.*	corteza,*f.*	skorpa,*nn.*	skorinke,*f.*
crutch	béquille,*f.*	Krücke,*f.*	gruccia,*f.*	muleta,*f.*	krycka,*nn.*	kule,*f.*
cry (utterance)	cri,*m.*	Ruf,*m.*	grido,*m.*	grito,*m.*	skrik,*n.*	geshrey,*m.*
cry (shout), to	crier	schreien	gridare	gritar	skrika	shrayen
cry (weep), to	pleurer	weinen	piangere	llorar	gråta	veynen
crystal (*min.*)	cristal,*m.*	Kristall,*m.*	cristallo,*m.*	cristal,*m.*	kristall,*nn.*	krishtol,*n.*
Cuba	Cuba,*f.*	Kuba,*n.*	Cuba,*f.*	Cuba	Cuba,*n.*	Kuba,*f.*
cube (*geom.*)	cube,*m.*	Würfel,*m.*	cubo,*m.*	cubo,*m.*	kub,*nn.*	kub,*m.*
cuckoo (bird)	coucou,*m.*	Kuckuck,*m.*	cuculo,*m.*	cuclillo,*m.*	gök,*nn.*	kukavke,*f.*
cucumber	concombre,*m.*	Gurke,*f.*	cetriolo,*m.*	pepino,*m.*	gurka,*nn.*	ugerke,*f.*
cuff (of sleeve)	manchette,*f.*	Manschette,*f.*	polsino,*m.*	puño,*m.*	manschett,*nn.*	manket,*m.*
cuff (of trouser)	bord (du panta-lon)	Umschlag,*m.*	orlo dei calzoni,*m.*	vuelta,*f.*	slag,*n.*	manket,*m.*
cultivate (till), to	cultiver	bebauen	coltivare	cultivar	odla	kultivirn
culture (refinement)	culture,*f.*	Bildung,*f.*	cultura,*f.*	cultura,*f.*	kultur,*nn.*	kultur,*f.*
culture (stage of civiliza-tion)	civilisation,*f.*	Kultur,*f.*	civilizzazione,*f.*	cultura,*f.*	kultur,*nn.*	kultur,*f.*
cunning (sly)	rusé	listig	furbo	astuto	listig	khitre
cup	tasse,*f.*	Tasse,*f.*	tazza,*f.*	taza,*f.*	kopp,*nn.*	kubik,*m.*
cupboard	armoire,*f.*	Schrank,*m.*	credenza,*f.*	armario,*m.*	skåp,*n.*	shrank,*m.*
curator	conservateur,*m.*	Kurator,*m.*	curatore,*m.*	curador,*m.*	kurator,*nn.*	kurator,*m.*
curb (edge of street)	bordure,*f.*	Prellstein,*m.*	cordone,*m.*	bordillo,*m.*	trottoarkant,*nn.*	trotuar-shvel,*f.*
curb (restraint)	frein,*m.*	Zügel,*m.*	freno,*m.*	freno,*m.*	band,*n.*	tsam,*f.*
curb (restrain), to	refréner	zügeln	frenare	reprimir	tygla	tsamen
cure (healing)	guérison,*f.*	Heilung,*f.*	guarigione,*f.*	curación,*f.*	bot,*nn.*	refue,*f.*
cure (remedy)	remède,*m.*	Heilmittel,*n.*	rimedio,*m.*	remedio,*m.*	botemedel,*n.*	refue,*f.*
cure (heal), to	guérir	heilen	guarire	curar	bota	oysheyln
curiosity (inquisitiveness)	curiosité,*f.*	Neugier(de),*f.*	curiosità,*f.*	curiosidad,*f.*	nyfikenhet,*nn.*	naygerikayt,*f.*
curious	curieux, -rieuse	neugierig	curioso	curioso	nyfiken	naygerik
curl (ringlet)	boucle (de che-veux),*f.*	Locke,*f.*	ricciolo,*m.*	rizo,*m.*	lock,*nn.*	grayzl,*n.*
currency (money)	monnaie,*f.*	Währung,*f.*	moneta,*f.*	moneda cor-riente,*f.*	valuta,*nn.*	gelt,*n.*
current (contemporary, *adj.*)	courant	laufend	attuale	corriente	innevarande	loyfik
current (of electricity)	courant,*m.*	Strom,*m.*	corrente,*f.*	corriente eléc-trica,*f.*	ström,*nn.*	shtrom,*m.*
current (of water)	courant,*m.*	Strömung,*f.*	corrente,*f.*	corriente,*f.*	strömdrag,*n.*	shtrom,*m.*
curse	malédiction,*f.*	Fluch,*m.*	maledizione,*f.*	maldición,*f.*	förbannelse,*nn.*	klole,*f.*
curse (damn), to	maudire	verfluchen	maledire	maldecir	förbanna	sheltn
curse (swear), to	jurer	fluchen	bestemmiare	blasfemar	svära	zidlen zikh
curtain (drape)	rideau,*m.*	Vorhang,*m.*	tendina,*f.*	cortina,*f.*	gardin,*nn.*	forhang,*m.*
curve	courbe,*f.*	Kurve,*f.*	curva,*f.*	curva,*f.*	kurva,*nn.*	boygn,*m.*
cushion (pillow)	coussin,*m.*	Kissen,*n.*	cuscino,*m.*	cojín,*m.*	dyna,*nn.*	kishn,*f.*
custom (habit)	coutume,*f.*	Sitte,*f.*	costume, *m.*	costumbre,*f.*	sed,*nn.*	minheg,*m.*
customer (buyer)	chaland,*m.*	Kunde,*m.*	cliente,*m.,f.*	cliente,*m.,f*	kund,*nn.*	koyne,*m.*
customhouse	douane,*f.*	Zollamt,*n.*	dogana,*f.*	aduana,*f.*	tullkammare,*nn.*	tsolamt,*n.*
customs (tax)	droits de douane,*m.pl.*	Zoll,*m.*	dogana,*f.*	derechos de aduana,*m.pl.*	tull,*nn.*	tsol,*m.*
cut (divide into parts), to	couper	schneiden	tagliare	cortar	skära	tseshnaydn
cut (reduce), to	réduire	verringern	ridurre	rebajar	beskära	shnaydn
cut (wound), to	couper	schneiden	tagliare	herir	skära	tseshnaydn
cylinder (*geom.*)	cylindre,*m.*	Zylinder,*m.*	cilindro,*m.*	cilindro,*m.*	cylinder,*nn.*	tsilinder,*m.*

English	French	German	Italian	Spanish	Swedish	Yiddish
Czechoslovakia	Tchécoslo-vaquie,*f.*	Tschechoslo-wakei,*f.*	Ceco-Slovakia,*f.*	Checoeslovaquia	Tjeckoslo-vakien,*n.*	Tshekhoslo-vakay,*f.*
dad	papa,*m.*	Vati,*m.*	babbo,*m.*	papá,*m.*	pappa,*nn.*	tate,*m.*
dagger	poignard,*m.*	Dolch,*m.*	pugnale,*m.*	puñal,*m.*	dolk,*nn.*	shtilet,*m.*
daily (*adj.*)	quotidien, -ne	täglich	quotidiano	diario	daglig	togteglekh
dainty	délicat	zierlich	delicato	delicado	utsökt	delikat
dairy	laiterie,*f.*	Molkerei,*f.*	latteria,*f.*	lechería,*f.*	mejeri,*n.*	milkhikeray,*f.*
daisy	marguerite,*f.*	Gänseblümchen, *n.*	margherita,*f.*	margarita,*f.*	tusensköna,*nn.*	margeritke,*f.*
dam (dike)	digue,*f.*	(Stau)Damm,*m.*	sbarramento,*m.*	represa,*f.*	damm,*nn.*	dambe,*f.*
damage (injury)	dommage,*m.*	Schaden,*m.*	danno,*m.*	daño,*m.*	skada,*nn.*	shodn,*m.*
damage (injure), to	endommager	beschädigen	danneggiare	dañar	skada	tseshedikn
damages (indemnification)	dommages-inté-rêts,*m.pl.*	Schadenersatz,*m.*	indennizzo,*m.*	daños y perjui-cios,*m.pl.*	skadestånd,*n.*	antshedikung,*f.*
damn, to	damner	verdammen	dannare	condenar	förbanna	farshelten
damp (moist)	humide	feucht	umido	húmedo	fuktig	faykht
dance (movement to music)	danse,*f.*	Tanz,*m.*	danza,*f.*	baile,*m.*	dans,*nn.*	tants,*m.*
dance (party)	bal,*m.*	Tanzgesellschaft, *f.*	ballo,*m.*	baile,*m.*	danstillställning, *nn.*	tants,*m.*
dance, to	danser	tanzen	ballare	bailar	dansa	tantsn
dandelion	pissenlit,*m.*	Löwenzahn,*m.*	radicchiella,*f.*	diente de león,*m.*	maskros,*nn.*	luftl,*n.*
danger	danger,*m.*	Gefahr,*f.*	pericolo,*m.*	peligro,*m.*	fara,*nn.*	sakone,*f.*
dangerous	dangereux, -reuse	gefährlich	pericoloso	peligroso	farlig	sakonesdik
Danish (*adj.*)	danois	dänisch	danese	danés, -nesa	dansk	denish
Danube	Danube,*m.*	Donau,*f.*	Danubio,*m.*	Danubio,*m.*	Donau,*nn.*	Dunay,*m.*
dare (venture), to	oser	wagen	osare	atreverse	våga	dervegn zikh
dark (in color, *adj.*)	foncé	dunkel	oscuro	o(b)scuro	mörk	tunkl
dark (without light, *adj.*)	sombre	dunkel	buio	o(b)scuro	mörk	fintster
darken (make dark), to	obscurcir	verdunkeln	oscurare	o(b)scurecer	göra mörk	fartunklen
darkness	obscurité,*f.*	Dunkelheit,*f.*	oscurità,*f.*	o(b)scuridad,*f.*	mörker,*n.*	fintsternish,*f.*
darling	chéri,*m.*	Liebling,*m.*	carino,*m.*	querido,*m.*	älskling,*nn.*	lyubenyu,*n.*
darn (mend), to	repriser	stopfen	rammendare	zurcir	stoppa	tsireven
dash (rush), to	précipiter, se	stürzen	precipitarsi	lanzarse	rusa	a loz ton zikh
date (appointment)	rendez-vous,*m.*	Verabredung,*f.*	appuntamento,*m.*	cita,*f.*	avtal,*n.*	bashtelung,*f.*
date (calendar designation)	date,*f.*	Datum,*n.*	data,*f.*	fecha,*f.*	datum,*n.* (*pl.* data)	date,*f.*
date (fruit)	datte,*f.*	Dattel,*f.*	dattero,*m.*	dátil,*m.*	dadel,*nn.*	teytl,*m.*
daughter	fille,*f.*	Tochter,*f.*	figlia,*f.*	hija,*f.*	dotter,*nn.* (*pl.* döttrar)	tokhter,*f.*
daughter-in-law	belle-fille,*f.*	Schwieger-tochter,*f.*	nuora,*f.*	nuera,*f.*	svärdotter,*nn.* (*pl.* -döttrar)	shnur,*f.*
dawn (daybreak)	aurore,*f.*	Morgendäm-merung,*f.*	alba,*f.*	alba,*f.*	gryning,*nn.*	kayor,*m.*
day (daytime)	journée,*f.*	Tag,*m.*	giorno,*m.*	día,*m.*	dag,*nn.*	tog,*m.*
day (24-hour period)	jour,*m.*	Tag,*m.*	giorno,*m.*	día,*m.*	dygn,*n.*	mesles,*m.*
daylight	jour,*m.*	Tageslicht,*n.*	luce del giorno,*f.*	luz del día, *f.*	dagsljus,*n.*	toglikht,*n.*
dazzle, to	éblouir	blenden	abbagliare	deslumbrar	blända	farblendn
dead	mort	tot	morto	muerto	död	toyt
deadly	mortel, -le	tödlich	mortale	mortal	dödlig	toyt-...
deaf	sourd	taub	sordo	sordo	döv	toyb
deal (trade), to	commercer	handeln	trattare	tratar	handla	handlen
dealer (trader)	commerçant,*m.*	Händler,*m.*	distributore,*m.*	negociante,*m.*	handlande,*nn.*	soykher,*m.*
dealings (relations)	relations,*f.pl.*	Verkehr,*m.*	relazioni,*f.pl.*	relaciones,*f.pl.*	förbindelse,*nn.*	magemase,*m.*
dear (beloved, *adj.*)	cher, chère	lieb	caro	querido	kär	lib
death	mort,*f.*	Tod,*m.*	morte,*f.*	muerte,*f.*	död,*nn.*	toyt,*m.*
debate	débat,*m.*	Debatte,*f.*	dibattito,*m.*	debate,*m.*	debatt,*nn.*	debate,*f.*
debenture	obligation,*f.*	Schuldverschrei-bung,*f.*	obbligazione,*f.*	obligación,*f.*	obligation,*nn.*	shtar-khoyv,*m.*
debit, to	débiter	belasten	addebitare	adeudar	debitera	aroprekhenen
debt	dette,*f.*	Schuld,*f.*	debito,*m.*	deuda,*f.*	skuld,*nn.*	khoyv,*m.*
debtor (*bus.*)	débiteur,*m.*	Schuldner,*m.*	debitore,*m.*	deudor,*m.*	gäldenär,*nn.*	bal-khoyv,*m.*
decay (decline)	décadence,*f.*	Zerfall,*m.*	decadenza,*f.*	decadencia,*f.*	förfall,*n*	tsefal,*m.*
decay (rottenness)	pourriture,*f.*	Fäulnis,*f.*	putridume,*m.*	podredura,*f.*	förruttnelse,*nn.*	foylung,*f.*
deceit	tromperie,*f.*	Betrug,*m.*	inganno,*m.*	engaño,*m.*	bedrägeri,*n.*	opnar,*m.*
deceive (delude), to	tromper	betrügen	deludere	engañar	bedra(ga)	opnarn
decent (fairly good)	passable	leidlich	decente	regular	hygglig	orntlekh
decent (respectable)	décent	anständig	decente	decente	anständig	orntlekh
decide (make up one's mind), to	décider, se	entschliessen, sich	decidersi	decidir	besluta (sig)	bashlisn
decision (judgment)	décision,*f.*	Entscheidung,*f.*	decisione,*f.*	decisión,*f.*	beslut,*n.*	bashlus,*m.*
deck (of cards)	jeu (de cartes),*m.*	Pack,*n.*	mazzo (di carte),*m.*	baraja,*f.*	kortlek,*nn.*	peshl,*n.*
deck (of ship)	pont,*m.*	Deck,*n.*	ponte,*m.*	cubierta,*f.*	däck,*n.*	dek,*m.*
declaration (announce-ment)	déclaration,*f.*	Erklärung,*f.*	dichiarazione,*f.*	declaración,*f.*	tillkännagivande, *n.*	deklaratsye,*f.*
declare (state), to	déclarer	erklären	dichiarare	declarar	förklara	derklern
decline (deterioration)	déclin,*m.*	Verfall,*m.*	decadenza,*f.*	decadencia,*f.*	nedgång,*nn.*	yeride,*f.*
decline (deteriorate), to	décliner	verfallen	decadere	declinar	gå utför	opfaln
decline (refuse), to	décliner	ablehnen	declinare	rehusar	avslå	opzogn zikh fun
decorate (adorn), to	décorer	schmücken	decorare	decorar	pryda	baputsn
decoration (décor)	décor,*m.*	Dekoration,*f.*	decorazione,*f.*	decoración,*f.*	dekorering,*nn.*	baputsung,*f.*
decoration (ornament)	décoration,*f.*	Verzierung,*f.*	decorazione,*f.*	decoración,*f.*	dekoration,*nn.*	baputsung,*f.*
decrease	diminution,*f.*	Abnahme,*f.*	diminuzione,*f.*	disminución,*f.*	minskning,*nn.*	farminerung,*f.*

English	French	German	Italian	Spanish	Swedish	Yiddish
decree (edict)	décret,*m.*	Verordnung,*f.*	decreto,*m.*	decreto,*m.*	förordning,*nn.*	dekret,*m.*
deduct, to	déduire	abziehen	dedurre	descontar	avdra(ga)	aroprekhenen
deed (act)	action,*f.*	Tat,*f.*	atto,*m.*	hecho,*m.*	gärning,*nn.*	aroprekhenen
deed (transfer agreement)	acte,*m.*	Urkunde,*f.*	atto,*m.*	escritura,*f.*	handling,*nn.*	akt,*m.*
						shtar,*m.*
deem (regard), to	juger	halten, für...	ritenere	considerar	anse	haltn far
deep (in color)	foncé	tief	carico	subido	djup	tif
deep (in extent)	profond	tief	profondo	hondo	djup	tif
deep (in tone)	grave	tief	grave	grave	djup	tif
deer	cerf,*m.*	Hirsch,*m.*	cervo,*m.*	ciervo,*m.*	rådjur,*n.*	sarne,*f.*
defeat	défaitè,*f.*	Niederlage,*f.*	sconfitta,*f.*	derrota,*f.*	nederlag,*n.*	mapole,*f.*
defeat (conquer), to	vaincre	besiegen	sconfiggere	vencer	besegra	bazign
defeat (thwart), to	frustrer	vereiteln	frustrare	frustrar	omintetgöra	bazign
defect (flaw)	defaut,*m.*	Mangel,*m.*	difetto,*m.*	defecto,*m.*	brist,*nn.*	goyver zayn
defend (protect), to	défendre	verteidigen	difendere	defender	försvara	pgam,*m.*
defense	défense,*f.*	Verteidigung,*f.*	difesa,*f.*	defensa,*f.*	försvar,*n.*	farteydikn
						farteydikung,*f.*
deficit (*bus.*)	déficit,*m.*	Fehlbetrag,*m.*	deficit,*m.*	déficit,*m.*	underskott,*n.*	defitsit,*m.*
define, to	définir	definieren	definire	definir	definiera	definirn
definite	défini	bestimmt	definito	definido	bestämd	bashtimt
defy, to	défier	trotzen	sfidare	desafiar	trotsa	ton antkegn
degree (unit of measurement)	degré,*m.*	Grad,*m.*	grado,*m.*	grado,*m.*	grad,*nn.*	grad,*m.*
delay	retard,*m.*	Verzögerung,*f.*	ritardo,*m.*	retraso,*m.*	dröjsmål,*n.*	ophalt,*m.*
delay (postpone), to	remettre	verzögern	differire	diferir	uppskjuta	opleygn
delay (retard), to	retarder	aufhalten	ritardare	demorar	fördröja	ophaltn
delegate	délégué,*m.*	Abgeordnete,*m.*, *f.*	delegato,*m.*	delegado,*m.*	ombud,*n.*	delegat,*m.*
deliberate (intentional)	intentionnel, -le	absichtlich	deliberato	deliberado	avsiktlig	bekivndik
delicate (dainty)	délicat	zart	delicato	delicado	delikat	delikat
delicate (sickly)	délicat	schwächlich	delicato	débil	klen	delikat
delicious	délicieux, -cieuse	köstlich	delizioso	delicioso	läcker	bataamt
delight	joie,*f.*	Entzücken,*n.*	delizia,*f.*	deleite,*m.*	glädje,*nn.*	tayneg,*m.*
delight (give pleasure to), to	délecter	entzücken	dilettare	deleitar	glädja	mekhaye zayn
delightful	délicieux, -cieuse	entzückend	dilettevole	deleitoso	förtjusande	mekhayedik
deliver (hand over), to	livrer	(über)liefern	consegnare	entregar	överlämna	ibergebn
delivery (handing over)	livraison,*f.*	Überlieferung, *f.*	consegna,*f.*	entrega,*f.*	overlämnande, *n.*	ibergebn,*n.*
demand (econ.)	demande,*f.*	Nachfrage,*f.*	domanda,*f.*	demanda,*f.*	efterfrågan,*nn.*	nokhfreg,*m.*
demand (request)	demande,*f.*	Verlangen,*n.*	domanda,*f.*	exigencia,*f.*	krav,*n.*	foderung,*f.*
demand (ask for), to	réclamer	verlangen	richiedere	exigir	begära	fodern
democracy	démocratie,*f.*	Demokratie,*f.*	democrazia,*f.*	democracia,*f.*	demokrati,*nn.*	demokratye,*f.*
democrat	démocrate,*m.*,*f.*	Demokrat,*m.*	democratico,*m.*	demócrata,*m.*,*f.*	demokrat,*nn.*	demokrat,*m.*
democratic	démocratique	demokratisch	democratico	democrático	demokratisk	demokratish
demonstrate (show), to	montrer	vorführen	dimostrare	demostrar	demonstrera	bavayzn
demonstration (proof)	démonstration,*f.*	Beweis,*m.*	dimostrazione,*f.*	demostración,*f.*	bevis,*n.*	bavayz,*m.*
den (animal lair)	tanière,*f.*	Höhle,*f.*	antro,*m.*	guarida,*f.*	lya,*nn.*	nore,*f.*
Denmark	Danemark,*m.*	Dänemark,*n.*	Danimarca,*f.*	Dinamarca	Danmark,*n.*	Denmark,*n.*
dense	dense	dicht	denso	denso	tät	gedikht
dentist	dentiste,*m.*	Zahnarzt,*m.*	dentista,*m.*	dentista,*m.*	tandläkare,*nn.*	tsondokter,*m.*
deny (contradict), to	nier	leugnen	negare	negar	förneka	leykenen
deny (refuse), to	refuser	verweigern	rifiutare	negar	vägra	opzogn
depart (leave), to	partir	abreisen	partire	partir	avresa	avekforn
department (administrative unit)	département,*m.*	Abteilung,*f.*	reparto,*m.*	departamento,*m.*	avdelning,*nn.*	opteylung,*f.*
department store	(grand) magasin, *m.*	Warenhaus,*n.*	grande magazzino,*m.*	almacén,*m.*	varuhus,*n.*	universal-krom, *f.*
departure (deviation)	déviation,*f.*	Abweichung,*f.*	deviamento,*m.*	desviación,*f.*	avvikelse,*nn.*	opvaykh,*m.*
departure (setting out)	départ,*m.*	Abfahrt,*f.*	partenza,*f.*	partida,*f.*	avresa,*nn.*	opfor,*m.*
dependent (reliant)	dépendant	abhängig	dipendente	dependiente	beroende	ophengik
depend (be contingent) on, to	dépendre de	abhängen von...	dipendere da	depender de	bero på	vendn zikh
depend (rely) on, to	compter sur	verlassen, sich auf...	contare su	contar con	lita på	farlozn zikh
deposit (money deposited)	dépôt,*m.*	Einzahlung,*f.*	deposito,*m.*	depósito,*m.*	inbetalning,*nn.*	ayntsolung,*f.*
deposit, to (*fin.*)	déposer	einzahlen	depositare	depositar	imbetala	ayntsoln
depositor (*fin.*)	déposant,*m.*	Kontoinhaber,*m.*	depositante,*m.*,*f.*	depositador,*m.*	insättare,*nn.*	ayntsoler,*m.*
depot (station)	gare,*f.*	Bahnhof,*m.*	stazione,*f.*	estación,*f.*	station,*nn.*	vokzal,*m.*
depression (econ.)	dépression (économique),*f.*	Depression,*f.*	crisi economica, *f.*	depresión,*f.*	depression,*nn.*	depresye,*f.*
depression (sadness)	abattement,*m.*	Niedergeschlagenheit,*f.*	depressione,*f.*	abatimiento,*m.*	nedslagenhet,*nn.*	more-shkhoyre, *f.*
deprive (divest), to	priver	entziehen	privare	privar	beröva	tsunemen
depth (deepness)	profondeur,*f.*	Tiefe,*f.*	profondità,*f.*	profundidad,*f.*	djup,*n.*	tif,*f.*
derive (get), to	tirer	erhalten	derivare	derivar	erhålla	aroyskrign
descend (move downward), to	descendre	hin-, her- absteigen	discendere	descender	gå ned	aropnidern
descendant (offspring)	descendant,*m.*	Nachkomme,*m.*	discendente,*m.*,*f.*	descendiente,*m.*,*f.*	avkomling,*nn.*	kinds kind,*n.*
describe (portray), to	décrire	beschreiben	descrivere	describir	beskriva	bashraybn
description (account)	description,*f.*	Beschreibung,*f.*	descrizione,*f.*	descripción,*f.*	beskrivning,*nn.*	bashraybung,*f.*
desert	désert,*m.*	Wüste,*f.*	deserto,*m.*	desierto,*m.*	öken,*nn.*	midber,*f.*
deserve, to	mériter	verdienen	meritare	merecer	förtjäna	midber,*f.*
design (intention)	dessein,*m.*	Absicht,*f.*	proposito,*m.*	propósito,*m.*	avsikt,*nn.*	fardinen
						kavone,*f.*
design (pattern)	dessin,*m.*	Entwurf,*m.*	disegno,*m.*	diseño,*m.*	mönster,*n.*	muster,*m.*
desirable	désirable	wünschenswert	desiderabile	deseable	önskvärd	ongeleygt

English	French	German	Italian	Spanish	Swedish	Yiddish
desire	désir,*m.*	Lust,*f.*	desiderio,*m.*	deseo,*m.*	begär,*n.*	bager,*m.*
desire (long for), to	désirer	begehren	desiderare	desear	önska	bagern
desk	bureau,*m.*	Schreibtisch,*m.*	scrivania,*f.*	escritorio,*m.*	skrivbord,*n.*	shraybtish,*m.*
despair (hopelessness)	désespoir,*m.*	Verzweiflung,*f.*	disperazione,*f.*	desesperación,*f.*	förtvivlan,*nn.*	yiush,*m.*
despair, to	désespérer	verzweifeln	disperare	desesperarse	förtvivla	zayn in yiush
desperate	désespéré	verzweifelt	disperato	desesperado	förtvivlad	fartsveyflt
despise, to	mépriser	verachten	disprezzare	despreciar	förakta	farakhtn
despite (*prep.*)	malgré	trotz	malgrado	a despecho de	trots	nit kukndik oyf
dessert	dessert,*m.*	Nachtisch,*m.*	dolce,*m.*	postre,*m.*	efterrätt,*nn.*	desert,*m.*
destination	destination,*f.*	Bestimmungs-ort,*m.*	destinazione,*f.*	destino,*m.*	bestämmelseort, *nn.*	tsil,*m.*
destiny	destin,*m.*	Schicksal,*n.*	destino,*m.*	destino,*m.*	öde,*n.*	goyrl,*m.*
destroy (demolish), to	détruire	zerstören	distruggere	destruir	förstöra	tseshtern
destroyer (ship)	contre-torpilleur,*m.*	Zerstörer,*m.*	esploratore,*m.*	destructor,*m.*	jagare,*nn.*	destroyer,*m.*
destruction (demolition)	destruction,*f.*	Zerstörung,*f.*	distruzione,*f.*	destrucción,*f.*	förstörelse,*nn.*	khurbn,*m.*
detail (minor item)	détail,*m.*	Einzelheit,*f.*	dettaglio,*m.*	detalle,*m.*	detalj,*nn.*	prat,*m.*
detect, to	découvrir	aufdecken	rilevare	descubrir	upptäcka	dershpirn
determination (fixed intent)	détermination,*f.*	Entschlossenheit, *f.*	determinazione, *f.*	empeño,*m.*	föresats,*nn.*	antshlosnkayt,*f.*
determine (ascertain), to	déterminer	feststellen	determinare	determinar	fastslå	festshteln
determine (make up one's mind), to	décider, (se)	entschliessen, sich	determinarsi	decidir	besluta (sig)	bashlisn bay zikh
detour	déviation,*f.*	Umleitung,*f.*	deviazione,*f.*	desviación,*f.*	omväg,*nn.*	umveg,*m.*
develop, to	développer	entwickeln	sviluppare	desarrollar	utveckla	antviklen
development	développement, *m.*	Entwicklung,*f.*	sviluppo,*m.*	desarrollo,*m.*	utveckling,*nn.*	antviklung,*f.*
deviate (diverge), to	dévier	abweichen	deviare	desviarse	avvika	opvaykhn
device (apparatus)	appareil,*m.*	Vorrichtung,*f.*	apparato,*m.*	dispositivo,*m.*	apparat,*nn.*	mitl,*n.*
devil	diable,*m.*	Teufel,*m.*	diavolo,*m.*	diablo,*m.*	djävul,*nn.*	tayvl,*m.*
devise (contrive), to	inventer	erdenken	inventare	idear	hitta på	oystrakhtn
devote oneself, to	consacrer, se	widmen, sich	dedicarsi	dedicarse	ägna sig	opgebn zikh
devotion (loyal attachment)	dévouement,*m.*	Hingebung,*f.*	devozione,*f.*	devoción,*f.*	hängivenhet,*nn.*	getrayshaft,*f.*
devour (eat), to	dévorer	verschlingen	divorare	devorar	sluka	farshlingen
dew	rosée,*f.*	Tau,*m.*	rugiada,*f.*	rocío,*m.*	dagg,*nn.*	toy,*m.*
dexterity	dextérité,*f.*	Gewandtheit,*f.*	destrezza,*f.*	destreza,*f.*	händighet,*nn.*	beryeshaft,*f.*
diabetes	diabète,*m.*	Zuckerkrank-heit,*f.*	diabete,*m.*	diabetes,*f.*	sockersjuka,*nn.*	tsuker-krankayt,*f.*
dial (graduated face)	cadran,*m.*	Zifferblatt,*n.*	quadrante,*m.*	disco graduado, *m.*	nummerskiva,*nn.*	tsiferblat,*n.*
diameter	diamètre,*m.*	Durchmesser,*m.*	diametro,*m.*	diámetro,*m.*	diameter,*nn.*	diameter,*m.*
diamond (gem)	diamant,*m.*	Diamant,*m.*	diamante,*m.*	diamante,*m.*	diamant,*nn.*	diment,*m.*
dice (marked cubes)	dés,*m.pl.*	Würfel,*m.pl.*	dadi,*m.pl.*	dados,*m.pl.*	tärningar,*nn.pl.*	toplshteyner,*m. pl.*
dictate (for transcription), to	dicter	diktieren	dettare	dictar	diktera	diktirn
dictate (give orders), to	dicter	diktieren	dettare	mandar	diktera	diktirn
dictionary	dictionnaire,*m.*	Wörterbuch,*n.*	dizionario,*m.*	diccionario,*m.*	ordbok,*nn.* (*pl.* -böcker)	verterbukh,*n.*
die, to	mourir	sterben	morire	morir(se)	dö	shtarbn
diet (restricted food allowance)	régime,*m.*	Diät,*f.*	dieta,*f.*	dieta,*f.*	diet,*nn.*	diete,*f.*
diet (total food consumed)	nourriture,*f.*	Diät,*f.*	alimentazione,*f.*	alimentación,*f.*	föda,*nn.*	diete,*f.*
differ (be unlike), to	différer	unterscheiden, sich	differire	diferenciar(se)	vara olik	zayn andersh
difference (dissimilarity)	différence,*f.*	Unterschied,*m.*	differenza,*f.*	diferencia,*f.*	olikhet,*nn.*	khilek,*m.*
difference (*math.*)	différence,*f.*	Rest,*m.*	resto,*m.*	residuo,*m.*	skillnad,*nn.*	diferents,*f.*
different (unlike)	différent	verschieden	differente	diferente	olika	ander
difficult	difficile	schwer	difficile	difícil	svår	shver
difficulty (hardness)	difficulté,*f.*	Schwierigkeit,*f.*	difficoltà,*f.*	dificultad,*f.*	besvärlighet,*nn.*	shverkayt,*f.*
difficulty (obstacle)	difficulté,*f.*	Schwierigkeit,*f.*	difficoltà,*f.*	obstáculo,*m.*	svårighet,*nn.*	menie,*f.*
dig (excavate), to	creuser	graben	scavare	cavar	gräva	grobn
digest, to	digérer	verdauen	digerire	digerir	smälta	fardayen
dignity	dignité,*f.*	Würde,*f.*	dignità,*f.*	dignidad,*f.*	värdighet,*nn.*	verde,*f.*
diligence	diligence,*f.*	Fleiss,*m.*	diligenza,*f.*	diligencia,*f.*	flit,*nn.*	hasmode,*f.*
diligent	diligent	fleissig	diligente	diligente	flitig	flaysik
dim	obscur	trübe	oscuro	semio(b)scuro	oklar	tunkl
diminish (make smaller), to	diminuer	verkleinern	diminuire	disminuir	förminska	farklenern
din	vacarme,*m.*	Getöse,*n.*	chiasso,*m.*	estrépito,*m.*	dån,*n.*	larem,*m.*
dine, to	dîner	(zu Mittag) essen	pranzare	comer	äta middag	esn mitik
diner (railway dining car)	wagon-restau-rant,*m.*	Speisewagen,*m.*	vagone risto-rante,*m.*	coche comedor, *m.*	restaurangvagn, *nn.*	vagon-restoran, *m.*
dining room	salle à manger,*f.*	Speisezimmer,*n.*	sala da pranzo,*f.*	comedor,*m.*	matsal,*nn.*	estsimer,*m.*
dinner	dîner,*m.*	Mittagessen,*n.*	pranzo,*m.*	comida,*f.*	middag,*nn.*	mitik,*m.*
dip (immerse), to	plonger	(ein)tauchen	immergere	sumergir	doppa	tunken
diphtheria	diphtérie,*f.*	Diphtherie,*f.*	difterite,*f.*	difteria,*f.*	difteri,*nn.*	difterit,*m.*
direct (immediate)	direct	unmittelbar	immediato	directo	omedelbar	direkt
direct (aim), to	diriger	richten	dirigere	dirigir	rikta	tsiln
direct (manage), to	diriger	leiten	dirigere	dirigir	leda	onfirn mit
direction (course)	direction,*f.*	Richtung,*f.*	direzione,*f.*	dirección,*f.*	riktning,*nn.*	rikhtung,*f.*
director	directeur,*m.*	Direktor,*m.*	direttore,*m.*	director,*m.*	ledare,*nn.*	direktor,*m.*
dirt (soil)	terre,*f.*	Erde,*f.*	terra,*f.*	tierra,*f.*	jord,*nn.*	erd,*f.*
dirt (unclean matter)	saleté,*f.*	Schmutz,*m.*	sporcizia,*f.*	suciedad,*f.*	smuts,*nn.*	shmuts,*n.*
dirty (soiled)	sale	schmutzig	sporco	sucio	smutsig	shmutsik
disagree (differ), to	être en désaccord	nicht überein-stimmen	non essere d'ac-cordo	disentir	vara oense	khoylek zayn
disagreeable	désagréable	unangenehm	sgradevole	desagradable	obehaglig	prikre

English	French	German	Italian	Spanish	Swedish	Yiddish
disappear, to	disparaître	verschwinden	sparire	desaparecer	försvinna	farshvundn vern
disappoint, to	désappointer	enttäuschen	deludere	decepcionar	göra besviken	anttoyshn
disappointment	désappointe-ment,*m.*	Enttäuschung,*f.*	delusione,*f.*	decepción,*f.*	besvikelse,*nn.*	anttoyshung,*f.*
disaster	désastre,*m.*	Katastrophe,*f.*	disastro,*m.*	desastre,*m.*	katastrof,*nn.*	katastrofe,*f.*
disbursement (*bus.*)	débours,*m.pl.*	Auslage,*f.*	sborso,*m.*	desembolso,*m.*	utbetalning,*nn.*	oystsolung,*f.*
discharge (dismissal)	congé,*m.*	Entlassung,*f.*	congedo,*m.*	despedida,*f.*	avsked,*nn.*	opzog,*m.*
discipline (training)	discipline,*f.*	Disziplin,*f.*	disciplina,*f.*	disciplina,*f.*	skolning,*nn.*	distsiplin,*f.*
discount (*n.*)	remise,*f.*	Rabatt,*m.*	sconto,*m.*	descuento,*m.*	rabatt,*nn.*	hanokhe,*f.*
discount, to (*bus.*)	escompter	rabattieren	scontare	descontar	ge rabatt	diskontirn
discourage (dishearten), to	décourager	entmutigen	scoraggiare	desanimar	göra modfälld	antmutikn
discover, to	découvrir	entdecken	scoprire	descubrir	upptäcka	oyfdekn
discovery	découverte,*f.*	Entdeckung,*f.*	scoperta,*f.*	descubrimiento,*m.*	upptäckt,*nn.*	oyfdekung,*f.*
discuss, to	discuter	besprechen	discutere	discutir	diskutera	arumredn
discussion	discussion,*f.*	Besprechung,*f.*	discussione,*f.*	discusión,*f.*	diskussion,*nn.*	diskusye,*f.*
disease	maladie,*f.*	Krankheit,*f.*	malattia,*f.*	enfermedad,*f.*	sjukdom,*nn.*	krankayt,*f.*
disgrace (shame)	honte,*f.*	Schmach,*f.*	vergogna,*f.*	ignominia,*f.*	skam,*nn.*	kharpe,*f.*
disguise	déguisement,*m.*	Verkleidung,*f.*	travestimento,*m.*	disfraz,*m.*	förklädnad,*nn.*	farshtelung,*f.*
disgust	dégoût,*m.*	Ekel,*m.*	disgusto,*m.*	aversión,*f.*	avsky,*nn.*	ekl,*m.*
dish (food)	mets,*m.*	Gericht,*n.*	piatto,*m.*	plato,*m.*	rätt,*nn.*	maykhl,*m.*
dishes (tableware)	vaisselle,*f.*	Geschirr,*n.*	stoviglie,*f.pl.*	vajilla,*f.*	servis,*nn.*	keylim,*pl.*
dishonor	déshonneur,*m.*	Unehre,*f.*	disonore,*m.*	deshonra,*f.*	vanära,*nn.*	umkoved,*m.*
dislike	aversion,*f.*	Abneigung,*f.*	antipatia,*f.*	aversión,*f.*	motvilja,*nn.*	antipatye,*f.*
dislike, to	ne pas aimer	nicht mögen	...non piacere (see p. 2955)	tener aversión a	tycka illa om	nit lib hobn
disloyalty	déloyauté,*f.*	Treulosigkeit,*f.*	slealtà,*f.*	deslealtad,*f.*	illojalitet,*nn.*	umloyalkayt,*f.*
dismal	morne	düster	lugubre	triste	dyster	vist
dismay	consternation,*f.*	Bestürzung,*f.*	sgomento,*m.*	desaliento,*m.*	bestörtning,*nn.*	shrek,*m.*
dismiss (discharge), to	congédier	entlassen	licenziare	despedir	avskeda	opzogn
disobey, to	désobéir (à)	nicht gehorchen	disobbedire	desobedecer	vara olydig mot	nit folgn
disorder (confusion)	désordre,*m.*	Unordnung,*f.*	disordine,*m.*	desorden,*m.*	oordning,*nn.*	umordenung,*f.*
dispatch (communication)	dépêche,*f.*	Meldung,*f.*	dispaccio,*m.*	parte,*m.*	rapport,*nn.*	depesh,*f.*
display (exhibit), to	étaler	ausstellen	esibire	exhibir	skylta med	oysshteln
dispose of (put away), to	disposer de	beseitigen	disfarsi di	acabar con	göra sig av med	poter vern fun
disposition (arrangement)	disposition,*f.*	Anordnung,*f.*	disposizione,*f.*	disposición,*f.*	anordning,*nn.*	dispozitsye,*f.*
disposition (disposal)	disposition,*f.*	Erledigung,*f.*	disposizione,*f.*	disposición,*f.*	avyttrande,*n.*	bazaytikung,*f.*
disposition (temperament)	caractère,*m.*	Gemütsart,*f.*	disposizione,*f.*	genio,*m.*	lynne,*n.*	temperament,*m.*
dispute	dispute,*f.*	Streit,*m.*	disputa,*f.*	disputa,*f.*	dispyt,*nn.*	vikuakh,*m.*
dispute (oppose by argument), to	contester	bestreiten	contestare	disputar	disputera	opfregn
dissolve (make end), to	dissoudre	auflösen	sciogliere	disolver	upplösa	funanderlozn
dissolve (make liquefy), to	(faire) dis-soudre	auflösen	sciogliere	disolver	upplösa	tselozn
distance	distance,*f.*	Entfernung,*f.*	distanza,*f.*	distancia,*f.*	avstånd,*n.*	mehalekh,*m.*
distant (far off)	lointain	entfernt	distante	lejano	avlägsen	vayt
distinct (different)	distinct	verschieden	distinto	distinto	olik	farsheydn
distinct (unmistakable)	distinct	deutlich	distinto	preciso	tydlig	boylet
distinction (difference)	distinction,*f.*	Unterschied,*m.*	distinzione,*f.*	distinción,*f.*	åtskillnad,*nn.*	nafke-mine,*f.*
distinction (eminence)	distinction,*f.*	Vornehmheit,*f.*	distinzione,*f.*	distinción,*f.*	betydenhet,*nn.*	oystseykhe-nung,*f.*
distinguish (differentiate), to	distinguer	unterscheiden	distinguere	distinguir	särskilja	funandersheydn
distinguished (notable)	distingué	ausgezeichnet	distinto	distinguido	framstående	ongezen
distract (divert), to	distraire	ablenken	distrarre	distraer	distrahera	tsemishn
distress	détresse,*f.*	Not,*f.*	afflizione,*f.*	apuro,*m.*	nöd,*nn.*	noyt,*f.*
distribute (allot), to	distribuer	verteilen	distribuire	repartir	fördela	farteyln
distribution (allotment)	distribution,*f.*	Verteilung,*f.*	distribuzione,*f.*	reparto,*m.*	fördelning,*nn.*	farteylung,*f.*
distribution (*bus.*)	distribution,*f.*	Verteilung,*f.*	distribuzione,*f.*	distribución,*f.*	distribution,*nn.*	farshpreytung,*f.*
district (locality)	district,*m.*	Bezirk,*m.*	distretto,*m.*	comarca,*f.*	distrikt,*n.*	distrikt,*m.*
disturb, to	déranger	stören	disturbare	perturbar	störa	shtern
ditch	fossé,*m.*	Graben,*m.*	fosso,*m.*	zanja,*f.*	dike,*n.*	rov,*m.*
dive, to	plonger	einen Kopf-sprung machen	precipitarsi	zambullirse	dyka	shpringen dem kop foroys
divide, to (*arith.*)	diviser	teilen	dividere	dividir	dividera	teyln
divide (become separate), to	diviser, se	teilen, sich	dividersi	dividirse	dela sig	teyln zikh
divide (make separate), to	diviser	teilen	dividere	dividir	dela	teyln
dividend (*bus.*)	dividende,*m.*	Dividende,*f.*	dividendo,*m.*	dividendo,*m.*	dividend,*nn.*	dividend,*m.*
divine (*adj.*)	divin	göttlich	divino	divino	gudomlig	getlekh
division (*mil.*)	division,*f.*	Division,*f.*	divisione,*f.*	división,*f.*	division,*nn.*	divizye,*f.*
division (portion)	division,*f.*	Abteilung,*f.*	divisione,*f.*	división,*f.*	avdelning,*nn.*	kheylek,*m.*
divorce (*law*)	divorce,*m.*	Ehescheidung,*f.*	divorzio,*m.*	divorcio,*m.*	skilsmässa,*nn.*	get,*m.*
dizzy (unsteady)	pris d'étourdisse-ment	schwindlig	(avere) le vertigini (see p. 2946)	aturdido	yr	shvindldik
do, to	faire	tun; machen	fare	hacer	göra	ton
dock	embarcadère,*m.*	Dock,*n.*	calata,*f.*	muelle,*m.*	docka,*nn.*	dok,*m.*
doctor	docteur,*m.*	Doktor,*m.*	dottore,*m.*	médico,*m.*	doktor,*nn.*	dokter,*m.*
doctrine	doctrine,*f.*	Lehre,*f.*	dottrina,*f.*	doctrina,*f.*	lära,*nn.*	shite,*f.*
document	document,*m.*	Dokument,*n.*	documento,*m.*	documento,*m.*	dokument,*nn.*	dokument,*m.*
dog	chien,*m.*	Hund,*m.*	cane,*m.*	perro,*m.*	hund,*nn.*	hunt,*m.*
doll	poupée,*f.*	Puppe,*f.*	bambola,*f.*	muñeca,*f.*	docka,*nn.*	lalke,*f.*

English	French	German	Italian	Spanish	Swedish	Yiddish
dome (cupola)	dôme,*m.*	Kuppel,*f.*	cupola,*f.*	cúpula,*f.*	kupol,*nn.*	kupol,*m.*
domestic (household, *adj.*)	domestique	häuslich	domestico	doméstico	huslig	shtubik
domestic (not foreign)	domestique	einheimisch	indigeno	nacional	inhemsk	inlendish
Dominican Republic	République Dominicaine,*f.*	Dominikanische Republik,*f.*	Repubblica Dominicana,*f.*	República Dominicana	Dominikanska republiken,*nn.*	Dominikaner Republik,*f.*
dominion (rule)	dominion,*m.*	Herrschaft,*f.*	dominio,*m.*	dominio,*m.*	välde,*n.*	mamshole,*f.*
donate, to	donner	spenden	donare	donar	skänka	shenken
donkey	âne,*m.*	Esel,*m.*	asino,*m.*	asno,*m.*	åsna,*nn.*	eyzl,*m.*
doom (ruin)	perte,*f.*	Untergang,*m.*	rovina,*f.*	perdición,*f.*	undergång,*nn.*	untergang,*m.*
doom (condemn), to	condamner	verurteilen	condannare	condenar	döma	farmishpetn
door	porte,*f.*	Tür,*f.*	porta,*f.*	puerta,*f.*	dörr,*nn.*	tir,*f.*
dose (*med.*)	dose,*f.*	Dosis,*f.*	dose,*f.*	dosis,*f.*	dos,*nn.*	doze,*f.*
dot (point)	point,*m.*	Punkt,*m.*	punto,*m.*	punto,*m.*	prick,*nn.*	pintele,*n.*
double (*adj.*)	double	doppelt	doppio	doble	dubbel	topl
doubt	doute,*m.*	Zweifel,*m.*	dubbio,*m.*	duda,*f.*	tvivel,*n.*	sofek,*m.*
doubt (be uncertain about), to	douter de	bezweifeln	dubitare	dudar	tvivla på	sofekn in
doubtful	douteux, -teuse	zweifelhaft	dubbioso	dudoso	tvivelaktig	sofekdik
doubtless	sans doute	zweifellos	senza dubbio	sin duda	otvivelaktig	on sofek
dove	colombe,*f.*	Taube,*f.*	colomba,*f.*	paloma,*f.*	duva,*nn.*	toyb,*f.*
down (downward, *adv.*)	(de haut) en bas	hinab; herab	giù	abajo	nedåt	arop
down (in lower place, *adv.*)	plus bas	unten	in basso	más abajo	nere	untn
down payment (*bus.*)	acompte,*m.*	Anzahlung,*f.*	acconto,*m.*	primer pago,*m.*	handpengar, *nn.pl.*	aderoyf,*m.*
downstairs (downward)	en bas (de l'escalier)	die Treppe hin-, her- unter	giù per la scala	escalera abajo	nedför trappan	arop di trep
downstairs (on a lower floor)	en bas	unten	in basso	abajo	i våningen under	untn
downward (*adv.*)	(de haut) en bas	hinunter; her- unter	giù	hacia abajo	nedåt	arunter
dozen	douzaine,*f.*	Dutzend,*n.*	dozzina,*f.*	docena,*f.*	dussin,*n.*	tuts,*m.*
draft (air current)	courant d'air,*m.*	(Luft)Zug,*m.*	corrente d'aria,*f.*	corriente de aire,*f.*	drag,*n.*	tsugvint,*m.*
draft (check)	traite,*f.*	Tratte,*f.*	tratta,*f.*	giro,*m.*	tratta,*nn.*	onvayzung,*f.*
draft (conscription)	conscription,*f.*	Wehrpflicht,*f.*	coscrizione,*f.*	leva,*f.*	värnplikt,*nn.*	tsvangdinst,*n.*
draft (sketch)	ébauche,*f.*	Entwurf,*m.*	abbozzo,*m.*	bosquejo,*m.*	utkast,*n.*	skitse,*f.*
draft (conscript), to	enrôler	ausheben	arrolare	reclutar	utta(ga) till värnplikt	nemen dinen
draft (sketch), to	ébaucher	zeichnen	abbozzare	bosquejar	göra utkast till	onvarfn
drag (pull), to	traîner	ziehen	trascinare	arrastrar	släpa	shlepn
dragon	dragon,*m.*	Drache,*m.*	drago,*m.*	dragón,*m.*	drake,*nn.*	piper-noter,*m.*
drain (conduit)	égout,*m.*	Abflussrohr,*n.*	tubo di scolo,*m.*	desagüe,*m.*	avlopp,*n.*	opflisrer,*f.*
drain (make dry), to	drainer	entwässern	prosciugare	desaguar	tappa ur	oystrikenen
drama	drame,*m.*	Drama,*n.*	dramma,*m.*	drama,*m.*	drama,*n.*	drame,*f.*
draw (pull along), to	tirer	ziehen	trarre	tirar	dra(ga)	tsien
draw (sketch), to	dessiner	zeichnen	disegnare	dibujar	teckna	tseykhenen
drawer (sliding box)	tiroir,*m.*	Schublade,*f.*	cassetto,*m.*	cajón,*m.*	(byrå)låda,*nn.*	shuflod,*m.*
drawing (sketch)	dessin,*m.*	Zeichnung,*f.*	disegno,*m.*	dibujo,*m.*	teckning,*nn.*	tseykhenung,*f.*
dread	effroi,*m.*	Furcht,*f.*	terrore,*m.*	miedo,*m.*	fruktan,*nn.*	eyme,*f.*
dreadful	effroyable	furchtbar	terribile	horrendo	fruktansvärd	eymedik
dream	rêve,*m.*	Traum,*m.*	sogno,*m.*	sueño,*m.*	dröm,*nn.*	kholem,*m.*
dream, to	rêver	träumen	sognare	soñar	drömma	kholemen
dreary	morne	öde	triste	lúgubre	dyster	trib
dress (frock)	robe,*f.*	Kleid,*n.*	veste,*f.*	vestido,*m.*	klänning,*nn.*	kleyd,*n.*
dress (clothe), to	habiller	anziehen	vestire	vestir	klä(da) på	onton
dress (decorate), to	parer	aufputzen	ornare	adornar	smycka	baputsn
dress (get dressed), to	habiller, s'	anziehen, sich	vestirsi	vestirse	klä(da) sig	onton zikh
dress, to (*med.*)	panser	verbinden	medicare	curar	förbinda	bandazhirn
dresser (bureau)	commode- toilette,*f.*	Kommode,*f.*	comò,*m.*	tocador,*m.*	toalettbyrå,*nn.*	komod,*m.*
dressing (sauce)	sauce,*f.*	Salatsosse,*f.*	condimento,*m.*	salsa,*f.*	salladsås,*nn.*	sous,*m.*
drift (float), to	dériver	treiben	andare alla deriva	ir a la deriva	driva	trogn zikh
drill (bore), to	forer	bohren	perforare	perforar	borra	ekbern
drink (beverage)	boisson,*f.*	Getränk,*n.*	bibita,*f.*	bebida,*f.*	dryck,*nn.*	getrank,*m.*
drink, to	boire	trinken	bere	beber	dricka	trinken
drip, to	dégoutter	tropfen	gocciolare	gotear	droppa	kapen
drive (a vehicle), to	conduire	fahren	condurre	guiar	köra	firn
drive (propel), to	pousser	(an)treiben	spingere	impeler	driva	traybn
driver (of automobile)	chauffeur,*m.*	Fahrer,*m.*	autista,*m.,f.*	chofer,*m.*	förare,*nn.*	firer,*m.*
drop (droplet)	goutte,*f.*	Tropfen,*m.*	goccia,*f.*	gota,*f.*	droppe,*nn.*	tropn,*m.*
drop (sudden fall)	chute,*f.*	Sturz,*m.*	caduta,*f.*	caída,*f.*	fall,*n.*	fal,*m.*
drop (fall), to	tomber	(um)fallen	cascare	caer	falla	faln
drop (let fall), to	lâcher	fallen lassen	lasciar cadere	dejar caer	släppa	lozn faln
drown (die by drowning), to	noyer, se	ertrinken	affogare	ahogarse	drunkna	dertrunken vern
drown (kill by drowning), to	noyer	ertränken	affogare	ahogar	dränka	dertrinken
drug (medicine)	drogue,*f.*	Droge,*f.*	medicamento,*m.*	droga,*f.*	drog,*nn.*	meditsin,*f.*
drug (narcotic)	stupéfiant,*m.*	Rauschgift,*n.*	narcotico,*m.*	narcótico,*m.*	narkotika,*nn.pl.*	narkotik,*m.*
drum (*mus.*)	tambour,*m.*	Trommel,*f.*	tamburo,*m.*	tambor,*m.*	trumma,*nn.*	poyk,*f.*

English	French	German	Italian	Spanish	Swedish	Yiddish
drunk (intoxicated)	ivre	betrunken	ubriaco	borracho	drucken	shiker
dry	sec, sèche	trocken	secco	seco	torr	trukn
dry (become dry), to	sécher, (se)	trocknen	asciugarsi	secarse	torka	trikenen zikh
dry (make dry), to	sécher	austrocknen	asciugare	secar	torka	trikenen
duck	canard,*m.*	Ente,*f.*	anitra,*f.*	pato,*m.*	anka,*nn.*	katshke,*f.*
due (payable)	dû, due	fällig	scaduto	pagadero	betalbar	felik
due (proper)	dû, due	gebührend	dovuto	debido	vederbörlig	geherik
dull (blunt)	émoussé	stumpf	smussato	embotado	slö	temp
dull (boring)	ennuyeux, -yeuse	langweilig	noioso	aburrido	tråkig	nudne
dumb (mute)	muet, -te	stumm	muto	mudo	stum	shtum
dumb (stupid)	bête	dumm	sciocco	estúpido	dum	narish
duplicate (copy, *n.*)	double,*m.*	Kopie,*f.*	duplicato,*m.*	duplicado,*m.*	kopia,*nn.*	duplikat,*m.*
duration	durée,*f.*	Dauer,*f.*	durata,*f.*	duración,*f.*	varaktighet,*nn.*	doyer,*m.*
during	pendant	während	durante	durante	under	beshas
dust	poussière,*f.*	Staub,*m.*	polvere,*f.*	polvo,*m.*	damm,*n.*	shtoyb,*m.*
dusty	poussiéreux, -reuse	staubig	polveroso	polvoriento	dammig	shtoybik
Dutch (*adj.*)	hollandais	holländisch	olandese	holandés,-desa	holländsk	holendish
duty (obligation)	devoir,*m.*	Pflicht,*f.*	dovere,*m.*	deber,*m.*	plikt,*nn.*	khoyv,*m.*
duty (tax)	droits de douane, *m.pl.*	Zoll,*m.*	dazio,*m.*	derechos de aduana,*m.pl.*	tull,*nn.*	tsol,*m.*
duty-free	franc de tout droit	zollfrei	esente da dazio	libre de derechos	tullfri	tsolfray
dwarf	nain,*m.*	Zwerg,*m.*	nano,*m.*	enano,*m.*	dvärg,*nn.*	karlik,*m.*
dwell (reside), to	habiter	wohnen	dimorare	residir	bo	voynen
dwelling	habitation,*f.*	Wohnung,*f.*	abitazione,*f.*	habitación,*f.*	bostad,*nn.* (*pl.* -städer)	voynung,*f.*
dye, to	teindre	färben	tingere	teñir	färga	farbn
dysentery	dysenterie,*f.*	Ruhr,*f.*	dissenteria,*f.*	disentería,*f.*	dysenteri,*nn.*	disenterye,*f.*
each (apiece, *adv.*)	(la) pièce,*f.*	je	al pezzo	por cada uno	var	yederer
each (every, *adj.*)	chaque	jeder	ogni	cada	varje	yeder
each one (*pron.*)	chacun	jeder	ognuno	cada uno	var och en	yederer
eager	ardent	eifrig	ardente	deseoso	ivrig	yederer
eagle	aigle,*m.*	Adler,*m.*	aquila,*f.*	águila,*f.*	örn,*nn.*	lohet
ear (external ear)	oreille,*f.*	Ohr,*n.*	orecchio,*m.*	oreja,*f.*	öra,*n.* (*pl.* öron)	odler,*m.*
ear (organ of hearing)	oreille,*f.*	Ohr,*n.*	orecchio,*m.*	oído,*m.*	öra,*n.* (*pl.* öron)	oyer,*m.*
earache	mal d'oreille,*m.*	Ohrenschmerzen,*m.*	mal d'orecchi,*m.*	dolor de oído,*m.*	örsprång,*n.*	oyer-veytik,*m.*
early (ahead of time, *adv.*)	de bonne heure	za früh	di buon'ora	temprano	tidigt	fri
early (before-time, *adj.*)	avancé	früh	di buon'ora	temprano	tidig	friik
earn (be paid), to	gagner	verdienen	guadagnare	ganar	tjäna	fardinen
earn (deserve), to	mériter	verdienen	meritare	merecer	förtjäna	fardinen
earnest	sérieux, -rieuse	ernst	zeloso	serio	allvarlig	erntst
earring	boucle d'oreille, *f.*	Ohrring,*m.*	orecchino,*m.*	arete,*m.*	örhänge,*n.*	oyringl,*n.*
earth (land)	terre,*f.*	Boden,*m.*	terra,*f.*	tierra,*f.*	jord,*nn.*	erd,*f.*
earth (planet)	terre,*f.*	Erde,*f.*	terra,*f.*	tierra,*f.*	jord,*nn.*	erd,*f.*
earthquake	tremblement de terre,*m.*	Erdbeben,*n.*	terremoto,*m.*	terremoto,*m.*	jordbävning,*nn.*	erd-tsiternish,*f.*
ease (comfort)	aise,*f.*	Behagen,*n.*	agio,*m.*	comodidad,*f.*	bekvämlighet, *nn.*	gringkayt,*f.*
ease (effortlessness)	facilité,*f.*	Leichtigkeit,*f.*	facilità,*f.*	facilidad,*f.*	lätthet,*nn.*	gringkayt,*f.*
ease (relieve), to	soulager	erleichtern	alleviare	aliviar	lätta	fargringern
east	est,*m.*	Osten,*m.*	est,*m.*	este,*m.*	öster,*nn.*	mizrakh,*m.*
Easter	Pâques,*m.*	Ostern,*n.*	Pasqua,*f.*	Pascua de Resurrección,*f.*	påsk,*nn.*	paskhe,*f.*
eastern	oriental	östlich	orientale	oriental	östlig	mizrakhdik
easy (not difficult)	facile	leicht	facile	fácil	lätt	gring
eat, to	manger	essen	mangiare	comer	äta	esn
echo	écho,*m.*	Widerhall,*m.*	eco,*m.*	eco,*m.*	eko,*n.*	viderkol,*m.*
economical (thrifty)	économe	sparsam	economico	económico	sparsam	shporevdik
economics	économie politique,*f.*	Volkswirtschaft, *f.*	scienza economica,*f.*	economía,*f.*	nationalekonomi,*nn.*	ekonomik,*f.*
economy (thrift)	économie,*f.*	Sparsamkeit,*f.*	economia,*f.*	economía,*f.*	sparsamhet,*nn.*	shporevdikayt, *f.*
Ecuador	Écuador,*m.*	Ekuador,*n.*	Equatore,*m.*	el Ecuador	Ecuador,*n.*	Ekvador,*n.*
edge (border)	bord,*m.*	Rand,*m.*	orlo,*m.*	borde,*m.*	kant,*nn.*	kant,*m.*
edge (sharp side)	tranchant,*m.*	Schneide,*f.*	filo,*m.*	filo,*m.*	egg,*nn.*	sharf,*f.*
Edinburgh	Édimbourg,*m.*	Edinburgh,*n.*	Edimburgo	Edimburgo	Edinburgh,*n.*	Edinburg,*n.*
edition	édition,*f.*	Ausgabe,*f.*	edizione,*f.*	edición,*f.*	upplaga,*nn.*	oysgabe,*f.*
editor	rédacteur,*m.*	Redakteur,*m.*	redattore,*m.*	redactor,*m.*	redaktör,*nn.*	redaktor,*m.*
educate, to	éduquer	erziehen	educare	educar	uppfostra	oysbildn
education (schooling process)	éducation,*f.*	Erziehung,*f.*	educazione,*f.*	educación,*f.*	utbildning,*nn.*	bildung,*f.*
eel	anguille,*f.*	Aal,*m.*	anguilla,*f.*	anguila,*f.*	ål,*nn.*	venger,*m.*
effect	effet,*m.*	Wirkung,*f.*	effetto,*m.*	efecto,*m.*	verkan,*nn.*	efekt,*m.*
effective (effectual)	efficace	wirksam	efficace	efectivo	verkan	efektiv
efficient (competent)	compétent	tüchtig	competente	eficiente	duglig	beryesh
efficient (producing desired results)	efficace	leistungsfähig	efficace	eficaz	effektiv	efektiv
effort	effort,*m.*	Anstrengung,*f.*	sforzo,*m.*	esfuerzo,*m.*	ansträngning,*nn.*	tirkhe,*f.*
egg	oeuf,*m.*	Ei,*n.*	uovo,*m.* (*pl.* uova,*f.*)	huevo,*m.*	ägg,*n.*	ey,*n.*
Egypt	Égypte,*f.*	Ägypten,*n.*	Egitto,*m.*	Egipto	Egypten,*n.*	Mitsraim,*n.*
Egyptian (*adj.*)	égyptien, -ne	ägyptisch	egiziano	egipcio	egyptisk	mitsrish

English	French	German	Italian	Spanish	Swedish	Yiddish
either (one or the other, *adj.*)	l'un ou l'autre	einer (von beiden)	l'uno o l'altro	uno u otro	endera	oder der oder yener
either (either one, *pron.*)	l'un ou l'autre	Einer (von Beiden)	l'uno o l'altro	uno u otro	vilken som helst	oder der oder yener
either (not...either, *adv.*)	(ne)...non plus	auch nicht	neanche	tampoco	heller	oykh nit
either...or (*conj.*)	ou...ou	entweder...oder	o...o	o...o	antingen... eller	oder...oder
elastic (springy)	élastique	elastisch	elastico	elástico	elastisk	elastish
elbow	coude,*m.*	Ellbogen,*m.*	gomito,*m.*	codo,*m.*	armbåge,*nn.*	eln-boygn,*m.*
elect, to	élire	wählen	eleggere	elegir	välja	oysklaybn
election	élection,*f.*	Wahl,*f.*	elezione,*f.*	elección,*f.*	val,*n.*	valn,*pl.*
electric	électrique	elektrisch	eléttrico	eléctrico	elektrisk	elektrish
electricity	électricité,*f.*	Elektrizität,*f.*	elettricità,*f.*	electricidad,*f.*	elektricitet,*nn.*	elektre,*f.*
electronics	électronique,*f.*	Elektronik,*f.*	elettronica,*f.*	electrónica,*f.*	elektronik,*nn.*	elektronik,*f.*
element	élément,*m.*	Element,*n.*	elemento,*m.*	elemento,*m.*	element,*n.*	element,*m.*
elementary (rudimentary)	élémentaire	elementar	elementare	rudimentario	elementär	elementar
elephant	éléphant,*m.*	Elefant,*m.*	elefante,*m.*	elefante,*m.*	elefant,*nn.*	helfant,*m.*
elevate (lift up), to	élever	erhöhen	elevare	elevar	upphöja	oyfheybn
elevator (passenger lift)	ascenseur,*m.*	Fahrstuhl,*m.*	ascensore,*m.*	ascensor,*m.*	hiss,*nn.*	lift,*m.*
eliminate, to	éliminer	ausscheiden	eliminare	eliminar	eliminera	poter vern
elm	orme,*m.*	Ulme,*f.*	olmo,*m.*	olmo,*m.*	alm,*nn.*	ulme,*f.*
eloquent	éloquent	beredt	eloquente	elocuente	vältalig	elokvent
else (different, *adj.*)	...d'autre	anders	altro	otro	annan	andersh
else (if not, *adv.*)	autrement	sonst	altrimenti	si no	annars	anit
else (in addition, *adj.*)	encore	(sonst) noch	altro	más	mera	nokh
else (instead, *adv.*)	...d'autre	sonst	altro	de otro modo	annars	anit
elsewhere	ailleurs	anderswo	altrove	a, de, en otra parte	annorstädes	andersh vu
embarrassment	embarras,*m.*	Verlegenheit,*f.*	imbarazzo,*m.*	desconcierto,*m.*	förlägenhet,*nn.*	farlegnhayt,*f.*
embrace (hug), to	étreindre	umarmen	abbracciare	abrazar	omfamna	arumnemen
embrace (include), to	embrasser	umfassen	abbracciare	abrazar	innesluta	araynnemen
emerald	émeraude,*f.*	Smaragd,*m.*	smeraldo,*m.*	esmeralda,*f.*	smaragd,*nn.*	shmaragd,*m.*
emerge, to	émerger	auftauchen	emergere	surgir	dyka upp	aroyskumen
emergency (*n.*)	cas d'urgence,*m.*	Notfall,*m.*	emergenza,*f.*	emergencia,*f.*	nödfall,*n.*	noytfal,*m.*
emotion	émotion,*f.*	Gefühl,*n.*	emozione,*f.*	emoción,*f.*	rörelse,*nn.*	emotsye,*f.*
emperor	empereur,*m.*	Kaiser,*m.*	imperatore,*m.*	emperador,*m.*	kejsare,*nn.*	keyser,*m.*
empire	empire,*m.*	(Kaiser)Reich,*n.*	impero,*m.*	imperio,*m.*	imperium,*n.*	imperye,*f.*
employ (hire), to	engager	anstellen	impiegare	emplear	anställa	onshteln
employ (use), to	employer	verwenden	impiegare	emplear	använda	nitsn
employee	employé,*m.*	Angestellte, *m.,f.*	impiegato,*m.*	empleado,*m.*	anställd,*nn.* (*pl. -a*)	ongeshtelter,*m.*
employer (boss)	patron,*m.*	Arbeitsgeber,*m.*	padrone,*m.*	patrono,*m.*	arbetsgivare,*nn.*	arbet-geber,*m.*
employment (work)	emploi,*m.*	Beschäftigung,*f.*	impiego,*m.*	empleo,*m.*	anställning,*nn.*	basheftikung,*f.*
empress	impératrice,*f.*	Kaiserin,*f.*	imperatrice,*f.*	emperatriz,*f.*	kejsarinna,*nn.*	keyserin,*f.*
empty	vide	leer	vuoto	vacío	tom	pust
empty (remove contents of), to	vider	(ent)leeren	vuotare	vaciar	tömma	oysleydikn
enable (make able), to	rendre capable	ermöglichen	mettere in grado di	capacitar	möjliggöra	gebn di miglekhkayt
enclose (include in envelope), to	inclure	beilegen	accludere	incluir	bifoga	bayleygn
enclose (surround), to	enceindre	einschliessen	cingere	encerrar	omge	arumtsamen
enclosure (addition)	annexe,*f.*	Beilage,*f.*	acclusa,*f.*	anexo,*m.*	bilaga,*nn.*	baylage,*f.*
encounter, to	rencontrer	begegnen	incontrare	encontrarse con	möta	trefn
encourage, to	encourager	ermutigen	incoraggiare	animar	uppmuntra	tsugebn mut
encyclopaedia	encyclòpédie,*f.*	Enzyklopädie,*f.*	enciclopedia,*f.*	enciclopedia,*f.*	konversations-lexikon,*n.*	entsiklopedye,*f.*
end (conclusion)	fin,*f.*	Schluss,*m.*	fine,*f.*	fin,*m.*	slut,*n.*	sof,*m.*
end (purpose)	fin,*m.*	Ziel,*n.*	fine,*m.*	propósito,*m.*	mål,*n.*	tsil,*m.*
end (bring to an end), to	finir	beenden	terminare	terminar	sluta	endikn
end (come to an end), to	terminer, se	enden	terminarsi	terminarse	sluta	endikn zikh
endeavor	effort,*m.*	Bestrebung,*f.*	sforzo,*m.*	empeño,*m.*	strävan,*nn.*	bamiung,*f.*
endeavor, to	efforcer de, s'	bemühen, sich	sforzarsi di	empeñarse	sträva	bamien zikh
ending (conclusion)	fin,*f.*	Ende,*n.*	conclusione,*f.*	terminación,*f.*	slut,*n.*	oysloz,*m.*
endless	sans fin	endlos	senza fine	sin fin	ändlös	on a sof
endorse (sign), to	endosser	girieren	girare	endosar	endossera	indorsirn
endorsement (signature)	endos,*m.*	Giro,*n.*	girata,*f.*	endoso,*m.*	påteckning,*nn.*	indorsirung,*f.*
endure (bear), to	supporter	ertragen	sopportare	soportar	uthärda	fartrogn
enema	lavement,*m.*	Klistier,*n.*	clistere,*m.*	enema,*f.*	lavemang,*n.*	kane,*f.*
enemy	ennemi,*m.*	Feind,*m.*	nemico,*m.*	enemigo,*m.*	fiende,*nn.*	soyne,*m.*
energy	énergie,*f.*	Energie,*f.*	energia,*f.*	energía,*f.*	energi,*nn.*	energye,*f.*
engage (employ), to	engager	anstellen	assumere	emplear	anställa	dingen
engage (be occupied) in, to	occuper (à, de), s'	beschäftigen, sich mit...	occuparsi di	ocuparse de	hålla på med	farnemen zikh mit
engagement (appointment)	rendez-vous,*m.*	Verabredung,*f.*	appuntamento, *m.*	cita,*f.*	avtal,*n.*	bashtelung,*f.*
engagement (betrothal)	fiançailles,*f.pl.*	Verlobung,*f.*	fidanzamento,*m.*	palabra de casamiento,*f.*	förlovning,*nn.*	farknasung,*f.*
engine (locomotive)	locomotive,*f.*	Lokomotive,*f.*	locomotiva,*f.*	locomotora,*f.*	lokomotiv,*n.*	lokomotiv,*m.*
engine (motor)	moteur,*m.*	Motor,*m.*	motore,*m.*	motor,*m.*	motor,*nn.*	motor,*m.*
engineer (professional engineer)	ingénieur,*m.*	Ingenieur,*m.*	ingegnere,*m.*	ingeniero,*m.*	ingenjör,*nn.*	inzhenir,*m.*

English	French	German	Italian	Spanish	Swedish	Yiddish
engineer (railroad engineman)	mécanicien,*m.*	Lokomotiv-führer,*m.*	macchinista,*m.*	maquinista,*m.*	lokomotivförare, *nn.*	mashinist,*m.*
England	Angleterre,*f.*	England,*n.*	Inghilterra,*f.*	Inglaterra	England,*n.*	England,*n.*
English (*adj.*)	anglais	englisch	inglese	inglés, -glesa	engelsk	english
enjoy (derive joy from), to	jouir de	geniessen	godere	gozar de	njuta av	hanoe hobn fun
enlarge (make larger), to	agrandir	vergrössern	ingrandire	ampliar	förstora	fargresern
enormous	énorme	ungeheuer	enorme	enorme	oerhörd	umgehayer
enough (*adj.*)	assez de	genügend	abbastanza	bastante	tillräcklig	genug
enough (*adv.*)	assez	genug	bastantemente	bastante	nog	genug
enough (*n.*)	assez	genug	abbastanza,*f.*	lo bastante	tillräcklig mängd,*nn.*	genug
ensign (*Nav.*)	enseigne,*m.*	Leutnant zur See,*m.*	guardiama-rina,*m.*	alférez,*m.*	fänrik,*nn.*	ensayn,*m.*
enter, to (*acctg.*)	porter en compte	verbuchen	inscrivere	asentar	bokföra	araynshraybn
enter (come or go into), to	entrer	eintreten, in...	entrare in	entrar	komma (gå) in i	arayngeyn in
enter (join), to	entrer (à, dans)	beitreten	entrare in	ingresar (en)	gå in i	arayngeyn in
enter (make record of), to	inscrire	eintragen	inscrivere	inscribir	anteckna	araynshraybn
enterprise (undertaking)	entreprise,*f.*	Unternehmen,*n.*	impresa,*f.*	empresa,*f.*	företag,*n.*	unternemung,*f.*
entertain (amuse), to	divertir	unterhalten	divertire	divertir	underhålla	farvayln
entertain (be host to), to	recevoir	bewirten	ricevere	agasajar	bjuda	oyfnemen
entertainment	divertissement,*m.*	Unterhaltung,*f.*	trattenimento,*m.*	entretenimiento,*m.*	underhållning,*nn.*	farvaylung,*f.*
enthusiasm	enthousiasme,*m.*	Begeisterung,*f.*	entusiasmo,*m.*	entusiasmo,*m.*	entusiasm,*nn.*	entuzyazm,*m.*
entire	entier, -tière	ganz	intero	entero	hel	gants
entitle (give a right to), to	donner droit	berechtigen	dare diritto	dar derecho	berättiga	barekhtikn
entrance	entrée,*f.*	Eingang,*m.*	entrata,*f.*	entrada,*f.*	ingång,*nn.*	arayngang,*m.*
entry (*acctg.*)	article,*m.*	Posten,*m.*	scrittura,*f.*	partida,*f.*	post,*nn.*	araynshray-bung,*f.*
envelope (folded wrapper)	enveloppe,*f.*	Briefumschlag,*m.*	busta,*f.*	sobre,*m.*	kuvert,*n.*	konvert,*m.*
envy	envie,*f.*	Neid,*m.*	invidia,*f.*	envidia,*f.*	avund,*nn.*	kine,*f.*
envy, to	envier	beneiden	invidiare	envidiar	avundas	mekane zayn
epidemic	épidémie,*f.*	Epidemie,*f.*	epidemia,*f.*	epidemia,*f.*	epidemi,*nn.*	mekane zayn
equal (*adj.*)	égal	gleich	eguale	igual	lika	epidemye,*f.*
equipment	équipement,*m.*	Ausrüstung,*f.*	attrezzamento,*m.*	equipo,*m.*	utrustning,*nn.*	glaykh
erase, to	effacer	ausradieren	cancellare	borrar	utplåna	oysshtayer,*m.*
eraser (rubber eraser)	gomme à effacer,*f.*	Radiergummi,*m.*	gomma,*f.*	goma,*f.*	radergummi,*n.*	mekn
erect (*adj.*)	droit	aufrecht	eretto	enhiesto	upprätt	meker,*m.*
erect (build), to	ériger	errichten	erigere	erigir	uppföra	glaykh
err, to	tromper, se	irren, sich	errare	errar	missta(ga) sig	oyfshteln
errand (commission)	commission,*f.*	Auftrag,*m.*	commissione,*f.*	mandado,*m.*	ärende,*n.*	toye zayn zikh
error	erreur,*f.*	Irrtum,*m.*	errore,*m.*	error,*m.*	fel,*n.*	shlikhes,*f.* toes,*m.*
escape, to	échapper, (s')	entgehen	scappare	escapar(se)	undgå	antloyfn
escort (social companion)	cavalier,*m.*	Begleiter,*m.*	cavaliere,*m.*	acompañante,*m.*	eskort,*nn.*	bagleyter,*m.*
especially	spécialement	besonders	specialmente	especialmente	särskilt	spetsyel
espionage	espionnage,*m.*	Spionage,*f.*	spionaggio,*m.*	espionaje,*m.*	spionage,*n.*	shpyonazh,*m.*
essential (*adj.*)	essentiel, -le	wesentlich	essenziale	esencial	väsentlig	ikerdik
establish (found), to	fonder	gründen	fondare	fundar	grunda	grindn
establish (prove), to	établir	nachweisen	stabilire	establecer	bevisa	dervayzn
establishment (firm)	établissement,*m.*	Unternehmen,*n.*	stabilimento,*m.*	establecimiento,*m.*	företag,*n.*	firme,*f.*
establishment (founding)	fondation,*f.*	Gründung,*f.*	stabilimento,*m.*	fundación,*f.*	grundande,*n.*	grindung,*f.*
estate (total possessions)	biens,*m.pl.*	Besitz,*m.*	beni,*m.pl.*	bienes,*m.pl.*	egendom,*nn.*	mayontik,*m.*
esteem, to	estimer	schätzen	stimare	estimar	uppskatta	leygn koved
estimate (calculate), to	estimer	schätzen	stimare	calcular	uppskatta	shatsn
eternal	éternel, -le	ewig	eterno	eterno	evig	eybik
etiquette	étiquette,*f.*	Etikette,*f.*	buona educa-zione,*f.*	etiqueta,*f.*	etikett,*nn.*	etiket,*m.*
Europe	Europe,*f.*	Europa,*n.*	Europa,*f.*	Europa	Europa,*n.*	Eyrope,*m.*
European (*adj.*)	européen, -ne	europäisch	europeo	europeo	europeisk	eyropeish
even (level, *adj.*)	égal	eben	piano	parejo	jämn	grod
evening	soir,*m.*	Abend,*m.*	sera,*f.*	anochecer,*m.*	kväll,*nn.*	ovnt,*m.*
event (happening)	événement,*m.*	Ereignis,*n.*	evento,*m.*	suceso,*m.*	händelse,*nn.*	gesheenish,*f.*
ever (at all times)	toujours	immer	sempre	siempre	alltid	tomid
ever (at any time)	jamais	je(mals)	sempre	alguna vez	någonsin	ven es iz
everlasting	éternel, -le	ewig	sempiterno	eterno	beständig	eybik
every	tout	jeder	ogni	cada	varje	yeder
everybody	tout le monde	jeder(mann)	ognuno	todo el mundo	var och en	yeder eyner
everyone	chacun	jeder(mann)	ciascuno	cada uno	var och en	yeder eyner
everything (*pron.*)	tout	alles	tutto	todo	allting	altsding
everywhere	partout	überall	dappertutto	en todas partes	överallt	umetum
evidence (indication)	évidence,*f.*	Zeichen,*n.*	evidenza,*f.*	evidencia,*f.*	tecken,*n.*	bavayz,*m.*
evidence (*law*)	preuve,*f.*	Beweis,*m.*	prova,*f.*	evidencia,*f.*	bevis,*n.*	bavayz,*m.*
evident	évident	offenbar	evidente	evidente	uppenbar	kentik
evil (*adj.*)	mauvais	übel	cattivo	mal(o)	ond	beyz
evil (*n.*)	mal,*m.*	Übel,*n.*	male,*m.*	mal,*m.*	ont,*n.*	beyz,*n.*
exact (precise)	exact	genau	esatto	exacto	exakt	genoy
exaggerate, to	exagérer	übertreiben	esagerare	exagerar	överdriva	megazem zayn
exalt, to	exalter	erheben	esaltare	exaltar	förhärliga	derheybn
examination (test)	examen,*m.*	Prüfung,*f.*	esame,*m.*	examen,*m.*	prövning,*nn.*	ekzamen,*m.*

English	French	German	Italian	Spanish	Swedish	Yiddish
examine (investigate), to	examiner	untersuchen	esaminare	examinar	undersöka	durkhkukn
example	exemple,*m.*	Beispiel,*n.*	esempio,*m.*	ejemplo,*m.*	exempel,*n.*	moshl,*m.*
exceed, to	dépasser	überschreiten	eccedere	exceder	övergå	aribergeyn
excellent	excellent	vortrefflich	eccellente	excelente	utmärkt	oysgetseykhnt
except (*prep.*)	sauf	ausser	salvo	excepto	utom	khuts
exception (unusual case)	exception,*f.*	Ausnahme,*f.*	eccezione,*f.*	excepción,*f.*	undantag,*n.*	oysnem,*m.*
excess	excès,*m.*	Übermass,*n.*	eccesso,*m.*	exceso,*m.*	övermått,*n.*	oydef,*m.*
excessive	excessif, -sive	übermässig	eccessivo	excesivo	överdriven	iberik
exchange (barter)	échange,*m.*	(Aus)Tausch,*m.*	scambio,*m.*	trueque,*m.*	utbyte,*n.*	oysbayt,*m.*
exchange, stock	bourse,*f.*	Börse,*f.*	Borsa,*f.*	bolsa,*f.*	börs,*nn.*	berze,*f.*
exchange (interchange), to	échanger	(aus)tauschen	scambiare	trocar	utbyta	oysbaytn
excite, to	exciter	aufregen	eccitare	excitar	uppegga	oyfregn
excitement	agitation,*f.*	Aufregung,*f.*	eccitazione,*f.*	animación,*f.*	uppståndelse, *nn.*	oyfregung,*f.*
exclaim, to	exclamer, (s')	ausrufen	esclamare	exclamar	utropa	oysshrayen
exclamation (*n.*)	exclamation,*f.*	Ausruf,*m.*	esclamazione,*f.*	exclamación,*f.*	utrop,*n.*	oysgeshrey,*m.*
exclude, to	exclure	ausschliessen	escludere	excluir	utesluta	oysshlisn
exclusive (not including)	exclusif, -sive	ausschliesslich	esclusivo	exclusivo	uteslutande	oysshlisndik
excuse (pretext)	excuse,*f.*	Vorwand,*m.*	scusa,*f.*	excusa,*f.*	förevändning,*nn.*	terets,*m.*
excuse (pardon), to	excuser	entschuldigen	scusare	excusar	ursäkta	antshuldikn
execute (carry out), to	exécuter	ausführen	eseguire	ejecutar	verkställa	oysfirn
execute (put to death), to	exécuter	hinrichten	giustiziare	ejecutar	avrätta	mekayem zayn dem psak
executive (*adj.*)	exécutif, -tive	Exekutiv-...	esecutivo	ejecutivo	verkställande	oysfir-...
exempt (*adj.*)	exempt	befreit	esente	exento	befriad	poter
exercise (drill)	exercice,*m.*	Übung,*f.*	esercizio,*m.*	ejercicio,*m.*	övning,*nn.*	genitung,*f.*
exercise (physical exertion)	exercice,*m.*	Leibesübungen, *f.pl.*	esercizio fisico, *m.*	ejercicio,*m.*	motion,*nn.*	gimnastik,*f.*
exercise (employ), to	exercer	ausüben	esercitare	ejercitar	utöva	oysnitsn
exhaust (use up), to	épuiser	erschöpfen	esaurire	agotar	förbruka	oysshepn
exhibit (show)	exposé,*m.*	Ausstellung,*f.*	mostra,*f.*	exhibición,*f.*	utställning,*nn.*	oysshtelung,*f.*
exhibit, to	exposer	ausstellen	esibire	exhibir	utställa	oysshteln
exhibition (exposition)	exposition,*f.*	Ausstellung,*f.*	esposizione,*f.*	exposición,*f.*	utställning,*nn.*	oysshtelung,*f.*
exile (banishment)	exil,*m.*	Verbannung,*f.*	esilio,*m.*	destierro,*m.*	landsförvisning, *nn.*	goles,*m.*
exist, to	exister	bestehen	esistere	existir	existera	eksistirn
existence	existence,*f.*	Dasein,*n.*	esistenza,*f.*	existencia,*f.*	tillvaro,*nn.*	eksistents,*f.*
exit	sortie,*f.*	Ausgang,*m.*	uscita,*f.*	salida,*f.*	utgång,*nn.*	aroysgang,*m.*
expand (make larger), to	étendre	ausbreiten	espandere	dilatar	utvidga	farbreytern
expect, to	attendre (à), (s')	erwarten	attendere	esperar	vänta sig	rikhtn zikh oyf
expectation	attente,*f.*	Erwartung,*f.*	attesa,*f.*	expectación,*f.*	förväntning,*nn.*	aroyskuk,*m.*
expedition (journey)	expédition,*f.*	Expedition,*f.*	spedizione,*f.*	expedición,*f.*	expedition,*nn.*	ekspeditsye,*f.*
expel (eject), to	expulser	ausstossen	espellere	expeler	fördriva	aroystraybn
expenditure (outlay)	dépense,*f.*	Ausgabe,*f.*	spesa,*f.*	gasto,*m.*	utgift,*nn.*	hoytsoe,*f.*
expense (cost)	frais,*m.pl.*	Unkosten,*pl.*	spesa,*f.*	costo,*m.*	omkostnad,*nn.*	hoytsoe,*f.*
expensive	coûteux, -teuse	teuer	costoso	costoso	dyr	tayer
experience (conscious event)	expérience,*f.*	Erlebnis,*n.*	esperienza,*f.*	experiencia,*f.*	upplevelse,*nn.*	iberlebung,*f.*
experience (skill)	pratique,*f.*	Erfahrung,*f.*	perizia,*f.*	práctica,*f.*	erfarenhet,*nn.*	praktik,*f.*
experiment	expérience,*f.*	Versuch,*m.*	esperimento,*m.*	experimento,*m.*	experiment,*n.*	eksperiment,*m.*
expert (*n.*)	expert,*m.*	Sachverständige, *m.,f.*	esperto,*m.*	experto,*m.*	expert,*nn.*	mumkhe,*m.*
expire (become void, *bus.*), to	expirer	ablaufen	scadere	expirar	utlöpa	oysgeyn
explain (account for), to	expliquer	erklären	spiegare	explicar	redogöra för	farentfern
explain (clarify), to	expliquer	erläutern	spiegare	explicar	förklara	derklern
explanation	explication,*f.*	Erklärung,*f.*	spiegazione,*f.*	explicación,*f.*	förklaring,*nn.*	derklerung,*f.*
explore, to	explorer	(er)forschen	esplorare	explorar	utforska	forshn
explosive (*n.*)	explosif,*m.*	Sprengstoff,*m.*	esplosivo,*m.*	explosivo,*m.*	sprängämne,*n.*	oyfrays-materyal,*m.*
export, to	exporter	ausführen	esportare	exportar	exportera	eksportirn
exportation	exportation,*f.*	Ausfuhr,*f.*	esportazione,*f.*	exportación,*f.*	export,*nn.*	eksport,*m.*
exporter	exportateur,*m.*	Exporteur,*m.*	esportatore,*m.*	exportador,*m.*	exportör,*nn.*	eksportirer,*m.*
expose (disclose), to	exposer	enthüllen	esporre	exponer	avslöja	oyfdekn
expose (lay open), to	exposer	aussetzen	esporre	exponer	utsätta	antplekn
express (state), to	exprimer	ausdrücken	esprimere	expresar	uttrycka	aroyszogn
expression (sign of feeling; word or phrase)	expression,*f.*	Ausdruck,*m.*	espressione,*f.*	expresión,*f.*	uttryck,*n.*	oysdruk,*m.*
exquisite	exquis	auserlesen	squisito	exquisito	utsökt	mehuderdik
extend (enlarge), to	étendre	erweitern	estendere	extender	utvidga	farbreytern
extend (stretch out), to	étendre	ausstrecken	allungare	extender	utsträcka	farlengern
extension (enlargement)	extension,*f.*	Erweiterung,*f.*	estensione,*f.*	extensión,*f.*	utvidgning,*nn.*	farlengerung,*f.*
extensive	étendu	ausgedehnt	esteso	extenso	vidsträckt	breyt
extent (magnitude)	étendue,*f.*	Ausmass,*n.*	estensione,*f.*	grado,*m.*	utsträckning,*nn.*	greys,*f.*
exterior (*adj.*)	extérieur	äusserlich	esterno	exterior	yttre	droysndik
extra (additional)	supplémentaire	extra	addizionale	de sobra	extra	ekstre
extraordinary	extraordinaire	ausserordentlich	straordinario	extraordinario	utomordentlig	oysergeveynt-lekh
extreme (farthest)	extrême	äusserst	estremo	extremo	ytterst	ekst
extreme (intense)	extrême	äusserst	estremo	extremo	intensiv	ekstrem
eye (*anat.*)	oeil,*m.*	Auge,*n.*	occhio,*m.*	ojo,*m.*	öga,*n.* (*pl.* ögon)	oyg,*n.*

English	French	German	Italian	Spanish	Swedish	Yiddish
eyebrow	sourcil,*m.*	Augenbraue,*f.*	sopracciglio,*m.* (*pl.* -glia,*f.*)	ceja,*f.*	ögonbryn,*n.*	brem,*f.*
eyelash	cil,*m.*	Wimper,*f.*	ciglio,*m.* (*pl.* -glia,*f.*)	pestaña,*f.*	ögonfrans,*nn.*	vie,*f.*
eyelid	paupière,*f.*	Augenlid,*n.*	palpebra,*f.*	párpado,*m.*	ögonlock,*n.*	ledl,*n.*
fable	fable,*f.*	Fabel,*f.*	favola,*f.*	fábula,*f.*	fabel,*nn.*	moshl,*m.*
fabric (cloth)	tissu,*m.*	Stoff,*m.*	tessuto,*m.*	tela,*f.*	tyg,*n.*	geveb,*n.*
face (*anat.*)	visage,*m.*	Gesicht,*n.*	faccia,*f.*	cara,*f.*	ansikte,*n.*	ponim,*n.*
face (surface)	surface,*f.*	Seite,*f.*	superficie,*f.*	faz,*f.*	framsida,*nn.*	droysn,*m.*
face value (*bus.*)	valeur nominale,*f.*	Nennwert,*m.*	valore nominale,*m.*	valor nominal,*m.*	nominellt värde,*n.*	nominale vert,*f.*
fact	fait,*m.*	Tatsache,*f.*	fatto,*m.*	hecho,*m.*	faktum,*n.* (*pl.* fakta)	fakt,*m.*
factor (element)	facteur,*m.*	Faktor,*m.*	fattore,*m.*	factor,*m.*	faktor,*nn.*	faktor,*m.*
factory	fabrique,*f.*	Fabrik,*f.*	fabbrica,*f.*	fábrica,*f.*	fabrik,*nn.*	fabrik,*f.*
faculty (ability)	faculté,*f.*	Fähigkeit,*f.*	facoltà,*f.*	facultad,*f.*	förmåga,*nn.*	feikayt,*f.*
faculty (teaching staff)	faculté,*f.*	Lehrkörper,*m.*	Facoltà,*f.*	facultad,*f.*	lärarkår,*nn.*	profesornshaft,*f.*
fade (disappear), to	évanouir, s'	(ver)schwinden	svanire	desvanecerse	försvinna	farshvundn vern
fade (lose color), to	faner, se	verblassen	sbiadire	descolorar	blekna	blakirn
fail (be unsuccessful), to	échouer	misslingen	non riuscire	fracasar	misslyckas	durkhfaln
fail (neglect) to, to	manquer de	versäumen	mancare di	dejar de	underlåta	farfeln
failure (bankruptcy, *bus.*)	faillite,*f.*	Bankrott,*m.*	fallimento,*m.*	quiebra,*f.*	konkurs,*nn.*	bankrot,*m.*
failure (lack of success)	échec,*m.*	Misslingen,*n.*	insuccesso,*m.*	fracaso,*m.*	misslyckande,*n.*	durkhfal,*m.*
failure (neglect)	manquement,*m.*	Unterlassung,*f.*	mancanza,*f.*	descuido,*m.*	försummelse,*nn.*	farfeln,*n.*
faint (dim, *adj.*)	faible	matt	debole	tenue	svag	shvakh
faint (swoon, *n.*)	évanouissement,*m.*	Ohnmacht,*f.*	svenimento,*m.*	desmayo,*m.*	svimning,*nn.*	khaloshes,*f.*
faint, to	évanouir, s'	in Ohnmacht fallen	svenire	desmayarse	svimma	khaleshn
fair (blond)	blond	hell(farbig)	biondo	rubio	ljus	hel
fair (impartial)	juste	fair	giusto	justo	rättvis	yoysherdik
fair (not cloudy)	beau	schön	chiaro	despejado	klar	sheyn
fair (passable)	passable	leidlich	passabile	regular	skaplig	nishkoshedik
fairly (impartially)	impartialement	fair	imparzialmente	justamente	rättvist	yoysherdik
fairly (somewhat)	assez	ziemlich	alquanto	medianamente	ganska	gants
fairy (*n.*)	fée,*f.*	Fee,*f.*	fata,*f.*	hada,*f.*	fe,*nn.*	feye,*f.*
fairy tale	conte de fées,*m.*	Märchen,*n.*	favola,*f.*	cuento de hadas,*m.*	saga,*nn.*	maysele,*n.*
faith (creed)	foi,*f.*	Glaubensbekenntnis,*n.*	fede,*f.*	credo,*m.*	tro,*nn.*	emune,*f.*
faith (trust)	confiance,*f.*	Vertrauen,*n.*	fiducia,*f.*	fe,*f.*	förtröstan,*nn.*	bitokhn,*m.*
faithful (loyal)	fidèle	treu	fedele	fiel	trogen	getray
fall (autumn, *n.*)	automne,*m.*	Herbst,*m.*	autunno,*m.*	otoño,*m.*	höst,*nn.*	harbst,*m.*
fall (drop)	chute,*f.*	Sturz,*m.*	caduta,*f.*	caída,*f.*	fall,*n.*	fal,*m.*
fall, to	tomber	fallen	cadere	caer	falla	faln
falls (waterfall)	chutes,*f.pl.*	Wasserfall,*m.*	cascata,*f.*	cascada,*f.*	vattenfall,*n.*	vaserfal,*m.*
false (deceitful)	infidèle	falsch	falso	falso	falsk	falsh
false (erroneous)	faux, fausse	falsch	erroneo	erróneo	falsk	falsh
falsehood (lie)	mensonge,*m.*	Unwahrheit,*f.*	menzogna,*f.*	falsedad,*f.*	felaktig	falsh
fame	renommée,*f.*	Ruhm,*m.*	fama,*f.*	fama,*f.*	osanning,*nn.* ryktbarhet,*nn.*	sheker,*m.* shem,*m.*
familiar (intimate)	familier, -lière	vertraut	familiare	familiar	förtrolig	noent
familiar (well-known)	familier, -lière	bekannt	conosciuto	familiar	välbekant	bakant
family	famille,*f.*	Familie,*f.*	famiglia,*f.*	familia,*f.*	familj,*nn.*	mishpokhe,*f.*
famous	fameux, -meuse	berühmt	famoso	famoso	berömd	barimt
fan, electric	ventilateur,*m.*	Ventilator,*m.*	ventilatore,*m.*	abanico eléctrico,*m.*	fläkt,*nn.*	ventilator,*m.*
fancy (fantasy)	fantaisie,*f.*	Einbildung,*f.*	fantasia,*f.*	fantasía,*f.*	fantasi,*nn.*	fantazye,*f.*
fancy (notion)	fantaisie,*f.*	Grille,*f.*	capriccio,*m.*	capricho,*m.*	infall,*n.*	aynfal,*m.*
fancy (imagine), to	imaginer, s'	einbilden, sich	immaginare	figurarse	föreställa sig	moln zikh
fancy (ornamental, *adj.*)	d'agrément	gemustert	ornato	de ornato	fin	getsatsket
far (afar, *adv.*)	loin	weit	lontano	lejos	långt borta	vayt
far (distant, *adj.*)	lointain	weit	lontano	lejano	fjärran	vayt
fare (*transp.*)	prix,*m.*	Fahrgeld,*n.*	prezzo del viaggio,*m.*	pasaje,*m.*	avgift,*nn.*	forgelt,*n.*
farewell (leave-taking)	adieu,*m.*	Abschied,*m.*	addio,*m.*	adiós,*m.*	farväl,*n.*	gezegenung,*f.*
farm	ferme,*f.*	Bauerngut,*n.*	podere,*m.*	granja,*f.*	bondgård,*nn.*	farm,*f.*
farmer	fermier,*m.*	Bauer,*m.*	coltivatore,*m.*	agricultor,*m.*	bonde,*nn.* (*pl.* bönder)	farmer,*m.*
farther (*adj.*)	plus lointain	weiter	più lontano	más lejano	avlägsnare	vayter
farther (*adv.*)	plus loin	weiter	più lontano	más lejos	längre bort	vayter
Fascism	fascisme,*m.*	Faschismus,*m.*	Fascismo,*m.*	fascismo,*m.*	fascism,*nn.*	fashizm,*m.*
fashion (current style)	mode,*f.*	Mode,*f.*	moda,*f.*	moda,*f.*	mod,*n.*	mode,*f.*
fashion (manner)	mode,*f.*	Weise,*f.*	maniera,*f.*	modo,*m.*	sätt,*n.*	oyfn,*m.*
fast (firm, *adj.*)	ferme	fest	fisso	fijo	fast	fest
fast (quick, *adj.*)	rapide	schnell	rapido	rápido	snabb	gikh
fast (quickly, *adv.*)	vite	geschwind	rapidamente	de prisa	fort	gikh
fasten, to	attacher	befestigen	attaccare	fijar	fästa	tsufestikn
fat (fatty tissue, *n.*)	graisse,*f.*	Fett,*n.*	grasso,*m.*	grasa,*f.*	fett,*n.*	fets,*n.*
fat (obese, *adj.*)	gras, -se	dick	grasso	gordo	fet	fet
fatal (deadly)	mortel, -le	tödlich	mortale	mortal	dödlig	toyt-...
fatal (fateful)	fatal	verhängnisvoll	fatale	fatal	ödesdiger	fatal
fate	sort,*m.*	Schicksal,*n.*	destino,*m.*	destino,*m.*	öde,*n.*	goyrl,*m.*
father	père,*m*	Vater,*m.*	padre,*m.*	padre,*m.*	fa(de)r,*nn.* (*pl.* fäder)	foter,*m.*

English	French	German	Italian	Spanish	Swedish	Yiddish
father-in-law	beau-père,*m.*	Schwieger-vater,*m.*	suocero,*m.*	suegro,*m.*	svärfa(de)r,*nn.* (*pl.* -fäder)	shver,*m.*
fatigue	fatigue,*f.*	Ermüdung,*f.*	fatica,*f.*	fatiga,*f.*	trötthet,*nn.*	midkayt,*f.*
faucet	robinet,*m.*	Wasserhahn,*m.*	rubinetto,*m.*	llave,*f.*	vattenkran,*nn.*	kran,*m.*
fault (cause for blame)	faute,*f.*	Schuld,*f.*	colpa,*f.*	culpa,*f.*	fel,*n.*	shuld,*f.*
fault (defect)	défaut,*m.*	Fehler,*m.*	difetto,*m.*	falta,*f.*	fel,*n.*	khisorn,*m.*
favor (approval)	faveur,*f.*	Gunst,*f.*	favore,*m.*	favor,*m.*	gillande,*n.*	tsushtimung,*f.*
favor (kindness)	grâce,*f.*	Gefallen,*m.*	favore,*m.*	favor,*m.*	gunst,*nn.*	toyve,*f.*
favorable	favorable	günstig	favorevole	favorable	gynnsam	gintsik
favorite (*adj.*)	favori, -te	Lieblings-...	favorito	favorito	favorit-...	balibt
fear	crainte,*f.*	Furcht,*f.*	paura,*f.*	temor,*m.*	fruktan,*nn.*	moyre,*f.*
fear (be afraid of), to	craindre	fürchten	temere	temer	frukta	moyre hobn far
fearful (afraid)	craintif, -tive	furchtsam	pauroso	temeroso	rädd	dershrokn
fearful (terrible)	terrible	fürchterlich	terribile	espantoso	fruktansvärd	moyredik
feast (meal)	festin,*m.*	Festmahl,*n.*	banchetto,*m.*	festín,*m.*	kalas,*n.*	sude,*f.*
feat	exploit,*m.*	Leistung,*f.*	azione straor-dinaria,*f.*	hazaña,*f.*	bedrift,*nn.*	gvure,*f.*
feather	plume,*f.*	Feder,*f.*	piuma,*f.*	pluma,*f.*	fjäder,*nn.*	feder,*f.*
feature (attribute)	trait,*m.*	Eigenschaft,*f.*	tratto carat-teristico,*m.*	rasgo,*m.*	egenskap,*nn.*	shtrikh,*m.*
feature (part of face)	trait,*m.*	(Gesichts)Zug,*m.*	fatezza,*f.*	facciones,*f.pl.*	anletsdrag,*n.*	shtrikh,*m.*
federal	fédéral	Bundes-...	federale	federal	federal	federal
fee	honoraires,*m.pl.*	Gebühr,*f.*	onorario,*m.*	honorario,*m.*	arvode,*n.*	optsol,*m.*
feeble	faible	schwach	debole	endeble	svag	shvakh
feed (give food to), to	nourrir	füttern	nutrire	dar de comer	föda	kormen
feel (experience), to	sentir, (se)	fühlen, (sich)	sentire	sentir	känna (sig)	shpirn
feel (touch), to	toucher	fühlen	toccare	tocar	känna	tapn
feel (grope) for, to	tâtonner vers	tasten, nach...	cercare a tastoni	buscar a tientas	treva efter	tapn
feeling (emotion)	sentiment,*m.*	Gefühl,*n.*	sentimento,*m.*	sentimiento,*m.*	känsla,*nn.*	gefil,*n.*
feeling (sensation)	sensation,*f.*	Empfindung,*f.*	sensazione,*f.*	sensación,*f.*	känsla,*nn.*	gefil,*n.*
fellow (person)	type,*m.*	Kerl,*m.*	persona,*f.*	individuo,*m.*	karl,*nn.*	khevre-man,*m.*
felt (*n.*)	feutre,*m.*	Filz,*m.*	feltro,*m.*	fieltro,*m.*	filt,*nn.*	poysht,*m.*
female (*adj.*)	femelle	weiblich	femminile	hembra	kvinnlig	vayblekh
female (*zool., n.*)	femelle,*f.*	Weibchen,*n.*	femmina,*f.*	hembra,*f.*	hona,*nn.*	nekeyve,*f.*
feminine	féminin	weiblich	femminile	feminino	feminin	vayblekh
fence (barrier)	clôture,*f.*	Zaun,*m.*	barriera,*f.*	cerca,*f.*	stängsel,*n.*	parkan,*m.*
fern	fougère,*f.*	Farn(kraut),*n.*	felce,*f.*	helecho,*m.*	ormbunke,*n.*	federgroz,*n.*
ferry (boat)	bac,*m.*	Fähre,*f.*	barca di passag-gio,*f.*	barco de tras-bordo,*m.*	färja,*nn.*	parom,*m.*
fertile	fertile	fruchtbar	fertile	fértil	bördig	frukhperdik
festival	fête,*f.*	Fest,*n.*	festa pubblica,*f.*	festival,*m.*	fest,*nn.*	yontev,*m.*
fetch (bring), to	apporter	holen	portare	traer	hämta	geyn brengen
fever	fièvre,*f.*	Fieber,*n.*	febbre,*f.*	fiebre,*f.*	feber,*nn.*	hits,*f.*
few (not many, *adj.*)	peu (de)	wenige	pochi, -che	pocos	få	vintsik
few, a	quelques-uns,*m.*, -unes,*f.*	ein paar	alcuni,*m.*, -cune, *f.*	algunos,*m.*, -nas, *f.*	några	a por
field (cleared land)	champ,*m.*	Feld,*n.*	campo,*m.*	campo,*m.*	fält,*n.*	feld,*n.*
field (sphere of action)	domaine,*m.*	Gebiet,*n.*	campo,*m.*	campo,*m.*	område,*n.*	shetakh,*m.*
fierce	féroce	wild	feroce	feroz	våldsam	retsikhedik
fig	figue,*f.*	Feige,*f.*	fico,*m.*	higo,*m.*	fikon,*n.*	fayg,*f.*
fight	combat,*m.*	Kampf,*m.*	lotta,*f.*	pelea,*f.*	kamp,*nn.*	kamf,*m.*
fight (contend), to	battre, se	kämpfen	battersi	pelear	kämpa	kemfn
fight (struggle against), to	combattre	bekämpfen	combattere contro	luchar contra	kämpa mot	bakemfn
figure (human form)	figure,*f.*	Gestalt,*f.*	persona,*f.*	figura,*f.*	figur,*nn.*	figur,*f.*
figure (numeral)	chiffre,*m.*	Zahl,*f.*	cifra,*f.*	cifra,*f.*	siffra,*nn.*	tsifer,*f.*
file (collection of papers)	dossier,*m.*	Akten,*m.pl.*	incartamento,*m.*	archivo,*m.*	dossier,*nn.*	aktn,*pl.*
file (tool)	lime,*f.*	Feile,*f.*	lima,*f.*	lima,*f.*	fil,*nn.*	fayl,*f.*
fill (make full), to	remplir	füllen	empire	llenar	fylla	onfiln
film (*photog.*)	pellicule,*f.*	Film,*m.*	pellicola,*f.*	película,*f.*	film,*nn.*	film,*m.*
film (thin coating)	pellicule,*f.*	Häutchen,*n.*	velo,*m.*	película,*f.*	hinna,*nn.*	haytl,*n.*
final (last)	final	endgültig	finale	final	sist	letst
finally	finalement	endlich	finalmente	por fin	slutligen	sofklsof
finances	finances,*f.pl.*	Finanzen,*pl.*	finanze,*f.pl.*	finanzas,*f.pl.*	finanser,*nn.pl.*	finantsn,*pl.*
financial	financier, -cière	finanziell	finanziario	financiero	finansiell	finantsyel
find (discover), to	trouver	finden	trovare	hallar	finna	gefinen
fine (good)	parfait	schön	buono	bueno	fin	fayn
fine (penalty, *n.*)	amende,*f.*	Geldstrafe,*f.*	ammenda,*f.*	multa,*f.*	böter,*nn.pl.*	geltshtrof,*f.*
fine (very small)	fin	fein	fino	menudo	fin	drobne
finger	doigt,*m.*	Finger,*m.*	dito,*m.*	dedo,*m.*	finger,*nn.,n.*	finger,*m.*
finish (complete), to	finir	vollenden	finire	terminar	avsluta	endikn
finish (reach the end), to	terminer, se	enden	terminarsi	terminar	sluta	endikn zikh
Finland	Finlande,*f.*	Finnland,*n.*	Finlandia,*f.*	Finlandia	Finland,*n.*	Finland,*n.*
Finnish (*adj.*)	finlandais	finnländisch	findlandese	finlandés	finsk	finish
fir	sapin,*m.*	Fichte,*f.*	abete,*m.*	abeto,*m.*	gran,*nn.*	tenenboym,*m.*
fire	feu,*m.*	Feuer,*n.*	fuoco,*m.*	fuego,*m.*	eld,*nn.*	fayer,*n.*
fire insurance	assurance-incendie,*f.*	Feuerversiche-rung,*f.*	assicurazione contro l'incendio,*f.*	seguro contra incendios,*m.*	brandförsäkring, *nn.*	strakhirung,*f.*
fireman	pompier,*m.*	Feuerwehrmann, *m.*	pompiere,*m.*	bombero,*m.*	brandsoldat,*nn.*	fayer-lesher,*m.*
fireplace	cheminée,*f.*	Kamin,*m.*	camino,*m.*	chimenea,*f.*	eldstad,*nn.* (*pl.* -städer)	kamin,*m.*

English	French	German	Italian	Spanish	Swedish	Yiddish
firm (adj.)	ferme	fest	fermo	firme	fast	fest
firm (business company)	maison,f.	Firma,f.	ditta,f.	casa,f.	firma,nn.	firme,f.
first (adj.)	premier, -mière	erst	primo	primer(o)	först(a)	ersht
first aid (med.)	premiers secours, m.pl.	erste Hilfe,f.	soccorsi d'urgenza,m.pl.	primeros auxilios, m.pl.	första förband,n.	gikhe hilf,f.
fish (animal)	poisson,m.	Fisch,m.	pesce,m.	pez,m.	fisk,nn.	fish,m.
fish (food)	poisson,m.	Fisch,m.	pesce,m.	pescado,m.	fisk,nn.	fish,m.
fish, to	pêcher	fischen	pescare	pescar	fiska	fishn
fisherman	pêcheur,m.	Fischer,m.	pescatore,m.	pescador,m.	fiskare,nn.	fisher,m.
fist	poing,m.	Faust,f.	pugno,m.	puño,m.	näve,nn.	foyst,f.
fit (suitable)	convenable	passend	adatto	adecuado	passande	pasik
fix (repair), to	réparer	reparieren	riparare	reparar	laga	farrikhtn
fix (settle), to	arranger	festsetzen	accomodare	arreglar	ordna	bashtimen
flag	drapeau,m.	Fahne,f.	bandiera,f.	bandera,f.	flagga,nn.	fon,f.
flame	flamme,f.	Flamme,f.	fiamma,f.	llama,f.	låga,nn.	flam,m.
flash (burst of light)	éclair,m.	Blitz,m.	lampo,m.	destello,m.	blixt,nn.	blits,m.
flashlight	lampe de poche, f.	Taschenlampe,f.	lampadina tascabile,f.	linterna eléctrica, f.	ficklampa,nn.	batereyke,f.
flat (level, adj.)	plat	flach	piano	plano	jämn	flakh
flatter (praise insincerely), to	flatter	schmeicheln	adulare	lisonjear	smickra	khanfenen
flavor (savor)	saveur,f.	Geschmack,m.	sapore,m.	sabor,m.	smak,nn.	aromat,m.
flax	lin,m.	Flachs,m.	lino.m.	lino,m.	lin,n.	flaks,m.
flee (run from), to	fuir	fliehen	fuggire	huir	fly	antloyfn
fleece	toison,f.	Vlies,n.	vello,m.	vellón,m.	(no equiv.)	fel,f.
fleet (group of vessels)	flotte,f.	Flotte,f.	flotta,f.	flota,f.	flotta,nn.	flot,m.
flesh	chair,f.	Fleisch,n.	carne,f.	carne,f.	kött,n.	fleysh,n.
flight (hasty departure)	fuite,f.	Flucht,f.	fuga,f.	fuga,f.	flygning,nn.	antloyfn,n.
flight (journey by air)	vol,m.	Flug,m.	volo,m.	vuelo,m.	flykt,nn.	fli,m.
fling, to	jeter	schmeissen	gettare	arrojar	slänga	shlaydern
flint	silex,m.	Feuerstein,n.	pietra focaia,f.	pedernal,m.	flinta,nn.	fayershteyn,m
float (be buoyant), to	flotter	schwimmen	galleggiare	flotar	flyta	haltn zikh oyfn vaser
flock	troupeau,m.	Herde,f.	gregge,m.	rebaño,m.	flock,nn.	stade,f.
flood	inondation,f.	Überschwemmung,f.	inondazione,f.	inundación,f.	översvämning, nn.	farfleytsung,f.
floor (bottom surface)	plancher,m.	(Fuss)Boden,m.	pavimento,m.	piso,m.	golv,n.	podloge,f.
floor (story)	étage,m.	Stock,m.	piano,m.	piso,m.	våning,nn.	gorn,m.
flour	farine,f.	Mehl,n.	farina,f.	harina,f.	mjöl,n.	mel,f.
flourish (thrive), to	fleurir	gedeihen	fiorire	florecer	blomstra	blien
flow (circulate), to	couler	fliessen	scorrere	fluir	flyta	flisn
flower (blossom)	fleur,f.	Blume,f.	fiore,m.	flor,f.	blomma,nn.	blum,f.
flute (mus.)	flûte,f.	Flöte,f.	flauto,m.	flauta,f.	flöjt,nn.	fleyt,f.
flutter (flap), to	flotter	flattern	sbattere	aletear	fladdra	fokhen
fly (housefly)	mouche,f.	Fliege,f.	mosca,f.	mosca,f.	fluga,nn.	flig,f.
fly, to	voler	fliegen	volare	volar	flyga	flien
foam	écume,f.	Schaum,m.	spuma,f.	espuma,f.	skum,n.	shoym,m.
foam rubber	caoutchouc-mousse,m.	Schaumgummi, m.	gommapiuma,f.	caucho esponjoso,m.	skumgummi,n.	shoymgume,f.
foe	ennemi,m.	Feind,m.	nemico,m.	enemigo,m.	fiende,nn.	faynd,m.
fog (mist)	brouillard,m.	Nebel,m.	nebbia,f.	niebla,f.	dimma,nn.	nepl,m.
foil (frustrate), to	déjouer	vereiteln	frustrare	frustrar	omintetgöra	shtern
fold (plait, n.)	pli,m.	Falte,f.	piego,m.	pliegue,m.	veck,nn.	kneytsh,m.
fold (lap over), to	plier	falten	piegare	doblar	vika	tsunoyfleygn
follow (go or come after), to	suivre	folgen	seguire	seguir	följa	nokhgeyn
follow (result), to	ensuivre, s'	folgen	seguire	resultar	följa	aroyskumen
follower (adherent)	partisan,m.	Anhänger,m.	partigiano,m.	partidario,m.	anhängare,nn.	onhenger,m.
following (followers)	partisans,m.pl.	Anhängerschaft, f.	aderenti,m.pl.	partidarios, m.pl.	anhängare,nn. pl.	onhengershaft, f.
folly	folie,f.	Torheit,f.	sciochezza,f.	locura,f.	dårskap,nn.	tipshes,f.
food	nourriture,f.	Nahrung,f.	cibo,m.	alimento,m.	föda,nn.	esnvarg,n.
fool	sot,m.	Narr,m.	sciocco,m.	tonto,m.	tok,nn.	nar,m.
foolish	sot, -te	töricht	imprudente	bobo	dum	narish
foot (anat.)	pied,m.	Fuss,m.	piede,m.	pie,m.	fot,nn. (pl. fötter)	fus,m.
for (conj.)	car	denn	perchè	porque	för	vorem
for (prep.)	pour	für	per	por, para	för	far
forbid, to	défendre	verbieten	proibire	prohibir	förbjuda	farvern
forbidden	défendu	verboten	proibito	prohibido	förbjuden	farvert
force (coercion)	force,f.	Gewalt,f.	forza,f.	fuerza,f.	tvång,n.	gvald,f.
force (power)	force,f.	Kraft,f.	forza,f.	fuerza,f.	kraft,nn.	koyakh,m.
force, to	forcer	zwingen	forzare	forzar	tvinga	neytn
ford, to	passer à gué	durchwaten	guadare	vadear	vada över	durkhbrodyen
forehead	front,m.	Stirn,f.	fronte,f.	frente,f.	panna,nn.	shtern,m.
foreign	étranger, -gère	ausländisch	straniero	extranjero	utländsk	oyslendish
foreigner	étranger,m.	Ausländer,m.	straniero,m.	extranjero,m.	utlänning,nn.	oyslender,m.
foreman (overseer)	contremaître,m.	Vorarbeiter,m.	capolavorante, m.	capataz,m.	förman,f. (pl. -män)	oyfzeer,m.
forest	forêt,f.	Wald,m.	foresta,f.	bosque,m.	skog,nn.	vald,m.
forever	à jamais	für immer	sempre	para siempre	för alltid	oyf tomid
forge (counterfeit), to	contrefaire	fälschen	contraffare	falsear	förfalska	nokhmakhn
forge (shape), to	forger	schmieden	forgiare	forjar	smida	shmidn
forget, to	oublier	vergessen	dimenticare	olvidar	glömma	shmidn
forgive, to	pardonner	verzeihen	perdonare	perdonar	förlåta	moykhl zayn

English	French	German	Italian	Spanish	Swedish	Yiddish
forgiveness	pardon,*m.*	Verzeihung,*f.*	perdono,*m.*	perdón,*m.*	förlåtelse,*nn.*	mekhile,*f.*
forgotten	oublié	vergessen	dimenticato	olvidado	glömd	fargesn
fork (eating utensil)	fourchette,*f.*	Gabel,*f.*	forchetta,*f.*	tenedor,*m.*	gaffel,*nn.*	gopl,*m.*
form (shape)	forme,*f.*	Form,*f.*	forma,*f.*	forma,*f.*	form,*nn.*	form,*f.*
form (shape), to	former	bilden	formare	formar	forma	furemen
formality	formalité,*f.*	Förmlichkeit,*f.*	formalità,*f.*	formalidad,*f.*	formalitet,*nn.*	formelkayt,*f.*
formation (creation)	formation,*f.*	Bildung,*f.*	formazione,*f.*	formación,*f.*	bildning,*nn.*	furemung,*f.*
former (first of two, *adj.*)	premier, -mière	erstere	primo	primer(o)	förra	frierdik
former (preceding, *adj.*)	antérieur	früher	precedente	anterior	föregående	frierdik
formula (prescribed guide)	formule,*f.*	Formel,*f.*	formula,*f.*	fórmula,*f.*	formel,*nn.*	forml,*f.*
forsake, to	abandonner	verlassen	abbandonare	abandonar	överge	farlozn
fort	fort,*m.*	Fort,*n.*	forte,*m.*	fuerte,*m.*	fort,*n.*	fort,*m.*
fortress	forteresse,*f.*	Festung,*f.*	fortezza,*f.*	fortaleza,*f.*	fästning,*nn.*	festung,*f.*
fortunate	heureux, -reuse	glücklich	fortunato	afortunado	lycklig	mazldik
fortune (luck)	fortune,*f.*	Glück,*n.*	fortuna,*f.*	fortuna,*f.*	tur,*nn.*	mazl,*n.*
fortune (wealth)	fortune,*f.*	Vermögen,*n.*	fortuna,*f.*	fortuna,*f.*	förmögenhet,*nn.*	ashires,*f.*
forward (*adv.*)	en avant	vorwärts	avanti	hacia adelante	framåt	foroys
forward (send by mail), to	transmettre	nachschicken	inoltrare	remitir	vidarebefordra	ibershikn
foster (encourage), to	encourager	fördern	incoraggiare	promover	gynna	shtitsn
foster child	enfant adopté,*m.*	Pflegling,*m.*	figlio adottivo,*m.*	hijo adoptivo,*m.*	fosterbarn,*n.*	oyftsikind,*n.*
foul (filthy)	immonde	schmutzig	sudicio	inmundo	smutsig	brudik
found (originate), to	fonder	gründen	fondare	fundar	grunda	grindn
foundation (base)	fondement,*m.*	Fundament,*n.*	fondamento,*m.*	fundamento,*m.*	grundval,*nn.*	fundament,*m.*
founder (*n.*)	fondateur,*m.*	Gründer,*m.*	fondatore,*m.*	fundador	grundläggare,*nn.*	grinder,*m.*
fountain	fontaine,*f.*	Springbrunnen, *m.*	fontana,*f.*	fuente,*f.*	fontän,*f.*	fontan,*m.*
fowl (poultry)	volaille,*f.*	Geflügel,*n.*	pollo,*m.*	pollo,*m.*	fågel,*nn.*	of,*n.*
fox	renard,*m.*	Fuchs,*m.*	volpe,*f.*	zorra,*f.*	räv,*nn.*	fuks,*m.*
fraction (part)	fraction,*f.*	Bruchteil,*m.*	frazione,*f.*	fracción,*f.*	bråkdel,*nn.*	brukhteyl,*m.*
fracture (*med.*)	fracture,*f.*	Bruch,*m.*	frattura,*f.*	fractura,*f.*	brott,*n.*	brokh,*m.*
fragment	fragment,*m.*	Bruchstück,*n.*	frammento,*m.*	fragmento,*m.*	fragment,*n.*	fragment,*m.*
frail (fragile)	frêle	zerbrechlich	fragile	débil	bräcklig	eydl
France	France,*f.*	Frankreich,*n.*	Francia,*f.*	Francia	Frankrike,*n.*	Frankraykh,*n.*
frank (*adj.*)	franc, franche	offen	franco	franco	uppriktig	ofn
fraud (deception)	fraude,*f.*	Schwindel,*m.*	frode,*f.*	fraude,*m.*	bedrägeri,*n.*	shvindl,*m.*
free (gratuitous)	gratuit	unentgeltlich	gratis	gratuito	gratis	umzist
free (independent)	libre	frei	libero	libre	fri	fray
free, to	libérer	befreien	liberare	librar	befria	bafrayen
freedom	liberté,*f.*	Freiheit,*f.*	libertà,*f.*	libertad,*f.*	frihet,*nn.*	frayhayt,*f.*
freeze (turn to ice), to	geler	(ge)frieren	gelare	congelar	frysa	farfroyrn vern
freight	marchandises, *f.pl.*	Fracht,*f.*	merci,*f.pl.*	flete,*m.*	frakt,*nn.*	frakht,*f.*
French (*adj.*)	français	französisch	francese	francés, -cesa	fransk	frantseyzish
frequent	fréquent	häufig	frequente	frecuente	vanlig	oft
fresh (new)	nouveau, -velle	frisch	fresco	fresco	ny	frish
fresh (not stale)	frais, fraîche	frisch	fresco	fresco	färsk	frish
fret (worry), to	faire du mauvais sang, se	grämen, sich	darsi pensiero	impacientarse	oroa sig	oysesn zikh dos harts
friend	ami,*m.*	Freund,*m.*	amico,*m.*	amigo,*m.*	vän,*nn.*	guter fraynd,*m.*
friendly	amical	freundlich	amichevole	amistoso	vänlig	frayndlekh
friendship	amitié,*f.*	Freundschaft,*f.*	amicizia,*f.*	amistad,*f.*	vänskap,*nn.*	gutfrayndshaft, *f.*
fright (alarm)	effroi,*m.*	Schreck,*m.*	spavento,*m.*	espanto,*m.*	skräck,*nn.*	ibershrek,*m.*
frighten (make afraid), to	effrayer	erschrecken	spaventare	espantar	skrämma	ibershrekn
fringe	frange,*f.*	Franse,*f.*	frangia,*f.*	fleco,*m.*	frans,*nn.*	frandz,*m.*
frog	grenouille,*f.*	Frosch,*m.*	rana,*f.*	rana,*f.*	groda,*nn.*	zhabe,*f.*
from	de	von; aus	da	de	från	fun
front (battle front)	front,*m.*	Front,*f.*	fronte,*f.*	frente,*f.*	front,*nn.*	front,*m.*
front (forward part)	devant,*m.*	Vorderseite,*f.*	davanti,*m.*	frente,*f.*	framsida,*nn.*	fornt,*m.*
frontier	frontière,*f.*	Grenze,*f.*	frontiera,*f.*	frontera,*f.*	gräns,*nn.*	grenets,*m.*
frost	gelée,*f.*	Frost,*m.*	brina,*f.*	escarcha,*f.*	frost,*nn.*	frost,*m.*
frown, to	froncer les sourcils	die Stirn runzeln	aggrottare le ciglia	fruncir el ceño	rynka pannan	krimen zikh
frozen	gelé	gefroren	gelato	congelado	frusen	farfroyrn
fruit	fruit,*m.*	Frucht,*f.*	frutto,*m.* (*pl.* frutta,*f.*)	fruta,*f.*	frukt,*nn.*	frukht,*f.*
fry (be cooked in fat), to	frire	braten, sich	friggere	freír	steka	preglen zikh
fuel	combustible,*m.*	Brennstoff,*m.*	combustibile,*m.*	combustible,*m.*	bränsle,*n.*	brenvarg,*n.*
fulfill, to	accomplir	erfüllen	adempiere	cumplir	uppfylla	mekayem zayn
full (ample)	ample	voll(ständig)	ampio	amplio	riklig	ful
full (complete)	complet, -plète	vollkommen	completo	completo	fullständig	ful
full (filled)	plein	voll	pieno	lleno	full	ful
fun	amusement,*m.*	Spass,*m.*	spasso,*m.*	diversión,*f.*	nöje,*n.*	hanoe,*f.*
function	fonction,*f.*	Funktion,*f.*	funzione,*f.*	función,*f.*	funktion,*nn.*	funktsye,*f.*
fund	fonds,*m.*	Fonds,*m.*	fondo,*m.*	fondo,*m.*	fond,*nn.*	fond,*m.*
fundamental	fondamental	grundlegend	fondamentale	fundamental	grundläggande	fundamental
funds	fonds,*m.pl.*	Kapital,*n.*	fondi,*m.pl.*	fondos,*m.pl.*	medel,*n.pl.*	fondn,*pl.*
funeral	funérailles,*f.pl.*	Begräbnis,*n.*	esequie,*f.pl.*	funerales,*m.pl.*	begravning,*nn.*	levaye,*f.*
funny (comical)	drôle	komisch	comico	cómico	rolig	komish
funny (odd)	drôle	seltsam	bizzarro	raro	konstig	modne
fur	fourrure,*f.*	Pelz,*m.*	pelliccia,*f.*	piel,*f.*	pälsverk,*n.*	futer,*m.*

English	French	German	Italian	Spanish	Swedish	Yiddish
furious	furieux, -rieuse	wütend	furioso	furioso	rasande	oyfgekokht
furnace (home heater)	calorifère,*m.*	Ofen,*m.*	calorifero,*m.*	horno,*m.*	värmepanna,*nn.*	oyvn,*m.*
furnish (put furniture in), to	meubler	ausstatten	ammobiliare	amueblar	möblera	oysshtayern
furnish (supply), to	fournir	liefern,*n.*	fornire	proveer	skaffa	farzorgn
furniture	meubles,*m.pl.*	Möbel,*n.pl.*	mobilia,*f.*	muebles,*m.pl.*	möbler,*nn.pl.*	mebl,*pl.*
furrow (*agric.*)	sillon,*m.*	Furche,*f.*	solco,*m.*	surco,*m.*	fåra,*nn.*	gare,*f.*
further (additional, *adj.*)	supplémentaire	ferner	altro	adicional	ytterligare	vayter
further (to greater extent, *adv.*)	plus	überdies	(di) più	más	vidare	dertsu
fury	fureur,*f.*	Wut,*f.*	furia,*f.*	furia,*f.*	raseri,*n.*	tsorn,*m.*
fuse (*elec.*)	plomb,*m.*	Sicherung,*f.*	valvola (elettrica),*f.*	fusible,*m.*	propp,*nn.*	korek,*m.*
fuss (ado)	histoire(s),*f.* (*pl.*)	Lärm,*m.*	storie,*f.pl.*	melindres,*m.pl.*	fjäsk,*n.*	tareram,*m.*
future (*adj.*)	futur	(zu)künftig	futuro	futuro	kommande	kumedik
future (n.)	avenir,*m.*	Zukunft,*f.*	futuro,*m.*	porvenir,*m.*	framtid,*nn.*	tsukunft,*f.*
gain (increase)	accroissement,*m.*	Gewinn,*m.*	aumento,*m.*	aumento,*m.*	ökning,*nn.*	gevins,*n.*
gain (get), to	gagner	gewinnen	ottenere	ganar	vinna	gevinen
gale (wind)	gros vent,*m.*	Sturm(wind),*m.*	bufera,*f.*	ventarrón,*m.*	blåst,*nn.*	shturemvint,*m.*
gallery (balcony)	galerie,*f.*	Galerie,*f.*	galleria,*f.*	galería,*f.*	läktare,*nn.*	galerye,*f.*
gallop (n.)	galop,*m.*	Galopp,*m.*	galoppo,*m.*	galope,*m.*	galopp,*nn.*	galop,*m.*
galoshes	galoches,*f.pl.*	Gummischuhe, *m.pl.*	galosce,*f.pl.*	chanclos,*m.pl.*	bottiner,*nn.pl.*	kaloshn,*pl.*
game (contest)	jeu,*m.*	Spiel,*n.*	giuoco,*m.*	juego,*m.*	spel,*n.*	shpil,*f.*
gang	bande,*f.*	Bande,*f.*	banda,*f.*	pandilla,*f.*	gäng,*n.*	bande,*f.*
gap	trouée,*f.*	Lücke,*f.*	apertura,*f.*	hueco,*m.*	öppning,*nn.*	bloyz,*m.*
garage	garage,*m.*	Garage,*f.*	autorimessa,*f.*	garaje,*m.*	garage,*n.*	garazh,*m.*
garbage	ordures,*f.pl.*	Abfall,*m.*	rifiuti,*m.pl.*	desperdicios, *m.pl.*	avskräde,*n.*	opfal,*m.*
garden	jardin,*m.*	Garten,*m.*	giardino,*m.*	jardín,*m.*	trädgård,*nn.*	gortn,*m.*
gardener	jardinier,*m.*	Gärtner,*m.*	giardiniere,*m.*	jardinero,*m.*	trädgårdsmästare,*nn.*	gertner,*m.*
garlic	ail,*m.*	Knoblauch,*m.*	aglio,*m.*	ajo,*m.*	vitlök,*nn.*	knobl,*m.*
garment	vêtement,*m.*	Kleidungsstück, *n.*	abito,*m.*	prenda de vestir, *f.*	klädesplagg,*n.*	malbush,*n.*
garrison	garnison,*f.*	Garnison,*f.*	guarnigione,*f.*	guarnición,*f.*	garnison,*nn.*	garnizon,*m.*
garter	jarretière,*f.*	Strumpfband,*n.*	giarrettiera,*f.*	liga,*f.*	strumpeband,*n.*	zoknbendl,*n.*
gas	gaz,*m.*	Gas,*n.*	gas,*m.*	gas,*m.*	gas,*nn.*	gaz,*m.*
gasoline	essence,*f.*	Benzin,*n.*	benzina,*f.*	gasolina,*f.*	bensin,*nn.*	gazolin,*f.*
gasp, to	haleter	keuchen	ansare	boquear	flämta	dishen
gate	porte,*f.*	Tor,*n.*	cancello,*m.*	portón,*m.*	port,*nn.*	toyer,*m.*
gather (bring together), to	ramasser	zusammenbringen	raccogliere	recoger	samla	klaybn
gather (congregate), to	assembler, s'	(ver)sammeln, sich	riunirsi	reunir	samlas	klaybn zikh
gay (merry)	gai	lustig	gaio	alegre	glad	freylekh
gaze, to	contempler	anstarren	guardare fissamente	mirar fijamente	stirra	aynkukn zikh
gear (*mech.*)	engrenage,*m.*	Gang,*m.*	ingranaggio,*m.*	engranaje,*m.*	växel,*nn.*	gang,*m.*
gem	gemme,*f.*	Edelstein,*m.*	gemma,*f.*	gema,*f.*	ädelsten,*nn.*	eydlshteyn,*m.*
general (*adj.*)	général	allgemein	generale	general	allmän	algemeyn
general (officer)	général,*m.*	General,*m.*	generale,*m.*	general,*m.*	general,*nn.*	general,*m.*
generation (period of time)	génération,*f.*	Generation,*f.*	generazione,*f.*	generación,*f.*	mansålder,*nn.*	dor,*m.*
generous	généreux, -reuse	freigebig	generoso	generoso	frikostig	breythartsik
Geneva	Genève,*f.*	Genf,*n.*	Ginevra,*f.*	Ginebra	Genève,*n.*	Zhenev,*n.*
genius	génie,*m.*	Genie,*n.*	genio,*m.*	genio,*m.*	geni,*n.*	goen,*m.*
gentle (soothing)	doux, douce	sanft	soave	suave	mild	tsart
gentleman	galant homme,*m.*	Herr,*m.*	galantuomo,*m.*	caballero,*m.*	gentleman,*nn.* (*pl.* -män)	dzhentlman,*m.*
genuine	authentique	echt	genuino	genuino	äkta	ekht
geography	géographie,*f.*	Erdkunde,*f.*	geografia,*f.*	geografía,*f.*	geografi,*nn.*	geografye,*f.*
geology	géologie,*f.*	Geologie,*f.*	geologia,*f.*	geología,*f.*	geologi,*nn.*	geologye,*f.*
germ (micro-organism)	microbe,*m.*	Bakterium,*n.*	microbo,*m.*	microbio,*m.*	bakterie,*nn.*	mikrob,*m.*
German (*adj.*)	allemand	deutsch	tedesco	alemán, -mana	tysk	daytsh
Germany	Allemagne,*f.*	Deutschland,*n.*	Germania,*f.*	Alemania	Tyskland,*n.*	daytshland,*n.*
gesture (motion)	geste,*m.*	Gebärde,*f.*	gesto,*m.*	ademán,*m.*	gest,*nn.*	tnue,*f.*
get (obtain), to	obtenir	bekommen	ottenere	obtener	få	krign
ghost	spectre,*m.*	Gespenst,*n.*	spettro,*m.*	fantasma,*m.*	spöke,*n.*	gayst,*m.*
giant	géant,*m.*	Riese,*m.*	gigante,*m.*	gigante,*m.*	jätte,*nn.*	riz,*m.*
gift (present)	cadeau,*m.*	Geschenk,*n.*	dono,*m.*	regalo,*m.*	gåva,*nn.*	matone,*f.*
gifted (talented)	doué	begabt	di talento	talentoso	begåvad	bashonken
ginger (spice)	gingembre,*m.*	Ingwer,*m.*	zenzero,*m.*	jengibre,*m.*	ingefära,*nn.*	ingber,*m.*
girdle (corset)	gaine,*f.*	Korsett,*n.*	fascetta,*f.*	corsé,*m.*	höfthållare,*nn.*	korset,*m.*
girl	jeune fille,*f.*	Mädchen,*n.*	ragazza,*f.*	muchacha,*f.*	flicka,*nn.*	meydl,*f.*
Girl Scout	(enfant) éclaireuse,*f.*	Pfadfinderin,*f.*	Guida,*f.*	Niña Exploradora,*f.*	flickscout,*nn.*	skoytin,*f.*
give (bestow), to	donner	geben	dare	dar	ge	gebn
give (deliver), to	rendre	übergeben	consegnare	dar	ge	derlangen
glad	heureux, -reuse	froh	allegro	contento	glad	tsufridn
gladness	joie,*f.*	Freude,*f.*	allegrezza,*f.*	alegría,*f.*	glädje,*nn.*	tsufridnkayt,*f.*
glance (quick look)	coup d'oeil,*m.*	Blick,*m.*	occhiata,*f.*	mirada,*f.*	blick,*nn.*	blik,*m.*

English	French	German	Italian	Spanish	Swedish	Yiddish
glance, to	jeter un coup d'oeil	flüchtig blicken	dare un'occhiata	echar una mirada	kasta en blick	a blik ton
glare (stare), to	regarder furieusement	(an) starren	guardare ferocemente	mirar fijamente	stirra	oyfshteln a por oygn
glass (material)	verre,*m.*	Glas,*n.*	vetro,*m.*	vidrio,*m.*	glas,*n.*	gloz,*n.*
glass (vessel)	verre,*m.*	(Trink)Glas,*n.*	bicchiere,*m.*	vaso,*m.*	glas,*n.*	gloz,*f.*
glasses (spectacles)	lunettes,*f.pl.*	Brille,*f.*	occhiali,*m.pl.*	anteojos,*m.pl.*	glasögon,*n.pl.*	briln,*pl.*
gleam (shine), to	luire	glänzen	brillare	fulgurar	glänsa	glantsn
glee (joy)	allégresse,*f.*	Heiterkeit,*f.*	allegria,*f.*	regocijo,*m.*	munterhet,*nn.*	simkhe,*f.*
glide, to	glisser	gleiten	scivolare	deslizarse	glida	glitshn zikh
glimpse	vue momentanée,*f.*	flüchtiger Blick, *m.*	visione momentanea,*f.*	vistazo,*m.*	glimt,*nn.*	blik,*m.*
glitter, to	étinceler	glitzern	rilucere	relucir	glittra	finklen
globe	globe,*m.*	Globus,*m.*	globo,*m.*	globo,*m.*	glob,*nn.*	globus,*m.*
gloom (depression)	mélancolie,*f.*	Trübsinn,*m.*	melanconia,*f.*	melancolía,*f.*	dysterhet,*nn.*	umer,*m.*
gloomy (melancholy)	lugubre	trübsinnig	melanconico	melancólico	dyster	farumert
glorious (resplendent)	resplendissant	herrlich	glorioso	glorioso	lysande	glorraykh
glory (renown)	gloire,*f.*	Ruhm,*m.*	gloria,*f.*	gloria,*f.*	ryktbarhet,*nn.*	glorye,*f.*
glossary	glossaire,*m.*	Wörterverzeichnis,*n.*	glossario,*m.*	glosario,*m.*	ordförteckning, *nn.*	glosar,*m.*
glove	gant,*m.*	Handschuh,*m.*	guanto,*m.*	guante,*m.*	handske,*nn.*	hentshke,*f.*
glow (shine), to	rayonner	glühen	essere incandescente	brillar	glöda	glien
glue	colle,*f.*	Leim,*m.*	colla,*f.*	cola,*f.*	lim,*n.*	kley,*f.*
gnaw (bite), to	ronger	nagen	rodere	roer	gnaga	grizhen
go (ride), to	aller	fahren	andare	ir	fara	forn
go (walk), to	aller	gehen	andare	ir	gå	geyn
goal (objective)	but,*m.*	Ziel,*n.*	meta,*f.*	meta,*f*	mål,*n.*	tsil,*m.*
goat	chèvre,*f.*	Ziege,*f.*	capra,*f.*	cabra,*f.*	get,*nn.* (*pl.* -ter)	tsig,*f.*
God	Dieu,*m.*	Gott,*m.*	Dio,*m.*	Dios,*m.*	Gud,*m.*	Got,*m.*
gold	or,*m.*	Gold,*n.*	oro,*m.*	oro,*m.*	guld,*n.*	gold,*n.*
golden	d'or	golden	d'oro	dorado	gyllene	goldn
golf	golf,*m.*	Golf(spiel),*n.*	golf,*m.*	golf,*m.*	golf,*nn.*	golf,*m.*
good, better, best	bon, meilleur, (le) meilleur	gut, besser, (der) beste	buono, migliore, (il) migliore	bueno, mejor, (lo) mejor	bra, bättre, bäst	gut, beser, best
good-by	au revoir	auf Wiedersehen	addio	adiós	adjö	zay(t) gezunt
Good Friday	Vendredi Saint,*m.*	Karfreitag,*m.*	Venerdì Santo,*m.*	Viernes Santo,*m.*	långfredag,*nn.*	guter fraytik,*m.*
goodness (kindliness)	bonté,*f.*	Güte,*f.*	bontà,*f.*	bondad,*f.*	godhet,*nn.*	gutskayt,*f.*
goods	marchandises, *f.pl.*	Waren,*f.pl.*	merci,*f.pl.*	mercancías,*f.pl.*	varor,*nn.pl.*	skhoyre,*f.*
goose	oie,*f.*	Gans,*f.*	oca,*f.*	ganso,*m.*	gås,*nn.* (*pl.* gäss)	gandz,*f.*
gorgeous	splendide	prächtig	magnifico	primoroso	praktfull	prekhtik
gossip (idle talk)	commérages, *m.pl.*	Geschwätz,*n.*	pettegolezzo,*m.*	chisme,*m.*	skvaller,*n.*	rekhiles,*f.*
govern (rule over), to	gouverner	regieren	governare	gobernar	regera över	regirn
government	gouvernement,*m.*	Regierung,*f.*	governo,*m.*	gobierno,*m.*	regering,*nn.*	regirung,*f.*
governor	gouverneur,*m.*	Gouverneur,*m.*	governatore,*m.*	gobernador,*m.*	guvernör,*nn.*	gubernator,*m.*
gown (dress)	robe,*f.*	Kleid,*n.*	abito,*m.*	vestido,*m.*	dräkt,*nn.*	kleyd,*n.*
grab, to	saisir	packen	afferrare	arrebatar	gripa	khapn
grace (gracefulness)	grâce,*f.*	Anmut,*f.*	grazia,*f.*	donaire,*m.*	behag,*n.*	gratsye,*f.*
graceful	gracieux, -cieuse	anmutig	grazioso	gracioso	graciös	gratsyez
gracious	gracieux, -cieuse	liebenswürdig	gentile	afable	älskvärd	laytzelik
grade (academic rating)	note,*f.*	Note,*f.*	voto,*m.*	calificación,*f.*	betyg,*n.*	tseykhn,*m.*
grade (relative position)	grade,*m.*	Rang,*m.*	grado,*m.*	grado,*m.*	grad,*nn.*	madreyge,*f.*
grade (school division)	année,*f.*	Klasse,*f.*	classe,*f.*	año,*m.*	klass,*nn.*	klas,*m.*
gradual	graduel, -le	allmählich	graduale	gradual	gradvis	behadrogedik
grain (cereal)	grains,*m.pl.*	Getreide,*n.*	cereale,*m.*	grano,*m.*	säd,*nn.*	tvue,*f.*
grammar	grammaire,*f.*	Grammatik,*f.*	grammatica,*f.*	gramática,*f.*	grammatik,*nn.*	gramatik,*f.*
grand (imposing)	grandiose	grossartig	grandioso	grandioso	storartad	grandyez
granddaughter	petite-fille,*f.*	Enkelin,*f.*	nipote,*f.*	nieta,*f.*	son-, dotterdotter,*nn.* (*pl.* -döttrar)	eynikl,*n.*
grandfather	grand-père,*m.*	Grossvater,*m.*	nonno,*m.*	abuelo,*m.*	far-, morfa(de)r,*nn.* (*pl.* -fäder)	zeyde,*m.*
grandmother	grand-mère,*f.*	Grossmutter,*f.*	nonna,*f.*	abuela,*f.*	far-, mormo(de)r,*nn.* (*pl.* -mödrar)	bobe,*f.*
grandson	petit-fils,*m.*	Enkel,*m.*	nipote,*m.*	nieto,*m.*	son-, dotterson,*nn.* (*pl.* -söner)	eynikl,*n.*
granite	granit,*m.*	Granit,*m.*	granito,*m.*	granito,*m.*	granit,*nn.*	granit,*m.*
grant (bestow), to	accorder	gewähren	accordare	conceder	bevilja	bavilikn
grape	grain de raisin,*m.*	Traube,*f.*	uva,*f.*	uva,*f.*	vindruva,*nn.*	vayntroyb,*f.*
graph	graphique,*m.*	graphische Darstellung,*f.*	grafico,*m.*	gráfico,*m.*	diagram,*n.*	krume,*f.*
grasp (grip), to	empoigner	(er)greifen	impugnare	agarrar	fatta	onkhapn
grasp (understand), to	saisir	begreifen	afferrare	comprender	fatta	toyfes zayn
grass	herbe,*f.*	Gras,*n.*	erba,*f.*	hierba,*f.*	gräs,*n.*	groz,*n.*
grasshopper	sauterelle,*f.*	Heuschrecke,*f.*	cavalletta,*f.*	saltamontes,*m.*	gräshoppa,*nn.*	shpringer,*m.*
grate (of furnace)	grille,*f.*	Rost,*m.*	graticola,*f.*	parrilla,*f.*	galler,*n.*	grate,*f.*
grateful	reconnaissant	dankbar	riconoscente	agradecido	tacksam	dankbar
gratitude	reconnaissance, *f.*	Dankbarkeit,*f.*	gratitudine,*f.*	gratitud,*f.*	tacksamhet,*nn.*	dankbarkayt,*f.*
grave (serious)	grave	ernst	grave	grave	allvarlig	erntst
grave (tomb)	tombe,*f.*	Grab,*n.*	tomba,*f.*	tumba,*f.*	grav,*nn.*	keyver,*m.*
gravel	gravier,*m.*	Kies,*m.*	ghiaia,*f.*	grava,*f.*	grus,*n.*	zhvir,*m.*
gravy	sauce,*f.*	Bratsaft,*m.*	sugo,*m.*	salsa,*f.*	sås,*nn.*	yoykh,*f.*

English	French	German	Italian	Spanish	Swedish	Yiddish
gray	gris	grau	grigio	gris	grå	groy
graze (feed), to	paître	weiden	pascersi	pacer	beta	pashen zikh
grease (cooking fat)	graisse,*f.*	Fett,*n.*	grasso,*m.*	grasa,*f.*	fett,*n.*	fets,*n.*
great	grand	gross	grande	grande	stor	groys
Great Britain	Grande Bretagne,*f.*	Grossbritannien, *n.*	Gran Brettagna, *f.*	Gran Bretaña	Storbritannien, *n.*	Groys-Britanye, *f.*
greatness (eminence)	grandeur,*f.*	Grösse,*f.*	grandezza,*f.*	grandeza,*f.*	storhet,*nn.*	groyskayt,*f.*
Greece	Grèce,*f.*	Griechenland,*n.*	Grecia,*f.*	Grecia	Grekland,*n.*	Grikhnland,*n.*
greedy	avide	gierig	avido	ávido	girig	girik
Greek (*adj.*)	grec, -que	griechisch	greco	griego	grekisk	girik
green (color)	vert	grün	verde	verde	grön	grikhish
greet (salute), to	saluer	(be)grüssen	salutare	saludar	hälsa (på)	grin
greeting	accueil,*m.*	Begrüssung,*f.*	accoglienza,*f.*	saludo,*m.*	hälsning,*nn.*	bagrisn
grief	chagrin,*m.*	Kummer,*m.*	afflizione,*f.*	aflicción,*f.*	sorg,*nn.*	bagrisung,*f.*
grieve (mourn), to	affliger, s'	trauern	affliggersi	afligirse	sörja	tsaar,*m.*
grim (stern)	sévère	hart	duro	torvo	hård	troyern
grin, to	sourire largement	grinsen	ghignare	disimular una sonrisa	grina	farbisn
grind (crush), to	moudre	mahlen	macinare	moler	mala	breyt shmeykh-len
grip (grasp)	prise,*f.*	Griff,*m.*	stretta,*f.*	apretón,*m.*	grepp,*n.*	tsemoln
groan (moan), to	gémir	stöhnen	gemere	gemir	stöna	khap,*m.*
grocery	épicerie,*f.*	Lebensmittel-geschäft,*n.*	bottega dei comestibili,*f.*	tienda de comestibles,*f.*	speceriaffär,*nn.*	krekhtsn
						shpayzkrom,*f.*
groom (bridegroom)	marié,*m.*	Bräutigam,*m.*	sposo,*m.*	novio,*m.*	brudgum,*nn.*	khosn,*m.*
gross (before deductions, *adj.*)	brut	brutto	lordo	bruto	brutto	bruto
gross (flagrant)	gros, -se	grob	flagrante	craso	grov	grob
gross (twelve dozen)	grosse,*f.*	Gros,*n.*	grossa,*f.*	gruesa,*f.*	gross,*n.*	gros,*m.*
ground (basis)	raison,*f.*	Grund,*m.*	ragione,*f.*	base,*f.*	grundval,*nn.*	grund,*m.*
ground (earth)	terre,*f.*	Boden,*m.*	terra,*f.*	tierra,*f.*	mark,*nn.*	grunt,*m.*
group	groupe,*m.*	Gruppe,*f.*	gruppo,*m.*	grupo,*m.*	grupp,*nn.*	grupe,*f.*
grove (small woods)	bosquet,*m.*	Wäldchen,*n.*	boschetto,*m.*	arboleda,*f.*	dunge,*nn.*	veldl,*n.*
grow, to (*biol.*)	croître	wachsen	crescere	crecer	växa	vaksn
grow (cultivate), to	cultiver	(an)bauen	coltivare	cultivar	odla	hodeven
grow (expand), to	croître	wachsen	crescere	crecer	tillta(ga)	vaksn
growl, to	gronder	knurren	ringhiare	gruñir	morra	vortshen
growth (development)	croissance,*f.*	Wachstum,*n.*	crescita,*f.*	desarrollo,*m.*	växt,*nn.*	vuks,*m.*
grow up (mature), to	grandir	erwachsen	farsi grande	desarrollarse	växa upp	oyfvaksn
grumble, to	grommeler	brummen	brontolare	refunfuñar	knorra	burtshen
guarantee (warrant)	garantie,*f.*	Bürgschaft,*f.*	garanzia,*f.*	garantía,*f.*	garanti,*nn.*	garantye,*f.*
guarantee, to	garantir	haften, für…	garantire	garantizar	garantera	garantirn
guarantor	garant,*m.*	Bürge,*m.*	garante,*m.*,*f.*	fiador,*m.*	garant,*nn.*	orev,*m.*
guard (watcher)	garde,*f.*	Wache,*f.*	guardiano,*m.*	guarda,*m.*	vakt,*nn.*	shoymer,*m.*
guard (watch over), to	protéger	hüten	custodire	custodiar	vakta	hitn
guardian	tuteur,*m.*	Vormund,*m.*	tutore,*m.*	tutor,*m.*	förmyndare,*nn.*	bashitser,*m.*
Guatemala	Guatemala,*m.*	Guatemala,*n.*	Guatemala,*m.*	Guatemala	Guatemala,*n.*	Gvatemala,*f.*
guess (divine), to	deviner	raten	indovinare	adivinar	gissa	trefn
guess (suppose), to	supposer	vermuten	supporre	suponer	anta(ga)	meshaer zayn
guest (visitor)	invité,*m.*	Gast,*m.*	ospite,*m.*,*f.*	huésped,*m.*	gäst,*nn.*	gast,*m.*
guide (one who guides)	guide,*m.*	Führer,*m.*	guida,*f.*	guía,*m.*	ciceron,*nn.*	firer,*m.*
guided missile	engin télé-guidé,*m.*	ferngelenktes Geschoss,*n.*	proiettile teleguidato,*m.*	proyectil dirigido,*m.*	styrbar projek-til,*nn.*	gekereveter proyektil,*m.*
guilt	culpabilité,*f.*	Schuld,*f.*	colpabilità,*f.*	culpa,*f.*	skuld,*nn.*	shuld,*f.*
guilty	coupáble	schuldig	colpevole	culpable	skyldig	shuldik
guitar	guitare,*f.*	Gitarre,*f.*	chitarra,*f.*	guitarra,*f.*	gitarr,*nn.*	gitare,*f.*
gulf (large bay)	golfe,*m.*	Golf,*m.*	golfo,*m.*	golfo,*m.*	havsbukt,*nn.*	ayngos,*m.*
gum (*anat.*)	gencive,*f.*	Zahnfleisch,*n.*	gengiva,*f.*	encía,*f.*	tandkött,*n.*	yasle,*f.*
gum (chewing gum)	gomme à mâcher,*f.*	Kaugummi,*m.*	gomma da masticare,*f.*	chicle,*m.*	tuggummi,*n.*	kaygume,*f.*
gun	fusil,*m.*	Gewehr,*n.*	fucile,*m.*	arma de fuego,*f.*	bössa,*nn.*	biks,*f.*
gutter (of street)	ruisseau,*m.*	Rinnstein,*m.*	cunetta,*f.*	arroyo,*m.*	rännsten,*nn.*	rinshtok,*m.*
guy (fellow)	type,*m.*	Kerl,*m.*	individuo,*m.*	tipo,*m.*	karl,*nn.*	khevre-man,*m.*
gymnasium (athletic arena)	gymnase,*m.*	Turnhalle,*f.*	palestra,*f.*	gimnasio,*m.*	gymnastiksal, *nn.*	gimnastisher zal,*m.*
gypsy	bohémien,*m.*	Zigeuner,*m.*	zingaro,*m.*	gitano,*m.*	zigenare,*nn.*	Tsigayner,*m.*
habit (custom)	habitude,*f.*	Gewohnheit,*f.*	abitudine,*f.*	hábito,*m.*	vana,*nn.*	gevoynhayt,*f.*
hail (ice)	grêle,*f.*	Hagel,*m.*	grandine,*f.*	granizo,*m.*	hagel,*nn.*	hogl,*m.*
hail (precipitate hail), to	grêler	hageln	grandinare	granizar	hagla	hoglen
hair	cheveux,*m.pl.*	Haar,*n.*	capelli,*m.pl.*	cabello,*m.*	hår,*n.*	hor,*m.*
Haiti	Haïti,*f.*	Haiti,*n.*	Haiti,*m.*	Haití	Haiti,*n.*	Haiti,*n.*
half (*adj.*)	demi	halb	mezzo	medio	halv	halb
half (*n.*)	moitié,*f.*	Hälfte,*f.*	metà,*f.*	mitad,*f.*	hälft,*nn.*	helft,*f.*
halibut	flétan,*m.*	Heilbutt,*m.*	rombo,*m.*	hipogloso,*m.*	helgeflundra,*nn.*	halibut,*m.*
hall (corridor)	corridor,*m.*	Gang,*m.*	corridoio,*m.*	pasillo,*m.*	korridor,*nn.*	koridor,*m.*
hall (meeting room)	salle,*f.*	Saal,*m.*	sala,*f.*	salón,*m.*	sal,*nn.*	zal,*m.*
halt (come to a stop), to	arrêter, s'	(an)halten	fermarsi	pararse	stanna	opshteln
ham (food)	jambon,*m.*	Schinken,*m.*	prosciutto,*m.*	jamón,*m.*	skinka,*nn.*	shinke,*f.*
hammer (tool)	marteau,*m.*	Hammer,*m.*	martello,*m.*	martillo,*m.*	hammare,*nn.*	hamer,*m.*
hand (*anat.*)	main,*f.*	Hand,*f.*	mano,*f.*	mano,*f.*	hand,*nn.* (*pl.* händer)	hant,*f.*
handful	poignée,*f.*	Handvoll,*f.*	pugno,*m.*	puñado,*m.*	handfull,*nn.*	hant,*f.*
handkerchief	mouchoir,*m.*	Taschentuch,*n.*	fazzoletto,*m.*	pañuelo,*m.*	näsduk,*nn.*	noztikhl,*n.*
handle	manche,*f.*	Griff,*m.*	manico,*m.*	mango,*m.*	handtag,*n.*	hentl,*n.*
handsome (attractive)	beau, belle	schön	bello	hermoso	handtag,*n.*	sheyn
handy (near at hand)	sous la main	bei der Hand	comodo	a la mano	vacker	
hang (be suspended), to	pendre	hängen	pendere	colgarse	till hands	tsu der hant
					hänga	hengen

English	French	German	Italian	Spanish	Swedish	Yiddish
hang (suspend), to	pendre	hängen	appendere	colgar	hänga	hengen
happen (occur), to	passer, se	geschehen	accadere	acontecer	hända	geshen
happily (luckily)	heureusement	glücklicherweise	fortunatamente	felizmente	lyckligtvis	tsum glik
happiness	bonheur,*m.*	Glück,*n.*	felicità,*f.*	felicidad,*f.*	lycka,*nn.*	glik,*n.*
happy (glad)	heureux, -reuse	glücklich	felice	feliz	glad	gliklekh
harbor	port,*m.*	Hafen,*m.*	porto,*m.*	puerto,*m.*	hamn,*nn.*	port,*m.*
hard (difficult)	difficile	schwer	difficile	difícil	svår	shver
hard (not soft)	dur	hart	duro	duro	hård	hart
harden (make hard), to	durcir	härten	indurire	endurecer	härda	harteven
hardly (barely)	à peine	kaum	appena	apenas	knappast	koym
hardship (privation)	privation,*f.*	Not,*f.*	privazione,*f.*	privación,*f.*	umbärande,*n.*	noyt,*f.*
hardware	quincaillerie,*f.*	Metallwaren,*pl.*	chincaglieria,*f.*	quincalla,*f.*	järnvaror,*nn.pl.*	ayznvarg,*n.*
hare	lièvre,*m.*	Hase,*m.*	lepre,*f.*	liebre,*f.*	hare,*nn.*	hoz,*m.*
harm (damage), to	nuire à	schaden	nuocere a	dañar	skada	shatn
harmony (*mus.*)	harmonie,*f.*	Harmonie,*f.*	armonia,*f.*	armonía,*f.*	harmoni,*nn.*	harmonye,*f.*
harness	harnais,*m.*	Geschirr,*n.*	bardatura,*f.*	guarniciones,*f. pl.*	sele,*nn.*	geshpan,*n.*
harp	harpe,*f.*	Harfe,*f.*	arpa,*f.*	arpa,*f.*	harpa,*nn.*	harf,*f.*
harsh (grating)	âpre	rauh	aspro	áspero	sträv	griltsndik
harsh (severe)	dur	rauh	rude	severo	sträng	roy
harvest	moisson,*f.*	Ernte,*f.*	raccolto,*m.*	cosecha,*f.*	skörd,*nn.*	shnit,*m.*
haste	hâte,*f.*	Hast,*f.*	fretta,*f.*	prisa,*f.*	brådska,*nn.*	aylenish,*f.*
hasten (expedite), to	hâter	beschleunigen	accelerare	acelerar	påskynda	tsuayln
hasten (hurry), to	hâter, se	beeilen, sich	affrettarsi	apresurarse	skynda sig	tsuayln zikh
hasty (hurried)	précipité	eilig	frettoloso	apresurado	hastig	aylik
hasty (rash)	irréfléchi	voreilig	precipitato	precipitado	förhastad	tsugeaylt
hat	chapeau,*m.*	Hut,*m.*	cappello,*m.*	sombrero,*m.*	hatt,*nn.*	hut,*m.*
hatch, to	faire éclore	brüten	fare schiudere	empollar	kläcka	oysbrien
hatchet	hachette,*f.*	Beil,*n.*	accetta,*f.*	hacha,*f.*	yxa,*nn.*	hak,*f.*
hate (hatred)	haine,*f.*	Hass,*m.*	odio,*m.*	odio,*m.*	hat,*n.*	sine,*f.*
hate, to	haïr	hassen	odiare	odiar	hata	faynt hobn
haul (pull), to	tirer	schleppen	tirare	arrastrar	hala	shlepn
haunt (visit often), to	hanter	häufig besuchen	frequentare	frecuentar	besöka ofta	nit oplozn
have, to	avoir	haben	avere	tener	ha(va)	hobn
Hawaii	Hawaii,*m.*	Hawaii,*n.*	Hawaii,*m.*	Hawaii	Hawaii,*n.*	Havai,*n.*
hawk	faucon,*m.*	Habicht,*m.*	falco,*m.*	halcón,*m.*	hök,*nn.*	falk,*m.*
hay	foin,*m.*	Heu,*n.*	fieno,*m.*	heno,*m.*	hö,*n.*	hey,*n.*
he	il	er	egli	él	han	er
	(see p. 2826 ff.)	*(see p. 2890)*	*(see p. 2947 ff.)*	*(see p. 3012 ff.)*	*(see p. 3075)*	*(see p. 3132)*
head (*anat.*)	tête,*f.*	Kopf,*m.*	testa,*f.*	cabeza,*f.*	huvud,*n.*	kop,*m.*
head (leader)	chef,*m.*	Vorsteher,*m.*	capo,*m.*	jefe,*m.*	chef,*nn.*	rosh,*m.*
head (lead), to	mener	leiten	essere a capo di	encabezar	leda	shteyn berosh
headache	mal de tête,*m.*	Kopfweh,*n.*	mal di capo,*m.*	dolor de cabeza, *m.*	huvudvärk,*nn.*	kopveytik,*m.*
heading (title)	intitulé,*m.*	Überschrift,*f.*	rubrica,*f.*	encabezamiento, *m.*	rubrik,*nn.*	kepl,*n.*
headquarters	quartier général, *m.*	Hauptquartier, *n.*	quartiere gene- rale,*m.*	cuartel general, *m.*	högkvarter,*n.*	hoyptkvartir,*f.*
heal (cure), to	guérir	heilen	guarire	curar	bota	heyln
health	santé,*f.*	Gesundheit,*f.*	salute,*f.*	salud,*f.*	hälsa,*nn.*	gezunt,*n.*
healthy	sain	gesund	sano	sano	frisk	gezunt
heap (pile)	tas,*m.*	Haufen,*m.*	mucchio,*m.*	montón,*m.*	hög,*nn.*	kupe,*f.*
hear, to	entendre	hören	udire	oir	höra	hern
heart	coeur,*m.*	Herz,*n.*	cuore,*m.*	corazón,*m.*	hjärta,*n.*	harts,*n.*
hearth	foyer,*m.*	Herd,*m.*	focolare,*m.*	fogón,*m.*	härd,*nn.*	heymbrand,*m.*
hearty (cordial)	cordial	herzlich	cordiale	cordial	hjärtlig	hartsik
heat	chaleur,*f.*	Hitze,*f.*	calore,*m.*	calor,*m.*	värme,*nn.*	hits,*f.*
heat, to	chauffer	heizen	riscaldare	calentar	uppvärma	heytsn
heave (lift), to	soulever	heben	sollevare	levantar	lyfta	heybn
heaven	ciel,*m.*	Himmel,*m.*	cielo,*m.*	cielo,*m.*	himmel,*nn.*	ganeydn,*m.*
heavy	lourd	schwer	pesante	pesado	tung	shver
Hebrew (*adj.*)	hébreu, -braï- que	hebräisch	ebreo	hebreo	hebreisk	hebreish
hedge (bushes)	haie,*f.*	Hecke,*f.*	siepe,*f.*	seto,*m.*	häck,*nn.*	lebediker ployt, *m.*
heed (mind), to	faire attention à	beachten	badare a	hacer caso de	bry sig om	nemen in akht
heel (*anat.*)	talon,*m.*	Ferse,*f.*	calcagno,*m.*	talón,*m.*	häl,*nn.*	pyate,*f.*
height (highness)	hauteur,*f.*	Höhe,*f.*	altezza,*f.*	altura,*f.*	höjd,*nn.*	heykh,*f.*
heir	héritier,*m.*	Erbe,*m.*	erede,*m.,f.*	heredero,*m.*	arvinge,*nn.*	yoyresh,*m.*
helicopter	hélicoptère,*m.*	Hubschrauber,*m.*	elicottero,*m.*	helicóptero,*m.*	helikopter,*nn.*	helikopter,*m.*
hell	enfer,*m.*	Hölle,*f.*	inferno,*m.*	infierno,*m.*	helvete,*n.*	gehenem,*n.*
helmet	casque,*m.*	Helm,*m.*	elmetto,*m.*	yelmo,*m.*	hjälm,*nn.*	kaske,*f.*
help (assistance)	aide,*f.*	Hilfe,*f.*	aiuto,*m.*	ayuda,*f.*	hjälp,*nn.*	hilf,*f.*
help, to	aider	helfen	aiutare	ayudar	hjälpa	helfn
helper	aide,*m.,f.*	Helfer,*m.*	aiutante,*m.,f.*	ayudante,*m.*	medhjälpare,*nn.*	gehilf,*m.*
helpful (useful)	utile	hilfreich	utile	útil	nyttig	nutsik
helpful (volunteering help)	secourable	hilfreich	soccorrevole	servicial	hjälpsam	oyshelfik
helpless	sans ressource	hilflos	impotente	desvalido	hjälplös	umbaholfn
Helsinki	Helsinki,*m.*	Helsinki,*n.*	Helsinki	Helsinki	Helsingfors,*n.*	Helsingfors,*n.*
hem	ourlet,*m.*	Saum,*m.*	orlo,*m.*	bastilla,*f.*	fåll,*nn.*	zoym,*m.*
hemisphere (*geog.*)	hémisphère,*m.*	Halbkugel,*f.*	emisfero,*m.*	hemisferio,*m.*	halvklot,*n.*	halbkaylekh,*m.*
hemorrhage	hémorragie,*f.*	Blutsturz,*m.*	emorragia,*f.*	hemorragia,*f.*	blödning,*nn.*	blutoysgos,*m.*

English	French	German	Italian	Spanish	Swedish	Yiddish
hen	poule,*f.*	Henne,*f.*	gallina,*f.*	gallina,*f.*	höna,*nn.*	hun,*f.*
hence (consequently)	de là	daher	quindi	por lo tanto	följaktligen	bekheyn
henceforth	désormais	von nun an	d'ora in avanti	de aquí en adelante	hädanefter	fun itst on
her	(*see p. 2826 ff.*)	(*see p. 2890 ff.*)	(*see p. 2947 ff.*)	(*see p. 3012*)	(*see p. 3075*)	(*see p. 3132*)
herb	herbe,*f.*	Kraut,*n.*	erba,*f.*	hierba,*f.*	ört,*nn.*	kraytekhts,*n.*
herd (of animals)	troupeau,*m.*	Herde,*f.*	mandria,*f.*	rebaño,*m.*	hjord,*nn.*	stade,*f.*
here (in this place, *adv.*)	ici	hier	qui	aquí	här	do
here (to this place, *adv.*)	ici	hierher	qui	aquí	hit	aher
hereafter (after this, *adv.*)	dorénavant	hernach	d'ora innanzi	de aquí en adelante	hädanefter	fun itst on
heredity	hérédité,*f.*	Erblichkeit,*f.*	eredità,*f.*	herencia,*f.*	ärftlighet,*nn.*	yerushedikayt,*f.*
hero	héros,*m.*	Held,*m.*	eroe,*m.*	héroe,*m.*	hjälte,*nn.*	held,*m.*
heroine	héroïne,*f.*	Heldin,*f.*	eroina,*f.*	heroína,*f.*	hjältinna,*nn.*	heldin,*f.*
herring	hareng,*m.*	Hering,*m.*	aringa,*f.*	arenque,*m.*	sill,*nn.*	hering,*m.*
hers	(*see p. 2827*)	(*see p. 2890*)	(*see p. 2948*)	(*see p. 3012*)	(*see p. 3075*)	(*see p. 3132*)
herself	(*see p. 2826 ff.*)	(*see p. 2890*)	(*see p. 2948 ff.*)	(*see p. 3012*)	(*see p. 3012*)	(*see p. 3132*)
hesitate, to	hésiter	zögern	esitare	vacilar	tveka	kvenklen zikh
hide (skin)	peau,*f.*	Fell,*n.*	pelle,*f.*	piel,*f.*	hud,*nn.*	fel,*f.*
hide (conceal), to	cacher	verstecken	nascondere	esconder	gömma	bahaltn
high	haut	hoch	alto	alto	hög	hoykh
high school	lycée,*m.*	höhere Schule,*f.*	scuola media superiore,*f.*	escuela secundaria,*f.*	(*no equiv.*)	mitlshul,*f.*
highway	grand-route,*f.*	Landstrasse,*f.*	autostrada,*f.*	carretera,*f.*	landsväg,*nn.*	shosey,*m.*
hike (march)	excursion à pied, *f.*	Wanderung,*f.*	camminata,*f.*	caminata,*f.*	(fot)vandring, *nn.*	shpatsir,*m.*
hill	colline,*f.*	Hügel,*m.*	collina,*f.*	colina,*f.*	backe,*nn.*	bergl,*n.*
hillside	flanc de colline, *m.*	Hügelabhang,*m.*	versante,*m.*	ladera,*f.*	sluttning,*nn.*	zayt fun bergl,*f.*
him	(*see p. 2826 ff.*)	(*see p. 2890 ff.*)	(*see p. 2948 ff.*)	(*see p. 3012*)	(*see p. 3075*)	(*see p. 3132*)
himself	(*see p. 2826 ff.*)	(*see p. 2890*)	(*see p. 2947 ff.*)	(*see p. 3012*)	(*see p. 3075*)	(*see p. 3132*)
hind (posterior, *adj.*)	de derrière	hintere	posteriore	trasero	bakre	hintersht
hinder, to	gêner	(ver)hindern	impedire	estorbar	hindra	shtern
hint (inkling)	indication,*f.*	Andeutung,*f.*	cenno,*m.*	indirecta,*f.*	vink,*nn.*	ontsuherenish,*f.*
hip	hanche,*f.*	Hüfte,*f.*	anca,*f.*	cadera,*f.*	höft,*nn.*	lend,*f.*
hire (employ), to	engager	anstellen	impiegare	emplear	anställa	dingen
his (*poss. adj.*)	(*see p. 2827*)	(*see p. 2891*)	(*see p. 2948*)	(*see p. 3012*)	(*see p. 3075*)	(*see p. 3132*)
his (*poss. pron.*)	(*see p. 2827*)	(*see p. 2890*)	(*see p. 2948*)	(*see p. 3012*)	(*see p. 3075*)	(*see p. 3132*)
hiss, to	siffler	zischen	fischiare	sisear	väsa	tsishen
historical	historique	historisch	storico	histórico	historisk	historish
history	histoire,*f.*	Geschichte,*f.*	storia,*f.*	historia,*f.*	historia,*nn.*	geshikhte,*f.*
hit (strike), to	frapper	schlagen	colpire	golpear	slå	shlogn
hitherto (thus far)	jusqu'ici	bisher	fino ad ora	hasta ahora	hittills	lesate
hive (beehive)	ruche,*f.*	Bienenkorb,*m.*	alveare,*m.*	colmena,*f.*	bikupa,*nn.*	binshtok,*m.*
hoe	houe,*f.*	Hacke,*f.*	zappa,*f.*	azada,*f.*	hacka,*nn.*	motike,*f.*
hoe, to	houer	hacken	zappare	cavar	hacka	motikeven
hog (animal)	porc,*m.*	Schwein,*n.*	maiale,*m.*	puerco,*m.*	svin,*n.*	khazer,*m.*
hold, to	tenir	halten	tenere	tener	hålla	haltn
holdings (possessions)	propriétés,*f.pl.*	Vermögen,*n.*	avere,*m.*	pertenencia,*f.*	innehav,*n.*	farmegn,*n.*
hole (cavity)	trou,*m.*	Loch,*n.*	buco,*m.*	hoyo,*m.*	hål,*n.*	lokh,*f.*
holiday	jour férié,*m.*	Feiertag,*m.*	giorno festivo,*m.*	día festivo,*m.*	fridag,*nn.*	yontev,*m.*
Holland	Hollande,*f.*	Holland,*n.*	Olanda,*f.*	Holanda	Holland,*n.*	Holand,*n.*
hollow (*adj.*)	creux, creuse	hohl	cavo	hueco	ihålig	hoyl
holy	saint	heilig	santo	sagrado	helig	heylik
home	demeure,*f.*	Heim,*n.*	casa,*f.*	hogar,*m.*	hem,*n.*	heym,*f.*
homely (everyday)	simple	heimelig	semplice	sencillo	vardaglig	heymish
homesick	nostalgique	Heimweh,*n.*	nostalgico	nostálgico	hemsjuk	farbenkt
homeward	vers sa demeure	heim	verso casa	a casa	hemåt	aheym
Honduras	Honduras,*m.*	Honduras,*n.*	Honduras,*m.*	Honduras	Honduras,*n.*	Honduras,*n.*
honest	honnête	ehrlich	onesto	honrado	ärlig	erlekh
honesty	honnêteté,*f.*	Redlichkeit,*f.*	onestà,*f.*	honradez,*f.*	ärlighet,*nn.*	erlekhkayt,*f.*
honey	miel,*m.*	Honig,*m.*	miele,*m.*	miel,*f.*	honung,*nn.*	honik,*m.*
honor	honneur,*m.*	Ehre,*f.*	onore,*m.*	honor,*m.*	ära,*nn.*	koved,*m.*
honor (respect), to	honorer	(ver)ehren	onorare	honrar	hedra	opgebn koved
honorable (upright)	d'honneur	rechtschaffen	onorevole	honorable	hederlig	bekovedik
hood (*auto.*)	capot,*m.*	Motorhaube,*f.*	cofano,*m.*	cubierta,*f.*	huv,*nn.*	motordek,*f.*
hood (cowl)	capuchon,*m.*	Kapuze,*f.*	cappuccio,*m.*	capucha,*f.*	huva,*nn.*	kaptur,*m.*
hoof	sabot,*m.*	Huf,*m.*	zoccolo,*m.*	pezuña,*f.*	hov,*nn.*	kopete,*f.*
hook	crochet,*m.*	Haken,*m.*	gancio,*m.*	gancho,*m.*	krok,*nn.*	kruk,*m.*
hop, to	sautiller	hüpfen	saltellare	saltar	hoppa	untershpringen
hope	espoir,*m.*	Hoffnung,*f.*	speranza,*f.*	esperanza,*f.*	hopp,*nn.*	hofenung,*f.*
hope, to	espérer	hoffen	sperare	esperar	hoppas	hofn
hopeful	plein d'espoir	hoffnungsvoll	speranzoso	lleno de esperanza	förhoppningsfull	ful mit hofenung
hopeless	sans espoir	hoffnungslos	disperato	sin esperanza	utan hopp	on hofenung
horizon	horizon,*m.*	Horizont,*m.*	orizzonte,*m.*	horizonte,*m.*	horisont,*nn.*	horizont,*m.*
horizontal (*adj.*)	horizontal	horizontal	orizzontale	horizontal	vågrät	horizontal
horn (*anat.*)	corne,*f.*	Horn,*n.*	corno,*m.*	cuerno,*m.*	horn,*n.*	horn,*m.*
horn (*auto.*)	corne (d'auto),*f.*	Hupe,*f.*	tromba,*f.*	bocina,*f.*	signalhorn,*n.*	trumeyt,*m.*
horn (*mus.*)	cor,*m.*	Horn,*n.*	corno,*m.*	corneta,*f.*	horn,*n.*	horn,*m.*
horrible	horrible	entsetzlich	orribile	horrible	fruktansvärd	groylik
horror (dread)	horreur,*f.*	Entsetzen,*n.*	orrore,*m.*	horror,*m.*	skräck,*nn.*	groyl,*m.*

English	French	German	Italian	Spanish	Swedish	Yiddish
horse	cheval,*m.*	Pferd,*n.*	cavallo,*m.*	caballo,*m.*	häst,*nn.*	ferd,*n.*
horsepower	puissance (en chevaux),*f.*	Pferdekraft,*f.*	cavallo vapore, *m.*	caballos de fuerza,*m.pl.*	hästkraft,*nn.*	ferdkraft,*f.*
hose (tube)	tuyau,*m.*	Schlauch,*m.*	tubo,*m.*	manguera,*f.*	slang,*nn.*	kishke,*f.*
hospital	hôpital,*m.*	Krankenhaus,*n.*	ospedale,*m.*	hospital,*m.*	sjukhus,*n.*	shpitol,*m.*
host	hôte,*m.*	Gastgeber,*m.*	ospite,*m.*,*f.*	anfitrión,*m.*	värd,*nn.*	gastgeber,*m.*
hostile	hostile	feindlich	ostile	hostil	fientlig	fayntlekh
hot	chaud	heiss	caldo	caliente	het	heys
hotel	hôtel,*m.*	Hotel,*n.*	albergo,*m.*	hotel,*m.*	hotell,*n.*	hotel,*m.*
hound	chien de meute, *m.*	Jagdhund,*m.*	bracco,*m.*	perro de caza,*m.*	jakthund,*nn.*	shpirhunt,*m.*
hour	heure,*f.*	Stunde,*f.*	ora,*f.*	hora,*f.*	timme,*nn.*	sho,*f.*
house	maison,*f.*	Haus,*n.*	casa,*f.*	casa,*f.*	hus,*n.*	hoyz,*n.*
household	ménage,*m.*	Haushalt,*m.*	famiglia,*f.*	casa,*f.*	hushåll,*n.*	balebatishkayt, *f.*
housewife	ménagère,*f.*	Hausfrau,*f.*	massaia,*f.*	ama de casa,*f.*	husmo(de)r,*nn.* (*pl.* -mödrar)	baleboste,*f.*
how (*interrog. adv.*)	comment	wie	come	cómo	hur	vi
how (*rel. adv.*)	comment	wie	come	como	hur	vi
however (nevertheless)	cependant	jedoch	però	sin embargo	emellertid	fun dest vegn
howl (wail), to	hurler	heulen	urlare	aullar	tjuta	voyen
hue	teinte,*f.*	Farbton,*m.*	tinta,*f.*	matiz,*m.*	färgton,*nn.*	shatirung,*f.*
hug, to	étreindre	umarmen	abbracciare	abrazar	omfamna	haldzn
huge	énorme	riesig	enorme	enorme	väldig	rizik
hum (murmur)	bourdonnement, *m.*	Summen,*n.*	ronzio,*m.*	susurro,*m.*	surr,*n.*	brum,*m.*
human (*adj.*)	humain	menschlich	umano	humano	mänsklig	mentshlekh
humanity (mankind)	humanité,*f.*	Menschheit,*f.*	umanità,*f.*	humanidad,*f.*	mänsklighet,*nn.*	mentshhayt,*f.*
humble (lowly)	humble	demütig	umile	humilde	ödmjuk	shofl
humility	humilité,*f.*	Demut,*f.*	umiltà,*f.*	humildad,*f.*	ödmjukhet,*nn.*	anives,*f.*
humor (drollery)	humour,*m.*	Humor,*m.*	umore faceto,*m.*	fantasía,*f.*	humor,*nn.*	humor,*m.*
hump	bosse,*f.*	Buckel,*m.*	gobba,*f.*	joroba,*f.*	puckel,*nn.*	hoyker,*m.*
Hungary	Hongrie,*f.*	Ungarn,*n.*	Ungheria,*f.*	Hungría	Ungern,*n.*	Ungern,*n.*
hunger	faim,*f.*	Hunger,*m.*	fame,*f.*	hambre,*f.*	hunger,*nn.*	hunger,*m.*
hungry	affamé	hungrig	affamato	hambriento	hungrig	hungerik
hungry, to be	avoir faim	Hunger haben	aver fame	tener hambre	vara hungrig	zayn hungerik
hunter	chasseur,*m.*	Jäger,*m.*	cacciatore,*m.*	cazador,*m.*	jägare,*nn.*	yeger,*m.*
hunting (sport)	chasse,*f.*	Jagd,*f.*	caccia,*f.*	la caza,*f.*	jakt,*nn.*	geyeg,*n.*
hurl, to	lancer	schleudern	lanciare	lanzar	slunga	shlaydern
hurry (haste)	hâte,*f.*	Eile,*f.*	fretta,*f.*	prisa,*f.*	brådska,*nn.*	aylenish,*f.*
hurry (hasten), to	hâter, se	beeilen, sich	affrettarsi	apresurarse	skynda sig	ayln zikh
hurt (be painful), to	avoir mal	schmerzen	dolere	dolerle (a uno)	göra ont	vey ton
hurt (inflict pain upon), to	faire (du) mal à	weh tun	fare male a	perjudicar	skada	vey ton
husband	mari,*m.*	Mann,*m.*	marito,*m.*	marido,*m.*	make,*nn.*	man,*m.*
hush (make quiet), to	faire taire	zum Schweigen bringen	far tacere	acallar	tysta ned	aynshtiln
hut	hutte,*f.*	Hütte,*f.*	capanna,*f.*	choza,*f.*	hydda,*nn.*	khate,*f.*
hymn (religious song)	hymne,*f.*	Kirchenlied,*n.*	inno,*m.*	himno,*m.*	psalm,*nn.*	kloysterlid,*n.*
hyphen	trait d'union,*m.*	Bindestrich,*m.*	tratto d'unione, *m.*	guión,*m.*	bindestreck,*n.*	makef,*m.*
I	je; moi	ich	io	yo	jag	ikh
ice (frozen water)	glace,*f.*	Eis,*n.*	ghiaccio,*m.*	hielo,*m.*	is,*nn.*	ayz,*n.*
icebox	glacière,*f.*	Eisschrank,*m.*	ghiacciaia,*f.*	nevera,*f.*	isskåp,*n.*	ayzkastn,*m.*
ice-cream	(crème à la) glace,*f.*	(Speise)Eis,*n.*	gelato,*m.*	helado,*m.*	glass,*nn.*	ayzkrem,*m.*
icy	glacial	eisig	ghiacciato	helado	isig	ayzik
idea	idée,*f.*	Idee,*f.*	idea,*f.*	idea,*f.*	idé,*nn.*	idee,*f.*
ideal (*n.*)	idéal,*m.*	Ideal,*n.*	ideale,*m.*	ideal,*m.*	ideal,*n.*	ideal,*m.*
identify, to	identifier	identifizieren	identificare	identificar	identifiera	identifitsirn
idle (not busy)	oisif, -sive	müssig	ozioso	desocupado	sysslolös	pust un pas
idle (useless)	oiseux, -seuse	unnütz	ozioso	inútil	onyttig	aroysgevorfn
idleness (inactivity)	oisiveté,*f.*	Müssiggang,*m.*	ozio,*m.*	ociosidad,*f.*	sysslolöshet,*nn.*	pust-un-paskayt, *f.*
idol	idole,*f.*	Götze,*m.*	idolo,*m.*	ídolo,*m.*	idol,*nn.*	gets,*m.*
if (supposing that)	si	wenn	se	si	om	oyb
if (whether)	si	ob	se	si	om	tsi
ignorance	ignorance,*f.*	Unwissenheit,*f.*	ignoranza,*f.*	ignorancia,*f.*	okunnighet,*nn.*	umvisn,*n.*
ignorant	ignorant	unwissend	ignorante	ignorante	okunnig	umvisndik
ill (sick)	malade	krank	ammalato	enfermo	sjuk	krank
illegal	illégal	ungesetzlich	illegale	ilegal	olaglig	umlegal
illness	maladie,*f.*	Krankheit,*f.*	malattia,*f.*	enfermedad,*f.*	sjukdom,*nn.*	krankayt,*f.*
illuminate (elucidate), to	illuminer	erleuchten	chiarire	esclarecer	belysa	balaykhtn
illuminate (light up), to	illuminer	beleuchten	illuminare	iluminar	upplysa	balaykhtn
illusion	illusion,*f.*	Illusion,*f.*	illusione,*f.*	ilusión,*f.*	illusion,*nn.*	iluzye,*f.*
illustrate (exemplify), to	éclairer par des exemples	illustrieren	illustrare	ejemplificar	illustrera	ilustrirn
illustration (example)	exemple,*m.*	Illustration,*f.*	illustrazione,*f.*	ejemplo,*m.*	illustration,*nn.*	ilustratsye,*f.*
illustration (pictorial representation)	illustration,*f.*	Abbildung,*f.*	disegno,*m.*	estampa,*f.*	illustration,*nn.*	gemel,*n.*
imagination	imagination,*f.*	Einbildungskraft, *f.*	immaginazione,*f.*	imaginación,*f.*	fantasi,*nn.*	fantazye,*f.*
imagine (picture mentally), to	imaginer, (s')	vorstellen, sich	figurarsi	imaginar	föreställa sig	moln zikh
imitate, to	imiter	nachahmen	imitare	imitar	imitera	nokhmakhn
immediate (instant)	immédiat	augenblicklich	immediato	inmediato	omedelbar	teykefdik
immediately (instantly)	immédiatement	(so)gleich	subito	inmediatamente	omedelbart	teykef

English	French	German	Italian	Spanish	Swedish	Yiddish
immense	immense	unermesslich	immenso	inmenso	otantlig	eyn-leshaer
immortal (*adj.*)	immortel, -le	unsterblich	immortale	inmortal	odödlig	umshterblekh
impatience	impatience,*f.*	Ungeduld,*f.*	impazienza,*f.*	impaciencia,*f.*	otålighet,*nn.*	umgeduld,*f.*
impatient	impatient	ungeduldig	impaziente	impaciente	otålig	umgeduldik
imperfect (defective)	imparfait	unvollkommen	imperfetto	imperfecto	bristfällig	pgimedik
imperial	impérial	kaiserlich	imperiale	imperial	kejserlig	keyserlekh
import, to (*bus.*)	importer	einführen	importare	importar	importera	importirn
importance	importance,*f.*	Wichtigkeit,*f.*	importanza,*f.*	importancia,*f.*	vikt,*nn.*	khshives,*f.*
important	important	wichtig	importante	importante	viktig	vikhtik
importation	importation,*f.*	Einfuhr,*f.*	importazione,*f.*	importación,*f.*	import,*nn.*	import,*m.*
importer	importateur,*m.*	Importeur,*m.*	importatore,*m.*	importador,*m.*	importör,*nn.*	importirer,*m.*
impose (inflict), to	imposer	auferlegen	imporre	imponer	ålägga	onton
impossibility	impossibilité,*f.*	Unmöglichkeit,*f.*	impossibilità,*f.*	imposibilidad,*f.*	omöjlighet,*nn.*	ummiglekhkayt, *f.*
impossible	impossible	unmöglich	impossibile	imposible	omöjlig	ummiglekh
impress (affect deeply), to	impressionner	eindrücken	commuovere	impresionar	imponera på	imponirn
impression (effect)	impression,*f.*	Eindruck,*m.*	impressione,*f.*	impresión,*f.*	intryck,*n.*	royshem,*m.*
improve (make better), to	améliorer	verbessern	migliorare	mejorar	förbättra	farbesern
improvement (betterment)	amélioration,*f.*	Verbesserung,*f.*	miglioramento,*m.*	mejoramiento,*m.*	förbättring,*nn.*	farbeserung,*f.*
impulse (sudden incitement)	impulsion,*f.*	Anregung,*f.*	impulso,*m.*	repente,*m.*	impuls,*nn.*	shtoys,*m.*
impure	impur	unrein	impuro	impuro	oren	umreyn
in (during, *prep.*)	pendant	bei	durante	en	om	in
in (inside, *prep.*)	dans	in	dentro	en	i	in
in (into, *prep.*)	dans	in	in	en	in i	in...arayn
inaccurate	inexact	ungenau	inesatto	inexacto	felaktig	umgenoy
inadequate	inadéquat	unzulänglich	inadeguato	inadecuado	otillräcklig	umadekvat
incident (event)	incident,*m.*	Vorfall,*m.*	avvenimento,*m.*	incidente,*m.*	händelse,*nn.*	intsident,*m.*
inclination (tendency)	inclination,*f.*	Neigung,*f.*	inclinazione,*f.*	inclinación,*f.*	böjelse,*nn.*	netie,*f.*
incline (tend), to	incliner	neigen	inclinare	inclinarse	vara böjd	noyte zayn
include (contain), to	comprendre	einschliessen	includere	incluir	innefatta	araynnemen
income	revenu,*m.*	Einkommen,*n.*	entrata,*f.*	ingreso,*m.*	inkomst,*nn.*	hakhnose,*f.*
income tax	impôt sur le revenu,*m.*	Einkommensteuer,*f.*	imposta sul reddito,*f.*	impuesto sobre rentas,*m.*	inkomstskatt,*nn.*	hakhnose-shtayer,*m.*
inconvenience	inconvénient,*m.*	Lästigkeit,*f.*	inconvenienza,*f.*	inconveniencia,*f.*	olägenhet,*nn.*	umbakvemkayt, *f.*
incorrect	inexact	unrichtig	erroneo	incorrecto	oriktig	nit-rikhtik
increase (increment)	augmentation,*f.*	Zunahme,*f.*	aumento,*m.*	aumento,*m.*	ökning,*nn.*	tsukum,*m.*
increase (add to), to	augmenter	vermehren	moltiplicare	aumentar	öka	farmern
increase (grow), to	accroître, s'	zunehmen	aumentarsi	aumentar	ökas	vaksn
indeed (*adv.*)	vraiment	zwar	veramente	de veras	sannerligen	take
indemnity (compensation)	indemnité,*f.*	Entschädigung,*f.*	indennizzo,*m.*	indemnización,*f.*	skadeständ,*n.*	antshedikung,*f.*
independence	indépendance,*f.*	Unabhängigkeit, *f.*	independenza,*f.*	independencia,*f.*	oberoende,*n.*	umophengikayt, *f.*
independent	indépendant	unabhängig	independente	independiente	oberoende	umophengik
index (list)	index,*m.*	Register,*n.*	indice,*m.*	índice,*m.*	register,*n.*	zukhtsetl,*n.*
India	Inde,*f.*	Indien,*n.*	India,*f.*	India	Indien,*n.*	Indye,*f.*
Indian, American	Indien,*m.*	Indianer,*m.*	pellirossa,*m.*,*f.*	indio americano, *m.*	indian,*nn.*	Indyaner,*m.*
indicate (point out), to	indiquer	(an)zeigen	indicare	indicar	visa	onvayzn
indicate (suggest), to	indiquer	andeuten	indicare	indicar	antyda	gebn tsu farshteyn
indifferent (unconcerned)	indifférent	gleichgültig	indifferente	indiferente	likgiltig	glaykhgiltik
indigestion	indigestion,*f.*	Verdauungsstörung,*f.*	indigestione,*f.*	indigestión,*f.*	dålig matsmältning,*nn.*	nit-fardayung,*f.*
indignation	indignation,*f.*	Entrüstung,*f.*	indignazione,*f.*	indignación,*f.*	indignation,*nn.*	oyfgebrakhtkayt,*f.*
indirect	indirect	mittelbar	indiretto	indirecto	indirekt	umdirekt
individual (particular, *adj.*)	particulier, -lière	besonder	particolare	particular	särskild	umdirekt
individual (person, *n.*)	individu,*m.*	Individuum,*n.*	individuo,*m.*	individuo,*m.*	individ,*nn.*	individuel
indoors (*adv.*)	dans la maison	drinnen	dentro	bajo techo	inomhus	yokhid,*m.*
induce (persuade), to	persuader	bewegen	persuadere	inducir	övertala	inveynik
industrial	industriel	industriell	industriale	industrial	industriell	poyeln
industrious	industrieux, -euse	fleissig	industrioso	industrioso	flitig	industriel
industry (trade)	industrie,*f.*	Industrie,*f.*	industria,*f.*	industria,*f.*	industri,*nn.*	flaysik
inevitable (*adj.*)	inévitable	unvermeidlich	inevitabile	inevitable	oundviklig	industrye,*f.*
infant (*n.*)	bébé,*m.*	Säugling,*m.*	bambino,*m.*	infante,*m.*	spädbarn,*n.*	umfarmaydlekh
infantile paralysis	paralysie infantile,*f.*	Kinderlähmung, *f.*	paralisi infantile, *f.*	parálisis infantil, *f.*	barnförlamning, *nn.*	oyfele,*n.* kinder-paraliz, *m.*
infection	infection,*f.*	Ansteckung,*f.*	infezione,*f.*	infección,*f.*	infektion,*nn.*	infektsye,*f.*
inferior (mediocre)	inférieur	minderwertig	inferiore	inferior	sämre	derunterdik
infinite	infini	unendlich	infinito	infinito	oändlig	umendlekh
inflammation	inflammation,*f.*	Entzündung,*f.*	infiammazione, *f.*	inflamación,*f.*	inflammation,*nn.*	ontsindung,*f.*
inflation (*econ.*)	inflation,*f.*	Inflation,*f.*	inflazione,*f.*	inflación,*f.*	inflation,*nn.*	inflatsye,*f.*
influence	influence,*f.*	Einfluss,*m.*	influenza,*f.*	influencia,*f.*	inflytande,*n.*	hashpoe,*f.*
influenza	influenza,*f.*	Grippe,*f.*	influenza,*f.*	influenza,*f.*	influensa,*nn.*	gripe,*f.*
inform (apprise), to	informer	Auskunft geben	informare	informar	underrätta	onzogn
information (knowledge)	informations,*f.* *pl.*	Auskunft,*f.*	informazioni,*f.* *pl.*	información,*f.*	kunskap,*nn.*	informatsye,*f.*
information (news)	informations,*f.* *pl.*	Nachricht,*f.*	informazioni,*f.* *pl.*	noticias,*f.pl.*	upplysning,*nn.*	informatsye,*f.*
inhabit, to	habiter	bewohnen	abitare	habitar	bebo	bavoynen

English	French	German	Italian	Spanish	Swedish	Yiddish
inhabitant	habitant,*m.*	Einwohner,*m.*	abitante,*m.,f.*	habitante,*m.*	invånare,*nn.*	aynvoyner,*m.*
inherit, to	hériter de	(er)erben	ereditare	heredar	ärva	yarshenen
initial (first, *adj.*)	initial	Anfangs-...	iniziale	inicial	begynnelse-...	tkhilesdik
initial (letter)	initiale,*f.*	Anfangsbuch-stabe,*m.*	iniziale,*f.*	letra inicial,*f.*	initial,*nn.*	initsyal,*m.*
injection (*med.*)	piqûre,*f.*	Einspritzung,*f.*	iniezione,*f.*	inyección,*f.*	insprutning,*nn.*	aynshpritsung,*f.*
injure, to	blesser	verletzen	ferire	lisiar	skada	tsekaletshen
injury	blessure,*f.*	Verletzung,*f.*	ferita,*f.*	lesión,*f.*	skada,*nn.*	vund,*f.*
injustice	injustice,*f.*	Ungerechtigkeit,*f.*	ingiustizia,*f.*	injusticia,*f.*	orättvisa,*nn.*	umyoysher,*m.*
ink	encre,*f.*	Tinte,*f.*	inchiostro,*m.*	tinta,*f.*	bläck,*n.*	tint,*f.*
inn	auberge,*f.*	Gasthof,*m.*	albergo,*m.*	posada,*f.*	värdshus,*n.*	kretshme,*f.*
inner	intérieur	inner	interno	interior	inre	inveynikst
innocent (guiltless)	innocent	unschuldig	innocente	inocente	oskyldig	umshuldik
inquire (ask), to	demander	nachfragen	domandare	preguntar	fråga	onfreg n
inquiry (question)	question,*f.*	Nachfrage,*f.*	domanda,*f.*	pregunta,*f.*	förfrågan,*nn.*	onfreg,*m.*
inscription	inscription,*f.*	Inschrift,*f.*	iscrizione,*f.*	inscripción,*f.*	inskrift,*nn.*	aynshrift,*f.*
insect	insecte,*m.*	Kerbtier,*n.*	insetto,*m.*	insecto,*m.*	insekt,*nn.*	insekt,*m.*
insert, to	insérer	einsetzen	inserire	insertar	insätta	araynton
inside (inner, *adj.*)	(d')intérieur	innen-...	interno	interior	inre	inveynikst
inside (interior, *n.*)	dedans,*m.*	Innere,*n.*	interno,*m.*	interior,*m.*	det inre,*n.*	inveynik,*m.*
inside (within, *adv.*)	dedans	drinnen	dentro	dentro	inne	inveynik
inside (within, *prep.*)	à l'intérieur de	innerhalb	dentro	dentro de	inuti	in
insignificant (trivial)	insignifiant	unbedeutend	insignificante	insignificante	obetydlig	nishtik
insist, to	insister	bestehen	insistere	insistir	yrka	bashteyn
insolvency (*bus.*)	insolvabilité,*f.*	Zahlungsunfähig-keit,*f.*	insolvenza,*f.*	insolvencia,*f.*	insolvens,*nn.*	umfeikayt tsu tsoln,*f.*
inspect, to	inspecter	besichtigen	ispezionare	inspeccionar	inspektera	onkukn
inspection (scrutiny)	inspection,*f.*	Kontrolle,*f.*	ispezione,*f.*	inspección,*f.*	inspektion,*nn.*	onkukn,*n.*
inspiration	inspiration,*f.*	Inspiration,*f.*	ispirazione,*f.*	inspiración,*f.*	inspiration,*nn.*	inspiratsye,*f.*
inspire, to	inspirer	begeistern	ispirare	inspirar	inspirera	inspirirn
install (set up for use), to	installer	aufstellen	installare	instalar	installera	instalirn
installment (payment, *bus.*)	acompte,*m.*	Rate,*f.*	rata,*f.*	plazo,*m.*	avbetalning,*nn.*	rate,*f.*
instance (example)	exemple,*m.*	Beispiel,*n.*	esempio,*m.*	ejemplo,*m.*	exempel,*n.*	bayshpil,*m.*
instant (*n.*)	instant,*m.*	Augenblick,*n.*	istante,*m.*	instante,*m.*	ögonblick,*n.*	rege,*f.*
instead of	au lieu de	statt	invece di	en lugar de	i stället för	anshtot
instinct	instinct,*m.*	Instinkt,*m.*	istinto,*m.*	instinto,*m.*	instinkt,*nn.*	instinkt,*m.*
institute	institut,*m.*	Anstalt,*f.*	istituto,*m.*	instituto,*m.*	institut,*n.*	institut,*m.*
institution (establishment)	institution,*f.*	Institution,*f.*	istituzione,*f.*	institución,*f.*	institution,*nn.*	institutsye,*f.*
instruct (direct), to	charger	anweisen	dare istruzioni (a)	dar instrucciones	visa	onzogn
instruct (teach), to	instruire	unterrichten	istruire	instruir	undervisa	lernen
instruction (teaching)	instruction,*f.*	Unterricht,*m.*	istruzione,*f.*	instrucción,*f.*	undervisning,*nn.*	lernen,*n.*
instrument (implement)	instrument,*m.*	Instrument,*n.*	strumento,*m.*	instrumento,*m.*	instrument,*n.*	instrument,*m.*
insufficient	insuffisant	ungenügend	insufficiente	insuficiente	otillräcklig	nit genugik
insult	insulte,*f.*	Beleidigung,*f.*	insulto,*m.*	insulto,*m.*	förolämpning,*nn.*	baleydikung,*f.*
insurance	assurance,*f.*	Versicherung,*f.*	assicurazione,*f.*	seguro,*m.*	försäkring,*nn.*	asekuratsye,*f.*
insure (buy insurance on), to	(faire) assurer	versichern	assicurare	asegurar	försäkra	asekurirn
insure (make sure), to	assurer	versichern	assicurare	asegurar	försäkra	farzikhern zikh
intellectual (*adj.*)	intellectuel, -le	geistig	intellettuale	intelectual	intellektuell	intelektuel
intelligence (understanding)	intelligence,*f.*	Verstand,*m.*	intelligenza,*f.*	inteligencia,*f.*	intelligens,*nn.*	inteligents,*f.*
intelligent	intelligent	verständig	intelligente	inteligente	intelligent	inteligent
intend (propose), to	avoir l'intention de	beabsichtigen	avere l'intenzione di	intentar	ämna	bedeye hobn
intense	intense	intensiv	intenso	intenso	intensiv	intensiv
intent (engrossed)	absorbé	bedacht auf	intento	atento	ivrigt upptagen	arayngeton
intention	intention,*f.*	Absicht,*f.*	intenzione,*f.*	intención,*f.*	avsikt,*nn.*	kavone,*f.*
interest (attention)	attention,*f.*	Interesse,*n.*	attenzione,*f.*	atención,*f.*	intresse,*n.*	interes,*m.*
interest (engaging quality)	intérêt,*m.*	Anziehungskraft,*f.*	attrazione,*f.*	atracción,*f.*	intresse,*n.*	interes,*m.*
interest (money rate)	intérêt,*m.*	Zinsen,*m.pl.*	interesse,*m.*	interés,*m.*	ränta,*nn.*	protsent,*m.*
interest (share)	intérêt,*m.*	Teilnahme,*f.*	parte,*f.*	participación,*f.*	andel,*nn.*	kheylek,*m.*
interest, to	intéresser	interessieren	interessare	interesar	intressera	interesirn
interesting	intéressant	interessant	interessante	interesante	intressant	interesant
interfere (meddle), to	mêler, se	einmischen, sich	immischiarsi	intervenir	lägga sig i	araynmishn zikh
interior (inside, *n.*)	intérieur,*m.*	Innere,*n.*	interno,*m.*	interior,*m.*	det inre,*n.def.*	inveynik,*m.*
internal	intérieur	inner(lich)	interno	interno	inre	inveynikst
international	international	international	internazionale	internacional	internationell	internatsyonal
interpret (explain), to	interpréter	deuten	interpretare	interpretar	tolka	oystaytshn
interrupt, to	interrompre	unterbrechen	interrompere	interrumpir	avbryta	iberraysn
interval (period of time)	intervalle,*m.*	Zwischenraum,*m.*	intervallo,*m.*	intervalo,*m.*	mellantid,*nn.*	tsivshntsayt,*f.*
interview	interview,*f.*	Interview,*n.*	intervista,*f.*	entrevista,*f.*	intervju,*nn.*	intervyu,*m.*
intimate (personal)	intime	vertraut	intimo	íntimo	intim	intim
into (to the inside)	dans	in	in	adentro	in i	in...arayn
intoxication (drunkenness)	ivresse,*f.*	Rausch,*m.*	ubriachezza,*f.*	embriaguez,*f.*	berusning,*nn.*	shikres,*f.*
introduce (bring in), to	introduire	einführen	introdurre	introducir	införa	araynfirn
introduce (make acquainted), to	présenter	vorstellen	presentare	presentar	presentera	bakenen
introduction (preliminary part)	introduction,*f.*	Einführung,*f.*	introduzione,*f.*	introducción,*f.*	inledning,*nn.*	araynfir,*m.*
introduction (presentation)	présentation,*f.*	Bekanntma-chung,*f.*	presentazione,*f.*	presentación,*f.*	presentation,*nn.*	forshteln,*n.*

English	French	German	Italian	Spanish	Swedish	Yiddish
intuition	intuition, *f.*	Intuition, *f.*	intuizione, *f.*	intuición, *f.*	intuition, *nn.*	intuitsye, *f.*
invade, to (*mil.*)	envahir	einfallen in	invadere	invadir	infalla i	araynraysn zikh in
invent, to	inventer	erfinden	inventare	inventar	uppfinna	oysgefinen
invention	invention, *f.*	Erfindung, *f.*	invenzione, *f.*	invención, *f.*	uppfinning, *nn.*	oysgefins, *n.*
inventory (*bus.*)	inventaire, *m.*	Inventar, *n.*	inventario, *m.*	inventario, *m.*	inventarieförteckning, *nn.*	inventar, *m.*
invest, to (*bus.*)	placer (de l'argent)	anlegen	investire	invertir	investera	investirn
investigate, to	examiner	untersuchen	indagare	investigar	undersöka	oysforshn
investigation	investigation, *f.*	Untersuchung, *f.*	investigazione, *f.*	investigación, *f.*	undersökning, *nn.*	oysforshung, *f.*
investment (*bus.*)	placement, *m.*	Geldanlage, *f.*	investimento, *m.*	inversión, *f.*	investering, *nn.*	investitsye, *f.*
invisible	invisible	unsichtbar	invisibile	invisible	osynlig	umzikhtbar
invitation	invitation, *f.*	Einladung, *f.*	invito, *m.*	invitación, *f.*	inbjudan, *nn.*	farbetung, *f.*
invite, to	inviter	einladen	invitare	invitar	inbjuda	farbetn
invoice	facture, *f.*	Rechnung, *f.*	fattura, *f.*	factura, *f.*	faktura, *nn.*	khezbn, *m.*
involve (entail), to	entraîner	zur Folge haben	richiedere	envolver	medföra	zayn farbundn mit
iodine (antiseptic)	teinture d'iode, *f.*	Jodtinktur, *f.*	tintura d'iodio, *f.*	yodo, *m.*	jod, *nn.*	yod, *m.*
Ireland	Irlande, *f.*	Irland, *n.*	Irlanda, *f.*	Irlanda	Irland, *n.*	Irland, *n.*
Irish (*adj.*)	irlandais	irisch	irlandese	irlandés, -desa	irländsk	irish
iron (metal)	fer, *m.*	Eisen, *n.*	ferro, *m.*	hierro, *m.*	järn, *n.*	ayzn, *n.*
iron, electric	fer à repasser électrique, *m.*	Bügeleisen, *n.*	ferro elettrico (per stirare), *m.*	plancha eléctrica, *f.*	strykjärn, *n.*	presayzn, *n.*
irregular (asymmetrical)	irrégulier, -lière	unregelmässig	asimmetrico	irregular	oregelbunden	umreguler
irregular (not conforming)	irrégulier, -lière	regelwidrig	irregolare	irregular	oregelbunden	umreguler
irrigation	irrigation, *f.*	Bewässerung, *f.*	irrigazione, *f.*	riego, *m.*	bevattning, *nn.*	bavaserung, *f.*
irritate (annoy), to	irriter	(auf)reizen	irritare	irritar	irritera	reytsn zikh mit
island (*geog.*)	île, *f.*	Insel, *f.*	isola, *f.*	isla, *f.*	ö, *nn.*	indzl, *m.*
Israel	Israël, *m.*	Israel, *n.*	Israele, *m.*	Israel	Israel, *n.*	Yisroel, *n.*
Israeli (*adj.*)	israéli	israelisch	israeli	israelito	israelisk	yisroeylish
issue (question)	question, *f.*	Streitfrage, *f.*	questione, *f.*	punto en cuestión, *m.*	fråga, *nn.*	inyen, *m.*
isthmus	isthme, *m.*	Landenge, *f.*	istmo, *m.*	istmo, *m.*	landtunga, *nn.*	istmos, *m.*
it	(*see p. 2826 ff.*)	(*see p. 2890*)	(*see p. 2947 ff.*)	(*see p. 3012*)	(*see p. 3075*)	(*see p. 3132*)
Italian (*adj.*)	italien, -ne	italienisch	italiano	italiano	italiensk	italyenish
Italy	Italie, *f.*	Italien, *n.*	Italia, *f.*	Italia	Italien, *n.*	Italye, *f.*
item (detail)	détail, *m.*	Einzelheit, *f.*	dettaglio, *m.*	detalle, *m.*	post, *nn.*	prat, *m.*
its (*poss. adj.*)	(*see p. 2827*)	(*see p. 2891*)	(*see p. 2948*)	(*see p. 3012*)	(*see p. 3075*)	(*see p. 3132*)
its (*poss. pron.*)	(*see p. 2827*)	(*see p. 2890*)	(*see p. 2948*)	(*see p. 3012*)	(*see p. 3075*)	(*see p. 3132*)
itself	(*see p. 2826 ff.*)	(*see p. 2890*)	(*see p. 2947 ff.*)	(*see p. 3012*)	(*see p. 3075*)	(*see p. 3132*)
ivory	ivoire, *m.*	Elfenbein, *n.*	avorio, *m.*	marfil, *m.*	elfenben, *n.*	helfantbeyn, *m.*
ivy	lierre, *m.*	Efeu, *n.*	edera, *f.*	hiedra, *f.*	murgröna, *nn.*	vilder vayn, *m.*
jacket (short coat)	jaquette, *f.*	Jacke, *f.*	giacca, *f.*	chaqueta, *f.*	jacka, *nn.*	yak, *m.*
jail	prison, *f.*	Gefängnis, *n.*	carcere, *m.*	cárcel, *f.*	fängelse, *n.*	turme, *f.*
jam (preserve)	confiture, *f.*	Marmelade, *f.*	marmellata, *f.*	compota, *f.*	sylt, *nn.*	ayngemakhts, *n.*
Japan	Japon, *m.*	Japan, *n.*	Giappone, *m.*	Japón	Japan, *n.*	Yapan, *n.*
Japanese (*adj.*)	japonais	japanisch	giapponese	japonés, -nesa	japansk	yapanish
jar (vessel)	bocal, *m.*	Krug, *m.*	barattolo, *m.*	jarra, *f.*	burk, *nn.*	sloy, *m.*
jaw	mâchoire, *f.*	Kiefer, *m.*	mascella, *f.*	quijada, *f.*	käke, *nn.*	kin, *f.*
jazz	jazz, *m.*	Jazz, *m.*	jazz, *m.*	jazz, *m.*	jazz, *nn.*	dzhez, *m.*
jealous	jaloux, -louse	eifersüchtig	geloso	celoso	avundsjuk	eyferzikhtik
jelly	gelée, *f.*	Gelee, *n.*	gelatina, *f.*	jalea, *f.*	gelé, *nn., n.*	galaret, *m.*
Jerusalem	Jérusalem, *f.*	Jerusalem, *n.*	Gerusalemme, *f.*	Jerusalén	Jerusalem, *n.*	Yerusholaim, *n.*
jest (joke)	plaisanterie, *f.*	Scherz, *m.*	scherzo, *m.*	broma, *f.*	skämt, *n.*	katoves, *m.*
jest (joke), to	plaisanter	scherzen	scherzare	bromear	skämta	traybn katoves
Jesus	Jésus	Jesus	Gesù	Jesús	Jesus	Yezus
jet engine	moteur à réaction, *f.*	Düsenantrieb, *m.*	motore a reazione, *m.*	motor de propulsión a chorro, *m.*	reaktionsmotor, *nn.*	dzhet-motor, *m.*
Jew (*n.*)	Juif, *m.*	Jude, *m.*	ebreo, *m.*	judío, *m.*	jude, *nn.*	Yid, *m.*
jewel	bijou, *m.*	Juwel, *n.*	gioiello, *m.*	joya, *f.*	juvel, *nn.*	brilyant, *m.*
jewelry	bijouterie, *f.*	Schmuck, *m.*	gioielli, *m.pl.*	joyas, *f.pl.*	smycken, *n.pl.*	tsirung, *f.*
Jewish (*adj.*)	juif, -ive	jüdisch	ebreo	judío	judisk	yidish
job (employment)	emploi, *m.*	Arbeit, *f.*	impiego, *m.*	empleo, *m.*	arbete, *n.*	shtele, *f.*
job (task)	travail, *m.*	Aufgabe, *f.*	compito, *m.*	tarea, *f.*	arbete, *n.*	uvde, *f.*
join (become a member of), to	entrer à, dans	beitreten	associarsi (a)	asociarse a	bli(va) medlem av	onshlisn zikh in
join (bring together), to	joindre	verbinden	unire	juntar	förena	fareynikn
joint (combined)	commun	gemeinsam	collettivo	conjunto	förenad	beshutfesdik
joke (jest)	plaisanterie, *f.*	Witz, *m.*	scherzo, *m.*	chiste, *m.*	skämt, *n.*	vits, *m.*
joke (jest), to	plaisanter	Spass machen	scherzare	chancearse	skämta	vitslen zikh
jolly (*adj.*)	jovial	lustig	gioviale	alegre	glad	freylekh
journal (magazine)	journal, *m.*	Zeitschrift, *f.*	giornale, *m.*	revista, *f.*	tidskrift, *nn.*	zhurnal, *m.*
journey	voyage, *m.*	Reise, *f.*	viaggio, *m.*	viaje, *m.*	resa, *nn.*	nesie, *f.*
joy	joie, *f.*	Freude, *f.*	gioia, *f.*	júbilo, *m.*	glädje, *nn.*	freyd, *f.*
joyful	joyeux, -euse	froh	lieto	jubiloso	glad	freydik
judge	juge, *m.*	Richter, *m.*	giudice, *m.*	juez, *m.*	domare, *nn.*	rikhter, *m.*
judge, to	juger	(be)urteilen	giudicare	juzgar	döma	mishpetn
judgment (estimation)	jugement, *m.*	Urteil, *n.*	discernimento, *m.*	juicio, *m.*	omdöme, *n.*	opshatsung, *f.*
judgment (*law*)	jugement, *m.*	Urteil, *n.*	sentenza, *f.*	juicio, *m.*	dom, *nn.*	psak-din, *m.*
jug	cruche, *f.*	Krug, *m.*	brocca, *f.*	jarro, *m.*	kanna, *nn.*	krug, *m.*
juice	jus, *m.*	Saft, *m.*	succo, *m.*	jugo, *m.*	saft, *nn.*	zaft, *m.*
jump (bound)	saut, *m.*	Sprung, *m.*	salto, *m.*	salto, *m.*	hopp, *n.*	shprung, *m.*
jump (bound), to	sauter	springen	saltare	saltar	hoppa	shpringen

English	French	German	Italian	Spanish	Swedish	Yiddish
junior (younger)	cadet, -te	jünger	minore	menor	yngre	yinger
jury	jury,*m.*	Geschworenen, *pl.*	giurati,*m.pl.*	jurado,*m.*	nämnd,*nn.*	zhuri,*f.*
just (equitable, *adj.*)	juste	gerecht	giusto	justo	rättvis	gerekhtik
just (merely)	seulement	bloss	semplicemente	solamente	bara	nor
justice (administration of law)	justice,*f.*	Justiz,*f.*	giustizia,*f.*	justicia,*f.*	rättskipning,*nn.*	gerekhtikayt,*f.*
justice (rightfulness)	justice,*f.*	Gerechtigkeit,*f.*	giustizia,*f.*	justicia,*f.*	rättvisa,*nn.*	gerekhtikayt,*f.*
justify (defend), to	justifier	rechtfertigen	giustificare	justificar	försvara	barekhtikn
justify (exonerate), to	justifier	rechtfertigen	giustificare	justificar	frita(ga)	matsdik zayn
Karachi	Karachi,*n.*	Karachi,*n.*	Karachi,*f.*	Karachi	Karachi,*n.*	Karatshi,*n.*
keen (eager)	ardent	eifrig	ardente	ansioso	ivrig	eyferdik
keen (sharp)	aigu, -ë	scharf	aguzzo	agudo	skarp	sharf
keep (continue), to	continuer (à, de)	einhalten	continuare a	seguir	fortsätta	haltn in eyn
keep (prevent), to	empêcher	abhalten	trattenere	impedir	hindra	ophaltn
keep (retain), to	garder	behalten	ritenere	guardar	behålla	lozn bay zikh
keeper (guard)	gardien,*m.*	Wärter,*m.*	custode,*m.*	guarda,*m.*	vakt,*nn.*	shoymer,*m.*
kernel	graine,*f.*	Kern,*m.*	chicco,*m.*	grano,*m.*	kärna,*nn.*	kerndl,*n.*
kerosene	pétrole,*m.*	Leuchtpetroleum,*n.*	petrolio illuminante,*m.*	keroseno,*m.*	fotogen,*nn.* or *n.*	naft,*m.*
kettle	bouilloire,*f.*	Kessel,*m.*	caldaia,*f.*	caldera,*f.*	kittel,*nn.*	kesl,*m.*
key (for lock)	clef,*f.*	Schlüssel,*m.*	chiave,*f.*	llave,*f.*	nyckel,*nn.*	shlisl,*m.*
kick (boot)	coup de pied,*m.*	Fusstritt,*m.*	calcio,*m.*	patada,*f.*	spark,*nn.*	brike,*m.*
kick (boot), to	botter	einen Fusstritt geben	colpire col piede	patear	sparka	briken
kid (goat)	chevreau,*m.*	Zicklein,*n.*	capretto,*m.*	cabrito,*m.*	killing,*nn.*	tsigele,*n.*
kidney (*anat.*)	rein,*m.*	Niere,*f.*	rene,*m.*	riñon,*m.*	njure,*nn.*	nir,*f.*
kill, to	tuer	töten	uccidere	matar	döda	derhargenen
kind (*adj.*)	bon, -ne	gütig	gentile	bondadoso	snäll	lib
kind (*n.*)	espèce,*f.*	Art,*f.*	specie,*f.*	especie,*f.*	slag,*n.*	min,*m.*
kindergarten	école maternelle,*f.*	Kindergarten,*m.*	giardino d'infanzia,*m.*	escuela de párvulos,*f.*	kindergarten,*nn.*	kinder-gortn,*m.*
kindness (favor)	bonté,*f.*	Freundlichkeit,*f.*	gentilezza,*f.*	favor,*m.*	vänlighet,*nn.*	frayndlekhkayt,*f.*
kindness (goodness)	bonté,*f.*	Güte,*f.*	gentilezza,*f.*	bondad,*f.*	godhet,*nn.*	gutskayt,*f.*
king	roi,*m.*	König,*m.*	re,*m.*	rey,*m.*	kung,*nn.*	kinig,*m.*
kingdom	royaume,*m.*	Königreich,*n.*	regno,*m.*	reino,*m.*	kungarike,*n.*	kinigraykh,*n.*
kiss	baiser,*m.*	Kuss,*m.*	bacio,*m.*	beso,*m.*	kyss,*nn.*	kush,*m.*
kiss, to	embrasser	küssen	baciare	besar	kyssa	kushn
kitchen	cuisine,*f.*	Küche,*f.*	cucina,*f.*	cocina,*f.*	kök,*n.*	kikh,*f.*
kite	cerf-volant,*m.*	(Flug)Drache,*m.*	cervo volante,*m.*	cometa,*f.*	(pappers)drake,*nn.*	flishlang,*f.*
kitten	chaton,*m.*	Kätzchen,*n.*	gattino,*m.*	gatito,*m.*	kattunge,*nn.*	ketsl,*n.*
knee	genou,*m.*	Knie,*n.*	ginocchio,*m.* (*pl.* ginocchia,*f.*)	rodilla,*f.*	knä,*n.*	kni,*m.*
kneel, to	agenouiller, s'	knien	inginocchiarsi	arrodillarse	knäböja	knien
knife	couteau,*m.*	Messer,*n.*	coltello,*m.*	cuchillo,*m.*	kniv,*nn.*	meser,*n.*
knight	chevalier,*m.*	Ritter,*m.*	cavaliere,*m.*	caballero,*m.*	riddare,*nn.*	riter,*m.*
knit, to	tricoter	stricken	lavorare a maglia	tejer	sticka	shtrikn
knitting	tricotage,*m.*	Strickarbeit,*f.*	lavoro a maglia,*m.*	tejido de punto,*m.*	stickning,*nn.*	shtrikeray,*f.*
knock (hit), to	frapper	klopfen	picchiare	tocar	slå	klapn
knot	noeud,*m.*	Knoten,*m.*	nodo,*m.*	nudo,*m.*	knut,*nn.*	knup,*m.*
know (be acquainted with), to	connaître	kennen	conoscere	conocer	känna	kenen
know (have knowledge), to	savoir	wissen	sapere	saber	veta	visn
knowledge (information)	connaissance,*f.*	(Er)Kenntnisse,*f.pl.*	conoscenza,*f.*	conocimiento,*m.*	vetskap,*nn.*	visn,*n.*
knowledge (understanding)	connaissance,*f.*	Wissen,*n.*	conoscenza,*f.*	entendimiento,*m.*	kunskap,*nn.*	kentenish,*f.*
known (familiar)	connu	bekannt	conosciuto	conocido	bekant	bavust
label	étiquette,*f.*	Etikett,*n.*	etichetta,*f.*	rótulo,*m.*	etikett,*nn.*	etiket,*m.*
labor (exertion)	labeur,*m.*	Anstrengung,*f.*	fatica,*f.*	labor,*f.*	möda,*nn.*	mi,*f.*
labor (labor force)	travail,*m.*	Arbeitskraft,*f.*	lavoro,*m.*	la fuerza obrera,*f.*	arbetskraft,*nn.*	arbetkraft,*f.*
laboratory	laboratoire,*m.*	Laboratorium,*n.*	laboratorio,*m.*	laboratorio,*m.*	laboratorium,*n.*	laboratorye,*f.*
laborer	manoeuvre,*m.*	Arbeiter,*m.*	bracciante,*m.*	obrero,*m.*	grovarbetare,*nn.*	shvartser arbeter,*m.*
lace (fabric)	dentelle,*f.*	Spitze,*f.*	merletto,*m.*	encaje,*m.*	spets,*nn.*	shpitsn,*pl.*
lace (shoelace)	lacet,*m.*	Schnürsenkel,*m.*	laccio,*m.*	cordón,*m.*	snörband,*n.*	shnirl,*n.*
lack (deficiency)	manque,*m.*	Mangel,*m.*	mancanza,*f.*	falta,*f.*	brist,*nn.*	doykhek,*m.*
lack (be without), to	manquer de	fehlen	mancare di	faltar	sakna	feln
lad	garçon,*m.*	Junge,*m.*	giovanetto,*m.*	mozalbete,*m.*	pojke,*nn.*	yung,*m.*
ladder	échelle,*f.*	Leiter,*f.*	scala,*f.*	escalera,*f.*	stege,*nn.*	leyter,*m.*
lady	dame,*f.*	Dame,*f.*	signora,*f.*	dama,*f.*	dam,*nn.*	dame,*f.*
lag (fall behind), to	traîner	zurückbleiben	indugiare	retrasarse	bli(va) efter	opshteyn
lake	lac,*m.*	See,*m.*	lago,*m.*	lago,*m.*	sjö,*nn.*	ozere,*f.*
lamb	agneau,*m.*	Lamm,*n.*	agnello,*m.*	cordero,*m.*	lamm,*n.*	lam,*f.*
lamb chop	côtelette d'agneau,*f.*	Hammelkotelett,*n.*	costoletta d'agnello,*f.*	chuleta de carnero,*f.*	lammkotlett,*nn.*	shepsener kotlet,*m.*
lame	boiteux, -teuse	lahm	zoppo	cojo	ofärdig	lom
lamp	lampe,*f.*	Lampe,*f.*	lampada,*f.*	lámpara,*f.*	lampa,*nn.*	lomp,*m.*
land (ground)	terre,*f.*	Land,*n.*	terra,*f.*	tierra,*f.*	land,*n.*	yaboshe,*f.*
land (property)	biens-fonds,*m.pl.*	Grundstück,*n.*	terreno,*m.*	bienes raíces,*m. pl.*	jord,*nn.*	erd,*f.*
land (region)	contrée,*f.*	Landschaft,*f.*	terra,*f.*	territorio,*m.*	trakt,*nn.*	land,*n.*

English	French	German	Italian	Spanish	Swedish	Yiddish
land (an airplane), to	atterrir	landen	atterrare	aterrizar	landa	landn
land (from a ship), to	débarquer	landen	sbarcare	desembarcar	landa	landn
landscape (scenery)	paysage,*m.*	Landschaft,*f.*	paesaggio,*m.*	paisaje,*m.*	landskap,*n.*	landshaft,*f.*
lane (narrow path)	allée,*f.*	(Fuss)Weg,*m.*	sentiero,*m.*	senda,*f.*	smal väg,*nn.*	shtegl,*n.*
language	langue,*f.*	Sprache,*f.*	lingua,*f.*	lengua,*f.*	språk,*n.*	shprakh,*f.*
lantern	lanterne,*f.*	Laterne,*f.*	lanterna,*f.*	linterna,*f.*	lykta,*nn.*	lamtern,*m.*
lap (of seated person)	giron,*m.*	Schoss,*m.*	grembo,*m.*	regazo,*m.*	knä,*n.*	shoys,*f.*
lapse (become void), to	périmer	verfallen	scadere	caducar	förfalla	oysloyfn
lard	saindoux,*m.*	Schmalz,*m.*	lardo,*m.*	manteca,*f.*	flott,*n.*	khazer-shmalts, *n.*
large	grand	gross	largo	grande	stor	groys
lark (bird)	alouette,*f.*	Lerche,*f.*	allodola,*f.*	alondra,*f.*	lärka,*nn.*	trilerl,*n.*
lash (eyelash)	cil,*m.*	Wimper,*f.*	ciglio,*m.* (*pl.* ciglia,*f.*)	pestaña,*f.*	ögonfrans,*nn.*	vie,*f.*
lash (whip)	fouet,*m.*	Peitschenhieb,*m.*	frusta,*f.*	látigo,*m.*	snärt,*nn.*	baytsh,*f.*
lash (fasten), to	lier	festbinden	legare	amarrar	surra	tsubindn
lash (whip), to	cingler	geisseln	frustare	dar latigazos	piska	shmaysn
lass	jeune fille,*f.*	Mädchen,*n.*	ragazza,*f.*	doncella,*f.*	tös,*nn.*	moyd,*f.*
last (after all others, *adv.*)	en dernier lieu	zuletzt	finalmente	al final	sist	tsu letst
last (final, *adj.*)	dernier, -nière	letzte(r, -s)	ultimo	último	sist	letst
last (most recent, *adj.*)	dernier, -nière	vorig	ultimo	último	senast	fargangen
last (most recently, *adv.*)	en dernier lieu	am letzten	ultimamente	últimamente	senast	tsu letst
last (continue), to	durer	dauern	durare	durar	vara	gedoyern
last (withstand use), to	tenir	bewähren, sich	conservarsi	durar	hålla sig	haltn zikh
latch	loquet,*m.*	Klinke,*f.*	stanghetta,*f.*	pestillo,*m.*	dörrklinka,*nn.*	ruker,*m.*
late (at relative time, *adv.*)	tard	spät	tardi	tarde	sent	shpet
late (deceased, *adj.*)	feu	selig	defunto	difunto	avliden	farshtorbn
late (overdue, *adj.*)	en retard	verspätet	in ritardo	tardío	försenad	farshpetikt
late (tardily, *adv.*)	en retard	spät	in ritardo	tardíamente	för sent	shpet
Latin (*adj.*)	latin	lateinisch	latino	latino	latinsk	lataynish
latter (second of two, *adj.*)	dernier, -nière	letztere	secondo	último	senare	letster
laugh, to	rire	lachen	ridere	reír	skratta	lakhn
laughter	rire,*m.*	Gelächter,*n.*	risa,*f.pl.*	risa,*f.*	skratt,*n.*	gelekhter,*n.*
launch (set afloat), to	lancer	vom Stapel lassen	varare	botar al agua	sjösätta	aroplozn
launch (start), to	lancer	in Gang setzen	lanciare	dar principio a	sätta i gång	lozn in gang
laundry (articles laundered)	lessive,*f.*	Wäsche,*f.*	bucato,*m.*	ropa lavada,*f.*	tvätt,*nn.*	vesh,*f.*
laundry (commercial plant)	buanderie,*f.*	Wäscherei,*f.*	lavanderia,*f.*	lavandería,*f.*	tvättinrättning, *nn.*	vesheray,*f.*
law (governing code)	droit,*m.*	Recht,*n.*	legge,*f.*	ley,*f.*	lag,*nn.*	gezets,*n.*
law (statute)	loi,*f.*	Gesetz,*n.*	legge,*f.*	derecho escrito, *m.*	lag,*nn.*	gezets,*n.*
lawful	légal	gesetzmässig	legittimo	legal	laglig	gezetslekh
lawn	pelouse,*f.*	Rasen,*m.*	tappeto verde,*m.*	césped,*m.*	gräsmatta,*nn.*	lonke,*f.*
lawyer	avocat,*m.*	Advokat,*m.*	avvocato,*m.*	abogado,*m.*	advokat,*nn.*	advokat,*m.*
lay (put down), to	poser	legen	collocare	colocar	lägga	leygn
layer (thickness)	couche,*f.*	Schicht,*f.*	strato,*m.*	capa,*f.*	lager,*n.*	shikht,*f.*
lazy	paresseux, -seuse	faul	pigro	perezoso	lat	foyl
lead (metal)	plomb,*m.*	Blei,*n.*	piombo,*m.*	plomo,*m.*	bly,*n.*	blay,*n.*
lead (be in advance), to	mener	(vor)führen	precedere	ser el primero	leda	firn
lead (guide), to	conduire	führen	condurre	guiar	leda	firn
leadership (authority)	direction,*f.*	Führung,*f.*	direzione,*f.*	dirección,*f.*	ledning,*nn.*	firershaft,*f.*
leaf (*bot.*)	feuille,*f.*	Blatt,*n.*	foglia,*f.*	hoja,*f.*	löv,*n.*	blat,*n.*
league	ligue,*f.*	Bund,*m.*	lega,*f.*	liga,*f.*	förbund,*n.*	lige,*f.*
lean (thin)	maigre	mager	magro	magro	mager	moger
lean (bend), to	pencher, (se)	hinneigen, (sich)	inclinarsi	inclinarse	luta (sig)	beygn zikh
leap (bound)	bond,*m.*	Sprung,*m.*	balzo,*m.*	salto,*m.*	språng,*n.*	shprung,*m.*
leap (jump), to	sauter	springen	saltare	saltar	hoppa	shpringen
learn (acquire knowledge), to	apprendre	lernen	imparare	aprender	lära sig	lernen zikh
learn (find out), to	apprendre	erfahren	apprendere	enterarse de	få veta	dervisn zikh
lease (hold by lease), to	louer	mieten	affittare	arrendar	hyra	dingen
least (*adj.*)	(le) moindre	geringst	(il) minimo	mínimo	minst	mindst
least (*adv.*)	(le) moins	am wenigsten	(il) meno	menos	minst	tsum mindstn
least (*n.*)	moins,*m.*	Wenigste,*n.*	minimo,*m.*	mínimo,*m.*	(det) minsta,*n.*	(dos) mindste,*n.*
leather (*n.*)	cuir,*m.*	Leder,*n.*	cuoio,*m.*	cuero,*m.*	läder,*n.*	leder,*f.*
leave (depart), to	partir	abreisen	partire	partir	resa	avekgeyn
leave (let remain), to	laisser	(übrig)lassen	lasciare	dejar	lämna	iberlozn
lecture (speech)	conférence,*f.*	Vorlesung,*f.*	conferenza,*f.*	conferencia,*f.*	föredrag,*n.*	lektsye,*f.*
ledge	rebord,*m.*	Gesims,*n.,m.*	orlo,*m.*	borde,*m.*	list,*nn.*	rand,*m.*
left (*adj.*)	gauche	link	sinistro	izquierdo	vänster	link
left (*adv.*)	(à) gauche	links	a sinistra	a la izquierda	till vänster	links
left (*n.*)	gauche,*f.*	Linke,*f.*	sinistra,*f.*	izquierda,*f.*	vänster hand	links
leg (*anat.*)	jambe,*f.*	Bein,*n.*	gamba,*f.*	pierna,*f.*	ben,*n.*	fus,*m.*
legal	légal	gesetzlich	legale	legal	laglig	legal
legend (story)	légende,*f.*	Legende,*f.*	leggenda,*f.*	leyenda,*f.*	legend,*nn.*	legende,*f.*
legislation	législation,*f.*	Gesetzgebung,*f.*	legislazione,*f.*	legislación,*f.*	lagstifning,*nn.*	gezets-gebung,*f.*
legislature	législature,*f.*	gesetzgebende Körperschaft,*f.*	legislatura,*f.*	legislatura,*f.*	lagstiftande församling,*nn.*	legislatur,*f.*
leisure	loisir,*m.*	Musse,*f.*	agio,*m.*	ocio,*m.*	fritid,*nn.*	fraytsayt,*f.*
lemon	citron,*m.*	Zitrone,*f.*	limone,*m.*	limón,*m.*	citron,*nn.*	limene,*f.*
lemonade	citronnade,*f.*	Limonade,*f.*	limonata,*f.*	limonada,*f.*	lemonad,*nn.*	limonad,*m.*

English	French	German	Italian	Spanish	Swedish	Yiddish
lend, to	prêter	(ver)leihen	prestare	prestar	låna (ut)	layen
length	longueur, f.	Länge, f.	lunghezza, f.	largo, m.	längd, nn.	leng, f.
Lent	Carême, m.	Fastenzeit, f.	quaresima, f.	cuaresma, f.	fastan, nn. def.	fasttsayt, f.
leopard	léopard, m.	Leopard, m.	leopardo, m.	leopardo, m.	leopard, nn.	lempert, m.
leprosy	lèpre, f.	Aussatz, m.	lebbra, f.	lepra, f.	spetälska, nn.	tsoraas, f.
less (adj.)	moindre	weniger	meno	menos	mindre	vintsiker
less (adv.)	moins	weniger	meno	menos	mindre	vintsiker
less (minus, prep.)	moins	weniger	meno	menos	minus	minus
lessen (make less), to	amoindrir	vermindern	diminuire	disminuir	minska	farminern
lesson (assignment)	leçon, f.	Aufgabe, f.	lezione, f.	lección, f.	läxa, nn.	lektsye, f.
lest	de peur que	damit...nicht	per tema che	para que no	för att inte	kedey nit
let (permit), to	laisser	lassen	permettere	dejar	låta	lozn
letter (character)	lettre, f.	Buchstabe, m.	lettera, f.	letra, f.	bokstav, nn. (pl. -stäver)	os, m.
letter (epistle)	lettre, f.	Brief, m.	lettera, f.	carta, f.	brev, n.	briv, m.
lettuce	laitue, f.	(Kopf)Salat, m.	lattuga, f.	lechuga, f.	(grön)sallad, nn.	salat, m.
level (flat)	plat	eben	piano	plano	jämn	glaykh
level (plane, n.)	niveau, m.	Höhe, f.	livello, m.	nivel, m.	plan, n.	madreyge, f.
lever	levier, m.	Hebel, m.	leva, f.	palanca, f.	spak, nn.	heyber, m.
liability (responsibility)	responsabilité, f.	Haftpflicht, f.	responsabilità, f.	responsabilidad, f.	ansvar, n.	akhrayes, f.
liable (responsible)	responsable	haftbar	responsabile	responsable	ansvarig	olel
liar	menteur, m.	Lügner, m.	bugiardo, m.	embustero, m.	lögnare, nn.	ligner, m.
liberal (polit., adj.)	libéral	liberal	liberale	liberal	liberal	liberal
liberate, to	libérer	befreien	liberare	libertar	befria	bafrayen
liberty (freedom)	liberté, f.	Freiheit, f.	libertà, f.	libertad, f.	frihet, nn.	frayhayt, f.
librarian	bibliothécaire, m.	Bibliothekar, m.	bibliotecario, m.	bibliotecario, m.	bibliotekarie, nn.	bibliotekar, m.
library	bibliothèque, f.	Bibliothek, f.	biblioteca, f.	biblioteca, f.	bibliotek, n.	bibliotek, f.
license (permit)	permis, m.	Bescheinigung, f.	patente, f.	licencia, f.	licens, nn.	litsents, f.
lick (lap), to	lécher	lecken	leccare	lamer	slicka	lekn
lid (cover)	couvercle, m.	Deckel, m.	coperchio, m.	tapa, f.	lock, n.	dek, f.
lie	mensonge, m.	Lüge, f.	bugia, f.	embuste, m.	lögn, nn.	lign, m.
lie (be located), to	trouver, se	liegen	trovarsi	estar	ligga	lign
lie (be prone), to	être étendu	liegen	giacere	tenderse	ligga	lign
lie (prevaricate), to	mentir	lügen	mentire	mentir	ljuga	lign zogn
lie down, to	étendre, s'	hinlegen, sich	coricarsi	acostarse	lägga sig	leygn zikh
lieutenant	lieutenant, m.	Leutnant, m.	tenente, m.	teniente, m.	löjtnant, nn.	leytenant, m.
life	vie, f.	Leben, n.	vita, f.	vida, f.	liv, n.	lebn, n.
lift (raise), to	lever	(auf)heben	sollevare	levantar	lyfta	heybn
light (bright)	clair	hell	chiaro	claro	ljus	likhtik
light (illumination)	lumière, f.	Licht, n.	luce, f.	luz, f.	ljus, n.	likht, n.
light (of little weight)	léger, -gère	leicht	leggero	ligero	lätt	gring
light (illuminate), to	éclairer	beleuchten	illuminare	iluminar	upplysa	balaykhtn
light (set fire to), to	allumer	anzünden	accendere	encender	tända	ontsindn
lightning	foudre, f.	Blitz, m.	fulmine, m.	relámpago, m.	blixt, nn.	blits, m.
like (adj.)	semblable	gleich	simile	semejante	lik	enlekh
like (adv.)	comme	wie	come	como	på samma sätt	vi
like (be fond of), to	aimer	gern haben	...piacere (a) (see p. 2955)	gustarle (a uno) (see p. 3019)	tycka om	lib hobn
likely (probable, adj.)	probable	wahrscheinlich	probabile	probable	sannolik	mashmoes
likewise (also)	de même	ebenfalls	similmente	también	också	des glaykhn
lilac (flower)	lilas, m.	Flieder, m.	lillà, f.	lila, f.	syren, nn.	bez, m.
lily	lis, m.	Lilie, f.	giglio, m.	lirio, m.	lilja, nn.	lilye, f.
Lima	Lima, f.	Lima, n.	Lima, f.	Lima	Lima, n.	Lima, n.
limb (anat.)	membre, m.	Glied, n.	membro, m.	miembro, m.	lem, nn.	eyver, m.
lime (fruit)	lime, f.	Limette, f.	cedro, m.	limón, m.	limon, nn.	laym, m.
limestone	pierre à chaux, f.	Kalkstein, m.	calcare, m.	piedra caliza, f.	kalksten, nn.	kalkhshteyn, m.
limit	limite, f.	Grenze, f.	limite, m.	límite, m.	gräns, nn.	gvul, m.
limit, to	limiter	beschränken	limitare	limitar	begränsa	bagrenetsn
limp (flaccid)	flasque	schlaff	floscio	flojo	slapp	shlaberik
limp (walk lamely), to	boiter	hinken	zoppicare	cojear	halta	hinken
line (cord)	ligne, f.	Leine, f.	corda, f.	cuerda, f.	lina, nn.	shtrik, m.
line (mark)	ligne, f.	Linie, f.	linea, f.	línea, f.	streck, n.	linye, f.
line (row)	ligne, f.	Reihe, f.	fila, f.	fila, f.	rad, nn.	shure, f.
linen (fabric)	toile (de lin), f.	Leinen, n.	tela di lino, f.	lino, m.	linne, n.	layvnt, m.
liner, ocean	paquebot trans- atlantique, m.	Überseedamp- fer, m.	piroscafo, m.	vapor de travesía, m.	oceanbåt, nn.	okean-shif, f.
linger (tarry), to	attarder, s'	verweilen	soffermarsi	demorarse	dröja	zamen zikh
lining	doublure, f.	Futter, n.	fodera, f.	forro, m.	foder, n.	untershlok, m.
link (connecting part)	lien, m.	(Ketten)Glied, n.	anello, m.	eslabón, m.	länk, nn.	bindglid, m.
linoleum	linoléum, m.	Linoleum, n.	linoleo, m.	linóleo, m.	linoleum, n.	linoleum, n.
lion	lion, m.	Löwe, m.	leone, m.	león, m.	lejon, n.	leyb, m.
lip (anat.)	lèvre, f.	Lippe, f.	labbro, m. (pl. labbra, f.)	labio, m.	läpp, nn.	lip, f.
lipstick	rouge à lèvres, m.	Lippenstift, m.	matita per labbra, f.	lápiz para los labios, m.	läppstift, n.	lipnshtift, m.
liqueur	liqueur, f.	Likör, m.	liquore, m.	pluscafé, m.	likör, nn.	liker, m.
liquid (n.)	liquide, m.	Flüssigkeit, f.	liquido, m.	líquido, m.	vätska, nn.	flisikayt, f.
liquor (alcoholic beverage)	alcool, m.	geistiges Get- ränk, n.	bibita alcolica, f.	licor, m.	sprit, nn.	alkohol, m.
list	liste, f.	Liste, f.	lista, f.	lista, f.	lista, nn.	reshime, f.
listen (hearken), to	écouter	zuhören	ascoltare	escuchar	lyssna	aynhern zikh

English	French	German	Italian	Spanish	Swedish	Yiddish
literary	littéraire	literarisch	letterario	literario	litterär	literarish
literature (belles-lettres)	littérature, f.	Literatur, f.	letteratura, f.	literatura, f.	litteratur, nn.	literatur, f.
lithography	lithographie, f.	Lithographie, f.	litografia, f.	litografía, f.	litografi, nn.	litografye, f.
litigation	litige, m.	Streitigkeit, f.	litigio, m.	litigación, f.	rättstvist, nn.	lodenish, f.
litter (stretcher)	civière, f.	Tragbahre, f.	barella, f.	camilla, f.	bår, nn.	trogbetl, n.
little (not much, adj.)	peu de	wenig	poco	poco	lite(t)	vintsik
little (slightly, adv.)	(un) peu	wenig	poco	poco	lite(t)	vintsik
little (small, adj.)	petit	klein	piccolo	pequeño	liten	kleyn
little (small amount, n.)	peu, m.	wenig	poco, m.	poco, m.	smula, nn.	vintsik
live (adj.)	vivant	lebendig	vivo	vivo	levande	lebedik
live (be alive), to	vivre	leben	vivere	vivir	leva	lebn
live (dwell), to	demeurer	wohnen	abitare	vivir	bo	voynen
lively (adj.)	animé	lebhaft	vivace	vivo	livlig	rirevdik
liver (anat.)	foie, m.	Leber, f.	fegato, m.	hígado, m.	lever, nn.	leber, f.
living (livelihood)	vie, f.	(Lebens)Unterhalt, m.	(la) vita, f.	subsistencia, f.	uppehälle, n.	parnose, f.
load (burden)	charge, f.	Last, f.	carico, m.	carga, f.	börda, nn.	mase, f.
load (fill), to	charger	laden	caricare	cargar	lasta	onlodn
loaf	pain, m.	Laib, m.	pane, m.	hogaza, f.	lev, nn.	labn, m.
loaf, to	flâner	faulenzen	oziare	holgazanear	slå dank	geyn leydik
loan	prêt, m.	Anleihe, f.	prestito, m.	préstamo, m.	lån, n.	halvoe, f.
lobster	homard, m.	Hummer, m.	aragosta, f.	langosta, f.	hummer, nn.	homar, m.
local (regional)	local	örtlich	locale	local	lokal	lokal
locality (place)	localité, f.	Ort, m.	località, f.	localidad, f.	plats, nn.	ort, n.
locate (find), to	trouver	ausfindig machen	trovare	encontrar	finna	gefinen
location (place)	situation, f.	Lage, f.	luogo, m.	colocación, f.	läge, n.	ort, n.
lock (fastening)	serrure, f.	Schloss, n.	serratura, f.	cerradura, f.	lås, n.	shlos, m.
lock (fasten with key), to	fermer à clef	(ver)schliessen	chiudere a chiave	cerrar con llave	låsa	farshlisn
locomotive	locomotive, f.	Lokomotive, f.	locomotiva, f.	locomotora, f.	lokomotiv, n.	lokomotiv, m.
lodge (cabin)	maisonnette, f.	Jagdhaus, n.	cabina, f.	casa de campo, f.	stuga, nn.	hayzl, n.
lodge (reside), to	demeurer	wohnen	alloggiare	vivir	bo	aynshteyn
lodging (temporary quarters)	logement, m.	Unterkunft, f.	alloggio, m.	hospedaje, m.	logi, n.	kvartir, f.
lofty (high)	élevé	hoch	elevato	elevado	hög	gehoybn
log (rough timber)	bûche, f.	Klotz, m.	ceppo, m.	leño, m.	stock, nn.	klots, m.
London	Londres, m.	London, n.	Londra, f.	Londres	London, n.	London, n.
lone (solitary)	solitaire	einsam	solo	solitario	ensam	eyntsik
lonely (lonesome)	solitaire	einsam	solitario	solo	enslig	elnt
lonely (unfrequented)	désert	verlassen	solitario	solitario	enslig	elnt
lonesome	seul	einsam	solitario	solo	ensam	elnt
long (not short)	long, -ue	lang	lungo	largo	lång	lang
long (of a specified length)	long, -ue	lang	lungo…	de largo	lång	lang
long for, to	avoir grande envie de	sehnen, sich	desiderare	anhelar	längta efter	benken nokh
look (aspect)	aspect, m.	Aussehen, n.	aspetto, m.	aspecto, m.	utseende, n.	oysze, m.
look (glance)	regard, m.	Blick, m.	sguardo, m.	mirada, f.	blick, nn.	kuk, m.
look (gaze), to	regarder	ansehen	guardare	mirar	titta	kukn
look (seem), to	avoir l'air	aussehen	sembrare	parecer	synas	oyszen
look for, to	chercher	suchen	cercare	buscar	leta efter	zukhn
loom	métier à tisser, m.	Webstuhl, m.	telaio, m.	telar, m.	vävstol, nn.	vebshtul, m.
loose (unbound)	délié	locker	sciolto	suelto	lös	loyz
lord (master)	seigneur, m.	Herr, m.	padrone, m.	señor, m.	herre, nn.	har, m.
lose, to	perdre	verlieren	perdere	perder	förlora	onvern
loss	perte, f.	Verlust, m.	perdita, f.	pérdida, f.	förlust, nn.	onver, m.
lot (salable items, bus.)	partie, f.	Partie, f.	partita, f.	lote, m.	parti, n.	skhum, m.
loud (resounding)	fort	laut	forte	fuerte	högljudd	hoykh
love	amour, m.	Liebe, f.	amore, m.	amor, m.	kärlek, nn.	libshaft, f.
love, to	aimer	lieben	amare	amar	älska	lib hobn
lover	amoureux, m.	Geliebte, m.,f.	innamorato, m.	amante, m.,f.	tillbedjare, nn.	libhober, m.
low	bas, -se	niedrig	basso	bajo	låg	niderik
lower (decrease), to	diminuer	herabsetzen	abbassare	disminuir	sänka	aroplozn
lower (let down), to	baisser	niederlassen	abbassare	bajar	sänka	aroplozn
loyal	loyal	treu	leale	leal	lojal	loyal
loyalty	loyauté, f.	Treue, f.	lealtà, f.	lealtad, f.	lojalitet, nn.	loyalkayt, f.
luck	chance, f.	Glück, n.	fortuna, f.	suerte, f.	tur, nn.	mazl, n.
lucky (fortunate)	heureux, -reuse	glücklich	fortunato	afortunado	lycklig	mazldik
luggage	bagages, m.pl.	Gepäck, n.	bagaglio, m.	equipaje, m.	bagage, n.	bagazh, m.
lull (calm)	accalmie, f.	(Ruhe)Pause, f.	calma, f.	calma, f.	lugnt ögonblick, n.	hafsoke, f.
lull (quiet), to	calmer	einschläfern	calmare	calmar	lugna	aynshtiln
lumber (timber)	bois de charpente, m.	Bauholz, n.	legname, m.	madera, f.	timmer, n.	gehilts, n.
lump (shapeless piece)	masse, f.	Klumpen, m.	blocco, m.	terrón, m.	klump, nn.	shtik, n.
lunch (midday meal)	déjeuner, m.	Mittagessen, n.	(seconda) colazione, f.	almuerzo, m.	lunch, nn.	onbaysn, m.
lung	poumon, m.	Lunge, f.	polmone, m.	pulmón, m.	lunga, nn.	lung, f.
lust (desire)	luxure, f.	Wollust, f.	concupiscenza, f.	lujuria, f.	åtrå, nn.	tayve, f.
luster (sheen)	lustre, m.	Glanz, m.	lustro, m.	lustre, m.	glans, nn.	glants, m.

English	French	German	Italian	Spanish	Swedish	Yiddish
luxury	luxe,*m.*	Luxus,*m.*	lusso,*m.*	lujo,*m.*	lyx,*nn.*	luksus,*m.*
machine	machine,*f.*	Maschine,*f.*	macchina,*f.*	máquina,*f.*	maskin,*nn.*	mashin,*f.*
machinery	machinerie,*f.*	Maschinerie,*f.*	macchinario,*m.*	maquinaria,*f.*	maskineri,*n.*	mashinerye,*f.*
mad (insane)	fou, folle	wahnsinnig	pazzo	loco	vansinnig	meshuge
madness (insanity)	folie,*f.*	Wahnsinn,*m.*	pazzia,*f.*	locura,*f.*	vansinne,*n.*	meshugaas,*f.*
Madrid	Madrid,*m.*	Madrid,*n.*	Madrid,*f.*	Madrid	Madrid,*n.*	Madrid,*m.*
magazine (periodical)	revue,*f.*	Zeitschrift,*f.*	rivista,*f.*	revista,*f.*	magasin,*n.*	zhurnal,*m.*
magic (*n.*)	magie,*f.*	Magie,*f.*	magia,*f.*	magia,*f.*	magi,*nn.*	kishef,*m.*
magician	magicien,*m.*	Zauberer,*m.*	mago,*m.*	mágico,*m.*	trollkarl,*nn.*	kishef-makher, *m.*
magnet	aimant,*m.*	Magnet,*m.*	calamita,*f.*	imán,*m.*	magnet,*nn.*	magnet,*m.*
magnificent	magnifique	herrlich	magnifico	magnífico	storartad	prakhtik
maid (servant)	bonne,*f.*	Dienstmädchen, *n.*	cameriera,*f.*	sirvienta,*f.*	hembiträde,*n.*	dinst,*f.*
maiden	jeune fille,*f.*	Jungfrau,*f.*	fanciulla,*f.*	joven soltera,*f.*	mö,*nn.*	bsule,*f.*
maiden name	nom de jeune fille,*m.*	Mädchenname, *m.*	nome di fan-ciulla,*m.*	apellido de sol-tera,*m.*	flicknamn,*n.*	meydlsher nomen,*m.*
mail (letters exchanged)	courrier,*m.*	Post,*f.*	corriere,*m.*	correspondencia, *f.*	post,*nn.*	post,*f.*
mail (postal system)	service des postes,*m.*	Postdienst,*m.*	posta,*f.*	correo,*m.*	post,*nn.*	post,*f.*
mail (post), to	mettre à la poste	mit der Post sen-den	impostare	echar al correo	posta	avekshikn
main (principal)	principal	Haupt-...	principale	principal	huvudsaklig	hoypt-...
maintain (preserve), to	maintenir	(bei)behalten	mantenere	mantener	bibehålla	oyfhitn
majesty	majesté,*f.*	Majestät,*f.*	maestà,*f.*	majestad,*f.*	majestät,*n.*	mayestet,*f.*
major (larger)	majeur	grösser	maggiore	mayor	större	greser
majority (greater number)	majorité,*f.*	Mehrheit,*f.*	maggioranza,*f.*	mayoría,*f.*	flertal,*n.*	merhayt,*f.*
make, to	faire	machen	fare	hacer	göra	makhn
malaria	paludisme,*m.*	Sumpffieber,*n.*	malaria,*f.*	malaria,*f.*	malaria,*nn.*	malarye,*f.*
male (*adj.*)	mâle	männlich	maschio	macho	manlig	menlekh
male (*zool., n.*)	mâle,*m.*	Männchen,*n.*	maschio,*m.*	macho,*m.*	hanne,*nn.*	zokher,*m.*
malice	malice,*f.*	Bosheit,*f.*	malizia,*f.*	malicia,*f.*	illvilja,*nn.*	rishes,*f.*
man	homme,*m.*	Mann,*m.*	uomo,*m.*	hombre,*m.*	man,*nn.(pl.* män)	man,*m.*
manage (administer), to	gérer	leiten	gestire	dirigir	sköta	onfirn mit
manage (contrive), to	arriver	zustandebringen	arrivare	manejar	lyckas	gerotn
management (administra-tion)	direction,*f.*	Leitung,*f.*	direzione,*f.*	dirección,*f.*	ledning,*nn.*	onfirung,*f.*
manager (administrator)	directeur,*m.*	(Betriebs)Leiter, *m.*	direttore,*m.*	administrador, *m.*	chef,*nn.*	farvalter,*m.*
mane (of horse)	crinière,*f.*	Mähne,*f.*	criniera,*f.*	crin,*f.*	man,*nn.*	grive,*f.*
manifest (*adj.*)	manifeste	offenkundig	manifesto	manifiesto	uppenbar	bashaymperlekh
mankind	humanité,*f.*	Menschheit,*f.*	genere umano,*m.*	humanidad,*f.*	mänskligheten, *nn. def.*	mentshhayt,*f.*
manly	viril	mannhaft	virile	varonil	manlig	gvuredik
manner (mode)	manière,*f.*	Weise,*f.*	maniera,*f.*	manera,*f.*	sätt,*n.*	oyfn,*m.*
manners (polite behavior)	manières,*f.pl.*	Manieren,*pl.*	maniere,*f.pl.*	modales,*m.pl.*	hyfsning,*nn.*	manirn,*pl.*
manual (by hand)	manuel, -le	mit der Hand	manuale	manual	hand-...	hant-...
manual (small book)	manuel,*m.*	Handbuch,*n.*	manuale,*m.*	manual,*m.*	handbok,*nn. (pl.* -böcker)	hantbukh,*n.*
manufacture, to	fabriquer	herstellen	fabbricare	fabricar	tillverka	oysarbetn
manufacturer	fabricant,*m.*	Fabrikant,*m.*	fabbricante,*m.,f.*	fabricante,*m.*	fabrikant,*nn.*	fabrikant,*m.*
many, more, most	beaucoup (de), plus (de), (la) plupart (de)	viele, mehr, (die) meist(en)	molti, più, (il) più di	muchos, más, (el) más	många, flera, (de) flesta	a sakh, merer, (dos) merste
map	carte,*f.*	(Land)Karte,*f.*	carta,*f.*	mapa,*m.*	karta,*nn.*	klon,*m.*
maple (tree)	érable,*m.*	Ahorn,*m.*	acero,*m.*	arce,*m.*	lönn,*nn.*	tsekrimen
mar (disfigure), to	gâcher	entstellen	sfigurare	desfigurar	vanpryda	tsekrimen
marble (mineral)	marbre,*m.*	Marmor,*m.*	marmo,*m.*	mármol,*m.*	marmor,*nn.*	mirmlshteyn,*m.*
march, to	marcher	marschieren	marciare	marchar	marschera	marshirn
mare	jument,*f.*	Stute,*f.*	cavalla,*f.*	yegua,*f.*	sto,*n.*	klatshe,*f.*
margarine	margarine,*f.*	Margarine,*f.*	margarina,*f.*	margarina,*f.*	margarin,*n.*	margarin,*m.*
margin (edge)	bord,*m.*	Rand,*m.*	margine,*f.*	margen,*m.*	kant,*nn.*	gilyen,*m.*
margin (surplus)	marge,*f.*	Spielraum,*m.*	soprappiù,*m.*	sobrante,*m.*	marginal,*nn.*	oydef,*m.*
marine (oceanic)	marin	See-...	marino	marino	havs-...	yam-...
mark (evidence)	marque,*f.*	Spur,*f.*	marca,*f.*	huella,*f.*	spår,*n.*	simen,*m.*
mark (symbol)	marque,*f.*	Merkmal,*n.*	segno,*m.*	símbolo,*m.*	märke,*n.*	simen,*m.*
mark (designate), to	marquer	bezeichnen	marcare	señalar	markera	batseykhenen
market (trading center)	marché,*m.*	Markt,*m.*	mercato,*m.*	mercado,*m.*	marknad(splats), *nn.*	mark,*m.*
marriage	mariage,*m.*	Ehe,*f.*	matrimonio,*m.*	matrimonio,*m.*	äktenskap,*n.*	zivegshaft,*f.*
married	marié	verheiratet	sposato	casado	gift	khasene gehat
marry, to	marier (avec), se	vermählen, sich mit...	sposare	casarse (con)	gifta sig med	khasene hobn (mit)
marsh	marais,*m.*	Sumpf,*f.*	palude,*f.*	pantano,*m.*	kärr,*n.*	zump,*m.*
marvel	merveille,*f.*	Wunder,*n.*	maraviglia,*f.*	maravilla,*f.*	under,*n.*	vunder,*m.*
marvelous	merveilleux, -leuse	wunderbar	maraviglioso	maravilloso	underbar	vunderlekh
masculine	masculin	männlich	maschile	masculino	maskulin	menlekh
mask (face covering)	masque,*m.*	Larve,*f.*	maschera,*f.*	máscara,*f.*	mask,*nn.*	maske,*f.*
mason (stonelayer)	maçon,*m.*	Maurer,*m.*	muratore,*m.*	albañil,*m.*	murare,*nn.*	muler,*m.*
mass (matter)	masse,*f.*	Masse,*f.*	massa,*f.*	masa,*f.*	massa,*nn.*	mase,*f.*
mass (*rel.*)	messe,*f.*	Messe,*f.*	messa,*f.*	misa,*f.*	mässa,*nn.*	mese,*f.*
mast	mât,*m.*	Mast,*m.*	albero,*m.*	mástil,*m.*	mast,*nn.*	mastboym,*m.*
master (great artist)	maître,*m.*	Meister,*m.*	maestro,*m.*	maestro,*m.*	mästare,*nn.*	mayster,*m.*

English	French	German	Italian	Spanish	Swedish	Yiddish
master (one in authority)	maître,*m.*	Herr,*m.*	padrone,*m.*	amo,*m.*	herre,*nn.*	balebos,*m.*
master (learn), to	maîtriser	beherrschen	vincere le diffi-coltà di	dominar	lära sig	bahershn
match (lucifer)	allumette,*f.*	Streichholz,*n.*	fiammifero,*m.*	fósforo,*m.*	tändsticka,*nn.*	shvebele,*n.*
match (equal), to	égaler	angleichen	eguagliare	igualar a	motsvara	pasn zikh
mate (find mate for), to	apparier	paaren	accoppiare	aparear	para	tsunoyfporn
material (substance)	matière,*f.*	Stoff,*m.*	materia,*f.*	material,*m.*	material,*n.*	tsunoyfporn
mathematics	mathématiques, *f.pl.*	Mathematik,*f.*	matematica,*f.*	matemática,*f.*	matematik,*nn.*	materyal,*m.* matematik,*f.*
matinee (theater performance)	matinée,*f.*	Nachmittagsvor-stellung,*f.*	recita diurna,*f.*	matiné,*m.*	matiné,*nn.*	matine,*m.*
matter (affair)	affaire,*f.*	Sache,*f.*	affare,*m.*	asunto,*m.*	sak,*nn.*	inyen,*m.*
matter (substance)	matière,*f.*	Stoff,*m.*	materia,*f.*	materia,*f.*	ämne,*n.*	materye,*f.*
mattress	matelas,*m.*	Matratze,*f.*	materasso,*m.*	colchón,*m.*	madrass,*nn.*	matrats,*m.*
mature (fall due), to	échoir	fällig werden	scadere	vencer	förfalla	felik vern
mature (ripen), to	mûrir	reifen	maturare	madurar	mogna	tsaytik vern
maturity (due date, *bus.*)	échéance,*f.*	Fälligkeit,*f.*	scadenza,*f.*	vencimiento,*m.*	förfallodag,*nn.*	termin,*m.*
may (*v.*)	(*see p. 2832*)	(*see p. 2895*)	(*see p. 2954*)	(*see p. 3017 ff.*)	(*see p. 3078*)	(*no equiv.*)
maybe	peut-être	vielleicht	forse	quizás	kanske	efsher
mayor	maire,*m.*	Bürgermeister, *m.*	sindaco,*m.*	alcalde,*m.*	borgmästare,*nn.*	birger-mayster, *m.*
me	me; moi (*see p. 2826 ff.*)	mich; mir (*see p. 2890 ff.*)	mi; me (*see p. 2947 ff.*)	me; mi (*see p. 3012*)	mig (*see p. 3075*)	mir; mikh (*see p. 3132*)
meadow	prairie,*f.*	Wiese,*f.*	prato,*m.*	pradera,*f.*	äng,*nn.*	lonke,*f.*
meal (repast)	repas,*m.*	Mahlzeit,*f.*	pasto,*m.*	comida,*f.*	måltid,*nn.*	moltsayt,*m.*
mean (malicious)	vilain	boshaft	meschino	maléfico	elak	rishesdik
mean (have in mind), to	vouloir dire	meinen	voler dire	querer decir	mena	meynen
mean (intend), to	avoir l'intention de	beabsichtigen	avere l'intenzione	tener intención	ämna	rekhenen
meaning (sense)	sens,*m.*	Sinn,*m.*	significato,*m.*	sentido,*m.*	betydelse,*nn.*	batayt,*m.*
means (method)	moyen(s),*m.*(*pl.*)	Mittel,*n.*	mezzo,*m.*	modo,*m.*	sätt,*nn.*	mitl,*n.*
meantime (*n.*)	entre-temps,*m.*	Zwischenzeit,*f.*	frattempo,*m.*	ínterin,*m.*	mellantid,*nn.*	tsvishntsayt,*f.*
meanwhile (*adv.*)	en attendant	inzwischen	intanto	mientras tanto	under tiden	dervayl
measles	rougeole,*f.*	Masern,*pl.*	rosolia,*f.*	sarampion,*m.*	mässlingen (*def.*),*nn.*	mozlen,*pl.*
measure (dimensions)	mesure,*f.*	Mass,*n.*	misura,*f.*	medida,*f.*	mått,*n.*	mos,*f.*
measure (find size of), to	mesurer	messen	misurare	medir	mäta	mestn
meat	viande,*f.*	Fleisch,*n.*	carne,*f.*	carne,*f.*	kött,*n.*	fleysh,*n.*
mechanic	mécanicien,*m.*	Mechaniker,*m.*	meccanico,*m.*	mecánico,*m.*	mekaniker,*nn.*	mekhaniker,*m.*
mechanical	mécanique	mechanisch	meccanico	mecánico	mekanisk	mekhanish
medal	médaille,*f.*	Orden,*m.*	medaglia,*f.*	medalla,*f.*	medalj,*nn.*	medal,*m.*
meddle, to	mêler (de), se	einmischen, sich	immischiarsi	meterse	lägga sig i	mishn zikh
medical	médical	ärztlich	medico	médico	medicinsk	meditsinish
medicine (medical science)	médecine,*f.*	Medizin,*f.*	medicina,*f.*	medicina,*f.*	medicin,*nn.*	meditsin,*f.*
medicine (medicament)	médicament,*m.*	Arznei,*f.*	medicina,*f.*	medicina,*f.*	medicin,*nn.*	meditsin,*f.*
meditate (reflect), to	méditer	nachdenken	meditare	meditar	meditera	denken
Mediterranean Sea	Mer Méditer-ranée,*f.*	Mittelländisches Meer,*n.*	Mare Mediter-raneo,*m.*	mar Mediter-ráneo,*m.*	Medelhavet,*n.*	Mitlendisher Yam,*m.*
medium (means)	moyen,*m.*	Mittel,*n.*	mezzo,*m.*	medio,*m.*	medel,*n.*	medyum,*m.*
meet (be introduced to), to	faire la connais-sance de	kennenlernen	essere presentato a	ser presentado a	träffa	bakenen zikh mit
meet (come together), to	réunir, se	zusammentreffen	incontrarsi (con)	reunirse	träffas	trefn zikh
meet (encounter), to	rencontrer	treffen, (sich)	incontrare	encontrar	möta	trefn
meeting (assembly)	réunion,*f.*	Tagung,*f.*	riunione,*f.*	reunión,*f.*	möte,*n.*	farzamlung,*f.*
melancholy (dejection)	mélancolie,*f.*	Schwermut,*m.*	malinconia,*f.*	melancolía,*f.*	melankoli,*nn.*	melankholye,*f.*
melt (become liquid), to	fondre	schmelzen	fondere	derretirse	smälta	tseshmoltsn vein
member (one of a group)	membre,*m.*	Mitglied,*n.*	membro,*m.*	miembro,*m.*	medlem,*nn.*	mitglid,*m.*
memorandum	mémorandum,*m.*	Merkzettel,*m.*	pro-memoria,*m.*	memorándum,*m.*	promemoria,*nn.*	memorandum, *m.*
memorial (*n.*)	monument,*m.*	Denkmal,*n.*	commemora-zione,*f.*	obra conmemo-rativa,*f.*	minnesmärke,*n.*	denkmol,*m.*
memory (ability to recall)	mémoire,*f.*	Gedächtnis,*n.*	memoria,*f.*	memoria,*f.*	minne,*n.*	zikorn,*m.*
memory (recollection)	souvenir,*m.*	Erinnerung,*f.*	ricordo,*m.*	memoria,*f.*	minne,*n.*	zikhroynes,*pl*
mend (repair), to	réparer	flicken	accomodare	reparar	laga	farrikhtn
mental	mental	geistig	mentale	mental	själslig	gaystik
mention, to	mentionner	erwähnen	menzionare	mencionar	nämna	dermonen
menu	carte,*f.*	Speisekarte,*f.*	lista (delle vivande),*f.*	menú,*m.*	matsedel,*nn.*	menyu,*m.*
mercantile	mercantile	kaufmännisch	commerciale	mercantil	merkantil	handls-...
merchandise	marchandise(s), *f.*(*pl.*)	Ware,*f.*	merce,*f.*	mercaderías,*f. pl.*	varor,*nn.pl.*	skhoyre,*f.*
merchant	commerçant,*m.*	Kaufmann,*m.*	mercante,*m.*	comerciante,*m.*	köpman,*nn.*(*pl. -män*)	soykher,*m.*
merciful	clément	barmherzig	clemente	misericordioso	barmhärtig	merakhemdik
mercury	mercure,*m.*	Quecksilber,*n.*	mercurio,*m.*	mercurio,*m.*	kvicksilver,*n.*	kvekzilber,*n.*
mercy	miséricorde,*f.*	Gnade,*f.*	misericordia,*f.*	misericordia,*f.*	barmhärtighet, *nn.*	rakhmim,*pl.*
mere	seul	bloss	semplice	mero	bara	bloyz
merely	seulement	bloss	semplicemente	meramente	bara	bloyz
merit	mérite,*m.*	Verdienst,*n.*	merito,*m.*	mérito,*m.*	förtjänst,*nn.*	mayle,*f.*
merit, to	mériter	verdienen	meritare	merecer	förtjäna	fardinen
merry	gai	fröhlich	allegro	alegre	munter	freylekh
mess (muddle)	gâchis,*m.*	Unordnung,*f.*	imbroglio,*m.*	confusión,*f.*	röra,*nn.*	balagan,*m.*
message (communication)	message,*m.*	Mitteilung,*f.*	comunicazione,*f.*	mensaje,*m.*	meddelande,*n.*	yedie,*f.*
messenger (courier)	messager,*m.*	Bote,*m.*	messaggero,*m.*	mensajero,*m.*	bud,*n.*	sholiakh,*m.*
metal (*n.*)	métal,*m.*	Metall,*n.*	metallo,*m.*	metal,*m.*	metall,*nn.*	metal,*m.*
method	méthode,*f.*	Methode,*f.*	metodo,*m.*	método,*m.*	metod,*nn.*	metod,*m.*

English	French	German	Italian	Spanish	Swedish	Yiddish
Mexican (*adj.*)	mexicain	mexikanisch	messicano	mejicano	mexikansk	meksikanish
Mexico	Mexique,*m.*	Mexiko,*n.*	Messico,*m.*	Méjico	Mexiko,*n.*	Meksike,*f.*
Mexico City	Mexico,*m.*	Mexiko,*n.*	Messico,*m.*	Méjico	Mexiko City,*n.*	Shtot Meksike, *f.*
middle (center)	milieu,*m.*	Mitte,*f.*	mezzo,*m.*	medio,*m.*	mitt,*nn.*	mitn,*m.*
midnight	minuit,*m.,f.*	Mitternacht,*f.*	mezzanotte,*f.*	medianoche,*f.*	midnatt,*nn.*	halbe nakht,*f.*
might (*n.*)	puissance,*f.*	Macht,*f.*	potere,*m.*	poder,*m.*	makt,*nn.*	makht,*f.*
might (*v.*)	(*see p.* 2835)	(*see p.* 2895)	(*see p.* 2954)	(*see p.* 3017)	(*see p.* 3078)	(*see p.* 3134)
mighty (powerful)	puissant	mächtig	potente	poderoso	mäktig	mekhtik
mighty (vast)	vaste	mächtig	vasto	enorme	väldig	gvaldik
military (*adj.*)	militaire	militärisch	militare	militar	militär	militerish
milk	lait,*m.*	Milch,*f.*	latte,*m.*	leche,*f.*	mjölk,*nn.*	milkh,*f.*
mind (opinion)	avis,*m.*	Meinung,*f.*	avviso,*m.*	parecer,*m.*	mening,*nn.*	meynung,*f.*
mine (explosive)	mine,*f.*	Mine,*f.*	mina,*f.*	mina,*f.*	mina,*nn.*	mine,*f.*
mine (*poss. pron.*)	(*see p.* 2827)	mein	(*see p.* 2948)	(*see p.* 3012)	(*see p.* 3075)	mayner
mine (pit)	mine,*f.*	Bergwerk,*n.*	miniera,*f.*	mina,*f.*	gruva,*nn.*	grub,*f.*
mine (dig for), to	creuser	graben	scavare	extraer (minerales)	gräva	grobn
miner	mineur,*m.*	Bergmann,*m.*	minatore,*m.*	minero,*m.*	gruvarbetare,*nn.*	greber,*m.*
mineral	minéral,*m.*	Mineral,*n.*	minerale,*m.*	mineral,*m.*	mineral,*n.*	mineral,*m.*
minister (cabinet member)	ministre,*m.*	Minister,*m.*	ministro,*m.*	ministro,*m.*	minister,*nn.*	minister,*m.*
minister (clergyman)	pasteur,*m.*	Pfarrer,*m.*	ministro,*m.*	pastor,*m.*	präst,*nn.*	gaystlekher,*m.*
minor (lesser)	moindre	gering(er)	minore	menor	mindre	klener
minority (smaller number)	minorité,*f.*	Minderheit,*f.*	minoranza,*f.*	minoría,*f.*	minoritet,*nn.*	minderhayt,*f.*
minute (unit of time)	minute,*f.*	Minute,*f.*	minuto,*m.*	minuto,*m.*	minut,*nn.*	minut,*f.*
minutes (record)	procès-verbal,*m.*	Protokoll,*n.*	(processo) verbale,*m.*	actas,*f.pl.*	protokoll,*n.*	protokol,*m.*
miracle	miracle,*m.*	Wunder,*n.*	miracolo,*m.*	milagro,*m.*	under,*n.*	nes,*m.*
mire (bog)	bourbier,*m.*	Sumpf,*m.*	fango,*m.*	cieno,*m.*	kärr,*n.*	tvan,*m.*
mirror	miroir,*m.*	Spiegel,*m.*	specchio,*m.*	espejo,*m.*	spegel,*nn.*	shpigl,*m.*
mirth	hilarité,*f.*	Lustigkeit,*f.*	ilarità,*f.*	júbilo,*m.*	munterhet,*nn.*	simkhe,*f.*
miscellaneous	varié	vermischt	miscellaneo	misceláneo	diverse	farsheydn
mischief (harm)	mal,*m.*	Unfug,*m.*	danno,*m.*	daño,*m.*	ofog,*n.*	shodn,*m.*
miser	avare,*m.*	Geizhals,*m.*	avaro,*m.*	avaro,*m.*	gnidare,*nn.*	kamtsn,*m.*
miserable (unhappy)	malheureux, -reuse	elend	infelice	miserable	olycklig	oyf tsores
misery (grief)	désolation,*f.*	Elend,*n.*	afflizione,*f.*	miseria,*f.*	bedrövelse,*nn.*	tsores,*pl.*
misfortune	malheur,*m.*	Unglück,*n.*	sfortuna,*f.*	desgracia,*f.*	otur,*nn.*	umglik,*n.*
mislay, to	égarer	verlegen	smarrire	extraviar	förlägga	farleygn
Miss	Mlle.; Mademoiselle,*f.* (*pl.* Mlles.; Mesdemoiselles)	Fräulein,*n.*	(la) signorina,*f.*	srita.; (la) señorita,*f.*	Fröken,*nn.*	frayln,*n.*
miss (fail to do), to	rater	verfehlen	non riuscire a	dejar de	missa	farfeln
miss (feel the loss of), to	regretter	vermissen	sentire la mancanza di	echar de menos	sakna	benken nokh
missionary	missionnaire,*m.*	Missionar,*m.*	missionario,*m.*	misionero,*m.*	missionär,*nn.*	misyoner,*m.*
mist	brume,*f.*	Nebel,*m.*	nebbia,*f.*	neblina,*f.*	dimma,*nn.*	nepl,*m.*
mistake	erreur,*f.*	Fehler,*m.*	sbaglio,*m.*	error,*m.*	misstag,*n.*	toes,*m.*
mistress (paramour)	maîtresse,*f.*	Mätresse,*f.*	amante,*f.*	concubina,*f.*	älskarinna,*nn.*	metrese,*f.*
mitten	mitaine,*f.*	Fausthandschuh, *m.*	mezzo-guanto,*m.*	mitón,*m.*	vante,*nn.*	hentshke on finger,*f.*
mix (make blend), to	mêler	mischen	mischiare	mezclar	blanda	mishn
mixture	mélange,*m.*	Mischung,*f.*	mistura,*f.*	mezcla,*f.*	blandning,*nn.*	gemish,*m.*
moan, to	gémir	stöhnen	gemere	gemir	stöna	okhtsn
mob (disorderly crowd)	foule,*f.*	Pöbel,*m.*	turba,*f.*	populacho,*m.*	pöbel,*nn.*	hamoyn,*m.*
mock (deride), to	railler	verhöhnen	deridere	mofar	håna	khoyzekn fun
mode (manner)	mode,*f.*	Art,*f.*	modo,*m.*	modo,*m.*	sätt,*n.*	oyfn,*m.*
model (exemplar)	modèle,*m.*	Muster,*n.*	modello,*m.*	modelo,*m.*	mönster,*n.*	model,*m.*
model (small copy)	modèle,*m.*	Modell,*n.*	modello,*m.*	modelo,*m.*	modell,*nn.*	model,*m.*
moderate (not extreme)	moyen, -ne	mässig	moderato	moderado	medelmåttig	mesik
modern	moderne	modern	moderno	moderno	modern	modern
modest	modeste	bescheiden	modesto	modesto	blygsam	basheydn
moist	moite	feucht	umido	húmedo	fuktig	faykht
moisture	humidité,*f.*	Feuchtigkeit,*f.*	umidità,*f.*	humedad,*f.*	fuktighet,*nn.*	faykhtkayt,*f.*
molasses	mélasse,*f.*	Melasse,*f.*	melassa,*f.*	miel de caña,*f.*	melass,*nn.*	patike,*f.*
moldy	moisi	schimmelig	ammuffito	mohoso	möglig	farshimlt
mole (animal)	taupe,*f.*	Maulwurf,*m.*	talpa,*f.*	topo,*m.*	mullvad,*nn.*	krot,*m.*
moment (instant)	moment,*m.*	Augenblick,*m.*	momento,*m.*	momento,*m.*	ögonblick,*n.*	moment,*m.*
monarch	monarque,*m.*	Monarch,*m.*	monarca,*m.*	monarca,*m.*	monark,*nn.*	monarkh,*m.*
monastery	monastère,*m.*	Kloster,*n.*	monastero,*m.*	monasterio,*m.*	kloster,*n.*	monastir,*m.*
money	argent,*m.*	Geld,*n.*	denaro,*m.*	dinero,*m.*	pengar,*nn.pl.*	gelt,*n.*
money order	mandat,*m.*	Geldanweisung,*f.*	vaglia,*m.*	giro postal,*m.*	postanvisning, *nn.*	gelt-onvayzung, *f.*
monk	moine,*m.*	Mönch,*m.*	monaco,*m.*	monje,*m.*	munk,*nn.*	monakh,*m.*
monkey	singe,*m.*	Affe,*m.*	scimmia,*f.*	mono,*m.*	apa,*nn.*	malpe,*f.*
monotonous (boring)	monotone	eintönig	monotono	monótono	enformig	monoton
monster (beast)	monstre,*m.*	Ungeheuer,*n.*	mostro,*m.*	monstruo,*m.*	odjur,*n.*	farzeenish,*f.*
monstrous (horrible)	monstrueux, -euse	ungeheuer	mostruoso	monstruoso	gräslig	meuyemdik
Montevideo	Montevideo,*m.*	Montevideo,*n.*	Montevideo,*f.*	Montevideo	Montevideo,*n.*	Montevideo,*n.*
month	mois,*m.*	Monat,*m.*	mese,*m.*	mes,*m.*	månad,*nn.*	khoydesh,*m.*
monthly (every month, *adj.*)	mensuel, -le	monatlich	mensile	mensual	månatlig	khoydeshlekh

English	French	German	Italian	Spanish	Swedish	Yiddish
monument	monument,*m.*	Denkmal,*n.*	monumento,*m.*	monumento,*m.*	monument,*n.*	denkmol,*m.*
mood (humor)	humeur,*f.*	Stimmung,*f.*	umore,*m.*	humor,*m.*	humör,*n.*	shtimung,*f.*
moon	lune,*f.*	Mond,*m.*	luna,*f.*	luna,*f.*	måne,*nn.*	levone,*f.*
moonlight	clair de lune,*m.*	Mondlicht,*n.*	chiaro di luna,*m.*	luz de la luna,*f.*	månsken,*n.*	levone-likht,*n.*
moor (waste land)	lande,*f.*	Moor,*n.*	landa,*f.*	páramo,*m.*	hed,*nn.*	zump,*m.*
moral (ethical)	moral	sittlich	morale	moral	moralisk	moralish
morale	moral,*m.*	Mut,*m.*	morale,*f.*	moral,*f.*	anda,*nn.*	moral,*f.*
morals	moeurs,*f.pl.*	Moral,*f.*	moralità,*f.*	moral,*f.*	moral,*nn.*	moral,*f.*
more (*adj.*)	plus (de)	mehr	più	más	mer	merer
moreover	de plus	ausserdem	inoltre	además	dessutom	dertsu
morning	matin,*m.*	Morgen,*m.*	mattino,*m.*	mañana,*f.*	morgon,*nn.*(*pl.* morgnar)	frimorgn,*m.*
morrow	lendemain,*m.*	folgender Tag,*m.*	giorno dopo,*m.*	mañana,*f.*	följande dag,*nn.*	morgn,*m.*
morsel (small bit)	morceau,*m.*	Stückchen,*n.*	boccone,*m.*	bocado,*m.*	smula,*nn.*	shtikl,*n.*
mortal (*adj.*)	mortel, -le	sterblich	mortale	mortal	dödlig	shterblekh
mortgage	hypothèque,*f.*	Hypothek,*f.*	ipoteca,*f.*	hipoteca,*f.*	inteckning,*nn.*	hipotek,*f.*
Moscow	Moscou,*m.*	Moskau,*n.*	Mosca,*f.*	Moscú	Moskva,*n.*	Moskve,*f.*
mosquito	moustique,*m.*	Moskito,*m.*	zanzara,*f.*	mosquito,*m.*	mygga,*nn.*	komar,*m.*
moss	mousse,*f*	Moos,*n.*	muschio,*m.*	musgo,*m.*	mossa,*nn.*	mokh,*m.*
most (*adv.*)	(le) plus	am meisten	(il) più	más	mest	tsum merstn
most (almost all, *adj.*)	presque tout	meist	quasi tutto	casi todo	(de) flesta	s'rov
most (greatest quantity, *adj.*)	(la) plupart de	grösst-...	(la) massima parte di	(la) mayor parte de	mest	merste
most (*n.*)	(la) plupart,*f.*	(das) Meiste,*n.*	(la) massima parte,*f.*	(el) más,*m.*	(det) mesta,*n.*	(dos) merste,*n.*
mostly	pour la plupart	meistens	per la massima parte	principalmente	för det mesta	merstns
moth	mite,*f.*	Motte,*f.*	tarma,*f*	polilla,*f.*	mal,*nn.*	mol,*m.*
mother	mère,*f.*	Mutter,*f.*	madre,*f.*	madre,*f.*	mo(de)r,*nn.*(*pl.* mödrar)	muter,*f.*
mother-in-law	belle-mère,*f.*	Schwiegermutter,*f.*	suocera,*f.*	suegra,*f.*	svärmo(de)r,*nn.* (*pl.* -mödrar)	shviger,*f.*
motion (movement)	mouvement,*m.*	Bewegung,*f.*	movimento,*m.*	movimiento,*m.*	rörelse,*nn.*	bavegung,*f.*
motive (*n.*)	motif,*m.*	Beweggrund,*m.*	motivo,*m.*	motivo,*m.*	motiv,*n.*	motiv,*m.*
motley (diverse)	bigarré	bunt	misto	variado	brokig	farsheydn-farbik
motor (engine)	moteur,*m.*	Motor,*m.*	motore,*m.*	motor,*m.*	motor,*nn.*	motor,*m.*
motto	devise,*f.*	Wahlspruch,*m.*	motto,*m.*	mote,*m.*	motto,*n.*	moto,*m.*
mound (hill)	tertre,*m.*	Erdhügel,*m.*	poggio,*m.*	montículo,*m.*	kulle,*nn.*	bergele,*n.*
mount (climb upon), to	monter sur	besteigen	montare	montar	bestiga	aroyfkrikhn oyf
mountain	montagne,*f.*	Berg,*m.*	montagna,*f.*	montaña,*f.*	berg,*n.*	barg,*m.*
mountainous	montagneux, -neuse	gebirgig	montagnoso	montañoso	bergig	bargik
mourn (feel grief), to	pleurer	trauern	piangere	lamentar	sörja	troyern
mournful (saddening)	triste	traurig	lugubre	triste	sorglig	troyerik
mouse	souris,*f.*	Maus,*f.*	topo,*m.*	ratón,*m.*	mus,*nn.*(*pl.* möss)	moyz,*f.*
mouth (*anat.*)	bouche,*f.*	Mund,*m.*	bocca,*f.*	boca,*f.*	mun,*nn.*	moyl,*n.*
move (change residence), to	déménager	umziehen	sgomberare	mudarse	flytta	ariberklaybn zikh
move (shift one's position), to	déplacer, se	bewegen, sich	muoversi	moverse	flytta sig	iberrukn zikh
move (shift the position of), to	déplacer	bewegen	muovere	mover	flytta	iberrukn
movement (motion)	mouvement,*m.*	Bewegung,*f.*	movimento,*m.*	movimiento,*m.*	rörelse,*nn.*	bavegung,*f.*
movies	cinéma,*m.*	Kino,*n.*	cinema,*m.*	cine,*m.*	bio,*nn.*	kino,*m.*
Mr. (Mister)	M.; Monsieur, *m.*	Herr,*m.*	(il) signore,*m.*	sr.; (el) señor,*m.*	Herr,*nn.*	her,*m.*
Mrs. (Mistress)	Mme.; Madame,*f.*	Frau,*f.*	(la) signora,*f.*	sra.; (la) señora,*f.*	Fru,*nn.*	froy,*f.*
much, more, most	beaucoup (de), plus (de), (la) plupart (de)	viel, mehr, (der) meist(e)	molto, più, (il) più di	mucho, más, (el) más	mycket, mera, mest	a sakh, merer, tsum merstn
mud	boue,*f.*	Schlamm,*m.*	fango,*m.*	lodo,*m.*	smörja,*nn.*	blote,*f.*
mule	mulet,*m.*	Maulesel,*m.*	mulo,*m.*	mula,*f.*	mulåsna,*nn.*	moyleyzl,*m.*
multiply, to (*arith.*)	multiplier	multiplizieren	moltiplicare	multiplicar	multiplicera	keyflen
multiply (grow numerous), to	multiplier, se	vermehren, sich	moltiplicarsi	multiplicar	ökas	mern zikh
multitude	multitude,*f.*	Menge,*f.*	moltitudine,*f.*	multitud,*f.*	mängd,*nn.*	mase,*f.*
mumps	oreillons,*m.pl.*	Ziegenpeter,*m.*	orecchioni,*m.pl.*	parótidas,*f.pl.*	påssjuka,*nn.*	svinke,*f.*
murder	meurtre,*m.*	Mord,*m.*	assassinio,*m.*	asesinato,*m.*	mord,*n.*	mord,*m.*
murderer	meurtrier,*m.*	Mörder,*m.*	assassino,*m.*	asesino,*m.*	mördare,*nn.*	merder,*m.*
murmur, to	murmurer	murmeln	mormorare	murmurar	mumla	murmlen
muscle	muscle,*m.*	Muskel,*m.*	muscolo,*m.*	músculo,*m.*	muskel,*nn.*	muskl,*m.*
muse (meditate), to	méditer	nachsinnen	meditare	meditar	fundera	klern
museum	musée,*m.*	Museum,*n.*	museo,*m.*	museo,*m.*	museum,*nn.*	muzey,*m.*
mushroom (*n.*)	champignon,*m.*	Pilz,*m.*	fungo,*m.*	seta,*f.*	svamp,*nn.*	shveml,*n.*
music	musique,*f.*	Musik,*f.*	musica,*f.*	música,*f.*	musik,*nn.*	muzik,*f.*
musical	musical	musikalisch	musicale	musical	musikalisk	muzikalish
musician	musicien,*m.*	Musiker,*m.*	musicista,*m.*	músico,*m.*	musiker,*nn.*	muziker,*m.*
must (*v.*)	(*see* falloir, p. 2835)	(*see* müssen, p. 2892 ff.)	(*see* dovere, p. 2957)	deber	(*see* måste, p. 3078)	muzn
mustache	moustache(s),*f.* (*pl.*)	Schnurrbart,*m.*	baffi,*m.pl.*	bigote,*m.*	mustasch,*nn.*	vontses,*pl.*
mustard	moutarde,*f.*	Senf,*m.*	senape,*m.*	mostaza,*f.*	senap,*nn.*	zeneft,*m.*
mute (silent)	muet, -te	stumm	muto	mudo	stum	shtum
mutter (mumble), to	marmotter	murren	borbottare	murmurar	muttra	preplen

English	French	German	Italian	Spanish	Swedish	Yiddish
mutton	mouton,*m.*	Hammelfleisch,*n.*	carne di montone,*f.*	carne de carnero,*f.*	fårkött,*n.*	shepsnfleysh,*n.*
mutual	mutuel, -le	gegenseitig	mutuo	mutuo	ömsesidig	kegnzaytik
my	(*see p.* 2827)	mein (*see p.* 2891)	(*see p.* 2948)	(*see p.* 3012)	min (*see p.* 3075)	mayn (*see p.* 3132)
myself	(*see p.* 2826 ff.)	(*see p.* 2890)	(*see p.* 2947)	(*see p.* 3012)	(*see p.* 3075)	(*see p.* 3132)
mysterious	mystérieux, -rieuse	geheimnisvoll	misterioso	misterioso	mystisk	soydesdik
mystery (enigma)	mystère,*m.*	Geheimnis,*n.*	mistero,*m.*	misterio,*m.*	mysterium,*n.*	retenish,*f.*
myth (legend)	mythe,*m.*	Mythos,*n.*	mito,*m.*	mito,*m.*	myt,*nn.*	mitos,*m.*
nail (*anat.*)	ongle,*m.*	Nagel,*m.*	unghia,*f.*	uña,*f.*	nagel,*nn.*	nogl,*m.*
nail (hardware)	clou,*m.*	Nagel,*m.*	chiodo,*m.*	clavo,*m.*	spik,*nn.*	tshvok,*m.*
naked	nu	nackt	nudo	desnudo	naken	naket
name	nom,*m.*	Name,*m.*	nome,*m.*	nombre,*m.*	namn,*n.*	nomen,*m.*
namely	(à) savoir	nämlich	cioè	a saber	nämligen	dehayne
nap (doze,*n.*)	somme,*m.*	Schläfchen,*n.*	pisolino,*m.*	siesta,*f.*	lur,*nn.*	driml,*m.*
nape	nuque,*f.*	Nacken,*m.*	nuca,*f.*	nuca,*f.*	nacke,*nn.*	patilnitse,*f.*
napkin	serviette,*f.*	Serviette,*f.*	tovagliolo,*m.*	servilleta,*f.*	servett,*nn.*	servetke,*f.*
Naples	Naples,*m.*	Neapel,*n.*	Napoli,*f.*	Nápoles	Neapel,*n.*	Neapl,*n.*
narrow	étroit	schmal	stretto	estrecho	smal	shmol
nation	nation,*f.*	Nation,*f.*	nazione,*f.*	nación,*f.*	nation,*nn.*	natsye,*f.*
national (*adj.*)	national	national	nazionale	nacional	nationell	natsyonal
native (indigenous)	natif, -tive	(ein)heimisch	indigeno	nativo	infödd	ayngeboyrn
native (*n.*)	natif,*m.*	gebürtig (*adj.*)	indigeno,*m.*	natural,*m.,f.*	inföding,*nn.*	geboyrener,*m.*
natural	naturel, -le	natürlich	naturale	natural	naturlig	natirlekh
nature (character)	nature,*f.*	Wesen,*n.*	naturale,*f.*	naturaleza,*f.*	natur,*nn.*	teve,*f.*
nature (physical world)	nature,*f.*	Nature,*f.*	natura,*f.*	naturaleza,*f.*	natur,*nn.*	natur,*f.*
naughty (disobedient)	méchant	unartig	cattivo	travieso	stygg	shtiferish
navigation	navigation,*f.*	Schiffahrt,*f.*	navigazione,*f.*	navegación,*f.*	navigation,*nn.*	navigatsye,*f.*
navy (*n.*)	marine,*f.*	Kriegsmarine,*f.*	marina,*f.*	marina de guerra,*f.*	flotta,*nn.*	krigsflot,*m.*
near (not far, *adv.*)	près	nah	vicino	cerca	nära	noent
near (*prep.*)	près de	neben; bei	vicino a	cerca de	nära	lebn
nearly (almost)	presque	fast	quasi	casi	nästan	kimat
neat (tidy)	propre	sauber	pulito	ordenado	snygg	tsikhtik
necessary	nécessaire	nötig	necessario	necesario	nödvändig	neytik
necessity	nécessité,*f.*	Notwendigkeit,*f.*	necessità,*f.*	necesidad,*f.*	nödvändighet,*nn.*	neytikayt,*f.*
neck (*anat.*)	cou,*m.*	Hals,*m.*	collo,*m.*	cuello,*m.*	hals,*nn.*	kark,*m.*
necklace	collier,*m.*	Halskette,*f.*	collana,*f.*	collar,*m.*	halsband,*n.*	haldzband,*m.*
need	besoin,*m.*	Not,*f.*	bisogno,*m.*	necesidad,*f.*	behov,*n.*	neytikayt,*f.*
need (require), to	avoir besoin de	brauchen	avere bisogno di	necesitar	behöva	darfn
needle	aiguille,*f.*	Nadel,*f.*	ago,*m.*	aguja,*f.*	synål,*nn.*	nodl,*f.*
needless	inutile	unnötig	inutile	innecesario	onödig	umneytik
neglect (slight), to	négliger	vernachlässigen	trascurare	despreciar	försumma	nit leygn genug oyf akht
negotiable (*bus.*)	négociable	übertragbar	negoziabile	negociable	säljbar	farkoyfevdik
negotiate, to	négocier	verhandeln über	trattare	negociar	underhandla om	farhandlen vegn
negotiation	négociation,*f.*	Verhandlung,*f.*	negoziato,*m.*	negociación,*f.*	underhandling,*nn.*	farhandlung *f.*
Negro	nègre,*m.*	Neger,*m.*	negro,*m.*	negro,*m.*	neger,*nn.*	Neger,*m.*
neigh, to	hennir	wiehern	nitrire	relinchar	gnägga	hirzhen
neighbor	voisin,*m.*	Nachbar,*m.*	vicino,*m.*	vecino,*m.*	granne,*nn.*	shokhn,*m.*
neighborhood	voisinage,*m.*	Nähe,*f.*	vicinato,*m.*	vecindad,*f.*	grannskap,*n.*	shkheyneshaft, *f.*
neither (*adj.*)	ni l'un...	kein...	nè l'uno...	ni el uno...	ingendera	nit der; nit yener
neither (*pron.*)	ni l'un...	kein...	nè l'uno...	ninguno	ingendera	nit der; nit yener
neither...nor (*conj.*)	ni...ni	weder...noch	(non)...nè...nè	ni...ni	varken	nit...nit
nephew	neveu,*m.*	Neffe,*m.*	nipote,*m.*	sobrino,*m.*	bror-, systerson,*nn.* (*pl.* -söner)	plimenik,*m.*
nerve (*anat.*)	nerf,*m.*	Nerv,*m.*	nervo,*m.*	nervio,*m.*	nerv,*nn.*	nerv,*m.*
nervous (high-strung)	nerveux, -veuse	nervös	nervoso	nervioso	nervös	nervez
nest (bird home)	nid,*m.*	Nest,*n.*	nido,*m.*	nido,*m.*	bo,*n.*	nest,*f.*
net (*adj.*)	net, -te	netto	netto	neto	netto	neto
net (mesh)	filet,*m.*	Netz,*n.*	rete,*f.*	red,*f.*	nät,*n.*	nets,*f.*
Netherlands, The	les Pays-Bas,*m. pl.*	die Niederlande, *pl.*	Olanda,*f.*	los Países Bajos, *m.pl.*	Nederländerna, *def.pl.*	Niderland,*n.*
neutral	neutre	neutral	neutrale	neutral	neutral	neytral
never	jamais	nie(mals)	mai	nunca	aldrig	keyn mol nit
nevertheless	néanmoins	trotzdem	nondimeno	sin embargo	inte dess mindre	fun dest vegn
new	nouveau, -velle	neu	nuovo	nuevo	ny	nay
New Delhi	New-Delhi,*m.*	Neudelhi,*n.*	Nuova Delhi,*f.*	Nueva Delhi	New Delhi,*n.*	Nay-Delhi,*n.*
newspaper	journal,*m.*	Zeitung,*f.*	giornale,*m.*	periódico,*m.*	tidning,*nn.*	tsaytung,*f.*
newsreel	actualités,*f.pl.*	Wochenschau,*f.*	cinegiornale,*m.*	película noticiera, *f.*	journalfilm,*nn.*	naysfilm,*m.*
newsstand	kiosque à journaux,*m.*	Zeitungskiosk,*m.*	edicola,*f.*	puesto de periódicos,*m.*	tidningskiosk, *nn.*	kiosk,*m.*
New Year's Day	jour de l'an,*m.*	Neujahrstag,*m.*	Capodanno,*m.*	día de año nuevo, *m.*	nyårsdag,*nn.*	nayyor-tog,*m.*
New York	New-York,*m.*	Neuyork,*n.*	Nuova York,*n.*	Nueva York	New York,*n.*	Nyu-York,*n.*
next (*adv.*)	ensuite	anschliessend	in sequito	luego	nästa	vayter
next (following, *adj.*)	suivant	nächst	seguente	siguiente	näst(a)	kumendik
next to (alongside of, *prep.*)	à côté de	neben	accanto a	junto a	näst intill	lebn

English	French	German	Italian	Spanish	Swedish	Yiddish
Nicaragua	Nicaragua,*m.*	Nicaragua,*n.*	Nicaragua,*m.*	Nicaragua	Nicaragua,*n.*	Nikaragva,*f.*
nice (agreeable)	agréable	nett	gentile	agradable	trevlig	voyl
nickel (*chem.*)	nickel,*m.*	Nickel,*n.*	nichel,*m.*	níquel,*m.*	nickel,*nn.*	nikl,*n.*
nickname	surnom,*m.*	Spitzname,*m.*	soprannome,*m.*	mote,*m.*	öknamn,*n.*	tsunemenish,*n.*
niece	nièce,*f.*	Nichte,*f.*	nipote,*f.*	sobrina,*f.*	brors-, syster-dotter,*nn.* (*pl.* -döttrar)	plimenitse,*f.*
night	nuit,*f.*	Nacht,*f.*	notte,*f.*	noche,*f.*	natt,*nn.* (*pl.* nätter)	nakht,*f.*
nightgown	chemise de nuit, *f.*	Nachthemd,*n.*	camicia da notte, *f.*	camisa de dormir, *f.*	nattdräkt,*nn.*	nakhthemd,*n.*
nightingale	rossignol,*m.*	Nachtigall,*f.*	usignolo,*m.*	ruiseñor,*m.*	näktergal,*nn.*	solovey,*m.*
Nile	Nil,*m.*	Nil,*m.*	Nilo,*m.*	Nilo	Nilen,*nn.*	Nilus,*m.*
nimble (agile)	agile	behend	agile	ágil	vig	shmaydik
no (nay)	non	nein	no	no	nej	neyn
no (not any, *adj.*)	aucun	kein	nessuno	ninguno	ingen	keyn
no (not any, *adv.*)	pas	gar nicht	non	ningún, -guna	inte	nit
nobility	noblesse,*f.*	Adel,*m.*	nobiltà,*f.*	nobleza,*f.*	adel,*nn.*	adl,*m.*
noble (*adj.*)	noble	edel	nobile	noble	förnäm	eydl
nobody (*pron.*)	personne	niemand	nessuno	nadie	ingen	keyner nit
nod, to	incliner la tête	nicken	inclinare la testa	cabecear	nicka	shoklen
noise (din)	bruit,*m.*	Lärm,*m.*	rumore,*m.*	ruido,*m.*	larm,*n.*	tuml,*m.*
noisy	bruyant	geräuschvoll	rumoroso	ruidoso	bullersam	tumldik
nominate, to	nommer	zur Wahl vorsch-lagen	nominare	nombrar	föreslå	nominirn
nomination	nomination,*f.*	Aufstellung,*f.*	nominazione,*f.*	nombramiento, *m.*	föreslående,*n.*	nominatsye,*f.*
none (*pron.*)	aucun	keine	nessuno	ninguno	ingen	keyner nit
nonsense	bêtise,*f.*	Unsinn,*m.*	sciochezza,*f.*	disparate,*m.*	dumheter,*nn.pl.*	umzin,*m.*
noon	midi,*m.*	Mittag,*m.*	mezzogiorno,*m.*	mediodía,*m.*	middag,*nn.*	halber tog,*m.*
nor	ni	noch	nè	ni	eller	oykh nit
normal (*adj.*)	normal	normal	normale	normal	normal	normal
north (*adv.*)	au nord	nördlich	a nord	al norte	norr	oyf tsofn
north (*n.*)	nord,*m.*	Norden,*m.*	settentrione,*m.*	norte,*m.*	nord,*nn.*	tsofn,*m.*
North America	Amérique du Nord,*f.*	Nordamerika,*m.*	America del Nord,*f.*	Norte América	Nordamerika,*n.*	Tsofn-Amerike, *f.*
northeast (*adj.*)	(du) nord-est	nordöstlich	del nord-est	nordeste	nordöstlig	tsofn-mizrakh-dik
northern	(du) nord	nördlich	settentrionale	septentrional	nordlig	tsofndik
northwest (*adj.*)	(du) nord-ouest	nordwestlich	del nord-ovest	noroeste	nordvästlig	tsofn-mayrevdik
Norway	Norvège,*f.*	Norwegen,*n.*	Norvegia,*f.*	Noruega	Norge,*n.*	Norvegye,*f.*
Norwegian (*adj.*)	norvégien, -ne	norwegisch	norvegese	noruego	norsk	norvegish
nose (*anat.*)	nez,*m.*	Nase,*f.*	naso,*m.*	nariz,*f.*	näsa,*nn.*	noz,*f.*
nostril	narine,*f.*	Nasenloch,*n.*	narice,*f.*	ventana de la nariz,*f.*	näsborre,*nn.*	nozlokh,*f.*
not	(ne)...pas	nicht	non	no	inte	nit; nisht
notable (*adj.*)	notable	bemerkenswert	notevole	notable	märklig	merkverdik
notary	notaire,*m.*	Notar,*m.*	notaio,*m.*	notario,*m.*	notarie,*nn.*	notar,*m.*
note (letter)	billet,*m.*	Briefchen,*n.*	biglietto,*m.*	billete,*m.*	kort brev,*n.*	brivl,*n.*
note (*mus.*)	note,*f.*	Note,*f.*	nota,*f.*	nota,*f.*	not,*nn.*	note,*f.*
note (promise to pay, *bus.*)	billet à ordre,*m.*	Schuldschein,*m.*	pagherò,*m.*	pagaré,*m.*	revers,*nn.*	veksl,*m.*
note (mention), to	noter	bemerken	rilevare	notar	framhålla	dermonen
note (perceive), to	noter	merken	notare	notar	märka	bamerkn
notebook	cahier,*m.*	(Schreib)Heft,*n.*	quaderno,*m.*	libreta,*f.*	anteckningsbok, *nn.* (*pl.* -böcker)	heft,*f.*
nothing (*n.*)	rien	nichts	niente	nada	intet	gornit
notice (attention)	attention,*f.*	Kenntnis,*f.*	attenzione,*f.*	atención,*f.*	uppmärksamhet, *nn.*	akht,*f.*
notice (notification)	avis,*m.*	Ankündigung,*f.*	avviso,*m.*	notificación,*f.*	tillkännagivande, *n.*	meldung,*f.*
notice (see), to	remarquer	bemerken	osservare	observar	märka	bamerkn
notify, to	aviser	benachrichtigen	notificare	notificar	underrätta	onzogn
notion (idea)	notion,*f.*	Idee,*f.*	nozione,*f.*	noción,*f.*	idé,*nn.*	aynfal,*m.*
notorious	notoire	berüchtigt	malfamato	notorio	ökänd	troyerik barimt
noun	nom,*m.*	Hauptwort,*n.*	nome,*m.*	nombre,*m.*	substantiv,*n.*	substantiv,*m.*
nourish, to	nourrir	(er)nähren	nutrire	nutrir	nära	dernern
nourishment	nourriture,*f.*	Nahrung,*f.*	nutrimento,*m.*	nutrimento,*m.*	näring,*nn.*	dernerung,*f.*
novel (book)	roman,*m.*	Roman,*m.*	romanzo,*m.*	novela,*f.*	roman,*nn.*	roman,*m.*
now (*adv.*)	maintenant	jetzt	ora	ahora	nu	itst; atsind
nowhere	nulle part	nirgends	in nessuna parte	en ninguna parte	ingenstans	in ergets nit
numb	engourdi	starr	insensibile	entumecido	domnad	geleymt
number (numeral)	numéro,*m.*	Nummer,*f.*	numero,*m.*	número,*m.*	siffra,*nn.*	numer,*m.*
number (quantity)	nombre,*m.*	(An)Zahl,*f.*	quantità,*f.*	número,*m.*	antal,*n.*	tsol,*f.*
number (assign numbers to), to	numéroter	numerieren	numerare	numerar	numrera	numerirn
numerous	nombreux, -breuse	zahlreich	numeroso	numeroso	talrik	tsolraykh
nun	religieuse,*f.*	Nonne,*f.*	monaca,*f.*	monja,*f.*	nunna,*nn.*	monashke,*f.*
nurse (medical assistant)	infirmière,*f.*	Kranken-schwester,*f.*	infermiera,*f.*	enfermera,*f.*	sjuksköterska, *nn.*	krankn-shvester,*f.*
nurse (give treatment to), to	soigner	pflegen	curare	cuidar	vårda	pileven
nursery (children's room)	chambre d'enfants,*f.*	Kinderstube,*f.*	stanza dei bambini,*f.*	habitación para niños,*f.*	barnkammare, *nn.*	kinder-tsimer, *m.*

English	French	German	Italian	Spanish	Swedish	Yiddish
nut (food)	noix,*f.*	Nuss,*f.*	noce,*f.*	nuez,*f.*	nöt,*nn.* (*pl.* nötter)	nus,*m.*
nut (*mech.*)	écrou,*m.*	(Schrauben) Mutter,*f.*	dado,*m.*	tuerca,*f.*	skruvmutter,*nn.*	muter,*f.*
nutmeg	muscade,*f.*	Muskatnuss,*f.*	noce moscata,*f.*	nuez moscada,*f.*	muskot,*nn.*	mushkat,*m.*
nylon (*n.*)	nylon,*m.*	Nylon,*n.*	nailon,*m.*	nilón,*m.*	nylon,*n.*,*nn.*	naylon,*m.*
oak	chêne,*m.*	Eiche,*f.*	quercia,*f.*	roble,*m.*	ek,*nn.*	demb,*m.*
oar (*n.*)	rame,*f.*	Ruder,*n.*	remo,*m.*	remo,*m.*	åra,*nn.*	ruder,*f.*
oasis	oasis,*f.*	Oase,*f.*	oasi,*f.*	oasis,*m.*	oas,*nn.*	oaze,*f.*
oath (vow)	serment,*m.*	Eid,*m.*	giuramento,*m.*	juramento,*m.*	ed,*nn.*	shvue,*f.*
oats	avoine,*f.*	Hater,*m.*	avena,*f.*	avena,*f.*	havre,*nn.*	hober,*m.*
obedience (compliance)	obéissance,*f.*	Gehorsam,*m.*	obbedienza,*f.*	obediencia,*f.*	lydnad,*nn.*	folgn,*n.*
obedient	obéissant	gehorsam	obbediente	obediente	lydig	folgevdik
obey, to	obéir (à)	gehorchen	obbedire a	obedecer	lyda	folgn
obituary (*n.*)	nécrologe,*m.*	Todesanzeige,*f.*	necrologia,*f.*	necrología,*f.*	dödsnotis,*nn.*	nekrolog,*m.*
object (aim)	but,*m.*	Ziel,*n.*	oggetto,*m.*	propósito,*m.*	syfte,*n.*	tsil,*m.*
object (thing)	objet,*m.*	Gegenstand,*m.*	oggetto,*m.*	objeto,*m.*	föremål,*n.*	obyekt,*m.*
object, to	opposer, (s')	einwenden	obbiettare	objetar	invända	aynvendn
objection	objection,*f.*	Einwand,*m.*	obbiezione,*f.*	objeción,*f.*	invändning,*nn.*	aynvendung,*f.*
objective (aim)	but,*m.*	Ziel,*n.*	oggettivo,*m.*	objetivo,*m.*	mål,*n.*	tsil,*m.*
obligation (duty)	obligation,*f.*	Verpflichtung,*f.*	obbligazione,*f.*	obligación,*f.*	skyldighet,*nn.*	hiskhayves,*f.*
obligatory (binding)	obligatoire	bindend	obbligatorio	obligatorio	obligatorisk	obligatorish
oblige (compel), to	obliger	verpflichten	obbligare	obligar	tvinga	neytn
oboe	hautbois,*m.*	Oboe,*f.*	oboe,*m.*	oboe,*m.*	oboe,*nn.*	oboe,*f.*
obscure (dim)	obscur	dunkel	oscuro	obscuro	dunkel	tunkl
obscure (unrenowned)	obscur	unbekannt	oscuro	obscuro	okänd	umbakant
observation (watching)	observation,*f.*	Beobachtung,*f.*	osservazione,*f.*	observación,*f.*	iakttagande,*n.*	observatsye,*f.*
observe (remark), to	observer	bemerken	osservare	observar	anmärka	bamerkn
observe (watch), to	observer	beobachten	osservare	observar	iaktta(ga)	observirn
observer	observateur,*m.*	Beobachter,*m.*	osservatore,*m.*	observador,*m.*	iakttagare,*nn.*	observator,*m.*
obstacle	obstacle,*m.*	Hindernis,*n.*	ostacolo,*m.*	obstáculo,*m.*	hinder,*n.*	mikhshl,*m.*
obtain (get), to	obtenir	erhalten	ottenere	obtener	erhålla	krign
obvious	évident	offenbar	ovvio	obvio	tydlig	klor vi der tog
occasion	occasion,*f.*	Gelegenheit,*f.*	occasione,*f.*	ocasión,*f.*	tillfälle,*n.*	gelegnhayt,*f.*
occasional	de temps en temps	gelegentlich	saltuario	ocasional	tillfällig	fun tsayt tsu tsayt
occasionally	de temps en temps	ab und zu	di quando in quando	de vez en cuando	emellanåt	fun tsayt tsu tsayt
occupation (calling)	métier,*m.*	Beruf,*m.*	occupazione,*f.*	ocupación,*f.*	yrke,*n.*	fakh,*m.*
occupation (*mil.*)	occupation,*f.*	Besetzung,*f.*	occupazione,*f.*	ocupación,*f.*	ockupation,*nn.*	okupatsye,*f.*
occupy (fill), to	occuper	einnehmen	occupare	ocupar	uppta(ga)	farnemen
occupy (live in), to	occuper	bewohnen	occupare	ocupar	bebo	voynen in
occupy (make busy), to	occuper	beschäftigen	occupare	ocupar	sysselsätta	basheftikn
occur (happen), to	avoir lieu	vorkommen	accadere	ocurrir	hända	geshen
ocean	océan,*m.*	Ozean,*m.*	oceano,*m.*	océano,*m.*	ocean,*nn.*	okean,*m.*
odd (not even)	impair	ungerade	impari	impar	udda	umgrod
odd (queer)	singulier, -lière	sonderbar	strano	raro	konstig	modne
odor (scent)	odeur,*f.*	Geruch,*m.*	odore,*m.*	olor,*m.*	lukt,*nn.*	reyakh,*m.*
of	de	von	di	de	av	fun
offend (affront), to	offenser	beleidigen	offendere	ofender	förnärma	baleydikn
offense (attack)	offensive,*f.*	Angriff,*m.*	offensiva,*f.*	ofensa,*f.*	anfall,*n.*	atake,*f.*
offense (transgression)	offense,*f.*	Vergehen,*n.*	offesa,*f.*	ofensa,*f.*	överträdelse,*nn.*	khet,*m.*
offer	offre,*f.*	Angebot,*n.*	offerta,*f.*	ofrecimiento,*m.*	anbud,*n.*	onbot,*m.*
offer (tender), to	offrir	anbieten	offrire	ofrecer	erbjuda	onbotn
office (place of business)	bureau,*m.*	Büro,*n.*	ufficio,*m.*	oficina,*f.*	kontor,*n.*	byuro,*n.*
office (position)	office,*m.*	Amt,*n.*	ufficio,*m.*	oficio,*m.*	ämbete,*n.*	amt,*m.*
officer (*mil.*)	officier,*m.*	Offizier,*m.*	ufficiale,*m.*	oficial,*m.*	officer,*nn.* (*pl.* -are)	ofitsir,*m.*
official (*adj.*)	officiel, -le	amtlich	ufficiale	oficial	officiell	ofitsyel
official (*n.*)	fonctionnaire,*m.*	Beamte,*m.*	funzionario,*m.*	funcionario,*m.*	tjänsteman,*nn.* (*pl.* -män)	baamter,*m.*
often	souvent	oft	spesso	a menudo	ofta	oft
oil	huile,*f.*	Öl,*n.*	olio,*m.*	aceite,*m.*	olja,*nn.*	eyl,*m.*
ointment	onguent,*m.*	Salbe,*f.*	unguento,*m.*	ungüento,*m.*	salva,*nn.*	zalb,*f.*
old (elderly)	vieux (vieil), vieille	alt	anziano	viejo	gammal	alt
old (not new)	vieux (vieil), vieille	alt	vecchio	viejo	gammal	alt
olive (fruit)	olive,*f.*	Olive,*f.*	oliva,*f.*	aceituna,*f.*	oliv,*nn.*	masline,*f.*
olive oil	huile d'olive,*f.*	Olivenöl,*n.*	olio d'oliva,*m.*	aceite de oliva,*m.*	olivolja,*nn.*	boyml,*m.*
omit (leave out), to	omettre	auslassen	omettere	omitir	utelämna	oyslozn
on (*prep.*)	sur	auf	su (*see p. 2946*)	en	på	oyf
once (one time, *adv.*)	une fois	einmal	una volta	una vez	en gång	eyn mol
once (formerly, *adv.*)	autrefois	einst	un tempo	en otro tiempo	en gång	a mol
onion	oignon,*m.*	Zwiebel,*f.*	cipolla,*f.*	cebolla,*f.*	lök,*nn.*	tsibele,*f.*
only (merely)	seulement	bloss	soltanto	solamente	bara	nor
only (sole)	seul	einzig	unico	único	bara	nor
onward (*adv.*)	en avant	vorwärts	avanti	hacia adelante	enda	eyntsik
open (*adj.*)	ouvert	offen	aperto	abierto	fram(åt)	foroys
open (make open), to	ouvrir	öffnen	aprire	abrir	öppen	ofn
opening (aperture)	ouverture,*f.*	Öffnung,*f.*	apertura,*f.*	abertura,*f.*	öppna	efenen
opening (beginning,*n.*)	commencement,*m.*	Eröffnung,*f.*	inizio,*m.*	inauguración,*f.*	öppning,*nn.* öppnande,*n.*	efenung,*f.* haskhole,*f.*

English	French	German	Italian	Spanish	Swedish	Yiddish
opera	opéra,*m.*	Oper,*f.*	opera,*f.*	ópera,*f.*	opera,*nn.*	opere,*f.*
operate (handle), to	faire marcher	betreiben	fare funzionare	manejar	sköta	arbetn bay; firn
operate (perform surgery), to	opérer	operieren	operare	operar	operera	operirn
operating expenses (*bus.*)	frais d'exploita-tion,*m.pl.*	Betriebskosten, *pl.*	spese d'azienda, *f.pl.*	gastos de explo-tación,*m.pl.*	driftskostnader, *nn.pl.*	arbet-hoytsoes, *pl.*
operation (functioning)	fonctionnement, *m.*	Betrieb,*m.*	funzionamento, *m.*	funcionamiento, *m.*	gång,*nn.*	gang,*m.*
operation (*med.*)	opération,*f.*	Operation,*f.*	operazione,*f.*	operación,*f.*	operation,*nn.*	operatsye,*f.*
opinion	opinion,*f.*	Meinung,*f.*	opinione,*f.*	opinión,*f.*	åsikt,*nn.*	meynung,*f.*
opponent (*n.*)	adversaire,*m.*	Gegner,*m.*	avversario,*m.*	adversario,*m.*	motståndare,*nn.*	kegener,*m.*
opportunity	occasion,*f.*	Gelegenheit,*f.*	occasione,*f.*	oportunidad,*f.*	tillfälle,*n.*	gelegnhayt,*f.*
oppose (combat), to	combattre	bestreiten	opporsi a	oponerse a	bekämpa	antkegnshteln zikh
opposite (*adj.*)	opposé	gegenübersteh-end	opposto	opuesto	motsatt	farkert
opposite (*n.*)	opposé,*m.*	Gegenteil,*n.*	opposto,*m.*	contrario,*m.*	motsats,*nn.*	heypekh,*m.*
opposite (*prep.*)	en face de	gegenüber	in faccia a	frente a	mitt emot	antkegn
opposition (resistance)	opposition,*f.*	Widerstand,*m.*	opposizione,*f.*	oposición,*f.*	motstånd,*n.*	kegnshtel,*m.*
oppress (tyrannize), to	opprimer	unterdrücken	opprimere	oprimir	förtrycka	badrikn
oppress (weigh down), to	oppresser	bedrängen	opprimere	oprimir	betunga	badrikn
optimistic	optimiste	optimistisch	ottimistico	optimista	optimistisk	optimistish
optional	facultatif, -tive	wahlfrei	a scelta	discrecional	valfri	nit-obligatorish
or	ou	oder	o	o, u	eller	oder
oral (spoken)	oral	mündlich	orale	oral	muntlig	balpe
orange (color)	orange	orange(farbig)	arancione	anaranjado	orange	oranzh
orange (fruit)	orange,*f.*	Orange,*f.*	arancia,*f.*	naranja,*f.*	apelsin,*nn.,n.*	marants,*m.*
orchard	verger,*m.*	Obstgarten,*m.*	frutteto,*m.*	huerto,*m.*	fruktträdgård, *nn.*	sod,*m.*
orchestra (*mus.*)	orchestre,*m.*	Orchester,*n.*	orchestra,*f.*	orquesta,*f.*	orkester,*nn.*	orkester,*m.*
orchid (flower)	orchidée,*f.*	Orchidee,*f.*	orchidea,*f.*	orquídea,*f.*	orkidé,*nn.*	orkhidee,*f.*
order (command)	ordre,*m.*	Befehl,*m.*	ordine,*m.*	orden,*f.*	order,*nn.*	bafel,*m.*
order (orderliness)	ordre,*m.*	Ordnung,*f.*	ordine,*m.*	orden,*m.*	ordning,*nn.*	ordenung,*f.*
order (purchase)	commande,*f.*	Auftrag,*m.*	ordinazione,*f.*	pedido,*m.*	order,*nn.*	bashtelung,*f.*
order (sequence)	ordre,*m.*	Reihenfolge,*f.*	ordine,*m.*	orden,*m.*	ordning,*nn.*	seyder,*m.*
order (command), to	ordonner	befehlen	comandare	ordenar	befalla	bafeln
order (purchase), to	commander	bestellen	comandare	pedir	beställa	bashteln
ordinary (usual)	ordinaire	gewöhnlich	usuale	ordinario	vanlig	geveyntlekh
ore	minerai,*m.*	Erz,*n.*	minerale,*m.*	mineral,*m.*	malm,*nn.*	arts,*n.*
organ (*anat.*)	organe,*m.*	Organ,*n.*	organo,*m.*	órgano,*m.*	organ,*n.*	organ,*m.*
organ (*mus.*)	orgue,*m.*	Orgel,*f.*	organo,*m.*	órgano,*m.*	orgel,*nn.*	orgl,*f.*
organization (association)	association,*f.*	Vereinigung,*f.*	organizzazione,*f.*	sociedad,*f.*	organisation,*nn.*	organizatsye,*f.*
organize (systematize), to	organiser	einrichten	organizzare	organizar	organisera	organizirn
Orient	Orient,*m.*	Osten,*m.*	Oriente,*m.*	Oriente,*m.*	Orienten,*nn. def.*	Oryent,*m.*
origin (source)	origine,*f.*	Ursprung,*m.*	origine,*f.*	origen,*m.*	ursprung,*n.*	moker,*m.*
original (first)	original	ursprünglich	originale	original	ursprunglig	lekhatkhiledik
ornament	ornement,*m.*	Zierde,*f.*	ornamento,*m.*	ornamento,*m.*	ornament,*n.*	ornament,*m.*
orphan (*n.*)	orphelin,*m.*	Waise,*m.,f.*	orfano,*m.*	huérfano,*m.*	föräldralöst barn, *n.*	yosem,*m.*
Oslo	Oslo,*m.*	Oslo,*n.*	Oslo,*f.*	Oslo	Oslo,*n.*	Oslo,*n.*
other (*adj.*)	autre	ander	altro	otro	annan (*see p.* 3076)	ander
other (*pron.*)	autre	Andere	altro	otro	annan (*see p.* 3076)	anderer
otherwise (contrarily)	autrement	anders	altrimenti	de otro modo	annorlunda	andersh
otherwise (under other conditions)	par ailleurs	sonst	altrimenti	de otro modo	annars	anit
Ottawa	Ottawa,*m.*	Ottawa,*n.*	Ottawa,*f.*	Ottawa	Ottawa,*n.*	Otava,*n.*
ought (*v.*)	devoir (*see p.* 2834)	sollen (*see p.* 2892 ff.)	dovere (*see p.* 2957)	deber	böra (*see p.* 3078)	darfn
our	notre; nos (*see p.* 2827)	unser (*see p.* 2891)	nostro (*see p.* 2948)	nuestro (*see p.* 3012)	vår (*see p.* 3075)	undzer (*see p.* 3132)
ours	(*see p.* 2827)	unser(e) (*see p.* 2890)	(*see p.* 2948)	(*see p.* 3012)	(*see p.* 3075)	undzerer (*see p.* 3132)
ourselves	(*see p.* 2826 ff.)	(*see p.* 2890)	(*see p.* 2947 ff.)	(*see p.* 3012)	(*see p.* 3075)	(*see p.* 3132)
out (forth, *adv.*)	dehors	heraus	fuori	fuera	ut	aroys
out (not in, *adv.*)	(au) dehors	aus	fuori	afuera	ute	nit inveynik
outdoors (*adv.*)	au dehors	draussen	all'aria libera	al aire libre	utomhus	in droysn
outer	extérieur	äussere	esteriore	exterior	yttre	droysndik
outfit (equipment)	attirail,*m.*	Ausrüstung,*f.*	equipaggia-mento,*m.*	equipo,*m.*	utrustning,*nn.*	oysshtayer,*m.*
outlet (*elec.*)	prise de courant, *f.*	Steckdose,*f.*	presa,*f.*	toma,*f.*	kontakt,*nn.*	shtepsl,*m.*
outlet (exit)	issue,*f.*	Ausgang,*m.*	uscita,*f.*	salida,*f.*	utgång,*nn.*	oysveg,*m.*
outlet (market, *bus.*)	débouché,*m.*	Absatzgebiet,*n.*	mercato,*m.*	salida,*f.*	marknad,*nn.*	mark,*m.*
outline (general plan)	esquisse,*f.*	Entwurf,*m.*	abbozzo,*m.*	bosquejo,*m.*	utkast,*n.*	onvorf,*m.*
outlook (attitude)	attitude,*f.*	Ausblick,*m.*	modo di pensare, *m.*	perspectiva,*f.*	syn,*nn.*	kuk,*m.*
output	rendement,*m.*	Produktion,*f.*	produzione,*f.*	producción total, *f.*	produktion,*nn.*	produktsye,*f.*
outside (*adj.*)	extérieur	äussere	esterno	exterior	yttre	droysndik
outside (*adv.*)	dehors	draussen	fuori	afuera	ute	in droysn
outside (*n.*)	dehors,*m.*	Aussenseite,*f.*	di fuori,*m.*	exterior,*m.*	utsida,*nn.*	droysn,*m.*
oven	four,*m.*	Backofen,*m.*	forno,*m.*	horno,*m.*	ugn,*nn.*	droysn,*m.*
over (above, *prep.*)	par-dessus	über	sopra	sobre	över	iber

English	French	German	Italian	Spanish	Swedish	Yiddish
over (across, *prep.*)	sur	quer über	attraverso	allende	över	ariber
overcoat	pardessus,*m.*	Mantel,*m.*	soprabito,*m.*	sobretodo,*m.*	ytterrock,*nn.*	mantl,*m.*
overcome (conquer), to	vaincre	überwältigen	vincere	vencer	övervinna	baykumen
overdue (in arrears)	arriéré	überfällig	in sofferenza	vencido y no pagado	förfallen	ariber dem termin
overhead (expenses, *bus.*)	frais généraux, *m.pl.*	allgemeine Unkosten,*pl.*	spese fisse,*f.pl.*	gastos generales, *m.pl.*	administrations-kostnader,*nn. pl.*	generale hoytsoes,*pl.*
overlook (disregard), to	passer sur	übersehen	passare sopra	pasar por alto	ignorera	farkukn
oversea(s) (*adj.*)	d'outre-mer	überseeisch	d'oltremare	ultramar	transmarin	meeyver-leyam
oversight (error)	inadvertence,*f.*	Versehen,*n.*	svista,*f.*	descuido,*m.*	förbiseende,*n.*	farze,*m.*
overtime (*bus.,n.*)	heures supplémentaires,*f.pl.*	Überstunden,*f. pl.*	ore straordinarie, *f.pl.*	horas adicionales, *f.pl.*	övertid,*nn.*	ibershoen,*pl.*
overturn (upset), to	renverser	umstürzen	rovesciare	volcar	välta	iberkern
owe, to	devoir	schuldig sein	dovere	deber	vara skyldig	kumen
owl	hibou,*m.*	Eule,*f.*	gufo,*m.*	buho,*m.*	uggla,*nn.*	sove,*f.*
own (*adj.*)	propre	eigen	proprio	propio	egen	eygn
own (possess), to	posséder	besitzen	possedere	poseer	äga	farmogn
owner	propriétaire,*m.*	Eigentümer,*m.*	proprietario,*m.*	propietario,*m.*	ägare,*nn.*	bazitser,*m.*
ox	boeuf,*m.*	Ochs,*m.*	bue,*m.*(*pl.* buoi)	buey,*m.*	oxe,*nn.*	oks,*m.*
oxygen	oxygène,*m.*	Sauerstoff,*m.*	ossigeno,*m.*	oxígeno,*m.*	syre,*n.*	zoyershtof,*m.*
oyster	huître,*f.*	Auster,*f.*	ostrica,*f.*	ostra,*f.*	ostron,*n.*	oyster,*m.*
pace (rate)	train,*m.*	Tempo,*n.*	andamento,*m.*	paso,*m.*	fart,*nn.*	tempo,*m.*
Pacific (*n.*)	Pacifique,*m.*	Stiller Ozean,*m.*	Pacifico,*m.*	Pacífico,*m.*	Stilla havet,*n. def.*	patsifik,*m.*
pack (wrap), to	emballer	verpacken	impaccare	empacar	packa in	aynpakn
package	colis,*m.*	Paket,*n.*	pacco,*m.*	paquete,*m.*	paket,*n.*	pekl,*n.*
packing (*n.*)	garniture,*f.*	Packmaterial,*n.*	imballaggio,*m.*	embalaje,*m.*	packning,*nn.*	aynpakung,*f.*
pad (cushion)	bourrelet,*m.*	Polster,*n.*	cuscinetto,*m.*	cojinete,*m.*	dyna,*nn.*	kishele,*n.*
paddle (oar)	pagaie,*f.*	Paddel,*n.*	pagaia,*f.*	canalete,*m.*	paddel,*nn.*	ruder,*f.*
page (leaf)	page,*f.*	Seite,*f.*	pagina,*f.*	página,*f.*	sida,*nn.*	zayt,*f.*
pail	seau,*m.*	Eimer,*m.*	secchia,*f.*	balde,*m.*	hink,*nn.*	emer,*m.*
pain (ache)	douleur,*f.*	Schmerz,*m.*	dolore,*m.*	dolor,*m.*	smärta,*nn.*	veytik,*m.*
painful	douloureux, -reuse	schmerzhaft	doloroso	doloroso	smärtsam	veytikdik
paint	peinture,*f.*	Farbe,*f.*	colore,*m.*	pintura,*f.*	färg,*nn.*	farb,*f.*
paint (represent), to	dépeindre	malen	dipingere	pintar	måla	moln
paint (spread color), to	peindre	anstreichen	dipingere	pintar	måla	farbn
painter (artist)	peintre,*m.*	Maler,*m.*	pittore,*m.*	pintor,*m.*	målare,*nn.*	moler,*m.*
painting (picture)	peinture,*f.*	Gemälde,*n.*	pittura,*f.*	pintura,*f.*	målning,*nn.*	gemel,*n.*
pair	paire,*f.*	Paar,*n.*	paio,*m.*(*pl.* paia, *f.*)	par,*m.*	par,*n.*	por,*f.*
pajamas	pyjama,*m.*	Pyjama,*n.*	pigiama,*m.*	pijamas,*m.pl.*	pyjamas,*nn.*	pizhame,*f.*
Pakistan	Pakistan,*m.*	Pakistan,*n.*	Pakistan,*m.*	Pakistán	Pakistan,*n.*	Pakistan,*n.*
Pakistani (*adj.*)	pakistani	pakistanisch	pakistano	pakistano	pakistansk	pakistanish
pal	copain,*m.*	Kamerad,*m.*	amico,*m.*	compañero,*m.*	kamrat,*nn.*	khaver,*m.*
palace	palais,*m.*	Palast,*m.*	palazzo,*m.*	palacio,*m.*	palats,*n.*	palats,*m.*
pale (wan)	pâle	blass	pallido	pálido	blek	blas
Palestine	Palestine,*f.*	Palästina,*n.*	Palestina,*f.*	Palestina	Palestina,*n.*	Erets-Yisroel,*n.*
palm (of hand)	paume,*f.*	Handfläche,*f.*	palmo,*m.*	palma,*f.*	handflata,*nn.*	dlonye,*f.*
palm (tree)	palmier,*m.*	Palme,*f.*	palma,*f.*	palma,*f.*	palm,*nn.*	palme,*f.*
Palm Sunday	dimanche des Rameaux,*m.*	Palmsonntag,*m.*	Domenica delle Palme,*f.*	Domingo de Ramos,*m.*	palmsöndagen, *nn.def.*	palmen-zuntik, *m.*
pan, frying	poêle,*f.*	Pfanne,*f.*	padella,*f.*	sartén,*f.*	stekpanna,*nn*	skovrode,*f.*
Panama	Panama,*m.*	Panama,*n.*	Panamà,*m.*	Panamá	Panama,*n.*	Paname,*f.*
pane, window	vitre,*f.*	Fensterscheibe,*f.*	vetro,*m.*	cuadro de vidrio, *m.*	fönsterruta,*nn.*	shoyb,*f.*
panic (fear)	panique,*f.*	Panik,*f.*	panico,*m.*	pánico,*m.*	panik,*nn.*	panik,*f.*
pansy	pensée,*f.*	Stiefmütterchen, *n.*	viola del pensiero,*f.*	pensamiento,*m.*	pensé,*nn.*	khaneles eygele, *n.*
pant (puff), to	haleter	keuchen	ansare	jadear	flämta	sopen
panther	panthère,*f.*	Panther,*m.*	pantera,*f.*	pantera,*f.*	panter,*nn.*	pantere,*f.*
paper	papier,*m.*	Papier,*n.*	carta,*f.*	papel,*m.*	papper,*n.*	papir,*n.*
parachute	parachute,*m.*	Fallschirm,*m.*	paracadute,*f.*	paracaídas,*m.*	fallskärm,*nn.*	parashut,*m.*
parade (procession)	défilé,*m.*	Parade,*f.*	sfilata,*f.*	desfile,*m.*	parad,*nn.*	parad,*m.*
paradise	paradis,*m.*	Paradies,*n.*	paradiso,*m.*	paraíso,*m.*	paradis,*n.*	ganeydn,*m.*
paragraph	paragraphe,*m.*	Absatz,*m.*	paragrafo,*m.*	párrafo,*m.*	paragraf,*nn.*	paragraf,*m.*
Paraguay	Paraguay,*m.*	Paraguay,*n.*	Paraguai,*m.*	el Paraguay	Paraguay,*n.*	Paragvay,*n.*
parallel (*adj.*)	parallèle	parallel	parallelo	paralelo	parallell	paralel
paralysis	paralysie,*f.*	Lähmung,*f.*	paralisi,*f.*	parálisis,*f.*	förlamning,*nn.*	paraliz,*m.*
parcel (package)	colis,*m.*	Paket,*n.*	pacco,*m.*	paquete,*m.*	paket,*n.*	pekl,*n.*
parcel post	(par) colis postal	Paketpost,*f.*	pacco postale,*m.*	paquete postal,*m.*	paketpost,*nn.*	peklpost,*f.*
pardon (forgiveness)	pardon,*m.*	Verzeihung,*f.*	perdono,*m.*	perdón,*m.*	förlåtelse,*nn.*	mekhile,*f.*
pardon (*law*)	grâce,*f.*	Begnadigung,*f.*	grazia,*f.*	indulto,*m.*	benådning,*nn.*	bagnedikung,*f.*
pardon (forgive), to	pardonner	verzeihen	perdonare	perdonar	förlåta	antshuldikn
parentheses	parenthèses,*f.pl.*	Klammern,*f.pl.*	parentesi,*f.pl.*	paréntesis,*m.*	parentes,*nn.*	halbe levones,*pl.*
parents	parents,*m.pl.*	Eltern,*pl.*	genitori,*m.pl.*	padres,*m.pl.*	föräldrar,*nn.pl.*	tate-mame,*pl.*
Paris	Paris,*m.*	Paris,*n.*	Parigi,*f.*	París	Paris,*n.*	Pariz,*n.*
parish	paroisse,*f.*	Kirchspiel,*n.*	parrocchia,*f.*	parroquia,*f.*	socken,*nn.*	parafye,*f.*
park	parc,*m.*	Park,*m.*	parco,*m.*	parque,*m.*	park,*nn.*	park,*m.*
park (put in place), to	stationner	parken	parcare	estacionar	parkera	parkn
parliament	parlement,*m.*	Parlament,*n.*	Parlamento,*m.*	parlamento,*m.*	parlament,*n.*	parlament,*m.*
parlor (living room)	salon,*m.*	Wohnzimmer,*n.*	salotto,*m.*	sala,*f.*	vardagsrum,*n.*	salon,*m.*
parrot	perroquet,*m.*	Papagei,*m.*	pappagallo,*m.*	loro,*m.*	papegoja,*nn.*	papugay,*m.*

English	French	German	Italian	Spanish	Swedish	Yiddish
parson	curé, *m.*	Pfarrer, *m.*	ministro, *m.*	clérigo, *m.*	kyrkoherde, *nn.*	gaystlekher, *m.*
part (portion)	part, *f.*	Teil, *m.*	parte, *f.*	parte, *f.*	del, *nn.*	teyl, *m.*
part (leave each other), to	séparer, se	trennen, sich	separarsi	separarse	skiljas	sheydn zikh
partial (incomplete)	partiel, -le	teilweise	parziale	parcial	ofullständig	teylvayz
participate, to	prendre part	teilnehmen	partecipare	participar	delta (ga)	onteyl nemen
particular (detail, *n.*)	détail, *m.*	Einzelheit, *f.*	dettaglio, *m.*	detalle, *m.*	detalj, *nn.*	prat, *m.*
particular (specific, *adj.*)	particulier, -lière	besonder	particolare	particular	särskild	spetsifish
partly	en partie	teils	parzialmente	en parte	delvis	tsum teyl
partner (*bus.*)	associé	Teilhaber, *m.*	socio, *m.*	socio, *m.*	kompanjon, *nn.*	shutef, *m.*
party (*pol.*)	parti, *m.*	Partei, *f.*	partito, *m.*	partido, *f.*	parti, *n.*	partey, *f.*
party (social gathering)	soirée, *f.*	Versammlung, *f.*	ricevimento, *m.*	tertulia, *f.*	bjudning, *nn.*	simkhe, *f.*
pass (go by), to	passer	vorbeigehen	passare	pasar	passera	farbaygeyn
pass (not fail in), to	être reçu (à, en)	bestehen	superare	salir aprobado	klara (sig)	oyshaltn
passage (passageway)	passage, *m.*	Gang, *m.*	passaggio, *m.*	pasaje, *m.*	gång, *nn.*	durkhgang, *m.*
passenger	voyageur, *m.*	Passagier, *m.*	passeggiero, *m.*	pasajero, *m.*	passagerare, *nn.*	pasazhir, *m.*
passion (emotion)	passion, *f.*	Leidenschaft, *f.*	passione, *f.*	pasión, *f.*	lidelse, *nn.*	laydnshaft, *f.*
passionate	passionné	leidenschaftlich	appassionato	apasionado	lidelsefull	laydnshaftlekh
Passover	Pâque, *f.*	Passahfest, *n.*	Pasqua degli Israeliti, *f.*	pascua de los hebreos, *f.*	(*no equiv.*)	Peysakh, *m.*
passport	passeport, *m.*	Pass, *m.*	passaporto, *m.*	pasaporte, *m.*	pass, *n.*	pas, *m.*
past (beyond, *prep.*)	au delà de	über	al di là di	más allá de	förbi	farbay
past (bygone, *adj.*)	passé	vergangen	passato	pasado	förfluten	farbay
past (*n.*)	passé, *m.*	Vergangenheit, *f.*	passato, *m.*	pasado, *m.*	det förflutna, *n. def.*	over, *m.*
paste (adhesive)	colle, *f.*	Kleister, *m.*	colla, *f.*	engrudo, *m.*	klister, *n.*	pap, *m.*
pastime	passe-temps, *m.*	Zeitvertreib, *m.*	passatempo, *m.*	pasatiempo, *m.*	tidsfördriv, *n.*	tsaytfartrayb, *m.*
pastor	pasteur, *m.*	Pastor, *m.*	pastore, *m.*	pastor, *m.*	pastor, *nn.*	pastor, *m.*
pasture (grassland)	pâturage, *m.*	Weide, *f.*	pascolo, *m.*	pastura, *f.*	betesmark, *nn.*	pashe, *f.*
pat (tap)	tape, *f.*	Klaps, *m.*	colpetto, *m.*	golpecito, *m.*	klapp, *nn.*	laykhter klap, *m.*
pat (tap), to	taper	patschen	battere legger-mente	golpear ligera-mente	klappa	laykht klapn
patch (repair)	pièce, *f.*	Flicken, *m.*	pezza, *f.*	parche, *m.*	lapp, *nn.*	late, *f.*
patent (*n.*)	brevet, *m.*	Patent, *m.*	patente, *f.*	brevetto, *f.*	patent, *n.*	patent, *m.*
path	sentier, *m.*	Pfad, *m.*	sentiero, *m.*	sendero, *m.*	stig, *nn.*	shteg, *m.*
patience	patience, *f.*	Geduld, *f.*	pazienza, *f.*	paciencia, *f.*	tålamod, *n.*	geduld, *f.*
patient (forbearing)	patient	geduldig	paziente	paciente	tålig	geduldik
patient (invalid)	malade, *m., f.*	Kranke, *m., f.*	paziente, *m., f.*	paciente, *m., f.*	patient, *nn.*	patsyent, *m.*
patriot	patriote, *m., f.*	Patriot, *m.*	patriota, *m., f.*	patriota, *m.*	patriot, *nn.*	patriot, *m.*
patron (customer)	client, *m.*	Kunde, *m.*	cliente, *m., f.*	cliente, *m., f.*	kund, *nn.*	shtendiker koyne, *m.*
pattern (design)	dessin, *m.*	Muster, *n.*	disegno, *m.*	diseño, *m.*	mönster, *n.*	muster, *m.*
pause (wait), to	marquer un temps	pausieren	soffermarsi	pausar	göra en paus	blaybn shteyn
pave, to	paver	pflastern	lastricare	pavimentar	stenlägga	brukirn
pavement	pavé, *m.*	Strassenpflaster, *n.*	pavimento, *m.*	pavimento, *m.*	stenläggning, *nn.*	bruk, *m.*
paw	patte, *f.*	Pfote, *f.*	zampa, *f.*	pata, *f.*	tass, *nn.*	lape, *f.*
pawn, to	mettre en gage	verpfänden	dare in pegno	empeñar	pantsätta	farzetsn
pawnshop	crédit municipal, *m.*	Leihhaus, *n.*	Monte di Pietà, *m.*	casa de empeños, *f.*	pantlånekontor, *nn.*	lombard, *m.*
pay, to	payer	bezahlen	pagare	pagar	betala	tsoln
payable (due)	payable	zahlbar	pagabile	pagadero	betalbar	tsu tsoln
payment	paiement, *m.*	Zahlung, *f.*	pagamento, *m.*	pago, *m.*	betalning, *nn.*	tsolung, *f.*
pea	petit pois, *m.*	Erbse, *f.*	pisello, *m.*	guisante, *m.*	ärt, *nn.*	arbes, *m.*
peace	paix, *f.*	Frieden, *m.*	pace, *f.*	paz, *f.*	fred, *nn.*	sholem, *m.*
peaceful (tranquil)	paisible	ruhig	tranquillo	tranquilo	stilla	fridlekh
peach	pêche, *f.*	Pfirsich, *m.*	pesca, *f.*	melocotón, *m.*	persika, *nn.*	fershke, *f.*
peacock	paon, *m.*	Pfau (hahn), *m.*	pavone, *m.*	pavo real, *m.*	påfågel, *nn.*	pave, *f.*
peak (mountain top)	cime, *f.*	Spitze, *f.*	vetta, *f.*	cumbre, *f.*	bergstopp, *nn.*	shpits, *m.*
peal, to	sonner	erschallen	risuonare	repicar	skalla	klingen
peanut	cacahuète, *f.*	Erdnuss, *f.*	arachide, *f.*	maní, *m.*	jordnöt, *nn.* (*pl.* -nötter)	fistashke, *f.*
pear	poire, *f.*	Birne, *f.*	pera, *f.*	pera, *f.*	päron, *n.*	barne, *f.*
pearl (gem)	perle, *f.*	Perle, *f.*	perla, *f.*	perla, *f.*	pärla, *nn.*	perl, *m.*
peasant	paysan, *m.*	Bauer, *m.*	contadino, *m.*	campesino, *m.*	bonde, *nn.* (*pl.* bönder)	poyer, *m.*
pebble	caillou, *m.*	Kiesel, *m.*	ciottolo, *m.*	piedrecilla, *f.*	småsten, *nn.*	shteyndl, *n.*
peck, to	picoter	picken	beccare	picotear	hacka	pikn
peculiar (odd)	singulier, -lière	eigentümlich	strano	singular	egendomlig	modne
peel (take skin from), to	peler	(ab)schälen	sbucciare	descortezar	skala	sheyln
peer (equal)	pareil, *m.*	Gleiche, *m.*	pari, *m.*	par, *m.*	(jäm)like, *nn.*	glaykher, *m.*
peer (look intently), to	regarder atten-tivement	spähen	guardare atten-tamente	mirar atenta-mente	stirra	aynkukn zikh
peg (pin)	cheville, *f.*	Pflock, *m.*	piolo, *m.*	clavija, *f.*	pinne, *nn.*	flekl, *n.*
Peiping	Peï-Ping, *f.*	Peking, *n.*	Pechino, *m.*	Peiping	Peking, *n.*	Peyping, *n.*
pen	porte-plume, *m.*	Schreibfeder, *f.*	penna, *f.*	pluma, *f.*	penna, *nn.*	pen, *f.*
pen, fountain	stylo (graphe), *m.*	Füllfeder, *f.*	penna stilogra-fica, *f.*	pluma fuente, *f.*	reservoarpenna, *nn.*	eybike feder, *f.*
penalty	peine, *f.*	Strafe, *f.*	pena, *f.*	penalidad, *f.*	straff, *n.*	shtrof, *f.*
pencil	crayon, *m.*	Bleistift, *m.*	matita, *f.*	lápiz, *m.*	blyerts, *nn.*	blayer, *m.*
penetrate (pierce), to	pénétrer	durchdringen	penetrare	penetrar	genomtränga	durkhdringen
penicillin	pénicilline, *f.*	Penizillin, *n.*	penicillina, *f.*	penicilina, *f.*	penicillin, *n.*	penitsilin, *m.*
peninsula	péninsule, *f.*	Halbinsel, *f.*	penisola, *f.*	península, *f.*	halvö, *nn.*	halbindzl, *m.*

English	French	German	Italian	Spanish	Swedish	Yiddish
people (persons)	gens,*m.pl.*	Leute,*f. pl.*	gente,*f.*	gente,*f.*	folk,*n.*	layt,*pl.*
people (populace)	peuple,*m.*	Volk,*n.*	popolo,*m.*	pueblo,*m.*	folk,*n.*	folk,*n.*
pepper (green vegetable)	poivron,*m.*	Pfeffer,*m.*	peperone,*m.*	pimiento,*m.*	(*no equiv.*)	fefer,*m.*
pepper (seasoning)	poivre,*m.*	Pfeffer,*m.*	pepe,*m.*	pimienta,*f.*	peppar,*nn.*	fefer,*m.*
per (for each)	par	für	per	por	per	a
perceive, to	apercevoir (de), (s')	wahrnehmen	accorgersi	percibir	märka	dershpirn
percent (n.)	pour-cent,*m.*	Prozent,*n.*	per cento,*m.*	por ciento,*m.*	procent,*nn.*	protsent,*m.*
percentage	pourcentage,*m.*	Prozentsatz,*m.*	percentuale,*f.*	porcentaje,*m.*	procent,*nn.*	protsent,*m.*
perch (sit), to	percher, (se)	aufsitzen	posarsi	posarse	sitta uppflugen	zitsn
perfect (flawless)	parfait	vollkommen	perfetto	perfecto	fullkomlig	perfekt
perfection (flawlessness)	perfection,*f.*	Vollkommenheit, *f.*	perfezione,*f.*	perfección,*f.*	fullkomlighet, *nn.*	shleymes,*f.*
perform (do), to	accomplir	verrichten	compiere	ejecutar	utföra	durkhfirn
performance (action)	exécution,*f.*	Verrichtung,*f.*	esecuzione,*f.*	ejecución,*f.*	utförande,*n.*	funktsyonirung, *f.*
performance (stage presentation)	représentation,*f.*	Aufführung,*f.*	rappresentazione, *f.*	representación, *f.*	föreställning,*nn.*	forshtelung,*f.*
perfume (fragrance)	parfum,*m.*	Parfüm,*n.*	profumo,*m.*	perfume,*m.*	parfym,*nn.*	parfum,*m.*
perhaps	peut-être	vielleicht	forse	tal vez	kanske	efsher
peril	péril,*m.*	Gefahr,*f.*	pericolo,*m.*	peligro,*m.*	fara,*nn.*	sakone,*f.*
period (of time)	période,*f.*	Zeitraum,*m.*	periodo,*m.*	período,*m.*	period,*nn.*	peryod,*m.*
period (*punct.*)	point,*m.*	Punkt,*m.*	punto,*m.*	punto,*m.*	punkt,*nn.*	punkt,*m.*
perish, to	périr	umkommen	perire	perecer	omkomma	umkumen
perjury	parjure,*m.*	Meineid,*m.*	spergiuro,*m.*	perjurio,*m.*	mened,*nn.*	falshe shvue,*f.*
permanent (*adj.*)	permanent	dauernd	permanente	permanente	permanent	shtendik
permission	permission,*f.*	Erlaubnis,*f.*	permesso,*m.*	permiso,*m.*	tillåtelse,*nn.*	derloybenish,*f.*
permit (allow), to	permettre	erlauben	permettere	permitir	tillåta	derloybn
perpetual	perpétuel, -le	fortwährend	perpetuo	perpetuo	ständig	eybik
persist (persevere), to	persister	beharren	persistere	persistir	framhärda	durkhhaltn
person	personne,*f.*	Person,*f.*	persona,*f.*	persona,*f.*	person,*nn.*	perzon,*f.*
personal	personnel, -le	persönlich	personale	personal	personlig	perzenlekh
personality	personnalité,*f.*	Persönlichkeit,*f.*	personalità,*f.*	personalidad,*f.*	personlighet,*nn.*	perzenlekhkayt, *f.*
perspire, to	transpirer	schwitzen	sudare	sudar	svettas	shvitsn
persuade, to	persuader	überreden	persuadere	persuadir	övertala	iberredn
Peru	Pérou,*m.*	Peru,*n.*	Peru,*m.*	el Perú	Peru,*n.*	Peru,*m.*
Peruvian (*adj.*)	péruvien, -ne	peruanisch	peruviano	peruano	peruansk	peruanish
pervert (distort), to	pervertir	verdrehen	pervertire	pervertir	förvränga	farkrimen
pessimistic	pessimiste	pessimistisch	pessimistico	pesimista	pessimistisk	pesimistish
pest (nuisance)	peste,*f.*	Pest,*f.*	peste,*f.*	molestia,*f.*	plågoris,*n.*	ontshepenish,*f.*
pester, to	importuner	plagen	infastidire	molestar	besvära	tshepen zikh tsu
pet (animal)	animal choyé,*m.*	Haustier,*n.*	animale favorito, *m.*	animal mimado, *m.*	(*no equiv.*)	glet-khayele,*n.*
petition (written request)	pétition,*f.*	Bittschrift,*f.*	istanza,*f.*	petición,*f.*	petition,*nn.*	petitsye,*f.*
petticoat	jupon,*m.*	Unterrock,*m.*	sottana,*f.*	enaguas,*f.pl.*	underkjol,*nn.*	unterkleyd,*n.*
petty (minor)	petit	geringfügig	insignificante	mezquino	obetydlig	nishtik
pharmacist	pharmacien,*m.*	Apotheker,*m.*	farmacista,*m.*	farmacéutico,*m.*	farmaceut,*nn.*	apteyker,*m.*
pharmacy (drug store)	pharmacie,*f.*	Apotheke,*f.*	farmacia,*f.*	farmacia,*f.*	apotek,*n.*	apteyk,*f.*
phase (stage)	phase,*f.*	Phase,*f.*	fase,*f.*	fase,*f.*	skede,*n.*	faze,*f.*
Philippines	Philippines,*f.pl.*	Philippinen, die,*pl.*	Filippine,*f.pl.*	Filipinas,*f.pl.*	Filippinerna *def.pl.*	Filipinen,*pl.*
philosophy	philosophie,*f.*	Philosophie,*f.*	filosofia,*f.*	filosofía,*f.*	filosofi,*nn.*	filosofye,*f.*
phone, to	téléphoner	telephonieren	telefonare	telefonear	telefonera	telefonirn
phonograph	phonographe,*m.*	Phonograph,*m.*	fonografo,*m.*	fonógrafo,*m.*	grammofon,*nn.*	fonograf,*m.*
photograph	photographie,*f.*	Photographie,*f.*	fotografia,*f.*	fotografía,*f.*	fotografi,*n.*	fotografye,*f.*
phrase (*gram.*)	locution (de phrase),*f.*	Phrase,*f.*	frase,*f.*	frase,*f.*	fras,*nn.*	fraze,*f.*
physical (bodily)	physique	physisch	fisico	corporal	kroppslig	fizish
physical (material)	physique	körperlich	fisico	físico	fysisk	fizish
physician	médecin,*m.*	Arzt,*m.*	medico,*m.*	médico,*m.*	läkare,*nn.*	dokter,*m.*
physics (science)	physique,*f.*	Physik,*f.*	fisica,*f.*	física,*f.*	fysik,*nn.*	fizik,*f.*
piano (n.)	piano,*m.*	Klavier,*n.*	pianoforte,*m.*	piano,*m.*	piano,*n.*	pyane,*f.*
pick (choose), to	choisir	auswählen	scegliere	escoger	välja	klaybn
pickle (preserve), to	mariner	einpökeln	marinare	escabechar	lägga in i lag	zayern
pick up (lift), to	relever	aufpicken	alzare	alzar	ta(ga) upp	oyfheybn
picnic	pique-nique,*m.*	Picknik,*n.*	picnic,*m.*	jira campestre,*f.*	picknick,*nn.*	piknik,*f.*
picture (depiction)	image,*f.*	Bild,*n.*	quadro,*m.*	cuadro,*m.*	bild,*nn.*	bild,*n.*
picturesque	pittoresque	malerisch	pittoresco	pintoresco	pittoresk	bilderish
pie	tarte,*f.*	Obstkuchen,*m.*	torta,*f.*	pastel,*m.*	paj,*nn.*	pay,*m.*
piece (bit)	morceau,*m.*	Stück,*n.*	pezzo,*m.*	pedazo,*m.*	stycke,*n.*	shtik,*n.*
piecemeal (*adv.*)	pièce à pièce	stückweise	pezzo a pezzo	a pedazos	styckevis	shtiklekhvayz
piecework (n.)	travail à la tâche, *m.*	Stückarbeit,*f.*	lavoro a cottimo, *m.*	trabajo a destajo, *m.*	ackordsarbete,*n.*	shtikarbet,*f.*
pierce, to	percer	durchstechen	perforare	penetrar	genomborra	durkhshtekhn
pig (animal)	cochon,*m.*	Schwein,*n.*	porco,*m.*	cerdo,*m.*	gris,*nn.*	khazer,*m.*
pigeon	pigeon,*m.*	Taube,*f.*	piccione,*m.*	paloma,*f.*	duva,*nn.*	toyb,*f.*
pile (heap)	tas,*m.*	Haufen,*m.*	mucchio,*m.*	montón,*m.*	hög,*nn.*	kupe,*f.*
pill	pilule,*f.*	Pille,*f.*	pillola,*f.*	píldora,*f.*	piller,*n.*	pil,*f.*
pillar (column)	pilier,*m.*	Pfeiler,*m.*	pilastro,*m.*	pilar,*m.*	pelare,*nn.*	zayl,*m.*
pillow	oreiller,*m.*	Kissen,*n.*	guanciale,*m.*	almohada,*f.*	kudde,*nn.*	kishn,*f.*
pilot (flier)	pilote,*m.*	Pilot,*m.*	pilota,*m.*	piloto,*m.*	pilot,*nn.*	pilot,*m.*

English	French	German	Italian	Spanish	Swedish	Yiddish
pin (sewing accessory)	épingle, *f.*	Stecknadel, *f.*	spillo, *m.*	alfiler, *m.*	knappnål, *nn.*	skpilke, *f.*
pinch (squeeze), to	pincer	kneifen	pizzicare	apretar	nypa	knaypn
pine (tree)	pin, *m.*	Kiefer, *f.*	pino, *m.*	pino, *m.*	tall, *nn.*	sosne, *f.*
pink (color)	rose	blassrot	color di rosa	rosado	skär	rozeve
pioneer	pionnier, *m.*	Pionier, *m.*	pioniere, *m.*	pionero, *m.*	pionjär, *nn.*	pyoner, *m.*
pipe (tobacco pipe)	pipe, *f.*	Pfeife, *f.*	pipa, *f.*	pipa, *f.*	pipa, *nn.*	lulke, *f.*
pipe (tube)	tuyau, *m.*	Röhre, *f.*	tubo, *m.*	tubo, *m.*	rör, *n.*	rer, *f.*
pirate	pirate, *m.*	Seeräuber, *m.*	pirata, *m.*	pirata, *m.*	pirat, *nn.*	pirat, *m.*
pistol	pistolet, *m.*	Pistole, *f.*	pistola, *f.*	pistola, *f.*	pistol, *nn.*	pistoyl, *m.*
pit (hole)	fosse, *f.*	Grube, *f.*	fossa, *f.*	hoyo, *m.*	grop, *nn.*	grub, *f.*
pitch (tar)	poix, *f.*	Pech, *n.*	pece, *f.*	brea, *f.*	beck, *n.*	smole, *f.*
pitch (throw), to	lancer	werfen	lanciare	lanzar	kasta	varfn
pitcher (container)	broc, *m.*	Krug, *m.*	brocca, *f.*	jarro, *m.*	tillbringare, *nn.*	krug, *m.*
pity (compassion)	pitié, *f.*	Mitleid, *n.*	compassione, *f.*	compasión, *f.*	medlidande, *n.*	rakhmones, *n.*
pity, to	plaindre	bedauern	compatire	compadecer	ömka	rakhmones hobn oyf
place (locality)	lieu, *m.*	Platz, *m.*	luogo, *m.*	lugar, *m.*	plats, *nn.*	plats, *m.*
place (lay), to	poser	legen	collocare	colocar	lägga	leygn
plain (clear)	clair	deutlich	chiaro	claro	tydlig	klor
plain (level land)	plaine, *f.*	Ebene, *f.*	pianura, *f.*	llanura, *f.*	slätt, *nn.*	ployn, *m.*
plan (scheme)	plan, *m.*	Plan, *m.*	piano, *m.*	plan, *m.*	plan, *nn.*	plan, *m.*
plan (prearrange), to	projeter	entwerfen	progettare	planear	planera	planeven
plane (airplane)	avion, *m.*	Flugzeug, *n.*	aeroplano, *m.*	aeroplano, *m.*	flygplan, *n.*	aeroplan, *m.*
plane (surface)	plan, *m.*	Fläche, *f.*	piano, *m.*	plano, *m.*	plan yta, *nn.*	flakh, *f.*
planet	planète, *f.*	Planet, *m.*	pianeta, *m.*	planeta, *m.*	planet, *nn.*	planet, *m.*
plank (timber)	planche, *f.*	Brett, *n.*	tavola, *f.*	tabla, *f.*	planka, *nn.*	plankn, *m.*
plant (factory)	usine, *f.*	Betriebsanlage, *f.*	stabilimento, *m.*	fábrica, *f.*	fabrik, *nn.*	fabrik, *f.*
plant (flora)	plante, *f.*	Pflanze, *f.*	pianta, *f.*	planta, *f.*	växt, *nn.*	geviks, *n.*
plant (sow), to	planter	pflanzen	piantare	plantar	plantera	farzetsn
plaster (wall coating)	plâtre, *m.*	Mörtel, *m.*	intonaco, *m.*	yeso, *m.*	murbruk, *n.*	tink, *m.*
plastic (*n.*)	plastique, *m.*	Kunststoff, *m.*	plastico, *m.*	plástico, *m.*	plast, *nn.*	plastik, *m.*
plate (shallow dish)	assiette, *f.*	Teller, *m.*	piatto, *m.*	plato, *m.*	tallrik, *nn.*	teler, *m.*
plateau (tableland)	plateau, *m.*	Hochebene, *f.*	altipiano, *m.*	mesa, *f.*	platå, *nn.*	plato, *m.*
platform, railroad	quai, *m.*	Bahnsteig, *m.*	marciapiede, *m.*	andén, *m.*	plattform, *nn.*	peron, *m.*
platinum (*chem.*)	platine, *m.*	Platin, *n.*	platino, *m.*	platino, *m.*	platina, *nn.*	platin, *n.*
play (stage presentation)	pièce de théâtre, *f.*	Schauspiel, *n.*	spettacolo, *m.*	representación, *f.*	pjäs, *nn.*	pyese, *f.*
play (engage in recreation), to	jouer	spielen	giocare	jugar	leka	shpiln zikh
play (perform music upon), to	jouer de	spielen	suonare	tocar	spela	shpiln
play (take the role of), to	jouer	spielen	recitare	hacer (el papel de)	spela	shpiln
player (in a game)	joueur, *m.*	Spieler, *m.*	giocatore, *m.*	jugador, *m.*	spelare, *nn.*	shpiler, *m.*
playground	cour de récréation, *f.*	Spielplatz, *m.*	campo di ricreazione, *m.*	campo de recreo, *m.*	lekplats, *nn.*	shpilplats, *m.*
playmate	camarade de jeux, *m.*, *f.*	Spielgefährte, *m.*	compagno di giuoco, *m.*	compañero de juego, *m.*	lekkamrat, *nn.*	shpil-khaver, *m.*
plead (appeal earnestly), to	supplier	flehen	supplicare	suplicar	be	betn zikh
pleasant	agréable	angenehm	piacevole	agradable	angenäm	ayngenem
please (satisfy), to	plaire (à)	belieben	accontentare	complacer	tillfredsställa	tsufridn shteln
pleasure	plaisir, *m.*	Vergnügen, *n.*	piacere, *m.*	placer, *m.*	nöje, *n.*	fargenign, *m.*
pledge (vow)	voeu, *m.*	Gelöbnis, *n.*	voto, *m.*	promesa, *f.*	löfte, *n.*	havtokhe, *f.*
plentiful	abondant	reichlich	abbondante	abundante	riklig	shefedik
plenty (*n.*)	abondance, *f.*	Fülle, *f.*	abbondanza, *f.*	abundancia, *f.*	överflöd, *n.*	shefe, *f.*
plight (predicament)	état, *m.*	missliche Lage, *f.*	guaio, *m.*	aprieto, *m.*	belägenhet, *nn.*	klem, *f.*
plot (conspiracy)	complot, *m.*	Verschwörung, *f.*	complotto, *m.*	complot, *m.*	komplott, *nn.*	farshverung, *f.*
plow (*n.*)	charrue, *f.*	Pflug, *m.*	aratro, *m.*	arado, *m.*	plog, *nn.*	aker, *m.*
plow (till), to	labourer	pflügen	arare	arar	plöja	akern
pluck (pull off), to	arracher	pflücken	strappare	coger	plocka	flikn
plug (*elec.*)	bouchon de prise de courant, *m.*	Stecker, *m.*	spina, *f.*	enchufe, *m.*	stickkontakt, *nn.*	gopl, *m.*
plug (stopper)	tampon, *m.*	Stöpsel, *m.*	turacciolo, *m.*	tapón, *m.*	propp, *nn.*	farshtekl, *n.*
plum (fruit)	prune, *f.*	Pflaume, *f.*	prugna, *f.*	ciruela, *f.*	plommon, *n.*	floym, *f.*
plump (chubby)	dodu	rundlich	grassetto	rechoncho	fyllig	oysgepashet
plunge (hurl oneself), to	plonger, (se)	tauchen	precipitare	arrojarse	störta (sig)	araynvarfn zikh
plural (*adj.*)	pluriel, -le	Mehrzahl-...	plurale	plural	plural	mertsol-...
plus (*prep.*)	plus	plus	più	más	plus	plus
pneumonia	pneumonie, *f.*	Lungenentzündung, *f.*	polmonite, *f.*	pulmonía, *f.*	lunginflammation, *nn.*	lungen-ontsindung, *f.*
pocket	poche, *f.*	Tasche, *f.*	tasca, *f.*	bolsillo, *m.*	ficka, *nn.*	keshene, *f.*
poem	poème, *m.*	Gedicht, *n.*	poesia, *f.*	poema, *m.*	dikt, *nn.*	poeme, *f.*
poet	poète, *m.*	Dichter, *m.*	poeta, *m.*	poeta, *m.*	diktare, *nn.*	poet, *m.*
poetry	poésie, *f.*	Dichtung, *f.*	poesia, *f.*	poesía, *f.*	poesi, *nn.*	poezye, *f.*
point (in space)	point, *m.*	Ort, *m.*	punto, *m.*	punto, *m.*	udde, *nn.*	punkt, *m.*
point (item)	point, *m.*	Punkt, *m.*	punto, *m.*	punto, *m.*	punkt, *nn.*	punkt, *m.*
point (sharp end)	pointe, *f.*	Spitze, *f.*	punta, *f.*	punta, *f.*	spets, *nn.*	shpits, *m.*
point (indicate), to	indiquer	hinweisen	indicare	indicar	peka	onvayzn
pointed (tapered)	pointu	spitzig	a punta	puntiagudo	spetsig	shpitsik
poison	poison, *m.*	Gift, *n.*	veleno, *m.*	veneno, *m.*	gift, *n.*	sam, *m.*
poison, to	empoisonner	vergiften	avvelenare	envenenar	förgifta	farsamen
Poland	Pologne, *f.*	Polen, *n.*	Polonia, *f.*	Polonia	Polen, *n.*	Poyln, *n.*

English	French	German	Italian	Spanish	Swedish	Yiddish
pole (end of axis)	pôle,*m.*	Pol,*m.*	polo,*m.*	polo,*m.*	pol,*nn.*	polus,*m.*
pole (rod)	perche,*f.*	Stange,*f.*	palo,*m.*	pértiga,*f.*	stång,*nn.*(*pl.* stänger)	drong,*m.*
police	police,*f.*	Polizei,*f.*	polizia,*f.*	policía,*f.*	polis,*nn.*	politsey,*f.*
policeman	agent de police, *m.*	Polizist,*m.*	vigile,*m.*	policía,*m.*	polis,*nn.*	politsyant,*m.*
policy (contract of insurance)	police,*f.*	Polize,*f.*	polizza,*f.*	póliza,*f.*	försäkringsbrev, *n.*	polis,*m.*
policy (course)	ligne de conduite, *f.*	Politik,*f.*	linea di condotta, *f.*	política,*f.*	politik,*nn.*	politik,*f.*
polish	poli,*m.*	Glanz,*m.*	lucido,*m.*	lustre,*m.*	polityr,*nn.*	polir,*m.*
Polish (*adj.*)	polonais	polnisch	polacco	polaco	polsk	poylish
polish, to	polir	polieren	lucidare	pulir	polera	polirn
polite	poli	höflich	garbato	cortés, -tesa	artig	eydl
political	politique	politisch	politico	político	politisk	politish
political science	science politique, *f.*	Staatswissenschaft,*f.*	scienza politica,*f.*	ciencia política, *f.*	statsvetenskap, *nn.*	politishe visnshaft,*f.*
politician	politicien,*m.*	Politiker,*m.*	uomo politico,*m.*	político,*m.*	politiker,*nn.*	politikant,*m.*
politics	politique,*f.*	Politik,*f.*	politica,*f.*	política,*f.*	politik,*nn.*	politik,*f.*
poll (survey)	sondage,*m.*	Umfrage,*f.*	scrutinio,*m.*	encuesta,*f.*	röstning,*nn.*	oysfreg,*m.*
pond	étang,*m.*	Teich,*m.*	stagno,*m.*	estanque,*m.*	damm,*nn.*	stav,*m.*
pony (animal)	poney,*m.*	Pferdchen,*n.*	cavallino,*m.*	caballito,*m.*	ponny,*nn.*	poni,*m.*
pool (standing water)	mare,*f.*	Pfuhl,*m.*	pozzo,*m.*	charco,*m.*	pöl,*nn.*	kaluzhe,*f.*
poor (needy)	pauvre	dürftig	...povero	pobre	fattig	orem
poor (unfortunate)	pauvre	arm	povero...	pobre	stackars	nebekh
pope	pape,*m.*	Papst,*m.*	papa,*m.*	papa,*m.*	påve,*nn.*	poyps,*m.*
popular (prevalent)	en vogue	verbreitet	popolare	popular	allmän	populer
popular (well-liked)	populaire	populär	popolare	popular	populär	balibt
population (number of people)	population,*f.*	Bevölkerung,*f.*	popolazione,*f.*	población,*f.*	folkmängd,*nn.*	bafelkerung,*f.*
porcelain (*n.*)	porcelaine,*f.*	Porzellan,*n.*	porcellana,*f.*	porcelana,*f.*	porslin,*n.*	portselay,*n.*
porch	véranda,*f.*	Vorhalle,*f.*	loggia,*f.*	pórtico,*m.*	veranda,*nn.*	ganik,*m.*
pork	porc,*m.*	Schweinefleisch,*n.*	carne di maiale,*f.*	carne de cerdo,*f.*	fläsk,*n.*	khazer-fleysh,*n.*
pork chop	côtelette de porc, *f.*	Schweinsrippchen,*n.pl.*	costoletta di maiale,*f.*	chuleta de cerdo, *f.*	fläskkotlett,*nn.*	khazer-kotlet,*m.*
port (harbor)	port,*m.*	Hafen,*m.*	porto,*m.*	puerto,*m.*	hamn,*nn.*	port,*m.*
porter (baggage carrier)	porteur,*m.*	Gepäckträger,*m.*	portabagagli,*m.*	cargador,*m.*	bärare,*nn.*	treger,*m.*
portion (part)	portion,*f.*	Teil,*m.*	porzione,*f.*	porción,*f.*	del,*nn.*	kheylek,*m.*
portrait	portrait,*m.*	Bildnis,*n.*	ritratto,*m.*	retrato,*m.*	porträtt,*n.*	portret,*m.*
Portugal	Portugal,*m.*	Portugal,*n.*	Portogallo,*m.*	Portugal	Portugal,*n.*	Portugal,*n.*
position (location)	position,*f.*	Lage,*f.*	posizione,*f.*	posición,*f.*	läge,*n.*	pozitsye,*f.*
positive (decisive)	positif, -tive	entscheidend	positivo	positivo	avgörande	befeyresh
possess, to	posséder	besitzen	possedere	poseer	äga	farmogn
possession (ownership)	possession,*f.*	Besitz,*m.*	possessione,*f.*	posesión,*f.*	besittning,*nn.*	farmogn,*n.*
possibility	possibilité,*f.*	Möglichkeit,*f.*	possibilità,*f.*	posibilidad,*f.*	möjlighet,*nn.*	miglekhkayt,*f.*
possible	possible	möglich	possibile	posible	möjlig	miglekh
post (pole)	poteau,*m.*	Pfosten,*m.*	palo,*m.*	poste,*m.*	stolpe,*nn.*	slup,*m.*
post (position)	poste,*m.*	Posten,*m.*	posto,*m.*	puesto,*m.*	post,*nn.*	postn,*m.*
postage (postal charge)	port,*m.*	Porto,*n.*	porto,*m.*	franqueo,*m.*	porto,*n.*	postgelt,*n.*
postman	facteur,*m.*	Briefträger,*m.*	postino,*m.*	cartero,*m.*	brevbärare,*nn.*	brivn-treger,*m.*
post office	bureau de poste, *m.*	Postamt,*n.*	ufficio postale,*m.*	correo,*m.*	postkontor,*n.*	postamt,*m.*
postpone, to	remettre	verschieben	posporre	posponer	uppskjuta	opleygn
postscript	post-scriptum,*m.*	Nachschrift,*f.*	poscritto,*m.*	posdata,*f*	postskriptum,*n.* (*pl.* -skripta)	nokhvort,*n.*
pot (container)	pot,*m.*	Topf,*m.*	pentola,*f.*	pote,*m.*	kruka,*nn.*	top,*m.*
potato (white)	pomme de terre, *f.*	Kartoffel,*f.*	patata,*f.*	papa,*f.*	potatis,*nn.,n.*	kartofl,*m.*
poultry	volaille,*f.*	Federvieh,*n.*	pollame,*m.*	aves de corral,*f. pl.*	fjäderfä,*n.*	oyfes,*pl.*
pound (pummel), to	cogner	stossen	pestare	machacar	banka	tseshtoysn
pour (make flow), to	verser	einschenken	versare	verter	hälla	gisn
poverty	pauvreté,*f.*	Armut,*f.*	povertà,*f.*	pobreza,*f.*	fattigdom,*nn.*	dales,*m.*
powder (cosmetic)	poudre,*f.*	Puder,*m.*	cipria,*f.*	polvos,*m.pl.*	puder,*n.*	puder,*m.*
powder (dust)	poudre,*f.*	Staub,*m.*	polvere,*f.*	polvo,*m.*	stoft,*n.*	proshik,*m.*
power (authority)	pouvoir,*m.*	Macht,*f.*	potere,*m.*	poder,*m.*	makt,*nn.*	makht,*f.*
powerful	puissant	mächtig	potente	poderoso	mäktig	makhtik
power of attorney	pouvoir,*m.*	Vollmacht,*f.*	procura,*f.*	poder,*m.*	fullmakt,*nn.*	fulmakht,*f.*
practical (not theoretical)	pratique	praktisch	pratico	práctico	praktisk	praktish
practice (custom)	usage,*m.*	Brauch,*m.*	uso,*m.*	práctica,*f.*	bruk,*n.*	firung,*f.*
practice (performance)	exercice,*m.*	Ausübung,*f.*	esercizio,*m.*	práctica,*f.*	utövning,*nn.*	praktik,*f.*
practice (put to practice), to	pratiquer	ausüben	praticare	practicar	utöva	praktitsirn
prairie	prairie,*f.*	Prärie,*f.*	prateria,*f.*	pradera,*f.*	prärie,*nn.*	prerye,*f.*
praise	louange,*f.*	Lob,*n.*	lode,*f.*	alabanza,*f.*	beröm,*n.*	shvakh,*m.*
praise, to	louer	loben	lodare	elogiar	berömma	loybn
pray, to	prier	beten	pregare	rezar	be(dja)	mispalel zayn
prayer (petition)	prière,*f.*	Gebet,*n.*	preghiera,*f.*	oración,*f.*	bön,*nn.*	tfile,*f.*
preach, to	prêcher	predigen	predicare	predicar	predika	preydikn
preacher	prédicateur,*m.*	Prediger,*m.*	predicatore,*m.*	predicador,*m.*	predikant,*nn.*	preydiker,*m.*
precious (costly)	précieux, -cieuse	kostbar	prezioso	precioso	dyrbar	tayer
precipice	précipice,*m.*	Abgrund,*m.*	precipizio,*m.*	precipicio,*m.*	brant,*nn.*	thom,*m.*
precise (exact)	précis	genau	preciso	preciso	precis	pretsiz

English	French	German	Italian	Spanish	Swedish	Yiddish
predict, to	prédire	voraussagen	predire	predecir	förutsäga	foroyszogn
preface	préface,f.	Vorwort,n.	prefazione,f.	prefacio,m.	förord,n.	hakdome,f.
prefer (like better), to	préférer	vorziehen	preferire	preferir	föredra(ga)	helter hobn
prejudice	préjugé,m.	Vorurteil,n.	pregiudizio,m.	prejuicio,m.	fördom,nn.	forurteyl,m.
preliminary (adj.)	préliminaire	vorläufig	preliminare	preliminar	förberedande	preliminar
premium (payment)	prime,f.	Prämie,f.	premio,m.	prima,f.	premie,nn.	premye,f.
preparation (preparatory act)	préparation,f.	Vorbereitung,f.	preparazione,f.	preparación,f.	förberedelse,nn.	tsugreytung,f.
prepare (make ready), to	préparer	vorbereiten	preparare	preparar	förbereda	tsugreytn
preposition (gram.)	préposition,f.	Verhältniswort,n.	preposizione,f.	preposición,f.	preposition,nn.	prepozitsye,f.
prescription (med.)	ordonnance,f.	Rezept,n.	ricetta,f.	receta,f.	recept,n.	retsept,m.
presence (being present)	présence,f.	Anwesenheit,f.	presenza,f.	presencia,f.	närvaro,nn.	bayzayn,n.
present (current, adj.)	actuel, -le	gegenwärtig	attuale	actual	närvarande	itstik
present (present time, n.)	présent,m.	Gegenwart,f.	presente,m.	presente,m.	närvarande tid, nn.	itstikayt,f.
present (give), to	donner	überreichen	presentare	regalar	skänka	derlangen
present (introduce), to	présenter	vorstellen	presentare	presentar	presentera	forshteln
present (set forth), to	présenter	darlegen	presentare	exponer	framlägga	prezentirn
preserve, to	conserver	erhalten	conservare	preservar	bevara	oyfhitn
president	président,m.	Präsident,m.	presidente,m.,f.	presidente,m.	president,nn.	prezident,m.
press (newspapers and periodicals)	presse,f.	Presse,f.	stampa,f.	prensa,f.	press,nn.	prese,f.
press (bear upon), to	presser	drücken	premere	apretar	pressa	drikn
press (iron), to	repasser	bügeln	stirare	planchar	pressa	presn
pressure (force)	pression,f.	Druck,m.	pressione,f.	presión,f.	tryck,n.	druk,m.
presume (assume), to	supposer	vermuten	assumere	presumir	anta(ga)	meshaer zayn
pretend (feign), to	feindre	heucheln	fingere	fingir	låtsa(s)	makhn dem onshtel
pretense (pretending)	semblant,m.	Vorgeben,n.	finta,f.	pretensión,f.	förevändning,nn.	onshtel,m.
pretext	prétexte,m.	Vorwand,m.	pretesto,m.	pretexto,m.	förevändning,nn.	terets,m.
pretty	joli	hübsch	grazioso	bonito	vacker	sheyn
prevail (exist widely), to	prédominer	vorherrschen	essere prevalente	prevalecer	råda	hershn
prevent (stop), to	empêcher	verhüten	prevenire	prevenir	förhindra	farhitn
previous	antérieur	vorhergehend	anteriore	previo	föregående	frierdik
prey (victim)	proie,f.	Beute,f.	preda,f.	presa,f.	byte,n.	royb,m.
price (bus.)	prix,m.	Preis,m.	prezzo,m.	precio,m.	pris,n.	prayz,m.
prick, to	piquer	stechen	pungere	picar	sticka	shtekhn
pride (self-esteem)	orgueil,m.	Stolz,m.	orgoglio,m.	orgullo,m.	stolthet,nn.	shtolts,m.
priest	prêtre,m.	Priester,m.	prete,m.	sacerdote,m.	präst,nn.	prister,m.
primary (first, adj.)	premier, -mière	erst	primario	primario	först(a)	ershtik
prime (first, adj.)	premier, -mière	erst	primo	primero	först(a)	ersht
primitive (early)	primitif, -tive	primitiv	primitivo	primitivo	primitiv	primitiv
prince	prince,m.	Prinz,m.	principe,m.	príncipe,m.	prins,nn.	prints,m.
princess	princesse,f.	Prinzessin,f.	principessa,f.	princesa,f.	prinsessa,nn.	printsesin,f.
principal (main)	principal	hauptsächlich	principale	principal	förnämst	hoypt-...
principle (basic truth)	principe,m.	Grundsatz,m.	principio,m.	principio,m.	grundsats,nn.	printsip,m.
print (printed reproduction)	estampe,f.	Abdruck	incisione,f.	impresión,f.	tryck,n.	opdruk,m.
print, to	imprimer	drucken	stampare	imprimir	trycka	drukn
printer	imprimeur,m.	Drucker,m.	tipografo,m.	impresor,m.	tryckare,nn.	druker,m.
prison	prison,f.	Gefängnis,n.	prigione,f.	prisión,f.	fängelse,n.	turme,f.
prisoner	prisonnier,m.	Gefangene,m.,f.	prigioniero,m.	prisionero,m.	fånge,nn.	arestant,m.
private (personal)	privé	privat	particolare	privado	privat	privat
private (mil.)	soldat (du rang),m.	Gemeiner,m.	soldato (semplice),m.	soldado raso,m.	menig,nn. (pl. -a)	soldat,m.
privilege	privilège,m.	Vorrecht,n.	privilegio,m.	privilegio,m.	privilegium,nn.	privilegye,f.
prize (trophy)	prix,m.	Preis,m.	premio,m.	premio,m.	pris,n.	priz,m.
probable (likely)	probable	wahrscheinlich	probabile	probable	trolig	mashmoes
problem	problème,m.	Problem,n.	problema,m.	problema,m.	problem,n.	problem,f.
process (set of operations)	procédé,m.	Verfahren,n.	processo,m.	proceso,m.	procedur,nn.	protses,m.
procession (parade)	procession,f.	(feierliche) Zug,m.	processione,f.	procesión,f.	procession,nn.	protsesye,f.
proclaim, to	proclamer	verkünd(ig)en	proclamare	proclamar	tillkännage	proklamirn
procure (obtain), to	obtenir	verschaffen	procurare	obtener	skaffa	farshafn
produce (yield)	rendement,m.	Ertrag,m.	prodotto,m.	producción,f.	avkastning,nn.	produkt,m.
produce (make), to	produire	hervorbringen	produrre	producir	producera	produtsirn
product	produit,m.	Erzeugnis,n.	prodotto,m.	producto,m.	produkt,m.	produkt,m.
production (manufacture)	production,f.	Herstellung,f.	produzione,f.	producción,f.	produktion,nn.	produktsye,f.
productive	productif, -tive	produktiv	produttivo	productive	produktiv	produktiv
profane (blasphemous)	profane	schändlich	blasfematorio	profano	profan	grob
profession (occupation)	profession,f.	Beruf,m.	professione,f.	profesión,f.	yrke,n.	profesye,f.
professional	professionnel, -le	fachmännisch	professionale	profesional	professionell	profesyonel
professor (teacher)	professeur,m.	Professor,m.	professore,m.	profesor,m.	professor,nn.	profesor,m.
profit (bus.)	bénéfice,m.	Gewinn,m.	profitto,m.	ganancia,f.	vinst,nn.	revakh,m.
profitable	profitable	einträglich	profittevole	provechoso	lönande	revokhimdik
profound	profond	tief	profondo	profundo	djup	tif
program (plan)	programme,m.	Programm,n.	programma,m.	programa,m.	program,n.	program,f.
progress	progrès,m.	Fortschritt,m.	progresso,m.	progreso,m.	framsteg,n.	progres,m.
progressive (advancing)	progressif, -sive	fortschrittlich	progressivo	progresivo	framåtgående	progresiv
prohibition	prohibition,f.	Verbot,m.	proibizione,f.	prohibición,f.	förbud,m.	farver,m.

English	French	German	Italian	Spanish	Swedish	Yiddish
project	projet,*m.*	Entwurf,*m.*	progetto,*m.*	proyecto,*m.*	projekt,*n.*	proyekt,*m.*
prolong, to	prolonger	verlängern	prolungare	prolongar	förlänga	farlengern
prominent (eminent)	éminent	hervorragend	eminente	sobresaliente	framstående	prominent
prominent (jutting)	saillant	hervorragend	prominente	prominente	utskjutande	aroysshtartsndik
promise (pledge)	promesse,*f.*	Versprechen,*n.*	promessa,*f.*	promesa,*f.*	löfte,*n.*	tsuzog,*m.*
promise (pledge), to	promettre	versprechen	promettere	prometer	lova	tsuzogn
promote (further), to	encourager	fördern	promuovere	promover	främja	protezhirn
promote (raise in rank), to	élever	befördern	promuovere	ascender	befordra	hekhern
promotion (advance)	promotion,*f.*	Beförderung,*f.*	promozione,*f.*	ascenso,*m.*	befordran,*nn.*	hekherung,*f.*
prompt (punctual)	ponctuel, -le	pünktlich	puntuale	puntual	punktlig	pinktlekh
prompt (quick)	prompt	unverzüglich	pronto	pronto	snabb	teykefdik
pronounce (declare), to	déclarer	verkünd(ig)en	dichiarare	declarar	förklara	aroysgebn a psak
pronounce (enunciate), to	prononcer	aussprechen	pronunziare	pronunciar	uttala	aroysredn
proof (demonstration)	preuve,*f.*	Beweis,*m.*	prova,*f.*	comprobación,*f.*	bevis,*n.*	bavayz,*m.*
proper (acceptable)	convenable	geziehmend	corretto	correcto	passande	orntlekh
property (possession)	biens,*m.pl.*	Eigentum,*n.*	avere,*m.*	propiedad,*f.*	egendom,*nn.*	farmegn,*n.*
prophet (religious teacher)	prophète,*m.*	Prophet,*m.*	profeta,*m.*	profeta,*m.*	profet,*nn.*	novi,*m.*
proportion (part)	partie,*f.*	Anteil,*m.*	porzione,*f.*	parte,*f.*	del,*nn.*	proports,*f.*
proportion (ratio)	proportion,*f.*	Verhältnis,*n.*	proporzione,*f.*	proporción,*f.*	förhållande,*n.*	farheltenish,*f.*
proposal (suggestion)	proposition,*f.*	Vorschlag,*m.*	proposta,*f.*	propuesta,*f.*	förslag,*n.*	forshlog,*m.*
propose (offer marriage), to	faire une demande en mariage	einen Heiratsantrag machen	domandare la mano (di)	declararse	fria	forleygn khasene tsu hobn
propose (suggest), to	proposer	vorschlagen	proporre	proponer	föreslå	forleygn
prose	prose,*f.*	Prosa,*f.*	prosa,*f.*	prosa,*f.*	prosa,*nn.*	proze,*f.*
prospect (thing expected)	perspective,*f.*	Aussicht,*f.*	prospetto,*m.*	expectativa,*f.*	utsikt,*nn.*	oyskuk,*m.*
prosper, to	prospérer	gedeihen	prosperare	prosperar	blomstra	matsliakh zayn
prosperity	prospérité,*f.*	Wohlstand,*m.*	prosperità,*f.*	prosperidad,*f.*	välstånd,*n.*	prosperitet,*f.*
prosperous	prospère	gedeihlich	prospero	próspero	blomstrande	bliendik
protect, to	protéger	schützen	proteggere	proteger	skydda	bashitsn
protection	protection,*f.*	Schutz,*m.*	protezione,*f.*	protección,*f.*	beskydd,*n.*	bashitsung,*f.*
protest	protestation,*f.*	Einspruch,*m.*	protesta,*f.*	protesta,*f.*	protest,*nn.*	protest,*m.*
protest, to	protester	beteuern	protestare	protestar	protestera	protestirn
proud (taking pride in)	fier, -ère	stolz	orgoglioso	orgulloso	stolt	shtolts
prove (verify), to	prouver	beweisen	provare	probar	bevisa	dervayzn
proverb	proverbe,*m.*	Sprichwort,*n.*	proverbio,*m.*	proverbio,*m.*	ordspråk,*n.*	shprikhvort,*n.*
provide (supply), to	fournir	versehen	provvedere	proveer	förse	farzorgn
province (*pol.*)	province,*f.*	Provinz,*f.*	provincia,*f.*	provincia,*f.*	provins,*nn.*	provints,*f.*
provision (stipulation)	stipulation,*f.*	Bedingung,*f.*	condizione,*f.*	estipulación,*f.*	bestämmelse,*nn.*	bading,*m.*
prune	pruneau,*m.*	Backpflaume,*f.*	prugna secca,*f.*	ciruela pasa,*f.*	katrinplommon,*n.*	getriknte floym,*f.*
psychiatry	psychiatrie,*f.*	Psychiatrie,*f.*	psichiatria,*f.*	psiquiatría,*f.*	psykiatri,*nn.*	psikhyatrye,*f.*
psychology	psychologie,*f.*	Psychologie,*f.*	psicologia,*f.*	psicología,*f.*	psykologi,*nn.*	psikhologye,*f.*
public (common, *adj.*)	public, -blique	öffentlich	pubblico	público	allmän	efntlekh
public (populace, *n.*)	public,*m.*	Publikum,*n.*	pubblico,*m.*	público,*m.*	allmänhet,*nn.*	oylem,*m.*
publication (published work)	publication,*f.*	Veröffentlichung,*f.*	pubblicazione,*f.*	publicación,*f.*	publikation,*nn.*	publikatsye,*f.*
publicity (notoriety)	publicité,*f.*	Offenkundigkeit,*f.*	pubblicità,*f.*	publicidad,*f.*	publicitet,*nn.*	pirsum,*m.*
publish, to	publier	herausgeben	pubblicare	publicar	publicera	aroysgebn
publisher	éditeur,*m.*	Verleger,*m.*	editore,*m.*	editor,*m.*	förläggare,*nn.*	aroysgeber,*m.*
pudding (dessert)	pouding,*m.*	Pudding,*m.*	bodino,*m.*	budín,*m.*	pudding,*nn.*	puding,*m.*
pull (draw), to	tirer	ziehen	tirare	tirar de	dra(ga)	tsien
pulse (*physiol.*)	pouls,*m.*	Puls,*m.*	polso,*m.*	pulso,*m.*	puls,*nn.*	deyfek,*m.*
pump	pompe,*f.*	Pumpe,*f.*	pompa,*f.*	bomba,*f.*	pump,*nn.*	pompe,*f.*
punch (blow)	coup,*m.*	Knuff,*m.*	pugno,*m.*	puñetazo,*m.*	slag,*n.*	zets,*m.*
punctual	ponctuel, -le	pünktlich	puntuale	puntual	punktlig	pinktlekh
punish, to	punir	strafen	punire	castigar	straffa	shtrofn
punishment	punition,*f.*	Strafe,*f.*	punizione,*f.*	castigo,*m.*	straff,*n.*	shtrof,*f.*
pupil (of eye)	pupille,*f.*	Pupille,*f.*	pupilla,*f.*	pupila,*f.*	pupill,*nn.*	shvartsapl,*n.*
pupil (student)	élève,*m.,f.*	Schüler,*m.*	allievo,*m.*	discípulo,*m.*	elev,*nn.*	talmid,*m.*
purchase (act of buying)	achat,*m.*	Kauf,*m.*	compra,*f.*	compra,*f.*	köp,*n.*	aynkoyf,*m.*
pure (unadulterated)	pur	rein	puro	puro	ren	reyn
purity (cleanness)	pureté,*f.*	Reinheit,*f.*	purità,*f.*	pureza,*f.*	renhet,*nn.*	reynkayt,*f.*
purple (color)	pourpre	purpurn	violetto	purpúreo	purpurfärgad	lila
purpose (aim)	but,*m.*	Absicht,*f.*	scopo,*m.*	propósito,*m.*	syfte,*n.*	tsil,*m.*
purse (coin pouch)	bourse,*f.*	Geldbeutel,*m.*	borsa,*f.*	portamonedas,*m.*	portmonnä,*nn.*	baytl,*n.*
pursue (chase), to	poursuivre	verfolgen	inseguire	perseguir	förfölja	nokhyogn
pursuit (chase)	poursuite,*f.*	Verfolgung,*f.*	inseguimento,*m.*	persecución,*f.*	förföljande,*n.*	yog,*f.*
push (shove)	poussée,*f.*	Stoss,*m.*	spinta,*f.*	empuje,*m.*	knuff,*nn.*	shtup,*m.*
push (shove), to	pousser	stossen	spingere	empujar	knuffa	shtupn
put (place), to	mettre	stellen	mettere	colocar	sätta	shteln
puzzle (game)	casse-tête,*m.*	Geduldspiel,*n.*	enigma,*m.*	rompecabezas,*m.*	pussel,*n.*	trefshpil,*f.*
quaint (unusual)	original	seltsam	originale	raro	sällsam	alt-frenkish
quake (shake), to	trembler	beben	tremare	temblar	skälva	tsitern
qualify (modify), to	modifier	einschränken	modificare	calificar	modifiera	aynengen
quality (attribute)	qualité,*f.*	Eigenschaft,*f.*	qualità,*f.*	calidad,*f.*	egenskap,*nn.*	eygnshaft,*f.*
quandary	embarras,*m.*	Verlegenheit,*f.*	impiccio,*m.*	perplejidad,*f.*	bryderi,*n.*	farlegnhayt,*f.*
quantity (amount)	quantité,*f.*	Menge,*f.*	quantità,*f.*	cantidad,*f.*	kvantitet,*nn.*	skhum,*m.*
quarrel (dispute)	querelle,*f.*	Streit,*m.*	alterco,*m.*	riña,*f.*	gräl,*n.*	krig,*f.*
quarrel (dispute), to	quereller, se	streiten	litigare	reñirse	gräla	krign zikh

English	French	German	Italian	Spanish	Swedish	Yiddish
quarter (one-fourth)	quart,*m.*	Viertel,*n.*	quarto,*m.*	cuarto	fjärdedel,*nn.*	fertl,*n.*
quarterly (four times a year)	trimestriel, -le	vierteljährlich	trimestrale	trimestral	kvartals-...	fertl-yorik
queen	reine,*f.*	Königin,*f.*	regina,*f.*	reina,*f.*	drottning,*nn.*	kinigin,*f.*
queer	bizarre	sonderbar	bizzarro	extraño	besynnerlig	oysterlish
quench, to	étancher	löschen	estinguere	apagar	släcka	shtiln
quest (search)	recherche,*f.*	Suche,*f.*	cerca,*f.*	busca,*f.*	sökande,*n.*	zukhn,*n.*
question (query)	question,*f.*	Frage,*f.*	domanda,*f.*	pregunta,*f.*	fråga,*nn.*	frage,*f.*
question (doubt), to	douter de	bezweifeln	mettere in dubbio	dudar	betvivla	sofekn
question (query), to	interroger	befragen	interrogare	interrogar	fråga	oysfregn
quick (rapid)	rapide	schnell	rapido	rápido	snabb	shnel
quicken, to	hâter	beschleunigen	affrettare	acelerar	påskynda	fargikhern
quiet (silent, *adj.*)	silencieux, -cieuse	still	silenzioso	silencioso	tyst	shtil
quiet (stillness)	tranquillité,*f.*	Ruhe,*f.*	quiete,*f.*	quietud,*f.*	stillhet,*nn.*	shtilkayt,*f.*
quiet (without motion, *adj.*)	tranquille	ruhig	quieto	quieto	stilla	ruik
quilt (bedcover)	courtepointe,*f.*	Steppdecke,*f.*	coltrone,*m.*	colcha,*f.*	täcke,*n.*	geshtepte koldre,*f.*
quit (stop), to	cesser	aufhören	smettere di	dejar	upphöra med	oyfhern
quite (considerably)	bien	ganz	abbastanza	bastante	riktigt	gants
Quito	Quito,*m.*	Quito,*n.*	Quito,*m.*	Quito	Quito,*n.*	Kito,*n.*
quiver, to	frémir	zittern	fremere	temblar	skälva	tsitern
quota	quote-part,*f.*	Quote,*f.*	quota,*f.*	cuota,*f.*	kvot,*nn.*	kvote,*f.*
quotation (price)	cotation,*f.*	Preisnotierung,*f.*	quotazione,*f.*	cotización,*f.*	notering,*nn.*	prayz-notirung, *f.*
quotation (selection)	citation,*f.*	Zitat,*n.*	citazione,*f.*	citación,*f.*	citat,*n.*	tsitat,*m.*
quote (cite), to	citer	zitieren	citare	citar	citera	tsitirn
rabbi	rabbin,*m.*	Rabbiner,*m.*	rabino,*m.*	rabí,*m.*	rabbin,*nn.*	rov,*m.*
rabbit	lapin,*m.*	Kaninchen,*n.*	coniglio,*m.*	conejo,*m.*	kanin,*nn.*	kinigl,*n.*
race (*anthrop.*)	race,*f.*	Rasse,*f.*	razza,*f.*	raza,*f.*	ras,*nn.*	rase,*f.*
race (contest)	course,*f.*	Wettlauf,*m.*	corsa,*f.*	carrera,*f.*	tävling,*nn.*	farmest,*m.*
radar (*n.*)	radar,*m.*	Radar,*n.*	radar,*m.*	radar,*m.*	radar,*nn.*	radar,*m.*
radiant	radieux, -dieuse	strahlend	radiante	radiante	strålande	shtralndik
radiator (heater)	radiateur,*m.*	Heizkörper,*m.*	termosifone,*m.*	radiador,*m.*	värmeelement,*n.*	radyator,*m.*
radical (basic)	radical	gründlich	radicale	radical	grundlig	radikal
radio (receiving set)	poste (de réception de T.S.F.), *m.*	Radio,*n.*	radio,*f.*	radio,*m.*	radio,*nn.*	radyo,*m.*
radioactivity	radio-activité,*f.*	Radioaktivität,*f.*	radioattività,*f.*	radiactividad,*f.*	radioaktivitet,*nn.*	radioaktiv-kayt,*f.*
rag (piece of cloth)	chiffon,*m.*	Lumpen,*m.*	straccio,*m.*	trapo,*m.*	trasa,*nn.*	shmate,*f.*
rage (wrath)	fureur,*f.*	Wut,*f.*	furore,*m.*	rabia,*f.*	raseri,*n.*	tsorn,*m.*
rage (rave), to	rager	wüten	arrabbiarsi	rabiar	rasa	busheven
rail (bar on track)	rail,*m.*	Schiene,*f.*	rotaia,*f.*	riel,*m.*	skena,*nn.*	rels,*m.*
railroad	chemin de fer,*m.*	Eisenbahn,*f.*	ferrovia,*f.*	ferrocarril,*m.*	järnväg,*nn.*	ban,*f.*
rain	pluie,*f.*	Regen,*m.*	pioggia,*f.*	lluvia,*f.*	regn,*n.*	regn,*m.*
rain, to	pleuvoir	regnen	piovere	llover	regna	regenen
rainbow	arc-en-ciel,*m.*	Regenbogen,*m.*	arcobaleno,*m.*	arco iris,*m.*	regnbåge,*nn.*	regn-boygn,*m.*
raincoat	imperméable,*m.*	Regenmantel,*m.*	impermeabile,*m.*	impermeable,*m.*	regnrock,*nn.*	regn-mantl,*m.*
rainy	pluvieux, -vieuse	regnerisch	piovigginoso	lluvioso	regnig	regndik
raise (collect), to	réunir	aufbringen	raccogliere	reunir	insamla	shafn
raise (lift up), to	lever	heben	alzare	alzar	lyfta upp	oyfheybn
raisin	raisin sec,*m.*	Rosine,*f.*	uva secca,*f.*	pasa,*f.*	russin,*n.*	rozhinke,*f.*
rake (tool)	râteau,*m.*	Harke,*f.*	rastrello,*m.*	rastrillo,*m.*	kratta,*nn.*	grable,*f.*
ram (animal)	bélier,*m.*	Widder,*m.*	montone,*m.*	morueco,*m.*	bagge,*nn.*	baran,*m.*
ram (butt), to	heurter	rammen	cozzare	topetar	stöta mot	farforn
range (of mountains)	chaîne,*f.*	Bergkette,*f.*	catena,*f.*	cordillera,*f.*	bergskedja,*nn.*	bargkeyt,*f.*
range (scope)	portée,*f.*	Bereich,*m.*	sfera (d'attività), *f.*	alcance,*m.*	område,*n.*	greykh,*m.*
rank (row)	rang,*m.*	Reihe,*f.*	fila,*f.*	fila,*f.*	rad,*nn.*	rey,*f.*
rank (standing)	rang,*m.*	Rang,*m.*	rango,*m.*	rango,*m.*	rang,*nn.*	rang,*m.*
ransom (*n.*)	rançon,*f.*	Lösegeld,*n.*	riscatto,*m.*	rescate,*m.*	lösen,*nn.*	oysleyzgelt,*n.*
rap, to	frapper	anklopfen	picchiare	golpear	knacka	onklapn
rapid (*adj.*)	rapide	schnell	rapido	rápido	snabb	geshvind
rapture	ravissement,*m.*	Entzücken,*n.*	rapimento,*m.*	rapto,*m.*	hänryckning,*nn.*	hispayles,*f.*
rare (uncommon)	rare	selten	raro	raro	sällsynt	zeltn
rash (*adj.*)	téméraire	vorschnell	imprudente	temerario	obetänksam	umbatrakht
raspberry	framboise,*f.*	Himbeere,*f.*	lampone,*m.*	frambuesa,*f.*	hallon,*n.*	maline,*f.*
rat	rat,*m.*	Ratte,*f.*	topo,*m.*	rata,*f.*	råtta,*nn.*	shtshur,*m.*
rate (degree of speed)	train,*m.*	Geschwindigkeit, *f.*	passo,*m.*	velocidad,*f.*	hastighet,*nn.*	tempo,*m.*
rate (exchange)	taux,*m.*	Kurs,*m.*	corso,*m.*	tipo de cambio, *m.*	kurs,*nn.*	kurs,*m.*
rate (price)	tarif,*m.*	Preis,*m.*	prezzo,*m.*	precio fijo,*m.*	pris,*n.*	prayz,*m.*
rather (preferably)	plutôt	eher	piuttosto	más bien	snarare	libersht
rather (somewhat)	assez	ziemlich	assai	algo	ganska	gants
rating (evaluation)	évaluation,*f.*	Schätzung,*f.*	valutazione,*f.*	evaluación,*f.*	värdering,*nn.*	shatsung,*f.*
ratio	raison,*f.*	Verhältnis,*n.*	rapporto,*m.*	razón,*f.*	förhållande,*n.*	farheltenish,*f.*
ration (allotment)	ration,*f.*	Ration,*f.*	razione,*f.*	ración,*f.*	ranson,*nn.*	ratsye,*f.*
rattle, to	cliqueter	klappern	risuonare	golpetear	skramla	gragern
rave (rant), to	tempêter	rasen	delirare	desvariar	väsnas	gvaldeven
raw (in natural state)	cru	roh	grezzo	crudo	rå	roy
ray (beam)	rayon,*m.*	Strahl,*m.*	raggio,*m.*	rayo,*m.*	stråle,*nn.*	shtral,*m.*
rayon	rayonne,*f.*	Kunstseide,*f.*	seta artificiale,*f.*	rayón,*m.*	konstsilke,*n.*	kunstzayd,*n.*

English	French	German	Italian	Spanish	Swedish	Yiddish
razor	rasoir,*m.*	Rasiermesser,*n.*	rasoio,*m.*	navaja de afeitar,*f.*	rakkniv,*nn.*	golmeser,*n.*
razor blade	lame de rasoir,*f.*	Rasierklinge,*f.*	lama di rasoio,*f.*	hoja de afeitar,*f.*	rakblad,*n.*	britve,*f.*
reach (arrive at), to	arriver à	erreichen	giungere	llegar a	komma till	derforn biz
reach (extend to), to	étendre à, s'	reichen	stendersi fino a	extenderse	sträcka sig	dergreykhn
reaction	réaction,*f.*	Reaktion,*f.*	reazione,*f.*	reacción,*f.*	reaktion,*nn.*	opruf,*m.*
read, to	lire	lesen	leggere	leer	läsa	leyenen
reader	lecteur,*m.*	Leser,*m.*	lettore,*m.*	lector,*m.*	läsare,*nn.*	leyener,*m.*
ready (prepared)	prêt	bereit	pronto	listo	färdig	greyt
real (actual)	réel, -le	wirklich	vero	real	verklig	real
real estate	biens-fonds,*m. pl.*	Grundeigentum, *n.*	beni immobili,*m. pl.*	bienes raíces,*m. pl.*	fastighet,*nn.*	grunteygns,*n.*
reality	réalité,*f.*	Wirklichkeit,*f.*	realtà,*f.*	realidad,*f.*	verklighet,*nn.*	vor,*f.*
realize (accomplish), to	réaliser	verwirklichen	realizzare	realizar	förverkliga	mekayem zayn
realize (recognize), to	rendre compte, se	vergegenwärtigen, sich	rendersi conto	darse cuenta de	inse	aynzen
really (actually)	vraiment	wirklich	in realtà	realmente	verkligen	beemes
really (indeed)	vraiment	in der Tat	veramente	realmente	verkligen	beemes
realm (field)	domaine,*m.*	Gebiet,*n.*	campo,*m.*	campo,*m.*	domän,*nn.*	sfere,*f.*
realm (kingdom)	royaume,*m.*	Reich,*n.*	reame,*m.*	reino,*m.*	rike,*n.*	melukhe,*f.*
reap, to	moissonner	ernten	mietere	cosechar	skörda	shnaydn
rear (*adj.*)	(d')arrière	Hinter-...	di dietro	posterior	bakre	hintersht
reason (ground)	raison,*f.*	Grund,*m.*	ragione,*f.*	razón,*f.*	orsak,*nn.*	taam,*m.*
reason (intellect)	raison,*f.*	Vernunft,*f.*	ragione,*f.*	razón,*f.*	förnuft,*n.*	seykhl,*m.*
reasonable (rational)	raisonnable	vernünftig	ragionevole	razonable	förnuftig	seykhldik
rebate (*bus.*)	remise,*f.*	Rabatt,*m.*	rimborso,*m.*	reintegro,*m.*	återbetalning,*nn.*	tsuriktsolung,*f.*
rebel (*n.*)	rebelle,*m.,f.*	Rebell,*m.*	ribelle,*m.,f.*	rebelde,*m.,f.*	rebell,*nn.*	rebel,*m.*
rebellion	rébellion,*f.*	Empörung,*f.*	ribellione,*f.*	rebelión,*f.*	uppror,*n.*	meride,*f.*
recall (remember), to	rappeler, se	erinnern, sich	ricordarsi	recordar	erinra sig	dermonen zikh
receipt (receiving)	réception,*f.*	Empfang,*m.*	ricevimento,*m.*	recibo,*m.*	mottagande,*n.*	bakumen,*n.*
receipt (voucher)	reçu,*m.*	Quittung,*f.*	ricevuta,*f.*	recibo,*m.*	kvitto,*n.*	kabole,*f.*
receipt, to (*bus.*)	quittancer	quittieren	quietanzare	extender recibo	kvittera	kvitirn
receive, to	recevoir	empfangen	ricevere	recibir	motta(ga)	bakumen
recent	récent	neu	recente	reciente	ny	anumltik
recently	récemment	unlängst	recentemente	recientemente	nyligen	anumlt
reception	accueil,*m.*	Empfang,*m.*	accoglienza,*f.*	recepción,*f.*	mottagande,*n.*	oyfnem,*m.*
recess (school intermission)	récréation,*f.*	Pause,*f.*	ricreazione,*f.*	hora de recreo,*f.*	rast,*nn.*	hafsoke,*f.*
recipe	recette,*f.*	Rezept,*n.*	ricetta,*f.*	receta,*f.*	recept,*n.*	retsept,*m.*
recite (repeat something learned), to	réciter	vortragen	recitare	recitar	föredra(ga)	aroysgerufn vern
reckless	téméraire	rücksichtslos	temerario	temerario	hänsynslös	hefkerdik
reckon (compute), to	compter	rechnen	comptuare	computar	beräkna	khezhbenen
reckon (consider), to	estimer	meinen	considrare	considerar	anse	haltn
recognition (acknowledgment)	reconnaissance,*f.*	Anerkennung,*f.*	riconoscimento *m.*	reconocimiento, *m.*	erkännande,*n.*	onerkenung,*f.*
recognition (identification)	reconnaissance, *f.*	Wiedererkennung,*f.*	riconoscimento, *m.*	reconocimiento, *m.*	igenkännande,*n.*	derkenen,*n.*
recognize (identify), to	reconnaître	wiedererkennen	riconoscere	reconocer	känna igen	derkenen
recommend (advise), to	recommander	empfehlen	raccomandare	recomendar	tillråda	rekomendirn
recommendation	recommandation, *f.*	Empfehlung,*f.*	raccomandazione,*f.*	recomendación, *f.*	rekommendation, *nn.*	rekomendatsye, *f.*
record (disk)	disque,*m.*	(Grammophon)- Platte,*f.*	disco,*m.*	disco,*m.*	grammofonskiva, *nn.*	rekord,*m.*
record (set down), to	enregistrer	aufzeichnen	registrare	inscribir	uppteckna	fartseykhenen
records (files)	registres,*m.pl.*	Akten,*m.pl.*	registri,*m.pl.*	registros,*m.pl.*	handlingar,*nn.pl.*	aktn,*pl.*
recover (get back), to	récupérer	wiedererlangen	ricuperare	recobrar	återfå	tsurikkrign
recover (get well), to	rétablir, se	erholen, sich	guarire	recuperar	tillfriskna	kumen tsu zikh
rectangle	rectangle,*m.*	Rechteck,*m.*	rettangolo,*m.*	rectángulo,*m.*	rektangel,*nn.*	grodek,*m.*
red	rouge	rot	rosso	rojo	röd	royt
redeem (buy back), to	racheter	loskaufen	riscattare	rescatar	återköpa	oyskoyfn
reduce (diminish), to	réduire	verringern	ridurre	reducir	minska	minern
reduction (lessening)	réduction,*f.*	Verminderung,*f.*	riduzione,*f.*	reducción,*f.*	minskning,*nn.*	minerung,*f.*
reed (grass)	roseau,*m.*	Rohr,*n.*	canna,*f.*	junco,*m.*	vass,*nn.*	ror,*m.*
reel (stagger), to	tituber	taumeln	barcollare	bambolearse	vackla	vign zikh
refer (allude), to	faire allusion	beziehen, sich	riferire	referirse	syfta	farrufn zikh
reference (allusion)	allusion,*f.*	Verweisung,*f.*	riferimento,*m.*	referencia,*f.*	hänsyftning,*nn.*	farrufn zikh,*n.*
refine (purify), to	raffiner	raffinieren	raffinare	refinar	rena	rafinirn
reflect (throw back), to	refléter	zurückwerfen	riflettere	reflejar	återspegla	opshpiglen
reflection (image)	reflet,*m.*	Spiegelbild,*n.*	riflessione,*f.*	reflejo,*m.*	spegelbild,*nn.*	opshpiglung,*f.*
reflection (meditation)	réflexion,*f.*	Überlegung,*f.*	riflessione,*f.*	reflexión,*f.*	eftertanke,*nn.*	yishev,*m.*
reform (*n.*)	réforme,*f.*	Reform,*f.*	riforma,*f.*	reforma,*f.*	reform,*nn.*	reform,*f.*
refresh, to	rafraîchir	erfrischen	ristorare	refrescar	uppfriska	oyffrishn
refreshments	rafraîchissements,*m.pl.*	Erfrischungen,*f. pl.*	rinfreschi,*m.pl.*	refrescos,*m.pl.*	förfriskningar, *nn.pl.*	kibed,*m.*
refrigerator	réfrigérateur,*m.*	Eisschrank,*m.*	frigorifero,*m.*	nevera,*f.*	kylskåp,*n.*	fridzhider,*m.*
refuge	refuge,*m.*	Zuflucht,*f.*	rifugio,*m.*	refugio,*m.*	tillflykt,*nn.*	mokem-miklet, *m.*
refugee	réfugié,*m.*	Flüchtling,*m.*	rifugiato,*m.*	refugiado,*m.*	flykting,*nn.*	polit,*m.*
refund (*bus.*)	remboursement, *m.*	Rückzahlung,*f.*	rimborso,*m.*	reembolso,*m.*	återbetalning,*nn.*	tsuriktsolung,*f.*
refuse (make a refusal), to	refuser	ablehnen	rifiutare	rehusar	vägra	opzogn zikh
refute, to	réfuter	widerlegen	confutare	refutar	vederlägga	opfregn
regal	royal	königlich	regale	real	kunglig	kiniglekh

English	French	German	Italian	Spanish	Swedish	Yiddish
regard (consider), to	considérer	betrachten	considerare	considerar	betrakta	batrakhtn
regarding (concerning)	à l'égard de	betreffs	(con) riguardo a	tocante a	beträffande	mikoyakh
regiment (n.)	régiment,m.	Regiment,n.	reggimento,m.	regimiento,m.	regemente,n.	regiment,m.
region (area)	région,f.	Gegend,f.	regione,f.	región,f.	trakt,nn.	rayon,m.
register (record)	registre,m.	Verzeichnis,n.	registro,m.	registro,m.	förteckning,nn.	register,m.
register, to	enregistrer	einschreiben	registrare	registrar	registrera	register,m.
registered (postal designation)	recommandé	eingeschrieben	raccomandato	certificado	rekommenderad	registrirn registrirt
regret (sorrow)	regret,m.	Bedauern,n.	rincrescimento, m.	pesadumbre,f.	ledsnad,nn.	badoyern,n.
regret, to	regretter	bedauern	...rincrescere (see p. 2955)	sentir	vara ledsen över	badoyern
regular (normal)	régulier, -lière	regelmässig	ordinario	regular	vanlig	reguler
regularity	régularité,f.	Regelmässigkeit, f.	regolarità,f.	regularidad,f.	regelbundenhet, nn.	regulerkayt,f.
regulation (rule)	règlement,m.	Vorschrift,f.	regolamento,m.	regla,f.	föreskrift,nn.	takone,f.
rehearsal	répétition,f.	Probe,f.	ripetizione,f.	ensayo,m.	repetition,nn.	repetitsye,f.
reign (period of rule)	règne,m.	Herrschaft,f.	regno,m.	reinado,m.	regeringstid,nn.	mamshole,f.
reimburse, to	rembourser	entschädigen	rimborsare	reintegrar	ersätta	umkern di hoytsoes
rein (strap)	rêne,m.	Zügel,m.	redine,f.	rienda,f.	tygel,nn.	leytse,f.
reindeer	renne,m.	Renntier,n.	renna,f.	reno,m.	ren,nn.	renifer,m.
reject, to	rejeter	ablehnen	rigettare	rechazar	avvisa	opvarfn
rejoice, to	réjouir, se	freuen, sich	rallegrarsi	regocijarse	glädja sig	freyen zikh
relapse, to	retomber	zurückfallen	ricadere	recaer	återfalla	tsurikfaln
relate (tell), to	raconter	erzählen	raccontare	relatar	berätta	ibergebn
related (connected)	apparenté	verwandt	connesso	relacionado	besläktad	kroyvish
relate (pertain) to, to	avoir rapport à	beziehen, sich	riferirsi a	relacionarse a	hänföra sig till	zayn shayekh
relation (connection)	rapport,m.	Beziehung,f.	rapporto,m.	relación,f.	förhållande,n.	shaykhes,f
relative (comparative)	relatif, -tive	verhältnismässig	relativo	relativo	relativ	relativ
relative (kinsman)	parent,m.	Verwandte,m.,f.	parente,m.	pariente,m.,f.	släkting,nn.	korev,m.
release (let go of), to	lâcher	freilassen	rilasciare	soltar	släppa lös	oplozn
reliable	sûr	zuverlässig	sicuro	digno de confianza	pålitlig	farlozlekh
relief (aid)	secours,m.	Unterstützung,f.	soccorso,m.	ayuda,f.	understöd,n.	hilf,f.
relief (alleviation)	soulagement,m.	Erleichterung,f.	sollievo,m.	alivio,m.	lättnad,nn.	fargringerung,f.
relieve (ease), to	soulager	erleichtern	sollevare	aliviar	lindra	fargringern
relieve (free), to	délivrer	befreien	liberare	librar	befria	bafrayen
religion	religion,f.	Religion,f.	religione,f.	religión,f.	religion,nn.	religye,f.
religious (adj.)	religieux, -gieuse	religiös	religioso	religioso	religiös	religyez
remain (be left), to	rester	übrigbleiben	rimanere	quedar	återstå	blaybn
remain (continue unchanged), to	rester	bleiben	rimanere	persistir	förbli	blaybn
remain (stay behind), to	rester	bleiben	rimanere	quedarse	stanna	blaybn
remainder	reste,m.	Rest,m.	resto,m.	resto,m.	återstod,nn.	resht,m.
remark (comment)	remarque,f.	Bemerkung,f.	osservazione,f.	advertencia,f.	yttrande,n.	bamerkung,f.
remark (say), to	constater	bemerken	osservare	comentar	yttra	bamerkn
remarkable (extraordinary)	remarquable	merkwürdig	straordinario	extraordinario	märkvärdig	merkverdik
remedy	remède,m.	Hilfsmittel,n.	rimedio,m.	remedio,m.	botemedel,n.	sgule,f.
remember (recollect), to	souvenir (de), se	erinnern, sich	ricordarsi (di)	recordar	minnas	dermonen zikh
remembrance (recollection)	souvenir,m.	Erinnerung,f.	ricordo,m.	recuerdo,m.	minne,n.	dermonung,f.
remind, to	rappeler à	erinnern	ricordare a	recordar	påminna	dermonen
remit (send payment), to	remettre	überweisen	rimettere	remesar	översända	ibershikn
remittance	remise,f.	(Geld)Sendung,f.	rimessa,f.	remesa,f.	remissa,nn.	geltshikung,f.
remote (far-off)	lointain	entlegen	remoto	remoto	avlägsen	vayt
remove (take away), to	enlever	beseitigen	togliere	quitar	avlägsna	tsunemen
render (cause to become), to	rendre	machen	rendere	hacer	göra	makhn far
renew, to	renouveler	erneuern	rinnovare	renovar	förnya	banayen
renounce (give up), to	renoncer à	verzichten auf	rinunciare	abandonar	uppge	opzogn zikh fun
rent (payment)	loyer,m.	Miete,f.	affitto,m.	alquiler,m.	hyra,nn.	dire-gelt,n.
rent (charge rent for), to	louer	vermieten	affittare	alquilar	hyra ut	fardingen
rent (pay rent for), to	louer	mieten	affittare	alquilar	hyra	dingen
repair (n.)	réparation,f.	Ausbesserung,f.	riparazione,f.	reparo,m.	reparation,nn.	reparatur,f.
repair (fix), to	réparer	ausbessern	riparare	reparar	reparera	farrikhtn
repay (reimburse), to	rembourser	zurückzahlen	rimborsare	reembolsar	återbetala	optsoln
repeat (reiterate), to	répéter	wiederholen	ripetere	repetir	upprepa	iberkhazern
repent, to	repentir, se	bereuen	pentirsi	arrepentirse	ångra	kharote hobn
replace (be a substitute for), to	remplacer	ersetzen	rimpiazzare	reemplazar	ersätta	farbaytn
reply	réponse,f.	Erwiderung,f.	risposta,f.	respuesta,f.	svar,n.	tshuve,f.
reply, to	répondre	erwidern	rispondere	responder	svara	entfern
report (account)	rapport,m.	Bericht,m.	rapporto,m.	informe,m.	rapport,nn.	barikht,m.
report (account formally), to	rendre compte	berichten	fare un rapporto (di)	presentar informe	rapportera	referirn
reporter (journalist)	reporter,m.	Berichterstatter, m.	cronista,m.,f.	reportero,m.	reporter,nn.(pl. -s)	reporter,m.
repose (calm)	repos,m.	Ruhe,f.	riposo,m.	calma,f.	lugn,n.	menukhe,f.
represent (act for), to	représenter	vertreten	rappresentare	representar	representera	menukhe,f.
represent (symbolize), to	symboliser	darstellen	rappresentare	representar	föreställa	reprezentirn
representation (pol.)	représentation,f.	Vertretung,f.	rappresentazione, f.	representación,f.	representation, nn.	reprezentirung,f.

English	French	German	Italian	Spanish	Swedish	Yiddish
representative (deputy)	représentant,*m.*	Vertreter,*m.*	deputato,*m.*	representante,*m.*	representant,*nn.*	forshteyer,*m.*
reproach	reproche,*m.*	Vorwurf,*m.*	rimprovero,*m.*	reproche,*m.*	förebråelse,*nn.*	tayne,*f.*
reproach, to	reprocher	vorwerfen	rimproverare	reprochar	förebrå	hobn taynes
republic	république,*f.*	Republik,*f.*	repubblica,*f.*	república,*f.*	republik,*nn.*	republik,*f.*
republican (*adj.*)	républicain	republikanisch	repubblicano	republicano	republikansk	republikanish
reputation	réputation,*f.*	Ruf,*m.*	riputazione,*f.*	reputación,*f.*	anseende,*n.*	shem,*m.*
request	demande,*f.*	Bitte,*f.*	richiesta,*f.*	solicitud,*f.*	begäran,*nn.*	bakoshe,*f.*
request, to	demander	ersuchen	richiedere	solicitar	begära	betn
require (need), to	avoir besoin de	erfordern	...occorrere (*see p.* 2955)	requerir	kräva	badarfn
resale (*bus.*)	revente,*f.*	Wiederverkauf, *m.*	rivendita,*f.*	reventa,*f.*	återförsäljning, *nn.*	viderfarkoyf,*m.*
rescue	sauvetage,*m.*	Rettung,*f.*	salvataggio,*m.*	rescate,*m.*	räddning,*nn.*	retung,*f.*
rescue, to	sauver	retten	salvare	rescatar	rädda	rateven
research	recherche(s),*f.* (*pl.*)	Forschung,*f.*	indagine,*f.*	investigación,*f.*	forskning,*nn.*	forshung,*f.*
resemble, to	ressembler à	ähneln	assomigliare a	asemejarse a	likna	zayn enlekh
resent, to	offenser de, s'	übelnehmen	offendersi di	resentirse de	uppta(ga) illa	faribl hobn
reservation (advance order)	réservation,*f.*	Vorausbestel-lung,*f.*	prenotazione,*f.*	reservación,*f.*	förutbeställning, *nn.*	rezervatsye,*f.*
reservation (mental qualifi-cation)	restriction,*f.*	Vorbehalt,*m.*	riserva,*f.*	restricción men-tal,*f.*	förbehåll,*n.*	bavorenish,*f.*
reserve (*bus.*)	réserve,*f.*	Reserven,*f.pl.*	riserva,*f.*	reserva,*f.*	reservfond,*nn.*	rezerv,*m.*
reserve (order in advance), to	retenir	vorausbestellen	prenotare	reservar	beställa	rezervirn
reserve (withhold), to	réserver	vorbehalten	detenere	reservar	reservera	iberlozn zikh
reservoir (water reserve)	réservoir,*m.*	Reservoir,*n.*	serbatoio,*m.*	depósito,*m.*	reservoar,*nn.*	rezervuar,*m.*
residence (abode)	résidence,*f.*	Wohnsitz,*m.*	residenza,*f.*	residencia,*f.*	bostad,*nn.* (*pl.* -städer)	voynort,*n.*
resident (*n.*)	habitant,*m.*	Ansässige,*m.,f.*	abitante,*m.,f.*	residente,*m.*	bofast person,*nn.*	aynvoyner,*m.*
resign (tender resignation), to	démissionner	zurücktreten	dimettersi	dimitir	avgå	rezignirn
resist, to	résister (à)	widerstehen	resistere a	resistir	motstå	antkegnshteln zikh
resistance	résistance,*f.*	Widerstand,*m.*	resistenza,*f.*	resistencia,*f.*	motstånd,*n.*	kegnshtel,*m.*
resolution (formal expres-sion)	résolution,*f.*	Beschluss,*m.*	deliberazione,*f.*	resolución,*f.*	resolution,*nn.*	rezolutsye,*f.*
resolve (determine), to	résoudre, (se)	beschliessen	risolversi	resolver(se)	bestämma	bashtimen
resort (spa)	station clima-tique,*f.*	Kurort,*m.*	stazione clima-tica,*f.*	lugar de tempo-rada,*m.*	kurort,*nn.*	kurort,*n.*
resort (have recourse), to	recourir (à)	Zuflucht nehmen zu	ricorrere	acudir	ta(ga) sin tillflykt	onkumen
resources (wealth)	ressources,*f.pl.*	Reichtümer,*m. pl.*	ricchezze,*f.pl.*	recursos,*m.pl.*	tillgångar,*nn.pl.*	oytsres,*pl.*
respect (esteem)	respect,*m.*	Achtung,*f.*	rispetto,*m.*	respeto,*m.*	respekt,*nn.*	derekh-erets,*m.*
respect (esteem), to	respecter	achten	rispettare	respetar	respektera	respektirn
respectable	respectable	anständig	rispettabile	respetable	respektabel	laytish
respective (*adj.*)	respectif, -tive	jeweilig	rispettivo	respectivo	respektive	geherik
respond (react), to	réagir	reagieren	reagire	responder	reagera	oprufn zikh
respond (reply), to	répondre	antworten	rispondere	responder	svara	entfern
response (reply)	réponse,*f.*	Antwort,*f.*	risposta,*f.*	respuesta,*f.*	svar,*n.*	entfer,*m.*
responsibility (account-ability)	responsabilité,*f.*	Verantwortung, *f.*	responsabilità,*f.*	responsabilidad, *f.*	ansvar,*n.*	akhrayes,*f.*
responsible (answerable)	responsable	verantwortlich	responsabile	responsable	ansvarig	farantvortlekh
rest (remainder)	reste,*m.*	Rest,*m.*	resto,*m.*	resto,*m.*	rest,*nn.*	resht,*m.*
rest (repose)	repos,*m.*	Ruhe,*f.*	riposo,*m.*	descanso,*m.*	vila,*nn.*	ru,*f.*
rest (repose), to	reposer, se	ruhen	riposarsi	descansar	vila	ruen
restaurant	restaurant,*m.*	Restaurant,*n.*	ristorante,*m.*	restaurante,*m.*	restaurang,*nn.*	restoran,*m.*
restless	agité	unruhig	agitato	inquieto	orolig	umruik
restore (reestablish), to	restaurer	wiederherstellen	ristabilire	restaurar	återställa	tsurik oyfshteln
restrain (check), to	refréner	zurückhalten	frenare	refrenar	hålla tillbaka	aynhaltn
result (consequence)	résultat,*m.*	Ergebnis,*n.*	conseguenza,*f.*	resultado,*m.*	resultat,*n.*	rezultat,*m.*
resume (recommence), to	reprendre	wiederanfangen	ricominciare	recomenzar	återuppta(ga)	vider nemen
retail (*bus., n.*)	détail,*m.*	Einzelhandel,*m.*	dettaglio,*m.*	venta al por me-nor,*f.*	detaljhandel,*nn.*	lakhodim-handl, *m.*
retailer (*bus.*)	détaillant,*m.*	Einzelhändler,*m.*	dettagliante,*m., f.*	detallista,*m.*	detaljhandlare, *nn.*	lakhodim-hend-ler,*m.*
retain (keep), to	conserver	behalten	ritenere	retener	behålla	lozn bay zikh
retire (stop working), to	prendre sa re-traite	zurückziehen, sich	ritirarsi	retirarse	dra(ga) sig till-baka	tsuriktsien zikh
retreat (*mil.*)	retraite,*f.*	Rückzug,*m.*	ritirata,*f.*	retiro,*m.*	reträtt,*nn.*	tsuriktsi,*m.*
return (coming or going back)	retour,*m.*	Rückkehr,*f.*	ritorno,*m.*	regreso,*m.*	återvändande,*n.*	tsurikker,*m.*
return (give back), to	rendre	zurückgeben	restituire	devolver	återlämna	umkern
return (go back), to	retourner	zurückkehren	ritornare	regresar	återvända	umkern zikh
reveal (divulge), to	révéler	enthüllen	rivelare	revelar	avslöja	oyszogn
revenge	vengeance,*f.*	Rache,*f.*	vendetta,*f.*	venganza,*f.*	hämnd,*nn.*	nekome,*f.*
revenue (*govt.*)	revenus,*m.pl.*	Staatseinnah-men,*f.pl.*	entrate pub-bliche,*f.pl.*	renta,*f.*	statsinkomster, *nn.pl.*	hakhnose,*f.*
reverence (respect)	révérence,*f.*	Verehrung,*f.*	reverenza,*f.*	reverencia,*f.*	vördnad,*nn.*	opshay,*m.*
reverse (contrary, *n.*)	contraire,*m.*	Gegenteil,*n.*	contrario,*m.*	lo contrario,*m.,f.*	motsats,*nn.*	heypekh,*m.*
review (critique)	compte rendu,*m.*	Besprechung,*f.*	recensione,*f.*	crítica,*f.*	recension,*nn.*	retsenzye,*f.*
review (look over again), to	revoir	überblicken	rivedere	repasar	åter granska	iberkukn
revive, to	ressusciter	wiederbeleben	risuscitare	resucitar	återuppliva	oyflebn
revolt	révolte,*f.*	Aufruhr,*f.*	rivolta,*f.*	rebelión,*f.*	uppror,*n.*	revolt,*m.*

English	French	German	Italian	Spanish	Swedish	Yiddish
revolution (*pol.*)	révolution, *f.*	Revolution, *f.*	rivoluzione, *f.*	revolución, *f.*	revolution, *nn.*	revolutsye, *f.*
revolver (weapon)	revolver, *m.*	Revolver, *m.*	revolver, *m.*	revólver, *m.*	revolver, *nn.*	revolver, *m.*
reward (recompense)	récompense, *f.*	Belohnung, *f.*	ricompensa, *f.*	recompensa, *f.*	belöning, *nn.*	skhar, *m.*
reward, to	récompenser	belohnen	ricompensare	recompensar	belöna	baloynen
rheumatism	rhumatisme, *m.*	Rheumatismus, *m.*	reumatismo, *m.*	reumatismo, *m.*	reumatism, *nn.*	revmatizm, *m.*
Rhine	Rhin, *m.*	Rhein, *m.*	Reno, *m.*	Rin, *m.*	Rhen, *nn.*	Reyn, *m.*
rhyme	rime, *f.*	Reim, *m.*	rima, *f.*	rima, *f.*	rim, *n.*	gram, *m.*
rib (*anat.*)	côte, *f.*	Rippe, *f.*	costola, *f.*	costilla, *f.*	revben, *n.*	rip, *f.*
ribbon	ruban, *m.*	Band, *n.*	nastro, *m.*	listón, *m.*	band, *n.*	lente, *f.*
rice	riz, *m.*	Reis, *m.*	riso, *m.*	arroz, *m.*	ris, *n.*	rayz, *m.*
rich	riche	reich	ricco	rico	rik	raykh
riches	richesses, *f.pl.*	Reichtum, *m.*	ricchezze, *f.pl.*	riquesa, *f.*	rikedom, *nn.*	ashires, *f.*
rid (free), to	débarrasser	befreien	sbarazzarsi di	librar	befria	bafrayen
riddle (*n.*)	énigme, *f.*	Rätsel, *n.*	indovinello, *m.*	acertijo, *m.*	gåta, *nn.*	retenish, *f.*
ride (in a car)	promenade (en voiture), *f.*	Fahrt, *f.*	passeggiata (in automobile), *f.*	paseo en auto, *m.*	åktur, *nn.*	for, *m.*
ride (in a car), to	aller en voiture	fahren	andare (in automobile)	pasear en auto	åka	forn
rider (horseman)	cavalier, *m.*	Reiter, *m.*	cavaliere, *m.*	jinete, *m.*	ryttare, *nn.*	rayter, *m.*
ridge (of mountains)	chaîne, *f.*	(Berg)Kette, *f.*	catena, *f.*	sierra, *f.*	bergås, *nn.*	bargkeyt, *f.*
ridge (raised area)	crête, *f.*	Rücken, *m.*	rilievo, *m.*	arruga, *f.*	upphöjning, *nn.*	rukn, *m.*
ridicule	ridicule, *m.*	Spott, *m.*	ridicolo, *m.*	ridículo, *m.*	åtlöje, *n.*	khoyzek, *m.*
ridiculous	ridicule	lächerlich	ridicolo	ridículo	löjlig	lekherlekh
rifle	fusil, *m.*	Gewehr, *n.*	fucile, *m.*	rifle, *m.*	gevär, *n.*	biks, *f.*
right (claim)	droit, *m.*	Recht, *n.*	diritto, *m.*	derecho, *m.*	rätt, *nn.*	rekht, *n.*
right (correct)	correct	richtig	esatto	correcto	rätt	rikhtik
right (on the right, *adj.*)	droit	recht	destro	a la derecha	höger	rekht
right (right-hand side)	droite, *f.*	Rechte, *f.*	destra, *f.*	derecho, *m.*	höger sida, *nn.*	rekhts
right (to the right, *adv.*)	à droite	rechts	a destra	a la derecha	till höger	rekhts
rim	bord, *m.*	Rand, *m.*	orlo, *m.*	borde, *m.*	kant, *nn.*	rand, *m.*
ring (circle)	anneau, *m.*	Ring, *m.*	cerchio, *m.*	círculo, *m.*	ring, *nn.*	ring, *m.*
ring (jewelry)	bague, *f.*	Ring, *m.*	anello, *m.*	anillo, *m.*	ring, *nn.*	fingerl, *n.*
ring (resound), to	sonner	klingen	risuonare	resonar	ringa	klingen
Rio de Janeiro	Rio-de-Janeiro, *m.*	Rio de Janeiro, *n.*	Rio de Janeiro, *m.*	Río de Janeiro	Rio de Janeiro, *n.*	Rio de Zhaneyro, *n.*
riot (disturbance)	émeute, *f.*	Aufruhr, *f.*	tumulto, *m.*	motín, *m.*	tumult, *n.*	mehume, *f.*
rip (tear away), to	déchirer	abreissen	strappare	arrancar	slita	raysn
ripe	mûr	reif	maturo	maduro	mogen	tsaytik
ripple	ride, *f.*	Kräuselung, *f.*	crespa, *f.*	ondulación, *f.*	krusning, *nn.*	runtsl, *n.*
rise (ascend), to	élever, s'	steigen	salire	elevarse	stiga	shtaygn
rise (increase), to	monter	steigen	aumentare	alzarse	ökas	heybn zikh
rise (in sky), to	lever, se	aufgehen	levarsi	salir	gå upp	oyfgeyn
rise (stand up), to	lever, se	aufstehen	levarsi	ponerse de pie	stiga upp	oyfshteyn
risk (danger)	risque, *m.*	Gefahr, *f.*	rischio, *m.*	riesgo, *m.*	risk, *nn.*	rizike, *f.*
rite	rite, *m.*	Ritus, *m.*	rito, *m.*	rito, *m.*	rit, *nn.*	ritus, *m.*
rival (competitor)	rival, *m.*	Konkurrent, *m.*	rivale, *m.,f.*	rival, *m.,f.*	rival, *nn.*	konkurent, *m.*
river	rivière, *f.*	Fluss, *m.*	fiume, *m.*	río, *m.*	flod, *nn.*	taykh, *m.*
road	route, *f.*	Strasse, *f.*	strada, *f.*	camino, *m.*	väg, *nn.*	veg, *m.*
roam, to	errer	umherstreifen	errare	vagar	ströva	voglen
roar (*n.*)	rugissement, *m.*	Gebrüll, *n.*	ruggito, *m.*	rugido, *m.*	rytande, *n.*	bril, *m.*
roast	rôti, *m.*	Braten, *m.*	arrosto, *m.*	asado, *m.*	stek, *nn.*	gebrotns, *n.*
roast (be roasted), to	rôtir	braten, sich	arrostirsi	asarse	ugnsteka	brotn zikh
rob (steal from), to	voler	berauben	rubare	robar	råna	baganvenen
robber	voleur, *m.*	Räuber, *m.*	ladro, *m.*	ladrón, *m.*	rånare, *nn.*	gazlen, *m.*
robe (dressing gown)	robe de chambre, *f.*	Schlafrock, *m.*	vestaglia, *f.*	bata, *f.*	morgonrock, *nn.*	shlofrok, *m.*
robin	rouge-gorge, *m.*	Rotkehlchen, *n.*	pettirosso, *m.*	petirrojo, *m.*	rödhakesångare, *nn.*	roytheldzl, *n.*
rock (large stone)	roc, *m.*	Felsen, *m.*	roccia, *f.*	roca, *f.*	stenblock, *n.*	feldz, *m.*
rocket	fusée, *f.*	Rakete, *f.*	razzo, *m.*	cohete, *m.*	raket, *nn.*	rakete, *f.*
rocky (rock-covered)	rocheux, -cheuse	felsig	roccioso	rocoso	klippig	shteynerdik
rod (bar)	verge, *f.*	Stange, *f.*	asta, *f.*	vara, *f.*	stång, *nn.* (*pl.* stänger)	prent, *m.*
role	rôle, *m.*	Rolle, *f.*	ruolo, *m.*	papel, *m.*	roll, *nn.*	role, *f.*
roll (bread)	petit pain, *m.*	Brötchen, *n.*	panino, *m.*	panecillo, *m.*	bulle, *nn.*	zeml, *f.*
roll (cylinder)	rouleau, *m.*	Walze, *f.*	rotolo, *m.*	rollo, *m.*	rulle, *nn.*	rolke, *f.*
roll (impel), to	rouler	rollen	rotolare	rodar	rulla	kayklen
roller (cylinder)	rouleau, *m.*	Walze, *f.*	rullo, *m.*	rodillo, *m.*	vals, *nn.*	valts, *m.*
Roman (*adj.*)	romain	römisch	romano	romano	romersk	roymish
romantic	romanesque	romantisch	romantico	romántico	romantisk	romantish
Rome	Rome, *f.*	Rom, *n.*	Roma, *f.*	Roma	Rom, *n.*	Roym, *n.*
roof	toit, *m.*	Dach, *n.*	tetto, *m.*	techo, *m.*	tak, *n.*	dakh, *m.*
room (of house)	pièce, *f.*	Zimmer, *n.*	stanza, *f.*	cuarto, *m.*	rum, *n.*	tsimer, *m.*
room (space)	place, *f.*	Raum, *m.*	spazio, *m.*	espacio, *m.*	utrymme, *n.*	ort, *n.*
rooster	coq, *m.*	Hahn, *m.*	gallo, *m.*	gallo, *m.*	tupp, *nn.*	hon, *m.*
root (*bot.*)	racine, *f.*	Wurzel, *f.*	radice, *f.*	raíz, *f.*	rot, *nn.* (*pl.* rötter)	vortsl, *m.*
rope	corde, *f.*	Tau, *n.*	fune, *f.*	soga, *f.*	rep, *n.*	shtrik, *m.*
rose (flower)	rose, *f.*	Rose, *f.*	rosa, *f.*	rosa, *f.*	ros, *nn.*	royz, *f.*

English	French	German	Italian	Spanish	Swedish	Yiddish
rot, to	pourrir	faulen	marcire	pudrirse	ruttna	foyln
rotten (decayed)	pourri	faul	marcio	podrido	rutten	farfoylt
rouge	rouge,*m.*	Schminke,*f.*	rossetto,*m.*	colorete,*m.*	rouge,*n.*	shminke,*f.*
rough (harsh)	dur	grob	aspro	grosero	hård	grob
rough (uneven)	rude	rauh	scabro	áspero	ojämn	roy
round (*adj.*)	rond	rund	rotondo	redondo	rund	kaylekhdik
rouse (awaken), to	éveiller	wecken	destare	despertar	väcka	oyfvekn
route	route,*f.*	Route,*f.*	itinerario,*m.*	ruta,*f.*	rutt,*m.*	marshrut,*m.*
rove, to	rôder	umherstreifen	vagare	vagar	ströva omkring	arumvandern
row (series)	rangée,*f.*	Reihe,*f.*	serie,*f.*	fila,*f.*	rad,*nn.*	shure,*f.*
royal	royal	königlich	reale	real	kunglig	kiniglekh
royalty (fee)	redevance,*f.*	Tantieme,*f.*	percentuale,*f.*	derechos,*m.pl.*	royalty,*nn.*(*pl.* -ties)	honorar,*m.*
rub, to	frotter	reiben	strofinare	frotar	gnida	raybn
rubber	caoutchouc,*m.*	Gummi,*n.*	gomma,*f.*	caucho,*m.*	gummi,*n.*	gume,*f.*
rubbers (overshoes)	caoutchoucs,*m.* *pl.*	Gummischuhe, *pl.*	soprascarpe,*f.pl.*	chanclos,*m.pl.*	galoscher,*nn.pl.*	kaloshn,*pl.*
rubbish (litter)	immondices,*f.pl.*	Abfall,*m.*	rifiuti,*m.pl.*	basura,*f.*	skräp,*n.*	mist,*n.*
ruby (gem)	rubis,*m.*	Rubin,*m.*	rubino,*m.*	rubí,*m.*	rubin,*nn.*	rubin,*m.*
rudder (of a boat)	gouvernail,*m.*	Ruder,*n.*	timone,*m.*	timón,*m.*	roder,*n.*	kerme,*f.*
rude (impolite)	impoli	grob	sgarbato	rudo	ohövlig	grob
rug	tapis,*m.*	Teppich,*m.*	tappeto,*m.*	alfombra,*f.*	matta,*un.*	divan,*m.*
ruin, to	ruiner	zerstören	rovinare	arruinar	ruinera	khorev makhn
ruins (remains)	ruine(s),*f.*	Ruine,*f.*	rovina,*f.*	ruinas,*f.pl.*	ruin,*nn.*	khurve,*f.*
rule (political control)	empire,*m.*	Herrschaft,*f.*	dominio,*m.*	dominio,*m.*	herravälde,*n.*	hershaft,*f.*
rule (regulation)	règle,*f.*	Regel,*f.*	regola,*f.*	regla,*f.*	regel,*nn.*	takone,*f.*
rule (usual case)	règle,*f.*	Regel,*f.*	regola,*f.*	regla general,*f.*	regel,*nn.*	klal,*m.*
rule (govern), to	gouverner	herrschen	governare	gobernar	härska över	hershn
ruler (measuring instrument)	règle,*f.*	Lineal,*n.*	riga,*f.*	regla,*f.*	linjal,*nn.*	vire,*f.*
ruler (sovereign)	souverain,*m.*	Herrscher,*m.*	sovrano,*m.*	soberano,*m.*	härskare,*nn.*	hersher,*m.*
rum	rhum,*m.*	Rum,*m.*	rum,*m.*	ron,*m.*	rom,*nn.*	rom,*m.*
Rumania	Roumanie,*f.*	Rumänien,*n.*	Romania,*f.*	Rumania	Rumänien,*n.*	Rumenye,*f.*
rumor	rumeur,*f.*	Gerücht,*n.*	rumore,*m.*	rumor,*m.*	rykte,*n.*	klang,*m.*
run (extend), to	étendre, s'	erstrecken, sich	estendersi	extenderse	sträcka sig	tsien zikh
run (flow), to	couler	fliessen	correre	correr	rinna	flisn
run (sprint), to	courir	rennen	correre	correr	springa	loyfn
rural	rural	ländlich	rurale	rural	lands-...	dorfish
rush (rapid motion)	ruée,*f.*	Sausen,*n.*	slancio,*m.*	prisa,*f.*	rusning,*nn.*	yog,*m.*
rush (dash), to	ruer, se	stürzen, sich	slanciarsi	apresurarse	rusa	ayln zikh
Russia	Russie,*f.*	Russland,*n.*	Russia,*f.*	Rusia	Ryssland,*n.*	Rusland,*n.*
Russian (*adj.*)	russe	russisch	russo	ruso	rysk	rusish
rust	rouille,*f.*	Rost,*m.*	ruggine,*f.*	orín,*m.*	rost,*nn.*	zhaver,*m.*
rustle	bruissement,*m.*	Rascheln,*n.*	fruscio,*m.*	susurro,*m.*	prassel,*n.*	shorkh,*m.*
rusty	rouillé	rostig	arrugginito	oxidado	rostig	farzhavert
rye (grain)	seigle,*m.*	Roggen,*m.*	segale,*f.*	centeno,*m.*	råg,*nn.*	korn,*m.*
sack (bag)	sac,*m.*	Sack,*m.*	sacco,*m.*	saco,*m.*	säck,*nn.*	zak,*m.*
sacred	sacré	heilig	sacro	sagrado	helig	heylik
sacrifice (giving up)	sacrifice,*m.*	Opfer,*n.*	sacrificio,*m.*	sacrificio,*m.*	uppoffrande,*n.*	makriv zayn,*n.*
sacrifice (forego), to	sacrifier	opfern	sacrificare	sacrificar	uppoffra	mevater zayn oyf
sad (sorrowful)	triste	traurig	triste	triste	sorgsen	umetik
saddle (seat)	selle,*f.*	Sattel,*m.*	sella,*f.*	silla de montar,*f.*	sadel,*nn.*	zotl,*m.*
sadness	tristesse,*f.*	Schwermut,*f.*	tristezza,*f.*	tristeza,*f.*	sorgsenhet,*nn.*	umet,*m.*
safe (unharmed)	sauf, sauve	heil	salvo	seguro	säker	besholem
safe (without risk)	sûr	sicher	sicuro	seguro	trygg	zikher
safety (*n.*)	sûreté,*f.*	Sicherheit,*f.*	sicurezza,*f.*	seguridad,*f.*	säkerhet,*nn.*	zikherkayt,*f.*
safety pin	épingle de sûreté,*f.*	Sicherheitsnadel, *f.*	spillo di sicurezza,*m.*	imperdible,*m.*	säkerhetsnål,*nn.*	zikher-nodl,*f.*
sage (*adj.*)	sage	weise	saggio	sabio	vis	khakhomish
sailor	marin,*m.*	Matrose,*m.*	marinaio,*m.*	marinero,*m.*	sjöman,*nn.*(*pl.* -män)	matroz,*m.*
saint	saint,*m.*	Heilige,*m.,f.*	santo,*m.*	santo,*m.*	helgon,*n.*	heyliker,*m.*
salad	salade,*f.*	Salat,*m.*	insalata,*f.*	ensalada,*f.*	sallad,*nn.*	salat,*m.*
salary	appointements, *m. pl.*	Gehalt,*n.*	stipendio,*m.*	salario,*m.*	lön,*nn.*	skhires,*pl.*
sale (exchange)	vente,*f.*	Verkauf,*m.*	vendita,*f.*	venta,*f.*	försäljning,*nn.*	farkoyf,*m.*
salesman	(commis) vendeur,*m.*	Verkäufer,*m.*	venditore,*m.*	vendedor,*m.*	handelsresande, *nn.*	farkoyfer,*m.*
salmon	saumon,*m.*	Lachs,*m.*	salmone,*m.*	salmón,*m.*	lax,*nn.*	laks,*m.*
salt	sel,*m.*	Salz,*n.*	sale,*m.*	sal,*f.*	salt,*n.*	zalts,*f.*
salute, to	saluer	grüssen	salutare	saludar	hälsa	salutirn
Salvador, El	Salvador,*m.*	Salvador,*n.*	Salvador,*m.*	Salvador, El	Salvador,*n.*	Salvador,*m.*
salvation	salut,*m.*	Heil,*n.*	salvezza,*f.*	salvación,*f.*	räddning,*nn.*	geule,*f.*
same (*adj.*)	même	der-, die-, dasselbe	stesso	mismo	samma	zelbik
sample	échantillon,*m.*	Muster,*n.*	campione,*m.*	muestra,*f.*	prov,*n.*	muster,*m.*
sand	sable,*m.*	Sand,*m.*	sabbia,*f.*	arena,*f.*	sand,*nn.*	zamd,*n.*
sandwich	sandwich,*m.*	Butterbrot,*n.*	sandwich,*m.*	emparedado,*m.*	smörgås,*nn.*	sendvitsh,*m.*
sandy	sablonneux, -neuse	sandig	sabbioso	arenoso	sandig	zamdik
sane	raisonnable	vernünftig	sano di mente	sano de mente	normal	baym zinen
Santiago	Santiago,*m.*	Santiago,*n.*	Santiago,*f.*	Santiago	Santiago,*n.*	Santyago,*n.*
sap (fluid)	sève,*f.*	Saft,*m.*	linfa,*f.*	savia,*f.*	sav,*nn.*	sok,*m.*
sapphire (gem)	saphir,*m.*	Saphir,*m.*	zaffiro,*m.*	zafiro,*m.*	safir,*nn.*	shafir,*m.*

English	French	German	Italian	Spanish	Swedish	Yiddish
sardine	sardine,*f.*	Sardine,*f.*	sardina,*f.*	sardina,*f.*	sardin,*nn.*	sardinke,*f.*
satin (*n.*)	satin,*m.*	Atlas,*m.*	raso,*m.*	raso,*m.*	satäng,*nn.*	atles,*m.*
satisfaction (contentment)	satisfaction,*f.*	Zufriedenheit,*f.*	soddisfazione,*f.*	satisfacción,*f.*	belåtenhet,*nn.*	bafridikung,*f.*
satisfaction (gratification)	satisfaction,*f.*	Befriedigung,*f.*	soddisfazione,*f.*	satisfacción,*f.*	tillfredsställelse, *nn.*	bafridikung,*f.*
satisfactory	satisfaisant	befriedigend	soddisfacente	satisfactorio	tillfredsställande	bafridikndik
satisfied (contented)	satisfait	zufrieden	soddisfatto	satisfecho	belåten	bafridikt
satisfy, to	satisfaire	befriedigen	soddisfare	satisfacer	tillfredsställa	bafridikn
sauce	sauce,*f.*	Sauce,*f.*	salsa,*f.*	salsa,*f.*	sås,*nn.*	sous,*m.*
saucer	soucoupe,*f.*	Untertasse,*f.*	sottotazza,*f.*	platillo,*m.*	tefat,*n.*	tetsl,*n.*
sausage	saucisse,*f.*	Wurst,*f.*	salsiccia,*f.*	salchicha,*f.*	korv,*nn.*	vursht,*f.*
savage (*adj.*)	sauvage	wild	selvaggio	salvaje	vild	vild
save (rescue), to	sauver	retten	salvare	salvar	rädda	rateven
save (store up), to	économiser	sparen	economizzare	ahorrar	spara	shporn
savings account	compte d'épar- gne,*m.*	Sparkonto,*n.*	conto di rispar- mio,*m.*	cuenta de aho rros,*f.*	sparkasseräk- ning,*nn.*	shporkonte,*f.*
savings (money)	économies,*f.pl.*	Ersparnis,*n.*	risparmio,*m.*	ahorros,*m.pl.*	besparingar,*nn. pl.*	opshporung,*f.*
savior	sauveur,*m.*	Heiland,*m.*	salvatore,*m.*	salvador,*m.*	frälsare,*nn.*	goyel,*m.*
saw (tool)	scie,*f.*	Säge,*f.*	sega,*f.*	sierra,*f.*	såg,*nn.*	zeg,*f.*
saxophone	saxophone,*m*	Saxophon,*n.*	sassofono,*m.*	saxofón,*m.*	saxofon,*nn.*	saksofon,*m.*
say, to	dire	sagen	dire	decir	säga	zogn
scale (graduated measure)	échelle,*f.*	Masstab,*m.*	scala,*f.*	escala,*f.*	skala,*nn.*	skale,*f.*
scale (proportion)	échelle,*f.*	Masstab,*m.*	scala,*f.*	escala,*f.*	skala,*nn.*	masshtab,*m.*
scales (balance)	balance,*f.*	Waage,*f.*	bilancia,*f.*	balanza,*f.*	våg,*nn.*	vog,*f.*
scandal	scandale,*m.*	Skandal,*m.*	scandalo,*m.*	escándalo,*m.*	skandal,*nn.*	skandal,*m.*
scar	cicatrice,*f.*	Narbe,*f.*	cicatrice,*f.*	cicatriz,*f.*	ärr,*n.*	shram,*m.*
scarce	rare	knapp	scarso	escaso	knapp	knap
scarcity	rareté,*f.*	Knappheit,*f.*	scarsità,*f.*	escasez,*f.*	knapphet,*nn.*	knapkayt,*f.*
scare (frighten), to	effrayer	erschrecken	spaventare	espantar	skrämma	ibershrekn
scarf (neck cloth)	écharpe,*f.*	Schal,*m.*	sciarpa,*f.*	bufanda,*f.*	halsduk,*nn.*	sharf,*f.*
scarlet (*adj.*)	écarlate	scharlachrot	scarlatto	escarlata	scharlakansröd	purpl
scarlet fever	scarlatine,*f.*	Scharlachfieber, *n.*	scarlattina,*f.*	escarlata,*f.*	scharlakansfeber, *nn.*	skarlatin,*m.*
scatter (strew), to	éparpiller	ausstreuen	spargere	esparcir	strö (ut)	tseshitn
scenario	scénario,*m.*	Drehbuch,*n.*	scenario,*m.*	argumento,*m.*	scenario,*n.*	stsenar,*m.*
scene (dramatic unit)	scène,*f.*	Auftritt,*m.*	scena,*f.*	cuadro,*m.*	scen,*nn.*	stsene,*f.*
scent (odor)	odeur,*f.*	Geruch,*m.*	odore,*m.*	olor,*m.*	doft,*nn.*	reyakh,*m.*
schedule (timetable)	horaire,*m.*	Stundenplan,*m.*	orario,*m.*	horario,*m.*	tidtabell,*nn.*	shoen-plan,*m.*
scheme (plan)	plan,*m.*	Plan,*m.*	progetto,*m.*	plan,*m.*	plan,*nn.*	plan,*m.*
scholar (savant)	érudit,*m.*	Gelehrte,*m.*	studioso,*m.*	sabio,*m.*	vetenskapsman, *nn.* (*pl.* -män)	gelernter,*m.*
school	école,*f.*	Schule,*f.*	scuola,*f.*	escuela,*f.*	skola,*nn.*	shul,*f.*
schoolhouse	(maison d') école, *f.*	Schulhaus,*n.*	scuola,*f.*	escuela,*f.*	skolhus,*n.*	shul,*f.*
schooling (instruction)	instruction,*f.*	Schulunterricht, *m.*	istruzione,*f.*	instrucción,*f.*	skolundervis- ning,*nn.*	oysshulung,*f.*
schoolroom	(salle de) classe, *f.*	Klassenzimmer, *n.*	aula,*f.*	sala de clase,*f.*	skolrum,*n.*	shultsimer,*m.*
science	science,*f.*	Wissenschaft,*f.*	scienza,*f.*	ciencia,*f.*	vetenskap,*nn.*	visnshaft,*f.*
scientific	scientifique	wissenschaftlich	scientifico	científico	vetenskaplig	visnshaftlekh
scientist	savant,*m.*	Wissenschaftler, *m.*	scienziato,*m.*	científico,*m.*	(natur)veten- skapsman,*nn.* (*pl.* -män)	visnshaftler,*m.*
scissors	ciseaux,*m.pl.*	Schere,*f.*	forbici,*f.pl.*	tijeras,*f.pl.*	sax,*nn.*	sher,*f.*
scold, to	gronder	schelten	sgridare	regañar	gräla på	musern
score (gain points), to	marquer	Punkte machen	ottenere punti	ganar tantos	vinna poäng	gevinen punktn
scorn	mépris,*m.*	Verachtung,*f.*	disprezzo,*m.*	desdén,*m.*	förakt,*n.*	bitl,*m.*
scorn (despise), to	mépriser	verachten	disprezzare	desdeñar	förakta	hobn bitl
Scotch (*adj.*)	écossais	schottisch	scozzese	escocés, -cesa	skotsk	shotish
Scotland	Écosse,*f.*	Schottland,*n.*	Scozia,*f.*	Escocia	Skottland,*n.*	Shotland,*n.*
scout (lookout)	éclaireur,*m.*	Späher,*m.*	esploratore,*m.*	explorador,*m.*	spanare,*nn.*	oysshpirer,*m.*
scrambled eggs	oeufs brouillés, *m.pl.*	Rührei,*n.*	uova strapazzate, *f.pl.*	huevos revueltos, *m.pl.*	äggröra,*nn.*	faynkukhn,*m.*
scrap (fragment)	bout,*m.*	Brocken,*m.*	pezzetto,*m.*	pedacito,*m.*	bit,*nn.*	brekl,*n.*
scrape (make smooth or clean), to	racler	schaben	raschiare	raspar	skrapa	shobn
scratch, to	gratter	kratzen	grattare	rascar	riva	kratsn
scream, to	crier	kreischen	urlare	chillar	skrika	gvaldeven
screen (for movies)	écran,*m.*	Leinwand,*f.*	schermo,*m.*	pantalla,*f.*	duk,*nn.*	ekran,*m.*
screen (partition)	paravent,*m.*	Schirm,*m.*	paravento,*m.*	mampara,*f.*	skärm,*nn.*	shirme,*f.*
screw (threaded nail)	vis,*f.*	Schraube,*f.*	vite,*f.*	tornillo,*m.*	skruv,*nn.*	shroyf,*m.*
screw driver	tournevis,*m.*	Schraubenzieher, *m.*	cacciavite,*f.*	destornillador,*m.*	skruvmejsel,*nn.*	shroyfn-tsier,*m.*
scrub, to	frotter	scheuern	strofinare	fregar	skura	shayern
sculptor	sculpteur,*m.*	Bildhauer,*m.*	scultore,*m.*	escultor,*m.*	skulptör,*nn.*	skulptor,*m.*
sea	mer,*f.*	Meer,*n.*	mare,*m.*	mar,*m.,f.*	hav,*n.*	yam,*m.*
seal (animal)	phoque,*m.*	Seehund,*m.*	foca,*f.*	foca,*f.*	säl,*nn.*	yam-hunt,*m.*
seal (mark)	sceau,*m.*	Siegel,*m.*	timbro,*m.*	sello,*m.*	sigill,*n.*	zigl,*m.*
seam (line of stitches)	couture,*f.*	Naht,*f.*	cucitura,*f.*	costura,*f.*	söm,*nn.*	not,*f.*
search (hunt)	recherche,*f.*	Suche,*f.*	ricerca,*f.*	búsqueda,*f.*	sökande,*n.*	zukhenish,*f.*
season (of year)	saison,*f.*	Jahreszeit,*f.*	stagione,*f.*	estación,*f.*	årstid,*nn.*	tsayt fun yor,*f.*
seat	siège,*m.*	Sitz,*m.*	sedile,*m.*	asiento,*m.*	sittplats,*nn.*	zitsort,*n.*
second (*adj.*)	deuxième	zweite	secondo	segundo	andra	tsveyt

English	French	German	Italian	Spanish	Swedish	Yiddish
second (time unit)	seconde,*f.*	Sekunde,*f.*	secondo,*m.*	segundo,*m.*	sekund,*nn.*	sekunde,*f.*
secret (*adj.*)	secret, -crète	geheim	segreto	secreto	hemlig	geheym
secret (*n.*)	secret,*m.*	Geheimnis,*n.*	segreto,*m.*	secreto,*m.*	hemlighet,*nn.*	sod,*m.*
secretary (stenographer)	secrétaire,*m.,f.*	Sekretärin,*f.*	segretaria,*f.*	secretaria,*f.*	sekreterare,*nn.*	sekretarshe,*m.*
section (part)	section,*f.*	Teil,*m.*	parte,*f.*	sección,*f.*	del,*nn.*	opteyl,*m.*
secure (safe)	sûr	sicher	sicuro	seguro	säker	zikher
secure (obtain), to	obtenir	erlangen	ottenere	obtener	skaffa	aynshafn
securities (stocks, etc.)	titres,*m.pl.*	Wertpapiere,*pl.*	titoli,*m.pl.*	valores,*m.pl.*	värdepapper,*n. pl.*	vertpapirn,*pl.*
security (safety)	sécurité,*f.*	Sicherheit,*f.*	sicurezza,*f.*	seguridad,*f.*	säkerhet,*nn.*	zikherkayt,*f.*
see, to	voir	sehen	vedere	ver	se	zen
seed (ovule)	grain,*m.*	Samen,*m.*	seme,*m.*	semilla,*f.*	frö,*n.*	zomen,*m.*
seem (appear), to	sembler	scheinen	parere	parecer	tyckas	oyszen
seize (capture), to	prendre	ergreifen	catturare	apoderarse de	gripa	khapn
seize (clutch), to	saisir	anpacken	afferrare	agarrar	fatta	onkhapn
seldom	rarement	selten	raramente	rara vez	sällan	zeltn
select, to	choisir	wählen	scegliere	seleccionar	välja	oysklaybn
selection (things chosen)	choix,*m.*	Auswahl,*f.*	selezione,*f.*	selección,*f.*	urval,*n.*	oysklayb,*m.*
self (*pron.*)	(...-)même *(see p. 2827)*	selber *(see p. 2890)*	sè stesso *(see p. 2948)*	mismo *(see p. 3012)*	själv	zikh *(see p. 3132)*
selfish	égoïste	selbstsüchtig	egoistico	egoísta	självisk	egoistish
sell, to	vendre	verkaufen	vendere	vender	sälja	farkoyfn
semicolon	point-virgule,*m.*	Strichpunkt,*m.*	punto e virgola,*m.*	punto y coma,*m.*	semikolon,*n.*	punktkome,*f.*
senate	sénat,*m.*	Senat,*m.*	senato,*m.*	senado,*m.*	senat,*nn.*	senat,*m.*
senator	sénateur,*m.*	Senator,*m.*	senatore,*m.*	senador,*m.*	senator,*nn.*	senator,*m.*
send, to	envoyer	senden	mandare	enviar	sända	shikn
senior (older)	aîné	älter	maggiore	mayor	äldre	elter
sensation (feeling)	sensation,*f.*	Empfindung,*f.*	sensazione,*f.*	sensación,*f.*	känsla,*nn.*	gefil,*n.*
sense (intelligence)	bon sens,*m.*	Vernunft,*f.*	giudizio,*m.*	entendimiento,*m.*	förstånd,*n.*	seykhl,*m.*
sense (signification)	sens,*m.*	Sinn,*m.*	senso,*m.*	significado,*m.*	betydelse,*nn.*	pshat,*m.*
sensible (reasonable)	sensé	vernünftig	ragionevole	sensato	förnuftig	seykhldik
sensitive (susceptible)	sensible	empfindlich	sensibile	sensible	känslig	shpirevdik
sentence (*gram.*)	phrase,*f.*	Satz,*m.*	frase,*f.*	frase,*f.*	mening,*nn.*	zats,*m.*
sentence, to	condamner	verurteilen	condannare	sentenciar	döma	farmishpetn
sentiment	sentiment,*m.*	Gefühl,*n.*	sentimento,*m.*	sentimiento,*m.*	känsla,*nn.*	sentiment,*m.*
separate	séparé	getrennt	separato	separado	särskild	bazunder
separate (come apart), to	séparer, se	trennen, sich	separarsi	separarse	skiljas	tseteyln zikh
separate (disconnect), to	séparer	trennen	separare	separar	skilja	opteyln
separation	séparation,*f.*	Trennung,*f.*	separazione,*f.*	separación,*f.*	skiljande,*n.*	tseteylung,*f.*
sergeant	sergent,*m.*	Sergeant,*m.*	sergente,*m.*	sargento,*m.*	sergeant,*nn.*	serzhant,*m.*
series	série,*f.*	Reihe,*f.*	serie,*f.*	serie,*f.*	serie,*nn.*	serye,*f.*
serious	sérieux, -rieuse	ernst	serio	serio	allvarlig	erntst
sermon	sermon,*m.*	Predigt,*f.*	sermone,*m.*	sermón,*m.*	predikan,*nn.*	preydik,*f.*
serpent	serpent,*m.*	Schlange,*f.*	serpente,*m.*	serpiente,*f.*	orm,*nn.*	shlang,*f.*
servant (in a household)	domestique,*m.,f.*	Dienstbote,*m.*	domestico,*m.*	sirviente,*m.*	tjänare,*nn.*	diner,*m.*
serve, to	servir	dienen	servire	servir	tjäna	dinen
service	service,*m.*	Dienst,*m.*	servizio,*m.*	servicio,*m.*	tjänst,*nn.*	dinst,*n.*
session	séance,*f.*	Sitzung,*f.*	seduta,*f.*	sesión,*f.*	sammanträde,*n.*	sesye,*f.*
set (in sky), to	coucher, se	untergehen	tramontare	ponerse	gå ned	untergeyn
set (put), to	mettre	setzen	collocare	poner	sätta	shteln
settle (agree on), to	décider	abmachen	fissare	convenir	göra upp	durkhkumen
settle (arrange), to	régler	festsetzen	accomodare	arreglar	ordna	opredn
settle (make one's home), to	établir, s'	niederlassen, sich	stabilirsi	establecerse	slå sig ned	bazetsn zikh
settlement (colony)	colonie,*f.*	Ansiedlung,*f.*	colonia,*f.*	colonia,*f.*	nybygge,*n.*	yishev,*m.*
settlement (compromise, *bus.*)	transaction,*f.*	Schlichtung,*f.*	transazione,*f.*	ajuste,*m.*	uppgörelse,*nn.*	silek,*m.*
settler	colon,*m.*	Ansiedler,*m.*	colono,*m.*	colono,*m.*	nybyggare,*nn.*	kolonist,*m.*
sever, to	couper	trennen	dividere	desunir	skilja	opraysn
several (a few, *adj.*)	plusieurs	mehrere	parecchi	varios	flera	etlekhe
severe (austere)	sévère	schmucklos	austero	austero	sträng	on baputsungen
severe (strict)	sévère	streng	severo	severo	sträng	shtreng
severity (sternness)	sévérité,*f.*	Strenge,*f.*	severità,*f.*	severidad,*f.*	stränghet,*nn.*	shtrengkayt,*f.*
sew, to	coudre	nähen	cucire	coser	sy	neyen
sewer (conduit)	égout,*m.*	Abzugskanal,*m.*	fogna,*f.*	albañal,*m.*	kloak,*nn.*	kanal,*m.*
sewing machine	machine à coudre,*f.*	Nähmaschine,*f.*	macchina da cucire,*f.*	máquina de coser,*f.*	symaskin,*nn.*	neymashin,*f.*
sex	sexe,*m.*	Geschlecht,*n.*	sesso,*m.*	sexo,*m.*	kön,*n.*	geshlekht,*n.*
shade (shadow)	ombre,*f.*	Schatten,*m.*	ombra,*f.*	sombra,*f.*	skugga,*nn.*	shotn,*m.*
shade (window blind)	store,*m.*	Rouleau,*n.*	tendina,*f.*	cortina,*f.*	rullgardin,*nn.*	shtore,*f.*
shadow	ombre,*f.*	Schatten,*m.*	ombra,*f.*	sombra,*f.*	skugga,*nn.*	shotn,*m.*
shady	ombragé	schattig	ombreggiante	sombreado	skuggig	shotndik
shaft (*mech.*)	arbre,*m.*	Stiel,*m.*	asta,*f.*	vara,*f.*	skaft,*n.*	shtil,*f.*
shake, to	secouer *(see p. 2830 ff.)*	schütteln *(see p. 2892 ff.)*	scuotere *(see p. 2951 ff.)*	sacudir *(see p. 3015)*	skaka *(see skola, p. 3078)*	shoklen *(see p. 3134)*
shall (*v.*)						
shallow	plat	seicht	poco profondo	poco profundo	flat	flakh
shame	honte,*f.*	Schande,*f.*	vergogna,*f.*	verguenza,*f.*	skam,*nn.*	kharpe,*f.*
shameful	honteux, -teuse	schändlich	vergognoso	vergonzoso	skamlig	shendlekh
shape (contour)	forme,*f.*	Form,*f.*	forma,*f.*	forma,*f.*	form,*nn.*	geshtalt,*n.*

English	French	German	Italian	Spanish	Swedish	Yiddish
share (part)	part,*f.*	Anteil,*m.*	parte,*f.*	porción,*f.*	del,*nn.*	kheylek,*m.*
share (stock)	action,*f.*	Aktie,*f.*	azione,*f.*	acción,*f.*	aktie,*nn.*	aktsye,*f.*
share, to	partager	teilen	condividere	compartir	dela	teyln zikh mit
sharp	aigu, -ë	scharf	affilato	afilado	skarp	sharf
sharpen, to	aiguiser	schärfen	affilare	afilar	vässa	shlayfn
shatter (smash in pieces), to	fracasser	zerschmettern	frantumare	hacer pedazos	splittra	tsepitslen
shave (oneself), to	raser, se	rasieren, sich	farsi la barba	afeitarse	raka sig	razirn zikh
shaver, electric	rasoir électrique, *m.*	elektrischer Rasierapparat, *m.*	rasoio elettrico, *m.*	afeitadora eléctrica,*f.*	elektrisk rakapparat,*nn.*	elektrisher razirer,*m.*
shaving cream	savon à barbe,*m.*	Rasiercreme,*f.*	sapone per la barba,*m.*	crema de afeitar, *f.*	rakkräm,*nn.*	razirzeyf,*f.*
she	elle	sie	ella	ella	hon	zi
shear, to	tondre	scheren	tosare	trasquilar	klippa	shern
shed (shelter)	hangar,*m.*	Schuppen,*m.*	tettoia,*f.*	cobertizo,*m.*	skjul,*n.*	saray,*m.*
shed (cast off), to	jeter	abwerfen	gettare	quitarse	fälla	aropvarfn
sheep	mouton,*m.*	Schaf,*n.*	pecora,*f.*	oveja,*f.*	får,*n.*	shof,*f.*
sheer (pure)	pur	schier	puro	puro	ren	gole
sheet (bedding)	drap,*m.*	Bettuch,*n.*	lenzuolo,*m.* (*pl.* -la,*f.*)	sábana,*f.*	lakan,*n.*	laylekh,*m.*
sheet (of paper)	feuille,*f.*	Bogen,*m.*	foglio,*m.*	hoja,*f.*	ark,*n.*	boygn,*m.*
shelf	rayon,*m.*	Fach,*n.*	palchetto,*m.*	anaquel,*m.*	hylla,*nn.*	politse,*f.*
shell (covering)	coquille,*f.*	Schale,*f.*	guscio,*m.*	cáscara,*f.*	skal,*n.*	sholekhts,*f.*
shelter	abri,*m.*	Schutz,*m.*	riparo,*m.*	abrigo,*m.*	skydd,*n.*	opdakh,*m.*
shelter, to	abriter	schützen	riparare	abrigar	skydda	gebn a dakh ibern kop
shepherd	berger,*m.*	Hirt,*m.*	pastore,*m.*	pastor,*m.*	herde,*nn.*	pastekh,*m.*
shield, to	protéger	beschirmen	riparare	proteger	skydda	bashitsn
shift (crew)	équipe,*f.*	Schicht,*f.*	squadra,*f.*	tanda,*f.*	skift,*n.*	shikht,*f.*
shine (gleam), to	briller	glänzen	luccicare	brillar	skina	blishtshen
shine (polish), to	polir	blank putzen	lucidare	dar brillo	blanka	polirn
ship	navire,*m.*	Schiff,*n.*	nave,*f.*	barco,*m.*	skepp,*n.*	shif,*f.*
ship (send goods), to	expédier	versenden	spedire	despachar	sända	ibershikn
shipment (goods)	envoi,*m.*	Sendung,*f.*	spedizione,*f.*	embarque,*m.*	sändning,*nn.*	shikung,*f.*
shipping agent	expéditeur,*m.*	Spediteur,*m.*	spedizioniere,*m.*	expedidor,*m.*	speditör,*nn.*	ibershiker,*m.*
shipyard	chantier,*m.*	Schiffswerft,*f.*	cantiere navale, *m.*	astillero,*m.*	skeppsvarv,*n.*	shifboy-hoyf,*m.*
shirt	chemise,*f.*	Hemd,*n.*	camicia,*f.*	camisa,*f.*	skjorta,*nn.*	hemd,*n.*
shiver (quake), to	frissonner	schauern	tremare	temblar	darra	tsitern
shock (mental jolt)	choc,*m.*	Erschütterung,*f.*	scossa,*f.*	susto,*m.*	chock,*nn.*	shok,*m.*
shock (jar), to	choquer	erschüttern	urtare	sacudir	chockera	shok,*m.*
shoe (footwear)	soulier,*m.*	Schuh,*m.*	scarpa,*f.*	zapato,*m.*	sko,*nn.*	shokirn
shoemaker	cordonnier,*m.*	Schuster,*m.*	calzolaio,*m.*	zapatero,*m.*	skomakare,*nn.*	shukh,*m.*
shoot (fire at), to	tirer sur	schiessen	tirare su	tirar a	skjuta	shuster,*m.*
shop (store)	boutique,*f.*	Laden,*m.*	negozio,*m.*	tienda,*f.*	butik,*nn.*	shisn
shop, to	faire des achats	einkaufen	fare compere	ir de compras	handla	krom,*f.*
shore	rive,*f.*	Ufer,*n.*	riva,*f.*	ribera,*f.*	strand,*nn.* (*pl.* stränder)	aynkoyfn breg,*m.*
short (brief)	court	kurz	breve	corto	kort	kurts
short (not long)	court	kurz	corto	corto	kort	kurts
shortage (lack)	manque,*m.*	Mangel,*m.*	deficienza,*f.*	escasez,*f.*	brist,*nn.*	doykhek,*m.*
shorthand (stenography, *n.*)	sténographie,*f.*	Schnellschrift,*f.*	stenografia,*f.*	taquigrafía,*f.*	stenografi,*nn.*	stenografye,*f.*
short story	conte,*m.*	Novelle,*f.*	novella,*f.*	cuento,*m.*	novell,*nn.*	novele,*f.*
shot (from firearm)	coup de feu,*m.*	Schuss,*m.*	sparo,*m.*	tiro,*m.*	skott,*n.*	shos,*m.*
should (*v.*)	(*see* devoir, *p.* 2834)	(*see* sollen, *p.* 2892)	(*see* dovere, *p.* 2957)	deber	(*see* skola, *p.* 3078)	zoln
shoulder (*anat.*)	épaule,*f.*	Schulter,*f.*	spalla,*f.*	hombro,*m.*	skuldra,*nn.*	aksl,*m.*
shout (cry)	cri,*m.*	Schrei,*m.*	grido,*m.*	grito,*m.*	rop,*n.*	geshrey,*m.*
shout (say loudly), to	crier	schreien	gridare	gritar	ropa	shrayen
shovel (tool)	pelle,*f.*	Schaufel,*f.*	pala,*f.*	pala,*f.*	skovel,*nn.*	shufl,*f.*
show (exhibit)	exposition,*f.*	Ausstellung,*f.*	mostra,*f.*	exhibición,*f.*	utställning,*nn.*	oysshtelung,*f.*
show (be visible), to	montrer, se	zeigen, sich	mostrarsi	mostrarse	visa sig	vayzn zikh
show (make visible), to	montrer	zeigen	mostrare	mostrar	visa	vayzn
shower (bath)	douche,*f.*	Brausebad,*n.*	doccia,*f.*	ducha,*f.*	dusch,*nn.*	shprits,*m.*
shower (rainfall)	averse,*f.*	Regenschauer,*m.*	acquazzone,*m.*	aguacero,*m.*	skur,*nn.*	regndl,*n.*
shrewd	fin	scharfsinnig	scaltro	astuto	slug	farshayt
shriek, to	hurler	kreischen	strillare	chillar	skrika	kvitshen
shrill	aigu, -ë	schrill	acuto	chillón	gäll	shrayik
shrimp	crevette,*f.*	Garnele,*f.*	gamberetto,*m.*	camarón,*m.*	räka,*nn.*	rakl,*n.*
shrink (become contracted), to	rétrécir, se	einlaufen	raccorciarsi	contraer(se)	krympa	ayntsien zikh
shrub	arbuste,*m.*	Strauch,*m.*	arbusto,*m.*	arbusto,*m.*	buske,*nn.*	kshak,*m.*
shudder, to	frémir	schaudern	rabbrividire	estremecerse	rysa	oyfshoydern
shut (make close), to	fermer	schliessen	chiudere	cerrar	stänga	farmakhn
shy (bashful)	timide	schüchtern	timido	tímido	blyg	shemevdik
sick (ailing)	malade	krank	malato	enfermo	sjuk	krank
sickness	maladie,*f.*	Krankheit,*f.*	malattia,*f.*	enfermedad,*f.*	sjukdom,*nn.*	krenk,*f.*
side	côté,*m.*	Seite,*f.*	lato,*m.*	lado,*m.*	sida,*nn.*	zayt,*f.*
sidewalk	trottoir,*m.*	Bürgersteig,*m.*	marciapiede,*m.*	acera,*f.*	trottoar,*nn.*	trotuar,*m.*
siege (*mil.*)	siège,*m.*	Belagerung,*f.*	assedio,*m.*	sitio,*m.*	belägring,*nn.*	balegerung,*f.*
sift (separate), to	passer au tamis	sieben	stacciare	cerner	sålla	zipn
sigh, to	soupirer	seufzen	sospirare	suspirar	sucka	ziftsn

English	French	German	Italian	Spanish	Swedish	Yiddish
sight (eyesight)	vue,*f.*	Sehkraft,*f.*	vista,*f.*	vista,*f.*	syn,*nn.*	riye,*f.*
sight (range of view)	vue,*f.*	Sehweite,*f.*	vista,*f.*	vista,*f.*	synhåll,*n.*	oygngreykh,*m.*
sight (spectacle)	spectacle,*m.*	Anblick,*m.*	spettacolo,*m.*	espectáculo,*m.*	syn,*nn.*	spektakl,*m.*
sight draft (*bus.*)	traite à vue,*f.*	Sichttratte,*f.*	tratta a vista,*f.*	letra a la vista,*f.*	avistaväxel,*nn.*	viste-onvay-zung,*f.*
sign (indication)	signe,*m.*	Zeichen,*n.*	segno,*m.*	signo,*m.*	tecken,*n.*	simen,*m.*
sign (endorse), to	signer	unterschreiben	firmare	firmar	underteckna	untershraybn
signal	signal,*m.*	Signal,*n.*	segnale,*m.*	señal,*f.*	signal,*nn.*	signal,*m.*
signature (name)	signature,*f.*	Unterschrift,*f.*	firma,*f.*	firma,*f.*	namnteckning,*nn.*	khsime,*f.*
significance (importance)	importance,*f.*	Bedeutung,*f.*	importanza,*f.*	significación,*f.*	betydelse,*nn.*	batayt,*m.*
significant (meaningful)	significatif, -tive	bedeutsam	significativo	significativo	betydelsefull	bataytik
signify (denote), to	signifier	bedeuten	significare	significar	beteckna	bataytn
silence (stillness)	silence,*m.*	Stille,*f.*	silenzio,*m.*	silencio,*m.*	tystnad,*nn.*	shtilkayt,*f.*
silent (mute)	silencieux, -cieuse	still	silenzioso	silencioso	tyst	shtil
silk (*n.*)	soie,*f.*	Seide,*f.*	seta,*f.*	seda,*f.*	silke,*n.*	zayd,*n.*
silly	sot, -te	albern	sciocco	necio	fånig	narish
silver (metal, *n.*)	argent,*m.*	Silber,*n.*	argento,*m.*	plata,*f.*	silver,*n.*	zilber,*n.*
similar	semblable	ähnlich	simile	similar	liknande	enlekh
similarity	similarité,*f.*	Ähnlichkeit,*f.*	similarità,*f.*	semejanza,*f.*	likhet,*nn.*	enlekhkayt,*f.*
simple (uninvolved)	simple	einfach	semplice	simple	enkel	poshet
simplicity	simplicité,*f.*	Einfachheit,*f.*	semplicità,*f.*	simplicidad,*f.*	enkelhet,*nn.*	pashtes,*f.*
sin	péché,*m.*	Sünde,*f.*	peccato,*m.*	pecado,*m.*	synd,*nn.*	zind,*f.*
sin, to	pécher	sündigen	peccare	pecar	synda	zindikn
since (after, *prep.*)	depuis	seit	da	desde	sedan	zint
since (because, *conj.*)	puisque	da	siccome	puesto que	emedan	vayl
since (from then to now, *adv.*)	depuis	seitdem	da allora	desde entonces	sedan dess	fun demolt on
sincere	sincère	aufrichtig	sincero	sincero	uppriktig	oyfrikhtik
sing, to	chanter	singen	cantare	cantar	sjunga	zingen
singer	chanteur,*m.*	Sänger,*m.*	cantante,*m.,f.*	cantante,*m.,f.*	sångare,*nn.*	zinger,*m.*
single (sole)	seul	einzeln	solo	solo	enda	eyntsik
single (unmarried)	célibataire	ledig	celibe	soltero	ogift	frayleydik
singular (*gram., n.*)	singulier,*m.*	Einzahl,*f.*	singolare,*m.*	singular,*m.*	singularis,*n.*	eyntsol,*f.*
singular (peculiar)	singulier, -lière	einzigartig	originale	singular	säregen	modne
sink (*n.*)	évier,*m.*	Ausguss,*m.*	acquaio,*m.*	fregadero,*m.*	vask,*nn.*	opgos,*m.*
sink (become submerged), to	couler	(ver)sinken	affondare	hundirse	sjunka	aynzinken
sink (fall slowly), to	baisser	(ver)sinken	calare lenta-mente	caer por grados	sjunka	zinken
sinner	pécheur,*m.*	Sünder,*m.*	peccatore,*m.*	pecador,*m.*	syndare,*nn.*	zindiker,*m.*
sip, to	siroter	schlürfen	sorseggiare	sorber	smutta på	zupn
sir	monsieur,*m.*	Herr,*m.*	signore,*m.*	señor,*m.*	min herre,*nn.*	ser,*m.*
sister (*n.*)	soeur,*f.*	Schwester,*f.*	sorella,*f.*	hermana,*f.*	syster,*nn.*	shvester,*f.*
sister-in-law	belle-soeur,*f.*	Schwägerin,*f.*	cognata,*f.*	cuñada,*f.*	svägerska,*nn.*	shvegerin,*f.*
sit (be sitting), to	être assis	sitzen	sedere	estar sentado	sitta	zitsn
sit down, to	asseoir, s'	setzen, sich	sedersi	sentarse	sätta sig	zetsn zikh
site	emplacement,*m.*	Lage,*f.*	posto,*m.*	sitio,*m.*	läge,*n.*	ort,*n.*
situation (circumstances)	situation,*f.*	Lage,*f.*	situazione,*f.*	situación,*f.*	situation,*nn.*	situatsye,*f.*
size (magnitude)	grandeur,*f.*	Grösse,*f.*	dimensione,*f.*	tamaño,*m.*	storlek,*nn.*	greys,*f.*
size (of hats)	tour de tête,*m.*	Grösse,*f.*	misura,*f.*	medida,*f.*	storlek,*nn.*	numer,*m.*
size (of shoes, gloves)	pointure,*f.*	Grösse,*f.*	numero,*m.*	número,*m.*	storlek,*nn.*	numer,*m.*
size (of suits, dresses, coats)	taille,*f.*	Grösse,*f.*	misura,*f.*	talla,*f.*	storlek,*nn.*	numer,*m.*
skate, ice	patin,*m.*	Schlittschuh,*m.*	pattino,*m.*	patín de hielo,*m.*	skridsko,*nn.*	glitsher,*m.*
skeleton (*anat.*)	squelette,*m.*	Skelett,*n.*	scheletro,*m.*	esqueleto,*m.*	skelett,*n.*	skelet,*m.*
sketch (rough drawing)	esquisse,*f.*	Entwurf,*m.*	schizzo,*m.*	boceto,*m.*	skiss,*nn.*	skitse,*f.*
ski, to	faire du ski	Schi laufen	sciare	esquiar	åka skidor	nartlen zikh
skilful	adroit	geschickt	abile	experto	skicklig	geshikt
skill (proficiency)	adresse,*f.*	Geschicklichkeit,*f.*	destrezza,*f.*	destreza,*f.*	skicklighet,*nn.*	beryeshaft,*f.*
skin (animal hide)	peau,*f.*	Fell,*n.*	pelle,*f.*	piel,*f.*	skinn,*n.*	fel,*f.*
skin (human skin)	peau,*f.*	Haut,*f.*	pelle,*f.*	cutis,*m.*	hud,*nn.*	hoyt,*f.*
skip (caper), to	gambader	hüpfen	saltare	saltar	skutta	hopken
skip (omit), to	sauter	überspringen	saltare	pasar por alto	hoppa över	iberhipern
skirt (garment)	jupe,*f.*	Rock,*m.*	gonnella,*f.*	falda,*f.*	kjol,*nn.*	rekl,*n.*
skull	crâne,*m.*	Schädel,*m.*	cranio,*m.*	cráneo,*m.*	skalle,*nn.*	sharbn,*m.*
sky	ciel,*m.*	Himmel,*m.*	cielo,*m.*	cielo,*m.*	himmel,*nn.*	himl,*m.*
skyscraper	gratte-ciel,*m.*	Wolkenkratzer,*m.*	grattacielo,*m.*	rascacielos,*m.*	skyskrapa,*nn.*	volkn-kratser,*m.*
slang (*n.*)	argot,*m.*	Slang,*n.*	gergo,*m.*	jerga,*f.*	slang,*nn.*	sleng,*m.*
slant (slope), to	être en pente	schräg liegen	inclinarsi	inclinarse	slutta	beygn zikh
slaughter	abattage,*m.*	Schlachten,*n.*	macello,*m.*	matanza,*f.*	slakt,*nn.*	shkhite,*f.*
Slavic (*adj.*)	slave	slawisch	slavo	eslavo	slavisk	slavish
slave	esclave,*m.,f.*	Sklave,*m.*	schiavo,*m.*	esclavo,*m.*	slav,*nn.*	shklaf,*m.*
slavery	esclavage,*m.*	Sklaverei,*f.*	schiavitù,*f.*	esclavitud,*f.*	slaveri,*n.*	shklaferay,*f.*
slay, to	tuer	erschlagen	uccidere	matar	slå ihjäl	teytn
sled	luge,*f.*	Schlitten,*m.*	slitta,*f.*	trineo,*m.*	kälke,*nn.*	shlitn,*m.*
sleep	sommeil,*m.*	Schlaf,*m.*	sonno,*m.*	sueño,*m.*	sömn,*nn.*	shlof,*m.*
sleep, to	dormir	schlafen	dormire	dormir	sova	shlofn
sleeve	manche,*f.*	Ärmel,*m.*	manica,*f.*	manga,*f.*	ärm,*nn.*	arbl,*m.*
sleigh	traineau,*m.*	Schlitten,*m.*	slitta,*f.*	trineo,*m.*	släde,*nn.*	shlitn,*m.*

English	French	German	Italian	Spanish	Swedish	Yiddish
slender (lean)	mince	schlank	slanciato	delgado	smärt	shlank
slice	tranche, *f.*	Schnitte, *f.*	fetta, *f.*	rebanada, *f.*	skiva, *nn.*	penets, *m.*
slide, to	glisser	gleiten	scivolare	deslizarse	glida	penets, *m.*
slight (*adj.*)	léger, -gère	gering	leggero	pequeño	obetydlig	glitshn zikh
slip (petticoat)	jupon, *m.*	Unterrock, *m.*	sottogonna, *f.*	combinación, *f.*	underkjol, *nn.*	knap
slip (slide), to	glisser	ausgleiten	sdrucciolare	deslizar	halka	unterkleyd, *n.*
						oysglitshn zikh
slipper	pantoufle, *f.*	Hausschuh, *m.*	pantofola, *f.*	zapatilla, *f.*	toffel, *nn.*	shtekshukh, *m.*
slippery	glissant	schlüpfrig	sdrucciolevole	resbaloso	hal	glitshik
slope (slant)	pente, *f.*	Neigung, *f.*	pendenza, *f.*	pendiente, *f.*	sluttning, *nn.*	shipue, *m.*
slow (not fast)	lent	langsam	lento	lento	långsam	pamelekh
slow (tardy)	tardif, -dive	nachgehend	in ritardo	tardo	sen(färdig)	farshpetikt
slumber	sommeil, *m.*	Schlummer, *m.*	sonno, *m.*	sueño, *m.*	slummer, *nn.*	dreml, *m.*
sly (crafty)	rusé	verschlagen	furbo	astuto	slug	khitre
small	petit	klein	piccolo	pequeño	liten	kleyn
smallpox	variole, *f.*	Blattern, *f.pl.*	vaiolo, *m.*	viruela, *f.*	smittkoppor, *nn. pl.*	pokn, *pl.*
smart (chic)	élégant	schick	elegante	elegante	stilig	modish
smart (clever)	habile	klug	accorto	listo	duktig	klug
smash, to	fracasser	zerschmettern	fracassare	aplastar	krossa	tseshmetern
smell (odor)	odeur, *f.*	Geruch, *m.*	odore, *m.*	olor, *m.*	lukt, *nn.*	reyakh, *m.*
smell (perceive odor), to	sentir	riechen	odorare	oler	känna lukten av	shmekn
smile	sourire, *m.*	Lächeln, *n.*	sorriso, *m.*	sonrisa, *f.*	leende, *n.*	shmeykhl, *m.*
smile, to	sourire	lächeln	sorridere	sonreírse	le	shmeykhlen
smoke	fumée, *f.*	Rauch, *m.*	fumo, *m.*	humo, *m.*	rök, *nn.*	roykh, *m.*
smoke, to	fumer	rauchen	fumare	fumar	röka	reykhern
smooth (*adj.*)	lisse	glatt	liscio	liso	slät	glat
smooth (level), to	aplanir	glätten	spianare	aplanar	jämna	oysgletn
snail	escargot, *m.*	Schnecke, *f.*	lumaca, *f.*	caracol, *m.*	snigel, *nn.*	shnek, *m.*
snake	serpent, *m.*	Schlange, *f.*	serpente, *m.*	culebra, *f.*	orm, *nn.*	shlang, *f.*
snap (crackle), to	pétiller	knacken	crepitare	chasquear	smälla	knakn
snare (trap)	piège, *m.*	Schlinge, *f.*	laccio, *m.*	trampa, *f.*	snara, *nn.*	siltse, *f.*
snatch, to	happer	erhaschen	afferrare	arrebatar	rycka till sig	khapn
sneeze, to	éternuer	niesen	starnutare	estornudar	nysa	nisn
sniff, to	renifler	schnüffeln	annusare	resollar hacia adentro	vädra	tsien mit der noz
snow	neige, *f.*	Schnee, *m.*	neve, *f.*	nieve, *f.*	snö, *nn.*	shney, *m.*
so (also, *adv.*)	aussi	auch	anche	también lo	också	oykh
so (in order that, *conj.*)	de sorte que	damit	acciocchè	para que	så att	kedey
so (therefore, *adv.*)	donc	also	dunque	por lo tanto	så	iz
so (to such a degree, *adv.*)	si	so	così	tan	så	azoy
soak (saturate), to	tremper	durchnässen	impregnare	empapar	blöta	aynveykn
soap	savon, *m.*	Seife, *f.*	sapone, *m.*	jabón, *m.*	tvål, *nn.*	zeyf, *f.*
soar (rise), to	prendre son essor	aufschwingen, sich	salire	remontarse	stiga	shvebn
sob, to	sangloter	schluchzen	singhiozzare	sollozar	snyfta	khlipen
sober (serious)	sérieux, -rieuse	nüchtern	serio	serio	allvarsam	nikhter
soccer	football, *m.*	Fussball, *m.*	giuoco del calcio, *m.*	fútbol, *m.*	fotboll, *nn.*	fusbol, *m.*
sociable (companionable)	sociable	gesellig	socievole	sociable	sällskaplig	gezelshaftlekh
social (societal)	social	gesellschaftlich	sociale	social	social	sotsyal
socialism	socialisme, *m.*	Sozialismus, *m.*	socialismo, *m.*	socialismo, *m.*	socialism, *nn.*	sotsyalizm, *m.*
socialist (*n.*)	socialiste, *m., f.*	Sozialist, *m.*	socialista, *m., f.*	socialista, *m.*	socialist, *nn.*	sotsyalist, *m.*
sociology	sociologie, *f.*	Soziologie, *f.*	sociologia, *f.*	sociología, *f.*	sociologi, *nn.*	sotsyologye, *f.*
society (association)	société, *f.*	Gesellschaft, *f.*	società, *f.*	sociedad, *f.*	förening, *nn.*	gezelshaft, *f.*
society (the public)	société, *f.*	Gesellschaft, *f.*	società, *f.*	sociedad, *f.*	samhälle, *n.*	gezelshaft, *f.*
sock (garment)	chaussette, *f.*	Socke, *f.*	calzino, *m.*	calcetín, *m.*	(kort) strumpa, *nn.*	skarpet, *m.*
sofa	sofa, *m.*	Sofa, *n.*	sofà, *m.*	sofá, *m.*	soffa, *nn.*	sofe, *f.*
soft (not hard)	mou, molle	weich	soffice	blando	mjuk	veykh
soften (mitigate), to	amollir	erweichen	mitigare	ablandar	mildra	farveykhern
soil (ground)	sol, *m.*	Boden, *m.*	suolo, *m.*	suelo, *m.*	jord, *nn.*	bodn, *m.*
soil (make dirty), to	souiller	beschmutzen	sporcare	ensuciar	smutsa ned	aynrikhtn
soldier	soldat, *m.*	Soldat, *m.*	soldato, *m.*	soldado, *m.*	soldat, *nn.*	zelner, *m.*
sole (of shoe)	semelle, *f.*	Sohle, *f.*	suola, *f.*	suela, *f.*	sula, *nn.*	padeshve, *f.*
sole (only)	seul	einzig	solo	único	enda	eyntsik
solemn (grave)	solennel, -le	feierlich	grave	solemne	högtidlig	fayerlekh
solicit (ask for), to	solliciter	erbitten	sollecitare	solicitar	be om	vendn zikh
solid (compact)	solide	fest	solido	sólido	solid	solid
solitary (unaccompanied)	solitaire	einsam	solitario	solitario	ensam	opgezundert
solitude	solitude, *f.*	Einsamkeit, *f.*	solitudine, *f.*	soledad, *f.*	ensamhet, *nn.*	eynzamkayt, *f.*
solution (solving)	solution, *f.*	Lösung, *f.*	soluzione, *f.*	solución, *f.*	lösning, *nn.*	farentferung, *f.*
solve, to	résoudre	lösen	risolvere	resolver	lösa	farentfern
some (a few, *adj.*)	quelques	einige	alcuni	algunos	några	etlekhe
some (unspecified, *adj.*)	quelque	irgend ein	qualche	algún, -guna	någon	epes a
some (a quantity, *pron.*)	en	etwas	ne	algunos	något	a bisl
some (a quantity of, *adj.*)	de (*see p.* 2826)	etwas	del (*see p.* 2946)	algo de	någon	a bisl
some (certain, *adj.*)	certains	manche	certo	algunos	en del	teyl
some (certain ones, *pron.*)	certains	manche	alcuni	algunos	somliga	a teyl
somebody	quelqu'un	jemand	qualcuno	alguien	någon	a teyl
somehow	de façon ou d'autre	irgendwie	in qualche modo	de algún modo	på något sätt	vi es iz

English	French	German	Italian	Spanish	Swedish	Yiddish
someone	quelqu'un	jemand	qualcuno	alguien	någon	emetser
something	quelque chose	etwas	qualche cosa	algo	någonting	epes
sometimes	quelquefois	manchmal	qualche volta	algunas veces	ibland	teyl mol
somewhat (*adv.*)	quelque peu	etwas	un poco	algo	något	a bisl
somewhere	quelque part	irgendwo	in qualche luogo	en alguna parte	någonstans	ergets
son	fils, *m.*	Sohn, *m.*	figlio, *m.*	hijo, *m.*	son, *nn.* (*pl.* söner)	zun, *m.*
song	chanson, *f.*	Lied, *n.*	canzone, *f.*	canción, *f.*	sång, *nn.*	lid, *n.*
son-in-law	gendre, *m.*	Schwiegersohn, *m.*	genero, *m.*	yerno, *m.*	svärson, *nn.* (*pl.* -söner)	eydem, *m.*
soon (early)	tôt	früh	presto	temprano	tidigt	fri
soon (shortly)	bientôt	bald	tra poco	pronto	snart	bald
soothe (calm), to	calmer	besänftigen	calmare	calmar	lugna	baruikn
sore (*adj.*)	douloureux, -reuse	wund	indolenzito	dolorido	öm	tseveytikt
sore throat	mal de gorge, *m.*	Halsweh, *n.*	mal di gola, *m.*	mal de garganta, *m.*	ont i halsen, *n.*	haldzveytik, *m.*
sorrow (sadness)	chagrin, *m.*	Kummer, *m.*	dolore, *m.*	pesar, *m.*	sorg, *nn.*	troyer, *m.*
sorry, to be	regretter	bedauern	...dispiacere a (*see p.* 2955)	sentir	vara ledsen	badoyern
sort	sorte, *f.*	Sorte, *f.*	sorta, *f.*	clase, *f.*	sort, *nn.*	sort, *m.*
soul	âme, *f.*	Seele, *f.*	anima, *f.*	alma, *f.*	själ, *nn.*	neshome, *f.*
sound (healthy)	sain	gesund	sano	sano	frisk	gezunt
sound (noise)	son, *m.*	Laut, *m.*	suono, *m.*	sonido, *m.*	ljud, *n.*	klang, *m.*
sound (make heard), to	sonner	ertönen lassen	suonare	sonar	ringa	klingen
soup	soupe, *f.*	Suppe, *f.*	minestra, *f.*	sopa, *f.*	soppa, *nn.*	zup, *f.*
sour (tart)	aigre	sauer	agro	agrio	sur	zoyer
source (origin)	source, *f.*	Quelle, *f.*	fonte, *f.*	fuente, *f.*	källa, *nn.*	moker, *m.*
south (*n.*)	sud, *m.*	Süden, *m.*	sud, *m.*	sur, *m.*	söder, *nn.*	dorem, *m.*
South America	Amérique du Sud, *f.*	Südamerika, *n.*	America del Sud, *f.*	América del Sur	Sydamerika, *n.*	dorem-amerike, *f.*
southeast (*adj.*)	(¹¹) sud-est	südöstlich	del sud-est	sudeste	sydöstlig	dorem-mizrakh-dik
southern	méridional	südlich	meridionale	meridional	sydlig	doremdik
southwest (*adj.*)	(du) sud-ouest	südwestlich	del sud-ovest	sudoeste	sydvästlig	dorem-mayrev-dik
souvenir	souvenir, *m.*	Andenken, *n.*	ricordo, *m.*	recuerdo, *m.*	suvenir, *nn.*	ondenk, *m.*
sovereign (ruler)	souverain, *m.*	Herrscher, *m.*	sovrano, *m.*	soberano, *m.*	suverän, *nn.*	eyberhar, *m.*
sow, to	semer	säen	seminare	sembrar	så	zeyen
space (area)	espace, *m.*	Raum, *m.*	spazio, *m.*	espacio, *m.*	utrymme, *n.*	shetakh, *m.*
spade (tool)	bêche, *f.*	Spaten, *m.*	vanga, *f.*	azada, *f.*	spade, *nn.*	lopete, *f.*
Spain	Espagne, *f.*	Spanien, *n.*	Spagna, *f.*	España	Spanien, *n.*	Shpanye, *f.*
span (spread)	envergure, *f.*	Spanne, *f.*	estensione, *f.*	trecho, *m.*	spännvidd, *nn.*	shpan, *m.*
Spanish (*adj.*)	espagnol	spanisch	spagnuolo	español	spansk	shpanish
spank, to	fesser	prügeln	sculacciare	zurrar	smiska	shmaysn
spare (not harm), to	épargner	schonen	risparmiare	hacer gracia de	skona	shaneven
spark	étincelle, *f.*	Funke, *m.*	scintilla, *f.*	chispa, *f.*	gnista, *nn.*	funk, *m.*
sparkle, to	étinceler	funkeln	scintillare	chispear	gnistra	finklen
sparrow	moineau, *m.*	Spatz, *m.*	passero, *m.*	gorrión, *m.*	sparv, *nn.*	shperl, *m.*
speak (talk), to	parler	sprechen	parlare	hablar	tala	redn
speaker (orator)	orateur, *m.*	Redner, *m.*	oratore, *m.*	orador, *m.*	talare, *nn.*	redner, *m.*
spear (weapon)	lance, *f.*	Speer, *m.*	lancia, *f.*	lanza, *f.*	spjut, *n.*	shpiz, *f.*
special	spécial	besonder	speciale	especial	speciell	spetsyel
spectacle (pageant)	spectacle, *m.*	Schauspiel, *n.*	spettacolo pub-blico, *m.*	espectáculo, *m.*	skådespel, *n.*	spektakl, *m.*
spectacles (glasses)	lunettes, *f.pl.*	Brille, *f.*	occhiali, *m.pl.*	anteojos, *m.pl.*	glasögon, *n.pl.*	briln, *pl.*
spectator	spectateur, *m.*	Zuschauer, *m.*	spettatore, *m.*	espectador, *m.*	åskådare, *nn.*	tsukuker, *m.*
speech (address)	discours, *m.*	Rede, *f.*	discorso, *m.*	discurso, *m.*	tal, *n.*	rede, *f.*
speech (oral expression)	parole, *f.*	Sprechen, *n.*	favella, *f.*	habla, *f.*	tal, *n.*	reyd, *pl.*
speed (rapidity)	vitesse, *f.*	Geschwindig-keit, *f.*	velocità, *f.*	velocidad, *f.*	fart, *nn.*	gikhkayt, *f.*
spell (charm)	charme, *m.*	Zauber, *m.*	incanto, *m.*	encanto, *m.*	förtrollning, *nn.*	kishef, *m.*
spell, to	épeler	buchstabieren	scrivere	deletrear	stava	oysleygn
spend (pay out), to	dépenser	ausgeben	spendere	gastar	ge ut	oysgebn
sphere (globe)	sphère, *f.*	Kugel, *f.*	sfera, *f.*	esfera, *f.*	glob, *nn.*	kaylekh, *m.*
sphere (range)	sphère, *f.*	Kreis, *m.*	sfera, *f.*	esfera, *f.*	område, *n.*	sfere, *f.*
spice	épice, *f.*	Gewürz, *n.*	spezia, *f.*	especia, *f.*	krydda, *nn.*	gevirts, *n.*
spider	araignée, *f.*	Spinne, *f.*	ragno, *m.*	araña, *f.*	spindel, *nn.*	shpin, *f.*
spill (let pour out), to	répandre	vergiessen	versare	derramar	spilla	fargisn
spin (form thread), to	filer	spinnen	filare	hilar	spinna	shpinen
spin (revolve), to	tournoyer	drehen, sich	girare	girar	snurra	dreyen zikh
spinach	épinards, *m.pl.*	Spinat, *m.*	spinaci, *m.pl.*	espinaca, *f.*	spenat, *nn.*	shpinat, *m.*
spine (*anat.*)	épine dorsale, *f.*	Rückgrat, *n.*	spina dorsale, *f.*	espina dorsal, *f.*	ryggrad, *nn.*	ruknbeyn, *m.*
spirit	esprit, *m.*	Geist, *m.*	spirito, *m.*	espíritu, *m.*	anda, *nn.*	gayst, *m.*
spiritual (*adj.*)	spirituel, -le	geistig	spirituale	espiritual	andlig	gaystik
spit, to	cracher	spucken	sputare	escupir	spotta	shpayen
spite (ill will)	malveillance, *f.*	Bosheit, *f.*	dispetto, *m.*	despecho, *m.*	ondska, *nn.*	lehakhes, *m.*
splash, to	faire jaillir	spritzen	schizzare	chapotear	stänka	shpritsn
splendid	splendide	prächtig	splendido	espléndido	glänsande	glentsndik
splendor	splendeur, *f.*	Pracht, *f.*	splendore, *m.*	esplendor, *m.*	prakt, *nn.*	glants, *m.*
split (rend), to	fendre	spalten	fendere	hender	splittra	shpaltn
spoil (mar), to	gâter	verderben	guastare	dañar	fördärva	kalye makhn
sponge	éponge, *f.*	Schwamm, *m.*	spugna, *f.*	esponja, *f.*	svamp, *nn.*	shvom, *m.*

English	French	German	Italian	Spanish	Swedish	Yiddish
spoon (tablespoon)	cuillère à soupe,*f.*	Esslöffel,*m.*	cucchiaio,*m.*	cuchara,*f.*	matsked,*nn.*	eslefl,*m.*
spoon (teaspoon)	cuillère à thé,*f.*	Teelöffel,*m.*	cucchiaino,*m.*	cucharita,*f.*	tesked,*nn.*	teylefl,*m.*
sport (game)	sport,*m.*	Sport,*m.*	giuoco,*m.*	deporte,*m.*	sport,*nn.*	sport,*m.*
spot (place)	endroit,*m.*	Stelle,*f.*	luogo,*m.*	sitio,*m.*	ställe,*n.*	plats,*m.*
spot (stain)	tache,*f.*	Fleck,*m.*	macchia,*f.*	mancha,*f.*	fläck,*nn.*	flek,*m.*
sprain, to	attraper une entorse à	verrenken	storcersi	torcer	vricka	oyslinken
spray, to	arroser	besprengen	spruzzare	rociar	bespruta	bashpritsn
spread (diffuse), to	répandre	verbreiten	spargere	esparcir	sprida	farshpreytn
spring (coil)	ressort,*m.*	Feder,*f.*	molla,*f.*	resorte,*m.*	fjäder,*nn.*	sprunzhine,*f.*
spring (season)	printemps,*m.*	Frühling,*m.*	primavera,*f.*	primavera,*f.*	vår,*nn.*	friling,*m.*
spring (leap), to	sauter	springen	saltare	saltar	hoppa	a shprung ton
sprinkle (scatter), to	répandre	sprenkeln	spargere	esparcir	strö	bashprenklen
spur (spike)	éperon,*m.*	Sporn,*m.*	sperone,*m.*	espuela,*f.*	sporre,*nn.*	shpor,*m.*
spy	espion,*m.*	Spion,*m.*	spia,*f.*	espía,*f.*	spion,*nn.*	shpyon,*m.*
square (*adj.*)	carré	quadratisch	quadrato	cuadrado	fyrkantig	kvadratish
square (plaza)	place,*f.*	Platz,*m.*	piazza,*f.*	plaza,*f.*	torg,*n.*	plats,*m.*
squeeze, to	serrer	drücken	stringere	apretar	krama	kvetshn
squirrel	écureuil,*m.*	Eichhörnchen,*n.*	scoiattolo,*m.*	ardilla,*f.*	ekorre,*nn.*	veverke,*f.*
squirt, to	faire gicler	spritzen	schizzare	echar un chisquete	spruta	shpritsn
stab, to	poignarder	(er)stechen	pugnalare	dar de puñaladas	sticka	dershtekhn
stable (shelter)	écurie,*f.*	Stall,*m.*	stalla,*f.*	establo,*m.*	stall,*n.*	shtal,*m.*
stable (steadfast)	stable	standfest	stabile	estable	stadig	stabil
stadium	stade,*m.*	Kampfbahn,*f.*	stadio,*m.*	estadio,*m.*	stadion,*n.*	stadyon,*m.*
staff (personnel)	personnel,*m.*	Personal,*n.*	personale,*m.*	personal,*m.*	personal,*nn.*	shtab,*m.*
staff (stick)	bâton,*m.*	Stab,*m.*	bastone,*m.*	báculo,*m.*	stav,*nn.*	shtab,*m.*
stage (dais)	estrade,*f.*	Bühne,*f.*	palcoscenico,*m.*	tablado,*m.*	scen,*nn.*	stsene,*f.*
stage (period)	étape,*f.*	Stufe,*f.*	fase,*f.*	etapa,*f.*	stadium,*n.*	stadye,*f.*
stagger (totter), to	chanceler	wanken	barcollare	tambalearse	vackla	vaklen zikh
stain	tache,*f.*	Fleck,*m.*	macchia,*f.*	mancha,*f.*	fläck,*nn.*	plame,*f.*
stainless steel	acier inoxydable, *m.*	rostfreier Stahl, *m.*	acciaio inossidabile,*m.*	acero inoxidable, *m.*	rostfritt stål,*n.*	zhaverfray shtol,*n.*
stairway	escalier,*m.*	Treppe,*f.*	scala,*f.*	escalera,*f.*	trappa,*nn.*	trep,*pl.*
stake (post)	poteau,*m.*	Pfahl,*m.*	palo,*m.*	estaca,*f.*	stake,*nn.*	slup,*m.*
stake (thing wagered)	enjeu,*m.*	Einsatz,*m.*	messa,*f.*	apuesta,*f.*	insats,*nn.*	kon,*m.*
stale	rassis	altbacken	stantio	añejo	gammal	alt-gebakn
stalk (stem)	tige,*f.*	Stengel,*m.*	gambo,*m.*	tallo,*m.*	stjälk,*nn.*	shtengl,*n.*
stall (stop going), to	caler	aussetzen	indugiare	pararse	stanna	farhakn zikh
stallion	étalon,*m.*	Hengst,*m.*	stallone,*m.*	caballo padre,*m.*	hingst,*nn.*	oger,*m.*
stammer, to	bégayer	stammeln	balbettare	tartamudear	stamma	fariken zikh
stamp, postage	timbre-poste,*m.*	Marke,*f.*	francobollo,*m.*	sello,*m.*	frimärke,*n.*	marke,*f.*
stamp (mark), to	timbrer	stempeln	timbrare	timbrar	stämpla	shtemplen
stamp (tread heavily), to	trépigner	stampfen	pestare	patear	stampa	tupen
stand (bear), to	supporter	ertragen	resistere a	soportar	stå ut med	fartrogn
stand (be upright), to	être debout	stehen	tenersi in piedi	estar de pie	stå	shteyn
standard (regular)	normal	normal	normale	normal	standard-...	standard-...
stand up, to	lever, se	aufstehen	levarsi	ponerse de pie	resa sig	oyfshteyn
star (*astron.*)	étoile,*f.*	Stern,*m.*	stella,*f.*	estrella,*f.*	stjärna,*nn.*	shtern,*m.*
starch (in food)	fécule,*f.*	Stärke,*f.*	amido,*m.*	almidón,*m.*	stärkelse,*nn.*	krokhmal,*m.*
stare, to	regarder fixement	starren	guardare fisso	mirar fijamente	stirra	glotsn
start (beginning)	commencement, *m.*	Anfang,*m.*	inizio,*m.*	comienzo,*m.*	början,*nn.*	onheyb,*m.*
start (initiate), to	commencer	anfangen	iniziare	comenzar	börja	onheybn
start (set out), to	mettre en route, se	losgehen	avviarsi	salir	starta	aroyslozn zikh
starve (die of hunger), to	mourir de faim	verhungern	morire di fame	morirse de hambre	svälta	shtarbn fun hunger
state (condition)	état,*m.*	Zustand,*m.*	stato,*m.*	estado,*m.*	tillstånd,*n.*	matsev,*m.*
state (nation)	état,*m.*	Staat,*m.*	stato,*m.*	estado,*m.*	stat,*nn.*	melukhe,*f.*
state (say), to	déclarer	angeben	dichiarare	declarar	uppge	derklern
statement (accounting, bus.)	relevé,*m.*	Aufstellung,*f.*	estratto di conto, *m.*	estado de cuenta, *m.*	redovisning,*nn.*	konte-barikht, *m.*
statement (declaration)	déclaration,*f.*	Behauptung,*f.*	dichiarazione,*f.*	declaración,*f.*	förklaring,*nn.*	derklerung,*f.*
statesman	homme d'état, *m.*	Staatsmann,*m.*	uomo di stato,*m.*	estadista,*m.*	statsman,*nn.* (*pl.* -män)	melukhe-man,*m.*
station, railroad	gare,*f.*	Bahnhof,*m.*	stazione,*f.*	estación,*f.*	station,*nn.*	stantsye,*f.*
stationary (unmoving)	stationnaire	feststehend	stazionario	estacionario	stillastående	fest
stationery (writing paper)	papier à lettres, *m.*	Schreibpapier,*n.*	carta da lettere,*f.*	papelería,*f.*	skrivpapper,*n.*	shraybpapir,*n.*
statue	statue,*f.*	Bildsäule,*f.*	statua,*f.*	estatua,*f.*	staty,*nn.*	statue,*f.*
stature (height)	stature,*f.*	Wuchs,*m.*	statura,*f.*	estatura,*f.*	längd,*nn.*	heykh,*f.*
stay (sojourn)	séjour,*m.*	Aufenthalt,*m.*	soggiorno,*m.*	estada,*f.*	vistelse,*nn.*	oyfhalt,*m.*
stay (remain), to	rester	bleiben	restare	permanecer	stanna	blaybn
stead (place)	lieu,*m.*	Stelle,*f.*	luogo,*m.*	lugar,*m.*	ställe,*n.*	ort,*n.*
steady (firm)	ferme	fest	fermo	firme	stadig	fest
steady (regular)	soutenu	stetig	costante	constante	jämn	shtendik
steal, to	voler	stehlen	rubare	robar	stjäla	ganvenen
steam	vapeur,*f.*	Dampf,*m.*	vapore,*m.*	vapor,*m.*	ånga,*nn.*	pare,*f.*
steel	acier,*m.*	Stahl,*m.*	acciaio,*m.*	acero,*m.*	stål,*n.*	shtol,*n.*

English	French	German	Italian	Spanish	Swedish	Yiddish
steep (*adj.*)	raide	steil	erto	empinado	brant	shtotsik
steeple	clocher,*m.*	Kirchturm,*m.*	campanile,*m.*	torre,*f.*	kyrktorn,*n.*	kloyster-turem, *m.*
steer, to	conduire	steuern	guidare	conducir	styra	kereven
stem (*bot.*)	tige,*f.*	Stiel,*m.*	stelo,*m.*	tallo,*m.*	stam,*nn.*	shtengl,*n.*
stencil	stencil,*m.*	Schablone,*f.*	lastra metallica, *f.*	estarcido,*m.*	stencil,*nn.*	shablon,*m.*
stenographer	sténographe,*m.,f.*	Stenografin,*f.*	stenografa,*f.*	estenógrafa,*f.*	stenograf,*nn.*	stenografin,*m.*
step (stair)	marche,*f.*	Stufe,*f.*	gradino,*m.*	escalón,*m.*	trappsteg,*n.*	trepl,*n.*
step (stride)	pas,*m.*	Schritt,*m.*	passo,*m.*	paso,*m.*	steg,*n.*	trot,*m.*
step, to	faire un pas	treten	fare un passo	dar un paso	stiga	tretn
stepdaughter	belle-fille,*f.*	Stieftochter,*f.*	figliastra,*f.*	hijastra,*f.*	styvdotter,*nn.* (*pl.* -döttrar)	shtiftokhter,*f.*
stepfather	beau-père,*m.*	Stiefvater,*m.*	padrigno,*m.*	padrastro,*m.*	styvfa(de)r,*nn.* (*pl.* -fäder)	shtiftate,*m.*
stepmother	belle-mère,*f.*	Stiefmutter,*f.*	matrigna,*f.*	madrastra,*f.*	styvmo(de)r,*nn.* (*pl.* -mödrar)	shtifmame,*f.*
stepson	beau-fils,*m.*	Stiefsohn,*m.*	figliastro,*m.*	hijastro,*m.*	styvson,*nn.* (*pl.* -söner)	shtifzun,*m*
stern (*adj.*)	sévère	streng	severo	severo	sträng	shtreng
steward (attendant on ship)	steward,*m.*	Steward,*m.*	cameriere (di bordo),*m.*	camarero,*m.*	steward.*nn.*	styuard,*m.*
stick (small branch)	rameau,*m.*	Stock,*m.*	rametto,*m.*	palo,*m.*	pinne,*nn.*	shtekn,*m.*
stick (adhere), to	coller, (se)	kleben	aderire	pegarse	sitta fast	klepn zikh
stick (thrust), to	fourrer	stecken	introdurre	meter	sticka	araynshtekn
stiff (inflexible)	raide	steif	rigido	rígido	styv	shtayf
still (*adv.*)	encore	noch	ancora	aún	ännu	nokh
still (motionless, *adj.*)	tranquille	ruhig	immobile	inmóvil	stilla	ruik
still (nevertheless, *conj.*)	cependant	dennoch	tuttavia	no obstante	ändå	dokh
stimulate (incite), to	stimuler	anregen	stimolare	estimular	stimulera	stimulirn
sting (pierce skin), to	piquer	stechen	pungere	picar	sticka	shtekhn
stingy	chiche	geizig	tirchio	mezquino	snål	karg
stink, to	puer	stinken	puzzare	apestar	stinka	shtinken
stir (mix), to	remuer	rühren	mescolare	revolver	röra om	mishn
stitch (of sewing)	point,*m.*	Stich,*m.*	punto,*m.*	puntada,*f.*	stygn,*n.*	shtokh,*m.*
stock (livestock)	bétail,*m.*	Viehstand,*m.*	bestiame,*m.*	ganado,*m.*	kreatursbesätt-ning,*nn.*	fikh,*n.*
stock (shares)	actions,*f.pl.*	Aktien,*f.pl.*	azioni,*f.pl.*	acciones,*m.pl.*	aktier,*nn.pl.*	aktsyes,*pl.*
stock (supply)	provision,*f.*	Vorrat,*m.*	provvista,*f.*	existencias,*f.pl.*	förråd,*n.*	zapas,*m.*
stockholder	actionnaire,*m.,f.*	Aktienbesitzer, *m.*	azionista,*m.,f.*	accionista,*m.*	aktieägare,*nn.*	aktsyoner,*m.*
Stockholm	Stockholm,*m.*	Stockholm,*n.*	Stoccolma,*f.*	Estocolmo	Stockholm,*n.*	Shtokholm,*n.*
stocking	bas,*m.*	Strumpf,*m.*	calza,*f.*	media,*f.*	strumpa,*nn.*	zok,*m.*
stomach	estomac,*m.*	Magen,*m.*	stomaco,*m.*	estómago,*m.*	mage,*nn.*	mogn,*m.*
stone (piece of rock)	pierre,*f.*	Stein,*m.*	pietra,*f.*	piedra,*f.*	sten,*nn.*	shteyn,*m.*
stool (seat)	escabeau,*m.*	Schemel,*m.*	sgabello,*m.*	taburete,*m.*	pall,*nn.*	taburet,*m.*
stoop (bend forward), to	pencher, se	bücken, sich	chinarsi	doblarse	böja sig	onbeygn zikh
stop (halt)	arrêt,*m.*	Halt,*m.*	fermata,*f.*	parada,*f.*	uppehåll,*n.*	opshtel,*m.*
stop (cease), to	cesser	aufhören	cessare	dejar de	upphöra	oyfhern
stop (come to a standstill), to	arrêter, s'	anhalten	fermarsi	pararse	stanna	opshteln zikh
stop (make halt), to	arrêter	aufhalten	fermare	detener	göra uppehåll	opshteln
storage	emmagasinage, *m.*	Lagerung,*f.*	immagazzinag-gio,*m.*	almacenaje,*m.*	magasinering,*nn.*	lign in lager,*n.*
store (shop)	boutique,*f.*	Laden,*m.*	negozio,*m.*	tienda,*f.*	butik,*nn.*	krom,*f.*
store (accumulate), to	emmagasiner	lagern	accumulare	acumular	lagra	haltn oyfn lager
stork	cigogne,*f.*	Storch,*m.*	cicogna,*f.*	cigueña,*f.*	stork,*nn.*	bushl,*m.*
storm	orage,*m.*	Sturm,*m.*	tempesta,*f.*	tormenta,*f.*	storm,*nn.*	shturem,*m.*
stormy	orageux, -geuse	stürmisch	tempestoso	tempestuoso	stormig	shturemdik
story (account)	histoire,*f.*	Geschichte,*f.*	racconto,*m.*	cuento,*m.*	berättelse,*nn.*	mayse,*f.*
story (floor)	étage,*m.*	Stockwerk,*n.*	piano,*m.*	piso,*m.*	våning,*nn.*	gorn,*m.*
stout (corpulent)	corpulent	stark	corpulento	corpulento	fetlagd	balaybt
stout (strong)	fort	stark	robusto	fuerte	kraftig	shtark
stove (for cooking)	fourneau (de cuisine),*m.*	Herd,*m.*	fornello,*m.*	estufa,*f.*	spis,*nn.*	plite,*f.*
stove (for heating)	poêle,*m.*	Ofen,*m.*	stufa,*f.*	estufa,*f.*	kamin,*nn.*	oyvn,*m.*
straight (directly, *adv.*)	directement	geradewegs	direttamente	directamente	direkt	glaykh
straight (not crooked, *adj.*)	droit	gerade	diritto	derecho	rak	glaykh
straighten (put in order), to	ranger	in Ordnung bringen	mettere in ordine	arreglar	ordna	oysglaykhn
strain (exertion)	effort,*m.*	Anstrengung,*f.*	sforzo,*m.*	esfuerzo,*m.*	ansträngning,*nn.*	onshtrengung,*f.*
strain (filter), to	filtrer	durchseihen	passare	colar	sila	zayen
strand (thread)	brin,*m.*	Strähne,*f.*	filo,*m.*	hilo,*m.*	sträng,*nn.*	shnirl,*f.*
strange (peculiar)	étrange	seltsam	strano	extraño	underlig	modne
stranger (unknown person)	inconnu,*m.*	Fremde,*m.,f.*	estraneo,*m.*	desconocido,*m.*	främling,*nn.*	fremder,*m.*
strap	courroie,*f.*	Riemen,*m.*	cinghia,*f.*	correa,*f.*	rem,*nn.*	rimen,*m.*
straw (dry grain stalks)	paille,*f.*	Stroh,*n.*	paglia,*f.*	paja,*f.*	halmstrå,*n.*	shtroy,*f.*
strawberry	fraise,*f.*	Erdbeere,*f.*	fragola,*f.*	fresa,*f.*	jordgubbe,*nn.*	truskavke,*f.*
stray (roam), to	vaguer	umherschweifen	errare	vagar	ströva	blondzhen
streak	raie,*f.*	Streifen,*m.*	striscia,*f.*	raya,*f.*	strimma,*nn.*	pas,*m.*
stream (rivulet)	ruisseau,*m.*	Strom,*m.*	corrente,*f.*	arroyo,*m.*	ström,*nn.*	taykhl,*n.*

English	French	German	Italian	Spanish	Swedish	Yiddish
stream, to	ruisseler	strömen	scorrere	fluir	strömma	shtromen
street	rue,*f.*	Strasse,*f.*	strada,*f.*	calle,*f.*	gata,*nn.*	gas,*f.*
strength	force(s),*f.* (*pl.*)	Kraft,*f.*	forza,*f.*	fuerza,*f.*	styrka,*nn.*	koyakh,*m.*
strengthen, to	fortifier	stärken	rinforzare	fortalecer	stärka	shtarkn
stress (physical tension)	tension,*f.*	Druck,*m.*	tensione,*f.*	tensión,*f.*	tryck,*n.*	druk,*m.*
stretch (draw out), to	étendre	ausdehnen	stendere	estirar	sträcka	oystsien
stretch (extend), to	étendre, s'	erstrecken, sich	stendersi	extenderse	sträcka sig	tsien zikh
strict (stringent)	strict	streng	rigoroso	estricto	sträng	shtreng
stride (walk), to	marcher à grands pas	schreiten	camminare a grandi passi	andar a zancadas	kliva	shpanen
strike (work stoppage)	grève,*f.*	Streik,*m.*	sciopero,*m.*	huelga,*f.*	strejk,*nn.*	strayk,*m.*
strike (hit), to	frapper	schlagen	colpire	golpear	slå	shlogn
strike (stop work), to	mettre en grève, se	streiken	scioperare	declararse en huelga	strejka	straykn
string (cord)	ficelle,*f.*	Schnur,*f.*	spago,*m.*	cordel,*m.*	snöre,*n.*	shnur,*m.*
strip (band)	bande,*f.*	Streifen,*m.*	lista,*f.*	tira,*f.*	remsa,*nn.*	shtreyf,*m.*
strip (denude), to	dépouiller	abstreifen	spogliare	desnudar	klä(da) av	aroptsien
stripe (streak)	raie,*f.*	Streifen,*m.*	striscia,*f.*	raya,*f.*	strimma,*nn.*	pas,*m.*
strive (exert oneself), to	efforcer (de), s'	streben	sforzarsi	esforzarse	sträva	shtrebn
stroke (attack of paralysis)	coup de sang,*m.*	Schlaganfall,*m.*	colpo,*m.*	ataque fulminante,*m.*	slag,*n.*	shlak,*m.*
stroke (blow)	coup,*m.*	Schlag,*m.*	colpo,*m.*	golpe,*m.*	slag,*n.*	klap,*m.*
stroke (rub gently), to	caresser	streicheln	passare la mano su	frotar suavemente	stryka	gletn
stroll, to	promener, se	schlendern	passeggiare	pasearse	vandra omkring	shpatsirn
strong	fort	stark	forte	fuerte	stark	shtark
structure (arrangement of parts)	structure,*f.*	Struktur,*f.*	struttura,*f.*	estructura,*f.*	struktur,*nn.*	struktur,*f.*
structure (thing built)	édifice,*m.*	Bau,*m.*	costruzione,*f.*	construcción,*f.*	byggnad,*nn.*	binyen,*m.*
struggle (great effort)	lutte,*f.*	Ringen,*n.*	lotta,*f.*	lucha,*f.*	möda,*nn.*	gerangl,*m.*
stubborn	obstiné	hartnäckig	testardo	terco	envis	farakshnt
student	étudiant,*m.*	Student,*m.*	studente,*m.*	estudiante,*m.*,*f.*	student,*nn.*	talmid,*m.*
study (active learning)	étude,*f.*	Studium,*n.*	studio,*m.*	estudio,*m.*	studium,*n.*	lernen,*n.*
study, to	étudier	studieren	studiare	estudiar	studera	lernen
stuff (substance)	matière(s),*f.* (*pl.*)	Stoff,*m.*	materia,*f.*	materia,*f.*	ämne,*n.*	shtof,*m.*
stumble (trip), to	trébucher	stolpern	inciampare	tropezar	snava	geshtroykhlt vern
stump (of tree)	souche,*f.*	Stumpf,*m.*	ceppo,*m.*	tocón,*m.*	stubbe,*nn.*	pnyak,*m.*
stupid	stupide	dumm	stupido	estúpido	dum	narish
sturdy	robuste	kräftig	robusto	robusto	kraftig	kreftik
stutter, to	bégayer	stottern	balbettare	tartamudear	stamma	shtamlen
style (manner)	style,*m.*	Stil,*m.*	maniera,*f.*	estilo,*m.*	sätt,*n.*	stil,*m.*
subdue (conquer), to	subjuguer	unterwerfen	domare	vencer	underkuva	unterdrikn
subject (citizen)	sujet,*m.*	Untertan,*m.*	suddito,*m.*	súbdito,*m.*	undersåte,*nn.*	untertaner,*m.*
subject (topic)	sujet,*m.*	Gegenstand,*m.*	argomento,*m.*	tema,*m.*	ämne,*n.*	teme,*f.*
subjective	subjectif, -tive	subjektiv	soggettivo	subjetivo	subjektiv	subyektiv
submarine	sousmarin,*m.*	Unterseeboot,*n.*	sommergibile,*m.*	submarino,*m.*	undervattensbåt,*nn.*	tunkshif,*f.*
submit (offer), to	offrir	vorlegen	sottoporre	someter	förelägga	forleygn
subscription (for periodicals, etc.)	abonnement,*m.*	Abonnement,*n.*	abbonamento,*m.*	subscripción,*f.*	abonnemang,*n.*	abonement,*m.*
subsequent	subséquent	folgend	susseguente	subsecuente	följande	shpeterdik
substance (matter)	substance,*f.*	Stoff,*m.*	sostanza,*f.*	substancia,*f.*	substans,*nn.*	substants,*f.*
substantial (sizable)	substantiel, -le	beträchtlich	sostanziale	substancial	betydlig	hipsh
substitute (thing replacing another)	succédané,*m.*	Ersatzmittel,*n.*	surrogato,*m.*	substituto,*m.*	surrogat,*n.*	bimkem,*m.*
substitute (put in place of), to	substituer	an die Stelle setzen	sostituire	substituir	sätta i stället	farbaytn
subtract, to	soustraire	abziehen	sottrarre	restar	subtrahera	aropnemen
subway (underground railway)	métro,*m.*	Untergrundbahn,*f.*	metropolitana,*f.*	subterráneo,*m.*	tunnelbana,*nn.*	unterban,*f.*
succeed (attain goal), to	réussir	Erfolg haben	riuscire (a)	tener éxito	lyckas	matsliakh zayn
succeed (follow), to	succéder (à)	folgen	succedere	seguir	följa	kumen nokh
success (attainment)	succès,*m.*	Erfolg,*m.*	successo,*m.*	éxito,*m.*	framgång,*nn.*	hatslokhe,*f.*
successful	heureux, -reuse	erfolgreich	felice	próspero	framgångsrik	matsliakhdik
succumb (yield), to	succomber	unterliegen	cedere	rendirse	duka under	faln
such (of that kind, *adj.*)	tel, -le	solch	tale	tal	sådan	aza
suck, to	sucer	saugen	succhiare	chupar	suga	zoygn
sudden (unexpected)	soudain	plötzlich	improvviso	imprevisto	plötslig	plutsemdik
sue (bring action against), to	appeler en justice	verklagen	citare in giudizio	demandar	stämma	lodn
suede (*n.*)	(peau de) suède,*f.*	Ziegenleder,*n.*	pelle camosciata,*f.*	gamuza,*f.*	mockaskinn,*n.*	shvedish leder,*n.*
suffer (undergo), to	subir	leiden	soffrire	sufrir	genomgå	laydn
suffering	souffrance,*f.*	Leiden,*n.*	sofferenza,*f.*	sufrimiento,*m.*	lidande,*n.*	laydn,*n.*
sufficient	suffisant	genügend	sufficiente	suficiente	tillräcklig	genugik
sugar	sucre,*m.*	Zucker,*m.*	zucchero,*m.*	azúcar,*m.*	socker,*n.*	tsuker,*m.*
suggest (bring to mind), to	suggérer	nahelegen	suggerire	sugerir	föra tanken till	dermonen
suggest (recommend), to	proposer	vorschlagen	suggerire	sugerir	föreslå	forshlogn
suggestion (proposal)	suggestion,*f.*	Vorschlag,*m.*	suggerimento,*m.*	sugestión,*f.*	förslag,*n.*	forshlog,*m.*
suicide	suicide,*m.*	Selbstmord,*m.*	suicida,*m.*	suicidio,*m.*	självmord,*n.*	zelbstmord,*m.*
suit (lawsuit)	procès,*m.*	Prozess,*m.*	causa,*f.*	pleito,*m.*	åtal,*n.*	protses,*m.*
suit, man's	complet,*m.*	Anzug,*m.*	abito,*m.*	traje,*m.*	kostym,*nn.*	garniter,*m.*
suit, woman's	tailleur,*m.*	Kostüm,*n.*	vestito,*m.*	traje,*m.*	dräkt,*nn.*	kostyum,*m.*
suitable	convenable	angemessen	adatto	apropiado	lämplig	pasik
sulphur	soufre,*m.*	Schwefel,*m.*	zolfo,*m.*	azufre,*m.*	svavel,*n.*	shvebl,*m.*
sum (quantity)	somme,*f.*	Summe,*f.*	somma,*f.*	suma,*f.*	summa,*nn.*	sume,*f.*

English	French	German	Italian	Spanish	Swedish	Yiddish
summary (synopsis)	sommaire,*m.*	Zusammenfass-ung,*f.*	sommario,*m.*	resumen,*m.*	resumé,*nn.*	kitser,*m.*
summer (*n.*)	été,*m.*	Sommer,*m.*	estate,*f.*	verano,*m.*	sommar,*nn.* (*pl.* somrar)	zumer,*m.*
summit	sommet,*m.*	Gipfel,*m.*	sommità,*f.*	cumbre,*f.*	topp,*nn.*	shpits,*m.*
summon (send for), to	faire venir	auffordern	chiamare	llamar	tillkalla	aroysrufn
sun	soleil,*m.*	Sonne,*f.*	sole,*m.*	sol,*m.*	sol,*nn.*	zun,*f.*
sunburn	brûlure de soleil,*f.*	Sonnenbrand,*m.*	bruciatura di sole,*f.*	quemadura de sol,*f.*	solbränna,*nn.*	opbren,*m.*
sunglasses	lunettes de soleil,*f.pl.*	Sonnenbrille,*f.*	occhiali da sole,*m.pl.*	gafas contra el sol,*f.pl.*	solglasögon, *pl.*	zunbriln, *pl.*
sunlight	lumière du soleil, *f.*	Sonnenlicht,*n.*	luce del sole,*f.*	luz solar,*f.*	solljus,*n.*	zunlikht,*f.*
sunny	ensoleillé	sonnig	soleggiato	asoleado	solig	zunik
sunrise	lever du soleil,*m.*	Sonnenaufgang, *m.*	levata del sole,*f.*	salida del sol,*f.*	soluppgång,*nn.*	zunoyfgang,*m.*
sunset	coucher du soleil, *m.*	Sonnenunter-gang,*m.*	tramonto,*m.*	puesta del sol,*f.*	solnedgång,*nn.*	zun-untergang, *m.*
sunshine	soleil,*m.*	Sonnenschein,*m.*	sole,*m.*	luz del sol,*f.*	solsken,*n.*	zunenshayn,*f.*
superior (excellent)	supérieur	vorzüglich	superiore	superior	utmärkt	oysgetseykhnt
superstition	superstition,*f.*	Aberglaube,*m.*	superstizione,*f.*	superstición,*f.*	vidskepelse,*nn.*	ayngleybenish,*f.*
superstitious	superstitieux, -tieuse	abergläubisch	superstizioso	supersticioso	vidskeplig	ayngegleybt
supper (light evening meal)	souper,*m.*	Abendbrot,*n.*	cena,*f.*	cena,*f.*	kvällsmat,*nn.*	vetshere,*f.*
supplier (*bus.*)	fournisseur,*m.*	Lieferant,*m.*	fornitore,*m.*	proveedor,*m.*	leverantör,*nn.*	liverant,*m.*
supply (amount available)	provision,*f.*	Vorrat,*m.*	provvista,*f.*	provisión,*f.*	tillgång,*nn.*	zapas,*m.*
supply (provide), to	fournir	versehen	provvedere	proveer	anskaffa	tsushteln
support (approval)	soutien,*m.*	Unterstützung,*f.*	sostegno,*m.*	apoyo,*m.*	stöd,*n.*	untershtitsung, *f.*
support (livelihood)	soutien,*m.*	Lebensunterhalt, *m.*	sostegno,*m.*	sustento,*m.*	uppehälle,*n.*	khiyune,*f.*
support (hold up), to	soutenir	(unter)stützen	sostenere	sostener	stödja	unterhaltn
suppose (assume), to	supposer	vermuten	supporre	suponer	anta(ga)	meshaer zayn
suppress (subdue), to	supprimer	unterdrücken	sopprimere	suprimir	undertrycka	dershtikn
supreme	suprême	höchst	supremo	supremo	högst	hekhst
surcharge (*bus.*)	surtaxe,*f.*	Zuschlag,*m.*	sopraprezzo,*m.*	recargo,*m.*	tilläggsavgift,*nn.*	tsugob-optsol,*m.*
sure	sûr	sicher	sicuro	seguro	säker	zikher
surface	surface,*f.*	Oberfläche,*f.*	superficie,*f.*	superficie,*f.*	yta,*nn.*	eyberflakh,*f.*
surgeon	chirurgien,*m.*	Chirurg,*m.*	chirurgo,*m.*	cirujano,*m.*	kirurg,*nn.*	khirurg,*m.*
Surinam	Surinam,*m.*	Surinam,*m.*	Surinam,*m.*	Surinam	Surinam,*m.*	Surinam,*n.*
surname	nom de famille,*m.*	Zuname,*m.*	cognome,*n.*	apellido,*m.*	tillnamn,*n.*	familye,*f.*
surpass, to	surpasser	übertreffen	sorpassare	sobrepasar	överträffa	aribershtaygn
surplus (*n.*)	surplus,*m.*	Überschuss,*m.*	soprappiù,*m.*	sobrante,*m.*	överskott,*n.*	oydef,*m.*
surprise	surprise,*f.*	Überraschung,*f.*	sorpresa,*f.*	sorpresa,*f.*	förvåning,*nn.*	khidesh,*m.*
surprise (astonish), to	surprendre	überraschen	sorprendere	sorprender	förvåna	farkhideshn
surprise (come upon suddenly), to	surprendre	überraschen	sorprendere	sorprender	överraska	umgerikht onkumen
surrender (*mil.*)	reddition,*f.*	Übergabe,*f.*	resa,*f.*	rendición,*f.*	kapitulation,*nn.*	kapitulatsye,*f.*
surrender (give oneself up), to	rendre, se	ergeben, sich	arrendersi	rendirse	ge sig	untergebn zikh
surrender (relinquish), to	abandonner	aufgeben	cedere	rendir	uppge	iberentfern
surround (enclose), to	entourer	umgeben	circondare	rodear	omge	arumringlen
surroundings	environs,*m.pl.*	Umgebung,*f.*	dintorni,*m.pl.*	alrededores,*m.pl.*	omgivning,*nn.*	arum,*m.*
survey (inspection)	inspection,*f.*	Besichtigung,*f.*	esame,*m.*	examen,*m.*	granskning,*nn.*	iberblik,*m.*
survive (remain alive), to	survivre	am Leben bleiben	sopravvivere	sobrevivir	överleva	blaybn lebn
suspect (distrust), to	soupçonner	beargwöhnen	sospettare	sospechar	misstänka	khoyshed zayn
suspect (surmise), to	douter (de), se	vermuten	sospettare	imaginar	förmoda	hobn a khshad
suspend (terminate), to	suspendre	einstellen	sospendere	suspender	suspendera	opshteln
suspenders	bretelles,*f.pl.*	Hosenträger, *m.pl.*	bretelle,*f.pl.*	tirantes,*m.pl.*	hängslen,*n.pl.*	shleykes,*pl.*
suspicion	soupçon,*m.*	Verdacht,*m.*	sospetto,*m.*	sospecha,*f.*	misstanke,*nn.*	khshad,*m.*
sustain (maintain), to	soutenir	aushalten	sostenere	sostener	uppehålla	oyshaltn
swallow (bird)	hirondelle,*f.*	Schwalbe,*f.*	rondine,*f.*	golondrina,*f.*	svala,*nn.*	shvalb,*f.*
swallow, to	avaler	schlucken	inghiottire	tragar	svälja	shlingen
swamp (*n.*)	marais,*m.*	Sumpf,*m.*	palude,*f.*	pantano,*m.*	träsk,*n.*	zump,*m.*
swan	cygne,*m.*	Schwan,*m.*	cigno,*m.*	cisne,*m.*	svan,*nn.*	shvan,*m.*
sway (influence)	empire,*m.*	Einfluss,*m.*	dominio,*m.*	influjo,*m.*	inflytande,*n.*	deye,*f.*
sway (swing), to	balancer, se	schwanken	oscillare	mecerse	svänga	vign zikh
swear (curse), to	jurer	fluchen	bestemmiare	blasfemar	svära	shiltn
swear (vow), to	jurer	schwören	giurare	jurar	svära	shvern
sweat	sueur,*f.*	Schweiss,*m.*	sudore,*m.*	sudor,*m.*	svett,*nn.*	shveys,*m.*
sweater	chandail,*m.*	Sweater,*m.*	maglia,*f.*	suéter,*m.*	ylletröja,*nn.*	sveter,*m.*
Sweden	Suède,*f.*	Schweden,*n.*	Svezia,*f.*	Suecia	Sverige,*n.*	Shvedn,*n.*
Swedish (*adj.*)	suédois	schwedisch	svedese	sueco	svensk	shvedish
sweep (clean), to	balayer	fegen	spazzare	barrer	sopa	oyskern
sweet (pleasant tasting)	doux, douce	süss	dolce	dulce	söt	zis
sweetheart	bien-aimé,*m.*	Liebchen,*n.*	innamorato,*m.*	novio,*m.*	älskling,*nn.*	gelibter,*m.*
sweetness	douceur,*f.*	Süssigkeit,*f.*	dolcezza,*f.*	dulzura,*f.*	sötma,*nn.*	ziskayt,*f.*
swell (bulge), to	enfler, s'	schwellen	ingrossare	hincharse	svälla	oyfblozn zikh
swift	rapide	geschwind	rapido	rápido	snabb	bistre
swim, to	nager	schwimmen	nuotare	nadar	simma	shvimen
swine	cochon,*m.*	Schwein,*m.*	maiale,*m.*	marrano,*m.*	svin,*n.*	khazer,*m.*
swing (oscillate), to	osciller	schwingen	oscillare	oscilarse	svänga	vign zikh
Swiss (*adj.*)	suisse	schweizerisch	svizzero	suizo	schweizisk	shveytserish
switch (*elec.*)	interrupteur,*m.*	Schalter,*m.*	interruttore,*m.*	interruptor,*m.*	strömbrytare,*nn.*	oysshliser,*m.*
Switzerland	Suisse,*f.*	Schweiz,*f.*	Svizzera,*f.*	Suiza	Schweiz,*n.*	Shveyts,*f.*

English	French	German	Italian	Spanish	Swedish	Yiddish
sword	épée, f.	Schwert, n.	spada, f.	espada, f.	svärd, n.	shverd, f.
syllable	syllabe, f.	Silbe, f.	sillaba, f.	sílaba, f.	stavelse, nn.	traf, m.
sympathy (accord)	sympathie, f.	Übereinstimmung, f.	simpatia, f.	simpatía, f.	överensstämmelse, nn.	simpatye, f.
sympathy (compassion)	compassion, f.	Mitgefühl, n.	pietà, f.	compasión, f.	deltagande, n.	mitgefil, n.
symphony	symphonie, f.	Symphonie, f.	sinfonia, f.	sinfonía, f.	symfoni, nn.	simfonye, f.
symptom	symptôme, m.	Symptom, n.	sintomo, m.	síntoma, m.	symptom, n.	simptom, m.
syringe	seringue, f.	Spritze, f.	siringa, f.	jeringa, f.	spruta, nn.	shprits, f.
system (method)	système, m.	System, n.	sistema, m.	sistema, m.	system, n.	sistem, f.
table (furniture)	table, f.	Tisch, m.	tavola, f.	mesa, f.	bord, n.	tish, m.
table (tabulation)	tableau, m.	Tabelle, f.	tavola, f.	tabla, f.	tabell, nn.	tabele, f.
tablecloth	nappe, f.	Tischtuch, n.	tovaglia, f.	mantel, m.	bordduk, nn.	tishtekh, m.
tail (of animal)	queue, f.	Schwanz, m.	coda, f.	cola, f.	svans, nn.	ek, m.
tailor	tailleur, m.	Schneider, m.	sarto, m.	sastre, m.	skräddare, nn.	shnayder, m.
take, to	prendre	nehmen	prendere	tomar	ta(ga)	nemen
tale (narrative)	conte, m.	Erzählung, f.	racconto, m.	cuento, m.	berättelse, nn.	dertseylung, f.
talent	talent, m.	Talent, n.	talento, m.	talento, m.	talang, nn.	talant, m.
talk (conversation)	conversation, f.	Gespräch, n.	conversazione, f.	conversación, f.	samtal, n.	shmues, m.
talk, to	parler	reden	parlare	hablar	tala	redn
tall (of persons)	grand	gross	alto	alto	lång	hoykh
tall (of things)	haut	hoch	alto	alto	hög	hoykh
tame	domestiqué	zahm	domestico	domesticado	tam	shtubik
tank (container)	réservoir, m.	Zisterne, f.	serbatoio, m.	tanque, m.	tank, nn.	bak, m.
tap (faucet)	robinet, m.	Hahn, m.	rubinetto, m.	grifo, m.	kran, nn.	kran, m.
tap (rap), to	taper	klopfen	battere leggermente	golpear ligeramente	knacka	kleplen
tape recorder	magnétophone, m.	Bandregistrierapparat, n.	registratore a nastro, m.	grabador de cinta, m.	bandinspelningsapparat, nn.	bandrekordirer, m.
tar	goudron, m.	Teer, m.	catrame, m.	brea, f.	tjära, nn.	smole, f.
tardy (adj.)	tardif, -dive	spät	tardivo	tardío	sen	shpet
tariff (duty)	tarif, m.	Zoll, m.	dazio, m.	tarifa, f.	tulltariff, nn.	tsol, m.
task	tâche, f.	Aufgabe, f.	compito, m.	tarea, f.	uppgift, nn.	uvde, f.
taste (flavor)	goût, m.	Geschmack, m.	gusto, m.	sabor, m.	smak, nn.	taam, m.
taste (sample), to	goûter	kosten	assaggiare	probar	smaka	farzukhn
tax (n.)	impôt, m.	Steuer, f.	imposta, f.	impuesto, m.	skatt, nn.	shtayer, m.
taxi	taxi, m.	Taxi, n.	tassì, m.	taxímetro, m.	taxi, nn.	taksi, m.
tea	thé, m.	Tee, m.	tè, m.	té, m.	te, n.	tey, f.
teach, to	enseigner	lehren	insegnare	enseñar	lära	lernen
teacher	instituteur, m.	Lehrer, m.	maestro (di scuola), m.	maestro, m.	lärare, nn.	lerer, m.
team (in sports)	équipe, f.	Mannschaft, f.	squadra, f.	equipo, m.	lag, n.	manshaft, f.
tear (teardrop)	larme, f.	Träne, f.	lagrima, f.	lágrima, f.	tår, nn.	trer, f.
tear (rip), to	déchirer	reissen	strappare	rasgar	riva (sönder)	raysn
tease, to	taquiner	necken	stuzzicare	embromar	reta	reytsn zikh mit
Tel Aviv	Tel-Aviv, m.	Tel Aviv, n.	Tel Aviv, f.	Tel Aviv	Tel Aviv, n.	Tel-Aviv, n.
telegram	télégramme, m.	Telegramm, n.	telegramma, m.	telegrama, m.	telegram, n.	telegram, f.
telegraph, to	télégraphier	telegraphieren	telegrafare	telegrafiar	telegrafera	telegrafirn
telephone	téléphone, m.	Fernsprecher, m.	telefono, m.	teléfono, m.	telefon, nn.	telefon, m.
telephone, to	téléphoner	anrufen	telefonare	telefonear	telefonera	telefonirn
telescope	télescope, m.	Fernrohr, n.	telescopio, m.	telescopio, m.	teleskop, n.	teleskop, m.
television	télévision, f.	Fernsehen, n.	televisione, f.	televisión, f.	television, nn.	televizye, f.
tell (inform), to	dire	sagen	informare	decir	tala om	zogn
tell (narrate), to	raconter	erzählen	raccontare	contar	berätta	dertseyln
temper (mood)	humeur, f.	Laune, f.	umore, m.	humor, m.	humör, n.	temperament, m.
temperature	température, f.	Temperatur, f.	temperatura, f.	temperatura, f.	temperatur, nn.	temperatur, f.
tempest	tempête, f.	Gewitter, n.	tempesta, f.	tempestad, f.	storm, nn.	shturemvint, m.
temple (anat.)	tempe, f.	Schläfe, f.	tempia, f.	sien, f.	tinning, nn.	shleyf, f.
temple (place of worship)	temple, m.	Tempel, m.	tempio, m.	templo, m.	tempel, n.	templ, m.
temporary	provisoire	vorläufig	provvisorio	provisional	tillfällig	dervaylik
tempt, to	tenter	versuchen	tentare	tentar	fresta	pruvn
temptation	tentation, f.	Versuchung, f.	tentazione, f.	tentación, f.	frestelse, nn.	nisoyen, m.
tenant	locataire, m., f.	Mieter, m.	inquilino, m.	inquilino, m.	hyresgäst, nn.	lokator, m.
tend (be apt), to	être enclin	neigen	tendere	tender	tendera	noyte zayn
tendency	tendance, f.	Neigung, f.	tendenza, f.	tendencia, f.	tendens, nn.	tendents, f.
tender (loving)	tendre	zärtlich	tenero	tierno	öm	tsertlekh
tenderness (love)	tendresse, f.	Zärtlichkeit, f.	tenerezza, f.	ternura, f.	ömhet, nn.	tsertlekhkayt, f.
tennis	tennis, m.	Tennis, n.	tennis, m.	tenis, m.	tennis, nn.	tenis, m.
tension (anxiety)	tension (des nerfs), f.	Spannung, f.	ansietà, f.	ansiedad, f.	spänning, nn.	shpanung, f.
tension (stretching)	tension, f.	Spannung, f.	tensione, f.	tensión, f.	spänning, nn.	shpanung, f.
tent	tente, f.	Zelt, n.	tenda, f.	tienda de campaña, f.	tält, n.	getselt, n.
term (duration)	terme, m.	Frist, f.	periodo, m.	plazo, m.	termin, nn.	period, m.
term (expression)	terme, m.	Ausdruck, m.	termine, m.	término, m.	term, nn.	termin, m.
terms (conditions)	conditions, f. pl.	Bedingungen, f. pl.	patti, m. pl.	condiciones, f. pl.	villkor, n. pl.	tnoyim, pl.
terrace	terrasse, f.	Terrasse, f.	terrazza, f.	terraza, f.	terrass, nn.	terase, f.
terrible	terrible	schrecklich	terribile	terrible	förskräcklig	shreklekh
terrify, to	terrifier	erschrecken	atterrire	aterrorizar	skrämma	shrekn
territory	territoire, m.	Gebiet, n.	territorio, m.	territorio, m.	territorium, n.	teritorye, f.
terror	terreur, f.	Schrecken, m.	terrore, m.	terror, m.	skräck, nn.	moyre, f.
test (educ.)	examen, m.	Prüfung, f.	esame, m.	examen, m.	prov, n.	test, m.

English	French	German	Italian	Spanish	Swedish	Yiddish
test (trial)	épreuve,*f.*	Probe,*f.*	prova,*f.*	prueba,*f.*	prov,*n.*	probe,*f.*
test (try), to	éprouver	probieren	provare	probar	pröva	oyspruvn
testify, to	témoigner	bezeugen	attestare	atestiguar	intyga	eydes zogn
testimony	témoignage,*m.*	Zeugnis,*n.*	testimonianza,*f.*	testimonio,*m.*	vittnesmål,*n.*	gvias-eydes,*m.*
text	texte,*m.*	Text,*m.*	testo,*m.*	texto,*m.*	text,*nn.*	tekst,*m.*
textbook	manuel,*m.*	Lehrbuch,*n.*	libro di testo,*m.*	libro de texto,*m.*	lärobok,*nn.*(*pl.* -böcker)	lernbukh,*n.*
textile (*n.*)	textile,*m.*	Webwaren,*f.pl.*	tessuto,*m.*	tejido,*m.*	vävnad,*nn.*	tekstil,*m.*
than	que	als	che	que	än	eyder
thank, to	remercier	danken	ringraziare	dar gracias a	tacka	danken
thankful	reconnaissant	dankbar	grato	agradecido	tacksam	dankbar
thanks (gratitude)	remerciements, *m.pl.*	Dank,*m.*	ringraziamenti, *m.pl.*	gracias,*f.pl.*	tack,*nn.,n.*	dank,*m.*
that (*conj.*)	que	dass	che	que	att	az
that (*dem. adj.*)	(*see p.* 2828)	(*see p.* 2891)	(*see p.* 2949)	(*see p.* 3013)	(*see p.* 3076)	(*see p.* 3133)
that (*dem. pron.*)	(*see p.* 2828)	(*see p.* 2891)	(*see p.* 2948 ff.)	(*see p.* 3013)	(*see p.* 3076)	(*see p.* 3133)
that (*rel. pron.*)	(*see p.* 2828)	(*see p.* 2891)	che	que	som	vos
thaw, to	dégeler	tauen	sgelarsi	deshelarse	töa	tsegeyn
the	(*see p.* 2825 ff.)	(*see p.* 2887)	(*see p.* 2945)	(*see p.* 3010 ff.)	(*see p.* 3074)	(*see p.* 3130)
theater	théâtre,*m.*	Theater,*n.*	teatro,*m.*	teatro,*m.*	teater,*nn.*	teater,*m.*
their	(*see p.* 2827)	(*see p.* 2891)	(*see p.* 2948)	(*see p.* 3012)	(*see p.* 3075)	zeyer
theirs	(*see p.* 2827)	(*see p.* 2890)	(*see p.* 2948)	(*see p.* 3012)	(*see p.* 3075)	zeyerer
them	(*see p.* 2826 ff.)	(*see p.* 2890)	(*see p.* 2947 ff.)	(*see p.* 3012)	(*see p.* 3075)	zey
theme (subject)	thème,*m.*	Thema,*n.*	tema,*m.*	tema,*m.*	tema,*n.*	teme,*f.*
themselves	(*see p.* 2826 ff.)	(*see p.* 2890)	(*see p.* 2947 ff.)	(*see p.* 3012)	(*see p.* 3075)	zikh
then (at that time)	alors	dann	allora	entonces	då	demolt
then (in that case)	donc	dann	allora	en tal caso	då	oyb azoy
then (subsequently)	puis	dann	poi	luego	sedan	shpeter
theory	théorie,*f.*	Theorie,*f.*	teoria,*f.*	teoría,*f.*	teori,*nn.*	teorye,*f.*
there (at that place)	y, là	dort	là	allá	där	dortn
thereafter	après (cela)	danach	da allora in poi	después de eso	därefter	dernokhdem
thereby	par ce moyen	damit	con tal mezzo	con eso	därigenom	dermit
therefore	donc	daher	perciò	por lo tanto	därför	deriber
thereof	en	davon	di ciò	de eso	därom	derfun
thermometer	thermomètre,*m.*	Thermometer,*n.*	termometro,*m.*	termómetro,*m.*	termometer,*nn.*	termometer,*m.*
these (*adj.*)	ces	(*see p.* 2891)	questi (queste)	estos (estas)	dessa	di
these (*pron.*)	(*see p.* 2828)	(*see p.* 2891)	questi (queste)	éstos (éstas)	dessa	di
they	(*see p.* 2826 ff.)	sie	(*see p.* 2947)	(*see p.* 3012)	de	zey
thick (not thin)	épais, -se	dick	spesso	espeso	tjock	dik
thicket	hallier,*m.*	Dickicht,*n.*	macchia,*f.*	maleza,*f.*	snår,*n.*	gedikhtenish,*f.*
thickness (dimension)	épaisseur,*f.*	Dicke,*f.*	spessore,*m.*	espesor,*m.*	tjocklek,*nn.*	greb,*f.*
thief	voleur,*m.*	Dieb,*m.*	ladro,*m.*	ladrón,*m.*	tjuv,*nn.*	ganev,*m.*
thigh	cuisse,*f.*	Schenkel,*m.*	coscia,*f.*	muslo,*m.*	lår,*n.*	dikh,*f.*
thin (not fat)	maigre	mager	magro	flaco	mager	dar
thin (not thick)	mince	dünn	sottile	delgado	tunn	din
thing (material object)	chose,*f.*	Ding,*n.*	cosa,*f.*	cosa,*f.*	sak,*nn.*	zakh,*f.*
think (reason), to	penser	denken	pensare	pensar	tänka	trakhtn
thirst	soif,*f.*	Durst,*m.*	sete,*f.*	sed,*f.*	törst,*nn.*	dorsht,*m.*
thirsty	altéré	durstig	assetato	sediento	törstig	dorshtik
this (*adj.*)	(*see p.* 2828)	(*see p.* 2891)	(*see p.* 2949)	(*see p.* 3013)	(*see p.* 3076)	(*see p.* 3133)
this (*pron.*)	(*see p.* 2828)	(*see p.* 2891)	(*see p.* 2949)	(*see p.* 3013)	(*see p.* 3076)	(*see p.* 3133)
thorn	épine,*f.*	Dorn,*m.*	spina,*f.*	espina,*f.*	tagg,*nn.*	dorn,*m.*
thorough (complete)	complet, -plète	gründlich	completo	completo	grundlig	gruntik
thoroughly	complètement	gründlich	completamente	completamente	grundligt	durkh un durkh
those (*adj.*)	ces	(*see p.* 2891)	quei (*see p.* 2949)	(*see p.* 3013)	de där	yene
those (*pron.*)	(*see p.* 2828)	(*see p.* 2891)	(*see p.* 2949)	(*see p.* 3013)	de där	yene
though (*conj.*)	quoique	obwohl	sebbene	aunque	fast (än)	khotsh
thought (contemplation)	pensée,*f.*	Nachdenken,*n.*	pensiero,*m.*	meditación,*f.*	tankar,*nn.pl.*	trakhtn,*n.*
thought (idea)	idée,*f.*	Gedanke,*m.*	idea,*f.*	idea,*f.*	tanke,*nn.*	gedank,*m.*
thoughtful (reflective)	pensif, -sive	nachdenklich	riflessivo	pensativo	tankfull	fartrakht
thread (sewing thread)	fil,*m.*	Faden,*m.*	filo,*m.*	hilo,*m.*	tråd,*nn.*	fodem,*m.*
threat	menace,*f.*	Drohung,*f.*	minaccia,*f.*	amenaza,*f.*	hot,*n.*	strashunik,*m.*
threaten, to	menacer	drohen	minacciare	amenazar	hota	strashen
thrive (grow vigorously), to	développer, se	gedeihen	fiorire	crecer con vigor	frodas	gedayen
thrive (succeed), to	prospérer	Glück haben	prosperare	tener buen éxito	lyckas	blien
throat	gorge,*f.*	Hals,*m.*	gola,*f.*	garganta,*f.*	hals,*nn.*	haldz,*m.*
throne	trône,*m.*	Thron,*m.*	trono,*m.*	trono,*m.*	tron,*nn.*	tron,*m.*
throng	foule,*f.*	Gedränge,*n.*	calca,*f.*	multitud,*f.*	mängd,*nn.*	gedrang,*m.*
through (by means of, *prep.*)	par	durch	a mezzo di	por medio de	genom	durkh
through (from end to end of, *prep.*)	à travers	durch	attraverso	a través de	igenom	durkh
throughout (from start to finish of, *prep.*)	pendant tout	durch...hindurch	durante tutto	durante todo	genom hela	durkh
throughout (in every part of, *prep.*)	dans tout	überall in	dappertutto	por todo	överallt i	in gor
throw, to	jeter	werfen	gettare	tirar	kasta	varfn
thrust (push), to	enfoncer	stossen	spingere	empujar	stöta	praln
thumb	pouce,*m.*	Daumen,*m.*	pollice,*m.*	pulgar,*m.*	tumme,*nn.*	grober finger,*m.*
thunder	tonnerre,*m.*	Donner,*m.*	tuono,*m.*	trueno,*m.*	åska,*nn.*	duner,*m.*

English	French	German	Italian	Spanish	Swedish	Yiddish
thus (in this way)	ainsi	so	così	así	så	azoy
thus (therefore)	donc	also	così	por eso	således	al-keyn
ticket (entitling card)	billet,*m.*	Karte,*f.*	biglietto,*m.*	billete,*m.*	biljett,*nn.*	bilet,*m.*
tickle (touch lightly), to	chatouiller	kitzeln	solleticare	hacer cosquillas a	kittla	kitslen
tide, high	marée haute,*f.*	Flut,*f.*	marea alta,*f.*	marea alta,*f.*	flod,*nn.*	tsuflus,*m.*
tide, low	marée basse,*f.*	Ebbe,*f.*	marea bassa,*f.*	marea baja,*f.*	ebb,*nn.*	opflus,*m.*
tie (bond)	lien,*m.*	Band,*n.*	vincolo,*m.*	vínculo,*m.*	band,*n.*	bund,*m.*
tie (necktie)	cravate,*f.*	Krawatte,*f.*	cravatta,*f.*	corbata,*f.*	slips,*nn.*	shnips,*m.*
tie (fasten), to	lier	binden	legare	amarrar	knyta	bindn
tiger	tigre,*m.*	Tiger,*m.*	tigre,*f.*	tigre,*m.*	tiger,*nn.*	tiger,*m.*
tight (close-fitting)	juste	(zu) eng	stretto	muy ajustado	trång	eng
tight (taut)	tendu	straff	teso	tirante	spänd	shtayf
till (cultivate), to	labourer	bebauen	coltivare	labrar	odla	baarbetn
timber (standing trees)	bois (sur pied), *m.*	Holz,*n.*	bosco,*m.*	árboles de monte, *m.pl.*	timmerskog,*nn.*	gehilts,*n.*
time (hour determined by clock)	heure,*f.*	Zeit,*f.*	ora,*f.*	hora,*f.*	tid,*nn.*	zeyger,*m.*
time (interval)	temps,*m.*	Zeit,*f.*	tempo,*m.*	tiempo,*m.*	tid,*nn.*	tsayt,*f.*
timetable	horaire,*m.*	Fahrplan,*m.*	orario,*m.*	horario,*m.*	tidtabell,*nn.*	forplan,*m.*
timid	timide	furchtsam	timido	tímido	blyg	shrekevdik
tin (metal)	étain,*m.*	Zinn,*n.*	stagno,*m.*	estaño,*m.*	tenn,*n.*	tsin,*n.*
tiny	tout petit	winzig	piccolino	diminuto	liten	montshinker
tip (gratuity)	pourboire,*m.*	Trinkgeld,*n.*	mancia,*f.*	propina,*f.*	dricks,*nn.*	trinkgelt,*n.*
tip (point)	bout,*m.*	Spitze,*f.*	punta,*f.*	punta,*f.*	spets,*nn.*	shpits,*m.*
tire	pneu,*m.*	Reifen,*m.*	pneumatico,*m.*	neumático,*m.*	däck,*n.*	reyf,*m.*
tire (become weary), to	fatiguer, se	müde werden	stancarsi	cansarse	tröttna	mid vern
tire (make weary), to	fatiguer	ermüden	stancare	cansar	trötta	farmatern
tired	fatigué	müde	stanco	cansado	trött	farmatert
tissue (*biol.*)	tissu,*m.*	Gewebe,*n.*	tessuto,*m.*	tejido,*m.*	vävnad,*nn.*	geveb,*n.*
title (name)	titre,*m.*	Überschrift,*f.*	titolo,*m.*	título,*m.*	titel,*nn.*	titl,*m.*
to (indicating destination, *prep.*)	à; en	nach	a; in	a; hasta	till	tsu
to (indicating direction, *prep.*)	à	zu	a	a	till	keyn
to (in order to, *prep.*)	pour	um zu	per	para	för att	kedey
to (used with indirect object, *prep.*)	à (*see p.* 2827)	zu	a (*see p.* 2947)	a (*see p.* 3012)	till	tsu
toad	crapaud,*m.*	Kröte,*f.*	rospo,*m.*	sapo,*m.*	padda,*nn.*	zhabe,*f.*
toast (bread)	pain grillé,*m.*	geröstete Brot-schnitte,*f.*	pane tostato,*m.*	tostada,*f.*	rostat bröd,*n.*	toust,*m.*
tobacco	tabac,*m.*	Tabak,*m.*	tabacco,*m.*	tabaco,*m.*	tobak,*nn.*	tabak,*m.*
today	aujourd'hui	heute	oggi	hoy	i dag	haynt
toe	orteil,*m.*	Zehe,*f.*	dito del piede,*m.*	dedo del pie,*m.*	tå,*nn.*	finger (fun fus), *m.*
together	ensemble	zusammen	insieme	juntos	tillsammans	tsuzamen
toilet (water closet)	cabinet(s),*m.* (*pl.*)	Toilette,*f.*	gabinetto,*m.*	inodoro,*m.*	toalett,*nn.*	klozet,*m.*
Tokyo	Tokyo,*m.*	Tokio,*n.*	Tokio,*f.*	Tokio	Tokyo,*n.*	Tokyo,*n.*
tolerate (permit), to	tolérer	dulden	tollerare	tolerar	tillåta	derlozn
tomato	tomate,*f.*	Tomate,*f.*	pomodoro,*m.*	tomate,*m.*	tomat,*nn.*	pomidor,*m.*
tomb	tombe,*f.*	Grabstätte,*f.*	tomba,*f.*	tumba,*f.*	grav(vård),*nn.*	keyver,*m.*
tomorrow	demain	morgen	domani	mañana	i morgon	morgn
tone (quality of sound)	ton,*m.*	Ton,*m.*	tono,*m.*	tono,*m.*	ton,*nn.*	ton,*m.*
tongue (*anat.*)	langue,*f.*	Zunge,*f.*	lingua,*f.*	lengua,*f.*	tunga,*nn.*	tsung,*f.*
tonight	ce soir	heute abend	stasera	esta noche	i kväll	haynt in ovnt
tonsillitis	amygdalite,*f.*	Mandelentzün-dung,*f.*	tonsillite,*f.*	tonsilitis,*f.*	mandelinflam-mation,*nn.*	mandl-ontsindung,*f.*
too (also)	aussi	auch	anche	también	också	oykh
too (overly)	trop	zu	troppo	demasiado	alltför	tsu
tool	outil,*m.*	Werkzeug,*n.*	arnese,*m.*	herramienta,*f.*	verktyg,*n.*	makhshir,*m.*
tooth	dent,*f.*	Zahn,*m.*	dente,*m.*	diente,*m.*	tand,*nn.*(*pl.* tänder)	tson,*m.*
toothache	mal de dents,*m.*	Zahnweh,*n.*	mal di dente,*m.*	dolor de diente, *m.*	tandvärk,*nn.*	tsonveytik,*m.*
toothbrush	brosse à dents,*f.*	Zahnbürste,*f.*	spazzolino per i denti,*m.*	cepillo de diente, *m.*	tandborste,*nn.*	tsonbershtl,*n.*
tooth paste	pâte dentifrice,*f.*	Zahnpaste,*f.*	pasta dentifricia, *f.*	pasta dentífrica, *f.*	tandkräm,*nn.*	tsonpaste,*f.*
top (highest, *adj.*)	plus haut	höchst	più alto	más alto	högst	hekhst
top (summit)	haut,*m.*	Gipfel,*m.*	sommità,*f.*	cima,*f.*	topp,*nn.*	shpits,*m.*
top (upper surface)	dessus,*m.*	obere Seite,*f.*	superficie,*f.*	superficie,*f.*	översida,*nn.*	oybn,*f.*
topic	sujet,*m.*	Thema,*n.*	soggetto,*m.*	tema,*m.*	ämne,*n.*	teme,*f.*
torch	torche,*f.*	Fackel,*f.*	torcia,*f.*	antorcha,*f.*	fackla,*nn.*	shturkats,*m.*
torment	tourment,*m.*	Qual,*f.*	tormento,*m.*	tormento,*m.*	pina,*nn.*	maternish,*f.*
torment, to	tourmenter	quälen	tormentare	atormentar	plåga	matern
torpedo	torpille,*f.*	Torpedo,*n.*	siluro,*m.*	torpedo,*m.*	torped,*nn.*	torpede,*f.*
torrent	torrent,*m.*	reissender Strom, *m.*	torrente,*f.*	torrente,*m.*	ström,*nn.*	shtrom,*m.*
torture	torture,*f.*	Folter,*f.*	tortura,*f.*	tortura,*f.*	tortyr,*nn.*	paynikung,*f.*
toss (throw), to	jeter	werfen	lanciare	tirar	slänga	varfn
total (complete)	total	gänzlich	totale	total	total	gants
total (sum)	total,*m.*	Gesamtbetrag,*m.*	totale,*m.*	suma,*f.*	slutsumma,*nn.*	sakhakl,*m.*
touch, to	toucher	berühren	toccare	tocar	beröra	onrirn
tough (resistant)	dur	zäh(e)	resistente	duro	seg	hart

English	French	German	Italian	Spanish	Swedish	Yiddish
tour	tour,*m.*	Tour,*f.*	giro,*m.*	jira,*f.*	tur,*nn.*	tur,*nn.*
tourist (*n.*)	touriste,*m.,f.*	Tourist,*m.*	turista,*m.,f.*	turista,*m.,f.*	turist,*nn.*	turist,*m.*
toward	vers	auf...zu	verso	hacia	mot	tsu
towel, hand	serviette,*f.*	Handtuch,*n.*	asciugamani,*m.*	toalla,*f.*	handduk,*nn.*	hantekh,*n.*
tower	tour,*f.*	Turm,*m.*	torre,*f.*	torre,*f.*	torn,*n.*	turem,*m.*
town	ville,*f.*	Stadt,*f.*	città,*f.*	pueblo,*m.*	stad,*nn.* (*pl.* städer)	shtetl,*n.*
toy	jouet,*m.*	Spielzeug,*n.*	giocattolo,*m.*	juguete,*m.*	leksak,*nn.*	shpilkhl,*n.*
trace (vestige)	trace,*f.*	Spur,*f.*	traccia,*f.*	vestigio,*m.*	spår,*n.*	shpur,*f.*
track (rails)	voie,*f.*	Geleise,*n.*	binario,*m.*	vía,*f.*	spår,*n.*	relsveg,*m.*
tractor (farm machine)	tracteur agricole, *m.*	Traktor,*m.*	trattore,*m.*	tractor,*m.*	traktor,*nn.*	traktor,*m.*
trade (commerce)	commerce,*m.*	Handel,*m.*	commercio,*m.*	comercio,*m.*	handel,*nn.*	handl,*m.*
trade (craft)	métier,*m.*	Gewerbe,*n.*	mestiere,*m.*	oficio,*m.*	yrke,*n.*	melokhe,*f.*
trade mark	marque de commerce,*f.*	Handelsmarke,*f.*	marca di fabbrica,*f.*	marca de fábrica, *f.*	varumärke,*n.*	handls-marke,*f.*
tradition	tradition,*f.*	Überlieferung,*f.*	tradizione,*f.*	tradición,*f.*	tradition,*nn.*	traditsye,*f.*
traffic (flow of vehicles)	circulation,*f.*	Verkehr,*m.*	traffico,*m.*	tráfico,*m.*	trafik,*nn.*	farker,*m.*
tragedy	tragédie,*f.*	Tragödie,*f.*	tragedia,*f.*	tragedia,*f.*	tragedi,*nn.*	tragedye,*f.*
tragic	tragique	tragisch	tragico	trágico	tragisk	tragish
trail (path)	piste,*f.*	Pfad,*m.*	pista,*f.*	sendero,*m.*	stig,*nn.*	veg,*m.*
train, railroad	train,*m.*	Zug,*m.*	treno,*m.*	tren,*m.*	tåg,*n.*	tsug,*m.*
training (instruction)	instruction,*f.*	Erziehung,*f.*	istruzione,*f.*	instrucción,*f.*	utbildning,*nn.*	oysshulung,*f.*
traitor	traître,*m.*	Verräter,*m.*	traditore,*m.*	traidor,*m.*	förrädare,*nn.*	farreter,*m.*
trample, to	piétiner	trampeln	calpestare	atropellar	trampa sönder	tsetretn
transform, to	transformer	verwandeln	trasformare	transformar	förvandla	ibermakhn
transit (passage)	cours de route,*m.*	Transport,*m.*	transito,*m.*	tránsito,*m.*	transport,*nn.*	ariberfirn,*n.*
translate, to	traduire	übersetzen	tradurre	traducir	översätta	iberzetsn
transparent	transparent	durchsichtig	trasparente	transparente	genomskinlig	durkhzeevdik
transport, to	transporter	befördern	trasportare	transportar	transportera	ariberfirn
transportation (conveying)	transport,*m.*	Beförderung,*f.*	trasporto,*m.*	transporte,*m.*	transport,*nn.*	ariberfirn,*n.*
trap (snare)	piège,*m.*	Falle,*f.*	trappola,*f.*	trampa,*f.*	fälla,*nn.*	pastke,*f.*
travel, to	voyager	reisen	viaggiare	viajar	resa	arumforn
traveler	voyageur,*m.*	Reisende,*m.,f.*	viaggiatore,*m.*	viajero,*m.*	resande,*nn.*	rayznder,*m.*
traveling salesman	voyageur de commerce,*m.*	Handelsreisende, *m.*	viaggiatore (di commercio),*m.*	viajante de comercio,*m.*	handelsresande, *nn.*	komivoyazhor, *m.*
tray	plateau,*m.*	Tablett,*n.*	vassoio,*m.*	bandeja,*f.*	bricka,*nn.*	tats,*f.*
treason	trahison,*f.*	Verrat,*m.*	tradimento,*m.*	traición,*f.*	förräderi,*n.*	farrat,*m.*
treasure	trésor,*m.*	Schatz,*m.*	tesoro,*m.*	tesoro,*m.*	skatt,*nn.*	oytser,*m.*
treasury (*govt.*)	trésorerie,*f.*	Schatz,*m.*	Tesoro,*m.*	tesorería,*f.*	finansdepartement,*n.*	melukhe-oytser, *m.*
treat (behave toward), to	traiter	behandeln	trattare	tratar	behandla	bahandeln
treatment (behavior toward)	traitement,*m.*	Behandlung,*f.*	trattamento,*m.*	manera de tratar, *f.*	behandling,*nn.*	bahandlung,*f.*
treatment (medical care)	traitement,*m.*	Behandlung,*f.*	cura,*f.*	tratamiento,*m.*	behandling,*nn.*	bahandlung,*f.*
treaty	traité,*m.*	Vertrag,*m.*	trattato,*m.*	tratado,*m.*	fördrag,*n.*	traktat,*m.*
tree	arbre,*m.*	Baum,*m.*	albero,*m.*	árbol,*m.*	träd,*n.*	boym,*m.*
tremble, to	trembler	zittern	tremare	estremecerse	darra	tsitern
trench (*mil.*)	tranchée,*f.*	Graben,*m.*	trincea,*f.*	trinchera,*f.*	skyttegrav,*nn.*	transhee,*f.*
trial (court proceeding)	procès,*m.*	Gerichtsverhandlung,*f.*	processo,*m.*	proceso,*m.*	rättegång,*nn.*	protses,*m.*
triangle (*geom.*)	triangle,*m.*	Dreieck,*n.*	triangolo,*m.*	triángulo,*m.*	triangel,*nn.*	drayek,*m.*
tribe	tribu,*f.*	Stamm,*m.*	tribù,*f.*	tribu,*f.*	stam,*nn.*	sheyvet,*m.*
tribute (money)	tribut,*m.*	Zins,*m.*	tributo,*m.*	tributo,*m.*	tribut,*nn.*	tribut,*m.*
trick (knack)	truc,*m.*	Kniff,*m.*	trucco,*m.*	maña,*f.*	konst,*nn.*	kunts,*f.*
trick (ruse)	tour,*m.*	Trick,*m.*	trucco,*m.*	engaño,*m.*	knep,*n.*	shpitsl,*n.*
trifle	bagatelle,*f.*	Kleinigkeit,*f.*	bagatella,*f.*	bagatela,*f.*	småsak,*nn.*	kleynikayt,*f.*
trim (decorate), to	orner	aufputzen	ornare	adornar	dekorera	baputsn
trip (journey)	voyage,*m.*	Reise,*f.*	viaggio,*m.*	viaje,*m.*	tur,*nn.*	nesie,*f.*
trip (stumble), to	trébucher	stolpern	inciampare	tropezar	snava	spotiken zikh
triumph	triomphe,*m.*	Triumph,*m.*	trionfo,*m.*	triunfo,*m.*	triumf,*nn.*	triumf,*m.*
trolley (street car)	tramway,*m.*	Strassenbahn,*f.*	tranvia,*f.*	tranvía de trole, *m.*	spårvagn,*nn.*	tramvay,*m.*
trombone	trombone,*m.*	Posaune,*f.*	trombone,*m.*	trombón,*m.*	basun,*nn.*	trombon,*m.*
troops (*mil.*)	troupes,*f.pl.*	Truppen,*f.pl.*	truppe,*f.pl.*	tropas,*m.pl.*	trupper,*nn.pl.*	militer,*n.*
trot	trot,*m.*	Trab,*m.*	trotto,*m.*	trote,*m.*	trav,*n.*	tlis,*m.*
trouble (distress)	ennui,*m.*	Schwierigkeiten, *f.pl.*	guaio,*m.*	aflicción,*f.*	bekymmer,*n.*	tsore,*f.*
trouble (exertion)	peine,*f.*	Mühe,*f.*	fatica,*f.*	pena,*f.*	möda,*nn.*	tirkhe,*f.*
trouble (disquiet), to	inquiéter	stören	disturbare	perturbar	oroa	shver makhn dos harts
trouble (inconvenience), to	déranger	belästigen	incomodare	molestar	besvära	matriakh zayn
trousers	pantalon(s),*m.* (*pl.*)	Hose(n),*f.pl.*	pantaloni,*m.pl.*	pantalones,*m.pl.*	byxor,*nn.pl.*	hoyzn,*pl.*
trout	truite,*f.*	Forelle,*f.*	trota,*f.*	trucha,*f.*	forell,*nn.*	forel,*f.*
truck (automobile)	camion,*m.*	Lastwagen,*m.*	autocarro,*m.*	camión,*m.*	lastbil,*nn.*	lastoyto,*m.*
true	vrai	wahr	vero	verdadero	sann	emes
trumpet (*mus.*)	trompette,*f.*	Trompete,*f.*	tromba,*f.*	trompeta,*f.*	trumpet,*nn.*	trumeyt,*m.*
trunk (baggage)	malle,*f.*	Koffer,*m.*	baule,*m.*	baúl,*m.*	koffert,*nn.*	kufert,*m.*
trunk (stem)	tronc,*m.*	Stamm,*m.*	tronco,*m.*	tronco,*m.*	stam,*nn.*	shtam,*m.*
trust (cartel)	trust,*m.*	Trust,*m.*	trust,*m.*	trust,*m.*	trust,*nn.*	trost,*m.*
trust (confidence)	confiance,*f.*	Vertrauen,*n.*	fiducia,*f.*	confianza,*f.*	förtroende,*n.*	tsutroy,*m.*
trust (rely on), to	fier,se	vertrauen	fidarsi di	confiar en	lita på	getroyen
truth	vérité,*f.*	Wahrheit,*f.*	verità,*f.*	verdad,*f.*	sanning,*nn.*	emes,*m.*
try (attempt), to	essayer	versuchen	tentare	intentar	försöka	pruvn

English	French	German	Italian	Spanish	Swedish	Yiddish
try (test), to	éprouver	prüfen	provare	probar	pröva	oyspruvn
tub (bathtub)	baignoire, f.	Wanne, f.	vasca, f.	bañera, f.	kar, n.	vane, f.
tube (pipe)	tube, m.	Röhre, f.	tubo, m.	tubo, m.	rör, n.	rer, f.
tuberculosis	tuberculose, f.	Tuberkulose, f.	tubercolosi, f.	tuberculosis, f.	tuberkulos, nn.	tuberkuloz, m.
tuck (slip inside), to	rentrer	stecken	fare entrare	remeter	stoppa in	farshtekn
tug (drag), to	tirer	schleppen	tirare	arrastrar	dra(ga)	shlepn
tuition (school fee)	frais d'inscrip-tion, m.pl.	Schulgeld, n.	tasse scolastiche, f.pl.	derechos de ense-ñanza, m.pl.	kursavgift, nn.	skhar-limud, m.
tulip	tulipe, f.	Tulpe, f.	tulipano, m.	tulipán, m.	tulpan, nn.	tulpan, m.
tumble (fall), to	tomber	fallen	cascare	caer	ramla	faln
tumbler (glass)	verre, m.	Becher, m.	bicchiere, m.	vaso, m.	dricksglas, n.	kelishek, m.
tumor	tumeur, f.	Geschwulst, f.	tumore, m.	tumor, m.	tumör, nn.	tumor, m.
tune (melody)	air, m.	Melodie, f.	aria, f.	tonada, f.	melodi, nn.	nign, m.
tunnel	tunnel, m.	Tunnel, m.	galleria, f.	túnel, m.	tunnel, nn.	tunel, m.
turkey	dindon, m.	Truthahn, m.	tacchino, m.	pavo, m.	kalkon, nn.	indik, m.
Turkey	Turquie, f.	Türkei, f.	Turchia, f.	Turquía	Turkiet, n.	Terkay, f.
Turkish (adj.)	turc, turque	türkisch	turchese	turco	turkisk	terkish
turn (change of direction)	virage, m.	Wendung, f.	giro, m.	vuelta, f.	vändning, nn.	ker, m.
turn (convert), to	changer	verwandeln	trasformare	convertir	förvandla	farvandlen
turn (face about), to	retourner, se	umdrehen, sich	voltarsi	volverse	vända sig	oysdreyen zikh
turn (make rotate), to	tourner	drehen	far girare	hacer girar	snurra	dreyen
turnip (white)	navet, m.	weisse Rübe, f.	navone, m.	nabo, m.	rova, nn.	brukve, f.
turtle	tortue, f.	Schildkröte, f.	tartaruga, f.	tortuga, f.	sköldpadda, nn.	tsherepakhe, f.
tweed (cloth)	tweed, m.	Tweed, m.	tweed, m.	mezclilla de lana, f.	tweed, nn.	tvidshtof, m.
twice	deux fois	zweimal	due volte	dos veces	två gånger	tsvey mol
twig	brindille, f.	Zweig, m.	rametto, m.	ramita, f.	kvist, nn.	tsvaygl, n.
twilight	crépuscule, m.	Dämmerung, f.	crepuscolo, m.	crepúsculo, m.	skymning, nn.	beyn-hashmo-shes, m.
twin (n.)	jumeau, m.	Zwilling, m.	gemello, m.	gemelo, m.	tvilling, nn.	tsviling, m.
twinkle, to	scintiller	blinken	scintillare	titilar	tindra	finklen
twist (wind), to	tordre	winden	torcere	torcer	tvinna	ayndreyen
type (kind)	genre, m.	Art, f.	tipo, m.	tipo, m.	slag, n.	tip, m.
type (typewrite), to	taper à la ma-chine	tippen	scrivere a mac-china	escribir en má-quina	skriva maskin	tipirn
typewriter	machine à écrire, f.	Schreibmaschine, f.	macchina da scri-vere, f.	máquina de escri-bir, f.	skrivmaskin, nn.	shraybmashin, f.
typhoid fever	fièvre typhoïde, f.	Unterleibs-typhus, m.	tifoide, f.	fiebre tifoidea, f.	tyfus, nn.	boykhtifus, m.
typical	typique	typisch	tipico	típico	typisk	tipish
typist	dactylographe, m., f.	Maschinen-schreiber, m.	dattilografo, m.	mecanógrafo, m.	maskinskrivare, nn.	tipist, m.
tyrant	tyran, m.	Tyrann, m.	tiranno, m.	tirano, m.	tyrann, nn.	tiran, m.
ugly	laid	hässlich	brutto	feo	ful	mies
ulcer	ulcère, m.	Geschwür, n.	ulcera, f.	úlcera, f.	magsår, n.	mogn-geshvir, m.
umbrella	parapluie, m.	(Regen)Schirm, m.	ombrello, m.	paraguas, m.	paraply, n., nn.	shirem, m.
uncle	oncle, m.	Onkel, m.	zio, m.	tío, m.	far-, mor-, bro-(de)r, nn. (pl. -bröder)	feter, m.
under (prep.)	sous	unter	sotto	bajo	under	unter
underground (below-ground, adj.)	souterrain	unterirdisch	sotteraneo	subterráneo	underjordisk	untererdish
underground (secret, adj.)	souterrain	unterirdisch	clandestino	secreto	hemlig	untererdish
underneath (prep.)	au-dessous de	unter	disotto	debajo de	under	unter
understand (comprehend), to	comprendre	verstehen	capire	comprender	förstå	farshteyn
understanding (compre-hension)	compréhension, f.	Verständnis, n.	comprensione, f.	comprensión, f.	förståelse, nn.	farshtendenish, n.
undertake (attempt), to	entreprendre	unternehmen	intraprendere	intentar	företa(ga) sig	unternemen zikh
undertaking (enterprise)	entreprise, f.	Unternehmung, f.	impresa, f.	empresa, f.	företag, n.	unternemung, f.
underwear	sous-vêtements, m.pl.	Unterkleidung, f.	biancheria (in-tima), f.	ropa interior, f.	underkläder, nn. pl.	untervesh, pl.
undoubtedly	indubitablement	zweifellos	indubbiamente	sin duda	otvivelaktigt	bli-sofek
uneasy (anxious)	inquiet, -quiète	unruhig	inquieto	inquieto	orolig	umruik
unemployed	en chômage	müssig	senza lavoro	desocupado	arbetslös	arbetsloz
unemployment	chômage, m.	Arbeitslosigkeit, f.	disoccupazione, f.	desempleo, m.	arbetslöshet, nn.	arbetslozikayt, f.
unequal	inégal	ungleich	ineguale	desigual	olika	umglaykh
unexpected (adj.)	inattendu	unerwartet	imprevisto	inesperado	oväntad	umgerikht
unfortunate	malheureux, -reuse	unglücklich	sfortunato	desventurado	olycklig	umgliklekh
unhappy (sorrowful)	malheureux, -reuse	unglücklich	infelice	infeliz	olycklig	umgliklekh
uniform (adj.)	uniforme	einheitlich	uniforme	uniforme	enhetlig	eynhaytlekh
uniform (n.)	uniforme, m.	Uniform, f.	uniforme, f.	uniforme, m.	uniform, nn.	mundir, m.
union (league)	union, f.	Bund, m.	unione, f.	unión, f.	förbund, n.	farband, m.
union (trade union)	syndicat, m.	Gewerkschaft, f.	sindacato, m.	sindicato, m.	fackförening, nn.	fareyn, m.
unite (make one), to	unir	vereinigen	unire	unir	förena	fareynikn
United Nations	Nations Unies, f.pl.	Vereinigten Na-tionen, f.pl.	Nazioni Unite, f.pl.	Naciones Unidas, f.pl.	Förenta na-tionerna, nn.pl.	Fareynikte Natsyes, pl.
United States	États-Unis, m.pl.	Vereinigten Staa-ten, m.pl.	Stati Uniti, m.pl.	Estados Unidos, m.pl.	Förenta staterna, nn.pl.	Fareynikte Shtatn, pl.
unity (accord)	unité, f.	Einigkeit, f.	unità, f.	concordia, f.	enighet, nn.	akhdes, f.
universal (adj.)	universel, -le	allgemein	universale	universal	allmän	universal

English	French	German	Italian	Spanish	Swedish	Yiddish
universe	univers,*m.*	Weltall,*n.*	universo,*m.*	universo,*m.*	universum,*n.*	univers,*m.*
university	université,*f.*	Universität,*f.*	università,*f.*	universidad,*f.*	universitet,*n.*	universitet,*m.*
unjust (inequitable)	injuste	ungerecht	ingiusto	injusto	orättfärdig	umgerekht
unknown	inconnu	unbekannt	sconosciuto	desconocido	okänd	umbakant
unless (*conj.*)	à moins que	wenn nicht	a meno che	a menos que	såvida inte	saydn
unlike (*adj.*)	dissemblable	unähnlich	dissimile	desemejante	olik	nit-enlekh
unload, to	décharger	abladen	scaricare	descargar	lasta av	oyslodn
unlucky	malchanceux, -ceuse	unglücklich	sfortunato	desgraciado	olycklig	shlimazldik
unnecessary	inutile	unnötig	inutile	innecesario	onödig	umneytik
unpaid (due)	impayé	unbezahlt	allo scoperto	no pagado	obetald	nit-batsolt
unpleasant	désagréable	unangenehm	sgradevole	desagradable	obehaglig	umayngenem
unreasonable (unreasoning)	déraisonnable	unvernünftig	irragionevole	irrazonable	oförnuftg	on aynzeenish
until (before, *prep.*)	avant	bis	prima di	antes de	förrän	biz
until (*conj.*)	jusqu'à ce que	bis	fino a che	hasta que	tills	biz
until (up to the time of, *prep.*)	jusqu'à	bis	fino a	hasta	till	biz
unworthy	indigne	unwürdig	indegno	indigno	ovärdig	umverdik
up (*adv.*)	(en) haut	oben	su	arriba	upp(e)	hekher
upon	sur	auf	sopra	sobre	på	oyf
upset (knock over), to	renverser	umstürzen	capovolgere	volcar	stjälpa	iberkern
upstairs (at upper story, *adv.*)	en haut	oben	al piano superiore	arriba	däruppe	oybn
upstairs (to upper story, *adv.*)	en haut	die Treppe hinauf	al piano superiore	hacia arriba	upp	aroyf di trep
upward (to a higher level, *adv.*)	en haut	aufwärts	inalto	hacia arriba	uppåt	aroyf
uranium	uranium,*m.*	Uran,*n.*	uranio,*m.*	uranio,*m.*	uran,*n.* or *nn.*	uranyum,*n.*
urban	urbain	städtlich	urbano	urbano	stads-...	shtotish
urge (try to persuade), to	exhorter	zureden	sollecitare	insistir en	uppmana	tsuredn
urgent	urgent	dringend	urgente	urgente	viktig	dringlekh
Uruguay	Uruguay,*m.*	Uruguay,*n.*	Uruguay,*m.*	el Uruguay	Uruguay,*n.*	Urugvay,*n.*
us	nous (*see p.* 2826 ff.)	uns (*see p.* 2890)	ci; noi (*see p.* 2947 ff.)	nosotros; nos (*see p.* 3012)	oss (*see p.* 3075)	undz
use (usefulness)	utilité,*f.*	Anwendung,*f.*	utilità,*f.*	utilidad,*f.*	nytta,*nn.*	nuts,*m.*
use (utilization)	usage,*m.*	Gebrauch,*m.*	uso,*m.*	uso,*m.*	användning,*nn.*	banuts,*m.*
use (utilize), to	employer	benutzen	usare	usar	använda	nutsn
useful	utile	nützlich	utile	útil	nyttig	nutsik
useless	inutile	nutzlos	inutile	inútil	onyttig	on a nutsn
usual	habituel, -le	gewöhnlich	solito	usual	vanlig	geveyntlekh
utility (usefulness)	utilité,*f.*	Nützlichkeit,*f.*	utilità,*f.*	utilidad,*f.*	nytta,*nn.*	nutsikayt,*f.*
utmost (extreme, *adj.*)	extrême	äusserst	massimo	extremo	ytterst	ekst
utter (*adj.*)	complet, -plète	völlig	completo	completo	ytterlig	fulshtendik
vacant (untenanted)	libre	leerstehend	vacante	vacante	ledig	leydik
vacation (work holidays)	vacances,*f.pl.*	Ferien,*pl.*	vacanze,*f.pl.*	vacaciones,*f.pl.*	semester,*nn.*	vakatsye,*f.*
vaccination	vaccination,*f.*	Impfung,*f.*	vaccinazione,*f.*	vacunación,*f.*	vaccination,*nn.*	vaktsinirung,*f.*
vacuum cleaner	aspirateur,*m.*	Staubsauger,*m.*	aspiratore,*m.*	aspirador de polvo,*m.*	dammsugare,*nn.*	shtoybzoyger,*m.*
vague (not precise)	vague	vag	vago	vago	obestämd	metushtesh
vain (conceited)	vaniteux, -teuse	eitel	vanitoso	vanidoso	fåfäng	fargleybt in zikh
vain (futile)	vain	vergeblich	vano	vano	fruktlös	aroysgevorfn
valley	vallée,*f.*	Tal,*n.*	vallata,*f.*	valle,*m.*	dal,*nn.*	tol,*m.*
valuable	de valeur	wertvoll	di valore	de valor	värdefull	vertful
value	valeur,*f.*	Wert,*m.*	valore,*m.*	valor,*m.*	värde,*n.*	vert,*f.*
value (appraise), to	évaluer	schätzen	valutare	valuar	värdera	shatsn
value (prize), to	priser	schätzen	apprezzare	valuar	värdera	tayer haltn
van (vehicle)	fourgon,*m.*	Transportwagen, *m.*	carro,*m.*	camión,*m.*	transportvagn, *nn.*	meblfur,*f.*
vanish (cease to be), to	évanouir, s'	verschwinden	svanire	desvanecerse	försvinna	farshvundn vern
vanish (go out of sight), to	évanouir, s'	verschwinden	scomparire	desvanecerse	försvinna	nelm vern
vanity (self-conceit)	vanité,*f.*	Eitelkeit,*f.*	vanità,*f.*	vanidad,*f.*	fåfänga,*nn.*	gadles,*f.*
vapor	vapeur,*f.*	Dunst,*m.*	vapore,*m.*	vapor,*m.*	dunst,*nn.*	pare,*f.*
variety (assortment)	assortiment,*m.*	Auswahl,*f.*	assortimento,*m.*	surtido,*m.*	sortering,*nn.*	oysklayb,*m.*
variety (diversity)	variété,*f.*	Mannigfaltigkeit, *f.*	varietà,*f.*	variedad,*f.*	mångfald,*nn.*	farsheydnkayt,*f.*
various (different)	varié	verschieden	diverso	varios	olika	farsheydn
varnish	vernis,*m.*	Firnis,*m.*	vernice,*f.*	barniz,*m.*	fernissa,*nn.*	pokost,*m.*
vary (differ), to	varier	abweichen	variare	diferir	vara olik	zayn andersh
vary (undergo change), to	varier	verändern, sich	mutarsi	variar	skifta	baytn zikh
vase	vase,*m.*	Vase,*f.*	vaso,*m.*	jarrón,*m.*	vas,*nn.*	vaze,*f.*
vast	vaste	unermesslich	vasto	vasto	vidsträckt	rizik
veal	veau,*m.*	Kalbfleisch,*n.*	vitello,*m.*	carne de ternera, *f.*	kalvkött,*n.*	kelberns,*n.*
veal chop	côtelette de veau, *f.*	Kalbskotelett,*n.*	costoletta di vitello,*f.*	chuleta de ternera,*f.*	kalvkotlett,*nn.*	kelberner kotlet, *m.*
vegetable	légume,*m.*	Gemüse,*n.*	verdura,*f.*	legumbre,*f.*	grönsak,*nn.*	grins,*n.*
vehicle (conveyance)	véhicule,*m.*	Fahrzeug,*n.*	veicolo,*m.*	vehículo,*m.*	åkdon,*n.*	formitl,*n.*
veil (*n.*)	voile,*m.*	Schleier,*m.*	velo,*m.*	velo,*m.*	flor,*n.*	shleyer,*m.*
vein (*anat.*)	veine,*f.*	Ader,*f.*	vena,*f.*	vena,*f.*	åder,*nn.*	vene,*f.*
velvet (*n.*)	velours,*m.*	Samt,*m.*	velluto,*m.*	terciopelo,*m.*	sammet,*nn.*	samet,*m.*
velveteen (*n.*)	veloutine,*f.*	Baumwollen-samt,*m.*	velluto di cotone, *m.*	pana,*f.*	bomullssammet, *nn.*	plis,*m.*
vendor (seller)	vendeur,*m.*	Verkäufer,*m.*	venditore,*m.*	vendedor,*m.*	säljare,*nn.*	farkoyfer,*m.*
Venezuela	Venezuela,*m.*	Venezuela,*n.*	Venezuela,*f.*	Venezuela	Venezuela,*n.*	Venetsuele,*f.*

English	French	German	Italian	Spanish	Swedish	Yiddish
Venezuelan (*adj.*)	vénézuélien, -ne	venezuelanisch	venezuelano	venezolano	(*no equiv.*)	venetsuelish
vengeance (revenge)	vengeance,*f.*	Rache,*f.*	vendetta,*f.*	venganza,*f.*	hämnd,*nn.*	nekome,*f.*
Venice	Venise,*f.*	Venedig,*n.*	Venezia,*f.*	Venecia	Venedig,*n.*	Venetsye,*f.*
venture	aventure,*f.*	Wagnis,*n.*	affare rischioso, *m.*	ventura,*f.*	vågstycke,*n.*	aynshtelenish,*f.*
venture (dare), to	risquer (à), se	wagen	arrischiarsi	atreverse	våga	aynshteln
verb	verbe,*m.*	Zeitwort,*n.*	verbo,*m.*	verbo,*m.*	verb,*n.*	verb,*m.*
verse (poetic writing)	vers,*m.*	Verse,*m.pl.*	versi,*m.pl.*	verso,*m.*	vers,*nn.*	ferzn,*pl.*
vertical (*adj.*)	vertical	senkrecht	verticale	vertical	vertikal	vertikal
very (extremely)	très	sehr	molto	muy	myckst	zeyer
vessel (receptacle)	récipient,*m.*	Gefäss,*n.*	recipiente,*m.*	vasija,*f.*	kärl,*n.*	keyle,*f.*
vessel (ship)	vaisseau,*m.*	Schiff,*n.*	bastimento,*m.*	barco,*m.*	fartyg,*n.*	shif,*f.*
vest	gilet,*m.*	Weste,*f.*	panciotto,*m.*	chaleco,*m.*	väst,*nn.*	vest,*f.*
veteran (experienced, *adj.*)	vieux (vieil), vieille	erprobt	esperimentato	veterano	erfaren	genit
veteran (*mil., n.*)	ancien combattant,*m.*	Veteran,*m.*	ex combattente, *m.*	veterano,*m.*	veteran,*nn.*	veteran,*m.*
vex (anger), to	vexer	ärgern	irritare	enfadar	förarga	denervirn
vice (moral fault)	vice,*m.*	Laster,*n.*	vizio,*m.*	vicio,*m.*	last,*nn.*	moralisher khisorn,*m.*
vicinity	voisinage,*m.*	Nähe,*f.*	vicinanza,*f.*	vecindad,*f.*	grannskap,*n.*	shkheynes,*f.*
victim	victime,*f.*	Opfer,*n.*	vittima,*f.*	víctima,*f.*	offer,*n.*	korbn,*m.*
victor	vainqueur,*m.*	Sieger,*m.*	vincitore,*m.*	vencedor,*m.*	segrare,*nn.*	bal-nitsokhn,*m.*
victorious	victorieux, -rieuse	siegreich	vittorioso	victorioso	segerrik	nitsokhndik
victory	victoire,*f.*	Sieg,*m.*	vittoria,*f.*	victoria,*f.*	seger,*nn.*	nitsokhn,*m.*
Vienna	Vienne,*f.*	Wien,*n.*	Vienna,*f.*	Viena	Wien,*n.*	Vin,*n.*
Viennese (*adj.*)	viennois	wienerisch	viennese	vienés, -nesa	wiensk	Vin,*n.*
view (opinion)	vue,*f.*	Ansicht,*f.*	opinione,*f.*	parecer,*m.*	åsikt,*nn.*	viner
view (scene)	vue,*f.*	Aussicht,*f.*	veduta,*f.*	vista,*f.*	utsikt,*nn.*	meynung,*f.* oysblik,*m.*
vigor (strength)	vigueur,*f.*	Kraft,*f.*	vigore,*m.*	vigor,*m.*	kraft,*nn.*	kraft,*f.*
vigorous	vigoureux, -reuse	kräftig	vigoroso	vigoroso	kraftig	kraftik
village	village,*m.*	Dorf,*n.*	villaggio,*m.*	aldea,*f.*	by,*nn.*	dorf,*n.*
villain	scélérat,*m.*	Schurke,*m.*	scellerato,*m.*	villano,*m.*	skurk,*nn.*	roshe,*m.*
vine (grapevine)	vigne,*f.*	Weinstock,*m.*	vite,*f.*	vid,*f.*	vinranka,*nn.*	vaynshtok,*m.*
vinegar	vinaigre,*m.*	Essig,*m.*	aceto,*m.*	vinagre,*m.*	ättika,*nn.*	esik,*m.*
vineyard	vignoble,*m.*	Weingarten,*m.*	vigneto,*m.*	viña,*f.*	vingård,*nn.*	vayngortn,*m.*
viola	alto (à cordes), *m.*	Viole,*f.*	viola,*f.*	viola,*f.*	altfiol,*nn.*	viole,*f.*
violate (infringe upon), to	violer	verletzen	contravvenire a	violar	överträda	oyver zayn oyf
violence	violence,*f.*	Gewalt,*f.*	violenza,*f.*	violencia,*f.*	våld,*n.*	gvald,*f.*
violent	violent	gewaltsam	violente	violento	våldsam	gvald-...
violet (flower)	violette,*f.*	Veilchen,*n.*	violetta,*f.*	violeta,*f.*	viol,*nn.*	faylkhl,*n.*
violin	violon,*m.*	Geige,*f.*	violino,*m.*	violín,*m.*	fiol,*nn.*	fidl,*m.*
virgin (*n.*)	vierge,*f.*	Jungfrau,*f.*	vergine,*f.*	virgen,*f.*	jungfru,*nn.*	bsule,*f.*
virtue (moral excellence)	vertu,*f.*	Tugend,*f.*	virtù,*f.*	virtud,*f.*	dygd,*nn.*	gute mides,*pl.*
visible	visible	sichtbar	visibile	visible	synlig	kentik
vision (eyesight)	vision,*f.*	Sehkraft,*f.*	vista,*f.*	vista,*f.*	syn,*nn.*	riye,*f.*
vision (foresight)	prévoyance,*f.*	Einsicht,*f.*	previdenza,*f.*	previsión,*f.*	vision,*nn.*	vizye,*f.*
visit (social call)	visite,*f.*	Besuch,*m.*	visita,*f.*	visita,*f.*	visit,*nn.*	vizit,*m.*
visit (stay)	séjour,*m.*	Besuch,*m.*	soggiorno,*m.*	visita,*f.*	besök,*n.*	bazukh,*m.*
visit (call on), to	rendre visite à	besuchen	visitare	visitar	besöka	kumen tsu gast tsu
visit (go to view), to	visiter	besuchen	visitare	visitar	besöka	bazukhn
visitor	visiteur,*m.*	Besucher,*m.*	ospite,*m.,f.*	visita,*f.*	besökande,*nn.*	bazukher,*m.*
vital (essential)	vital	wesentlich	essenziale	vital	väsentlig	neytik in lebn
vitamin	vitamine,*f.*	Vitamin,*n.*	vitamina,*f.*	vitamina,*f.*	vitamin,*nn.*	vitamin,*m.*
vivid	vif, vive	lebhaft	vivido	vívido	livfull	lebedik
voice	voix,*f.*	Stimme,*f.*	voce,*f.*	voz,*f.*	röst,*nn.*	kol,*n.*
void (null)	nul, -le	nichtig	nullo	nulo	ogiltig	posl
volcano	volcan,*m.*	Vulkan,*m.*	vulcano,*m.*	volcán,*m.*	vulkan,*nn.*	vulkan,*m.*
volume (book)	volume,*m.*	Band,*m.*	volume,*m.*	volumen,*m.*	band,*nn.*	band,*m.*
volume (quantity)	volume,*m.*	Volumen,*n.*	volume,*m.*	cantidad,*f.*	volym,*nn.*	skhum,*m.*
volume (space occupied)	volume,*m.*	Rauminhalt,*m.*	volume,*m.*	volumen,*m.*	volym,*nn.*	farnem,*m.*
volunteer (*mil.*)	volontaire,*m.*	Freiwillige,*m.*	volontario,*m.*	voluntario,*m.*	frivillig,*nn.* (*pl. -a*)	volontir,*m.*
vomit, to	vomir	erbrechen	vomitare	vomitar	kräkas	oysbrekhn
vote	vote,*m.*	Stimme,*f.*	voto,*m.*	voto,*m.*	röst,*nn.*	shtim,*f.*
vote, to	voter	stimmen	votare	votar	rösta	shtimen
voter	électeur,*m.*	Wähler,*m.*	votante,*m.,f.*	votante,*m.,f.*	väljare,*nn.*	veyler,*m.*
vow	voeu,*m.*	Gelübde,*n.*	voto,*m.*	voto,*m.*	högtidligt löfte, *n.*	neyder,*m.*
voyage	voyage,*m.*	Reise,*f.*	viaggio,*m.*	viaje por mar,*m.*	(sjö)resa,*nn.*	nesie,*f.*
vulgar (ill-bred)	vulgaire	gemein	volgare	vulgar	vulgär	vulgar
wade, to	patauger	waten	sguazzare	vadear	vada	brodzhen
wages	salaire,*m.*	Lohn,*m.*	salario,*m.*	salario,*m.*	lön,*nn.*	loyn,*m.*
wail, to	gémir	wehklagen	gemere	gemir	jämra sig	makhn yeloles
waist (*anat.*)	taille,*f.*	Taille,*f.*	vita,*f.*	cintura,*f.*	midja,*nn.*	talye,*f.*
wait (defer action), to	attendre	warten	aspettare	esperar	vänta	vartn
waiter	garçon (de restaurant),*m.*	Kellner,*m.*	cameriere,*m.*	camarero,*m.*	kypare,*nn.*	kelner,*m.*
wait for, to	attendre	warten auf	aspettare	esperar	vänta på	vartn oyf
wake (make awaken), to	réveiller	wecken	svegliare	despertar	väcka	oyfvekn
wake (rouse oneself), to	réveiller, se	erwachen	svegliarsi	despertarse	vakna	oyfvekn zikh

English	French	German	Italian	Spanish	Swedish	Yiddish
Wales	Galles,*f.*	Wales,*n.*	Galles,*m.*	Gales,*f.*	Wales,*n.*	Velyz,*n.*
walk (stroll)	promenade,*f.*	Spaziergang,*m.*	passeggiata,*f.*	paseo,*m.*	promenad,*nn.*	shpatsir,*m.*
walk, to	marcher	gehen	camminare	andar	gå	geyn
wall (inside)	mur,*m.*	Wand,*f.*	parete,*f.*	pared,*f.*	vägg,*nn.*	vant,*f.*
wall (outside)	mur,*m.*	Mauer,*f.*	muro,*m.*	pared,*f.*	vägg,*nn.*	vant,*f.*
walnut (*n.*)	noix,*f.*	Walnuss,*f.*	noce,*f.*	nogal,*m.*	valnöt,*nn.* (*pl.* -nötter)	velisher nus,*m.*
waltz (dance step)	valse,*f.*	Walzer,*m.*	valzer,*m.*	vals,*m.*	vals,*nn.*	vals,*m.*
wander, to	errer	wandern	vagare	vagar	vandra	vandern
want (lack)	manque,*m.*	Mangel,*m.*	mancanza,*f.*	falta,*f.*	brist,*nn.*	doykhek,*m.*
want (need)	manque,*m.*	Bedürftigkeit,*f.*	bisogno,*m.*	necesidad,*f.*	behov,*n.*	baderfenish,*f.*
want (desire), to	vouloir	begehren	volere	querer	önska	veln
war	guerre,*f.*	Krieg,*m.*	guerra,*f.*	guerra,*f.*	krig,*n.*	milkhome,*f.*
ward (sickroom)	salle d'hôpital,*f.*	Krankensaal,*m.*	corsia,*f.*	sala de hospital, *f.*	sjuksal,*nn.*	palate,*f.*
wardrobe (apparel)	garde-robe,*f.*	Garderobe,*f.*	vestiario,*m.*	vestuario,*m.*	garderob,*nn.*	garderob,*m.*
warehouse	entrepôt,*m.*	Lagerhaus,*n.*	magazzino,*m.*	almacén,*m.*	varuupplag,*n.*	sklad,*m.*
wares	marchandise(s), *f.(pl.)*	Ware,*f.*	mercanzia,*f.*	mercancías,*f.pl.*	varor,*nn.pl.*	skhoyre,*f.*
warm	chaud	warm	caldo	caliente	varm	varem
warm, to	chauffer	wärmen	riscaldare	calentar	värma	varemen
warmth	chaleur,*f.*	Wärme,*f.*	calore,*m.*	calor,*m.*	värme,*nn.*	varemkayt,*f.*
warn, to	avertir	warnen	avvertire	advertir	varna	vorenen
warp (become misshapen), to	déjeter, se	werfen, sich	deformarsi	deformarse	slå sig	oyskrimen zikh
warrant (justify), to	justifier	rechtfertigen	giustificare	justificar	berättiga	barekhtikn
Warsaw	Varsovie,*f.*	Warschau,*n.*	Varsavia,*f.*	Varsovia	Warszawa,*n.*	Varshe,*f.*
wash (cleanse), to	laver	waschen	lavare	lavar	tvätta	vashn
wash (cleanse oneself), to	laver, se	waschen, sich	lavarsi	lavarse	tvätta sig	vashn zikh
wasp	guêpe,*f.*	Wespe,*f.*	vespa,*f.*	avispa,*f.*	geting,*nn.*	vesp,*f.*
waste (squandering)	gaspillage,*m.*	Verschwendung, *f.*	sciupo,*m.*	derroche,*m.*	slöseri,*n.*	patern,*n.*
waste (squander), to	gaspiller	verschwenden	sciupare	derrochar	slösa	patern
watch (timepiece)	montre,*f.*	Uhr,*f.*	orologio,*m.*	reloj,*m.*	klocka,*nn.*	zeyger,*m.*
watch (guard), to	veiller	bewachen	vigilare	vigilar	bevaka	bavakhn
watch (observe), to	regarder	beobachten	stare a guardare	observar	iaktta(ga)	batrakhtn
water	eau,*f.*	Wasser,*n.*	acqua,*f.*	agua,*f.*	vatten,*n.*	vaser,*n.*
waterproof	imperméable	wasserdicht	impermeabile	impermeable	vattentät	vaser-zikher
wave (billow)	vague,*f.*	Welle,*f.*	onda,*f.*	ola,*f.*	våg,*nn.*	khvalye,*f.*
wave (flutter), to	agiter, s'	flattern	sventolare	agitarse	vaja	flatern
wax (beeswax)	cire,*f.*	Wachs,*m.*	cera,*f.*	cera,*f.*	vax,*n.*	vaks,*m.*
way (manner)	facon,*f.*	Weise,*f.*	modo,*m.*	manera,*f.*	sätt,*f.*	oyfn,*m.*
way (route)	chemin,*m.*	Weg,*m.*	via,*f.*	ruta,*f.*	väg,*nn.*	veg,*m.*
we	nous (*see p.* 2826 ff.)	wir (*see p.* 2890)	noi (*see p.* 2947 ff.)	nosotros (*see p.* 3012)	vi (*see p.* 3075)	mir
weak	faible	schwach	debole	débil	svag	shvakh
weaken (make weak), to	affaiblir	schwächen	indebolire	debilitar	försvaga	opshvakhn
weakness	faiblesse,*f.*	Schwäche,*f.*	debolezza,*f.*	debilidad,*f.*	svaghet,*nn.*	shvakhkayt,*f.*
wealth	richesse(s),*f.(pl.)*	Reichtum,*m.*	ricchezze,*f.pl.*	riqueza,*f.*	rikedom,*nn.*	ashires,*f.*
wealthy	riche	reich	ricco	rico	förmögen	raykh
weapon	arme,*f.*	Waffe,*f.*	arma,*f.*	arma,*f.*	vapen,*n.*	kley-zayin,*n.*
wear (have on), to	porter	tragen	portare	llevar	ha på sig	trogn
weary	las, -se	müde	affaticato	cansado	trött	farmatert
weather	temps,*m.*	Wetter,*n.*	tempo,*m.*	tiempo,*m.*	väder,*n.*	veter,*n.*
weave, to	tisser	weben	tessere	tejer	väva	vebn
wedding	mariage,*m.*	Hochzeit,*f.*	sposalizio,*m.*	boda,*f.*	bröllop,*n.*	khasene,*f.*
wee	tout petit	winzig	piccino	chiquitico	mycket liten	pitsl
weed	mauvaise herbe, *f.*	Unkraut,*n.*	erbaccia,*f.*	mala hierba,*f.*	ogräs,*n.*	vildgroz,*n.*
week	semaine,*f.*	Woche,*f.*	settimana,*f.*	semana,*f.*	vecka,*nn.*	vokh,*f.*
weekend (*n.*)	fin de semaine,*f.*	Wochenende,*n.*	fine di settimana, *f.*	fin de semana,*m.*	veckoslut,*n.*	sof-vokh,*m.*
weekly (*adj.*)	hebdomadaire	wöchentlich	settimanale	semanal	vecko-...	vokhn-...
weep, to	pleurer	weinen	piangere	llorar	gråta	veynen
weigh, to	peser	wiegen	pesare	pesar	väga	vegn
weight (scale weight)	poids,*m.*	Gewicht,*n.*	peso,*m.*	peso,*m.*	vikt,*nn.*	vog,*f.*
weird (unearthly)	surnaturel, -le	unheimlich	soprannaturale	sobrenatural	övernaturlig	tshudne
welcome (*n.*)	accueil,*m.*	Willkommen,*n.*	accoglienza,*f.*	bienvenida,*f.*	välkommen,*n.*	kabolas-ponem, *m.*
welcome (receive hospitably), to	souhaiter la bienvenue	begrüssen	accogliere cordialmente	dar la bienvenida a	välkomna	bagrisn
welfare (well-being)	bien-être,*m.*	Wohlfahrt,*f.*	benessere,*m.*	bienestar,*m.*	välfärd,*nn.*	voylshtand,*m.*
well (and then?, *interj.*)	alors	nun	ebbene	bueno	nå	nu
well (commendably, *adv.*)	bien	gut	bene	bien	bra	gut
well (in health, *adj.*)	bien portant	wohl	sano	sano	frisk	gezunt
well (oil, gas shaft, *n.*)	puits,*m.*	Bohrloch,*n.*	pozzo,*m.*	pozo,*m.*	källa,*nn.*	brunem,*m.*
well (water pit, *n.*)	puits,*m.*	Brunnen,*m.*	pozzo,*m.*	pozo,*m.*	brunn,*nn.*	brunem,*m.*
west (*n.*)	ouest,*m.*	Westen,*m.*	ovest,*m.*	oeste,*m.*	väster,*nn.*	mayrev,*m.*
western	occidental	westlich	occidentale	occidental	västlig	mayrevdik
wet	mouillé	nass	bagnato	mojado	våt	nas
wet, to	mouiller	nässen	bagnare	mojar	väta	aynnetsn
whale	baleine,*f.*	Walfisch,*m.*	balena,*f.*	ballena,*f.*	val,*nn.*	valfish,*m.*
what (*interrog. adj.*)	(*see p.* 2828)	welche(r, -s)	che	qué	(*see p.* 3076)	velkher
what (*interrog. pron.*)	(*see p.* 2828)	was	che cosa	qué	(*see p.* 3076)	vos

English	French	German	Italian	Spanish	Swedish	Yiddish
what (*rel. pron.*)	ce qui; ce que (*see p.* 2828)	was	quel che	lo que	vad (som) (*see p.* 3076)	vos
whatever (*adj.*)	quelque…que (qui)	welche(r, -s)… auch	qualunque	cual(es)quier(a)	vilken, vilket, vilka…än	velkher nor
whatever (*pron.*)	tout ce qui; tout ce que	was auch	qualsiasi cosa	cualquier cosa que	vad än	vos nor
wheat	blé,*m.*	Weizen,*m.*	grano,*m.*	trigo,*m.*	vete,*n.*	veyts,*m.*
wheel	roue,*f.*	Rad,*n.*	ruota,*f.*	rueda,*f.*	hjul,*n.*	rod,*n.*
when (any time that, *conj.*)	quand	wenn immer	quando	cuando	när	ven
when (at the time that, *conj.*)	lorsque	als	allorchè	mientras (que)	när	ven
when (at what time, *adv.*)	quand	wann	quando	cuándo	när	ven
when (which time, *pron.*)	quand	wann	quando	cuándo	när	ven
whenever	toutes les fois que	so oft	quandunque	siempre que	närhelst	ven nor
where (in, at the place that, *conj.*)	où	wo	dove	donde	där	vu
where (in, at what place, *adv.*)	où	wo	dove	dónde	var	vu
where (to what place, *adv.*)	où	wohin	dove	adónde	vart	vuhin
wherever (at, in whatever place)	partout où	wo immer	dovunque	a-, en- donde- quiera que	varhelst	vu nor
wherever (no matter where)	n'importe où	wo immer	non importa dove	dondequiera que	var…än	vu s'zol nit zayn
whether (either, *conj.*)	soit	ob	sia	sea que…o que	vare sig	tsi
whether (if, *conj.*)	si	ob	se	si	om	tsi
which	(*see p.* 2828)	(*see p.* 2891)	(*see p.* 2948)	(*see p.* 3012 ff.)	(*see p.* 3076)	velkher
whichever (*adj.*)	n'importe quel, -le	welche(r, -s)… auch	qualsiasi	cual(es)quiera (que)	vilken, vilket, vilka…än	velkher nor
while (during the time that, *conj.*)	pendant que	während	mentre	mientras (que)	medan	beshas
while (short time, *n.*)	(espace de) temps,*m.*	Weile,*f.*	breve tempo,*m.*	rato,*m.*	stund,*nn.*	vayle,*f.*
whip	fouet,*m.*	Peitsche,*f.*	frusta,*f.*	látigo,*m.*	piska,*nn.*	baytsh,*f.*
whip (flog), to	fouetter	peitschen	frustare	azotar	piska	shmaysn
whirl (make revolve), to	faire tournoyer	wirbeln	far girare	dar vueltas	snurra	a drey ton
whiskey	whisk(e)y,*m.*	Whisky,*m.*	whiskey,*m.*	whisky,*m.*	visky,*nn.*	branfn,*m.*
whisper	chuchotement,*m.*	Geflüster,*n.*	bisbiglio,*m.*	cuchicheo,*m.*	viskning,*nn.*	sheptsh,*m.*
whisper (utter softly), to	chuchoter	flüstern	bisbigliare	cuchichear	viska	sheptshen
whistle, to	siffler	pfeifen	fischiare	silbar	vissla	fayfn
white (*adj.*)	blanc, -he	weiss	bianco	blanco	vit	vays
who (*interrog. pron.*)	qui; qui est-ce qui	wer	chi	quién	vem; vilken (*see p.* 3076)	ver
who (*rel. pron.*)	qui	(*see p.* 2891)	che	quien; que (*see p.* 3012)	som; vilken (*see p.* 3075)	vos
whoever (any person who)	celui qui	wer auch immer	chiunque	quienquiera que	vem än	ver nor
whoever (no matter who)	n'importe qui	wer auch immer	non importa chi	quienquiera que	vem än	ver s'zol nit zayn
whole (entire, *adj.*)	entier, -tière	ganz	intero	entero	hel	gants
whole (entirety, *n.*)	tout,*m.*	Ganze,*n.*	tutto,*m.*	todo,*m.*	helhet,*nn.*	gantse,*n.*
wholesale (*adj., bus.*)	en gros	Engros-…	all'ingrosso	al por mayor	parti-…	hurt-…
wholesaler (*bus.*)	grossiste,*m.,f.*	Grosshändler,*m.*	grossista,*m.,f.*	mayorista,*m.,f.*	grossist,*nn.*	hurtovnik,*m.*
wholesome (beneficial)	sain	gesund	sano	saludable	hälsosam	gezunt
whom (*interrog. pron.*)	qui; qui est-ce que (*see p.* 2828)	wem; wen	chi	a quién	vem; vilken (*see p.* 3076)	vemen
whom (*rel. pron.*)	que	(*see p.* 2891)	cui, che (*see p.* 2948 ff.)	a quien	som; vilken (*see p.* 3075 ff.)	vos
whooping cough	coqueluche,*f.*	Keuchhusten,*m.*	tosse canina,*f.*	tos ferina,*f.*	kikhosta,*nn.*	kaykhhust,*m.*
whose (*interrog. pron.*)	à qui, de qui (*see p.* 2828)	wessen	di chi	de quién	vems; vilkens (*see p.* 3076)	vemes
whose (*rel. pron.*)	(*see p.* 2828)	(*see p.* 2891)	il cui (*see p.* 2948)	(*see p.* 3013)	vars; vilkens (*see p.* 3076)	(*see p.* 3133)
why	pourquoi	warum	perchè	por qué	varför	far vos
wide (comprehensive)	étendu	umfangreich	largo	comprensivo	vidsträckt	koyleldik
wide (not narrow)	large	breit	largo	ancho	vid	breyt
wide (of specified width)	large	breit	largo	de ancho	bred	breyt
widow	veuve,*f.*	Witwe,*f.*	vedova,*f.*	viuda,*f.*	änka,*nn.*	almone,*f.*
widower	veuf,*m.*	Witwer,*m.*	vedovo,*m.*	viudo,*m.*	änkling,*nn.*	almen,*m.*
width	largeur,*f.*	Breite,*f.*	larghezza,*f.*	anchura,*f.*	bredd,*nn.*	breyt,*f.*
wife	femme,*f.*	Frau,*f.*	moglie,*f.*	esposa,*f.*	hustru,*nn.*	froy,*f.*
wild (undomesticated)	sauvage	wild	selvaggio	salvaje	vild	vild
wilderness	désert,*m.*	Wildnis,*f.*	deserto,*m.*	yermo,*m.*	vildmark,*nn.*	vildland,*n.*
will (document)	testament,*m.*	Testament,*n.*	testamento,*m.*	testamento,*m.*	testamente,*n.*	tsavoe,*f.*
will (power of choice)	volonté,*f.*	Wille,*m.*	volontà,*f.*	voluntad,*f.*	vilja,*nn.*	viln,*m.*
will (*v.*)	(*see p.* 2830)	(*see p.* 2892)	(*see p.* 2951)	(*see p.* 3015)	(*see p.* 3077)	(*see p.* 3134)
willing (favorably disposed)	(bien) disposé	bereitwillig	disposto	dispuesto	villig	gern
willow	saule,*m.*	Weide,*f.*	salce,*m.*	sauce,*m.*	vide,*n.*	verbe,*f.*
wilt, to	flétrir, se	welken	languire	marchitarse	vissna	farvyanet vern
win (be victor in), to	gagner	gewinnen	vincere	vencer	vinna	gevinen
wind	vent,*m.*	Wind,*m.*	vento,*m.*	viento,*m.*	vind,*nn.*	vint,*m.*
window	fenêtre,*f.*	Fenster,*m.*	finestra,*f.*	ventana,*f.*	fönster,*n.*	fentster,*m.*
windshield	pare-brise,*m.*	Windschutz- scheibe,*f.*	parabrezza,*f.*	parabrisa,*m.*	vindruta,*nn.*	vintshoyb,*f.*
windy (windswept)	balayé par le vent	windig	ventoso	ventoso	blåsig	vintik

English	French	German	Italian	Spanish	Swedish	Yiddish
wine (beverage)	vin,*m.*	Wein,*m.*	vino,*m.*	vino,*m.*	vin,*n.*	vayn,*m.*
wing (*zool.*)	aile,*f.*	Flügel,*m.*	ala,*f.*	ala,*f.*	vinge,*nn.*	fligl,*m.*
wink, to	cligner de l'oeil	blinzeln	ammiccare	pestañear	blinka	vinken
winter (*n.*)	hiver,*m.*	Winter,*m.*	inverno,*m.*	invierno,*m.*	vinter,*nn.*	vinter,*m.*
wipe (make dry by wiping), to	essuyer	wischen	asciugare	secar	torka	vishn
wire (metal thread)	fil de fer,*m.*	Draht,*m.*	filo metallico,*m.*	alambre,*m.*	metalltråd,*nn.*	drot,*m.*
wire (telegram)	télégramme,*m.*	Telegramm,*n.*	telegramma,*m.*	telegrama,*m.*	telegram,*n.*	depesh,*f.*
wisdom	sagesse,*f.*	Weisheit,*f.*	saggezza,*f.*	sabiduría,*f.*	klokhet,*nn.*	khokhme,*f.*
wise	sage	weise	saggio	sabio	klok	klug
wish	désir,*m.*	Wunsch,*m.*	desiderio,*m.*	deseo,*m.*	önskan,*nn.*	bager,*m.*
wish for, to	désirer	wünschen, sich	desiderare	desear	önska (sig)	veln
wish (desire on behalf of), to	souhaiter	wünschen	augurare	desear	tillönska	vintshn
wit (humor)	esprit,*m.*	Witz,*m.*	spirito,*m.*	sal,*f.*	kvickhet,*nn.*	vitsikayt,*f.*
witch	sorcière,*f.*	Hexe,*f.*	strega,*f.*	bruja,*f.*	häxa,*nn.*	makhsheyfe,*f.*
with (*prep.*)	avec	mit	cón	con	med	mit
withdraw (depart), to	retirer, se	zurückziehen, sich	ritirarsi	separarse	dra(ga) sig till-baka	tsuriktsien zikh
withdraw (take back), to	retirer	zurückziehen	ritirare	retirar	ta(ga) tillbaka	tsuriktsien
wither, to	flétrir, se	verwelken	appassire	marchitarse	vissna	farvelkn
within (in less time than, *prep.*)	dans	innerhalb	entro	dentro de	inom	in meshekh fun
within (inside, *prep.*)	dans	innerhalb	dentro	dentro de	inne i	inveynik in
within (on the inside, *adv.*)	à l'intérieur	drinnen	all'interno	adentro	därinne	inveynik
without (failing to, *prep.*)	sans	ohne zu	senza	sin	utan att	nit ...-ndik
without (lacking, *prep.*)	sans	ohne	senza	sin	utan	on
witness (one who testifies)	témoin,*m.*	Zeuge,*m.*	testimone,*m.*	testigo,*m.*,*f.*	vittne,*n.*	eydes,*m.*
witty	spirituel, -le	geistreich	spiritoso	ingenioso	kvick	vitsik
wizard (sorcerer)	sorcier,*m.*	Zauberer,*m.*	mago,*m.*	brujo,*m.*	trollkarl,*nn.*	mekhashef,*m.*
woe	malheur,*m.*	Weh,*n.*	dolore,*m.*	aflicción,*f.*	ve,*n.*	tsore,*f.*
wolf	loup,*m.*	Wolf,*m.*	lupo,*m.*	lobo,*m.*	varg,*nn.*	volf,*m.*
woman	femme,*f.*	Frau,*f.*	donna,*f.*	mujer,*f.*	kvinna,*nn.*	froy,*f.*
womb	matrice,*f.*	Gebärmutter,*f.*	utero,*m.*	útero,*m.*	livmoder,*nn.*	trakht,*f.*
wonder	étonnement,*m.*	Verwunderung,*f.*	maraviglia,*f.*	pasmo,*m.*	häpnad,*nn.*	khidesh,*m.*
wonder (ask oneself), to	demander, se	fragen, sich	domandarsi	preguntarse	undra	fregn zikh
wonderful	merveilleux, -leuse	wunderbar	maraviglioso	maravilloso	underbar	vunderlekh
woo, to	faire la cour à	werben um	fare la corte a	cortejar	gilja	shadkhenen zikh tsu
wood (forest)	bois,*m.*	Wald,*m.*	bosco,*m.*	bosque,*m.*	skog,*nn.*	vald,*m.*
wood (lumber)	bois,*m.*	Holz,*n.*	legno,*m.*	madera,*f.*	trä,*n.*	holts,*n.*
wool (cloth)	laine,*f.*	Wolle,*f.*	tessuto di lana,*m.*	paño,*m.*	ylle,*n.*	vol,*f.*
wool (fleece)	laine,*f.*	Wolle,*f.*	lana,*f.*	lana,*f.*	ull,*nn.*	vol,*f.*
word	mot,*m.*	Wort,*n.*	parola,*f.*	palabra,*f.*	ord,*n.*	vort,*n.*
work (labor)	travail,*m.*	Arbeit,*f.*	lavoro,*m.*	trabajo,*m.*	arbete,*n.*	arbet,*f.*
work (opus)	oeuvre,*f.*	Werk,*n.*	lavoro,*m.*	obra,*f.*	verk,*n.*	verk,*n.*
work (labor), to	travailler	arbeiten	laborare	trabajar	arbeta	arbetn
worker	ouvrier,*m.*	Arbeiter,*m.*	operaio,*m.*	trabajador,*m.*	arbetare,*nn.*	arbeter,*m.*
world	monde,*m.*	Welt,*f.*	mondo,*m.*	mundo,*m.*	värld,*nn.*	velt,*f.*
worm	ver,*m.*	Wurm,*n.*	verme,*m.*	gusano,*m.*	mask,*nn.*	vorem,*m.*
worry (anxiety)	inquiétude,*f.*	Sorge,*f.*	preoccupazione,*f.*	ansiedad,*f.*	oro,*nn.*	dayge,*f.*
worry (feel anxious), to	inquiéter, s'	ängstigen, sich	stare in pensiero	inquietarse	oroa sig	daygen
worse (*adj.*)	pire	schlimmer	peggiore	peor	sämre	erger
worse (*adv.*)	pis	schlimmer	peggio	peor	värre	erger
worship (*rel.*)	culte,*m.*	Anbetung,*f.*	adorazione,*f.*	adoración,*f.*	dyrkan,*nn.*	fargeterung,*f.*
worship, to (*rel.*)	adorer	anbeten	adorare	adorar	dyrka	dinen
worst (*adj.*)	(le) pire	schlimmst	(il) peggiore	(el) peor	sämst	ergst
worst (*adv.*)	(le) pis	am schlimmsten	(il) peggio	(lo) peor	värst	tsum ergstn
worst (*n.*)	pis,*m.*	Schlimmste,*n.*	peggio,*m.*	(lo) peor,*n.*	(det) värsta,*n.*	ergste,*n.*
worth (value)	valeur,*f.*	Wert,*m.*	valore,*m.*	valor,*m.*	värde,*n.*	vert,*f.*
worthless (valueless)	sans valeur	wertlos	senza valore	sin valor	värdelös	on a vert
worthy (deserving)	digne	würdig	meritevole	digno	värdig	roe
would (*v.*)	(*see p.* 2830 ff.)	(*see p.* 2892)	(*see p.* 2951 ff.)	(*see p.* 3016)	(*see* skulle, *p.* 3078)	(*see p.* 3134)
wound (injury)	blessure,*f.*	Wunde,*f.*	ferita,*f.*	herida,*f.*	sår,*n.*	vund,*f.*
wound, to	blesser	verwunden	ferire	herir	såra	farvundn
wrap (envelop), to	envelopper	einwickeln	avvolgere	envolver	slå in	aynviklen
wrath	colère,*f.*	Zorn,*m.*	collera,*f.*	ira,*f.*	vrede,*nn.*	tsorn,*m.*
wreath	couronne,*f.*	Kranz,*m.*	ghirlanda,*f.*	corona,*f.*	krans,*nn.*	krants,*m.*
wreck (ruins)	ruine(s),*f.*	Wrack,*n.*	rovina,*f.*	destrozos,*m.pl.*	spillror,*nn.pl.*	vrak,*m.*
wreck, to	démolir	zum Scheitern bringen	rovinare	arruinar	förstöra	tseshtern
wrench (wrest), to	arracher	entreissen	strappare	arrancar	vrida	aroysraysn
wrestle, to	lutter	ringen	lottare	luchar a brazo partido	brottas	ranglen zikh
wretch (hapless person)	misérable,*m.*,*f.*	Elende,*m.*,*f.*	disgraziato,*m.*	miserable,*m.*,*f.*	stackare,*nn.*	umgliklekher,*m.*
wrinkle (fold)	pli,*m.*	Falte,*f.*	grinza,*f.*	arruga,*f.*	rynka,*nn.*	kneytsh,*m.*
wrist	poignet,*m.*	Handgelenk,*n.*	polso,*m.*	muñeca,*f.*	handled,*nn.*	hantgelenk,*n.*
write, to	écrire	schreiben	scrivere	escribir	skriva	shraybn
writer (author)	écrivain,*m.*	Schriftsteller,*m.*	scrittore,*m.*	escritor,*m.*	författare,*nn.*	shrayber,*m.*
writing (art of writing)	écrire,*m.*	Schriftstellerei,*f.*	l'arte di scrivere,*m.*	arte de escribir,*m.*	författande,*n.*	shraybn,*n.*

English	French	German	Italian	Spanish	Swedish	Yiddish
writing (handwriting)	écriture,*f.*	Schrift,*f.*	scrittura,*f.*	letra,*f.*	handstil,*nn.*	ksav,*m.*
wrong (amiss, *adv.*)	mal	verkehrt	male	mal	galet	kalye
wrong (erroneous, *adj.*)	erroné	falsch	sbagliato	incorrecto	felaktig	falsh
wrong (injustice)	mal,*m.*	Unrecht,*n.*	ingiustizia,*f.*	injusticia,*f.*	orättvisa,*nn.*	avle,*f.*
wrong (unjust, *adj.*)	mal	unrecht	ingiusto	injusto	orättvis	umgerekht
X-ray (Roentgen ray)	rayon X,*m.*	Röntgenstrahlen, *m.pl.*	raggio X,*m.*	rayo X,*m.*	röntgen,*nn.*	rentgen-shtral, *m.*
X-ray (X-ray picture)	radiographie,*f.*	Röntgenauf-nahme,*f.*	radiografia,*f.*	radiografía,*f.*	röntgen,*nn.*	rentgen-bild,*n.*
X-ray (examine), to	radiographier	durchleuchten	radiografare	radiografiar	röntga	durkhlaykhtn
yard (enclosure near house)	cour (de maison), *f.*	Hof,*m.*	cortile,*m.*	cercado,*m.*	gård,*nn.*	hoyf,*m.*
yarn (fiber)	fil,*m.*	Garn,*n.*	filato,*m.*	hilado,*m.*	garn,*n.*	garn,*m.*
yawn, to	bâiller	gähnen	sbadigliare	bostezar	gäspa	genetsn
year	an,*m.*	Jahr,*n.*	anno,*m.*	año,*m.*	år,*n.*	yor,*n.*
yearly (*adj.*)	annuel, -le	jährlich	annuale	anual	årlig	yorik
yearly (*adv.*)	annuellement	jährlich	annualmente	anualmente	årligen	ale yor
yeast	levain,*m.*	Hefe,*f.*	lievito,*m.*	levadura,*f.*	jäst,*nn.*	heyvn,*pl.*
yell, to	hurler	gellend schreien	gridare	gritar	skrika	shrayen
yellow (*adj.*)	jaune	gelb	giallo	amarillo	gul	gel
yellow fever	fièvre jaune,*f.*	gelbe Fieber,*n.*	febbre gialla,*f.*	fiebre amarilla,*f.*	gula febern,*nn. def.*	geler fiber,*m.*
yes	oui	ja	sì	sí	ja	yo
yes (after negative question)	si	doch	sì	sí	jo	yo aderabe
yesterday	hier	gestern	ieri	ayer	i går	nekhtn
yet (nevertheless, *adv.*)	cependant	dennoch	nondimeno	no obstante	ändå	dokh
yet (now, until now, *adv.*)	encore	noch	ancora	todavía	ännu	nokh
yield (product)	rendement,*m.*	Ertrag,*m.*	rendimento,*m.*	rendimiento,*m.*	avkastning,*nn.*	getrog,*n.*
yield (give in), to	céder	nachgeben	cedere	ceder	ge efter	nokhgebn
yoke (wooden frame)	joug,*m.*	Joch,*n.*	giogo,*m.*	yugo,*m.*	ok,*n.*	yokh,*m.*
you	(*see p.* 2826 ff.)	(*see p.* 2890)	(*see p.* 2947 ff.)	(*see p.* 3012)	(*see p.* 3075)	(*see p.* 3132)
young (*adj.*)	jeune	jung	giovane	joven	ung	yung
youngster	garçon,*m.*	Kind,*n.*	ragazzo,*m.*	jovencito,*m.*	unge,*nn.*	bokherl,*n.*
your	(*see p.* 2827)	(*see p.* 2891)	(*see p.* 2948)	(*see p.* 3012)	(*see p.* 3075)	(*see p.* 3132)
yours	(*see p.* 2827)	(*see p.* 2890)	(*see p.* 2948)	(*see p.* 3012)	(*see p.* 3075)	(*see p.* 3132)
yourself	(*see p.* 2826 ff.)	(*see p.* 2890)	(*see p.* 2948)	(*see p.* 3012)	(*see p.* 3075)	zikh
yourselves	(*see p.* 2826 ff.)	(*see p.* 2890)	(*see p.* 2948)	(*see p.* 3012)	(*see p.* 3075)	zikh
youth (period of life)	jeunesse,*f.*	Jugend,*f.*	gioventù,*f.*	juventud,*f.*	ungdom,*nn.*	yugnt,*f.*
youth (young man)	jeune homme,*m.*	Jüngling,*m.*	giovanotto,*m.*	joven,*m.*	yngling,*nn.*	yunger-man,*m.*
youthful	jeune	jugendlich	giovane	joven	ungdomlig	yugntlekh
youthfulness	jeunesse,*f.*	Jugend,*f.*	giovinezza,*f.*	juventud,*f.*	ungdomlighet, *nn.*	yugnt,*f.*
Yugoslavia	Yougoslavie,*f.*	Jugoslawien,*n.*	Iugoslavia,*f.*	Yugoeslavia	Jugoslavien,*n.*	Yugoslavye,*f.*
zeal	zèle,*m.*	Eifer,*m.*	zelo,*m.*	celo,*m.*	iver,*nn.*	bren,*m.*
zebra	zèbre,*m.*	Zebra,*n.*	zebra,*f.*	cebra,*f.*	sebra,*nn.*	zebre,*f.*
zero (*n.*)	zéro,*m.*	Null,*f.*	zero,*m.*	cero,*m.*	nolla,*nn.*	nul,*m.*
zinc	zinc,*m.*	Zink,*n.*	zinco,*m.*	cinc,*m.*	zink,*nn.*	tsink,*n.*
zipper	fermeture éclair, *f.*	Reissverschluss, *m.*	chiusura lampo, *f.*	cierre relámpago, *m.*	blixtlås,*n.*	shlesl,*n.*
zone	zone,*f.*	Zone,*f.*	zona,*f.*	zona,*f.*	zon,*nn.*	zone,*f.*
zoo	jardin zoolo-gique,*m.*	Zoo,*m.*	giardino zoolo-gico,*m.*	parque zoológico, *m.*	djurpark,*nn.*	zoologisher gortn,*m.*
zoology	zoologie,*f.*	Zoologie,*f.*	zoologia,*f.*	zoología,*f.*	zoologi,*nn.*	zoologye f.

Special Lists

Alphabet

English Alphabet	French Pronunciation	German Pronunciation	Italian Pronunciation	Spanish Pronunciation	Swedish Pronunciation	Yiddish
a	AH	AH	AH	AH	AW	
b	BAY	BAY	BEE	BEH	BAY	
c	SAY	TSAY	CHEE	SEH	SAY	
d	DAY	DAY	DEE	DEH	DAY	
e	UH	AY	EH	EH	EH	
f	EFF	EFF	EHF-*feh*	EH-*feh*	EF	
g	ZHAY	GAY	JEE	HEH	GAY	
h	AHSH	HAH	AHK-*kah*	AH-*cheh*	HOH	(*Yiddish is writ-*
i	EE	EE	EE	EE	EE	*ten in a modified*
j	ZHEE	YAWT	*ee* LOONG-*goh*	HO-*tah*	YEE	*Hebrew alpha-*
						bet. When Latin
k	KAH	KAH	KAHP-*pah*	KAH	KOH	*letters are men-*
l	ELL	ELL	ELL-*leh*	EH-*leh*	ELL	*tioned (e.g., in*
m	EM	EM	EMM-*meh*	EH-*meh*	EM	*referring to*
n	EN	EN	ENN-*neh*	EH-*neh*	EN	*chemical formu-*
o	OH	OH	OH	OH	OO	*las, government*
						institutions,
p	PAY	PAY	PEE	PEH	PAY	*etc.), it is*
q	KÜ	KOO	KOO	KOO	KUH	*customary in all*
r	EHR	EHR	EHR-*reh*	EH-*reh*	AIRR	*English-speak-*
s	ESS	ESS	ESS-*seh*	EH-*seh*	ESS	*ing areas to use*
						the English
t	TAY	TAY	TEE	TEH	TAY	*pronunciation*)
u	Ü	OO	OO	OO	UH	
v	VAY	FOW	VEE; VOO	VEH	VAY	
w	*doo-bl(ih)* VAY	VAY	DOHP-*p_yoh vee*; DOHP-*p_yoh voo*	*doh-vleh* OO	DUHB-*ell-vay*	
x	EEX	IX	EEKS	EH-*keess*	ECKS	
y	*ee* GRECK	IP-*see-lawnn*	*ee* GREH-*koh*	EE *gree* EH-*gah*	Ü	
z	ZEDD	TSET	DZEH-*tah*	SEH-*tah*	SAY-*tah*	

Cardinal numbers

English	French	German	Italian	Spanish	Swedish	Yiddish
one	un, une	eins	uno	uno	en, ett	eyns
two	deux	zwei	due	dos	två	tsvey
three	trois	drei	tre	tres	tre	dray
four	quatre	vier	quattro	cuatro	fyra	fir
five	cinq	fünf	cinque	cinco	fem	finf
six	six	sechs	sei	seis	sex	zeks
seven	sept	sieben	sette	siete	sju	zibn
eight	huit	acht	otto	ocho	åtta	akht
nine	neuf	neun	nove	nueve	nio	nayn
ten	dix	zehn	dieci	diez	tio	tsen
eleven	onze	elf	undici	once	elva	elf
twelve	douze	zwölf	dodici	doce	tolv	tsvelf
thirteen	treize	dreizehn	tredici	trece	tretton	draytsn
fourteen	quatorze	vierzehn	quattordici	catorce	fjorton	fertsn
fifteen	quinze	fünfzehn	quindici	quince	femton	fuftsn
sixteen	seize	sechzehn	sedici	dieciséis	sexton	zekhtsn
seventeen	dix-sept	siebzehn	diciassette	diecisiete	sjutton	zibetsn
eighteen	dix-huit	achtzehn	diciotto	dieciocho	arton	akhtsn
nineteen	dix-neuf	neunzehn	diciannove	diecinueve	nitton	nayntsn
twenty	vingt	zwanzig	venti	veinte	tjugo	tsvantsik
twenty-one	vingt et un	einundzwanzig	ventuno	veintiuno	tjugoen	eyn un tsvantsik
twenty-two	vingt-deux	zweiundzwanzig	ventidue	veintidós	tjugotvå	tsvey un tsvant-sik
thirty	trente	dreissig	trenta	treinta	trettio	draysik
forty	quarante	vierzig	quaranta	cuarenta	fyrtio	fertsik
fifty	cinquante	fünfzig	cinquanta	cincuenta	femtio	fuftsik
sixty	soixante	sechzig	sessanta	sesenta	sextio	zekhtsik
seventy	soixante-dix	siebzig	settanta	setenta	sjuttio	zibetsik
eighty	quatre-vingts	achtzig	ottanta	ochenta	åttio	akhtsik
ninety	quatre-vingt-dix	neunzig	novanta	noventa	nittio	nayntsik
one hundred	cent	hundert	cento	cien	hundra	hundert
one hundred one	cent un	hundert und eins	cento uno	ciento uno	hundraen	hundert eyns
two hundred	deux cents	zweihundert	duecento	doscientos	tvåhundra	tsvey hundert
two hundred one	deux cent un	zweihundert und eins	duecento uno	doscientos uno	tvåhundraen	tsvey hundert eyns
one thousand	mille	(ein) tausend	mille	mil	tusen	toyznt
one thousand one	mille un	tausend und eins	mille uno	mil uno	ett tusen en	toyznt un eyns
two thousand	deux mille	zweitausend	due mila	dos mil	två tusen	tsvey toyznt
two thousand one	deux mille un	zweitausend und eins	due mila uno	dos mil uno	två tusen en	tsvey toyznt un eyns
one million	un million	eine Million	un milione	un millón	en miljon	eyn milyon
one billion	un milliard	eine Milliarde	un bilione	mil millones	en miljard	eyn milyard

Ordinal numbers

English	French	German	Italian	Spanish	Swedish	Yiddish
first	premier, -mière	erste	primo	primero	första	ershter
second	deuxième; second, -e	zweite	secondo	segundo	andra	tsveyter
third	troisième	dritte	terzo	tercero	tredje	driter
fourth	quatrième	vierte	quarto	cuarto	fjärde	ferter
fifth	cinquième	fünfte	quinto	quinto	femte	finfter
sixth	sixième	sechste	sesto	sexto	sjätte	zekster
seventh	septième	siebente	settimo	séptimo	sjunde	zibeter
eighth	huitième	achte	ottavo	octavo	åttonde	akhter
ninth	neuvième	neunte	nono	noveno	nionde	naynter
tenth	dixième	zehnte	decimo	décimo	tionde	tsenter
eleventh	onzième	elfte	undicesimo	undécimo	elfte	elfter
twelfth	douzième	zwölfte	dodicesimo	duodécimo	tolfte	tsvelfter

Days of the week

English	French	German	Italian	Spanish	Swedish	Yiddish
Sunday	dimanche,*m.*	Sonntag,*m.*	domenica,*f.*	domingo,*m.*	söndag,*nn.*	zuntik,*m.*
Monday	lundi,*m.*	Montag,*m.*	lunedì,*m.*	lunes,*m.*	måndag,*nn.*	montik,*m.*
Tuesday	mardi,*m.*	Dienstag,*m.*	martedì,*m.*	martes,*m.*	tisdag,*nn.*	dinstik,*m.*
Wednesday	mercredi,*m.*	Mittwoch,*m.*	mercoledì,*m.*	miércoles,*m.*	onsdag,*nn.*	mitvokh,*m.*
Thursday	jeudi,*m.*	Donnerstag,*m.*	giovedì,*m.*	jueves,*m.*	torsdag,*nn.*	donershtik,*m.*
Friday	vendredi,*m.*	Freitag,*m.*	venerdì,*m.*	viernes,*m.*	fredag,*nn.*	fraytik,*m.*
Saturday	samedi,*m.*	Samstag (Sonnabend),*m.*	sabato,*m.*	sábado,*m.*	lördag,*nn.*	shabes,*m.*

Months of the year

English	French	German	Italian	Spanish	Swedish	Yiddish
January	janvier,*m.*	Januar,*m.*	gennaio,*m.*	enero,*m.*	januari,*nn.*	Yanuar,*m.*
February	février,*m.*	Februar,*m.*	febbraio,*m.*	febrero,*m.*	februari,*nn.*	Februar,*m.*
March	mars,*m.*	März,*m.*	marzo,*m.*	marzo,*m.*	mars,*nn.*	Marts,*m.*
April	avril,*m.*	April,*m.*	aprile,*m.*	abril,*m.*	april,*nn.*	April,*m.*
May	mai,*m.*	Mai,*m.*	maggio,*m.*	mayo,*m.*	maj,*nn.*	May,*m.*
June	juin,*m.*	Juni,*m.*	giugno,*m.*	junio,*m.*	juni,*nn.*	Yuni,*m.*
July	juillet,*m.*	Juli,*m.*	luglio,*m.*	julio,*m.*	juli,*nn.*	Yuli,*m.*
August	août,*m.*	August,*m.*	agosto,*m.*	agosto,*m.*	augusti,*nn.*	Oygust,*m.*
September	septembre,*m.*	September,*m.*	settembre,*m.*	septiembre,*m.*	september,*nn.*	September,*m.*
October	octobre,*m.*	Oktober,*m.*	ottobre,*m.*	octubre,*m.*	oktober,*m.*	Oktober,*m.*
November	novembre,*m.*	November,*m*	nobembre,*m.*	noviembre,*m.*	november,*nn.*	November,*m.*
December	décembre,*m.*	Dezember,*m.*	dicembre,*m.*	diciembre,*m.*	december,*nn.*	Detsember,*m.*

Common first names

English	French	German	Italian	Spanish	Swedish	Yiddish
Abraham	Abraham	Abraham	Abramo	Abrahan	Abraham	Avrohom
Adam	Adam	Adam	Adamo	Adán	Adam	Odom
Agnes	Agnès	Agnes	Agnese	Inés	Agnes	Agnes
Albert	Albert	Albert	Alberto	Alberto	Albert	Albert
Alexander	Alexandre	Alexander	Alessandro	Alejandro	Alexander	Aleksander
Alfred	Alfred	Alfred	Alfredo	Alfredo	Alfred	Alfred
Alice	Alice	Alice	Alice	Alicia	Alice	Alise
Andrew	André	Andreas	Andrea	Andrés	Anders	Andreas
Ann, Anne	Anne	Anna	Anna	Ana	Anna	Anne
Anthony	Antoine	Anton	Antonio	Antonio	Anton	Anton
Arnold	Arnaud	Arnold	Arnaldo	Arnaldo	Arnold	Arnold
Arthur	Arthur	Artur	Arturo	Arturo	Artur	Artur
Barbara	Barbe	Barbara	Barbara	Bárbara	Barbara	Barbare
Beatrice	Béatrice	Beatrice	Beatrice	Beatriz	(*no equiv.*)	Beatritse
Benjamin	Benjamin	Benjamin	Beniamino	Benjamín	Benjamin	Binyomin
Bernard	Bernard	Bernhard	Bernardo	Bernardo	Bernhard	Bernard
Bertha	Berthe	Berta	Berta	Berta	Berta	Berte
Caroline	Caroline	Karoline	Carolina	Carolina	Karolina	Karoline
Charles	Charles	Karl	Carlo	Carlos	Karl	Karl
Charlotte	Charlotte	Charlotte	Carlotta	Carlota	Charlotta	Sharlote
Christine	Christine	Christine	Cristina	Cristina	Kristina	Kristine
Christopher	Christophe	Christoph	Cristoforo	Cristóbal	Kristofer	Kristofer
Clara	Claire	Klara	Clara	Clara	Klara	Klare
Clare	Claire	Kläre	Clara	Clara	Klara	Kleyr
Conrad	Conrad	Konrad	Corrado	Conrado	Konrad	Konrad
Constance	Constance	Konstanze	Costanza	Constanza	(*no equiv.*)	Konstantsyus
Daniel	Daniel	Daniel	Daniele	Daniel	Daniel	Doniel
David	David	David	Davide	David	David	Dovid
Dorothy	Dorothée	Dorothea	Dorotea	Dorotea	Dorotea	Dorotee
Edith	Édith	Edith	Editta	(*no equiv.*)	Edit	Edit
Edmund	Edmond	Edmund	Edmondo	Edmundo	Edmund	Edmund

English	French	German	Italian	Spanish	Swedish	Yiddish
Edward	Édouard	Eduard	Edoardo	Eduardo	Edvard	Eduard
Eleanor	Éléonore	Eleonore	Eleonora	Leonor	Eleonora	Eleonore
Elizabeth	Élisabeth	Elisabeth	Elisabetta	Isabel	Elisabet, Lisa	Elizabet
Emily	Émilie	Emilie	Emilia	Emilia	Emilia	Emilye
Emma	Emma	Emma	Emma	Ema	Emma	Eme
Ernest	Ernest	Ernst	Ernesto	Ernesto	Ernst	Ernst
Eugene	Eugène	Eugen	Eugenio	Eugenio	Eugen	Eygenyus
Felix	Félix	Felix	Felice	Félix	Felix	Feliks
Ferdinand	Ferdinand	Ferdinand	Ferdinando	Fernando	Ferdinand	Ferdinand
Florence	Florence	Flora	Florenza	Florencia	(*no equiv.*)	Florens
Frances	Françoise	Franziska	Francesca	Francisca	(*no equiv.*)	Frantsiske
Francis	François	Franz	Francesco	Francisco	Frans	Frants
Frederick	Frédéric	Friederich	Federico	Federico	Fredrik	Fridrikh
George	Georges	Georg	Giorgio	Jorge	Georg	Georg
Gertrude	Gertrude	Gertrud	Gertrude	Gertrudis	Gertrud	Gertrude
Gustav	Gustave	Gustav	Gustavo	Gustavo	Gustav	Gustav
Harold	Harold	Harold	Aroldo	Haroldo	Harald	Harold
Harry	Henri	Heinrich (Heini)	Arrigo	Enrique	Harry	Hari
Helen	Hélène	Helene	Elena	Elena	Helena, Lena	Helene
Henrietta	Henriette	Henriette	Enrichetta	Enriqueta	Henrietta	Henriete
Henry	Henri	Heinrich	Enrico	Enrique	Henrik	Henri
Herbert	Herbert	Herbert	Erberto	Heriberto	Herbert	Herbert
Herman	Hermann	Hermann	Ermanno	Germán	Herman	Herman
Horace	Horace	Horaz	Orazio	Horacio	Horatius	Horatsyus
Hugh	Hugues	Hugo	Ugo	Hugo	Hugo	Hugo
Irene	Irène	Irene	Irene	Irene	(*no equiv.*)	Irene
Isaac	Isaak	Isaak	Isacco	Isaac	Isak	Ayzik, Yitskhok
Isabel	Isabelle	Isabella	Isabella	Isabel	Isabella	Izabele
Jacob	Jacob	Jakob	Giacobbe	Jacobo	Jakob	Yankev
James	Jacques	Jakob	Giacomo	Jaime	Jakob	Dzheymz
Jane	Jeanne	Johanna	Giovanna	Juana	(*no equiv.*)	Dzheyn
Jean	Jeanne	Johanna	Giovanna	Juana	(*no equiv.*)	Dzhin
Joan	Jeanne	Johanna	Giovanna	Juana	(*no equiv.*)	Dzhoun
John	Jean	Johann	Giovanni	Juan	John, Johan	Yohan
Joseph	Joseph	Joseph	Giuseppe	José	Josef	Yoysef
Josephine	Joséphine	Josephine	Giuseppina	Josefina	Josefina	Yosefine
Judith	Judith	Judith	Giuditta	Judit	Judit	Yehudis
Julian	Julien	Julian	Giuliano	Julián	(*no equiv.*)	Yulyan
Kate	Catherine	Käthe	Caterina	Catalina	(*no equiv.*)	Keyt
Katharine	Catherine	Katharina	Caterina	Catalina	Karin, Katarina	Katarine
Laura	Laure	Laura	Laura	Laura	Laura	Laure
Leo	Léo	Leo	Leone	León	Leo	Leyb
Leon	Léon	Leo	Leone	León	Leon	Leon
Leonard	Léonard	Leonhard	Leonardo	Leonardo	Leonard	Leonard
Leonora	Léonore	Leonore	Leonora	Leonor	(*no equiv.*)	Leonore
Leopold	Léopold	Leopold	Leopoldo	Leopoldo	Leopold	Leopold
Louis	Louis	Ludwig	Luigi	Luis	Ludvig	Ludvig
Louise	Louise	Luise	Luisa	Luisa	Lovisa	Luize
Margaret	Marguerite	Margarete	Margherita	Margarita	Greta, Margareta	Margaret
Marie	Marie	Marie	Maria	María	Maria	Marie
Mark	Marc	Markus	Marco	Marcos	Markus	Markus
Martha	Marthe	Martha	Marta	Marta	Marta, Märta	Marte
Martin	Martin	Martin	Martino	Martín	Martin	Martin
Mary	Marie	Maria	Maria	María	Maria	Marie
Matthew	Mathieu	Matthias	Matteo	Mateo	Matteus	Matias
Michael	Michel	Michael	Michele	Miguel	Mikael	Mikhoel
Nicholas	Nicolas	Nikolas	Nicola	Nicolás	Nicklas, Nikolaus	Nikolay
Olga	Olga	Olga	Olga	Olga	Olga	Olge
Otto	Othon	Otto	Ottone	Otón	Otto	Oto
Patrick	Patrice	Patricius	Patrizio	Patricio	Patrik	Patrik
Paul	Paul	Paul	Paolo	Pablo	Paul	Paul
Paula	Paule	Paula	Paola	Paula	Paula	Paule
Peter	Pierre	Peter	Pietro	Pedro	Per, Petrus, Petter	Peter
Philip	Philippe	Philipp	Filippo	Felipe	Filip	Filip
Ralph	Raoul	Ralf	Raulo	Rafael	Rolf	Ralf
Raymond	Raymond	Raimund	Raimondo	Raimundo	(*no equiv.*)	Raymund
Rebecca	Rébecca	Rebekka	Rebecca	Rebeca	Rebecka	Rivke
Richard	Richard	Richard	Riccardo	Ricardo	Rickard	Rikhard
Robert	Robert	Robert	Roberto	Roberto	Robert	Robert
Rosalie	Rosalie	Rosalie	Rosalia	Rosalía	(*no equiv.*)	Rozalye
Rose	Rose	Rosa	Rosa	Rosa	Rosa	Roze
Rosemary	Rose-Marie	Rosemarie	Rosamaria	Rosa María	(*no equiv.*)	Rozmari
Rudolph	Rudolph	Rudolf	Rodolfo	Rodolfo	Rudolf	Rudolf
Ruth	Ruth	Ruth	Ruth	Rut	Rut	Rus
Samuel	Samuel	Samuel	Samuele	Samuel	Samuel	Shmuel
Sarah	Sarah	Sara	Sara	Sara	Sara	Sore

English	French	German	Italian	Spanish	Swedish	Yiddish
Saul	Saül	Saul	Saul	Saúl	Saul	Shoul
Stephen	Étienne	Stefan	Stefano	Esteban	Stefan	Stefan
Susan	Susanne	Susanne	Susanna	Susana	Susanna	Suzane
Sylvia	Sylvie	Sylvia	Silvia	Silvia	Sylvia	Silvye
Theresa	Thérèse	Therese	Teresa	Teresa	Teresia	Tereze
Thomas	Thomas	Thomas	Tomaso	Tomás	Tomas	Tomas
Victor	Victor	Viktor	Vittorio	Víctor	Viktor	Viktor
Vincent	Vincent	Vinzenz	Vincenzo	Vicente	Vincent	Vintsent
Virginia	Virginie	Virginie	Virginia	Virginia	Virginia	Virdzhinye
Walter	Gautier	Walter	Gualtiero	Gualterio	Valter	Valter
William	Guillaume	Wilhelm	Guglielmo	Guillermo	Vilhelm	Vilyam

English	French	German	Italian	Spanish	Swedish	Yiddish

Britannica
World Language Dictionary

Part I I

Other Languages

French · German · Italian · Spanish · Swedish · Yiddish

to

English

French

to English

Note on Symbols. For a list of abbreviations used in the main word list, see p. 2674. The number indicated for each French verb in the word list is the key to its conjugation. Verbs numbered (1), (2) and (3) are considered regular; they are conjugated according to models bearing the corresponding numbers under *Present Tense, Past Tense, Future Tense*, etc., pp. 2829–33 of the French grammar. Verbs numbered (4) through (63) are irregular; for their forms, see the corresponding numbers in the *List of irregular verbs*, pp. 2833–36 of the French grammar.

French nouns with both masculine and feminine forms appear in the following list in the masculine form only. Irregular feminine forms of adjectives are included in the list. See the pronunciation column for changes effected solely by addition of final -e to the masculine.

Notes on Pronunciation. The pronunciation of words in the following list is indicated wherever possible by words or syllables easily recognized by English-speaking persons. However, the English transliterations given are not to be considered as completely accurate representations of French pronunciation, since French sounds have no exact equivalents. The transliterations are based on the following principles:

Stress. Stress in French is expressed by lengthening the stressed syllable rather than by increasing the intensity of the voice, as in English. In the French spoken chain, stress falls on the final syllable of a sense group (see pp. 2822–25, pronunciation of *Useful Expressions*), or group of words making up a unit of meaning. In the case of individual words, stress has been indicated by printing final syllables in capital letters.

Syllabic division. In the chain of speech, French syllables tend to end on vowel sounds and to begin on consonant sounds, as opposed to English. The transliterations have been divided into syllables accordingly; for example, the word *abdomen* has been divided, for purposes of closest possible approximation to French pronunciation, *ah-bduh-*MENN.

Representation of sounds. The transliterations represent the sounds of vowels in English words as follows: *ah* as in *ah*; *eh* as in *peck*; *ay* as in *late*; *oh* as in *note*; *uh* (when transliterating French spellings *au* or *o*) as in *love*; *uh* (when transliterating French spellings *eu, oeu, oe*) as in *curb* (see "Basic Key to French Pronunciation," p. 2837); *ih* as in *typical*; *ee* as in *machine*; *oo* as in *moon*. Consonants in transliterations are pronounced as in easily recognized English words or syllables. In most unfamiliar combinations of consonants occurring in the transliterations, each letter is to be given its separate value; for example, *ps* is to be pronounced as in la*ps*e, not as in *ps*ychology. Exceptions are the combinations *ng* (see below, *Special Cases*) and *zh* which is to be pronounced as *z* is in a*z*ure.

Special cases. See "Basic Key to French Pronunciation," pp. 2837–38, for explanation of the following French spellings: *u* transliterated *ü; eu, oeu, oe* transliterated *uh; en, in, im, yn, ym, ain, aim, ein* transliterated *ang; an, am, en, em* transliterated *ahng; on, om* transliterated *ohng; un, um* transliterated *uhng; r; h* (mute) and *h* (aspirate). (Note that the *n* and *g* are merely indications of nasal vowels and *are not to be pronounced;* when the nasal vowel is not the final sound of a sense group, the *g* in the transliteration has generally been omitted.)

French	Pronunciation	English
à	AH	at (by, for the price of, in, to, toward, *prep.*)
"	"	to (indicating destination, *prep.*)
"	"	to (indicating direction, *prep.*)
"	"	to (used with indirect object, *prep.*)
abandonner (1)	*ah-bahn-duh-*NAY	abandon, to
"	"	forsake, to
"	"	surrender (relinquish), to
abattement, *m.*	*ah-bah-*TMAHNG	depression (sadness)
abattage, *m.*	*ah-bah-*TAHZH	slaughter
abdomen, *m.*	*ah-bduh-*MENN	abdomen
abeille, *f.*	*ah-*BAY	bee
abolir (2)	*ah-buh-*LEER	abolish, to
abondance, *f.*	*ah-bohn-*DAHNSS	abundance
"	"	plenty (*n.*)
abondant	*ah-bohn-*DAHNG, -DAHNT	abundant
"	"	plentiful
abonnement, *m.*	*ah-bun-*MAHNG	subscription (for periodicals, etc.)
aboyer (1)	*ah-bwah-*YAY	bark (bay), to
abréviation, *f.*	*ah-bray-v yah-s* YOHNG	abbreviation
abri, *m.*	*ah-*BREE	shelter
abricot, *m.*	*ah-bree-*KOH	apricot
abriter (1)	*ah-bree-*TAY	shelter, to
absence, *f.*	*ah-*PSAHNSS	absence
absent	*ah-*PSAHNG, -PSAHNT	absent
absent	*ah-*PSAHNG, -PSAHNT	away
absolu	*ah-psuh-*LÜ	absolute (complete)
absorbé	*ah-psor-*BAY	intent (engrossed)
absorber (1)	*ah-psor-*BAY	absorb (suck up), to
abuser de (1)	*ah-bü-*ZAY *dih*	abuse (misuse), to
accalmie, *f.*	*ah-kahl-*MEE	lull (calm)
accent, *m.*	*ah-*KSAHNG	accent
"	"	stress (emphasis)
acceptation, *f.*	*ah-kseh-ptah-s* YOHNG	acceptance (receipt)
accepter (1)	*ah-kseh-*PTAY	accept, to
accident, *m.*	*ah-ksee-*DAHNG	accident (mishap)
acclamer (1)	*ah-klah-*MAY	cheer (applaud), to
accompagner (1)	*ah-kohm-pah-*N YAY	accompany (go along with), to
accomplir (2)	*ah-kohm-*PLEER	accomplish, to
"	"	fulfill, to
"	"	perform (do), to
accord, *m.*	*ah-*KOR	accord
"	"	agreement (mutual understanding)
accordéon, *m.*	*ah-kor-day-*OHNG	accordion
accorder (1)	*ah-kor-*DAY	bestow, to
"	"	grant, to
accroissement, *m.*	*ah-krwah-*SMAHNG	gain (increase)
accroître, s'	*sah-*KRWAH-*tr(ih)*	increase (grow), to
accueil, *m.*	*ah-*KUH *y*	greeting
"	"	reception
"	"	welcome (*n.*)
accumulateur, *m.*	*ah-kü-mü-lah-*TUHR	battery (storage)
accumuler (1)	*ah-kü-mü-*LAY	accumulate (amass), to
accusation, *f.*	*ah-kü-zah-s* YOHNG	accusation
"	"	charge
accuser (1)	*ah-kü-*ZAY	accuse, to
accuser réception (de)	*ah-kü-zay ray-sehp-s* YOHNG *(dih)*	acknowledge (note receipt of), to
achat, *m.*	*ah-*SHAH	purchase (act of buying)
acheter (1)	*ah-*SHTAY	buy, to
acheteur, *m.*	*ah-*SHTUHR	buyer
achever (1)	*ah-*SHVAY	complete (finish), to
acide, *m.*	*ah-*SEED	acid
acier, *m.*	*ah-s* YAY	steel
acier inoxydable, *m.*	*ah-s yay ee-nuh-ksee-*DAH-*bl(ih)*	stainless steel
acompte, *m.*	*ah-*KOHNT	down payment (*bus.*)
"	"	installment (*bus.*)
acquérir (4)	*ah-kay-*REER	acquire, to
acte, *m.*	AHKT	act
"	"	deed (transfer agreement)
acteur, *m.*	*ah-*KTUHR	actor (player)
actif, -tive	*ah-*KTEEF, -KTEEV	active (energetic)

French	Pronunciation	English	French	Pronunciation	English
action, *f.*	*ahk-*S_YOHNG	action	aigu, -ë	*ay-*GÜ	keen
"	"	agency (instrumentality)	"	"	sharp
"	"	deed	"	"	shrill
"	"	share (stock)	aiguille, *f.*	*ay-*GÜ_EE	needle
actionnaire, *m., f.*	*ahk-s_yuh-*NEHR	stockholder	aiguiser (1)	*ay-ghee-*ZAY	sharpen, to
actions, *f.pl.*	*ahk-*S_YOHNG	stock (shares)	ail, *m.*	AH_y	garlic
activité, *f.*	*ah-ktee-vee-*TAY	activity (exertion of energy)	aile, *f.*	ELL	wing (*zool.*)
actrice, *f.*	*ah-*KTREESS	actress	ailleurs	*ah-*YUHR	elsewhere
actualités, *f.pl.*	*ahk-tü_ah-lee-*TAY	newsreel	aimant, *m.*	*ay-*MAHNG	magnet
actuel, -le	*ah-*KTÜ_ELL	present (current, *adj.*)	aimer (1)	*ay-*MAY	like (be fond of), to
adapter (1)	*ah-dah-*PTAY	adapt, to	"	"	love, to
addition, *f.*	*ah-dee-s_*YOHNG	addition (process of adding)	aîné	*ay-*NAY	senior (older)
additionnel, -le	*ah-dee-s_yuh-*NELL	additional	ainsi	*an-*SEE	thus (in this way)
additionner (1)	*ah-dee-s_yuh-*NAY	add (find sum of), to	air, *m.*	AIR	air
additionneuse, *f.*	*ah-dee-s_yuh-*NUHZ	adding machine	"	"	tune (melody)
adieu, *m.*	*ah-*D_YUH	farewell (leave-taking)	aise, *f.*	EZZ	ease (comfort)
adjectif, *m.*	*ah-dzheh-*KTEEF	adjective	ajouter (1)	*ah-zhoo-*TAY	add (include), to
administration, *f.*	*ah-dmee-nee-strah-*S_YOHNG	administration (*bus.*)	ajuster (1)	*ah-zhü-*STAY	adjust (regulate), to
admiration, *f.*	*ah-dmee-rah-s_*YOHNG	admiration	alarme, *f.*	*ah-*LAHRM	alarm (fear)
admirer (1)	*ah-dmee-*RAY	admire, to	Alaska, *f.*	*ah-lah-*SKAH	Alaska
adopter (1)	*ah-duh-*PTAY	adopt (embrace), to	Albanie, *f.*	*ahl-bah-*NEE	Albania
adorable	*ah-duh-*RAH-bl(*ih*)	adorable	alcool, *m.*	*ahl-*KUHL	alcohol
adorer (1)	*ah-duh-*RAY	adore, to	"	"	liquor
"	"	worship, to (*rel.*)	allée, *f.*	*ah-*LAY	lane (narrow path)
adresse, *f.*	*ah-*DRESS	address (postal directions)	allégresse, *f.*	*ah-lay-*GRESS	glee (joy)
"	"	skill (proficiency)	Allemagne, *f.*	*ahl-*MAH-n_yih	Germany
adroit	*ah-*DRWAH	skilful	allemand	*ahl-*MAHNG, -MAHND	German (*adj.*)
adverbe, *m.*	*ah-*DVEHRB	adverb	aller (5)	*ah-*LAY	go, to
adversaire, *m.*	*ah-dvehr-*SEHR	opponent (*n.*)	aller en voiture	*ah-lay ahn vwah-*TÜR	ride (in a car), to
aéroport, *m.*	*ah-ay-ruh-*POR	airport	allergie, *f.*	*ah-lehr-*ZHEE	allergy (*med.*)
affaiblir (2)	*ah-feh-*BLEER	weaken (make weak), to	alliage, *m.*	*ah-L_*YAHZH	alloy (metal)
affaire, *f.*	*ah-*FAIR	affair	alliance, *f.*	*ah-L_*YAHNSS	alliance
"	"	matter	allié, *m.*	*ah-L_*YAY	ally
affaires, *f.pl.*	*ah-*FAIR	business (commerce)	allumer (1)	*ah-lü-*MAY	light (set fire to), to
affamé	*ah-fah-*MAY	hungry	allumette, *f.*	*ah-lü-*METT	match (lucifer)
affecter (1)	*ah-feh-*KTAY	affect (pretend), to	allusion, *f.*	*ah-lü-z_*YOHNG	reference (allusion)
affection, *f.*	*ah-fehk-s_*YOHNG	affection (love)	alors	*ah-*LOR	then (at that time)
affectueux, -tueuse	*ah-fehk-*TÜ_UH, -TÜ_UHZ	affectionate (loving)	"	"	well (and then?, *interj.*)
affliger, s' (1)	*sah-flee-*ZHAY	grieve (mourn), to	alouette, *f.*	*ah-loo-*ETT	lark (bird)
africain	*ah-free-*KANG, -KENN	African (*adj.*)	alphabet, *m.*	*ahl-fah-*BEH	alphabet
Afrique, *f.*	*ah-*FREEK	Africa	altéré	*ahl-tay-*RAY	thirsty
âge, *m.*	AHZH	age (accumulated years)	alto (à cordes), *m.*	*ahl-*TOH (*ah* KORD)	viola
agence, *f.*	*ah-*ZHAHNSS	agency (business firm)	aluminium	*ah-lü-mee-N_*YUMM	aluminum
agenouiller, s' (1)	*sah-zhnoo-*YAY	kneel, to	amande, *f.*	*ah-*MAHND	almond
agent, *m.*	*ah-*ZHAHNG	agent (representative)	ambassadeur, *m.*	*ahm-bah-sah-*DUHR	ambassador
agent de police, *m.*	*ah-zhahng d(ih) puh-*LEESS	policeman	ambitieux, -tieuse	*ahm-bee-*S_YUH, -S_YUHZ	ambitious (aspiring)
agile	*ah-*ZHEEL	nimble (agile)	ambition, *f.*	*ahm-bee-*S_YOHNG	ambition
agir (2)	*ah-*ZHEER	act (do), to	ambré	*ahm-*BRAY	amber (*adj.*)
agitation, *f.*	*ah-zhee-tah-s_*YOHNG	excitement	ambulance, *f.*	*ahm-bü-*LAHNSS	ambulance
agité	*ah-zhee-*TAY	restless	âme, *f.*	AHM	soul
agiter, s' (1)	*sah-zhee-*TAY	wave (flutter), to	amélioration, *f.*	*ah-may-l_yuh-rah-s_*YOHNG	improvement (betterment)
agneau, *m.*	*ah-N_*YOH	lamb	améliorer (1)	*ah-may-l_yuh-*RAY	improve (make better), to
agrandir (2)	*ah-grahn-*DEER	enlarge (make larger), to	amende, *f.*	*ah-*MAHND	fine (penalty, *n.*)
agréable	*ah-gray-*AH-bl(*ih*)	agreeable (pleasing)	amendement, *m.*	*ah-mahn-*DMAHNG	amendment (enacted change)
"	"	nice	amer, -mère	*ah-*MEHR	bitter
"	"	pleasant	américain	*ah-may-ree-*KANG, -KENN	American (*adj.*)
agrément, *m.*	*ah-gray-*MAHNG	acceptance (approval)	Amérique, *f.*	*ah-may-*REEK	America
agriculture, *f.*	*ah-gree-kül-*TÜR	agriculture	Amérique du Nord, *f.*	*ah-may-reek dü* NOR	North America
ahurir (2)	*ah-ü-*REER	bewilder, to	Amérique du Sud, *f.*	*ah-may-reek dü* SÜD	South America
aide, *f.*	EDD	aid	ami, *m.*	*ah-*MEE	friend
"	"	assistance	amical	*ah-mee-*KAHL	friendly
"	"	help	amiral, *m.*	*ah-mee-*RAHL	admiral
aide, *m., f.*	EDD	assistant	amitié, *f.*	*ah-mee-t_*YAY	friendship
"	"	helper	amoindrir (2)	*ah-mwan-*DREER	lessen (make less), to
aider (1)	*ay-*DAY	aid, to	amollir (2)	*ah-muh-*LEER	soften (mitigate), to
"	"	assist, to	amortir (2)	*ah-mor-*TEER	amortize, to
"	"	help, to	amortissement, *m.*	*ah-mor-tee-*SMAHNG	amortization (*bus.*)
aigle, *m.*	EH-gl(*ih*)	eagle	amour, *m.*	*ah-*MOOR	love
aigre	EH-gr(*ih*)	sour (tart)	amoureux, *m.*	*ah-moo-*RUH	lover
			ample	AHM-pl(*ih*)	ample
			"	"	full
			ampoule, *f.*	*ahm-*POOL	blister
			"	"	bulb (light bulb)
			Amsterdam, *m.*	*ahm-stehr-*DAHM	Amsterdam

French	Pronunciation	English
amusement, *m.*	*ah-mü*-ZMAHNG	amusement
"	"	fun
amuser (1)	*ah-mü*-ZAY	amuse, to
amygdalite, *f.*	*ah-mee-gdah*-LEET	tonsillitis
an, *m.*	AHNG	year
ancêtre, *m.,f.*	*ahn*-SEH-*tr(ih)*	ancestor
ancien, -ne	*ahn*-S YANG, -S YENN	ancient
ancien combattant, *m.*	*ahn-s yan kohm-bah-*TAHNG	veteran (*mil., n.*)
ancre, *f.*	AHN-*kr(ih)*	anchor
âne, *m.*	AHNN	donkey
ange, *m.*	AHNZH	angel
anglais	*ahn*-GLEH, -GLEZZ	English (*adj.*)
angle, *m.*	AHN-*gl(ih)*	angle (*geom.*)
Angleterre, *f.*	*ahn-glih*-TEHR	England
angoisse, *f.*	*ahn*-GWAHSS	agony (mental pain)
"	"	anguish
anguille, *f.*	*ahn*-GHEE	eel
animal, *m.*	*ah-nee*-MAHL	animal
animal choyé, *m.*	*ah-nee-mahl shwah*-YAY	pet (animal)
animé	*ah-nee*-MAY	lively (*adj.*)
anneau, *m.*	*ah*-NOH	ring (circle)
année, *f.*	*ah*-NAY	grade (school division)
annexe, *f.*	*ah*-NEX	enclosure (addition)
anniversaire, *m.*	*ah-nee-vehr*-SEHR	anniversary
"	"	birthday
annonce, *f.*	*ah*-NOHNSS	advertisement
annoncer (1)	*ah-nohn*-SAY	announce, to
annoncer, (faire)	*ah-nohn*-SAY	advertise (give notice of), to
annuel, -le	*ah*-NÜ ELL	annual
"	"	yearly (*adj.*)
annuellement	*ah-nü ell*-MAHNG	yearly (*adv.*)
annuler (1)	*ah-nü*-LAY	annul, to
"	"	cancel (revoke), to
antenne, *f.*	*ahn*-TENN	aerial (antenna)
antérieur	*ahn-tay*-R YUHR	former (preceding)
"	"	previous
anthologie, *f.*	*ahn-tuh-luh*-ZHEE	anthology
anthropologie, *f.*	*ahn-truh-puh-luh*-ZHEE	anthropology
antibiotique, *m.*	*ahn-tee-b yuh*-TEEK	antibiotic
antiquité, *f.*	*ahn-tee-kee*-TAY	antiquity (ancientness)
apaiser (1)	*ah-peh*-ZAY	appease (calm), to
apercevoir (de), (s') (49)	*(s)ah-pehr-sih*-VWAHR *(dih)*	perceive, to
aplanir	*ah-plah*-NEER	smooth (level), to
apôtre, *m.*	*ah*-POH-*tr(ih)*	apostle
apparaître (17)	*ah-pah*-REH-*tr(ih)*	appear (come in sight), to
appareil, *m.*	*ah-pah*-RAY	device (apparatus)
appareil photographique, *f.*	*ah-pah-ray fuh-tuh-grah*-FEEK	camera
apparenté	*ah-pah-rahn*-TAY	related (connected)
apparier (1)	*ah-pah*-R YAY	mate (find mate for), to
appartement, *m.*	*ah-pahr-tih*-MAHNG	apartment
appartenir à (55)	*ah-pahr-tih*-NEER *ah*	belong to (be the property of), to
appât, *m.*	*ah*-PAH	bait (for animals)
appel, *m.*	*ah*-PELL	appeal (entreaty)
appeler (1)	*ah*-PLAY	call (summon), to
appeler de	*ah*-PLAY *dih*	appeal (ask reconsideration of), to
appeler en justice	*ah-play ahn zhü-*STEESS	sue (bring action against), to
appendicite, *f.*	*ah-pan-dee*-SEET	appendicitis
appétit, *m.*	*ah-pay*-TEE	appetite
applaudir (2)	*ah-ploh*-DEER	clap (applaud), to
applaudissements, *m.pl.*	*ah-ploh-dee*-SMAHNG	applause
application, *f.*	*ah-plee-kah*-S YOHNG	application (use)
appliquer (1)	*ah-plee*-KAY	apply (put to use), to
appointements, *m.pl.*	*ah-pwan*-TMAHNG	salary
apporter (1)	*ah-por*-TAY	bring, to
"	"	fetch, to
apprécier (1)	*ah-pray*-S YAY	appreciate (perceive fully), to
apprendre (48)	*ah*-PRAHN-*dr(ih)*	learn, to
apprenti, *m.*	*ah-prahn*-TEE	apprentice (trade student)
approbation, *f.*	*ah-pruh-bah*-S YOHNG	approval
approcher de, s' (1)	*sah-pruh*-SHAY *dih*	approach (come near to), to
approuver (1)	*ah-proo*-VAY	approve, to
"	"	assent, to
âpre	AH-*pr(ih)*	harsh (grating)
après	*ah*-PREH	after (*prep.*)
après (cela)	*ah*-PREH (S[*ih*]LAH)	thereafter
après-midi, *m.*	*ah-preh-mee*-DEE	afternoon
après que	*ah*-PREH *kih*	after (*conj.*)
araignée, *f.*	*ah-reh*-N YAY	spider
arbre, *m.*	AHR-*br(ih)*	shaft (*mech.*)
"	"	tree
arbuste, *m.*	*ahr*-BÜST	shrub
arc-en-ciel, *m.*	*ahr-kahn*-S YELL	rainbow
architecte, *m.*	*ahr-shee*-TECKT	architect
ardent	*ahr*-DAHNG, -DAHNT	eager
"	"	keen
argent, *m.*	*ahr*-ZHAHNG	money
"	"	silver (metal, *n.*)
argentin	*ahr-zhahn*-TANG, -TEEN	Argentinian (*adj.*)
Argentine, *f.*	*ahr-zhahn*-TEEN	Argentina
argile, *f.*	*ahr*-ZHEEL	clay
argot, *m.*	*ahr*-GOH	slang (*n.*)
arithmétique, *f.*	*ah-ree-tmay*-TEEK	arithmetic
arme, *f.*	AHRM	weapon
armée, *f.*	*ahr*-MAY	army
armer (1)	*ahr*-MAY	arm, to
armoire, *f.*	*ahr*-MWAHR	cupboard
armure, *f.*	*ahr*-MÜR	armor (protective clothing)
arracher (1)	*ah-rah*-SHAY	pluck (pull off), to
"	"	wrench (wrest), to
arrangement, *m.*	*ah-rahn*-ZHMAHNG	arrangement (order)
arranger (1)	*ah-rahn*-ZHAY	arrange, to
"	"	fix (settle), to
arrêt, *m.*	*ah*-REH	stop (halt)
arrêter (1)	*ah-reh*-TAY	arrest, to
"	"	check, to
"	"	stop (make halt), to
arrêter, s'	*sah-reh*-TAY	halt (come to a stop), to
"	"	stop (come to a standstill), to
arriéré	*ah-r yay*-RAY	overdue (in arrears)
arrière, (d')	*(d)ah-*R YEHR	rear (*adj.*)
arrière, en	*ahn-nah-*R YEHR	back (*adv.*)
"	"	backward (rearward, *adv.*)
"	"	behind (in the rear, *adv.*)
arrivée, *f.*	*ah-ree*-VAY	arrival
arriver (1)	*ah-ree*-VAY	arrive, to
"	"	manage (contrive), to
arriver à	*ah-ree*-VAY *ah*	reach (arrive at), to
arroser (1)	*ah-roh*-ZAY	spray, to
art, *m.*	AHR	art
artère, *f.*	*ahr*-TEHR	artery (*anat.*)
arthrite, *f.*	*ahr*-TREET	arthritis
article, *m.*	*ahr*-TEE-*kl(ih)*	article
"	"	entry (*acctg.*)
artificiel, -le	*ahr-tee-fee*-S YELL	artificial (synthetic)
artiste, *m.,f.*	*ahr*-TEEST	artist
artistique	*ahr-tee*-STEEK	artistic (tasteful)
ascenseur, *m.*	*ah-sahn*-SUHR	elevator (passenger lift)
asiatique	*ah-z yah*-TEEK	Asiatic (*adj.*)
Asie, *f.*	*ah*-ZEE	Asia
asile, *m.*	*ah*-ZEEL	asylum (institution)
aspect, *m.*	*ah*-SPEH	appearance
"	"	aspect (phase)
"	"	look
asperges, *f.pl.*	*ah*-SPEHRZH	asparagus
aspirateur, *m.*	*ah-spee-rah*-TUHR	vacuum cleaner
aspirine, *f.*	*ah-spee*-REEN	aspirin
assemblée, *f.*	*ah-sahm*-BLAY	convention (meeting)
assembler (1)	*ah-sahm*-BLAY	assemble (bring together), to
"	"	collect (bring together), to
assembler, s'	*sah-sahm*-BLAY	assemble (meet), to
"	"	gather (congregate), to
asseoir, s' (6)	*sah*-SWAHR	sit down, to

French	Pronunciation	English
assertion, *f.*	*ah-sehr*-S YOHNG	assertion (declaration)
assez	*ah-*SAY	enough (*adv., n.*)
"	"	fairly (somewhat)
"	"	rather
assez de	*ah-*SAY *dih*	enough (*adj.*)
assiette, *f.*	*ah-*S YETT	plate (shallow dish)
assigner (1)	*ah-see-*N YAY	assign (prescribe lesson), to
assister à (1)	*ah-see-*STAY *ah*	attend (be present at), to
association, *f.*	*ah-suh-s yah-*S YOHNG	organization (association)
associé	*ah-suh-*S YAY	partner (*bus.*)
associer (1)	*ah-suh-*S YAY	associate (relate), to
assortiment, *m.*	*ah-sor-tee-*MAHNG	variety (assortment)
assurance, *f.*	*ah-sü-*RAHNSS	insurance
assurance-incendie, *f.*	*ah-sü-rahnss-an-sahn-*DEE	fire insurance
assuré	*ah-sü-*RAY	confident (self-assured)
assurer (1)	*ah-sü-*RAY	assure, to
"	"	insure (make sure), to
assurer, (faire)	*ah-sü-*RAY	insure (buy insurance on), to
Athènes, *f.*	*ah-*TENN	Athens
athlète, *m., f.*	*ah-*TLETT	athlete
athlétique	*ah-tlay-*TEEK	athletic
Atlantique, *m.*	*ah-tlahn-*TEEK	Atlantic (*n.*)
atlas, *m.*	*ah-*TLAHSS	atlas
atmosphère, *f.*	*ah-tmuh-*SFEHR	atmosphere
atome, *m.*	*ah-*TOHM	atom
attacher (1)	*ah-tah-*SHAY	attach (join), to
"	"	fasten, to
attaque, *f.*	*ah-*TAHK	attack (personal assault)
attaquer (1)	*ah-tah-*KAY	assault, to
"	"	attack, to
attarder, s' (1)	*sah-tahr-*DAY	linger (tarry), to
atteindre (19)	*ah-*TAN-*dr(ih)*	achieve, to
"	"	attain, to
attendant, en	*ahn-nah-tahn-*DAHNG	meanwhile
attendre (3)	*ah-*TAHN-*dr(ih)*	await, to
"	"	wait (defer action), to
"	"	wait for, to
attendre (à), (s')	*(s)ah-*TAHN-*dr(ah)*	expect, to
attendre à, s'	*sah-*TAHN-*drah*	anticipate (expect), to
attente, *f.*	*ah-*TAHNT	expectation
attentif, -tive	*ah-tahn-*TEEF, -TEEV	attentive (heedful)
attention, *f.*	*ah-tahn-*S YOHNG	attention
"	"	care (heed)
"	"	interest
"	"	notice
atterrir (2)	*ah-teh-*REER	land (an airplane), to
attirail, *m.*	*ah-tee-*RYE	outfit (equipment)
attirer (1)	*ah-tee-*RAY	attract, to
attitude, *f.*	*ah-tee-*TÜD	attitude (manner)
"	"	outlook
attraction, *f.*	*ah-trahk-*S YOHNG	attraction
attraper (1)	*ah-trah-*PAY	catch (nab), to
attraper une entorse à	*ah-trah-pay ün ahn-*TORSS *ah*	sprain, to
attrayant	*ah-treh-*YAHNG, -YAHNT	attractive (pleasing)
attribut, *m.*	*ah-tree-*BÜ	attribute (characteristic)
auberge, *f.*	*oh-*BEHRZH	inn
aucun	*oh-*KUHNG, -KÜN	no (not any, *adj.*)
"	"	none (*pron.*)
au-delà de	*oh-*D(*ih*)LAH *dih*	across (beyond)
"	"	beyond (farther on than, *prep.*)
"	"	past (*prep.*)
au-dessous	*oh-*D(*ih*)SOO	beneath (below, *adv.*)
au-dessous de	*oh-*D(*ih*)SOO *dih*	below (*prep.*)
"	"	beneath (*prep.*)
"	"	underneath (*prep.*)
au-dessus de	*oh-*D(*ih*)SÜ *dih*	above (higher than, *prep.*)
"	"	beyond (out of reach of, *prep.*)

French	Pronunciation	English
auditoire, *m.*	*oh-dee-*TWAHR	audience
augmentation, *f.*	*uh-gmahn-tah-s* YOHNG	increase (increment)
augmenter (1)	*uh-gmahn-*TAY	increase (add to), to
aujourd'hui	*oh-zhoor-*DÜ EE	today
auparavant	*oh-pah-rah-*VAHNG	before (in the past, *adv.*)
aurore, *f.*	*uh-*ROR	dawn (daybreak)
aussi	*oh-*SEE	also
"	"	as (equally, *adv.*)
"	"	so (*adv.*)
"	"	too
Australie, *f.*	*oh-strah-*LEE	Australia
australien, -ne	*oh-strah-*L YANG, -L YENN	Australian (*adj.*)
autel, *m.*	*oh-*TELL	altar
auteur, *m., f.*	*oh-*TUHR	author
authentique	*oh-tahn-*TEEK	genuine
autobiographie, *f.*	*uh-tuh-b yuh-grah-*FEE	autobiography
autobus, *m.*	*uh-tuh-*BÜS	bus
automne, *m.*	*oh-*TUNN	autumn
"	"	fall
automobile, *f.*	*uh-tuh-muh-*BEEL	automobile
autorisation, *f.*	*oh-tuh-ree-zah-s* YOHNG	authorization
autorité, *f.*	*oh-tuh-ree-*TAY	authority
autour de	*oh-*TOOR *dih*	around (*prep.*)
autre	OH-*tr(ih)*	other (*adj., pron.*)
autrefois	*oh-trih-*FWAH	once (formerly, *adv.*)
autrement	*oh-trih-*MAHNG	else (if not, *adv.*)
"	"	otherwise (contrarily)
Autriche, *f.*	*oh-*TREESH	Austria
autrichien, -ne	*oh-tree-*SH YANG, -SH YENN	Austrian (*adj.*)
avaler (1)	*ah-vah-*LAY	swallow, to
avancé	*ah-vahn-*SAY	early (before-time, *adj.*)
avance, par	*pahr ah-*VAHNSS	beforehand (*adv.*)
avancer (1)	*ah-vahn-*SAY	advance (go forward), to
avant	*ah-*VAHNG	before (ahead, *adv.*)
"	"	by (prior to, *prep.*)
"	"	until (before, *prep.*)
avant, en	*ahn-nah-*VAHNG	ahead
"	"	forward (*adv.*)
"	"	onward (*adv.*)
avant, *m.*	*ah-*VAHNG	bow (of ship)
avant (de)	*ah-*VAHNG (*dih*)	before (earlier than, *prep.*)
avantage, *m.*	*ah-vahn-*TAHZH	advantage
avant que	*ah-*VAHN *kih*	before (prior to the time when, *conj.*)
avare, *m.*	*ah-*VAHR	miser
avec	*ah-*VEHK	with
avenir, *m.*	*ah-*VNEER	future (*n.*)
aventure, *f.*	*ah-vahn-*TÜR	adventure
"	"	venture
avenue, *f.*	*ah-*VNÜ	avenue (street)
averse, *f.*	*ah-*VEHRSS	shower (rainfall)
aversion, *f.*	*ah-vehr-*S YOHNG	dislike
averti	*ah-vehr-*TEE	aware
avertir (2)	*ah-vehr-*TEER	caution, to
"	"	warn, to
aveugle	*ah-*VUH-*gl(ih)*	blind (lacking sight)
aveugler (1)	*ah-vuh-*GLAY	blind, to
aviateur, *m.*	*ah-v yah-*TUHR	aviator
avide	*ah-*VEED	greedy
avion, *m.*	*ah-*V YOHNG	airplane
"	"	plane
avis, *m.*	*ah-*VEE	mind (opinion)
"	"	notice (notification)
aviser (1)	*ah-vee-*ZAY	notify, to
avocat, *m.*	*ah-vuh-*KAH	attorney
"	"	counsel
avoine, *f.*	*ah-*VWAHNN	oats
avoir (7)	*ah-*VWAHR	have, to
avoir besoin de	*ah-vwahr bih-*ZWANG *dih*	need, to
"	"	require, to
avoir faim	*ah-vwahr* FANG	hungry, to be
avoir grande envie de	*ah-vwahr grahnd ahn-*VEE *dih*	long for, to

French	Pronunciation	English	French	Pronunciation	English
avoir l'air	*ah-vwahr* LAIR	look (seem), to	batterie,*f.*	*bah-*TREE	battery (artillery)
avoir lieu	*ah-vwahr* L_YUH	occur (happen), to	battre (8)	BAH-*tr(ih)*	beat, to
avoir l'intention de	*ah-vwahr lan-tahn-*S_YOHNG *dih*	intend (propose), to	battre, se	BAH-*tr(ih)*	fight (contend), to
"	"	mean, to	bavarder (1)	*bah-vahr-*DAY	chatter, to
avoir mal	*ah-vwahr* MAHL	ache, to	Bavière,*f.*	*bah-*V_YEHR	Bavaria
"	"	hurt (be painful), to	beau, belle	BOH, BELL	beautiful
avoir rapport à	*ah-vwahr rah-*POR *ah*	relate (pertain) to, to	"	"	fair (not cloudy)
avouer (1)	*ah-*VWAY	confess (admit), to	"	"	handsome (attractive)
axe radiobalisé,*m.*	*ahx rah-d_yuh-bah-lee-*ZAY	beam (radio signal)	beaucoup (de)	*boh-*KOO *(dih)*	many
bac,*m.*	BAHK	ferry (boat)	"	"	much
bagages,*m.pl.*	*bah-*GAHZH	baggage	beau-fils,*m.*	*boh-*FEESS	stepson
"	"	luggage	beau-frère,*m.*	*boh-*FREHR	brother-in-law
bagatelle,*f.*	*bah-gah-*TELL	trifle	beau-père,*m.*	*boh-*PEHR	father-in-law
bague,*f.*	BAHG	ring (jewelry)			stepfather
baie,*f.*	BAY	bay (inlet)	beauté,*f.*	*boh-*TAY	beauty
"	"	berry (fruit)	bébé,*m.*	*bay-*BAY	baby
baignoire,*f.*	*beh-*NWAHR	bathtub	"	"	infant (*n.*)
"	"	tub	bec,*m.*	BECK	bill (beak)
bâiller (1)	*bah-*YAY	yawn, to	bêche,*f.*	BESH	spade (tool)
bain,*m.*	BANG	bath	bégayer (1)	*bay-geh-*YAY	stammer, to
baisser (1)	*beh-*SAY	lower (let down), to	"	"	stutter, to
"	"	sink (fall slowly), to	bêler (1)	*beh-*LAY	bleat, to
baiser,*m.*	*bay-*ZAY	kiss	belge	BELLZH	Belgian (*adj.*)
bal,*m.*	BAHL	dance (party)	Belgique,*f.*	*bell-*ZHEEK	Belgium
balai,*m.*	*bah-*LAY	broom	bélier,*m.*	*beh-*L_YAY	ram (animal)
balance,*f.*	*bah-*LAHNSS	scales (balance)	belle (see beau)		
balancer, se	*sih bah-lahn-*SAY	sway (swing), to	belle-fille,*f.*	*bell-*FEE	daughter-in-law
balayé par le vent	*bah-leh-yay pahr lih* VAHNG	windy (windswept)	"	"	stepdaughter
balayer (1)	*bah-leh-*YAY	sweep (clean), to	belle-mère,*f.*	*bell-*MEHR	mother-in-law
Bâle,*f.*	BAHL	Basle	"	"	stepmother
baleine,*f.*	*bah-*LENN	whale	belle-soeur,*f.*	*bell-*SUHR	sister-in-law
balle,*f.*	BAHL	ball (sphere)	bénéfice,*m.*	*bay-ñay-*FEESS	profit (*bus.*)
"	"	bullet	bénir (9)	*bay-*NEER	bless, to
ballon,*m.*	*bah-*LOHNG	balloon	béquille,*f.*	*bay-*KEE	crutch
banane,*f.*	*bah-*NAH_N	banana	berceau,*m.*	*behr-*SOH	cradle
banc,*m.*	BAHNG	bench (long seat)	berger,*m.*	*behr-*ZHAY	shepherd
bandage,*m.*	*bahn-*DAHZH	bandage	Berlin,*m.*	*behr-*LANG	Berlin
bande,*f.*	BAHND	band	Berne,*f.*	BEHRN	Berne
"	"	gang	besoin,*m.*	*bih-*ZWANG	need
"	"	strip	bétail,*m.*	*bay-*TYE	cattle
bandit,*m.*	*bahn-*DEE	bandit	"	"	stock (livestock)
banjo,*m.*	*bahn-*ZHOH	banjo	bête	BEHT	dumb (stupid)
bannière,*f.*	*bah-*N_YEHR	banner	bête,*f.*	BEHT	beast (animal)
banque,*f.*	BAHNK	bank (treasury)	bêtise,*f.*	*bay-*TEEZ	nonsense
banquet,*m.*	*bahn-*KEH	banquet	béton,*m.*	*bay-*TOHNG	concrete (artificial stone)
banquier,*m.*	*bahn-*K_YAY	banker	betterave,*f.*	*beh-*TRAHV	beet (red root)
baptême,*m.*	*bah-*TEMM	baptism	beurre,*m.*	BURR	butter
bar,*m.*	BAHR	bar (barroom)	bévue,*f.*	*bay-*VÜ	blunder
barbe,*f.*	BAHRB	beard	Bible,*f.*	BEE-*bl(ih)*	Bible
baromètre,*m.*	*bah-ruh-*MEH-*tr(ih)*	barometer	bibliographie,*f.*	*bee-blee-yuh-grah-*FEE	bibliography
barre,*f.*	BAHR	bar (pole)	bibliothécaire,*m.*	*bee-blee-uh-teh-*KEHR	librarian
barrer (1)	*bah-*RAY	bar (block), to	bibliothèque,*f.*	*bee-blee-uh-*TECK	library
barrière,*f.*	*bah-*R_YEHR	barrier	bicyclette,*f.*	*bee-see-*KLETT	bicycle
bas,*m.*	BAH	stocking	bien	B_YANG	quite (considerably)
bas, -se	BAH, BAHSS	low	"	"	well (commendably, *adv.*)
bas, en	*ahn* BAH	below (lower down, *adv.*)	bien-aimé	*b_yan-nay-*MAY	beloved (*adj.*)
bas, en	*ahn* BAH	downstairs (on a lower floor)	bien-aimé,*m.*	*b_yan-nay-*MAY	sweetheart
bas, (de haut) en	*(dih oh-t)ahn* BAH	down (*adv.*)	bien-être,*m.*	*b_yan-*NEH-*tr(ih)*	welfare (well-being)
"	"	downward (*adv.*)	bienfaisance,*f.*	*b_yan-fih-*ZAHNSS	charity (philanthropy)
bas, plus	*plü* BAH	down (in lower place, *adv.*)	bienfait,*m.*	*b_yan-*FEH	blessing (boon)
bas (de l'escalier), en	*ahn* BAH *(dih leh-skah-*L_YAY)	downstairs (downward)	bien portant	*b_yan por-*TAHNG	well (in health, *adj.*)
base,*f.*	BAHZ	base (foundation)	bien que	B_YAN *kih*	although
"	"	basis	bien sûr	*b_yan* SÜR	course, of
base-ball,*m.*	*behz-*BOHL	baseball	biens,*m.pl.*	B_YANG	estate (total possessions)
basket-ball,*m.*	*bah-skeht-*BOHL	basketball	biens,*m.pl.*	B_YANG	property (possession)
bataille,*f.*	*bah-*TYE	battle	biens-fonds,*m.pl.*	*b_yan-*FOHNG	land (property)
bateau,*m.*	*bah-*TOH	boat	"	"	real estate
bâtiment,*m.*	*bah-tee-*MAHNG	building	bientôt	*b_yan-*TOH	soon (shortly)
bâtir (2)	*bah-*TEER	build, to	bière,*f.*	B_YEHR	beer
bâton,*m.*	*bah-*TOHNG	staff	bigarré	*bee-gah-*RAY	motley (diverse)
batte,*f.*	BAHT	bat (club)	bijou,*m.*	*bee-*ZHOO	jewel
			bijouterie,*f.*	*bee-zhoo-*TREE	jewelry
			billard,*m.*	*bee-*YAHR	billiards

French	Pronunciation	English
billet,*m.*	*bee*-YEH	bill (currency)
"	"	note (letter)
"	"	ticket (entitling card)
billet à ordre,*m.*	*bee-yeh ah* OR-*dr(ih)*	note (promise to pay, *bus.*)
biographie,*f.*	*b_yuh-grah*-FEE	biography
biologie,*f.*	*b_yuh-luh*-ZHEE	biology
bizarre	*bee*-ZAHR	queer
blaireau,*m.*	*blay*-ROH	badger (animal)
blâmer (1)	*blah*-MAY	blame, to
blanc, -he	BLAHNG, BLAHNSH	blank (unmarked)
"	"	white (*adj.*)
blanchir (2)	*blahn*-SHEER	bleach (make white), to
blé,*m.*	BLAY	wheat
blesser (1)	*bleh*-SAY	injure, to
"	"	wound, to
blessure,*f.*	*bleh*-SÜR	injury
"	"	wound
bleu	BLUH	blue
bloc,*m.*	BLUCK	block (solid piece)
blond	BLOHNG, BLOHND	blond
"	"	fair
bloquer (1)	*bluh*-KAY	block (obstruct), to
blouse,*f.*	BLOOZ	blouse (shirtwaist)
bobine,*f.*	*buh*-BEEN	coil (*elec.*)
bocal,*m.*	*buh*-KAHL	jar (vessel)
boeuf,*m.*	BUHF	beef
"	"	ox
bohémien,*m.*	*buh-ay*-M_YANG	gypsy
boire (10)	BWAHR	drink, to
bois,*m.*	BWAH	wood
bois de charpente,*m.*	*bwah dih shahr*-PAHNT	lumber (timber)
boisson,*f.*	*bwah*-SOHNG	drink (beverage)
bois (sur pied),*m.*	BWAH (*sür* P_YAY)	timber (standing trees)
boîte,*f.*	BWAHT	box (container)
"	"	can (tin)
boiter (1)	*bwah*-TAY	limp, to
boiteux, -teuse	*bwah*-TUH, -TUHZ	lame
bol,*m.*	BUHL	bowl (dish)
Bolivie,*f.*	*buh-lee*-VEE	Bolivia
bombe,*f.*	BOHMB	bomb (projectile)
bombe atomique,*f.*	*bohmb ah-tuh*-MEEK	atomic bomb
bon, -ne	BOHNG, BUNN	good
"	"	kind (*adj.*)
bonbons,*m.pl.*	*bohn*-BOHNG	candy
bond,*m.*	BOHNG	bound
"	"	leap
bondir (2)	*bohn*-DEER	bounce, to
bonheur,*m.*	*buh*-NUHR	happiness
bon marché, (à)	(*ah*) *bohn mahr*-SHAY	cheap (inexpensive)
bonne,*f.*	BUNN	maid (servant)
bonne heure, de	*dih buh*-NUHR	early (ahead of time, *adv.*)
bonté,*f.*	*bohn*-TAY	goodness
"	"	kindness
boom,*m.*	BOOM	boom (*bus.*)
bord,*m.*	BOR	border
"	"	brink (verge)
"	"	edge
"	"	margin
"	"	rim
bord, à	*ah* BOR	aboard
bord (du pantalon),*m.*	BOR (*dü pahn-tah-*LOHNG)	cuff (of trouser)
bordure,*f.*	*bor*-DÜR	curb (edge of street)
bosquet,*m.*	*buh*-SKEH	grove (small woods)
bosse,*f.*	BUSS	hump
botanique,*f.*	*buh-tah*-NEEK	botany
botte,*f.*	BUTT	boot (footgear)
botter (1)	*buh*-TAY	kick (boot), to
bouche,*f.*	BOOSH	mouth (*anat.*)
boucher,*m.*	*boo*-SHAY	butcher
bouchon,*m.*	*boo*-SHOHNG	cork (stopper)
bouchon de prise de courant,*m.*	*boo-shohn dih preez dih koo*-RAHNG	plug (*elec.*)
boucle (de cheveux),*f.*	BOO-*kl(ih)* (*dih* SH(*ih*)-VUH)	curl (ringlet)
boucle d'oreille,*f.*	*boo-klih duh*-RAY	earring
boue,*f.*	BOO	mud
bougie,*f.*	*boo*-ZHEE	candle
bouillir (26)	*boo*-YEER	boil (bubble up), to
bouilloire,*f.*	*boo-ee*-WAHR	kettle
bouillonner (1)	*boo-yuh*-NAY	bubble, to
boulanger,*m.*	*boo-lahn*-ZHAY	baker
bouleau,*m.*	*boo*-LOH	birch (tree)
boulon,*m.*	*boo*-LOHNG	bolt (long metal fastener)
bourbier,*m.*	*boor*-B_YAY	mire (bog)
bourdonnement,*m.*	*boor-dun*-MAHNG	hum (murmur)
bourgeon,*m.*	*boor*-ZHOHNG	bud (*bot.*)
bourrelet,*m.*	*boor*-LEH	pad (cushion)
bourse,*f.*	BOORSS	exchange, stock
"	"	purse (coin pouch)
boussole,*f.*	*boo*-SUHL	compass (magnetic instrument)
bout,*m.*	BOO	scrap (fragment)
"	"	tip (point)
bouteille,*f.*	*boo*-TAY	bottle
boutique,*f.*	*boo*-TEEK	shop
"	"	store
bouton,*m.*	*boo*-TOHNG	button
boxer (1)	*buh*-KSAY	box (fight), to
boy-scout,*m.*	*boy*-SKOOT	Boy Scout
bracelet,*m.*	*brah*-SLEH	bracelet
branche,*f.*	BRAHNSH	branch (bough)
bras,*m.*	BRAH	arm (*anat.*)
brave	BRAHV	brave
bref, brève	BREFF, BREHV	brief (fleeting)
Brésil,*m.*	*bray*-ZEEL	Brazil
brésilien, -ne	*bray-zee*-L_YANG, -L_YENN	Brazilian (*adj.*)
bretelles,*f.pl.*	*brih*-TELL	suspenders
brevet,*m.*	*brih*-VEH	patent (*n.*)
bride,*f.*	BREED	bridle (harness)
bridge au plafond,*m.*	*breedzh oh plah*-FOHNG	bridge, contract
brillant	*bree*-YAHNG, -YAHNT	bright (shining)
"	"	brilliant
briller (1)	*bree*-YAY	shine (gleam), to
brin,*m.*	BRANG	strand (thread)
brindille,*f.*	*bran*-DEE	twig
brique,*f.*	BREEK	brick (building material)
brise,*f.*	BREEZ	breeze
britannique	*bree-tah*-NEEK	British (*adj.*)
broc,*m.*	BROH	pitcher (container)
broche,*f.*	BRUSH	brooch
bronchite,*f.*	*brohn*-SHEET	bronchitis
bronze,*m.*	BROHNZ	bronze (*n.*)
brosse,*f.*	BRUSS	brush (scrubbing utensil)
brosse à dents,*f.*	*bruss ah* DAHNG	toothbrush
brouillard,*m.*	*broo*-YAHR	fog (mist)
bruissement,*m.*	*brü_ee*-SMAHNG	rustle
bruit,*m.*	BRÜ_EE	noise (din)
brûler (1)	*brü*-LAY	burn, to
brûlure de soleil,*f.*	*brü-lür dih suh*-LAY	sunburn
brume,*f.*	BRÜM	mist
brun	BRUHNG, BRÜN	brown
brune	BRÜN	brunette (*adj.*)
brut	BRÜT	crude
"	"	gross (before deductions, *adj.*)
brute,*f.*	BRÜT	brute (animal, *n.*)
Bruxelles,*f.*	*brü*-SELL	Brussels
bruyant	*brü_ee*-YAHNG, -YAHNT	noisy
buanderie,*f.*	*bü-ahn*-DREE	laundry (commercial plant)
bûche,*f.*	BÜSH	log (rough timber)
budget,*m.*	*bü*-DZHEH	budget (*n.*)
Buenos-Aires,*m.*	*bway-noh*-ZEHR	Buenos Aires
buffle,*m.*	BÜ-*fl(ih)*	buffalo
buisson,*m.*	*bü_ee*-SOHNG	bush (plant)
Bulgarie,*f.*	*bül-gah*-REE	Bulgaria
bureau,*m.*	*bü*-ROH	bureau
"	"	desk
"	"	office (place of business)
bureau de poste,*m.*	*bü-roh d(ih)* PUHST	post office
buste,*m.*	BÜST	bust (statue)

French	Pronunciation	English
but,*m.*	BÜ(T)	aim
"	"	goal
"	"	object
"	"	objective
"	"	purpose
ça	SAH	that (*dem. pron.*)
cabine,*f.*	kah-BEEN	cabin (of ship)
cabinet,*m.*	kah-bee-NEH	cabinet (*govt.*)
cabinet(s),*m.(pl.)*	kah-bee-NEH	toilet (water closet)
câble,*m.*	KAH-bl(ih)	cable (rope)
câbler (1)	kah-BLAY	cable, to
câblogramme,*m.*	kah-bluh-GRAHM	cablegram
cacahuète,*f.*	kah-kah-WETT	peanut
cacao,*m.*	kah-kah-OH	cocoa
cacher (1)	kah-SHAY	conceal, to
"	"	hide, to
cadavre,*m.*	kah-DAH-vr(ih)	corpse
cadeau,*m.*	kah-DOH	gift (present)
cadet, -te	kah-DEH, -DETT	junior (younger)
cadran,*m.*	kah-DRAHNG	dial (graduated face)
café,*m.*	kah-FAY	coffee
cafetière,*f.*	kahf-T_YEHR	coffee pot
cage,*f.*	KAHZH	cage
cahier,*m.*	kah-YAY	notebook
caillou,*m.*	kah-YOO	pebble
caissier,*m.*	keh-S_YAY	cashier
calcul,*m.*	kahl-KÜL	account (calculation)
calculer (1)	kahl-kü-LAY	calculate (compute), to
calendrier,*m.*	kah-lahn-dree-YAY	calendar
caler (1)	kah-LAY	stall (stop going), to
calme	KAHLM	calm (*adj.*)
calmer (1)	kah-LMAY	lull (quiet), to
"	"	soothe (calm), to
calorie,*f.*	kah-luh-REE	calorie
calorifère,*m.*	kah-luh-ree-FEHR	furnace (home heater)
camarade,*m.,f.*	kah-mah-RAHD	comrade
camarade de jeux, *m.,f.*	kah-mah-rahd dih ZHUH	playmate
cambrioleur,*m.*	kahm-bree-yuh-LUHR	burglar
camion,*m.*	kah-M_YOHNG	truck (automobile)
camp,*m.*	KAHNG	camp (encampment, mil.)
campagne,*f.*	kahm-PAH-n_yih	campaign (*mil.*)
"	"	country (country-side)
Canada,*m.*	kah-nah-DAH	Canada
canadien, -ne	kah-nah-D_YANG, -D_YENN	Canadian (*adj.*)
canal,*m.*	kah-NAHL	canal
"	"	channel (strait)
canapé,*m.*	kah-nah-PAY	couch
canard,*m.*	kah-NAHR	duck
cancer,*m.*	kahn-SEHR	cancer
candidat,*m.*	kahn-dee-DAH	candidate
canne,*f.*	KAH_N	cane (walking stick)
cannelle,*f.*	kah-NELL	cinnamon
canoë,*m.*	kah-nuh-AY	canoe
canon,*m.*	kah-NOHNG	cannon
caoutchouc,*m.*	kah-oo-CHOO	rubber
caoutchouc-mousse,*m.*	kah-oo-choo-MOOSS	foam rubber
caoutchoucs,*m.pl.*	kah-oo-CHOO	rubbers (overshoes)
cap,*m.*	KAHP	cape (headland)
capable	kah-PAH-bl(ih)	able
"	"	capable (competent)
capacité,*f.*	kah-pah-see-TAY	ability
"	"	capacity (volume)
capitaine,*m.*	kah-pee-TENN	captain (officer)
capital,*m.*	kah-pee-TAHL	capital (wealth)
capitale,*f.*	kah-pee-TAHL	capital (city)
caporal,*m.*	kah-puh-RAHL	corporal (*mil.*)
capot,*m.*	kah-POH	hood (*auto.*)
captif,*m.*	kah-PTEEF	captive (prisoner)
capturer (1)	kah-ptü-RAY	capture (seize), to
capuchon,*m.*	kah-pü-SHOHNG	hood (cowl)
car	KAHR	for (*conj.*)
caractère,*m.*	kah-rah-KTEHR	character (nature)
"	"	disposition (temperament)

French	Pronunciation	English
caractéristique	kah-rah-kteh-ree-STEEK	characteristic (typical)
carbone,*m.*	kahr-BUNN	carbon (*chem.*)
Carême,*m.*	kah-REMM	Lent
caresser (1)	kah-reh-SAY	stroke (rub gently), to
cargaison,*f.*	kahr-gay-ZOHNG	cargo
caricature,*f.*	kah-ree-kah-TÜR	cartoon (caricature)
carnaval,*m.*	kahr-nah-VAHL	carnival
carotte,*f.*	kah-RUTT	carrot
carré	kah-RAY	square (*adj.*)
carrefour,*m.*	kahr-FOOR	crossroads
carrière,*f.*	kah-R_YEHR	career
carte,*f.*	KAHRT	map
"	"	menu
carte (à jouer),*f.*	kahrt (ah ZHWAY)	card, playing
carte (de visite),*f.*	kahrt (dih vee-ZEET)	card, calling
carte postale,*f.*	kahrt puh-STAHL	card, postal
carton,*m.*	kahr-TOHNG	cardboard
cas,*m.*	KAH	case (instance)
cas d'urgence,*m.*	kah dür-ZHAHNSS	emergency (*n.*)
casque,*m.*	KAHSK	helmet
casquette,*f.*	kah-SKETT	cap (hat)
casser (1)	kah-SAY	break (make smash), to
casser, se	sih kah-SAY	break (come apart), to
casse-tête,*m.*	kahss-TETT	puzzle (game)
castor,*m.*	kah-STOR	beaver (animal)
catalogue,*m.*	kah-tah-LUGG	catalogue
cathédrale,*f.*	kah-tay-DRAHL	cathedral
catholique	kah-tuh-LEEK	Catholic (*adj.*)
cause,*f.*	KOHZ	cause
cause de, à	ah KOHZ dih	because of (*adv.*)
causer (1)	koh-ZAY	cause, to
"	"	chat, to
cavalier,*m.*	kah-vah-L_YAY	escort (social companion)
"	"	rider (horseman)
cave,*f.*	KAHV	cellar
caverne,*f.*	kah-VEHRN	cave
ce	SIH	he
"	"	it
"	"	that (*adj.*)
"	"	this (*adj.*)
ceci	sih-SEE	this (*dem. pron.*)
céder (1)	say-DAY	cede, to
"	"	yield (give in), to
cèdre,*m.*	SEH-dr(ih)	cedar (tree)
ceinture,*f.*	san-TÜR	belt (article of clothing)
cela	S(ih)LAH	this, that (*dem. pron.*)
célébrer (1)	say-lay-BRAY	celebrate, to
céleri,*m.*	sell-REE	celery
célibataire	say-lee-bah-TEHR	single (unmarried)
célibataire,*m.*	say-lee-bah-TEHR	bachelor (unmarried man)
celles(-ci)	SELL(-SEE)	these (*pron.*)
celles(-là)	SELL(-LAH)	these, those (*pron.*)
cellule,*f.*	seh-LÜL	cell (*biol.*)
celui	sih-LÜ_EE	he
"	"	him
celui qui	sih-LÜ_EE KEE	whoever (any person who)
cendres,*f.pl.*	SAHN-dr(ih)	ashes
cendrier,*m.*	sahn-dree-YAY	ash tray
central	sahn-TRAHL	central
centre,*m.*	SAHN-tr(ih)	center
cependant	sih-pahn-DAHNG	however
"	"	still (*conj.*)
"	"	yet (nevertheless, adv.)
ce que	s(ih)KIH	what (*rel. pron.*)
ce qui	s(ih)KEE	what (*rel. pron.*)
cercle,*m.*	SEHR-kl(ih)	circle (*geom.*)
"	"	club (association)
cercueil,*m.*	sehr-KUH_y	coffin
céréale,*f.*	say-ray-AHL	cereal
cérémonie,*f.*	say-ray-muh-NEE	ceremony
cerf,*m.*	SEHRF	deer

French	Pronunciation	English
cerf-volant,*m.*	*sehr-vuh-*LAHNG	kite
cerise,*f.*	*sih-*REEZ	cherry (fruit)
certain	*sehr-*TANG, -TENN	certain
certainement	*sehr-tehn-*MAHNG	certainly (of course!, *interj.*)
certains	*sehr-*TANG, -TENN	some (certain, *adj.*)
certains	*sehr-*TANG, -TENN	some (certain ones, *pron.*)
certificat,*m.*	*sehr-tee-fee-*KAH	certificate
certifier (1)	*sehr-tee-*F_YAY	certify, to
cerveau,*m.*	*sehr-*VOH	brain (*anat.*)
ces	SAY	these (*adj.*)
"	"	those (*adj.*)
cesser (1)	*seh-*SAY	cease, to
"	"	quit, to
"	"	stop, to
cession,*f.*	*seh-*S_YOHNG	assignment (legal transfer)
cet, -te	SET	that, this (*adj.*)
ceux(-ci)	SUH(-SEE)	these (*pron.*)
ceux(-là)	SUH(-LAH)	these, those (*pron.*)
chacun,*m.*	*shah-*KUHNG	each one (*pron.*)
"	"	everyone
chagrin,*m.*	*shah-*GRANG	grief
"	"	sorrow (sadness)
chaîne,*f.*	SHENN	chain
"	"	range (of mountains)
"	"	ridge (of mountains)
chair,*f.*	SHEHR	flesh
chaise,*f.*	SHEZZ	chair
chaland,*m.*	*shah-*LAHNG	customer (buyer)
chaleur,*f.*	*shah-*LUHR	heat
"	"	warmth
chambre à coucher,*f.*	*shahm-brah-koo-*SHAY	bedroom
chambre de commerce,*f.*	*shahm-brih dih kuh-*MEHRSS	chamber of commerce
chambre d'enfants,*f.*	*shahm-brih dahn-*FAHNG	nursery (children's room)
chameau,*m.*	*shah-*MOH	camel
champ,*m.*	SHAHNG	field (cleared land)
champignon,*m.*	*shahm-pee-*N_YOHNG	mushroom (*n.*)
champion,*m.*	*shahm-*P_YOHNG	champion
chance,*f.*	SHAHNSS	chance (possibility)
"	"	luck
chanceler (1)	*shahn-*SLAY	stagger (totter), to
chandail,*m.*	*shahn-*DYE	sweater
changement,*m.*	*shahn-*ZHMAHNG	change (alteration)
changer (1)	*shahn-*ZHAY	alter (make different), to
"	"	change, to
"	"	turn (convert), to
chanson,*f.*	*shahn-*SOHNG	song
chanter (1)	*shahn-*TAY	sing, to
chanteur,*m.*	*shahn-*TUHR	singer
chantier,*m.*	*shahn-*T_YAY	shipyard
chapeau,*m.*	*shah-*POH	hat
chapelle,*f.*	*shah-*PELL	chapel
chapitre,*m.*	*shah-*PEE-*tr(ih)*	chapter (of book)
chaque	SHAHK	each (every, *adj.*)
charbon,*m.*	*shahr-*BOHNG	coal
charge,*f.*	SHAHRZH	care (custody)
"	"	charge (responsibility)
"	"	load (burden)
charger (1)	*shahr-*ZHAY	charge, to
"	"	instruct (direct), to
"	"	load (fill), to
charmant	*shahr-*MAHNG	charming
charme,*m.*	SHAHRM	charm (attraction)
"	"	spell
charmer (1)	*shahr-*MAY	charm (delight), to
charpentier,*m.*	*shahr-pahn-*T_YAY	carpenter
charrette,*f.*	*shah-*RETT	cart
charrue,*f.*	*shah-*RÜ	plow (*n.*)
charte,*f.*	SHAHRT	charter (act of incorporation)
chasse,*f.*	SHAHSS	hunting (sport)
chasseur,*m.*	*shah-*SUHR	hunter
chaste	SHAHST	chaste
chat,*m.*	SHAH	cat

French	Pronunciation	English
châtaignier,*m.*	*shah-teh-*N_YAY	chestnut (tree)
château,*m.*	*shah-*TOH	castle
chaton,*m.*	*shah-*TOHNG	kitten
chatouiller (1)	*shah-too-*YAY	tickle (touch lightly), to
chaud	SHOH, SHOHD	hot
"	"	warm
chauffer (1)	*shoh-*FAY	heat, to
"	"	warm, to
chauffeur,*m.*	*shoh-*FUHR	driver (of automobile)
chaussette,*f.*	*shoh-*SETT	sock (garment)
chauve	SHOHV	bald (hairless)
chauve-souris,*f.*	*shohv-soo-*REE	bat (animal)
chef,*m.*	SHEFF	head (leader)
chef de train,*m.*	*sheff dih* TRANG	conductor (ticket collector)
chemin,*m.*	SH*(ih)*MANG	way (route)
chemin de fer,*m.*	*sh(ih)mang d(ih)* FEHR	railroad
cheminée,*f.*	*sh(ih) mee-*NAY	chimney
"	"	fireplace
chemise,*f.*	SH*(ih)*MEEZ	shirt
chemise de nuit,*f.*	*sh(ih)meez dih* NÜ_EÉ	nightgown
chêne,*m.*	SHENN	oak
chenille,*f.*	SH*(ih)*NEE	caterpillar
chèque,*m.*	SHECK	check (bank check)
cher, chère	SHEHR	dear (beloved, *adj.*)
chercher (1)	*shehr-*SHAY	look for, to
chéri,*m.*	*shay-*REE	darling
chérir (2)	*shay-*REER	cherish, to
cheval,*m.*	SH*(ih)*VAHL	horse
chevalier,*m.*	*sh(ih)vah-*L_YAY	knight
cheveux,*m.pl.*	SH*(ih)*VUH	hair
cheville,*f.*	SH*(ih)*VEE	ankle
"	"	peg (pin)
chèvre,*f.*	SHEH-*vr(ih)*	goat
chevreau,*m.*	*shih-*VROH	kid (goat)
chiche	SHEESH	stingy
chien,*m.*	SH_YANG	dog
chien de meute,*m.*	*sh_yang d(ih)* MUHT	hound
chiffon,*m.*	*shee-*FOHNG	rag (piece of cloth)
chiffre,*m.*	SHEE-*fr(ih)*	figure (numeral)
Chili,*m.*	*shee-*LEE	Chile
chilien, -ne	*shee-*L_YANG, -L_YENN	Chilean (*adj.*)
chimie,*f.*	*shee-*MEE	chemistry
Chine,*f.*	SHEEN	China
chinois	*shee-*NWAH, -NWAHZ	Chinese (*adj.*)
chirurgien,*m.*	*shee-rür-*ZH_YANG	surgeon
choc,*m.*	SHUCK	shock (mental jolt)
chocolat,*m.*	*shuh-kuh-*LAH	chocolate
choeur,*m.*	KUHR	choir
choisi	*shwah-*ZEE	chosen
choisir (2)	*shwah-*ZEER	choose, to
"	"	pick, to
"	"	select, to
choix,*m.*	SHWAH	choice
"	"	selection
choléra,*m.*	*kuh-lay-*RAH	cholera
chômage,*m.*	*shuh-*MAHZH	unemployment
chômage, en	*ahn shuh-*MAHZH	unemployed
choquer (1)	*shuh-*KAY	shock (jar), to
chose,*f.*	SHOHZ	thing (material object)
chou,*m.*	SHOO	cabbage
chou-fleur,*m.*	*shoo-*FLUHR	cauliflower
chrétien,*m.*	*kray-*T_YANG	Christian (*n.*)
Christ,*m.*	KREEST	Christ
chrome,*m.*	KROHM	chromium
chronique,*f.*	*kruh-*NEEK	chronicle
chuchotement,*m.*	*shü-shuh-*TMAHNG	whisper
chuchoter (1)	*shü-shuh-*TAY	whisper (utter softly), to
chute,*f.*	SHÜT	drop
"	"	fall
chutes,*f.pl.*	SHÜT	falls (waterfall)
cicatrice,*f.*	*see-kah-*TREESS	scar
ciel,*m.*	S_YELL	heaven
"	"	sky
cigare,*m.*	*see-*GAHR	cigar

French	Pronunciation	English
cigarette,*f.*	*see-gah-*RETT	cigarette
cigogne,*f.*	*see-*GUH-*n_yih*	stork
cil,*m.*	SEEL	eyelash
cime,*f.*	SEEM	peak (mountain top)
ciment,*m.*	*see-*MAHNG	cement
cimetière,*m.*	*seem-*T_YEHR	cemetery
cinéma,*m.*	*see-nay-*MAH	movies
cingler (1)	*san-*GLAY	lash (whip), to
cirage,*m.*	*see-*RAHZH	polish
circonférence,*f.*	*seer-kohn-fay-*RAHNSS	circumference
circonstance,*f.*	*seer-kohn-*STAHNSS	circumstance (external condition)
circulaire	*seer-kü-*LEHR	circular (*adj.*)
circulaire,*f.*	*seer-kü-*LEHR	circular (letter or brochure, *bus.*)
circulation,*f.*	*seer-kü-lah-*S_YOHNG	circulation
"	"	traffic (flow of vehicles)
cire,*f.*	SEER	wax (beeswax)
cirer (1)	*see-*RAY	polish, to
cirque,*m.*	SEERK	circus
ciseau,*m.*	*see-*ZOH	chisel (tool)
ciseaux,*m.pl.*	*see-*ZOH	scissors
citation,*f.*	*see-tah-*S_YOHNG	quotation (selection)
citer (1)	*see-*TAY	quote (cite), to
citoyen,*m.*	*see-twah-*YANG	citizen
citron,*m.*	*see-*TROHNG	lemon
citronnade,*f.*	*see-truh-*NAHD	lemonade
civière,*f.*	*see-*V_YEHR	litter (stretcher)
civil	*see-*VEEL	civil (secular)
civilisation,*f.*	*see-vee-lee-zah-*S_YOHNG	civilization
"	"	culture (stage of civilization)
clair	KLEHR	clear
"	"	light (bright)
"	"	plain (clear)
clair de lune,*m.*	*klehr dih* LÜN	moonlight
clairon,*m.*	*kleh-*ROHN	bugle
clarinette,*f.*	*klah-ree-*NETT	clarinet
classe,*f.*	KLAHSS	class (kind)
classe, (salle de),*f.*	(*sahl dih*) KLAHSS	schoolroom
classique	*klah-*SEEK	classic (first-class, *adj.*)
classique,*m.*	*klah-*SEEK	classic (first-class work)
clause,*f.*	KLOHZ	clause (stipulation)
clef,*f.*	KLAY	key (for lock)
clément	*klay-*MAHNG, -MAHNT	merciful
client,*m.*	*klee-*YAHNG	patron (customer)
cligner de l'oeil (1)	*klee-*N_YAY *d*(*ih*) LUH_*y*	wink, to
climat,*m.*	*klee-*MAH	climate (weather)
climatisation,*f.*	*klee-mah-tee-zah-*S_YOHNG	air conditioning
cliqueter (1)	*klee-*KTAY	rattle, to
cloche,*f.*	KLUHSH	bell
clocher,*m.*	*kluh-*SHAY	steeple
clôture,*f.*	*kloh-*TÜR	fence (barrier)
clou,*m.*	KLOO	nail (hardware)
clou de girofle,*m.*	*kloo dih zhee-*RUH-*fl*(*ih*)	clove
coassociation,*f.*	*koh-ah-suh-*s_*yah-*S_YOHNG	copartnership (*bus.*)
cochon,*m.*	*kuh-*SHOHNG	pig (animal)
"	"	swine
cocktail,*m.*	*kuh-*KTELL	cocktail
coco, (noix de),*m.*	(*nwah dih*) *kuh-*KOH	coconut
code,*m.*	KUHD	code (law)
coeur,*m.*	KUHR	heart
coffre,*m.*	KUH-*fr*(*ih*)	chest (box)
cogner (1)	*kuh-*N_YAY	pound (pummel), to
coiffeur,*m.*	*kwah-*FUHR	barber
coin,*m.*	KWANG	corner
coke,*m.*	KUHK	coke
col,*m.*	KUHL	collar
colère,*f.*	*kuh-*LEHR	anger
"	"	wrath
colère, en	*ahn kuh-*LEHR	angry
colis,*m.*	*kuh-*LEE	package
"	"	parcel
colis postal, (par)	(*pahr*) *kuh-lee puh-*STAHL	parcel post
colle,*f.*	KUHL	glue
"	"	paste (adhesive)
collection,*f.*	*kuh-lehk-*S_YOHNG	collection

French	Pronunciation	English
coller, (se) (1)	(*sih*) *kuh-*LAY	stick (adhere), to
collier,*m.*	*kuh-*L_YAY	necklace
colline,*f.*	*kuh-*LEEN	hill
colombe,*f.*	*kuh-*LOHMB	dove
Colombie,*f.*	*kuh-lohm-*BEE	Colombia
colon,*m.*	*kuh-*LOHNG	colonist
"	"	settler
colonel,*m.*	*kuh-luh-*NELL	colonel
colonial	*kuh-luh-*N_YAHL	colonial
colonie,*f.*	*kuh-luh-*NEE	colony
"	"	settlement
colonne,*f.*	*kuh-*LUNN	column
combat,*m.*	*kohm-*BAH	combat
"	"	fight
combattre (8)	*kohm-*BAH-*tr*(*ih*)	fight (struggle against), to
"	"	oppose (combat), to
combinaison,*f.*	*kohm-bee-neh-*ZOHNG	combination
combiner (1)	*kohm-bee-*NAY	combine (make join), to
combiner, se	*sih kohm-bee-*NAY	combine (coalesce), to
combustible,*m.*	*kohm-bü-*STEE-*bl*(*ih*)	fuel
comédie,*f.*	*kuh-may-*DEE	comedy (comic play)
comité,*m.*	*kuh-mee-*TAY	committee
commandant,*m.*	*kuh-mahn-*DAHNG	commander (officer)
commande,*f.*	*kuh-*MAHND	order (purchase)
commandement,*m.*	*kuh-mahn-*DMAHNG	command (authority)
commander (1)	*kuh-mahn-*DAY	order (purchase), to
comme	KUHM	as (in the same way, *conj.*)
"	"	like (*adv.*)
commencement,*m.*	*kuh-mahn-*SMAHNG	beginning
"	"	opening
"	"	start
commencer (1)	*kuh-mahn-*SAY	begin, to
"	"	commence, to
"	"	start, to
comment	*kuh-*MAHNG	how
commenter (1)	*kuh-mahn-*TAY	comment, to
commérages,*m.pl.*	*kuh-may-*RAHZH	gossip (idle talk)
commerçant,*m.*	*kuh-mehr-*SAHNG	dealer (trader)
"	"	merchant
commerce,*m.*	*kuh-*MEHRSS	commerce
"	"	trade
commercer (1)	*kuh-mehr-*SAY	deal (trade), to
commercial	*kuh-mehr-*S_YAHL	commercial
commettre (39)	*kuh-*MEH-*tr*(*ih*)	commit (perpetrate), to
commissaire,*m.*	*kuh-mee-*SEHR	commissioner (deputized person)
commission,*f.*	*kuh-mee-*S_YOHNG	commission
"	"	errand
commode	*kuh-*MUHD	convenient
commode,*f.*	*kuh-*MUHD	bureau (chest)
commode-toilette,*f.*	*kuh-muhd-twah-*LETT	dresser (bureau)
commodité,*f.*	*kuh-muh-dee-*TAY	convenience
commun	*kuh-*MUHNG, -MÜN	joint (combined)
communication,*f.*	*kuh-mü-nee-kah-*S_YOHNG	communication
communiquer (1)	*kuh-mü-nee-*KAY	convey (communicate), to
communisme,*m.*	*kuh-mü-*NEE-*sm*(*ih*)	communism
compact	*kohm-*PAHKT	compact (packed firmly)
compagnie,*f.*	*kohm-pah-*N_YEE	company
compagnon,*m.*	*kohm-pah-*N_YOHNG	companion
comparaison,*f.*	*kohm-pah-ray-*ZOHNG	comparison
comparer (1)	*kohm-pah-*RAY	compare (consider relatively), to
compartiment,*m.*	*kohm-pahr-tee-*MAHNG	compartment (of train)
compas,*m.*	*kohm-*PAH	compass (drawing instrument)
compassion,*f.*	*kohm-pah-*S_YOHNG	sympathy (compassion)
compensation,*f.*	*kohm-pahn-sah-*S_YOHNG	compensation (*bus.*)
compétent	*kohm-pay-*TAHNG, -TAHNT	competent (able)
"	"	efficient
complet,*m.*	*kohm-*PLEH	suit, man's

French	Pronunciation	English
complet, -plète	*kohm*-PLEH, -PLETT	complete
"	"	full
"	"	thorough
"	"	utter (*adj.*)
complètement	*kohm-pleh*-TMAHNG	altogether (entirely)
"	"	thoroughly
complexe	*kohm*-PLEX	complex (complicated)
compliment,*m.*	*kohm-plee*-MAHNG	compliment
complot,*m.*	*kohm*-PLOH	plot (conspiracy)
composé,*m.*	*kohm-poh*-ZAY	compound (mixture)
composer (1)	*kohm-poh*-ZAY	compose, to (*mus.*)
composition,*f.*	*kohm-poh-zee*-S YOHNG	composition (make-up)
compréhension,*f.*	*kohm-pray-ahn-*S YOHNG	understanding (comprehension)
comprendre (48)	*kohm*-PRAHN-*dr*(*ih*)	comprehend, to
"	"	include (contain), to
"	"	understand, to
compromis,*m.*	*kohm-pruh*-MEE	compromise (mutual concessions)
comptable,*m.*	*kohn*-TAH-*bl*(*ih*)	accountant
comptant, (argent), *m.*	(*ahr-zhahng*) *kohm*-TAHNG	cash (money)
compte,*m.*	KOHNT	account (bank account)
compte courant,*m.*	*kohnt koo*-RAHNG	charge account
compte d'épargne, *m.*	*kohnt day*-PAHR-*n yih*	savings account
compter (1)	*kohn*-TAY	count, to
"	"	reckon (compute), to
compte rendu,*m.*	*kohnt rahn*-DÜ	review (critique)
compter sur (1)	*kohn*-TAY *sür*	count on, to
"	"	depend (rely) on, to
comptoir,*m.*	*kohn*-TWAHR	counter (table)
concentrer (1)	*kohn-sahn*-TRAY	concentrate (make converge), to
conception,*f.*	*kohn-sehp*-S YOHNG	conception (*physiol.*)
concernant	*kohn-sehr*-NAHNG	concerning (regarding)
concerner (1)	*kohn-sehr*-NAY	concern (affect), to
concert,*m.*	*kohn*-SEHR	concert (musical performance)
concevoir (49)	*kohn-sih*-VWAHR	conceive (imagine), to
concis	*kohn*-SEE, -SEEZ	compact (brief)
conclure (13)	*kohn*-KLÜR	conclude (make end), to
conclusion,*f.*	*kohn-klü-z* YOHNG	conclusion
concombre,*m.*	*kohn*-KOHM-*br*(*ih*)	cucumber
concours,*m.*	*kohn*-KOOR	contest
concret, -crète	*kohn*-KREH, -KRETT	concrete (real)
concurrence,*f.*	*kohn-kü*-RAHNSS	competition (*bus.*)
concurrent,*m.*	*kohn-kü*-RAHNG	competitor (*bus.*)
condamner (1)	*kohn-dah*-NAY	condemn, to
"	"	doom, to
"	"	sentence, to
condenser (1)	*kohn-dahn*-SAY	condense (compress), to
condition,*f.*	*kohn-dee-s* YOHNG	condition (stipulation)
conditions,*f.pl.*	*kohn-dee-s* YOHNG	terms (conditions)
conduire (14)	*kohn*-DÜ_EER	conduct (manage), to
"	"	drive (a vehicle), to
"	"	lead (guide), to
"	"	steer, to
conduire, se (14)	*sih kohn*-DÜ_EER	act, to
"	"	behave (conduct oneself), to
conduite,*f.*	*kohn*-DÜ_EET	behavior
conférence,*f.*	*kohn-fay*-RAHNSS	conference (meeting)
"	"	lecture (speech)
conférer (1)	*kohn-fay*-RAY	confer (bestow), to
confiance,*f.*	*kohn*-F_YAHNSS	confidence
"	"	faith
"	"	trust
confidentiel, -le	*kohn-fee-dahn-s* YELL	confidential (private)
confiture,*f.*	*kohn-fee*-TÜR	jam (preserve)
conflit,*m.*	*kohn*-FLEE	conflict
confort,*m.*	*kohn*-FOR	comfort (ease)
confortable	*kohn-for*-TAH-*bl*(*ih*)	comfortable (affording comfort)

French	Pronunciation	English
confusion,*f.*	*kohn-fü-z* YOHNG	confusion (disorder)
congé,*m.*	*kohn*-ZHAY	discharge (dismissal)
congédier (1)	*kohn-zhay-D* YAY	dismiss (discharge), to
congrégation,*f.*	*kohn-gray-gah-s* YOHNG	congregation (religious community)
congrès,*m.*	*kohn*-GREH	congress (legislature)
conjonction,*f.*	*kohn-zhohnk-s* YOHNG	conjunction (*gram.*)
connaissance,*f.*	*kuh-neh*-SAHNSS	acquaintance
"	"	knowledge
connaissement,*m.*	*kuh-neh*-SMAHNG	bill of lading
connaître (16)	*kuh*-NEH-*tr*(*ih*)	know (be acquainted with), to
connu	*kuh*-NÜ	known (familiar)
conquête,*f.*	*kohn*-KETT	conquest
consacrer, se (1)	*sih kohn-sah*-KRAY	devote oneself, to
conscience,*f.*	*kohn-s* YAHNSS	conscience
conscient	*kohn-s* YAHNG, -S YAHNT	conscious (aware)
conscription,*f.*	*kohn-skreep-s* YOHNG	draft (conscription)
conseil,*m.*	*kohn*-SAY	advice
"	"	board
"	"	council
"	"	counsel
conseiller (1)	*kohn-seh*-YAY	advise, to
"	"	counsel, to
consentir (26)	*kohn-sahn*-TEER	agree (assent), to
"	"	consent, to
conséquence,*f.*	*kohn-say*-KAHNSS	consequence
conséquent, par	*pahr kohn-say*-KAHNG	consequently
conservateur,*m.*	*kohn-sehr-vah*-TUHR	curator
conserver (1)	*kohn-sehr*-VAY	preserve, to
"	"	retain (keep), to
considérable	*kohn-see-day*-RAH-*bl*(*ih*)	considerable (*adj.*)
considération,*f.*	*kohn-see-day-rah-*S YOHNG	consideration
considérer (1)	*kohn-see-day*-RAY	consider (reflect on), to
"	"	regard, to
considérer comme admis	*kohn-see-day-ray kuhm ah*-DMEE	assume (take for granted), to
consignataire,*m.,f.*	*kohn-see-n yah*-TEHR	consignee (*bus.*)
consister en (dans) (1)	*kohn-see*-STAY *ahng* (*dahng*)	consist of (comprise), to
consolation,*f.*	*kohn-suh-lah-s* YOHNG	comfort (solace)
"	"	consolation
consoler (1)	*kohn-suh*-LAY	comfort (console), to
consommation,*f.*	*kohn-suh-mah-s* YOHNG	consumption (using up)
consommer (1)	*kohn-suh*-MAY	consume, to
constater (1)	*kohn-stah*-TAY	remark (say), to
consternation,*f.*	*kohn-stehr-nah-s* YOHNG	dismay
constituer (1)	*kohn-stee*-TÜ_AY	constitute (make up), to
constitution,*f.*	*kohn-stee-tü-s* YOHNG	constitution
construction,*f.*	*kohn-strük-s* YOHNG	construction (fabrication)
construire (14)	*kohn*-STRÜ_EER	construct, to
consul,*m.*	*kohn*-SÜL	consul
consulter (1)	*kohn-sül*-TAY	consult (seek professional advice of), to
contact,*m.*	*kohn*-TAHKT	contact (meeting)
conte,*m.*	KOHNT	short story
"	"	tale (narrative)
conte de fées,*m.*	*kohnt dih* FAY	fairy tale
contempler (1)	*kohn-tahm*-PLAY	gaze, to
contemporain	*kohn-tahm-puh*-RANG, -RENN	contemporary (modern)
contenir (55)	*kohn-t*(*ih*)NEER	contain, to
content	*kohn*-TAHNG, -TAHNT	content (satisfied)
contenu,*m.*	*kohn-t*(*ih*)NÜ	contents
contester (1)	*kohn-teh*-STAY	contest (dispute), to
"	"	dispute (oppose by argument), to
continent,*m.*	*kohn-tee*-NAHNG	continent (*geog.*)
continu	*kohn-tee*-NÜ	continuous
continuel, -le	*kohn-tee*-NÜ_ELL	constant
"	"	continual
continuer (1)	*kohn-tee*-NÜ_AY	continue, to
continuer (à, de)	*kohn-tee*-NÜ_AY (*ah*, *dih*)	keep (continue), to
contracter (1)	*kohn-trah*-KTAY	contract (make shrink), to
contraire	*kohn*-TREHR	contrary (opposite)
contraire,*m.*	*kohn*-TREHR	reverse (contrary, *n.*)
contraste,*m.*	*kohn*-TRAHST	contrast

French	Pronunciation	English
contrat, *m.*	*kohn*-TRAH	contract
contrat de vente, *m.*	*kohn-trah d(ih)* VAHNT	bill of sale
contre	KOHN-*tr(ih)*	against
contrebande, *f.*	*kohn-trih*-BAHND	contraband
contrée, *f.*	*kohn*-TRAY	land (region)
contrefaire (32)	*kohn-trih*-FEHR	forge (counterfeit), to
contremaître, *m.*	*kohn-trih*-MEH-*tr(ih)*	foreman (overseer)
contreseing, *m.*	*kohn-trih*-SANG	countersignature (*bus.*)
contre-torpilleur, *m.*	*kohn-trih-tor-pee*-YUHR	destroyer (ship)
contribuer (1)	*kohn-tree*-BÜ AY	contribute, to
contribution, *f.*	*kohn-tree-bü*-S YOHNG	contribution
convaincre (57)	*kohn*-VAN-*kr(ih)*	convince, to
convenable	*kohn-v(ih)*NAH-*bl(ih)*	fit
"	"	proper (acceptable)
"	"	suitable
convenir (59)	*kohn-v(ih)*NEER	agree (concur), to
"	"	apply (be fitting), to
conversation, *f.*	*kohn-vehr-sah*-S YOHNG	conversation
"	"	talk
conversion, *f.*	*kohn-vehr*-S YOHNG	conversion
"	"	conversion rate (*bus.*)
converti, *m.*	*kohn-vehr*-TEE	convert (proselyte)
convertir (2)	*kohn-vehr*-TEER	convert (transform), to
conviction, *f.*	*kohn-veek*-S YOHNG	conviction (belief)
convoi, *m.*	*kohn*-VWAH	convoy (*mil.*)
coopération, *f.*	*kuh-uh-pay-rah*-S YOHNG	cooperation
coopérative, *f.*	*kuh-uh-pay-rah*-TEEV	cooperative (*n.*)
copain, *m.*	*kuh*-PANG	pal
Copenhague, *f.*	*kuh-peh*-NAHG	Copenhagen
copie, *f.*	*kuh*-PEE	copy (duplicate)
copie au carbone, *f.*	*kuh-pee oh kahr*-BUNN	carbon copy
copier (1)	*kuh*-P YAY	copy (imitate), to
copropriétaire, *m.*, *f.*	*koh-pruh-pree-ay*-TEHR	co-owner (*bus.*)
copyright, *m.*	*kuh-pee*-RITE	copyright (*n.*)
coq, *m.*	KUHK	cock
"	"	rooster
coqueluche, *f.*	*kuh*-KLÜSH	whooping cough
coquille, *f.*	*kuh*-KEE	shell (covering)
cor, *m.*	KOR	horn (*mus.*)
corbeau, *m.*	*kor*-BOH	crow (bird)
corde, *f.*	KORD	cord
"	"	rope
cordial	*kor*-D YAHL	cordial (*adj.*)
"	"	hearty
cordonnier, *m.*	*kor-duh*-N YAY	shoemaker
corne, *f.*	KORN	horn (*anat.*)
corne (d'auto), *f.*	KORN (*doh*-TOH)	horn (*auto.*)
corps, *m.*	KOR	body (*anat.*)
corpulent	*kor-pü*-LAHNG, -LAHNT	stout (corpulent)
correct	*kuh*-RECKT	right (correct)
correspondance, *f.*	*kuh-reh-spohn*-DAHNSS	correspondence (letters)
correspondant, *m.*	*kuh-reh-spohn*-DAHNG	correspondent (letter writer)
correspondre (3)	*kuh-reh*-SPOHN-*dr(ih)*	correspond (agree), to
correspondre avec	*kuh-reh*-SPOHN-*drah-veck*	correspond with (write to), to
corridor, *m.*	*kuh-ree*-DOR	hall (corridor)
corroboration, *f.*	*kuh-ruh-buh-rah*-S YOHNG	confirmation (corroboration)
corroborer (1)	*kuh-ruh-buh*-RAY	confirm (corroborate), to
cosmétique, *m.*	*kuh-smeh*-TEEK	cosmetic (*n.*)
Costa-Rica, *f.*	*kuh-stah-ree*-KAH	Costa Rica
costume, *m.*	*kuh*-STÜM	costume
cotation, *f.*	*kuh-tah*-S YOHNG	quotation (price)
côte, *f.*	KOHT	coast (seaboard)
"	"	rib (*anat.*)
côté, *m.*	*kuh*-TAY	side
côté de, à	*ah kuh*-TAY *dih*	beside (*prep.*)
"	"	next to (alongside of, *prep.*)
côtelette d'agneau, *f.*	*kuh-tlett dah*-N YOH	lamb chop

French	Pronunciation	English
côtelette de porc, *f.*	*kuh-tlett dih* POR	pork chop
côtelette de veau, *f.*	*kuh-tlett dih* VOH	veal chop
coton, *m.*	*kuh*-TOHNG	cotton (boll)
cotonnade, *f.*	*kuh-luh*-NAHD	cotton (fabric)
cou, *m.*	KOO	neck (*anat.*)
couche, *f.*	KOOSH	layer (thickness)
coucher, se (1)	*sih koo*-SHAY	go to bed, to
"	"	set (in sky), to
coucher du soleil, *m.*	*koo-shay dü suh*-LAY	sunset
couchette, *f.*	*koo*-SHETT	berth (train bunk)
coucou, *m.*	*koo*-KOO	cuckoo (bird)
coude, *m.*	KOOD	elbow
coudre (17)	KOO-*dr(ih)*	sew, to
couler (1)	*koo*-LAY	flow (circulate), to
"	"	run, to
"	"	sink (become submerged), to
couleur, *f.*	*koo*-LUHR	color
coup, *m.*	KOO	blow
"	"	punch
"	"	stroke
coupable	*koo*-PAH-*bl(ih)*	guilty
coup de dents, *m.*	*koo d(ih)* DAHNG	bite
coup de feu, *m.*	*koo d(ih)* FUH	shot (from firearm)
coup de pied, *m.*	*koo d(ih)* P YAY	kick (boot)
coup de sang, *m.*	*koo d(ih)* SAHNG	stroke (attack of paralysis)
coup d'oeil, *m.*	*koo* DUH_y	glance (quick look)
couper (1)	*koo*-PAY	cut, to
"	"	sever, to
couple, *m.*	KOO-*pl(ih)*	couple (pair, *n.*)
coupon, *m.*	*koo*-POHNG	coupon (detachable certificate)
cour, *f.*	KOOR	court (of ruler)
courage, *m.*	*koo*-RAHZH	courage
courant	*koo*-RAHNG, -RAHNT	current (contemporary, *adj.*)
courant, *m.*	*koo*-RAHNG	current
courant d'air, *m.*	*koo-rahn* DEHR	draft (air current)
courbé	*koor*-BAY	bent (curved)
courbe, *f.*	KOORB	curve
courber, (se) (1)	(*sih*) *koor*-BAY	bend (be bent), to
cour (de maison), *f.*	KOOR (*dih may*-ZOHNG)	yard (enclosure near house)
cour de récréation, *f.*	*koor dih ray-kray-ah*-S YOHNG	playground
courir (2)	*koo*-REER	run (sprint), to
couronne, *f.*	*koo*-RUNN	crown
"	"	wreath
couronner (1)	*koo-ruh*-NAY	crown, to
courrier, *m.*	*koo*-R YAY	mail (letters exchanged)
courroie, *f.*	*koo*-RWAH	strap
cours de route, *m.*	*koor dih* ROOT	transit (passage)
course, *f.*	KOORSS	race (contest)
court	KOOR	short
courtepointe, *f.*	*koor-tih*-PWANT	quilt (bedcover)
courtier, *m.*	*koor*-T YAY	broker (*bus.*)
courtois	*koor*-TWAH, -TWAHZ	courteous (polite)
courtoisie, *f.*	*koor-twah*-ZEE	courtesy
cousin, *m.*	*koo*-ZANG	cousin
coussin, *m.*	*koo*-SANG	cushion (pillow)
couteau, *m.*	*koo*-TOH	knife
coûter (1)	*koo*-TAY	cost, to
coûteux, -teuse	*koo*-TUH, -TUHZ	costly
"	"	expensive
coutume, *f.*	*koo*-TÜM	custom (habit)
couture, *f.*	*koo*-TÜR	seam (line of stitches)
couvercle, *m.*	*koo*-VEHR-*kl(ih)*	cover
"	"	lid
couverture, *f.*	*koo-vehr*-TÜR	blanket
couvrir (44)	*koo*-VREER	cover, to
crabe, *m.*	KRAHB	crab (shellfish)
cracher (1)	*krah*-SHAY	spit, to
craie, *f.*	KREH	chalk
craindre (19)	KRAN-*dr(ih)*	fear (be afraid of), to
crainte, *f.*	KRANT	fear
crainte (respectueuse), *f.*	KRANT (*reh-speck-tü*_UHZ)	awe
craintif, -tive	*kran*-TEEF, -TEEV	fearful (afraid)
cramoisi	*krah-mwah*-ZEE	crimson
crampe, *f.*	KRAHMP	cramp (*med.*)

French	Pronunciation	English
crâne, *m.*	KRAH_N	skull
crapaud, *m.*	*krah*-POH	toad
cravate, *f.*	*krah*-VAHT	tie (necktie)
crayon, *m.*	*kreh*-YOHNG	pencil
crayon de couleur, *m.*	*kreh-yohng dih koo-*LUHR	crayon
créancier, *m.*	*kray-ahn*-S_YAY	creditor (*bus.*)
création, *f.*	*kray-ah*-S_YOHNG	creation
créature, *f.*	*kray-ah*-TÜR	creature (living being)
crédit, *m.*	*kray*-DEE	credit (*bus.*)
créditer (1)	*kray-dee*-TAY	credit, to (*bus.*)
crédit municipal, *m.*	*kray-dee mü-nee-see-*PAHL	pawnshop
créer (1)	*kray*-AY	create, to
crème, *f.*	KREHM	cream
crépuscule, *m.*	*kray-pü*-SKÜL	twilight
crête, *f.*	KRETT	crest (summit)
"	"	ridge (raised area)
creuser (1)	*kruh*-ZAY	dig (excavate), to
"	"	mine, to
creux, creuse	KRUH, KRUHZ	hollow (*adj.*)
crevette, *f.*	*krih*-VETT	shrimp
cri, *m.*	KREE	call
"	"	cry (utterance)
"	"	shout
crier (1)	*kree*-YAY	call, to
"	"	cry, to
"	"	scream, to
"	"	shout (say loudly), to
crime, *m.*	KREEM	crime
criminel, *m.*	*kree-mee*-NELL	criminal (*n.*)
criminel, -le	*kree-mee*-NELL	criminal (*adj.*)
crinière, *f.*	*kree*-N_YEHR	mane (of horse)
crise, *f.*	KREEZ	crisis
cristal, *m.*	*kree*-STAHL	crystal (*min.*)
critique, *f.*	*kree*-TEEK	criticism
critique, *m.*	*kree*-TEEK	critic
crochet, *m.*	*kruh*-SHEH	hook
croire (20)	KRWAHR	believe (accept), to
croisement, *m.*	*krwah*-ZMAHNG	crossing (intersection)
croiser (1)	*krwah*-ZAY	cross (crossbreed), to
croiseur, *m.*	*krwah*-ZUHR	cruiser (ship)
croisière, *f.*	*krwah*-Z_YEHR	cruise (voyage)
croissance, *f.*	*krwah*-SAHNSS	growth (development)
croître (21)	KRWAH-*tr(ih)*	grow (expand), to
"	"	grow, to (*biol.*)
croix, *f.*	KRWAH	cross (crucifix)
croquant	*kruh*-KAHNG, -KAHNT	crisp (brittle)
croûte, *f.*	KROOT	crust
cru	KRÜ	raw (in natural state)
cruche, *f.*	KRÜSH	jug
cruel, -le	*krü*-ELL	cruel
Cuba, *f.*	*kü*-BAH	Cuba
cube, *m.*	KÜB	cube (*geom.*)
cuillère à soupe, *f.*	*kü_ee-yehr ah* SOOP	spoon (tablespoon)
cuillère à thé, *f.*	*kü_ee-yehr ah* TAY	spoon (teaspoon)
cuir, *m.*	KÜ_EER	leather (*n.*)
cuirassé (de ligne), *m.*	*kü_ee-rah*-SAY (*dih* LEE-*n_yih*)	battleship
cuire (14), (faire)	KÜ_EER	cook (heat food), to
cuire (au four)	KÜ_EER (*oh* FOOR)	bake (be cooking), to
cuisine, *f.*	*kü_ee*-ZEEN	kitchen
cuisinier, *m.*	*kü_ee-zee*-N_YAY	cook
cuisse, *f.*	KÜ_EESS	thigh
cuivre, *m.*	KÜ_EE-*vr(ih)*	copper
culpabilité, *f.*	*kül-pah-bee-lee*-TAY	guilt
culte, *m.*	KÜLT	worship (*rel.*)
cultiver (1)	*kül-tee*-VAY	cultivate, to
"	"	grow, to
culture, *f.*	*kül*-TÜR	culture (refinement)
curé, *m.*	*kü*-RAY	parson
curieux, -rieuse	*kü*-R_YUH, -R_YUHZ	curious (inquisitive)
curiosité, *f.*	*kü-r_yoh-zee*-TAY	curiosity (inquisitiveness)
cygne, *m.*	SEE-*n_yih*	swan
cylindre, *m.*	*see*-LAN-*dr(ih)*	cylinder (*geom.*)
dactylographe, *m.*, *f.*	*dah-ktee-luh*-GRAHF	typist
d'agrément	*dah-gray*-MAHNG	fancy (ornamental, *adj.*)
daim, *m.*	DANG	buck (male deer)

French	Pronunciation	English
dame, *f.*	DAHM	lady
damner (1)	*dah*-NAY	damn, to
Danemark, *m.*	*dah*-NMAHRK	Denmark
danger, *m.*	*dahn*-ZHAY	danger
dangereux, -reuse	*dahn*-ZHRUH, -ZHRUHZ	dangerous
danois	*dah*-NWAH, -NWAHZ	Danish (*adj.*)
dans	DAHNG	in (inside, into, *prep.*)
"	"	into (to the inside)
"	"	within (in less time than, inside, *prep.*)
danse, *f.*	DAHNSS	dance (movement to music)
danser (1)	*dahn*-SAY	dance, to
dans la maison	*dahng lah may*-ZOHNG	indoors (*adv.*)
dans tout	*dahn* TOO	throughout (in every part of, *prep.*)
Danube, *m.*	*dah*-NÜB	Danube
date, *f.*	DAHT	date (calendar designation)
datte, *f.*	DAHT	date (fruit)
...d'autre	...DOH-*tr(ih)*	else (*adj., adv.*)
de	DIH	about (concerning)
"	"	from
"	"	of
de (d'); du, de la (de l'); des	*dih* (*d'*); *dü, dih lah* (*dih l'*); *day*	any (a quantity of, *adj.*)
"	"	some (a quantity of, *adj.*)
débarquer (1)	*day-bahr*-KAY	land (from a ship), to
débarrasser (1)	*day-bah-rah*-SAY	rid (free), to
débat, *m.*	*day*-BAH	debate
débiter (1)	*day-bee*-TAY	debit, to
débiteur, *m.*	*day-bee*-TUHR	debtor (*bus.*)
débouché, *m.*	*day-boo*-SHAY	outlet (market, *bus.*)
débours, *m.pl.*	*day*-BOOR	disbursement (*bus.*)
décadence, *f.*	*day-kah*-DAHNSS	decay (decline)
décent	*day*-SAHNG, -SAHNT	decent (respectable)
décharger (1)	*day-shahr*-ZHAY	unload, to
déchirer (1)	*day-shee*-RAY	rip, to
"	"	tear, to
décider (1)	*day-see*-DAY	settle (agree on), to
décider, (se)	(*sih*) *day-see*-DAY	determine (make up one's mind), to
décider, se	*sih day-see*-DAY	decide (make up one's mind), to
décision, *f.*	*day-see*-Z_YOHNG	decision (judgment)
déclaration, *f.*	*day-klah-rah*-S_YOHNG	announcement
"	"	declaration
"	"	statement
déclarer (1)	*day-klah*-RAY	declare, to
"	"	pronounce, to
"	"	state (say), to
déclin, *m.*	*day*-KLANG	decline (deterioration)
décliner (1)	*day-klee*-NAY	decline, to
décor, *m.*	*day*-KOR	decoration (décor)
décoration, *f.*	*day-kuh-rah*-S_YOHNG	decoration (ornament)
décorer (1)	*day-kuh*-RAY	decorate (adorn), to
décourager (1)	*day-koo-rah*-ZHAY	discourage (dishearten), to
découverte, *f.*	*day-koo*-VEHRT	discovery
découvrir (44)	*day-koo*-VREER	detect, to
"	"	discover, to
décret, *m.*	*day*-KREH	decree (edict)
décrire (28)	*day*-KREER	describe (portray), to
dedans	*dih*-DAHNG	inside (within, *adv.*)
dedans, *m.*	*dih*-DAHNG	inside (interior, *n.*)
dédouanement, *m.*	*day-dwah*-MAHNG	clearance (customs clearance)
déduire (14)	*day*-DÜ_EER	deduct, to
défaite, *f.*	*day*-FETT	defeat
défaut, *m.*	*day*-FOH	defect (flaw)
"	"	fault
défendre (3)	*day*-FAHN-*dr(ih)*	defend (protect), to
"	"	forbid, to
défendu	*day-fahn*-DÜ	forbidden
défense, *f.*	*day*-FAHNSS	defense
défi, *m.*	*day*-FEE	challenge
déficit, *m.*	*day-fee*-SEET	deficit (*bus.*)
défier (1)	*day*-F_YAY	defy, to
défilé, *m.*	*day-fee*-LAY	parade (procession)

French	Pronunciation	English
défini	*day-fee*-NEE	definite
définir (2)	*day-fee*-NEER	define, to
dégeler (1)	*day*-ZHLAY	thaw, to
dégoût, *m.*	*day*-GOO	disgust
dégoutter (1)	*day-goo*-TAY	drip, to
degré, *m.*	*dih*-GRAY	degree (unit of measurement)
déguisement, *m.*	*day-ghee*-ZMAHNG	disguise
dehors	*dih*-OR	out (forth, *adv.*)
"	"	outside (*adv.*)
dehors, *m.*	*dih*-OR	outside (*n.*)
dehors, (au)	(*oh*) *dih*-OR	out (not in, *adv.*)
dehors, au	*oh dih*-OR	outdoors (*adv.*)
déjà	*day*-ZHAH	already
déjeter, se (1)	*sih day*-ZH(*ih*)TAY	warp (become misshapen), to
déjeuner, *m.*	*day-zhuh*-NAY	lunch (midday meal)
déjouer (1)	*day*-ZHWAY	foil (frustrate), to
de la (see de)		
délecter (1)	*day-leck*-TAY	delight (give pleasure to), to
délégué, *m.*	*day-lay*-GAY	delegate
délicat	*day-lee-*KAH, -KAHT	dainty
"	"	delicate
délicieux, -cieuse	*day-lee-*S_YUH, -S_YUHZ	delicious
"	"	delightful
délié	*day-*L_YAY	loose (unbound)
délivrer (1)	*day-lee-*VRAY	relieve (free), to
déloyauté, *f.*	*day-lwah-yoh-*TAY	disloyalty
demain	*dih-*MANG	tomorrow
demande, *f.*	*dih-*MAHND	application
"	"	demand
"	"	request
demander (1)	*dih-mahn-*DAY	request, to
demander, se	*sih dih-mahn-*DAY	wonder (ask oneself), to
demander (à)	*dih-mahn-*DAY (*ah*)	ask (put question to), to
demander à	*dih-mahn-*DAY *ah*	ask (request), to
déménager (1)	*day-may-nah-*ZHAY	move (change residence), to
démentir (26)	*day-mahn-*TEER	contradict (deny), to
demeure, *f.*	*dih-*MUHR	home
demeurer (1)	*dih-muh-*RAY	live (dwell), to
"	"	lodge (reside), to
demi	*dih-*MEE	half (*adj.*)
démissionner (1)	*day-mee-s_yuh-*NAY	resign (tender resignation), to
démocrate, *m., f.*	*day-muh-*KRAHT	democrat
démocratie, *f.*	*day-muh-krah-*TEE	democracy
démocratique	*day-muh-krah-*TEEK	democratic
démolir (2)	*day-muh-*LEER	wreck, to
démonstration, *f.*	*day-mohn-strah-*S_YOHNG	demonstration (proof)
dense	DAHNSS	dense
dent, *f.*	DAHNG	tooth
dentelle, *f.*	*dahn-*TELL	lace (fabric)
dentiste, *m.*	*dahn-*TEEST	dentist
départ, *m.*	*day-*PAHR	departure (setting out)
département, *m.*	*day-pahr-tih-*MAHNG	department (administrative unit)
dépasser (1)	*day-pah-*SAY	exceed, to
dépêche, *f.*	*day-*PESH	dispatch (communication)
dépeindre (19)	*day-*PAN-*dr*(*ih*)	paint (represent), to
dépendant	*day-pahn-*DAHNG, -DAHNT	dependent (reliant)
dépendre de (3)	*day-*PAHN-*drih dih*	depend (be contingent) on, to
dépense, *f.*	*day-*PAHNSS	expenditure (outlay)
dépenser (1)	*day-pahn-*SAY	spend (pay out), to
déplacer (1)	*day-plah-*SAY	move (shift the position of), to
déplacer, se	*sih day-plah-*SAY	move (shift one's position), to
déposant, *m.*	*day-poh-*ZAHNG	depositor (*fin.*)
déposer (1)	*day-poh-*ZAY	deposit, to (*fin.*)
dépôt, *m.*	*day-*POH	deposit (money deposited)
dépouiller (1)	*day-poo-*YAY	strip (denude), to
dépression (économique), *f.*	*day-preh-*S_YOHNG (*ay-kuh-nuh-*MEEK)	depression (*econ.*)
depuis	*dih-*PÜ_EE	since (*adv., prep.*)
déraisonnable	*day-ray-zuh-*NAH-*bl*(*ih*)	unreasonable (unreasoning)

French	Pronunciation	English
déranger (1)	*day-rahn-*ZHAY	disturb, to
"	"	trouble (inconvenience), to
dériver (1)	*day-ree-*VAY	drift (float), to
dernier, -nière	*dehr-*N_YAY, -N_YEHR	last (*adj.*)
"	"	latter (second of two)
dernier lieu, en	*ahn dehr-n_yay* L_YUH	last (*adv.*)
derrière	*deh-*R_YEHR	behind (*prep.*)
derrière, de	*dih deh-*R_YEHR	hind (posterior, *adj.*)
des (see de)		
dés, *m. pl.*	DAY	dice (marked cubes)
désagréable	*day-zah-gray-*AH-*bl*(*ih*)	disagreeable
"	"	unpleasant
désappointement, *m.*	*day-zah-pwan-*TMAHNG	disappointment
désappointer (1)	*day-zah-pwan-*TAY	disappoint, to
désastre, *m.*	*day-*ZAH-*str*(*ih*)	disaster
descendant, *m.*	*day-sahn-*DAHNG	descendant (offspring)
descendre (3)	*day-*SAHN-*dr*(*ih*)	descend (move downward), to
description, *f.*	*deh-skreep-*S_YOHNG	description (account)
désert	*day-*ZEHR, -ZEHRT	lonely (unfrequented)
désert, *m.*	*day-*ZEHR	desert
"	"	wilderness
désespéré	*day-zeh-spay-*RAY	desperate
désespérer (1)	*day-zeh-spay-*RAY	despair, to
désespoir, *m.*	*day-zeh-*SPWAHR	despair (hopelessness)
déshonneur, *m.*	*day-zuh-*NUHR	dishonor
désir, *m.*	*day-*ZEER	desire
"	"	wish
désirable	*day-zee-*RAH-*bl*(*ih*)	desirable
désirer (1)	*day-zee-*RAY	desire (long for), to
"	"	wish for, to
désireux, -reuse	*day-zee-*RUH, -RUHZ	anxious (wanting very much)
désobéir (à) (2)	*day-zuh-bay-*EER (*ah*)	disobey, to
désolation, *f.*	*day-zuh-lah-*S_YOHNG	misery (grief)
désordre, *m.*	*day-*ZOR-*dr*(*ih*)	disorder (confusion)
désormais	*day-zor-*MEH	henceforth
desquels, desquelles	*day-*KELL	whose (*rel. pron.*)
dessein, *m.*	*day-*SANG	design (intention)
dessert, *m.*	*day-*SEHR	dessert
dessin, *m.*	*day-*SANG	design
"	"	drawing (sketch)
"	"	pattern
dessiner (1)	*day-see-*NAY	draw (sketch), to
dessus, *m.*	*dih-*SÜ	top (upper surface)
destin, *m.*	*deh-*STANG	destiny
destinataire, *m., f.*	*deh-stee-nah-*TEHR	addressee
destination, *f.*	*deh-stee-nah-*S_YOHNG	destination
destruction, *f.*	*deh-strük-*S_YOHNG	destruction (demolition)
détaché	*day-tah-*SHAY	casual (offhand)
détail, *m.*	*day-*TYE	detail (minor item)
"	"	item
"	"	particular
"	"	retail (*bus., n.*)
détaillant, *m.*	*day-tah-*YAHNG	retailer (*bus.*)
détermination, *f.*	*day-tehr-mee-nah-*S_YOHNG	determination (fixed intent)
déterminer (1)	*day-tehr-mee-*NAY	determine (ascertain), to
détourner (1)	*day-toor-*NAY	avert (prevent), to
détresse, *f.*	*day-*TRESS	distress
détruire (14)	*day-*TRÜ_EER	destroy (demolish), to
dette, *f.*	DETT	debt
deux, les	*lay* DUH	both (*adj.*)
deux fois	*duh* FWAH	twice
deuxième	*duh-*Z_YEMM	second (*adj.*)
deux-points, *m. pl.*	*duh-*PWANG	colon (*punct.*)
devant	*dih-*VAHNG	ahead (in front)
"	"	before (in front of, *prep.*)
devant, *m.*	*dih-*VAHNG	front (forward part)
développement, *m.*	*day-vluhp-*MAHNG	development
développer (1)	*day-vluh-*PAY	develop, to
développer, se	*sih day-vluh-*PAY	thrive (grow vigorously), to

French	Pronunciation	English
devenir (59)	*dih-*V(*ih*)NEER	become, to
"	"	become of (happen to), to
déviation, *f.*	*day-v_yah-*S_YOHNG	departure (deviation)
"	"	detour
dévier (1)	*day-v_yay*	deviate (diverge), to
deviner (1)	*dih-vee-*NAY	guess (divine), to
devise, *f.*	*dih-*VEEZ	motto
devoir (24)	*dih-*VWAHR	ought (*v.*)
"	"	owe, to
devoir, *m.*	*dih-*VWAHR	assignment (*educ.*)
"	"	duty (obligation)
dévorer (1)	*day-vuh-*RAY	devour (eat), to
dévouement, *m.*	*day-voo-*MAHNG	devotion (loyal attachment)
dextérité, *f.*	*dex-tay-ree-*TAY	dexterity
d'honneur	*duh-*NUHR	honorable (upright)
diabète, *m.*	*d_yah-*BETT	diabetes
diable, *m.*	D_YAH-*bl*(*ih*)	devil
diamant, *m.*	*d_yah-*MAHNG	diamond (gem)
diamètre, *m.*	*d_yah-*MEH-*tr*(*ih*)	diameter
dicter (1)	*dee-*KTAY	dictate, to
dictionnaire, *m.*	*deek-s_yuh-*NEHR	dictionary
Dieu, *m.*	D_YUH	God
différence, *f.*	*dee-fay-*RAHNSS	difference
différent	*dee-fay-*RAHNG, -RAHNT	different (unlike)
différer (1)	*dee-fay-*RAY	differ (be unlike), to
difficile	*dee-fee-*SEEL	difficult
"	"	hard
difficulté, *f.*	*dee-fee-kül-*TAY	difficulty
digérer (1)	*dee-zhay-*RAY	digest, to
digne	DEE-*n_yih*	worthy (deserving)
dignité, *f.*	*dee-n_yee-*TAY	dignity
digue, *f.*	DEEG	dam (dike)
diligence, *f.*	*dee-lee-*ZHAHNSS	diligence
diligent	*dee-lee-*ZHAHNG, -ZHAHNT	diligent
dimanche des Rameaux, *m.*	*dee-mahnsh day rah-*MOH	Palm Sunday
diminuer (1)	*dee-mee-*NÜ_AY	diminish (make less), to
"	"	lower (decrease), to
diminution, *f.*	*dee-mee-nü-*S_YOHNG	decrease
dindon, *m.*	*dan-*DOHNG	turkey
dîner (1)	*dee-*NAY	dine, to
dîner, *m.*	*dee-*NAY	dinner
diphtérie, *f.*	*dee-ftay-*REE	diphtheria
dire (25)	DEER	say, to
"	"	tell (inform), to
direct	*dee-*RECKT	direct (immediate)
directement	*dee-reh-ktih-*MAHNG	straight (directly, *adv.*)
directeur, *m.*	*dee-reh-*KTUHR	conductor (*mus.*)
"	"	director
"	"	manager (administrator)
direction, *f.*	*dee-reck-*S_YOHNG	direction (course)
"	"	leadership (authority)
"	"	management (administration)
diriger (1)	*dee-ree-*ZHAY	beam (direct, *rad.*), to
"	"	control, to
"	"	direct, to
discipline, *f.*	*dee-see-*PLEEN	discipline (training)
discours, *m.*	*dee-*SKOOR	address
"	"	speech
discussion, *f.*	*dee-skü-*S_YOHNG	discussion
discuter (1)	*dee-skü-*TAY	discuss, to
disparaître (16)	*dee-spah-*REH-*tr*(*ih*)	disappear, to
disponible	*dee-spuh-*NEE-*bl*(*ih*)	available
disposé, (bien)	(*b_yang*) *dee-spoh-*ZAY	willing (favorably disposed)
disposer de (1)	*dee-spoh-*ZAY *dih*	dispose of (put away), to
disposition, *f.*	*dee-spoh-zee-*S_YOHNG	arrangement (preparation)
"	"	disposition
dispute, *f.*	*dee-*SPÜT	argument
"	"	dispute
disque, *m.*	DEESK	record (disk)
dissemblable	*dee-sahm-*BLAH-*bl*(*ih*)	unlike (*adj.*)
dissoudre, (faire) (50)	*dee-*SOO-*dr*(*ih*)	dissolve, to
distance, *f.*	*dee-*STAHNSS	distance
distinct	*dee-*STANKT	distinct
distinction, *f.*	*dee-stank-*S_YOHNG	distinction
distingué	*dee-stan-*GAY	distinguished (notable)
distinguer (1)	*dee-stan-*GAY	distinguish (differentiate), to
distraire (56)	*dee-*STREHR	distract (divert), to
distribuer (1)	*dee-stree-*BÜ_AY	distribute (allot), to
distribution, *f.*	*dee-stree-bü-*S_YOHNG	distribution
district, *m.*	*dee-*STREEKT	district (locality)
divertir (2)	*dee-vehr-*TEER	entertain (amuse), to
divertissement, *m.*	*dee-vehr-tee-*SMAHNG	entertainment
dividende, *m.*	*dee-vee-*DAHND	dividend (*bus.*)
divin	*dee-*VANG, -VEEN	divine (*adj.*)
diviser (1)	*dee-vee-*ZAY	divide, to (*arith.*)
"	"	divide (make separate), to
diviser, se	*sih dee-vee-*ZAY	divide (become separate), to
division, *f.*	*dee-vee-z_*YOHNG	division
divorce, *m.*	*dee-*VORSS	divorce (*law*)
docteur, *m.*	*duh-*KTUHR	doctor
doctrine, *f.*	*duh-*KTREEN	doctrine
document, *m.*	*duh-kü-*MAHNG	document
dodu	*duh-*DÜ	plump (chubby)
doigt, *m.*	DWAH	finger
domaine, *m.*	*duh-*MENN	field (sphere of action)
"	"	realm
dôme, *m.*	DOHM	dome (cupola)
domestique	*duh-meh-*STEEK	domestic
domestiqué	*duh-meh-stee-*KAY	tame
domestique, *m.,f.*	*duh-meh-*STEEK	servant (in a household)
dominion, *m.*	*duh-mee-n_*YOHNG	dominion (rule)
dommage, *m.*	*duh-*MAHZH	damage (injury)
dommages-intérêts, *m.pl.*	*duh-mah-zhan-tay-*REH	damages (indemnification)
donc	DOHN(K)	so (therefore, *adv.*)
"	"	then (in that case)
"	"	therefore
"	"	thus
donner (1)	*duh-*NAY	donate, to
"	"	give (bestow), to
"	"	present, to
donner droit	*duh-nay* DRWAH	entitle (give a right to), to
dont	DOHNG	whose (*rel. pron.*)
dorénavant	*duh-ray-nah-*VAHNG	hereafter (after this, *adv.*)
dormir (26)	*dor-*MEER	sleep, to
dos, *m.*	DOH	back (*anat.*)
dose, *f.*	DOHZ	dose (*med.*)
dossier, *m.*	*duh-s_*YAY	file (collection of papers)
douane, *f.*	DWANN	customhouse
double	DOO-*bl*(*ih*)	double (*adj.*)
double, *m.*	DOO-*bl*(*ih*)	duplicate (copy, *n.*)
doublure, *f.*	*doo-*BLÜR	lining
douceur, *f.*	*doo-*SUHR	sweetness
douche, *f.*	DOOSH	shower (bath)
doué	*doo-*AY	gifted (talented)
douleur, *f.*	*doo-*LUHR	pain (ache)
douloureux, -reuse	*doo-loo-*RUH, -RUHZ	painful
"	"	sore (*adj.*)
doute, *m.*	DOOT	doubt
douter (de), se (1)	*sih doo-*TAY (*dih*)	suspect (surmise), to
douter de	*doo-*TAY *dih*	doubt (be uncertain about), to
"	"	question, to
douteux, -teuse	*doo-*TUH, -TUHZ	doubtful
doux, douce	DOO, DOOSS	gentle (soothing)
"	"	sweet (pleasant tasting)
douzaine, *f.*	*doo-*ZENN	dozen
dragon, *m.*	*drah-*GOHNG	dragon
drainer (1)	*dreh-*NAY	drain (make dry), to
drame, *m.*	DRAHM	drama
drap, *m.*	DRAH	sheet (bedding)
drapeau, *m.*	*drah-*POH	flag
drogue, *f.*	DRUG	drug (medicine)
droit	DRWAH, DRWAHT	erect (*adj.*)
"	"	right (on the right, *adj.*)
"	"	straight (not crooked, *adj.*)

French	Pronunciation	English
droit,*m.*	DRWAH	law (governing code)
"	"	right (claim)
droite,*f.*	DRWAHT	right (right-hand side)
droite, à	*ah* DRWAHT	right (to the right, *adv.*)
droits de douane, *m.pl.*	*drwah dih* DWANN	customs
"	"	duty (tax)
drôle	DROHL	funny
du (see de)		
dû, due	DÜ	due
duquel, de laquelle	*dü-*KELL, *dih lah-*KELL	whose (*rel. pron.*)
dur	DÜR	hard (not soft)
"	"	harsh (severe)
"	"	rough
"	"	tough (resistant)
durcir (2)	*dür-*SEER	harden (make hard), to
durée,*f.*	*dü-*RAY	duration
durer (1)	*dü-*RAY	last (continue), to
dysenterie,*f.*	*dee-sahn-*TREE	dysentery
eau,*f.*	OH	water
eau-de-vie,*f.*	*oh-d(ih)-*VEE	brandy
ébauche,*f.*	*ay-*BOHSH	draft (sketch)
ébaucher (1)	*ay-boh-*SHAY	draft (sketch), to
éblouir (2)	*ay-bloo-*EER	dazzle, to
écarlate	*ay-kahr-*LAHT	scarlet (*adj.*)
échange,*m.*	*ay-*SHAHNZH	exchange (barter)
échanger (1)	*ay-shahn-*ZHAY	exchange (interchange), to
échantillon,*m.*	*ay-shahn-tee-*YOHNG	sample
échapper, (s') (1)	*(s)ay-shah-*PAY	escape, to
écharpe,*f.*	*ay-*SHAHRP	scarf (neck cloth)
échéance,*f.*	*ay-shay-*AHNSS	maturity (due date, *bus.*)
échec,*m.*	*ay-*SHECK	failure (lack of success)
échecs,*m.pl.*	*ay-*SHECK	chess
échelle,*f.*	*ay-*SHELL	ladder
"	"	scale
écho,*m.*	*ay-*KOH	echo
échoir (27)	*ay-*SHWAHR	mature (fall due), to
échouer (1)	*ay-*SHWAY	fail (be unsuccessful), to
éclair,*m.*	*ay-*KLEHR	flash (burst of light)
éclairer (1)	*ay-klay-*RAY	light (illuminate), to
éclairer par des exemples	*ay-klay-ray pahr day-zeh-*GZAHM-*pl(ih)*	illustrate (exemplify), to
éclaireur,*m.*	*ay-klay-*RUHR	scout (lookout)
éclaireuse, (enfant),*f.*	*(ahn-fahn) ay-klay-*RUHZ	Girl Scout
éclater (1)	*ay-klah-*TAY	burst, to
école,*f.*	*ay-*KUHL	school
école, (maison d'), *f.*	*(may-zohn d)ay-*KUHL	schoolhouse
école maternelle,*f.*	*ay-ĸuhl mah-tehr-*NELL	kindergarten
école par correspondance,*f.*	*ay-ĸuhl pahr kuh-reh-spohn-*DAHNSS	correspondence school
économe	*ay-kuh-*NUMM	economical (thrifty)
économie,*f.*	*ay-kuh-nuh-*MEE	economy (thrift)
économie politique, *f.*	*ay-kuh-nuh-mee puh-lee-*TEEK	economics
économies,*f.pl.*	*ay-kuh-nuh-*MEE	savings (money)
économiser (1)	*ay-kuh-nuh-mee-*ZAY	save (store up), to
écorce,*f.*	*ay-*KORSS	bark (of tree)
écossais	*ay-kuh-*SEH, -SEZZ	Scotch (*adj.*)
Écosse,*f.*	*ay-*KUHSS	Scotland
écouter (1)	*ay-koo-*TAY	listen (hearken), to
écran,*m.*	*ay-*KRAHNG	screen (for movies)
écraser (1)	*ay-krah-*ZAY	crush, to
écraser, s'	*say-krah-*ZAY	crash (be smashed), to
écrire (28)	*ay-*KREER	write, to
écrire,*m.*	*ay-*KREER	writing (art of writing)
écriture,*f.*	*ay-kree-*TÜR	writing (handwriting)
écrivain,*m.*	*ay-kree-*VANG	writer (author)
écrou,*m.*	*ay-*KROO	nut (*mech.*)
Écuador,*m.*	*ay-kwah-*DOR	Ecuador
écume,*f.*	*ay-*KÜM	foam
écureuil,*m.*	*ay-kü-*RUH*_y*	squirrel
écurie,*f.*	*ay-kü-*REE	stable (shelter)
édifice,*m.*	*ay-dee-*FEESS	structure (thing built)
Édimbourg,*m.*	*ay-dam-*BOOR	Edinburgh
éditeur,*m.*	*ay-dee-*TUHR	publisher

French	Pronunciation	English
édition,*f.*	*ay-dee-*S_YOHNG	edition
éducation,*f.*	*ay-dü-kah-*S_YOHNG	education (schooling process)
éduquer (1)	*ay-dü-*KAY	educate, to
effacer (1)	*ay-fah-*SAY	blot out, to
"	"	erase, to
effet,*m.*	*ay-*FEH	effect
efficace	*ay-fee-*KAHSS	effective (effectual)
"	"	efficient (producing desired results)
effondrer, s' (1)	*say-fohn-*DRAY	collapse (cave in), to
efforcer (de), s' (1)	*say-for-*SAY (*dih*)	strive (exert oneself), to
efforcer de, s'	*say-for-*SAY *dih*	endeavor, to
effort,*m.*	*ay-*FOR	effort
"	"	endeavor
"	"	strain (exertion)
effrayer (1)	*ay-freh-*YAY	frighten (make afraid), to
"	"	scare, to
effriter (1)	*ay-free-*TAY	crumble, to
effroi,*m.*	*ay-*FRWAH	dread
"	"	fright (alarm)
effroyable	*ay-frwah-*YAH-*bl(ih)*	dreadful
égal	*ay-*GAHL	equal (*adj.*)
"	"	even (level, *adj.*)
égaler (1)	*ay-gah-*LAY	match (equal), to
égarer (1)	*ay-gah-*RAY	mislay, to
égayer (1)	*ay-geh-*YAY	cheer (gladden), to
église,*f.*	*ay-*GLEEZ	church
égoïste	*ay-goh-*EEST	selfish
égoût,*m.*	*ay-*GOO	drain (conduit)
"	"	sewer
Égypte,*f.*	*ay-*ZHEEPT	Egypt
égyptien, -ne	*ay-zheep-*S_YANG, -S_YENN	Egyptian (*adj.*)
élastique	*ay-lah-*STEEK	elastic (springy)
électeur,*m.*	*ay-leh-*KTUHR	voter
élection,*f.*	*ay-leck-*S_YOHNG	election
électricité,*f.*	*ay-leck-tree-see-*TAY	electricity
électrique	*ay-leck-*TREEK	electric
électronique,*f.*	*ay-leck-truh-*NEEK	electronics
égard de, à l'	*ah lay-*GAHR *dih*	regarding (concerning)
élégant	*ay-lay-*GAHNG, -GAHNT	smart (chic)
élément,*m.*	*ay-lay-*MAHNG	element
élémentaire	*ay-lay-mahn-*TEHR	elementary (rudimentary)
éléphant,*m.*	*ay-lay-*FAHNG	elephant
élevé	*ell-*VAY	lofty (high)
élève,*m.,f.*	*ay-*LEHV	pupil (student)
élever (1)	*ell-*VAY	elevate (lift up), to
"	"	promote (raise in rank), to
élever, s'	*sell-*VAY	arise (come about), to
"	"	rise (ascend), to
éliminer (1)	*ay-lee-mee-*NAY	eliminate, to
élire (38)	*ay-*LEER	elect, to
elle	ELL	her, it, she
elle, à	*ah* ELL	hers, its (*poss. pron.*)
elle-même	*ell-*MEMM	herself, itself
elles	ELL	they
elles-mêmes	*ell-*MEMM	themselves
éloquent	*ay-luh-*KAHNG, -KAHNT	eloquent
emballer (1)	*ahm-bah-*LAY	pack (wrap), to
embarcadère,*m.*	*ahm-bahr-kah-*DEHR	dock
embarcation,*f.*	*ahm-bahr-kah-*S_YOHNG	craft (vessel)
embarras,*m.*	*ahm-bah-*RAH	embarrassment
"	"	quandary
embrasser (1)	*ahm-brah-*SAY	embrace, to
"	"	kiss, to
embrayage,*m.*	*ahm-breh-*YAHZH	clutch (automotive device)
embrouiller (1)	*ahm-broo-*YAY	confuse (mix up), to
émeraude,*f.*	*em-*ROHD	emerald
émerger (1)	*ay-mehr-*ZHAY	emerge, to
émeute,*f.*	*ay-*MUHT	riot (disturbance)
éminent	*ay-mee-*NAHNG, -NAHNT	prominent (eminent)
emmagasinage,*m.*	*ahm-mah-gah-zee-*NAHZH	storage
emmagasiner (1)	*ahm-mah-gah-zee-*NAY	store (accumulate), to
émotion,*f.*	*ay-moh-*S_YOHNG	emotion

French	Pronunciation	English
émoussé	ay-moo-SAY	blunt
"	"	dull
empêcher (1)	ahm-peh-SHAY	keep (prevent), to
"	"	prevent (stop), to
empereur, *m.*	ahm-PRUHR	emperor
empire, *m.*	ahm-PEER	empire
"	"	rule (political control)
"	"	sway (influence)
emplacement, *m.*	ahm-plah-SMAHNG	site
emploi, *m.*	ahm-PLWAH	employment (work)
"	"	job
employé, *m.*	ahm-plwah-YAY	employee
employer (1)	ahm-plwah-YAY	employ, to
"	"	use (utilize), to
empoigner (1)	ahm-pwah-N YAY	grasp (grip), to
empoisonner (1)	ahm-pwah-zuh-NAY	poison, to
emprunter (1)	ahm-pruhn-TAY	borrow, to
emprunteur, *m.*	ahm-pruhn-TUHR	borrower (*bus.*)
en	AHNG	any (*pron.*)
"	"	as (in the role of, *prep.*)
"	"	some (a quantity, *pron.*)
"	"	to (indicating destination, *prep.*)
"	"	thereof
encaisser (1)	ahn-keh-SAY	collect, to (*bus.*)
enceindre (19)	ahn-SAN-dr(*ih*)	enclose (surround), to
enchérisseur, *m.*	ahn-shay-ree-SUHR	bidder (*bus.*)
enclin à	ahn-KLANG, -KLEEN *ah*	apt to (prone to)
encore	ahn-KOR	again
"	"	else (in addition, *adj.*)
"	"	still (*adv.*)
"	"	yet (now, until now, *adv.*)
encore un	ahn-KOR-*uhng*, -*ün*	another (one more, *adj., pron.*)
encourager (1)	ahn-koo-rah-ZHAY	encourage, to
"	"	foster, to
"	"	promote (further), to
encre, *f.*	AHN-kr(*ih*)	ink
encyclopédie, *f.*	ahn-see-kluh-pay-DEE	encyclopaedia
endommager (1)	ahn-duh-mah-ZHAY	damage (injure), to
endormi	ahn-dor-MEE	asleep (sleeping)
endos, *m.*	ahn-DOH	endorsement (signature)
endosser (1)	ahn-duh-SAY	endorse (sign), to
endroit, *m.*	ahn-DRWAH	spot (place)
énergie, *f.*	ay-nehr-ZHEE	energy
enfance, *f.*	ahn-FAHNSS	childhood
enfant, *m., f.*	ahn-FAHNG	child
enfant adopté, *m.*	ahn-fahn ah-duh-PTAY	foster child
enfanter (1)	ahn-fahn-TAY	bear (give birth to), to
enfer, *m.*	ahn-FEHR	hell
enfler, s' (1)	sahn-FLAY	swell (bulge), to
enfoncer (1)	ahn-fohn-SAY	thrust (push), to
engagement, *m.*	ahn-gah-ZHMAHNG	commitment (*bus.*)
engager (1)	ahn-gah-ZHAY	employ, to
"	"	engage, to
"	"	hire, to
engin téléguidé, *m.*	ahn-zhan tay-lay-ghee-DAY	guided missile
engourdi	ahn-goor-DEE	numb
engrenage, *m.*	ahn-grih-NAHZH	gear (*mech.*)
énigme, *f.*	ay-NEE-gm(*ih*)	riddle (*n.*)
enjeu, *m.*	ahn-ZHUH	stake (thing wagered)
enlever (1)	ahn-L(*ih*)VAY	remove (take away), to
ennemi, *m.*	enn-MEE	enemy
"	"	foe
ennui, *m.*	ahn-NÜ EE	boredom
"	"	trouble (distress)
ennuyer (1)	ahn-nü ee-YAY	annoy (irk), to
"	"	bother, to
ennuyeux, -yeuse	ahn-nü ee-YUH, -YUHZ	dull (boring)
énorme	ay-NORM	enormous
"	"	huge
enregistrer (1)	ahn-rih-zhee-STRAY	record (set down), to
"	"	register, to
en retard	ahn *rih*-TAHR	behind (late, *adv.*)
"	"	late (overdue, *adj.*)
"	"	late (tardily, *adv.*)
"	"	tardy (*adv.*)

French	Pronunciation	English
enrôler (1)	ahn-roh-LAY	draft (conscript), to
enseigne, *m.*	ahn-SEN-yih	ensign (*Nav.*)
enseigner (1)	ahn-seh-N YAY	teach, to
ensemble	ahn-SAHM-bl(*ih*)	together
ensevelir (2)	ahn-sih-v(*ih*)LEER	bury (entomb), to
ensoleillé	ahn-suh-leh-YAY	sunny
ensuite	ahn-SÜ EET	afterward (later)
"		next (*adv.*)
ensuivre, s' (54)	sahn-SÜ EE-vr(*ih*)	follow (result), to
entendre (3)	ahn-TAHN-dr(*ih*)	hear, to
enterrement, *m.*	ahn-tehr-MAHNG	burial
enthousiasme, *m.*	ahn-too-z YAH-sm(*ih*)	enthusiasm
entier, -tière	ahn-T YAY, -T YEHR	entire
"	"	whole (*adj.*)
entourer (1)	ahn-too-RAY	surround (enclose), to
entraîner (1)	ahn-treh-NAY	involve (entail), to
entre	AHN-tr(*ih*)	between (*prep.*)
entrée, *f.*	ahn-TRAY	admission (right to enter)
"	"	entrance
entrepôt, *m.*	ahn-trih-POH	warehouse
entreprendre (3)	ahn-trih-PRAHN-dr(*ih*)	undertake (attempt), to
entreprise, *f.*	ahn-trih-PREEZ	enterprise
"		undertaking
entrer (1)	ahn-TRAY	enter (come or go into), to
entrer à	ahn-TRAY *ah*	enter (join), to
"	"	join (become a member of), to
entrer dans	ahn-TRAY *dahng*	enter (join), to
"	"	join (become a member of), to
entre-temps, *m.*	ahn-trih-TAHNG	meantime (*n.*)
envahir (2)	ahn-vah-EER	invade, to (*mil.*)
enveloppe, *f.*	ahn-VLUHP	envelope (folded wrapper)
envelopper (1)	ahn-v(*ih*)luh-PAY	wrap (envelop), to
envergure, *f.*	ahn-vehr-GÜR	span (spread)
envie, *f.*	ahn-VEE	envy
envier (1)	ahn-V YAY	envy, to
environ	ahn-vee-ROHNG	about (approximately)
environs, *m. pl.*	ahn-vee-ROHNG	surroundings
envoi, *m.*	ahn-VWAH	consignment (*bus.*)
"	"	shipment (goods)
envoyer (29)	ahn-vwah-YAY	send, to
épais, -se	ay-PEH, -PESS	thick (not thin)
épaisseur, *f.*	ay-peh-SUHR	thickness (dimension)
épargner (1)	ay-pahr-N YAY	spare (not harm), to
éparpiller (1)	ay-pahr-pee-YAY	scatter (strew), to
épaule, *f.*	ay-POHL	shoulder (*anat.*)
épée, *f.*	ay-PAY	sword
épeler (1)	ay-PLAY	spell, to
éperon, *m.*	ay-PROHNG	spur (spike)
épice, *f.*	ay-PEESS	spice
épicerie, *f.*	ay-pee-SREE	grocery
épidémie, *f.*	ay-pee-day-MEE	epidemic
épinards, *m. pl.*	ay-pee-NAHR	spinach
épine, *f.*	ay-PEEN	thorn
épine dorsale, *f.*	ay-peen dor-SAHL	spine (*anat.*)
épingle, *f.*	ay-PAN-gl(*ih*)	pin (sewing accessory)
épingle de sûreté, *f.*	ay-pan-glih dih sür-TAY	safety pin
éponge, *f.*	ay-POHNZH	sponge
épreuve, *f.*	ay-PRUHV	test (trial)
éprouver (1)	ay-proo-VAY	test, to
"		try, to
épuiser (1)	ay-pü ee-ZAY	exhaust (use up), to
équilibre, *m.*	ay-kee-LEE-br(*ih*)	balance (equilibrium)
équipage, *m.*	ay-kee-PAHZH	crew
équipe, *f.*	ay-KEEP	shift (crew)
"		team (in sports)
équipement, *m.*	ay-keep-MAHNG	equipment
érable, *m.*	ay-RAH-bl(*ih*)	maple (tree)
ériger (1)	ay-ree-ZHAY	erect (build), to
errer (1)	eh-RAY	roam, to
"	"	wander, to
erreur, *f.*	eh-RUHR	error
"	"	mistake

French	Pronunciation	English
erroné	*eh-ruh-*NAY	wrong (erroneous, *adj.*)
érudit,*m.*	*ay-rü-*DEE	scholar (savant)
escabeau,*m.*	*eh-skah-*BOH	stool (seat)
escalier,*m.*	*eh-skah-*L YAY	stairway
escargot,*m.*	*eh-skahr-*GOH	snail
esclavage,*m.*	*eh-sklah-*VAHZH	slavery
esclave,*m.,f.*	*eh-*SKLAHV	slave
escompter (1)	*eh-skohn-*TAY	discount, to (*bus.*)
espace,*m.*	*eh-*SPAHSS	space (area)
Espagne,*f.*	*eh-*SPAH-*n yih*	Spain
espagnol	*eh-spah-*N YULL	Spanish (*adj.*)
espèce,*f.*	*eh-*SPESS	kind (*n.*)
espérer (1)	*eh-spay-*RAY	hope, to
espion,*m.*	*eh-*SP YOHNG	spy
espionnage,*m.*	*eh-sp yuh-*NAHZH	espionage
espoir,*m.*	*eh-*SPWAHR	hope
esprit,*m.*	*eh-*SPREE	mind (intellect)
"	"	spirit
"	"	wit (humor)
esquisse,*f.*	*eh-*SKEESS	outline (general plan)
"	"	sketch (rough drawing)
essayer (1)	*ay-seh-*YAY	try (attempt), to
essence,*f.*	*ay-*SAHNSS	gasoline
essentiel, -le	*ay-sahn-*S YELL	essential (*adj.*)
essuyer (1)	*ay-sü ee-*YAY	wipe (make dry by wiping), to
est,*m.*	ESST	east
estampe,*f.*	*eh-*STAHMP	print (printed reproduction)
estimer (1)	*eh-stee-*MAY	esteem, to
"	"	estimate (calculate), to
"	"	reckon (consider), to
estomac,*m.*	*eh-stuh-*MAH	stomach
estrade,*f.*	*eh-*STRAHD	stage (dais)
estropié,*m.*	*eh-struh-*P YAY	cripple
et	AY	and
étable,*f.*	*ay-*TAH-*bl(ih)*	barn
établir (2)	*ay-tah-*BLEER	establish (prove), to
établir, s'	*say-tah-*BLEER	settle (make one's home), to
établissement,*m.*	*ay-tah-blee-*SMAHNG	establishment (firm)
étage,*m.*	*ay-*TAHZH	floor
"	"	story
étain,*m.*	*ay-*TANG	tin (metal)
étaler (1)	*ay-tah-*LAY	display (exhibit), to
étalon,*m.*	*ay-tah-*LOHNG	stallion
étancher (1)	*ay-tahn-*SHAY	quench, to
étang,*m.*	*ay-*TAHNG	pond
étape,*f.*	*ay-*TAHP	stage (period)
état,*m.*	*ay-*TAH	condition
"	"	plight (predicament)
"	"	state
États-Unis,*m.pl.*	*ay-tah-zü-*NEE	United States
été,*m.*	*ay-*TAY	summer (*n.*)
étendre (3)	*ay-*TAHN-*dr(ih)*	expand (make larger), to
"	"	extend, to
"	"	stretch (draw out), to
étendre, s'	*say-*TAHN-*dr(ih)*	lie down, to
"	"	run (extend), to
"	"	stretch (extend), to
étendre à, s'	*say-*TAHN-*drah*	reach (extend to), to
étendu	*ay-tahn-*DÜ	extensive
"	"	wide (comprehensive)
étendue,*f.*	*ay-tahn-*DÜ	area
"	"	extent (magnitude)
éternel, -le	*ay-tehr-*NELL	eternal
"	"	everlasting
éternuer (1)	*ay-tehr-*NÜ AY	sneeze, to
étinceler (1)	*ay-tan-*SLAY	glitter, to
"	"	sparkle, to
étincelle,*f.*	*ay-tan-*SELL	spark
étiquette,*f.*	*ay-tee-*KETT	etiquette
"	"	label
étoffe,*f.*	*ay-*TUFF	cloth
étoile,*f.*	*ay-*TWAHL	star (*astron.*)

French	Pronunciation	English
étonnement,*m.*	*ay-tuhn-*MAHNG	amazement
"	"	astonishment
"	"	wonder
étonner (1)	*ay-tuh-*NAY	amaze, to
"	"	astonish, to
étouffer (1)	*ay-too-*FAY	choke, to
étrange	*ay-*TRAHNZH	strange (peculiar)
étranger,*m.*	*ay-trahn-*ZHAY	foreigner
étranger, -gère	*ay-trahn-*ZHAY, -ZHEHR	foreign
étranger, à l'	*ah lay-trahn-*ZHAY	abroad (in foreign land)
être (30)	EH-*tr(ih)*	be, to
être affamé (de)	*eh-trah-fah-*MAY (*dih*)	crave (desire), to
être assis	*eh-trah-*SEE	sit (be sitting), to
être d'accord avec	*eh-trih dah-*KOR *ah-veck*	agree with, to
être debout	*eh-trih* D(*ih*)BOO	stand (be upright), to
être enclin	*eh-trahn-*KLANG, -KLEEN	tend (be apt), to
être en désaccord	*eh-trahn day-zah-*KOR	disagree (differ), to
être en pente	*eh-trahn-*PAHNT	slant (slope), to
être étendu	*eh-tray-tahn-*DÜ	lie (be prone), to
étreindre (19)	*ay-*TRAN-*dr(ih)*	embrace, to
"	"	hug, to
être reçu (a, en)	*eh-trih rih-*SÜ (*ah, ahng*)	pass (not fail in), to
étroit	*ay-*TRWAH, -TRWAHT	narrow
étude,*f.*	*ay-*TÜD	study (active learning)
étudiant,*m.*	*ay-tü-*D YAHNG	student
étudier (1)	*ay-tü-*D YAY	study, to
Europe,*f.*	*uh-*RUHP	Europe
européen, -ne	*uh-ruh-pay-*ANG, -ENN	European (*adj.*)
eux	UH	them
"	"	they
eux, à	*ah* UH	theirs
eux-mêmes	*uh-*MEMM	themselves
évaluation,*f.*	*ay-vah-lü ah-*S YOHNG	rating (evaluation)
évaluer (1)	*ay-vah-*LÜ AY	value (appraise), to
évanouir, s' (2)	*say-vah-*NWEER	fade (disappear), to
"	"	faint, to
"	"	vanish, to
évanouissement,*m.*	*ay-vah-nwee-*SMAHNG	faint (swoon, *n.*)
éveillé	*ay-veh-*YAY	awake
éveiller (1)	*ay-veh-*YAY	rouse (awaken), to
événement,*m.*	*ay-venn-*MAHNG	event (happening)
évêque,*m.*	*ay-*VECK	bishop
évidence,*f.*	*ay-vee-*DAHNSS	evidence (indication)
évident	*ay-vee-*DAHNG, -DAHNT	apparent
"	"	evident
"	"	obvious
évier,*m.*	*ay-*V YAY	sink (*n.*)
éviter (1)	*ay-vee-*TAY	avoid, to
exact	*eh-*GZAH(KT)	accurate
"	"	correct
"	"	exact (precise)
exagérer (1)	*eh-gzah-zhay-*RAY	exaggerate, to
exalter (1)	*eh-gzahl-*TAY	exalt, to
examen,*m.*	*eh-gzah-*MANG	examination
"	"	test (*educ.*)
examiner (1)	*eh-gzah-mee-*NAY	examine, to
"	"	investigate, to
excellent	*eh-kseh-*LAHNG, -LAHNT	excellent
exception,*f.*	*eh-ksehp-*S YOHNG	exception (unusual case)
excès,*m.*	*eh-*KSEH	excess
excessif, -sive	*eh-kseh-*SEEF, -SEEV	excessive
exciter (1)	*eh-ksee-*TAY	arouse, to
"	"	excite, to
exclamation,*f.*	*ex-klah-mah-*S YOHNG	exclamation (*n.*)
exclamer, (s') (1)	(*s*)*ex-klah-*MAY	exclaim, to
exclure (13)	*ex-*KLÜR	exclude, to
exclusif, -sive	*ex-klü-*ZEEF, -ZEEV	exclusive (not including)
excursion à pied,*f.*	*ex-kür-s yohng ah* P YAY	hike (march)
excuse,*f.*	*ex-*KÜZ	excuse (pretext)
excuser (1)	*ex-kü-*ZAY	excuse (pardon), to
excuser, s'	*sex-kü-*ZAY	apologize, to
exécuter (1)	*eh-gzeh-kü-*TAY	execute, to

French	Pronunciation	English
exécutif, -tive	*eh-gzeh-kü-*TEEF, -TEEV	executive (*adj.*)
exécution, *f.*	*eh-gzeh-kü-*SYOHNG	performance (action)
exemplaire, *m.*	*eh-gzahm-*PLEHR	copy (of a publication)
exemple, *m.*	*eh-*GZAHM-*pl(ih)*	example
"	"	illustration
"	"	instance
exempt	*eh-*GZAHNG, -GZAHNT	exempt (*adj.*)
exercer (1)	*eh-gzehr-*SAY	exercise (employ), to
exercice, *m.*	*eh-gzehr-*SEESS	exercise
"	"	practice (performance)
exhorter (1)	*eh-gzor-*TAY	urge (try to persuade), to
exil, *m.*	*eh-*GZEEL	exile (banishment)
exiler (1)	*eh-gzee-*LAY	banish (exile), to
existence, *f.*	*eh-gzee-*STAHNSS	existence
exister (1)	*eh-gzee-*STAY	exist, to
expédier (1)	*ex-pay-*DYAY	ship (send goods), to
expéditeur, *m.*	*ex-pay-dee-*TUHR	shipping agent
expédition, *f.*	*ex-pay-dee-*SYOHNG	expedition (journey)
expérience, *f.*	*ex-pay-*RYAHNSS	experience (conscious event)
"	"	experiment
expert, *m.*	*ex-*PEHR	expert (*n.*)
expertise, *f.*	*ex-pehr-*TEEZ	appraisal (*bus.*)
expirer (1)	*ex-pee-*RAY	expire (become void *bus.*), to
explication, *f.*	*ex-plee-kah-*SYOHNG	explanation
expliquer (1)	*ex-plee-*KAY	account for, to
"	"	explain, to
exploit, *m.*	*ex-*PLWAH	feat
explorer (1)	*ex-pluh-*RAY	explore, to
explosif, *m.*	*ex-ploh-*ZEEF	explosive (*n.*)
exportateur, *m.*	*ex-por-tah-*TUHR	exporter
exportation, *f.*	*ex-por-tah-*SYOHNG	exportation
exporter (1)	*ex-por-*TAY	export, to
exposé, *m.*	*ex-poh-*ZAY	exhibit (show)
exposer (1)	*ex-poh-*ZAY	exhibit, to
"	"	expose, to
exposition, *f.*	*ex-poh-zee-*SYOHNG	exhibition (exposition)
"	"	show (exhibit)
expression, *f.*	*ex-preh-*SYOHNG	expression
exprimer (1)	*ex-pree-*MAY	express (state), to
expulser (1)	*ex-pül-*SAY	expel (eject), to
exquis	*ex-*KEE, -KEEZ	exquisite
extension, *f.*	*ex-tahn-*SYOHNG	extension (enlargement)
extérieur	*ex-tay-*RYUHR	exterior (*adj.*)
"	"	outer
"	"	outside (*adj.*)
extraordinaire	*ex-tr(ah-)or-dee-*NEHR	extraordinary
extrême	*ex-*TREMM	extreme
"	"	utmost
fable, *f.*	FAH-*bl(ih)*	fable
fabricant, *m.*	*fah-bree-*KAHNG	manufacturer
fabrique, *f.*	*fah-*BREEK	factory
fabriquer (1)	*fah-bree-*KAY	manufacture, to
face de, en	*ahn* FAHSS *dih*	opposite (*prep.*)
facile	*fah-*SEEL	easy (not difficult)
facilité, *f.*	*fah-see-lee-*TAY	ease (effortlessness)
façon, *f.*	*fah-*SOHNG	way (manner)
façon ou d'autre, de	*dih fah-sohng oo* DOH-*tr(ih)*	somehow
facteur, *m.*	*fah-*KTUHR	factor (element)
"	"	postman
facture, *f.*	*fah-*KTÜR	bill
"	"	invoice
facultatif, -tive	*fah-kül-tah-*TEEF, -TEEV	optional
faculté, *f.*	*fah-kül-*TAY	faculty
faible	FEH-*bl(ih)*	faint (dim)
"	"	feeble
"	"	weak
faiblesse, *f.*	*feh-*BLESS	weakness
faillite, *f.*	*fah-*YEET	bankruptcy
"	"	failure (*bus.*)
faim, *f.*	FANG	hunger

French	Pronunciation	English
faire (32)	FEHR	do, to
"	"	make, to
faire allusion	*fehr ah-lü-z*YOHNG	refer (allude), to
faire attention à	*fehr ah-tahn-*SYOHNG *ah*	heed (mind), to
faire de la publicité	*fehr dih lah pü-blee-see-*TAY	advertise (sponsor advertising), to
faire des achats	*fehr day-zah-*SHAH	shop, to
faire (du) mal à	*fehr (dü)* MAHL *ah*	hurt (inflict pain upon), to
faire du mauvais sang, se	*sih fehr dü muh-veh* SAHNG	fret (worry), to
faire du ski	*fehr dü* SKEE	ski, to
faire éclore	*fehr ay-*KLOR	hatch, to
faire gicler	*fehr zhee-*KLAY	squirt, to
faire jaillir	*fehr zhah-*YEER	splash, to
faire la connaissance de	*fehr lah kuh-neh-*SAHNSS *dih*	meet (be introduced to), to
faire la cour à	*fehr lah* KOOR *ah*	woo, to
faire la cuisine	*fehr lah kü_ee-*ZEEN	cook (prepare meals) to
faire marcher	*fehr mahr-*SHAY	operate (handle), to
faire partie de	*fehr pahr-*TEE *dih*	belong (be a part of), to
faire sauter	*fehr soh-*TAY	blast (explode), to
faire taire	*fehr* TEHR	hush (make quiet), to
faire tournoyer	*fehr toor-nwah-*YAY	whirl (make revolve), to
faire une demande en mariage	*fehr ün dih-mahnd ahn mah-r*YAHZH	propose (offer marriage), to
faire un pas	*fehr uhn* PAH	step, to
faire venir	*fehr vih-*NEER	summon (send for), to
fait, *m.*	FEH(T)	fact
falaise, *f.*	*fah-*LEZZ	cliff
falloir (33)	*fah-*LWAHR	must (*v.*)
fameux, -meuse	*fah-*MUH, -MUHZ	famous
familier, -lière	*fah-mee-L*YAY, -L*YEHR*	familiar
famille, *f.*	*fah-*MEE	family
faner, se (1)	*sih fah-*NAY	fade (lose color), to
fantaisie, *f.*	*fahn-tay-*ZEE	fancy
fardeau, *m.*	*fahr-*DOH	burden (load)
farine, *f.*	*fah-*REEN	flour
fascisme, *m.*	*fah-*SHEE-*sm(ih)*	Fascism
fatal	*fah-*TAHL	fatal (fateful)
fatigué	*fah-tee-*GAY	tired
fatigue, *f.*	*fah-*TEEG	fatigue
fatiguer (1)	*fah-tee-*GAY	tire (make weary), to
fatiguer, se	*sih fah-tee-*GAY	tire (become weary), to
faucon, *m.*	*foh-*KOHNG	hawk
faute, *f.*	FOHT	blame
"	"	fault
faux, fausse	FOH, FOHSS	counterfeit (*adj.*)
"	"	false (erroneous)
faveur, *f.*	*fah-*VUHR	favor (approval)
favorable	*fah-vuh-*RAH-*bl(ih)*	favorable
favori, -te	*fah-vuh-*REE, -REET	favorite (*adj.*)
fécule, *f.*	*fay-*KÜL	starch (in food)
fédéral	*fay-day-*RAHL	federal
fée, *f.*	FAY	fairy (*n.*)
feindre (19)	FAN-*dr(ih)*	pretend (feign), to
félicité, *f.*	*fay-lee-see-*TAY	bliss
féliciter (1)	*fay-lee-see-*TAY	congratulate, to
femelle	*fih-*MELL	female (*adj.*)
femelle, *f.*	*fih-*MELL	female (*zool., n.*)
féminin	*fay-mee-*NANG, -NEEN	feminine
femme, *f.*	FAHM	wife
"	"	woman
fendre (3)	FAHN-*dr(ih)*	crack, to
"	"	split (rend), to
fenêtre, *f.*	*f(ih)*NEH-*tr(ih)*	window
fente, *f.*	FAHNT	crack (fissure)
fer, *m.*	FEHR	iron (metal)
fer à repasser électrique, *m.*	*fehr ah rih-pah-*SAY *ay-leh-*KTREEK	iron, electric
ferme	FEHRM	fast (firm)
"	"	firm
"	"	steady
ferme, *f.*	FEHRM	farm
fermer (1)	*fehr-*MAY	close, to
"	"	shut (make close), to

French	Pronunciation	English
fermer à clef	*fehr-may ah* KLAY	lock (fasten with key), to
fermeture éclair, *f.*	*fehr-mih-tür ay*-KLEHR	zipper
fermier, *m.*	*fehr*-M_YAY	farmer
féroce	*fay*-RUSS	fierce
fertile	*fehr*-TEEL	fertile
fesser (1)	*feh*-SAY	spank, to
festin, *m.*	*feh*-STANG	feast (meal)
fête, *f.*	FETT	festival
feu	FUH	late (deceased, *adj.*)
feu, *m.*	FUH	fire
feuille, *f.*	FUH_y	leaf (*bot.*)
"	"	sheet (of paper)
feutre, *m.*	FUH-*tr(ih)*	felt (*n.*)
fiançailles, *f.pl.*	*f_yahn*-SYE	engagement (betrothal)
ficelle, *f.*	*fee*-SELL	string (cord)
fidèle	*fee*-DELL	faithful (loyal)
fidélité, *f.*	*fee-day-lee*-TAY	allegiance
fier, -ère	F_YEHR	proud (taking pride in)
fier à, se	*sih* F_YAY *ah*	trust (rely on), to
fièvre, *f.*	F_YEH-*vr(ih)*	fever
fièvre jaune, *f.*	*f_yeh-vrih* ZHOH_N	yellow fever
fièvre typhoïde, *f.*	*f_yeh-vrih tee-foh*-EED	typhoid fever
figue, *f.*	FEEG	fig
figure, *f.*	*fee*-GÜR	figure (human form)
fil, *m.*	FEEL	thread (sewing thread)
"	"	yarn (fiber)
fil de fer, *m.*	*feel dih* FEHR	wire (metal thread)
filer (1)	*fee*-LAY	spin (form thread), to
filet, *m.*	*fee*-LEH	net (mesh)
fille, *f.*	FEE	daughter
fils, *m.*	FEESS	son
filtrer (1)	*feel*-TRAY	strain (filter), to
fin	FANG, FEEN	fine (very small)
"	"	shrewd
fin, *f.*	FANG	end
"	"	ending (conclusion)
final	*fee*-NAHL	final (last)
finalement	*fee-nahl*-MAHNG	finally
finances, *f.pl.*	*fee*-NAHNSS	finances
financier, -cière	*fee-nahn*-S_YAY -S_YEHR	financial
fin de semaine, *f.*	*fan dih* SMENN	weekend (*n.*)
finir (2)	*fee*-NEER	end (bring to an end), to
"	"	finish (complete), to
finlandais	*fan-lahn*-DEH, -DEZZ	Finnish (*adj.*)
Finlande, *f.*	*fan*-LAHND	Finland
flamber (1)	*flahm*-BAY	blaze (burn brightly), to
flamme, *f.*	FLAHM	flame
flanc de colline, *m.*	*flahn dih kuh*-LEEN	hillside
flâner (1)	*flah*-NAY	loaf, to
flasque	FLAHSK	limp (flaccid)
flatter (1)	*flah*-TAY	flatter, to
flèche, *f.*	FLESH	arrow
flétan, *m.*	*flay*-TAHNG	halibut
flétrir, se (2)	*sih flay*-TREER	wilt, to
"	"	wither, to
fleur, *f.*	FLUHR	blossom
"	"	flower
fleurir (2)	*fluh*-REER	bloom, to
"	"	flourish (thrive), to
flotte, *f.*	FLUHT	fleet (group of vessels)
flotter (1)	*fluh*-TAY	float (be buoyant), to
"	"	flutter (flap), to
flûte, *f.*	FLÜT	flute (*mus.*)
foi, *f.*	FWAH	faith (creed)
foie, *m.*	FWAH	liver (*anat.*)
foin, *m.*	FWANG	hay
folie, *f.*	*fuh*-LEE	folly
"	"	madness (insanity)
foncé	*fohn*-SAY	dark (in color)
"	"	deep (in color)
fonction, *f.*	*fohnk*-S_YOHNG	function
fonctionnaire, *m.*	*fohnk-s_yuh*-NEHR	official (*n.*)

French	Pronunciation	English
fonctionnement, *m.*	*fohnk-s_yuhn*-MAHNG	operation (functioning)
fond, *m.*	FOHNG	bottom
fondamental	*fohn-dah-mahn*-TAHL	fundamental
fondateur, *m.*	*fohn-dah*-TUHR	founder (*n.*)
fondation, *f.*	*fohn-dah*-S_YOHNG	establishment (founding)
fondement, *m.*	*fohn*-D(*ih*)MAHNG	foundation (base)
fonder (1)	*fohn*-DAY	base, to
"	"	establish, to
"	"	found, to
fondre (3)	FOHN-*dr(ih)*	melt (become liquid), to
fonds, *m.*	FOHNG	fund
fonds, *m.pl.*	FOHNG	funds
fontaine, *f.*	*fohn*-TENN	fountain
football, *m.*	*foo_t*-BOHL	soccer
force, *f.*	FORSS	force
forcer (1)	*for*-SAY	compel, to
"	"	force, to
force(s), *f.(pl.)*	FORSS	strength
forer (1)	*fuh*-RAY	drill (bore), to
forêt, *f.*	*fuh*-REH	forest
forger (1)	*for*-ZHAY	forge (shape), to
forgeron, *m.*	*for-zhih*-ROHNG	blacksmith
formalité, *f.*	*for-mah-lee*-TAY	formality
formation, *f.*	*for-mah*-S_YOHNG	formation (creation)
forme, *f.*	FORM	form
"	"	shape (contour)
former (1)	*for*-MAY	form (shape), to
formule, *f.*	*for*-MÜL	formula (prescribed guide)
fort	FOR, FORT	loud
"	"	stout (strong)
"	"	strong
fort, *m.*	FOR	fort
forteresse, *f.*	*for-tih*-RESS	fortress
fortifier (1)	*for-tee*-F_YAY	strengthen, to
fortune, *f.*	*for*-TÜN	fortune
fosse, *f.*	FUSS	pit (hole)
fossé, *m.*	*fuh*-SAY	ditch
fou, folle	FOO, FUHL	crazy
"	"	mad (insane)
foudre, *f.*	FOO-*dr(ih)*	lightning
fouet, *m.*	FWEH	lash
"	"	whip
fouetter (1)	*fweh*-TAY	whip (flog), to
fougère, *f.*	*foo*-ZHEHR	fern
foule, *f.*	FOOL	crowd
"	"	mob (disorderly crowd)
"	"	throng
four, *m.*	FOOR	oven
fourchette, *f.*	*foor*-SHETT	fork (eating utensil)
fourgon, *m.*	*foor*-GOHNG	van (vehicle)
fourmi, *f.*	*foor*-MEE	ant
fourneau (de cuisine), *m.*	*foor*-NOH (*dih kü_ee-*ZEEN)	stove (for cooking)
fournir (2)	*foor*-NEER	furnish, to
"	"	provide, to
"	"	supply, to
fournisseur, *m.*	*foor-nee*-SUHR	supplier (*bus.*)
fourrer (1)	*foo*-RAY	stick (thrust), to
fourrure, *f.*	*foo*-RÜR	fur
foyer, *m.*	*fwah*-YAY	hearth
fracas, *m.*	*frah*-KAH	crash (loud noise)
fracasser (1)	*frah-kah*-SAY	shatter, to
"	"	smash, to
fraction, *f.*	*frahk*-S_YOHNG	fraction (part)
fracture, *f.*	*frah*-KTÜR	fracture (*med.*)
fragile	*frah*-ZHEEL	brittle
fragment, *m.*	*frah*-GMAHNG	fragment
frais, fraîche	FREH, FRESH	chilly
"	"	cool
"	"	fresh (not stale)
frais, *m.pl.*	FREH	expense (cost)
frais de courtage, *m.pl.*	*freh dih koor*-TAHZH	brokerage (fee)
frais d'exploitation, *m.pl.*	*freh dex-plwah-tah*-S_YOHNG	operating expenses (*bus.*)
frais d'inscription, *m.pl.*	*freh dan-skreep*-S_YOHNG	tuition (school fee)

French	Pronunciation	English
frais généraux,*m. pl.*	*freh zhay-nay-*ROH	overhead (expenses, *bus.*)
fraise,*f.*	FREZZ	strawberry
framboise,*f.*	*frahm-*BWAHZ	raspberry
franc, franche	FRAHNG, FRAHNSH	frank (*adj.*)
français	*frahn-*SEH, -SEZZ	French (*adj.*)
franc de tout droit	*frahng dih too* DRWAH	duty-free
France,*f.*	FRAHNSS	France
frange,*f.*	FRAHNZH	fringe
frapper (1)	*frah-*PAY	hit, to
"	"	knock, to
"	"	rap, to
"	"	strike, to
fraude,*f.*	FROHD	fraud (deception)
frauder (1)	*froh-*DAY	cheat (defraud), to
frayer (1)	*freh-*YAY	pave (prepare), to
frein,*m.*	FRANG	brake
"	"	check
"	"	curb (restraint)
frêle	FRELL	frail (fragile)
frémir (2)	*fray-*MEER	quiver, to
"	"	shudder, to
fréquent	*fray-*KAHNG, -KAHNT	frequent
frère,*m.*	FREHR	brother
frire (34)	FREER	fry (be cooked in fat), to
frisson,*m.*	*free-*SOHNG	chill (shivering sensation)
frissonner (1)	*free-suh-*NAY	shiver (quake), to
froid	FRWAH, FRWAHD	cold (*adj.*)
froid,*m.*	FRWAH	cold (low temperature)
froideur,*f.*	*frwah-*DUHR	chill (coldness)
fromage,*m.*	*fruh-*MAHZH	cheese
froncer les sourcils (1)	*frohn-say lay soor-*SEE	frown, to
front,*m.*	FROHNG	forehead
"	"	front (battle front)
frontière,*f.*	*frohn-*T_YEHR	border
"	"	frontier
frotter (1)	*fruh-*TAY	rub, to
"	"	scrub, to
fruit,*m.*	FRÜ_EE	fruit
frustrer (1)	*frü-*STRAY	defeat (thwart), to
fuir (35)	FÜ_EER	flee (run from), to
fuite,*f.*	FÜ_EET	flight (hasty departure)
fumée,*f.*	*fü-*MAY	smoke
fumer (1)	*fü-*MAY	smoke, to
funérailles,*f.pl.*	*fü-nay-*RYE	funeral
fureur,*f.*	*fü-*RUHR	fury
"	"	rage (wrath)
furieux, -rieuse	*fü-*R_YUH, -R_YUHZ	furious
fusée,*f.*	*fü-*ZAY	rocket
fusil,*m.*	*fü-*ZEE	gun
"	"	rifle
futur	*fü-*TÜR	future (*adj.*)
gâcher (1)	*gah-*SHAY	mar (disfigure), to
gâchis,*m.*	*gah-*SHEE	mess (muddle)
gagner (1)	*gah-*N_YAY	earn (be paid), to
"	"	gain (get), to
"	"	win (be victor in), to
gai	GAY	cheerful (joyful)
"	"	gay
"	"	merry
gaine,*f.*	GHENN	girdle (corset)
galant homme,*m.*	*gah-lahn-*TUMM	gentleman
galerie,*f.*	*gahl-*REE	gallery (balcony)
Galles,*f.*	GAHL	Wales
galoches,*f.pl.*	*gah-*LUSH	galoshes
galop,*m.*	*gah-*LOH	gallop (*n.*)
gambader (1)	*gahm-bah-*DAY	skip (caper), to
gant,*m.*	GAHNG	glove
garage,*m.*	*gah-*RAHZH	garage
garant,*m.*	*gah-*RAHNG	guarantor
garantie,*f.*	*gah-rahn-*TEE	guarantee (warrant)
garantir (2)	*gah-rahn-*TEER	guarantee, to
garçon,*m.*	*gahr-*SOHNG	boy
"	"	lad
"	"	youngster
garçon (de restaurant),*m.*	*gahr-*SOHNG (*dih reh-stuh-*RAHNG)	waiter
garde,*f.*	GAHRD	guard (watcher)
garder (1)	*gahr-*DAY	keep (retain), to
garde-robe,*f.*	*gahr-*D(*ih*)RUB	wardrobe (apparel)
gardien,*m.*	*gahr-*D_YANG	keeper (guard)
gare,*f.*	GAHR	depot
"	"	station, railroad
garnison,*f.*	*gahr-nee-*ZOHNG	garrison
garniture,*f.*	*gahr-nee-*TÜR	packing (*n.*)
gaspillage,*m.*	*gah-spee-*YAHZH	waste (squandering)
gaspiller (1)	*gah-spee-*YAY	waste (squander), to
gâteau,*m.*	*gah-*TOH	cake (dessert)
gâter (1)	*gah-*TAY	spoil (mar), to
gauche	GOHSH	left (*adj.*)
gauche, (à)	(*ah*) GOHSH	left (*adv.*)
gauche,*f.*	GOHSH	left (*n.*)
gaz,*m.*	GAHZ	gas
géant,*m.*	*zhay-*AHNG	giant
gelé	*zhih-*LAY	frozen
gelée,*f.*	*zhih-*LAY	frost
"	"	jelly
geler (1)	*zhih-*LAY	freeze (turn to ice), to
gémir (2)	*zhay-*MEER	groan, to
"	"	moan, to
"	"	wail, to
gemme,*f.*	ZHEMM	gem
gencive,*f.*	*zhahn-*SEEV	gum (*anat.*)
gendre,*m.*	ZHAHN-*dr(ih)*	son-in-law
gêner (1)	*zheh-*NAY	hinder, to
général	*zhay-nay-*RAHL	general (*adj.*)
général,*m.*	*zhay-nay-*RAHL	general (officer)
génération,*f.*	*zhay-nay-rah-*S_YOHNG	generation (period of time)
généreux, -reuse	*zhay-nay-*RUH, -RUHZ	generous
Genève,*f.*	*zhih-*NEHV	Geneva
génie,*m.*	*zhay-*NEE	genius
genou,*m.*	*zhih-*NOO	knee
genre,*m.*	ZHAHN-*rih*	type (kind)
gens,*m.pl.*	ZHAHNG	people (persons)
géographie,*f.*	*zhay-uh-grah-*FEE	geography
géologie,*f.*	*zhay-uh-luh-*ZHEE	geology
gérer (1)	*zhay-*RAY	manage (administer), to
geste,*m.*	ZHEST	gesture (motion)
gilet,*m.*	*zhee-*LEH	vest
gingembre,*m.*	*zhan-*ZHAHM-*br(ih)*	ginger (spice)
giron,*m.*	*zhee-*ROHNG	lap (of seated person)
glace,*f.*	GLAHSS	ice (frozen water)
glace, (crème à la) *f.*	(*kremm ah lah*) GLAHSS	ice-cream
glacial	*glah-*S_YAHL	icy
glacière,*f.*	*glah-*S_YEHR	icebox
gland,*m.*	GLAHNG	acorn
glissant	*glee-*SAHNG, -SAHNT	slippery
glisser (1)	*glee-*SAY	glide, to
"	"	slide, to
"	"	slip, to
globe,*m.*	GLUBB	globe
gloire,*f.*	GLWAHR	glory (renown)
glossaire,*m.*	*gluh-*SEHR	glossary
golf,*m.*	GULF	golf
golfe,*m.*	GULF	gulf (large bay)
gomme à effacer,*f.*	*gum ah ay-fah-*SAY	eraser (rubber eraser)
gomme à mâcher	*gum ah mah-*SHAY	gum (chewing gum)
gorge,*f.*	GORZH	throat
goudron,*m.*	*goo-*DROHNG	tar
goût,*m.*	GOO	taste (flavor)
goûter (1)	*goo-*TAY	taste (sample), to
goutte,*f.*	GOOT	drop (droplet)
gouvernail,*m.*	*goo-vehr-*NYE	rudder (of a boat)
gouvernement,*m.*	*goo-vehr-nih-*MAHNG	government
gouverner (1)	*goo-vehr-*NAY	govern, to
"	"	rule, to
gouverneur,*m.*	*goo-vehr-*NUHR	governor
grâce,*f.*	GRAHSS	favor (kindness)
"	"	grace
"	"	pardon (*law*)

French	Pronunciation	English
gracieux, -cieuse	*grah-*S_YUH, -S_YUHZ	graceful
"	"	gracious
grade,*m.*	GRAHD	grade (relative position)
graduel, -le	*grah-*DÜ_ELL	gradual
grain,*m.*	GRANG	seed (ovule)
grain de raisin,*m.*	*gran dih ray-*ZANG	grape
graine,*f.*	GRENN	kernel
grains,*m.pl.*	GRANG	grain (cereal)
graisse,*f.*	GRESS	fat (fatty tissue, *n.*)
"	"	grease (cooking fat)
grammaire,*f.*	*grah-*MEHR	grammar
grand	GRAHNG, GRAHND	big
"	"	great
"	"	large
"	"	tall (of persons)
Grande Bretagne, *f.*	*grahnd brih-*TAH-*n_yih*	Great Britain
grandeur,*f.*	*grahn-*DUHR	greatness (eminence)
"	"	size (magnitude)
grandiose	*grahn-*D_YOHZ	grand (imposing)
grandir (2)	*grahn-*DEER	grow up (mature), to
grand-mère,*f.*	*grahn-*MEHR	grandmother
grand-père,*m.*	*grahn-*PEHR	grandfather
grand-route,*f.*	*grahn-*ROOT	highway
granit,*m.*	*grah-*NEE(T)	granite
graphique,*m.*	*grah-*FEEK	chart
"		graph
gras, -se	GRAH, GRAHSS	fat (obese)
gratte-ciel,*m.*	*graht-*S_YELL	skyscraper
gratter (1)	*grah-*TAY	scratch, to
gratuit	*grah-*TÜ_EE, -TÜ_EET	free (gratuitous)
grave	GRAHV	deep (in tone)
"	"	grave (serious)
graver (1)	*grah-*VAY	carve (cut designs), to
gravier,*m.*	*grah-*V_YAY	gravel
gravir (2)	*grah-*VEER	climb (scale), to
grec, -que	GRECK	Greek (*adj.*)
Grèce,*f.*	GRESS	Greece
grêle,*f.*	GRELL	hail (ice)
grêler (1)	*greh-*LAY	hail (precipitate hail), to
grenouille,*f.*	*grih-*NOO_*y*	frog
grève,*f.*	GREHV	strike (work stoppage)
griffe,*f.*	GREEF	claw (of animal)
grille,*f.*	GREE	grate (of furnace)
grillon,*m.*	*gree-*YOHNG	cricket (insect)
gris	GREE, GREEZ	gray
grommeler (1)	*gruh-*MLAY	grumble, to
gronder (1)	*grohn-*DAY	growl, to
"	"	scold, to
gros,*m.*	GROH	bulk (largest part)
gros, -se	GROH, GROHSS	gross (flagrant)
gros, en	*ahn* GROH	wholesale (*adj.*, *bus.*)
grosse,*f.*	GROHSS	gross (twelve dozen)
grossier, -sière	*groh-*S_YAY, S_YEHR	coarse
grossiste,*m.*,*f.*	*groh-*SEEST	wholesaler (*bus.*)
gros vent,*m.*	*groh* VAHNG	gale (wind)
groupe,*m.*	GROOP	group
Guatemala,*m.*	*gwah-tay-mah-*LAH	Guatemala
guêpe,*f.*	GHEP	wasp
guérir (2)	*gay-*REER	cure, to
"	"	heal, to
guérison,*f.*	*gay-ree-*ZOHNG	cure (healing)
guerre,*f.*	GHEHR	war
guide,*m.*	GHEED	guide (one who guides)
guitare,*f.*	*ghee-*TAHR	guitar
gymnase,*m.*	*zheem-*NAHZ	gymnasium (athletic arena)
habile	*ah-*BEEL	clever
"		smart
habiller (1)	*ah-bee-*YAY	clothe, to
"	"	dress, to
habiller, s'	*sah-bee-*YAY	dress (get dressed), to
habitant,*m.*	*ah-bee-*TAHNG	inhabitant
"	"	resident (*n.*)
habitation,*f.*	*ah-bee-tah-*S_YOHNG	dwelling

French	Pronunciation	English
habiter (1)	*ah-bee-*TAY	dwell (reside), to
"	"	inhabit, to
habitude,*f.*	*ah-bee-*TÜD	habit
habituel, -le	*ah-bee-*TÜ_ELL	usual
habituer, s' (1)	*sah-bee-*TÜ_AY	accustom oneself, to
* hache,*f.*	AHSH	axe
* hachette,*f.*	*ah-*SHETT	hatchet
* haie,*f.*	EH	hedge (bushes)
Haïti,*f.*	*ah-ee-*TEE	Haiti
* haine,*f.*	ENN	hate (hatred)
* haïr (37)	*ah-*EER	hate, to
haleine,*f.*	*ah-*LENN	breath
* haleter (1)	*ahl-*TAY	gasp, to
"	"	pant (puff), to
* hallier,*m.*	*ah-*L_YAY	thicket
* hanche,*f.*	AHNSH	hip
* hangar,*m.*	*ahn-*GAHR	shed (shelter)
* hanter (1)	*ahn-*TAY	haunt (visit often), to
* happer (1)	*ah-*PAY	snatch, to
* hardi	*ahr-*DEE	bold (courageous)
* hareng,*m.*	*ah-*RAHNG	herring
* haricot vert,*m.*	*ah-ree-koh* VEHR	bean (string bean)
harmonie,*f.*	*ahr-muh-*NEE	harmony (*mus.*)
* harnais,*m.*	*ahr-*NEH	harness
* harpe,*f.*	AHRP	harp
* hasard,*m.*	*ah-*ZAHR	accident
"		chance (fate)
* hâte,*f.*	AHT	haste
"	"	hurry
* hâter (1)	*ah-*TAY	hasten (expedite), to
"	"	quicken, to
* hâter, se (1)	*sih ah-*TAY	hasten, to
"	"	hurry, to
* haut	OH	high
"	"	tall (of things)
* haut,*m.*	OH	top (summit)
* haut, (en)	(*ahng*) OH	up (*adv.*)
* haut, en	*ahng* OH	above (overhead, *adv.*)
"	"	upstairs
"	"	upward (to a higher level, *adv.*)
* haut, plus	*plü* OH	top (highest, *adj.*)
* hautbois,*m.*	*oh-*BWAH	oboe
* hauteur,*f.*	*oh-*TUHR	height (highness)
Hawaii,*m.*	*hah-wah-*EE	Hawaii
hebdomadaire	*eh-bduh-mah-*DEHR	weekly (*adj.*)
hébreu, -braïque	*ay-*BRUH, -*brah-*EEK	Hebrew (*adj.*)
hélicoptère,*m.*	*ay-lee-kuh-*PTEHR	helicopter
Helsinki,*m.*	*ell-san-*KEE	Helsinki
hémisphère,*m.*	*ay-mee-*SFEHR	hemisphere (*geog.*)
hémorragie,*f.*	*ay-muh-rah-*ZHEE	hemorrhage
* hennir (2)	*eh-*NEER	neigh, to
herbe,*f.*	EHRB	grass
"	"	herb
hérédité,*f.*	*ay-ray-dee-*TAY	heredity
hériter de (1)	*ay-ree-*TAY *dih*	inherit, to
héritier,*m.*	*ay-ree-*T_YAY	heir
héroïne,*f.*	*ay-roh-*EEN	heroine
* héros,*m.*	*ay-*ROH	hero
hésiter (1)	*ay-zee-*TAY	hesitate, to
* hêtre,*m.*	EH-*tr*(*ih*)	beech (tree)
heure,*f.*	UHR	hour
"	"	time (hour determined by clock)
heures supplémentaires,*f.pl.*	*uhr sü-play-mahn-*TEHR	overtime (*bus.*, *n.*)
heureusement	*uh-ruh-*ZMAHNG	happily (luckily)
heureux, -reuse	*uh-*RUH, -RUHZ	fortunate
"	"	glad
"	"	happy
"	"	lucky
"	"	successful
* heurter (1)	*uhr-*TAY	ram (butt), to

* These words require the full rather than the elided form of articles, pronouns, prepositions, etc., and permit no linking in pronunciation with consonant sounds preceding them; for example, *l'*homme, but *le* héros; *un_*hôtel (*uhn noh-*TELL), but un héros (*uhng ay-*ROH).

French	Pronunciation	English
* hibou,*m.*	*ee*-BOO	owl
hier	YEHR	yesterday
hilarité,*f.*	*ee-lah-ree*-TAY	mirth
hirondelle,*f.*	*ee-rohn*-DELL	swallow (bird)
histoire,*f.*	*ee*-STWAHR	history
"	"	story (account)
histoire(s),*f.(pl.)*	*ee*-STWAHR	fuss (ado)
historique	*ee-stuh*-REEK	historical
hiver,*m.*	*ee*-VEHR	winter (*n.*)
* hollandais	*uh-lahn*-DEH, -DEZZ	Dutch (*adj.*)
* Hollande,*f.*	*uh*-LAHND	Holland
* homard,*m.*	*uh*-MAHR	lobster
homme,*m.*	UMM	man
homme d'affaires,*m.*	*umm dah*-FEHR	businessman
homme d'état,*m.*	*umm day*-TAH	statesman
Honduras,*m.*	*ohn-doo*-RAHSS	Honduras
Hongrie,*f.*	*ohn*-GREE	Hungary
honnête	*uh*-NET	honest
honnêteté,*f.*	*uh-net*-TAY	honesty
honneur,*m.*	*uh*-NUHR	honor
honoraires,*m.pl.*	*uh-nuh*-REHR	fee
honorer (1)	*uh-nuh*-RAY	honor (respect), to
* honte,*f.*	OHNT	disgrace
"	"	shame
* honteux, -teuse	*ohn*-TUH, -TUHZ	ashamed (mortified)
"	"	shameful
hôpital,*m.*	*uh-pee*-TAHL	hospital
horaire,*m.*	*uh*-REHR	schedule
"	"	timetable
horizon,*m.*	*uh-ree*-ZOHNG	horizon
horizontal	*uh-ree-zohn*-TAHL	horizontal (*adj.*)
horloge,*f.*	*or*-LUHZH	clock
horreur,*f.*	*uh*-RUHR	horror (dread)
horrible	*uh*-REE-*bl(ih)*	horrible
hostile	*uh*-STEEL	hostile
hôte,*m.*	OHT	host
hôtel,*m.*	*oh*-TELL	hotel
* houe,*f.*	OO	hoe
* houer (1)	*oo*-AY	hoe, to
huile,*f.*	Ü EEL	oil
huile d'olive,*f.*	*ü eel duh*-LEEV	olive oil
huître,*f.*	Ü EE-*tr(ih)*	oyster
humain	*ü*-MANG, -MENN	human (*adj.*)
humanité,*f.*	*ü-mah-nee*-TAY	humanity
"	"	mankind
humble	UHM-*bl(ih)*	humble (lowly)
humeur,*f.*	*ü*-MUHR	mood (humor)
"	"	temper
humide	*ü*-MEED	damp (moist)
humidité,*f.*	*ü-mee-dee*-TAY	moisture
humilité,*f.*	*ü-mee-lee*-TAY	humility
humour,*m.*	*ü*-MOOR	humor (drollery)
* hurler (1)	*ür*-LAY	howl (wail), to
"	"	shriek, to
"	"	yell, to
* hutte,*f.*	ÜT	hut
hymne,*f.*	EE-*mn(ih)*	hymn (religious song)
hypothèque,*f.*	*ee-puh*-TECK	mortgage
ici	*ee*-SEE	here (*adv.*)
idéal,*m.*	*ee-day*-AHL	ideal (*n.*)
idée,*f.*	*ee*-DAY	conception (notion)
"	"	idea
"	"	thought
identifier (1)	*ee-dahn-tee*-F YAY	identify, to
idole,*f.*	*ee*-DULL	idol
ignorance,*f.*	*ee-n yuh*-RAHNSS	ignorance
ignorant	*ee-n yuh*-RAHNG, -RAHNT	ignorant
il	EEL	he
il	EEL	it
île,*f.*	EEL	island (geog.)
illégal	*ee-lay*-GAHL	illegal
illuminer (1)	*ee-lü-mee*-NAY	illuminate, to
illusion,*f.*	*ee-lü-z* YOHNG	illusion

French	Pronunciation	English
illustration,*f.*	*ee-lü-strah*-S YOHNG	illustration (pictorial representation)
ils	EEL	they
il y a ...	*ee*-L YAH ...	ago (past, *adj.*)
image,*f.*	*ee*-MAHZH	picture (depiction)
imagination,*f.*	*ee-mah-zhee-nah*-S YOHNG	imagination
imaginer, (s') (1)	(*s*)*ee-mah-zhee*-NAY	imagine (picture mentally), to
imaginer, s'	*see-mah-zhee*-NAY	fancy (imagine), to
imiter (1)	*ee-mee*-TAY	imitate, to
immédiat	*ee-may*-D YAH, -D YAHT	immediate (instant)
immédiatement	*ee-may-d yah*-TMAHNG	immediately (instantly)
immense	*ee*-MAHNSS	immense
immonde	*ee*-MOHND	foul (filthy)
immondices,*f.pl.*	*ee-mohn*-DEESS	rubbish (litter)
immortel, -le	*ee-mor*-TELL	immortal (*adj.*)
impair	*am*-PEHR	odd (not even)
imparfait	*am-pahr*-FEH, -FETT	imperfect (defective)
impartialement	*am-pahr-s yahl*-MAHNG	fairly (impartially)
impatience,*f.*	*am-pah*-S YAHNSS	impatience
impatient	*am-pah*-S YAHNG, -S YAHNT	impatient
impayé	*am-peh*-YAY	unpaid (due)
impératrice,*f.*	*am-pay-rah*-TREESS	empress
impérial	*am-pay*-R YAHL	imperial
imperméable	*am-pehr-may*-AH-*bl(ih)*	waterproof
imperméable,*m.*	*am-pehr-may*-AH-*bl(ih)*	raincoat
impoli	*am-puh*-LEE	rude (impolite)
importance,*f.*	*am-por*-TAHNSS	importance
"	"	significance
important	*am-por*-TAHNG, -TAHNT	important
importateur,*m.*	*am-por-tah*-TUHR	importer
importation,*f.*	*am-por-tah*-S YOHNG	importation
importer (1)	*am-por*-TAY	import, to (bus.)
importuner (1)	*am-por-tü*-NAY	pester, to
imposer (1)	*am-poh*-ZAY	assess (impose tax), to
"	"	impose (inflict), to
impossibilité,*f.*	*am-puh-see-bee-lee*-TAY	impossibility
impossible	*am-puh*-SEE-*bl(ih)*	impossible
impôt,*m.*	*am*-POH	tax (*n.*)
impôt sur le revenu,*m.*	*am-poh sür lih rih*-VNÜ	income tax
impression,*f.*	*am-preh*-S YOHNG	impression (effect)
impressionner (1)	*am-preh-s yuh*-NAY	impress (affect deeply), to
imprimer (1)	*am-pree*-MAY	print, to
imprimeur,*m.*	*am-pree*-MUHR	printer
impulsion,*f.*	*am-pül*-S YOHNG	impulse (sudden incitement)
impur	*am*-PÜR	impure
imputer (1)	*am-pü*-TAY	charge (debit), to
inadéquat	*ee-nah-day*-KWAH, -KWAHT	inadequate
inadvertence,*f.*	*ee-nah-dvehr*-TAHNSS	oversight (error)
inattendu	*ee-nah-tahn*-DÜ	unexpected (*adj.*)
incident,*m.*	*an-see*-DAHNG	incident (event)
inclination,*f.*	*an-klee-nah*-S YOHNG	inclination (tendency)
incliner (1)	*an-klee*-NAY	incline (tend), to
incliner, s'	*san-klee*-NAY	bow (in greeting), to
incliner la tête	*an-klee-nay lah* TETT	nod, to
inclure (13)	*an*-KLÜR	enclose (include in envelope), to
inconnu	*an-kuh*-NÜ	unknown
inconnu,*m.*	*an-kuh*-NÜ	stranger (unknown person)
inconvénient,*m.*	*an-kohn-vay*-N YAHNG	inconvenience
Inde,*f.*	AND	India
indemnité,*f.*	*an-dem-nee*-TAY	indemnity (compensation)
indépendance,*f.*	*an-day-pahn*-DAHNSS	independence
indépendant	*an-day-pahn*-DAHNG, -DAHNT	independent
index,*m.*	*an*-DEX	index (list)
indication,*f.*	*an-dee-kah*-S YOHNG	hint (inkling)
Indien,*m.*	*an*-D YANG	Indian, American
indifférent	*an-dee-fay*-RAHNG, -RAHNT	indifferent (unconcerned)
indigestion,*f.*	*an-dee-zheh*-ST YOHNG	indigestion
indignation,*f.*	*an-dee-n yah*-S YOHNG	indignation
indigne	*an*-DEE-*n yih*	unworthy
indiquer (1)	*an-dee*-KAY	indicate, to
"	"	point, to

* These words require the full rather than the elided form of articles, pronouns, prepositions, etc., and permit no linking in pronunciation with consonant sounds preceding them; for example, *l'*homme, but *le* héros; un hôtel (*uhn noh*-TELL), but un héros (*uhng ay*-ROH).

French	Pronunciation	English
indirect	*an-dee-*RECKT	indirect
individu, *m.*	*an-dee-vee-*DÜ	individual (person, *n.*)
indubitablement	*an-dü-bee-tah-blih-*MAHNG	undoubtedly
industrie, *f.*	*an-dü-*STREE	industry (trade)
industriel, -le	*an-dü-stree-*YELL	industrial
industrieux, -ieuse	*an-dü-stree-*YUH, -YUHZ	industrious
inégal	*ee-nay-*GAHL	unequal
inévitable	*ee-nay-vee-*TAH-*bl(ih)*	inevitable (*adj.*)
inexact	*ee-neh-*GZAH(KT)	inaccurate
"	"	incorrect
infection, *f.*	*ahn-feck-*S YOHNG	infection
inférieur	*an-fay-*R YUHR	inferior (mediocre)
infidèle	*an-fee-*DELL	false (deceitful)
infini	*an-fee-*NEE	infinite
infirmière, *f.*	*an-feer-*M YEHR	nurse (medical assistant)
inflammation, *f.*	*an-flah-mah-*S YOHNG	inflammation
inflation, *f.*	*an-flah-*S YOHNG	inflation (*econ.*)
influence, *f.*	*an-flü-*AHNSS	influence
influenza, *f.*	*an-flü-ahn-*ZAH	influenza
influer sur (1)	*an-flü-*AY *sür*	affect (influence), to
informations, *f.pl.*	*an-for-mah-*S YOHNG	information
informer (1)	*an-for-*MAY	acquaint, to
"	"	inform (apprise), to
informer sur, s'	*san-for-*MAY *sür*	ask about, to
ingénieur, *m.*	*an-zhay-*N YUHR	engineer (professional engineer)
inhabituel, -le	*ee-nah-bee-*TÜ ELL	unusual
initial	*ee-nee-*S YAHL	initial (first, *adj.*)
initiale, *f.*	*ee-nee-*S YAHL	initial (letter)
injuste	*an-*ZHÜST	unjust (prejudiced)
injustice, *f.*	*an-zhü-*STEESS	injustice
innocent	*ee-nuh-*SAHNG, -SAHNT	innocent (guiltless)
inondation, *f.*	*ee-nohn-dah-*S YOHNG	flood
inquiet, -quiète	*an-*K YEH, -K YETT	anxious
"	"	uneasy
inquiéter (1)	*an-k yay-*TAY	trouble (disquiet), to
inquiéter, s'	*san-k yay-*TAY	worry (feel anxious), to
inquiétude, *f.*	*an-k yay-*TÜD	worry (anxiety)
inscription, *f.*	*an-skreep-*S YOHNG	inscription
inscrire (28)	*an-*SKREER	enter (make record of), to
insecte, *m.*	*an-*SECKT	bug
"	"	insect
insérer (1)	*an-say-*RAY	insert, to
insignifiant	*an-see-n yee-*F YAHNG, -F YAHNT	insignificant (trivial)
insister	*an-see-*STAY	insist, to
insolvabilité, *f.*	*an-sull-vah-bee-lee-*TAY	insolvency (*bus.*)
inspecter (1)	*an-speh-*KTAY	inspect, to
inspection, *f.*	*an-speck-*S YOHNG	inspection (scrutiny)
"	"	survey
inspiration, *f.*	*an-spee-rah-*S YOHNG	inspiration
inspirer (1)	*an-spee-*RAY	inspire, to
installer (1)	*an-stah-*LAY	install (set up for use), to
instant, *m.*	*an-*STAHNG	instant (*n.*)
instinct, *m.*	*an-*STANG	instinct
institut, *m.*	*an-stee-*TÜ	institute
instituteur, *m.*	*an-stee-tü-*TUHR	teacher
institution, *f.*	*an-stee-tü-*S YOHNG	institution (establishment)
instruction, *f.*	*an-strük-*S YOHNG	instruction (teaching)
"	"	schooling
"	"	training
instruire (14)	*an-*STRÜ EER	coach (train), to
"	"	instruct (teach), to
instrument, *m.*	*an-strü-*MAHNG	instrument (implement)
insuffisant	*an-sü-fee-*ZAHNG, -ZAHNT	insufficient
insulte, *f.*	*an-*SÜLT	insult
intellectuel, -le	*an-teh-leck-*TÜ ELL	intellectual (*adj.*)
intelligence, *f.*	*an-teh-lee-*ZHAHNSS	intelligence (understanding)
intelligent	*an-teh-lee-*ZHAHNG, -ZHAHNT	intelligent
intense	*an-*TAHNSS	intense
intention, *f.*	*an-tahn-*S YOHNG	intention
intentionnel, -le	*an-tahn-s yuh-*NELL	deliberate (intentional)
intéressant	*an-tay-reh-*SAHNG, -SAHNT	interesting

French	Pronunciation	English
intéresser (1)	*an-tay-reh-*SAY	interest, to
intérêt, *m.*	*an-tay-*REH	interest
intérêts composés, *m.pl.*	*an-tay-reh kohm-poh-*ZAY	compound interest
intérieur	*an-tay-*R YUHR	inner
"	"	internal
intérieur, *m.*	*an-tay-*R YUHR	interior (inside, *n.*)
intérieur, (d')	*(d)an-tay-*R YUHR	inside (inner, *adj.*)
intérieur, à l'	*ah lan-tay-*R YUHR	within (on the inside, *adv.*)
intérieur de, à l'	*ah lan-tay-*R YUHR *dih*	inside (within, *prep.*)
international	*an-tehr-nah-s yuh-*NAHL	international
interpréter (1)	*an-tehr-pray-*TAY	interpret (explain), to
interroger (1)	*an-tay-ruh-*ZHAY	question (query), to
interrompre (52)	*an-tay-*ROHM-*pr(ih)*	interrupt, to
interrupteur, *m.*	*an-tay-rü-*PTUHR	switch (*elec.*)
intervalle, *m.*	*an-tehr-*VAHL	interval (period of time)
interview, *f.*	*an-tehr-*V YOO	interview
intestins, *m.pl.*	*an-teh-*STANG	bowels (*anat.*)
intime	*an-*TEEM	close
"	"	intimate (personal)
intitulé, *m.*	*an-tee-tü-*LAY	heading (title)
introduction, *f.*	*an-truh-dük-*S YOHNG	introduction (preliminary part)
introduire (14)	*an-truh-*DÜ EER	introduce (bring in), to
intuition, *f.*	*an-tü ee-*S YOHNG	intuition
inutile	*ee-nü-*TEEL	needless
"	"	unnecessary
"	"	useless
inventaire, *m.*	*an-vahn-*TEHR	inventory (*bus.*)
inventer (1)	*an-vahn-*TAY	devise (contrive), to
"	"	invent, to
invention, *f.*	*an-vahn-*S YOHNG	invention
investigation, *f.*	*an-veh-stee-gah-*S YOHNG	investigation
invisible	*an-vee-*ZEE-*bl(ih)*	invisible
invitation, *f.*	*an-vee-tah-*S YOHNG	invitation
invité, *m.*	*an-vee-*TAY	guest (visitor)
inviter (1)	*an-vee-*TAY	invite, to
invités, *m.pl.*	*an-vee-*TAY	company (guests)
irlandais	*eer-lahn-*DEH, -DEZZ	Irish (*adj.*)
Irlande, *f.*	*eer-*LAHND	Ireland
irréfléchi	*ee-ray-flay-*SHEE	hasty (rash)
irrégulier, -lière	*ee-ray-gü-*L YAY, -L YEHR	irregular
irrigation, *f.*	*ee-ree-gah-*S YOHNG	irrigation
irriter (1)	*ee-ree-*TAY	irritate (annoy), to
Israël, *m.*	*ee-srah-*ELL	Israel
israéli	*ee-srah-ay-*LEE	Israeli (*adj.*)
issue, *f.*	*ee-*SÜ	outlet (exit)
isthme, *m.*	EE-*sm(ih)*	isthmus
Italie, *f.*	*ee-tah-*LEE	Italy
italien, -ne	*ee-tah-*L YANG, -L YENN	Italian (*adj.*)
ivoire, *m.*	*ee-*VWAHR	ivory
ivre	EE-*vr(ih)*	drunk (intoxicated)
ivresse, *f.*	*ee-*VRESS	intoxication (drunkenness)
jaloux, -louse	*zhah-*LOO, -LOOZ	jealous
jamais	*zhah-*MEH	ever (at any time)
"	"	never
jamais, à	*ah zhah-*MEH	forever
jambe, *f.*	ZHAHMB	leg (*anat.*)
jambon, *m.*	*zhahm-*BOHNG	ham (food)
Japon, *m.*	*zhah-*POHNG	Japan
japonais	*zhah-puh-*NEH, -NEZZ	Japanese (*adj.*)
jaquette, *f.*	*zhah-*KETT	jacket (short coat)
jardin, *m.*	*zhahr-*DANG	garden
jardinier, *m.*	*zhahr-dee-*N YAY	gardener
jardin zoologique, *m.*	*zhahr-dan zuh-luh-*ZHEEK	zoo
jarretière, *f.*	*zhahr-*T YEHR	garter
jaune	ZHOH N	yellow (*adj.*)
jazz, *m.*	JAZZ	jazz
je	ZHIH	I
Jérusalem, *f.*	*zhay-rü-zah-*LEMM	Jerusalem
Jésus	*zhay-*ZÜ	Jesus
jeter (1)	*zhih-*TAY	fling, to
"	"	shed (cast off), to
"	"	toss, to
"	"	throw, to
jeter un coup d'oeil (1)	*zhih-tay uhn koo* DUH *y*	glance, to

French	Pronunciation	English
jeu, *m.*	ZHUH	game (contest)
jeu (de cartes), *m.*	ZHUH (*dih* KAHRT)	deck (of cards)
jeune	ZHUH_N	young (*adj.*)
"	"	youthful
jeune fille, *f.*	*zhuh_n* FEE	girl
"	"	lass
"	"	maiden
jeune homme, *m.*	*zhuh*-NUMM	youth (young man)
jeunesse, *f.*	*zhuh*-NESS	youth (period of life)
"	"	youthfulness
joie, *f.*	ZHWAH	delight
"	"	gladness
"	"	joy
joindre (19)	ZHWAN-*dr*(*ih*)	connect (link), to
"	"	join (bring together), to
joindre, se	*sih* ZHWAN-*dr*(*ih*)	connect (be joined), to
joli	*zhuh*-LEE	pretty
joue, *f.*	ZHOO	cheek
jouer (1)	*zhoo*-AY	play (engage in recreation), to
"	"	play (take the role of), to
jouer de	*zhoo*-AY *dih*	play (perform music upon), to
jouet, *m.*	ZHWEH	toy
joueur, *m.*	*zhoo*-UHR	player (in a game)
joug, *m.*	ZHOO	yoke (wooden frame)
jouir de (2)	ZHWEER *dih*	enjoy (derive joy from), to
jour, *m.*	ZHOOR	day (24-hour period)
"	"	daylight
jour de l'an, *m.*	*zhoor dih* LAHNG	New Year's Day
jour férié, *m.*	*zhoor feh*-R_YAY	holiday
journal, *m.*	*zhoor*-NAHL	journal (magazine)
"		newspaper
journée, *f.*	*zhoor*-NAY	day (daytime)
jovial	*zhuh*-V_YAHL	jolly (*adj.*)
joyeux, -yeuse	*zhwah*-YUH, -YUHZ	joyful
juge, *m.*	ZHÜZH	judge
jugement, *m.*	*zhü*-ZHMAHNG	judgment
juger (1)	*zhü*-ZHAY	deem (regard), to
"	"	judge, to
Juif, *m.*	ZHÜ_EEF	Jew (*n.*)
juif, -ive	ZHÜ_EEF, -EEV	Jewish (*adj.*)
jumeau, *m.*	*zhü*-MOH	twin (*n.*)
jument, *f.*	*zhü*-MAHNG	mare
jupe, *f.*	ZHÜP	skirt (garment)
jupon, *m.*	*zhü*-POHNG	petticoat
"	"	slip
jurer (1)	*zhü*-RAY	curse, to
"	"	swear, to
jury, *m.*	*zhü*-REE	jury
jus, *m.*	ZHÜ	juice
jusqu'à	ZHÜ-SKAH	until (up to the time of, *prep.*)
jusqu'à ce que	ZHÜ-SKAH-SKIH	until (*conj.*)
jusqu'ici	*zhü*-skee-SEE	hitherto (thus far)
juste	ZHÜST	fair (impartial)
"	"	just (equitable, *adj.*)
"	"	tight (close-fitting)
justice, *f.*	*zhü*-STEESS	justice
justifier (1)	*zhü*-stee-F_YAY	justify, to
"	"	warrant, to
Karachi, *m.*	*kah-rah*-SHEE	Karachi
kiosque à journaux, *m.*	*k_yussk ah zhoor*-NOH	newsstand
la	LAH	her
"	"	it
"	"	per (for each)
"	"	the
là	LAH	there (at that place)
là, de	*dih* LAH	hence (consequently)
labeur, *m.*	*lah*-BUHR	labor (exertion)
laboratoire, *m.*	*lah-buh-rah*-TWAHR	laboratory
labourer (1)	*lah-boo*-RAY	plow, to
"	"	till (cultivate), to
lac, *m.*	LAHK	lake
lacet, *m.*	*lah*-SEH	lace (shoelace)
lâche, *m.*, *f.*	LAHSH	coward
lâcher (1)	*lah*-SHAY	drop (let fall), to
"	"	release (let go of), to
laid	LEH, LED	ugly
laine, *f.*	LENN	wool
laisser (1)	*leh*-SAY	leave (let remain), to
"	"	let (permit), to
laisser passer	*leh-say pah*-SAY	admit (permit to enter), to
lait, *m.*	LEH	milk
laiterie, *f.*	*leh*-TREE	dairy
laiton, *m.*	*leh*-TOHNG	brass (metal, *n.*)
laitue, *f.*	*lay*-TÜ	lettuce
lame, *f.*	LAHM	blade (cutting tool)
lame de rasoir, *f.*	*lahm dih rah*-ZWAHR	razor blade
lampe, *f.*	LAHMP	lamp
lampe de poche, *f.*	*lahmp dih* PUHSH	flashlight
lance, *f.*	LAHNSS	spear (weapon)
lancer (1)	*lahn*-SAY	cast (throw), to
"	"	hurl, to
"	"	launch, to
"	"	pitch (throw), to
lande, *f.*	LAHND	moor (waste land)
langue, *f.*	LAHN_G	language
"	"	tongue (*anat.*)
lanterne, *f.*	*lahn*-TEHRN	lantern
lapin, *m.*	*lah*-PANG	rabbit
laquelle (see lequel)		
laquelle, de (see duquel)		
lard, *m.*	LAHR	bacon
large	LAHRZH	broad
"	"	wide
largeur, *f.*	*lahr*-ZHUHR	breadth
"	"	width
larme, *f.*	LAHRM	tear (teardrop)
las, -se	LAH, LAHSS	weary
latin	*lah*-TANG, -TEEN	Latin (*adj.*)
lavement, *m.*	*lah*-VMAHNG	enema
laver (1)	*lah*-VAY	wash (cleanse), to
laver, se	*sih lah*-VAY	wash (cleanse oneself), to
le	LIH	him, it
"	"	per (for each)
"	"	the
Le Caire, *m.*	*lih* KEHR	Cairo
lécher (1)	*lay*-SHAY	lick (lap), to
leçon, *f.*	*lih*-SOHNG	lesson
lecteur, *m.*	*leh*-KTUHR	reader
légal	*lay*-GAHL	lawful
"	"	legal
légende, *f.*	*lay*-ZHAHND	legend (story)
léger, -gère	*lay*-ZHAY, -ZHEHR	light (of little weight)
"	"	slight (*adj.*)
législation, *f.*	*lay-zhee-slah*-S_YOHNG	legislation
législature, *f.*	*lay-zhee-slah*-TÜR	legislature
légume, *m.*	*lay*-GÜM	vegetable
lendemain, *m.*	*lahn*-D(*ih*)MANG	morrow
lent	LAHNG	slow (not fast)
léopard, *m.*	*lay-uh*-PAHR	leopard
lèpre, *f.*	LEH-*pr*(*ih*)	leprosy
lequel, laquelle	*lih*-KELL, *lah*-KELL	that (*rel. pron.*)
"	"	which (*interrog., rel. pron.*)
les	LAY	the
"	"	them
lesquels, lesquelles	*lay*-KELL	that (*rel. pron.*)
"	"	which (*interrog., rel. pron.*)
lessive, *f.*	*leh*-SEEV	laundry (articles laundered)
lettre, *f.*	LEH-*tr*(*ih*)	letter
leur	LUHR	their
"	"	(to) them
leur, le (la)	*lih* (*lah*) LUHR	theirs
leurs	LUHR	their
leurs, les	*lay* LUHR	theirs

French	Pronunciation	English	French	Pronunciation	English
levain, *m.*	*lih*-VANG	yeast	lointain	*lwan*-TANG, -TENN	distant
lever (1)	*lih*-VAY	lift, to	"	"	far (*adj.*)
"	"	raise, to			remote (far-off)
lever, se	*sih* L(*ih*)VAY	rise, to	lointain, plus	*plü lwan*-TANG, -TENN	farther (*adj.*)
"	"	stand up, to	loisir, *m.*	*lwah*-ZEER	leisure
lever du soleil, *m.*	*lih-vay dü suh*-LAY	sunrise	Londres, *m.*	LOHN-*dr*(*ih*)	London
			long, -ue	LOHNG, LOHN_G	long
levier, *m.*	*lih*-V_YAY	lever	long de, le	*lih* LOHNG *dih*	along (lengthwise of)
lèvre, *f.*	LEH-*vr*(*ih*)	lip (*anat.*)	longueur, *f.*	*lohn*-GUHR	length
libéral	*lee-bay*-RAHL	liberal (*polit., adj.*)	loquet, *m.*	*luh*-KEH	latch
libérer (1)	*lee-bay*-RAY	free, to	lorsque	LOR-SKIH	when (at the time
"	"	liberate, to			that, *conj.*)
liberté, *f.*	*lee-behr*-TAY	freedom	louange, *f.*	*loo*-AHNZH	praise
"	"	liberty	louer (1)	*loo*-AY	lease, to
libre	LEE-*br*(*ih*)	free (independent)	"	"	praise, to
"	"	vacant (untenanted)	"	"	rent, to
			loup, *m.*	LOO	wolf
lien, *m.*	L_YANG	bond	lourd	LOOR, LOORD	heavy
"	"	link (connecting part)	loyal	*lwah*-YAHL	loyal
"	"	tie	loyauté, *f.*	*lwah-yoh*-TAY	loyalty
lier (1)	*lee*-YAY	bind, to	loyer, *m.*	*lwah*-YAY	rent (payment)
"	"	lash (fasten), to	luge, *f.*	LÜZH	sled
"	"	tie, to	lugubre	*lü*-GÜ-*br*(*ih*)	gloomy (melancholy)
lierre, *m.*	L_YEHR	ivy	lui	LÜ_EE	he
lieu, *m.*	L_YUH	place (locality)	"	"	(to) her
"	"	stead	"	"	(to) him
lieu de, au	*oh* L_YUH *dih*	instead of	"	"	(to) it
lieutenant, *m.*	*l_yuh*-T(*ih*)NAHNG	lieutenant	lui, à	*ah* LÜ_EE	his, its (*poss. pron.*)
lièvre, *m.*	L_YEH-*vr*(*ih*)	hare	lui-même	*lü_ee*-MEMM	himself, itself
ligne, *f.*	LEE-*n_yih*	line	luire (14)	LÜ_EER	gleam (shine), to
ligne de conduite, *f.*	*lee-n_yih dih kohn-dü_EET*	policy (course)	lumière, *f.*	*lü*-M_YEHR	light (illumination)
ligue, *f.*	LEEG	league	lumière du soleil, *f.*	*lü-m_yehr dü suh*-LAY	sunlight
lilas, *m.*	*lee*-LAH	lilac (flower)	lune, *f.*	LÜN	moon
Lima, *f.*	*lee*-MAH	Lima	lunettes, *f.pl.*	*lü*-NETT	glasses
lime, *f.*	LEEM	file (tool)	"	"	spectacles
"	"	lime (fruit)	lunettes de soleil, *f.pl.*	*lü-nett dih suh*-LAY	sunglasses
limite, *f.*	*lee*-MEET	boundary	lustre, *m.*	LÜ-*str*(*ih*)	luster (sheen)
"	"	limit	lutte, *f.*	LÜT	struggle (great effort)
limiter (1)	*lee-mee*-TAY	confine, to	lutter (1)	*lü*-TAY	wrestle, to
"	"	limit, to	luxe, *m.*	LÜX	luxury
lin, *m.*	LANG	flax	luxure, *f.*	*lü*-KSÜR	lust (desire)
linoléum, *m.*	*lee-nuh-lay*-UMM	linoleum	lycée, *m.*	*lee*-SAY	high school
lion, *m.*	L_YOHNG	lion	M.; Monsieur, *m.* (*pl.* MM.; Messieurs)	*mih*-S_YUH (*may*-S_YUH)	Mr. (Mister)
liqueur, *f.*	*lee*-KUHR	liqueur	ma	MAH	my
liquide, *m.*	*lee*-KEED	liquid (*n.*)	mâcher (1)	*mah*-SHAY	chew, to
lire (38)	LEER	read, to	machine, *f.*	*mah*-SHEEN	machine
lis, *m.*	LEESS	lily	machine à coudre, *f.*	*mah-sheen ah* KOO-*dr*(*ih*)	sewing machine
lisse	LEESS	smooth (*adj.*)	machine à écrire, *f.*	*mah-sheen ah ay*-KREER	typewriter
liste, *f.*	LEEST	list	machinerie, *f.*	*mah-sheen*-REE	machinery
lit, *m.*	LEE	bed	mâchoire, *f.*	*mah*-SHWAHR	jaw
lit de camp, *m.*	*lee dih* KAHNG	cot (bed)	maçon, *m.*	*mah*-SOHNG	mason (stonelayer)
lithographie, *f.*	*lee-tuh-grah*-FEE	lithography	Madrid, *m.*	*mah*-DREED	Madrid
litige, *m.*	*lee*-TEEZH	litigation	magasin, (grand), *m.*	(*grahn*) *mah-gah*-ZANG	department store
littéraire	*lee-tay*-REHR	literary	magicien, *m.*	*mah-zhee*-S_YANG	magician
littérature, *f.*	*lee-tay-rah*-TÜR	literature (belles-lettres)	magie, *f.*	*mah*-ZHEE	magic (*n.*)
livraison, *f.*	*lee-vray*-ZOHNG	delivery (handing over)	magnétophone, *m.*	*mah-n_yeh-tuh*-FUN	tape recorder
livre, *m.*	LEE-*vr*(*ih*)	book	magnifique	*mah-n_yee*-FEEK	magnificent
livrer (1)	*lee*-VRAY	deliver (hand over), to	maigre	MEH-*gr*(*ih*)	lean
livret, *m.*	*lee*-VREH	booklet	"	"	thin (not fat)
local	*luh*-KAHL	local (regional)	maillot de bain, *m.*	*mah-yoh d*(*ih*) BANG	bathing suit
localité, *f.*	*luh-kah-lee*-TAY	locality (place)	main, *f.*	MANG	hand (*anat.*)
locataire, *m.,f.*	*luh-kah*-TEHR	tenant	maintenant	*man*-T(*ih*)NAHNG	now (*adv.*)
locomotive, *f.*	*luh-kuh-muh*-TEEV	engine (locomotive)	maintenir (55)	*man*-T(*ih*)NEER	argue, to
"	"	locomotive	"	"	assert (declare), to
locution (de phrase), *f.*	*luh-kü*-S_YOHNG (*dih* FRAHZ)	phrase (*gram.*)	"	"	maintain, to
logement, *m.*	*luh*-ZHMAHNG	lodging (temporary quarters)	maire, *m.*	MEHR	mayor
loger (1)	*luh*-ZHAY	accommodate (have room for), to	mais	MEH	but (yet, *conj.*)
loi, *f.*	LWAH	law (statute)	maïs, *m.*	*mah*-EESS	corn (maize)
loin	LWANG	away (from a place, *adv.*)	maison, *f.*	*may*-ZOHNG	concern
"	"	far (afar, *adv.*)	"	"	firm
loin, plus	*plü* LWANG	farther (*adv.*)	"	"	house
			maisonnette, *f.*	*may-zuh*-NETT	lodge (cabin)
			maître, *m.*	MEH-*tr*(*ih*)	master
			maîtresse, *f.*	*may*-TRESS	mistress (paramour)
			maîtriser (1)	*meh-tree*-ZAY	master (learn), to
			majesté, *f.*	*mah-zheh*-STAY	majesty

French	Pronunciation	English
majeur	*mah*-ZHUHR	major (larger)
majorité,*f.*	*mah-zhuh-ree*-TAY	majority (greater number)
mal	MAHL	wrong (*adj., adv.*)
mal,*m.*	MAHL	ache
"	"	evil (*n.*)
"	"	mischief (harm)
"	"	wrong (injustice)
malade	*mah*-LAHD	ill
"	"	sick (ailing)
malade,*m.,f.*	*mah*-LAHD	patient (invalid)
maladie,*f.*	*mah-lah*-DEE	disease
"	"	illness
"	"	sickness
maladroit	*mah-lah*-DRWAH, -DRWAHT	awkward
malchanceux, -ceuse	*mahl-shahn*-SUH, -SUHZ	unlucky
mal de dents,*m.*	*mahl dih* DAHNG	toothache
mal de gorge,*m.*	*mahl dih* GORZH	sore throat
mal d'oreille,*m.*	*mahl duh*-RAY	earache
mal de tête,*m.*	*mahl dih* TETT	headache
mâle	MAHL	male (*adj.*)
malédiction,*f.*	*mah-lay-deek*-S_YOHNG	curse
malgré	*mahl*-GRAY	despite (*prep.*)
malheur,*m.*	*mah*-LUHR	misfortune
"		woe
malheureux, -reuse	*mah-luh*-RUH, -RUHZ	miserable
"	"	unfortunate
"	"	unhappy (sorrowful)
malice,*f.*	*mah*-LEESS	malice
malle,*f.*	MAHL	trunk (baggage)
malveillance,*f.*	*mahl-veh*-YAHNSS	spite (ill will)
manche,*f.*	MAHNSH	sleeve
manche,*m.*	MAHNSH	handle
manchette,*f.*	*mahn*-SHETT	cuff (of sleeve)
mandat,*m.*	*mahn*-DAH	money order
manger (1)	*mahn*-ZHAY	eat, to
manie,*f.*	*mah*-NEE	craze (fad)
manière,*f.*	*mah*-N_YEHR	manner (mode)
manières,*f.pl.*	*mah*-N_YEHR	manners (polite behavior)
manifeste	*mah-nee*-FEST	manifest (*adj.*)
manoeuvre,*m.*	*mah*-NUH-*vr(ih)*	laborer
manque,*m.*	MAHNK	lack (deficiency)
"	"	shortage
"	"	want
manquement,*m.*	*mahnk*-MAHNG	failure (neglect)
manquer de (1)	*mahn*-KAY *dih*	fail (neglect) to, to
"	"	lack (be without), to
mansarde,*f.*	*mahn*-SAHRD	attic
manteau,*m.*	*mahn*-TOH	cloak (apparel)
"	"	coat (woman's overcoat)
manuel,*m.*	*mah*-NÜ_ELL	manual (small book)
"	"	textbook
manuel, -le	*mah*-NÜ_ELL	manual (by hand)
marais,*m.*	*mah*-REH	marsh
"	"	swamp (*n.*)
marbre,*m.*	MAHR-*br(ih)*	marble (mineral)
marchandise,*f.*	*mahr-shahn*-DEEZ	commodity
marchandise(s),*f.* (*pl.*)	*mahr-shahn*-DEEZ	merchandise
"	"	wares
marchandises,*f.pl.*	*mahr-shahn*-DEEZ	freight
"	"	goods
marche,*f.*	MAHRSH	step (stair)
marché,*m.*	*mahr*-SHAY	bargain (agreement)
"	"	market (trading center)
marcher (1)	*mahr*-SHAY	march, to
"	"	walk, to
marcher à grands pas	*mahr-shay ah grahn* PAH	stride (walk), to
mare,*f.*	MAHR	pool (standing water)
marée haute,*f.*	*mah-ray* OHT	tide, high
marée basse,*f.*	*mah-ray* BAHSS	tide, low
margarine,*f.*	*mahr-gah*-REEN	margarine
marge,*f.*	MAHRZH	margin (surplus)
marguerite,*f.*	*mahr-ghih*-REET	daisy
mari,*m.*	*mah*-REE	husband

French	Pronunciation	English
mariage,*m.*	*mah*-R_YAHZH	marriage
"	"	wedding
marié	*mah*-R_YAY	married
marié,*m.*	*mah*-R_YAY	groom (bridegroom)
mariée,*f.*	*mah*-R_YAY	bride
marier (avec), se (1)	*sih mah*-R_YAY (*ah-veck*)	marry, to
marin	*mah*-RANG, -REEN	marine (oceanic)
marin,*m.*	*mah*-RANG	sailor
marine,*f.*	*mah*-REEN	navy (*n.*)
mariner (1)	*mah-REE*-NAY	pickle (preserve), to
marmotter (1)	*mahr-muh*-TAY	mutter (mumble), to
marque,*f.*	MAHRK	brand (trade mark)
"	"	mark
marque de commerce,*f.*	*mahrk dih kuh*-MEHRSS	trade mark
marquer (1)	*mahr*-KAY	mark (designate), to
"	"	score (gain points), to
marquer un temps	*mahr-kay uhn* TAHNG	pause (wait), to
marteau,*m.*	*mahr*-TOH	hammer (tool)
masculin	*mah-skü*-LANG, -LEEN	masculine
masque,*m.*	MAHSK	mask (face covering)
masse,*f.*	MAHSS	lump (shapeless piece)
"	"	mass (matter)
massue,*f.*	MAH-SÜ	club (cudgel)
mât,*m.*	MAH	mast
matelas,*m.*	*mah*-TLAH	mattress
mathématiques,*f. pl.*	*mah-tay-mah*-TEEK	mathematics
matière,*f.*	*mah*-T_YEHR	material (substance)
"		matter
matière(s),*f.(pl.)*	*mah*-T_YEHR	stuff (substance)
matin,*m.*	*mah*-TANG	morning
matinée,*f.*	*mah-tee*-NAY	matinee (theater performance)
matrice,*f.*	*mah*-TREESS	womb
maudire (25)	*moh*-DEER	curse (damn), to
mauvais	*muh*-VEH, -VEHZ	bad
"		evil (*adj.*)
mauvaise herbe,*f.*	*muh-veh*-ZEHRB	weed
me	MIH	(to) me
"	"	(to) myself
mécanicien,*m.*	*may-kah-nee*-S_YANG	engineer (railroad engineman)
"	"	mechanic
mécanique	*may-kah*-NEEK	mechanical
méchant	*may*-SHAHNG, -SHAHNT	naughty (disobedient)
médaille,*f.*	*may*-DYE	medal
médecin,*m.*	*med*-SANG	physician
médecine,*f.*	*med*-SEEN	medicine (medical science)
médical	*may-dee*-KAHL	medical
médicament,*m.*	*may-dee-kah*-MAHNG	medicine (medicament)
méditer (1)	*may-dee*-TAY	meditate (reflect), to
"	"	muse, to
meilleur	*meh*-YUHR	better (*adj.*)
meilleur, (le)	(*lih*) *meh*-YUHR	best (*adj.*)
mélancolie,*f.*	*may-lahn-kuh*-LEE	gloom (depression)
"	"	melancholy (dejection)
mélange,*m.*	*may*-LAHNZH	blend
"	"	mixture
mélanger (1)	*may-lahn*-ZHAY	blend (make combine), to
mélasse,*f.*	*may*-LAHSS	molasses
mêler (1)	*meh*-LAY	mix (make blend), to
mêler, se	*sih meh*-LAY	interfere (meddle), to
mêler (de), se	*sih meh*-LAY (*dih*)	meddle, to
membre,*m.*	MAHM-*br(ih)*	limb (*anat.*)
"	"	member (one of a group)
même	MEMM	same (*adj.*)
(...-)même	(...-)MEMM	self (*pron.*)
même, de	*dih* MEMM	likewise (also)
mémoire,*f.*	*may*-MWAHR	memory (ability to recall)
mémorandum,*m.*	*may-muh-rahn*-DUMM	memorandum
menace,*f.*	*mih*-NAHSS	threat
menacer (1)	*mih-nah*-SAY	threaten, to
ménage,*m.*	*may*-NAHZH	household
ménagère,*f.*	*may-nah*-ZHEHR	housewife

French	Pronunciation	English
mendiant, *m.*	*mahn-*D_YAHNG	beggar
mendier (1)	*mahn-*D_YAY	beg (solicit alms), to
mener (1)	*mih-*NAY	head, to
"	"	lead (be in advance), to
mensonge, *m.*	*mahn-*SOHNZH	falsehood
"	"	lie
mensuel, -le	*mahn-*SÜ_ELL	monthly (every month, *adj.*)
mental	*mahn-*TAHL	mental
menteur, *m.*	*mahn-*TUHR	liar
mentionner (1)	*mahn-s_yuh-*NAY	mention, to
mentir (26)	*mahn-*TEER	lie (prevaricate), to
menton, *m.*	*mahn-*TOHNG	chin
mépris, *m.*	*may-*PREE	contempt
"	"	scorn
mépriser (1)	*may-pree-*ZAY	despise, to
"	"	scorn, to
mer, *f.*	MEHR	sea
mercantile	*mehr-kahn-*TEEL	mercantile
mercredi des Cendres, *m.*	*mehr-krih-dee day* SAHN-*dr(ih)*	Ash Wednesday
mercure, *m.*	*mehr-*KÜR	mercury
mère, *f.*	MEHR	mother
méridional	*may-ree-d_yuh-*NAHL	southern
mérite, *m.*	*may-*REET	credit (commendation)
"	"	merit
mériter (1)	*may-ree-*TAY	deserve, to
"	"	earn, to
"	"	merit, to
merle, *m.*	MEHRL(*ih*)	blackbird
Mer Méditerranée, *f.*	*mehr may-dee-teh-rah-*NAY	Mediterranean Sea
merveille, *f.*	*mehr-*VAY	marvel
merveilleux, -leuse	*mehr-veh-*YUH, -YUHZ	marvelous
"	"	wonderful
mes	MAY	my
message, *m.*	*meh-*SAHZH	message (communication)
messager, *m.*	*meh-sah-*ZHAY	messenger (courier)
messe, *f.*	MESS	mass (*rel.*)
mesure, *f.*	*mih-*ZÜR	measure (dimensions)
mesurer (1)	*mih-zü-*RAY	measure (find size of), to
métal, *m.*	*may-*TAHL	metal (*n.*)
méthode, *f.*	*may-*TUHD	method
métier, *m.*	*may-*T_YAY	craft
"	"	occupation (calling)
"	"	trade
métier à tisser, *m.*	*may-t_yay ah tee-*SAY	loom
métro, *m.*	*may-*TROH	subway (underground railway)
mets, *m.*	MEH	dish (food)
mettre (39)	MEH-*tr(ih)*	put (place), to
"	"	set, to
mettre à la poste	*meh-trah lah* PUHST	mail (post), to
mettre en gage	*meh-trahn* GAHZH	pawn, to
mettre en grève, se	*sih meh-trahn-*GREHV	strike (stop work), to
mettre en route, se	*sih meh-trahn* ROOT	start (set out), to
meubler (1)	*muh-*BLAY	furnish (put furniture in), to
meubles, *m.pl.*	MUH-*bl(ih)*	furniture
meunier, *m.*	*muh-*N_YAY	miller
meurtre, *m.*	MUHR-*tr(ih)*	murder
meurtrier, *m.*	*muhr-tree-*YAY	murderer
meurtrissure, *f.*	*muhr-tree-*SÜR	bruise
mexicain	*meh-ksee-*KANG, -KENN	Mexican (*adj.*)
Mexico, *m.*	*meh-ksee-*KOH	Mexico City
Mexique, *m.*	*meh-*KSEEK	Mexico
microbe, *m.*	*mee-*KRUBB	germ (microorganism)
midi, *m*	*mee-*DEE	noon
miel, *m.*	M_YELL	honey
mien, le	*lih* M_YANG	mine (*poss. pron.*)
mienne, la	*lah* M_YENN	mine (*poss. pron.*)
miennes, les	*lay* M_YENN	mine (*poss. pron.*)
miens, les	*lay* M_YANG	mine (*poss. pron.*)
miette, *f.*	M_YETT	crumb
mieux	M_YUH	better (*adv.*)
milieu, *m.*	*mee-*L_YUH	middle (center)
milieu de, au	*oh mee-*L_YUH *dih*	amid
militaire	*mee-lee-*TEHR	military (*adj.*)

French	Pronunciation	English
mince	MANSS	slender (lean)
"	"	thin (not thick)
mine, *f.*	MEEN	mine (*n.*)
minerai, *m.*	*meen-*RAY	ore
minéral, *m.*	*mee-nay-*RAHL	mineral
mineur, *m.*	*mee-*NUHR	miner
ministre, *m.*	*mee-*NEE-*str(ih)*	minister (cabinet member)
minorité, *f.*	*mee-nuh-ree-*TAY	minority (smaller number)
minuit, *m.,f.*	*mee-*NÜ_EE	midnight
minute, *f.*	*mee-*NÜT	minute (unit of time)
miracle, *m.*	*mee-*RAH-*kl(ih)*	miracle
miroir, *m.*	*mee-*RWAHR	mirror
misérable, *m.,f.*	*mee-zay-*RAH-*bl(ih)*	wretch (hapless person)
miséricorde, *f.*	*mee-zay-ree-*KORD	mercy
missionnaire, *m.*	*mee-s_yuh-*NEHR	missionary
mitaine, *f.*	*mee-*TENN	mitten
mite, *f.*	MEET	moth
Mlle.; Mademoiselle, *f.* (*pl.* Mlles.; Mesdemoiselles)	*mah-d(ih)-mwah-*ZELL (*may-d[ih]-mwah-*ZELL)	Miss
Mme.; Madame, *f.* (*pl.* Mmes.; Mesdames)	*mah-*DAHM (*may-*DAHM)	Mrs. (Mistress)
mode, *f.*	MUD	fashion
"	"	mode (manner)
modèle, *m.*	*muh-*DELL	model
moderne	*muh-*DEHRN	modern
modeste	*muh-*DESST	modest
modifier (1)	*muh-dee-*F_YAY	qualify (modify), to
moeurs, *f.pl.*	MUHRSS	morals
moi	MWAH	I
"	"	(to) me
moi, à	*ah* MWAH	mine (*poss. pron.*)
moi(-même)	MWAH(-MEMM)	myself
moindre	MWAN-*dr(ih)*	less (*adj.*)
"	"	minor (lesser)
moindre, (le)	(*lih*) MWAN-*dr(ih)*	least (*adj.*)
moine, *m.*	MWAH_N	monk
moineau, *m.*	*mwah-*NOH	sparrow
moins	MWANG	less (*adv., prep.*)
moins, (le)	(*lih*) MWANG	least (*adv.*)
moins, *m.*	MWANG	least (*n.*)
moins que, à	*ah* MWANG *kih*	unless (*conj.*)
mois, *m.*	MWAH	month
moisi	*mwah-*ZEE	moldy
moisson, *f.*	*mwah-*SOHNG	harvest
moissonner (1)	*mwah-suh-*NAY	reap, to
moite	MWAHT	moist
moitié, *f.*	*mwah-*T_YAY	half (*n.*)
mollet, *m.*	*muh-*LEH	calf (*anat.*)
moment, *m.*	*muh-*MAHNG	moment (instant)
mon	MOHNG	my
monarque, *m.*	*muh-*NAHRK	monarch
monastère, *m.*	*muh-nah-*STEHR	monastery
monde, *m.*	MOHND	world
monnaie, *f.*	*muh-*NEH	currency (money)
monotone	*muh-nuh-*TUNN	monotonous (boring)
monsieur, *m.*	*mih-*S_YUH	sir
monstre, *m.*	MOHN-*str(ih)*	monster (beast)
monstrueux, -euse	*mohn-strü-*UH, -UHZ	monstrous (horrible)
montagne, *f.*	*mohn-*TAH-*n_yih*	mountain
montagneux, -neuse	*mohn-tah-*N_YUH, -N_YUHZ	mountainous
monter (1)	*mohn-*TAY	ascend (go upward along), to
"	"	climb, to
"	"	rise (increase), to
monter à, se	*sih mohn-*TAY *ah*	amount to, to
monter sur	*mohn-*TAY *sür*	mount (climb upon), to
Montevideo, *m.*	*mohn-tay-vee-day-*OH	Montevideo
montre, *f.*	MOHN-*tr(ih)*	watch (timepiece)
montrer (1)	*mohn-*TRAY	demonstrate, to
"	"	show (make visible), to
montrer, se	*sih mohn-*TRAY	show (be visible), to
monument, *m.*	*muh-nü-*MAHNG	memorial (*n.*)
"	"	monument

French	Pronunciation	English
moral	*muh*-RAHL	moral (ethical)
moral, *m.*	*muh*-RAHL	morale
morceau, *m.*	*mor*-SOH	bit (small part)
"	"	morsel (small bit)
"	"	piece
mordre (52)	MOR-*dr(ih)*	bite, to
morne	MORN	dismal
"	"	dreary
mort	MOR, MORT	dead
mort, *f.*	MOR	death
mortel, -le	*mor*-TELL	deadly
"	"	fatal
"	"	mortal (*adj.*)
Moscou, *m.*	*muh*-SKOO	Moscow
mot, *m.*	MOH	word
moteur, *m.*	*muh*-TUHR	motor (engine)
moteur à réaction, *f.*	*muh-tuhr ah ray-ahk-*S_YOHNG	jet engine
motif, *m.*	*muh*-TEEF	motive (*n.*)
mou, molle	MOO, MULL	soft (not hard)
mouche, *f.*	MOOSH	fly (housefly)
mouchoir, *m.*	*moo*-SHWAHR	handkerchief
moudre (40)	MOO-*dr(ih)*	grind (crush), to
mouillé	*moo*-YAY	wet
mouiller (1)	*moo*-YAY	wet, to
mourir (41)	*moo*-REER	die, to
mourir de faim	*moo-reer dih* FANG	starve (die of hunger), to
mousse, *f.*	MOOSS	moss
moustache(s), *f.* (*pl.*)	*moo*-STAHSH	mustache
moustique, *m.*	*moo*-STEEK	mosquito
moutarde, *f.*	*moo*-TAHRD	mustard
mouton, *m.*	*moo*-TOHNG	mutton
"	"	sheep
mouvement, *m.*	*moo*-VMAHNG	motion
"	"	movement
moyen, *m.*	*mwah*-YANG	medium (means)
moyen, -ne	*mwah*-YANG, -YENN	average (ordinary, *adi.*)
"	"	moderate (not extreme)
moyenne, *f.*	*mwah*-YENN	average (mean, *n.*)
moyen(s), *m.*(*pl.*)	*mwah*-YANG	means (method)
muet, -te	MÜ_EH, _ETT	dumb
"	"	mute (silent)
mugir (2)	*mü*-ZHEER	bellow (roar), to
mulet, *m.*	*mü*-LEH	mule
multiplier (1)	*mül-tee-plee*-YAY	multiply, to (*arith.*)
multiplier, se	*sih mül-tee-plee*-YAY	multiply (grow numerous), to
multitude, *f.*	*mül-tee*-TÜD	multitude
mûr	MÜR	ripe
mur, *m.*	MÜR	wall
mûre sauvage, *f.*	*mür soh*-VAHZH	blackberry
mûrir (2)	*mü*-REER	mature (ripen), to
murmurer (1)	*mür-mü*-RAY	murmur, to
muscade, *f.*	*mü*-SKAHD	nutmeg
muscle, *m.*	MÜ-*skl(ih)*	muscle
musée, *m.*	*mü*-ZAY	museum
musical	*mü-zee*-KAHL	musical
musicien, *m.*	*mü-zee*-S_YANG	musician
musique, *f.*	*mü*-ZEEK	band (instrumental group)
"	"	music
mutuel, -le	*mü*-TÜ_ELL	mutual
myrtille, *f.*	*meer*-TEE	blueberry
mystère, *m.*	*mee*-STEHR	mystery (enigma)
mystérieux, -rieuse	*mee-stay*-R_YUH, -R_YUHZ	mysterious
mythe, *m.*	MEET	myth (legend)
nager (1)	*nah*-ZHAY	swim, to
nain, *m.*	NANG	dwarf
naissance, *f.*	*neh*-SAHNSS	birth
naître (43)	NEH-*tr(ih)*	born, to be
Naples, *m.*	NAH-*pl(ih)*	Naples
nappe, *f.*	NAHP	tablecloth
narine, *f.*	*nah*-REEN	nostril
natif, *m.*	*nah*-TEEF	native (*n.*)
natif, -tive	*nah*-TEEF, -TEEV	native (indigenous)
nation, *f.*	*nah*-S_YOHNG	nation

French	Pronunciation	English
Nations Unies, *f.* *pl.*	*nah-s_yohn-zü*-NEE	United Nations
national	*nah-s_yuh*-NAHL	national (*adj.*)
nature, *f.*	*nah*-TÜR	nature
naturel, -le	*nah-tü*-RELL	natural
navet, *m.*	*nah*-VEH	turnip (white)
navigation, *f.*	*nah-vee-gah*-S_YOHNG	navigation
navire, *m.*	*nah*-VEER	ship
néanmoins	*nay-ahn*-MWANG	nevertheless
nécessaire	*nay-seh*-SEHR	necessary
nécessité, *f.*	*nay-seh-see*-TAY	necessity
nécrologe, *m.*	*nay-kruh*-LUHZH	obituary (*n.*)
négligent	*nay-glee*-ZHAHNG, -ZHAHNT	careless (negligent)
négliger (1)	*nay-glee*-ZHAY	neglect (slight), to
négociable	*nay-guh-s_yah-bl(ih)*	negotiable (*bus.*)
négociation, *f.*	*nay-guh-s_yah-s_yohng*	negotiation
négocier (1)	*nay-guh-s_yay*	bargain, to
"	"	negotiate, to
nègre, *m.*	NEH-*gr(ih)*	Negro
neige, *f.*	NEHZH	snow
ne...non plus	*nih...nohn* PLÜ	either (not...either, *adv.*)
ne...pas	*nih...*PAH	not
ne pas aimer (1)	*nih pah-zay*-MAY	dislike, to
nerf, *m.*	NEHR	nerve (*anat.*)
nerveux, -veuse	*nehr*-VUH, -VUHZ	nervous (high-strung)
net, -te	NET	net (*adj.*)
nettoyer (1)	*neh-twah*-YAY	clean, to
neutre	NUH-*tr(ih)*	neutral
neveu, *m.*	*nih*-VUH	nephew
New-Delhi, *m.*	*n_yoo-deh*-LEE	New Delhi
New-York, *m.*	*n_yoo*-YORK	New York
nez, *m.*	NAY	nose (*anat.*)
ni	NEE	nor
ni...ni	NEE...NEE	neither...nor (*conj.*)
Nicaragua, *m.*	*nee-kah-rah*-GWAH	Nicaragua
nickel, *m.*	*nee*-KELL	nickel (*chem.*)
nid, *m.*	NEE	nest (bird home)
nièce, *f.*	N_YESS	niece
nier (1)	*nee*-AY	deny (contradict), to
Nil, *m.*	NEEL	Nile
ni l'un...	*nee* LUHNG...	neither (*adj.*, *pron.*)
n'importe où	*nam-por*-TOO	anywhere (wheresoever)
"	"	wherever (no matter where)
n'importe quel, -le	*nam-port(ih)* KELL	any (any at all, *adj.*)
"	"	any (any one, *adj.*)
"	"	whichever (*adj.*)
n'importe qui	*nam-port(ih)* KEE	anybody (anybody whosoever)
"	"	anyone (anyone whosoever)
"	"	whoever (no matter who)
n'importe quoi	*nam-port(ih)* KWAH	anything (anything whatever)
niveau, *m.*	*nee*-VOH	level (plane, *n.*)
noble	NUH-*bl(ih)*	noble (*adj.*)
noblesse, *f.*	*nuh*-BLESS	nobility
Noël, *m.*	*nuh*-ELL	Christmas
noeud, *m.*	NUH	knot
noir	NWAHR	black
noix, *f.*	NWAH	nut (food)
"	"	walnut (*n.*)
nom, *m.*	NOHNG	name
"	"	noun
nombre, *m.*	NOHM-*br(ih)*	number (quantity)
nombreux, -breuse	*nohm*-BRUH, -BRUHZ	numerous
nom de famille, *m.*	*nohm d(ih) fah*-MEE	surname
nom de jeune fille, *m.*	*nohm dih zhuh_n* FEE	maiden name
nomination, *f.*	*nuh-mee-nah*-S_YOHNG	appointment
"	"	nomination
nommer (1)	*nuh*-MAY	appoint, to
"	"	nominate, to
non	NOHNG	no (nay)
non plus	*nohn* PLÜ	either (not...either, *adv.*)
nord, *m.*	NOR	north (*n.*)
nord, (du)	(*dü*) NOR	northern
nord, au	*oh* NOR	north (*adv.*)
nord-est, (du)	(*dü*) *nor*-ESST	northeast (*adj.*)

French	Pronunciation	English
nord-ouest, (du)	(dü) nor-WEST	northwest (adj.)
normal	nor-MAHL	normal (adj.)
"	"	standard (regular)
Norvège, f.	nor-VEHZH	Norway
norvégien, -ne	nor-vay-ZH YANG, -ZH YENN	Norwegian (adj.)
nos	NOH	our
nostalgique	nuh-stahl-ZHEEK	homesick
notable	nuh-TAH-bl(ih)	notable (adj.)
notaire, m.	nuh-TEHR	notary
note, f.	NUTT	grade (academic rating)
"	"	note (mus.)
noter (1)	nuh-TAY	note, to
notion, f.	nuh-S YOHNG	notion (idea)
notoire	nuh-TWAHR	notorious
notre	NUH-tr(ih)	our
nôtre, le (la)	lih (lah) NOH-tr(ih)	ours
nôtres, les	lay NOH-tr(ih)	ours
nourrir (2)	noo-REER	feed (give food to), to
"	"	nourish, to
nourriture, f.	noo-ree-TÜR	diet (total food consumed)
"	"	food
"	"	nourishment
nous	NOO	(to) us
"	"	we
nous, à	ah NOO	ours
nous(-mêmes)	NOO(-MEMM)	(to) ourselves
nouveau, -velle	noo-VOH, -VELL	fresh
"	"	new
noyer (1)	nwah-YAY	drown (kill by drowning), to
noyer, se	sih nwah-YAY	drown (die by drowning), to
nu	NÜ	bare (nude)
"	"	naked
nuage, m.	NÜ_AHZH	cloud
nuageux, -geuse	nü_ah-ZHUH, -ZHUHZ	cloudy (overcast)
nuire à (14)	NÜ_EER ah	harm (damage), to
nuit, f.	NÜ_EE	night
nul, -le	NÜL	void (null)
nulle part	nül PAHR	anywhere (not...anywhere)
"	"	nowhere
numéro, m.	nü-may-ROH	number (numeral)
numéroter (1)	nü-may-ruh-TAY	number (assign numbers to), to
nuque, f.	NÜK	nape
nylon, m.	nee-LOHNG	nylon (n.)
oasis, f.	oh-ah-ZEESS	oasis
obéir (à) (2)	uh-bay-EER (ah)	obey, to
obéissance, f.	uh-bay-ee-SAHNSS	obedience (compliance)
obéissant	uh-bay-ee-SAHNG, -SAHNT	obedient
objection, f.	uh-bzheck-S YOHNG	objection
objet, m.	uh-BZHEH	object (thing)
obligation, f.	uh-blee-gah-S YOHNG	bond
"	"	debenture
"	"	obligation (duty)
obligatoire	uh-blee-gah-TWAHR	obligatory (binding)
obliger (1)	uh-blee-ZHAY	oblige (compel), to
obscur	uh-PSKÜR	dim
"	"	obscure
obscurcir (2)	uh-pskür-SEER	darken (make dark), to
obscurité, f.	uh-pskü-ree-TAY	darkness
observateur, m.	uh-psehr-vah-TUHR	observer
observation, f.	uh-psehr-vah-S YOHNG	comment (remark)
"	"	observation (watching)
observer (1)	uh-psehr-VAY	observe, to
obstacle, m.	uh-PSTAH-kl(ih)	obstacle
obstiné	uh-pstee-NAY	stubborn
obtenir (55)	uh-ptih-NEER	get, to
"	"	obtain, to
"	"	procure, to
"	"	secure, to
occasion, f.	uh-kah-z YOHNG	bargain (advantageous purchase)
"	"	chance
"	"	occasion
"	"	opportunity

French	Pronunciation	English
occidental	uh-ksee-dahn-TAHL	western
occupation, f.	uh-kü-pah-S YOHNG	occupation (mil.)
occupé	uh-kü-PAY	busy (occupied)
occuper (1)	uh-kü-PAY	occupy, to
occuper (à, de), s'	suh-kü-PAY (ah, dih)	engage (be occupied) in, to
océan, m.	uh-say-AHNG	ocean
odeur, f.	uh-DUHR	odor
"	"	scent
"	"	smell
oeil, m.	UH_y	eye (anat.)
oeillet, m.	uh-YEH	carnation
oeuf, m.	UFF (pl. UH)	egg
oeufs brouillés, m. pl.	uh broo-YAY	scrambled eggs
oeuvre, f.	UH-vr(ih)	work (composition)
offense, f.	uh-FAHNSS	offense (transgression)
offenser (1)	uh-fahn-SAY	offend (affront), to
offenser de, s'	suh-fahn-SAY dih	resent, to
offensive, f.	uh-fahn-SEEV	offense (attack)
office, m.	uh-FEESS	office (position)
officiel, -le	uh-fee-S YELL	official (adj.)
officier, m.	uh-fee-S YAY	officer (mil.)
offre, f.	UH-fr(ih)	bid (amount offered)
"	"	offer
offrir (44)	uh-FREER	offer (tender), to
"	"	submit (offer), to
oie, f.	WAH	goose
oignon, m.	uh-N YOHNG	onion
oiseau, m.	wah-ZOH	bird
oiseux, -seuse	wah-ZUH, -ZUHZ	idle (useless)
oisif, -sive	wah-ZEEF, -ZEEV	idle (not busy)
oisiveté, f.	wah-zee-VTAY	idleness (inactivity)
olive, f.	uh-LEEV	olive (fruit)
ombragé	ohm-brah-ZHAY	shady
ombre, f.	OHM-br(ih)	shade
"	"	shadow
omettre (39)	uh-MEH-tr(ih)	omit (leave out), to
oncle, m.	OHN-kl(ih)	uncle
ongle, m.	OHN-gl(ih)	nail (anat.)
onguent, m.	ohn-GAHNG	ointment
opéra, m.	uh-pay-RAH	opera
opération, f.	uh-pay-rah-S YOHNG	operation (med.)
opérations de banque, f. pl.	uh-pay-rah-s_yohng dih BAHNK	banking
opérer (1)	uh-pay-RAY	operate (perform surgery), to
opinion, f.	uh-pee-N YOHNG	belief
"	"	opinion
opposé	uh-poh-ZAY	opposite (adj.)
opposé, m.	uh-poh-ZAY	opposite (n.)
opposer, (s') (1)	(s)uh-poh-ZAY	object, to
opposition, f.	uh-poh-zee-S YOHNG	opposition (resistance)
oppresser (1)	uh-preh-SAY	oppress, to
optimiste	uh-ptee-MEEST	optimistic
or, m.	OR	gold
or, d'	DOR	golden
orage, m.	uh-RAHZH	storm
orageux, -geuse	uh-rah-ZHUH, -ZHUHZ	stormy
oral	uh-RAHL	oral (spoken)
orange	uh-RAHNZH	orange (color)
orange, f.	uh-RAHNZH	orange (fruit)
orateur, m.	uh-rah-TUHR	speaker (orator)
orchestre, m.	or-KEH-str(ih)	orchestra (mus.)
orchidée, f.	or-kee-DAY	orchid (flower)
ordinaire	or-dee-NEHR	common (usual)
"	"	ordinary
ordonnance, f.	or-duh-NAHNSS	prescription (med.)
ordonner (1)	or-duh-NAY	command, to
"	"	order, to
ordre, m.	OR-dr(ih)	command
"	"	order
ordures, f. pl.	or-DÜR	garbage
oreille, f.	uh-RAY	ear
oreiller, m.	uh-reh-YAY	pillow
oreillons, m. pl.	uh-reh-YOHNG	mumps

French	Pronunciation	English
organe, *m.*	or-GAH_N	organ (*anat.*)
organiser (1)	or-gah-nee-ZAY	organize (systematize), to
orge, *f.*	ORZH	barley
orgue, *m.*	ORG	organ (*mus.*)
orgueil, *m.*	or-GUH_y	pride (self-esteem)
Orient, *m.*	uh-R_YAHNG	Orient
oriental	uh-r_yahn-TAHL	eastern
original	uh-ree-zhee-NAHL	original (first)
"	"	quaint (unusual)
origine, *f.*	uh-ree-ZHEEN	origin (source)
orme, *m.*	ORM	elm
ornement, *m.*	or-nih-MAHNG	ornament
orner (1)	or-NAY	adorn (beautify), to
"	"	trim (decorate), to
orphelin, *m.*	or-fih-LANG	orphan (*n.*)
orteil, *m.*	or-TAY	toe
os, *m.*	UHSS (OH, pl.)	bone
osciller (1)	uh-see-YAY	swing (oscillate), to
oser (1)	oh-ZAY	dare (venture), to
Oslo, *m.*	uh-SLOH	Oslo
Ottawa, *m.*	uh-tah-WAH	Ottawa
ou	OO	or
où	OO	where (*adv., conj.*)
ou...ou	OO...OO	either...or (*conj.*)
oublié	oo-blee-YAY	forgotten
oublier (1)	oo-blee-YAY	forget, to
ouest, *m.*	WEST	west (*n.*)
oui	WEE	yes
ourlet, *m.*	oor-LEH	hem
ours, *m.*	OORSS	bear (animal)
outil, *m.*	oo-TEE	tool
outre, en	ahn-NOO-tr(ih)	besides (moreover, *adv.*)
outre-mer, d'	doo-trih-MEHR	oversea(s) (*adj.*)
ouvert	oo-VEHR, -VEHRT	open (*adj.*)
ouverture, *f.*	oo-vehr-TÜR	opening (aperture)
ouvrier, *m.*	oo-vree-YAY	worker
ouvrir (2)	oo-VREER	open (make open), to
oxygène, *m.*	uh-ksee-ZHENN	oxygen
Pacifique, *m.*	pah-see-FEEK	Pacific (*n.*)
pagaie, *f.*	pah-GAY	paddle (oar)
page, *f.*	PAHZH	page (leaf)
paiement, *m.*	pay-MAHNG	payment
paille, *f.*	PYE	straw (dry grain stalks)
pain, *m.*	PANG	bread
"	"	loaf
pain grillé, *m.*	pan gree-YAY	toast (bread)
paire, *f.*	PEHR	pair
paisible	pay-ZEE-bl(ih)	peaceful (tranquil)
paître (16)	PEH-tr(ih)	graze (feed), to
paix, *f.*	PEH	peace
Pakistan, *m.*	pah-kee-STAHNG	Pakistan
pakistani	pah-kee-stah-NEE	Pakistani (*adj.*)
palais, *m.*	pah-LEH	palace
pâle	PAHL	pale (wan)
Palestine, *f.*	pah-leh-STEEN	Palestine
palmier, *m.*	pahl-M_YAY	palm (tree)
palourde, *f.*	pah-LOORD	clam
paludisme, *m.*	pah-lü-DEE-sm(ih)	malaria
Panama, *m.*	pah-nah-MAH	Panama
panier, *m.*	pah-N_YAY	basket
panique, *f.*	pah-NEEK	panic (fear)
panser (1)	pahn-SAY	dress, to (*med.*)
pantalon(s), *m.(pl.)*	pahn-tah-LOHNG	trousers
panthère, *f.*	pahn-TEHR	panther
pantoufle, *f.*	pahn-TOO-fl(ih)	slipper
paon, *m.*	PAHNG	peacock
papa, *m.*	pah-PAH	dad
pape, *m.*	PAHP	pope
papier, *m.*	pah-P_YAY	paper
papier à lettres, *m.*	pah-p_yay ah LEH-tr(ih)	stationery (writing paper)
papillon, *m.*	pah-pee-YOHNG	butterfly
Pâque, *f.*	PAHK	Passover
paquebot transatlantique, *m.*	pahk-boh trahn-zah-tlahn-TEEK	liner, ocean
Pâques, *m.*	PAHK	Easter
paquet, *m.*	pah-KEH	bundle (parcel)

French	Pronunciation	English
par	PAHR	by (*prep., math.*)
"	"	by (via, *prep.*)
"	"	per (for each)
"	"	through (by means of, *prep.*)
parachute, *m.*	pah-rah-SHÜT	parachute
paradis, *m.*	pah-rah-DEE	paradise
paragraphe, *m.*	pah-rah-GRAHF	paragraph
Paraguay, *m.*	pah-rah-GAY	Paraguay
par ailleurs	pahr ah-YUHR	otherwise (under other conditions)
paraître (16)	pah-REH-tr(ih)	appear (seem), to
parallèle	pah-rah-LELL	parallel (*adj.*)
paralysie, *f.*	pah-rah-lee-ZEE	paralysis
paralysie infantile, *f.*	pah-rah-lee-zee an-fahn-TEEL	infantile paralysis
parapluie, *m.*	pah-rah-PLÜ_EE	umbrella
paravent, *m.*	pah-rah-VAHNG	screen (partition)
parc, *m.*	PAHRK	park
par ce moyen	pahr sih mwah-YANG	thereby
parce que	PAHR-s(ih)KIH	because (*conj.*)
par-dessus	pahr-dih-SÜ	over (above, *prep.*)
pardessus, *m.*	pahr-dih-SÜ	coat
"	"	overcoat
pardon, *m.*	pahr-DOHNG	forgiveness
"	"	pardon
pardonner (1)	pahr-duh-NAY	forgive, to
"	"	pardon, to
pare-brise, *m.*	pahr-BREEZ	windshield
pareil, *m.*	pah-RAY	peer (equal)
pareil, -le	pah-RAY	alike (similar)
pareillement	pah-ray-MAHNG	alike (similarly)
parent, *m.*	pah-RAHNG	relative (kinsman)
parents, *m.pl.*	pah-RAHNG	parents
parenthèses, *f.pl.*	pah-rahn-TEZZ	parentheses
parer (1)	pah-RAY	dress (decorate), to
paresseux, -seuse	pah-reh-SUH, -SUHZ	lazy
parfait	pahr-FEH, -FETT	fine (good)
"	"	perfect (flawless)
parfum, *m.*	pahr-FUHNG	perfume (fragrance)
pari, *m.*	pah-REE	bet
parier (1)	pah-R_YAY	bet, to
Paris, *m.*	pah-REE	Paris
parjure, *m.*	pahr-ZHÜR	perjury
parlement, *m.*	pahr-lih-MAHNG	parliament
parler (1)	pahr-LAY	speak, to
"	"	talk, to
parmi	pahr-MEE	among
paroisse, *f.*	pah-RWAHSS	parish
parole, *f.*	pah-RULL	speech (oral expression)
part, *f.*	PAHR	part (portion)
"	"	share
part, à	ah PAHR	apart
"	"	aside (away)
"	"	beside (other than, *prep.*)
partager (1)	pahr-tah-ZHAY	share, to
parti, *m.*	pahr-TEE	party (*pol.*)
particulier, -lière	pahr-tee-kü-L_YAY, -L_YEHR	individual (particular, *adj.*)
"	"	particular (*adj.*)
partie, *f.*	pahr-TEE	lot (salable items, *bus.*)
"	"	proportion (part)
partie, en	ahn pahr-TEE	partly
partiel, -le	pahr-S_YELL	partial (incomplete)
partir (26)	pahr-TEER	depart, to
"	"	leave, to
partisan, *m.*	pahr-tee-ZAHNG	follower (adherent)
partisans, *m.pl.*	pahr-tee-ZAHNG	following (followers)
partout	pahr-TOO	everywhere
partout où	pahr-TOO oo	wherever (at, in whatever place)
pas	PAH	no (not any, *adv.*)
"	"	not
pas, *m.*	PAH	step (stride)
passable	pah-SAH-bl(ih)	decent (fairly good)
"	"	fair (passable)
passage, *m.*	pah-SAHZH	aisle (passageway)
"	"	passage
passé	pah-SAY	past (bygone, *adj.*)
passé, *m.*	pah-SAY	past (*n.*)

French	Pronunciation	English
passeport,*m.*	*pah*-SPOR	passport
passer (1)	*pah*-SAY	pass (go by), to
passer, se	*sih pah*-SAY	happen (occur), to
passer à gué	*pah-say ah* GAY	ford, to
passer au tamis	*pah-say oh tah*-MEE	sift (separate), to
passer sur	*pah*-SAY *sür*	overlook (disregard), to
passe-temps,*m.*	*pah*-STAHNG	pastime
passion,*f.*	*pah*-S_YOHNG	passion (emotion)
passionné	*pah-s_yuh*-NAY	passionate
pasteur,*m.*	*pah*-STUHR	minister (clergyman)
"	"	pastor
patauger (1)	*pah-toh*-ZHAY	wade, to
pâte,*f.*	PAHT	batter (flour mixture)
pâte dentifrice,*f.*	*paht dahn-tee*-FREESS	tooth paste
patience,*f.*	*pah*-S_YAHNSS	patience
patient	*pah*-S_YAHNG, -S_YAHNT	patient (forbearing)
patin,*m.*	*pah*-TANG	skate, ice
patriote,*m.,f.*	*pah-tree*-YUTT	patriot
patron,*m.*	*pah*-TROHNG	boss (master)
"	"	employer
patte,*f.*	PAHT	paw
pâturage,*m.*	*pah-tü*-RAHZH	pasture (grassland)
paume,*f.*	POHM	palm (of hand)
paupière,*f.*	*poh*-P_YEHR	eyelid
pauvre	POH-*vr(ih)*	poor
pauvreté,*f.*	*poh-vrih*-TAY	poverty
pavé,*m.*	*pah*-VAY	pavement
paver (1)	*pah*-VAY	pave, to
payable	*peh*-YAH-*bl(ih)*	payable (due)
payement,*m.*	*pay*-MAHNG	payment
payer (1)	*peh*-YAY	pay, to
pays,*m.*	*peh*-YEE	country (nation)
paysage,*m.*	*peh-ee*-ZAHZH	landscape (scenery)
paysan,*m.*	*peh-ee*-ZAHNG	peasant
Pays-Bas, les,*m. pl.*	*lay peh-yee*-BAH	Netherlands, The
peau,*f.*	POH	hide
"	"	skin
pêche,*f.*	PESH	peach
péché,*m.*	*pay*-SHAY	sin
pêcher (1)	*peh*-SHAY	fish, to
pécher	*pay*-SHAY	sin, to
pêcheur,*m.*	*peh*-SHUHR	fisherman
pécheur,*m.*	*pay*-SHUHR	sinner
peigne,*m.*	PEN-*yih*	comb (for hair)
peindre (19)	PAN-*dr(ih)*	paint (spread color), to
peine,*f.*	PEN	penalty
"	"	trouble (exertion)
peine, à	*ah* PEN	hardly (barely)
peintre,*m.*	PAN-*tr(ih)*	painter (artist)
peinture,*f.*	*pan*-TÜR	paint
"	"	painting (picture)
Peï-Ping,*f.*	*peh-ee*-PANG	Peiping
peler (1)	*pih*-LAY	peel (take skin from), to
pelle,*f.*	PELL	shovel (tool)
pellicule,*f.*	*peh-lee*-KÜL	film
pelouse,*f.*	*pih*-LOOZ	lawn
penchant,*m.*	*pahn*-SHAHNG	bent (penchant)
pencher, (se) (1)	*(sih) pahn*-SHAY	lean (bend), to
pencher, se	*sih pahn*-SHAY	stoop (bend forward), to
pendant	*pahn*-DAHNG	during
"	"	in
pendant que	*pahn*-DAHN *kih*	as
"	"	while
pendant tout	*pahn-dahn* TOO	throughout (from start to end of, *prep.*)
pendre (3)	PAHN-*dr(ih)*	hang, to
pénétrer (1)	*pay-nay*-TRAY	penetrate (pierce), to
pénicilline,*f.*	*pay-née-see*-LEEN	penicillin
péninsule,*f.*	*pay-nan*-SÜL	peninsula
pensée,*f.*	*pahn*-SAY	pansy
"	"	thought (contemplation)
pensif, -sive	*pahn*-SEEF, -SEEV	thoughtful (reflective)

French	Pronunciation	English
pension (de famille),*f.*	*pahn*-S_YOHNG *(dih fah*-MEE)	boarding house
pente,*f.*	PAHNT	slope (slant)
percer (1)	*pehr*-SAY	pierce, to
perche,*f.*	PEHRSH	pole (rod)
percher, (se) (1)	*(sih) pehr*-SHAY	perch (sit), to
perdre (3)	PEHR-*dr(ih)*	lose, to
père,*m.*	PEHR	father
perfection,*f.*	*pehr-feck*-S_YOHNG	perfection (flawlessness)
péril,*m.*	*pay*-REEL	peril
périmer (1)	*pay-ree*-MAY	lapse (become void), to
période,*f.*	*pay*-R_YUHD	period (of time)
périr (2)	*pay*-REER	perish, to
perle,*f.*	PEHR-*lih*	pearl (gem)
perle (de collier),*f.*	PEHR-*lih (dih kuh*-L_YAY)	bead (jewelry)
permanent	*pehr-mah*-NAHNG, -NAHNT	permanent (*adj.*)
permettre (39)	*pehr*-MEH-*tr(ih)*	allow, to
"	"	permit, to
permettre, se	*sih pehr*-MEH-*tr(ih)*	afford (have the means), to
permis,*m.*	*pehr*-MEE	license (permit)
permission,*f.*	*pehr-mee*-S_YOHNG	permission
Pérou,*m.*	*pay*-ROO	Peru
perpétuel, -le	*pehr-pay-tü*-ELL	perpetual
perroquet,*m.*	*peh-ruh*-KEH	parrot
persister (1)	*pehr-see*-STAY	persist (persevere), to
personnage,*m.*	*pehr-suh*-NAHZH	character (person portrayed)
personnalité,*f.*	*pehr-suh-nah-lee*-TAY	personality
personne	*pehr*-SUN	anybody (not...anybody)
"	"	anyone (not...anyone)
"	"	nobody
personne,*f.*	*pehr*-SUN	person
personnel,*m.*	*pehr-suh*-NELL	staff (personnel)
personnel, -le	*pehr-suh*-NELL	personal
perspective,*f.*	*pehr-speh*-KTEEV	prospect (thing expected)
persuader (1)	*pehr-sü_ah*-DAY	induce, to
"	"	persuade, to
perte,*f.*	PEHRT	doom (ruin)
"	"	loss
péruvien, -ne	*pay-rü*-V_YANG, -V_YENN	Peruvian (*adj.*)
pervertir (2)	*pehr-vehr*-TEER	pervert (distort), to
peser (1)	*pih*-ZAY	weigh, to
pessimiste	*peh-see*-MEEST	pessimistic
peste,*f.*	PEST	pest (nuisance)
pétiller (1)	*pay-tee*-YAY	snap (crackle), to
petit	*pih*-TEE, -TEET	little
"	"	petty (minor)
"	"	small
petit déjeuner,*m.*	*p(ih)-tee day-zhuh*-NAY	breakfast
petite-fille,*f.*	*p(ih)-teet*-FEE	granddaughter
petit-fils,*m.*	*p(ih)-tee*-FEESS	grandson
pétition,*f.*	*pay-tee*-S_YOHNG	petition (written request)
petit pain,*m.*	*p(ih)-tee* PANG	roll (bread)
petit pois,*m.*	*p(ih)-tee* PWAH	pea
pétrole,*m.*	*pay*-TRULL	kerosene
peu,*m.*	PUH	little (small amount, *n.*)
peu, (un)	*(uhn)* PUH	little (slightly, *adv.*)
peu (de)	PUH *(dih)*	few (not many, *adj.*)
peu de	PUH *dih*	little (not much, *adj.*)
peuple,*m.*	PUH-*pl(ih)*	people (populace)
peur que, de	*dih* PUHR *kih*	lest
peut-être	*puh*-TEH-*tr(ih)*	maybe
"	"	perhaps
pharmacie,*f.*	*fahr-mah*-SEE	pharmacy (drug store)
pharmacien,*m.*	*fahr-mah*-S_YANG	pharmacist
phase,*f.*	FAHZ	phase (stage)
Philippines,*f.pl.*	*fee-lee*-PEEN	Philippines
philosophie,*f.*	*fee-luh-zuh*-FEE	philosophy
phonographe,*m.*	*fuh-nuh*-GRAHF	phonograph
phoque,*m.*	FUHK	seal (animal)
photocalque,*m.*	*fuh-tuh*-KAHLK	blueprint
photographie,*f.*	*fuh-tuh-grah*-FEE	photograph
phrase,*f.*	FRAHZ	sentence (*gram.*)

French	Pronunciation	English
physique	*fee*-ZEEK	physical
physique,*f.*	*fee*-ZEEK	physics (science)
piano,*m.*	*p_yah*-NOH	piano (*n.*)
picoter (1)	*pee-kuh*-TAY	peck, to
pièce,*f.*	P_YESS	patch (repair)
"	"	room (of house)
pièce, (la),*f.*	(*lah*) P_YESS	each (apiece, *adv.*)
pièce à pièce	*p_yess ah* P_YESS	piecemeal (*adv.*)
pièce (de mon-	*p_yess* (*dih muh*-NEH)	coin
naie),*f.*		
pièce de théâtre,*f.*	*p_yess dih tay*-AH-*tr*(*ih*)	play (stage presenta-
		tion)
pied,*m.*	P_YAY	foot (*anat.*)
piège,*m.*	P_YEHZH	snare
"	"	trap
pierre,*f.*	P_YEHR	stone (piece of rock)
pierre à chaux,*f.*	*p_yehr ah* SHOH	limestone
piétiner (1)	*p_yay-tee*-NAY	trample, to
pigeon,*m.*	*pee*-ZHOHNG	pigeon
pile,*f.*	PEEL	battery (primary
		cell)
pilier,*m.*	*pee*-L_YAY	pillar (column)
pilote,*m.*	*pee*-LUHT	pilot (flier)
pilule,*f.*	*pee*-LÜL	pill
pin,*m.*	PANG	pine (tree)
pincer (1)	*pan*-SAY	pinch (squeeze), to
pionnier,*m.*	*p_yuh*-N_YAY	pioneer
pipe,*f.*	PEEP	pipe (tobacco pipe)
pique-nique,*m.*	*peek*-NEEK	picnic
piquer (1)	*pee*-KAY	prick, to
"	"	sting (pierce skin),
		to
piqûre,*f.*	*pee*-KÜR	injection (*med.*)
pirate,*m.*	*pee*-RAHT	pirate
pire	PEER	worse
pire, (le)	(*lih*) PEER	worst (*adj.*)
pires, (les)	(*lay*) PEER	worst (*adj.*)
pis	PEE	worse (*adv.*)
pis, (le)	(*lih*) PEE	worst (*adv.*)
pis,*m.*	PEE	worst (*n.*)
pissenlit,*m.*	*pee-sahn*-LEE	dandelion
piste,*f.*	PEEST	trail (path)
pistolet,*m.*	*pee-stuh*-LEH	pistol
pitié,*f.*	*pee*-T_YAY	pity (compassion)
pittoresque	*pee-tuh*-RESK	picturesque
place,*f.*	PLAHSS	room (space)
"	"	square (plaza)
placement,*m.*	*plah*-SMAHNG	investment (*bus.*)
placer (de l'argent)	*plah*-SAY (*dih lahr*-	invest, to (*bus.*)
	ZHAHNG)	
placier,*m.*	*plah*-S_YAY	canvasser (*bus.*)
plafond,*m.*	*plah*-FOHNG	ceiling (of room)
plage,*f.*	PLAHZH	beach (strand)
plaindre (19)	PLAN-*dr*(*ih*)	pity, to
plaindre, se	*sih* PLAN-*dr*(*ih*)	complain, to
plaine,*f.*	PLENN	plain (level land)
plainte,*f.*	PLANT	complaint
plaire (à) (45)	PLEHR (*ah*)	please (satisfy), to
plaisanter (1)	*play-zahn*-TAY	jest, to
"	"	joke, to
plaisanterie,*f.*	*play-zahn*-TREE	jest
"	"	joke
plaisir,*m.*	*play*-ZEER	pleasure
plan,*m.*	PLAHNG	plan
"	"	plane (surface)
"	"	scheme
planche,*f.*	PLAHNSH	board
"	"	plank
plancher,*m.*	*plahn*-SHAY	floor (bottom sur-
		face)
planète,*f.*	*plah*-NETT	planet
plante,*f.*	PLAHNT	plant (flora)
planter (1)	*plahn*-TAY	plant (sow), to
plastique,*m.*	*plah*-STEEK	plastic (*n.*)
plat	PLAH, PLAHT	flat
"	"	level
"	"	shallow
plateau,*m.*	*plah*-TOH	plateau (tableland)
"	"	tray
platine,*m.*	*plah*-TEEN	platinum
plâtre,*m.*	PLAH-*tr*(*ih*)	plaster (wall coating)

French	Pronunciation	English
plein	PLANG, PLENN	full (filled)
plein d'espoir	*plan deh*-SPWAHR	hopeful
pleurer (1)	*pluh*-RAY	cry, to
"	"	mourn (feel grief), to
		weep, to
pleuvoir (46)	*pluh*-VWAHR	rain, to
pli,*m.*	PLEE	fold (plait)
"	"	wrinkle
plier (1)	*plee*-YAY	bend (make bend),
		to
"	"	fold (lap over), to
"	"	fuse (*elec.*)
plomb,*m.*	PLOHNG	lead (metal)
plonger (1)	*plohn*-ZHAY	dip (immerse), to
"	"	dive, to
plonger, (se)	(*sih*) *plohn*-ZHAY	plunge (hurl one-
		self), to
pluie,*f.*	PLÜ_EE	rain
plume,*f.*	PLÜM	feather
plupart, la,*f.*	*lah plü*-PAHR	most (*n.*)
plupart, pour la	*poor lah plü*-PAHR	mostly
plupart de, la	*lah plü*-PAHR *dih*	most (greatest
		quantity, *adj.*)
pluriel, -le	*plü*-R_YELL	plural (*adj.*)
plus	PLÜ	further (to greater
		extent, *adv.*)
plus	PLÜSS	plus (*prep.*)
plus (de)	PLÜ (*dih*)	more (*adj.*)
plus, de	*dih* PLÜSS	moreover
plus, le (la)	*lih* (*lah*) PLÜ	most (*adv.*)
plus, les	*lay* PLÜ	most (*adv.*)
plusieurs	*plü*-Z_YUHR	several (a few, *adj.*)
plutôt	*plü*-TOH	rather (preferably)
pluvieux, -vieuse	*plü*-V_YUH, -V_YUHZ	rainy
pneu,*m.*	PNUH	tire
pneumonie,*f.*	*pnuh-muh*-NEE	pneumonia
poche,*f.*	PUHSH	pocket
poêle,*f.*	PWAHL	pan, frying
poêle,*m.*	PWAHL	stove (for heating)
poème,*m.*	*puh*-EMM	poem
poésie,*f.*	*puh-ay*-ZEE	poetry
poète,*m.*	*puh*-ETT	poet
poids,*m.*	PWAH	weight (scale weight)
poignard,*m.*	*pwah*-N_YAHR	dagger
poignarder (1)	*pwah-n_yahr*-DAY	stab, to
poignée,*f.*	*pwah*-N_YAY	handful
poignet,*m.*	*pwah*-N_YEH	wrist
poing,*m.*	PWANG	fist
point,*m.*	PWANG	dot
"	"	period (*punct.*)
"	"	point
"	"	stitch (of sewing)
pointe,*f.*	PWANT	point (sharp end)
pointu	*pwan*-TÜ	pointed (tapered)
pointure,*f.*	*pwan*-TÜR	size (of shoes, gloves)
point-virgule,*m.*	*pwan-veer*-GÜL	semicolon
poire,*f.*	PWAHR	pear
poison,*m.*	*pwah*-ZOHNG	poison
poisson,*m.*	*pwah*-SOHNG	fish
poitrine,*f.*	*pwah*-TREEN	chest (*anat.*)
poivre,*m.*	PWAH-*vr*(*ih*)	pepper (seasoning)
poivron,*m.*	*pwah*-VROHNG	pepper (green vege-
		table)
poix,*f.*	PWAH	pitch (tar)
pôle,*m.*	POHL	pole (end of axis)
poli	*puh*-LEE	civil
"	"	polite
poli,*m.*	*puh*-LEE	polish
police,*f.*	*puh*-LEESS	police
"	"	policy (contract of
		insurance)
polir (2)	*puh*-LEER	polish, to
"	"	shine, to
politicien,*m.*	*puh-lee-tee*-S_YANG	politician
politique	*puh-lee*-TEEK	political
politique,*f.*	*puh-lee*-TEEK	politics
Pologne,*f.*	*puh*-LUH-*n_yih*	Poland
polonais	*puh-luh*-NEH, -NEZZ	Polish (*adj.*)
pomme,*f.*	PUHM	apple
pomme de terre,*f.*	*puhm dih* TEHR	potato (white)
pompe,*f.*	POHMP	pump
pompier,*m.*	*pohm*-P_YAY	fireman
ponctuel, -le	*pohn*-KTÜ_ELL	prompt
"	"	punctual

French	Pronunciation	English
poney, *m.*	*puh*-NEH	pony (animal)
pont, *m.*	POHNG	bridge (span)
"	"	deck (of ship)
populaire	*puh-pü*-LEHR	popular (well-liked)
population, *f.*	*puh-pü-lah* S_YOHNG	population (number of people)
porc, *m.*	POR	hog
"	"	pork
porcelaine, *f.*	*por-sih*-LENN	porcelain (*n.*)
port, *m.*	POR	carriage (posture)
"	"	harbor
"	"	port
"	"	postage (postal charge)
porte, *f.*	PORT	door
"	"	gate
porte-avions, *m.*	*por-tah*-V_YOHNG	aircraft carrier
portée, *f.*	*por*-TAY	range (scope)
porte-plume, *m.*	*port*-PLÜM	pen
porter (1)	*por*-TAY	bear, to
"	"	carry, to
"	"	wear (have on), to
porter en compte	*por-tay ahn* KOHNT	enter, to (*acctg.*)
porteur, *m.*	*por*-TUHR	bearer (*banking*)
"	"	porter (baggage carrier)
portion, *f.*	*por*-S_YOHNG	portion (part)
portrait, *m.*	*por*-TREH	portrait
Portugal, *m.*	*por-tü*-GAHL	Portugal
poser (1)	*poh*-ZAY	lay (put down), to
"	"	place (lay), to
positif, -tive	*poh-zee*-TEEF, -TEEV	positive (decisive)
position, *f.*	*poh-zee*-S_YOHNG	position (location)
posséder (1)	*puh-say*-DAY	own, to
"	"	possess, to
possession, *f.*	*puh-seh*-S_YOHNG	possession (ownership)
possibilité, *f.*	*puh-see-bee-lee*-TAY	possibility
possible	*puh*-SEE-bl(*ih*)	possible
poste, *m.*	PUHST	post (position)
poste (de réception de T.S.F.), *m.*	PUHST (*dih ray-sehp*-S_YOHNG *dih* TAY ESS EFF)	radio (receiving set)
poste aérienne, *f.*	*puhst-ah-ay*-R_YENN	air mail
post-scriptum, *m.*	*puhst-skree*-PTUMM	postscript
pot, *m.*	POH	pot (container)
poteau, *m.*	*puh*-TOH	post (pole)
"	"	stake
pouce, *m.*	POOSS	thumb
pouding, *m.*	*poo*-DAN_G	pudding (dessert)
poudre, *f.*	POO-dr(*ih*)	powder
poulain, *m.*	*poo*-LANG	colt
poule, *f.*	POOL	hen
poulet, *m.*	*poo*-LEH	chicken
pouls, *m.*	POO	pulse (*physiol.*)
poumon, *m.*	*poo*-MOHNG	lung
poupée, *f.*	*poo*-PAY	doll
pour	POOR	for (*prep.*)
"	"	to (in order to, *prep.*)
pourboire, *m.*	*poor*-BWAHR	tip (gratuity)
pour-cent, *m.*	*poor*-SAHNG	percent
pourcentage, *m.*	*poor-sahn*-TAHZH	percentage
pourpre	POOR-*pr*(*ih*)	purple (color)
pourquoi	*poor*-KWAH	why
pourri	*poo*-REE	rotten (decayed)
pourrir (2)	*poo*-REER	rot, to
pourriture, *f.*	*poo-ree*-TÜR	decay (rottenness)
poursuite, *f.*	*poor*-SÜ_EET	pursuit (chase)
poursuivre (54)	*poor*-SÜ_EE-*vr*(*ih*)	chase, to
"	"	pursue, to
poussée, *f.*	*poo*-SAY	push (shove)
pousser (1)	*poo*-SAY	blow (make move), to
"	"	drive (propel), to
"	"	push (shove), to
poussière, *f.*	*poo*-S_YEHR	dust
poussiéreux, -reuse	*poo-s_yeh*-RUH, -RUHZ	dusty
poutre, *f.*	POO-*tr*(*ih*)	beam (rafter)
pouvoir (47)	*poo*-VWAHR	can (be able to)
"	"	may (be able to)

French	Pronunciation	English
pouvoir, *m.*	*poo*-VWAHR	power (control)
"	"	power of attorney
prairie, *f.*	*pray*-REE	meadow
"	"	prairie
pratique	*prah*-TEEK	practical (not theoretical)
pratique, *f.*	*prah*-TEEK	experience (skill)
pratiquer (1)	*prah-tee*-KAY	practice (put to practice), to
prêcher (1)	*preh*-SHAY	preach, to
précieux, -cieuse	*pray*-S_YUH, -S_YUHZ	precious
précipice, *m.*	*pray-see*-PEESS	precipice
précipité	*pray-see-pee*-TAY	hasty (hurried)
précipiter, se (1)	*sih pray-see-pee*-TAY	dash (rush), to
précis	*pray*-SEE, -SEEZ	precise (exact)
prédicateur, *m.*	*pray-dee-kah*-TUHR	preacher
prédire (25)	*pray*-DEER	predict, to
prédominer (1)	*pray-duh-mee*-NAY	prevail (exist widely), to
préface, *f.*	*pray*-FAHSS	preface
préférer (1)	*pray-fay*-RAY	prefer (like better), to
préjugé, *m.*	*pray-zhü*-ZHAY	prejudice
préliminaire	*pray-lee-mee*-NEHR	preliminary (*adj.*)
premier, -mière	*prih*-M_YAY, -M_YEHR	first (*adj.*)
"	"	former (first of two, *adj.*)
"	"	primary
"	"	prime (*adj.*)
premiers secours, *m.pl.*	*prih-m_yay sih*-KOOR	first aid (*med.*)
prendre (48)	PRAHN-*dr*(*ih*)	seize (capture), to
"	"	take, to
prendre garde à	*prahn-drih* GAHRD *ah*	beware of, to
prendre part	*prahn-drih* PAHR	participate, to
prendre sa retraite	*prahn-drih sah rih*-TRETT	retire (stop working), to
prendre son essor	*prahn-drih sohn-nay*-SOR	soar (rise), to
prendre un bain	*prahn-druhn*-BANG	bathe (take a bath), to
préparation, *f.*	*pray-pah-rah*-S_YOHNG	preparation (preparatory act)
préparer (1)	*pray-pah*-RAY	prepare (make ready), to
préposition, *f.*	*pray-poh-zee*-S_YOHNG	preposition (*gram.*)
près	PREH	close (*adv.*)
"	"	near (not far, *adv.*)
près de	PREH *dih*	at
"	"	by
"	"	near (*prep.*)
présence, *f.*	*pray*-ZAHNSS	attendance
"	"	presence
présent, *m.*	*pray*-ZAHNG	present (present time, *n.*)
présentation, *f.*	*pray-zahn-tah*-S_YOHNG	introduction (presentation)
présenter (1)	*pray-zahn*-TAY	introduce (make acquainted), to
présenter (1)	*pray-zahn*-TAY	present, to
président, *m.*	*pray-zee*-DAHNG	chairman
"	"	president
presque	PREH-SKIH	almost
"	"	nearly
presque tout	*preh-skih* TOO	most (almost all, *adj.*)
presse, *f.*	PRESS	press (newspapers and periodicals)
presser (1)	*preh*-SAY	press (bear upon), to
"	"	squeeze, to
pression, *f.*	*preh*-S_YOHNG	pressure (force)
prêt	PREH	ready (prepared)
prêt, *m.*	PREH	loan
prêter (1)	*preh*-TAY	lend, to
prétexte, *m.*	*pray*-TEXT	pretext
prêtre, *m.*	PREH-*tr*(*ih*)	priest
preuve, *f.*	PRUHV	evidence (*law*)
"	"	proof (demonstration)
prévoyance, *f.*	*pray-vwah*-YAHNSS	vision (foresight)
prier (1)	*pree*-YAY	pray, to
prière, *f.*	*pree*-YEHR	prayer (petition)
prime, *f.*	PREEM	premium (payment)
primitif, -tive	*pree-mee*-TEEF, -TEEV	primitive (early)
prince, *m.*	PRANSS	prince
princesse, *f.*	*pran*-SESS	princess

French	Pronunciation	English
principal	*pran-see-*PAHL	chief (leading)
"	"	main
"	"	principal
principe, *m.*	*pran-*SEEP	principle (basic truth)
printemps, *m.*	*pran-*TAHNG	spring (season)
pris de peur	*pree dih* PUHR	afraid
pris d'étourdissement	*pree day-toor-dee-*SMAHNG	dizzy (unsteady)
prise, *f.*	PREEZ	grip (grasp)
prise de courant, *f.*	*preez dih koo-*RAHNG	outlet (*elec.*)
priser (1)	*pree-*ZAY	value (prize), to
prison, *f.*	*pree-*ZOHNG	jail
"	"	prison
prisonnier, *m.*	*pree-zuh-*N_YAY	prisoner
privation, *f.*	*pree-vah-*S_YOHNG	hardship (privation)
privé	*pree-*VAY	private (personal)
priver (1)	*pree-*VAY	deprive (divest), to
privilège, *m.*	*pree-vee-*LEHZH	privilege
prix, *m.*	PREE	charge
"	"	cost
"	"	fare (*transp.*)
"	"	price (*bus.*)
"	"	prize (trophy)
probable	*pruh-*BAH-*bl*(*ih*)	likely
"	"	probable
problème, *m.*	*pruh-*BLEMM	problem
procédé, *m.*	*pruh-say-*DAY	process (set of operations)
procès, *m.*	*pruh-*SEH	suit (lawsuit)
"	"	trial (court proceeding)
procession, *f.*	*pruh-seh-*S_YOHNG	procession (parade)
procès-verbal, *m.*	*pruh-seh-vehr-*BAHL	minutes (record)
proclamer (1)	*pruh-klah-*MAY	proclaim, to
productif, -tive	*pruh-dü-*KTEEF, -KTEEV	productive
production, *f.*	*pruh-dük-*S_YOHNG	production
produire (14)	*pruh-*DÜ_EER	produce (make), to
produit, *m.*	*pruh-*DÜ_EE	product
profane	*pruh-*FAH_N	profane (blasphemous)
professeur, *m.*	*pruh-feh-*SUHR	professor (teacher)
profession, *f.*	*pruh-feh-*S_YOHNG	profession (occupation)
professionnel, -le	*pruh-feh-s_yuh-*NELL	professional
profit, *m.*	*pruh-*FEE	benefit (advantage)
profitable	*pruh-fee-*TAH-*bl*(*ih*)	profitable
profond	*pruh-*FOHNG, -FOHND	deep (in extent)
"	"	profound
profondeur, *f.*	*pruh-fohn-*DUHR	depth (deepness)
programme, *m.*	*pruh-*GRAHM	program (plan)
progrès, *m.*	*pruh-*GREH	advance
"	"	progress
progressif, -sive	*pruh-greh-*SEEF, -SEEV	progressive
prohibition, *f.*	*proh-ee-bee-*S_YOHNG	prohibition
proie, *f.*	PRWAH	prey (victim)
projet, *m.*	*pruh-*ZHEH	project
projeter (1)	*pruh-*ZHTAY	plan (prearrange), to
prolonger (1)	*pruh-lohn-*ZHAY	prolong, to
promenade, *f.*	*pruh-*M(*ih*)NAHD	walk (stroll)
promenade (en voiture), *f.*	*pruh-*M(*ih*)NAHD (*ahn vwah-*TÜR)	ride (in a car)
promener, se (1)	*sih pruh-*MNAY	stroll, to
promesse, *f.*	*pruh-*MESS	promise (pledge)
promettre (39)	*pruh-*MEH-*tr*(*ih*)	promise (pledge), to
promotion, *f.*	*pruh-moh-*S_YOHNG	promotion (advance)
prompt	PROHNG, PROHNT	prompt (quick)
prononcer (1)	*pruh-nohn-*SAY	pronounce (enunciate), to
prophète, *m.*	*pruh-*FETT	prophet (religious teacher)
proportion, *f.*	*pruh-por-*S_YOHNG	proportion (ratio)
proposer (1)	*pruh-poh-*ZAY	propose, to
"	"	suggest (recommend), to
proposition, *f.*	*pruh-poh-zee-*S_YOHNG	proposal (suggestion)
propre	PRUH-*pr*(*ih*)	clean
"	"	neat (tidy)
"	"	own (*adj.*)
propriétaire, *m.*	*pruh-pree-ay-*TEHR	owner
propriétés, *f.pl.*	*pruh-pree-ay-*TAY	holdings (possessions)
prose, *f.*	PROHZ	prose

French	Pronunciation	English
prospère	*pruh-*SPEHR	prosperous
prospérer (1)	*pruh-spay-*RAY	prosper, to
"	"	thrive (succeed), to
prospérité, *f.*	*pruh-spay-ree-*TAY	prosperity
protection, *f.*	*pruh-teck-*S_YOHNG	protection
protéger (1)	*pruh-teh-*ZHAY	guard (watch over), to
"	"	protect, to
"	"	shield, to
protestation, *f.*	*pruh-teh-stah-*S_YOHNG	protest
protester (1)	*pruh-teh-*STAY	protest, to
prouver (1)	*proo-*VAY	prove (verify), to
proverbe, *m.*	*pruh-*VEHRB	proverb
province, *f.*	*pruh-*VANSS	province (*pol.*)
provision, *f.*	*pruh-vee-z*_YOHNG	stock
"	"	supply (amount available)
provisoire	*pruh-vee-*ZWAHR	temporary
prudence, *f.*	*prü-*DAHNSS	caution (heed)
prudent	*prü-*DAHNG	careful
"	"	conservative (cautious)
prune, *f.*	PRÜN	plum (fruit)
pruneau, *m.*	*prü-*NOH	prune
psychiatrie, *f.*	*psee-k_yah-*TREE	psychiatry
psychologie, *f.*	*psee-kuh-luh-*ZHEE	psychology
public, *m.*	*pü-*BLEEK	community
"	"	public (populace, *n.*)
public, -blique	*pü-*BLEEK	public (common, *adj.*)
publication, *f.*	*pü-blee-kah-*S_YOHNG	publication (published work)
publicité, *f.*	*pü-blee-see-*TAY	publicity (notoriety)
publier (1)	*pü-blee-*YAY	publish, to
puer (1)	PÜ_AY	stink, to
puis	PÜ_EE	then (subsequently)
puisque	PÜ_EE-SKIH	since (because, *conj.*)
puissance, *f.*	*pü_ee-*SAHNSS	might (*n.*)
puissance (en chevaux), *f.*	*pü_ee-sahnss* (*ahn* SH[*ih*]VOH)	horsepower
puissant	*pü_ee-*SAHNG	mighty
"	"	powerful
puits, *m.*	PÜ_EE	well (*n.*)
punir (2)	*pü-*NEER	punish, to
punition, *f.*	*pü-nee-*S_YOHNG	punishment
pupille, *f.*	*pü-*PEE	pupil (of eye)
pur	PÜR	pure
"	"	sheer
pureté, *f.*	*pür-*TAY	purity (cleanness)
pyjama, *m.*	*pee-zhah-*MAH	pajamas
quai, *m.*	KAY	platform, railroad
qualité, *f.*	*kah-lee-*TAY	quality (attribute)
quand	KAHNG	when (*adv., pron.*)
"	"	when (any time that, *conj.*)
quantité, *f.*	*kahn-tee-*TAY	quantity (amount)
quart, *m.*	KAHR	quarter (one-fourth)
quartier, *m.*	*kahr-*T_YAY	community (neighborhood)
quartier général, *m.*	*kahr-t_yay zhay-nay-*RAHL	headquarters
que	KIH	than
"	"	that (*conj.*)
"	"	that (*rel. pron.*)
"	"	what (*interrog. pron.*)
"	"	which (*rel. pron.*)
"	"	whom (*rel. pron.*)
quel, -le	KELL	what (*interrog. adj.*)
"	"	which (*interrog. adj.*)
quelque	KELL-KIH	some (unspecified, *adj.*)
quelque chose	*kell-kih* SHOHZ	anything
"	"	something
quelquefois	*kell-kih-*FWAH	sometimes
quelque part	*kell-kih* PAHR	somewhere
quelque peu	*kell-kih* PUH	somewhat (*adv.*)
quelque...que	KELL-KIH...KIH	whatever (*adj.*)
quelque...qui	*kell-kih...*KEE	whatever (*adj.*)
quelques	KELL-KIH	some (a few, *adj.*)
quelqu'un	*kell-*KUHNG	anybody
"	"	anyone
"	"	somebody
"	"	someone

French	Pronunciation	English
quelques-uns, -unes	kell-kih-ZUHNG, -ZÜN	few, a
querelle, f.	kih-RELL	quarrel (dispute)
quereller, se (1)	kih-reh-LAY	quarrel (dispute), to
qu'est-ce que	KEH-SKIH	what (*interrog. pron.*)
qu'est-ce qui	KEH-SKEE	what (*interrog. pron.*)
question, f.	keh-ST YOHNG	inquiry
"	"	issue
		question
queue, f.	KUH	tail (of animal)
qui	KEE	that (*rel. pron.*)
"	"	which (*rel. pron.*)
"	"	who
"	"	whom (*interrog. pron.*)
qui, à	ah KEE	whose (*interrog. pron.*)
qui, de	dih KEE	whose (*interrog., rel. pron.*)
qui est-ce que	KEE_EH-SKIH	whom (*interrog. pron.*)
qui est-ce qui	KEE_EH-SKEE	who (*interrog. pron.*)
quincaillerie, f.	kan-kye-REE	hardware
Quito, m.	kee-TOH	Quito
quittancer (1)	kee-tahn-SAY	receipt, to (*bus.*)
quoi	KWAH	what (*interrog. pron.*)
quoique	KWAH-KIH	though (*conj.*)
quote-part, f.	kuht-PAR	quota
quotidien, -ne	kuh-tee-D YANG, -D YENN	daily (*adj.*)
rabbin, m.	rah-BANG	rabbi
race, f.	RAHSS	breed (stock)
"	"	race (*anthrop.*)
racheter (1)	rah-SHTAY	redeem (buy back), to
racine, f.	rah-SEEN	root (*bot.*)
racler (1)	rah-KLAY	scrape (make smooth or clean), to
raconter (1)	rah-kohn-TAY	relate, to
"	"	tell (narrate), to
radar, m.	rah-DAHR	radar (*n.*)
radiateur, m.	rah-d yah-TUHR	radiator (heater)
radical	rah-dee-KAHL	radical (basic)
radieux, -dieuse	rah-D YUH, -D YUHZ	radiant
radio-activité, f.	rah-d yoh-ah-ktee-vee-TAY	radioactivity
radio-diffusion, f.	rah-d yoh-dee-fü-Z YOHNG	broadcasting (*rad.*)
radiographie, f.	rah-d yuh-grah-FEE	X-ray (X-ray picture)
radiographier (1)	rah-d yuh-grah-F YAY	X-ray (examine), to
raffiner (1)	rah-fee-NAY	refine (purify), to
rafraîchir (2)	rah-freh-SHEER	cool (make less hot), to
"	"	refresh, to
refraîchissements, m.pl.	rah-freh-shee-SMAHNG	refreshments
rager (1)	rah-ZHAY	rage (rave), to
raid aérien, m.	red ah-ay-R YANG	air raid
raide	RED	steep (*adj.*)
"	"	stiff (inflexible)
raie, f.	RAY	streak
"	"	stripe
rail, m.	RYE	rail (bar on track)
railler (1)	rah-YAY	mock (deride), to
raisin sec, m.	ray-zan SECK	raisin
raison, f.	ray-ZOHNG	ground (basis)
"	"	ratio
"	"	reason
raisonnable	ray-zuh-NAH-bl(ih)	reasonable (rational)
"	"	sane
ramasser (1)	rah-mah-SAY	gather (bring together), to
rame, f.	RAHM	oar (*n.*)
rameau, m.	rah-MOH	bough
"	"	stick (small branch)
ramper (1)	rahm-PAY	crawl, to
		creep, to
rançon, f.	rahn-SOHNG	ransom (*n.*)
rang, m.	RAHNG	rank
rangée, f.	rahn-ZHAY	row (series)
ranger (1)	rahn-ZHAY	straighten (put in order), to
rapide	rah-PEED	fast
"	"	quick
"	"	rapid
"	"	swift

French	Pronunciation	English
rappeler à (1)	rah-PLAY ah	remind, to
rappeler, se (1)	sih rah-PLAY	recall (remember), to
rapport, m.	rah-POR	account
"	"	connection (relationship)
"	"	relation
"	"	report
rare	RAHR	rare (uncommon)
"		scarce
rarement	rahr-MAHNG	seldom
rareté, f.	rahr-TAY	scarcity
raser, se (1)	sih rah-ZAY	shave (oneself), to
rasoir, m.	rah-ZWAHR	razor
rasoir électrique, m.	rah-zwahr ay-leck-TREEK	shaver, electric
rassis	rah-SEE, -SEEZ	stale
rat, m.	RAH	rat
râteau, m.	rah-TOH	rake (tool)
rater (1)	rah-TAY	miss (fail to do), to
ration, f.	rah-S YOHNG	ration (allotment)
ravissement, m.	rah-vee-SMAHNG	rapture
rayon, m.	reh-YOHNG	beam
"	"	ray
"	"	shelf
rayon X, m.	reh-yohn EEX	X-ray (Roentgen ray)
rayonne, f.	reh-YUNN	rayon
rayonner (1)	reh-yuh-NAY	beam (shine), to
"	"	glow, to
réaction, f.	ray-ahk-S YOHNG	reaction
réagir (2)	ray-ah-ZHEER	respond (react), to
réaliser	ray-ah-lee-ZAY	realize (accomplish), to
réalité, f.	ray-ah-lee-TAY	reality
rebelle, m., f.	rih-BELL	rebel (*n.*)
rébellion, f.	ray-beh-L YOHNG	rebellion
rebord, m.	rih-BOR	ledge
récemment	ray-sah-MAHNG	recently
recensement, m.	rih-sahn-SMAHNG	census
récent	ray-SAHNG, -SAHNT	recent
réception, f.	ray-sehp-S YOHNG	receipt (receiving)
recette, f.	rih-SETT	recipe
recevoir (49)	rih-sih-VWAHR	entertain (be host to), to
"	"	receive, to
recherche, f.	rih-SHEHRSH	quest
"	"	search (hunt)
recherche(s), f.(pl.)	rih-SHEHRSH	research
récipient, m.	ray-see-P YAHNG	vessel (receptacle)
réciter (1)	ray-see-TAY	recite (repeat something learned), to
réclamer (1)	ray-klah-MAY	demand (ask for), to
récolte, f.	ray-KUHLT	crop (produce)
recommandation, f.	rih-kuh-mahn-dah-S YOHNG	recommendation
recommandé	rih-kuh-mahn-DAY	registered (postal designation)
recommander (1)	rih-kuh-mahn-DAY	advocate, to
"	"	recommend, to
récompense, f.	ray-kohm-PAHNSS	reward (recompense)
récompenser (1)	ray-kohm-pahn-SAY	reward, to
reconnaissance, f.	rih-kuh-neh-SAHNSS	gratitude
"	"	recognition
reconnaissant	rih-kuh-neh-SAHNG, -SAHNT	grateful
"	"	thankful
reconnaître (16)	rih-kuh-NEH-tr(ih)	acknowledge, to
"	"	admit (concede), to
"	"	appreciate (be grateful for), to
"	"	recognize (identify), to
recourir (à) (18)	rih-koo-REER (ah)	resort (have recourse), to
récréation, f.	ray-kray-ah-S YOHNG	recess (school intermission)
rectangle, m.	reh-KTAHN-gl(ih)	rectangle
reçu, m.	rih-SÜ	receipt (voucher)
reculons, (à)	(ah) r(ih)-kü-LOHNG	backward (in reverse, *adv.*)
récupérer (1)	ray-kü-pay-RAY	recover (get back), to
rédacteur, m.	ray-dah-KTUHR	editor
reddition, f.	reh-dee-S YOHNG	surrender (*mil.*)
redevance, f.	rih-dih-VAHNSS	royalty (fee)
réduction, f.	ray-dük-S YOHNG	reduction (lessening)
réduire (14)	ray-DÜ_EER	cut, to
"	"	reduce (diminish), to

French	Pronunciation	English
réel, -le	*ray*-ELL	actual
réel, -le	*ray*-ELL	real
reflet, *m.*	*rih*-FLEH	reflection (image)
refléter (1)	*rih-flay*-TAY	reflect (throw back), to
réflexion, *f.*	*ray-fleck*-S_YOHNG	reflection (meditation)
réforme, *f.*	*ray*-FORM	reform (*n.*)
refréner (1)	*rih-fray*-NAY	curb, to
"	"	restrain (check), to
réfrigérateur, *m.*	*ray-free-zhay-rah*-TUHR	refrigerator
refuge, *m.*	*rih*-FÜZH	refuge
réfugié, *m.*	*ray-fü-*ZH_YAY	refugee
refuser (1)	*rih-fü*-ZAY	deny, to
"	"	refuse (make a refusal), to
réfuter (1)	*ray-fü*-TAY	refute, to
regard, *m.*	*rih*-GAHR	look (glance)
regarder (1)	*rih-gahr*-DAY	look (gaze), to
"	"	watch (observe), to
regarder attentivement	*rih-gahr-day ah-tahn-tee-*VMAHNG	peer (look intently), to
regarder fixement	*rih-gahr-day feex-*MAHNG	stare, to
regarder furieusement (1)	*rih-gahr-day fü-r_yuh-*ZMAHNG	glare (stare), to
régime, *m.*	*ray*-ZHEEM	diet (restricted food allowance)
régiment, *m.*	*ray-zhee-*MAHNG	regiment (*n.*)
région, *f.*	*ray*-ZH_YOHNG	area
"	"	region
registre, *m.*	*rih-*ZHEE-*str(ih)*	register
registres, *m. pl.*	*rih-*ZHEE-*str(ih)*	records (files)
règle, *f.*	REH-*gl(ih)*	rule
"	"	ruler (measuring instrument)
règlement, *m.*	*reh-glih-*MAHNG	regulation (rule)
régler (1)	*ray*-GLAY	settle (arrange), to
règne, *m.*	REH-*n_yih*	reign (period of rule)
regret, *m.*	*rih*-GREH	regret (sorrow)
regretter (1)	*rih-greh*-TAY	miss (feel the loss of), to
"	"	regret, to
"	"	sorry, to be
régularité, *f.*	*ray-gü-lah-ree*-TAY	regularity
régulier, -lière	*ray-gü-*L_YAY, -L_YEHR	regular (normal)
rein, *m.*	RANG	kidney (*anat.*)
reine, *f.*	RENN	queen
rejeter (1)	*rih-*ZHTAY	reject, to
réjouir, se (2)	*sih ray-*ZHWEER	rejoice, to
relatif, -tive	*rih-lah-*TEEF, -TEEV	comparative
"	"	relative
relations, *f. pl.*	*rih-lah-*S_YOHNG	dealings (relations)
relevé, *m.*	*rih-*L*(ih)*VAY	statement (accounting, *bus.*)
relever (1)	*rih-*LVAY	pick up (lift), to
religieuse, *f.*	*rih-lee-*ZH_YUHZ	nun
religieux, -gieuse	*rih-lee-*ZH_YUH, -ZH_YUHZ	religious (*adj.*)
religion, *f.*	*rih-lee-*ZH_YOHNG	religion
remâcher (1)	*rih-mah-*SHAY	brood over, to
remarquable	*rih-mahr-*KAH-*bl(ih)*	remarkable (extraordinary)
remarque, *f.*	*rih-*MAHRK	remark (comment)
remarquer (1)	*rih-mahr-*KAY	notice (see), to
remboursement, *m.*	*rahm-boor-*SMAHNG	refund (*bus.*)
rembourser (1)	*rahm-boor-*SAY	reimburse, to
"	"	repay, to
remède, *m.*	*rih-*MEDD	cure
"	"	remedy
remerciements, *m.pl.*	*rih-mehr-see-*MAHNG	thanks (gratitude)
remercier (1)	*rih-mehr-*S_YAY	thank, to
remettre (39)	*rih-*MEH-*tr(ih)*	delay, to
"	"	postpone, to
"	"	remit (send payment), to
remise, *f.*	*rih-*MEEZ	discount (*n.*)
"	"	rebate (*bus.*)
"	"	remittance
remplacer (1)	*rahm-plah-*SAY	replace (be a substitute for), to
remplir (2)	*rahm-*PLEER	fill (make full), to
remuer (1)	*rih-*MÜ_AY	stir (mix), to
renard, *m.*	*rih-*NAHR	fox
rencontrer (1)	*rahn-kohn-*TRAY	encounter, to
"	"	meet, to

French	Pronunciation	English
rendement, *m.*	*rahn-*D*(ih)*MAHNG	output
"	"	produce
"	"	yield (product)
rendez-vous, *m.*	*rahn-day-*VOO	appointment (meeting)
"	"	date
"	"	engagement
rendre (3)	RAHN-*dr(ih)*	give (deliver), to
"	"	render (cause to become), to
"	"	return (give back), to
rendre, se	*sih* RAHN-*dr(ih)*	surrender (give oneself up), to
rendre capable	*rahn-drih kah-*PAH-*bl(ih)*	enable, (make able), to
rendre compte	*rahn-drih* KOHNT	report (account formally), to
rendre compte, se	*sih rahn-drih* KOHNT	realize (recognize), to
rendre visite à	*rahn-drih vee-*ZEET *ah*	visit (call on), to
rêne, *m.*	RENN	rein (strap)
renifler (1)	*rih-nee-*FLAY	sniff, to
renne, *m.*	RENN	reindeer
renommée, *f.*	*rih-nuh-*MAY	fame
renoncer à (1)	*rih-nohn-*SAY *ah*	renounce (give up), to
renouveler (1)	*rih-noo-*VLAY	renew, to
rente, *f.*	RAHNT	annuity
rentrer (1)	*rahn-*TRAY ·	go home, to
"	"	tuck (slip inside), to
renverser (1)	*rahn-vehr-*SAY	overturn, to
"	"	upset (knock over), to
répandre (3)	*ray-*PAHN-*dr(ih)*	spill (let pour out), to
"	"	spread (diffuse), to
"	"	sprinkle (scatter), to
réparation, *f.*	*ray-pah-rah-*S_YOHNG	repair (*n.*)
réparer (1)	*ray-pah-*RAY	fix, to
"	"	mend, to
"	"	repair, to
repas, *m.*	*rih-*PAH	meal (repast)
repasser (1)	*rih-pah-*SAY	press (iron), to
repentir, se (26)	*sih rih-pahn-*TEER	repent, to
répéter (1)	*ray-pay-*TAY	repeat (reiterate), to
répétition, *f.*	*ray-pay-tee-*S_YOHNG	rehearsal
"	"	repetition
répondre (3)	*ray-*POHN-*dr(ih)*	reply, to
"	"	respond, to
répondre à	*ray-*POHN-*drah*	answer, to
réponse, *f.*	*ray-*POHNSS	answer
"	"	reply
"	"	response
reporter, *m.*	*rih-por-*TEHR	reporter (journalist)
repos, *m.*	*rih-*POH	repose
"	"	rest
reposer, se (1)	*sih rih-poh-*ZAY	rest (repose), to
reprendre (48)	*rih-*PRAHN-*dr(ih)*	resume (recommence), to
représentant, *m.*	*rih-pray-zahn-*TAHNG	representative (deputy)
représentation, *f.*	*rih-pray-zahn-tah-*S_YOHNG	performance (stage presentation)
représentation, *f.*	*rih-pray-zahn-tah-*S_YOHNG	representation (*pol.*)
représenter (1)	*rih-pray-zahn-*TAY	represent (act for), to
repriser (1)	*rih-pree-*ZAY	darn (mend), to
reproche, *m.*	*rih-*PRUHSH	reproach
reprocher (1)	*rih-pruh-*SHAY	reproach, to
républicain	*ray-pü-blee-*KANG, -KENN	republican (*adj.*)
république, *f.*	*ray-pü-*BLEEK	commonwealth
"	"	republic
République Dominicaine, *f.*	*ray-pü-bleek duh-mee-nee-*KENN	Dominican Republic
réputation, *f.*	*ray-pü-tah-*S_YOHNG	reputation
réservation, *f.*	*ray-zehr-vah-*S_YOHNG	reservation (advance order)
réserve, *f.*	*ray-*ZEHRV	reserve (*bus.*)
réserver (1)	*ray-zehr-*VAY	reserve (withhold), to
réservoir, *m.*	*ray-zehr-*VWAHR	reservoir (water reserve)
"	"	tank (container)
résidence, *f.*	*ray-zee-*DAHNSS	residence (abode)
résistance, *f.*	*ray-zee-*STAHNSS	resistance

French	Pronunciation	English
résister (à) (1)	*ray-zee*-STAY (*ah*)	resist, to
résolution, *f.*	*ray-zuh-lü*-S_YOHNG	resolution (formal expression)
résonner (1)	*ray-zuh*-NAY	clang, to
résoudre (50)	*ray*-ZOO-*dr*(*ih*)	solve, to
résoudre, (se)	(*sih*) *ray*-ZOO-*dr*(*ih*)	resolve (determine), to
respect, *m.*	*reh*-SPEH	respect (esteem)
respectable	*reh-speh*-KTAH-*bl*(*ih*)	respectable
respecter (1)	*reh-speh*-KTAY	respect (esteem), to
respectif, -tive	*reh-speh*-KTEEF, -KTEEV	respective (*adj.*)
respirer (1)	*reh-spee*-RAY	breathe (draw breath), to
resplendissant	*reh-splahn-dee*-SAHNG, -SAHNT	glorious (resplendent)
responsable	*reh-spohn*-SAH-*bl*(*ih*)	liable
"	"	responsible (answerable)
responsabilité, *f.*	*reh-spohn-sah-bee-lee*-TAY	liability
"	"	responsibility (accountability)
ressembler à (1)	*rih-sahm*-BLAY *ah*	resemble, to
ressort, *m.*	*rih*-SOR	spring (coil)
ressources, *f. pl.*	*rih*-SOORSS	resources (wealth)
ressusciter (1)	*ray-sü-see*-TAY	revive, to
restaurant, *m.*	*reh-stuh*-RAHNG	restaurant
restaurer (1)	*reh-stuh*-RAY	restore (reestablish), to
reste, *m.*	REST	remainder
"	"	rest (remainder)
rester (1)	*reh*-STAY	abide, to
"	"	remain, to
"	"	stay, to
restriction, *f.*	*reh-streek*-S_YOHNG	reservation (mental qualification)
résultat, *m.*	*ray-zül*-TAH	result (consequence)
résulter (1)	*ray-zül*-TAY	result, to
rétablir, se (2)	*sih ray-tah*-BLEER	recover (get well), to
retard, *m.*	*rih*-TAHR	delay
retarder (1)	*rih-tahr*-DAY	delay (retard), to
retenir (55)	*rih*-T(*ih*)NEER	book (engage space), to
"	"	reserve (order in advance), to
retirer (1)	*rih-tee*-RAY	withdraw (take back), to
retirer, se	*sih rih-tee*-RAY	withdraw (depart), to
retomber (1)	*rih-tohm*-BAY	relapse, to
retour, *m.*	*rih*-TOOR	return (coming or going back)
retourner (1)	*rih-toor*-NAY	return (go back), to
retourner, se	*sih rih-toor*-NAY	turn (face about), to
retraite, *f.*	*rih*-TRETT	retreat (*mil.*)
rétrécir, se (2)	*sih ray-tray*-SEER	shrink (become contracted), to
réunion, *f.*	*ray-ü*-N_YOHNG	assembly
"	"	meeting
réunir (2)	*ray-ü*-NEER	raise (collect), to
réunir, se	*sih ray-ü*-NEER	meet (come together), to
réussir (2)	*ray-ü*-SEER	succeed (attain goal), to
rêve, *m.*	REHV	dream
réveiller (1)	*ray-veh*-YAY	awaken (make awaken), to
"	"	wake (make awaken), to
réveiller, se	*sih ray-veh*-YAY	awaken (rouse oneself), to
"	"	wake (rouse oneself), to
révéler (1)	*ray-vay*-LAY	reveal (divulge), to
revendication, *f.*	*rih-vahn-dee-kah*-S_YOHNG	claim
revendiquer (1)	*rih-vahn-dee*-KAY	claim, to
revente, *f.*	*rih*-VAHNT	resale (*bus.*)
revenu, *m.*	*rih*-V(*ih*)NÜ	income
revenus, *m.pl.*	*rih*-V(*ih*)NÜ	revenue (*govt.*)
rêver (1)	*reh*-VAY	dream, to
révérence, *f.*	*ray-vay*-RAHNSS	reverence (respect)
revers, *m.*	*rih*-VEHR	back (reverse side)
revoir (62)	*rih*-VWAHR	review (look over again), to
revoir, au	*oh* R(*ih*)VWAHR	good-by
révolte, *f.*	*ray*-VUHLT	revolt
révolution, *f.*	*ray-vuh-lü*-S_YOHNG	revolution (*pol.*)

French	Pronunciation	English
revolver, *m.*	*ray-vuh*-LVEHR	revolver (weapon)
revue, *f.*	*rih*-VÜ	magazine (periodical)
Rhin, *m.*	RANG	Rhine
rhum, *m.*	RUM	rum
rhumatisme, *m.*	*rü-mah*-TEE-*sm*(*ih*)	rheumatism
rhume, *m.*	RÜM	cold (disease)
riche	REESH	rich
"	"	wealthy
richesse(s), *f.*(*pl.*)	*ree*-SHESS	wealth
richesses, *f. pl.*	*ree*-SHESS	riches
ride, *f.*	REED	ripple
rideau, *m.*	*ree*-DOH	curtain (drape)
ridicule	*ree-dee*-KÜL	ridiculous
ridicule, *m.*	*ree-dee*-KÜL	ridicule
rien	R_YANG	anything (not...anything)
"	"	nothing (*n.*)
rime, *f.*	REEM	rhyme
Río-de-Janeiro, *m.*	*ree-oh dih zhah-nay*-ROH	Rio de Janeiro
rire (51)	REER	laugh, to
rire, *m.*	REER	laughter
risque, *m.*	REESK	risk (danger)
risquer (à), se (1)	*sih ree*-SKAY (*ah*)	venture (dare), to
rite, *m.*	REET	rite
rival, *m.*	*ree*-VAHL	rival (competitor)
rive, *f.*	REEV	bank
"	"	shore
rivière, *f.*	*ree*-V_YEHR	river
riz, *m.*	REE	rice
robe, *f.*	RUB	dress (frock)
"	"	gown
robe de chambre, *f.*	*rub dih* SHAHM-*br*(*ih*)	robe (dressing gown)
robinet, *m.*	*ruh-bee*-NEH	faucet
"	"	tap
robuste	*ruh*-BÜST	sturdy
roc, *m.*	RUCK	rock (large stone)
rocheux, -cheuse	*ruh*-SHUH, -SHUHZ	rocky (rock-covered)
rôder (1)	*roh*-DAY	rove, to
roi, *m.*	RWAH	king
rôle, *m.*	ROHL	role
romain	*ruh*-MANG, -MENN	Roman (*adj.*)
roman, *m.*	*ruh*-MAHNG	novel (book)
romanesque	*ruh-mah*-NESSK	romantic
Rome, *f.*	RUM	Rome
rompre (52)	ROHM-*pr*(*ih*)	break (make divide), to
rond	ROHNG	round (*adj.*)
ronger (1)	*rohn*-ZHAY	gnaw (bite), to
rose	ROHZ	pink (color)
rose, *f.*	ROHZ	rose (flower)
roseau, *m.*	*roh*-ZOH	reed (grass)
rosée, *f.*	*roh*-ZAY	dew
rossignol, *m.*	*ruh-see*-N_YUHL	nightingale
rôti, *m.*	*ruh*-TEE	roast
rôtir (2)	*ruh*-TEER	roast (be roasted), to
roue, *f.*	ROO	wheel
rouge	ROOZH	red
rouge, *m.*	ROOZH	rouge
rouge à lèvres, *m.*	*roozh ah* LEH-*vr*(*ih*)	lipstick
rouge-gorge, *m.*	*roozh*-GORZH	robin
rougeole, *f.*	*roo*-ZHULL	measles
rougir (2)	*roo*-ZHEER	blush, to
rouille, *f.*	ROO_*y*	rust
rouillé	*roo*-YAY	rusty
rouleau, *m.*	*roo*-LOH	roll (cylinder)
"	"	roller
rouler (1)	*roo*-LAY	roll (impel), to
Roumanie, *f.*	*roo-mah*-NEE	Rumania
route, *f.*	ROOT	road
"	"	route
royal	*rwah*-YAHL	regal
"	"	royal
royaume, *m.*	*rwah*-YOH_M	kingdom
"	"	realm
ruban, *m.*	*rü*-BAHNG	band
"	"	ribbon
rubis, *m.*	*rü*-BEE	ruby (gem)
ruche, *f.*	RÜSH	hive (beehive)
rude	RÜD	rough (uneven)
rue, *f.*	RÜ	street
ruée, *f.*	RÜ_AY	rush (rapid motion)

French	Pronunciation	English
ruer, se (1)	*sih* RÜ_AY	rush (dash), to
rugissement, *m.*	*rü-zhee*-SMAHNG	roar (*n.*)
ruine(s), *f.*	RÜ_EEN	ruins (remains)
"	"	wreck
ruiner (1)	*rü_ee*-NAY	ruin, to
ruisseau, *m.*	*rü_ee*-SOH	brook
"	"	creek
"	"	gutter (of street)
"	"	stream
ruisseler (1)	*rü_ee*-SLAY	stream, to
rumeur, *f.*	*rü*-MUHR	rumor
rupture de contrat, *f.*	*rü-ptür dih kohn*-TRAH	breach of contract (*bus.*)
rural	*rü*-RAHL	rural
rusé	*rü*-ZAY	cunning
"	"	sly (crafty)
russe	RÜSS	Russian (*adj.*)
Russie, *f.*	*rü*-SEE	Russia
sa	SAH	her (*poss. pron.*)
"	"	his (*poss. adj.*)
"	"	its (*poss. adj.*)
sable, *m.*	SAH-*bl(ih)*	sand
sablonneux, -neuse	*sah-bluh*-NUH, -NUHZ	sandy
sabot, *m.*	*sah*-BOH	hoof
sac, *m.*	SAHK	bag (sack)
"	"	sack
sac à main, *m.*	*sah-kah*-MANG	bag (purse)
sacré	*sah*-KRAY	sacred
sacrifice, *m.*	*sah-kree*-FEESS	sacrifice (giving up)
sacrifier (1)	*sah-kree-F_YAY*	sacrifice (forego), to
sage	SAHZH	sage (*adj.*)
"	"	wise
sagesse, *f.*	*sah*-ZHESS	wisdom
saigner (1)	*seh-N_YAY*	bleed (lose blood), to
saillant	*sah*-YAHNG	prominent (jutting)
sain	SANG, SENN	healthy
"	"	sound
"	"	wholesome (beneficial)
saindoux, *m.*	*san*-DOO	lard
saint	SANG, SANT	holy
saint, *m.*	SANG	saint
saisie, *f.*	*say*-ZEE	attachment (legal seizure)
saisir (2)	*say*-ZEER	grab, to
"	"	grasp (understand), to
"	"	seize (clutch), to
saison, *f.*	*say*-ZOHNG	season (of year)
salade, *f.*	*sah*-LAHD	salad
salaire, *m.*	*sah*-LEHR	wages
sale	SAHL	dirty (soiled)
saleté, *f.*	*sahl*-TAY	dirt (unclean matter)
salle, *f.*	SAHL	auditorium
"	"	hall (meeting room)
salle à manger, *f.*	*sah-lah-mahn*-ZHAY	dining room
salle de bain, *f.*	*sahl dih* BANG	bathroom
salle de classe, *f.*	*sahl dih* KLAHSS	classroom
salle d'hôpital, *f.*	*sahl duh-pee*-TAHL	ward (sickroom)
salon, *m.*	*sah*-LOHNG	parlor (living room)
saluer (1)	*sah-LÜ_AY*	greet, to
"	"	salute, to
salut, *m.*	*sah*-LÜ	bow (nod)
"	"	salvation
Salvador, *m.*	*sahl-vah*-DOR	Salvador, El
sandwich, *m.*	*sahn*-DWEECH	sandwich
sang, *m.*	SAHNG	blood
sangloter (1)	*sahn-gluh*-TAY	sob, to
sans	SAHNG	without (*prep.*)
sans doute	*sahn* DOOT	doubtless
sans espoir	*sahn-zeh*-SPWAHR	hopeless
sans fin	*sahn* FANG	endless
sans ressource	*sahn rih*-SOORSS	helpless
sans valeur	*sahn vah*-LUHR	worthless (valueless)
santé, *f.*	*sahn*-TAY	health
Santiago, *m.*	*sahn-t_yah*-GOH	Santiago
saphir, *m.*	*sah*-FEER	sapphire (gem)
sapin, *m.*	*sah*-PANG	fir
sardine, *f.*	*sahr*-DEEN	sardine
satin, *m.*	*sah*-TANG	satin (*n.*)
satisfaction, *f.*	*sah-tee-sfahk-S_YOHNG*	satisfaction

French	Pronunciation	English
satisfaire (32)	*sah-tee*-SFEHR	satisfy, to
satisfaisant	*sah-tee-sfih*-ZAHNG	satisfactory
satisfait	*sah-tee*-SFEH	satisfied (contented)
sauce, *f.*	SOHSS	dressing
"	"	gravy
"	"	sauce
saucisse, *f.*	*soh*-SEESS	sausage
sauf	SOHF	except (*prep.*)
sauf, sauve	SOHF, SOHV	safe (unharmed)
saule, *m.*	SOHL	willow
saumon, *m.*	*soh*-MOHNG	salmon
saut, *m.*	SOH	jump (bound)
sauter (1)	*soh*-TAY	jump (bound), to
"	"	leap, to
"	"	skip (omit), to
"	"	spring, to
sauterelle, *f.*	*soh*-TRELL	grasshopper
sautiller (1)	*soh-tee*-YAY	hop, to
sauvage	*soh*-VAHZH	savage (*adj.*)
"	"	wild (undomesticated)
sauver (1)	*soh*-VAY	rescue, to
"	"	save, to
sauvetage, *m.*	*soh*-VTAHZH	rescue
sauveur, *m.*	*soh*-VUHR	savior
savant, *m.*	*sah*-VAHNG	scientist
saveur, *f.*	*sah*-VUHR	flavor (savor)
savoir (53)	*sah*-VWAHR	know (have knowledge), to
savoir, (à)	(*ah*) *sah*-VWAHR	namely
savon, *m.*	*sah*-VOHNG	soap
savon à barbe, *m.*	*sah-vohn ah* BAHRB	shaving cream
saxophone, *m.*	*sah-ksuh*-FUNN	saxophone
scandale, *m.*	*skahn*-DAHL	scandal
scarabée, *m.*	*skah-rah*-BAY	beetle
scarlatine, *f.*	*skahr-lah*-TEEN	scarlet fever
sceau, *m.*	SOH	seal (mark)
scélérat, *m.*	*say-lay*-RAH	villain
scénario, *m.*	*say-nah-R_YOH*	scenario
scène, *f.*	SENN	scene (dramatic unit)
scie, *f.*	SEE	saw (tool)
science, *f.*	S_YAHNSS	science
science politique, *f.*	*s_yahnss puh-lee*-TEEK	political science
scientifique	*s_yahn-tee*-FEEK	scientific
scintiller (1)	*san-tee*-YAY	twinkle, to
scrutin, *m.*	*skrü*-TANG	ballot
sculpteur, *m.*	*skül*-TUHR	sculptor
se	SIH	(to) herself, himself, itself, themselves
séance, *f.*	*say*-AHNSS	session
seau, *m.*	SOH	bucket
"	"	pail
sec, sèche	SECK, SESH	dry
sécher (1)	*seh*-SHAY	dry (make dry), to
sécher, (se)	(*sih*) *seh*-SHAY	dry (become dry), to
seconde, *f.*	*sih*-GOHND	second (time unit)
secouer (1)	*sih*-KWAY	shake, to
secourable	*sih-koo*-RAH-*bl(ih)*	helpful (volunteering help)
secours, *m.*	*sih*-KOOR	relief (aid)
secret, -crète	*sih*-KREH, -KRETT	secret (*adj.*)
secret, *m.*	*sih*-KREH	secret (*n.*)
secrétaire, *m., f.*	*sih-kray*-TEHR	secretary (stenographer)
section, *f.*	*seck-S_YOHNG*	section (part)
sécurité, *f.*	*say-kü-ree*-TAY	security (safety)
seigle, *m.*	SEH-*gl(ih)*	rye (grain)
seigneur, *m.*	*say-N_YUHR*	lord (master)
sein, *m.*	SANG	bosom
"	"	breast
séjour, *m.*	*say*-ZHOOR	stay (sojourn)
"	"	visit
sel, *m.*	SELL	salt
selle, *f.*	SELL	saddle (seat)
selon	*s(ih)*-LOHNG	according to (in accordance with)
semaine, *f.*	*sih*-MENN	week
semblable	*sahm*-BLAH-*bl(ih)*	like (*adj.*)
"	"	similar
semblant, *m.*	*sahm*-BLAHNG	pretense (pretending)
sembler (1)	*sahm*-BLAY	seem (appear), to
semelle, *f.*	*sih*-MELL	sole (of shoe)

French	Pronunciation	English	French	Pronunciation	English
semer (1)	*sih*-MAY	sow, to	siens, les	*lay* S_YANG	hers (*poss. pron.*)
sénat, *m.*	*say*-NAH	senate	"	"	his (*poss. pron.*)
sénateur, *m.*	*say-nah*-TUHR	senator	"	"	its (*poss. pron.*)
sens, *m.*	SAHNSS	meaning	siffler (1)	*see*-FLAY	hiss, to
"	"	sense (signification)	"	"	whistle, to
sens, bon, *m.*	*bohn* SAHNSS	sense (intelligence)	signal, *m.*	*see*-N_YAHL	signal
sensation, *f.*	*sahn-sah*-S_YOHNG	feeling	signature, *f.*	*see-n_yah*-TÜR	signature (name)
"	"	sensation	signe, *m.*	SEE-*n_yih*	sign (indication)
sensé	*sahn*-SAY	sensible	signer (1)	*see*-N_YAY	sign (endorse), to
sensible	*sahn*-SEE-*bl*(*ih*)	sensitive (suscepti-	significatif, -tive	*see-n_yee-fee-kah*-TEEF,	significant (meaning-
		ble)		-TEEV	ful)
sentier, *m.*	*sahn*-T_YAY	path	signifier (1)	*see-n_yee*-F_YAY	signify (denote), to
sentiment, *m.*	*sahn-tee*-MAHNG	feeling (emotion)	silence, *m.*	*see*-LAHNSS	silence (stillness)
"	"	sentiment	silencieux, -cieuse	*see-lahn*-S_YUH, -S_YUHZ	quiet
sentir	*sahn*-TEER	smell (perceive odor),	"	"	silent
		to	silex, *m.*	*see*-LEX	flint
sentir, (se) (26)	(*sih*) *sahn*-TEER	feel (experience), to	sillon, *m.*	*see*-YOHNG	furrow (*agric.*)
séparation, *f.*	*say-pah-rah*-S_YOHNG	separation	similarité, *f.*	*see-mee-lah-ree*-TAY	similarity
séparé	*say-pah*-RAY	separate	simple	SAM-*pl*(*ih*)	homely (everyday)
séparer (1)	*say-pah*-RAY	separate (discon-	"	"	simple (uninvolved)
		nect), to	simplicité, *f.*	*sam-plee-see*-TAY	simplicity
séparer, se	*sih suy-pah*-RAY	part (leave each	sincère	*san*-SEHR	sincere
		other), to	singe, *m.*	SANZH	monkey
"	"	separate (come	singulier, -lière	*san-gü*-L_YAY, -LYEHR	odd (queer)
		apart), to	"	"	peculiar
sergent, *m.*	*sehr*-ZHAHNG	sergeant	"	"	singular
série, *f.*	*say*-REE	series	singulier, *m.*	*san-gü*-L_YAY	singular (*gram.*, *n.*)
sérieux, -rieuse	*say*-R_YUH, -R_YUHZ	earnest	sinon	*see*-NOHNG	but (if not, *conj.*)
"	"	serious	siroter (1)	*see-ruh*-TAY	sip, to
"	"	sober	situation, *f.*	*see-tü_ah*-S_YOHNG	location (place)
serin, *m.*	*sih*-RANG	canary	"	"	situation (circum-
seringue, *f.*	*sih*-RAN_G	syringe			stances)
serment, *m.*	*sehr*-MAHNG	oath (vow)	slave	SLAHV	Slavic (*adj.*)
sermon, *m.*	*sehr*-MOHNG	sermon	sociable	*suh*-S_YAH-*bl*(*ih*)	sociable (companion-
serpent, *m.*	*sehr*-PAHNG	serpent			able)
"	"	snake	social	*suh*-S_YAHL	social (societal)
serre, *f.*	SEHR	claw (of bird)	socialisme, *m.*	*suh-s_yah*-LEE-*sm*(*ih*)	socialism
serrer (1)	*seh*-RAY	clasp (embrace), to	socialiste, *m.*, *f.*	*suh-s_yah*-LEEST	socialist (*n.*)
"	"	squeeze, to	société, *f.*	*suh-s_yay*-TAY	association (body of
serrure, *f.*	*seh*-RÜR	lock (fastening)			persons)
service, *m.*	*sehr*-VEESS	service	"	"	society
service des postes,	*sehr-veess day* PUHST	mail (postal system)	société (enregi-	*suh-s_yay-tay* (*ahn-rih-*	corporation
m.			strée), *f.*	*zhee*-STRAY)	
serviette, *f.*	*sehr*-V_YETT	briefcase	sociologie, *f.*	*suh-s_yuh-luh*-ZHEE	sociology
"	"	napkin	soeur, *f.*	SUHR	sister (*n.*)
"	"	towel, hand	sofa, *m.*	*suh*-FAH	sofa
servir (26)	*sehr*-VEER	serve, to	soie, *f.*	SWAH	silk (*n.*)
ses	SAY	her, his, its (*poss.*	soif, *f.*	SWAHF	thirst
		adj.)	soigner (1)	*swah*-N_YAY	nurse (give treat-
seul	SUHL	alone			ment to), to
"	"	lonesome	soi-même	*swah*-MEMM	herself, himself, it-
"	"	mere			self, oneself
"	"	only	soir, *m.*	SWAHR	evening
"	"	single	soir, ce	*sih* SWAHR	tonight
"	"	sole	soirée, *f.*	*swah*-RAY	party (social gather-
seulement	*suhl*-MAHNG	just			ing)
"	"	merely	soit	SWAH	whether (either,
"	"	only			*conj.*)
sève, *f.*	SEHV	sap (fluid)	sol, *m.*	SULL	soil (ground)
sévère	*say*-VEHR	grim	soldat, *m.*	*sull*-DAH	soldier
"	"	severe	soldat (du rang),	*sull*-DAH (*dü* RAHNG)	private (*mil.*)
"	"	stern (*adj.*)	*m.*		
sévérité, *f.*	*say-vay-ree*-TAY	severity (sternness)	soleil, *m.*	*sun*-LAY	sun
sexe, *m.*	SEX	sex	"	"	sunshine
si	SEE	if	solennel, -le	*suh-lah*-NELL	solemn (grave)
"	"	so (to such a degree,	solide	*suh*-LEED	solid (compact)
		adv.)	solitaire	*suh-lee*-TEHR	lone
"	"	whether (if, *conj.*)	"	"	lonely (lonesome)
"	"	yes (in contradic-	"	"	solitary
		tion)	solitude, *f.*	*suh-lee*-TÜD	solitude
siècle, *m.*	S_YEH-*kl*(*ih*)	century	solliciter (1)	*suh-lee-see*-TAY	solicit (ask for), to
siège, *m.*	S_YEHZH	seat	solution, *f.*	*suh-lü*-S_YOHNG	solution (solving)
"	"	siege (*mil.*)	sombre	SOHM-*br*(*ih*)	dark (without light,
sien, le	*lih* S_YANG	hers (*poss. pron.*)			*adj.*)
"	"	his (*poss. pron.*)	sommaire, *m.*	*suh*-MEHR	summary (synopsis)
"	"	its (*poss. pron.*)	somme, *f.*	SUM	amount
sienne, la	*lah* S_YENN	hers (*poss. pron.*)	"		sum (quantity)
"	"	his (*poss. pron.*)	somme, *m.*	SUM	nap (doze)
"	"	its (*poss. pron.*)	sommeil, *m.*	*suh*-MAY	sleep
siennes, les	*lay* S_YENN	hers (*poss. pron.*)	"	"	slumber
"	"	his (*poss. pron.*)	sommet, *m.*	*suh*-MEH	summit
"	"	its (*poss. pron.*)	son	SOHNG	her, his, its (*poss.*
					adj.)
			son, *m.*	SOHNG	sound (noise)

French	Pronunciation	English
sondage, *m.*	*sohn*-DAHZH	poll (survey)
sonner (1)	*suh*-NAY	peal, to
"	"	ring (resound), to
"	"	sound (make heard), to
sorcier, *m.*	*sor*-S_YAY	wizard (sorcerer)
sorcière, *f.*	*sor*-S_YEHR	witch
sort, *m.*	SOR	fate
sorte, *f.*	SORT	sort
sorte que, de	*dih* SORT *kih*	so (in order that, *conj.*)
sortie, *f.*	*sor*-TEE	exit
sot, -te	SOH, SUHT	foolish
"	"	silly
sot, *m.*	SOH	fool
souche, *f.*	SOOSH	stump (of tree)
souci, *m.*	*soo*-SEE	care (concern)
soucier, se (1)	*sih soo*-S_YAY	care (be concerned), to
soucoupe, *f.*	*soo*-KOOP	saucer
soudain	*soo*-DANG, -DENN	sudden (unexpected)
souffler (1)	*soo*-FLAY	blow (breathe out), to
souffrance, *f.*	*soo*-FRAHNSS	suffering
soufre, *m.*	SOO-*fr(ih)*	sulphur
souhaiter (1)	*sweh*-TAY	wish (desire on behalf of), to
souhaiter la bienvenue	*sweh-tay lah b_yan-vih-*NÜ	welcome (receive hospitably), to
souiller (1)	*soo*-YAY	soil (make dirty), to
soulagement, *m.*	*soo-lah*-ZHMAHNG	relief (alleviation)
soulager (1)	*soo-lah*-ZHAY	ease, to
"	"	relieve, to
soulever (1)	*soo*-L(*ih*)VAY	heave (lift), to
soulier, *m.*	*soo*-L_YAY	shoe (footwear)
soumettre, se (39)	*sih soo*-MEH-*tr(ih)*	comply (acquiesce), to
soupçon, *m.*	*soo*-PSOHNG	suspicion
soupçonner (1)	*soo-psuh*-NAY	suspect (distrust), to
soupe, *f.*	SOOP	soup
souper, *m.*	*soo*-PAY	supper (light evening meal)
soupirer (1)	*soo-pee*-RAY	sigh, to
source, *f.*	SOORSS	source (origin)
sourcil, *m.*	*soor*-SEE	eyebrow
sourd	SOOR, SOORD	deaf
sourire (51)	*soo*-REER	smile, to
sourire, *m.*	*soo*-REER	smile
sourire largement	*soo-reer lahr-zhih-*MAHNG	grin, to
souris, *f.*	*soo*-REE	mouse
sous	SOO	under (*prep.*)
sous la main	*soo lah* MANG	handy (near at hand)
sousmarin, *m.*	*soo-mah*-RANG	submarine
sous-produit, *m.*	*soo-pruh*-DÜ_EE	by-product
sous-sol, *m.*	*soo*-SUHL	basement
soustraire (56)	*soo*-STREHR	subtract, to
sous-vêtements, *m. pl.*	*soo-veh*-TMAHNG	underwear
soutenir (55)	*soo*-T(*ih*)NEER	contend (maintain), to
soutenir (55) "	*soo*-T(*ih*)NEER "	support (hold up), to sustain, to
soutenu	*soo*-T(*ih*)NÜ	steady (regular)
souterrain	*soo-teh*-RANG, -RENN	underground (*adj.*)
soutien, *m.*	*soo*-T_YANG	support
soutien-gorge, *m.*	*soo-t_yan*-GORZH	brassiere
souvenir, *m.*	*soo*-V(*ih*)NEER	memory (recollection)
"	"	remembrance
"	` "	souvenir
souvenir (de), se (59)	*sih soo*-V(*ih*)NEER (*dih*)	remember (recollect), to
souvent	*soo*-VAHNG	often
souverain, *m.*	*soo*-V(*ih*)RANG	ruler
"		sovereign
spécial	*spay*-S_YAHL	special
spécialement	*spay-s_yahl*-MAHNG	especially
spectacle, *m.*	*speh*-KTAH-*kl(ih)*	sight
"	"	spectacle (pageant)
spectateur, *m.*	*speh-ktah*-TUHR	spectator
spectre, *m.*	SPECK-*tr(ih)*	ghost
sphère, *f.*	SFEHR	sphere

French	Pronunciation	English
spirituel, -le	*spee-ree*-TÜ_ELL	spiritual (*adj.*)
"		witty
splendeur, *f.*	*splahn*-DUHR	splendor
splendide	*splahn*-DEED	gorgeous
"		splendid
sport, *m.*	SPOR	sport (game)
squelette, *m.*	*skih*-LETT	skeleton (*anat.*)
stable	STAH-*bl(ih)*	stable (steadfast)
stade, *m.*	STAHD	stadium
station climatique, *f.*	*stah-s_yohn klee-mah-*TEEK	resort (spa)
stationnaire	*stah-s_yuh*-NEHR	stationary (unmoving)
stationner (1)	*stah-s_yuh*-NAY	park (put in place), to
statue, *f.*	*stah*-TÜ	statue
stature, *f.*	*stah*-TÜR	stature (height)
statut, *m.*	*stah*-TÜ	by-law
stencil, *m.*	*sten*-SEEL	stencil
sténographe, *m., f.*	*stay-nuh*-GRAHF	stenographer
sténographie, *f.*	*stay-nuh-grah*-FEE	shorthand (stenography, *n.*)
stérile	*stay*-REEL	barren
steward, *m.*	*st_yoo*-WAHRD	steward (attendant on ship)
stimuler (1)	*stee-mü*-LAY	stimulate (incite), to
stipulation, *f.*	*stee-pü-lah*-S_YOHNG	provision (stipulation)
Stockholm, *m.*	*stuh*-KUHLM	Stockholm
store, *m.*	STOR	shade (window blind)
strict	STREEKT	strict (stringent)
structure, *f.*	*strü*-KTÜR	structure (arrangement of parts)
stupéfiant, *m.*	*stü-pay*-F_YAHNG	drug (narcotic)
stupide	*stü*-PEED	stupid
style, *m.*	STEEL	style (manner)
stylo à bille, *m.*	*stee-loh ah* BEE	ball-point pen
stylo(graphe), *m.*	*stee-loh*(-GRAHF)	pen, fountain
subir (2)	*sü*-BEER	suffer (undergo), to
subjectif, -tive	*süb-zheh*-KTEEF, -KTEEV	subjective
subjuguer (1)	*süb-zhü*-GAY	subdue (conquer), to
suborner (1)	*sü-bor*-NAY	bribe, to
subséquent	*sü-psay*-KAHNG, -KAHNT	subsequent
substance, *f.*	*sü*-PSTAHNSS	substance (matter)
substantiel, -le	*sü-pstahn*-S_YELL	substantial (sizable)
substituer (1)	*sü-pstee*-TÜ_AY	substitute (put in place of), to
succédané, *m.*	*sü-ksay-dah*-NAY	substitute (thing replacing another)
succéder (à) (1)	*sü-ksay*-DAY (*ah*)	succeed (follow), to
succès, *m.*	*sü*-KSEH	success (attainment)
succomber (1)	*sü-kohm*-BAY	succumb (yield), to
sucer (1)	*sü*-SAY	suck, to
sucre, *m.*	SÜ-*kr(ih)*	sugar
sud, *m.*	SÜD	south (*n.*)
sud-est, (du)	(*dü*) *sü*-DESST	southeast (*adj.*)
sud-ouest, (du)	(*dü*) *sü*-DWEST	southwest (*adj.*)
Suède, *f.*	SÜ_EDD	Sweden
suède, (peau de), *f.*	(*poh dih*) SÜ_EDD	suede (*n.*)
suédois	*sü_eh*-DWAH, -DWAHZ	Swedish (*adj.*)
sueur, *f.*	SÜ_UHR	sweat
suffisant	*sü-fee*-ZAHNG, -ZAHNT	adequate
"	"	sufficient
suggérer (1)	*sü-gzhay*-RAY	suggest (bring to mind), to
suggestion, *f.*	*sü-gzheh*-ST_YOHNG	suggestion (proposal)
suicide, *m.*	*sü_ee*-SEED	suicide
suisse	SÜ_EESS	Swiss (*adj.*)
Suisse, *f.*	SÜ_EESS	Switzerland
suite, *f.*	SÜ_EET	continuation
suivant	*sü_ee*-VAHNG, -VAHNT	next (following, *adj.*)
suivre (54)	SÜ_EE-*vr(ih)*	follow (go or come after), to
sujet, *m.*	*sü*-ZHEH	subject
"	"	topic
supérieur	*sü-pay*-R_YUHR	superior (excellent)
superstitieux, -tieuse	*sü-pehr-stee*-S_YUH, -S_YUHZ	superstitious
superstition, *f.*	*sü-pehr-stee*-S_YOHNG	superstition
supplément, *m.*	*sü-play*-MAHNG	addition (supplement)
supplémentaire	*sü-play-mahn*-TEHR	extra (additional)
"	"	further (*adj.*)

French	Pronunciation	English
supplier (1)	*sü-plee-*YAY	appeal to (entreat), to
"	"	beg, to
"	"	plead (appeal earnestly), to
supporter (1)	*sü-por-*TAY	bear, to
"	"	endure, to
"	"	stand (bear), to
supposer (1)	*sü-poh-*ZAY	guess, to
"	"	presume (assume), to
"	"	suppose (assume), to
suprême	*sü-*PREMM	supreme
supprimer (1)	*sü-pree-*MAY	suppress (subdue), to
sur	SÜR	across (from side to side)
"	"	at
"	"	on (*prep.*)
"	"	over
"	"	upon
sûr	SÜR	reliable
"	"	safe (without risk)
"	"	secure
"	"	sure
sûrement	*sür-*MAHNG	certainly (surely, *adv.*)
sûreté,*f.*	*sür-*TAY	safety (*n.*)
surface,*f.*	*sür-*FAHSS	face
"	"	surface
Surinam,*m.*	*soo-ree-*NAHM	Surinam
surnaturel,-le	*sür-nah-tü-*RELL	weird (unearthly)
surnom,*m.*	*sür-*NOHNG	nickname
surpasser (1)	*sür-pah-*SAY	surpass, to
surpaye,*f.*	*sür-*PAY	bonus (extra wages)
surplus,*m.*	*sür-*PLÜ	surplus (*n.*)
surprendre (48)	*sür-*PRAHN-*dr(ih)*	surprise, to
surprise,*f.*	*sür-*PREEZ	surprise
surtaxe,*f.*	*sür-*TAHX	surcharge (*bus.*)
surtout	*sür-*TOO	chiefly (mainly)
survivre (61)	*sür-*VEE-*vr(ih)*	survive (remain alive), to
suspendre (3)	*sü-*SPAHN-*dr(ih)*	suspend (terminate), to
syllabe,*f.*	*see-*LAHB	syllable
symboliser (1)	*sam-buh-lee-*ZAY	represent (symbolize), to
sympathie,*f.*	*sam-pah-*TEE	sympathy (accord)
symphonie,*f.*	*sam-fuh-*NEE	symphony
symptôme,*m.*	*sam-*PTOHM	symptom
syndicat,*m.*	*san-dee-*KAH	union (trade union)
système,*m.*	*see-*STEM	system (method)
ta	TAH	your
tabac,*m.*	*tah-*BAH	tobacco
table,*f.*	TAH-*bl(ih)*	table (furniture)
tableau,*m.*	*tah-*BLOH	table (tabulation)
tableau noir,*m.*	*tah-bloh* NWAHR	blackboard
tablier,*m.*	*tah-blee-*YAY	apron (garment)
tache,*f.*	TAHSH	blot
"	"	spot
"	"	stain
tâche,*f.*	TAHSH	task
tacher (1)	*tah-*SHAY	blot (stain), to
taille,*f.*	TYE	size (of suits, dresses, coats)
"	"	waist (*anat.*)
tailleur,*m.*	*tah-*YUHR	suit, woman's
"	"	tailor
talent,*m.*	*tah-*LAHNG	talent
talon,*m.*	*tah-*LOHNG	heel (*anat.*)
tambour,*m.*	*tahm-*BOOR	drum (*mus.*)
tampon,*m.*	*tahm-*POHNG	plug (stopper)
tanière,*f.*	*tah-*N_YEHR	den (animal lair)
tante,*f.*	TAHNT	aunt
tape,*f.*	TAHP	pat (tap)
taper (1)	*tah-*PAY	pat, to
"	"	tap (rap), to
taper à la machine	*tah-pay ah lah mah-*SHEEN	type (typewrite), to
tapis,*m.*	*tah-*PEE	carpet
"	"	rug
taquiner (1)	*tah-kee-*NAY	tease, to
tard	TAHR	late (at relative time, *adv.*)
tardif, -dive	*tahr-*DEEF, -DEEV	slow
		tardy (*adj.*)

French	Pronunciation	English
tarif,*m.*	*tah-*REEF	rate (price)
"	"	tariff (duty)
tarte,*f.*	TAHRT	pie
tas,*m.*	TAH	heap
"	"	pile
tasse,*f.*	TAHSS	cup
tâtonner vers (1)	*tah-tuh-*NAY *vehr*	feel (grope) for, to
taupe,*f.*	TOHP	mole (animal)
taureau,*m.*	*tuh-*ROH	bull (male bovine)
taux,*m.*	TOH	rate (exchange)
taxi,*m.*	*tah-*KSEE	cab
		taxi
Tchécoslovaquie,*f.*	*cheh-kuh-sluh-vah-*KEE	Czechoslovakia
te	TIH	(to) you
teindre (19)	TAN-*dr(ih)*	dye, to
teinte,*f.*	TANT	hue
teinture d'iode,*f.*	*tan-tür* D_YUHD	iodine (antiseptic)
tel, -le	TELL	such (of that kind, *adj.*)
Tel-Aviv,*m.*	*teh-lah-*VEEV	Tel Aviv
télégramme,*m.*	*tay-lay-*GRAHM	telegram
		wire (telegram)
télégraphier (1)	*tay-lay-grah-*F_YAY	telegraph, to
téléphone,*m.*	*tay-lay-*FUN	telephone
téléphoner (1)	*tay-lay-fuh-*NAY	phone, to
		telephone, to
télescope,*m.*	*tay-leh-*SKUPP	telescope
télévision,*f.*	*tay-lay-vee-z_*YOHNG	television
téméraire	*tay-may-*REHR	rash (*adj.*)
téméraire	*tay-may-*REHR	reckless
témoignage,*m.*	*tay-mwah-*N_YAHZH	testimony
témoigner (1)	*tay-mwah-*N_YAY	testify, to
témoin,*m.*	*tay-*MWANG	witness (one who testifies)
tempe,*f.*	TAHMP	temple (*anat.*)
température,*f.*	*tahm-pay-rah-*TÜR	temperature
tempête,*f.*	*tahm-*PET	tempest
tempête de neige,*f.*	*tahm-pet dih* NEHZH	blizzard
tempêter (1)	*tahm-peh-*TAY	rave (rant), to
temple,*m.*	TAHM-*pl(ih)*	temple (place of worship)
temps,*m.*	TAHNG	time (interval)
"	"	weather
(espace de) temps,*m.*	*(eh-spahss dih)* TAHNG	while (short time, *n.*)
temps en temps, de	*dih tahn-zahn-*TAHNG	occasional
"	"	occasionally
tendance,*f.*	*tahn-*DAHNSS	tendency
tendre (3)	TAHN-*dr(ih)*	strain (stretch), to
tendre	TAHN-*dr(ih)*	tender (loving)
tendresse,*f.*	*tahn-*DRESS	tenderness (love)
tendu	*tahn-*DÜ	tight (taut)
teneur de livres,*m.*	*tih-nuhr dih* LEE-*vr(ih)*	bookkeeper (*bus.*)
tenir (55)	*tih-*NEER	hold, to
"	"	last (withstand use), to
tennis,*m.*	*teh-*NEESS	tennis
tension,*f.*	*tahn-*S_YOHNG	stress
		tension (stretching)
tension (des nerfs),*f.*	*tahn-*S_YOHNG *(day* NEHR*)*	tension (anxiety)
tentation,*f.*	*tahn-tah-*S_YOHNG	temptation
tentative,*f.*	*tahn-tah-*TEEV	attempt
tente,*f.*	TAHNT	tent
tenter (1)	*tahn-*TAY	attempt, to
"	"	tempt, to
tenue des livres,*f.*	*tih-nü day* LEE-*vr(ih)*	bookkeeping (*bus.*)
terme,*m.*	TEHRM	term
terminer (1)	*tehr-mee-*NAY	close (finish), to
terminer, se	*sih tehr-mee-*NAY	end (come to an end), to
"	"	finish (reach the end), to
terrasse,*f.*	*teh-*RAHSS	terrace
terre,*f.*	TEHR	dirt (soil)
"	"	earth
"	"	ground
"	"	land
terreur,*f.*	*teh-*RUHR	terror
terrible	*teh-*REE-*bl(ih)*	awful
"	"	fearful
"	"	terrible

French	Pronunciation	English
terrifier (1)	*teh-ree-*F_YAY	terrify, to
territoire,*m.*	*teh-ree-*TWAHR	territory
tertre,*m.*	TEHR-*tr(ih)*	mound (hill)
tes	TAY	your
testament,*m.*	*teh-stah-*MAHNG	will (document)
tête,*f.*	TETT	head (*anat.*)
texte,*m.*	TEXT	text
textile,*m.*	*teh-*KSTEEL	textile (*n.*)
thé,*m.*	TAY	tea
théâtre,*m.*	*tay-*AH-*tr(ih)*	theater
thème,*m.*	TEMM	theme (subject)
théorie,*f.*	*tay-uh-*REE	theory
thermomètre,*m.*	*tehr-muh-*MEH-*tr(ih)*	thermometer
tien, le	*lih* T_YANG	yours
tienne, la	*lah* T_YENN	yours
tiennes, les	*lay* T_YENN	yours
tiens, les	*lay* T_YANG	yours
tige,*f.*	TEEZH	stalk
tige,*f.*	TEEZH	stem (*bot.*)
tigre,*m.*	TEE-*gr(ih)*	tiger
timbre-poste,*m.*	*tam-brih-*PUHST	stamp, postage
timbrer (1)	*tam-*BRAY	stamp (mark), to
timide	*tee-*MEED	bashful
"	"	shy
"	"	timid
tirer (1)	*tee-*RAY	derive (get), to
"	"	draw, to
"	"	haul (pull), to
tirer (1)	*tee-*RAY	pull, to
"	"	tug (drag), to
tirer sur	*tee-*RAY *sür*	shoot (fire at), to
tiroir,*m.*	*tee-*RWAHR	drawer (sliding box)
tisser (1)	*tee-*SAY	weave, to
tissu,*m.*	*tee-*SÜ	fabric (cloth)
"	"	tissue (*biol.*)
titre,*m.*	TEE-*tr(ih)*	title (name)
titres,*m.pl.*	TEE-*tr(ih)*	securities (stocks, etc.)
tituber (1)	*tee-tü-*BAY	reel (stagger), to
toi	TWAH	you
toi(-même)	TWAH(-MEMM)	yourself
toile,*f.*	TWAHL	canvas (cloth)
toile (de lin),*f.*	TWAHL (*dih* LANG)	linen (fabric)
toison,*f.*	*twah-*ZOHNG	fleece
toit,*m.*	TWAH	roof
Tokyo,*m.*	*tuh-*K_YOH	Tokyo
tolérer (1)	*tuh-lay-*RAY	tolerate (permit), to
tomate,*f.*	*tuh-*MAHT	tomato
tombe,*f.*	TOHMB	grave (tomb)
tomber (1)	*tohm-*BAY	drop (fall), to
"	"	fall, to
"	"	tumble, to
ton	TOHNG	your
ton,*m.*	TOHNG	tone (quality of sound)
tondre (3)	TOHN-*dr(ih)*	shear, to
tonneau,*m.*	*tuh-*NOH	barrel (cask)
tonnerre,*m.*	*tuh-*NEHR	thunder
torche,*f.*	TORSH	torch
tordre (3)	TOR-*dr(ih)*	twist (wind), to
torpille,*f.*	*tor-*PEE	torpedo
torrent,*m.*	*tuh-*RAHNG	torrent
tortu	*tor-*TÜ	crooked
tortue,*f.*	*tor-*TÜ	turtle
torture,*f.*	*tor-*TÜR	torture
tôt	TOH	soon (early)
tôt, plus	*plü* TOH	before (earlier, *adv.*)
total	*tuh-*TAHL	total (complete)
total,*m.*	*tuh-*TAHL	total (sum)
toucher (1)	*too-*SHAY	cash (receive cash for), to
"	"	feel, to
"	"	touch, to
toujours	*too-*ZHOOR	always
"		ever (at all times)
tour,*f.*	TOOR	tower
tour,*m.*	TOOR	tour
"	"	trick (ruse)
tour de tête,*m.*	*toor dih* TETT	size (of hats)

French	Pronunciation	English
touriste,*m.,f.*	*too-*REEST	tourist (*n.*)
tourment,*m.*	*toor-*MAHNG	torment
tourmenter (1)	*toor-mahn-*TAY	torment, to
tourner (1)	*toor-*NAY	turn (make rotate), to
tournevis,*m.*	*toor-nih-*VEESS	screw driver
tournoyer (1)	*toor-nwah-*YAY	spin (revolve), to
tous, toutes (les) deux	*too, toot* (*lay*) DUH	both (*pron.*)
tout	TOO	all (entirely, *adv.*)
tout	TOO, TOOT	all (*adj.*)
"	"	any (*adj.*)
"	"	every
tout	TOO	everything (*pron.*)
tout,*m.*	TOO	all (everything, *n.*)
"	"	whole (entirety, *n.*)
tout cas, en	*ahn too* KAH	anyway (in any case)
tout ce que	TOO S(*ih*)KIH	whatever (*pron.*)
tout ce qui	TOO S(*ih*)KEE	whatever (*pron.*)
toute facon, de	*dih toot fah-*SOHNG	anyhow (in any case)
toutes les fois que	*toot lay* FWAH *kih*	whenever
tout le monde	*too l(ih)* MOHND	everybody
tout petit	TOO P(*ih*)TEE	tiny
"	"	wee
toux,*f.*	TOO	cough
trace,*f.*	TRAHSS	trace (vestige)
tracteur agricole, *m.*	*trah-*KTUHR *ah-gree-*KUHL	tractor (farm machine)
tradition,*f.*	*trah-dee-*S_YOHNG	tradition
traduire (14)	*trah-*DÜ_EER	translate, to
tragédie,*f.*	*trah-zhay-*DEE	tragedy
tragique	*trah-*ZHEEK	tragic
trahir (2)	*trah-*EER	betray, to
trahison,*f.*	*trah-ee-*ZOHNG	treason
train,*m.*	TRANG	pace
"	"	rate (degree of speed)
"	"	train, railroad
traineau,*m.*	*treh-*NOH	sleigh
traîner (1)	*treh-*NAY	drag (pull), to
"	"	lag (fall behind), to
trait,*m.*	TREH	feature
trait d'union,*m.*	*treh dü-*N_YOHNG	hyphen
traite,*f.*	TRETT	bill of exchange
"	"	draft (check)
traité,*m.*	*treh-*TAY	treaty
traite à vue,*f.*	*trett ah* VÜ	sight draft (*bus.*)
traitement,*m.*	*treh-*TMAHNG	treatment
traiter (1)	*treh-*TAY	treat (behave toward), to
traître,*m.*	TREH-*tr(ih)*	traitor
tramway,*m.*	*trah-*MWAY	trolley (street car)
tranchant,*m.*	*trahn-*SHAHNG	edge (sharp side)
tranche,*f.*	TRAHNSH	slice
tranchée,*f.*	*trahn-*SHAY	trench (*mil.*)
tranquille	*trahn-*KEEL	quiet (without motion, *adj.*)
"	"	still (*adj.*)
tranquillité,*f.*	*trahn-kee-lee-*TAY	quiet (stillness)
transaction,*f.*	*trahn-zahk-*S_YOHNG	settlement (compromise, *bus.*)
transformer (1)	*trahn-sfor-*MAY	transform, to
transmettre (39)	*trahn-*SMEH-*tr(ih)*	forward (send by mail), to
transparent	*trahn-spah-*RAHNG, -RAHNT	transparent
transpirer (1)	*trahn-spee-*RAY	perspire, to
transport,*m.*	*trahn-*SPOR	transportation (conveying)
transporter (1)	*trahn-spor-*TAY	convey, to
"	"	transport, to
transporteur,*m.*	*trahn-spor-*TUHR	carrier (*bus.*)
travail,*m.*	*trah-*VYE	job (task)
"	"	labor (labor force)
"	"	work
travail à la tâche, *m.*	*trah-vye ah lah* TAHSH	piecework (*n.*)
travailler (1)	*trah-vah-*YAY	work (labor), to
travers, à	*ah trah-*VEHR	across (to the other side)
"	"	through (from end to end of, *prep.*)

French	Pronunciation	English
traversée, f.	trah-vehr-SAY	crossing (ocean voyage)
traverser (1)	trah-vehr-SAY	cross (traverse), to
trébucher (1)	tray-bü-SHAY	stumble, to
"	"	trip, to
trèfle, m.	TREH-fl(ih)	clover
tremblement de terre, m.	trahm-blih-mahn dih TEHR	earthquake
trembler (1)	trahm-BLAY	quake (shake), to
"	"	tremble, to
tremper (1)	trahm-PAY	soak (saturate), to
trépigner (1)	tray-pee-N_YAY	stamp (tread heavily), to
très	TREH	very (extremely)
trésor, m.	tray-ZOR	treasure
trésorerie, f.	tray-zor-REE	treasury (govt.)
tresser (1)	treh-SAY	braid (plait), to
triangle, m.	tree-YAHN-gl(ih)	triangle (geom.)
tribu, f.	tree-BÜ	tribe
tribunal, m.	tree-bü-NAHL	court (of law)
tribut, m.	tree-BÜ	tribute (money)
tricotage, m.	tree-kuh-TAHZH	knitting
tricoter (1)	tree-kuh-TAY	knit, to
trimestriel, -le	tree-meh-stree-YELL	quarterly (four times a year)
triomphe, m.	tree-YOHMF	triumph
triste	TREEST	mournful (saddening)
"	"	sad (sorrowful)
tristesse, f.	tree-STESS	sadness
trombone, m.	trohm-BUN	trombone
tromper (1)	trohm-PAY	deceive, to
tromper, se	sih trohm-PAY	err, to
tromperie, f.	trohm-PREE	deceit
trompette, f.	trohm-PET	trumpet (mus.)
tronc, m.	TROHNG	trunk (stem)
trône, m.	TROH_N	throne
trop	TROH	too (overly)
trot, m.	TROH	trot
trottoir, m.	truh-TWAHR	sidewalk
trou, m.	TROO	hole (cavity)
trouée, f.	troo-AY	gap
troupeau, m.	troo-POH	flock
"	"	herd (of animals)
troupes, f.pl.	TROOP	troops (mil.)
trouver (1)	troo-VAY	find (discover), to
"	"	locate, to
trouver, se	sih troo-VAY	lie (be located), to
truc, m.	TRÜK	trick (knack)
truite, f.	TRÜ_EET	trout
trust, m.	TRUST	trust (cartel)
tu	TÜ	you
tube, m.	TÜB	tube (pipe)
tuberculose, f.	tü-behr-kü-LOHZ	tuberculosis
tuer (1)	TÜ_AY	kill, to
"	"	slay, to
tulipe, f.	tü-LEEP	tulip
tumeur, f.	tü-MUHR	tumor
tunnel, m.	tü-NELL	tunnel
turc, turque	TÜRK	Turkish (adj.)
Turquie, f.	tür-KEE	Turkey
tuteur, m.	tü-TUHR	guardian (protector)
tuyau, m.	tü_ee-YOH	hose
"	"	pipe (tube)
tweed, m.	TWEED	tweed (cloth)
type, m.	TEEP	chap
"	"	fellow
typique	tee-PEEK	typical
tyran, m.	tee-RAHNG	tyrant
ulcère, m.	ül-SEHR	ulcer
un, une	UHNG, ÜN	a (an)
un autre	uh-NOH-tr(ih)	another (different, adj.)
"	"	another (different one, pron.)
une fois	ün FWAH	once (one time, adv.)
uniforme	ü-nee-FORM	uniform (adj.)
uniforme, m.	ü-nee-FORM	uniform (n.)
union, f.	ü-N_YOHNG	union (league)
unir (2)	ü-NEER	unite (make one), to
unité, f.	ü-nee-TAY	unity (accord)

French	Pronunciation	English
univers, m.	ü-nee-VEHR	universe
universel, -le	ü-nee-vehr-SELL	universal (adj.)
université, f.	ü-nee-vehr-see-TAY	university
un moment	uhn muh-MAHNG	awhile (adv.)
un ou l'autre, l'	luh-noo-LOH-tr(ih)	either (adj., pron.)
uranium, m.	ü-rah-N_YUMM	uranium
urbain	ür-BANG, -BENN	urban
urgent	ür-ZHAHNG	urgent
Uruguay, m.	ü-rü-GAY	Uruguay
usage, m.	ü-ZAHZH	practice (custom)
"	"	use (utilization)
usine, f.	ü-ZEEN	plant (factory)
utile	ü-TEEL	helpful
"	"	useful
utilité, f.	ü-tee-lee-TAY	use (usefulness)
"	"	utility
vacances, f.pl.	vah-KAHNSS	vacation (work holidays)
vacarme, m.	vah-KAHRM	din
vaccination, f.	vah-ksee-nah-S_YOHNG	vaccination
vache, f.	VAHSH	cow
vague	VAHG	vague (not precise)
vague, f.	VAHG	wave (billow)
vaguer (1)	vah-GAY	stray (roam), to
vain	VANG, VENN	vain (futile)
vaincre (57)	VAN-kr(ih)	conquer, to
"	"	defeat, to
"	"	overcome, to
vainqueur, m.	van-KUHR	victor
vaisseau, m.	veh-SOH	vessel (ship)
vaisselle, f.	veh-SELL	dishes (tableware)
valeur, f.	vah-LUHR	asset (bus.)
"	"	value
"	"	worth
valeur, de	dih vah-LUHR	valuable
valeur nominale, f.	vah-luhr nuh-mee-NAHL	face value (bus.)
vallée, f.	vah-LAY	valley
valse, f.	VAHLSS	waltz (dance step)
vanité, f.	vah-nee-TAY	vanity (self-conceit)
vaniteux, -teuse	vah-nee-TUH, -TUHZ	vain (conceited)
vanter, se (1)	sih vahn-TAY	boast, to
vapeur, f.	vah-PUHR	steam
"	"	vapor
varicelle, f.	vah-ree-SELL	chicken pox
varié	vah-R_YAY	miscellaneous
"	"	various (different)
varier (1)	vah-R_YAY	vary (differ), to
"	"	vary (undergo change), to
variété, f.	vah-r_yay-TAY	variety (diversity)
variole, f.	vah-R_YULL	smallpox
Varsovie, f.	vahr-suh-VEE	Warsaw
vase, m.	VAHZ	vase
vaste	VAHST	mighty
"	"	vast
veau, m.	VOH	calf (animal)
"	"	veal
véhicule, m.	vay-ee-KÜL	vehicle (conveyance)
veiller (1)	veh-YAY	watch (guard), to
veine, f.	VENN	vein (anat.)
velours, m.	vih-LOOR	velvet (n.)
veloutine, f.	vih-loo-TEEN	velveteen (n.)
vendeur, m.	vahn-DUHR	clerk (salesperson)
"	"	vendor (seller)
vendeur, (commis), m.	(kuh-mee) vahn-DUHR	salesman
vendre (3)	VAHN-dr(ih)	sell, to
Vendredi Saint, m.	vahn-drih-dee SANG	Good Friday
Venezuela, m.	vay-nay-zway-LAH	Venezuela
vénézuélien, -ne	vay-nay-zü_ay-L_YANG, -L_YENN	Venezuelan (adj.)
vengeance, f.	vahn-ZHANSS	revenge
"	"	vengeance
venir (59)	vih-NEER	come, to
Venise, f.	vih-NEEZ	Venice
vent, m.	VAHNG	wind
vente, f.	VAHNT	sale (exchange)
vente à l'enchère, f.	vahnt ah-lahn-SHEHR	auction (sale)
vente de soldes, f.	vahnt dih SUHLD	clearance sale
ventilateur, m.	vahn-tee-lah-TUHR	fan, electric
ventre, m.	VAHN-tr(ih)	belly (abdomen)

French	Pronunciation	English
ver,m.	VEHR	worm
véranda,f.	vay-rahn-DAH	porch
verbe,m.	VEHRB	verb
verge,f.	VEHRZH	rod (bar)
verger,m.	vehr-ZHAY	orchard
vérificateur des comptes,m.	vay-ree-fee-kah-tuhr day KOHNT	auditor
vérification,f.	vay-ree-fee-kah-s_YOHNG	check (examination)
vérification de comptes,f.	vay-ree-fee-kah-s_yohng dih KOHNT	audit (n.)
vérifier (1)	vay-ree-F_YAY	check (test), to
vérité,f.	vay-ree-TAY	truth
vernis,m.	vehr-NEE	varnish
verre,m.	VEHR	glass
"	"	tumbler
verrou,m.	veh-ROO	bolt (lock)
vers	VEHR	toward
vers,m.	VEHR	verse (poetic writing)
vers sa demeure	vehr sah D(ih)MUHR	homeward
verser (1)	vehr-SAY	pour (make flow), to
vert	VEHR, VEHRT	green (color)
vertu,f.	vehr-TÜ	virtue (moral excellence)
vessie,f.	veh-SEE	bladder (anat.)
vêtement,m.	veh-TMAHNG	garment
vêtements,m.pl.	veh-TMAHNG	attire (apparel)
"	"	clothing
veuf,m.	VUHF	widower
veuve,f.	VUHV	widow
vexer (1)	veh-KSAY	vex (anger), to
viande,f.	V_YAHND	meat
vice,m.	VEESS	vice (moral fault)
victime,f.	vee-KTEEM	victim
victoire,f.	vee-KTWAHR	victory
victorieux, -rieuse	vee-ktuh-R_YUH, -R_YUHZ	victorious
vide	VEED	empty
vider (1)	vee-DAY	empty (remove contents of), to
vie,f.	VEE	life
"	"	living (livelihood)
Vienne,f.	V_YENN	Vienna
viennois	v_yeh-NWAH, -NWAHZ	Viennese (adj.)
vierge,f.	V_YEHRZH	virgin (n.)
vieux (vieil), vieille	V_YUH (V_YAY), V_YAY	old
vieux (vieil), vieille	V_YUH (V_YAY), V_YAY	veteran (experienced)
vif, vive	VEEF, VEEV	vivid
vigne,f.	VEE-n_yih	vine (grapevine)
vignoble,m.	vee-N_YUH-bl(ih)	vineyard
vigoureux, -reuse	vee-goo-RUH, -RUHZ	vigorous
vigueur,f.	vee-GUHR	vigor (strength)
vigueur, en	ahn vee-GUHR	active (in force)
vilain	vee-LANG, -LENN	mean (malicious)
village,m.	vee-LAHZH	village
ville,f.	VEEL	city
"	"	town
vin,m.	VANG	wine (beverage)
vinaigre,m.	vee-NEH-gr(ih)	vinegar
violence,f.	v_yuh-LAHNSS	violence
violent	v_yuh-LAHNG	violent
violer (1)	v_yuh-LAY	violate (infringe upon), to
violette,f.	v_yuh-LETT	violet (flower)
violon,m.	v_yuh-LOHNG	violin
violoncelle,m.	v_yuh-lohn-SELL	cello
virage,m.	vee-RAHZH	turn (change of direction)
virgule,f.	veer-GÜL	comma
viril	vee-REEL	manly
vis,f.	VEESS	screw (threaded nail)
visage,m.	vee-ZAHZH	countenance
"	"	face (anat.)
viser (1)	vee-ZAY	aim (direct), to
visible	vee-ZEE-bl(ih)	visible
vision,f.	vee-Z_YOHNG	vision (eyesight)
visite,f.	vee-ZEET	visit (social call)
visiter (1)	vee-zee-TAY	visit (go to view), to
visiteur,m.	vee-zee-TUHR	visitor
vital	vee-TAHL	vital (essential)
vitamine,f.	vee-lah-MEEN	vitamin
vite	VEET	fast (quickly)
vitesse,f.	vee-TESS	speed (rapidity)
vitre,f.	VEE-tr(ih)	pane, window
vivant	vee-VAHNG	alive
"	"	live (adj.)
vivre (61)	VEE-vr(ih)	live (be alive), to
voeu,m.	VUH	pledge
"	"	vow
vogue, en	ahn VUHG	popular (prevalent)
voie,f.	VWAH	track (rails)
voile,m.	VWAHL	veil (n.)
voir (62)	VWAHR	behold, to
"	"	see, to
voisin,m.	vwah-ZANG	neighbor
voisinage,m.	vwah-zee-NAHZH	neighborhood
"	"	vicinity
voiture,f.	vwah-TÜR	car (auto)
"	"	carriage (horse-drawn vehicle)
"	"	coach, railroad
voiture d'enfant,f.	vwah-tür dahn-FAHNG	carriage (baby buggy)
voiturée,f.	vwah-tü-RAY	carload (bus.)
voix,f.	VWAH	voice
voix, à haute	ah oht VWAH	aloud
vol,m.	VUHL	flight (journey by air)
volaille,f.	vuh-LYE	fowl
"	"	poultry
volcan,m.	vull-KAHNG	volcano
voler (1)	vuh-LAY	fly, to
"	"	rob, to
"	"	steal, to
voleur,m.	vuh-LUHR	robber
voleur,m.	vuh-LUHR	thief
volontaire,m.	vuh-lohn-TEHR	volunteer (mil.)
volonté,f.	vuh-lohn-TAY	will (power of choice)
volume,m.	vuh-LÜM	volume
vomir (2)	vuh-MEER	vomit, to
vos	VOH	your
vote,m.	VUHT	vote
voter (1)	vuh-TAY	vote, to
votre	VUH-tr(ih)	your
vôtre, la	lah VOH-tr(ih)	yours
vôtre, le	lih VOH-tr(ih)	yours
vôtres, les	lay VOH-tr(ih)	yours
vouloir (63)	voo-LWAHR	want (desire), to
vouloir dire	voo-lwahr DEER	mean (have in mind), to
vous	VOO	you
vous(-même)	VOO(-MEMM)	yourself
vous(-mêmes)	VOO(-MEMM)	yourselves
voûte,f.	VOOT	arch (curved structure)
voyage,m.	vwah-YAHZH	journey
"	"	trip
"	"	voyage
voyager (1)	vwah-yah-ZHAY	travel, to
voyageur,m.	vwah-yah-ZHUHR	passenger
"	"	traveler
voyageur de commerce,m.	vwah-yah-zhuhr dih kuh-MEHRSS	traveling salesman
vrai	VRAY	true
vraiment	vray-MAHNG	indeed (adv.)
"	"	really
vue,f.	VÜ	sight (eyesight)
"	"	sight (range of view)
"	"	view
vue momentanée, f.	vü muh-mahn-tah-NAY	glimpse
vulgaire	vül-GEHR	common
"	"	vulgar (ill-bred)
wagon,m.	vah-GOHNG	car, railroad
wagon-restaurant, m.	vah-gohn-reh-stuh-RAHNG	diner (railway dining car)
whisk(e)y,m.	wee-SKEE	whiskey
y	EE	it
"	"	there (at that place)
Yougoslavie,f.	yoo-guh-slah-VEE	Yugoslavia
zèbre,m.	ZEH-br(ih)	zebra
zèle,m.	ZELL	zeal
zéro,m.	zay-ROH	zero (n.)
zinc,m.	ZAN_GH	zinc
zone,f.	ZONE	zone
zoologie,f.	zuh-luh-ZHEE	zoology

French Special Lists

Alphabet

a	AH		j	ZHEE		s	ESS
b	BAY		k	KAH		t	TAY
c	SAY		l	ELL		u	Ü
d	DAY		m	EM		v	VAY
e	UH (AY, EH)		n	EN		w	doo-bl(ih) VAY
f	EFF		o	OH		x	EEX
g	ZHAY		p	PAY		y	ee GRECK
h	AHSH		q	KÜ		z	ZEDD
i	EE		r	EHR			

Cardinal Numbers

French	Pronunciation	English	French	Pronunciation	English
un, une	UHNG, ÜN	one	vingt et un	van-tay-UHNG	twenty-one
deux	DUH	two	vingt-deux	vant-DUH	twenty-two
trois	TRWAH	three	trente	TRAHNT	thirty
quatre	KAH-tr(ih)	four	quarante	kah-RAHNT	forty
cinq	SANK	five	cinquante	san-KAHNT	fifty
six	SEESS	six	soixante	swah-SAHNT	sixty
sept	SET	seven	soixante-dix	swah-sahnt-DEESS	seventy
huit	Ü_EET	eight	quatre-vingts	kah-tr(ih)-VANG	eighty
neuf	NUFF	nine	quatre-vingt-dix	kah-tr(ih)-van-DEESS	ninety
dix	DEESS	ten	cent	SAHNG	one hundred
onze	OHNZ	eleven	cent un	sahng UHNG	one hundred one
douze	DOOZ	twelve	deux cents	duh SAHNG	two hundred
treize	TREZZ	thirteen	deux cent un	duh sahng UHNG	two hundred one
quatorze	kah-TORZ	fourteen	mille	MEEL	one thousand
quinze	KANZ	fifteen	mille un	meel UHNG	one thousand one
seize	SEZ	sixteen	deux mille	duh MEEL	two thousand
dix-sept	deess-SET	seventeen	deux mille un	duh meel UHNG	two thousand one
dix-huit	dee-zü_EET	eighteen	un million	uhn mee-L YOHNG	one million
dix-neuf	dee-ZNUFF	nineteen	un milliard	uhn mee-L YAHR	one billion
vingt	VANG	twenty			

Ordinal Numbers

French	Pronunciation	English	French	Pronunciation	English
premier, -mière	prih-M YAY, -M YEHR	first	septième	seh-T YEMM	seventh
deuxième; second, -e	duh-Z YEMM; sih-GOHNG, -GOHND	second	huitième	ü_ee-T YEMM	eighth
troisième	trwah-Z YEMM	third	neuvième	nuh-V YEMM	ninth
quatrième	kah-tree-YEMM	fourth	dixième	dee-Z YEMM	tenth
cinquième	san-K YEMM	fifth	onzième	ohn-Z YEMM	eleventh
sixième	see-Z YEMM	sixth	douzième	doo-Z YEMM	twelfth

Days of the Week

French	Pronunciation	English	French	Pronunciation	English
dimanche,m.	dee-MAHNSH	Sunday	jeudi,m.	zhuh-DEE	Thursday
lundi,m.	luhn-DEE	Monday	vendredi,m.	vahn-drih-DEE	Friday
mardi,m.	mahr-DEE	Tuesday	samedi,m.	sah-MDEE	Saturday
mercredi,m.	mehr-krih-DEE	Wednesday			

Months of the Year

French	Pronunciation	English	French	Pronunciation	English
janvier,m.	zhahn-V YAY	January	juillet,m.	zhü_ee-YAY	July
février,m.	feh-vree-YAY	February	août,m.	OO	August
mars,m.	MARSS	March	septembre,m.	seh-PTAHM-br(ih)	September
avril,m.	ah-VREEL	April	octobre,m.	uh-KTUH-br(ih)	October
mai,m.	MAY	May	novembre,m.	nuh-VAHM-br(ih)	November
juin,m.	ZHÜ_ANG	June	décembre,m.	day-SAHM-br(ih)	December

First Names

French	Pronunciation	English	French	Pronunciation	English
Abraham	ah-brah-AHM	Abraham	Benjamin	ban-zhah-MANG	Benjamin
Adam	ah-DAHNG	Adam	Bernard	behr-NAHR	Bernard
Agnès	ah-N YESS	Agnes	Berthe	BEHRT	Bertha
Albert	ahl-BEHR	Albert	Caroline	kah-ruh-LEEN	Caroline
Alexandre	ah-lch-KSAHN-dr(ih)	Alexander			
Alfred	ahl-FRED	Alfred	Catherine	kah-TREEN	Kate
Alice	ah-LEESS	Alice	"	"	Katharine
André	ahn-DRAY	Andrew			
Anne	AH_N	Ann, Anne	Charles	SHAHRL	Charles
Antoine	ahn-TWAH_N	Anthony	Charlotte	shahr-LUHT	Charlotte
Arnaud	ahr-NO	Arnold	Christine	kree-STEEN	Christine
Arthur	ahr-TÜR	Arthur	Christophe	kree-STUFF	Christopher
			Claire	KLEHR	Clara
Barbe	BAHRB	Barbara	"	"	Clare
Béatrice	bay-ah-TREESS	Beatrice	Conrad	kohn-RAHD	Conrad

French	Pronunciation	English	French	Pronunciation	English
Constance	*kohn*-STAHNSS	Constance	**Judith**	*zhü*-DEET	Judith
Daniel	*dah-n͟_YELL*	Daniel	**Julien**	*zhü-L͟_YANG*	Julian
David	*dah*-VEED	David	**Laure**	LOR	Laura
			Léo	*lay*-OH	Leo
Dorothée	*duh-ruh*-TAY	Dorothy	**Léon**	*lay*-OHNG	Leon
Édith	*ay*-DEET	Edith	**Léonard**	*lay-uh*-NAHR	Leonard
Edmond	*ed*-MOHNG	Edmund			
Édouard	*ay*-DWAHR	Edward	**Léonore**	*lay-uh*-NOR	Leonora
Éléonore	*ay-lay-uh*-NOR	Eleanor	**Léopold**	*lay-uh*-PUHLD	Leopold
Élisabeth	*ay-lee-zah*-BET	Elizabeth	**Louis**	L͟_WEE	Louis
			Louise	L͟_WEEZ	Louise
Émilie	*ay-mee*-LEE	Emily	**Marc**	MAHRK	Mark
Emma	*eh*-MAH	Emma	**Marguerite**	*mahr-ghih*-REET	Margaret
Ernest	*ehr*-NEST	Ernest	**Marie**	*mah*-REE	Marie
Étienne	*ay-t͟_YENN*	Stephen	"	"	Mary
Eugène	*uh*-ZHENN	Eugene	**Marthe**	MAHRT	Martha
Félix	*fay*-LIX	Felix	**Martin**	*mahr*-TANG	Martin
			Mathieu	*mah-t͟_YUH*	Matthew
Ferdinand	*fehr-dee*-NAHNG	Ferdinand	**Michel**	*mee*-SHELL	Michael
Florence	*fluh*-RAHNSS	Florence			
François	*frahn*-SWAH	Francis	**Nicolas**	*nee-kuh*-LAH	Nicholas
Françoise	*frahn*-SWAHZZ	Frances	**Olga**	*uhl*-GAH	Olga
Frédéric	*fray-day*-REEK	Frederick	**Othon**	*oh*-TOHNG	Otto
Gautier	*goh-t͟_YAY*	Walter	**Patrice**	*pah*-TREESS	Patrick
			Paul	PUHL	Paul
Georges	ZHORZH	George	**Paule**	POHL	Paula
Gertrude	*zhehr*-TRÜD	Gertrude			
Guillaume	*ghee*-YOHM	William	**Philippe**	*fee*-LEEP	Philip
Gustave	*gü*-STAHV	Gustav	**Pierre**	P͟_YEHR	Peter
Harold	*ah*-RUHLD	Harold	**Raoul**	*rah*-OOL	Ralph
Hélène	*ay*-LEN	Helen	**Raymond**	*ray*-MOHNG	Raymond
			Rébecca	*ray-beh*-KAH	Rebecca
Henri	*ahn*-REE	Harry	**Richard**	*ree*-SHAHR	Richard
"	"	Henry			
Henriette	*ahn-R͟_YETT*	Henrietta	**Robert**	*ruh*-BEHR	Robert
Herbert	*ehr*-BEHR	Herbert	**Rosalie**	*ro-zah*-LEE	Rosalie
Hermann	*ehr-MAH_N*	Herman	**Rose**	ROHZ	Rose
Horace	*uh*-RAHSS	Horace	**Rose-Marie**	*rohz-mah*-REE	Rosemary
			Rudolph	*rü*-DUHLF	Rudolph
Hugues	ÜG	Hugh	**Ruth**	RÜT	Ruth
Irène	*ee*-REN	Irene			
Isaak	*ee*-ZAHK	Isaac	**Samuel**	*sah-MÜ_ELL*	Samuel
Isabelle	*ee-zah*-BELL	Isabel	**Sarah**	*sah*-RAH	Sarah
Jacob	*zhah*-KUBB	Jacob	**Saül**	*sah*-ÜL	Saul
Jacques	ZHAHK	James	**Susanne**	*sü-ZAH_N*	Susan
			Sylvie	*seel*-VEE	Sylvia
Jean	ZHAHNG	John			
Jeanne	ZHAH_N	Jane	**Thérèse**	*tay*-REZZ	Theresa
"	"	Jean	**Thomas**	*tuh*-MAH	Thomas
"	"	Joan	**Victor**	*vee*-KTOR	Victor
Joseph	*zho*-ZEFF	Joseph	**Vincent**	*van*-SAHNG	Vincent
Joséphine	*zho-zay*-FEEN	Josephine	**Virginie**	*veer-zhee*-NEE	Virginia

USEFUL EXPRESSIONS

Greetings

English	Pronunciation	French
How are you?	*kuh-mahn-tah-lay*-VOO?	**Comment allez-vous?**
Well, thanks, and you?	*b͟_yan, mehr-see, ay* VOO?	**Bien, merci, et vous?**
Good morning.	*bohn*-ZHOOR.	**Bonjour.**
Good afternoon.	*bohn*-ZHOOR.	**Bonjour.**
Good evening.	*bohn*-SWAHR.	**Bonsoir.**
Good night.	*bun* NÜ_EE.	**Bonne nuit.**
See you again.	*oh play*-ZEER.	**Au plaisir.**
So long.	*ah b͟_yan*-TOH.	**A bientôt.**
Good luck!	*bun* SHAHNSS!	**Bonne chance!**
Good-by.	*oh* R(ih)VWAHR.	**Au revoir.**
Glad to meet you.	*ahn-shahn-tay dih fehr vuh-trih kuh-neh*-SAHNSS.	**Enchanté de faire votre connaissance.**
Congratulations.	*toot may fay-lee-see-tah-s͟_YOHNG.*	**Toutes mes félicitations.**
Happy Birthday.	*bohn ah-nee-vehr*-SEHR.	**Bon anniversaire.**
Merry Christmas.	*zhwah-yuh nuh*-ELL.	**Joyeux Noël.**
Happy New Year.	*bun ah*-NAY.	**Bonne Année.**

Ordinary Conversation

English	Pronunciation	French
Thank you.	*mehr*-SEE.	**Merci.**
Please.	*vuh*-YAY.	**Veuillez.**
You're welcome.	*zhih voo-zahn* PREE.	**Je vous en prie.**
Pardon me.	*ex-kü-zay*-MWAH.	**Excusez-moi.**
What do you call this?	*kuh-mahn ah-pell-tohn sih*-SEE?	**Comment appelle-t-on ceci?**
I'm sorry.	*zhih rih*-GRETT.	**Je regrette.**
Allow me.	*pehr-meh-tay*-MWAH.	**Permettez-moi.**
I would like...	*zhih voo*-DRAY...	**Je voudrais...**

English	Pronunciation	French
Come in.	*ahn*-TRAY.	Entrez.
May I introduce...	*pehr-meh-lay-mwah d(ih) voo pray-zahn-*TAY...	Permettez-moi de vous présenter...
What is your name?	*kuh-mahn voo-zah-play-*VOO?	Comment vous appelez-vous?
My name is...	*zhih mah-*PELL...	Je m'appelle...
I don't know.	*zhih n(ih) say* PAH.	Je ne sais pas.
I'm thirsty.	*zhay* SWAHF.	J'ai soif.
I'm hungry.	*zhay* FANG.	J'ai faim.
I'm an American.	*zhih sü_ee-zah-may-ree-*KANG (-KENN).	Je suis Américain(e).
Where can I find...?	*oo pü_eezh troo-*VAY...?	Où puis-je trouver...?
What is this?	*keh-skih say kih sih-*SEE?	Qu'est-ce que c'est que ceci?

Foreign Languages

English	Pronunciation	French
Do you speak...?	*pahr-lay-*VOO...?	Parlez-vous...?
I speak (understand) a little...	*zhih pahrl (kohm-prahng) uhn* PUH...	Je parle (comprends) un peu...
I do not speak...	*zhih n(ih) pahrl* PAH...	Je ne parle pas...
Is there someone here who speaks English?	*yah-teel kell-kuhng ee-see kee pahr-lahn-*GLEH?	Y a-t-il quelqu'un ici qui parle anglais?
I understand you.	*zhih voo kohm-*PRAHNG.	Je vous comprends.
I don't understand.	*zhih n(ih) kohm-prahng* PAH.	Je ne comprends pas.
Please speak more slowly.	*pahr-lay plü lahnt-*MAHNG, *seel voo* PLEH.	Parlez plus lentement, s'il vous plaît.
Please repeat.	*ray-pay-*TAY, *seel voo* PLEH.	Répétez, s'il vous plaît.

Asking Directions

English	Pronunciation	French
In which direction is...?	*dih kell kuh-*TAY *eh...*?	De quel côté est...?
Please take me to...	*voo-lay-voo b_yan mah-mnay ah...*	Voulez-vous bien m'emmener à...
Please take me there.	*voo-lay-voo b_yan mee ah-mnay.*	Voulez-vous bien m'y emmener.
Where can I mail this?	*oo pü_eezh meh-trih sih-see ah lah* PUHST?	Où puis-je mettre ceci à la poste?
Please direct me to...	*voo-lay-voo b_yan man-dee-kay oo s(ih)* TROOV...	Voulez-vous bien m'indiquer où se trouve...
...the telephone.	*...lih tay-lay-*FUN.	...le téléphone.
...the toilet.	*...lay lah-vah-*BOH.	...les lavabos.
...the post office.	*...lah* PUHST.	...la poste.
...the bank.	*...lah* BAHNK.	...la banque.
...the police station.	*...lih kuh-mee-sah-r_yah d(ih) puh-*LEESS.	...le commissariat de police.
...the U. S. consulate.	*...lih kohn-sü-lah ah-may-ree-*KANG.	...le consulat américain.
Please point.	*mohn-tray dü* DWAH, *seel voo* PLEH.	Montrez du doigt, s'il vous plaît.

The Hotel

English	Pronunciation	French
I would like a room...	*zhih voo-dray-(z)ün* SHAHM-*br(ih)*...	Je voudrais une chambre...
...with a single bed.	*...ah uhn* LEE.	...à un lit.
...with two beds.	*...ah duh* LEE.	...à deux lits.
...with bath.	*...ah-veck sahl dih* BANG.	...avec salle de bain.
...without meals.	*...sahn rih-*PAH.	...sans repas.
Please, the key for Room...	*lah klay poor lih nü-may-roh..., seel voo* PLEH.	La clef pour le numéro..., s'il vous plaît.
Please call me at...o'clock.	*voo-lay-voo b_yan mih ray-veh-yay ah...*UHR.	Voulez-vous bien me réveiller à...heures.
I want this...	*zhih voo-dray fehr...*	Je voudrais faire...
...pressed.	*...rih-pah-say sih-*SEE.	...repasser ceci.
...cleaned.	*...neh-twah-yay sih-*SEE.	...nettoyer ceci.
...washed.	*...lah-vay sih-*SEE.	...laver ceci.
...repaired.	*...ray-pah-ray sih-*SEE.	...réparer ceci.
When will (my suit) be returned?	*kahn-teh-skohn rah-por-tih-rah (mohn kohm-*PLEH)?	Quand est-ce qu'on rapportera (mon complet)?
Please return (my suit) at...	*voo-lay-voo b_yan rah-por-tay (mohn kohm-*PLEH) *ah...*	Voulez-vous bien rapporter (mon complet) à...

The Restaurant

English	Pronunciation	French
A table for two, please.	*ün tah-bl(ih) poor* DUH, *seel voo* PLEH.	Une table pour deux, s'il vous plaît.
I would like to see the menu.	*zhih voo-dray vwahr lah* KAHRT.	Je voudrais voir la carte.
I want it...	*zhih l(ih)* VUH...	Je le veux...
...rare.	*...seh-*N_YAHNG.	...saignant.
...medium.	*...ah* PWANG.	...à point.
...well done.	*...b_yan* KÜ_EE.	...bien cuit.
Check, please!	*lah-dee-s_*YOHNG, *seel voo* PLEH!	L'addition, s'il vous plaît!

Telephoning

English	Pronunciation	French
I wish to telephone.	*zhih day-zeer tay-lay-fuh-*NAY.	Je désire téléphoner.
Please get me this number.	*voo-lay-voo b_yan mih duh-nay sih nü-may-*ROH.	Voulez-vous bien me donner ce numéro.

English	Pronunciation	French
Please give me the number of...	*voo-lay-voo b̯yan mih duh-nay lih nü-may-roh dih tay-lay-*FUN *dih...*	Voulez-vous bien me donner le numéro de téléphone de...
What did you say?	*kuh-*MAHNG?	Comment?
The line is busy.	*lah lee-n̯yeh-tuh-kü-*PAY.	La ligne est occupé.
What is the charge?	*kohm-b̯yan* ESS?	Combien est-ce?

Time

English	Pronunciation	French
What time is it?	*kell uhr eh-*TEEL?	Quelle heure est-il?
It is...	*eel eh...*	Il est...
...five o'clock.	*...san-*KUHR.	...cinq heures.
...ten past eight.	*...ü_ee-tuhr* DEESS.	...huit heures dix.
...a quarter past six.	*...see-zuhr ay* KAHR.	...six heures et quart.
...half past five.	*...san-kuhr ay* D(*ih*)MEE.	...cinq heures et demie.
...five to seven.	*...seh-tuhr mwan* SANK.	...sept heures moins cinq.
The day before yesterday	*ah-vahn-*T̯YEHR	Avant-hier
Yesterday evening	*yehr* SWAHR	Hier soir
This morning	*sih mah-*TANG	Ce matin
At noon	*ah mee-*DEE	À midi
In the afternoon	*(pahn-dahn) lah-preh-mee-*DEE	(Pendant) l'après-midi
In the evening	*lih* SWAHR	Le soir
At night	*(pahn-dahn) lah* NÜ_EE	(Pendant) la nuit
At midnight	*ah mee-*NÜ_EE	À minuit
Tomorrow morning	*dih-man mah-*TANG	Demain matin
Tomorrow evening	*dih-man* SWAHR	Demain soir
The day after tomorrow	*ah-preh-*D(*ih*)MANG	Après-demain

Weather

English	Pronunciation	French
It's hot.	*eel feh* SHOH.	Il fait chaud.
It's cold.	*eel feh* FRWAH.	Il fait froid.
It's raining.	*eel* PLUH.	Il pleut.
It's snowing.	*eel* NEHZH.	Il neige.
What fine weather!	*kell boh* TAHNG!	Quel beau temps!

Postal Information

English	Pronunciation	French
How much is the postage on this?	*ah kohm-*B̯YAN *dwah-tohn ah-frahn-*SHEER *sih-*SEE?	A combien doit-on affranchir ceci?
Give me...worth of stamps.	*duh-nay-mwah day* TAM-*brah...*	Donnez-moi des timbres à...
Please send this letter...	*voo-lay-voo b̯yan ahn-vwah-yay set* LEH-*tr(ih)...*	Voulez-vous bien envoyer cette lettre...
...airmail.	*...pahr ah-v̯*YOHNG.	...par avion.
...special delivery.	*...pahr ex-*PREH.	...par exprès.
...registered.	*...rih-kuh-mahn-*DAY.	...recommandée.
Please send this parcel post.	*voo-lay-voo b̯yan ahn-vwah-yay sih-see pahr kuh-lee puh-*STAHL.	Voulez-vous bien envoyer ceci par colis postal.

Barber and Beauty Shop

English	Pronunciation	French
I want a haircut.	*zhih voo-dray-(z)ün koop dih* SHVUH.	Je voudrais une coupe de cheveux.
Not too short.	*pah troh* KOOR.	Pas trop courts.
No hair oil, thank you.	*pah d(ih) kuh-smay-*TEEK, *mehr-see.*	Pas de cosmétique, merci.
I want a shave.	*zhih voo-dray mih fehr rah-*ZAY.	Je voudrais me faire raser.
I want a shampoo.	*zhih voo-dray-zuhn shahm-*PWANG.	Je voudrais un shampoing.
I want my hair set.	*zhih voo-dray-(z)ün mee-zahn-*PLEE.	Je voudrais une mise-en-plis.

Transportation

English	Pronunciation	French
Where is the ticket office?	*oo ay l(ih) ghee-*SHEH?	Où est le guichet?
When does...arrive?	*ah kell uhr ah-reev...*	À quelle heure arrive...
...the train...	*...lih* TRANG?	...le train?
...the plane...	*...lah-v̯*YOHNG?	...l'avion?
...the bus...	*...loh-tuh-*BÜSS?	...l'autobus?
At what time does the train leave for...?	*ah kell uhr pahr lih trang poor...?*	À quelle heure part le train pour...?
From which track does the train for...leave?	*sür kell vwah pahr lih trang poor...?*	Sur quelle voie part le train pour...?
Is this the right train for...?	*say b̯yan lih tran poor...?*	C'est bien le train pour...?
Where is my baggage?	*oo sohn may bah-*GAHZH?	Où sont mes bagages?
Where is the baggage room?	*oo ay lahn-rih-zhee-strih-mahn day bah-*GAHZH?	Où est l'enregistrement des bagages?
Please call a taxi.	*ah-play uhn tah-*KSEE, *seel voo* PLEH.	Appelez un taxi, s'il vous plait.

Auto Travel

English	Pronunciation	French
What place is this?	*kell ahn-drwah* ESS?	Quel endroit est-ce?
Where is the town?	*oo s(ih) troov lah* VEEL?	Où se trouve la ville?
Which is the best road for...?	*kell ay lih meh-yuhr shih-man poor ah-lay ah...?*	Quel est le meilleur chemin pour aller à...?
Turn to the right.	*ah-lay ah* DRWAHT.	Allez à droite.
Turn to the left.	*ah-lay ah* GOHSH.	Allez à gauche.
Go straight on.	*ah-lay too* DRWAH.	Allez tout droit.
Go back.	*rih-toor-*NAY.	Retournez.
This way.	*pahr ee-*SEE.	Par ici.
That way.	*pahr* LAH.	Par là.
How far is it to...?	*ah kell dee-stahnss sih troov...?*	À quelle distance se trouve...?
Is this the road to...?	*eh-skih set root men ah...?*	Est-ce que cette route mène à...?
Is it...	*eh-skih seh...*	Est-ce que c'est...
...near?	...PREH?	...près?
...far?	...LWANG?	...loin?
...very far?	*...treh* LWANG?	...très loin?
Which way is...	*dih kell kuh-tay eh...*	De quel côté est...
...north?	*...lih* NOR?	...le nord?
...south?	*...lih* SÜD?	...le sud?
...east?	...LEST?	...l'est?
...west?	...LWEST?	...l'ouest?
Is the road...?	*lah roo t eh-tell...?*	La route est-elle...?
Is there a detour?	*eh-skee-l yah iin day-v yah-s* YOHNG?	Est-ce qu'il y a une déviation?
What is the speed limit?	*kell eh lah vee-tess mah-ksee-*MAH?	Quelle est la vitesse maxima?
Where is the nearest gas station?	*oo eh lih puhst day-sahnss lih plü* PRUHSH?	Où est le poste d'essence le plus proche?
Where can I find a garage (for repairs)?	*oo pü eezh troo-vay uhn gah-*RAHZH?	Où puis-je trouver un garage?
I need...	*zhay bih-*ZWANG...	J'ai besoin...
...oil.	...DÜ_EEL.	...d'huile.
...gasoline.	*...day-*SAHNSS.	...d'essence.
...a tire.	*...duhn* PNUH.	...d'un pneu.

Public Signs

English	Pronunciation	French
Keep Out	*day-fahnss dahn-*TRAY	Défense d'entrer
For Hire	*ah* LWAY	À louer
No Parking	*day-fahnss dih stah-s yuh-*NAY	Défense de stationner
No Smoking	*day-fahnss dih fü-*MAY	Défense de fumer
Sale	SULLD	Soldes
Women	DAHM	Dames
Men	UMM	Hommes
No Spitting	*day-fahnss dih krah-*SHAY	Défense de cracher
Railroad	*sh(ih)mang d(ih)* FEHR	Chemin de fer
Dangerous Curve	*toor-nahn dahn-*ZHRUH	Tournant dangereux
Keep to the Right (Left)	*tih-nay vuh-trih* DRWAHT (GOHSH)	Tenez votre droite (gauche)
Dead End	*am-*PAHSS	Impasse
Men Working	*trah-*VOH	Travaux
No Thoroughfare	*sahn-san-tehr-*DEE	Sens interdit
One-way Street	*sahn-sü-*NEEK	Sens unique
Go Slow	*rah-lahn-*TEER	Ralentir
Toilet	*doo-blih vay* SAY	W.C.
Entrance	*ahn-*TRAY	Entrée
Exit	*sor-*TEE	Sortie

French Grammar

ARTICLES

Definite article

	Sing.		*Pl.*	
Masc.	le	the		
Fem.	la	the	*Masc. and Fem.* les the
(*l'* before vowel or mute *h*) *				

le garçon	the boy	les garçons	the boys
l'alphabet	the alphabet	les alphabets	the alphabets
l'hôtel	the hotel	les hôtels	the hotels
la pomme	the apple	les pommes	the apples
l'orange	the orange	les oranges	the oranges
l'herbe	the grass	les herbes	the grasses

* Words beginning with aspirate *h* require the full rather than the elided form of articles, pronouns, prepositions, etc., and permit no linking in pronunciation with consonant sounds preceding them; for example, *l'homme*, but *le héros*; *un hôtel* (*uhn noh-*TELL), but *un héros* (*uhng ay-*ROH).

Contractions of the definite article. The prepositions *de* and *à* are always contracted with the articles *le* and *les* as follows:

de and *le* = *du*	le nom *du* garçon	the name *of the* boy
	loin *du* théâtre	far *from the* theater
de and *les* = *des*	le prix *des* chambres	the price *of the* rooms
à and *le* = *au*	Je vais *au* théâtre.	I am going *to the* theater.
	Il est *au* restaurant.	He is *at the* restaurant.
à and *les* = *aux*	Je parle *aux* garçons.	I speak *to the* boys.

With nouns in the general sense

Nouns used with the meaning of "all," "every," "in general" regularly have the definite article in French, though not always in English.

| J'aime *le* café. | I like coffee. |

Le chien est l'ami de *l'*homme.   *The* dog is man's friend.
La bonté est une vertu.   Kindness is a virtue.

With nouns in the partitive sense

Nouns with the words "some" or "any" expressed or implied are said to be used in a partitive sense. This is regularly expressed in French by *de* and the definite article before the noun.

A-t-il *de l'*argent?   Has he (*some, any*) money?
Voulez-vous *du* pain?   Do you want (*some, any*) bread?

J'ai *de la* monnaie.   I have (*some*) change.
Il est avec *des* amis.   He is with friends.

Indefinite article

Masc.	un	a, an	un garçon	a boy
Fem.	une	a, an	un bras	an arm
			une maison	a house
			une pomme	an apple
Masc. and Fem. Pl.	des	(some)	des garçons	(some) boys

NOUNS

Plural of nouns

The plural of nouns is regularly formed by adding *-s* to the singular.

le garçon	the boy	les garçons	the boys
la pomme	the apple	les pommes	the apples
l'hôtel	the hotel	les hôtels	the hotels

Nouns ending in *-s*, *-x* or *-z* remain unchanged in the plural.

le pas	the step	les pas	the steps
la voix	the voice	les voix	the voices
le nez	the nose	les nez	the noses

Most nouns ending in *-al* change the *-al* to *-au* and add *-x* to form the plural.

le cheval	the horse	les chevaux	the horses
le journal	the newspaper	les journaux	the newspapers

Nouns ending in *-au* and *-eu* add *-x* to form the plural.

le château	the castle	les châteaux	the castles
le jeu	the game	les jeux	the games

Exceptions to these rules are given in the word list.

Gender of nouns

Nouns in French are masculine or feminine and thus are modified by the corresponding adjectives and articles.

le garçon	un hôtel
la pomme	une orange

Some nouns, usually denoting persons, are both masculine and feminine.

un (une) enfant	a child
un (une) camarade	a comrade
un (une) élève	a pupil

Most nouns denoting living beings distinguish the two genders by changes in the ending of the noun, as follows:

The feminine is generally formed by adding *-e* to the masculine.

Masc.	*Fem.*	
candidat	candidate	candidate
ami	amie	friend
ours	ourse	bear
voisin	voisine	neighbor

Masculine nouns ending in *-el* and *-eau* form the feminine by changing the endings to *-elle*.

criminel	criminelle	criminal
chameau	chamelle	camel

Masculine nouns ending in *-en* and *-on* double the *n* before adding the feminine *e*.

gardien	gardienne	guardian
baron	baronne	baron, baroness

Masculine nouns ending in *-er* have *-ère* for the feminine.

boulanger	boulangère	baker
berger	bergère	shepherd, shepherdess

Some masculine nouns ending in *-eur* change the final *r* to *s* before the feminine *e*.

danseur	danseuse	dancer
chanteur	chanteuse	singer

A few masculine nouns ending in *-eur* change the *-eur* to *-eresse* in the feminine

pécheur	pécheresse	sinner

Some masculine nouns change final *-teur* to *-trice* in the feminine.

acteur	actrice	actor, actress
lecteur	lectrice	reader

Other irregular feminine endings are given in the French-to-English word list.

PRONOUNS

The personal pronouns are usually classified as *unstressed* (or *conjunctive* = joined with) and *stressed* (or *disjunctive* = disjoined, separated from). The unstressed forms are connected immediately to the verb. The stressed forms are usually found removed from the verb, used as objects of prepositions, etc.

Personal pronouns—unstressed forms

Subject of the verb

je	I	nous	we
tu	you	vous	you
il	he, it	ils	they
elle	she, it	elles	they
on	we, you, one, people, they		

Je vais au théâtre.   *I* am going to the theater.
Elles chantent bien.   *They* sing well.

The pronoun *on* is used indefinitely with the meanings listed. It is always the subject of a third person singular verb.

On voit cela tous les jours.   *You see* (*we see, one sees*) that every day.
On va au cinéma ce soir.   *We* (*the folks*) *are going* to the movies tonight.
On parle portugais au Brésil.   *They speak* Portuguese (Portuguese *is spoken*) in Brazil.

Direct object of the verb

me	me, myself	nous	us, ourselves
te	you, yourself	vous	you, yourself, yourselves
le	him, it	les	them
la	her, it	se	themselves
se	himself, herself, itself		

Il *me* voit.   He sees *me*.
Nous *nous* croyons.   We believe *ourselves*.
Elle *se* voit.   She sees *herself*.
Vous *les* entendez.   You hear *them*.

Indirect object of the verb

me	(to) me, myself	nous	(to) us, ourselves
te	(to) you, yourself	vous	(to) you, yourself, -selves
lui	(to) him, her, it	leur	(to) them
se	(to) himself, herself, itself	se	(to) themselves

Il *me* donne le livre.   He gives *me* the book.
Je *lui* ai donné le livre.   I gave *him* (*her*) the book.
Ils *nous* parlent.   They are speaking *to us*.
Il *se* parle.   He is talking *to himself*.

Forms *y* and *en*

Y means: to (at, on, in, into) it, them; there; to (at, in, on, into) that place.

En means: of (from) it, them; some, any, some of it, some of them; from there; from that place.

The forms *y* and *en* were originally adverbs. They are sometimes classified as pronominal adverbs. Their position and connection to the verb are like those of the direct and indirect object pronouns.

Y replaces the preposition *à* (*en, dans, sur*) plus a noun of either number or gender. *Y* usually stands for things.

A-t-il répondu *à la lettre?*	Has he answered (*to*) *the letter?*
Il *y* a répondu.	He has answered (*to*) *it.*
Est-ce que le livre est *sur la table?*	Is the book *on the table?*
Il *y* est.	It is (*there*).

En replaces the preposition *de* plus a noun of either number or gender. It usually stands for things, ideas or statements.

Nous parlons *des livres.*	We are speaking *of the books.*
Nous *en* parlons.	We are speaking *of them.*

The use of *en* to express some, any, some of it, some of them gives it the classification of partitive pronoun. It thus replaces nouns used in the partitive sense.

A-t-elle *des livres?*	Has she (*some, any*) *books?*
Elle *en* a.	She has (*some*).

Position of unstressed object pronouns. In general, the unstressed object pronouns—direct, indirect or both—stand immediately before the verb of which they are the object.

Je *vous* vois.	I see *you.*
Je *vous* parle.	I'm speaking *to you.*
Je veux *vous le* donner.	I want to give *it to you.*

When the verb is an *affirmative command*, its object pronouns—direct, indirect or both—follow it immediately.

Parlez-*moi.*	Speak *to me.*
Lisez-*le.*	Read *it.*
Donnez-*le-lui.*	Give *it to him* (*her*).
Donnez-*m'en.*	Give *me some* (*of it, of them*).

Note: When the verb is an affirmative command, the stressed forms *moi* and *toi* (see below) are used instead of *me* and *te*, except before *en.*

Donnez-*moi* du pain.	Give *me* some bread.
Donnez-*m'en.*	Give *me some.*

Relative position of object pronouns. When two pronoun objects precede the verb, the following table gives their relative positions.

me		le		lui		y before en
te	before	la	before	leur	before	
se		les				
nous						
vous						

Il *me le* donne.	He gives *it to me.*
Je *le lui* donne.	I give it *to him.*
Vous *nous en* parlez.	You speak *to us of it.*
Nous *l'y* avons vu.	We saw *him there.*

When two pronoun objects follow the verb, the direct object precedes the indirect. *Y* and *en*, in that order, are always last.

Donnez-*le-moi.*	Give *it to me.*
Donnez-*nous-en.*	Give *us some.*

Formal address. In direct address to one person, the form *vous* is used formally and to express respect. The forms *tu, te, toi* are generally used within the family, between close friends, between children, by grownups to children, by everybody to animals.

Elision. The dropping of a vowel takes place when the following forms stand before words beginning with a vowel or mute *h: je, me, te, le, la.*

J'ai	I have
Il *m'*a donné le livre.	He gave *me* the book.
Je *t'*ai donné le livre.	I gave *you* the book.
Je *l'*ai donné à mon frère.	I gave *it* to my brother.

Reflexive and reciprocal use. The direct and indirect object forms *se, nous, vous,* are used both reflexively and reciprocally (see also below, section on *Reflexive Verbs*).

Ils *se* voient.	They see *themselves.* (direct object, reflexive)
Ils *se* voient.	They see *each other.* (direct object, reciprocal)
Nous *nous* parlons.	We talk *to ourselves.* (indirect object, reflexive)
Nous *nous* parlons.	We talk *to each other.* (indirect object, reciprocal)

Personal pronouns—stressed forms

moi	I, me, myself	nous	we, us, ourselves
toi	you, yourself	vous	you, yourself, yourselves
lui	he, himself, him	eux	they, them, themselves
elle	she, her, herself	elles	they, them, themselves
soi	himself, herself, oneself		

Use of the stressed forms

When a verb is implied but not expressed.

Qui est là? —*Moi.*	Who is there? —*I.*
Qui voyez-vous? —*Eux.*	Whom do you see? —*Them.*

For emphasis, in apposition.

Je l'ai vu, *moi.*	*I* saw it.
Lui, il ne me croit pas.	*He* doesn't believe me.

-même(s) attached to the stressed forms makes them more emphatic.

Il le fait *lui-même.*	He does it *himself.*

As logical subject of the verb after *ce,* plus form of verb *être* (to be).

C'est *moi.*	It is *I.*
C'est *vous.*	It is *you.*

When one element of a compound subject or object is a pronoun.

Son père et *lui* viendront.	His father and *he* will come.

As object of a preposition.

Je vais avec *eux.*	I'm going with *them.*
Chacun pour *soi.*	Everyone for *himself.*
On parle de *moi.*	People are talking about *me.*

Possessive adjectives and pronouns

Possessive adjectives *

Masc. Sing.		*Fem. Sing.*		*Masc. and Fem. Pl.*	
mon	my	ma	my	mes	my
ton	your	ta	your	tes	your
son	his, her, its, one's	sa	his, her, its, one's	ses	his, her, its, one's
notre	our	notre	our	nos	our
votre	your	votre	your	vos	your
leur	their	leur	their	leurs	their

Possessive pronouns

Masc. Sing.		*Fem. Sing.*	
le mien	mine	la mienne	mine
le tien	yours	la tienne	yours
le sien	his, hers, its, one's own	la sienne	his, hers, its, one's own
le nôtre	ours	la nôtre	ours
le vôtre	yours	la vôtre	yours
le leur	theirs	la leur	theirs

Masc. Pl.		*Fem. Pl.*	
les miens	mine	les miennes	mine
les tiens	yours	les tiennes	yours
les siens	his, hers, its, one's own	les siennes	his, hers, its, one's own
les nôtres	ours	les nôtres	ours
les vôtres	yours	les vôtres	yours
les leurs	theirs	les leurs	theirs

Possessives, both adjectives and pronouns, agree in *number and gender* with *the thing possessed,* in *person* with *the possessor.*

Elle a *son* livre et *le sien.*	She has *his* book and *hers.*
Elle a *ses* livres et *les nôtres.*	She has *her* books and *ours.*

Note: The forms *mon, ton, son* are used instead of *ma, ta, sa* before a vowel or mute *h.*

son histoire	*his* (*her*) story
ton enfance	*your* childhood

The prepositions *de* and *à* contract with the masculine singular and the masculine and feminine plural possessive pronouns.

Vous avez répondu à votre père; je vais répondre *au mien.*	You have answered your father; I'm going to answer *mine.*
Si vous donnez vos opinions, il va parler *des siennes.*	If you give your opinions, he's going to speak *of his.*

---

* For convenience, possessive, demonstrative and interrogative adjectives are treated in this section on pronouns.

Relative pronouns

qui	who, which, that; whom (object of a preposition)
ce qui	that which, what, which
que	whom, which, that
ce que	that which, what, which
dont	whose, of whom, of which
lequel (*masc. sing.*)	
laquelle (*fem. sing.*)	which, that
lesquels (*masc. pl.*)	
lesquelles (*fem. pl.*)	
quoi	which, what

Relative pronouns agree in gender, number and person with their antecedents.

Qui is used:
  As subject of a verb.

l'homme *qui* arrive	the man *who* is arriving

  As object of a preposition.

l'homme *avec qui* je parlais	the man *with whom* I was speaking

Ce qui is the *compound* relative form (*ce* is the antecedent of *qui*) which is used as subject of a verb.

ce qui est vrai	*what* (that which) is true

Que is used as direct object of a verb.

le livre *que* j'ai	the book *that* I have

Ce que is the *compound* relative form (*ce* is the antecedent of *que*) which is used as direct object of a verb.

J'aime *ce que* vous m'apportez.	I like *what* (that which) you bring me.

Dont equals the preposition *de* plus the relative pronouns *qui* or *que*.

les hommes *dont* je parle	the men *of whom* I'm speaking
la dame *dont* le fils est ici	the lady *whose* son is here

Lequel, laquelle, lesquels, lesquelles are used as objects of prepositions when the relative pronoun stands for a thing.

le stylo *avec lequel* j'écris	the pen *with which* I'm writing
les livres *sur lesquels* je compte	the books I'm counting on (*on which* I'm counting)

Quoi is the relative pronoun used when the antecedent is indefinite, and is usually the object of a preposition.

Vous savez *à quoi* je pense.	You know what I'm thinking of.

Note: The adverb *où* is frequently used instead of the prepositions *dans, à, sur, par* plus a relative pronoun.

la ville *où* je demeure	the city *where* (in which) I live

Interrogative adjectives and pronouns

Interrogative adjectives *

	Sing.	Pl.	
Masc.	quel	quels	what?, which?
Fem.	quelle	quelles	what?, which?

Quel chapeau voulez-vous?	*Which* hat do you want?
Quelle est votre adresse?	*What* is your address?

Interrogative pronouns

Variable forms:

	Sing.		Pl.		
Masc.	lequel	which?	lesquels	which? which ones?
	lesquels	which one?	lesquelles	

Voici des pommes. *Lesquelles* voulez-vous?	Here are some apples. *Which* do you want?

The prepositions *à* and *de* contract with *lequel, lesquels* and *lesquelles*.

Desquels avez-vous parlé?	*Which* (ones) did you speak about?
Auquel pensez-vous?	*Which one* are you thinking of?

Invariable forms:

qui	who?, whom?
que	what?
quoi	what?

Qui êtes-vous?	*Who* are you?
Qui voyez-vous?	*Whom* do you see?
De *qui* parlez-vous?	Of *whom* are you speaking?

Qui is used:

  As subject of a verb

Qui êtes-vous?	*Who* are you?

  As object of a verb

Qui voyez-vous?	*Whom* do you see?

---

* For convenience, possessive, demonstrative and interrogative adjectives are treated in this section on pronouns.

  As object of a preposition

De *qui* parlez-vous?	Of *whom* are you speaking?

Que is the unstressed (conjunctive) form used as direct object or predicate of a verb.

Que dites-vous?	*What* are you saying?
Que sont-ils devenus?	*What* has become of them? (*What* have they become?)

Note: The form *qu'est-ce qui*...("what...?") is regularly used as subject of a verb.

Qu'est-ce qui se passe?	*What* is going on?

Quoi is the stressed (disjunctive) form used:
  When the verb is understood

J'ai quelque chose pour vous.	I have something for you.
Quoi?	*What?*

  As object of a preposition

De *quoi* parlez-vous?	*What* are you talking *about*?

Demonstrative adjectives and pronouns

Demonstrative adjectives *

Masc. Sing.
ce (before consonant or aspirate h)	this, that
cet (before vowel or mute h)	this, that

Fem. Sing.
cette	this, that

Masc. and Fem. Pl.
ces	these, those

The demonstrative adjective agrees in number and gender with the noun which it modifies.

ce livre	this (that) book
cet arbre	this (that) tree
cet hôtel	this (that) hotel
cette pomme	this (that) apple
cet autre livre	this (that) other book

To distinguish the meanings of *this* and *that, these* and *those,* *-ci* and *-là*, respectively, are attached to the noun modified.

Donnez-moi *ce livre-ci.*	Give me *this* book.
Gardez *ce livre-là.*	Keep *that* book.

Demonstrative pronouns

Masc. Sing.
celui(-ci; -là)	this one, that one, the one, he

Fem. Sing.
celle(-ci; -là)	this one, that one, the one, she

Masc. Pl.
ceux(-ci; -là)	these, those, the ones, they

Fem. Pl.
celles(-ci; -là)	these, those, the ones, they

Neuter
ce	this, that, he, she, it
ceci	this
cela	that

Masculine and feminine forms are regularly:
Accompanied by *-ci* or *-là*

Donnez-moi *celles-ci;* gardez *celles-là.*	Give me *these;* keep *those.*

Followed by a *de* phrase

mon livre et *celui de mon frère*	my book and *my brother's*

Followed by a relative clause

J'aime *ceux qui* sont sur la table.	I like *the ones that* are on the table.
Donnez-moi *celui que* vous avez.	Give me *the one that* you have.

Neuter forms:

Ce is used as subject of *être* when the predicate is a proper noun, a modified noun, a pronoun.

*C'*est Jean.	*It'*s John.
*C'*est un grand homme.	*He'*s a great man.
*C'*est lui.	*It'*s he.

Ce is used as subject of *être* when it refers back to a situation, fact or idea.

*C'*est vrai.	*That* (it) is true.

Note: The *e* of *ce* elides before a vowel.

Ceci and *cela* stand for something indicated although not specifically named, or to ideas, facts, situations.

Prenez *ceci;* laissez *cela.*	Take *this;* leave *that.*
Regardez *cela.*	Look at *that.*

Note: cela is contracted to *ça* in familiar speech.

Ça ne fait rien.	*That* doesn't matter.

ADJECTIVES *

Adjectives regularly agree in number and gender with the nouns that they modify.

Gender of adjectives

The feminine of·an adjective is regularly formed by adding -*e* to the masculine singular. Adjectives whose masculine ends in -*e* remain unchanged in the feminine.

Masc.	*Fem.*	
joli	jolie	pretty
grand	grande	big
jeune	jeune	young

Irregular formations include the following changes in the masculine stem upon adding the feminine -*e*:

Final -*f* becomes *v*
" -*x* " *s*
" -*c* " sometimes *ch*, sometimes *qu*
" -*g* " *gu*

acti*f*	acti*ve*	active
dangereu*x*	dangereu*se*	dangerous
blan*c*	blan*che*	white
publi*c*	publi*que*	public
lon*g*	lon*gue*	long

Masculine adjectives ending in -*el*, -*eil*, -*ien*, -*on*, -*s*, -*t* usually double the final consonant before adding the feminine -*e*.

cru*el*	cru*elle*	cruel
par*eil*	par*eille*	alike
anci*en*	anci*enne*	ancient
b*on*	b*onne*	good
épai*s*	épai*sse*	thick
so*t*	so*tte*	silly

Note: The adjectives *beau*, fine, beautiful; *fou*, mad, foolish; *mou*, soft; *nouveau*, new; *vieux*, old, have the following additional forms for the masculine singular, used only when the adjective comes immediately before a word beginning with a vowel or mute *h*: *bel; fol; mol; nouvel; vieil.*

The *e* of final -*er* and -*et* of some adjectives becomes *è* in the feminine.

ch*er*	ch*ère*	dear
lég*er*	lég*ère*	light, slight
premi*er*	premi*ère*	first
compl*et*	compl*ète*	complete

Some adjectives ending in -*eur* form the feminine by changing the -*r* to -*s* and adding -*e*.

rêv*eur*	rêv*euse*	dreamy
tromp*eur*	tromp*euse*	deceiving, deceitful

Some adjectives ending in -*teur* change the -*teur* to -*trice* to form the feminine.

cré*ateur*	cré*atrice*	creative

Plural of adjectives

Most masculine adjectives and all feminine adjectives form the plural by adding -*s* to the singular.

* For convenience, possessive, demonstrative and interrogative adjectives are treated in the section on pronouns.

Masc. Sing.	*Masc. Pl.*	*Fem. Sing.*	*Fem. Pl.*	
grand	grand*s*	grande	grande*s*	big
joli	joli*s*	jolie	jolie*s*	pretty

Special cases include the following:

Masculine adjectives ending in -*eau* add -*x* to form the plural.

Masc. Sing.	*Masc. Pl.*	
beau	beau*x*	beautiful
nouveau	nouveau*x*	new

Masculine adjectives ending in -*s* or -*x* remain unchanged.

bas	bas	low
gris	gris	gray

Masculine adjectives ending in -*al* regularly have a plural ending in -*aux*.

libéral	libér*aux*	liberal
légal	lég*aux*	legal

A small number of masculine adjectives ending in -*al* form the plural by adding -*s*.

naval	naval*s*	naval
fatal	fatal*s*	fatal
final	final*s*	final

Other special cases are given in the word list.

Comparison of adjectives

The comparative degree is regularly expressed by placing *plus*, more (comparison of superiority); *moins*, less (comparison of inferiority); or *aussi*, as (comparison of equality) before the adjective compared.

grand	big
plus grand	bigger
moins grand	less big
aussi grand	as big

The adjectives *bon*, *mauvais* and *petit* have special forms in the comparative degree.

bon	good	meilleur	better
mauvais	bad	pire	worse
petit	little	moindre	lesser (in importance)

Note: The form *plus petit* is also used, to mean smaller, or lesser in size.

The superlative degree is regularly expressed by placing the definite article or a possessive adjective before the forms used to express comparisons of superiority or inferiority.

Marie et Jeanne sont *les plus belles* jeunes filles de la classe. — Marie and Jean are *the most beautiful* girls in the class.

C'est *sa meilleure* robe. — It's *her best* dress.

When expressing the superlative degree of an adjective following the noun, the definite article remains.

Jean est l'étudiant *le plus intelligent* de la classe. — John is *the most intelligent* student in the class.

mon chien *le plus fidèle* — my *most faithful* dog

VERBS

Numbering of verbs

Each verb in the French-to-English list is followed by a number in parentheses. These numbers refer to verbs (1) through (63) whose forms are given for the most important tenses in this French grammar section (pp. 2829–36).

Conjugation of verbs

Every verb form has two elements: the *stem* and the *ending*.

Classification of regular verbs. There are three regular classes of conjugations of verbs. They are numbered (1), (2) and (3) in the French-to-English word list (pp. 2777–2820) according to their infinitive endings.

Model verbs:

Verb	*Stem*	*Infinitive ending*	*Conjugation*
chanter (to sing)	chant-	-er	(1)
finir (to finish)	fin-	-ir	(2)
vendre (to sell)	vend-	-re	(3)

The forms for these model verbs have been given in full in all the commonly used tenses (see pp. 2829–33). These will serve as models for all verbs numbered (1), (2) and (3) in the French-to-English word list.

Classification of irregular verbs. Other verbs, which possess certain irregular forms, are numbered in classes (4) through (63). A sample for each class is conjugated in the commonly used tenses (see pp. 2833–36). These will serve as models for all verbs bearing the same numbers in the French-to-English word list.

Moods of the verbs

The moods are the different ways of conceiving and presenting the action expressed by the verb. The following moods will be distinguished here: (1) the indicative, (2) the imperative and (3) the subjunctive.

Indicative mood

The indicative mood presents action or state objectively. It is the mood of direct or indirect statements and questions. It is used in both main and subordinate clauses of the sentence. It possesses the following commonly used tenses:

Present tense. Its use indicates that the action or state is taking place at the moment of speech. To form the present tense of regular verbs, the following endings are added to the infinitive stem:

(1) chanter

je chante	I sing	nous chant*ons*	we sing
tu chant*es*	you sing	vous chant*ez*	you sing
il chante	he, it sings	ils chant*ent*	they sing
elle chante	she, it sings	elles chant*ent*	they sing

(2) finir

je fin*is*	I finish	nous fin*issons*	we finish

tu fin*is*	you finish	vous fin*issez*	you finish
il fin*it*	he, it finishes	ils fin*issent*	they finish
elle fin*it*	she, it finishes	elles fin*issent*	they finish

(3) vendre

je vend*s*	I sell	nous vend*ons*	we sell
tu vend*s*	you sell	vous vend*ez*	you sell
il vend	he sells	ils vend*ent*	they sell
elle vend	she sells	elles vend*ent*	they sell

The present tense of irregular verbs is given in the list of models for irregular verbs (see pp. 2833–36).

Imperfect tense. Its use indicates that the action or state was in progress, but not yet completed, at some point in the past to which the speaker is referring. The imperfect tense of regular verbs and most irregular verbs is formed by dropping the *-ons* from the first person plural form of the present tense and adding the following endings:

(1) chanter

je chant*ais*	I was singing (used to sing)
tu chant*ais*	you were singing (used to sing)
il chant*ait*	he, it was singing (used to sing)
elle chant*ait*	she, it was singing (used to sing)
nous chant*ions*	we were singing (used to sing)
vous chant*iez*	you were singing (used to sing)
ils chant*aient*	they were singing (used to sing)
elles chant*aient*	they were singing (used to sing)

(2) finir

je finiss*ais*	I was finishing (used to finish)
tu finiss*ais*	you were finishing (used to finish)
il finiss*ait*	he, it was finishing (used to finish)
elle finiss*ait*	she, it was finishing (used to finish)
nous finiss*ions*	we were finishing (used to finish)
vous finiss*iez*	you were finishing (used to finish)
ils finiss*aient*	they were finishing (used to finish)
elles finiss*aient*	they were finishing (used to finish)

(3) vendre

je vend*ais*	I was selling (used to sell)
tu vend*ais*	you were selling (used to sell)
il vend*ait*	he was selling (used to sell)
elle vend*ait*	she was selling (used to sell)
nous vend*ions*	we were selling (used to sell)
vous vend*iez*	you were selling (used to sell)
ils vend*aient*	they were selling (used to sell)
elles vend*aient*	they were selling (used to sell)

The imperfect tense is primarily a descriptive tense and may be termed also the past descriptive tense. Its use is illustrated as follows:

To express what was happening when something else happened or was happening.

Nous *parlions* quand il est entré.	We *were speaking* when he came in.
Il *parlait* pendant qu'elle *chantait*.	He *was talking* while she *was singing*.

To express what used to happen (habitual or repeated action in the past).

Il *se levait* tard.	He *used to get up* late.
Il nous *parlait* souvent de son père.	He *would* often *talk* to us of his father.

To express a condition or state of mind at some time in the past.

Je *voulais* aller en France avec vous.	I *wanted* to go to France with you.

In the if-clause of conditional sentences, when the verb in the result clause is in the conditional tense.

Si j'*avais* de l'argent, j'irais en France.	If I *had* the money, I'd go to France.

Simple past tense. This is a narrative tense. It expresses actions completed in the past without reference to the present time. Its use is limited to literary French and formal public address. It is almost never used in conversation. The simple past tense of regular verbs is formed by adding the following endings to the infinitive stem:

(1) chanter

je chant*ai*	I sang
tu chant*as*	you sang
il chant*a*	he, it sang
elle chant*a*	she, it sang
nous chant*âmes*	we sang
vous chant*âtes*	you sang
ils chant*èrent*	they sang
elles chant*èrent*	they sang

(2) finir

je fin*is*	I finished
tu fin*is*	you finished
il fin*it*	he, it finished
elle fin*it*	she, it finished
nous fin*îmes*	we finished
vous fin*îtes*	you finished
ils fin*irent*	they finished
elles fin*irent*	they finished

(3) vendre

je vend*is*	I sold
tu vend*is*	you sold
il vend*it*	he sold
elle vend*it*	she sold
nous vend*îmes*	we sold
vous vend*îtes*	you sold
ils vend*irent*	they sold
elles vend*irent*	they sold

The following endings are added to the infinitive stem of **most** irregular verbs: *-us, -us, -ut, -ûmes, -ûtes, -urent*.

The forms for irregular verbs are given in the list of model verbs, pp. 2833–36.

Future tense. This tense is used to express actions that will take place at some future time. The future tense of regular verbs is formed by adding the following endings to the infinitive of the first and second conjugations and to the infinitive minus final *-e* of the third conjugation.

(1) chanter

je chanter*ai*	I shall (will) sing
tu chanter*as*	you will sing
il chanter*a*	he, it will sing
elle chanter*a*	she, it will sing
nous chanter*ons*	we shall (will) sing
vous chanter*ez*	you will sing
ils chanter*ont*	they will sing
elles chanter*ont*	they will sing

(2) finir

je finir*ai*	I shall (will) finish
tu finir*as*	you will finish
il finir*a*	he, it will finish
elle finir*a*	she, it will finish
nous finir*ons*	we shall (will) finish
vous finir*ez*	you will finish
ils finir*ont*	they will finish
elles finir*ont*	they will finish

(3) vendre

je vendr*ai*	I shall (will) sell
tu vendr*as*	you will sell
il vendr*a*	he will sell
elle vendr*a*	she will sell
nous vendr*ons*	we shall (will) sell
vous vendr*ez*	you will sell
ils vendr*ont*	they will sell
elles vendr*ont*	they will sell

The future tense of irregular verbs is given in the list of model irregular verbs, pp. 2833–36.

Conditional tense. This is used to express a result which depends on certain conditions implied or expressed in the imperfect tense.

Si j'avais de l'argent, j'*irais* en France.	If I had money, I *would go* to France.

In indirect discourse, to express what was once future and is now past.

Il a dit qu'il *viendrait*.	He said that he *would come*.

To express polite statements or requests.

Je *voudrais* voir un chapeau.	I *would like* to see a hat.
Auriez-vous la bonté de faire cela?	*Would you* be kind enough to do that?

The conditional tense of regular verbs is formed by adding the endings of the imperfect tense to the infinitive of the first and second conjugations and to the infinitive minus final *-e* of the third conjugation.

(1) chanter

je chanter*ais*	I would sing
tu chanter*ais*	you would sing
il chanter*ait*	he, it would sing
elle chanter*ait*	she, it would sing
nous chanter*ions*	we would sing
vous chanter*iez*	you would sing
ils chanter*aient*	they would sing
elles chanter*aient*	they would sing

(2) finir

je finir*ais*	I would finish
tu finir*ais*	you would finish
il finir*ait*	he, it would finish
elle finir*ait*	she, it would finish
nous finir*ions*	we would finish

vous finiriez	you would finish
ils finiraient	they would finish
elles finiraient	they would finish

(3) vendre

je vendrais	I would sell
tu vendrais	you would sell
il vendrait	he would sell
elle vendrait	she would sell
nous vendrions	we would sell
vous vendriez	you would sell
ils vendraient	they would sell
elles vendraient	they would sell

The conditional tense of irregular verbs is given in the list of model irregular verbs, pp. 2833–36.

Present participle. The present participle is used as a verbal adjective or verbal noun, with or without the preposition *en*, to express cause, action, manner, motive simultaneous to the main verb, or means.

Riant, elle a fini l'histoire.	*Laughing*, she finished the story.
Étant malade, elle ne sort pas.	*Being* ill, she does not go out.
En faisant ceci, vous gagnerez.	*By doing* this, you will win.
(*En*) *disant* cela, il est sorti.	*Saying* that, he went out.

The present participle of regular verbs is formed by adding -*ant* to the infinitive stem of the 1st and 3rd conjugations -*issant* to the infinitive stem of the 2nd conjugation.

(1) chanter

chant*ant*	singing

(2) finir

fin*issant*	finishing

(3) vendre

vend*ant*	selling

The present participles of irregular verbs are given in the list of irregular verbs, pp. 2833–36.

Past participle. The past participle is used as an attributive or predicate adjective and, with the auxiliary verbs *avoir* and *être*, as the second element in the compound tenses (see below). As an adjective, it follows the regular rules for formation of the feminine singular and the masculine and feminine plural (see above, p. 2829).

des livres *donnés* par le professeur	books *given* by the teacher
Tenez la porte *ouverte*.	Hold the door *open*.

Note: The compound tenses are: the present perfect, past perfect, future perfect and conditional perfect.

The past participle of regular verbs is formed by adding -*é* to the infinitive stem of the 1st conjugation; -*i* to the infinitive stem of the 2nd conjugation; -*u* to the infinitive stem of the 3rd conjugation.

(1) chanter

chant*é*	sung

(2) finir

fin*i*	finished

(3) vendre

vend*u*	sold

The past participle of irregular verbs is given in the list of models of irregular verbs, pp. 2833–36.

Present perfect tense. The present perfect is a narrative tense. It is used in the following ways:

To express what has happened with respect to the present time.

J'ai lu ce livre.	*I have read* that book.

As the conversational equivalent of the simple past tense (see above, p. 2830).

J'ai lu ce livre la semaine dernière.	*I read* that book last week.

The present perfect tense is formed by compounding the present tense of the verb *avoir*, to have (of the verb *être* in the case of all reflexive verbs and those listed below), with the past participle.

j'ai chanté	I sang (*have* sung)
nous nous *sommes* vus	we saw (*have* seen) each other
elle *est* partie	she left (*has* left)

(1) chanter

j'ai chanté	I sang (have sung)
tu as chanté	you sang (have sung)
il a chanté	he, it sang (has sung)
elle a chanté	she, it sang (has sung)
nous avons chanté	we sang (have sung)
vous avez chanté	you sang (have sung)
ils ont chanté	they sang (have sung)
elles ont chanté	they sang (have sung)

(2) finir

j'ai fini, etc.	I (have) finished, etc.

(3) vendre

j'ai vendu, etc.	I (have) sold, etc.

The verb *être* is used as the auxiliary of all reflexive verbs (see below, p. 2833, for discussion of reflexive verbs).

je me *suis* levé	I got up

The verb *être* is also used as the auxiliary of the following intransitive verbs and their compounds:

aller	to go	naître	to be born
arriver	to arrive, happen	partir	to leave
descendre	to go down	rester	to stay, remain
devenir	to become	retourner	to return
entrer	to enter, go in, come in	sortir	to go out
		tomber	to fall
mourir	to die	venir	to come

je *suis* allé	I went (*have* gone)
je *suis* tombé	I fell (*have* fallen)
vous *êtes* venu	you came (*have* come)

Verbs Compounded with *Être*

se flatter

je me suis flatté(e)	I (have) flattered myself
tu t'es flatté(e)	you (have) flattered yourself
il s'est flatté	he (has) flattered himself
elle s'est flattée	she (has) flattered herself
nous nous sommes flatté(e)s	we (have) flattered ourselves
vous vous êtes flatté(e)(s)	you (have) flattered yourself (-selves)
ils se sont flattés	they (have) flattered themselves
elles se sont flattées	they (have) flattered themselves

aller

je suis allé, etc.	I went (have gone), etc.

Note: The past participle of verbs compounded with *avoir* agrees in gender and number with the preceding direct object of the verb.

Où est la robe? Je *l'*ai vendue.	Where is the dress? I sold it.

The past participle of reflexive verbs usually agrees in gender and number with the preceding direct object of the verb.

Elles *se* sont vu*es*.	They saw themselves.

The past participle of other verbs compounded with *être* agrees in gender and number with the subject of the verb.

Elle est entré*e*.	She went (came) in.
Ils sont parti*s*.	They (have) left.

Past perfect (pluperfect) tense. The past perfect or pluperfect tense is used to express actions completed in the past before some other time in the past. It is formed as is the present perfect tense, with the exception that the imperfect tense of the auxiliary verb, *avoir* or *être*, is used in every case.

j'*avais* chanté	I *had* sung
nous nous *étions* vus	we *had* seen each other
elles *étaient* parties	they *had* left

(1) chanter

j'avais chanté	I had sung
tu avais chanté	you had sung
il avait chanté	he, it had sung
elle avait chanté	she, it had sung
nous avions chanté	we had sung
vous aviez chanté	you had sung
ils avaient chanté	they had sung
elles avaient chanté	they had sung

(2) finir

j'avais fini, etc.	I had finished, etc.

(3) vendre

j'avais vendu, etc.	I had sold, etc.

Verbs Compounded with *Être*

aller

j'étais allé(e)	I had gone
tu étais allé(e)	you had gone
il était allé	he had gone
elle était allée	she had gone
nous étions allé(e)s	we had gone
vous étiez allé(e)(s)	you had gone
ils étaient allés	they had gone
elles étaient allées	they had gone

Future perfect tense. The future perfect tense is used to express actions which will be completed after some time in the future. It is formed as is the present perfect, with the exception that the future tense of the auxiliary verb, *avoir* or *être*, is used

in every case.

j'*aurai* chanté	I *will have* sung
nous nous *serons* vus	we *will have* seen each other
elle *sera* partie	she *will have* left

(1) chanter

j'aurai chanté	I will have sung
tu auras chanté	you will have sung
il aura chanté	he will have sung
elle aura chanté	she will have sung
nous aurons chanté	we will have sung
vous aurez chanté	you will have sung
ils auront chanté	they will have sung
elles auront chanté	they will have sung

(2) finir

j'aurai fini, etc.	I will have finished, etc.

(3) vendre

j'aurai vendu, etc.	I will have sold, etc.

Verbs Compounded with *Être*

aller

je serai allé(e)	I will have gone
tu seras allé(e)	you will have gone
il sera allé	he, it will have gone
elle sera allée	she, it will have gone
nous serons allé(e)s	we will have gone
vous serez allé(e)(s)	you will have gone
ils seront allés	they will have gone
elles seront allées	they will have gone

Conditional perfect tense. The uses of the conditional perfect tense are parallel to those of the conditional, to express actions that would have taken place. It is formed as is the present perfect, with the exception that the conditional tense of the auxiliary verb, *avoir* or *être*, is used in every case.

j'*aurais* chanté	I *would have* sung
nous nous *serions* vus	we *would have* seen each other
elle *serait* partie	she *would have* left

(1) chanter

j'aurais chanté	I would have sung
tu aurais chanté	you would have sung
il aurait chanté	he, it would have sung
elle aurait chanté	she, it would have sung
nous aurions chanté	we would have sung
vous auriez chanté	you would have sung
ils auraient chanté	they would have sung
elles auraient chanté	they would have sung

(2) finir

j'aurais fini, etc.	I would have finished, etc.

(3) vendre

j'aurais vendu, etc.	I would have sold, etc.

Verbs Compounded with *Être*

aller

je serais allé(e)	I would have gone
tu serais allé(e)	you would have gone
il serait allé	he, it would have gone
elle serait allée	she, it would have gone
nous serions allé(e)s	we would have gone
vous seriez allé(e)(s)	you would have gone
ils seraient allés	they would have gone
elles seraient allées	they would have gone

Imperative mood

The imperative mood expresses action in the form of a command, a request or a prayer. It is always distinguished by the absence of any pronoun subject.

The familiar imperative (see above, p. 2827, note on the use of *tu*, *te* and *toi*) for second and third conjugation verbs has the same form as the second person singular, present indicative.

Finis-le.	Finish it.
Vends-le.	Sell it.

The familiar imperative for 1st conjugation verbs except *aller* has the same form as the first person singular, present indicative.

Donne-le-moi.	Give it to me.

Note: 1st conjugation familiar imperatives add an -*s* when the verb is followed by *y* or *en*.

Penses-y.	Think of it.
Parles-en.	Speak of it.

Note: The familiar imperative of the verb *aller* is *va*. This form also adds an -*s* when followed by *y*.

Vas-y.	Go ahead; go there.

The first person plural imperative has the same form as the first person plural, present indicative.

Chantons-le.	Let's sing it.
Finissons-le.	Let's finish it.
Vendons-le.	Let's sell it.

The second person plural or polite imperative has the same form as the second person plural, present indicative.

Chantez-le.	Sing it.
Finissez-le.	Finish it.
Vendez-le.	Sell it.

The following verbs have irregular imperatives which have the same form as the second person singular and first and second person plural, present subjunctive (see below for explanation of the subjunctive):

	Familiar		First Person Pl.		Polite	
être	sois	be	soyons	let's be	soyez	be
avoir	aie	have	ayons	let's have	ayez	have
savoir	sache	know	sachons	let's know	sachez	know

Subjunctive mood

The subjunctive mood expresses action regarded in the mind as uncertain, desirable or undesirable, dependent. It occurs usually in subordinate clauses. It is used:

After verbal expressions of wishing, willing, preferring.

Je *veux qu'il reste* à la maison.   I *want him to stay* at home.

After verbal expressions of necessity and judgment involving approval and disapproval.

Il *faut que nous soyons* là à l'heure.	We *must* (*it is necessary that we*) *be* there on time.

After verbal expressions of emotion such as joy, sorrow, anger, surprise, fear.

Je *suis content que vous soyez venu.*	I *am happy that you have come.*

After verbal expressions of doubt, denial, possibility.

Je *doute qu'il soit* riche.   I *doubt that he is* rich.

After verbal expressions of thinking, perceiving, knowing, when uncertainty or doubt is implied.

Croyez-vous qu'il vienne?   *Do you think* that he will come?

In adverbial clauses after the following conjunctions expressing time, purpose, condition, concession.

avant que	before	jusqu'à ce que	until
à moins que	unless	afin que	in order that
bien que	although	de peur que	for fear that

Donnez-lui le livre *avant qu'il parte.*	Give him the book *before he goes.*
Je resterai *jusqu'à ce qu'il revienne.*	I'll stay *until he comes back.*
Je le lui montrerai *afin qu'il sache* la vérité.	I'll show it to him *so that he may know* the truth.
Nous commencerons à huit heures, *à moins qu'il soit en retard.*	We'll begin at eight o'clock, *unless he is late.*
J'irai avec vous, *bien que je n'aie pas* beaucoup d'argent.	I'll go with you, *although I don't have* much money.

Only the present and the present perfect tenses are in common use in the subjunctive mood. Their forms are given below.

Present subjunctive. The present subjunctive tense is formed by adding the following endings to the stem of the third person plural, present indicative.

(1) chanter

(que) je chant*e*	(that) I (may) sing
(que) tu chant*es*	(that) you (may) sing
(qu')il chant*e*	(that) he (may) sing
(qu')elle chant*e*	(that) she (may) sing
(que) nous chant*ions*	(that) we (may) sing
(que) vous chant*iez*	(that) you (may) sing
(qu')ils chant*ent*	(that) they (may) sing
(qu')elles chant*ent*	(that) they (may) sing

(2) finir

(que) je fin*isse*	(that) I (may) finish
(que) tu fin*isses*	(that) you (may) finish
(qu')il fin*isse*	(that) he (may) finish
(qu')elle fin*isse*	(that) she (may) finish
(que) nous fin*issions*	(that) we (may) finish
(que) vous fin*issiez*	(that) you (may) finish
(qu')ils fin*issent*	(that) they (may) finish
(qu')elles fin*issent*	(that) they (may) finish

(3) vendre

(que) je vend*e*, etc.	(that) I (may) sell, etc.

The present subjunctive of irregular verbs is given in the list of models of irregular verbs, pp. 2833–36.

Present perfect subjunctive. The present perfect tense of the subjunctive is formed as is the present perfect of the indicative, with the exception that the present subjunctive of the auxiliary verb, *avoir* or *être*, is used in every case.

(que) j'*aie* chanté	(that) I *have* sung
(que) je me *sois* dépêché	(that) I *have* hurried
(que) vous *soyez* venu	(that) you *have* come

(1) chanter

(que) j'aie chanté	(that) I have sung
(que) tu aies chanté	(that) you have sung
(qu')il ait chanté	(that) he has sung
(qu')elle ait chanté	(that) she has sung
(que) nous ayons chanté	(that) we have sung
(que) vous ayez chanté	(that) you have sung
(qu')ils aient chanté	(that) they have sung
(qu')elles aient chanté	(that) they have sung

(2) finir

(que) j'aie fini, etc.	(that) I have finished, etc.

(3) vendre

(que) j'aie vendu, etc.	(that) I have sold, etc.

Verbs Compounded with *Être*

aller

(que) je sois allé(e)	(that) I have gone
(que) tu sois allé(e)	(that) you have gone
(qu')il soit allé	(that) he has gone
(qu')elle soit allée	(that) she has gone
(que) nous soyons allé(e)s	(that) we have gone
(que) vous soyez allé(e)(s)	(that) you have gone
(qu')ils soient allés	(that) they have gone
(qu')elles soient allées	(that) they have gone

Reflexive verbs

Reflexive verbs are those in which the subject acts upon itself.

Je *me* lave.	I wash *myself*.
Je *me* parle	I talk *to myself*.

When the subject acts upon only a part of itself, the reflexive verb is said to be used reciprocally.

Ils *se* voient.	They see *themselves* (*each other*).

Most transitive verbs can be made reflexive by using the proper reflexive object pronouns with them. These may be construed as direct or indirect object. (See above, section on unstressed object pronouns, pp. 2826–27.)

me	nous
te	vous
se	se

parler	to speak
se parler	to speak *to oneself*
laver	to wash
se laver	to wash *oneself*

The reflexive verb is used much more frequently in French because:

It often expresses what would be rendered by the passive voice in English.

Cela ne *se dit* pas.	That is not said.

It often expresses what would be rendered in English by an intransitive verb.

Arrêtez-vous!	Stop!
Il se lève.	He gets up.

Some French verbs, with meanings corresponding to intransitive verbs in English, are always accompanied by a reflexive pronoun. These are sometimes known as essentially pronominal verbs. Examples are:

s'agenouiller	to kneel
s'écrouler	to collapse
s'efforcer	to strive
s'enfuir	to flee
s'évanouir	to faint; vanish
se méfier	to mistrust
se souvenir	to remember

Negation

Negative sentences or clauses are formed in French by the use of *ne* and some other word, usually an adverb or indefinite adjective or pronoun, attached to the verb. The following is the principal list of words used thus negatively:

pas	not
point	not
guère	hardly, scarcely
jamais	never
plus	no more, no longer, not...any longer, not...any more
aucun	no, none, none at all
personne	no one, nobody, not...anybody
rien	nothing, not anything
ni...ni	neither...nor

Ne stands immediately before the verb and any unstressed object pronouns it may have. The other negative expressions will follow the verb if they constitute its complement, or precede it if they constitute its subject. *Jamais, aucun, personne, rien* and *ni...ni* are frequently construed as subject of the verb.

Je *ne* le vois *pas*.	I do *not* see him.
Je *n'*y vais *guère*.	I *scarcely* go there.
Je *ne* le fais *jamais*.	I *never* do it.
Je *ne* le vois *plus*.	I *no longer* see him.
Je *n'*en ai *aucun*.	I haven't *any* at all.
Je *ne* vois *personne*.	I see *no one*.
Je *n'*ai *rien*.	I have *nothing*.
Je *n'*ai *ni* argent *ni* amis.	I have *neither* money *nor* friends.
*Personne n'*est venu.	*No one* came.
*Rien n'*est perdu.	*Nothing* is lost.
Ni l'un *ni* l'autre *n'*est venu.	*Neither* one *nor* the other came.

Negation may be expressed with two or more of these adverbs or indefinites placed after the same verb.

Il *ne* donnera *jamais plus rien* à *personne*.	He will *never* give *anything* to *anyone any more*.
Je *n'*ai *plus rien* à faire.	I have *nothing* to do *any more*.

Irregular verbs

Following is a list of irregular verbs. Except where its absence would cause confusion, the subject pronoun (*je, tu,* etc.) has been omitted.

(4) Acquérir (to acquire); also *conquérir*
Present: acquiers, acquiers, acquiert, acquérons, acquérez, acquièrent
Future: acquerrai, etc.; *Conditional:* acquerrais, etc.
Present Perfect: ai acquis, etc.
Present Participle: acquérant
Past Participle: acquis

(5) Aller (to go)
Present: vais, vas, va, allons, allez, vont
Future: irai, etc.; *Conditional:* irais, etc.
Present Perfect: suis allé, etc.
Present Participle: allant
Past Participle: allé

(6) Asseoir (to seat) (generally employed reflexively: *s'asseoir,* to sit down)
Present: assieds, assieds, assied, asseyons, asseyez, asseyent; *or* assois, assois, assoit, assoyons, assoyez, assoient
Future: assiérai, etc.; *or* assoirai, etc. *Conditional:* assiérais, etc.; *or* assoirais, etc.
Present Perfect: ai assis, etc.
Present Participle: asseyant *or* assoyant
Past Participle: assis

(7) Avoir (to have)
Present: ai, as, a, avons, avez, ont
Imperfect: avais, avais, avait, avions, aviez, avaient
Past Definite: eus, eus, eut, eûmes, eûtes, eurent
Future: aurai, auras, aura, aurons, aurez, auront; *Conditional:* aurais, etc.
Present Perfect: ai eu, etc.
Present Subjunctive: aie, aies, ait, ayons, ayez, aient
Imperfect Subjunctive: eusse, eusses, eût, eussions, eussiez, eussent
Present Participle: ayant
Past Participle: eu

(8) Battre (to beat)
Present: bats, bats, bat, battons, battez, battent
Future: battrai, etc.; *Conditional:* battrais, etc.
Present Perfect: ai battu, etc.
Present Participle: battant
Past Participle: battu

(9) Bénir (to bless) is regular except for the past participle; benit is used only as an adjective. Example: de l'eau bénite (holy water, *f.*); du pain bénit (holy bread, *m.*).

(10) Boire (to drink)
Present: bois, bois, boit, buvons, buvez, boivent
Future: boirai, etc.; *Conditional:* boirais, etc.
Present Perfect: ai bu, etc.
Present Subjunctive: boive, boives, boive, buvions, buviez, boivent
Present Participle: buvant
Past Participle: bu

(11) Bruire (to murmur, rustle) (generally used impersonally)
Present: il bruit
Imperfect: il bruissait, (ils) bruissaient
Present Participle: bruissant; bruyant (used only as adjective)
Past Participle: bruit

(12) Clore (to close); also *déclore, éclore, enclore, forclore*
Present: clos, clos, clôt, closons, closez, closent
Future: clorai, etc.; *Conditional:* clorais, etc.
Present Perfect: ai clos, etc.
Present Subjunctive: close, closes, close, closions, closiez, closent
Past Participle: clos

(13) Conclure (to conclude); also *exclure*
Present: conclus, conclus, conclut, concluons, concluez, concluent
Future: conclurai, etc.; *Conditional:* conclurais, etc.
Present Perfect: ai conclu, etc.
Present Participle: concluant
Past Participle: conclu

(14) Conduire (to conduct); also *déduire, détruire, cuire, construire, instruire, introduire, nuire, produire, réduire, traduire*
Present: conduis, conduis, conduit, conduisons, conduisez, conduisent
Future: conduirai, etc.; *Conditional:* conduirais, etc.
Present Perfect: ai conduit, etc.
Present Participle: conduisant
Past Participle: conduit

(15) Confire (to preserve); also *suffire*
Present: confis, confis, confit, confisons, confisez, confisent
Imperfect: confisais, etc.
Future: confirai, etc.; *Conditional:* confirais, etc.
Present Perfect: ai confit, etc.
Present Subjunctive: confise, confises, confise, confisions, confisiez, confisent
Present Participle: confisant
Past Participle: confit

(16) Connaître (to know); also *apparaître, disparaître, paraître, paître, reconnaître*
Present: connais, connais, connaît, connaissons, connaissez, connaissent
Future: connaîtrai, etc.; *Conditional:* connaîtrais, etc.
Present Perfect: ai connu, etc.
Present Participle: connaissant
Past Participle: connu

(17) Coudre (to sew)
Present: couds, couds, coud, cousons, cousez, cousent
Future: coudrai, etc.; *Conditional:* coudrais, etc.
Present Perfect: ai cousu, etc.
Present Participle: cousant
Past Participle: cousu

(18) Courir (to run); also *accourir, concourir, secourir*
Present: cours, cours, court, courons, courez, courent
Future: courrai, etc.; *Conditional:* courrais, etc.
Present Perfect: ai couru, etc.
Present Participle: courant
Past Participle: couru

(19) Craindre (to fear); also *atteindre, étreindre, feindre, geindre, joindre, peindre, plaindre, teindre*
Present: crains, crains, craint, craignons, craignez, craignent
Future: craindrai, etc.; *Conditional:* craindrais, etc.
Present Perfect: ai craint, etc.
Present Participle: craignant
Past Participle: craint

(20) Croire (to believe)
Present: crois, crois, croit, croyons, croyez, croient
Future: croirai, etc.; *Conditional:* croirais, etc.
Present Perfect: ai cru, etc.
Present Participle: croyant
Past Participle: cru

(21) Croître (to grow)
Present: croîs, croîs, croît, croissons, croissez, croissent
Future: croîtrai, etc.; *Conditional:* croîtrais, etc.
Present Perfect: ai crû, etc.
Present Participle: croissant
Past Participle: crû, *m.*, crue, *f.*

(22) Cueillir (to gather); also *accueillir, assaillir, tressaillir*
Present: cueille, cueilles, cueille, cueillons, cueillez, cueillent
Future: cueillerai, etc.; *Conditional:* cueillerais, etc.
Present Perfect: ai cueilli, etc.
Present Participle: cueillant
Past Participle: cueilli

(23) Déchoir (to decline)
Present: déchois, déchois, déchoit, déchoyons, déchoyez, déchoient
Past: déchus, déchus, déchut, déchûmes, déchûtes, déchurent
Future: décherrai, etc.; *Conditional:* décherrais, etc.
Present Perfect: ai déchu *or* suis déchu, etc.
Present Subjunctive: déchoie, déchoies, déchoie, déchoyions, déchoyiez, déchoient
Present Participle: déchoyant
Past Participle: déchu

(24) Devoir (ought)
Present: dois, dois, doit, devons, devez, doivent
Past: dus, dus, dut, dûmes, dûtes, durent
Future: devrai, etc.; *Conditional:* devrais, etc.
Present Perfect: ai dû, etc.
Present Subjunctive: doive, doives, doive, devions, deviez, doivent
Present Participle: devant
Past Participle: dû, *m.*, due, *f.*, du(e)s, *pl.*

(25) Dire (to say, tell); also *contredire, dédire, prédire, redire*
Present: dis, dis, dit, disons, dites, disent
Future: dirai, etc.; *Conditional:* dirais, etc.
Present Perfect: ai dit, etc.
Present Participle: disant
Past Participle: dit

(26) Dormir (to sleep); also *bouillir, consentir, assortir, mentir, partir, sentir, servir, sortir, repentir*
Present: dors, dors, dort, dormons, dormez, dorment
Future: dormirai, etc.; *Conditional:* dormirais, etc.
Present Perfect: ai dormi, etc.
Present Participle: dormant
Past Participle: dormi

(27) Échoir (to fall due)
Present: il échoit *or* échet; ils échoient *or* échéent
Imperfect: il échoyait
Future: il écherra *or* échoira; *Conditional:* il écherrait *or* échoirait
Present Perfect: il est échu, etc.
Present Subjunctive: il échoie
Present Participle: échéant
Past Participle: échu

(28) Écrire (to write); also *décrire, inscrire, prescrire*
Present: écris, écris, écrit, écrivons, écrivez, écrivent
Future: écrirai, etc.; *Conditional:* écrirais, etc.
Present Perfect: ai écrit, etc.
Present Participle: écrivant
Past Participle: écrit

(29) Envoyer (to send); also *renvoyer*
Present: envoie, envoies, envoie, envoyons, envoyez, envoient
Future: enverrai, etc.; *Conditional:* enverrais, etc.
Present Perfect: ai envoyé, etc.
Present Participle: envoyant
Past Participle: envoyé

(30) Être (to be)
Present: suis, es, est, sommes, êtes, sont
Imperfect: étais, étais, était, étions, étiez, étaient
Past: fus, fus, fut, fûmes, fûtes, furent
Future: serai, etc.; *Conditional:* serais, etc.
Present Perfect: ai été, etc.
Present Subjunctive: sois, sois, soit, soyons, soyez, soient
Imperfect Subjunctive: fusse, fusses, fût, fussions, fussiez, fussent
Present Participle: étant
Past Participle: été

(31) Faillir (to fail); also *défaillir*
Present: faux, faux, faut, faillons, faillez, faillent
Imperfect: faillais, etc.
Past: faillis, faillis, faillit, faillîmes, faillîtes, faillirent
Future: faudrai, faudras, etc.; *Conditional:* faudrais, etc.

Present Perfect: ai failli, etc.
Present Subjunctive: faille, failles, faille, faillions, failliez, faillent
Present Participle: faillant
Past Participle: failli

(32) Faire (to do, make); also *contrefaire, défaire, refaire, satisfaire*
Present: fais, fais, fait, faisons, faites, font
Future: ferai, etc.; *Conditional:* ferais, etc.
Present Perfect: ai fait, etc.
Present Subjunctive: fasse, etc.
Present Participle: faisant
Past Participle: fait

(33) Falloir (must) (impersonal)
Present: il faut
Imperfect: il fallait
Past: il fallut
Future: il faudra; *Conditional:* il faudrait
Present Perfect: il a fallu
Present Subjunctive: il faille
Past Participle: fallu

(34) Frire (to fry)
Present: fris, fris, frit, frions, friez, frient
Future: frirai, etc.; *Conditional:* frirais, etc.
Present Perfect: ai frit, etc.
Present Participle: friant
Past Participle: frit

(35) Fuir (to flee); also *s'enfuir*
Present: fuis, fuis, fuit, fuyons, fuyez, fuient
Future: fuirai, etc.; *Conditional:* fuirais, etc.
Present Perfect: ai fui, etc.
Present Participle: fuyant
Past Participle: fui

(36) Gésir (to lie, lie buried)
Present: gis, gis, gît, gisons, gisez, gisent
Imperfect: gisais, etc.
Present Participle: gisant

(37) Haïr (to hate)
Present: hais, hais, hait, haïssons, haïssez, haïssent
Future: haïrai, etc.; *Conditional:* haïrais, etc.
Present Perfect: ai haï, etc.
Present Subjunctive: haïsse, etc.
Present Participle: haïssant
Past Participle: haï

(38) Lire (to read); also *élire, relire*
Present: lis, lis, lit, lisons, lisez, lisent
Future: lirai, etc.; *Conditional:* lirais, etc.
Present Perfect: ai lu, etc.
Present Participle: lisant
Past Participle: lu

(39) Mettre (to place, put); also *admettre, commettre, permettre, promettre, remettre, soumettre*
Present: mets, mets, met, mettons, mettez, mettent
Future: mettrai, etc.; *Conditional:* mettrais, etc.
Present Perfect: ai mis, etc.
Present Participle: mettant
Past Participle: mis

(40) Moudre (to grind)
Present: mouds, mouds, moud, moulons, moulez, moulent
Future: moudrai, etc.; *Conditional:* moudrais, etc.
Present Perfect: ai moulu, etc.
Present Participle: moulant
Past Participle: moulu

(41) Mourir (to die)
Present: meurs, meurs, meurt, mourons, mourez, meurent
Future: mourrai, etc.; *Conditional:* mourrais, etc.
Present Perfect: suis mort, etc.
Present Participle: mourant
Past Participle: mort

(42) Mouvoir (to move); also *émouvoir, promouvoir*
Present: meus, meus, meut, mouvons, mouvez, meuvent
Imperfect: mouvais, etc.
Past: mus, mus, mut, mûmes, mûtes, murent
Future: mouvrai, etc.; *Conditional:* mouvrais, etc.
Present Perfect: ai mû, etc.
Present Subjunctive: meuve, meuves, meuve, mouvions, mouviez, meuvent
Present Participle: mouvant
Past Participle: mû, *m.*, mue, *f.*, mu(e)s, *pl.*

(43) Naître (to be born); also *renaître*
Present: nais, nais, naît, naissons, naissez, naissent
Imperfect: naissais, etc.
Past: naquis, naquis, naquit, naquîmes, naquîtes, naquirent
Future: naîtrai, etc.; *Conditional:* naîtrais, etc.
Present Perfect: suis né, etc.
Present Subjunctive: naisse, naisses, naisse, naissions, naissiez, naissent
Present Participle: naissant
Past Participle: né

(44) Ouvrir (to open); also *couvrir, découvrir, offrir, souffrir*
Present: ouvre, ouvres, ouvre, ouvrons, ouvrez, ouvrent
Future: ouvrirai, etc.; *Conditional:* ouvrirais, etc.
Present Perfect: ai ouvert, etc.
Present Participle: ouvrant
Past Participle: ouvert

(45) Plaire (to please); also *déplaire, taire*
Present: plais, plais, plaît, plaisons, plaisez, plaisent
Future: plairai, etc.; *Conditional:* plairais, etc.
Present Perfect: ai plu, etc.
Present Participle: plaisant
Past Participle: plu

(46) Pleuvoir (impersonal) (to rain)
Present: il pleut
Future: il pleuvra; *Conditional:* il pleuvrait
Present Perfect: il a plu
Present Subjunctive: il pleuve
Present Participle: pleuvant
Past Participle: plu

(47) Pouvoir (to be able)
Present: puis *or* peux, peux, peut, pouvons, pouvez, peuvent
Imperfect: pouvais, etc.
Past: pus, pus, put, pûmes, pûtes, purent
Future: pourrai, etc.; *Conditional:* pourrais, etc.
Present Perfect: ai pu, etc.
Present Subjunctive: puisse, puisses, puisse, puissions, puissiez, puissent
Present Participle: pouvant
Past Participle: pu

(48) Prendre (to take); also *apprendre, comprendre, entreprendre, reprendre, surprendre*
Present: prends, prends, prend, prenons, prenez, prennent
Future: prendrai, etc.; *Conditional:* prendrais, etc.
Present Perfect: ai pris, etc.
Present Participle: prenant
Past Participle: pris

(49) Recevoir (to receive); also *concevoir, apercevoir, décevoir*
Present: reçois, reçois, reçoit, recevons, recevez, reçoivent
Future: recevrai, etc.; *Conditional:* recevrais, etc.
Present Perfect: ai reçu, etc.
Present Subjunctive: reçoive, etc.
Present Participle: recevant
Past Participle: reçu

(50) Résoudre (to resolve); also *absoudre, dissoudre*
Present: résous, résous, résout, résolvons, résolvez, résolvent
Imperfect: résolvais, etc.
Future: résoudrai, etc.; *Conditional:* résoudrais, etc.
Present Perfect: ai résolu, etc.
Present Subjunctive: résolve, résolves, résolve, résolvions, résolviez, résolvent
Present Participle: résolvant
Past Participle: résolu *and* résous
Past Participle (absoudre): absous, absoute
Past Participle (dissoudre): dissous, dissoute

(51) Rire (to laugh); also *sourire*
Present: ris, ris, rit, rions, riez, rient
Future: rirai, etc.; *Conditional:* rirais, etc.
Present Perfect: ai ri, etc.
Present Participle: riant
Past Participle: ri

(52) Rompre (to break); also *corrompre*
Present: romps, romps, rompt, rompons, rompez, rompent
Future: romprai, etc.; *Conditional:* romprais, etc.
Present Perfect: ai rompu, etc.
Present Participle: rompant
Past Participle: rompu

(53) Savoir (to know)
Present: sais, sais, sait, savons, savez, savent
Future: saurai, etc.
Present Perfect: ai su, etc.
Present Subjunctive: sache, saches, sache, sachions, sachiez, sachent
Present Participle: sachant
Past Participle: su

(54) Suivre (to follow); also *s'ensuivre, poursuivre*
Present: suis, suis, suit, suivons, suivez, suivent
Future: suivrai, etc.
Present Perfect: ai suivi, etc.
Present Participle: suivant
Past Participle: suivi

(55) Tenir (to hold); also *appartenir, contenir, maintenir, obtenir, retenir, soutenir*
Present: tiens, tiens, tient, tenons, tenez, tiennent
Future: tiendrai, etc.
Present Perfect: ai tenu, etc.
Present Subjunctive: (que) je tienne, etc.
Present Participle: tenant
Past Participle: tenu

(56) Traire (to milk); also *abstraire, attraire, distraire, extraire, rentraire, retraire, soustraire, braire*
Present: trais, trais, trait, trayons, trayez, traient
Imperfect: trayais, etc.
Future: trairai, etc.; *Conditional:* trairais, etc.
Present Perfect: ai trait, etc.
Present Subjunctive: traie, traies, traie, trayions, trayiez, traient
Present Participle: trayant
Past Participle: trait

(57) Vaincre (to conquer); also *convaincre*
Present: vaincs, vaincs, vainc, vainquons, vainquez, vainquent
Future: vaincrai, etc.; *Conditional:* vaincrais, etc.
Present Perfect: ai vaincu, etc.
Present Participle: vainquant
Past Participle: vaincu

(58) Valoir (to be worth); also *équivaloir, prévaloir, revaloir*
Present: vaux, vaux, vaut, valons, valez, valent
Imperfect: valais, etc.
Past: valus, valus, valut, valûmes, valûtes, valurent

Future: vaudrai, etc.; *Conditional:* vaudrais, etc.
Present Subjunctive: vaille, vailles, vaille, valions, valiez, vaillent
Present Participle: valant
Past Participle: valu

(59) Venir (to come); also *convenir, devenir, parvenir, revenir*
Present: viens, viens, vient, venons, venez, viennent
Future: viendrai, etc.; *Conditional:* viendrais, etc.
Present Perfect: suis venu, etc.
Present Subjunctive: (que) je vienne, etc.
Present Participle: venant
Past Participle: venu

(60) Vêtir (to clothe)
Present: vêts, vêts, vêt, vêtons, vêtez, vêtent
Future: vêtirai, etc.; *Conditional:* vêtirais, etc.
Present Perfect: ai vêtu, etc.
Present Participle: vêtant
Past Participle: vêtu

(61) Vivre (to live); also *survivre*
Present: vis, vis, vit, vivons, vivez, vivent
Future: vivrai, etc.; *Conditional:* vivrais, etc.
Present Perfect: ai vécu, etc.
Present Participle: vivant
Past Participle: vécu

(62) Voir (to see); also *entrevoir, prévoir, revoir*
Present: vois, vois, voit, voyons, voyez, voient
Future: verrai, etc.; *Conditional:* verrais, etc.
Present Perfect: ai vu, etc.
Present Participle: voyant
Past Participle: vu

(63) Vouloir (to wish)
Present: veux, veux, veut, voulons, voulez, veulent
Imperfect: voulais, etc.
Past: voulus, voulus, voulut, voulûmes, voulûtes, voulurent
Future: voudrai, etc.; *Conditional:* voudrais, etc.
Present Perfect: ai voulu
Present Subjunctive: veuille, veuilles, veuille, voulions, vouliez, veuillent
Present Participle: voulant
Past Participle: voulu
Imperative: veuillez

French Pronunciation

English pronunciation differs fundamentally from French in tension, frontal articulation and syllabic division. English is characterized by very relaxed pronunciation, French by very tense pronunciation. Tension of the muscles of articulation prevents wavering or diphthongized vowels in French, whereas the relaxed articulation of English produces vowels which waver constantly and change timbre. The presence of this tension in French also accounts for the absence of friction in the pronunciation of French consonants, whereas the lack of tension produces this friction in English.

French is characterized by a frontal resonance, because (1) all consonants pronounced with the tip of the tongue are articulated farther forward in the mouth than in English, (2) most French vowels are pronounced with lips rounded, whereas in English less than twenty-five per cent of the vowels are so pronounced, (3) French has a series of vowels which have frontal resonance by means of both tongue and lips, which English does not possess.

VOWELS

French Spelling Group	English Words with the Approximate Vowel Sound	French Examples
a, à, â	ah	la, pas, classe
ai	peck	française, aime, américaine
	late	j'ai, gai, mai
ain, aim †	hang, thank	main, pain, faim, daim
an, am †	gong, honk	an, dans, champ, camp, manque
au	note, wrote	au, haut, gauche
	love, blood	automobile, restaurant, augmenter
è	peck	mère, cèdre, après
ê	peck	être, même, bête
é	late	été, déjà, Amérique
e	peck	certain, avec, quel, cher, belle
	late	parler, nez, chez
	typical	petit, tenir, de, le
	ah	femme, évidemment, récemment
ei	peck	neige, veine, Seine
ein †	hang, thank	plein, ceinture
en †	gong, honk	vent, entrer, comment
	hang, thank	rien, bien, examen
em †	gong, honk	sembler, Luxembourg, trembler

French Spelling Group	English Words with the Approximate Vowel Sound	French Examples
eu ‡	curb, hurt	bleu, deux, heure, jeune
i	machine	il, qui, rire, tranquille
	yes	bien, lieu, nation, rien
in, im †	hang, thank	vin, fin, Inde, médecin, simple, important
o	note, wrote	chose, métro, stylo
	love, blood	docteur, obtenir, moteur
ô	note, wrote	plutôt, le nôtre, le vôtre
oe, oeu ‡	curb, hurt	oeil, oeuf, boeuf
oi	wad, waffle	moi, bois, voir, loi
oin †	wangle	moins, loin, coin
on, om †	only	mon, bon, nom, ombre
ou	moon	ou, pour, nous, trou
	we, way	oui, louer, jouer
u ¶	(no equivalent— see below)	du, une, rue, étudier, lui, nuit, huit, depuis
ue	curb, hurt	cueillir, orgueil
un, um †	sung, hung	un, chacun, parfum, humble
y	machine	stylo, système
	yes	yeux, bruyant
yn, ym †	hang, thank	syncope, symbole

CONSONANTS

Consonants which do not appear in the list below are to be given approximately the same sound as in English (see "Notes on Pronunciation," p. 2777).

French Spelling Group	English Words Possessing the Approximate Consonant Sound	French Examples
c (except before e, i, y)	come, coat, cat	comme, cours, car, curé
(before e, i, y)	certain, citrus, Cyrus	cent, cinq, cylindre
ç	certain, citrus	français, garçon
cc (except before e, i, y)	occur, raccoon	accord, occuliste
(before e, i, y)	accident, accent	accident, accent
ch	champagne, chandelier	chercher, acheter, champ
	orchestra	orchestre, Christ
g (except before e, i, y)	go, garb, gun	gauche, garçon, légume
(before e, i, y)	measure, pleasure, azure	gentil, agent, potage

French Spelling Group	English Words Possessing the Approximate Consonant Sound	French Examples
gg (except before e, i, y)	go, garb, gun	aggraver
(before e, i, y)	(the sound g in go plus the sound s in measure)	suggérer
gn	canyon, banyan	campagne, gagner
gu (before e, i, y)	go, garb, gun	guerre, guère, Guy
h (mute)	Entirely silent	homme, heure, heureux
(aspirate)	Entirely silent, but prevents elision and linking. See below.	* hâte, * héros, * haut
il (final after vowel)	play	travail, fauteuil, soleil
ill (between vowels)	play	travailler, meilleur

---

* H is always silent. Mute h, however, permits the following:

linking of the final consonant sound of the preceding word with the vowel immediately following; for example, un hôtel (uhn noh-TELL).

elision of the final vowel sound of the preceding word; for example, l'hôtel (loh-TELL).

Aspirate h, indicated here and in the French to English list by *, prevents both linking and elision; for example, un héros (uhng ay-ROH), le héros (lih ay-ROH).

† The spellings in, im, yn, ym, ain, aim, ein, oin, an, am, en, em, on, om, un, um all represent nasal vowels, except when followed immediately by a vowel or by another n or m. They are so-called because their resonance is produced in the mouth and nose simultaneously. The mouth remains open at the end of their pronunciation, and the n or m is entirely silent. The nasal resonance of these vowels resembles somewhat the sound of the vowel plus n in the English words "hang," "hank" (for the transliteration ang), "bong," "conk" (for the transliteration ahng), "sung," "sunk" (for the transliteration uhng).

‡ The spellings eu, oeu, oe represent two distinct vowel sounds in French, depending upon whether they are in syllables which end in vowel sounds or in consonant sounds. The closest equivalent in English is perhaps the sound of the vowel in some New England pronunciations of words like "first," "third," "hurt," "curb," with no r consonant pronounced.

¶ The spelling u represents both a vowel and a consonant in French, the latter when it is the initial sound of a syllable. The vowel sound is produced approximately by pronouncing ee in English while the lips are rounded as in whistling. The consonant sound ü is produced by beginning to produce the vowel ü and then abruptly drawing the corners of the lips apart for the pronunciation of the following vowel.

French Spelling Group	English Words Possessing the Approximate Consonant Sound	French Examples	French Spelling Group	English Words Possessing the Approximate Consonant Sound	French Examples
j	measure, azure	jardin, jaune, jour	s (between written vowels)	rose, nose	rose, maison, besoin
q	pe*ck*	cinq, coq	t (before i plus vowel)	mi*ss*	nation, portion
qu	*c*at, *c*ut, *k*it	que, quart, qui	th	*t*ake	théâtre, bibliothèque
r §			w	*v*ain	wagon
s (except between written vowels)	*s*it, *s*ell	sans, soeur, monsieur	x (in "ex" before vowel)	e*x*act	examen, exact, exister

§ There are two distinct *r* sounds found in France. The first is generally known as the tip-trill *r* because it is pronounced with the tip of the tongue. It resembles the *r* commonly heard in Italian and Spanish and used by singers on the concert stage for clarity. The second, known generally as the French *r*, is heard commonly in the area around Paris as well as in certain other regions of France. It differs considerably from the characteristic American *r* as heard in the midwest, which is produced by turning the tip of the tongue up and back against the middle of the soft palate in the roof of the mouth. The French *r* is produced by creating friction between the back of the tongue and the back of the soft palate while the vocal chords vibrate. The tip of the tongue is down and does not enter at all into the production of the sound. The French *r* has been rendered below by the transliteration *r*.

German

to English

CONTENTS

Note on Symbols. For a list of abbreviations used in the main word list, see p. 2674. The number indicated for each German verb in the word list is the key to its conjugation. Verbs numbered (1) are weak verbs and are conjugated according to models under *Present Tense, Simple Past Tense, Compound Past Tense,* etc., pp. 2892–93 of the German grammar. Verbs numbered (2) through (162) are strong, (163) through (169) modal auxiliaries, (170) through (177) weak but irregular in some way, (178) through (181) irregular; for their patterns of conjugation, see the corresponding numbers, pp. 2893–95 of the German grammar.

Notes on Pronunciation, Spelling, etc. The pronunciation in the following list is indicated wherever possible by words or syllables easily recognized by English-speaking persons. Thus, the German word *Problem* is rendered *pro*-BLAME. There are some sounds in the German language, however, which cannot be reproduced in this manner: *ü*, shown in the pronunciation column as *ü*, is pronounced like the English *ee* but with rounded lips; *ö*, rendered as *ö*, is pronounced like the *a* in the English word "make," but pronounced with rounded lips; *ch*, rendered as *kh*, is pronounced like the gargling sound in the Scottish word *loch* when it follows *a, o* or *u;* but, when it follows any other letter, or when it begins a word, it is pronounced correctly by shaping the mouth to say the English word "hue" and creating friction for the *h* by pressing the tip of the tongue against the lower front teeth. *Ei*, shown in the phonetics as *ye, ie, y* or *i*-consonant-*e* as in "line," is pronounced like the *ie* in the English word "tie." Double consonants in the pronunciation column indicate that the vowel preceding them should be short. *G* is always pronounced hard as in "go"; *ow* always as in "cow." Readers who are interested in more detailed rules of German pronunciation are referred to "Basic Key to German Pronunciation," p. 2896.

All German nouns are spelled with capital initial letters. German adjectives which form compounds with the nouns they modify are indicated in the lists as prefixes; for example, Exekutiv-..., executive (*adj.*).

German	Pronunciation	English
Aal, *m.*	AHL	eel
Abbildung, *f.*	AHPP-*bill-doong*	illustration (pictorial representation)
abbrechen (20)	AHPP-*breh-kh_en*	break (make divide), to
Abdruck, *m.*	AHPP-*droo_k*	print (printed reproduction)
Abend, *m.*	AH-*bent*	evening
Abendbrot, *n.*	AH-*bent-brote*	supper (light evening meal)
Abenteuer, *n.*	AH-*ben-toy-ehr*	adventure
aber	AH-*behr*	but (yet, *conj.*)
Aberglaube, *m.*	AH-*behr-gl_ow-buh*	superstition
abergläubisch	AH-*behr-gloy-bish*	superstitious
Abfahrt, *f.*	AHPP-*fahrrt*	departure (setting out)
Abfall, *m.*	AHPP-*fahll*	garbage
"	"	rubbish (litter)
Abflussrohr, *n.*	AHPP-*flooss-roar*	drain (conduit)
Abgeordnete, *m.,f.*	AHPP-*guh-ord-nuh-tuh*	delegate
Abgrund, *m.*	AHPP-*groonnt*	precipice
abhalten (59)	AHPP-*hahl-ten*	keep (prevent), to
abhängen von... (60)	AHPP-*heng-en fun...*	depend (be contingent) on, to
abhängig	AHPP-*heng-ick*	dependent (reliant)
Abkürzung, *f.*	AHPP-*kürts-oong*	abbreviation
abladen (70)	AHPP-*lah-den*	unload, to
ablaufen (72)	AHPP-*l_ow-fen*	expire (become void, *bus.*), to
ablehnen (1)	AHPP-*lay-nen*	decline, to
"	"	refuse (make a refusal), to
"	"	reject, to
ablenken (1)	AHPP-*leng-ken*	distract (divert), to
abmachen (1)	AHPP-*mah_kh-en*	settle (agree on), to
Abmachung, *f.*	AHPP-*mah_kh-oong*	bargain (agreement)
Abnahme, *f.*	AHPP-*nah-muh*	decrease
Abneigung, *f.*	AHPP-*nye-goong*	dislike
Abonnement, *n.*	*ah-bawnn-ay-*MAHNG	subscription (for periodicals, etc.)
abreisen (1)	AHPP-*rye-zenn*	depart, to
"	"	leave, to
abreissen (85)	AHPP-*rice-en*	rip (tear away), to
Absatz, *m.*	AHPP-*zahtts*	paragraph
Absatzgebiet, *n.*	AHPP-*zahtts-guh-beet*	outlet (market, *bus.*)
abschaffen (92)	AHPP-*shahff-en*	abolish, to
Abschied, *m.*	AHPP-*sheet*	farewell (leave-taking)
Abschnitt, *m.*	AHPP-*shnitt*	coupon (detachable certificate)
Absicht, *f.*	AHPP-*zikht*	design
"	"	intention
"	"	purpose (aim)
absichtlich	AHPP-*zikht-likh*	deliberate (intentional)

German	Pronunciation	English
abstreifen (1)	AHPP-*shtrye-fen*	strip (denude), to
abstürzen (1)	AHPP-*shtürts-en*	crash (be smashed), to
Abteil, *n.*	AHPP-*tile*	compartment (of train)
Abteilung, *f.*	AHPP-*tile-oong*	department (administrative unit)
"	"	division (portion)
Abtretung, *f.*	AHPP-*tray-toong*	assignment (legal transfer)
ab und zu	AHPP *oont* TSOO	occasionally
abweichen (154)	AHPP-*vye-kh_en*	deviate (diverge), to
"	"	vary (differ), to
Abweichung, *f.*	AHPP-*vye-kh oong*	departure (deviation)
abwenden (177)	AHPP-*venn-den*	avert (prevent), to
abwesend	AHPP-*vay-zent*	absent
Abwesenheit, *f.*	AHPP-*vay-zen-hite*	absence
abwerfen (157)	AHPP-*vehr-fen*	shed (cast off), to
abziehen (161)	AHPP-*tsee-en*	deduct, to
"	"	subtract, to
Abzugskanal, *m.*	AHPP-*tsooks-kah-nahl*	sewer (conduit)
Acht, *f.*	AH_KHT	care (heed)
achten (1)	AH_KH-*ten*	respect (esteem), to
Achtung, *f.*	AH_KH-*toong*	respect (esteem)
addieren (1)	*ahd-*DEER-*en*	add (find sum of), to
Addition, *f.*	*ahd-deet-tsee-*YOHN	addition (process of adding)
Adel, *m.*	AH-*del*	nobility
Ader, *f.*	AH-*dehr*	vein (*anat.*)
Adler, *m.*	AHD-*lehr*	eagle
Admiral, *m.*	*ahd-mee-*RAHL	admiral
Adressat, *m.*	*ah-dress-*SAHT	addressee
Advokat, *m.*	*ahd-voh-*KAH_T	lawyer
Affe, *m.*	AHFF-*uh*	monkey
Afrika, *n.*	AH-*free-kah*	Africa
afrikanisch	*ah-free-*KAH-*nish*	African (*adj.*)
A. G. (Aktiengesellschaft), *f.*	AH-GAY (AHK-*tsee-yen-guh-zell-shahfft*)	corporation
Ägypten, *n.*	*ay-*GÜP-*ten*	Egypt
ägyptisch	*ay-*GÜP-*tish*	Egyptian (*adj.*)
ähneln (1)	AY-*nel'n*	resemble, to
ähnlich	AYN-*likh*	similar
Ähnlichkeit, *f.*	AYN-*likh-kite*	similarity
Ahorn, *m.*	AH-*horn*	maple (tree)
Akkumulator, *m.*	*ahk-koom-muh-*LAH-*tor*	battery (storage)
Akten, *m.pl.*	AHK-*ten*	file (collection of papers)
"	"	records (files)
Aktenmappe, *f.*	AHK-*ten-mah-puh*	briefcase
Aktie, *f.*	AHK-*tsee-uh*	share (stock)
Aktien, *f.pl.*	AHK-*tsee-en*	stock (shares)
Aktienbesitzer, *m.*	AHK-*tsee-en-buh-zitt-sehr*	stockholder
Aktivposten, *m.*	*ahk-*TEEF-*pawss-ten*	asset (*bus.*)

German	Pronunciation	English
Alaska, *n.*	*ah*-LAHSS-*kah*	Alaska
Albanien, *n.*	*ahl*-BAHN-*yen*	Albania
albern	AHLL-*behrn*	silly
Alkohol, *m.*	AHLL-*koh-hohl*	alcohol
Allee, *f.*	*ahl*-LAY	avenue (street)
allein	*ahl*-LINE	alone
Allergie, *f.*	*ahl-lehr*-G EE	allergy (*med.*)
alles	AHLL-*less*	all (everything, *n.*)
"	"	everything (*pron.*)
allgemein	AHLL-*guh-mine*	general (*adj.*)
"	"	universal (*adj.*)
allgemeine Un-kosten, *pl.*	AHLL-*guh-mine-uh* OON-*kawss-ten*	overhead (expenses, *bus.*)
allmählich	*ahll*-MAY-*likh*	gradual
Alphabet, *n.*	*ahl-fah*-BAIT	alphabet
als	AHLLSS	as (in the role of, *prep.*)
"	"	than
"	"	when' (at the time that, *conj.*)
also	AHLL-*zoh*	so (therefore, *adv.*)
"	"	thus (therefore)
alt	AHLLT	old
Altar, *m.*	*ahl*-TAHR	altar
altbacken	AHLLT-*bahk-ken*	stale
älter	ELL-*tehr*	senior (older)
Alter, *n.*	AHL-*tehr*	age (accumulated years)
Altertümlichkeit, *f.*	AHLL-*tehr-tüm-likh-kite*	antiquity (ancientness)
Aluminium, *n.*	*ah-loo*-MEEN-*ee-oom*	aluminum
Ameise, *f.*	AH-*my-zuh*	ant
Amerika, *n.*	*ah*-MAY-*ree-kah*	America
amerikanisch	*ah-may-ree*-KAH-*nish*	American (*adj.*)
amortisieren (1)	*ah-more-tih*-ZEE-*ren*	amortize, to
Amsterdam, *n.*	*ahmm-stehr*-DAHM	Amsterdam
Amt, *n.*	AHMMT	office (position)
amtlich	AHMMT-*likh*	official (*adj.*)
an	AHNN	at (by)
anbeten (1)	AHNN-*bay-ten*	adore, to
"	"	worship, to (*rel.*)
Anbetung, *f.*	AHNN-*bay-toong*	worship (*rel.*)
anbieten (13)	AHNN-*bee-ten*	offer (tender), to
Anblick, *m.*	AHNN-*blick*	sight (spectacle)
Andenken, *n.*	AHNN-*deng-ken*	souvenir
ander	AHNN-*dehr*	other (*adj.*)
Andere	AHNN-*dehr-uh*	other (*pron.*)
anderer, ein	INE AHNN-*dehr-ehr*	another (*adj., pron.*)
(ver)ändern (1)	(*fehr-*)ENN-*dehrn*	alter (make different), to
ändern, sich	ZIKH ENN-*dehrn*	change (become different), to
anders	AHNN-*dehrss*	else (different, *adj.*)
"	"	otherwise (contrarily)
anderswo	AHNN-*dehrss-voh*	elsewhere
(Ver)Änderung, *f.*	(*fehr-*)ENN-*duh-roong*	change (alteration)
andeuten (1)	AHNN-*doy-ten*	indicate (suggest), to
Andeutung, *f.*	AHNN-*doy-toong*	hint (inkling)
anerkennen (173)	AHNN-*ehr-ken-nen*	acknowledge (admit), to
Anerkennung, *f.*	AHNN-*ehr-ken-noong*	recognition (acknowledgment)
Anfang, *m.*	AHNN-*fahnng*	beginning
"	"	start
anfangen (33)	AHNN-*fahnng-en*	begin (start to do), to
"	"	commence (make a start), to
"	"	start (initiate), to
Anfangs-...	AHNN-*fahnngss-...*	initial (first, *adj.*)
Anfangsbuchstabe, *m.*	AHNN-*fahnngs-boo kh-shtah-buh*	initial (letter)
angeben (43)	AHNN-*gay-ben*	state (say), to
Angebot, *n.*	AHNN-*guh-boht*	bid (amount offered)
"	"	offer
angehen (46)	AHNN-*gay-en*	concern (affect), to
angemessen	AHNN-*guh-mess-en*	suitable
angenehm	AHNN-*guh-name*	agreeable (pleasing)
"	"	pleasant
Angestellte, *m., f.*	AHNN-*guh-shtell-tuh*	employee
angleichen (55)	AHNN-*glye kh-en*	match (equal), to
angreifen (58)	AHNN-*grife-en*	assault, to
"	"	attack (assault physically), to

German	Pronunciation	English
Angriff, *m.*	AHNN-*griff*	attack (personal assault)
"	"	offense
Angst, *f.*	AHNNGST	anxiety
ängstigen, sich (1)	*zikh* ENG-*stee-gen*	worry (feel anxious), to
ängstlich	ENGST-*likh*	afraid
anhalten (59)	AHNN-*hahl-ten*	stop (come to a standstill), to
anhängen (60)	AHNN-*heng-en*	attach (join), to
Anhänger, *m.*	AHNN-*heng-ehr*	follower (adherent)
Anhängerschaft, *f.*	AHNN-*heng-ehr-shahfft*	following (followers)
anhäufen (1)	AHNN-*hoy-fen*	accumulate (amass), to
Anker, *m.*	AHNN-*kehr*	anchor
Anklage, *f.*	AHNN-*klah-guh*	accusation
"	"	charge
anklagen (1)	AHNN-*klah-gen*	accuse, to
"	"	charge, to
ankleiden (1)	AHNN-*klye-den*	clothe, to
anklopfen (1)	AHNN-*klawpp-fen*	rap, to
ankommen (68)	AHNN-*kawm-men*	arrive, to
Ankündigung, *f.*	AHNN-*kün-dee-goong*	notice (notification)
Ankunft, *f.*	AHNN-*koonft*	arrival
anlegen (1)	AHNN-*lay-gen*	invest, to (*bus.*)
Anleihe, *f.*	AHNN-*lye-uh*	loan
Anmut, *f.*	AHNN-*moot*	grace (gracefulness)
anmutig	AHNN-*moo-tikh*	graceful
Annahme, *f.*	AHNN-*nah-muh*	acceptance (receipt)
annehmen (80)	AHNN-*nay-men*	accept, to
"	"	adopt (embrace), to
"	"	assume (take for granted), to
annoncieren (1)	*ahnn-nohn*-SEE-*renn*	advertise (give notice of), to
Anordnung, *f.*	AHNN-*ord-noong*	disposition (arrangement)
anpacken (1)	AHNN-*pahk-en*	seize (clutch), to
anpassen (1)	AHNN-*pahss-sen*	adapt, to
anregen (1)	AHNN-*ray-gen*	stimulate (incite), to
Anregung, *f.*	AHNN-*ray-goong*	impulse (sudden incitement)
anrufen (89)	AHNN-*roo-fen*	telephone, to
Ansässige, *m., f.*	AHNN-*zess-eeg-uh*	resident (*n.*)
anschliessend	AHNN-*shlee-sent*	next (*adv.*)
anschreiben (109)	AHNN-*shrye-ben*	charge (debit), to
Anschrift, *f.*	AHNN-*shrift*	address (postal directions)
ansehen (118)	AHNN-*zay-en*	behold, to
"	"	look (gaze), to
Ansicht, *f.*	AHNN-*zikht*	view (opinion)
Ansiedler, *m.*	AHNN-*zeed-lehr*	settler
Ansiedlung, *f.*	AHNN-*zeed-loong*	settlement (colony)
Anspruch, *m.*	AHNN-*shprookh*	claim
Anstalt, *f.*	AHNN-*shtahlt*	asylum (institution)
"	"	institute
anständig	AHNN-*shten-dick*	decent
"	"	respectable
anstarren (1)	AHNN-*shtahr-en*	gaze, to
Ansteckung, *f.*	AHNN-*shteck-oong*	infection
anstellen (1)	AHNN-*shtell-len*	employ, to
"	"	engage, to
"	"	hire, to
anstreichen (135)	AHNN-*shtrye-kh en*	paint (spread color), to
Anstrengung, *f.*	AHNN-*shtreng-oong*	effort
"	"	labor (exertion)
"	"	strain
Anteil, *m.*	AHNN-*tile*	proportion (part)
"	"	share
Antenne, *f.*	*ahn*-TEN-*nuh*	aerial (antenna)
Anthologie, *f.*	*ahn-toh-lo*-G EE	anthology
Anthropologie, *f.*	*ahn-troh-po-lo*-G EE	anthropology
Antibiotikum, *n.*	*ahn-tee-bee*-OH-*tee-koom*	antibiotic
Antlitz, *n.*	AHNNT-*litts*	countenance (face)
Antwort, *f.*	AHNNT-*vort*	answer
"	"	response (reply)
antworten (1)	AHNNT-*vor-ten*	answer (address reply to), to
"	"	respond (reply), to
Anwalt, *m.*	AHNN-*vahlt*	counsel (lawyer)
(Rechts)Anwalt, *m.*	(*rehkhts-*)AHNN-*vahlt*	attorney

German	Pronunciation	English	German	Pronunciation	English
anweisen (155)	AHNN-*vye-zenn*	instruct (direct), to	**auf**	OWF	at (on)
anwenden (177)	AHNN-*ven-den*	apply (put to use), to	"	"	on (*prep.*)
Anwendung, *f.*	AHNN-*ven-doong*	application	"	"	upon
"	"	use (usefulness)	**aufbringen (171)**	OWF-*bring-en*	raise (collect), to
Anwesenheit, *f.*	AHNN-*vay-zen-hite*	attendance	**aufdecken (1)**	OWF-*deck-en*	detect, to
"	"	presence (being present)	**Aufenthalt,** *m.*	OWF-*ent-hahlt*	stay (sojourn)
Anzahlung, *f.*	AHNN-*tsah-loong*	down payment (*bus.*)	**auferlegen (1)**	OWF-*ehr-lay-gen*	impose (inflict), to
Anzeige, *f.*	AHNN-*tsye-guh*	advertisement	**auffordern (1)**	OWF-*for-dehrn*	summon (send for), to
anziehen (161)	AHNN-*tsee-en*	attract, to			
"	"	dress (clothe), to	**Aufführung,** *f.*	OWF-*fü-roong*	performance (stage presentation)
anziehen, sich	*zikh* AHNN-*tsee-en*	dress (get dressed), to	**Aufgabe,** *f.*	OWF-*gah-buh*	assignment (*educ.*)
anziehend	AHNN-*tsee-ent*	attractive (pleasing)	"	"	job
Anziehung, *f.*	AHNN-*tsee-oong*	attraction	"	"	lesson (assignment)
Anziehungskraft, *f.*	AHNN-*tsee-oongs-krahfft*	interest (engaging quality)	"	"	task
			aufgeben (43)	OWF-*gay-ben*	abandon (give up), to
Anzug, *m.*	AHNN-*tsook*	suit, man's	"	"	assign (prescribe lesson), to
anzünden (1)	AHNN-*tsün-den*	light (set fire to), to	"	"	surrender (relinquish), to
Apfel, *m.*	AHPP-*fel*	apple			
Apostel, *m.*	*ah-*PAWSS-*tel*	apostle	**aufgehen (46)**	OWF-*gay-en*	rise (in sky), to
Apotheke, *f.*	*ah-poh-*TAY-*kuh*	pharmacy (drug store)	**aufhalten (59)**	OWF-*hahl-ten*	arrest (halt), to
Apotheker, *m.*	*ah-poh-*TAY-*kehr*	pharmacist	"	"	check, to
appellieren (1)	*ahp-pell-*LEE-*ren*	appeal (ask reconsideration of), to	"	"	delay (retard), to
			"	"	stop (make halt), to
Appetit, *m.*	*ahp-puh-*TEET	appetite	**aufheben (62)**	OWF-*hay-ben*	annul, to
Aprikose, *f.*	*ahp-ree-*KOH-*zuh*	apricot	"	"	cancel (revoke), to
Arbeit, *f.*	AHR-*bite*	job (employment)			
"	"	work (labor)	**aufheitern (1)**	OWF-*hy-tehrn*	cheer (gladden), to
arbeiten (1)	AHR-*by-ten*	work (labor), to	**aufhören (1)**	OWF-*hö-ren*	cease, to
Arbeiter, *m.*	AHR-*by-tehr*	laborer	"	"	quit, to
"	"	worker	"	"	stop, to
Arbeitgeber, *m.*	AHR-*bite-gay-behr*	employer (boss)	**auflösen (1)**	OWF-*lö-zenn*	dissolve, to
Arbeitskraft, *f.*	AHR-*bites-krahft*	labor (labor force)			
Arbeitslosigkeit, *f.*	AHR-*bites-loh-zikh-kite*	unemployment	**aufmerksam**	OWF-*mehrk-zahmm*	attentive (heedful)
Argentinien, *n.*	*ahr-gen-*TEEN-*yen*	Argentina	**Aufmerksamkeit,** *f.*	OWF-*mehrk-zahmm-kite*	attention (heed)
			aufnehmen (80)	OWF-*nay-men*	absorb (suck up), to
argentinisch	*ahr-gen-*TEEN-*ish*	Argentinian (*adj.*)	**aufpicken (1)**	OWF-*pick-en*	pick up (lift), to
ärgern (1)	EHR-*gehrn*	annoy (irk), to			
"	"	vex (anger), to	**aufputzen (1)**	OWF-*poott-sen*	dress (decorate), to
Arithmetik, *f.*	*ah-ritt-may-*TEEK	arithmetic	"	"	trim, to
arm	ARM	poor (unfortunate)	**aufrecht**	OWF-*rehkht*	erect (*adj.*)
Arm, *m.*	ARM	arm (*anat.*)	**aufregen (1)**	OWF-*ray-gen*	arouse, to
Armband, *n.*	ARM-*bahnt*	bracelet	"	"	excite, to
Ärmel, *m.*	EHR-*mel*	sleeve	**Aufregung,** *f.*	OWF-*ray-goong*	excitement
Armut, *f.*	AHR-*moot*	poverty	**aufrichtig**	OWF-*rikh-tikh*	sincere
Art, *f.*	ART	kind (*n.*)	**Aufruhr,** *f.*	OWF-*roor*	revolt
"	"	mode (manner)	"	"	riot (disturbance)
"	"	type	**aufschwingen, sich (116)**	*zikh* OWF-*shving-en*	soar (rise), to
Arthritis, *f.*	*ahr-*TREE-*tiss*	arthritis	**Aufsicht,** *f.*	OWF-*zikht*	charge (responsibility)
Artikel, *m.*	*ahr-*TEE-*kell*	article (literary composition)	**aufsitzen (122)**	OWF-*zit-sen*	perch (sit), to
Arznei, *f.*	*arts-*NYE	medicine (medicament)	**aufstehen (129)**	OWF-*shtay-en*	rise, to
			"	"	stand up, to
Arzt, *m.*	ARTST	physician	**aufstellen (1)**	OWF-*shtell-en*	install (set up for use), to
ärztlich	EHRTS-*likh*	medical	**Aufstellung,** *f.*	OWF-*shtell-oong*	nomination
Asche, *f.*	AHSH-*uh*	ashes	"	"	statement (accounting, *bus.*)
Aschenbecher, *m.*	AHSH-*en-beh_kh-ehr*	ash tray			
Aschermittwoch, *m.*	AHSH-*ehr-mitt-vawkh*	Ash Wednesday	**auftauchen (1)**	OWF-*t_ow_kh-en*	emerge, to
asiatisch	*ah-zee-*AH-*tish*	Asiatic (*adj.*)	**Auftrag,** *m.*	OWF-*trahk*	errand (commission)
Asien, *n.*	AH-*zee-en*	Asia	"	"	order (purchase)
Aspirin, *n.*	*ahss-pih-*REEN	aspirin	**Auftritt,** *m.*	OWF-*tritt*	act (dramatic unit)
Ast, *m.*	AHSST	bough	"	"	scene
Atem, *m.*	AH-*tem*	breath	**aufwachen (1)**	OWF-*vahkh-en*	awaken (rouse oneself), to
Athen, *n.*	*ah-*TAYN	Athens			
Athlet, *m.*	*aht-*LATE	athlete	**aufwärts**	OWF-*vehrts*	upward (to a higher level, *adv.*)
athletisch	*aht-*LAY-*tish*	athletic	**aufwecken (1)**	OWF-*veck-en*	awaken (make awaken), to
Atlantische Ozean, *m.*	*aht-*LAHNN-*tish-uh* OATS-*ay-ahnn*	Atlantic (*n.*)	**aufzeichnen (1)**	OWF-*tsye_kh-nen*	record (set down), to
Atlas, *m.*	AHT-*lahss*	atlas	**Auge,** *n.*	*ow-guh*	eye (*anat.*)
"	"	satin (*n.*)	**Augenblick,** *n.*	*ow-gen-blick*	instant (*n.*)
atmen (1)	AHT-*men*	breathe (draw breath), to	"	"	moment
Atmosphäre, *f.*	*aht-mawss-*FAIR-*uh*	atmosphere (environment)	**augenblicklich**	*ow-gen-blick-likh*	immediate (instant)
Atom, *n.*	*ah-*TOHM	atom	**Augenbraue,** *f.*	*ow-gen-brow-uh*	eyebrow
atomische Bombe, *f.*	*ah-*TOH-*mish-uh* BAWMM-*buh*	atomic bomb	**Augenlid,** *n.*	*ow-gen-leet*	eyelid
			aus	OWSS	from
auch	OW_KH	also	"	"	out (not in, *adv.*)
"	"	so (also, *adv.*)			
"	"	too	**ausbessern (1)**	*owss-bess-ehrn*	repair (fix), to
auch nicht	OW_KH NIKHT	either (not...either, *adv.*)	**Ausbesserung,** *f.*	*owss-bess-uh-roong*	repair (*n.*)
			Ausblick, *m.*	*owss-blick*	outlook (attitude)

German	Pronunciation	English	German	Pronunciation	English
ausbreiten (1)	owss-*brite-en*	expand (make larger), to	ausstatten (1)	owss-*shtahtt-en*	furnish (put furniture in), to
ausdehnen (1)	owss-*day-nen*	stretch (draw out), to	ausstellen (1)	owss-*shtell-len*	display, to
Ausdruck, *m.*	owss-*droock*	expression			exhibit, to
"	"	term	Ausstellung, *f.*	owss-*shtell-oong*	exhibit
ausdrücken (1)	owss-*drück-en*	express (state), to			exhibition (exposition)
Auseinandersetzung, *f.*	owss-*ine-*AHNN*-dehr-zet-tsoong*	argument (dispute)	. "	"	show
			ausstossen (134)	owss-*shtoh-sen*	expel (eject), to
auserlesen	owss-*ehr-lay-zenn*	exquisite	ausstrecken (1)	owss-*shtreck-en*	extend (stretch out), to
auserwählt	owss-*ehr-vale_t*	chosen	ausstreuen (1)	owss-*shtroy-en*	scatter (strew), to
ausfindig machen (1)	owss-*fin-dikh* MAH_KH-*en*	locate (find), to	Auster, *f.*	owss-*tehr*	oyster
			austilgen (1)	owss-*till-gen*	blot out (efface), to
Ausfuhr, *f.*	owss-*foor*	exportation	Australien, *n.*	owss-TRAHL-*yen*	Australia
ausführen (1)	owss-*fü-ren*	execute (carry out), to			
"	"	export, to	australisch	owss-TRAHL-*ish*	Australian (*adj.*)
Ausgabe, *f.*	owss-*gah-buh*	edition	austrocknen (1)	owss-*trawk-nen*	dry (make dry), to
"	"	expenditure (outlay)	ausüben (1)	owss-*ü-ben*	exercise (employ), to
Ausgang, *m.*	owss-*gahng*	exit			practice (put to practice), to
"	"	outlet	Ausübung, *f.*	owss-*ü-boong*	practice (performance)
ausgeben (43)	owss-*gay-ben*	spend (pay out), to	Auswahl, *f.*	owss-*vahl*	selection
ausgedehnt	owss-*guh-dane_t*	extensive	"	"	variety (assortment)
ausgezeichnet	owss-*guh-tsye_kh-net*	distinguished (notable)	auswählen (1)	owss-*vay-len*	pick (choose), to
			Ausverkauf, *m.*	owss-*fehr-kowf*	clearance sale
ausgleiten (56)	owss-*glye-ten*	slip (slide), to	Auto, *n.*	ow-*toh*	car (auto)
Ausguss, *m.*	owss-*gooss*	sink	Axt, *f.*	AHXT	axe
aushalten (59)	owss-*hahl-ten*	sustain (maintain), to	Bach, *m.*	BAHKH	brook
ausheben (62)	owss-*hay-ben*	draft (conscript), to	"	"	creek (stream)
Auskunft, *f.*	owss-*koonft*	information (knowledge)	Backe, *f.*	BAHK-*uh*	cheek
			backen (2)	BAHK-*ken*	bake (be cooking), to
Auskunft geben (43)	owss-*koonft* GAY-*ben*	inform (apprise), to	Bäcker, *m.*	BECK-*ehr*	baker
Auslage, *f.*	owss-*lah-guh*	disbursement (*bus.*)	Backofen, *m.*	BAHK-*oh-fen*	oven
Ausland, im	*imm* owss-*lahnt*	abroad (in foreign land)	Backpflaume, *f.*	BAHK-*pfl_ow-muh*	prune
Ausländer, *m.*	owss-*len-der*	foreigner	Bad, *n.*	BAHT	bath
ausländisch	owss-*len-dish*	foreign	Badeanzug, *m.*	BAH-*duh-ahnn-tsook*	bathing suit
auslassen (71)	owss-*lahss-sen*	omit (leave out), to	baden (1)	BAH-*den*	bathe (take a bath), to
Ausmass, *n.*	owss-*mahss*	extent (magnitude)	Badewanne, *f.*	BAH-*duh-vahn-nuh*	bathtub
Ausnahme, *f.*	owss-*nah-muh*	exception (unusual case)	Badezimmer, *n.*	BAH-*duh-tsim-mehr*	bathroom
ausradieren (1)	owss-*rah-deer-en*	erase, to	Bahnhof, *m.*	BAHN-*hohf*	depot
Ausruf, *m.*	owss-*roo_f*	exclamation (*n.*)	"	"	station, railroad
ausrufen (89)	owss-*roo-fen*	exclaim, to	Bahnsteig, *m.*	BAHN-*shtye_k*	platform, railroad
			Bakterium, *n.*	*bahk-*TARE*-ee-oom*	germ (micro-organism)
Ausrüstung, *f.*	owss-*rüss-toong*	equipment	bald	BAHLLT	soon (shortly)
"	"	outfit	Balken, *m.*	BAHL-*ken*	beam (rafter)
Aussatz, *m.*	owss-*zahtts*	leprosy	Ball, *m.*	BAHLL	ball (sphere)
ausscheiden (93)	owss-*shy-den*	eliminate, to	Ballon, *m.*	*bah-*LONG	balloon
ausschliessen (104)	owss-*shlee-sen*	exclude, to	Banane, *f.*	*bah-*NAH*-nuh*	banana
ausschliesslich	owss-*shleess-likh*	exclusive (not including)	Band, *n.* (*pl.* Bänder)	BAHNNT (BEND-*ehr*)	band
Ausschuss, *m.*	owss-*shooss*	board (council)	"	"	ribbon
"	"	commission (group)	Band, *n.* (*pl.* Bande)	BAHNNT (BAHNN-*duh*)	bond (emotional tie)
"	"	committee	"	"	tie
Aussehen, *n.*	owss-*zay-en*	appearance	Band, *m.* (*pl.* Bände)	BAHNNT	volume (book)
"	"	look (aspect)	Bande, *f.*	BAHNN-*duh*	band
			"	"	gang
aussehen (118)	owss-*zay-en*	look (seem), to	Bandregistrierapparat, *n.*	BAHNNT-*ray-g_eess-treer-ah-pah-*RAHT	tape recorder
Aussenseite, *f.*	owss-*en-zite-uh*	outside (*n.*)	Bandit, *m.*	*bahn-*DEET	bandit
ausser	owss-*ehr*	beside (other than, *prep.*)	Banjo, *n.*	BAN-*jo*	banjo
"	"	except (*prep.*)	Bank, *f.*	BAHNNK	bank (treasury)
ausser dass	owss-*ehr dahss*	but (if not, *conj.*)	"	"	bench (long seat)
ausserdem	owss-*ehr-dame*	besides (*adv.*)	Bankier, *m.*	*bahnnk-*YAY	banker
"	"	moreover	Bankrott, *m.*	*bahnnk-*RAWTT	bankruptcy
			"	"	failure (*bus.*)
äussere	OYSS-*ehr-uh*	outer	Bankwesen, *n.*	BAHNNK-*vay-zen*	banking
"	"	outside (*adj.*)	Banner, *n.*	BAHNN-*nehr*	banner
äusserlich	OYSS-*ehr-likh*	exterior (*adj.*)	Bar, *f.*	BAR	bar (barroom)
ausserordentlich	owss-*ehr-or-dent-likh*	extraordinary	Bär, *m.*	BARE	bear (animal)
äusserst	OYSS-*ehrst*	extreme	Bargeld, *n.*	BAR-*gellt*	cash (money)
"	"	utmost (*adj.*)	barmherzig	*barm-*HEHRT*-sikh*	merciful
			Bart, *m.*	BAHRRT	beard
aussetzen (1)	owss-*zett-sen*	expose (lay open), to	Baseball, *m.*	BASE-*ball*	baseball
"	"	stall (stop going), to	Basel, *n.*	BAHZL	Basle
Aussicht, *f.*	ows-*zikht*	chance (possibility)	Batterie, *f.*	*baht-teh-*REE	battery (artillery)
"	"	prospect (thing expected)	"	"	battery (primary cell)
"	"	view (scene)	Bau, *m.*	B_OW	construction (fabrication)
Aussprache, *f.*	owss-*shprah-kh_uh*	accent (speech)	"	"	structure (thing built)
aussprechen (125)	owss-*shprekh-en*	pronounce (enunciate), to			

German	Pronunciation	English
Bauch, *m.*	B_OWKH	abdomen
,,	,,	belly
bauen (1)	B_OW-*en*	build, to
(an)bauen	(AHNN-)*b_ow-en*	grow (cultivate), to
(er)bauen	(*ehr*-)B_OW-*en*	construct, to
Bauer, *m.*	B_OW-*er*	farmer
,,	,,	peasant
Bauerngut, *n.*	B_OW-*ehrn-goot*	farm
Bauholz, *n.*	B_OW-*hawlts*	lumber (timber)
Baukünstler, *m.*	B_OW-*künst-lehr*	architect
Baum, *m.*	B_OWM	tree
Baumwolle, *f.*	B_OWM-*vawll-uh*	cotton
Baumwollensamt, *m.*	B_OWM-*vawll-en-zahmmt*	velveteen (*n.*)
Bayern, *n.*	BY-*ehrn*	Bavaria
beabsichtigen (1)	*buh*-AHPP-*zikh-tih-gen*	mean, to
,,	,,	intend (propose), to
beachten (1)	*buh*-AHKH-*ten*	heed (mind), to
Beamte, *m.*	*buh*-AHMM-*tuh*	official (*n.*)
beanspruchen (1)	*buh*-AHNN-*shprookh-en*	claim, to
beantworten (1)	*buh*-AHNNT-*vor-ten*	answer (give answer to), to
beargwöhnen (1)	*buh*-ARG-*vö-nen*	suspect (distrust), to
bebauen (1)	*buh*-B_OW-*en*	cultivate, to
,,	,,	till, to
beben (1)	BAY-*ben*	quake (shake), to
Becher, *m.*	BEHKH-*ehr*	tumbler (glass)
bedacht auf	*buh*-DAHKH_T OWF	intent (engrossed)
Bedauern, *n.*	*buh*-D_OW-*ehrn*	regret (sorrow)
bedauern (1)	*buh*-D_OW-*ehrn*	pity, to
,,	,,	regret, to
,,	,,	sorry, to be
bedeuten (1)	*buh*-DOY-*ten*	signify (denote), to
bedeutsam	*buh*-DOYT-*zahm*	significant (meaningful)
Bedeutung, *f.*	*buh*-DOY-*toong*	significance (importance)
Bedingung, *f.*	*buh*-DING-*oong*	condition
,,	,,	provision
Bedingungen, *f.pl.*	*buh*-DING-*oong-en*	terms (conditions)
bedrängen (1)	*buh*-DRENG-*en*	oppress (weigh down), to
Bedürftigkeit, *f.*	*buh*-DÜRF-*tikh-kite*	want (need)
beeilen, sich (1)	*zikh buh*-EYE-*len*	hasten, to
,,	,,	hurry, to
beenden (1)	*buh*-ENN-*den*	end (bring to an end), to
Beere, *f.*	BARE-*ruh*	berry (fruit)
Befehl, *m.*	*buh*-FAIL	command
,,	,,	order
befehlen (3)	*buh*-FAIL-*en*	command, to
,,	,,	order, to
Befehlshaber, *m.*	*buh*-FAILS-*hah-behr*	commander (officer)
befestigen (1)	*buh*-FESS-*tee-gen*	fasten, to
beflecken (1)	*buh*-FLECK-*en*	blot (stain), to
befördern (1)	*buh*-FÖR-*dehrn*	convey, to
,,	,,	promote (raise in rank), to
,,	,,	transport, to
Beförderung, *f.*	*buh*-FÖR-*duh-roong*	promotion (advance)
,,	,,	transportation (conveying)
befragen (1)	*buh*-FRAHG-*en*	question (query), to
befreien (1)	*buh*-FRY-*en*	free, to
,,	,,	liberate, to
,,	,,	relieve, to
,,	,,	rid, to
befreit	*buh*-FRITE	exempt
befriedigen (1)	*buh*-FREE-*dee-gen*	satisfy, to
befriedigend	*buh*-FREE-*dee-g_ent*	satisfactory
Befriedigung, *f.*	*buh*-FREE-*dee-goong*	satisfaction (gratification)
befürworten (1)	*buh*-FÜR-*vor-ten*	advocate, to
begabt	*buh*-GAHPT	gifted (talented)
begegnen (1)	*buh*-GAYG-*nen*	encounter, to
begehen (46)	*buh*-GAY-*en*	commit (perpetrate), to
begehren (1)	*buh*-GAY-*ren*	desire (long for), to
,,	,,	want, to
begeistern (1)	*buh*-GICE-*tehrn*	inspire, to

German	Pronunciation	English
Begeisterung, *f.*	*buh*-GICE-*tehr-oong*	enthusiasm
beginnen (5)	*buh*-GINN-*nen*	begin (come into being), to
beglaubigen (1)	*buh*-GL_OW-*bee-gen*	certify, to
begleiten (1)	*buh*-GLITE-*en*	accompany (go along with), to
Begleiter, *m.*	*buh*-GLYE-*tehr*	escort (social companion)
Begnadigung, *f.*	*buh*-G_NAH-*dee-goong*	pardon (*law*)
begraben (57)	*buh*-GRAH-*ben*	bury (entomb), to
Begräbnis, *n.*	*buh*-GRAYP-*niss*	burial
,,	,,	funeral
begreifen (58)	*buh*-GRIFE-*en*	comprehend, to
,,	,,	grasp, to
Begriff, *m.*	*buh*-GRIFF	conception (notion)
begründen (1)	*buh*-GRÜNN-*den*	base (found), to
begrüssen (1)	*buh*-GRÜ-*sen*	welcome (receive hospitably), to
Begrüssung, *f.*	*buh*-GRÜ-*soong*	greeting
Behagen, *n.*	*buh*-HAH-*gen*	ease (comfort)
behaglich	*buh*-HAHG-*likh*	comfortable (affording comfort)
behalten (59)	*buh*-HAHLL-*ten*	keep, to
,,	,,	retain, to
(bei)behalten (6)	(BY-)*buh*-HAHLL-*ten*	maintain (preserve), to
behandeln (1)	*buh*-HAHNN-*del'n*	treat (behave toward), to
Behandlung, *f.*	*buh*-HAHNND-*loong*	treatment (behavior toward)
,,	,,	treatment (medical care)
beharren (1)	*buh*-HAHR-*renn*	persist (persevere), to
behaupten (1)	*buh*-HOWP-*ten*	argue (maintain), to
,,	,,	assert (declare), to
,,	,,	contend, to
Behauptung, *f.*	*buh*-HOWP-*toong*	assertion
,,	,,	statement
behende	*buh*-HEN-*duh*	nimble (agile)
beherrschen (1)	*buh*-HEHR-*shen*	master (learn), to
bei	BY	at (in)
,,	,,	at (by)
,,	,,	by (*prep.*)
,,	,,	in (during, *prep.*)
,,	,,	near (*prep.*)
beide	BY-*duh*	both
Beifall, *m.*	BY-*fahll*	applause
Beifall rufen (89)	BY-*fahll* ROO-*fen*	cheer (applaud), to
beifügen (1)	BY-*fü-gen*	add (include), to
Beil, *n.*	BILE	hatchet
Beilage, *f.*	BY-*lah-guh*	enclosure (addition)
beiläufig	BY-*loy-fikh*	casual (offhand)
beilegen (1)	BY-*lay-gen*	enclose (include in envelope), to
Bein, *n.*	BINE	leg (*anat.*)
beiseite	*by*-ZITE-*uh*	aside (away)
Beispiel, *n.*	BY-*shpeel*	example
,,	,,	instance
beissen (7)	BICE-*en*	bite, to
Beistand, *m.*	BY-*shtahnt*	assistance
beistehen (129)	BY-*shtay-en*	assist, to
beistimmen (1)	BY-*shtim-men*	agree, to
,,	,,	assent, to
Beitrag, *m.*	BY-*trahk*	contribution
beitragen (137)	BY-*trah-gen*	contribute, to
beitreten (140)	BY-*tray-ten*	enter (join), to
,,	,,	join (become a member of), to
beiwohnen (1)	BY-*voh-nen*	attend (be present at), to
Beiwort, *n.*	BY-*vort*	adjective
Bejahung, *f.*	*buh*-YAH-*oong*	acceptance (approval)
bekämpfen (1)	*buh*-KEMP-*fen*	fight (struggle against), to
bekannt	*buh*-KAHNNT	familiar
,,	,,	known
Bekannte, *m., f.*	*buh*-KAHNN-*tuh*	acquaintance (person known)
bekannt machen (1)	*buh*-KAHNNT MAH-*kh_en*	acquaint (inform), to

German	Pronunciation	English
Bekanntmachung, *f.*	*buh*-KAHNNT-*mahkh-oong*	introduction (presentation)
Bekehrte, *m.,f.*	*buh*-CARE-*tuh*	convert (proselyte)
bekommen (68)	*buh*-KAWMM-*en*	get (obtain), to
Belagerung, *f.*	*buh*-LAH-*guh-roong*	siege (*mil.*)
belasten (1)	*buh*-LAHSS-*ten*	debit, to
belästigen (1)	*buh*-LESS-*tih-gen*	trouble (inconvenience), to
beleidigen (1)	*buh*-LYE-*dih-gen*	offend (affront), to
Beleidigung, *f.*	*buh*-LYE-*dih-goong*	insult
beleuchten (1)	*buh*-LOY_KH-*ten*	illuminate, to
″	″	light, to
Belgien, *n.*	BELG-*ee-en*	Belgium
belgisch	BELL-*gish*	Belgian (*adj.*)
belieben (1)	*buh*-LEEB-*en*	please (satisfy), to
bellen (1)	BELL-*en*	bark (bay), to
belohnen (1)	*buh*-LOAN-*en*	reward, to
Belohnung, *f.*	*buh*-LOAN-*oong*	reward (recompense)
bemerken (1)	*buh*-MEHR-*ken*	note (mention), to
″	″	notice (see), to
″	″	observe, to
″	″	remark (say), to
bemerkenswert	*buh*-MEHR-*kenns-vehrt*	notable (*adj.*)
Bemerkung, *f.*	*buh*-MEHR-*koong*	comment
″	″	remark
Bemerkungen machen (1)	*buh*-MEHR-*koong-en* MAH-*kh_en*	comment, to
bemühen, sich (1)	*zikh buh*-MÜ-*en*	endeavor, to
benachrichtigen (1)	*buh*-NAHKH-*rikh-tih-gen*	notify, to
Benehmen, *n.*	*buh*-NAY-*men*	behavior
benehmen, sich (80)	*zikh buh*-NAY-*men*	behave (conduct oneself), to
beneiden (1)	*buh*-NIDE-*en*	envy, to
benutzen (1)	*buh*-NOOTT-*sen*	use (utilize), to
Benzin, *n.*	*ben*-TSEEN	gasoline
beobachten (1)	*buh*-OHB-*ah_kh-ten*	observe, to
″	″	watch, to
Beobachter, *m.*	*buh*-OHB-*ah_kh-tehr*	observer
Beobachtung, *f.*	*buh*-OHB-*ah_kh-toong*	observation (watching)
bequem	*buh*-KVAYM	convenient
Bequemlichkeit, *f.*	*buh*-KVAYM-*likh-kite*	comfort (ease)
″	″	convenience
beraten (83)	*buh*-RAH-*ten*	counsel, to
berauben (1)	*buh*-R_OWB-*en*	rob (steal from), to
berechnen (1)	*buh*-REHKH-*nen*	calculate (compute), to
berechtigen (1)	*buh*-REHKH-*tih-gen*	entitle (give a right to), to
beredt	*buh*-RATE	eloquent
Bereich, *m.*	*buh*-RYE_KH	range (scope)
bereit	*buh*-RITE	ready (prepared)
bereitwillig	*buh*-RITE-*vill-ick*	willing (favorably disposed)
bereuen (1)	*buh*-ROY-*en*	repent, to
Berg, *m.*	BEHRK	mountain
Bergkette, *f.*	BEHRK-*ket-tuh*	range (of mountains)
Bergmann, *m.*	BEHRK-*mahnn*	miner
Bergwerk, *n.*	BEHRK-*vehrk*	mine (pit)
Bericht, *m.*	*buh*-RIKH_T	report (account)
berichten (1)	*buh*-RIKH-*ten*	report (account formally), to
Berichterstatter, *m.*	*buh*-RIKH_T-*ehr-shtahtt-ehr*	reporter (journalist)
Berlin, *n.*	*behr*-LEEN	Berlin
Bern, *n.*	BEHRN	Berne
bernsteinfarbig	BEHRN-*shtine-fahr-bikh*	amber (*adj.*)
bersten (9)	BEHR-*stenn*	burst, to
berüchtigt	*buh*-RÜKH-*tickt*	notorious
Beruf, *m.*	*buh*-ROOF	occupation (calling)
″	″	profession
berühmt	*buh*-RÜMT	famous
berühren (1)	*buh*-RÜ-*ren*	touch, to
Berührung, *f.*	*buh*-RÜ-*roong*	contact (meeting)
besänftigen (1)	*buh*-ZENF-*tih-gen*	soothe (calm), to
beschädigen (1)	*buh*-SHAY-*dih-gen*	damage (injure), to
beschäftigen (1)	*buh*-SHEFF-*tih-gen*	occupy (make busy), to
beschäftigen, sich mit...	*zikh mit...buh*-SHEFF-*tih-gen*	engage (be occupied) in, to
beschäftigt	*buh*-SHEFF-*tickt*	busy (occupied)
Beschäftigung, *f.*	*buh*-SHEFF-*tih-goong*	employment (work)
beschämt	*buh*-SHAME_T	ashamed (mortified)
bescheiden (93)	*buh*-SHY-*den*	modest
Bescheinigung, *f.*	*buh*-SHY-*nee-goong*	certificate
″	″	license (permit)
beschirmen (1)	*buh*-SHEERR-*men*	shield, to
Beschlagnahme, *f.*	*buh*-SHLAHK-*nah-muh*	attachment (legal seizure)
beschleunigen (1)	*buh*-SHLOY-*nih-gen*	hasten (expedite), to
″	″	quicken, to
beschliessen (104)	*buh*-SHLEE-*sen*	resolve (determine), to
Beschluss, *m.*	*buh*-SHLOOS	resolution (formal expression)
beschmutzen (1)	*buh*-SHMOOTT-*sen*	soil (make dirty), to
beschränken (1)	*buh*-SHRENG-*ken*	confine (limit), to
″	″	limit, to
beschreiben (109)	*buh*-SHRY-*ben*	describe (portray), to
Beschreibung, *f.*	*buh*-SHRY-*boong*	description (account)
beschwichtigen (1)	*buh*-SHVIKH-*tih-gen*	appease (calm), to
beseitigen (1)	*buh*-ZITE-*tih-gen*	dispose of (put away), to
″	″	remove (take away), to
Besen, *m.*	BAY-*zen*	broom
Besetzung, *f.*	*buh*-ZETTS-*oong*	occupation (*mil.*)
besichtigen (1)	*buh*-ZIKH-*tih-gen*	inspect, to
Besichtigung, *f.*	*buh*-ZIKH-*tih-goong*	survey (inspection)
besiegen (1)	*buh*-ZEE-*gen*	beat (defeat), to
″	″	defeat (conquer), to
Besitz, *m.*	*buh*-ZITTS	estate (total possessions)
″	″	possession (ownership)
besitzen (122)	*buh*-ZITT-*sen*	own, to
″	″	possess, to
besonder	*buh*-ZAWNN-*dehr*	individual (*adj.*)
″	″	particular (specific, *adj.*)
″	″	special
besonders	*buh*-ZAWNN-*dehrss*	especially
besprechen (125)	*buh*-SHPREH_KH-*en*	discuss, to
Besprechung, *f.*	*buh*-SHPREH_KH-*oong*	discussion
″	″	review (critique)
besprengen (1)	*buh*-SHPRENG-*en*	spray, to
besser	BESS-*sehr*	better (*adj., adv.*)
bestätigen (1)	*buh*-SHTAY-*tih-gen*	acknowledge (note receipt of), to
″	″	confirm (corroborate), to
Bestätigung, *f.*	*buh*-SHTAY-*tih-goong*	confirmation (corroboration)
beste, (der)	(*dehr*) BESS-*tuh*	best
bestechen (128)	*buh*-SHTEH_KH-*en*	bribe, to
bestehen (129)	*buh*-SHTAY-*en*	exist, to
″	″	insist, to
″	″	pass (not fail in), to
bestehen aus	*buh*-SHTAY-*en* OWSS	consist of (comprise), to
be steigen (131)	*buh*-SHTYE-*gen*	ascend (go upward along), to
″	″	climb (scale), to
″	″	mount (climb upon), to
bestellen (1)	*buh*-SHTELL-*en*	book (engage space), to
″	″	order (purchase), to
besteuern (1)	*buh*-SHTOY-*ehrn*	assess (impose tax), to
bestimmt	*buh*-SHTIMMT	definite
Bestimmungsort, *m.*	*buh*-SHTIMM-*oongs-ort*	destination
Bestrebung, *f.*	*buh*-SHTRAY-*boong*	endeavor
bestreiten (136)	*buh*-SHTRYE-*ten*	contest, to
″	″	dispute (oppose by argument), to
″	″	oppose (combat), to
Bestürzung, *f.*	*buh*-SHTÜR-*tsoong*	dismay
Besuch, *m.*	*buh*-ZOO_KH	visit (social call)
″	″	visit (stay)
besuchen (1)	*buh*-ZOO-*kh_en*	visit, to
besuchen, häufig	HOY-*fikh buh*-ZOO-*kh_en*	haunt (visit often), to
Besucher, *m.*	*buh*-ZOO-*kh_ehr*	visitor
beten (1)	BAY-*ten*	pray, to
beteuern (1)	*buh*-TOY-*ehrn*	protest, to
Beton, *m.*	*bay*-TOHNG	concrete (artificial stone)

German	Pronunciation	English
Betonung, *f.*	*buh*-TONE-*oong*	accent (stress)
betrachten (1)	*buh*-TRAH_KH-*ten*	regard (consider), to
beträchtlich	*buh*-TREH_KHT-*likh*	considerable (*adj.*)
"	"	substantial (sizable)
Betrag, *m.*	*buh*-TRAHK	amount
betragen (137)	*buh*-TRAH-*gen*	amount to, to
betreffen (138)	*buh*-TREFF-*fen*	affect (influence), to
betreffend	*buh*-TREFF-*ent*	concerning
betreffs	*buh*-TREFFS	regarding
betreiben (139)	*buh*-TRY-*ben*	operate (handle), to
Betrieb, *m.*	*buh*-TREEP	operation (functioning)
Betriebsanlage, *f.*	*buh*-TREEPS-*ahn-lah-guh*	plant (factory)
Betriebskosten, *pl.*	*buh*-TREEPS-*kawss-ten*	operating expenses (*bus.*)
Betrug, *m.*	*buh*-TROOK	deceit
betrügen (10)	*buh*-TRÜ-*gen*	cheat (defraud), to
"	"	deceive (delude), to
betrunken	*buh*-TROONG-*ken*	drunk (intoxicated)
Bett, *n.*	BET	bed
(Schlafwagen)Bett, *n.*	(SHLAHF-*vahg-en*-)BET	berth (train bunk)
betteln (1)	BET-*tel'n*	beg (solicit alms), to
Bettler, *m.*	BET-*lehr*	beggar
Bettuch, *n.*	BET-*too_kh*	sheet (bedding)
beugen, sich (1)	*zikh* BOY-*gen*	bend (be bent), to
beunruhigt	*buh*-OONN-*roo-ickt*	anxious (uneasy)
Beute, *f.*	BOY-*tuh*	prey (victim)
Bevölkerung, *f.*	*buh*-FÖL-*kehr-oong*	population (number of people)
Bevollmächtigte, *m., f.*	*buh*-FAWLL-*meh_kh-tick-tuh*	authority (person with power)
Bevollmächtigung, *f.*	*buh*-FAWLL-*meh_kh-tih-goong*	authorization
bevor	*buh*-FOR	before (prior to the time when, *conj.*)
bewachen (1)	*buh*-VAH_KH-*en*	watch (guard), to
bewaffnen (1)	*buh*-VAHFF-*nen*	arm, to
bewähren, sich (1)	*zikh buh*-VARE-*en*	last (withstand use), to
Bewässerung, *f.*	*buh*-VESS-*uh-roong*	irrigation
bewegen (11)	*buh*-VAY-*gen*	induce (persuade), to
"	"	move (shift the position of), to
bewegen, sich	*zikh buh*-VAY-*gen*	move (shift one's position), to
Beweggrund, *m.*	*buh*-VAKE-*groont*	motive (*n.*)
Bewegung, *f.*	*buh*-VAY-*goong*	motion
"	"	movement
Beweis, *m.*	*buh*-VICE	demonstration
"	"	evidence (*law*)
"	"	proof (demonstration)
beweisen (155)	*buh*-VIZE-*en*	prove (verify), to
bewirten (1)	*buh*-VEERR-*ten*	entertain (be host to), to
bewohnen (1)	*buh*-VOH-*nen*	inhabit, to
"	"	occupy (live in), to
bewundern (1)	*buh*-VOONN-*dehrn*	admire, to
Bewunderung, *f.*	*buh*-VOONN-*duh-roong*	admiration
bewusst	*buh*-VOOSST	aware
"	"	conscious
bezahlen (1)	*buh*-TSAH-*len*	pay, to
bezaubern (1)	*buh*-TS_OW-*behrn*	charm (delight), to
bezeichnen (1)	*buh*-TSYE_KH-*nen*	mark (designate), to
bezeichnend	*buh*-TSYE_KH-*nent*	characteristic (typical)
bezeugen (1)	*buh*-TSOY-*gen*	testify, to
beziehen, sich (161)	*zikh buh*-TSEE-*en*	refer (allude), to
"	"	relate (pertain) to, to
Beziehung, *f.*	*buh*-TSEE-*oong*	relation (connection)
Bezirk, *m.*	*buh*-TSEERRK	district (locality)
bezweifeln (1)	*buh*-TSVYE-*fel'n*	doubt (be uncertain about), to
"	"	question, to
Bibel, *f.*	BEE-*bel*	Bible
Biber, *m.*	BEE-*behr*	beaver (animal)
Bibliothek, *f.*	*bee-blee-oh*-TAKE	library
Bibliothekar, *m.*	*bee-blee-oh-tay*-KAHR	librarian
biegen (12)	BEE-*gen*	bend (make bend), to
Biene, *f.*	BEE-*nuh*	bee
Bienenkorb, *m.*	BEE-*nen-kawrp*	hive (beehive)
Bier, *n.*	BEER	beer
Bieter, *m.*	BEAT-*ehr*	bidder (*bus.*)

German	Pronunciation	English
Bild, *n.*	BILLT	picture (depiction)
bilden (1)	BILL-*den*	constitute (make up), to
"	"	form (shape), to
Bilderserie, *f.*	BILL-*dehr-sare-yeh*	comic strip
Bildhauer, *m.*	BILLT-*how-ehr*	sculptor
Bildnis, *n.*	BILLT-*niss*	portrait
Bildsäule, *f.*	BILLT-*zoy-luh*	statue
Bildung, *f.*	BILL-*doong*	culture (refinement)
"	"	formation (creation)
billard, *n.*	BILL-*yart*	billiards
billig	BILL-*ikh*	cheap (inexpensive)
billigen (1)	BILL-*ig-en*	approve (think well of), to
Billigung, *f.*	BILL-*ig-oong*	approval
binden (14)	BINN-*den*	bind, to
"	"	tie (fasten), to
bindend	BINN-*dent*	obligatory (binding)
Bindestrich, *m.*	BINN-*duh-shtrikh*	hyphen
Bindewort, *n.*	BINN-*duh-vort*	conjunction (*gram.*)
Biologie, *f.*	*bee-o-loh*-G_EE	biology
Birke, *f.*	BEERR-*kuh*	birch (tree)
Birne, *f.*	BEERR-*nuh*	pear
bis	BISS	until (*conj.*)
"	"	until (before, *prep.*)
"	"	until (up to the time of, *prep.*)
Bischof, *m.*	BISH-*ohf*	bishop
bisher	*biss*-HARE	hitherto (thus far)
Biss, *m.*	BISS	bite
Bisschen, *n.*	BISS-*kh_en*	bit (small part)
Bitte, *f.*	BIT-*tuh*	appeal (entreaty)
"	"	request
bitten (15)	BIT-*ten*	beg (entreat), to
bitten um	BIT-*ten oom*	ask (request), to
bitter	BIT-*lehr*	bitter
Bittschrift, *f.*	BIT-*shrifft*	petition (written request)
blank putzen (1)	BLAHNNK POOTT-*sen*	shine (polish), to
Blase, *f.*	BLAH-*zuh*	blister
blasen (1)	BLAH-*zen*	blow, to
blass	BLAHSS	pale (wan)
blassrot	BLAHSS-*rote*	pink (color)
Blatt, *n.*	BLAHTT	leaf (*bot.*)
Blattern, *f.pl.*	BLAHTT-*ehrn*	smallpox
blau	BL_OW	blue
Blaupause, *f.*	BL_OW-*p_ow-zuh*	blueprint
Blei, *n.*	BLYE	lead (metal)
bleiben (17)	BLIBE-*en*	abide, to
"	"	remain (continue unchanged), to
"	"	remain (stay behind), to
"	"	stay, to
bleichen (18)	BLYE-*kh_en*	bleach (make white), to
Bleistift, *m.*	BLYE-*shtift*	pencil
blenden (1)	BLENN-*den*	blind, to
"	"	dazzle, to
Blick, *m.*	BLICK	glance
"	"	look
Blick, flüchtiger, *m.*	FLÜKH-*lih-gehr* BLICK	glimpse
blind	BLINNT	blind (lacking sight)
Blinddarmentzündung, *f.*	BLINNT-*dahrm-ent-tsün-doong*	appendicitis
blinken (1)	BLING-*ken*	twinkle, to
blinzeln (1)	BLINN-*tsel'n*	wink, to
Blitz, *m.*	BLITTS	flash (burst of light)
"	"	lightning
Block, *m.*	BLAWK	block (solid piece)
blöken (1)	BLÖ-*ken*	bleat, to
blond	BLAWNNT	blond
bloss	BLOHSS	just
"	"	mere
"	"	merely
"	"	only
blühen (1)	BLÜ-*en*	bloom, to
Blume, *f.*	BLOO-*muh*	flower (blossom)
Blumenkohl, *m.*	BLOO-*men-kole*	cauliflower
Bluse, *f.*	BLOO-*zuh*	blouse (shirtwaist)

German	Pronunciation	English
Blut,*n.*	BLOOT	blood
Blüte,*f.*	BLÜ-*tuh*	blossom
bluten (1)	BLOO-*ten*	bleed (lose blood), to
Blutsturz,*m.*	BLOOT-*shtoorts*	hemorrhage
Bock,*m.*	BAWK	buck (male deer)
Boden,*m.*	BOH-*den*	bottom
"	"	earth (land)
"	"	ground
"	"	soil
(Fuss)Boden,*m.*	(FOOSS-)BOH-*den*	floor (bottom surface)
Bogen,*m.*	BOH-*gen*	arch (curved structure)
"	"	sheet (of paper)
(grüne) Bohne,*f.*	(GRÜ-*nuh*) BOH-*nuh*	bean (string bean)
bohren (1)	BOH-*ren*	drill (bore), to
Bohrloch,*n.*	BORE-*law_kh*	well (oil, gas shaft, *n.*)
Bolivien,*n.*	*boh*-LEAVE-*yen*	Bolivia
Bolzen,*m.*	BAWLL-*tsen*	bolt (long metal fastener)
Bombe,*f.*	BAWMM-*buh*	bomb (projectile)
Boot,*n.*	BOAT	boat
Bord, an	AHNN BORT	aboard
borgen (1)	BOR-*gen*	borrow, to
Borger,*m.*	BOR-*gehr*	borrower (*bus.*)
Börse,*f.*	BÖR-*zuh*	exchange, stock
boshaft	BOHSS-*hahft*	mean (malicious)
Bosheit,*f.*	BOHSS-*hite*	malice
"	"	spite (ill will)
Botanik,*f.*	*boh*-TAH-*nick*	botany
Bote,*m.*	BOH-*tuh*	messenger (courier)
Botschafter,*m.*	BOAT-*shahf-tehr*	ambassador
boxen (1)	BAWX-*en*	box (fight), to
brasilianisch	*brah-zeel-ee*-AHN-*ish*	Brazilian (*adj.*)
Brasilien,*n.*	*brah*-ZEEL-*yen*	Brazil
Braten,*m.*	BRAH-*ten*	roast
braten, sich (19)	*zikh* BRAH-*ten*	fry (be cooked in fat), to
"	"	roast (be roasted), to
Bratsaft,*m.*	BRAHT-*zahfft*	gravy
Brauch,*m.*	BROW_KH	practice (custom)
brauchen (1)	BROW_KH-*en*	need (require), to
braun	BROWN	brown
Brausebad,*n.*	BROW-*zuh-baht*	shower (bath)
Braut,*f.*	BROWT	bride
Bräutigam,*m.*	BROY-*tih-gahm*	groom (bridegroom)
brechen (20)	BREH-*kh_en*	break (come apart), to
breit	BRIGHT	broad
"	"	wide (of specified width)
Breite,*f.*	BRIGHT-*uh*	breadth
"	"	width
Bremse,*f.*	BREMM-*zuh*	brake (*n.*)
brennen (170)	BRENN-*en*	burn (be on fire), to
Brennstoff,*m.*	BRENN-*shtawf*	fuel
Brett,*n.*	BRETT	board
"	"	-plank (timber)
Bridge,*n.*	BRIDGE	bridge, contract
Brief,*m.*	BREEF	letter (epistle)
Briefchen,*n.*	BREEF-*kh_en*	note (letter)
Briefträger,*m.*	BREEF-*tray-gehr*	postman
Briefumschlag,*m.*	BREEF-*oom-shlahk*	envelope (folded wrapper)
Briefwechsel,*m.*	BREEF-*vex'l*	correspondence (letters)
Brille,*f.*	BRILL-*uh*	glasses
"	"	spectacles
bringen (171)	BRING-*en*	bring, to
britisch	BREE-*tish*	British (*adj.*)
Brocken,*m.*	BRAWCK-*en*	scrap (fragment)
Brombeere,*f.*	BRAWMM-*bare-uh*	blackberry
Bronchitis,*f.*	*brawn*-KH_EE-*liss*	bronchitis
Bronze,*f.*	BRAWNG-*zuh*	bronze (*n.*)
Brosche,*f.*	BRAWSH-*uh*	brooch
Broschüre,*f.*	*braw*-SHÜ-*ruh*	booklet
Brot,*n.*	BROH_T	bread
Brötchen,*n.*	BRÖT-*kh_en*	roll (bread)
Brotschnitte, geröstete,*f.*	*guh*-RÖ-*stuh-tuh* BROH_T-*shnitt-tuh*	toast (bread)
Bruch,*m.*	BROOKH	fracture (*med.*)
Bruchstück,*n.*	BROOKH-*shtük*	fragment
Bruchteil,*m.*	BROOKH-*tile*	fraction (part)
Brücke,*f.*	BRÜK-*uh*	bridge (span)
Bruder,*m.*	BROO-*dehr*	brother
brüllen (1)	BRÜLL-*en*	bellow (roar), to
brummen (1)	BRUHMM-*en*	grumble, to
brünett	*brü*-NET	brunette (*adj.*)
Brunnen,*m.*	BROONN-*en*	well (water pit, *n.*)
Brüssel,*n.*	BRÜSS-*el*	Brussels
Brust,*f.*	BROOSST	breast
"	"	chest (*anat.*)
brüten (1)	BRÜ-*ten*	hatch, to
brüten, über	BRÜ-*ten ü-behr*	brood over, to
brutto	BROOTT-*toh*	gross (before deductions, *adj.*)
Buch,*n.*	BOOKH	book
Buche,*f.*	BOO-*kh uh*	beech (tree)
Bücherrevision,*f.*	BÜKH-*ehr-ray-veez-YOHN*	audit (*n.*)
Buchführer,*m.*	BOOKH-*fü-rehr*	accountant
Buchhalter,*m.*	BOOKH-*hahl-tehr*	bookkeeper (*bus.*)
Buchhaltung,*f.*	BOOKH-*hahl-toong*	bookkeeping (*bus.*)
(Konserven)Büchse,*f.*	(*kawn*-ZEHR-*ven*-) BÜKH-*suh*	can (tin)
Buchstabe,*m.*	BOOKH-*shtah-buh*	letter (character)
buchstabieren (1)	*bookh-shtah*-BEE-*ren*	spell, to
Bucht,*f.*	BOOKHT	bay (inlet)
Buckel,*m.*	BOOK-*el*	hump
bücken, sich (1)	*zikh* BÜCK-*en*	stoop (bend forward), to
Budget,*n.*	*bü*-JAY	budget (*n.*)
Buenos Aires,*n.*	BWEH-*nohss* EYE-*ress*	Buenos Aires
Büffel,*m.*	BÜF-*fel*	buffalo
Bug,*m.*	BOO_K	bow (of ship)
Bügeleisen,*n.*	BÜ-*gel-eye-zen*	iron, electric
bügeln (1)	BÜ-*gel'n*	press (iron), to
Bühne,*f.*	BÜ-*nuh*	stage (dais)
Bulgarien,*n.*	*booll*-GAR-*yen*	Bulgaria
Bund,*m.*	BOONNT	league
"	"	union
Bundes-...	BOONN-*dess-...*	federal
Bündnis,*n.*	BÜNNT-*niss*	alliance
bunt	BOONNT	motley (diverse)
Buntstift,*m.*	BOONNT-*shtift*	crayon
Bürge,*m.*	BÜRR-*guh*	guarantor
(Staats)Bürger,*m.*	(SHTAHTS-)BÜR-*gehr*	citizen
bürgerlich	BÜR-*gehr-likh*	civil (secular)
Bürgermeister,*m.*	BÜR-*gehr-mice-tehr*	mayor
Bürgersteig,*m.*	BÜR-*gehr-shtike*	sidewalk
Bürgschaft,*f.*	BÜRG-*shahft*	guarantee (warrant)
Büro,*n.*	*bü*-ROH	bureau
"	"	office (place of business)
Bürste,*f.*	BÜR-*stuh*	brush (scrubbing utensil)
Busch,*m.*	BUSH	bush (plant)
Busen,*m.*	BOO-*zen*	bosom
Büste,*f.*	BÜSS-*tuh*	bust (statue)
Büstenhalter,*m.*	BÜSS-*ten-hahl-tehr*	brassiere
Butter,*f.*	BOOTT-*tehr*	butter
Butterbrot,*n.*	BOOTT-*tehr-broht*	sandwich
Cello,*n.*	CHELL-*oh*	cello
Charakter,*m.*	*kahr*-AHK-*tehr*	character (nature)
Chef,*m.*	SHEFF	boss (master)
Chemie,*f.*	*kh_ay*-MEE	chemistry
Chile,*n.*	CHEE-*lay*	Chile
chilenisch	*chee*-LAY-*nish*	Chilean (*adj.*)
China,*n.*	KH_EE-*nah*	China
chinesisch	*kh_ee*-NAY-*zish*	Chinese (*adj.*)
Chirurg,*m.*	*kh_ee*-ROORRK	surgeon
Cholera,*f.*	KOHL-*uh-rah*	cholera
Chor,*m.*	CORE	choir
Christ,*m.*	KRISST	Christian (*n.*)
Christus,*m.*	KRISS-*tooss*	Christ
Chrom,*m.*	KROAM	chromium
Chronik,*f.*	KROH-*nick*	chronicle
Cocktail,*m.*	COCK-*tail*	cocktail
Couch,*f.*	KOWTCH	couch
da	DAH	since (because, *conj.*)
Dach,*n.*	DAH_KH	roof
Dachboden,*m.*	DAH_KH-*boh-den*	attic
Dachs,*m.*	DAHX	badger (animal)
danach	*dah*-NAH_KH	thereafter
daher	*dah*-HAIR	hence (consequently)
"	"	therefore

German	Pronunciation	English
Dame,*f.*	DAH-*muh*	lady
damit	*dah*-MITT	so (in order that, *conj.*)
"	"	thereby
damit...nicht	*dah*-MITT...NIKHT	lest
(Stau)Damm,*m.*	(SHTOW-)DAHMM	dam (dike)
Dämmerung,*f.*	DEM-*muh-roong*	twilight
Dampf,*m.*	DAHMMPF	steam
Dänemark,*n.*	DAY-*nuh-mark*	Denmark
dänisch	DAY-*nish*	Danish (*adj.*)
Dank,*m.*	DAHNNK	thanks (gratitude)
dankbar	DAHNNK-*bar*	grateful
"	"	thankful
Dankbarkeit,*f.*	DAHNNK-*bar-kite*	gratitude
danken (1)	DAHNNG-*ken*	thank, to
dann	DAHNN	then (at that time)
"	"	then (in that case)
"	"	then (subsequently)
darlegen (1)	DAHR-*lay-gen*	present (set forth), to
darstellen (1)	DAHR-*shtell-en*	represent (symbolize), to
Darstellung, graphische,*f.*	GRAH-*fish-uh* DAHR-*shtel-loong*	graph
das	DAHSS	that (*rel. pron.*)
"	"	the
"	"	which (*rel. pron.*)
"	"	who (*rel. pron.*)
"	"	whom (*rel. pron.*)
Dasein,*n.*	DAH-*zine*	existence
dass	DAHSS	that (*conj.*)
dasselbe	*dahss*-ZELL-*buh*	same (*adj.*)
Dattel,*f.*	DAHTT-*tel*	date (fruit)
Datum,*n.*	DAH-*toomm*	date (calendar designation)
Dauer,*f.*	DOW-*ehr*	duration
dauern (1)	DOW-*ehrn*	last (continue), to
dauernd	DOW-*ehrnt*	constant
"	"	continual
"	"	continuous
"	"	permanent (*adj.*)
Daumen,*m.*	DOW-*men*	thumb
davon	*dah*-FAWNN	thereof
Debatte,*f.*	*day*-BAHTT-*tuh*	debate
Deck,*n.*	DECK	deck (of ship)
Decke,*f.*	DECK-*uh*	blanket
"	"	ceiling (of room)
Deckel,*m.*	DECK-*el*	cover
"	"	lid
(be)decken (1)	(*buh*-)DECK-*en*	cover, to
definieren (1)	*day-fih*-NEAR-*en*	define, to
dein	DINE	your
deine(r, -s)	DYE-*neh*(*r, -s*)	yours
Dekoration,*f.*	*day-ko-rahts*-YOHN	decoration (décor)
dem	DAME	the
"	"	whom (*rel. pron.*)
Demokrat,*m.*	*day-moh*-KRAHT	democrat
Demokratie,*f.*	*day-moh-krah*-TEE	democracy
demokratisch	*day-moh*-KRAH-*tish*	democratic
Demut,*f.*	DAY-*moot*	humility
demütig	DAY-*mü-tick*	humble (lowly)
den	DANE	the
"	"	whom (*rel. pron.*)
denken (172)	DENG-*ken*	think (reason), to
Denkmal,*n.*	DENG_K-*mahl*	memorial (*n.*)
"	"	monument
denn	DENN	for (*conj.*)
dennoch	DENN-*naw_kh*	still (nevertheless, *conj.*)
"	"	yet (nevertheless, *adv.*)
Depression,*f.*	*day-press*-YOHN	depression (*econ.*)
der	DAIR	that (*rel. pron.*)
"	"	the
"	"	which (*rel. pron.*)
"	"	who (*rel. pron.*)
"	"	whom (*rel. pron.*)
deren	DAIR-*en*	whose (*rel. pron.*)
derselbe	*dair*-ZELL-*buh*	same (*adj.*)
dessen	DESS-*en*	whose (*rel. pron.*)
deuten (1)	DOY-*ten*	interpret (explain), to

German	Pronunciation	English
deutlich	DOYT-*likh*	distinct (unmistakable)
"	"	plain (clear)
deutsch	DOYTSH	German (*adj.*)
Deutschland,*n.*	DOYTSH-*lahnt*	Germany
Diagramm,*n.*	*dee-ah*-GRAHMM	chart (graph)
Diamant,*m.*	*dee-ah*-MAHNNT	diamond (gem)
Diät,*f.*	*dee*-ATE	diet
dich	DIKH	you (*sing.*), yourself
dicht	DIKHT	dense
Dichter,*m.*	DIKH-*tehr*	poet
Dichtung,*f.*	DIKH-*toong*	poetry
dick	DICK	fat (obese, *adj.*)
"	"	thick (not thin)
Dicke,*f.*	DICK-*uh*	thickness (dimension)
Dickicht,*n.*	DICK-*ikht*	thicket
die	DEE	that (*rel. pron.*)
"	"	the
"	"	which (*rel. pron.*)
"	"	who (*rel. pron.*)
"	"	whom (*rel. pron.*)
Dieb,*m.*	DEEP	thief
dienen (1)	DEE-*nen*	serve, to
Dienst,*m.*	DEENST	service
Dienstbote,*m.*	DEENST-*boh-tuh*	servant (in a household)
Dienstmädchen,*n.*	DEENST-*maid-kh_en*	maid (servant)
diese	DEE-*zuh*	these (*adj., pron.*)
diese(r, -s)	DEE-*zeh*(*r, -s*)	this (*adj., dem. pron.*)
dieselbe	*dee*-ZELL-*buh*	same (*adj.*)
diktieren (1)	*dick*-TEER-*ren*	dictate, to
Ding,*n.*	DING	thing (material object)
Diphtherie,*f.*	*dif-tay*-REE	diphtheria
dir	DEER	you (*sing.*)
Direktor,*m.*	*dee*-RECK-*tor*	director
Dirigent,*m.*	*deer-rih*-G_ENT	conductor (*mus.*)
Disziplin,*f.*	*dis-tsip*-LEEN	discipline (training)
Dividende,*f.*	*dee-vee*-DEN-*duh*	dividend (*bus.*)
Division,*f.*	*dee-veez*-YOHN	division (*mil.*)
doch	DAW_KH	yes (after negative question)
Dock,*n.*	DAWCK	dock (wharf)
Doktor,*m.*	DAWCK-*tohr*	doctor
Dokument,*n.*	*doh-koo*-MENT	document
Dolch,*m.*	DAWLKH	dagger
Dom,*m.*	DOME	cathedral
Dominikanische Republik,*f.*	*doh-mee-nee*-KAH-*nish-uh ray-poo*-BLEEK	Dominican Republic
Donau,*f.*	DOH-*now*	Danube
Donner,*m.*	DAWNN-*ehr*	thunder
Doppelpunkt,*m.*	DAWPP-*pel-poonk_t*	colon (*punct.*)
doppelt	DAWPP-*elt*	double (*adj.*)
Dorf,*n.*	DORF	village
Dorn,*m.*	DORN	thorn
dort	DORT	there (at that place)
Dosis,*f.*	DOH-*sis*	dose (*med.*)
Drache,*m.*	DRAH_KH-*uh*	dragon
(Flug)Drache,*m.*	(FLOOK-)DRAH_KH-*uh*	kite
Draht,*m.*	DRAHT	wire (metal thread)
Drama,*n.*	DRAH-*mah*	drama
draussen	DROWSS-*en*	outdoors (*adv.*)
"	"	outside (*adv.*)
Drehbuch,*n.*	DRAY-*boo_kh*	scenario
drehen (1)	DRAY-*en*	turn (make rotate), to
drehen, sich	*zikh* DRAY-*en*	spin (revolve), to
Dreieck,*n.*	DRY-*eck*	triangle (*geom.*)
dringend	DRING-*ent*	urgent
drinnen	DRINN-*en*	indoors (*adv.*)
"	"	inside (within, *adv.*)
"	"	within (on the inside, *adv.*)
Droge,*f.*	DROH-*guh*	drug (medicine)
drohen (1)	DROH-*en*	threaten, to
Drohung,*f.*	DROH-*oong*	threat
Druck,*m.*	DROOCK	pressure (force)
"	"	stress (physical tension)
drucken (1)	DROOCK-*en*	print, to
drücken (1)	DRÜCK-*en*	press (bear upon), to
"	"	squeeze, to
Drucker,*m.*	DROOCK-*ehr*	printer
du	DOO	you

German	Pronunciation	English	German	Pronunciation	English
dulden (1)	DOOLL-*den*	tolerate (permit), to	**einbilden, sich (1)**	*zikh* INE-*bill-den*	fancy (imagine), to
			Einbildung, *f.*	INE-*bill-doong*	fancy (fantasy)
dumm	DOOMM	stupid	**Einbildungskraft,**	INE-*bill-doongs-krahft*	imagination
"	"	dumb	*f.*		
dunkel	DOONNG-*kell*	dark (in color, *adj.*)	**Einbrecher,** *m.*	INE-*breh_kh-ehr*	burglar
"	"	dark (without light, *adj.*)	**Eindruck,** *m.*	INE-*droock*	impression (effect)
			eindrücken (1)	INE-*drük-ken*	impress (affect deeply), to
"	"	obscure (unclear)			
Dunkelheit, *f.*	DOONNG-*kel-hite*	darkness	**einer (von beiden)**	EYE-*nehr* (*fun* BY-*den*)	either (one or the other, *adj.*)
dünn	DÜNN	thin (not thick)			
Dunst, *m.*	DOONNST	vapor	**Einer (von Beiden)**	EYE-*nehr* (*fun* BY-*den*)	either (either one, *pron.*)
durch	DOORRKH	through (by means of, *prep.*)			
			einfach	INE-*fahkh*	simple (uninvolved)
"	"	through (from end to end of, *prep.*)	**Einfachheit,** *f.*	INE-*fahkh-hite*	simplicity
			einfallen in (32)	INE-*fahll-en inn*	invade, to (*mil.*)
durchdringen (22)	*doorrkh*-DRING-*en*	penetrate (pierce), to	**Einfluss,** *m.*	INE-*flooss*	influence
durch...hindurch	DOORRKH...*hin*-DOORRKH	throughout (from start to finish of, *prep.*)	"	"	sway
			Einfuhr, *f.*	INE-*foor*	importation
			einführen (1)	INE-*fü-ren*	import, to (*bus.*)
durchleuchten (1)	*doorrkh*-LOY_KH-*ten*	X-ray (examine), to	"	"	introduce (bring in), to
Durchmesser, *m.*	DOORRKH-*mess-sehr*	diameter			
durchnässen (1)	*doorrkh*-NESS-*en*	soak (saturate), to	**Einführung,** *f.*	INE-*fü-roong*	introduction (preliminary part)
Durchschlag, *m.*	DOORRKH-*shlahk*	carbon copy			
Durchschnitt, *m.*	DOORRKH-*shnitt*	average (mean, *n.*)	**Eingang,** *m.*	INE-*gahng*	entrance
durchschnittlich	DOORRKH-*shnitt-likh*	average (ordinary, *adj.*)	**eingeschlafen**	INE-*guh-shlah-fen*	asleep (sleeping)
			eingeschrieben	INE-*guh-shree-ben*	registered (postal designation)
durchseihen (1)	DOORRKH-*zye-en*	strain (filter), to			
durchsichtig	DOORRKH-*zikh-tikh*	transparent	**Eingeweide,** *n.*	INE-*guh-vye-duh*	bowels (*anat.*)
durchstechen (128)	*doorrkh*-SHTEH_KH-*en*	pierce, to	**einhalten (59)**	INE-*hahll-ten*	keep (continue), to
			einheimisch	INE-*hime-ish*	domestic (not foreign)
durchwaten (1)	*doorkh*-VAH-*ten*	ford, to			
dürfen (163)	DÜR-*fen*	may (*v.*)	**einheitlich**	INE-*hite-likh*	uniform (*adj.*)
dürftig	DÜRF-*tick*	poor (needy)	**einige**	INE-*ee-guh*	some (a few, *adj.*)
Durst, *m.*	DOORSST	thirst	**Einigkeit,** *f.*	INE-*ick-kite*	unity (accord)
durstig	DOORSS-*tick*	thirsty	**einkaufen (1)**	INE-*kow-fen*	shop, to
Düsenantrieb, *m.*	DÜ-*zenn-ahnn-treep*	jet engine	**Einkommen,** *n.*	INE-*kawmm-en*	income
düster	DÜS-*tehr*	dismal	**Einkommensteuer,** *f.*	INE-*kawmm-en-shtoy-ehr*	income tax
Dutzend, *n.*	DOOTT-*sent*	dozen			
Ebbe, *f.*	EBB-*uh*	tide, low	**einladen (70)**	INE-*lah-den*	invite, to
eben	AY-*ben*	even (*adj.*)	**Einladung,** *f.*	INE-*lah-doong*	invitation
"	"	level (flat)	**einlaufen (72)**	INE-*l_ow-fen*	shrink (become contracted), to
Ebene, *f.*	AY-*ben-uh*	plain (level land)			
ebenfalls	AY-*ben-fahllss*	likewise (also)	**einlösen (1)**	INE-*lö-zen*	cash (receive cash for), to
echt	EH_KHT	genuine	**einmal**	INE-*mahl*	once (one time, *adv.*)
Ecke, *f.*	ECK-*uh*	corner	**einmischen, sich (1)**	*zikh* INE-*mish-en*	interfere, to
edel	AY-*del*	noble (*adj.*)			
Edelstein, *m.*	AY-*del-shtine*	gem	"	"	meddle, to
Edinburgh, *n.*	AY-*dinn-boork*	Edinburgh	**einnehmen (80)**	INE-*nay-men*	occupy (fill), to
			einordnen (1)	INE-*ord-nen*	arrange (place), to
Efeu, *n.*	EFF-*foy*	ivy	**Einordnung,** *f.*	INE-*ord-noong*	arrangement (order)
Ehe, *f.*	AY-*uh*	marriage			
eher	AY-*ehr*	rather (preferably)	**einpacken (1)**	INE-*pahck-en*	wrap (envelop), to
Ehescheidung, *f.*	AY-*uh-shy-doong*	divorce (*law*)	**einpökeln (1)**	INE-*pök-el'n*	pickle (preserve), to
Ehre, *f.*	AY-*ruh*	credit (commendation)	**einrichten (1)**	INE-*rikh-ten*	arrange (plan), to
			"	"	organize (systematize), to
"	"	honor			
(ver)ehren (1)	(*fehr*-)AIR-*en*	honor (respect), to	**einsam**	INE-*zahm*	lone
Ehrfurcht, *f.*	AIR-*foorkht*	awe	"	"	lonely
Ehrgeiz, *m.*	AIR-*gites*	ambition	"	"	lonesome
ehrgeizig	AIR-*gites-sick*	ambitious (aspiring)	"	"	solitary (unaccompanied)
ehrlich	AIR-*likh*	honest	**Einsamkeit,** *f.*	INE-*zahm-kite*	solitude
Ei, *n.*	EYE	egg	**Einsatz,** *m.*	INE-*zahts*	stake (thing wagered)
Eiche, *f.*	EYE_KH-*uh*	oak			
Eichel, *f.*	EYE-*kh_ell*	acorn	**einschenken (1)**	INE-*sheng-ken*	pour (make flow), to
Eichhörnchen, *n.*	EYE_KH-*hörn-kh_en*	squirrel	**einschläfern (1)**	INE-*shlay-fehrn*	lull (quiet), to
			einschliessen (104)	INE-*shlee-sen*	enclose (surround), to
Eid, *m.*	ITE	oath (vow)			
Eifer, *m.*	EYE-*fehr*	zeal	"	"	include (contain), to
eifersüchtig	EYE-*fehr-sükh-tick*	jealous	**einschränken (1)**	INE-*shreng-ken*	qualify (modify), to
eifrig	EYE-*frick*	anxious (wanting very much)	**einschreiben (109)**	INE-*shribe-en*	register, to
			einsetzen (1)	INE-*zets-en*	insert, to
"	"	eager	**Einsicht,** *f.*	INE-*zikht*	vision (foresight)
"	"	keen			
eigen	EYE-*gen*	own (*adj.*)	**Einspritzung,** *f.*	INE-*shprits-oong*	injection (*med.*)
Eigenschaft, *f.*	EYE-*gen-shahft*	attribute (characteristic)	**Einspruch,** *m.*	INE-*shprookh*	protest
			einst	INE_ST	once (formerly, *adv.*)
"	"	feature	**einstellen (1)**	INE-*shtell-en*	adjust (regulate), to
"	"	quality	"	"	suspend (terminate), to
Eigentum, *n.*	EYE-*gen-toomm*	property (possession)			
Eigentümer, *m.*	EYE-*gen-tü-mehr*	owner	**einstürzen (1)**	INE-*shtür-tsen*	collapse (cave in), to
eigentümlich	EYE-*gen-tüm-likh*	peculiar (odd)	**eintönig**	INE-*tö-nick*	monotonous (boring)
Eile, *f.*	EYE-*luh*	hurry (haste)	**eintragen (137)**	INE-*trah-gen*	enter (make record of), to
eilig	EYE-*lick*	hasty (hurried)			
			einträglich	INE-*tray-glikh*	profitable
Eimer, *m.*	EYE-*mehr*	bucket	**eintreten, in... (140)**	*inn*...INE-*tray-ten*	enter (come or go into), to
"	"	pail			
ein, eine	INE, INE-*uh*	a (an)			

German	Pronunciation	English
einverstanden sein, mit... (179)	*mitt...*INE-*fehr-shtahn-den* ZINE	agree with, to
Einwand, *m.*	INE-*vahnt*	objection
einwenden (177)	INE-*ven-den*	object, to
Einwohner, *m.*	INE-*voh-nehr*	inhabitant
Einzahl, *f.*	INE-*tsahl*	singular (*gram., n.*)
einzahlen (1)	INE-*tsah-len*	deposit, to (*fin.*)
Einzahlung, *f.*	INE-*tsah-loong*	deposit (money deposited)
Einzelhandel, *m.*	INE-*tsell-hahnn-del*	retail (*bus., n.*)
Einzelhändler, *m.*	INE-*tsell-hennd-lehr*	retailer (*bus.*)
Einzelheit, *f.*	INE-*tsell-hite*	detail (minor item)
"	"	item (detail)
		particular (*n.*)
einzeln	INE-*tsel'n*	single (sole)
einziehen (161)	INE-*tsee-en*	collect, to (*bus.*)
einzig	INE-*tsick*	only
"		sole
einzigartig	INE-*tsick-ahr-tick*	singular (peculiar)
Eis, *n.*	ICE	ice (frozen water)
(Speise) Eis, *n.*	(SHPYE-*zuh-*)ICE	ice-cream
Eisen, *n.*	EYE-*zen*	iron (metal)
Eisenbahn, *f.*	EYE-*zen-bahn*	railroad
eisig	EYE-*zick*	icy
Eisschrank, *m.*	ICE-*shrahnk*	icebox
"		refrigerator
eitel	EYE-*tell*	vain (conceited)
Eitelkeit, *f.*	EYE-*tell-kite*	vanity (self-conceit)
Ekel, *m.*	AY-*kel*	disgust
Ekuador, *n.*	*eck-vah-*DOOR	Ecuador
elastisch	*ay-*LAHSS-*tish*	elastic (springy)
Elefant, *m.*	*el-luh-*FAHNNT	elephant
elektrisch	*el-*LECK-*trish*	electric
Elektrizität, *f.*	*el-leck-trih-tsih-*TATE	electricity
Elektronik, *f.*	*el-leck-*TRO-*nick*	electronics
Element, *n.*	*el-luh-*MENT	element
elementar	*el-luh-men-*TAR	elementary (rudimentary)
elend	AY-*lent*	miserable (unhappy)
Elend, *n.*	AY-*lent*	misery (grief)
Elende, *m., f.*	AY-*len-duh*	wretch (hapless person)
Elfenbein, *n.*	ELL-*fen-bine*	ivory
Ellbogen, *m.*	ELL-*boh-gen*	elbow
Eltern, *pl.*	ELL-*tehrn*	parents
Empfang, *m.*	*emp-*FAHNNG	receipt (receiving)
"	"	reception
empfangen (33)	*emp-*FAHNNG-*en*	receive, to
Empfänger, *m.*	*emp-*FENG-*ehr*	consignee (*bus.*)
Empfängnis, *f.*	*emp-*FENG-*niss*	conception (*physiol.*)
empfehlen (24)	*emp-*FAY-*len*	recommend (advise), to
Empfehlung, *f.*	*emp-*FAY-*loong*	recommendation
empfindlich	*emp-*FINND-*likh*	sensitive (susceptible)
Empfindung, *f.*	*emp-*FINN-*doong*	feeling
"	"	sensation
Empörung, *f.*	*em-*PÖ-*roong*	rebellion
Ende, *n.*	ENN-*duh*	ending (conclusion)
enden (1)	ENN-*den*	end (come to an end), to
"	"	finish (reach the end), to
endgültig	END-*gül-tick*	final (last)
endlich	END-*likh*	finally
endlos	END-*lohss*	endless
Energie, *f.*	*enn-ehr-*G_EE	energy
eng, (zu)	(*tsoo*) ENG	tight (close-fitting)
Engel, *m.*	ENG-*el*	angel
England, *n.*	ENG-*lahnt*	England
englisch	ENG-*lish*	English (*adj.*)
Engros-...	*ahng-*GROH-*...*	wholesale (*adj., bus.*)
Enkel, *m.*	ENG-*kell*	grandson
Enkelin, *f.*	ENG-*kell-lin*	granddaughter
entdecken (1)	*ent-*DECK-*en*	discover, to
Entdeckung, *f*	*ent-*DECK-*oong*	discovery
Ente, *f.*	ENN-*tuh*	duck
entfernt	*ent-*FEHRNT	distant (far-off)
"	"	away (from a place, *adv.*)
Entfernung, *f.*	*ent-*FEHR-*noong*	distance

German	Pronunciation	English
entgegengesetzt	*ent-*GAY-*gen-guh-zettst*	contrary (opposite)
entgehen (46)	*ent-*GAY-*en*	escape, to
enthalten (59)	*ent-*HAHLL-*ten*	contain, to
enthüllen (1)	*ent-*HÜLL-*len*	expose (disclose), to
"		reveal (divulge), to
entlang	*ent-*LAHNG	along (lengthwise of)
entlassen (71)	*ent-*LAHSS-*sen*	dismiss (discharge), to
Entlassung, *f.*	*ent-*LAHSS-*oong*	discharge (dismissal)
entlegen	*ent-*LAY-*gen*	remote (far-off)
entmutigen (1)	*ent-*MOO-*tih-gen*	discourage (dishearten), to
entreissen (85)	*ent-*RYE-*sen*	wrench (wrest), to
Entrüstung, *f.*	*ent-*RÜSS-*toong*	indignation
entschädigen (1)	*ent-*SHAY-*dih-gen*	reimburse, to
Entschädigung, *f.*	*ent-*SHAY-*dih-goong*	indemnity (compensation)
entscheidend	*ent-*SHY-*dent*	positive (decisive)
Entscheidung, *f.*	*ent-*SHY-*doong*	decision (judgment)
entschliessen, sich (104)	*zikh ent-*SHLEE-*sen*	decide (make up one's mind), to
"	"	determine (make up one's mind), to
Entschlossenheit, *f.*	*ent-*SHLAWSS-*en-hite*	determination (fixed intent)
entschuldigen (1)	*ent-*SHOOL-*dih-gen*	excuse (pardon), to
entschuldigen, sich	*zikh ent-*SHOOL-*dih-gen*	apologize, to
Entsetzen, *n.*	*ent-*ZETTS-*en*	horror (dread)
entsetzlich	*ent-*ZETTS-*likh*	horrible
entsprechen (125)	*ent-*SHPREH_KH-*en*	correspond (agree), to
entstehen (129)	*ent-*SHTAY-*en*	arise (come about), to
entstellen (1)	*ent-*SHTELL-*len*	mar (disfigure), to
enttäuschen (1)	*ent-*TOY-*shen*	disappoint, to
Enttäuschung, *f.*	*ent-*TOY-*shoong*	disappointment
entwässern (1)	*ent-*VESS-*ehrn*	drain (make dry), to
entweder...oder	ENT-*vay-dehr...*OH-*dehr*	either...or (*conj.*)
entwerfen (157)	*ent-*VEHR-*fen*	plan (prearrange), to
entwickeln (1)	*ent-*VICK-*el'n*	develop, to
Entwicklung, *f.*	*ent-*VICK-*loong*	development
Entwurf, *m.*	*ent-*VOORRF	design (pattern)
"	"	draft
"	"	outline (general plan)
"	"	project
"	"	sketch (rough drawing)
entziehen (161)	*ent-*TSEE-*en*	deprive (divest), to
entzücken (1)	*ent-*TSÜK-*ken*	delight (give pleasure to), to
Entzücken, *n.*	*ent-*TSÜK-*ken*	delight
"	"	rapture
entzückend	*ent-*TSÜK-*ent*	delightful
Entzündung, *f.*	*ent-*TSÜN-*doong*	inflammation
Enzyklopädie, *f.*	*enn-tsü-kloh-pay-*DEE	encyclopaedia
Epidemie, *f.*	*eh-pih-duh-*MEE	epidemic
er	AIR	he
"	"	it
Erbe, *m.*	EHR-*buh*	heir
(er)erben (1)	(*ehr-*)EHR-*ben*	inherit, to
erbitten (15)	*ehr-*BITT-*en*	solicit, to
Erblichkeit, *f.*	EHRP-*likh-kite*	heredity
erbrechen (20)	*ehr-*BREHKH-*en*	vomit, to
Erbse, *f.*	EHRP-*suh*	pea
Erdbeben, *n.*	AIRT-*bay-ben*	earthquake
Erdbeere, *f.*	AIRT-*bay-ruh*	strawberry
Erde, *f.*	AIR-*duh*	dirt (soil)
"	"	earth (planet)
erdenken (172)	*ehr-*DENG-*ken*	devise (contrive), to
Erdhügel, *m.*	AIRT-*hü-gel*	mound (hill)
Erdkunde, *f.*	AIRT-*koon-duh*	geography
Erdnuss, *f.*	AIRT-*nooss*	peanut
Ereignis, *n.*	*ehr-*IKE-*niss*	event (happening)
erfahren (31)	*ehr-*FAR-*en*	learn (find out), to
Erfahrung, *f.*	*ehr-*FAR-*oong*	experience (skill)
erfinden (35)	*ehr-*FIN-*den*	invent, to
Erfindung, *f.*	*ehr-*FIN-*doong*	invention
Erfolg, *m.*	*ehr-*FAWLLK	success (attainment)
Erfolg haben (178)	*ehr-*FAWLLK *hah-ben*	succeed (attain goal), to
erfolgreich	*ehr-*FAWLLG-*rye_kh*	successful

German	Pronunciation	English
erfordern (1)	*ehr*-FOR-*dehrn*	require (need), to
erfrischen (1)	*ehr*-FRISH-*shen*	refresh, to
Erfrischungen, *f.pl.*	*ehr*-FRISH-*shoong-en*	refreshments
erfüllen (1)	*ehr*-FÜLL-*len*	fulfill, to
ergeben, sich (43)	*zikh ehr*-GAY-*ben*	surrender (give one-self up), to
Ergebnis, *n.*	*ehr*-GAPE-*niss*	result (consequence)
ergreifen (58)	*ehr*-GRIFE-*en*	seize (capture), to
erhalten (59)	*ehr*-HAHLL-*ten*	derive (get), to
"	"	obtain, to
"	"	preserve, to
erhaschen (1)	*ehr*-HAHSH-*en*	snatch, to
erheben (62)	*ehr*-HAY-*ben*	exalt, to
erhöhen (1)	*ehr*-HÖ-*en*	elevate (lift up), to
erholen, sich (1)	*zikh ehr*-HOLE-*en*	recover (get well), to
erinnern (1)	*ehr*-IN-*ehrn*	remind, to
erinnern, sich	*zikh ehr*-IN-*ehrn*	recall (remember), to
"	"	remember (recollect), to
Erinnerung, *f.*	*ehr*-IN-*uh-roong*	memory
"	"	remembrance (recollection)
Erkältung, *f.*	*ehr*-KELL-*toong*	cold (disease)
erklären (1)	*ehr*-KLAIR-*ren*	declare (state), to
"	"	explain (account for), to
Erklärung, *f.*	*ehr*-KLAIR-*roong*	declaration (announcement)
"	"	explanation
erlangen (1)	*ehr*-LAHNNG-*en*	secure (obtain), to
erlauben (1)	*ehr*-L OW-*ben*	allow, to
"	"	permit, to
Erlaubnis, *f.*	*ehr*-L OWP-*niss*	permission
erläutern (1)	*ehr*-LOY-*tehrn*	explain (clarify), to
Erlebnis, *n.*	*ehr*-LAPE-*niss*	experience (conscious event)
Erledigung, *f.*	*ehr*-LAY-*dih-goong*	disposition (disposal)
erleichtern (1)	*ehr*-LYE_KH-*tehrn*	ease, to
"	"	relieve, to
Erleichterung, *f.*	*ehr*-LYE_KH-*tuh-roong*	relief (alleviation)
erleuchten (1)	*ehr*-LOY_KH-*ten*	illuminate (elucidate), to
ermöglichen (1)	*ehr*-MÖG-*lee-kh_en*	enable (make able), to
ermüden (1)	*ehr*-MÜ-*den*	tire (make weary), to
Ermüdung, *f.*	*ehr*-MÜ-*doong*	fatigue
ermutigen (1)	*ehr*-MOO-*tih-gen*	encourage, to
ernennen (174)	*ehr*-NENN-*nen*	appoint, to
Ernennung, *f.*	*ehr*-NENN-*noong*	appointment (nomination)
erneuern (1)	*ehr*-NOY-*ehrn*	renew, to
ernst	EHRNST	earnest
"	"	grave
"	"	serious
Ernte, *f.*	EHRN-*tuh*	crop (produce)
"	"	harvest
ernten (1)	EHRN-*ten*	reap, to
erobern (1)	*ehr*-OH-*behrn*	conquer, to
Eroberung, *f.*	*ehr*-OH-*behr-oong*	conquest
Eröffnung, *f.*	*ehr*-ÖFF-*noong*	opening (beginning, *n.*)
erprobt	*ehr*-PROHPT	veteran (experienced)
erreichen (1)	*ehr*-RYE-*kh_en*	attain (arrive at), to
"	"	reach, to
errichten (1)	*ehr*-RIKH-*ten*	erect (build), to
erröten (1)	*ehr*-RÖ-*ten*	blush, to
Ersatzmittel, *n.*	*ehr*-ZAHTTS-*mitt-el*	substitute (thing replacing another)
erschallen (27)	*ehr*-SHAHLL-*len*	peal, to
erscheinen (94)	*ehr*-SHY-*nen*	appear (come in sight), to
erschlagen (100)	*ehr*-SHLAHG-*en*	slay, to
erschöpfen (1)	*ehr*-SHÖPP-*fen*	exhaust (use up), to
erschrecken (28)	*ehr*-SHRECK-*en*	frighten (make afraid), to
"	"	terrify, to
"	"	scare, to
erschüttern (1)	*ehr*-SHÜTT-*ehrn*	shock (jar), to
Erschütterung, *f.*	*ehr*-SHÜTT-*tuh-roong*	shock (mental jolt)
ersetzen (1)	*ehr*-ZET-*sen*	replace (be a substitute for), to
Ersparnis, *n.*	*ehr*-SHPAHR-*niss*	savings (money)
erst	EHRST	first (*adj.*)
"	"	primary (*adj.*)
"	"	prime (*adj.*)

German	Pronunciation	English
erstaunen (1)	*ehr*-SHT_OW-*nen*	amaze, to
"	"	astonish, to
Erstaunen, *n.*	*ehr*-SHT_OW-*nen*	amazement
"		astonishment
erstere	EHRSS-*teh-ruh*	former (first of two, *adj.*)
erstrecken, sich (1)	*zikh ehr*-SHTRECK-*en*	run (extend), to
"	"	stretch (extend), to
ersuchen (1)	*ehr*-ZOO-*kh_en*	appeal to (entreat), to
"	"	request, to
ertönen lassen (71)	*ehr*-TÖ-*nen lahss-en*	sound (make heard), to
Ertrag, *m.*	*ehr*-TRAHK	produce
"		yield (product)
ertragen (137)	*ehr*-TRAH-*gen*	bear, to
"	"	endure, to
"	"	stand, to
ertränken (1)	*ehr*-TRENG-*ken*	drown (kill by drowning), to
ertrinken (142)	*ehr*-TRING-*ken*	drown (die by drowning), to
erwachen (1)	*ehr*-VAH_KH-*en*	wake (rouse oneself), to
erwachsen (151)	*ehr*-VAHX-*en*	grow up (mature), to
erwähnen (1)	*ehr*-VAY-*nen*	mention, to
erwarten (1)	*ehr*-VAR-*ten*	anticipate, to
"	"	await, to
"	"	expect, to
Erwartung, *f.*	*ehr*-VAR-*toong*	expectation
erweichen (154)	*ehr*-VIE-*kh_en*	soften (mitigate), to
erweitern (1)	*ehr*-VITE-*ehrn*	extend (enlarge), to
Erweiterung, *f.*	*ehr*-VIE-*tuh-roong*	extension (enlargement)
erwerben (156)	*ehr*-VEHR-*ben*	acquire, to
erwidern (1)	*ehr*-VEE-*dehrn*	reply, to
Erwiderung, *f.*	*ehr*-VEE-*duh-roong*	reply
Erz, *n.*	EHRTS	ore
erzählen (1)	*ehr*-TSAY-*len*	relate, to
"	"	tell (narrate), to
Erzählung, *f.*	*ehr*-TSAY-*loong*	tale (narrative)
Erzeugnis, *n.*	*ehr*-TSOYG-*niss*	product
erziehen (161)	*ehr*-TSEE-*en*	educate, to
Erziehung, *f.*	*ehr*-TSEE-*oong*	education (schooling process)
"	"	training (instruction)
erzielen (1)	*ehr*-TSEE-*len*	achieve (attain), to
es	ESS	it
Esel, *m.*	AY-*zel*	donkey
essen (30)	ESS-*sen*	eat, to
essen, (zu Mittag)	(*tsoo* MITT-*tahk*) ESS-*en*	dine, to
Essig, *m.*	ESS-*ikh*	vinegar
Esslöffel, *m.*	ESS-*löff-el*	spoon (tablespoon)
Etikett, *n.*	*eh-tee*-KETT	label
Etikette, *f.*	*eh-tee*-KETT-*tuh*	etiquette
etwas	ETT-*vahss*	some (a quantity, *pron.*)
"	"	some (a quantity of, *adj.*)
"	"	something
"	"	somewhat (*adv.*)
euch	OYKH	you (*pl.*), yourselves
euer	OY-*ehr*	your
euere(r, -s)	OY-*uh-reh*(r, -s)	yours
Eule, *f.*	OY-*luh*	owl
Europa, *n.*	*oy*-ROH-*pah*	Europe
europäisch	*oy-roh*-PAY-*ish*	European (*adj.*)
ewig	AY-*vick*	eternal
"	"	everlasting
Exekutiv-...	*ex-eck-koo*-TEEF-...	executive (*adj.*)
Exemplar, *n.*	*ex-emm*-PLAHR	copy (of a publication)
Expedition, *f.*	*ex-pay-deets*-YOHN	expedition (journey)
Exporteur, *m.*	*ex-pawr*-TÖR	exporter
extra	EX-*trah*	extra (additional)
Fabel, *f.*	FAH-*bel*	fable
Fabrik, *f.*	*fah*-BREEK	factory
Fabrikant, *m.*	*fah-bree*-KAHNNT	manufacturer
Fach, *n.*	FAHKH	shelf
fachmännisch	FAHKH-*men-ish*	professional
Fackel, *f.*	FAHCK-*el*	torch
Faden, *m.*	FAH-*den*	thread (sewing thread)

German	Pronunciation	English
fähig	FAY-*ick*	able (capable)
Fähigkeit,*f.*	FAY-*ick-kite*	ability
"	"	faculty
Fahne,*f.*	FAH-*nuh*	flag
Fähre,*f.*	FARE-*uh*	ferry (boat)
fahren (31)	FAH-*ren*	drive (a vehicle), to
		go, to
"	"	ride (in a car), to
Fahrer,*m.*	FAR-*ehr*	driver (of auto-mobile)
Fahrgeld,*n.*	FAR-*gelt*	fare (*transp.*)
Fahrplan,*m.*	FAR-*plahn*	timetable
Fahrstuhl,*m.*	FAR-*shtool*	elevator (passenger lift)
Fahrt,*f.*	FAHRRT	ride (in a car)
Fahrzeug,*n.*	FAR-*tsoyg*	vehicle (conveyance)
fair	FARE	fair (impartial)
"	"	fairly (impartially)
Faktor,*m.*	FAHK-*tor*	factor (element)
Fall,*m.*	FAHLL	case (instance)
Falle,*f.*	FAHLL-*uh*	trap (snare)
fallen (32)	FAHLL-*en*	fall, to
"	"	tumble, to
(um)fallen	(OOMM-)FAHLL-*en*	drop, to
fallen lassen (71)	FAHLL-*en* LAHSS-*senn*	drop (let fall), to
fällig	FELL-*ick*	due (payable)
Fälligkeit,*f.*	FELL-*ick-kite*	maturity (due date, *bus.*)
fällig werden (181)	FELL-*ick* VARE-*den*	mature (fall due), to
Fallschirm,*m.*	FAHLL-*sheerm*	parachute
falsch	FAHLLSH	false
"	"	wrong (erroneous, *adj.*)
fälschen (1)	FELSH-*en*	forge (counterfeit), to
Falte,*f.*	FAHLL-*tuh*	fold (plait,*n.*)
"	"	wrinkle
falten (1)	FAHLL-*ten*	fold (lap over), to
Familie,*f.*	*fah*-MEEL-*yuh*	family
fangen (33)	FAHNNG-*en*	catch (nab), to
Farbe,*f.*	FAR-*buh*	color
"	"	paint
färben (1)	FARE-*ben*	dye, to
Farbton,*m.*	FAHRP-*tone*	hue
Farn(kraut),*n.*	FAHRN(-*krowt*)	fern
Faschismus,*m.*	*fah*-SHISS-*mooss*	Fascism
Fass,*n.*	FAHSS	barrel (cask)
fast	FAHSST	almost
"	"	nearly
Fastenzeit,*f.*	FAHSST-*en-tsite*	Lent
faul	FOWL	lazy
"	"	rotten (decayed)
faulen (1)	FOW-*len*	rot, to
faulenzen (1)	FOW-*lents-en*	loaf, to
Fäulnis,*f.*	FOIL-*niss*	decay (rottenness)
Faust,*f.*	FOWST	fist
Fausthandschuh,*m.*	FOWST-*hahnnt-shoo*	mitten
Feder,*f.*	FAY-*dehr*	feather
"	"	spring (coil)
Federvieh,*n.*	FAY-*dehr-fee*	poultry
Fee,*f.*	FAY	fairy (*n.*)
fegen (1)	FAY-*gen*	sweep (clean), to
Fehlbetrag,*m.*	FAIL-*buh-trahk*	deficit (*bus.*)
fehlen (1)	FAY-*len*	lack (be without), to
Fehler,*m.*	FAY-*lehr*	blunder
"	"	fault (defect)
"	"	mistake
feierlich	FIRE-*likh*	solemn (grave)
feiern (1)	FYE-*ehrn*	celebrate, to
Feiertag,*m.*	FYE-*ehr-tahk*	holiday
Feige,*f.*	FYE-*guh*	fig
Feigling,*m.*	FIGE-*ling*	coward
Feile,*f.*	FYE-*luh*	file (tool)
fein	FINE	fine (very small)
Feind,*m.*	FINE_T	enemy
"	"	foe
feindlich	FINE_T-*likh*	hostile
Feld,*n.*	FELT	field (cleared land)
Feldbett,*n.*	FELD-*bet*	cot (bed)
Feldzug,*m.*	FELT-*tsoo_k*	campaign (*mil.*)
Fell,*n.*	FELL	hide
"	"	skin (animal hide)

German	Pronunciation	English
Felsen,*m.*	FELL-*zen*	rock (large stone)
felsig	FELL-*zikh*	rocky (rock-covered)
Fenster,*n.*	FENN-*stehr*	window
Fensterscheibe,*f.*	FENN-*stehr-shy-buh*	pane, window
Ferien,*pl.*	FEHR-*yen*	vacation (work holi-days)
ferner	FEHR-*nehr*	further (additional, *adj.*)
ferngelenktes Geschoss,*n.*	FEHRN-*guh*-LENK-*tess guh*-SHAWSS	guided missile
Fernrohr,*n.*	FEHRN-*roar*	telescope
Fernsehen,*n.*	FEHRN-*zay-en*	television
Fernsprecher,*m.*	FEHRN-*sprehkh-ehr*	telephone
Fernunterrichts-schule,*f.*	FEHRN-*oon-tehr-rikhts-* SHOO-*luh*	correspondence school
Ferse,*f.*	FEHR-*suh*	heel (*anat.*)
fest	FEST	fast
"	"	firm (*adj.*)
"	"	solid (compact)
"	"	steady
Fest,*n.*	FEST	festival
festbinden (14)	FEST-*bin-den*	lash (fasten), to
Festmahl,*n.*	FEST-*mahl*	banquet
"	"	feast (meal)
festnehmen (80)	FEST-*nay-men*	capture (seize), to
festsetzen (1)	FEST-*zett-sen*	fix (settle), to
"	"	settle (arrange), to
feststehend	FEST-*shtay-ent*	stationary (unmov-ing)
feststellen (1)	FEST-*shte-llen*	determine (ascer-tain), to
Festung,*f.*	FESS-*toong*	fortress
Fett,*n.*	FETT	fat (fatty tissue,*n.*)
"	"	grease (cooking fat)
feucht	FOYKHT	damp
"	"	moist
Feuchtigkeit,*f.*	FOYKH-*tick-kite*	moisture
Feuer,*n.*	FOY-*ehr*	fire
Feuerstein,*m.*	FOY-*ehr-shtine*	flint
Feuerversicher-ung,*f.*	FOY-*ehr-fehr-zikh-ehr-oong*	fire insurance
Feuerwehrmann,*m.*	FOY-*ehr-vare-mahnn*	fireman
Fichte,*f.*	FIKH-*tuh*	fir
Fieber,*n.*	FEE-*behr*	fever
Film,*m.*	FILM	film (*photog.*)
Filz,*m.*	FILTS	felt (*n.*)
Finanzen,*pl.*	*fee*-NAHNN-*tsen*	finances
finanziell	*fee*-NAHNN-*tsee-el*	financial
finden (35)	FINN-*den*	find (discover), to
Finger,*m.*	FING-*ehr*	finger
Finnland,*n.*	FINN-*lahnt*	Finland
finnländisch	FINN-*lenn-dish*	Finnish (*adj.*)
Firma,*f.*	FEERR-*muh*	firm (business com-pany)
Firnis,*m.*	FEERR-*niss*	varnish
Fisch,*m.*	FISH	fish
fischen (1)	FISH-*en*	fish, to
Fischer,*m.*	FISH-*ehr*	fisherman
flach	FLAHKH	flat (level, *adj.*)
Fläche,*f.*	FLEH_KH-*uh*	plane (surface)
Flachs,*m.*	FLAHX	flax
Flamme,*f.*	FLAHMM-*uh*	flame
Flasche,*f.*	FLAHSH-*uh*	bottle
flattern (1)	FLAHTT-*ehrn*	flutter (flap), to
"	"	wave, to
flechten (36)	FLEH_KH-*ten*	braid (plait), to
Fleck,*m.*	FLECK	spot
"	"	stain
Fledermaus,*f.*	FLAY-*dehr-mouse*	bat (animal)
flehen (1)	FLAY-*en*	plead (appeal ear-nestly), to
Fleisch,*n.*	FLY_SH	flesh
"	"	meat
Fleischer,*m.*	FLY_SH-*ehr*	butcher
Fleiss,*m.*	FLICE	diligence
fleissig	FLICE-*ick*	diligent
"	"	industrious
flicken (1)	FLICK-*en*	mend (repair), to
Flicken,*m.*	FLICK-*en*	patch (repair)
Flieder,*m.*	FLEE-*dehr*	lilac (flower)
Fliege,*f.*	FLEE-*guh*	fly (housefly)
fliegen (37)	FLEE-*gen*	fly, to

German	Pronunciation	English
Flieger,*m.*	FLEE-*gehr*	aviator
fliehen (38)	FLEE-*en*	flee (run from), to
fliessen (39)	FLEE-*sen*	flow (circulate), to
"	"	run, to
Flöte,*f.*	FLÖ-*tuh*	flute (*mus.*)
Flotte,*f.*	FLAWTT-*tuh*	fleet (group of vessels)
Fluch,*m.*	FLOO_KH	curse
fluchen (1)	FLOO-*kh_en*	curse, to
"	"	swear, to
Flucht,*f.*	FLOO_KHT	flight (hasty departure)
flüchtig blicken (1)	FLÜKH-*tick* BLICK-*ken*	glance, to
Flüchtling,*m.*	FLÜKHT-*ling*	refugee
Flug,*m.*	FLOOCK	flight (journey by air)
Flügel,*m.*	FLÜ-*gel*	wing (*zool.*)
Flughafen,*m.*	FLOO_K-*hah-fen*	airport
Flugzeug,*n.*	FLOO_K-*tsoyk*	airplane
Flugzeugträger,*m.*	FLOOCK-*tsoyg-tray-gehr*	aircraft carrier
Fluss,*m.*	FLOOSS	river
Flüssigkeit,*f.*	FLÜSS-*ick-kite*	liquid (*n.*)
flüstern (1)	FLÜSS-*tehrn*	whisper (utter softly), to
Flut,*f.*	FLOO_T	tide, high
Folge,*f.*	FAWLL-*guh*	consequence
Folge haben, zur (178)	*tsoor* FAWLL-*guh hah-ben*	involve (entail), to
folgen (1)	FAWLL-*gen*	follow, to
"	"	succeed, to
folgend	FAWLL-*g_ent*	subsequent
Folter,*f.*	FAWLL-*tehr*	torture
Fonds,*m.*	FOHNG	fund
fördern (1)	FÖR-*dehrn*	foster (encourage), to
"	"	promote (further), to
Forelle,*f.*	*foh*-RELL-*uh*	trout
Form,*f.*	FORM	form
"	"	shape (contour)
Formel,*f.*	FOR-*mel*	formula (prescribed guide)
Förmlichkeit,*f.*	FÖRM-*likh-kite*	formality
(er)forschen (1)	(*ehr*-)FOR-*shen*	explore, to
Forschung,*f.*	FOR-*shoong*	research
Fort,*n.*	FORT	fort
fortschreiten (111)	FORT-*shrye-ten*	proceed (advance), to
Fortschritt,*m.*	FORT-*shritt*	advance
"	"	progress
fortschrittlich	FORT-*shritt-likh*	progressive
fortsetzen (1)	FORT-*zetts-en*	continue, to
Fortsetzung,*f.*	FORT-*zetts-soong*	continuation
fortwährend	FORT-*vare-ent*	perpetual
Fracht,*f.*	FRAHKHT	freight
Frachtbrief,*m.*	FRAHKHT-*breef*	bill of lading
Frage,*f.*	FRAH-*guh*	question (query)
fragen (1)	FRAHG-*en*	ask (put question to), to
fragen, sich	*zikh* FRAH-*gen*	wonder (ask oneself), to
fragen über	FRAH-*gen* Ü-*behr*	ask about, to
Frankreich,*n.*	FRAHNNK-*rye_kh*	France
Franse,*f.*	FRAHNN-*zuh*	fringe
französisch	*frahn*-TSÖ-*zish*	French (*adj.*)
Frau,*f.*	FR_OW	Mrs. (Mistress)
"	"	wife
"	"	woman
Fräulein,*n.*	FROY-*line*	Miss
frei	FRY	free (independent)
freigebig	FRY-*gay-bick*	generous
Freiheit,*f.*	FRY-*hite*	freedom
"	"	liberty
freilassen (71)	FRY-*lahss-sen*	release (let go of), to
Freiwillige,*m.*	FRY-*vill-ee-guh*	volunteer (*mil.*)
Fremde,*m.,f.*	FREM-*duh*	stranger (unknown person)
Freude,*f.*	FROY-*duh*	gladness
"	"	joy
freuen, sich (1)	*zikh* FROY-*en*	rejoice, to
Freund,*m.*	FROYNT	friend
freundlich	FROYNT-*likh*	friendly
Freundlichkeit,*f.*	FROYNT-*likh-kite*	kindness (favor)

German	Pronunciation	English
Freundschaft,*f.*	FROYNT-*shahft*	friendship
Frieden,*m.*	FREE-*den*	peace
Friedhof,*m.*	FREET-*hohf*	cemetery
(ge)frieren (41)	(*guh*-)FREE-*ren*	freeze (turn to ice), to
frisch	FRISH	fresh
Frisör,*m.*	*frih*-ZÖR	barber
Frist,*f.*	FRISST	term (duration)
froh	FRO	glad
"	"	joyful
fröhlich	FRÖ-*likh*	merry
Front,*f.*	FRAWNNT	front (battle front)
Frosch,*m.*	FRAWSH	frog
Frost,*m.*	FRAWSST	frost
Frösteln,*n.*	FRÖSS-*tel'n*	chill (shivering sensation)
Frucht,*f.*	FROOKHT	fruit
fruchtbar	FROOKHT-*bar*	fertile
früh	FRÜ	early (before-time, *adj.*)
"	"	soon
früh, zu	*tsoo* FRÜ	early (ahead of time, *adv.*)
früher	FRÜ-*ehr*	before (earlier, *adv.*)
"	"	former (preceding, *adj.*)
Frühling,*m.*	FRÜ-*ling*	spring (season)
Frühstück,*n.*	FRÜ-*shtück*	breakfast
Fuchs,*m.*	FOOX	fox
fügen, sich (1)	*zikh* FÜ-*gen*	comply (acquiesce), to
fühlen (1)	FÜ-*len*	feel (touch), to
fühlen, (sich)	(*zikh*) FÜ-*len*	feel (experience), to
führen (1)	FÜ-*ren*	lead (guide), to
(vor)führen (1)	(FOR-)FÜ-*ren*	lead (be in advance), to
Führer,*m.*	FÜ-*rehr*	guide (one who guides)
Führung,*f.*	FÜ-*roong*	leadership (authority)
Fülle,*f.*	FÜLL-*uh*	abundance
"	"	plenty (*n.*)
füllen (1)	FÜLL-*en*	fill (make full), to
Füllen,*n.*	FÜLL-*en*	colt
Füllfeder,*f.*	FÜLL-*fay-dehr*	pen, fountain
Fundament,*n.*	*foon-dah*-MENT	foundation (base)
Funke,*m.*	FOONG-*kuh*	spark
funkeln (1)	FOONG-*kel'n*	sparkle, to
Funktion,*f.*	*foonk-tsee*-OHN	function
für	FÜR	for (*prep.*)
"	"	per (for each)
Furche,*f.*	FOORR-*kh_uh*	furrow (*agric.*)
Furcht,*f.*	FOORRKHT	alarm
"	"	dread
"	"	fear
furchtbar	FOORRKHT-*bar*	awful
"	"	dreadful
fürchten (1)	FÜRKH-*ten*	fear (be afraid of), to
fürchterlich	FÜRKH-*tehr-likh*	fearful (terrible)
furchtsam	FOORRKHT-*zahm*	fearful (afraid)
"	"	timid
für sich allein	*für* ZIKH *ahl*-LINE	apart
Fürsorge,*f.*	FÜR-*zor-guh*	care (custody)
Fuss,*m.*	FOOSS	foot (*anat.*)
Fussball,*m.*	FOOSS-*bahll*	soccer
Fusstritt,*m.*	FOOSS-*tritt*	kick (boot)
Fusstritt geben, einen (43)	*ine-en* FOOSS-*tritt* GAY-*ben*	kick (boot), to
Futter,*n.*	FOOTT-*tehr*	lining
füttern (1)	FÜTT-*ehrn*	feed (give food to), to
Gabel,*f.*	GAH-*bel*	fork (eating utensil)
gähnen (1)	GAY-*nen*	yawn, to
Galerie,*f.*	*gah-luh*-REE	gallery (balcony)
Galopp,*m.*	*gah*-LAWPP	gallop (*n.*)
Gang,*m.*	GAHNNG	aisle (passageway)
"	"	gear (*mech.*)
"	"	hall (corridor)
"	"	passage
Gang setzen, in (1)	*in* GAHNNG ZETTS-*en*	launch (start), to
Gans,*f.*	GAHNSS	goose
Gänseblümchen,*n.*	GENN-*zuh-blüm-kh_en*	daisy

German	Pronunciation	English
ganz	GAHNNTS	all (entirely, *adv.*)
"	"	all (whole of, *adj.*)
ganz	GAHNNTS	altogether (entirely)
"	"	entire
"	"	quite (considerably)
Ganze,*n.*	GAHNNT-*suh*	whole (*adj.*)
		whole (entirety, *n.*)
gänzlich	G_ENTS-*likh*	total (complete)
Garage,*f.*	gah-RAH-*zhuh*	garage
Garderobe,*f.*	gahr-duh-ROH-*buh*	wardrobe (apparel)
Garn,*n.*	GAHRN	yarn (fiber)
Garnele,*f.*	gahr-NAY-*luh*	shrimp
gar nicht	GAHR NIKHT	no (not any, *adv.*)
Garnison,*f.*	gahr-nee-ZONE	garrison
Garten,*m.*	GAHRR-*ten*	garden
Gärtner,*m.*	GEHRT-*nehr*	gardener
Gas,*n.*	GAH_SS	gas
Gast,*m.*	GAH_SST	guest (visitor)
Gastgeber,*m.*	GAH_SST-*gay-behr*	host
Gasthof,*m.*	GAH_SST-*hohf*	inn
Gebärde,*f.*	guh-BARE-*duh*	gesture (motion)
gebären (42)	guh-BARE-*en*	bear (give birth to), to
Gebärmutter,*f.*	guh-BARE-*moott-ehr*	womb
Gebäude,*n.*	guh-BOY-*duh*	building
geben (43)	GAY-*ben*	give (bestow), to
Gebet,*n.*	guh-BATE	prayer (petition)
Gebiet,*n.*	guh-BEET	area (region)
"	"	field (sphere of action)
"	"	realm (field)
"	"	territory
gebirgig	guh-BEER-*gick*	mountainous
gebogen	guh-BOH-*gen*	bent (curved)
geboren sein (werden) (179)	guh-BORE-*ren* ZINE (VARE-*den*)	born, to be
Gebrauch,*m.*	guh-BROW_KH	use (utilization)
Gebrüll,*n.*	guh-BR_ÜLL	roar (*n.*)
Gebühr,*f.*	guh-B_ÜR	fee
gebürend	guh-B_ÜR-*ent*	due (proper)
Geburt,*f.*	guh-BOO_RT	birth
gebürtig (*adj.***)**	guh-B_ÜR-*tick*	native
Geburtstag,*m.*	guh-BOO_RTS-*tahk*	birthday
Gedächtnis,*n.*	guh-DEKHT-*niss*	memory (ability to recall)
Gedanke,*m.*	guh-DAHNNG-*kuh*	thought (idea)
gedeihen (44)	guh-DYE-*en*	flourish, to
"	"	prosper, to
"	"	thrive (grow vigorously), to
gedeihlich	guh-DYE-*likh*	prosperous
Gedicht,*n.*	guh-DIKHT	poem
Gedränge,*n.*	guh-DRENG-*uh*	throng
gedrungen	guh-DROONG-*en*	compact (packed firmly)
Geduld,*f.*	guh-DOOLLT	patience
geduldig	guh-DOOLL-*dick*	patient (forbearing)
Geduldspiel,*n.*	guh-DOOLLT-*shpeel*	puzzle (game)
Gefahr,*f.*	guh-FAR	danger
"	"	peril
"	"	risk
gefährlich	guh-FAIR-*likh*	dangerous
Gefährte,*m.*	guh-FAIR-*tuh*	companion
Gefallen,*m.*	guh-FAHLL-*en*	favor (kindness)
gefälscht	guh-FELSHT	counterfeit (*adj.*)
Gefangene,*m.,f.*	guh-FAHNNG-*en-uh*	captive
"	"	prisoner
Gefängnis,*n.*	guh-FENG-*niss*	jail
"	"	prison
Gefäss,*n.*	guh-FACE	vessel (receptacle)
Geflügel,*n.*	guh-FLÜ-*gel*	fowl (poultry)
Geflüster,*n.*	guh-FLÜSS-*tehr*	whisper
gefroren	guh-FROH-*ren*	frozen
Gefühl,*n.*	guh-FÜL	emotion
"	"	feeling
"	"	sentiment
gegen	GAY-*gen*	against
"	"	at (to, toward)
"	"	toward
Gegend,*f.*	GAY-*g_ent*	region (area)

German	Pronunciation	English
Gegensatz,*m.*	GAY-*gen-zahtts*	conflict (opposition)
"	"	contrast
gegenseitig	GAY-*gen-zile-tick*	mutual
Gegenstand,*m.*	GAY-*gen-shtahnt*	object (thing)
"		subject (topic)
Gegenteil,*n.*	GAY-*gen-tile*	opposite (*n.*)
"	"	reverse (contrary, *n.*)
gegenüber	gay-gen-ü-*behr*	opposite (*prep.*)
gegenüberstehend	gay-gen-ü-*behr-shtay-ent*	opposite (*adj.*)
Gegenwart,*f.*	GAY-*gen-vahrt*	present (present time, *n.*)
gegenwärtig	GAY-*gen-vare-tick*	present (current, *adj.*)
Gegenzeichnung,*f.*	GAY-*gen-*TSYEKH-*noong*	countersignature (*bus.*)
Gegner,*m.*	GAYG-*nehr*	opponent (*n.*)
Gehalt,*n.*	guh-HAHLLT	salary
geheim	guh-HIME	secret (*adj.*)
Geheimnis,*n*	guh-HIME-*niss*	mystery (enigma)
"		secret (*n.*)
geheimnisvoll	guh-HIME-*niss-fawll*	mysterious
gehen (46)	GAY-*en*	go (walk), to
"	"	walk, to
Gehilfe,*m.*	guh-HILL-*fuh*	assistant
Gehirn,*n.*	guh-HEERN	brain (*anat.*)
gehorchen (1)	guh-HOAR-*kh_en*	obey, to
gehorchen, nicht	NIKHT guh-HOAR-*kh_en*	disobey, to
gehören (1)	guh-HÖR-*en*	belong, to
"		belong to, to
gehorsam	guh-HOAR-*zahm*	obedient
Gehorsam,*m.*	guh-HOAR-*zahm*	obedience (compliance)
Geige,*f.*	GUY-*guh*	violin
geisseln (1)	GUY-*sel'n*	lash (whip), to
Geist,*m.*	GUY_ST	mind (intellect)
"	"	spirit
geistig	GUY-*stick*	intellectual (*adj.*)
"		mental
"	"	spiritual (*adj.*)
geistiges Getränk,*n.*	GUY_SS-*tih-gess* guh-TRENG_K	liquor (alcoholic beverage)
geistreich	GUY_ST-*rye_kh*	witty
Geizhals,*m.*	GITES-*hahlss*	miser
geizig	GUY-*tsick*	stingy
Gelächter,*n.*	guh-LEKH-*tehr*	laughter
gelb	GELP	yellow (*adj.*)
gelbe Fieber,*n.*	GELL-*buh* FEE-*behr*	yellow fever
Geld,*n.*	GELT	money
Geldanlage,*f.*	GELT-*ahnn-lah-guh*	investment (*bus.*)
Geldanweisung,*f.*	GELT-*ahnn-vize-oong*	money order
Geldbeutel,*m.*	GELT-*boy-tel*	purse (coin pouch)
Geldschein,*m.*	GELT-*shine*	bill (currency)
Geldstrafe,*f.*	GELT-*shtrah-fuh*	fine (penalty, *n.*)
Gelee,*n.*	zhuh-LAY	jelly
Gelegenheit,*f.*	guh-LAY-*gen-hite*	chance
"	"	occasion
"	"	opportunity
Gelegenheitskauf,*m.*	guh-LAY-*gen-hites-kowf*	bargain (advantageous purchase)
gelegentlich	guh-LAY-*g_ent-likh*	occasional
Gelehrte,*m.*	guh-LAIR-*tuh*	scholar (savant)
Geleise,*n.*	guh-LYE-*zuh*	track (rails)
(Schutz)Geleit,*n.*	(SHUHTS-)guh-LITE	convoy (*mil.*)
geliebt	guh-LEEBT	beloved (*adj.*)
Geliebte,*m.,f.*	guh-LEEB-*tuh*	lover
gellend schreien (110)	GELL-*ent* SHRYE-*en*	yell, to
Gelöbnis,*n.*	guh-LÖP-*niss*	pledge
Gelübde,*n.*	guh-LÜPP-*duh*	vow
Gemälde,*n.*	guh-MEL-*duh*	painting (picture)
gemein	guh-MINE	common
"		vulgar (ill-bred)
Gemeinde,*f.*	guh-MINE-*duh*	community (neighborhood)
"	"	congregation (religious community)
Gemeiner,*m.*	guh-MY-*nehr*	private (*mil.*)
gemeinsam	guh-MINE-*zahm*	joint (combined)
Gemeinschaft,*f.*	guh-MINE-*shahfft*	community (the public)
Gemüse,*n.*	guh-MÜ-*zuh*	vegetable

German	Pronunciation	English
gemustert	*guh*-MOOSS-*tehrt*	fancy (ornamental, *adj.*)
Gemütsart,*f.*	*guh*-MÜHTS-*art*	disposition (temperament)
genau	*guh*-NOW	accurate
"	"	exact
"	"	precise
genehmigen (1)	*guh*-NAY-*mih-gen*	approve (sanction), to
geneigt	*guh*-NIKE_T	apt to (prone to)
General,*m.*	*gay-nay*-RAHL	general (officer)
Generation,*f.*	*gay-nuh-rahts*-YOHN	generation (period of time)
Genf,*n.*	GENF	Geneva
Genie,*n.*	*zhay*-NEE	genius
geniessen (50)	*guh*-NEE-*senn*	enjoy (derive joy from), to
Genossenschaft,*f.*	*guh*-NAWSS-*sen-shahft*	cooperative (*n.*)
genug	*guh*-NOO_K	enough (*adv.*)
"	"	enough (*n.*)
genügend	*guh*-NÜ-*g_ent*	adequate
"	"	enough (*adj.*)
"	"	sufficient
Geologie,*f.*	*gay-oh-loh*-G_EE	geology
Gepäck,*n.*	*guh*-PECK	baggage
"	"	luggage
Gepäckträger,*m.*	*guh*-PECK-*tray-gehr*	porter (baggage carrier)
gerade	*guh*-RAH-*duh*	straight (not crooked, *adj.*)
geradewegs	*guh*-RAH-*duh-vake_ss*	straight (directly, *adv.*)
geräuschvoll	*guh*-ROYSH-*fawll*	noisy
gerecht	*guh*-REHKHT	just (equitable, *adj.*)
Gerechtigkeit,*f.*	*guh*-REHKH-*tick-kite*	justice (rightfulness)
Gericht,*n.*	*guh*-RIKHT	court (of law)
"	"	dish (food)
Gerichtsverhandlung,*f.*	*guh*-RIKHTS-*fehr-hahnnd-loong*	trial (court proceeding)
gering	*guh*-RING	slight (*adj.*)
gering(er)	*guh*-RING(-*ehr*)	minor (lesser)
geringfügig	*guh*-RING-*füg-ick*	petty (minor)
geringst	*guh*-RINGSST	least (*adj.*)
gern haben (178)	GEHRN *hah-ben*	like (be fond of), to
Gerste,*f.*	GEHR-*stuh*	barley
Geruch,*m.*	*guh*-ROO_KH	odor
"	"	scent
"	"	smell
Gerücht,*n.*	*guh*-RÜKHT	rumor
Gesamtbetrag,*m.*	*guh*-ZAHMMT-*buh-trahk*	total (sum)
Geschäft,*n.*	*guh*-SHEFFT	business (commerce)
Geschäftsmann,*m.*	*guh*-SHEFFTS-*mahnn*	businessman
geschehen (52)	*guh*-SHAY-*en*	happen (occur), to
Geschenk,*n.*	*guh*-SHENK	gift (present)
Geschichte,*f.*	*guh*-SHIKH-*tuh*	history
"	"	story (account)
Geschicklichkeit,*f.*	*guh*-SHICK-*likh-kite*	skill (proficiency)
geschickt	*guh*-SHICKT	skilful
Geschirr,*n.*	*guh*-SHEERR	dishes (tableware)
"	"	harness
Geschlecht,*n.*	*guh*-SHLEH_KHT	sex
Geschmack,*m.*	*guh*-SHMAHCK	flavor (savor)
"	"	taste
Geschwätz,*n.*	*guh*-SHVETTS	gossip (idle talk)
geschwind	*guh*-SHVINNT	fast (quickly)
"		swift
Geschwindigkeit,*f.*	*guh*-SHVINN-*dick-kite*	rate (degree of speed)
"	"	speed (rapidity)
Geschworenen,*pl.*	*guh*-SHVOR-*uh-nen*	jury
Geschwulst,*f.*	*guh*-SHVOOLST	tumor
Geschwür,*n.*	*guh*-SHVÜR	ulcer
gesellig	*guh*-ZELL-*lick*	sociable (companionable)
Gesellschaft,*f.*	*guh*-ZELL-*shahft*	company
"	"	society
gesellschaftlich	*guh*-ZELL-*shahft-likh*	social (societal)
Gesetz,*n.*	*guh*-ZETTS	law (statute)
Gesetzbuch,*n.*	*guh*-ZETTS-*boo_kh*	code (law)
gesetzgebende Körperschaft,*f.*	*guh*-ZETTS-*gay-ben-duh* KÖR-*pehr-shahft*	legislature
Gesetzgebung,*f.*	*guh*-ZETTS-*gay-boong*	legislation
gesetzlich	*guh*-ZETTS-*likh*	legal
gesetzmässig	*guh*-ZETTS-*may-sick*	lawful
Gesicht,*n.*	*guh*-ZIKHT	face (*anat.*)

German	Pronunciation	English
Gesims,*n.*	*guh*-ZIMMSS	ledge
Gespenst,*n.*	*guh*-SHPENNST	ghost
Gespräch,*n.*	*guh*-SPREH_KH	talk (conversation)
Gestalt,*f.*	*guh*-SHTAHLLT	figure (human form)
gestehen (129)	*guh*-SHTAY-*en*	confess (admit), to
gestern	GUESS-*tehrn*	yesterday
Gesuch,*n.*	*guh*-ZOOKH	application (request)
gesund	*guh*-ZOONNT	healthy
"	"	sound
"	"	wholesome (beneficial)
Gesundheit,*f.*	*guh*-ZOONNT-*hite*	health
Getöse,*n.*	*guh*-TÖ-*zuh*	din
Getränk,*n.*	*guh*-TRENGK	drink (beverage)
Getreide,*n.*	*guh*-TRY-*duh*	cereal
"	"	grain
getrennt	*guh*-TRENT	separate
gewähren (1)	*guh*-VARE-*en*	grant (bestow), to
Gewalt,*f.*	*guh*-VAHLLT	force (coercion)
"	"	violence
gewaltsam	*guh*-VAHLLT-*zahm*	violent
Gewandtheit,*f.*	*guh*-VAHNNT-*hite*	dexterity
Gewebe,*n.*	*guh*-VAY-*buh*	tissue (*biol.*)
Gewehr,*n.*	*guh*-VARE	gun
"	"	rifle
Gewerbe,*n.*	*guh*-VEHR-*buh*	trade (craft)
Gewerkschaft,*f.*	*guh*-VEHRK-*shahfft*	union (trade union)
Gewicht,*n.*	*guh*-VIKHT	weight (scale weight)
Gewinn,*m.*	*guh*-VINN	gain (increase)
"	"	profit (*bus.*)
gewinnen (53)	*guh*-VINN-*nen*	gain (get), to
"	"	win (be victor in), to
gewiss	*guh*-VISS	certain (particular)
Gewissen,*n.*	*guh*-VISS-*sen*	conscience
Gewitter,*n.*	*guh*-VITT-*ehr*	tempest
gewöhnen, sich (1)	*zikh guh*-VÖ-*nen*	accustom oneself, to
Gewohnheit,*f.*	*guh*-VOHN-*hite*	habit (custom)
gewöhnlich	*guh*-VÖN-*likh*	common
"	"	ordinary
"	"	usual
Gewürz,*n.*	*guh*-VÜRTS	spice
geziehmend	*guh*-TSEE-*ment*	proper (acceptable)
gierig	GEAR-*ick*	greedy
Gift,*n.*	GIFT	poison
Gipfel,*m.*	GIPP-*fel*	crest
"	"	summit
"	"	top
girieren (1)	*zhee*-REE-*ren*	endorse (sign), to
Giro,*n.*	ZHEE-*ro*	endorsement (signature)
Gitarre,*f.*	*g_ee*-TAHR-*ruh*	guitar
Glanz,*m.*	GLAHNNTS	luster (sheen)
"	"	polish
glänzen (1)	GLENNT-*sen*	gleam, to
"	"	shine, to
glänzend	GLENNT-*sent*	brilliant (remarkable)
Glas,*n.*	GLAHSS	glass (material)
(Trink)Glas,*n.*	(TRING_K-)GLAHSS	glass (vessel)
glatt	GLAHTT	smooth (*adj.*)
glätten	GLETT-*ten*	smooth (level), to
Glaube,*m.*	GL_OW-*buh*	belief (opinion)
glauben (1)	GL_OW-*ben*	believe (accept), to
Glaubensbekenntnis,*n.*	GL_OW-*bens-buh-kennt-niss*	faith (creed)
Gläubiger,*m.*	GLOY-*bih-gehr*	creditor (*bus.*)
gleich	GLYE_KH	alike
"	"	equal (*adj.*)
"		like (*adj.*)
(so)gleich	(*zoh*-)GLYE_KH	immediately (instantly)
Gleiche,*m.*	GLYE-*khuh*	peer (equal)
Gleichgewicht,*n.*	GLYE_KH-*guh-vikht*	balance (equilibrium)
gleichgültig	GLYE_KH-*gül-tick*	indifferent (unconcerned)
gleiten (56)	GLITE-*en*	glide, to
"	"	slide, to
Glied,*n.*	GLEET	limb (*anat.*)
(Ketten)Glied,*n.*	(KETT-*ten*-)GLEET	link (connecting part)

German	Pronunciation	English
glitzern (1)	GLITTS-*ehrn*	glitter, to
Globus,*m.*	GL_OW-*buhss*	globe
Glocke,*f.*	GLAWK-*uh*	bell
Glück,*n.*	GLÜCK	fortune
"	"	happiness
"	"	luck
Glück haben (178)	GLÜCK *hah-ben*	thrive (succeed), to
glücklich	GLÜCK-*likh*	fortunate
"	"	happy (glad)
"	"	lucky
glücklicherweise	GLÜCK-*likh-ehr-vize-uh*	happily (luckily)
Glühbirne,*f.*	GLÜ-*beer-nuh*	bulb (light bulb)
glühen (1)	GLÜ-*en*	glow (shine), to
Gnade,*f.*	G_NAH-*duh*	mercy
Gold,*n.*	GAWLT	gold
golden	GAWLL-*den*	golden
Golf,*m.*	GAWLF	gulf (large bay)
Golf(spiel),*n.*	GAWLF-(*shpeel*)	golf
Gott,*m.*	GAWTT	God
göttlich	GÖTT-*likh*	divine (*adj.*)
Götze,*m.*	GÖTT-*suh*	idol
Gouverneur,*m.*	*goo-vehr*-NÖR	governor
Grab,*n.*	GRAHP	grave (tomb)
graben (57)	GRAH-*ben*	dig (excavate), to
"	"	mine (dig for), to
Graben,*m.*	GRAH-*ben*	ditch
"	"	trench (*mil.*)
Grabstätte,*f.*	GRAHP-*shtett-uh*	tomb
Grad,*m.*	GRAHT	degree (unit of measurement)
grämen, sich (1)	*zikh* GRAY-*men*	fret (worry), to
Grammatik,*f.*	*grahm*-MAH-*tick*	grammar
Granit,*m.*	*grah*-NEET	granite
Gras,*n.*	GRAHSS	grass
gratulieren (1)	*grah-too*-LEE-*ren*	congratulate, to
grau	GR_OW	gray
grausam	GR_OW-*zahm*	cruel
(er)greifen (58)	(*ehr*-)GRIFE-*en*	grasp (grip), to
Grenze,*f.*	GRENT-*suh*	border
"	"	frontier
"	"	limit
Griechenland,*n.*	GREE_KH-*en-lahnt*	Greece
griechisch	GREE_KH-*ish*	Greek (*adj.*)
Griff,*m.*	GRIFF	grip (grasp)
"	"	handle
Grille,*f.*	GRILL-*luh*	cricket (insect)
"	"	fancy (notion)
grinsen (1)	GRIN-*zen*	grin, to
Grippe,*f.*	GRIPP-*uh*	influenza
grob	GRAWPP	coarse
"	"	gross (flagrant)
"	"	rough (harsh)
"	"	rude (impolite)
Gros,*n.*	GRAWSS	gross (twelve dozen)
gross	GROHSS	big
"	"	great
"	"	large
grossartig	GROHSS-*ahr-tick*	grand (imposing)
Grossbritannien,*n.*	*grohss-britt*-TAHN-*yen*	Great Britain
Grösse,*f.*	GRÖ-*suh*	greatness (eminence)
"	"	size
grösser	GRÖ-*sehr*	major (larger)
Grosshändler,*m.*	GROHSS-*hend-lehr*	wholesaler (*bus.*)
Grossmutter,*f.*	GROHSS-*moott-tehr*	grandmother
grösst	GRÖSST	most (greatest quantity, *adj.*)
Grossvater,*m.*	GROHSS-*fah-tehr*	grandfather
Grube,*f.*	GROO-*buh*	pit (hole)
grün	GRÜN	green (color)
Grund,*m.*	GROONNT	ground (basis)
"	"	reason
Grundeigentum,*n.*	GROONNT-*eye-gen-toomm*	real estate
gründen (1)	GRÜNN-*den*	establish (found), to
"	"	found (originate), to
Gründer,*m.*	GRÜNN-*dehr*	founder (*n.*)
Grundfläche,*f.*	GROONNT-*fleh_kh-uh*	area (extent)
Grundkapital,*n.*	GROONNT-*kah-pee-*TAHL	capital (wealth)
Grundlage,*f.*	GROONNT-*lah-guh*	basis
grundlegend	GROONNT-*lay-g_ent*	fundamental

German	Pronunciation	English
gründlich	GRÜNT-*likh*	radical (basic)
"	"	thorough (complete)
"	"	thoroughly
Grundsatz,*m.*	GROONNT-*zahtts*	principle (basic truth)
Grundstück,*n.*	GROONNT-*shtück*	land (property)
Gründung,*f.*	GRÜNN-*doong*	establishment (founding)
Gruppe,*f.*	GROOPP-*uh*	group
grüssen (1)	GRÜSS-*sen*	salute, to
(be)grüssen (1)	(*buh*-)GRÜSS-*sen*	greet (salute), to
Guatemala,*n.*	*gwah-tay*-MAH-*lah*	Guatemala
gültig	GÜL-*tick*	active (in force)
Gummi,*n.*	GOOMM-*ee*	rubber
Gummischuhe,*m. pl.*	GOOMM-*ee-shoo-uh*	galoshes
"	"	rubbers (overshoes)
Gunst,*f.*	GOONNST	favor (approval)
günstig	GÜNN-*stick*	favorable
Gurke,*f.*	GOORR-*kuh*	cucumber
Gürtel,*m.*	GÜRR-*tel*	belt (article of clothing)
gut	GOOT	good
"	"	well (commendably, *adv.*)
Güte,*f.*	GÜ-*tuh*	goodness (kindliness)
"	"	kindness
gütig	GÜ-*tick*	kind (*adj.*)
gutschreiben (109)	GOOT-*shrye-ben*	credit, to (*bus.*)
Haar,*n.*	HAHR	hair
haben (178)	HAH-*ben*	have, to
Habicht,*m.*	HAH-*bikht*	hawk
Hacke,*f.*	HAHCK-*kuh*	hoe
hacken (1)	HAHCK-*en*	hoe, to
Hafen,*m.*	HAH-*fen*	harbor
"	"	port
Hafer,*m.*	HAH-*fehr*	oats
haftbar	HAHFFT-*bar*	liable (responsible)
haften, für... (1)	*für...* HAHFF-*ten*	guarantee, to
Haftpflicht,*f.*	HAHFFT-*pflikht*	liability (responsibility)
Hagel,*m.*	HAH-*gel*	hail (ice)
hageln (1)	HAH-*gel'n*	hail (precipitate hail), to
Hahn,*m.*	HAHN	cock
"	"	rooster
"	"	tap (faucet)
Haiti,*n.*	*hah*-EE-*tee*	Haiti
Haken,*m.*	HAH-*ken*	hook
halb	HAHLLP	half (*adj.*)
Halbinsel,*f.*	HAHLLP-*in-zel*	peninsula
Halbkugel,*f.*	HAHLLP-*koo-gel*	hemisphere (*geog.*)
Hälfte,*f.*	HELFF-*tuh*	half (*n.*)
Hals,*m.*	HAHLLSS	neck (*anat.*)
"	"	throat
Halskette,*f.*	HAHLLSS-*kett-tuh*	necklace
Halsweh,*n.*	HAHLLSS-*vay*	sore throat
Halt,*m.*	HAHLLT	stop (halt)
halten (59)	HAHLL-*ten*	hold, to
(an)halten	(AHNN-)HAHLL-*ten*	halt (come to a stop), to
halten, für...	*für...* HAHLL-*ten*	deem (regard), to
Haltung,*f.*	HAHLL-*toong*	attitude (manner)
(Körper)Haltung,*f.*	(KÖR-*pehr*-)HAHLL-*toong*	carriage (posture)
Hammelfleisch,*n.*	HAHMM-*mel-fly_sh*	mutton
Hammelkotelett,*n.*	HAHMM-*mel-kaw-tell-let*	lamb chop
Hammer,*m.*	HAHMM-*mehr*	hammer (tool)
Hand,*f.*	HAHNNT	hand (*anat.*)
Hand, bei der	BY *dehr* HAHNNT	handy (near at hand)
Hand, mit der	*mit dehr* HAHNNT	manual (by hand)
Handbuch,*n.*	HAHNNT-*bookh*	manual (small book)
Handel,*m.*	HAHNN-*del*	commerce
"	"	trade
handeln (1)	HAHNN-*del'n*	act (do), to
"	"	deal (trade), to
Handelsgesellschaft, offene,*f.*	AWF-*fen-nuh* HAHNN-*delss-guh-zell-shahft*	copartnership (*bus.*)
Handelskammer,*f.*	HAHNN-*delss-kahmm-mehr*	chamber of commerce
Handelsmarke,*f.*	HAHNN-*delss-mahr-kuh*	trade mark
Handelsreisende,*m.*	HAHNN-*delss-rye-zen-duh*	traveling salesman
Handfläche,*f.*	HAHNNT-*fleh_kh-uh*	palm (of hand)
Handgelenk,*n.*	HAHNNT-*guh-lenk*	wrist

German	Pronunciation	English
Händler, *m.*	HENND-*lehr*	dealer (trader)
Handlung, *f.*	HAHNND-*loong*	action (deed)
Handschuh, *m.*	HAHNNT-*shoo*	glove
Handtasche, *f.*	HAHNNT-*tahsh-uh*	bag (purse)
Handtuch, *n.*	HAHNNT-*too_kh*	towel, hand
Handvoll, *f.*	HAHNNT-*fawll*	handful
Handwerk, *n.*	HAHNND-*vehrk*	craft (trade)
hängen (60)	HENG-*en*	hang, to
Harfe, *f.*	HAHR-*fuh*	harp
Harke, *f.*	HAHR-*kuh*	rake (tool)
Harmonie, *f.*	*hahr-moh-*NEE	harmony (*mus.*)
Harnblase, *f.*	HAHRN-*blah-zuh*	bladder (*anat.*)
hart	HAHRT	grim (stern)
"	"	hard (not soft)
härten (1)	HEHR-*ten*	harden (make hard), to
hartnäckig	HAHRT-*neck-ick*	stubborn
Hase, *m.*	HAH-*zuh*	hare
Hass, *m.*	HAHSS	hate (hatred)
hassen (1)	HAHSS-*sen*	hate, to
hässlich	HESS-*likh*	ugly
Hast, *f.*	HAHSST	haste
Haufen, *m.*	HOW-*fen*	heap
"	"	pile
häufig	HOY-*fick*	frequent
Haupt-...	HOWPT-*...*	chief (leading)
"	"	main
"	"	principal
Hauptquartier, *n.*	HOWPT-*kvahr-teer*	headquarters
hauptsächlich	HOWPT-*zeh_kh-likh*	chiefly (mainly)
Hauptstadt, *f.*	HOWPT-*shtaht*	capital (city)
Hauptteil, *m.*	HOWPT-*tile*	bulk (largest part)
Hauptwort, *n.*	HOWPT-*vort*	noun
Haus, *n.*	HOWSS	house
Hausfrau, *f.*	HOWSS-*fr_ow*	housewife
Haushalt, *m.*	HOWSS-*hahlt*	household
Hausierer, *m.*	*how-*ZEE-*rehr*	canvasser (*bus.*)
häuslich	HOYSS-*likh*	domestic (household, *adj.*)
Hausschuh, *m.*	HOWSS-*shoo*	slipper
Haustier, *n.*	HOWSS-*teer*	pet (animal)
Haut, *f.*	HOWT	skin (human skin)
Häutchen, *n.*	HOYT-*kh_en*	film (thin coating)
Hawaii, *n.*	*hah-*VAH-*ee*	Hawaii
Hebel, *m.*	HAY-*bel*	lever
heben (62)	HAY-*ben*	heave, to
"	"	raise, to
(auf)heben	(OWF-)HAY-*ben*	lift (raise), to
hebräisch	*h.th-*BRAY-*ish*	Hebrew (*adj.*)
Hecke, *f.*	HECK-*kuh*	hedge (bushes)
Heer, *n.*	HAIR	army
Hefe, *f.*	HAY-*fuh*	yeast
(Schreib)Heft, *n.*	(SHRIPE-)HEFFT	notebook
hegen (1)	HAY-*gen*	cherish, to
Heidelbeere, *f.*	HYE-*del-bay-ruh*	blueberry
heil	HILE	safe (unharmed)
Heil, *n.*	HILE	salvation
Heiland, *m.*	HYE-*lahnt*	savior
Heilbutt, *m.*	HILE-*boott*	halibut
heilen (1)	HYE-*len*	cure, to
"	"	heal, to
heilig	HYE-*lick*	holy
"	"	sacred
Heilige, *m.,f.*	HILE-*ee-guh*	saint
Heilmittel, *n.*	HILE-*mit-tel*	cure (remedy)
Heilung, *f.*	HYE-*loong*	cure (healing)
heim	HIME	homeward
Heim, *n.*	HIME	home
heimelig	HIME-*uh-lick*	homely (everyday)
(ein)heimisch	(INE-)HIME-*ish*	native (indigenous)
Heimweh, *n.*	HIME-*vay*	homesick
Heiratsantrag machen, einen (1)	*eye-nen* HYE-*rahts-ahnn-trahk* MAH_KH-*en*	propose (offer marriage), to
heiss	HICE	hot
heiter	HYE-*tehr*	cheerful (joyful)
Heiterkeit, *f.*	HYE-*tehr-kite*	glee (joy)
heizen (1)	HITES-*en*	heat, to
Heizkörper, *m.*	HITES-*kör-pehr*	radiator (heater)
Held, *m.*	HELLT	hero
Heldin, *f.*	HELL-*din*	heroine

German	Pronunciation	English
helfen (64)	HELL-*fen*	aid, to
"	"	help, to
Helfer, *m.*	HELL-*fehr*	helper
hell	HELL	bright (shining)
"	"	light
hell(farbig)	HELL(-*fahr-bick*)	fair (blond)
Helm, *m.*	HELM	helmet
Helsinki, *n.*	HELL-*sing-kee*	Helsinki
Hemd, *n.*	HEMM_T	shirt
Hemmung, *f.*	HEMM-*moong*	check (restraint)
Hengst, *m.*	HENGST	stallion
Henne, *f.*	HENN-*nuh*	hen
herab	*hehr-*AHPP	down (downward, *adv.*)
herabsetzen (1)	*hehr-*AHPP-*zetts-en*	lower (decrease), to
herabsteigen (131)	*hehr-*AHPP-*shtye-gen*	descend (move downward), to
heraus	*hehr-*OWSS	out (forth, *adv.*)
Herausforderung, *f.*	*hehr-*OWSS-*for-dehr-oong*	challenge
herausgeben (43)	*hehr-*OWSS-*geh-ben*	publish, to
Herbst, *m.*	HEHRPST	autumn
"	"	fall
Herd, *m.*	HEHRT	hearth
"	"	stove (for cooking)
Herde, *f.*	HEHR-*duh*	flock
"	"	herd (of animals)
hereinlassen (71)	*hehr-*INE-*lahss-sen*	admit (permit to enter), to
Hering, *m.*	HEHR-*ing*	herring
hernach	*hehr-*NAH_KH	hereafter (after this, *adv.*)
Herr, *m.*	HEHRR	gentleman
"	"	lord
"	"	master (one in authority)
"	"	Mr. (Mister)
"	"	sir
herrlich	HEHRR-*likh*	glorious (resplendent)
"	"	magnificent
Herrschaft, *f.*	HEHRR-*shahft*	dominion
"	"	reign (period of rule)
"	"	rule (political control)
herrschen (1)	HEHRR-*shen*	rule (govern), to
Herrscher, *m.*	HEHRR-*shehr*	ruler
"	"	sovereign
herstellen (1)	HEHR-*shtell-en*	manufacture, to
Herstellung, *f.*	*hehr-*SHTELL-*oong*	production (manufacture)
herunter	*hehr-*OONN-*tehr*	downward (*adv.*)
hervorbringen (171)	*hehr-*FOR-*bring-en*	produce (make), to
hervorragend	*hehr-*FOR-*rahg-ent*	prominent
Herz, *n.*	HEHRRTS	heart
herzlich	HEHRRTS-*likh*	cordial (*adj.*)
"	"	hearty
Heu, *n.*	HOY	hay
heucheln (1)	HOY-*kh_el'n*	affect, to
"	"	pretend (feign), to
heulen (1)	HOY-*len*	howl (wail), to
Heuschrecke, *f.*	HOY-*shreck-uh*	grasshopper
heute	HOY-*tuh*	today
heute abend	HOY-*tuh* AH-*bent*	tonight
heutig	HOY-*tick*	contemporary (modern)
Hexe, *f.*	HEX-*uh*	witch
hier	HEER	here (in this place, *adv.*)
hierher	HEER-*hehr*	here (to this place, *adv.*)
Hilfe, *f.*	HILL-*fuh*	aid
"	"	help (assistance)
Hilfe, erste, *f.*	EHR-*stuh* HILL-*fuh*	first aid (*med.*)
hilflos	HILLF-*lohss*	helpless
hilfreich	HILLF-*rye_kh*	helpful
Hilfsmittel, *n.*	HILLFS-*mit-tel*	remedy
Himbeere, *f.*	HIMM-*bay-ruh*	raspberry
Himmel, *m.*	HIMM-*mel*	heaven
"	"	sky
hinab	*hinn-*AHPP	down (downward, *adv.*)
hinabsteigen (131)	*hinn-*AHPP-*shtye-gen*	descend (move downward), to

German	Pronunciation	English
(ver)hindern (1)	(fehr-)HINN-dehrn	hinder, to
Hindernis, n.	HINN-dehr-niss	obstacle
hineinlassen (71)	hinn-INE-lahss-sen	admit (permit to enter), to
Hingebung, f.	HINN-gay-boong	devotion (loyal attachment)
hinken (1)	HING-ken	limp, to
hiniegen, sich (1)	zikh HINN-lay-gen	lie down, to
hinneigen, (sich)	(zikh) HINN-nye-gen	lean (bend), to
hinrichten (1)	HINN-rikh-ten	execute (put to death), to
Hinsicht, f.	HINN-zikht	aspect (phase)
hinten	HINN-ten	behind (in the rear, adv.)
hinter	HINN-tehr	behind (prep.)
Hinter-...	HINN-tehr-...	rear (adj.)
hintere	HINN-tuh-ruh	hind (posterior, adj.)
hinterher	hinn-tehr-HEHR	behind (late, adv.)
hinunter	hinn-OONN-tehr	downward (adv.)
hinweisen (155)	HINN-vye-zen	point (indicate), to
Hirsch, m.	HEERRSH	deer
Hirt, m.	HEERRT	shepherd
historisch	hiss-TOH-rish	historical
Hitze, f.	HIT-suh	heat
hoch	HOH_KH	high
"	"	lofty
"	"	tall
Hochebene, f.	HOH_KH-ay-buh-nuh	plateau (tableland)
höchst	HÖKH_ST	supreme
"	"	top (highest, adj.)
Hochzeit, f.	HOH_KH-tsyte	wedding
Hof, m.	HOHF	court (of ruler)
"	"	yard (enclosure near house)
hoffen (1)	HAWFF-en	hope, to
Hoffnung, f.	HAWFF-noong	hope
hoffnungslos	HAWFF-noongs-lohss	hopeless
hoffnungsvoll	HAWFF-noongs-fawll	hopeful
höflich	HÖF-likh	civil
"	"	courteous
"	"	polite
Höflichkeit, f.	HÖF-likh-kite	courtesy
Höhe, f.	HÖ-yuh	height (highness)
"	"	level (plane, n.)
höhere Schule, f.	HÖ-ehr-uh SHOO-luh	high school
hohl	HOLE	hollow (adj.)
Höhle, f.	HÖ-luh	cave
"	"	den (animal lair)
holen (1)	HOH-len	fetch (bring), to
Holland, n.	HAWLL-lahnt	Holland
holländisch	HAWLL-en-dish	Dutch (adj.)
Hölle, f.	HÖLL-uh	hell
Holz, n.	HAWLLTS	timber (standing trees)
"	"	wood (lumber)
Honduras, n.	hawnn-DOO-rahss	Honduras
Honig, m.	HOH-nick	honey
hören (1)	HÖ-ren	hear, to
Horizont, m.	haw-ree-TSAWNT	horizon
horizontal	haw-ree-tsawn-TAHL	horizontal (adj.)
Horn, n.	HORN	horn (anat.)
"	"	horn (mus.)
Hörsaal, m.	HÖR-zah_l	auditorium
Hose(n), f.pl.	HOH-zuh(n)	trousers
Hosenträger, m.pl.	HOH-zen-tray-gehr	suspenders
Hotel, n.	ho-TELL	hotel
hübsch	HÜPSH	pretty
Hubschrauber, m.	HOOP-shr_ow-bchr	helicopter
Huf, m.	HOO_F	hoof
Hüfte, f.	HÜFF-tuh	hip
Hügel, m.	HÜ-gel	hill
Hügelabhang, m.	HÜ-gel-ahpp-hahng	hillside
Huhn, n.	HOON	chicken
Hund, m.	HOONT	dog
Hunger, m.	HOONN-gchr	hunger
Hunger haben (178)	HOONN-gchr HAH-ben	hungry, to be
hungrig	HOONNG-rick	hungry
Hummer, m.	HOOMM-mehr	lobster
Humor, m.	hoo-MORE	humor (drollery)
hüpfen (1)	HÜPP-fen	hop, to
"	"	skip (caper), to

German	Pronunciation	English
Hupe, f.	HOO-puh	horn (auto.)
Husten, m.	HOO-sten	cough
Hut, m.	HOO_T	hat
hüten (1)	HÜ-len	guard (watch over), to
hüten vor, sich	zikh HÜ-ten for	beware of, to
Hütte, f.	HÜTT-tuh	hut
Hypothek, f.	hü-po-TAKE	mortgage
ich	IKH	I
Ideal, n.	ee-day-AHL	ideal (n.)
Idee, f.	ee-DAY	idea
"	"	notion
identifizieren (1)	ee-den-tih-fih-TSEE-ren	identify, to
ihm	EEM	him
ihn	EEN	him
"	"	it
ihr	EAR	her
"	"	its
"	"	their
"	"	your
Ihr	EAR	their
"	"	your
ihre(r)	EAR-eh(r)	theirs
Ihre(r, -s)	EAR-eh(r, -s)	yours
ihrer	EAR-ehr	hers
Illusion, f.	ill-looz-YOHN	illusion
Illustration, f.	ill-looss-trahts-YOHN	illustration (example)
illustrieren (1)	ill-looss-TREE-ren	illustrate (exemplify), to
immer	IMM-mehr	always
"	"	ever (at all times)
immer, für	für IMM-mehr	forever
Impfung, f.	IMP-foong	vaccination
Importeur, m.	im-pawr-TÖR	importer
in	INN	at
"	"	in (inside, prep.)
"	"	into (to the inside)
Indianer, m.	in-dee-AHNN-ehr	Indian, American
Indien, n.	IND-yen	India
Individuum, n.	in-dih-VEE-doo-oomm	individual (person, n.)
Industrie, f.	in-dooss-TREE	industry (trade)
industriell	in-dooss-tree-YELL	industrial
Inflation, f.	in-flah-tsee-YOHN	inflation (econ.)
infolgedessen	inn-fawll-guh-DESS-en	consequently
Ingenieur, m.	inn-zhenn-YÖR	engineer (professional engineer)
Ingwer, m.	INNG-vehr	ginger (spice)
Inhalt, m.	INN-hahlt	capacity (volume)
"	"	contents
innen-...	INN-en-...	inside (inner, adj.)
inner	INN-ehr	inner
Innere, n.	INN-ehr-uh	inside
"	"	interior
innerhalb	INN-ehr-hahlp	inside (prep.)
"	"	within (prep.)
inner(lich)	INN-chr(-likh)	internal
Inschrift, f.	INN-shrift	inscription
Insel, f.	INN-zcl	island (geog.)
Inspiration, f.	inn-spce-rahts-YOHN	inspiration
Instinkt, m.	in-STINKT	instinct
Institution, f.	in-stce-toots-YOHN	institution (establishment)
Instrument, n.	in-stroo-MENT	instrument (implement)
intensiv	in-tcn-SEEFF	intense
interessant	in-tchr-ruh-SAHNNT	interesting
Interesse, n.	in-tchr-ESS-uh	interest (attention)
interessieren (1)	in-tchr-ruh-SEE-ren	interest, to
international	in-tehr-nahts-yoh-NAHL	international
Interview, n.	in-tehr-VIEW	interview
Intuition, f.	in-too-its-YOHN	intuition
Inventar, n.	in-venn-TAHR	inventory (bus.)
inzwischen	in-TSVISH-en	meanwhile (adv.)
irgend ein	EAR-g_ent ine	any (any one, adj.)
"	"	some (unspecified, adj.)
irgendeiner	EAR-g_ent-INE-ehr	anyone (someone)
irgendetwas	EAR-g_ent-ETT-vahss	anything (something)
irgend jemand	EAR-g_ent YAY-mahnt	anybody (somebody)

German	Pronunciation	English
irgendwelche	EAR-*g_ent*-VELL-*kh_uh*	any (any at all, *adj.*)
"	"	any (a quantity of, *adj.*)
irgendwie	EERR-*g_ent*-vee	somehow
irgendwo	EERR-*g_ent*-voh	somewhere
irisch	EERR-*ish*	Irish (*adj.*)
Irland,*n.*	EERR-*lahnt*	Ireland
irren, sich (1)	*zikh* EERR-*en*	err, to
Irrtum,*m.*	EERR-*toomm*	error
Israel,*n.*	IZZ-*rah-ale*	Israel
israelisch	*iz-rah-*ALE-*ish*	Israeli (*adj.*)
Italien,*n.*	*ee-*TAHL-*yen*	Italy
italienisch	*ee-tahl-*YAY-*nish*	Italian (*adj.*)
ja	YAH	yes
Jacke,*f.*	YAHCK-*uh*	jacket (short coat)
Jagd,*f.*	YAHGT	hunt (sport)
Jagdhaus,*n.*	YAHGT-*howss*	lodge (cabin)
Jagdhund,*m.*	YAHGT-*hoont*	hound
jagen (1)	YAH-*gen*	chase, to
Jäger,*m.*	YAY-*gehr*	hunter
Jahr,*n.*	YAHR	year
Jahresrente,*f.*	YAH-*ress-ren-tuh*	annuity
Jahrestag,*m.*	YAH-*ress-tahk*	anniversary
Jahreszeit,*f.*	YAH-*ress-tsite*	season (of year)
Jahrhundert,*n.*	*yahr-*HOONN-*dehrt*	century
jährlich	YEHR-*likh*	annual
"	"	yearly (*adv., adj.*)
Japan,*n.*	YAH-*pahn*	Japan
japanisch	*yah-*PAH-*nish*	Japanese (*adj.*)
Jazz,*m.*	JAZZ	jazz
je	YAY	each (apiece, *adv.*)
jedenfalls	YAY-*den-fahlls*	anyhow (in any case)
"	"	anyway (in any case)
jede(r, -s)	YAY-*deh*(r, -s)	all (every, *adj.*)
"	"	any (every, *adj.*)
"	"	each (every, *adj.*)
"	"	each one (*pron.*)
"	"	every (*adj.*)
jeder(mann)	YAY-*dehr*(-*mahnn*)	everybody
"	"	everyone
jedoch	YAY-*dawkh*	however (nevertheless)
je(mals)	YAY(-*mahlss*)	ever (at any time)
jemand	YAY-*mahnt*	somebody
"	"	someone
jene	YAY-*nuh*	those (*adj., pron.*)
jene(r, -s)	YAY-*nch*(r, -s)	that (*dem. adj., dem. pron.*)
jenseits	YANE-*ziles*	across (beyond)
"	"	beyond (out of reach of, *prep.*)
Jerusalem,*n.*	*yeh-*ROO-*zah-lem*	Jerusalem
Jesus	YAY-*zooss*	Jesus
jetzt	YETTST	now (*adv.*)
jeweilig	YAY-*vile-ick*	respective (*adj.*)
Joch,*n.*	YAW_KH	yoke (wooden frame)
Jodtinktur,*f.*	YOHT-*tink-toor*	iodine (antiseptic)
Jude,*m.*	YOO-*duh*	Jew (*n.*)
jüdisch	YÜ-*dish*	Jewish (*adj.*)
Jugend,*f.*	YOO-*g_ent*	youth (period of life)
"	"	youthfulness
jugendlich	YOO-*g_ent-likh*	youthful
Jugoslawien,*n.*	*yoo-go-*SLAHV-*yen*	Yugoslavia
jung	YOONNG	young (*adj.*)
Junge,*m.*	YOONNG-*uh*	boy
"	"	lad
jünger	YÜNNG-*ehr*	junior (younger)
Jungfrau,*f.*	YOONNG-*fr_ow*	maiden
"	"	virgin (*n.*)
Junggeselle,*m.*	YOONNG-*guh-zell-uh*	bachelor (unmarried man)
Jüngling,*m.*	YÜNNG-*ling*	youth (young man)
Justiz,*f.*	*yooss-*TEETS	justice (administration of law)
Juwel,*n.*	*yoo-*VALE	jewel
Kabel,*n.*	KAH-*bel*	cable (rope)
Kabelgramm,*n.*	KAH-*bel-grahmm*	cablegram
kabeln (1)	KAH-*bel'n*	cable, to
Kabine,*f.*	*kah-*BEE-*nuh*	cabin (of ship)
Kabinett,*n.*	*kah-bee-*NET	cabinet (*govt.*)
Kaffee,*m.*	KAHFF-*ay*	coffee

German	Pronunciation	English
Kaffeekanne,*f.*	KAHFF-*ay-kahn-nuh*	coffee pot
Käfer,*m.*	KAY-*fehr*	beetle
Käfig,*m.*	KAY-*fick*	cage
kahl	KAHL	bald (hairless)
Kairo,*n.*	KYE-*ro*	Cairo
Kaiser,*m.*	KYE-*zehr*	emperor
Kaiserin,*f.*	KYE-*zehr-inn*	empress
kaiserlich	KYE-*zehr-likh*	imperial
Kakao,*m.*	*kah-*KAH-*oh*	cocoa
Kalb,*n.*	KAHLLP	calf (animal)
Kalbsfleisch,*n.*	KAHLLPS-*fly_sh*	veal
Kalbskotelett,*n.*	KAHLLPS-*koht-let*	veal chop
Kalender,*m.*	*kah-*LEN-*dehr*	calendar
Kalkstein,*m.*	KAHLLK-*shtine*	limestone
Kalorie,*f.*	*kah-loh-*REE	calorie
kalt	KAHLLT	cold (*adj.*)
Kälte,*f.*	KELL-*tuh*	chill (coldness)
"	"	cold (low temperature)
Kamel,*n.*	*kah-*MAIL	camel
Kamera,*f.*	KAH-*muh-rah*	camera
Kamerad,*m.*	*kah-muh-*RAHT	comrade
"	"	pal
Kamin,*m.*	*kah-*MEEN	fireplace
Kamm,*m.*	KAHMM	comb (for hair)
Kampf,*m.*	KAHMMPF	combat
"	"	fight
(Wett)Kampf,*m.*	(*vet-*)KAHMMPF	contest
Kampfbahn,*f.*	KAHMMPF-*bahn*	stadium
kämpfen (1)	KEMP-*fen*	fight (contend), to
Kanada,*n.*	KAH-*nah-dah*	Canada
kanadisch	*kah-*NAH-*dish*	Canadian (*adj.*)
Kanal,*m.*	*kah-*NAHL	canal
"	"	channel (strait)
Kanarienvogel,*m.*	*kah-*NAHR-*yen-foh-gel*	canary
Kandidat,*m.*	*kahn-dee-*DAHT	candidate
Kaninchen,*n.*	*kah-*NEEN-*kh_en*	rabbit
Kanone,*f.*	*kah-*NO-*nuh*	cannon
Kanu,*n.*	*kah-*NOO	canoe
Kap,*n.*	KAHP	cape (headland)
Kapelle,*f.*	*kah-*PELL-*uh*	band (instrumental group)
"	"	chapel
Kapital,*n.*	*kah-pee-*TAHL	funds
Kapitän,*m.*	*kah-pee-*TAYN	captain (officer)
Kapitel,*n.*	*kah-*PIT-*tel*	chapter (of book)
Kapuze,*f.*	*kah-*POO-*tsuh*	hood (cowl)
Karachi,*n.*	*kah-*RAH-*tschee*	Karachi
Karfreitag,*m.*	*car-*FRY-*tahck*	Good Friday
Karikatur,*f.*	*kahr-ih-kah-*TOOR	cartoon (caricature)
karmesinrot	*kahr-muh-*ZEEN-*rote*	crimson
Karneval,*m.*	KAHR-*nuh-vahl*	carnival
Karren,*m.*	KAHRR-*en*	cart
Karte,*f.*	KAHRR-*tuh*	ticket (entitling card)
(Land)Karte,*f.*	(LAHNNT-)KAHRR-*tuh*	map
Kartoffel,*f.*	*kahr-*TAWFF-*fell*	potato (white)
Käse,*m.*	KAY-*zuh*	cheese
Kassierer,*m.*	*kahss-*SEER-*ehr*	cashier
Kastanie,*f.*	*kahss-*TAHN-*yeh*	chestnut (tree)
Katalog,*m.*	*kah-tah-*LOHK	catalogue
Katastrophe,*f.*	*kah-tah-*STROH-*fuh*	disaster
katholisch	*kah-*TOH-*lish*	Catholic (*adj.*)
Kätzchen,*n.*	KETTS-*kh_en*	kitten
Katze,*f.*	KAHT-*suh*	cat
kauen (1)	KOW-*en*	chew, to
Kauf,*m.*	KOWF	purchase (act of buying)
kaufen (1)	KOW-*fen*	buy, to
Käufer,*m.*	KOY-*fehr*	buyer
Kaufmann,*m.*	KOWF-*mahnn*	merchant
kaufmännisch	KOWF-*men-nish*	mercantile
Kaugummi,*m.*	KOW-*goomm-mee*	gum (chewing gum)
kaum	KOWM	hardly (barely)
kein	KINE	neither (*adj., pron.*)
"	"	no (not any, *adj.*)
keine	KINE-*uh*	none (*pron.*)
keiner	KINE-*ehr*	anyone (not...anyone)
Keller,*m.*	KELL-*ehr*	basement
"	"	cellar
Kellner,*m.*	KELL-*nehr*	waiter

German	Pronunciation	English
kennen (173)	KENN-*nen*	know (be acquainted with), to
kennenlernen (1)	KENN-*nen-lehr-nen*	meet (be introduced to), to
Kenntnis, *f.*	KENNT-*niss*	acquaintance (knowledge)
"	"	notice (attention)
(Er)Kenntnisse, *f. pl.*	(*ehr-*)KENNT-*niss-uh*	knowledge (information)
Kerbtier, *m.*	KEHRP-*teer*	bug
"	"	insect
Kerl, *m.*	KEHRL	chap
"	"	fellow (person)
"	"	guy
Kern, *m.*	KEHRN	kernel
Kerze, *f.*	KEHR-*tsuh*	candle
Kessel, *m.*	KESS-*el*	kettle
Kette, *f.*	KET-*tuh*	chain
(Berg)Kette, *f.*	(BEHRG-)KET-*tuh*	ridge (of mountains)
keuchen (1)	KOY-*kh_en*	gasp, to
		pant (puff), to
Keuchhusten, *m.*	KOYKH-*hoo_ss-ten*	whooping cough
Keule, *f.*	KOY-*luh*	club (cudgel)
keusch	KOYSH	chaste
Kiefer, *f.*	KEE-*fehr*	pine (tree)
Kiefer, *m.*	KEE-*fehr*	jaw
Kies, *m.*	KEESS	gravel
Kiesel, *m.*	KEE-*zell*	pebble
Kind, *n.*	KINNT	child
"	"	youngster
Kindergarten, *m.*	KINN-*dehr-gahr-ten*	kindergarten
Kinderlähmung, *f.*	KINN-*dehr-lay-moong*	infantile paralysis
Kinderstube, *f.*	KINN-*dehr-shtoo-buh*	nursery (children's room)
Kinderwagen, *m.*	KINN-*dehr-vah-gen*	carriage (baby buggy)
Kindheit, *f.*	KINNT-*hite*	childhood
Kindlein, *n.*	KINNT-*line*	baby
Kinn, *n.*	KINN	chin
Kino, *n.*	KEE-*no*	movies
Kirche, *f.*	KEERR_KH-*uh*	church
Kirchenlied, *n.*	KEERR_KH-*en-leet*	hymn (religious song)
Kirchspiel, *n.*	KEERR_KH-*shpeel*	parish
Kirchturm, *m.*	KEERR_KH-*toorm*	steeple
Kirsche, *f.*	KEERR-*shuh*	cherry (fruit)
Kissen, *n.*	KISS-*en*	cushion
"	"	pillow
Kiste, *f.*	KISS-*tuh*	chest (box)
kitzeln (1)	KITT-*sel'n*	tickle (touch lightly), to
Klage, *f.*	KLAH-*guh*	complaint
klagen (1)	KLAH-*gen*	complain, to
Klammern, *f. pl.*	KLAHMM-*ehrn*	parentheses
klappern (1)	KLAHPP-*ehrn*	rattle, to
Klaps, *m.*	KLAHPSS	pat (tap)
klar	KLAHR	clear
Klarinette, *f.*	*klahrr-ih-*NETT-*tuh*	clarinet
Klasse, *f.*	KLAHSS-*uh*	class (kind)
"	"	grade (school division)
Klassenzimmer, *n.*	KLAHSS-*en-tsim-mehr*	classroom
"	"	schoolroom
klassisch	KLAHSS-*ish*	classic (first-class, *adj.*)
klatschen (1)	KLAHTCH-*en*	clap (applaud), to
Klaue, *f.*	KLOW-*uh*	claw (of animal)
Klausel, *f.*	KLOW-*zel*	clause (stipulation)
Klavier, *n.*	*klah-*VEER	piano (*n.*)
kleben (1)	KLAY-*ben*	stick (adhere), to
Klecks, *m.*	KLEX	blot (stain)
Klee, *m.*	KLAY	clover
Kleid, *n.*	KLITE	dress (frock)
"	"	gown
Kleidung, *f.*	KLYE-*doong*	attire (apparel)
"	"	clothing
Kleidungsstück, *n.*	KLYE-*doongs-shtük*	garment
klein	KLINE	little (*adj.*)
"	"	small
Kleinigkeit, *f.*	KLYE-*nick-kite*	trifle
Kleister, *m.*	KLICE-*tehr*	paste (adhesive)
Klima, *n.*	KLEE-*mah*	climate (weather)

German	Pronunciation	English
Klimaanlage, *f.*	KLEE-*mah-ahnn-lah-guh*	air conditioning
Klinge, *f.*	KLINNG-*uh*	blade (cutting tool)
klingen (66)	KLINNG-*en*	ring (resound), to
Klinke, *f.*	KLINNG-*kuh*	latch
Klippe, *f.*	KLIP-*puh*	cliff
klirren (1)	KLEERR-*en*	clang, to
Klistier, *n.*	*kliss-*TEER	enema
klopfen (1)	KLAWPP-*fen*	knock (hit), to
"	"	tap (rap), to
Kloster, *n.*	KLOHSS-*tehr*	monastery
Klotz, *m.*	KLAWTSS	log (rough timber)
klug	KLOOK	clever
"	"	smart
Klumpen, *m.*	KLOOMM-*pen*	lump (shapeless piece)
knacken (1)	K_NAHCK-*en*	snap (crackle), to
knapp	K_NAHPP	scarce
Knappheit, *f.*	K_NAHPP-*hite*	scarcity
kneifen (67)	K_NIFE-*en*	pinch (squeeze), to
Knie, *n.*	K_NEE	knee
knien (1)	K_NEE-*en*	kneel, to
Kniff, *m.*	K_NIFF	trick (knack)
Knoblauch, *m.*	K_NAWP-*l_owkh*	garlic
Knöchel, *m.*	K_NÖCK-*el*	ankle
Knochen, *m.*	K_NAW-*kh_en*	bone
Knopf, *m.*	K_NAWPF	button
Knospe, *f.*	K_NAWSS-*puh*	bud (*bot.*)
Knoten, *m.*	K_NOH-*ten*	knot
Knuff, *m.*	K_NOOFF	punch (blow)
knurren (1)	K_NOORR-*ren*	growl, to
knusperig	K_NOOSS-*puh-rick*	crisp (brittle)
Koch, *m.*	KAWKH	cook
kochen (1)	KAW-*kh_en*	boil (bubble up), to
"	"	cook, to
Köder, *m.*	KÖ-*dehr*	bait (for animals)
Koffer, *m.*	KAWFF-*fehr*	trunk (baggage)
Kognak, *m.*	KAWNN-*yahck*	brandy
Kohl, *m.*	KOLE	cabbage
Kohle, *f.*	KOLE-*uh*	coal
Kohlenstoff, *m.*	KOLE-*en-shtawff*	carbon (*chem.*)
Kokosnuss, *m.*	KOH-*kohss-nooss*	coconut
Koks, *m.*	COKES	coke
kolonial	*koh-lohn-*YAHL	colonial
Kolonie, *f.*	*koh-loh-*NEE	colony
Kolumbien, *n.*	*koh-*LOOMM-*bee-en*	Colombia
komisch	KOH-*mish*	funny (comical)
Komma, *n.*	KAWMM-*ah*	comma
kommen (68)	KAWMM-*en*	come, to
kommerziell	*kawmm-ehrts-*YELL	commercial
Kommissar, *m.*	*kawmm-miss-*SAHR	commissioner (deputized person)
Kommode, *f.*	*kawmm-*MOH-*duh*	bureau (chest)
"	"	dresser
Kommunismus, *m.*	*kawmm-moo-*NISS-*mooss*	communism
Komödie, *f.*	*koh-*MÖD-*yuh*	comedy (comic play)
Kompanie, *f.*	*kawmm-pah-*NEE	company (*mil.*)
Kompass, *m.*	KAWMM-*pahss*	compass (magnetic instrument)
Kompliment, *n.*	*kawmm-plee-*MENT	compliment
komponieren (1)	*kawmm-poh-*NEE-*ren*	compose, to (*mus.*)
Kompromiss, *m.*	*kawmm-pro-*MISS	compromise (mutual concessions)
Konferenz, *f.*	*kawnn-fuh-*RENTS	conference (meeting)
Kongress, *m.*	*kawng-*GRESS	congress (legislature)
König, *m.*	KÖ-*nig*	king
Königin, *f.*	KÖ-*nig-in*	queen
königlich	KÖ-*nig-likh*	regal
"	"	royal
Königreich, *n.*	KÖ-*nig-rye_kh*	kingdom
Konjunktur, *f.*	*kawnn-yoonk-*TOOR	boom (*bus.*)
konkret	*kawnn-*KRATE	concrete (real)
Konkurrent, *m.*	*kawnn-koo-*RENT	competitor (*bus.*)
"	"	rival
Konkurrenz, *f.*	*kawnn-koo-*RENTS	competition (*bus.*)
können (164)	KÖNN-*en*	can (*v.*)
konnte (164)	KAWNN-*tuh*	could (*v.*)
konservativ	*kawnn-zehr-vah-*TEEF	conservative (cautious)

German	Pronunciation	English
Konstitution, *f.*	*kawnn-stee-toots-*YOHN	constitution (nature)
Konsul, *m.*	KAWNN-*zooll*	consul
Konterbande, *f.*	*kawnn-tehr-*BAHNN-*duh*	contraband
Konto, *n.*	KAWNN-*toh*	account (bank account)
Kontoinhaber, *m.*	KAWNN-*toh-inn-hah-behr*	depositor (*fin.*)
Kontrolle, *f.*	*kawnn-*TRAWLL-*uh*	check (examination)
"	"	inspection (scrutiny)
konzentrieren (1)	*kawnn-tsenn-*TREE-*ren*	concentrate (make converge), to
Konzert, *n.*	*kawnn-*TSEHRRT	concert (musical performance)
Kopenhagen, *n.*	*koh-pen-*HAH-*gen*	Copenhagen
Kopf, *m.*	KAWPPF	head (*anat.*)
Kopfsprung machen, einen (1)	*eye-nen* KAWPPF-*shproong mah_kh-en*	dive, to
Kopfweh, *n.*	KAWPPF-*vay*	headache
Kopie, *f.*	*kow-*PEE	copy
"	"	duplicate (*n.*)
Korb, *m.*	KAWRP	basket
Korbball, *m.*	KAWRP-*bahll*	basketball
Kork, *m.*	KAWRK	cork (stopper)
Körper, *m.*	KÖR-*pehr*	body (*anat.*)
körperlich	KÖR-*pehr-likh*	physical (material)
Korporal, *m.*	*core-po-*RAHL	corporal (*mil.*)
Korrespondent, *m.*	*kaw-res-pawnn-*DENNT	correspondent (letter writer)
korrespondieren (1)	*kaw-res-pawnn-*DEE-*ren*	correspond with (write to), to
Korsett, *n.*	*kor-*SET	girdle (corset)
Kostarika, *n.*	*coast-ah-*REE-*kuh*	Costa Rica
kostbar	KAWSST-*bar*	costly
"	"	precious
kosten (1)	KAWSS-*ten*	cost, to
"	"	taste (sample), to
Kosten, *pl.*	KAWSS-*ten*	cost (price)
köstlich	KÖST-*likh*	delicious
Kostüm, *n.*	*kawss-*TÜM	costume
"	"	suit, woman's
Krach, *m.*	KRAH_KH	crash (loud noise)
Kraft, *f.*	KRAHFFT	force (power)
"	"	strength
"	"	vigor
kräftig	KREHFF-*tick*	sturdy
"	"	vigorous
Kragen, *m.*	KRAH-*gen*	collar
Krähe, *f.*	KRAY-*uh*	crow (bird)
Kralle, *f.*	KRAHLL-*uh*	claw (of bird)
Krampf, *m.*	KRAHMMPF	cramp (*med.*)
krank	KRAHNNK	ill
"	"	sick (ailing)
Kranke, *m.*, *f.*	KRAHNNG-*kuh*	patient (invalid)
Krankenhaus, *n.*	KRAHNNG-*ken-house*	hospital
Krankensaal, *m.*	KRAHNNG-*ken-zahl*	ward (sickroom)
Krankenschwester, *f.*	KRAHNNG-*ken-shvess-tehr*	nurse (medical assistant)
Krankenwagen, *m.*	KRAHNNG-*ken-vah-gen*	ambulance
Krankheit, *f.*	KRAHNNK-*hite*	disease
"	"	illness
"	"	sickness
Kranz, *m.*	KRAHNNTS	wreath
Kräuselung, *f.*	KROY-*zel-oong*	ripple
kratzen (1)	KRAHTT-*sen*	scratch, to
Kraut, *n.*	KR_OWT	herb
Krawatte, *f.*	*krah-*VAHTT-*tuh*	tie (necktie)
Krebs, *m.*	KRAYBSS	cancer
"	"	crab (shellfish)
Kredit, *m.*	*kray-*DEET	credit (*bus.*)
Kreide, *f.*	KRYE-*duh*	chalk
Kreis, *m.*	KRICE	circle (*geom.*)
"	"	sphere (range)
kreischen (1)	KRYE-*shen*	scream, to
"	"	shriek, to
kreisförmig	KRICE-*för-mick*	circular (*adj.*)
Kreuz, *n.*	KROYTS	cross (crucifix)
kreuzen (1)	KROYTS-*sen*	cross (crossbreed), to
Kreuzer, *m.*	CROY-*tsehr*	cruiser (ship)
Kreuzung, *f.*	KROYTS-*soong*	crossing (intersection)
kriechen (68)	KREE-*kh_en*	crawl (creep), to
Krieg, *m.*	KREEK	war
Kriegsmarine, *f.*	KREEKS-*mah-*REE-*nuh*	navy (*n.*)
Kriminal-...	*krimm-ee-*NAHL-...	criminal (*adj.*)

German	Pronunciation	English
Krise, *f.*	KREE-*zuh*	crisis
Kristall, *m.*	*kriss-*TAHLL	crystal (*min.*)
Kritik, *f.*	*krih-*TEEK	criticism (judgment)
Kritiker, *m.*	KREE-*tick-ehr*	critic
Krone, *f.*	KROH-*nuh*	crown (headdress)
krönen (1)	KRÖN-*en*	crown, to
Kröte, *f.*	KRÖ-*tuh*	toad
Krücke, *f.*	KRÜCK-*kuh*	crutch
Krug, *m.*	KROO_K	jar (vessel)
"	"	jug
"	"	pitcher (container)
Krume, *f.*	KROO-*muh*	crumb
krumm	KROOMM	crooked
Krüppel, *m.*	KRÜPP-*el*	cripple
Kruste, *f.*	KROOS-*tuh*	crust
Kuba, *n.*	COO-*bah*	Cuba
Küche, *f.*	KÜ-*kh_uh*	kitchen
Kuchen, *m.*	KOO-*kh_en*	cake (dessert)
Kuckuck, *m.*	KOOCK-*koock*	cuckoo (bird)
Kugel, *f.*	KOO-*gel*	bullet
"	"	sphere (globe)
Kugelschreiber, *m.*	KOO-*gel-shrye-behr*	ball-point pen
Kuh, *f.*	KOO	cow
kühl	KÜL	chilly
"	"	cool (having low temperature)
kühlen (1)	KÜ-*len*	cool (make less hot), to
kühn	KÜN	bold (courageous)
Kultur, *f.*	*kooll-*TOOR	civilization
"	"	culture (stage of civilization)
Kummer, *m.*	KOOMM-*ehr*	grief
"	"	sorrow (sadness)
kümmern, sich (1)	*zikh* KÜMM-*ehrn*	care (be concerned), to
Kunde, *m.*	KOONN-*duh*	customer (buyer)
"	"	patron
(zu)künftig	(TSOO-)KÜNNF-*tick*	future (*adj.*)
Kunst, *f.*	KOONST	art
Künstler, *m.*	KÜNST-*lehr*	artist
künstlerisch	KÜNST-*lehr-ish*	artistic (tasteful)
künstlich	KÜNNST-*likh*	artificial (synthetic)
Kunstseide, *f.*	KOONST-*zye-duh*	rayon
Kunststoff, *m.*	KOONNST-*shtawff*	plastic (*n.*)
Kupfer, *n.*	KOOPP-*fehr*	copper
Kuppel, *f.*	KOOPP-*ell*	dome (cupola)
Kupplung, *f.*	KOOPP-*loong*	clutch (automotive device)
Kurator, *m.*	*koor-*AH-*tor*	curator
Kurort, *m.*	KOOR-*ort*	resort (spa)
Kurs, *m.*	KOORRSS	conversion rate (*bus.*)
"	"	rate (exchange)
Kurve, *f.*	KOOR-*vuh*	curve
kurz	KOORTS	brief (fleeting)
"	"	compact
"	"	short
Kuss, *m.*	KOOSS	kiss
küssen	KÜSS-*en*	kiss, to
Küste, *f.*	KÜSS-*tuh*	coast (seaboard)
Laboratorium, *n.*	*lah-boh-rah-*TOR-*yoomm*	laboratory
Lächeln, *n.*	LEH_KH-*el'n*	smile
lächeln (1)	LEH_KH-*el'n*	smile, to
lachen (1)	LAH_KH-*en*	laugh, to
lächerlich	LEH_KH-*ehr-likh*	ridiculous
Lachs, *m.*	LAH_KHS	salmon
Laden, *m.*	LAH-*den*	shop
"	"	store
laden (70)	LAH-*den*	charge, to (*elec.*)
"	"	load (fill), to
Ladentisch, *m.*	LAH-*den-tish*	counter (table)
Ladung, *f.*	LAH-*doong*	cargo
Lage, *f.*	LAH-*guh*	location (place)
"	"	position
"	"	site
"	"	situation (circumstances)
Lager, *n.*	LAH-*gehr*	camp (encampment, *mil.*)
Lagerhaus, *n.*	LAH-*gehr-howss*	warehouse
lagern (1)	LAHG-*ehrn*	store (accumulate), to
Lagerung, *f.*	LAH-*guh-roong*	storage
lahm	LAHM	lame

German	Pronunciation	English
Lähmung,*f.*	LAME-*oong*	paralysis
Laib,*m.*	LIPE	loaf
Lamm,*n.*	LAHMM	lamb
Lampe,*f.*	LAHMM-*puh*	lamp
Land,*n.*	LAHNNT	country
"	"	land (ground)
landen (1)	LAHNN-*den*	land, to
Landenge,*f.*	LAHNND-*eng-uh*	isthmus
ländlich	LEND-*likh*	rural
Landschaft,*f.*	LAHNNT-*shahfft*	land (region)
"	"	landscape (scenery)
Landstrasse,*f.*	LAHNNT-*shtrah-suh*	highway
Landwirtschaft,*f.*	LAHNNT-*veert-shahfft*	agriculture
lang	LAHNNG	long
Länge,*f.*	LENG-*uh*	length
langsam	LAHNNG-*zahm*	slow (not fast)
Lang(e)weile,*f.*	LAHNG(-*uh*)-*vye-luh*	boredom
langweilig	LAHNNG-*vile-ick*	dull (boring)
Lärm,*m.*	LAIRM	fuss (ado)
"	"	noise (din)
Larve,*f.*	LAHR-*vuh*	mask (face covering)
lassen (71)	LAHSS-*senn*	let (permit), to
(übrig)lassen	(Ü-*brick*-)LAHSS-*senn*	leave (let remain), to
Last,*f.*	LAHSST	burden
"	"	load
Laster,*n.*	LAHSS-*tehr*	vice (moral fault)
Lästigkeit,*f.*	LEHSS-*tick-kite*	inconvenience
Lastwagen,*m.*	LAHSST-*vah-gen*	truck (automobile)
lateinisch	lah-TINE-*ish*	Latin (*adj.*)
Laterne,*f.*	lah-TEHR-*nuh*	lantern
Laufbahn,*f.*	L_OWF-*bahn*	career
laufend	L_OWF-*ent*	current (contemporary, *adj.*)
Laune,*f.*	L_OW-*nuh*	temper (mood)
laut	L_OWT	aloud
"	"	loud (resounding)
Laut,*m.*	L_OWT	sound (noise)
Leben,*n.*	LAY-*ben*	life
leben (1)	LAY-*ben*	live (be alive), to
Leben bleiben, am (1)	*ahmm* LAY-*ben bly-ben*	survive (remain alive), to
lebendig	*lay*-BEN-*dick*	alive
"	"	live (*adj.*)
Lebensgeschichte, *f.*	LAY-*benss-guh-shikh-tuh*	biography
Lebensmittelgeschäft,*n.*	LAY-*bens-mit-tell-guh-shefft*	grocery
Lebensunterhalt, *m.*	LAY-*benss-oonn-tehr-hahllt*	support (livelihood)
Leber,*f.*	LAY-*behr*	liver (*anat.*)
lebhaft	LAPE-*hahfft*	lively (*adj.*)
"	"	vivid
lecken (1)	LECK-*en*	lick (lap), to
Leder,*n.*	LAY-*dehr*	leather (*n.*)
ledig	LAY-*dick*	single (unmarried)
leer	LAIR	blank (unmarked)
"	"	empty
(ent)leeren (1)	(*ent*-)LAIR-*en*	empty (remove contents of), to
leerstehend	LAIR-*shtay-ent*	vacant (untenanted)
legen (1)	LAY-*gen*	lay (put down), to
"	"	place, to
Legende,*f.*	*lay*-GENN-*duh*	legend (story)
Legierung,*f.*	*luh*-GEER-*oong*	alloy (metal)
Lehrbuch,*n.*	LAIR-*boo_kh*	textbook
Lehre,*f.*	LAIR-*uh*	doctrine
lehren (1)	LAY-*ren*	teach, to
Lehrer,*m.*	LAY-*rehr*	teacher
Lehrkörper,*m.*	LAIR-*kör-pehr*	faculty (teaching staff)
Lehrling,*m.*	LAIR-*ling*	apprentice (trade student)
Leibesübungen,*f. pl.*	LYE-*bess-ü-boong-en*	exercise (physical exertion)
Leiche,*f.*	LYE-*kh_uh*	corpse
leicht	LYE_KHT	easy (not difficult)
"	"	light (of little weight)
Leichtigkeit,*f.*	LYE_KH-*tick-kite*	ease (effortlessness)
leiden (73)	LYE-*den*	suffer (undergo), to
Leiden,*n.*	LYE-*den*	suffering
Leidenschaft,*f.*	LYE-*den-shahfft*	passion (emotion)

German	Pronunciation	English
leidenschaftlich	LYE-*den-shahfft-likh*	passionate
leidlich	LITE-*likh*	decent (fairly good)
"	"	fair (passable)
(ver)leihen (74)	(*fehr*-)LYE-*en*	lend, to
Leihhaus,*n.*	LYE-*howss*	pawnshop
Leim,*m.*	LIME	glue
Leine,*f.*	LYE-*nuh*	line (cord)
Leinen,*n.*	LINE-*en*	linen (fabric)
Leinwand,*f.*	LINE-*vahnnt*	canvas (cloth)
"	"	screen (for movies)
leisten, sich (1)	*zikh* LICE-*ten*	afford (have the means), to
Leistung,*f.*	LICE-*toong*	feat
leistungsfähig	LICE-*toongs-fay-ick*	competent (able)
"	"	efficient (producing desired results)
leiten (1)	LYE-*ten*	conduct, to
"	"	direct, to
"	"	head (lead), to
"	"	manage (administer), to
Leiter,*f.*	LYE-*tehr*	ladder
(Betriebs)Leiter, *m.*	(*buh*-TREEPS-)LYE-*tehr*	manager (administrator)
Leitung,*f.*	LYE-*toong*	management (administration)
Leopard,*m.*	*lay-oh*-PART	leopard
Lerche,*f.*	LEHR-*kh_uh*	lark (bird)
lernen (1)	LEHR-*nen*	learn (acquire knowledge), to
lesen (75)	LAY-*zen*	read, to
Leser,*m.*	LAY-*zehr*	reader
letzte(r, -s)	LETTS-*tuh*(*r, -s*)	last (final, *adj.*)
letzten, am	AHMM LETTS-*ten*	last (most recently, *adv.*)
letztere	LETTS-*teh-ruh*	latter (second of two, *adj.*)
Leuchtpetroleum, *n.*	LOYKHT-*peh-troh-lee-oom*	kerosene
leugnen (1)	LOYG-*nen*	deny (contradict), to
Leute,*f.pl.*	LOY-*tuh*	people (persons)
Leutnant,*m.*	LOYT-*nahnt*	lieutenant
Leutnant zur See, *m.*	LOYT-*nahnnt tsoor* ZAY	ensign (*Nav.*)
liberal	*lee-buh*-RAHL	liberal (*polit., adj.*)
Licht,*n.*	LIKHT	light (illumination)
lieb	LEEP	dear (beloved, *adj.*)
Liebchen,*n.*	LEEP-*kh_en*	sweetheart
Liebe,*f.*	LEE-*buh*	love
lieben (1)	LEE-*ben*	love, to
liebenswürdig	LEE-*bens-vür-dick*	gracious
lieblich	LEEB-*likh*	adorable
Liebling,*m.*	LEEB-*ling*	darling
Lieblings-...	LEEB-*lingss-...*	favorite (*adj.*)
Lied,*n.*	LEET	song
Lieferant,*m.*	*lee-feh*-RAHNNT	supplier (*bus.*)
liefern (1)	LEE-*fehrn*	furnish (supply), to
(über)liefern	(*ü-behr*-)LEE-*fehrn*	deliver (hand over), to
liegen (76)	LEE-*gen*	lie (be located), to
"	"	lie (be prone), to
Likör,*m.*	*lee*-KÖR	liqueur
Lilie,*f.*	LEEL-*yuh*	lily
Lima,*n.*	LEE-*mah*	Lima
Limette,*f.*	*lee*-MET	lime (fruit)
Limonade,*f.*	*lee-moh*-NAH-*duh*	lemonade
Lineal,*n.*	*leen*-YAHL	ruler (measuring instrument)
Linie,*f.*	LEEN-*yuh*	line (mark)
Linienschiff,*n.*	LEEN-*yen-shiff*	battleship
link	LINK	left (*adj.*)
Linke,*f.*	LING-*kuh*	left (*n.*)
links	LINKS	left (*adv.*)
Linoleum,*n.*	*lee*-NOH-*lee-oom*	linoleum
Lippe,*f.*	LIP-*puh*	lip (*anat.*)
Lippenstift,*m.*	LIP-*en-shtifft*	lipstick
Liste,*f.*	LISS-*tuh*	list
listig	LISS-*lick*	cunning (sly)
literarisch	*lih-tehr*-AHR-*rish*	literary
Literatur,*f.*	*lih-tuh-rah*-TOOR	literature (belles-lettres)
Lithographie,*f.*	*lih-toh-grah*-FEE	lithography
Lob,*n.*	LOHP	praise
loben (1)	LOH-*ben*	praise, to
Loch,*n.*	LAWKH	hole (cavity)
Locke,*f.*	LAWCKK-*uh*	curl (ringlet)
locker	LAWCKK-*ehr*	loose (unbound)

German	Pronunciation	English	German	Pronunciation	English
lodern (1)	LOH-*dehrn*	blaze (burn brightly), to	Manschette,*f.*	*mahnn*-SHETT-*uh*	cuff (of sleeve)
Lohn,*m.*	LOHN	wages	Mantel,*m.*	MAHNN-*tell*	coat
Lokomotive,*f.*	*loh-kuh-moh*-TEE-*vuh*	engine	"	"	overcoat
"	"	locomotive	Märchen,*n.*	MARE-*kh en*	fairy tale
Lokomotivführer, *m.*	*loh-kuh-moh*-TEEF-*fü-rehr*	engineer (railroad engineman)	Marke,*f.*	MAHRR-*kuh*	brand (trade mark)
London,*n.*	LAWN-*done*	London	"	"	stamp, postage
löschen (1)	LÖSH-*en*	quench, to	Markt,*m.*	MAHRRKT	market (trading center)
Lösegeld,*n.*	LÖ-*zuh-gellt*	ransom (*n.*)	Margarine,*f.*	*mahr-guh*-REE-*nuh*	margarine
lösen (1)	LÖ-*zen*	solve, to	Marmelade,*f.*	*mahr-muh*-LAH-*duh*	jam (preserve)
losgehen (46)	LOHSS-*gay-en*	start (set out), to	Marmor,*m.*	MAHR-*more*	marble (mineral)
loskaufen (1)	LOHSS-*kow-fen*	redeem (buy back), to	marschieren (1)	*mahr*-SHEE-*ren*	march, to
			Maschine,*f.*	*mah*-SHEE-*nuh*	machine
Lösung,*f.*	LÖ-*zoong*	solution (solving)	Maschinenschrei-ber,*m.*	*mah*-SHEE-*nen-shry-behr*	typist
Löwe,*m.*	LÖ-*vuh*	lion			
Löwenzahn,*m.*	LÖ-*venn-tsahn*	dandelion	Maschinerie,*f.*	*ham-shee-nuh*-REE	machinery
Lücke,*f.*	LÜCK-*kuh*	gap	Masern,*pl.*	MAH-*zehrn*	measles
Luft,*f.*	LOOFFT	air	Mass,*n.*	MAHSS	measure (dimensions)
"	"	atmosphere			
Luftangriff,*m.*	LOOFFT-*ahnn-griff*	air raid	mässig	MACE-*ick*	moderate (not extreme)
Lüftchen,*n.*	LÜFFT-*kh en*	breeze			
Luftdruckmesser, *m.*	LOOFFT-*droock-mess-sehr*	barometer	Masse,*f.*	MAHSS-*uh*	mass (matter)
			Masstab,*m.*	MAHSS-*shtahp*	scale
Luftpost,*f.*	LOOFFT-*pawsst*	airmail	Mast,*m.*	MAHSST	mast
Lüge,*f.*	LÜ-*guh*	lie	Mathematik,*f.*	*mah-tuh-mah*-TEEK	mathematics
lügen (77)	LÜ-*gen*	lie (prevaricate), to	Matratze,*f.*	*mah*-TRAHT-*suh*	mattress
Lügner,*m.*	LÜG-*nehr*	liar	Mätresse,*f.*	*may*-TRESS-*suh*	mistress (paramour)
Lumpen,*m.*	LOOMM-*pen*	rag (piece of cloth)	Matrose,*m.*	*mahtt*-ROH-*zuh*	sailor
Lunge,*f.*	LOONNG-*uh*	lung	matt	MAHTT	faint (dim, *adj.*)
Lungenentzün-dung,*f.*	LOONNG-*en-ent-tsün-doong*	pneumonia	Mauer,*f.*	M_OW-*ehr*	wall (outside)
			Maulesel,*m.*	M_OWL-*ay-zel*	mule
Lust,*f.*	LOOSST	desire	Maulwurf,*m.*	M_OWL-*voorrf*	mole (animal)
lustig	LOOSS-*tick*	gay (merry)			
"	"	jolly (*adj.*)	Maurer,*m.*	M_OW-*rehr*	mason (stonelayer)
Lustigkeit,*f.*	LOOSS-*tick-kite*	mirth	Maus,*f.*	MOUSE	mouse
Luxus,*m.*	LOOX-*ooss*	luxury	Mechaniker,*m.*	*muh*-KAHN-*ee-kehr*	mechanic
machen (1)	MAH_KH-*en*	do, to	mechanisch	*muh*-KAH-*nish*	mechanical
"	"	make, to	Medizin,*f.*	*may-dih*-TSEEN	medicine (medical science)
machen (1)	MAH_KH-*en*	render (cause to become), to	Meer,*n.*	MAIR	sea
			Mehl,*n.*	MAIL	flour
Macht,*f.*	MAH_KHT	might (*n.*)	mehr	MAIR	more (*adj.*)
"	"	power (authority)	mehrere	MAY-*ruh-ruh*	several (a few, *adj.*)
mächtig	MEH_KH-*tick*	mighty	Mehrheit,*f.*	MAIR-*hite*	majority (greater number)
"	"	powerful			
Mädchen,*n.*	MAID-*kh en*	girl	Mehrzahl-...	MAIR-*tsahl*-...	plural (*adj.*)
"	"	lass	mein	MINE	mine (*poss. pron.*)
Mädchenname,*m.*	MAID-*kh en-nah-muh*	maiden name	"	"	my
Madrid,*n.*	*mah*-DREED	Madrid	Meineid,*m.*	MINE-*ite*	perjury
Magen,*m.*	MAH-*gen*	stomach	meinen (1)	MY-*nen*	mean (have in mind), to
mager	MAH-*gehr*	lean			
"	"	thin (not fat)	"	"	reckon (consider), to
Magie,*f.*	*mah*-G_EE	magic (*n.*)	Meinung,*f.*	MINE-*oong*	mind (opinion)
Magnet,*m.*	*mahg*-NATE	magnet	"	"	opinion
			Meissel,*f.*	MY-*sel*	chisel (tool)
mahlen (1)	MAH-*len*	grind (crush), to	meist	MICE_T	most (almost all, *adj.*)
Mähne,*f.*	MAY-*nuh*	mane (of horse)			
Mahlzeit,*f.*	MAHL-*tsite*	meal (repast)	Meiste, (das),*n.*	(*dahss*) MICE-*tuh*	most (*n.*)
Mais,*m.*	MICE	corn (maize)	meisten, am	*ahm* MICE-*ten*	most (*adv.*)
Majestät,*f.*	*mah-yes*-TATE	majesty	meistens	MICE-*tenss*	mostly
Makler,*m.*	MAHK-*lehr*	broker (*bus.*)	Meister,*m.*	MICE-*tehr*	champion
Maklergebühr,*f.*	MAHK-*lehr-guh*-BÜR	brokerage (fee)	"	"	master (great artist)
mal	MAHLL	by (*prep., math.*)	Meisterwerk,*n.*	MICE-*tehr-vehrk*	classic (first-class work)
malen (1)	MAHL-*en*	paint (represent), to			
Maler,*m.*	MAHL-*ehr*	painter (artist)	Melasse,*f.*	*may*-LAHSS-*suh*	molasses
malerisch	MAH-*luh-rish*	picturesque	melden (1)	MELL-*den*	announce, to
manche	MAHNN-*kh eh*	some (certain, *adj.*)	Meldung,*f.*	MELL-*doong*	announcement
"	"	some (certain ones, *pron.*)	"	"	dispatch (communication)
manchmal	MAHNNKH-*mahl*	sometimes			
Mandel,*f.*	MAHNN-*del*	almond	Melodie,*f.*	*may-loh*-DEE	tune (melody)
Mandelentzün-dung,*f.*	MAHNN-*del-ent*-TSÜNN-*doong*	tonsillitis	Menge,*f.*	MENNG-*uh*	crowd
			"	"	multitude
Mangel,*m.*	MAHNNG-*el*	defect (flaw)	"	"	quantity (amount)
"	"	lack (deficiency)	Menschheit,*f.*	MENNSH-*hite*	humanity
"	"	shortage	"	"	mankind
"	"	want	menschlich	MENNSH-*likh*	human (*adj.*)
Manieren,*pl.*	*mahnn*-EAR-*en*	manners (polite behavior)	merken (1)	MAIR-*kenn*	note (perceive), to
			Merkmal,*n.*	MAIRK-*mahl*	mark (symbol)
Mann,*m.*	MAHNN	husband	merkwürdig	MAIRK-*vür-dick*	remarkable (extraordinary)
"	"	man			
Männchen,*n.*	MEHN-*kh en*	male (*zool., n.*)	Merkzettel,*m.*	MAIRK-*tset-tell*	memorandum
mannhaft	MAHNN-*hahfft*	manly	Messe,*f.*	MESS-*uh*	mass (*rel.*)
Mannigfaltigkeit, *f.*	MAHNN-*ick-fahll-tick-kite*	variety (diversity)	messen (79)	MESS-*en*	measure (find size of), to
männlich	MEHN-*likh*	male (*adj.*)	Messer,*n.*	MESS-*ehr*	knife
"	"	masculine	Messing,*n.*	MESS-*ing*	brass (metal, *n.*)
Mannschaft,*f.*	MAHNN-*shahfft*	crew	Metall,*n.*	*may*-TAHLL	metal (*n.*)
"	"	team (in sports)	Metallwaren,*pl.*	*may*-TAHL-*vahr-en*	hardware
			Methode,*f.*	*may*-TOH-*duh*	method

German	Pronunciation	English	German	Pronunciation	English
Mexiko,*n.*	MEX-*ee-ko*	Mexico	Morgen,*m.*	MOR-*gen*	morning
"	"	Mexico City	morgen	MOR-*gen*	tomorrow
mexikanisch	*mex-ee-*KAH-*nish*	Mexican (*adj.*)	Morgendämme-rung,*f.*	MOR-*gen-*DEM-*muh-roong*	dawn (daybreak)
mich	MIKH	me	Mörtel,*m.*	MÖR-*tel*	plaster (wall coating)
"	"	myself	Moskau,*n.*	MAWSS-*kòw*	Moscow
Miete,*f.*	MEE-*tuh*	rent (payment)	Moskito,*m.*	*moss-*KEE-*toh*	mosquito
mieten (1)	MEE-*ten*	lease (hold by lease), to	Motor,*m.*	MOH-*tor*	engine
"	"	rent (pay rent for), to	"	"	motor
Mieter,*m.*	MEE-*tehr*	tenant	Motorhaube,*f.*	MOH-*tor-how-buh*	hood (*auto.*)
Milch,*f.*	MILL_KH	milk	Motte,*f.*	MAWT-*tuh*	moth
militärisch	*mill-ee-*TARE-*ish*	military (*adj.*)	müde	MÜ-*duh*	tired
Minderheit,*f.*	MINN-*dehr-hite*	minority (smaller number)	"	"	weary
minderwertig	MINN-*dehr-vare-tick*	inferior (mediocre)	müde werden (181)	MÜ-*duh* VAIR-*den*	tire (become weary), to
Mine,*f.*	MEE-*nuh*	mine (explosive)	Mühe,*f.*	MÜ-*uh*	trouble (exertion)
Mineral,*n.*	*mee-nuh-*RAHL	mineral	Müller,*m.*	MÜLL-*lehr*	miller
Minister,*m.*	*mee-*NISS-*tehr*	minister (cabinet member)	multiplizieren (1)	*mooll-tee-plee-*TSEE-*ren*	multiply, to (*arith.*)
Minute,*f.*	*mee-*NOO-*tuh*	minute (unit of time)	Mund,*m.*	MOONNT	mouth (*anat.*)
mir	MEER	me	mündlich	MÜNND-*likh*	oral (spoken)
"	"	myself	Münze,*f.*	MÜNT-*suh*	coin
mischen (1)	MISH-*en*	blend (make combine), to	murmeln (1)	MOORR-*mel'n*	murmur, to
"	"	mix (make blend), to	murren (1)	MOORR-*ren*	mutter (mumble), to
Mischung,*f.*	MISH-*oong*	blend	Museum,*n.*	*moo-*ZAY-*oomm*	museum
"	"	mixture	Muskatnuss,*f.*	*mooss-*KAHT-*nooss*	nutmeg
missbrauchen (1)	*miss-*BROW-*kh_en*	abuse (misuse), to	Musik,*f.*	*moo-*ZEEK	music
Missionar,*m.*	*miss-yo-*NAHR	missionary	musikalisch	*moo-zee-*KAH-*lish*	musical
missliche Lage,*f.*	MISS-*leekh-uh* LAH-*guh*	plight (predicament)	Musiker,*m.*	MOO-*zee-kehr*	musician
misslingen (47)	*miss-*LING-*en*	fail (be unsuccessful), to	Muskel,*m.*	MOOSS-*kel*	muscle
Misslingen,*n.*	*miss-*LING-*en*	failure (lack of success)	Musse,*f.*	MOO-*suh*	leisure
mit	MITT	with	müssen (166)	MÜSS-*en*	must (*v.*)
Miteigentümer,*m.*	MITT-*eye-gen-tü-mehr*	co-owner (*bus.*)	müssig	MÜ-*sick*	idle (not busy)
Mitgefühl,*n.*	MITT-*guh-fül*	sympathy (compassion)	"	"	unemployed
Mitglied,*n.*	MITT-*gleet*	member (one of a group)	Müssiggang,*m.*	MÜ-*sick-gahng*	idleness (inactivity)
Mitleid,*n.*	MITT-*lite*	pity (compassion)	Muster,*n.*	MOOSS-*tehr*	model (exemplar)
Mittag,*m.*	MITT-*tahk*	noon	"	"	pattern (design)
Mittagessen,*n.*	MITT-*tahg-ess-senn*	dinner	"	"	sample
"	"	lunch (midday meal)	Mut,*m.*	MOOT	courage
Mitte,*f.*	MITT-*tuh*	middle (center)	"	"	morale
mitteilen (1)	MITT-*tile-en*	convey (communicate), to	Mutter,*f.*	MOOTT-*ehr*	mother
Mitteilung,*f.*	MITT-*tile-oong*	account (report)	(Schrauben)Mutter,*f.*	(SHR_OW-*ben-*)MOOTT-*ehr*	nut (*mech.*)
"	"	communication	Mütze,*f.*	MÜTT-*suh*	cap (hat)
"	"	message	Mythos,*n.*	MÜ-*tawss*	myth (legend)
Mittel,*n.*	MITT-*tel*	agency (instrumentality)	nach	NAH_KH	according to (in accordance with)
"	"	means (method)	"	"	after (*prep.*)
"	"	medium	"	"	to (indicating destination, *prep.*)
Mittelländisches Meer,*n.*	MITT-*el-len-dish-es* MARE	Mediterranean Sea	nachahmen (1)	NAH_KH-*ah-men*	copy, to
mittelbar	MITT-*tel-bar*	indirect	"	"	imitate, to
Mittelpunkt,*m.*	MITT-*tel-poonk_t*	center	Nachbar,*m.*	NAH_KH-*bar*	neighbor
mitten in	MITT-*ten inn*	amid	nachdem	NAH_KH-*dame*	after (*conj.*)
			nachdenken (172)	NAH_KH-*deng-ken*	meditate (reflect), to
Mitternacht,*f.*	MITT-*tehr-nahkht*	midnight	Nachdenken,*n.*	NAH_KH-*deng-ken*	thought (contemplation)
Mitwirkung,*f.*	MIT-*veer-koong*	cooperation	nachdenklich	NAH_KH-*dengk-likh*	thoughtful (reflective)
Möbel,*n.pl.*	MÖ-*bel*	furniture			
Mode,*f.*	MOH-*duh*	fashion (current style)	Nachfrage,*f.*	NAH_KH-*frah-guh*	demand (*econ.*)
Modell,*n.*	*moh-*DELL	model (small copy)	"	"	inquiry (question)
modern	*moh-*DEHRN	modern	nachfragen (1)	NAH_KH-*frah-gen*	inquire (ask), to
mögen (165)	MÖ-*gen*	may (*v.*)	nachgeben (43)	NAH_KH-*gay-ben*	yield (give in), to
"	"	might(*v.*)			
mögen, nicht	NIKHT MÖ-*gen*	dislike, to	nachgehend	NAH_KH-*gay-ent*	slow (tardy)
möglich	MÖG-*likh*	possible	nachher	NAH_KH-*hehr*	afterward (later)
Möglichkeit,*f.*	MÖG-*likh-kite*	possibility	Nachkomme,*m.*	NAH_KH-*kawmm-muh*	descendant (offspring)
Mohrrübe,*f.*	MORE-*rü-buh*	carrot	nachlässig	NAH_KH-*less-ick*	careless (negligent)
Molkerei,*f.*	*mawl-kuh-*RYE	dairy	Nachmittag,*m.*	NAH_KH-*mit-tahk*	afternoon
Monarch,*m.*	*moh-*NAHRKH	monarch	Nachmittagsvorstellung,*f.*	NAH_KH-*mit-tahks-for-shtell-oong*	matinee (theater performance)
Monat,*m.*	MOH-*naht*	month	Nachricht,*f.*	NAH_KH-*rikht*	information (news)
monatlich	MOH-*naht-likh*	monthly (every month, *adj.*)	nachschicken (1)	NAH_KH-*shick-ken*	forward (send by mail), to
Mönch,*m.*	MÖN_KH	monk	Nachschrift,*f.*	NAH_KH-*shrifft*	postscript
Mond,*m.*	MOHNT	moon	nachsinnen (121)	NAH_KH-*zinn-en*	muse (meditate), to
Mondlicht,*n.*	MOHND-*likht*	moonlight	nächst	NEXT	next (following, *adj.*)
Montevideo,*n.*	*mohn-tay-vee-*DAY-*oh*	Montevideo	Nacht,*f.*	NAH_KHT	night
Moor,*n.*	MOHR	moor (waste land)	Nachthemd,*n.*	NAH_KHT-*hemm_t*	nightgown
Moos,*n.*	MOHSS	moss	Nachtigall,*f.*	NAH_KH-*tee-gahll*	nightingale
Moral,*f.*	*mo-*RAHL	morals			
Mord,*m.*	MORT	murder	Nachtisch,*m.*	NAH_KH-*tish*	dessert
Mörder,*m.*	MÖR-*dehr*	murderer	nachweisen (155)	NAH_KH-*vize-en*	establish (prove), to
			Nacken,*m.*	NAHCK-*en*	nape
			nackt	NAHKT	bare (nude)
			"	"	naked

German	Pronunciation	English
Nadel,*f.*	NAH-*del*	needle
Nagel,*m.*	NAH-*gel*	nail
nagen (1)	NAH-*gen*	gnaw (bite), to
nah	NAH	close (*adj., adv.*)
"	"	near (not far, *adv.*)
Nähe,*f.*	NAY-*uh*	neighborhood
"	"	vicinity
nahelegen (1)	NAH-*uh-lay-gen*	suggest (bring to mind), to
nähen (1)	NAY-*en*	sew, to
nähern, sich (1)	zikh NAY-*ehrn*	approach (come near to), to
Nähmaschine,*f.*	NAY-*mah-shee-nuh*	sewing machine
(er)nähren (1)	(*ehr-*)NAIR-*en*	nourish, to
Nahrung,*f.*	NAH-*roong*	food
"	"	nourishment
Naht,*f.*	NAHT	seam (line of stitches)
Name,*m.*	NAH-*muh*	name
nämlich	NAME-*likh*	namely
Narbe,*f.*	NAHRR-*buh*	scar
Narr,*m.*	NAHRR	fool
Nase,*f.*	NAH-*zuh*	nose (*anat.*)
Nasenloch,*n.*	NAH-*zen-lawkh*	nostril
nass	NAHSS	wet
nässen (1)	NEHSS-*en*	wet, to
Nation,*f.*	*nahts-*YOHN	nation
national	*nahts-yoh-*NAHL	national (*adj.*)
Natur,*f.*	*nah-*TOOR	nature (physical world)
natürlich	*nah-*TÜR-*likh*	natural
Neapel,*n.*	*nay-*AH-*pel*	Naples
Nebel,*m.*	NAY-*bel*	fog
"	"	mist
neben	NAY-*ben*	at (near)
"	"	beside (*prep.*)
"	"	near (*prep.*)
"	"	next to (alongside of, *prep.*)
Nebenprodukt,*n.*	NAY-*ben-pro-doockt*	by-product
necken (1)	NECK-*en*	tease, to
Neffe,*m.*	NEFF-*uh*	nephew
Neger,*m.*	NAY-*gehr*	Negro
nehmen (80)	NAY-*men*	take, to
Neid,*m.*	NYE_T	envy
neigen (1)	NYE-*gen*	incline, to
"	"	tend (be apt), to
Neigung,*f.*	NYE-*goong*	bent (penchant)
"	"	inclination
"	"	slope (slant)
"	"	tendency
nein	NINE	no (nay)
Nelke,*f.*	NELL-*kuh*	carnation
(Gewürz)Nelke,*f.*	(*guh-*VÜRTS-)NELL-*kuh*	clove
Nennwert,*m.*	NENN-*vehrt*	face value (*bus.*)
Nerv,*m.*	NEHRF	nerve (*anat.*)
nervös	*nehr-*VÖSS	nervous (high-strung)
Nest,*n.*	NESST	nest (bird home)
nett	NETT	nice (agreeable)
netto	NETT-*toh*	net (*adj.*)
Netz,*n.*	NETTS	net (mesh)
neu	NOY	new
"	"	recent
Neudelhi,*n.*	*noy-*DELL-*hee*	New Delhi
Neugier(de),*f.*	NOY-*gear*(-*duh*)	curiosity (inquisitiveness)
neugierig	NOY-*gear-ick*	curious (inquisitive)
Neujahrstag,*m.*	NOY-*yahrs-tahk*	New Year's Day
neutral	*noy-*TRAHL	neutral
Neuyork,*n.*	NOY-*yawrk*	New York
Nicaragua,*n.*	*nee-kah-*RAHG-*wah*	Nicaragua
nicht	NIKHT	not
Nichte,*f.*	NIKH-*tuh*	niece
nichtig	NIKH-*tick*	void (null)
nichts	NIKHTS	anything (not...anything)
"	"	nothing (*n.*)
Nickel,*n.*	NICK-*kel*	nickel (*chem.*)
nicken (1)	NICK-*en*	nod, to
nie(mals)	NEE(-*mahlss*)	never

German	Pronunciation	English
Niedergeschlagen-heit,*f.*	NEE-*dehr-guh-shlah-gen-hite*	depression (sadness)
Niederlage,*f.*	NEE-*dehr-lah-guh*	defeat
Niederlande, die, *pl.*	*dee* NEE-*dehr-lahnn-duh*	Netherlands, The
niederlassen (71)	NEE-*dehr-lahss-en*	lower (let down), to
niederlassen, sich	*zikh* NEE-*dehr-lahss-en*	settle (make one's home), to
niedrig	NEE-*drick*	low
niemand	NEE-*mahnnt*	anybody (not...anybody)
"	"	nobody (*pron.*)
Niere,*f.*	NEAR-*uh*	kidney (*anat.*)
niesen (1)	NEE-*zen*	sneeze, to
Nil,*m.*	NEEL	Nile
nirgends	NEERR-*g_ents*	anywhere (not...anywhere)
"	"	nowhere
noch	NAW_KH	nor
"	"	still (*adv.*)
"	"	yet (now, until now, *adv.*)
noch, (sonst)	(ZAWNNST) NAW_KH	else (in addition, *adj.*)
noch ein	NAW_KH INE	another (one more, more, *adj., pron.*)
Nonne,*f.*	NAWNN-*uh*	nun
Nordamerika,*m.*	NORD-*ah-*MAY-*ree-kah*	North America
Norden,*m.*	NOR-*den*	north (*n.*)
nördlich	NÖRD-*likh*	north (*adv.*)
"	"	northern
nordöstlich	*nord-*ÖSST-*likh*	northeast (*adj.*)
nordwestlich	*nord-*VEST-*likh*	northwest (*adj.*)
normal	*nor-*MAHL	normal (*adj.*)
"	"	standard (regular)
Norwegen,*n.*	NOR-*vay-gen*	Norway
norwegisch	NOR-*vay-gish*	Norwegian (*adj.*)
Not,*f.*	NOTE	distress
"	"	hardship (privation)
"	"	need
Notar,*m.*	*no-*TAR	notary
Note,*f.*	NO-*tuh*	grade (academic rating)
"	"	note (*mus.*)
Notfall,*m.*	NOTE-*fahll*	emergency (*n.*)
nötig	NÖ-*tick*	necessary
Notwendigkeit,*f.*	NOTE-*venn-dick-kite*	necessity
Novelle,*f.*	*noh-*VEL-*luh*	short story
nüchtern	NÜKH-*tehrn*	sober (serious)
Null,*f.*	NOOLL	zero (*n.*)
numerieren (1)	*noomm-ehr-*EAR-*en*	number (assign numbers to), to
Nummer,*f.*	NOOMM-*ehr*	number (numeral)
nun	NOONN	well (and then?, *interj.*)
nun an, von	*fawnn* NOON AHNN	henceforth
Nuss,*f.*	NOOSS	nut (food)
nützlich	NÜTTS-*likh*	useful
Nützlichkeit,*f.*	NÜTTS-*likh-kite*	utility (usefulness)
nutzlos	NOOTTS-*lohss*	useless
Nylon,*n.*	NYE-*lawnn*	nylon (*n.*)
Oase,*f.*	*oh-*AH-*zuh*	oasis
ob	OHP	if
"	"	whether (*conj.*)
oben	OH-*ben*	above (overhead, *adv.*)
"	"	up (*adv.*)
"	"	upstairs (at upper story, *adv.*)
obere Seite,*f.*	OH-*beh-ruh* ZYE-*tuh*	top (upper surface)
Oberfläche,*f.*	OH-*behr-fleh_kh-uh*	surface
Oberst,*m.*	OH-*behrst*	colonel
obgleich	*ohp-*GLYE_KH	although
Oboe,*f.*	*oh-*BOH-*eh*	oboe
Obstgarten,*m.*	OHPST-*gahr-ten*	orchard
Obstkuchen,*m.*	OHPST-KOO-*kh_en*	pie
obwohl	*ohp-*VOHL	though (*conj.*)
Ochs,*m.*	AWX	ox
öde	Ö-*duh*	dreary
oder	OH-*dehr*	or
Ofen,*m.*	OH-*fen*	furnace (home heater)
"	"	stove (for heating)
offen	AWFF-*fen*	frank (*adj.*)
"	"	open (*adj.*)

German	Pronunciation	English
offenbar	AWFF-*fen-bar*	apparent
"	"	evident
		obvious
offenkundig	AWFF-*fen-koon-dick*	manifest (*adj.*)
Offenkundigkeit,*f.*	AWFF-*en-koon-dick-kite*	publicity (notoriety)
öffentlich	ÖFF-*ent-likh*	public (common, adj.)
Offizier,*m.*	*awff-fee*-TSEER	officer (*mil.*)
öffnen (1)	ÖFF-*nen*	open (make open), to
Öffnung,*f.*	ÖFF-*noong*	opening (aperture)
oft	AWFFT	often
ohne	OH-*nuh*	without (lacking, prep.)
ohne zu	OH-*nuh tsoo*	without (failing to, prep.)
Ohnmacht,*f.*	OHN-*mah_kht*	faint (swoon, n.)
Ohnmacht fallen, in (32)	*in* OHN-*mah_kht* FAHLL-*len*	faint, to
Ohr,*n.*	OAR	ear
Ohrenschmerzen, *m.*	OAR-*en-shmehr-tsen*	earache
Ohrring,*m.*	OAR-*ring*	earring
Öl,*n.*	ÖL	oil
Olive,*f.*	*oh-*LEE-*vuh*	olive (fruit)
Olivenöl,*n.*	*oh-*LEE-*ven-öl*	olive oil
Omnibus,*m.*	AWMM-*nee-booss*	bus
Onkel,*m.*	AWNG-*kel*	uncle
Oper,*f.*	OH-*pehr*	opera
Operation,*f.*	*aw-pehr-rahts-*YOHN	operation (*med.*)
operieren (1)	*aw-peh-*REAR-*en*	operate (perform surgery), to
Opfer,*n.*	AWPP-*fehr*	sacrifice (giving up)
"	"	victim
opfern (1)	AWPP-*fehrn*	sacrifice (forego), to
optimistisch	*awpp-tih-*MISS-*tish*	optimistic
Orange,*f.*	*oh-*RAHNZH-*uh*	orange (fruit)
orange(farbig)	*oh-*RAHNZH-*uh(-far-bick)*	orange (color)
Orchester,*n.*	*awr-*KEHSST-*ehr*	orchestra (*mus.*)
Orchidee,*f.*	*awrkh-ee-*DAY	orchid (flower)
Orden,*m.*	AWR-*den*	medal
Ordnung,*f.*	AWRD-*noong*	order (orderliness)
Ordnung bringen, in (171)	*in* AWRT-*noong* BRING-*en*	straighten (put in order), to
Organ,*n.*	*or-*GAHN	organ (*anat.*)
Orgel,*f.*	OR-*gel*	organ (*mus.*)
Ort,*m.*	ORT	locality (place)
"	"	point (in space)
örtlich	ÖRT-*likh*	local (regional)
Oslo,*n.*	AWSS-*loh*	Oslo
Osten,*m.*	OHSS-*ten*	east
"	"	Orient
Ostern,*n.*	OHSS-*tehrn*	Easter
Österreich,*n.*	Ös-*tuh-rye_kh*	Austria
Österreichisch	ÖS-*tuh-rye_kh-ish*	Austrian (*adj.*)
östlich	ÖST-*likh*	eastern
Ottawa,*n.*	AW-*tuh-vah*	Ottawa
Ozean,*m.*	OH-*tsay-ahn*	ocean
Paar,*n.*	PAHR	couple
"	"	pair
paar, ein	INE PAHR	few, a
paaren (1)	PAHR-*ren*	mate (find mate for), to
Pack,*n.*	PAHCK	deck (of cards)
packen (1)	PAHCK-*en*	grab, to
Packmaterial,*n.*	PAHCK-*mah-tehr-yahl*	packing (*n.*)
Paddel,*n.*	PAHDD-*el*	paddle (oar)
Paket,*n.*	*pah-*KATE	bundle
"	"	package
"	"	parcel
Paketpost,*f.*	*pah-*KATE-*pawsst*	parcel post
Pakistan,*n.*	PAH-*kee-stahn*	Pakistan
pakistanisch	*pah-kee-*STAH-*nish*	Pakistani (*adj.*)
Palast,*m.*	*pah-*LAHSST	palace
Palästina,*n.*	*pah-less-*TEE-*nah*	Palestine
Palme,*f.*	PAHLL-*muh*	palm (tree)
Palmsonntag,*m.*	*pahllm-*ZAWNN-*tahk*	Palm Sunday
Panama,*n.*	PAH-*nah-mah*	Panama
Panik,*f.*	PAH-*nick*	panic (fear)
Panther,*m.*	PAHNN-*tehr*	panther
Panzer,*m.*	PAHNN-*tsehr*	armor (protective clothing)
Papagei,*m.*	*pah-pah-*GUY	parrot
Papier,*n.*	*pah-*PEER	paper
Pappe,*f.*	PAHPP-*puh*	cardboard

German	Pronunciation	English
Papst,*m.*	PAHPST	pope
Parade,*f.*	*pah-*RAH-*duh*	parade (procession)
Paradies,*n.*	*pah-rah-*DEESS	paradise
Paraguay,*n.*	PAH-*rah-gwah_ee*	Paraguay
parallel	*pah-rah-*LAYL	parallel (*adj.*)
Parfüm,*n.*	*pahr-*FÜM	perfume (fragrance)
Paris,*n.*	*pah-*REESS	Paris
Park,*m.*	PAHRRK	park
parken (1)	PAHRR-*ken*	park (put in place), to
Parlament,*n.*	*pahr-lah-*MENT	parliament
Partie,*f.*	*pahr-*TEE	lot (salable items, bus.)
Partei,*f.*	*pahr-*TYE	party (*pol.*)
Pass,*m.*	PAHSS	passport
Passagier,*m.*	*pahss-sah-*ZHEER	passenger
Passahfest,*n.*	PAHSS-*sah-fest*	Passover
passend	PAHSS-*ent*	fit (suitable)
Pastor,*m.*	PAHSS-*tohr*	pastor
Patent,*n.*	*pah-*TENT	patent (*n.*)
Patriot,*m.*	*pah-tree-*OHT	patriot
patschen (1)	PAHTT-*shen*	pat (tap), to
Pause,*f.*	POW-*zuh*	recess (school intermission)
(Ruhe)Pause,*f.*	(ROO-*uh-*)POW-*zuh*	lull (calm)
pausieren (1)	*pow-*ZEE-*ren*	pause (wait), to
Pech,*n.*	PEH_KH	pitch (tar)
Peitsche,*f.*	PITE-*shuh*	whip
peitschen (1)	PITE-*shen*	whip (flog), to
Peitschenhieb,*m.*	PITE-*shen-heep*	lash (whip)
Peking,*n.*	PEH-*king*	Peiping
Pelz,*m.*	PELTS	fur
Penizillin,*n.*	*penn-ih-tsih-*LEEN	penicillin
Pension,*f.*	*pahn-see-*YOHNG	boarding house
Perle,*f.*	PEHR-*luh*	bead (jewelry)
"	"	pearl (gem)
Person,*f.*	*pehr-*ZOHN	character (person portrayed)
"	"	person
Personal,*n.*	*pehr-zoh-*NAHL	staff (personnel)
Personenwagen,*m.*	*pehr-*ZOHN-*en-vah-gen*	coach, railroad
persönlich	*pehr-*ZÖN-*likh*	personal
Persönlichkeit,*f.*	*pehr-*ZÖN-*likh-kite*	personality
Peru,*n.*	*pay-*ROO	Peru
peruanisch	*pay-roo-*AH-*nish*	Peruvian (*adj.*)
pessimistisch	*pess-ih-*MISS-*tish*	pessimistic
Pest,*f.*	PEST	pest (nuisance)
Pfad,*m.*	PFAHT	path
"	"	trail
Pfadfinder,*m.*	PFAHT-*finn-dehr*	Boy Scout
Pfadfinderin,*f.*	PFAHT-*finn-dehr-in*	girl scout
Pfahl,*m.*	PFAHL	stake (post)
Pfanne,*f.*	PFAHNN-*uh*	pan, frying
Pfarrer,*m.*	PFAHRR-*ehr*	minister (clergyman)
"	"	parson
Pfau(hahn),*m.*	PFOW(-*hahnn*)	peacock
Pfeffer,*m.*	PFEFF-*ehr*	pepper
Pfeife,*f.*	PFIFE-*uh*	pipe (tobacco pipe)
pfeifen (81)	PFIFE-*en*	whistle, to
Pfeil,*m.*	PFILE	arrow
Pfeiler,*m.*	PFYE-*lehr*	pillar (column)
Pferd,*n.*	PFAIRT	horse
Pferdchen,*n.*	PFAIRD-*kh_en*	pony (animal)
Pferdekraft,*f.*	PFAIR-*duh-krahft*	horsepower
Pfirsich,*m.*	PFEER-*zikh*	peach
Pflanze,*f.*	PFLAHNN-*tsuh*	plant (flora)
pflanzen (1)	PFLAHNN-*tsen*	plant (sow), to
pflastern (1)	PFLAHSS-*tehrn*	pave, to
Pflaume,*f.*	PFL_OW-*muh*	plum (fruit)
pflegen (1)	PFLAY-*gen*	nurse (give treatment to), to
Pflegling,*m.*	PFLAYG-*ling*	foster child
Pflicht,*f.*	PFLIKHT	duty (obligation)
Pflock,*m.*	PFLAWCK	peg (pin)
pflücken (1)	PFLÜCK-*en*	pluck (pull off), to
Pflug,*m.*	PFLOO_K	plow (*n.*)
pflügen (1)	PFLÜ-*gen*	plow (till), to
Pfosten,*m.*	PFAWSS-*ten*	post (pole)
Pfote,*f.*	PFOH-*tuh*	paw
Pfuhl,*m.*	PFOOL	pool (standing water)
Phase,*f.*	FAH-*zuh*	phase (stage)

German	Pronunciation	English
Philippinen, die, *pl.*	DEE *fee-lip*-PEE-*nen*	Philippines
Philosophie, *f.*	*fee-loh-zoh*-FEE	philosophy
Phonograph, *m.*	*foh-noh*-GRAHF	phonograph
Photographie, *f.*	*foh-toh-grah*-FEE	photograph
Phrase, *f.*	FRAH-*zuh*	phrase (*gram.*)
Physik, *f.*	*fü*-ZEEK	physics (science)
physisch	FÜ-*zish*	physical (bodily)
picken (1)	PICK-*en*	peck, to
Picknik, *n.*	PICK-*nick*	picnic
Pille, *f.*	PILL-*luh*	pill
Pilot, *m.*	*pee*-LOHT	pilot (flier)
Pilz, *m.*	PILLTS	mushroom (*n.*)
Pionier, *m.*	*pee-oh*-NEER	pioneer
Pistole, *f.*	*piss*-TOH-*luh*	pistol
plagen (1)	PLAH-*gen*	pester, to
Plan, *m.*	PLAHN	plan
"	"	scheme
Planet, *m.*	*plah*-NAYT	planet
plappern (1)	PLAHPP-*ehrn*	chatter, to
Platin, *n.*	*plah*-TEEN	platinum
(Grammophon)-	(*grahmm-o*-PHONE-)	record (disk)
Platte, *f.*	PLAHTT-*tuh*	
Platz, *m.*	PLAHTTS	place (locality)
"	"	square (plaza)
plaudern (1)	PLOW-*dehrn*	chat, to
plötzlich	PLÖTTS-*likh*	sudden (unexpected)
plus	PLOOSS	plus (*prep.*)
Pöbel, *m.*	PÖ-*bel*	mob (disorderly crowd)
Pol, *m.*	POLE	pole (end of axis)
Polen, *n.*	POH-*len*	Poland
polieren (1)	*poh*-LEE-*ren*	polish, to
Politik, *f.*	*poh-lee*-TEEK	policy (course)
"	"	politics
Politiker, *m.*	*poh*-LEE-*tee-kehr*	politician
politisch	*poh*-LEE-*lish*	political
Polize, *f.*	*poh*-LEE-*tsuh*	policy (contract of insurance)
Polizei, *f.*	*poh-lee-*T_SYE	police
Polizist, *m.*	*poh-lee*-TSIST	policeman
polnisch	PAWLL-*nish*	Polish (*adj.*)
Polster, *n.*	PAWLL-*stehr*	pad (cushion)
populär	*poh-poo*-LEHR	popular (well-liked)
Porto, *n.*	POR-*toh*	postage (postal charge)
Portugal, *n.*	POR-*too-gahl*	Portugal
Porzellan, *n.*	*por*-TSELL-*lahn*	porcelain (*n.*)
Posaune, *f.*	*poh*-ZOW-*nuh*	trombone
Post, *f.*	PAWSST	mail (letters exchanged)
Postamt, *n.*	PAWSST-*ahmmt*	postoffice
Postdienst, *m.*	PAWSST-*deenst*	mail (postal system)
Posten, *m.*	PAWSS-*ten*	entry (*acctg.*)
"	"	post (position)
Postkarte, *f.*	PAWSST-*kahr-tuh*	card, postal
Pracht, *f.*	PRAH_KHT	splendor
prächtig	PREH_KH-*lick*	gorgeous
"	"	splendid
prahlen (1)	PRAH-*len*	boast, to
praktisch	PRAHCK-*lish*	practical (not theoretical)
Prämie, *f.*	PRAY-*mee-yuh*	premium (payment)
Prärie, *f.*	PRAY-*ree*	prairie
Präsident, *m.*	*pray-zee*-DENT	president
predigen (1)	PRAY-*dih-gen*	preach, to
Prediger, *m.*	PRAY-*dih-gehr*	preacher
Predigt, *f.*	PRAY-*dickt*	sermon
Preis, *m.*	PRICE	charge
"	"	cost
"	"	price (*bus.*)
"	"	prize (trophy)
"	"	rate
Preisnotierung, *f.*	PRICE-*no-tee-roong*	quotation (price)
Prellstein, *m.*	PRELL-*shtine*	curb (edge of street)
Presse, *f.*	PRESS-*uh*	press (newspapers and periodicals)
Priester, *m.*	PREESS-*tehr*	priest
primitiv	*primm-ih*-TEEF	primitive (early)
Prinz, *m.*	PRINNTS	prince
Prinzessin, *f.*	*prin*-TSESS-*inn*	princess
privat	*pree*-VAHT	private (personal)

German	Pronunciation	English
Probe, *f.*	PRO-*buh*	rehearsal
"	"	test (trial)
probieren (1)	*pro*-BEE-*ren*	test (try), to
Problem, *n.*	*pro*-BLAME	problem
Produktion, *f.*	*pro-doockts*-YOHN	output
produktiv	*pro-doock*-TEEF	productive
Professor, *m.*	*pro*-FESS-*ohr*	professor (teacher)
Programm, *n.*	*pro*-GRAHMM	program (plan)
Prophet, *m.*	*pro*-FATE	prophet (religious teacher)
Prosa, *f.*	PRO-*zah*	prose
Protokoll, *n.*	*pro-toh*-KAWLL	minutes (record)
Provinz, *f.*	*pro*-VINNTS	province (*pol.*)
Provision, *f.*	*pro-veez*-YOHN	commission (fee)
Prozent, *n.*	*pro*-TSENT	percent (*n.*)
Prozentsatz, *m.*	*pro*-TSENT-*zahttss*	percentage
Prozess, *m.*	*pro*-TSESS	suit (lawsuit)
prüfen (1)	PRÜ-*fen*	check, to
"	"	try (test), to
Prüfung, *f.*	PRÜ-*foong*	examination (test)
"	"	test (*educ.*)
prügeln (1)	PRÜ-*gel'n*	spank, to
Psychiatrie, *f.*	*p_sükh-yahtt*-REE	psychiatry
Psychologie, *f.*	*p_sü-kh_oh-loh*-G_EE	psychology
Publikum, *n.*	POO-*blee-koomm*	audience
"	"	public (populace, *n.*)
Pudding, *m.*	POODD-*ing*	pudding (dessert)
Puder, *m.*	POO-*dehr*	powder (cosmetic)
Puls, *m.*	POOLLSS	pulse (*physiol.*)
Pumpe, *f.*	POOMM-*puh*	pump
Punkt, *m.*	POONKT	dot
"	"	period (*punct.*)
"	"	point (item)
Punkte machen (1)	POONK-*tuh mah_kh-en*	score (gain points), to
pünktlich	PÜNKT-*likh*	prompt
"	"	punctual
Pupille, *f.*	*poo*-PILL-*uh*	pupil (of eye)
Puppe, *f.*	POOPP-*puh*	doll
purpurn	POORR-*poorn*	purple (color)
Pyjama, *n.*	*pee*-JAH-*mah*	pajamas
quadratisch	*kvah*-DRAH-*tish*	square (*adj.*)
Qual, *f.*	KVAHL	agony (mental pain)
"	"	anguish
"	"	torment
quälen (1)	KVAY-*len*	torment, to
Quecksilber, *n.*	KVECK-*zill-behr*	mercury
Quelle, *f.*	KVELL-*uh*	source (origin)
quer über	*kvehr ü-behr*	over (across, *prep.*)
Quetschung, *f.*	KVET-*shoong*	bruise
Quito, *n.*	KEE-*toh*	Quito
quittieren (1)	*kvitt*-TEE-*ren*	receipt, to (*bus.*)
Quittung, *f.*	KVITT-*toong*	receipt (voucher)
Quote, *f.*	KVOH-*tuh*	quota
Rabatt, *m.*	*rah*-BAHTT	discount (*n.*)
"	"	rebate (*bus.*)
rabattieren (1)	*rah-baht*-TEE-*ren*	discount, to (*bus.*)
Rabbiner, *m.*	*rah*-BEE-*nehr*	rabbi
Rache, *f.*	RAH_KH-*uh*	revenge
"	"	vengeance
Rad, *n.*	RAHT	wheel
(Fahr)Rad, *n.*	(FAR-)RAHT	bicycle
Radar, *n.*	RAH-*dahr*	radar (*n.*)
Radiergummi, *m.*	*rah*-DEER-*goomm-mee*	eraser (rubber eraser)
Radio, *n.*	RAHD-*yoh*	radio (receiving set)
Radioaktivität, *f.*	*rahd-yo-ahck-tee-vee*-TATE	radioactivity
raffinieren (1)	*rahff-ee*-NEE-*ren*	refine (purify), to
Rakete, *f.*	*rah*-KAY-*tuh*	rocket
rammen (1)	RAHMM-*men*	ram (butt), to
Rand, *m.*	RAHNNT	border
"	"	brink (verge)
"	"	edge
"	"	margin
"	"	rim
Rang, *m.*	RAHNNG	grade (relative position)
"	"	rank (standing)
Rascheln, *n.*	RAHSH-*el'n*	rustle
rasen (1)	RAH-*zen*	rave (rant), to
Rasen, *m.*	RAH-*zen*	lawn
Rasierapparat, elektrischer, *m.*	*eh*-LECK-*trish-ehr rah-*ZEER-*ahp-pah-raht*	shaver, electric

German	Pronunciation	English
Rasiercreme, *f.*	*rah*-ZEER-*kray-muh*	shaving cream
rasieren, sich	*zikh rah*-ZEE-*ren*	shave (oneself), **to**
Rasierklinge, *f.*	*rah*-ZEER-*kling-uh*	razor blade
Rasiermesser, *n.*	*rah*-ZEER-*mess-ehr*	razor
Rasse, *f.*	RAHSS-*suh*	breed (stock)
"	"	race (*anthrop.*)
Rat, *m.*	RAHT	advice
"	"	council
Rat(schlag), *m.*	RAHT(-*shlahk*)	counsel (advice)
Rate, *f.*	RAH-*tuh*	installment (payment, *bus.*)
raten (83)	RAH-*ten*	advise (counsel), to
"		guess (divine), to
Rate ziehen, zu (161)	*tsoo* RAH-*tuh tsee-en*	consult (seek professional advice of), to
Ration, *f.*	*rahts*-YOHN	ration (allotment)
Rätsel, *n.*	RATE-*sel*	riddle (*n.*)
Ratte, *f.*	RAHTT-*tuh*	rat
Räuber, *m.*	ROY-*behr*	robber
Rauch, *m.*	R_OWKH	smoke
rauchen (1)	R_OWKH-*en*	smoke, to
rauh	R_OW	harsh
"	"	rough (uneven)
Raum, *m.*	R_OWM	room
"	"	space (area)
Rauminhalt, *m.*	R_OWM-*in-hahlt*	volume (space occupied)
Raupe, *f.*	R_OW-*puh*	caterpillar
Rausch, *m.*	R_OWSH	intoxication (drunkenness)
Rauschgift, *n.*	R_OWSH-*gift*	drug (narcotic)
reagieren (1)	*ray-ah*-G_EE-*ren*	respond (react), to
Reaktion, *f.*	*ray-ahkts*-YOHN	reaction
Rebell, *m.*	*ray*-BELL	rebel (*n.*)
Rechenmaschine, *f.*	REH_KH-*en-mah-shee-nuh*	adding machine
Rechenschaft geben über (43)	REH_KH-*en-shahft* GAY-*ben* ü-*behr*	account for (explain), to
rechnen (1)	REH_KH-*nen*	reckon (compute), to
Rechnung, *f.*	REH_KH-*noong*	account (calculation)
"	"	bill
"	"	invoice
Rechnung, laufende, *f.*	L_OW-*fenn-duh* REH_KH-*noong*	charge account
recht	REH_KHT	right (on the right, *adj.*)
Recht, *n.*	REH_KHT	law (governing code)
"		right (claim)
Rechte, *f.*	REH_KH-*tuh*	right (right-hand side)
Rechteck, *m.*	REH_KHT-*eck*	rectangle
rechtfertigen (1)	REH_KHT-*fehr-tee-gen*	justify, to
"	"	warrant, to
rechts	REH_KHTS	right (to the right, *adv.*)
rechtschaffen	REH_KHT-*shahff-en*	honorable (upright)
Redakteur, *m.*	*ray-dahck*-TÖR	editor
Rede, *f.*	RAY-*duh*	address
"	"	speech
reden (1)	RAY-*den*	talk, to
Redlichkeit, *f.*	RAID-*likh-kite*	honesty
Redner, *m.*	RAID-*nehr*	speaker (orator)
Reform, *f.*	*ray*-FORM	reform (*n.*)
Regel, *f.*	RAY-*gel*	rule (regulation)
"	"	rule (usual case)
regelmässig	RAY-*gel-may-sick*	regular (normal)
Regelmässigkeit, *f.*	RAY-*gel-may-sick-kite*	regularity
regelwidrig	RAY-*gel-veed-rick*	irregular (not conforming)
Regen, *m.*	RAY-*gen*	rain
Regenbogen, *m.*	RAY-*gen-boh-gen*	rainbow
Regenmantel, *m.*	RAY-*gen-mahnn-tel*	raincoat
Regenschauer, *m.*	RAY-*gen-sh_ow-ehr*	shower (rainfall)
regieren (1)	*ray*-GEAR-*ren*	govern, to
Regierung, *f.*	*ray*-GEAR-*oong*	government
Regiment, *n.*	*ray-g_ee*-MENT	regiment (*n.*)
Register, *n.*	*ray*-GISS-*tehr*	index (list)
regnen (1)	RAYG-*nen*	rain, to
regnerisch	RAYG-*nuh-rish*	rainy·
reiben (84)	RYE-*ben*	rub, to
reich	RYE_KH	rich
"	"	wealthy
Reich, *n.*	RYE_KH	realm (kingdom)

German	Pronunciation	English
(Kaiser)Reich, *n.*	(KYE-*zehr*-)RYE_KH	empire
reichen (1)	RYE-*kh_en*	reach (extend to), to
reichlich	RYE_KH-*likh*	abundant
"	"	ample
		plentiful
Reichtum, *m.*	RYE_KH-*toom*	riches
"	"	wealth
Reichtümer, *m.pl.*	RYE_KH-*tü-mehr*	resources (wealth)
reif	RIFE	ripe
reifen (1)	RYE-*fen*	mature (ripen), to
Reifen, *m.*	RYE-*fen*	tire
Reihe, *f.*	RYE-*uh*	line
"	"	rank
"	"	row
"	"	series
Reihenfolge, *f.*	RYE-*en-fawl-guh*	order (sequence)
Reim, *m.*	RIME	rhyme
rein	RINE	clean
"	"	pure (unadulterated)
Reinheit, *f.*	RINE-*hite*	purity (cleanness)
reinigen (1)	RINE-*ih-gen*	clean, to
Reis, *m.*	RICE	rice
Reise, *f.*	RYE-*zuh*	journey
"	"	trip
"	"	voyage
reisen (1)	RYE-*zen*	travel, to
Reisende, *m.*,*f.*	RYE-*zen-duh*	traveler
reissen (85)	RYE-*sen*	tear (rip), to
reissender Strom, *m.*	RYE-*sen-dehr* SHTROHM	torrent
Reissverschluss, *m.*	RICE-*fehr-shlooss*	zipper
Reiter, *m.*	RYE-*tehr*	rider (horseman)
Reiz, *m.*	RITES	charm (attraction)
(auf)reizen (1)	(OWF-)RITES-*en*	irritate (annoy), to
reizend	RYE-*tsent*	charming
Reklame machen (1)	*ray*-KLAH-*muh* MAH_KH-*en*	advertise (sponsor advertising), to
Religion, *f.*	*ray-lig*-YOHN	religion
religiös	*ray-lig*-YÖS	religious (*adj.*)
rennen (175)	REN-*nen*	run (sprint), to
Renntier, *n.*	RENN-*teer*	reindeer
reparieren (1)	*reh-par*-REER-*en*	fix (repair), to
Republik, *f.*	*ray-poo*-BLEEK	republic
republikanisch	*ray-poo-blee*-KAH-*nish*	republican (*adj.*)
Reserven, *f.pl.*	*ray*-ZEHR-*ven*	reserve (*bus.*)
Reservoir, *n.*	*ray-zehr-vo*-AR	reservoir (water reserve)
Rest, *m.*	REST	difference (*math.*)
"	"	remainder
"	"	rest
Restaurant, *n.*	*ress-toh*-RAHNG	restaurant
retten (1)	RET-*ten*	rescue, to
		save, to
Rettung, *f.*	RETT-*oong*	rescue
Revisor, *m.*	*ray-vee*-ZOR	auditor
Revolution, *f.*	*ray-voh-loots*-YOHN	revolution (*pol.*)
Revolver, *m.*	*ray*-VAWLL-*vehr*	revolver (weapon)
Rezept, *n.*	*ray*-TSEPT	prescription (*med.*)
"		recipe
Rhein, *m.*	RINE	Rhine
Rheumatismus, *m.*	*roy-mah*-TISS-*mooss*	rheumatism
richten (1)	RIKH-*ten*	direct (aim), to
Richter, *m.*	RIKH-*tehr*	judge
richtig	RIKH-*tick*	correct
"	"	right (correct, *adj.*)
Richtstrahl, *m.*	RIKHT-*shtrahl*	beam (radio signal)
Richtung, *f.*	RIKH-*toong*	direction (course)
riechen (87)	REE-*kh_en*	smell (perceive odor), to
Riegel, *m.*	REE-*gel*	bolt (lock)
Riemen, *m.*	REE-*men*	strap
Riese, *m.*	REE-*zuh*	giant
riesig	REE-*zick*	huge
(Baum)Rinde, *f.*	(B_OWM-)RINN-*duh*	bark (of tree)
Rindfleisch, *n.*	RINNT-*fly_sh*	beef
Rindvieh, *n.*	RINNT-*fee*	cattle
Ring, *m.*	RING	ring
ringen (88)	RING-*en*	wrestle, to
Ringen, *n.*	RING-*en*	struggle (great effort)
Rinnstein, *m.*	RINN-*shtine*	gutter (of street)

German	Pronunciation	English
Rio de Janeiro, *n.*	REE-*oh day zhah*-NAY-*roh*	Rio de Janeiro
Rippe, *f.*	RIP-*puh*	rib (anat.)
Riss, *m.*	RISS	crack (fissure)
Ritter, *m.*	RITT-*ehr*	knight
Ritus, *m.*	REE-*tooss*	rite
Rock, *m.*	RAWCK	skirt (garment)
Roggen, *m.*	RAWG-*gen*	rye (grain)
roh	ROH	crude
"	"	raw (in natural state)
Rohr, *n.*	ROHR	reed (grass)
Röhre, *f.*	RÖ-*ruh*	pipe
"	"	tube
Rolle, *f.*	RAWLL-*luh*	role
rollen (1)	RAWLL-*len*	roll (impel), to
Rom, *n.*	ROME	Rome
Roman, *m.*	*roh*-MAHN	novel (book)
romantisch	*roh*-MAHNN-*tish*	romantic
römisch	RÖ-*mish*	Roman (adj.)
Röntgenaufnahme, *f.*	RÖNT-*gen-owf-nah-muh*	X-ray (X-ray picture)
Röntgenstrahlen, *m.pl.*	RÖNT-*gen-shtrahl-en*	X-ray (Roentgen ray)
Rose, *f.*	ROH-*zuh*	rose (flower)
Rosine, *f.*	*roh*-ZEE-*nuh*	raisin
Rost, *m.*	RAWSST	grate (of furnace)
"	"	rust
rostfreier Stahl, *m.*	RAWSST-*fry-ehr* SHTAHL	stainless steel
rostig	RAWSS-*tick*	rusty
rot	ROHT	red
rote Rübe, *f.*	ROH-*tuh* RÜ-*buh*	beet (red root)
Rotkehlchen, *n.*	ROTE-*kale-kh en*	robin
Rouleau, *n.*	*roo*-LOH	shade (window blind)
Route, *f.*	ROO-*tuh*	route
Rubin, *m.*	*roo*-BEE N	ruby (gem)
Rücken, *m.*	RÜCK-*ken*	back (anat.)
"	"	ridge (raised area)
Rückgrat, *n.*	RÜCK-*graht*	spine (anat.)
Rückkehr, *f.*	RÜCK-*kair*	return (coming or going back)
Rückseite, *f.*	RÜCK-*zite-uh*	back (reverse side)
Rücksicht, *f.*	RÜCK-*zikht*	consideration (regard)
rücksichtslos	RÜCK-*zikhts-lohss*	reckless
rückwärts	RÜCK-*vehrts*	backward (rearward, adv.)
Rückzahlung, *f.*	RÜCK-*tsah-loong*	refund (bus.)
Rückzug, *m.*	RÜCK-*tsook*	retreat (mil.)
Ruder, *n.*	ROO-*dehr*	oar (n.)
"	"	rudder (of a boat)
Ruf, *m.*	ROO_F	call (shout)
"	"	cry (utterance)
"	"	reputation
rufen (88)	ROO-*fen*	call (shout), to
rufen lassen (70)	ROO-*fen* LAHSS-*en*	call (summon), to
Ruhe, *f.*	ROO-*uh*	quiet (stillness)
"	"	repose (calm)
"	"	rest
ruhen (1)	ROO-*en*	rest (repose), to
ruhig	ROO-*ick*	calm (adj.)
"	"	peaceful (tranquil)
"	"	quiet (without motion, adj.)
"	"	still (adj.)
Ruhm, *m.*	ROOM	fame
"	"	glory (renown)
Ruhr, *f.*	ROOR	dysentery
Rührei, *n.*	RÜR-*eye*	scrambled eggs
rühren (1)	RÜ-*ren*	stir (mix), to
Ruine, *f.*	*roo*-EE-*nuh*	ruins (remains)
Rum, *m.*	ROOMM	rum
Rumänien, *n.*	*roo*-MANE-*yen*	Rumania
rund	ROONNT	round (adj.)
Rundfunkübertragung, *f.*	ROONNT-*foonk-ü-behr-trah-goong*	broadcasting (rad.)
rundlich	ROONND-*likh*	plump (chubby)
Rundschreiben, *n.*	ROONNT-*shrye-ben*	circular (letter or brochure, bus.)
russisch	ROOSS-*ish*	Russian (adj.)
Russland, *n.*	ROOSS-*lahnnt*	Russia
Saal, *m.*	ZAHL	hall (meeting room)
Sache, *f.*	ZAH_KH-*uh*	affair
"	"	article (thing)
"	"	matter

German	Pronunciation	English
Sachverständige, *m., f.*	ZAH_KH-*fehr-shtenn-dih-guh*	expert (n.)
Sack, *m.*	ZAHCK	bag
"	"	sack
säen (1)	ZAY-*en*	sow, to
Saft, *m.*	ZAHFFT	juice
"	"	sap (fluid)
Säge, *f.*	ZAY-*guh*	saw (tool)
sagen (1)	ZAH-*gen*	say, to
"	"	tell (inform), to
Sahne, *f.*	ZAH-*nuh*	cream
Salat, *m.*	*zah*-LAHT	salad
(Kopf)Salat, *m.*	(KAWPF-)*zah*-LAHT	lettuce
Salatsosse, *f.*	*zah*-LAHT-*zoh-suh*	dressing (sauce)
Salbe, *f.*	ZAHLL-*buh*	ointment
Salvador, *n.*	*zahl-vah*-DORE	Salvador, El
Salz, *n.*	ZAHLLTS	salt
Samen, *m.*	ZAH-*men*	seed (ovule)
sammeln (1)	ZAHMM-*mel'n*	collect (bring together), to
(ver)sammeln, sich	*zikh (fehr-)*ZAHMM-*mel'n*	gather (congregate), to
Sammlung, *f.*	ZAHMM-*loong*	collection
Samt, *m.*	ZAHMMT	velvet (n.)
Sand, *m.*	ZAHNNT	sand
sandig	ZAHNN-*dick*	sandy
sanft	ZAHNFFT	gentle (soothing)
Sänger, *m.*	ZENG-*ehr*	singer
Santiago, *n.*	*sahnnt*-YAH-*go*	Santiago
Saphir, *m.*	ZAH-*fear*	sapphire (gem)
Sardine, *f.*	*zahr*-DEE-*nuh*	sardine
Sarg, *m.*	ZARK	coffin
Sattel, *m.*	ZAHTT-*tel*	saddle (seat)
Satz, *m.*	ZAHTTS	sentence (gram.)
sauber	ZOW-*behr*	neat (tidy)
Sauce, *f.*	ZOH-*suh*	sauce
sauer	ZOW-*ehr*	sour (tart)
Sauerstoff, *m.*	ZOW-*ehr-shtawf*	oxygen
saugen (91)	ZOW-*gen*	suck, to
Säugling, *m.*	ZOYG-*ling*	infant (n.)
Säule, *f.*	ZOY-*luh*	column (pillar)
Saum, *m.*	Z_OWM	hem
Säure, *f.*	ZOY-*ruh*	acid
Sausen, *n.*	ZOW-*zen*	rush (rapid motion)
Saxophon, *n.*	*zahck-so*-PHONE	saxophone
schaben (1)	SHAH-*ben*	scrape (make smooth or clean), to
Schablone, *f.*	*shahb*-LOH-*nuh*	stencil
Schach, *n.*	SHAHKH	chess
Schachtel, *f.*	SHAH_KH-*tel*	box (container)
Schädel, *m.*	SHAY-*del*	skull
schaden (1)	SHAH-*den*	harm (damage), to
Schaden, *m.*	SHAH-*den*	damage (injury)
Schadenersatz, *m.*	SHAH-*den-ehr*-ZAHTTS	damages (indemnification)
Schaf, *n.*	SHAHF	sheep
(er)schaffen (92)	(*ehr*-)SHAHFF-*en*	create, to
Schaffner, *m.*	SHAHFF-*nehr*	conductor (ticket collector)
Schal, *m.*	SHAHL	scarf (neck cloth)
Schale, *f.*	SHAH-*luh*	shell (covering)
(ab)schälen (1)	(AHPP-)SHALE-*len*	peel (take skin from), to
Schalter, *m.*	SHAHLLT-*ehr*	switch (elec.)
Schande, *f.*	SHAHNN-*duh*	shame
schändlich	SHEND-*likh*	profane (blasphemous)
"	"	shameful
scharf	SHAHRRF	keen
"	"	sharp
schärfen (1)	SHARE-*fen*	sharpen, to
scharfsinnig	SHAHRRF-*zin-nick*	shrewd
Scharlachfieber, *n.*	SHAHRR-*lah_kh-fee-behr*	scarlet fever
scharlachrot	SHAHRR-*lah_kh-rote*	scarlet (adj.)
Schatten, *m.*	SHAHTT-*en*	shade
"	"	shadow
schattig	SHAHTT-*ick*	shady
Schatz, *m.*	SHAHTTS	treasure
"	"	treasury (govt.)
schätzen (1)	SHETT-*sen*	appreciate, to
"	"	esteem, to
"	"	estimate (calculate), to
"	"	value, to

German	Pronunciation	English
Schätzung, *f.*	SHETT-*soong*	rating (evaluation)
schaudern (1)	SH_OW-*dehrn*	shudder, to
schauern (1)	SH_OW-*ehrn*	shiver (quake), to
Schaufel, *f.*	SH_OW-*fel*	shovel (tool)
Schaum, *m.*	SH_OWM	foam
Schaumgummi, *m.*	SH_OWM-*goomm-mee*	foam rubber
Schauspiel, *n.*	SH_OW-*shpeel*	play (stage presentation)
"	"	spectacle (pageant)
Schauspieler, *m.*	SH_OW-*shpeel-ehr*	actor (player)
Schauspielerin, *f.*	SH_OW-*shpeel-ehr-in*	actress
Scheck, *m.*	SHECK	check (bank check)
scheinen (94)	SHY-*nen*	appear, to
"	"	seem, to
Scheitern bringen, zum (171)	*tsoom* SHY-*tehrn bring-en*	wreck, to
schelten (95)	SHELL-*ten*	scold, to
Schemel, *m.*	SHAY-*mel*	stool (seat)
Schenkel, *m.*	SHENNG-*kel*	thigh
Schere, *f.*	SHAY-*ruh*	scissors
scheren (96)	SHARE-*en*	shear, to
Scherz, *m.*	SHEHRTS	jest (joke)
scherzen (1)	SHEHRTS-*en*	jest (joke), to
scheuern (1)	SHOY-*ehrn*	scrub, to
Scheune, *f.*	SHOY-*nuh*	barn
Schicht, *f.*	SHEE_KHT	layer (thickness)
"	"	shift (crew)
schick	SHICK	smart (chic)
Schicksal, *n.*	SHICK-*zahl*	destiny
"	"	fate
Schiene, *f.*	SHEE-*nuh*	rail (bar on track)
schier	SHEER	sheer (pure)
schiessen (98)	SHEE-*sen*	shoot (fire at), to
Schiff, *m.*	SHIFF	craft
"	"	ship
"	"	vessel
Schiffahrt, *f.*	SHIFF-*fahrt*	navigation
Schiffswerft, *f.*	SHIFFS-*vehrft*	shipyard
Schi laufen (72)	SHEE *l_ow-fen*	ski, to
Schildkröte, *f.*	SHILT-*krö-tuh*	turtle
schimmelig	SHIMM-*mel-lick*	moldy
Schinken, *m.*	SHINNG-*ken*	ham (food)
Schirm, *m.*	SHEERM	screen (partition)
(Regen)Schirm, *m.*	(RAY-*gen-*)SHEERM	umbrella
Schlacht, *f.*	SHLAH_KHT	battle
Schlachten, *n.*	SHLAH_KH-*ten*	slaughter
Schlaf, *m.*	SHLAHF	sleep
Schläfchen, *n.*	SHLAFE-*kh_en*	nap (doze, *n.*)
Schläfe, *f.*	SHLAY-*fuh*	temple (*anat.*)
schlafen (99)	SHLAH-*fen*	sleep, to
schlaff	SHLAHFF	limp (flaccid)
Schlafrock, *m.*	SHLAHF-*rawck*	robe (dressing gown)
Schlafzimmer, *n.*	SHLAHF-*tsim-mehr*	bedroom
Schlag, *m.*	SHLAHK	blow
"	"	stroke
Schlagader, *f.*	SHLAHG-*ahd-dehr*	artery (*anat.*)
Schlaganfall, *m.*	SHLAHG-*ahnn-fahll*	stroke (attack of paralysis
schlagen (100)	SHLAH-*gen*	beat (thrash), to
"	"	hit, to
"	"	strike, to
Schläger, *m.*	SHLAY-*gehr*	bat (club)
Schlamm, *m.*	SHLAHMM	mud
Schlange, *f.*	SHLAHNNG-*uh*	serpent
"	"	snake
schlank	SHLAHNNK	slender (lean)
Schlauch, *m.*	SHL_OWKH	hose (tube)
schleichen (101)	SHLYE-*kh_en*	creep, to
Schleier, *m.*	SH_LYE-*ehr*	veil (*n.*)
schlendern (1)	SHLENN-*dehrn*	stroll, to
schleppen (1)	SHLEPP-*en*	haul (pull), to
"	"	tug (drag), to
schleudern (1)	SHLOY-*dehrn*	hurl, to
Schlichtung, *f.*	SHLEE_KH-*toong*	settlement (compromise, *bus.*)
schliessen (104)	SHLEE-*sen*	close (finish), to
"	"	close (shut), to
"	"	conclude (make end), to
"	"	shut (make close), to

German	Pronunciation	English
(ver)schliessen	(*fehr-*)SHLEE-*sen*	lock (fasten), to
schlimm	SHLIMM	bad
schlimmer	SHLIMM-*mehr*	worse (*adj., adv.*)
schlimmst	SHLIMMST	worst (*adj.*)
Schlimmste, *n.*	SHLIMM-*stuh*	worst (*n.*)
schlimmsten, am	*ahmm* SHLIMM-*sten*	worst (*adv.*)
Schlinge, *f.*	SHLINNG-*uh*	snare (trap)
Schlitten, *m.*	SHLITT-*en*	sled
"	"	sleigh
Schlittschuh, *m.*	SHLITT-*shoo*	skate, ice
Schloss, *n.*	SHLAWSS	castle
"	"	lock (fastening)
schluchzen (1)	SHLOOKH-*tsen*	sob, to
schlucken (1)	SHLOOCK-*en*	swallow, to
Schlummer, *m.*	SHLOOMM-*ehr*	slumber
schlüpfrig	SHLÜPP-*frick*	slippery
schlürfen (1)	SHLÜR-*fen*	sip, to
Schluss, *m.*	SHLOOSS	conclusion
"	"	end
Schlüssel, *m.*	SHLÜSS-*el*	key (for lock)
Schmach, *f.*	SHMAH_KH	disgrace (shame)
schmal	SHMAHL	narrow
Schmalz, *m.*	SHMAHLLTS	lard
schmeicheln (1)	SHMYE_KH-*el'n*	flatter (praise insincerely), to
schmeissen (106)	SHMICE-*en*	fling, to
schmelzen (107)	SHMELLT-*sen*	melt (become liquid), to
Schmerz, *m.*	SHMEHRTS	ache
"	"	pain
schmerzen (1)	SHMEHR-*tsen*	ache, to
"	"	hurt (be painful), to
schmerzhaft	SHMEHRTS-*hahfft*	painful
Schmetterling, *m.*	SHMET-*tehr-ling*	butterfly
Schmied, *m.*	SHMEET	blacksmith
schmieden (1)	SHMEE-*den*	forge (shape), to
Schminke, *f.*	SHMINN-*kuh*	rouge
Schmuck, *m.*	SHMOOCK	jewelry
schmücken (1)	SHMÜCK-*en*	decorate (adorn), to
schmucklos	SHMOOCK-*lohss*	severe (austere)
Schmutz, *m.*	SHMOOTTS	dirt (unclean matter)
schmutzig	SHMOOTTS-*ick*	dirty (soiled)
"	"	foul (filthy)
Schnabel, *m.*	SHNAH-*bel*	bill (beak)
Schnecke, *f.*	SHNECK-*kuh*	snail
Schnee, *m.*	SHNAY	snow
Schneesturm, *m.*	SHNAY-*shtoorm*	blizzard
Schneide, *f.*	SHNYE-*duh*	edge (sharp side)
schneiden (108)	SHNYE-*den*	cut (divide into parts), to
"	"	cut (wound), to
Schneider, *m.*	SHNYE-*dehr*	tailor
schnell	SHNELL	fast
"	"	quick
"	"	rapid (*adj.*)
Schnellschrift, *f.*	SHNELL-*shrift*	shorthand (stenography, *n.*)
Schnitte, *f.*	SHNITT-*tuh*	slice
schnitzen (1)	SHNITT-*zen*	carve (cut designs), to
schnüffeln (1)	SHNÜFF-*el'n*	sniff, to
Schnur, *f.*	SHNOOR	string (cord)
Schnurrbart, *m.*	SHNOOR-*bahrrt*	mustache
Schnürsenkel, *m.*	SHNÜR-*zeng-kel*	lace (shoelace)
Schokolade, *f.*	*shoh-koh-*LAH-*duh*	chocolate
schon	SHONE	already
schön	SHÖN	beautiful
"	"	fair (not cloudy)
"	"	fine (good)
"	"	handsome (attractive)
schonen	SHOH-*nen*	spare (not harm), to
Schönheit, *f.*	SHÖN-*hite*	beauty
Schönheitsmittel, *n.*	SHÖN-*hites-mit-tel*	cosmetic (*n.*)
Schöpfung, *f.*	SHÖPP-*foong*	creation
Schornstein, *m.*	SHORN-*shtine*	chimney
Schoss, *m.*	SHOHSS	lap (of seated person)
schottisch	SHAWTT-*ish*	Scotch (*adj.*)
Schottland, *n.*	SHAWTT-*lahnnt*	Scotland
schräg liegen (76)	SHRAYG *leeg-en*	slant (slope), to

German	Pronunciation	English
Schrank, *m.*	SHRAHNNK	cupboard
Schranke, *f.*	SHRAHNN-*kuh*	barrier
Schraube, *f.*	SHR_OW-*buh*	screw (threaded nail)
Schraubenzieher, *m.*	SHR_OW-*ben-tsee-ehr*	screw driver
Schreck, *m.*	SHRECK	fright (alarm)
Schrecken, *m.*	SHRECK-*en*	terror
schrecklich	SHRECK-*likh*	terrible
Schrei, *m.*	SHRYE	shout (cry)
schreiben (109)	SHRIBE-*en*	write, to
Schreibfeder, *f.*	SHRIPE-*fay-dehr*	pen
Schreibmaschine, *f.*	SHRIBE-*mah-shee-nuh*	typewriter
Schreibpapier, *n.*	SHRIPE-*pah*-PEER	stationery (writing paper)
Schreibtisch, *m.*	SHRIPE-*tish*	desk
schreien (110)	SHRYE-*en*	cry (shout), to
"	"	shout (say loudly), to
schreiten (111)	SHRITE-*en*	stride (walk), to
Schrift, *f.*	SHRIFT	writing (handwriting)
Schriftsteller, *m.*	SHRIFT-*shtell-ehr*	writer (author)
Schriftstellerei, *f.*	SHRIFT-*shtell-uh*-RYE	writing (art of writing)
Schrifttum, *n.*	SHRIFT-*toom*	bibliography
schrill	SHRILL	shrill
Schritt, *m.*	SHRITT	step (stride)
Schublade, *f.*	SHOOP-*lah-duh*	drawer (sliding box)
schüchtern	SHÜKH-*tehrn*	bashful
"	"	shy
Schuh, *m.*	SHOO	shoe (footwear)
Schuld, *f.*	SHOOLLT	blame
"	"	debt
"	"	fault (cause for blame)
"	"	guilt
schulden (1)	SHOOLL-*den*	owe, to
schuldig	SHOOLL-*dick*	guilty
Schuldner, *m.*	SHOOLLD-*nehr*	debtor (*bus.*)
Schuldschein, *m.*	SHOOLLT-*shine*	bond (debenture)
"	"	note (promise to pay, *bus.*)
Schuldverschreibung, *f.*	SHOOLLT-*fehr-shrye-boong*	debenture
Schule, *f.*	SHOO-*luh*	school
Schüler, *m.*	SHÜ-*lehr*	pupil (student)
Schulgeld, *n.*	SHOOL-*gelt*	tuition (school fee)
Schulhaus, *n.*	SHOOL-*howss*	schoolhouse
Schulter, *f.*	SHOOLL-*tehr*	shoulder (*anat.*)
Schulunterricht, *m.*	SHOOL-*oonn-tehr-rikht*	schooling (instruction)
Schuppen, *m.*	SHOOPP-*en*	shed (shelter)
Schurke, *m.*	SHOORR-*kuh*	villain
Schürze, *f.*	SHÜR-*tsuh*	apron (garment)
Schuss, *m.*	SHOOSS	shot (from firearm)
Schüssel, *f.*	SHÜSS-*sel*	bowl (dish)
Schuster, *m.*	SHOO_SS-*tehr*	shoemaker
schütteln (1)	SHÜTT-*tel'n*	shake, to
Schutz, *m.*	SHOOTTS	protection
"	"	shelter
schützen (1)	SHÜTT-*sen*	protect, to
"	"	shelter, to
schwach	SHVAH_KH	feeble
"	"	weak
Schwäche, *f.*	SHVEH_KH-*uh*	weakness
schwächen (1)	SHVEH_KH-*en*	weaken (make weak), to
schwächlich	SHVEH_KH-*likh*	delicate (sickly)
Schwager, *m.*	SHVAH-*gehr*	brother-in-law
Schwägerin, *f.*	SHVAY-*guh-rin*	sister-in-law
Schwalbe, *f.*	SHVAHLL-*buh*	swallow (bird)
Schwamm, *m.*	SHVAHMM	sponge
Schwan, *m.*	SHVAHN	swan
schwanken (1)	SHVAHNNG-*ken*	sway (swing), to
Schwanz, *m.*	SHVAHNNTS	tail (of animal)
schwarz	SHVAHRRTS	black
Schweden, *n.*	SHVAY-*den*	Sweden
schwedisch	SHVAY-*dish*	Swedish (*adj.*)
Schwefel, *m.*	SHVAY-*fel*	sulphur
Schweigen bringen, zum (171)	*tsoom* SHVYE-*gen* BRINNG-*en*	hush (make quiet), to
Schwein, *n.*	SHVINE	hog
"	"	pig
"	"	swine
Schweinefleisch, *n.*	SHVINE-*uh-fly_sh*	pork

German	Pronunciation	English
Schweinsrippchen, *pl.*	SHVINES-*rip-kh_en*	pork chop
Schweiss, *m.*	SHVICE	sweat
Schweiz, *f.*	SHVITES	Switzerland
schweizerisch	SHVITE-*suh-rish*	Swiss (*adj.*)
schwellen (113)	SHVEL-*len*	swell (bulge), to
schwer	SHVAIR	difficult
"	"	hard
"	"	heavy
Schwermut, *m.*	SHVAIR-*moot*	melancholy (dejection)
"	"	sadness
Schwert, *n.*	SHVAIRT	sword
Schwester, *f.*	SHVESS-*tehr*	sister (*n.*)
Schwiegermutter, *f.*	SHVEE-*gehr-moott-ehr*	mother-in-law
Schwiegersohn, *m.*	SHVEE-*gehr-zohn*	son-in-law
Schwiegertochter, *f.*	SHVEE-*gehr-tawkht-ehr*	daughter-in-law
Schwiegervater, *m.*	SHVEE-*gehr-fah-tehr*	father-in-law
Schwierigkeit, *f.*	SHVEE-*rick-kite*	difficulty
Schwierigkeiten, *f. pl.*	SHVEE-*rick-kye-ten*	trouble (distress)
schwimmen (114)	SHVIMM-*men*	float (be buoyant), to
"	"	swim, to
Schwindel, *m.*	SHVINN-*del*	fraud (deception)
(ver)schwinden (115)	(*fehr*-)SHVINN-*den*	fade (disappear), to
schwindlig	SHVINND-*lick*	dizzy (unsteady)
schwingen (116)	SHVINNG-*en*	swing (oscillate), to
schwitzen (1)	SHVITT-*sen*	perspire, to
schwören (117)	SHVÖ-*ren*	swear (vow), to
See, *m.*	ZAY	lake
See-...	ZAY-...	marine (oceanic)
Seehund, *m.*	ZAY-*hoont*	seal (animal)
Seele, *f.*	ZAY-*luh*	soul
Seeräuber, *m.*	ZAY-*roy-behr*	pirate
Segen, *m.*	ZAYG-*en*	blessing (boon)
segnen (1)	ZAYG-*nen*	bless, to
sehen (118)	ZAY-*en*	see, to
Sehkraft, *f.*	ZAY-*krahfft*	sight (eyesight)
"	"	vision (eyesight)
sehnen, sich (1)	*zikh* ZAY-*nen*	long for, to
sehr	ZAIR	very (extremely)
Sehweite, *f.*	ZAY-*vye-tuh*	sight (range of view)
seicht	ZYE_KHT	shallow
Seide, *f.*	ZIDE-*uh*	silk (*n.*)
Seife, *f.*	ZIFE-*uh*	soap
sein (179)	ZINE	be, to
sein	ZINE	his (*poss. adj., poss. pron.*)
"	"	its (*poss. adj., poss. pron.*)
seit	ZITE	since (after, *prep.*)
seitdem	*zite*-DAME	since (from then to now, *adv.*)
Seite, *f.*	ZITE-*tuh*	face (surface)
"	"	page (leaf)
"	"	side
Sekretärin, *f.*	*zeck-ray*-TAIR-*een*	secretary (stenographer)
Sekunde, *f.*	*zay*-KOONN-*duh*	second (time unit)
selber	ZELL-*behr*	myself, yourself, etc.
"	"	oneself
"	"	self (*pron.*)
selbst	ZELLPST	itself
"	"	myself, yourself, etc.
"	"	oneself
selbstbewusst	ZELLPST-*buh-voost*	confident (self-assured)
Selbstbiographie, *f.*	ZELLPST-*bee-oh-grah-fee*	autobiography
Selbstmord, *m.*	ZELLPST-*mort*	suicide
selbstsüchtig	ZELLPST-*zükh-tick*	selfish
selbstverständlich	ZELLPST-*fehr*-SHTENNT-*likh*	certainly (*interj.*)
"	"	course, of
selig	ZAY-*lick*	late (deceased, *adj.*)
Sellerie, *m.*	ZELL-*uh-ree*	celery
selten	ZELL-*ten*	rare (uncommon)
"	"	seldom
seltsam	ZELLT-*zahm*	funny (odd)
"	"	quaint (unusual)
"	"	strange (peculiar)

German	Pronunciation	English
Senat,*m.*	*zay*-NAHT	senate
Senator,*m.*	*zay*-NAH-*tor*	senator
senden (176)	ZENN-*den*	beam (direct, *rad.*), to
"	"	send, to
senden, mit der Post (176)	MITT *dehr*-PAWSST ZENN-*den*	mail (post), to
Sendung,*f.*	ZENN-*doong*	consignment (*bus.*)
"	"	shipment (goods)
(Geld)Sendung,*f.*	(GELLT-)ZENN-*doong*	remittance
Senf,*m.*	ZENF	mustard
senkrecht	ZENK-*rekht*	vertical (*adj.*)
Sergeant,*m.*	*zehr*-ZHAHNNT	sergeant
Serviette,*f.*	*zehrv*-YET-*tuh*	napkin
setzen (1)	ZET-*sen*	set (put), to
setzen, sich	*zikh* ZET-*sen*	sit down, to
seufzen (1)	ZOYF-*lsen*	sigh, to
sich	ZIKH	itself
"	"	myself, yourself, etc.
		oneself
sicher	ZIKH-*ehr*	certain (sure)
"	"	certainly (surely, *adv.*)
"	"	safe (without risk)
"	"	secure
"	"	sure
Sicherheit,*f.*	ZIKH-*ehr-hite*	safety (*n.*)
"	"	security
Sicherheitsnadel,*f.*	ZIKH-*ehr-hite_s-nah-del*	safety pin
Sicherung,*f.*	ZIKH-*ehr-roong*	fuse (*elec.*)
sichtbar	ZIKHT-*bar*	visible
Sichttratte,*f.*	ZIKHT-*traht-tuh*	sight draft (*bus.*)
sie	ZEE	her
"	"	it
"	"	she
"	"	them
"	"	they
Sie	ZEE	you
sieben (1)	ZEE-*ben*	sift (separate), to
(An)Siedler,*m.*	(AHNN-)ZEED-*lehr*	colonist
Sieg,*m.*	ZEEK	victory
Siegel,*m.*	ZEEG-*el*	seal (mark)
Sieger,*m.*	ZEEG-*ehr*	victor
siegreich	ZEEG-*rye_kh*	victorious
Signal,*n.*	*zig*-NAHL	signal
Signalhorn,*n.*	*zig*-NAHL-*horn*	bugle
Silbe,*f.*	ZILL-*buh*	syllable
Silber,*n.*	ZILL-*behr*	silver (metal,*n.*)
singen (119)	ZING-*en*	sing, to
(ver)sinken (120)	(*fehr*-)ZING-*ken*	sink, to
Sinn,*m.*	ZINN	meaning
"	"	sense (signification)
Sitte,*f.*	ZITT-*luh*	custom (habit)
sittlich	ZITT-*likh*	moral (ethical)
Sitz,*m.*	ZITTS	seat
sitzen (122)	ZITT-*sen*	sit (be sitting), to
Sitzung,*f.*	ZITT-*soong*	session
Skandal,*m.*	*skahn*-DAHL	scandal
Skelett,*n.*	*skay*-LETT	skeleton (*anat.*)
Sklave,*m.*	SKLAH-*vuh*	slave
Sklaverei,*f.*	SKLAH-*vuh-rye*	slavery
Slang,*m.*	SLANG	slang (*n.*)
slawisch	SLAH-*vish*	Slavic (*adj.*)
Smaragd,*m.*	*smah*-RAHCKT	emerald
so	ZOH	so (to such a degree, *adv.*)
"	"	thus (in this way)
Socke,*f.*	ZAWCK-*uh*	sock (garment)
Sockel,*m.*	ZAWCK-*el*	base (foundation)
Sofa,*n.*	ZOH-*fah*	sofa
Sohle,*f.*	ZOH-*luh*	sole (of shoe)
Sohn,*m.*	ZONE	son
solch	ZOHLKH	such (of that kind, *adj.*)
Soldat,*m.*	*zawll*-DAHT	soldier
sollen (167)	ZAWLL-*en*	ought (*v.*)
"	"	should (*v.*)
Sommer,*m.*	ZAWMM-*ehr*	summer (*n.*)
sonderbar	ZAWNN-*dehr-bar*	odd
"	"	queer
Sondervergütung,*f.*	ZAWNN-*dehr-fehr*-GÜ-*toong*	bonus (extra wages)

German	Pronunciation	English
Sonne,*f.*	ZAWNN-*uh*	sun
Sonnenaufgang,*m.*	ZAWNN-*en-owf-gahnng*	sunrise
Sonnenbrand,*m.*	ZAWNN-*en-brahnnt*	sunburn
Sonnenbrille,*f.*	ZAWNN-*en-brill-uh*	sunglasses
Sonnenlicht,*n.*	ZAWNN-*en-likht*	sunlight
Sonnenschein,*m.*	ZAWNN-*en-shine*	sunshine
Sonnenuntergang,*m.*	ZAWNN-*en-oonn-tehr-gähnng*	sunset
sonnig	ZAWNN-*ick*	sunny
sonst	ZAWNNST	else (if not, *adv.*)
"	"	else (instead, *adv.*)
"	"	otherwise (under other conditions)
so oft	zo AWFFT	whenever
Sorge,*f.*	ZAWR-*guh*	care (concern)
"	"	worry (anxiety)
Sorte,*f.*	ZAWR-*tuh*	sort
Sozialismus,*m.*	*zohts-yah*-LISS-*mooss*	socialism
Sozialist,*n.*	*zohts-yah*-LIST	socialist (*n.*)
Soziologie,*f.*	*zohts-yoh-loh*-G_EE	sociology
spähen (1)	SHPAY-*en*	peer (look intently), to
Späher,*m.*	SHPAY-*ehr*	scout (lookout)
Spalte,*f.*	SHPAHLL-*tuh*	column (*print.*)
spalten (1)	SHPAHLL-*ten*	crack (make split), to
"	"	split (rend), to
Spanien,*n.*	SHPAHN-*yen*	Spain
spanisch	SHPAH-*nish*	Spanish (*adj.*)
Spanne,*f.*	SHPAHNN-*nuh*	span (spread)
Spannung,*f.*	SHPAHNN-*noong*	tension
sparen (1)	SHPAH-*ren*	save (store up), to
Spargel,*m.*	SHPAHR-*gel*	asparagus
Sparkonto,*n.*	SHPAHR-*kawnn-toh*	savings account
sparsam	SHPAHR-*zahm*	economical (thrifty)
Sparsamkeit,*f.*	SHPAHR-*zahm-kite*	economy (thrift)
Spass,*m.*	SHPAHSS	fun
Spass machen (1)	SHPAHSS MAH_KH-*en*	joke (jest), to
spät	SHPATE	late (at relative time, *adv.*)
"	"	late (tardily, *adv.*)
"	"	tardy (*adj.*)
Spaten,*m.*	SHPAH-*ten*	spade (tool)
Spatz,*m.*	SHPAHTTS	sparrow
Spaziergang,*m.*	*shpah*-TSEER-*gahng*	walk (stroll)
Spazierstock,*m.*	*shpah*-TSEER-*shtawck*	cane (walking stick)
Speck,*m.*	SHPECK	bacon
Spediteur,*m.*	*shpay-dee*-TÖR	carrier (*bus.*)
"	"	shipping agent
Speer,*m.*	SHPAIR	spear (weapon)
Speisekarte,*f.*	SHPYE-*zuh-kahr-tuh*	menu
Speisewagen,*m.*	SHPYE-*zuh-vah-gen*	diner (railway dining car)
Speisezimmer,*n.*	SHPYE-*zuh-tsimm-ehr*	dining room
spenden (1)	SHPENN-*den*	donate, to
(ver)sperren (1)	(*fehr*-)SHPEHRR-*ren*	bar, to
"	"	block (obstruct), to
Spiegel,*m.*	SHPEE-*gel*	mirror
Spiegelbild,*n.*	SHPEE-*gel-billt*	reflection (image)
Spiel,*n.*	SHPEEL	game (contest)
spielen (1)	SHPEE-*len*	play, to
Spieler,*m.*	SHPEE-*lehr*	player (in a game)
Spielgefährte,*m.*	SHPEEL-*guh-fair-tuh*	playmate
Spielkarte,*f.*	SHPEEL-*kahr-tuh*	card, playing
Spielplatz,*m.*	SHPEEL-*plahtts*	playground
Spielraum,*m.*	SHPEEL-*r_owm*	margin (surplus)
Spielzeug,*n.*	SHPEEL-*tsoyk*	toy
Spinat,*m.*	*shpee*-NAHT	spinach
Spinne,*f.*	SHPINN-*nuh*	spider
spinnen (124)	SHPINN-*nen*	spin (form thread), to
Spion,*m.*	*shpee*-OHN	spy
Spionage,*f.*	*shpee-oh*-NAH-*zhuh*	espionage
Spitze,*f.*	SHPITT-*suh*	lace (fabric)
"	"	peak (mountain top)
"	"	point (sharp end)
"	"	tip
spitzig	SHPITT-*sick*	pointed (tapered)
Spitzname,*m.*	SHPITTS-*nah-muh*	nickname
Sporn,*m.*	SHPAWRN	spur (spike)
Sport,*m.*	SHPAWRT	sport (game)
Spott,*m.*	SHPAWTT	ridicule
Sprache,*f.*	SHPRAH_KH-*uh*	language

German	Pronunciation	English
sprechen (125)	SHPREH_KH-*en*	speak (talk), to
Sprechen,*n.*	SHPREH_KH-*en*	speech (oral expression)
sprengen (1)	SHPRENG-*en*	blast (explode), to
Sprengstoff,*m.*	SHPRENG-*shtawff*	explosive (*n.*)
sprenkeln (1)	SHPRENG-*kel'n*	sprinkle (scatter), to
Sprichwort,*n.*	SHPRIKH-*vort*	proverb
Springbrunnen,*m.*	SHPRING-*broonn-en*	fountain
springen (127)	"	bounce, to
"	"	jump (bound), to
"	"	leap, to
"	"	spring, to
Spritze,*f.*	SHPRITT-*suh*	syringe
spritzen (1)	SHPRITT-*sen*	splash, to
"	"	squirt, to
spröde	SHPRÖ-*duh*	brittle
sprudeln (1)	SHPROO-*del'n*	bubble, to
Sprung,*m.*	SHPROONNG	bound
"	"	jump
"	"	leap
spucken (1)	SHPOOCK-*en*	spit, to
Spule,*f.*	SHPOO-*luh*	coil (*elec.*)
Spur,*f.*	SHPOOR	mark (evidence)
"	"	trace (vestige)
Staat,*m.*	SHTAHT	state (nation)
Staatenbund,*m.*	SHTAH-*ten-boonnt*	commonwealth
Staatseinnahmen, *f.pl.*	SHTAHTS-*ine-nah-men*	revenue (*govt.*)
Staatsmann,*m.*	SHTAHTS-*mahnn*	statesman
Staatswissen- schaft,*f.*	SHTAHTS-*viss-en- shahfft*	political science
Stab,*m.*	SHTAHP	staff (stick)
Stadt,*f.*	SHTAHTT	city
"	"	town
städtlich	SHTETT-*likh*	urban
Stahl,*m.*	SHTAHL	steel
Stall,*m.*	SHTAHLL	stable (shelter)
Stamm,*m.*	SHTAHMM	tribe
"	"	trunk (stem)
stammeln (1)	SHTAHMM-*el'n*	stammer, to
stampfen (1)	SHTAHMMP-*fen*	stamp (tread heavily), to
standfest	SHTAHNNT-*fest*	stable (steadfast)
Stange,*f.*	SHTAHNNG-*uh*	bar
"	"	pole
"	"	rod
Stapel lassen, vom (71)	*fawmm* SHTAH-*pel* LAHSS-*senn*	launch (set afloat), to
Star,*m.*	SHTAHRR	blackbird
stark	SHTARK	stout
"	"	strong
Stärke,*f.*	SHTEHR-*kuh*	starch (in food)
stärken (1)	SHTEHR-*ken*	strengthen, to
starr	SHTAHRR	numb
starren (1)	SHTAHRR-*en*	stare, to
(an)starren	(AHNN-)SHTAHRR-*en*	glare (stare), to
statt	SHTAHTT	instead of
Statut,*n.*	*shtah*-TOO_T	by-law
Staub,*m.*	SHT_OWP	dust
"	"	powder
staubig	SHT_OW-*bick*	dusty
Staubsauger,*m.*	SHTOWB-*zow-gehr*	vacuum cleaner
stechen (128)	SHTEH_KH-*en*	prick, to
"	"	sting (pierce skin), to
(er)stechen	(*ehr*-)SHTEH_KH-*en*	stab, to
Steckdose,*f.*	SHTECK-*doh-zuh*	outlet (*elec.*)
stecken (1)	SHTECK-*en*	stick (thrust), to
"	"	tuck (slip inside), to
Stecker,*m.*	SHTECK-*ehr*	plug (*elec.*)
Stecknadel,*f.*	SHTECK-*nah-del*	pin (sewing accessory)
stehen (129)	SHTAY-*en*	stand (be upright), to
stehlen (130)	SHTAY-*len*	steal, to
steif	SHTIFE	stiff (inflexible)
steigen (131)	SHTYE-*gen*	climb (rise), to
"	"	rise (ascend), to
"	"	rise (increase), to
steil	SHTILE	steep (*adj.*)
Stein,*m.*	SHTINE	stone (piece of rock)
Stelle,*f.*	SHTELL-*uh*	spot (place)
"	"	stead (place)
stellen (1)	SHTELL-*en*	put (place), to

German	Pronunciation	English
Stelle setzen, an die (1)	*ahn dee* SHTELL-*uh* *zett-sen*	substitute (put in place of), to
stempeln (1)	SHTEMM-*pel'n*	stamp (mark), to
Stengel,*m.*	SHTENG-*el*	stalk (stem)
Stenografin,*f.*	*shtay-noh*-GRAHF-*in*	stenographer
Steppdecke,*f.*	SHTEPP-*deck-uh*	quilt (bedcover)
sterben (132)	SHTEHR-*ben*	die, to
sterblich	SHTEHRP-*likh*	mortal (*adj.*)
Stern,*m.*	SHTEHRN	star (*astron.*)
stetig	SHTAY-*tick*	steady (regular)
Steuer,*f.*	SHTOY-*ehr*	tax (*n.*)
steuern (1)	SHTOY-*ehrn*	control (direct), to
"	"	steer, to
Steward,*m.*	STOO-*art*	steward (attendant on ship)
Stich,*m.*	SHTIKH	stitch (of sewing)
Stiefel,*m.*	SHTEE-*fel*	boot (footgear)
Stiefmutter,*f.*	SHTEEF-*moott-tehr*	stepmother
Stiefmütterchen,*n.*	SHTEEF-*mütt-tehr-kh_en*	pansy
Stiefsohn,*m.*	SHTEEF-*zohn*	stepson
Stieftochter,*f.*	SHTEEF-*tawkh-tehr*	stepdaughter
Stiefvater,*m.*	SHTEEF-*fah-tehr*	stepfather
Stiel,*m.*	SHTEEL	shaft (*mech.*)
"	"	stem (*bot.*)
Stier,*m.*	SHTEER	bull (male bovine)
Stil,*m.*	SHTEEL	style (manner)
still	SHTILL	quiet (*adj.*)
"	"	silent (mute)
Stille,*f.*	SHTILL-*uh*	silence (stillness)
Stiller Ozean,*m.*	SHTILL-*ehr* OH-*tsay-ahn*	Pacific (*n.*)
Stimme,*f.*	SHTIMM-*muh*	voice
"	"	vote
stimmen (1)	SHTIMM-*men*	vote, to
Stimmung,*f.*	SHTIMM-*oong*	mood (humor)
stinken (133)	SHTING-*ken*	stink, to
Stirn,*f.*	SHTEERN	forehead
Stirn runzeln, die (1)	*dee* SHTEERN ROONTS-*el'n*	frown, to
Stock,*m.*	SHTAWCK	floor (story)
"	"	stick (small branch)
Stockholm,*n.*	SHTAWCK-*hawlm*	Stockholm
Stockwerk,*n.*	SHTAWCK-*vehrk*	story (floor)
Stoff,*m.*	SHTAWFF	cloth
"	"	fabric
"	"	material
"	"	matter
"	"	stuff
"	"	substance
stöhnen (1)	SHTÖ-*nen*	groan, to
"	"	moan, to
stolpern (1)	SHTAWLL-*pehrn*	stumble, to
"	"	trip, to
stolz	SHTAWLLTS	proud (taking pride in)
Stolz,*m.*	SHTAWLLTS	pride (self-esteem)
stopfen (1)	SHTAWP-*fen*	darn (mend), to
Stöpsel,*m.*	SHTÖPP-*sel*	plug (stopper)
Storch,*m.*	SHTAWRKH	stork
stören (1)	SHTÖ-*ren*	bother (annoy), to
"	"	disturb, to
"	"	trouble (disquiet), to
Stoss,*m.*	SHTAWSS	push (shove)
stossen (134)	SHTOH-*sen*	pound (pummel), to
"	"	push (shove), to
"	"	thrust, to
stottern (1)	SHTAWTT-*ehrn*	stutter, to
Strafe,*f.*	SHTRAH-*fuh*	penalty
"	"	punishment
strafen (1)	SHTRAH-*fen*	punish, to
straff	SHTRAHFF	tight (taut)
Strahl,*m.*	SHTRAHL	beam
"	"	ray
strahlen (1)	SHTRAH-*len*	beam (shine), to
strahlend	SHTRAH-*lent*	radiant
Strähne,*f.*	SHTRAY-*nuh*	strand (thread)
Strand,*m.*	SHTRAHNNT	beach (strand)
Strasse,*f.*	SHTRAH-*suh*	road
"	"	street
Strassenbahn,*f.*	SHTRAH-*sen-bahn*	trolley (street car)

German	Pronunciation	English
Strassenkreuzung, *f.*	SHTRAH-*sen-kroyts-soong*	crossroads
Strassenpflaster,*n.*	SHTRAH-*sen-pflahss-tehr*	pavement
Strauch,*m.*	SHTR_OWKH	shrub
streben (1)	SHTRAY-*ben*	strive (exert oneself), to
streicheln (1)	SHTRYE-*kh_el'n*	stroke (rub gently), to
Streichholz,*n.*	SHTRYE_KH-*hawllts*	match (lucifer)
Streifen,*m.*	SHTRYE-*fen*	streak
"	"	strip (band)
		stripe
Streik,*m.*	SHTRIKE	strike (work stoppage)
streiken (1)	SHTRIKE-*en*	strike (stop work), to
Streit,*m.*	SHTRITE	conflict (struggle)
"	"	dispute
		quarrel
streiten (136)	SHTRYE-*ten*	quarrel (dispute), to
Streitfrage,*f.*	SHTRITE-*frah-guh*	issue (question)
Streitigkeit,*f.*	SHTRITE-*ick-kite*	litigation
streng	SHTRENG	severe
"	"	stern (*adj.*)
"	"	strict (stringent)
Strenge,*f.*	SHTRENG-*uh*	severity (sternness)
Strichpunkt,*m.*	SHTRIKH-*poonkt*	semicolon
Strick,*m.*	SHTRICK	cord (rope)
Strickarbeit,*f.*	SHTRICK-*ahrr-bite*	knitting
stricken (1)	SHTRICK-*en*	knit, to
Stroh,*n.*	SHTROH	straw (dry grain stalks)
Strom,*m.*	SHTROHM	current (of electricity)
"	"	stream (rivulet)
strömen (1)	SHTRÖ-*men*	stream, to
Strömung,*f.*	SHTRÖ-*moong*	current (of water)
Struktur,*f.*	*shtroock*-TOOR	structure (arrangement of parts)
Strumpf,*m.*	SHTROOMPF	stocking
Strumpfband,*n.*	SHTROOMPF-*bahnnt*	garter
Stück,*n.*	SHTÜCK	piece (bit)
Stückarbeit,*f.*	SHTÜCK-*ahr-bite*	piecework (*n.*)
Stückchen,*n.*	SHTÜCK-*kh_en*	morsel (small bit)
stückweise	SHTÜCK-*vize-uh*	piecemeal (*adv.*)
Student,*m.*	*shtoo*-DENT	student
studieren (1)	*shtoo*-DEE-*ren*	study, to
Studium,*n.*	SHTOOD-*yoomm*	study (active learning)
Stufe,*f.*	SHTOO-*fuh*	stage (period)
"	"	step (stair)
Stuhl,*m.*	SHTOOL	chair
stumm	SHTOOMM	dumb
"	"	mute (silent)
stumpf	SHTOOMPF	blunt
"	"	dull
Stumpf,*m.*	SHTOOMPF	stump (of tree)
Stunde,*f.*	SHTOONN-*duh*	hour
Stundenplan,*m.*	SHTOONN-*den-plahn*	schedule (timetable)
Sturm,*m.*	SHTOORM	storm
Sturm(wind),*m.*	SHTOORM(-*vinnt*)	gale (wind)
stürmisch	SHTÜRR-*mish*	stormy
Sturz,*m.*	SHTOORTS	drop (sudden fall)
"	"	fall
stürzen (1)	SHTÜR-*tsen*	dash (rush), to
stürzen, sich	*zikh* SHTÜR-*tsen*	rush (dash), to
Stute,*f.*	SHTOO-*tuh*	mare
(unter)stützen (1)	(*oonn-tehr-*)SHTÜTT-*sen*	support (hold up), to
subjektiv	*zoob-yeck*-TEEF	subjective
Suche,*f.*	ZOOKH-*uh*	quest
"	"	search (hunt)
suchen (1)	ZOOKH-*en*	look for, to
Südamerika,*n.*	ZÜD-*ah*-MAY-*ree-kah*	South America
Süden,*m.*	*zü-den*	south (*n.*)
südlich	ZÜD-*likh*	southern
südöstlich	*züd*-ÖST-*likh*	southeast (*adj.*)
südwestlich	*züd*-VEST-*likh*	southwest (*adj.*)
Summe,*f.*	ZOOMM-*uh*	sum (quantity)
Summen,*n.*	ZOOMM-*en*	hum (murmur)
Sumpf,*m.*	ZOOMPF	marsh
"	"	mire (bog)
		swamp (*n.*)

German	Pronunciation	English
Sumpffieber,*n.*	ZOOMPF-*fee-behr*	malaria
Sünde,*f.*	ZÜNN-*duh*	sin
Sünder,*m.*	ZÜNN-*dehr*	sinner
sündigen (1)	ZÜNN-*dee-gen*	sin, to
Suppe,*f.*	ZOOPP-*uh*	soup
Surinam,*n.*	ZOO-*ree-nahm*	Surinam
süss	ZÜSS	sweet (pleasant tasting)
Süssigkeit,*f.*	*zü-sick-kite*	candy
"	"	sweetness
Sweater,*m.*	SVAY-*tehr*	sweater
Symphonie,*f.*	*zim-foh*-NEE	symphony
Symptom,*n.*	*zimp*-TOME	symptom
System,*n.*	*züs*-TAME	system (method)
Tabelle,*f.*	*tah*-BELL-*luh*	table (tabulation)
Tablett,*n.*	*tah*-BLETT	tray
Tabak,*m.*	TAH-*bahck*	tobacco
Tadel,*m.*	TAH-*del*	criticism (censure)
tadeln (1)	TAH-*del'n*	blame, to
Tag,*m.*	TAHK	day
Tag, folgender,*m.*	FAWLL-*gen-dehr* TAHK	morrow
Tageslicht,*n.*	TAH-*gess-likht*	daylight
täglich	TAYG-*likh*	daily (*adj.*)
Tagung,*f.*	TAH-*goong*	convention
"	"	meeting (assembly)
Taille,*f.*	TAHLL-*yuh*	waist (*anat.*)
Tal,*n.*	TAHL	valley
Talent,*n.*	*tah*-LENT	talent
Tante,*f.*	TAHNN-*tuh*	aunt
Tantieme,*f.*	*tahng-tee*-EH-*muh*	royalty (fee)
Tanz,*m.*	TAHNNTS	dance (movement to music)
tanzen (1)	TAHNNTS-*sen*	dance, to
Tanzgesellschaft,*f.*	TAHNNTS-*guh-zell-shahfft*	dance (party)
tapfer	TAHPP-*fehr*	brave
Tasche,*f.*	TAHSH-*uh*	pocket
Taschenlampe,*f.*	TAHSH-*en-lahm-puh*	flashlight
Taschentuch,*n.*	TAHSH-*en-too_kh*	handkerchief
Tasse,*f.*	TAHSS-*suh*	cup
tasten, nach... (1)	NAH_KH... TAHSS-*ten*	feel (grope) for, to
Tat,*f.*	TAHT	act
"	"	deed
Tat, in der	*in dare* TAHT	really (indeed)
tätig	TAY-*tick*	active (energetic)
Tätigkeit,*f.*	TAY-*tick-kite*	activity (exertion of energy)
Tatsache,*f.*	TAHT-*zahkh-uh*	fact
Tau,*n.*	T_OW	dew
"	"	rope
taub	T_OWP	deaf
Taube,*f.*	T_OW-*buh*	dove
"	"	pigeon
tauchen (1)	T_OW-*kh_en*	plunge (hurl oneself), to
(ein)tauchen	(INE-)T_OW-*kh_en*	dip (immerse), to
tauen (1)	T_OW-*en*	thaw, to
Taufe,*f.*	T_OW-*fuh*	baptism
taumeln (1)	T_OW-*mel'n*	reel (stagger), to
(Aus)Tausch,*m.*	(OWSS-)T_OWSH	exchange (barter)
(aus)tauschen (1)	(OWSS-)T_OW-*shen*	exchange (interchange), to
Taxi,*n.*	TAHCK-*see*	cab
"	"	taxi
Tee,*m.*	TAY	tea
Teelöffel,*m.*	TAY-*löff-el*	spoon (teaspoon)
Teer,*m.*	TAIR	tar
Teich,*m.*	TYE_KH	pond
Teig,*m.*	TIKE	batter (flour mixture)
Teil,*m.*	TILE	part
"	"	portion
"	"	section
teilen (1)	TIE-*len*	divide, to (*arith.*)
"	"	divide (make separate), to
"	"	share, to
teilen, sich	*zikh* TILE-*en*	divide (become separate), to
Teilhaber,*m.*	TILE-*hah-behr*	partner (*bus.*)
Teilnahme,*f.*	TILE-*nah-muh*	interest (share)
teilnehmen (80)	TILE-*nay-men*	participate, to
teils	TILES	partly
teilweise	TILE-*vize-uh*	partial (incomplete)
Tel Aviv,*n.*	*tell ah*-VEEF	Tel Aviv

German	Pronunciation	English
Telegramm,*n.*	*tay-luh*-GRAHMM	telegram
"	"	wire
telegraphieren (1)	*tay-luh-grah*-FEE-*ren*	telegraph, to
telephonieren (1)	*tay-luh-foh*-NEE-*ren*	phone, to
Teller,*m.*	TELL-*ehr*	plate (shallow dish)
Tempel,*m.*	TEMM-*pel*	temple (place of worship)
Temperatur,*f.*	*temm-puh-rah*-TOOR	temperature
Tempo,*n.*	TEMM-*po*	pace (rate)
Tennis,*n.*	TENN-*niss*	tennis
Teppich,*m.*	TEPP-*ikh*	carpet
"	"	rug
Terrasse,*f.*	*tehr*-RAHSS-*uh*	terrace
Testament,*n.*	*tess-tah*-MENT	will (document)
teuer	TOY-*ehr*	expensive
Teufel,*m.*	TOY-*fel*	devil
Text,*m.*	TEXT	text
Theater,*n.*	*tay*-AH-*tehr*	theater
Thema,*n.*	TAY-*mah*	theme (subject)
"	"	topic
Theorie,*f.*	*tay-oh*-REE	theory
Thermometer,*n.*	*tehr-moh*-MAY-*tehr*	thermometer
Thron,*m.*	TROHN	throne
tief	TEEF	deep
"	"	profound
Tiefe,*f.*	TEE-*fuh*	depth (deepness)
Tier,*n.*	TEER	animal
"	"	beast
"	"	brute (*n.*)
Tiger,*m.*	TEE-*gehr*	tiger
Tilgung,*f.*	TILL-*goong*	amortization (*bus.*)
Tinte,*f.*	TINN-*tuh*	ink
tippen (1)	TIPP-*pen*	type (typewrite), to
Tisch,*m.*	TISH	table (furniture)
Tischtuch,*n.*	TISH-*too_kh*	tablecloth
Tochter,*f.*	TAWKH-*tehr*	daughter
Tod,*m.*	TOTE	death
Todesanzeige,*f.*	TOH-*dess-ahnn-tsye-guh*	obituary (*n.*)
tödlich	TÖD-*likh*	deadly
"	"	fatal
Toilette,*f.*	*too-ah*-LETT-*tuh*	toilet (water closet)
Tokio,*n.*	TOHK-*yoh*	Tokyo
Tomate,*f.*	*toh*-MAH-*tuh*	tomato
Ton,*m.*	TONE	clay
"	"	tone (quality of sound)
Topf,*m.*	TAWPPF	pot (container)
Tor,*n.*	TOHR	gate
Torheit,*f.*	TOHR-*hite*	folly
töricht	TÖ-*rikht*	foolish
Torpedo,*n.*	*tohr*-PAY-*doh*	torpedo
tot	TOTE	dead
töten (1)	TÖ-*ten*	kill, to
Tour,*f.*	TOOR	tour
Tourist,*m.*	*too*-RIST	tourist (*n.*)
Trab,*m.*	TRAHP	trot
Tragbahre,*f.*	TRAHK-*bar-uh*	litter (stretcher)
tragen (137)	TRAH-*gen*	bear, to
"	"	carry, to
"	"	wear (have on), to
tragisch	TRAH-*gish*	tragic
Tragödie,*f.*	*trah*-GÖD-*yuh*	tragedy
trainieren (1)	*tray*-NEE-*ren*	coach (train), to
Traktor,*m.*	TRAHCK-*tor*	tractor (farm machine)
trampeln (1)	TRAHMM-*pel'n*	trample, to
Träne,*f.*	TRAY-*nuh*	tear (teardrop)
Transport,*m.*	*trahnns*-PORT	transit (passage)
Transportwagen,*m.*	*trahnns*-PORT-*vahg-en*	van (vehicle)
Tratte,*f.*	TRAHT-*tuh*	draft (check)
Traube,*f.*	TR_OW-*buh*	grape
trauern (1)	TR_OW-*ehrn*	grieve, to
"	"	mourn (feel grief), to
Traum,*m.*	TR_OWM	dream
träumen (1)	TROY-*men*	dream, to
traurig	TR_OW-*rick*	mournful (saddening)
"	"	sad (sorrowful)

German	Pronunciation	English
treffen, (sich) (138)	(*zikh*) TREFF-*en*	meet (encounter), to
treiben (139)	TRY-*ben*	drift (float), to
(an)treiben	(AHNN-)TRY-*ben*	drive (propel), to
trennen (1)	TRENN-*en*	separate (disconnect), to
"	"	sever, to
trennen, sich	*zikh* TRENN-*en*	part (leave each other), to
"	"	separate (come apart), to
Trennung,*f.*	TRENN-*oong*	separation
Treppe,*f.*	TREPP-*puh*	stairway
Treppe hinauf, die	*dee* TREPP-*puh hin*-OWF	upstairs (to upper story, *adv.*)
Treppe hinunter (herunter), die	*dee* TREPP-*puh hin*-OONN-*tehr* (*hair*-OONN-*tehr*)	downstairs (downward)
treten (140)	TRAY-*len*	step, to
treu	TROY	faithful
"	"	loyal
Treue,*f.*	TROY-*uh*	allegiance
"	"	loyalty
Treulosigkeit,*f.*	TROY-*loh-zick-kite*	disloyalty
Trick,*m.*	TRICK	trick (ruse)
trinken (142)	TRING-*ken*	drink, to
Trinkgeld,*n.*	TRINK-*gelt*	tip (gratuity)
Triumph,*m.*	*tree*-OOMMF	triumph
trocken	TRAWCK-*en*	dry
trocknen (1)	TRAWCK-*nen*	dry (become dry), to
tropfen (1)	TRAWPP-*fen*	drip, to
Tropfen,*m.*	TRAWPP-*fen*	drop (droplet)
Trommel,*f.*	TRAWMM-*el*	drum (*mus.*)
Trompete,*f.*	*trawm*-PAY-*tuh*	trumpet (*mus.*)
Trost,*m.*	TROHST	comfort (solace)
"	"	consolation
trösten (1)	TRÖS-*ten*	comfort (console), to
trotz	TRAWTTS	despite (*prep.*)
trotzdem	TRAWTTS-*dame*	nevertheless
trotzen (1)	TRAWTT-*sen*	defy, to
trübe	TRÜ-*buh*	dim
Trübsinn,*m.*	TRÜB-*zin*	gloom (depression)
trübsinnig	TRÜB-*zin-ick*	gloomy (melancholy)
Truppen,*f.pl.*	TROOPP-*en*	troops (*mil.*)
Trust,*m.*	TROOSST	trust (cartel)
Truthahn,*m.*	TROOT-*hahn*	turkey
Tschechoslowakei,*f.*	*cheh-kho-slo-vah*-KIE	Czechoslovakia
Tuberkulose,*f.*	*too-behr-koo*-LOH-*zuh*	tuberculosis
tüchtig	TÜKH-*tick*	capable
"	"	efficient
Tugend,*f.*	TOO-*g_ent*	virtue (moral excellence)
Tulpe,*f.*	TOOLL-*puh*	tulip
tun (180)	TOON	do, to
Tunnel,*m.*	TOONN-*el*	tunnel
Tür,*f.*	TÜRR	door
Türkei,*f.*	*türr*-KYE	Turkey
türkisch	TÜRR-*kish*	Turkish (*adj.*)
Turm,*m.*	TOORRM	tower
Turnhalle,*f.*	TOORRN-*hahll-luh*	gymnasium (athletic arena)
Tweed,*m.*	TWEED	tweed (cloth)
typisch	TÜ-*pish*	typical
Tyrann,*m.*	*tü*-RAHNN	tyrant
übel	Ü-*bel*	evil (*adj.*)
Übel,*n.*	Ü-*bel*	evil (*n.*)
übelnehmen (80)	Ü-*bel-nay-men*	resent, to
über	Ü-*behr*	about (concerning)
"	"	above (higher than, *prep.*)
"	"	across (from side to side)
"	"	across (to the other side)
"	"	by (via, *prep.*)
"	"	over (above, *prep.*)
"	"	past (beyond, *prep.*)
überall	*ü-behr*-AHLL	everywhere
überall in	*ü-behr*-AHLL *in*	throughout (in every part of, *prep.*)
überblicken (1)	*ü-behr*-BLICK-*en*	review (look over again), to
Überbringer,*m.*	*ü-behr*-BRING-*ehr*	bearer (*banking*)
überdies	*ü-behr*-DEESS	further (to greater extent), to

German	Pronunciation	English
Übereinkunft, *f.*	*ü-behr-*INE*-koonnft*	agreement (mutual understanding)
übereinstimmen (1)	*ü-behr-*INE*-shtimm-men*	agree (concur), to
übereinstimmen, nicht	NIKHT *ü-behr-*INE*-shtimm-en*	disagree (differ), to
Übereinstimmung, *f.* ,,	*Ü-behr-*INE*-shtimm-oong* ,,	accord (agreement) sympathy
Überfahrt, *f.*	*Ü-behr-fahrrt*	crossing (ocean voyage)
überfällig	*Ü-behr-fell-ick*	overdue (in arrears)
Übergabe, *f.*	*Ü-behr-gah-buh*	surrender (*mil.*)
übergeben (43) ,,	*ü-behr-*GAY*-ben* ,,	cede, to give (deliver), to
über...hinaus	*ü-behr...hin-*OWSS	beyond (farther on than, *prep.*)
überlegen, sich (1)	*zikh ü-behr-*LAY*-gen*	consider (reflect on), to
Überlegung, *f.* ,, ,,	*ü-behr-*LAY*-goong* ,, ,,	consideration (thought) reflection (meditation)
Überlieferung, *f.* ,, ,,	*ü-behr-*LEE*-fehr-oong* ,, ,,	delivery (handing over) tradition
Übermass, *n.*	*Ü-behr-mahss*	excess
übermässig	*Ü-behr-may-sick*	excessive
überraschen (1)	*ü-behr-*RAHSH*-en*	surprise, to
Überraschung, *f.*	*ü-behr-*RAHSH*-oong*	surprise
überreden (1)	*ü-behr-*RAY*-den*	persuade, to
überreichen (1)	*ü-behr-*RYE*-kh_en*	present (give), to
überschreiten (111) ,, ,,	*ü-behr-*SHRYE*-ten* ,, ,,	cross (traverse), to exceed, to
Überschrift, *f.* ,,	*Ü-behr-shrift* ,,	heading title (name)
Überschuss, *m.*	*Ü-behr-shooss*	surplus (*n.*)
Überschwemmung, *f.*	*ü-behr-*SHVEMM*-moong*	flood
Überseedampfer, *m.*	*Ü-behr-zay-*DAHMMP*-fehr*	liner, ocean
überseeisch	*Ü-behr-zay-ish*	oversea(s) (*adj.*)
übersehen (1)	*ü-behr-*ZAY*-en*	overlook (disregard), to
übersetzen (1)	*ü-behr-*ZET*-sen*	translate, to
überspringen (127)	*ü-behr-*SHPRING*-en*	skip (omit), to
Überstunden, *f.pl.*	*Ü-behr-shtoonn-den*	overtime (*bus.*, *n.*)
übertragbar	*ü-behr-*TRAHG*-bar*	negotiable (*bus.*)
übertreffen (138)	*ü-behr-*TREFF*-en*	surpass, to
übertreiben (139)	*ü-behr-*TRY*-ben*	exaggerate, to
überwältigen (1)	*ü-behr-*VELL*-tih-gen*	overcome (conquer), to
überweisen (155)	*ü-behr-*VIZE*-en*	remit (send payment), to
überzeugen (1)	*ü-behr-*TSOY*-gen*	convince, to
Überzeugung, *f.*	*ü-behr-*TSOY*-goong*	conviction (belief)
übrigbleiben (17)	*ÜB-rick-blibe-en*	remain (be left), to
Übung, *f.*	*Ü-boong*	exercise (drill)
Ufer, *n.* ,,	*OO-fehr* ,,	bank shore
Uhr, *f.* ,,	OOR ,,	clock watch (timepiece)
Ulme, *f.*	OOLL*-muh*	elm
um ,, ,,	OOMM ,, ,,	around (*prep.*) at (to, toward) at (for the price of)
umarmen (1) ,, ,,	*oomm-*ARM*-en* ,, ,,	clasp, to embrace (hug), to hug, to
umdrehen, sich (1)	*zikh* OOMM*-dray-en*	turn (face about), to
(Kreis)Umfang, *m.*	(CRISE-)OOMM*-fahnng*	circumference
umfangreich	OOMM*-fahnng-rye_kh*	wide (comprehensive)
umfassen (1)	*oomm-*FAHSS*-en*	embrace (include), to
Umfrage, *f.*	OOMM*-frah-guh*	poll (survey)
umgeben (43)	*oomm-*GAY*-ben*	surround (enclose), to
Umgebung, *f.*	*oomm-*GAY*-boong*	surroundings
umgekehrt	OOMM*-guh-kehrt*	backward (in reverse, *adv.*)
Umhang, *m.*	OOMM*-hahng*	cloak (apparel)
umherschweifen (1)	*oomm-*HAIR*-shvye-fen*	stray (roam), to
umherstreifen (1) ,, ,,	*oomm-*HAIR*-shtrye-fen* ,, ,,	roam, to rove, to

German	Pronunciation	English
umkommen (68)	OOMM*-kawmm-men*	perish, to
Umlauf, *m.*	OOMM*-l_owf*	circulation (dissemination)
Umleitung, *f.*	OOMM*-lye-toong*	detour
Umschlag, *m.*	*oomm-*SHLAHK	cuff (of trouser)
Umstand, *m.*	OOMM*-shtahnt*	circumstance (external condition)
Umstandswort, *n.*	OOMM*-shtahnts-vort*	adverb
umstürzen (1) ,,	OOMM*-shtür-tsen* ,,	overturn (upset), to upset (knock over), to
umwandeln (1)	OOMM*-vahn-del'n*	convert (transform), to
umziehen (161)	OOMM*-tsee-en*	move (change residence), to
um zu	OOMM *tsoo*	to (in order to, *prep.*)
unabhängig	OONN*-ahpp-heng-ick*	independent
Unabhängigkeit, *f.*	OONN*-ahpp-heng-ick-kite*	independence
unähnlich	OONN*-ane-likh*	unlike (*adj.*)
unangenehm ,,	OONN*-ahnn-guh-name* ,,	disagreeable unpleasant
unartig	OONN*-ahr-tick*	naughty (disobedient)
unbedeutend	OONN*-buh-doy-tent*	insignificant (trivial)
unbekannt ,,	OONN*-buh-kahnnt* ,,	obscure (unrenowned) unknown
unbezahlt	OONN*-buh-tsahlt*	unpaid (due)
und	OONNT	and
Unehre, *f.*	OONN*-air-uh*	dishonor
unendlikh	OONN*-ent-likh*	infinite
unentgeltlich	OONN*-ent-*GELT*-likh*	free (gratuitous)
unermesslich ,,	OONN*-ehr-*MESS*-likh* ,,	immense vast
unerwartet	OONN*-ehr-*VAHRR*-tet*	unexpected (*adj.*)
Unfall, *m.*	OONN*-fahll*	accident (mishap)
unfruchtbar	OONN*-frookht-bar*	barren
Unfug, *m.*	OONN*-foock*	mischief (harm)
Ungarn, *n.*	ONN*-garn*	Hungary
Ungeduld, *f.*	OONN*-guh-doollt*	impatience
ungeduldig	OONN*-guh-dooll-dick*	impatient
ungefähr	OONN*-guh-*FARE	about (approximately)
ungeheuer ,,	OONN*-guh-hoy-ehr* ,,	enormous monstrous (horrible)
Ungeheuer, *n.*	OONN*-guh-hoy-ehr*	monster (beast)
ungenau	OONN*-guh-now*	inaccurate
ungenügend	OONN*-guh-nü-g_ent*	insufficient
ungerade	OONN*-guh-rah-duh*	odd (not even)
ungerecht	OONN*-guh-reh_kht*	unjust (inequitable)
Ungerechtigkeit, *f.*	OONN*-guh-rehh_kh-tick-kite*	injustice
ungeschickt	OONN*-guh-shickt*	awkward
ungesetzlich	OONN*-guh-zetts-likh*	illegal
ungleich	OONN*-glye_kh*	unequal
Unglück, *n.*	OONN*-glück*	misfortune
unglücklich ,, ,,	OONN*-glück-likh* ,, ,,	unfortunate unhappy (sorrowful) unlucky
unheimlich	OONN*-hime-likh*	weird (unearthly)
Uniform, *f.*	*oo-nee-*FORM	uniform (*n.*)
Universität, *f.*	*oo-nee-vehr-zee-*TAYT	university
Unkosten, *pl.*	OONN*-kawss-ten*	expense (cost)
Unkraut, *n.*	OONN*-krowt*	weed
unlängst	OONN*-lengst*	recently
unmittelbar	OONN*-mitt-tell-bar*	direct (immediate)
unmöglich	OONN*-*MÖG*-likh*	impossible
Unmöglichkeit, *f.*	OONN*-*MÖG*-likh-kite*	impossibility
unnötig ,,	OONN*-nö-tikh* ,,	needless unnecessary
unnütz	OONN*-nütts*	idle (useless)
Unordnung, *f.* ,,	OONN*-ord-noong* ,,	disorder (confusion) mess (muddle)
unrecht	OONN*-reh_kht*	wrong (unjust, *adj.*)
Unrecht, *n.*	OONN*-reh_kht*	wrong (injustice)
unrein	OONN*-rine*	impure
unregelmässig	OONN*-ray-gel-may-sick*	irregular (asymmetrical)
unrichtig	OONN*-rikh-tick*	incorrect
unruhig ,,	OONN*-roo-ick* ,,	restless uneasy (anxious)
uns	OONNS	us
unschuldig	OONN*-shooll-dick*	innocent (guiltless)

German	Pronunciation	English
unser	OONN-*zehr*	our
unser(e)	OONN-*zehr(-uh)*	ours
unsichtbar	OONN-*zikht-bar*	invisible
Unsinn, *m.*	OONN-*zin*	nonsense
unsterblich	OONN-*shtehrp-likh*	immortal (*adj.*)
unten	OONN-*ten*	beneath (below, *adv.*)
"	"	below (lower down, *adv.*)
"	"	down (in lower place, *adv.*)
"	"	downstairs (on a lower floor)
unter	OONN-*tehr*	among
"	"	beneath (below, *prep.*)
"	"	below (less than, *prep.*)
"	"	under
"	"	underneath (*prep.*)
unterbrechen (20)	*oonn-tehr*-BREH_KH-*en*	interrupt, to
unterbringen (171)	*oonn-tehr*-BRING-*en*	accommodate (have room for), to
unterdrücken (1)	*oonn-tehr*-DRÜCK-*en*	oppress (tyrannize), to
"	"	suppress (subdue), to
Untergang, *m.*	OONN-*tehr-gahng*	doom (ruin)
untergehen (46)	OONN-*tehr-gay-en*	set (in sky), to
Untergrundbahn, *f.*	OONN-*tehr-groonnt-bahn*	subway (underground railway)
unter(halb)	OONN-*tehr(-hahlp)*	below (lower than, *prep.*)
(Lebens)Unterhalt, *m.*	(LAY-*bens*-)OONN-*tehr-hahlt*	living (livelihood)
unterhalten (59)	*oonn-tehr*-HAHLL-*ten*	amuse, to
"	"	entertain, to
Unterhaltung, *f.*	*oonn-tehr*-HAHLL-*toong*	conversation
"	"	entertainment
unterirdisch	OONN-*tehr-eerr-dish*	underground (*adj.*)
Unterkleidung, *f.*	OONN-*tehr-klye-doong*	underwear
Unterkunft, *f.*	OONN-*tehr-koonnft*	lodging (temporary quarters)
Unterlassung, *f.*	*oonn-tehr*-LAHSS-*oong*	failure (neglect)
Unterleibstyphus, *m.*	OONN-*tehr-lipes-tü-fooss*	typhoid fever
unterliegen (76)	*oonn-tehr*-LEEG-*en*	succumb (yield), to
Unternehmen, *n.*	*oonn-tehr*-NAY-*men*	concern (business firm)
"	"	enterprise (undertaking)
"	"	establishment (firm)
unternehmen (80)	*oonn-tehr*-NAY-*men*	undertake (attempt), to
Unternehmung, *f.*	*oonn-tehr*-NAY-*moong*	undertaking (enterprise)
Unterricht, *m.*	OONN-*tehr-rikht*	instruction (teaching)
unterrichten (1)	*oonn-tehr*-RIKH-*ten*	instruct (teach), to
Unterrock, *m.*	OONN-*tehr-rawck*	petticoat
"	"	slip
unterscheiden (93)	*oonn-tehr*-SHY-*den*	distinguish (differentiate), to
unterscheiden, sich	*zikh oonn-tehr*-SHY-*den*	differ (be unlike), to
Unterschied, *m.*	OONN-*tehr-sheet*	difference (dissimilarity)
"	"	distinction (difference)
unterschreiben (109)	*oonn-tehr*-SHRIBE-*en*	sign (endorse), to
Unterschrift, *f.*	OONN-*tehr-shrift*	signature (name)
Unterseeboot, *n.*	OONN-*tehr-zay-boat*	submarine
Unterstützung, *f.*	*oonn-tehr*-SHTÜTT-*soong*	relief (aid)
"	"	support (approval)
untersuchen (1)	*oonn-tehr*-ZOO_KH-*en*	examine, to
"	"	investigate, to
Untersuchung, *f.*	*oonn-tehr*-ZOO_KH-*oong*	investigation
Untertan, *m.*	OONN-*tehr-tahn*	subject (citizen)
Untertasse, *f.*	OONN-*tehr-tahss-suh*	saucer
unterwerfen (157)	*oonn-tehr*-VEHR-*fen*	subdue (conquer), to
unvermeidlich	OONN-*fehr-mide-likh*	inevitable (*adj.*)
unvernünftig	OONN-*fehr-nünf-tikh*	unreasonable (unreasoning)
unverzüglich	OONN-*fehr*-TSÜG-*likh*	prompt (quick)
unvollkommen	OONN-*fawl-kawmm-en*	imperfect (defective)
Unwahrheit, *f.*	OONN-*vahr-hite*	falsehood (lie)
unwissend	OONN-*viss-ent*	ignorant
Unwissenheit, *f.*	OONN-*viss-en-hite*	ignorance
unwürdig	OONN-*vür-dick*	unworthy
unzulänglich	OONN-*tsoo-leng-likh*	inadequate
uralt	OOR-*ahlt*	ancient
Uran, *n.*	*oo*-RAHN	uranium
Urheberrecht, *n.*	OOR-*hay-behr-reh_kht*	copyright (*n.*)
Urkunde, *f.*	OOR-*koonn-duh*	charter (act of incorporation)
"	"	deed (transfer agreement)
Ursache, *f.*	OOR-*zah_kh-uh*	cause
Ursprung, *m.*	OOR-*shproong*	origin (source)
ursprünglich	OOR-*shprüng-likh*	original (first)
Urteil, *n.*	OOR-*tile*	judgment (*law*)
"		judgment (estimation)
(be)urteilen (1)	(*buh*-)OOR-*tie-len*	judge, to
Uruguay, *n.*	*oo-roog*-WYE	Uruguay
vag	VAHK	vague (not precise)
Vase, *f.*	VAH-*zuh*	vase
Vater, *m.*	FAH-*tehr*	father
Vati, *m.*	FAH-*tee*	dad
Veilchen, *n.*	FILE-*kh_en*	violet (flower)
Venedig, *n.*	*vay*-NAY-*dick*	Venice
Venezuela, *n.*	*vay-nay-tsoo*-AY-*lah*	Venezuela
venezuelanisch	*vay-nay-tsoo-eh*-LAH-*nish*	Venezuelan (*adj.*)
Ventilator, *m.*	*ven-tee*-LAH-*tor*	fan, electric
Venusmuschel, *f.*	VAY-*nooss-moosh-el*	clam
Verabredung, *f.*	*fehr*-AHPP-*ray-doong*	appointment (meeting)
"	"	date
"	"	engagement
verachten (1)	*fehr*-AH_KH-*ten*	despise, to
"	"	scorn, to
Verachtung, *f.*	*fehr*-AH_KH-*toong*	contempt
"	"	scorn
verändern (1)	*fehr*-ENN-*dehrn*	change (make different), to
verändern, sich	*zikh fehr*-ENN-*dehrn*	vary (undergo change), to
verantwortlich	*fehr*-AHNNT-*vort-likh*	responsible (answerable)
Verantwortung, *f.*	*fehr*-AHNNT-*vor-toong*	responsibility (accountability)
Verband, *m.*	*fehr*-BAHNNT	bandage
verbannen (1)	*fehr*-BAHNN-*nen*	banish (exile), to
Verbannung, *f.*	*fehr*-BAHNN-*oong*	exile (banishment)
verbergen (145)	*fehr*-BEHR-*gen*	conceal, to
verbessern (1)	*fehr*-BESS-*ehrn*	improve (make better), to
Verbesserung, *f.*	*fehr*-BESS-*ehr-oong*	improvement (betterment)
verbeugen, sich (1)	*zikh fehr*-BOY-*gen*	bow (in greeting), to
Verbeugung, *f.*	*fehr*-BOY-*goong*	bow (nod)
verbieten (13)	*fehr*-BEE-*ten*	forbid, to
verbinden (14)	*fehr*-BINN-*den*	associate (relate), to
"	"	combine (make join), to
"	"	connect (link), to
"	"	dress, to (*med.*)
"	"	join (bring together), to
Verbindung, *f.*	*fehr*-BINN-*doong*	combination
"	"	communication (intercourse)
"	"	compound (mixture)
verblassen (1)	*fehr*-BLAHSS-*sen*	fade (lose color), to
Verbot, *m.*	*fehr*-BOAT	prohibition
verboten	*fehr*-BOH-*ten*	forbidden
Verbrauch, *m.*	*fehr*-BROWKH	consumption (using up)
verbrauchen (1)	*fehr*-BROW-*kh_en*	consume, to
Verbrechen, *n.*	*fehr*-BREH_KH-*en*	crime
Verbrecher, *m.*	*fehr*-BREH_KH-*ehr*	criminal (*n.*)
verbreiten (1)	*fehr*-BRYE-*ten*	spread (diffuse), to
verbreitet	*fehr*-BRYE-*tet*	popular (prevalent)
verbrennen (170)	*fehr*-BRENN-*nen*	burn (set fire to), to
verbuchen (1)	*fehr*-BOO-*kh_en*	enter, to (*acctg.*)
Verbündete, *m.,f.*	*fehr*-BÜNN-*duh-tuh*	ally
Verdacht, *m.*	*fehr*-DAH_KHT	suspicion
verdammen (1)	*fehr*-DAHMM-*men*	damn, to
verdauen (1)	*fehr*-DOW-*en*	digest, to
Verdauungsstörung, *f.*	*fehr*-DOW-*oongs-shtör-oong*	indigestion
verderben (146)	*fehr*-DEHR-*ben*	spoil (mar), to
verdichten (1)	*fehr*-DIKH-*ten*	condense (compress), to

German	Pronunciation	English
verdienen (1)	*fehr*-DEE-*nen*	deserve, to
"	"	earn (be paid), to
		merit, to
Verdienst, *n.*	*fehr*-DEENST	merit
verdrehen (1)	*fehr*-DRAY-*en*	pervert (distort), to
verdunkeln (1)	*fehr*-DOON-*kel'n*	darken (make dark), to
Verehrung, *f.*	*fehr*-AIR-*oong*	reverence (respect)
Verein, *m.*	*fehr*-INE	association (body of persons)
"	"	club
vereinigen (1)	*fehr*-INE-*ee-gen*	unite (make one), to
vereinigen, sich	*zikh fehr*-INE-*ee-gen*	combine (coalesce), to
Vereinigten Nationen, *f.pl.*	*fehr*-INE-*ick-ten nahts*-YOH-*nen*	United Nations
Vereinigten Staaten, *m.pl.*	*fehr*-INE-*ick-ten* SHTAH-*ten*	United States
Vereinigung, *f.*	*fehr*-INE-*ee-goong*	organization (association)
vereiteln (1)	*fehr*-EYE-*tel'n*	defeat (thwart), to
"	"	foil (frustrate), to
Verfahren, *n.*	*fehr*-FAH-*ren*	process (set of operations)
Verfall, *m.*	*fehr*-FAHLL	decline (deterioration)
verfallen (32)	*fehr*-FAHLL-*len*	decline (deteriorate), to
"	"	lapse (become void), to
Verfasser, *m.*	*fehr*-FAHSS-*sehr*	author
Verfassung, *f.*	*fehr*-FAHSS-*oong*	constitution (law)
verfehlen (1)	*fehr*-FAY-*len*	miss (fail to do), to
verfluchen (1)	*fehr*-FLOO-*kh_en*	curse (damn), to
verfolgen (1)	*fehr*-FAWLL-*gen*	pursue (chase), to
Verfolgung, *f.*	*fehr*-FAWLL-*goong*	pursuit (chase)
Verfügung stehen, zur	*tsoor fehr*-FÜ-*goong* SHTAY-*en*	available
vergangen	*fehr*-GAHNNG-*en*	past (bygone, *adj.*)
Vergangenheit, *f.*	*fehr*-GAHNNG-*en-hite*	past (*n.*)
vergeblich	*fehr*-GABE-*likh*	vain (futile)
vergegenwärtigen, sich (1)	*zikh fehr*-GAY-*gen-vehr-tee-gen*	realize (recognize), to
Vergehen, *n.*	*fehr*-GAY-*en*	offense (transgression)
vergessen	*fehr*-GESS-*en*	forgotten
vergessen (148)	*fehr*-GESS-*en*	forget, to
vergiessen (54)	*fehr*-G_EE-*sen*	spill (let pour out), to
vergiften (1)	*fehr*-GIFF-*ten*	poison, to
Vergleich, *m.*	*fehr*-GLYE_KH	comparison
vergleichen (55)	*fehr*-GLYE_KH-*en*	compare (consider relatively), to
Vergnügen, *n.*	*fehr*-G_NÜ-*gen*	pleasure
Vergnügung, *f.*	*fehr*-G_NÜ-*goong*	amusement
Vergnügungsreise, *f.*	*fehr*-G_NÜ-*goongs*-RYE-*zuh*	cruise (voyage)
vergrössern (1)	*fehr*-GRÖ-*sehrn*	enlarge (make larger), to
Vergütung, *f.*	*fehr*-GÜ-*toong*	compensation (*bus.*)
verhaften (1)	*fehr*-HAHFF-*ten*	arrest (take into custody), to
verhalten, sich (59)	*zikh fehr*-HAHLL-*ten*	act (behave), to
Verhältnis, *n.*	*fehr*-HELLT-*niss*	proportion
"	"	ratio
verhältnismässig	*fehr*-HELLT-*niss-may-sick*	comparative
"	"	relative (*adj.*)
Verhältniswort, *n.*	*fehr*-HELLT-*niss-vawrt*	preposition (*gram.*)
verhandeln (1)	*fehr*-HAHNN-*del'n*	bargain (negotiate), to
verhandeln über	*fehr*-HAHNN-*del'n ü-behr*	negotiate, to
Verhandlung, *f.*	*fehr*-HAHNNT-*loong*	negotiation
verhängnisvoll	*fehr*-HENG-*niss-fawll*	fatal (fateful)
verheiratet	*fehr*-HYE-*rah-tett*	married
verhöhnen (1)	*fehr*-HÖ-*nen*	mock (deride), to
verhungern (1)	*fehr*-HOONNG-*ehrn*	starve (die of hunger), to
verhüten (1)	*fehr*-HÜ-*ten*	prevent (stop), to
Verkauf, *m.*	*fehr*-KOWF	sale (exchange)
verkaufen (1)	*fehr*-KOW-*fen*	sell, to
Verkäufer, *m.*	*fehr*-KOY-*fehr*	clerk (salesperson)
"	"	salesman
"	"	vendor (seller)
Verkaufsschein, *m.*	*fehr*-KOWFS-*shine*	bill of sale

German	Pronunciation	English
Verkehr, *m.*	*fehr*-KAIR	dealings (relations)
"	"	traffic (flow of vehicles)
verkehrt	*fehr*-KAIRT	wrong (amiss, *adv.*)
verklagen (1)	*fehr*-KLAHG-*en*	sue (bring action against), to
Verkleidung, *f.*	*fehr*-KLYE-*doong*	disguise
verkleinern (1)	*fehr*-KLYE-*nehrn*	diminish (make smaller), to
verkünd(ig)en (1)	*fehr*-KÜND-(*ig*-)*en*	proclaim, to
"	"	pronounce (declare), to
verlangen (1)	*fehr*-LAHNNG-*en*	demand (ask for), to
verlangen, nach...	NAH_KH...*fehr*-LAHNNG-*en*	crave (desire), to
Verlangen, *n.*	*fehr*-LAHNNG-*en*	demand (request)
verlängern (1)	*fehr*-LENG-*chrn*	prolong, to
verlassen	*fehr*-LAHSS-*sen*	lonely (unfrequented)
verlassen (71)	*fehr*-LAHSS-*sen*	forsake, to
verlassen, sich auf...	*zikh* OWF...*fehr*-LAHSS-*sen*	count (rely) on, to
"	"	depend (rely) on, to
verlegen (1)	*fehr*-LAY-*gen*	mislay, to
Verlegenheit, *f.*	*fehr*-LAY-*gen-hite*	embarrassment
"	"	quandary
Verleger, *m.*	*fehr*-LAY-*gehr*	publisher
verleihen (74)	*fehr*-LYE-*en*	bestow, to
"	"	confer, to
verletzen (1)	*fehr*-LET-*sen*	injure, to
"	"	violate (infringe upon), to
Verletzung, *f.*	*fehr*-LET-*soong*	injury
verlieren (149)	*fehr*-LEE-*ren*	lose, to
Verlobung, *f.*	*fehr*-LOH-*boong*	engagement (betrothal)
Verlust, *m.*	*fehr*-LOOSST	loss
vermählen, sich mit...(1)	*zikh mitt...fehr*-MAY-*len*	marry, to
vermehren (1)	*fehr*-MARE-*en*	increase (add to), to
vermehren, sich	*zikh fehr*-MARE-*en*	multiply (grow numerous), to
vermeiden (78)	*fehr*-MY-*den*	avoid, to
vermieten (1)	*fehr*-MEE-*ten*	rent (charge rent for), to
vermindern (1)	*fehr*-MIN-*dehrn*	lessen (make less), to
Verminderung, *f.*	*fehr*-MIN-*duh-roong*	reduction (lessening)
vermischt	*fehr*-MISHT	miscellaneous
vermissen (1)	*fehr*-MISS-*en*	miss (feel the loss of), to
Vermögen, *n.*	*fehr*-MÖ-*gen*	fortune (wealth)
"	"	holdings (possessions)
vermuten (1)	*fehr*-MOO-*ten*	guess, to
"	"	presume (assume), to
"	"	suppose, to
"	"	suspect (surmise), to
vernachlässigen (1)	*fehr*-NAH_KH-*less-ih-gen*	neglect (slight), to
Vernunft, *f.*	*fehr*-NOONNFT	reason (intellect)
"	"	sense (intelligence)
vernünftig	*fehr*-NÜNF-*tick*	reasonable (rational)
"	"	sane
"	"	sensible
Veröffentlichung, *f.*	*fehr*-ÖFF-*ent-likh-oong*	publication (published work)
Verordnung, *f.*	*fehr*-ORD-*noong*	decree (edict)
verpacken (1)	*fehr*-PAHCK-*en*	pack (wrap), to
verpfänden (1)	*fehr*-PFENN-*den*	pawn, to
verpflichten (1)	*fehr*-PFLIKH-*ten*	oblige (compel), to
Verpflichtung, *f.*	*fehr*-PFLIKH-*toong*	commitment (*bus.*)
"	"	obligation (duty)
Verrat, *m.*	*fehr*-RAHT	treason
verraten (82)	*fehr*-RAH-*ten*	betray, to
Verräter, *m.*	*fehr*-RAY-*tchr*	traitor
verrenken (1)	*fehr*-RENG-*ken*	sprain, to
verrichten (1)	*fehr*-RIKH-*ten*	perform (do), to
Verrichtung, *f.*	*fehr*-RIKH-*toong*	performance (action)
verringern (1)	*fehr*-RING-*chrn*	cut (reduce), to
"		reduce (diminish), to
verrückt	*fehr*-RÜCKT	crazy
Verrücktheit, *f.*	*fehr*-RÜCKT-*hite*	craze (fad)
versammeln, sich (1)	*zikh fehr*-SAHMM-*el'n*	assemble (meet), to
Versammlung, *f.*	*fehr*-SAHMM-*loong*	assembly (meeting)
"	"	party (social gathering)

German	Pronunciation	English
versäumen (1)	*fehr*-ZOY-*men*	fail (neglect) to, to
verschaffen (1)	*fehr*-SHAHFF-*en*	procure (obtain), to
verschieben (97)	*fehr*-SHEE-*ben*	postpone, to
verschieden	*fehr*-SHEE-*den*	different (unlike)
"	"	distinct
"	"	various
verschlagen	*fehr*-SHLAH-*gen*	sly (crafty)
verschlingen (105)	*fehr*-SHLING-*en*	devour (eat), to
verschwenden (1)	*fehr*-SHVENN-*den*	waste (squander), to
Verschwendung, *f.*	*fehr*-SHVENN-*doong*	waste (squandering)
verschwinden (115)	*fehr*-SHVINN-*den*	disappear, to
"	"	vanish, to
Verschwörung, *f.*	*fehr*-SHVÖR-*oong*	plot (conspiracy)
Verse, *m.pl.*	FEHR-*zuh*	verse (poetic writing)
versehen (118)	*fehr*-ZAY-*en*	provide, to
"	"	supply, to
Versehen, *n.*	*fehr*-ZAY-*en*	oversight (error)
versenden (176)	*fehr*-ZEND-*en*	ship (send goods), to
versichern (1)	*fehr*-ZIKH-*ehrn*	assure, to
"	"	insure, to
Versicherung, *f.*	*fehr*-ZIKH-*ehr-oong*	insurance
verspätet	*fehr*-SHPAY-*tet*	late (overdue, *adj.*)
versprechen (125)	*fehr*-SHPREH_KH-*en*	promise (pledge), to
Versprechen, *n.*	*fehr*-SHPREH_KH-*en*	promise (pledge)
Verstand, *m.*	*fehr*-SHTAHNNT	intelligence (under-standing)
verständig	*fehr*-SHTENN-*dick*	intelligent
Verständnis, *n.*	*fehr*-SHTEND-*niss*	understanding (comprehension)
verstecken (1)	*fehr*-SHTECK-*en*	hide (conceal), to
verstehen (129)	*fehr*-SHTAY-*en*	understand (com-prehend), to
Versteigerung, *f.*	*fehr*-SHTYE-*guh-roong*	auction (sale)
Versuch, *m.*	*fehr*-ZOOKH	attempt
"	"	experiment
versuchen (1)	*fehr*-ZOO-*kh_en*	attempt, to
"	"	tempt, to
"	"	try, to
Versuchung, *f.*	*fehr*-ZOO-*kh_oong*	temptation
verteidigen (1)	*fehr*-TYE-*dih-gen*	defend (protect), to
Verteidigung, *f.*	*fehr*-TYE-*dih-goong*	defense
verteilen (1)	*fehr*-TILE-*en*	distribute (allot), to
Verteilung, *f.*	*fehr*-TILE-*oong*	distribution
Vertrag, *m.*	*fehr*-TRAHK	contract
"	"	treaty
Vertragsbruch, *m.*	*fehr*-TRAHKS-*brookh*	breach of contract (*bus.*)
Vertrauen, *n.*	*fehr*-TR_OW-*en*	confidence
"	"	faith
"	"	trust
vertrauen (1)	*fehr*-TR_OW-*en*	trust (rely on), to
vertraulich	*fehr*-TR_OW-*likh*	confidential (private)
vertraut	*fehr*-TR_OWT	familiar
"	"	intimate (personal)
vertreten (140)	*fehr*-TRAY-*ten*	represent (act for), to
Vertreter, *m.*	*fehr*-TRAY-*tehr*	agent
"	"	representative (deputy)
Vertretung, *f.*	*fehr*-TRAY-*toong*	agency (business firm)
"	"	representation (*pol.*)
verursachen (1)	*fehr*-OOR-*zahkh-en*	cause, to
verurteilen (1)	*fehr*-OOR-*ti_e-len*	condemn (censure), to
"	"	doom (condemn), to
"	"	sentence, to
Verwaltung, *f.*	*fehr*-VAHLL-*toong*	administration (*bus.*)
verwandeln (1)	*fehr*-VAHNN-*del'n*	transform, to
"		turn (convert), to
verwandt	*fehr*-VAHNNT	related (connected)
Verwandte, *m., f.*	*fehr*-VAHNNT-*tuh*	relative (kinsman)
verweigern (1)	*fehr*-VYE-*gehrn*	deny (refuse), to
verweilen (1)	*fehr*-VILE-*en*	linger (tarry), to
Verweisung, *f.*	*fehr*-VIE-*zoong*	reference (allusion)
verwelken (1)	*fehr*-VELL-*ken*	wither, to
verwenden (177)	*fehr*-VENN-*den*	employ (use), to
verwickelt	*fehr*-VICK-*elt*	complex (compli-cated)

German	Pronunciation	English
verwirklichen (1)	*fehr*-VEERRK-*likh-en*	realize (accomplish), to
verwirren (1)	*fehr*-VEERR-*en*	bewilder, to
"	"	confuse (mix up), to
Verwirrung, *f.*	*fehr*-VEERR-*roong*	confusion (disorder)
verwunden (1)	*fehr*-VOONN-*den*	wound, to
Verwunderung, *f.*	*fehr*-VOONN-*duh-roong*	wonder
Verzeichnis, *n.*	*fehr*-TSYE_KH-*niss*	register (record)
verzeihen (160)	*fehr*-TSYE-*en*	forgive, to
"	"	pardon (forgive), to
Verzeihung, *f.*	*fehr*-TSYE-*oong*	forgiveness
"	"	pardon (forgiveness)
verzichten auf (1)	*fehr*-TSIKH-*ten owff*	renounce (give up), to
verzieren (1)	*fehr*-TSEE-*ren*	adorn (beautify), to
Verzierung, *f.*	*fehr*-TSEE-*roong*	decoration (orna-ment)
verzögern (1)	*fehr*-TSÖ-*gehrn*	delay (postpone), to
Verzögerung, *f.*	*fehr*-TSÖ-*guh-roong*	delay
verzweifeln (1)	*fehr*-TSVIFE-*el'n*	despair, to
verzweifelt	*fehr*-TSVIFE-*elt*	desperate
Verzweiflung, *f.*	*fehr*-TSVIFE-*loong*	despair (hopeless-ness)
Veteran, *m.*	*vay-tuh*-RAHN	veteran (*mil., n.*)
Vetter, *m.*	FET-*tehr*	cousin
Viehstand, *m.*	FEE-*shtahnnt*	stock (livestock)
viel	FEEL	much
viele	FEE-*luh*	many
vielleicht	*feel*-LYE_KHT	maybe
"	"	perhaps
Viertel, *n.*	FEERR-*tel*	quarter (one-fourth)
vierteljährlich	*feerr-tel*-YAIR-*likh*	quarterly (four times a year)
Viole, *f.*	*vee*-OH-*luh*	viola
Visitenkarte, *f.*	*vee*-ZEE-*ten-kahr-tuh*	card, calling
Vitamin, *n.*	*vee-tah*-MEEN	vitamin
Vlies, *n.*	FLEECE	fleece
Vogel, *m.*	FOH-*gel*	bird
Volk, *n.*	FAWLLK	people (populace)
Volkswirtschaft, *f.*	FAWLLX-*veert-shahfft*	economics
Volkszählung, *f.*	FAWLLX-*tsay-loong*	census
voll	FAWLL	full (filled)
voll(ständig)	FAWLL(-*shtenn-dick*)	full (ample)
vollbringen (171)	*fawll*-BRING-*en*	accomplish, to
vollenden (1)	*fawll*-ENN-*den*	complete, to
"	"	finish, to
		utter (*adj.*)
völlig	FÖLL-*ick*	
vollkommen	FAWLL-*kawm-men*	absolute
"	"	full (complete)
"	"	perfect (flawless)
Vollkommenheit, *f.*	FAWLL-*kawm-men-hite*	perfection (flawless-ness)
Vollmacht, *f.*	FAWLL-*mah_kht*	authority (power)
"	"	power of attorney
vollständig	FAWLL-*shtenn-dick*	complete (entire)
Volumen, *n.*	*vo*-LOO-*men*	volume (quantity)
von	FAWNN	from
"	"	of
vor	FOR	ago (past, *adj.*)
"	"	before (*prep.*)
"	"	by (prior to, *prep.*)
Vorarbeiter, *m.*	FOR-*ahr-bite-tehr*	foreman (overseer)
voraus	*for*-OWSS	ahead (in front)
voraus, (im)	(*imm*) *for*-OWSS	beforehand (*adv.*)
vorausbestellen (1)	*for*-OWSS-*buh-shtell-en*	reserve (order in ad-vance), to
Vorausbestellung, *f.*	*for*-OWSS-*buh-shtell-oong*	reservation (advance order)
voraussagen (1)	*for*-OWSS-*zah-gen*	predict, to
Vorbehalt, *m.*	FOR-*buh*-HAHLLT	reservation (mental qualification)
vorbehalten (6)	FOR-*buh-hahll-ten*	reserve (withhold), to
vorbeigehen (46)	*for*-BY-*gay-en*	pass (go by), to
vorbereiten (1)	FOR-*buh*-RYE-*ten*	prepare (make ready), to
Vorbereitung, *f.*	FOR-*buh-rye-toong*	arrangement
"	"	preparation (pre-paratory act)
Vorderseite, *f.*	FOR-*dehr-zite-uh*	front (forward part)
voreilig	FOR-*eye-lick*	hasty (rash)
Vorfahr, *m.*	FOR-*far*	ancestor
Vorfall, *m.*	FOR-*fahll*	incident (event)
vorführen (1)	FOR-*für-en*	demonstrate (show), to

German	Pronunciation	English
Vorgeben,*n.*	*for-*GAY*-ben*	pretense (pretending)
Vorhalle,*f.*	FOR*-hahll-uh*	porch
Vorhang,*m.*	FOR*-hahng*	curtain (drape)
vorher	FOR*-hair*	before (in the past, *adv.*)
vorhergehend	*for-*HAIR*-gay-ent*	previous
vorherrschen (1)	FOR*-*HEHRR*-shen*	prevail (exist widely), to
vorig	FO*-rick*	last (most recent, *adj.*)
vorkommen (68)	FOR*-kawm-men*	occur (happen), to
vorläufig	FOR*-loy-fick*	preliminary (*adj.*)
"	"	temporary
vorlegen (1)	FOR*-lay-gen*	submit (offer), to
Vorlesung,*f.*	FOR*-lay-zoong*	lecture (speech)
Vormund,*m.*	FOR*-moonnt*	guardian (protector)
vorn(e)	FORN(*-uh*)	before (ahead, *adv.*)
Vornehmheit,*f.*	FOR*-name-hite*	distinction (eminence)
Vorrat,*m.*	FOR*-raht*	stock
"	"	supply (amount available)
Vorrecht,*n.*	FOR*-reh_kht*	privilege
Vorrichtung,*f.*	FOR*-rikh-toong*	device (apparatus)
vorrücken (1)	FOR*-rück-en*	advance (go forward), to
Vorschlag,*m.*	FOR*-shlahk*	proposal
"	"	suggestion
vorschlagen (100)	FOR*-shlah-gen*	propose, to
"	"	suggest (recommend), to
vorschlagen, zur Wahl	*tsoor* VAHL FOR*-shlah-gen*	nominate, to
vorschnell	FOR*-shnell*	rash (*adj.*)
Vorschrift,*f.*	FOR*-shrift*	regulation (rule)
Vorsicht,*f.*	FOR*-zikht*	caution (heed)
vorsichtig	FOR*-zikh-tick*	careful (cautious)
Vorsitzende,*m.,f.*	FOR*-zits-en-duh*	chairman
Vorsteher,*m.*	FOR*-shtay-ehr*	head (leader)
vorstellen (1)	FOR*-shtell-en*	introduce (make acquainted), to
"	"	present (introduce), to
vorstellen, sich	*zikh* FOR*-shtell-en*	conceive, to
"	"	imagine (picture mentally), to
Vorteil,*m.*	FOR*-tile*	advantage
"	"	benefit
vortragen (137)	FOR*-trahg-en*	recite (repeat something learned), to
vortrefflich	*for-*TREFF*-likh*	excellent
Vorurteil,*n.*	FOR*-oor-tile*	prejudice
Vorwand,*m.*	FOR*-vahnnt*	excuse
"	"	pretext
vorwärts	FOR*-vehrts*	ahead
"	"	forward (*adv.*)
"	"	onward (*adv.*)
vorwerfen (157)	FOR*-vehr-fen*	reproach, to
Vorwort,*n.*	FOR*-vawrt*	preface
Vorwurf,*m.*	FOR*-voorrf*	reproach
vorziehen (161)	FOR*-tsee-en*	prefer (like better), to
vorzüglich	FOHR*-tsüg-likh*	superior (excellent)
Vulkan,*m.*	*vooll-*KAHN	volcano
Waage,*f.*	VAH*-guh*	scales (balance)
wach	VAH KH	awake
Wache,*f.*	VAH_KH*-uh*	guard (watcher)
Wachs,*m.*	VAHX	wax (beeswax)
wachsen (151)	VAHX*-en*	grow, to (*biol.*)
"	"	grow (expand), to
Wachstum,*n.*	VAHX*-toom*	growth (development)
Wade,*f.*	VAH*-duh*	calf (*anat.*)
Waffe,*f.*	VAHFF*-uh*	weapon
wagen (1)	VAH*-gen*	dare, to
"	"	venture, to
Wagen,*m.*	VAH*-gen*	carriage (horse-drawn vehicle)
(Eisenbahn)Wagen	(EYE*-zen-bahn-*)VAH*-gen*	car, railroad
(Kraft)Wagen,*m.*	(*krahfft-*)VAH*-gen*	automobile
Wagenladung,*f.*	VAH*-gen-lah-doong*	carload (*bus.*)
Wagnis,*n.*	VAHG*-niss*	venture
Wahl,*f.*	VAHL	choice (act of choosing)
"	"	election

German	Pronunciation	English
wählen (1)	VAY*-len*	choose, to
"	"	elect, to
"	"	select, to
Wähler,*m.*	VAY*-lehr*	voter
wahlfrei	VAHL*-fry*	optional
Wahlspruch,*m.*	VAHL*-shprookh*	motto
Wahlzettel,*m.*	VAHL*-tset-tel*	ballot
Wahnsinn,*m.*	VAHN*-zin*	madness (insanity)
wahnsinnig	VAHN*-zin-ick*	mad (insane)
wahr	VAHR	true
während	VAY*-rent*	as (while, *conj.*)
"	"	during
"	"	while (during the time that, *conj.*)
Wahrheit,*f.*	VAHR*-hite*	truth
wahrnehmen (80)	VAHR*-nay-men*	perceive, to
wahrscheinlich	*vahr-*SHINE*-likh*	likely
"	"	probable
Währung,*f.*	VARE*-oong*	currency (money)
Waise,*m.,f.*	VIZE*-uh*	orphan (*n.*)
Wald,*m.*	VAHLLT	forest
"	"	wood (forest)
Wäldchen,*n.*	VELT*-kh_en*	grove (small woods)
Wales,*n.*	VEHLS	Wales
Walfisch,*m.*	VAHLL*-fish*	whale
Walnuss,*f.*	VAHLL*-nooss*	walnut (*n.*)
Walze,*f.*	VAHLL*-tsuh*	roll (cylinder)
"	"	roller
Walzer,*m.*	VAHLL*-tsehr*	waltz (dance step)
Wand,*f.*	VAHNNT	wall (inside)
wandern (1)	VAHNN*-dehrn*	wander, to
Wanderung,*f.*	VAHNN*-duh-roong*	hike (march)
Wandtafel,*f.*	VAHNNT*-tah-fel*	blackboard
wanken (1)	VAHNNG*-ken*	stagger (totter), to
wann	VAHNN	when (at what time, *adv.*)
"	"	when (which time, *pron.*)
Wanne,*f.*	VAHNN*-nuh*	tub (bathtub)
Ware,*f.*	VAHR*-uh*	commodity
"	"	merchandise
"	"	wares
Waren,*f.pl.*	VAHR*-en*	goods
Warenhaus,*n.*	VAHR*-en-house*	department store
warm	VAHRRM	warm
Wärme,*f.*	VEHR*-muh*	warmth
wärmen (1)	VEHR*-men*	warm, to
warnen (1)	VAHRR*-nen*	caution, to
"	"	warn, to
Warschau,*n.*	VAHR*-sh_ow*	Warsaw
warten (1)	VAHRR*-ten*	wait (defer action), to
warten auf	VAHR*-ten owff*	wait for, to
Wärter,*m.*	VEHR*-tehr*	keeper (guard)
warum	*vah-*ROOMM	why
was	VAHSS	what (*pron.*)
was auch	VAHSS *ow_kh*	whatever (*pron.*)
Wäsche,*f.*	VESH*-uh*	laundry (articles laundered)
waschen (152)	VAHSH*-en*	wash (cleanse), to
waschen, sich	*zikh* VAHSH*-en*	wash (cleanse oneself), to
Wäscherei,*f.*	*vesh-uh-*RYE	laundry (commercial plant)
was immer	VAHSS IMM*-mehr*	anything (anything whatever)
Wasser,*n.*	VAHSS*-ehr*	water
wasserdicht	VAHSS*-ehr-dikht*	waterproof
Wasserfall,*m.*	VAHSS*-ehr-fahll*	falls (waterfall)
Wasserhahn,*m.*	VAHSS*-ehr-hahn*	faucet
waten (1)	VAH*-ten*	wade, to
weben (153)	VAY*-ben*	weave, to
Webstuhl,*m.*	VAPE*-shtool*	loom
Webwaren,*f.pl.*	VAPE*-vah-ren*	textile (*n.*)
Wechsel,*m.*	VECK*-sel*	bill of exchange
wecken (1)	VECK*-en*	rouse (awaken), to
"	"	wake (make awaken), to
weder...noch	VAY*-dehr...*NAW_KH	neither...nor (*conj.*)
weg	VECK	away (absent, *adj.*)
Weg,*m.*	VAYK	way (route)
(Fuss)Weg,*m.*	(FOO_SS*-*)VAYK	lane (narrow path)

German	Pronunciation	English
wegen	VAY-*gen*	because of (*adv.*)
Weh, *n.*	VAY	woe
wehklagen (1)	VAY-*klah-gen*	wail, to
Wehrpflicht, *f.*	VARE-*pflikht*	draft (conscription)
weh tun (180)	VAY *toon*	hurt (inflict pain upon), to
Weibchen, *n.*	VIBE-*kh_en*	female (*zool., n.*)
weiblich	VIBE-*likh*	female (*adj.*)
"		feminine
weich	VYE_KH	soft (not hard)
Weide, *f.*	VYE-*duh*	pasture (grassland)
"	"	willow
weiden (1)	VYE-*den*	graze (feed), to
Weihnachten, *f.pl.*	VYE-*nah_kh-ten*	Christmas
weil	VILE	because (*conj.*)
Weile, *f.*	VYE-*luh*	while (short time, *n.*)
Weile, eine	*ine-uh* VYE-*luh*	awhile (*adv.*)
Wein, *m.*	VINE	wine (beverage)
weinen (1)	VINE-*en*	cry, to
"	"	weep, to
Weingarten, *m.*	VINE-*gahr-ten*	vineyard
Weinstock, *m.*	VINE-*shtawck*	vine (grapevine)
weise	VYE-*zuh*	sage (*adj.*)
"		wise
Weise, *f.*	VYE-*zuh*	fashion
"	"	manner (mode)
"	"	way
Weisheit, *f.*	VIZE-*hite*	wisdom
weiss	VICE	white (*adj.*)
weisse Rübe, *f.*	VYE-*suh* RÜ-*buh*	turnip (white)
weit	VITE	far
weiter	VYE-*tehr*	farther
Weizen, *m.*	VITE-*sen*	wheat
welche	VELL-*kh_uh*	any (*pron.*)
welche(r, -s)	VELL-*kh_eh*(r, -s)	what (*interrog. adj.*)
"	"	which (*interrog. adj.*)
welche(r, -s)... auch	VELL-*kh_eh*(r, -s)... OW_KH	whatever (*adj.*)
"	"	whichever (*adj.*)
welches	VEL-*kh_ess*	which (*interrog. pron.*)
welken (1)	VELL-*ken*	wilt, to
Welle, *f.*	VELL-*uh*	wave (billow)
Welt, *f.*	VELT	world
Weltall, *n.*	VELT-*ahll*	universe
Weltteil, *n.*	VELT-*tile*	continent (*geog.*)
wem	VAIM	whom (*interrog. pron.*)
wen	VAIN	whom (*interrog. pron.*)
Wendung, *f.*	VENN-*doong*	turn (change of direction)
wenig	VAY-*nick*	little (not much, *adj.*)
"	"	little (slightly, *adv.*)
"	"	little (small amount, *n.*)
wenige	VAIN-*ih-guh*	few (not many), *adj.*
weniger	VAIN-*ih-gehr*	less (*adj., adv.*)
"	"	less (minus, *prep.*)
Wenigste, *n.*	VAY-*nick-stuh*	least (*n.*)
wenigsten, am	AHMM VAY-*nick-sten*	least (*adv.*)
wenn	VENN	if (supposing that)
wenn immer	VENN *imm-ehr*	when (any time that, *conj.*)
wenn nicht	*venn* NIKHT	unless (*conj.*)
wer	VAIR	who (*interrog. pron.*)
wer auch immer	VAIR *ow_kh imm-mehr*	whoever
werben um (156)	VEHR-*ben oomm*	woo, to
werden (181)	VAIR-*den*	become, to
"	"	will (*v.*)
werden aus	VAIR-*den* OWSS	become of (happen to), to
werfen (157)	VEHR-*fen*	cast, to
"	"	pitch, to
"	"	throw, to
"	"	toss, to
werfen, sich	*zikh* VEHR-*fen*	warp (become misshapen), to
wer immer	VAIR IMM-*mehr*	anybody (anybody whosoever)
"	"	anyone (anyone whosoever)

German	Pronunciation	English
Werk, *n.*	VEHRK	work (opus)
Werkzeug, *n.*	VEHRK-*tsoyk*	tool
Wert, *m.*	VAIRT	value
"		worth
wertlos	VAIRT-*lohss*	worthless (valueless)
Wertpapiere, *pl.*	VAIRT-*pah-pee-ruh*	securities (stocks, etc.)
Wertschätzung, *f.*	VAIRT-*shett-soong*	appraisal (*bus.*)
wertvoll	VAIRT-*fawll*	valuable
Wesen, *n.*	VAY-*zen*	nature (character)
(Lebe)Wesen, *n.*	(LAY-*buh-*)VAY-*zen*	creature (living being)
wesentlich	VAY-*zent-likh*	essential (*adj.*)
"	"	vital
Wespe, *f.*	VESS-*puh*	wasp
wessen	VESS-*en*	whose (*interrog. pron.*)
Weste, *f.*	VESS-*tuh*	vest
Westen, *m.*	VESS-*ten*	west (*n.*)
westlich	VEST-*likh*	western
Wette, *f.*	VET-*tuh*	bet
wetten (1)	VET-*len*	bet, to
Wetter, *n.*	VET-*tehr*	weather
Wettlauf, *m.*	VET-*l_owf*	race (contest)
Whisky, *m.*	VISS-*kee*	whiskey
wichtig	VIKH-*tick*	important
Wichtigkeit, *f.*	VIKH-*tick-kite*	importance
Widder, *m.*	VID-*dehr*	ram (animal)
Widerhall, *m.*	VEE-*dehr-hahll*	echo
widerlegen (1)	*vee-dehr-*LAY-*gen*	refute, to
widersprechen (125)	*vee-dehr-*SHPREH_KH-*en*	contradict (deny), to
Widerstand, *m.*	VEE-*dehr-shtahnnt*	opposition
"	"	resistance
widerstehen (129)	*vee-dehr-*SHTAY-*en*	resist, to
widmen, sich (1)	*zikh* VID-*men*	devote oneself, to
wie	VEE	as (in the same way, *conj.*)
"	"	as (equally, *adv.*)
"	"	how
"	"	like (*adv.*)
wieder	VEE-*dehr*	again
wiederanfangen (33)	VEE-*dehr-*AHNN-*fahnng-en*	resume (recommence), to
wiederbeleben (1)	VEE-*dehr-buh-*LAY-*ben*	revive, to
wiedererkennen (173)	VEE-*dehr-ehr-ken-nen*	recognize (identify), to
Wiedererkennung, *f.*	VEE-*dehr-ehr-ken-noong*	recognition (identification)
wiedererlangen (1)	VEE-*dehr-ehr-lahnng-en*	recover (get back), to
wiederherstellen (1)	*vee-dehr-*HAIR-*shtell-en*	restore (reestablish), to
wiederholen (1)	*vee-dehr-*HOLE-*en*	repeat (reiterate), to
Wiedersehen, auf	OWFF VEE-*dehr-zay-en*	good-by
Wiederverkauf, *m.*	VEE-*dehr-fehr-kowf*	resale (*bus.*)
Wiege, *f.*	VEE-*guh*	cradle
wiegen (158)	VEE-*gen*	weigh, to
wiehern (1)	VEE-*ehrn*	neigh, to
Wien, *n.*	VEEN	Vienna
wienerisch	VEE-*nuh-rish*	Viennese (*adj.*)
Wiese, *f.*	VEE-*zuh*	meadow
wild	VILLT	fierce
"	"	savage (*adj.*)
"	"	wild
Wildnis, *f.*	VILLT-*niss*	wilderness
Wille, *m.*	VILL-*uh*	will (power of choice)
Willkommen, *n.*	*vill-*KAWMM-*men*	welcome (*n.*)
Wimper, *f.*	VIMM-*pehr*	eyelash
"	"	lash
Wind, *m.*	VINNT	wind
winden (159)	VIN-*den*	twist (wind), to
windig	VIN-*dick*	windy (windswept)
Windpocken, *f.pl.*	VINNT-*paw-kenn*	chicken-pox
Windschutzscheibe, *f.*	VINT-*shoots-shy-buh*	windshield
Winkel, *m.*	VING-*kel*	angle (*geom.*)
Winter, *m.*	VIN-*tehr*	winter (*n.*)
winzig	VINT-*sick*	tiny
"	"	wee
wir	VEER	we
wirbeln (1)	VEERR-*bel'n*	whirl (make revolve), to
wirklich	VEERR-*klikh*	actual
"	"	real
"	"	really (actually)

German	Pronunciation	English
Wirklichkeit, *f.*	VEERR-*klikh-kite*	reality
wirksam	VEERRK-*zahm*	effective (effectual)
Wirkung, *f.*	VEERR-*koong*	effect
wischen (1)	VISH-*en*	wipe (make dry by wiping), to
wissen (169)	VISS-*en*	know (have knowledge), to
Wissen, *n.*	VISS-*en*	knowledge (understanding)
Wissenschaft, *f.*	VISS-*en-shahfft*	science
Wissenschaftler, *m.*	VISS-*en-shahfft-lehr*	scientist
wissenschaftlich	VISS-*en-shahfft-likh*	scientific
Witwe, *f.*	VIT-*vuh*	widow
Witwer, *m.*	VIT-*vehr*	widower
Witz, *n.*	VITTS	joke (jest)
"	"	wit (humor)
wo	VOH	where (in, at the place that, *conj.*)
"	"	where (in, at what place, *adv.*)
Woche, *f.*	VAWKH-*uh*	week
Wochenende, *n.*	VAWKH-*en-en-duh*	weekend (*n.*)
Wochenschau, *f.*	VAWKH-*en-sh_ow*	newsreel
wöchentlich	VÖKH-*ent-likh*	weekly (*adj.*)
wohin	*voh*-HIN	where (to what place, *adv.*)
wohl	VOHL	well (in health, *adj.*)
Wohlfahrt, *f.*	VOHL-*fahrt*	welfare (well-being)
Wohlstand, *m.*	VOHL-*shtahnnt*	prosperity
Wohltätigkeit, *f.*	VOHL-*tay-tick-kite*	charity (philanthropy)
wohnen (1)	VOH-*nen*	dwell, to
"	"	live, to
"	"	lodge (reside), to
Wohnsitz, *m.*	VOHN-*zitts*	residence (abode)
Wohnung, *f.*	VOH-*noong*	apartment
"	"	dwelling
Wohnzimmer, *n.*	VOHN-*tsimm-ehr*	parlor (living room)
wo immer	VOH IMM-*mehr*	anywhere (wheresoever)
"	"	wherever (at, in whatever place)
Wolf, *m.*	VAWLLF	wolf
Wolke, *f.*	VAWLL-*kuh*	cloud
Wolkenkratzer, *m.*	VAWLL-*ken-krahtt-sehr*	skyscraper
wolkig	VAWLL-*kick*	cloudy (overcast)
Wolle, *f.*	VAWLL-*uh*	wool
Wollust, *f.*	VAWLL-*loosst*	lust (desire)
Wonne, *f.*	VAWNN-*nuh*	bliss
Wort, *n.*	VAWRT	word
Wörterbuch, *n.*	VÖR-*tehr-bookh*	dictionary
Wörterverzeichnis, *n.*	VÖR-*tehr-fehr-tsye_kh-niss*	glossary
Wrack, *n.*	VRAHCK	wreck (ruins)
Wuchs, *m.*	VOOX	stature (height)
wund	VOONNT	sore (*adj.*)
Wunde, *f.*	VOONN-*duh*	wound (injury)
Wunder, *n.*	VOONN-*dehr*	marvel
"	"	miracle
wunderbar	VOONN-*dehr-bar*	marvelous
"	"	wonderful
Wunsch, *m.*	VOONNSH	wish
wünschen (1)	VÜN-*shen*	wish (desire on behalf of), to
wünschen, sich	*zikh* VÜN-*shen*	wish for, to
wünschenswert	VÜN-*shenns-vairt*	desirable
würde	VÜRR-*duh*	would (*v.*)
Würde, *f.*	VÜRR-*duh*	dignity
würdig	VÜRR-*dick*	worthy (deserving)
würdigen (1)	VÜRR-*dih-gen*	appreciate (perceive fully), to
Würfel, *m.*	VÜRR-*fel*	cube (*geom.*)
Würfel, *m.pl.*	VÜRR-*fel*	dice (marked cubes)
(er)würgen (1)	(*ehr*-)VÜRR-*gen*	choke, to
Wurm, *n.*	VOORRM	worm
Wurst, *f.*	VOORRST	sausage
Wurzel, *f.*	VOORR-*tsel*	root (*bot.*)
Wüste, *f.*	VÜ-*stuh*	desert
Wut, *f.*	VOO_T	fury
"	"	rage (wrath)
wüten (1)	VÜ-*ten*	rage (rave), to
wütend	VÜ-*tent*	furious
zäh(e)	TSAY(-*uh*)	tough (resistant)
Zahl, *f.*	TSAHL	figure (numeral)
(An)Zahl, *f.*	(AHNN-)TSAHL	number (quantity)
zahlbar	TSAHL-*bar*	payable (due)
zählen (1)	TSAY-*len*	count (enumerate), to
zahlreich	TSAHL-*rye_kh*	numerous
Zahlung, *f.*	TSAH-*loong*	payment
Zahlungsunfähigkeit, *f.*	TSAH-*loongs-oon-fay-ick-kite*	insolvency (*bus.*)
zahm	TSAHM	tame
Zahn, *m.*	TSAHN	tooth
Zahnarzt, *m.*	TSAHN-*artst*	dentist
Zahnbürste, *f.*	TSAHN-*bür-stuh*	toothbrush
Zahnfleisch, *n.*	TSAHN-*fly_sh*	gum (*anat.*)
Zahnpaste, *f.*	TSAHN-*pahss-tuh*	tooth paste
Zahnweh, *n.*	TSAHN-*vay*	toothache
zart	TSAHRRT	delicate (dainty)
zärtlich	TSEHRT-*likh*	affectionate
"	"	tender (loving)
Zärtlichkeit, *f.*	TSEHRT-*likh-kite*	tenderness (love)
Zauber, *m.*	TS_OW-*behr*	spell (charm)
Zauberer, *m.*	TS_OW-*buh-rehr*	magician
"	"	wizard (sorcerer)
Zaum, *m.*	TS_OWM	bridle (harness)
Zaun, *m.*	TS_OW_N	fence (barrier)
Zebra, *n.*	TSABE-*rah*	zebra
Zeder, *f.*	TSAY-*dehr*	cedar (tree)
Zehe, *f.*	TSAY-*uh*	toe
Zeichen, *n.*	TSYE-*kh_en*	evidence
"	"	sign (indication)
zeichnen (1)	TSYE_KH-*nen*	draft (sketch), to
"	"	draw (sketch), to
Zeichnung, *f.*	TSYE_KH-*noong*	drawing (sketch)
zeigen (1)	TSYE-*gen*	show (make visible), to
(an)zeigen	(AHNN-)TSYE-*gen*	indicate (point out), to
zeigen, sich	*zikh* TSYE-*gen*	show (be visible), to
Zeit, *f.*	TSITE	time
Zeitraum, *m.*	TSITE-*r_owm*	period (of time)
Zeitschrift, *f.*	TSITE-*shrift*	journal (magazine)
"	"	magazine (periodical)
Zeitung, *f.*	TSYE-*toong*	newspaper
Zeitungskiosk, *m.*	TSYE-*toongs-kee-awssk*	newsstand
Zeitvertreib, *m.*	TSITE-*fehr-tripe*	pastime
Zeitwort, *n.*	TSITE-*vawrt*	verb
Zelle, *f.*	TSEL-*luh*	cell (*biol.*)
Zelt, *n.*	TSELT	tent
Zement, *m.*	*tsay*-MENT	cement
zentral	*tsen*-TRAHL	central
zerbrechen (20)	*tsehr*-BREH-*kh_en*	break (make smash), to
zerbrechlich	*tsehr*-BREH_KH-*likh*	frail (fragile)
Zeremonie, *f.*	*tsehr-uh-moh*-NEE	ceremony
Zerfall, *m.*	*tsehr*-FAHLL	decay (decline)
zerkrümeln (1)	*tsehr*-KRÜ-*mel'n*	crumble, to
zerquetschen (1)	*tsehr*-KVETCH-*en*	crush, to
zerschmettern (1)	*tsehr*-SHMETT-*ehrn*	shatter (smash in pieces), to
"	"	smash, to
zerstören (1)	*tsehr*-SHTÖ-*ren*	destroy (demolish), to
"	"	ruin, to
Zerstörer, *m.*	*tsehr*-SHTÖH-*rer*	destroyer (ship)
Zerstörung, *f.*	*tsehr*-SHTÖ-*roong*	destruction (demolition)
Zeuge, *m.*	TSOY-*guh*	witness (one who testifies)
Zeugnis, *n.*	TSOYK-*niss*	testimony
Zicklein, *n.*	TSICK-*line*	kid (goat)
Ziege, *f.*	TSEE-*guh*	goat
Ziegel, *m.*	TSEE-*gel*	brick (building material)
Ziegenleder, *n.*	TSEE-*gen-lay-dehr*	suede (*n.*)
Ziegenpeter, *m.*	TSEE-*gen-pay-tehr*	mumps
ziehen (161)	TSEE-*en*	drag, to
"	"	draw (pull along), to
"	"	pull, to
Ziehharmonika, *f.*	TSEE-*hahr-moh-nee-kah*	accordion
Ziel, *n.*	TSEEL	end (purpose)
"	"	goal
"	"	object (aim)
"	"	objective

German	Pronunciation	English
zielen (1)	TSEEL-*en*	aim (direct), to
ziemlich	TSEEM-*likh*	fairly (somewhat)
"	"	rather
Zierde,*f.*	TSEER-*duh*	ornament
zierlich	TSEER-*likh*	dainty
Zifferblatt,*n.*	TSIFF-*fehr-blahtt*	dial (graduated face)
Zigarette,*f.*	*tsee-gah*-RET-*tuh*	cigarette
Zigarre,*f.*	*tsee*-GAHRR-*uh*	cigar
Zigeuner,*m.*	*tsih*-GOY-*nehr*	gypsy
Zimmer,*n.*	TSIMM-*mehr*	room (of house)
Zimmermann,*m.*	TSIMM-*mehr-mahnn*	carpenter
Zimt,*m.*	TSIMMT	cinnamon
Zink,*n.*	TSINK	zinc
Zinn,*n.*	TSIN	tin (metal)—
Zins,*m.*	TSINSS	tribute (money)
Zinsen,*m.pl.*	TSIN-*zen*	interest (money rate)
Zinseszinsen,*m.pl.*	TSIN-*zess-tsin-zen*	compound interest
Zirkel,*m.*	TSEERR-*kel*	compass (drawing instrument)
Zirkus,*m.*	TSEERR-*kooss*	circus
zischen (1)	TSISH-*en*	hiss, to
Zisterne,*f.*	*tsiss-*TEHR-*nuh*	tank (container)
Zitat,*n.*	*tsee-*TAHT	quotation (selection)
zitieren (1)	*tsee-*TEE-*ren*	quote (cite), to
Zitrone,*f.*	*tsee-*TROH-*nuh*	lemon
zittern (1)	TSIT-*ehrn*	quiver, to
"	"	tremble, to
Zivilisation,*f.*	*tsee-vee-lee-zahts-*YOHN	civilization (civilized condition)
zögern (1)	TSÖ-*gehrn*	hesitate, to
Zoll,*m.*	TSAWLL	customs (tax)
"	"	duty (tax)
"	"	tariff
Zollabfertigung,*f.*	TSAWLL-*ahpp-fehr-tee-goong*	clearance (customs clearance)
Zollamt,*n.*	TSAWLL-*ahmmt*	customhouse
zollfrei	TSAWLL-*fry*	duty-free
Zone,*f.*	TSO-*nuh*	zone
Zoo,*m.*	TSO	zoo
Zoologie,*f.*	*tso-oh-loh-*G_EE	zoology
Zorn,*m.*	TSAWRN	anger
"		wrath
zornig	TSAWR-*nick*	angry
zu	TSOO	to (indicating direction, *prep.*)
zu	TSOO	to (used with indirect object, *prep.*)
"	"	too (overly)
Zucker,*m.*	TSOOCK-*ehr*	sugar
Zuckerkrankheit,*f.*	TSOOCK-*ehr-krahnnk-hite*	diabetes
Zufall,*m.*	TSOO-*fahll*	accident (chance)
"	"	chance (fate)
Zuflucht,*f.*	TSOO-*flookht*	refuge
Zuflucht nehmen zu (80)	*tsoo-flookht* NAY-*men tsoo*	resort (have recourse), to
zufrieden	*tsoo-*FREE-*den*	content
"	"	satisfied (contented)
Zufriedenheit,*f.*	*tsoo-*FREE-*den-hite*	satisfaction (contentment)
Zug,*m.*	TSOOK	train, railroad
Zug, (feierliche),*m.*	(FYE-*ehr-lee-kh_eh*) TSOOK	procession (parade)
(Gesichts)Zug,*m.*	(*guh-*ZIKHTS-)TSOOK	feature (part of face)
(Luft)Zug,*m.*	(LOOFFT-)TSOOK	draft (air current)
zugeben (43)	TSOO-*gay-ben*	admit (concede), to
Zügel,*m.*	TSÜ-*gel*	curb (restraint)
"	"	rein (strap)
zügeln (1)	TSÜ-*gel'n*	curb (restrain), to
zuhören (1)	TSOO-*hö-ren*	listen (hearken), to
Zukunft,*f.*	TSOO-*koonft*	future (*n.*)
zuletzt	*tsoo-*LETTST	last (after all others, *adv.*)
Zunahme,*f.*	TSOO-*nah-muh*	increase (increment)
Zuname,*m.*	TSOO-*nah-muh*	surname

German	Pronunciation	English
zunehmen (80)	TSOO-*nay-men*	increase (grow), to
Zuneigung,*f.*	TSOO-*nye-goong*	affection (love)
Zunge,*f.*	TSOONNG-*uh*	tongue (*anat.*)
zureden (1)	TSOO-*ray-den*	urge (try to persuade), to
zurück	*tsoo-*RÜCK	back (rearward, *adv.*)
zurückbleiben (17)	*tsoo-*RÜCK-*blye-ben*	lag (fall behind), to
zurückfallen (32)	*tsoo-*RÜCK-*fahll-len*	relapse, to
zurückgeben (43)	*tsoo-*RÜCK-*gay-ben*	return (give back), to
zurückhalten (59)	*tsoo-*RÜCK-*hahll-ten*	restrain (check), to
zurückkehren (1)	*tsoo-*RÜCK-*kay-ren*	return (go back), to
zurücktreten (140)	*tsoo-*RÜCK-*tray-ten*	resign (tender resignation), to
zurückwerfen (157)	*tsoo-*RÜCK-*vehr-fen*	reflect (throw back), to
zurückzahlen (1)	*tsoo-*RÜCK-*tsah-len*	repay (reimburse), to
zurückziehen (161)	*tsoo-*RÜCK-*tsee-en*	withdraw (take back), to
zurückziehen, sich	*zikh tsoo-*RÜCK-*tsee-en*	retire (stop working), to
"	"	withdraw (depart), to
zusammen	*tsoo-*ZAHMM-*en*	together
zusammenbringen (171)	*tsoo-*ZAHMM-*en-bring-en*	assemble (bring together), to
"	"	gather (bring together), to
Zusammenfassung,*f.*	*tsoo-*ZAHMM-*en-fahss-oong*	summary (synopsis)
Zusammenhang,*m.*	*tsoo-*ZAHMM-*en-hahng*	connection (relationship)
Zusammensetzung,*f.*	*tsoo-*ZAHMM-*en-zets-oong*	composition (make-up)
zusammentreffen (138)	*tsoo-*ZAHMM-*en-treff-en*	meet (come together), to
zusammenziehen (161)	*tsoo-*ZAHMM-*men-tsee-en*	contract (make shrink), to
Zusatz,*m.*	TSOO-*zahts*	addition (supplement)
Zusatzartikel,*m.*	TSOO-*zahts-ahr-tee-kell*	amendment (enacted change)
zusätzlich	TSOO-*zetts-likh*	additional
Zuschauer,*m.*	TSOO-*sh_ow-ehr*	spectator
Zuschlag,*m.*	TSOO-*shlahk*	surcharge (*bus.*)
Zustand,*m.*	TSOO-*shtahnnt*	condition
"	"	state
zustandebringen (171)	*tsoo-*SHTAHNN-*duh-bring-en*	manage (contrive), to
zustimmen (1)	TSOO-*shtimm-men*	consent, to
zutreffen (138)	TSOO-*treff-fen*	apply (be fitting), to
Zutritt,*m.*	TSOO-*tritt*	admission (right to enter)
zuverlässig	TSOO-*fehr-less-ick*	reliable
zwar	TSVAHR	indeed (*adv.*)
Zweck,*m.*	TSVECK	aim (purpose)
Zweifel,*m.*	TSVIFE-*el*	doubt
zweifelhaft	TSVIFE-*el-hahfft*	doubtful
zweifellos	TSVIFE-*el-lohss*	doubtless
"	"	undoubtedly
Zweig,*m.*	TSVIKE	branch (bough)
"		twig
zweimal	TSVYE-*mahl*	twice
zweite	TSVYE-*tuh*	second (*adj.*)
Zwerg,*m.*	TSVEHRK	dwarf
Zwiebel,*f.*	TSVEE-*bel*	onion
Zwilling,*m.*	TSVILL-*ing*	twin (*n.*)
zwingen (162)	TSVING-*en*	compel, to
"	"	force, to
zwischen	TSVISH-*en*	between (*prep.*)
Zwischenraum,*m.*	TSVISH-*en-r_owm*	interval (period of time)
Zwischenzeit,*f.*	TSVISH-*en-tsite*	meantime (*n.*)
Zylinder,*m.*	*tsee-*LIN-*dehr*	cylinder (*geom.*)

German Special Lists

Alphabet

a	AH	j	YAWT	s	ESS
b	BAY	k	KAH	t	TAY
c	TSAY	l	ELL	u	OO
d	DAY	m	EM	v	F_OW
e	AY	n	EN	w	VAY
f	EFF	o	OH	x	IX
g	GAY	p	PAY	y	IP-see-lawnn
h	HAH	q	KOO	z	TSET
i	EE	r	EHR		

Cardinal Numbers

German	Pronunciation	English	German	Pronunciation	English
eins	EYE_NSS	one	zweiundzwanzig	TS_VYE-oont-TSVAHNN-tsick	twenty-two
zwei	TS_VYE	two			
drei	DRY	three	dreissig	DRY-sick	thirty
vier	FEAR	four	vierzig	FEERR-tsick	forty
fünf	FÜNF	five	fünfzig	FÜNF-tsick	fifty
sechs	ZEX	six	sechzig	ZEH_KH-tsick	sixty
sieben	ZEE-ben	seven	siebzig	ZEEP-tsick	seventy
acht	AH_KHT	eight	achtzig	AH_KH-tsick	eighty
neun	NOYN	nine	neunzig	NOYN-tsick	ninety
zehn	TSAYN	ten	hundert	HOONN-dehrt	one hundred
elf	ELF	eleven	hundert und eins	HOONN-dehrt oont EYE_NSS	one hundred one
zwölf	TSVÖLF	twelve			
dreizehn	DRY-tsayn	thirteen	zweihundert	TS_VYE-hoonn-dehrt	two hundred
vierzehn	FEERR-tsayn	fourteen	zweihundert und eins	TS_VYE-hoonn-dehrt oont EYE_NSS	two hundred one
fünfzehn	FÜNF-tsayn	fifteen			
sechzehn	ZEH_KH-tsayn	sixteen	(ein) tausend	(ine) T_OW-zent	one thousand
siebzehn	ZEEP-tsayn	seventeen	tausend und eins	T_OW-zent oont EYE_NSS	one thousand one
achtzehn	AH_KHT-tsayn	eighteen	zweitausend	TS_VYE-t_ow-zent	two thousand
neunzehn	NOYN-tsayn	nineteen	zweitausend und eins	TS_VYE-t_ow-zent oont EYE_NSS	two thousand one
zwanzig	TSVAHNN-tsick	twenty			
einundzwanzig	INE-oont-TSVAHNN-tsick	twenty-one	eine Million	EYE-nuh mill-YOHN	one million
			eine Milliarde	EYE-nuh mill-YAHR-duh	one billion

Ordinal Numbers

German	Pronunciation	English	German	Pronunciation	English
erste	AIR-stuh	first	siebente	ZEE-ben-tuh	seventh
zweite	TS_VYE-tuh	second	achte	AH_KH-tuh	eighth
dritte	DRIT-tuh	third	neunte	NOYN-tuh	ninth
vierte	FEAR-tuh	fourth	zehnte	TSAYN-tuh	tenth
fünfte	FÜNF-tuh	fifth	elfte	ELF-tuh	eleventh
sechste	ZEH_KH-stuh	sixth	zwölfte	TSVÖLF-tuh	twelfth

Days of the Week

German	Pronunciation	English	German	Pronunciation	English
Sonntag, m.	ZAWNN-tahk	Sunday	Donnerstag, m.	DAWNN-ehrss-tahk	Thursday
Montag, m.	MOHN-tahk	Monday	Freitag, m.	FRY-tahk	Friday
Dienstag, m.	DEENSS-tahk	Tuesday	Samstag (Sonna-bend), m.	ZAHMMS-tahk (ZAWNN-ah-bent)	Saturday
Mittwoch, m.	MIT-vawkh	Wednesday			

Months of the Year

German	Pronunciation	English	German	Pronunciation	English
Januar, m.	YAH-noo-ahr	January	Juli, m.	YOO-lee	July
Februar, m.	FAY-broo-ahr	February	August, m.	ow-GOOST	August
März, m.	MEHRTS	March	September, m.	zep-TEM-behr	September
April, m.	ah-PRILL	April	Oktober, m.	awck-TOH-behr	October
Mai, m.	MY	May	November, m.	no-VEM-behr	November
Juni, m.	YOO-nee	June	Dezember, m.	day-TSEM-behr	December

First Names

German	Pronunciation	English	German	Pronunciation	English
Abraham	AH-brah-hahm	Abraham	Beatrice	bay-ah-TREE-suh	Beatrice
Adam	AH-dahm	Adam	Benjamin	BEN-yah-meen	Benjamin
Agnes	AHGG-ness	Agnes	Bernhard	BEHRN-hart	Bernard
Albert	AHLL-behrt	Albert	Berta	BEHR-tah	Bertha
Alexander	ah-leck-ZAHNN-dehr	Alexander	Charlotte	shahr-LAWTT-uh	Charlotte
Alfred	AHLL-frait	Alfred			
			Christine	kriss-TEE-nuh	Christine
Alice	ah-LEE-suh	Alice	Christoph	KRISS-tawff	Christopher
Andreas	ahnn-DRAY-ahss	Andrew	Daniel	DAH-nee-ell	Daniel
Anna	AHNN-ah	Ann, Anne	David	DAH-feet	David
Anton	AHNN-tone	Anthony	Dorothea	doh-roh-TAY-ah	Dorothy
Arnold	AHR-nawlt	Arnold			
Artur	AHR-toor	Arthur	Edith	AY-dit	Edith
			Edmund	ED-moont	Edmund
Barbara	BAR-bah-rah	Barbara	Eduard	AY-doo-art	Edward

German	Pronunciation	English	German	Pronunciation	English
Eleonore	*ay-lay-oh-*NO-*ruh*	Eleanor	Leo	LAY-*oh*	Leo
Elisabeth	*ay-*LEE-*zah-bet*	Elizabeth	"	"	Leon
Emilie	*ay-*MEEL-*yuh*	Emily	Leonhard	LAY-*ohn-hart*	Leonard
			Leonore	*lay-oh-*NO-*ruh*	Leonora
Emma	EM-*ah*	Emma	Leopold	LAY-*oh-pawlt*	Leopold
Ernst	EHRNST	Ernest			
Eugen	*oy-*GAIN	Eugene	Ludwig	LOOT-*vick*	Louis
Felix	FAY-*lix*	Felix	Luise	LOO-*ee-zuh*	Louise
Ferdinand	FEHR-*dee-nahnt*	Ferdinand	Margarete	*mahr-guh-*RAY-*tuh*	Margaret
Flora	FLOH-*rah*	Florence	Maria	*mah-*REE-*ah*	Mary
			Marie	*mah-*REE	Marie
Franz	FRAHNNTS	Francis	Markus	MAHR-*kooss*	Mark
Franziska	*frahn-*TSISS-*kah*	Frances			
Friedrich	FREE-*duh-rikh*	Frederick	Martha	MAHR-*tah*	Martha
Georg	*gay-*AWRK	George	Martin	MAHR-*teen*	Martin
Gertrud	GEHR-*troot*	Gertrude	Matthias	*maht-*TEE-*ahss*	Matthew
Gustav	GOOSS-*tahff*	Gustav	Michael	MEEKH-*ah-ell*	Michael
			Nikolas	NICK-*o-lahss*	Nicholas
Hans	HAHNNS	John	Olga	AWL-*gah*	Olga
Harold	HAH-*rawlt*	Harold			
Heinrich (Heini)	HINE-*rikh* (HI-*nee*)	Harry	Otto	AWT-*toh*	Otto
"	"	Henry	Patricius	*pah-*TRITS-*yooss*	Patrick
Helene	*hay-*LAY-*nuh*	Helen	Paul	POWL	Paul
Henriette	*hen-ree-*ET-*uh*	Henrietta	Paula	POW-*lah*	Paula
			Peter	PAY-*tehr*	Peter
Herbert	HEHR-*behrt*	Herbert	Philipp	FEE-*lip*	Philip
Hermann	HEHR-*mahnn*	Herman			
Horaz	*hoh-*RAHTS	Horace	Ralf	RAHLLF	Ralph
Hugo	HOO-*go*	Hugh	Raimund	RYE-*moont*	Raymond
Irene	*ee-*RAY-*nuh*	Irene	Rebekka	*ray-*BECK-*ah*	Rebecca
Isaak	EE-*zahck*	Isaac			
			Richard	RIKH-*art*	Richard
Isabella	*ee-zah-*BELL-*ah*	Isabel	Robert	ROH-*behrt*	Robert
Jakob	YAH-*kawp*	Jacob	Rosa	ROH-*zah*	Rose
"	"	James			
Johann	*yoh-*HAHNN	John	Rosalie	*roh-*ZAHL-*yuh*	Rosalie
Johanna	*yoh-*HAHNN-*ah*	Jane	Rosemarie	ROH-*zuh-mah-ree*	Rosemary
"	"	Jean	Rudolf	ROO-*dawlf*	Rudolph
"	"	Joan	Ruth	ROO_T	Ruth
			Samuel	ZAH-*moo-ell*	Samuel
Joseph	YOH-*zeff*	Joseph	Sara	ZAH-*rah*	Sarah
Josephine	*yoh-zeh-*FEE-*nuh*	Josephine			
Judith	YOO-*ditt*	Judith	Saul	ZOWL	Saul
Julian	YOOL-*yahn*	Julian	Stefan	SHTEFF-*ahn*	Stephen
Karl	KARL	Charles	Susanne	*zoo-*ZAHNN-*uh*	Susan
Karoline	*kah-roh-*LEE-*nuh*	Caroline	Sylvia	ZEEL-*vee-ah*	Sylvia
			Therese	*tay-*RAY-*zuh*	Theresa
Katharina	*kah-tah-*REE-*nah*	Katharine			
Käthe	KAY-*tuh*	Kate	Thomas	TOH-*mahss*	Thomas
Klara	KLAH-*rah*	Clara	Viktor	VICK-*tor*	Victor
Kläre	KLAY-*ruh*	Clare	Vinzenz	VIN-*tsents*	Vincent
Konrad	KAWNN-*raht*	Conrad	Virginie	*veer-*G_EE-*nee*	Virginia
Konstanze	*kawnn-*STAHNN-*tsuh*	Constance	Walter	VAHLL-*tehr*	Walter
Laura	L_OW-*rah*	Laura	Wilhelm	VILL-*helm*	William

USEFUL EXPRESSIONS

Greetings

English	Pronunciation	German
How are you?	*vee* GATE *ess* EE-*nen*?	Wie geht es Ihnen?
Well, thanks, and you?	GOOT, DAHNNG-*kuh, oont* EE-*nen*?	Gut, danke, und Ihnen?
Good morning.	*goo-ten* MAWR-*gen.*	Guten Morgen.
Good afternoon.	*goo-ten* TAHK.	Guten Tag.
Good evening.	*goo-ten* AH-*bent.*	Guten Abend.
Good night.	*goo-tuh* NAH_KHT.	Gute Nacht.
See you again.	*owf* VEE-*dehr-zay-en.*	Auf Wiedersehen.
So long.	*ahd-*YÖ.	Adieu.
Good luck!	*feel* GLÜCK!	Viel Glück!
Good-by.	*owf* VEE-*dehr-zay-en.*	Auf Wiedersehen.
Glad to meet you.	ZAIR AHNN-*guh-name.*	Sehr angenehm.
Congratulations.	*ikh grah-too-*LEE-*ruh.*	Ich gratuliere.
Happy birthday.	HEHRTS-*likhs-tuh guh-*BOORTS-*tahks-*VÜN-*shuh.*	Herzlichste Geburtstagswünsche.
Merry Christmas.	FRÖ-*likh-uh* VIE-*nah_kh-ten.*	Fröhliche Weihnachten.
Happy New Year.	*ine* GLÜCK-*likh-ess* NOY-*ess* YAHR.	Ein glückliches neues Jahr.

Ordinary Conversation

English	Pronunciation	German
Thank you.	DAHNG-*kuh (shön).*	Danke (schön).
Please.	BIT-*tuh.*	Bitte.
You're welcome.	BIT-*tuh (shön).*	Bitte (schön).
Pardon me.	*ent-*SHOOLL-*dee-gen* ZEE.	Entschuldigen Sie.
What do you call this?	*vee* NENT *mahn dahss*?	Wie nennt man das?
I'm sorry.	*ess toot meer* LITE.	Es tut mir leid.

English	*Pronunciation*	*German*
Allow me.	ehr-L_OW-ben zee MEER.	Erlauben Sie mir.
I would like…	ikh MÖKH-tuh…	Ich möchte…
Come in.	hehr-RINE.	Herein.
May I introduce…	DARF ikh FOR-shtell-en…	Darf ich vorstellen…
What is your name?	vee HICE-sen zee?	Wie heissen Sie?
My name is…	ikh HICE-suh…; mine NAH-muh ist…	Ich heisse…; Mein Name ist…
I don't know.	ich VICE nikht.	Ich weiss nicht.
I'm thirsty.	ikh hah-buh DOORST.	Ich habe Durst.
I'm hungry.	ikh hah-buh HOONG-ehr.	Ich habe Hunger.
I'm an American.	ikh bin ah-may-ree-KAH-nehr(-in).	Ich bin Amerikaner(in).
Where can I find…?	VOH kahnn ikh…FIN-den?	Wo kann ich…finden?
What is this?	VAHSS ist DAHSS?	Was ist das?

Foreign Languages

English	*Pronunciation*	*German*
Do you speak…?	SHPREH_KH-en zee…?	Sprechen Sie…?
I speak (understand) a little…	ikh SHPREH_KH-uh (fehr-SHTAY-uh) ET-vahss…	Ich spreche (verstehe) etwas…
I do not speak…	ikh SHPREH_KH-uh kine…	Ich spreche kein…
Is there someone here who speaks English?	ist YAY-mahnnt dah, dair ENG-lish SHPRIKHT?	Ist jemand da, der englisch spricht?
I understand you.	ikh fehr-SHTAY-uh zee.	Ich verstehe Sie.
I don't understand.	ikh fehr-SHTAY-uh nikht.	Ich verstehe nicht.
Please speak more slowly.	BIT-tuh SHPREH_KH-en zee LAHNNG-zah-mehr.	Bitte sprechen Sie langsamer.
Please repeat.	BIT-tuh vee-dehr-HOLE-en zee.	Bitte wiederholen Sie.

Asking Directions

English	*Pronunciation*	*German*
In which direction is…?	in VEL-kh_ehr RIKH-toong ist…?	In welcher Richtung ist…?
Please take me to…	BIT-tuh BRING-en zee mikh nah_kh…	Bitte bringen Sie mich nach…
Please take me there.	BIT-tuh BRING-en zee mikh DORT-hin.	Bitte bringen Sie mich dorthin.
Where can I mail this?	VOH kahnn ikh dee-zuh PAWSST OWF-gay-ben?	Wo kann ich diese Post aufgeben?
Please direct me to…	BIT-tuh T_SYE-gen zee meer, voh…	Bitte zeigen Sie mir, wo…
…the telephone.	…dahss tay-luh-FONE ist.	…das Telephon ist.
…the toilet.	…dee twah-LET-tuh ist.	…die Toilette ist.
…the post office.	…dahss PAWSST-ahmt ist.	…das Postamt ist.
…the bank.	…dee BAHNNK ist.	…die Bank ist.
…the police station.	…dahss pawll-ee-T_SYE-ahmt ist.	…das Polizeiamt ist.
…the U.S. consulate.	…dahss ah-may-ree-KAH-nish-uh kawnn-zoo-LAHT ist.	…das amerikanische Konsulat ist.
Please point.	T_SYE-gen zee meer BIT-tuh.	Zeigen Sie mir bitte.

The Hotel

English	*Pronunciation*	*German*
I would like a room…	ikh vün-shuh ine TSIMM-mehr…	Ich wünsche ein Zimmer…
…with a single bed.	…mit ine-em BET.	…mit einem Bett.
…with two beds.	…mit ts_vye BET-ten.	…mit zwei Betten.
…with bath.	…mit BAHT.	…mit Bad.
…without meals.	…OH-nuh MAHL-tsite-en.	…ohne Mahlzeiten.
Please, the key for Room…	BIT-tuh dane SHLÜSS-el tsoom TSIMM-ehr…	Bitte den Schlüssel zum Zimmer…
Please call me at…o'clock.	VECK-en zee mikh BIT-tuh oomm…OOR.	Wecken Sie mich bitte um…Uhr.
I want this…	ikh MÖKH-tuh deess…	Ich möchte dies…
…pressed.	…guh-BÜ-gelt HAH-ben.	…gebügelt haben.
…cleaned.	…guh-RINE-ickt HAH-ben.	…gereinigt haben.
…washed.	…guh-VAHSH-en HAH-ben.	…gewaschen haben.
…repaired.	…ray-pah-REERT HAH-ben.	…repariert haben.
When will (my suit) be returned?	VAHNN veert mahnn (my-nen AHNN-tsook) tsoo-RÜCK-bring-en?	Wann wird man (meinen Anzug) zurückbringen?
Please return (my suit) at…	BIT-tuh BRING-en zee (my-nen AHNN-tsook) oom…tsoo-RÜCK.	Bitte bringen Sie (meinen Anzug) um… zurück.

The Restaurant

English	*Pronunciation*	*German*
A table for two, please.	ine-ne TISH für TS_VYE pehr-ZOH-nen, BIT-tuh.	Einen Tisch für zwei Personen, bitte.
I would like to see the menu.	ikh MÖKH-tuh dee SHPYE-zuh-car-tuh ZAY-en.	Ich möchte die Speisekarte sehen.
I want it…	ikh MÖKH-tuh ess…	Ich möchte es…
…rare.	…NIKHT DOORKH-guh-brah-ten.	…nicht durchgebraten.
…medium.	…NIKHT ZAIR DOORKH-guh-brah-ten.	…nicht sehr durchgebraten.
…well done.	…GOOT DOORKH-guh-brah-ten.	…gut durchgebraten.
Check, please!	dee REH_KH-noong, BIT-tuh!	Die Rechnung, bitte!

Telephoning

English	*Pronunciation*	*German*
I wish to telephone.	ikh MÖKH-tuh tay-luh-fo-NEE-ren.	Ich möchte telephonieren.

English	Pronunciation	German
Please get me this number.	BIT-*tuh* fehr-BIN-*den* zee mikh dee-zehr NOOMM-*ehr*	Bitte verbinden Sie mich mit dieser Nummer.
Please give me the number of...	BIT-*tuh* GAY-*ben* zee meer dee NOOMM-*ehr* fawnn...	Bitte geben Sie mir die Nummer von...
What did you say?	VEE bit-*tuh?*	Wie bitte?
The line is busy.	buh-ZETST.	Besetzt.
What is the charge?	vee-FEEL buh-TRAIKT dee guh-BÜR?	Wieviel beträgt die Gebühr?

Time

English	Pronunciation	German
What time is it?	vee SHPAYT ist ess?	Wie spät ist es?
It is...	ess ist...	Es ist...
...five o'clock.	...FÜNF oor.	...fünf Uhr.
...ten past eight.	...TSAYN (mee-noo-ten) nah_kh AH_KHT.	...zehn (Minuten) nach acht.
...a quarter past six.	...FEERR-*tel* ZEE-*ben.*	...viertel sieben.
...half past five.	...hahllp ZEX.	...halb sechs.
...five to seven.	...FÜNF (mee-noo-ten) for ZEE-ben.	...fünf (Minuten) vor sieben.
The day before yesterday	FOR-*guess-tehrn*	Vorgestern
Yesterday evening	GUESS-*tehrn* AH-*bent*	Gestern abend
This morning	HOY-*tuh* MOR-*gen*	Heute morgen
At noon	MIT-*tahks*	Mittags
In the afternoon	ahmm NAH_KH-*mit-tahk*	Am Nachmittag
In the evening	ahmm AH-*bent*	Am Abend
At night	in dair NAH_KHT	In der Nacht
At midnight	oomm MIT-*tehr-nah_kht*	Um Mitternacht
Tomorrow morning	mawr-gen FRÜ	Morgen früh
Tomorrow evening	mawr-gen AH-*bent*	Morgen abend
The day after tomorrow	ü-behr-mawr-gen	Übermorgen

Weather

English	Pronunciation	German
It's hot.	ess ist HICE.	Es ist heiss.
It's cold.	ess ist KAHLLT.	Es ist kalt.
It's raining.	ess RAIG-*net.*	Es regnet.
It's snowing.	ess SHNITE.	Es schneit.
What fine weather!	vahss für SHÖ-*ness* VET-*tehr!*	Was für schönes Wetter!

Postal Information

English	Pronunciation	German
How much is the postage on this?	vee-feel buh-TRAYKT dahss POR-*toh?*	Wieviel beträgt das Porto?
Give me...worth of stamps.	GAY-*ben* zee meer für...MARK-*en.*	Geben Sie mir für...Marken.
Please send this letter...	BIT-*tuh* SHICK-*en* zee dee-zen BREEF...	Bitte schicken sie diesen Brief...
...air mail.	...pehr LOOFT-*pawst.*	...per Luftpost.
...special delivery.	...pehr ILE-*boh-tuh*	...per Eilbote.
...registered.	...ahls INE-*shribe-uh-breef.*	...als Einschreibebrief.
Please send this parcel post.	BIT-*tuh* SHICK-*en* zee deess pehr pah-KATE-*pawst.*	Bitte schicken sie dies per Paketpost.

Barber and Beauty Shop

English	Pronunciation	German
I want a haircut.	HAH-*ruh* SHNYE-*den,* BIT-*tuh.*	Haare schneiden, bitte.
Not too short.	NIKHT tsoo KOORTS.	Nicht zu kurz.
No hair oil, thank you.	KINE HAHR-*öl,* BIT-*tuh.*	Kein Haaröl, bitte.
I want a shave.	rah-ZEE-*ren,* BIT-*tuh.*	Rasieren, bitte.
I want a shampoo.	ikh MÖKH-*tuh* mine HAHR guh-VAHSH-*en* hah-ben.	Ich möchte mein Haar gewaschen haben.
I want my hair set.	ikh MÖKH-*tuh* mine HAHR guh-LAYKT HAH-*ben.*	Ich möchte mein Haar gelegt haben.

Transportation

English	Pronunciation	German
Where is the ticket office?	VOH ist dair FAR-*car-ten-shahll-tehr?*	Wo ist der Fahrkartenschalter?
When does...	VAHNN KAWMMT...	Wann kommt...
...the train arrive?	...dair TSOOK ahnn?	...der Zug an?
...the plane arrive?	...dahss FLOOK-*tsoyk* ahnn?	...das Flugzeug an?
...the bus arrive?	...dair AWMM-*nee-booss* ahnn?	...der Omnibus an?
At what time does the train leave for...?	oomm VEE-*feel* OOR fairt dair TSOOK näh_kh...ahpp?	Um wieviel Uhr fährt der Zug nach...ab?
From which track does the train for...leave?	fawn vell-shem BAHN-*shtike fairt dair* TSOO_K näh_kh...ahpp?	Von welchem Bahnsteig fährt der Zug nach...ab?
Is this the right train for...?	ist deess dair TSOO_K näh_kh...?	Ist dies der Zug nach...?
Where is my baggage?	VOH ist mine guh-PECK?	Wo ist mein Gepäck?
Where is the baggage room?	VOH ist dair guh-PECK-*r_owm?*	Wo ist der Gepäckraum?
Please call a taxi.	BIT-*tuh* ROO-*fen* zee ine TAHCK-*see.*	Bitte rufen Sie eine Taxi.

Auto Travel

English	Pronunciation	German
What place is this?	VEL-*kh ehr* ORT *ist dahss?*	Welcher Ort ist das?
Where is the town?	VOH *ist dee* SHTAHTT?	Wo ist die Stadt?
Which is the best road for...?	VEL-*kh ehr ist dair* BESS-*tuh* VAYK *nah kh*...?	Welcher ist der beste Weg nach...?
Turn to the right.	FAH-*ren zee* REH KHTS.	Fahren Sie rechts.
Turn to the left.	FAH-*ren zee* LINKS.	Fahren Sie links.
Go straight on.	FAH-*ren zee guh*-RAH-*duh*-OWSS.	Fahren Sie geradeaus.
Go back.	FAH-*ren zee tsoo*-RÜCK.	Fahren Sie zurück.
This way.	*in* DEE-*zehr* RIKH-*toong.*	In dieser Richtung.
That way.	*in* YAY-*nehr* RIKH-*toong.*	In jener Richtung.
How far is it to...?	*vee* VITE *ist ess biss*...?	Wie weit ist es bis...?
Is this the road to...?	*ist* DEESS *dair* VAYK *nah kh*...?	Ist dies der Weg nach...?
Is it...	*ist ess*...	Ist es...
...near?	...NAH?	...nah?
...far?	...VITE?	...weit?
...very far?	...ZAIR *vite?*	...sehr weit?
Which way is...	VOH *ist*...	Wo ist...
...north?	...NOR-*den?*	...Norden?
...south?	...zü-*den?*	...Süden?
...east?	...AWSS-*ten?*	...Osten?
...west?	...VESS-*ten?*	...Westen?
Is the road...?	*ist dee* SHTRAH-*suh*...?	Ist die Strasse...?
Is there a detour?	GIPT *ess ine-en* OOMM-*vayk?*	Gibt es einen Umweg?
What is the speed limit?	VAHSS *ist dee* HÖKH ST-*guh-shvinn-dikh-kite?*	Was ist die Höchstgeschwindigkeit?
Where is the nearest gas station?	VOH *ist dee* NEH KH-*stuh* TAHNNK-*shtell-uh?*	Wo ist die nächste Tankstelle?
Where can I find a garage (for repairs)?	VOH *kahnn ikh ine-uh gah*-RAH-*zhuh* FIN-*den?*	Wo kann ich eine Garage finden?
I need...	*ikh* BROW-*kh uh*...	Ich brauche...
...oil.	...ÖL.	...Öl.
...gasoline.	...*ben*-TSEEN.	...Benzin.
...a tire.	...*ine-en* RIFE-*en.*	...einen Reifen.

Public Signs

English	Pronunciation	German
Keep out	TSOO-*tritt fehr*-BOH-*ten*	Zutritt Verboten
For Hire	*tsoo fehr*-MEE-*ten*	Zu Vermieten
No Parking	PAR-*ken fehr*-BOH-*ten*	Parken Verboten
No Smoking	R OW-*kh en fehr*-BOH-*ten*	Rauchen Verboten
Sale	OWSS-*fehr-kowf*	Ausverkauf
Women	FROW-*en;* DAH-*men*	Frauen; Damen
Men	MEN-*nehr;* HEHR-*ren*	Männer; Herren
Detour	OOMM-*lye-toong*	Umleitung
Railroad	EYE-*zen-bahn*	Eisenbahn
Dangerous Curve	*guh*-FAIR-*likh-uh* KOORR-*vuh*	Gefährliche Kurve
Keep to the Right (Left)	REH KHTS (LINKS) *fah-ren*	Rechts (Links) Fahren
Dead End	ZAHCK-*gahss-uh*	Sackgasse
Men Working	AH KH-*toonk!* B OW-*shtell-uh!*	Achtung! Baustelle!
No Thoroughfare	KIE-*nuh* DOORKH-*fahrt*	Keine Durchfahrt
One-way Street	INE-*bahn-shtrah-suh*	Einbahnstrasse
Go Slow	LAHNNG-*zahm*	Langsam
Toilet	*twah*-LET-*tuh*	Toilette
Entrance	INE-*gahng*	Eingang
Exit	OWSS-*gahng*	Ausgang

German Grammar

ARTICLES

In German the article has the same gender, number and case as the noun with which it is used.

Definite article

	Masc. Sing.	Fem. Sing.	Neuter Sing.	Masc., Fem., Neuter Pl.
Nominative	der	die	das	die
Genitive	des	der	des	der
Dative	dem	der	dem	den
Accusative	den	die	das	die

Contractions of the definite article. The masculine and neuter definite article, in its dative form, *dem*, is commonly contracted with a preceding preposition, thus: *an dem = am, bei dem =* *beim, von dem = vom, zu dem = zum.* The neuter definite article in the accusative, *das*, may be contracted with prepositions, thus: *an das = ans, auf das = aufs, für das = fürs, in das = ins.* The feminine dative definite article, *der*, may be contracted with a preceding *zu*, thus: *zu der = zur.*

Indefinite article

	Masc. Sing.	Fem. Sing.	Neuter Sing.	Masc., Fem., Neuter Pl.
Nominative	ein	eine	ein	
Genitive	eines	einer	eines	
Dative	einem	einer	einem	*none*
Accusative	einen	eine	ein	

NOUNS

Plural of nouns

German nouns differ in the way they form their plurals. The nouns contained in this dictionary belong to the following categories:

Plural ending -er. If the stressed vowel of the noun in the singular is *a, o, u* or *au*, it is changed to *ä, ö, ü* or *äu*, respectively, thus: *Mann—Männer, Dorf—Dörfer, Buch—Bücher, Haus—Häuser.*

Amt	Feld	Kalb	Schulhaus
Armband	Feuerwehr-	Kaufmann	Schwert
Augenlid	mann	Kind	Signalhorn
Bad	Gehalt	Kirchenlied	Spiegelbild
Band	Geist	Kleid	Sprichwort
Bauerngut	Geld	Krankenhaus	Staatsmann
Beiwort	Geschäfts-	Kraut	Strauch
Bergmann	mann	Lagerhaus	Streichholz
Bettuch	Geschlecht	Lamm	Tal
Bild	Gesetzbuch	Land	Taschentuch
Bindewort	Gesicht	Lehrbuch	Tischtuch
Blatt	Gespenst	Leihhaus	Trinkgeld
Bohrloch	Glas	Licht	Umstandswort
Brett	Glied	Lied	Verhältniswort
Buch	Gott	Loch	Volk
Dach	Grab	Mann	Wald
Denkmal	Gras	Mitglied	Warenhaus
Dorf	Handbuch	Nasenloch	Wort
Dorn	Handtuch	Nest	Wörterbuch
Drehbuch	Hauptwort	Ort	Wurm
Ei	Haus	Postamt	Zeitwort
Fach	Holz	Rad	Zifferblatt
Fahrrad	Horn	Rand	Zimmermann
Farnkraut	Huhn	Schild	Zollamt
Fass	Jagdhaus	Schloss	

This pattern also applies to all nouns ending in *-tum;* e.g., *Irrtum—Irrtümer.*

No plural ending, but change of vowels *a, o, u* and *au*, respectively, to *ä, ö, ü* and *äu* (e.g., *Vater—Väter*).

Apfel	Hafen	Nagel	Schwieger-
Boden	Hammer	Obstgarten	tochter
Bruder	Kanarienvogel	Ofen	Schwiegervater
Dachboden	Kindergarten	Regenmantel	Stiefmutter
Faden	Kloster	Sattel	Stieftochter
Flughafen	Laden	Schaden	Tochter
Garten	Magen	Schnabel	Vater
Graben	Mangel	Schwager	Vogel
Grossmutter	Mantel	Schwieger-	Wasser
Grossvater	Mutter	mutter	

No plural ending. The plural is distinguished from the singular only by the form of the accompanying article or adjective(s).

Adler	Briefchen	Felsen	Gürtel
Aktivposten	Briefträger	Fenster	Haken
Andenken	Brocken	Fernsprecher	Händler
Anhänger	Brötchen	Feuer	Haufen
Anker	Brunnen	Finger	Hausierer
Ansiedler	Buchführer	Fleischer	Häutchen
Apostel	Buchhalter	Flicken	Hebel
Apotheker	Buckel	Flieder	Heilmittel
Arbeiter	Büffel	Flieger	Heizkörper
Arbeitsgeber	Bügeleisen	Flügel	Helfer
Ärmel	Bürgermeister	Flugzeugträger	Herrscher
Artikel	Busen	Fonds	Hilfsmittel
Aschenbecher	Daumen	Fräulein	Hüftgürtel
Bäcker	Deckel	Führer	Hügel
Badezimmer	Dichter	Futter	Hummer
Balken	Dienstmäd-	Gänseblüm-	Indianer
Banner	chen	chen	Jäger
Baukünstler	Drucker	Gärtner	Kabel
Becher	Durchmesser	Gastgeber	Käfer
Befehlshaber	Eichhörnchen	Gebäude	Kaiser
Begleiter	Eimer	Gegner	Kalender
Beobachter	Einbrecher	Geldbeutel	Kaninchen
Berichter-	Einwohner	Gelübde	Kapitel
statter	Ellbogen	Gemälde	Karren
Besen	Empfänger	Gemüse	Käse
Besucher	Engel	Gepäckträger	Kassierer
Bettler	Enkel	Gewebe	Kätzchen
Biber	Erdbeben	Gewerbe	Käufer
Bieter	Erdhügel	Gewissen	Keller
Bildhauer	Ersatzmittel	Gewitter	Kellner
Bogen	Esel	Gipfel	Kessel
Bolzen	Esslöffel	Gläubiger	Kiefer (jaw)
Borger	Fahrer	Grosshändler	Kiesel
Botschafter	Fehler	Gründer	Kinderwagen

Kindlein	Musiker	Schinken	Ufer
Kissen	Muster	Schlafzimmer	Ungeheuer
Klassenzimmer	Nacken	Schläger	Unternehmen
Kleinhändler	Nebel	Schleier	Veilchen
Klumpen	Neger	Schlitten	Verbrechen
Knöchel	Onkel	Schlüssel	Verbrecher
Knochen	Opfer	Schneider	Verfahren
Knoten	Orchester	Schnürsenkel	Verfasser
Koffer	Orden	Schönheits-	Vergehen
Kontoinhaber	Paddel	mittel	Vergnügen
Körper	Panther	Schrauben-	Verkäufer
Kragen	Panzer	zieher	Verleger
Krankenwagen	Personen-	Schrifsteller	Vermögen
Kritiker	wagen	Schuldner	Verräter
Krüppel	Pfadfinder	Schüler	Versehen
Kuchen	Pfarrer	Schuppen	Versprechen
Kugelschreiber	Pfeiler	Schuster	Vertreter
Künstler	Pferdchen	Seeräuber	Vetter
Lager	Pfosten	Segen	Viertel
Laster	Politiker	(An)Siedler	Vorarbeiter
Leben	Polster	Sieger	Vorsteher
Lehrer	Posten	Sommer	Wagen
Leiden	Prediger	Späher	Wähler
(Betriebs)-	Priester	Spaten	Wahlzettel
Leiter	Rabbiner	Speisewagen	Wäldchen
Leser	Rasen	Speisezimmer	Walzer
Liebchen	Rasiermesser	Spiegel	Wärter
Lokomotiv-	Rätsel	Spieler	Wechsel
führer	Räuber	Springbrunnen	Weibchen
Lüftchen	Redner	Staubsauger	Wesen
Luftdruck-	Regen	Stecker	Widder
messer	Regenbogen	Stengel	Winkel
Lügner	Regenschauer	Stiefel	Winter
Lumpen	Register	Stiefmütter-	Wissenschaft-
Mädchen	Reifen	chen	ler
Makler	Reiter	Stöpsel	Witwer
Maler	Revolver	Streifen	Wohnzimmer
Männchen	Richter	Stückchen	Wolkenkratzer
Märchen	Riegel	Sünder	Wunder
Maulesel	Riemen	Teelöffel	Würfel
Maurer	Ritter	Teilhaber	Zauber
Mechaniker	Rotkehlchen	Teller	Zauberer
Meister	Rücken	Tempel	Zeichen
Menschenalter	Ruder	Teufel	Zicklein
Merkzettel	Rundschreiben	Theater	Ziegel
Messer	Samen	Thermometer	Zigeuner
Mieter	Sänger	Tiger	Zimmer
Minister	Schaffner	Transport-	Zirkel
Miteigentümer	Schalter	wagen	Zügel
Mittel	Schatten	Tropfen	Zusatzartikel
Mörder	Schauspieler	Tunnel	Zuschauer
Mörtel	Schemel	Übel	Zweifel
Müller	Schenkel	Überbringer	Zylinder

Plural ending -e, and change of vowels *a, o, u* and *au* to *ä, ö, ü* and *äu*, respectively (e.g., *Arzt—Ärzte*).

Abdruck	Bauch	Empfang	General
Abfluss	Baum	Entwurf	Geruch
Abgrund	Beinbruch	Erdnuss	Geschmack
Absatz	Beitrag	Ertrag	Geschwulst
Abzugskanal	Betrag	Fahrplan	Grund
Admiral	Beweggrund	Fahrstuhl	Grundsatz
Altar	Bienenkorb	Fall	Gruss
Anfang	Bischof	Farbton	Hahn
Angst	Block	Faust	Hals
Anspruch	Blutsturz	Fehlbetrag	Hand
Antrag	Bock	Feldzug	Hauptstadt
Anwalt	Brand	Fledermaus	Haut
Anzug	Brauch	Fluch	Hof
Arbeitskraft	Braut	Flug	Hügelabhang
Arzt	Briefumschlag	Fluss	Hut
Ast	Brust	Friedhof	Kamm
Auftrag	Bund	Frosch	Kampf
Ausdruck	Busch	Frost	Kanal
Ausgang	Chor	Frucht	Kauf
Ausguss	Damm	Fuchs	Kirchturm
Auskunft	Dampf	Fuss	Klang
Ausschuss	Draht	Gang	Klotz
Ausverkauf	Duft	Gans	Knopf
Axt	Dunst	Gast	Knuff
Bach	Eindruck	Gasthof	Koch
Badeanzug	Einfluss	Gebrauch	Kokosnuss
Bahnhof	Eingang	Gegensatz	Kopf
Ball	Einsatz	Gegenstand	Korb
Band	Einspruch	Geizhals	Kraft
Bank	Einwand	Gelegenheits-	Krampf
Bart	Eisschrank	kauf	Kranz

Krug	Reissverschluss	Stab	Vertrag
Kuh	Rock	Stadt	Vorfall
Kunst	Rückzug	Stahl	Vorhang
Kuss	Sack	Stall	Vorrat
Leinwand	Saft	Stamm	Vorschlag
Lohn	Sarg	Stiefsohn	Vorwand
Löwenzahn	Satz	Stock	Vorwurf
Luft	Saum	Storch	Wahlspruch
Lust	Schatz	Stoss	Walnuss
Macht	Schaum	Strom	Wand
Markt	Schlafrock	Strumpf	Wasserfall
Masstab	Schlag	Stuhl	Wasserhahn
Maulwurf	Schlaganfall	Stumpf	Webstuhl
Maus	Schlauch	Stundenplan	Weinstock
Muskatnuss	Schluss	Sturm	Wettkampf
Nacht	Schneesturm	Sturz	Wettlauf
Naht	Schnurrbart	Sumpf	Wiederverkauf
Not	Schoss	Tanz	Wolf
Notfall	Schrank	Ton	Wollust
Nuss	Schuss	Topf	Wuchs
Palast	Schwamm	Traum	Wunsch
Papst	Schwan	Truthahn	Wurst
Pass	Schwanz	Turm	Zahn
Pfahl	Schwarm	Übereinkunft	Zahnarzt
Pferdekraft	Schwiegersohn	Überschuss	Zaum
Pflock	Sohn	(Kreis)-	Zaun
Pflug	Sonnenaufgang	Umfang	Zeitraum
Plan	Sonnenunter-	Umhang	Zoll
Platz	gang	Umschlag	Zufall
Prozentsatz	Spass	Umstand	Zug
Rang	Spaziergang	Unfall	Zusammen-
Rat	Spielplatz	Unterrock	hang
Ratschlag	Sprung	Unterkunft	Zusatz
Raum	Staatenbund	Ursprung	Zuschlag
Rausch		Verband	Zustand
		Verkauf	Zwischenraum

Konzert	Ozean	Salat	Talent
Kork	Paar	Salz	(Aus) Tausch
Kostüm	Paket	Sand	Teig
Krach	Papier	Saphir	Teil
Krebs	Paradies	Säugling	Telegramm
Kredit	Parfüm	Schaf	Teppich
Kreis	Park	Schauspiel	Testament
Kreuz	Parlament	Scherz	Text
Krieg	Passagier	Schicksal	Thron
Kristall	Patent	Schiff	Tier
Kuckuck	Peitschenhieb	Schirm	Tisch
Kurort	Pelz	Schlittschuh	Tod
Kurs	Personal	Schmetterling	Tor (gate)
Lachs	Pfad	Schornstein	Transport
Ladentisch	Pfeil	Schrei	Triumph
Laib	Pferd	Schreibheft	Umweg
Lebensmittel-	Pfirsich	Schreibtisch	Unterschied
geschäft	Pflegling	Schritt	Unterseeboot
Lehrling	Pfuhl	Schuh	Urteil
Leim	Picknik	Schuldschein	Verbot
Leutnant	Pilz	Schwein	Verdienst
Liebling	Pionier	Seehund	Verein
Likör	Pol	Senat	Vergleich
Lineal	Preis	Signal	Verkaufsschein
Lippenstift	Prellstein	Sinn	Verlust
Luftangriff	Problem	Sitz	Versuch
Magnet	Programm	Skandal	Vitamin
Mass	Protokoll	Skelett	Vliess
Mast	Prozent	Spediteur	Vorbehalt
Meer	Prozess	Speer	Vormund
Meineid	Pudding	Spiel	Vorrecht
Meisterwerk	Punkt	Spielzeug	Vorteil
Merkmal	Rabatt	Spion	Vorurteil
Metall	Rasierapparat	Sprengstoff	Vorwort
Mineral	Rauschgift	Star	Vulkan
Missionar	Recht	Stein	Walfisch
Mittelpunkt	Rechteck	Stern	Weg
Modell	Redakteur	Steward	Wein
Monat	Regiment	Stich	Weltteil
Mönch	(Kaiser) Reich	Stiel	Werk
Mond	Reim	Stier	Werkzeug
Moor	Reiz	Stil	Wert
Moos	Renntier	Stockwerk	Wind
Mord	Reservoir	Stoff	Witz
Nachmittag	Rest	Strand	Wohnsitz
Nachtisch	Rezept	Streik	Zeitungskiosk
Nebenprodukt	Ring	Streit	Zeitvertreib
Nennwert	Rinnstein	Strich	Zelt
Netz	Riss	Strichpunkt	Zement
Notar	Rohr	Strick	Ziel
Offizier	Roman	Stück	Zitat
Ohrring	Rost	Sturmwind	Zweck
Öl	Rubin	System	Zweig
Organ	Rückgrat	Tablett	Zwerg
Ort	Ruf	Tag	Zwilling

Plural ending -e and no change in vowel

Aal	Brennstoff	Fundament	Heim
Abend	Brief	Fusstritt	Helm
Abflussrohr	Bruchstück	Garn	Hengst
Absatzgebiet	Bruchteil	Gas	Herd
Abschied	Bug	Gebet	Hering
Abschnitt	Buntstift	Gebiet	Hirsch
Abteil	Bürgersteig	Geburtstag	Huf
Ahorn	Butterbrot	Gedicht	Hund
Alphabet	Charakter	Geduldspiel	Ideal
Anblick	Dachs	Gefäss	Importeur
Angebot	Diagramm	Gefühl	Ingenieur
Angriff	Dickicht	Gegenteil	Inhalt
Anteil	Dieb	Gehirn	Instinkt
Antlitz	Dienst	Geldschein	Instrument
Arm	Ding	(Schutz)-	Inventar
Atom	Dokument	Geleit	Jagdhund
Aufenthalt	Doppelpunkt	Gericht	Jahr
Auftritt	Dreieck	Gerücht	Jahrestag
Augenblick	Düsenantrieb	Geschäft	Jahrhundert
Ausblick	Dutzend	Geschenk	Joch
Ausmass	Edelstein	Geschirr	Jüngling
Ausruf	Eid	Geschwür	Kabelgramm
Bahnsteig	Element	Gesetz	Kabinett
Band	Erfolg	Gesims	Käfig
Bankrott	Ergebnis	Gespräch	Kamel
Bau	Erlebnis	Gesuch	Kamin
Befehl	Erz	Getränk	Kapitän
Begriff	Exemplar	Gewehr	Karneval
Beil	Exporteur	Gewicht	Katalog
Bein	Fahrzeug	Gewinn	Kerbtier
Beispiel	Fallschirm	Gewürz	Kerl
Bereich	Fausthand-	Gift	Kern
Berg	schuh	Golf	Kinn
Bergwerk	Feiertag	Grad	Kirchspiel
Bericht	Feigling	Granit	Klaps
Beruf	Feind	Griff	Klavier
Bestimmungs-	Fell	Grundstück	Klecks
ort	Fernrohr	Haar	Kleidungs-
Besuch	Fest	Habicht	stück
Betrieb	Festmahl	Halt	Klima (pl.
Beweis	Film	Handgelenk	Klimate)
Bezirk	Fisch	Handschuh	Klistier
Bibliothekar	Fleck	Handwerk	Kniff
Bindestrich	Flüchtling	Hauptquartier	Kommissar
Biss	Flugzeug	Hauptteil	Kompass
Bleistift	Frachtbrief	Haushalt	Kompliment
Blick	Freund	Hausschuh	Kompromiss
Blitz	Frisör	Haustier	Kongress
Boot	Frühling	Heer	König
Bräutigam	Frühstück	Heiland	Königreich

Plural ending -s and no change in vowel

Abonnement	Couch (pl.	Kap	Sofa
Auto	Couches)	Kino	Sweater
Ballon	Dock	Komma	Taxi
Banjo	Fort	Konto	Tee
Bankier	Gelee	Pyjama	Tempo
Bar	Genie	Radiergummi	Torpedo
Budget	Giro	Radio	Trick
Büro	Hotel	Rasiercreme	Trust
Chef	Interview	Restaurant	Zebra
Cocktail	Kamera	Rouleau	Ziehharmonika
	Kanu	Rum	

Plural ending -se and no change in vowel

Begräbnis	Erzeugnis	Glaubensbe-	Verzeichnis
Bildnis	Firnis	kenntnis	Wagnis
Ereignis	Gefängnis	Hindernis	Wörterver-
Ergebnis	Geheimnis	Kenntnis	zeichnis
Erlaubnis	Gelöbnis	Omnibus	Zeugnis
Ersparnis		Verhältnis	Zirkus

Plural ending -n or -en and no change in vowel. This classification includes all feminine nouns not listed in the previous groups, and the masculine and neuter nouns enumerated below. Plural forms in which the base undergoes a change are specified in parentheses.

Adressat	Atlas	Bär	Bevollmäch-
Advokat	(Atlanten)	Basis (Basen)	tigte
Affe	Auge	Bauer	Bote
Akkumulator	Auster	Beamte	Buchstabe
Angestellte	Bakterium	Bekannte	Bürge
Ansässige	(Bakterien)	Bett	Chirurg
Athlet	Bandit		Christ

Datum (Daten)	Handelsrei-	Monarch	Schmerz
Demokrat	sende	Motor	Schreck
Diamant	Hase	Museum (Mu-	Schurke
Dienstbote	Heilige	seen)	See
Dirigent	Held	Muskel	Senator
Doktor	Hemd	Mythos (My-	Sergeant
Dosis (Dosen)	Herr	then)	Soldat
Drache	Herz	Nachbar	Sozialist
Drama (Dra-	Hirt	Nachkomme	Spatz
men)	Interesse	Nachthemd	Spielgefährte
Eisenbahn	Jude	Name	Spitzname
Elefant	Junge	Narr	Staat
Ende	Junggeselle	Neffe	Statut
Erbe	Juwel	Nerv	Stirn
Ernte	Kalbskotelett	Oberst	Strahl
Etikett	Kamerad	Ochs	Student
Fabrikant	Kandidat	Ohr	Studium (Stu-
Faktor	Kartoffel	Pastor	dien)
Feldbett	Kiefer (pine)	Patriot	Thema (The-
Firma (Fir-	Konkurrent	Pfau	men)
men)	Konsul	Phonograph	Tourist
Freiwillige	Korrespondent	Pilot	Traktor
Fremde	Kranke	Planet	Tyrann
Funke	Kranken-	Polizist	Uniform
Gedanke	schwester	Präsident	Universität
Gefährte	Kunde	Prinz	Untertan
Gefangene	Kurator	Professor	Verbündete
Gehilfe	Laboratorium	Prophet	Verwandte
Gelehrte	(Labora-	Rebell	Veteran
Geliebte	torien)	Reisende	Vollmacht
Globus (Glo-	Leiter (ladder)	Revisor	Vorfahr
ben)	Leopard	Richtstrahl	Vorsitzende
Götze	Lieferant	Riese	Waise
Hammelkote-	Löwe	Ritus (Riten)	Zeuge
lett	Mädchenname	Sachverstän-	Zins
	Matrose	dige	Zuname

Gender of nouns

Every German noun is either masculine, feminine or neuter in gender. The article and adjectives, if any, which are used with a noun must be of the same gender as the noun. Gender of nouns is shown in the main word list by the designations *m.* for masculine, *f.* for feminine and *n.* for neuter.

To designate women German usually employs special feminine nouns even where English does not do this; for example, *Freund* means "friend," but for a girl or woman friend the feminine *Freundin* is used. Some of these special feminine nouns are listed in the dictionary. Other nouns may be made feminine by adding *-in;* e.g., if a "borrower" (*Borger*) is a woman, she is called a *Borgerin*.

Case of nouns

Nouns in German appear in one of four cases, according to their function in the sentence. The cases are nominative, geni-

tive, dative and accusative. Nouns appear in the dictionary in the nominative case. The other cases are formed from the nominative in several ways, according to the plural group to which the noun belongs.

Plural ending -er

	Sing.	Pl.
Nominative	Mann	Männer
Genitive	Mannes	Männer
Dative	Mann(e) *	Männern
Accusative	Mann	Männer

No plural ending

	Masc. and Neuter		Fem.	
	Sing.	Pl.	Sing.	Pl.
Nominative	Vater	Väter	Mutter	Mütter
Genitive	Vaters	Väter	Mutter	Mütter
Dative	Vater	Vätern	Mutter	Müttern
Accusative	Vater	Väter	Mutter	Mütter

Plural ending -e

	Masc. and Neuter		Fem.	
	Sing.	Pl.	Sing.	Pl.
Nominative	Baum	Bäume	Hand	Hände
Genitive	Baumes	Bäume	Hand	Hände
Dative	Baum(e) *	Bäumen	Hand	Händen
Accusative	Baum	Bäume	Hand	Hände

Plural ending -s

	Masc. and Neuter		Fem.	
	Sing.	Pl.	Sing.	Pl.
Nominative	Hotel	Hotels	Kamera	Kameras
Genitive	Hotels	Hotels	Kamera	Kameras
Dative	Hotel	Hotels	Kamera	Kameras
Accusative	Hotel	Hotels	Kamera	Kameras

Plural ending -en

	Masc.		Fem.	
	Sing.	Pl.	Sing.	Pl.
Nominative	Student	Studenten	Frau	Frauen
Genitive	Studenten	Studenten	Frau	Frauen
Dative	Studenten	Studenten	Frau	Frauen
Accusative	Studenten	Studenten	Frau	Frauen

Note: A few nouns in the last group are inflected in the singular as if they belonged to the first group; e.g., *Staat, Auge.*

* The (*e*) in parentheses means that in the dative this ending may, but need not, be added.

PRONOUNS

Personal pronouns

German has three pronouns meaning "you": *du,* which is used with a child, a relative or a close friend; *ihr,* which is used to more than one individual of the kind to whom one would say *du;* and *Sie,* which is used to either one or several persons with whom one is not on sufficiently familiar terms to say *du* or *ihr. Sie* also means "they," but in writing it is capitalized only when it means "you."

Subject of the verb (nominative)

ich	I	wir	we
du	you	ihr	you
er	he	sie	they
sie	she	Sie	you
es	it		

     Ich lese.   *I* am reading.

Direct object of the verb (accusative)

mich	me	uns	us
dich	you	euch	you
ihn	him	sie	them
sie	her	Sie	you
es	it		

     Er sieht *mich.*   He sees *me.*

These forms of the personal pronoun are also used after certain prepositions; see the section on *Prepositions,* below.

     Ein Buch für *mich.*   A book for *me.*

Indirect object of the verb (dative)

mir	me	uns	us
dir	you	euch	you
ihm	him	ihnen	them
ihr	her	Ihnen	you
ihm	it		

     Er hilft *mir.*   He helps *me.*

These forms of the personal pronoun are also used after certain prepositions; see the section on *Prepositions* for a list of them.

     Er kommt mit *mir.*   He is coming with *me.*

Object of a few special verbs and prepositions (genitive)

meiner	me	unser	us
deiner	you	euer	you
seiner	him	ihrer	them
ihrer	her	Ihrer	you
seiner	it		

     Er erinnert sich *meiner.*   He remembers *me.*

See the section on *Prepositions* (p. 2892) for a list of the prepositions that take the genitive.

Possessive pronouns

For the German words corresponding to "my," "your," etc., see the section on *Possessive Adjectives,* p. 2891.

Reflexive pronouns

mich	myself	uns	ourselves
dich	yourself	euch	yourselves
sich	himself, herself itself	sich	themselves, yourselves

     Ich rasiere *mich.*   I shave *myself.*

Relative pronouns

The German equivalents of English "who," "whom," "whose," "which" and "that" depend not on whether the reference is to a person or to a thing but on the gender of the noun referred to. The relative pronoun also has the same number—singular or plural—as the noun it refers to. Its case is determined by its own function in the relative clause.

	Masc. Sing.	Fem. Sing.	Neuter Sing.	Pl.
Nominative	der	die	das	die
Genitive	dessen	deren	dessen	deren
Dative	dem	der	dem	denen
Accusative	den	die	das	die

ein Mann, *der* dort war	a man *who* was there
eine Geschichte, *die* wahr ist	a story *that* is true
ein Kind, *dessen* Augen blau sind	a child *whose* eyes are blue
ein Buch, *das* ich brauche	a book *which* I need
die Freunde, mit *denen* ich sprach	the friends with *whom* I spoke

Interrogative pronouns

Who, whom, whose

Wer—used as the subject of a verb (nominative).

Wer ist das?	*Who* is this?

Wem—used as the indirect object of a verb and with certain prepositions (dative).

Wem begegnetest du?	*Whom* did you meet?
Mit *wem* sprachst du?	With *whom* did you speak?

Wen—used as the direct object of a verb and with certain prepositions (accusative).

Wen sahst du?	*Whom* did you see?
Auf *wen* wartest du?	For *whom* are you waiting?

Wessen—used as a possessive and as an object after certain verbs and prepositions (genitive).

Wessen Mantel ist das?	*Whose* coat is this?

What

Was will er?	*What* does he want?

Which, which one

Welcher, meaning "which" or "which one," is an adjective and has to agree in number, case and gender with the noun with which it is used (if any). For rules of its inflection, see the section on *Interrogative Adjectives*, below.

Welches Buch (sing., neuter, nom.) ist das beste?	*Which* book is the best?
In *welcher* Strasse (sing., fem., dat.) wohnen Sie?	On *which* street do you live?
Welche (pl., acc.) möchtest du haben?	*Which ones* would you like to have?

Demonstrative pronouns

This, this one

Dieser, meaning "this" or "this one," is an adjective and agrees in number, case and gender with the noun with which it is used (if any). For details of its inflection, see the section on *Demonstrative Adjectives*, below.

Dieser Mann (sing., masc., nom.) ist nicht alt.	*This* man is not old.
Mit *diesem* Auge (sing., neuter, dat.) sehe ich besser.	With *this* eye I see better.
Zeige es *dieser* (sing., fem., dat.).	Show it to *this one*.

That, that one

Jener, meaning "that" or "that one," is an adjective and agrees in number, case and gender with the noun with which it is used (if any). For details of its inflection, see the section on *Demonstrative Adjectives*, below.

in *jenem* Jahr (sing., neuter, dat.)	in *that* year
auf *jenen* (pl., dat.)	on *those*

ADJECTIVES

Declension of adjectives

In German, adjectives agree in number, gender and case with the nouns with which they are used. In addition, they are inflected differently depending on whether they are preceded by a definite article ("weak" inflection), by an indefinite article ("mixed" inflection) or by no article ("strong" inflection). Predicate adjectives are not inflected.

Strong inflection

	Masc. Sing.	Fem. Sing.	Neuter Sing.	Pl.
Nominative	guter	gute	gutes	gute
Genitive	guten	guter	guten	guter
Dative	gutem	guter	gutem	guten
Accusative	guten	gute	gutes	gute

Weak inflection

Nominative	gute	gute	gute	guten
Genitive	guten	guten	guten	guten
Dative	guten	guten	guten	guten
Accusative	guten	gute	gute	guten

This inflection is used if the adjective is preceded by a definite article or by *dieser, jener, jeder, welcher, mancher* or *solcher*.

Mixed inflection

Nominative	guter	gute	gutes	guten
Genitive	guten	guten	guten	guten
Dative	guten	guten	guten	guten
Accusative	guten	gute	gutes	guten

This inflection is used if the adjective is preceded by an indefinite article, by a possessive adjective or by *kein*.

ein *guter* Brief	a good letter
seine *guten* Wörter	his good words
kein *gutes* Zeichen	not a good sign

Comparison of adjectives

Regular comparison

Simple	reich	rich
Comparative	reicher	richer
Superlative	(der) reichst(e)	the richest

Most one-syllable adjectives which have the vowels *a, o* or *u* change them to *ä, ö* or *ü*, respectively, in the comparative and superlative. Thus *alt, älter, der älteste; dumm, dümmer, der dümmste.*

Irregular comparison

A few common adjectives have irregular comparisons. The most important are the following:

Simple	Comparative	Superlative
gut	besser	der besste
hoch	höher	der höchste
nah	näher	der nächste
viel	mehr	der meiste

Interrogative adjectives

The interrogative adjective *welcher*, meaning "which," is inflected like a regular adjective in the strong inflection, except that the genitive singular of the masculine and neuter takes the ending *-es*, thus: *welches*.

Demonstrative adjectives

The demonstrative adjectives *dieser*, "this," and *jener*, "that," are inflected like regular adjectives in the strong inflection, except that the genitive singular of the masculine and neuter takes the ending *-es*, thus: *dieses, jenes*.

Possessive adjectives

Forms

mein	my	unser	our
dein	your	euer	your
sein	his	ihr	their
ihr	her	Ihr	your
sein	its		

Inflection

	Masc. Sing.	Fem. Sing.	Neuter Sing.	Pl.
Nominative	mein	meine	mein	meine
Genitive	meines	meiner	meines	meiner
Dative	meinem	meiner	meinem	meinen
Accusative	meinen	meine	mein	meine

The numeral *ein* and the adjective *kein*, meaning "no," "not any," are also inflected like possessive adjectives.

PREPOSITIONS

The following prepositions require the dative case: *aus, bei, dank, entgegen, gegenüber, längs, mit, nach, seit, von, zu;* for example: *zu dem Knaben, zu mir, zu ihm.*

The following prepositions require the accusative case: *bis, durch, für, gegen, ohne, um;* for example: *für den Knaben, für mich, für ihn.*

The following prepositions require the dative case when they denote location and the accusative when they denote direction:

an, auf, ausser, hinter, in, neben, über, unter, vor, zwischen; for example: *auf dem Tisch* (on the table: location), *auf den Tisch* (onto the table: direction).

The following prepositions require the genitive case: *anstatt, ausserhalb, betreffs, bezüglich, infolge, innerhalb, laut, statt, trotz, um...willen, während, zwecks;* for example: *anstatt des Lehrers* (instead of the teacher), *während der Jahre* (during the years).

VERBS

Types of verbs

German verbs are classified as "weak," "strong," modal auxiliaries and irregular. Each type of verb may also have a prefix which is either separable or inseparable (see section on *Prefixes*, p. 2893).

Numbering of verbs

Each verb in the German-to-English list is followed by a number in parentheses. Number (1) means a weak verb. Other numbers correspond to models (2) through (181) in this German grammar section, pp. 2893–95.

Infinitive and verb root

Each verb in the main word list appears in its infinitive form. The infinitive is made up of a verb root and an infinitive ending.

Infinitive	Root	Ending
lieben	lieb-	-en

Present tense

Weak verbs

ich liebe	I love	wir lieben	we love
du liebst	you love	ihr liebt	you love
er liebt	he loves	sie lieben	they love

Strong verbs. Strong verbs are inflected in the present tense like weak ones, except that if the vowel is *a* it is changed to *ä* in the second and third persons singular, while *e* is changed to *i* or *ie*. Thus:

ich trage	ich helfe	ich befehle
du trägst	du hilfst	du befiehlst
er trägt	er hilft	er befiehlt

Modal auxiliaries

Infinitive	ich	du	er	wir	ihr	sie
dürfen	darf	darfst	darf	dürfen	dürft	dürfen
können	kann	kannst	kann	können	könnt	können
mögen	mag	magst	mag	mögen	mögt	mögen
müssen	muss	musst	muss	müssen	müsst	müssen
sollen	soll	sollst	soll	sollen	sollt	sollen
wollen	will	willst	will	wollen	wollt	wollen

The following verb is also conjugated like a modal auxiliary:

wissen	weiss	weisst	weiss	wissen	wisst	wissen

Irregular verbs

Infinitive	ich	du	er	wir	ihr	sie
haben	habe	hast	hat	haben	habt	haben
sein	bin	bist	ist	sind	seid	sind
werden	werde	wirst	wird	werden	werdet	werden

Simple past tense

The simple past tense is ordinarily used to describe past events with reference to other past events, but without reference to the present.

Weak verbs. To form the simple past tense, endings are added to the verb root, as follows:

ich liebte	I loved	wir liebten	we loved
du liebtest	you loved	ihr liebtet	you loved
er liebte	he loved	sie liebten	they loved

Strong verbs. To form the simple past tense, the reader can look up the simple past tense form in the list of verbs at the end of this section, and add the appropriate ending.

tragen—simple past tense form: *trug*

ich trug	I carried	wir trugen	we carried
du trugst	you carried	ihr trugt	you carried
er trug	he carried	sie trugen	they carried

Past participle

Weak verbs. To form the past participle, add *ge-* before the verb root and *-t* (or *-et*) after it; for example: *lieb, geliebt.*

Some verbs which are not stressed on the first syllable of the verb root do not add *ge-*; for example: *marschier, marschiert.*

Strong verbs, modal auxiliaries and irregular verbs. The past participles may be found in the list at the end of this section.

Verbs with prefix. See section on *Prefixes*, p. 2893.

Compound past tense

The compound past tense is used to describe past events with some reference to the present; e.g., events that are still going on, events that are no longer going on and the like. The compound past tense is made up of an auxiliary and the past participle. The auxiliary is generally the appropriate form of the verb *haben*, but a few verbs, mostly indicating motion, use *sein* as the auxiliary.

ich habe geliebt	I loved	ich bin gekommen	I came
du hast geliebt	you loved	du bist gekommen	you came
er hat geliebt	he loved	er ist gekommen	he came
wir haben geliebt	we loved	wir sind gekommen	we came
ihr habt geliebt	you loved	ihr seid gekommen	you came
sie haben geliebt	they loved	sie sind gekommen	they came

Future tense

The future tense is formed by using the irregular verb *werden* (see section on *Irregular Verbs*, above) as an auxiliary with the infinitive of the main verb.

ich werde lieben	I *shall* love
du wirst kommen	you *will* come
er wird aufstehen	he *will* rise

Present participle

The present participle is formed by adding *-d* to the infinitive:

lieben
liebend — loving
kommen
kommend — coming

Imperative mood

Weak verbs. The singular of the imperative is identical in form with the first person singular of the present tense. The plural is identical with the second person plural of the present tense; for example: *liebe, liebt.*

Strong verbs. The singular of the imperative is identical with the verb root. If it is a verb whose vowel changes from *e* to *i* or *ie* in the second and third persons singular of the present tense, the imperative also uses the changed vowel; for example: *trag, hilf.*

The plural of the imperative is identical with the second person plural of the present tense; for example: *tragt, helft.*

Present subjunctive

The chief use of the present subjunctive is in reporting things for the truth of which the speaker does not wish to take responsibility.

Er sagt, er *sei* krank.　　He says he *is* sick (but I can't vouch for it).

The present subjunctive is formed by adding endings to the verb root, as follows:

ich helfe	(that) I help	wir helfen	(that) we help
du helfest	(that) you help	ihr helfet	(that) you help
er helfe	(that) he helps	sie helfen	(that) they help

The only verb which has an irregular present subjunctive is *sein.* It is formed as follows:

ich sei	(that) I am	wir seien	(that) we are
du seiest	(that) you are	ihr seiet	(that) you are
er sei	(that) he is	sie seien	(that) they are

Past subjunctive

The chief use of the past subjunctive is in conditional clauses.

Wenn es warm *wäre, trüge* ich keinen Mantel.　　If it *were* warm, I *would* not *wear* an overcoat.

Weak verbs. The past subjunctive of weak verbs is exactly

like the simple past tense.

Strong verbs, modal auxiliaries and irregular verbs. The past subjunctive is formed by adding endings to the simple past tense form of the verb and by changing its vowel, if it is *a, o* or *u*, to *ä, ö* or *ü*, respectively.

Infinitive:	halten	tragen	sein
Past tense:	hielt	trug	war
Past subjunctive:	ich hielte	ich trüge	ich wäre
	du hieltest	du trügest	du wärest
	er hielte	er trüge	er wäre
	wir hielten	wir trügen	wir wären
	ihr hieltet	ihr trüget	ihr wäret
	sie hielten	sie trügen	sie wären

Reflexive verbs

When the subject and the object of a verb are the same, the verb is called reflexive.

Er rasiert *sich*.   He shaves *himself*.

In German, reflexive verbs are commoner than in English.

sich waschen   to wash
sich verändern   to change

Verbs which must be used reflexively to translate the English meaning are indicated as follows in the vocabulary lists:

freuen, sich   to rejoice

For verbs which are used both reflexively and nonreflexively for the meaning of the English verb, the reflexive pronoun appears in parentheses after the verb in the vocabulary lists:

rasieren, (sich)   to shave

For the reflexive pronoun, see the section on *Reflexive Pronouns*, p. 2890.

Prefixes

There are two kinds of prefixes, separable and inseparable.

Separable prefixes. The separable prefixes are *ab, an, auf, aus, bei, dar, ein, entgegen, fort, heim, herab, hinab, los, mit, nach, nieder, vor, weg, zu, zurück* and *zusammen.*

In normal word order, the separable prefix is detached and placed after the verb in the present tense, the simple past tense, the present subjunctive and the past subjunctive; for example: *er kommt an, er kam an, er komme an, er käme an.* It is attached before the infinitive and the past participle: *ankommen, angekommen.*

In certain kinds of subordinate clauses the prefix is attached to the verb even in the other tenses.

Inseparable prefixes. The inseparable prefixes are *be, ent, ge, miss, ver, wider* and *zer.* They are never separated from the verb. In the past participle of verbs with inseparable prefixes, *ge* is not added; for example: *er besucht, er besuchte, er besuche; besuchen, besucht.*

Separable or inseparable prefixes. Some prefixes are separable when stressed and inseparable when unstressed. These are *durch, über, um* and *wieder;* for example: *er überreicht* (ü-behr-RYE-kht) but *er setzt über* (ZETST Ü-behr).

Strong and irregular verbs and modal auxiliaries

Below is a list of verbs, numbered (2) through (181) in the German-to-English word list. Verbs numbered (1) are weak and are conjugated according to patterns found under *Present Tense, Simple Past Tense, Compound Past Tense,* etc., above. Verbs numbered (2) through (162) are strong; numbers (163) through (169) are modal auxiliaries; (170) through (177) are weak, but irregular in some way; (178) through (181) are irregular.

STRONG VERBS

Infinitive	Present Tense Third Person Sing.	Past Tense First Person Sing.	Past Participle
(2) **Backen** (to bake)	bäckt	buk	gebacken
(3) **Befehlen** (to order, command)	befiehlt	befahl	befohlen
(4) **Befleissen (sich)** (to apply oneself)	befleisst	befliss	beflissen
(5) **Beginnen** (to begin)	beginnt	begann	begonnen
(6) **Behalten** (to retain)	behält	behielt	behalten
(7) **Beissen** (to bite)	beisst	biss	gebissen
(8) **Bergen** (to hide)	birgt	barg	geborgen
(9) **Bersten** (to burst)	birst	barst	geborsten
(10) **Betrügen** (to cheat, deceive)	betrügt	betrog	betrogen
(11) **Bewegen** (to induce) (*Note:* Weak verb as, to move)	bewegt	bewog	bewogen
(12) **Biegen** (to bend)	biegt	bog	gebogen
(13) **Bieten** (to bid, offer)	bietet	bot	geboten
(14) **Binden** (to bind)	bindet	band	gebunden
(15) **Bitten** (to beg, ask)	bittet	bat	gebeten
(16) **Blasen** (to blow)	bläst	blies	geblasen
(17) **Bleiben** (to stay, remain)	bleibt	blieb	geblieben
(18) **Bleichen** (to fade, pale)	bleicht	blich	geblichen
(19) **Braten** (to roast, fry)	brät	briet	gebraten
(20) **Brechen** (to break)	bricht	brach	gebrochen
(21) **Dingen** (to hire, engage)	dingt	dang	gedungen
(22) **Dringen** (to urge, press)	dringt	drang	gedrungen
(23) **Dreschen** (to thrash)	drischt	drosch	gedroschen
(24) **Empfehlen** (to recommend)	empfiehlt	empfahl	empfohlen
(25) **Erbleichen** (to grow pale)	erbleicht	erblich	erblichen
(26) **Erlöschen** (to extinguish)	erlöscht	erlosch	erloschen
(27) **Erschallen** (to resound)	erschallt	erscholl	erschollen
(28) **Erschrecken** (to frighten, terrify)	erschreckt	erschrak	erschrocken
(29) **Erwägen** (to consider)	erwägt	erwog	erwogen
(30) **Essen** (to eat)	isst	ass	gegessen
(31) **Fahren** (to drive)	fährt	fuhr	gefahren
(32) **Fallen** (to fall)	fällt	fiel	gefallen
(33) **Fangen** (to catch)	fängt	fing	gefangen
(34) **Fechten** (to fight)	ficht	focht	gefochten
(35) **Finden** (to find)	findet	fand	gefunden
(36) **Flechten** (to plait)	flicht	flocht	geflochten
(37) **Fliegen** (to fly)	fliegt	flog	geflogen
(38) **Fliehen** (to flee)	flieht	floh	geflohen
(39) **Fliessen** (to flow)	fliesst	floss	geflossen
(40) **Fressen** (to eat—of animals)	frisst	frass	gefressen
(41) **Frieren** (to freeze)	friert	fror	gefroren
(42) **Gebären** (to bear)	gebiert	gebar	geboren
(43) **Geben** (to give)	gibt	gab	gegeben
(44) **Gedeihen** (to thrive)	gedeiht	gedieh	gediehen
(45) **Gefallen** (to please)	gefällt	gefiel	gefallen
(46) **Gehen** (to go)	geht	ging	gegangen
(47) **Gelingen** (to succeed)	gelingt	gelang	gelungen
(48) **Gelten** (to be worth, valid)	gilt	galt	gegolten
(49) **Genesen** (to recover)	genest	genas	genesen
(50) **Geniessen** (to enjoy)	geniesst	genoss	genossen
(51) **Geraten** (to thrive)	gerät	geriet	geraten
(52) **Geschehen** (to happen)	geschieht	geschah	geschehen
(53) **Gewinnen** (to win, obtain)	gewinnt	gewann	gewonnen
(54) **Giessen** (to pour)	giesst	goss	gegossen
(55) **Gleichen** (to resemble)	gleicht	glich	geglichen
(56) **Gleiten** (to glide)	gleitet	glitt	geglitten

Infinitive	Present Tense Third Person Sing.	Past Tense First Person Sing.	Past Participle
(57) Graben (to dig)	gräbt	grub	gegraben
(58) Greifen (to grasp, seize)	greift	griff	gegriffen
(59) Halten (to hold, stop)	hält	hielt	gehalten
(60) Hängen (to hang)	hängt	hing	gehangen
(61) Hauen (to hew, hit)	haut	hieb	gehauen
(62) Heben (to raise, lift)	hebt	hob	gehoben
(63) Heissen (to be called, bid)	heisst	hiess	geheissen
(64) Helfen (to help)	hilft	half	geholfen
(65) Klimmen (to climb)	klimmt	klomm	geklommen
(66) Klingen (to sound, ring)	klingt	klang	geklungen
(67) Kneifen (to pinch)	kneift	kniff	gekniffen
(68) Kommen (to come)	kommt	kam	gekommen
(69) Kriechen (to creep)	kriecht	kroch	gekrochen
(70) Laden (to load)	ladet	lud	geladen
(71) Lassen (to let, allow, permit)	lässt	liess	gelassen
(72) Laufen (to run)	läuft	lief	gelaufen
(73) Leiden (to suffer, endure)	leidet	litt	gelitten
(74) Leihen (to lend)	leiht	lieh	geliehen
(75) Lesen (to read)	liest	las	gelesen
(76) Liegen (to lie—place)	liegt	lag	gelegen
(77) Lügen (to lie—untruth)	lügt	log	gelogen
(78) Meiden (to avoid)	meidet	mied	gemieden
(79) Messen (to measure)	misst	mass	gemessen
(80) Nehmen (to take)	nimmt	nahm	genommen
(81) Pfeifen (to whistle)	pfeift	pfiff	gepfiffen
(82) Quellen (to gush, well up)	quillt	quoll	gequollen
(83) Raten (to advise)	rät	riet	geraten
(84) Reiben (to rub)	reibt	rieb	gerieben
(85) Reissen (to tear)	reisst	riss	gerissen
(86) Reiten (to ride)	reitet	ritt	geritten
(87) Riechen (to smell)	riecht	roch	gerochen
(88) Ringen (to wrestle, struggle)	ringt	rang	gerungen
(89) Rufen (to call, exclaim)	ruft	rief	gerufen
(90) Saufen (to swill, drink to excess)	säuft	soff	gesoffen
(91) Saugen (to suck)	säugt	sog	gesogen
(92) Schaffen (to create, make, work)	schafft	schuf	geschaffen
(93) Scheiden (to part, separate)	scheidet	schied	geschieden
(94) Scheinen (to seem, shine)	scheint	schien	geschienen
(95) Schelten (to scold)	schilt	schalt	gescholten
(96) Scheren (to shear, clip)	schiert *or* schert	schor	geschoren
(97) Schieben (to shove, push)	schiebt	schob	geschoben
(98) Schiessen (to shoot)	schiesst	schoss	geschossen
(99) Schlafen (to sleep)	schläft	schlief	geschlafen
(100) Schlagen (to strike, beat, hit)	schlägt	schlug	geschlagen
(101) Schleichen (to sneak, slink, skulk)	schleicht	schlich	geschlichen
(102) Schleifen (to grind)	schleift	schliff	geschliffen
(103) Schleissen (to slit, split)	schleisst	schliss	geschlissen
(104) Schliessen (to close, shut)	schliesst	schloss	geschlossen
(105) Schlingen (to wind, devour)	schlingt	schlang	geschlungen
(106) Schmeissen (to throw, cast, smite)	schmeisst	schmiss	geschmissen
(107) Schmelzen (to melt)	schmilzt	schmolz	geschmolzen
(108) Schneiden (to cut)	schneidet	schnitt	geschnitten
(109) Schreiben (to write)	schreibt	schrieb	geschrieben
(110) Schreien (to scream)	schreit	schrie	geschrien
(111) Schreiten (to step, stride, proceed)	schreitet	schritt	geschritten
(112) Schweigen (to be silent)	schweigt	schwieg	geschwiegen
(113) Schwellen (to swell)	schwillt	schwoll	geschwollen
(114) Schwimmen (to swim)	schwimmt	schwamm	geschwommen
(115) Schwinden (to vanish, disappear)	schwindet	schwand	geschwunden
(116) Schwingen (to swing)	schwingt	schwang	geschwungen
(117) Schwören (to swear)	schwört	schwur	geschworen
(118) Sehen (to see)	sieht	sah	gesehen
(119) Singen (to sing)	singt	sang	gesungen
(120) Sinken (to sink)	sinkt	sank	gesunken
(121) Sinnen (to reflect, meditate)	sinnt	sann	gesonnen
(122) Sitzen (to sit)	sitzt	sass	gesessen
(123) Speien (to spew)	speit	spie	gespien
(124) Spinnen (to spin)	spinnt	spann	gesponnen
(125) Sprechen (to speak)	spricht	sprach	gesprochen
(126) Spriessen (to sprout)	spriesst	spross	gesprossen
(127) Springen (to jump, leap, spring)	springt	sprang	gesprungen
(128) Stechen (to sting, prick, stab, pierce)	sticht	stach	gestochen
(129) Stehen (to stand)	steht	stand	gestanden
(130) Stehlen (to steal)	stiehlt	stahl	gestohlen
(131) Steigen (to rise, mount)	steigt	stieg	gestiegen
(132) Sterben (to die)	stirbt	starb	gestorben
(133) Stinken (to stink)	stinkt	stank	gestunken
(134) Stossen (to push)	stösst	stiess	gestossen
(135) Streichen (to stroke)	streicht	strich	gestrichen
(136) Streiten (to dispute)	streitet	stritt	gestritten
(137) Tragen (to carry, bear, wear)	trägt	trug	getragen
(138) Treffen (to meet)	trifft	traf	getroffen
(139) Treiben (to drive)	treibt	trieb	getrieben
(140) Treten (to tread, step)	tritt	trat	getreten
(141) Triefen (to drip)	trieft	troff	getroffen
(142) Trinken (to drink)	trinkt	trank	getrunken
(143) Trügen (to deceive, mislead)	trügt	trog	getrogen
(144) Verbleichen (to fade)	verbleicht	verblich	verblichen
(145) Verbergen (to conceal, hide)	verbirgt	verbarg	verborgen

Infinitive	Present Tense Third Person Sing.	Past Tense First Person Sing.	Past Participle
(146) Verderben (to spoil, corrupt)	verdirbt	verdarb	verdorben
(147) Verdriessen (to vex)	verdriesst	verdross	verdrossen
(148) Vergessen (to forget)	vergisst	vergass	vergessen
(149) Verlieren (to lose)	verliert	verlor	verloren
(150) Verschallen (to die away—of sound)	verschallt	verscholl	verschollen
(151) Wachsen (to grow)	wächst	wuchs	gewachsen
(152) Waschen (to wash)	wäscht	wusch	gewaschen
(153) Weben (to weave)	webt	wob	gewoben
(154) Weichen (to yield)	weicht	wich	gewichen
(155) Weisen (to show, direct)	weist	wies	gewiesen
(156) Werben (to enlist, court, sue)	wirbt	warb	geworben
(157) Werfen (to throw)	wirft	warf	geworfen
(158) Wiegen (to weigh)	wiegt	wog	gewogen
(159) Winden (to wind)	windet	wand	gewunden
(160) Zeihen (to accuse)	zeiht	zieh	geziehen
(161) Ziehen (to pull, draw)	zieht	zog	gezogen
(162) Zwingen (to force, compel)	zwingt	zwang	gezwungen

MODAL AUXILIARIES

Infinitive	Present Tense Third Person Sing.	Past Tense First Person Sing.	Past Participle
(163) Dürfen (permission: to be allowed, may, dare)	darf	durfte	gedurft
(164) Können (ability: can, be able to)	kann	konnte	gekonnt
(165) Mögen (possibility: may, dare to, like to)	mag	mochte	gemocht
(166) Müssen (necessity: must, have to)	muss	musste	gemusst

Infinitive	Present Tense Third Person Sing.	Past Tense First Person Sing.	Past Participle
(167) Wollen (intention: will, want to, intend to)	will	wollte	gewollt
(168) Sollen (obligation: shall, is to)	soll	sollte	gesollt

LIKE MODAL AUXILIARIES

Infinitive	Present Tense Third Person Sing.	Past Tense First Person Sing.	Past Participle
(169) Wissen (to know)	weiss	wusste	gewusst

IRREGULAR WEAK VERBS

Infinitive	Present Tense Third Person Sing.	Past Tense First Person Sing.	Past Participle
(170) Brennen (to burn)	brennt	brannte	gebrannt
(171) Bringen (to bring)	bringt	brachte	gebracht
(172) Denken (to think)	denkt	dachte	gedacht
(173) Kennen (to know)	kennt	kannte	gekannt
(174) Nennen (to name)	nennt	nannte	genannt
(175) Rennen (to run)	rennt	rannte	gerannt
(176) Senden (to send)	sendet	sandte	gesandt
(177) Wenden (to turn)	wendet	wandte	gewandt

IRREGULAR VERBS

(178) Haben (to have)
　Present: ich habe, du hast, er hat, wir haben, ihr habt, sie haben
　Simple Past: ich hatte, etc.
　Past Participle: gehabt

(179) Sein (to be)
　Present: ich bin, du bist, er ist, wir sind, ihr seid, sie sind
　Simple Past: ich war, etc.
　Imperative: sei, seid
　Present Subjunctive: ich sei, du seiest, er sei, wir seien, ihr seiet, sie seien
　Past Participle: gewesen

(180) Tun (to do)
　Present: ich tue, du tust, er tut, wir tun, ihr tut, sie tun
　Simple Past: ich tat, etc.
　Past Participle: getan

(181) Werden (to become)
　Present: ich werde, du wirst, er wird, wir werden, ihr werdet, sie werden
　Simple Past: ich wurde, etc.
　Past Participle: geworden

German Pronunciation

VOWELS

In general German vowels are pronounced long when they come at the end of a syllable, when followed by an *h* and/or one consonant, and when doubled. Double consonants or any two consonants are usually preceded by a short vowel.

German Vowel	Closest English Equivalent	German Example
long a	*a* as in f*a*ther	Vater, Zahn
short a	*a* as in f*a*ther, only shorter	Stadt, Mann
long e, ee	*a* as in m*a*ke, but without the final diphthongal glide	ewig, Seele
short e	*e* as in s*e*t	Brett, wenn
short e in unstressed syllable	*e* as in tak*e*n	Gebirge, bezahlen
long i, and ie	*ee* as in b*ee*	sie, Krise
short i	*i* as in st*i*ll	still, Himmel
long o, oo	*o* as in *o*bey	Boden, Sohn, Boot
short o	*o* as in c*o*rn	Korn, kommen
long ä	*ai* as in *ai*r	Käse, mässig
short ä	*e* as in s*e*t	Hände, kälter
long ö	like the English *a*, as in m*a*ke, without the final diphthongal glide, but pronounced with rounded lips	Öl, schön
short ö	same as long ö, only shorter	Hölle, können
long ü, y	like the English *ee*, but pronounced with rounded lips; like the *u* in the French l*u*ne	kühn, müde
short ü	same as long ü, only shorter	stürzen, Künstler
ei, ai	*i* as in s*i*de, *ye* as in r*ye*	Seide, Waise
au	*ow* as in c*ow*	kauen, Haus
äu, eu	*oy* as in t*oy*	täuschen, Freude

CONSONANTS

Many consonants (for example, *f, m, t*) have approximately the same values in English and German. Those German consonants whose pronunciations differ are listed below (special cases are indicated in parentheses):

German Consonant	Closest English Equivalent	German Example
b	*b* as in *b*ear (or, if final, *p* as in car*p*)	Bär (Korb)
ch	*ch* as in the Scottish lo*ch*, or *ch* as in Gret*ch*en *	Koch, ich
d	*d* as in *d*oor (or, if final, *t* as in cour*t*)	Dank (Band)
g	*g* as in *g*o (or, if final, sometimes *k* as in mar*k*; and, if final and preceded by an *i*, *ch* as in Gret*ch*en) *	gut (Tag, König)
h	*h* as in *h*ouse (or silent when following a vowel; *h* then indicates that the vowel is long)	Haus (Zahl)
j	*y* as in *y*es	ja
qu	*kv*	Qualität
s	before a vowel *z* as in *z*oo, finally *ss* as in le*ss*	sagen, Haus
sch	*sh* as in *sh*oe	Scham
sp	initially *shp* otherwise *sp* as in ra*sp*	spät, Knospe
st	initially *sht*, otherwise *st* as in la*st*	Stadt, Last
v	usually *f* as in *f*ather (sometimes *v* as in *v*ase)	Vater (Vase)
w	*v* as in *v*est	Westen
z	*ts* as in ca*ts*	Zigarre

* For a more detailed explanation of these sounds see the introduction to the German-to-English word list on p. 2839.

Italian

to English

CONTENTS

Note on Symbols. For a list of abbreviations used in the main word list, see p. 2674. The number indicated for each Italian verb in the word list is the key to its conjugation. Verbs numbered (1), (2), (3) and (4) are considered regular; they are conjugated according to models bearing the corresponding numbers under *Present Tense, Imperfect Tense, Simple Past Tense*, etc., pp. 2950–55 of the Italian grammar. Verbs numbered (5) through (118) are irregular; for their forms, see the corresponding numbers in the list of irregular verbs, pp. 2955–59 of the Italian grammar.

Notes on Pronunciation. The pronunciation of words in the following list is indicated wherever possible by words or syllables easily recognized by English-speaking persons. Thus, the Italian word *circa* is rendered CHEER-*kah*. The vowels *a, e* and *o* are rendered *ah, eh* and *oh*, respectively, in the pronunciation column, except where clear equivalents in English words or syllables can be formed without the inclusion of the *h*. In some cases, for instance, the *eh* sound has been obtained by inserting a double consonant after *e*, as in *vendita* (VENN-*dee-tah*). In both instances (*eh-* or *venn-*, etc.) the *e* is to be pronounced the same; *i.e.*, without the final glide sound (*y*) of the interjection "eh?" The transcription *oh* is to be pronounced without the final glide sound (*w*). Because of practical limitations no attempt has been made to indicate the differences between "open" and "close" *o* and *e*. Wherever the letters *ow* appear in the pronunciation column, they are to be pronounced as they are in the English word "cow." Wherever *g* appears in the pronunciation column it is to be pronounced with a hard sound as in the English word "go."

Readers who are interested in more detailed rules of Italian pronunciation are referred to "Basic Key to Italian Pronunciation," p. 2960.

Italian	Pronunciation	English
a	AH	at (by)
"	"	at (for the price of)
"	"	to (indicating destination, *prep.*)
"	"	to (indicating direction, *prep.*)
"	"	to (used with indirect object, *prep.*)
abbagliare (1)	ahb-bah-L_YAH-*reh*	dazzle, to
abbaiare (1)	ahb-bah-YAH-*reh*	bark (bay), to
abbandonare (1)	ahb-bahn-doh-NAH-*reh*	abandon (give up), to
"	"	forsake, to
abbassare (1)	ahb-bahss-SAH-*reh*	lower, to
abbastanza	ahb-bah-STAHN-*tsah*	enough (*adj.*)
"	"	quite (considerably)
abbastanza,*f.*	abh-bah-STAHN-*tsah*	enough (*n.*)
abbigliamento,*m.*	ahb-bee-l_yah-MENN-*toh*	attire (apparel)
abbigliare (1)	ahb-bee-L_YAH-*reh*	clothe, to
abbonamento,*m.*	ahb-boh-nah-MENN-*toh*	subscription (for periodicals, etc.)
abbondante	ahb-bohn-DAHN-*teh*	abundant
"	"	plentiful
abbondanza,*f.*	ahb-bohn-DAHN-*tsah*	abundance
"	"	plenty (*n.*)
abbozzare (1)	ahb-boht-TSAH-*reh*	draft (sketch), to
abbozzo,*m.*	ahb-BOHT-*tsoh*	draft (sketch)
"	"	outline
abbracciare (1)	ahb-braht-CHAH-*reh*	clasp, to
"	"	embrace, to
"	"	hug, to
abbreviazione,*f.*	ahb-breh-v_yah-TS_YOH-*neh*	abbreviation
abete,*m.*	ah-BEH-*teh*	fir
abile	AH-*bee-leh*	skilful
abilità,*f.*	ah-bee-lee-TAH	skill (proficiency)
abitante,*m.,f.*	ah-bee-TAHN-*teh*	inhabitant
"	"	resident (*n.*)
abitare (1)	ah-bee-TAH-*reh*	inhabit, to
"	"	live (dwell), to
abitazione,*f.*	ah-bee-tah-TS_YOH-*neh*	dwelling
abito,*m.*	AH-*bee-toh*	garment
"	"	gown (dress)
"	"	suit, man's
abituarsi (1)	ah-bee-TWAHR-*see*	accustom oneself, to
abitudine,*f.*	ah-bee-TOO-*dee-neh*	habit (custom)
abolire (3)	ah-boh-LEE-*reh*	abolish, to
abusare di (1)	ah-boo-ZAH-*reh dee*	abuse (misuse), to
accadere (21)	ahk-kah-DEH-*reh*	happen, to
"	"	occur, to
accampamento,*m.*	ahk-kahm-pah-MENN-*toh*	camp (encampment, *mil.*)
accanto a	ahk-KAHN-*toh ah*	beside (next to, *prep.*)
"	"	next (alongside of, *prep.*)
accecare (1)	aht-cheh-KAH-*reh*	blind, to
accelerare (1)	aht-cheh-leh-RAH-*reh*	hasten (expedite), to
accendere (5)	aht-CHENN-*deh-reh*	light (set fire to), to
accento,*m.*	aht-CHENN-*toh*	accent
accetta,*f.*	aht-CHETT-*tah*	hatchet
accettare (1)	aht-chett-TAH-*reh*	accept, to
accettazione,*f.*	aht-chett-tah-TS_YOH-*neh*	acceptance (receipt)
acchiappare (1)	ahk-k_yahp-PAH-*reh*	catch (nab), to
acciaio,*m.*	aht-CHAH-*yoh*	steel
acciaio inossidabile,*m.*	aht-CHAH-*yoh ee-nohss-see-DAH-bee-leh*	stainless steel
accidente,*m.*	aht-chee-DENN-*teh*	accident (mishap)
acciocchè	aht-chohk-KEH	so (in order that, *conj.*)
acclamare (1)	ahk-klah-MAH-*reh*	cheer (applaud), to
accludere(23)	ahk-KLOO-*deh-reh*	enclose (include in envelope), to
acclusa,*f.*	ahk-KLOO-*sah*	enclosure (addition)
accoglienza,*f.*	ahk-koh-L_YENN-*tsah*	greeting
"	"	reception
"	"	welcome (*n.*)
accogliere cordialmente (25)	ahk-KOH-*l_yeh-reh* kohr-d_yahl-MENN-*teh*	welcome (receive hospitably), to
accomodare (1)	ahk-koh-moh-DAH-*reh*	accommodate (have room for), to
"	"	fix, to
"	"	mend (repair), to
"	"	settle (arrange), to
accompagnare (1)	ahk-kohm-pah-N_YAH-*reh*	accompany (go along with), to
acconsentire (4)	ahk-kohn-senn-TEE-*reh*	agree (assent), to
accontentare (1)	ahk-kohn-tenn-TAH-*reh*	please (satisfy), to
acconto,*m.*	ahk-KOHN-*toh*	down payment (*bus.*)
accoppiare (1)	ahk-kohp-P_YAH-*reh*	mate (find mate for), to
accordare (1)	ahk-kohr-DAH-*reh*	grant (bestow), to
accordo,*m.*	ahk-KOHR-*doh*	accord
"	"	agreement (mutual understanding)
accorgersi (95)	ahk-KOHR-*jehr-see*	perceive, to
accorto	ahk-KOHR-*toh*	clever
"	"	smart
accreditare (1)	ahk-kreh-dee-TAH-*reh*	credit, to (*bus.*)
accumulare (1)	ahk-koo-moo-LAH-*reh*	accumulate (amass), to
"	"	store, to
accumulatore,*m.*	ahk-koo-moo-lah-TOH-*reh*	battery (storage)
accurato	ahk-koo-RAH-*toh*	accurate
accusa,*f.*	ahk-KOO-*zah*	accusation
"	"	charge
accusare (1)	ahk-koo-ZAH-*reh*	accuse, to
accusare ricevuta (di)	ahk-koo-ZAH-*reh ree-cheh-*VOO-*tah (dee)*	acknowledge (note receipt of), to
acero,*m.*	AH-*cheh-roh*	maple (tree)
aceto,*m.*	ah-CHEH-*toh*	vinegar

ITALIAN

Italian	Pronunciation	English
acido, *m.*	AH-*chee-doh*	acid
acqua, *f.*	AHK-*kwah*	water
acquaio, *m.*	*ahk*-KWAH-*yoh*	sink (*n.*)
acquavite, *f.*	*ahk-kwah*-VEE-*teh*	brandy
acquazzone, *m.*	*ahk-kwaht*-TSOH-*neh*	shower (rainfall)
acquistare (1)	*ahk-kwee*-STAH-*reh*	acquire, to
acuto	*ah*-KOO-*toh*	shrill
adattare (1)	*ah-daht*-TAH-*reh*	adapt, to
adatto	*ah*-DAHT-*toh*	fit
"	"	suitable
addebitare (1)	*ahd-deh-bee*-TAH-*reh*	charge, to
"	"	debit, to
addio	*ahd*-DEE-*oh*	good-by
addio, *m.*	*ahd*-DEE-*oh*	farewell (leave-taking)
addizionale	*ahd-dee-ts_yoh*-NAH-*leh*	extra (additional)
addizionare (1)	*ahd-dee-ts_yoh*-NAH-*reh*	add (find sum of), to
addizione, *f.*	*ahd-dee*-TS_YOH-*neh*	addition (process of adding)
addome, *m.*	*ahd*-DOH-*meh*	abdomen
addormentato	*ahd-dohr-menn*-TAH-*toh*	asleep (sleeping)
adeguato	*ah-deh*-GWAH-*toh*	adequate (sufficient)
adempiere (45)	*ah*-DEMM-*p_yeh-reh*	fulfill, to
aderenti, *m.pl.*	*ah-deh*-RENN-*tee*	following (followers)
aderire (3)	*ah-deh*-REE-*reh*	stick (adhere), to
adirato	*ah-dee*-RAH-*toh*	angry
adorabile	*ah-doh*-RAH-*bee-leh*	adorable
adorare (1)	*ah-doh*-RAH-*reh*	adore, to
"	"	worship, to (*rel.*)
adorazione, *f.*	*ah-doh-rah*-TS_YOH-*neh*	worship (*rel.*)
adottare (1)	*ah-doht*-TAH-*reh*	adopt (embrace), to
adulare (1)	*ah-doo*-LAH-*reh*	flatter (praise insincerely), to
adunanza, *f.*	*ah-doo*-NAHN-*tsah*	assembly (meeting)
adunarsi (1)	*ah-doo*-NAHR-*see*	assemble (meet), to
aeroplano, *m.*	*ah_eh-roh*-PLAH-*noh*	airplane
"	"	plane
aeroporto, *m.*	*ah_eh-roh*-POHR-*toh*	airport
affamato	*ahf-fah*-MAH-*toh*	hungry
affare, *m.*	*ahf*-FAH-*reh*	affair
"	"	matter
affare rischioso, *m.*	*ahf*-FAH-*reh ree-*SK_YOH-*soh*	venture
affari, *m.pl.*	*ahf*-FAH-*ree*	business (commerce)
affaticato	*ahf-fah-tee*-KAH-*toh*	weary
affermare (1)	*ahf-fehr*-MAH-*reh*	assert (declare), to
afferrare (1)	*ahf-fehr*-RAH-*reh*	grab, to
"	"	seize (clutch), to
"	"	snatch, to
affettare (1)	*ahf-fett*-TAH-*reh*	affect (pretend), to
affetto, *m.*	*ahf*-FETT-*toh*	affection (love)
affettuoso	*ahf-fett*-TWOH-*soh*	affectionate (loving)
affilare (1)	*ahf-fee*-LAH-*reh*	sharpen, to
affilato	*ahf-fee*-LAH-*toh*	sharp
affittare (1)	*ahf-feet*-TAH-*reh*	lease, to
"	"	rent, to
affitto, *m.*	*ahf*-FEET-*toh*	rent (payment)
affliggersi (9)	*ahf*-FLEED-*jehr-see*	grieve (mourn), to
afflizione, *f.*	*ahf-flee*-TS_YOH-*neh*	distress
"	"	grief
"	"	misery
affogare (1)	*ahf-foh*-GAH-*reh*	drown, to
affondare (1)	*ahf-fohn*-DAH-*reh*	sink (become submerged), to
affrettare (1)	*ahf-frett*-TAH-*reh*	quicken, to
affrettarsi	*ahf-frett*-TAHR-*see*	hasten, to
"	"	hurry, to
Africa, *f.*	AH-*free-kah*	Africa
africano	*ah-free*-KAH-*noh*	African (*adj.*)
agenzia, *f.*	*ah-jenn*-TSEE-*ah*	agency (business firm)
aggettivo, *m.*	*ahd-jett*-TEE-*voh*	adjective
aggiungere (57)	*ahd*-JOON-*jeh-reh*	add (include), to
aggiunta, *f.*	*ahd*-JOON-*tah*	addition (supplement)
aggiustare (1)	*ahd-joo*-STAH-*reh*	adjust (regulate), to
aggredire (3)	*ahg-greh*-DEE-*reh*	attack (assault physically), to
aggressione, *f.*	*ahg-gress*-S_YOH-*neh*	attack (personal assault)

Italian	Pronunciation	English
aggrottare le ciglia (1)	*ahg-groht*-TAH-*reh leh* CHEE-*l_yah*	frown, to
agile	AH-*jee-leh*	nimble (agile)
agio, *m.*	AH-*joh*	ease (comfort)
"	"	leisure
agire (3)	*ah*-JEE-*reh*	act (do), to
agitato	*ah-jee*-TAH-*toh*	restless
aglio, *m.*	AH-*l_yoh*	garlic
agnello, *m.*	*ah*-N_YELL-*loh*	lamb
ago, *m.*	AH-*goh*	needle
agricoltura, *f.*	*ah-gree-kohl*-TOO-*rah*	agriculture
agro	AH-*groh*	sour (tart)
aguzzo	*ah*-GOOT-*tsoh*	keen (sharp)
aiutante, *m., f.*	*ah-yoo*-TAHN-*teh*	helper
aiutare (1)	*ah-yoo*-TAH-*reh*	aid, to
"	"	help, to
aiuto, *m.*	*ah*-YOO-*toh*	aid
"	"	help (assistance)
ala, *f.*	AH-*lah*	wing (*zool.*)
Alaska, *m.*	*ah*-LAH-*skah*	Alaska
alba, *f.*	AHL-*bah*	dawn (daybreak)
Albania, *f.*	*ahl-bah*-NEE-*ah*	Albania
albergo, *m.*	*ahl*-BEHR-*goh*	hotel
"	"	inn
albero, *m.*	AHL-*beh-roh*	mast
"	"	tree
albicocca, *f.*	*ahl-bee*-KOHK-*kah*	apricot
alcool, *m.*	AHL-*kohl*	alcohol
alcuni, alcune	*ahl*-KOO-*nee, ahl*-KOO-*neh*	few, a
"	"	some (a few, *adj.*)
"	"	some (certain ones, *pron.*)
alfabeto, *m.*	*ahl-fah*-BEH-*toh*	alphabet
alimentazione, *f.*	*ah-lee-menn-tah*-TS_YOH-*neh*	diet (total food consumed)
allarme, *m.*	*ahl*-LAHR-*meh*	alarm (fear)
alleanza, *f.*	*ahl-leh*-AHN-*tsah*	alliance
alleato, *m.*	*ahl-leh*-AH-*toh*	ally
allegrezza, *f.*	*ahl-leh*-GRETT-*tsah*	gladness
allegria, *f.*	*ahl-leh*-GREE-*ah*	glee (joy)
allegro	*ahl*-LEH-*groh*	glad
"	"	merry
allergia, *f.*	*ahl-lehr*-JEE-*ah*	allergy (*med.*)
alleviare (1)	*ahl-leh*-V_YAH-*reh*	ease (relieve), to
allievo, *m.*	*ahl*-L_YEH-*voh*	pupil (student)
allodola, *f.*	*ahl*-LOH-*doh-lah*	lark (bird)
alloggiare (1)	*ahl-lohd*-JAH-*reh*	lodge (reside), to
alloggio, *m.*	*ahl*-LOHD-*joh*	lodging (temporary quarters)
allora	*ahl*-LOH-*rah*	then (at that time)
"	"	then (in that case)
allorchè	*ahl-lohr*-KEH	when (at the time that, *conj.*)
alluminio, *m.*	*ahl-loo*-MEE-*n_yoh*	aluminum
allungare (1)	*ahl-loong*-GAH-*reh*	extend (stretch out), to
alquanto	*ahl*-KWAHN-*toh*	fairly (somewhat)
altare, *m.*	*ahl*-TAH-*reh*	altar
alterare (1)	*ahl-teh*-RAH-*reh*	alter (make different), to
alterco, *m.*	*ahl*-TEHR-*koh*	quarrel (dispute)
altezza, *f.*	*ahl*-TETT-*tsah*	height (highness)
altipiano, *m.*	*ahl-tee*-P_YAH-*noh*	plateau (tableland)
alto	AHL-*toh*	high
"	"	tall
alto, in	*een* AHL-*toh*	above (overhead, *adv.*)
"	"	upward (to a higher level, *adv.*)
alto, più	*p_yoo* AHL-*toh*	top (highest, *adj.*)
altrimenti	*ahl-tree*-MENN-*tee*	else (if not, *adv.*)
"	"	otherwise
altro	AHL-*troh*	else (*adj.*)
"	"	else (instead, *adv.*)
"	"	further (additional, *adj.*)
"	"	other (*adj., pron.*)
altro, un	*oon* AHL-*troh*	another
altrove	*ahl*-TROH-*veh*	elsewhere
alveare, *m.*	*ahl-veh*-AH-*reh*	hive (beehive)
alzare (1)	*ahl*-TSAH-*reh*	pick up, to
"	"	raise (lift up), to

Italian	Pronunciation	English
amante, *f.*	ah-MAHN-*teh*	mistress (paramour)
amare (1)	ah-MAH-*reh*	love, to
amaro	ah-MAH-*roh*	bitter
amato	ah-MAH-*toh*	beloved (*adj.*)
ambasciatore, *m.*	ahm-bah-shah-TOH-*reh*	ambassador
ambizione, *f.*	ahm-bee-TS_YOH-*neh*	ambition
ambizioso	ahm-bee-TS_YOH-*soh*	ambitious (aspiring)
ambra, del colore dell'	dell koh-LOH-*reh* dell-LAHM-*brah*	amber (*adj.*)
America, *f.*	ah-MEH-*ree-kah*	America
America del Nord, *f.*	ah-MEH-*ree-kah* dell NOHRD	North America
America del Sud, *f.*	ah-MEH-*ree-kah* dell SOOD	South America
americano	ah-meh-ree-KAH-*noh*	American (*adj.*)
amichevole	ah-mee-KEH-*voh-leh*	friendly
amicizia, *f.*	ah-mee-CHEE-ts_yah	friendship
amico, *m.*	ah-MEE-*koh*	friend
"	"	pal
amido, *m.*	AH-*mee-doh*	starch (in food)
ammaccatura, *f.*	ahm-mahk-kah-TOO-*rah*	bruise
ammalato	ahm-mah-LAH-*toh*	ill (sick)
ammenda, *f.*	ahm-MENN-*dah*	fine (penalty, *n.*)
ammettere (60)	ahm-MET-*teh-reh*	admit, to
ammiccare (1)	ahm-meek-KAH-*reh*	wink, to
amministrazione, *f.*	ahm-mee-nee-strah-TS_YOH-*neh*	administration (*bus.*)
ammiraglio, *m.*	ahm-mee-RAH-*l_yoh*	admiral
ammirare (1)	ahm-mee-RAH-*reh*	admire, to
ammirazione, *f.*	ahm-mee-rah-TS_YOH-*neh*	admiration
ammissione, *f.*	ahm-mees-s_YOH-*neh*	admission (right to enter)
ammobiliare (1)	ahm-moh-bee-L_YAH-*reh*	furnish (put furniture in), to
ammontare a (1)	ahm-mohn-TAH-*reh* ah	amount to, to
ammortizzare (1)	ahm-mohr-teed-DZAH-*reh*	amortize, to
ammortizzazione, *f.*	ahm-mohr-teed-dzah-TS_YOH-*neh*	amortization (*bus.*)
ammuffito	ahm-moof-FEE-*toh*	moldy
amore, *m.*	ah-MOH-*reh*	love
ampio	AHM-*p_yoh*	full (ample)
Amsterdam, *f.*	ahm-stehr-DAHM	Amsterdam
anca, *f.*	AHNG-*kah*	hip
anche	AHNG-*keh*	also
"	"	so (*adv.*)
"	"	too
ancora	ahng-KOH-*rah*	still (as yet, *adv.*)
"	"	still (even more, *adv.*)
"	"	yet (now, until now, *adv.*)
ancora, *f.*	AHNG-*koh-rah*	anchor
andamento, *m.*	ahn-dah-MENN-*toh*	pace (rate)
andare (10)	ahn-DAH-*reh*	go, to
andare (in automobile)	ahn-DAH-*reh* (een ow-toh-MOH-*bee-leh*)	ride (in a car), to
andare alla deriva	ahn-DAH-*reh* ahl-lah deh-REE-*vah*	drift (float), to
andazzo, *m.*	ahn-DAHT-*tsoh*	craze (fad)
anello, *m.*	ah-NELL-*loh*	link (connecting part)
"	"	ring (jewelry)
angelo, *m.*	AHN-*jeh-loh*	angel
angolo, *m.*	AHNG-*goh-loh*	angle (*geom.*)
"	"	corner
angoscia, *f.*	ahng-GOH-*shah*	agony (mental pain)
"	"	anguish
anguilla, *f.*	ahng-GWEEL-*lah*	eel
anima, *f.*	AH-*nee-mah*	soul
animale, *m.*	ah-nee-MAH-*leh*	animal
animale favorito, *m.*	ah-nee-MAH-*leh* fah-voh-REE-*toh*	pet (animal)
anitra, *f.*	AH-*nee-trah*	duck
anniversario, *m.*	ahn-nee-vehr-SAH-*r_yoh*	anniversary
anno, *m.*	AHN-*noh*	year
annoiare (1)	ahn-noh-YAH-*reh*	annoy (irk), to
annuale	ahn-NWAH-*leh*	annual
"	"	yearly (*adj.*)
annualmente	ahn-nwahl-MENN-*teh*	yearly (*adv.*)
annullare (1)	ahn-nool-LAH-*reh*	annul, to
"	"	cancel (revoke), to
annunziare (1)	ahn-noon-TS_YAH-*reh*	advertise (give notice of), to
"	"	announce, to
annunzio, *m.*	ahn-NOON-*ts_yoh*	advertisement
"	"	announcement
annusare (1)	ahn-noo-ZAH-*reh*	sniff, to
ansare (1)	ahn-SAH-*reh*	gasp, to
"	"	pant (puff), to
ansia, *f.*	AHN-s_yah	anxiety
ansietà, *f.*	ahn-s_yeh-TAH	tension (anxiety)
ansioso	ahn-S_YOH-*soh*	anxious (uneasy)
antenato, *m.*	ahn-teh-NAH-*toh*	ancestor
antenna, *f.*	ahn-TENN-*nah*	aerial (antenna)
anteriore	ahn-teh-R_YOH-*reh*	previous
antibiotico, *m.*	ahn-tee-bee-OH-*tee-koh*	antibiotic
antichità, *f.*	ahn-tee-kee-TAH	antiquity (ancientness)
anticipo, in	een ahn-TEE-*chee-poh*	beforehand (*adv.*)
antico	ahn-TEE-*koh*	ancient
antipatia, *f.*	ahn-tee-pah-TEE-*ah*	dislike
antologia, *f.*	ahn-toh-loh-JEE-*ah*	anthology
antro, *m.*	AHN-*troh*	den (animal lair)
antropologia, *f.*	ahn-troh-poh-loh-JEE-*ah*	anthropology
anziano	ahn-TS_YAH-*noh*	old (elderly)
ape, *f.*	AH-*peh*	bee
aperto	ah-PEHR-*toh*	open (*adj.*)
apertura, *f.*	ah-pehr-TOO-*rah*	gap
"	"	opening (aperture)
apostolo, *m.*	ah-POH-*stoh-loh*	apostle
apparato, *m.*	ahp-pah-RAH-*toh*	device (apparatus)
apparecchio fotografico, *m.*	ahp-pah-REKK-*k_yoh* foh-toh-GRAH-*fee-koh*	camera
apparenza, *f.*	ahp-pah-RENN-*tsah*	appearance (aspect)
apparire (12)	ahp-pah-REE-*reh*	appear (come in sight), to
appartamento, *m.*	ahp-pahr-tah-MENN-*toh*	apartment
appartenere (112)	ahp-pahr-teh-NEH-*reh*	belong (be a part of), to
appartenere a	ahp-pahr-teh-NEH-*reh* ah	belong to (be the property of), to
appassionato	ahp-pahss-s_yoh-NAH-*toh*	passionate
appassire (3)	ahp-pahss-SEE-*reh*	wither, to
appellare contro (1)	ahp-pell-LAH-*reh* KOHN-*troh*	appeal (ask reconsideration of), to
appello, *m.*	ahp-PELL-*loh*	appeal (entreaty)
appena	ahp-PEH-*nah*	hardly (barely)
appendere (13)	ahp-PENN-*deh-reh*	hang (suspend), to
appendicite, *f.*	ahp-penn-dee-CHEE-*teh*	appendicitis
appetito, *m.*	ahp-peh-TEE-*toh*	appetite
applaudire (4)	ahp-plow-DEE-*reh*	clap (applaud), to
applauso, *m.*	ahp-PLOW-*soh*	applause
applicare (1)	ahp-plee-KAH-*reh*	apply (put to use), to
applicazione, *f.*	ahp-plee-kah-TS_YOH-*neh*	application (use)
apprendere (78)	ahp-PRENN-*deh-reh*	learn (find out), to
apprendista, *m.,f.*	ahp-prenn-DEE-*stah*	apprentice (trade student)
apprezzare (1)	ahp-prett-TSAH-*reh*	appreciate (perceive fully), to
"	"	value (prize), to
approvare (1)	ahp-proh-VAH-*reh*	approve, to
approvazione, *f.*	ahp-proh-vah-TS_YOH-*neh*	acceptance
"	"	approval
appuntamento, *m.*	ahp-poon-tah-MENN-*toh*	appointment (meeting)
"	"	date
"	"	engagement
appuramento, *m.*	ahp-poo-rah-MEN-*toh*	audit (*n.*)
aprire (14)	ah-PREE-*reh*	open (make open), to
aquila, *f.*	AH-*kwee-lah*	eagle
arachide, *f.*	ah-RAH-*kee-deh*	peanut
aragosta, *f.*	ah-rah-GOH-*stah*	lobster
arancia, *f.*	ah-RAHN-*chah*	orange (fruit)
arancione	ah-rahn-CHOH-*neh*	orange (color)
arare (1)	ah-RAH-*reh*	plow (till), to
aratro, *m.*	ah-RAH-*troh*	plow (*n.*)
arbusto, *m.*	ahr-BOO-*stoh*	shrub
architetto, *m.*	ahr-kee-TETT-*toh*	architect
arco, *m.*	AHR-*koh*	arch (curved structure)
arcobaleno, *m.*	ahr-koh-bah-LEH-*noh*	rainbow

Italian	Pronunciation	English
ardente	*ahr*-DENN-*teh*	eager
"	"	keen
ardito	*ahr*-DEE-*toh*	bold (courageous)
area, *f.*	AH-*reh-ah*	area (extent)
Argentina, *f.*	*ahr-jenn*-TEE-*nah*	Argentina
argentino	*ahr-jenn*-TEE-*noh*	Argentinian (*adj.*)
argento, *m.*	*ahr*-JENN-*toh*	silver (metal, *n.*)
argilla, *f.*	*ahr*-JEEL-*lah*	clay
argomento, *m.*	*ahr-goh*-MENN-*toh*	subject (topic)
aria, *f.*	AH-*r_yah*	air
"	"	tune (melody)
aria condizionata, *f.*	*ahr-r_yah kohn-dee-ts_yoh*-NAH-*tah*	air conditioning
aria libera, all'	*ahl*-LAH-*r_yah* LEE-*beh-rah*	outdoors (*adv.*)
aringa, *f.*	*ah*-REENG-*gah*	herring
aritmetica, *m.*	*ah-reet*-MEH-*tee-kah*	arithmetic
arma, *f.*	AHR-*mah*	weapon
armare (1)	*ahr*-MAH-*reh*	arm, to
armatura, *f.*	*ahr-mah*-TOO-*rah*	armor (protective clothing)
armonia, *f.*	*ahr-moh*-NEE-*ah*	harmony (*mus.*)
arnese, *m.*	*ahr*-NEH-*zeh*	tool
arpa, *f.*	AHR-*pah*	harp
arrabbiarsi (1)	*ahr-rahb*-B_YAHR-*see*	rage (rave), to
arrendersi (84)	*ahr*-RENN-*dehr-see*	surrender (give oneself up), to
arrestare (1)	*ahr-reh*-STAH-*reh*	arrest, to
arrischiarsi (1)	*ahr-ree*-SK_YAHR-*see*	venture (dare), to
arrivare (1)	*ahr-ree*-VAH-*reh*	arrive, to
"	"	manage (contrive), to
arrivo, *m.*	*ahr*-REE-*voh*	arrival
arrolare (1)	*ahr-roh*-LAH-*reh*	draft (conscript), to
arrossire (3)	*ahr-rohss*-SEE-*reh*	blush, to
arrostirsi (3)	*ahr-roh*-STEER-*see*	roast (be roasted), to
arrosto, *m.*	*ahr*-ROH-*stoh*	roast
arrugginito	*ahr-rood-jee*-NEE-*toh*	rusty
arte, *f.*	AHR-*teh*	art
arte di scrivere, l', *m.*	LAHR-*teh dee* SKREE-*veh-reh*	writing (art of writing)
arteria, *f.*	*ahr*-TEH-*r_yah*	artery (*anat.*)
articolo, *m.*	*ahr*-TEE-*koh-loh*	article (literary composition)
"	"	item (particular)
artificiale	*ahr-tee-fee*-CHAH-*leh*	artificial (synthetic)
artiglio, *m.*	*ahr*-TEE-*l_yoh*	claw
artista, *m.*, *f.*	*ahr*-TEE-*stah*	artist
artrite, *f.*	*ahr*-TREE-*teh*	arthritis
ascensore, *m.*	*ah-shenn*-SOH-*reh*	elevator (passenger lift)
ascia, *f.*	AH-*shah*	axe
asciugamani, *m.*	*ah-shoo-gah*-MAH-*nee*	towel, hand
asciugare (1)	*ah-shoo*-GAH-*reh*	dry (make dry), to
"	"	wipe (make dry by wiping), to
asciugarsi	*ah-shoo*-GAHR-*see*	dry (become dry), to
ascoltare (1)	*ah-skohl*-TAH-*reh*	listen (hearken), to
Asia, *f.*	AH-*z_yah*	Asia
asiatico	*ah-z_*YAH-*tee-koh*	Asiatic (*adj.*)
asimmetrico	*ah-seem*-MEH-*tree-koh*	irregular (asymmetrical)
asino, *m.*	AH-*see-noh*	donkey
asparago, *m.*	*ah*-SPAH-*rah-goh*	asparagus
aspettare (1)	*ah-spett*-TAH-*reh*	wait (defer action), to
"	"	wait for, to
aspettarsi	*ah-spett*-TAHR-*see*	anticipate (expect), to
aspetto, *m.*	*ah*-SPETT-*toh*	aspect (phase)
"	"	look
aspiratore, *m.*	*ah-spee-rah*-TOH-*reh*	vacuum cleaner
aspirina, *f.*	*ah-spee*-REE-*nah*	aspirin
aspro	AH-*sproh*	harsh (grating)
"	"	rough
assaggiare (1)	*ahss-sahd*-JAH-*reh*	taste (sample), to
assai	*ahss*-SYE	rather (somewhat)
assalire (90)	*ahss-sah*-LEE-*reh*	assault, to
assassinio, *m.*	*ahss-sahss*-SEE-*n_yoh*	murder
assassino, *m.*	*ahss-sahss*-SEE-*noh*	murderer
assedio, *m.*	*ahss*-SEH-*d_yoh*	siege (*mil.*)
assegnare (1)	*ahss-seh*-N_YAH-*reh*	assign (prescribe lesson), to
assegno, *m.*	*ahss*-SEH-*n_yoh*	check (bank check)

Italian	Pronunciation	English
assente	*ahss*-SENN-*teh*	absent
"	"	away (*adj.*)
assentire (4)	*ahss-senn*-TEE-*reh*	assent, to
assenza, *f.*	*ahss*-SENN-*tsah*	absence
asserzione, *f.*	*ahss-sehr*-TS_YOH-*neh*	assertion (declaration)
assetato	*ahss-seh*-TAH-*ion*	thirsty
assicurare (1)	*ahss-see-koo*-RAH-*reh*	assure, to
"	"	insure, to
assicurazione, *f.*	*ahss-see-koo-rah-*TS_YOH-*neh*	insurance
assicurazione contro l'inçendio, *f.*	*ahss-see-koo-rah-*TS_YOH-*neh* KOHN-*troh leen-*CHENN-*d_yoh*	fire insurance
assistente, *m.*, *f.*	*ahss-see-*STENN-*teh*	assistant
assistenza, *f.*	*ahss-see-*STENN-*tsah*	assistance
"	"	attendance (presence)
assistere (16)	*ahss*-SEE-*steh-reh*	assist, to
assistere a	*ahss*-SEE-*steh-reh ah*	attend (be present at), to
associarsi (a) (1)	*ahss-soh*-CHAHR-*see* (*ah*)	join (become a member of), to
associazione, *f.*	*ahss-soh-chah*-TS_YOH-*neh*	association (body of persons)
assoluto	*ahss-soh*-LOO-*toh*	absolute (complete)
assomigliare a (1)	*ahss-soh-mee*-L_YAH-*reh*	resemble, to
assorbire (3)	*ahss-sohr*-BEE-*reh*	absorb (suck up), to
assortimento, *m.*	*ahss-sohr-tee*-MENN-*toh*	variety (assortment)
assumere (18)	*ahss*-SOO-*meh-reh*	assume (take for granted), to
"	"	engage (employ), to
"	"	presume, to
asta, *f.*	AH-*stah*	rod (bar)
"	"	shaft (*mech.*)
Atene, *f.*	*ah*-TEH-*neh*	Athens
atlante, *m.*	*aht*-LAHN-*teh*	atlas
Atlantico, *m.*	*aht*-LAHN-*tee-koh*	Atlantic (*n.*)
atleta, *m.*, *f.*	*aht*-LEH-*tah*	athlete
atletico	*aht*-LEH-*tee-koh*	athletic
atmosfera, *f.*	*aht-moh*-SFEH-*rah*	atmosphere
atomo, *m.*	AH-*toh-moh*	atom
attaccare (1)	*aht-tahk*-KAH-*reh*	attach (join), to
"	"	fasten, to
atteggiamento, *m.*	*aht-tehd-jah*-MENN-*toh*	attitude (manner)
attendere (111)	*aht*-TENN-*deh-reh*	await, to
"	"	expect, to
attento	*aht*-TENN-*toh*	attentive (heedful)
attenzione, *f.*	*aht-tenn*-TS_YOH-*neh*	attention
"	"	care (heed)
"	"	interest
"	"	notice
atterrare (1)	*aht-tehr*-RAH-*reh*	land (an airplane), to
atterrire (3)	*aht-tehr*-REE-*reh*	terrify, to
attesa, *f.*	*aht*-TEH-*sah*	expectation
attestare (1)	*aht-teh*-STAH-*reh*	testify, to
attività, *f.*	*aht-tee-vee*-TAH	activity (exertion of energy)
attivo	*aht*-TEE-*voh*	active (energetic)
atto, *m.*	AHT-*toh*	act
"	"	deed
atto di vendita, *m.*	AHT-*toh dee* VENN-*dee-tah*	bill of sale
attore, *m.*	*aht*-TOH-*reh*	actor (player)
attraente	*aht-trah*-ENN-*teh*	attractive (pleasing)
attrarre (116)	*aht*-TRAHR-*reh*	attract, to
attrattiva, *f.*	*aht-traht*-TEE-*vah*	attraction
"	"	charm
attraverso	*aht-trah*-VEHR-*soh*	across (to the other side)
"	"	through (from end to end of, *prep.*)
"	"	over (across, *prep.*)
attrazione, *f.*	*aht-trah*-TS_YOH-*neh*	interest (engaging quality)
attrezzamento, *m.*	*aht-trett-tsah*-MENN-*toh*	equipment
attributo, *m.*	*aht-tree*-BOO-*toh*	attribute (characteristic)
attrice, *f.*	*aht*-TREE-*cheh*	actress
attuale	*aht*-TWAH-*leh*	current (contemporary, *adj.*)
"	"	present (*adj.*)
auditorio, *m.*	*ow-dee*-TOH-*r_yoh*	auditorium

Italian	Pronunciation	English
augurare (1)	ow-goo-RAH-reh	wish (desire on be-half of), to
aula, *f.*	OW-lah	classroom
"	"	schoolroom
aumentare (1)	ow-menn-TAH-reh	rise (increase), to
aumentarsi	ow-menn-TAHR-see	increase (grow), to
aumento, *m.*	ow-MENN-toh	gain
"	"	increase (increment)
austero	ow-STEH-roh	severe (austere)
Australia, *f.*	ow-STRAH-l_yah	Australia
australiano	ow-strah-L_YAH-noh	Australian (*adj.*)
Austria, *f.*	OW-str_yah	Austria
austriaco	ow-STREE-ah-koh	Austrian (*adj.*)
autista, *m.,f.*	ow-TEE-stah	driver (of auto-mobile)
auto, *f.*	OW-toh	car (auto)
autoambulanza, *f.*	ow-toh-ahm-boo-LAHN-tsah	ambulance
autobiografia, *f.*	ow-toh-bee-oh-grah-FEE-ah	autobiography
autobus, *m.*	ow-toh-BOOSS	bus
autocarro, *m.*	ow-toh-KAHR-roh	truck (automobile)
automobile, *f.*	ow-toh-MOH-bee-leh	automobile
autore, *m.*	ow-TOH-reh	author
autorimessa, *f.*	ow-toh-ree-MESS-sah	garage
autorità, *f.*	ow-toh-ree-TAH	authority
autorizzazione, *f.*	ow-toh-reed-dzah-TS_YOH-neh	authorization
autostrada, *f.*	ow-toh-STRAH-dah	highway
autunno, *m.*	ow-TOON-noh	autumn
"	"	fall (*n.*)
avanti	ah-VAHN-tee	ahead (*adv.*)
"	"	forward (*adv.*)
"	"	onward (*adv.*)
avanti, d'ora in	DOH-rah een ah-VAHN-tee	henceforth
avanzare (1)	ah-vahn-TSAH-reh	advance (go for-ward), to
avaro, *m.*	ah-VAH-roh	miser
avena, *f.*	ah-VEH-nah	oats
avere (19)	ah-VEH-reh	have, to
avere, *m.*	ah-VEH-reh	holdings (posses-sions)
"	"	property
avere bisogno di	ah-VEH-reh bee-ZOH-n_yoh dee	need (require), to
avere l'intenzione	ah-VEH-reh leen-tenn-TS_YOH-neh	mean (intend), to
avere l'intenzione di	ah-VEH-reh leen-tenn-TS_YOH-neh dee	intend (propose), to
aver fame	ah-vehr FAH-meh	hungry, to be
aviatore, *m.*	ah-v_yah-TOH-reh	aviator
avido	AH-vee-doh	greedy
avorio, *m.*	ah-VOH-r_yoh	ivory
avvelenare (1)	ahv-veh-leh-NAH-reh	poison, to
avvenimento, *m.*	ahv-veh-nee-MENN-toh	incident (event)
avvenire (123)	ahv-veh-NEE-reh	become of (happen to), to
avventura, *f.*	ahv-venn-TOO-rah	adventure
avverbio, *m.*	ahv-VEHR-b_yoh	adverb
avversario, *m.*	ahv-vehr-SAH-r_yoh	opponent (*n.*)
avvertire (4)	ahv-vehr-TEE-reh	caution, to
"	"	warn, to
avviarsi (1)	ahv-V_YAHR-see	start (set out), to
avvicinarsi a (1)	ahv-vee-chee-NAHR-see ah	approach (come near to), to
avviso, *m.*	ahv-VEE-zoh	mind (opinion)
"	"	notice (notification)
avvocato, *m.*	ahv-voh-KAH-toh	attorney
"	"	counsel
"	"	lawyer
avvolgere (127)	ahv-VOHL-jeh-reh	wrap (envelop), to
azione, *f.*	ah-TS_YOH-neh	action (deed)
"	"	share (stock)
azione straordina-ria, *f.*	ah-TS_YOH-neh strah-ohr-dee-NAH-r_yah	feat
azioni, *f.pl.*	ah-TS_YOH-nee	stock (shares)
azionista, *m.,f.*	ah-ts_yoh-NEE-stah	stockholder
azzurro	ahd-DZOOR-roh	blue
babbo, *m.*	BAHB-boh	dad
bacca, *f.*	BAHK-kah	berry (fruit)
bacca di mirtillo, *f.*	BAHK-kah dee meer-TEEL-loh	blueberry
baciare (1)	bah-CHAH-reh	kiss, to
bacio, *m.*	BAH-choh	kiss
badare a (1)	bah-DAH-reh ah	heed (mind), to
baffi, *m.pl.*	BAHF-fee	mustache
bagaglio, *m.*	bah-GAH-l_yoh	baggage
"	"	luggage
bagatella, *f.*	bah-gah-TELL-lah	trifle
bagnare (1)	bah-N_YAH-reh	wet, to
bagnato	bah-N_YAH-toh	wet
bagno, *m.*	BAH-n_yoh	bath
baia, *f.*	BAH-yah	bay (inlet)
balbettare (1)	bahl-bett-TAH-reh	stammer, to
"	"	stutter, to
balena, *f.*	bah-LEH-nah	whale
ballare (1)	bahl-LAH-reh	dance, to
ballo, *m.*	BAHL-loh	dance (party)
balordaggine, *f.*	bah-lohr-DAHD-jee-neh	blunder
balzare (1)	bahl-TSAH-reh	bounce, to
balzo, *m.*	BAHL-tsoh	bound
"	"	leap
bambino, *m.*	bahm-BEE-noh	baby
"	"	child
"	"	infant (*n.*)
bambola, *f.*	BAHM-boh-lah	doll
banana, *f.*	bah-NAH-nah	banana
banca, *f.*	BAHN-kah	bank (treasury)
banchetto, *m.*	bahng-KETT-toh	banquet
"	"	feast (meal)
banchiere, *m.*	bahng-K_YEH-reh	banker
banco, *m.*	BAHNG-koh	bench (long seat)
"	"	counter (table)
banda, *f.*	BAHN-dah	band
"	"	gang
banda musicale, *f.*	BAHN-dah moo-zee-KAH-leh	band (instrumental group)
bandiera, *f.*	bahn-D_YEH-rah	banner
"	"	flag
bandire (3)	bahn-DEE-reh	banish (exile), to
bandito, *m.*	bahn-DEE-toh	bandit
banjo, *m.*	BAHN-joh	banjo
bar, *m.*	BAHR	bar (barroom)
bara, *f.*	BAH-rah	coffin
barattolo, *m.*	bah-RAHT-toh-loh	jar (vessel)
barba, *f.*	BAHR-bah	beard
barbabietola rossa, *f.*	bahr-bah-B_YEH-toh-lah ROHS-sah	beet (red root)
barbiere, *m.*	bahr-B_YEH-reh	barber
barca, *f.*	BAHR-kah	craft (vessel)
barca di passaggio, *f.*	BAHR-kah dee pahss-SAHD-joh	ferry (boat)
barcollare (1)	bahr-kohl-LAH-reh	reel, to
"	"	stagger (totter), to
bardatura, *f.*	bahr-dah-TOO-rah	harness
barella, *f.*	bah-RELL-lah	litter (stretcher)
barile, *m.*	bah-REE-leh	barrel (cask)
barometro, *m.*	bah-ROH-meh-troh	barometer
barra, *f.*	BAHR-rah	bar (pole)
barriera, *f.*	bahr-R_YEH-rah	barrier
"	"	fence
basare (1)	bah-ZAH-reh	base (found), to
base, *f.*	BAH-zeh	base (foundation)
"	"	basis
Basilea, *f.*	bah-zee-LEH-ah	Basle
basso	BAHSS-soh	low
basso, in	een BAHSS-soh	down (in lower place, *adv.*)
"	"	downstairs (on a lower floor)
bastantemente	bah-stahn-teh-MENN-teh	enough (*adv.*)
bastimento, *m.*	bah-stee-MENN-toh	vessel (ship)
bastone, *m.*	bah-STOH-neh	bat
"	"	cane (walking stick)
"	"	club (cudgel)
"	"	staff (stick)
battaglia, *f.*	baht-TAH-l_yah	battle
battello, *m.*	baht-TELL-loh	boat
battere (2)	BAHT-teh-reh	beat (thrash), to
battere legger-mente	BAHT-teh-reh ledd-jehr-MENN-teh	pat, to
"	"	tap (rap), to
batteria, *f.*	baht-teh-REE-ah	battery (artillery)
battersi	BAHT-tehr-see	fight (contend), to

Italian	Pronunciation	English
battesimo, *m.*	baht-TEH-zee-moh	baptism
baule, *m.*	bah-OO-leh	trunk (baggage)
Baviera, *f.*	bah-V_YEH-rah	Bavaria
beccare (1)	bekk-KAH-reh	peck, to
becco, *m.*	BEKK-koh	bill (beak)
belare (1)	beh-LAH-reh	bleat, to
belga	BELL-gah	Belgian (*adj.*)
Belgio, *m.*	BELL-joh	Belgium
bellezza, *f.*	bell-LETT-tsah	beauty
bello	BELL-loh	beautiful
"	"	handsome (attractive)
benchè	beng-KEH	although
benda, *f.*	BENN-dah	bandage
bene	BEH-neh	well (commendably, *adv.*)
bene, *m.*	BEH-neh	asset (*bus.*)
benedire (36)	beh-neh-DEE-reh	bless, to
beneficenza, *f.*	beh-neh-fee-CHENN-tsah	charity (philanthropy)
benessere, *m.*	beh-NESS-seh-reh	welfare (well-being)
beni, *m.pl.*	BEH-nee	estate (total possessions)
beni immobili, *m. pl.*	BEH-nee eem-MOH-bee-lee	real estate
benzina, *f.*	benn-DZEE-nah	gasoline
bere (20)	BEH-reh	drink, to
Berlino, *m.*	behr-LEE-noh	Berlin
Berna, *f.*	BEHR-nah	Berne
berretto, *m.*	behr-RETT-toh	cap (hat)
bestemmiare (1)	beh-stemm-M_YAH-reh	curse, to
"	"	swear, to
bestia, *f.*	BEH-st_yah	beast
"	"	brute (animal, *n.*)
bestiame, *m.*	beh-ST_YAH-meh	cattle
"	"	stock (livestock)
betulla, *f.*	beh-TOOL-lah	birch (tree)
biancheria (intima), *f.*	b_yahng-keh-REE-ah (EEN-tee-mah)	underwear
bianco	B_YAHNG-koh	white (*adj.*)
bianco, in	een B_YAHNG-koh	blank (unmarked)
biasimare (1)	b_yah-zee-MAH-reh	blame, to
Bibbia, *f.*	BEEB-b_yah	Bible
bibita, *f.*	BEE-bee-tah	drink (beverage)
bibita alcolica, *f.*	BEE-bee-tah ahl-KOH-lee-kah	liquor (alcoholic beverage)
bibliografia, *f.*	bee-blee-oh-grah-FEE-ah	bibliography
biblioteca, *f.*	bee-bl_yoh-TEH-kah	library
bibliotecario, *m.*	bee-bl_yoh-teh-KAH-r_yoh	librarian
bicchiere, *m.*	beek-K_YEH-reh	glass (vessel)
"	"	tumbler
bicicletta, *f.*	bee-chee-KLETT-tah	bicycle
bigliardo (giuoco del), *m.*	bee-L_YAHR-doh (JWOH-koh dell)	billiards
biglietto, *m.*	bee-L_YETT-toh	note (letter)
"	"	ticket (entitling card)
biglietto (di banca) *m.*	bee-L_YETT-toh (dee BAHN-kah)	bill (currency)
bilancia, *f.*	bee-LAHN-chah	scales (balance)
bilancio, *m.*	bee-LAHN-choh	budget (*n.*)
binario, *m.*	bee-NAH-r_yoh	track (rails)
biografia, *f.*	bee-oh-grah-FEE-ah	biography
biologia, *f.*	bee-oh-loh-JEE-ah	biology
biondo	B_YOHN-doh	blond
"	"	fair
birra, *f.*	BEER-rah	beer
bisbigliare (1)	bee-zbee-L_YAH-reh	whisper (utter softly), to
bisbiglio, *m.*	bee-ZBEE-l_yoh	whisper
bisogno, *m.*	bee-ZOH-n_yoh	need
"	"	want (need)
bizzarro	beed-DZAHR-roh	funny (odd)
"	"	queer
blasfematorio	blah-sfeh-mah-TOH-r_yoh	profane (blasphemous)
blocco, *m.*	BLOHK-koh	block (solid piece)
"	"	lump (shapeless piece)
blusa, *f.*	BLOO-zah	blouse (shirtwaist)
bobina, *f.*	boh-BEE-nah	coil (*elec.*)
bocca, *f.*	BOHK-kah	mouth (*anat.*)
boccone, *m.*	bohk-KOH-neh	morsel (small bit)
bodino, *m.*	boh-DEE-noh	pudding (dessert)
Bolivia, *m.*	boh-LEE-v_yah	Bolivia
bollire (4)	bohl-LEE-reh	boil (bubble up), to
bollone, *m.*	bohl-LOH-neh	bolt (long metal fastener)
bomba, *f.*	BOHM-bah	bomb (projectile)
bomba atomica, *f.*	BOHM-bah ah-TOH-mee-kah	atomic bomb
bontà, *f.*	bohn-TAH	goodness (kindliness)
borbottare (1)	bohr-boht-TAH-reh	mutter (mumble), to
bordo, *m.*	BOHR-doh	border (edge)
bordo, a	ah BOHR-doh	aboard
borsa, *f.*	BOHR-sah	bag (purse)
"	"	purse (coin pouch)
Borsa, *f.*	BOHR-sah	exchange, stock
boschetto, *m.*	boh-SKETT-toh	grove (small woods)
bosco, *m.*	BOH-skoh	timber (standing trees)
"	"	wood (forest)
botanica, *f.*	boh-TAH-nee-kah	botany
bottega dei comestibili, *f.*	boht-TEH-gah day koh-meh-STEE-bee-lee	grocery
bottiglia, *f.*	boht-TEE-l_yah	bottle
bottone, *m.*	boht-TOH-neh	button
Boy Scout, *m.*	BOY SKOWT	Boy Scout
braccialetto, *m.*	braht-chah-LETT-toh	bracelet
bracciante, *m.*	braht-CHAHN-teh	laborer
braccio, *m.*	BRAHT-choh	arm (*anat.*)
bracco, *m.*	BRAHK-koh	hound
Brasile, *m.*	brah-ZEE-leh	Brazil
brasiliano	brah-zee-L_YAH-noh	Brazilian (*adj.*)
bretelle, *f.pl.*	breh-TELL-leh	suspenders
breve	BREH-veh	brief (fleeting)
"	"	short
brevetto, *m.*	breh-VETT-toh	patent (*n.*)
brezza, *f.*	BREDD-dzah	breeze
briciola, *f.*	BREE-choh-lah	crumb
bridge a contratto, *m.*	BRIDGE ah kohn-TRAHT-toh	bridge, contract
briglia, *f.*	BREE-l_yah	bridle (harness)
brillante	breel-LAHN-teh	bright (shining)
"	"	brilliant
brillare (1)	breel-LAH-reh	beam, to
"	"	gleam (shine), to
brina, *f.*	BREE-nah	frost
britannico	bree-TAHN-nee-koh	British (*adj.*)
brividi, *m.pl.*	BREE-vee-dee	chill (shivering sensation)
brocca, *f.*	BROHK-kah	jug
"	"	pitcher (container)
bronchite, *f.*	brohn-KEE-teh	bronchitis
brontolare (1)	brohn-toh-LAH-reh	grumble, to
bronzo, *m.*	BROHN-dzoh	bronze
bruciare (1)	broo-CHAH-reh	burn, to
bruciatura di sole, *f.*	broo-chah-TOO-rah dee SOH-leh	sunburn
bruco, *m.*	BROO-koh	caterpillar
bruna	BROO-nah	brunette (*adj.*)
brutto	BROOT-toh	ugly
Bruxelles, *f.*	broos-SELL-less	Brussels
bucato, *m.*	boo-KAH-toh	laundry (articles laundered)
buco, *m.*	BOO-koh	hole (cavity)
bue, *m.* (*pl.* buoi)	BOO-eh (BWOY)	ox
Buenos Aires, *f.*	BWEH-nohss EYE-ress	Buenos Aires
bufalo, *m.*	BOO-fah-loh	buffalo
bufera, *f.*	boo-FEH-rah	gale (wind)
bugia, *f.*	boo-JEE-ah	lie
bugiardo, *m.*	boo-JAHR-doh	liar
buio	BOO-yoh	dark (without light, *adj.*)
Bulgaria, *f.*	bool-gah-REE-ah	Bulgaria
buono	BWOH-noh	fine
"	"	good
buona educazione, *f.*	BWOH-nah eh-doo-kah-TS_YOH-neh	etiquette
buon mercato, a	ah BWOHN mehr-KAH-toh	cheap (inexpensive)
buon'ora, di	dee bwoh-NOH-rah	early (*adj., adv.*)
burro, *m.*	BOOR-roh	butter
bussola, *f.*	BOOSS-soh-lah	compass (magnetic instrument)
busta, *f.*	BOO-stah	envelope (folded wrapper)
busto, *m.*	BOO-stoh	bust (statue)
cabina, *f.*	kah-BEE-nah	cabin
"	"	lodge
cablografare (1)	kah-bloh-grah-FAH-reh	cable, to
cablogramma, *m.*	kah-bloh-GRAHM-mah	cablegram

Italian	Pronunciation	English
cacao, *m.*	*kah*-KAH-*oh*	cocoa
caccia, *f.*	KAHT-*chah*	hunt (sport)
cacciatore, *m.*	*kaht-chah*-TOH-*reh*	hunter
cacciavite, *f.*	*kaht-chah*-VEE-*teh*	screw driver
cadavere, *m.*	*kah*-DAH-*veh-reh*	corpse
cadere (21)	*kah*-DEH-*reh*	fall, to
caduta, *f.*	*kah*-DOO-*tah*	drop
"	"	fall
caffè, *m.*	*kahf*-FEH	coffee
caffetiera, *f.*	*kahf-feh-*T_YEH-*rah*	coffee pot
Cairo, Il	*eel* KYE-*roh*	Cairo
calamita, *f.*	*kah-lah*-MEE-*tah*	magnet
calare lentamente (1)	*kah*-LAH-*reh lenn-tah*-MENN-*teh*	sink (fall slowly), to
calata, *f.*	*kah*-LAH-*tah*	dock
calca, *f.*	KAHL-*kah*	throng
calcagno, *m.*	*kahl*-KAH-*n_yoh*	heel (*anat.*)
calcare, *m.*	*kahl*-KAH-*reh*	limestone
calcestruzzo, *m.*	*kahl-cheh-*STROOT-*tsoh*	concrete (artificial stone)
calcio, *m.*	KAHL-*choh*	kick (boot)
calcolare (1)	*kahl-koh*-LAH-*reh*	calculate (compute), to
caldaia, *f.*	*kahl*-DAH-*yah*	kettle
caldo	KAHL-*doh*	hot
"	"	warm
calendario, *m.*	*kah-lenn*-DAH-*r_yoh*	calendar
calma, *f.*	KAHL-*mah*	lull (calm)
calmare (1)	*kahl*-MAH-*reh*	lull (quiet), to
"	"	soothe (calm), to
calmo	KAHL-*moh*	calm (*adj.*)
calore, *m.*	*kah*-LOH-*reh*	heat
"	"	warmth
caloria, *f.*	*kah-loh*-REE-*ah*	calorie
calorifero, *m.*	*kah-loh*-REE-*feh-roh*	furnace (home heater)
calpestare (1)	*kahl-peh-*STAH-*reh*	trample, to
calvo	KAHL-*voh*	bald (hairless)
calza, *f.*	KAHL-*tsah*	stocking
calzino, *m.*	*kahl*-TSEE-*noh*	sock (garment)
calzolaio, *m.*	*kahl-tsoh*-LAH-*yoh*	shoemaker
cambiale, *f.*	*kahm*-B_YAH-*leh*	bill of exchange
cambiamento, *m.*	*kahm-b_yah*-MENN-*toh*	change (alteration)
cambiare (1)	*kahm*-B_YAH-*reh*	change, to
camera, *f.*	KAH-*meh-rah*	bedroom
camera di commercio, *f.*	KAH-*meh-rah dee kohm*-MEHR-*choh*	chamber of commerce
cameriera, *f.*	*kah-meh-r_*YEH-*rah*	maid (servant)
cameriere, *m.*	*kah-meh-r_*YEH-*reh*	waiter
cameriere (di bordo), *m.*	*kah-meh-r_*YEH-*reh (dee* BOHR-*doh)*	steward (attendant on ship)
camicia, *f.*	*kah*-MEE-*chah*	shirt
camicia da notte, *f.*	*kah*-MEE-*chah dah* NOHT-*teh*	nightgown
camino, *m.*	*kah*-MEE-*noh*	chimney
"	"	fireplace
cammello, *m.*	*kahm*-MELL-*loh*	camel
camminare (1)	*kahm-mee*-NAH-*reh*	walk, to
camminare a grandi passi	*kahm-mee*-NAH-*reh ah* GRAHN-*dee* PAHSS-*see*	stride (walk), to
camminata, *f.*	*kahm-mee*-NAH-*tah*	hike (march)
campagna, *f.*	*kahm*-PAH-*n_yah*	campaign (*mil.*)
"	"	country (countryside)
campanello, *m.*	*kahm-pah*-NELL-*loh*	bell
campanile, *m.*	*kahm-pah*-NEE-*leh*	steeple
campione, *m.*	*kahm*-P_YOH-*neh*	champion
"	"	sample
campo, *m.*	KAHM-*poh*	field
"	"	realm
campo di ricreazione, *m.*	KAHM-*poh dee ree-kreh-ah-*TS_YOH-*neh*	playground
Canadà, *m.*	*kah-nah*-DAH	Canada
canadese	*kah-nah*-DEH-*seh*	Canadian (*adj.*)
canale, *m.*	*kah*-NAH-*leh*	canal
canarino, *m.*	*kah-nah*-REE-*noh*	canary
cancellare (1)	*kahn-chell*-LAH-*reh*	blot out (efface), to
"	"	erase, to
cancello, *m.*	*kahn*-CHELL-*loh*	gate
cancro, *m.*	KAHNG-*kroh*	cancer
candela, *f.*	*kahn*-DEH-*lah*	candle
candidato, *m.*	*kahn-dee*-DAH-*toh*	candidate
cane, *m.*	KAH-*neh*	dog
canna, *f.*	KAHN-*nah*	reed (grass)

Italian	Pronunciation	English
cannella, *f.*	*kahn*-NELL-*lah*	cinnamon
cannone, *m.*	*kahn*-NOH-*neh*	cannon
canoa, *f.*	*kah*-NOH-*ah*	canoe
cantante, *m., f.*	*kahn*-TAHN-*teh*	singer
cantare (1)	*kahn*-TAH-*reh*	sing, to
cantiere navale, *m.*	*kahn*-T_YEH-*reh nah-*VAH-*leh*	shipyard
cantina, *f.*	*kahn*-TEE-*nah*	cellar
canzone, *f.*	*kahn*-TSOH-*neh*	song
capace	*kah*-PAH-*cheh*	able
"	"	capable (competent)
capacità, *f.*	*kah-pah-chee-*TAH	ability
"	"	capacity (volume)
capanna, *f.*	*kah*-PAHN-*nah*	hut
capelli, *m. pl.*	*kah*-PELL-*lee*	hair
capire (3)	*kah*-PEE-*reh*	understand (comprehend), to
capitale, *f.*	*kah-pee*-TAH-*leh*	capital (city)
capitale, *m.*	*kah-pee*-TAH-*leh*	capital (wealth)
capitano, *m.*	*kah-pee*-TAH-*noh*	captain (officer)
capitolo, *m.*	*kah-*PEE-*toh-loh*	chapter (of book)
capo, *m.*	KAH-*poh*	cape (headland)
"	"	head (leader)
Capodanno, *m.*	*kah-poh-*DAHN-*noh*	New Year's Day
capolavorante, *m.*	*kah-poh-lah-voh-*RAHN-*teh*	foreman (overseer)
caporale, *m.*	*kah-poh-*RAH-*leh*	corporal (*mil.*)
capovolgere (127)	*kah-poh-*VOHL-*jeh-reh*	upset (knock over), to
cappella, *f.*	*kah-*PELL-*lah*	chapel
cappello, *m.*	*kahp-*PELL-*loh*	hat
cappuccio, *m.*	*kahp-*POOT-*choh*	hood (cowl)
capra, *f.*	KAH-*prah*	goat
capretto, *m.*	*kah-*PRETT-*toh*	kid (goat)
capriccio, *m.*	*kah-*PREET-*choh*	fancy (notion)
carattere, *m.*	*kah-*RAHT-*teh-reh*	character (nature)
caratteristico	*kah-raht-teh-*REE-*stee-koh*	characteristic (typical)
carbone (fossile), *m.*	*kahr-*BOH-*neh (fohss-*SEE-*leh)*	coal
carbonio, *m.*	*kahr-*BOH-*n_yoh*	carbon (*chem.*)
carcere, *m.*	KAHR-*cheh-reh*	jail
caricare (1)	*kah-ree-*KAH-*reh*	charge, to (*elec.*)
"	"	load (fill), to
caricatura, *f.*	*kah-ree-kah-*TOO-*rah*	cartoon (caricature)
carico	KAH-*ree-koh*	deep (in color)
carico, *m.*	KAH-*ree-koh*	burden
"	"	cargo
"	"	load
carino, *m.*	*kah-*REE-*noh*	darling
carne, *f.*	KAHR-*neh*	flesh
"	"	meat
carne di maiale, *f.*	KAHR-*neh dee mah-*YAH-*leh*	pork
carne di montone, *f.*	KAHR-*neh dee mohn-*TOH-*neh*	mutton
carnesecca, *f.*	*kahr-neh-*SEKK-*kah*	bacon
carnevale, *m.*	*kahr-neh-*VAH-*leh*	carnival
caro	KAH-*roh*	dear (beloved, *adj.*)
carota, *f.*	*kah-*ROH-*tah*	carrot
carrata, *f.*	*kahr-*RAH-*tah*	carload (*bus.*)
carretta, *f.*	*kahr-*RETT-*tah*	cart
carriera, *f.*	*kahr-*R_YEH-*rah*	career
carro, *m.*	KAHR-*roh*	van (vehicle)
carrozza, *f.*	*kahr-*ROHT-*tsah*	carriage (horse-drawn vehicle)
"	"	coach, railroad
carrozzina, *f.*	*kahr-roht-*TSEE-*nah*	carriage (baby buggy)
carta, *f.*	KAHR-*tah*	map
"	"	paper
carta (da giuoco), *f.*	KAHR-*tah (dah* JWOH-*koh)*	card, playing
carta da lettere, *f.*	KAHR-*tah dah* LETT-*teh-reh*	stationery (writing paper)
carta (da visita), *f.*	KAHR-*tah (dah* VEE-*zee-tah)*	card, calling
cartolina, *f.*	*kahr-toh-*LEE-*nah*	card, postal
cartone, *m.*	*kahr-*TOH-*neh*	cardboard
casa, *f.*	KAH-*sah*	home
"	"	house
casa, verso	VEHR-*soh* KAH-*sah*	homeward
casa di salute, *f.*	KAH-*sah dee sah-*LOO-*teh*	asylum (institution)

Italian	Pronunciation	English
cascare (1)	kah-SKAH-reh	drop (fall), to
"	"	tumble, to
cascata, f.	kah-SKAH-tah	falls (waterfall)
caso, m.	KAH-zoh	accident
"	"	case (instance)
		chance (fate)
cassa, f.	KAHSS-sah	chest (box)
cassetto, m.	kahss-SETT-toh	drawer (sliding box)
cassettone, m.	kahss-sett-TOH-neh	bureau (chest)
cassiere, m., f.	kahss-S_YEH-reh	cashier
castagno, m.	kah-STAH-n_yoh	chestnut (tree)
castello, m.	kah-STELL-loh	castle
casto	KAH-stoh	chaste
castoro, m.	kah-STOH-roh	beaver (animal)
catalogo, m.	kah-TAH-loh-goh	catalogue
catena, f.	kah-TEH-nah	chain
"	"	range (of mountains)
"	"	ridge (of mountains)
catino, m.	kah-TEE-noh	basin (small bowl)
catrame, m.	kah-TRAH-meh	tar
cattedrale, f.	kaht-teh-DRAH-leh	cathedral
cattivo	kaht-TEE-voh	bad
"	"	evil (adj.)
"	"	naughty (disobedi-ent)
cattolico	kaht-TOH-lee-koh	Catholic (adj.)
catturare (1)	kaht-too-RAH-reh	capture, to
"	"	seize, to
causa, f.	KOW-zah	cause
"	"	suit (lawsuit)
causa di, a	ah KOW-zah dee	because of (adv.)
causare (1)	kow-ZAH-reh	cause, to
cautela, f.	kow-TEH-lah	caution (heed)
cauto	KOW-toh	careful (cautious)
cavaliere, m.	kah-vah-L_YEH-reh	escort (social com-panion)
"	"	knight
"	"	rider (horseman)
cavalla, f.	kah-VAHL-lah	mare
cavalletta, f.	kah-vahl-LETT-tah	grasshopper
cavallino, m.	kah-vahl-LEE-noh	pony (animal)
cavallo, m.	kah-VAHL-loh	horse
cavallo vapore, m.	kah-VAHL-loh vah-POH-reh	horsepower
caverna, f.	kah-VEHR-nah	cave
caviglia, f.	kah-VEE-l_yah	ankle
cavo	KAH-voh	hollow (adj.)
cavolfiore, m.	kah-vohl-F_YOH-reh	cauliflower
cavolo, m.	KAH-voh-loh	cabbage
Ceco-Slovakia, f.	CHEH-koh zloh-VAH-k_yah	Czechoslovakia
cedere (2)	CHEH-deh-reh	cede, to
"	"	succumb, to
"	"	surrender (relin-quish), to
"	"	yield (give in), to
cedro, m.	CHEH-droh	cedar (tree)
"	"	lime (fruit)
celare (1)	cheh-LAH-reh	conceal, to
celebrare (1)	cheh-leh-BRAH-reh	celebrate, to
celibe	CHEH-lee-beh	single (unmarried)
cellula, f.	CHELL-loo-lah	cell (biol.)
cemento, m.	cheh-MEN-toh	cement
cena, f.	CHEH-nah	supper (light evening meal)
cenere, f.	CHEH-neh-reh	ashes
cenno, m.	CHENN-noh	hint (inkling)
censimento, m.	chenn-see-MENN-toh	census
centrale	chenn-TRAH-leh	central
centro, m.	CHENN-troh	center
ceppo, m.	CHEPP-poh	log (rough timber)
"	"	stump (of tree)
cera, f.	CHEH-rah	wax (beeswax)
cerca, f.	CHEHR-kah	quest (search)
cercare (1)	chehr-KAH-reh	look for, to
cercare a tastoni	chehr-KAH-reh ah tah-STOH-nee	feel (grope) for, to
cerchio, m.	CHEHR-k_yoh	ring (circle)
cereale, m.	cheh-reh-AH-leh	cereal
"	"	grain
cereale confezion-ato, m.	cheh-reh-AH-leh kohn-feh-ts_yoh-NAH-toh	cereal (prepared food)

Italian	Pronunciation	English
cerimonia, f.	cheh-ree-MOH-n_yah	ceremony
certamente	chehr-tah-MENN-teh	certainly
certificare (1)	chehr-tee-fee-KAH-reh	certify, to
certificato, m.	chehr-tee-fee-KAH-toh	certificate
certo	CHEHR-toh	certain (particular)
"	"	some (certain, adj.)
cervello, m.	chehr-VELL-loh	brain (anat.)
cervo, m.	CHEHR-voh	deer
cervo volante, m.	CHEHR-voh voh-LAHN-teh	kite
cesello, m.	cheh-ZELL-loh	chisel (tool)
cespuglio, m.	cheh-SPOO-l_yoh	bush (plant)
cessare (1)	chess-SAH-reh	cease, to
"	"	stop, to
cessione, f.	chess-S_YOH-neh	assignment (legal transfer)
cetriolo, m.	cheh-TR_YOH-loh	cucumber
che	KEH	than
"	"	that (conj., rel. pron.)
"	"	what (interrog. adj.)
"	"	which (rel. pron.)
"	"	who (rel. pron.)
"	"	whom (rel. pron.)
che cosa	keh KOH-sah	what (interrog. pron.)
chi	KEE	who (interrog. pron.)
"	"	(person) who (rel. pron.)
"	"	whom (interrog. pron.)
"	"	(person) whom (rel. pron.)
chi, di	dee KEE	whose (interrog. pron., rel. pron.)
chiacchierare (1)	k_yahk-k_yeh-RAH-reh	chatter, to
chiamare (1)	k_yah-MAH-reh	call, to
"	"	summon (send for), to
chiamata, f.	k_yah-MAH-tah	call (shout)
chiarire (3)	k_yah-REE-reh	illuminate (eluci-date), to
chiaro	K_YAH-roh	clear
"	"	fair (not cloudy)
"	"	light (bright)
"	"	plain
chiaro di luna, m.	K_YAH-roh dee LOO-nah	moonlight
chiasso, m.	K_YAHSS-soh	din
chiave, f.	K_YAH-veh	key (for lock)
chicco, m.	KEEK-koh	kernel
chiedere (22)	K_YEH-deh-reh	ask (request), to
chiesa, f.	K_YEH-zah	church
chimica, f.	KEE-mee-kah	chemistry
chinarsi (1)	kee-NAHR-see	stoop (bend for-ward), to
chincaglieria, f.	keeng-kah-l_yeh-REE-ah	hardware
chiodo, m.	K_YOH-doh	nail (hardware)
chirurgo, m.	kee-ROOR-goh	surgeon
chitarra, f.	kee-TAHR-rah	guitar
chiudere (23)	K_YOO-deh-reh	close, to
"	"	shut (make close), to
chiudere a chiave	K_YOO-deh-reh ah K_YAH-veh	lock (fasten with key), to
chiunque	kee-OONG-kweh	anybody (anybody whosoever)
"	"	anyone (anyone whosoever)
"	"	whoever (any person who)
chiusura lampo, f.	k_yoo-SOO-rah LAHM-poh	zipper
ci	CHEE	ourselves
"	"	(to) us
cianografia, f.	chah-noh-grah-FEE-ah	blueprint
ciascuno	chah-SKOO-noh	everyone
cibo, m.	CHEE-boh	food
cicatrice, f.	chee-kah-TREE-cheh	scar
cicogna, f.	chee-KOH-n_yah	stork
cieco	CH_YEH-koh	blind (lacking sight)
cielo, m.	CH_YEH-loh	heaven
"	"	sky
cifra, f.	CHEE-frah	figure (numeral)
ciglio, m. (pl. -glia, f.)	CHEE-l_yoh	eyelash
cigno, m.	CHEE-n_yoh	swan
Cile, m.	CHEE-leh	Chile
cileno	chee-LEH-noh	Chilean (adj.)

Italian	Pronunciation	English
ciliegia, *f.*	*chee-L_YEH-jah*	cherry (fruit)
cilindro, *m.*	*chee-LEEN-droh*	cylinder (*geom.*)
cimitero, *m.*	*chee-mee-TEH-roh*	cemetery
Cina, *f.*	CHEE-*nah*	China
cinegiornale, *m.*	*chee-neh-johr-*NAH-*leh*	newsreel
cinema, *m.*	CHEE-*neh-mah*	movies
cinese	*chee-*NEH-*seh*	Chinese (*adj.*)
cingere (24)	CHEEN-*jeh-reh*	enclose (surround), to
cinghia, *f.*	CHEENG-*g_yah*	strap
cintura, *f.*	*cheen-*TOO-*rah*	belt (article of clothing)
ciò	CHOH	it
"	"	this (*dem. pron.*)
ciò, di	*dee* CHOH	thereof
ciò che	CHOH *keh*	that which
cioccolata, *f.*	*chohk-koh-*LAH-*tah*	chocolate
cioè	*choh-*EH	namely
ciottolo, *m.*	CHOHT-*toh-loh*	pebble
cipolla, *f.*	*chee-*POHL-*lah*	onion
cipria, *f.*	CHEE-*pr_yah*	powder (cosmetic)
circa	CHEER-*kah*	about
circo, *m.*	CHEER-*koh*	circus
circolare	*cheer-koh-*LAH-*reh*	circular (*adj.*)
circolare, *f.*	*cheer-koh-*LAH-*reh*	circular (letter or brochure, *bus.*)
circolo, *m.*	CHEER-*koh-loh*	circle (*geom.*)
"		club (association)
circondare (1)	*cheer-kohn-*DAH-*reh*	surround (enclose), to
circonferenza, *f.*	*cheer-kohn-feh-*RENN-*tsah*	circumference
circonstanza, *f.*	*cheer-kohn-*STAHN-*tsah*	circumstance (external condition)
citare (1)	*chee-*TAH-*reh*	quote (cite), to
citare in giudizio	*chee-*TAH-*reh een joo-*DEE-*ts_yoh*	sue (bring action against), to
citazione, *f.*	*chee-tah-*TS_YOH-*neh*	quotation (selection)
città, *f.*	*cheet-*TAH	city
"		town
cittadino, *m.*	*cheet-tah-*DEE-*noh*	citizen
civile	*chee-*VEE-*leh*	civil
civilizzazione, *f.*	*chee-vee-leed-dzah-*TS_YOH-*neh*	civilization (civilized condition)
"		culture (stage of civilization)
civiltà, *f.*	*chee-veel-*TAH	civilization (culture)
clandestino	*klahn-deh-*STEE-*noh*	underground (secret, *adj.*)
clarinetto, *m.*	*klah-ree-*NETT-*toh*	clarinet
classe, *f.*	KLAHSS-*seh*	grade (school division)
classico	KLAHSS-*see-koh*	classic (first-class, *adj.*)
classico, *m.*	KLAHSS-*see-koh*	classic (first-class work)
clausola, *f.*	KLOW-*zoh-lah*	clause (stipulation)
clemente	*kleh-*MENN-*teh*	merciful
cliente, *m., f.*	*klee-*ENN-*teh*	buyer
"	"	customer
"		patron
clima, *m.*	KLEE-*mah*	climate (weather)
clistere, *m.*	*klee-*STEH-*reh*	enema
cocco, *m.*	KOHK-*koh*	coconut
cocktail, *m.*	KOHK-*tell*	cocktail
coda, *f.*	KOH-*dah*	tail (of animal)
codardo, *m.*	*koh-*DAHR-*doh*	coward
codesti	*koh-*DEH-*stee*	those
codesto	*koh-*DEH-*stoh*	that
codice, *m.*	KOH-*dee-cheh*	code (law)
cofano, *m.*	KOH-*fah-noh*	hood (*auto.*)
cognata, *f.*	*koh-*N_YAH-*tah*	sister-in-law
cognato, *m.*	*koh-*N_YAH-*toh*	brother-in-law
cognome, *m.*	*koh-*N_YOH-*meh*	surname
coke, *m.*	KOHK	coke
colazione (prima), *f.*	(PREE *mah*) *koh-lah-*TS_YOH-*neh*	breakfast
colazione, (seconda), *f.*	(*seh-*KOHN-*dah*) *koh-lah-*TS_YOH-*neh*	lunch (midday meal)
colera, *f.*	*koh-*LEH-*rah*	cholera
colla, *f.*	KOHL-*lah*	glue
"	"	paste (adhesive)
collana, *f.*	*kohl-*LAH-*nah*	necklace

Italian	Pronunciation	English
collera, *f.*	KOHL-*leh-rah*	anger
"	"	wrath
collettivo	*kohl-lett-*TEE-*voh*	joint (combined)
colletto, *m.*	*kohl-*LETT-*toh*	collar
collina, *f.*	*kohl-*LEE-*nah*	hill
collo, *m.*	KOHL-*loh*	neck (*anat.*)
collocare (1)	*kohl-loh-*KAH-*reh*	lay (put down), to
"	"	place, to
"	"	set (put), to
colomba, *f.*	*koh-*LOHM-*bah*	dove
Colombia, *f.*	*koh-*LOHM-*b_yah*	Colombia
colonia, *f.*	*koh-*LOH-*n_yah*	colony
"	"	settlement
coloniale	*koh-loh-*N_YAH-*leh*	colonial
colonna, *f.*	*koh-*LOHN-*nah*	column
colonnello, *m.*	*koh-lohn-*NELL-*loh*	colonel
colono, *m.*	*koh-*LOH-*noh*	colonist
"	"	settler
color di rosa	*koh-*LOHR *dee* ROH-*zah*	pink (color)
colore, *m.*	*koh-*LOH-*reh*	color
"	"	paint
coloro che	*koh-*LOH-*roh keh*	those who
colpa, *f.*	KOHL-*pah*	blame
"	"	fault (cause for blame)
colpabilità, *f.*	*kohl-pah-bee-lee-*TAH	guilt
colpetto, *m.*	*kohl-*PETT-*toh*	pat (tap)
colpevole	*kohl-*PEH-*voh-leh*	guilty
colpire (3)	*kohl-*PEE-*reh*	hit, to
"	"	strike, to
colpire col piede	*kohl-*PEE-*reh kohl* P_YEH-*deh*	kick (boot), to
colpo, *m.*	KOHL-*poh*	blow
"	"	stroke
coltello, *m.*	*kohl-*TELL-*loh*	knife
coltivare (1)	*kohl-tee-*VAH-*reh*	cultivate, to
"	"	grow, to
"	"	till, to
coltivatore, *m.*	*kohl-tee-vah-*TOH-*reh*	farmer
coltrone, *m.*	*kohl-*TROH-*neh*	quilt (bedcover)
colui	*koh-*LOO-*ee*	that
colui che	*koh-*LOO-*ee keh*	he who
comandante, *m.*	*koh-mahn-*DAHN-*teh*	commander (officer)
comandare (1)	*koh-mahn-*DAH-*reh*	command, to
"	"	order, to
comando, *m.*	*koh-*MAHN-*doh*	command
combattere contro (2)	*kohm-*BAHT-*teh-reh* KOHN-*troh*	fight (struggle against), to
combattimento, *m.*	*kohm-baht-tee-*MENN-*toh*	combat
combinare (1)	*kohm-bee-*NAH-*reh*	combine (make join), to
combinarsi	*kohm-bee-*NAHR-*see*	combine (coalesce), to
combinazione, *f.*	*kohm-bee-nah-*TS_YOH-*neh*	combination
combustibile, *m.*	*kohm-boo-*STEE-*bee-leh*	fuel
come	KOH-*meh*	as (in the role of, *prep.*)
"	"	as (in the same way, *conj.*)
"	"	how
"	"	like (*adv.*)
comico	KOH-*mee-koh*	funny (comical)
cominciare (1)	*koh-meen-*CHAH-*reh*	begin, to
comitato, *m.*	*koh-mee-*TAH-*toh*	committee
commedia, *f.*	*kohm-*MEH-*d_yah*	comedy (comic play)
commemorazione, *f.*	*kohm-meh-moh-rah-*TS_YOH-*neh*	memorial (*n.*)
commentare (1)	*kohm-menn-*TAH-*reh*	comment, to
commerciale	*kohm-mehr-*CHAH-*leh*	commercial
"	"	mercantile
commercio, *m.*	*kohm-*MEHR-*choh*	commerce
"	"	trade
commercio bancario, *m.*	*kohm-*MEHR-*choh bahng-*KAH-*r_yoh*	banking
commesso, *m.*	*kohm-*MESS-*soh*	clerk (salesperson)
commettere (60)	*kohm-*METT-*teh-reh*	commit (perpetrate), to
commissario, *m.*	*kohm-mees-*SAH-*r_yoh*	commissioner (deputized person)

Italian	Pronunciation	English
commissione, *f.*	*kohm-meess-*S_YOH-*neh*	commission
"	"	errand
commuovere (64)	*kohm-*MWOH-*veh-reh*	impress (affect deeply), to
comò, *m.*	*koh-*MOH	dresser (bureau)
comodità, *f.*	*koh-moh-dee-*TAH	comfort (ease)
"	"	convenience
comodo	KOH-*moh-doh*	comfortable (affording comfort)
"	"	convenient
"	"	handy (near at hand)
compagnia, *f.*	*kohm-pah-*N_YEE-*ah*	company (*mil.*)
compagno, *m.*	*kohm-*PAH-*n_yoh*	companion
"	"	comrade
compagno di giuoco, *m.*	*kohm-*PAH-*n_yoh dee* JWOH-*koh*	playmate
compartimento, *m.*	*kohm-pahr-tee-*MENN-*to*	compartment (of train)
compassi, *m.pl.*	*kohm-*PAHSS-*see*	compass (drawing instrument)
compassione, *f.*	*kohm-pahss-*S_YOH-*neh*	pity (compassion)
compatire (3)	*kohm-pah-*TEE-*reh*	pity, to
compatto	*kohm-*PAHT-*toh*	compact (packed firmly)
competente	*kohm-peh-*TENN-*teh*	competent (able)
"	"	efficient
compiere (45)	KOHM-*p_yeh-reh*	accomplish, to
"	"	perform (do), to
compito, *m.*	KOHM-*pee-toh*	assignment (*educ.*)
compito, *m.*	KOHM-*pee-toh*	job
"	"	task
compleanno, *m.*	*kohm-pleh-*AHN-*noh*	birthday
completamente	*kohm-pleh-tah-*MENN-*teh*	thoroughly
completare (1)	*kohm-pleh-*TAH-*reh*	complete (finish), to
completo	*kohm-*PLEH-*toh*	complete (entire)
"	"	full
"	"	thorough
"	"	utter (*adj.*)
complicato	*kohm-plee-*KAH-*toh*	complex (complicated)
complimento, *m.*	*kohm-plee-*MEN-*toh*	compliment
complotto, *m.*	*kohm-*PLOHT-*toh*	plot (conspiracy)
comporre (76)	*kohm-*POHR-*reh*	compose, to (*mus.*)
comportamento, *m.*	*kohm-pohr-tah-*MEN-*toh*	behavior
comportarsi (1)	*kohm-pohr-*TAHR-*see*	act, to
"	"	behave (conduct oneself), to
composizione, *f.*	*kohm-poh-zee-*TS_YOH-*neh*	composition (make-up)
composto, *m.*	*kohm-*POH-*stoh*	compound (mixture)
compra, *f.*	KOHM-*prah*	purchase (act of buying)
comprare (1)	*kohm-*PRAH-*reh*	buy, to
comprendere (78)	*kohm-*PRENN-*deh-reh*	comprehend (understand), to
comprensione, *f.*	*kohm-prenn-*S_YOH-*neh*	understanding (comprehension)
compromissione, *f.*	*kohm-proh-meess-*S_YOH-*neh*	compromise (mutual concessions)
comproprietà, *f.*	*kohm-proh-pr_yeh-*TAH	copartnership (*bus.*)
comproprietario, *m.*	*kohm-proh-pr_yeh-*TAH-*r_yoh*	co-owner (*bus.*)
computare (1)	*kohm-poo-*TAH-*reh*	reckon (compute), to
comune	*koh-*MOO-*neh*	common (usual)
comunicare (1)	*koh-moo-nee-*KAH-*reh*	convey (communicate), to
comunicazione, *f.*	*koh-moo-nee-kah-*TS_YOH-*neh*	communication
"	"	message
comunicazioni, *f. pl.*	*koh-moo-nee-kah-*TS_YOH-*nee*	communication (intercourse)
comunismo, *m.*	*koh-moo-*NEE-*zmoh*	communism
comunque	*koh-*MOONG-*kweh*	anyway (in any case)
còn	KOHN	with
concentrare (1)	*kohn-chenn-*TRAH-*reh*	concentrate (make converge), to
concepire (3)	*kohn-cheh-*PEE-*reh*	conceive (imagine), to
concerto, *m.*	*kohn-*CHEHR-*toh*	concert (musical performance)
concetto, *m.*	*kohn-*CHETT-*toh*	conception (notion)
concezione, *f.*	*kohn-cheh-*TS_YOH-*neh*	conception (*physiol.*)
conciso	*kohn-*CHEE-*zoh*	compact (brief)
concludere (6)	*kohn-*KLOO-*deh-reh*	conclude (make end), to
conclusione, *f.*	*kohn-kloo-*Z_YOH-*neh*	conclusion
"	"	ending
concorrente, *m.,f.*	*kohn-kohr-*RENN-*teh*	competitor (*bus.*)

Italian	Pronunciation	English
concorrenza, *f.*	*kohn-kohr-*RENN-*tsah*	competition (*bus.*)
concorso, *m.*	*kohn-*KOHR-*soh*	contest
concreto	*kohn-*KREH-*toh*	concrete (real)
concupiscenza, *f.*	*kohn-koo-pee-*SHENN-*tsah*	lust (desire)
condannare (1)	*kohn-dahn-*NAH-*reh*	condemn, to
"	"	doom, to
"		sentence, to
condensare (1)	*kohn-denn-*SAH-*reh*	condense (compress), to
condimento, *m.*	*kohn-dee-*MENN-*toh*	dressing (sauce)
condividere (40)	*kohn-dee-*VEE-*deh-reh*	share, to
condizione, *f.*	*kohn-dee-*TS_YOH-*neh*	condition
"	"	provision (stipulation)
condurre (7)	*kohn-*DOO_R-*reh*	conduct, to
"	"	drive (a vehicle), to
"		lead (guide), to
conferenza, *f.*	*kohn-feh-*RENN-*tsah*	conference (meeting)
"	"	lecture (speech)
conferire (3)	*kohn-feh-*REE-*reh*	bestow, to
"		confer, to
confermare (1)	*kohn-fehr-*MAH-*reh*	confirm (corroborate), to
confermazione, *f.*	*kohn-fehr-mah-*TS_YOH-*neh*	confirmation (corroboration)
confessare (1)	*kohn-fess-*SAH-*reh*	confess (admit), to
confidente	*kohn-fee-*DENN-*teh*	confident (self-assured)
confidenza, *f.*	*kohn-fee-*DENN-*tsah*	confidence (trust)
confidenziale	*kohn-fee-den-*TS_YAH-*leh*	confidential (private)
confine, *m.*	*kohn-*FEE-*neh*	border (frontier)
conflitto, *m.*	*kohn-*FLEET-*toh*	conflict
confondere (54)	*kohn-*FOHN-*deh-reh*	bewilder, to
"	"	confuse (mix up), to
confortare (1)	*kohn-fohr-*TAH-*reh*	comfort (console), to
conforto, *m.*	*kohn-*FOHR-*toh*	comfort (solace)
confrontare (1)	*kohn-frohn-*TAH-*reh*	compare (consider relatively), to
confronto, *m.*	*kohn-*FROHN-*toh*	comparison
confusione, *f.*	*kohn-foo-z_*YOH-*neh*	confusion (disorder)
confutare (1)	*kohn-foo-*TAH-*reh*	refute, to
congedo, *m.*	*kohn-*JEH-*doh*	discharge (dismissal)
congiunzione, *f.*	*kohn-joon-*TS_YOH-*neh*	conjunction (*gram.*)
congratulare con (1)	*kohn-grah-too-*LAH-*reh kohn*	congratulate, to
congresso, *m.*	*kohn-*GRESS-*soh*	convention (meeting)
coniglio, *m.*	*koh-*NEE-*l_yoh*	rabbit
connesso	*kohn-*NESS-*soh*	related (connected)
connettere (11)	*kohn-*NETT-*teh-reh*	connect (link), to
conoscenza, *f.*	*koh-noh-*SHENN-*tsah*	acquaintance
"	"	knowledge
conoscere (28)	*koh-*NOH-*sheh-reh*	know (be acquainted with), to
conosciuto	*koh-noh-*SHOO-*toh*	familiar (well-known)
"	"	known
conquista, *f.*	*kohn-*KWEE-*stah*	conquest
conscio	KOHN-*shoh*	aware
"	"	conscious
consegna, *f.*	*kohn-*SEH-*n_yah*	consignment (*bus.*)
"	"	delivery (handing over)
consegnare (1)	*koh-seh-*N_YAH-*reh*	deliver (hand over), to
"	"	give, to
consegnatario, *m.*	*kohn-seh-n_yah-*IAH-*r_yoh*	consignee (*bus.*)
conseguenza, *f.*	*kohn-seh-*GWENN-*tsah*	consequence
"	"	result
conseguenza, in	*een kohn-seh-*GWENN-*tsah*	consequently
consentire (4)	*kohn-senn-*TEE-*reh*	consent, to
consentire (a)	*kohn-senn-*TEE-*reh* (*ah*)	comply (acquiesce), to
conservare (1)	*kohn-sehr-*VAH-*reh*	preserve, to
conservarsi	*kohn-sehr-*VAHR-*see*	last (withstand use), to
considerare (1)	*kohn-see-deh-*RAH-*reh*	consider, to
"	"	reckon, to
"	"	regard, to
considerazione, *f.*	*kohn-see-deh-rah-*TS_YOH-*neh*	consideration (thought)
considerevole	*kohn-see-deh-*REH-*voh-leh*	considerable (*adj.*)

Italian	Pronunciation	English
consigliare (1)	*kohn-see-*L_YAH*-reh*	advise, to
"	"	counsel, to
consiglio, *m.*	*kohn-*SEE*-l_yoh*	advice
"	"	board
"	"	council
"	"	counsel
consistere in (16)	*kohn-*SEE*-steh-reh een*	consist of (comprise), to
consolazione, *f.*	*kohn-soh-lah-*TS_YOH*-neh*	consolation (comfort)
console, *m.*	KOHN*-soh-leh*	consul
consultare (1)	*kohn-sool-*TAH*-reh*	consult (seek professional advice of), to
consumare (1)	*kohn-soo-*MAH*-reh*	consume, to
consumo, *m.*	*kohn-*SOO*-moh*	consumption (using up)
contabile, *m.,f.*	*kohn-*TAH*-bee-leh*	accountant
"	"	bookkeeper (*bus.*)
contabilità, *f.*	*kohn-tah-bee-lee-*TAH	bookkeeping (*bus.*)
contadino, *m.*	*kohn-tah-*DEE*-noh*	peasant
contanti, *m.pl.*	*kohn-*TAHN*-tee*	cash (money)
contare (1)	*kohn-*TAH*-reh*	count (enumerate), to
contare su	*kohn-*TAH*-reh soo*	count (rely) on, to
"	"	depend (rely) on, to
contatto, *m.*	*kohn-*TAHT*-toh*	contact (meeting)
contemporaneo	*kohn-temm-poh-*RAH*-neh-oh*	contemporary (modern)
contenere (112)	*kohn-teh-*NEH*-reh*	contain, to
contento	*kohn-*TENN*-toh*	content (satisfied)
contenuto, *m.*	*kohn-teh-*NOO*-toh*	contents
contestare (1)	*kohn-teh-*STAH*-reh*	contest, to
"	"	dispute (oppose by argument), to
continente, *m.*	*kohn-tee-*NENN*-teh*	continent (*geog.*)
continuare (1)	*kohn-tee-*NWAH*-reh*	continue, to
continuare a	*kohn-tee-*NWAH*-reh ah*	keep (continue), to
continuazione, *f.*	*kohn-tee-nwah-*TS_YOH*-neh*	continuation
continuo	*kohn-*TEE*-nwoh*	constant
"	"	continual
"	"	continuous
conto, *m.*	KOHN*-toh*	account (bank account)
"	"	account (calculation)
conto corrente, *m.*	KOHN*-toh kohr-*RENN*-teh*	charge account
conto di risparmio, *m.*	KOHN*-toh dee ree-*SPAHR*-m_yoh*	savings account
contrabbando, *m.*	*kohn-trahb-*BAHN*-doh*	contraband
contraddire (36)	*kohn-trahd-*DEE*-reh*	contradict (deny), to
contraffare (51)	*kohn-trahf-*FAH*-reh*	forge (counterfeit), to
contraffatto	*kohn-trahf-*FAHT*-toh*	counterfeit (*adj.*)
contrario	*kohn-*TRAH*-r_yoh*	contrary (opposite)
contrario, *m.*	*kohn-*TRAH*-r_yoh*	reverse (contrary, *n.*)
contrarre (116)	*kohn-*TRAHR*-reh*	contract (make shrink), to
contrasto, *m.*	*kohn-*TRAH*-stoh*	contrast
contrattare (1)	*kohn-traht-*TAH*-reh*	bargain (negotiate), to
contratto, *m.*	*kohn-*TRAHT*-toh*	contract
contravvenire a (123)	*kohn-trahv-veh-*NEE*-reh ah*	violate (infringe upon), to
contribuire (3)	*kohn-tree-*BWEE*-reh*	contribute, to
contribuzione, *f.*	*kohn-tree-boo-*TS_YOH*-neh*	contribution
contro	KOHN*-troh*	against
controfirma, *f.*	*kohn-troh-*FEER*-mah*	countersignature (*bus.*)
controllare (1)	*kohn-trohl-*LAH*-reh*	check (test), to
controllo, *m.*	*kohn-*TROHL*-loh*	check (examination)
controllore, *m.*	*kohn-trohl-*LOH*-reh*	conductor (ticket collector)
convenire (123)	*kohn-veh-*NEE*-reh*	apply (be fitting), to
conversare (1)	*kohn-vehr-*SAH*-reh*	chat, to
conversazione, *f.*	*kohn-vehr-sah-*TS_YOH*-neh*	conversation
"	"	talk
conversione, *f.*	*kohn-vehr-*S_YOH*-neh*	conversion rate (*bus.*)
convertire (4)	*kohn-vehr-*TEE*-reh*	convert (transform), to
convertito, *m.*	*kohn-vehr-*TEE*-toh*	convert (proselyte)
convincere (124)	*kohn-*VEEN*-cheh-reh*	convince, to
convinzione, *f.*	*kohn-veen-*TS_YOH*-neh*	conviction (belief)
convoglio, *m.*	*kohn-*VOH*-l_yoh*	convoy (*mil.*)

Italian	Pronunciation	English
cooperazione, *f.*	*koh-oh-peh-rah-*TS_YOH*-neh*	cooperation
Copenaghen, *f.*	*koh-peh-*NAH*-gen*	Copenhagen
coperchio, *m.*	*koh-*PEHR*-k_yoh*	cover
"	"	lid
coperta, *f.*	*koh-*PEHR*-tah*	blanket
copia, *f.*	KOH*-p_yah*	copy (duplicate)
copia (a carta carbone), *f.*	KOH*-p_yah (ah* KAHR*-tah kahr-*BOH*-neh)*	carbon copy
copiare (1)	*koh-p*YAH*-reh*	copy (imitate), to
coppia, *f.*	KOHP*-p_yah*	couple (pair, *n.*)
coprire (14)	*koh-*PREE*-reh*	cover, to
coraggio, *m.*	*koh-*RAHD*-joh*	courage
coraggioso	*koh-rahd-*JOH*-soh*	brave
corazzata, *f.*	*koh-raht-*TSAH*-tah*	battleship
corda, *f.*	KOHR*-dah*	cord (rope)
"	"	line
cordiale	*kohr-*D_YAH*-leh*	cordial (*adj.*)
"		hearty
cordone, *m.*	*kohr-*DOH*-neh*	curb (edge of street)
coricarsi (1)	*koh-ree-*KAHR*-see*	lie down, to
corno, *m.*	KOHR*-noh*	horn
coro, *m.*	KOH*-roh*	choir
corona, *f.*	*koh-*ROH*-nah*	crown
coronare (1)	*koh-roh-*NAH*-reh*	crown, to
corpo, *m.*	KOHR*-poh*	body (*anat.*)
corpulento	*kohr-poo-*LENN*-toh*	stout (corpulent)
corrente, *f.*	*kohr-*RENN*-teh*	current
"	"	stream (rivulet)
corrente d'aria, *f.*	*kohr-*RENN*-teh* DAH*-r_yah*	draft (air current)
correre (29)	KOHR*-reh-reh*	run, to
corretto	*kohr-*RETT*-toh*	correct
"		proper (acceptable)
corridoio, *m.*	*kohr-ree-*DOH*-yoh*	hall (corridor)
corriere, *m.*	*koh-*R_YEH*-reh*	mail (letters exchanged)
corrispondente, *m.,f.*	*kohr-ree-spohn-*DENN*-teh*	correspondent (letter writer)
corrispondenza, *f.*	*kohr-ree-spohn-*DENN*-tsah*	correspondence (letters)
corrispondere (87)	*kohr-ree-*SPOHN*-deh-reh*	correspond (agree), to
corrispondere con	*kohr-ree-*SPOHN*-deh-reh kohn*	correspond with (write to), to
corrompere (89)	*koh-*ROHM*-peh-reh*	bribe, to
corsa, *f.*	KOHR*-sah*	race (contest)
corsia, *f.*	*kohr-*SEE*-ah*	ward (sickroom)
corso, *m.*	KOHR*-soh*	avenue (street)
"	"	rate (exchange)
corte, *f.*	KOHR*-teh*	court (of ruler)
corteccia, *f.*	*kohr-*TETT*-chah*	bark (of tree)
cortese	*kohr-*TEH*-zeh*	courteous (polite)
cortesia, *f.*	*kohr-teh-*ZEE*-ah*	courtesy
cortile, *m.*	*kohr-*TEE*-leh*	yard (enclosure near house)
corto	KOHR*-toh*	short (not long)
corvo, *m.*	KOHR*-voh*	crow (bird)
cosa, *f.*	KOH*-sah*	thing (material object)
coscia, *f.*	KOH*-shah*	thigh
coscienza, *f.*	*koh-*SH_YENN*-tsah*	conscience
coscrizione, *f.*	*koh-skree-*TS_YOH*-neh*	draft (conscription)
così	*koh-*SEE	as (equally, *adv.*)
"	"	so (to such a degree, *adv.*)
"	"	thus
cosmetico, *m.* (*pl.* -ci)	*koh-*ZMEH*-tee-koh*	cosmetic (*n.*)
costa, *f.*	KOH*-stah*	coast (seaboard)
costante	*koh-*STAHN*-teh*	steady (regular)
costare (1)	*koh-*STAH*-reh*	cost, to
Costa Rica, *f.*	KOH*-stah* REE*-kah*	Costa Rica
costituire (3)	*koh-stee-*TWEE*-reh*	constitute (make up), to
costituzione, *f.*	*koh-stee-too-*TS_YOH*-neh*	constitution
costo, *m.*	KOH*-stoh*	cost (price)
costola, *f.*	KOH*-stoh-lah*	rib (*anat.*)
costoletta d'agnello, *f.*	*koh-stoh-*LETT*-tah dah-*N_YELL*-loh*	lamb chop
costoletta di maiale, *f.*	*koh-stoh-*LETT*-tah dee mah-*YAH*-leh*	pork chop
costoletta di vitello, *f.*	*koh-stoh-*LETT*-tah dee vee-*TELL*-loh*	veal chop
costoso	*koh-*STOH*-soh*	costly
"	"	expensive
costringere (107)	*koh-*STREEN*-jeh-reh*	compel, to

Italian	Pronunciation	English	Italian	Pronunciation	English
costruire (30)	koh-STRWEE-reh	construct, to	custode, m.	koo-STOH-deh	keeper (guard)
costruzione, f.	koh-stroo-TS_YOH-neh	construction (fabrication)	custodia, f.	koo-STOH-d_yah	care (custody)
"	"	structure (thing built)	custodire (3)	koo-stoh-DEE-reh	guard (watch over), to
costume, m.	koh-STOO-meh	costume	da	DAH	from
"	"	custom (habit)	"	"	since (after, prep.)
costume da bagno, m.	koh-STOO-meh dah BAH-n_yoh	bathing suit	da allora	dah ahl-LOH-rah	since (from then to now, adv.)
cotone, m.	koh-TOH-neh	cotton (boll)	da allora in poi	dah ahl-LOH-rah een POY	thereafter
cozzare (1)	koht-TSAH-reh	ram (butt), to	dadi, m. pl.	DAH-dee	dice (marked cubes)
crampo, m.	KRAHM-poh	cramp (med.)	dado, m.	DAH-doh	nut (mech.)
cranio, m.	KRAH-n_yoh	skull	daino, m.	DYE-noh	buck (male deer)
cravatta, f.	krah-VAHT-tah	tie (necktie)	danese	dah-NEH-seh	Danish (adj.)
creare (1)	kreh-AH-reh	create, to	Danimarca, f.	dah-nee-MAHR-kah	Denmark
creatura, f.	kreh-ah-TOO-rah	creature (living being)	dannare (1)	dahn-NAH-reh	damn, to
creazione, f.	kreh-ah-TS_YOH-neh	creation	danno, m.	DAHN-noh	damage (injury)
credenza, f.	kreh-DENN-tsah	cupboard	"	"	mischief (harm)
credere (2)	KREH-deh-reh	believe (accept), to	Danubio, m.	dah-NOO-b_yoh	Danube
credito, m.	KREH-dee-toh	credit (bus.)	danza, f.	DAHN-tsah	dance (movement to music)
creditore, m.	kreh-dee-TOH-reh	creditor (bus.)	dappertutto	dahp-pehr-TOOT-toh	everywhere
cremisino	kreh-mee-ZEE-noh	crimson	"	"	throughout (in every part of, prep.)
crepitare (1)	kreh-pee-TAH-reh	snap (crackle), to	dare (33)	DAH-reh	give (bestow), to
crepuscolo, m.	kreh-POO-skoh-loh	twilight	dare diritto	DAH-reh dee-REET-toh	entitle (give a right to), to
crescere (31)	KREH-sheh-reh	grow, to	dare in pegno	DAH-reh een PEH-n_yoh	pawn, to
crescita, f.	KREH-shee-tah	growth (development)	dare istruzioni (a)	DAH-reh ee-stroo-TS_YOH-nee (ah)	instruct (direct), to
crespa, f.	KREH-spah	ripple	dare un'occhiata	DAH-reh oo-nohk-K_YAH-tah	glance, to
criminale	kree-mee-NAH-leh	criminal (adj.)	darsi pensiero	DAHR-see penn-S_YEH-roh	fret (worry), to
criniera, f.	kree-N_YEH-rah	mane (of horse)	data, f.	DAH-tah	date (calendar designation)
crisi, f. (pl. crisi)	KREE-zee	crisis			
crisi economica, f.	KREE-zee eh-koh-NOH-mee-kah	depression (econ.)	dattero, m.	DAHT-teh-roh	date (dried fruit)
cristallo, m.	kree-STAHL-loh	crystal (min.)	dattilografo, m.	daht-tee-LOH-grah-foh	typist
cristiano, m.	kree-ST_YAH-noh	Christian (n.)	davanti	dah-VAHN-tee	ahead (in front)
Cristo, m.	KREE-stoh	Christ	"	"	before (adv.)
critica, f.	KREE-tee-kah	criticism	davanti, m.	dah-VAHN-tee	front (forward part)
critico, m.	KREE-tee-koh	critic	davanti a	dah-VAHN-tee ah	before (in front of, prep.)
croccante	krohk-KAHN-teh	crisp (brittle)			
croce, f.	KROH-cheh	cross (crucifix)	dazio, m.	DAH-ts_yoh	duty (tax)
crociera, f.	kroh-CH_YEH-rah	cruise (voyage)	"	"	tariff
crollare (1)	krohl-LAH-reh	collapse (cave in), to	debito, m.	DEH-bee-toh	debt
cromo, m.	KROH-moh	chromium	debitore, m.	deh-bee-TOH-reh	debtor (bus.)
cronaca, f.	KROH-nah-kah	chronicle	debole	DEH-boh-leh	faint (dim, adj.)
cronista, m.,f.	kroh-NEE-stah	reporter (journalist)	"	"	feeble
crosta, f.	KROH-stah	crust	"	"	weak
crudele	kroo-DEH-leh	cruel	debolezza, f.	deh-boh-LETT-tsah	weakness
Cuba, f.	KOO-bah	Cuba	decadenza, f.	deh-kah-DENN-tsah	decay
cubo, m.	KOO-boh	cube (geom.)	"	"	decline (deterioration)
cucchiaino, m.	kook-k_yah-EE-noh	spoon (teaspoon)			
cucchiaio, m.	kook-K_YAH-yoh	spoon (tablespoon)	decadere (21)	deh-kah-DEH-reh	decline (deteriorate), to
cucetta, f.	koo-CHETT-tah	berth (train bunk)	decente	deh-CHENN-teh	decent
cucina, f.	koo-CHEE-nah	kitchen	decidersi (34)	deh-CHEE-dehr-see	decide (make up one's mind), to
cucinare (1)	koo-chee-NAH-reh	cook (prepare meals), to	decisione, f.	deh-chee-S_YOH-neh	decision (judgment)
cucire (4)	koo-CHEE-reh	sew, to	declinare (1)	deh-klee-NAH-reh	decline (refuse), to
cucitura, f.	koo-chee-TOO-rah	seam (line of stiches)	decorare (1)	deh-koh-RAH-reh	decorate (adorn), to
cuculo, m.	KOO-koo-loh	cuckoo (bird)	decorazione, f.	deh-koh-rah-TS_YOH-neh	decoration
cugino, m.	koo-JEE-noh	cousin	decreto, m.	deh-KREH-toh	decree (edict)
cui	KOO-ee	that (rel. pron.)	dedicarsi (1)	deh-dee-KAHR-see	devote oneself, to
"	"	which (rel. pron.)	dedurre (7)	deh-DOO_R-reh	deduct, to
"	"	whom (rel. pron.)	deficienza, f.	deh-fee-CHENN-tsah	shortage (lack)
cui, il	eel KOO-ee	whose (rel. pron.)	deficit, m.	DEH-fee-cheet	deficit (bus.)
culla, f.	KOOL-lah	cradle	definire (3)	deh-fee-NEE-reh	define, to
cultura, f.	kool-TOO-rah	culture (refinement)	definito	deh-fee-NEE-toh	definite
cunetta, f.	koo-NETT-tah	gutter (of street)	deformarsi (1)	deh-fohr-MAHR-see	warp (become misshapen), to
cuocere (32)	KWOH-cheh-reh	cook (heat food), to	defunto	deh-FOON-toh	late (deceased, adj.)
cuocere al forno	KWOH-cheh-reh ahl FOHR-noh	bake (be cooking), to	del, dei, degli, della, delle, dell'	DELL, DAY, DEH-l_yee, DELL-lah, DELL-leh, DELL	any (a quantity of, adj.)
cuoco, m.	KWOH-koh	cook	"	"	some (a quantity of, adj.)
cuoio, m.	KWOH-yoh	leather (n.)	delegato, m.	deh-leh-GAH-toh	delegate
cuore, m.	KWOH-reh	heart	deliberato	deh-lee-beh-RAH-toh	deliberate (intentional)
cupola, f.	KOO-poh-lah	dome (cupola)			
cupone, m.	koo-POH-neh	coupon (detachable certificate)	deliberazione, f.	deh-lee-beh-rah-TS_YOH-neh	resolution (formal expression)
cura, f.	KOO-rah	care (concern)	delicato	deh-lee-KAH-toh	dainty
"	"	treatment (medical care)	"	"	delicate
curare (1)	koo-RAH-reh	nurse (give treatment to), to	delinquente, m.,f.	deh-leeng-KWENN-teh	criminal (n.)
curatore, m.	koo-rah-TOH-reh	curator			
curiosità, f.	koo-r_yoh-see-TAH	curiosity			
curioso	koo-R_YOH-soh	curious			
curva, f.	KOOR-vah	curve			
curvo	KOOR-voh	bent (curved)			
cuscinetto, m.	koo-shee-NETT-toh	pad (cushion)			
cuscino, m.	koo-SHEE-noh	cushion (pillow)			

Italian	Pronunciation	English
delirare (1)	*deh-lee-*RAH*-reh*	rave (rant), to
delitto,*m.*	*deh-*LEET*-toh*	crime
delizia,*f.*	*deh-*LEE*-ts_yah*	delight
delizioso	*deh-lee-*TS_YOH*-soh*	delicious
della (see **del**)		
delle (see **del**)		
deludere (6)	*deh-*LOO*-deh-reh*	deceive, to
"	"	disappoint, to
delusione,*f.*	*deh-loo-z_*YOH*-neh*	disappointment
democratico	*deh-moh-*KRAH*-tee-koh*	democratic
democratico,*m.*	*deh-moh-*KRAH*-tee-koh*	democrat
democrazia,*f.*	*deh-moh-krah-*TSEE*-ah*	democracy
denaro,*m.*	*deh-*NAH*-roh*	money
denso	DENN*-soh*	dense
dente,*m.*	DENN*-teh*	tooth
dentista,*m.*	*denn-*TEE*-stah*	dentist
dentro	DENN*-troh*	in (inside, *prep.*)
"	"	indoors (*adv.*)
"	"	inside (*adv., prep.*)
"	"	within (inside, *prep.*)
depositante,*m.,f.*	*deh-poh-zee-*TAHN*-teh*	depositor (*fin.*)
depositare (1)	*deh-poh-zee-*TAH*-reh*	deposit, to (*fin.*)
deposito,*m.*	*deh-*POH*-zee-toh*	deposit (money deposited)
depressione,*f.*	*deh-press-s_*YOH*-neh*	depression (sadness)
deputato,*m.*	*deh-poo-*TAH*-toh*	representative (deputy)
deridere (85)	*deh-*REE*-deh-reh*	mock (deride), to
derivare (1)	*deh-ree-*VAH*-reh*	derive (get), to
derrata,*f.*	*dehr-*RAH*-tah*	commodity
descrivere (96)	*deh-*SKREE*-veh-reh*	describe (portray), to
descrizione,*f.*	*deh-skree-*TS_YOH*-neh*	description (account)
deserto,*m.*	*deh-*ZEHR*-toh*	desert
"	"	wilderness
desiderabile	*deh-see-deh-*RAH*-bee-leh*	desirable
desiderare (1)	*deh-see-deh-*RAH*-reh*	desire, to
"	"	long for, to
"	"	wish for, to
desiderare ardentemente	*deh-see-deh-*RAH*-reh ahr-denn-teh-*MENN*-teh*	crave (desire), to
desiderio,*m.*	*deh-see-*DEH*-r_yoh*	desire
		wish
destare (1)	*deh-*STAH*-reh*	arouse (excite), to
"	"	rouse (awaken), to
destinatario,*m.*	*deh-stee-nah-*TAH*-r_yoh*	addressee
destinazione,*f.*	*deh-stee-nah-*TS_YOH*-neh*	destination
destino,*m.*	*deh-*STEE*-noh*	destiny
"	"	fate
destra,*f.*	DEH*-strah*	right (right-hand side)
destra, a	*ah* DEH*-strah*	right (to the right, *adv.*)
destrezza,*f.*	*deh-*STRETT*-tsah*	dexterity
destro	DEH*-stroh*	right (on the right, *adj.*)
detenere (112)	*deh-teh-*NEH*-reh*	reserve (withhold), to
determinare (1)	*deh-tehr-mee-*NAH*-reh*	determine (ascertain), to
determinarsi	*deh-tehr-mee-*NAHR*-see*	determine (make up one's mind), to
determinazione,*f.*	*deh-tehr-mee-nah-*TS_YOH*-neh*	determination (fixed intent)
dettagliante,*m.,f.*	*dett-tah-*L_YAHN*-teh*	retailer (*bus.*)
dettaglio,*m.*	*dett-*TAH*-l_yoh*	detail
"	"	item
"	"	particular (*n.*)
"	"	retail (*bus., n.*)
dettare (1)	*dett-*TAH*-reh*	dictate, to
deviamento,*m.*	*deh-v_yah-*MENN*-toh*	departure (deviation)
deviare (1)	*deh-v_*YAH*-reh*	deviate (diverge), to
deviazione,*f.*	*deh-v_yah-ts_*YOH*-neh*	detour
devozione,*f.*	*deh-voh-*TS_YOH*-neh*	devotion (loyal attachment)
di	DEE	of
diabete,*m.*	*dee ah-*BEH*-teh*	diabetes
diagramma,*m.*	*dee-ah-*GRAHM*-mah*	chart (graph)
diamante,*m.*	*dee-ah-*MAHN*-teh*	diamond (gem)
diametro,*m.*	*dee-*AH*-meh-troh*	diameter
diavolo,*m.*	D_YAH*-voh-loh*	devil
dibattito,*m.*	*dee-*BAHT*-tee-toh*	debate
dichiarare (1)	*dee-k_yah-*RAH*-reh*	declare, to
"	"	pronounce, to
"	"	state (say), to

Italian	Pronunciation	English
dichiarazione,*f.*	*dee-k_yah-rah-*TS_YOH*-neh*	declaration (announcement)
"	"	statement
dieta,*f.*	D_YEH*-tah*	diet (restricted food allowance)
dietro, di	*dee* D_YEH*-troh*	behind (in the rear, *adv.*)
"	"	rear (*adj.*)
dietro a	D_YEH*-troh ah*	behind (*prep.*)
difendere (35)	*dee-*FENN*-deh-reh*	defend (protect), to
difesa,*f.*	*dee-*FEH*-sah*	defense
difetto,*m.*	*dee-*FEHT*-toh*	defect (flaw)
"	"	fault
differente	*deef-feh-*RENN*-teh*	different (unlike)
differenza,*f.*	*deef-feh-*RENN*-tsah*	difference (dissimilarity)
differire (3)	*deef-feh-*REE*-reh*	delay (postpone), to
"	"	differ (be unlike), to
difficile	*deef-*FEE*-chee-leh*	difficult
"	"	hard
difficoltà,*f.*	*deef-fee-kohl-*TAH	difficulty
diffusione,*f.*	*deef-foo-z_*YOH*-neh*	circulation (dissemination)
difterite,*f.*	*deef-teh-*REE*-teh*	diphtheria
digerire (3)	*dee-jeh-*REE*-reh*	digest, to
dignità,*f.*	*dee-n_yee-*TAH	dignity
dilettare (1)	*dee-lett-*TAH*-reh*	delight (give pleasure to), to
dilettevole	*dee-lett-*TEH*-voh-leh*	delightful
diligente	*dee-lee-*JENN*-teh*	diligent
diligenza,*f.*	*dee-lee-*JENN*-tsah*	diligence
dimensione,*f.*	*dee-menn-s_*YOH*-neh*	size (magnitude)
dimenticare (1)	*dee-menn-tee-*KAH*-reh*	forget, to
dimenticato	*dee-menn-tee-*KAH*-toh*	forgotten
dimettersi (60)	*dee-*METT*-tehr-see*	resign (tender resignation), to
diminuire (3)	*dee-mee-*NWEE*-reh*	diminish (make smaller), to
"	"	lessen (make less), to
diminuzione,*f.*	*dee-mee-noo-ts_*YOH*-neh*	decrease
dimorare (1)	*dee-moh-*RAH*-reh*	abide (stay), to
"	"	dwell (reside), to
dimostrare (1)	*dee-moh-*STRAH*-reh*	demonstrate (show), to
dimostrazione,*f.*	*dee-moh-strah-*TS_YOH*-neh*	demonstration (proof)
dintorni,*m.pl.*	*deen-*TOHR*-nee*	surroundings
Dio,*m.*	DEE*-oh*	God
dipendente	*dee-penn-*DENN*-teh*	dependent (reliant)
dipendere da (13)	*dee-*PENN*-deh-reh dah*	depend (be contingent) on, to
dipingere (73)	*dee-*PEEN*-jeh-reh*	paint, to
dire (36)	DEE*-reh*	say, to
direttamente	*dee-rett-tah-*MENN*-teh*	straight (directly, *adv.*)
direttore,*m.*	*dee-rett-*TOH*-reh*	conductor (*mus.*)
"	"	director
"	"	manager (administrator)
direzione,*f.*	*dee-reh-*TS_YOH*-neh*	direction (course)
"	"	leadership (authority)
"	"	management administration
dirigere (37)	*dee-*REE*-jeh-reh*	control, to
"	"	direct, to
diritto	*dee-*REET*-toh*	straight (not crooked, *adj.*)
diritto,*m.*	*dee-*REET*-toh*	right (claim)
disastro,*m.*	*dee-*ZAH*-stroh*	disaster
discendente,*m.,f.*	*dee-shenn-*DENN*-teh*	descendant (offspring)
discendere (93)	*dee-*SHENN*-deh-reh*	descend (move downward), to
discernimento,*m.*	*dee-shehr-nee-*MENN*-toh*	judgment (estimation)
disciplina,*f.*	*dee-shee-*PLEE*-nah*	discipline (training)
disco,*m.*	DEE*-skoh*	record (disk)
discorso,*m.*	*dee-*SKOHR*-soh*	address
"	"	speech
discussione,*f.*	*dee-skooss-s_*YOH*-neh*	discussion
discutere (38)	*dee-*SKOO*-teh-reh*	discuss, to
disegnare (1)	*dee-seh-n_*YAH*-reh*	draw (sketch), to
disegni a fumetti, *m.pl.*	*dee-*SEH*-n_yee ah foo-*METT*-tee*	comic strip

Italian	Pronunciation	English
disegno, m.	dee-SEH-n_yoh	design
"	"	drawing (sketch)
"	"	illustration (pictorial representation)
"	"	pattern
disfarsi di (51)	dee-SFAHR-see dee	dispose of (put away), to
disgraziato, m.	dee-zgrah-TS_YAH-toh	wretch (hapless person)
disgusto, m.	dee-ZGOO-stoh	disgust
disinvolto	dee-zeen-VOHL-toh	casual (offhand)
disobbedire (3)	dee-zohb-beh-DEE-reh	disobey, to
disoccupazione, f.	dee-zohk-koo-pah-TS_YOH-neh	unemployment
disonore, m.	dee-zoh-NOH-reh	dishonor
disordine, m.	dee-ZOHR-dee-neh	disorder (confusion)
disotto	dee-SOHT-toh	underneath (prep.)
dispaccio, m.	dee-SPAHT-choh	dispatch (communication)
disperare (1)	dee-speh-RAH-reh	despair, to
disperato	dee-speh-RAH-toh	desperate
"	"	hopeless
disperazione, f.	dee-speh-rah-TS_YOH-neh	despair (hopelessness)
dispetto, m.	dee-SPETT-toh	spite (ill will)
...dispiacere a (imp.) (71)	...dee-sp_yah-CHEH-reh ah	sorry, to be
disponibile	dee-spoh-NEE-bee-leh	available
disporre (76)	dee-SPOHR-reh	arrange (place), to
disposizione, f.	dee-spoh-zee-TS_YOH-neh	arrangement (order)
"	"	bent (penchant)
"	"	disposition
disposto	dee-SPOH-stoh	willing (favorably disposed)
disprezzare (1)	dee-sprett-TSAH-reh	despise, to
"	"	scorn, to
disprezzo, m.	dee-SPRETT-tsoh	contempt
"	"	scorn
disputa, f.	DEE-spoo-tah	argument
"	"	dispute
dissenteria, f.	dees-senn-teh-REE-ah	dysentery
dissimile	dees-SEE-mee-leh	unlike (adj.)
distante	dee-STAHN-teh	distant (far-off)
distanza, f.	dee-STAHN-tsah	distance
distinguere (39)	dee-STEENG-gweh-reh	distinguish (differentiate), to
distinto	dee-STEEN-toh	distinct
"	"	distinguished (notable)
distinzione, f.	dee-steen-TS_YOH-neh	distinction
distrarre (116)	dee-STRAHR-reh	distract (divert), to
distretto, m.	dee-STRETT-toh	district (locality)
distribuire (3)	dee-stree-BWEE-reh	distribute (allot), to
distributore, m.	dee-stree-boo-TOH-reh	dealer (trader)
distribuzione, f.	dee-stree-boo-TS_YOH-neh	distribution
distruggere (108)	dee-STROOD-jeh-reh	destroy (demolish), to
distruzione, f.	dee-stroo-TS_YOH-neh	destruction (demolition)
disturbare (1)	dee-stoor-BAH-reh	disturb, to
"	"	trouble (disquiet), to
dito, m.	DEE-toh	finger
dito del piede, m.	DEE-toh del P_YEH-deh	toe
ditta, f.	DEET-tah	company (bus.)
"	"	concern
"	"	firm
diventare (1)	dee-venn-TAH-reh	become, to
diverso	dee-VEHR-soh	various
divertimento, m.	dee-vehr-tee-MENN-toh	amusement
divertire (4)	dee-vehr-TEE-reh	amuse, to
"	"	entertain, to
dividendo, m.	dee-vee-DENN-doh	dividend (bus.)
dividere (40)	dee-VEE-deh-reh	divide, to (arith.)
"	"	divide (make separate), to
"	"	sever, to
dividersi	dee-VEE-dehr-see	divide (become separate), to
divino	dee-VEE-noh	divine (adj.)
divisione, f.	dee-vee-z_YOH-neh	division
divorare (1)	dee-voh-RAH-reh	devour (eat), to
divorzio, m.	dee-VOHR-ts_yoh	divorce (law)
dizionario, m.	dee-ts_yoh-NAH-r_yoh	dictionary
doccia, f.	DOHT-chah	shower (bath)
documento, m.	doh-koo-MENN-toh	document

Italian	Pronunciation	English
dogana, f.	doh-GAH-nah	customhouse
"	"	customs (tax)
dolce	DOHL-cheh	sweet (pleasant tasting)
dolce, m.	DOHL-cheh	dessert
dolcezza, f.	dohl-CHETT-tsah	sweetness
dolci, m. pl.	DOHL-chee	candy
dolere (41)	doh-LEH-reh	ache, to
"	"	hurt (be painful), to
dolore, m.	doh-LOH-reh	ache
"	"	pain
"	"	sorrow (sadness)
"	"	woe
doloroso	doh-loh-ROH-soh	painful
domanda, f.	doh-MAHN-dah	application (request)
"	"	demand
"	"	inquiry
"	"	question (query)
domandare (1)	doh-mahn-DAH-reh	inquire, to
domandare la mano (di)	doh-mahn-DAH-reh lah MAH-noh (dee)	propose (offer marriage), to
domandarsi	doh-mahn-DAHR-see	wonder (ask oneself), to
domani	doh-MAH-nee	tomorrow
domare (1)	doh-MAH-reh	subdue (conquer), to
Domenica delle Palme, f.	doh-MEH-nee-kah dell-leh PAHL-meh	Palm Sunday
domestico	doh-MEH-stee-koh	domestic (household, adj.)
"	"	tame
domestico, m.	doh-MEH-stee-koh	servant (in a household)
dominio, m.	doh-MEE-n_yoh	dominion
"	"	rule (political control)
"	"	sway (influence)
donare (1)	doh-NAH-reh	donate, to
donna, f.	DOHN-nah	woman
dono, m.	DOH-noh	gift (present)
dopo	DOH-poh	after (prep.)
"	"	afterward (later)
dopo che	DOH-poh keh	after (conj.)
doppio	DOHP-p_yoh	double (adj.)
dormire (4)	dohr-MEE-reh	sleep, to
dorso, m.	DOHR-soh	back (n.)
dose, f.	DOH-zeh	dose (med.)
dottore, m.	doht-TOH-reh	doctor
dottrina, f.	doht-TREE-nah	doctrine
dove	DOH-veh	where
dovere (42)	doh-VEH-reh	must (v.)
"	"	ought (v.)
"	"	owe, to
"	"	should (v.)
dovere, m.	doh-VEH-reh	duty (obligation)
dovunque	doh-VOONG-kweh	wherever (at, in whatever place)
dovuto	doh-VOO-toh	due (proper)
dozzina, f.	dohd-DZEE-nah	dozen
drago, m.	DRAH-goh	dragon
dramma, m.	DRAHM-mah	drama
dubbio, m.	DOOB-b_yoh	doubt
dubbioso	doob-B_YOH-soh	doubtful
dubitare (1)	doo-bee-TAH-reh	doubt (be uncertain about), to
due punti, m. pl.	doo-eh POON-tee	colon (punct.)
due volte	doo-eh VOHL-teh	twice
dunque	DOONG-kweh	so (therefore, adv.)
duplicato, m.	doo-plee-KAH-toh	duplicate (copy, n.)
durante	doo-RAHN-teh	during
"	"	in (during, prep.)
durante tutto	doo-RAHN-teh TOOT-toh	throughout (from start to finish of, prep.)
durare (1)	doo-RAH-reh	last (continue), to
durata, f.	doo-RAH-tah	duration
duro	DOO-roh	grim (stern)
"	"	hard (not soft)
e	EH	and
ebbene	ebb-BEH-neh	well (and then?, interj.)
ebreo	eh-BREH-oh	Hebrew (adj.)
"	"	Jewish (adj.)
ebreo, m.	eh-BREH-oh	Jew (n.)
eccedere (2)	ett-CHEH-deh-reh	exceed, to

Italian	Pronunciation	English
eccellente	*ett-chell-*LENN-*teh*	excellent
eccessivo	*ett-chess-*SEE-*voh*	excessive
eccesso,*m.*	*ett-*CHESS-*soh*	excess
eccezione,*f.*	*ett-cheh-*TS_YOH-*neh*	exception (unusual case)
eccitare (1)	*ett-chee-*TAH-*reh*	excite, to
eccitazione,*f.*	*ett-chee-tah-*TS_YOH-*neh*	excitement
eco,*m.*	EH-*koh*	echo
economia,*f.*	*eh-koh-noh-*MEE-*ah*	economy
economico	*eh-koh-*NOH-*mee-koh*	economical (thrifty)
economizzare (1)	*eh-koh-noh-meed-*DZAH-*reh*	save (store up), to
ed	*edd*	and
edera,*f.*	EH-*deh-rah*	ivy
edicola,*f.*	*eh-*DEE-*koh-lah*	newsstand
Edimburgo	*eh-deem-*BOOR-*goh*	Edinburgh
editore,*m.*	*eh-dee-*TOH-*reh*	publisher
edizione,*f.*	*eh-dee-*TS_YOH-*neh*	edition
educare (1)	*eh-doo-*KAH-*reh*	educate, to
educazione,*f.*	*eh-doo-kah-*TS_YOH-*neh*	education (schooling process)
effetto,*m.*	*ehf-*FETT-*toh*	effect
efficace	*ehf-fee-*KAH-*cheh*	effective (effectual)
"	"	efficient (producing desired results)
Egitto,*m.*	*eh-*JEET-*toh*	Egypt
egiziano	*eh-jee-*TS_YAH-*noh*	Egyptian (*adj.*)
egli	EH-*l_yee*	he
egoistico	*eh-goh-*EE-*stee-koh*	selfish
eguagliare (1)	*eh-gwah-*L_YAH-*reh*	match (equal), to
eguale	*eh-*GWAH-*leh*	equal (*adj.*)
elastico	*eh-*LAH-*stee-koh*	elastic (springy)
elefante,*m.*	*eh-leh-*FAHN-*teh*	elephant
elegante	*eh-leh-*GAHN-*teh*	artistic (tasteful)
"	"	smart (chic)
eleggere (59)	*eh-*LEDD-*jeh-reh*	elect, to
elementare	*eh-leh-menn-*TAH-*reh*	elementary (rudimentary)
elemento,*m.*	*eh-leh-*MENN-*toh*	element
elettricità,*f.*	*eh-lett-tree-chee-*TAH	electricity
elettrico	*eh-*LETT-*tree-koh*	electric
elettronica,*f.*	*eh-lett-*TROH-*nee-kah*	electronics
elevare (1)	*eh-leh-*VAH-*reh*	elevate (lift up), to
elevato	*eh-leh-*VAH-*toh*	lofty (high)
elezione,*f.*	*eh-leh-*TS_YOH-*neh*	election
elicottero,*m.*	*eh-lee-*KOHT-*teh-roh*	helicopter
eliminare (1)	*eh-lee-mee-*NAH-*reh*	eliminate, to
ella	ELL-*lah*	she
elmetto,*m.*	*ell-*METT-*toh*	helmet
eloquente	*eh-loh-*KWENN-*teh*	eloquent
emendamento,*f.*	*eh-menn-dah-*MENN-*toh*	amendment (enacted change)
emergenza,*f.*	*eh-mehr-*JENN-*tsah*	emergency (*n.*)
emergere (44)	*eh-*MEHR-*jeh-reh*	emerge, to
eminente	*eh-mee-*NENN-*teh*	prominent (eminent)
emisfero,*m.*	*eh-mee-*SFEH-*roh*	hemisphere (*geog.*)
emorragia,*f.*	*eh-mohr-rah-*JEE-*ah*	hemorrhage
emozione,*f.*	*eh-moh-*TS_YOH-*neh*	emotion
empire (3)	*emm-*PEE-*reh*	fill (make full), to
enciclopedia,*f.*	*enn-chee-kloh-peh-*DEE-*ah*	encyclopaedia
energia,*f.*	*eh-nehr-*JEE-*ah*	energy
enigma,*m.*	*eh-*NEE-*gmah*	puzzle (game)
enorme	*eh-*NOHR-*meh*	enormous
"	"	huge
entrambi	*enn-*TRAHM-*bee*	both (*pron.*)
entrare in (1)	*enn-*TRAH-*reh een*	enter (come or go into), to
"	"	enter (join), to
entrata,*f.*	*enn-*TRAH-*tah*	entrance
"	"	income
entrate pubbliche, *f.pl.*	*enn-*TRAH-*teh* POOB-*blee-keh*	revenue (*govt.*)
entro	ENN-*troh*	within (in less time than, *prep.*)
entusiasmo,*m.*	*enn-too-*Z_YAH-*zmoh*	enthusiasm
epidemia,*f.*	*eh-pee-deh-*MEE-*ah*	epidemic
Equatore,*m.*	*eh-kwah-*TOH-*reh*	Ecuador
equilibrio,*m.*	*eh-kwee-*LEE-*br_yoh*	balance (equilibrium)
equipaggiamento, *m.*	*eh-kwee-pahd-jah-*MENN-*toh*	outfit
equipaggio,*m.*	*eh-kwee-*PAHD-*joh*	crew
erba,*f.*	EHR-*bah*	grass
"	"	herb

Italian	Pronunciation	English
erbaccia,*f.*	*ehr-*BAHT-*chah*	weed
erede,*m.,f.*	*eh-*REH-*deh*	heir
eredità,*f.*	*eh-reh-dee-*TAH	heredity
ereditare (1)	*eh-reh-dee-*TAH-*reh*	inherit, to
eretto	*eh-*RETT-*toh*	erect (*adj.*)
erigere (37)	*eh-*REE-*jeh-reh*	erect (build), to
eroe,*m.*	*eh-*ROH-*eh*	hero
eroina,*f.*	*eh-roh-*EE-*nah*	heroine
errare (1)	*ehr-*RAH-*reh*	err, to
"	"	roam, to
"	"	stray, to
erroneo	*ehr-*ROH-*neh-oh*	false (erroneous)
"	"	incorrect
errore,*m.*	*ehr-*ROH-*reh*	error
erto	EHR-*toh*	steep (*adj.*)
esagerare (1)	*eh-zah-jeh-*RAH-*reh*	exaggerate, to
esalare (1)	*eh-zah-*LAH-*reh*	blow (breathe out), to
esaltare (1)	*eh-zahl-*TAH-*reh*	exalt, to
esame,*m.*	*eh-*ZAH-*meh*	examination
"	"	survey (inspection)
"	"	test (*educ.*)
esaminare (1)	*eh-zah-mee-*NAH-*reh*	examine (investigate), to
esatto	*eh-*ZAHT-*toh*	exact (precise)
"	"	right (correct)
esaurire (3)	*eh-zow-*REE-*reh*	exhaust (use up), to
esca,*f.*	EH-*skah*	bait (for animals)
esclamare (1)	*eh-sklah-*MAH-*reh*	exclaim, to
esclamazione,*f.*	*eh-sklah-mah-*TS_YOH-*neh*	exclamation (*n.*)
escludere (6)	*eh-*SKLOO-*deh-reh*	exclude, to
esclusivo	*eh-skloo-*SEE-*voh*	exclusive (not including)
esecutivo	*eh-zeh-koo-*TEE-*voh*	executive (*adj.*)
esecuzione,*f.*	*eh-zeh-koo-*TS_YOH-*neh*	performance (action)
eseguire (3)	*eh-zeh-*GWEE-*reh*	execute (carry out), to
esempio,*m.*	*eh-*ZEMM-*p_yoh*	example
"	"	instance
esemplare,*m.*	*eh-zemm-*PLAH-*reh*	copy (of a publication)
esente	*eh-*ZENN-*teh*	exempt
esente da dazio	*eh-*ZENN-*teh dah* DAH-*ts_yoh*	duty-free
esequie,*f.pl.*	*eh-*ZEH-*kw_yeh*	funeral
esercitare (1)	*eh-zehr-chee-*TAH-*reh*	exercise (employ), to
esercito,*m.*	*eh-*ZEHR-*chee-toh*	army
esercizio,*m.*	*eh-zehr-*CHEE-*ts_yoh*	exercise (drill)
"	"	practice (performance)
esercizio fisico,*m.*	*eh-zehr-*CHEE-*ts_yoh* FEE-*zee-koh*	exercise (physical exertion)
esibire (3)	*eh-zee-*BEE-*reh*	display, to
"	"	exhibit, to
esilio,*m.*	*eh-*ZEE-*l_yoh*	exile (banishment)
esistenza,*f.*	*eh-zee-*STENN-*tsah*	existence
esistere (16)	*eh-*ZEE-*steh-reh*	exist, to
esitare (1)	*eh-zee-*TAH-*reh*	hesitate, to
espandere (101)	*eh-*SPAHN-*deh-reh*	expand (make larger), to
espellere (47)	*eh-*SPELL-*leh-reh*	expel (eject), to
esperienza,*f.*	*eh-speh-*R_YENN-*tsah*	experience (conscious event)
esperimentato	*eh-speh-ree-menn-*TAH-*toh*	veteran (experienced)
esperimento,*m.*	*eh-speh-ree-*MENN-*toh*	experiment
esperto,*m.*	*eh-*SPEHR-*toh*	expert (*n.*)
esplorare (1)	*eh-sploh-*RAH-*reh*	explore, to
esploratore,*m.*	*eh-sploh-rah-*TOH-*reh*	destroyer (ship)
esploratore,*m.*	*eh-sploh-rah-*TOH-*reh*	scout (lookout)
esplosivo,*m.*	*eh-sploh-*SEE-*voh*	explosive (*n.*)
esporre (76)	*eh-*SPOHR-*reh*	expose, to
esportare (1)	*eh-spohr-*TAH-*reh*	export, to
esportatore,*m.*	*eh-spohr-tah-*TOH-*reh*	exporter
esportazione,*f.*	*eh-spohr-tah-*TS_YOH-*neh*	exportation
esposizione,*f.*	*eh-spoh-zee-*TS_YOH-*neh*	exhibition (exposition)
espressione,*f.*	*eh-spress-*S_YOH-*neh*	expression
esprimere (26)	*eh-*SPREE-*meh-reh*	express (state), to
essa	ESS-*sah*	it, her
essa stessa	ESS-*sah* STESS-*sah*	itself, herself
esse	ESS-*seh*	they

Italian	Pronunciation	English
essenziale	*ess-senn-*TS_YAH*-leh*	essential (*adj.*)
"	"	vital
essere (49)	ESS-*seh-reh*	be, to
essere a capo di	ESS-*seh-reh* ah KAH-*poh dee*	head (lead), to
essere d'accordo	ESS-*seh-reh dah-*KOHR-*doh*	agree (concur), to
essere d'accordo, non	*nohn* ESS-*seh-reh dah-*KOHR-*doh*	disagree (differ), to
essere d'accordo con	ESS-*seh-reh dah-*KOHR-*doh kohn*	agree with, to
essere incandescente	ESS-*seh-reh een-kahn-deh-*SHENN-*teh*	glow (shine), to
essere presentato a	ESS-*seh-reh preh-zenn-*TAH-*toh ah*	meet (be introduced to), to
essere prevalente	ESS-*seh-reh preh-vah-*LENN-*teh*	prevail (exist widely), to
essi	ESS-*see*	they
esso	ESS-*soh*	it
esso stesso	ESS-*soh* STESS-*soh*	itself
est, *m.*	EST	east
estate, *f.*	*eh-*STAH-*teh*	summer (*n.*)
estendere (111)	*eh-*STENN-*deh-reh*	extend (enlarge), to
estendersi	*eh-*STENN-*dehr-see*	run (extend), to
estensione, *f.*	*eh-stenn-*S_YOH-*neh*	extension
"	"	extent (magnitude)
"	"	span (spread)
esteriore	*eh-steh-*R_YOH-*reh*	outer
esterno	*eh-*STEHR-*noh*	exterior (*adj.*)
"	"	outside (*adj.*)
estero, all'	*ahl-*LEH-*steh-roh*	abroad (in foreign land)
esteso	*eh-*STEH-*soh*	extensive
estinguere (39)	*eh-*STEEN-*gweh-reh*	quench, to
estraneo, *m.*	*eh-*STRAH-*neh-oh*	stranger (unknown person)
estratto di conto, *m.*	*eh-*STRAHT-*toh dee* KOHN-*toh*	statement (accounting, *bus.*)
estremo	*eh-*STREH-*moh*	extreme
età, *f.*	*eh-*TAH	age (accumulated years)
eterno	*eh-*TEHR-*noh*	eternal
etichetta, *f.*	*eh-tee-*KETT-*tah*	label
Europa, *f.*	*eh_oo-*ROH-*pah*	Europe
europeo	*eh_oo-roh-*PEH-*oh*	European (*adj.*)
evento, *m.*	*eh-*VENN-*toh*	event (happening)
evidente	*eh-vee-*DENN-*teh*	apparent (obvious)
"	"	evident
evidenza, *f.*	*eh-vee-*DENN-*tsah*	evidence (indication)
evitare (1)	*eh-vee-*TAH-*reh*	avoid, to
ex combattente, *m.*	*ex kohm-baht-*TENN-*teh*	veteran (*mil.*, *n.*)
fa	FAH	ago (past, *adj.*)
fabbrica, *f.*	FAHB-*bree-kah*	factory
fabbricante, *m.*, *f.*	*fahb-bree-*KAHN-*teh*	manufacturer
fabbricare (1)	*fahb-bree-*KAH-*reh*	build, to
"	"	manufacture, to
fabbricato, *m.*	*fahb-bree-*KAH-*toh*	building
fabbro ferraio, *m.*	FAHB-*broh fehr-*RAH-*yoh*	blacksmith
faccia, *f.*	FAHT-*chah*	face (*anat.*)
faccia a, in	*een* FAHT-*chah ah*	opposite (*prep.*)
facile	FAH-*chee-leh*	easy (not difficult)
facilità, *f.*	*fah-chee-lee-*TAH	ease (effortlessness)
facoltà, *f.*	*fah-kohl-*TAH	faculty (ability)
Facoltà, *f.*	*fah-kohl-*TAH	faculty (teaching staff)
faggio, *m.*	FAHD-*joh*	beech (tree)
fagiolino, *m.*	*fah-joh-*LEE-*noh*	bean (string bean)
falco, *m.*	FAHL-*koh*	hawk
falegname, *m.*	*fah-leh-*N_YAH-*meh*	carpenter
fallimento, *m.*	*fahl-lee-*MENN-*toh*	bankruptcy
"	"	failure (*bus.*)
falso	FAHL-*soh*	false (deceitful)
fama, *f.*	FAH-*mah*	fame
fame, *f.*	FAH-*meh*	hunger
famiglia, *f.*	*fah-*MEE-*l_yah*	family
"	"	household
familiare	*fah-mee-*L_YAH-*reh*	familiar (intimate)
famoso	*fah-*MOH-*soh*	famous
fanciulla, *f.*	*fahn-*CHOOL-*lah*	maiden
fango, *m.*	FAHNG-*goh*	mire (bog)
"	"	mud
fantasia, *f.*	*fahn-tah-*ZEE-*ah*	fancy (fantasy)

Italian	Pronunciation	English
fare (51)	FAH-*reh*	do, to
"	"	make, to
fare compere	FAH-*reh* KOHM-*peh-reh*	shop, to
fare della pubblicità	FAH-*reh dell-lah poob-blee-chee-*TAH	advertise (sponsor advertising), to
fare entrare	FAH-*reh enn-*TRAH-*reh*	tuck (slip inside), to
fare funzionare	FAH-*reh foon-ts_yoh-*NAH-*reh*	operate (handle), to
fare il pugilato	FAH-*reh eel poo-jee-*LAH-*toh*	box (fight), to
fare la corte a	FAH-*reh lah* KOHR-*teh ah*	woo, to
fare male a	FAH-*reh* MAH-*leh ah*	hurt (inflict pain upon), to
fare schiudere	FAH-*reh* SK_YOO-*deh-reh*	hatch, to
fare un inchino	FAH-*reh oon een-*KEE-*noh*	bow (in greeting), to
fare un passo	FAH-*reh oon* PAHSS-*soh*	step, to
fare un rapporto (di)	FAH-*reh oon rahp-*POHR-*toh (dee)*	report (account formally), to
fare volare	FAH-*reh voh-*LAH-*reh*	blow (make move), to
farfalla, *f.*	*fahr-*FAHL-*lah*	butterfly
far girare	FAHR *jee-*RAH-*reh*	turn (make rotate), to
"	"	whirl (make revolve), to
farina, *f.*	*fah-*REE-*nah*	flour
farmacia, *f.*	*fahr-mah-*CHEE-*ah*	pharmacy (drug store)
farmacista, *m.*	*fahr-mah-*CHEE-*stah*	pharmacist
far male a	FAHR MAH-*leh ah*	hurt (inflict pain upon), to
far saltare	FAHR *sahl-*TAH-*reh*	blast (explode), to
farsi grande	FAHR-*see* GRAHN-*deh*	grow up (mature), to
farsi la barba	FAHR-*see lah* BAHR-*bah*	shave (oneself), to
far tacere	*fahr tah-*CHEH-*reh*	hush (make quiet), to
fascetta, *f.*	*fah-*SHETT-*tah*	girdle (corset)
Fascismo, *m*	*fah-*SHEE-*zmoh*	Fascism
fase, *f.*	FAH-*zeh*	phase
"	"	stage (period)
fata, *f.*	FAH-*tah*	fairy (*n.*)
fatale	*fah-*TAH-*leh*	fatal (fateful)
fatica, *f.*	*fah-*TEE-*kah*	fatigue
fatica, *f.*	*fah-*TEE-*kah*	labor (exertion)
"	"	trouble (exertion)
fattezza, *f.*	*faht-*TETT-*tsah*	feature (part of face)
fatto, *m.*	FAHT-*toh*	fact
fattore, *m.*	*faht-*TOH-*reh*	factor (element)
fattura, *f.*	*faht-*TOO-*rah*	bill
"	"	invoice
favella, *f.*	*fah-*VELL-*lah*	speech (oral expression)
favola, *f.*	FAH-*voh-lah*	fable
"	"	fairy tale
favore, *m.*	*fah-*VOH-*reh*	favor
favorevole	*fah-voh-*REH-*voh-leh*	favorable
favorito	*fah-voh-*REE-*toh*	favorite (*adj.*)
fazzoletto, *m.*	*faht-tsoh-*LETT-*toh*	handkerchief
febbre, *f.*	FEBB-*breh*	fever
febbre gialla, *f.*	FEBB-*breh* JAHL-*lah*	yellow fever
fede, *f.*	FEH-*deh*	faith (creed)
fedele	*feh-*DEH-*leh*	faithful (loyal)
fedeltà, *f.*	*feh-dehl-*TAH	allegiance
federale	*feh-deh-*RAH-*leh*	federal
fegato, *m.*	FEH-*gah-toh*	liver (*anat.*)
felce, *f.*	FELL-*cheh*	fern
felice	*feh-*LEE-*cheh*	happy (glad)
"	"	successful
felicità, *f.*	*feh-lee-chee-*TAH	bliss
"	"	happiness
feltro, *m.*	FELL-*troh*	felt (*n.*)
femmina, *f.*	FEMM-*mee-nah*	female (*zool.*, *n.*)
femminile	*femm-mee-*NEE-*leh*	female (*adj.*)
"	"	feminine
fendere (52)	FENN-*deh-reh*	crack (make split), to
"	"	split (rend), to
ferire (3)	*feh-*REE-*reh*	injure, to
"	"	wound, to
ferita, *f.*	*feh-*REE-*tah*	injury
"	"	wound
fermare (1)	*fehr-*MAH-*reh*	stop (make halt), to

Italian	Pronunciation	English
fermarsi	*fehr*-MAHR-*see*	halt (come to a stop), to
"	"	stop (come to a standstill), to
fermata, *f.*	*fehr*-MAH-*tah*	stop (halt)
fermo	FEHR-*moh*	firm (*adj.*)
"	"	steady
feroce	*feh*-ROH-*cheh*	fierce
ferro, *m.*	FEHR-*roh*	iron (metal)
ferro elettrico (per stirare), *m.*	FEHR-*roh eh*-LETT-*tree-koh (pehr stee*-RAH-*reh)*	iron, electric
ferrovia, *f.*	*fehr-roh*-VEE-*ah*	railroad
fertile	FEHR-*tee-leh*	fertile
fessura, *f.*	*fehss*-SOO-*rah*	crack (fissure)
festa pubblica, *f.*	FEH-*stah* POOB-*blee-kah*	festival
fetta, *f.*	FETT-*tah*	slice
fiamma, *f.*	F_YAHM-*mah*	flame
fiammeggiare (1)	*f_yahm-medd*-JAH-*reh*	blaze (burn brightly), to
fiammifero, *m.*	*f_yahm*-MEE-*feh-roh*	match (lucifer)
fiato, *m.*	F_YAH-*toh*	breath
fico, *m.*	FEE-*koh*	fig
fidanzamento, *m.*	*fee-dahn-tsah*-MENN-*toh*	engagement (betrothal)
fidarsi di (1)	*fee*-DAHR-*see dee*	trust (rely on), to
fiducia, *f.*	*fee*-DOO-*chah*	faith
"	"	trust (confidence)
fieno, *m.*	F_YEH-*noh*	hay
figlia, *f.*	FEE-*l_yah*	daughter
figliastra, *f.*	*fee*-L_YAH-*strah*	stepdaughter
figliastro, *m.*	*fee*-L_YAH-*stroh*	stepson
figlio, *m.*	FEE-*l_yoh*	son
figlio adottivo, *m.*	FEE-*l_yoh ah-doht*-TEE-*voh*	foster child
figurarsi (1)	*fee-goo*-RAHR-*see*	imagine (picture mentally), to
fila, *f.*	FEE-*lah*	line (row)
"	"	rank
filare (1)	*fee*-LAH-*reh*	spin (form thread), to
filato, *m.*	*fee*-LAH-*toh*	yarn (fiber)
Filippine, *f.pl.*	*fee-leep*-PEE-*neh*	Philippines
filo, *m.*	FEE-*loh*	edge (sharp side)
"	"	strand
"	"	thread (sewing thread)
filo metallico, *m.*	FEE-*loh meh*-TAHL-*lee-koh*	wire (metal thread)
filosofia, *f.*	*fee-loh-zoh*-FEE-*ah*	philosophy
finale	*fee*-NAH-*leh*	final (last)
finalmente	*fee-nahl*-MENN-*teh*	finally
"	"	last (after all others, *adv.*)
finanze, *f.pl.*	*fee*-NAHN-*tseh*	finances
finanziario	*fee-nahn*-TS_YAH-*r_yoh*	financial
fine, *f.*	FEE-*neh*	end
fine di settimana, *f.*	FEE-*neh dee sett-tee*-MAH-*nah*	weekend (*n.*)
finestra, *f.*	*fee*-NEH-*strah*	window
fingere (24)	FEEN-*jeh-reh*	pretend (feign), to
finire (3)	*fee*-NEE-*reh*	finish (complete), to
finlandese	*feen-lahn*-DEH-*seh*	Finnish (*adj.*)
Finlandia, *f.*	*feen*-LAHN-*d_yah*	Finland
fino	FEE-*noh*	fine (very small)
fino a	FEE-*noh ah*	until (up to the time of, *prep.*)
fino a che	FEE-*noh ah keh*	until (*conj.*)
fino ad ora	FEE-*noh ah*-DOH-*rah*	hitherto (thus far)
finta, *f.*	FEEN-*tah*	pretense (pretending)
fiore, *m.*	F_YOH-*reh*	blossom
"	"	flower
fiorire (3)	*f_yoh*-REE-*reh*	bloom, to
"	"	flourish, to
"	"	thrive (grow vigorously), to
firma, *f.*	FEER-*mah*	signature (name)
firmare (1)	*feer*-MAH-*reh*	sign (endorse), to
fisarmonica, *f.*	*fee-zahr*-MOH-*nee-kah*	accordion
fischiare (1)	*fee*-SK_YAH-*reh*	hiss, to
"	"	whistle, to
fisica, *f.*	FEE-*zee-kah*	physics (science)
fisico	FEE-*zee-koh*	physical
fissare (1)	*feess*-SAH-*reh*	settle (agree on), to
fissare le tasse	*feess*-SAH-*reh leh* TAHSS-*seh*	assess (impose tax), to
fisso	FEESS-*soh*	fast (firm)

Italian	Pronunciation	English
fiume, *m.*	F_YOO-*meh*	river
flagrante	*flah*-GRAHN-*teh*	gross (flagrant)
flauto, *m.*	FL_OW-*toh*	flute (*mus.*)
floscio	FLOH-*shoh*	limp (flaccid)
flotta, *f.*	FLOHT-*tah*	fleet (group of vessels)
foca, *f.*	FOH-*kah*	seal (animal)
focolare, *m.*	*foh-koh*-LAH-*reh*	hearth
fodera, *f.*	FOH-*deh-rah*	lining
foglia, *f.*	FOH-*l_yah*	leaf (*bot.*)
foglio, *m.*	FOH-*l_yoh*	sheet (of paper)
fogna, *f.*	FOH-*n_yah*	sewer (conduit)
folla, *f.*	FOHL-*lah*	crowd
fondamentale	*fohn-dah-menn*-TAH-*leh*	fundamental
fondamento, *m.*	*fohn-dah*-MENN-*toh*	foundation (base)
fondare (1)	*fohn*-DAH-*reh*	establish, to
"	"	found, to
fondatore, *m.*	*fohn-dah*-TOH-*reh*	founder (*n.*)
fondere (54)	FOHN-*deh-reh*	melt (become liquid), to
fondi, *m.pl.*	FOHN-*dee*	funds
fondo, *m.*	FOHN-*doh*	bottom
"	"	fund
fonografo, *m.*	*foh*-NOH-*grah-foh*	phonograph
fontana, *f.*	*fohn*-TAH-*nah*	fountain
fonte, *f.*	FOHN-*teh*	source (origin)
forbici, *f.pl.*	FOHR-*bee-chee*	scissors
forchetta, *f.*	*fohr*-KETT-*tah*	fork (eating utensil)
foresta, *f.*	*foh*-REH-*stah*	forest
forgiare (1)	*fohr*-JAH-*reh*	forge (shape), to
forma, *f.*	FOHR-*mah*	form
"	"	shape (contour)
formaggio, *m.*	*fohr*-MAHD-*joh*	cheese
formalità, *f.*	*fohr-mah-lee*-TAH	formality
formare (1)	*fohr*-MAH-*reh*	form (shape), to
formare bolle	*fohr*-MAH-*reh* BOHL-*leh*	bubble, to
formazione, *f.*	*fohr-mah*-TS_YOH-*neh*	formation (creation)
formica, *f.*	*fohr*-MEE-*kah*	ant
formula, *f.*	FOHR-*moo-lah*	formula (prescribed guide)
fornello, *m.*	*fohr*-NELL-*loh*	stove (for cooking)
fornire (3)	*fohr*-NEE-*reh*	furnish (supply), to
fornitore, *m.*	*fohr-nee*-TOH-*reh*	supplier (*bus.*)
forno, *m.*	FOHR-*noh*	oven
forse	FOHR-*seh*	maybe
"	"	perhaps
forte	FOHR-*teh*	loud (resounding)
"	"	strong
forte, *m.*	FOHR-*teh*	fort
fortezza, *f.*	*fohr*-TETT-*tsah*	fortress
fortuna, *f.*	*fohr*-TOO-*nah*	fortune
"	"	luck
fortunatamente	*fohr-too-nah-tah*-MENN-*teh*	happily (luckily)
fortunato	*fohr-too*-NAH-*toh*	fortunate
"	"	lucky
forza, *f.*	FOHR-*tsah*	force
"	"	strength
forzare (1)	*fohr*-TSAH-*reh*	force, to
fossa, *f.*	FOHSS-*sah*	pit (hole)
fosso, *m.*	FOHSS-*soh*	ditch
fotografia, *f.*	*foh-toh-grah*-FEE-*ah*	photograph
fra	FRAH	among
"	"	between (*prep.*)
fracassare (1)	*frah-kahss*-SAH-*reh*	smash, to
fracassarsi	*frah-kahss*-SAHR-*see*	crash (be smashed), to
fracasso, *m.*	*frah*-KAHSS-*soh*	crash (loud noise)
fragile	FRAH-*jee-leh*	brittle
"	"	frail (fragile)
fragola, *f.*	FRAH-*goh-lah*	strawberry
frammento, *m.*	*frahm*-MENN-*toh*	fragment
francese	*frahn*-CHEH-*zeh*	French (*adj.*)
Francia, *f.*	FRAHN-*chah*	France
franco	FRAHNG-*koh*	frank (*adj.*)
francobollo, *m.*	*frahng-koh*-BOHL-*loh*	stamp, postage
frangia, *f.*	FRAHN-*jah*	fringe
frantumare (1)	*frahn-too*-MAH-*reh*	shatter (smash in pieces), to
frase, *f.*	FRAH-*zeh*	phrase (*gram.*)
"	"	sentence (*gram.*)

Italian	Pronunciation	English
fratello, m.	frah-TELL-loh	brother
frattempo, m.	fraht-TEMM-poh	meantime (n.)
frattura, f.	fraht-TOO-rah	fracture (med.)
frazione, f.	frah-TS_YOH-neh	fraction (part)
freccia, f.	FRETT-chah	arrow
freddezza, f.	fredd-DETT-tsah	chill (coldness)
freddo	FREDD-doh	chilly
"	"	cold (adj.)
freddo, m.	FREDD-doh	cold (low temperature)
fremere (2)	FREH-meh-reh	quiver, to
frenare (1)	freh-NAH-reh	check (stop), to
frenare (1)	freh-NAH-reh	curb, to
"	"	restrain, to
freno, m.	FREH-noh	brake
"	"	check
"	"	curb (restraint)
frequentare (1)	freh-kwenn-TAH-reh	haunt (visit often), to
frequente	freh-KWENN-teh	frequent
fresco	FREH-skoh	cool (having low temperature)
"	"	fresh
fretta, f.	FRETT-tah	haste
"	"	hurry
frettoloso	frett-toh-LOH-soh	hasty (hurried)
friggere (55)	FREED-jeh-reh	fry (be cooked in fat), to
frigorifero, m.	free-goh-REE-feh-roh	refrigerator
frizione, f.	free-TS_YOH-neh	clutch (automotive device)
frode, f.	FROH-deh	fraud (deception)
fronte, f.	FROHN-teh	forehead
"	"	front (battle front)
frontiera, f.	frohn-T_YEH-rah	frontier
fruscio, m.	froo-SHEE-oh	rustle
frusta, f.	FROO-stah	lash
"	"	whip
frustare (1)	froo-STAH-reh	lash, to
"	"	whip (flog), to
frustrare (1)	froo-STRAH-reh	defeat (thwart), to
"	"	foil (frustrate), to
frutteto, m.	froot-TEH-toh	orchard
frutto, m. (pl. frutta, f.)	FROOT-toh	fruit
fucile, m.	foo-CHEE-leh	gun
"	"	rifle
fuga, f.	FOO-gah	flight (hasty departure)
fuggire (4)	food-JEE-reh	flee (run from), to
fulmine, m.	FOOL-mee-neh	lightning
fumare (1)	foo-MAH-reh	smoke, to
fumo, m.	FOO-moh	smoke
fune, f.	FOO-neh	rope
fungo, m.	FOONG-goh	mushroom (n.)
funzionamento, m.	foon-ts_yoh-nah-MENN-toh	operation (functioning)
funzionario, m.	foon-ts_yoh-NAH-r_yoh	official (n.)
funzione, f.	foon-TS_YOH-neh	function
fuoco, m.	FWOH-koh	fire
fuori	FWOH-ree	out (adv.)
"	"	outside (adv.)
fuori, di, m.	dee FWOH-ree	outside (n.)
furbo	F_OOR-boh	sly (crafty)
furia, f.	FOO-r_yah	fury
furioso	foo-r_YOH-soh	furious
furore, m.	foo-ROH-reh	rage (wrath)
futuro	foo-TOO-roh	future (adj.)
futuro, m.	foo-TOO-roh	future (n.)
gabbia, f.	GAHB-b_yah	cage
gabinetto, m.	gah-bee-NETT-toh	cabinet (govt.)
"	"	toilet (water closet)
gaio	GAH-yoh	gay (merry)
"	"	cheerful (joyful)
galantuomo, m.	gah-lahn-TWOH-moh	gentleman
galleggiare (1)	gahl-ledd-JAH-reh	float (be buoyant), to
galleria, f.	gahl-leh-REE-ah	gallery (balcony)
"	"	tunnel
Galles, m.	GAHL-less	Wales
gallina, f.	gahl-LEE-nah	hen
gallo, m.	GAHL-loh	cock
"	"	rooster

Italian	Pronunciation	English
galoppo, m.	gah-LOHP-poh	gallop (n.)
galosce, f. pl.	gah-LOH-sheh	galoshes
gamba, f.	GAHM-bah	leg (anat.)
gamberetto, m.	gahm-beh-RETT-toh	shrimp
gambo, m.	GAHM-boh	stalk (stem)
gancio, m.	GAHN-choh	hook
garante, m., f.	gah-RAHN-teh	guarantor
garantire (3)	gah-rahn-TEE-reh	guarantee, to
garanzia, f.	gah-rahn-TSEE-ah	guarantee (warrant)
garbato	gahr-BAH-toh	polite
garofano, m.	gah-ROH-fah-noh	carnation
"	"	clove
gas, m.	GAHZ	gas
gattino, m.	gaht-TEE-noh	kitten
gatto, m.	GAHT-toh	cat
gelare (1)	jeh-LAH-reh	freeze (turn to ice), to
gelatina, f.	jeh-lah-TEE-nah	jelly
gelato	jeh-LAH-toh	frozen
gelato, m.	jeh-LAH-toh	ice-cream
geloso	jeh-LOH-soh	jealous
gemello, m.	jeh-MELL-loh	twin (n.)
gemere (2)	JEH-meh-reh	groan, to
"	"	moan, to
"	"	wail, to
gemma, f.	JEMM-mah	gem
generale	jeh-neh-RAH-leh	general (adj.)
generale, m.	jeh-neh-RAH-leh	general (officer)
generazione, f.	jeh-neh-rah-TS_YOH-neh	generation (period of time)
genere, m.	JEH-neh-reh	class (kind)
genere umano, m.	JEH-neh-reh oo-MAH-noh	mankind
genero, m.	JEH-neh-roh	son-in-law
generoso	jeh-neh-ROH-soh	generous
gengiva, f.	jenn-JEE-vah	gum (anat.)
genio, m.	JEH-n_yoh	genius
genitori, m. pl.	jeh-nee-TOH-ree	parents
gente, f.	JENN-teh	people (persons)
gentile	jenn-TEE-leh	gracious
"	"	nice (agreeable)
"	"	kind (adj.)
gentilezza, f.	jenn-tee-LETT-tsah	kindness
genuino	jeh-NWEE-noh	genuine
geografia, f.	jeh-oh-grah-FEE-ah	geography
geologia, f.	jeh-oh-loh-JEE-ah	geology
gergo, m.	JEHR-goh	slang (n.)
Germania, f.	jehr-MAH-n_yah	Germany
germoglio, m.	jehr-MOH-l_yoh	bud (bot.)
Gerusalemme, f.	jeh-roo-zah-LEMM-meh	Jerusalem
gesso, m.	JESS-soh	chalk
gestire (3)	jeh-STEE-reh	manage (administer), to
gesto, m.	JEH-stoh	gesture (motion)
Gesù	jeh-ZOO	Jesus
gettare (1)	jett-TAH-reh	cast, to
"	"	fling, to
"	"	shed (cast off), to
"	"	throw, to
ghiacciaia, f.	g_yaht-CHAH-yah	icebox
ghiacciato	g_yaht-CHAH-toh	icy
ghiaccio, m.	G_YAHT-choh	ice (frozen water)
ghiaia, f.	G_YAH-yah	gravel
ghianda, f.	G_YAHN-dah	acorn
ghignare (1)	ghee-N_YAH-reh	grin, to
ghirlanda, f.	gheer-LAHN-dah	wreath
già	JAH	already
giacca, f.	JAHK-kah	jacket (short coat)
giacere (56)	jah-CHEH-reh	lie (be prone), to
giallo	JAHL-loh	yellow (adj.)
Giappone, m.	jahp-POH-neh	Japan
giapponese	jahp-poh-NEH-seh	Japanese (adj.)
giardiniere, m.	jahr-dee-N_YEH-reh	gardener
giardino, m.	jahr-DEE-noh	garden
giardino d'infanzia, m.	jahr-DEE-noh deen-FAHN-ts_yah	kindergarten
giardino zoologico, m.	jahr-DEE-noh dzoh-oh-LOH-jee-koh	zoo
giarrettiera, f.	jahr-rett-T_YEH-rah	garter
gigante, m.	jee-GAHN-teh	giant
giglio, m.	JEE-l_yoh	lily
Ginevra, f.	jee-NEH-vrah	Geneva

Italian	Pronunciation	English
ginocchio,*m.* (*pl.* ginocchia,*f.*)	*jee*-NOHK-*k_yoh*	knee
giocare (1)	*joh*-KAH-*reh*	play (engage in recreation), to
giocatore,*m.*	*joh-kah*-TOH-*reh*	player (in a game)
giocattolo,*m.*	*joh*-KAHT-*toh-loh*	toy
giogo,*m.*	JOH-*goh*	yoke (wooden frame)
gioia,*f.*	JOH-*yah*	joy
gioielli,*m.pl.*	*joh*-YELL-*lee*	jewelry
gioiello,*m.*	*joh*-YELL-*loh*	jewel
giornale,*m.*	*johr*-NAH-*leh*	journal
"	"	newspaper
giorno,*m.*	JOHR-*noh*	day
giorno delle Ceneri,*m.*	JOHR-*noh dell-leh* CHEH-*neh-ree*	Ash Wednesday
giorno dopo,*m.*	JOHR-*noh* DOH-*poh*	morrow
giorno festivo,*m.*	JOHR-*noh feh*-STEE-*voh*	holiday
giovane	JOH-*vah-neh*	young (*adj.*)
"	"	youthful
giovanetto,*m.*	*joh-vah*-NETT-*toh*	lad
giovanotto,*m.*	*joh-vah*-NOHT-*toh*	youth (young man)
gioventù,*f.*	*joh-venn*-TOO	youth (period of life)
gioviale	*joh*-V_YAH-*leh*	jolly (*adj.*)
giovinezza,*f.*	*joh-vee*-NETT-*tsah*	youthfulness
girare (1)	*jee*-RAH-*reh*	endorse (sign), to
"	"	spin (revolve), to
girata,*f.*	*jee*-RAH-*tah*	endorsement (signature)
giro,*m.*	JEE-*roh*	tour
"	"	turn (change of direction)
giù	JOO	down (*adv.*)
"	"	downward (*adv.*)
giudicare (1)	*joo-dee*-KAH-*reh*	judge, to
giudice,*m.*	JOO-*dee-cheh*	judge
giudizio,*m.*	*joo*-DEE-*ts_yoh*	sense (intelligence)
giungere (57)	JOON-*jeh-reh*	reach (arrive at), to
giuoco,*m.*	JWOH-*koh*	game (contest)
"	"	sport
giuoco a palla,*m.*	JWOH-*koh ah* PAHL-*lah*	baseball
giuoco del calcio,*m.*	JWOH-*koh dell* KAHL-*choh*	soccer
giù per la scala	JOO *pehr lah* SKAH-*lah*	downstairs (downward)
giuramento,*m.*	*joo-rah*-MENN-*toh*	oath (vow)
giurare (1)	*joo*-RAH-*reh*	swear (vow), to
giurati,*m.pl.*	*joo*-RAH-*tee*	jury
giustificare (1)	*joo-stee-fee*-KAH-*reh*	justify, to
"	"	warrant, to
giustizia,*f.*	*joo*-STEE-*ts_yah*	justice
giustiziare (1)	*joo-stee*-TS_YAH-*reh*	execute (put to death), to
giusto	JOO-*stoh*	fair (impartial)
"	"	just (equitable, *adj.*)
gli (*art.,m.pl.*)	L_YEE	the
gli (*pron.*)	L_YEE	(to) him
globo,*m.*	GLOH-*boh*	globe
gloria,*f.*	GLOH-*r_yah*	glory (renown)
glorioso	*gloh*-R_YOH-*soh*	glorious (resplendent)
glossario,*m.*	*glohss*-SAH-*r_yoh*	glossary
gobba,*f.*	GOHB-*bah*	hump
goccia,*f.*	GOHT-*chah*	drop (droplet)
gocciolare (1)	*goht-choh*-LAH-*reh*	drip, to
godere (2)	*goh*-DEH-*reh*	enjoy (derive joy from), to
goffo	GOHF-*foh*	awkward
gola,*f.*	GOH-*lah*	throat
golf,*m.*	GOHLF	golf
golfo,*m.*	GOHL-*foh*	gulf (large bay)
gomena,*f.*	GOH-*meh-nah*	cable (rope)
gomito,*m.*	GOH-*mee-toh*	elbow
gomma,*f.*	GOHM-*mah*	eraser (rubber eraser)
"	"	rubber
gomma da masticare,*f.*	GOHM-*mah dah mah-stee*-KAH-*reh*	gum (chewing gum)
gommapiuma,*f.*	*gohm-mah*-P_YOO-*mah*	foam rubber
gonnella,*f.*	*gohn*-NELL-*lah*	skirt (garment)
governare (1)	*goh-vehr*-NAH-*reh*	govern, to
"	"	rule, to
governatore,*m.*	*goh-vehr-nah*-TOH-*reh*	governor

Italian	Pronunciation	English
governo,*m.*	*goh*-VEHR-*noh*	government
gradevole	*grah*-DEH-*voh-leh*	agreeable (pleasing)
gradino,*m.*	*grah*-DEE-*noh*	step (stair)
gradire (3)	*grah*-DEE-*reh*	appreciate (be grateful for), to
grado,*m.*	GRAH-*doh*	degree (unit of measurement)
"	"	grade (relative position)
graduale	*grah*-DWAH-*leh*	gradual
grafico,*m.*	GRAH-*fee-koh*	graph
grammatica,*f.*	*grahm*-MAH-*tee-kah*	grammar
Gran Brettagna,*f.*	*grahn brett*-TAHN-*n_yah*	Great Britain
granchio,*m.*	GRAHNG-*k_yoh*	crab (shellfish)
grande	GRAHN-*deh*	big
"	"	great
grande magazzino,*m.*	GRAHN-*deh mah-gahd*-DZEE-*noh*	department store
grandezza,*f.*	*grahn*-DETT-*tsah*	greatness (eminence)
grandinare (1)	*grahn-dee*-NAH-*reh*	hail (precipitate hail), to
grandine,*f.*	GRAHN-*dee-neh*	hail (ice)
grandioso	*grahn*-D_YOH-*soh*	grand (imposing)
granito,*m.*	*grah*-NEE-*toh*	granite
grano,*m.*	GRAH-*noh*	wheat
granturco,*m.*	*grahn*-TOOR-*koh*	corn (maize)
grassetto	*grahss*-SETT-*toh*	plump (chubby)
grasso	GRAHSS-*soh*	fat (obese, *adj.*)
grasso,*m.*	GRAHSS-*soh*	fat (fatty tissue, *n.*)
"	"	grease (cooking fat)
graticola,*f.*	*grah*-TEE-*koh-lah*	grate (of furnace)
gratis	GRAH-*teess*	free (gratuitous)
gratitudine,*f.*	*grah-tee*-TOO-*dee-neh*	gratitude
grato	GRAH-*toh*	thankful
grattacielo,*m.*	*graht-tah*-CH_YEH-*loh*	skyscraper
grattare (1)	*graht*-TAH-*reh*	scratch, to
grave	GRAH-*veh*	deep (in tone)
"	"	grave (serious)
"	"	solemn
grazia,*f.*	GRAH-*ts_yah*	blessing (boon)
"	"	grace (gracefulness)
"	"	pardon (*law*)
grazioso	*grah*-TS_YOH-*soh*	graceful
"	"	pretty
greco	GREH-*koh*	Greek (*adj.*)
Grecia,*f.*	GREH-*chah*	Greece
gregge,*m.*	GREDD-*jeh*	flock
grembiale,*m.*	*gremm*-B_YAH-*leh*	apron (garment)
grembo,*m.*	GREMM-*boh*	lap (of seated person)
grezzo	GREDD-*dzoh*	crude
"	"	raw (in natural state)
gridare (1)	*gree*-DAH-*reh*	cry, to
"	"	shout (say loudly), to
"	"	yell, to
grido,*m.*	GREE-*doh*	cry (utterance)
"	"	shout
grigio	GREE-*joh*	gray
grillo,*m.*	GREEL-*loh*	cricket (insect)
grinza,*f.*	GREEN-*tsah*	wrinkle (fold)
grossa,*f.*	GROHSS-*sah*	gross (twelve dozen)
grossista,*m.,f.*	*grohss*-SEE-*stah*	wholesaler (*bus.*)
grosso,*m.*	GROHSS-*soh*	bulk (largest part)
grossolano	*grohss-soh*-LAH-*noh*	coarse
gruccia,*f.*	GROOT-*chah*	crutch
gruppo,*m.*	GROOP-*poh*	group
guadagnare (1)	*gwah-dah*-N_YAH-*reh*	earn (be paid), to
guadare (1)	*gwah*-DAH-*reh*	ford, to
guaio,*m.*	GWAH-*yoh*	plight (predicament)
"	"	trouble (distress)
guancia,*f.*	GWAHN-*chah*	cheek
guanciale,*m.*	*gwahn*-CHAH-*leh*	pillow
guanto,*m.*	GWAHN-*toh*	glove
guardare (1)	*gwahr*-DAH-*reh*	look (gaze), to
guardare attentamente	*gwahr*-DAH-*reh aht-tenn-tah*-MENN-*teh*	peer (look intently), to
guardare ferocemente	*gwahr*-DAH-*reh feh-roh-cheh*-MENN-*teh*	glare (stare), to
guardare fissamente	*gwahr*-DAH-*reh feess-sah*-MENN-*teh*	gaze, to
guardare fisso	*gwahr*-DAH-*reh* FEESS-*soh*	stare, to
guardarsi da	*gwahr*-DAHR-*see dah*	beware of, to

Italian	Pronunciation	English
guardiamarina, *m.*	*gwahr-d_yah-mah-*REE-*nah*	ensign (*Nav.*)
guardiano, *m.*	*gwahr-*D_YAH-*noh*	guard (watcher)
guarigione, *f.*	*gwah-ree-*JOH-*neh*	cure (healing)
guarire (3)	*gwah-*REE-*reh*	cure, to
"	"	heal, to
"	"	recover (get well), to
guarnigione, *f.*	*gwahr-nee-*JOH-*neh*	garrison
guastare (1)	*gwah-*STAH-*reh*	spoil (mar), to
Guatemala, *m.*	*gwah-teh-*MAH-*lah*	Guatemala
guerra, *f.*	GWEHR-*rah*	war
gufo, *m.*	GOO-*foh*	owl
Guida, *f.*	GWEE-*dah*	Girl Scout
guida, *f.*	GWEE-*dah*	guide (one who guides)
guidare (1)	*gwee-*DAH-*reh*	steer, to
guscio, *m.*	GOO-*shoh*	shell (covering)
gusto, *m.*	GOO-*stoh*	taste (flavor)
Haiti, *m.*	EYE-*tee*	Haiti
Hawaii, *m.*	*ah-*WAH-*yee*	Hawaii
Helsinki	*ell-*SEENG-*kee*	Helsinki
Honduras, *m.*	*ohn-*DOO-*rahss*	Honduras
i	EE	the
idea, *f.*	*ee-*DEH-*ah*	idea
"	"	thought
ideale, *m.*	*ee-deh-*AH-*leh*	ideal (*n.*)
identificare (1)	*ee-denn-tee-fee-*KAH-*reh*	identify, to
idolo, *m.*	EE-*doh-loh*	idol
ieri	YEH-*ree*	yesterday
ignorante	*ee-n_yoh-*RAHN-*teh*	ignorant
ignoranza, *f.*	*ee-n_yoh-*RAHN-*tsah*	ignorance
il	EEL	the
ilarità, *f.*	*ee-lah-ree-*TAH	mirth
illegale	*eel-leh-*GAH-*leh*	illegal
illuminare (1)	*eel-loo-mee-*NAH-*reh*	illuminate, to
"	"	light, to
illusione, *f.*	*eel-loo-z_*YOH-*neh*	illusion
illustrare (1)	*eel-loo-*STRAH-*reh*	illustrate, to
illustrazione, *f.*	*eel-loo-strah-*TS_YOH-*neh*	illustration
imballaggio, *m.*	*eem-bahl-*LAHD-*joh*	packing (*n.*)
imbarazzo, *m.*	*eem-bah-*RAHT-*tsoh*	embarrassment
imbiancare (1)	*eem-b_yahng-*KAH-*reh*	bleach (make white), to
imbroglio, *m.*	*eem-*BROH-*l_yoh*	mess (muddle)
imitare (1)	*ee-mee-*TAH-*reh*	imitate, to
immagazzinaggio, *m.*	*eem-mah-gahd-dzee-*NAHD-*joh*	storage
immaginare (1)	*eem-mah-jee-*NAH-*reh*	fancy, to
immaginazione, *f.*	*eem-mah-jee-nah-*TS_YOH-*neh*	imagination
immediato	*eem-meh-*D_YAH-*toh*	direct
"	"	immediate (instant)
immenso	*eem-*MENN-*soh*	immense
immergere (44)	*eem-*MEHR-*jeh-reh*	dip (immerse), to
immischiarsi (1)	*eem-mee-*SK_YAHR-*see*	interfere, to
"	"	meddle, to
immobile	*eem-*MOH-*bee-leh*	still (motionless, *adj.*)
immortale	*eem-mohr-*TAH-*leh*	immortal (*adj.*)
impaccare (1)	*eem-pahk-*KAH-*reh*	pack (wrap), to
imparare (1)	*eem-pah-*RAH-*reh*	learn (acquire knowledge), to
impari	*eem-*PAH-*ree*	odd (not even)
imparzialmente	*eem-pahr-ts_yahl-*MENN-*teh*	fairly (impartially)
impaurito	*eem-pah-oo-*REE-*toh*	afraid
impaziente	*eem-pah-*TS_YENN-*teh*	impatient
impazienza, *f.*	*eem-pah-*TS_YENN-*tsah*	impatience
impedire (3)	*eem-peh-*DEE-*reh*	avert (prevent), to
"	"	hinder, to
impegno, *m.*	*eem-*PEH-*n_yoh*	commitment (*bus.*)
imperatore, *m.*	*eem-peh-rah-*TOH-*reh*	emperor
imperatrice, *f.*	*eem-peh-rah-*TREE-*cheh*	empress
imperfetto	*eem-pehr-*FETT-*toh*	imperfect (defective)
imperiale	*eem-peh-*R_YAH-*leh*	imperial
impermeabile	*eem-pehr-meh-*AH-*bee-leh*	waterproof
impermeabile, *m.*	*eem-pehr-meh-*AH-*bee-leh*	raincoat
impero, *m.*	*eem-*PEH-*roh*	empire
impiccio, *m.*	*eem-*PEET-*choh*	quandary
impiegare (1)	*eem-p_yeh-*GAH-*reh*	employ, to
"	"	hire, to
impiegato, *m.*	*eem-p_yeh-*GAH-*toh*	employee
impiego, *m.*	*eem-p_*YEH-*goh*	employment (work)
		job
imporre (76)	*eem-*POHR-*reh*	impose (inflict), to
importante	*eem-pohr-*TAHN-*teh*	important
importanza, *f.*	*eem-pohr-*TAHN-*tsah*	importance
"	"	significance
importare (1)	*eem-pohr-*TAH-*reh*	import, to (*bus.*)
importatore, *m.*	*eem-pohr-tah-*TOH-*reh*	importer
importazione, *f.*	*eem-pohr-tah-*TS_YOH-*neh*	importation
impossibile	*eem-pohss-*SEE-*bee-leh*	impossible
impossibilità, *f.*	*eem-pohss-see-bee-lee-*TAH	impossibility
imposta, *f.*	*eem-*POH-*stah*	tax (*n.*)
impostare (1)	*eem-poh-*STAH-*reh*	mail (post), to
imposta sul reddito, *f.*	*eem-*POH-*stah sool* REDD-*dee-toh*	income tax
impotente	*eem-poh-*TENN-*teh*	helpless
impregnare (1)	*eem-preh-*N_YAH-*reh*	soak (saturate), to
impresa, *f.*	*eem-*PREH-*sah*	enterprise
"	"	undertaking
impressione, *f.*	*eem-press-*S_YOH-*neh*	impression
imprevisto	*eem-preh-*VEE-*stoh*	unexpected (*adj.*)
improvviso	*eem-prohv-*VEE-*zoh*	sudden (unexpected)
imprudente	*eem-proo-*DENN-*teh*	foolish
"	"	rash (*adj.*)
impugnare (1)	*eem-poo-*N_YAH-*reh*	grasp (grip), to
impulso, *m.*	*eem-*POOL-*soh*	impulse (sudden incitement)
impuro	*eem-*POO-*roh*	impure
in	EEN	at (in)
"	"	in (into, *prep.*)
"	"	into (to the inside)
"	"	to (indicating destination, *prep.*)
inadeguato	*ee-nah-deh-*GWAH-*toh*	inadequate
incantare (1)	*een-kahn-*TAH-*reh*	charm (delight), to
incantevole	*een-kahn-*TEH-*voh-leh*	charming
incanto, *m.*	*een-*KAHN-*toh*	spell (charm)
incarico, *m.*	*een-*KAH-*ree-koh*	charge (responsibility)
incartamento, *m.*	*een-kahr-tah-*MENN-*toh*	file (collection of papers)
incassare (1)	*een-kahss-*SAH-*reh*	cash (receive cash for), to
inchino, *m.*	*een-*KEE-*noh*	bow (nod)
inchiostro, *m.*	*een-k_*YOH-*stroh*	ink
inciampare (1)	*een-chahm-*PAH-*reh*	stumble, to
"	"	trip, to
incisione, *f.*	*een-chee-z_*YOH-*neh*	print (printed reproduction)
inclinare (1)	*een-klee-*NAH-*reh*	incline (tend), to
inclinare la testa	*een-klee-*NAH-*reh lah* TEH-*stah*	nod, to
inclinarsi	*een-klee-*NAHR-*see*	lean (bend), to
"	"	slant (slope), to
inclinazione, *f.*	*een-klee-nah-*TS_YOH-*neh*	inclination (tendency)
includere (6)	*een-*KLOO-*deh-reh*	include (contain), to
incolpare (1)	*een-kohl-*PAH-*reh*	charge (accuse), to
incomodare (1)	*een-koh-moh-*DAH-*reh*	trouble (inconvenience), to
incontrare (1)	*een-kohn-*TRAH-*reh*	encounter, to
"	"	meet, to
incontrarsi (con)	*een-kohn-*TRAHR-*see (kohn)*	meet (come together), to
inconvenienza, *f.*	*een-kohn-veh-*N_YENN-*tsah*	inconvenience
incoraggiare (1)	*een-koh-rahd-*JAH-*reh*	encourage, to
"	"	foster, to
incrociare (1)	*een-kroh-*CHAH-*reh*	cross (crossbreed), to
incrociatore, *m.*	*een-kroh-chah-*TOH-*reh*	cruiser (ship)
incrocio, *m.*	*een-*KROH-*choh*	crossing (intersection)
"	"	crossroads
incursione aerea, *f.*	*een-koor-*S_YOH-*neh ah-*EH-*reh-ah*	air raid
indagare (1)	*een-dah-*GAH-*reh*	investigate, to
indagine, *f.*	*een-*DAH-*jee-neh*	research
indebolire (3)	*een-deh-boh-*LEE-*reh*	weaken (make weak), to
indegno	*een-*DEH-*n_yoh*	unworthy
indennizzo, *m.*	*een-denn-*NEED-*dzoh*	damages (indemnification)
"	"	indemnity (compensation)
independente	*een-deh-penn-*DENN-*teh*	independent
independenza, *f.*	*een-deh-penn-*DENN-*tsah*	independence
India, *f.*	EEN-*d_yah*	India

Italian	*Pronunciation*	*English*
indicare (1)	*een-dee-*KAH-*reh*	indicate, to
"	"	point, to
indice, *m.*	EEN-*dee-cheh*	index (list)
indietro	*een-D* YEH-*troh*	back (rearward, adv.)
"	"	backward (rearward, adv.)
indifferente	*een-deef-feh-*RENN-*teh*	indifferent (unconcerned)
indigeno	*een-*DEE-*jeh-noh*	domestic (not foreign)
"	"	native (indigenous)
indigeno, *m.*	*een-*DEE-*jeh-noh*	native (*n.*)
indigestione, *f.*	*een-dee-jeh-*ST YOH-*neh*	indigestion
indignazione, *f.*	*een-dee-n yah-*TS YOH-*neh*	indignation
indiretto	*een-dee-*RETT-*toh*	indirect
indirizzo, *m.*	*een-dee-*REET-*tsoh*	address (postal directions)
individuale	*een-dee-vee-*DWAH-*leh*	individual (particular, adj.)
individuo, *m.*	*een-dee-*VEE-*dwoh*	guy (fellow)
"	"	individual (person, *n.*)
indolenzito	*een-doh-lenn-*TSEE-*toh*	sore (adj.)
indovinare (1)	*een-doh-vee-*NAH-*reh*	guess (divine), to
indovinello, *m.*	*een-doh-vee-*NELL-*loh*	riddle (*n.*)
indubbiamente	*een-doob-b yah-*MENN-*teh*	undoubtedly
indugiare (1)	*een-doo-*JAH-*reh*	lag (fall behind), to
"	"	stall (stop going), to
indurire (3)	*een-doo-*REE-*reh*	harden (make hard), to
industria, *f.*	*een-*DOO-*str yah*	industry (trade)
industriale	*een-doo-*STR YAH-*leh*	industrial
industrioso	*een-doo-*STR YOH-*soh*	industrious
ineguale	*ee-neh-*GWAH-*leh*	unequal
inesatto	*ee-neh-*ZAHT-*toh*	inaccurate
inevitabile	*ee-neh-vee-*TAH-*bee-leh*	inevitable (adj.)
infanzia, *f.*	*een-*FAHN-*ts yah*	childhood
infastidire (3)	*een-fah-stee-*DEE-*reh*	bother (annoy), to
"	"	pester, to
infelice	*een-feh-*LEE-*cheh*	miserable
"		unhappy (sorrowful)
inferiore	*een-feh-*R YOH-*reh*	inferior (mediocre)
infermiera, *f.*	*een-fehr-*M YEH-*rah*	nurse (medical assistant)
inferno, *m.*	*een-*FEHR-*noh*	hell
infezione, *f.*	*een-feh-*TS YOH-*neh*	infection
infiammazione, *f.*	*een-f yahm-mah-*TS YOH-*neh*	inflammation
infinito	*een-fee-*NEE-*toh*	infinite
inflazione, *f.*	*een-flah-*TS YOH-*neh*	inflation (econ.)
influenza, *f.*	*een-floo-*ENN-*tsah*	influence
"	"	influenza
influenzare (1)	*een-floo-enn-*TSAH-*reh*	affect (influence), to
informare (1)	*een-fohr-*MAH-*reh*	acquaint, to
"	"	inform (apprise), to
"	"	tell, to
informazioni, *f.pl.*	*een-fohr-mah-*TS YOH-*nee*	information
inganno, *m.*	*een-*GAHN-*noh*	deceit
ingegnere, *m.*	*een-jeh-*N YEH-*reh*	engineer (professional engineer)
Inghilterra, *f.*	*een-gheel-*TEHR-*rah*	England
inghiottire (3)	*een-g yoht-*TEE-*reh*	swallow, to
inginocchiarsi (1)	*een-jee-nohk-*K YAHR-*see*	kneel, to
ingiustizia, *f.*	*een-joo-*STEE-*ts yah*	injustice
"	"	wrong
ingiusto	*een-*JOO-*stoh*	unjust (inequitable)
"	"	wrong (adj.)
inglese	*een-*GLEH-*seh*	English (adj.)
ingombrare (1)	*een-gohm-*BRAH-*reh*	block (obstruct), to
ingranaggio, *m.*	*een-grah-*NAHD-*joh*	gear (mech.)
ingrandire (3)	*een-grahn-*DEE-*reh*	enlarge (make larger), to
ingrossare (1)	*een-grohss-*SAH-*reh*	swell (bulge), to
ingrosso, all'	*ahl-leeng-*GROHSS-*soh*	wholesale (adj., bus.)
iniezione, *f.*	*ee-n yeh-*TS YOH-*neh*	injection (med.)
iniziale	*ee-nee-*TS YAH-*leh*	initial (first, adj.)
iniziale, *f.*	*ee-nee-*TS YAH-*leh*	initial (letter)
iniziare (1)	*ee-nee-*TS YAH-*reh*	start (initiate), to
inizio, *m.*	*ee-*NEE-*ts yoh*	opening (beginning, *n.*)
"	"	start

Italian	*Pronunciation*	*English*
innamorato, *m.*	*een-nah-moh-*RAH-*toh*	lover
		sweetheart
innanzi, d'ora	DOH-*rah een-*NAHN-*tsee*	hereafter (after this, adv.)
inno, *m.*	EEN-*noh*	hymn (religious song)
innocente	*een-noh-*CHENN-*teh*	innocent (guiltless)
inoltrare (1)	*ee-nohl-*TRAH-*reh*	forward (send by mail), to
inoltre	*ee-*NOHL-*treh*	besides (adv.)
"	"	moreover
inondazione, *f.*	*ee-nohn-dah-*TS YOH-*neh*	flood
inquieto	*een-*KW YEH-*toh*	uneasy (anxious)
inquilino, *m.*	*ecn-kwee-*LEE-*noh*	tenant
insalata, *f.*	*een-sah-*LAH-*tah*	salad
inscrivere (96)	*een-*SKREE-*veh-reh*	enter (make record of), to
insegnare (1)	*een-seh-*N YAH-*reh*	coach (train), to
"		teach, to
inseguimento, *m.*	*een-seh-gwee-*MENN-*toh*	pursuit (chase)
inseguire (4)	*een-seh-*GWEE-*reh*	chase, to
"	"	pursue, to
insensibile	*een-senn-*SEE-*bee-leh*	numb
inserire (3)	*een-seh-*REE-*reh*	insert, to
insetto, *m.*	*een-*SETT-*toh*	bug
"		insect
insieme	*een-S* YEH-*meh*	together
insignificante	*een-see-n yee-fee-*KAHN-*teh*	insignificant (trivial)
"		petty (minor)
insistere (16)	*een-*SEE-*steh-reh*	insist, to
insolvenza, *f.*	*een-sohl-*VENN-*tsah*	insolvency (bus.)
installare (1)	*een-stahl-*LAH-*reh*	install (set up for use), to
insuccesso, *m.*	*een-soot-*CHESS-*soh*	failure (lack of success)
insufficiente	*een-soof-fee-*CHENN-*teh*	insufficient
insulto, *m.*	*een-*SOOL-*toh*	insult
intagliare (1)	*een-tah-*L YAH-*reh*	carve (cut designs), to
intanto	*een-*TAHN-*toh*	meanwhile (adv.)
intelletto, *m.*	*een-tell-*LETT-*toh*	mind (intellect)
intellettuale	*een-tell-lett-*TWAH-*leh*	intellectual (adj.)
intelligente	*een-tell-lee-*JENN-*teh*	intelligent
intelligenza, *f.*	*een-tell-lee-*JENN-*tsah*	intelligence (understanding)
intenso	*een-*TENN-*soh*	intense
intento	*een-*TENN-*toh*	intent (engrossed)
intenzione, *f.*	*een-tenn-*TS YOH-*neh*	intention
interamente	*een-teh-rah-*MENN-*teh*	altogether (entirely)
interessante	*een-teh-ress-*SAHN-*teh*	interesting
interessare (1)	*een-teh-ress-*SAH-*reh*	interest, to
interesse, *m.*	*een-teh-*RESS-*seh*	interest (money rate)
interesse composto, *m.*	*een-teh-*RESS-*seh kohm-*POH-*stoh*	compound interest
internazionale	*een-tehr-nah-ts yoh-*NAH-*leh*	international
interno	*een-*TEHR-*noh*	inner
"	"	inside (adj.)
"	"	internal
interno, *m.*	*een-*TEHR-*noh*	inside (*n.*)
"	"	interior (*n.*)
interno, all'	*ahl-leen-*TEHR-*noh*	within (on the inside, adv.)
intero	*een-*TEH-*roh*	entire
"	"	whole (adj.)
interpretare (1)	*een-tehr-preh-*TAH-*reh*	interpret (explain), to
interrogare (1)	*een-tehr-roh-*GAH-*reh*	question (query), to
interrogare circa	*een-tehr-roh-*GAH-*reh* CHEER-*kah*	ask about, to
interrompere (89)	*een-tehr-*ROHM-*peh-reh*	interrupt, to
interruttore, *m.*	*een-tehr-root-*TOH-*reh*	switch (elec.)
intervallo, *m.*	*een-tehr-*VAHL-*loh*	interval (period of time)
intervento, *m.*	*een-tehr-*VENN-*toh*	agency (instrumentality)
intervista, *f.*	*een-tehr-*VEE-*stah*	interview
intimo	EEN-*tee-moh*	close (intimate)
"	"	intimate (personal)
intonaco, *m.*	*een-*TOH-*nah-koh*	plaster (wall coating)
intorno a	*een-*TOHR-*noh ah*	around (prep.)
intraprendere (78)	*een-trah-*PRENN-*deh-reh*	undertake (attempt), to
intrecciare (1)	*een-trett-*CHAH-*reh*	braid (plait), to
introdurre (7)	*een-troh-*DOO_R-*reh*	introduce (bring in), to
"	"	stick (thrust), to

Italian	Pronunciation	English
introduzione,*f.*	*een-troh-doo*-TS YOH-*neh*	introduction (preliminary part)
intuizione,*f.*	*een-too ee*-TS YOH-*neh*	intuition
inutile	*ee*-NOO-*tee-leh*	needless
"	"	unnecessary
"	"	useless
invadere (50)	*een*-VAH-*deh-reh*	invade, to (*mil.*)
invece di	*een*-VEH-*cheh dee*	instead of
inventare (1)	*een-venn*-TAH-*reh*	devise (contrive), to
"	"	invent, to
inventario,*m.*	*een-venn*-TAH-*r yoh*	inventory (*bus.*)
invenzione,*f.*	*een-venn*-TS YOH-*neh*	invention
inverno,*m.*	*een*-VEHR-*noh*	winter (*n.*)
investigazione,*f.*	*een-veh-stee-gah*-TS YOH-*neh*	investigation
investimento,*m.*	*een-veh-stee*-MENN-*toh*	investment (*bus.*)
investire (4)	*een-veh*-STEE-*reh*	invest, to (*bus.*)
invidia,*f.*	*een*-VEE-*d yah*	envy
invidiare (1)	*een-vee*-D YAH-*reh*	envy, to
invisibile	*een-vee*-ZEE-*bee-leh*	invisible
invitare (1)	*een-vee*-TAH-*reh*	invite, to
invito,*m.*	*een*-VEE-*toh*	invitation
io	EE-*oh*	I
ipoteca,*f.*	*ee-poh*-TEH-*kah*	mortgage
Irlanda,*f.*	*eer*-LAHN-*dah*	Ireland
irlandese	*eer-lahn*-DEH-*seh*	Irish (*adj.*)
irragionevole	*eer-rah-joh*-NEH-*voh-leh*	unreasonable (unreasoning)
irregolare (1)	*eer-reh-goh*-LAH-*reh*	irregular (not conforming)
irrigazione,*f.*	*eer-ree-gah*-TS YOH-*neh*	irrigation
irritare (1)	*eer-ree*-TAH-*reh*	irritate (annoy), to
"	"	vex (anger), to
iscrizione,*f.*	*ee-skree*-TS YOH-*neh*	inscription
isola,*f.*	EE-*zoh-lah*	island (*geog.*)
ispezionare (1)	*ee-speh-ts yoh*-NAH-*reh*	inspect, to
ispezione,*f.*	*ee-speh*-TS YOH-*neh*	inspection (scrutiny)
ispirare (1)	*ee-spee*-RAH-*reh*	inspire, to
ispirazione,*f.*	*ee-spee-rah*-TS YOH-*neh*	inspiration
Israele,*m.*	*ee-zrah*-EH-*leh*	Israel
israeli	*ee-zrah*-EH-*lee*	Israeli (*adj.*)
istante,*m.*	*ee*-STAHN-*teh*	instant (*n.*)
istanza,*f.*	*ee*-STAHN-*tsah*	petition (written request)
istinto,*m.*	*ee*-STEEN-*toh*	instinct
istituto,*m.*	*ee-stee*-TOO-*toh*	institute
istituzione,*f.*	*ee-stee-too*-TS YOH-*neh*	institution (establishment)
istmo,*m.*	EE-*stmoh*	isthmus
istruire (30)	*ee*-STRWEE-*reh*	instruct (teach), to
istruzione,*f.*	*ee-stroo*-TS YOH-*neh*	instruction (teaching)
"	"	schooling
"	"	training
Italia,*f.*	*ee*-TAH-*l yah*	Italy
italiano	*ee-tah-*L YAH-*noh*	Italian (*adj.*)
itinerario,*m.*	*ee-tee-neh*-RAH-*r yoh*	route
Iugoslavia,*f.*	*yoo-goh*-ZLAH-*v yah*	Yugoslavia
jazz,*m.*	*jahz*	jazz
Karachi,*f.*	*kah*-RAH-*kee*	Karachi
là	LAH	there (at that place)
la (*art.,f.sing.*)	LAH	the
la (*pron.*)	LAH	her, it, you
là di, al di	*ahl dee* LAH *dee*	across (beyond)
"	"	past (*prep.*)
labbro,*m.* (*pl.* labbra,*f.*)	LAHB-*broh*	lip (*anat.*)
laboratorio,*m.*	*lah-boh-rah*-TOH-*r yoh*	laboratory
laccio,*m.*	LAHT-*choh*	lace (shoelace)
"	"	snare (trap)
ladro,*m.*	LAH-*droh*	burglar
"	"	robber
"	"	thief
lagnanza,*f.*	*lah-*N YAHN-*tsah*	complaint
lagnarsi (1)	*lah-*N YAHR-*see*	complain, to
lago,*m.*	LAH-*goh*	lake
lagrima,*f.*	LAH-*gree-mah*	tear (teardrop)
lama,*f.*	LAH-*mah*	blade (cutting tool)
lama di rasoio,*f.*	LAH-*mah dee rah*-SOH-*yoh*	razor blade
lampada,*f.*	LAHM-*pah-dah*	lamp
lampada (incandescente),*f.*	LAHM-*pah-dah (een-kahn-deh*-SHENN-*teh*)	bulb (light bulb)
lampadina tascabile,*f.*	*lahm-pah*-DEE-*nah tah*-SKAH-*bee-leh*	flashlight
lampo,*m.*	LAHM-*poh*	flash (burst of light)
lampone,*m.*	*lahm*-POH-*neh*	raspberry

Italian	Pronunciation	English
lana,*f.*	LAH-*nah*	wool (fleece)
lancia,*f.*	LAHN-*chah*	spear (weapon)
lanciare (1)	*lahn*-CHAH-*reh*	hurl, to
"	"	launch (start), to
"	"	pitch (throw), to
"	"	toss, to
landa,*f.*	LAHN-*dah*	moor (waste land)
languire (3)	*lahng*-GWEE-*reh*	wilt, to
lanterna,*f.*	*lahn*-TEHR-*nah*	lantern
lardo,*m.*	LAHR-*doh*	lard
larghezza,*f.*	*lahr*-GET-*tsah*	breadth
"		width
largo	LAHR-*goh*	broad
"	"	large
"	"	wide
lasciar cadere (1)	*lah*-SHAHR *kah*-DEH-*reh*	drop (let fall), to
lasciare	*lah*-SHAH-*reh*	leave (let remain), to
lastra metallica,*f.*	LAH-*strah meh*-TAHL-*lee-kah*	stencil
lastricare (1)	*lah-stree*-KAH-*reh*	pave, to
latino	*lah*-TEE-*noh*	Latin (*adj.*)
lato,*m.*	LAH-*toh*	side
latta,*f.*	LAHT-*tah*	can (tin)
latte,*m.*	LAHT-*teh*	milk
latteria,*f.*	*laht-teh*-REE-*ah*	dairy
lattuga,*f.*	*laht*-TOO-*gah*	lettuce
làvagna,*f.*	*lah*-VAH-*n yah*	blackboard
lavanderia,*f.*	*lah-vahn-deh*-REE-*ah*	laundry (commercial plant)
lavare (1)	*lah*-VAH-*reh*	wash (cleanse), to
lavarsi	*lah*-VAHR-*see*	wash (cleanse oneself), to
lavorare (1)	*lah-voh*-RAH-*reh*	work (labor), to
lavorare a maglia	*lah-voh*-RAH-*reh ah* MAH-*l yah*	knit, to
lavoro,*m.*	*lah*-VOH-*roh*	labor (labor force)
"	"	work
lavoro a cottimo,*m.*	*lah*-VOH-*roh ah* KOHT-*tee-moh*	piecework (*n.*)
lavoro a maglia,*m.*	*lah*-VOH-*roh ah* MAH-*l yah*	knitting
le (*art.,f.pl.*)	LEH	the
le (*pron.*)	LEH	(to) her, you
"	"	them, you
leale	*leh*-AH-*leh*	loyal
lealtà,*f.*	*leh-ahl*-TAH	loyalty
lebbra,*f.*	LEBB-*brah*	leprosy
leccare (1)	*lekk*-KAH-*reh*	lick (lap), to
lega,*f.*	LEH-*gah*	alloy (metal)
"	"	league
legale	*leh*-GAH-*leh*	legal
legame,*m.*	*leh*-GAH-*meh*	bond (emotional tie)
legare (1)	*leh*-GAH-*reh*	bind, to
"	"	lash (fasten), to
"	"	tie, to
legge,*f.*	LEDD-*jeh*	law
leggenda,*f.*	*ledd*-JENN-*dah*	legend (story)
leggere (59)	LEDD-*jeh-reh*	read, to
leggero	*ledd*-JEH-*roh*	light (of little weight)
"	"	slight (*adj.*)
legislatura,*f.*	*leh-jee-zlah*-TOO-*rah*	congress
"	"	legislature
legislazione,*f.*	*leh-jee-zlah*-TS YOH-*neh*	legislation
legittimo	*leh*-JEET-*tee-moh*	lawful
legname,*m.*	*leh-*N YAH-*meh*	lumber (timber)
legno,*m.*	LEH-*n yoh*	wood (lumber)
lei	LAY	her (*pers. pron.*)
Lei	LAY	you
lei stessa	LAY STESS-*sah*	herself
Lei stesso	LAY STESS-*soh*	yourself
lento	LENN-*toh*	slow (not fast)
lenzuolo,*m.* (*pl.* -la,*f.*)	*lenn*-TS WOH-*loh*	sheet (bedding)
leone,*m.*	*leh*-OH-*neh*	lion
leopardo,*m.*	*leh-oh*-PAHR-*doh*	leopard
lepre,*f.*	LEH-*preh*	hare
lettera,*f.*	LETT-*teh-rah*	letter
letterario	*lett-teh*-RAH-*r yoh*	literary
letteratura,*f.*	*lett-teh-rah*-TOO-*rah*	literature (belleslettres)

Italian	Pronunciation	English
lettino, *m.*	*lett-*TEE*-noh*	cot (bed)
letto, *m.*	LETT-*toh*	bed
lettore, *m.*	*lett-*TOH*-reh*	reader
leva, *f.*	LEH-*vah*	lever
levarsi (1)	*leh-*VAHR*-see*	rise (in sky), to
"	"	rise (stand up), to
"	"	stand up, to
levata del sole, *f.*	*leh-*VAH*-tah dell* SOH-*leh*	sunrise
lezione, *f.*	*leh-*TS_YOH*-neh*	lesson (assignment)
li	LEE	them, you
liberale	*lee-beh-*RAH*-leh*	liberal (*polit., adj.*)
liberare (1)	*lee-beh-*RAH*-reh*	free, to
"	"	liberate, to
"	"	relieve (free), to
libero	LEE-*beh-roh*	free (independent)
libertà, *f.*	*lee-behr-*TAH	freedom
"	"	liberty
libretto, *m.*	*lee-*BRETT*-toh*	booklet
libro, *m.*	LEE-*broh*	book
libro di testo, *m.*	LEE-*broh dee* TEH-*stoh*	textbook
licenziare (1)	*lee-chenn-*TS_YAH*-reh*	dismiss (discharge), to
lieto	L_YEH-*toh*	joyful
lievito, *m.*	L_YEH-*vee-toh*	yeast
lillà, *f.*	*leel-*LAH	lilac (flower)
lima, *f.*	LEE-*mah*	file (tool)
Lima, *f.*	LEE-*mah*	Lima
limitare (1)	*lee-mee-*TAH*-reh*	confine, to
"	"	limit, to
limite, *m.*	LEE-*mee-teh*	boundary
"	"	limit
limonata, *f.*	*lee-moh-*NAH*-tah*	lemonade
limone, *m.*	*lee-*MOH*-neh*	lemon
linea, *f.*	LEE-*neh-ah*	line (mark)
linea di condotta, *f.*	LEE-*neh-ah dee kohn-*DOHT-*tah*	policy (course)
linfa, *f.*	LEEN-*fah*	sap (fluid)
lingua, *f.*	LEENG-*gwah*	language
"	"	tongue (*anat.*)
lino, *m.*	LEE-*noh*	flax
linoleo, *m.*	*lee-*NOH*-leh-oh*	linoleum
liquido, *m.*	LEE-*kwee-doh*	liquid (*n.*)
liquore, *m.*	*lee-*KWOH*-reh*	liqueur
liscio	LEE-*shoh*	smooth (*adj.*)
lista, *f.*	LEE-*stah*	list
"	"	strip (band)
lista (delle vivande), *f.*	LEE-*stah (dell-leh vee-*VAHN*-deh)*	menu
litigare (1)	*lee-tee-*GAH*-reh*	quarrel (dispute), to
litigio, *m.*	*lee-*TEE*-joh*	litigation
litografia, *f.*	*lee-toh-grah-*FEE*-ah*	lithography
livello, *m.*	*lee-*VELL*-loh*	level (plane, *n.*)
lo (*pron.*)	LOH	him, it
lo (*art., m.sing.*)	LOH	the
locale	*loh-*KAH*-leh*	local (regional)
località, *f.*	*loh-kah-lee-*TAH	locality (place)
locomotiva, *f.*	*loh-koh-moh-*TEE*-vah*	engine
"	"	locomotive
lodare (1)	*loh-*DAH*-reh*	praise, to
lode, *f.*	LOH-*deh*	praise
loggia, *f.*	LOHD-*jah*	porch
Londra, *f.*	LOHN-*drah*	London
lontano	*lohn-*TAH*-noh*	far (*adj., adv.*)
lontano, più	P_YOO *lohn-*TAH*-noh*	farther (*adj., adv.*)
lordo	LOHR-*doh*	gross (before deductions, *adj.*)
loro	LOH-*roh*	their, your
"	"	(to) them
"	"	(to) you
Loro	LOH-*roh*	you
loro, il (la, i, le)	*eel (lah, ee, leh)* LOH-*roh*	theirs, yours
Loro stessi	LOH-*roh* STESS-*see*	yourselves
lotta, *f.*	LOHT-*tah*	fight
"	"	struggle (great effort)
lottare (1)	*loht-*TAH*-reh*	wrestle, to
luccicare (1)	*loot-chee-*KAH*-reh*	shine (gleam), to
luce, *f.*	LOO-*cheh*	light (illumination)
luce del giorno, *f.*	LOO-*cheh dell* JOHR-*noh*	daylight

Italian	Pronunciation	English
luce del sole, *f.*	LOO-*cheh dell* SOH-*leh*	sunlight
lucidare (1)	*loo-chee-*DAH*-reh*	polish, to
"	"	shine, to
lucido, *m.*	LOO-*chee-doh*	polish
lugubre	LOO-*goo-breh*	dismal
"	"	mournful (saddening)
lui	LOO-*ee*	him
lui stesso	LOO-*ee* STESS-*soh*	himself
lumaca, *f.*	*loo-*MAH*-kah*	snail
luna, *f.*	LOO-*nah*	moon
lunghezza, *f.*	*loong-*GETT*-tsah*	length
lungo	LOONG-*goh*	along (lengthwise of)
"	"	long (not short)
lungo...	LOONG-*goh...*	long (of a specified length)
luogo, *m.*	LWOH-*goh*	location
"	"	place (locality)
"	"	spot
"	"	stead
lupo, *m.*	LOO-*poh*	wolf
lusso, *m.*	LOOSS-*soh*	luxury
lustro, *m.*	LOO-*stroh*	luster (sheen)
ma	MAH	but (yet, *conj.*)
macchia, *f.*	MAHK-*k_yah*	blot
"	"	spot
"	"	stain
"	"	thicket
macchiare (1)	*mahk-*K_YAH*-reh*	blot (stain), to
macchina, *f.*	MAHK-*kee-nah*	machine
macchina calcolatrice, *f.*	MAHK-*kee-nah kahl-koh-lah-*TREE*-cheh*	adding machine
macchina da cucire, *f.*	MAHK-*kee-nah dah koo-*CHEE*-reh*	sewing machine
macchina da scrivere, *f.*	MAHK-*kee-nah dah* SKREE-*veh-reh*	typewriter
macchinario, *m.*	*mahk-kee-*NAH*-r_yoh*	machinery
macchinista, *m.*	*mahk-kee-*NEE*-stah*	engineer (railroad engineman)
macellaio, *m.*	*mah-chell-*LAH*-yoh*	butcher
macello, *m.*	*mah-*CHELL*-loh*	slaughter
macinare (1)	*mah-chee-*NAH*-reh*	grind (crush), to
madre, *f.*	MAH-*dreh*	mother
Madrid, *f.*	*mah-*DREED	Madrid
maestà, *f.*	*mah-eh-*STAH	majesty
maestro, *m.*	*mah-*EH-*stroh*	master (great artist)
maestro (di scuola), *m.*	*mah-*EH-*stroh (dee* SKWOH-*lah)*	teacher
magazzino, *m.*	*mah-gahd-*DZEE*-noh*	warehouse
maggioranza, *f.*	*mahd-joh-*RAHN*-tsah*	majority (greater number)
maggiore	*mahd-*JOH*-reh*	major (larger)
"	"	senior (older)
magia, *f.*	*mah-*JEE*-ah*	magic (*n.*)
maglia, *f.*	MAH-*l_yah*	sweater
magnifico	*mah-*N_YEE*-fee-koh*	gorgeous
"	"	magnificent
mago, *m.*	MAH-*goh*	magician
"	"	wizard (sorcerer)
magro	MAH-*groh*	lean
"	"	thin (not fat)
mai	MY	never
maiale, *m.*	*mah-*YAH*-leh*	hog (animal)
"	"	swine
malaria, *f.*	*mah-*LAH*-r_yah*	malaria
malato	*mah-*LAH*-toh*	sick (ailing)
malattia, *f.*	*mah-laht-*TEE*-ah*	disease
"	"	illness
"	"	sickness
mal di capo, *m.*	MAHL *dee* KAH-*poh*	headache
mal di dente, *m.*	MAHL *dee* DENN-*teh*	toothache
mal di gola, *m.*	MAHL *dee* GOH-*lah*	sore throat
mal d'orecchi, *m.*	*mahl doh-*REKK*-kee*	earache
male	MAH-*leh*	wrong (amiss, *adv.*)
male, *m.*	MAH-*leh*	evil (*n.*)
maledire (36)	*mah-leh-*DEE*-reh*	curse (damn), to
maledizione, *f.*	*mah-leh-dee-*TS_YOH*-neh*	curse
malfamato	*mahl-fah-*MAH*-toh*	notorious
malgrado	*mahl-*GRAH*-doh*	despite (*prep.*)
malinconia, *f.*	*mah-leen-koh-*NEE*-ah*	gloom (depression)
"	"	melancholy (dejection)
malinconico	*mah-leen-*KOH*-nee-koh*	gloomy (melancholy)

Italian	Pronunciation	English
malizia, *f.*	*mah-*LEE-*ts yah*	malice
mancanza, *f.*	*mahng-*KAHN-*tsah*	failure (neglect)
"	"	lack (deficiency)
"	"	want (lack)
mancare di (1)	*mahn-*KAH-*reh dee*	fail (neglect) to, to
"	"	lack (be without), to
mancia, *f.*	MAHN-*chah*	tip (gratuity)
mandare (1)	*mahn-*DAH-*reh*	send, to
mandorla, *f.*	MAHN-*dohr-lah*	almond
mandria, *f.*	MAHN-*dr yah*	herd (of animals)
mangiare (1)	*mahn-*JAH-*reh*	eat, to
manica, *f.*	MAH-*nee-kah*	sleeve
manico, *m.*	MAH-*nee-koh*	handle
maniera, *f.*	*mah-*N YEH-*rah*	fashion
"	"	manner (mode)
"	"	style
maniere, *f.pl.*	*mah-*N YEH-*reh*	manners (polite behavior)
manifesto	*mah-nee-*FEH-*stoh*	manifest (*adj.*)
mano, *f.*	MAH-*noh*	hand (*anat.*)
mantello, *m.*	*mahn-*TELL-*loh*	cloak (apparel)
mantenere (112)	*mahn-teh-*NEH-*reh*	maintain (preserve), to
manuale	*mah-*NWAH-*leh*	manual (by hand)
manuale, *m.*	*mah-*NWAH-*leh*	manual (small book)
manzo, *m.*	MAHN-*dzoh*	beef
maraviglia, *f.*	*mah-rah-*VEE-*l yah*	marvel
"	"	wonder
maraviglioso	*mah-rah-vee-*L YOH-*soh*	marvelous
"	"	wonderful
marca, *f.*	MAHR-*kah*	brand (trade mark)
"	"	mark (evidence)
marca di fabbrica, *f.*	MAHR-*kah dee* FAHB-*bree-kah*	trade mark
marcare (1)	*mahr-*KAH-*reh*	mark (designate), to
marciapiede, *m.*	*mahr-chah-*P YEH-*deh*	platform, railroad
"	"	sidewalk
marciare (1)	*mahr-*CHAH-*reh*	march, to
marcio	MAHR-*choh*	rotten (decayed)
marcire (3)	*mahr-*CHEE-*reh*	rot, to
mare, *m.*	MAH-*reh*	sea
marea alta, *f.*	*mah-*REH-*ah* AHL-*tah*	tide, high
marea bassa, *f.*	*mah-*REH-*ah* BAHSS-*sah*	tide, low
Mare Mediterraneo, *m.*	MAH-*reh meh-dee-tehr-*RAH-*neh-oh*	Mediterranean Sea
margarina, *f.*	*mahr-gah-*REE-*nah*	margarine
margherita, *f.*	*mahr-geh-*REE-*tah*	daisy
margine, *f.*	MAHR-*jee-neh*	margin (edge)
marina, *f.*	*mah-*REE-*nah*	navy (*n.*)
marinaio, *m.*	*mah-ree-*NAH-*yoh*	sailor
marinare (1)	*mah-ree-*NAH-*reh*	pickle (preserve), to
marino	*mah-*REE-*noh*	marine (oceanic)
marito, *m.*	*mah-*REE-*toh*	husband
marmellata, *f.*	*mahr-mell-*LAH-*tah*	jam (preserve)
marmo, *m.*	MAHR-*moh*	marble (mineral)
marrone	*mahr-*ROH-*neh*	brown
martello, *m.*	*mahr-*TELL-*loh*	hammer (tool)
mascella, *f.*	*mah-*SHELL-*lah*	jaw
maschera, *f.*	MAH-*skeh-rah*	mask (face covering)
maschile	*mah-*SKEE-*leh*	masculine
maschio	MAH-*sk yoh*	male (*adj.*)
massa, *f.*	MAHSS-*sah*	mass (matter)
massaia, *f.*	*mahss-*SAH-*yah*	housewife
massima parte, la, *f.*	*lah* MAHSS-*see-mah* PAHR-*teh*	most (*n.*)
massima parte, per la	*pehr lah* MAHSS-*see-mah* PAHR-*teh*	mostly
massima parte di, la	*lah* MAHSS-*see-mah* PAHR-*teh dee*	most (greatest quantity, *adj.*)
massimo	MAHSS-*see-moh*	utmost (extreme, *adj.*)
masticare (1)	*mah-stee-*KAH-*reh*	chew, to
matematica, *f.*	*mah-teh-*MAH-*tee-kah*	mathematics
materasso, *m.*	*mah-teh-*RAHSS-*soh*	mattress
materia, *f.*	*mah-*TEH-*r yah*	material (substance)
"	"	matter
"	"	stuff (substance)
matita, *f.*	*mah-*TEE-*tah*	pencil
matita per labbra, *f.*	*mah-*TEE-*tah pehr* LAHB-*brah*	lipstick
matrigna, *f.*	*mah-*TREE-*n yah*	stepmother
matrimonio, *m.*	*mah-tree-*MOH-*n yoh*	marriage
mattino, *m.*	*maht-*TEE-*noh*	morning
mattone, *m.*	*maht-*TOH-*neh*	brick (building material)
maturare (1)	*mah-too-*RAH-*reh*	mature (ripen), to
maturo	*mah-*TOO-*roh*	ripe
mazzo (di carte), *m.*	MAHT-*tsoh (dee* KAHR-*teh)*	deck (of cards)
me	MEH	me
meccanico	*mekk-*KAH-*nee-koh*	mechanical
meccanico, *m.*	*mekk-*KAH-*nee-koh*	mechanic
medaglia, *f.*	*meh-*DAH-*l yah*	medal
media, *f.*	MEH-*d yah*	average (mean, *n.*)
medicamento, *m.*	*meh-dee-kah-*MENN-*toh*	drug (medicine)
medicare (1)	*meh-dee-*KAH-*reh*	dress, to (*med.*)
medicina, *f.*	*meh-dee-*CHEE-*nah*	medicine (medical science)
medico	MEH-*dee-koh*	medical
medico, *m.*	MEH-*dee-koh*	physician
mediocre	*meh-*D YOH-*kreh*	average (ordinary, *adj.*)
meditare (1)	*meh-dee-*TAH-*reh*	meditate (reflect), to
"	"	muse, to
meglio	MEH-*l yoh*	better (*adv.*)
mela, *f.*	MEH-*lah*	apple
melassa, *f.*	*meh-*LAHSS-*sah*	molasses
membro, *m.*	MEMM-*broh*	limb (*anat.*)
"	"	member (one of a group)
memoria, *f.*	*meh-*MOH-*r yah*	memory (ability to recall)
mendicante, *m.*	*menn-dee-*KAHN-*teh*	beggar
mendicare (1)	*menn-dee-*KAH-*reh*	beg (solicit alms), to
meno	MEH-*noh*	less (*adj., adv., prep.*)
meno che, a	*ah* MEH-*noh keh*	unless (*conj.*)
meno, (il)	*(eel)* MEH-*noh*	least (*adv.*)
mensile	*menn-*SEE-*leh*	monthly (every month, *adj.*)
mentale	*menn-*TAH-*leh*	mental
mentire (3)	*menn-*TEE-*reh*	lie (prevaricate), to
mento, *m.*	MENN-*toh*	chin
mentre	MENN-*treh*	as (while, *conj.*)
"	"	while (during the time that, *conj.*)
menzionare (1)	*menn-ts yòh-*NAH-*reh*	mention, to
menzogna, *f.*	*menn-*TSOH-*n yah*	falsehood (lie)
mercante, *m.*	*mehr-*KAHN-*teh*	merchant
mercanzia, *f.*	*mehr-kahn-*TSEE-*ah*	wares
mercato, *m.*	*mehr-*KAH-*toh*	market (trading center)
"	"	outlet (market, *bus.*)
merce, *f.*	MEHR-*cheh*	merchandise
merci, *f.pl.*	MEHR-*chee*	freight
"	"	goods
mercurio, *m.*	*mehr-*KOO-*r yoh*	mercury
meridionale	*meh-ree-d yoh-*NAH-*leh*	southern
meritare (1)	*meh-ree-*TAH-*reh*	deserve, to
"	"	earn, to
"	"	merit, to
meritevole	*meh-ree-*TEH-*voh-leh*	worthy (deserving)
merito, *m.*	MEH-*ree-toh*	credit (commendation)
"	"	merit
merletto, *m.*	*mehr-*LETT-*toh*	lace (fabric)
merlo, *m.*	MEHR-*loh*	blackbird
meschino	*meh-*SKEE-*noh*	mean (malicious)
mescolare (1)	*meh-skoh-*LAH-*reh*	blend (make combine), to
"	"	stir (mix), to
mese, *m.*	MEH-*seh*	month
messa, *f.*	MESS-*sah*	mass (*rel.*)
"	"	stake (thing wagered)
messaggero, *m.*	*mess-sahd-*JEH-*roh*	messenger (courier)
messicano	*mess-see-*KAH-*noh*	Mexican (*adj.*)
Messico, *f.*	MESS-*see-koh*	Mexico City
Messico, *m.*	MESS-*see-koh*	Mexico
me stesso	MEH STESS-*soh*	myself
mestiere, *m.*	*meh-*ST YEH-*reh*	craft
"	"	trade
meta, *f.*	MEH-*tah*	goal (objective)
metà, *f.*	*meh-*TAH	half (*n.*)
metallo, *m.*	*meh-*TAHL-*loh*	metal (*n.*)
metodo, *m.*	MEH-*toh-doh*	method
metropolitana, *f.*	*meh-troh-poh-lee-*TAH-*nah*	subway (underground railway)

Italian	Pronunciation	English
mettere (60)	METT-*teh-reh*	put (place), to
mettere in dubbio	METT-*teh-reh een* DOOB-*b_yoh*	question (doubt), to
mettere in grado di	METT-*teh-reh een* GRAH-*doh dee*	enable (make able), to
mettere in ordine	METT-*teh-reh een* OHR-*dee-neh*	straighten (put in order), to
mettere in relazione	METT-*teh-reh een reh-lah-*TS_YOH-*neh*	associate (relate), to
mezzanotte,*f.*	*medd-dzah-*NOHT-*teh*	midnight
mezzo	MEDD-*dzoh*	half (*adj.*)
mezzo,*m.*	MEDD-*dzoh*	means (method)
"	"	medium
mezzo,*m.*	MEDD-*dzoh*	middle (center)
mezzo di, a	*ah* MEDD-*dzoh dee*	through (by means of, *prep.*)
mezzo, con tal	*kohn tahl* MEDD-*dzoh*	thereby
mezzo di, in	*een* MEDD-*dzoh dee*	amid
mezzogiorno,*m.*	*medd-dzoh-*JOHR-*noh*	noon
mezzo-guanto,*m.*	MEDD-*dzoh-*GWAHN-*toh*	mitten
mi	MEE	(to) me, myself
mia (see mio, il)		
microbo,*m.*	MEE-*kroh-boh*	germ (micro-organism)
mie (see mio, il)		
miei (see mio, il)		
miele,*m.*	M_YEH-*leh*	honey
mietere (2)	M_YEH-*teh-reh*	reap, to
miglioramento,*m.*	*mee-l_yoh-rah-*MENN-*toh*	improvement (betterment)
migliorare (1)	*mee-l_yoh-*RAH-*reh*	improve (make better), to
migliore	*mee-*L_YOH-*reh*	better (*adj.*)
migliore, (il)	(*eel*) *mee-*L_YOH-*reh*	best (*adj.*)
militare	*mee-lee-*TAH-*reh*	military (*adj.*)
mina,*f.*	MEE-*nah*	mine (explosive)
minaccia,*f.*	*mee-*NAHT-*chah*	threat
minacciare (1)	*mee-naht-*CHAH-*reh*	threaten, to
minatore,*m.*	*mee-nah-*TOH-*reh*	miner
minerale,*m.*	*mee-neh-*RAH-*leh*	mineral
"	"	ore
minestra,*f.*	*mee-*NEH-*strah*	soup
miniera,*f.*	*mee-*N_YEH-*rah*	mine (pit)
minimo, (il)	(*eel*) MEE-*nee-moh*	least (*adj.*)
minimo,*m.*	MEE-*nee-moh*	least (*n.*)
ministro,*m.*	*mee-*NEE-*stroh*	minister
"	"	parson
minoranza,*f.*	*mee-noh-*RAHN-*tsah*	minority (smaller number)
minore	*mee-*NOH-*reh*	junior (younger)
"		minor (lesser)
minuto,*m.*	*mee-*NOO-*toh*	minute (unit of time)
mio, il	*eel* MEE-*oh*	mine (*poss. pron.*)
"	"	my
miracolo,*m.*	*mee-*RAH-*koh-loh*	miracle
mirare (1)	*mee-*RAH-*reh*	behold, to
miscela,*f.*	*mee-*SHEH-*lah*	blend (mixture)
miscellaneo	*mee-shell-*LAH-*neh-oh*	miscellaneous
mischiare (1)	*mee-*SK_YAH-*reh*	mix (make blend), to
misericordia,*f.*	*mee-zeh-ree-*KOHR-*d_yah*	mercy
missionario,*m.*	*meess-s_yoh-*NAH-*r_yoh*	missionary
misterioso	*mee-steh-*R_YOH-*soh*	mysterious
mistero,*m.*	*mee-*STEH-*roh*	mystery (enigma)
misto	MEE-*stoh*	motley (diverse)
mistura,*f.*	*mee-*STOO-*rah*	mixture
misura,*f.*	*mee-*ZOO-*rah*	measure (dimensions)
"	"	size (of hats, suits, dresses, coats)
misurare (1)	*mee-zoo-*RAH-*reh*	measure (find size of), to
mitigare (1)	*mee-tee-*GAH-*reh*	soften (mitigate), to
mito,*m.*	MEE-*toh*	myth (legend)
mobilia,*f.*	*moh-*BEE-*l_yah*	furniture
moda,*f.*	MOH-*dah*	fashion (current style)
modello,*m.*	*moh-*DELL-*loh*	model
moderato	*moh-deh-*RAH-*toh*	moderate (not extreme)
moderno	*moh-*DEHR-*noh*	modern
modesto	*moh-*DEH-*stoh*	modest
modificare (1)	*moh-dee-fee-*KAH-*reh*	qualify (modify), to
modo,*m.*	MOH-*doh*	mode
"	"	way (manner)

Italian	Pronunciation	English
modo di pensare,*m.*	MOH-*doh dee penn-*SAH-*reh*	outlook (attitude)
moglie,*f.*	MOH-*l_yeh*	wife
molla,*f.*	MOHL-*lah*	spring (coil)
molti	MOHL-*tee*	many
moltiplicare (1)	*mohl-tee-plee-*KAH-*reh*	increase (add to), to
"	"	multiply, to (*arith.*)
moltiplicarsi	*mohl-tee-plee-*KAHR-*see*	multiply (grow numerous), to
moltitudine,*f.*	*mohl-tee-*TOO-*dee-neh*	multitude
molto	MOHL-*toh*	much
"	"	very (extremely)
molto desideroso	MOHL-*toh deh-see-deh-*ROH-*soh*	anxious (wanting very much)
momento,*m.*	*moh-*MENN-*toh*	moment (instant)
monaca,*f.*	MOH-*nah-kah*	nun
monaco,*m.*	MOH-*nah-koh*	monk
monarca,*m.*	*moh-*NAHR-*kah*	monarch
monastero,*m.*	*moh-nah-*STEH-*roh*	monastery
mondo,*m.*	MOHN-*doh*	world
moneta,*f.*	*moh-*NEH-*tah*	coin
"	"	currency (money)
monotono	*moh-*NOH-*toh-noh*	monotonous (boring)
montagna,*f.*	*mohn-*TAH-*n_yah*	mountain
montagnoso	*mohn-tah-*N_YOH-*soh*	mountainous
montare (1)	*mohn-*TAH-*reh*	mount (climb upon), to
Monte di Pietà,*m.*	MOHN-*teh dee p_yeh-*TAH	pawnshop
Montevideo,*f.*	*mohn-teh-vee-*DEH-*oh*	Montevideo
montone,*m.*	*mohn-*TOH-*neh*	ram (animal)
monumento,*m.*	*moh-noo-*MENN-*toh*	monument
mora di rovo,*f.*	MOH-*rah dee* ROH-*voh*	blackberry
morale	*moh-*RAH-*leh*	moral (ethical)
morale,*m.*	*moh-*RAH-*leh*	morale
moralità,*f.*	*moh-rah-lee-*TAH	morals
mordere (61)	MOHR-*deh-reh*	bite, to
morire (62)	*moh-*REE-*reh*	die, to
morire di fame	*moh-*REE-*reh dee* FAH-*meh*	starve (die of hunger), to
mormorare (1)	*mohr-moh-*RAH-*reh*	murmur, to
mormorio,*m.*	*mohr-moh-*REE-*oh*	hum (murmur)
morso,*m.*	MOHR-*soh*	bite
mortale	*mohr-*TAH-*leh*	deadly
"	"	fatal
"	"	mortal (*adj.*)
morte,*f.*	MOHR-*teh*	death
morto	MOHR-*toh*	dead
mosca,*f.*	MOH-*skah*	fly (housefly)
Mosca,*f.*	MOH-*skah*	Moscow
mostra,*f.*	MOH-*strah*	exhibit
"	"	show
mostrare (1)	*moh-*STRAH-*reh*	show (make visible), to
mostrarsi	*moh-*STRAHR-*see*	show (be visible), to
mostro,*m.*	MOH-*stroh*	monster (beast)
mostruoso	*moh-*STRWOH-*soh*	monstrous (horrible)
motivo,*m.*	*moh-*TEE-*voh*	motive (*n.*)
motore,*m.*	*moh-*TOH-*reh*	engine
"	"	motor
motore a reazione,*m.*	*moh-*TOH-*reh ah reh-ah-*TS_YOH-*neh*	jet engine
motto,*m.*	MOHT-*toh*	motto
movimento,*m.*	*moh-vee-*MENN-*toh*	motion
"	"	movement
mucchio,*m.*	MOOK-*k_yoh*	heap
"	"	pile
muggire (3)	*mood-*JEE-*reh*	bellow (roar), to
mugnaio,*m.*	*moo-*N_YAH-*yoh*	miller
mulo,*m.*	MOO-*loh*	mule
muovere (64)	MWOH-*veh-reh*	move (shift the position of), to
muoversi	MWOH-*vehr-see*	move (shift one's position), to
muratore,*m.*	*moo-rah-*TOH-*reh*	mason (stonelayer)
muro,*m.*	MOO-*roh*	wall (outside)
muschio,*m.*	MOO-*sk_yoh*	moss
muscolo,*m.*	MOO-*skoh-loh*	muscle
museo,*m.*	*moo-*ZEH-*oh*	museum
musica,*f.*	MOO-*zee-kah*	music
musicale	*moo-zee-*KAH-*len*	musical
musicista,*m.*	*moo-zee-*CHEE-*stah*	musician

Italian	Pronunciation	English
mutarsi (1)	moo-TAHR-see	vary (undergo change), to

muto
  "
	MOO-toh
	  "
		dumb
		mute (silent)

mutuatario,*m.*	moo-twah-TAH-r_yoh	borrower (*bus.*)
mutuo	MOO-twoh	mutual
nailon,*m.*	NYE-lohn	nylon (*n.*)
nano,*m.*	NAH-noh	dwarf
Napoli,*f.*	NAH-poh-lee	Naples
narcotico,*m.*	nahr-KOH-tee-koh	drug (narcotic)
narice,*f.*	nah-REE-cheh	nostril
nascere (65)	NAH-sheh-reh	arise (come about), to born, to be
nascita,*f.*	NAH-shee-tah	birth
nascondere (66)	nah-SKOHN-deh-reh	hide (conceal), to
naso,*m.*	NAH-soh	nose (*anat.*)

nastro,*m.*
  "
	NAH-stroh
	  "
		band
		ribbon

Natale,*m.*	nah-TAH-leh	Christmas
natura,*f.*	nah-TOO-rah	nature (physical world)
naturale	nah-too-RAH-leh	natural
naturale,*m.*	nah-too-RAH-leh	nature (character)
naturalmente	nah-too-rahl-MENN-teh	course, of
nave,*f.*	NAH-veh	ship
nave portaerei,*f.*	NAH-veh pohr-tah-EH-ray	aircraft carrier
navigazione,*f.*	nah-vee-gah-TS_YOH-neh	navigation
navone,*m.*	nah-VOH-neh	turnip (white)
nazionale	nah-ts_yoh-NAH-leh	national (*adj.*)
nazione,*f.*	nah-TS_YOH-neh	nation
Nazioni Unite,*f.pl.*	nah-TS_YOH-nee oo-NEE-teh	United Nations

ne
  "
	NEH
	  "
		any (*pron.*)
		some (a quantity, *pron.*)

nè	NEH	nor
neanche	neh-AHNG-keh	either (not...either, *adv.*)

nebbia,*f.*
  "
	NEBB-b_yah
	  "
		fog
		mist

necessario	neh-chess-SAH-r_yoh	necessary
necessità,*f.*	neh-chess-see-TAH	necessity
necrologia,*f.*	neh-kroh-loh-JEE-ah	obituary (*n.*)
negare (1)	neh-GAH-reh	deny (contradict), to
negoziabile	neh-goh-TS_YAH-bee-leh	negotiable (*bus.*)
negoziato,*m.*	neh-goh-TS_YAH-toh	negotiation

negozio,*m.*
  "
	neh-GOH-ts_yoh
	  "
		shop
		store

negro,*m.*	NEH-groh	Negro
nè l'uno nè l'altro	neh LOO-noh neh LAHL-troh	neither (*adj., pron.*)

nemico,*m.*
  "
	neh-MEE-koh
	  "
		enemy
		foe

(non)...nè...nè	(NOHN)...NEH...NEH	neither...nor (*conj.*)
nero	NEH-roh	black
nervo,*m.*	NEHR-voh	nerve (*anat.*)
nervoso	nehr-VOH-soh	nervous (high-strung)
nessuna parte, in	een ness-SOO-nah PAHR-teh	anywhere (not...anywhere) nowhere
nessuno	ness-SOO-noh	anybody (not...anybody)
"	"	anyone (not...anyone)

nessuno
  "
  "
	ness-SOO-noh
	  "
	  "
		no (not any, *adj.*)
		nobody (*pron.*)
		none (*pron.*)

netto	NEHT-toh	net (*adj.*)
neutrale	neh_oo-TRAH-leh	neutral
neve,*f.*	NEH-veh	snow
Nicaragua,*m.*	nee-kah-RAH-gwah	Nicaragua
nichel,*m.*	NEE-kell	nickel (*chem.*)
nido,*m.*	NEE-doh	nest (bird home)
niente	N_YENN-teh	anything (not...anything)
"	"	nothing (*n.*)
Nilo,*m.*	NEE-loh	Nile

nipote,*f.*
  "
	nee-POH-teh
	  "
		granddaughter
		niece

nipote,*m.*
  "
	nee-POH-teh
	  "
		grandson
		nephew

nitrire (3)	nee-TREE-reh	neigh, to
no	NOH	no (nay)

Italian	Pronunciation	English
nobile	NOH-bee-leh	noble (*adj.*)
nobiltà,*f.*	noh-beel-TAH	nobility

noce,*f.*
  "
	NOH-cheh
	  "
		nut (food)
		walnut (*n.*)

noce moscata,*f.*	NOH-cheh moh-SKAH-tah	nutmeg
nodo,*m.*	NOH-doh	knot

noi
  "
	NOY
	  "
		us
		we

noia,*f.*	NOH-yah	boredom
noioso	noh-YOH-soh	dull (boring)
noi stessi	NOY STESS-see	ourselves
nome,*m.*	NOH-meh	name
		noun
nome di fanciulla,*m.*	NOH-meh dee fahn-CHOOL-lah	maiden name
nomina,*f.*	NOH-mee-nah	appointment (nomination)
nominare (1)	noh-mee-NAH-reh	appoint, to nominate, to
nominazione,*f.*	noh-mee-nah-TS_YOH-neh	nomination

non
  "
	NOHN
	  "
		no (not any, *adv.*)
		not

nondimeno
  "
	nohn-dee-MEH-noh
	  "
		nevertheless
		yet (*adv.*)

non importa chi	nohn eem-POHR-tah KEE	whoever (no matter who)
non importa dove	nohn eem-POHR-tah DOH-veh	wherever (no matter where)
nonna,*f.*	NOHN-nah	grandmother
nonno,*m.*	NOHN-noh	grandfather
non riuscire (120)	nohn ree-oo-SHEE-reh	fail (be unsuccessful), to
non riuscire a	nohn ree-oo-SHEE-reh ah ah NOHRD	miss (fail to do), to
nord, a		north (*adv.*)
nord-est, del	dell nohr-DEST	northeast (*adj.*)
nord-ovest, del	dell nohr-DOH-vest	northwest (*adj.*)

normale
  "
	nohr-MAH-leh
	  "
		normal (*adj.*)
		standard (regular)

norvegese	nohr-veh-JEH-seh	Norwegian (*adj.*)
Norvegia,*f.*	nohr-VEH-jah	Norway
nostalgico	noh-STAHL-jee-koh	homesick
nostra (see **nostro, il**)		
nostre (see **nostro, il**)		
nostri (see **nostro, il**)		

nostro, il
  "
	eel NOH-stroh
	  "
		our
		ours

nota,*f.*	NOH-tah	note (*mus.*)
notaio,*m.*	no-TAH-yoh	notary
notare (1)	noh-TAH-reh	note (perceive), to
notevole	noh-TEH-voh-leh	notable (*adj.*)
notificare (1)	noh-tee-fee-KAH-reh	notify, to
notte,*f.*	NOHT-teh	night
novella,*f.*	noh-VELL-lah	short story
nozione,*f.*	noh-TS_YOH-neh	notion (idea)
nuca,*f.*	NOO-kah	nape

nudo
  "
	NOO-doh
	  "
		bare (nude)
		naked

nullo	NOOL-loh	void (null)
numerare (1)	noo-meh-RAH-reh	number (assign numbers to), to

numero,*m.*
  "
	NOO-meh-roh
	  "
		number (numeral)
		size (of shoes, gloves)

numeroso	noo-meh-ROH-soh	numerous
nuocere a	NWOH-cheh-reh ah	harm (damage), to
nuora,*f.*	NWOH-rah	daughter-in-law
nuotare (1)	nwoh-TAH-reh	swim, to
Nuova Delhi,*f.*	NWOH-vah DEH-lee	New Delhi
Nuova York,*f.*	NWOH-vah YOHRK	New York
nuovo	NWOH-voh	new
nuovo, di	dee NWOH-voh	again
nutrimento,*m.*	noo-tree-MENN-toh	nourishment

nutrire (3)
  "
  "
	noo-TREE-reh
	  "
	  "
		cherish, to
		feed (give food to), to
		nourish, to

nuvola,*f.*	NOO-voh-lah	cloud
nuvoloso	noo-voh-LOH-soh	cloudy (overcast)
o	OH	or

Italian	Pronunciation	English
oasi, *f.*	OH-*ah-zee*	oasis
obbediente	*ohb-beh-*D_YENN-*teh*	obedient
obbedienza, *f.*	*ohb-beh-*D_YENN-*tsah*	obedience (compliance)
obbedire a (3)	*ohb-beh-*DEE-*reh ah*	obey, to
obbiettare (1)	*ohb-b_yett-*TAH-*reh*	object, to
obbiezione, *f.*	*ohb-b_yeh-*TS_YOH-*neh*	objection
obbligare (1)	*ohb-blee-*GAH-*reh*	oblige (compel), to
obbligatorio	*ohb-blee-gah-*TOH-*r_yoh*	obligatory (binding)
obbligazione, *f.*	*ohb-blee-gah-*TS_YOH-*neh*	bond
"	"	debenture
"	"	obligation (duty)
oboe, *m.*	OH-*boh-eh*	oboe
oca, *f.*	OH-*kah*	goose
occasione, *f.*	*ohk-kah-z*YOH-*neh*	bargain (advantageous purchase)
"	"	chance
"	"	occasion
"	"	opportunity
occhiali, *m.pl.*	*ohk-*K_YAH-*lee*	glasses
"	"	spectacles
occhiali da sole, *m. pl.*	*ohk-*K_YAH-*lee dah* SOH-*leh*	sunglasses
occhiata, *f.*	*ohk-*K_YAH-*tah*	glance (quick look)
occhio, *m.*	OHK-*k_yoh*	eye (*anat.*)
occidentale	*oht-chee-denn-*TAH-*leh*	western
...occorrere (*imp.*) (29)	...*ohk-*KOHR-*reh-reh*	require (need), to
occupare (1)	*ohk-koo-*PAH-*reh*	occupy, to
occuparsi di	*ohk-koo-*PAHR-*see dee*	engage (be occupied) in, to
occupato	*ohk-koo-*PAH-*toh*	busy (occupied)
occupazione, *f.*	*ohk-koo-pah-*TS_YOH-*neh*	occupation
oceano, *m.*	*oh-*CHEH-*ah-noh*	ocean
odiare (1)	*oh-*D_YAH-*reh*	hate, to
odio, *m.*	OH-*d_yoh*	hate (hatred)
odorare (1)	*oh-doh-*RAH-*reh*	smell (perceive odor), to
odore, *m.*	*oh-*DOH-*reh*	odor
"	"	scent
"	"	smell
offendere (35)	*ohf-*FENN-*deh-reh*	offend (affront), to
offendersi di	*ohf-*FENN-*dehr-see dee*	resent, to
offensiva, *f.*	*ohf-fenn-*SEE-*vah*	offense (attack)
offerente, *m., f.*	*ohf-feh-*RENN-*teh*	bidder (*bus.*)
offerta, *f.*	*ohf-*FEHR-*tah*	bid (amount offered)
"	"	offer .
offesa, *f.*	*ohf-*FEH-*sah*	offense (transgression)
offrire (14)	*ohf-*FREE-*reh*	offer (tender), to
oggettivo, *m.*	*ohd-jett-*TEE-*voh*	objective (aim)
oggetto, *m.*	*ohd-*JETT-*toh*	article (thing)
"	"	object
oggi	OHD-*jee*	today
ogni	OH-*n_yee*	all (every, *adj.*)
"	"	any (every, *adj.*)
"	"	each (*adj.*)
"	"	every
ogni caso, in	*een* OH-*n_yee* KAH-*zoh*	anyhow (in any case)
ognuno	*oh-*N_YOO-*noh*	each one (*pron.*)
"	"	everybody
Olanda, *f.*	*oh-*LAHN-*dah*	Holland
"	"	Netherlands, The
olandese	*oh-lahn-*DEH-*seh*	Dutch (*adj.*)
olio, *m.*	OH-*l_yoh*	oil
olio d'oliva, *m.*	OH-*l_yoh doh-*LEE-*vah*	olive oil
oliva, *f.*	*oh-*LEE-*vah*	olive (fruit)
olmo, *m.*	OHL-*moh*	elm
oltre	OHL-*treh*	beyond (farther on than, *prep.*)
oltre a	OHL-*treh ah*	beside (other than, *prep.*)
oltremare, d'	*dohl-treh-*MAH-*reh*	oversea(s) (*adj.*)
ombra, *f.*	OHM-*brah*	shade
"	"	shadow
ombreggiante	*ohm-bredd-*JAHN-*teh*	shady
ombrello, *m.*	*ohm-*BRELL-*loh*	umbrella
omettere (60)	*oh-*METT-*teh-reh*	omit (leave out), to
onda, *f.*	OHN-*dah*	wave (billow)
onestà, *f.*	*oh-neh-*STAH	honesty
onesto	*oh-*NEH-*stoh*	honest
onorare (1)	*oh-noh-*RAH-*reh*	honor (respect), to
onorario, *m.*	*oh-noh-*RAH-*r_yoh*	fee
onore, *m.*	*oh-*NOH-*reh*	honor
onorevole	*oh-noh-*REH-*voh-leh*	honorable (upright)
o...o	OH...OH	either...or (*conj.*)
opera, *f.*	OH-*peh-rah*	opera
operai, *m.pl.*	*oh-peh-*RYE	worker
operare (1)	*oh-peh-*RAH-*reh*	operate (perform surgery), to
operazione, *f.*	*oh-peh-rah-*TS_YOH-*neh*	operation (*med.*)
opinione, *f.*	*oh-pee-*N_YOH-*neh*	belief
"	"	opinion
"	"	view
opporsi a (76)	*ohp-*POHR-*see*	oppose (combat), to
opposizione, *f.*	*ohp-poh-zee-*TS_YOH-*neh*	opposition (resistance)
opposto	*okp-*POH-*stoh*	opposite (*adj.*)
opposto, *m.*	*okp-*POH-*stoh*	opposite (*n.*)
opprimere (26)	*ohp-*PREE-*meh-reh*	oppress, to
ora	OH-*rah*	now (*adv.*)
ora, *f.*	OH-*rah*	hour
"	"	time (hour determined by clock)
orale	*oh-*RAH-*leh*	oral (spoken)
orario, *m.*	*oh-*RAH-*r_yoh*	schedule
"	"	timetable
oratore, *m.*	*oh-rah-*TOH-*reh*	speaker (orator)
orchestra, *f.*	*ohr-*KEH-*strah*	orchestra (*mus.*)
orchidea, *f.*	*ohr-kee-*DEH-*ah*	orchid (flower)
ordinare (1)	*ohr-dee-*NAH-*reh*	arrange (plan), to
ordinario	*ohr-dee-*NAH-*r_yoh*	regular (normal)
ordinazione, *f.*	*ohr-dee-nah-*TS_YOH-*neh*	order (purchase)
ordine, *m.*	OHR-*dee-neh*	order (command)
ordine, *m.*	OHR-*dee-neh*	order (orderliness)
"	"	order (sequence)
orecchino, *m.*	*oh-rekk-*KEE-*noh*	earring
orecchio, *m.*	*oh-*REKK-*k_yoh*	ear
orecchioni, *m.pl.*	*oh-rekk-*K_YOH-*nee*	mumps
ore straordinarie, *f.pl.*	OH-*reh strah-ohr-dee-*NAH-*r_yeh*	overtime (*bus., n.*)
orfano, *m.*	OHR-*fah-noh*	orphan (*n.*)
organizzare (1)	*ohr-gah-need-*DZAH-*reh*	organize (systematize), to
organizzazione, *f.*	*ohr-gah-need-dzah-*TS_YOH-*neh*	organization (association)
organo, *m.*	OHR-*gah-noh*	organ
orgoglio, *m.*	*ohr-*GOH-*l_yoh*	pride (self-esteem)
orgoglioso	*ohr-goh-*L_YOH-*soh*	proud (taking pride in)
orientale	*oh-r_yenn-*TAH-*leh*	eastern
Oriente, *m.*	*oh-*R_YENN-*teh*	Orient
originale	*oh-ree-jee-*NAH-*leh*	original
"	"	quaint (unusual)
"	"	singular (peculiar)
origine, *f.*	*oh-*REE-*jee-neh*	origin (source)
orizzontale	*oh-reed-dzohn-*TAH-*leh*	horizontal (*adj.*)
orizzonte, *m.*	*oh-reed-*DZOHN-*teh*	horizon
orlo, *m.*	OHR-*loh*	brink (verge)
"	"	edge (border)
"	"	hem
"	"	ledge
"	"	rim
orlo dei calzoni, *m.*	OHR-*loh day kahl-*TSOH-*nee*	cuff (of trouser)
ornamento, *m.*	*ohr-nah-*MENN-*toh*	ornament
ornare (1)	*ohr-*NAH-*reh*	adorn (beautify), to
"	"	dress (decorate), to
"	"	trim, to
ornato	*ohr-*NAH-*toh*	fancy (ornamental, *adj.*)
oro, *m.*	OH-*roh*	gold
oro, d'	DOH-*roh*	golden
orologio, *m.*	*oh-roh-*LOH-*joh*	clock
"	"	watch (timepiece)
orribile	*ohr-*REE-*bee-leh*	horrible
orrore, *m.*	*ohr-*ROH-*reh*	horror (dread)
orso, *m.*	OHR-*soh*	bear (animal)
orzo, *m.*	OHR-*dzoh*	barley
osare (1)	*oh-*ZAH-*reh*	dare (venture), to
oscillare (1)	*oh-sheel-*LAH-*reh*	sway, to
"	"	swing (oscillate), to

Italian	Pronunciation	English
oscurare (1)	*oh-skoo-*RAH*-reh*	darken (make dark), to
oscurità, *f.*	*oh-skoo-ree-*TAH	darkness
oscuro	*oh-*SKOO*-roh*	dark (in color, *adj.*)
"	"	dim
"	"	obscure
Oslo, *f.*	OH*-zloh*	Oslo
ospedale, *m.*	*oh-speh-*DAH*-leh*	hospital
ospite, *m.,f.*	OH*-spee-teh*	guest
"	"	host
"	"	visitor
ospiti, *m.pl.*	OH*-spee-tee*	company (guests)
osservare (1)	*ohss-sehr-*VAH*-reh*	notice (see), to
"	"	observe, to
"	"	remark (say), to
osservatore, *m.*	*ohss-sehr-vah-*TOH*-reh*	observer
osservazione, *f.*	*ohss-sehr-vah-*TS_YOH*-neh*	comment
"	"	observation
"	"	remark
ossigeno, *m.*	*ohs-*SEE*-jeh-noh*	oxygen
osso, *m.*	OHSS*-soh*	bone
ostacolo, *m.*	*oh-*STAH*-koh-loh*	obstacle
ostile	*oh-*STEE*-leh*	hostile
ostrica, *f.*	OH*-stree-kah*	oyster
Ottawa, *f.*	OHT*-tah-wah*	Ottawa
ottenere (112)	*oht-teh-*NEH*-reh*	gain, to
"	"	get, to
"	"	obtain, to
"	"	secure, to
ottenere punti	*oht-teh-*NEH*-reh* POON*-tee*	score (gain points), to
ottimistico	*oht-tee-*MEE*-stee-koh*	optimistic
ottone, *m.*	*oht-*TOH*-neh*	brass (metal, *n.*)
ovest, *m.*	OH*-vest*	west (*n.*)
ovvio	OHV*-v_yoh*	obvious
oziare (1)	*oh-*TS_YAH*-reh*	loaf, to
ozio, *m.*	OH*-ts_yoh*	idleness (inactivity)
ozioso	*oh-*TS_YOH*-soh*	idle
pacco, *m.*	PAHK*-koh*	bundle
"	"	package
"	"	parcel
pacco postale, *m.*	PAHK*-koh* *pohss-*TAH*-leh*	parcel post
pace, *f.*	PAH*-cheh*	peace
Pacifico, *m.*	*pah-*CHEE*-fee-koh*	Pacific (*n.*)
padella, *f.*	*pah-*DELL*-lah*	pan, frying
padre, *m.*	PAH*-dreh*	father
padrigno, *m.*	*pah-*DREE*-n_yoh*	stepfather
padrone, *m.*	*pah-*DROH*-neh*	boss
"	"	employer
"	"	lord
"	"	master (one in authority)
paesaggio, *m.*	*pah-eh-*ZAHD*-joh*	landscape (scenery)
paese, *m.*	*pah-*EH*-zeh*	country (nation)
pagabile	*pah-*GAH*-bee-leh*	payable (due)
pagaia, *f.*	*pah-*GAH*-yah*	paddle (oar)
pagamento, *m.*	*pah-gah-*MENN*-toh*	payment
pagare (1)	*pah-*GAH*-reh*	pay, to
pagherò, *m.*	*pah-geh-*ROH	note (promise to pay, *bus.*)
pagina, *f.*	PAH*-jee-nah*	page (leaf)
paglia, *f.*	PAH*-l_yah*	straw (dry grain stalks)
paio, *m.* (*pl.* paia, *f.*)	PAH*-yoh*	pair
Pakistan, *m.*	*pah-kee-*STAHN	Pakistan
pakistano	*pah-kee-*STAH*-noh*	Pakistani (*adj.*)
pala, *f.*	PAH*-lah*	shovel (tool)
palazzo, *m.*	*pah-*LAHT*-tsoh*	palace
palchetto, *m.*	*pah-*KETT*-toh*	shelf
palcoscenico, *m.*	*pahl-koh-*SHEH*-nee-koh*	stage (dais)
Palestina, *f.*	*pah-leh-*STEE*-nah*	Palestine
palestra, *f.*	*pah-*LEH*-strah*	gymnasium (athletic arena)
palla, *f.*	PAHL*-lah*	ball (sphere)
pallacanestro, *m.*	*pahl-lah-kah-*NEH*-stroh*	basketball
pallido	PAHL*-lee-doh*	pale (wan)
pallone, *m.*	*pahl-*LOH*-neh*	balloon
pallottola, *f.*	*pahl-*LOHT*-toh-lah*	bullet
palma, *f.*	PAHL*-mah*	palm (tree)
palmo, *m.*	PAHL*-moh*	palm (of hand)
palpebra, *f.*	*pahl-*PEH*-brah*	eyelid

Italian	Pronunciation	English
palo, *m.*	PAH*-loh*	pole (rod)
"	"	post
"	"	stake
paltò, *m.*	*pahl-*TOH	coat (woman's overcoat)
palude, *f.*	*pah-*LOO*-deh*	marsh
"		swamp (*n.*)
Panamà, *m.*	*pah-nah-*MAH	Panama
pancia, *f.*	PAHN*-chah*	belly (abdomen)
panciotto, *m.*	*pahn-*CHOHT*-toh*	vest
panico, *m.*	PAH*-nee-koh*	panic (fear)
pane, *m.*	PAH*-neh*	bread
"	"	loaf
pane tostato, *m.*	PAH*-neh* *toh-*STAH*-toh*	toast (bread)
panettiere, *m.*	*pah-nett-*T_YEH*-reh*	baker
paniere, *m.*	*pah-*N_YEH*-reh*	basket
panino, *m.*	*pah-*NEE*-noh*	roll (bread)
panna, *f.*	PAHN*-nah*	cream
pantaloni, *m.pl.*	*pahn-tah-*LOH*-nee*	trousers
pantera, *f.*	*pahn-*TEH*-rah*	panther
pantofola, *f.*	*pahn-*TOH*-foh-lah*	slipper
papa, *m.*	PAH*-pah*	pope
pappagallo, *m.*	*pahp-pah-*GAHL*-loh*	parrot
parabrezza, *f.*	*pah-rah-*BREDD*-dzah*	windshield
paracadute, *f.*	*pah-rah-kah-*DOO*-teh*	parachute
paradiso, *m.*	*pah-rah-*DEE*-zoh*	paradise
paragrafo, *m.*	*pah-*RAH*-grah-foh*	paragraph
Paraguai, *m.*	*pah-rah-*GWAH*_y*	Paraguay
paralisi, *f.*	*pah-*RAH*-lee-zee*	paralysis
paralisi infantile, *f.*	*pah-*RAH*-lee-zee een-fahn-*TEE*-leh*	infantile paralysis
parallelo	*pah-rahl-*LEH*-loh*	parallel (*adj.*)
paravento, *m.*	*pah-rah-*VENN*-toh*	screen (partition)
parcare (1)	*pahr-*KAH*-reh*	park (put in place), to
parco, *m.*	PAHR*-koh*	park
parecchi	*pah-*REKK*-kee*	several (a few, *adj.*)
parente, *m.*	*pah-*RENN*-teh*	relative (kinsman)
parentesi, *f.pl.*	*pah-*RENN*-teh-zee*	parentheses
parere (68)	*pah-*REH*-réh*	seem (appear), to
parete, *f.*	*pah-*REH*-teh*	wall (inside)
pari, *m.*	PAH*-ree*	peer (equal)
Parigi, *f.*	*pah-*REE*-jee*	Paris
Parlamento, *m.*	*pahr-lah-*MENN*-toh*	parliament
parlare (1)	*pahr-*LAH*-reh*	speak, to
"	"	talk, to
parola, *f.*	*pah-*ROH*-lah*	word
parrocchia, *f.*	*pahr-*ROHK*-k_yah*	parish
parrocchiani, *m. pl.*	*pahr-rohk-*K_YAH*-nee*	congregation (religious community)
parte, *f.*	PAHR*-teh*	interest
"	"	part (portion)
"	"	section
"	"	share
parte, a	*ah* PAHR*-teh*	apart
parte, da	*dah* PAHR*-teh*	aside (away)
partecipare (1)	*pahr-teh-chee-*PAH*-reh*	participate, to
partenza, *f.*	*pahr-*TENN*-tsah*	departure (setting out)
particolare	*pahr-tee-koh-*LAH*-reh*	individual (particular, *adj.*)
"	"	particular (*adj.*)
"	"	private (personal)
partigiano, *m.*	*pahr-tee-*JAH*-noh*	follower (adherent)
partire (4)	*pahr-*TEE*-reh*	depart, to
"	"	leave, to
partita, *f.*	*pahr-*TEE*-tah*	lot (salable items, *bus.*)
partito, *m.*	*pahr-*TEE*-toh*	party (*pol.*)
partorire (3)	*pahr-toh-*REE*-reh*	bear (give birth to), to
parziale	*pahr-*TS_YAH*-leh*	partial (incomplete)
parzialmente	*pahr-ts_yahl-*MENN*-teh*	partly
pascersi (2)	PAH*-shehr-see*	graze (feed), to
pascolo, *m.*	PAH*-skoh-loh*	pasture (grassland)
Pasqua, *f.*	PAH*-skwah*	Easter
Pasqua degli Israeliti, *f.*	PAH*-skwah* *deh-l_yee ee-zrah_eh-*LEE*-tee*	Passover
passabile	*pahss-*SAH*-bee-leh*	fair (passable)
passaggio, *m.*	*pahss-*SAHD*-joh*	aisle
"	"	passage
passaporto, *m.*	*pahss-sah-*POHR*-toh*	passport

Italian	Pronunciation	English
passare (1)	*pahss-*SAH-*reh*	pass (go by), to
"	"	strain (filter), to
passare la mano su	*pahss-*SAH-*reh lah* MAH-*noh soo*	stroke (rub gently), to
passare sopra	*pahss-*SAH-*reh* SOH-*prah*	overlook (disregard), to
passatempo,*m.*	*pahss-sah-*TEMM-*poh*	pastime
passato	*pahss-*SAH-*toh*	past (bygone, *adj.*)
passato,*m.*	*pahss-*SAH-*toh*	past (*n.*)
passeggiare (1)	*pahss-sedd-*JAH-*reh*	stroll, to
passeggiata,*f.*	*pahss-sedd-*JAH-*tah*	walk (stroll)
passeggiata (in automobile),*f.*	*pahss-sedd-*JAH-*tah (een ow-toh-*MOH-*bee-leh)*	ride (in a car)
passeggiero,*m.*	*pahss-sedd-*JEH-*roh*	passenger
passero,*m.*	PAHSS-*seh-roh*	sparrow
passione,*f.*	*pahss-s_*YOH-*neh*	passion (emotion)
passo,*m.*	PAHSS-*soh*	rate (degree of speed)
"	"	step (stride)
pasta,*f.*	PAH-*stah*	batter (flour mixture)
pasta dentifricia,*f.*	PAH-*stah denn-tee-*FREE-*chah*	tooth paste
pastello,*m.*	*pah-*STELL-*loh*	crayon
pasto,*m.*	PAH-*stoh*	meal (repast)
pastore,*m.*	*pah-*STOH-*reh*	pastor
"	"	shepherd
patata,*f.*	*pah-*TAH-*tah*	potato (white)
patente,*f.*	*pah-*TENN-*teh*	license (permit)
patriota,*m.,f.*	*pah-*TR_YOH-*tah*	patriot
patti,*m.pl.*	PAHT-*tee*	terms (conditions)
pattino,*m.*	PAHT-*tee-noh*	skate, ice
patto,*m.*	PAHT-*toh*	bargain (agreement)
paura,*f.*	*pah-*OO-*rah*	fear
pauroso	*pah_oo_*ROH-*soh*	fearful (afraid)
pavimento,*m.*	*pah-vee-*MENN-*toh*	floor (bottom surface)
"	"	pavement
pavone,*m.*	*pah-*VOH-*neh*	peacock
paziente	*pah-ts_*YENN-*teh*	patient (forbearing)
paziente,*m.,f.*	*pah-ts_*YENN-*teh*	patient (invalid)
pazienza,*f.*	*pah-ts_*YENN-*tsah*	patience
pazzia,*f.*	*paht-*TSEE-*ah*	madness (insanity)
pazzo	PAHT-*tsoh*	crazy
"	"	mad (insane)
peccare (1)	*pekk-*KAH-*reh*	sin, to
peccato,*m.*	*pekk-*KAH-*toh*	sin
peccatore,*m.*	*pekk-kah-*TOH-*reh*	sinner
pece,*f.*	PEH-*cheh*	pitch (tar)
Pechino,*m.*	*peh-*KEE-*noh*	Peiping
pecora,*f.*	PEH-*koh-rah*	sheep
peggio	PEDD-*joh*	worse (*adv.*)
peggio,*m.*	PEDD-*joh*	worst (*n.*)
peggio, il	*eel* PEDD-*joh*	worst (*adv.*)
peggiore	*pedd-*JOH-*reh*	worse (*adj.*)
peggiore, (il)	*(eel) pedd-*JOH-*reh*	worst (*adj.*)
pelle,*f.*	PELL-*leh*	hide
"	"	skin
pelle camosciata,*f.*	PELL-*leh kah-moh-*SHAH-*tah*	suede (*n.*)
pelliccia,*f.*	*pell-*LEET-*chah*	fur
pellicola,*f.*	*pell-*LEE-*koh-lah*	film (*photog.*)
pellirossa,*m.,f.*	*pell-lee-*ROHSS-*sah*	Indian, American
pena,*f.*	PEH-*nah*	penalty
pendenza,*f.*	*penn-*DENN-*tsah*	slope (slant)
pendere (2)	PENN-*deh-reh*	hang (be suspended), to
penetrare (1)	*peh-neh-*TRAH-*reh*	penetrate (pierce), to
penicillina,*f.*	*peh-nee-cheel-*LEE-*nah*	penicillin
penisola,*f.*	*peh-*NEE-*zoh-lah*	peninsula
penna,*f.*	PENN-*nah*	pen
penna a sfera,*f.*	PENN-*nah ah* SFEH-*rah*	ball-point pen
penna stilografica, *f.*	PENN-*nah stee-loh-*GRAH-*fee-kah*	pen, fountain
pensare (1)	*penn-*SAH-*reh*	think (reason), to
pensiero,*m.*	*penn-s_*YEH-*roh*	thought (contemplation)
pensione,*f.*	*penn-s_*YOH-*neh*	boarding house
pentirsi (3)	*penn-*TEER-*see*	repent, to
pentola,*f.*	PENN-*toh-lah*	pot (container)
pepe,*m.*	PEH-*peh*	pepper (seasoning)
peperone,*m.*	*peh-peh-*ROH-*neh*	pepper (green vegetable)

Italian	Pronunciation	English
per	PEHR	by (*prep., math.*)
"	"	by (via, *prep.*)
"	"	for (*prep.*)
"	"	per (for each)
"	"	to (in order to, *prep.*)
pera,*f.*	PEH-*rah*	pear
percento,*m.*	*pehr-*CHENN-*toh*	percent (*n.*)
percentuale,*f.*	*pehr-chenn-*TWAH-*leh*	percentage
"	"	royalty (fee)
perchè	*pehr-*KEH	because (*conj.*)
"	"	for (*conj.*)
"	"	why
perciò	*pehr-*CHOH	therefore
perdere (69)	PEHR-*deh-reh*	lose, to
perdita,*f.*	PEHR-*dee-tah*	loss
perdonare (1)	*pehr-doh-*NAH-*reh*	forgive, to
"	"	pardon, to
perdono,*m.*	*pehr-*DOH-*noh*	forgiveness
"	"	pardon
perfetto	*pehr-*FETT-*toh*	perfect (flawless)
perfezione,*f.*	*pehr-feh-ts_*YOH-*neh*	perfection (flawlessness)
perforare (1)	*pehr-foh-*RAH-*reh*	drill (bore), to
"	"	pierce, to
pericolo,*m.*	*peh-*REE-*koh-loh*	danger
"	"	peril
pericoloso	*peh-ree-koh-*LOH-*soh*	dangerous
periodo,*m.*	*peh-*REE-*oh-doh*	period (of time)
"	"	term (duration)
perire (3)	*peh-*REE-*reh*	perish, to
perizia,*f.*	*peh-*REE-*ts_yah*	experience (skill)
perla,*f.*	PEHR-*lah*	bead (jewelry)
"	"	pearl (gem)
permanente	*pehr-mah-*NENN-*teh*	permanent (*adj.*)
permesso,*m.*	*pehr-*MESS-*soh*	permission
permettere (60)	*pehr-*METT-*teh-reh*	allow, to
"	"	let, to
"	"	permit, to
permettersi	*pehr-*METT-*tehr-see*	afford (have the means), to
però	*peh-*ROH	however (nevertheless)
perpetuo	*pehr-*PEH-*twoh*	perpetual
persistere	*pehr-*SEE-*steh-reh*	persist (persevere), to
persona,*f.*	*pehr-*SOH-*nah*	fellow (person)
"	"	figure (human form)
"	"	person
personaggio,*m.*	*pehr-soh-*NAHD-*joh*	character (person portrayed)
personale	*pehr-soh-*NAH-*leh*	personal
personale,*m.*	*pehr-soh-*NAH-*leh*	staff (personnel)
personalità,*f.*	*pehr-soh-nah-lee-*TAH	personality
persuadere (70)	*pehr-swah-*DEH-*reh*	induce, to
"	"	persuade, to
Peru,*m.*	*peh-*ROO	Peru
peruviano	*peh-roo-*V_YAH-*noh*	Peruvian (*adj.*)
pervertire (3)	*pehr-vehr-*TEE-*reh*	pervert (distort), to
pesante	*peh-*SAHN-*teh*	heavy
pesare (1)	*peh-*SAH-*reh*	weigh, to
pesca,*f.*	PEH-*skah*	peach
pescare (1)	*peh-*SKAH-*reh*	fish, to
pescatore,*m.*	*peh-skah-*TOH-*reh*	fisherman
pesce,*m.*	PEH-*sheh*	fish
peso,*m.*	PEH-*soh*	weight (scale weight)
pessimistico	*pess-see-*MEE-*stee-koh*	pessimistic
pestare (1)	*peh-*STAH-*reh*	pound (pummel), to
"	"	stamp (tread heavily), to
peste,*f.*	PEH-*steh*	pest (nuisance)
petrolio il- luminante,*m.*	*peh-*TROH-*l_yoh eel-loo-mee-*NAHN-*teh*	kerosene
pettegolezzo,*m.*	*pett-teh-goh-*LETT-*tsoh*	gossip (idle talk)
pettine,*m.*	PETT-*tee-neh*	comb (for hair)
pettirosso,*m.*	*pett-tee-*ROHSS-*soh*	robin
petto,*m.*	PETT-*toh*	breast
"	"	chest (*anat.*)
pezza,*f.*	PETT-*tsah*	patch (repair)
pezzetto,*m.*	*pett-*TSETT-*toh*	bit (small part)
"	"	scrap (fragment)
pezzo,*m.*	PETT-*tsoh*	piece (bit)
pezzo, al	*ahl* PETT-*tsoh*	each (apiece, *adv.*)

Italian	Pronunciation	English
pezzo a pezzo	PETT-*tsoh ah* PETT-*tsoh*	piecemeal (*adv.*)
piacere, *m.*	*p̶ yah*-CHEH-*reh*	pleasure
...piacere (a) (*imp.*) (71)	...*p̶ yah*-CHEH-*reh* (*ah*)	like (be fond of), to
piacere, ...non (*imp.*) (71)	...*nohn p̶ yah*-CHEH-*reh*	dislike, to
piacevole	*p̶ yah*-CHEH-*voh-leh*	pleasant
pianeta, *m.*	*p̶ yah*-NEH-*tah*	planet
piangere (72)	P̶ YAHN-*jeh-reh*	cry, to
"	"	mourn (feel grief), to
		weep, to
piano	P̶ YAH-*noh*	even (level, *adj.*)
"	"	flat (*adj.*)
"	"	level
piano, *m.*	P̶ YAH-*noh*	floor
"	"	plan (scheme)
"	"	plane (surface)
"	"	story
pianoforte, *m.*	*p̶ yah-noh*-FOHR-*teh*	piano (*n.*)
piano superiore, al	*ahl* P̶ YAH-*noh soo-peh-* R̶ YOH-*reh*	upstairs (*adv.*)
pianta, *f.*	P̶ YAHN-*tah*	plant (flora)
piantare (1)	*p̶ yahn*-TAH-*reh*	plant (sow), to
pianura, *f.*	*p̶ yah*-NOO-*rah*	plain (level land)
piatto, *m.*	P̶ YAHT-*toh*	dish (food)
"	"	plate (shallow dish)
piazza, *f.*	P̶ YAHT-*tsah*	square (plaza)
picchiare (1)	*peek*-K̶ YAH-*reh*	knock (hit), to
"	"	rap, to
piccino	*peet*-CHEE-*noh*	wee
piccione, *m.*	*peet*-CHOH-*neh*	pigeon
piccolino	*peek-koh*-LEE-*noh*	tiny
piccolo	PEEK-*koh-loh*	little (small, *adj.*)
"	"	small
picnic, *m.*	*pick-nick*	picnic
piede, *m.*	P̶ YEH-*deh*	foot (*anat.*)
piegare (1)	*p̶ yeh*-GAH-*reh*	bend (make bend), to
"	"	fold (lap over), to
piegarsi (1)	*p̶ yeh*-GAHR-*see*	bend (be bent), to
piego, *m.*	P̶ YEH-*goh*	fold (plait, *n.*)
pieno	P̶ YEH-*noh*	full (filled)
pietà, *f.*	*p̶ yeh*-TAH	sympathy (compassion)
pietra, *f.*	P̶ YEH-*trah*	stone (piece of rock)
pietra focaia, *f.*	P̶ YEH-*trah foh*-KAH-*yah*	flint
pigiama, *m.*	*pee*-JAH-*mah*	pajamas
pigro	PEE-*groh*	lazy
pila elettrica, *f.*	PEE-*lah eh*-LETT-*tree-kah*	battery (primary cell)
pilastro, *m.*	*pee*-LAH-*stroh*	pillar (column)
pillola, *f.*	PEEL-*loh-lah*	pill
pilota, *m.*	*pee*-LOH-*tah*	pilot (flier)
pino, *m.*	PEE-*noh*	pine (tree)
pioggia, *f.*	P̶ YOHD-*jah*	rain
piolo, *m.*	P̶ YOH-*loh*	peg (pin)
piombo, *m.*	P̶ YOHM-*boh*	lead (metal)
pioniere, *m.*	*p̶ yoh*-N̶ YEH-*reh*	pioneer
piovere (74)	P̶ YOH-*veh-reh*	rain, to
piovigginoso	*p̶ yoh-veed-jee*-NOH-*soh*	rainy
pipa, *f.*	PEE-*pah*	pipe (tobacco pipe)
pipistrello, *m.*	*pee-pee*-STRELL-*loh*	bat (animal)
pirata, *m.*	*pee*-RAH-*tah*	pirate
piroscafo, *m.*	*pee*-ROH-*skah-foh*	liner, ocean
pisello, *m.*	*pee*-SELL-*loh*	pea
pisolino, *m.*	*pee-soh*-LEE-*noh*	nap (doze, *n.*)
pista, *f.*	PEE-*stah*	trail (path)
pistola, *f.*	*pee*-STOH-*lah*	pistol
pittore, *m.*	*peet*-TOH-*reh*	painter (artist)
pittoresco	*peet-toh*-REH-*skoh*	picturesque
pittura, *f.*	*peet*-TOO-*rah*	painting (picture)
più	P̶ YOO	more (*adj.*)
"	"	plus (*prep.*)
più, (di)	(*dee*) P̶ YOO	further (to greater extent, *adv.*)
più, (il)	(*eel*) P̶ YOO	most (*adv.*)
piuma, *f.*	P̶ YOO-*mah*	feather
piuttosto	*p̶ yoot*-TOH-*stoh*	rather (preferably)
pizzicare (1)	*peet-tsee*-KAH-*reh*	pinch (squeeze), to
placare (1)	*plah*-KAH-*reh*	appease (calm), to
plastico, *m.*	PLAH-*stee-koh*	plastic (*n.*)
platino, *m.*	PLAH-*tee-noh*	platinum
plurale	*ploo*-RAH-*leh*	plural (*adj.*)
pneumatico, *m.*	*pneh̶ oo*-MAH-*tee-koh*	tire

Italian	Pronunciation	English
poche	POH-*keh*	few (not many, *adj.*)
pochi	POH-*kee*	few (not many, *adj.*)
poco	POH-*koh*	little (not much, *adj.*)
"	"	little (slightly, *adv.*)
poco, *m.*	POH-*koh*	little (small amount, *n.*)
poco, tra	*trah* POH-*koh*	soon (shortly)
poco, un	*oon* POH-*koh*	somewhat (*adv.*)
poco profondo	POH-*koh proh*-FOHN-*doh*	shallow
podere, *m.*	*poh*-DEH-*reh*	farm
poesia, *f.*	*poh-eh*-ZEE-*ah*	poem
"	"	poetry
poeta, *m.*	*poh*-EH-*tah*	poet
poggio, *m.*	POHD-*joh*	mound (hill)
poi	POY	then (subsequently)
polacco	*poh*-LAHK-*koh*	Polish (*adj.*)
politica, *f.*	*poh*-LEE-*tee-kah*	politics
politico	*poh*-LEE-*tee-koh*	political
polizia, *f.*	*poh-lee*-TSEE-*ah*	police
polizza, *f.*	POH-*leet-tsah*	policy (contract of insurance)
polizza di carico, *f.*	POH-*leet-tsah dee* KAH-*ree-koh*	bill of lading
pollame, *m.*	*pohl*-LAH-*meh*	poultry
pollice, *m.*	POHL-*lee-cheh*	thumb
pollo, *m.*	POHL-*loh*	chicken
"	"	fowl (poultry)
polmone, *m.*	*pohl*-MOH-*neh*	lung
polmonite, *f.*	*pohl-moh*-NEE-*teh*	pneumonia
polo, *m.*	POH-*loh*	pole (end of axis)
Polonia, *f.*	*poh*-LOH-*n̶ yah*	Poland
polpaccio, *m.*	*pohl*-PAHT-*choh*	calf (*anat.*)
polsino, *m.*	*pohl*-SEE-*noh*	cuff (of sleeve)
polso, *m.*	POHL-*sòh*	pulse (*physiol.*)
"	"	wrist
polvere, *f.*	POHL-*veh-reh*	dust
"	"	powder
polverizzare (1)	*pohl-veh-reed*-DZAH-*reh*	crumble, to
polveroso	*pohl-veh*-ROH-*soh*	dusty
pomeriggio, *m.*	*poh-meh*-REED-*joh*	afternoon
pomodoro, *m.*	*poh-moh*-DOH-*roh*	tomato
pompa, *f.*	POHM-*pah*	pump
pompiere, *m.*	*pohm*-P̶ YEH-*reh*	fireman
ponte, *m.*	POHN-*teh*	bridge (span)
"	"	deck (of ship)
popolare	*poh-poh*-LAH-*reh*	popular
popolazione, *f.*	*poh-poh-lah*-TS̶ YOH-*neh*	population (number of people)
popolo, *m.*	POH-*poh-loh*	people (populace)
porcellana, *f.*	*pohr-chell*-LAH-*nah*	porcelain (*n.*)
porco, *m.*	POHR-*koh*	pig (animal)
porta, *f.*	POHR-*tah*	door
portabagagli, *m.*	*pohr-tah-bah*-GAH-*l̶ yee*	porter (baggage carrier)
portacenere, *m.*	*pohr-tah*-CHEH-*neh-reh*	ash tray
portafoglio, *m.*	*pohr-tah*-FOH-*l̶ yoh*	briefcase
portamento, *m.*	*pohr-tah*-MENN-*toh*	carriage (posture)
portare (1)	*pohr*-TAH-*reh*	bear, to
"	"	bring, to
"	"	carry, to
"	"	fetch, to
"	"	wear (have on), to
portatore, *m.*	*pohr-tah*-TOH-*reh*	bearer (*banking*)
"	"	carrier (*bus.*)
porto, *m.*	POHR-*toh*	harbor
"	"	port
"	"	postage (postal charge)
Portogallo, *m.*	*pohr-toh*-GAHL-*loh*	Portugal
porzione, *f.*	*pohr*-TS̶ YOH-*neh*	portion
"	"	proportion (part)
posarsi (1)	*poh*-SAHR-*see*	perch (sit), to
poscritto, *m.*	*poh*-SKREET-*toh*	postscript
positivo	*poh-zee*-TEE-*voh*	positive (decisive)
posizione, *f.*	*poh-zee*-TS̶ YOH-*neh*	position
posporre (76)	*poh*-SPOHR-*reh*	postpone, to
possedere (98)	*pohss-seh*-DEH-*reh*	own, to
"	"	possess, to
possessione, *f.*	*pohss-sess*-S̶ YOH-*neh*	possession (ownership)
possibile	*pohss*-SEE-*bee-leh*	possible

Italian	Pronunciation	English
possibilità,*f.*	*pohss-see-bee-lee-*TAH	chance possibility
posta,*f.*	POH-*stah*	mail (postal system)
Posta Aerea,*f.*	POH-*stah ah-*EH*-reh-ah*	air mail
posteriore	*poh-steh-*R_YOH*-reh*	hind (posterior, *adj.*)
postino,*m.*	*poh-*STEE*-noh*	postman
posto,*m.*	POH-*stoh*	post (position) site
potente	*poh-*TENN*-teh*	mighty powerful
potere (77)	*poh-*TEH*-reh*	can (*v.*) may (*v.*)
potere,*m.*	*poh-*TEH*-reh*	might (*n.*) power (authority)
...povero	...POH-*veh-roh*	poor (needy)
povero...	POH-*veh-roh*...	poor (unfortunate)
povertà,*f.*	*poh-vehr-*TAH	poverty
pozzo,*m.*	POHT-*tsoh*	pool (standing water) well (*n.*)
pranzare (1)	*prahn-*DZAH*-reh*	dine, to
pranzo,*m.*	PRAHN-*dzoh*	dinner
prateria,*f.*	*prah-teh-*REE*-ah*	prairie
praticare (1)	*prah-tee-*KAH*-reh*	practice (put to practice), to
pratico	PRAH-*tee-koh*	practical (not theoretical)
prato,*m.*	PRAH-*toh*	meadow
precedente	*preh-cheh-*DENN*-teh*	former (preceding, *adj.*)
precedere (2)	*preh-*CHEH*-deh-reh*	lead (be in advance), to
precipitare (1)	*preh-chee-pee-*TAH*-reh*	plunge (hurl oneself), to
precipitarsi	*preh-chee-pee-*TAHR*-see*	dash (rush), to dive, to
precipitato	*preh-chee-pee-*TAH*-toh*	hasty (rash)
precipizio,*m.*	*preh-chee-*PEE*-ts_yoh*	cliff precipice
preciso	*preh-*CHEE*-zoh*	precise (exact)
preda,*f.*	PREH-*dah*	prey (victim)
predicare (1)	*preh-dee-*KAH*-reh*	preach, to
predicatore,*m.*	*preh-dee-kah-*TOH*-reh*	preacher
predire (36)	*preh-*DEE*-reh*	predict, to
prefazione,*f.*	*preh-fah-*TS_YOH*-neh*	preface
preferire (3)	*preh-feh-*REE*-reh*	prefer (like better), to
pregare (1)	*preh-*GAH*-reh*	pray, to
preghiera,*f.*	*preh-*G_YEH*-rah*	prayer (petition)
pregiudizio,*m.*	*preh-joo-*DEE*-ts_yoh*	prejudice
preliminare	*preh-lee-mee-*NAH*-reh*	preliminary (*adj.*)
premere (2)	PREH-*meh-reh*	press (bear upon), to
premio,*m.*	PREH-*m_yoh*	bonus (extra wages) premium (payment) prize (trophy)
prendere (78)	PRENN-*deh-reh*	take, to
prendere a prestito	PRENN-*deh-reh ah* PREH-*stee-toh*	borrow, to
prendere un bagno	PRENN-*deh-reh oon* BAH-*n_yoh*	bathe (take a bath), to
prenotare (1)	*preh-noh-*TAH*-reh*	book (engage space), to reserve (order in advance), to
prenotazione,*f.*	*preh-noh-tah-*TS_YOH*-neh*	reservation (advance order)
preoccuparsi (di) (1)	*preh-ohk-koo-*PAHR*-see (dee)*	care (be concerned), to
preoccupazione,*f.*	*preh-ohk-koo-pah-*TS_YOH*-neh*	worry (anxiety)
preparare (1)	*preh-pah-*RAH*-reh*	prepare (make ready), to
preparativo,*m.*	*preh-pah-rah-*TEE*-voh*	arrangement (preparation)
preparazione,*f.*	*preh-pah-rah-*TS_YOH*-neh*	preparation (preparatory act)
preposizione,*f.*	*preh-poh-zee-*TS_YOH*-neh*	preposition (*gram.*)
presa,*f.*	PREH-*sah*	outlet (*elec.*)
presentare (1)	*preh-zenn-*TAH*-reh*	introduce (make acquainted), to present, to
presentazione,*f.*	*preh-zenn-tah-*TS_YOH*-neh*	introduction (presentation)
presente,*m.*	*preh-*ZENN*-teh*	present (present time, *n.*)
presenza,*f.*	*preh-*ZENN*-tsah*	presence (being present)
presidente,*m.,f.*	*preh-see-*DENN*-teh*	chairman president
pressione,*f.*	*press-*S_YOH*-neh*	pressure (force)
presso	PRESS-*soh*	at (near) by (near, *prep.*)
prestare (1)	*preh-*STAH*-reh*	lend, to
prestito	PREH-*stee-toh*	loan
presto	PREH-*stoh*	soon (early)
prete,*m.*	PREH-*teh*	priest
pretendere (111)	*preh-*TENN*-deh-reh*	contend (maintain), to
pretesto,*m.*	*preh-*TEH*-stoh*	pretext
prevenire (123)	*preh-veh-*NEE*-reh*	prevent (stop), to
previdenza,*f.*	*preh-vee-*DENN*-tsah*	vision (foresight)
prezioso	*preh-*TS_YOH*-soh*	precious (costly)
prezzo,*m.*	PRETT-*tsoh*	charge price (*bus.*) rate
prezzo del viaggio, *m.*	PRETT-*tsoh dell* V_YAHD-*joh*	fare (*transp.*)
prigione,*f.*	*pree-*JOH*-neh*	prison
prigioniero,*m.*	*pree-joh-*N_YEH*-roh*	captive prisoner
prima	PREE-*mah*	before (earlier, *adv.*)
prima che	PREE-*mah keh*	before (prior to the time when, *conj.*)
prima di	PREE-*mah dee*	before (earlier than, *prep.*) by (prior to, *prep.*) until (before, *prep.*)
primario	*pree-*MAH*-r_yoh*	primary (first, *adj.*)
primavera,*f.*	*pree-mah-*VEH*-rah*	spring (season)
primitivo	*pree-mee-*TEE*-voh*	primitive (early)
primo	PREE-*moh*	chief (leading) first (*adj.*) former (first of two, *adj.*) prime (*adj.*)
principale	*preen-chee-*PAH*-leh*	main principal
principalmente	*preen-chee-pahl-*MENN*-teh*	chiefly (mainly)
principe,*m.*	PREEN-*chee-peh*	prince
principessa,*f.*	*preen-chee-*PESS*-sah*	princess
principiare (1)	*preen-chee-*P_YAH*-reh*	commence (make a start), to
principio,*m.*	*preen-*CHEE*-p_yoh*	beginning principle (basic truth)
privare (1)	*pree-*VAH*-reh*	deprive (divest), to
privazione,*f.*	*pree-vah-*TS_YOH*-neh*	hardship (privation)
privilegio,*m.*	*pree-vee-*LEH*-joh*	privilege
probabile	*proh-*BAH*-bee-leh*	likely (*adj.*) probable
problema,*m.*	*proh-*BLEH*-mah*	problem
processione,*f.*	*proh-chess-*S_YOH*-neh*	procession (parade)
processo,*m.*	*proh-*CHESS*-soh*	trial (court proceeding) process (set of operations)
proclamare (1)	*proh-klah-*MAH*-reh*	proclaim, to
procura,*f.*	*proh-*KOO*-rah*	power of attorney
procurare (1)	*proh-koo-*RAH*-reh*	procure (obtain), to
prodotto,*m.*	*proh-*DOHT*-toh*	produce (yield) product
produrre (7)	*proh-*DOO-R_*reh*	produce (make), to
produttivo	*proh-doot-*TEE*-voh*	productive
produzione,*f.*	*proh-doo-*TS_YOH*-neh*	output production (manufacture)
professionale	*proh-fess-s_yoh-*NAH*-leh*	professional
professione,*f.*	*proh-fess-*S_YOH*-neh*	profession (occupation)
professore,*m.*	*proh-fess-*SOH*-reh*	professor (teacher)
profeta,*m.*	*proh-*FEH*-tah*	prophet (religious teacher)
profittevole	*proh-feet-*TEH*-voh-leh*	profitable
profitto,*m.*	*proh-*FEET*-toh*	benefit (advantage) profit (*bus.*)
profondità,*f.*	*proh-fohn-dee-*TAH	depth (deepness)

Italian	Pronunciation	English
profondo	*proh*-FOHN-*doh*	deep (in extent)
"	"	profound
profumo,*m.*	*proh*-FOO-*moh*	perfume (fragrance)
progettare (1)	*proh-jett*-TAH-*reh*	plan (prearrange), to
progetto,*m.*	*proh*-JETT-*toh*	project
"	"	scheme (plan)
programma,*m.*	*proh*-GRAHM-*mah*	program (plan)
progressivo	*proh-gress*-SEE-*voh*	progressive
progresso,*m.*	*proh*-GRESS-*so*	advance
"	"	progress
proibire (3)	*proh-ee*-BEE-*reh*	forbid, to
proibito	*proh-ee*-BEE-*toh*	forbidden
proibizione,*f.*	*proh-ee-bee-*TS_YOH-*neh*	prohibition
proiettile tele-guidato,*m.*	*proh-*YET-*tee-leh teh-leh-gwee-*DAH-*toh*	guided missile
prolungare	*proh-loong-*GAH-*reh*	prolong, to
pro-memoria,*m.*	*proh-meh-*MOH-*r_yah*	memorandum
promessa,*f.*	*proh-*MESS-*sah*	promise (pledge)
promettere (60)	*proh-*METT-*teh-reh*	promise (pledge), to
prominente	*proh-mee-*NENN-*teh*	prominent (jutting)
promozione,*f.*	*proh-moh-*TS_YOH-*neh*	promotion (advance)
promuovere (64)	*proh-*MWOH-*veh-reh*	promote, to
pronto	PROHN-*toh*	prompt (quick)
"	"	ready (prepared)
pronunziare (1)	*proh-noon-*TS_YAH-*reh*	pronounce (enunciate), to
propenso a	*proh-*PENN-*soh ah*	apt to (prone to)
proporre (76)	*proh-*POHR-*reh*	propose (suggest), to
proporzione,*f.*	*proh-pohr-*TS_YOH-*neh*	proportion (ratio)
proposito,*m.*	*proh-*POH-*zee-toh*	design (intention)
proposta,*f.*	*proh-*POH-*stah*	proposal (suggestion)
proprietà letteraria,*f.*	*proh-pr_yeh-*TAH *lett-teh-*RAH-*r_yah*	copyright (*n.*)
proprietario,*m.*	*proh-pr_yeh-*TAH-*r_yoh*	owner
proprio	PROH-*pr_yoh*	own (*adj.*)
prora,*f.*	PROH-*rah*	bow (of ship)
prosa,*f.*	PROH-*zah*	prose
prosciugare (1)	*proh-shoo-*GAH-*reh*	drain (make dry), to
prosciutto,*m.*	*proh-*SHOOT-*toh*	ham (food)
prosperare (1)	*proh-speh-*RAH-*reh*	prosper, to
"	"	thrive (succeed), to
prosperità,*f.*	*proh-speh-ree-*TAH	boom (*bus.*)
"	"	prosperity
prospero	PROH-*speh-roh*	prosperous
prospetto,*m.*	*proh-*SPETT-*toh*	prospect (thing expected)
proteggere (79)	*proh-*TEDD-*jeh-reh*	protect, to
protesta,*f.*	*proh-*TEH-*stah*	protest
protestare (1)	*proh-teh-*STAH-*reh*	protest, to
protezione,*f.*	*proh-teh-*TS_YOH-*neh*	protection
prova,*f.*	PROH-*vah*	evidence (*law*)
"	"	proof (demonstration)
"	"	test (trial)
provare (1)	*proh-*VAH-*reh*	prove (verify), to
"	"	test, to
"	"	try, to
proverbio,*m.*	*proh-*VEHR-*b_yoh*	proverb
provincia,*f.*	*proh-*VEEN-*chah*	province (*pol.*)
provvedere (122)	*prohv-veh-*DEH-*reh*	provide, to
"	"	supply, to
provvigione (di sensale),*f.*	*prohv-vee-*JOH-*neh (dee senn-*SAH-*leh)*	brokerage (fee)
provvisorio	*prohv-vee-*ZOH-*r_yoh*	temporary
provvista,*f.*	*prohv-*VEE-*stah*	stock
"	"	supply (amount available)
prudente	*proo-*DENN-*teh*	conservative (cautious)
prugna,*f.*	PROO-*n_yah*	plum (fruit)
prugna secca,*f.*	PROO-*n_yah* SEKK-*kah*	prune
psichiatria,*f.*	*psee-k_yah-*TREE-*ah*	psychiatry
psicologia,*f.*	*psee-koh-loh-*JEE-*ah*	psychology
pubblicare (1)	*poob-blee-*KAH-*reh*	publish, to
pubblicazione,*f.*	*poob-blee-kah-*TS_YOH-*neh*	publication (published work)
pubblicità,*f.*	*poob-blee-chee-*TAH	publicity (notoriety)
pubblico	POOB-*blee-koh*	public (common, *adj.*)
pubblico,*m.*	POOB-*blee-koh*	public (populace, *n.*)
pugnalare (1)	*poo-n_yah-*LAH-*reh*	stab, to
pugnale,*m.*	*poo-*N_YAH-*leh*	dagger
pugno,*m.*	POO-*n_yoh*	fist
"	"	handful
"	"	punch (blow)
puledro,*m.*	*poo-*LEH-*droh*	colt
pulire (3)	*poo-*LEE-*reh*	clean, to
pulito	*poo-*LEE-*toh*	clean
"		neat (tidy)
pungere (80)	POON-*jeh-reh*	prick, to
"	"	sting (pierce skin), to
punire (3)	*poo-*NEE-*reh*	punish, to
punizione,*f.*	*poo-nee-*TS_YOH-*neh*	punishment
punta,*f.*	POON-*tah*	point (sharp end)
"	"	tip
punta, a	*ah* POON-*tah*	pointed (tapered)
puntare (1)	*poon-*TAH-*reh*	aim (direct), to
punto,*m.*	POON-*toh*	dot
"	"	period (*punct.*)
"	"	point
"	"	stitch (of sewing)
punto e virgola,*m.*	POON-*toh eh* VEER-*goh-lah*	semicolon
puntuale	*poon-*T_WAH-*leh*	prompt
"	"	punctual
pupilla,*f.*	*poo-*PEEL-*lah*	pupil (of eye)
purità,*f.*	*poo-ree-*TAH	purity (cleanness)
puro	POO-*roh*	pure (unadulterated)
"	"	sheer
putridume,*m.*	*poo-tree-*DOO-*meh*	decay (rottenness)
puzzare (1)	*poot-*TSAH-*reh*	stink, to
quaderno,*m.*	*kwah-*DEHR-*noh*	notebook
quadrante,*m.*	*kwah-*DRAHN-*teh*	dial (graduated face)
quadrato	*kwah-*DRAH-*toh*	square (*adj.*)
quadro,*m.*	KWAH-*droh*	picture (depiction)
qualche	KWAHL-*keh*	some (unspecified, *adj.*)
qualche cosa	KWAHL-*keh* KOH-*sah*	anything
"	"	something
qualche luogo, in	*een* KWAHL-*keh* LWOH-*goh*	somewhere
qualche modo, in	*een* KWAHL-*keh* MOH-*doh*	somehow
qualche tempo, per	*pehr* KWAHL-*keh* TEMM-*poh*	awhile (*adv.*)
qualche volta	KWAHL-*keh* VOHL-*tah*	sometimes
qualcuno	*kwahl-*KOO-*noh*	anybody (somebody)
"	"	anyone (someone)
"	"	somebody
"	"	someone
quale	KWAH-*leh*	which (*interrog. adj., pron.*)
quale, del (della, dei, delle)	*dell (dell-lah, day, dell-leh)* KWAH-*leh*	whose (*rel. pron.*)
quale, il (la, i, le)	*eel (lah, ee, leh)* KWAH-*leh*	which (*rel. pron.*)
qualità,*f.*	*kwah-lee-*TAH	quality
qualsiasi	*kwahl-*SEE-*ah-see*	any (any at all, *adj.*)
"	"	any (any one, *adj.*)
"	"	whichever (*adj.*)
qualsiasi cosa	*kwahl-*SEE-*ah-see* KOH-*sah*	whatever (*pron.*)
qualunque	*kwah-*LOONG-*kweh*	whatever (*adj.*)
qualunque cosa	*kwah-*LOONG-*kweh* KOH-*sah*	anything (anything whatever)
qualunque luogo, in	*een kwah-*LOONG-*kweh* LWOH-*goh*	anywhere (wheresoever)
quando	KWAHN-*doh*	when (any time that, *conj.*)
"	"	when (at what time, *adv.*)
"	"	when (which time, *pron.*)
quando in quando, di	*dee* KWAHN-*doh een* KWAHN-*doh*	occasionally
quandunque	*kwahn-*DOONG-*kweh*	whenever
quantità,*f.*	*kwahn-tee-*TAH	number
"	"	quantity (amount)
quaresima,*f.*	*kwah-*REH-*zee-mah*	Lent
quartiere generale,*m.*	*kwahr-*T_YEH-*reh jeh-neh-*RAH-*leh*	headquarters
quarto,*m.*	KWAHR-*toh*	quarter (one-fourth)
quasi	KWAH-*zee*	almost
"	"	nearly

Italian	Pronunciation	English
quasi tutto	KWAH-*zee* TOOT-*toh*	most (almost all, *adj.*)
quegli	KWEH-*l yee*	that
"	"	those (*adj.*)
quei	KWAY	those (*adj.*)
quel	KWELL	that (*adj.*)
quel che	KWELL *keh*	what (*rel. pron.*)
quella (see quello)		
quelle (see quei)		
quelli	KWELL-*lee*	those (*adj., pron.*)
quello	KWELL-*loh*	that (*adj., pron.*)
quercia, *f.*	KWEHR-*chah*	oak
questa (see questo)		
queste (see questi)		
questi	KWEH-*stee*	these (*adj., pron.*)
"	"	this
questione, *f.*	kweh-ST YOH-*neh*	issue (question)
questo	KWEH-*stoh*	this (*adj., pron.*)
qui	KWEE	here (*adv.*)
quietanzare (1)	kw yeh-tahn-TSAH-*reh*	receipt, to (*bus.*)
quiete, *f.*	KW YEH-*teh*	quiet (stillness)
quieto	KW YEH-*toh*	quiet (without motion, *adj.*)
quindi	KWEEN-*dee*	hence (consequently)
Quito, *f.*	KEE-*toh*	Quito
quota, *f.*	KWOH-*tah*	quota
quotazione, *f.*	kwoh-tah-TS YOH-*neh*	quotation (price)
quotidiano	kwoh-tee-D YAH-*noh*	daily (*adj.*)
rabbrividire (3)	rahb-bree-vee-DEE-*reh*	shudder, to
rabino, *m.*	rah-BEE-*noh*	rabbi
raccogliere (25)	rahk-KOH-*l yeh-reh*	collect, to
"	"	gather (bring together), to
"	"	raise (collect), to
raccolta, *f.*	rahk-KOHL-*tah*	collection
raccolto, *m.*	rahk-KOHL-*toh*	crop (produce)
"	"	harvest
raccomandare (1)	rahk-koh-mahn-DAH-*reh*	advocate, to
"	"	recommend (advise), to
raccomandato	rahk-koh-mahn-DAH-*toh*	registered (postal designation)
raccomandazione, *f.*	rahk-koh-mahn-dah-TS YOH-*neh*	recommendation
raccontare (1)	rahk-kohn-TAH-*reh*	relate, to
"	"	tell (narrate), to
racconto, *m.*	rahk-KOHN-*toh*	story (account)
"	"	tale (narrative)
raccorciarsi (1)	rahk-kohr-CHAHR-*see*	shrink (become contracted), to
radar, *m.*	RAH-*dahr*	radar (*n.*)
radiante	rah-D YAHN-*teh*	radiant
radicale	rah-dee-KAH-*leh*	radical (basic)
radicchiella, *f.*	rah-deek-K YELL-*lah*	dandelion
radice, *f.*	rah-DEE-*cheh*	root (*bot.*)
radio, *f.*	RAH-*d yoh*	radio (receiving set)
radioattività, *f.*	rah-d yoh-aht-tee-vee-TAH	radioactivity
radio diffusione, *f.*	RAH-*d yoh* deef-foo-Z YOH-*neh*	broadcasting (*rad.*)
radiografare (1)	rah-d yoh-grah-FAH-*reh*	X-ray (examine), to
radiografia, *f.*	rah-d yoh-grah-FEE-*ah*	X-ray (X-ray picture)
raffinare (1)	rahf-fee-NAH-*reh*	refine (purify), to
raffreddore, *m.*	rahf-fredd-DOH-*reh*	cold (disease)
ragazza, *f.*	rah-GAHT-*tsah*	girl
"	"	lass
ragazzo, *m.*	rah-GAHT-*tsoh*	boy (lad)
"	"	youngster
raggio, *m.*	RAHD-*joh*	beam
"	"	ray
raggio X, *m.*	RAHD-*joh* EE-*kess*	X-ray (Roentgen ray)
raggiungere (57)	rahd-JOON-*jeh-reh*	attain (arrive at), to
ragione, *f.*	rah-JOH-*neh*	ground (basis)
"	"	reason
ragionevole	rah-joh-NEH-*voh-leh*	reasonable (rational)
"	"	sensible
ragno, *m.*	RAH-*n yoh*	spider
rallegrare (1)	rahl-leh-GRAH-*reh*	cheer (gladden), to
rallegrarsi	rahl-leh-GRAHR-*see*	rejoice, to
rame, *m.*	RAH-*meh*	copper

Italian	Pronunciation	English
rametto, *m.*	rah-METT-*toh*	stick (small branch)
"	"	twig
rammendare (1)	rahm-menn-DAH-*reh*	darn (mend), to
ramo, *m.*	RAH-*moh*	bough
"	"	branch
rana, *f.*	RAH-*nah*	frog
rango, *m.*	RAHNG-*goh*	rank (standing)
rapidamente	rah-pee-dah-MENN-*teh*	fast (quickly)
rapido	RAH-*pee-doh*	fast
"	"	quick
"	"	rapid (*adj.*)
"	"	swift
rapimento, *m.*	rah-pee-MENN-*toh*	rapture
rapporto, *m.*	rahp-POHR-*toh*	account
"	"	connection (relationship)
"	"	ratio
"	"	relation
"	"	report
rappresentante, *m., f.*	rahp-preh-zenn-TAHN *teh*	agent (representative)
rappresentare (1)	rahp-preh-zenn-TAH-*reh*	represent (act for), to
rappresentazione, *f.*	rahp-preh-zenn-tah-TS YOH-*neh*	performance
"	"	representation
raramente	rah-rah-MENN-*teh*	seldom
raro	RAH-*roh*	rare (uncommon)
raschiare (1)	rah-SK YAH-*reh*	scrape (make smooth or clean), to
raso, *m.*	RAH-*soh*	satin (*n.*)
rasoio, *m.*	rah-ZOH-*yoh*	razor
rasoio elettrico, *m.*	rah-ZOH-*yoh* eh-LETT-*tree-koh*	shaver, electric
rastrello, *m.*	rah-STRELL-*loh*	rake (tool)
rata, *f.*	RAH-*tah*	installment (payment, *bus.*)
razione, *f.*	rah-TS YOH-*neh*	ration (allotment)
razza, *f.*	RAHT-*tsah*	breed (stock)
"	"	race (*anthrop.*)
razzo, *m.*	RAHD-*dzoh*	rocket
re, *m.*	REH	king
reagire (3)	reh-ah-JEE-*reh*	respond (react), to
reale	reh-AH-*leh*	royal
realizzare (1)	reh-ah-leed-DZAH-*reh*	achieve (attain), to
"	"	realize (accomplish), to
realtà, *f.*	reh-ahl-TAH	reality
realtà, in	een reh-ahl-TAH	really (actually)
reame, *m.*	reh-AH-*meh*	realm (kingdom)
reazione, *f.*	reh-ah-TS YOH-*neh*	reaction
recensione, *f.*	reh-chenn-S YOH-*neh*	review (critique)
recente	reh-CHENN-*teh*	recent
recentemente	reh-chenn-teh-MENN-*teh*	recently
recipiente, *m.*	reh-chee-P YENN-*teh*	vessel (receptacle)
recita diurna, *f.*	REH-*chee-tah* D YOOR-*nah*	matinee (theater performance)
recitare (1)	reh-chee-TAH-*reh*	play (take the role of), to
"	"	recite, to
reclamare (1)	reh-klah-MAH-*reh*	claim, to
reclamo, *m.*	reh-KLAH-*moh*	claim
redattore, *m.*	reh-daht-TOH-*reh*	editor
redine, *f.*	REH-*dee-neh*	rein (strap)
regale	reh-GAH-*leh*	regal
reggimento, *m.*	redd-jee-MENN-*toh*	regiment (*n.*)
reggipetto, *m.*	red-jee-PETT-*toh*	brassiere
regina, *f.*	reh-JEE-*nah*	queen
regione, *f.*	reh-JOH-*neh*	area
"	"	region
registrare (1)	reh-jee-STRAH-*reh*	record (set down), to
"	"	register, to
registratore a nastro, *m.*	reh-jee-strah-TOH-*reh* *ah* NAH-*stroh*	tape recorder
registri, *m. pl.*	reh-JEE-*stree*	records (files)
registro, *m.*	reh-JEE-*stroh*	register (record)
regno, *m.*	REH-*n yoh*	kingdom
"	"	reign (period of rule)
regola, *f.*	REH-*goh-lah*	rule (regulation)
"	"	rule (usual case)
regolamento, *m.*	reh-goh-lah-MENN-*toh*	regulation (rule)
regolarità, *f.*	reh-goh-lah-ree-TAH	regularity
relativo	reh-lah-TEE-*voh*	comparative
"	"	relative
relazioni, *f. pl.*	reh-lah-TS YOH-*nee*	dealings (relations)

Italian	Pronunciation	English
religione, *f.*	*reh-lee-*JOH*-neh*	religion
religioso	*reh-lee-*JOH*-soh*	religious (*adj.*)
remo, *m.*	REH*-moh*	oar (*n.*)
remoto	*reh-*MOH*-toh*	remote (far-off)
render conto di (2)	RENN*-dehr* KOHN*-toh dee*	account for (explain), to
rendere	RENN*-deh-reh*	render (cause to become), to
rendersi conto	RENN*-dehr-see* KOHN*-toh*	realize (recognize), to
rendimento, *m.*	*renn-dee-*MENN*-toh*	yield (product)
rendita, *f.*	RENN*-dee-tah*	annuity
rene, *m.*	REH*-neh*	kidney (*anat.*)
renna, *f.*	RENN*-nah*	reindeer
Reno, *m.*	REH*-noh*	Rhine
reparto, *m.*	*reh-*PAHR*-toh*	department (administrative unit)
repubblica, *f.*	*reh-*POOB*-blee-kah*	commonwealth
"	"	republic
Repubblica Dominicana, *f.*	*reh-*POOB*-blee-kah doh-mee-nee-*KAH*-nah*	Dominican Republic
repubblicano	*reh-poob-blee-*KAH*-noh*	republican (*adj.*)
resa, *f.*	REH*-sah*	surrender (*mil.*)
residenza, *f.*	*reh-see-*DENN*-tsah*	residence (abode)
resistente	*reh-see-*STENN*-teh*	tough (resistant)
resistenza, *f.*	*reh-see-*STENN*-tsah*	resistance
resistere a (16)	*reh-*SEE*-steh-reh ah*	resist, to
"	"	stand (bear), to
respirare (1)	*reh-spee-*RAH*-reh*	breathe (draw breath), to
responsabile	*reh-spohn-*SAH*-bee-leh*	liable
"	"	responsible (answerable)
responsabilità, *f.*	*reh-spohn-sah-bee-lee-*TAH	liability
"	"	responsibility
restare (1)	*reh-*STAH*-reh*	stay (remain), to
restituire (3)	*reh-stee-*TWEE*-reh*	return (give back), to
resto, *m.*	REH*-stoh*	difference (*math.*)
"	"	remainder
"	"	rest
rete, *f.*	REH*-teh*	net (mesh)
rettangolo, *m.*	*rett-*TAHNG*-goh-loh*	rectangle
reumatismo, *m.*	*reh_oo-mah-*TEE*-zmoh*	rheumatism
reverenza, *f.*	*reh-veh-*RENN*-tsah*	reverence
revolver, *m.*	*reh-*VOHL*-vehr*	revolver (weapon)
ribelle, *m., f.*	*ree-*BELL*-leh*	rebel (*n.*)
ribellione, *f.*	*ree-bell-l_*YOH*-neh*	rebellion
ricadere (21)	*ree-kah-*DEH*-reh*	relapse, to
ricchezze, *f.pl.*	*reek-*KETT*-tseh*	resources
"	"	riches
"	"	wealth
ricciolo, *m.*	REET*-choh-loh*	curl (ringlet)
ricco	REEK*-koh*	rich
"	"	wealthy
ricerca, *f.*	*ree-*CHEHR*-kah*	search (hunt)
ricetta, *f.*	*ree-*CHETT*-tah*	prescription (*med.*)
"	"	recipe
ricevere (2)	*ree-*CHEH*-veh-reh*	entertain (be host to), to
"	"	receive, to
ricevimento, *m.*	*ree-cheh-vee-*MENN*-toh*	party (social gathering)
"	"	receipt (receiving)
ricevuta, *f.*	*ree-cheh-*VOO*-tah*	receipt (voucher)
richiedere (22)	*ree-*K_YEH*-deh-reh*	demand (ask for), to
"	"	involve (entail), to
"	"	request, to
richiesta, *f.*	*ree-*K_YEH*-stah*	request
ricominciare (1)	*ree-koh-meen-*CHAH*-reh*	resume (recommence), to
ricompensa, *f.*	*ree-kohm-*PENN*-sah*	reward (recompense)
ricompensare (1)	*ree-kohm-penn-*SAH*-reh*	reward, to
riconoscente	*ree-koh-noh-*SHENN*-teh*	grateful
riconoscere (28)	*ree-koh-*NOH*-sheh-reh*	acknowledge (admit), to
"	"	recognize (identify), to
riconoscimento, *m.*	*ree-koh-noh-shee-*MENN*-toh*	recognition
ricordare a (1)	*ree-kohr-*DAH*-reh ah*	remind, to
ricordarsi	*ree-kohr-*DAHR*-see*	recall (remember), to
ricordarsi (di)	*ree-kohr-*DAHR*-see (dee)*	remember (recollect), to

Italian	Pronunciation	English
ricordo, *m.*	*ree-*KOHR*-doh*	memory (recollection)
"	"	remembrance
"	"	souvenir
ricorrere (29)	*ree-*KOHR*-reh-reh*	resort (have recourse), to
ricreazione, *f.*	*ree-kreh-ah-*TS_YOH*-neh*	recess (school intermission)
ricuperare (1)	*ree-koo-peh-*RAH*-reh*	recover (get back), to
ridere (85)	REE*-deh reh*	laugh, to
ridicolo	*ree-*DEE*-koh-loh*	ridiculous
ridicolo, *m.*	*ree-*DEE*-koh-loh*	ridicule
ridurre (7)	*ree-*DOO_R*-reh*	cut (reduce), to
"	"	reduce, to
riduzione, *f.*	*ree-doo-*TS_YOH*-neh*	reduction (lessening)
riferimento, *m.*	*ree-feh-ree-*MENN*-toh*	reference (allusion)
riferire (3)	*ree-feh-*REE*-reh*	refer (allude), to
riferirsi a	*ree-feh-*REER*-see ah*	relate (pertain) to, to
rifiutare (1)	*ree-f_yoo-*TAH*-reh*	deny (refuse), to
"	"	refuse, to
rifiuti, *m.pl.*	*ree-*F_YOO*-tee*	garbage
"	"	rubbish (litter)
riflessione, *f.*	*ree-fless-*S_YOH*-neh*	reflection (image)
riflessivo	*ree-fless-*SEE*-voh*	thoughtful (reflective)
riflettere (2)	*ree-*FLETT*-teh-reh*	reflect (throw back), to
riforma, *f.*	*ree-*FOHR*-mah*	reform (*n.*)
rifugiato, *m.*	*ree-foo-*JAH*-toh*	refugee
rifugio, *m.*	*ree-*FOO*-joh*	refuge
riga, *f.*	REE*-gah*	ruler (measuring instrument)
rigettare (1)	*ree-jett-*TAH*-reh*	reject, to
rigido	REE*-jee-doh*	stiff (inflexible)
rigoroso	*ree-goh-*ROH*-soh*	strict (stringent)
riguardare (1)	*ree-gwahr-*DAH*-reh*	concern (affect), to
riguardo, *m.*	*ree-*GWAHR*-doh*	consideration (regard)
riguardo a, (con)	(*kohn*) *ree-*GWAHR*-doh ah*	concerning
"	"	regarding
rilasciare (1)	*ree-lah-*SHAH*-reh*	release (let go of), to
rilevare (1)	*ree-leh-*VAH*-reh*	detect, to
"	"	note (mention), to
rilievo, *m.*	*ree-l_*YEH*-voh*	ridge (raised area)
rilucere (2)	*ree-*LOO*-cheh-reh*	glitter, to
rima, *f.*	REE*-mah*	rhyme
rimanere (86)	*ree-mah-*NEH*-reh*	remain, to
rimborsare (1)	*reem-bohr-*SAH*-reh*	reimburse, to
"	"	repay, to
rimborso, *m.*	*reem-*BOHR*-soh*	rebate (*bus.*)
"	"	refund (*bus.*)
rimedio, *m.*	*ree-*MEH*-d_yoh*	cure
"	"	remedy
rimessa, *f.*	*ree-*MESS*-sah*	remittance
rimettere (60)	*ree-*METT*-teh-reh*	remit (send payment), to
rimpiazzare (1)	*reem-p_yaht-*TSAH*-reh*	replace (be a substitute for), to
rimproverare (1)	*reem-proh-veh-*RAH*-reh*	reproach, to
rimprovero, *m.*	*reem-*PROH*-veh-roh*	reproach
...rincrescere (imp.) (31)	...*reeng-*KREH*-sheh-reh*	regret, to
rincrescimento, *m.*	*reeng-kreh-shee-*MENN*-toh*	regret (sorrow)
rinforzare (1)	*reen-fohr-*TSAH*-reh*	strengthen, to
rinfrescare (1)	*reen-freh-*SKAH*-reh*	cool (make less hot), to
rinfreschi, *m.pl.*	*reen-*FREH*-skee*	refreshments
ringhiare (1)	*reeng-G_*YAH*-reh*	growl, to
ringraziamenti, *m.pl.*	*reeng-grah-ts_yah-*MENN*-tee*	thanks (gratitude)
ringraziare (1)	*reeng-grah-*TS_YAH*-reh*	thank, to
rinnovare (1)	*reen-noh-*VAH*-reh*	renew, to
rinunciare (1)	*ree-noon-*CHAH*-reh*	renounce (give up), to
Rio de Janeiro, *m.*	REE*-oh deh jah-*NAY*-roh*	Rio de Janeiro
riparare (1)	*ree-pah-*RAH*-reh*	fix, to
"	"	repair, to
"	"	shelter, to
"	"	shield, to

Italian	Pronunciation	English
riparazione,*f.*	*ree-pah-rah-*TS_YOH-*neh*	repair (*n.*)
riparo,*m.*	*ree-*PAH-*roh*	shelter
ripetere (2)	*ree-*PEH-*teh-reh*	repeat (reiterate), to
ripetizione,*f.*	*ree-peh-tee-*TS_YOH-*neh*	rehearsal
riposarsi (1)	*ree-poh-*SAHR-*see*	rest (repose), to
riposo,*m.*	*ree-*POH-*soh*	repose (calm)
"	"	rest
riputazione,*f.*	*ree-poo-tah-*TS_YOH-*neh*	reputation
risa,*f.pl.*	REE-*sah*	laughter
risarcimento,*m.*	*ree-sahr-chee-*MENN-*toh*	compensation (*bus.*)
riscaldare (1)	*ree-skahl-*DAH-*reh*	heat, to
"	"	warm, to
riscattare (1)	*ree-skaht-*TAH-*reh*	redeem (buy back), to
riscatto,*m.*	*ree-*SKAHT-*toh*	ransom (*n.*)
rischio,*m.*	REE-*sk_yoh*	risk (danger)
riscuotere (97)	*ree-*SKWOH-*teh-reh*	collect, to (*bus.*)
riserva,*f.*	*ree-*SEHR-*vah*	reservation (mental qualification)
"	"	reserve (*bus.*)
riso,*m.*	REE-*soh*	rice
risolvere (17)	*ree-*SOHL-*veh-reh*	solve, to
risolversi	*ree-*SOHL-*vehr-see*	resolve (determine), to
risparmiare (1)	*ree-spahr-*M_YAH-*reh*	spare (not harm), to
risparmio,*m.*	*ree-*SPAHR-*m_yoh*	savings (money)
rispettabile	*ree-spett-*TAH-*bee-leh*	respectable
rispettare (1)	*ree-spett-*TAH-*reh*	respect (esteem), to
rispettivo	*ree-spett-*TEE-*voh*	respective (*adj.*)
rispetto,*m.*	*ree-*SPETT-*toh*	respect (esteem)
rispondere (87)	*ree-*SPOHN-*deh-reh*	reply, to
"	"	respond, to
rispondere a	*ree-*SPOHN-*deh-reh ah*	answer (reply to), to
risposta,*f.*	*ree-*SPOH-*stah*	answer
"	"	reply
"	"	response
ristabilire (3)	*ree-stah-bee-*LEE-*reh*	restore (reestablish), to
ristorante,*m.*	*ree-stoh-*RAHN-*teh*	restaurant
ristorare (1)	*ree-stoh-*RAH-*reh*	refresh, to
risuonare (1)	*ree-swoh-*NAH-*reh*	clang, to
"	"	peal, to
"	"	rattle, to
"	"	ring (resound), to
risuscitare (1)	*ree-soo-shee-*TAH-*reh*	revive, to
ritardare (1)	*ree-tahr-*DAH-*reh*	delay (retard), to
ritardo,*m.*	*ree-*TAHR-*doh*	delay
ritardo, in	*een ree-*TAHR-*doh*	behind (late, *adv.*)
"	"	late (tardily, *adv.*)
"	"	late (overdue, *adj.*)
"	"	slow (tardy)
ritenere (112)	*ree-teh-*NEH-*reh*	deem (regard), to
"	"	keep, to
"	"	retain, to
ritirare (1)	*ree-tee-*RAH-*reh*	withdraw (take back), to
ritirarsi	*ree-tee-*RAHR-*see*	retire (stop working), to
"	"	withdraw (depart), to
ritirata,*f.*	*ree-tee-*RAH-*tah*	retreat (*mil.*)
rito,*m.*	REE-*toh*	rite
ritornare (1)	*ree-tohr-*NAH-*reh*	return (go back), to
ritorno,*m.*	*ree-*TOHR-*noh*	return (coming or going back)
ritratto,*m.*	*ree-*TRAHT-*toh*	portrait
ritroso	*ree-*TROH-*soh*	bashful
ritroso, a	*ah ree-*TROH-*soh*	backward (in reverse, *adv.*)
riunione,*f.*	*ree_oo-*N_YOH-*neh*	meeting (assembly)
riunire (3)	*ree_oo-*NEE-*reh*	assemble (bring together), to
riunirsi	*ree_oo-*NEER-*see*	gather (congregate), to
riuscire, non (120)	*nohn ree_oo-*SHEE-*reh*	fail (be unsuccessful), to
riuscire (a)	*ree_oo-*SHEE-*reh* (*ah*)	succeed (attain goal), to
riuscire a, non	*nohn ree-oo-*SHEE-*reh ah*	miss (fail to do), to
riva,*f.*	REE-*vah*	bank
"		shore
rivale,*m.,f.*	*ree-*VAH-*leh*	rival (competitor)
rivedere (122)	*ree-veh-*DEH-*reh*	review (look over again), to

Italian	Pronunciation	English
rivelare (1)	*ree-veh-*LAH-*reh*	reveal (divulge), to
rivendita,*f.*	*ree-*VENN-*dee-tah*	resale (*bus.*)
rivista,*f.*	*ree-*VEE-*stah*	magazine (periodical)
rivolta,*f.*	*ree-*VOHL-*tah*	revolt
rivoluzione,*f.*	*ree-voh-loo-*TS_YOH-*neh*	revolution (*pol.*)
robusto	*roh-*BOO-*stoh*	stout (strong)
"	"	sturdy
roccia,*f.*	ROHT-*chah*	rock (large stone)
roccioso	*roht-*CHOH-*soh*	rocky (rock-covered)
rodere (88)	ROH-*deh-reh*	gnaw (bite), to
Roma,*f.*	ROH-*mah*	Rome
Romania,*f.*	*roh-mah-*NEE-*ah*	Rumania
romano	*roh-*MAH-*noh*	Roman (*adj.*)
romantico	*roh-*MAHN-*tee-koh*	romantic
romanzo,*m.*	*roh-*MAHN-*dzoh*	novel (book)
rombo,*m.*	ROHM-*boh*	halibut
rompere (89)	ROHM-*peh-reh*	break (make divide), to
"	"	break (make smash), to
rompersi	ROHM-*pehr-see*	break (come apart), to
rondine,*f.*	ROHN-*dee-neh*	swallow (bird)
rosa,*f.*	ROH-*zah*	rose (flower)
rospo,*m.*	ROH-*spoh*	toad
rosolia,*f.*	*roh-zoh-*LEE-*ah*	measles
rossetto,*m.*	*rohss-*SETT-*toh*	rouge
rosso	ROHSS-*soh*	red
rotaia,*f.*	*roh-*TAH-*yah*	rail (bar on track)
rotolare (1)	*roh-toh-*LAH-*reh*	roll (impel), to
rotolo,*m.*	ROH-*toh-loh*	roll (cylinder)
rotondo	*roh-*TOHN-*doh*	round (*adj.*)
rottura di contratto,*f.*	*roht-*TOO-*rah dee kohn-*TRAHT-*toh*	breach of contract (*bus.*)
rovesciare (1)	*roh-veh-*SHAH-*reh*	overturn (upset), to
rovina,*f.*	*roh-*VEE-*nah*	doom (ruin)
"	"	ruins (remains)
"	"	wreck
rovinare (1)	*roh-vee-*NAH-*reh*	ruin, to
"	"	wreck, to
rubare (1)	*roo-*BAH-*reh*	rob (steal from), to
"	"	steal, to
rubinetto,*m.*	*roo-bee-*NETT-*toh*	faucet
"	"	tap
rubino,*m.*	*roo-*BEE-*noh*	ruby (gem)
rubrica,*f.*	ROO-*bree-kah*	heading (title)
rude	ROO-*deh*	harsh (severe)
ruggine,*f.*	ROOD-*jee-neh*	rust
ruggito,*m.*	*rood-*JEE-*toh*	roar (*n.*)
rugiada,*f.*	*roo-*JAH-*dah*	dew
rullo,*m.*	ROOL-*loh*	roller (cylinder)
rum,*m.*	ROOM	rum
ruminare tristamente (1)	*roo-mee-*NAH-*reh tree-stah-*MENN-*teh*	brood over, to
rumore,*m.*	*roo-*MOH-*reh*	noise (din)
"	"	rumor
rumoroso	*roo-moh-*ROH-*soh*	noisy
ruolo,*m.*	RWOH-*loh*	role
ruota,*f.*	RWOH-*tah*	wheel
rurale	*roo-*RAH-*leh*	rural
ruscello,*m.*	*roo-*SHELL-*loh*	brook
"	"	creek (stream)
Russia,*f.*	ROOSS-*s_yah*	Russia
russo	ROOSS-*soh*	Russian (*adj.*)
sabbia,*f.*	SAHB-*b_yah*	sand
sabbioso	*sahb-*B_YOH-*soh*	sandy
sacco,*m.*	SAHK-*koh*	bag
"	"	sack
sacrificare (1)	*sah-kree-fee-*KAH-*reh*	sacrifice (forgo), to
sacrificio,*m.*	*sah-kree-*FEE-*choh*	sacrifice (giving up)
sacro	SAH-*kroh*	sacred
saggezza,*f.*	*sahd-*JETT-*tsah*	wisdom
saggio	SAHD-*joh*	sage (*adj.*)
"		wise
sala,*f.*	SAH-*lah*	hall (meeting room)
sala da pranzo,*f.*	SAH-*lah dah* PRAHN-*dzoh*	dining room
salario,*m.*	*sah-*LAH-*r_yoh*	wages
salce,*m.*	SAHL-*cheh*	willow
sale,*m.*	SAH-*leh*	salt
salire (90)	*sah-*LEE-*reh*	climb, to
"	"	rise (ascend), to
"		soar, to
salmone,*m.*	*sahl-*MOH-*neh*	salmon

Italian	Pronunciation	English	Italian	Pronunciation	English
salotto,*m.*	*sah*-LOHT-*toh*	parlor (living room)	scatola,*f.*	SKAH-*toh-lah*	box (container)
salsa,*f.*	SAHL-*sah*	sauce	scavare (1)	*skah*-VAH-*reh*	dig (excavate), to
salsiccia,*f.*	*sahl*-SEET-*chah*	sausage	"	"	mine (dig for), to
saltare (1)	*sahl*-TAH-*reh*	jump (bound), to	scegliere (92)	SHEH-*l̸ yeh-reh*	choose, to
"	"	leap, to	"	"	pick, to
"	"	skip, to	"	"	select, to
"	"	spring (leap), to	scellerato,*m.*	*shell-leh*-RAH-*toh*	villain
saltellare (1)	*sahl-tell*-LAH-*reh*	hop, to	scelta,*f.*	SHELL-*tah*	choice (act of choos-
salto,*m.*	SAHL-*toh*	jump (bound)			ing)
saltuario	*sahl*-TWAH-*r̸ yoh*	occasional	scelta, a	*ah* SHELL-*tah*	optional
salutare (1)	*sah-loo*-TAH-*reh*	greet, to	scelto	SHELL-*toh*	chosen
"	"	salute, to	scena,*f.*	SHEH-*nah*	scene (dramatic unit)
salute,*f.*	*sah*-LOO-*teh*	health ·	scenario,*m.*	*sheh*-NAH-*r̸ yoh*	scenario
Salvador,*m.*	*sahl-vah*-DOHR	Salvador, El	scheda di	SKEH-*dah dee voh-tah-*	ballot
salvare (1)	*sahl*-VAH-*reh*	rescue, to	votazione,*f.*	TS YOH-*neh*	
"	"	save, to	scheletro,*m.*	SKEH-*leh-troh*	skeleton (*anat.*)
salvataggio,*m.*	*sahl-vah*-TAHD-*joh*	rescue	schermo,*m.*	SKEHR-*moh*	screen (for movies)
salvatore,*m.*	*sahl-vah*-TOH-*reh*	savior	scherzare (1)	*skehr*-TSAH-*reh*	jest, to
salvezza,*f.*	*sahl*-VETT-*tsah*	salvation	"	"	joke, to
salvo	SAHL-*voh*	except (*prep.*)	scherzo,*m.*	SKEHR-*tsoh*	jest
"	"	safe (unharmed)	"	"	joke
sandwich,*m.*	SEND-*weech*	sandwich	schiacciare (1)	*sk̸ yaht*-CHAH-*reh*	crush, to
sangue,*m.*	SAHNG-*gweh*	blood	schiavitù,*f.*	*sk̸ yah-vee*-TOO	slavery
sanguinare (1)	*sahng-gwee*-NAH-*reh*	bleed (lose blood), to	schiavo,*m.*	SK̸ YAH-*voh*	slave
sano	SAH-*noh*	healthy	schizzare (1)	*skeet*-TSAH-*reh*	splash, to
"	"	sound	"	"	squirt, to
"	"	well (*adj.*)	schizzo,*m.*	SKEET-*tsoh*	sketch (rough draw-
"	"	wholesome (bene-			ing)
		ficial)	sciare (1)	*shee*-AH-*reh*	ski, to
sano di mente	SAH-*noh dee* MENN-*teh*	sane	sciarpa,*f.*	SHAHR-*pah*	scarf (neck cloth)
Santiago,*f.*	*sahn*-T̸ YAH-*goh*	Santiago	scientifico	*sh̸ yenn*-TEE-*fee-koh*	scientific
santo	SAHN-*toh*	holy	scienza,*f.*	SH̸ YENN-*tsah*	science
santo,*m.*	SAHN-*toh*	saint	scienza economica,	SH̸ YENN-*tsah eh-koh-*	economics
sapere (91)	*sah*-PEH-*reh*	know (have knowl-	*f.*	NOH-*mee-kah*	
		edge), to	scienza politica,*f.*	SH̸ YENN-*tsah poh*-LEE-	political science
sapone,*m.*	*sah*-POH-*neh*	soap		*tee-kah*	
sapone per la	*sah*-POH-*neh pehr lah*	shaving cream	scienziato,*m.*	*sh̸ yenn*-TS̸ YAH-*toh*	scientist
barba,*m.*	BAHR-*bah*		scimmia,*f.*	SHEEM-*m̸ yah*	monkey
sapore,*m.*	*sah*-POH-*reh*	flavor (savor)	scintilla,*f.*	*sheen*-TEEL-*lah*	spark
sardina,*f.*	*sahr*-DEE-*nah*	sardine	scintillare (1)	*sheen-teel*-LAH-*reh*	sparkle, to
sarto,*m.*	SAHR-*toh*	tailor	"	"	twinkle, to
sassofono,*m.*	*sahss*-SOH-*foh-noh*	saxophone	sciochezza,*f.*	*shoh*-KETT-*tsah*	folly
sbadigliare (1)	*zbah-dee*-L̸ YAH-*reh*	yawn, to	"	"	nonsense
sbagliato	*zbah*-L̸ YAH-*toh*	wrong (erroneous,	sciocco	SHOHK-*koh*	dumb (stupid)
		adj.)	"	"	silly
sbaglio,*m.*	ZBAH-*l̸ yoh*	mistake	sciocco,*m.*	SHOHK-*koh*	fool
sbarazzarsi di (1)	*zbah-raht*-TSAHR-*see dee*	rid (free), to	sciogliere (94)	SHOH-*l̸ yeh-reh*	dissolve, to
sbarcare (1)	*zbahr*-KAH-*reh*	bar (block), to	sciolto	SHOHL-*toh*	loose (unbound)
"	"	land (from a ship), to	scioperare (1)	*shoh-peh*-RAH-*reh*	strike (stop work), to
sbarramento,*m.*	*zbahr-rah*-MENN-*toh*	dam (dike)	sciopero,*m.*	SHOH-*peh-roh*	strike (work stop-
sbattere (2)	ZBAHT-*teh-reh*	flutter (flap), to			page)
sbiadire (3)	*zb̸ yah*-DEE-*reh*	fade (lose color), to	sciupare (1)	*shoo*-PAH-*reh*	waste (squander), to
sborso,*m.*	ZBOHR-*soh*	disbursement (*bus.*)	sciupo,*m.*	SHOO-*poh*	waste (squandering)
sbucciare (1)	*zboot*-CHAH-*reh*	peel (take skin from),	scivolare (1)	*shee-voh*-LAH-*reh*	glide, to
		to	"	"	slide, to
scabro	SKAH-*broh*	rough (uneven)	"	"	slip, to
scacchi (giuoco	SKAHK-*kee* (JWOH-*koh*	chess	scodella,*f.*	*skoh*-DELL-*lah*	bowl (dish)
degli),*m.pl.*	*deh-l̸ yee*)		scoiattolo,*m.*	*skoh*-YAHT-*toh-loh*	squirrel
scadenza,*f.*	*skah*-DENN-*tsah*	maturity (due date,	scomessa,*f.*	*skoh*-MESS-*sah*	bet
		bus.)	scommettere (60)	*skoh*-METT-*teh-reh*	bet, to
scadere (21)	*skah*-DEH-*reh*	expire (become void,	scomparire (12)	*skohm-pah*-REE-*reh*	vanish (go out of
		bus.), to			sight), to
"	"	lapse (become void),	sconfiggere (53)	*skohn*-FEED-*jeh-reh*	defeat (conquer), to
		to	sconfitta,*f.*	*skohn*-FEET-*tah*	defeat
"	"	mature (fall due), to	sconosciuto	*skoh-noh*-SHOO-*toh*	unknown
scaduto	*skah*-DOO-*toh*	due (payable)	scontare (1)	*skohn*-TAH-*reh*	discount, to (*bus.*)
scala,*f.*	SKAH-*lah*	ladder	sconto,*m.*	SKOHN-*toh*	discount (*n.*)
"	"	scale (graduated	scopa,*f.*	SKOH-*pah*	broom
		measure)	scoperta,*f.*	*skoh*-PEHR-*tah*	discovery
"	"	scale (proportion)	scoperto, allo	AHL-*loh skoh*-PEHR-*toh*	unpaid (due)
"	"	stairway	scopo,*m.*	SKOH-*poh*	aim
scaltro	SKAHL-*troh*	shrewd	"	"	purpose
scambiare (1)	*skahm*-B̸ YAH-*reh*	exchange (inter-	scoppiare (1)	*skohp*-P̸ YAH-*reh*	burst, to
		change), to	scoprire (14)	*skoh*-PREE-*reh*	discover, to
scambio,*m.*	SKAHM-*b̸ yoh*	exchange (barter)	scoraggiare (1)	*skoh-rahd*-JAH-*reh*	discourage (dis-
scandalo,*m.*	SKAHN-*dah-loh*	scandal			hearten), to
scapolo,*m.*	SKAH-*poh-loh*	bachelor (unmarried	scorrere (29)	SKOHR-*reh-reh*	flow (circulate), to
		man)	"	"	stream, to
scappare (1)	*skahp*-PAH-*reh*	escape, to	scossa,*f.*	SKOHSS-*sah*	shock (mental jolt)
scarafaggio,*m.*	*skah-rah*-FAHD-*joh*	beetle	Scozia,*f.*	SKOH-*ts̸ yah*	Scotland
scaricare (1)	*skah-ree*-KAH-*reh*	unload, to	scozzese	*skoht*-TSEH-*seh*	Scotch (*adj.*)
scarlattina,*f.*	*skahr-laht*-TEE-*nah*	scarlet fever	scrittore,*m.*	*skreet*-TOH-*reh*	writer (author)
scarlatto	*skahr*-LAHT-*toh*	scarlet (*adj.*)	scrittura,*f.*	*skreet*-TOO-*rah*	entry (*acctg.*)
scarpa,*f.*	SKAHR-*pah*	shoe (footwear)	"	"	writing (handwrit-
scarsità,*f.*	*skahr-see*-TAH	scarcity			ing)
scarso	SKAHR-*soh*	scarce			

Italian	Pronunciation	English
scrivania, *f.*	*skree-vah-*NEE-*ah*	desk
scrivere (96)	SKREE-*veh-reh*	spell, to
"	"	write, to
scrivere a macchina	SKREE-*veh-reh ah* MAHK-*kee-nah*	type (typewrite), to
scrutinio, *m.*	*skroo-*TEE-*n yoh*	poll (survey)
sculacciare (1)	*skoo-laht-*CHAH-*reh*	spank, to
scultore, *m.*	*skool-*TOH-*reh*	sculptor
scuola, *f.*	SKWOH-*lah*	school
"	"	schoolhouse
scuola media superiore, *f.*	SKWOH-*lah* MEH-*d yah soo-peh-*R YOH-*reh*	high school
scuola per corrispondenza, *f.*	SKWOH-*lah pehr kohr-ree-spohn-*DENN-*tsah*	correspondence school
scuotere (97)	SKWOH-*teh-reh*	shake, to
scusa, *f.*	SKOO-*zah*	excuse (pretext)
scusare (1)	*skoo-*ZAH-*reh*	excuse (pardon), to
scusarsi	*skoo-*ZAHR-*see*	apologize, to
sdoganamento, *m.*	*zdoh-gah-nah-*MENN-*toh*	clearance (customs clearance)
sdrucciolare (1)	*zdroot-choh-*LAH-*reh*	slip (slide), to
sdrucciolevole	*zdroot-choh-*LEH-*voh-leh*	slippery
se	SEH	if
"	"	whether
sebbene	*sebb-*BEH-*neh*	though (*conj.*)
secchia, *f.*	SEKK-*k yah*	bucket
"	"	pail
secco	SEKK-*koh*	dry
secolo, *m.*	SEH-*koh-loh*	century
secondo	*seh-*KOHN-*doh*	according to (in accordance with)
"	"	latter (second of two, *adj.*)
"	"	second (*adj.*)
secondo, *m.*	*seh-*KOHN-*doh*	second (time unit)
sedano, *m.*	SEH-*dah-noh*	celery
sedere (98)	*seh-*DEH-*reh*	sit (be sitting), to
sedersi	*seh-*DEHR-*see*	sit down, to
sedia, *f.*	SEH-*d yah*	chair
sedile, *m.*	*seh-*DEE-*leh*	seat
seduta, *f.*	*seh-*DOO-*tah*	session
sega, *f.*	SEH-*gah*	saw (tool)
segale, *f.*	SEH-*gah-leh*	rye (grain)
segnale, *m.*	*seh-*N YAH-*leh*	beam (radio signal)
"	"	signal
segno, *m.*	SEH-*n yoh*	mark (symbol)
"	"	sign (indication)
segretaria, *f.*	*seh-greh-*TAH-*r yah*	secretary (stenographer)
segreto	*seh-*GREH-*toh*	secret (*adj.*)
segreto, *m.*	*seh-*GREH-*toh*	secret (*n.*)
seguente	*seh-*GWENN-*teh*	next (following, *adj.*)
seguire (4)	*seh-*GWEE-*reh*	follow, to
seguito, in	*een* SEH-*gwee-toh*	next (*adv.*)
selezione, *f.*	*seh-leh-*TS YOH-*neh*	selection
sella, *f.*	SELL-*lah*	saddle (seat)
selvaggio	*sell-*VAHD-*joh*	savage (*adj.*)
"	"	wild (undomesticated)
sembrare (1)	*semm-*BRAH-*reh*	look (seem), to
seme, *m.*	SEH-*meh*	seed (ovule)
seminare (1)	*seh-mee-*NAH-*reh*	sow, to
sempiterno	*semm-pee-*TEHR-*noh*	everlasting
semplice	SEMM-*plee-cheh*	homely (everyday)
"	"	mere
"	"	simple (uninvolved)
semplicemente	*semm-plee-cheh-*MENN-*teh*	just
"	"	merely
semplicità, *f.*	*semm-plee-chee-*TAH	simplicity
sempre	SEMM-*preh*	always
"	"	ever
"	"	forever
senape, *m.*	SEH-*nah-peh*	mustard
senato, *m.*	*seh-*NAH-*toh*	senate
senatore, *m.*	*seh-nah-*TOH-*reh*	senator
seno, *m.*	SEH-*noh*	bosom
se non	*seh* NOHN	but (if not, *conj.*)
sensale, *m.*	*senn-*SAH-*leh*	broker (*bus.*)
sensazione, *f.*	*senn-sah-*TS YOH-*neh*	feeling
"	"	sensation

Italian	Pronunciation	English
sensibile	*senn-*SEE-*bee-leh*	sensitive (susceptible)
senso, *m.*	SENN-*soh*	sense (signification)
sentenza, *f.*	*senn-*TENN-*tsah*	judgment (*law*)
sentiero, *m.*	*senn-*T YEH-*roh*	lane
"	"	path
sentimento, *m.*	*senn-tee-*MENN-*toh*	feeling (emotion)
"	"	sentiment
sentire (4)	*senn-*TEE-*reh*	feel (experience), to
sentire la mancanza di	*senn-*TEE-*reh lah mahng-*KAHN-*tsah dee*	miss (feel the loss of), to
senza	SENN-*tsah*	without (*prep.*)
senza dubbio	SENN-*tsah* DOOB-*b yoh*	doubtless
senza fine	SENN-*tsah* FEE-*neh*	endless
senza lavoro	SENN-*tsah lah-*VOH-*roh*	unemployed
senza valore	SENN-*tsah vah-*LOH-*reh*	worthless (valueless)
separare (1)	*seh-pah-*RAH-*reh*	separate (disconnect), to
separarsi	*seh-pah-*RAHR-*see*	part (leave each other), to
"	"	separate (come apart), to
separato	*seh-pah-*RAH-*toh*	separate
separazione, *f.*	*seh-pah-rah-*TS YOH-*neh*	separation
sepoltura, *f.*	*seh-pohl-*TOO-*rah*	burial
seppellire (3)	*sepp-pell-*LEE-*reh*	bury (entomb), to
sequestro, *m.*	*seh-*KWEH-*stroh*	attachment (legal seizure)
sera, *f.*	SEH-*rah*	evening
serbatoio, *m.*	*sehr-bah-*TOH-*yoh*	reservoir (water reserve)
"	"	tank (container)
sergente, *m.*	*sehr-*JENN-*teh*	sergeant
serie, *f.*	SEH-*r yeh*	row
"	"	series
serio	SEH-*r yoh*	serious
sermone, *m.*	*sehr-*MOH-*neh*	sermon
serpente, *m.*	*sehr-*PENN-*teh*	serpent
"	"	snake
serratura, *f.*	*sehr-rah-*TOO-*rah*	lock (fastening)
servire (4)	*sehr-*VEE-*reh*	serve, to
servizio, *m.*	*sehr-*VEE-*ts yoh*	service
sesso, *m.*	SESS-*soh*	sex
sè stessi	*seh* STESS-*see*	themselves
sè stesso	SEH STESS-*soh*	self (*pron.*)
seta, *f.*	SEH-*tah*	silk (*n.*)
seta artificiale, *f.*	SEH-*tah ahr-tee-fee-*CHAH-*leh*	rayon
sete, *f.*	SEH-*teh*	thirst
settentrionale	*sett-tenn-tr yoh-*NAH-*leh*	northern
settentrione, *m.*	*sett-tenn-*TR YOH-*neh*	north (*n.*)
settimana, *f.*	*sett-tee-*MAH-*nah*	week
settimanale	*sett-tee-mah-*NAH-*leh*	weekly (*adj.*)
severità, *f.*	*seh-veh-ree-*TAH	severity (sternness)
severo	*seh-*VEH-*roh*	severe
"	"	stern (*adj.*)
sfera, *f.*	SFEH-*rah*	sphere
sfera (d'attività), *f.*	SFEH-*rah (daht-tee-vee-*TAH)	range (scope)
sfida, *f.*	SFEE-*dah*	challenge
sfidare (1)	*sfee-*DAH-*reh*	defy, to
sfigurare (1)	*sfee-goo-*RAH-*reh*	mar (disfigure), to
sfilata, *f.*	*sfee-*LAH-*tah*	parade (procession)
sfortuna, *f.*	*sfohr-*TOO-*nah*	misfortune
sfortunato	*sfohr-too-*NAH-*toh*	unfortunate
"	"	unlucky
sforzarsi (1)	*sfohr-*TSAHR-*see*	strive (exert oneself), to
sforzarsi di	*sfohr-*TSAHR-*see dee*	endeavor, to
sforzo, *m.*	SFOHR-*tsoh*	effort
"	"	endeavor
"	"	strain (exertion)
sgabello, *m.*	*zgah-*BELL-*loh*	stool (seat)
sgarbato	*zgahr-*BAH-*toh*	rude (impolite)
sgelarsi (1)	*zjeh-*LAHR-*see*	thaw, to
sgomberare (1)	*zgohm-beh-*RAH-*reh*	move (change residence), to
sgomento, *m.*	*zgoh-*MENN-*toh*	dismay
sgradevole	*zgrah-*DEH-*voh-leh*	disagreeable
"	"	unpleasant
sgridare (1)	*zgree-*DAH-*reh*	scold, to
sguardo, *m.*	ZGWAHR-*doh*	look (glance)
sguazzare (1)	*zgwaht-*TSAH-*reh*	wade, to

Italian	Pronunciation	English
si	SEE	herself, himself, it-self, themselves, yourself, your-selves
sì	SEE	yes
sia	SEE-*ah*	whether (either, *conj.*)
siccome	*seek*-KOH-*meh*	since (because, *conj.*)
sicurezza, *f.*	*see-koo*-RETT-*tsah*	safety (*n.*)
"	"	security
sicuro	*see*-KOO-*roh*	certain
"	"	reliable
"	"	safe (without risk)
"	"	secure
"	"	sure
siepe, *f.*	S YEH-*peh*	hedge (bushes)
sigaretta, *f.*	*see-gah*-RETT-*tah*	cigarette
sigaro, *m.*	SEE-*gah-roh*	cigar
significare (1)	*see-n yee-fee*-KAH-*reh*	signify (denote), to
significativo	*see-n yee-fee-kah*-TEE-*voh*	significant (meaning-ful)
significato, *m.*	*see-n yee-fee*-KAH-*toh*	meaning (sense)
signora, *f.*	*see*-N YOH-*rah*	lady
signora, (la), *f.*	(*lah*) *see*-N YOH-*rah*	Mrs. (Mistress)
signore, *m.*	*see*-N YOH-*reh*	sir
signore, (il), *m.*	(*eel*) *see*-N YOH-*reh*	Mr. (Mister)
signorina, (la), *f.*	(*lah*) *see-n yoh*-REE-*nah*	Miss
silenzio, *m.*	*see*-LENN-*ts yoh*	silence (stillness)
silenzioso	*see-lenn*-TS YOH-*soh*	quiet (*adj.*)
"	"	silent
sillaba, *f.*	SEEL-*lah-bah*	syllable
siluro, *m.*	*see*-LOO-*roh*	torpedo
similarità, *f.*	*see-mee-lah-ree*-TAH	similarity
simile	SEE-*mee-leh*	alike
"	"	like (*adj.*)
"	"	similar
similmente	*see-meel*-MENN-*teh*	alike (similarly)
"	"	likewise (also)
simpatia, *f.*	*seem-pah*-TEE-*ah*	sympathy (accord)
sincero	*seen*-CHEH-*roh*	sincere
sindacato, *m.*	*seen-dah*-KAH-*toh*	union (trade union)
sindaco, *m.*	SEEN-*dah-koh*	auditor
"	"	mayor
sinfonia, *f.*	*seen-foh*-NEE-*ah*	symphony
singhiozzare (1)	*seeng-g yoht*-TSAH-*reh*	sob, to
singolare, *m.*	*seeng-goh*-LAH-*reh*	singular (*gram., n.*)
sinistra, *f.*	*see*-NEE-*strah*	left (*n.*)
sinistra, a	*ah see*-NEE-*strah*	left (*adv.*)
sinistro	*see*-NEE-*stroh*	left (*adj.*)
sintomo, *m.*	SEEN-*toh-moh*	symptom
siringa, *f.*	*see*-REENG-*gah*	syringe
sistema, *m.*	*see*-STEH-*mah*	system (method)
situazione, *f.*	*see-twah*-TS YOH-*neh*	situation (circum-stances)
slanciarsi (1)	*zlahn*-CHAHR-*see*	rush (dash), to
slanciato	*zlahn*-CHAH-*toh*	slender (lean)
slancio, *m.*	ZLAHN-*choh*	rush (rapid motion)
slavo	ZLAH-*voh*	Slavic (*adj.*)
slealtà, *f.*	*zleh-ahl*-TAH	disloyalty
slitta, *f.*	ZLEET-*tah*	sled
"	"	sleigh
smarrire (3)	*zmahr*-REE-*reh*	mislay, to
smeraldo, *m.*	*zmeh*-RAHL-*doh*	emerald
smettere di (60)	ZMETT-*teh-reh dee*	quit (stop), to
smussato	*zmooss*-SAH-*toh*	blunt
"	"	dull
soave	*soh*-AH-*veh*	gentle (soothing)
sobrio	SOH-*bree_oh*	sober
soccorrevole	*sohk-kohr*-REH-*voh-leh*	helpful (volunteering help)
soccorsi d'urgenza, *m.pl.*	*sohk*-KOHR-*see doo r*-JENN-*tsah*	first aid (*med.*)
soccorso, *m.*	*sohk*-KOHR-*soh*	relief (aid)
sociale	*soh*-CHAH-*leh*	social (societal)
socialismo, *m.*	*soh-chah*-LEE-*zmoh*	socialism
socialista, *m., f.*	*soh-chah*-LEE-*stah*	socialist (*n.*)
società, *f.*	*soh-ch yeh*-TAH	community (the public)
"	"	society
società anonima, *f.*	*soh-ch yeh*-TAH *ah*-NOH-*nee-mah*	corporation
società coopera-tiva, *f.*	*soh-ch yeh*-TAH *koh-oh-peh-rah*-TEE-*vah*	cooperative (*n.*)

Italian	Pronunciation	English
socievole	*soh*-CH YEH-*voh-leh*	sociable (companion-able)
socio, *m.*	SOH-*choh*	partner (*bus.*)
sociologia, *f.*	*soh-choh-loh*-JEE-*ah*	sociology
soddisfacente	*sohd-dee-sfah*-CHENN-*teh*	satisfactory
soddisfare (51)	*sohd-dee*-SFAH-*reh*	satisfy, to
soddisfatto	*sohd-dee*-SFAHT-*toh*	satisfied (contented)
soddisfazione, *f.*	*sohd-dee-sfah*-TS YOH-*neh*	satisfaction
sofà, *m. (pl.* sofà)	*soh*-FAH	couch
"	"	sofa
sofferenza, *f.*	*sohf-feh*-RENN-*tsah*	suffering
sofferenza, in	*een sohf-feh*-RENN-*tsah*	overdue (in arrears)
soffermarsi (1)	*sohf-fehr*-MAHR-*see*	linger (tarry), to
"	"	pause (wait), to
soffice	SOHF-*fee-cheh*	soft (not hard)
soffitta, *f.*	*sohf*-FEET-*tah*	attic
soffitto, *m.*	*sohf*-FEET-*toh*	ceiling (of room)
soffocare (1)	*sohf-foh*-KAH-*reh*	choke, to
soffrire (14)	*sohf*-FREE-*reh*	suffer (undergo), to
soggettivo	*sohd-jett*-TEE-*voh*	subjective
soggetto, *m.*	*sohd*-JETT-*toh*	topic
soggiorno, *m.*	*sohd*-JOHR-*noh*	stay (sojourn)
"	"	visit
sognare (1)	*soh*-N YAH-*reh*	dream, to
sogno, *m.*	SOH-*n yoh*	dream
solco, *m.*	SOHL-*koh*	furrow (*agric.*)
soldato, *m.*	*sohl*-DAH-*toh*	soldier
soldato (semplice), *m.*	*sohl*-DAH-*toh* (SEMM-*plee-cheh*)	private (*mil.*)
sole, *m.*	SOH-*leh*	sun
"	"	sunshine
soleggiato	*soh-ledd*-JAH-*toh*	sunny
solido	SOH-*lee-doh*	solid (compact)
solitario	*soh-lee*-TAH-*r yoh*	lonely
"	"	lonesome
"	"	solitary (unaccom-panied)
solito	SOH-*lee-toh*	usual
solitudine, *f.*	*soh-lee*-TOO-*dee-neh*	solitude
sollecitare (1)	*sohl-leh-chee*-TAH-*reh*	solicit (ask for), to
"	"	urge (try to per-suade), to
solleticare	*sohl-leh-tee*-KAH-*reh*	tickle (touch lightly), to
sollevare (1)	*sohl-leh*-VAH-*reh*	heave, to
"	"	lift (raise), to
"	"	relieve (ease), to
sollievo, *m.*	*sohl*-L YEH-*voh*	relief (alleviation)
solo	SOH-*loh*	alone
"	"	lone (solitary)
"	"	single
"	"	sole (only)
soltanto	*sohl*-TAHN-*toh*	only (merely)
soluzione, *f.*	*soh-loo*-TS YOH-*neh*	solution (solving)
somma, *f.*	SOHM-*mah*	amount
"	"	sum (quantity)
sommario, *m.*	*sohm*-MAH-*r yoh*	summary (synopsis)
sommergibile, *m.*	*sohm-mehr*-JEE-*bee-leh*	submarine
sommità, *f.*	*sohm-mee*-TAH	summit
"	"	top
sonno, *m.*	SOHN-*noh*	sleep
"	"	slumber
sopportare (1)	*sohp-pohr*-TAH-*reh*	bear, to
"	"	endure, to
sopprimere (26)	*sohp*-PREE-*meh-reh*	suppress (subdue), to
sopra	SOH-*prah*	across (from side to side)
"	"	over (above, *prep.*)
"	"	upon
soprabito, *m.*	*soh*-PRAH-*bee-toh*	coat (man's over-coat)
"	"	overcoat
sopracciglio, *m.* (*pl.* -glia, *f.*)	*soh-praht*-CHEE-*l yoh*	eyebrow
sopra di, al di	*ahl dee* SOH-*prah dee*	above (higher than, *prep.*)
"	"	beyond (out of reach of, *prep.*)
soprannaturale	*soh-prahn-nah-too*-RAH-*leh*	weird (unearthly)
soprannome, *m.*	*soh-prahn*-NOH-*meh*	nickname

Italian	Pronunciation	English
soprappiù, *m.*	soh-prahp-P_YOO	margin (surplus)
"	"	surplus (*n.*)
sopraprezzo, *m.*	soh-prah-PRETT-tsoh	surcharge (*bus.*)
soprascarpe, *f.pl.*	soh-prah-SKAHR-peh	rubbers (overshoes)
sopravvivere (125)	soh-prahv-VEE-veh-reh	survive (remain alive), to
sordo	SOHR-doh	deaf
sorella, *f.*	soh-RELL-lah	sister (*n.*)
sorpassare (1)	sohr-pahss-SAH-reh	surpass, to
sorprendere (78)	sohr-PRENN-deh-reh	surprise, to
sorpresa, *f.*	sohr-PREH-sah	surprise
sorridere (85)	sohr-REE-deh-reh	smile, to
sorriso, *m.*	sohr-REE-soh	smile
sorseggiare (1)	sohr-sedd-JAH-reh	sip, to
sorta, *f.*	SOHR-tah	sort
sospendere (13)	soh-SPENN-deh-reh	suspend (terminate), to
sospettare (1)	soh-spett-TAH-reh	suspect, to
sospetto, *m.*	soh-SPETT-toh	suspicion
sospirare (1)	soh-spee-RAH-reh	sigh, to
sostanza, *f.*	soh-STAHN-tsah	substance (matter)
sostanziale	soh-stahn-TS_YAH-leh	substantial (sizable)
sostegno, *m.*	soh-STEH-n_yoh	support
sostenere (112)	soh-steh-NEH-reh	argue (maintain), to
"	"	support (hold up), to
"	"	sustain, to
sostituire (3)	soh-stee-TWEE-reh	substitute (put in place of), to
sottana, *f.*	soht-TAH-nah	petticoat
sotteraneo	soht-teh-RAH-neh-oh	underground (below-ground, *adj.*)
sottile	soht-TEE-leh	thin (not thick)
sotto	SOHT-toh	beneath (below, *prep.*)
"	"	under (*prep.*)
sotto (a)	SOHT-toh (ah)	below (lower than, *prep.*)
sotto, di	dee SOHT-toh	below (lower down, *adv.*)
"	"	beneath (*adv.*)
sottogonna, *f.*	soht-toh-GOHN-nah	slip (petticoat)
sottoporre (76)	soht-toh-POHR-reh	submit (offer), to
sottoprodotto, *m.*	soht-toh-proh-DOHT-toh	by-product
sottosuolo, *m.*	soht-toh-SWOH-loh	basement
sottotazza, *f.*	soht-toh-TAHT-tsah	saucer
sottrarre (116)	soht-TRAHR-reh	subtract, to
sovrano, *m.*	soh-VRAH-noh	ruler
"	"	sovereign
spada, *f.*	SPAH-dah	sword
Spagna, *f.*	SPAH-n_yah	Spain
spagnuolo	spah-N_YWOH-loh	Spanish (*adj.*)
spago, *m.*	SPAH-goh	string (cord)
spalla, *f.*	SPAHL-lah	shoulder (*anat.*)
spargere (102)	SPAHR-jeh-reh	scatter (strew), to
"	"	spread (diffuse), to
"		sprinkle, to
sparire (3)	spah-REE-reh	disappear, to
sparo, *m.*	SPAH-roh	shot (from firearm)
spasso, *m.*	SPAHSS-soh	fun
spaventare (1)	spah-venn-TAH-reh	frighten (make afraid), to
"	"	scare, to
spavento, *m.*	spah-VENN-toh	fright (alarm)
spazio, *m.*	SPAH-ts_yoh	room
"	"	space (area)
spazzare (1)	spaht-TSAH-reh	sweep (clean), to
spazzola, *f.*	SPAHT-tsoh-lah	brush (scrubbing utensil)
spazzolino per i denti, *m.*	spaht-tsoh-LEE-noh pehr ee DENN-tee	toothbrush
specchio, *m.*	SPEKK-k_yoh	mirror
speciale	speh-CHAH-leh	special
specialmente	speh-chahl-MENN-teh	especially
specie, *f.*	SPEH-cheh	kind (*n.*)
spedire (3)	speh-DEE-reh	ship (send goods), to
spedizione, *f.*	speh-dee-TS_YOH-neh	expedition (journey)
"	"	shipment (goods)
spedizioniere, *m.*	speh-dee-ts_yoh-N_YEH-reh	shipping agent
spendere (104)	SPENN-deh-reh	spend (pay out), to
speranza, *f.*	speh-RAHN-tsah	hope
speranzoso	speh-rahn-TSOH-soh	hopeful
sperare (1)	speh-RAH-reh	hope, to
spergiuro, *m.*	spehr-JOO-roh	perjury
sperone, *m.*	speh-ROH-neh	spur (spike)
spesa, *f.*	SPEH-sah	expenditure (outlay)
"	"	expense (cost)
spese d'azienda, *f.pl.*	SPEH-seh dah-TS_YENN-dah	operating expenses (*bus.*)
spese fisse, *f.pl.*	SPEH-seh FEESS-seh	overhead (expenses, *bus.*)
spesso	SPESS-soh	often
"	"	thick (not thin)
spessore, *m.*	spess-SOH-reh	thickness (dimension)
spettacolo, *m.*	spett-TAH-koh-loh	play (stage presentation)
"	"	sight (spectacle)
spettacolo pubblico, *m.*	spett-TAH-koh-loh POOB-blee-koh	spectacle (pageant)
spettatore, *m.*	spett-tah-TOH-reh	spectator
spettro, *m.*	SPETT-troh	ghost
spezia, *f.*	SPEH-ts_yah	spice
spia, *f.*	SPEE-ah	spy
spiaggia, *f.*	SP_YAHD-jah	beach (strand)
spianare (1)	sp_yah-NAH-reh	smooth (level), to
spiegare (1)	sp_yeh-GAH-reh	explain, to
spiegazione, *f.*	sp_yeh-gah-TS_YOH-neh	explanation
spillo, *m.*	SPEEL-loh	pin (sewing accessory)
spillo di sicurezza, *m.*	SPEEL-loh dee see-koo-RETT-tsah	safety pin
spillone, *m.*	speel-LOH-neh	brooch
spina, *f.*	SPEE-nah	plug (*elec.*)
"	"	thorn
spinaci, *m.pl.*	spee-NAH-chee	spinach
spina dorsale, *f.*	SPEE-nah dohr-SAH-leh	spine (*anat.*)
spingere (105)	SPEEN-jeh-reh	drive (propel), to
"	"	push (shove), to
"		thrust (push), to
spinta, *f.*	SPEEN-tah	push (shove)
spionaggio, *m.*	sp_yoh-NAHD-joh	espionage
spirito, *m.*	SPEE-ree-toh	spirit
"	"	wit (humor)
spiritoso	spee-ree-TOH-soh	witty
spirituale	spee-ree-TWAH-leh	spiritual (*adj.*)
splendido	SPLENN-dee-doh	splendid
splendore, *m.*	splenn-DOH-reh	splendor
spogliare (1)	spoh-L_YAH-reh	strip (denude), to
sporcare (1)	spohr-KAH-reh	soil (make dirty), to
sporcizia, *f.*	spohr-CHEE-ts_yah	dirt (unclean matter)
sporco	SPOHR-koh	dirty (soiled)
sposa, *f.*	SPOH-zah	bride
sposalizio, *m.*	spoh-zah-LEE-ts_yoh	wedding
sposare (1)	spoh-ZAH-reh	marry, to
sposato	spoh-ZAH-toh	married
sposo, *m.*	SPOH-zoh	groom (bridegroom)
spruzzare (1)	sproot-TSAH-reh	spray, to
spugna, *f.*	SPOO-n_yah	sponge
spuma, *f.*	SPOO-mah	foam
sputare (1)	spoo-TAH-reh	spit, to
squadra, *f.*	SKWAH-drah	shift (crew)
"	"	team (in sports)
squisito	skwee-ZEE-toh	exquisite
stabile	STAH-bee-leh	stable (steadfast)
stabilimento, *m.*	stah-bee-lee-MENN-toh	establishment
"	"	plant (factory)
stabilire (3)	stah-bee-LEE-reh	establish, to
stabilirsi	stah-bee-LEER-see	settle (make one's home), to
stacciare (1)	staht-CHAH-reh	sift (separate), to
stadio, *m.*	STAH-d_yoh	stadium
stagione, *f.*	stah-JOH-neh	season (of year)
stagno, *m.*	STAH-n_yoh	pond
"	"	tin (metal)
stalla, *f.*	STAHL-lah	barn
"	"	stable
stallone, *m.*	stahl-LOH-neh	stallion
stampa, *f.*	STAHM-pah	press (newspapers and periodicals)
stampare (1)	stahm-PAH-reh	print, to
stancare (1)	stahng-KAH-reh	tire (make weary), to
stancarsi	stahng-KAHR-see	tire (become weary), to
stanco	STAHNG-koh	tired
stanghetta, *f.*	stahng-GETT-tah	bolt (lock)
"	"	latch

Italian	Pronunciation	English
stantio	STAHN-*t yoh*	stale
stanza, *f.*	STAHN-*tsah*	room (of house)
stanza da bagno, *f.*	STAHN-*tsah dah* BAH-*n yoh*	bathroom
stanza dei bambini, *f.*	STAHN-*tsah day bahm-*BEE-*nee*	nursery (children's room)
stare a guardare (106)	STAH-*reh ah gwahr-*DAH-*reh*	watch (observe), to
stare in pensiero	STAH-*reh een penn-*S YEH-*roh*	worry (feel anxious), to
starnutare (1)	*stahr-noo-*TAH-*reh*	sneeze, to
stasera	*stah-*SEH-*rah*	tonight
Stati Uniti, *m.pl.*	STAH-*tee oo-*NEE-*tee*	United States
stato, *m.*	STAH-*toh*	state
statua, *f.*	STAH-*twah*	statue
statura, *f.*	*stah-*TOO-*rah*	stature (height)
statuto, *m.*	*stah-*TOO-*toh*	by-law
"	"	charter (act of incorporation)
stazionario	*stah-ts yoh-*NAH-*r yoh*	stationary (unmoving)
stazione, *f.*	*stah-*TS YOH-*neh*	depot
"	"	station, railroad
stazione climatica, *f.*	*stah-*TS YOH-*neh klee-*MAH-*tee-kah*	resort (spa)
stella, *f.*	STELL-*lah*	star (*astron.*)
stelo, *m.*	STEH-*loh*	stem (*bot.*)
stendere (111)	STENN-*deh-reh*	stretch (draw out), to
stendersi	STENN-*dehr-see*	stretch (extend), to
stendersi fino a	STENN-*dehr-see* FEE-*noh ah*	reach (extend to), to
stenografa, *f.*	*steh-*NOH-*grah-fah*	stenographer
stenografia, *f.*	*steh-noh-grah-*FEE-*ah*	shorthand (stenography, *n.*)
sterile	STEH-*ree-leh*	barren
stesso, *m.*	STESS-*soh*	same (*adj.*)
stimare (1)	*stee-*MAH-*reh*	esteem, to
"	"	estimate (calculate), to
stimolare (1)	*stee-moh-*LAH-*reh*	stimulate (incite), to
stipendio, *m.*	*stee-*PENN-*d yoh*	salary
stirare (1)	*stee-*RAH-*reh*	press (iron), to
stivale, *m.*	*stee-*VAH-*leh*	boot (footgear)
Stoccolma, *f.*	*stohk-*KOHL-*mah*	Stockholm
stoffa, *f.*	STOHF-*fah*	cloth
stomaco, *m.*	STOH-*mah-koh*	stomach
storcersi (115)	STOHR-*chehr-see*	sprain, to
storia, *f.*	STOH-*r yah*	history
storico	STOH-*ree-koh*	historical
storie, *f.pl.*	STOH-*r yeh*	fuss (ado)
storpio	STOHR-*p yoh*	cripple
stoviglie, *f.pl.*	*stoh-*VEE-*l yeh*	dishes (tableware)
straccio, *m.*	STRAHT-*choh*	rag (piece of cloth)
strada, *f.*	STRAH-*dah*	road
"	"	street
straniero	*strah-*N YEH-*roh*	foreign
straniero, *m.*	*strah-*N YEH-*roh*	foreigner
strano	STRAH-*noh*	odd (queer)
"	"	peculiar
"	"	strange
straordinario	*strah-ohr-dee-*NAH-*r yoh*	extraordinary
"	"	remarkable
strappare (1)	*strahp-*PAH-*reh*	pluck (pull off), to
"	"	rip (tear away), to
"	"	tear, to
"	"	wrench (wrest), to
strato, *m.*	STRAH-*toh*	layer (thickness)
strega, *f.*	STREH-*gah*	witch
stretta, *f.*	STRETT-*tah*	grip (grasp)
stretto	STRETT-*toh*	narrow
"	"	tight (close-fitting)
stretto, *m.*	STRETT-*toh*	channel (strait)
strillare (1)	*streel-*LAH-*reh*	shriek, to
stringere (107)	STREEN-*jeh-reh*	squeeze, to
striscia, *f.*	STREE-*shah*	streak
"	"	stripe
strisciare (1)	*stree-*SHAH-*reh*	crawl, to
"	"	creep, to
strofinare (1)	*stroh-fee-*NAH-*reh*	rub, to
"	"	scrub, to

Italian	Pronunciation	English
strumento, *m.*	*stroo-*MENN-*toh*	instrument (implement)
struttura, *f.*	*stroot-*TOO-*rah*	structure (arrangement of parts)
studente, *m.*	*stoo-*DENN-*teh*	student
studiare (1)	*stoo-*D YAH-*reh*	study, to
studio, *m.*	STOO-*d yoh*	study (active learning)
studioso, *m.*	*stoo-*D YOH-*soh*	scholar (savant)
stufa, *f.*	STOO-*fah*	stove (for heating)
stupido	STOO-*pee-doh*	stupid
stupire (3)	*stoo-*PEE-*reh*	amaze, to
"	"	astonish, to
stupore, *m.*	*stoo-*POH-*reh*	amazement
"	"	astonishment
stuzzicare (1)	*stoots-tsee-*KAH-*reh*	tease, to
su	SOO	at (on)
"	"	on (*prep.*)
"	"	up (*adv.*)
sua (see suo, il)		
subito	SOO-*bee-toh*	immediately (instantly)
succedere (27)	*soot-*CHEH-*deh-reh*	succeed (follow), to
successo, *m.*	*soot-*CHESS-*soh*	success (attainment)
succhiare (1)	*sook-*K YAH-*reh*	suck, to
succo, *m.*	SOOK-*koh*	juice
sud, *m.*	SOOD	south (*n.*)
sudare (1)	*soo-*DAH-*reh*	perspire, to
suddito, *m.*	SOOD-*dee-toh*	subject (citizen)
sud-est, del	*dell soo-*DEST	southeast (*adj.*)
sudicio	SOO-*dee-choh*	foul (filthy)
sudore, *m.*	*soo-*DOH-*reh*	sweat
sud-ovest, del	*dell soo-*DOH-*vest*	southwest (*adj.*)
sue (see suo, il)		
sufficiente	*soof-fee-*CH YENN-*teh*	ample
"	"	sufficient
suggerimento, *m.*	*sood-jeh-ree-*MENN-*toh*	suggestion (proposal)
suggerire (3)	*sood-jeh-*REE-*reh*	suggest, to
sugo, *m.*	SOO-*goh*	gravy
suicida, *m.*	*soo-ee-*CHEE-*dah*	suicide
suo, il	*eel* SOO-*oh*	her, his, its, your
"		hers, his, its, yours
suocera, *f.*	SWOH-*cheh-rah*	mother-in-law
suocero, *m.*	SWOH-*cheh-roh*	father-in-law
suoi (see suo, il)		
suola, *f.*	SWOH-*lah*	sole (of shoe)
suolo, *m.*	SWOH-*loh*	soil (ground)
suonare (1)	*swoh-*NAH-*reh*	play (perform music upon), to
"	"	sound (make heard), to
suono, *m.*	SWOH-*noh*	sound (noise)
superare (1)	*soo-peh-*RAH-*reh*	pass (not fail in), to
superficie, *f.*	*soo-pehr-*FEE-*ch yeh*	face (surface)
"	"	surface
"	"	top (upper surface)
superiore	*soo-peh-*R YOH-*reh*	superior (excellent)
superstizione, *f.*	*soo-pehr-stee-*TS YOH-*neh*	superstition
superstizioso	*soo-pehr-stee-*TS YOH-*soh*	superstitious
supplementare (1)	*soop-pleh-menn-*TAH-*reh*	additional
supplicare (1)	*soop-plee-*KAH-*reh*	appeal to (entreat), to
"	"	beg (entreat), to
"	"	plead, to
supporre (76)	*soop-*POHR-*reh*	guess, to
"	"	suppose (assume), to
supremo	*soo-*PREH-*moh*	supreme
Surinam	*soo-ree-*NAHM	Surinam
surrogato, *m.*	*soor-roh-*GAH-*toh*	substitute (thing replacing another)
susseguente	*sooss-seh-*GWENN-*teh*	subsequent
svanire (3)	*zvah-*NEE-*reh*	fade (disappear), to
"	"	vanish (cease to be), to
svedese	*zveh-*DEH-*seh*	Swedish (*adj.*)
svegliare (1)	*zveh-*L YAH-*reh*	awaken (make awaken), to
"	"	wake (make awaken), to

Italian	Pronunciation	English
svegliarsi	zveh-L_YAHR-*see*	awaken (rouse one-self), to
"	"	wake (rouse oneself), to
sveglio	ZVEH-*l yoh*	awake
svenimento,*m.*	zveh-nee-MENN-*toh*	faint (swoon, *n.*)
svenire (123)	zveh-NEE-*reh*	faint, to
sventolare (1)	zvenn-toh-LAH-*reh*	wave (flutter), to
Svezia,*f.*	ZVEH-*ts yah*	Sweden
sviluppare (1)	zvee-loop-PAH-*reh*	develop, to
sviluppo,*m.*	zvee-LOOP-*poh*	development
svista,*f.*	ZVEE-*stah*	oversight (error)
Svizzera,*f.*	ZVEET-*tseh-rah*	Switzerland
svizzero	ZVEET-*tseh-roh*	Swiss (*adj.*)
tabacco,*m.*	*tah*-BAHK-*koh*	tobacco
tacchino,*m.*	*tahk*-KEE-*noh*	turkey
tagliare (1)	*tah*-L_YAH-*reh*	cut (divide into parts), to
"	"	cut (wound), to
tale	TAH-*leh*	such (of that kind, *adj.*)
talento,*m.*	*tah*-LENN-*toh*	talent
talento, di	*dee tah*-LENN-*toh*	gifted (talented)
talpa,*f.*	TAHL-*pah*	mole (animal)
tamburo,*m.*	*tahm*-BOO-*roh*	drum (*mus.*)
tappeto,*m.*	*tahp*-PEH-*toh*	carpet
"	"	rug
tappeto verde,*m.*	*tahp*-PEH-*toh* VEHR-*deh*	lawn
tappo,*m.*	TAHP-*poh*	cork (stopper)
tardi	TAHR-*dee*	late (at relative time, *adv.*)
tardivo	*tahr*-DEE-*voh*	tardy (*adj.*)
tarma,*f.*	TAHR-*mah*	moth
tartaruga,*f.*	*tahr-tah*-ROO-*gah*	turtle
tasca,*f.*	TAH-*skah*	pocket
tasse scolastiche, *f.pl.*	TAHSS-*seh skoh*-LAH-*stee-keh*	tuition (school fee)
tassì,*m.*	*tahss*-SEE	cab
"	"	taxi
tasso,*m.*	TAHSS-*soh*	badger (animal)
tavola,*f.*	TAH-*voh-lah*	board
"	"	plank (timber)
"	"	table
tazza,*f.*	TAHT-*tsah*	cup
tè,*m.*	TEH	tea
teatro,*m.*	*teh*-AH-*troh*	theater
tedesco	*teh*-DEH-*skoh*	German (*adj.*)
tela di canapa,*f.*	TEH-*lah dee* KAH-*nah-pah*	canvas (cloth)
tela di cotone,*f.*	TEH-*lah dee koh*-TOH-*neh*	cotton (fabric)
tela di lino,*f.*	TEH-*lah dee* LEE-*noh*	linen (fabric)
telaio,*m.*	*teh*-LAH-*yoh*	loom
Tel Aviv,*f.*	*tell ah*-VEEV	Tel Aviv
telefonare (1)	*teh-leh-foh*-NAH-*reh*	phone, to
"	"	telephone, to
telefono,*m.*	*teh*-LEH-*foh-noh*	telephone
telegrafare (1)	*teh-leh-grah*-FAH-*reh*	telegraph, to
telegramma,*m.*	*teh-leh*-GRAHM-*mah*	telegram
"	"	wire
telescopio,*m.*	*teh-leh*-SKOH-*p yoh*	telescope
televisione,*f.*	*teh-leh-vee*-Z_YOH-*neh*	television
tema,*m.*	TEH-*mah*	theme (subject)
tema che, per	*pehr* TEH-*mah keh*	lest
temerario	*teh-meh*-RAH-*r yoh*	reckless
temere (2)	*teh*-MEH-*reh*	fear (be afraid of), to
temperatura,*f.*	*temm-peh-rah*-TOO-*rah*	temperature
tempesta,*f.*	*temm*-PEH-*stah*	storm
"	"	tempest
tempesta di neve,*f.*	*temm*-PEH-*stah dee* NEH-*veh*	blizzard
tempestoso	*temm-peh*-STOH-*soh*	stormy
tempia,*f.*	TEMM-*p yah*	temple (*anat.*)
tempio,*m.*	TEMM-*p yoh*	temple (place of worship)
tempo,*m.*	TEMM-*poh*	time (interval)
"	"	weather
tempo, breve,*m.*	BREH-*veh* TEMM-*poh*	while (short time,*n.*)
tempo, un	*oon* TEMM-*poh*	before (in the past, *adv.*)
"	"	once (formerly, *adv.*)
tenda,*f.*	TENN-*dah*	tent

Italian	Pronunciation	English
tendenza,*f.*	*tenn*-DENN-*tsah*	tendency
tendere (111)	TENN-*deh-reh*	tend (be apt), to
tendina,*f.*	*tenn*-DEE-*nah*	curtain (drape)
"	"	shade (window blind)
tenente,*m.*	*teh*-NENN-*teh*	lieutenant
tenere (112)	*teh*-NEH-*reh*	hold, to
tenerezza,*f.*	*teh-neh*-RETT-*tsah*	tenderness (love)
tenero	TEH-*neh-roh*	tender (loving)
tenersi in piedi	*teh*-NEHR-*see een* P_YEH-*dee*	stand (be upright), to
tennis,*m.*	TENN-*neess*	tennis
tensione,*f.*	*tenn*-S_YOH-*neh*	stress (physical tension)
"	"	tension
tentare (1)	*tenn*-TAH-*reh*	attempt, to
"	"	tempt, to
"	"	try, to
tentativo,*m.*	*tenn-tah*-TEE-*voh*	attempt
tentazione,*f.*	*tenn-tah*-TS_YOH-*neh*	temptation
teoria,*f.*	*teh-oh*-REE-*ah*	theory
terminare (1)	*tehr-mee*-NAH-*reh*	close (finish), to
"	"	end (bring to an end), to
terminarsi	*tehr-mee*-NAHR-*see*	end (come to an end), to
"	"	finish (reach the end), to
termine,*m.*	TEHR-*mee-neh*	term (expression)
termometro,*m.*	*tehr*-MOH-*meh-troh*	thermometer
termosifone,*m.*	*tehr-moh-see*-FOH-*neh*	radiator (heater)
terra,*f.*	TEHR-*rah*	dirt (soil)
"	"	earth
"	"	ground
"	"	land (ground)
"	"	land (region)
terrazza,*f.*	*tehr*-RAHT-*tsah*	terrace
terremoto,*m.*	*tehr-reh*-MOH-*toh*	earthquake
terreno,*m.*	*tehr*-REH-*noh*	land (property)
terribile	*tehr*-REE-*bee-leh*	awful
"	"	dreadful
"	"	fearful
"	"	terrible
territorio,*m.*	*tehr-ree*-TOH-*r yoh*	territory
terrore,*m.*	*tehr*-ROH-*reh*	dread
"	"	terror
teso	TEH-*soh*	tight (taut)
tesoro,*m.*	*teh*-ZOH-*roh*	treasure
Tesoro,*m.*	*teh*-ZOH-*roh*	treasury (*govt.*)
tessere (2)	TESS-*seh-reh*	weave, to
tessuto,*m.*	*tess*-SOO-*toh*	fabric (cloth)
"	"	textile (*n.*)
"	"	tissue (*biol.*)
tessuto di lana,*m.*	*tess*-SOO-*toh dee* LAH-*nah*	wool (cloth)
testa,*f.*	TEH-*stah*	head (*anat.*)
testamento,*m.*	*teh-stah*-MENN-*toh*	will (document)
testardo	*teh*-STAHR-*doh*	stubborn
te stesso	TEH STESS-*soh*	yourself
testimone,*m.*	*teh-stee*-MOH-*neh*	witness (one who testifies)
testimonianza,*f.*	*teh-stee-moh*-N_YAHN-*tsah*	testimony
testo,*m.*	TEH-*stoh*	text
tetto,*m.*	TETT-*toh*	roof
tettoia,*f.*	*tett*-TOH-*yah*	shed (shelter)
ti	TEE	(to) you, yourself
tifoide,*f.*	*tee*-FOY-*deh*	typhoid fever
tigre,*f.*	TEE-*greh*	tiger
timbrare (1)	*teem*-BRAH-*reh*	stamp (mark), to
timbro,*m.*	TEEM-*broh*	seal (mark)
timido	TEE-*mee-doh*	shy (bashful)
"	"	timid
timone,*m.*	*tee*-MOH-*neh*	rudder (of a boat)
timore,*m.*	*tee*-MOH-*reh*	awe
tingere (113)	TEEN-*jeh-reh*	dye, to
tinta,*f.*	TEEN-*tah*	hue
tintura d'iodio,*f.*	*teen*-TOO-*rah* D_YOH-*d yoh*	iodine (antiseptic)
tipico	TEE-*pee-koh*	typical
tipo,*m.*	TEE-*poh*	type (kind)
tipografo,*m.*	*tee*-POH-*grah-foh*	printer

Italian	Pronunciation	English
tiranno,*m.*	*tee-*RAHN*-noh*	tyrant
tirare (1)	*tee-*RAH*-reh*	haul (pull), to
"	"	pull (draw), to
"	"	tug (drag), to
tirare su	*tee-*RAH*-reh soo*	shoot (fire at), to
tirchio	TEER*-k yoh*	stingy
titoli,*m.*	TEE*-toh-lee*	securities (stocks, etc.)
titolo,*m.*	TEE*-toh-loh*	title (name)
Tizio,*m.*	TEE*-ts yoh*	chap (fellow)
toccare (1)	*tohk-*KAH*-reh*	feel (touch), to
"	"	touch, to
togliere (114)	TOH*-l yeh-reh*	remove (take away), to
Tokio,*f.*	TOH*-k yoh*	Tokyo
tollerare (1)	*tohl-leh-*RAH*-reh*	tolerate (permit), to
tomba,*f.*	TOHM*-bah*	grave
"	"	tomb
tono,*m.*	TOH*-noh*	tone (quality of sound)
tonsillite,*f.*	*tohn-seel-*LEE*-teh*	tonsillitis
topo,*m.*	TOH*-poh*	mouse
"	"	rat
torcere (115)	TOHR*-cheh-reh*	twist (wind), to
torcia,*f.*	TOHR*-chah*	torch
tormentare (1)	*tohr-menn-*TAH*-reh*	torment, to
tormento,*m.*	*tohr-*MENN*-toh*	torment
toro,*m.*	TOH*-roh*	bull (male bovine)
torre,*f.*	TOHR*-reh*	tower
torrente,*f.*	*tohr-*RENN*-teh*	torrent
torta,*f.*	TOHR*-tah*	cake (dessert)
"	"	pie
torto	TOHR*-toh*	crooked
tortura,*f.*	*tohr-*TOO*-rah*	torture
tosare (1)	*toh-*ZAH*-reh*	shear, to
tosse,*f.*	TOHSS*-seh*	cough
tosse canina,*f.*	TOHSS*-seh kah-*NEE*-nah*	whooping cough
totale	*toh-*TAH*-leh*	total (complete)
totale,*m.*	*toh-*TAH*-leh*	total (sum)
tovaglia,*f.*	*toh-*VAH*-l yah*	tablecloth
tovagliolo,*m.*	*toh-vah-*L YOH*-loh*	napkin
traccia,*f.*	TRAHT*-chah*	trace (vestige)
tradimento,*m.*	*trah-dee-*MENN*-toh*	treason
tradire (3)	*trah-*DEE*-reh*	betray, to
traditore,*m.*	*trah-dee-*TOH*-reh*	traitor
tradizione,*f.*	*trah-dee-*TS YOH*-neh*	tradition
tradurre (7)	*trah-*D OOR*-reh*	translate, to
traffico,*m.*	TRAHF*-fee-koh*	traffic (flow of vehicles)
tragedia,*f.*	*trah-*JEH*-d yah*	tragedy
tragico	TRAH*-jee-koh*	tragic
tramontare (1)	*trah-mohn-*TAH*-reh*	set (in sky), to
tramonto,*m.*	*trah-*MOHN*-toh*	sunset
tranquillo	*trahn-*KWEEL*-loh*	peaceful (tranquil)
transazione,*f.*	*trahn-zah-*TS YOH*-neh*	settlement (compromise, *bus.*)
transito,*m.*	TRAHN*-see-toh*	transit (passage)
tranvia,*f.*	*trahn-*VEE*-ah*	trolley (street car)
trappola,*f.*	TRAHP*-poh-lah*	trap (snare)
trarre (116)	TRAHR*-reh*	draw (pull along), to
trascinare (1)	*trah-shee-*NAH*-reh*	drag (pull), to
trascurare (1)	*trah-skoo-*RAH*-reh*	neglect (slight), to
trascurato	*trah-skoo-*RAH*-toh*	careless (negligent)
trasformare (1)	*trah-sfohr-*MAH*-reh*	transform, to
"	"	turn (convert), to
trasmettere (60)	*trah-*ZMETT*-teh-reh*	beam (direct, *rad.*), to
trasparente	*trah-spah-*RENN*-teh*	transparent
trasportare (1)	*trah-spohr-*TAH*-reh*	convey, to
"	"	transport, to
trasporto,*m.*	*trah-*SPOHR*-toh*	transportation (conveying)
tratta,*f.*	TRAHT*-tah*	draft (check)
tratta a vista,*f.*	TRAHT*-tah ah* VEE*-stah*	sight draft (*bus.*)
trattamento,*m.*	*traht-tah-*MENN*-toh*	treatment (behavior toward)
trattare (1)	*traht-*TAH*-reh*	deal (trade), to
"	"	negotiate, to
"	"	treat (behave toward), to
trattato,*m.*	*traht-*TAH*-toh*	treaty
trattenere (112)	*traht-teh-*NEH*-reh*	keep (prevent), to
trattenimento,*m.*	*traht-teh-nee-*MENN*-toh*	entertainment

Italian	Pronunciation	English
tratto caratteristico,*m.*	TRAHT*-toh kah-raht-teh-*REE*-stee-koh*	feature (attribute)
tratto d'unione,*m.*	TRAHT*-toh doo-n* YOH*-neh*	hyphen
trattore,*m.*	*traht-*TOH*-reh*	tractor (farm machine)
trave,*f.*	TRAH*-veh*	beam (rafter)
traversare (1)	*trah-vehr-*SAH*-reh*	cross (traverse), to
traversata,*f.*	*trah-vehr-*SAH*-tah*	crossing (ocean voyage)
travestimento,*m.*	*trah-veh-stee-*MENN*-toh*	disguise
tremare (1)	*treh-*MAH*-reh*	quake (shake), to
"	"	shiver, to
"	"	tremble, to
treno,*m.*	TREH*-noh*	train, railroad
triangolo,*m.*	*tree-*AHNG*-goh-loh*	triangle (*geom.*)
tribù,*f.*	*tree-*BOO	tribe
tribunale,*m.*	*tree-boo-*NAH*-leh*	court (of law)
tributo,*m.*	*tree-*BOO*-toh*	tribute (money)
trifoglio,*m.*	*tree-*FOH*-l yoh*	clover
trimestrale	*tree-meh-*STRAH*-leh*	quarterly (four times a year)
trincea,*f.*	*treen-*CHEH*-ah*	trench (*mil.*)
trionfo,*m.*	*tree-*OHN*-foh*	triumph
triste	TREE*-steh*	dreary
"	"	sad (sorrowful)
tristezza,*f.*	*tree-*STETT*-tsah*	sadness
tromba,*f.*	TROHM*-bah*	bugle
"	"	horn (*auto.*)
"	"	trumpet (*mus.*)
trombone,*m.*	*trohm-*BOH*-neh*	trombone
tronco,*m.*	TROHNG*-koh*	trunk (stem)
trono,*m.*	TROH*-noh*	throne
troppo	TROHP*-poh*	too (overly)
trota,*f.*	TROH*-tah*	trout
trotto,*m.*	TROHT*-toh*	trot
trovare (1)	*troh-*VAH*-reh*	find (discover), to
"	"	locate, to
trovarsi	*troh-*VAHR*-see*	lie (be located), to
trucco,*m.*	TROOK*-koh*	trick
truffare (1)	*troof-*FAH*-reh*	cheat (defraud), to
truppe,*f.pl.*	TROOP*-pęh*	troops (*mil.*)
trust,*m.*	TRUST	trust (cartel)
tu	TOO	you
tua (see tuo, il)		
tubercolosi,*f.*	*too-behr-koh-*LOH*-zee*	tuberculosis
tubo,*m.*	TOO*-boh*	hose
"	"	pipe
"	"	tube
tubo di scolo,*m.*	TOO*-boh dee* SKOH*-loh*	drain (conduit)
tue (see tuo, il)		
tulipano,*m.*	*too-lee-*PAH*-noh*	tulip
tumore,*m.*	*too-*MOH*-reh*	tumor
tumulto,*m.*	*too-*MOOL*-toh*	riot (disturbance)
tuo, il	*eel* TOO*-oh*	your
"	"	yours
tuoi (see tuo, il)		
tuono,*m.*	TWOH*-noh*	thunder
turacciolo,*m.*	*too-*RAHT*-choh-loh*	plug (stopper)
turba,*f.*	TOOR*-bah*	mob (disorderly crowd)
turchese	*toor-*KEH*-seh*	Turkish (*adj.*)
Turchia,*f.*	*toor-*KEE*-ah*	Turkey
turista,*m.,f.*	*too-*REE*-stah*	tourist (*n.*)
tutore,*m.*	*too-*TOH*-reh*	guardian (protector)
tuttavia	*toot-tah-*VEE*-ah*	still (nevertheless, *conj.*)
tutti e due	TOOT*-tee eh* DOO*-eh*	both (*adj.*)
tutto	TOOT*-toh*	all (entirely, *adv.*)
"	"	all (whole of, *adj.*)
"	"	everything (*pron.*)
tutto,*m.*	TOOT*-toh*	all (everything, *n.*)
"	"	whole (entirety, *n.*)
tweed,*m.*	TWEED	tweed (cloth)
ubriachezza,*f.*	*oo-br yah-*KETT*-tsah*	intoxication (drunkenness)
ubriaco	*oo-*BR YAH*-koh*	drunk (intoxicated)
uccello,*m.*	*oot-*CHELL*-loh*	bird
uccidere (117)	*oot-*CHEE*-deh-reh*	kill, to
"	"	slay, to
udire (118)	*oo-*DEE*-reh*	hear, to

Italian	Pronunciation	English
uditorio, *m.*	*oo-dee-*TOH-*r_yoh*	audience
ufficiale	*oof-fee-*CHAH-*leh*	official (*adj.*)
ufficiale, *m.*	*oof-fee-*CHAH-*leh*	officer (*mil.*)
ufficio, *m.*	*oof-*FEE-*choh*	bureau
"	"	office
ufficio postale, *m.*	*oof-*FEE-*choh poh-*STAH-*leh*	post office
ulcera, *f.*	OOL-*cheh-rah*	ulcer
ultimamente	*ool-tee-mah-*MENN-*teh*	last (most recently, *adv.*)
ultimo	OOL-*tee-moh*	last (*adj.*)
umanità, *f.*	*oo-mah-nee-*TAH	humanity (mankind)
umano	*oo-*MAH-*noh*	human (*adj.*)
umidità, *f.*	*oo-mee-dee-*TAH	moisture
umido	OO-*mee-doh*	damp
"	"	moist
umile	OO-*mee-leh*	humble (lowly)
umiltà, *f.*	*oo-meel-*TAH	humility
umore, *m.*	*oo-*MOH-*reh*	mood (humor)
"	"	temper
umore faceto, *m.*	*oo-*MOH-*reh fah-*CHEH-*toh*	humor (drollery)
un	OON	a (an)
un'	OON	a (an)
una	OO-*nah*	a (an)
una volta	*oo-nah* VOHL-*tah*	once (one time, *adv.*)
Ungheria, *f.*	*oong-gheh-*REE-*ah*	Hungary
unghia, *f.*	OONG-*g_yah*	nail (*anat.*)
unguento, *m.*	*oong-*GWENN-*toh*	ointment
unico	OO-*nee-koh*	only (sole)
uniforme	*oo-nee-*FOHR-*meh*	uniform (*adj.*)
uniforme, *f.*	*oo-nee-*FOHR-*meh*	uniform (*n.*)
unione, *f.*	*oo-*N_YOH-*neh*	union (league)
unire (3)	*oo-*NEE-*reh*	join (bring together), to
"	"	unite (make one), to
unità, *f.*	*oo-nee-*TAH	unity (accord)
universale	*oo-nee-vehr-*SAH-*leh*	universal (*adj.*)
università, *f.*	*oo-nee-vehr-see-*TAH	university
universo, *m.*	*oo-nee-*VEHR-*soh*	universe
uno	OO-*noh*	a (an)
uno o l'altro, l'	LOO-*noh oh* LAHL-*troh*	either (*adj., pron.*)
uomo, *m.*	WOH-*moh*	man
uomo d'affari, *m.*	WOH-*moh dah-*FAH-*ree*	businessman
uomo di stato, *m.*	WOH-*moh dee* STAH-*toh*	statesman
uomo politico, *m.*	WOH-*moh poh-*LEE-*tee-koh*	politician
uova strapazzate, *f.pl.*	WOH-*vah strah-paht-*TSAH-*teh*	scrambled eggs
uovo, *m.* (*pl.* uova, *f.*)	WOH-*voh*	egg
uranio, *m.*	*oo-*RAH-*n_yoh*	uranium
urbano	*oor-*BAH-*noh*	urban
urgente	*oor-*JENN-*teh*	urgent
urlare (1)	*oor-*LAH-*reh*	howl (wail), to
"	"	scream, to
urtare (1)	*oor-*TAH-*reh*	shock (jar), to
Uruguay, *m.*	*oo-roo-*GWAH_*y*	Uruguay
usare (1)	*oo-*ZAH-*reh*	use (utilize), to
uscita, *f.*	*oo-*SHEE-*tah*	exit
"	"	outlet
usignolo, *m.*	*oo-zee-*N_YOH-*loh*	nightingale
uso, *m.*	OO-*zoh*	practice (custom)
"	"	use (utilization)
usuale	*oo-*ZWAH-*leh*	ordinary (usual)
utero, *m.*	OO-*teh-roh*	womb
utile	OO-*tee-leh*	helpful
"	"	useful
utilità, *f.*	*oo-tee-lee-*TAH	use (usefulness)
"	"	utility
uva, *f.*	OO-*vah*	grape
uva secca, *f.*	OO-*vah* SEKK-*kah*	raisin
vacante	*vah-*KAHN-*teh*	vacant (untenanted)
vacanze, *f.pl.*	*vah-*KAHN-*tseh*	vacation (work holidays)
vacca, *f.*	VAHK-*kah*	cow
vaccinazione, *f.*	*vaht-chee-nah-*TS_YOH-*neh*	vaccination
vagare (1)	*vah-*GAH-*reh*	rove, to
"	"	wander, to
vaglia, *m.*	VAH-*l_yah*	money order
vago	VAH-*goh*	vague (not precise)

Italian	Pronunciation	English
vagone, *m.*	*vah-*GOH-*neh*	car, railroad
vagone ristorante, *m.*	*vah-*GOH-*neh ree-stoh-*RAHN-*teh*	diner (railway dining car)
vaiolo, *m.*	*vah-*YOH-*loh*	smallpox
vallata, *f.*	*vahl-*LAH-*tah*	valley
valore, *m.*	*vah-*LOH-*reh*	value
"	"	worth
valore, di	*dee vah-*LOH-*reh*	valuable
valore nominale, *m.*	*vah-*LOH-*reh noh-mee-*NAH-*leh*	face value (*bus.*)
valutare (1)	*vah-loo-*TAH-*reh*	value (appraise), to
valutazione, *f.*	*vah-loo-tah-*TS_YOH-*neh*	appraisal (*bus.*)
"	"	rating (evaluation)
valvola (elettrica) *f.*	VAHL-*voh-lah* (*eh-*LETT-*tree-kah*)	fuse (*elec.*)
valzer, *m.*	VAHL-*tsehr*	waltz (dance step)
vanga, *f.*	VAHNG-*gah*	spade (tool)
vanità, *f.*	*vah-nee-*TAH	vanity (self conceit)
vanitoso	*vah-nee-*TOH-*soh*	vain (conceited)
vano	VAH-*noh*	vain (futile)
vantaggio, *m.*	*vahn-*TAHD-*joh*	advantage
vantarsi (1)	*vahn-*TAHR-*see*	boast, to
vapore, *m.*	*vah-*POH-*reh*	steam
"	"	vapor
varare (1)	*vah-*RAH-*reh*	launch (set afloat), to
variare (1)	*vah-r_*YAH-*reh*	vary (differ), to
varicella, *f.*	*vah-ree-*CHELL-*lah*	chicken pox
varietà, *f.*	*vah-r_yeh-*TAH	variety (diversity)
Varsavia, *f.*	*vahr-*SAH-*v_yah*	Warsaw
vasca, *f.*	VAH-*skah*	tub (bathtub)
vasca da bagno, *f.*	VAH-*skah dah* BAH-*n_yoh*	bathtub
vaso, *m.*	VAH-*zoh*	vase
vassoio, *m.*	*vahss-*SOH-*yoh*	tray
vasto	VAH-*stoh*	mighty
"	"	vast
vecchio	VEKK-*k_yoh*	old (not new)
vedere (122)	*veh-*DEH-*reh*	see, to
vedova, *f.*	VEH-*doh-vah*	widow
vedovo, *m.*	VEH-*doh-voh*	widower
veduta, *f.*	*veh-*DOO-*tah*	view (scene)
veicolo, *m.*	*veh-*EE-*koh-loh*	vehicle (conveyance)
veleno, *m.*	*veh-*LEH-*noh*	poison
vello, *m.*	VELL-*loh*	fleece
velluto, *m.*	*vell-*LOO-*toh*	velvet (*n.*)
velluto di cotone, *m.*	*vell-*LOO-*toh dee koh-*TOH-*neh*	velveteen (*n.*)
velo, *m.*	VEH-*loh*	film (thin coating)
"	"	veil (*n.*)
velocità, *f.*	*veh-loh-chee-*TAH	speed (rapidity)
vena, *f.*	VEH-*nah*	vein (*anat.*)
vendere (2)	VENN-*deh-reh*	sell, to
vendetta, *f.*	*venn-*DETT-*tah*	revenge
"	"	vengeance
vendita, *f.*	VENN-*dee-tah*	sale (exchange)
vendita all'asta, *f.*	VENN-*dee-tah ahl-*LAH-*stah*	auction (sale)
vendita di liquidazione, *f.*	VENN-*dee-tah dee lee-kwee-dah-*TS_YOH-*neh*	clearance sale
venditore, *m.*	*venn-dee-*TOH-*reh*	salesman
"	"	vendor (seller)
venditore ambulante, *m.*	*venn-dee-*TOH-*reh ahm-boo-*LAHN-*teh*	canvasser (*bus.*)
Venerdi Santo, *m.*	*veh-nehr-*DEE SAHN-*toh*	Good Friday
Venezia, *f.*	*veh-*NEH-*ts_yah*	Venice
Venezuela, *f.*	*veh-neh-*ZWEH-*lah*	Venezuela
venezuelano	*veh-neh-zweh-*LAH-*noh*	Venezuelan (*adj.*)
venire (123)	*veh-*NEE-*reh*	come, to
ventilatore, *m.*	*venn-tee-lah-*TOH-*reh*	fan, electric
vento, *m.*	VENN-*toh*	wind
ventoso	*venn-*TOH-*soh*	windy (windswept)
veramente	*veh-rah-*MENN-*teh*	indeed (*adv.*)
"	"	really
verbale, (processo), *m.*	(*proh-*CHESS-*soh*) *vehr-*BAH-*leh*	minutes (record)
verbo, *m.*	VEHR-*boh*	verb
verde	VEHR-*deh*	green (color)
verdura, *f.*	*vehr-*DOO-*rah*	vegetable
vergine, *f.*	VEHR-*jee-neh*	virgin (*n.*)
vergogna, *f.*	*vehr-*GOH-*n_yah*	disgrace
"	"	shame

Italian	Pronunciation	English
vergognoso	*vehr-goh-*N_YOH*-soh*	ashamed (mortified)
"	"	shameful
verità,*f.*	*veh-ree-*TAH	truth
verme,*m.*	VEHR-*meh*	worm
vernice,*f.*	*vehr-*NEE-*cheh*	varnish
vero	VEH-*roh*	actual
"	"	real
"	"	true
versante,*m.*	*vehr-*SAHN-*teh*	hillside
versare (1)	*vehr-*SAH-*reh*	pour (make flow), to
"	"	spill (let pour out), to
versi,*m.pl.*	VEHR-*see*	verse (poetic writing)
verso	VEHR-*soh*	at (to, toward)
"	"	toward
verticale	*vehr-tee-*KAH-*leh*	vertical (*adj.*)
vertigini,*f.pl.*	*vehr-*TEE-*jee-nee*	dizziness
vescica,*f.*	*veh-*SHEE-*kah*	bladder (*anat.*)
vescichetta,*f.*	*veh-shee-*KETT-*tah*	blister
vescovo,*m.*	VESS-*koh-voh*	bishop
vespa,*f.*	VEH-*spah*	wasp
vestaglia,*f.*	*veh-*STAH-*l_yah*	robe (dressing gown)
veste,*f.*	VEH-*steh*	dress (frock)
vestiario,*m.*	*veh-*ST_YAH-*r_yoh*	clothing
"	"	wardrobe (apparel)
vestire (4)	*veh-*STEE-*reh*	dress (clothe), to
vestirsi	*veh-*STEER-*see*	dress (get dressed), to
vestito,*m.*	*veh-*STEE-*toh*	suit, woman's
vetro,*m.*	VEH-*troh*	glass (material)
"	"	pane (window)
vetta,*f.*	VETT-*tah*	crest (summit)
"	"	peak (mountain top)
vi	VEE	(to) you, yourself, yourselves
via	VEE-*ah*	away (from a place, *adv.*)
via,*f.*	VEE-*ah*	way (route)
viaggiare (1)	*v_yahd-*JAH-*reh*	travel, to
viaggiatore,*m.*	*v_yahd-jah-*TOH-*reh*	traveler
viaggiatore (di commercio),*m.*	*v_yahd-jah-*TOH-*reh (dee kohm-*MEHR-*choh)*	traveling salesman
viaggio,*m.*	V_YAHD-*joh*	journey
"	"	trip
"	"	voyage
vicinanza,*f.*	*vee-chee-*NAHN-*tsah*	community (neighborhood)
"	"	vicinity
vicinato,*m.*	*vee-chee-*NAH-*toh*	neighborhood
vicino	*vee-*CHEE-*noh*	near (not far, *adv.*)
vicino,*m.*	*vee-*CHEE-*noh*	neighbor
vicino (a)	*vee-*CHEE-*noh (ah)*	close (near, *adv.*)
vicino a	*vee-*CHEE-*noh ah*	near (*prep.*)
Vienna,*f.*	V_YENN-*nah*	Vienna
viennese	*v_yenn-*NEH-*seh*	Viennese (*adj.*)
vigilare (1)	*vee-jee-*LAH-*reh*	watch (guard), to
vigile,*m.*	VEE-*jee-leh*	policeman
vigneto,*m.*	*vee-*N_YEH-*toh*	vineyard
vigore,*m.*	*vee-*GOH-*reh*	vigor (strength)
vigore, in	*een vee-*GOH-*reh*	active (in force)
vigoroso	*vee-goh-*ROH-*soh*	vigorous
villaggio,*m.*	*veel-*LAHD-*joh*	village
violoncello,*m.*	*v_yoh-lohn-*CHELL-*loh*	cello
vincere (124)	VEEN-*cheh-reh*	beat (defeat), to
"	"	conquer, to
"	"	overcome, to
"	"	win (be victor in), to
vincere le difficoltà di	VEEN-*cheh-reh leh deef-fee-kohl-*TAH *dee*	master (learn), to
vincitore,*m.*	*veen-chee-*TOH-*reh*	victor
vincolo,*m.*	VEENG-*koh-loh*	tie (bond)
vino,*m.*	VEE-*noh*	wine (beverage)
viola,*f.*	V_YOH-*lah*	viola
viola del pensiero,*f.*	V_YOH-*lah dell penn-*S_YEH-*roh*	pansy
violente	*v_yoh-*LENN-*teh*	violent
violenza,*f.*	*v_yoh-*LENN-*tsah*	violence
violetta,*f.*	*v_yoh-*LETT-*tah*	violet (flower)
violetto	*v_yoh-*LETT-*toh*	purple (color)
violino,*m.*	*v_yoh-*LEE-*noh*	violin
virgola,*f.*	VEER-*goh-lah*	comma
virile	*vee-*REE-*leh*	manly
virtù,*f.*	*veer-*TOO	virtue (moral excellence)
viscere,*f.pl.*	VEE-*sheh-reh*	bowels (*anat.*)
visibile	*vee-*ZEE-*bee-leh*	visible

Italian	Pronunciation	English
visione momentanea,*f.*	*vee-z*_YOH-*neh moh-menn-*TAH-*neh-ah*	glimpse
visita,*f.*	VEE-*zee-tah*	visit (social call)
visitare (1)	*vee-zee-*TAH-*reh*	visit, to
viso,*m.*	VEE-*zoh*	countenance (face)
vista,*f.*	VEE-*stah*	sight (eyesight)
"	"	sight (range of view)
"	"	vision (eyesight)
vita,*f.*	VEE-*tah*	life
"	"	waist (*anat.*)
vita, (la),*f.*	*(lah)* VEE-*tah*	living (livelihood)
vitamina,*f.*	*vee-tah-*MEE-*nah*	vitamin
vite,*f.*	VEE-*teh*	screw (threaded nail)
"	"	vine (grapevine)
vitello,*m.*	*vee-*TELL-*loh*	calf (animal)
"	"	veal
vittima,*f.*	VEET-*tee-mah*	victim
vittoria,*f.*	*veet-*TOH-*r_yah*	victory
vittorioso	*veet-toh-*R_YOH-*soh*	victorious
vivace	*vee-*VAH-*cheh*	lively (*adj.*)
vivere (125)	VEE-*veh-reh*	live (be alive), to
vivido	VEE-*vee-doh*	vivid
vivo	VEE-*voh*	alive
"	"	live (*adj.*)
vizio,*m.*	VEE-*ts_yoh*	vice (moral fault)
voce,*f.*	VOH-*cheh*	voice
voce, ad alta	*ahd* AHL-*tah* VOH-*cheh*	aloud
voi stessi	VOY STESS-*see*	yourselves
volare (1)	*voh-*LAH-*reh*	fly, to
voler dire (126)	*voh-*LEHR DEE-*reh*	mean (have in mind), to
volere	*voh-*LEH-*reh*	want (desire), to
volgare	*vohl-*GAH-*reh*	common (vulgar)
"	"	vulgar (ill-bred)
volo,*m.*	VOH-*loh*	flight (journey by air)
volontà,*f.*	*voh-lohn-*TAH	will (power of choice)
volontario,*m.*	*voh-lohn-*TAH-*r_yoh*	volunteer (*mil.*)
volpe,*f.*	VOHL-*peh*	fox
voltarsi (1)	*vohl-*TAHR-*see*	turn (face about), to
volume,*m.*	*voh-*LOO-*meh*	volume
vomitare (1)	*voh-mee-*TAH-*reh*	vomit, to
vongola,*f.*	VOHN-*goh-lah*	clam
vostra (see vostro)		
vostre (see vostro)		
vostri (see vostro)		
vostro, il	*eel* VOH-*stroh*	your
"	"	yours
votante,*m.,f.*	*voh-*TAHN-*teh*	voter
votare (1)	*voh-*TAH-*reh*	vote, to
voto,*m.*	VOH-*toh*	grade (academic rating)
"	"	pledge
"	"	vote
"	"	vow
vulcano,*m.*	*vool-*KAH-*noh*	volcano
vuotare (1)	*vwoh-*TAH-*reh*	empty (remove contents of), to
vuoto	VWOH-*toh*	empty
whiskey,*m.*	WEE-*skee*	whiskey
zaffiro,*m.*	*dzahf-*FEE-*roh*	sapphire (gem)
zampa,*f.*	TSAHM-*pah*	paw
zanzara,*f.*	*dzahn-*DZAH-*rah*	mosquito
zappa,*f.*	TSAHP-*pah*	hoe
zappare (1)	*tsahp-*PAH-*reh*	hoe, to
zebra,*f.*	DZEH-*brah*	zebra
zelo,*m.*	DZEH-*loh*	zeal
zeloso	*dzeh-*LOH-*soh*	earnest
zenzero,*m.*	DZENN-*dzeh-roh*	ginger (spice)
zero,*m.*	DZEH-*roh*	zero (*n.*)
zia,*f.*	TSEE-*ah*	aunt
zinco,*m.*	DZEENG-*koh*	zinc
zingaro,*m.*	TSEENG-*gah-roh*	gypsy
zio,*m.*	TSEE-*oh*	uncle
zoccolo,*m.*	TSOHK-*koh-loh*	hoof
zolfo,*m.*	DZOHL-*foh*	sulphur
zona,*f.*	DZOH-*nah*	zone
zoologia,*f.*	*dzoh-oh-loh-*JEE-*ah*	zoology
zoppicare (1)	*tsohp-pee-*KAH-*reh*	limp, to
zoppo	TSOHP-*poh*	lame
zucchero,*m.*	TSOOK-*keh-roh*	sugar

Italian Special Lists

Alphabet

a	AH		j	*ee* LOONG-*goh*		s	ESS-*seh*
b	BEE		k	KAHP-*pah*		t	TEE
c	CHEE		l	ELL-*leh*		u	OO
d	DEE		m	EMM-*meh*		v	VOO
e	EH		n	ENN-*neh*		w	DOHP-*p_yoh voo*
f	EHF-*feh*		o	OH		x	EEKS
g	JEE		p	PEE		y	EE-*psee-lohn*
h	AHK-*kah*		q	KOO		z	DZEH-*tah*
i	EE		r	EHR-*reh*			

Cardinal Numbers

Italian	Pronunciation	English	Italian	Pronunciation	English
uno	OO-*noh*	one	ventuno	*venn*-TOO-*noh*	twenty-one
due	DOO-*eh*	two	ventidue	*venn-tee*-DOO-*eh*	twenty-two
tre	TREH	three	trenta	TRENN-*tah*	thirty
quattro	KWAHT-*troh*	four	quaranta	*kwah*-RAHN-*tah*	forty
cinque	CHEEN-*kweh*	five	cinquanta	*cheen*-KWAHN-*tah*	fifty
sei	SAY	six	sessanta	*sess*-SAHN-*tah*	sixty
sette	SET-*teh*	seven	settanta	*set*-TAHN-*tah*	seventy
otto	OHT-*toh*	eight	ottanta	*oht*-TAHN-*tah*	eighty
nove	NOH-*veh*	nine	novanta	*noh*-VAHN-*tah*	ninety
dieci	D_YEH-*chee*	ten	cento	CHENN-*toh*	one hundred
undici	OON-*dee-chee*	eleven	cento uno	CHENN-*toh* OO-*noh*	one hundred one
dodici	DOH-*dee-chee*	twelve	duecento	*doo-eh*-CHENN-*toh*	two hundred
tredici	TREH-*dee-chee*	thirteen	duecento uno	*doo-eh*-CHENN-*toh* OO-*noh*	two hundred one
quattordici	*kwaht*-TOHR-*dee-chee*	fourteen			
quindici	KWEEN-*dee-chee*	fifteen	mille	MEEL-*leh*	one thousand
sedici	SEH-*dee-chee*	sixteen	mille uno	MEEL-*leh* OO-*noh*	one thousand one
diciassette	*dee-chahss*-SET-*teh*	seventeen	due mila	DOO-*eh* MEE-*lah*	two thousand
diciotto	*dee*-CHOHT-*toh*	eighteen	due mila uno	DOO-*eh* MEE-*lah* OO-*noh*	two thousand one
diciannove	*dee-chahn*-NOH-*veh*	nineteen	un milione	*oon mee*-L_YOH-*neh*	one million
venti	VENN-*tee*	twenty	un miliardo	*oon mee*-L_YAHR-*doh*	one billion

Ordinal Numbers

Italian	Pronunciation	English	Italian	Pronunciation	English
primo	PREE-*moh*	first	settimo	SETT-*tee-moh*	seventh
secondo	*seh*-KOHN-*doh*	second	ottavo	*oht*-TAH-*voh*	eighth
terzo	TEHR-*tsoh*	third	nono	NOH-*noh*	ninth
quarto	KWAHR-*toh*	fourth	decimo	DEH-*chee-moh*	tenth
quinto	KWEEN-*toh*	fifth	undicesimo	*oon-dee*-CHEH-*zee-moh*	eleventh
sesto	SEH-*stoh*	sixth	dodicesimo	*doh-dee*-CHEH-*zee-moh*	twelfth

Days of the Week

Italian	Pronunciation	English	Italian	Pronunciation	English
domenica, *f.*	*doh*-MEH-*nee-kah*	Sunday	giovedì, *m.*	*joh-veh*-DEE	Thursday
lunedì, *m.*	*loo-neh*-DEE	Monday	venerdì, *m.*	*veh-nehr*-DEE	Friday
martedì, *m.*	*mahr-teh*-DEE	Tuesday	sabato, *m.*	SAH-*bah-toh*	Saturday
mercoledì, *m.*	*mehr-koh-leh*-DEE	Wednesday			

Months of the Year

Italian	Pronunciation	English	Italian	Pronunciation	English
gennaio, *m.*	*jenn*-NAH-*yoh*	January	luglio, *m.*	LOO-*l_yoh*	July
febbraio, *m.*	*fehb*-BRAH-*yoh*	February	agosto, *m.*	*ah*-GOH-*stoh*	August
marzo, *m.*	MAHR-*tsoh*	March	settembre, *m.*	*set*-TEMM-*breh*	September
aprile, *m.*	*ah*-PREE-*leh*	April	ottobre, *m.*	*oht*-TOH-*breh*	October
maggio, *m.*	MAHD-*joh*	May	novembre, *m.*	*noh*-VEMM-*breh*	November
giugno, *m.*	JOO-*n_yoh*	June	dicembre, *m.*	*dee*-CHEMM-*breh*	December

First Names

Italian	Pronunciation	English	Italian	Pronunciation	English
Abramo	*ah*-BRAH-*moh*	Abraham	Barbara	BAHR-*bah-rah*	Barbara
Adamo	*ah*-DAH-*moh*	Adam	Beatrice	*beh-ah*-TREE-*cheh*	Beatrice
Agnese	*ah*-N_YEH-*seh*	Agnes	Beniamino	*behn-yah*-MEE-*noh*	Benjamin
Alberto	*ahl*-BEHR-*toh*	Albert	Bernardo	*behr*-NAHR-*doh*	Bernard
Alessandro	*ah-lehss*-SAHN-*droh*	Alexander			
Alfredo	*ahl*-FREH-*doh*	Alfred	Berta	BEHR-*tah*	Bertha
Alice	*ah*-LEE-*cheh*	Alice	Carlo	KAHR-*loh*	Charles
Andrea	*ahn*-DREH-*ah*	Andrew	Carlotta	*kahr*-LOHT-*tah*	Charlotte
Anna	AHN-*nah*	Ann, Anne	Carolina	*kah-roh*-LEE-*nah*	Caroline
Antonio	*ahn*-TOH-*n_yoh*	Anthony	Caterina	*kah-teh*-REE-*nah*	Kate
Arnaldo	*ahr*-NAHL-*doh*	Arnold	"	"	Katharine
Aroldo	*ah*-ROHL-*doh*	Harold			
Arrigo	*ahr*-REE-*goh*	Harry	Clara	KLAH-*rah*	Clara
Arturo	*ahr*-TOO-*roh*	Arthur	"		Clare

Italian	Pronunciation	English	Italian	Pronunciation	English
Corrado	kohr-RAH-doh	Conrad	Laura	L_OW-rah	Laura
Costanza	koh-STAHN-tsah	Constance	Leonardo	leh-oh-NAHR-doh	Leonard
Cristina	kree-STEE-nah	Christine	Leone	leh-OH-neh	Leo
Cristoforo	kree-STOH-foh-roh	Christopher	"	"	Leon
			Leonora	leh-oh-NOH-rah	Leonora
Daniele	dah-N_YEH-leh	Daniel	Leopoldo	leh-oh-POHL-doh	Leopold
Davide	DAH-vee-deh	David			
Dorotea	doh-roh-TEH-ah	Dorothy	Luigi	loo-EE-jee	Louis
Editta	eh-DEET-tah	Edith	Luisa	loo-EE-zah	Louise
Edmondo	ehd-MOHN-doh	Edmund	Marco	MAHR-koh	Mark
Edoardo	eh-doh-AHR-doh	Edward	Margherita	mahr-geh-REE-tah	Margaret
			Maria	mah-REE-ah	Marie
Elena	EH-leh-nah	Helen	"	"	Mary
Eleonora	eh-leh-oh-NOH-rah	Eleanor			
Elisabetta	eh-lee-zah-BETT-tah	Elizabeth	Marta	MAHR-tah	Martha
Emilia	eh-MEE-l_yah	Emily	Martino	mahr-TEE-noh	Martin
Emma	EMM-mah	Emma	Matteo	maht-TEH-oh	Matthew
Enrichetta	enn-ree-KEHT-tah	Henrietta	Michele	mee-KEH-leh	Michael
			Nicola	nee-KOH-lah	Nicholas
Enrico	enn-REE-koh	Henry	Olga	OHL-gah	Olga
Erberto	ehr-BEHR-toh	Herbert			
Ermanno	ehr-MAHN-noh	Herman	Orazio	oh-RAH-ts_yoh	Horace
Ernesto	ehr-NEH-stoh	Ernest	Ottone	oht-TOH-neh	Otto
Eugenio	eh_oo-JEH-n_yoh	Eugene	Paola	PAH_oh-lah	Paula
Federico	feh-deh-REE-koh	Frederick	Paolo	PAH_oh-loh	Paul
			Patrizio	pah-TREE-ts_yoh	Patrick
Felice	feh-LEE-cheh	Felix	Pietro	P_YEH-troh	Peter
Ferdinando	fehr-dee-NAHN-doh	Ferdinand			
Filippo	fee-LEEP-poh	Philip	Raimondo	rah_ee-MOHN-doh	Raymond
Fiorenza	f_yoh-REHN-tsah	Florence	Raulo	RAH-oo-loh	Ralph
Francesca	frahn-CHEH-skah	Frances	Rebecca	reh-BEHK-kah	Rebecca
Francesco	frahn-CHEH-skoh	Francis	Riccardo	reek-KAHR-doh	Richard
			Roberto	roh-BEHR-toh	Robert
Gertrude	gehr-TROO-deh	Gertrude	Rodolfo	roh-DOHL-foh	Rudolph
Giacobbe	jah-KOHB-beh	Jacob			
Giacomo	JAH-koh-moh	James	Rosa	ROH-zah	Rose
Giorgio	JOHR-joh	George	Rosalia	roh-zah-LEE-ah	Rosalie
Giovanna	joh-VAHN-nah	Jane	Rosamaria	roh-zah-mah-REE-ah	Rosemary
"	"	Jean	Ruth	ROOT	Ruth
			Samuele	sah-M_WEH-leh	Samuel
Giovanna	joh-VAHN-nah	Joan	Sara	SAH-rah	Sarah
Giovanni	joh-VAHN-nee	John			
Giuditta	joo-DEET-tah	Judith	Saul	SAH-ool	Saul
Giuliano	joo-L_YAH-noh	Julian	Silvia	SEEL-v_yah	Sylvia
Giuseppe	joo-ZEPP-peh	Joseph	Stefano	STEH-fah-noh	Stephen
Giuseppina	joo-zepp-PEE-nah	Josephine	Susanna	soo-ZAHN-nah	Susan
			Teresa	teh-REH-zah	Theresa
Gualtiero	gwahl-T_YEH-roh	Walter			
Guglielmo	goo-L_YELL-moh	William	Tomaso	toh-MAH-soh	Thomas
Gustavo	goo-STAH-voh	Gustav	Ugo	OO-goh	Hugh
Irene	ee-REH-neh	Irene	Vincenzo	veen-CHENN-tsoh	Vincent
Isabella	ee-zah-BELL-lah	Isabel	Virginia	veer-JEE-n_yah	Virginia
Isacco	ee-ZAHK-koh	Isaac	Vittorio	veet-TOH-r_yoh	Victor

USEFUL EXPRESSIONS

Greetings

English	Pronunciation	Italian
How are you?	KOH-meh STAH?	Come sta?
Well, thanks, and you?	BEH-neh, GRAH-ts_yeh, eh LAY?	Bene, grazie, e Lei?
Good morning.	bwohn JOHR-noh.	Buon giorno.
Good afternoon.	bwohn JOHR-noh.	Buon giorno.
Good evening.	BWOH-nah SEH-rah.	Buona sera.
Good night.	BWOH-nah NOHT-teh.	Buona notte.
See you again.	ahr-ree-veh-DEHR-lah.	Arrivederla.
So long.	CHOW.	Ciao.
Good luck!	BWOH-nah fohr-TOO-nah!	Buona fortuna!
Good-by.	ahd-DEE-oh.	Addio.
Glad to meet you.	p_yah-CHEH-reh (dee FAH-reh lah SOO-ah koh-noh-SHENN-tsah).	Piacere (di fare la sua conoscenza).
Congratulations.	kohn-grah-too-lah-TS_YOH-nee	Congratulazioni
Happy Birthday.	bwohn kohm-pleh-AHN-noh.	Buon compleanno.
Merry Christmas.	bwohn nah-TAH-leh.	Buon Natale.
Happy New Year.	feh-LEE-cheh kah-poh DAHN-noh.	Felice capo d'anno.

Ordinary Conversation

English	Pronunciation	Italian
Thank you.	GRAH-ts_yeh.	Grazie.
Please.	pehr fah-VOH-reh.	Per favore.
You're welcome.	PREH-goh.	Prego.
Pardon me.	SKOO-zee.	Scusi.
What do you call this?	KOH-meh see K_YAH-mah KWEH-stoh?	Come si chiama questo?
I'm sorry.	mee dee-SP_YAH-cheh.	Mi dispiace.

English	Pronunciation	Italian
Allow me.		Mi permetta.
I would like...	*mee pehr-*MET*-tah.*	Vorrei...
Come in.	VOHR-*ray...*	Avanti.
May I introduce...	*ah-*VAHN*-tee.*	Le presento...
What is your name?	*leh preh-*ZENN*-toh...*	Come si chiama?
	KOH-*meh see* K_YAH*-mah?*	
My name is...	*mee* K_YAH*-moh...*	Mi chiamo...
I don't know.	*nohn* SO.	Non so.
I'm thirsty.	*oh* SEH*-teh.*	Ho sete.
I'm hungry.	*oh* FAH*-meh.*	Ho fame.
I'm an American.	SOH*-noh ah-meh-ree-*KAH*-noh (ah-meh-ree-* KAH*-nah).*	Sono americano (americana).
Where can I find...?	DOH*-veh poh-*TRAY *troh-*VAH*-reh...?*	Dove potrei trovare...?
What is this?	*keh* KOH*-sah eh* KWEH*-stoh?*	Che cosa è questo?

Foreign Languages

English	Pronunciation	Italian
Do you speak...?	PAHR*-lah...?*	Parla...?
I speak (understand) a little...	PAHR*-loh (kah-*PEE*-skoh) oon poh...*	Parlo (capisco) un po'...
I do not speak...	*nohn* PAHR*-loh...*	Non parlo...
Is there someone here who speaks English?	CHEH *kwahl-*KOO*-noh keh* PAHR*-lah eeng-*GLEH*-seh* KWEE?	C'è qualcuno che parla inglese qu
I understand you.	*lah kah-*PEE*-skoh.*	La capisco.
I don't understand.	*nohn kah-*PEE*-skoh.*	Non capisco.
Please speak more slowly.	*pehr fah-*VOH*-reh,* PAHR*-lee p_yoo lenn-tah-* MENN*-teh.*	Per favore, parli più lentamente.
Please repeat.	*pehr fah-*VOH*-reh, ree-*PEH*-tah.*	Per favore, ripeta.

Asking Directions

English	Pronunciation	Italian
In which direction is...	*een* KEH *dee-reh-*TS_YOH*-neh eh...*	In che direzione è...
Please take me to...	*pehr fah-*VOH*-reh, mee* POHR*-tee ah...*	Per favore, mi porti a...
Please take me there.	*pehr fah-*VOH*-reh, mee* POHR*-tee lah.*	Per favore, mi porti là.
Where can I mail this?	DOH*-veh* POHSS*-soh eem-poh-*STAH*-reh* KWEH*-stoh?*	Dove posso impostare questo?
Please direct me...	*pehr fah-*VOH*-reh, poh-*TREBB*-beh dee-*REE*-jehr-mee...*	Per favore, potrebbe dirigermi...
...to the telephone.	*...ahl teh-*LEH*-foh-noh.*	...al telefono.
...to the toilet.	*...ahl gah-bee-*NETT*-toh.*	...al gabinetto.
...the post office.	AHL*-lah* POH*-stah.*	...alla posta.
...the bank.	AHL*-lah* BAHNG*-kah.*	...alla banca.
...the police station.	*...*AHL*-lah kweh-*STOO*-rah.*	...alla questura.
...the U. S. consulate.	*...ahl kohn-soh-*LAH*-toh ah-meh-ree-*KAH*-noh.*	...al consolato americano.
Please point.	EEN*-dee-kee, pehr fah-*VOH*-reh.*	Indichi, per favore.

The Hotel

English	Pronunciation	Italian
I would like a room...	*vohr-*RAY OO*-nah* KAH*-meh-rah...*	Vorrei una camera...
...with a single bed.	*...ah oon* LETT*-toh.*	...a un letto.
...with two beds.	*...ah* DOO*-eh* LETT*-tee.*	...a due letti.
...with bath.	*...kohn* BAH*-n_yoh.*	...con bagno.
...without meals.	*...*SENN*-tsah penn-s_*YOH*-neh.*	...senza pensione.
Please, the key for Room...	*pehr fah-*VOH*-reh, lah* K_YAH*-veh dell* NOO*-meh-roh...*	Per favore, la chiave del numero...
Please call me at...o'clock.	*pehr fah-*VOH*-reh, mee* SVEH*-l_yee* AHL*-leh...*	Per favore, mi svegli alle...
I want this...	*deh-*SEE*-deh-roh keh* KWEH*-stoh* SEE*-ah...*	Desidero che questo sia...
...pressed.	*...stee-*RAH*-toh.*	...stirato.
...cleaned.	*...poo-*LEE*-toh.*	...pulito.
...washed.	*...lah-*VAH*-toh.*	...lavato.
...repaired.	*...rahm-menn-*DAH*-toh.*	...rammendato.
When will (my suit) be returned?	KWAHN*-doh ree-pohr-teh-*RAHN*-noh (eel* MEE*-oh veh-*STEE*-toh)?*	Quando riporteranno (il mio vestito)?
Please return (my suit) at...	*pehr fah-*VOH*-reh, ree-pohr-*TAH*-teh (eel* MEE*-oh veh-*STEE*-toh) ah...*	Per favore, riportate (il mio vestito) a...

The Restaurant

English	Pronunciation	Italian
A table for two, please.	*oo-nah* TAH*-voh-lah pehr* DOO*-eh, pehr fah-*VOH*-reh.*	Una tavola per due, per favore.
I would like to see the menu.	*vohr-*RAY *veh-*DEH*-reh lah* LEE*-stah.*	Vorrei vedere la lista.
I want it...	*loh deh-*SEE*-deh-roh...*	Lo desidero...
...rare.	*...*POH*-koh* KOHT*-toh.*	...poco cotto.
...medium.	*...ah* MEDD*-dzah koht-*TOO*-rah.*	...a mezza cottura.
...well-done.	*...ben* KOHT*-toh.*	...ben cotto.
Check, please!	*eel* KOHN*-toh, pehr fah-*VOH*-reh!*	Il conto, per favore!

Telephoning

English	Pronunciation	Italian
I wish to telephone.	deh-SEE-deh-roh teh-leh-foh-NAH-reh.	Desidero telefonare.
Please get me this number.	pehr fah-VOH-reh, mee METT-tah een koh-moo-nee-kah-TS_YOH-neh kohn KWEH-stoh NOO-meh-roh.	Per favore, mi metta in comunicazione con questo numero.
Please give me the number of...	pehr fah-VOH-reh, mee DEE-ah eel NOO-meh-roh dee...	Per favore, mi dia il numero di...
What did you say?	KOH-meh, PREH-goh?	Come, prego?
The line is busy.	lah LEE-neh_ah eh ohk-koo-PAH-tah.	La linea è occupata.
What is the charge?	KWAHL eh lah tah-REEF-fah?	Qual è la tariffa?

Time

English	Pronunciation	Italian
What time is it?	keh OH-rah eh?	Che ora è?
It is...	SOH-noh...	Sono...
...five o'clock.	...leh CHEEN-kweh.	...le cinque.
...ten past eight.	...leh OHT-toh eh D_YEH-chee.	...le otto e dieci.
...a quarter past six.	...leh SAY eh oon KWAHR-toh.	...le sei e un quarto.
...half past five.	...leh CHEEN-kweh eh MEDD-dzah.	...le cinque e mezza.
...five to seven.	...leh SETT-teh MEH-noh CHEEN-kweh.	...le sette meno cinque.
The day before yesterday	LAHL-troh YEH-ree	L'altro ieri
Yesterday evening	YEH-ree SEH-rah	Ieri sera
This morning	stah-MAH-nee	Stamani
At noon	ah medd-dzoh-JOHR-noh	A mezzogiorno
In the afternoon	nell poh-meh-REED-joh	Nel pomeriggio
In the evening	dee SEH-rah	Di sera
At night	dee NOHT-teh	Di notte
At midnight	ah medd-dzah-NOHT-teh	A mezzanotte
Tomorrow morning	doh-MAH-nee maht-TEE-nah	Domani mattina
Tomorrow evening	doh-MAH-nee SEH-rah	Domani sera
The day after tomorrow	DOH-poh doh-MAH-nee	Dopo domani

Weather

English	Pronunciation	Italian
It's hot.	fah KAHL-doh.	Fa caldo.
It's cold.	fah FREDD-doh.	Fa freddo.
It's raining.	P_YOH-veh.	Piove.
It's snowing.	NEH-vee-kah.	Nevica.
What fine weather!	keh bell TEMM-poh!	Che bel tempo!

Postal Information

English	Pronunciation	Italian
How much is the postage on this?	KWAHN-toh pehr ahf-frahn-KAH-reh KWEH-stoh?	Quanto per affrancare questo?
Give me...worth of stamps.	mee DEE-ah...dee frahn-koh-BOHL-lee.	Mi dia...di francobolli.
Please send this letter...	pehr fah-VOH-reh, speh-DEE-skah KWEH-stah LETT-teh-rah	Per favore, spedisca questa lettera...
...airmail.	...pehr VEE-ah ah_EH-reh_ah.	...per via aerea.
...special delivery.	...pehr eh-SPRESS-soh.	...per espresso.
...registered.	...rahk-koh-mahn-DAH-tah.	...raccomandata.
Please send this parcel post.	pehr fah-VOH-reh, loh speh-DEE-skah PAHK-koh poh-STAH-leh.	Per favore, lo spedisca pacco postale.

Barber and Beauty Shop

English	Pronunciation	Italian
I want a haircut.	deh-SEE-deh-roh FAHR-mee tah-L_YAH-reh ee kah-PELL-lee.	Desidero farmi tagliare i capelli.
Not too short.	NOHN TROHP-poh KOHR-tee.	Non troppo corti.
No hair oil, thank you.	NOH, GRAH-ts_yeh, N_YENN-teh breel-lahn-TEE-nah.	No, grazie, niente brillantina.
I want a shave.	deh-SEE-deh-roh FAHR-mee FAH-reh lah BAHR-bah.	Desidero farmi fare la barba.
I want a shampoo.	deh-SEE-deh-roh FAHR-mee lah-VAH-reh ee kah-PELL-lee.	Desidero farmi lavare i capelli.
I want my hair set.	deh-SEE-deh-roh oo-nohn-doo-lah-TS_YOH-neh.	Desidero un'ondulazione.

Transportation

English	Pronunciation	Italian
Where is the ticket office?	DOH-veh EH lah bee-l_yett-teh-REE-ah?	Dove è la biglietteria?
When does...arrive?	KWAHN-doh ahr-REE-vah...	Quando arriva...
...the plane...	...lah_eh-roh-PLAH-noh?	...l'aeroplano?
...the train...	...eel TREH-noh?	...il treno?

English	Pronunciation	Italian
...the bus...	...L_OW-*toh-booss*?	...l'autobus?
At what time does the train leave for...?	ah *keh* OH-*rah* PAHR-*teh eel* TREH-*noh pehr*...?	A che ora parte il treno per...?
From which track does the train for... leave?	dah KWAH-*leh* bee-NAH-*r_yoh* PAHR-*teh eel* TREH-*noh pehr*...?	Da quale binario parte il treno per...?
Is this the right train for...?	eh KWEH-*stoh eel* TREH-*noh pehr*...?	È questo il treno per...?
Where is my baggage?	DOH-*veh eh eel* MEE-*oh bah*-GAH-*l_yoh*?	Dove è il mio bagaglio?
Where is the baggage room?	DOH-*veh eh eel deh*-POH-*zee-toh bah*-GAH-*l_yee*?	Dove è il deposito bagagli?
Please call a taxi.	*pehr fah*-VOH-*reh, mee* K_YAH-*mee oon tahs*-SEE.	Per favore, mi chiami un tassì.

Auto Travel

English	Pronunciation	Italian
What place is this?	*keh* POH-*stoh eh* KWEH-*stoh*?	Che posto è questo?
Where is the town?	DOH-*veh eh lah cheet*-TAH?	Dove è la città?
Which is the best road for...?	KWAHL *eh lah mee-l_yohr* STRAH-*dah pehr*...?	Qual è la miglior strada per...?
Turn to the right.	VOHL-*tee ah* DEH-*strah*.	Volti a destra.
Turn to the left.	VOHL-*tee ah see*-NEE-*strah*.	Volti a sinistra.
Go straight on.	*kohn*-TEE-*n_wee dee*-REET-*toh*.	Continui diritto.
Go back.	*ree*-TOHR-*nee*.	Ritorni.
This way.	*dee* KWEE.	Di qui.
That way.	*dee* LEE.	Di lì.
How far is it to...?	KWAHN-*toh eh lohn*-TAH-*noh*...*dee* KWEE?	Quanto è lontano...di qui?
Is this the road to...?	*eh* KWEH-*stah lah* STRAH-*dah pehr*...?	È questa la strada per...?
Is it...	*eh*...	È...
...near?	...*vee*-CHEE-*noh*?	...vicino?
...far?	...*lohn*-TAH-*noh*?	...lontano?
...very far?	...MOHL-*toh lohn*-TAH-*noh*?	...molto lontano?
Which way is...	*een* KWAH-*leh dee-reh* TS_YOH-*neh eh*...	In quale direzione è...
...north?	...*eel* NORD?	...il nord?
...south?	...*eel* SOOD?	...il sud?
...east?	...LEST?	...l'est?
...west?	...LOH-*vest*?	...l'ovest?
Is the road...?	*eh lah* STRAH-*dah*...?	È la strada...?
Is there a detour?	CHEH *oo-nah dvh-v_yah*-TS_YOH-*neh*?	C'è una deviazione?
What is the speed limit?	*kwah*-LEH *lah* MAHSS-*see-mah veh-loh-chee*-TAH?	Qual'è la massima velocità?
Where is the nearest gas station?	DOH-*veh see* TROH-*vah lah stah*-TS_YOH-*neh dee ree-fohr-nee*-MENN-*toh p_yoo vee*-CHEE-*nah*?	Dove si trova la stazione di rifornimento più vicina?
Where can I find a garage (for repairs)?	DOH-*veh* POHSS-*soh troh*-VAH-*reh oon-ow-toh-ree*-MESS-*sah*?	Dove posso trovare un'autorimessa?
I need...	*oh bee*-ZOH-*n_yoh dee*...	Ho bisogno di...
...oil.	...OH-*l_yoh*.	...olio.
...gasoline.	...*ben*-DZEE-*nah*.	...benzina.
...a tire.	...OO-*nah* GOHM-*mah*.	...una gomma.

Public Signs

English	Pronunciation	Italian
Keep Out	*v_yeh*-TAH-*toh leen*-GRESS-*soh*	Vietato l'Ingresso
For Hire	*ahf*-FEET-*tah-see*	Affittasi
No Parking	*dee-v_yeh*-TOH-*toh dee* SOH-*stah*	Divieto di Sosta
No Smoking	*v_yeh*-TAH-*toh foo*-MAH-*reh*	Vietato Fumare
Sale	VENN-*dee-tah*	Vendita
Women	*see*-N_YOH-*reh*	Signore
Men	*see*-N_YOH-*ree*	Signori
No Spitting	EH *proh-ee*-BEE-*toh spoo*-TAH-*reh*	È Proibito Sputare
Railroad	*fehr-roh*-VEE-*ah*	Ferrovia
Dangerous Curve	KOOR-*vah peh-ree-koh*-LOH-*sah*	Curva Pericolosa
Keep to the Right (Left)	*mahn-teh*-NEH-*reh lah* DEH-*strah (see*-NEE-*strah)*	Mantenere la Destra (Sinistra)
Dead End	VEE-*ah* CH_YEH-*kah*	Via Cieca
Men Working	*lah*-VOH-*ree een eh-zeh-koo*-TS_YOH-*neh*	Lavori in Esecuzione
No Thoroughfare	VEE-*ah* K_YOO-*sah*	Via Chiusa
One-way Street	SENN-*soh* OO-*nee-koh*	Senso Unico
Go Slow	*rahl-lenn*-TAH-*reh*	Rallentare
Toilet	*gah-bee*-NETT-*toh*	Gabinetto
Entrance	*enn*-TRAH-*tah*	Entrata
Exit	*oo*-SHEE-*tah*	Uscita

Italian Grammar

ARTICLES

Definite article

Masc. Sing.	il	the	il re	the king
	l' (before a vowel)	the	l'uomo	the man
	lo (before *z*, or *s* followed by a consonant)	the	lo zio	the uncle
Fem. Sing.	la	the	la sposa	the bride
	l' (before a vowel)	the	l'anima	the soul

Masc. Pl.	i	the	i muri	the walls
	gli (before *z*, or *s* followed by consonant; before vowels, except *i*)	the	gli zii	the uncles
	gl' (before *i*)	the	gl'Italiani	the Italians
Fem. Pl.	le	the	le madri	the mothers
	l' (before *e*)	the	l'erbe	the grasses

Contractions of the definite article. Certain prepositions are usually contracted with the forms of the definite article:

Article:	*il*	*lo*	*i*	*gli*	*la*	*le*	*l'*
a to, at	al	allo	ai	agli	alla	alle	all'
da by, from	dal	dallo	dai	dagli	dalla	dalle	dall'
di of	del	dello	dei	degli	della	delle	dell'
in in	nel	nello	nei	negli	nella	nelle	nell'
su on	sul	sullo	sui	sugli	sulla	sulle	sull'

Less frequently, the prepositions *per* and *con* are contracted with the article.

al re	*to the* king	dalle madri	*by the* mothers
allo zio	*to the* uncle	dalla madre	*from the* mother
agli zii	*to the* uncles	dall'anima	*from the* soul
dai ragazzi	*by the* boys	dall'uomo	*from the* man

Indefinite article

Masc.	un	a, an	un albero	a tree
	uno (before *z*, or *s* followed by a consonant)	a, an	uno sbaglio	a mistake
Fem.	una	a, an	una penna	a pen
	un' (before a vowel)	a, an	un'aquila	an eagle

Masc. Pl.	dei, etc. (see *With Nouns in the Partitive Sense*, below)	some	dei ragazzi	(some) boys
Fem. Pl.	delle, etc.	some	delle ragazze	(some) girls

With nouns in the general sense

Nouns used with the meaning of "all," "every," "in general" regularly have the definite article in Italian, although not always in English.

Mi piace *il* caffè.	I like coffee.
Il cane è l'amico d*ell'*uomo.	*The* dog is man's friend.
*L'*avarizia è un vizio.	Avarice is a vice.

With nouns in the partitive sense

Nouns with the words "some" or "any" expressed or implied are said to be used in the partitive sense. This is very often expressed in Italian by *di* and the definite article contracted before the noun.

Avete *dei* libri?	Have you (*some, any*) books?
Vuole Lei *del* pane?	Do you want (*some, any*) bread?
Andai con *degli* amici.	I went with friends.

NOUNS

Gender of nouns

The characteristic ending for a masculine noun in Italian is *-o*, while the characteristic ending for the feminine is *-a*. Another large group of nouns end in *-e* and may be masculine or feminine. The adjectives and articles that modify the nouns in Italian agree with the noun they modify in number and gender.

lo zio	the uncle	uno scaffale	a bookshelf
il padre	the father	una madre	a mother
la nonna	the grandmother	un'alunna	a student, *f.*
la madre	the mother	l'estate, *f.*	(the) summer
un albergo	a hotel	l'odore, *m.*	the odor

Other, smaller groups of nouns have characteristic endings of their own. Nouns ending with a stressed *-à* or a stressed *-ù* are feminine. Nouns of Greek origin (usually similar in English) ending in *-i* are feminine; nouns of Greek origin ending in *-a* are masculine.

la virtù	virtue	la tesi	the thesis
la bontà	goodness	il programma	the program
la crisi	the crisis	il poeta	the poet, *m.*

Some nouns, usually denoting persons, are either masculine or feminine. Many have the same suffixes as the following nouns:

Masc.	*Fem.*	
un cantante	una cantante	a singer
un pezzente	una pezzente	a beggar
un artista	un'artista	an artist
un suicida	una suicida	a suicide

Most nouns denoting living beings distinguish the two genders by changes in the ending of the noun, as shown below. (In the word list, generally, only the masculine forms of such nouns are given.)

By changing the masculine ending *-o* or *-e* to *-a*.

un professore	una professora	a professor
un bambino	una bambina	a boy baby, a girl baby
un giardiniere	una giardiniera	a gardener

By changing the masculine ending to *-essa*.

il poeta	la poetessa	the poet
il dottore	la dottoressa	the doctor
il conte	la contessa	the count, the countess

By changing the masculine ending *-tore* to *-trice*.

aviatore	aviatrice	aviator, aviatrix
attore	attrice	actor, actress
peccatore	peccatrice	sinner

A few nouns do not fit any of the classifications given above.

il brindisi	the toast	un dì	one day
l'eco, *f.*	the echo	la radio	the radio
un dio	a god	il boia	the executioner
una dea	a goddess	il tranvai	the streetcar
la mano	the hand	il vaglia	the money order

In other cases, a feminine noun may also (and sometimes almost exclusively) represent a person of the male sex.

la guida	the guide, *m.*	la recluta	the recruit, *m.*
la sentinella	the sentinel, *m.*	la spia	the spy, *m.*
la persona	the person, *m.*	la vittima	the victim, *m.*

Plural of nouns

Masculine nouns ending in *-o, -e, -a, -i* in the singular take the ending *-i* to form their plural.

Sing.		*Pl.*	
il fratello	the brother	i fratelli	the brothers
il padre	the father	i padri	the fathers
il pianista	the pianist	i pianisti	the pianists

Feminine nouns ending in *-a* in the singular take the ending *-e* in the plural. Those ending in *-e* in the singular take the ending *-i* in the plural.

la guida	the guide	le guide	the guides
la pianista	the pianist	le pianiste	the pianists
la madre	the mother	le madri	the mothers

Certain nouns do not change their form in the plural, remaining invariable:

Those ending in *-i*.

la tesi	the thesis	le tesi	the theses
il brindisi	the toast	i brindisi	the toasts

Those ending in *-à* and *-ù* (feminine).

la bontà	the kindness	le bontà	the kindnesses
la virtù	the virtue	le virtù	the virtues

Nouns of one syllable, nouns ending in *-ie*, nouns of foreign origin ending in a consonant, and the noun *vaglia* do not change in the plural.

il re	the king	i re	the kings
la specie	the species, *sing.*	le specie	the species, *pl.*
il revolver	the revolver	i revolver	the revolvers
il film	the film	i film	the films
il vaglia	the money order	i vaglia	the money orders

The consonant preceding the final vowel may be affected by the vowel change in the plural.

The change may be simply a *spelling* change, made necessary to preserve the original consonant sound.

The endings *-ca* and *-ga* preserve the velar (hard) sound of their consonants by adding an *h*.

il collega	the colleague	i colleghi	the colleagues
la formica	the ant	le formiche	the ants
la sega	the saw	le seghe	the saws

For the same reason, nouns ending in *-co* take the plural ending *-chi* if the stress is on the syllable before the last.

il sacco	the sack	i sacchi	the sacks
il fico	the fig	i fichi	the figs

The endings *-cia, -gia* and *-io*, with unstressed *i*, lose this *i* when they take the vowel ending of the plural form, since it is no longer needed to indicate the palatal (soft) sound of the preceding consonant.

la faccia	the face	le facce	the faces
il faggio	the beech	i faggi	the beeches
la spiaggia	the shore	le spiagge	the shores

The consonant preceding the final vowel may change in sound, although not in the spelling. The velar (hard) sound of the ending -*co* will become palatal (soft) when the stress is not on the syllable before the last. (Here and following, the irregular stresses—those not falling on the next-to-last syllable—are indicated by a vowel set in boldface type.)

il mo**na**co	the monk	i mo**na**ci	the monks
il **sin**daco	the mayor	i **sin**daci	the mayors

The rule for the ending -*co* does not apply in the following cases (the stressed syllable, as indicated by the boldface vowel, would ordinarily indicate the opposite phenomenon):

Soft c		*Hard ch*	
gli a**mi**ci	the friends	i **ca**richi	the loads
i **Gre**ci	the Greeks	gli **sto**machi	the stomachs
i **por**ci	the pigs		
i ne**mi**ci	the enemies		

Certain nouns may be said to have irregular plural forms. A number of nouns ending in -*o* may take a plural denoting a collective group or pairs of parts, or combined multiple; the plural ending in this case is -*a* and the plural word is feminine. *Il braccio* (the arm) becomes *le braccia*, etc.

braccio	arm	ciglio	eyelash
centinaio	about 100	dito	finger

frutto	fruit	osso	bone (*pl.*, bones of the body)
ginocchio	knee		
labbro	lip	paio	pair
lenzuolo	sheet	riso	laugh (*pl.*, laughter)
membro	(body) member	sopracciglio	eyebrow
		uovo	egg
migliaio	about 1,000		
miglio	mile		

Plurals of these nouns may be considered irregular:

Sing.		*Pl.*	
il bue	the ox	i buoi	the oxen
l'uomo	the man	gli uomini	the men
la moglie	the wife	le mogli	the wives

Note: In certain very common Italian expressions, nouns are used where an adjective is to be found in the corresponding English expression. These nouns are used in conjunction with the verb *avere* (to have).

aver(e) sonno	to be sleepy	aver sete	to be thirsty
aver(e) fretta	to be in a hurry	aver fame	to be hungry
aver voglia	to want (to be wanting)	aver paura	to be afraid
		aver freddo	to be cold
aver caldo	to be warm	aver pazienza	to be patient
aver coraggio	to be courageous	aver torto	to be wrong
aver ragione	to be right		
avere le vertigini	to be dizzy		

PRONOUNS

The personal pronouns are usually classified as *unstressed* (or *conjunctive* = joined with) and *stressed* (or *disjunctive* = disjoined, separated from). The unstressed forms are placed immediately before (or in some cases) after the verb. The stressed forms are usually found removed from the verb, used as objects of prepositions, etc. (See below.)

Personal pronouns—unstressed forms

Subject of the verb

io	I	noi	we
tu	you	voi	you
egli	he		
esso	he, it	essi	they (*masc.*)
ella	she		
essa	she, it	esse	they (*fem.*)
Lei†	you (*sing.*)	Loro	you (*pl.*)
Ella	you (*sing.*)		

Io vado al teatro. — I am going to the theater.
Esse cantano bene. — *They* sing well.

Since the verb endings usually indicate person and number, the subject pronouns are seldom necessary for clearness. Unless emphasis is desired they may be omitted where no ambiguity will result.

Vado al teatro. — I am going to the theater.
Cantano bene. — *They* sing well.
But: Anch'*io* canto bene. — *I*, too, sing well.

Direct object of the verb

mi	me, myself	ci	us, ourselves
ti	you, yourself	vi	you, yourself, yourselves
lo	him, it	li	them (*masc.*)
la	her, it	le	them (*fem.*)
si	himself, herself, itself	si	themselves
la†	you	li	you (*masc.*)
—	—	le	you (*fem.*)
si	yourself	si	yourselves

Mi vede. — He (or she) sees *me*.
Noi *ci* crediamo. — We believe *ourselves*.
Essa *si* vede. — She sees *herself*.
Voi *li* capite. — You understand *them*.
Io *la* vedo. — I see *you*. or I see *her*.

Indirect object of the verb

mi	(to) me, myself	ci	(to) us, ourselves
ti	(to) you, yourself	vi	(to) you, yourself, yourselves
gli	(to) him	* loro	(to) them
le	(to) her		
le	(to) you	* loro	(to) you
si	(to) yourself	si	(to) yourselves

* The conjunctive pronoun *loro* is placed after the verb.
† See *Direct Address*, p. 2948.

Egli *mi* dà il libro. — He gives *me* the book.
Io *le* ho dato il libro. — I have given *her* the book. *or* I have given *you* the book.
Essi *vi* parlano. — They are speaking *to you*.
Egli *si* vede. — He sees *himself*.

Note: The prepositional relationship contained in the indirect object pronoun may be translatable in English by a word other than "to." In some cases (parts of the body, clothing, etc.) it may indicate possession and obviate the need for a possessive pronoun, which is replaced by the definite article.

Le comprai un libro. — I bought a book *for* her.
Gli ho lavato la camicia. — I have washed *his* shirt.
Mi son lavato la faccia. — I have washed *my* face.

The forms *ci* and *ne*. *Ci* as pronominal adverb refers to things, and means: "to (at, on, in, into) it"; "to (at, on, in, into) them"; "there"; "to (at, on, in, into) that place." It replaces the prepositions *a, in, su* plus a noun. (Alternate: *vi*.)

Non *ci* badi. — Don't pay any attention *to it*.
Ci sono entrati? — Did you go *into it* (*in there*)?
Ci mette la tovaglia. — He is putting the tablecloth *on it*.
Ci penso. — I am thinking *of* (*to*) *it*.
Ci vado. — I am going *to that place* (*there*).

Ne usually refers to things, and means: "of (from) it," "of (from) them"; "some," "any," "some of it," "some of them"; "from there"; "from that place." It replaces the preposition *di* plus a noun. (It may also refer to persons with the meanings of "of him," "of her," "of them.") With the meaning "some," "any," "some of it," "some of them," "of them," it replaces a noun used in the partitive sense, and may refer to persons.

Ne ho uno. — I have one (*of them*).
Ne ho abbastanza. — I have enough (*of it*).
Io *ne* sono uscito. — I have come out *from that place*.
Ne abbiamo. — We have *some*.
Ne parlavamo. — We were speaking *of it*.

Position of unstressed object pronouns. In general, the unstressed object pronouns—direct, indirect or both—stand immediately before the verb of which they are the object, when that verb is finite or personal, and not an affirmative imperative (command). However, *loro* follows the verb.

Ti vedo. — I see *you*.
Vi parlo. — I am speaking *to you*.
Te lo davo. — I was giving *it to you*.
Scriverò *loro*. — I will write *to them*.

When the verb is an affirmative imperative, an infinitive or a participle, its object pronouns are appended to it and are written as one word with it (except *loro*). The stress is retained on the same syllable of the verb. If it follows immediately after a stressed syllable, the beginning consonant of the pronoun doubles (except *gli*).

Dammi. — Give *me*.
Dagli. — Give *him*.

Fate*lo*.	Do *it*.
Date*gli*.	Give to *him*.
Desidero veder*lo*.	I wish to see *him*.
fatto*lo*...	having done *it*.
Mostra*lo loro*.	Show *it* to *them*.

Note: This does not apply to the subjunctive used in the place of an imperative.

When two pronoun objects are used, the indirect object precedes the direct, and the *-i* of the indirect object changes to *-e*. *Gli* and *le* become *glie*, which is written as one word with the following pronoun.

Me lo da.	He gives *it* to *me*.
Dam*melo*.	Give *it* to *me*.
Date*glielo*.	Give *it* to *him*.
Glieli daremo.	We shall give *them* to her (*him*).
Ce lo mando.	I send *it* there (*to that place*).
Date*mene*.	Give *me* some.

Direct address. In direct address to one or several persons, the forms *Lei* (you, *sing.*) and *Loro* (you, *pl.*) are used formally and to express respect. The forms *tu*, *ti*, *te* (*sing.*) and *voi*, *vi* (*pl.*) are used within the family, between close friends, between children, by adults to children, by everybody to animals. However, *voi* is used by a speaker or writer addressing an audience; it is also used in some parts of Italy and by some speakers in place of *Lei* and *Loro*. The pronoun itself may often be omitted, but the personal ending of the verb will indicate the form of address.

Andate via!	(to children: *voi*)	Go away!
(*Loro*) Non parlano.	(formal address, *pl.*)	You do not speak.
(*Lei*) Vede.	(formal address, *sing.*)	You see.
Sai bene.	(to a friend: *tu*)	You know well.
Tu sai.	(to a child)	You know.

Lei and *Loro* are used in direct address but take verbs in the third person. They derive from ceremonial forms similar to the English "Your Excellency *is* indeed most kind." In order to avoid confusion with a "true" third person, *Lei* and *Loro* are omitted from the sentence only when the context has clearly established that the verb is being used in direct address.

When the third person is used as direct address, the object pronouns (often capitalized) are:

(one person)	la	you	le	(to) you
(men, or men and women)	li	you	loro	(to) you
(women)	le	you	loro	(to) you

Io *la* conosco.	I know *you*. (a man or woman)
Io *le* vedo.	I see *you*. (women)
Le parlo.	I am speaking *to you*. (a man or woman)
Parlo *loro*.	I am speaking *to you*. (men or women)

Elision. The dropping of a vowel usually takes place when *lo* and *la* stand before a vowel or silent *h*. Elision also occurs frequently with *mi*, *ti*, *si*.

*L'*ho veduta.	I have seen *her*.
*T'*ho parlato.	I have spoken *to you*.
*S'*avvicinò a lei.	He drew (*himself*) near (to) her.

Reflexive and reciprocal use. The direct and indirect object forms *si*, *ci*, *vi* are used both reflexively and reciprocally (see p. 2955 *Reflexive Verbs*).

Essi *si* vedono.	They see *themselves*. (direct object, reflexive)
Essi *si* vedono.	They see *each other*. (direct object, reciprocal)
Noi *ci* parliamo.	We talk *to ourselves*. (indirect object, reflexive)
Noi *ci* parliamo.	We talk *to each other*. (indirect object, reciprocal)

Personal pronouns—stressed forms

me	I, me, myself	noi	we, us, ourselves
te	you, yourself	voi	you, yourself, yourselves
lui	he, him, himself	loro	them, themselves
lei	she, her, herself		
esso	he, him, himself, it	essi	them, themselves (*masc.*)
essa	she, her, herself, it	esse	them, themselves (*fem.*)
sè	himself, herself, itself, oneself	sè	themselves
Lei	you, yourself	Loro	you, yourselves

Use of the stressed forms

After prepositions.

Andate con *lui*.	Go with *him*.
Lavora da *sè*.	He works by *himself*.

After comparatives.

Essa è più alta di *me*.	She is taller than *I*.

In the place of the conjunctive pronouns, when the verb has two or more direct or two or more indirect objects.

Visiterò *lui* e *lei*.	I shall visit *him* and *her*.
Parlo a *te* e a *lei*.	I am speaking to *you* and to *her*.

In place of the conjunctive pronoun for emphasis, clearness or contrast.

Amo *te*, non *lui*.	I love *you*, not *him*.

In place of the subject pronouns, for emphasis, but only if the pronoun to be used is of the third person, singular or plural. The adjective *stesso* may be added for emphasis.

Io parlerò, ma non *lui*.	I shall speak, but not *he*.
Chi parla? *Lui*.	Who is speaking? *He*.
But: L'ho fatto *io stesso*.	I did it *myself*.

In exclamations.

Beata *lei!*	*She's* the happy one!

When the pronoun is in the predicate after the verb *essere* (to be).

Se fosse *lui*.	If it were *he*.

Possessive pronouns and adjectives *

Masc.		*Fem.*			
Sing.	*Pl.*	*Sing.*	*Pl.*		
il mio	i miei	la mia	le mie		my, mine
il tuo	i tuoi	la tua	le tue		your, yours
il suo	i suoi	la sua	le sue		his, her, hers, its
il suo	i suoi	la sua	le sue	(Lei)	your, yours
il nostro	i nostri	la nostra	le nostre		our, ours
il vostro	i vostri	la vostra	le vostre		your, yours
il loro	i loro	la loro	le loro		their, theirs
il loro	i loro	la loro	le loro	(Loro)	your, yours

The possessives are used both as adjectives and pronouns. They agree in number and gender with the thing possessed, in person with the possessor.

Essa ha *il suo* libro e *il vostro*.	She has *her* book and *yours*.
Essa ha *i suoi* libri e *i nostri*.	She has *her* books and *ours*.

Note: Suo has four different meanings ("his," "her," "its," "your"), but the gender of the possessor is usually made clear in the context; while the person, if not clear in the context, may be indicated by the subject. When the possessor is not the subject of the sentence, ambiguity is avoided by the use of *di lui* for "his," *di lei* for "her," *di Lei* (or *di Loro*) for "your" and *di loro* for "their."

Egli legge *il suo* libro.	He is reading *his* book.
Egli legge il libro *di Lei*.	He is reading *your* book.
Egli legge il libro *di lei*.	He is reading *her* book.

The articles *il* and *la* are omitted before singular nouns denoting a family relationship. However, they remain in the case of *nonno* (grandfather), *nonna* (grandmother), *babbo* (daddy), *mamma* (mother) (from infants' speech); and whenever the noun carries a suffix.

mio padre	my father	mio zio	my uncle
mia cugina	my cousin	mio fratello	my brother
But: il mio nonno	my grandfather	la mia mamma	my mother
la tua nonna	my grandmother	il mio cugin*etto*	my *little* cousin

Relative pronouns

che	who, whom, which, that
cui	whom, which, that
il quale (*masc. sing.*) la quale (*fem. sing.*) i quali (*masc. pl.*) le quali (*fem. pl.*)	who, whom, that, which
chi	he who, him who, one who (whom), a person who (whom), those who (whom)
colui che	(same as above; *sing.*)
coloro che	(same as above; *pl.*)
quel che (*or* quello che) ciò che	that which, what (for the definite "the one," "the ones," see *Demonstrative Pronouns*, below)
il cui la cui i cui le cui	whose, of which (whose)
quale, quali	which (one), which (ones)

Che is used as a subject or as a direct object.

l'uomo *che* arriva	the man *who* is arriving
l'uomo *che* vedi	the man *whom* you see

---

* For convenience, possessive, demonstrative and interrogative adjectives are treated in this section on pronouns.

Cui is used chiefly as the object of prepositions (but note *il cui*, below).

l'uomo *con cui* parlavo	the man *with whom* I was speaking

Il quale, etc., agrees in gender and number with its antecedent. Certain prepositions preceding it combine with the article (*di + il quale = del quale*, etc.; see p. 2946). It is used for emphasis, or to avoid ambiguity, in place of the more frequent *che* and *cui*. It may be used as subject, direct object or object of a preposition. As object of *di* it means "whose" ("of which") when the phrase modifies a noun.

il marito di Maria, *al quale* parlavo	Mary's husband, *to whom* I was speaking
Maria e Giovanni, *il quale* parla così bene	Mary and John, *who* speaks so well
Parlo alla sorella di Giovanni, *della quale* ho letto il libro.	I am speaking to John's sister, *whose* book I have read.

Chi, colui che, coloro che are used when the antecedent is an indefinite person or persons. They are used as subjects and objects of a verb and as objects of a preposition.

Chi cerca, trova.	He who (*whoever*) looks, finds.

Quel che or *quello che* (with an indefinite antecedent) and *ciò che* translate the English relative pronoun "what" ("that which"):

Prendi *ciò che* vuoi.	Take *what* you want.
Quello che vuoi non c'è.	*What* you want isn't there.

Il cui, etc., translates the English relative pronoun "whose" ("of which"). The article varies in gender and number according to the thing possessed.

un palazzo *le cui* finestre eran chiuse	a building *whose* windows were closed

Quale is the pronominal form corresponding to the interrogative adjective.

Dimmi *quali* vuoi.	Tell me *which* (ones) you want.

Interrogative adjectives and pronouns *

Interrogative adjectives

	Sing.	Pl.	
Masc. and *fem.*	quale	quali	what? which?
Invariable		che	what?
Masc.	quanto	quanti	how much? how many?
Fem.	quanta	quante	

Quale cappello vuole Lei?	*Which* hat do you want?
Che libro vuoi?	*What* book do you want?
Quanta carta vuoi?	*How much* paper do you want?

Interrogative pronouns

Variable forms: The interrogative adjectives *quale* and *quanto*, shown above, may be used as interrogative pronouns.

Quante ne vuoi?	*How many* (of them) do you want?
Quali vuoi?	*Which* (ones) do you want?

Invariable forms:	chi	who? whom?
	che	what?

Chi is used:
   As subject of a verb

Chi sei?	*Who* are you?

   As object of a verb

Chi vedi?	*Whom* do you see?

   As object of a preposition

Di *chi* parli?	*Of whom* are you speaking?
Di *chi* è questo libro?	*Whose* book is this?

---

* For convenience, possessive, demonstrative and interrogative adjectives are treated in this section on pronouns.

Che or *che cosa* is used:
   As subject of a verb

Che cosa è accaduto?	*What* has happened?

   As direct object or predicate of a verb

Che dite?	*What* are you saying?
Che sono diventati?	*What* has become of them? (*What* have they become?)

   As object of a preposition

In *che* posso servirla?	(*In what*) can I be of service?

Demonstrative adjectives and pronouns *

Demonstrative adjectives

Masc. Sing.	*Fem. Sing.*	
questo	questa	this
codesto	codesta	that (near the person addressed)
quel	quella	that (over there)
quello		that
quell'	quell'	that

Masc. Pl.	*Fem. Pl.*	
questi	queste	these
codesti	codeste	those (near the person addressed)
quei	quelle	those (over there)
quegli		those

Demonstrative adjectives agree in number and gender with the noun they modify. The demonstrative adjective *quello* is irregular and takes endings corresponding to those of the definite article. (Similarly, the adjective *bello*; see *Adjectives*, below.) *Questo, codesto* and their feminine forms elide with a following vowel.

quel ragazzo	*that* boy	*quello* sbaglio	*that* mistake
quei ragazzi	*those* boys	*codesto* scaffale	*that* bookcase
quegli uomini	*those* men	*codest'*armadio	*that* wardrobe

Demonstrative pronouns. The demonstrative pronouns most often used are similar in form to the demonstrative adjectives. However, *quel, quello* and *quell'* are reduced to *quello*, and *quei* and *quegli* to *quelli*.

Prenderò *quello* e *quelli*.	I shall take *that* and *those*.
Mi dia *codeste*.	Give me *those* (near you).

Note: The demonstrative pronouns listed above may refer to persons or things.

Quelli non sono bravi ragazzi.	*Those* are not good boys.

Certain other demonstrative pronouns refer only to persons.

questi, costui	this man	costei this woman	costoro these men *or* women
quegli, colui	that man	colei that woman	coloro those men *or* women

Questi non sa dove andare.	*This man* doesn't know where to go.

Note: Costui, costei and *costoro* usually convey an idea of disparagement.

Costui è un ladro.	*This fellow* is a thief.

Demonstrative pronouns are often followed by a *di* phrase or a relative clause. In the latter case they are usually translated as "the one," "the ones."

Il mio libro e *quello di mio padre*.	My book and *my father's*.
Mi piacciono *quelli che sono sulla tavola*.	I like *the ones on the table*.

The neuter forms *ciò* and *lo* are equivalent to *questo* or *questa cosa*. They may be translated by "this" or "that."

Ciò non sembra vero.	*This* doesn't seem true.
Siate*lo* per noi.	Be *that* for us.

ADJECTIVES

Adjectives in Italian vary in gender and number in agreement with the nouns they modify, and in the same manner as the Italian nouns. (See *Gender of Nouns* and *Plural of Nouns* p. 2946.)

Gender and number of adjectives

Certain adjectives, while regular when placed after a noun or in the predicate, are irregular when placed before the noun.

The forms of *bello* are similar to those of the definite article.

il	bel	un *bel* ragazzo	a *handsome* boy
lo	bello	un *bello* specchio	a *fine* mirror
i	bei	i *bei* quadri	the *beautiful* pictures
gli	begli	i *begli* specchi	the *fine* mirrors
la	bella	una *bella* ragazza	a *beautiful* girl
le	belle	le *belle* donne	the *beautiful* women
l'	bell'	un *bell'*uomo	a *handsome* man
		una *bell'*azione (*f.*)	a *fine* deed

The forms of *buono* are similar to those of the indefinite article.

un	buon	un *buon* ragazzo	a *good* boy
		un *buon* amico	a *good* friend
uno	buono	un *buono* zio	a *good* uncle
una	buona	una *buona* ragazza	a *good* girl
un'	buon'	una *buon'*azione (*f.*)	a *good* deed

The adjectives *grande* and *santo* become *gran* and *san* before a consonant (except *s* plus consonant and *z*) and elide before a vowel.

un *grande* specchio	a *big* mirror	*Santo* Stefano	*Saint* Stephen
un *gran* chiasso	a *great* noise	*San* Luigi	*Saint* Louis
un *grand'*amore	a *great* love	*Sant'*Antonio	*Saint* Anthony

Position of adjectives

Most adjectives follow the noun in Italian when their usual meaning is intended. However certain adjectives of very common use, listed below, generally precede the noun, if not modified by an adverb.

bello	beautiful	giovane	young	breve	short
brutto	ugly	nuovo	new	lungo	long
buono	good	vecchio	old	piccolo	small
cattivo	bad	antico	ancient	grande	large

Note: If used emphatically, the adjectives which usually precede may follow the noun.

È una madre *buona!* She is a *good* mother!

Comparison of adjectives

The comparison of equality is expressed by the forms *così...come* or *tanto...quanto*, equivalent to "as (so)...as" in English.

| Maria non è *così* bella *come* Anna. | Mary isn't *so* beautiful *as* Ann. |
| Giovanni è *tanto* buono *qaunto* diligente. | John is *as* good *as* he is diligent. |

The comparison of inequality is expressed by *più* (more) and *meno* (less) placed before the adjective.

| Anna è *più* bella. | Ann is *more* beautiful. |
| Anna è *meno* studiosa. | Ann is *less* studious. |

In comparisons of inequality the equivalent of the conjunc-tion "than" before a noun or a pronoun is *di*.

| Anna è *più* bella *di* Maria. | Ann is more beautiful *than* Mary. |
| È *più* alto *di* quel che sembra. | He is taller *than* (that which) he seems. |

Note: Che is used where the use of *di* would result in a different meaning.

| Egli non è *più* invidioso *che* Pietro. | He is not more envious *than* Peter. |
| (Egli non è *più* invidioso *di* Pietro.) | (He is no longer envious *of* Peter.) |

Certain adjectives are often compared irregularly.

buono	good	migliore	better
cattivo	bad	peggiore	worse
alto	high	superiore	higher †
basso	low	inferiore	lower †
grande	big	maggiore	bigger †
piccolo	small	minore	smaller †

The superlative degree is regularly expressed by placing the definite article or a possessive pronoun before the forms used to express comparisons. If the superlative follows a noun already modified by a definite article, the definite article need not be repeated.

Paolo è *il meno* diligente della classe.	Paul is *the least* diligent (student) in the class.
Paolo è *il peggiore* studente della classe.	Paul is *the worst* student in the class.
Paolo è *lo* studente *meno* diligente.	Paul is *the least* diligent student.

---

† The comparatives *superiore, inferiore, maggiore, minore* are usually figurative.

ADVERBS

Adverbs in Italian usually follow the word they modify.

Comparison of adverbs. Adverbs are compared like adjectives. The following adverbs are compared irregularly.

bene	well	meglio	better	il meglio	best
male	badly	peggio	worse	il peggio	worst
molto	much	più	more	il più	most
poco	little	meno	less	il meno	least

VERBS

Numbering of verbs

Each verb in the Italian-to-English list is followed by a number in parentheses. These numbers refer to verbs (1) through (127) whose forms are given for the most important tenses in this Italian grammar section.

Conjugation of verbs *

Every verb form has two elements: the *stem* and the *ending*.
Classification of regular verbs. There are three regular classes or conjugations of verbs. They are numbered (1), (2) and (3) in the Italian-to-English word list according to their infinitive endings. Certain verbs with the same infinitive ending as the 3rd conjugation (and usually considered part of that conjugation) have been numbered (4). Unlike the other verbs of the 3rd conjugation, they do not contain the syllable *-isc-* in the present indicative, present subjunctive and imperative.

Model verbs		*Stem*	*Infinitive ending*	*Conjugation*
parlare	(to speak)	parl-	-are	(1)
vendere	(to sell)	vend-	-ere	(2)
finire	(to finish)	fin-	-ire	(3)
servire	(to serve)	serv-	-ire	(4)

The forms for these verbs are given in full below in all the commonly used tenses. These will serve as models for all verbs numbered (1), (2), (3) and (4) in the Italian-to-English list.
Classification of irregular verbs. Other verbs, which possess certain irregular forms, are numbered (5) through (127) in the word list. Each of these verb types is conjugated in its irregular tenses in the list of irregular verbs, pp. 2955–59. These will serve as models for all verbs bearing the same numbers in the Italian-to-English word list.

Moods of the verbs

The moods are the different ways of conceiving and presenting the action expressed by the verb. The indicative, imperative and subjunctive moods will be distinguished here.

Indicative mood

The indicative mood presents action or state objectively. It is the mood of direct or indirect statements and questions. It is used in both main and subordinate clauses of the sentence. It possesses the following commonly used tenses:

Present tense. This indicates that the action is taking place, or that the state exists, at the moment of speech. To form the present tense of regular verbs, the following endings are added to the infinitive stem:

(1) parlare
	parl*o*	I speak		parl*iamo*	we speak
	parl*i*	you speak		parl*ate*	you speak
	parl*a*	he, she, it speaks		parl*ano*	they speak
(Lei)	parl*a*	you speak	(Loro)	parl*ano*	you speak

(2) vendere
	vend*o*	I sell		vend*iamo*	we sell
	vend*i*	you sell		vend*ete*	you sell
	vend*e*	he, she, it sells		vend*ono*	they sell
(Lei)	vend*e*	you sell	(Loro)	vend*ono*	you sell

(3) finire
	fin*isco*	I finish		fin*iamo*	we finish
	fin*isci*	you finish		fin*ite*	you finish
	fin*isce*	he, she, it finishes		fin*iscono*	they finish
(Lei)	fin*isce*	you finish	(Loro)	fin*iscono*	you finish

(4) servire (like *finire*)
	serv*o*	I serve		serv*iamo*	we serve
	serv*i*	you serve		serv*ite*	you serve
	serv*e*	he, she, it serves		serv*ono*	they serve
(Lei)	serv*e*	you serve	(Loro)	serv*ono*	you serve

The present tense of irregular verbs is given in the list of irregular verbs (see pp. 2955–59).

Imperfect tense. This indicates that the action or state was in progress, but not yet completed, at some point in the past to which the speaker is referring. To form the imperfect tense of all verbs in Italian (except *essere*, "to be") the following endings are added to the infinitive stem:

(1) parlare
	parl*avo*	I was speaking		parl*avamo*	we were speaking
	parl*avi*	you were speaking		parl*avate*	you were speaking
	parl*ava*	he, she, it was speaking		parl*avano*	they were speaking
(Lei)	parl*ava*	you were speaking	(Loro)	parl*avano*	you were speaking

(2) vendere
| | vend*evo* | I was selling | | vend*evamo* | we were selling |

vend*evi*	you were selling	vend*evate*	you were selling
vend*eva*	he, she, it was selling	vend*evano*	they were selling
(Lei) vend*eva*	you were selling	(Loro) vend*evano*	you were selling

(3) finire

fin*ivo*	I was finishing	fin*ivamo*	we were finishing
fin*ivi*	you were finishing	fin*ivate*	you were finishing
fin*iva*	he, she, it was finishing	fin*ivano*	they were finishing
(Lei) fin*iva*	you were finishing	(Loro) fin*ivano*	you were finishing

(4) servire (like *finire*)
serv*ivo*, I was serving, etc.
etc.

The imperfect tense is primarily a descriptive tense and may be termed also the past descriptive tense. Its use is illustrated as follows:

To express what was happening when something else was happening or happened.

Noi *parlavamo* mentre ella cantava.	We *were talking* while she *was singing.*
Noi *parlavamo* quando egli entrò.	We *were speaking* when he entered.

To express what used to happen (habitual or repeated action in the past).

Si *alzava* tardi.	He *used to get up* late.
Ci *parlava* spesso di suo padre.	He *used to speak* to us often of his father.
	or He *would* often *talk* to us of his father.

To express a condition or state of mind at some time in the past.

Si *vedeva* molta gente nella via.	One *saw* many people on the street.
Non lo *sapevo.*	I *did* not *know* it.
Volevo andare in Francia con Lei.	I *wanted* to go to France with you.

Simple past tense. This is a narrative tense. It expresses actions completed in the past, without reference to the present time (compare the imperfect tense, above, and the present perfect, below). The simple past tense of regular verbs is formed by adding the following endings to the infinitive stem:

(1) parlare

parl*ai*	I spoke	parl*ammo*	we spoke
parl*asti*	you spoke	parl*aste*	you spoke
parl*ò*	he, she, it spoke	parl*arono*	they spoke
(Lei) parl*ò*	you spoke	(Loro) parl*arono*	you spoke

(2) vendere

vend*ei*	I sold	vend*emmo*	we sold
vend*esti*	you sold	vend*este*	you sold
vend*è*	he, she, it sold	vend*erono*	they sold
(Lei) vend*è*	you sold	(Loro) vend*erono*	you sold

(3) finire

fin*ii*	I finished	fin*immo*	we finished
fin*isti*	you finished	fin*iste*	you finished
fin*ì*	he, she, it finished	fin*irono*	they finished
(Lei) fin*ì*	you finished	(Loro) fin*irono*	you finished

(4) servire (like *finire*)
serv*ii*, I served, etc.
etc.

Most irregular verbs form the simple past upon both an irregular and a regular stem in a definite pattern. The irregular stem is used for the first person singular and the third person singular and plural. This pattern is found, for example, in the simple past of the verb *prendere.*

pres*i*	I took	prend*emmo*	we took
prend*esti*	you took	prend*este*	you took
pres*e*	he, she, it took	pres*ero*	they took

Where such a pattern occurs, the simple past is shown in the list of irregular verbs as follows: *presi, prendesti,* etc.; *posi, ponesti,* etc.; *rasi, radesti,* etc.

Future tense. This is used to express actions that will take place at some future time. The future tense of regular verbs is formed by adding the future endings to the infinitive minus the final vowel; however, in the 1st conjugation the infinitive ending *-are* changes to *-er-*.

(1) parlare

parler*ò*	I shall speak	parler*emo*	we shall speak
parler*ai*	you will speak	parler*ete*	you will speak
parler*à*	he, she, it will speak	parler*anno*	they will speak
(Lei) parler*à*	you will speak	(Loro) parler*anno*	you will speak

(2) vendere

vender*ò*	I shall sell	vender*emo*	we shall sell
vender*ai*	you will sell	vender*ete*	you will sell
vender*à*	he, she, it will sell	vender*anno*	they will sell
(Lei) vender*à*	you will sell	(Loro) vender*anno*	you will sell

(3) finire

finir*ò*	I shall finish	finir*emo*	we shall finish
finir*ai*	you will finish	finir*ete*	you will finish
finir*à*	he, she, it will finish	finir*anno*	they will finish
(Lei) finir*à*	you will finish	(Loro) finir*anno*	you will finish

(4) servire (like *finire*)
servir*ò*, I shall serve, etc.
etc.

Only the stem on which the future tense is formed is ever irregular. The endings shown above are to be added to the irregular future stem, shown in the irregular verb list with the first person singular ending.

Note: The future tense is used in Italian to express probability in the present.

Saranno in casa.	They *are probably* at home.
Canterà.	He *probably sings.*

Conditional tense. This is used as follows:

To express a result which depends on certain conditions expressed or implied.

Se avessi del denaro, *andrei* in Italia.	If I had money I *would go* to Italy.
Lo *comprerei.*	I *would buy* it.

In indirect discourse, to express what was once future and is now past.

Ha detto che lo *comprerebbe.*	He said *he would buy* it.

To express polite statements or requests.

Vorrei vedere un cappello.	I *would like to see* a hat.

To express what is reported by others, or on the authority of another.

Secondo sua moglie, *guadagnerebbe* poco denaro.	According to his wife, *he earns* little money.

The conditional tense of regular verbs is formed by adding the endings of the conditional tense to the infinitive minus the final vowel; however, in the 1st conjugation the infinitive ending *-are* changes to *-er-*.

(1) parlare

parler*ei*	I would speak
parler*esti*	you would speak
parler*ebbe*	he, she, it would speak
(Lei) parler*ebbe*	you would speak
parler*emmo*	we would speak
parler*este*	you would speak
parler*ebbero*	they would speak
(Loro) parler*ebbero*	you would speak

(2) vendere

vender*ei*	I would sell
vender*esti*	you would sell
vender*ebbe*	he, she, it would sell
(Lei) vender*ebbe*	you would sell
vender*emmo*	we would sell
vender*este*	you would sell
vender*ebbero*	they would sell
(Loro) vender*ebbero*	you would sell

(3) finire

finir*ei*	I would finish
finir*esti*	you would finish
finir*ebbe*	he, she, it would finish
(Lei) finir*ebbe*	you would finish
finir*emmo*	we would finish
finir*este*	you would finish

finir*ebbero*	they would finish
(Loro) finir*ebbero*	you would finish

(4) servire (like *finire*)
servir*ei*, etc.   I would serve, etc.

Only the stem on which the conditional tense is formed is ever irregular, and it is the same as that used for the future. The endings shown above are to be added to the irregular stem, shown in the irregular verb list with the first person singular ending.

Present participle. The present participle is used as a verbal adjective or verbal noun to express means, or to express cause, action, manner or motive, simultaneous to the action of the main verb.

Essendo malata, essa non esce.	*Being* ill, she does not go out.
Facendo ciò, vincerete.	By *doing* that, you will win.
Dicendo questo, egli uscì.	*Saying* this, he went out.

The present participle of regular verbs is formed by adding *-ando* to the infinitive stem of the verbs of the 1st conjugation and *-endo* to the infinitive stem of the verbs of the other conjugations.

(1) parlare
parl*ando*   speaking

(2) vendere
vend*endo*   selling

(3) finire
fin*endo*   finishing

(4) servire
serv*endo*   serving

The present participle of irregular verbs is not given in the list of irregular verbs, since it may readily be formed from the infinitive stem.

Past participle. The past participle is used as an attributive or predicate adjective and, with the auxiliary verbs *avere* and *essere*, as the second element in the compound tenses. As an adjective, it follows the regular rules for formation of the feminine singular and the masculine and feminine plural (see p. 2949).

dei libri *dati* dal professore	books *given* by the teacher
Tenga la porta *aperta.*	Hold the door *open.*

Note: The compound tenses are the present perfect, past perfect, future perfect, conditional perfect and (see p. 2954) the subjunctive perfect.

The past participle of regular verbs is formed by adding *-ato* to the infinitive stem of the 1st conjugation; *-uto* to the infinitive stem of the 2nd conjugation; and *-ito* to the infinitive stem of the 3rd and 4th conjugations.

(1) parlare
parl*ato*   spoken

(2) vendere
vend*uto*   sold

(3) finire
fin*ito*   finished

(4) servire
serv*ito*   served

The past participle is given in the list of irregular verbs whenever it is irregular.

Present perfect tense. The present perfect is a narrative tense. It is used to express what has happened with respect to the present time. The action has taken place:

The very same day.

Stamane *ho parlato* con Luigi.	This morning *I spoke* with Louis.

In a period of time extending into the present.

Non l'*ho portata* ancora quest'anno.	I *haven't worn* it yet this year.

At an indefinite time, but with effects lasting into the present.

Io *ho letto* quel libro.	I *have read* that book.
Egli *ha imparato* a divertirsi.	He *has learned* to have a good time.

The present perfect is formed by compounding the present tense of the verb *avere* (of the verb *essere* in the case of the verbs listed below) with the past participle.

Io *ho parlato.*	I *have spoken. or* I *spoke.*
Ci *siamo visti.*	We *have seen* (*saw*) each other.
Ella *è partita.*	She (*has*) *left.*

(1) parlare
ho parlato	I have spoken *or* I spoke
hai parlato	you have spoken *or* you spoke
ha parlato	he, she, it has spoken *or* spoke
(Lei) ha parlato	you have spoken *or* you spoke
abbiamo parlato	we have spoken *or* we spoke
avete parlato	you have spoken *or* you spoke
hanno parlato	they have spoken *or* they spoke
(Loro) hanno parlato	you have spoken *or* you spoke

(2) vendere
ho venduto, etc.   I have sold *or* I sold, etc.

(3) finire
ho finito, etc.   I have finished *or* I finished, etc.

(4) servire
ho servito, etc.   I have served *or* I served, etc.

The verb *essere* is used as the auxiliary of:

All reflexive verbs (see p. 2955).

Io mi *sono* alzato   I got up

Intransitive verbs of movement, rest or being or condition; the past participle describes the result of the displacement (or lack of it), the change of being or condition, etc.

io *sono* andato	I have gone *or* I went
egli *è* caduto	he has fallen *or* he fell
siamo ritornati	we have returned *or* we returned
essi *sono* stati	they have been *or* they were

Verbs of this type (intransitive meaning) are:

andare	to go	rimanere	to remain
arrivare	to arrive	ritornare	to return
cadere	to fall	salire	to go up
correre	to run	saltare	to jump
diventare	to become	sbarcare	to land
durare	to last	scendere	to go down
entrare	to enter	stare	to stay, be, stand
giungere	to arrive		
morire	to die	uscire	to go out, come out
nascere	to be born		
partire	to leave, depart	venire	to come
restare	to remain	vivere	to live

Impersonal intransitive verbs.

dispiacere	to displease	parere	to seem
piacere	to please	sembrare	to seem
m'*è* sembrato		it seemed to me	

Impersonal verbs describing the weather.

piovere	to rain	nevicare	to snow
lampeggiare	to lighten	tuonare	to thunder
è piovuto		it rained *or* it has rained	

Note: The past participle of verbs compounded with *avere* agrees in gender and number with the preceding direct object.

Dov'è la veste?	Where is the dress?
L'ho vendut*a.*	I have sold it.

The past participle of reflexive verbs (compounded with *essere*) agrees in gender and number with the preceding direct object of the verb.

Esse si sono vist*e.*	They saw themselves (each other).

The past participle of other verbs compounded with *essere* agrees in gender and number with the subject of the verb.

Ella è entrat*a.*	She has entered.
Essi sono partit*i.*	They have left.

Verbs Compounded with Essere

andare
sono andato (-a)	I have gone *or* I went
sei andato (-a)	you have gone *or* you went
è andato (-a)	he, she, it has gone *or* went
(Lei) è andato (-a)	you have gone *or* you went
siamo andati (-e)	we have gone *or* we went
siete andati (-e)	you have gone *or* you went
sono andati (-e)	they have gone *or* they went
(Loro) sono andati (-e)	you have gone *or* you went

Past perfect tense. The past perfect tense is used to express actions completed in the past before some other time in the past. It is formed as is the present perfect tense, with the exception that the imperfect tense of the auxiliary verb, *avere* or *essere*, is used in every case.

io *avevo* cantato	I *had* sung
noi ci *eravamo* veduti	we *had* seen ourselves (each other)
esse *erano* partite	they *had* left

(1) parlare
avevo parlato	I had spoken
avevi parlato	you had spoken
aveva parlato	he, she, it had spoken
(Lei) aveva parlato	you had spoken

avevamo parlato	we had spoken
avevate parlato	you had spoken
avevano parlato	they had spoken
(Loro) avevano parlato	you had spoken

(2) vendere

avevo venduto, etc.	I had sold, etc.

(3) finire

avevo finito, etc.	I had finished, etc.

(4) servire

avevo servito, etc.	I had served, etc.

Verbs Compounded with Essere

andare

ero andato (-a)	I had gone
eri andato (-a)	you had gone
era andato (-a)	he, she, it had gone
(Lei) era andato (-a)	you had gone
eravamo andati (-e)	we had gone
eravate andati (-e)	you had gone
erano andati (-e)	they had gone
(Loro) erano andati (-e)	you had gone

Future perfect. The future perfect tense is used to express actions which will be completed after some time in the future. It is formed as is the present perfect, with the exception that the future tense of the auxiliary verb, *avere* or *essere*, is always used.

avrò cantato	I *shall have* sung
ci *saremo* veduti	we *shall have* seen each other
sarà partita	*she will have* left

The future perfect tense may also express probability in the past (see *Future Tense*, p. 2951).

sarà partita	*she has probably* left

(1) parlare

avrò parlato	I shall have spoken
avrai parlato	you will have spoken
avrà parlato	he, she, it will have spoken
(Lei) avrà parlato	you will have spoken
avremo parlato	we shall have spoken
avrete parlato	you will have spoken
avranno parlato	they will have spoken
(Loro) avranno parlato	you will have spoken

(2) vendere

avrò venduto, etc.	I shall have sold, etc.

(3) finire

avrò finito, etc.	I shall have finished, etc.

(4) servire

avrò servito, etc.	I shall have served, etc.

Verbs Compounded with Essere

andare

sarò andato (-a)	I shall have gone
sarai andato (-a)	you will have gone
sarà andato (-a)	he, she, it will have gone
(Lei) sarà andato (-a)	you will have gone
saremo andati (-e)	we shall have gone
sarete andati (-e)	you will have gone
saranno andati (-e)	they will have gone
(Loro) saranno andati (-e)	you will have gone

Conditional perfect tense. The uses of the conditional perfect tense are parallel to those of the conditional, to express actions that would have taken place. The conditional perfect tense is formed as is the present perfect, with the exception that the conditional tense of the auxiliary verb, *avere* or *essere*, is used in every case.

avrei cantato	I *would have* sung
noi ci *saremmo* visti	we *would have* seen each other
essa *sarebbe* andata	she *would have* gone

(1) parlare

avrei parlato	I would have spoken
avresti parlato	you would have spoken
avrebbe parlato	he, she, it would have spoken
(Lei) avrebbe parlato	you would have spoken
avremmo parlato	we would have spoken
avreste parlato	you would have spoken
avrebbero parlato	they would have spoken
(Loro) avrebbero parlato	you would have spoken

(2) vendere

avrei venduto, etc.	I would have sold, etc.

(3) finire

avrei finito, etc.	I would have finished, etc.

(4) servire

avrei servito, etc.	I would have served, etc.

Verbs Compounded with Essere

andare

sarei andato (-a)	I would have gone
saresti andato (-a)	you would have gone
sarebbe andato (-a)	he, she, it would have gone
(Lei) sarebbe andato (-a)	you would have gone
saremmo andati (-e)	we would have gone
sareste andati (-e)	you would have gone
sarebbero andati (-e)	they would have gone
(Loro) sarebbero andati (-e)	you would have gone

Imperative mood

The imperative mood expresses action in the form of a command, a request or a prayer. It is usually distinguished by the absence of any pronoun subject.

The second person singular imperative (see p. 2948, *Direct Address*) for 1st conjugation verbs has the same form as the third person singular, present indicative.

Parla!	Speak!

The second person singular imperative for verbs of the other conjugations has the same form as the second person singular, present indicative.

Vendi!	Sell!
Finisci!	Finish!
Servi!	Serve!

The negative of the second person singular imperative for all the conjugations is formed with *non* and the infinitive.

Non parlare!	Don't speak!
Non vendere!	Don't sell!
Non finire!	Don't finish!
Non servire!	Don't serve!

The first person plural imperative has the same form as the first person plural, present indicative.

Parliamo!	Let us speak!
Vendiamo!	Let us sell!
Finiamo!	Let us finish!
Serviamo!	Let us serve!

The second person plural imperative has the same form as the second person plural, present indicative.

Parlate!	Speak!
Vendete!	Sell!
Finite!	Finish!

No "true" imperative exists for the "polite" or "formal" third person used in direct address (see *Direct Address*, p. 2948). An equivalent is obtained, however, with the use of subjunctive forms (see *Subjunctive Mood*, below).

Parli.	(Lei)	(Please) speak.
Venda.	(Lei)	(Please) sell.
Parlino.	(Loro)	(Please) speak.
Finisca.	(Lei)	(Please) finish.
Servano.	(Loro)	(Please) serve.

Note: See pp. 2947–48 for information concerning pronoun objects used with imperative forms.

Pronoun objects follow an affirmative imperative and (except *loro*) are attached to the verb, which does not alter its stress pattern. (Following one-syllable verbs, the initial consonant of the pronoun doubles [except *gli*].)

Note: This rule does not apply in the case of the subjunctive equivalent of the imperative.

Parlatecene.	Speak to us of it.
Vendiamolo.	Let us sell it.
Fallo.	Do it.

In the case of the negative imperative, the pronoun objects precede.

Non mi parlare.	Don't speak to me.
Non me lo dite.	Don't tell it to me.

Subjunctive mood

The subjunctive mood expresses action regarded in the mind as uncertain, desirable or undesirable, dependent. It occurs usually in subordinate clauses.

It is used after verbal expressions of wishing, willing, preferring.

Voglio che tu rimanga a casa.	I *want you to stay* at home.
Egli *ordina che tu sia* a casa.	He *orders you to be* at home.
Preferisco che sia qui.	I *prefer that he be* here.

It is used after verbal expressions of necessity and judgment involving approval and disapproval.

Bisogna che Lei ci vada.	It *is necessary for you to go* there.

È meglio che tu rimanga. | It's better that you stay.

It is used after verbal expressions of emotion such as joy, sorrow, anger, surprise, fear.

Son contento che Lei sia venuto. | I am happy that you have come.

Mi dispiace che tuo fratello sia malato. | I am sorry your brother is ill.

It is used after verbal expressions of doubt, denial, possibility.

Dubito che sia ricco. | I doubt that he is rich.

È possibile che abbia ragione. | It is possible that he is right.

Egli nega che sia vero. | He denies it is right.

It is used after verbal expressions of thinking, perceiving, hoping, knowing, when uncertainty is implied.

Credo che siano arrivati. | I think they have arrived.

It is frequently used in adverbial clauses after the following conjunctions expressing time, purpose, condition, concession.

prima che	before	finchè	until
avanti che	before	perchè	in order that
benchè	although	affinchè	in order that
sebbene	although	purchè	provided that
a meno che	unless		

Dagli il libro prima che parta. | Give him the book *before he leaves.*

Rimarrò qui finchè venga. | I'll stay here *until he comes.*

Glielo mostrerò perchè sappia la verità. | I'll show it to him *so that he may know* the truth.

Andrò con voi, benchè io abbia poco denaro. | I'll go with you, *although I have* little money.

Note: When "may" and "might" indicate subjunctive meanings in English they are not translated; the appropriate subjunctive form of the Italian verb is used instead.

Ho paura che *venga.* | I am afraid that *he may come.*

Avevano paura che *venisse.* | They were afraid that *he might come.*

When "may" and "might" indicate permission (i.e., have the meanings of "can" and "could") they are translated by forms of *potere* (see list of irregular verbs, p. 2958).

Egli *può* venire. | He *may (can)* come.

Gli fu detto che *potera* venire. | He was told *he might (could)* come.

Present subjunctive. The present subjunctive is formed by adding the following endings to the infinitive stem.

(1) parlare

par*li*	(that) I (may) speak
par*li*	(that) you (may) speak
par*li*	(that) he, she, it (may) speak
(Lei) par*li*	(that) you (may) speak
par*liamo*	(that) we (may) speak
par*liate*	(that) you (may) speak
par*lino*	(that) they (may) speak
(Loro) par*lino*	(that) you (may) speak

(2) vendere

vend*a*	(that) I (may) sell
vend*a*	(that) you (may) sell
vend*a*	(that) he, she, it (may) sell
(Lei) vend*a*	(that) you (may) sell
vend*iamo*	(that) we (may) sell
vend*iate*	(that) you (may) sell
vend*ano*	(that) they (may) sell
(Loro) vend*ano*	(that) you (may) sell

(3) finire

fin*isca*	(that) I (may) finish
fin*isca*	(that) you (may) finish
fin*isca*	(that) he, she, it (may) finish
(Lei) fin*isca*	(that) you (may) finish
fin*iamo*	(that) we (may) finish
fin*iate*	(that) you (may) finish
fin*iscano*	(that) they (may) finish
(Loro) fin*iscano*	(that) you (may) finish

(4) servire

serv*a*	(that) I (may) serve
serv*a*	(that) you (may) serve
serv*a*	(that) he, she, it (may) serve
(Lei) serv*a*	(that) you (may) serve
serv*iamo*	(that) we (may) serve
serv*iate*	(that) you (may) serve
serv*ano*	(that) they (may) serve
(Loro) serv*ano*	(that) you (may) serve

The present subjunctive of irregular verbs is given in the list of the irregular verbs. Since the three persons of the singular are the same in all Italian verbs, both regular and irregular, only one form is shown for the singular in the list of irregular verbs.

Present perfect subjunctive. The present perfect of the subjunctive is formed as is the present perfect of the indicative, with the exception that the present subjunctive of the auxiliary verb, *avere* or *essere*, is used in every case.

È possibile che abbia cantato. | It is possible that *he may have sung.*

Non credo che essi *siano* venuti. | I don't believe that they *have* come.

(1) parlare

abbia parlato	(that) I (may) have spoken
abbia parlato	(that) you (may) have spoken
abbia parlato	(that) he, she, it may have spoken *or* has spoken
(Lei) abbia parlato	(that) you (may) have spoken
abbiamo parlato	(that) we (may) have spoken
abbiate parlato	(that) you (may) have spoken
abbiano parlato	(that) they (may) have spoken
(Loro) **a**bbiano parlato	(that) you (may) have spoken

(2) vendere

abbia venduto, etc.	(that) I (may) have sold, etc.

(3) finire

abbia finito, etc.	(that) I (may) have finished, etc.

(4) servire

abbia servito, etc.	(that) I (may) have served, etc.

Verbs Compounded with Essere

andare

sia andato (-a)	(that) I (may) have gone
sia andato (-a)	(that) you (may) have gone
sia andato (-a)	(that) he, she, it may have gone *or* has gone
(Lei) sia andato (-a)	(that) you (may) have gone
siamo andati (-e)	(that) we (may) have gone
siate andati (-e)	(that) you (may) have gone
siano andati (-e)	(that) they (may) have gone
(Loro) siano andati (-e)	(that) you (may) have gone

Past subjunctive. When the verbal expression in the main clause of a sentence is in a past tense or in the conditional, it is followed by the past (or past perfect, see below) subjunctive.

Pensavo che *fossero* in cucina. | I thought *they might be* in the kitchen.

Pensavo che *fossero* venuti. | I thought *they had* come.

Voleva che lo *facessi* io. | He wanted me *to do* it.

Non credeva che li *avessi* fatti. | He didn't believe that *I had done* them.

(1) parlare

parl*assi*	(that) I spoke
parl*assi*	(that) you spoke
parl*asse*	(that) he, she, it spoke
(Lei) parl*asse*	(that) you spoke
parl*assimo*	(that) we spoke
parl*aste*	(that) you spoke
parl*assero*	(that) they spoke
(Loro) parl*assero*	(that) you spoke

(2) vendere

vend*essi*	(that) I sold
vend*essi*	(that) you sold
vend*esse*	(that) he, she, it sold
(Lei) vend*esse*	(that) you sold
vend*essimo*	(that) we sold
vend*este*	(that) you sold
vend*essero*	(that) they sold
(Loro) vend*essero*	(that) you sold

(3) finire

fin*issi*	(that) I finished
fin*issi*	(that) you finished
fin*isse*	(that) he, she, it finished
(Lei) fin*isse*	(that) you finished
fin*issimo*	(that) we finished
fin*iste*	(that) you finished
fin*issero*	(that) they finished
(Loro) fin*issero*	(that) you finished

(4) servire (like *finire*)

serv*issi*, etc.	(that) I served, etc.

There are no irregular forms of the past subjunctive.

Past perfect subjunctive. The past perfect of the subjunctive is formed as is the past perfect of the indicative, with the exception that the past subjunctive of the auxiliary verb, *avere* or *essere*, is used in every case.

(1) parlare

avessi parlato	(that) I had spoken
avessi parlato	(that) you had spoken
avesse parlato	(that) he, she, it had spoken
(Lei) avesse parlato	(that) you had spoken

avessimo parlato	(that) we had spoken
aveste parlato	(that) you had spoken
avessero parlato	(that) they had spoken
(Loro) avessero parlato	(that) you had spoken

(2) vendere

| avessi venduto, etc. | (that) I had sold, etc. |

(3) finìre

| avessi finito, etc. | (that) I had finished, etc. |

(4) servìre (like *finìre*)

| avessi servito, etc. | (that) I had served, etc. |

Verbs Compounded with Essere

andare

fossi andato (-a)	(that) I had gone
fossi andato (-a)	(that) you had gone
fosse andato (-a)	(that) he, she, it had gone
(Lei) fosse andato (-a)	(that) you had gone
fossimo andati (-e)	(that) we had gone
foste andati (-e)	(that) you had gone
fossero andati (-e)	(that) they had gone
(Loro) fossero andati (-e)	(that) you had gone

Note: If the result, or principal clause, of a conditional sentence is in the conditional tense, the verb in the "if" clause will be in the past (or past perfect) subjunctive.

| Ci sarei andato se Lei me l'*avesse detto*. | I would have gone there if you *had told* me. |
| Parlerei se *potessi*. | I would speak if *I could*. |

Reflexive verbs

A reflexive verb is a verb whose subject acts upon itself.

| Io mi lavo. | I wash myself. |
| Io mi parlo. | I speak to myself. |

When the subject acts upon only a part of itself, the reflexive verb is said to be used reciprocally.

| Essi si vedono. | They see themselves (each other). |

Most transitive verbs can be made reflexive by using the proper reflexive object pronouns with them. These may be construed as direct or indirect objects. (See above, section on unstressed object pronouns, pp. 2947–48.)

mi	ci
ti	vi
si	si

lavare	to wash
lavarsi	to wash *oneself*
parlare	to speak
parlarsi	to speak *to oneself*

The reflexive verb is used more frequently in Italian because:

It expresses what would be rendered in English by the indefinite pronoun "one" (or the indefinite "you").

| Non *si* sa mai. | One never knows. |

It often expresses what would be rendered by the passive voice in English.

| Ciò non *si* dice. | That is not said. |

It often expresses what would be rendered in English by an intransitive verb.

| Fermate*vi!* | Stop! |
| Egli *si* alza. | He gets up. |

Note: Thus, the English verb "to stop (make halt)" is translated in the word list as *fermare*, while the verb "to stop (come to a standstill)" is translated *fermarsi*. Other Italian verbs, with meanings corresponding to intransitive verbs in English, are always accompanied by a reflexive pronoun; e.g., inginocchiarsi (to kneel).

Impersonal verbal expressions

Certain verbal expressions are impersonal in Italian, while their corresponding forms in English are not impersonal.

Mi occorre vederlo.	I *need* to see him.
Mi rincresce.	I *regret* (it).
Mi dispiace.	I *am sorry.*

With similar expressions the subject of the English sentence becomes the object in Italian.

| *Mi piace* il suo vestito. | *I like* his suit. (His suit *is pleasing to me.*) |

Negation of verbs

The equivalent of "not" is *non*, placed before the verb and any object pronouns it may have. Other negative expressions used in connection with negative verbs are:

mai	never	neanche	not even
niente	nothing	nemmeno	not even
nulla	nothing	nessuno	nobody, not one, not any
nè...nè	neither...nor	più	no more, no longer

When the above expressions follow the verb, *non* precedes the verb; when one of the above-mentioned expressions precedes the verb, *non* is omitted.

Non ho *nulla*.	I have *nothing*.
Non ho *nemmeno* una casa.	I *don't even* have a house.
Nessuno arriva.	*No one* arrives.

The negative expressions used with the verb may be two or more.

| *Non* darò *più niente* a *nessuno*. | I *won't* give *anyone anything any more*. |

Pronunciation changes

The pronunciation of the *c* or *g* of verbs ending in *-cere* or *-gere* will be determined by the vowel following the *c* or *g*. When the vowel is *a, o, u*, the consonant is velar (hard), and when the vowel is *e* or *i*, the consonant is palatal (soft).

vincere	VEEN-*cheh-reh*	crescere	KREH-*sheh-reh*
vinco	VEEN-*koh*	cresco	KREH-*skoh*
vincono	VEEN-*koh-noh*	crescono	KREH-*skoh-noh*

However, in the case of verbs ending in *-cere*, when regular, will show an orthographical (spelling) change indicating that the *c* is palatal (soft). An *i* is inserted before the *u* of the past participle. (See "Basic Key to Italian Pronunciation," p. 2960.)

| crescere | KREH-*sheh-reh* | cresciuto | kreh-SHOO-*toh* |

Verbs ending in *-care* and *-gare* show no pronunciation change from the *c* and *g* of the infinitive, and the necessary orthographical change takes place in the personal forms.

toccare	tohk-KAH-*reh*	pagare	pah-GAH-*reh*
tocco	TOHK-*koh*	paga	PAH-*gah*
tocchino	TOHK-*kee-noh*	paghi	PAH-*g̱ee*

IRREGULAR VERBS

In the following list of irregular verbs only the irregular features of each verb are shown. Certain parts of any verb may be regular (the present participle, the imperfect tense and the past subjunctive of almost all verbs, for instance), and the appropriate ending for such forms of irregular verbs may be obtained by consulting the forms of model verbs (1), (2), (3) and (4), pp. 2950–55.

In the simple past tense the forms follow a definite pattern; the forms of the first and second person singular, shown here, provide the basis for constructing the other forms according to the pattern explained above (see p. 2950). Where only the stem of a tense form is irregular, the first person singular is the only form shown (for example, *Future:* dirò, etc.; *Conditional:* direi, etc.). In the present subjunctive the three personal forms in the singular are identical, so the singular form is shown only once (for example, *dica, diciamo, diciate, dicano.*)

All the forms are shown for the auxiliary verbs, *avere* and *essere*.

Note: Stress in spoken Italian usually falls on the penultimate (next-to-last) syllable of a word. Irregularities of stress are indicated (1) in the Italian spelling by a grave accent (`) on the final vowel, if stressed; and (2) conventionally and in the following list by a vowel set in boldface type.

(5) Accèndere (to light)
　Simple Past: accesi, accendesti, etc.
　Past Participle: acceso

(6) Acclùdere (to enclose); also *alludere, concludere, deludere, disilludere, eludere, escludere, illudere, includere*
　Simple Past: acclusi, accludesti, etc.
　Past Participle: accluso

(7) Addurre (contracted from *adducere*) (to convey); also *condurre, dedurre, indurre, introdurre, produrre, ridurre, riprodurre, sedurre, tradurre*
　Present: adduco, etc.
　Imperfect: adducevo, etc.
　Simple Past: addussi, adducesti, etc.
　Future: addurrò, etc.; *Conditional:* addurrei, etc.
　Past Participle: addotto

(8) Affìggere (to stick, fasten); also *prefiggersi*
　Simple Past: affissi, affiggesti, etc.
　Past Participle: affisso

(9) Affliggere (to afflict); also *infliggere*
Simple Past: afflissi, affliggesti, etc.
Past Participle: afflitto

(10) Andare (to go)
Present: vado, vai, va, andiamo, andate, vanno
Future: andrò, etc.; *Conditional:* andrei, etc.
Present Subjunctive: vada, andiamo, andiate, vadano
Imperative: va', andiamo, andate

(11) Annettere (to annex); also *connettere, sconnettere*
Simple Past: annessi, annettesti, etc.
Past Participle: annesso

(12) Apparere or **apparire,** regular (3) (to appear); also *comparire, scomparire, trasparire*
Present: appaio, appari, appare, appariamo, apparite, appaiono
Simple Past: apparsi, apparisti, etc.
Present Subjunctive: appaia, appariamo, appariate, appaiano
Imperative: appari, appariamo, apparite
Past Participle: apparso

(13) Appendere (to hang); also *dipendere, sospendere*
Simple Past: appesi, appendesti, etc.
Past Participle: appeso

(14) Aprire (to open); also *coprire, offrire, ricoprire, scoprire*
Simple Past: apersi *or* aprii, apristi, etc.
Past Participle: aperto

(15) Ardere (to burn)
Simple Past: arsi, ardesti, etc.
Past Participle: arso

(16) Assistere (to assist, be present); also *consistere, esistere, insistere, resistere*
Past Participle: assistito.

(17) Assolvere (to absolve): also *risolvere*
Simple Past: assolsi *or* assolvei, assolvesti, etc.
Past Participle: assolto *or* assoluto

(18) Assumere (to assume); also *presumere*
Simple Past: assunsi, assumesti, etc.
Past Participle: assunto

(19) Avere (to have)
Present: ho, hai, ha, abbiamo, avete, hanno
Imperfect: avevo, avevi, aveva, avevamo, avevate, avevano
Simple Past: ebbi, avesti, ebbe, avemmo, aveste, ebbero
Future: avrò, avrai, avrà, avremo, avrete, avranno
Conditional: avrei, avresti, avrebbe, avremmo, avreste, avrebbero
Present Subjunctive: abbia, abbia, abbia, abbiamo, abbiate, abbiano
Past Subjunctive: avessi, avessi, avesse, avessimo, aveste, avessero
Imperative: abbi, abbiamo, abbiate
Present Participle: avendo
Past Participle: avuto

(20) Bere (contracted from *bevere*) (to drink)
Present: bevo, etc.
Imperfect: bevevo, etc.
Simple Past: bevvi, bevesti, etc.
Future: berrò *or* beverò, etc.; *Conditional:* berrei *or* beverei, etc.
Past Participle: bevuto

(21) Cadere (to fall); also *accadere, decadere, ricadere, scadere*
Simple Past: caddi, cadesti, etc.
Future: cadrò, etc.; *Conditional:* cadrei, etc.

(22) Chiedere (to ask, request); also *richiedere*
Present: chiedo *or* chieggo, chiedi, chiede, chiediamo, chiedete, chiedono *or* chieggono
Simple Past: chiesi, chiedesti, etc.
Past Participle: chiesto

(23) Chiudere (to close); also *acchiudere, conchiudere, dischiudere, racchiudere, rinchiudere, schiudere, socchiudere*
Simple Past: chiusi, chiudesti, etc.
Past Participle: chiuso

(24) Cingere (to gird, embrace); also *fingere*
Simple Past: cinsi, cingesti, etc.
Past Participle: cinto

(25) Cogliere (to gather); also *accogliere, raccogliere*
Present: colgo, cogli, coglie, cogliamo, cogliete, colgono
Simple Past: colsi, cogliesti, etc.
Present Subjunctive: colga, cogliamo, cogliate, colgano
Past Participle: colto

(26) Comprimere (to compress); also *deprimere, esprimere, imprimere, opprimere, reprimere, sopprimere*
Simple Past: compressi, comprimesti, etc.
Past Participle: compresso

(27) Concedere (to concede, grant); also *retrocedere, succedere*
Simple Past: concessi *or* concedei, concedesti, etc.
Past Participle: concesso *or* conceduto

(28) Conoscere (to know); also *riconoscere, sconoscere*
Simple Past: conobbi, conoscesti, etc.

(29) Correre (to run); also *accorrere, concorrere, discorrere, incorrere, occorrere, percorrere, ricorrere, scorrere, soccorrere, trascorrere*
Simple Past: corsi, corresti, etc.
Past Participle: corso

(30) Costruire (to construct, build); also *istruire*
Simple Past: costrussi *or* costruisti, etc.
Past Participle: costrutto *or* costruito

(31) Crescere (to grow); also *accrescere, decrescere, increscere, rincrescere*
Simple Past: crebbi, crescesti, etc.

(32) Cuocere (to cook)
Present: cuocio, cuoci, cuoce, cociamo, cocete, cuociono
Simple Past: cossi, cocesti, etc.
Present Subjunctive: cuocia, cociamo, cociate, cuociano
Past Participle: cotto

(33) Dare (to give); also *ridare*
Present: do, dai, dà, diamo, date, danno
Simple Past: detti *or* diedi, desti, etc.
Future: darò, etc.; *Conditional:* darei, etc.
Present Subjunctive: dia, diamo, diate, diano
Past Subjunctive: dessi, etc.
Imperative: da', diamo, date
Past Participle: dato

(34) Decidere (to decide); also *incidere, recidere*
Simple Past: decisi, decidesti, etc.
Past Participle: deciso

(35) Difendere (to defend); also *offendere*
Simple Past: difesi, difendesti, etc.
Past Participle: difeso

(36) Dire (contracted from *dicere*) (to say, tell); also *addirsi, benedire, contraddire, maledire, predire, ridire*
Present: dico, dici, dice, diciamo, dite, dicono
Imperfect: dicevo, etc.
Simple Past: dissi, dicesti, etc.
Future: dirò, etc.; *Conditional:* direi, etc.
Present Subjunctive: dica, diciamo, diciate, dicano
Imperative: di', diciamo, dite
Past Participle: detto

(37) Dirigere (to direct); also *erigere*
Simple Past: diressi, dirigesti, etc.
Past Participle: diretto

(38) Discutere (to discuss); also *incutere*
Simple Past: discussi, discutesti, etc.
Past Participle: discusso

(39) Distinguere (to distinguish); also *estinguere*
Simple Past: distinsi, distinguesti, etc.
Past Participle: distinto

(40) Dividere (to divide); also *condividere*

Simple Past: divisi, dividesti, etc.
Past Participle: diviso

(41) Dolere (to ache, pain); also *condolersi*
Present: dolgo, duoli, duole, doliamo, dolete, dolgono
Simple Past: dolsi, dolesti, etc.
Future: dorrò, etc.; *Conditional:* dorrei, etc.
Present Subjunctive: dolga, doliamo, doliate, dolgano

(42) Dovere (to have to, be obliged, must)
Present: devo *or* debbo, devi, deve, dobbiamo, dovete,
    devono *or* debbono.
Future: dovrò, etc.; *Conditional:* dovrei, etc.
Present Subjunctive: deva *or* debba, dobbiamo, doviate
    or dobbiate, devano *or* debbano.

(43) Elidere (to elide)
Simple Past: elisi, elidesti, etc.
Past Participle: eliso

(44) Emergere (to emerge); also *immergere, sommergere*
Simple Past: emersi, emergesti, etc.
Past Participle: emerso

(45) Empiere, like *empire,* regular (3); also *adempiere, compiere*

(46) Esigere (to exact, collect); also *redigere, transigere*
Past Participle: esatto

(47) Espellere (to expel)
Simple Past: espulsi, espellesti, etc.
Past Participle: espulso

(48) Esplodere (to explode)
Simple Past: esplosi, esplodesti, etc.
Past Participle: esploso

(49) Essere (to be)
Present: sono, sei, è, siamo, siete, sono
Imperfect: ero, eri, era, eravamo, eravate, erano
Simple Past: fui, fosti, fu, fummo, foste, furono
Future: sarò, sarai, sarà, saremo, sarete, saranno
Conditional: sarei, saresti, sarebbe, saremmo, sareste,
    sarebbero
Present Subjunctive: sia, sia, sia, siamo, siate, siano
Past Subjunctive: fossi, fossi, fosse, fossimo, foste, fossero
Imperative: sii, siamo, siate
Present Participle: essendo
Past Participle: stato

(50) Evadere (to evade); also *invadere*
Simple Past: evasi, evadesti, etc.
Past Participle: evaso

(51) Fare (contracted from *facere*) (to do, make); also *contraf-
    fare, disfare, rifare, soddisfare, sopraffare*
Present: faccio *or* fo, fai, fa, facciamo, fate, fanno
Imperfect: facevo, etc.
Simple Past: feci, facesti, etc.
Future: farò, etc.; *Conditional:* farei, etc.
Present Subjunctive: faccia, facciamo, facciate, facciano
Imperative: fa', facciamo, fate
Past Participle: fatto

(52) Fendere (to split)
Past Participle: fesso

(53) Figgere (to fix); also *configgere, sconfiggere, trafiggere*
Simple Past: fissi, figgesti, etc.
Past Participle: fitto

(54) Fondere (to melt); also *confondere, diffondere, profondere*
Simple Past: fusi, fondesti, etc.
Past Participle: fuso

(55) Friggere (to fry)
Simple Past: frissi, friggesti, etc.
Past Participle: fritto

(56) Giacere (to lie)
Present: giaccio, giaci, giace, giaciamo, giacete, giacciono
Simple Past: giacqui, giacesti, etc.
Present Subjunctive: giaccia, giaciamo, giaciate, giac-
    ciano

(57) Giungere (to arrive, join the hands); also *aggiungere,
    congiungere, disgiungere, raggiungere, soggiungere*
Simple Past: giunsi, giungesti, etc.
Past Participle: giunto

(58) Ledere (to hurt, offend)
Simple Past: lesi, ledesti, etc.
Past Participle: leso

(59) Leggere (to read); also *eleggere*
Simple Past: lessi, leggesti, etc.
Past Participle: letto

(60) Mettere (to put); also *ammettere, commettere, dimettere,
    emettere, omettere, permettere, premettere, promettere,
    rimettere, scommettere, smettere, sottomettere, tras-
    mettere*
Simple Past: misi, mettesti, etc.
Past Participle: messo

(61) Mordere (to bite); also *rimordere*
Simple Past: morsi, mordesti, etc.
Past Participle: morso

(62) Morire (to die)
Present: muoio, muori, muore, moriamo, morite,
    muoiono
Future: morrò *or* morirò, etc.; *Conditional:* morrei *or*
    morirei, etc.
Past Participle: morto

(63) Mungere (to milk)
Simple Past: munsi, mungesti, etc.
Past Participle: munto

(64) Muovere *or* **movere** (to move); also *commuovere, promuo-
    vere, rimuovere, smuovere*
Present: muovo *or* movo, muovi *or* movi, muove *or*
    move, moviamo, movete, muovono *or* movono
Simple Past: mossi, movesti, etc.
Past Participle: mosso

(65) Nascere (to be born); also *rinascere*
Simple Past: nacqui, nascesti, etc.
Past Participle: nato

(66) Nascondere (to hide, conceal)
Simple Past: nascosi, nascondesti, etc.
Past Participle: nascosto

(67) Nuocere *or* **nocere** (to hurt, harm)
Present: noccio, nuoci, nuoce, nociamo, nocete, nocciono
Simple Past: nocqui, nocesti, etc.
Present Subjunctive: noccia, nociamo, nociate, nocciano

(68) Parere (to seem, appear)
Present: paio, pari, pare, paiamo *or* pariamo, parete,
    paiono
Simple Past: parvi *or* parsi, paresti, etc.
Future: parrò, etc.; *Conditional:* parrei, etc.
Present Subjunctive: paia, paiamo, pariate, paiano
Past Participle: parso

(69) Perdere (to lose); also *disperdere, sperdersi*
Simple Past: persi *or* perdei *or* perdetti, perdesti, etc.
Past Participle: perso *or* perduto

(70) Persuadere (to persuade); also *dissuadere*
Simple Past: persuasi, persuadesti, etc.
Past Participle: persuaso

(71) Piacere (to be pleasing); also *compiacere, dispiacere*
Present: piaccio, piaci, piace, piacciamo, piacete,
    piacciono
Simple Past: piacqui, piacesti, etc.
Present Subjunctive: piaccia, piacciamo, piacciate,
    piacciano

(72) Piangere (to cry, weep); also *compiangere, rimpiangere*
Simple Past: piansi, piangesti, etc.
Past Participle: pianto

(73) Pingere (to paint); also *dipingere*
Simple Past: pinsi, pingesti, etc.
Past Participle: pinto

(74) Piovere (to rain) (impersonal)
Simple Past: piovve

(75) Porgere (to present, offer); also *sporgere*
Simple Past: porsi, porgesti, etc.
Past Participle: porto

(76) Porre (contracted from *ponere*) (to put, place); also *apporre, comporre, deporre, disporre, esporre, frapporre, imporre, interporre, opporre, posporre, preporre, proporre, riporre, scomporre, sottoporre, supporre*
Present: pongo, poni, pone, poniamo, ponete, pongono
Simple Past: posi, ponesti, etc.
Future: porrò, etc.; *Conditional:* porrei, etc.
Present Subjunctive: ponga, poniamo, poniate, pongano
Past Participle: posto

(77) Potere (to be able, may, can)
Present: posso, puoi, può, possiamo, potete, possono
Future: potrò, etc.; *Conditional:* potrei, etc.
Present Subjunctive: possa, possiamo, possiate, possano

(78) Prendere (to take); also *apprendere, comprendere, intraprendere, rapprendere, riprendere, sorprendere*
Simple Past: presi, prendesti, etc.
Past Participle: preso

(79) Proteggere (to protect)
Simple Past: protessi, proteggesti, etc.
Past Participle: protetto

(80) Pungere (to sting, prick)
Simple Past: punsi, pungesti, etc.
Past Participle: punto

(81) Radere (to shave)
Simple Past: rasi, radesti, etc.
Past Participle: raso

(82) Redimere (to redeem)
Simple Past: redensi, redimesti, etc.
Past Participle: redento

(83) Reggere (to support); also *correggere, sorreggere*
Simple Past: ressi, reggesti, etc.
Past Participle: retto

(84) Rendere (to render); also *arrendersi*
Simple Past: resi, rendesti, etc.
Past Participle: reso

(85) Ridere (to laugh); also *deridere, sorridere*
Simple Past: risi, ridesti, etc.
Past Participle: riso

(86) Rimanere (to remain)
Present: rimango, rimani, rimane, rimaniamo, rimanete, rimangono
Simple Past: rimasi, rimanesti, etc.
Future: rimarrò, etc.; *Conditional:* rimarrei, etc.
Present Subjunctive: rimanga, rimaniamo, rimaniate, rimangano
Past Participle: rimasto

(87) Rispondere (to answer, reply); also *corrispondere*
Simple Past: risposi, rispondesti, etc.
Past Participle: risposto

(88) Rodere (to gnaw)
Simple Past: rosi, rodesti, etc.
Past Participle: roso

(89) Rompere (to break); also *corrompere, interrompere, irrompere, prorompere*
Simple Past: ruppi, rompesti, etc.
Past Participle: rotto

(90) Salire (to ascend, climb, go up, get on); also *assalire*
Present: salgo, sali, sale, saliamo, salite, salgono
Present Subjunctive: salga, saliamo, saliate, salgano

(91) Sapere (to know, know how)
Present: so, sai, sa, sappiamo, sapete, sanno
Simple Past: seppi, sapesti, etc.
Future: saprò, etc.; *Conditional:* saprei, etc.
Present Subjunctive: sappia, sappiamo, sappiate, sappiano
Imperative: sappi, sappiamo, sappiate

(92) Scegliere (to select); also *prescegliere*
Present: scelgo, scegli, sceglie, scegliamo, scegliete, scelgono
Simple Past: scelsi, scegliesti, etc.
Present Subjunctive: scelga, scegliamo, scegliate, scelgano
Past Participle: scelto

(93) Scendere (to descend, go down, get down); also *ascendere, condiscendere, discendere*
Simple Past: scesi, scendesti, etc.
Past Participle: sceso

(94) Sciogliere (to untie, dissolve); also *disciogliere*
Present: sciolgo, sciogli, scioglie, sciogliamo, sciogliete, sciolgono
Simple Past: sciolsi, sciogliesti, etc.
Present Subjunctive: sciolga, sciogliamo, sciogliate, sciolgano
Past Participle: sciolto

(95) Scorgere (to perceive); also *accorgersi*
Simple Past: scorsi, scorgesti, etc.
Past Participle: scorto

(96) Scrivere (to write); also *descrivere, inscrivere, iscrivere, prescrivere, proscrivere, trascrivere*
Simple Past: scrissi, scrivesti, etc.
Past Participle: scritto

(97) Scuotere (to shake); also *percuotere, ripercuotere, riscuotere*
Present: scuoto, scuoti, scuote, scotiamo, scotete, scuotono
Simple Past: scossi, scotesti, etc.
Future: scoterò, etc.; *Conditional:* scoterei, etc.
Past Participle: scosso

(98) Sedere (to sit); also *possedere*
Present: siedo *or* seggo, siedi, siede, sediamo, sedete, siedono *or* seggono
Present Subjunctive: sieda *or* segga, sediamo, sediate, siedano *or* seggano

(99) Solere (to be accustomed)
Present: soglio, suoli, suole, sogliamo, solete, sogliono
Present Subjunctive: soglia, sogliamo, sogliate, sogliano
Past Participle: solito

(100) Sorgere (to arise); also *risorgere*
Simple Past: sorsi, sorgesti, etc.
Past Participle: sorto

(101) Spandere (to spread, spill); also *espandere*
Past Participle: spanto

(102) Spargere (to spread, scatter)
Simple Past: sparsi, spargesti, etc.
Past Participle: sparso

(103) Spegnere *or* **spengere** (to extinguish)
Simple Past: spensi, spengesti, etc.
Past Participle: spento

(104) Spendere (to spend)
Simple Past: spesi, spendesti, etc.
Past Participle: speso

(105) Spingere (to push); also *respingere*
Simple Past: spinsi, spingesti, etc.
Past Participle: spinto

(106) Stare (to stay, stand, be)
Present: sto, stai, sta, stiamo, state, stanno
Simple Past: stetti, stesti, stette, stemmo, steste, stettero
Future: starò, etc.; *Conditional:* starei, etc.
Present Subjunctive: stia, stiamo, stiate, stiano
Past Subjunctive: stessi, etc.
Imperative: sta', stiamo, state
Past Participle: stato

(107) Stringere (to bind fast); also *costringere, ristringere*
Simple Past: strinsi, stringesti, etc.
Past Participle: stretto

(108) Struggere (to melt, pine away); also *distruggere*
Simple Past: strussi, struggesti, etc.
Past Participle: strutto

(109) Svellere (to uproot)
Present: svello *or* svelgo, svelli *or* svelgi, svelle *or* svelge, svelliamo *or* svelgiamo, svellete *or* svelgete, svellono *or* svelgono
Simple Past: svelsi, svelgesti, etc.
Present Subjunctive: svelga, svelliamo, svelliate, svelgano
Past Participle: svelto

(110) Tacere (to be silent)
Present: taccio, taci, tace, taciamo, tacete, **tac**ciono
Simple Past: tacqui, tacesti, etc.

(111) Tendere (to tend); also *attendere, contendere, distendere, estendere, intendere, pretendere, sottintendere, stendere*
Simple Past: tesi, tendesti, etc.
Past Participle: teso

(112) Tenere (to hold, have); also *appartenere, astenersi, contenere, detenere, mantenere, ottenere, rattenere, ritenere, sostenere, trattenere*
Present: tengo, tieni, tiene, teniamo, tenete, **ten**gono
Simple Past: tenni, tenesti, etc.
Future: terrò etc.; *Conditional:* terrei, etc.
Present Subjunctive: tenga, teniamo, teniate, **ten**gano

(113) Tingere (to dye); also *attingere*
Simple Past: tinsi, tingesti, etc.
Past Participle: tinto

(114) Togliere *or* **torre** (to take from); also *distogliere* or *distorre*
Present: tolgo, togli, toglie, togliamo, togliete, **tol**gono
Simple Past: tolsi, togliesti, etc.
Future: toglierò *or* torrò, etc.; *Conditional:* toglierei *or* torrei, etc.
Present Subjunctive: tolga, togliamo, togliate, **tol**gano
Past Participle: tolto

(115) Torcere (to twist, writhe); also *attorcere, rattorcere, scontorcere, torcere*
Simple Past: torsi, torcesti, etc.
Past Participle: torto

(116) Trarre (contracted from *traere*) (to draw, pull); also *attrarre, contrarre, distrarre, estrarre, rattrarsi, ritrarre, sottrarre*
Present: traggo, trai, trae, traiamo, traete, **trag**gono
Simple Past: trassi, traesti, etc.
Future: trarrò, etc.; *Conditional:* trarrei, etc.
Present Subjunctive: tragga, traiamo, traiate, **trag**gano
Past Participle: tratto

(117) Uccidere (to kill)
Simple Past: uccisi, uccidesti, etc.
Past Participle: ucciso

(118) Udire (to hear)
Present: odo, odi, ode, udiamo, udite, **o**dono
Present Subjunctive: oda, udiamo, udiate, **o**dano

(119) Ungere (to grease)
Simple Past: unsi, ungesti, etc.
Past Participle: unto

(120) Uscire (to go out); also *riuscire*
Present: esco, esci, esce, usciamo, uscite, **e**scono
Present Subjunctive: esca, usciamo, usciate, **e**scano

(121) Valere (to be worth); also *equivalere*
Present: valgo, vali, vale, valiamo, valete, **val**gono
Simple Past: valsi, valesti, etc.
Future: varrò, etc.; *Conditional:* varrei, etc.
Present Subjunctive: valga, valiamo, valiate, **val**gano
Past Participle: valso

(122) Vedere (to see); also *avvedersi, prevedere, provvedere, ravvedersi, rivedere*
Simple Past: vidi, vedesti, etc.
Future: vedrò, etc.; *Conditional:* vedrei, etc.
Past Participle: visto *or* veduto

(123) Venire (to come); also *avvenire, contravvenire, convenire, devenire, intervenire, pervenire, prevenire, provenire, rinvenire, svenire*
Present: vengo, vieni, viene, veniamo, venite, **ven**gono
Simple Past: venni, venisti, etc.
Future: verrò, etc.; *Conditional:* verrei, etc.
Past Participle: venuto

(124) Vincere (to win); also *convincere*
Simple Past: vinsi, vincesti, etc.
Past Participle: vinto

(125) Vivere (to live); also *convivere, rivivere, sopravvivere*
Simple Past: vissi, vivesti, etc.
Future: vivrò, etc.; *Conditional:* vivrei, etc.
Past Participle: vissuto

(126) Volere (to will, wish, want)
Present: voglio, vuoi, vuole, vogliamo, volete, **vo**gliono
Simple Past: volli, volesti, etc.
Future: vorrò, etc.; *Conditional:* vorrei, etc.
Present Subjunctive: voglia, vogliamo, vogliate, **vo**gliano
Imperative: vogli, vogliamo, vogliate

(127) Volgere (to turn, revolve); also *avvolgere, capovolgere, involgere, ravvolgere, rivolgere, sconvolgere, svolgere, travolgere*
Simple Past: volsi, volgesti, etc.
Past Participle: volto

Italian Pronunciation

The English equivalents given below cannot be exact transcriptions of the Italian sounds. The latter differ from those of English because the vocal organs are in a different "set." Compared to Italian, English is a "consonantal" language pronounced with a slack mouth which returns to the closed position of the consonants. As a result, stressed vowels are not held firmly, but change in quality and pitch while being pronounced; and unstressed vowels are slurred (road = roh_ood; feel = fee_ill; savor = saver). Italian is a "vowel" language, and a greater tension is developed in the muscles of the lips and mouth. The vowel openings are anticipated, quickly attained and firmly held, so that the vowel does not waver in quality or pitch and is not slurred. In addition, the sounds of Italian, especially the consonants, are generally pronounced farther forward in the mouth.

VOWELS

Italian Vowel	Closest English Equivalent	Italian Example
a	a as in father	carta, sala
e (close)	a as in late *	cena, mente
e (open)	e as in met	tema, bello
i	i as in machine	il, cima
i (unstressed before another vowel)	y as in yet	ieri, aiuto

Italian Vowel	Closest English Equivalent	Italian Example
o (close)	o as in rope *	ogni, corso
o (open)	o as in soft	può, porta
u	oo as in moon *	fumo, luna
u (unstressed before another vowel)	w as in well	uomo, nuovo

* Italian e, pronounced "close," is a pure vowel without the y sound at the end of the a of "late"; the "close" o is pronounced without the w sound at the end of the English long o. Italian u is pronounced farther back in the mouth than English oo, and is more rounded.

CONSONANTS

Consonants which do not appear in the list below are to be given approximately the same sound as in English, with the exception of r, which is trilled. The letter n, when it precedes a hard c, g or q, is pronounced as in English ("anchor," "hunger"), Italian dentals t, d, l, n are pronounced farther forward in the mouth with the tongue touching the teeth.

Italian Consonant	Closest English Equivalent	Italian Example
c	c as in carry	carne, sicuro
c (before e, i)	ch as in chin	vicino, aceto
ch	k as in kill	chiave, schiavo
ci (before a, o, u)	ch as in chin	provincia, ciarla
g	g as in gun	gallo, grande
g (before e, i)	g as in general	gentile, regina
gh	g as in go	laghi
gi (before a, o, u)	j as in joke	giallo, ragione, giusto
gli	lli as in million	egli, paglia
gn	ni as in onion	bagno, ogni
h (always silent)	silent as in honest	ha, ahi
qu	qu as in quiet	quattro, questo

Italian Consonant	Closest English Equivalent	Italian Example
s (when initial before a vowel, when doubled, when followed by c, f, p, q, t)	s as in sand	santo, basso, sforzo
s	s as in muse	sbaglio, vaso
sc (before e, i)	sh as in ship	scena, scimmia
sch	sk as in skill	schivo, scheda
sc	sk as in skip	oscuro, escluso
sci (before a, o, u)	sh as in ship	sciocco, sciame
z	ts as in bets	grazie, vizio
z	dz as in adze	analizzare

A marked distinction is made in Italian between single and double consonants. A double consonant is held twice as long as a single consonant, like the two t's or n's in the English words "at times" or "then neither," pronounced without pause. Double c and double g before e or i are pronounced as one sound, quite like the t ch in "at church" and the d-j in "mid-journey" (faccio, faggio). Before double consonants a stressed vowel is short. Before a single consonant a stressed vowel is longer, while the single consonant always begins the following syllable (senno = sen-no, seno = se-no; nonno = non-no, nono = no-no).

Spanish

to English

CONTENTS

Note on Symbols. For a list of abbreviations used in the main word list, see p. 2674. The number indicated for each Spanish verb in the word list is the key to its conjugation. Verbs numbered (1), (2) and (3) are considered regular; they are conjugated according to models bearing the corresponding numbers under *Present Tense, Imperfect Tense, Simple Past Tense,* etc., pp. 3014–18 of the grammar. Verbs numbered (4) through (39) are irregular; for their forms, see the corresponding numbers in the list of irregular verbs, pp. 3019–23 of the grammar.

Nouns with masculine and feminine forms appear in the masculine only unless irregularities appear in the feminine, in which case both forms appear. No genders are given with geographical names because the article is rarely used with place names in Spanish. In the few cases where the article is used, it appears in the text together with the noun.

Notes on Pronunciation. The pronunciation of words in the following list is indicated wherever possible by one-syllable English words or syllables easily recognized by English-speaking persons. For example, the Spanish word *hora* is rendered OH-*rah; fulgurar* is rendered *fool-goo-*RAHR.

While the great majority of Spanish sounds are capable of approximate renderings in English syllables, certain sounds are either only vaguely suggested by means of such syllables or call for special devices for their clear designation. For example, *r* and *rr* have only vague equivalents in the English letters R and RR. To pronounce these sounds correctly, a trilling sound must be created by tapping the tip of the tongue several times against the front palate. The Spanish consonant *d* when transliterated TH has the value of the unaspirated *th* in *this.* The transliterations for *z*, soft *c* and *ll*, as given in the "Basic Key to Spanish Pronunciation," p. 3024, reflect the common pronunciation of these letters in Hispanic America, and not the sounds they are given in central Spain (*th, th* and *ly* respectively).

Certain Spanish diphthongs, such as *ei* and *eu*, must be approximated by rendering the value of each separate vowel and linking these together with a ligature (EH‿ee and EH‿oo).

The same vowel occurring twice together in the same word is to be pronounced in such a way that the second vowel has the value of an echo of the first. In *cooperar* the second *o* is to be given a half-value both united with and distinguished from the value of the first *o*. This is suggested by placing the second *o* in parentheses, as in *koh(oh)-peh-*RAHR.

The vowels *a, e* and *o* are rendered with an *h* in order to show that they are always given a broad and full value. In all cases the *h* so used is unaspirated. The consonant *g* is transliterated *gh* to give a hard sound in such words as *ghee-*OHN (*guión*). A more detailed guide to pronunciation is found in the "Basic Key to Spanish Pronunciation."

Spanish	Pronunciation	English
a	AH	at (by)
"	"	at (for the price of)
"	"	at (near)
"	"	at (to, toward)
"	"	to (indicating destination, *prep.*)
"	"	to (indicating direction, *prep.*)
"	"	to (used with indirect object, *prep.*)
abajo	*ah-*VAH-*hoh*	below (lower down, *adv.*)
"	"	beneath (*adv.*)
"	"	down (*adv.*)
"	"	downstairs (on a lower floor)
"	"	downward (*adv.*)
abajo, más	MAHSS *ah-*VAH-*hoh*	down (in lower place, *adv.*)
abandonar (1)	*ah-vahn-doh-*NAHR	abandon, to
"	"	forsake, to
"	"	renounce (give up), to
abanico eléctrico, m.	*ah-vah-*NEE-*koh eh-*LEHK-*tree-koh*	fan, electric
abatimiento, m.	*ah-vah-tee-*M‿YEHN-*toh*	depression (sadness)
abdomen, m.	*ahv-*THOH-*mehn*	abdomen
abedul, m.	*ah-beh-*THOOL	birch (tree)
abeja, f.	*ah-*VEH-*hah*	bee
abertura, f.	*ah-vehr-*TOO-*rah*	opening (aperture)
abeto, m.	*ah-*VEH-*toh*	fir
abierto	*ah-*V‿YEHR-*toh*	open (*adj.*)
ablandar (1)	*ah-vlahn-*DAHR	soften (mitigate), to
abogado, m.	*ah-voh-*GAH-*thoh*	attorney
"	"	counsel
"	"	lawyer
abogar por (1)	*ah-voh-*GAHR *pohr*	advocate, to
abolir (3)	*ah-voh-*LEER	abolish, to
abonar en cuenta (1)	*ah-voh-*NAH‿*rehn* KWEHN-*tah*	credit, to (*bus.*)
a bordo	*ah* VOHR-*thoh*	aboard
abrazar (1)	*ah-vrah-*SAHR	clasp, to
"	"	embrace, to
"	"	embrace (include), to
"	"	hug, to
abreviatura, f.	*ah-vreh-*V‿*yah-*TOO-*rah*	abbreviation
abrigar (1)	*ah-vree-*GAHR	cherish, to
"	"	shelter, to
abrigo, m.	*ah-*VREE-*goh*	shelter

Spanish	Pronunciation	English
abrigo de mujer, m.	*ah-*VREE-*goh theh moo-*HEHR	coat (woman's overcoat)
abrir (3)	*ah-*VREER	open (make open), to
absoluto	*ahv-soh-*LOO-*toh*	absolute (complete)
absorber (2)	*ahv-sohr-*VEHR	absorb (suck up), to
abuela, f.	*ah-*VWEH-*lah*	grandmother
abuelo, m.	*ah-*VWEH-*loh*	grandfather
abundancia, f.	*ah-voon-*DAHN-*s‿yah*	abundance
"	"	plenty (*n.*)
abundante	*ah-voon-*DAHN-*teh*	abundant
"	"	plentiful
aburrido	*ah-voo-*RREE-*thoh*	dull (boring)
aburrimiento, m.	*ah-voo-rree-*M‿YEHN-*toh*	boredom
abusar de (1)	*ah-voo-*SAHR *theh*	abuse (misuse), to
acabar con (1)	*ah-kah-*VAHR *kohn*	dispose of (put away), to
acallar (1)	*ah-kah-*YAHR	hush (make quiet), to
accidente, m.	*ahk-see-*THEHN-*teh*	accident (mishap)
acción, f.	*ahk-*S‿YOHN	action (deed)
"	"	share (stock)
acciones, m.pl.	*ahk-s‿*YOH-*nehss*	stock (shares)
accionista, m.	*ahk-s‿yoh-*NEESS-*tah*	stockholder
aceite, m.	*ah-*SAY-*teh*	oil
aceite de oliva, m.	*ah-*SAY-*teh theh oh-*LEE-*vah*	olive oil
aceituna, f.	*ah-say-*TOO-*nah*	olive (fruit)
acelerar (1)	*ah-seh-leh-*RAHR	hasten (expedite), to
acelerar (1)	*ah-seh-leh-*RAHR	quicken, to
acento, m.	*ah-*SEHN-*toh*	accent
aceptación, f.	*ah-sehp-tah-*S‿YOHN	acceptance (receipt)
aceptar (1)	*ah-sehp-*TAHR	accept, to
acera, f.	*ah-*SEH-*rah*	sidewalk
acercarse (a) (1)	*ah-sehr-*KAHR-*seh* (*ah*)	approach (come near to), to
acero, m.	*ah-*SEH-*roh*	steel
acero inoxidable, m.	*ah-*SEH-*roh ee-noh-gsee-*THAH-*vleh*	stainless steel
acertijo, m.	*ah-sehr-*TEE-*hoh*	riddle (*n.*)
ácido, m.	AH-*see-thoh*	acid
acompañante, m.	*ah-kohm-pah-*N‿YAHN-*teh*	escort (social companion)
acompañar (1)	*ah-kohm-pah-*N‿YAHR	accompany (go along with), to
"	"	attach (join), to
acondicionamiento del aire, m.	*ah-kohn-dee-s‿yoh-nah-*M‿YEHN-*toh theh-*LAH‿*ee-reh*	air conditioning
aconsejar (1)	*ah-kohn-seh-*HAHR	advise, to
"	"	counsel, to

Spanish	Pronunciation	English
acontecer (11)	*ah-kohn-teh-*SEHR	happen (occur), to
acorazado,*m.*	*ah-koh-rah-*SAH*-thoh*	battleship
acordeón,*m.*	*ah-kohr-theh-*OHN	accordion
acostarse (5)	*ah-kohss-*TAHR*-seh*	lie down, to
acostumbrarse (1)	*ah-kohss-toom-*BRAHR*-seh*	accustom oneself, to
acreedor,*m.*	*ah-kreh(eh)-*THOHR	creditor (*bus.*)
actas,*f.pl.*	AHK*-tahss*	minutes (record)
actitud,*f.*	*ahk-tee-*TOO_TH	attitude (manner)
actividad,*f.*	*ahk-tee-vee-*THAHTH	activity (exertion of energy)
activo	*ahk-*TEE*-voh*	active (energetic)
acto,*m.*	AHK*-toh*	act
actor,*m.*	*ahk-*TOHR	actor (player)
actriz,*f.*	*ahk-*TREESS	actress
actual	*ahk-*TWAHL	present (current, *adj.*)
acudir (3)	*ah-koo-*THEER	resort (have recourse), to
acuerdo,*m.*	*ah-*KWEHR*-thoh*	accord
"	"	agreement (mutual understanding)
acumulador (eléctrico),*m.*	*ah-koo-moo-lah-*THOHR (*eh-*LEHK*-tree-koh*)	battery (storage)
acumular (1)	*ah-koo-moo-*LAHR	accumulate (amass), to
"	"	store, to
acusación,*f.*	*ah-koo-sah-*S_YOHN	accusation
"	"	charge
acusar (1)	*ah-koo-*SAHR	accuse, to
"	"	charge, to
acusar recibo	*ah-koo-*SAHR *rreh-*SEE*-voh*	acknowledge (note receipt of), to
adaptar (1)	*ah-thahp-*TAHR	adapt, to
adecuado	*ah-theh-*KWAH*-thoh*	adequate (sufficient)
"	"	fit (suitable)
adelante	*ah-theh-*LAHN*-teh*	ahead (forward)
"	"	before (ahead, *adv.*)
adelanto,*m.*	*ah-theh-*LAHN*-toh*	advance (progress)
ademán,*m.*	*ah-theh-*MAHN	gesture (motion)
además	*ah-theh-*MAHSS	besides (*adv.*)
"	"	moreover
además de	*ah-theh-*MAHZ *theh*	beside (other than, *prep.*)
adentro	*ah-*THEHN*-troh*	into (to the inside)
"	"	within (on the inside, *adv.*)
adeudar (1)	*ah-theh_oo-*THAHR	debit, to
adición,*f.*	*ah-thee-*S_YOHN	addition (supplement)
adicional	*ah-thee-s_yoh-*NAHL	additional
"	"	further (*adj.*)
adiós	*ah-*TH_YOHSS	good-by
adiós, *m.*	*ah-*TH_YOHSS	farewell (leave-taking)
adivinar (1)	*ah-thee-vee-*NAHR	guess (divine), to
adjetivo,*m.*	*ahth-heh-*TEE*-voh*	adjective
administración,*f.*	*ahth-mee-nee-strah-*S_YOHN	administration (*bus.*)
administrador,*m.*	*ahth-mee-nee-strah-*THOHR	manager (administrator)
admiración,*f.*	*ahth-mee-rah-*S_YOHN	admiration
admirar (1)	*ahth-mee-*RAHR	admire, to
adónde	*ah-*THOHN*-deh*	where (to what place, *adv.*)
adoptar (1)	*ah-thohp-*TAHR	adopt (embrace), to
adorable	*ah-thoh-*RAH*-vleh*	adorable
adoración,*f.*	*ah-thoh-rah-*S_YOHN	worship (*rel.*)
adorar (1)	*ah-thoh-*RAHR	adore, to
"	"	worship, to (*rel.*)
adornar (1)	*ah-thohr-*NAHR	adorn (beautify), to
"	"	dress (decorate), to
"	"	trim, to
adquirir (6)	*ahth-kee-*REER	acquire, to
aduana,*f.*	*ah-*THWAH*-nah*	customhouse
adverbio,*m.*	*ahth-*VEHR*-v_yoh*	adverb
adversario,*m.*	*ahth-vehr-*SAH*-r_yoh*	opponent (*n.*)
advertencia,*f.*	*ahth-vehr-*TEHN*-s_yah*	remark (comment)
advertir (7)	*ahth-vehr-*TEER	caution, to
"	"	warn, to
aeroplano,*m.*	*ah_eh-roh-*PLAH*-noh*	airplane
"	"	plane
aeropuerto,*m.*	*ah_eh-roh-*PWEHR*-toh*	airport
afable	*ah-*FAH*-vleh*	gracious
afectar (1)	*ah-fehk-*TAHR	affect (pretend), to

Spanish	Pronunciation	English
afeitadora eléctrica,*f.*	*ah-feh-ee-tah-*THOH*-rah eh-*LEHK*-tree-kah*	shaver, electric
afeitarse (1)	*ah-feh_ee-*TAHR*-seh*	shave (oneself), to
afilado	*ah-fee-*LAH*-thoh*	sharp
afilar (1)	*ah-fee-*LAHR	sharpen, to
afirmación,*f.*	*ah-feer-mah-*S_YOHN	assertion (declaration)
afirmar (1)	*ah-feer-*MAHR	assert (declare), to
aflicción,*f.*	*ah-fleek-*S_YOHN	grief
"	"	trouble (distress)
"	"	woe
afligirse (3)	*ah-flee-*HEER*-seh*	grieve (mourn), to
afortunado	*ah-fohr-too-*NAH*-thoh*	fortunate
"	"	lucky
África	AH*-free-kah*	Africa
africano	*ah-free-*KAH*-noh*	African (*adj.*)
afuera	*ah-*FWEH*-rah*	out (not in, *adv.*)
"	"	outside (*adv.*)
agarrar (1)	*ah-gah-*RRAHR	grasp (grip), to
"	"	seize (clutch), to
agasajar (1)	*ah-gah-sah-*HAHR	entertain (be host to), to
agencia,*f.*	*ah-*HEHN*-s_yah*	agency (business firm)
agente,*m.*	*ah-*HEHN*-teh*	agent (representative)
ágil	AH*-heel*	nimble (agile)
agitarse (1)	*ah-hee-*TAHR*-seh*	wave (flutter), to
agonía,*f.*	*ah-goh-*NEE*-ah*	agony (mental pain)
agotar (1)	*ah-goh-*TAHR	exhaust (use up), to
agradable	*ah-grah-*THAH*-vleh*	agreeable
"	"	nice
"	"	pleasant
agradecer (11)	*ah-grah-theh-*SEHR	appreciate (be grateful for), to
agradecido	*ah-grah-theh-*SEE*-thoh*	grateful
"	"	thankful
agredir (3)	*ah-greh-*THEER	attack (assault physically), to
agresión,*f.*	*ah-greh-*S_YOHN	attack (personal assault)
agricultor,*m.*	*ah-gree-kool-*TOHR	farmer
agricultura,*f.*	*ah-gree-kool-*TOO*-rah*	agriculture
agrio	AH*-gr_yoh*	sour (tart)
agua,*f.*	AH*-gwah*	water
aguacero,*m.*	*ah-gwah-*SEH*-roh*	shower (rainfall)
aguardiente,*m.*	AH*-gwahr-*TH_YEHN*-teh*	brandy
agudo	*ah-*GOO*-thoh*	keen (sharp)
águila,*f.*	AH*-ghee-lah*	eagle
aguja,*f.*	*ah-*GOO*-hah*	needle
ahogar (1)	*ah_oh-*GAHR	choke, to
"	"	drown (kill by drowning), to
ahogarse	*ah_oh-*GAHR*-seh*	drown (die by drowning), to
ahora	*ah-*OH*-rah*	now (*adv.*)
ahorrar (1)	*ah-oh-*RRAHR	save (store up), to
ahorros,*m.pl.*	*ah-*OH*-rrohss*	savings (money)
aire,*m.*	AH_*ee-reh*	air (atmosphere)
aire libre, al	*ahl ah-*EE*-reh* LEE*-vreh*	outdoors (*adv.*)
ajedrez,*m.*	*ah-heh-*THREHSS	chess
ajo,*m.*	AH*-hoh*	garlic
ajustar (1)	*ah-hooss-*TAHR	adjust (regulate), to
ajuste,*m.*	*ah-*HOOSS*-teh*	settlement (compromise, *bus.*)
ala,*f.*	AH*-lah*	wing (*zool.*)
alabanza,*f.*	*ah-lah-*VAHN*-sah*	praise
alambre,*m.*	*ah-*LAHM*-breh*	wire (metal thread)
alarma,*f.*	*ah-*LAHR*-mah*	alarm (fear)
Alaska	*ah-*LAHSS*-kah*	Alaska
alba,*f.*	AHL*-bah*	dawn (daybreak)
albañal,*m.*	*ahl-bah-*N_YAHL	sewer (conduit)
Albania	*ahl-*BAH*-n_yah*	Albania
albañil,*m.*	*ahl-bah-*N_YEEL	mason (stonelayer)
albaricoque,*m.*	*ahl-bah-ree-*KOH*-keh*	apricot
alcalde,*m.*	*ahl-*KAHL*-theh*	mayor
alcance,*m.*	*ahl-*KAHN*-seh*	range (scope)
alcanzar (1)	*ahl-kahn-*SAHR	attain (arrive at), to
alcoba,*f.*	*ahl-*KOH*-vah*	bedroom
alcohol,*m.*	*ahl-*KOH(*oh*)L	alcohol
aldea,*f.*	*ahl-*DEH*-ah*	village
aleación,*f.*	*ah-leh-ah-*S_YOHN	alloy (metal)

Spanish	Pronunciation	English
alegrar (1)	*ah-leh*-GRAHR	cheer (gladden), to
alegre	*ah*-LEH-*greh*	gay
"	"	jolly
"	"	merry
alegría, *f.*	*ah-leh*-GREE-*ah*	gladness
alemán, -mana	*ah-leh*-MAHN, -MAH-*nah*	German (*adj.*)
Alemania	*ah-leh*-MAH-*n yah*	Germany
alergia, *f.*	*ah*-LEHR-*h yah*	allergy (*med.*)
aletear (1)	*ah-leh-teh*-AHR	flutter (flap), to
alfabeto, *m.*	*ahl-fah*-VEH-*toh*	alphabet
alférez, *m.*	*ahl*-FEH-*rehss*	ensign (*Nav.*)
alfiler, *m.*	*ahl-fee*-LAHR	pin (sewing accessory)
alfombra, *f.*	*ahl*-FOHM-*brah*	carpet
"	"	rug
algo	AHL-*goh*	anything
"	"	rather
"	"	something
"	"	somewhat (*adv.*)
algo de	AHL-*goh theh*	any (a quantity of, *adj.*)
"	"	some (a quantity of, *adj.*)
algodón, *m.*	*ahl-goh*-THOHN	cotton (boll)
algodón, (tela de), (*f.*) *m.*	(TEH-*lah theh*) *ahl-goh*-THOHN	cotton (fabric)
alguien	AHL-*g yehn*	somebody
"	"	someone
algún, -guna	*ahl*-GOON, -GOO-*nah*	some (unspecified, *adj.*)
alguna parte, en	*ehn ahl*-GOO-*nah* PAHR-*teh*	somewhere
algunas (see algunos)		
algunas veces	*ahl*-GOO-*nahss* VEH-*sehss*	sometimes
alguna vez	*ahl*-GOO-*nah* VEHSS	ever (at any time)
algún modo, de	*deh ahl*-GOON MOH-*thoh*	somehow
alguno	*ahl*-GOO-*noh*	anyone (someone)
algunos, -gunas	*ahl*-GOO-*nohss*, -GOO-*nahss*	few, a
"	"	some (a few, *adj.*)
"	"	some (a quantity, *pron.*)
"	"	some (certain *adj.*)
"	"	some (certain ones, *pron.*)
aliado, *m.*	*ah*-L *YAH-thoh*	ally
alianza, *f.*	*ah*-L *YAHN-sah*	alliance
aliento, *m.*	*ah*-L *YEHN-toh*	breath
alimentacion, *f.*	*ah-lee-mehn-tah*-S YOHN	diet (food regularly consumed)
alimento, *m.*	*ah-lee*-MEHN-*toh*	food
aliviar (1)	*ah-lee*-V *YAHR*	ease, to
"	"	relieve, to
alivio, *m.*	*ah*-LEE-*v yoh*	relief (alleviation)
allá	*ah*-YAH	there (at that place)
allá de, más	MAHSS *ah*-YAH *theh*	beyond (*prep.*)
"	"	past (*prep.*)
allende	*ah*-YEHN-*deh*	over (across, *prep.*)
alma, *f.*	AHL-*mah*	soul
almacén, *m.*	*ahl-mah*-SEHN	department store
"	"	warehouse
almacenaje, *m.*	*ahl-mah-seh*-NAH-*heh*	storage
almeja, *f.*	*ahl*-MEH-*hah*	clam
almendra, *f.*	*ahl*-MEHN-*drah*	almond (*fruit*)
almidón, *m.*	*ahl-mee*-THOHN	starch (in food)
almirante, *m.*	*ahl-mee*-RAHN-*teh*	admiral
almohada, *f.*	*ahl-moh*-AH-*thah*	pillow
almuerzo, *m.*	*ahl*-M WEHR-*soh*	lunch (midday meal)
alondra, *f.*	*ah*-LOHN-*drah*	lark (bird)
alquilar (1)	*ahl-kee*-LAHR	rent, to
alquiler, *m.*	*ahl-kee*-LEHR	rent (payment)
alrededor de	*ahl-reh-theh*-THOHR *theh*	around (*prep.*)
alrededores, *m.pl.*	*ahl-reh-theh*-THOH-*rehss*	surroundings
altar, *m.*	*ahl*-TAHR	altar
alterar (1)	*ahl-teh*-RAHR	alter (make different), to
alterarse	*ahl-teh*-RAHR-*seh*	change (become different), to
alto	AHL-*toh*	high
"	"	tall
alto, más	*mahss*-AHL-*toh*	top (highest, *adj.*)
altura, *f.*	*ahl*-TOO-*rah*	height (highness)
aluminio, *m.*	*ah-loo*-MEE-*n yoh*	aluminum
alumno, *m.*	*ah*-LOOM-*noh*	pupil (student)
alzar (1)	*ahl*-SAHR	pick up (lift), to
"	"	raise (lift up), to

Spanish	Pronunciation	English
alzarse	*ahl*-SAHR-*seh*	rise (increase), to
ama de casa, *f.*	AH-*mah theh* KAH-*sah*	housewife
amante, *m., f.*	*ah*-MAHN-*teh*	lover
amar (1)	*ah*-MAHR	love, to
amargo	*ah*-MAHR-*goh*	bitter
amarillo	*ah-mah*-REE-*yoh*	yellow (*adj.*)
amarrar (1)	*ah-mah*-RRAHR	lash (fasten), to
"	"	tie (fasten), to
ambición, *f.*	*ahm-bee*-S YOHN	ambition
ambicioso	*ahm-bee*-S YOH-*soh*	ambitious (aspiring)
ambiente, *m.*	*ahm*-B YEHN-*teh*	atmosphere (environment)
ambulancia, *f.*	*ahm-boo*-LAHN-*s yah*	ambulance
amenaza, *f.*	*ah-meh*-NAH-*sah*	threat
amenazar (1)	*ah-meh-nah*-SAHR	threaten, to
América	*ah*-MEH-*ree-kah*	America
América del Sur	*ah*-MEH-*ree-kah thehl* SOOR	South America
amigo, *m.*	*ah*-MEE-*goh*	friend
amistad, *f.*	*ah-meess*-TAHTH	friendship
amistoso	*ah-meess*-TOH-*soh*	friendly
amo, *m.*	AH-*moh*	master (one in authority)
amor, *m.*	*ah*-MOHR	love
amortización, *f*	*ah-mohr-tee-sah*-S YOHN	amortization (*bus.*)
amortizar (1)	*ah-mohr-tee*-SAHR	amortize, to
ampliar (1)	*ahm*-PL YAHR	enlarge (make larger), to
amplio	AHM-*pl yoh*	full (ample)
ampolla, *f.*	*ahm*-POH-*yah*	blister
Amsterdam	*ahm-stehr*-THAHM	Amsterdam
amueblar (1)	*ah-mweh*-VLAHR	furnish (put furniture in), to
añadir (3)	*ah-n yah*-THEER	add (include), to
anaquel, *m.*	*ah-nah*-KEHL	shelf
anaranjado	*ah-nah-rahn*-HAH-*thoh*	orange (color)
ancho	AHN-*choh*	broad
"	"	wide (not narrow)
ancho, de	*deh* AHN-*choh*	wide (of specified width)
anchura, *f.*	*ahn*-CHOO-*rah*	breadth (width)
"	"	width
ancla, *f.*	AHN-*klah*	anchor
andar (16)	*an*-DAHR	walk, to
andar a zancadas	*ahn*-DAH-*rah sahn*-KAH-*thahss*	stride (walk), to
andén, *m.*	*ahn*-DEHN	platform, railroad
añejo	*ah*-N YEH-*hoh*	stale
anexo, *m.*	*ah*-NEHK-*soh*	enclosure (addition)
anfitrión, *m.*	*ahn-fee*-TR YOHN	host
ángel, *m.*	AHN-*hehl*	angel
anguila, *f.*	*ahn*-GHEE-*lah*	eel
ángulo, *m.*	AHN-*goo-loh*	angle (*geom.*)
angustia, *f.*	*ahn*-GOOSS-*t yah*	anguish
anhelar (1)	*ah-neh*-LAHR	crave (desire), to
"	"	long for, to
anillo, *m.*	*ah*-NEE-*yoh*	ring (jewelry)
animación, *f.*	*ah-nee-mah*-S YOHN	excitement
animal, *m.*	*ah-nee*-MAHL	animal
animal mimado, *m.*	*ah-nee*-MAHL *mee*-MAH-*thoh*	pet (animal)
animar (1)	*ah-nee*-MAHR	encourage, to
aniversario, *m.*	*ah-nee-vehr*-SAH-*r yoh*	anniversary
año, *m.*	AH-*n yoh*	grade (school division)
"	"	year
anochecer, *m.*	*ah-noh-cheh*-SEHR	evening
ansiedad, *f.*	*ahn*-S *yeh*-THAHTH	anxiety
"	"	tension
"	"	worry
ansioso	*ahn*-S YOH-*soh*	keen (eager)
antena, *f.*	*ahn*-TEH-*nah*	aerial (antenna)
anteojos, *m.pl.*	*ahn-teh*-OH-*hohss*	glasses
"	"	spectacles
anterior	*ahn-teh*-R YOHR	former (preceding, *adj.*)
antes	AHN-*tehss*	before (earlier, *adv.*)
"	"	before (in the past, *adv.*)
"	"	beforehand (*adv.*)
antes de	AHN-*tehz-theh*	before (earlier than, *prep.*)
"	"	by (prior to, *prep.*)
"	"	until (*prep.*)

Spanish	Pronunciation	English
antes (de) que	AHN-*tehss* (*theh*) *keh*	before (prior to the time when, *conj.*)
antibiótico,*m.*	*ahn-tee-*B_YOH-*tee-koh*	antibiotic
anticipar(se) (1)	*ahn-tee-see-*PAHR(-*seh*)	anticipate (expect), to
antigüedad,*f.*	*ahn-tee-gweh-*THAHTH	antiquity (ancientness)
antiguo	*ahn-*TEE-*gwoh*	ancient
antología,*f.*	*ahn-toh-loh-*HEE-*ah*	anthology
antorcha,*f.*	*ahn-*TOHR-*chah*	torch
antropología,*f.*	*ahn-troh-poh-loh-*HEE-*ah*	anthropology
anual	*ah-*NWAHL	annual
"	"	yearly (*adj.*)
anualmente	*ah-nwahl-*MEHN-*teh*	yearly (*adv.*)
anular (1)	*ah-noo-*LAHR	annul, to
anunciar (1)	*ah-noon-*S_YAHR	advertise (give notice of), to
"	"	announce, to
anuncio,*m.*	*ah-*NOON-*s_yoh*	advertisement
"	"	announcement
apagar (1)	*ah-pah-*GAHR	quench, to
aparear (1)	*ah-pah-reh-*AHR	mate (find mate for), to
aparecer (11)	*ah-pah-reh-*SEHR	appear (come in sight), to
aparente	*ah-pah-*REHN-*teh*	apparent (obvious)
apariencia,*f.*	*ah-pah-*R_YEHN-*s_yah*	appearance (aspect)
aparte	*ah-*PAHR-*teh*	apart
"	"	aside (away)
apasionado	*ah-pah-s_yoh-*NAH-*thoh*	passionate
apelar (1)	*ah-peh-*LAHR	appeal (ask reconsideration of), to
apellido,*m.*	*ah-peh-*YEE-*thoh*	surname
apellido de soltera, *m.*	*ah-peh-*YEE-*thoh theh sohl-*TEH-*rah*	maiden name
apenas	*ah-*PEH-*nahss*	hardly (barely)
apendicitis,*f.*	*ah-pehn-dee-*SEE-*teess*	appendicitis
apestar (1)	*ah-pehss-*TAHR	stink, to
apetito,*m.*	*ah-peh-*TEE-*toh*	appetite
apio,*m.*	AH-*p_yoh*	celery
aplacar (1)	*ah-plah-*KAHR	appease (calm), to
aplanar (1)	*ah-plah-*NAHR	smooth (level), to
aplastar (1)	*ah-plahss-*TAHR	smash, to
aplaudir (3)	*ah-plah_oo-*THEER	cheer (applaud), to
"	"	clap (applaud), to
aplauso,*m.*	*ah-*PLAH_OO-*soh*	applause
aplicación,*f.*	*ah-plee-kah-*S_YOHN	application (use)
aplicar (1)	*ah-plee-*KAHR	apply (put to use), to
aplicarse	*ah-plee-*KAHR-*seh*	apply (be fitting), to
apoderarse de (1)	*ah-poh-theh-*RAHR-*seh theh*	seize (capture), to
apostar (1)	*ah-pohss-*TAHR	bet, to
apóstol,*m.*	*ah-*POHSS-*tohl*	apostle
apoyo,*m.*	*ah-*POH-*yoh*	support (approval)
apreciar (1)	*ah-preh-*S_YAHR	appreciate (perceive fully), to
aprender (2)	*ah-prehn-*DEHR	learn (acquire knowledge), to
aprendiz,*m.*	*ah-prehn-*DEESS	apprentice (trade student)
apresurado	*ah-preh-soo-*RAH-*thoh*	hasty (hurried)
apresurarse (1)	*ah-preh-soo-*RAHR-*seh*	hasten, to
"	"	hurry, to
"	"	rush (dash), to
apretar (4)	*ah-preh-*TAHR	pinch, to
"	"	press (bear upon), to
"	"	squeeze, to
apretón,*m.*	*ah-preh-*TOHN	grip (grasp)
aprieto,*m.*	*ah-*PR_YEH-*toh*	plight (predicament)
aprobación,*f.*	*ah-proh-vah-*S_YOHN	acceptance
"		approval
aprobar (5)	*ah-proh-*VAHR	approve, to
apropiado	*ah-proh-*P_YAH-*thoh*	suitable
apuesta,*f.*	*ah-*PWEHSS-*tah*	bet
"	"	stake (thing wagered)
apuntar (1)	*ah-poon-*TAHR	aim (direct), to
apuro,*m.*	*ah-*POO-*roh*	distress
aquel, aquella	*ah-*KEHL, *ah-*KEH-*yah*	that (*dem. adj.*)
aquél (aquello), aquélla	*ah-*KEHL (*ah-*KEH-*yoh*), *ah-*KEH-*yah*	that (*dem. pron.*)

Spanish	Pronunciation	English
aquellos, aquellas	*ah-*KEH-*yohss, ah-*KEH-*yahss*	those (*adj.*)
aquéllos, aquéllas	*ah-*KEH-*yohss, ah-*KEH-*yahss*	those (*pron.*)
aquí	*ah-*KEE	here (*adv.*)
aquí en adelante, de	*deh ah-*KEE *ehn ah-theh-*LAHN-*teh*	henceforth
"	"	hereafter (after this, *adv.*)
arado,*m.*	*ah-*RAH-*thoh*	plow (*n.*)
araña,*f.*	*ah-*RAH-*n_yah*	spider
arándano,*m.*	*ah-*RAHN-*dah-noh*	blueberry
arar (1)	*ah-*RAHR	plow (till), to
árbol,*m.*	AHR-*vohl*	tree
arboleda,*f.*	*ahr-voh-*LEH-*thah*	grove (small woods)
árboles de monte, *m.pl.*	AHR-*voh-lehss theh* MOHN-*teh*	timber (standing trees)
arbusto,*m.*	*ahr-*BOOSS-*toh*	bush (plant)
"	"	shrub
arca,*f.*	AHR-*kah*	chest (box)
arce,*m.*	AHR-*seh*	maple (tree)
archivo,*m.*	*ahr-*CHEE-*voh*	file (collection of papers)
arcilla,*f.*	*ahr-*SEE-*yah*	clay
arco,*m.*	AHR-*koh*	arch (curved structure)
arco iris,*m.*	AHR-*koh* EE-*reess*	rainbow
arder (2)	*ahr-*THEHR	blaze (burn brightly), to
"	"	burn (be on fire), to
ardilla,*f.*	*ahr-*THEE-*yah*	squirrel
área,*f.*	AH-*reh-ah*	area (extent)
arena,*f.*	*ah-*REH-*nah*	sand
arenoso	*ah-reh-*NOH-*soh*	sandy
arenque,*m.*	*ah-*REHN-*keh*	herring
arete,*m.*	*ah-*REH-*teh*	earring
Argentina, la	*lah ahr-hehn-*TEE-*nah*	Argentina
argentino	*ahr-hehn-*TEE-*noh*	Argentinian (*adj.*)
argumento,*m.*	*ahr-goo-*MEHN-*toh*	scenario
aritmética,*f.*	*ah-reet-*MEH-*tee-kah*	arithmetic
arma,*f.*	AHR-*mah*	weapon
arma de fuego,*f.*	AHR-*mah theh* FWEH-*goh*	gun
armadura,*f.*	*ahr-mah-*THOO-*rah*	armor (protective clothing)
armar (1)	*ahr-*MAHR	arm, to
armario,*m.*	*ahr-*MAH-*r_yoh*	cupboard
armonía,*f.*	*ahr-moh-*NEE-*ah*	harmony (*mus.*)
arpa,*f.*	AHR-*pah*	harp
arquitecto,*m.*	*ahr-kee-*TEHK-*toh*	architect
arrancar (1)	*ah-rrahn-*KAHR	rip (tear away), to
"	"	wrench (wrest), to
arrastrar (1)	*ah-rahss-*TRAHR	haul (pull), to
"	"	tug (drag), to
arrastrarse (1)	*ah-rrahss-*TRAHR-*seh*	crawl (creep), to
arrebatar (1)	*ah-rreh-vah-*TAHR	grab, to
"	"	snatch, to
arreglar (1)	*ah-rreh-*GLAHR	fix, to
"	"	settle, to
"	"	straighten (put in order), to
arrendar (4)	*ah-rrehn-*DAHR	lease (hold by lease), to
arrepentirse (4)	*ah-rreh-pehn-*TEER-*seh*	repent, to
arrestar (1)	*ah-rrehss-*TAHR	arrest (take into custody), to
arriba	*ah-*RREE-*vah*	above (overhead, *adv.*)
"	"	up (*adv.*)
"	"	upstairs (at upper story, *adv.*)
arrodillarse (1)	*ah-rroh-thee-*YAHR-*seh*	kneel, to
arrojar (1)	*ah-rroh-*HAHR	cast (throw), to
"	"	fling, to
arrojarse	*ah-rroh-*HAHR-*seh*	plunge (hurl oneself), to
arroyo,*m.*	*ah-*RROH-*yoh*	brook
"	"	creek
"	"	gutter (of street)
"	"	stream (rivulet)
arroz,*m.*	*ah-*RROHSS	rice
arruga,*f.*	*ahr-*RROO-*gah*	ridge (raised area)
"	"	wrinkle (fold)
arruinar (1)	*ah-rr_wee-*NAHR	ruin, to
"		wreck, to

Spanish	Pronunciation	English	Spanish	Pronunciation	English
arte,*f.*	AHR-*teh*	art (work of art)	atento	ah-TEHN-*toh*	attentive (heedful)
			"		intent (engrossed)
arte,*m.*	AHR-*teh*	art (activity)	aterrizar (1)	ah-teh-rree-SAHR	land (an airplane), to
arte de escribir,*m.*	AHR-*teh th_ehss-kree-* VEER	writing (art of writing)	aterrorizar (1)	ah-teh-rroh-ree-SAHR	terrify, to
			atestiguar (1)	ah-tehss-tee-GWAHR	testify, to
arteria,*f.*	ahr-teh-REE-*ah*	artery (*anat.*)			
artículo,*m.*	ahr-TEE-*koo-loh*	article (literary composition)	Atlántico,*m.*	aht-LAHN-tee-koh	Atlantic (*n.*)
			atlas,*m.*	AHT-*lahss*	atlas
artificial	ahr-tee-fee-S_YAHL	artificial (synthetic)	atleta,*m.*	aht-LEH-*tah*	athlete
artista,*m.*,*f.*	ahr-TEESS-*tah*	artist	atlético	aht-LEH-tee-koh	athletic
artístico	ahr-TEESS-*tee-koh*	artistic (tasteful)	atmósfera,*f.*	aht-MOHSS-*feh-rah*	atmosphere (air)
artritis,*f.*	ahr-TREE-*leess*	arthritis			
			átomo,*m.*	AH-*toh-moh*	atom
asado,*m.*	ah-SAH-*thoh*	roast	atormentar (1)	ah-tohr-mehn-TAHR	torment, to
asaltar (1)	ah-sahl-TAHR	assault, to	atracción,*f.*	ah-trahk-S_YOHN	attraction
asarse (1)	ah-SAHR-*seh*	roast (be roasted), to	"	"	interest (engaging quality)
ascender (4)	ahss-sehn-DEHR	ascend (go upward along), to	atractivo	ah-trahk-TEE-*voh*	attractive (pleasing)
"	"	promote (raise in rank), to	atraer (36)	ah-trah-EHR	attract, to
			atrás	ah-TRAHSS	back (rearward, *adv.*)
ascender a	ahss-sehn-DEHR	number (amount to), to	atravesar (4)	ah-trah-veh-SAHR	cross (traverse), to
ascendiente,*m.*	ahss-sehn-D_YEHN-*teh*	ancestor	atreverse (2)	ah-treh-VEHR-*seh*	dare, to
ascenso,*m.*	ahss-SEHN-*soh*	promotion (advance)	"	"	venture, to
ascensor,*m.*	ahss-sehn-SOHR	elevator (passenger lift)	atrevido	ah-treh-VEE-*thoh*	bold (courageous)
			atributo,*m.*	ah-tree-VOO-*toh*	attribute (charac- teristic)
asegurar (1)	ah-seh-goo-RAHR	assure, to			
"	"	insure (buy insur- ance on), to	atropellar (1)	ah-troh-peh-YAHR	trample, to
"	"	insure (make sure), to	aturdido	ah-toor-THEE-*thoh*	dizzy (unsteady)
asemejarse a (1)	ah-seh-meh-HAHR-*seh* *ah*	resemble, to	aturdir (3)	ah-toor-THEER	bewilder, to
			auditorio,*m.*	ow-thee-TOH-*r_yoh*	audience
asentar (4)	ah-sehn-TAHR	enter, to (*acctg.*)	aula,*f.*	OW-*lah*	classroom
asentir (7)	ah-sehn-TEER	agree, to			
"	"	assent, to	aullar (1)	ow-YAHR	howl (wail), to
asesinato,*m.*	ah-seh-see-NAH-*toh*	murder	aumentar (1)	ow-mehn-TAHR	increase, to
asesino,*m.*	ah-seh-SEE-*noh*	murderer	aumento,*m.*	ow-MEHN-*toh*	gain
así	ah-SEE	thus (in this way)	"	"	increase (increment)
			aún	ah-OON	still (*adv.*)
Asia	AH-s_yah	Asia			
asiático	ah-S_YAH-*tee-koh*	Asiatic (*adj.*)	aunque	OW_N-keh	although
asiento,*m.*	ah-S_YEHN-*toh*	seat	"	"	though (*conj.*)
asignar (1)	ah-seeg-NAHR	assign (prescribe lesson), to	ausencia,*f.*	ow-SEHN-s_yah	absence
asilo,*m.*	ah-SEE-*loh*	asylum (institution)	ausente	ow-SEHN-*teh*	absent
asistencia,*f.*	ah-seess-TEHN-s_yah	attendance (pres- ence)	"	"	away (*adj.*)
			austero	ow-STEH-*roh*	severe (austere)
asistir (3)	ah-seess-TEER	attend (be present at), to	Australia	owss-TRAH-l_yah	Australia
asno,*m.*	AHZ-*noh*	donkey	australiano	owss-trah-L_YAH-*noh*	Australian (*adj.*)
asociación,*f.*	ah-soh-s_yah-S_YOHN	association (body of persons)	Austria	OWSS-tr_yah	Austria
			austríaco	owss-TREE-ah-koh	Austrian (*adj.*)
asociación co- operativa,*f.*	ah-soh-s_yah-S_YOHN koh(oh)-peh-rah-TEE- vah	cooperative (*n.*)	autobiografía,*f.*	ow-toh-vee-oh-grah-FEE- ah	autobiography
			automóvil,*m.*	ow-toh-MOH-veel	automobile
asociar (1)	ah-soh-S_YAHR	associate (relate), to	autor,*m.*	ow-TOHR	author
asociarse a	ah-soh-S_YAHR-*seh ah*	join (become a mem- ber of), to	autoridad,*f.*	ow-toh-ree-THAHTH	authority
			autorización,*f.*	ow-toh-ree-sah-s_YOHN	authorization
asoleado	ah-soh-leh-AH-*thoh*	sunny	avanzar (1)	ah-vahn-SAHR	advance (go for- ward), to
asombrar (1)	ah-sohm-BRAHR	amaze, to			
"	"	astonish, to	avaro,*m.*	ah-VAH-*roh*	miser
asombro,*m.*	ah-SOHM-*broh*	amazement	ave,*f.*	AH-*veh*	bird
"	"	astonishment	avena,*f.*	ah-VEH-*nah*	oats
aspecto,*m.*	ahss-PEHK-*toh*	aspect (phase)	avenida,*f.*	ah-veh-NEE-*thah*	avenue (street)
"	"	look (aspect)	aventura,*f.*	ah-vehn-TOO-*rah*	adventure
			avergonzado	ah-vehr-gohn-SAH-*thoh*	ashamed (mortified)
áspero	AHSS-*peh-roh*	harsh (grating)			
"	"	rough (uneven)	aversión,*f.*	ah-vehr-S_YOHN	disgust
aspirador de polvo, *m.*	ah-spee-rah-THOHR *theh* POHL-*voh*	vacuum cleaner	"	"	dislike
			aves de corral,*f.pl.*	AH-*vehss theh* koh-RAHL	poultry
aspirina,*f.*	ahss-pee-REE-*nah*	aspirin	aviador,*m.*	ah-v_yah-THOHR	aviator
astillero,*m.*	ah-stee-YEH-*roh*	shipyard	ávido	AH-*vee-thoh*	greedy
astuto	ahss-TOO-*toh*	cunning	avispa,*f.*	ah-VEESS-*pah*	wasp
"	"	shrewd	ayer	ah-YEHR	yesterday
"	"	sly (crafty)	ayuda,*f.*	ah-YOO-*thah*	aid
			"	"	assistance
asunto,*m.*	ah-SOON-*toh*	affair	"	"	help
"	"	matter	"	"	relief
ataque fulminante, *m.*	ah-TAH-*keh fool-mee-* NAHN-*teh*	stroke (attack of paralysis)	ayudante,*m.*	ah-yoo-THAHN-*teh*	assistant
			"	"	helper
atar (1)	ah-TAHR	bind (tie), to	ayudar (1)	ah-yoo-THAHR	aid, to
ataúd,*m.*	ah-tah-OOTH	coffin	"	"	assist, to
atavío,*m.*	ah-tah-VEE-*oh*	attire (apparel)	"	"	help, to
Atenas	ah-TEH-*nahss*	Athens	azada,*f.*	ah-SAH-*thah*	hoe
atención,*f.*	ah-tehn-S_YOHN	attention (heed)	"	"	spade (tool)
"	"	care (heed)	azotar (1)	ah-soh-TAHR	whip (flog), to
"	"	interest	azúcar,*m.*	ah-SOO-*kahr*	sugar
"	"	notice	azufre,*m.*	ah-SOO-*freh*	sulphur

Spanish	Pronunciation	English
azul	*ah*-SOOL	blue
báculo,*m.*	BAH-*koo-loh*	staff (stick)
bagatela,*f.*	*bah-gah*-TEH-*lah*	trifle
bahía,*f.*	*bah-*EE-*ah*	bay (inlet)
bailar (1)	*bah_ee*-LAHR	dance, to
baile,*m.*	BAH_*ee-leh*	dance
bajar (1)	*bah*-HAHR	lower (let down), to
bajo	BAH-*hoh*	beneath (*prep.*)
"	"	low
		under (subject to, *prep.*)
"	"	under (*prep.*)
bajo techo	BAH-*hoh* TEH-*choh*	indoors (*adv.*)
bala,*f.*	BAH-*lah*	bullet
balanza,*f.*	*bah*-LAHN-*sah*	scales (balance)
balar (1)	*bah*-LAHR	bleat, to
balde,*m.*	BAHL-*deh*	pail
ballena,*f.*	*bah*-YEH-*nah*	whale
baloncesto,*m.*	*bah-lohn*-SEHSS-*toh*	basketball
bambolearse (1)	*bahm-boh-leh*-AHR-*seh*	reel (stagger), to
bañarse (1)	*bah-*N_YAHR-*seh*	bathe (take a bath), to
banca,*f.*	BAHN-*kah*	banking
banco,*m.*	BAHN-*koh*	bank (treasury)
"	"	bench (long seat)
banda,*f.*	BAHN-*dah*	band (instrumental group)
bandeja,*f.*	*bahn*-DEH-*hah*	tray
bandera,*f.*	*bahn*-DEH-*rah*	flag
bandido,*m.*	*bahn*-DEE-*thoh*	bandit
bañera,*f.*	*bah-*N_YEH-*rah*	bathtub
"	"	tub
banjo,*m.*	BAHN-*hoh*	banjo
baño,*m.*	BAH-*n_yoh*	bath
baño, (cuarto de), *m.*	(KWAHR-*toh theh*) VAH-*n_yoh*	bathroom
banquero,*m.*	*bahn*-KEH-*roh*	banker
banquete,*m.*	*bahn*-KEH-*teh*	banquet
baraja,*f.*	*bah*-RAH-*hah*	deck (of cards)
barato	*bah*-RAH-*toh*	cheap (inexpensive)
barba,*f.*	BAHR-*vah*	beard
"	"	chin
barbero,*m.*	*bahr*-VEH-*roh*	barber
barco,*m.*	BAHR-*koh*	boat
"	"	ship
"	"	vessel
barco de trasbordo, *m.*	BAHR-*koh theh trahss*-VOHR-*thoh*	ferry (boat)
barniz,*m.*	*bahr*-NEESS	varnish
barómetro,*m.*	*bah*-ROH-*meh-troh*	barometer
barrer (2)	*bah*-RREHR	sweep (clean), to
barrera,*f.*	*bah*-RREH-*rah*	barrier
barril,*m.*	*bah*-RREEL	barrel (cask)
basar (1)	*bah*-SAHR	base (found), to
base,*f.*	BAH-*seh*	base (foundation)
"	"	basis
"	"	ground
Basilea	*bah-see*-LEH_*ah*	Basle
bastante	*bah*-STAHN-*teh*	considerable (*adj.*)
"	"	enough
"	"	quite (considerably)
bastilla,*f.*	*bah*-STEE-*yah*	hem
bastón,*m.*	*bah*-STOHN	cane (walking stick)
basura,*f.*	*bah*-SOO-*rah*	rubbish (litter)
bata,*f.*	BAH-*tah*	robe (dressing gown)
batalla,*f.*	*bah*-TAH-*yah*	battle
bate,*m.*	BAH-*teh*	bat (club)
batería,*f.*	*bah-teh*-REE-*ah*	battery (artillery)
batido,*m.*	*bah*-TEE-*thoh*	batter (flour mixture)
baúl,*m.*	*bah-*OOL	trunk (baggage)
bautismo,*m.*	*bah_oo*-TEESS-*moh*	baptism
Baviera	*bah-*v_YEH-*rah*	Bavaria
baya,*f.*	BAH-*yah*	berry
beber (2)	*beh*-VEHR	drink, to
bebida,*f.*	*beh*-VEE-*thah*	drink (beverage)
béisbol,*m.*	BEH_*eez-vohl*	baseball
belga	BEHL-*gah*	Belgian (*adj.*)
Bélgica	BEHL-*hee-kah*	Belgium
belleza,*f.*	*beh*-YEH-*sah*	beauty
bello	BEH-*yoh*	beautiful
bellota,*f.*	*beh*-YOH-*tah*	acorn
bendecir (22)	*behn-deh*-SEER	bless, to

Spanish	Pronunciation	English
bendición,*f.*	*behn-dee-*S_YOHN	blessing (boon)
Berlín	*behr*-LEEN	Berlin
Berna	BEHR-*nah*	Berne
besar (1)	*beh*-SAHR	kiss, to
beso,*m.*	BEH-*soh*	kiss
bestia,*f.*	BEHSS-*t_yah*	beast (animal)
Biblia,*f.*	BEE-*vl_yah*	Bible
bibliografía,*f.*	*bee-vl_yoh-grah-*FEE-*ah*	bibliography
biblioteca,*f.*	*bee-vl_yoh-*TEH-*kah*	library
bibliotecario,*m.*	*bee-vl_yoh-teh-*KAH-*r_yoh*	librarian
bicho,*m.*	BEE-*choh*	bug (insect)
bicicleta,*f.*	*bee-see-*KLEH-*tah*	bicycle
bien	B_YEHN	well (commendably, *adv.*)
bien, más	MAHSS-B_YEHN	rather (preferably)
bienes,*m.pl.*	B_YEH-*nehss*	estate (total possessions)
bienes raíces,*m.pl.*	B_YEH-*nehss rah-*EE-*sehss*	land (property
"	"	real estate
bienestar,*m.*	*b_yeh-nehss-*TAHR	welfare (well-being)
bienvenida,*f.*	*b_yehn-veh-*NEE-*thah*	welcome (*n.*)
bigote,*m.*	*bee-*GOH-*teh*	mustache
billar,*m.*	*bee-*YAHR	billiards
billete,*m.*	*bee-*YEH-*teh*	bill (currency)
"	"	note (letter)
		ticket (entitling card)
biografía,*f.*	*b_yoh-grah-*FEE-*ah*	biography
biología,*f.*	*b_yoh-loh-*HEE-*ah*	biology
bisonte,*m.*	*bee-*SOHN-*teh*	buffalo
blanco	BLAHN-*koh*	white (*adj.*)
blanco, en	*ehm* BLAHN-*koh*	blank (unmarked)
blando	BLAHN-*doh*	soft (not hard)
blanquear (1)	*blahn_keh-*AHR	bleach (make white), to
blasfemar (1)	*blahss-feh-*MAHR	curse, to
"	"	swear, to
bloque,*m.*	BLOH-*keh*	block (solid piece)
blusa,*f.*	BLOO-*sah*	blouse (shirtwaist)
bobo	BOH-*voh*	foolish
boca,*f.*	BOH-*kah*	mouth (*anat.*)
bocado,*m.*	*boh*-KAH-*thoh*	morsel (small bit)
boceto,*m.*	*boh*-SEH-*toh*	sketch (rough drawing)
bocina,*f.*	*boh*-SEE-*nah*	horn (*auto.*)
boda,*f.*	BOH-*thah*	wedding
bodega,*f.*	*boh*-THEH-*gah*	cellar
Bolivia	*boh-*LEE-*v_yah*	Bolivia
bolsa,*f.*	BOHL-*sah*	bag (purse)
"	"	exchange, stock
bolsillo,*m.*	*bohl*-SEE-*yoh*	pocket
bomba,*f.*	BOHM-*bah*	bomb (projectile)
"	"	pump
bomba atómica,*f.*	BOHM-*bah ah-*TOH-*mee-kah*	atomic bomb
bombero,*m.*	*bohm*-BEH-*roh*	fireman
bombilla,*f.*	*bohm*-BEE-*yah*	bulb (light bulb)
bondad,*f.*	*bohn*-DATH	goodness
"	"	kindness
bondadoso	*bohn-dah*-THOH-*soh*	kind (*adj.*)
bonito	*boh*-NEE-*toh*	pretty
bono,*m.*	BOH-*noh*	bond (debenture)
boquear (1)	*boh-keh-*AHR	gasp, to
borde,*m.*	BOHR-*theh*	border
"	"	brink (verge)
"	"	edge
"	"	ledge
"	"	rim
bordillo,*m.*	*bohr*-THEE-*yoh*	curb (edge of street)
borracho	*boh*-RRAH-*choh*	drunk (intoxicated)
borrar (1)	*boh*-RRAHR	erase, to
bosque,*m.*	BOHSS-*keh*	forest
"	"	wood
bosquejar (1)	*bohss-keh*-HAHR	draft (sketch), to
bosquejo,*m.*	*bohss*-KEH-*hoh*	draft (sketch)
"	"	outline
bostezar (1)	*bohss-teh*-SAHR	yawn, to
bota,*f.*	BOH-*tah*	boot (footgear)
botánica,*f.*	*boh*-TAH-*nee-kah*	botany
botar al agua (1)	*boh*-TAHR *ahl* AH-*gwah*	launch (set afloat), to
botella,*f.*	*boh*-TEH-*yah*	bottle

Spanish	Pronunciation	English	Spanish	Pronunciation	English
botón, *m.*	boh-TOHN	bud (*bot.*)	caerse	kah-EHR-seh	collapse (cave in), to
"	"	button	café, *m.*	kah-FEH	coffee
boxear (1)	bohk-seh-AHR	box (fight), to	cafetera, *f.*	kah-feh-TEH-rah	coffee pot
bramar (1)	brah-MAHR	bellow (roar), to	caída, *f.*	kah-EE-thah	drop
			"	"	fall
Brasil, el	ehl brah-SEEL	Brazil	Cairo	KAH_ee-roh	Cairo
brasileño	brah-see-LEH-n_yoh	Brazilian (*adj.*)	caja, *f.*	KAH-hah	box (container)
brazo, *m.*	BRAH-soh	arm (*anat.*)	cajero, *m.*	kah-HEH-roh	cashier
brea, *f.*	BREH-ah	pitch	cajón, *m.*	kah-HOHN	drawer (sliding box)
"	"	tar	calambre, *m.*	kah-LAHM-breh	cramp (*med.*)
			calcetín, *m.*	kahl-seh-TEEN	sock (garment)
breve	BREH-veh	brief (fleeting)	calcular (1)	kahl-koo-LAHR	calculate (compute),
brida, *f.*	BREE-thah	bridle (harness)			to
brillante	bree-YAHN-teh	bright (shining)	"	"	estimate, to
"	"	brilliant (remark-	caldera, *f.*	kahl-THEH-rah	kettle
		able)	calendario, *m.*	kah-lehn-DAH-r_yoh	calendar
brillar (1)	bree-YAHR	glow, to	calentar (4)	kah-lehn-TAHR	heat, to
		shine (gleam), to	"	"	warm, to
brisa, *f.*	BREE-sah	breeze			
británico	bree-TAH-nee-koh	British (*adj.*)	calidad, *f.*	kah-lee-THAHTH	quality (attribute)
broche, *m.*	BROH-cheh	brooch	caliente	kah-L_YEHN-teh	hot
broma, *f.*	BROH-mah	jest (joke)	"	"	warm
			calificación, *f.*	kah-lee-fee-kah-S_YOHN	grade (academic rat-
bromear (1)	broh-MEH-ahr	jest (joke), to			ing)
bronce, *m.*	BROHN-seh	bronze (*n.*)	calificar (1)	kah-lee-fee-KAHR	qualify (modify), to
bronquitis, *f.*	brohn-KEE-teess	bronchitis	calle, *f.*	KAH-yeh	street
bruja, *f.*	BROO-hah	witch	calma, *f.*	KAHL-mah	lull
brujo, *m.*	BROO-hoh	wizard (sorcerer)	"	"	repose (calm)
brújula, *f.*	BROO-hoo-lah	compass (magnetic			
		instrument)	calmar (1)	kahl-MAHR	lull (quiet), to
Bruselas	broo-SEH-lahss	Brussels	"	"	soothe (calm), to
bruto	BROO-toh	gross (before deduc-	calor, *m.*	kah-LOHR	heat
		tions, *adj.*)	"	"	warmth
bruto, *m.*	BROO-toh	brute (animal, *n.*)	caloría, *f.*	kah-loh-REE-ah	calorie
budín, *m.*	boo-THEEN	pudding (dessert)	calvo	KAHL-voh	bald (hairless)
bueno	BWEH-noh	fine (good)			
"	"	well (and then?,	cama, *f.*	KAH-mah	bed
		interj.)	cámara, *f.*	KAH-mah-rah	camera
bueno, mejor, lo	BWEH-noh, meh-HOHR,	good, better, best	camarada, *m., f.*	kah-mah-RAH-thah	comrade
mejor	loh meh-HOHR		cámara de comer-	KAH-mah-rah theh koh-	chamber of com-
Buenos Aires	BWEH-nohss AH_ee-rehss	Buenos Aires	cio, *f.*	MEHR-s_yoh	merce
buey, *m.*	BWEH	ox	camarero, *m.*	kah-mah-REH-roh	steward (attendant
bufanda, *f.*	boo-FAHN-dah	scarf (neck cloth)			on ship)
buho, *m.*	BOO-oh	owl	"	"	waiter
Bulgaria	bool-GAH-r_yah	Bulgaria	camarón, *m.*	kah-mah-ROHN	shrimp
			camarote, *m.*	kah-mah-ROH-teh	cabin (of ship)
burbujear (1)	boor-voo-heh-AHR	bubble, to	cambiar (1)	kahm-B_YAHR	change (make dif-
busca, *f.*	BOOSS-kah	quest (search)			ferent), to
buscar (1)	booss-KAHR	look for, to	cambio, *m.*	KAHM-b_yoh	change (alteration)
buscar a tientas	booss-KAHR ah T_YEHN-	feel (grope) for, to	camello, *m.*	kah-MEH-yoh	camel
	tahss		camilla, *f.*	kah-MEE-yah	litter (stretcher)
búsqueda, *f.*	BOOSS-keh-thah	search (hunt)	caminata, *f.*	kah-mee-NAH-tah	hike (march)
busto, *m.*	BOOSS-toh	bust (statue)	camino, *m.*	kah-MEE-noh	road
caballero, *m.*	kah-vah-YEH-roh	gentleman			
"	"	knight	camión, *m.*	kah-M_YOHN	truck (automobile)
			"	"	van (vehicle)
caballito, *m.*	kah-vah-YEE-toh	pony (animal)	camisa, *f.*	kah-MEE-sah	shirt
caballo, *m.*	kah-VAH-yoh	horse	camisa de dormir,	kah-MEE-sah theh dohr-	nightgown
caballo padre, *m.*	kah-VAH-yoh PAH-	stallion	*f.*	MEER	
	th_reh		campamento, *m.*	kahm-pah-MEHN-toh	camp (encampment,
caballos de fuerza,	kah-VAH-yohss theh	horsepower			*mil.*)
m.pl.	FWEHR-sah		campana, *f.*	kahm-PAH-nah	bell
cabecear (1)	kah-veh-seh-AHR	nod, to	campaña, *f.*	kahm-PAH-n_yah	campaign (*mil.*)
cabello, *m.*	kah-VEH-yoh	hair	campeón, *m.*	kahm-peh-OHN	champion
cabeza, *f.*	kah-VEH-sah	head (*anat.*)			
cable, *m.*	KAH-vleh	cable (rope)	campesino, *m.*	kahm-peh-SEE-noh	peasant
cablegrafiar (1)	kah-vleh-grah-F_YAHR	cable, to	campo, *m.*	KAHM-poh	country (country-
cablegrama, *m.*	kah-vleh-GRAH-mah	cablegram			side)
cabo, *m.*	KAH-voh	cape (headland)	"	"	field
cabo, *m.*	KAH-voh	corporal (*mil.*)	"	"	realm (field)
cabra, *f.*	KAH-vrah	goat			
cabrito, *m.*	kah-VREE-toh	kid (goat)	campo de recreo,	KAHM-poh theh reh-	playground
cacao, *m.*	kah-KAH-oh	cocoa	*m.*	KREH-oh	
cada	KAH-thah	each (*adj.*)	Canadá, (el)	(ehl) kah-nah-THAH	Canada
"	"	every	canadiense	kah-nah-TH_YEHN-seh	Canadian (*adj.*)
cada uno	KAH-thah_OO-noh	each one (*pron.*)	canal, *m.*	kah-NAHL	canal
		everyone	"	"	channel (strait)
cada uno, por	pohr KAH-thah_oo-noh	each (apiece, *adv.*)	canalete, *m.*	kah-nah-LEH-teh	paddle (oar)
cadáver, *m.*	kah-THAH-vehr	corpse	canario, *m.*	kah-NAH-r_yoh	canary
cadena, *f.*	kah-THEH-nah	chain			
cadera, *f.*	kah-THEH-rah	hip	cancelar (1)	kahn-seh-LAHR	cancel (revoke), to
caducar (1)	kah-thoo-KAHR	lapse (become void),	cáncer, *m.*	KAHN-sehr	cancer
		to	canción, *f.*	kahn-S_YOHN	song
caer (19)	kah-EHR	drop, to	candidato, *m.*	kahn-dee-THAH-toh	candidate
"	"	fall, to	canela, *f.*	kah-NEH-lah	cinnamon
"	"	tumble, to	cangrejo, *m.*	kahn-GREH-hoh	crab (shellfish)
caer por grados	kah-EHR pohr GRAH-	sink (fall slowly), to			
	thohss		canoa, *f.*	kah-NOH-ah	canoe
			cañón, *m.*	kah-N_YOHN	cannon

Spanish	Pronunciation	English
cansado	*kahn*-SAH-*thoh*	tired
"	"	weary
cansar (1)	*kahn*-SAHR	tire (make weary), to
cansarse	*kahn*-SAHR-*seh*	tire (become weary), to
cantante, *m.,f.*	*kahn*-TAHN-*teh*	singer
cantar (1)	*kahn*-TAHR	sing, to
cantidad, *f.*	*kahn*-tee-THAHTH	amount
"	"	quantity
"	"	volume
cantina, *f.*	*kahn*-TEE-*nah*	bar (barroom)
capa, *f.*	KAH-*pah*	cloak (apparel)
"	"	layer (thickness)
capacidad, *f.*	*kah-pah-see*-THATH	capacity (volume)
capacitar (1)	*kah-pah-see*-TAHR	enable (make able), to
capataz, *m.*	*kah-pah*-TAHSS	foreman (overseer)
capaz	*kah*-PAHSS	able
"	"	capable
capilla, *f.*	*kah*-PEE-*yah*	chapel
capital, *f.*	*kah-pee*-TAHL	capital (city)
capital, *m.*	*kah-pee*-TAHL	capital (wealth)
capitán, *m.*	*kah-pee*-TAHN	captain (officer)
capítulo, *m.*	*kah*-PEE-*too-loh*	chapter (of book)
capricho, *m.*	*kah*-PREE-*choh*	fancy (notion)
capucha, *f.*	*kah*-POO-*chah*	hood (cowl)
cara, *f.*	KAH-*rah*	face (*anat.*)
caracol, *m.*	*kah-rah*-KOHL	snail
carácter, *m.*	*kah*-RAHK-*tehr*	character (nature)
característico	*kah-rahk-teh*-REESS-*tee-koh*	characteristic (typical)
carbón, *m.*	*kahr*-VOHN	coal
carbono, *m.*	*kahr*-VOH-*noh*	carbon (*chem.*)
cárcel, *f.*	KAHR-*sehl*	jail
cardenal, *m.*	*kahr-theh*-NAHL	bruise
carga, *f.*	KAHR-*gah*	burden
"	"	load
cargador, *m.*	*kahr-gah*-THOHR	porter (baggage carrier)
cargamento, *m.*	*kahr-gah*-MEHN-*toh*	cargo
cargar (1)	*kahr*-GAHR	charge, to (*elec.*)
"	"	charge (debit), to
"	"	load (fill), to
cargo, *m.*	KAHR-*goh*	charge (responsibility)
caricatura, *f.*	*kah-ree-kah*-TOO-*rah*	cartoon (caricature)
caridad, *f.*	*kah-ree*-THAHTH	charity (philanthropy)
cariño, *m.*	*kah*-REE-*n yoh*	affection (love)
cariñoso	*kah-ree-n* YOH-*soh*	affectionate (loving)
carmesí	*kahr-meh*-SEE	crimson
carnaval, *m.*	*kahr-nah*-VAHL	carnival
carne, *f.*	KAHR-*neh*	flesh
"	"	meat
carne de carnero, *f.*	KAHR-*neh theh kahr*-NEH-*roh*	mutton
carne de cerdo, *f.*	KAHR-*neh theh* SEHR-*thoh*	pork
carne de ternera, *f.*	KAHR-*neh theh tehr*-NEH-*rah*	veal
carne de vaca, *f.*	KAHR-*neh theh* VAH-*kah*	beef
carnicero, *m.*	*kahr-nee*-SEH-*roh*	butcher
carpintero, *m.*	*kahr-peen*-TEH-*roh*	carpenter
carrera, *f.*	*kah*-RREH-*rah*	career
"	"	race (contest)
carretada, *f.*	*kah*-RREH-*tah-thah*	carload (*bus.*)
carrete, *m.*	*kah*-RREH-*teh*	coil (*elec.*)
carretera, *f.*	*kah-rreh*-TEH-*rah*	highway
carro, *m.*	KAH-*rroh*	cart
carta, *f.*	KAHR-*tah*	letter (epistle)
carta de venta, *f.*	KAHR-*tah theh* VEHN-*tah*	bill of sale
cartera, *f.*	*kahr*-TEH-*rah*	briefcase
cartero, *m.*	*kahr*-TEH-*roh*	postman
cartón, *m.*	*kahr*-TOHN	cardboard
casa, *f.*	KAH-*sah*	concern
"	"	firm (business company)
"	"	house
"	"	household
casa, a	*ah* KAH-*sah*	homeward

Spanish	Pronunciation	English
casa de campo, *f.*	KAH-*sah theh* KAHM-*poh*	lodge (cabin)
casa de empeños, *f.*	KAH-*sah th ehm*-PEH-*n yohss*	pawnshop
casado	*kah*-SAH-*thoh*	married
casarse (con) (1)	*kah*-SAHR-*seh* (*kohn*)	marry, to
cascada, *f.*	*kahss*-KAH-*thah*	falls (waterfall)
cáscara, *f.*	KAHSS-*kah-rah*	shell (covering)
casi	KAH-*see*	almost
"	"	nearly
caso, *m.*	KAH-*soh*	case (instance)
caso, en tal	*ehn tahl* KAH-*soh*	then (in that case)
castaño, *m.*	*kahss*-TAH-*n yoh*	chestnut (tree)
castigar (1)	*kahss-tee*-GAHR	punish, to
castigo, *m.*	*kahss*-TEE-*goh*	punishment
castillo, *m.*	*kahss*-TEE-*yoh*	castle
casto	KAHSS-*toh*	chaste
castor, *m.*	*kahss*-TOHR	beaver (animal)
casual	*kah*-SWAHL	casual (offhand)
casualidad, *f.*	*kah-swah-lee*-THAHTH	accident
"	"	chance (fate)
catálogo, *m.*	*kah*-TAH-*loh-goh*	catalogue
catedral, *f.*	*kah-teh*-THRAHL	cathedral
católico	*kah*-TOH-*lee-koh*	Catholic (*adj.*)
catre, *m.*	KAH-*treh*	cot (bed)
caucho, *m.*	KOW-*choh*	rubber
caucho esponjoso, *m.*	KOW-*choh ehss-pohn*-HOH-*soh*	foam rubber
causa, *f.*	KOW-*sah*	cause
causa de, a	*ah* KOW-*sah-theh*	because of (*adv.*)
causar (1)	*kow*-SAHR	cause, to
cautivo, *m.*	*kow*-TEE-*voh*	captive (prisoner)
cavar (1)	*kah*-VAHR	dig (excavate), to
"	"	hoe, to
cavilar (1)	*kah-vee*-LAHR	brood over, to
caza, *f.*	KAH-*sah*	hunt (sport)
cazador, *m.*	*kah-sah*-THOHR	hunter
cebada, *f.*	*seh*-VAH-*thah*	barley
cebo, *m.*	SEH-*voh*	bait (for animals)
cebolla, *f.*	*seh*-VOH-*yah*	onion
cebra, *f.*	SEH-*vrah*	zebra
ceder (2)	*seh*-THEHR	cede, to
"	"	yield (give in), to
cedro, *m.*	SEH-*throh*	cedar (tree)
cegar (4)	*seh*-GAHR	blind, to
ceja, *f.*	SEH-*hah*	eyebrow
celebrar (1)	*seh-leh*-VRAHR	celebrate, to
celo, *m.*	SEH-*loh*	zeal
celoso	*seh*-LOH-*soh*	jealous
célula, *f.*	SEH-*loo-lah*	cell (*biol.*)
cementerio, *m.*	*seh-mehn*-TEH-*r yoh*	cemetery
cemento, *m.*	*seh*-MEHN-*toh*	cement
cena, *f.*	SEH-*nah*	supper (light evening meal)
cenicero, *m.*	*seh-nee*-SEH-*roh*	ash tray
cenizas, *f.pl.*	*seh*-NEE-*sahss*	ashes
censo, *m.*	SEHN-*soh*	census
centeno, *m.*	*sehn*-TEH-*noh*	rye (grain)
central	*sehn*-TRAHL	central
centro, *m.*	SEHN-*troh*	center
cepillo, *m.*	*seh*-PEE-*yoh*	brush (scrubbing utensil)
cepillo de diente, *m.*	*seh*-PEE-*yoh theh* TH YEHN-*teh*	toothbrush
cera, *f.*	SEH-*rah*	wax (beeswax)
cerca	SEHR-*kah*	close (*adv.*)
"	"	near (not far, *adv.*)
cerca, *f.*	SEHR-*kah*	fence (barrier)
cerca de	SEHR-*kah theh*	about (approximately)
"	"	near (*prep.*)
cercado, *m.*	*sehr*-KAH-*thoh*	yard (enclosure near house)
cerdo, *m.*	SEHR-*thoh*	pig (animal)
cereal, *m.*	*seh-reh*-AHL	cereal
cerebro, *m.*	*seh*-REH-*vroh*	brain (*anat.*)
ceremonia, *f.*	*seh-reh*-MOH-*n yah*	ceremony
cereza, *f.*	*seh*-REH-*sah*	cherry (fruit)
cerner (4)	*sehr*-NEHR	sift (separate), to
cero, *m.*	SEH-*roh*	zero (*n.*)
cerradura, *f.*	*seh-rrah*-THOO-*rah*	lock (fastening)

Spanish	Pronunciation	English
cerrar (4)	*seh*-RRAHR	close, to
"	"	shut, to
cerrar con llave (4)	*seh*-RRAHR *kohn* YAH-*veh*	lock (fasten with key), to
cerrojo,*m.*	*seh*-RROH-*hoh*	bolt (lock)
certificado	*sehr-tee-fee*-KAH-*thoh*	registered (postal designation)
certificado,*m.*	*sehr-tee-fee*-KAH-*thoh*	certificate
certificar (1)	*sehr-tee-fee*-KAHR	certify, to
cerveza,*f.*	*sehr*-VEH-*sah*	beer
cesar (1)	*seh*-SAHR	cease (be at an end), to
cesión,*f.*	*seh*-S YOHN	assignment (legal transfer)
césped,*m.*	SEHSS-*peth*	lawn
cesta,*f.*	SEHSS-*tah*	basket
chaleco,*m.*	*chah*-LEH-*koh*	vest
chancearse (1)	*chahn-seh*-AHR-*seh*	joke (jest), to
chanclos,*m.pl.*	CHAHN-*klohss*	galoshes
"	"	rubbers (overshoes)
chapotear (1)	*chah-poh-teh*-AHR	splash, to
chaqueta,*f.*	*chah*-KEH-*tah*	jacket (short coat)
charco,*m.*	CHAHR-*koh*	pool (standing water)
charlar (1)	*chahr*-LAHR	chat, to
chasquear (1)	*chahss-keh*-AHR	snap (crackle), to
Checoeslovaquia	*cheh-koh-ehss-loh*-VAH-*k yah*	Czechoslovakia
cheque,*m.*	CHEH-*keh*	check (bank check)
chicle,*m.*	CHEE-*kleh*	gum (chewing gum)
chico,*m.*	CHEE-*koh*	chap (fellow)
Chile	CHEE-*leh*	Chile
chileno	*chee*-LEH-*noh*	Chilean (*adj.*)
chillar (1)	*chee*-YAHR	scream, to
"	"	shriek, to
chillón	*chee*-YOHN	shrill
chimenea,*f.*	*chee-meh*-NEH-*ah*	chimney
"	"	fireplace
China	CHEE-*nah*	China
chino	CHEE-*noh*	Chinese (*adj.*)
chiquitico	*chee-kee*-TEE-*koh*	wee
chisme,*m.*	CHEEZ-*meh*	gossip (idle talk)
chispa,*f.*	CHEESS-*pah*	spark
chispear (1)	*cheess-peh*-AHR	sparkle, to
chiste,*m.*	CHEESS-*teh*	joke (jest)
chocolate,*m.*	*choh-koh*-LAH-*teh*	chocolate
chofer,*m.*	*choh*-FEHR	driver (of automobile)
choza,*f.*	CHOH-*sah*	hut
chuleta de carnero, *f.*	*choo*-LEH-*tah theh kahr*-NEH-*roh*	lamb chop
chuleta de cerdo,*f.*	*choo*-LEH-*tah theh* SEHR-*thoh*	pork chop
chuleta de ternera, *f.*	*choo*-LEH-*tah theh tehr*-NEH-*rah*	veal chop
chupar (1)	*choo*-PAHR	suck, to
cicatriz,*f.*	*see-kah*-TREESS	scar
ciego	S YEH-*goh*	blind (lacking sight)
cielo,*m.*	S YEH-*loh*	heaven
"	"	sky
cielo raso,*m.*	S YEH-*loh* RAH-*soh*	ceiling (of room)
ciencia,*f.*	S YEHN-*s yah*	science
ciencia política,*f.*	S YEHN-*s yah poh*-LEE-*tee-kah*	political science
cieno,*m.*	S YEH-*noh*	mire (bog)
científico	*s yehn*-TEE-*fee-koh*	scientific
científico,*m.*	*s yehn*-TEE-*fee-koh*	scientist
cierre relámpago, *m.*	S YEH-*rreh reh*-LAHM-*pah-goh*	zipper
ciertamente	*s yehr-tah*-MEHN-*teh*	certainly (surely, *adv.*)
cierto	S YEHR-*toh*	certain (particular)
"	"	certain (sure)
ciervo,*m.*	S YEHR-*voh*	deer
cifra,*f.*	SEE-*frah*	figure (numeral)
cigarrillo,*m.*	*see-gah*-RREE-*yoh*	cigarette
cigarro,*m.*	*see*-GAH-*rroh*	cigar
cigüeña,*f.*	*see*-GWEH-*n yah*	stork
cilindro,*m.*	*see*-LEEN-*droh*	cylinder (*geom.*)
cima,*f.*	SEE-*mah*	top (summit)
cinc,*m.*	SEENK	zinc
cincel,*m.*	*seen*-SEHL	chisel (tool)
cine,*m.*	SEE-*neh*	movies
cinta,*f.*	SEEN-*tah*	band (ribbon)
cinto,*m.*	SEEN-*toh*	belt (article of **cloth**ing)

Spanish	Pronunciation	English
cintura,*f.*	*seen*-TOO-*rah*	waist (*anat.*)
circo,*m.*	SEER-*koh*	circus
circulación,*f.*	*seer-koo-lah*-S YOHN	circulation (dissemination)
circular	*seer-koo*-LAHR	circular (*adj.*)
circular,*f.*	*seer-koo*-LAHR	circular (letter or brochure, *bus.*)
círculo,*m.*	SEER-*koo-loh*	circle (*geom.*)
"	"	ring (circle)
circunferencia,*f.*	*seer-koon-feh*-REHN-*s yah*	circumference
circunstancia,*f.*	*seer-koon*-STAHN-*s yah*	circumstance (external condition)
ciruela,*f.*	*see-r* WEH-*lah*	plum (fruit)
ciruela pasa,*f.*	*see-r* WEH-*lah* PAH-*sah*	prune
cirujano,*m.*	*see-roo*-HAH-*noh*	surgeon
cisne,*m.*	SEESS-*neh*	swan
cita,*f.*	SEE-*tah*	appointment (meeting)
"	"	date
"	"	engagement
citación,*f.*	*see-tah*-S YOHN	quotation (selection)
citar (1)	*see*-TAHR	quote (cite), to
ciudad,*f.*	*s yoo*-THAHTH	city
ciudadano,*m.*	*s yoo-thah*-THAH-*noh*	citizen
civil	*see*-VEEL	civil
civilización,*f.*	*see-vee-lee-sah*-S YOHN	civilization (civilized condition)
"	"	civilization (culture)
clarinete,*m.*	*klah-ree*-NEH-*teh*	clarinet
claro	KLAH-*roh*	clear
"	"	light (bright)
"	"	plain (clear)
clase,*f.*	KLAH-*seh*	class
"	"	sort
clásico	KLAH-*see-koh*	classic (first-class, *adj.*)
cláusula,*f.*	KLAH-OO-*soo-lah*	clause (stipulation)
clavel,*m.*	*klah*-VEHL	carnation
clavija,*f.*	*klah*-VEE-*hah*	peg (pin)
clavo,*m.*	KLAH-*voh*	clove
"	"	nail (hardware)
clérigo,*m.*	KLEH-*ree-goh*	parson
cliente,*m.,f.*	KL YEHN-*teh*	customer (buyer)
"	"	patron
clima,*m.*	KLEE-*mah*	climate (weather)
club,*m.*	KLOOV	club (association)
cobarde,*m.*	*koh*-VAHR-*theh*	coward
cobertizo,*m.*	*koh-vehr*-TEE-*soh*	shed (shelter)
cobrar (1)	*koh*-VRAHR	collect, to (*bus.*)
cobre,*m.*	KOH-*vreh*	copper
cocer (20)	*koh*-SEHR	cook (heat food), to
cocer en horno (20)	*koh*-SEH *reh* NOHR-*noh*	bake (be cooking), to
coche,*m.*	KOH-*cheh*	car (auto)
"	"	carriage (horse-drawn vehicle)
coche (para niños), *m.*	KOH-*cheh* (PAH-*rah* NEE-*n yohss*)	carriage (baby buggy)
coche comedor,*m.*	KOH-*cheh koh-meh*-THOHR	diner (train)
cocina,*f.*	*koh*-SEE-*nah*	kitchen
cocinar (1)	*koh-see*-NAHR	cook (prepare meals), to
cocinero,*m.*	*koh-see*-NEH-*roh*	cook
coco,*m.*	KOH-*koh*	coconut
coctel,*m.*	*kohk*-TEHL	cocktail
código,*m.*	KOH-*thee-goh*	code (law)
codo,*m.*	KOH-*thoh*	elbow
coger (2)	*koh*-HEHR	catch (nab), to
"	"	pluck (pull off), to
cohete,*m.*	*koh*-HEH-*teh*	rocket
cojear (1)	*koh-heh*-AHR	limp, to
cojín,*m.*	*koh*-HEEN	cushion (pillow)
cojinete,*m.*	*koh-hee*-NEH-*teh*	pad (cushion)
cojo	KOH-*hoh*	lame
cojo,*m.*	KOH-*hoh*	cripple
col,*f.*	KOHL	cabbage
cola,*f.*	KOH-*lah*	glue
"	"	tail (of animal)
colar (5)	*koh*-LAHR	strain (filter), to
colcha,*f.*	KOHL-*chah*	quilt (bedcover)
colchón,*m.*	*kohl*-CHOHN	mattress
colección,*f.*	*koh-lehk*-S YOHN	collection

Spanish	Pronunciation	English
cólera (asiático), *m.*	KOH-*leh-rah* (*ah*-S_YAH-*tee-koh*)	cholera
colgar (5)	*kohl*-GAHR	hang (suspend), to
colgarse (5)	*kohl*-GAHR-*seh*	hang (be suspended), to
coliflor, *f.*	*koh-lee*-FLOHR	cauliflower
colina, *f.*	*koh*-LEE-*nah*	hill
collar, *m.*	*koh*-YAHR	necklace
colmena, *f.*	*kohl*-MEH-*nah*	hive (beehive)
colocación, *f.*	*koh-loh-kah*-S_YOHN	arrangement (order)
"	"	location (place)
colocar (1)	*koh-loh*-KAHR	arrange (place), to
"	"	lay, to
"	"	place, to
"	"	put, to
Colombia	*koh*-LOHM-*b_yah*	Colombia
colonia, *f.*	*koh*-LOH-*n_yah*	colony
		settlement
colonial	*koh-loh*-N_YAHL	colonial
colono, *m.*	*koh*-LOH-*noh*	colonist
"	"	settler
color, *m.*	*koh*-LOHR	color
color de ámbar, *m.*	*koh*-LOHR *theh* AHM-*bahr*	amber (*adj.*)
colorete, *m.*	*koh-loh*-REH-*teh*	rouge
columna, *f.*	*koh*-LOOM-*nah*	column (*print.*)
coma, *f.*	KOH-*mah*	comma
comandante, *m.*	*koh-mahn*-DAHN-*teh*	commander (officer)
comarca, *f.*	*koh*-MAHR-*kah*	district (locality)
combate, *m.*	*kohm*-BAH-*teh*	combat
combinación, *f.*	*kohm-bee-nah*-S_YOHN	combination
"	"	slip (petticoat)
combinar (1)	*kohm-bee*-NAHR	combine (make join), to
combinarse	*kohm-bee*-NAHR-*seh*	combine (coalesce), to
combustible, *m.*	*kohm-booss*-TEE-*vleh*	fuel
comedia, *f.*	*koh*-MEH-*th_yah*	comedy (comic play)
comedor, *m.*	*koh-meh*-THOHR	dining room
comentar (1)	*koh-mehn*-TAHR	comment, to
"	"	remark (say), to
comenzar (4)	*koh-mehn*-SAHR	begin (start to do), to
"	"	commence, to
"	"	start (initiate), to
comer (2)	*koh*-MEHR	dine, to
"	"	eat, to
comercial	*koh-mehr*-S_YAHL	commercial
comerciante, *m.*	*koh-mehr*-S_YAHN-*teh*	merchant
comercio, *m.*	*koh*-MEHR-*s_yoh*	commerce
"	"	trade
cometa, *f.*	*koh*-MEH-*tah*	kite
cometer (2)	*koh-meh*-TEHR	commit (perpetrate), to
cómico	KOH-*mee-koh*	funny (comical)
comida, *f.*	*koh*-MEE-*thah*	dinner
"	"	meal (repast)
comienzo, *m.*	*koh*-M_YEHN-*soh*	start (beginning)
comisario, *m.*	*koh-mee*-SAH-*r_yoh*	commissioner (deputized person)
comisión, *f.*	*koh-mee*-S_YOHN	commission
comité, *m.*	*koh-mee*-TEH	committee
como	KOH-*moh*	as (in the role of, *prep.*)
"	"	as (in the same way, *conj.*)
"	"	how (*rel. adv.*)
"	"	like (*adv.*)
cómo	KOH-*moh*	how (*interrog. adv.*)
cómoda, *f.*	KOH-*moh-thah*	bureau (chest)
comodidad, *f.*	*koh-moh-thee*-THAHTH	comfort
"	"	convenience
"	"	ease
cómodo	KOH-*moh-thoh*	comfortable (affording comfort)
"	"	convenient
compacto	*kohm*-PAHK-*toh*	compact (packed firmly)
compadecer (11)	*kohm-pah-theh*-SEHR	pity, to
compañero, *m.*	*kohm-pah*-N_YEH-*roh*	companion
"	"	pal
compañero de juego, *m.*	*kohm-pah*-N_YEH-*roh theh* HWEH-*goh*	playmate
compañía, *f.*	*kohm-pah*-N_YEE-*ah*	company (*bus.*)
"	"	company (*mil.*)
comparación, *f.*	*kohm-pah-rah*-S_YOHN	comparison
comparar (1)	*kohm-pah*-RAHR	compare (consider relatively), to
compartimiento, *m.*	*kohm-pahr-tee*-M_YEHN-*toh*	compartment (of train)
compartir (3)	*kohm-pahr*-TEER	share, to
compás, *m.*	*kohm*-PAHSS	compass (drawing instrument)
compasión, *f.*	*kohm-pah*-S_YOHN	pity (compassion)
"	"	sympathy
competencia, *f.*	*kohm-peh*-TEHN-*s_yah*	competition (*bus.*)
competente	*kohm-peh*-TEHN-*teh*	competent (able)
complacer (11)	*kohm-plah*-SEHR	please (satisfy), to
complejo	*kohm*-PLEH-*hoh*	complex (complicated)
completamente	*kohm-pleh-tah*-MEHN-*teh*	thoroughly
completar (1)	*kohm-pleh*-TAHR	complete (finish), to
completo	*kohm*-PLEH-*toh*	complete (entire)
"	"	full
"	"	thorough
completo	*kohm*-PLEH-*toh*	utter (*adj.*)
complot, *m.*	*kohm*-PLOHT	plot (conspiracy)
componer (31)	*kohm-poh*-NEHR	compose, to (*mus.*)
composición, *f.*	*kohm-poh-see*-S_YOHN	composition (make-up)
compota, *f.*	*kohm*-POH-*tah*	jam (preserve)
compra, *f.*	KOHM-*prah*	purchase (act of buying)
comprar (1)	*kohm*-PRAHR	buy, to
comprender (2)	*kohm-prehn*-DEHR	comprehend, to
"	"	grasp, to
"	"	understand, to
comprensión, *f.*	*kohm-prehn*-S_YOHN	understanding (comprehension)
comprensivo	*kohm-prehn*-SEE-*voh*	wide (comprehensive)
comprobación, *f.*	*kohm-proh-vah*-S_YOHN	proof (demonstration)
comprobar (5)	*kohm-proh*-VAHR	check (test), to
compromiso, *m.*	*kohm-proh*-MEE-*soh*	commitment (*bus.*)
compuesto, *m.*	*kohm*-PWEHSS-*toh*	compound (mixture)
computar (1)	*kohm-poo*-TAHR	reckon (compute), to
comunicación, *f.*	*koh-moo-nee-kah*-S_YOHN	communication
comunicar (1)	*koh-moo-nee*-KAHR	convey (communicate), to
comunismo, *m.*	*koh-moo*-NEEZ-*moh*	communism
con	KOHN	with
concebir (9)	*kohn-seh*-VEER	conceive (imagine), to
conceder (2)	*kohn-seh*-THEHR	admit (concede), to
"	"	grant (bestow), to
concepción, *f.*	*kohn-sehp*-S_YOHN	conception (*physiol.*)
concepto, *m.*	*kohn*-SEHP-*toh*	conception (notion)
concernir (4)	*kohn-sehr*-NEER	concern (affect), to
conciencia, *f.*	*kohn*-S_YEHN-*s_yah*	conscience
concierto, *m.*	*kohn*-S_YEHR-*toh*	concert (musical performance)
conciso	*kohn*-SEE-*soh*	compact (brief)
concluir (14)	*kohn-kloo*-EER	close (finish) to
"	"	conclude (make end), to
conclusión, *f.*	*kohn-kloo*-S_YOHN	conclusion (decision)
"	"	conclusion (end)
concordia, *f.*	*kohn*-KOHR-*d_yah*	unity (accord)
concreto	*kohn*-KREH-*toh*	concrete (real)
concubina, *f.*	*kohn-koo*-VEE-*nah*	mistress (paramour)
concurso, *m.*	*kohn*-KOOR-*soh*	contest
condenar (1)	*kohn-deh*-NAHR	condemn (censure), to
"	"	damn, to
"	"	doom (condemn), to
condensar (1)	*kohn-dehn*-SAHR	condense (compress), to
condición, *f.*	*kohn-dee*-S_YOHN	condition
condiciones, *f.pl.*	*kohn-dee*-S_YOH-*nehss*	terms (conditions)
conducir (12)	*kohn-doo*-SEER	conduct (manage), to
"	"	steer, to
conducirse	*kohn-doo*-SEER-*seh*	behave (conduct oneself), to
conducta, *f.*	*kohn*-DOOK-*tah*	behavior
conectar (1)	*koh-nehk*-TAHR	connect (link), to
conejo, *m.*	*koh*-NEH-*hoh*	rabbit
con eso	*kohn* EH-*soh*	thereby
conferencia, *f.*	*kohn-feh*-REHN-*s_yah*	conference (meeting)
"	"	lecture (speech)
conferir (7)	*kohn-feh*-REER	confer (bestow), to
confesar (4)	*kohn-feh*-SAHR	confess (admit), to

Spanish	Pronunciation	English
confiado en sí mismo	kohn-F YAH-thoh ehn see MEEZ-moh	confident (self-assured)
confianza, f.	kohn-F YAHN-sah	confidence trust
confiar en (1)	kohn-F YAHR ehn	trust (rely on), to
confidencial	kohn-fee-dehn-S YAHL	confidential (private)
confirmación, f.	kohn-feer-mah-S YOHN	confirmation (corroboration)
confirmar (1)	kohn-feer-MAHR	confirm (corroborate), to
conflicto, m.	kohn-FLEEK-toh	conflict
confundir (3)	kohn-foon-DEER	confuse (mix up), to
confusión, f.	kohn-foo-S YOHN	confusion (disorder) mess (muddle)
congelado	kohn-heh-LAH-thoh	frozen
congelar (1)	kohn-heh-LAHR	freeze (turn to ice), to
congreso, m.	kohn-GREH-soh	convention (meeting)
conjunción, f.	kohn-hoon-S YOHN	conjunction (gram.)
conjunto	kohn-HOON-toh	joint (combined)
conocer (11)	koh-noh-SEHR	know (be acquainted with), to
conocido	koh-noh-SEE-thoh	known (familiar)
conocido, m.	koh-noh-SEE-thoh	acquaintance (person known)
conocimiento, m.	koh-noh-see-M YEHN-toh	acquaintance
"	"	knowledge (information)
conocimiento de embarque, m.	koh-noh-see-M YEHN-toh theh ehm-BAHR-keh	bill of lading
conquista, f.	kohn-KEESS-tah	conquest
conquistar (1)	kohn-keess-TAHR	conquer, to
consciente	kohn-S YEHN-teh	conscious (aware)
consecuencia, f.	kohn-seh-KWEHN-s yah	consequence
consejo, m.	kohn-SEH-hoh	advice
"	"	council
"	"	counsel
consentir (7)	kohn-sehn-TEER	consent, to
conservador	kohn-sehr-vah-THOHR	conservative (cautious)
consideración, f.	kohn-see-theh-rah-S YOHN	consideration
considerar (1)	kohn-see-theh-RAHR	consider (reflect on), to
"	"	deem, to
"	"	reckon, to
"	"	regard, to
consignatario, m.	kohn-seeg-nah-TAHR-yoh	consignee (bus.)
consiguiente, por	pohr kohn-see-GH YEHN-teh	consequently
consistir en (3)	kohn-seess-TEE rehn	consist of (comprise), to
consolar (5)	kohn-soh-LAHR	comfort (console), to
constante	kohn-STAHN-teh	constant (continual)
"	"	steady (regular)
constitución, f.	kohn-stee-too-S YOHN	constitution
constituir (14)	kohn-stee-TWEER	constitute (make up), to
construcción, f.	kohn-strook-S YOHN	construction (fabrication)
"	"	structure (thing built)
construir (14)	kohn-STR WEER	construct, to
consuelo, m.	kohn-SWEH-loh	comfort (solace) consolation
cónsul, m.	KOHN-sool	consul
consultar (1)	kohn-sool-TAHR	consult (seek professional advice of), to
consumir (3)	kohn-soo-MEER	consume, to
consumo, m.	kohn-soo-moh	consumption (using up)
contabilidad, f.	kohn-tah-vee-lee-THAHTH	bookkeeping (bus.)
contacto, m.	kohn-TAHK-toh	contact (meeting)
contador, m.	kohn-tah-THOHR	accountant
contar (5)	kohn-TAHR	count (enumerate), to
"	"	tell (narrate), to
contar con	kohn-TAHR kohn	count (rely) on, to depend on, to
contemporáneo	kohn-tehm-poh-RAH-neh-oh	contemporary (modern)
contener (35)	kohn-teh-NEHR	contain, to

Spanish	Pronunciation	English
contenido, m.	kohn-teh-NEE-thoh	contents
contento	kohn-TEHN-toh	content (satisfied)
"	"	glad
contestar (1)	kohn-tehss-TAHR	answer (give answer to), to
continente, m.	kohn-tee-NEHN-teh	continent (geog.)
continuación, f.	kohn-tee-nwah-S YOHN	continuation
continuar (1)	kohn-tee-NWAHR	continue, to
continuo	kohn-TEE-nwoh	continual
"	"	continuous
contra	KOHN-trah	against
contrabando, m.	kohn-trah-VAHN-doh	contraband
contradecir (22)	kohn-trah-theh-SEER	contradict (deny), to
contraer (36)	kohn-trah-EHR	contract (make shrink), to
contraer(se)	kohn-trah-EHR(-seh)	shrink (become contracted), to
contrafirma, f.	kohn-trah-FEER-mah	countersignature (bus.)
contrario	kohn-TRAH-r yoh	contrary
contrario, m.	kohn-TRAH-r yoh	opposite (n.)
contrario, lo	loh kohn-TRAH-r yoh	reverse (contrary, n.)
contraste, m.	kohn-TRAHSS-teh	contrast
contrato, m.	kohn-TRAH-toh	contract
contravención del contrato, f.	kohn-trah-vehn-S YOHN dehl kohn-TRAH-toh	breach of contract (bus.)
contribución, f.	kohn-tree-voo-S YOHN	contribution
contribuir (14)	kohn-tree-BWEER	contribute, to
convencer (2)	kohm-behn-SEHR	convince, to
convenir (37)	kohm-beh-NEER	settle (agree on), to
conversación, f.	kohm-behr-sah-S YOHN	conversation
"	"	talk
conversión, f.	kohm-behr-S YOHN	conversion rate (bus.)
convertir (7)	kohm-behr-TEER	convert (transform), to
"	"	turn, to
convicción, f.	kohm-beek-S YOHN	conviction (belief)
convoy, m.	kohm-BOY	convoy (mil.)
cooperación, f.	koh(oh)-peh-rah-S YOHN	cooperation
Copenhague	koh-peh-NAH-gheh	Copenhagen
copia, f.	KOH-p yah	copy (duplicate)
copia (en papel carbón), f.	KOH-p yah (ehm pah-PEHL kahr-VOHN)	carbon copy
copiar (1)	koh-P YAHR	copy (imitate), to
copropietario, m.	koh-proh-p yeh-TAH-r yoh	co-owner (bus.)
coque, m.	KOH-keh	coke
corazón, m.	koh-rah-SOHN	heart
corbata, f.	kohr-VAH-tah	tie (necktie)
corcho, m.	KOHR-choh	cork (stopper)
cordel, m.	kohr-THEHL	string (cord)
cordero, m.	kohr-THEH-roh	lamb
cordial	kohr-TH YAHL	cordial (adj.)
"	"	hearty
cordillera, f.	kohr-thee-YEH-rah	range (of mountains)
cordón, m.	kohr-THOHN	lace (shoelace)
corneta, f.	kohr-NEH-tah	bugle
"	"	horn (mus.)
coro, m.	KOH-roh	choir
corona, f.	koh-ROH-nah	crown (headdress)
"	"	crown (sovereignty)
"	"	wreath
coronar (1)	koh-roh-NAHR	crown, to
coronel, m.	koh-roh-NEHL	colonel
corporal	kohr-poh-RAHL	physical (bodily)
corpulento	kohr-poo-LEHN-toh	stout (corpulent)
correa, f.	koh-RREH-ah	strap
correcto	koh-RREHK-toh	correct
"	"	proper (acceptable)
"	"	right (adj.)
corredor, m.	koh-rreh-THOHR	broker (bus.)
correo, m.	koh-RREH-oh	mail (postal system)
"	"	post office
correo aéreo, m.	koh-RREH-oh ah-EH-reh-oh	air mail
correr (2)	koh-RREHR	run (flow), to
"	"	run (sprint), to
correspondencia, f.	koh-rrehss-pohn-DEHN-s yah	correspondence (letters)
"	"	mail (letters exchanged)
corresponder (2)	koh-rrehss-pohn-DEHR	correspond (agree), to

Spanish	Pronunciation	English
corresponderse con	*koh-rrehss-pohn-*DEHR-*seh kohn*	correspond with (write to), to
correspondiente, *m.*	*koh-rrehss-pohn-*D_YEHN-*teh*	correspondent (letter writer)
corretaje, *m.*	*koh-rreh-*TAH-*heh*	brokerage (fee)
corriente	*koh-*RR_YEHN-*teh*	current (contemporary, *adj.*)
corriente, *f.*	*koh-*RR_YEHN-*teh*	current (of water)
corriente de aire, *f.*	*koh-*RR_YEHN-*teh theh* AH_*ee-reh*	draft (air current)
corriente eléctrica, *f.*	*koh-*RR_YEHN-*teh eh-*LEHK-*tree-kah*	current (of electricity)
corsé, *m.*	*kohr-*SEH	girdle (corset)
cortar (1)	*kohr-*TAHR	cut (divide into parts), to
corte, *f.*	KOHR-*teh*	court (of ruler)
cortejar (1)	*kohr-teh-*HAHR	woo, to
cortés	*kohr-*TEHSS	courteous
"	"	polite
cortesía, *f.*	*kohr-teh-*SEE-*ah*	courtesy
corteza, *f.*	*kohr-*TEH-*sah*	bark (of tree)
"	"	crust
cortina, *f.*	*kohr-*TEE-*nah*	curtain (drape)
"	"	shade (window blind)
corto	KOHR-*toh*	short (brief)
cosa, *f.*	KOH-*sah*	article
"	"	thing (material object)
cosecha, *f.*	*koh-*SEH-*chah*	crop (produce)
"	"	harvest
cosechar (1)	*koh-seh-*CHAHR	reap, to
coser (2)	*koh-*SEHR	sew, to
cosmético, *m.*	*kohz-*MEH-*tee-koh*	cosmetic (*n.*)
costa, *f.*	KOHSS-*tah*	coast (seaboard)
"	"	cost (price)
costar (5)	*kohss-*TAHR	cost, to
Costa Rica	KOHSS-*tah* REE-*kah*	Costa Rica
costilla, *f.*	*kohss-*TEE-*yah*	rib (*anat.*)
costo, *m.*	KOHSS-*toh*	expense (cost)
costoso	*kohss-*TOH-*soh*	costly
"	"	expensive
costumbre, *f.*	*kohss-*TOOM-*breh*	custom (habit)
costura, *f.*	*kohss-*TOO-*rah*	seam (line of stitches)
cotización, *f.*	*koh-tee-sah-*S_YOHN	quotation (price)
cráneo, *m.*	KRAH-*neh-oh*	skull
craso	KRAH-*soh*	gross (flagrant)
creación, *f.*	*kreh-ah-*S_YOHN	creation
crear (1)	*kreh-*AHR	create, to
crecer (11)	*kreh-*SEHR	grow, to
crecer con vigor	*kreh-*SEHR *kohn bee-*GOHR	thrive (grow vigorously), to
crédito, *m.*	KREH-*thee-toh*	credit (*bus.*)
"	"	credit (commendation)
credo, *m.*	KREH-*thoh*	faith (creed)
creer (2)	KR(*eh*)EHR	believe (accept), to
crema de afeitar, *f.*	KREH-*mah theh ah-feh_ee-*TAHR	shaving cream
crepúsculo, *m.*	*kreh-*POO-*skoo-loh*	twilight
criatura, *f.*	*kr_yah-*TOO-*rah*	baby
"	"	creature (living being)
crimen, *m.*	KREE-*mehn*	crime
criminal	*kree-mee-*NAHL	criminal (*adj.*)
crin, *f.*	KREEN	mane (of horse)
crisis, *f.*	KREE-*seess*	crisis
cristal, *m.*	*kreess-*TAHL	crystal (*min.*)
cristiano, *m.*	*kreess-*T_YAH-*noh*	Christian (*n.*)
Cristo, *m.*	KREESS-*toh*	Christ
crítica, *f.*	KREE-*tee-kah*	criticism (censure)
"	"	criticism (judgment)
"	"	review (critique)
crítico, *m.*	KREE-*tee-koh*	critic
cromo, *m.*	KROH-*moh*	chromium
crónica, *f.*	KROH-*nee-kah*	chronicle
crucero, *m.*	*kroo-*SEH-*roh*	cruiser (ship)
crudo	KROO-*thoh*	raw (in natural state)
cruel	*kroo-*EHL	cruel
crujiente	*kroo-*H_YEHN-*teh*	crisp (brittle)
cruz, *f.*	KROOSS	cross (crucifix)
cruzar (1)	*kroo-*SAHR	cross (crossbreed), to
cuadrado	*kwah-*THRAH-*thoh*	square (*adj.*)
cuadrilla, *f.*	*kwah-*TH_REE-*yah*	band (gang)
cuadro, *m.*	KWAH-*throh*	chart (graph)
"	"	picture (depiction)
"	"	scene (dramatic unit)

Spanish	Pronunciation	English
cuadro de vidrio, *m.*	KWAH-*throh theh* VEETH-*r_yoh*	pane, window
cuál	KWAHL	which (*interrog. adj., pron.*)
cual, el (la)	*ehl (lah)* KWAHL	who (*rel. pron.*)
cuáles	KWAH-*lehss*	which (*interrog. adj., pron.*)
cuales, los (las)	*lohss (lahss)* K_WAH-*lehss*	who (*rel. pron.*)
cualquier(a)	*kwahl-*K_YEHR(-*ah*)	any (any one, *adj.*)
cual(es)quier(a)	*kwahl(-lehss)-*K_YEHR(-*ah*)	any (any at all, *adj.*)
"	"	whatever (*adj.*)
cualquiera	*kwahl-*K_YEH-*rah*	anybody (somebody)
cual(es)quier(a) (que)	*kwahl(-lehss)-*K_YEHR(-*ah*) (*keh*)	whichever (*adj.*)
cualquier cosa	*kwahl-*K_YEHR KOH-*sah*	anything (anything whatever)
cualquier cosa que	*kwahl-*K_YEHR KOH-*sah keh*	whatever (*pron.*)
cualquier modo, de	*deh kwahl-*K_YEHR MOH-*thoh*	anyway (in any case)
cualquier persona	*kwahl-*K_YEHR *pehr-*SOH-*nah*	anybody (anybody whosoever)
"	"	anyone (anyone whosoever)
cuando	KWAHN-*doh*	when (any time that, *conj.*)
cuándo	KWAHN-*doh*	when (at what time, *adv.*)
"	"	when (which time, *pron.*)
cuaresma, *f.*	*kwah-*REHSS-*mah*	Lent
cuartel general, *m.*	*kwahr-*TEHL *heh-neh-*RAHL	headquarters
cuarto	KWAHR-*toh*	quarter (one-fourth)
cuarto, *m.*	KWAHR-*toh*	room (of house)
Cuba	KOO-*vah*	Cuba
cubeta, *f.*	*koo-*VEH-*tah*	bucket
cubierta, *f.*	*koo-*V_YEHR-*tah*	deck (of ship)
"	"	hood (*auto.*)
cubo, *m.*	KOO-*voh*	cube (*geom.*)
cuchara, *f.*	*koo-*CHAH-*rah*	spoon (tablespoon)
cucharita, *f.*	*koo-chah-*REE-*tah*	spoon (teaspoon)
cuchichear (1)	*koo-chee-cheh-*AHR	whisper (utter softly), to
cuchicheo, *m.*	*koo-chee-*CHEH-*oh*	whisper
cuchillo, *m.*	*koo-*CHEE-*yoh*	knife
cuclillo, *m.*	*koo-*KLEE-*yoh*	cuckoo (bird)
cuello, *m.*	KWEH-*yoh*	collar
"	"	neck (*anat.*)
cuenco, *m*	KWEHN-*koh*	bowl (dish)
cuenta, *f.*	KWEHN-*tah*	account (bank account)
"	"	account (calculation)
"	"	bead (jewelry)
cuenta corriente, *f.*	KWEHN-*tah koh-*RR_YEHN-*teh*	charge account
cuenta de ahorros, *f.*	KWEHN-*tah theh ah_*OH-*rrohss*	savings account
cuento, *m.*	KWEHN-*toh*	short story
"	"	story (account)
"	"	tale (narrative)
cuento de hadas, *m.*	KWEHN-*toh theh* AH-*thass*	fairy tale
cuerda, *f.*	KWEHR-*thah*	cord (rope)
"	"	line (cord)
cuerno, *m.*	KWEHR-*noh*	horn (*anat.*)
cuero, *m.*	KWEH-*roh*	leather (*n.*)
cuerpo, *m.*	KWEHR-*poh*	body (*anat.*)
cuervo, *m.*	KWEHR-*voh*	crow (bird)
cueva, *f.*	KWEH-*vah*	cave
cuidado, *m.*	*kwee-*THAH-*thoh*	care (concern)
cuidadoso	*kwee-thah-*THOH-*soh*	careful (cautious)
cuidar (1)	*kwee-*THAHR	nurse (give treatment to), to
culebra, *f.*	*koo-*LEH-*vrah*	snake
culpa, *f.*	KOOL-*pah*	blame
"	"	fault (cause for blame)
"	"	guilt
culpable	*kool-*PAH-*vleh*	guilty
culpar (1)	*kool-*PAHR	blame, to
cultivar (1)	*kool-tee-*VAHR	cultivate (till), to
"	"	grow, to

Spanish	Pronunciation	English
cultura,*f.*	*kool*-TOO-*rah*	culture
cumbre,*f.*	KOOM-*breh*	crest
"	"	peak (mountain top)
		summit
cumpleaños,*m.*	*koom-pleh*_AH-*n yohss*	birthday
cumplimiento,*m.*	*koom-plee*-M_YEHN-*toh*	compliment
cumplir (3)	*koom*-PLEER	accomplish, to
"	"	comply (acquiesce), to
		to
"	"	fulfill, to
cuna,*f.*	KOO-*nah*	cradle
cuñada,*f.*	*koo*-N_YAH-*thah*	sister-in-law
cuñado,*m.*	*koo*-N_YAH-*thoh*	brother-in-law
cuota,*f.*	KWOH-*tah*	quota
cupón,*m.*	*koo*-POHN	coupon (detachable certificate)
cúpula,*f.*	KOO-*poo-lah*	dome (cupola)
curación,*f.*	*koo-rah*-S_YOHN	cure (healing)
curador,*m.*	*koo-rah*-THOHR	curator
curar (1)	*koo*-RAHR	cure, to
"	"	dress, to (*med.*)
"	"	heal, to
curiosidad,*f.*	*koo-r_yoh-see*-THAHTH	curiosity (inquisitiveness)
curioso	*koo*-R_YOH-*soh*	curious (inquisitive)
curva,*f.*	KOOR-*vah*	curve
custodia,*f.*	*kooss*-TOH-*th_yah*	care (custody)
custodiar (1)	*kooss-toh*-TH_YAHR	guard (watch over), to
cutis,*m.*	KOO-*teess*	skin (human skin)
cuyo, cuya	KOO-*yoh,* KOO-*yah*	whose (*rel. pron.*)
cuyos, cuyas	KOO-*yohss,* KOO-*yahss*	whose (*rel. pron.*)
dados,*m.pl.*	DAH-*thohss*	dice (marked cubes)
dama,*f.*	DAH-*mah*	lady
dañar (1)	*dah*-N_YAHR	damage (injure), to
"	"	harm, to
"	"	spoil (mar), to
danés, -nesa	*dah*-NEHSS, -NEH-*sah*	Danish (*adj.*)
daño,*m.*	DAH-*n_yoh*	damage (injury)
"	"	mischief (harm)
daños y perjuicios,*m.pl.*	DAH-*n_yoh see pehr*-HWEE-*s_yohss*	damages (indemnification)
Danubio	*dah*-NOO-*v_yoh*	Danube
dar (21)	DAHR	give, to
dar brillo	*dahr* BREE-*yoh*	shine (polish), to
dar de comer	DAHR *theh koh*-MEHR	feed (give food to), to
dar de puñaladas	DAHR *theh poo-n_yah*-LAH-*thahss*	stab, to
dar derecho	DAHR *deh*-REH-*choh*	entitle (give a right to), to
dar entrada	DAHR *ehn*-TRAH-*thah*	admit (permit to enter), to
dar gracias a	*dahr* GRAH-*s_yahss ah*	thank, to
dar instrucciones	DAHR *een-strook*-S_YOH-*nehss*	instruct (direct), to
dar la bienvenida a	DAHR *lah b_yehn-veh*-NEE-*thah ah*	welcome (receive hospitably), to
dar latigazos	DAHR *lah-tee*-GAH-*sohss*	lash (whip), to
dar por sentado	DAHR *pohr sehn*-TAH-*thoh*	assume (take for granted), to
dar principio a	DAHR *preen*-SEE-*p_yoh ah*	launch (start), to
darse cuenta de	DAHR-*seh* KWEHN-*tah theh*	realize (recognize), to
dar un paso	DAHR *oon* PAH-*soh*	step, to
dar vueltas	*dahr* VWEHL-*tahss*	whirl (make revolve), to
dátil,*m.*	DAH-*teel*	date (fruit)
de	*deh*	from
"	"	of
debajo de	*deh*-VAH-*hoh theh*	below (less than, *prep.*)
"	"	below (lower than, *prep.*)
"	"	underneath (*prep.*)
debate,*m.*	*deh*-VAH-*teh*	debate
deber,*m.*	*deh*-VEHR	duty (obligation)
deber (2)	*deh*-VEHR	must (*v.*)
"	"	ought (*v.*)
"	"	owe, to
"	"	should (*v.*)
debido	*deh*-VEE-*thoh*	due (proper)
débil	DEH-*veel*	delicate (sickly)
"	"	frail (fragile)
"	"	weak

Spanish	Pronunciation	English
debilidad,*f.*	*deh-vee-lee*-THATH	weakness
debilitar (1)	*deh-vee-lee*-TAHR	weaken (make weak), to
decadencia,*f.*	*deh-kah*-THEHN-*s_yah*	decay
"	"	decline (deterioration)
decente	*deh*-SEHN-*teh*	decent (respectable)
decepción,*f.*	*deh-sehp*-S_YOHN	disappointment
decepcionar (1)	*deh-sehp-s_yoh*-NAHR	disappoint, to
decidir (3)	*deh-see*-THEER	decide (make up one's mind), to
"	"	determine, to
decir (22)	*deh*-SEER	say, to
		tell (inform), to
decisión,*f.*	*deh-see*-S_YOHN	decision (judgment)
declaración,*f.*	*deh-klah-rah*-S_YOHN	declaration (announcement)
"	"	statement
declarar (1)	*deh-klah*-RAHR	declare, to
"	"	pronounce, to
"	"	state (say), to
declararse	*deh-klah*-RAHR-*seh*	propose (offer marriage), to
declararse en huelga	*dehk-lah*-RAHR-*seh ehn* WEHL-*gah*	strike (stop work), to
declinar (1)	*deh-klee*-NAHR	decline (deteriorate), to
decoración,*f.*	*deh-koh-rah*-S_YOHN	decoration
decorar (1)	*deh-koh*-RAHR	decorate (adorn), to
decreto,*m.*	*deh*-KREH-*toh*	decree (edict)
dedicarse (1)	*deh-thee*-KAHR-*seh*	devote oneself, to
dedo,*m.*	DEH-*thoh*	finger
dedo del pie,*m.*	DEH-*thoh thehl* P_YEH	toe
defecto,*m.*	*deh*-FEHK-*toh*	defect (flaw)
defender (4)	*deh-fehn*-DEHR	defend (protect), to
defensa,*f.*	*deh*-FEHN-*sah*	defense
déficit,*m.*	DEH-*fee-seet*	deficit (*bus.*)
definido	*deh-fee*-NEE-*thoh*	definite
definir (3)	*deh-fee*-NEER	define, to
deformarse (1)	*deh-fohr*-MAHR-*seh*	warp (become misshapen), to
dejar (1)	*deh*-HAHR	leave (let remain), to
"	"	let (permit), to
"	"	quit (stop), to
dejar caer	*deh*-HAHR *kah*-EHR	drop (let fall), to
dejar de	*deh*-HAHR *theh*	cease (desist), to
"	"	fail (neglect) to, to
"	"	miss (fail to do), to
"	"	stop, to
delantal,*m.*	*deh-lahn*-TAHL	apron (garment)
delante	*deh*-LAHN-*teh*	ahead (in front)
delante de	*deh*-LAHN-*teh theh*	before (in front of, *prep.*)
delegado,*m.*	*deh-leh*-GAH-*thoh*	delegate
deleitar (1)	*deh-lay*-TAHR	delight (give pleasure to), to
deleite,*m.*	*deh*-LAY-*teh*	delight
deleitoso	*deh-lay*-TOH-*soh*	delightful
deletrear (1)	*deh-leh-treh*-AHR	spell, to
delgado	*dehl*-GAH-*thoh*	slender (lean)
"	"	thin (not thick)
deliberado	*deh-lee-veh*-RAH-*thoh*	deliberate (intentional)
delicado	*deh-lee*-KAH-*thoh*	dainty
"	"	delicate
delicioso	*deh-lee*-S_YOH-*soh*	delicious
demanda,*f.*	*deh*-MAHN-*dah*	demand (*econ.*)
demandar (1)	*deh-mahn*-DAHR	sue (bring action against), to
demasiado	*deh-mah*-S_YAH-*thoh*	too (overly)
democracia,*f.*	*deh-moh*-KRAH-*s_yah*	democracy
demócrata,*m.,f.*	*deh*-MOH-*krah-tah*	democrat
democrático	*deh-moh*-KRAH-*tee-koh*	democratic
demorar (1)	*deh-moh*-RAHR	delay (retard)
demorarse	*deh-moh*-RAHR-*seh*	linger (tarry), to
demostración,*f.*	*deh-mohss-trah*-S_YOHN	demonstration (proof)
demostrar (5)	*deh-mohss*-TRAHR	demonstrate (show), to
denso	DEHN-*soh*	dense
dentista,*m.*	*dehn*-TEESS-*tah*	dentist
dentro	DEHN-*troh*	inside (within, *adv.*)
dentro de	DEHN-*troh-theh*	inside (*prep.*)
"	"	within (*prep.*)
"	"	within (in less time than, *prep.*)

Spanish	Pronunciation	English
departamento,*m.*	*deh-pahr-tah-*MEHN-*toh*	apartment
"	"	department (administrative unit)
depender de (2)	*deh-pehn-*DEHR *theh*	depend (be contingent) on, to
dependiente	*deh-pehn-*D_YEHN-*teh*	dependent (reliant)
dependiente,*m.*	*deh-pehn-*D_YEHN-*teh*	clerk (salesperson)
deporte,*m.*	*deh-*POHR-*teh*	sport (game)
depositador,*m.*	*deh-poh-see-tah-*THOHR	depositor (*fin.*)
depositar (1)	*deh-poh-see-*TAHR	deposit, to (*fin.*)
depósito,*m.*	*deh-*POH-*see-toh*	deposit (money deposited)
"	"	reservoir (water reserve)
depresión,*f.*	*deh-preh-*S_YOHN	depression (*econ.*)
derecha, a la	*ah lah theh-*REH-*chah*	right (on the right, *adj.*)
derecha, a la	*ah lah theh-*REH-*chah*	right (to the right, *adv.*)
derecho	*deh-*REH-*choh*	right (right-hand side)
"	"	straight (not crooked, *adj.*)
derecho,*m.*	*deh-*REH-*choh*	right (claim)
derecho escrito,*m.*	*deh-*REH-*choh ehss-*KREE-*toh*	law (statute)
derechos,*m.pl.*	*deh-*REH-*chohss*	royalty (fee)
derechos de aduana,*m.pl.*	*deh-*REH-*chohss theh ah-*THWAH-*nah*	customs (tax)
"	"	duty
derechos de enseñanza,*m.pl.*	*deh-*REH-*chohss theh ehn-sehn-*YAHN-*sah*	tuition (school fee)
derivado,*m.*	*deh-ree-*VAH-*thoh*	by-product
derivar (1)	*deh-ree-*VAHR	derive (get), to
derramar (1)	*deh-rrah-*MAHR	spill (let pour out), to
derretirse (9)	*deh-rreh-*TEER-*seh*	melt (become liquid), to
derrochar (1)	*deh-rroh-*CHAHR	waste (squander), to
derroche,*m.*	*deh-*RROH-*cheh*	waste (squandering)
derrota,*f.*	*deh-*RROH-*tah*	defeat
desafiar (1)	*deh-sah-*F_YAHR	defy, to
desafío,*m.*	*deh-sah-*FEE-*oh*	challenge
desagradable	*deh-sah-grah-*THAH-*vleh*	disagreeable
"	"	unpleasant
desaguar (1)	*deh-sah-*GWAHR	drain (make dry), to
desagüe,*m.*	*deh-*SAH-*gweh*	drain (conduit)
desaliento,*m.*	*deh-sah-*L_YEHN-*toh*	dismay
desanimar (1)	*deh-sah-nee-*MAHR	discourage (dishearten), to
desaparecer (11)	*deh-sah-pah-reh-*SEHR	disappear, to
desarrollar (1)	*deh-sah-rroh-*YAHR	develop, to
desarrollarse	*deh-sah-rroh-*YAHR-*seh*	grow up (mature), to
desarrollo,*m.*	*deh-sah-*RROH-*yoh*	development
"	"	growth
desastre,*m.*	*deh-*SAHSS-*treh*	disaster
desayuno,*m.*	*deh-sah-*YOO-*noh*	breakfast
descansar (1)	*dehss-kahn-*SAHR	rest (repose), to
descanso,*m.*	*dehss-*KAHN-*soh*	rest (repose)
descargar (1)	*dehss-kahr-*GAHR	unload, to
descender (4)	*dehss-sehn-*DEHR	descend (move downward), to
descendiente,*m.*	*dehss-sehn-*D_YEHN-*teh*	descendant (offspring)
descolorar (1)	*dehss-koh-loh-*RAHR	fade (lose color), to
desconcierto,*m.*	*dehss-kohn-*S_YEHR-*toh*	embarrassment
desconocido	*dehss-koh-noh-*SEE-*thoh*	unknown
desconocido,*m.*	*dehss-koh-noh-*SEE-*thoh*	stranger (unknown person)
descontar (5)	*dehss-kohn-*TAHR	deduct, to
"	"	discount, to (*bus.*)
descortezar (1)	*dehss-kohr-teh-*SAHR	peel (take skin from), to
describir	*dehss-kree-*VEER	describe (portray), to
descripción,*f.*	*dehss-kreep-*S_YOHN	description (account)
descubrimiento,*m.*	*dehss-koo-vree-*M_YEHN-*toh*	discovery
descubrir (3)	*dehss-koo-*VREER	betray (reveal), to
"	"	detect, to
"	"	discover, to
descuento,*m.*	*dehss-*KWEHN-*toh*	discount (*n.*)
descuidado	*dehss-kwee-*THAH-*thoh*	careless (negligent)
descuido,*m.*	*dehss-*KWEE-*thoh*	failure (neglect)
"	"	oversight (error)
desde	DEHSS-*deh*	since (after, *prep.*)
desde entonces	DEHSS-*deh ehn-*TOHN-*sehss*	since (from then to now, *adv.*)
desdén,*m.*	*dehss-*DEHN	scorn
desdeñar (1)	*dehss-dehn-*YAHR	scorn (despise), to
deseable	*deh-seh-*AH-*vleh*	desirable
desear (1)	*deh-seh-*AHR	desire (long for), to
"	"	wish (desire on behalf of), to
"	"	wish for, to
desembarcar (1)	*deh-sehm-bahr-*KAHR	land (from a ship), to
desembolso,*m.*	*deh-sehm-*BOHL-*soh*	disbursement (*bus.*)
desemejante	*deh-seh-meh-*HAHN-*teh*	unlike (*adj.*)
desempleo,*m.*	*deh-sehm-*PLEH-*oh*	unemployment
deseo,*m.*	*deh-*SEH-*oh*	desire
"	"	wish
deseoso	*deh-seh-*OH-*soh*	anxious (wanting very much)
"	"	eager
desesperación,*f.*	*deh-sehss-peh-rah-*S_YOHN	despair (hopelessness)
desesperado	*deh-sehss-peh-*RAH-*thoh*	desperate
desesperarse (1)	*deh-sehss-peh-*RAHR-*seh*	despair, to
desfigurar (1)	*dehss-fee-goo-*RAHR	mar (disfigure), to
desfile,*m.*	*dehss-*FEE-*leh*	parade (procession)
desgracia,*f.*	*dehss-*GRAH-*s_yah*	misfortune
desgraciado	*dehss-grah-*S_YAH-*thoh*	unlucky
deshelarse (4)	*dehss-eh-*LAHR-*seh*	thaw, to
deshonra,*f.*	*deh-*SOHN-*rah*	dishonor
desierto,*m.*	*deh-*S_YEHR-*toh*	desert
desigual	*deh-see-*GWAHL	unequal
deslealtad,*f.*	*dehz-leh-ahl-*TATH	disloyalty
deslizar (1)	*dehz-lee-*SAHR	slip (slide), to
deslizarse	*dehz-lee-*SAHR-*seh*	glide, to
"	"	slide, to
deslumbrar (1)	*dehz-loom-*BRAHR	dazzle, to
desmayarse (1)	*dehz-mah-*YAHR-*seh*	faint, to
desmayo,*m.*	*dehz-*MAH-*yoh*	faint (swoon, *n.*)
desmenuzar (1)	*dehz-meh-noo-*SAHR	crumble, to
desnudar (1)	*dehz-noo-*THAHR	strip (denude), to
desnudo	*dehz-*NOO-*thoh*	bare (nude)
"	"	naked
desobedecer (11)	*deh-soh-veh-theh-*SEHR	disobey, to
desocupado	*deh-soh-koo-*PAH-*thoh*	unemployed
desorden,*m.*	*deh-*SOHR-*thehn*	disorder (confusion)
despachar (1)	*dehss-pah-*CHAHR	ship (send goods), to
despacho de aduana,*m.*	*dehss-*PAH-*choh theh ah-*THWAH-*nah*	clearance (customs clearance)
despecho,*m.*	*dehss-*PEH-*choh*	spite (ill will)
despecho de, a	*ah dehss-*PEH-*choh theh*	despite (*prep.*)
despedida,*f.*	*dehss-peh-*THEE-*thah*	discharge (dismissal)
despedir (9)	*dehss-peh-*THEER	dismiss (discharge), to
despejado	*dehss-peh-*HAH-*thoh*	fair (not cloudy)
desperdicios,*m.pl.*	*dehss-pehr-*THEE-*s_yohss*	garbage
despertar (4)	*dehss-pehr-*TAHR	awaken (make awaken), to
"	"	rouse, to
"	"	wake (make awaken), to
despertarse	*dehss-pehr-*TAHR-*seh*	awaken (rouse oneself), to
"	"	wake (rouse oneself), to
despierto	*dehss-*P_YEHR-*toh*	awake
despreciar (1)	*dehss-preh-*S_YAHR	despise, to
"	"	neglect (slight), to
desprecio,*m.*	*dehss-*PREH-*s_yoh*	contempt (scorn)
después	*dehss-*PWEHSS	afterward (later)
después de	*dehss-*PWEHSS *theh*	after (*prep.*)
después de eso	*dehss-*PWEHSS *theh* EH-*soh*	thereafter
después (de) que	*dehss-*PWEHSS (*theh*) *keh*	after (*conj.*)
destello,*m.*	*dehss-*TEH-*yoh*	flash (burst of light)
desterrar (4)	*dehss-teh-*RRAHR	banish (exile), to
destierro,*m.*	*dehss-*T_YEH-*rroh*	exile (banishment)
destinatario,*m.*	*dehss-tee-nah-*TAH-*r_yoh*	addressee
destino,*m.*	*dehss-*TEE-*noh*	destination
"	"	destiny
"	"	fate
destornillador,*m.*	*dehss-tohr-nee-yah-*THOHR	screw driver
destreza,*f.*	*dehss-*TREH-*sah*	dexterity
"	"	skill (proficiency)
destrozos,*m.pl.*	*dehss-*TROH-*sohss*	wreck (ruins)

Spanish	Pronunciation	English
destrucción, f.	dehss-trook-S̲ YOHN	destruction (demolition)
destructor, m.	dehss-trook-TOHR	destroyer (ship)
destruir (14)	dehss-troo_EER	destroy (demolish), to
desunir (3)	deh-soo-NEER	sever, to
desvalido	dehz-vah-LEE-thoh	helpless
desván, m.	dehz-VAHN	attic
desvanecerse (11)	dehz-vah-neh-SEHR-seh	fade (disappear), to; vanish, to
desvariar (1)	dehz-vah-R̲ YAHR	rave (rant), to
desventurado	dehz-vehn-too-RAH-thoh	unfortunate
desviación, f.	dehz-v̲ yah-S̲ YOHN	departure (deviation); detour
desviarse (1)	dehz-V̲ YAHR-seh	deviate (diverge), to
detalle, m.	deh-TAH-yeh	detail (minor item); item (detail); particular (n.)
detallista, m.	deh-tah-YEESS-tah	retailer (bus.)
detener (35)	deh-teh-NEHR	arrest (halt), to; stop (make halt), to
determinar (1)	deh-tehr-mee-NAHR	determine (ascertain), to
detrás	deh-TRAHSS	behind (in the rear, adv.)
detrás de	deh-TRAHZ theh	behind (prep.)
deuda, f.	DEH̲ oo-thah	debt
deudor, m.	deh̲ oo-THOHR	debtor (bus.)
de un lado a atro	deh̲ oon LAH-thoh̲ ah̲ OH-troh	across (from side to side)
de veras	deh VEH-rahss	indeed (adv.)
devoción, f.	deh-voh-S̲ YOHN	devotion (loyal attachment)
devolver (5)	deh-vohl-VEHR	return (give back), to
devorar (1)	deh-voh-RAHR	devour (eat), to
día, m.	DEE-ah	day
diabetes, f.	d̲ yah-BEH-tehss	diabetes
diablo, m.	D̲ YAH-vloh	devil
día de año nuevo, m.	DEE-ah theh AH-n̲ yoh N̲ WEH-voh	New Year's Day
día festivo, m.	DEE-ah fehss-TEE-voh	holiday
diamante, m.	d̲ yah-MAHN-teh	diamond (gem)
diámetro, m.	D̲ YAH-meh-troh	diameter
diario	D̲ YAH-r̲ yoh	daily (adj.)
dibujar (1)	dee-voo-HAHR	draw (sketch), to
dibujo, m.	dee-VOO-hoh	drawing (sketch)
diccionario, m.	deek-s̲ yoh-NAH-r̲ yoh	dictionary
dictar (1)	deek-TAHR	dictate (for transcription), to
diente, m.	D̲ YEHN-teh	tooth
diente de león, m.	D̲ YEHN-teh theh leh̲-OHN	dandelion
dieta, f.	D̲ YEH-tah	diet (restricted allowance of food)
diferencia, f.	dee-feh-REHN-s̲ yah	difference (dissimilarity)
diferenciar(se) (1)	dee-feh-rehn-S̲ YAHR-(-seh)	differ (be unlike), to
diferente	dee-feh-REHN-teh	different (unlike)
diferir (7)	dee-feh-REER	delay (postpone), to; vary (differ), to
difícil	dee-FEE-seel	difficult; hard
dificultad, f.	dee-fee-kool-TAHTH	difficulty (hardness)
difteria, f.	deef-TEH-r̲ yah	diphtheria
difunto	dee-FOON-toh	late (deceased, adj.)
digerir (7)	dee-heh-REER	digest, to
dignidad, f.	deeg-nee-THAHTH	dignity
digno	DEEG-noh	worthy (deserving)
digno de confianza	DEEG-noh theh kohn-F̲ YAHN-sah	reliable
dilatar (1)	dee-lah-TAHR	expand (make larger), to
diligencia, f.	dee-lee-HEHN-s̲ yah	diligence
diligente	dee-lee-HEHN-teh	diligent
diminuto	dee-mee-NOO-toh	tiny
dimitir (3)	dee-mee-TEER	resign (tender resignation), to
Dinamarca	dee-nah-MAHR-kah	Denmark
dinero, m.	dee-NEH-roh	money
Dios, m.	D̲ YOHSS	God
dirección, f.	dee-rehk-S̲ YOHN	address (postal directions); direction (course); leadership (authority); management (administration)
directamente	dee-rehk-tah-MEHN-teh	straight (directly, adv.)
directo	dee-REHK-toh	direct (immediate)
director, m.	dee-rehk-TOHR	conductor (mus.); director
dirigir (3)	dee-ree-HEER	control, to; direct (aim), to; direct (manage), to; manage (administer), to
dirigir (una radiodifusión)	dee-ree-HEER (oo-nah RRAH-th̲ yoh-thee-foo-S̲ YOHN)	beam (direct, rad.), to
disciplina, f.	deess-see-PLEE-nah	discipline (training)
disco, m.	DEESS-koh	record (disk)
disco graduado, m.	DEES-koh grah-TH̲ WAH-thoh	dial (graduated face)
discrecional	deess-kreh-s̲ yoh-NAHL	optional
disculparse (1)	deess-kool-PAHR-seh	apologize, to
discurso, m.	deess-KOOR-soh	address; speech
discusión, f.	deess-koo-S̲ YOHN	discussion
discutir (3)	deess-koo-TEER	discuss, to
diseño, m.	dee-SEH-n̲ yoh	design; pattern
disentería, f.	dee-sehn-teh-REE-ah	dysentery
disentir (7)	dee-sehn-TEER	disagree (differ), to
disfraz, m.	deess-FRAHSS	disguise
disimular una sonrisa (1)	dee-see-moo-LAHR oo-nah sohn-REE-sah	grin, to
disminución, f.	deez-mee-noo-S̲ YOHN	decrease
disminuir (14)	deez-mee-NWEER	diminish (make smaller), to; lessen, to; lower (decrease), to
disolver (5)	dee-sohl-VEHR	dissolve
disparate, m.	deess-pah-RAH-teh	blunder; nonsense
disponible	deess-poh-NEE-vleh	available
disposición, f.	deess-poh-see-S̲ YOHN	disposition (arrangement); disposition (disposal)
dispositivo, m.	deess-poh-see-TEE-voh	device (apparatus)
dispuesto	deess-PWESS-toh	willing (favorably disposed)
dispuesto a	deess-PWEHSS-toh̲ ah	apt to (prone to)
disputa, f.	deess-POO-tah	argument; dispute
disputar (1)	deess-poo-TAHR	contest (dispute), to; dispute (oppose by argument), to
distancia, f.	deess-TAHN-s̲ yah	distance
distinción, f.	deess-teen-S̲ YOHN	distinction
distinguido	deess-teen-GHEE-thoh	distinguished (notable)
distinguir (3)	deess-teen-GHEER	distinguish (differentiate), to
distinto	deess-TEEN-toh	distinct (different)
distraer (36)	deess-trah-EHR	distract (divert), to
distribución, f.	deess-tree-voo-S̲ YOHN	distribution (bus.)
diversión, f.	dee-vehr-S̲ YOHN	amusement; fun
divertir (7)	dee-vehr-TEER	amuse, to; entertain (amuse), to
dividendo, m.	dee-vee-THEHN-doh	dividend (bus.)
dividir (3)	dee-vee-THEER	divide (make separate), to; divide, to (arith.)
dividirse	dee-vee-THEER-seh	divide (become separate), to
divino	dee-VEE-noh	divine (adj.)
división, f.	dee-vee-S̲ YOHN	division
divorcio, m.	dee-VOHR-s̲ yoh	divorce (law)
doblar (1)	doh-VLAHR	bend (make bend), to; fold (lap over), to
doblarse	doh-VLAHR-seh	stoop (bend forward), to
doble	DOH-vleh	double (adj.)
docena, f.	doh-SEH-nah	dozen
doctrina, f.	dohk-TREE-nah	doctrine
documento, m.	doh-koo-MEHN-toh	document
dolerle (a uno) (5)	doh-LEHR-leh (ah oo-noh)	ache, to; hurt (be painful), to
dolor, m.	doh-LOHR	ache; pain

Spanish	Pronunciation	English
dolor de cabeza,*m.*	*doh*-LOHR *theh kah*-VEH-*sah*	headache
dolor de diente,*m.*	*doh*-LOHR *theh* TH YEHN-*teh*	toothache
dolor de oído,*m.*	*doh*-LOHR *theh oh* EE-*thoh*	earache
dolorido	*doh-loh*-REE-*thoh*	sore (*adj.*)
doloroso	*doh-loh*-ROH-*soh*	painful
domesticado	*doh-mehss-tee*-KAH-*thoh*	tame
doméstico	*doh*-MEHSS-*tee-koh*	domestic (household, *adj.*)
Domingo de Ramos,*m.*	*doh*-MEEN-*goh theh* RAH-*mohss*	Palm Sunday
dominar (1)	*doh-mee*-NAHR	master (learn), to
dominio,*m.*	*doh*-MEE-*n yoh*	dominion
"	"	rule (political control)
donaire,*m.*	*doh*-NAH EE-*reh*	grace (gracefulness)
donar (1)	*doh*-NAHR	donate, to
doncella,*f.*	*dohn*-SEH-*yah*	lass
donde	DOHN-*deh*	where (in, at the place that, *conj.*)
dónde	DOHN-*deh*	where (in, at what place, *adv.*)
dondequiera	*dohn-deh*-K YEH-*rah*	anywhere (wheresoever)
dondequiera que	*dohn-deh*-K YEH-*rah keh*	wherever (no matter where)
dondequiera que, a-, en-	*ah-, ehn- dohn-deh-*K YEH-*rah keh*	wherever (at, in whatever place)
dorado	*doh*-RAH-*thoh*	golden
dormido	*dohr*-MEE-*thoh*	asleep (sleeping)
dormir (8)	*dohr*-MEER	sleep, to
dorso,*m.*	DOHR-*soh*	back (reverse side)
dos, los	*lohz* THOHSS	both (*adj.*)
dosis,*f.*	DOH-*seess*	dose (*med.*)
dos puntos,*m.pl.*	DOHSS POON-*tohss*	colon (*punct.*)
dos veces	DOHSS VEH-*sehss*	twice
dragón,*m.*	*drah*-GOHN	dragon
drama,*m.*	DRAH-*mah*	drama
droga,*f.*	DROH-*gah*	drug (medicine)
ducha,*f.*	DOO-*chah*	shower (bath)
duda,*f.*	DOO-*thah*	doubt
dudar (1)	*doo*-THAHR	doubt (be uncertain about), to
"	"	question, to
dudoso	*doo*-THOH-*soh*	doubtful
dulce,*m.*	DOOL-*seh*	candy
"	"	sweet (pleasant tasting)
dulzura,*f.*	*dool*-SOO-*rah*	sweetness
duplicado,*m.*	*doo-plee*-KAH-*thoh*	duplicate (copy, *n.*)
duración,*f.*	*doo-rah*-S YOHN	duration
durante	*doo*-RAHN-*teh*	during
durante todo	*doo*-RAHN-*teh* TOH-*thoh*	throughout (from start to finish of, *prep.*)
durar (1)	*doo*-RAHR	last (continue), to
"	"	last (withstand use), to
duro	DOO-*roh*	hard (not soft)
"	"	tough (resistant)
e	EH	and
echar al correo (1)	*eh*-CHAHR *ahl koh-*RREH-*oh*	mail (post), to
echar de menos	*eh*-CHAHR *theh*-MEH-*nohss*	miss (feel the loss of), to
echar una mirada	*eh*-CHAHR OO-*nah mee-*RAH-*thah*	glance, to
echar un chisquete	*eh*-CHAHR *oon cheess-*KEH-*teh*	squirt, to
eco,*m.*	EH-*koh*	echo
economía,*f.*	*eh-koh-noh*-MEE-*ah*	economics
"	"	economy (thrift)
económico	*eh-koh*-NOH-*mee-koh*	economical (thrifty)
Ecuador, el	*eh leh-kwah*-THOHR	Ecuador
edad,*f.*	*eh*-THAHTH	age (accumulated years)
edición,*f.*	*eh-thee*-S YOHN	edition
edificar (1)	*eh-thee-fee*-KAHR	build, to
edificio,*m.*	*eh-thee*-FEE-*s yoh*	building
Edimburgo	*eh-theem*-BOOR-*goh*	Edinburgh
editor,*m.*	*eh-thee*-TOHR	publisher
educación,*f.*	*eh-thoo-kah*-S YOHN	education (schooling process)
educar (1)	*eh-thoo*-KAHR	educate, to
efectivo,*m.*	*eh-fehk*-TEE-*voh*	cash (money)
efectivo	*eh-fehk*-TEE-*voh*	effective (effectual)
efecto,*m.*	*eh*-FEHK-*toh*	effect
eficaz	*eh-fee*-KAHSS	efficient (producing desired results)
eficiente	*eh-fee*-S YEHN-*teh*	efficient (competent)
egipcio	*eh*-HEEP-*s yoh*	Egyptian (*adj.*)
Egipto,*m.*	*eh*-HEEP-*toh*	Egypt
egoísta	*eh*-GWEESS-*tah*	selfish
ejecución,*f.*	*eh-heh-koo*-S YOHN	performance (action)
ejecutar (1)	*eh-heh-koo*-TAHR	execute (carry out), to
"	"	execute (put to death), to
"	"	perform (do), to
ejecutivo	*eh-heh-koo*-TEE-*voh*	executive (*adj.*)
ejemplar,*m.*	*eh-hehm*-PLAHR	copy (of a publication)
ejemplificar (1)	*eh-hehm-plee-fee*-KAHR	illustrate (exemplify), to
ejemplo,*m.*	*eh*-HEHM-*ploh*	example
"	"	illustration (example)
"	"	instance (example)
eje radiodirector,*m.*	EH-*heh rah-th yoh-thee-rehk*-TOHR	beam (radio signal)
ejercicio,*m.*	*eh-hehr*-SEE-*s yoh*	exercise (drill)
"	"	exercise (physical exertion)
ejercitar (1)	*eh-hehr-see*-TAHR	exercise (employ), to
ejército,*m.*	*eh*-HEHR-*see-toh*	army
él	EHL	he
"	"	it
el	EHL	the
él, a	*ah* EHL	(to) him
él, de	*deh* EHL	his
elástico	*eh*-LAHSS-*tee-koh*	elastic (springy)
elección,*f.*	*eh-lehk*-S YOHN	election
electricidad,*f.*	*eh-lehk-tree-see*-THAHTH	electricity
eléctrico	*eh*-LEHK-*tree-koh*	electric
electrónica,*f.*	*eh-lehk*-TROH-*nee-kah*	electronics
elefante,*m.*	*eh-leh*-FAHN-*teh*	elephant
elegante	*eh-leh*-GAHN-*teh*	smart (chic)
elegir (9)	*eh-leh*-HEER	elect, to
elemento,*m.*	*eh-leh*-MEHN-*toh*	element
elevado	*eh-leh*-VAH-*thoh*	lofty (high)
elevar (1)	*eh-leh*-VAHR	elevate (lift up), to
elevarse	*eh-leh*-VAHR-*seh*	rise (ascend), to
eliminar (1)	*eh-lee-mee*-NAHR	eliminate, to
ella	EH-*yah*	it
"	"	she
ella, a	*ah* EH-*yah*	(to) her
ella, de	*deh* EH-*yah*	her
"	"	hers
ella misma	EH-*yah* MEEZ-*mah*	herself
"	"	itself
ellas	EH-*yahss*	they
ellas mismas	EH-*yahss* MEEZ-*mahss*	themselves
ello	EH-*yoh*	it
ellos	EH-*yohss*	they
ellos (ellas), a	*ah* EH-*yohss* (EH-*yahss*)	(to) them
ellos (ellas), de	DEH EH-*yohss* (EH-*yahss*)	their
"	"	theirs
ellos mismos	EH-*yohss* MEEZ-*mohss*	themselves
él mismo	EHL MEEZ-*moh*	himself
elocuente	*eh-loh*-KWEHN-*teh*	eloquent
elogiar (1)	*eh-loh*-H YAHR	praise, to
embajador,*m.*	*ehm-bah-hah*-THOHR	ambassador
embalaje,*m.*	*ehm-bah*-LAH-*heh*	packing (*n.*)
embarcación,*f.*	*ehm-bahr-kah*-S YOHN	craft (vessel)
embargo,*m.*	*ehm*-BAHR-*goh*	attachment (legal seizure)
embarque,*m.*	*ehm*-BAHR-*keh*	shipment (goods)
embotado	*ehm-boh*-TAH-*thoh*	blunt
"	"	dull
embrague,*m.*	*ehm*-BRAH-*geh*	clutch (automotive device)
embriaguez,*f.*	*ehm-br yah*-GEHSS	intoxication (drunkenness)
embromar (1)	*ehm-broh*-MAHR	tease, to
embuste,*m.*	*ehm*-BOOSS-*teh*	lie
embustero,*m.*	*ehm-booss-teh*-roh	liar
emergencia,*f.*	*eh-mehr*-HEHN-*s yah*	emergency (*n.*)
emoción,*f.*	*eh-moh*-S YOHN	emotion
empacar (1)	*ehm-pah*-KAHR	pack (wrap), to
empapar (1)	*ehm-pah*-PAHR	soak (saturate), to

Spanish	Pronunciation	English
emparedado, *m.*	*ehm-pah-reh-*THAH-*thoh*	sandwich
empeñar (1)	*ehm-peh-*N_YAHR	pawn, to
empeñarse	*ehm-peh-*N_YAHR-*seh*	endeavor, to
empeño, *m.*	*ehm-*PEH-*n_yoh*	determination (fixed intent)
"	"	endeavor
emperador, *m.*	*ehm-peh-rah-*THOHR	emperor
emperatriz, *f.*	*ehm-peh-rah-*TREESS	empress
empezar (4)	*ehm-peh-*SAHR	begin (come into being), to
empinado	*ehm-pee-*NAH-*thoh*	steep (*adj.*)
empleado, *m.*	*ehm-pleh-*AH-*thoh*	employee
emplear (1)	*ehm-pleh-*AHR	employ, to
"	"	engage, to
"	"	hire, to
empleo, *m.*	*ehm-*PLEH-*oh*	employment (work)
"	"	job
empollar (1)	*ehm-poh-*YAHR	hatch, to
empresa, *f.*	*ehm-*PREH-*sah*	enterprise
"	"	undertaking
empujar (1)	*ehm-poo-*HAHR	push (shove), to
"	"	thrust, to
empuje, *m.*	*ehm-*POO-*heh*	push (shove)
en	*ehn*	at (in)
"	"	at (on)
"	"	in
"	"	on (*prep.*)
enaguas, *f.pl.*	*eh-*NAH-*gwahss*	petticoat
enano, *m.*	*eh-*NAH-*noh*	dwarf
encabezamiento, *m.*	*ehn-kah-veh-sah-*M_YEHN-*toh*	heading (title)
encabezar	*ehn-kah-veh-*SAHR	head (lead), to
encaje, *m.*	*ehn-*KAH-*heh*	lace (fabric)
encantador	*ehn-kahn-tah-*THOHR	charming
encantar (1)	*ehn-kahn-*TAHR	charm (delight), to
encanto, *m.*	*ehn-*KAHN-*toh*	charm (attraction)
"	"	spell
encender (4)	*ehn-sehn-*THEHR	light (set fire to), to
encerrar (4)	*ehn-seh-*RRAHR	enclose (surround), to
enchufe, *m.*	*ehn-*CHOO-*feh*	plug (*elec.*)
encía, *f.*	*ehn-*SEE-*ah*	gum (*anat.*)
enciclopedia, *f.*	*ehn-see-kloh-*PEH-*th_yah*	encyclopaedia
encontrar (5)	*ehn-kohn-*TRAHR	encounter, to
"	"	locate (find), to
"	"	meet, to
encorvado	*ehn-kohr-*VAH-*thoh*	bent (curved)
encorvarse (1)	*ehn-kohr-*VAHR-*seh*	bend (be bent), to
encrucijada, *f.*	*ehn-kroo-see-*HAH-*thah*	crossing (intersection)
"	"	crossroads
encuesta, *f.*	*ehn-*KWEHSS-*tah*	poll (survey)
endeble	*ehn-*DEH-*vleh*	feeble
endosar (1)	*ehn-doh-*SAHR	endorse (sign), to
endoso, *m.*	*ehn-*DOH-*soh*	endorsement (signature)
endurecer (11)	*ehn-doo-reh-*SEHR	harden (make hard), to
enema, *f.*	*eh-*NEH-*mah*	enema
enemigo, *m.*	*eh-neh-*MEE-*goh*	enemy
"	"	foe
energía, *f.*	*eh-nehr-*HEE-*ah*	energy
enfadar (1)	*ehn-fah-*THAHR	vex (anger), to
enfermedad, *f.*	*ehn-fehr-meh-*THAHTH	disease
"	"	illness
"	"	sickness
enfermera, *f.*	*ehn-fehr-*MEH-*rah*	nurse (medical assistant)
enfermo	*ehn-*FEHR-*moh*	ill
"	"	sick (ailing)
enfriar (1)	*ehn-free-*AHR	cool (make less hot), to
engañar (1)	*ehn-gah-*N_YAHR	cheat (defraud), to
"	"	deceive (delude), to
engaño, *m.*	*ehn-*GAH-*n_yoh*	deceit
"	"	trick (ruse)
engranaje, *m.*	*ehn-grah-*NAH-*heh*	gear (*mech.*)
engrudo, *m.*	*ehn-*GROO-*thoh*	paste (adhesive)
enhiesto	*ehn-*YEHSS-*toh*	erect (*adj.*)
enmienda, *f.*	*ehm-*M_YEHN-*dah*	amendment (enacted change)

Spanish	Pronunciation	English
enojado	*eh-noh-*HAH-*thoh*	angry
enojo, *m.*	*eh-*NOH-*hoh*	anger
enorme	*eh-*NOHR-*meh*	enormous
"	"	huge
"	"	mighty (vast)
ensalada, *f.*	*ehn-sah-*LAH-*thah*	salad
ensayo, *m.*	*ehn-*SAH-*yoh*	rehearsal
enseñar (1)	*ehn-seh-*N_YAHR	teach, to
ensuciar (1)	*ehn-soo-*S_YAHR	soil (make dirty), to
entendimiento, *m.*	*ehn-tehn-dee-*M_YEHN-*toh*	knowledge (understanding)
"	"	sense (intelligence)
enterado	*ehn-teh-*RAH-*thoh*	aware
enteramente	*ehn-teh-rah-*MEHN-*teh*	all (entirely, *adv.*)
"	"	altogether
enterar (1)	*ehn-teh-*RAHR	acquaint (inform), to
enterarse de	*ehn-teh-*RAHR-*seh theh*	learn (find out), to
entero	*ehn-*TEH-*roh*	entire
"	"	whole (*adj.*)
enterrar (4)	*ehn-teh-*RRAHR	bury (entomb), to
entierro, *m.*	*ehn-*T_YEH-*rroh*	burial
entonces	*ehn-*TOHN-*sehss*	then (at that time)
entrada, *f.*	*ehn-*TRAH-*thah*	admission (right to enter)
"	"	entrance
entrar (1)	*ehn-*TRAHR	enter (come or go into), to
entre	EHN-*treh*	among
"	"	between (*prep.*)
entrega, *f.*	*ehn-*TREH-*gah*	delivery (handing over)
entregar (1)	*ehn-treh-*GAHR	deliver (hand over), to
entrenar (1)	*ehn-treh-*NAHR	coach (train), to
entretenimiento, *m.*	*ehn-treh-teh-nee-*M_YEHN-*toh*	entertainment
entrevista, *f.*	*ehn-treh-*VEESS-*tah*	interview
entumecido	*ehn-too-meh-*SEE-*thoh*	numb
entusiasmo, *m.*	*ehn-too-*S_YAHZ-*moh*	enthusiasm
envenenar (1)	*ehn-beh-neh-*NAHR	poison, to
enviar (1)	*ehn-*B_YAHR	send, to
envidia, *f.*	*ehn-*BEE-*th_yah*	envy
envidiar (1)	*ehn-bee-*TH_YAHR	envy, to
envolver (5)	*ehn-bohl-*VEHR	involve (entail), to
"	"	wrap (envelop), to
epidemia, *f.*	*eh-pee-*THEH-*m_yah*	epidemic
equilibrio, *m.*	*eh-kee-*LEE-*vr_yoh*	balance (equilibrium)
equipaje, *m.*	*eh-kee-*PAH-*heh*	baggage
"	"	luggage
equipo, *m.*	*eh-*KEE-*poh*	equipment
"	"	outfit
"	"	team (in sports)
erigir (3)	*eh-ree-*HEER	erect (build), to
errar (4)	*eh-*RRAHR	err, to
erróneo	*eh-*RROH-*neh-oh*	false (erroneous)
error, *m.*	*eh-*RROHR	error
"	"	mistake
esa (see ese)		
ésa (see ése)		
esas (see esos)		
ésas (see ésos)		
escabechar (1)	*ehss-kah-veh-*CHAHR	pickle (preserve), to
escala, *f.*	*ehss-*KAH-*lah*	scale
escalar (1)	*ehss-kah-*LAHR	climb (scale), to
escalera, *f.*	*ehss-kah-*LEH-*rah*	ladder
"	"	stairway
escalera abajo	*ehss-kah-*LEH-*rah-*VAH-*hoh*	downstairs (downward)
escalofrío, *m.*	*ehss-kah-loh-*FREE-*oh*	chill (shivering sensation)
escalón, *m.*	*ehss-kah-*LOHN	step (stair)
escándalo, *m.*	*ehss-*KAHN-*dah-loh*	scandal
escapar(se) (1)	*ehss-kah-*PAHR(*seh*)	escape, to
escarabajo, *m.*	*ehss-kah-rah-*VAH-*hoh*	beetle
escarcha, *f.*	*ehss-*KAHR-*chah*	frost
escarlata	*ehss-kahr-*LAH-*tah*	scarlet (*adj.*)
escarlata, *f.*	*ehss-kahr-*LAH-*tah*	scarlet fever
escasez, *f.*	*ehss-kah-*SEHSS	scarcity
"	"	shortage (lack)
escaso	*ehss-*KAH-*soh*	scarce
esclarecer (11)	*ehss-klah-rah-*SEHR	illuminate (elucidate), to

Spanish	Pronunciation	English
esclavitud, f.	ehss-klah-vee-TOOTH	slavery
esclavo, m.	ehss-KLAH-voh	slave
escoba, f.	ehss-KOH-vah	broom
escocés, -cesa	ehss-koh-SEHSS, -SEH-sah	Scotch (adj.)
Escocia	ehss-KOH-s_yah	Scotland
escoger (2)	ehss-koh-HEHR	choose (select), to
"	"	pick, to
escogido	ehss-koh-HEE-thoh	chosen
esconder (2)	ehss-kohn-DEHR	hide (conceal), to
escribir (3)	ehss-kree-VEER	write, to
escribir en máquina	ehss-kree-VEER ehn MAH-kee-nah	type (typewrite), to
escritor, m.	ehss-kree-TOHR	writer (author)
escritorio, m.	ehss-kree-TOH-r_yoh	desk
escritura, f.	ehss-kree-TOO-rah	deed (transfer agreement)
escritura de constitución, f.	ehss-kree-TOO-rah theh kohn-stee-too-S_YOHN	charter (act of incorporation
escuchar (1)	ehss-koo-CHAHR	listen (hearken), to
escuela, f.	ehss-KWEH-lah	school
"	"	schoolhouse
escuela de párvulos, f.	ehss-K_WEH-lah theh PAHR-voo-lohss	kindergarten
escuela por correspondencia, f.	ehss-KWEH-lah pohr KOH-rrehss-pohn-DEHN-s_yah	correspondence school
escuela secundaria, f.	ehss-KWEH-lah seh-koon-DAH-r_yah	high school
escultor, m.	ehss-kool-TOHR	sculptor
escupir (3)	ehss-koo-PEER	spit, to
ese, esa	EH-seh, EH-sah	that (dem. adj.)
ése (eso), ésa	EH-seh (EH-soh), EH-sah	that (dem. pron.)
esencial	eh-sehn-S_YAHL	essential (adj.)
esfera, f.	ehss-FEH-rah	sphere
esforzarse (5)	ehss-fohr-SAHR-seh	strive (exert oneself), to
esfuerzo, m.	ehss-FWEHR-soh	effort
"	"	strain (exertion)
eslabón, m.	ehss-lah-VOHN	link (connecting part)
eslavo	ehss-LAH-voh	Slavic (adj.)
esmeralda, f.	ehss-meh-RAHL-thah	emerald
eso (see ése)		
eso, de	deh EH-soh	thereof
eso, por	poh_REH-soh	thus (therefore)
esos, esas	EH-sohss, EH-sahss	those (adj.)
ésos, ésas	EH-sohss, EH-sahss	those (pron.)
espacio, m.	ehss-PAH-s_yoh	room
"	"	space (area)
espada, f.	ehss-PAH-thah	sword
espalda, f.	ehss-PAHL-dah	back (anat.)
España	ehss-PAH-n_yah	Spain
español	ehss-pah-N_YOHL	Spanish (adj.)
espantar (1)	ehss-pahn-TAHR	frighten (make afraid), to
"	"	scare, to
espanto, m.	ehss-PAHN-toh	fright (alarm)
espantoso	ehss-pahn-TOH-soh	fearful (terrible)
esparcir (3)	ehss-pahr-SEER	scatter (strew), to
"	"	spread (diffuse), to
"	"	sprinkle, to
espárrago, m.	ehss-PAH-rrah-goh	asparagus
especia, f.	ehss-PEH-s_yah	spice
especial	ehss-peh-S_YAHL	special
especialmente	ehss-peh-s_yahl-MEHN-teh	especially
especie, f.	ehss-PEH-s_yeh	kind (n.)
espectáculo, m.	ehss-pehk-TAH-koo-loh	sight
"	"	spectacle (pageant)
espectador, m.	ehss-pehk-tah-THOHR	spectator
espejo, m.	ehss-PEH-hoh	mirror
esperanza, f.	ehss-peh-RAHN-sah	hope
esperar (1)	ehss-peh-RAHR	await, to
"	"	expect, to
"	"	hope, to
esperar (1)	ehss-peh-RAHR	wait (defer action), to
"	"	wait for, to
espeso	ehss-PEH-soh	thick (not thin)
espesor, m.	ehss-peh-SOHR	thickness (dimension)
espía, m.	ehss-PEE-ah	spy
espina, f.	ehss-PEE-nah	thorn

Spanish	Pronunciation	English
espinaca, f.	ehss-pee-NAH-kah	spinach
espina dorsal, f.	ehss-PEE-nah thohr-SAHL	spine (anat.)
espionaje, m.	ehss-p_yoh-NAH-heh	espionage
espíritu, m.	ehss-PEE-ree-too	spirit
espiritual	ehss-pee-ree-TWAHL	spiritual (adj.)
espléndido	ehss-PLEHN-dee-thoh	splendid
esplendor, m.	ehss-plehn-DOHR	splendor
esponja, f.	ehss-POHN-hah	sponge
esponsales, m. pl.	ehss-pohn-SAH-lehss	engagement (betrothal)
esposa, f.	ehss-POH-sah	wife
espuela, f.	ehss-PWEH-lah	spur (spike)
espuma, f.	ehss-POO-mah	foam
esqueleto, m.	ehss-keh-LEH-toh	skeleton (anat.)
esquiar (1)	ehss-K_YAHR	ski, to
esquina, f.	ehss-KEE-nah	corner (street intersection)
esta	EHSS-tah	this (adj.)
ésta	EHSS-tah	this (dem. pron.)
estable	ehss-TAH-vleh	stable (steadfast)
establecer (11)	ehss-tah-vleh-SEHR	establish (prove), to
establecerse	ehss-tah-vleh-SEHR-seh	settle (make one's home), to
establecimiento, m.	ehss-tah-vleh-see-M_YEHN-toh	establishment (firm)
establo, m.	ehss-TAH-vloh	barn
"	"	stable (shelter)
estaca, f.	ehss-TAH-kah	stake (post)
estación, f.	ehss-tah-S_YOHN	depot (station)
"	"	season (of year)
"	"	station, railroad
estacionar (1)	ehss-tah-s_yoh-NAHR	park (put in place), to
estacionario	ehss-tah-s_yoh-NAH-r_yoh	stationary (unmoving)
estada, f.	ehss-TAH-thah	stay (sojourn)
estadio, m.	ehss-TAH-d_yoh	stadium
estadista, m.	ehss-tah-THEESS-tah	statesman
estado, m.	ehss-TAH-thoh	commonwealth
"	"	state
estado de cuenta, m.	ehss-TAH-thoh theh KWEHN-tah	statement (accounting, bus.)
Estados Unidos, m. pl.	ehss-TAH-thohss oo-NEE-thohss	United States
estallar (1)	ehss-tah-YAHR	burst, to
estampa, f.	ehss-TAHM-pah	illustration (pictorial representation)
estaño, m.	ehss-TAH-n_yoh	tin (metal)
esta noche	EHSS-tah NOH-cheh	tonight
estanque, m.	ehss-TAHN-keh	pond
estar (24)	ehss-TAHR	be, to
"	"	lie (be located), to
estarcido, m.	ehss-tahr-SEE-thoh	stencil
estar de acuerdo	ehss-TAHR theh_ah-KWEHR-thoh	agree (concur), to
estar de acuerdo con	ehss-TAHR theh_ah-KWEHR-thoh kohn	agree with, to
estar de pie	ehss-TAHR theh P_YEH	stand (be upright), to
estar ocupado en	ehss-TAH_roh-koo-PAH-thoh_ehn	engage (be occupied) in, to
estar radiante	ehss-TAHR rrah-TH_YAHN-teh	beam (shine), to
estar sentado	ehss-TAHR sehn-TAH-thoh	sit (be sitting), to
estas	EHSS-tahss	these (adj.)
éstas	EHSS-tahss	these (pron.)
estatua, f.	ehss-tah-TWAH	statue
estatura, f.	ehss-tah-TOO-rah	stature (height)
estatuto, m.	ehss-tah-TOO-toh	by-law
este	EHSS-teh	this (adj.)
éste	EHSS-teh	this (dem. pron.)
este, m.	EHSS-teh	east
estenógrafa, f.	ehss-teh-NOH-grah-fah	stenographer
estéril	ehss-TEH-rreel	barren
estilo, m.	ehss-TEE-loh	style (manner)
estimar (1)	ehss-tee-MAHR	esteem, to
estimular (1)	ehss-tee-moo-LAHR	stimulate (incite), to
estipulación, f.	ehss-tee-poo-lah-S_YOHN	provision (stipulation)
estirar (1)	ehss-tee-RAHR	stretch (draw out), to
esto	EHSS-toh	this (dem. pron.)
Estocolmo	ehss-toh-KOHL-moh	Stockholm

Spanish	Pronunciation	English
estómago, *m.*	ehss-TOH-*mah-goh*	stomach
estorbar (1)	ehss-*tohr*-VAHR	hinder, to
estornudar (1)	ehss-*tohr-noo*-THAHR	sneeze, to
estos	EHSS-*tohss*	these (*adj.*)
éstos	EHSS-*tohss*	these (*pron.*)
estrecho	ehss-TREH-*choh*	narrow
estrella, *f.*	ehss-TREH-*yah*	star (*astron.*)
estrellarse (1)	ehss-*treh*-YAHR-*seh*	crash (be smashed), to
estremecerse (11)	ehss-*treh-meh*-SEHR-*seh*	shudder, to
"	"	tremble, to
estrépito, *m.*	ehss-TREH-*pee-toh*	din
estricto	ehss-TREEK-*toh*	strict (stringent)
estructura, *f.*	ehss-*trook*-TOO-*rah*	structure (arrangement of parts)
estruendo, *m.*	ehss-*troo* EHN-*doh*	crash (loud noise)
estudiante, *m., f.*	ehss-*too*-TH_YAHN-*teh*	student
estudiar (1)	ehss-*too*-TH_YAHR	study, to
estudio, *m.*	ehss-TOO-*th_yoh*	study (active learning)
estufa, *f.*	ehss-TOO-*fah*	stove
estúpido	ehss-TOO-*pee-thoh*	dumb
"	"	stupid
etapa, *f.*	eh-TAH-*pah*	stage (period)
eterno	eh-TEHR-*noh*	eternal
"	"	everlasting
etiqueta, *f.*	eh-tee-KEH-*tah*	etiquette
Europa	eh_oo-ROH-*pah*	Europe
europeo	eh_oo-roh-PEH-*oh*	European (*adj.*)
evaluación, *f.*	eh-vah-loo-ah-S_YOHN	rating (evaluation)
evidencia, *f.*	eh-vee-THEHN-*s_yah*	evidence (*law*)
evidente	eh-vee-THEHN-*teh*	evident
evitar (1)	eh-vee-TAHR	avoid, to
exacto	ehg-SAHK-*toh*	accurate
"	"	exact (precise)
exagerar (1)	ehg-*sah-heh*-RAHR	exaggerate, to
exaltar (1)	ehg-*sahl*-TAHR	exalt, to
examen, *m.*	ehg-SAH-*mehn*	examination (test)
"	"	survey (inspection)
"	"	test (*educ.*)
examinar (1)	ehg-*sah-mee*-NAHR	examine (investigate), to
exceder (2)	ehss-*seh*-THEHR	exceed, to
excelente	ehss-*seh*-LEHN-*teh*	excellent
excepción, *f.*	ehss-*sehp*-S_YOHN	exception (unusual case)
excepto	ehss-SEHP-*toh*	except (*prep.*)
excesivo	ehss-*seh*-SEE-*voh*	excessive
exceso, *m.*	ehss-SEH-*soh*	excess
excitar (1)	ehss-*see*-TAHR	arouse, to
"	"	excite, to
exclamación, *f.*	ehss-*klah-mah*-S_YOHN	exclamation (*n.*)
exclamar (1)	ehss-*klah*-MAHR	exclaim, to
excluir (14)	ehss-*kloo* EER	exclude, to
exclusivo	ehss-*kloo*-SEE-*voh*	exclusive (not including)
excusa, *f.*	ehss-KOO-*sah*	excuse (pretext)
excusar (1)	ehss-*koo*-SAHR	excuse (pardon), to
exento	ehg-SEHN-*toh*	exempt
exhibición, *f.*	ehg-*see-vee*-S_YOHN	exhibit
"	"	show
exhibir (3)	ehg-*see*-VEER	display, to
"	"	exhibit, to
exigencia, *f.*	ehg-*see*-HEHN-*s_yah*	demand (request)
exigir (3)	ehg-*see*-HEER	demand (ask for), to
existencia, *f.*	ehg-*seess*-TEHN-*s_yah*	existence
existencias, *f.pl.*	ehg-*seess*-TEHN-*s_yahss*	stock (supply)
existir (3)	ehg-*seess*-TEER	exist, to
éxito, *m.*	EHG-*see-toh*	success (attainment)
expectación, *f.*	ehss-*pehk-tah*-S_YOHN	expectation
expectativa, *f.*	ehss-*pek-tah*-TEE-*vah*	prospect (thing expected)
expedición, *f.*	ehss-*peh-thee*-S_YOHN	expedition (journey)
expedidor, *m.*	ehss-*peh-thee*-THOHR	shipping agent
expeler (2)	ehss-*peh*-LEHR	expel (eject), to
experiencia, *f.*	ehss-*peh*-R_YEHN-*s_yah*	experience (conscious event)
experimento, *m.*	ehss-*peh-ree*-MEHN-*toh*	experiment
experto	ehss-PEHR-*toh*	skilful
experto, *m.*	ehss-PEHR-*toh*	expert (*n.*)
expirar (1)	ehss-*pee*-RAHR	expire (become void, *bus.*), to

Spanish	Pronunciation	English
explicación, *f.*	ehss-*plee-kah*-S_YOHN	explanation
explorador, *m.*	ehss-*ploh-rah*-THOHR	scout (lookout)
explorar (1)	ehss-*ploh*-RAHR	explore, to
explosivo, *m.*	ehss-*ploh*-SEE-*voh*	explosive (*n.*)
exponer (31)	ehss-*poh*-NEHR	expose, to
"	"	present (set forth), to
exportación, *f.*	ehss-*pohr-tah*-S_YOHN	exportation
exportador, *m.*	ehss-*pohr-tah*-THOHR	exporter
exportar (1)	ehss-*pohr*-TAHR	export, to
exposicion, *f.*	ehss-*poh-see*-S_YOHN	exhibition (exposition)
expresar (1)	ehss-*preh*-SAHR	express (state), to
expresión, *f.*	ehss-*preh*-S_YOHN	expression
exquisito	ehss-*kee*-SEE-*toh*	exquisite
extender (4)	ehss-*tehn*-DEHR	extend, to
extender recibo	ehss-*tehn*-DEHR *reh-*SEE-*voh*	receipt, to (*bus.*)
extenderse	ehss-*tehn*-DEHR-*seh*	reach (extend to), to
"	"	run (extend), to
"	"	stretch (extend), to
extensión, *f.*	ehss-*tehn*-S_YOHN	extension (enlargement)
extenso	ehss-TEHN-*soh*	extensive
exterior	ehss-*teh*-R_YOHR	exterior (*adj.*)
"	"	outer
"	"	outside (*adj.*)
exterior, *m.*	ehss-*teh*-R_YOHR	outside (*n.*)
extraer (minerales) (36)	ehss-*trah*-EHR (*mee-neh*-RAH-*lehss*)	mine (dig for), to
extranjero	ehss-*trahn*-HEH-*roh*	foreign
extranjero, *m.*	ehss-*trahn*-HEH-*roh*	foreigner
extranjero, en el	eh_neh_lehss-*trahn*-HEH-*roh*	abroad (in foreign land)
extraño	ehss-TRAH-*n_yoh*	queer
"	"	strange (peculiar)
extraordinario	ehss-*trah_ohr-thee*-NAH-*r_yoh*	extraordinary
"	"	remarkable
extraviar (1)	ehss-*trah*-V_YAHR	mislay, to
extremo	ehss-TREH-*moh*	extreme
"	"	utmost (*adj.*)
fábrica, *f.*	FAH-*vree-kah*	factory
"	"	plant
fabricante, *m.*	*fah-vree*-KAHN-*teh*	manufacturer
fabricar (1)	*fah-vree*-KAHR	manufacture, to
fábula, *f.*	FAH-*voo-lah*	fable
facciones, *f.pl.*	*fahk*-S_YOHN-*chss*	feature (part of face)
fácil	FAH-*seel*	easy (not difficult)
facilidad, *f.*	*fah-see-lee*-THAHTH	ease (effortlessness)
factor, *m.*	*fahk*-TOHR	factor (element)
factura, *f.*	*fahk*-TOO-*rah*	bill
"	"	invoice
facultad, *f.*	*fah-kool*-TAHTH	faculty (ability)
"	"	faculty (teaching staff)
falda, *f.*	FAHL-*dah*	skirt (garment)
falsear (1)	*fahl-seh*-_AHR	forge (counterfeit), to
falsedad, *f.*	*fahl-seh*-THAHTH	falsehood (lie)
falso	FAHL-*soh*	counterfeit (*adj.*)
"	"	false (deceitful)
falta, *f.*	FAHL-*tah*	fault (defect)
"	"	lack (deficiency)
"	"	want
faltar (1)	*fahl*-TAHR	lack (be without), to
fama, *f.*	FAH-*mah*	fame
familia, *f.*	*fah*-MEE-*l_yah*	family
familiar	*fah-mee*-L_YAHR	familiar (intimate)
"	"	familiar (well-known)
famoso	*fah*-MOH-*soh*	famous
fantasía, *f.*	*fahn-tah*-SEE-*ah*	fancy (fantasy)
"	"	humor (drollery)
fantasma, *m.*	*fahn*-TAHSS-*mah*	ghost
farmacéutico, *m.*	*fahr-mah*-SEH-_oo-*tee-koh*	pharmacist
farmacia, *f.*	*fahr*-MAH-*s_yah*	pharmacy (drug store)
fascismo, *m.*	*fah*-SEEZ-*moh*	fascism
fase, *f.*	FAH-*seh*	phase (stage)
fastidiar (1)	*fahss-tee*-TH_YAHR	annoy (irk), to
fatal	*fah*-TAHL	fatal (fateful)
fatiga, *f.*	*fah*-TEE-*gah*	fatigue
favor, *m.*	*fah*-VOHR	favor
"	"	kindness

Spanish	Pronunciation	English
favorable	*fah-voh-*RAH*-vleh*	favorable
favorito	*fah-voh-*REE*-toh*	favorite (*adj.*)
faz, *f.*	FAHSS	face (surface)
fe, *f.*	FEH	faith (trust)
fecha, *f.*	FEH*-chah*	date (calendar designation)
federal	*feh-theh-*RAHL	federal
felicidad, *f.*	*feh-lee-see-*THAHTH	bliss
"	"	happiness
felicitar (1)	*feh-lee-see-*TAHR	congratulate, to
feligreses, *m.pl.*	*feh-lee-*GREH*-sehss*	congregation (religious community)
feliz	*feh-*LEESS	happy (glad)
felizmente	*feh-leess-*MEHN*-teh*	happily (luckily)
feminino	*feh-mee-*NEE*-noh*	feminine
feo	FEH*-oh*	ugly
feroz	*feh-*ROHSS	fierce
ferrocarril, *m.*	*feh-roh-kah-*REEL	railroad
fértil	FEHR*-teel*	fertile
festín, *m.*	*fehss-*TEEN	feast (meal)
festival, *m.*	*fehss-tee-*VAHL	festival
fiador, *m.*	*f_yah-*THOHR	guarantor
fiebre, *f.*	F_YEH*-vreh*	fever
fiebre amarilla, *f.*	F_YEH*-vreh ah-mah-*REE*-yah*	yellow fever
fiebre tifoidea, *f.*	F_YEH*-vreh tee-foh-*EE*-theh-ah*	typhoid fever
fiel	F_YEHL	faithful (loyal)
fieltro, *m.*	F_YEHL*-troh*	felt (*n.*)
figura, *f.*	*fee-*GOO*-rah*	figure (human form)
figurarse (1)	*fee-goo-*RAHR*-seh*	fancy (imagine), to
fijar (1)	*fee-*HAHR	fasten, to
fijo	FEE*-hoh*	fast (firm)
fila, *f.*	FEE*-lah*	line
fila, *f.*	FEE*-lah*	rank
"	"	row (series)
Filipinas, *f.pl.*	*fee-lee-*PEE*-nahss*	Philippines
filo, *m.*	FEE*-loh*	edge (sharp side)
filosofía, *f.*	*fee-loh-soh-*FEE*-ah*	philosophy
fin, *m.*	FEEN	end (conclusion)
fin, por	*pohr* FEEN	finally
final	*fee-*NAHL	final (last)
final, al	*ahl-fee-*NAHL	last (after all others, *adv.*)
financiero	*fee-nahn-*S_YEH*-roh*	financial
finanzas, *f.pl.*	*fee-*NAHN*-sahss*	finances
fin de semana, *m.*	FEEN *deh seh-*MAH*-nah*	weekend (*n.*)
fingir (3)	*feen-*HEER	pretend (feign), to
finlandés	*feen-lahn-*DEHSS	Finnish (*adj.*)
Finlandia	*feen-*LAHN*-d_yah*	Finland
firma, *f.*	FEER*-mah*	signature (name)
firmar (1)	*feer-*MAHR	sign (endorse), to
firme	FEER*-meh*	firm (*adj.*)
"	"	steady
física, *f.*	FEE*-see-kah*	physics (science)
físico	FEE*-see-koh*	physical (material)
flaco	FLAH*-koh*	thin (not fat)
flauta, *f.*	FLAH_OO*_tah*	flute (*mus.*)
flecha, *f.*	FLEH*-chah*	arrow
fleco, *m.*	FLEH*-koh*	fringe
flete, *m.*	FLEH*-teh*	freight
flojo	FLOH*-hoh*	limp (flaccid)
flor, *f.*	FLOHR	blossom
"	"	flower
florecer (11)	*floh-reh-*SEHR	bloom, to
"	"	flourish (thrive), to
flota, *f.*	FLOH*-tah*	fleet (group of vessels)
flotar (1)	*floh-*TAHR	float (be buoyant), to
fluir (14)	*floo-*EER	flow (circulate), to
"	"	stream, to
foca, *f.*	FOH*-kah*	seal (animal)
fogón, *m.*	*foh-*GOHN	hearth
folleto, *m.*	*foh-*YEH*-toh*	booklet
fondo, *m.*	FOHN*-doh*	bottom
"	"	fund
fondos, *m.pl.*	FOHN*-dohss*	funds
fonógrafo, *m.*	*foh-*NOH*-grah-foh*	phonograph
forjar (1)	*fohr-*HAHR	forge (shape), to
forma, *f.*	FOHR*-mah*	form
"	"	shape (contour)

Spanish	Pronunciation	English
formación, *f.*	*fohr-mah-*S_YOHN	formation (creation)
formalidad, *f.*	*fohr-mah-lee-*THATH	formality
formar (1)	*fohr-*MAHR	form (shape), to
fórmula, *f.*	FOHR*-moo-lah*	formula (prescribed guide)
forro, *m.*	FOH*-rroh*	lining
fortalecer (11)	*fohr-tah-leh-*SEHR	strengthen, to
fortaleza, *f.*	*fohr-tah-*LEH*-sah*	fortress
fortuna, *f.*	*fohr-*TOO*-nah*	fortune
forzar (5)	*fohr-*SAHR	force, to
fósforo, *m.*	FOHSS*-foh-roh*	match (lucifer)
fotografía, *f.*	*foh-toh-grah-*FEE*-ah*	photograph
fracasar (1)	*frah-kah-*SAHR	fail (be unsuccessful), to
fracaso, *m.*	*frah-*KAH*-soh*	failure (lack of success)
fracción, *f.*	*frahk-*S_YOHN	fraction (part)
fractura, *f.*	*frahk-*TOO*-rah*	fracture (*med.*)
fragmento, *m.*	*frahg-*MEHN*-toh*	fragment
frambuesa, *f.*	*frahm-*B_WEH*-sah*	raspberry
francés, -cesa	*frahn-*SEHSS, -SEH*-sah*	French (*adj.*)
Francia	FRAHN*-s_yah*	France
franco	FRAHN*-koh*	frank (*adj.*)
franqueo, *m.*	*frahn-*KEH*-oh*	postage (postal charge)
frase, *f.*	FRAH*-seh*	phrase (*gram.*)
"	"	sentence (*gram.*)
fraude, *m.*	FRAH_OO*-theh*	fraud (deception)
frecuentar (1)	*freh-kwehn-*TAHR	haunt (visit often), to
frecuente	*freh-*KWEHN*-teh*	frequent
fregadero, *m.*	*freh-gah-*THEH*-roh*	sink (basin)
fregar (4)	*freh-*GAHR	scrub, to
freír (10)	*freh-*EER	fry (be cooked in fat), to
freno, *m.*	FREH*-noh*	brake
"	"	curb (restraint)
frente, *f.*	FREHN*-teh*	forehead
"	"	front
frente a	FREHN*-teh ah*	opposite (*prep.*)
fresa, *f.*	FREH*-sah*	strawberry
fresco	FREHSS *-koh*	chilly
"	"	cool (having low temperature)
"	"	fresh
frío	FREE*-oh*	cold (*adj.*)
frío, *m.*	FREE*-oh*	chill (coldness)
"	"	cold (low temperature)
frontera, *f.*	*frohn-*TEH*-rah*	border
"	"	frontier
frotar (1)	*froh-*TAHR	rub, to
frotar suavemente	*froh-*TAHR *swah-veh-*MEHN*-teh*	stroke (rub gently), to
fruncir el ceño (3)	*froon-*SEER *ehl* SEH*-n_yoh*	frown, to
frustrar (1)	*frooss-*TRAHR	defeat (thwart), to
"	"	foil (frustrate), to
fruta, *f.*	FROO*-tah*	fruit
fuego, *m.*	FWEH*-goh*	fire
fuente, *f.*	FWEHN*-teh*	fountain
"	"	source (origin)
fuera	FWEH*-rah*	out (forth, *adv.*)
fuerte	FWEHR*-teh*	loud (resounding)
"	"	stout
"	"	strong
fuerte, *m.*	FWEHR*-teh*	fort
fuerza, *f.*	FWEHR*-sah*	force
"	"	strength
fuerza obrera, la, *f.*	*lah* FWEHR*-sah oh-*VREH*-rah*	labor (labor force)
fuga, *f.*	FOO*-gah*	flight (hasty departure)
fulgurar (1)	*fool-goo-*RAHR	gleam (shine), to
fumar (1)	*foo-*MAHR	smoke, to
función, *f.*	*foon-*S_YOHN	function
funcionamiento, *m.*	*foon-s_yohn-ah-*M_YEHN*-toh*	operation (functioning)
funcionario, *m.*	*foon-s_yoh-*NAH*-r_yoh*	official (*n.*)
fundación, *f.*	*foon-dah-*S_YOHN	establishment (founding)
fundador	*foon-dah-*THOHR	founder (*n.*)
fundamental	*foon-dah-mehn-*TAHL	fundamental

Spanish	Pronunciation	English
fundamento, *m.*	*foon-dah-*MEHN*-toh*	foundation (base)
fundar (1)	*foon-*DAHR	establish, to
"	"	found, (originate), to
funerales, *m.pl.*	*foo-neh-*RAH*-lehss*	funeral
furia, *f.*	FOO*-r yah*	fury
furioso	*foo-R YOH-soh*	furious
fusible, *m.*	*foo-*SEE*-vleh*	fuse (*elec.*)
fútbol, *m.*	FOOT*-bohl*	soccer
futuro	*foo-*TOO*-roh*	future (*adj.*)
gabán, *m.*	*gah-*VAHN	coat (man's over-coat)
gabinete, *m.*	*gah-bee-*NEH*-teh*	cabinet (*govt.*)
gafas contra el sol, *f.pl.*	GAH*-fahss* KOHN*-trah ehl* SOHL	sunglasses
galería, *f.*	*gah-leh-*REE*-ah*	gallery (balcony)
Gales, *f.*	GAH*-lehss*	Wales
gallina, *f.*	*gah-*YEE*-nah*	hen
gallo, *m.*	GAH*-yoh*	cock
"	"	rooster
galope, *m.*	*gah-*LOH*-peh*	gallop (*n.*)
gamuza, *f.*	*gah-*MOO*-sah*	suede (*n.*)
ganado, *m.*	*gah-*NAH*-thoh*	stock (livestock)
ganado vacuno, *m.*	*gah-*NAH*-thoh vah-*KOO*-noh*	cattle
ganancia, *f.*	*gah-nahn-*S YAH	profit (*bus.*)
ganar (1)	*gah-*NAHR	earn (be paid), to
"	"	gain (get), to
ganar tantos	*gah-*NAHR TAHN*-tohss*	score (gain points), to
gancho, *m.*	GAHN*-choh*	hook
ganga, *f.*	GAHN*-gah*	bargain (advanta-geous purchase)
ganso, *m.*	GAHN*-soh*	goose
garaje, *m.*	*gah-*RAH*-heh*	garage
garantía, *f.*	*gah-rahn-*TEE*-ah*	guarantee (warrant)
garantizar (1)	*gah-rahn-tee-*SAHR	guarantee, to
garganta, *f.*	*gahr-*GAHN*-tah*	throat
garra, *f.*	GAH*-rrah*	claw (of bird)
gas, *m.*	GAHSS	gas
gasolina, *f.*	*gah-soh-*LEE*-nah*	gasoline
gastar (1)	*gahss-*TAHR	spend (pay out), to
gasto, *m.*	GAHSS*-toh*	expenditure (outlay)
gastos de explo-tación, *m.pl.*	GAHSS*-tohss d ehss-ploh-tah-*S YOHN	operating expenses (*bus.*)
gastos generales, *m.pl.*	GAHSS*-tohss heh-neh-*RAH*-lehss*	overhead (expenses, *bus.*)
gatito, *m.*	*gah-*TEE*-toh*	kitten
gato, *m.*	GAH*-toh*	cat
gema, *f.*	HEH*-mah*	gem
gemelo, *m.*	*heh-*MEH*-loh*	twin (*n.*)
gemir (9)	*heh-*MEER	groan, to
"	"	moan, to
"	"	wail, to
generación, *f.*	*heh-neh-rah-*S YOHN	generation (period of time)
general	*heh-neh-*RAHL	general (*adj.*)
general, *m.*	*heh-neh-*RAHL	general (officer)
generoso	*heh-neh-*ROH*-soh*	generous
genio, *m.*	HEH*-n yoh*	disposition (tem-perament)
"	"	genius
gente, *f.*	HEHN*-teh*	people (persons)
genuino	*heh-n* WEE*-noh*	genuine
geografía, *f.*	*heh-oh-grah-*FEE*-ah*	geography
geología, *f.*	*heh-oh-loh-*HEE*-ah*	geology
gigante, *m.*	*hee-*GAHN*-teh*	giant
gimnasio, *m.*	*heem-*NAH*-s yoh*	gymnasium (athletic arena)
Ginebra	*hee-*NEH*-vrah*	Geneva
girar (1)	*hee-*RAHR	spin (revolve), to
giro, *m.*	HEE*-roh*	draft (check)
giro postal, *m.*	HEE*-roh pohss-*TAHL	money order
gitano, *m.*	*hee-*TAH*-noh*	gypsy
globo, *m.*	GLOH*-voh*	balloon
"	"	globe
gloria, *f.*	GLOH*-r yah*	glory (renown)
glorioso	*gloh-R YOH-soh*	glorious (resplend-ent)
glosario, *m.*	*gloh-*SAH*-r yoh*	glossary
gobernador, *m.*	*goh-vehr-nah-*THOHR	governor
gobernar (4)	*goh-vehr-*NAHR	govern, to
"	"	rule, to
gobierno, *m.*	*goh-*V YEHR*-noh*	government
golf, *m.*	GOHLF	golf
golfo, *m.*	GOHL*-foh*	gulf (large bay)
golondrina, *f.*	*goh-lohn-*DREE*-nah*	swallow (bird)

Spanish	Pronunciation	English
golpe, *m.*	GOHL*-peh*	blow
"	"	stroke
golpear (1)	*gohl-peh-*AHR	hit (strike), to
"	"	rap, to
"	"	strike (hit), to
golpear ligera-mente	*gohl-peh-*AHR *lee-heh-rah-*MEHN*-teh*	pat, to
golpecito, *m.*	*gohl-peh-*SEE*-toh*	tap (rap), to
golpetear (1)	*gohl-peh-teh-*AHR	pat (tap)
goma, *f.*	GOH*-mah*	rattle, to
"	"	eraser (rubber eraser)
gordo	GOHR*-thoh*	fat (obese, *adj.*)
gorra, *f.*	GOH*-rrah*	cap (hat)
gorrión, *m.*	*goh-*RR YOHN	sparrow
gota, *f.*	GOH*-tah*	drop (droplet)
gotear (1)	*goh-teh-*AHR	drip, to
gozar de (1)	*goh-*SAHR *theh*	enjoy (derive joy from), to
grabador de cinta, *m.*	*grah-vah-*THOHR *theh* SEEN*-tah*	tape recorder
gracias, *f.pl.*	GRAH*-s yahss*	thanks (gratitude)
gracioso	*grah-*S YOH*-soh*	graceful
grado, *m.*	GRAH*-thoh*	degree (unit of measurement)
"	"	extent (magnitude)
"	"	grade (relative posi-tion)
gradual	*grah-*THWAHL	gradual
gráfico, *m.*	GRAH*-fee-koh*	graph
gramática, *f.*	*grah-*MAH*-tee-kah*	grammar
Gran Bretaña	GRAHN *breh-*TAH*-n yah*	Great Britain
grande	GRAHN*-deh*	big
"	"	great
"	"	large
grandeza, *f.*	*grahn-*DEH*-sah*	greatness (eminence)
grandioso	*grahn-D YOH-soh*	grand (imposing)
granito, *m.*	*grah-*NEE*-toh*	granite
granizar (1)	*grah-nee-*SAHR	hail (precipitate hail), to
granizo, *m.*	*grah-*NEE*-soh*	hail (ice)
granja, *f.*	GRAHN*-hah*	farm
grano, *m.*	GRAH*-noh*	grain (cereal)
"	"	kernel
grasa, *f.*	GRAH*-sah*	fat (fatty tissue, *n.*)
"	"	grease (melted fat)
gratitud, *f.*	*grah-tee-*TOOTH	gratitude
gratuito	*grah-*TWEE*-toh*	free (gratuitous)
grava, *f.*	GRAH*-vah*	gravel
gravar (1)	*grah-*VAHR	assess (impose tax), to
grave	GRAH*-veh*	deep (in tone)
"	"	grave (serious)
Grecia	GREH*-s yah*	Greece
griego	GR YEH-goh*	Greek (*adj.*)
grieta, *f.*	GR YEH-tah*	crack (fissure)
grifo, *m.*	GREE*-foh*	tap (faucet)
grillo, *m.*	GREE*-yoh*	cricket (insect)
gris	GREESS	gray
gritar (1)	*gree-*TAHR	call (shout), to
"	"	cry (shout), to
"	"	shout (say loudly), to
"	"	yell, to
grito, *m.*	GREE*-toh*	call
"	"	cry (utterance)
"	"	shout
grosero	*groh-*SEH*-roh*	rough (harsh)
gruesa, *f.*	GROO *eh-sah*	gross (twelve dozen)
gruñir (13)	*groo-N* YEER	growl, to
grupo, *m.*	GROO*-poh*	group
guante, *m.*	GWAHN*-teh*	glove
guarda, *f.*	GWAHR*-thah*	guard (watcher)
"	"	keeper
guardar (1)	*gwahr-*THAHR	keep (retain), to
guardarse de	*gwahr-*THAHR*-seh theh*	beware of, to
guarida, *f.*	*gwah-*REE*-thah*	den (animal lair)
guarnición, *f.*	*gwahr-nee-*S YOHN	garrison
guarniciones, *f.pl.*	*gwahr-nee-*S YOH*-nehss*	harness
Guatemala	*gwah-teh-*MAH*-lah*	Guatemala
guerra, *f.*	GHEH*-rrah*	war
guía, *m.*	GHEE*-ah*	guide (one who guides)
guiar (1)	*ghee-*AHR	drive (a vehicle), to
"	"	lead (guide), to
guión, *m.*	*ghee-*OHN	hyphen

Spanish	Pronunciation	English
guisante, *m.*	*ghee-*SAHN*-teh*	pea
guitarra, *f.*	*ghee-*TAH*-rrah*	guitar
gusano, *m.*	*goo-*SAH*-noh*	worm
gustarle (a uno) (1)	*gooss-*TAHR*-leh (ah* OO*-noh)*	like (be fond of), to
haba, *f.*	AH*-vah*	bean (string bean)
hábil	AH*-veel*	clever
habilidad, *f.*	*ah-vee-lee-*THAHTH	ability
habitacion, *f.*	*hah-vee-tah-*S YOHN	dwelling
habitación para niños, *f.*	*ah-vee-tah-*S Y OHN PAH*-rah* NEE*-n yohss*	nursery (children's room)
habitante, *m.*	*ah-vee-*TAHN*-teh*	inhabitant
habitar (1)	*ah-vee-*TAHR	inhabit, to
hábito, *m.*	AH*-vee-toh*	habit (custom)
habla, *f.*	AH*-vlah*	speech (oral expression)
hablar (1)	*ah-*VLAHR	speak, to
"	"	talk, to
hace	AH*-seh*	ago (past, *adj.*)
hacer (26)	*ah-*SEHR	do, to
"	"	make, to
"	"	render (cause to become), to
hacer arreglos (para)	*ah-*SEHR *ah-*REHG*-lohss* (PAH*-rah*)	arrange (plan), to
hacer caso de	*ah-*SEHR KAH*-soh theh*	heed (mind), to
hacer cosquillas a	*ah-*SEHR *kohss-*KEE*-yahss ah*	tickle (touch lightly), to
hacer efectivo	*ah-*SEHR *eh-fehk-*TEE*-voh*	cash (receive cash for), to
hacer (el papel de)	*ah-*SEHR *(ehl pah-*PEHL *deh)*	play (take the role of), to
hacer girar	*ah-*SEHR *hee-*RAHR	turn (make rotate), to
hacer gracia de	*ah-*SEHR GRAH*-s yah theh*	spare (not harm), to
hacer pedazos	*ah-*SEHR *peh-*THAH*-sohss*	shatter (smash in pieces), to
hacer reverencia	*ah-*SEHR *rreh-veh-*REHN*-s yah*	bow (in greeting), to
hacerse	*ah-*SEHR*-seh*	become, to
hacer trenzas	*ah-*SEHR TREHN*-sahss*	braid (plait), to
hacha, *f.*	AH*-chah*	axe
"	"	hatchet
hacia	AH*-s yah*	ago (past, *adj.*)
"	"	toward
hacia adelante	AH*-s yah ah-theh-*LAHN*-teh*	forward (*adv.*)
"	"	onward (*adv.*)
hacia arriba	AH*-s yah ah-*RREE*-vah*	upstairs (to upper story, *adv.*)
"	"	upward (to a higher level, *adv.*)
hacia atrás	AH*-s yah ah-*TRAHSS	backward (in reverse, *adv.*)
"	"	backward (rearward, *adv.*)
hada, *f.*	AH*-thah*	fairy (*n.*)
Haití	*ah ee-*TEE	Haiti
halar (1)	*ah-*LAHR	drag (pull), to
halcón, *m.*	*ahl-*KOHN	hawk
hallar (1)	*ah-*YAHR	find (discover), to
hambre, *f.*	AHM*-breh*	hunger
hambriento	*ahm-*BR YEHN*-toh*	hungry
harina, *f.*	*ah-*REE*-nah*	flour
hasta	AHSS*-tah*	to (indicating destination, *prep.*)
hasta	AHSS*-tah*	until (up to the time of, *prep.*)
hasta ahora	AHSS*-t ah-*OH*-rah*	hitherto (thus far)
hasta que	AHSS*-tah keh*	until (*conj.*)
Hawaii	*hah-*WAI*-ee*	Hawaii
haya, *f.*	AH*-yah*	beech (tree)
hazaña, *f.*	*ah-*SAH*-n yah*	feat
hebreo	*eh-*VREH*-oh*	Hebrew (*adj.*)
hecho, *m.*	EH*-choh*	deed (act)
"	"	fact
helado, *m.*	*eh-*LAH*-thoh*	ice-cream
"	"	icy
helecho, *m.*	*eh-*LEH*-choh*	fern
helicoptero, *m.*	*eh-lee-kohp-*TEH*-roh*	helicopter
heliograbado, *m.*	EH*-l yoh-grah-*VAH*-thoh*	blueprint
Helsingfors	*ehl-*SEENG*-fohrss*	Helsinki
hembra	EHM*-brah*	female (*adj.*)
hembra, *f.*	EHM*-brah*	female (*zool.*, *n.*)
hemisferio, *m.*	*eh-meess-*FEH*-r yoh*	hemisphere (*geog.*)
hemorragia, *f.*	*eh-moh-*RRAH*-h yah*	hemorrhage

Spanish	Pronunciation	English
hender (4)	*ehn-*DEHR	crack, to
"		split (rend), to
heno, *m.*	EH*-noh*	hay
heredar (1)	*eh-reh-*THAHR	inherit, to
heredero, *m.*	*eh-reh-*THEH*-roh*	heir
herencia, *f.*	*eh-*REHN*-s yah*	heredity
herida, *f.*	*eh-*REE*-thah*	wound (injury)
herir (7)	*eh-*REER	cut, to
"	"	wound, to
hermana, *f.*	*ehr-*MAH*-nah*	sister (*n.*)
hermano, *m.*	*ehr-*MAH*-noh*	brother
hermoso	*ehr-*MOH*-soh*	handsome (attractive)
héroe, *m.*	EH*-roh-eh*	hero
heroína, *f.*	*ehr-oh-*EE*-nah*	heroine
herramienta, *f.*	*eh-rrah-*M YEHN*-tah*	tool
herrero, *m.*	*eh-*RREH*-roh*	blacksmith
hervir (7)	*ehr-*VEER	boil (bubble up), to
hiedra, *f.*	YEH*-thrah*	ivy
hielo, *m.*	YEH*-loh*	ice (frozen water)
hierba, *f.*	YEHR*-vah*	grass
"	"	herb
hierro, *m.*	YEH*-rroh*	iron (metal)
hígado, *m.*	EE*-gah-thoh*	liver (*anat.*)
higo, *m.*	EE*-goh*	fig
hija, *f.*	EE*-hah*	daughter
hijastra, *f.*	*ee-*HAHSS*-trah*	step-daughter
hijastro, *m.*	*ee-*HAHSS*-troh*	step-son
hijo, *m.*	EE*-hoh*	son
hijo adoptivo, *m.*	EE*-hoh ah-thohp-*TEE*-voh*	foster child
hilado, *m.*	*ee-*LAH*-thoh*	yarn (fiber)
hilar (1)	*ee-*LAHR	spin (form thread), to
hilo, *m.*	EE*-loh*	strand
"	"	thread (sewing thread)
himno, *m.*	EEM*-noh*	hymn (religious song)
hincharse (1)	*een-*CHAHR*-seh*	swell (bulge), to
hipogloso, *m.*	*ee-poh-*GLOH*-soh*	halibut
hipoteca, *f.*	*ee-poh-*TEH*-kah*	mortgage
historia, *f.*	*eess-*TOH*-r yah*	history
histórico	*eess-*TOH*-ree-koh*	historical
historieta cómica, *f.*	*eess-toh-*R YEH*-tah* KOH*-mee-kah*	comic strip
hogar, *m.*	*oh-*GAHR	home
hogaza, *f.*	*oh-*GAH*-sah*	loaf
hoja, *f.*	OH*-hah*	blade (cutting tool)
"	"	leaf (*bot.*)
"	"	sheet (of paper)
hoja de afeitar, *f.*	OH*-hah theh ah-feh-*TAHR	razor blade
Holanda	*oh-*LAHN*-dah*	Holland
holandés, -desa	*oh-lahn-*DEHSS, -DEH*-sah*	Dutch (*adj.*)
holgazanear (1)	*ohl-gah-sah-neh-*AHR	loaf, to
hombre, *m.*	OHM*-breh*	man
hombre de negocios, *m.*	OHM*-breh theh neh-*GOH*-s yohss*	businessman
hombro, *m.*	OHM*-broh*	shoulder (*anat.*)
hondo	OHN*-doh*	deep (in extent)
Honduras	*ohn-*DOO*-rahss*	Honduras
honor, *m.*	*oh-*NOHR	honor
honorable	*oh-noh-*RAH*-vleh*	honorable (upright)
honorario, *m.*	*oh-noh-*RAH*-r yoh*	fee
honradez, *f.*	*ohn-rah-*THEHSS	honesty
honrado	*ohn-*RAH*-thoh*	honest
honrar (1)	*ohn-*RAHR	honor (respect), to
hora, *f.*	OH*-rah*	hour
"	"	time (hour determined by clock)
hora de recreo, *f.*	OH*-rah theh reh-*KREH*-oh*	recess (school intermission)
horario, *m.*	*oh-*RAH*-r yoh*	schedule
"	"	timetable
horas adicionales, *f.pl.*	OH*-rahss ah-thee-s yoh-*NAH*-lehss*	overtime (*bus.*, *n.*)
horizontal	*oh-ree-sohn-*TAHL	horizontal (*adj.*)
horizonte, *m.*	*oh-ree-*SOHN*-teh*	horizon
hormiga, *f.*	*ohr-*MEE*-gah*	ant
hormigón, *m.*	*ohr-mee-*GOHN	concrete (artificial stone)
horno, *m.*	OHR*-noh*	furnace (home heater)
"	"	oven
horrendo	*oh-*RREHN*-doh*	dreadful
horrible	*oh-*RREE*-vleh*	horrible

Spanish	Pronunciation	English
horror,*m.*	oh-RROHR	horror (dread)
hospedaje,*m.*	ohss-peh-THAH-*heh*	lodging (temporary quarters)
hospedar (1)	ohss-peh-THAHR	accommodate (to have room for), to
hospital,*m.*	ohss-pee-TAHL	hospital
hostil	ohss-TEEL	hostile
hotel,*m.*	oh-TEHL	hotel
hoy	OY	today
hoyo,*m.*	OH-*yoh*	hole (cavity)
"	"	pit
hueco	WEH-*koh*	hollow (*adj.*)
hueco,*m.*	WEH-*koh*	gap
huelga,*f.*	WEHL-*gah*	strike (work stoppage)
huella,*f.*	WEH-*yah*	mark (evidence)
huérfano,*m.*	WEHR-*fah-noh*	orphan (*n.*)
huerto,*m.*	WEHR-*toh*	orchard
hueso,*m.*	WEH-*soh*	bone
huésped,*m.*	WEHSS-*peth*	guest (visitor)
huevo,*m.*	WEH-*voh*	egg
huevos revueltos, *m.pl.*	WEH-*vohss reh-*VWEHL-*tohss*	scrambled eggs
huir (14)	oo-EER	flee (run from), to
humanidad,*f.*	oo-mah-nee-THAHTH	humanity
"	"	mankind
humano	oo-MAH-*noh*	human (*adj.*)
humedad,*f.*	oo-meh-THAHTH	moisture
húmedo	OO-*meh-thoh*	damp
"	"	moist
humilde	oo-MEEL-*theh*	humble (lowly)
humildad,*f.*	oo-meel-THAHTH	humility
humo,*m.*	OO-*moh*	smoke
humor,*m.*	oo-MOHR	mood (humor)
"	"	temper
hundirse (3)	oon-DEER-*seh*	sink (become submerged), to
Hungría	oon-GREE-*ah*	Hungary
idea,*f.*	ee-THEH-*ah*	idea
"	"	thought
ideal,*m.*	ee-theh-AHL	ideal (*n.*)
idear (1)	ee-theh-AHR	devise (contrive), to
identificar (1)	ee-thehn-tee-fee-KAHR	identify, to
ídolo,*m.*	EE-*thoh-loh*	idol
iglesia,*f.*	eeg-LEH-*s_yah*	church
ignominia,*f.*	eeg-noh-MEE-*nee_ah*	disgrace (shame)
ignorancia,*f.*	eeg-noh-RAHN-*s_yah*	ignorance
ignorante	eeg-noh-RAHN-*teh*	ignorant
igual	ee-GWAHL	equal (*adj.*)
igualar a (1)	ee-gwah-LAHR *ah*	match (equal), to
ilegal	ee-leh-GAHL	illegal
iluminar (1)	ee-loo-mee-NAHR	illuminate (light up), to
"	"	light, to
ilusión,*f.*	ee-loo-S_YOHN	illusion
imaginación,*f.*	ee-mah-hee-nah-S_YOHN	imagination
imaginar (1)	ee-mah-hee-NAHR	imagine (picture mentally), to
"	"	suspect (surmise), to
imán,*m.*	ee-MAHN	magnet
imitar (1)	ee-mee-TAHR	imitate, to
impaciencia,*f.*	eem-pah-S_YEHN-*s_yah*	impatience
impacientarse (1)	eem-pah-S_yehn-TAHR-*seh*	fret (worry), to
impaciente	eem-pah-S_YEHN-*teh*	impatient
impar	EEM-*pahr*	odd (not even)
impedir (9)	eem-peh-THEER	avert (prevent), to
"	"	bar (block), to
"	"	check (stop), to
"	"	keep (prevent), to
impeler (2)	eem-peh-LEHR	drive (propel), to
imperdible,*m.*	eem-pehr-THEE-*vleh*	safety pin
imperfecto	eem-pehr-FEHK-*toh*	imperfect (defective)
imperial	eem-peh-R_YAHL	imperial
imperio,*m.*	eem-PEH-*r_yoh*	empire
impermeable,*m.*	eem-pehr-meh-AH-*vleh*	raincoat
"	"	waterproof
imponer (31)	eem-poh-NEHR	impose (inflict), to
importación,*f.*	eem-pohr-tah-S_YOHN	importation
importador,*m.*	eem-pohr-tah-THOHR	importer
importancia,*f.*	eem-pohr-TAHN-*s_yah*	importance
importante	eem-pohr-TAHN-*teh*	important
importar (1)	eem-pohr-TAHR	import, to (*bus.*)
imposibilidad,*f.*	eem-poh-see-vee-lee-THATH	impossibility

Spanish	Pronunciation	English
imposible	eem-poh-SEE-*vleh*	impossible
impresión,*f.*	eem-preh-S_YOHN	impression (effect)
"	"	print (printed reproduction)
impresionar (1)	eem-preh-s_yoh-NAHR	impress (affect deeply), to
impresor,*m.*	eem-preh-SOHR	printer
imprevisto	eem-preh-VEESS-*toh*	sudden (unexpected)
imprimir (3)	eem-pree-MEER	print, to
impuesto,*m.*	eem-PWEHSS-*toh*	tax (*n.*)
impuesto sobre rentas,*m.*	eem-PWEHSS-*toh* SOH-*vreh* REHN-*tahss*	income tax
impuro	eem-POO-*roh*	impure
inadecuado	ee-nah-theh-KWAH-*thoh*	inadequate
inauguración,*f.*	een-ah_oo-goo-rah-S_YOHN	opening (beginning, *n.*)
incidente,*m.*	een-see-THEHN-*teh*	incident (event)
inclinación,*f.*	een-klee-nah-S_YOHN	bow (nod)
"	"	inclination (tendency)
inclinarse (1)	een-klee-NAHR-*seh*	incline (tend), to
"	"	lean (bend), to
"	"	slant (slope), to
incluir (14)	een-KL_WEER	enclose (include in envelope), to
"	"	include (contain), to
inconveniencia,*f.*	een-kohn-veh-N_YEHN-*s_yah*	inconvenience
incorrecto	een-koh-RREHK-*toh*	incorrect
"	"	wrong (erroneous, *adj.*)
incursión aérea,*f.*	een-*koor*-S_YOH-*nah-EH-reh_ah*	air raid
indemnización,*f.*	een-dehm-nee-sah-S_YOHN	indemnity (compensation)
independencia,*f.*	een-deh-pehn-DEHN-*s_yah*	independence
independiente	een-deh-pehn-D_YEHN-*teh*	independent
India	EEN-*d_yah*	India
indicar (1)	een-dee-KAHR	indicate, to
"	"	point, to
índice,*m.*	EEN-*dee-seh*	index (list)
indiferente	een-dee-feh-REHN-*teh*	indifferent (unconcerned)
indigestión,*f.*	een-dee-hehss-T_YOHN	indigestion
indignación,*f.*	een-deeg-nah-S_YOHN	indignation
indigno	een-DEEG-*noh*	unworthy
indio americano,*m.*	EEN-*d_yoh ah-meh-ree-*KAH-*noh*	Indian, American
indirecta,*f.*	een-dee-REHK-*tah*	hint (inkling)
indirecto	een-dee-REHK-*toh*	indirect
individuo,*m.*	een-dee-VEE-*thwoh*	fellow
"	"	individual (person, *n.*)
inducir (12)	een-doo-SEER	induce (persuade), to
indulto,*m.*	een-DOOL-*toh*	pardon (*law*)
industria,*f.*	een-DOOSS-*tr_yah*	industry (trade)
industrial	een-dooss-TR_YAHL	industrial
industrioso	een-dooss-TR_YOH-*soh*	industrious
inesperado	ee-nehss-peh-RAH-*thoh*	unexpected (*adj.*)
inevitable	ee-neh-vee-TAH-*bleh*	inevitable (*adj.*)
inexacto	ee-nehg-SAHK-*toh*	inaccurate
infante,*m.*	een-FAHN-*teh*	infant (*n.*)
infección,*f.*	een-fehk-S_YOHN	infection
infeliz	een-feh-LEESS	unhappy (sorrowful)
inferior	een-feh-R_YOHR	inferior (mediocre)
infierno,*m.*	een-F_YEHR-*noh*	hell
infinito	een-fee-NEE-*toh*	infinite
inflación,*f.*	een-flah-S_YOHN	inflation (*econ.*)
inflamación,*f.*	een-flah-mah-S_YOHN	inflammation
influencia,*f.*	een-FL_WEHN-*s_yah*	influence
influenza,*f.*	een-FL_WEHN-*sah*	influenza
influir en (13)	in-FL_WEER *ehn*	affect (influence), to
influjo,*m.*	een-FLOO-*hoh*	sway (influence)
información,*f.*	een-fohr-mah-S_YOHN	information (knowledge)
informar (1)	een-fohr-MAHR	inform (apprise), to
informe,*m.*	een-FOHR-*meh*	report (account)
ingeniero,*m.*	een-heh-N_YEH-*roh*	engineer (professional engineer)
ingenioso	een-heh-N_YOH-*soh*	witty
Inglaterra,*f.*	een-glah-TEH-*rrah*	England
inglés, -glesa	een-GLEHSS, -GLEH-*sah*	English (*adj.*)
ingresar (en) (1)	een-greh-SAHR (*ehn*)	enter (join), to
ingreso,*m.*	een-GREH-*soh*	income
inicial	ee-nee-S_YAHL	initial (first, *adj.*)

Spanish	Pronunciación	English
injusticia, *f.*	*een-hooss-*TEE-*s yah*	injustice
"	"	wrong
injusto	*een-*HOOSS-*toh*	unjust (inequitable)
"		wrong (*adj.*)
inmediatamente	*een-meh-th yah-tah-* MEHN-*teh*	immediately (instantly)
inmediato	*een-meh-*TH YAH-*toh*	immediate (instant)
inmenso	*een-*MEHN-*soh*	immense
inmortal	*een-mohr-*TAHL	immortal (*adj.*)
inmóvil	*een-*MOH-*veel*	still (motionless, *adj.*)
inmundo	*een-*MOON-*doh*	foul (filthy)
innecesario	*een-neh-seh-*SAH-*r yoh*	needless
"	"	unnecessary
inocente, *m.*	*ee-noh-*SEHN-*teh*	innocent (guiltless)
inodoro, *m.*	*ee-noh-*THOH-*roh*	toilet (water closet)
inquietarse (1)	*een-k yeh-*TAHR-*seh*	worry (feel anxious), to
inquieto	*een-*K YEH-*toh*	anxious
"	"	restless
"	"	uneasy
inquilino, *m.*	*een-kee-*LEE-*noh*	tenant
inscribir (3)	*een-skree-*VEER	enter (make record of), to
"	"	record (set down), to
inscripción, *f.*	*een-skreep-*S YOHN	inscription
insecto, *m.*	*een-*SEHK-*toh*	insect
insertar (1)	*een-sehr-*TAHR	insert, to
insignificante	*een-seeg-nee-fee-*KAHN-*teh*	insignificant (trivial)
insistir (3)	*een-seess-*TEER	insist, to
insistir en	*een-seess-*TEER *ehn*	urge (try to persuade), to
insolvencia, *f.*	*een-sohl-*VEHN-*s yah*	insolvency (*bus.*)
inspección, *f.*	*een-spehk-*S YOHN	check (examination)
"	"	inspection (scrutiny)
inspeccionar (1)	*een-spehk-s yoh-*NAHR	inspect, to
inspiración, *f.*	*een-spee-rah-*S YOHN	inspiration
inspirar (1)	*een-spee-*RAHR	inspire, to
instalar (1)	*een-stah-*LAHR	install (set up for use), to
instante, *m.*	*een-*STAHN-*teh*	instant (*n.*)
instinto, *m.*	*een-*STEEN-*toh*	instinct
institución, *f.*	*een-stee-too-*S YOHN	institution (establishment)
instituto, *m.*	*een-stee-*TOO-*toh*	institute
instrucción, *f.*	*een-strook-*S YOHN	instruction (teaching)
"	"	schooling
"	"	training
instruir (14)	*eenss-*TR WEER	instruct (teach), to
instrumento, *m.*	*eenss-troo-*MEHN-*toh*	instrument (implement)
insuficiente	*een-soo-fee-*S YEHN-*teh*	insufficient
insulto, *m.*	*een-*SOOL-*toh*	insult
intelectual	*een-teh-lehk-*TWAHL	intellectual (*adj.*)
inteligencia, *f.*	*een-teh-lee-*HEHN-*s yah*	intelligence (understanding)
inteligente	*een-teh-lee-*HEHN-*teh*	intelligent
intención, *f.*	*een-tehn-*S YOHN	intention
intenso	*een-*TEHN-*soh*	intense
intentar (1)	*een-tehn-*TAHR	intend (propose), to
"	"	undertake (attempt), to
"	"	try (attempt), to
interés, *m.*	*een-teh-*REHSS	interest (money rate)
interesante	*een-teh-reh-*SAHN-*teh*	interesting
interesar (1)	*een-teh-reh-*SAHR	interest, to
interesarse (en)	*een-teh-reh-*SAHR-*seh* (*ehn*)	care (be concerned), to
interés compuesto, *m.*	*een-teh-*REHSS *kohm-* PWEHSS-*toh*	compound interest
ínterin, *m.*	EEN-*teh-reen*	meantime (*n.*)
interior	*een-teh-r YOHR*	inner
		inside (*adj.*)
interior, *m.*	*een-teh-r YOHR*	inside (*n.*)
"	"	interior (*n.*)
internacional	*een-tehr-nah-s yoh-* NAHL	international
interno	*een-*TEHR-*noh*	internal
interpretar (1)	*een-tehr-preh-*TAHR	interpret (explain), to
interrogar (5)	*een-teh-rroh-*GAHR	question (query), to
interrumpir (3)	*een-teh-rroom-*PEER	interrupt, to
interruptor, *m.*	*een-teh-rroop-*TOHR	switch (*elec.*)
intervalo, *m.*	*een-tehr-*VAH-*loh*	interval (period of time)
intervención, *f.*	*een-tehr-vehn-*S YOHN	audit (*n.*)

Spanish	Pronunciación	English
intervenir (37)	*een-tehr-veh-*NEER	interfere (meddle), to
interventor, *m.*	*een-tehr-vehn-*TOHR	auditor (*n.*)
intestinos, *m.pl.*	*een-tehss-*TEE-*nohss*	bowels (*anat.*)
íntimo	EEN-*tee-moh*	close
"		intimate (personal)
introducción, *f.*	*een-troh-thook-*S YOHN	introduction (preliminary part)
introducir (12)	*een-troh-thoo-*SEER	introduce (bring in), to
intuición, *f.*	*een-twee-*S YOHN	intuition
inundación, *f.*	*ee-noon-dah-*S YOHN	flood
inútil	*ee-*NOO-*teel*	idle
"		useless
invadir (3)	*een-bah-*THEER	invade, to (*mil.*)
invención, *f.*	*een-behn-*S YOHN	invention
inventar (1)	*een-behn-*TAHR	invent, to
inventario, *m.*	*een-behn-*TAH-*r yoh*	inventory (*bus.*)
inversión, *f.*	*een-behr-*S YOHN	investment (*bus.*)
invertir (7)	*een-behr-*TEER	invest, to (*bus.*)
investigación, *f.*	*een-behss-tee-gah-* S YOHN	investigation
"	"	research
investigar (1)	*een-behss-tee-*GAHR	investigate, to
invierno, *m.*	*een-*B YEHR-*noh*	winter (*n.*)
invisible	*een-bee-*SEE-*bleh*	invisible
invitación, *f.*	*een-bee-tah-*S YOHN	invitation
invitar (1)	*een-bee-*TAHR	invite, to
inyección, *f.*	*een-yehk-*S YOHN	injection (*med.*)
ir (27)	EER	go, to
ira, *f.*	EE-*rah*	wrath
ir a la deriva	EER *ah lah theh-*REE-*vah*	drift (float), to
ir de compras	EER *theh* KOHM-*prahss*	shop, to
Irlanda	*eer-*LAHN-*dah*	Ireland
irlandés, -desa	*eer-lahn-*DEHSS, -DEH-*sah*	Irish (*adj.*)
irrazonable	*eer-rrah-soh-*NAH-*vleh*	unreasonable (unreasoning)
irregular	*ee-rreh-goo-*LAHR	irregular
irritar (1)	*ee-rree-*TAHR	irritate (annoy), to
isla, *f.*	EESS-*lah*	island (*geog.*)
Israel	*eess-rah-*EHL	Israel
israelito	*eess-rah-eh-*LEE-*toh*	Israeli (*adj.*)
istmo, *m.*	EESST-*moh*	isthmus
Italia	*ee-*TAH-*l yah*	Italy
italiano, *m.*	*ee-tah-*L YAH-*noh*	Italian (*adj.*)
izquierda, *f.*	*eess-*K YEHR-*thah*	left (*n.*)
izquierda, a la	*ah lah eess-*K YEHR-*thah*	left (*adv.*)
izquierdo	*eess-*K YEHR-*thoh*	left (*adj.*)
jabón, *m.*	*hah-*VOHN	soap
jactarse (1)	*hahk-*TAHR-*seh*	boast, to
jadear (1)	*hah-theh-*AHR	pant (puff), to
jalea, *f.*	*hah-*LEH-*ah*	jelly
jamón, *m.*	*hah-*MOHN	ham (food)
Japón	*hah-*POHN	Japan
japonés, -nesa	*hah-poh-*NEHSS, -NEH-*sah*	Japanese (*adj.*)
jardín, *m.*	*hahr-*THEEN	garden
jardinero, *m.*	*hahr-thee-*NEH-*roh*	gardener
jarra, *f.*	HAH-*rrah*	jar (vessel)
jarro, *m.*	HAH-*rroh*	jug
"	"	pitcher (container)
jarrón, *m.*	*hah-*RROHN	vase
jaula, *f.*	HOW-*lah*	cage
jazz, *m.*	HAHSS	jazz
jefe, *m.*	HEH-*feh*	head (leader)
jengibre, *m.*	*hehn-*HEE-*vreh*	ginger (spice)
jerga, *f.*	HEHR-*gah*	slang (*n.*)
jeringa, *f.*	*heh-*REEN-*gah*	syringe
Jerusalén	*heh-roo-sah-*LEHN	Jerusalem
Jesús	*heh-*SOOSS	Jesus
jinete, *m.*	*hee-*NEH-*teh*	rider (horseman)
jira, *f.*	HEE-*rah*	tour
jira campestre, *f.*	HEE-*rah kahm-*PEHSS-*treh*	picnic
joroba, *f.*	*hoh-*ROH-*vah*	hump
joven	HOH-*vehn*	young (*adj.*)
"		youthful
joven, *m.*	HOH-*vehn*	youth (young man)
jovencito, *m.*	*hoh-vehn-*SEE-*toh*	youngster
joven soltera, *f.*	HOH-*vehn sohl-*TEH-*rah*	maiden

Spanish	Pronunciation	English
jovial	*hoh-V YAHL*	cheerful (joyful)
joya, *f.*	*HOH-yah*	jewel
joyas, *f.pl.*	*HOH-yahss*	jewelry
júbilo, *m.*	*HOO-vee-loh*	joy / mirth
jubiloso	*hoo-vee-LOH-soh*	joyful
judío	*hoo-THEE-oh*	Jewish (*adj.*)
judío, *m.*	*hoo-THEE-oh*	Jew (*n.*)
juego, *m.*	*HWEH-goh*	game (contest)
juego de naipes, *m.*	*HWEH-goh theh NAH ee-pehss*	bridge, contract
juez, *m.*	*H_WEHSS*	judge
jugador, *m.*	*hoo-gah-THOHR*	player (in a game)
jugar (6)	*hoo-GAHR*	play (engage in recreation), to
jugo, *m.*	*HOO-goh*	juice
juguete, *m.*	*hoo-GEH-teh*	toy
juicio, *m.*	*HWEE-s yoh*	judgment
junco, *m.*	*HOON-koh*	reed (grass)
junta, *f.*	*HOON-tah*	board (council)
juntar (1)	*hoon-TAHR*	join (bring together), to
junto a	*HOON-toh ah*	by (near, *prep.*) / next (alongside of, *prep.*)
juntos	*HOON-tohss*	together
jurado, *m.*	*hoo-RAH-thoh*	jury
juramento, *m.*	*hoo-rah-MEHN-toh*	oath (vow)
jurar (1)	*hoo-RAHR*	swear (vow), to
justamente	*hooss-tah-MEHN-teh*	fairly (impartially)
justicia, *f.*	*hooss-TEE-s yah*	justice
justificar (1)	*hooss-tee-fee-KAHR*	justify (defend), to / justify (exonerate), to / warrant (justify), to
justo	*HOOSS-toh*	fair (impartial) / just (equitable, *adj.*)
juventud, *f.*	*hoo-vehn-TOO TH*	youth (period of life)
juventud, *f.*	*hoo-vehn-TOO TH*	youthfulness
juzgar (1)	*hooss-GAHR*	judge, to
Karachi	*kah-RAH-chee*	Karachi
keroseno, *m.*	*keh-roh-SEH-noh*	kerosene
la (*def. art.*)	*LAH*	the
la (*pron.*)	*LAH*	her / it / you
labio, *m.*	*LAH-v yoh*	lip (*anat.*)
labor, *f.*	*lah-VOHR*	labor (exertion)
laboratorio, *m.*	*lah-voh-rah-TOH-r yoh*	laboratory
labrar (1)	*lah-VRAHR*	till (cultivate), to
ladera, *f.*	*lah-THEH-rah*	hillside
lado, *m.*	*LAH-thoh*	side
lado de, al	*ah LAH-thoh theh*	beside (next to, *prep.*)
ladrar (1)	*lah-THRAHR*	bark (bay), to
ladrillo, *m.*	*lah-TH REE-yoh*	brick (building material)
ladrón, *m.*	*lah-THROHN*	burglar / robber / thief
lago, *m.*	*LAH-goh*	lake
lágrima, *f.*	*LAH-gree-mah*	tear (teardrop)
lamentar (1)	*lah-mehn-TAHR*	mourn (feel grief), to
lamer (2)	*lah-MEHR*	lick (lap), to
la misma	*lah MEEZ-mah*	itself
lámpara, *f.*	*LAHM-pah-rah*	lamp
lana, *f.*	*LAH-nah*	wool (fleece)
langosta, *f.*	*lahn-GOHSS-tah*	lobster
lanza, *f.*	*LAHN-sah*	spear (weapon)
lanzar (1)	*lahn-SAHR*	hurl, to / pitch (throw), to
lanzarse	*lahn-SAHR-seh*	dash (rush), to
lápiz, *m.*	*LAH-peess*	crayon / pencil
lápiz para los labios, *m.*	*LAH-peess PAH-rah lohss LAH-v yohss*	lipstick
largo	*LAHR-goh*	long (not short)
largo, *m.*	*LAHR-goh*	length
largo, de	*deh-LAHR-goh*	long (of a specified length)
largo de, a lo	*ah loh LAHR-goh theh*	along (lengthwise of)
las	*LAHSS*	them
lata, *f.*	*LAH-tah*	can (tin)
látigo, *m.*	*LAH-tee-goh*	lash / whip
latino	*lah-TEE-noh*	Latin (*adj.*)
latón, *m.*	*lah-TOHN*	brass (metal, *n.*)
lavandería, *f.*	*lah-vahn-deh-REE-ah*	laundry (commercial plant)
lavar (1)	*lah-VAHR*	wash (cleanse), to
lavarse	*lah-VAHR-seh*	wash (cleanse oneself), to
lazo, *m.*	*LAH-soh*	bond (emotional tie)
le	*LEH*	(to) her / (to) him / (to) it / (to) you
leal	*leh-AHL*	loyal
lealtad, *f.*	*leh-ahl-TAHTH*	allegiance / loyalty
lección, *f.*	*lehk-S YOHN*	lesson (assignment)
leche, *f.*	*LEH-cheh*	milk
lechería, *f.*	*leh-cheh-REE-ah*	dairy
lechuga, *f.*	*leh-CHOO-gah*	lettuce
lector, *m.*	*lehk-TOHR*	reader
leer (2)	*LEH(eh)R*	read, to
legal	*leh-GAHL*	lawful / legal
legislación, *f.*	*leh-heess-lah-S YOHN*	legislation
legislatura, *f.*	*leh-heess-lah-TOO-rah*	congress / legislature
legumbre, *f.*	*leh-GOOM-breh*	vegetable
lejano	*leh-HAH-noh*	distant (far-off) / far (*adj.*)
lejano, más	*mahss leh-HAH-noh*	farther (*adj.*)
lejos	*LEH-hohss*	away (from a place, *adv.*) / far (afar, *adv.*)
lejos, más	*mahss LEH-hohss*	farther (*adv.*)
lengua, *f.*	*LEHN-gwah*	language / tongue (*anat.*)
leño, *m.*	*LEH-n yoh*	log (rough timber)
lento	*LEHN-toh*	slow (not fast)
león, *m.*	*leh-OHN*	lion
leopardo, *m.*	*lee-oh-PAHR-thoh*	leopard
lepra, *f.*	*LEH-prah*	leprosy
les	*LEHSS*	(to) them / (to) you
lesión, *f.*	*leh-S YOHN*	injury
letra, *f.*	*LEH-trah*	letter (character) / writing (handwriting)
letra a la vista, *f.*	*LEH-trah ah lah VEE-stah*	sight draft (*bus.*)
letra de cambio, *f.*	*LEH-trah theh KAHM-b yoh*	bill of exchange
letra inicial, *f.*	*LEH-trah ee-nee-S YAHL*	initial (letter)
leva, *f.*	*LEH-vah*	draft (conscription)
levadura, *f.*	*leh-vah-THOO-rah*	yeast
levantar (1)	*leh-vahn-TAHR*	heave, to / lift (raise), to
ley, *f.*	*LAY*	law (governing code)
leyenda, *f.*	*leh-YEHN-dah*	legend (story)
liberal	*lee-veh-RAHL*	liberal (*polit.*, *adj.*)
libertad, *f.*	*lee-vehr-TAHTH*	freedom / liberty
libertar (1)	*lee-vehr-TAHR*	liberate, to
librar (1)	*lee-VRAHR*	free, to / relieve, to / rid, to
libre	*LEE-vreh*	free (independent)
libre de derechos	*LEE-vreh theh theh-REH-chohss*	duty-free
libreta, *f.*	*lee-BREH-tah*	notebook
libro, *m.*	*LEE-vroh*	book
libro de texto, *m.*	*LEE-vroh theh TEHGSS-toh*	textbook
licencia, *f.*	*lee-SEHN-s yah*	license (permit)
licor, *m.*	*lee-KOHR*	liquor (alcoholic beverage)
liebre, *f.*	*L YEH-vreh*	hare
liga, *f.*	*LEE-gah*	garter / league
ligero	*lee-HEH-roh*	light (of little weight)
lila, *f.*	*LEE-lah*	lilac (flower)
Lima	*LEE-mah*	Lima
lima, *f.*	*LEE-mah*	file (tool)

Spanish	Pronunciation	English
limitar (1)	*lee-mee-*TAHR	confine, to
"	"	limit, to
límite,*m.*	LEE-*mee-teh*	boundary
"	"	limit
limón,*m.*	*lee-*MOHN	lemon
"	"	lime (fruit)
limonada,*f.*	*lee-moh-*NAH-*thah*	lemonade
limpiar (1)	*leem-p_*YAHR	clean, to
limpio	LEEM-*p_yoh*	clean
línea,*f.*	LEE-*neh-ah*	line (mark)
lino,*m.*	LEE-*noh*	flax
"	"	linen (fabric)
linóleo,*m.*	*lee-*NOH-*leh-oh*	linoleum
linterna,*f.*	*leen-*TEHR-*nah*	lantern
linterna eléctrica,*f.*	*leen-*TEHR-*nah eh-*LEHK-*tree-kah*	flashlight
liquidación, (venta de),*f.*	(BEHN-*tah-theh-*) *lee-kee-thah-*S_YOHN	clearance sale
líquido,*m.*	LEE-*kee-thoh*	liquid (*n.*)
lirio,*m.*	LEE-*r_yoh*	lily
lisiar (1)	*lee-*S_YAHR	injure, to
liso	LEE-*soh*	smooth (*adj.*)
lisonjear (1)	*lee-sohn-heh-*AHR	flatter (praise insincerely), to
lista,*f.*	LEESS-*tah*	list
listo	LEESS-*toh*	ready (prepared)
"	"	smart (clever)
listón,*m.*	*leess-*TOHN	ribbon
litera,*f.*	*lee-*TEH-*rah*	berth (train bunk)
literario	*lee-teh-*RAH-*r_yoh*	literary
literatura,*f.*	*lee-teh-rah-*TOO-*rah*	literature (belles-lettres)
litigación,*f.*	*lee-tee-gah-*S_YOHN	litigation
litografía,*f.*	*lee-toh-grah-*FEE-*ah*	lithography
llama,*f.*	YAH-*mah*	flame
llamar (1)	*yah-*MAHR	call, to
"	"	summon (send for), to
llanura,*f.*	*yah-*NOO-*rah*	plain (level land)
llave,*f.*	YAH-*veh*	faucet
"	"	key (for lock)
llegada,*f.*	*yeh-*GAH-*thah*	arrival
llegar (1)	*yeh-*GAHR	arrive, to
llegar a	*yeh-*GAHR *ah*	reach (arrive at), to
llenar (1)	*yeh-*NAHR	fill (make full), to
lleno	YEH-*noh*	full (filled)
lleno de esperanza	YEH-*noh theh_ss-peh-*RAHN-*sah*	hopeful
llevar (1)	*yeh-*VAHR	bear, to
"	"	carry, to
"	"	wear (have on), to
llorar (1)	*yoh-*RAHR	cry, to
"	"	weep, to
llover (5)	*yoh-*VEHR	rain, to
lluvia,*f.*	YOO-*v_yah*	rain
lluvioso	*yoo-*V_YOH-*soh*	rainy
lo (*def. art.*)	LOH	the
lo (*pron.*)	LOH	him
"	"	it
lobo,*m.*	LOH-*voh*	wolf
local	*loh-*KAHL	local (regional)
localidad,*f.*	*loh-kah-lee-*THATH	locality (place)
loco	LOH-*koh*	crazy
"	"	mad (insane)
locomotora,*f.*	*loh-koh-mah-*TOH-*rah*	engine
"	"	locomotive
locura,*f.*	*loh-*KOO-*rah*	folly
"	"	madness (insanity)
lodo,*m.*	LOH-*thoh*	mud
lograr (1)	*loh-*GRAHR	achieve (attain), to
lo más	*loh* MAHSS	most (almost all, *adj.*)
lo mismo	*loh* MEEZ-*moh*	itself
lona,*f.*	LOH-*nah*	canvas (cloth)
Londres	LOHN-*drehss*	London
lo que	*loh keh*	what (*rel. pron.*)
loro,*m.*	LOH-*roh*	parrot
los	LOHSS	them
los dos	*lohz* THOHSS	both (*pron.*)
los (las) que	LOHSS (LAHSS) KEH	who (*rel. pron.*)
lote,*m.*	LOH-*teh*	lot (salable items, *bus.*)

Spanish	Pronunciation	English
lucha,*f.*	LOO-*chah*	struggle (great effort)
luchar a brazo partido (1)	*loo-*CHAHR *ah* BRAH-*soh pahr-*TEE-*thoh*	wrestle, to
luchar contra	*loo-*CHAHR KOHN-*trah*	fight (struggle against), to
luego	L_WEH-*goh*	next (*adv.*)
"	"	then (subsequently)
lugar,*m.*	*loo-*GAHR	place (locality)
"	"	stead
lugar de, en	*ehn loo-*GAHR-*theh*	instead of
lugar de temporada,*m.*	*loo-*GAHR *theh tehm-poh-*RAH-*thah*	resort (spa)
lúgubre	LOO-*goo-vreh*	dreary
lujo,*m.*	LOO-*hoh*	luxury
lujuria,*f.*	*loo-*HOO-*r_yah*	lust (desire)
luna,*f.*	LOO-*nah*	moon
lustre,*m.*	LOOSS-*treh*	luster (sheen)
"	"	polish
luz,*f.*	LOOSS	light (illumination)
luz de la luna,*f.*	LOOSS *theh lah* LOO-*nah*	moonlight
luz del día,*f.*	*looss thehl* DEE-*ah*	daylight
luz del sol,*f.*	LOOSS *thehl* SOHL	sunshine
luz solar,*f.*	LOOSS *soh-*LAHR	sunlight
machacar (1)	*mah-chah-*KAHR	crush, to
"	"	pound (pummel), to
macho	MAH-*choh*	male (*adj.*)
macho del ciervo, *m.*	MAH-*choh thehl* S_YEHR-*voh*	buck (male deer)
madera,*f.*	*mah-*THEH-*rah*	lumber (timber)
"	"	wood
madrastra,*f.*	*mah-*THRAHSS-*trah*	step-mother
madre,*f.*	MAH-*threh*	mother
Madrid	*mah-*THREETH	Madrid
madurar (1)	*mah-thoo-*RAHR	mature (ripen), to
maduro	*mah-*THOO-*roh*	ripe
maestro,*m.*	*mah-*EHSS-*troh*	master (great artist)
"	"	teacher
magia,*f.*	MAH-*h_yah*	magic (*n.*)
mágico,*m.*	MAH-*hee-koh*	magician
magnífico	*mahg-*NEE-*fee-koh*	magnificent
magro	MAH-*groh*	lean (thin)
maíz,*m.*	*mah-*EESS	corn (maize)
majestad,*f.*	*mah-hehss-*TAHTH	majesty
mal	MAHL	evil (*adj.*)
"	"	wrong (amiss, *adv.*)
mal,*m.*	MAHL	evil (*n.*)
mala hierba,*f.*	MAH-*lah* YEHR-*vah*	weed
malaria,*f.*	*mah-*LAH-*r_yah*	malaria
maldecir (22)	*mahl-deh-*SEER	curse (damn), to
mal de garganta,*m.*	MAHL *deh gahr-*GAHN-*tah*	sore throat
maldición,*f.*	*mahl-dee-*S_YOHN	curse
maléfico	*mah-*LEH-*fee-koh*	mean (malicious)
maleza,*f.*	*mah-*LEH-*sah*	thicket
malicia,*f.*	*mah-*LEE-*s_yah*	malice
malo	MAH-*loh*	bad
"	"	evil (*adj.*)
mampara,*f.*	*mahm-*PAH-*rah*	screen (partition)
maña,*f.*	MAH-*n_yah*	trick (knack)
mañana	*mah-*N_YAH-*nah*	tomorrow
mañana,*f.*	*mah-*N_YAH-*nah*	morning
"	"	morrow
mancha,*f.*	MAHN-*chah*	blot
"	"	spot
"	"	stain
manchar (1)	*mahn-*CHAHR	blot (stain), to
mandado,*m.*	*mahn-*DAH-*thoh*	errand (commission)
mandar (1)	*mahn-*DAHR	command (order), to
"	"	dictate (give orders), to
mando,*m.*	MAHN-*doh*	command (authority)
manejar (1)	*mah-neh-*HAHR	manage (contrive), to
"	"	operate (handle), to
manera,*f.*	*mah-*NEH-*rah*	manner (mode)
"	"	way
manera de tratar, *f.*	*mah-*NEH-*rah theh trah-*TAHR	treatment (behavior toward)
manga,*f.*	MAHN-*gah*	sleeve

Spanish	Pronunciation	English
mango, *m.*	MAHN-*goh*	handle
manguera, *f.*	*mahn*-GEH-*rah*	hose (tube)
maní, *m.*	*mah*-NEE	peanut
manía, *f.*	*mah*-NEE-*ah*	craze (fad)
manifiesto	*mah-nee*-F_YEHSS-*toh*	manifest (*adj.*)
mano, *f.*	MAH-*noh*	hand (*anat.*)
mano, a la	*ah lah* MAH-*noh*	handy (near at hand)
manta, *f.*	MAHN-*tah*	blanket
manteca, *f.*	*mahn*-TEH-*kah*	butter
"	"	lard
mantel, *m.*	*mahn*-TEHL	tablecloth
mantener (35)	*mahn-teh*-NEHR	maintain (preserve), to
mantequilla, *f.*	*mahn-teh*-KEE-*yah*	butter
manual	*mahn*-WAHL	manual (by hand)
manual, *m.*	*mahn*-WAHL	manual (small book)
manzana, *f.*	*mahn*-SAH-*nah*	apple
mapa, *m.*	MAH-*pah*	map
máquina, *f.*	MAH-*kee-nah*	machine
máquina de coser, *f.*	MAH-*kee-nah theh koh*-SEHR	sewing machine
máquina de escribir, *f.*	MAH-*kee-nah thehss-kree*-VEER	typewriter
máquina de sumar, *f.*	MAH-*kee-nah theh soo*-MAHR	adding machine
maquinaria, *f.*	*mah-kee*-NAH-*r_yah*	machinery
maquinista, *m.*	*mah-kee*-NEESS-*tah*	engineer (railroad engineman)
mar, *m., f.*	MAHR	sea
maravilla, *f.*	*mah-rah*-VEE-*yah*	marvel
maravilloso	*mah-rah-vee*-YOH-*soh*	marvelous
"	"	wonderful
marca (de fábrica), *f.*	MAHR-*kah* (*theh* FAH-*vree-kah*)	brand (trade mark)
marca de fábrica, *f.*	MAHR-*kah theh* FAH-*vree-kah*	trade mark
marchar (1)	*mahr*-CHAHR	march, to
marchitarse (1)	*mahr-chee*-TAHR-*seh*	wilt, to
"	"	wither, to
marea alta, *f.*	*mah*-REH-*ah* AHL-*tah*	tide, high
marea baja, *f.*	*mah*-REH-*ah* VAH-*hah*	tide, low
marfil, *m.*	*mahr*-FEEL	ivory
margarina, *f.*	*mahr-gah*-REE-*nah*	margarine
margarita, *f.*	*mahr-gah*-REE-*tah*	daisy
margen, *f.*	MAHR-*hehn*	margin (edge)
marido, *m.*	*mah*-REE-*thoh*	husband
marina de guerra, *f.*	*mah*-REE-*nah theh* GHEH-*rah*	navy (*n.*)
marinero, *m.*	*mah-ree*-NEH-*roh*	sailor
marino	*mah-ree*-NEE-*noh*	marine (oceanic)
mariposa, *f.*	*mah-ree*-POH-*sah*	butterfly
mar Mediterráneo,	MAHR *meh-thee-teh*-RRAH-*neh-oh*	Mediterranean Sea
mármol, *m.*	MAHR-*mohl*	marble (mineral)
marrano, *m.*	*mah*-RRAH-*noh*	swine
martillo, *m.*	*mahr*-TEE-*yoh*	hammer (tool)
más	MAHSS	else (in addition, *adj.*)
"	"	further (to greater extent, *adv.*)
"	"	more (*adj., adv.*)
"	"	plus (*prep.*)
más (el)	(*ehl*) MAHSS	most (*n.*)
masa, *f.*	MAH-*sah*	mass (matter)
mascar (1)	*mahss*-KAHR	chew, to
máscara, *f.*	MAHSS-*kah-rah*	mask (face covering)
masculino	*mahss-koo*-LEE-*noh*	masculine
mástil, *m.*	MAHSS-*teel*	mast
matanza, *f.*	*mah*-TAHN-*sah*	slaughter
matar (1)	*mah*-TAHR	kill, to
"	"	slay, to
matemática, *f.*	*mah-teh*-MAH-*tee-kah*	mathematics
materia, *f.*	*mah*-TEH-*r_yah*	matter
"	"	stuff (substance)
material, *m.*	*mah-teh*-R_YAHL	material (substance)
matiné, *m.*	*mah-tee*-NEH	matinee (theater performance)
matiz, *m.*	*mah*-TEESS	hue
matrimonio, *m.*	*mah-tree*-MOH-*n_yoh*	marriage
mayor	*mah*-YOHR	major (larger)
"	"	senior (older)
mayor, al por	*ahl pohr mah*-YOHR	wholesale (*adj., bus.*)

Spanish	Pronunciation	English
mayoría, *f.*	*mah-yoh*-REE-*ah*	majority (greater number)
mayorista, *m., f.*	*mah-yoh*-REESS-*tah*	wholesaler (*bus.*)
mayor parte, *f.*	*mah*-YOHR PAHR-*teh*	bulk (largest part)
mayor parte de, la	*lah mah*-YOHR PAHR-*teh theh*	most (greatest quantity, *adj.*)
me	MEH	(to) me
mecánico	*meh*-KAH-*nee-koh*	mechanical
mecánico, *m.*	*meh*-KAH-*nee-koh*	mechanic
mecanógrafo, *m.*	*meh-kah*-NOH-*grah-foh*	typist
mecerse (2)	*meh*-SEHR-*seh*	sway (swing), to
medalla, *f.*	*meh*-THAH-*yah*	medal
media, *f.*	MEH-*th_yah*	stocking
medianamente	*me-th_yah-nah*-MEHN-*teh*	fairly (somewhat)
mediano	*meh*-TH_YAH-*noh*	average (ordinary, *adj.*)
medianoche, *f.*	*meh-th_yah*-NOH-*cheh*	midnight
medicina, *f.*	*meh-thee*-SEE-*nah*	medicine
médico	MEH-*thee-koh*	medical
médico, *m.*	MEH-*thee-koh*	doctor
"	"	physician
medida, *f.*	*meh*-THEE-*thah*	measure (dimensions)
"	"	size (of hats)
medio	MEH-*th_yoh*	half (*adj.*)
medio, *m.*	MEH-*th_yoh*	agency (instrumentality)
"	"	medium (means)
"	"	middle (center)
medio de, en	*ehm* MEH-*th_yoh theh*	amid
medio de, por	*pohr* MEH-*th_yoh theh*	through (by means of, *prep.*)
mediodía, *m.*	*meh-th_yoh*-THEE-*ah*	noon
medir (9)	*meh*-THEER	measure (find size of), to
meditación, *f.*	*meh-thee-tah*-S_YOHN	thought (contemplation)
meditar (1)	*meh-thee*-TAHR	meditate (reflect), to
"	"	muse (meditate), to
mejicano	*meh-hee*-KAH-*noh*	Mexican (*adj.*)
Méjico	MEH-*hee-koh*	Mexico
"	"	Mexico City
mejilla, *f.*	*meh*-HEE-*yah*	cheek
mejor	*meh*-HOHR	better (*adj.*)
"	"	better (*adv.*)
mejor, (el)	(*ehl*) *mah*-HOHR	best (*adj.*)
mejoramiento, *m.*	*meh-hoh-rah*-M_YEHN-*toh*	improvement (betterment)
mejorar (1)	*meh-hoh*-RAHR	improve (make better), to
melancolía, *f.*	*meh-lahn-koh*-LEE-*ah*	gloom (depression)
"	"	melancholy (dejection)
melancólico	*meh-lahn*-KOH-*lee-koh*	gloomy
melindres, *m.pl.*	*meh*-LEEN-*drehss*	fuss (ado)
melocotón, *m.*	*meh-loh-koh*-TOHN	peach
memorándum, *m.*	*meh-moh*-RAHN-*doom*	memorandum
memoria, *f.*	*meh*-MOH-*r_yah*	memory
mencionar (1)	*mehn-s_yoh*-NAHR	mention, to
mendigar (1)	*mendee*-GAHR	beg (solicit alms), to
mendigo, *m.*	*mehn*-DEE-*goh*	beggar
menor	*meh*-NOHR	junior (younger)
"	"	minor (lesser)
menos	MEH-*nohss*	least (*adv.*)
"	"	less (*adj., adv., prep.*)
menos que, a	*ah* MEH-*nohss keh*	but (if not, *conj.*)
"	"	unless (*conj.*)
mensaje, *m.*	*mehn*-SAH-*heh*	message (communication)
mensajero, *m.*	*mehn-sah*-HEH-*roh*	messenger (courier)
mensual	*mehn*-SWAHL	monthly (every month, *adj.*)
mental	*mehn*-TAHL	mental
mente, *f.*	MEHN-*teh*	mind (intellect)
mentir (7)	*mehn*-TEER	lie (prevaricate), to
menú, *m.*	*meh*-NOO	menu
menudo	*meh*-NOO-*thoh*	fine (very small)
menudo, a	*ah meh*-NOO-*thoh*	often
meramente	*meh-rah*-MEHN-*teh*	merely
mercaderías, *f.pl.*	*mehr-kah-theh*-REE-*ahss*	merchandise
mercado, *m.*	*mehr*-KAH-*thoh*	market (trading center)

Spanish	Pronunciation	English
mercancía, *f.*	*mehr-kahn-*SEE-*ah*	commodity
mercancías, *f.pl.*	*mehr-kahn-*SEE-*ahss*	goods
"	"	wares
mercantil	*mehr-kahn-*TEEL	mercantile
mercurio, *m.*	*mehr-*KOO-*r_yoh*	mercury
merecer (11)	*meh-reh-*SEHR	deserve, to
"	"	earn, to
		merit, to
meridional	*meh-ree-d_yoh-*NAHL	southern
mérito, *m.*	MEH-*ree-toh*	merit
mero	MEH-*roh*	mere
mes, *m.*	MEHSS	month
mesa, *f.*	MEH-*sah*	plateau (tableland)
"	"	table (furniture)
meta, *f.*	MEH-*tah*	goal (objective)
metal, *m.*	*meh-*TAHL	metal (*n.*)
meter (2)	*meh-*TEHR	stick (thrust), to
meterse	*meh-*TEHR-*seh*	meddle, to
método, *m.*	MEH-*toh-thoh*	method
mezcla, *f.*	MEHSS-*klah*	blend
"	"	mixture
mezclar (1)	*mehss-*KLAHR	blend (make combine), to
"	"	mix (make blend), to
mezclilla de lana, *f.*	*mehss-*KLEE-*yah theh* LAH-*nah*	tweed (cloth)
mezquino	*mehss-*KEE-*noh*	petty (minor)
"	"	stingy
mi	MEE	me
"	"	my
mía, (la)	(*lah*) MEE-*ah*	mine (*poss. pron.*)
mías, (las)	(*lahss*) MEE-*ahss*	mine (*poss. pron.*)
microbio, *m.*	*mee-*KROH-*v_yoh*	germ (micro-organism)
miedo, *m.*	M_YEH-*thoh*	dread
miel, *f.*	M_YEHL	honey
miel de caña, *f.*	M_YEHL *deh* KAH-*n_yah*	molasses
miembro, *m.*	M_YEHM-*broh*	limb (*anat.*)
"	"	member (one of a group)
mientras	M_YEHN-*trahss*	as (while, *conj.*)
mientras (que)	M_YEHN-*trahss* (*keh*)	when (at the time that, *conj.*)
"	"	while (during the time that, *conj.*)
mientras tanto	M_YEHN-*trahss* TAHN-*toh*	meanwhile (*adv.*)
miércoles de ceniza, *m.*	M_YEHR-*koh-lehz theh* seh-NEE-*sah*	Ash Wednesday
migaja, *f.*	*mee-*GAH-*hah*	crumb
milagro, *m.*	*mee-*LAH-*groh*	miracle
militar	*mee-lee-*TAHR	military (*adj.*)
mi mismo	MEE MEEZ-*moh*	myself
mina, *f.*	MEE-*nah*	mine (explosive)
"	"	mine (pit)
mineral, *m.*	*mee-neh-*RAHL	mineral
"	"	ore
minero, *m.*	*mee-*NEH-*roh*	miner
mínimo	MEE-*nee-moh*	least (*adj.*)
mínimo, *m.*	MEE-*nee-moh*	least (*n.*)
ministro, *m.*	*mee-*NEESS-*troh*	minister (cabinet member)
minoría, *f.*	*mee-noh-*REE-*ah*	minority (smaller number)
minuto, *m.*	*mee-*NOO-*toh*	minute (unit of time)
mío, (el, lo)	(*ehl, loh*) MEE-*oh*	mine (*poss. pron.*)
míos, (los)	(*lohss*) MEE-*ohss*	mine (*poss. pron.*)
mirada, *f.*	*mee-*RAH-*thah*	glance
"	"	look
mirar (1)	*mee-*RAHR	behold, to
"	"	look, to
mirar atentamente	*mee-*RAHR *ah-tehn-tah-*MEHN-*teh*	peer (look intently), to
mirar fijamente	*mee-*RAHR *fee-hah-*MEHN-*teh*	gaze, to
"	"	glare, to
"	"	stare, to
mirlo, *m.*	MEER-*loh*	blackbird
mis	MEESS	my
misa, *f.*	MEE-*sah*	mass (*rel.*)
misceláneo	*mee-seh-*LAH-*n_yoh*	miscellaneous
miserable	*mee-sch-*RAH-*vleh*	miserable (unhappy)
miserable, *m.,f.*	*mee-sch-*RAH-*vleh*	wretch (hapless person)

Spanish	Pronunciation	English
miseria, *f.*	*mee-*SEH-*r_yah*	misery (grief)
misericordia, *f.*	*mee-sch-ree-*KOHR-*th_yah*	mercy
misericordioso	*mee-sch-ree-kohr-*TH_YOH-*soh*	merciful
misionero, *m.*	*mee-s_yoh-*NEH-*roh*	missionary
mismo	MEEZ-*moh*	same (*adj.*)
"	"	self (*pron.*)
mismo modo, del	*dehl-*MEEZ-*moh-*MOH-*thoh*	alike (similarly)
misterio, *m.*	*meess-*TEH-*r_yoh*	mystery (enigma)
misterioso	*meess-teh-*R_YOH-*soh*	mysterious
mitad, *f.*	*mee-*TATH	half (*n.*)
mito, *m.*	MEE-*toh*	myth (legend)
mitón, *m.*	*mee-*TOHN	mitten
moda, *f.*	MOH-*thah*	fashion (current style)
modales, *m.pl.*	*moh-*THAH-*lehss*	manners (polite behavior)
modelo, *m.*	*moh-*THEH-*loh*	model (exemplar)
"	"	model (small copy)
moderado	*moh-theh-*RAH-*thoh*	moderate (not extreme)
moderno	*moh-*THEHR-*noh*	modern
modesto	*moh-*THEHSS-*toh*	modest
modo, *m.*	MOH-*thoh*	fashion (manner)
"	"	means (method)
"	"	mode (manner)
mofar (1)	*moh-*FAHR	mock (deride), to
mohoso	*moh-*HOH-*soh*	moldy
mojado	*moh-*HAH-*thoh*	wet
mojar (1)	*moh-*HAHR	wet, to
moler (5)	*moh-*LEHR	grind (crush), to
molestar (1)	*moh-lehss-*TAHR	bother (annoy), to
"	"	pester, to
"	"	trouble (inconvenience), to
molestia, *f.*	*moh-*LEHSS-*t_yah*	pest (nuisance)
molinero, *m.*	*moh-lee-*NEH-*roh*	miller
momento, *m.*	*moh-*MEHN-*toh*	moment (instant)
monarca, *m.*	*moh-*NAHR-*kah*	monarch
monasterio, *m.*	*moh-nahss-*TEH-*r_yoh*	monastery
moneda, *f.*	*moh-*NEH-*thah*	coin
moneda corriente, *f.*	*moh-*NEH-*thah koh-*RR_YEHN-*teh*	currency (money)
monja, *f.*	MOHN-*hah*	nun
monje, *m.*	MOHN-*heh*	monk
mono, *m.*	MOH-*noh*	monkey
monótono	*moh-*NOH-*toh-noh*	monotonous (boring)
monstruo, *m.*	MOHNSS-*tr_woh*	monster (beast)
monstruoso	*mohnss-*TR_WOH-*soh*	monstrous (horrible)
montaña, *f.*	*mohn-*TAH-*n_yah*	mountain
montañoso	*mohn-tah-n_*YOH-*soh*	mountainous
montar (1)	*mohn-*TAHR	mount (climb upon), to
montar a Montevideo	*mohn-*TAHR *ah* *mohn-teh-vee-*THEH-*oh*	amount to, to Montevideo
montículo, *m.*	*mohn-*TEE-*koo-loh*	mound (hill)
montón, *m.*	*mohn-*TOHN	heap
"	"	pile
monumento, *m.*	*moh-noo-*MEHN-*toh*	monument
mora, *f.*	MOH-*rah*	blackberry
moral	*moh-*RAHL	moral (ethical)
moral, *f.*	*moh-*RAHL	morale
"	"	morals
mordedura, *f.*	*mohr-theh-*THOO-*rah*	bite
morder (5)	*mohr-*THEHR	bite, to
morir(se) (8)	*moh-*REER(-*seh*)	die, to
morirse de hambre	*moh-*REER-*seh theh* AHM-*breh*	starve (die of hunger), to
mortal	*mohr-*TAHL	deadly
"	"	fatal
"	"	mortal (*adj.*)
morueco, *m.*	*moh-*R_WEH-*koh*	ram (animal)
mosca, *f.*	MOHSS-*kah*	fly (housefly)
Moscú	*mohss-*KOO	Moscow
mosquito, *m.*	*mohss-*KEE-*toh*	mosquito
mostaza, *f.*	*mohss-*TAH-*sah*	mustard
mostrador, *m.*	*mohss-trah-*THOHR	counter (table)
mostrar (5)	*mohss-*TRAHR	show (make visible), to
mostrarse	*mohss-*TRAHR-*seh*	show (be visible), to
mote, *m.*	MOH-*teh*	motto
"	"	nickname

Spanish	Pronunciation	English
motín,*m.*	*moh*-TEEN	riot (disturbance)
motivo,*m.*	*moh*-TEE-*voh*	motive (*n.*)
motor,*m.*	*moh*-TOHR	motor (engine)
motor de propulsión a chorro,*m.*	*moh*-TOHR *theh proh*-POOL-S‿YOHN *ah* CHOH-*rroh*	jet engine
mover (5)	*moh*-VEHR	move (shift the position of), to
moverse	*moh*-VEHR-*seh*	move (shift one's position), to
movimiento,*m.*	*moh*-*vee*-M‿YEHN-*toh*	motion
"	"	movement
mozalbete,*m.*	*moh*-*sahl*-BEH-*teh*	lad
muchacha,*f.*	*moo*-CHAH-*chah*	girl
muchacho,*m.*	*moo*-CHAH-*choh*	boy (lad)
muchedumbre,*f.*	*moo*-*cheh*-THOOM-*breh*	crowd
mucho, más, lo más	MOO-*choh*, MAHSS, *loh* MAHSS	much, more, most
muchos, más, lo más	MOO-*chohss*, MAHSS, *loh* MAHSS	many, more, most
mudarse (1)	*moo*-THAHR-*seh*	move (change residence), to
mudo	MOO-*thoh*	dumb
"	"	mute (silent)
muebles,*m.pl.*	MWEH-*vlehss*	furniture
muelle,*m.*	MWEH-*yeh*	dock
muerte,*f.*	MWEHR-*teh*	death
muerto	MWEHR-*toh*	dead
muestra,*f.*	MWEHSS-*trah*	sample
mujer,*f.*	*moo*-HEHR	woman
mula,*f.*	MOO-*lah*	mule
muleta,*f.*	*moo*-LEH-*tah*	crutch
multa,*f.*	MOOL-*tah*	fine (penalty, *n.*)
multiplicar (1)	*mool*-*tee*-*plee*-KAHR	multiply, to (*arith.*)
"	"	multiply (grow numerous), to
multitud,*f.*	*mool*-*tee*-TOOTH	multitude
"	"	throng
mundo,*m.*	MOON-*doh*	world
muñeca,*f.*	*moo*-N‿YEH-*kah*	doll
"		wrist
murciélago,*m.*	*moor*-*see*‿EH-*lah*-*goh*	bat (animal)
murmurar (1)	*moo*-*moo*-RAHR	murmur, to
"	"	mutter (mumble), to
músculo,*m.*	MOOSS-*koo*-*loh*	muscle
museo,*m.*	*moo*-SEH-*oh*	museum
musgo,*m.*	MOOSS-*goh*	moss
música,*f.*	MOO-*see*-*kah*	music
musical	*moo*-*see*-KAHL	musical
músico,*m.*	MOO-*see*-*koh*	musician
muslo,*m.*	MOOSS-*loh*	thigh
mutuo	MOO-*twoh*	mutual
muy	MOO-*ee*	very (extremely)
muy ajustado	MOO-*ee*-*ah*-*hooss*-TAH-*thoh*	tight (close-fitting)
nabo,*m.*	NAH-*voh*	turnip (white)
nacer (11)	*nah*-SEHR	born, to be
nacimiento,*m.*	*nah*-*see*-M‿YEHN-*toh*	birth
nación,*f.*	*nah*-S‿YOHN	nation
nacional	*nah*-*s*‿*yoh*-NAHL	domestic (not foreign)
"	"	national (*adj.*)
Naciones Unidas, *f.pl.*	*nah*-S‿YOH-*nehss oo*-NEE-*thahss*	United Nations
nada	NAH-*thah*	anything (not... anything)
"	"	nothing (*n.*)
nadar (1)	*nah*-THAHR	swim, to
nadie	NAH-*th*‿*yeh*	anybody (not... anybody
"	"	nobody (*pron.*)
naipe,*m.*	NAH‿*ee*-*peh*	card, playing
Nápoles	NAH-*poh*-*lehss*	Naples
naranja,*f.*	*nah*-RAHN-*hah*	orange (fruit)
narcótico,*m.*	*nahr*-KOH-*tee*-*koh*	drug (narcotic)
nariz,*f.*	*nah*-REESS	nose (*anat.*)
nata,*f.*	NAH-*tah*	cream
nativo	*nah*-TEE-*voh*	native (indigenous)
natural	*nah*-*too*-RAHL	natural
natural,*m.,f.*	*nah*-*too*-RAHL	native (*n.*)
naturaleza,*f.*	*nah*-*too*-*rah*-LEH-*sah*	nature
navaja de afeitar, *f.*	*nah*-VAH-*hah theh ah*-*fay*-TAHR	razor

Spanish	Pronunciation	English
navegación,*f.*	*nah*-*veh*-*gah*-S‿YOHN	navigation
Navidad,*f.*	*nah*-*vee*-THAHTH	Christmas
neblina,*f.*	*neh*-VLEE-*nah*	mist
necesario	*neh*-*seh*-SAH-*r*‿*yoh*	necessary
necesidad,*f.*	*neh*-*seh*-*see*-THAHTH	necessity
"	"	need
"	"	want
necesitar (1)	*neh*-*seh*-*see*-TAHR	need (require), to
necio	NEH-*s*‿*yoh*	silly
necrología,*f.*	*nehk*-*roh*-*loh*-HEE‿*ah*	obituary (*n.*)
negar (4)	*neh*-GAHR	deny (contradict), to
negociable	*neh*-*goh*-S‿YAH-*vleh*	negotiable (*bus.*)
negociación,*f.*	*neh*-*goh*-*s*‿*yah*-S‿YOHN	negotiation
negociante,*m.*	*neh*-*goh*-S‿YAHN-*teh*	dealer (trader)
negociar (1)	*neh*-*goh*-S‿YAHR	bargain, to
"	"	negotiate, to
negocio,*m.*	*neh*-GOH-*s*‿*yoh*	business (commerce)
negro	NEH-*groh*	black
negro,*m.*	NEH-*groh*	Negro
nervio,*m.*	NEHR-*v*‿*yoh*	nerve (*anat.*)
nervioso	*nehr*-V‿YOH-*soh*	nervous (high-strung)
neto	NEH-*toh*	net (*adj.*)
neumático,*m.*	*neh*-*oo*-MAH-*tee*-*koh*	tire
neutral	*neh*-*oo*-TRAHL	neutral
nevera,*f.*	*neh*-VEH-*rah*	icebox
"	"	refrigerator
ni	NEE	nor
Nicaragua	*nee*-*kah*-RAH-*gwah*	Nicaragua
nido,*m.*	NEE-*thoh*	nest (bird home)
niebla,*f.*	N‿YEH-*vlah*	fog (mist)
ni el uno...	NEE *ehl* OO-*noh*...	neither (*adj.*)
nieta,*f.*	N‿YEH-*tah*	granddaughter
nieto,*m.*	N‿YEH-*toh*	grandson
nieve,*f.*	N‿YEH-*veh*	snow
Nilo	NEE-*loh*	Nile
nilón,*m.*	*nee*-LOHN	nylon (*n.*)
Niña Exploradora, *f.*	NEE-*n*‿*yah ehss*-*ploh*-*rah*-THOH-*rah*	Girl Scout
niñez,*f.*	*nee*-N‿YEHSS	childhood
ningún, -guna	*neen*-GOON, GOO-*nah*	no (not any, *adj.*)
ninguna parte, en	*ehn neen*-GOO-*nah* PAHR-*teh*	anywhere (not... anywhere)
"	"	nowhere
ninguno	*neen*-GOO-*noh*	anyone (not... anyone)
"	"	neither (*pron.*)
"	"	none (*pron.*)
ni...ni	*nee*...*nee*	neither...nor (*conj.*)
niño,*m.*	NEE-*n*‿*yoh*	child
Niño Explorador, *m.*	NEEN-*yoh ehss*-*ploh*-*rah*-THOHR	Boy Scout
níquel,*m.*	NEE-*kehl*	nickel (*chem.*)
nivel,*m.*	*nee*-VEHL	level (plane, *n.*)
no	NOH	no (*adv.*)
"	"	not
noble	NOH-*vleh*	noble (*adj.*)
nobleza,*f.*	*noh*-VLEH-*sah*	nobility
noche,*f.*	NOH-*cheh*	night
noción,*f.*	*noh*-S‿YOHN	notion (idea)
nogal,*m.*	*noh*-GAHL	walnut (*n.*)
nombramiento,*m.*	*nohm*-*brah*-M‿YEHN-*toh*	appointment
"	"	nomination
nombrar (1)	*nohm*-BRAHR	appoint, to
"	"	nominate, to
nombre,*m.*	NOHM-*breh*	name
"	"	noun
no obstante	*n(oh)ohb*-STAHN-*teh*	still (nevertheless, *conj.*)
"	"	yet (nevertheless, *adv.*)
no pagado	NOH *pah*-GAH-*thoh*	unpaid (due)
nordeste	*nohr*-DEHSS-*teh*	northeast (*adj.*)
normal	*nohr*-MAHL	normal (*adj.*)
"	"	standard (regular)
noroeste	*noh*-R‿WEHSS-*teh*	northwest (*adj.*)
norte,*m.*	NOHR-*teh*	north (*n.*)
norte, al	*ahl* NOHR-*teh*	north (*adv.*)
Norte América	NOHR-*teh ah*-MEHR-*ee*-*kah*	North America
norteamericano	NOHR-*teh*-*ah*-*meh*-*ree*-KAH-*noh*	American (*adj.*)

Spanish	Pronunciation	English
Noruega	*noh-R_WEH-gah*	Norway
noruego	*noh-R_WEH-goh*	Norwegian (adj.)
nos	NOHSS	us
nosotros	*noh-SOH-trohss*	us
"	"	we
nosotros mismos	*noh-SOH-trohss* MEEZ-mohss	ourselves
nostálgico	*nohss-TAHL-hee-koh*	homesick
nota, f.	NOH-*tah*	note (mus.)
notable	*noh-TAH-vleh*	notable (adj.)
notar (1)	*noh-TAHR*	note, to
notario, m.	*noh-TAH-r_yoh*	notary
noticias, f.pl.	*noh-TEE-s_yahss*	information (news)
notificación, f.	*noh-tee-fee-kah-S_YOHN*	notice (notification)
notificar (1)	*noh-tee-fee-KAHR*	notify, to
notorio	*noh-TOH-r_yoh*	notorious
novela, f.	*noh-VEH-lah*	novel (book)
novia, f.	NOH-*v_yah*	bride
novio, m.	NOH-*v_yoh*	groom (bridegroom)
"	"	sweetheart
nube, f.	NOO-*veh*	cloud
nublado	*noo-VLAH-thoh*	cloudy (overcast)
nuca, f.	NOO-*kah*	nape
nudo, m.	NOO-*thoh*	knot
nuera, f.	NWEH-*rah*	daughter-in-law
nuestra, la	*lah* N_WEHSS-*trah*	ours
nuestras, las	*lahss* N_WEHSS-*trahss*	ours
nuestro, -tra	N_WEHSS-*troh, -trah*	our
"	"	ours
nuestro, el	*ehl* N_WEHSS-*troh*	ours
nuestros, -tras	N_WEHSS-*trohss, -trahss*	our
"	"	ours
nuestros, los	*lohss* N_WEHSS-*trohss*	ours
Nueva Delhi	N_WEH-*vah* THEHL-*ee*	New Delhi
Nueva York	N_WEH-*vah* YOHRK	New York
nuevo	N_WEH-*voh*	new
nuez, f.	N_WEHSS	nut (food)
nuez moscada, f.	N_WEHSS *mohss*-KAH-*thah*	nutmeg
nulo	NOO-*loh*	void (null)
numerar (1)	*noo-meh-RAHR*	number (assign numbers to), to
número, m.	NOO-*meh-roh*	number
"	"	size (of shoes, gloves)
numeroso	*noo-meh-ROH-soh*	numerous
nunca	NOON-*kah*	never
nutrimento, m.	*noo-tree-*M_YEHN-*toh*	nourishment
nutrir (3)	*noo-*TREER	nourish, to
o	OH	or
oasis, m.	*oh-AH-seess*	oasis
obedecer (11)	*oh-veh-theh-SEHR*	obey, to
obediencia, f.	*oh-veh-*TH_YEHN-*s_yah*	obedience (compliance)
obediente	*oh-beh-*TH_YEHN-*teh*	obedient
obispo, m.	*oh-VEESS-poh*	bishop
objeción, f.	*ohb-hehk-S_YOHN*	objection
objetar (1)	*ohb-heh-TAHR*	object, to
objetivo, m.	*ohb-heh-TEE-voh*	objective (aim)
objeto, m.	*ohb-HEH-toh*	object (thing)
obligación, f.	*oh-vlee-gah-S_YOHN*	debenture
"	"	obligation (duty)
obligar (1)	*oh-vlee-GAHR*	compel, to
"	"	oblige, to
obligatorio	*oh-vlee-gah-TOH-r_yoh*	obligatory (binding)
oboe, m.	*oh-VOH-eh*	oboe
obra, f.	OH-*vrah*	work (opus)
obra clásica, f.	OH-*vrah* KLAH-*see-kah*	classic (first-class work)
obra conmemorativa, f.	OH-*vrah kohn-meh-moh-rah*-TEE-*vah*	memorial
obrar (1)	*oh-*VRAHR	act (do), to
obrero, m.	*oh-*VREH-*roh*	laborer
o(b)scurecer	*ohss-koo-reh-SEHR*	darken (make dark), to
o(b)scuridad, f.	*ohss-koo-ree-THAHTH*	darkness
o(b)scuro	*ohss*-KOO-*roh*	dark (adj.)
"	"	obscure
observación, f.	*ohv-sehr-vah-S_YOHN*	comment (remark)
"	"	observation (watching)
observador, m.	*ohv-sehr-vah-THOHR*	observer

Spanish	Pronunciation	English
observar (1)	*ohv-sehr-VAHR*	notice (see), to
"	"	observe (remark), to
"	"	watch
obstáculo, m.	*ohv-STAH-koo-loh*	difficulty
"	"	obstacle
obstruir (14)	*ohv-STR_WEER*	block (obstruct), to
obtener (35)	*ohv-teh-NEHR*	get, to
"	"	obtain
"	"	procure, to
"	"	secure, to
obvio	OHB-*v_yoh*	obvious
ocasión, f.	*oh-kah-S_YOHN*	chance (opportunity)
"	"	occasion
ocasional	*oh-kah-s_yoh-NAHL*	occasional
occidental	*ohk-see-thehn-TAHL*	western
océano, m.	*oh-SEH-ah-noh*	ocean
ocio, m.	OH-*s_yoh*	leisure
ociosidad, f.	*oh-s_yoh-see-THAHTH*	idleness (inactivity)
ocultar (1)	*oh-kool-TAHR*	conceal, to
ocupación, f.	*oh-koo-pah-S_YOHN*	occupation
ocupado	*oh-koo-PAH-thoh*	busy (occupied)
ocupar (1)	*oh-koo-PAHR*	occupy, to
ocurrir (3)	*oh-koo-RREER*	occur (happen), to
odiar (1)	*oh-*TH_YAHR	hate, to
odio, m.	OH-*th_yoh*	hate (hatred)
oeste, m.	*oh-EHSS-teh*	west (n.)
ofender (2)	*oh-fehn-DEHR*	offend (affront), to
ofensa, f.	*oh-FEHN-sah*	offense
oficial	*oh-fee-S_YAHL*	official (adj.)
oficial, m.	*oh-fee-S_YAHL*	officer (mil.)
oficina, f.	*oh-fee-SEE-nah*	bureau
"	"	office (place of business)
oficio, m.	*oh-FEE-s_yoh*	craft
"	"	office (position)
"	"	trade
ofrecer (11)	*oh-freh-SEHR*	offer (tender), to
ofrecimiento, m.	*oh-freh-see-*M_YEHN-*toh*	offer
oído, m.	*oh-EE-thoh*	ear (organ of hearing)
oír (28)	*oh-EER*	hear, to
ojo, m.	OH-*hoh*	eye (anat.)
ola, f.	OH-*lah*	wave (billow)
oler (5)	*oh-LEHR*	smell (perceive odor), to
olmo, m.	OHL-*moh*	elm
olor, m.	*oh-LOHR*	odor
"	"	scent
"	"	smell
olvidado	*ohl-vee-THAH-thoh*	forgotten
olvidar (1)	*ohl-vee-THAHR*	forget, to
omitir (3)	*oh-mee-TEER*	omit (leave out), to
ómnibus, m.	OHM-*nee-vooss*	bus
ondulación, f.	*ohn-doo-lah-S_YOHN*	ripple
o...o	OH...OH	either...or (conj.)
ópera, f.	OH-*peh-rah*	opera
operación, f.	*oh-peh-rah-S_YOHN*	operation (med.)
operar (1)	*oh-peh-RAHR*	operate (perform surgery), to
opinión, f.	*oh-pee-*N_YOHN	belief
"	"	opinion
oponerse a (31)	*oh-poh-NEHR-seh ah*	oppose (combat), to
oportunidad, f.	*oh-pohr-too-nee-THAHTH*	opportunity
oposición, f.	*oh-poh-see-S_YOHN*	opposition (resistance)
oprimir (3)	*oh-pree-MEER*	oppress, to
optimista	*ohp-tee-MEESS-tah*	optimistic
opuesto	*oh-PWEHSS-toh*	opposite (adj.)
oración, f.	*oh-rah-S_YOHN*	prayer (petition)
orador, m.	*oh-rah-THOHR*	speaker (orator)
oral	*oh-RAHL*	oral (spoken)
orden, f.	OHR-*thehn*	command
"	"	order
ordenado	*ohr-theh-NAH-thoh*	neat (tidy)
ordenar (1)	*ohr-theh-NAHR*	order (command), to
ordinario	*ohr-thee-NAH-r_yoh*	common (usual)
"	"	ordinary
oreja, f.	*oh-REH-hah*	ear (external ear)
organizar (1)	*ohr-gah-nee-SAHR*	organize (systematize), to
órgano, m.	OHR-*gah-noh*	organ

Spanish	Pronunciation	English
orgullo,*m.*	ohr-GOO-yoh	pride (self-esteem)
orgulloso	ohr-goo-YOH-soh	proud (taking pride in)
oriental	oh-r yehn-TAHL	eastern
Oriente,*m.*	oh-R YEHN-teh	Orient
origen,*m.*	oh-REE-hehn	origin (source)
original	oh-ree-hee-NAHL	original (first)
orín,*m.*	oh-RREEN	rust
ornamento,*m.*	ohr-nah-MEHN-toh	ornament
ornato, de	ohr-NAH-toh, deh	fancy (ornamental, *adj.*)
oro,*m.*	OH-roh	gold
orquesta,*f.*	ohr-KEHSS-tah	orchestra (*mus.*)
orquídea,*f.*	ohr-KEE-*theh-ah*	orchid (flower)
oruga,*f.*	oh-ROO-gah	caterpillar
os	OHSS	you
oscilarse (1)	oh-see-LAHR-seh	swing (oscillate), to
Oslo	OHSS-loh	Oslo
oso,*m.*	OH-soh	bear (animal)
ostra,*f.*	OHSS-trah	oyster
otoño,*m.*	oh-TOH-*n yoh*	autumn
"	"	fall (*n.*)
otorgar (1)	oh-tohr-GAHR	bestow, to
otra parte, a	ah OH-trah PAHR-*tch*	elsewhere
otra parte, de	deh OH-trah PAHR-*tch*	elsewhere
otra parte, en	ehn OH-trah PAHR-*teh*	elsewhere
otra vez	OH-trah VEHSS	again
otro	OH-troh	another (*adj., pron.*)
"	"	else (different, *adj.*)
"	"	other (*adj., pron.*)
otro lado de, al	ah-LOH-troh LAH-*thoh theh*	across (beyond)
otro modo, de	deh OH-troh MOH-*thoh*	else (instead, *adv.*)
"	"	otherwise
otro tiempo, en	ehn OH-troh T YEHM-*poh*	once (formerly, *adv.*)
Ottawa	oh-TAH-wah	Ottawa
oveja,*f.*	oh-VEH-hah	sheep
oxidado	ohk-see-THAH-*thoh*	rusty
oxígeno,*m.*	ohk-SEE-heh-noh	oxygen
pacer (11)	*pah*-SEHR	graze (feed), to
paciencia,*f.*	*pah*-S YEHN-*s yah*	patience
paciente	*pah*-S YEHN-*teh*	patient (forbearing)
paciente,*m.,f.*	*pah*-S YEHN-*teh*	patient (invalid)
Pacífico,*m.*	*pah*-SEE-fee-koh	Pacific (*n.*)
padrastro,*m.*	*pah*-THRAHSS-*troh*	step-father
padre,*m.*	PAH-*threh*	father
padres,*m.pl.*	PAH-*threhss*	parents
pagadero	*pah*-gah-THEH-*roh*	due
"	"	payable
pagar (1)	*pah*-GAHR	pay, to
pagaré,*m.*	*pah*-gah-REH	note (promise to pay, *bus.*)
página,*f.*	PAH-*hee-nah*	page (leaf)
pago,*m.*	PAH-*goh*	payment
país,*m.*	*pah*-EESS	country (nation)
paisaje,*m.*	*pah*-ee-SAH-heh	landscape (scenery)
Países Bajos, los, *m.pl.*	lohss *pah*-EE-sehss BAH-hohss	Netherlands, The
paja,*f.*	PAH-*hah*	straw (dry grain stalks)
Pakistán	*pah*-keess-TAHN	Pakistan
pakistano	*pah*-kee-STAH-*noh*	Pakistani (*adj.*)
pala,*f.*	PAH-*lah*	shovel (tool)
palabra,*f.*	*pah*-LAH-*vrah*	word
palacio,*m.*	*pah*-LAH-*s yoh*	palace
palanca,*f.*	*pah*-LAHN-*kah*	bar (pole)
"	"	lever
Palestina	*pah*-lehss-TEE-*nah*	Palestine
pálido	PAH-*lee-thoh*	pale (wan)
palma,*f.*	PAHL-*mah*	palm
palo,*m.*	PAH-*loh*	club (cudgel)
"	"	stick (small branch)
paloma,*f.*	*pah*-LOH-*mah*	dove
"	"	pigeon
pan,*m.*	PAHN	bread
pana,*f.*	PAH-*nah*	velveteen (*n.*)
panadero,*m.*	*pah*-nah-THEH-*roh*	baker
Panamá	*pah*-nah-MAH	Panama
pandilla,*f.*	*pah*n-DEE-*yah*	gang
panecillo,*m.*	*pah*-neh-SEE-*yoh*	roll (bread)
pánico,*m.*	PAH-*nee-koh*	panic (fear)
paño,*m.*	PAH-*n yoh*	wool (cloth)

Spanish	Pronunciation	English
pantalla,*f.*	*pahn*-TAH-*yah*	screen (for movies)
pantalones,*m.pl.*	*pahn-tah*-LOH-*nehss*	trousers
pantano,*m.*	*pahn*-TAH-*noh*	marsh
"	"	swamp (*n.*)
pantera,*f.*	*pahn*-TEH-*rah*	panther
pantorrilla,*f.*	*pahn-toh*-RREE-*yah*	calf (*anat.*)
pañuelo,*m.*	*pah*-n YWEH-*loh*	handkerchief
papa,*f.*	PAH-*pah*	potato (white)
papa,*m.*	PAH-*pah*	pope
papá,*m.*	*pah*-PAH	dad
papel,*m.*	*pah*-PEHL	paper
"	"	role
papelería,*f.*	*pah-peh-leh*-REE-*ah*	stationery (writing paper)
papeleta,*f.*	*pah-peh*-LEH-*tah*	ballot
paquete,*m.*	*pah*-KEH-*teh*	bundle
"	"	package
"	"	parcel
paquete postal,*m.*	*pah*-KEH-*teh pohss*-TAHL	parcel post
par,*m.*	PAHR	pair
"	"	peer (equal)
para	PAH-*rah*	for (*prep.*)
"	"	to (in order to, *prep.*)
parabrisa,*m.*	*pah-rah*-VREE-*sah*	windshield
paracaídas,*m.*	*pah-rah-kah*-EE-*thahss*	parachute
parada,*f.*	*pah*-RAH-*thah*	stop (halt)
paraguas,*m.*	*pah*-RAH-*gwahss*	umbrella
Paraguay, el	ehl *pah-rah*-GWAH EE	Paraguay
paraíso,*m.*	*pah-rah*-EE-*soh*	paradise
paralelo	*pah-rah*-LEH-*loh*	parallel (*adj.*)
parálisis,*f.*	*pah*-RAH-*lee-seess*	paralysis
parálisis infantil,*f.*	*pah*-RAH-*lee-sees een-fahn*-TEEL	infantile paralysis
páramo,*m.*	PAH-*rah-moh*	moor (waste land)
para que	PAH-*rah* KEH	so (in order that, *conj.*)
para que no	PAH-*rah* keh noh	lest
pararse (1)	*pah*-RAHR-*seh*	halt (come to a stop), to
"	"	stall (stop going), to
"	"	stop (come to a standstill), to
parche,*m.*	PAHR-*cheh*	patch (repair)
parcial	*pahr*-S YAHL	partial (incomplete)
pardo (castaño)	PAHR-*thoh* (kahss-TAH-n yoh)	brown
parecer (11)	*pah-reh*-SEHR	appear, to
"	"	look, to
"	"	seem, to
parecer,*m.*	*pah-reh*-SEHR	mind (opinion)
"	"	view (opinion)
pared,*f.*	*pah*-REHTH	wall
pareja,*f.*	*pah*-REH-*hah*	couple (pair, *n.*)
parejo	*pah*-REH-*hoh*	even (level, *adj.*)
paréntesis,*m.*	*pah*-REHN-*teh-seess*	parentheses
pariente,*m.,f.*	*pah*-R YEHN-*teh*	relative (kinsman)
parir (3)	*pah*-REER	bear (give birth to), to
París	*pah*-REESS	Paris
parlamento,*m.*	*pahr-lah*-MEHN-*toh*	parliament
parlotear (1)	*pahr-loh-teh*-AHR	chatter, to
parótidas,*f.pl.*	*pah*-ROH-*tee-thahss*	mumps
párpado,*m.*	PAHR-*pah-thoh*	eyelid
parque,*m.*	PAHR-*keh*	park
parque zoológico, *m.*	PAHR-*keh s(oh)oh*-LOH-*hee-koh*	zoo
párrafo,*m.*	PAH-*rrah-foh*	paragraph
parrilla,*f.*	*pah*-RREE-*yah*	grate (of furnace)
parroquia,*f.*	*pah*-RROH-*k yah*	parish
parroquiano,*m.*	*pah*-rroh-K YAH-*noh*	buyer
parte,*f.*	PAHR-*teh*	part (portion)
"	"	proportion
parte,*m.*	PAHR-*teh*	dispatch (communication)
parte, en	ehn PAHR-*teh*	partly
participación,*f.*	*pahr-tee-see-pah*-S YOHN	interest (share)
participar (1)	*pahr-tee-see*-PAHR	participate, to
particular	*pahr-tee-koo*-LAHR	individual (*adj.*)
"	"	particular (specific, *adj.*)
partida,*f.*	*pahr*-TEE-*thah*	departure (setting out)
"	"	entry (*acctg.*)

Spanish	Pronunciation	English
partida del activo	*pahr*-TEE-*thah thehl ahk-* TEE-*voh*	asset (*bus.*)
partidario,*m.*	*pahr-tee-*THAH-*r yoh*	follower (adherent)
partidarios,*m.pl.*	*pahr-tee-*THAH-*r yohss*	following (followers)
partido,*f.*	*pahr*-TEE-*thoh*	party (*pol.*)
partir (3)	*pahr*-TEER	depart, to
"	"	leave, to
partirse	*pahr*-TEER-*seh*	break (come apart), to
pasa,*f.*	PAH-*sah*	raisin
pasado	*pah*-SAH-*thoh*	past (bygone, *adj.*)
pasado,*m.*	*pah*-SAH-*thoh*	past (*n.*)
pasaje,*m.*	*pah*-SAH-*heh*	fare (*transp.*)
"	"	passage (passage- way)
pasajero,*m.*	*pah-sah-*HEH-*roh*	passenger
pasaporte,*m.*	*pah-sah-*POHR-*teh*	passport
pasar (1)	*pah*-SAHR	pass (go by), to
pasar por alto	*pah*-SAHR *pohr* AHL-*toh*	overlook (disre- gard), to
"	"	skip (omit), to
pasatiempo,*m.*	*pah-sah-*T YEHM-*poh*	pastime
pascua de los hebreos,*f.*	PAHSS-*kwah theh lohss* *eh-*VREH-*ohss*	Passover
Pascua de Resur- rección,*f.*	PAHSS-*kwah theh rreh-* *soo-rrehk-*S YOHN	Easter
pasear en auto (1)	*pah-seh-*AHR *ehn* OW- *toh*	ride (in a car), to
pasearse	*pah-seh-*AHR-*seh*	stroll, to
paseo,*m.*	*pah-*SEH-*oh*	walk (stroll)
paseo en auto,*m.*	*pah-*SEH-*oh ehn* OW-*toh*	ride (in a car)
pasillo,*m.*	*pah-*SEE-*yoh*	aisle (passageway)
"	"	hall (corridor)
pasión,*f.*	*pah-*S YOHN	passion (emotion)
pasmo,*m.*	PAHSS-*moh*	wonder
paso,*m.*	PAH-*soh*	pace (degree of speed)
"	"	step (stride)
pasta dentífrica,*f.*	PAHSS-*tah thehn-*TEE- *free-kah*	tooth paste
pastel,*m.*	*pahss-*TEHL	pie
pastor,*m.*	*pahss-*TOHR	minister (clergy- man)
"	"	pastor
"	"	shepherd
pastura,*f.*	*pahss-*TOO-*rah*	pasture (grassland)
pata,*f.*	PAH-*tah*	paw
patada,*f.*	*pah-*TAH-*thah*	kick (boot)
patear (1)	*pah-teh-*AHR	kick (boot), to
"	"	stamp (tread heavily), to
patente,*f.*	*pah-*TEHN-*teh*	patent (*n.*)
patín de hielo,*m.*	*pah-*TEEN *deh* YEH-*loh*	skate, ice
pato,*m.*	PAH-*toh*	duck
patriota,*m.*	*pah-*TR YOH-*tah*	patriot
patrón,*m.*	*pah-*TROHN	boss (master)
patrono,*m.*	*pah-*TROH-*noh*	employer (boss)
pausar (1)	*pow-*SAHR	pause (wait), to
pavimentar (1)	*pah-vee-mehn-*TAHR	pave, to
pavimento,*m.*	*pah-vee-*MEHN-*toh*	pavement
pavo,*m.*	PAH-*voh*	turkey
pavor,*m.*	*pah-*VOHR	awe
pavo real,*m.*	PAH-*voh reh-*AHL	peacock
paz,*f.*	PAHSS	peace
pecado,*m.*	*peh-*KAH-*thoh*	sin
pecador,*m.*	*peh-kah-*THOHR	sinner
pecar (1)	*peh-*KAHR	sin, to
pecho,*m.*	PEH-*choh*	breast
"	"	chest (*anat.*)
pedacito,*m.*	*peh-thah-*SEE-*toh*	scrap (fragment)
pedazo,*m.*	*peh-*THAH-*soh*	piece (bit)
pedazos, a	*ah peh-*THAH-*sohss*	piecemeal (*adv.*)
pedernal,*m.*	*peh-thehr-*NAHL	flint
pedido,*m.*	*peh-*THEE-*thoh*	order (purchase)
pedir (9)	*peh-*THEER	ask (request), to
"	"	order (purchase), to
pedir prestado	*peh-*THEER *prehss-*TAH- *thoh*	borrow, to
pegar (1)	*peh-*GAHR	beat (thrash), to
pegarse	*peh-*GAHR-*seh*	stick (adhere), to
peine,*m.*	PEH *ee-neh*	comb (for hair)
Peiping	*pay-*PEENG	Peiping
pelea,*f.*	*peh-*LEH-*ah*	fight

Spanish	Pronunciation	English
pelear (1)	*peh-leh-*AHR	fight (contend), to
película,*f.*	*peh-*LEE-*koo-lah*	film
película noticiera, *f.*	*peh-*LEE-*koo-lah noh-* *tee-*S YEH-*rah*	newsreel
peligro,*m.*	*peh-*LEE-*groh*	danger
"	"	peril
peligroso	*peh-lee-*GROH-*soh*	dangerous
pelota,*f.*	*peh-*LOH-*tah*	ball (sphere)
pena,*f.*	PEH-*nah*	trouble (exertion)
penalidad,*f.*	*peh-nah-lee-*THAHTH	penalty
pendiente,*f.*	*pehn-*D YEHN-*teh*	slope (slant)
pendón,*m.*	*pehn-*DOHN	banner
penetrar (1)	*peh-neh-*TRAHR	penetrate, to
"	"	pierce, to
penicilina,*f.*	*peh-nee-see-*LEE-*nah*	penicillin
península,*f.*	*peh-*NEEN-*soo-lah*	peninsula
pensamiento,*m.*	*pehn-sah-*M YEHN-*toh*	pansy
pensar (4)	*pehn-*SAHR	think (reason), to
pensativo	*pehn-sah-*TEE-*voh*	thoughtful (reflec- tive)
pensión,*f.*	*pehn-*S YOHN	boarding house
peor	*peh-*OHR	worse (*adj., adv.*)
peor, (el)	(*ehl*) *peh-*OHR	worst (*adj.*)
peor, (lo)	(*loh*) *peh-*OHR	worst (*adv.*)
peor, (lo),*m.*	(*loh*) *peh-*OHR	worst (*n.*)
pepino,*m.*	*peh-*PEE-*noh*	cucumber
pequeño	*peh-*KEH-*n yoh*	little (*adj.*)
"	"	slight (*adj.*)
"	"	small
pera,*f.*	PEH-*rah*	pear
percibir (3)	*pehr-see-*VEER	perceive, to
perder (4)	*pehr-*THEHR	lose, to
perdición,*f.*	*pehr-thee-*S YOHN	doom (ruin)
pérdida,*f.*	PEHR-*thee-thah*	loss
perdón,*m.*	*pehr-*THOHN	forgiveness
"	"	pardon
perdonar (1)	*pehr-thoh-*NAHR	forgive, to
"	"	pardon, to
perecer (11)	*peh-reh-*SEHR	perish, to
perezoso	*peh-reh-*SOH-*soh*	lazy
perfección,*f.*	*pehr-fehk-*S YOHN	perfection (flawless- ness)
perfecto	*pehr-*FEHK-*toh*	perfect (flawless)
perforar (1)	*pehr-foh-*RAHR	drill (bore), to
perfume,*m.*	*pehr-*FOO-*meh*	perfume (fragrance)
periódico,*m.*	*peh-R yOH-thee-koh*	newspaper
período,*m.*	*peh-*REE-*oh-thoh*	period (of time)
perjudicar (1)	*pehr-hoo-thee-*KAHR	hurt (inflict pain upon), to
perjurio,*m.*	*pehr-*HOO-*r yoh*	perjury
perla,*f.*	PEHR-*lah*	pearl (gem)
permanecer (11)	*pehr-mah-neh-*SEHR	abide, to
"	"	stay (remain), to
permanente	*pehr-mah-*NEHN-*teh*	permanent (*adj.*)
permiso,*m.*	*pehr-*MEE-*soh*	permission
permitir (3)	*pehr-mee-*TEER	allow, to
"	"	permit, to
permitirse	*pehr-mee-*TEER-*seh*	afford (have the means), to
perno,*m.*	PEHR-*noh*	bolt (long metal fastener)
pero	PEH-*roh*	but (yet, *conj.*)
perpetuo	*pehr-*PEH-*twoh*	perpetual
perplejidad,*f.*	*pehr-pleh-hee-*THAHTH	quandary
perro,*m.*	PEH-*rroh*	dog
perro de caza,*m.*	PEH-*rroh theh* KAH-*sah*	hound
persecución,*f.*	*pehr-seh-koo-*S YOHN	pursuit (chase)
perseguir (9)	*pehr-seh-*GHEER	chase, to
"	"	pursue, to
persistir (3)	*pehr-seess-*TEER	persist (persevere), to
"	"	remain (continue unchanged), to
persona,*f.*	*pehr-*SOH-*nah*	person
personaje,*m.*	*pehr-soh-*NAH-*heh*	character (person portrayed)
personal	*pehr-soh-*NAHL	personal
personal,*m.*	*pehr-soh-*NAHL	staff (personnel)
personalidad,*f.*	*pehr-soh-nah-lee-* THAHTH	personality
perspectiva,*f.*	*pehr-spehk-*TEE-*vah*	outlook (attitude)
persuadir (3)	*pehr-swah-*THEER	persuade, to

Spanish	Pronunciation	English
pertenecer (11)	pehr-teh-neh-SEHR	belong, to
pertenencia,f.	pehr-teh-NEHN-s_yah	holdings (possessions)
pértiga,f.	PEHR-tee-gah	pole (rod)
perturbar (1)	pehr-toor-VAHR	disturb, to
"	"	trouble (disquiet), to
Perú, el	ehl peh-ROO	Peru
peruano	peh-RWAH-noh	Peruvian (adj.)
pervertir (7)	pehr-vehr-TEER	pervert (distort), to
pesado	peh-SAH-thoh	heavy
pesadumbre,f.	peh-sah-THOOM-breh	regret (sorrow)
pesar (1)	peh-SAHR	weigh, to
pesar,m.	peh-SAHR	sorrow (sadness)
pescado,m.	pehss-KAH-thoh	fish (food)
pescador,m.	pehss-kah-THOHR	fisherman
pescar (1)	pehss-KAHR	fish, to
pesimista	peh-see-MEESS-tah	pessimistic
peso,m.	PEH-soh	weight (scale weight)
pestaña,f.	pehss-TAH-n_yah	eyelash
pestañear (1)	pehss-tah-nyeh-AHR	wink, to
pestillo,m.	pehss-TEE-yoh	latch
petición,f.	peh-tee-s_YOHN	petition (written request)
petirrojo,m.	peh-tee-RROH-hoh	robin
pez,m.	PEHSS	fish (animal)
pezuña,f.	peh-SOO-n_yah	hoof
piano,m.	P_YAH-noh	piano (n.)
picar (1)	pee-KAHR	prick, to
"	"	sting (pierce skin), to
pico,m.	PEE-koh	bill (beak)
picotear (1)	pee-koh-teh-AHR	peck, to
pie,m.	P_YEH	foot (anat.)
piedra,f.	P_YEH-thrah	stone (piece of rock)
piedra caliza,f.	P_YEH-thrah kah-LEE-sah	limestone
piedrecilla,f.	p_yeh-threh-SEE-yah	pebble
piel,f.	P_YEHL	fur
"	"	hide
"	"	skin (animal hide)
pierna,f.	P_YEHR-nah	leg (anat.)
pijamas, m.pl.	pee-HAH-mahss	pajamas
pilar,m. (1)	pee-LAHR	pillar (column)
pila seca,f.	PEE-lah SEH-kah	battery (primary cell)
píldora,f.	PEEL-thoh-rah	pill
piloto,m.	pee-LOH-toh	pilot (flier)
pimienta,f.	pee-M_YEHN-tah	pepper (seasoning)
pimiento,m.	pee-M_YEHN-toh	pepper (green vegetable)
pino,m.	PEE-noh	pine (tree)
pintar (1)	peen-TAHR	paint, to
pintor,m.	peen-TOHR	painter (artist)
pintoresco	peen-toh-REHSS-koh	picturesque
pintura,f.	peen-TOO-rah	paint
"	"	painting (picture)
pionero,m.	p_yoh-NEH-roh	pioneer
pipa,f.	PEE-pah	pipe (tobacco pipe)
pirata,m.	pee-RAH-tah	pirate
piso,m.	PEE-soh	floor
pistola,f.	peess-TOH-lah	pistol
pizarra,f.	pee-SAH-rrah	blackboard
placer,m.	plah-SEHR	pleasure
plan,m.	PLAHN	plan
"	"	scheme
plancha eléctrica,f.	PLAHN-chah eh-LEHK-tree-kah	iron, electric
planchar (1)	plahn-CHAHR	press (iron), to
planear (1)	plah-neh-AHR	plan (prearrange), to
planeta,m.	plah-NEH-tah	planet
plano	PLAH-noh	flat (adj.)
"	"	level (adj.)
plano,m.	PLAH-noh	plane (surface)
planta,f.	PLAHN-tah	plant (flora)
plantar (1)	plahn-TAHR	plant (sow), to
plástico,m.	PLAHSS-tee-koh	plastic (n.)
plata,f.	PLAH-tah	silver (metal, n.)
plátano,m.	PLAH-tah-noh	banana
platillo,m.	plah-TEE-yoh	saucer
platino,m.	plah-TEE-noh	platinum
plato,m.	PLAH-toh	dish (food)
"	"	plate (shallow dish)

Spanish	Pronunciation	English
playa,f.	PLAH-yah	beach (strand)
plaza,f.	PLAH-sah	square (plaza)
plazo,m.	PLAH-soh	installment (payment, bus.)
"	"	term (duration)
pleito,m.	PLAY-toh	suit (lawsuit)
pliegue,m.	PL_YEH-geh	fold (plait, n.)
plomo,m.	PLOH-moh	lead (metal)
pluma,f.	PLOO-mah	feather
"	"	pen
pluma fuente,f.	PLOO-mah FWEHN-teh	pen, fountain
pluma fuente con punta de bola,f.	PLOO-mah FWEHN-teh kohn POON-tah theh VOH-lah	ball-point pen
plural	ploo-RAHL	plural (adj.)
pluscafé,m.	plooss-kah-FEH	liqueur
población,f.	pohv-lah-S_YOHN	population (number of people)
pobre	POH-vreh	poor
pobreza,f.	poh-VREH-sah	poverty
poco	POH-koh	little (not much, adj.)
poco	POH-koh	little (slightly, adv.)
poco,m.	POH-koh	little (small amount, n.)
poco profundo	POH-koh proh-FOON-doh	shallow
pocos	POH-kohss	few (not many, adj.)
pocos,m.pl.	POH-kohss	few (small number, n.)
poder (29)	poh-THEHR	can (v.)
"	"	may (v.)
poder,m.	poh-THEHR	might (n.)
"	"	power (authority)
"	"	power of attorney
poderoso	poh-theh-ROH-soh	mighty
"	"	powerful
podredura,f.	poh-threh-THOO-rah	decay (rottenness)
podrido	poh-TH_REE-thoh	rotten (decayed)
poema,m.	poh-EH-mah	poem
poesía,f.	poh-eh-SEE-ah	poetry
poeta,m.	poh-EH-tah	poet
polaco	poh-LAH-koh	Polish (adj.)
policía,f.	poh-lee-SEE-ah	police
policía,m.	poh-lee-SEE-ah	policeman
polilla,f.	poh-LEE-yah	moth
política,f.	poh-LEE-tee-kah	policy (course)
"	"	politics
político	poh-LEE-tee-koh	political
político,m.	poh-LEE-tee-koh	politician
póliza,f.	POH-lee-sah	policy (contract of insurance)
pollo,m.	POH-yoh	chicken
"	"	fowl (poultry)
polo,m.	POH-loh	pole (end of axis)
Polonia	poh-LOH-n_yah	Poland
polvo,m.	POHL-voh	dust
"	"	powder
polvoriento	pohl-voh-R_YEHN-toh	dusty
polvos,m.pl.	POHL-vohss	powder (cosmetic)
poner (31)	poh-NEHR	set (put), to
poner anuncios	poh-NEHR ah-NOON-s_yohss	advertise (sponsor advertising), to
ponerse	poh-NEHR-seh	set (in sky), to
ponerse de pie	poh-NEHR-seh theh P_YEH	rise, to
"	"	stand up, to
populacho,m.	poh-poo-LAH-choh	mob (disorderly crowd)
popular	poh-poo-LAHR	popular (prevalent)
"	"	popular (well-liked)
poquito,m.	poh-KEE-toh	bit (small part)
por	POHR	by (prep., math.)
"	"	by (via, prep.)
por	POHR	for (prep.)
"	"	per (for each)
porcelana,f.	pohr-seh-LAH-nah	porcelain (n.)
porcentaje,m.	pohr-sehn-TAH-heh	percentage
por ciento,m.	pohr S_YEHN-toh	percent (n.)
por cierto	pohr S_YEHR-toh	certainly (of course!, interj.)
porción,f.	pohr-S_YOHN	portion (part)
"	"	share

Spanish	Pronunciation	English
porqué	*pohr*-KEH	because (*conj.*)
"	"	for (*conj.*)
por qué	*pohr* KEH	why
portaaviones, *m.*	*pohr-tah(ah)*-V_YOH-nehss	aircraft carrier
portador, *m.*	*pohr-tah*-THOHR	bearer (*banking*)
"	"	carrier (*bus.*)
portamonedas, *m.*	*pohr-tah-moh*-NEH-thahss	purse (coin pouch)
portarse (1)	*pohr*-TAHR-*seh*	act (behave), to
porte, *m.*	POHR-*teh*	carriage (posture)
pórtico, *m.*	POHR-*tee-koh*	porch
portón, *m.*	*pohr*-TOHN	gate
Portugal	*pohr-too*-GAHL	Portugal
porvenir, *m.*	*pohr-veh*-NEER	future (*n.*)
posada, *f.*	*poh*-SAH-*thah*	inn
posarse (1)	*poh*-SAHR-*seh*	perch (sit), to
posdata, *f.*	*pohss*-DAH-*tah*	postscript
poseer (2)	*poh*-SEH(*eh*)R	own, to
"	"	possess, to
posesión, *f.*	*poh-seh*-S_YOHN	possession (ownership)
posibilidad, *f.*	*poh-see-vee-lee*-THAHTH	chance
"	"	possibility
posible	*poh*-SEE-*vleh*	possible
posición, *f.*	*poh-see*-S_YOHN	position (location)
positivo	*poh-see*-TEE-*voh*	positive (decisive)
posponer (31)	*pohss-poh*-NEHR	postpone, to
poste, *m.*	POHSS-*teh*	post (pole)
posterior	*pohss-teh*-R_YOHR	rear (*adj.*)
postor, *m.*	*pohss*-TOHR	bidder (*bus.*)
postre, *m.*	POHSS-*treh*	dessert
postura, *f.*	*pohss*-TOO-*rah*	bid (amount offered)
pote, *m.*	POH-*teh*	pot (container)
potro, *m.*	POH-*troh*	colt
pozo, *m.*	POH-*soh*	well (*n.*)
práctica, *f.*	PRAHK-*tee-kah*	experience (skill)
"	"	practice
practicar (1)	*prahk-tee*-KAHR	practice (put to practice), to
práctico	PRAHK-*tee-koh*	practical (not theoretical)
pradera, *f.*	*prah*-THEH-*rah*	meadow
"	"	prairie
precaución, *f.*	*preh-kah_oo*-S_YOHN	caution (heed)
precio, *m.*	PREH-*s_yoh*	charge
"	"	price (*bus.*)
precio fijo, *m.*	PREH-*s_yoh* FEE-*hoh*	rate (price)
precioso	*preh*-S_YOH-*soh*	precious (costly)
"	"	valuable
precipicio, *m.*	*preh-see*-PEE-*s_yoh*	precipice
precipitado	*preh-see-pee*-TAH-*thoh*	hasty (rash)
preciso	*preh*-SEE-*soh*	distinct (unmistakable)
"	"	precise (exact)
predecir (22)	*preh-theh*-SEER	predict, to
predicador, *m.*	*preh-thee-kah*-THOHR	preacher
predicar (1)	*preh-thee*-KAHR	preach, to
prefacio, *m.*	*preh*-FAH-*s_yoh*	preface
preferir (7)	*preh-feh*-REER	prefer (like better), to
pregunta, *f.*	*preh*-GOON-*tah*	inquiry
"	"	question (query)
preguntar (1)	*preh-goon*-TAHR	inquire, to
preguntar por	*preh-goon*-TAHR *pohr*	ask about, to
preguntarse	*preh-goon*-TAHR-*seh*	wonder (ask oneself), to
prejuicio, *m.*	*preh*-HWEE-*s_yoh*	prejudice
preliminar	*preh-lee-mee*-NAHR	preliminary (*adj.*)
premio, *m.*	PREH-*m_yoh*	prize (trophy)
prenda de vestir, *f.*	PREHN-*dah theh vehss*-TEER	garment
prender (2)	*prehn*-DEHR	capture (seize), to
prensa, *f.*	PREHN-*sah*	press (newspapers and periodicals)
preparación, *f.*	*preh-pah-rah*-S_YOHN	preparation (preparatory act)
preparar (1)	*preh-pah*-RAHR	prepare (make ready), to
preparativo, *m.*	*preh-pah-rah*-TEE-*voh*	arrangement
preposición, *f.*	*preh-poh-see*-S_YOHN	preposition (*gram.*)
presa, *f.*	PREH-*sah*	prey (victim)

Spanish	Pronunciation	English
presencia, *f.*	*preh*-SEHN-*s_yah*	presence (being present)
presentación, *f.*	*preh-sehn-tah*-S_YOHN	introduction (presentation)
presentar (1)	*preh-sehn*-TAHR	introduce (make acquainted), to
"	"	present, to
presentar informe	*preh-sehn*-TAHR *een*-FOHR-*meh*	report (account formally), to
presente, *m.*	*preh*-SEHN-*teh*	present (present time, *n.*)
preservar (1)	*preh-sehr*-VAHR	preserve, to
presidente, *m.*	*preh-see*-THEHN-*teh*	chairman
"	"	president
presión, *f.*	*preh*-S_YOHN	pressure (force)
préstamo, *m.*	PREHSS-*tah-moh*	loan
prestar (1)	*prehss*-TAHR	lend, to
prestatario, *m.*	*press-tah*-TAH-*r_yoh*	borrower (*bus.*)
presumir (3)	*preh-soo*-MEER	presume, to
presupuesto, *m.*	*preh-soo*-PWEHSS-*toh*	budget (*n.*)
pretensión, *f.*	*preh-tehn*-S_YOHN	pretense (pretending)
pretexto, *m.*	*preh*-TEHKSS-*toh*	pretext
prevalecer (11)	*preh-vah-leh*-SEHR	prevail (exist widely), to
prevenir (37)	*preh-veh*-NEER	prevent (stop), to
previo	PREH-*v_yoh*	previous
previsión, *f.*	*pre*-VEE-*s_yohn*	vision (foresight)
prima, *f.*	PREE-*mah*	bonus (extra wages)
"	"	premium (payment)
primario	*pree*-MAH-*r_yoh*	primary (first, *adj.*)
primavera, *f.*	*pree-mah*-VEH-*rah*	spring (season)
primer(o)	*pree*-MEHR(-*oh*)	first (*adj.*)
"	"	former (first of two, *adj.*)
"	"	prime (*adj.*)
primeros auxilios, *m.pl.*	*pree*-MEH-*rohss ow*-GSEE-*l_yohss*	first aid (*med.*)
primer pago, *m.*	*pree*-MEHR PAH-*goh*	down payment (*bus.*)
primitivo	*pree-mee*-TEE-*voh*	primitive (early)
primo, *m.*	PREE-*moh*	cousin
primoroso	*pree-moh*-ROH-*soh*	gorgeous
princesa, *f.*	*preen*-SEH-*sah*	princess
principal	*preen-see*-PAHL	chief (leading)
"	"	main
"	"	principal
principalmente	*preen-see-pahl*-MEHN-*teh*	chiefly (mainly)
"	"	mostly
príncipe, *m.*	PREEN-*see-peh*	prince
principio, *m.*	*preen*-SEE-*p_yoh*	beginning
"	"	principle (basic truth)
prisa, *f.*	PREE-*sah*	haste
"	"	hurry
"	"	rush (rapid motion)
prisa, de	*deh* PREE-*sah*	fast (quickly)
prisión, *f.*	*pree*-S_YOHN	prison
prisionero, *m.*	*pree-s_yoh*-NEH-*roh*	prisoner
privación, *f.*	*pree-vah*-S_YOHN	hardship (privation)
privado	*pree*-VAH-*thoh*	private (personal)
privar (1)	*pree*-VAHR	deprive (divest), to
privilegio, *m.*	*pree-vee*-LEH-*h_yoh*	privilege
proa, *f.*	PROH-*ah*	bow (of ship)
probable	*proh*-VAH-*vleh*	likely (*adj.*)
"	"	probable
probar (5)	*proh*-VAHR	prove (verify), to
"	"	taste (sample), to
"	"	test, to
"	"	try, to
problema, *m.*	*proh*-VLEH-*mah*	problem
procesión, *f.*	*proh-seh*-S_YOHN	procession (parade)
proceso, *m.*	*proh*-SEH-*soh*	process (set of operations)
"	"	trial (court proceeding)
proclamar (1)	*proh-klah*-MAHR	proclaim, to
procurar (1)	*proh-koo*-RAHR	attempt, to
producción, *f.*	*proh-thook*-S_YOHN	produce (yield)
"	"	production (manufacture)
producción total, *f.*	*proh-thook*-S_YOHN *toh*-TAHL	output

Spanish	Pronunciation	English
producir (12)	*proh-thoo-*SEER	produce (make), to
productivo	*proh-thook-*TEE-*voh*	productive
producto,*m.*	*proh-*THOOK-*toh*	product
profano	*proh-*FAH-*noh*	profane (blasphemous)
profesión,*f.*	*proh-feh-*S_YOHN	profession (occupation)
profesional	*proh-feh-s_yoh-*NAHL	professional
profesor,*m.*	*proh-feh-*SOHR	professor (teacher)
profeta,*m.*	*proh-*FEH-*tah*	prophet (religious teacher)
profundidad,*f.*	*proh-foon-dee-*THAHTH	depth (deepness)
profundo	*proh-*FOON-*doh*	profound
programa,*m.*	*proh-*GRAH-*mah*	program (plan)
progresivo	*proh-greh-*SEE-*voh*	progressive
progreso,*m.*	*proh-*GREH-*soh*	progress
prohibición,*f.*	*proh-ee-vee-*S_YOHN	prohibition
prohibido	*proh-ee-*VEE-*thoh*	forbidden
prohibir (3)	*proh-ee-*VEER	forbid, to
proyectil dirigido, *m.*	*proh-yehk-*TEEL *dee-ree-*HEE-*thoh*	guided missile
prolongar (1)	*proh-lohn-*GAHR	prolong, to
promesa,*f.*	*proh-*MEH-*sah*	pledge (vow)
"	"	promise
prometer (2)	*proh-meh-*TEHR	promise (pledge), to
prominente	*proh-mee-*NEHN-*teh*	prominent (jutting)
promover (5)	*proh-moh-*VEHR	foster (encourage), to
"	"	promote (further), to
pronto	PROHN-*toh*	prompt (quick)
"	"	soon (shortly)
pronunciar (1)	*proh-noon-*S_YAHR	pronounce (enunciate), to
propensión,*f.*	*proh-pehn-*S_YOHN	bent (penchant)
propiedad,*f.*	*proh-p_yeh-*THAHTH	copyright (*n.*)
"	"	property (possession)
propietario,*m.*	*proh-p_yeh-*TAH-*r_yoh*	owner
propina,*f.*	*proh-*PEE-*nah*	tip (gratuity)
propio	PROH-*p_yoh*	own (*adj.*)
proponer (31)	*proh-poh-*NEHR	propose (suggest), to
proporción,*f.*	*proh-pohr-*S_YOHN	proportion (ratio)
propósito,*m.*	*proh-*POH-*see-toh*	aim
"	"	design (intention)
"	"	end
"	"	object
"	"	purpose
propuesta,*f.*	*proh-*PWEHSS-*tah*	proposal (suggestion)
prosa,*f.*	PROH-*sah*	prose
proselíto,*m.*	*proh-*SEH-*lee-toh*	convert (proselyte)
prosperar (1)	*prohss-peh-*RAHR	prosper, to
prosperidad,*f.*	*prohss-peh-ree-*THAHTH	boom (*bus.*)
"	"	prosperity
próspero	PROHSS-*peh-roh*	prosperous
"	"	successful
protección,*f.*	*proh-tehk-*S_YOHN	protection
proteger (2)	*proh-teh-*HEHR	protect, to
"	"	shield, to
protesta,*f.*	*proh-*TEHSS-*tah*	protest
protestar (1)	*proh-tehss-*TAHR	protest, to
provechoso	*proh-veh-*CHOH-*soh*	profitable
proveedor,*m.*	*proh-veh(eh)-*THOHR	supplier (*bus.*)
proveer (2)	*proh-*V(*eh*)EHR	furnish, to
"	"	provide, to
"	"	supply, to
proverbio,*m.*	*proh-*VEHR-*b_yoh*	proverb
provincia,*f.*	*proh-*VEEN-*s_yah*	province (*pol.*)
provisión,*f.*	*proh-vee-*S_YOHN	supply (amount available)
provisional	*proh-vee-s_yoh-*NAHL	temporary
proyecto,*m.*	*proh-*YEHK-*toh*	project
prueba,*f.*	PR_WEH-*vah*	test (trial)
psicología,*f.*	*see-koh-loh-*HEE-*ah*	psychology
psiquiatría,*f.*	*see-kee-ah-*TREE-*ah*	psychiatry
publicación,*f.*	*poo-vlee-kah-*S_YOHN	publication (published work)
publicar (1)	*poo-vlee-*KAHR	publish, to
publicidad,*f.*	*poo-vlee-see-*THAHTH	publicity (notoriety)
público	POO-*vlee-koh*	public (common, *adj.*)
público,*m.*	POO-*vlee-koh*	community
"	"	public (populace)
pudrirse (3)	*poo-*THREER-*seh*	rot, to
pueblo,*m.*	PWEH-*vloh*	people (populace)
"	"	town
puente,*m.*	PWEHN-*teh*	bridge (span)
puerco,*m.*	PWEHR-*koh*	hog (animal)
puerta,*f.*	PWEHR-*tah*	door
puerto,*m.*	PWEHR-*toh*	harbor
"	"	port
puesta del sol,*f.*	PWEHSS-*tah thehl* SOHL	sunset
puesto,*m.*	PWEHSS-*toh*	post (position)
puesto de periódicos,*m.*	PWEHSS-*toh theh peh-ree-*OH-*thee-kohss*	newsstand
puesto que	PWEHSS-*toh keh*	since (because, *conj.*)
pulgar,*m.*	*pool-*GAHR	thumb
pulir (3)	*poo-*LEER	polish, to
pulmón,*m.*	*pool-*MOHN	lung
pulmonía,*f.*	*pool-moh-*NEE-*ah*	pneumonia
pulsera,*f.*	*pool-*SEH-*rah*	bracelet
pulso,*m.*	POOL-*soh*	pulse (*physiol.*)
puñado,*m.*	*poo-*N_YAH-*thoh*	handful
puñal,*m.*	*poo-*N_YAHL	dagger
puñetazo,*m.*	*poo-n_yeh-*TAH-*soh*	punch (blow)
puño,*m.*	POO-*n_yoh*	cuff (of sleeve)
"	"	fist
punta,*f.*	POON-*tah*	point (sharp end)
"	"	tip
puntada,*f.*	*poon-*TAH-*thah*	stitch (of sewing)
puntiagudo	*poon-t_yah-*GOO-*thoh*	pointed (tapered)
punto,*m.*	POON-*toh*	dot
"	"	period (*punct.*)
"	"	point
punto en cuestión, *m.*	POON-*toh ehn kwehss-*T_YOHN	issue (question)
punto y coma,*m.*	POON-*toh ee* KOH-*mah*	semicolon
puntual	*poon-*TWAHL	prompt
"	"	punctual
pupila,*f.*	*poo-*PEE-*lah*	pupil (of eye)
pureza,*f.*	*poo-*REH-*sah*	purity (cleanness)
puro	POO-*roh*	pure (unadulterated)
"	"	sheer
purpúreo	*poor-*POO-*reh-oh*	purple (color)
que	KEH	than
"	"	that (*conj. rel. pron.*)
que	KEH	who (*rel. pron.*)
qué	KEH	what (*interrog. adj., pron.*)
que, el (la)	*ehl* (*lah*) KEH	who (*rel. pron.*)
quebradizo	*keh-vrah-*THEE-*soh*	brittle
quedar (1)	*keh-*THAHR	remain (be left), to
quedarse	*keh-*THAHR-*seh*	remain (stay behind), to
queja,*f.*	KEH-*hah*	complaint
quejarse (1)	*keh-*HAHR-*seh*	complain, to
quemadura de sol, *f.*	*keh-mah-*THOO-*rah theh* SOHL	sunburn
quemar (1)	*keh-*MAHR	burn (set fireto), to
querer (32)	*keh-*REHR	want (desire), to
querer decir	*keh-*REHR *theh-*SEER	mean (have in, mind), to
querido	*keh-*REE-*thoh*	dear (*adj.*)
"	"	beloved (*adj.*)
querido,*m.*	*keh-*REE-*thoh*	darling
queso,*m.*	KEH-*soh*	cheese
quiebra,*f.*	K_YEH-*vrah*	bankruptcy
"	"	failure (*bus.*)
quien(es)	K_YEHN(-*ehss*)	who (*rel. pron.*)
quién(es)	K_YEHN(-*ehss*)	who (*interrog. pron.*)
quien, a	*ah* K_YEHN	whom (*rel. pron.*)
quién, a	*ah* K_YEHN	whom (*interrog. pron.*)
quien, de	*deh* K_YEHN	whose (*rel. pron.*)
quién, de	*deh* K_YEHN	whose (*interrog. pron.*)
quienquiera que	*k_yehn-*K_YEH-*rah keh*	whoever
quieto	K_YEH-*toh*	quiet (without motion, *adj.*)
quietud,*f.*	*k_yeh-*TOO_TH	quiet (stillness)
quijada,*f.*	*kee-*HAH-*thah*	jaw
química,*f.*	KEE-*mee-kah*	chemistry
quincalla,*f.*	*keen-*KAH-*yah*	hardware
quitar (1)	*kee-*TAHR	remove (take away), to
quitarse	*kee-*TAHR-*seh*	shed (cast off), to
Quito	KEE-*toh*	Quito
quizás	*kee-*SAHSS	maybe
rabí,*m.*	*rrah-*VEE	rabbi
rabia,*f.*	RRAH-*v_yah*	rage (wrath)

Spanish	Pronunciation	English
rabiar (1)	RRAH-*v yahr*	rage (rave), to
ración, *f.*	*rrah*-S YOHN	ration (allotment)
radar, *m.*	*rrah*-THAHR	radar (*n.*)
radiactividad, *f.*	*rrah-th yahk-tee-vee-*THATH	radioactivity
radiador, *m.*	*rrah-th yah*-THOHR	radiator (heater)
radiante	*rrah*-TH YAHN-*teh*	radiant
radical	*rrah-thee-*KAHL	radical (basic)
radio, *m.*	RRAH-*th yoh*	radio (receiving set)
radiodifusión, *f.*	RRAH-*th yoh-thee-foo-*S YOHN	broadcasting (*rad.*)
radiografía, *f.*	*rrah-th yoh-grah-*FEE-*ah*	X-ray (X-ray picture)
radiografiar (1)	*rrah-th yoh-grah-*F YAHR	X-ray (examine), to
raíz, *f.*	*rrah*-EESS	root (*bot.*)
rama, *f.*	RRAH-*mah*	bough
"	"	branch
ramita, *f.*	*rrah*-MEE-*tah*	twig
rana, *f.*	RRAH-*nah*	frog
rango, *m.*	RRAHN-*goh*	rank (standing)
rápido	RRAH-*pee-thoh*	fast
"	"	quick
"	"	rapid (*adj.*)
"	"	swift
rapto, *m.*	RRAHP-*toh*	rapture
rara vez	RRAH-*rah* VEHSS	seldom
raro	RRAH-*roh*	funny
"	"	odd (queer)
"	"	quaint (unusual)
"	"	rare (uncommon)
rascacielos, *m.*	*rrahss-kah-*S YEH-*lohss*	skyscraper
rascar (1)	*rrahss-*KAHR	scratch, to
rasgar (1)	*rrahss-*GAHR	tear (rip), to
rasgo, *m.*	RRAHSS-*goh*	feature (attribute)
raso, *m.*	RRAH-*soh*	satin (*n.*)
raspar (1)	*rrahss-*PAHR	scrape (make smooth or clean), to
rastrillo, *m.*	*rrah-*STREE-*yoh*	rake (tool)
rata, *f.*	RRAH-*tah*	rat
rato, *m.*	RRAH-*toh*	while (short time, *n.*)
rato, por un	*poh roon* RAH-*toh*	awhile (*adv.*)
ratón, *m.*	*rrah-*TOHN	mouse
raya, *f.*	RRAH-*yah*	streak
"	"	stripe
rayo, *m.*	RRAH-*yoh*	beam
"	"	ray
rayón, *m.*	*rrah-*YOHN	rayon
rayo X, *m.*	RRAH-*yoh* EEK-*ehss*	X-ray (Roentgen ray)
raza, *f.*	RRAH-*sah*	breed (stock)
"	"	race (*anthrop.*)
razón, *f.*	*rrah-*SOHN	ratio
"	"	reason
razonable	*rrah-soh-*NAH-*vleh*	reasonable (rational)
reacción, *f.*	*rreh-*AHK-S YOHN	reaction
real	*rreh-*AHL	real (actual)
"	"	regal
"	"	royal
realidad, *f.*	*rreh-ah-lee-*THAHTH	reality
realizar	*rreh-ah-lee-*SAHR	realize (accomplish), to
realmente	*rreh-ahl-*MEHN-*teh*	really (actually)
"	"	really (indeed)
rebajar (1)	*rreh-vah-*HAHR	cut (reduce), to
rebanada, *f.*	*rreh-vah-*NAH-*thah*	slice
rebaño, *m.*	*rreh-*VAH-*n yoh*	flock
"	"	herd (of animals)
rebelde, *m.,f.*	*rreh-*VEHL-*theh*	rebel (*n.*)
rebelión, *f.*	*rreh-veh-*L YOHN	rebellion
"	"	revolt
rebotar (1)	*rreh-voh-*TAHR	bounce, to
recaer (19)	*rreh-kah-*EHR	relapse, to
recargo, *m.*	*rreh-*KAHR-*goh*	surcharge (*bus.*)
recepción, *f.*	*rreh-sehp-*S YOHN	reception
receta, *f.*	*rreh-*SEH-*tah*	prescription (*med.*)
"	"	recipe
rechazar (1)	*rreh-chah-*SAHR	reject, to
rechoncho	*rreh-*CHOHN-*choh*	plump (chubby)
recibir (3)	*rreh-see-*VEER	receive, to
recibo, *m.*	*rreh-*SEE-*voh*	receipt
reciente	*rreh-*S YEHN-*teh*	recent

Spanish	Pronunciation	English
recientemente	*rreh-s yehn-teh-*MEHN-*teh*	recently
recitar (1)	*rreh-see-*TAHR	recite (repeat something learned)
reclamación, *f.*	*rreh-klah-mah-*S YOHN	claim
reclamar (1)	*rreh-klah-*MAHR	claim, to
reclutar (1)	*rreh-kloo-*TAHR	draft (conscript), to
recobrar (1)	*rreh-koh-*VRAHR	recover (get back), to
recoger (2)	*rreh-koh-*HEHR	gather (bring together), to
recomendación, *f.*	*rreh-koh-mehn-dah-*S YOHN	recommendation
recomendar (4)	*rreh-koh-mehn-*DAHR	recommend (advise), to
recomenzar (4)	*rreh-koh-mehn-*SAHR	resume (recommence), to
recompensa, *f.*	*rreh-kohm-*PEHN-*sah*	reward (recompense)
recompensar (1)	*rreh-kohm-pehn-*SAHR	reward, to
reconcentrar (1)	*rreh-kohn-sehn-*TRAHR	concentrate (make converge), to
reconocer (11)	*rreh-koh-noh-*SEHR	acknowledge (admit) to
"	"	recognize (identify), to
reconocimiento, *m.*	*rreh-koh-noh-see-*M YEHN-*toh*	recognition
recordar (5)	*rreh-kohr-*THAHR	recall, to
"	"	remember (recollect), to
"	"	remind, to
rectángulo, *m.*	*rrehk-*TAHN-*goo-loh*	rectangle
recuerdo, *m.*	*rreh-*KWEHR-*thoh*	remembrance (recollection)
"	"	souvenir
recuperar (1)	*rreh-koo-peh-*RAHR	recover (get well), to
recursos, *m.pl.*	*rreh-*KOOR-*sohss*	resources (wealth)
red, *f.*	RREHTH	net (mesh)
redactor, *m.*	*rreh-thahk-*TOHR	editor
redondo	*rreh-*THOHN-*doh*	round (*adj.*)
reducción, *f.*	*rreh-thook-*S YOHN	reduction (lessening)
reducir (12)	*rreh-thoo-*SEER	reduce (diminish), to
reembolsar (1)	*rr(eh)ehm-bohl-*SAHR	repay (reimburse), to
reembolso, *m.*	*rr(eh)ehm-*BOHL-*soh*	refund (*bus.*)
reemplazar (1)	*rr(eh)ehm-plah-*SAHR	replace (be a substitute for), to
referencia, *f.*	*rreh-feh-*REHN-*s yah*	reference (allusion)
referirse (7)	*rreh-feh-*REER-*seh*	refer (allude), to
refinar (1)	*rreh-fee-*NAHR	refine (purify), to
reflejar (1)	*rreh-fleh-*HAHR	reflect (throw back), to
reflejo, *m.*	*rreh-*FLEH-*hoh*	reflection (image)
reflexión, *f.*	*rreh-flehk-*S YOHN	reflection (meditation)
reforma, *f.*	*rreh-*FOHR-*mah*	reform (*n.*)
refrenar (1)	*rreh-freh-*NAHR	restrain (check), to
refrescar (1)	*rreh-frehss-*KAHR	refresh, to
refrescos, *m.pl.*	*rreh-*FREHSS-*kohss*	refreshments
refugiado, *m.*	*rreh-foo-*H YAH-*thoh*	refugee
refugio, *m.*	*rreh-*FOO-*h yoh*	refuge
refunfuñar (1)	*rreh-foon-foo-*N YAHR	grumble, to
refutar (1)	*rreh-foo-*TAHR	refute, to
regalar (1)	*rreh-gah-*LAHR	present (give), to
regalo, *m.*	*rreh-*GAH-*loh*	gift (present)
regañar (1)	*rreh-gahn-*YAHR	scold, to
regazo, *m.*	*rreh-*GAH-*soh*	lap (of seated person)
regimiento, *m.*	*rreh-hee-*M YEHN-*toh*	regiment (*n.*)
región, *f.*	*rreh-*H YOHN	area
"	"	region
registrar (1)	*rreh-heess-*TRAHR	register, to
registro, *m.*	*rreh-*HEESS-*troh*	register (record)
registros, *m.pl.*	*rreh-*HEESS-*trohss*	records (files)
regla, *f.*	RREH-*glah*	regulation
"	"	rule
"	"	ruler (measuring instrument)
regla general, *f.*	RREH-*glah heh-neh-*RAHL	rule (usual case)
regocijarse (1)	*rreh-goh-see-*HAHR-*seh*	rejoice, to
regocijo, *m.*	*rreh-goh-*SEE-*hoh*	glee (joy)
regresar (1)	*rreh-greh-*SAHR	return (go back), to
regreso, *m.*	*rreh-*GREH-*soh*	return (coming or going back)
regular	*rreh-goo-*LAHR	decent (fairly good)
"	"	fair (passable)
"	"	regular (normal)

Spanish	Pronunciation	English
regularidad, *f.*	*rreh-goo-lah-ree-*THAHTH	regularity
rehusar (1)	*rreh-oo-*SAHR	decline, to
"	"	deny, to
"	"	refuse (make a refusal), to
reina, *f.*	RREH *ee-nah*	queen
reinado, *m.*	RREH *ee-*NAH-*thoh*	reign (period of rule)
reino, *m.*	RREH *ee-noh*	kingdom
"	"	realm
reintegrar (1)	*rreh-een-teh-*GRAHR	reimburse, to
reintegro, *m.*	*rreh-een-*TEH-*groh*	rebate (*bus.*)
reír (10)	*rreh-*EER	laugh, to
relación, *f.*	*rreh-lah-*S YOHN	connection (relationship)
"	"	relation
relacionado	*rreh-lah-s yoh-*NAH-*thoh*	related (connected)
relacionarse a	*rreh-lah-s yoh-*NAHR-*seh ah*	relate (pertain) to, to
relaciones, *f.pl.*	*rreh-lah-*S YOH-*nehss*	dealings (relations)
relámpago, *m.*	*rreh-*LAHM-*pah-goh*	lightning
relatar (1)	*rreh-lah-*TAHR	relate (tell), to
relativo	*rreh-lah-*TEE-*voh*	comparative
"	"	relative
relato, *m.*	*rreh-*LAH-*toh*	account (report)
religión, *f.*	*rreh-lee-*H YOHN	religion
religioso	*rreh-lee-*H YOH-*soh*	religious (*adj.*)
relinchar (1)	*rreh-leen-*CHAHR	neigh, to
reloj, *m.*	*rreh-*LOH	clock
"	"	watch (timepiece)
relucir (11)	*rreh-loo-*SEER	glitter, to
remedio, *m.*	*rreh-*MEH-*th yoh*	cure
"	"	remedy
remesa, *f.*	*rreh-*MEH-*sah*	consignment (*bus.*)
"	"	remittance
remesar (1)	*rreh-meh-*SAHR	remit (send payment), to
remeter (2)	*rreh-meh-*TEHR	tuck (slip inside), to
remitir (3)	*rreh-mee-*TEER	forward (send by mail), to
remo, *m.*	RREH-*moh*	oar (*n.*)
remolacha, *f.*	*rreh-moh-*LAH-*chah*	beet (red root)
remontarse (1)	*rreh-mohn-*TAHR-*seh*	soar (rise), to
remoto	*rreh-*MOH-*toh*	remote (far-off)
remuneración, *f.*	*rreh-moo-neh-rah-*S YOHN	compensation (*bus.*)
rendición, *f.*	*rrehn-dee-*S YOHN	surrender (*mil.*)
rendimiento, *m.*	*rrehn-dee-*M YEHN-*toh*	yield (product)
rendir (9)	*rrehn-*DEER	surrender (relinquish), to
rendirse	*rrehn-*DEER-*seh*	succumb (yield), to
"	"	surrender (give oneself up), to
reñirse (10)	*rreh-*N YEER-*seh*	quarrel (dispute), to
reno, *m.*	RREH-*noh*	reindeer
renovar (5)	*rreh-noh-*VAHR	renew, to
renta, *f.*	RREHN-*tah*	revenue (*govt.*)
reo, *m.*	RREH-*oh*	criminal (*n.*)
reparar (1)	*rreh-pah-*RAHR	fix, to
"	"	mend, to
"	"	repair, to
reparo, *m.*	*rreh-*PAH-*roh*	repair (*n.*)
repartir (3)	*rreh-pahr-*TEER	distribute (allot), to
reparto, *m.*	*rreh-*PAHR-*toh*	distribution (allotment)
repasar (1)	*rreh-pah-*SAHR	review (look over again), to
repente, *m.*	*rreh-*PEHN-*teh*	impulse (sudden incitement)
repetir (9)	*rreh-peh-*TEER	repeat (reiterate), to
repicar (1)	*rreh-pee-*KAHR	peal, to
reportero, *m.*	*rreh-pohr-*TEH-*roh*	reporter (journalist)
represa, *f.*	*rreh-*PREH-*sah*	dam (dike)
representación, *f.*	*rreh-preh-sehn-tah-*S YOHN	performance (stage presentation)
"	"	play (stage presentation)
"	"	representation (*pol.*)
representante, *m.*	*rreh-preh-sehn-*TAHN-*teh*	representative (deputy)
representar (1)	*rreh-preh-sehn-*TAHR	represent (act for), to
"	"	represent (symbolize), to
represión, *f.*	*rreh-preh-*S YOHN	check (restraint)
reprimir (3)	*rreh-pree-*MEER	curb (restrain), to

Spanish	Pronunciation	English
reprochar (1)	*rreh-proh-*CHAHR	reproach, to
reproche, *m.*	*rreh-*PROH-*cheh*	reproach
república, *f.*	*rreh-*POO-*vlee-kah*	republic
República Dominicana	*rreh-*POOV-*lee-kah thoh-mee-nee-*KAH-*nah*	Dominican Republic
republicano	*rreh-poo-vlee-*KAH-*noh*	republican (*adj.*)
reputación, *f.*	*rreh-poo-tah-*S YOHN	reputation
requerir (7)	*rreh-keh-*REER	require (need), to
resbaloso	*rrehss-bah-*LOH-*soh*	slippery
rescatar (1)	*rrehss-kah-*TAHR	redeem (buy back), to
"	"	rescue, to
rescate, *m.*	*rrehss-*KAH-*teh*	ransom (*n.*)
"	"	rescue
resentirse de (4)	*rreh-sehn-*TEER-*seh theh*	resent, to
reserva, *f.*	*rreh-*SEHR-*vah*	reserve (*bus.*)
reservación, *f.*	*rreh-sehr-vah-*S YOHN	reservation (advance order)
reservar (1)	*rreh-sehr-*VAHR	book (engage space), to
"	"	reserve, to
resfriado, *m.*	*rrehss-*FR YAH-*thoh*	cold (disease)
residencia, *f.*	*rreh-see-*THEHN-*s yah*	residence (abode)
residente, *m.*	*rreh-see-*THEHN-*teh*	resident (*n.*)
residir (3)	*rreh-see-*THEER	dwell (reside), to
residuo, *m.*	*rreh-*SEE-*thwoh*	difference (*math.*)
resistencia, *f.*	*rreh-seess-*TEHN-*s yah*	resistance
resistir (3)	*rreh-seess-*TEER	resist, to
resollar hacia adentro (5)	*rreh-soh-*YAHR AH-*s yah-*THEHN-*troh*	sniff, to
resolución, *f.*	*rreh-soh-loo-*S YOHN	resolution (formal expression)
"	"	will (power of choice)
resolver (5)	*rreh-sohl-*VEHR	solve, to
resolver(se)	*rreh-sohl-*VEHR(-*seh*)	resolve (determine), to
resonar (5)	*rreh-soh-*NAHR	clang, to
"	"	ring (resound), to
resorte, *m.*	*rreh-*SOHR-*teh*	spring (coil)
respectivo	*rrehss-pehk-*TEE-*voh*	respective (*adj.*)
respecto a	*rrehss-*PEHK-*toh ah*	concerning (regarding)
respetable	*rrehss-peh-*TAH-*vleh*	respectable
respetar (1)	*rrehss-peh-*TAHR	respect (esteem), to
respeto, *m.*	*rrehss-*PEH-*toh*	respect (esteem)
respirar (1)	*rrehss-pee-*RAHR	breathe (draw breath), to
responder (2)	*rrehss-pohn-*DEHR	reply, to
"	"	respond (react), to
"	"	respond, to
responder a	*rrehss-pohn-*DEHR *ah*	answer (address reply to), to
responsabilidad, *f.*	*rrehss-pohn-sah-vee-lee-*THAHTH	liability
"	"	responsibility (accountability)
responsable	*rrehss-pohn-*SAH-*vleh*	liable
"	"	responsible (answerable)
respuesta, *f.*	*rrehss-*PWEHSS-*tah*	answer
"	"	reply
"	"	response
restar (1)	*rrehss-*TAHR	subtract, to
restaurante, *m.*	*rrehss-t ow-*RAHN-*teh*	restaurant
restaurar (1)	*rrehss-t ow-*RAHR	restore (re-establish), to
resto, *m.*	RREHSS-*toh*	remainder
"	"	rest
restricción mental, *f.*	*rrehss-treek-*S YOHN *mehn-*TAHL	reservation (mental qualification)
resucitar (1)	*reh-soo-see-*TAHR	revive, to
resultado, *m.*	*rreh-sool-*TAH-*thoh*	result (consequence)
resultar (1)	*rreh-sool-*TAHR	follow (result), to
resumen, *m.*	*rreh-*SOO-*mehn*	summary (synopsis)
retener (35)	*rreh-teh-*NEHR	retain (keep), to
retirar (1)	*rreh-tee-*RAHR	withdraw (take back), to
retirarse	*rreh-tee-*RAHR-*seh*	retire (stop working), to
retiro, *m.*	*rreh-*TEE-*roh*	retreat (*mil.*)
retrasarse (1)	*rreh-trah-*SAHR-*seh*	lag (fall behind), to
retraso, *m.*	*rreh-*TRAH-*soh*	delay
retraso, con	*kohn rreh-*TRAH-*soh*	behind (late, *adv.*)
retrato, *m.*	*rreh-*TRAH-*toh*	portrait
reumatismo, *m.*	*rreh-oo-mah-*TEESS-*moh*	rheumatism
reunión, *f.*	*rreh-oo-*N YOHN	assembly
"	"	meeting

Spanish	Pronunciation	English
reunir (3)	*rreh-oo*-NEER	assemble (bring together), to
"	"	collect (bring together), to
"	"	gather (congregate), to
"	"	raise, to
reunirse	*rreh-oo*-NEER-*seh*	assemble, to
"		meet (come together), to
revelar (1)	*rreh-veh*-LAHR	reveal (divulge), to
reventa, *f.*	*rreh*-VEHN-*tah*	resale (*bus.*)
reverencia, *f.*	*rreh-veh*-REHN-*s yah*	reverence (respect)
revisor, *m.*	*rreh-vee*-SOHR	conductor (ticket collector)
revista, *f.*	*rreh*-VEESS-*tah*	journal
"	"	magazine (periodical)
revolución, *f.*	*rreh-voh-loo*-S YOHN	revolution (*pol.*)
revólver, *m.*	*rreh-voh*l-*vehr*	revolver (weapon)
revolver (5)	*rreh-vohl*-VEHR	stir (mix), to
rey, *m.*	RREH	king
rezar (1)	*rreh*-SAHR	pray, to
ribera, *f.*	*rree-veh*-*rah*	bank
"	"	shore
rico	RREE-*koh*	rich
"	"	wealthy
"	"	ridiculous
ridículo, *m.*	*rree*-THEE-*koo-loh*	ridicule
riego, *m.*	RR YEH-*goh*	irrigation
riel, *m.*	RR YEHL	rail (bar on track)
rienda, *f.*	RR YEHN-*dah*	rein (strap)
riesgo, *m.*	RR YEHSS-*goh*	risk (danger)
rifle, *m.*	RREE-*fleh*	rifle
rígido	RREE-*hee-thoh*	stiff (inflexible)
rima, *f.*	RREE-*mah*	rhyme
Rin, *m.*	RREEN	Rhine
riña, *f.*	RREE-*n yah*	quarrel (dispute)
rincón, *m.*	*rreen*-KOHN	corner (angle)
riñon, *m.*	*rree*-N YOHN	kidney (*anat.*)
río, *m.*	RREE-*oh*	river
Río de Janeiro	RREE-*oh theh hah*-NEH-*ee-roh*	Rio de Janeiro
riquesa, *f.*	*rree*-KEH-*sah*	riches
"	"	wealth
risa, *f.*	RREE-*sah*	laughter
risco, *m.*	RREESS-*koh*	cliff
rito, *m.*	RREE-*toh*	rite
rival, *m.*	*rree*-VAHL	competitor (*bus.*)
"	"	rival
rizo, *m.*	RREE-*soh*	curl (ringlet)
robar (1)	*rroh*-VAHR	rob (steal from), to
"	"	steal, to
roble, *m.*	RROH-*vleh*	oak
robusto	*rroh*-BOOSS-*toh*	sturdy
roca, *f.*	RROH-*kah*	rock (large stone)
rociar (1)	*rroh*-S YAHR	spray, to
rocío, *m.*	*rroh*-SEE-*oh*	dew
rocoso	*rroh*-KOH-*soh*	rocky (rock-covered)
rodar (5)	*rroh*-THAHR	roll (impel), to
rodear (1)	*rroh-theh*-AHR	surround (enclose), to
rodilla, *f.*	*rroh*-THEE-*yah*	knee
rodillo, *m.*	*rroh*-THEE-*yoh*	roller (cylinder)
roer (2)	*rroh*-EHR	gnaw (bite), to
rogar (5)	*rroh*-GAHR	beg (entreat), to
rojo	RROH-*hoh*	red
rollo, *m.*	RROH-*yoh*	roll (cylinder)
Roma	RROH-*mah*	Rome
romano	*rroh*-MAH-*noh*	Roman (*adj.*)
romántico	*rroh*-MAHN-*tee-koh*	romantic
romper (2)	*rrohm*-PEHR	break (make divide), to
"	"	break (make smash), to
romperse	*rrohm*-PEHR-*seh*	break (come apart), to
ron, *m.*	RROHN	rum
ropa, *f.*	RROH-*pah*	clothing
ropa interior, *f.*	RROH-*pah een-teh*-R YOHR	underwear
ropa lavada, *f.*	RROH-*pah lah*-VAH-*thah*	laundry (articles laundered)
rosa, *f.*	RROH-*sah*	rose (flower)
rosado	*rroh*-SAH-*thoh*	pink (color)

Spanish	Pronunciation	English
rótulo, *m.*	RROH-*too-loh*	label
rubí, *m.*	*rroo*-VEE	ruby (gem)
rubio	RROO-*v yoh*	blond
"		fair
ruborizarse (1)	*rroo-voh-ree*-SAHR-*seh*	blush, to
rudimentario	*rroo-thee-mehn*-TAH-*r yoh*	elementary (rudimentary)
rudo	RROO-*thoh*	rude (impolite)
rueda, *f.*	RR WEH-*thah*	wheel
rugido, *m.*	*rroo*-HEE-*thoh*	roar (*n.*)
ruido, *m.*	RR WEE-*thoh*	noise (din)
ruidoso	*rr wee*-THOH-*soh*	noisy
ruinas, *f. pl.*	RR WEE-*nahss*	ruins (remains)
ruiseñor, *m.*	*rr wee-seh*-N YOHR	nightingale
Rumania	*rroo*-MAH-*n yah*	Rumania
rumor, *m.*	*rroo*-MOHR	rumor
rural	*rroo*-RAHL	rural
Rusia	RROO-*s yah*	Russia
ruso	RROO-*soh*	Russian (*adj.*)
ruta, *f.*	RROO-*tah*	route
"	"	way
sábana, *f.*	SAH-*vah-nah*	sheet (bedding)
saber (33)	*sah*-VEHR	know (have knowledge), to
saber, a	*ah sah*-VEHR	namely
sabiduría, *f.*	*sah-vee-thoo*-REE-*ah*	wisdom
sabio	SAH-*v yoh*	sage (*adj.*)
"		wise
sabio, *m.*	SAH-*v yoh*	scholar (savant)
sabor, *m.*	*sah*-VOHR	flavor (savor)
"	"	taste
sacerdote, *m.*	*sah-sehr*-THOH-*teh*	priest
saco, *m.*	SAH-*koh*	bag
"	"	sack
sacrificar (1)	*sahk-ree-fee*-KAHR	sacrifice (forego), to
sacrificio, *m.*	*sahk-ree*-FEE-*s yoh*	sacrifice (giving up)
sacudir (3)	*sah-koo*-THEER	shake, to
"	"	shock (jar), to
sagrado	*sah*-GRAH-*thoh*	holy
"	"	sacred
sal, *f.*	SAHL	salt
"	"	wit (humor)
sala, *f.*	SAH-*lah*	parlor (living room)
sala de clase, *f.*	SAH-*lah theh* KLAH-*seh*	schoolroom
sala de hospital, *f.*	SAH-*lah theh ohss-pee*-TAHL	ward (sickroom)
salario, *m.*	*sah*-LAH-*r yoh*	salary
"	"	wages
salchicha, *f.*	*sahl*-CHEE-*chah*	sausage
salida, *f.*	*sah*-LEE-*thah*	exit
"	"	outlet
"	"	outlet (market, *bus.*)
salida del sol, *f.*	*sah*-LEE-*thah thehl* SOHL	sunrise
salir (15)	*sah*-LEER	rise (in sky), to
"	"	start (set out), to
salir aprobado	*sah*-LEER *ah-proh*-VAH-*thoh*	pass (not fail in), to
salmón, *m.*	*sahl*-MOHN	salmon
salón, *m.*	*sah*-LOHN	hall (meeting room)
salón de actos, *m.*	*sah*-LOHN *theh* AHK-*tohss*	auditorium
salsa, *f.*	SAHL-*sah*	dressing
"	"	gravy
"	"	sauce
saltamontes, *m.*	*sahl-tah*-MOHN-*tehss*	grasshopper
saltar (1)	*sahl*-TAHR	hop, to
"	"	jump (bound), to
"	"	leap, to
"	"	skip (caper), to
"	"	spring, to
salto, *m.*	SAHL-*toh*	bound
"	"	jump
"	"	leap
salud, *f.*	*sah*-LOOTH	health
saludable	*sah-loo*-THAH-*vleh*	wholesome (beneficial)
saludar (1)	*sah-loo*-THAHR	greet, to
"	"	salute, to
saludo, *m.*	*sah*-LOO-*thoh*	greeting
salvación, *f.*	*sahl-vah*-S YOHN	salvation
salvador, *m.*	*sahl-vah*-THOHR	savior

Spanish	Pronunciation	English
Salvador, El	*ehl sahl-vah-*THOHR	Salvador, El
salvaje	*sahl-*VAH-*heh*	savage (*adj.*)
"	"	wild (undomesticated)
salvar (1)	*sahl-*VAHR	save (rescue), to
sangrar (1)	*sahn-*GRAHR	bleed (lose blood), to
sangre, *f.*	SAHN-*greh*	blood
sano	SAH-*noh*	healthy
"	"	sound
"	"	well (in health, *adj.*)
sano de mente	SAH-*noh theh* MEHN-*teh*	sane
Santiago	*sahn-*T_YAH-*goh*	Santiago
santo, *m.*	SAHN-*toh*	saint
sapo, *m.*	SAH-*poh*	toad
sarampion, *m.*	*sah-rahm-*P_YOHN	measles
sardina, *f.*	*sahr-*THEE-*nah*	sardine
sargento, *m.*	*sahr-*HEHN-*toh*	sergeant
sartén, *f.*	*sahr-*TEHN	pan, frying
sastre, *m.*	SAHSS-*treh*	tailor
satisfacción, *f.*	*sah-teess-fahk-*S_YOHN	satisfaction
satisfacer (26)	*sah-tees-fah-*SEHR	satisfy, to
satisfactorio	*sah-tees-fahk-*TOH-*r_yoh*	satisfactory
satisfecho	*sah-tees-*FEH-*choh*	satisfied (contented)
sauce, *m.*	SOW-*seh*	willow
savia, *f.*	SAH-*v_yah*	sap (fluid)
saxofón, *m.*	*sahk-soh-*FOHN	saxophone
se	SEH	herself, himself, itself, yourself, yourselves, themselves
sea que...o que	SEH_*ah keh...oh keh*	whether (either, *conj.*)
secar (1)	*seh-*KAHR	dry (make dry), to
"	"	wipe (make dry by wiping), to
secarse	*seh-*KAHR-*seh*	dry (become dry), to
sección, *f.*	*sehk-*S_YOHN	section (part)
seco	SEH-*koh*	dry
secretario, *m.*	*seh-kreh-*TAH-*r_yoh*	secretary (stenographer)
secreto	*seh-*KREH-*toh*	secret (*adj.*)
"	"	underground (*adj.*)
secreto, *m.*	*seh-*KREH-*toh*	secret (*n.*)
sed, *f.*	SEHTH	thirst
seda, *f.*	SEH-*thah*	silk (*n.*)
sediento	*seh-*TH_YEHN-*toh*	thirsty
seguir (9)	*seh-*GHEER	follow (go or come after), to
"	"	keep (continue), to
"	"	succeed, to
según	*seh-*GOON	according to (in accordance with)
segundo	*seh-*GOON-*doh*	second (*adj.*)
segundo, *m.*	*seh-*GOON-*doh*	second (time unit)
seguridad, *f.*	*seh-goo-ree-*THAHTH	safety (*n.*)
"	"	security
seguro	*seh-*GOO-*roh*	safe
"	"	secure
"	"	sure
seguro, *m.*	*seh-*GOO-*roh*	insurance
seguro contra incendios, *m.*	*seh-*GOO-*roh* KOHN-*trah een-*SEHN-*d_yohss*	fire insurance
selección, *f.*	*seh-lehk-*S_YOHN	choice (act of choosing)
"	"	selection
seleccionar (1)	*seh-lehk-s_yoh-*NAHR	select, to
sello, *m.*	SEH-*yoh*	seal (mark)
"	"	stamp, postage
semana, *f.*	*seh-*MAH-*nah*	week
semanal	*seh-mah-*NAHL	weekly (*adj.*)
semblante, *m.*	*sehm-*BLAHN-*teh*	countenance (face)
sembrar (4)	*sehm-*BRAHR	sow, to
semejante	*seh-meh-*HAHN-*teh*	alike (similar)
"	"	like (*adj.*)
semejanza, *f.*	*seh-meh-*HAHN-*sah*	similarity
semilla, *f.*	*seh-*MEE-*yah*	seed (ovule)
semio(b)scuro	*seh-mee-oh-*SKOO-*roh*	dim
senado, *m.*	*seh-*NAH-*thoh*	senate
senador, *m.*	*seh-nah-*THOHR	senator
señal, *f.*	*seh-*N_YAHL	signal
señalar (1)	*seh-n_yah-*LAHR	mark (designate), to
sencillo	*sehn-*SEE-*yoh*	homely (everyday)
senda, *f.*	SEHN-*dah*	lane (narrow path)
sendero, *m.*	*sehn-*DEH-*roh*	path
"	"	trail

Spanish	Pronunciation	English
seno, *m.*	SEH-*noh*	bosom
señor, *m.*	*seh-*N_YOHR	lord (master)
"	"	sir
sensación, *f.*	*sehn-sah-*S_YOHN	feeling
"	"	sensation
sensato	*sehn-*SAH-*toh*	sensible (reasonable)
sensible	*sehn-*SEE-*vleh*	sensitive (susceptible)
sentarse (4)	*sehn-*TAHR-*seh*	sit down, to
sentenciar (1)	*sehn-tehn-*S_YAHR	sentence, to
sentido, *m.*	*sehn-*TEE-*thoh*	meaning (sense)
sentimiento, *m.*	*sehn-tee-*M_YEHN-*toh*	feeling (emotion)
"	"	sentiment
sentir (7)	*sehn-*TEER	feel (experience), to
"	"	regret, to
"	"	sorry, to be
separación, *f.*	*seh-pah-rah-*S_YOHN	separation
separado	*seh-pah-*RAH-*thoh*	separate
separar (1)	*seh-pah-*RAHR	separate (disconnect), to
separarse	*seh-pah-*RAHR-*seh*	part (leave each other), to
"	"	separate (come apart), to
"	"	withdraw (depart), to
septentrional	*sehp-tehn-tr_yoh-*NAHL	northern
ser (34)	SEHR	be, to
ser de	SEHR *theh*	become of (happen to), to
ser el primero	SEHR *ehl pree-*MEH-*roh*	lead (be in advance), to
serie, *f.*	SEH-*r_yeh*	series
serio	SEH-*r_yoh*	earnest
"	"	serious
"	"	sober
sermón, *m.*	*sehr-*MOHN	sermon
serpiente, *f.*	*sehr-*P_YEHN-*teh*	serpent
ser presentado a	SEHR *preh-sehn-*TAH-*thoh ah*	meet (be introduced to), to
servicial	*sehr-vee-*S_YAHL	helpful (volunteering help)
servicio, *m.*	*sehr-*VEE-*s_yoh*	service
servilleta, *f.*	*sehr-vee-*YEH-*tah*	napkin
servir (7)	*sehr-*VEER	serve, to
sesión, *f.*	*seh-*S_YOHN	session
seta, *f.*	SEH-*tah*	mushroom (*n.*)
seto, *m.*	SEH-*toh*	hedge (bushes)
severidad, *f.*	*seh-veh-ree-*THAHTH	severity (sternness)
severo	*seh-*VEH-*roh*	harsh
"	"	severe (strict)
"	"	stern
sexo, *m.*	SEHG-*soh*	sex
si	SEE	if
"	"	whether (*conj.*)
sí	SEE	yes
sí (misma)	SEE (MEEZ-*mah*)	herself, itself
sí (mismo)	SEE (MEEZ-*moh*)	himself, itself
sí (mismos)	SEE (MEEZ-*mohss*)	themselves
siempre	S_YEHM-*preh*	always
"	"	ever (at all times)
siempre, por	*pohr* S_YEHM-*preh*	forever
siempre que	S_YEHM-*preh keh*	whenever
sien, *f.*	S_YEHN	temple (*anat.*)
sierra, *f.*	S_YEH-*rrah*	ridge (of mountains)
"	"	saw (tool)
siesta, *f.*	S_YEHSS-*tah*	nap (doze, *n.*)
siglo, *m.*	SEE-*gloh*	century
significación, *f.*	*seeg-nee-fee-kah-*S_YOHN	significance (importance)
significado, *m.*	*seeg-nee-fee-*KAH-*thoh*	sense (signification)
significar (1)	*seeg-nee-fee-*KAHR	signify (denote), to
significativo	*seeg-nee-fee-kah-*TEE-*voh*	significant (meaningful)
signo, *m.*	SEEG-*noh*	sign (indication)
siguiente	*see-*G_YEHN-*teh*	next (following, *adj.*)
sílaba, *f.*	SEE-*lah-vah*	syllable
silbar (1)	*seel-*BAHR	whistle, to
silencio, *m.*	*see-lehn-*S_YOH	silence (stillness)
silencioso	*see-lehn-*S_YOH-*soh*	quiet (*adj.*)
"	"	silent (mute)

Spanish	Pronunciation	English
silla, *f.*	SEE-*yah*	chair
silla de montar, *f.*	SEE-*yah theh* mohn-TAHR	saddle (seat)
símbolo, *m.*	SEEM-*boh-loh*	mark (symbol)
similar	*see-mee-*LAHR	similar
simpatía, *f.*	*seem-pah-*TEE-*ah*	sympathy (accord)
simple	SEEM-*pleh*	simple (uninvolved)
simplicidad, *f.*	*seem-plee-see-*THAHTH	simplicity
sin	SEEN	without (*prep.*)
sincero	*seen-*SEH-*roh*	sincere
sindicato, *m.*	*seen-dee-*KAH-*toh*	union (trade union)
sin duda	*seen* DOO-*thah*	doubtless
"	"	undoubtedly
sin embargo	SEEN *ehm-*BAHR-*goh*	however
"	"	nevertheless
sin esperanza	SEEN *ehss-peh-*RAHN-*sah*	hopeless
sin fin	SEEN FEEN	endless
sinfonía, *f.*	*seen-foh-*NEE-*ah*	symphony
singular	*seen-goo-*LAHR	peculiar (odd)
"	"	singular
singular, *m.*	*seen-goo-*LAHR	singular (*gram.*, *n.*)
si no	*see* NOH	else (if not, *adv.*)
síntoma, *m.*	SEEN-*toh-moh*	symptom
sin valor	*seen-bah-*LOHR	worthless (valueless)
sirvienta, *f.*	*seer-*V_YEHN-*tah*	maid (servant)
sirviente, *m.*	*seer-*V_YEHN-*teh*	servant (in a household)
sisear (1)	*see-seh-*AHR	hiss, to
sistema, *m.*	*seess-*TEH-*mah*	system (method)
sitio, *m.*	SEE-*t_yoh*	siege (*mil.*)
"	"	site
"	"	spot (place)
situación, *f.*	*see-twah-*S_YOHN	situation (circumstances)
soberano, *m.*	*soh-veh-*RAH-*noh*	sovereign
"	"	ruler
sobornar (1)	*soh-vohr-*NAHR	bribe, to
sobra, de	*deh* SOH-*vrah*	extra (additional)
sobrante, *m.*	*soh-*VRAHN-*teh*	margin
"	"	surplus (*n.*)
sobre	SOH-*vreh*	about (concerning)
"	"	above (higher than, *prep.*)
"	"	over (*prep.*)
"	"	upon
sobre, *m.*	SOH-*vreh*	envelope (folded wrapper)
sobrenatural	*soh-vreh-nah-too-*RAHL	weird (unearthly)
sobrepasar (1)	*soh-vreh-pah-*SAHR	surpass, to
sobresaliente	*soh-vreh-sah-*L_YEHN-*teh*	prominent (eminent)
sobretodo, *m.*	*soh-vreh-*TOH-*thoh*	overcoat
sobrevivir (3)	*soh-vreh-vee-*VEER	survive (remain alive), to
sobrina, *f.*	*soh-*VREE-*nah*	niece
sobrino, *m.*	*soh-*VREE-*noh*	nephew
sociable	*soh-*S_YAH-*vleh*	sociable (companionable)
social	*soh-*S_YAHL	social (societal)
socialismo, *m.*	*soh-s_yah-*LEESS-*moh*	socialism
socialista, *m.*	*soh-s_yah-*LEESS-*tah*	socialist (*n.*)
sociedad, *f.*	*soh-s_yeh-*THAHTH	organization (association)
"	"	society
sociedad anónima, *f.*	*soh-s_yeh-*THAHTH *ah-*NOH-*nee-mah*	corporation
sociedad regular colectiva, *f.*	*soh-s_yeh-*THAHTH *rreh-goo-*LAHR *koh-lehk-*TEE-*vah*	copartnership (*bus.*)
socio, *m.*	SOH-*s_yoh*	partner (*bus.*)
sociología, *f.*	*soh-s_yoh-loh-*HEE-*ah*	sociology
sofá, *m.*	*so-*FAH	couch
"	"	sofa
soga, *f.*	SOH-*gah*	rope
sol, *m.*	SOHL	sun
solamente	*soh-lah-*MEHN-*teh*	just (merely)
"	"	only (*adv.*)
soldado, *m.*	*sohl-*THAH-*thoh*	soldier
soldado raso, *m.*	*sohl-*THAH-*thoh* RRAH-*soh*	private (*mil.*)
soledad, *f.*	*soh-leh-*THAHTH	solitude
solemne	*soh-*LEHM-*neh*	solemn (grave)
solicitador, *m.*	*soh-lee-see-tah-*THOHR	canvasser (*bus.*)
solicitar (1)	*soh-lee-see-*TAHR	request, to
"	"	solicit (ask for), to

Spanish	Pronunciation	English
solicitud, *f.*	*soh-lee-see-*TOO_TH	application
"		request
sólido	SOH-*lee-thoh*	solid (compact)
solitario	*soh-lee-*TAH-*r_yoh*	lone
"	"	lonely (unfrequented)
"	"	solitary (unaccompanied)
sollozar (1)	*soh-yoh-*SAHR	sob, to
solo	SOH-*loh*	alone
"	"	lonely
"	"	lonesome
"	"	single (sole)
soltar (5)	*sohl-*TAHR	release (let go of), to
soltero	*sohl-*TEH-*roh*	single (unmarried)
soltero, *m.*	*sohl-*TEH-*roh*	bachelor (unmarried man)
solución, *f.*	*soh-loo-*S_YOHN	solution (solving)
sombra, *f.*	SOHM-*brah*	shade
"	"	shadow
sombreado	*sohm-breh-*AH-*thoh*	shady
sombrero, *m.*	*sohm-*BREH-*roh*	hat
someter (2)	*soh-meh-*TEHR	submit (offer), to
sonar (5)	*soh-*NAHR	sound (make heard), to
soñar (5)	*soh-*N_YAHR	dream, to
sonido, *m.*	*soh-*NEE-*thoh*	sound (noise)
sonreírse (10)	*sohn-reh-*EER-*seh*	smile, to
sonrisa, *f.*	*sohn-*REE-*sah*	smile
sopa, *f.*	SOH-*pah*	soup
soplar (1)	*soh-*PLAHR	blow (breathe out), to
"	"	blow (make move), to
soportar (1)	*soh-pohr-*TAHR	bear, to
"	"	endure, to
soportar (1)	*soh-pohr-*TAHR	stand (bear), to
sorber (2)	*sohr-*VEHR	sip, to
sordo	SOHR-*thoh*	deaf
sorprender (2)	*sohr-prehn-*DEHR	surprise, to
sorpresa, *f.*	*sohr-*PREH-*sah*	surprise
sospecha, *f.*	*sohss-*PEH-*chah*	suspicion
sospechar (1)	*sohss-peh-*CHAHR	suspect (distrust), to
sostén, *m.*	*sohss-*TEHN	brassiere
sostener (35)	*sohss-teh-*NEHR	argue (maintain), to
"	"	contend (maintain), to
"	"	support (hold up), to
"	"	sustain, to
sótano, *m.*	SOH-*tah-noh*	basement
sr.; (el) señor, *m.*	(*ehl*) *seh-*N_YOHR	Mr. (Mister)
sra.; (la) señora, *f.*	(*lah*) *seh-*N_YOH-*rah*	Mrs. (Mistress)
srita.; (la) señorita, *f.*	(*lah*) *seh-n_yoh-*REE-*tah*	Miss
su(s)	SOO(SS)	her, his, its, their, your
suave	SWAH-*veh*	gentle (soothing)
subasta, *f.*	*soo-*VAHSS-*tah*	auction (sale)
súbdito, *m.*	SOOB-*thee-toh*	subject (citizen)
subido	*soo-*VEE-*thoh*	deep (in color)
subir (3)	*soo-*VEER	climb (rise), to
subjetivo	*soob-heh-*TEE-*voh*	subjective
submarino, *m.*	*soob-mah-*REE-*noh*	submarine
subscripción, *f.*	*soob-skreep-*S_YOHN	subscription (for periodicals, etc.)
subsecuente	*soob-seh-*KWEHN-*teh*	subsequent
subsistencia, *f.*	*soob-seess-*TEHN-*s_yah*	living (livelihood)
substancia, *f.*	*soob-*STAHN-*s_yah*	substance (matter)
substancial	*soob-stahn-*S_YAHL	substantial (sizable)
substituir (14)	*soob-stee-*TWEER	substitute (put in place of), to
substituto, *m.*	*soob-stee-*TOO-*toh*	substitute (thing replacing another)
subterráneo	*soob-teh-*RRAH-*neh-oh*	underground (belowground, *adj.*)
subterráneo, *m.*	*soob-teh-*RRAH-*neh-oh*	subway (underground railway)
suceso, *m.*	*soo-*SEH-*soh*	event (happening)
suciedad, *f.*	*soo-s_yeh-*THAHTH	dirt (unclean matter)
sucio	SOO-*s_yoh*	dirty (soiled)
sudar (1)	*soo-*THAHR	perspire, to
sudeste	*soo-*THEHSS-*teh*	southeast (*adj.*)
sudoeste	*soo-thoh-*EHSS-*teh*	southwest (*adj.*)
sudor, *m.*	*soo-*THOHR	sweat

Spanish	Pronunciation	English	Spanish	Pronunciation	English
Suecia	SWEH-*s_yah*	Sweden	tal vez	*tahl* VEHSS	perhaps
sueco	SWEH-*koh*	Swedish (*adj.*)	tamaño,*m.*	*tah*-MAH-*n_yoh*	size (magnitude)
suegra,*f.*	SWEH-*grah*	mother-in-law	tambalearse (1)	*tahm-bah-leh-*AHR-*seh*	stagger (totter), to
suegro,*m.*	SWEH-*groh*	father-in-law	también	*tahm-*B_YEHN	also
suela,*f.*	SWEH-*lah*	sole (of shoe)	"	"	likewise
suelo,*m.*	SWEH-*loh*	soil (ground)	"	"	too
suelto	SWEHL-*toh*	loose (unbound)	también lo	*tahm-*B_YEHN *loh*	so (also, *adv.*)
sueño,*m.*	SWEH-*n_yoh*	dream	tambor,*m.*	*tahm-*BOHR	drum (*mus.*)
"	"	sleep	tampoco	*tahm-*POH-*koh*	either (not...either, *adv.*)
"	"	slumber	tan	TAHN	as (equally, *adv.*)
suerte,*f.*	SWEHR-*teh*	luck	"	"	so (to such a degree, *adv.*)
suéter,*m.*	SWEH-*tehr*	sweater	tanda,*f.*	TAHN-*dah*	shift (crew)
suficiente	*soo-fee-*S_YEHN-*teh*	ample	tanque,*m.*	TAHN-*keh*	tank (container)
"	"	sufficient	tanto, por lo	POHR *loh* TAHN-*toh*	hence (consequently)
suficiente, lo	*loh soo-fee-*S_YEHN-*teh*	enough (*n.*)	"	"	so (*adv.*)
sufrimiento,*m.*	*soo-free-*M_YEHN-*toh*	suffering	"	"	therefore
sufrir (3)	*soo-*FREER	suffer (undergo), to	tapa,*f.*	TAH-*pah*	cover
sugerir (7)	*soo-heh-*REER	suggest, to	"	"	lid
sugestión,*f.*	*soo-hehss-*T_YOHN	suggestion (proposal)	tapar (1)	*tah-*PAHR	cover, to
suicidio,*m.*	*soo_ee-*SEE-*th_yoh*	suicide	tapón,*m.*	*tah-*POHN	plug (stopper)
Suiza	SWEE-*sah*	Switzerland	taquigrafía,*f.*	*tah-kee-grah-*FEE-*ah*	shorthand (stenography, *n.*)
suizo	SWEE-*soh*	Swiss (*adj.*)	tarde	TAHR-*theh*	late (at relative time, *adv.*)
suma,*f.*	SOO-*mah*	addition (process of adding)	tarde,*f.*	TAHR-*theh*	afternoon
"	"	sum (quantity)	tardíamente	*tahr-*THEE-*ah-mehn-teh*	late (tardily, *adv.*)
suma,*f*	SOO-*mah*	total	tardío	*tahr-*THEE-*oh*	late (overdue, *adj.*)
sumar (1)	*soo-*MAHR	add (find sum of), to	"	"	tardy
sumergir (3)	*soo-mehr-*HEER	dip (immerse), to	tardo	TAHR-*thoh*	slow (tardy)
superficie,*f.*	*soo-pehr-*FEE-*s_yeh*	surface	tarea,*f.*	*tah-*REH-*ah*	job
"	"	top (upper surface)	"	"	task
superior	*soo-peh-*R_YOHR	superior (excellent)	tarea escolar,*f.*	*tah-*REH-*ah ehss-koh-*LAHR	assignment (*educ.*)
superstición	*soo-pehr-stee-*S_YOHN	superstition	tarifa,*f.*	*tah-*REE-*fah*	tariff (duty)
supersticioso	*soo-pehr-stee-*S_YOH-*soh*	superstitious	tarjeta de visita,*f.*	*tahr-*HEH-*tah theh vee-*SEE-*tah*	card, calling
súplica,*f.*	SOO-*plee-kah*	appeal (entreaty)	tarjeta postal,*f.*	*tahr-*HEH-*tah pohss-*TAHL	card, postal
suplicar (1)	*soo-plee-*KAHR	appeal to (entreat), to	tartamudear (1)	*tahr-tah-moo-theh-*AHR	stammer, to
"	"	plead (appeal earnestly), to	"	"	stutter, to
suponer (31)	*soo-poh-*NEHR	guess, to	taxi,*m.*	TAHG-*see*	cab (taxi)
"	"	suppose (assume), to	taxímetro,*m.*	*tahg-*SEE-*meh-troh*	taxi
supremo	*soo-*PREH-*moh*	supreme	taza,*f.*	TAH-*sah*	cup
suprimir (3)	*soo-pree-*MEER	suppress (subdue), to	te	TEH	you
supuesto, por	*pohr soo-*PWEHSS-*toh*	course, of	té,*m.*	TEH	tea
sur,*m.*	SOOR	south (*n.*)	teatro,*m.*	*teh-*AH-*troh*	theater
surco,*m.*	SOOR-*koh*	furrow (*agric.*)	techo,*m.*	TEH-*choh*	roof
surgir (3)	*soor-*HEER	arise (come about), to	tejer (2)	*teh-*HEHR	knit, to
"	"	emerge, to	"	"	weave, to
Surinam	*soo-ree-*NAHM	Surinam	tejido,*m.*	*teh-*HEE-*thoh*	textile (*n.*)
surtido,*m.*	*soor-*TEE-*thoh*	variety (assortment)	"	"	tissue (*biol.*)
suspender (2)	*sooss-pehn-*DEHR	suspend (terminate), to	tejido de punto,*m.*	*teh-*HEE-*thoh theh* POON-*toh*	knitting
suspirar (1)	*sooss-pee-*RAHR	sigh, to	tejón,*m.*	*teh-*HOHN	badger (animal)
sustento,*m.*	*sooss-*TEHN-*toh*	support (livelihood)	tela,*f.*	TEH-*lah*	cloth
susto,*m.*	SOOSS-*toh*	shock (mental jolt)	"	"	fabric
susurro,*m.*	*soo-*SOO-*rroh*	hum (murmur)	telar,*m.* (1)	*teh-*LAHR	loom
"	"	rustle	Tel Aviv	TEHL *ah-*VEEV	Tel Aviv
suya, (la)	(*lah*) SOO-*yah*	hers, his, its, theirs, yours	telefonear (1)	*teh-leh-foh-neh-*AHR	phone, to
suyas, (las)	(*lahss*) SOO-*yahss*	hers, his, its, theirs, yours	"	"	telephone, to
suyo, (el)	(*ehl*) SOO-*yoh*	hers, his, its, theirs, yours	teléfono,*m.*	*teh-*LEH-*foh-noh*	telephone
suyos, (los)	(*lohss*) SOO-*yohss*	hers, his, its, theirs, yours	telegrafiar (1)	*teh-leh-grah-*F_YAHR	telegraph, to
tabaco,*m.*	*tah-*VAH-*koh*	tobacco	telegrama,*m.*	*teh-leh-*GRAH-*mah*	telegram
tabla,*f.*	TAH-*vlah*	board	"	"	wire
"	"	plank (timber)	telescopio,*m.*	*teh-leh-*SKOH-*p_yoh*	telescope
"	"	table (tabulation)	televisión,*f.*	*teh-leh-vee-*S_YOHN	television
tablado,*m.*	*tah-*VLAH-*thoh*	stage (dais)	tema,*m.*	TEH-*mah*	subject
taburete,*m.*	*tah-voo-*REH-*teh*	stool (seat)	"	"	theme
tachar (1)	*tah-*CHAHR	blot out (efface), to	"	"	topic
tal	TAHL	such (of that kind, *adj.*)	temblar (4)	*tehm-*BLAHR	quake (shake), to
talento,*m.*	*tah-*LEHN-*toh*	talent	"	"	quiver, to
talentoso	*tah-lehn-*TOH-*soh*	gifted (talented)	"	"	shiver, to
tallar (1)	*tah-*YAHR	carve (cut designs), to	temer (2)	*teh-*MEHR	fear (be afraid of), to
talla,*f.*	TAH-*yah*	size (of suits, dresses, coats)	temerario	*teh-meh-*RAH-*r_yoh*	rash (*adj.*)
tallo,*m.*	TAH-*yoh*	stalk	"	"	reckless
"	"	stem (*bot.*)	temeroso	*teh-meh-*ROH-*soh*	afraid
talón,*m.*	*tah-*LOHN	heel (*anat.*)	"	"	fearful
			temor,*m.*	*teh-*MOHR	fear

Spanish	Pronunciation	English
temperatura, *f.*	*tehm-peh-rah-*TOO-*rah*	temperature
tempestad, *f.*	*tehm-pehss-*TAHTH	tempest
tempestuoso	*tehm-pehss-*TWOH-*soh*	stormy
templo, *m.*	TEHM-*ploh*	temple (place of worship)
temprano	*tehm-*PRAH-*noh*	early (ahead of time, *adv.*)
"	"	early (before-time, *adj.*)
"	"	soon
tendencia, *f.*	*tehn-*DEHN-*s_yah*	tendency
tender (4)	*tehn-*DEHR	tend (be apt), to
tenderse	*tehn-*DEHR-*seh*	lie (be prone), to
tenedor, *m.*	*teh-neh-*THOHR	fork (eating utensil)
tenedor de libros, *m.*	*teh-neh-*THOHR *theh* LEE-*vrohss*	bookkeeper (*bus.*)
tener (35)	*teh-*NEHR	have, to
"	"	hold, to
tener aversión a	*teh-*NEHR *ah-vehr-*S_YOH *nah*	dislike, to
tener buen éxito	*teh-*NEHR *bwehn* EHG-*see-toh*	thrive (succeed), to
tener éxito	*teh-*NEHR EHG-*see-toh*	succeed (attain goal), to
tener hambre	*teh-*NEHR AHM-*breh*	hungry, to be
tener intención	*teh-*NEHR *een-tehn-*S_YOHN	mean (intend), to
teniente, *m.*	*teh-*N_YEHN-*teh*	lieutenant
teñir (10)	*teh-*N_YEER	dye, to
tenis, *m.*	*teh-*NEESS	tennis
tensión, *f.*	*tehn-*S_YOHN	stress (physical tension)
"	"	tension (stretching)
tentación, *f.*	*tehn-tah-*S_YOHN	temptation
tentar (4)	*tehn-*TAHR	tempt, to
tentativa, *f.*	*tehn-tah-*TEE-*vah*	attempt
tenue	TEH-*n_weh*	faint (dim, *adj.*)
teoría, *f.*	*teh-oh-*REE-*ah*	theory
terciopelo, *m.*	*tehr-s_yoh-*PEH-*loh*	velvet (*n.*)
terco	TEHR-*koh*	stubborn
terminación, *f.*	*tehr-mee-nah-*S_YOHN	ending (conclusion)
terminar (1)	*tehr-mee-*NAHR	end (bring to an end), to
"	"	finish (reach the end), to
terminarse	*tehr-mee-*NAHR-*seh*	end (come to an end), to
término, *m.*	TEHR-*mee-noh*	term (expression)
término medio, *m.*	TEHR-*mee-noh* MEH-*th_yoh*	average (mean, *n.*)
termómetro, *m.*	*tehr-*MOH-*meh-troh*	thermometer
ternero, *m.*	*tehr-*NEH-*roh*	calf (animal)
ternura, *f.*	*tehr-*NOO-*rah*	tenderness (love)
terraza, *f.*	*teh-*RRAH-*sah*	terrace
terremoto, *m.*	*teh-rreh-*MOH-*toh*	earthquake
terrible	*teh-*RREE-*vleh*	awful
"	"	terrible
territorio, *m.*	*teh-rree-*TOH-*r_yoh*	land (region)
"	"	territory
terrón, *m.*	*teh-*RROHN	lump (shapeless piece)
terror, *m.*	*teh-*RROHR	terror
tertulia, *f.*	*tehr-*TOO-*l_yah*	party (social gathering)
tesorería, *f.*	*teh-soh-reh-*REE-*ah*	treasury (*govt.*)
tesoro, *m.*	*teh-*SOH-*roh*	treasure
testamento, *m.*	*tehss-tah-*MEHN-*toh*	will (document)
testigo, *m., f.*	*tehss-*TEE-*goh*	witness (one who testifies)
testimonio, *m.*	*tehss-tee-*MOH-*n_yoh*	testimony
texto, *m.*	TEHG-*stoh*	text
ti, a	*ah* TEE	you
tía, *f.*	TEE-*ah*	aunt
tiempo, *m.*	T_YEHM-*poh*	time (interval)
"	"	weather
tienda, *f.*	T_YEHN-*dah*	shop
"	"	store
tienda de campaña, *f.*	T_YEHN-*dah theh kahm-*PAH-*n_yah*	tent
tienda de comestibles, *f.*	T_YEHN-*dah theh koh-mehss-*TEE-*vlehss*	grocery
tierno	T_YEHR-*noh*	tender (loving)
tierra, *f.*	T_YEH-*rrah*	dirt (soil)
"	"	earth
"	"	ground
"	"	land

Spanish	Pronunciation	English
tigre, *m.*	TEE-*greh*	tiger
tijeras, *f.pl.*	*tee-*HEH-*rahss*	scissors
timbrar (1)	*teem-*BRAHR	stamp (mark), to
tímido	TEE-*mee-thoh*	shy (bashful)
"	"	timid
timón, *m.*	*tee-*MOHN	rudder (of a boat)
tinta, *f.*	TEEN-*tah*	ink
tío, *m.*	TEE-*oh*	uncle
típico	TEE-*pee-koh*	typical
tipo, *m.*	TEE-*poh*	guy (fellow)
"	"	type (kind)
tipo de cambio, *m.*	TEE-*poh theh* KAHM-*b_yoh*	rate (exchange)
tira, *f.*	TEE-*rah*	strip (band)
tirano, *m.*	*tee-*RAH-*noh*	tyrant
tirante	*tee-*RAHN-*teh*	tight (taut)
tirantes, *m.pl.*	*tee-*RAHN-*tehss*	suspenders
tirar (1)	*tee-*RAHR	draw (pull along), to
"	"	throw, to
"	"	toss, to
tirar a	*tee-*RAHR *ah*	shoot (fire at), to
tirar de	*tee-*RAHR *theh*	pull (draw), to
tiro, *m.*	TEE-*roh*	shot (from firearm)
titilar (1)	*tee-tee-*LAHR	twinkle, to
título, *m.*	TEE-*too-loh*	title (name)
tiza, *f.*	TEE-*sah*	chalk
toalla, *f.*	*toh-*AH-*yah*	towel, hand
tobillo, *m.*	*toh-*VEE-*yoh*	ankle
tocador, *m.*	*toh-kah-*THOHR	dresser (bureau)
tocante a	*toh-*KAHN-*teh ah*	regarding (concerning)
tocar (1)	*toh-*KAHR	feel, to
"	"	knock (hit), to
"	"	play (perform music upon), to
"	"	touch, to
tocino, *m.*	*toh-*SEE-*noh*	bacon
tocón, *m.*	*toh-*KOHN	stump (of tree)
todas partes, en	*ehn* TOH-*thahss* PAHR-*tehss*	everywhere
todavía	*toh-thah-*VEE-*ah*	yet (now, until now, *adv.*)
todo	TOH-*thoh*	all (*adj.*)
"	"	any (every, *adj.*)
"	"	everything (*pron.*)
todo, *m.*	TOH-*thoh*	all (everything, *n.*)
"	"	whole (entirety, *n.*)
todo, por	*pohr* TOH-*thoh*	throughout (in every part of, *prep.*)
todo el mundo	TOH-*thoh ehl* MOON-*doh*	everybody
todos modos, de	*deh* TOH-*thohz* MOH-*thohss*	anyhow (in any case)
Tokio	TOH-*k_yoh*	Tokyo
tolerar (1)	*toh-leh-*RAHR	tolerate (permit), to
toma, *f.*	TOH-*mah*	outlet (*elec.*)
tomar (1)	*toh-*MAHR	take, to
tomar prestado	*toh-*MAHR *prehss-*TAH-*thoh*	borrow, to
tomate, *m.*	*toh-*MAH-*teh*	tomato
tonada, *f.*	*toh-*NAH-*thah*	tune (melody)
tono, *m.*	TOH-*noh*	tone (quality of sound)
tonsilitis, *f.*	*tohn-see-*LEE-*teess*	tonsillitis
tonto, *m.*	TOHN-*toh*	fool
topetar (1)	*toh-peh-*TAHR	ram (butt), to
topo, *m.*	TOH-*poh*	mole (animal)
torcer (5)	*tohr-*SEHR	sprain, to
"	"	twist (wind), to
torcido	*tohr-*SEE-*thoh*	crooked
tormenta, *f.*	*tohr-*MEHN-*tah*	storm
tormento, *m.*	*tohr-*MEHN-*toh*	torment
tornillo, *m.*	*tohr-*NEE-*yoh*	screw (threaded nail)
toro, *m.*	TOH-*roh*	bull (male bovine)
torpe	TOHR-*peh*	awkward
torpedo, *m.*	*tohr-*PEH-*thoh*	torpedo
torre, *f.*	TOH-*rreh*	steeple
"	"	tower
torrente, *m.*	*toh-*RREHN-*teh*	torrent
torta, *f.*	TOHR-*tah*	cake (dessert)
tortuga, *f.*	*tohr-*TOO-*gah*	turtle
tortura, *f.*	*tohr-*TOO-*rah*	torture
torvo	TOHR-*voh*	grim (stern)
tos, *f.*	TOHSS	cough
tosco	TOHSS-*koh*	coarse
"	"	crude

Spanish	Pronunciation	English
tos ferina, f.	TOHSS feh-REE-nah	whooping cough
tostada, f.	tohss-TAH-thoh	toast (bread)
total	toh-TAHL	total (complete)
trabajador, m.	trah-vah-hah-THOHR	worker
trabajar (1)	trah-vah-HAHR	work (labor), to
trabajo, m.	trah-VAH-hoh	work (labor)
trabajo a destajo, m.	trah-VAH-hoh ah dehss-TAH-hoh	piecework (n.)
tractor, m.	trahk-TOHR	tractor (farm machine)
tradición, f.	trah-thee-S YOHN	tradition
traducir (12)	trah-thoo-SEER	translate, to
traer (36)	trah-EHR	bring, to
"	"	fetch, to
tráfico, m.	TRAH-fee-koh	traffic (flow of vehicles)
tragar (1)	trah-GAHR	swallow, to
tragedia, f.	trah-HEH-th yah	tragedy
trágico	TRAH-hee-koh	tragic
traición, f.	trah-ee-S YOHN	treason
traicionar (1)	trah-ee-s yoh-NAHR	betray (deceive), to
traidor, m.	trah-ee-THOHR	traitor
traje, m.	TRAH-heh	suit, man's
"	"	suit, woman's
traje de baño, m.	TRAH-heh theh VAH-n yoh	bathing suit
traje regional, m.	TRAH-heh reh-h yoh-NAHL	costume
trampa, f.	TRAHM-pah	snare
"	"	trap
tranquilo	trahn-KEE-loh	calm (adj.)
"	"	peaceful (tranquil)
transacción, f.	trahn-sahk-S YOHN	compromise (mutual concessions)
transformar (1)	trahn-sfohr-MAHR	transform, to
tránsito, m.	TRAHN-see-toh	transit (passage)
transparente	trahnss-pah-REHN-teh	transparent
transportar (1)	trahnss-pohr-TAHR	convey, to
"	"	transport, to
transporte, m.	trahnss-POHR-teh	transportation (conveying)
tranvía de trole, m.	trahn-VEE ah theh TROH-leh	trolley (street car)
trapo, m.	TRAH-poh	rag (piece of cloth)
trasero	trah-SEH-roh	hind (posterior, adj.)
trasquilar (1)	trahss-kee-LAHR	shear, to
tratado, m.	trah-TAH-thoh	treaty
tratamiento, m.	trah-tah-M YEHN-toh	treatment (medical care)
tratar (1)	trah-TAHR	deal (trade), to
"	"	treat (behave toward), to
trato, m.	TRAH-toh	bargain (agreement)
través de, a	ah trah-VEHSS theh	across (to the other side)
través de, a	ah trah-VEHSS theh	through (from end to end of, prep.)
travesía, f.	trah-veh-SEE-ah	crossing (ocean voyage)
travieso	trah-V YEH-soh	naughty (disobedient)
trébol, m.	TREH-vohl	clover
trecho, m.	TREH-choh	span (spread)
tren, m.	TREHN	train (railroad)
triángulo, m.	tree-AHN-goo-loh	triangle (geom.)
tribu, f.	TREE-voo	tribe
tribunal, m.	tree-voo-NAHL	court (of law)
tributo, m.	tree-VOO-toh	tribute (money)
trigo, m.	TREE-goh	wheat
trimestral	tree-mehss-TRAHL	quarterly (four times a year)
trinchera, f.	treen-CHEH-rah	trench (mil.)
trineo, m.	tree-NEH-oh	sled
"	"	sleigh
tripulación, f.	tree-poo-lah-S YOHN	crew
triste	TREESS-teh	dismal
"	"	mournful (saddening)
"	"	sad (sorrowful)
tristeza, f.	treess-TEH-sah	sadness
triunfo, m.	tree-OON-foh	triumph
trocar (1)	troh-KAHR	exchange (interchange), to

Spanish	Pronunciation	English
trombón, m.	trohm-BOHN	trombone
trompeta, f.	trohm-PEH-tah	trumpet (mus.)
tronco, m.	TROHN-koh	trunk (stem)
trono, m.	TROH-noh	throne
tropas, m. pl.	TROH-pahss	troops (mil.)
tropezar (4)	troh-peh-SAHR	stumble, to
"	"	trip, to
trote, m.	TROH-teh	trot
trucha, f.	TROO-chah	trout
trueno, m.	TR WEH-noh	thunder
trueque, m.	TR WEH-keh	exchange (barter)
trust, m.	TROOST	trust (cartel)
tú	TOO	you
tu(s)	TOO(ss)	your
tuberculosis, f.	too-vehr-koo-LOH-seess	tuberculosis
tubo, m.	TOO-voh	pipe
"	"	tube
tuerca, f.	TWEHR-kah	nut (mech.)
tulipán, m.	too-lee-PAHN	tulip
tumba, f.	TOOM-bah	grave
"	"	tomb
tú mismo	TOO MEEZ-moh	yourself
tumor, m.	too-MOHR	tumor
túnel, m.	TOO-nehl	tunnel
turco	TOOR-koh	Turkish (adj.)
turista, m., f.	too-REESS-tah	tourist (n.)
Turquía	toor-KEE-ah	Turkey
tutor, m.	too-TOHR	guardian
tuya(s), la(s)	lah(ss) TOO-yah(ss)	yours
tuyo(s), el (los)	ehl (lohss) TOO-yoh(ss)	yours
u	OO	or
úlcera, f.	OOL-seh-rah	ulcer
últimamente	OOL-tee-mah-mehn-teh	last (most recently, adv.)
último	OOL-tee-moh	last (adj.)
"	"	latter (second of two, adj.)
ultramar	ool-trah-MAHR	oversea(s) (adj.)
un	OON	a (an)
una	OO-nah	a (an)
uña, f.	OO-n yah	claw (of animal)
"	"	nail (anat.)
una vez	OO-nah VEHSS	once (one time, adv.)
ungüento, m.	oon-HWEHN-toh	ointment
único	OO-nee-koh	only
"	"	sole
uniforme	oo-nee-FOHR-meh	uniform (adj.)
uniforme, m.	oo-nee-FOHR-meh	uniform (n.)
unión, f.	oo-N YOHN	union (league)
unir (3)	oo-NEER	unite (make one), to
universal	oo-nee-vehr-SAHL	universal (adj.)
universidad, f.	oo-nee-vehr-see-THAHTH	university
universo, m.	oo-nee-VEHR-soh	universe
uno u otro	OO-noh oo OH-troh	either (either one, pron.)
"	"	either (one or the other, adj.)
uranio, m.	oo-RAH-n yoh	uranium
urbano	oor-VAH-noh	urban
urgente	oor-HEHN-teh	urgent
Uruguay, el	eh-l oo-roo-GWAH ee	Uruguay
usar (1)	oo-SAHR	use (utilize), to
uso, m.	OO-soh	use (utilization)
usted(es)	oo-STEHTH(-ehss)	you
usted(es), a	ah oo-STEHTH(-ehss)	you
de usted(es), (el, la)	(ehl, lah) theh oo-STEHTH(-ehss)	yours
(los, las) de usted(es)	(lohss, lahss) theh oo-STEHTH(-ehss)	yours
usted mismo	oo-STEHTH MEEZ-moh	yourself
ustedes mismos	oo-STEH-thehss MEEZ-mohss	yourselves
usual	oo-soo-AHL	usual
útero, m.	OO-teh-roh	womb
útil	OO-teel	helpful
"	"	useful
utilidad, f.	oo-tee-lee-THAHTH	use (usefulness)
"	"	utility (usefulness)
uva, f.	OO-vah	grape
vaca, f.	BAH-kah	cow
vacaciones, f. pl.	bah-kah-S YOH-nehss	vacation (work holidays)
vacante	bah-KAHN-teh	vacant (untenanted)

Spanish	Pronunciation	English
vaciar (1)	bah-S_YAHR	empty (remove contents of), to
vacilar (1)	bah-see-LAHR	hesitate, to
vacío	bah-SEE-oh	empty
vacunación, f.	bah-koo-nah-S_YOHN	vaccination
vadear (1)	bah-theh-AHR	ford, to
"	"	wade, to
vagar (1)	bah-GAHR	roam, to
"	"	rove, to
"	"	stray, to
"	"	wander, to
vago	BAH-goh	vague (not precise)
vagón, m.	bah-GOHN	car, railroad
"	"	coach, railroad
vajilla, f.	bah-HEE-yah	dishes (tableware)
valiente	bah-L_YEHN-teh	brave
valle, m.	BAH-yeh	valley
valor, m.	bah-LOHR	courage
"	"	value
"	"	worth
valor, de	theh bah-LOHR	valuable
valoración, f.	bah-loh-rah-S_YOHN	appraisal (bus.)
valores, m. pl.	bah-LOH-rehss	securities (stocks, etc.)
valor nominal, m.	bah-LOHR noh-mee-NAHL	face value (bus.)
vals, m.	BAHLSS	waltz (dance step)
valuar (1)	bah-L_WAHR	value, to
vanidad, f.	bah-nee-THAHTH	vanity (self-conceit)
vanidoso	bah-nee-THOH-soh	vain (conceited)
vano	BAH-noh	vain (futile)
vapor, m.	bah-POHR	steam
"	"	vapor
vapor de travesía, m.	bah-POHR theh trah-veh-SEE-ah	liner, ocean
vara, f.	BAH-rah	rod (bar)
"	"	shaft (mech.)
variado	bah-R_YAH-thoh	motley (diverse)
variar (1)	bah-R_YAHR	vary (undergo change), to
varicela, f.	bah-ree-SEH-lah	chicken-pox
variedad, f.	bah-r_yeh-THAHTH	variety (diversity)
varios	BAH-r_yohss	several (a few, adj.)
"	"	various
varonil	bah-roh-NEEL	manly
Varsovia	bahr-SOH-v_yah	Warsaw
vasija, f.	bah-SEE-hah	vessel (receptacle)
vaso, m.	BAH-soh	glass (vessel)
"	"	tumbler
vasto	BAHSS-toh	vast
vecindad, f.	beh-seen-DAHTH	community
"	"	neighborhood
"	"	vicinity
vecino, m.	beh-SEE-noh	neighbor
vehículo, m.	beh-HEE-koo-loh	vehicle (conveyance)
vejiga, f.	beh-HEE-gah	bladder (anat.)
vela, f.	BEH-lah	candle
vellón, m.	beh-YOHN	fleece
velo, m.	BEH-loh	veil (n.)
velocidad, f.	beh-loh-see-THAHTH	rate (degree of speed)
"	"	speed (rapidity)
vena, f.	BEH-nah	vein (anat.)
vencedor, m.	behn-seh-THOHR	victor
vencer (2)	behn-SEHR	beat, to
"	"	defeat, to
"	"	mature (fall due), to
"	"	overcome, to
"	"	subdue, to
"	"	win (be victor in), to
vencido y no pagado	behn-SEE-thoh ee NOH pah-GAH-thoh	overdue (in arrears)
vencimiento, m.	behn-see-M_YEHN-toh	maturity (due date, bus.)
venda, f.	BEHN-dah	bandage
vendedor, m.	behn-deh-THOHR	salesman
"	"	vendor (seller)
vender (2)	behn-DEHR	sell, to
Venecia	beh-NEH-s_yah	Venice
veneno, m.	beh-NEH-noh	poison
venezolano	beh-neh-soh-LAH-noh	Venezuelan (adj.)
Venezuela	beh-neh-SWEH-lah	Venezuela

Spanish	Pronunciation	English
venganza, f.	behn-GAHN-sah	revenge
"	"	vengeance
venir (37)	beh-NEER	come, to
venta, f.	BEHN-tah	sale (exchange)
venta al por menor, f.	BEHN-t_ahl pohr meh-NOHR	retail (bus., n.)
ventaja, f.	behn-TAH-hah	advantage
"	"	benefit
ventana, f.	behn-TAH-nah	window
ventana de la nariz, f.	behn-TAH-nah theh lah nah-REESS	nostril
ventarrón, m.	behn-tah-RROHN	gale (wind)
ventisca, f.	behn-TEESS-kah	blizzard
ventoso	behn-TOH-soh	windy (windswept)
ventura, f.	behn-TOO-rah	venture
ver (38)	BEHR	see, to
verano, m.	beh-RAH-noh	summer (n.)
verbo, m.	BEHR-boh	verb
verdad, f.	behr-THAHTH	truth
verdadero	behr-thah-THEH-roh	actual (real)
"	"	true
verde	BEHR-theh	green (color)
vergonzoso	behr-gohn-SOH-soh	bashful
"	"	shameful
verguenza, f.	behr-GWEHN-sah	shame
verso, m.	BEHR-soh	verse (poetic writing)
verter (4)	behr-TEHR	pour (make flow), to
vertical	behr-tee-KAHL	vertical (adj.)
vestido, m.	behss-TEE-thoh	dress (frock)
"	"	gown
vestigio, m.	behss-TEE-h_yoh	trace (vestige)
vestir (9)	behss-TEER	clothe, to
"	"	dress, to
vestirse	behss-TEER-seh	dress (get dressed), to
vestuario, m.	behss-TWAH-r_yoh	wardrobe (apparel)
veterano	beh-teh-RAH-noh	veteran (experienced)
veterano, m.	beh-teh-RAH-noh	veteran (mil., n.)
vez en cuando, de	deh VEHSS ehn KWAHN-doh	occasionally
vía, f.	BEE-ah	track (rails)
viajante de comercio, m.	b_yah-HAHN-teh theh koh-MEHR-s_yoh	traveling salesman
viajar (1)	b_yah-HAHR	travel, to
viaje, m.	B_YAH-heh	journey
"	"	trip
viaje por mar, m.	B_YAH-heh pohr MAHR	voyage
"	"	cruise
viajero, m.	b_yah-HEH-roh	traveler
vicio, m.	BEE-s_yoh	vice (moral fault)
víctima, f.	BEEK-tee-mah	victim
victoria, f.	beek-TOH-r_yah	victory
victorioso	beek-toh-R_YOH-soh	victorious
vid, f.	BEETH	vine (grapevine)
vida, f.	BEE-thah	life
vidrio, m.	BEE-dr_yoh	glass (material)
viejo	B_YEH-hoh	old
Viena	B_YEH-nah	Vienna
vienés, -nesa	b_yeh-NEHSS, -NEH-sah	Viennese (adj.)
viento, m.	B_YEHN-toh	wind
vientre, m.	B_YEHN-treh	belly (abdomen)
Viernes Santo, m.	B_YEHR-nehss SAHN-toh	Good Friday
viga, f.	BEE-gah	beam (rafter)
vigente	bee-HEHN-teh	active (in force)
vigilar (1)	bee-hee-LAHR	watch (guard), to
vigor, m.	bee-GOHR	vigor (strength)
vigoroso	bee-goh-ROH-soh	vigorous
villano, m.	bee-YAH-noh	villain
viña, f.	BEE-n_yah	vineyard
vinagre, m.	bee-NAH-greh	vinegar
vínculo, m.	BEEN-koo-loh	tie (bond)
vino, m.	BEE-noh	wine (beverage)
viola, f.	B_YOH-lah	viola
violar (1)	b_yoh-LAHR	violate (infringe upon), to
violencia, f.	b_yoh-LEHN-s_yah	violence
violento	b_yoh-LEHN-toh	violent
violeta, f.	b_yoh-LEH-tah	violet (flower)
violín, m.	b_yoh-LEEN	violin
violoncelo, m.	b_yoh-lohn-SEH-loh	cello
virgen, f.	BEER-hehn	virgin (n.)
virtud, f.	BEER-too_th	virtue (moral excellence)

Spanish	Pronunciation	English
viruela, *f.*	*bee*-R_WEH-*lah*	smallpox
visible	*bee*-SEE-*bleh*	visible
visita, *f.*	*bee*-SEE-*tah*	company (guests)
"	"	visit
"	"	visitor
visitar (1)	*bee-see*-TAHR	visit, to
vista, *f.*	BEESS-*tah*	sight (eyesight)
"	"	sight (range of view)
"	"	view (scene)
"	"	vision (eyesight)
vistazo, *m.*	*beess*-TAH-*soh*	glimpse
vital	*bee*-TAHL	vital (essential)
vitalicio, *m.*	*bee-tah*-LEE-*s_yoh*	annuity
vitamina, *f.*	*bee-tah*-MEEN-*ah*	vitamin
viuda, *f.*	B_YOO-*thah*	widow
viudo, *m.*	B_YOO-*thoh*	widower
vívido	BEE-*vee-thoh*	vivid
vivir (3)	*bee*-VEER	live (be alive), to
"	"	live (dwell), to
"	"	lodge (reside), to
vivo	BEE-*voh*	alive
"	"	live (*adj.*)
"	"	lively (*adj.*)
volar (5)	*boh*-LAHR	blast (explode), to
"	"	fly, to
volcán, *m.*	*bohl*-KAHN	volcano
volcar (5)	*bohl*-KAHR	overturn, to
"	"	upset (knock over), to
volumen, *m.*	*boh*-LOO-*mehn*	volume (book)
"	"	volume (space occupied)
voluntario, *m.*	*boh-loon*-TAH-*r_yoh*	volunteer (*mil.*)
volverse (5)	*bohl*-VEHR-*seh*	turn (face about), to
vomitar (1)	*boh-mee*-TAHR	vomit, to
vosotros	*boh*-SOH-*trohss*	you
"	"	yourselves
vosotros, a	*ah voh*-SOH-*trohss*	you
vosotros mismos	*boh*-SOH-*trohss* MEEZ-*mohss*	yourselves
votante, *m., f.*	*boh*-TAHN-*teh*	voter
votar (1)	*boh*-TAHR	vote, to
voto, *m.*	BOH-*toh*	vote
"	"	vow
voz, *f.*	BOHSS	voice
voz alta, en	*ehm boh*_SAHL-*tah*	aloud
vuelo, *m.*	BWEH-*loh*	flight (journey by air)
vuelta, *f.*	BWEHL-*tah*	cuff (of trouser)
"	"	turn (change of direction)
vuestra(s)	B_WEHSS-*trah*(*ss*)	yours
vuestra, la	*lah* V_WEHSS-*trah*	yours
vuestras las	*lahss* V_WEHSS-*trahss*	yours
vuestro(s)	B_WEHSS-*troh*(*ss*)	your
vuestro, el	*ehl* V_WEHSS-*troh*	yours
vuestros, los	*lohss* V_WEHSS-*trohss*	yours
vulgar	*bool*-GAHR	common
"	"	vulgar (ill-bred)
whisky, *m.*	WEESS-*kee*	whiskey
y	EE	and
ya	YAH	already
yegua, *f.*	YEH-*gwah*	mare
yelmo, *m.*	YEHL-*moh*	helmet
yermo, *m.*	YEHR-*moh*	wilderness
yerno, *m.*	YEHR-*noh*	son-in-law
yeso, *m.*	YEH-*soh*	plaster (wall coating)
yo	YOH	I
yodo, *m.*	YOH-*thoh*	iodine (antiseptic)
yo mismo	YOH MEEZ-*moh*	myself
yugo, *m.*	YOO-*goh*	yoke (wooden frame)
Yugoeslavia	*yoo-goh-ehss*-LAH-*v_yah*	Yugoslavia
zafiro, *m.*	*sah*-FEE-*roh*	sapphire (gem)
zambullirse (13)	*sahm-boo*-YEER-*seh*	dive, to
zanahoria, *f.*	*sah-nah*-OH-*r_yah*	carrot
zanja, *f.*	SAHN-*hah*	ditch
zapatero, *m.*	*sah-pah*-TEH-*roh*	shoemaker
zapatilla, *f.*	*sah-pah*-TEE-*yah*	slipper
zapato, *m.*	*sah*-PAH-*toh*	shoe (footwear)
zona, *f.*	SOH-*nah*	zone
zoología, *f.*	*s*(*oh*)*oh-loh*-HEE_*ah*	zoology
zorra, *f.*	SOH-*rrah*	fox
zurcir (3)	*soor*-SEER	darn (mend), to
zurrar (1)	*soo*-RRAHR	spank, to

Spanish Special Lists

Alphabet

a	AH	j	HO-*tah*	r	EH-*reh*
b	BEH	k	KAH	rr	EH-*rreh*
c	SEH	l	EH-*leh*	s	EH-*seh*
ch	CHEH	ll	EH-*l yeh*	t	TEH
d	DEH	m	EH-*meh*	u	OO
e	EH	n	EH-*neh*	v	VEH
f	EH-*feh*	ñ	EH-*n yeh*	w	*doh-vleh*-OO
g	HEH	o	OH	x	EH-*keess*
h	AH-*cheh*	p	PEH	y	EE *gree* EH-*gah*
i	EE	q	KOO	z	SEH-*tah*

Cardinal Numbers

Spanish	Pronunciation	English	Spanish	Pronunciation	English
uno	OO-*noh*	one	veintiuno	*beh een-tee*-OO-*noh*	twenty-one
dos	DOHSS	two	veintidós	*beh een-tee*-DOHSS	twenty-two
tres	TREHSS	three	treinta	TREH *een-tah*	thirty
cuatro	KWAH-*troh*	four	cuarenta	*kwah*-REHN-*tah*	forty
cinco	SEEN-*koh*	five	cincuenta	*seen*-KWEHN-*tah*	fifty
seis	SEH-*eess*	six	sesenta	*seh*-SEHN-*tah*	sixty
siete	*see*-EH-*teh*	seven	setenta	*seh*-TEHN-*tah*	seventy
ocho	OH-*choh*	eight	ochenta	*oh*-CHEHN-*tah*	eighty
nueve	NWEH-*veh*	nine	noventa	*noh*-VEHN-*tah*	ninety
diez	D YEHSS	ten	cien	*see*-EHN	one hundred
once	OHN-*seh*	eleven	ciento uno	*see*-EHN-*toh* OO-*noh*	one hundred one
doce	DOH-*seh*	twelve	doscientos	*doh-see*-EHN-*tohss*	two hundred
trece	TREH-*seh*	thirteen	doscientos uno	*doh-see*-EHN-*tohss* OO-*noh*	two hundred one
catorce	*kah*-TOHR-*seh*	fourteen			
quince	KEEN-*seh*	fifteen	mil	MEEL	one thousand
dieciséis	*d yehss-ee*-SEH-*eess*	sixteen	mil uno	*meel* OO-*noh*	one thousand one
diecisiete	*d yehss-ee-see*-EH-*teh*	seventeen	dos mil	*dohss* MEEL	two thousand
dieciocho	*d yehss-ee*-OH-*choh*	eighteen	dos mil uno	*dohss* MEEL OO-*noh*	two thousand one
diecinueve	*d yehss-ee*-NWEH-*veh*	nineteen	un millón	*oon mee*-YOHN	one million
veinte	BEH *een-teh*	twenty	mil millones	*meel mee*-YOH-*nehss*	one billion

Ordinal Numbers

Spanish	Pronunciation	English	Spanish	Pronunciation	English
primero	*pree*-MEH-*roh*	first	séptimo	SEHP-*tee-moh*	seventh
segundo	*seh*-GOON-*doh*	second	octavo	*ohk*-TAH-*voh*	eighth
tercero	*tehr*-SEH-*roh*	third	noveno	*noh*-VEH-*noh*	ninth
cuarto	KWAHR-*toh*	fourth	décimo	DEH-*see-moh*	tenth
quinto	KEEN-*toh*	fifth	undécimo	*oon*-DEH-*see-moh*	eleventh
sexto	SEHKSS-*toh*	sixth	duodécimo	*doo-oh*-THEH-*see-moh*	twelfth

Days of the Week

Spanish	Pronunciation	English	Spanish	Pronunciation	English
domingo,*m.*	*doh*-MEEN-*goh*	Sunday	jueves,*m.*	H WEH-*vehss*	Thursday
lunes,*m.*	LOO-*nehss*	Monday	viernes,*m.*	B YEHR-*nehss*	Friday
martes,*m.*	MAHR-*tehss*	Tuesday	sábado,*m.*	SAH-*vah-thoh*	Saturday
miércoles,*m.*	M YEHR-*koh-lehss*	Wednesday			

Months of the Year

Spanish	Pronunciation	English	Spanish	Pronunciation	English
enero,*m.*	*eh*-NEH-*roh*	January	julio,*m.*	HOO-*l yoh*	July
febrero,*m.*	*feh*-VREH-*roh*	February	agosto,*m.*	*ah*-GOHSS-*toh*	August
marzo,*m.*	MAHR-*soh*	March	septiembre,*m.*	*seh*-T YEHM-*breh*	September
abril,*m.*	*ah*-VREEL	April	octubre,*m.*	*ohk*-TOO-*vreh*	October
mayo,*m.*	MAH-*yoh*	May	noviembre,*m.*	*noh*-V YEHM-*breh*	November
junio,*m.*	HOO-*n yoh*	June	diciembre,*m.*	*dee*-S YEHM-*breh*	December

First Names

Spanish	Pronunciation	English	Spanish	Pronunciation	English
Abrahán	*ah*-BRAHN	Abraham	**Bernardo**	*behr*-NAHR-*thoh*	Bernard
Adán	*ah*-THAHN	Adam	**Berta**	BEHR-*tah*	Bertha
Alberto	*ahl*-BEHR-*toh*	Albert	**Carlos**	KAHR-*lohss*	Charles
Alejandro	*ah-leh*-HAHN-*droh*	Alexander	**Carlota**	*kahr*-LOH-*tah*	Charlotte
Alfredo	*ahl*-FREH-*thoh*	Alfred			
Alicia	*ah*-LEE-*s yah*	Alice	**Carolina**	*kah-roh*-LEE-*nah*	Caroline
Andrés	*ahn*-DRESS	Andrew	**Catalina**	*kah-tah*-LEE-*nah*	Kate
Ana	AH-*nah*	Ann, Anne	"		Katharine
Antonio	*ahn*-TOH-*n yoh*	Anthony	**Clara**	KLAH-*rah*	Clara
Arnaldo	*ahr*-NAHL-*doh*	Arnold	"		Clare
Arturo	*ahr*-TOO-*roh*	Arthur	**Conrado**	*kohn*-RAH-*thoh*	Conrad
Bárbara	BAHR-*bah-rah*	Barbara			
			Constanza	*kohn*-STAHN-*sah*	Constance
Beatriz	*beh-ah*-TREESS	Beatrice	**Cristina**	*kreess*-TEE-*nah*	Christine
Benjamín	*behn-hah*-MEEN	Benjamin	**Cristóbal**	*kreess*-TOH-*bahl*	Christopher

Spanish	Pronunciation	English
Daniel	*dah-N_YEHL*	Daniel
David	*dah-VEETH*	David
Dorotea	*doh-roh-TEH_ah*	Dorothy
Edmundo	*ehth-MOON-doh*	Edmund
Eduardo	*eh-THWAHR-thoh*	Edward
Elena	*eh-LEH-nah*	Helen
Ema	*EH-mah*	Emma
Emilia	*eh-MEE-l_yah*	Emily
Enrique	*ehn-REE-keh*	Harry
"	"	Henry
Enriqueta	*ehn-ree-KEH-tah*	Henrietta
Ernesto	*ehr-NEHSS-toh*	Ernest
Esteban	*ehss-TEH-vahn*	Stephen
Eugenio	*eh-oo-HEH-n_yoh*	Eugene
Federico	*feh-theh-REE-koh*	Frederick
Felipe	*feh-LEE-peh*	Philip
Félix	*FEH-leekss*	Felix
Fernando	*fehr-NAHN-doh*	Ferdinand
Florencia	*floh-REHN-s_yah*	Florence
Francisca	*frahn-SEESS-kah*	Frances
Francisco	*frahn-SEESS-koh*	Francis
Germán	*hehr-MAHN*	Herman
Gertrudis	*hehr-TROO-theess*	Gertrude
Gualterio	*gwahl-TEH-r_yoh*	Walter
Guillermo	*g_ee-YEHR-moh*	William
Gustavo	*gooss-TAH-voh*	Gustav
Haroldo	*ah-ROHL-thoh*	Harold
Heriberto	*eh-ree-VEHR-toh*	Herbert
Horacio	*oh-RAH-s_yoh*	Horace
Hugo	*OO-goh*	Hugh
Inés	*ee-NEHSS*	Agnes
Irene	*ee-REH-neh*	Irene
Isaac	*ee-SAHK*	Isaac
Isabel	*ee-sah-VEHL*	Elizabeth
"	"	Isabel
Jacobo	*hah-KOH-voh*	Jacob
Jaime	*hah_EE-meh*	James
Jorge	*HOHR-heh*	George
José	*hoh-SEH*	Joseph
Josefina	*hoh-seh-FEE-nah*	Josephine
Juan	*HWAHN*	John
Juana	*HWAH-nah*	Jane
"	"	Jean
"	"	Joan
Judit	*hoo-THEET*	Judith

Spanish	Pronunciation	English
Julián	*hoo-lee-AHN*	Julian
Laura	*LAH_oo-rah*	Laura
León	*leh-OHN*	Leo
"	"	Leon
Leonardo	*leh_oh-NAHR-thoh*	Leonard
Leonor	*leh_oh-NOHR*	Eleanor
"	"	Leonora
Leopoldo	*leh_oh-POHL-thoh*	Leopold
Luis	*loo_EESS*	Louis
Luisa	*loo_EE-sah*	Louise
Marcos	*MAHR-kohss*	Mark
Margarita	*mahr-gah-REE-tah*	Margaret
María	*mah-REE-ah*	Marie
"	"	Mary
Marta	*MAHR-tah*	Martha
Martín	*mahr-TEEN*	Martin
Mateo	*mah-TEH-oh*	Matthew
Miguel	*mee-GEHL*	Michael
Nicolás	*nee-koh-LAHSS*	Nicholas
Olga	*OHL-gah*	Olga
Otón	*oh-TOHN*	Otto
Pablo	*PAH-vloh*	Paul
Patricio	*pah-TREE-s_yoh*	Patrick
Paula	*PAH_oo-lah*	Paula
Pedro	*PEH-throh*	Peter
Rafael	*rrah-fah-EHL*	Ralph
Raimundo	*rrah_ee-MOON-doh*	Raymond
Rebeca	*rreh-VEH-kah*	Rebecca
Ricardo	*rree-KAHR-thoh*	Richard
Roberto	*rroh-VEHR-toh*	Robert
Rodolfo	*rroh-THOHL-foh*	Rudolph
Rosa	*RROH-sah*	Rose
Rosalía	*rroh-sah-LEE-ah*	Rosalie
Rosa María	*RROH-sah mah-REE-ah*	Rosemary
Rut	*RROOT*	Ruth
Samuel	*sah-MWEHL*	Samuel
Sara	*SAH-rah*	Sarah
Saúl	*sah-OOL*	Saul
Silvia	*SEEL-v_yah*	Sylvia
Susana	*soo-SAH-nah*	Susan
Teresa	*teh-REH-sah*	Theresa
Tomás	*toh-MAHSS*	Thomas
Vicente	*bee-SEHN-teh*	Vincent
Víctor	*BEEK-tohr*	Victor
Virginia	*beer-HEE-n_yah*	Virginia

USEFUL EXPRESSIONS

Greetings

English	Pronunciation	Spanish
How are you?	KOH-*moh_ehss*-TAH_oo-STEHTH?	¿Cómo está usted?
Well, thanks, and you?	B_YEHN, GRAH-*s_yahss*, *ee_oo*-STEHTH?	Bien, gracias, ¿y usted?
Good morning.	BWEH-*nohss* DEE-*ahss*.	Buenos días.
Good afternoon.	BWEH-*nahss* TAHR-*thehss*.	Buenas tardes.
Good evening (night).	BWEH-*nahss* NOH-*chehss*.	Buenas noches.
See you again.	AHSS-*tah lah* VEESS-*tah*.	Hasta la vista.
So long.	AHSS-*tah* L_WEH-*goh*.	Hasta luego.
Good luck!	BWEH-*nah* SWEHR-*teh!*	¡Buena suerte!
Good-by.	*ah*-TH_YOHSS.	Adiós.
Glad to meet you.	MOO-*choh* GOOSS-*toh theh koh-noh*-SEHR-*loh* (-*lah*).	Mucho gusto de conocerlo (-la).
Congratulations.	*feh-lee-see*-THAH-*thehss*.	Felicidades.
Happy Birthday.	*moo-chahss feh-lee-see*-THAH-*thehss*.	Muchas felicidades.
Merry Christmas.	*feh*-LEE-*sehss* PAHSS-*kwahss*.	Felices Pascuas.
Happy New Year.	*feh*-LEESS AH-*n_yoh* N_WEH-*voh*.	Feliz Año Nuevo.

Ordinary Conversation

English	Pronunciation	Spanish
Thank you.	GRAH-*s_yahss*.	Gracias.
Please.	*pohr fah*-VOHR.	Por favor.
You're welcome.	*noh* AH_*ee theh* KEH.	No hay de qué.
Pardon me.	*pehr*-THOH-*neh-meh*.	Perdóneme.
What do you call this?	KOH-*moh seh*, YAH-*mah_ehss*-*toh*?	¿Cómo se llama esto?
I'm sorry.	*loh* SYEHN-*toh*.	Lo siento.
Allow me.	*pehr*-MEE-*tah-meh*.	Permítame.

English	Pronunciation	Spanish
I would like...	*kee-*S YEH-*rah*...	Quisiera...
Come in.	*ah-theh-*LAHN-*teh.*	Adelante.
May I introduce...	*pehr-*MEE-*tah-meh preh-sehn-*TAHR-*leh*...	Permítame presentarle...
What is your name?	KOH-*moh seh* YAH-*mah* oo-STEHTH?	¿Cómo se llama usted?
My name is...	*meh* YAH-*moh*...	Me llamo...
I don't know.	*noh* SEH.	No sé.
I'm thirsty.	TEHN-*goh* SEHTH.	Tengo sed.
I'm hungry.	TEHN-*goh* AHM-*breh.*	Tengo hambre.
I'm an American.	SOY *nohr-teh-ah-meh-ree-*KAH-*noh (-nah).*	Soy norteamericano (-na).
Where can I find...?	DOHN-*deh* PWEH-*thoh ehn-kohn-*TRAHR...?	¿Dónde puedo encontrar...?
What is this?	KEH(*eh*)SS EHSS-*toh*?	¿Qué es esto?

Foreign Languages

English	Pronunciation	Spanish
Do you speak...?	AH-*vlah* oo-STEHTH...?	¿Habla usted...?
I speak (understand) a little...	AH-*vloh (ehn-*T YEHN-*doh)* oon POH-*koh theh*...	Hablo (entiendo) un poco de...
I do not speak...	*noh* AH-*vloh*...	No hablo...
Is there someone here who speaks English?	AH *ee* AHL-*g yehn ah-*KEE *keh* AHV-*leh een-*GLEHSS?	¿Hay alguien aquí que hable inglés?
I understand you.	*leh(eh)n-*T YEHN-*doh.*	Le entiendo.
I don't understand.	*noh ehn-*T YEHN-*doh.*	No entiendo.
Please speak more slowly.	AH-*vleh mahss dehss-*PAH-*s yoh, pohr fah-*VOHR.	Hable más despacio, por favor.
Please repeat.	*rreh-*PEE-*tah, pohr fah-*VOHR.	Repita, por favor.

Asking Directions

English	Pronunciation	Spanish
In which direction is...?	*ehn* KEH *thee-rehk-*S YOHN KEH-*thah*...?	¿En qué dirección queda...?
Please take me to...	YEH-*veh-meh ah..., pohr fah-*VOHR.	Lléveme a..., por favor.
Please take me there.	YEH-*veh-meh ah-*YAH, *pohr fah-*VOHR.	Lléveme allá, por favor.
Where can I mail this?	DOHN-*deh* PWEH-*thoh theh-poh-see-*TAHR EHSS-*toh ehn ehl koh-*RREH-*oh*?	¿Dónde puedo depositar esto en el correo?
Please direct me to...	AH-*gah-meh fah-*VOHR *theh theh-*SEER-*meh* DOHN-*deh(eh)ss-*TAH...	Hágame favor de decirme dónde está...
...the telephone.	...*ehl teh-*LEH-*foh-noh.*	...el teléfono.
...the toilet.	...*ehl ehss-koo-*SAH-*thoh.*	...el excusado.
...the post office.	...*ehl koh-*RREH-*oh.*	...el correo.
...the bank.	...*ehl* BAHN-*koh.*	...el banco.
...the police station.	...*lah koh-mee-sah-*REE-*ah.*	...la comisaría.
...the U. S. consulate.	...*ehl kohn-soo-*LAH-*thoh theh lohss ehss-*TAH-*thohss oo-*NEE-*thohss.*	...el Consulado de los Estados Unidos.
Please point.	*een-*DEE-*keh-meh, pohr fah-*VOHR.	Indíqueme, por favor.

The Hotel

English	Pronunciation	Spanish
I would like a room...	K YEH-*roh* oon KWAHR-*toh*...	Quiero un cuarto...
...with a single bed.	...*kohn* oo-*nah* SOH-*lah* KAH-*mah.*	...con una sola cama.
...with two beds.	...*kohn* DOHSS KAH-*mahss.*	...con dos camas.
...with bath.	...*kohn* BAH-*n yoh.*	...con baño.
...without meals.	...SEEN *koh-*MEE-*thahss.*	...sin comidas.
Please, the key for Room...	POHR *fah-*VOHR, *lah* YAH-*veh thehl* KWAHR-*toh*...	Por favor, la llave del cuarto...
Please call me at...o'clock.	*fah-*VOHR *theh yah-*MAHR-*meh ah lahss*...	Favor de llamarme a las...
I want this...	K YEH-*roh keh meh*...	Quiero que me...
...pressed.	...PLAHN-*chehn* EHSS-*toh.*	...planchen esto.
...cleaned.	...LEEM-*p yehn* EHSS-*toh.*	...limpien esto.
...washed.	...LAH-*vehn* EHSS-*toh.*	...laven esto.
...repaired.	...*ah-*RREH-*glehn* EHSS-*toh.*	...arreglen esto.
When will (my suit) be returned?	KWAHN-*doh seh meh theh-*VWEHL-*veh (ehl* TRAH-*heh)*?	¿Cuándo se me devuelve (el traje)?
Please return (my suit) at...	POHR *fah-*VOHR *theh-*VWEHL-*vah (ehl* TRAH-*heh) ah*...	Por favor, devuelva (el traje) a...

The Restaurant

English	Pronunciation	Spanish
A table for two, please.	OO-*nah* MEH-*sah* PAH-*rah* THOHSS, *pohr fah-*VOHR.	Una mesa para dos, por favor.
I would like to see the menu.	*meh gooss-tah-*REE-*ah vehr ehl meh-*NOO.	Me gustaría ver el menú.
I want it...	*loh* K YEH-*roh*...	Lo quiero...
...rare.	...MEH-*th yoh* KROO-*thoh.*	...medio crudo.
...medium.	...*noh moo* EE *koh-*SEE-*thoh.*	...no muy cocido.
...well-done.	B YEHN *koh-*SEE-*thoh.*	...bien cocido.
Check, please!	*lah* KWEHN-*tah pohr fah-*VOHR!	¡La cuenta, por favor!

Telephoning

English	Pronunciation	Spanish
I wish to telephone.	K YEH-*roh ah-*VLAHR *pohr teh-*LEH-*foh-noh.*	Quiero hablar por teléfono.

English	Pronunciation	Spanish
Please get me this number.	koh-NEHK-teh-meh kohn EHSS-teh NOO-meh-roh, pohr fah-VOHR.	Conécteme con este número, por favor.
Please give me the number of...	AH-gah-meh fah-VOHR theh THAHR-meh(eh)l NOO-meh-roh theh...	Hágame favor de darme el número de...
What did you say?	KOH-moh?	¿Cómo?
The line is busy.	ehss-TAH_oh-koo-PAH-thah lah LEE-neh-ah.	Está ocupada la línea.
What is the charge?	KWAHN-toh KWEHSS-tah?	¿Cuánto cuesta?

Time

English	Pronunciation	Spanish
What time is it?	KEH_OH-rah ehss?	¿Qué hora es?
It is...	SOHN lahss...	Son las...
...five o'clock.	...SEEN-koh...	...cinco.
...ten past eight.	...OH-choh_ee TH_YEHSS.	...ocho y diez.
...a quarter past six.	...SEH-eess ee KWAHR-toh.	...seis y cuarto.
...half past five.	...SEEN-koh_ee MEH-th_yah.	...cinco y media.
...five to seven.	...S_YEH-teh MEH-nohss SEEN-koh.	...siete menos cinco.
The day before yesterday	AHN-tehss theh_ah-YEHR	Antes de ayer
Yesterday evening	ah-NOH-cheh	Anoche
This morning	EHSS-tah mah-N_YAH-nah	Esta mañana
At noon	ah meh-th_yoh-THEE-ah	A mediodía
In the afternoon	ehn lah TAHR-theh	En la tarde
In the evening	ehn lah NOH-cheh	En la noche
At night	deh NOH-cheh	De noche
At midnight	ah meh-th_yah-NOH-cheh	A medianoche
Tomorrow morning	mah-N_YAH-nah ehn lah mah-N_YAH-nah	Mañana en la mañana
Tomorrow evening	mah-N_YAH-nah ehn lah NOH-cheh	Mañana en la noche
The day after tomorrow	pah-SAH-thoh mah-N_YAH-nah	Pasado mañana

Weather

English	Pronunciation	Spanish
It's hot.	AH-seh kah-LOHR.	Hace calor.
It's cold.	AH-seh FREE-oh.	Hace frío.
It's raining.	ehss-TAH yoh-V_YEHN-doh.	Está lloviendo.
It's snowing.	ehss-TAH neh-VAHN-doh.	Está nevando.
What fine weather!	keh LEEN-doh THEE-ah (LEEN-dah NOH-cheh)!	¡Qué lindo día (linda noche)!

Postal Information

English	Pronunciation	Spanish
How much is the postage on this?	KWAHN-toh KWEHSS-tah_ehl frahn-KEH-oh THEH(eh)SS-toh?	¿Cuánto cuesta el franqueo de esto?
Give me...worth of stamps.	DEH-meh...theh(eh)ss-tahm-PEE-yahss.	Déme...de estampillas.
Please send this letter...	fah-VOHR theh mahn-DAHR EHSS-tah KAHR-tah...	Favor de mandar esta carta...
...airmail.	...pohr VEE-ah(ah)-EH-reh-ah.	...por vía aérea.
...special delivery.	...kohn ehn-TREH-gah_een-meh-TH_YAH-tah.	...con entrega inmediata.
...registered.	...sehr-tee-fee-KAH-thah.	...certificada.
Please send this parcel post.	fah-VOHR theh mahn-DAHR EHSS-toh KOH-moh pah-KEH-teh pohss-TAHL.	Favor de mandar esto como paquete postal.

Barber and Beauty Shop

English	Pronunciation	Spanish
I want a haircut.	K_YEH-roh kohr-TAHR-meh(eh)l PEH-loh.	Quiero cortarme el pelo.
Not too short.	NOH MOO-ee KOHR-toh.	No muy corto.
No hair oil, thank you.	NOH theh-SEH-oh ah-SAY-teh, GRAH-s_yahss.	No deseo aceite, gracias.
I want a shave.	K_YEH-roh ah-feh_ee-TAHR-meh.	Quiero afeitarme.
I want a shampoo.	K_YEH-roh oon chahm-POO.	Quiero un champú.
I want my hair set.	K_YEH-roh peh_ee-NAHR-meh.	Quiero peinarme.

Transportation

English	Pronunciation	Spanish
Where is the ticket office?	DOHN-deh(eh)ss-TAH lah_oh-fee-SEE-nah theh boh-LEH-tohss?	¿Dónde está la oficina de boletos?
When does the...arrive?	ah KEH_OH-rah YEH-gah_ehl...	¿A qué hora llega el...
...train...	...TREHN?	...tren?
...plane...	...ah-V_YOHN?	...avión?
...bus...	...ow-toh-VOOSS?	...autobús?
At what time does the train leave for...?	ah KEH_OH-rah SAH-leh(eh)l TREHN PAH-rah...?	¿A qué hora sale el tren para...?
From which track does the train for... leave?	pohr KEH VEE-ah SAH-leh(eh)l TREHN PAH-rah...?	¿Por qué vía sale el tren para...?
Is this the right train for...?	ehss EHSS-teh(eh)l TREHN PAH-rah...?	¿Es éste el tren para...?
Where is my baggage?	DOHN-deh(eh)ss-TAH mee_eh-kee-PAH-heh?	¿Dónde está mi equipaje?
Where is the baggage room?	DOHN-deh(eh)ss-TAH_ehl KWAHR-toh theh(eh)-kee-PAH-heh?	¿Dónde está el cuarto de equipaje?

English	Pronunciation	Spanish
Please call a taxi.	YAH-*meh* oon TAHKSS-*ee pohr fah*-VOHR.	Llame un taxi, por favor.

Auto Travel

English	Pronunciation	Spanish
What place is this?	KEH *loo*-GAHR *ehss* EHSS-*teh*?	¿Qué lugar es éste?
Where is the town?	DOHN-*deh* KEH-*thah* ehl PWEH-*vloh*?	¿Dónde queda el pueblo?
Which is the best road for...?	KWAHL EHSS *ehl meh*-HOHR *kah*-MEE-*noh* PAH-*rah*...?	¿Cuál es el mejor camino para...?
Turn to the right.	DEH VWEHL-*tah(ah) lah theh*-REH-*chah*.	Dé vuelta a la derecha.
Turn to the left.	DEH VWEHL-*tah(ah) lah eess*-K YEHR-*thah*.	Dé vuelta a la izquierda.
Go straight on.	SEE-*gah theh*-REH-*choh*.	Siga derecho.
Go back.	*rreh*-GREH-*seh*.	Regrese.
This way.	*ehn* EHSS-*tah thee-rehk*-S YOHN.	En esta dirección.
That way.	*ehn* EH-*sah thee-rehk*-S YOHN.	En esa dirección.
How far is it to...?	*ah* KEH *theess*-TAHN-*s yah ehss*-TAH-*mohss theh*...?	¿A qué distancia estamos de...?
Is this the road to...?	*ehss* EHSS-*teh(eh)l kah*-MEE-*noh ah*...?	¿Es éste el camino a...?
Is it...	*ehss*...	¿Es...
...near?	...SEHR-*kah*?	...cerca?
...far?	...LEH-*hohss*?	...lejos?
...very far?	...*moo* EE LEH-*hohss*?	...muy lejos?
Which way is...	*ehn* KEH *thee-rehk*-S YOHN KEH-*thah* ehl...	¿En qué dirección queda el...
...north?	...NOHR-*teh*?	...norte?
...south?	...SOOR?	...sur?
...east?	...EHSS-*teh*?	...este?
...west?	...*oh*-EHSS-*teh*?	...oeste?
Is the road...?	*ehss*-TAH...*ehl kah*-MEE-*noh*?	¿Está...el camino?
Is there a detour?	*ah* EE *ahl*-GOO-*nah thess-v yah*-S YOHN?	¿Hay alguna desviación?
What is the speed limit?	KWAHL EHSS *ehl* LEE-*mee-teh theh veh-loh-see*-THAHTH?	¿Cuál es el límite de velocidad?
Where is the nearest gas station?	DOHN-*deh(eh)ss*-TAH *lah ss-tah*-S YOHN *theh gah-soh*-LEE-*nah* MAHSS *sehr*-KAH-*nah*?	¿Dónde está la estación de gasolina más cercana?
Where can I find a garage (for repairs)?	DOHN-*deh* PWEH-*thoh ehnn-kohn*-TRAHR *oon gah*-RAH-*heh*?	¿Dónde puedo encontrar un garaje?
I need...	*neh-seh*-SEE-*toh*...	Necesito...
...oil.	...*ah*-SAY-*teh*.	...aceite.
...gasoline.	...*gah-soh*-LEE-*nah*.	...gasolina.
...a tire.	...*oon neh-oo*-MAH-*tee-koh*.	...un neumático.

Public Signs

English	Pronunciation	Spanish
Keep Out	*seh proh*-EE-*veh pah*-SAHR	Se Prohibe Pasar
For Hire	*seh* ahl-KEE-*lah*	Se Alquila
No Parking	*ehss-tah-s yoh-nah*-M YEHNN-*toh proh*-ee-VEE-*thoh*	Estacionamiento Prohibido
No Smoking	*seh proh*-EE-*veh foo*-MAHR	Se Prohibe Fumar
Sale	*bah*-RAH-*tah*	Barata
Women	DAH-*mahss*	Damas
Men	*kah-vah*-YEH-*rohss*	Caballeros
No Spitting	*seh proh*-EE-*veh ehss-koo*-PEER	Se Prohibe Escupir
Railroad	*feh-rroh-kah*-RREEL	Ferrocarril
Dangerous Curve	KOOR-*vah peh-lee*-GROH-*sah*	Curva Peligrosa
Keep to the Right (Left)	*mahn*-TEHN-*gah-seh ah lah theh*-REH-*chah* (*eess*-K YEHR-*thah*)	Manténgase a la Derecha (Izquierda)
Dead End	*kah*-MEE-*noh seh*-RRAH-*thoh*	Camino Cerrado
Men Working	OHM-*brehss trah-vah*-HAHN-*doh*	Hombres Trabajando
No Thoroughfare	*noh ah* EE PAH-*soh*	No Hay Paso
One-way Street	*dee-rehk*-S YOHN OO-*nee-kah*	Dirección Unica
Go Slow	*dehss*-PAH-*s yoh*	Despacio
Toilet	*ehss-koo*-SAH-*thoh*	Excusado
Entrance	*ehn*-TRAH-*thah*	Entrada
Exit	*sah*-LEE-*thah*	Salida

Spanish Grammar

ARTICLES

Definite article

	Sing.			
Masc.	el	the	el hombre	the man
Fem.	la	the	la mujer	the woman
Neuter	lo	the	lo bueno	the good
	Pl.			
Masc.	los	the	los hombres	the men
Fem.	las	the	las mujeres	the women

Note: The masculine singular definite article combines with the preposition *a* to form the contraction *al* and with the preposition *de* to form *del*.

Llegó temprano *al* río.　　　He arrived early *at the* river.

The neuter article *lo* is used with adjectives, past participles and adverbs to express an abstract meaning.

No es bueno pensar en *lo* pasado.　　It is not good to think of *what is* past.

Special uses of the definite article. The Spanish definite article is used in many cases in which English commonly omits the article.

The definite article is used to denote a general class or species of objects in the abstract.

El oro es precioso.	Gold is valuable.

The definite article is used in expressions of time, before days of the week and seasons.

Es *la* una.	It is one o'clock.
¡Que salga el sol *el* lunes!	May the sun shine Monday!
El verano es mi estación predilecta.	Summer is my favorite season.

The definite article is used before certain geographical names and with adjectives denoting languages (except when these are preceded by *hablar*, to speak, or *de* or *en*).

El Perú es uno de los países más hermosos del continente.	Peru is one of the most beautiful countries on the continent.
El inglés tiene mucha influencia.	English has a good deal of influence.

But it is omitted in such expressions as:

Hablo español.	I speak Spanish.
No puedo escribir en alemán.	I cannot write in German.

The definite article is used before titles and with proper nouns.

el señor García Rodríguez	Mr. García Rodríguez
el doctor José Torres	Doctor José Torres

Indefinite article

Sing.

Masc.	un	a, an	un hombre, un artículo	a man, an article
Fem.	una	a, an	una mujer, una manzana	a woman, an apple

Pl.

Masc.	unos	some, several	unos hombres	some men, several men
Fem.	unas	some, several	unas mujeres	some women, several women

Agreement of articles

Both definite and indefinite articles agree with the noun they modify in gender and number.

Omission of the article

The definite and indefinite articles are generally omitted before nouns in apposition.

Juan, amigo de mi hermano, vino ayer.	John, a (the) friend of my brother, came yesterday.

The indefinite article is omitted before an unmodified predicate noun indicating rank, occupation, nationality, religion, etc.

El señor Mellado es puertorriqueño.	Mr. Mellado is a Puerto Rican.
Soy abogado.	I am a lawyer.
Es católico.	He is a Catholic.

The indefinite article is omitted with certain indefinite words and expressions such as *cierto* (a certain), *otro* (another), *tal*, *semejante* and *tan* (all meaning "such"), and with the numerals *ciento* (100) and *mil* (1,000).

No puedo darla a otra persona.	I cannot give it to another person.
Nunca he oído tal historia.	I have never heard such a story.
México dista mas de mil millas de Illinois.	Mexico is more than a thousand miles from Illinois.

NOUNS

Plural of nouns

To form the plural of nouns, add *s* or *es* to the singular, as follows:

With nouns ending in an unstressed vowel or diphthong, add *s*.

el perro	the dog	la especie	the kind
los perros	the dogs	las especies	the kinds

With nouns ending in a stressed vowel or a diphthong ending in *y*, add *es*.

el bambú	the bamboo	la ley	the law
los bambúes	the bamboos	las leyes	the laws

With nouns ending in a consonant, add *es*.

el patrón	the boss	el riel	the rail
los patrones	the bosses	los rieles	the rails

Exceptions to these rules may be found in the Spanish-to-English word list.

Gender of nouns

All nouns in Spanish are either masculine or feminine. These are distinguished by certain simple signs.

Masculine nouns. The following nouns are masculine:

Nouns representing male beings, regardless of word endings.

el actor	the actor	el general	the general
el cura	the priest	el león	the lion

Nouns ending in -*o* (with the single exception, *la mano*).

el toro	the bull	el libro	the book

A number of nouns associated with the masculine for a variety of reasons, such as: names of rivers, seas, oceans, days of the week, seasons and countries.

el Amazonas	the Amazon	el lunes	Monday
el Caribe	the Caribbean	el Perú	Peru
el Pacífico	the Pacific		

Feminine nouns. The following nouns are feminine:

Nouns representing female beings, regardless of endings:

la actriz	the actress	la madre	the mother
la hermana	the sister	la mujer	the woman

Nouns ending in -*a* (with certain exceptions, such as *el día* and *el mapa*).

la cosa	the thing	la cocina	the kitchen

Most nouns ending in -*dad*, -*tad*, -*tud*, -*ie*, -*ión* and -*umbre*.

la felicidad	happiness	la especie	kind
la mitad	half	la perfección	perfection
la virtud	virtue	la certidumbre	certainty

Nouns representing some cities, towns and provinces and letters of the alphabet.

la Asunción	Asuncion	la *a*	the *a*
la Plata	the Plate	la *be*	the *b*

Formation of feminine nouns. Masculine nouns ending in -*o* or -*e* drop the final letter and add -*a* in the feminine.

el hijo	the son	la hija	the daughter
el mono	the monkey	la mona	the monkey
el monje	the monk	la monja	the nun

Masculine nouns ending in -*d*, -*l*, -*n*, -*r*, -*s* or -*z* add -*a* in the feminine.

el huésped	the guest	la huéspeda	the guest
el león	the lion	la leona	the lioness
el profesor	the teacher	la profesora	the teacher

Generally only the masculine of nouns which form the feminine regularly appears in the word lists. Some nouns follow no set rule in forming the feminine, and they appear in both forms.

Gender and meaning. Certain nouns of identical form in the masculine and feminine change their meaning in passing from one gender to the other.

el capital	the capital (money)	la capital	the capital (city)
el corte	the cut, edge	la corte	the court
el papa	the pope	la papa	the potato

PRONOUNS

Personal pronouns

Personal pronouns are used in Spanish (1) as subjects, (2) as direct objects, (3) as indirect objects, (4) as reflexive pronouns and (5) as objects of prepositions. Each of these uses involves a set of pronoun forms for its peculiar rendering.

Subject of the verb

yo	I	nosotros	we
tú	you (familiar)	vosotros	you (familiar)
él	he	ellos	they
ella	she	ellas	they
ello *	it		
usted	you	ustedes	you

The subject pronoun is omitted in Spanish except where it is needed for clarity, emphasis or contrast.

Iba a la iglesia.	*He* went to church.
Hicimos el trabajo.	*We* did the work.

But:

Juan y María se fueron a Italia. *El* se quedó allá, pero *ella* regresó a casa.	John and Mary went to Italy. *He* stayed there, but *she* returned home.

The forms *tú* and *vosotros* are used only with members of the family, with children or with intimate friends. With others the proper forms are *usted* and *ustedes*.

¿Conoce *usted* a mi padre, señor Arias?	Do *you* know my father, Mr. Arias?
No hagas *tú* eso, hijo.	Don't do that, son.

Generally the subject "it" is unexpressed in Spanish.

Es probable que vengan hoy.	*It* is likely that they will come today.

Direct object of the verb

me	me	nos	us
te	you (familiar)	os	you (familiar)
le, lo*	him, it	les, los	them
la	her, it	les, las	them
le, lo; la	you	les, los; las	you
lo*	it		

Indirect object of the verb

me	(to) me	nos	(to) us
te	(to) you (familiar)	os	(to) you (familiar)
le	(to) him	les	(to) them
le	(to) her	les	(to) them
le	(to) you	les	(to) you

Position of object pronouns. The object pronoun in Spanish normally comes immediately before the verb.

Le dije que no pude venir.	I told *her* that I could not come.
Me ha pedido prestado un peso.	He has asked to borrow a peso from *me*.

In three cases the object pronoun comes after the verb:
When used with the infinitive:

No quería gastar*lo*.	I did not want to spend *it*.

When used with the present participle:

Están haciéndo*la* ahora.	They are doing *it* now.

When used with the imperative or with the subjunctive in commands:

Déme*lo*, niño.	Give *it* to me, child.
Hagámos*lo*.	Let us do *it!*

But when the infinitive or present participle depends upon an auxiliary, the object pronoun sometimes comes before the verb.

No *la* puedo llevar al cine hoy.	I cannot take *her* to the movies today.
Me estan mirando todavía.	They are still looking at *me*.

The indirect object pronoun always precedes the direct object pronoun when both are governed by the same verb.

Luis *me lo* ha prometido.	Louis has promised *it* to *me*.
Devuélve*nosla* cuando termines.	Return *it* to *us* when you are finished.

When two object pronouns are governed by the same verb, both being in the third person, the indirect object pronoun becomes *se*.

Entrégue*selo*.	Hand it to *her*.
El *se la* regaló.	He gave it to *her* (as a present).

Reflexive pronouns

me	myself	nos	ourselves
te	yourself (familiar)	os	yourselves (familiar)
se	himself, herself, yourself	se	themselves, yourselves

The reflexive pronoun is used to form reflexive verbs (see p. 3018).

---

* Spanish pronouns, like the nouns they stand for, are usually rendered by the masculine or feminine forms, even when these would be expressed by a neuter form in English.

La vela se hundió en el lago. *Ella* fue la última que tuvimos. — The candle sank in the lake. *It* was the last that we had.

Only in special cases do the neuter forms *ello* or *lo* find expression in Spanish speech or writing.

Me engañé.	I deceived *myself*.

The position of the reflexive pronoun is governed by the same rules that apply to regular object pronouns. When an object pronoun occurs alongside the reflexive pronoun, the reflexive pronoun always comes first.

El no *se lo* comió.	He did not eat *it*.

Emphatic pronoun forms *myself, yourself*, etc., are rendered in Spanish by *mismo, misma*, etc., rather than the reflexive pronoun.

Prepositional pronouns

mí	me	nosotros, -as	us
ti	you (familiar)	vosotros, -as	you (familiar)
él	he	ellos	them
ella	she	ellas	them
usted	you	ustedes	you

Prepositional pronouns are used after all prepositions.

El libro es para *ti*.	The book is for *you*.

With *con* (with) the first and second person singular prepositional pronouns form the words *contigo* and *conmigo*.

Venga usted *conmigo*.	Come *with me*.

Prepositional pronouns are used redundantly with *a* to give emphasis or clarity to the other pronouns.

Me dió una joya a *mí*.	He gave *me* a jewel.

Possessive adjectives and pronouns†

Possessive adjectives. Spanish has two forms of the possessive adjective, (1) a shorter form that precedes the noun and (2) a longer form that follows the noun. These are used interchangeably, except in direct address where the longer form is preferred.

Sing.		*Pl.*	
mi (mío, -a)	my	mis (míos, -as)	my
tu (tuyo, -a)	your (familiar)	tus (tuyos, -as)	your (familiar)
su (suyo, -a)	his, hers, its, your	sus (suyos, -as)	his, hers, its, your
nuestro, -a	our	nuestros, -as	our
vuestro, -a	your (familiar)	vuestros, -as	your (familiar)
su (suyo, -a)	their, your	sus (suyos, -as)	their, your

Possessive pronouns. The possessive pronouns derive from the long form of the possessive adjective and an appropriate form of the definite article.

Sing.		*Pl.*		
Masc.	*Fem.*	*Masc.*	*Fem.*	
el mío	la mía	los míos	las mías	mine
el tuyo	la tuya	los tuyos	las tuyas	yours (fam.)
el suyo	la suya	los suyos	las suyas	his, hers, its, yours
el nuestro	la nuestra	los nuestros	las nuestras	ours
el vuestro	la vuestra	los vuestros	las vuestras	yours (fam.)
el suyo	la suya	los suyos	las suyas	theirs, yours

Agreement of possessives. Possessive adjectives and pronouns agree in person with the possessor and in gender and number with that which is possessed.

La culpa es *mía*.	The blame is *mine*.
El se comió *su* pan, pero ella no se comió el suyo.	He ate *his* bread, but she did not eat *hers*.

Ambiguity in the short forms of the third person possessive adjectives (*su, sus*) is avoided by adding *de* and the prepositional pronoun or a possessive phrase after the noun.

su papel de *él*	*his* paper
sus libros *de ellos*	*their* books

With articles of clothing or parts of the body, the definite article is usually substituted for the possessive adjective.

El se cortó *el* dedo.	He cut *his* finger.
Las muchachas perdieron *los* zapatos.	The girls lost *their* shoes.

Relative pronouns

Sing.		*Pl.*	
que	that, which, who	que	that, which, who
quien	who, he who, the one who	quienes	who, those who, the ones who
el que, la que, lo que	who, which	los que, las que	who, which, those who, the ones who
el cual, la cual, lo	which, who, what, that	los cuales, las cuales	who, which, the ones who

---

† For convenience, possessive, demonstrative and interrogative adjectives are treated in this section on pronouns.

Sing.		Pl.	
cuyo, cuya	whose, of which	cuyos, cuyas	whose, of which
cuanto, cuanta	all that, as much as	cuantos, cuantas	all those, as many as

Que is used for both "who" and "which."

la tienda en *que* hacemos las compras	the store in *which* we shop
Ella es la muchacha *que* llegó ayer.	She is the girl *who* arrived yesterday.

Quien is used only for persons.

el hombre a *quien* yo detesto	the man *whom* I hate

El que (*la que*, etc.) and *el cual* (*la cual*, etc.) refer to both persons and things.

Cuyo, cuya, etc., are forms of possessive adjectives, referring to both persons and things.

Juan, *cuya* casa quedaba cerca, estaba enfermo.	Juan, *whose* house was near, was sick.

Cuanto, cuanta, etc., may be used either as a pronoun or adjective.

No sé *cuántos* vienen.	I don't know *how many* are coming.
No sé *cuántos* autos vienen.	I don't know *how many* cars are coming.

Interrogative pronouns and adjectives *

Sing.		Pl.	
qué	what? which?		
quién	who?	quiénes	who?
cuál	what? which?	cuáles	what? which?
cuánto, -a	how much?	cuántos, -as	how many?

Agreement of interrogatives. Interrogative adjectives agree with the noun they modify in number and gender.

¿*Cuántas* manzanas tiene usted?	*How many* apples do you have?

Interrogative pronouns agree with their antecedents in number and gender.

Tengo tres relojes. ¿*Cuántos* tiene usted?	I have three watches. *How many* do you have?

Qué is both an adjective and pronoun. As a pronoun it refers only to things.

¿*Qué* libro está leyendo ahora?	*What* book are you reading now?
¿*Qué* deseas tú?	*What* do you want?

Quién is only a pronoun. It refers only to persons.

¿*Quién* es aquel vendedor?	*Who* is that salesman?

De quién is used to express "whose," "of whom" and "from whom" in the interrogative.

¿*De quiénes* vinieron las flores?	*From whom* did the flowers come?

A quién is used to express "whom" and "to whom" in the interrogative.

¿*A quién* dió usted la boleta?	*To whom* did you give the ticket?

Cuál is both a pronoun and adjective. It generally has a selective meaning.

¿*Cuál* es su hermana?	*Which one* is your sister?

Cuánto is both a pronoun and adjective.

¿*Cuántas* flores crecen en Cuba?	*How many* flowers grow in Cuba?

¿*Cuántos* hay?	*How many* are there?

Demonstrative adjectives and pronouns *

Demonstrative adjectives

Sing.		Pl.	
este, esta	this	estos, estas	these
ese, esa	that (near)	esos, esas	those (near)
aquel, aquella	that (far)	aquellos, aquellas	those (far)

Demonstrative pronouns

Sing.		Pl.	
éste, ésta, esto	this	éstos, éstas	these
ése, ésa, eso	that (near)	ésos, ésas	those (near)
aquél, aquélla, aquello	that (far)	aquéllos, aquéllas	those (far)

Agreement of demonstratives. Demonstrative adjectives agree with the word they modify in gender and number. Demonstrative pronouns agree with their antecedents in gender and number.

Aquel caballo es fuerte.	*That* horse is strong.
María es una muchacha muy linda, pero prefiero a *ésta*.	Mary is a very pretty girl, but I prefer *this one*.

The neuter pronouns (*esto, eso* and *aquello*) refer to something unnamed or to a whole statement already expressed. They are always in the singular.

Eso no me gusta.	I don't like *that*.
Muchos hombres son embusteros. *Esto* explica el porqué de las leyes.	Many men are liars. *This* explains the reason for laws.

Este and *aquél* in certain contexts mean "the latter" and "the former," respectively.

El clima de San Juan y el de Ponce se parecen; *aquél* es más lluvioso, *éste* es más seco.	The climate of San Juan and that of Ponce are similar; *the former* is more rainy, *the latter* drier.

Indefinite pronouns

algo	something
alguien	someone, somebody
alguno, -a, -os, -as	someone, some
nada	nothing, not...anything
nadie	no one, not...anyone
ninguno, -a	no one, not...anyone

Algo and *nada* refer to things.

No tiene *nada*.	He has *nothing*.
Me dijo *algo* que no puedo recordar.	He told me *something* that I cannot remember.

Alguien and *nadie* refer to persons.

¿Hay *alguien* que sepa francés?	Does *anyone* know French?
Nadie sabe francés.	*No one* knows French.

Alguno, alguna, etc., and *ninguno* and *ninguna* refer to persons or things.

Ninguno de los perros lo cogió.	*None* of the dogs caught it.
Algunos saben leer, y *algunos* saben escribir.	*Some* know how to read, and *some* know how to write.

ADJECTIVES

Gender of adjectives

The feminine of adjectives is formed in the following ways:
With adjectives ending in -*o* in the masculine singular, substitute -*a* for -*o*.

Masc.	*Fem.*	
bonit*o*	bonit*a*	pretty
pequeñ*o*	pequeñ*a*	small

With adjectives of nationality ending in a consonant in the masculine singular, add -*a* and omit the accent, if one appears on the final syllable of the masculine form.

Masc.	*Fem.*	
inglés	inglesa	English
alemán	alemana	German

With adjectives ending in -*an*, -*on* or -*or* (except in comparative forms—*mayor, mejor*, etc.) in the masculine singular, add -*a*.

holgazán	holgazana	lazy
glotón	glotona	gluttonous
hablador	habladora	talkative

All other adjectives are the same in the masculine and feminine forms.

amable	amable	kind
triste	triste	sad
fácil	fácil	easy

Plural of adjectives

To form the plural of adjectives -*s* or -*es* is added to the singular form in exactly the same way as it is added to form the plural of nouns (see p. 3011).

Position of adjectives

Adjectives which describe or distinguish the noun that they modify usually follow the noun.

El hombre delgado es *feo*; el otro es más *atractivo*.	The thin man is *ugly*; the other is more *attractive*.

Adjectives which give the inherent quality of a noun or limit a noun usually precede the noun they modify.

la *hermosa* Helena de Troya	the *beautiful* Helen of Troy
los *dos* lápices de mi hermano	the *two* pencils of my brother

Some adjectives change their meanings depending on whether they precede or follow the noun.

un *gran* hombre	a *great* man
un hombre *grande*	a *large* man
pobre muchacho	*unfortunate* boy

---

* For convenience, possessive, demonstrative and interrogative adjectives are treated in this section on pronouns.

muchacho *pobre*   *poor* boy

A few adjectives, like *grande, malo, bueno, primero,* and *alguno* assume shortened forms (gran, mal, buen, primer, algún) before masculine, singular nouns.

Comparison of adjectives

The comparative of Spanish adjectives is formed by prefixing *más* (more) or *menos* (less) to the adjective form. The true superlative is formed by prefixing a form of the definite article to the comparative.

azul	blue	el (la, lo) *más* azul	blu*est*
más azul	blu*er*	los (las) *más* azules	blu*est*
espiritual	spiritual		
menos espiritual	*less* spiritual		
el (la, lo) *menos* espiritual	*least* spiritual		
los (las) *menos* espirituales	*least* spiritual		

Four adjectives have irregular comparisons that may be used alternately with regular comparisons. Two others have only irregular forms.

bueno, mejor, el (la, lo) mejor	good, better, best
malo, peor, el (la, lo) peor	bad, worse, worst
grande, mayor, el (la, lo) mayor	large, larger (greater), largest
pequeño, menor, el (la, lo) menor	small, smaller (lesser), smallest

Mucho and *poco* have only irregular forms.

mucho, más, lo (los, las) más   much, more, most

poco, menos, lo (los, las) menos little, less, least

Spanish has an absolute superlative (equivalent to the English "exceedingly") formed by adding -*ísimo* (-*ísima,* -*ísimos,* -*ísimas*) to the adjective.

Es un hombre inteligent-*ísimo*   He is an *exceedingly* intelligent man.

Comparatives of equality, such as "as...as" or "as many (much)...as," are formed by *tan...como* or *tanto...como.*

Es *tan* bueno *como* mi primo.   He is *as* good *as* my cousin.
Hoy en día no se venden *tantos* sombreros *como* antes.   Not *as many* hats are sold nowadays *as* formerly.

Comparatives of inequality, such as "more...than" or "less...than," are formed by using the regular comparative forms (or irregular forms with the irregular adjectives) with *que.*

El es *más alto que* yo.   He is *taller than* I.
Ella es *menos gorda que* su hermana.   She is *less corpulent than* her sister.

When the comparative of inequality is used with numerals, *de* is substituted for *que.*

Tengo mas *de* veinte pesos.   I have more *than* twenty pesos.

When the comparative of inequality refers to an entire thought or expression, the phrase *de lo que* is used in place of *que.*

El muchacho era más estúpido *de lo que* yo me imaginaba.   The boy was stupider *than* I thought.

VERBS

Infinitive and verb stem

The verbs in the main word list are given in their infinitive forms. The infinitive of each verb consists of a verb stem and an infinitive ending. For example:

Infinitive	*Stem*	*Ending*
amar	am	ar

Uses of the infinitive

The Spanish infinitive differs from the English infinitive in two of its uses:

It is used as the only form of the verbal noun. The use of the present participle for the verbal noun is not found in Spanish.

El comer es un deleite.   *Eating* is a joy.
Ella se ruborizó *al ver* a su marido.   She blushed *on seeing* her husband.

It is sometimes used in affirmative commands and exclamations.

Escribir las frases en inglés.   *Write* the sentences in English.

Regular and irregular verbs

All Spanish verbs have infinitives ending in *-ar, -er* or *-ir.* Verbs with the same infinitive endings and the same conjugated forms constitute classes or conjugations of verbs. All verbs fall into classes of either regular or irregular verbs.

Regular verbs. The largest number of Spanish verbs fall into three regular conjugations depending on the infinitive endings. Model verbs:

Verb	*Stem*	*Infinitive Ending*	*Conjugation*
amar (to love)	am-	-ar	(1)
temer (to fear)	tem-	-er	(2)
partir (to part)	part-	-ir	(3)

These verbs appear in the Spanish-to-English word list with the numbers (1), (2) and (3) and may be referred to the model conjugations of regular verbs (see pp. 3014–18) for their past, future, conditional and other forms.

Irregular verbs. A number of Spanish verbs vary from regular forms in certain moods, tenses or numbers both in vocal and written quality. The large majority of these verbs are subject to similar variations and may be classified into twelve irregular verb groups, numbered in the Spanish-to-English word list (4) to (16). The remaining irregular verbs, falling under no special classification owing to special irregularities, are numbered (17) to (39). Some of these verbs are the following:

Verb	*Class*	*Irregular Form*	*Irregularity*
perder	(4)	pierdo	stem *e > ie*
soñar	(5)	sueño	stem *o > ue*
hacer	(26)	haría	*ce* is dropped
poner	(31)	pongo	*g* is added

Models for all irregular verbs are found on pp. 3019–23 of this grammar.

Orthographic-changing verbs

Many Spanish verbs that are regular in their spoken forms change their spelling in special instances to agree with Spanish orthography.

Verb	*Orthographic Regularity*	*Irregular Form*
vencer	vencen	venzo
dirigir	dirigen	dirijo

These verbs, called orthographic-changing verbs, are listed in the model conjugation of regular verbs and receive a fuller treatment on p. 3019.

Defective verbs

Some Spanish verbs are regular in their conjugated forms but are lacking in certain of these forms. For example:

Verb	*Limited to*
soler	present and imperfect indicative, and present subjunctive.
atañer	the third person, singular and plural, in all tenses.

The defective forms of these verbs are indicated in the model conjugation of the regular verbs (see pp. 3014–18).

Present tense

Uses of the present tense. The Spanish present tense differs from the English equivalent in two respects:

The present tense is used in Spanish with either *hace* or *desde* to express the meaning of the English "to have been." For example:

Hace mucho que *estoy* aquí.   *I have been* here a long time.
Lee desde las nueve.   *He has been reading* since nine o'clock.

The present tense is used in Spanish with *por poco* and *acabar de* to give the meaning of the English expressions "almost" and "to have just." For example:

Por poco me mato.   *I almost killed* myself.
Acabo de terminar el libro.   *I have just* finished the book.

Regular verbs. To form the present tense of regular verbs (1), (2) and (3), the verb stem is used and the following endings are added:

(1) amar

yo am*o*	I love	nosotros am*amos*	we love
tú am*as*	you (familiar) love	vosotros am*áis*	you (familiar) love
él am*a*	he loves	ellos am*an*	they love
usted am*a*	you love	ustedes am*an*	you love

(2) temer

yo tem*o*	I fear	nosotros tem*emos*	we fear
tú tem*es*	you (familiar) fear	vosotros tem*éis*	you (familiar) fear
él tem*e*	he fears	ellos tem*en*	they fear
usted tem*e*	you fear	ustedes tem*en*	you fear

(3) partir

yo part*o*	I part	nosotros part*imos*	we part
tú part*es*	you (familiar) part	vosotros part*ís*	you (familiar) part
él part*e*	he parts	ellos part*en*	they part
usted part*e*	you part	ustedes part*en*	you part

Irregular verbs. The present tense of irregular verbs is given under the models for irregular verbs on pp. 3019–23.

Orthographic-changing and defective verbs. Verbs ending in *-cer, -cir, -ger, -gir, -guir* and *-quir* undergo changes of spelling in the first person singular form of the present, as follows: $c > z$, $g > j$, $gu > g$ and $qu > q$.

The following verbs have restricted forms in the present:

Verb	Limited to
agredir, abolir	first and second person plural
atañer, concernir, placer	third person, singular and plural
balbucir	second and third person singular, first, second and third person plural

Imperfect tense

Uses of the imperfect tense. The imperfect tense has the following uses:

To express past action regarded as continued or habitual.

Ella *temía* a los perros. — She *used to fear* dogs.

To express continuing action in relation to other action.

El entró mientras yo *estaba* allí. — He entered while I *was* there.

To give a descriptive setting for a narrative.

Las mujeres *lavaban* la ropa sucia y los niños *jugaban* en la orilla del río. — The women *were washing* the dirty clothes and the children *were playing* on the shore of the river.

To express emotion, thought or knowledge in the past.

Esperaban que vendría pronto. — *They expected* him to come soon.

Sabíamos la historia. — We *knew* the story.

With *por poco* and *acabar de* to express "almost" and "to have just" in the past.

Al encender el fuego mi hermano *por poco se quemaba.* — On lighting the fire my brother *almost burned himself.*

Acababa de sentarme cuando llegaron dos amigos. — *I had just* sat down when two friends arrived.

Regular verbs. To form the imperfect tense of all regular verbs (1), (2) and (3), the verb stem is used and the following endings are added:

(1) amar

yo am*aba*	I was loving
tú am*abas*	you (familiar) were loving
él am*aba*	he was loving
usted am*aba*	you were loving
nosotros am*ábamos*	we were loving
vosotros am*abais*	you (familiar) were loving
ellos am*aban*	they were loving
ustedes am*aban*	you were loving

(2) temer

yo tem*ía*	I was fearing
tú tem*ías*	you (familiar) were fearing
él tem*ía*	he was fearing
usted tem*ía*	you were fearing
nosotros tem*íamos*	we were fearing
vosotros tem*íais*	you (familiar) were fearing
ellos tem*ían*	they were fearing
ustedes tem*ían*	you were fearing

(3) partir

yo part*ía*	I was parting
tú part*ías*	you (familiar) were parting
él part*ía*	he was parting
usted part*ía*	you were parting
nosotros part*íamos*	we were parting
vosotros part*íais*	you (familiar) were parting
ellos part*ían*	they were parting
ustedes part*ían*	you were parting

Irregular verbs. The imperfect tense of irregular verbs is given under the models for irregular verbs on pp. 3019–23.

Orthographic-changing and defective verbs. No spelling changes occur in the forms of the imperfect tense. *Roer* (to gnaw) is lacking in forms in this tense. The following verbs are limited to the third person, singular and plural, of the imperfect tense: *atañer, concernir* and *placer.*

Simple past tense

Uses of the simple past. The simple past is used in Spanish to indicate a state or action completed in the past.

Regular verbs. To form the past tense of all regular verbs (1), (2) and (3), the verb stem is used and the following endings are added:

(1) amar

yo am*é*	I loved
tú am*aste*	you (familiar) loved
él am*ó*	he loved
usted am*ó*	you loved
nosotros am*amos*	we loved
vosotros am*asteis*	you (familiar) loved
ellos am*aron*	they loved
ustedes am*aron*	you loved

(2) temer

yo tem*í*	I feared
tú tem*iste*	you (familiar) feared
él tem*ió*	he feared
usted tem*ió*	you feared
nosotros tem*imos*	we feared
vosotros tem*isteis*	you (familiar) feared
ellos tem*ieron*	they feared
ustedes tem*ieron*	you feared

(3) partir

yo part*í*	I parted
tú part*iste*	you (familiar) parted
él part*ió*	he parted
usted part*ió*	you parted
nosotros part*imos*	we parted
vosotros part*isteis*	you (familiar) parted
ellos part*ieron*	they parted
ustedes part*ieron*	you parted

Irregular verbs. The simple past tense of irregular verbs is given under the models for irregular verbs on pp. 3019–23.

Orthographic-changing and defective verbs. Verbs of the 1st conjugation (1) ending in *-car, -gar, -guar* and *-zar* undergo changes of spelling in the first person singular of the simple past, as follows: $c > qu$, $gu > gü$, $g > gu$ and $z > c$.

The following verbs have no forms in the past: *placer, roer* and *soler.*

The following verbs are limited to the third person, singular and plural, of the simple past: *atañer* and *concernir.*

Future tense

Uses of the future tense. The future tense is used to indicate actions or states that will occur at some time after the present, as in English. It also is often employed to express probability or conjecture referring to the present. For example:

¿Qué hora es? *Serán* las nueve. — What time is it? *It must be* nine o'clock.

El presidente *tendrá* más de sesenta años. — The president *must be* more than sixty years of age.

Regular verbs. To form the future tense of all regular verbs (1), (2) and (3), the infinitive form is used and the following endings are added:

(1) amar

yo amar*é*	I shall (will) love
tú amar*ás*	you (familiar) will love
él amar*á*	he will love
usted amar*á*	you will love
nosotros amar*emos*	we shall (will) love
vosotros amar*éis*	you (familiar) will love
ellos amar*án*	they will love
ustedes amar*án*	you will love

(2) temer

yo temer*é*	I shall (will) fear
tú temer*ás*	you (familiar) will fear
él temer*á*	he will fear
usted temer*á*	you will fear
nosotros temer*emos*	we shall (will) fear
vosotros temer*éis*	you (familiar) will fear
ellos temer*án*	they will fear
ustedes temer*án*	you will fear

(3) partir

yo partir*é*	I shall (will) part
tú partir*ás*	you (familiar) will part
él partir*á*	he will part
usted partir*á*	you will part
nosotros partir*emos*	we shall (will) part
vosotros partir*éis*	you (familiar) will part
ellos partir*án*	they will part
ustedes partir*án*	you will part

Irregular verbs. The future tense of irregular verbs is given under the models for irregular verbs on pp. 3019–23.

Orthographic-changing and defective verbs. There are no orthographic changes in the future tense.

The following verbs have no future forms: *placer, roer* and *soler.*

The following verbs are limited to the third person, singular and plural, of the future tense: *atañer* and *concernir.*

Conditional tense

Uses of the conditional tense. The conditional tense has the following uses:

To state the result of conditions contrary to fact.

Yo *iría*, si mi madre me lo permitiese.	I *would go*, if my mother would let me.

To express willingness or desire.

Me *gustaría* comprar aquel automóvil.	I *would like* to buy that car.

To express probability in the past.

Serían las once cuando llegamos.	*It must have been* eleven o'clock when we arrived.

To express the future.

¿*Podría* usted venir a mi casa mañana?	*Would* you come to my house tomorrow?

Regular verbs. To form the conditional tense of all regular verbs (1), (2) and (3), the infinitive form is used and the following endings are added:

(1) amar

yo amar*ía*	I would love
tú amar*ías*	you (familiar) would love
él amar*ía*	he would love
usted amar*ía*	you would love
nosotros amar*íamos*	we would love
vosotros amar*íais*	you (familiar) would love
ellos amar*ían*	they would love
ustedes amar*ían*	you would love

(2) temer

yo temer*ía*	I would fear
tú temer*ías*	you (familiar) would fear
él temer*ía*	he would fear
usted temer*ía*	you would fear
nosotros temer*íamos*	we would fear
vosotros temer*íais*	you (familiar) would fear
ellos temer*ían*	they would fear
ustedes temer*ían*	you would fear

(3) partir

yo partir*ía*	I would part
tú partir*ías*	you (familiar) would part
él partir*ía*	he would part
usted partir*ía*	you would part
nosotros partir*íamos*	we would part
vosotros partir*íais*	you (familiar) would part
ellos partir*ían*	they would part
ustedes partir*ían*	you would part

Irregular verbs. The conditional tense of irregular verbs is given under the models for irregular verbs on pp. 3019–23.

Orthographic-changing and defective verbs. There are no orthographic changes in the conditional tense.

The following verbs have no conditional forms: *placer*, *roer* and *soler*.

The following verbs are limited to the third person, singular and plural, of the conditional tense: *atañer* and *concernir*.

Present participle

Uses of the present participle. The Spanish present participle is used as follows:

To form the progressive tenses with a form of *estar.* *

Estoy leyendo el libro.	I *am reading* the book.
El *estaba comprando* legumbres.	He *was buying* vegetables.

To express manner, means, cause, condition or time in a series of adverbial constructions. †

Vino *cantando*.	He came *singing*.
Comiendo engorda uno.	*By eating* one becomes fat.
Estando muy ocupada, no pudo acompañarnos.	*Being* very busy, she could not go with us.
Comiendo mucho por la mañana, no tendrá que comer tanto al mediodía.	*If you eat* a lot in the morning, you will not have to eat so much at noon.
Estando los padres en el cine, él se acostó.	*While* his parents *were* at the movies, he retired.

Regular verbs. To form the present participle of regular verbs (1), (2) and (3), the verb stem is used and the following endings are added:

(1) amar

am*ando*	loving

(2) temer

tem*iendo*	fearing
or	
caer	
ca*yendo* ‡	falling

(3) partir

part*iendo*	parting
or	
construir	
constru*yendo* ‡	constructing

Irregular verbs. The present participles of irregular verbs are given under the models for irregular verbs on pp. 3019–23.

Past participle

Uses of the past participle. The past participle has the following principal uses:

To form the compound tenses with *haber*.

El visitante *ha dejado* su dirección.	The visitor *has left* his address.

To form the true passive with *ser*.

Es prohibido gritar aquí.	Shouting *is prohibited* here.

To express completed action or a state resulting from such action with *estar, encontrarse, quedar(se), sentirse, hallarse*, etc.

El trabajo está *terminado*.	The work is *finished*.
Se encontraron *cansados* después del viaje.	They found themselves *tired* after the journey.

To express the time or circumstances of a state or action

Terminada la clase, los estudiantes se fueron.	The class *being over*, the students went away.

As an adjective.

los niños *cansados*	the *tired* children
el hombre *muerto*	the *dead* man

Regular past participles. To form the regular past participle of all verbs, the verb stem is used and the following endings are added:

(1) comprar

compr*ado*	bought

(2) temer

tem*ido*	feared

(3) partir

part*ido*	parted

Irregular past participles. Many regular and irregular verbs have past participles which differ from the *-ado* and *-ido* forms. Where these irregular participles exist alongside regular past participles, the irregular form is generally reserved for use as an adjective. Otherwise, the irregular form subserves all the functions of the past participle.

Some of the commonest irregularities in past participles are the following:

Infinitive	Regular Participle	Irregular Participle
abrir		abierto
cubrir		cubierto
decir		dicho
despertar	despertado	despierto
elegir	elegido	electo
escribir		escrito
freír	freído	frito
hacer		hecho
imprimir		impreso
morir		muerto
poner		puesto
prender	prendido	preso
proveer	proveído	provisto
romper	rompido	roto
ver		visto
volver		vuelto

Present perfect tense

Uses of the present perfect tense. The present perfect tense is used to express a state or action completed in relation to the present time. The present perfect tense in Spanish corresponds † to the English equivalent.

Regular verbs. To form the present perfect tense of regular verbs (1), (2) and (3), the past participle form of the verb is used, preceded by the present tense of *haber*, as follows:

(1) amar

yo he amado	I have loved
tú has amado	you (familiar) have loved
él ha amado	he has loved
usted ha amado	you have loved
nosotros hemos amado	we have loved
vosotros habéis amado	you (familiar) have loved
ellos han amado	they have loved
ustedes han amado	you have loved

(2) temer

yo he temido	I have feared
tú has temido	you (familiar) have feared
él ha temido	he has feared

---

* *Andar, ir, quedar(se), seguir* and *venir* are sometimes used in place of *estar* for emphasis.
† The present participle is never used as a verbal noun or adjective (see p. 3014).
‡ The unstressed letter *i* appearing between two vowels is written *y*.

usted ha temido	you have feared
nosotros hemos temido	we have feared
vosotros habéis temido	you (familiar) have feared
ellos han temido	they have feared
ustedes han temido	you have feared

(3) partir

yo he partido	I have parted
tú has partido	you (familiar) have parted
él ha partido	he has parted
usted ha partido	you have parted
nosotros hemos partido	we have parted
vosotros habéis partido	you (familiar) have parted
ellos han partido	they have parted
ustedes han partido	you have parted

Irregular verbs. The present perfect tense of irregular verbs is given under the models for irregular verbs on pp. 3019–23.

Orthographic-changing and defective verbs. There are no orthographic changes in the present perfect tense.

The following verbs have no present perfect forms: *placer*, *roer* and *soler*.

The following verbs are limited to the third person, singular and plural, of the present perfect tense: *atañer* and *concernir*.

Perfect of the imperfect (the pluperfect), perfect of the simple past, future perfect and conditional perfect

Uses of the remaining perfect tenses. The uses of the Spanish perfect tenses correspond to the uses of the English perfect tenses.*

Regular verbs. To form the remaining perfect tenses of regular verbs (1), (2) and (3), the past participle of the verb is used after an appropriate form of *haber*. † For example:

Pluperfect

yo había amado, etc.	I had (through a duration) loved, etc.

Perfect of the simple past

yo hube amado, etc.	I had (at a definite time) loved, etc.

Future perfect

yo habré amado, etc.	I will have loved, etc.

Conditional perfect

yo habría amado, etc.	I would have loved, etc.

Irregular verbs. The perfect tenses of irregular verbs are formed in the same way as are the perfect tenses of regular verbs.

Orthographic-changing and defective verbs. Orthographic changes and defective forms are the same in all perfect tenses. The model of the present perfect tense may serve for all perfect tenses (see pp. 3016–17).

Imperative mood

Uses of the imperative. The *tú* and *vosotros* forms of the imperative are found only in affirmative commands. Where a negative command is employed in these forms, the subjunctive must be used.

¡*Ve tú* a la casa de María!	*Go* to Mary's house!
¡*No te vayas* ya!	*Don't go* so soon!

The *usted* and *ustedes* forms are found in both affirmative and negative commands.

Regular verbs. To form the imperative of regular verbs (1), (2) and (3), the verb stem is used and the following endings are added:

(1) amar

ama tú	love	amad vosotros	love
ame usted	love	amen ustedes	love

(2) temer

teme tú	fear	temed vosotros	fear
tema usted	fear	teman ustedes	fear

(3) partir

parte tú	part	partid vosotros	part
parta usted	part	partan ustedes	part

Irregular verbs. The imperative for irregular verbs is given under the models for irregular verbs (see pp. 3019–23).

Orthographic-changing and defective verbs. There are no orthographic changes of imperative verb forms.

The following verbs have no imperative forms: *placer*, *balbucir*, *roer*, *soler*, *concernir* and *atañer*.

The following verbs lack the *tú* form of the imperative: *agredir* and *abolir*.

Subjunctive mood

The subjunctive in Spanish corresponds to certain usages in English, such as:

If I *were* king
I will give it to anyone who *might* use it.‡

The doubt and uncertainty of these expressions is characteristic of the subjunctive in all of its forms. The subjunctive is the mood of the indefinite and possible and is found in the following constructions:

In independent sentences or principal clauses expressing desire or command with *que* either present or implied.

¡*No haga usted* eso!	*Don't do* that!
¡*Que canten* las señoritas!	*Let* the girls *sing*!
Bajemos a la calle a ver lo que ha ocurrido.	*Let us go down* to the street to see what has happened.

In clauses beginning with *que*...(that...), when the clause depends on a verb of hope, fear, regret, etc.

El temió que el enemigo le *hubiese oído*.	He feared that the enemy *had heard* him.
Siento que *no pueda ir* con usted a México.	I am sorry that *I cannot go* with you to Mexico.

In clauses beginning with *que*...(that...), when the clause depends on an impersonal expression such as *es probable que*...(it is probable that...), *es necesario que*...(it is necessary that...), *conviene que*...(it is fitting that...).¶

Es necesario que *termines* ahora.	It is necessary that *you finish* now.
Conviene que *vaya* de etiqueta al baile.	It is fitting that *you wear* a formal suit to the dance.

In clauses beginning with indefinite expressions, such as *dondequiera que*...(wherever...), *quienquiera que*...(whoever...), *por menos que*...(however little...), etc.

Dondequiera que *vaya*, tenga la bondad de escribirme.	Wherever *you go*, be good enough to write me.
Le daré el regalo a quienquiera que me *quite* el saco.	I will give the gift to whoever *takes* my coat *off*.
Por más libros que *lea*, nunca podrá hacerse inteligente.	However many books he *reads*, he will never become intelligent.

In clauses denoting purpose, restriction, supposition, concession and so forth, beginning with such expressions as *a fin* (*de*) *que*...(in order that...), *de manera que*...(so that...), *dado que*...(granted that...), *a menos que*...(unless...).

A menos que me *escribas*, no vendré el lunes.	Unless *you write* me, I will not come on Monday.
Presentó su caso de manera que no *pudiese dudar*lo nadie.	He presented his case in such a way that no one *could doubt* it.
Me mandaron una docena de piñas, a fin de que los *recordase*.	They sent me a dozen pineapples, so that *I would remember* them.

In conditional clauses beginning with *si*...(if...) or equivalent expressions.

Si el libro *no fuera* tan grande, lo leería.	If the book *were not* so large, I would read it.
Aunque me *hubiera pagado* un millón pesos, no se lo habría dado.	Even though *he had paid* me a million pesos, I would not have given it to him.

Present subjunctive

Uses of the present subjunctive. The present subjunctive covers both the present and future tenses of the subjunctive. For example:

Espero que *esté* bien.	I hope *you are* well.
Espero que *esté* bien para mañana.	I hope *you will be* well tomorrow.

Regular verbs. To form the present subjunctive of regular verbs (1), (2) and (3), the verb stem is used and the following endings are added:

(1) amar

yo ame	(that) I (may) love
tú ames	(that) you (familiar) (may) love
él ame	(that) he (may) love

---

* With the one notable exception listed above (see p. 3015).

† Forms of the verb *haber* may be found under the conjugations of irregular verbs, number (25) (see p. 3023).

‡ When "may" and "might" carry the meaning of possibility, wish or desire, they are translated by the appropriate subjunctive form of the Spanish verb.

¡Ojalá, que *hubiera hablado* con ella!	Oh, that *I might have talked* with her!
¡Que *goce* usted de sus vacaciones!	*May you enjoy* your vacation!

When permission or freedom to do something is meant, an appropriate form of *poder* is used (see p. 3023).

¿Se *puede* entrar?	*May* one come in?
Pudo haber venido, pero no quiso.	He *might* have come, but he did not want to.

¶ Such expressions as *es cierto que*...(it is certain that...), *es claro que*...(it is clear that...) and so forth naturally take the indicative mood. *Acaso*, *quizá*(s) and *tal vez* (all meaning "perhaps") may take either the indicative or subjunctive.

usted am*e*	(that) you (may) love
nosotros am*emos*	(that) we (may) love
vosotros am*éis*	(that) you (familiar) (may) love
ellos am*en*	(that) they (may) love
ustedes am*en*	(that) you (may) love

(2) and (3) escribir

yo escrib*a*	(that) I (may) write
tú escrib*as*	(that) you (familiar) (may) write
él escrib*a*	(that) he (may) write
usted escrib*a*	(that) you (may) write
nosotros escrib*amos*	(that) we (may) write
vosotros escrib*áis*	(that) you (familiar) (may) write
ellos escrib*an*	(that) they (may) write
ustedes escrib*an*	(that) you (may) write

Irregular verbs. The present subjunctive of irregular verbs **is** given under the models for irregular verbs (see pp. 3019–23).

Orthographic-changing and defective verbs. All verbs in the 1st conjugation ending in *-car, -gar, -guar* and *-zar* undergo the following changes in the present subjunctive: *c > qu, g > gu, gu > gü* and *z > c.*

All verbs in the 2nd and 3rd conjugations ending in *-cer, -cir, -ger, -gir, -guir* and *-quir* undergo the following changes in the present subjunctive: *c > z, g > j, gu > g* and *qu > c.*

Certain verbs have no forms in the present subjunctive: *balbucir, placer, abolir* and *agredir.*

Certain verbs suffer limitations in the present subjunctive: *atañer* and *concernir,* limited to the third person, singular and plural.

Imperfect subjunctive

Uses of the imperfect subjunctive. The imperfect subjunctive is used for the past, the definite past and the conditional tenses. It normally follows principal verbs in these tenses. For example:

Esperaba que *estudiase.*	He hoped that *she would study* (at the time or over a period of time).
Me gustaría que *hiciese* sus compras ahora.	I would like you *to shop* now.

Regular verbs. To form the imperfect subjunctive of regular verbs (1), (2) and (3), the third person plural form of the simple past tense is used, the ending *-ron* is dropped and the following endings are added:

(1) amar

yo am*ara* or *-ase*	(that) I (might) love
tú am*aras* or *-ases*	(that) you (familiar) (might) love
él am*ara* or *-ase*	(that) he (might) love
usted am*ara* or *-ase*	(that) you (might) love
nosotros am*áramos* or *-ásemos*	(that) we (might) love
vosotros am*arais* or *-aseis*	(that) you (familiar) (might) love
ellos am*aran* or *-asen*	(that) they (might) love
ustedes am*aran* or *-asen*	(that) you (might) love

(2) and (3) escribir

yo escrib*iera* or *-iese*	(that) I (might) write
tú escrib*ieras* or *-ieses*	(that) you (familiar) (might) write
él escrib*iera* or *-iese*	(that) he (might) write
usted escrib*iera* or *-iese*	(that) you (might) write
nosotros escrib*iéramos* or *iésemos*	(that) we (might) write
vosotros escrib*ierais* or *-ieseis*	(that) you (familiar) (might) write
ellos escrib*ieran* or *-iesen*	(that) they (might) write
ustedes escrib*ieran* or *-iesen*	(that) you (might) write

Irregular verbs. The imperfect subjunctive of irregular verbs is given under the models for irregular verbs (see pp. 3019–23).

Orthographic-changing and defective verbs. There are no orthographic changes in imperfect subjunctive verb forms.

The following verbs have no imperfect subjunctive forms: *placer, roer* and *soler.*

The following verbs are limited to the third person, singular and plural, in the imperfect subjunctive: *atañer* and *concernir.*

Present perfect (and past perfect) of the subjunctive

Uses of the present and past perfect subjunctive. The present perfect subjunctive is used to give the subjunctive forms in the present and future perfect tenses. For example:

El espera que ella *haya venido.*	He hopes that she *has come.*
Habremos terminado antes de que *hayan llegado.*	We will have finished before *they (will) have arrived.*

The past perfect subjunctive is used to give the subjunctive forms in the pluperfect, the perfect of the simple past and the conditional perfect tenses. For example:

Ellos habían sentido que no *hubieran venido* sus padres.	They had regretted that their parents *had not come.*
Ella temió que el ladrón *hubiese entrado.*	She feared that the robber *had entered.*
Habrían mandado los libros si *hubiéramos pagado* el franqueo.	They would have sent the books if *we had paid* the postage.

Regular verbs. To form the perfect tenses, subjunctive, of regular verbs (1), (2) and (3), the past participle of the verb is used after an appropriate subjunctive form of *haber.** For example:

Present perfect

yo haya amado, etc.	(that) I (would) have loved, etc.

Past perfect

yo {hubiera *or* hubiese} amado, etc.	(that) I (might) have loved, etc.

Irregular verbs. The subjunctive perfect forms of irregular verbs follow the same rules that apply to regular forms.

Orthographic-changing and defective verbs. There are no orthographic changes in perfect subjunctive verb forms.

The following verbs have no perfect subjunctive forms: *placer, roer* and *soler.*

The following verbs are limited to the third person, singular and plural, of the perfect subjunctive forms: *atañer, concernir.*

Reflexive verbs

Uses of the reflexive verb form. The reflexive verb form is used in Spanish as follows:

To express an action which is directed toward the subject, even where this is not explicitly expressed in English. For example:

atreverse	to dare	desayunarse	to eat breakfast
quejarse	to complain	suicidarse	to commit suicide

To alter the meaning of certain verbs. The new meanings generally have a direct or indirect reference to the subject. For example:

ir	to go	irse	to go away
parecer	to appear	parecerse	to resemble each other
poner	to put	ponerse	to become; to put on (wearing apparel)

To give the passive. For example:

Se necesita un cuarto amueblado.	A furnished room *is wanted.*
En los Estados Unidos *se produce* mucho hierro.	A lot of iron *is produced* in the United States.

In impersonal commands and indefinite statements with subjects such as "one," "you," "we," "they" and "people." For example:

Primero, *se cuece* una taza de arroz en baño de María.	First, *you cook* a cup of rice in a double boiler.
En México *se hacen* platos muy ricos.	In Mexico *they prepare* excellent dishes.

Reflexive form of verbs. † To make verbs reflexive in all persons, tenses and moods, add the reflexive pronoun to the verb form desired, as follows:

me amo	I love myself	nos amamos	we love ourselves
te amas	you (familiar) love yourself	os amáis	you (familiar) love yourselves
se ama	he loves himself	se aman	they love themselves
se ama	you love yourself	se aman	you love yourselves

Negation

The negative in Spanish is generally formed by placing the adverb *no* before the principal verb.

El *no está* aquí.	He *is not* here.
No quiero ir al cine.	*I do not want to go* to the movies.

The negative may also be expressed with certain negative words like *nunca* (never), *jamás* (never), *nada* (nothing) and *nadie* (no one) placed before the principal verb without *no.* (These words are sometimes used with *no* to reinforce the negative expression; in such cases they always follow the verb.)

Nunca he visto tal cosa.	*I have never seen* such a thing.
(*No he visto* tal cosa *nunca.*	*I have never seen* such a thing.)

---

* Forms of the verb *haber* may be found under the conjugations of irregular verbs, number (25) (see p. 3023).

† A few Spanish verbs may carry a reflexive meaning without the addition of the reflexive pronoun; for example, *caer* and *llegar.*

Idiomatic uses of special verbs

Many Spanish verbs have ranges of significance which are quite different from those found in simple English translations. The most important of these require a brief description.

Impersonal expressions. With certain verbs Spanish uses impersonal expressions in which the subject of the corresponding English expression becomes the object of the Spanish verb. Some verbs occurring in these expressions are *agradar* (to please), *doler* (to pain), *gustar* (to like), *importar* (to concern), *molestar* (to bother) and *parecer* (to seem).

Me gusta la música.	*I like* music. (Music *pleases me*.)
Nos parece que sí.	*We think* so. (*It seems* so *to us*.)

Ser and Estar (to be)
Ser is always used:

   Where the meaning is one of ownership, membership, origin or material.

El señor Díaz *es* dueño de este negocio.	Mr. Diaz *is* owner of this business.
Juan *es* de Chile.	John *is* from Chile.
La silla *es* de madera.	The chair *is* wooden.

   In expressions of time.*

¿Qué hora *es?*	What time *is it?*
Son las diez.	*It is* ten o'clock.
¿Qué día *es* hoy? *Es* viernes.	What day *is* this? *It is* Friday.

   In most impersonal expressions.

Es necesario que...	*It is* necessary that...
Es bueno que...	*It is* well that...

   With all predicate nouns and pronouns and adjectives used as nouns.

El trineo *es* mío.	The sled *is* mine.
La lección para hoy *es* ésta.	The lesson for today *is* this (one).

Estar is always used:

   With references to position or location.

Maria *está* en el Brasil.	Maria *is* in Brazil.
El jefe no *está.*	The boss *is* not *here.*
Cuba *está* en el Caribe.	Cuba *is* in the Caribbean.

   To indicate a resultant state or condition.

Lo siento mucho. El taxi no *está* libre.	I am very sorry. The taxi *is* occupied.
El trabajo *está* terminado.	The work *is* finished.

   To form the progressive tenses.

Está durmiendo todavía.	He *is* still sleeping.
Estaba comiendo cuando llegué.	He *was* eating when I arrived.

   Certain adjectives change their meanings depending on whether *ser* or *estar* is used.

	with *ser*	with *estar*
bueno	good (in character)	well (in health)
cansado	boring	bored *or* tired
listo	clever	ready
malo	bad or wicked	ill
muerto	killed	dead
vivo	lively	alive

Haber
Haber is used in the following ways:

   As an auxiliary verb to form the compound tenses.

No *hemos* comprado el baúl.	We *have* not bought the trunk.

   To denote the presence or existence of something. In the present indicative the form *hay* is used for the singular and plural.

Hay mucha gente aquí.	*There are* many people here.
Habrá una fiesta el viernes.	*There will be* a party on Friday.

   To express obligation impersonally.

---
* With the exception of ¿A cuántos estamos? (What is the date?), etc.

Irregular verb types

(4) TYPE A

Verbs of this type change the stem vowel *e* to *ie* when accented. ‡

		Present
Alentar	yo	aliento
(to encourage)	tú	alientas
	él (usted)	alienta
	ellos (ustedes)	alientan
Entender	yo	entiendo
(to understand)	tú	entiendes
	él (usted)	entiende
	ellos (ustedes)	entienden

‡ The verb *errar*, which belongs to Type A, substitutes *ye* for *ie* in its irregular forms.

Después de comer, *hay que* descansar un rato.	After eating, *one should* rest a while.
Había que hacer la ropa en la casa, hace años.	*They had to* make their clothing at home, years ago.

   To express the future with the preposition *de*.

El tiempo *ha de* cambiar pronto.	The weather *will* change soon.

   To express certain conditions of the weather.

Hay niebla.	*It is* misty.

Tener
The verb *tener* is used:

   To indicate age.

El muchacho *tiene* siete años.	The boy *is* seven years old.

   With *que* to express strong obligation.

Los jóvenes *tienen que* limpiarse las manos.	The young men *have* to clean their hands.

   In a number of miscellaneous idioms.

tener sed	to be thirsty
tener miedo	to be afraid
tener prisa	to be in a hurry
tener razón	to be right
tener la culpa	to be at fault

Hacer
The verb *hacer* is found in various expressions of time and weather.

Hace mucho que no va al cine.	*It has been* a long time since he went to the movies.
Hace frío hoy.	*It is* cold today.
Hacía un tiempo pésimo la semana pasada.	The weather last week *was* terrible.

Deber
Deber used with the infinitive expresses moral obligation.

Usted *debe* ir con ella.	You *should* go with her.

   With *de* it is used to express strong probability or conjecture.

Debía de haber estudiado, porque su examen fué excelente.	*He must have* studied, because his examination was excellent.
Aunque llegó tarde, *debió de* haber empezado temprano.	Although he arrived late, he *must have* started early.

Table of orthographic changes in Spanish

Verb type	Ending	Change	Before
sacar	-car	$c > qu$	
pagar	-gar	$g > gu$	
averiguar	-guar	$gu > gü$	*e*
rezar	-zar	$z > c$	
vencer	-cer (after consonant)	$c > z$	
esparcir	-cir (after consonant)	$c > z$	
coger	-ger	$g > j$	*a, o*
dirigir	-gir	$g > j$	
distinguir	-guir	$gu > g$	
delinquir	-quir	$qu > c$	

Irregular verbs

The irregular verbs deviate from regular forms by involving some change either in their stem vowels, in their endings or in both. In the following twelve types † of irregular verbs, the first six—Types A to F, numbered (4) to (9) inclusive—undergo changes in their stem vowels; the last five—Types H to L, numbered (11) to (15) inclusive—undergo changes in their endings; and the seventh—Type G, numbered (10)—involves changes in both stem vowel and endings. In each type the changes are governed by clear-cut principles.

All verb forms not listed in the following classifications are regular.

† The twelve types listed here are those of the Academy of the Spanish Language. The order of listing, however, is not that of the academy.

Present Subjunctive	Imperative
aliente	
alientes	alienta tú
aliente	aliente usted
alienten	alienten ustedes
entienda	
entiendas	entiende tú
entienda	entienda usted
entiendan	entiendan ustedes

		Present	Present Subjunctive	Imperative
Discernir (to discern)	yo	discierno	discierna	
	tú	disciernes	disciernas	discierne tú
	él (usted)	discierne	discierna	discierna usted
	ellos (ustedes)	disciernen	disciernan	disciernan ustedes

(5) TYPE B

Verbs of this type change the stem vowel *o* to *ue* when accented.*

		Present	Present Subjunctive	Imperative
Contar (to count)	yo	cuento	cuente	
	tú	cuentas	cuentes	cuenta tú
	él (usted)	cuenta	cuente	cuente usted
	ellos (ustedes)	cuentan	cuenten	cuenten ustedes
Mover (to move)	yo	muevo	mueva	
	tú	mueves	muevas	mueve tú
	él (usted)	mueve	mueva	mueva usted
	ellos (ustedes)	mueven	muevan	muevan ustedes

(6) TYPE C

Verbs of this type change the stem vowel *i* to *ie* or the stem vowel *u* to *ue* when accented. Included in this type are *jugar* and all verbs ending in *-irir*.

		Present	Present Subjunctive	Imperative
Jugar (to play)	yo	juego	juegue	
	tú	juegas	juegues	juega tú
	él (usted)	juega	juegue	juegue usted
	ellos (ustedes)	juegan	jueguen	jueguen ustedes
Adquirir (to acquire)	yo	adquiero	adquiera	
	tú	adquieres	adquieras	adquiere tú
	él (usted)	adquiere	adquiera	adquiera usted
	ellos (ustedes)	adquieren	adquieran	adquieran ustedes

(7) TYPE D

Verbs of this type change the stem vowel *e* to *ie* when accented. When the stem vowel is unaccented and the ending begins with *a* or a diphthong, the *e* changes to *i*. Included in this type are all verbs ending in *-entir*, *-erir* and *-ertir*, as well as the verbs *hervir* and *rehervir*.

	Present Participle	Present	Past	Present Subjunctive	Imperfect Subjunctive	Future Subjunctive	Imperative
Sentir (to feel)	sintiendo						
yo		siento		sienta	sintiera *or* sintiese	sintiere	
tú		sientes		sientas	sintieras *or* sintieses	sintieres	siente tú
él (usted)		siente	sintió	sienta	sintiera *or* sintiese	sintiere	sienta usted
nosotros				sintamos	sintiéramos *or* sintiésemos	sintiéremos	
vosotros				sintáis	sintierais *or* sintieseis	sintiereis	
ellos (ustedes)		sienten	sintieron	sientan	sintieran *or* sintiesen	sintieren	sientan ustedes

(8) TYPE E

Verbs of this type change the stem vowel *o* to *ue* when accented. When the stem vowel is unaccented and the ending begins with *a* or a diphthong, the *o* changes to *u*. Included in this type are *dormir*, *morir* and their compounds.

	Present Participle	Present	Past	Present Subjunctive	Imperfect Subjunctive	Future Subjunctive	Imperative
Dormir (to sleep)	durmiendo						
yo		duermo		duerma	durmiera *or* durmiese	durmiere	
tú		duermes		duermas	durmieras *or* durmieses	durmieres	duerme tú
él (usted)		duerme	durmió	duerma	durmiera *or* durmiese	durmiere	duerma usted
nosotros				durmamos	durmiéramos *or* durmiésemos	durmiéremos	
vosotros				durmáis	durmierais *or* durmieseis	durmiereis	
ellos (ustedes)		duermen	durmieron	duerman	durmieran *or* durmiesen	durmieren	duerman ustedes

(9) TYPE F

Verbs of this type change the stem vowel *e* to *i* both when the stem vowel is accented and when the stem vowel is unaccented and the ending begins with *a* or a diphthong. Included in this type are all verbs ending in *-ebir*, *-edir* (except *agredir* and *transgredir*), *-egir*, *-eguir*, *-emir*, *-enchir*, *-endir*, *-estir* and *-etir*.

	Present Participle	Present	Past	Present Subjunctive	Imperfect Subjunctive	Future Subjunctive	Imperative
Pedir (to ask)	pidiendo						
yo		pido		pida	pidiera *or* pidiese	pidiere	
tú		pides		pidas	pidieras *or* pidieses	pidieres	pide tú
él (usted)		pide	pidió	pida	pidiera *or* pidiese	pidiere	pida usted
nosotros				pidamos	pidiéramos *or* pidiésemos	pidiéremos	

---

* The verb *oler*, which belongs to Type B, substitutes *hue* for *ue* in its irregular forms.

		Present Participle	Present	Past	Present Subjunctive	Imperfect Subjunctive	Future Subjunctive	Imperative
	vosotros				pidáis	pidierais *or* pidieseis	pidiereis	
	ellos (ustedes)		piden	pidieron	pidan	pidieran *or* pidiesen	pidieren	pidan ustedes

(10) TYPE G

Verbs of this type change the stem vowel *e* to *i* when accented. Also, the *i* of the ending is dropped whenever it forms part of a diphthong. Included in this type are all verbs ending in *-eír* and *-eñir*.

		Present Participle	Present	Past	Present Subjunctive	Imperfect Subjunctive	Future Subjunctive	Imperative
Reír (to laugh)	yo	riendo	río		ría	riera *or* riese	riere	
	tú		ríes		rías	rieras *or* rieses	rieres	ríe tú
	él (usted)		ríe	rió	ría	riera *or* riese	riere	ría usted
	nosotros				riamos	riéramos *or* riésemos	riéremos	
	vosotros				riáis	rierais *or* rieseis	riereis	
	ellos (ustedes)		ríen	rieron	rían	rieran *or* riesen	rieren	rían ustedes
Teñir (to dye)	yo	tiñendo	tiño		tiña	tiñera *or* tiñese	tiñere	
	tú		tiñes		tiñas	tiñeras *or* tiñeses	tiñeres	tiñe tú
	él (usted)		tiñe	tiñó	tiña	tiñera *or* tiñese	tiñere	tiña usted
	nosotros				tiñamos	tiñéramos *or* tiñésemos	tiñéremos	
	vosotros				tiñáis	tiñerais *or* tiñeseis	tiñereis	
	ellos (ustedes)		tiñen	tiñeron	tiñan	tiñeran *or* tiñesen	tiñeren	tiñan ustedes

(11) TYPE H

Verbs of this type change the final *c* of the verb stem to *z* when it precedes *a* or *o*. Included in this type are all verbs ending in *-acer* (except *hacer*, *placer*, *yacer* and their compounds), *-ecer* (except *mecer* and *remecer*), *-ocer* (except *cocer* and its compounds) and *-ucir* (except *-ducir*).

		Present	Present Subjunctive	Imperative
Agradecer (to appreciate)	yo	agradezco	agradezca	
	tú		agradezcas	
	él (usted)		agradezca	agradezca usted
	nosotros		agradezcamos	
	vosotros		agradezcáis	
	ellos (ustedes)		agradezcan	agradezcan ustedes
Conocer (to know)	yo	conozco	conozca	
	tú		conozcas	
	él (usted)		conozca	conozca usted
	nosotros		conozcamos	
	vosotros		conozcáis	
	ellos (ustedes)		conozcan	conozcan ustedes
Lucir (to glow)	yo	luzco	luzca	
	tú		luzcas	
	él (usted)		luzca	luzca usted
	nosotros		luzcamos	
	vosotros		luzcáis	
	ellos (ustedes)		luzcan	luzcan ustedes

(12) TYPE I

Verbs of this type change the final *c* of the verb stem to *z* before *a* or *o* in the present and present subjunctive. The *c* is changed to *j* in all forms of the past, the imperfect subjunctive and the future subjunctive. This type includes all verbs ending in *-ducir*.

		Present	Past	Present Subjunctive	Imperfect Subjunctive	Future Subjunctive	Imperative
Conducir (to lead)	yo	conduzco	conduje	conduzca	condujera *or* condujese	condujere	
	tú		condujiste	conduzcas	condujeras *or* condujeses	condujeres	
	él (usted)		condujo	conduzca	condujera *or* condujese	condujere	conduzca usted
	nosotros		condujimos	conduzcamos	condujéramos *or* condujésemos	condujéremos	
	vosotros		condujisteis	conduzcáis	condujerais *or* condujeseis	condujereis	
	ellos (ustedes)		condujeron	conduzcan	condujeran *or* condujesen	condujesen	conduzcan ustedes

(13) TYPE J

Verbs of this type drop the *i* of the ending when it forms part of a diphthong. Included in this type are all verbs ending in *-añer*, *-añir*, *-iñir*, *-uñir*, *-eller* and *-ullir*.

		Present Participle	Past	Imperfect Subjunctive	Future Subjunctive
Tañer		tañendo			
(to toll)	yo			tañera *or* tañese	tañere
	tú			tañeras *or* tañeses	tañeres
	él (usted)		tañó	tañera *or* tañese	tañere
	nosotros			tañéramos *or* tañésemos	tañéremos
	vosotros			tañerais *or* tañeseis	tañereis
	ellos (ustedes)		tañeron	tañeran *or* tañesen	tañeren
Mullir		mullendo			
(to fluff)	yo			mullera *or* mullese	mullere
	tú			mulleras *or* mulleses	mulleres
	él (usted)		mulló	mullera *or* mullese	mullere
	nosotros			mulléramos *or* mullésemos	mulléremos
	vosotros			mullerais *or* mulleseis	mullereis
	ellos (ustedes)		mulleron	mulleran *or* mullesen	mulleren

(14) TYPE K

Verbs of this type take *y* after the stem vowel *u* before *a*, *e* and *o*. Included in this type are all verbs ending in *-uir* (except *inmiscuir*).

		Present	Present Subjunctive	Imperative
Huir	yo	huyo	huya	
(to flee)	tú	huyes	huyas	huye tú
	él (usted)	huye	huya	huya usted
	nosotros		huyamos	
	vosotros		huyáis	
	ellos (ustedes)	huyen	huyan	huyan ustedes

(15) TYPE L

Verbs of this type take a *g* after the *l* of the stem when it is followed by *a* or *o*. In the future and conditional tenses the stem vowel *e* or *i* is changed to *d*, and the *e* of the imperative singular is dropped. This type includes *valer*, *salir* and their compounds.

		Present	Future	Conditional	Present Subjunctive	Imperative
Valer	yo	valgo	valdré	valdría	valga	
(to be worth)	tú		valdrás	valdrías	valgas	val *or* vale tú
	él (usted)		valdrá	valdría	valga	valga usted
	nosotros		valdremos	valdríamos	valgamos	
	vosotros		valdréis	valdríais	valgáis	
	ellos (ustedes)		valdrán	valdrían	valgan	valgan ustedes
Salir	yo	salgo	saldré	saldría	salga	
(to leave)	tú		saldrás	saldrías	salgas	sal tú
	él (usted)		saldrá	saldría	salga	salga usted
	nosotros		saldremos	saldríamos	salgamos	
	vosotros		saldréis	saldríais	salgáis	
	ellos (ustedes)		saldrán	saldrían	salgan	salgan ustedes

Special irregular verbs

Following is a list of verbs with irregularities which apply only to them and their compounds. These verbs are the models for all verbs in the Spanish-to-English word list numbered (16) to (39). Where all six forms are given, the subject pronoun (*yo*, *tú*, etc.) has been omitted.

(16) Andar (to walk)
Past: anduve, anduviste, anduvo, anduvimos, anduvisteis, anduvieron
Imperfect Subjunctive: anduviera *or* anduviese, anduvieras *or* anduvieses, anduviera *or* anduviese, anduviéramos *or* anduviésemos, anduvierais *or* anduvieseis, anduvieran *or* anduviesen

(17) Asir (to seize)
Present: yo asgo
Present Subjunctive: asga, asgas, asga, asgamos, asgáis, asgan
Imperative: asga usted, asgan ustedes

(18) Caber (to fit into)
Present: yo quepo
Past: cupe, cupiste, cupo, cupimos, cupisteis, cupieron
Future: cabré, cabrás, cabrá, cabremos, cabréis, cabrán
Conditional: cabría, cabrías, cabría, cabríamos, cabríais, cabrían
Present Subjunctive: quepa, quepas, quepa, quepamos, quepáis, quepan
Imperfect Subjunctive: cupiera *or* cupiese, cupieras *or* cupieses, cupiera *or* cupiese, cupiéramos *or* cupiésemos, cupierais *or* cupieseis, cupieran *or* cupiesen
Imperative: quepa usted, quepan ustedes

(19) Caer (to fall)
Present: yo caigo
Present Subjunctive: caiga, caigas, caiga, caigamos, caigáis, caigan

(20) Cocer (to cook)
Present: yo cuezo, tú cueces, él (usted) cuece, ellos (ustedes) cuecen
Present Subjunctive: yo cueza, tú cuezas, él (usted) cueza, ellos (ustedes) cuezan
Imperative: cuece tú, cueza usted, cuezan ustedes

(21) Dar (to give)
Present: yo doy
Past: di, diste, dio, dimos, disteis, dieron
Imperfect Subjunctive: diera *or* diese, dieras *or* dieses, diera *or* diese, diéramos *or* diésemos, dierais *or* dieseis, dieran *or* diesen

(22) Decir (to say)
Present Participle: diciendo
Present: yo digo, tú dices, él (usted) dice, ellos (ustedes) dicen
Past: dije, dijiste, dijo, dijimos, dijisteis, dijeron
Future: diré, dirás, dirá, diremos, diréis, dirán
Conditional: diría, dirías, diría, diríamos, diríais, dirían
Present Subjunctive: diga, digas, diga, digamos, digáis, digan
Imperfect Subjunctive: dijera *or* dijese, dijeras *or* dijeses, dijera *or* dijese, dijéramos *or* dijésemos, dijerais *or* dijeseis, dijeran *or* dijesen
Imperative: di tú, diga usted, digan ustedes

(23) Erguir (to set upright)
Present Participle: irguiendo
Present: yo irgo *or* yergo, tú irgues *or* yergues, él (usted) irgue *or* yergue, ellos (ustedes) irguen *or* yerguen
Past: él (usted) irguió, ellos (ustedes) irguieron
Present Subjunctive: irga *or* yerga, irgas *or* yergas, irga *or* yerga, irgamos *or* yergamos, irgáis *or* yergáis, irgan *or* yergan
Imperfect Subjunctive: irguiera *or* irguiese, irguieras *or* irguieses, irguiera *or* irguiese, irguiéramos *or* irguiésemos, irguierais *or* irguieseis, irguieran *or* irguiesen
Imperative: irgue *or* yergue tú, irga *or* yerga usted, irgan *or* yergan ustedes

(24) Estar (to be)
Present: yo estoy, tú estás, él (usted) está, ellos (ustedes) están
Past: estuve, estuviste, estuvo, estuvimos, estuvisteis, estuvieron

Present Subjunctive: yo esté, tú estés, él (usted) esté, ellos (ustedes) estén
Imperfect Subjunctive: estuviera *or* estuviese, estuvieras *or* estuvieses, estuviera *or* estuviese, estuviéramos *or* estuviésemos, estuvierais *or* estuvieseis, estuvieran *or* estuviesen
Imperative: está tú, esté usted, estén ustedes

(25) Haber (to have—auxiliary)
Present: yo he, tú has, él (usted) ha, nosotros hemos, ellos (ustedes) han
Past: hube, hubiste, hubo, hubimos, hubisteis, hubieron
Future: habré, habrás, habrá, habremos, habréis, habrán
Conditional: habría, habrías, habría, habríamos, habríais, habrían
Imperfect Subjunctive: hubiera *or* hubiese, hubieras *or* hubieses, hubiera *or* hubiese, hubiéramos *or* hubiésemos, hubierais *or* hubieseis, hubieran *or* hubiesen

(26) Hacer (to make *or* to do)
Present: yo hago
Past: hice, hiciste, hizo, hicimos, hicisteis, hicieron
Future: haré, harás, hará, haremos, haréis, harán
Conditional: haría, harías, haría, haríamos, haríais, harían
Present Subjunctive: haga, hagas, haga, hagamos, hagáis, hagan
Imperfect Subjunctive: hiciera *or* hiciese, hicieras *or* hicieses, hiciera *or* hiciese, hiciéramos *or* hiciésemos, hicierais *or* hicieseis, hicieran *or* hiciesen
Imperative: haz tú, haga usted, hagan ustedes

(27) Ir (to go)
Present Participle: yendo
Present: voy, vas, va, vamos, vais, van
Past: fui, fuiste, fue, fuimos, fuisteis, fueron
Imperfect: iba, ibas, iba, íbamos, íbais, iban
Future: iré, irás, irá, iremos, iréis, irán
Conditional: iría, irías, iría, iríamos, iríais, irían
Present Subjunctive: vaya, vayas, vaya, vayamos, vayáis, vayan
Imperfect Subjunctive: fuera *or* fuese, fueras *or* fueses, fuera *or* fuese, fuéramos *or* fuésemos, fuerais *or* fueseis, fueran *or* fuesen
Imperative: ve tú, vaya usted, id vosotros, vayan ustedes

(28) Oír (to hear)
Present: yo oigo, tú oyes, él (usted) oye, ellos (ustedes) oyen
Present Subjunctive: oiga, oigas, oiga, oigamos, oigáis, oigan
Imperative: oye tú, oiga usted, oigan ustedes

(29) Poder (to be able)
Present Participle: pudiendo
Present: yo puedo, tú puedes, él (usted) puede, ellos (ustedes) pueden
Past: pude, pudiste, pudo, pudimos, pudisteis, pudieron
Future: podré, podrás, podrá, podremos, podréis, podrán
Conditional: podría, podrías, podría, podríamos, podríais, podrían
Present Subjunctive: yo pueda, tú puedas, él (usted) pueda, ellos (ustedes) puedan
Imperfect Subjunctive: pudiera *or* pudiese, pudieras *or* pudieses, pudiera *or* pudiese, pudiéramos *or* pudiésemos, pudierais *or* pudieseis, pudieran *or* pudiesen
Imperative: puede tú, pueda usted, puedan ustedes

(30) Pudrir (to rot)
Past Participle: podrido

(31) Poner (to put)
Present: yo pongo
Past: puse, pusiste, puso, pusimos, pusisteis, pusieron
Future: pondré, pondrás, pondrá, pondremos, pondréis, pondrán
Conditional: pondría, pondrías, pondría, pondríamos, pondríais, pondrían
Present Subjunctive: ponga, pongas, ponga, pongamos, pongáis, pongan
Imperfect Subjunctive: pusiera *or* pusiese, pusieras *or* pusieses, pusiera *or* pusiese, pusiéramos *or* pusiésemos, pusierais *or* pusieseis, pusieran *or* pusiesen
Imperative: pon tú, ponga usted, pongan ustedes

(32) Querer (to want)
Present: yo quiero, tú quieres, él (usted) quiere, ellos (ustedes) quieren

Past: quise, quisiste, quiso, quisimos, quisisteis, quisieron
Future: querré, querrás, querrá, querremos, querréis, querrán
Conditional: querría, querrías, querría, querríamos, querríais, querrían
Present Subjunctive: yo quiera, tú quieras, él (usted) quiera, ellos (ustedes) quieran
Imperfect Subjunctive: quisiera *or* quisiese, quisieras *or* quisieses, quisiera *or* quisiese, quisiéramos *or* quisiésemos, quisierais *or* quisieseis, quisieran *or* quisiesen
Imperative: quiere tú, quiera usted, quieran ustedes

(33) Saber (to know)
Present: yo sé
Past: supe, supiste, supo, supimos, supisteis, supieron
Future: sabré, sabrás, sabrá, sabremos, sabréis, sabrán
Conditional: sabría, sabrías, sabría, sabríamos, sabríais, sabrían
Imperfect Subjunctive: supiera *or* supiese, supieras *or* supieses, supiera *or* supiese, supiéramos *or* supiésemos, supierais *or* supieseis, supieran *or* supiesen

(34) Ser (to be)
Present: soy, eres, es, somos, sois, son
Past: fui, fuiste, fue, fuimos, fuisteis, fueron
Imperfect: era, eras, era, éramos, erais, eran
Present Subjunctive: sea, seas, sea, seamos, seáis, sean
Imperfect Subjunctive: fuera *or* fuese, fueras *or* fueses, fuera *or* fuese, fuéramos *or* fuésemos, fuerais *or* fueseis, fueran *or* fuesen
Imperative: sé tú, sea usted, sean ustedes

(35) Tener (to have)
Present: yo tengo, tú tienes, él (usted) tiene, ellos (ustedes) tienen
Past: tuve, tuviste, tuvo, tuvimos, tuvisteis, tuvieron
Future: tendré, tendrás, tendrá, tendremos, tendréis, tendrán
Conditional: tendría, tendrías, tendría, tendríamos, tendríais, tendrían
Present Subjunctive: tenga, tengas, tenga, tengamos, tengáis, tengan
Imperfect Subjunctive: tuviera *or* tuviese, tuvieras *or* tuvieses, tuviera *or* tuviese, tuviéramos *or* tuviésemos, tuvierais *or* tuvieseis, tuvieran *or* tuviesen
Imperative: ten tú, tenga usted, tengan ustedes

(36) Traer (to bring)
Present: yo traigo
Past: traje, trajiste, trajo, trajimos, trajisteis, trajeron
Present Subjunctive: traiga, traigas, traiga, traigamos, traigáis, traigan
Imperfect Subjunctive: trajera *or* trajese, trajeras *or* trajeses, trajera *or* trajese, trajéramos *or* trajesemos, trajerais *or* trajeseis, trajeran *or* trajesen
Imperative: traiga usted, traigan ustedes

(37) Venir (to come)
Present Participle: viniendo
Present: yo vengo, tú vienes, él (usted) viene, ellos (ustedes) vienen
Past: vine, viniste, vino, vinimos, vinisteis, vinieron
Future: vendré, vendrás, vendrá, vendremos, vendréis, vendrán
Conditional: vendría, vendrías, vendría, vendríamos, vendríais, vendrían
Present Subjunctive: venga, vengas, venga, vengamos, vengáis, vengan
Imperfect Subjunctive: viniera *or* viniese, vinieras *or* vinieses, viniera *or* viniese, viniéramos *or* viniésemos, vinierais *or* vinieseis, vinieran *or* viniesen
Imperative: ven tú, venga usted, vengan ustedes

(38) Ver (to see)
Present: yo veo
Imperfect: veía, veías, veía, veíamos, veíais, veían
Present Subjunctive: vea, veas, vea, veamos, veáis, vean
Imperative: vea usted, vean ustedes

(39) Yacer (to lie down)
Present: yo yazco, yazgo *or* yago
Present Subjunctive: yazca, yazga *or* yaga; yazcas, yazgas *or* yagas; yazca, yazga *or* yaga; yazcamos, yazgamos *or* yagamos; yazcáis, yazgáis *or* yagáis; yazcan, yazgan *or* yagan
Imperative: yace *or* yaz tú; yazca, yazga *or* yaga usted; yazcan, yazgan *or* yagan ustedes

Spanish Pronunciation

VOWELS AND DIPHTHONGS

Spanish Vowel or Diphthong	Closest English Equivalent	Spanish Example
a	a as in father	la, drama
e	e as in let	del, moderno
i	i as in machine	si, final
o	o as in forty	con, norte
u	u as in rule	burro, fruta
y (alone or at end of word)	i as in machine	y, voy
ai (or ay at end of word)	i as in ice	aire, hay
au	ow as in cow	automóvil, jaula
ei (or ey at end of word)	a as in late	seis, ley

Spanish Vowel or Diphthong	Closest English Equivalent	Spanish Example
ia	ya as in yard	gracias
ie	ye as in yet	bien
io	yo as in yoke	junio
oi (or oy at end of word)	oy as in boy	boicot, voy
ua	wa as in water	agua, cuatro
ue (except after g or q)	we as in went	huevo, jueves
ui (except after g or q)	wee as in week	huir, genuino
uo (except after g or q)	wo as in woke	antiguo, cuota

CONSONANTS

Spanish Consonant	Closest English Equivalent	Spanish Example
b (at beginning of word or after m or n)	b as in boy	burro, cambio
b (in other cases)	v as in velvet	haber, libro
*c (before i and e)	c as in century	centro, cigarro
c (before a, o and u)	c as in car	cara, cosa
ch	ch as in chair	chico, rancho
d (at the beginning of word or after m or n)	d as in day	día, donde
d (in other cases)	th as in this	cada, red
g (before i and e)	h as in hoot	gente, original
g (before a, o, u; also before ui and ue when the u is silent)	g as in go	agosto, gato, gusto; guitarra, guerra
h	silent as h in ghost	hora, historia
j	h as in hoot	Juan, rojo
*ll	y as in yarn	llana, calle
ñ	ny as in canyon	mañana, niño
q (only used before diphthongs ue and ui)	c as in car	que, quieto

Spanish Consonant	Closest English Equivalent	Spanish Example
r (at beginning of word)	long trill as in ...rrrring	rosa, república
r (within word)	short trill as in ...rring	para, verano
rr	long trill as in ...rrrring	perro, terrible
s (before m or v)	s as in design	desmayo, desvalido
s (in other cases)	s as in sand	sembra, sin
v (at beginning of word or after m or n)	b as in boat	vocal, tranvía
v (in other cases)	v as in vat	novio, huevo
x (with e before any consonant but h)	s as in save	experto, exterior
x (in other cases)	x as in exact	taxi, texto
y (when preceding a vowel)	y as in yet	ayer, yo
*z	s as in sin	azul, plaza

* The transliterations for z, soft c and ll reflect the common pronunciations of these letters in Hispanic America, and not the sounds they are given in central Spain (th, th and ly respectively).

STRESS OR ACCENT

Words ending in a vowel or in n or s are regularly accented on the next to last syllable: hermano (ehr-MAH-noh), comen (KOH-mehn), entonces (ehn-TOHN-sehss). Words ending in a consonant other than n or s are regularly accented on the last syllable: prometer (proh-meh-TEHR), hospital (ohss-pee-TAHL), feliz (feh-LEESS).

Words not conforming to the above rules carry the written accent mark on the syllable to be stressed: holandés (oh-lahn-DEHSS), común (koh-MOON), sílaba (SEE-lah-vah). Some words carry accent marks to distinguish them from other words that are the same in form but carry different meanings: él (EHL) meaning "he," and el (EHL) meaning "the"; este (EHSS-teh) meaning "this," and éste (EHSS-teh) meaning "this one." In these cases the pronunciation is the same with or without the accent mark.

Swedish

to English

CONTENTS

Note on Symbols. For a list of abbreviations used in the main word list, see p. 2674. The number indicated for each Swedish verb in the word list is the key to its conjugation. Verbs numbered (1), (2) and 3 are weak verbs and are conjugated according to models bearing the corresponding numbers under *Present Tense, Past Tense, Future Tense,* etc., pp. 3077–78 of the Swedish grammar. Verbs numbered (4) are auxiliaries, (5) through (9) regular strong verbs, (10) irregular strong verbs and (11) irregular weak verbs; for their patterns of conjugation, see the corresponding numbers, pp. 3078–79 of the Swedish grammar. Roman numerals accompanying most nouns in the list refer to declension patterns described on p. 3075.

Notes on Pronunciation. The pronunciation in the following list is indicated wherever possible by a spelling which is read and pronounced as in English. Thus, the Swedish word *bredvid* is rendered *bred*-VEED, with the accent on the syllable in capital

letters. There are sounds in the Swedish language, however, which cannot be reproduced in this manner. Those sounds have been transcribed as follows: *aw* represents the long Swedish *a* which is pronounced like *a* in "far"; *ah* is used for short Swedish *a* and is to be pronounced like the first *a* in "aha"; *ay* represents long *e* which is similar to German long *e* and French *é; ö* is like German *ö* and French *eu; ai* is used for long *ä* which is approximately the same as the first sound in "air"; *oh* represents Swedish *å* (sometimes *o*) and is pronounced when long as *o* in "or" and when short as *o* in "boy"; *ü* is used for Swedish *y* which is similar to German *ü* and French *u* in *vue; u* and *uh* are used for Swedish *u* which when long is similar to *u* in "Yule" and when short to *u* in "put." Wherever *g* appears in the pronunciation column it is to be pronounced with a hard sound as in English "go"; *ng* is always pronounced as in "singer," never as in "finger"; *r* is usually trilled, resembling *r* in "through"; *s* is always unvoiced as in "so."

Double consonants have sometimes been used to indicate that a preceding vowel is short. An elision mark, ‿, is sometimes used to indicate that a preceding vowel sound is long, as *oo* in BOO‿K (*bok*), or that a consonant which might otherwise be silent is to be pronounced, as *k* in K‿NAI (*knä*).

More detailed rules are given in "Basic Key to Swedish Pronunciation," p. 3080.

Note on Alphabetizing. In Swedish, the letters *Å, Ä* and *Ö* are alphabetized following *Z*. In the following list, however, in order to facilitate its use by English-speaking peoples, these letters are alphabetized in the usual English order.

Swedish	Pronunciation	English
abonnemang,*n.* (V)	*ah-bohn-eh-*MAHNG	subscription (for periodicals, *etc.*)
absorbera (1)	*ahb-sohr-*BAY-*rah*	absorb (suck up), to
accent,*nn.* (III)	*ahck-*SENT	accent (stress)
ackordsarbete,*n.* (IV)	*ah-*KORDS-*ahr-*BAY-*teh*	piecework (*n.*)
addera (1)	*ah-*DAY-*rah*	add (find sum of), to
addition,*nn.*	*ah-dee-*SHOON	addition (process of adding)
adel,*nn.*	AW-*dell*	nobility
ädelsten,*nn.* (II)	AID-*el-stayn*	gem
åder,*nn.* (I)	OH-*dehr*	vein (*anat.*)
adjektiv,*n.* (V)	AHD-*yeck-teev*	adjective
adjö	*ah-*YÖ	good-by
administrations- kostnader,*nn.pl.*	*ahd-min-iss-trah-* SHOONS-*kohst-nah- dehr*	overhead (expenses, *bus.*)
adress,*nn.* (III)	*ah-*DRESS	address (postal directions)
adressat,*nn.* (III)	*ah-dreh-*SAWT	addressee
adverb,*n.* (V)	*ahd-*VAIRRB	adverb
advokat,*nn.* (III)	*ahd-voo-*KAWT	attorney
"	"	counsel
"	"	lawyer
affärer,*nn.pl.*	*ah-*FAIR-*ehr*	business (commerce)
affärsbiträde,*n.* (IV)	*ah-*FAISH-*bee-*TRAI-*deh*	clerk (salesperson)
affärsföretag,*n.* (V)	*ah-*FAISH-*för-eh-tawg*	concern (business firm)
affärsman, *nn.* (*pl.*-män)	*ah-*FAISH-*mahn*	businessman
Afrika,*n.*	AW-*frick-ah*	Africa
afrikansk	*ah-frick-*AWNSK	African (*adj.*)
äga (2)	AIG-*ah*	own, to
"	"	possess, to
ägare,*nn.* (V)	AIG-*ah-reh*	owner
agent,*nn.* (III)	*ah-*YENT	agent (representative)
agentur,*nn.* (III)	*ah-yen-*TU‿R	agency (business firm)
ägg,*n.* (V)	EGG	egg
äggröra,*nn.*	EGG-*rö-rah*	scrambled eggs
ägna sig (1)	ENG-*nah say*	devote oneself, to
åka (2)	OH-*kah*	ride (in a car), to
åka skidor	*oh-kah-*SHEE-*door*	ski, to
åkdon,*n.* (V)	OH‿K-*doon*	vehicle (conveyance)
akt,*nn.* (III)	AHCKT	act (dramatic unit)
äkta	ECK-*tah*	genuine
akta sig för (1)	AHCK-*tah say för*	beware of, to
äktenskap,*n.* (V)	ECK-*ten-skawp*	marriage
aktie,*nn.* (III)	AHKT-*see-eh*	share (stock)
aktieägare,*nn.* (V)	AHKT-*see-eh-aig-ah-reh*	stockholder
aktier,*nn.pl.*	AHKT-*see-ehr*	stock (shares)
aktiv	AHCK-*teev*	active
åktur,*nn.* (III)	OH‿K-*tu‿r*	ride (in a car)
ål,*nn.* (II)	OH‿L	eel
ålägga (11)	OH-*leg-ah*	impose (inflict), to
Alaska,*n.*	*ah-*LAHSS-*kah*	Alaska
Albanien,*n.*	*ahll-*BAW-*nee-en*	Albania
ålder,*nn.* (II)	OHLL-*dehr*	age (accumulated years)
ålderdomlighet,*nn.* (III)	OHLL-*dehr-doom-lig- hayt*	antiquity (ancientness)
äldre	ELL-*dreh*	senior (older)
aldrig	AHLL-*drig*	never
alfabet,*n.* (V)	*ahll-fah-*BAYT	alphabet
alkohol,*nn.*	*ahll-ko-*HOH‿L	alcohol
alla	AHLL-*ah*	all (every, *adj.*)
alldeles	AHLL-*day-less*	all (entirely, *adv.*) altogether
allergi,*nn.*	AHLL-*ehrg-*EE	allergy (*med.*)
allmän	AHLL-*men*	general (*adj.*)
"	"	popular (prevalent)
"	"	public (common, *adj.*)
allmän	AHLL-*men*	universal (*adj.*)
allmänhet,*nn.*	AHLL-*men-hayt*	public (populace, *n.*)
allt	AHLLT	all (everything, *n.*)
alltför	AHLLT-*för*	too (overly)
alltid	AHLL-*tid*	always
"	"	ever (at all times)
allting	AHLL-*ting*	everything (*pron.*)
allvarlig	AHLL-*vawr-lig*	earnest
"	"	grave
"	"	serious
allvarsam	AHLL-*vaw-shahm*	sober (serious)
alm,*nn.* (II)	AHLLM	elm
almanacka,*nn.* (I)	AHLL-*mah-nah-kah*	calendar
älska (1)	ELL-*skah*	love, to
älskad	ELL-*skahd*	beloved (*adj.*)
älskarinna,*nn.* (I)	*el-skahr-*IN-*ah*	mistress (paramour)
älskling,*nn.* (II)	ELSK-*ling*	darling
"	"	sweetheart
älskvärd	ELSK-*vaird*	gracious

Swedish	Pronunciation	English
altare,*n.* (IV)	AHLL-*tah-reh*	altar
altfiol,*nn.* (III)	AHLLT-*fee-ool*	viola
aluminium,*n.*	*ah-lu-*MEE-*nee-uhm*	aluminum
ambassadör,*nn.* (III)	*ahm-bah-sah-*DÖR	ambassador
ämbete,*n.* (IV)	EM-*bay-teh*	office (position)
ambulans,*nn.* (III)	*ahm-buh-*LAHNS	ambulance
Amerika,*n.*	*ah-*MEH-*ree-kah*	America
amerikansk	*ah-meh-ree-*KAWNSK	American (*adj.*)
amiral,*nn.* (III)	*ah-mee-*RAWL	admiral
ämna (1)	EM-*nah*	intend (propose), to
"	"	mean, to
ämne,*n.* (IV)	EM-*neh*	matter (substance)
"	"	stuff
"	"	subject
"	"	topic
amortera (1)	*ah-moor-*TAY-*rah*	amortize, to
amortering,*nn.* (II)	*ah-moor-*TAY-*ring*	amortization (*bus.*)
Amsterdam,*n.*	AHM-*stehr-dahm*	Amsterdam
än	EN	than
anbud,*n.* (V)	AHN-*buh_d*	bid (amount offered)
"	"	offer
ändå	EN-*doh*	still (nevertheless, *conj.*)
"	"	yet (*adv.*)
anda,*nn.*	AHN-*dah*	morale
"	"	spirit
andas (1)	AHN-*dahss*	breathe (draw breath), to
andedräkt,*nn.* (III)	AHN-*deh-dreckt*	breath
andel,*nn.* (II)	AHN-*dayl*	interest (share)
andlig	AHND-*lig*	spiritual (*adj.*)
ändlös	END-*lö_s*	endless
andra	AHN-*drah*	second (*adj.*)
ändra (1)	EN-*drah*	alter (make different), to
"	"	change (make different), to
ändras (1)	EN-*drahs*	change (become different), to
ändring,*nn.*(II)	END-*ring*	change (alteration)
anfall,*n.* (V)	AHN-*fahll*	offense (attack)
anförande,*n.* (IV)	AHN-*för-ahn-deh*	address (speech)
äng,*nn.* (II)	ENG	meadow
angå (10)	AHN-*goh*	concern (affect), to
ånga,*nn.* (I)	OHNG-*ah*	steam
angående	AHN-*goh-en-deh*	concerning (regarding)
ängel,*nn.* (II)	ENG-*el*	angel
angelägenhet,*nn.* (III)	AHN-*yeh-laig-en-hayt*	affair (matter)
angenäm	AHN-*yeh-naim*	agreeable (pleasing)
angenäm	AHN-*yeh-naim*	pleasant
ångra (1)	OHNG-*rah*	repent, to
ängslan,*nn.*	ENGS-*lahn*	anxiety
anhängare,*nn.* (V)	AHN-*heng-ah-reh*	follower (adherent)
anhängare,*nn.pl.*	AHN-*heng-ah-reh*	following (followers)
anka,*nn.* (I)	AHNG-*kah*	duck
änka,*nn.* (I)	ENG-*kah*	widow
ankare,*n.* (IV)	AHNG-*kah-reh*	anchor
anklaga (1)	AHN-*klaw-gah*	accuse, to
"	"	charge, to
anklagelse,*nn.* (III)	AHN-*klawg-el-seh*	accusation
"	"	charge
änkling,*nn.* (II)	ENK-*ling*	widower
ankomma (10)	AHN-*kohm-ah*	arrive, to
ankomst,*nn.*	AHN-*kohmst*	arrival
anletsdrag,*n.* (V)	AHN-*lets-drawg*	feature (part of face)
anmärka (2)	AHN-*mairrk-ah*	comment, to
"	"	observe (remark), to
anmärkning,*nn.* (II)	AHN-*mairrk-ning*	comment (remark)
annan	AHN-*ahn*	else (different, *adj.*)
"	"	other (*adj.*, *pron.*)
annan, en	*en* AHN-*ahn*	another (different, different one, *adj.*, *pron.*)
annars	AHN-*ahsh*	else (if not, *adv.*)
"	"	else (instead, *adv.*)
"	"	otherwise (under other conditions)

Swedish	Pronunciation	English
annons,*nn.* (III)	*ah-*NOHNGS	advertisement
annonsera (1)	*ah-nohng-*SAY-*rah*	advertise (sponsor advertising), to
annorlunda	AHN-*oor-luhn-dah*	otherwise (contrarily)
annorstädes	AHN-*oo-shtaid-es*	elsewhere
ännu	EN-*uh*	still (as yet, *adv.*)
"	"	still (even more, *adv.*)
"	"	yet (now, until now, *adv.*)
ännu en	EN-*nuh* EN	another (one more, *adj.*)
annulera (1)	*ah-nuh-*LAY-*rah*	cancel (revoke), to
anordning,*nn.* (II)	AHN-*ord-ning*	disposition (arrangement)
anse (10)	AHN-*say*	deem (regard), to
"	"	reckon (consider), to
anseende,*n.*	AHN-*say-en-deh*	reputation
ansikte,*n.* (IV)	AHN-*sick-teh*	countenance
"	"	face (*anat.*)
anskaffa (1)	AHN-*skahf-ah*	supply (provide), to
ansökan,*nn.*	AHN-*sö-kahn*	application (request)
anspråk,*n.* (V)	AHN-*sproh_k*	claim
anställa (2)	AHN-*stell-ah*	employ, to
"	"	engage, to
"	"	hire, to
anställd,*nn.* (*pl.*-a)	AHN-*steld*	employee
anställning,*nn.* (II)	AHN-*stell-ning*	employment (work)
anstalt,*nn.*(III)	AHN-*stahlt*	asylum (institution)
anständig	AHN-*sten-dig*	decent (respectable)
ansträngning,*nn.* (II)	AHN-*streng-ning*	effort
"	"	strain (exertion)
ansvar,*n.*	AHN-*svawr*	charge
"	"	liability
"	"	responsibility (accountability)
ansvarig	AHN-*svawr-ig*	liable
"	"	responsible (answerable)
anta(ga) (9)	AHN-*taw*(-*gah*)	accept, to
"	"	adopt (embrace), to
"	"	guess, to
"	"	presume (assume), to
anta(ga) (9)	AHN-*taw*(-*gah*)	suppose, to
antal,*n.* (V)	AHN-*tawl*	number (quantity)
anteckna (1)	AHN-*teck-nah*	enter (make record of), to
anteckningsbok, *nn.* (*pl.* -böcker)	AHN-*teck-nings-boo_k*	notebook
antenn,*nn.* (III)	*ahn-*TEN	aerial (antenna)
antibioticum,*n.* (*pl.* -tica)	*ahn-tee-bee-*OH-*tick-uhm*	antibiotic
antingen...eller	AHN-*ting-en*...ELL-*ehr*	either...or (*conj.*)
antologi,*nn.* (III)	*ahn-toh-log-*EE	anthology
antropologi,*nn.*	*ahn-troh-poh-log-*EE	anthropology
antyda (2)	AHN-*tü-dah*	indicate (suggest), to
använda (2)	AHN-*ven-dah*	employ, to
"	"	use (utilize), to
användning,*nn.* (II)	AHN-*vend-ning*	application
"	"	use (utilization)
apa,*nn.* (I)	AW-*pah*	monkey
apelsin,*nn.*,*n.* (III)	*ah-pell-*SEEN	orange (fruit)
apostel,*nn.* (II)	*ah-*POHSS-*tell*	apostle
apotek,*n.* (V)	*ah-poo-*TAYK	pharmacy (drug store)
apparat,*nn.* (III)	*ah-pah-*RAWT	device (apparatus)
applåd,*nn.* (III)	*ah-*PLOH_D	applause
äpple,*n.* (IV)	EP-*leh*	apple
aprikos,*nn.* (III)	*ah-prih-*KOO_S	apricot
aptit,*nn.*	*ahp-*TEET	appetite
år,*n.* (V)	OR	year
ära,*nn.*	AIR-*ah*	credit (commendation)
"	"	honor
åra,*nn.* (I)	OR-*ah*	oar (*n.*)
arbeta (1)	AHRR-*bay-tah*	work (labor), to
arbetare,*nn.* (V)	AHRR-*bay-tah-reh*	worker
arbete,*n.* (IV)	AHRR-*bay-teh*	job (employment)
"	"	work (labor)
arbetsgivare,*nn.* (V)	AHRR-*bets-yee-vah-reh*	employer (boss)
arbetskraft,*nn.* (III)	AHRR-*bets-krahft*	labor (labor force)
arbetslös	AHRR-*bets-lö_s*	unemployed

Swedish	Pronunciation	English
arbetslöshet,*nn.*	AHRR-*bets-lö̱_s*-HAYT	unemployment
ärelysten	AIR-*eh-lüst-en*	ambitious (aspiring)
ärelystnad,*nn.*	AIR-*eh-lüst-nahd*	ambition
ärende,*n.* (IV)	AIR-*en-deh*	errand (commission)
ärftlighet,*nn.*	AIRFT-*lig-hayt*	heredity
arg	AHRR-*yuh*	angry
Argentina,*n.*	*ahrg-en*-TEE-*nah*	Argentina
argentinsk	*ahrg-en*-TEENSK	Argentinian (*adj.*)
århundrade,*n.* (IV)	OR-*huhn-drah-deh*	century
ark,*n.* (V)	AHRRK	sheet (of paper)
arkitekt,*nn.* (III)	*ahr-kee*-TECKT	architect

årlig
    ″
	OR-*lig*
	    ″
		annual
		yearly (*adj.*)

ärlig	AIR-*lig*	honest
årligen	OR-*lig-en*	yearly (*adv.*)
ärlighet,*nn.*	AIR-*lig-hayt*	honesty
arm,*nn.* (II)	AHRRM	arm (*anat.*)
ärm,*nn.* (II)	AIRRM	sleeve
armbåge,*nn.* (II)	AHRRM-*boh_g-eh*	elbow
armband,*n.* (V)	AHRRM-*bahnd*	bracelet
armé,*nn.* (III)	*ahr*-MAY	army
ärr,*n.* (V)	AIRR	scar
arrangemang,*n.* (III, V)	*ah-rahng-sheh*-MAHNG	arrangement (preparation)
arrangera (1)	*ah-rahng*-SHAY-*rah*	arrange (plan), to
årsdag,*nn.* (II)	OH_SH-*dawg*	anniversary
årsränta,*nn.* (I)	OH_SH-*ren-tah*	annuity
årstid,*nn.* (III)	OH_SH-*teed*	season (of year)
ärt,*nn.* (III)	AIRRT	pea

artig
    ″
	ART-*ig*
	    ″
		civil
		courteous

artig	ART-*ig*	polite
artighet,*nn.* (III)	ART-*ig-hayt*	courtesy
artikel,*nn.* (II)	*ahr*-TICK-*el*	article (literary composition)
artistisk	*ahr*-TISS-*tisk*	artistic (tasteful)
ärva (2)	AIRR-*vah*	inherit, to
arvinge,*nn.* (II)	AHRR-*ving-eh*	heir
arvode,*n.* (IV)	AHRR-*voo-deh*	fee
asiatisk	*ah-see*-AW-*tisk*	Asiatic (*adj.*)
Asien,*n.*	AW-*see-en*	Asia

åsikt,*nn.* (III)
    ″
	OH-*sickt*
	    ″
		opinion
		view

ask,*nn.* (II)	AHSSK	box (container)
aska,*nn.*	AHSS-*kah*	ashes
åska,*nn.*	OHSS-*kah*	thunder
åskådare,*nn.* (V)	OH-*skoh-dah-reh*	spectator
askkopp,*nn.* (II)	AHSSK-*kohp*	ash tray
askonsdag,*nn.* (II)	AHSSK-*oons-dawg*	Ash Wednesday
åsna,*nn.* (I)	OH_S-*nah*	donkey
aspirin,*nn.*,*n.*	*ahss-pee*-REEN	aspirin
assistent,*nn.* (III)	*ah-siss*-TENT	assistant
associera (1)	*ah-soh-see*-AY-*rah*	associate (relate), to
äta (10)	A-*tah*	eat, to
åtal,*n.* (V)	OH-*tawl*	suit (lawsuit)
äta middag (10)	*a-tah*-MID-*dawg*	dine, to
Aten,*n.*	*ah*-TAYN	Athens
återbetala (1, 2)	OH-*tehr-beh-taw-lah*	repay, to

återbetalning,*nn.*
(II)
    ″
	OH-*tehr-beh-tawl-ning*
	
	    ″
		rebate (*bus.*)
		
		refund (*bus.*)

återfå (10)	OH-*tehr-foh*	recover (get back), to
återfalla (10)	OH-*tehr-fahll-ah*	relapse, to
återförsäljning,*nn.*	OH-*tehr-för-sell_yuh-ning*	resale (*bus.*)
åter granska (1)	OH-*tehr* GRAHN-*skah*	review (look over again), to
återköpa (2)	OH-*tehr-chö-pah*	redeem (buy back), to
återlämna (1)	OH-*tehr-lem-nah*	return (give back), to
återspegla (1)	OH-*teh-shpayg-lah*	reflect (throw back), to
återstå (10)	OH-*teh-shtoh*	remain (be left), to
återställa (2)	OH-*teh-shtell-ah*	restore (reestablish), to
återstod,*nn.*	OH-*teh-shtood*	remainder
återuppliva (1)	OH-*tehr-uhp-lee-vah*	revive, to
återuppta(ga) (9)	OH-*tehr-uhp-taw(-gah)*	resume (recommence), to
återvända (2)	OH-*tehr-ven-dah*	return (go back), to
återvändande,*n.*	OH-*tehr-ven-dahn-deh*	return (coming or going back)
Atlanten,*nn.*	*aht*-LAHN-*ten*	Atlantic (*n.*)

Swedish	Pronunciation	English
åtlöje,*n.*	OH_T-*löy-eh*	ridicule

atmosfär,*nn.* (III)
    ″
	aht-mooss-FAIR
	    ″
		atmosphere (air)
		atmosphere (environment)

atom,*nn.* (III)	*ah*-TOH_M	atom
atombomb,*nn.* (III)	*ah*-TOH_M-*bohm_b*	atomic bomb
åtrå,*nn.*	OH-*troh*	lust (desire)
åtskillnad,*nn.*	OH_T-*shill-nahd*	distinction (difference)
att	AHT	that (*conj.*)
ättika,*nn.*	ET-*tick-ah*	vinegar
attraktion,*nn.* (III)	*ah-trahck*-SHOON	attraction
auktion,*nn.* (III)	*owk*-SHOON	auction (sale)
auktoritet,*nn.* (III)	*owk-toh-ree*-TAYT	authority (person with power)
Australien,*n.*	*ah-uh*-STRAW-*lee-en*	Australia
australisk	*ah-uh*-STRAW-*lisk*	Australian (*adj.*)
automobil,*nn.* (III)	*oh-toh-moh*-BEEL	automobile
av	AWV	of
avbetalning,*nn.* (II)	AWV-*beh-tawl-ning*	installment (payment, *bus.*)
avbryta (7)	AWV-*brü-tah*	interrupt, to

avdelning,*nn.* (II)
    ″
	AWV-*dayl-ning*
	    ″
		department (administrative unit)
		division (portion)

avdra(ga) (9)	AWV-*draw(-gah)*	deduct, to
äventyr,*n.* (V)	AIV-*en-tür*	adventure
avgå (10)	AWV-*goh*	resign (tender resignation), to
avgift,*nn.* (III)	AWV-*yift*	fare (*transp.*)
avgörande	AWV-*yö-rahn-deh*	positive (decisive)
avistaväxel,*nn.*(II)	*ah*-VISS-*tah-vex-el*	sight draft (*bus.*)

avkastning,*nn.*
    ″
	AWV-*kahsst-ning*
	    ″
		produce
		yield (product)

avkomling,*nn.* (II)	AWV-*kohm-ling*	descendant (offspring)
avkyla (2)	AWV-*chü-lah*	cool (make less hot), to

avlägsen
    ″
	AWV-*lex-en*
	    ″
		distant (far-off)
		remote

avlägsna (1)	AWV-*lex-nah*	remove (take away), to
avlägsnare	AWV-*lex-nah-reh*	farther (*adj.*)
avliden	AWV-*lee-den*	late (deceased, *adj.*)
avlopp,*n.* (V)	AWV-*lohp*	drain (conduit)
avloppsledning,*nn.* (I)	AWV-*lohps*-LAYD-*ning*	sewer (conduit)
avresa (2)	AWV-*ray-sah*	depart (leave), to
avresa,*nn.* (I)	AWV-*ray-sah*	departure (setting out)
avrätta (1)	AWV-*ret-ah*	execute (put to death), to

avsikt,*nn.* (III)
    ″
	AWV-*sickt*
	    ″
		design (intention)
		intention

avsiktlig	AWV-*sickt-lig*	deliberate (intentional)
avskaffa (1)	AWV-*skahf-ah*	abolish, to
avsked,*nn.* (V)	AWV-*shayd*	discharge (dismissal)
avskeda (1)	AWV-*shay-dah*	dismiss (discharge), to
avskräde,*n.*	AWV-*skrai-deh*	garbage
avsky,*nn.*	AWV-*shü*	disgust
avslå (10)	AWV-*sloh*	decline (refuse), to

avslöja (1)
    ″
	AWV-*slöy-ah*
	    ″
		expose (disclose), to
		reveal (divulge), to

avsluta (1)
    ″
	AWV-*slu-tah*
	    ″
		complete, to
		finish (complete), to

avsluta (1, 6)	AWV-*slu-tah*	conclude (make end), to
avstå (10)	AWV-*stoh*	cede, to
avstånd,*n.* (V)	AWV-*stohnd*	distance

avtal,*n.* (V)
    ″
    ″
	AWV-*tawl*
	    ″
	    ″
		appointment (meeting)
		date
		engagement

avund,*nn.*	AWV-*uhnd*	envy
avundas (1)	AWV-*uhn-dahs*	envy, to
avundsjuk	AWV-*uhnd-shu_k*	jealous
avvärja (2)	AWV-*vairr-yah*	avert (prevent), to
avvika (5)	AWV-*vee-kah*	deviate (diverge), to
avvikelse,*nn.* (III)	AWV-*veek-el-seh*	departure (deviation)
avvisa (1)	AWV-*vee-sah*	reject, to
avyttrande,*n.*	AWV-*üt-rahn-deh*	disposition (disposal)

bäck,*nn.* (II)
    ″
	BECK
	    ″
		brook
		creek (stream)

backe,*nn.* (II)	BAHCK-*eh*	hill
bad,*n.* (V)	BAWD	bath

Swedish	Pronunciation	English
båda	BOH-*dah*	both (pron.)
"	"	both (adj.)
bada (1)	BAW-*dah*	bathe (take a bath), to
bädd,*nn.* (II)	BED	berth (train bunk)
baddräkt,*nn.* (III)	BAWD-*dreckt*	bathing suit
badkar,*n.* (V)	BAWD-*kawr*	bathtub
badrum,*n.* (V)	BAWD-*ruhm*	bathroom
bagage,*n.*	*bah*-GAWSH	baggage
"	"	luggage
bagare,*nn.* (V)	BAW-*gah-reh*	baker
bagge,*nn.* (II)	BAHGG-*eh*	ram (animal)
Bajern,*n.*	BAH-*yehrn*	Bavaria
bakåt	BAWK-*oht*	back (rearward, *adv.*)
"	"	backward
baklänges	BAWK-*leng-es*	backward (in reverse, *adv.*)
bakom	BAWK-*ohm*	behind (*prep.*)
"	"	behind (in the rear, *adv.*)
bakre	BAWK-*reh*	hind (posterior, *adj.*)
"	"	rear (*adj.*)
baksida,*nn.* (I)	BAWK-*see-dah*	back (reverse side)
bakterie,*nn.* (III)	*bahck*-TAY-*ree-eh*	germ (microorganism)
balans,*nn.*	*bah*-LAHNGS	balance (equilibrium)
ballong,*nn.* (III)	*bah*-LONG	balloon
bälte,*n.* (IV)	BELL-*teh*	belt (article of clothing)
banan,*nn.* (III)	*bah*-NAWN	banana
band,*n.* (V)	BAHND	band
"	"	bond (emotional tie)
"	"	curb (restraint)
"	"	ribbon
"	"	tie
"	"	volume (book)
bandage,*n.* (V)	*bahn*-DAWSH	bandage
bandinspelnings-apparat,*nn.* (III)	BAHND-*in-spayl-nings-ah-pah*-RAWT	tape recorder
bandit,*nn.* (III)	*bahn*-DEET	bandit
banjo,*nn.* (III)	BAHN-*yoo*	banjo
bank,*nn.* (III)	BAHNK	bank (treasury)
bänk,*nn.* (II)	BENK	bench (long seat)
banka (1)	BAHNK-*ah*	pound (pummel), to
bankett,*nn.* (III)	*bahng*-KET	banquet
bankir,*nn.* (III)	*bahng*-KEER	banker
bankrörelse,*nn.* (III)	BAHNK-*rör-el-seh*	banking
bar	BAR	bare (nude)
bar,*nn.* (III)	BAR	bar (barroom)
bår,*nn.* (II)	BOR	litter (stretcher)
bär,*n.* (V)	BAIR	berry (fruit)
bara	BAR-*ah*	just
"	"	mere
"	"	merely
"	"	only
bära (10)	BAIR-*ah*	bear, to
"	"	carry, to
bärare,*nn.* (V)	BAIR-*ah-reh*	porter (baggage carrier)
barberare,*nn.* (V)	*bahr*-BAY-*rah-reh*	barber
bark,*nn.*	BAHRRK	bark (of tree)
barm,*nn.* (II)	BAHRRM	bosom
barmhärtig	*bahrm*-HAIRT-*ig*	merciful
barmhärtighet,*nn.*	*bahrm*-HAIRT-*ig-hayt*	mercy
barn,*n.* (V)	BARN	child
barndom,*nn.*	BARN-*doom*	childhood
barnförlamning,*nn.*	BARN-*för-lawm-ning*	infantile paralysis
barnkammare,*nn.* (V)	BARN-*kahm-ah-reh*	nursery (children's room)
bärnstensgul	BAIRN-*stens-guh l*	amber (*adj.*)
barnvagn,*nn.* (II)	BARN-*vahngn*	carriage (baby buggy)
barometer,*nn.* (II)	*bah-roo*-MAY-*tehr*	barometer
baseboll,*nn.*	BASE-*bohll*	baseball
Basel,*n.*	BAW-*sell*	Basle
bäst	BEST	best (*adj.*)
basun,*nn.* (III)	*bah*-SU_N	trombone
båt,*nn.* (II)	BOH_T	boat
batteri,*n.* (III)	*bah-teh*-REE	battery (primary cell)
"	"	battery (storage)
bättre	BET-*reh*	better (*adj.,adv.*)
bäver,*nn.* (II)	BAI-*vehr*	beaver (animal)
be (10)	BAY	ask (request), to
"	"	plead (appeal earnestly), to

Swedish	Pronunciation	English
bebo (3)	*beh*-BOO	inhabit, to
"	"	occupy (live in), to
beck,*n.*	BECK	pitch (tar)
be(dja) (10)	BAY(D-*yah*)	pray, to
bedra(ga) (9)	*beh*-DRAW(-*gah*)	deceive (delude), to
bedrägeri,*n.* (III)	*beh-draig-eh*-REE	deceit
"	"	fraud
bedrift,*nn.* (III)	*beh*-DRIFT	feat
bedrövelse,*nn.* (III)	*beh*-DRÖ-*vell-seh*	misery (grief)
befälhavare,*nn.* (V)	*beh*-FAIL-*haw-vah-reh*	commander (officer)
befalla (2)	*beh*-FAHLL-*ah*	order, to
befordra (1)	*beh*-FOORD-*rah*	convey (transport), to
"	"	promote (raise in rank), to
befordran,*nn.*	*beh*-FOORD-*rahn*	promotion (advance)
befria (1)	*beh*-FREE-*ah*	free, to
"	"	liberate, to
"	"	relieve, to
"	"	rid, to
befriad	*beh*-FREE-*ahd*	exempt (*adj.*)
befruktning,*nn.* (II)	*beh*-FRUHKT-*ning*	conception (*physiol.*)
begå (10)	*be*-GOH	commit (perpetrate), to
begär,*n.* (V)	*beh*-YAIR	desire
begära (2)	*beh*-YAIR-*ah*	demand (ask for), to
"	"	request, to
begäran,*nn.*	*beh*-YAIR-*ahn*	request
begåvad	*beh*-GOH-*vahd*	gifted (talented)
begränsa (1)	*beh*-GREN-*sah*	confine, to
"	"	limit, to
begrava (2)	*be*-GRAW-*vah*	bury (entomb), to
begravning,*nn.* (II)	*be*-GRAWV-*ning*	burial
"	"	funeral
begynnelse-...	*beh*-YÜN-*el-seh-...*	initial (first, *adj.*)
behag,*n.*	*beh*-HAWG	grace (gracefulness)
behålla (10)	*beh*-HOHLL-*ah*	keep, to
"	"	retain, to
behandla (1)	*beh*-HAHND-*lah*	treat (behave toward), to
behandling,*nn.* (II)	*beh*-HAHND-*ling*	treatment
behov,*n.* (V)	*beh*-HOOV	need
"	"	want
behöva (2)	*beh*-HÖ-*vah*	need (require), to
bekämpa (1)	*beh*-CHEM-*pah*	oppose (combat), to
bekant	*beh*-KAHNT	known (familiar)
bekant,*nn.* (*pl.* bekanta)	*beh*-KAHNT	acquaintance (person known)
bekräfta (1)	*beh*-KREF-*tah*	confirm (corroborate), to
bekräftelse,*nn.* (III)	*beh*-KREF-*tell-seh*	confirmation (corroboration)
bekväm	*beh*-KVAIM	comfortable (affording comfort)
"	"	convenient
bekvämlighet,*nn.* (III)	*beh*-KVAIM-*lig-hayt*	comfort
"	"	convenience
"	"	ease
bekymmer,*n.* (V)	*beh*-CHÜM-*ehr*	care (concern)
"	"	trouble (distress)
belägenhet,*nn.*	*beh*-LAIG-*en-hayt*	plight (predicament)
belägring,*nn.* (II)	*beh*-LAIG-*ring*	siege (*mil.*)
belåten	*beh*-LOH-*ten*	satisfied (contented)
belåtenhet,*nn.*	*beh*-LOH-*ten-hayt*	satisfaction (contentment)
Belgien,*n.*	BELLG-*ee-en*	Belgium
belgisk	BELLG-*isk*	Belgian (*adj.*)
belöna (1)	*beh*-LÖ-*nah*	reward, to
belöning,*nn.* (II)	*beh*-LÖ-*ning*	reward (recompense)
belöpa sig till (2)	*beh*-LÖ-*pah say till*	amount to, to
belysa (2)	*beh*-LÜ-*sah*	illuminate (elucidate), to
bemyndigande,*n.* (IV)	*beh*-MÜN-*dig-ahn-deh*	authorization
ben,*n.* (V)	BAYN	bone
"	"	leg (*anat.*)
benådning,*nn.* (II)	*beh*-NOH_D-*ning*	pardon (*law*)
benägen att	*beh*-NAIG-*en aht*	apt to (prone to)
bensin,*nn.*	*ben*-SEEN	gasoline
be om (10)	BAY *ohm*	solicit (ask for), to
be om ursäkt	*bay ohm* UH-*sheckt*	apologize, to

Swedish	Pronunciation	English
beräkna (1)	*beh*-RAIK-*nah*	calculate (compute), to
"	"	reckon, to
beräkning,*nn.* (II)	*beh*-RAIK-*ning*	account (calculation)
berätta (1)	*beh*-RET-*ah*	relate, to
"	"	tell (narrate), to
berättelse,*nn.* (III)	*beh*-RET-*el-seh*	story (account)
		tale (narrative)
berättiga (1)	*beh*-RET-*ig-ah*	entitle (give a right to), to
"	"	warrant (justify), to
berg,*n.* (V)	BAIRR *yuh*	mountain
bergås,*nn.* (II)	BAIRR *yuh-oh_s*	ridge (of mountains)
bergig	BAIRR-*yig*	mountainous
bergskedja,*nn.* (I)	BAIRR *yuhs-chayd-yah*	range (of mountains)
bergstopp,*nn.* (II)	BAIRR *yuhs-tohp*	peak (mountain top)
Berlin,*n.*	*behr*-LEEN	Berlin
Bern,*n.*	BAIRN	Berne
beroende	*beh*-ROO-*en-deh*	dependent (reliant)
beröm,*n.*	*beh*-RÖM	praise
berömd	*beh*-RÖMD	famous
berömma (2)	*beh*-RÖM-*ah*	praise, to
bero på (3)	*beh*-ROO *poh*	depend (be contingent) on, to
beröra (2)	*beh*-RÖ-*rah*	touch, to
beröva (1)	*beh*-RÖ-*vah*	deprive (divest), to
berusning, *nn.*	*beh*-RU_S-*ning*	intoxication (drunkenness)
besättning,*nn.* (II)	*beh*-SET-*ning*	crew
besegra (1)	*beh*-SAYG-*rah*	beat, to
"	"	conquer, to
"	"	defeat, to
besegrande,*n.*	*beh*-SAYG-*rahn-deh*	conquest
besittning,*nn.*	*beh*-SIT-*ning*	possession (ownership)
beskära (10)	*beh*-SHAIR-*ah*	cut (reduce), to
beskriva (5)	*beh*-SKREE-*vah*	describe (portray), to
beskrivning,*nn.* (II)	*beh*-SKREEV-*ning*	description (account)
beskydd,*n.*	*beh*-SHÜD	protection
besläktad	*beh*-SLECK-*tahd*	related (connected)
beslut,*n.* (V)	*beh*-SLU_T	conclusion
"	"	decision (judgment)
besluta (sig) (1, 6)	*beh*-SLU-*tah* (*say*)	decide (make up one's mind), to
"	"	determine, to
besök,*n.* (V)	*beh*-SÖ_K	visit (stay)
besöka (2)	*beh*-SÖ-*kah*	visit (call on), to
"	"	visit (go to view), to
besöka ofta	*beh*-SÖ-*kah* OFF-*tah*	haunt (visit often), to
besökande,*nn.* (V)	*beh*-SÖ-*kahn-deh*	visitor
besparingar,*nn.pl.*	*beh*-SPAW-*ring-ahr*	savings (money)
bespruta (1)	*beh*-SPRU-*tah*	spray, to
best,*nn.* (II)	BEST	brute (animal, *n.*)
bestå av (10)	*beh*-STOH AWV	consist of (comprise), to
beställa (2)	*beh*-STELL-*ah*	order (purchase), to
"	"	reserve (order in advance), to
beställa biljett	*beh*-STELL-*ah bill*-YET	book (engage space), to
bestämd	*beh*-STEMD	definite
bestämma (2)	*beh*-STEM-*ah*	resolve (determine), to
bestämmelse,*nn.* (III)	*beh*-STEM-*el-seh*	provision (stipulation)
bestämmelseort, *nn.* (III)	*beh*-STEM-*el-seh-oort*	destination
beständig	*beh*-STEN-*dig*	everlasting
bestiga (5)	*beh*-STEE-*gah*	mount (climb upon), to
bestörtning,*nn.*	*beh*-STÖRT-*ning*	dismay
bestrida (5)	*beh*-STREE-*dah*	contest (dispute), to
"	"	contradict (deny), to
besvara (1)	*beh*-SVAW-*rah*	answer (give answer to), to
besvära (1)	*beh*-SVAI-*rah*	bother (annoy), to
"	"	pester, to
"	"	trouble (inconvenience), to
besvärlighet,*nn.* (III)	*beh*-SVAIR-*lig-hayt*	difficulty (hardness)
besvikelse,*nn.* (III)	*beh*-SVEEK-*el-seh*	disappointment
besynnerlig	*beh*-SÜN-*ehr-lig*	queer

Swedish	Pronunciation	English
beta (1)	BAY-*tah*	graze (feed), to
betala (1)	*beh*-TAW-*lah*	pay, to
betalbar	*beh*-TAWL-*bar*	due
"	"	payable
betalning,*nn.* (II)	*beh*-TAWL-*ning*	payment
bete,*n.* (IV)	BAY-*teh*	bait (for animals)
bete sig (3)	*beh*-TAY *say*	act (behave), to
beteckna (1)	*beh*-TECK-*nah*	signify (denote), to
betesmark,*nn.* (III)	BAY-*tes-mahrrk*	pasture (grassland)
betong,*nn.*	*beh*-TONG	concrete (artificial stone)
beträffande	*beh*-TREF-*ahn-deh*	regarding (concerning)
betrakta (1)	*beh*-TRAHCK-*tah*	regard (consider), to
betraktande,*n.*	*beh*-TRAHCK-*tahn-deh*	consideration (thought)
betsel,*n.* (V)	BET-*sell*	bridle (harness)
bett,*n.* (V)	BET	bite
betunga (1)	*beh*-TUHNG-*ah*	oppress (weigh down), to
betvivla (1)	*beh*-TVEEV-*lah*	question (doubt), to
betydelse,*nn.* (III)	*beh*-TÜ-*dell-seh*	meaning
"	"	sense (signification)
"	"	significance (importance)
betydelsefull	*beh*-TÜ-*dell-seh-fuhll*	significant (meaningful)
betydenhet,*nn.*	*beh*-TÜ-*den-hayt*	distinction (eminence)
betydlig	*beh*-TÜ_D-*lig*	considerable (*adj.*)
"	"	substantial (sizable)
betyg,*n.* (V)	*beh*-TÜ_G	grade (academic rating)
beundra (1)	*beh*-UHN-*drah*	admire, to
beundran,*nn.*	*beh*-UHN-*drahn*	admiration
bevaka (1)	*beh*-VAW-*kah*	watch (guard), to
beväpna (1)	*beh*-VAIP-*nah*	arm, to
bevara (1)	*beh*-VAW-*rah*	preserve, to
bevattning,*nn.*	*beh*-VAHT-*ning*	irrigation
bevilja (1)	*beh*-VILL-*yah*	grant (bestow), to
bevis,*n.* (V)	*beh*-VEES	demonstration
"	"	evidence (*law*)
"	"	proof
bevisa (1)	*beh*-VEE-*sah*	establish, to
"	"	prove (verify), to
bevista (1)	*beh*-VISS-*tah*	attend (be present at), to
bi,*n.* (IV)	BEE	bee
bibehålla (10)	BEE-*beh-hohll-ah*	maintain (preserve), to
bibel,*nn.* (II)	BEE-*bell*	Bible
bibliografi,*nn.* (III)	*bib-lee-oo-grah*-FEE	bibliography
bibliotek,*n.* (V)	*bib-lee-oo*-TAYK	library
bibliotekarie,*nn.* (III)	*bib-lee-oo-teh*-KAW-*ree-eh*	librarian
bidrag,*n.* (V)	BEE-*drawg*	contribution
bidra(ga) (9)	BEE-*draw*(-*gah*)	contribute, to
bifoga (1)	BEE-*foo-gah*	enclose (include in envelope), to
biljard,*nn.*	*bill*-YARD	billiards
bikupa,*nn.* (I)	BEE-*kuh-pah*	hive (beehive)
bil,*nn.* (II)	BEEL	car (auto)
bilaga,*nn.* (I)	BEE-*law-gah*	enclosure (addition)
bild,*nn.* (III)	BILLD	picture (depiction)
bildning,*nn.* (II)	BILLD-*ning*	formation (creation)
biljett,*nn.* (III)	*bill*-YET	ticket (entitling card)
billig	BILL-*ig*	cheap (inexpensive)
binda (8)	BIN-*dah*	bind (tie), to
bindestreck,*n.* (V)	BIN-*deh-streck*	hyphen
bio,*nn.*	BEE-*oo*	movies
biografi,*nn.* (III)	*bee-oh-grah*-FEE	biography
biologi,*nn.*	*bee-oh-log*-EE	biology
biprodukt,*nn.* (III)	BEE-*proh*-DUHKT	by-product
biskop,*nn.* (II)	BISS-*kohp*	bishop
bistå (10)	BEE-*stoh*	assist, to
bistånd,*n.*	BEE-*stohnd*	assistance
bit,*nn.* (II)	BEET	scrap (fragment)
bita (5)	BEE-*tah*	bite, to
bitter	BIT-*ehr*	bitter
bjälke,*nn.* (II)	B_YELL-*keh*	beam (rafter)
björk,*nn.* (II)	B_YÖRCK	birch (tree)
björn,*nn.* (II)	B_YÖRN	bear (animal)
björnbär,*n.* (V)	B_YÖRN-*bair*	blackberry
bjuda (6)	B_YU-*dah*	entertain (be host to), to

Swedish	Pronunciation	English
bjudning,*nn.* (II)	B_YU_D-*ning*	party (social gathering)
blå	BLOH	blue
blåbär,*n.* (V)	BLOH-*bair*	blueberry
bläck,*n.*	BLECK	ink
blad,*n.* (V)	BLAWD	blade (cutting tool)
blåkopia,*nn.* (I)	BLOH-*koh*-PEE-*ah*	blueprint
blåmärke,*n.* (IV)	BLOH-*mairr-keh*	bruise
bland	BLAHND	among
blanda (1)	BLAHND-*ah*	blend (make combine), to
"	"	mix (make blend), to
blända (1)	BLEN-*dah*	blind, to
"	"	dazzle, to
blandning,*nn.* (II)	BLAHND-*ning*	blend
"	"	mixture
blank	BLAHNK	blank (unmarked)
blanka (1)	BLAHNK-*ah*	shine (polish), to
blåsa,*nn.* (I)	BLOH-*sah*	bladder (*anat.*)
"	"	blister
blåsa (2)	BLOH-*sah*	blow, to
blåsig	BLOH-*sig*	windy (windswept)
blåst,*nn.*	BLOH_ST	gale (wind)
blek	BLAYK	pale (wan)
bleka (2)	BLAY-*kah*	bleach (make white), to
blekna (1)	BLAYK-*nah*	fade (lose color), to
blick,*nn.* (II)	BLICK	glance (quick look)
"	"	look
blind	BLINND	blind (lacking sight)
blindtarmsinflammation,*nn.* (III)	BLINND-*tahrms-in-flahm-ah*-SHOON	appendicitis
blinka (1)	BLINK-*ah*	wink, to
bli synlig	*blee* SÜ_N-*lig*	appear (come in sight), to
bli(va) (4)	BLEE(-*vah*)	become, to
bli(va) av	BLEE(-*vah*) AWV	become of (happen to), to
bli(va) efter	*blee*(-*vah*)-EF-*tehr*	lag (fall behind), to
bli(va) medlem av	*blee*(-*vah*) MAYD-*lem awv*	join (become a member of), to
blixt,*nn.* (II)	BLIXT	flash (burst of light)
"	"	lightning
blixtlås,*n.* (V)	BLIXT-*loh_s*	zipper
block,*n.* (V)	BLOHCK	block (solid piece)
blod,*n.*	BLOO_D	blood
blöda (2)	BLÖ-*dah*	bleed (lose blood), to
blödning,*nn.* (II)	BLÖ_D-*ning*	hemorrhage
blom,*nn.*	BLOOMM	blossom
blomkål,*nn.*	BLOOMM-*koh_l*	cauliflower
blomma (1)	BLOOMM-*ah*	bloom, to
blomma,*nn.* (I)	BLOOMM-*ah*	flower
blomstra (1)	BLOHM-*strah*	flourish (thrive), to
"	"	prosper, to
blomstrande	BLOHM-*strahn-deh*	prosperous
blond	BLOHND	blond
blöta (2)	BLÖ-*tah*	soak (saturate), to
blunder,*nn.*	BLUHN-*dehr*	blunder
blus,*nn.* (II)	BLUH_S	blouse (shirtwaist)
bly,*n.*	BLÜ	lead (metal)
blyerts,*nn.* (II)	BLÜ-*ehrtsh*	pencil
blyg	BLÜ_G	bashful
"	"	shy
"	"	timid
blygsam	BLÜ_G-*sahm*	modest
bo (3)	BOO	dwell (reside), to
"	"	live, to
"	"	lodge, to
bo,*n.* (IV)	BOO	nest (bird home)
bock,*nn.* (II)	BOHCK	buck (male deer)
bofast person,*nn.* (III)	BOO-*fahst pash*-OON	resident (*n.*)
böja (2)	BÖY-*ah*	bend (make bend), to
böja sig	BÖY-*ah say*	bend (be bent), to
"	"	stoop (bend forward), to
böjelse,*nn.* (III)	BÖY-*el-seh*	bent (penchant)
"	"	inclination (tendency)
bok,*nn.* (II)	BOO_K	beech (tree)
bok,*nn.* (*pl.* böcker)	BOO_K	book

Swedish	Pronunciation	English
bokföra (2)	BOO_K-*för-ah*	enter, to (*acctg.*)
bokföring,*nn.*	BOO_K-*för-ing*	bookkeeping (*bus.*)
bokhållare,*nn.* (V)	BOO_K-*hohll-ah-reh*	bookkeeper (*bus.*)
bokstav,*nn.* (*pl.* -stäver)	BOOK-*stawv*	letter (character)
bolag,*n.* (V)	BOO-*lawg*	company (*bus.*)
"	"	corporation
Bolivia,*n.*	*boh*-LEE-*vih-ah*	Bolivia
boll, *nn.* (II)	BOHLL	ball (sphere)
bomb,*nn.* (III)	BOHM_B	bomb (projectile)
bomull,*nn.*	BOOMM-*uhll*	cotton (boll)
bomullssammet, *nn.*	BOOMM-*uhlls-sahm-et*	velveteen (*n.*)
bomullstyg,*n.* (V)	BOOMM-*uhlls-tü_g*	cotton (fabric)
bön,*nn.* (III)	BÖ_N	prayer (petition)
böna,*nn.* (I)	BÖ-*nah*	bean (string bean)
bonde,*nn.* (*pl.* bönder)	BOOND-*eh*	farmer
"	"	peasant
bondgård,*nn.* (II)	BOOND-*gord*	farm
bönfalla (10)	BÖ_N-*fahll-ah*	beg (entreat), to
bonus,*nn.*	BOH-*nuhss*	bonus (extra wages)
böra (4)	BÖR-*ah*	ought (*v.*)
bord,*n.* (V)	BOORD	table (furniture)
börda,*nn.* (I)	BÖRD-*ah*	burden
"	"	load
bordduk,*nn.* (II)	BOORD-*du_k*	tablecloth
bördig	BÖRD-*ig*	fertile
borgerlig	BOHRR-*yehr-lig*	civil (secular)
borgmästare,*nn.* (V)	BOHRR_*yuh-mess-tah-reh*	mayor
börja (1)	BÖRR-*yah*	begin (come into being), to
"	"	begin (start to do), to
börja (1)	BÖRR-*yah*	commence, to
"	"	start (initiate), to
början,*nn.*	BÖRR-*yahn*	beginning
"	"	start
borra (1)	BOHRR-*ah*	drill (bore), to
börs,*nn.* (III)	BÖSH	exchange, stock
borste,*nn.* (II)	BOHSH-*teh*	brush (scrubbing utensil)
bort	BOHRT	away (from a place, *adv.*)
borta	BOHRT-*ah*	away (absent, *adj.*)
bortom	BOHRT-*ohm*	beyond (out of reach of, *prep.*)
boskap,*nn.*	BOO-*skawp*	cattle
bössa,*nn.* (I)	BÖSS-*ah*	gun
bostad,*nn.* (*pl.* -städer)	BOO-*stawd*	dwelling
"	"	residence (abode)
bot,*nn.*	BOOT	cure (healing)
bota (1)	BOO-*tah*	cure, to
"	"	heal, to
botanik,*nn.*	*boo-tah*-NEEK	botany
botemedel,*n.* (V)	BOO-*teh-may-dell*	cure
"	"	remedy
böter,*nn. pl.*	BÖ-*tehr*	fine (penalty, *n.*)
botten,*nn.* (II)	BOHT-*en*	bottom
bottiner,*nn.pl.*	*boh*-TEEN-*ehr*	galoshes
boxas (1)	BOOK-*sahs*	box (fight), to
boyscout,*nn.* (III)	BOY-*scout*	Boy Scout
bra	BRAW	good
"	"	well (commendably, *adv.*)
bräcklig	BRECK-*lig*	frail (fragile)
bräde,*n.* (III)	BRAI-*deh*	board (plank)
brådska,*nn.*	BROHSS-*kah*	haste
"	"	hurry
brak,*n.* (V)	BRAWK	crash (loud noise)
bräka (2)	BRAI-*kah*	bleat, to
bråkdel,*nn.* (II)	BROH_K-*dayl*	fraction (part)
brandförsäkring, *nn.* (II)	BRAHND-*fö*-SHAIK-*ring*	fire insurance
brandsoldat,*nn.* (III)	BRAHND-*sohll*-DAWT	fireman
bränna (2)	BREN-*ah*	burn (set fire to), to
bränsle,*n.* (IV)	BRENS-*leh*	fuel
brant	BRAHNT	steep (*adj.*)
brant,*nn.* (III)	BRAHNT	precipice
brasiliansk	*brah-sill-ee*-AWNSK	Brazilian (*adj.*)

Swedish	Pronunciation	English
Brasilien,*n.*	*brah-*SEEL*-ee-en*	Brazil
bred	BRAYD	broad
"	"	wide (of specified width)
bredd,*nn.* (III)	BRED	breadth
"	"	width
bredvid	*bred-*VEED	beside (next to, *prep.*)
brev,*n.* (V)	BRAYV	letter (epistle)
brevbärare,*nn.* (V)	BRAYV-*bair-ah-reh*	postman
brevkort,*n.* (V)	BRAYV-*koort*	card, postal
brevväxla med (1)	BRAYV-*vex-lah mayd*	correspond with (write to), to
brevväxling,*nn.*	BRAYV-*vex-ling*	correspondence (letters)
bricka,*nn.* (I)	BRICK-*ah*	tray
briljant	*brill-*YAHNT	brilliant (remarkable)
brinna (8)	BRIN-*ah*	burn (be on fire), to
bris,*nn.* (II, III)	BREES	breeze
brist,*nn.* (III)	BRIST	defect (flaw)
"	"	lack (deficiency)
"	"	shortage
"	"	want
brista (8)	BRISS-*tah*	burst, to
bristfällig	BRIST-*fell-ig*	imperfect (defective)
brittisk	BRIT-*isk*	British (*adj.*)
bro,*nn.* (II)	BROO	bridge (span)
bröd,*n.* (V)	BRÖD	bread
bro(de)r,*nn.* (*pl.* bröder)	BROO(*-deh*)R	brother
brokig	BROOK-*ig*	motley (diverse)
bröllop,*n.* (V)	BRÖLL-*lohp*	wedding
broms,*nn.* (II)	BROHMS	brake
bronkit,*nn.* (III)	*brohng-*KEET	bronchitis
brons,*nn.*	BROHNS	bronze (*n.*)
brorsdotter,*nn.* (*pl.* döttrar)	BROOSH-*doht-ehr*	niece (brother's daughter)
brorson,*nn.* (*pl.* -söner)	BROO-*shoh_n*	nephew (brother's son)
brosch,*nn.* (III)	BROHSH	brooch
broschyr,*nn.* (III)	*broo-*SHÜR	booklet
bröst,*n.* (V)	BRÖST	breast
brösthållare,*nn.* (V)	BRÖST-*hohll-ah-reh*	brassiere
bröstkorg,*nn.* (II)	BRÖST-*kohr_yuh*	chest (*anat.*)
brott,*n.* (V)	BROHT	crime
"	"	fracture (*med.*)
brottas (1)	BROHT-*ahs*	wrestle, to
brottslig	BROHTS-*lig*	criminal (*adj.*)
brottsling,*nn.* (II)	BROHTS-*ling*	criminal (*n.*)
brud,*nn.* (II)	BRUD	bride
brudgum,*nn.* (II)	BRUD-*guhm*	groom (bridegroom)
bruk,*n.* (V)	BRUK	practice (custom)
brun	BRUN	brown
brunett	*bru-*NET	brunette (*adj.*)
brunn,*nn.* (II)	BRUHN	well (water pit, *n.*)
brutto	BRUHT-*oh*	gross (before deductions, *adj.*)
bryderi,*n.* (III)	*brü-deh-*REE	quandary
bry sig om (3)	*brü-say-*OHM	care (be concerned), to
"	"	heed (mind), to
Bryssel,*n.*	BRÜSS-*el*	Brussels
bryta (6)	BRÜ-*tah*	break (make divide), to
brytning,*nn.* (II)	BRÜ_T-*ning*	accent (speech)
bubbla (1)	BUHB-*lah*	bubble, to
bud,*n.* (V)	BUH_D	messenger (courier)
budget,*nn.* (III)	BUHD-*yet*	budget (*n.*)
Buenos Aires,*n.*	*buh-*AY*-nohs* I*-res*	Buenos Aires
buffel,*nn.* (II)	BUHFF-*el*	buffalo
buga (sig) (1)	BUH-*gah* (*say*)	bow (in greeting), to
bugning,*nn.* (II)	BUH_G-*ning*	bow (nod)
buk,*nn.* (II)	BUH_K	abdomen
"	"	belly
Bulgarien,*n.*	*buhll-*GAW*-ree-en*	Bulgaria
bulle,*nn.* (II)	BUHLL-*eh*	roll (bread)
bullersam	BUHLL-*eh-shahm*	noisy
bult,*nn.* (II)	BUHLLT	bolt (long metal fastener)
bundsförvant,*nn.* (III)	BUHNDS-*för-vahnt*	ally

Swedish	Pronunciation	English
bur,*nn.* (II)	BUH_R	cage
burk,*nn.* (II)	BUHRRK	jar (vessel)
(konserv)burk,*nn.*	(*kohn-*SEHRV*-*)BUHRRK	can (tin)
buske,*nn.* (II)	BUHSS-*keh*	bush (plant)
"	"	shrub
buss,*nn.* (II)	BUHSS	bus
butik,*nn.* (III)	*buh-*TEEK	shop
"	"	store
by,*nn.* (II)	BÜ	village
bygga (2)	BÜG-*ah*	build, to
"	"	construct, to
byggnad,*nn.* (III)	BÜG-*nahd*	building
byggnad,*nn.*	BÜG-*nahd*	structure (thing built)
byrå,*nn.* (II)	BÜH-*roh*	bureau (chest)
byrå,*nn.* (III)	BÜH-*roh*	bureau (office)
byst,*nn.* (III)	BÜST	bust (statue)
byte,*n.* (IV)	BÜ-*teh*	prey (victim)
byxor,*nn.pl.*	BÜX-*oor*	trousers
ceder,*nn.* (II)	SAY-*dehr*	cedar (tree)
cell,*nn.* (III)	SELL	cell (*biol.*)
cello,*nn.* (*pl.* celli)	SELL-*oo*	cello
cement,*nn.*	*seh-*MENT	cement
central	*sen-*TRAWL	central
centrum,*n.* (*pl.* -tra)	SENT-*ruhm*	center
ceremoni,*nn.* (III)	*seh-reh-moh-*NEE	ceremony
charm,*nn.*	SHAHRRM	charm (attraction)
check,*nn.* (III)	CHECK	check (bank check)
chef,*nn.* (III)	SHAIF	boss (master)
"	"	head (leader)
"	"	manager (administrator)
Chile,*n.*	CHEE-*leh*	Chile
chilensk	*chee-*LAYNSK	Chilean (*adj.*)
chock,*nn.* (III)	SHOHCK	shock (mental jolt)
chockera (1)	*shoh-*KAY*-rah*	shock (jar), to
choklad,*nn.*	*shook-*LAWD	chocolate
ciceron,*nn.* (III)	*siss-eh-*ROON	guide (one who guides)
cigarett,*nn.* (III)	*sig-ah-*RET	cigarette
cigarr,*nn.* (III)	*sig-*AHRR	cigar
cirkel,*nn.* (II)	*seer-*KELL	circle (*geom.*)
cirkelrund	SEER-*kell-ruhnd*	circular (*adj.*)
cirkulär,*n.* (V)	*seer-kuh-*LAIR	circular (letter or brochure, *bus.*)
cirkus,*nn.* (II)	SEER-*kuhss*	circus
citat,*n.* (V)	*sit-*TAWT	quotation (selection)
citera (1)	*sit-*TAY*-rah*	quote (cite), to
citron,*nn.* (III)	*sit-*TROON	lemon
civilisation,*nn.*	*siv-ill-iss-ah-*SHOON	civilization (civilized condition)
cocktail,*nn.* (II)	KOHCK-*tail*	cocktail
Columbia,*n.*	*koh-*LUHM*-bee-ah*	Colombia
Costa Rica,*n.*	*kohss-tah* REE*-kah*	Costa Rica
Cuba,*n.*	KUH-*bah*	Cuba
cykel,*nn.* (II)	SÜCK-*el*	bicycle
cylinder,*nn.* (II)	*süh-*LIN*-dehr*	cylinder (*geom.*)
då	DOH	then (at that time)
"	"	then (in that case)
däck,*n.* (V)	DECK	deck (of ship)
"	"	tire
dadel,*nn.* (II)	DAHD-*el*	date (fruit)
dag, i	*ee-*DAWG	today
dag,*nn.* (II)	DAWG	day (daytime)
dagg,*nn.*	DAHGG	dew
daglig	DAWG-*lig*	daily (*adj.*)
dagsljus,*n.*	DAHX-*yu_s*	daylight
dal,*nn.* (II)	DAWL	valley
dålig	DOH-*lig*	bad
dålig matsmältning,*nn.*	DOH-*lig* MAWT*-smelt-ning*	indigestion
dam,*nn.* (III)	DAWM	lady
damm,*n.*	DAHMM	dust
damm,*nn.* (II)	DAHMM	dam (dike)
"	"	pond
dammig	DAHMM-*ig*	dusty
dammsugare,*nn.* (V)	DAHMM-*su-gah-reh*	vacuum cleaner
dån,*n.*	DOH_N	din
Danmark,*n.*	DAHNN-*mahrk*	Denmark
dans,*nn.* (III)	DAHNS	dance (movement to music)
dansa (1)	DAHNN-*sah*	dance, to
dansk	DAHNSK	Danish (*adj.*)

Swedish	Pronunciation	English
danstillställning, *nn.* (II)	DAHNS-*till-stell-ning*	dance (party)
där	DAIR	there (at that place)
"	"	where (in, at the place that)
därefter	DAIR-*ef-tehr*	thereafter
därför	DAIR-*för*	therefore
därigenom	DAIR-*ee*-YAY-*nohm*	thereby
därinne	*dair*-IN-*eh*	within (on the inside, *adv.*)
därom	*dair*-OHM	thereof
darra (1)	DAHRR-*ah*	shiver (quake), to tremble, to
"	"	
dårskap,*nn.* (III)	DOH-*shkawp*	folly
däruppe	*dair*-UHP-*eh*	above (overhead, *adv.*)
"	"	upstairs (at upper story, *adv.*)
datum,*n.* (*pl.* data)	DAW-*tuhm*	date (calendar designation)
de	DAY	the
"	"	they
debatt,*nn.* (III)	*deh*-BAHT	debate
debitera (1)	*deh-bit*-TAY-*rah*	charge, to
"	"	debit, to
de där	*day*-DAIR	those (*dem. adj., dem. pron.*)
definiera (1)	*deh-fin-ee*-AYR-*ah*	define, to
de här	*day*-HAIR	these (*dem. adj., dem. pron.*)
dekoration,*nn.* (III)	*deh-koh-rah*-SHOON	decoration (ornament)
dekorera (1)	*deh-koh*-RAY-*rah*	trim (decorate), to
dekorering,*nn.*	*deh-koh*-RAY-*ring*	decoration (décor)
del,*nn.* (II)	DAYL	part
"	"	portion
"	"	proportion
"	"	section
"	"	share
dela (1)	DAY-*lah*	divide (make separate), to
"	"	share, to
dela sig	DAY-*lah say*	divide (become separate), to
delägare,*nn.* (V)	DAYL-*ai-gah-reh*	co-owner (*bus.*)
delägarskap,*n.* (V)	DAYL-*ai-gah-shkawp*	copartnership (*bus.*)
delikat	*deh-lick*-KAWT	delicate (dainty)
delta(ga) (9)	DAYL-*taw(-gah)*	participate, to
deltagande,*n.*	DAYL-*taw-gahn-deh*	sympathy (compassion)
delvis	DAYL-*vees*	partly
dem	DEM	them
demokrat,*nn.* (III)	*deh-moo*-KRAWT	democrat
demokrati,*nn.* (III)	*deh-moo-krah*-TEE	democracy
demokratisk	*deh-moo*-KRAW-*tisk*	democratic
demonstrera (1)	*deh-mohn*-STRAY-*rah*	demonstrate (show), to
den	DEN	it
"	"	the
den där	*den* DAIR	that (*dem. adj., dem. pron.*)
den här	*den* HAIR	this (*dem. pron.*)
denna	DEN-*ah*	that (*dem. adj., dem. pron.*)
"	"	this (*dem. adj., dem. pron.*)
depression,*nn.* (III)	*deh-preh*-SHOON	depression (*econ.*)
deras	DAY-*rahs*	their
"	"	theirs
dess	DESS	its (*poss. adj.*)
dessa	DESS-*ah*	these (*dem. adj., dem. pron.*)
"	"	those (*dem. adj., dem. pron.*)
dessutom	*dess*-UH_T-*ohm*	besides (*adv.*)
"	"	moreover
det	DEH(T)	it
det	DEH(T)	the
detalj,*nn.* (III)	*deh*-TAHLL_*yuh*	detail (minor item)
"	"	particular
detaljhandel,*nn.*	*deh*-TAHLL_*yuh-hahn-dell*	retail (*bus., n.*)
detaljhandlare,*nn.* (V)	*deh*-TAHLL_*yuh-hahnd-lah-reh*	retailer (*bus.*)

Swedish	Pronunciation	English
detta	DET-*ah*	that (*dem. adj., dem. pron.*)
"	"	this (*dem. adj., dem. pron.*)
diagram,*n.* (V)	*dee-ah*-GRAHM	graph
diamant,*nn.* (III)	*dee-ah*-MAHNT	diamond (gem)
diameter,*nn.* (II)	*dee-ah*-MAY-*tehr*	diameter
diet,*nn.*	*dee*-AYT	diet (restricted food allowance)
difteri,*nn.*	*dif-teh*-REE	diphtheria
dig	DAY	you (*informal*)
"	"	yourself
dike,*n.* (IV)	DEE-*keh*	ditch
dikt,*nn.* (III)	DICKT	poem
diktare,*nn.* (V)	DICK-*tah-reh*	poet
diktera (1)	*dick*-TAY-*rah*	dictate, to
dimma,*nn.* (I)	DIM-*ah*	fog
"	"	mist
din, ditt, dina	DIN, DIT, DEE-*nah*	your (*informal*)
"	"	yours
direkt	*dee*-RECKT	straight (directly, *adv.*)
dirigent,*nn.* (III)	*dee-rig*-ENT	conductor (*mus.*)
disk,*nn.* (II)	DISK	counter (table)
diskussion,*nn.* (III)	*diss-kuh*-SHOON	discussion
diskutera (1)	*diss-kuh*-TAY-*rah*	discuss, to
disputera (1)	*diss-puh*-TAY-*rah*	dispute (oppose by argument), to
dispyt,*nn.* (III)	*dis*-PÜ_T	argument
"	"	dispute
distrahera (1)	*diss-trah*-HAY-*rah*	distract (divert), to
distribution,*nn.* (III)	*diss-trib-uh*-SHOON	distribution (*bus.*)
distrikt,*n.* (V)	*diss*-STRICKT	district (locality)
diverse	*dee*-VASH-*eh*	miscellaneous
dividend,*nn.* (III)	*dee-vee*-DEND	dividend (*bus.*)
dividera (1)	*dih-vih*-DAY-*rah*	divide, to (*arith.*)
division,*nn.* (III)	*dee-vee*-SHOON	division (*mil.*)
djärv	YAIRRV	bold (courageous)
djävul,*nn.* (II)	YAI-*vuhll*	devil
djup	YU_P	deep (in color)
"	"	deep (in extent)
"	"	deep (in tone)
"	"	profound
djup,*n.* (V)	YU_P	depth (deepness)
djur,*n.* (V)	YU_R	animal
djur (fyrfota),*n.* (V)	YU_R (FÜ_R-*foo_t-ah*)	beast
djurpark,*nn.* (III)	YU_R-*pahrrk*	zoo
dö (10)	DÖ	die, to
docka,*nn.* (I)	DOHCK-*ah*	dock
"	"	doll
död	DÖ_D	dead
död,*nn.*	DÖ_D	death
döda (1)	DÖ-*dah*	kill, to
dödlig	DÖ_D-*lig*	deadly
"	"	fatal
"	"	mortal (*adj.*)
dödsnotis,*nn.* (III)	DÖTS-*noh*-TEES	obituary (*n.*)
doft,*nn.* (III)	DOHFT	scent (odor)
doktor,*nn.* (III)	DOHCK-*tor*	doctor
dokument,*n.* (V)	*doh-kuh*-MENT	document
dölja (11)	DÖLL-*yah*	conceal, to
dolk,*nn.* (II)	DOHLL_K	dagger
dom,*nn.* (II)	DOOMM	judgment (*law*)
döma (2)	DÖM-*ah*	doom (condemn), to
"	"	judge, to
"	"	sentence, to
domän,*nn.* (III)	*doh*-MAIN	realm (field)
domare,*nn.* (V)	DOOMM-*ah-reh*	judge
Dominikanska republiken,*nn.*	*doh-mih-nih*-KAWN-*skah reh-puhb*-LEEK-*en*	Dominican Republic
domkyrka,*nn.* (I)	DOOMM-*chür-kah*	cathedral
domnad	DOHMM-*nahd*	numb
domstol,*nn.* (II)	DOOMM-*stool*	court (of law)
Donau,*nn.*	DOH-*now*	Danube
dop,*n.* (V)	DOOP	baptism
doppa (1)	DOHP-*ah*	dip (immerse), to
dörr,*nn.* (II)	DÖRR	door
dörrklinka,*nn.* (I)	DÖRR-*klink-ah*	latch

Swedish	Pronunciation	English
dos,*nn.* (III)	DOO_S	dose (*med.*)
dossier,*nn.* (III)	dohss-YAY	file (collection of papers)
dotter,*nn.* (*pl.* döttrar)	DOHT-*ehr*	daughter
dotterdotter,*nn.* (*pl.* -döttrar)	DOHT-*ehr-doht-ehr*	granddaughter
dotterson,*nn.* (*pl.* -söner)	DOHT-*eh-shoh_n*	grandson
döv	DÖ_V	deaf
drag,*n.*	DRAWG	draft (air current)
dra(ga) (9)	DRAW(-*gah*)	draw, to
"	"	pull, to
		tug (drag), to
dra(ga) sig tillbaka	draw(-*gah*)-say-till-BAW-kah	retire (stop working), to
"	"	withdraw (depart), to
dragspel,*n.* (V)	DRAWG-*spayl*	accordion
drake,*nn.* (II)	DRAW-*keh*	dragon
(pappers)drake,*nn.* (II)	(PAHP-*esh*-)DRAW-keh	kite
dräkt,*nn.* (III)	DREKT	gown (dress)
"	"	suit, woman's
drama,*n.* (III)	DRAW-*mah*	drama
dränka (2)	DRENK-*ah*	drown (kill by drowning), to
dricka (8)	DRICK-*ah*	drink, to
dricks,*nn.*	DRIX	tip (gratuity)
dricksglas,*n.* (V)	DRIX-*glaws*	tumbler (glass)
driftskostnader,*nn. pl.*	DRIFTS-*kohst-nah-dehr*	operating expenses (*bus.*)
driva (5)	DREE-*vah*	drift (float), to
"	"	drive (propel), to
drog,*nn.* (III)	DROH_G	drug (medicine)
dröja (2)	DRÖY-*ah*	linger (tarry), to
dröjsmål,*n.* (V)	DRÖYS-*moh_l*	delay
dröm,*nn.* (II)	DRÖM	dream
drömma (2)	DRÖM-*ah*	dream, to
droppa (1)	DROHP-*ah*	drip, to
droppe,*nn.* (II)	DROHP-*eh*	drop (droplet)
drottning,*nn.* (II)	DROHT-*ning*	queen
drucken	DRUHCK-*en*	drunk (intoxicated)
drunkna (1)	DRUHNK-*nah*	drown (die by drowning), to
dryck,*nn.* (III)	DRÜCK	drink (beverage)
du	DU	you (informal)
dubbel	DUHB-*el*	double (*adj.*)
duglig	DUH_G-*lig*	able
"	"	capable
"	"	competent
"	"	efficient
duk,*nn.* (II)	DUH_K	screen (for movies)
duka under (1)	duh-kah UHN-*dehr*	succumb (yield), to
duktig	DUHCK-*tig*	smart (clever)
dum	DUHM	dumb
"	"	foolish
dum	DUHM	stupid
dumheter,*nn. pl.*	DUHM-*hay-tehr*	nonsense
dunge,*nn.* (II)	DUHNG-*eh*	grove (small woods)
dunkel	DUHNK-*el*	obscure (unclear)
dunst,*nn.*	DUHNST	vapor
dusch,*nn.* (II)	DUHSH	shower (bath)
dussin,*n.* (V)	DUHSS-*in*	dozen
duva,*nn.* (I)	DU-*vah*	dove
"	"	pigeon
dvärg,*nn.* (II)	DVAIR_*yuh*	dwarf
dygd,*nn.* (III)	DÜGD	virtue (moral excellence)
dygn,*n.* (V)	DÜNGN	day (24-hour period)
dyka (2, 10)	DÜ-*kah*	dive, to
dyka upp	dü-kah-UHP	emerge, to
dyna,*nn.* (I)	DÜ-*nah*	cushion (pillow)
"	"	pad
dyr	DÜR	expensive
dyrbar	DÜR-*bar*	costly
"	"	precious
dyrka (1)	DÜRR-*kah*	worship, to (*rel.*)
dyrkan,*nn.*	DÜRR-*kahn*	worship (*rel.*)
dysenteri,*nn.*	dü-sen-teh-REE	dysentery
dyster	DÜSS-*tehr*	dismal
"	"	dreary
"	"	gloomy (melancholy)
dysterhet,*nn.*	DÜSS-*tehr-hayt*	gloom (depression)

Swedish	Pronunciation	English
ebb,*nn.*	EBB	tide, low
Ecuador,*n.*	eck-vah-DOHR	Ecuador
ed,*nn.* (III)	AYD	oath (vow)
Edinburgh,*n.*	ED-*in-börr-oh*	Edinburgh
effektiv	eh-feck-TEEV	efficient (producing desired results)
efter	EF-*tehr*	after (*prep.*)
"	"	behind (late, *adv.*)
efteråt	EF-*tehr-oh_t*	afterward (later)
efterfrågan,*nn.*	EF-*ter-froh-gahn*	demand (*econ.*)
eftermiddag,*nn.* (II)	EF-*tehr-mid-dawg*	afternoon
efterrätt,*nn.* (III)	EF-*tehr-ret*	dessert
eftertanke,*nn.*	EF-*tehr-tahnk-eh*	reflection (meditation)
egen	AYG-*en*	own (*adj.*)
egendom,*nn.* (II)	AYG-*en-doomm*	estate (total possessions)
"	"	property (possession)
egendomlig	AYG-*en-doomm-lig*	peculiar (odd)
egenskap,*nn.* (III)	AYG-*en-skawp*	attribute (characteristic)
"	"	feature (attribute)
"	"	quality
egg,*nn.* (II)	EGG	edge (sharp side)
Egypten,*n.*	eh-YÜP-*ten*	Egypt
egyptisk	eh-YÜP-*tisk*	Egyptian (*adj.*)
ehuru	eh-HU-*ru*	although .
ek,*nn.* (II)	AYK	oak
eko,*n.* (IV)	AYK-*oo*	echo
ekollon,*n.* (V)	AYK-*ohll-ohn*	acorn
ekorre,*nn.* (II)	ECK-*orr-eh*	squirrel
elak	AYL-*ahck*	mean (malicious)
elastisk	eh-LAHSS-*tisk*	elastic (springy)
eld,*nn.* (II)	ELD	fire
eldstad,*nn.* (*pl.* -städer)	ELD-*stawd*	fireplace
elefant,*nn.* (III)	eh-leh-FAHNT	elephant
elektricitet,*nn.*	eh-leck-triss-ee-TAYT	electricity
elektrisk	eh-LECK-*trisk*	electric
elektrisk rakapparat,*nn.* (III)	eh-LECK-*trisk* RAWK-*ah-pah*-RAWT	electric shaver
elektronik,*nn.*	eh-leck-troh-NEEK	electronics
element, *n.* (V)	eh-leh-MENT	element
elementär	eh-leh-men-TAIR	elementary (rudimentary)
elev,*nn.* (III)	eh-LAYV	pupil (student)
elfenben,*n.*	ELL-*fen-bayn*	ivory
eliminera (1)	eh-lim-ee-NAY-*rah*	eliminate, to
eller	ELL-*ehr*	nor
"	"	or
emedan	eh-MAY-*dahn*	because (*conj.*)
"	"	since (*conj.*)
emellanåt	eh-MELL-*ahn-oh_t*	occasionally
emellertid	eh-mel-ehr-TEED	however (nevertheless)
emot	eh-MOOT	against
en (*obj.*)	EN	you (*indef.*)
en, ett	EN, ET	a (an)
enda	EN-*dah*	only
"	"	single
"	"	sole
en del	en DAYL	some (certain, *adj.*)
endera	EN-*day-rah*	either (one or the other, *adj.*)
endossera (1)	ahng-doh-SAY-*rah*	endorse (sign), to
energi,*nn.*	eh-nehr-SHEE	energy
enformig	AYN-*fohrm-ig*	monotonous (boring)
engelsk	ENG-*elsk*	English (*adj.*)
England,*n.*	ENG-*lahnd*	England
enhetlig	AYN-*hayt-lig*	uniform (*adj.*)
enighet,*nn.*	AYN-*ig-hayt*	agreement (mutual understanding)
"	"	unity (accord)
enkel	ENK-*el*	simple (uninvolved)
enkelhet,*nn.*	ENK-*el-hayt*	simplicity
enligt	AYN-*lickt*	according to (in accordance with)
ens	ENS	your (*indef.*)
ensam	EN-*sahm*	alone
"	"	'lone
"	"	lonesome
"	"	solitary (unaccompanied)
ensamhet,*nn.*	EN-*sahm-hayt*	solitude

Swedish	Pronunciation	English
enslig	AYNS-*lig*	lonely
en stund	*en* STUHND	awhile (*adv.*)
en till	EN TILL	another (one more, *pron.*)
entusiasm,*nn.*	*ahng-tu-see*-AHSSM	enthusiasm
envis	EN-*vees*	stubborn
epidemi,*nn.* (III)	*eh-pid-deh*-MEE	epidemic
er	AYR	yourself
"	"	yourselves
er, ert, era	AYR, AYRT, AYR-*ah*	you
"	"	your
"	"	yours
erbjuda (6)	AIR-*b_yu-dah*	offer (tender), to
erfaren	AIR-*far-en*	veteran (experienced)
erfarenhet,*nn.*	AIR-*far-en-hayt*	experience (skill)
erhålla (10)	AIR-*hohll-ah*	derive (get), to
"	"	obtain, to
erinra sig (1)	AIR-*in-rah say*	recall (remember), to
erkänna (2)	AIR-*chen-ah*	confess (admit), to
"	"	acknowledge, to
erkänna mottagandet av	AIR-*chen-ah* MOOT-*tawg-ahn-det awv*	acknowledge (note receipt of), to
erkännande,*n.* (IV)	AIR-*chen-ah*	recognition (acknowledgment)
ersätta (11)	AIR-*shet-ah*	reimburse, to
"	"	replace (be a substitute for), to
ersättning,*nn.* (II)	AI-*shet-ning*	compensation (*bus.*)
eskort,*nn.* (III)	*eh*-SKOHRT	escort (social companion)
etikett,*nn.* (III)	*eh-tee*-KET	etiquette
"	"	label
Europa,*n.*	*eh-uh*-ROO-*pah*	Europe
europeisk	*eh-uh-roo*-PAY-*isk*	European (*adj.*)
evig	AYV-*ig*	eternal
exakt	*eck*-SAHKT	exact (precise)
exempel,*n.* (V)	*eck*-SEM-*pel*	example
"	"	instance
exemplar,*n.* (V)	*eck-sem*-PLAR	copy (of a publication)
existera (1)	*eck-siss*-TAY-*rah*	exist, to
expedition,*nn.* (III)	*eck-speh-dee*-SHOON	expedition (journey)
experiment,*n.* (V)	*eck-speh-ree*-MENT	experiment
expert,*nn.* (III)	*eck*-SPAIRT	expert (*n.*)
export,*nn.*	*eck*-SPOHRT	exportation
exportera (1)	*eck-spohrt*-TAY-*rah*	export, to
exportör,*nn.* (III)	*eck-spohrt*-TÖR	exporter
extra	ECK-*strah*	extra (additional)
få	FOH	few (not many, *adj.*)
få (10)	FOH	get (obtain), to
fabel,*nn.* (III)	FAW-*bell*	fable
fabrik,*nn.* (III)	*fah*-BREEK	factory
"	"	plant
fabrikant,*nn.* (III)	*fah-brick*-KAHNT	manufacturer
fackförening,*nn.* (II)	FAHCK-*för-ayn-ing*	union (trade union)
fackla,*nn.* (I)	FAHCK-*lah*	torch
fa(de)r,*nn.* (*pl.* fäder)	FAH(-*deh*)R	father
fåfäng	FOH-*feng*	vain (conceited)
fåfänga,*nn.*	FOH-*feng-ah*	vanity (self-conceit)
fågel,*nn.* (II)	FOH_G-*el*	bird
"	"	fowl (poultry)
faktor,*nn.* (III)	FAHCK-*tor*	factor (element)
faktum,*n.* (*pl.* fakta)	FAHCK-*tuhm*	fact
faktura,*nn.* (I)	*fahck*-TU-*rah*	invoice
fall,*n.* (V)	FAHLL	case (instance)
"	"	drop
"	"	fall
fåll,*nn.* (II)	FOHLL	hem
falla (10)	FAHLL-*ah*	drop, to
"	"	fall, to
fälla (2)	FELL-*ah*	shed (cast off), to
fälla,*nn.* (I)	FELL-*ah*	trap (snare)
fallskärm,*nn.* (II)	FAHLL-*shairm*	parachute
falsk	FAHLSK	counterfeit (*adj.*)
"	"	false (deceitful)
fält,*n.* (V)	FELT	field (cleared land)
fälttåg,*n.* (V)	FELT-*toh_g*	campaign (*mil.*)
familj,*nn.* (III)	*fah*-MILL_*yuh*	family
fana,*nn.* (I)	FAW-*nah*	banner

Swedish	Pronunciation	English
fånga (1)	FOHNG-*ah*	catch (nab), to
fånge,*nn.* (II)	FOHNG-*eh*	captive
"	"	prisoner
fängelse,*n.* (III)	FENG-*el-seh*	jail
"	"	prison
fånig	FOH-*nig*	silly
fänrik,*nn.* (II)	FAN-*rick*	ensign
fantasi,*nn.* (III)	*fahn-tah*-SEE	fancy (fantasy)
"	"	imagination
får,*n.* (V)	FOR	sheep
fara,*nn.* (I)	FAR-*ah*	danger
"	"	peril
fåra,*nn.* (I)	FOH-*rah*	furrow (*agric.*)
fara (9)	FAR-*ah*	go (ride), to
farbro(de)r,*nn.* (*pl.* -bröder)	FAHRR-*broo*(-*deh*)*r*	uncle (paternal)
färdas över (1)	FAIRD-*ahs* ö-*vehr*	cross (traverse), to
färdig	FAIRD-*ig*	ready (prepared)
farfa(de)r,*nn.* (*pl.* -fäder)	FAHRR-*fah*(-*deh*)*r*	grandfather (paternal)
färg,*nn.* (III)	FAIRR_*yuh*	color
"	"	paint
färga (1)	FAIRR-*yah*	dye, to
färgkrita,*nn.* (I)	*fairr_yuh-kree-tah*	crayon
färgton,*nn.* (III)	FAIRR_*yuh-toon*	hue
färja,*nn.* (I)	FAIRR-*yah*	ferry (boat)
fårkött,*n.*	FOR-*chöt*	mutton
farlig	FAR-*lig*	dangerous
farmaceut,*nn.* (III)	*fahr-mah*-SEVT	pharmacist
farmo(de)r,*nn.* (*pl.* -mödrar)	FAHRR-*moo*(-*deh*)*r*	grandmother (paternal)
färsk	FESHK	fresh (not stale)
fart,*nn.* (III)	FART	pace (rate)
"	"	speed (rapidity)
fartyg,*n.* (V)	FAR-*tü_g*	craft
"	"	vessel (ship)
farväl,*n.* (V)	*fahrr*-VAIL	farewell (leave-taking)
fascism,*nn.*	*fah*-SHISM	fascism
fast	FAHSST	fast
"	"	firm (*adj.*)
fast(än)	FAHSST (-*en*)	though (*conj.*)
fästa (2)	FESS-*tah*	attach (join), to
"	"	fasten, to
fastan,*nn. def.*	FAHSS-*tahn*	Lent
faster,*nn.* (II)	FAHSS-*tehr*	aunt (paternal)
fastighet,*nn.* (III)	FAHSS-*tig-hayt*	real estate
fästning,*nn.* (II)	FEST-*ning*	fortress
fastslå (10)	FAHSST-*sloh*	determine (ascertain), to
fat,*n.* (V)	FAWT	barrel (cask)
fatta (1)	FAHT-*ah*	grasp (grip), to
"	"	grasp (understand), to
"	"	seize (clutch), to
fattig	FAHT-*ig*	poor (needy)
fattigdom,*nn.*	FAHT-*ig-doomm*	poverty
få veta	*foh*-VAY-*tah*	learn (find out), to
favorit-...	*fah-voo*-REET-...	favorite (*adj.*)
fe,*nn.* (III)	FAY	fairy (*n.*)
feber,*nn.* (II)	FAY-*behr*	fever
federal	*feh-deh*-RAWL	federal
feg stackare,*nn.* (V)	FAYG STAHCK-*ah-reh*	coward
fel,*n.* (V)	FAYL	error
"	"	fault (cause for blame)
felaktig	FAYL-*ahck-tig*	inaccurate
"	"	false (erroneous)
"	"	wrong (*adj.*)
feminin	FAY-*min-een*	feminine
fernissa,*nn.* (I)	*fair*-NISS-*ah*	varnish
fest,*nn.* (III)	FEST	festival
fet	FAYT	fat (obese, *adj.*)
fetlagd	FAYT-*lahgd*	stout (corpulent)
fett,*n.*	FET	fat (fatty tissue, *n.*)
fett,*n.* (III)	FET	grease (melted fat)
ficka,*nn.* (I)	FICK-*ah*	pocket
ficklampa,*nn.* (I)	FICK-*lahm-pah*	flashlight
fiende,*nn.* (III)	FEE-*en-deh*	enemy
"	"	foe
fientlig	*fee*-ENT-*lig*	hostile
figur,*nn.* (III)	*fig*-GUH_R	figure (human form)
fikon,*n.* (V)	FEE-*kohn*	fig

Swedish	Pronunciation	English
fil,*nn.* (II)	FEEL	file (tool)
Filippinerna (*def. pl.*)	FIH-*lih*-PEE-*nehr-nah*	Philippines
film,*nn.* (III)	FILM	film (*photog.*)
filosofi,*nn.* (III)	*fill-oh-soh*-FEE	philosophy
filt,*nn.* (II)	FILT	blanket
"	"	felt (*n.*)
fin	FEEN	fine (good)
"	"	fine (very small)
fin	FEEN	fancy (ornamental, *adj.*)
finansdepartement, *n.* (V)	*fin*-AHNGS-*deh-pahrt-eh*-MENT	treasury (*govt.*)
finanser,*nn. pl.*	*fin*-AHNG-*sehr*	finances
finansiell	*fin-ahng-see*-ELL	financial
finger,*nn.,n.* (II)	FING-*ehr*	finger
Finland,*n.*	FIN-*lahnd*	Finland
finna (8)	FIN-*ah*	find (discover), to
"	"	locate, to
finsk	FINSK	Finnish (*adj.*)
fiol,*nn.* (III)	*fee*-OOL	violin
fira (1)	FEE-*rah*	celebrate, to
firma,*nn.* (I)	FIHRR-*mah*	firm (business company)
fisk,*nn.* (II)	FISK	fish
fiska (1)	FISS-*kah*	fish, to
fiskare,*nn.* (V)	FISS-*kah-reh*	fisherman
fjäder,*nn.* (II)	F_YAI-*dehr*	feather
"	"	spring (coil)
fjäderfä,*n.* (IV)	F_YAI-*dehr-fai*	poultry
fjärdedel,*nn.* (II)	F_YAIRD-*eh-dayl*	quarter (one-fourth)
fjäril,*nn.* (II)	F_YAIR-*il*	butterfly
fjärran	F_YAIRR-*ahn*	far (distant, *adj.*)
fjäsk,*n.*	F_YESK	fuss (ado)
fläck,*nn.* (II)	FLECK	blot
"	"	spot
"	"	stain
fläcka ner (1)	*fleck-ah*-NAYR	blot (stain), to
fladdermus,*nn.* (*pl.* -möss)	FLAHD-*ehr-muh_s*	bat (animal)
fladdra (1)	FLAHD-*rah*	flutter (flap), to
flagga,*nn.* (I)	FLAHG-*ah*	flag
fläkt,*nn.* (II)	FLECKT	fan, electric
flamma (1)	FLAHM-*ah*	blaze (burn brightly), to
flämta (1)	FLEM-*tah*	gasp, to
"	"	pant (puff), to
fläsk,*n.*	FLESK	pork
flaska,*nn.* (I)	FLAHS-*kah*	bottle
fläskkotlett,*nn.* (III)	FLESK-*koht-let*	pork chop
flat	FLAWT	shallow
fläta (1)	FLAI-*tah*	braid (plait), to
flertal,*n.*	FLAYR-*tawl*	majority (greater number)
flesta, (de)	(*day*) FLESS-*tah*	most (almost all, *adj.*)
flicka,*nn.* (I)	FLICK-*ah*	girl
flicknamn,*n.* (V)	FLICK-*nahmn*	maiden name
flickscout,*nn.* (III)	FLICK-*scout*	girl scout
flinta,*nn.* (I)	FLIN-*tah*	flint
flit,*nn.*	FLEET	diligence
flitig	FLEE-*tig*	diligent
"	"	industrious
flock,*nn.* (II)	FLOHCK	flock
flod,*nn.*	FLOO_D	tide, high
flod,*nn.* (III)	FLOO_D	river
flöjt,*nn.* (III)	FLÖYT	flute (*mus.*)
flor,*n.* (V)	FLOO_R	veil (*n.*)
flott,*n.*	FLOHT	lard
flotta,*nn.* (I)	FLOHT-*ah*	fleet (group of vessels)
"	"	navy (*n.*)
fluga,*nn.* (I)	FLU-*gah*	fly (housefly)
fly (3)	FLÜ	flee (run from), to
flyga (7)	FLÜ-*gah*	fly, to
flyganfall,*n.* (V)	FLÜ_G-*ahn-fahll*	air raid
flygare,*nn.* (V)	FLÜ-*gah-reh*	aviator
flygfält,*n.* (V)	FLÜ_G-*felt*	airport
flygmaskin,*nn.* (III)	FLÜ_G-*mah-sheen*	airplane
flygning,*nn.* (II)	FLÜ_G-*ning*	flight (hasty departure)

Swedish	Pronunciation	English
flygplan,*n.* (V)	FLÜ_G-*plawn*	plane
flygpost,*nn.*	FLÜ_G-*pohsst*	air mail
flykt,*nn.* (III)	FLÜCKT	flight (journey by air)
flykting,*nn.* (II)	FLÜCK-*ling*	refugee
flyta (7)	FLÜ-*tah*	float (be buoyant), to
"	"	flow (circulate), to
flytta (1)	FLÜT-*ah*	move (change residence), to
"	"	move (shift the position of), to
flytta sig	FLÜT-*ah say*	move (shift one's position), to
föda (2)	FÖ-*dah*	bear (give birth to), to
"	"	feed (give food to), to
föda,*nn.*	FÖ-*dah*	diet (total food consumed)
"	"	food
född	FÖD	born, to be
födelse,*nn.* (III)	FÖ-*dell-seh*	birth
födelsedag,*nn.* (II)	FÖ-*dell-seh-dawg*	birthday
foder,*n.* (V)	FOO-*dehr*	lining
föl,*n.* (V)	FÖ_L	colt
följa (2)	FÖLL-*yah*	follow (go or come after), to
"	"	follow (result), to
"	"	succeed (follow), to
följaktligen	FÖLL-*yahkt-lig-en*	consequently
"	"	hence
följa med	*föll-yah*-MAYD	accompany (go along with), to
följande	FÖLL-*yahn-deh*	subsequent
följande dag,*nn.*	FÖLL-*yahn-deh* DAWG	morrow
följd,*nn.* (III)	FÖLL_*yud*	consequence
folk,*n.* (V)	FOHLLK	people (populace)
folkmängd,*nn.* (III)	FOHLLK-*mengd*	population (number of people)
folkräkning,*nn.* (II)	FOHLL_K-*raik-ning*	census
fond,*nn.* (III)	FOHND	fund
fönster,*n.* (V)	FÖN-*stehr*	window
fönsterruta,*nn.* (I)	FÖN-*stehr-ru-tah*	pane, window
fontän,*nn.* (III)	*fohn*-TAIN	fountain
för	FÖR	at (for the price of)
"	"	for
för,*nn.*	FÖR	bow (of ship)
förakt,*n.*	*för*-AHKT	contempt
"	"	scorn
förakta (1)	*för*-AHCK-*tah*	despise, to
"	"	scorn, to
föräldralöst barn, *n.* (V)	*för*-ELL-*drah-lö_st* BARN	orphan (*n.*)
föräldrar,*nn. pl.*	*för*-ELL-*drahr*	parents
för alltid	*för*-AHLL-*teed*	forever
förare,*nn.* (V)	FÖR-*ah-reh*	driver (of automobile)
förarga (1)	*för*-AHRR-*yah*	annoy (irk), to
"	"	vex (anger), to
föra tanken till (2)	*för-ah*-TAHNK-*en till*	suggest (bring to mind), to
för att	*för*-AHT	to (in order to, *prep.*)
för att inte	*för-aht*-IN-*teh*	lest
förbanna (1)	*för*-BAHN-*ah*	curse, to
"	"	damn, to
förbannelse,*nn.* (III)	*för*-BAHN-*el-seh*	curse
förbättra (1)	*för*-BET-*rah*	improve (make better), to
förbättring,*nn.* (II)	*för*-BET-*ring*	improvement (betterment)
förbehåll,*n.* (V)	FÖR-*beh-hohll*	reservation (mental) qualification)
förbereda (2)	FÖR-*beh-ray-dah*	prepare (make ready), to
förberedande	FÖR-*beh-ray-dahn-deh*	preliminary (*adj.*)
förberedelse,*nn.* (III)	FÖR-*beh-ray-dell-seh*	preparation (preparatory act)
förbi	*för*-BEE	past (beyond, *prep.*)
förbigående, i	*ee*-FÖR-*bee-goh-en-deh*	casual (offhand)
förbinda (8)	*för*-BIN-*dah*	connect (link), to
"	"	dress, to (*med.*)
förbindelse,*nn.* (III)	*för*-BIN-*dell-seh*	communication (intercourse)
"	"	dealings (relations)

Swedish	Pronunciation	English
förbiseende,n. (IV)	FÖR-*bee-say-en-deh*	oversight (error)
förbjuda (6)	*för*-B_YU-*dah*	forbid, to
förbjuden	*för*-B_YU-*den*	forbidden
förbli (5)	*för*-BLEE	remain (continue unchanged), to
förbruka (1)	*för*-BRU-*kah*	consume, to
"	"	exhaust (use up), to
förbrukning,nn.	*för*-BRU_K-*ning*	consumption (using up)
förbud,n. (V)	*för*-BUH_D	prohibition
förbund,n. (V)	*för*-BUHND	alliance
"	"	league
"	"	union
fördärva (1)	*för*-DAIRR-*vah*	spoil (mar), to
fördel,nn. (II)	FÖR-*dayl*	advantage
"	"	benefit
fördela (1)	*för*-DAY-*lah*	distribute (allot), to
fördelning,nn.	*för*-DAYL-*ning*	distribution (allotment)
för det mesta	*för*-*deh*-MESS-*tah*	mostly
fördom,nn. (II)	FÖR-*doomm*	prejudice
fördöma (2)	*för*-DÖM-*ah*	condemn (censure), to
fordra (1)	FOORD-*rah*	claim, to
fördrag,n. (V)	*för*-DRAWG	treaty
fordringsägare,nn. (V)	FOORD-*rings-aig-ah-reh*	creditor (*bus.*)
fördriva (5)	*för*-DREE-*vah*	expel (eject), to
fördröja (2)	*för*-DRÖY-*ah*	delay (retard), to
före	FÖR-*eh*	ahead (in front)
"	"	before (*adv.*)
"	"	before (earlier than, *prep.*)
"	"	by (prior to, *prep.*)
förebrå (3)	FÖR-*eh-broh*	reproach, to
förebråelse,nn. (III)	FÖR-*eh-broh-el-seh*	reproach
föredrag,n. (V)	FÖR-*eh-drawg*	lecture (speech)
föredra(ga) (9)	FÖR-*eh-draw*(-*gah*)	prefer (like better), to
"	"	recite (repeat something learned), to
föregående	FÖR-*eh-goh-en-deh*	former (preceding, *adj.*)
"	"	previous
förelägga (11)	*för-eh*-LEG-*ah*	submit (offer), to
forell,nn. (III)	*foh*-RELL	trout
föremål,n. (V)	FÖR-*eh-moh_l*	object (thing)
förena (1)	*för*-AYN-*ah*	join (bring together), to
"	"	unite (make one), to
förenad	*för*-AYN-*ahd*	joint (combined)
förena sig	*för*-AYN-*ah say*	combine (coalesce), to
förening,nn. (II)	*för*-AYN-*ing*	association (body of persons)
"	"	society
Förenta nationerna,nn. pl.	*för*-AYN-*tah* naht-SHOO-*nehr-nah*	United Nations
Förenta staterna, nn. pl.	*för*-AYN-*tah* STAW-*tehr-nah*	United States
föresats,nn. (III)	FÖR-*eh-sahts*	determination (fixed intent)
föreskrift,nn. (III)	FÖR-*eh-skrift*	regulation (rule)
föreslå (10)	FÖR-*eh-sloh*	nominate, to
"	"	propose, to
"	"	suggest (recommend), to
föreslående,n.	FÖR-*eh-sloh-en-deh*	nomination
förestalla (2)	FÖR-*eh-stell-ah*	represent (symbolize), to
förestalla sig	FÖR-*eh-stell-ah say*	fancy, to
"	"	imagine (picture mentally), to
föreställning,nn. (II)	FÖR-*eh-stell-ning*	conception (notion)
"	"	performance (stage presentation)
företag,n. (V)	FÖR-*eh-tawg*	enterprise
"	"	establishment (firm)
"	"	undertaking
företa(ga) sig (9)	FÖR-*eh-taw*(-*gah*) say	undertake (attempt), to
förevändning,nn. (II)	FÖR-*eh-vend-ning*	excuse
"	"	pretense (pretending)
"	"	pretext

Swedish	Pronunciation	English
förfader,nn. (pl. -fäder)	FÖR-*faw-dehr*	ancestor
förfäkta (1)	*för*-FECK-*tah*	advocate, to
förfall,n.	*för*-FAHLL	decay (decline)
förfalla (10)	*för*-FAHLL-*ah*	lapse (become void), to
"	"	mature (fall due), to
förfallen	*för*-FAHLL-*en*	overdue (in arrears)
förfallodag,nn. (II)	*för*-FAHLL-*oo-dawg*	maturity (due date, *bus.*)
förfalska (1)	*för*-FAHLL-*skah*	forge (counterfeit), to
författande,n.	*för*-FAHT-*ahn-deh*	writing (art of writing)
författare,nn. (V)	*för*-FAHT-*ah-reh*	author
"	"	writer
författning,nn. (II)	*för*-FAHT-*ning*	constitution (law)
förfluten	*för*-FLU-*ten*	past (bygone, *adj.*)
förflutna, det,n. def.	*deh-för*-FLU_T-*nah*	past (*n.*)
förfölja (2)	*för*-FÖLL-*yah*	pursue (chase), to
förföljande,n.	*för*-FÖLL-*yahn-deh*	pursuit (chase)
förfrågan,nn.	*för*-FROH-*gahn*	inquiry (question)
förfriskningar,nn. pl.	*för*-FRISK-*ning-ahr*	refreshments
förgifta (1)	*för*-YIF-*tah*	poison, to
förhållande,n. (IV)	*för*-HOHLL-*ahn-deh*	proportion
"	"	ratio
"	"	relation (connection)
förhärliga	*för*-HAIR-*lig-ah*	exalt, to
förhastad	*för*-HAHSS-*tahd*	hasty (rash)
förhindra (1)	*för*-HIND-*rah*	prevent (stop), to
förhoppningsfull	*för*-HOHP-*nings-full*	hopeful
förkläde,n. (IV)	FÖR-*klai*(-*deh*)	apron (garment)
förklädnad,nn. (III)	*för*-KLAID-*nahd*	disguise
förklara (1)	*för*-KLAW-*rah*	declare (state), to
"	"	explain (clarify), to
"	"	pronounce, to
förklaring,nn. (II)	*för*-KLAW-*ring*	explanation
"	"	statement (declaration)
förkortning,nn. (II)	*för*-KOHRT-*ning*	abbreviation
förkylning,nn. (II)	*för*-CHÜ_L-*ning*	cold (disease)
förlägenhet,nn.	*för*-LAIG-*en-hayt*	embarrassment
förlägga (11)	*för*-LEG-*ah*	mislay, to
förläggare,nn. (V)	*för*-LEG-*ah-reh*	publisher
förlagsrätt,nn.	*för*-LAWGS-*ret*	copyright (*n.*)
förlamning,nn. (II)	*för*-LAWM-*ning*	paralysis
förlänga (2)	*för*-LENG-*ah*	prolong, to
förlåta (10)	*för*-LOH-*tah*	forgive, to
"	"	pardon, to
förlåtelse,nn.	*för*-LOH-*tell-seh*	forgiveness
"	"	pardon
förlora (1)	*för*-LOO-*rah*	lose, to
förlovning,nn. (II)	*för*-LOHV-*ning*	engagement (betrothal)
förlust,nn. (III)	*för*-LUHST	loss
form,nn. (III)	FOHRRM	form
"	"	shape (contour)
forma (1)	FOHRR-*mah*	form (shape), to
förmåga,nn.	*för*-MOH-*gah*	ability
"	"	faculty
formalitet,nn. (III)	*fohrr-mah-lee*-TAYT	formality
förman,nn. (pl. -män)	FÖR-*mahn*	foreman (overseer)
förmedling,nn.	*för*-MAYD-*ling*	agency (instrumentality)
formel,nn. (III)	FOHRR-*mell*	formula (prescribed guide)
förminska (1)	*för*-MIN-*skah*	diminish (make smaller), to
förmoda (1)	*för*-MOO-*dah*	suspect (surmise), to
förmögen	*för*-MÖ_G-*en*	wealthy
förmögenhet,nn. (III)	*för*-MÖ_G-*en-hayt*	fortune (wealth)
förmyndare,nn. (V)	FÖR-*mün-dah-reh*	guardian (protector)
förnäm	*för*-NAIM	noble (*adj.*)
förnämst	*för*-NEMST	chief (leading)
"	"	principal (main)
förnärma (1)	*för*-NAIRRM-*ah*	offend (affront), to
förneka (1)	*för*-NAY-*kah*	deny (contradict), to
forntida	FOORN-*tee-dah*	ancient
förnuft,n.	*för*-NUHFT	reason (intellect)
förnuftig	*för*-NUHF-*tig*	reasonable (rational)
"	"	sensible

Swedish	Pronunciation	English	Swedish	Pronunciation	English
förnya (1)	*för*-NÜ-*ah*	renew, to	förtröstan,*nn.*	*för*-TRÖST-*ahn*	faith (trust)
förolämpning,*nn.* (II)	FÖR-*oo-lemp-ning*	insult	förtrycka (2)	*för*-TRÜCK-*ah*	oppress (tyrannize), to
förord,*n.* (V)	FÖR-*oord*	preface	fortsätta (11)	FOORT-*set-ah*	continue, to
förordning,*nn.* (II)	*för*-ORD-*ning*	decree (edict)	"	"	keep (continue), to
förorsaka (1)	FÖR-*oo-shaw-kah*	cause, to	fortsättning,*nn.*	FOORT-*set-ning*	continuation
förpliktelse,*nn.* (III)	*för*-PLICK-*tell-seh*	commitment (*bus.*)			
			förtvivla (1)	*för*-TVEEV-*lah*	despair, to
förra	FÖRR-*ah*	former (first of two, *adj.*)	förtvivlad	*för*-TVEEV-*lahd*	desperate
			förtvivlan,*nn.*	*för*-TVEEV-*lahn*	despair (hopelessness)
förråd,*n.* (V)	*för*-ROH_D	stock (supply)			
förrädare,*nn.* (V)	*för*-RAI-*dah-reh*	traitor	förut	FÖR-*uht*	before (earlier, *adv.*)
förräderi,*n.* (III)	*för-rai-deh*-REE	treason	förutbeställning, *nn.* (II)	FÖR-*uh_t-beh-stell-ning*	reservation (advance order)
förrän	FÖRR-*en*	until (before, *prep.*)			
förruttnelse,*nn.*	*för*-RUHT-*nel-seh*	decay (rottenness)	förutsäga (11)	FÖR-*uht-say-ah*	predict, to
försäkra (1)	*fö*-SHAIK-*rah*	assert (declare), to	förutsätta (11)	FÖR-*uht-set-ah*	assume (take for granted), to
"	"	assure, to			
"	"	insure, to	förutse (10)	FÖR-*uht-say*	anticipate (expect), to
försäkran,*nn.*	*fö*-SHAIK-*rahn*	assertion (declaration)			
			förväg, i	*ee* FÖR-*vaig*	beforehand (*adv.*)
försäkring,*nn.* (II)	*fö*-SHAIK-*ring*	insurance	förvaltning,*nn.*	*för*-VAHLT-*ning*	administration (*bus.*)
försäkringsbrev,*n.* (V)	*fö*-SHAIK-*rings*-BRAYV	policy (contract of insurance)	förvåna (1)	*för*-VOH-*nah*	amaze, to
			"	"	astonish, to
försäljning,*nn.* (II)	*fö*-SHELL_*yuh-ning*	sale (exchange)	"	"	surprise, to
församling,*nn.* (II)	*fö*-SHAHM-*ling*	congregation (religious community)	förvandla (1)	*för*-VAHND-*lah*	convert, to
			"	"	transform, to
förse (10)	*fö*-SHAY	provide (supply), to	"	"	turn (convert), to
försenad	*fö*-SHAY-*nahd*	late (overdue, *adj.*)	förvåning,*nn.*	*för*-VOH-*ning*	astonishment
för sig själv	*fö-shay* SHELV	apart	"	"	surprise
försiktig	*fö*-SHICK-*tig*	careful (cautious)	förväntning,*nn.* (II)	*för*-VENT-*ning*	expectation
"	"	conservative	förvärva (1)	*för*-VAIRRV-*ah*	acquire, to
försiktighet,*nn.*	*fö*-SHICK-*tig-hayt*	caution (heed)			
			förverkliga (1)	*för*-VAIRRK-*lig-ah*	realize (accomplish), to
forskning,*nn.* (II)	FOHSHK-*ning*	research			
förskräcklig	*fö*-SHKRECK-*lig*	awful	förvirra (1)	*för*-VIHRR-*ah*	bewilder, to
"	"	terrible	"	"	confuse (mix up), to
förslag,*n.* (V)	*fö*-SHLAWG	proposal			
"	"	suggestion	förvirring,*nn.*	*för*-VIHRR-*ring*	confusion (disorder)
försök,*n.* (V)	*fö*-SHÖ_K	attempt	förvränga (2)	*för*-VRENG-*ah*	pervert (distort), to
			fosterbarn,*n.* (V)	FOOSS-*tehr-barn*	foster child
försöka (2)	*fö*-SHÖ-*kah*	attempt, to	fot,*nn.* (*pl.* fötter)	FOO_T	foot (*anat.*)
"	"	try, to	fotboll,*nn.*	FOO_T-*bohll*	soccer
först(a)	FÖSHT(-*ah*)	first (*adj.*)	fotled,*nn.* (III)	FOO_T-*layd*	ankle
"	"	primary (first, *adj.*)	fotogen,*nn.* or *n.*	*foh-toh*-SHAYN	kerosene
"	"	prime	fotografi,*n.* (III)	*foo-too-grah*-FEE	photograph
förstå (10)	*fö*-SHTOH	comprehend, to	fråga (1)	FROH-*gah*	ask (put question to), to
"		understand, to			
			"	"	inquire (ask), to
förståelse,*nn.*	*fö*-SHTOH-*el-seh*	understanding (comprehension)	"	"	question (query), to
första förband,*n.* (V)	FÖSH-*tah för*-BAHND	first aid (*med.*)	fråga,*nn.* (I)	FROH-*gah*	issue (question)
			"	"	question (query)
förstånd,*n.*	*fö*-SHTOHND	mind (intellect)	fråga om	FROH-*gah ohm*	ask about, to
"	"	sense (intelligence)	fragment,*n.* (V)	*frahg*-MENT	fragment
förstora (1)	*fö*-SHTOO-*rah*	enlarge (make larger), to	frakt,*nn.* (III)	FRAHCKT	freight
			fraktsedel,*nn.* (II)	FRAHCKT-*say-dell*	bill of lading
förstöra (2)	*fö*-SHTÖ-*rah*	destroy (demolish), to			
"	"	wreck, to	frälsare,*nn.* (V)	FRELL-*sah-reh*	savior
fö störelse,*nn.*	*fö*-SHTÖ-*rel-seh*	destruction (demolition)	framåt	FRAHM-*oht*	ahead
			"	"	forward (*adv.*)
försumma (1)	*fö*-SHUHM-*ah*	neglect (slight), to	fram(åt)	FRAHM(-*oht*)	onward (*adv.*)
försummelse,*nn.* (III)	*fö*-SHUHM-*el-seh*	failure (neglect)	framåtgående	FRAHM-*oht-goh-en-deh*	progressive (advancing)
försvaga (1)	*fö*-SHVAW-*gah*	weaken (make weak), to	framför	FRAHM-*för*	before (in front of, *prep.*)
försvar,*n.*	*fö*-SHVAWR	defense	framgång,*nn.* (II)	FRAHM-*gohng*	success (attainment)
försvara (1)	*fö*-SHVAW-*rah*	defend (protect), to	framgångsrik	FRAHM-*gohngs-reek*	successful
"	"	justify, to	framhålla (10)	FRAHM-*hohll-ah*	note (mention), to
försvinna (8)	*fö*-SHVIN-*ah*	disappear, to	framhärda (1)	FRAHM-*haird-ah*	persist (persevere), to
"	"	fade, to			
"	"	vanish (go out of sight), to	främja (1)	FREM-*yah*	promote (further), to
			framlägga (11)	FRAHM-*leg-ah*	present (set forth), to
fort	FOORT	fast (quickly)	främling,*nn.* (II)	FREM-*ling*	stranger (unknown person)
fort,*n.* (V)	FOHRT	fort			
förteckning,*nn.* (II)	*för*-TECK-*ning*	register (record)	framsida,*nn.* (I)	FRAHM-*see-dah*	face (surface)
förtjäna (1)	*för*-CHAI-*nah*	deserve, to	"	"	front (forward part)
"	"	earn, to	framstående	FRAHM-*stoh-en-deh*	distinguished (notable)
"	"	merit, to	"	"	prominent (eminent)
förtjänst,*nn.* (III)	*för*-CHENST	merit	framsteg,*n.* (V)	FRAHM-*stayg*	advance
förtjusande	*för*-CHU-*sahn-deh*	adorable	"	"	progress
"	"	charming	framtid,*nn.*	FRAHM-*teed*	future (*n.*)
"	"	delightful	från	FROH_N	from
förtroende,*n.* (IV)	*för*-TROO-*en-deh*	confidence			
"	"	trust	Frankrike,*n.*	FRAHNK-*ree-keh*	France
			frans,*nn.* (II)	FRAHNS	fringe
förtrolig	*för*-TROO-*lig*	familiar (intimate)	fransk	FRAHNSK	French (*adj.*)
förtrolla (1)	*för*-TROHLL-*ah*	charm (delight), to	frånvarande	FROH_N-*vaw-rahn-deh*	absent
förtrollning,*nn.*	*för*-TROHLL-*ning*	spell (charm)	frånvaro,*nn.*	FROH_N-*vaw-roo*	absence
			fras,*nn.* (III)	FRAWS	phrase (*gram.*)

Swedish	Pronunciation	English
fred,*nn.* (III)	FRAYD	peace
fresta (1)	FRES-*tah*	tempt, to
frestelse,*nn.* (III)	FRES-*tell-seh*	temptation
fri	FREE	free (independent)
fria (1)	FREE-*ah*	propose (offer marriage), to
fridag,*nn.* (II)	FREE-*dawg*	holiday
frihet,*nn.*	FREE-*hayt*	freedom
frihet,*nn.* (III)	FREE-*hayt*	liberty
frikostig	FREE-*kohs-tig*	generous
frimärke,*n.* (IV)	FREE-*mairr-keh*	stamp, postage
frisk	FRISK	healthy
"	"	sound
"		well (in health, *adj.*)
frita(ga) (9)	FREE-*taw* (-*gah*)	justify (exonerate), to
fritid,*nn.*	FREE-*teed*	leisure
frivillig,*nn.* (*pl.* -a)	FREE-*vill-ig*	volunteer (*mil.*)
frö,*n.* (IV)	FRÖ	seed (ovule)
frodas (1)	FROO-*dahs*	thrive (grow vigorously), to
Fröken,*nn.* (II)	FRÖ-*ken*	Miss
front,*nn.* (III)	FROHNT	front (battle front)
frost,*nn.* (III)	FROHSST	frost
Fru,*nn.* (II)	FRU	Mrs. (Mistress)
frukost,*nn.* (II)	FRUH-*kohst*	breakfast
frukt,*nn.* (III)	FRUHCKT	fruit
frukta (1)	FRUHCK-*tah*	fear (be afraid of), to
fruktan,*nn.*	FRUHCK-*tahn*	dread
"	"	fear
fruktansvärd	FRUHCK-*tahns-vaird*	dreadful
"	"	fearful (terrible)
"	"	horrible
fruktlös	FRUHCKT-*lö_s*	vain (futile)
fruktträdgård,*nn.* (II)	FRUHCKT-*traid-gord*	orchard
frusen	FRU-*sen*	frozen
frysa (7)	FRÜ-*sah*	freeze (turn to ice), to
fuktig	FUHCK-*tig*	damp
"	"	moist
fuktighet,*nn.*	FUHCK-*tig-hayt*	moisture
ful	FUH_L	ugly
full	FUHLL	full (filled)
fullkomlig	FUHLL-*kohm-lig*	perfect (flawless)
fullkomlighet,*nn.*	FUHLL-*kohm-lig-hayt*	perfection (flawlessness)
fullmakt,*nn.* (III)	FUHLL-*mahkt*	power of attorney
fullständig	FUHLL-*sten-dig*	absolute
"	"	complete (entire)
"	"	full (complete)
fundera (1)	*fuhn*-DAY-*rah*	muse (meditate), to
funktion,*nn.* (III)	*fuhnk*-SHOON	function
fylla (2)	FÜLL-*ah*	fill (make full), to
fyllig	FÜLL-*ig*	plump (chubby)
fyrkantig	FÜR-*kahn-tig*	square (*adj.*)
fysik,*nn.*	*fü*-SEEK	physics (science)
fysisk	FÜ-*sisk*	physical (material)
gå (10)	GOH	go, to
"	"	walk, to
gaffel,*nn.* (II)	GAHF-*el*	fork (eating utensil)
gå framåt	*goh*-FRAHM-*oht*	advance (go forward), to
gå in i	*goh*-IN *ee*	enter (join), to
gäldenär,*nn.* (III)	*yell-deh*-NAIR	debtor (*bus.*)
galet	GAW-*let*	wrong (amiss, *adv.*)
gäll	YELL	shrill
galler,*n.* (V)	GAHLL-*ehr*	grate (of furnace)
galopp,*nn.*	*gah*-LOHP	gallop (*n.*)
galoscher,*nn.pl.*	*gah*-LOHSH-*ehr*	rubbers (overshoes)
gammal	GAHM-*ahll*	old
"	"	stale
gå ned	*goh*-NAYD	descend (move downward), to
"	"	set (in sky), to
gäng,*n.* (V)	YENG	band
"	"	gang
gång,*nn.* (II)	GOHNG	aisle (passageway)
"	"	passage
gång,*nn.*	GOHNG	operation (functioning)

Swedish	Pronunciation	English
gång, en	*en*-GOHNG	once
gånger	GOHNG-*ehr*	by (*prep., math.*)
ganska	GAHN-*skah*	fairly (somewhat)
"	"	rather
går, i	*ee*-GOR	yesterday
garage,*n.* (V)	*gah*-RAWSH	garage
garant,*nn.* (III)	*gah*-RAHNT	guarantor
garantera (1)	*gah-rahn*-TAY-*rah*	guarantee, to
garanti,*nn.* (III)	*gah-rahn*-TEE	guarantee (warrant)
gård,*nn.* (II)	GORD	yard (enclosure near house)
garderob,*nn.* (III)	*gahrd-eh*-ROH_B	wardrobe (apparel)
gardin,*nn.* (III)	*gard*-DEEN	curtain (drape)
garn,*n.* (V)	GARN	yarn (fiber)
gärning,*nn.* (II)	YAIRN-*ing*	deed (act)
garnison,*nn.* (III)	*gar-nis*-SOON	garrison
gas,*nn.* (III)	GAWS	gas
gås,*nn.* (*pl.* gäss)	GOH_S	goose
gå sönder	*goh*-SÖN-*dehr*	break (come apart), to
gäspa (1)	YESS-*pah*	yawn, to
gäst,*nn.* (III)	YEST	guest (visitor)
gäster,*nn.pl.*	YESS-*tehr*	company (guests)
gata,*nn.* (I)	GAW-*tah*	avenue
"	"	street
gåta,*nn.* (I)	GOH-*tah*	riddle (*n.*)
gå upp	*goh*-UHP	rise (in sky), to
gå uppför	*goh*-UHP-*för*	ascend (go upward along)
gå utför	*goh*-UHT-*för*	decline (deteriorate), to
gåva,*nn.* (I)	GOH-*vah*	gift (present)
ge (10)	YAY	give (bestow), to
"	"	give (deliver), to
ge efter	*yay*-EF-*tehr*	yield (give in), to
ge i uppgift	*yay-ee*-UHP-*yift*	assign (prescribe lesson), to
gelé,*nn.* or *n.* (III)	*sheh*-LAY	jelly
general,*nn.* (III)	*yeh-neh*-RAWL	general (officer)
Genève,*n.*	*sheh*-NAIV	Geneva
geni,*n.* (III)	*sheh*-NEE	genius
genom	YAY-*nohm*	through (by means of, *prep.*)
genomborra (1)	YAY-*nohm-bohrr-ah*	pierce, to
genomgå (10)	YAY-*nohm-goh*	suffer (undergo), to
genom hela	YAY-*nohm* HAY-*lah*	throughout (from start to finish of, *prep.*)
genomskinlig	YAY-*nohm-sheen-lig*	transparent
genomslagskopia,*nn.* (I)	YAY-*nohm-slawgs-koh*-PEE-*ah*	carbon copy
genomsnittlig	YAY-*nohm-snit-lig*	average (ordinary, *adj.*)
genomtränga (2)	YAY-*nohm-treng-ah*	penetrate (pierce), to
gentleman,*nn.* (*pl.* -män)	YENT-*leh-mahn*	gentleman
geografi,*nn.*	*yay-oh-grah*-FEE	geography
geologi,*nn.*	*yay-oh-log*-EE	geology
ge rabatt	*yay-rah*-BAHT	discount, to (*bus.*)
ge sig	YAY *say*	surrender (give oneself up), to
gest,*nn.* (III)	SHEST	gesture (motion)
get,*nn.* (*pl.* -ter)	YAYT	goat
geting,*nn.* (II)	YAY-*ting*	wasp
ge ut	*yay*-UH_T	spend (pay out), to
gevär,*n.* (V)	*yeh*-VAIR	rifle
gift	YIFT	married
gift,*n.* (III)	YIFT	poison
gifta sig med (2)	YIF-*tah-say mayd*	marry, to
gilja (1)	YILL-*yah*	woo, to
gilla (1)	YILL-*ah*	approve (think well of), to
gillande,*n.* (IV)	YILL-*ahn-deh*	acceptance
"	"	approval
"	"	favor (approval)
girig	YEE-*rig*	greedy
gissa (1)	YISS-*ah*	guess (divine), to
gitarr,*nn.* (III)	*yih*-TAHRR	guitar
glad	GLAWD	cheerful
"	"	gay (merry)
"	"	glad
"	"	happy
"	"	jolly (*adj.*)
"	"	joyful
glädja (11)	GLAID-*yah*	delight (give pleasure to), to

Swedish	Pronunciation	English
glädja sig	GLAID-*yah say*	rejoice, to
glädje,*nn.*	GLAID-*yeh*	delight
glädje,*nn.*	GLAID-*yeh*	gladness
"	"	joy
glans,*nn.*	GLAHNS	luster (sheen)
glänsa (2)	GLEN-*sah*	gleam (shine), to
glänsande	GLEN-*sahn-deh*	splendid
glas,*n.* (V)	GLAWS	glass (material)
"	"	glass (vessel)
glasögon,*n.pl.*	GLAWS-*ö-gohn*	glasses
"	"	spectacles
glass,*nn.*	GLAHSS	ice-cream
glida (5)	GLEE-*dah*	glide, to
"	"	slide, to
glimt,*nn.* (II)	GLIMT	glimpse
glittra (1)	GLIT-*rah*	glitter, to
glob,*nn.* (III)	GLOOB	globe
"	"	sphere
glöda (2)	GLÖ-*dah*	glow (shine), to
glödlampa,*nn.* (I)	GLÖ_D-*lahm-pah*	bulb (light bulb)
glömd	GLÖMD	forgotten
glömma (2)	GLÖM-*ah*	forget, to
gnaga (1)	G_NAW-*gah*	gnaw (bite), to
gnägga (1)	G_NEG-*ah*	neigh, to
gnida (5)	G_NEE-*dah*	rub, to
gnidare,*nn.* (V)	G_NEE-*dah-reh*	miser
gnista,*nn.* (I)	G_NISS-*tah*	spark
gnistra (1)	G_NISS-*trah*	sparkle, to
godhet,*nn.*	GOO_D-*hayt*	goodness
"	"	kindness
godkänna (2)	GOOD-*chen-ah*	approve (sanction), to
gök,*nn.* (II)	YÖ_K	cuckoo (bird)
golf,*nn.*	GOHLLF	golf
golv,*n.* (V)	GOHLLV	floor (bottom surface)
gömma (2)	YÖM-*ah*	hide (conceal), to
göra (11)	YÖ-*rah*	do, to
"	"	make, to
"	"	render (cause to become), to
göra besviken	yö-*rah-beh-*SVEEK-*en*	disappoint, to
göra en paus	yö-*rah-en-*PAW-*uhs*	pause (wait), to
göra modfälld	yö-*rah-*MOOD-*feld*	discourage (dishearten), to
göra mörk	yö-*rah-*MÖRRK	darken (make dark), to
göra ont	yö-*rah-*OONNT	hurt (be painful), to
göra sig av med	yö-*rah-say-*AWV *mayd*	dispose of (put away), to
göra upp	yö-*rah-*UHP	settle (agree on), to
göra uppehåll	yö-*rah-*UHP-*eh-hohll*	stop (make halt), to
göra utkast till	yö-*rah-*UH_T-*kahst till*	draft (sketch), to
gott köp,*n.*	GOHT CHÖ_P	bargain (advantageous purchase)
grå	GROH	gray
grabb,*nn.* (II)	GRAHB	chap (fellow)
graciös	grah-*see-*ö_s	graceful
grad,*nn.* (III)	GRAWD	degree (unit of measurement)
"	"	grade (relative position)
grädde,*nn.*	GRED-*eh*	cream
gradvis	GRAWD-*vees*	gradual
gräl,*n.* (V)	GRAIL	quarrel (dispute)
gräla (1)	GRAI-*lah*	quarrel (dispute), to
gräla på	GRAI-*lah poh*	scold, to
grammatik,*nn.* (I)	grah-*mah-*TEEK	grammar
grammofon,*nn.* (III)	grah-*moo-*FOH_N	phonograph
grammofonskiva,*nn.* (I)	grah-*moo-*FOH_N-*shee-vah*	record (disk)
gran,*nn.* (II)	GRAWN	fir
granit,*nn.* (III)	grah-*NEET	granite
granne,*nn.* (II)	GRAHN-*eh*	neighbor
grannskap,*n.* (V)	GRAHN-*skawp*	neighborhood
"	"	vicinity
gräns,*nn.* (III)	GRENS	border
"	"	boundary
"	"	frontier
"	"	limit
granskning,*nn.* (II)	GRAHNSK-*ning*	survey (inspection)

Swedish	Pronunciation	English
gräs,*n.* (V)	GRAIS	grass
gräshoppa,*nn.* (I)	GRAIS-*hohp-ah*	grasshopper
gräslig	GRAIS-*lig*	monstrous (horrible)
gräsmatta,*nn.* (I)	GRAIS-*maht-ah*	lawn
gråta (10)	GROH-*tah*	cry, to
"	"	weep, to
gratis	GRAW-*tiss*	free (gratuitous)
gratulera (1)	grah-*tuh-*LAY-*rah*	congratulate, to
grav,*nn.* (II)	GRAWV	grave
grav(vård),*nn.* (II)	GRAWV(-*vord*)	tomb
gräva (2)	GRAI-*vah*	dig (excavate), to
"	"	mine (dig for), to
grävling,*nn.* (II)	GRAIV-*ling*	badger (animal)
grekisk	GRAY-*kisk*	Greek (*adj.*)
Grekland,*n.*	GRAYK-*lahnd*	Greece
gren,*nn.* (II)	GRAYN	bough
"	"	branch
grepp,*n.* (V)	GREP	grip (grasp)
grina (1)	GREE-*nah*	grin, to
gripa (5)	GREE-*pah*	capture, to
"	"	grab, to
"	"	seize, to
gris,*nn.* (II)	GREES	pig (animal)
groda,*nn.* (I)	GROO-*dah*	frog
grön	GRÖ_N	green (color)
grönsak,*nn.* (III)	GRÖ_N-*sawk*	vegetable
grop,*nn.* (II)	GROOP	pit (hole)
gross,*n.* (V)	GROHSS	gross (twelve dozen)
grossist,*nn.* (III)	groh-*SIST	wholesaler (*bus.*)
grotta,*nn.* (I)	GROHT-*ah*	cave
grov	GROOV	coarse
"	"	gross (flagrant)
grovarbetare,*nn.* (V)	GROOV-*ahrr-bay-tah-reh*	laborer
grubbla över (1)	GRUHB-*lah* ö-*vehr*	brood over, to
grund,*nn.* (III)	GRUHND	cause
grunda (1)	GRUHN-*dah*	base, to
"	"	establish, to
"	"	found (originate), to
grundande,*n.*	GRUHN-*dahn-deh*	establishment (founding)
grundläggande	GRUHND-*leg-ahn-deh*	fundamental
grundläggare,*nn.* (V)	GRUHND-*leg-ah-reh*	founder (*n.*)
grundlig	GRUHND-*lig*	radical (basic)
"	"	thorough (complete)
grundligt	GRUHND-*lickt*	thoroughly
grundsats,*nn.* (III)	GRUHND-*sahts*	principle (basic truth)
grundval,*nn.* (II)	GRUHND-*vawl*	basis
"	"	foundation
"	"	ground
grupp,*nn.* (III)	GRUHP	group
grus,*n.*	GRU_S	gravel
gruva,*nn.* (I)	GRU-*vah*	mine (pit)
gruvarbetare,*nn.* (V)	GRU_V-*ahrr-bay-tah-reh*	miner
grym	GRÜM	cruel
gryning,*nn.*	GRÜ-*ning*	dawn (daybreak)
Guatemala,*n.*	guh-*ah-teh-*MAW-*lah*	Guatemala
Gud,*m.*	GUH_D	God
gudomlig	guh-*DOOMM-lig*	divine (*adj.*)
gul	GU_L	yellow (*adj.*)
gula febern,*nn.def.*	gu-*lah-*FAY-*behrn*	yellow fever
guld,*n.*	GUHLD	gold
gummi,*n.*	GUHM-*ee*	rubber
gunst,*nn.*	GUHNST	favor (kindness)
gurka,*nn.* (I)	GUHRR-*kah*	cucumber
guvernör,*nn.* (III)	guh-*vehr-*NÖR	governor
gyllene	YÜLL-*eh-neh*	golden
gymnastiksal,*nn.* (II)	yüm-*nah-*STEEK-*sawl*	gymnasium (athletic arena)
gynna (1)	YÜN-*ah*	foster (encourage), to
gynnsam	YÜN-*sahm*	favorable
häck,*nn.* (II)	HECK	hedge (bushes)
hacka (1)	HAHCK-*ah*	hoe, to
"	"	peck, to
hacka,*nn.* (I)	HAHCK-*ah*	hoe
hädanefter	HAI-*dahn-ef-tehr*	henceforth
"	"	hereafter (after this, *adv.*)
hagel,*n.* (V)	HAWG-*el*	hail (ice)
hagla (1)	HAWG-*lah*	hail (precipitate hail), to

Swedish	Pronunciation	English
Haiti,*n.*	*hah*-EE-*tih*	Haiti
haka,*nn.* (I)	HAW-*kah*	chin
häkta (1)	HECK-*tah*	arrest (take into custody), to
hal	HAWL	slippery
hål,*n.* (V)	HOH_L	hole (cavity)
häl,*nn.* (II)	HAIL	heel (*anat.*)
hala (1)	HAW-*lah*	haul (pull), to
hälft,*nn.* (III)	HELFT	half (*n.*)
halka (1)	HAHLL-*kah*	slip (slide), to
hälla (2)	HELL-*ah*	pour (make flow), to
hålla (10)	HOHLL-*ah*	hold, to
hålla på med	*hohll-ah*-POH *mayd*	engage (be occupied) in, to
hålla sig	HOHLL-*ah say*	last (withstand use), to
hålla tillbaka	*hohll-ah-till-*BAW-*kah*	restrain (check), to
hållning,*nn.*	HOHLL-*ning*	attitude (manner) carriage (posture)
hallon,*n.* (V)	HAHLL-*ohn*	raspberry
halmstrå,*n.* (IV)	HAHLLM-*stroh*	straw (dry grain stalks)
hals,*nn.* (II)	HAHLLS	neck (*anat.*) throat
hälsa (1)	HELL-*sah*	salute, to
hälsa,*nn.*	HELL-*sah*	health
hälsa (på)	HELL-*sah* (*poh*)	greet (salute), to
halsband,*n.* (V)	HAHLLS-*bahnd*	necklace
halsduk,*nn.* (II)	HAHLLS-*duh_k*	scarf (neck cloth)
hälsning,*nn.* (II)	HELLS-*ning*	greeting
hälsosam	HELL-*soh-sahm*	wholesome (beneficial)
halta (1)	HAHLL-*tah*	limp, to
halv	HAHLLV	half (*adj.*)
halvklot,*n.* (V)	HAHLLV-*kloot*	hemisphere (*geog.*)
halvö,*nn.* (II)	HAHLLV-*ö*	peninsula
hammare,*nn.* (V)	HAHM-*ah-reh*	hammer (tool)
hamn,*nn.* (II)	HAHMN	harbor port
hämnd,*nn.*	HEMD	revenge vengeance
hämta (1)	HEM-*tah*	fetch (bring), to
han	HAHN	he
håna (1)	HOH-*nah*	mock (deride), to
hand-...	HAHND-...	manual (by hand)
hand,*nn.* (*pl.* händer)	HAHND	hand (*anat.*)
hända (2)	HEN-*dah*	happen, to occur, to
handbok,*nn.* (*pl.* -böcker)	HAHND-*boo_k*	manual (small book)
handduk,*nn.* (II)	HAHND-*duh_k*	towel, hand
handel,*nn.*	HAHN-*dell*	commerce trade
händelse,*nn.* (III)	HEN-*dell-seh*	event (happening) incident
handelskammare, *nn.* (V)	HAHN-*dells-kahm-ah-reh*	chamber of commerce
handelsresande, *nn.* (V)	HAHN-*dells-ray-sahn-deh*	traveling salesman
handflata,*nn.* (I)	HAHND-*flaw-tah*	palm (of hand)
handfull,*nn.*	HAHND-*fuhll*	handful
händighet,*nn.*	HEN-*dig-hayt*	dexterity
handla (1)	HAHND-*lah*	act (do), to deal (trade), to shop, to
handlande,*nn.* (V)	HAHND-*lahn-deh*	dealer (trader)
handled,*nn.* (III)	HAHND-*layd*	wrist
handling,*nn.* (II)	HAHND-*ling*	act action deed (transfer agreement)
handlingar,*nn.pl.*	HAHND-*ling-ahr*	records (files)
handpengar,*nn.pl.*	HAHND-*peng-ahr*	down payment (*bus.*)
handske,*nn.* (II)	HAHND-*skeh*	glove
handstil,*nn.* (II)	HAHND-*steel*	writing (handwriting)
handtag,*n.* (V)	HAHND-*tawg*	handle
handväska,*nn.* (I)	HAHND-*vess-kah*	bag (purse)
hänföra sig till (2)	HAIN-*fö-rah say till*	relate (pertain) to, to
hänga (2)	HENG-*ah*	hang (be suspended), to
hangarfartyg,*n.* (V)	*hahng-*GAWR-*fawr-tü_g*	aircraft carrier
hängivenhet,*nn.*	HAIN-*yee-ven-hayt*	devotion (loyal attachment)

Swedish	Pronunciation	English
hängslen,*n.pl.*	HENG-*slen*	suspenders
hanne,*nn.* (II)	HAHN-*eh*	male (*n.*)
hänryckning,*nn.*	HAIN-*rück-ning*	rapture
hans	HAHNS	his
hänsyftning,*nn.* (II)	HAIN-*süft-ning*	reference (allusion)
hänsyn,*nn.* (V)	HAIN-*sü_n*	consideration (regard)
hänsynslös	HAIN-*sü_ns-lö_s*	reckless
hantverk,*n.* (V)	HAHNT-*vairk*	craft
ha på sig	*haw-*POH *say*	wear (have on), to
häpnad,*nn.*	HAIP-*nahd*	amazement wonder
här	HAIR	here (in this place, *adv.*)
hår,*n.* (V)	HOHR	hair
ha råd	*haw-*ROH_D	afford (have the means), to
härbärgera	*hairr-bairr-*YAY-*rah*	accommodate (have room for), to
hård	HORD	grim (stern) hard (not soft) rough (harsh)
härd,*nn.* (II)	HAIRD	hearth
härda (1)	HAIRD-*ah*	harden (make hard), to
hare,*nn.* (II)	HAW-*reh*	hare
harmoni,*nn.* (III)	*hahr-moo-*NEE	harmony (*mus.*)
harpa,*nn.* (I)	HAHRR-*pah*	harp
härska över (1)	HASH-*kah* ö-*vehr*	rule (govern), to
härskare,*nn.* (V)	HASH-*kah-reh*	ruler (sovereign)
häst,*nn.* (II)	HEST	horse
hastig	HAHSS-*tig*	hasty (hurried)
hastighet,*nn.* (III)	HAHSS-*tig-hayt*	rate (degree of speed)
hästkraft,*nn.* (III)	HEST-*krahft*	horsepower
hat,*n.*	HAWT	hate (hatred)
hata (1)	HAW-*tah*	hate, to
hatt,*nn.* (II)	HAHTT	hat
hav,*n.* (V)	HAWV	sea
ha(va) (4)	HAW	have, to
haverera (1)	*hah-veh-*RAY-*rah*	crash (be smashed), to
havre,*nn.*	HAWV-*reh*	oats
havs-...	HAHFS-...	marine (oceanic)
havsbukt,*nn.* (III)	HAHFS-*buhkt*	gulf (large bay)
Hawaii,*n.*	*hah-*VAH-*yih*	Hawaii
häxa,*nn.* (I)	HEX-*ah*	witch
hebreisk	*heh-*BRAY-*isk*	Hebrew (*adj.*)
hed,*nn.* (II)	HAYD	moor (waste land)
hederlig	HAY-*dehr-lig*	honorable (upright)
hedra (1)	HAY-*drah*	honor (respect), to
hejda (1)	HAY-*dah*	arrest (halt), to check (stop), to
hejdande,*n.*	HAY-*dahn-deh*	check (restraint)
hel	HAYL	all entire whole
helgeflundra,*nn.* (I)	HELL-*yeh-fluhn-drah*	halibut
helgon,*n.* (V)	HELL-*gohn*	saint
helhet,*nn.* (III)	HAYL-*hayt*	whole (entirety, *n.*)
helig	HAY-*lig*	holy sacred
helikopter,*nn.* (II)	*heh-lee-*KOHP-*tehr*	helicopter
heller	HELL-*ehr*	either (not...either, *adv.*)
Helsingfors,*n.*	*hell-sing-*FOHSH	Helsinki
helvete,*n.* (IV)	HELL-*vay-teh*	hell
hem,*n.* (V)	HEM	home
hemåt	HEM-*oht*	homeward
hembiträde,*n.* (IV)	HEM-*bee-trai-deh*	maid (servant)
hemlig	HEM-*lig*	secret (*adj.*) underground
hemlighet,*nn.* (III)	HEM-*lig-hayt*	secret (*n.*)
hemsjuk	HEM-*shu_k*	homesick
henne	HEN-*eh*	her (*pers. pron.*)
hennes	HEN-*es*	her (*poss. adj.*) hers (*poss. pron.*)
herde,*nn.* (II)	HAYRD-*eh*	shepherd
Herr,*nn.* (II)	HAIRR	Mr. (Mister)
herravälde,*n.* (IV)	HAIRR-*ah-*VELL-*deh*	rule (political control)

Swedish	Pronunciation	English
herre,*nn.* (II)	HAIRR-*eh*	lord (master)
"	"	master (one in authority)
herre, min,*nn.*	*min*-HAIRR-*eh*	sir
het	HAYT	hot
himmel,*nn.* (II)	HIM-*el*	heaven
"	"	sky
hinder,*n.* (V)	HIN-*dehr*	obstacle
hindra (1)	HIN-*drah*	hinder, to
"	"	keep (prevent), to
hingst,*nn.* (II)	HINGST	stallion
hink,*nn.* (II)	HINK	bucket
"	"	pail
hinna,*nn.* (I)	HIN-*ah*	film (thin coating)
hiss,*nn.* (II)	HISS	elevator (passenger lift)
historia,*nn.*	*his*-TOO-*ree-ah*	history
historisk	*his*-TOO-*risk*	historical
hit	HEET	here (to this place, *adv.*)
hitta på (1)	*hit-ah*-POH	devise (contrive), to
hittills	HEET-*tills*	hitherto (thus far)
hjälm,*nn.* (II)	YELM	helmet
hjälp,*nn.*	YELP	aid
"	"	help (assistance)
hjälpa (2)	YELL-*pah*	aid, to
"	"	help, to
hjälplös	YELP-*lö̱ s*	helpless
hjälpsam	YELP-*sahm*	helpful (volunteering help)
hjälte,*nn.* (II)	YELL-*teh*	hero
hjältinna,*nn.* (I)	*yelt*-IN-*ah*	heroine
hjärna,*nn.* (I)	YAIRN-*ah*	brain (*anat.*)
hjärta,*n.* (IV)	YAIRT-*ah*	heart
hjärtlig	YAIRT-*lig*	cordial (*adj.*)
"	"	hearty
hjord,*nn.* (II)	YOORD	herd (of animals)
hjul,*n.* (V)	YU̱L	wheel
hö,*n.*	HÖ	hay
höft,*nn.* (III)	HÖFT	hip
höfthållare,*nn.* (V)	HÖFT-*hohll-ah-reh*	girdle (corset)
hög	HÖ̱G	high
"	"	lofty
"	"	tall (of things)
hög,*nn.* (II)	HÖ̱G	heap
"	"	pile
höger	HÖ̱G-*ehr*	right (on the right, *adj.*)
höger sida,*nn.* (I)	HÖ̱G-*ehr* SEE-*dah*	right (right-hand side)
högkonjunktur,*nn.* (III)	HÖ̱G-*kohn-yuhnk-*TUH̱R	boom (*bus.*)
högkvarter,*n.* (V)	HÖ̱G-*kvahrt-*TAYR	headquarters
högljudd	HÖ̱G-*yuhdd*	loud (resounding)
högröd	HÖ̱G-*rö̱ d*	crimson
högst	HÖXT	supreme
"	"	top (highest, *adj.*)
högt	HÖCKT	aloud
högtidlig	*höck*-TEED-*lig*	solemn (grave)
högtidligt löfte,*n.* (IV)	*höck*-TEED-*lickt* LÖFF-*teh*	vow
höjd,*nn.* (III)	HÖYD	height (highness)
hök,*nn.* (II)	HÖ̱K	hawk
Holland,*n.*	HOHLL-*lahnd*	Holland
holländsk	HOHLL-*lensk*	Dutch (*adj.*)
hon	HOONN	she
hona,*nn.* (I)	HOO-*nah*	female (*zool.*, *n.*)
höna,*nn.* (I)	HÖ-*nah*	hen
Honduras,*n.*	*hohn*-DUH-*rahs*	Honduras
honom	HOHN-*ohm*	him
honung,*nn.*	HOH-*nuhng*	honey
hopa (1)	HOO-*pah*	accumulate (amass), to
hopp,*n.* (V)	HOHP	bound (leap)
"	"	hope
"	"	jump
hoppa (1)	HOHP-*ah*	hop, to
"	"	jump (bound), to
"	"	leap, to
"	"	spring, to
hoppa över	*hohp-ah*-ö-*vehr*	skip (omit), to
hoppas (1)	HOHP-*ahs*	hope, to
höra (2)	HÖ-*rah*	hear, to

Swedish	Pronunciation	English
horisont,*nn.* (III)	*hoh-riss*-SOHNT	horizon
horn,*n.* (V)	HOORN	bugle
"	"	horn (*anat.*)
"	"	horn (*mus.*)
hörn,*n.* (V)	HÖRN	corner (angle)
"	"	corner (street intersection)
höst,*nn.* (II)	HÖST	autumn
"	"	fall
hosta,*nn.*	HOOSS-*tah*	cough
hot,*n.*	HOOT	threat
hota (1)	HOO-*tah*	threaten, to
hotell,*n.* (V)	*hoo*-TELL	hotel
hov,*n.* (V)	HOH̱V	court (of ruler)
hov,*n.* (II)	HOO̱V	hoof
hud,*nn.*	HUH̱D	skin (human skin)
hud,*nn.* (II)	HUH̱D	hide
hummer,*nn.* (II)	HUHM-*ehr*	lobster
humor,*nn.*	HUH̱M-*or*	humor (drollery)
humör,*n.*	*huh*-MÖR	mood
"	"	temper
hund,*nn.* (II)	HUHND	dog
hunger,*nn.*	HUHNG-*ehr*	hunger
hungrig	HUHNG-*rig*	hungry
hur	HUH̱R	how
hus,*n.* (V)	HUH̱S	house
hushåll,*n.* (V)	HUH̱S-*hohll*	household
huslig	HUH̱S-*lig*	domestic (in household, *adj.*)
husmo(de)r,*nn.* (*pl.* -mödrar)	HUH̱S-*moo(-deh)r*	housewife
hustru,*nn.* (II)	HUHS-*tru*	wife
huv,*nn.* (II)	HUH̱V	hood (*auto.*)
huva,*nn.* (I)	HUH̱V-*ah*	hood (cowl)
huvud,*n.* (IV, V)	HUH̱V-*uhd*	head (*anat.*)
huvuddel,*nn.* (II)	HUH̱V-*uhd-dayl*	bulk (largest part)
huvudsaklig	HUH̱V-*uhd-sawk-lig*	main (principal)
huvudsakligen	HUH̱V-*uhd-sawk-lig-en*	chiefly (mainly)
huvudstad,*nn.* (*pl.* -städer)	HUH̱V-*uhd-stawd*	capital (city)
huvudvärk,*nn.*	HUH̱V-*uhd-vairk*	headache
hydda,*nn.* (I)	HÜD-*ah*	hut
hyfsning,*nn.*	HÜFS-*ning*	manners (polite behavior)
hygglig	HÜG-*lig*	decent (fairly good)
hylla,*nn.* (I)	HÜLL-*ah*	shelf
hyra (2)	HÜ-*rah*	lease (hold by lease), to
"	"	rent (pay rent for), to
hyra,*nn.* (I)	HÜ-*rah*	rent (payment)
hyra ut	*hü-rah*-UH̱T	rent (charge rent for), to
hyresgäst,*nn.* (III)	HÜ-*rehs-yest*	tenant
hytt,*nn.* (III)	HÜT	cabin (of ship)
i	EE	at
"	"	in (inside, *prep.*)
iaktta(ga) (9)	EE-*ahkt-taw(-gah)*	observe, to
"	"	watch, to
iakttagande,*n.*	EE-*ahkt-taw-gahn-deh*	observation (watching)
iakttagare,*nn.* (V)	EE-*ahkt-taw-gah-reh*	observer
ibland	*ee*-BLAHND	sometimes
idé,*nn.* (III)	*ee*-DAY	idea
"	"	notion
ideal,*n.* (V)	*ee-day*-AWL	ideal (*n.*)
identifiera (1)	*ee-den-tee-fee*-AYR-*ah*	identify, to
idol,*nn.* (III)	*ee*-DOH̱L	idol
idrotts-...	EE-*drohts*-...	athletic
idrottsman,*nn.* (*pl.* -män)	EE-*drohts-mahn*	athlete
igen	*ee*-YEN	again
igenkännande,*n.*	*ee*-YEN-*chen-ahn-deh*	recognition (identification)
igenom	*ee*-YAY-*nohm*	through (from end to end of, *prep.*)
ignorera (1)	*ig-noo*-RAY-*rah*	overlook (disregard), to
ihålig	EE-*hoh-lig*	hollow (*adj.*)
ila (1)	EE-*lah*	flit (dart), to
illojalitet,*nn.*	*ill-loy-ah-lit*-TAYT	disloyalty
illusion,*nn.* (III)	*ill-uh*-SHOON	illusion
illustration,*nn.* (III)	*ill-uh-strah*-SHOON	illustration (example)
"	"	illustration (pictorial representation)

Swedish	Pronunciation	English
illustrera (1)	*ill-uh-*STRAY-*rah*	illustrate (exemplify), to
illvilja,*nn.*	ILL-*vill-yah*	malice
imitera (1)	*im-it-*TAY-*rah*	imitate, to
imperium,*n.* (III)	*im-*PAY-*ree-uhm*	empire
imponera på (1)	*im-poh-*NAY-*rah poh*	impress (affect deeply), to
import,*nn.*	*im-*POHRT	importation
importera (1)	*im-pohrt-*TAY-*rah*	import, to (*bus.*)
importör,*nn.* (III)	*im-pohrt-*TÖR	importer
impuls,*nn.* (III)	*im-*PUHLS	impulse (sudden incitement)
inälvor,*nn.pl.*	IN-*ell-voor*	bowels (*anat.*)
inbetala (1)	IN-*beh-taw-lah*	deposit, to (*fin.*)
inbetalning,*nn.* (II)	IN-*beh-tawl-ning*	deposit (money deposited)
inbjuda (7)	IN-*b̠ yu-dah*	invite, to
inbjudan,*nn.*	IN-*b̠ yu-dahn*	invitation
inbrottstjuv,*nn.* (II)	IN-*brohts-chu̠ v*	burglar
indian,*nn.* (III)	*in-dee-*AWN	Indian, American
Indien,*n.*	IN-*dee-en*	India
indignation,*nn.*	*in-dig-nah-*SHOON	indignation
indirekt	IN-*dee-reckt*	indirect
individ,*nn.* (III)	*in-dee-*VEED	individual (person, *n.*)
industri,*nn.* (III)	*in-duh-*STREE	industry (trade)
industriell	*in-duh-stree-*ELL	industrial
infall,*n.* (V)	IN-*fahll*	fancy (notion)
infalla i (10)	IN-*fahll-ah ee*	invade, to (*mil.*)
infektion,*nn.* (III)	*in-feck-*SHOON	infection
inflammation,*nn.* (III)	*in-flahm-ah-*SHOON	inflammation
inflation,*nn.*	*in-flah-*SHOON	inflation (*econ.*)
influensa,*nn.*	*in-flu-*EN-*sah*	influenza
inflytande,*n.* (IV)	IN-*flü-tahn-deh*	influence
"	"	sway
infödd	IN-*född*	native (indigenous)
inföding,*nn.* (II)	IN-*fö-ding*	native (*n.*)
införa (2)	IN-*fö-rah*	introduce (bring in), to
ingång,*nn.* (II)	IN-*gohng*	entrance (entryway)
ingefära,*nn.*	ING-*eh-fair-ah*	ginger (spice)
ingen	ING-*en*	no (not any, *adj.*)
"	"	nobody (*pron.*)
"	"	none (*pron.*)
ingendera	ING-*en-day-rah*	neither (*adj., pron.*)
ingenjör,*nn.* (III)	*in-shen-*YÖR	engineer (professional engineer)
ingenstans	ING-*en-stahns*	nowhere
inhemsk	IN-*hemsk*	domestic (not foreign)
in i	IN EE	into (to the inside)
initial,*nn.* (III)	*in-it-see-*AWL	initial (letter)
inkassera (1)	IN-*kah-say-rah*	cash (receive cash for), to
"	"	collect, to (*bus.*)
inkomst,*nn.* (III)	IN-*kohmst*	income
inkomstskatt,*nn.* (III)	IN-*kohmst-skaht*	income tax
inledning,*nn.* (II)	IN-*layd-ning*	introduction (preliminary part)
innan	IN-*ahn*	before (prior to the time when, *conj.*)
inne	IN-*eh*	inside (within, *adv.*)
innefatta (1)	IN-*eh-faht-ah*	include (contain), to
innehåll,*n.*	IN-*eh-hohll*	contents
innehålla (10)	IN-*eh-hohll-ah*	contain, to
innehav,*n.* (V)	IN-*eh-hawv*	holdings (possessions)
innehavare,*nn.* (V)	IN-*eh-haw-vah-reh*	bearer (*banking*)
inne i	IN-*ne ee*	within (inside, *prep.*)
innesluta (6)	IN-*eh-slu-tah*	embrace (include), to
innevarande	IN-*eh-vaw-rahn-deh*	current (contemporary, *adj.*)
inom	IN-*ohm*	within (in less time than, *prep.*)
inomhus	IN-*ohm-huh̠ s*	indoors (*adv.*)
inrätta (1)	IN-*ret-ah*	constitute (make up), to
inre	IN-*reh*	inner
"	"	inside
"	"	internal
inre, det,*n. def.*	*deh-*IN-*reh*	inside (interior, *n.*)
"	"	interior (inside, *n.*)
insamla (1)	IN-*sahm-lah*	raise (collect), to
insats,*nn.* (III)	IN-*sahts*	stake (thing wagered)

Swedish	Pronunciation	English
insätta (11)	IN-*set-ah*	insert, to
insättare,*nn.* (V)	IN-*set-ah-reh*	depositor (*fin.*)
inse (10)	IN-*say*	appreciate (perceive fully), to
"	"	realize (recognize), to
insekt,*nn.* (III)	IN-*seckt*	bug
"	"	insect
inskrift,*nn.* (III)	IN-*skrift*	inscription
insolvens,*nn.*	*in-sohl-*VENS	insolvency (*bus.*)
inspektera (1)	*in-speck-*TAY-*rah*	inspect, to
inspektion,*nn.* (III)	*in-speck-*SHOON	inspection (scrutiny)
inspiration,*nn.* (III)	*in-spee-rah-*SHOON	inspiration
inspirera (1)	*in-spee-*RAY-*rah*	inspire, to
insprutning,*nn.* (II)	IN-*spru̠ t-ning*	injection (*med.*)
installera (1)	*in-stah-*LAY-*rah*	install (set up for use), to
instinkt,*nn.* (III)	IN-*stinkt*	instinct
institut,*n.* (V)	*in-stit-*TU̠ T	institute
institution,*nn.* (III)	*in-stit-uh-*SHOON	institution (establishment)
instrument,*n.* (V)	*in-stru-*MENT	instrument (implement)
inte	IN-*teh*	no (not any, *adv.*)
"	"	not
inteckning,*nn.* (II)	IN-*teck-ning*	mortgage
inte dess mindre	IN-*teh dess-*MIN-*dreh*	nevertheless
intellektuell	*in-teh-leck-tuh-*ELL	intellectual (*adj.*)
intelligens,*nn.*	*in-teh-lig-*ENS	intelligence (understanding)
intelligent	*in-teh-lig-*ENT	intelligent
intensiv	*in-ten-*SEEV	extreme
"	"	intense
internationell	*in-tehr-naht-shoo-*NELL	international
intervju,*nn.* (III)	*in-tehr-*VIEW	interview
intet	IN-*tet*	nothing (*n.*)
intim	*in-*TEEM	intimate (personal)
intressant	*in-treh-*SAHNGT	interesting
intresse,*n.*	*in-*TRESS-*eh*	interest (attention)
intresse,*n.* (IV)	*in-*TRESS-*eh*	interest (engaging quality)
intressera (1)	*in-treh-*SAY-*rah*	interest, to
intryck,*n.* (V)	IN-*trück*	impression (effect)
intuition,*nn.*	*in-tuh-ee-*SHOON	intuition
intyg,*n.* (V)	IN-*tü̠ g*	certificate
intyga (1)	IN-*tü-gah*	certify, to
"	"	testify, to
inuti	IN-*uht-ee*	inside (within, *prep.*)
invånare,*nn.* (V)	IN-*voh-nah-reh*	inhabitant
invända (2)	IN-*ven-dah*	object, to
invändning,*nn.* (II)	IN-*vend-ning*	objection
invänta (1)	IN-*ven-tah*	await, to
invecklad	IN-*veck-lahd*	complex (complicated)
inventarieförteckning, *nn.* (II)	*in-ven-*TAW-*ree-eh-för-*TECK-*ning*	inventory (*bus.*)
investera (1)	*in-ves-*TAY-*rah*	invest, to (*bus.*)
investering,*nn.* (II)	*in-ves-*TAY-*ring*	investment (*bus.*)
Irland,*n.*	EER-*lahnd*	Ireland
irländsk	EER-*lensk*	Irish (*adj.*)
irritera (1)	*ihrr-it-*TAY-*rah*	irritate (annoy), to
is,*nn.*	EES	ice (frozen water)
isig	EES-*ig*	icy
Israel,*n.*	EES-*rah-el*	Israel
israelisk	*ees-rah-*AYL-*isk*	Israeli (*adj.*)
isskåp,*n.* (V)	EES-*skoh̠ p*	icebox
Italien,*n.*	*ee-*TAWL-*ee-en*	Italy
italiensk	*ee-tahll-*YAYNSK	Italian (*adj.*)
iver,*nn.*	EE-*vehr*	zeal
ivrig	EEV-*rig*	anxious (wanting very much)
"	"	eager
"	"	keen
ivrigt upptagen	EEV-*rickt* UHP-*tawg-en*	intent (engrossed)
ja	YAW	yes
jacka,*nn.* (I)	YAHCK-*ah*	jacket (short coat)
jag	YAWG	I
jaga (1)	YAW-*gah*	chase, to
jagare,*nn.* (V)	YAW-*gah-reh*	destroyer (ship)
jägare,*nn.* (V)	YAI-*gah-reh*	hunter
jakt,*nn.* (III)	YAHKT	hunt (sport)
jakthund,*nn.* (II)	YAHKT-*huhnd*	hound
jämföra (2)	YEM-*fö-rah*	compare (consider relatively), to
jämförelse,*nn.* (III)	YEM-*fö-rell-seh*	comparison

Swedish	Pronunciation	English
jämn	YEMN	even
"	"	flat
"	"	level
"	"	steady (regular)
jämna (1)	YEM-*nah*	smooth (level), to
jämra sig (1)	YEM-*rah say*	wail, to
Japan,*n.*	YAW-*pahn*	Japan
japansk	*yah*-PAWNSK	Japanese (*adj.*)
järn,*n.*	YAIRN	iron (metal)
järnväg,*nn.* (II)	YAIRN-*vaig*	railroad
järnvaror,*nn.pl.*	YAIRN-*vaw-ror*	hardware
jäst,*nn.*	YEST	yeast
jätte,*nn.* (II)	YET-*eh*	giant
javisst	*yah*-VIST	certainly (of course!, *interj.*)
jazz,*nn.*	YAHSS	jazz
Jerusalem,*n.*	*yeh*-RU-*sah-lem*	Jerusalem
Jesus	YAY-*suhs*	Jesus
jo	YOO	yes (after negative question)
jod,*nn.*	YOHD	iodine (antiseptic)
jord,*nn.*	YOORD	dirt
"	"	earth
"	"	earth (planet)
"	"	land (property)
"	"	soil (ground)
jordbävning,*nn.* (II)	YOORD-*baiv-ning*	earthquake
jordbruk,*n.*	YOORD-*bru̱k*	agriculture
jordgubbe,*nn.* (II)	YOORD-*guhb-eh*	strawberry
jordnöt,*nn.* (*pl.* -nötter)	YOORD-*nö̱t*	peanut
journalfilm,*nn.* (III)	*shoor*-NAWL-*film*	newsreel
jude,*nn.* (II)	YU-*deh*	Jew (*n.*)
judisk	YU-*disk*	Jewish (*adj.*)
Jugoslavien,*n.*	*yu h-goo*-SLAW-*vih-en*	Yugoslavia
jul,*nn.* (II)	YU̱L	Christmas
jungfru,*nn.* (III)	YUHNG-*fru*	virgin (*n.*)
justera (1)	*shuhss*-TAY-*rah*	adjust (regulate), to
juvel,*nn.* (III)	*yu*-VAYL	jewel
kabel,*nn.* (II)	KAW-*bell*	cable (rope)
kabeltelegram,*n.* (V)	KAW-*bell-tell-eh*-GRAHM	cablegram
kaffe,*n.*	KAHF-*eh*	coffee
kaffepanna,*nn.* (I)	KAHF-*eh-pahn-ah*	coffee pot
Kairo,*n.*	CAI-*roo*	Cairo
kakao,*nn.*	KAW-*kah-oo*	cocoa
käke,*nn.* (II)	CHAI-*keh*	jaw
kål,*nn.*	KOH̱L	cabbage
kalas,*n.* (V)	*kah*-LAWS	feast (meal)
kälke,*nn.* (II)	CHELL-*keh*	sled
kalkon,*nn.* (III)	*kahll*-KOON	turkey
kalksten,*nn.*	KAHLLK-*stayn*	limestone
kall	KAHLL	cold (*adj.*)
källa,*nn.* (I)	CHELL-*ah*	source (origin)
"	"	well (oil, gas shaft, *n.*)
källare,*nn.* (V)	CHELL-*ah-reh*	cellar
källarvåning,*nn.* (II)	CHELL-*ahr-voh-ning*	basement
kålmask,*nn.* (II)	KOH̱L-*mahssk*	caterpillar
kalori,*nn.* (III)	*kah-loo*-REE	calorie
kalv,*nn.* (II)	KAHLLV	calf (animal)
kalvkotlett,*nn.* (III)	KAHLLV-*koht*-LET	veal chop
kalvkött,*n.*	KAHLLV-*chöt*	veal
kam,*nn.* (II)	KAHM	comb (for hair)
kamel,*nn.* (III)	*kah*-MAYL	camel
kamera,*nn.* (I)	KAW-*meh-rah*	camera
kamin,*nn.* (III)	*kah*-MEEN	stove (for heating)
kamp,*nn.*	KAHMP	combat
"		fight
kämpa (1)	CHEM-*pah*	fight (contend), to
kämpa mot	CHEM-*pah* MOOT	fight (struggle against), to
kamrat,*nn.* (III)	*kahm*-RAWT	companion
"	"	comrade
"		pal
kamrer,*nn.* (III)	*kahm*-RAYR	accountant
kan (4)	KAHN	can (*v.*)
kan (kunde)	KAHN (KUHN-*deh*)	might (*v.*)
Kanada,*n.*	KAHN-*ah-dah*	Canada
kanadensisk	*kah-nah*-DEN-*sisk*	Canadian (*adj.*)
kanal,*nn.* (III)	*kah*-NAWL	canal

Swedish	Pronunciation	English
kanariefågel,*nn.* (II)	*kah*-NAW-*ree-eh*-FOH̱G-*el*	canary
kandidat,*nn.* (III)	*kahn-did*-DAWT	candidate
kanel,*nn.*	*kah*-NAYL	cinnamon
kanfas,*nn.*	KAHN-*fahss*	canvas (cloth)
kanin,*nn.* (III)	*kah*-NEEN	rabbit
känna (2)	CHEN-*ah*	feel (touch), to
"	"	know (be acquainted with), to
kanna,*nn.* (I)	KAHN-*ah*	jug
känna (sig)	CHEN-*ah* (*say*)	feel (experience), to
känna igen	*chen-ah-ee*-YEN	recognize (identify), to
känna lukten av	*chen-ah*-LUHCK-*ten awv*	smell (perceive odor), to
kännedom,*nn.*	CHEN-*eh-doomm*	acquaintance (knowledge)
kanon,*nn.* (III)	*kah*-NOON	cannon
kanot,*nn.* (III)	*kah*-NOOT	canoe
kanske	KAHN-*sheh*	maybe
"	"	perhaps
känsla,*nn.* (I)	CHENS-*lah*	feeling (emotion)
"	"	sensation
"	"	sentiment
känslig	CHENS-*lig*	sensitive (susceptible)
kant,*nn.* (III)	KAHNT	border
"	"	edge
"	"	margin
"	"	rim
kapell,*n.* (V)	*kah*-PELL	chapel
kapital,*n.*	*kah-pit*-TAWL	capital (wealth)
kapitel,*n.* (V)	*kah*-PIT-*el*	chapter (of book)
kapitulation,*nn.* (III)	*kah-pit-uh-lah*-SHOON	surrender (*mil.*)
käpp,*nn.* (II)	CHEP	cane (walking stick)
kappa,*nn.* (I)	KAHP-*ah*	cloak (apparel)
"		coat (woman's overcoat)
kapten,*nn.* (III)	*kahp*-TAYN	captain (officer)
kär,*n.* (V)	CHAIR	dear (beloved, *adj.*)
kar,*n.* (V)	KAR	tub (bathtub)
Karachi,*n.*	*kah*-RAH-*chee*	Karachi
karaktär,*nn.* (III)	*kah-rahck*-TAIR	character (nature)
karaktäristisk	*kah-rahck-tehr*-ISS-*tisk*	characteristic (typical)
karikatyrteckning, *nn.* (II)	*kah-rick-ah*-TÜR-*teck-ning*	cartoon (caricature)
karl,*nn.* (II)	KAWR	fellow (person)
"	"	guy
kärl,*n.* (V)	CHAIL	vessel (receptacle)
kärlek,*nn.*	CHAIR-*layk*	love
kärna,*nn.* (I)	CHAIRN-*ah*	kernel
karneval,*nn.* (III)	*kahrn-eh*-VAWL	carnival
kärr,*n.* (V)	CHAIRR	marsh
"		mire (bog)
kärra,*nn.* (I)	CHAIRR-*ah*	cart
karriär,*nn.* (III)	*kah-ree*-AIR	career
karta,*nn.* (I)	KART-*ah*	map
kartbok,*nn.* (*pl.* -böcker)	KART-*boo̱k*	atlas
kassör,*nn.* (III)	*kah*-SÖR	cashier
kasta (1)	KAHSS-*tah*	cast, to
"	"	pitch, to
"	"	throw, to
kasta en blick	KAHSS-*tah en* BLICK	glance, to
kastanj,*nn.* (III)	*kah*-STAHṈ_*yuh*	chestnut (tree)
katalog,*nn.* (III)	*kah-tah*-LOH̱G	catalogue
katastrof,*nn.* (III)	*kah-tah*-STROH̱F	disaster
katolsk	*kah*-TOOLSK	Catholic (*adj.*)
katrinplommon,*n.* (V)	*kah*-TREEN-*ploomm-ohn*	prune
katt,*nn.* (III)	KAHT	cat
kattunge,*nn.* (II)	KAHT-*uhng-eh*	kitten
kedja,*nn.* (I)	CHAYD-*yah*	chain
kejsare,*nn.* (V)	CHAY-*sah-reh*	emperor
kejsarinna,*nn.* (I)	CHAY-*sahr-in-ah*	empress
kejserlig	CHAY-*sehr-lig*	imperial
kemi,*nn.*	*cheh*-MEE	chemistry
kikhosta,*nn.*	CHEEK-*hooss-tah*	whooping cough
killing,*nn.* (II)	CHILL-*ing*	kid (goat)
Kina,*n.*	CHEE-*nah*	China
kind,*nn.* (III)	CHINND	cheek
kindergarten,*nn.* (V)	KIN-*dehr-gahrt-en*	kindergarten

Swedish	Pronunciation	English
kinesisk	*chee*-NAY-*sisk*	Chinese (*adj.*)
kirurg,*nn.* (III)	*chee*-RUHR_G	surgeon
kista,*nn.* (I)	CHISS-*tah*	chest (box)
kittel,*nn.* (II)	CHIT-*el*	kettle
kittla (1)	CHIT-*lah*	tickle (touch lightly), to
kjol,*nn.* (II)	CHOOL	skirt (garment)
kläcka (2)	KLECK-*ah*	hatch, to
klä(da) (2)	KLAI(-*dah*)	clothe, to
klä(da) av	*klai*(-*dah*)-AWV	strip (denude), to
klä(da) sig	KLAI(-*dah*) *say*	dress (get dressed), to
kläder,*nn. pl.*	KLAI-*dehr*	clothing
klädesplagg,*n.* (V)	KLAI-*des-plahg*	garment
klädsel,*nn.*	KLED-*sel*	attire (apparel)
klaga (1)	KLAW-*gah*	complain, to
klagomål,*n.* (V)	KLAW-*goo-moh_l*	complaint
klandra (1)	KLAHN-*drah*	blame, to
klänning,*nn.* (II)	KLEN-*ing*	dress (frock)
klapp,*nn.* (II)	KLAHP	pat (tap)
klappa (1)	KLAHP-*ah*	pat (tap), to
klappa händerna	KLAHP-*ah* HEN-*dehr-nah*	clap (applaud), to
klar	KLAWR	clear
"	"	fair (not cloudy)
klara (sig) (1)	KLAW-*rah* (*say*)	pass (not fail in), to
klarinett,*nn.* (III)	*klah-rin*-NET	clarinet
klass,*nn.* (III)	KLAHSS	class (kind)
"	"	grade (school division)
klassisk	KLAHSS-*isk*	classic (first-class, *adj.*)
klassiskt verk,*n.* (V)	KLAHSS-*iskt* VAIRRK	classic (first-class work)
klassrum,*n.* (V)	KLAHSS-*ruhm*	classroom
klättra uppför (1)	KLET-*rah* UHP-*för*	climb (scale), to
klausul,*nn.* (III)	*klah-uh*-SU_L	clause (stipulation)
klen	KLAYN	delicate (sickly)
klimat,*n.* (V)	*klee*-MAWT	climate (weather)
klinga (1)	KLING-*ah*	clang, to
klippa,*nn.* (I)	KLIP-*ah*	cliff
klippa (2)	KLIP-*ah*	shear, to
klippig	KLIP-*ig*	rocky (rock covered)
klister,*n.*	KLISS-*tehr*	paste (adhesive)
kliva (5)	KLEE-*vah*	stride (walk), to
klo,*nn.* (III)	KLOO	claw (of animal)
klo,*nn.* (III)	KLOO	claw (of bird)
klocka,*nn.* (I)	KLOHCK-*ah*	bell
"	"	clock
"	"	watch (timepiece)
klok	KLOO_K	wise
klokhet,*nn.*	KLOO_K-*hayt*	wisdom
kloster,*n.* (V)	KLOHSS-*tehr*	monastery
klöver,*nn.*	KLÖ-*vehr*	clover
klubb,*nn.*	KLUHB	club (association)
klubba,*nn.* (I)	KLUHB-*ah*	club (cudgel)
klump,*nn.* (II)	KLUHMP	lump (shapeless piece)
knä,*n.*	K_NAI	lap (of seated person)
knä,*n.* (IV)	K_NAI	knee
knäböja (2)	K_NAI-*böy-ah*	kneel, to
knacka (1)	K_NAHCK-*ah*	rap, to
"	"	tap, to
knapp	K_NAHP	scarce
knapp,*nn.* (II)	K_NAHP	button
knappast	K_NAHP-*ahst*	hardly (barely)
knapphet,*nn.*	K_NAHP-*hayt*	scarcity
knappnål,*nn.* (II)	K_NAHP-*noh_l*	pin (sewing accessory)
knep,*n.* (V)	K_NAYP	trick (ruse)
kniv,*nn.* (II)	K_NEEV	knife
knopp,*nn.* (II)	K_NOHP	bud (*bot.*)
knorra (1)	K_NOHRR-*ah*	grumble, to
knuff,*nn.* (II)	K_NUHF	push (shove)
knuffa (1)	K_NUHF-*ah*	push (shove), to
knut,*nn.* (II)	K_NU_T	knot
knyta (7)	K_NÜ-*tah*	tie (fasten), to
ko,*nn.* (III)	KOO	cow
kock,*nn.* (II)	KOHCK	cook
koffert,*nn.* (II)	KOHFF-*ehrt*	trunk (baggage)
kök,*n.* (V)	CHÖ_K	kitchen
koka (1, 2)	KOO-*kah*	boil (bubble up), to
"	"	cook (heat food), to

Swedish	Pronunciation	English
kokosnöt,*nn.* (*pl.* -nötter)	KOOCK-*ooss-nö_t*	coconut
koks,*nn.*	KOHX	coke
kol,*n.*	KOH_L	carbon (*chem.*)
kol,*n.* (V)	KOH_L	coal
kolera,*nn.*	KOO-*leh-rah*	cholera
kolon,*n.* (V)	KOO-*lohn*	colon (*punct.*)
koloni,*nn.* (III)	*koh-loh*-NEE	colony
kolonial	*koh-loh-nee*-AWL	colonial
kolonn,*nn.* (III)	*koh*-LOHNN	column (pillar)
koltrast,*nn.* (II)	KOH_L-*trahst*	blackbird
kombination,*nn.* (III)	*kohm-bin-ah*-SHOON	combination
kombinera (1)	*kohm-bin*-NAY-*rah*	combine (make join), to
komedi,*nn.* (III)	*koh-meh*-DEE	comedy (comic play)
komma (10)	KOHM-*ah*	come, to
komma,*n.* (IV)	KOHM-*ah*	comma
komma (gå) in i	*kohm-ah* (*goh*) IN *ee*	enter (come or go into), to
kommande	KOHM-*ahn-deh*	future (*adj.*)
kommando,*n.* (IV)	*koh*-MAHN-*doo*	command (authority)
komma till	KOHM-*ah till*	reach (arrive at), to
kommendera (1)	*koh-men*-DAY-*rah*	command (order), to
kommersiell	*koh-mesh-ee*-ELL	commercial
kommission,*nn.* (III)	*koh-mee*-SHOON	commission (group)
kommitté,*nn.* (III)	*koh-mit*-TAY	committee
kommunism,*nn.*	*koh-muh*-NISSM	communism
kompakt	*kohm*-PAHKT	compact (packed firmly)
kompani,*n.* (III)	*kohm-pah*-NEE	company (*mil.*)
kompanjon,*nn.* (III)	*kohm-pahn*-YOON	partner (*bus.*)
kompass,*nn.* (III)	*kohm*-PAHSS	compass (magnetic instrument)
komplimang,*nn.* (III)	*kohm-plee*-MAHNG	compliment
komplott,*nn.* (III)	*kohm*-PLOHT	plot (conspiracy)
komponera (1)	*kohm-poo*-NAY-*rah*	compose, to (*mus.*)
kompromiss,*nn.* (III)	*kohm-proo*-MISS	compromise (mutual concessions)
kön,*n.* (V)	CHÖ_N	sex
koncentrera (1)	*kohn-sen*-TRAY-*rah*	concentrate (make converge), to
kondensera (1)	*kohn-den*-SAY-*rah*	condense (compress), to
konduktör,*nn.* (III)	*kohn-duhck*-TÖR	conductor (ticket collector)
konferens,*nn.* (III)	*kohn-feh*-RENS	conference (meeting)
konfidentiell	*kohn-fee-dent-see*-ELL	confidential (private)
konfiskation,*nn.* (III)	*kohn-fiss-kah*-SHOON	attachment (legal seizure)
konflikt,*nn.* (III)	*kohn*-FLICKT	conflict (opposition)
kongress,*nn.* (III)	*kohn*-GRESS	congress (legislature)
konjak,*nn.*	KOHN-*yahck*	brandy
konjunktion,*nn.* (III)	*kohn-yuhnk*-SHOON	conjunction (*gram.*)
konkret	*kohn*-KRAYT	concrete (real)
konkurrens,*nn.*	*kohn-kuh*-RAHNGS	competition (*bus.*)
konkurrent,*nn.* (III)	*kohn-kuh*-RENT	competitor (*bus.*)
konkurs,*nn.* (III)	*kohn*-KUHSH	bankruptcy
"	"	failure (bankruptcy)
konsert,*nn.* (III)	*kohn*-SAIR	concert (musical performance)
konst-...	KOHNST-...	artificial (synthetic)
konst,*nn.* (III)	KOHNST	art
"	"	trick (knack)
konstig	KOHN-*stig*	funny
"	"	odd (queer)
konstitution,*nn.* (III)	*kohn-stit-uh*-SHOON	constitution (nature)
konstnär,*nn.* (III)	KOHNST-*nair*	artist
konstruktion,*nn.* (III)	*kohn-struhck*-SHOON	construction (fabrication)
konstsilke,*n.*	KOHNST-*sill-keh*	rayon
konsul,*nn.* (III)	KOHN-*suhl*	consul
kontakt,*nn.* (III)	*kohn*-TAHKT	contact (meeting)
"	"	outlet (*elec.*)
kontanter,*nn.pl.*	*kohn*-TAHN-*tehr*	cash (money)
kontinent,*nn.* (III)	*kohn-tin*-NENT	continent (*geog.*)
konto,*n.* (IV)	KOHN-*too*	account (bank account)
"	"	charge account

Swedish	Pronunciation	English
kontor,*n.* (V)	*kohn*-TOOR	office (place of business)
kontraband,*n.* (V)	KOHN-*trah-bahnd*	contraband
kontrakt,*n.* (V)	*kohn*-TRAHKT	contract
kontraktbridge,*nn.*	*kohn*-TRAHKT-*bridge*	bridge, contract
kontraktsbrott,*n.* (V)	*kohn*-TRAHKTS-*broht*	breach of contract (*bus.*)
kontrasignering, *nn.* (II)	KOHN-*trah-sing-nay-ring*	countersignature (*bus.*)
kontrast,*nn.* (III)	*kohn*-TRAHSST	contrast
kontroll,*nn.* (III)	*kohn*-TROHLL	check (examination)
kontrollera (1)	*kohn-troh*-LAY-*rah*	check (test), to
konversationslexikon,*n.* (V)	*kohn-vesh-ah*-SHOONS-*lex-ee-kohn*	encyclopaedia
konverteringsvärde,*n.* (IV)	*kohn-vehr*-TAY-*rings-vaird-eh*	conversion rate (*bus.*)
konvoj,*nn.* (III)	*kohn*-VOY	convoy (*mil.*)
kooperativ förening,*nn.* (II)	*koo-*OHP-*eh-rah-teev för-*AYN-*ing*	cooperative (*n.*)
köp,*n.* (V)	CHÖ_P	purchase (act of buying)
köpa (2)	CHÖ-*pah*	buy, to
köpare,*nn.* (V)	CHÖ-*pah-reh*	buyer
köpebrev,*n.* (V)	CHÖ-*peh-brayv*	bill of sale
Köpenhamn,*n.*	*chö-pen-*HAHMN	Copenhagen
kopia,*nn.* (I)	*koh*-PEE-*ah*	copy
"	"	duplicate (*n.*)
kopiera (1)	*koh-pee-*AYR-*ah*	copy (imitate), to
köpman,*nn.* (*pl.* -män)	CHÖ_P-*mahn*	merchant
"	"	trader
kopp,*nn.* (II)	KOHP	cup
koppar,*nn.*	KOHP-*ahr*	copper
koppling,*nn.* (II)	KOHP-*ling*	clutch (automotive device)
köpslå (10)	CHÖ_P-*sloh*	bargain (negotiate), to
kör,*nn.* (III)	KÖR	choir
köra (2)	CHÖ-*rah*	drive (a vehicle), to
korg,*nn.* (II)	KOR_yuh	basket
korgboll,*nn.*	KOR_yuh-*bohll*	basketball
kork,*nn.* (II)	KOHRRK	cork (stopper)
korn,*n.*	KOORN	barley
korpral,*nn.* (III)	*kohr*-PRAWL	corporal (*mil.*)
korrespondensinstitut,*n.* (V)	*koh-reh-spohn*-DAHNGS-*in-stit*-TU_T	correspondence school
korrespondent,*nn.* (III)	*koh-reh-spohn*-DENT	correspondent (letter writer)
korridor,*nn.* (III)	*koh-rid*-DOHR	hall (corridor)
kors,*n.* (V)	KOHSH	cross (crucifix)
korsa (1)	KOHSH-*ah*	cross (crossbreed), to
körsbär,*n.* (V)	CHÖSH-*bair*	cherry (fruit)
korsning,*nn.* (II)	KOHSH-*ning*	crossing (intersection)
korsväg,*nn.* (II)	KOHSH-*vaig*	crossroads
kort	KOHRRT	brief (fleeting)
"	"	short
kort brev,*n.* (V)	KOHRRT BRAYV	note (letter)
kortfattad	KOHRRT-*faht-ahd*	compact (brief)
kortlek,*nn.* (II)	KOORT-*layk*	deck (of cards)
korv,*nn.* (II)	KOHRRV	sausage
kosta (1)	KOHSS-*tah*	cost, to
kostnad,*nn.* (III)	KOHST-*nahd*	cost (price)
kostym,*nn.* (III)	*koh*-STÜ_M	costume
"	"	suit, man's
kött,*n.*	CHÖT	flesh
"	"	meat
krabba,*nn.* (I)	KRAHB-*ah*	crab (shellfish)
kraft,*nn.* (III)	KRAHFT	force (power)
"	"	vigor (strength)
kräfta,*nn.*	KREF-*tah*	cancer
kraftig	KRAHFF-*lig*	stout (strong)
"	"	sturdy
"	"	vigorous
krage,*nn.* (II)	KRAWG-*eh*	collar
kråka,*nn.* (I)	KROH-*kah*	crow (bird)
kräkas (2)	KRAI-*kahs*	vomit, to
krama (1)	KRAW-*mah*	squeeze, to
kramp,*nn.* (III)	KRAHMP	cramp (*med.*)
kran,*nn.* (II)	KRAWN	tap (faucet)
krans,*nn.* (II)	KRAHNS	wreath
kratta,*nn.* (I)	KRAHT-*ah*	rake (tool)
krav,*n.* (V)	KRAWV	demand (request)

Swedish	Pronunciation	English
kräva (2)	KRAI-*vah*	require (need), to
kreatursbesättning,*nn.* (II)	KRAY-*ah-tu_sh-beh*-SET-*ning*	stock (livestock)
kredit,*nn.* (III)	*kreh*-DEET	credit (*bus.*)
kreditera (1)	*kreh-dit*-TAY-*rah*	credit, to (*bus.*)
krig,*n.* (V)	KREEG	war
kris,*nn.* (III)	KREES	crisis
kristall,*nn.* (III)	*kriss*-STAHLL	crystal (*min.*)
kristen,*nn.* (*pl.* kristna)	KRISS-*ten*	Christian (*n.*)
Kristus,*m.*	KRISS-*tuhss*	Christ
krita,*nn.* (I)	KREE-*tah*	chalk
kritik,*nn.* (III)	*krit*-TEEK	criticism (censure)
kritiker,*nn.* (V)	KREE-*tick-ehr*	critic
krok,*nn.* (II)	KROO_K	hook
krokig	KROOK-*ig*	bent (curved)
"	"	crooked
krom,*nn.*	KROHM	chromium
krön,*n.* (V)	KRÖ_N	crest (summit)
kröna (2)	KRÖ-*nah*	crown, to
krona,*nn.* (I)	KROO-*nah*	crown (headdress)
krönika,*nn.* (I)	KRÖ-*nick-ah*	chronicle
kropp,*nn.* (II)	KROHP	body (*anat.*)
kroppslig	KROHPS-*lig*	physical (bodily)
krossa (1)	KROSS-*ah*	crush, to
"	"	smash, to
kruka,*nn.* (I)	KRU-*kah*	pot (container)
krusning,*nn.* (II)	KRU_S-*ning*	ripple
krycka,*nn.* (I)	KRÜCK-*ah*	crutch
krydda,*nn.* (I)	KRÜDD-*ah*	spice
kryddnejlika,*nn.* (I)	KRÜD-*nay-lick-ah*	clove
krympa (2)	KRÜM-*pah*	shrink (become contracted), to
krympling,*nn.* (II)	KRÜMP-*ling*	cripple
krypa (7)	KRÜ-*pah*	crawl, to
"	"	creep, to
kryssare,*nn.* (V)	KRÜSS-*ah-reh*	cruiser (ship)
kryssning,*nn.* (II)	KRÜSS-*ning*	cruise (voyage)
kub,*nn.* (III)	KUH_B	cube (*geom.*)
kubikinnehåll,*n.*	*kuh*-BEEK-*in-eh-hohll*	capacity (volume)
kudde,*nn.* (II)	KUHD-*eh*	pillow
kula,*nn.* (I)	KUH-*lah*	bullet
kulle,*nn.* (II)	KUHLL-*eh*	mound (hill)
kulpenna,*nn.* (I)	KUH_L-*pen-ah*	ball-point pen
kultur,*nn.*	*kuhll*-TUHR	civilization (culture)
"	"	culture (refinement)
kund,*nn.* (III)	KUHND	customer (buyer)
"	"	patron
kunde (4)	KUHN-*deh*	could (*v.*)
kung,*nn.* (II)	KUHNG	king
kungarike,*n.* (IV)	KUHNG-*ah-ree-keh*	kingdom
kunglig	KUHNG-*lig*	regal
"	"	royal
kunskap,*nn.* (III)	KUHN-*skawp*	information
"	"	knowledge (understanding)
kupé,*nn.* (III)	*kuh*-PAY	compartment (of train)
kupol,*nn.* (III)	*kuh*-POH_L	dome (cupola)
kupong,*nn.* (III)	*kuh*-POHNG	coupon (detachable certificate)
kurator,*nn.* (III)	*kuh*-RAW-*toor*	curator
kurort,*nn.* (III)	KU_R-*oort*	resort (spa)
kurs,*nn.* (III)	KUHSH	rate (exchange)
kursavgift,*nn.* (III)	KUHSH-*awv-yift*	tuition (school fee)
kurva,*nn.* (I)	KUHRR-*vah*	curve
kusin,*nn.* (III)	*kuh*-SEEN	cousin
kust,*nn.* (III)	KUHST	coast (seaboard)
kuvert,*n.* (V)	*kuh*-VAIR	envelope (folded wrapper)
kväll, i	*ee*-KVELL	tonight
kväll,*nn.* (II)	KVELL	evening
kvällsmat,*nn.*	KVELLS-*mawt*	supper (light evening meal)
kvantitet,*nn.* (III)	*kvahn-tit*-TAYT	quantity (amount)
kvartals-...	*kvahrt*-TAWLS-...	quarterly (four times a year)
kvast,*nn.* (II)	KVAHSST	broom
kväva (2)	KVAI-*vah*	choke, to
kvick	KVICK	witty
kvickhet,*nn.*	KVICK-*hayt*	wit (humor)
kvicksilver,*n.*	KVICK-*sill-vehr*	mercury
kvinna,*nn.* (I)	KVIN-*ah*	woman
kvinnlig	KVIN-*lig*	female (*adj.*)

Swedish	Pronunciation	English
kvist,*nn.* (II)	KVIST	twig
kvittera (1)	*kvit*-TAY-*rah*	receipt, to (*bus.*)
kvitto,*n.* (IV)	KVIT-*oo*	receipt (voucher)
kvot,*nn.* (III)	KVOOT	quota
kyckling,*nn.* (II)	CHÜCK-*ling*	chicken
kyla,*nn.*	CHÜ-*lah*	chill (coldness)
"	"	cold (low temperature)
kylig	CHÜ-*lig*	chilly
kylskåp,*n.* (V)	CHÜ_L-*skoh_p*	refrigerator
kypare,*nn.* (V)	CHÜ-*pah-reh*	waiter
kyrka,*nn.* (I)	CHÜRR-*kah*	church
kyrkogård,*nn.* (II)	CHÜRR-*koo-gord*	cemetery
kyrkoherde,*nn.* (II)	CHÜRR-*koo-hayrd-eh*	parson
kyrktorn,*n.* (V)	CHÜRRK-*toorn*	steeple
kysk	CHÜSK	chaste
kyss,*nn.* (II)	CHÜSS	kiss
kyssa (2)	CHÜSS-*ah*	kiss, to
laboratorium,*n.* (III)	*lah-boo-rah*-TOO-*ree-uhm*	laboratory
läcker	LECK-*ehr*	delicious
(byrå)låda,*nn.* (I)	(BÜ-*roh*)-LOH-*dah*	drawer (sliding box)
ladda (1)	LAHD-*ah*	charge, to (*elec.*)
läder,*n.*	LAI-*dehr*	leather (*n.*)
ladugård,*nn.* (II)	LAW(-*duh*)-*gord*	barn
låg	LOH_G	low
lag,*n.* (V)	LAWG	team (in sports)
lag,*nn.* (II)	LAWG	law (governing code)
laga (1)	LAW-*gah*	fix, to
"	"	mend (repair), to
låga,*nn.* (I)	LOH-*gah*	flame
laga mat (1)	*law-gah*-MAWT	cook (prepare meals), to
lagbok,*nn.* (*pl.* -böcker)	LAWG-*boo_k*	code (law)
läge,*n.* (IV)	LAIG-*eh*	location (place)
"	"	position (location)
		site
lägenhet,*nn.* (III)	LAIG-*en-hayt*	apartment
lager,*n.* (V)	LAWG-*ehr*	layer (thickness)
läger,*n.* (V)	LAIG-*ehr*	camp (encampment, *mil.*)
lägga (11)	LEG-*ah*	lay (put down), to
"	"	place (lay), to
lägga in i lag	*leg-ah*-IN *ee*-LAWG	pickle (preserve), to
lägga sig	LEG-*ah say*	lie down, to
lägga sig i	*leg-ah-say*-EE	interfere, to
"	"	meddle, to
laglig	LAWG-*lig*	lawful
"	"	legal
lagra (1)	LAWG-*rah*	store (accumulate), to
lagstiftande församling,*nn.* (II)	LAWG-*stif-tahn-deh fö*-SHAHM-*ling*	legislature
lagstiftning,*nn.*	LAWG-*stift-ning*	legislation
lakan,*n.* (V)	LAW-*kahn*	sheet (bedding)
läkare,*nn.* (V)	LAI-*kah-reh*	physician
läktare,*nn.* (V)	LECK-*tah-reh*	gallery (balcony)
lamm,*n.* (V)	LAHM	lamb
lammkotlett,*nn.* (III)	LAHM-*koht*-LET	lamb chop
lämna (1)	LEM-*nah*	leave (let remain), to
lämna tillträde	LEM-*nah* TILL-*trai-deh*	admit (permit to enter), to
lämpa (1)	LEM-*pah*	adapt, to
lampa,*nn.* (I)	LAHM-*pah*	lamp
lämplig	LEMP-*lig*	suitable
lån,*n.* (V)	LOH_N	loan
låna (1)	LOH-*nah*	borrow, to
låna (ut)	LOH-*nah* (UH_T)	lend, to
land,*n.*	LAHND	land (ground)
land,*n.* (*pl.* länder)	LAHND	country (nation)
landa (1)	LAHN-*dah*	land (an airplane), to
"	"	land (from a ship), to
lands-...	LAHNDS-...	rural
landsbygd,*nn.* (III)	LAHNDS-*bügd*	country (countryside)
landsförvisa (1)	LAHNDS-*för-vee-sah*	banish (exile), to
landsförvisning,*nn.*	LAHNDS-*för-vees-ning*	exile (banishment)
landskap,*n.* (V)	LAHND-*skawp*	landscape (scenery)
landsväg,*nn.* (II)	LAHNDS-*vaig*	highway

Swedish	Pronunciation	English
landtunga,*nn.* (I)	LAHND-*tuhng-ah*	isthmus
lång	LOHNG	long (not short)
"		long (of a specified length)
"	"	tall (of persons)
längd,*nn.*	LENGD	length
		stature (height)
långfredag,*nn.*	LOHN-*fray-dawg*	Good Friday
längre	LENG-*reh*	further (to greater degree, *adv.*)
längre bort	LENG-*reh* BOHRT	farther (*adv.*)
längs	LENGS	along (lengthwise of)
långsam	LOHNG-*sahm*	slow (not fast)
längta efter (1)	LENG-*tah* EF-*tehr*	crave (desire), to
"	"	long for, to
långt borta	LOHNGT BOHRT-*ah*	far (afar, *adv.*)
länk,*nn.* (II)	LENK	link (connecting part)
låntagare,*nn.* (V)	LOHN-*taw-gah-reh*	borrower (*bus.*)
lapp,*nn.* (II)	LAHP	patch (repair)
läpp,*nn.* (II)	LEP	lip (*anat.*)
läppstift,*n.* (V)	LEP-*stift*	lipstick
lår,*n.* (V)	LOR	thigh
lära (2)	LAIR-*ah*	teach, to
lära,*nn.* (I)	LAIR-*ah*	doctrine
lärare,*nn.* (V)	LAIR-*ah-reh*	teacher
lärarkår,*nn.* (III)	LAIR-*ahr-kor*	faculty (teaching staff)
lära sig	LAIR-*ah say*	learn (acquire knowledge), to
"	"	master, to
lärka,*nn.* (I)	LAIRR-*kah*	lark (bird)
lärling,*nn.* (II)	LAIR-*ling*	apprentice (trade student)
larm,*n.*	LAHRRM	noise (din)
lärobok,*nn.* (*pl.* -böcker)	LAIR-*oo-boo_k*	textbook
lås,*n.* (V)	LOH_S	lock (fastening)
låsa (2)	LOH-*sah*	lock (fasten with key), to
läsa (2)	LAI-*sah*	read, to
läsare,*nn.* (V)	LAI-*sah-reh*	reader
last,*nn.* (III)	LAHSST	cargo
"	"	vice (moral fault)
lasta (1)	LAHSS-*tah*	load (fill), to
lasta av	*lahss-tah*-AWV	unload, to
lastbil,*nn.* (II)	LAHSST-*beel*	truck (automobile)
lat	LAWT	lazy
låta (10)	LOH-*tah*	let (permit), to
latinsk	*lah*-TEENSK	Latin (*adj.*)
låtsa (1)	LOHT-*sah*	affect (pretend), to
"	"	pretend (feign), to
lätt	LET	easy (not difficult)
"	"	light (of little weight)
lätta (1)	LET-*ah*	ease (relieve), to
lätthet,*nn.*	LET-*hayt*	ease (effortlessness)
lättnad,*nn.* (III)	LET-*nahd*	relief (alleviation)
lavemang,*n.* (V)	*lah-veh*-MAHNG	enema
lax,*nn.* (II)	LAHX	salmon
läxa,*nn.* (I)	LEX-*ah*	assignment (*educ.*)
"	"	lesson
le (10)	LAY	smile, to
leda (2)	LAY-*dah*	conduct, to
"	"	direct (manage), to
"	"	head, to
"	"	lead (guide), to
ledare,*nn.* (V)	LAY-*dah-reh*	director
ledgångsreumatism,*nn.*	LAYD-*gohngs-rö-mah*-TISSM	arthritis
ledig	LAY-*dig*	vacant (untenanted)
ledning,*nn.*	LAYD-*ning*	leadership (authority)
"	"	management (administration)
ledsnad,*nn.*	LESS-*nahd*	regret (sorrow)
leende,*n.* (IV)	LAY-*en-deh*	smile
legend,*nn.* (III)	*leg*-END	legend (story)
legering,*nn.* (II)	*leg*-AYR-*ing*	alloy (metal)
lejon,*n.* (V)	LAY-*ohn*	lion
leka (2)	LAY-*kah*	play (engage in recreation), to
lekkamrat,*nn.* (III)	LAYK-*kahm*-RAWT	playmate
lekplats,*nn.* (III)	LAYK-*plahts*	playground
leksak,*nn.* (III)	LAYK-*sawk*	toy
lem,*nn.* (II)	LEM	limb (*anat.*)

Swedish	Pronunciation	English
lemonad,*nn.* (III)	*leh-moh-*NAWD	lemonade
leopard,*nn.* (III)	*lay-oo-*PARD	leopard
lera,*nn.* (1)	LAY-*rah*	clay
leta efter (1)	LAY-*tah-* EF-*tehr*	look for, to
lev,*nn.* (II)	LAYV	loaf
leva (2)	LAY-*vah*	live (be alive), to
levande	LAY-*vahn-deh*	alive
"	"	live (*adj.*)
lever,*nn.* (II)	LAY-*vehr*	liver (*anat.*)
leverantör,*nn.* (III)	*leh-vehr-ahn-*TÖR	supplier (*bus.*)
liberal	*lib-eh-*RAWL	liberal (*polit., adj.*)
licens,*nn.* (III)	*lee-*SENS	license (permit)
lidande,*n.* (IV)	LEE-*dahn-deh*	suffering
lidelse,*nn.* (III)	LEE-*dell-seh*	passion (emotion)
lidelsefull	LEE-*dell-seh-fuhll*	passionate
ligga (10)	LIG-*ah*	lie (be located), to
lik	LEEK	like (*adj.*)
lik,*n.* (V)	LEEK	corpse
lika	LEE-*kah*	alike (similar)
"	"	as (equally, *adv.*)
"	"	equal (*adj.*)
likaledes	LEE-*kah-lay-dess*	alike (similarly)
(jäm)like,*nn.* (II)	(YEM-)LEEK-*eh*	peer (equal)
likgiltig	LEEK-*yill-tig*	indifferent (unconcerned)
likhet,*nn.* (III)	LEEK-*hayt*	similarity
likkista,*nn.* (I)	LEEK-*chiss-tah*	coffin
likna (1)	LEEK-*nah*	resemble, to
liknande	LEEK-*nahn-deh*	similar
likör,*nn.* (III)	*lick-*KÖR	liqueur
lilja,*nn.* (I)	LILL-*yah*	lily
lim,*n.* (V)	LIM	glue
Lima,*n.*	LEE-*mah*	Lima
limon,*nn.* (III)	*lee-*MOON	lime (fruit)
lin,*n.*	LEEN	flax
lina,*nn.* (I)	LEE-*nah*	line (cord)
lindra (1)	LIND-*rah*	relieve (ease), to
linjal,*nn.* (III)	*lin-*YAWL	ruler (measuring instrument)
linne,*n.*	LIN-*eh*	linen (fabric)
linoleum,*n.*	*lin-*OH-*lee-uhm*	linoleum
list,*nn.* (III)	LIST	ledge
lista,*nn.* (I)	LISS-*tah*	list
listig	LISS-*tig*	cunning (sly)
lita på (1)	LEE-*tah poh*	depend (rely) on, to
"	"	trust, to
lite(t)	LEE-*teh*	little (not much, *adj.*)
"	"	little (slightly, *adv.*)
liten	LEE-*ten*	little (small, *adj.*)
"	"	small
"	"	tiny
litografi,*nn.* (III)	*lit-oh-grah-*FEE	lithography
litterär	*lit-teh-*RAIR	literary
litteratur,*nn.* (III)	*lit-teh-rah-*TUHR	literature (belleslettres)
liv,*n.* (V)	LEEV	life
livfull	LEEV-*fuhll*	vivid
livlig	LEEV-*lig*	lively (*adj.*)
livmoder,*nn.*	LEEV-*moo-dehr*	womb
ljud,*n.* (V)	YU_D	sound (noise)
ljuga (6)	YU-*gah*	lie (prevaricate), to
ljus	YU_S	bright (shining)
"	"	fair (blond)
"	"	light (not dark)
ljus,*n.* (V)	YU_S	light (illumination)
(stearin)ljus,*n.* (V)	(*steh-ah-*REEN-)YU_S	candle
lock,*n.* (V)	LOHCK	cover (lid)
"	"	lid
lock,*nn.* (II)	LOHCK	curl (ringlet)
löfte,*n.* (IV)	LÖF-*teh*	pledge (vow)
"	"	promise
logi,*n.* (III, IV)	*loh-*SHEE	lodging (temporary quarters)
lögn,*nn.* (III)	LÖNGN	lie
lögnare,*nn.* (V)	LÖNG-*nah-reh*	liar
lojal	*loh-*YAWL	loyal
lojalitet,*nn.*	*loy-yah-lit-*TAYT	loyalty
löjlig	LÖY-*lig*	ridiculous
löjtnant,*nn.* (III)	LÖYT-*nahnt*	lieutenant

Swedish	Pronunciation	English
lök,*nn.* (II)	LÖ_K	onion
lokal	*loo-*KAWL	local (regional)
lokomotiv,*n.* (V)	*loh-koh-moo-*TEEV	locomotive
lokomotivförare,*nn.* (V)	*loh-koh-moo-*TEEV-*fö-rah-reh*	engineer (railroad engineman)
lön,*nn.* (III)	LÖ_N	salary
"	"	wages
lönande	LÖ-*nahn-deh*	profitable
London,*n.*	LOHN-*dohn*	London
lönn,*nn.* (II)	LÖN	maple (tree)
lös	LÖ_S	loose (unbound)
lösa (2)	LÖ-*sah*	solve, to
lösen,*nn.*	LÖ-*sen*	ransom (*n.*)
lösning,*nn.* (II)	LÖ_S-*ning*	solution (solving)
löv,*n.* (V)	LÖ_V	leaf (*bot.*)
lova (1)	LOH-*vah*	promise (pledge), to
luft,*nn.*	LUHFT	air (atmosphere)
luftkonditionering,*nn.*	LUHFT-*kohn-dish-oh-*NAY-*ring*	air conditioning
lugn	LUHNGN	calm (*adj.*)
lugn,*n.*	LUHNGN	repose (calm)
lugna (1)	LUHNG-*nah*	appease (calm), to
"	"	lull (quiet), to
"	"	soothe, to
lugnt ögonblick,*n.* (V)	LUHNGT Ö-*gohn-blick*	lull (calm)
lukt,*nn.* (III)	LUHKT	odor (scent)
"	"	smell
lunch,*nn.* (III)	LUHNCH	lunch (midday meal)
lunga,*nn.* (I)	LUHNG-*ah*	lung
lunginflammation,*nn.*	LUHNG-*in-flahm-ah-*SHOON	pneumonia
lur,*nn.*	LU_R	nap (doze, *n.*)
lura (1)	LU-*rah*	cheat (defraud), to
luta (sig) (1)	LU-*tah* (*say*)	lean (bend), to
lya,*nn.* (I)	LÜ-*ah*	den (animal lair)
lycka,*nn.*	LÜCK-*ah*	happiness
lyckas (1)	LÜCK-*ahs*	manage (contrive), to
"	"	succeed (attain goal), to
"	"	thrive (succeed), to
lycklig	LÜCK-*lig*	fortunate
"	"	lucky
lyckligtvis	LÜCK-*lickt-vees*	happily (luckily)
lyda (2)	LÜ-*dah*	obey, to
lydig	LÜ-*dig*	obedient
lydnad,*nn.*	LÜ_D-*nahd*	obedience (compliance)
lyfta (2)	LÜF-*tah*	heave, to
"	"	lift, to
lyfta upp	*lüf-tah-*UHP	raise, to
lykta,*nn.* (I)	LÜCK-*tah*	lantern
lynne,*n.* (IV)	LÜN-*eh*	disposition (temperament)
lysande	LÜ-*sahn-deh*	glorious (resplendent)
lyssna (1)	LÜSS-*nah*	listen (hearken), to
lyx,*nn.*	LÜX	luxury
må (3)	MOH	may (*v.*)
madrass,*nn.* (III)	*mah-*DRAHSS	mattress
Madrid,*n.*	*mah-*DREED	Madrid
magasin,*n.* (V)	*mah-gah-*SEEN	magazine (periodical)
magasinering,*nn.* (II)	*mah-gah-sin-*NAY-*ring*	storage
mage,*nn.* (II)	MAWG-*eh*	stomach
mager	MAWG-*ehr*	lean
"	"	thin (not fat)
magi,*nn.*	*mahg-*EE	magic (*n.*)
magnet,*nn.* (III)	*mahng-*NAYT	magnet
magsår,*n.* (V)	MAWG-*sor*	ulcer
majestät,*n.* (III, V)	*mah-yeh-*STAIT	majesty
majs,*nn.*	MICE	corn (maize)
make,*nn.* (II)	MAW-*keh*	husband
mäklararvode,*n.* (IV)	MECK-*lahr-ahr-*VOO-*deh*	brokerage (fee)
mäklare,*nn.* (V)	MECK-*lah-reh*	broker (*bus.*)
makt,*nn.*	MAHKT	might (*n.*)
"	"	power (authority)
mäktig	MECK-*tig*	mighty
"	"	powerful
mål,*n.* (V)	MOH_L	aim (purpose)
"	"	end (purpose)
"	"	goal
"	"	objective
mal,*nn.* (II)	MAWL	moth

Swedish	Pronunciation	English	Swedish	Pronunciation	English
mala (2)	MAW-*lah*	grind (crush), to	medborgare,*nn.* (V)	MAYD-*bohr-yah-reh*	citizen
måla (1)	MOH-*lah*	paint (spread color), to	meddela (1)	MAYD-*day-lah*	convey (communicate), to
målare,*nn.* (V)	MOH-*lah-reh*	painter (artist)	meddelande,*n.* (IV)	MAYD-*dayl-ahn-deh*	communication
malaria,*nn.*	*mah-*LAWR*-ee-ah*	malaria	"	"	message
malm,*nn.* (III)	MAHLLM	ore	medel,*n.* (V)	MAY-*dell*	medium (means)
målning,*nn.* (II)	MOH̱L-*ning*	painting (picture)	medel,*n.pl.* (V)	MAY-*dell*	funds
måltid,*nn.* (III)	MOH̱L-*teed*	meal (repast)	Medelhavet,*n.*	MAY-*dell-haw-vet*	Mediterranean Sea
			medelmåttig	MAY-*dell-moht-ig*	moderate (not extreme)
man	MAHN	you (*indef.*)	medeltal,*n.* (V)	MAY-*dell-tawl*	average (mean, *n.*)
man,*nn.* (II)	MAWN	mane (of horse)	medföra (2)	MAYD-*för-ah*	involve (entail), to
man,*nn.* (*pl.* män)	MAHN	man	medge (10)	MAYD-*yay*	admit (concede), to
månad,*nn.* (III)	MOH-*nahd*	month	medhjälpare,*nn.* (V)	MAYD-*yell-pah-reh*	helper
månatlig	MOH-*nawt-lig*	monthly (every month, *adj.*)	medicin,*nn.* (III)	*meh-dis-*SEEN	medicine (medicament)
mandel,*nn.* (II)	MAHN-*dell*	almond	medicinsk	*meh-dis-*SEENSK	medical
mandelinflammation,*nn.*	MAHN-*dell-in-flahm-ah-*SHOON	tonsillitis	meditera (1)	*meh-dit-*TAY-*rah*	meditate (reflect), to
måne,*nn.* (II)	MOH-*neh*	moon	medlem,*nn.* (II)	MAYD-*lem*	member (one of a group)
många	MOHNG-*ah*	many	medlidande,*n.*	MAYD-*leed-ahn-deh*	pity (compassion)
mängd,*nn.* (III)	MENGD	crowd	medräkna (1)	MAYD-*raik-nah*	add (include), to
"	"	multitude	medveten	MAYD-*vay-ten*	aware
"	"	throng	"	"	conscious
mångfald,*nn.*	MOHNG-*fahlld*	variety (diversity)	mejeri,*n.* (III)	*meh-yeh-*REE	dairy
mani,*nn.* (III)	*mah-*NEE	craze (fad)	mekaniker,*nn.* (V)	*meh-*KAW-*nick-ehr*	mechanic
manlig	MAHN-*lig*	male (*adj.*)	mekanisk	*meh-*KAW-*nisk*	mechanical
"	"	manly	melankoli,*nn.*	*meh-lahn-koo-*LEE	melancholy (dejection)
mansålder,*nn.* (II)	MAHNS-*ohll-dehr*	generation (period of time)	melass,*nn.*	*meh-*LAHSS	molasses
manschett,*nn.* (III)	*mahn-*SHET	cuff (of sleeve)	mellan	MELL-*ahn*	between (*prep.*)
månsken,*n.*	MOH̱N-*shayn*	moonlight	mellantid,*nn.* (III)	MELL-*ahn-teed*	interval (period of time)
mänsklig	MENSK-*lig*	human (*adj.*)	"	"	meantime (*n.*)
mänsklighet,*nn.*	MENSK-*lig-hayt*	humanity (mankind)	melodi,*nn.* (III)	*meh-loh-*DEE	tune (melody)
mänskligheten,*nn. def.*	MENSK-*lig-hayt-en*	mankind	men	MEN	but (yet, *conj.*)
margarin,*n.*	*mahr-gah-*REEN	margarine	mena (1)	MAY-*nah*	mean (have in mind), to
marginal,*nn.* (III)	*mahrg-in-*NAWL	margin (surplus)	mened,*nn.* (III)	MAYN-*ayd*	perjury
marin,*nn.* (III)	*mah-*REEN	marine (oceanic)	menig,*nn.* (*pl.* -a)	MAY-*nig*	private (*mil.*)
mark,*nn.*	MAHRRK	ground (earth)	mening,*nn.* (II)	MAY-*ning*	mind (opinion)
märka (2)	MAIRR-*kah*	note, to	"	"	sentence (*gram.*)
"	"	notice (see), to	mer	MAYR	more (*adj.*)
"	"	perceive, to	mera	MAY-*rah*	else (in addition, *adj.*)
märke,*n.* (IV)	MAIRR-*keh*	mark (symbol)	merkantil	*mairr-kahn-*TEEL	mercantile
(varu)märke,*n.* (IV)	(VAW-*ruh-*)MAIRR-*keh*	brand (trade mark)	mest	MEST	most (*adv.*)
markera (1)	*mahrr-*KAY-*rah*	mark (designate), to	"	"	most (greatest quantity, *adj.*)
märklig	MAIRRK-*lig*	notable (*adj.*)	mesta, (det),*n.*	(*deh-*)MESS-*tah*	most (*n.*)
marknad,*nn.* (III)	MAHRRK-*nahd*	outlet	metall,*nn.* (III)	*meh-*TAHLL	metal (*n.*)
marknad(splats), *nn.* (III)	MAHRRK-*nahd*(-*splahts*)	market (trading center)	metalltråd,*nn.* (II)	*meh-*TAHLL-*troẖd*	wire (metal thread)
märkvärdig	MAIRRK-*vaird-ig*	remarkable (extraordinary)	metod,*nn.* (III)	*meh-*TOOD	method
marmor,*nn.*	MAHRR-*moor*	marble (mineral)	mexikansk	*meck-sick-*KAWNSK	Mexican (*adj.*)
marschera (1)	*mahr-*SHAY-*rah*	march, to	Mexiko,*n.*	MECK-*sick-koo*	Mexico
mask,*nn.* (III)	MAHSSK	mask (face covering)	Mexiko City,*n.*	MECK-*sick-koo* SIT-*tee*	Mexico City
mask,*nn.* (II)	MAHSSK	worm	middag,*nn.* (II)	MID-*dawg*	dinner
maskin,*nn.* (III)	*mah-*SHEEN	machine	"	"	noon
maskineri,*n.* (III)	*mah-shee-neh-*REE	machinery	midja,*nn.* (I)	MEED-*yah*	waist (*anat.*)
maskinskrivare,*nn.* (V)	*mah-*SHEEN-*skree-vah-reh*	typist	midnatt,*nn.*	MEED-*naht*	midnight
maskros,*nn.* (I)	MAHSSK-*roos*	dandelion	mig	MAY	me
maskulin	MAHSS-*kuh-leen*	masculine	mild	MILLD	gentle (soothing)
massa,*nn.* (I)	MAHSS-*ah*	mass (matter)	mildra (1)	MILL-*drah*	soften (mitigate), to
mässa,*nn.* (I)	MESS-*ah*	mass (*rel.*)	militär	*mill-it-*TAIR	military (*adj.*)
mässing,*nn.*	MESS-*ing*	brass (metal, *n.*)	min, mitt, mina	MIN, MIT, MEE-*nah*	mine (*poss. pron.*)
mässlingen (*def.*), *nn.*	MESS-*ling-en*	measles	"	"	my
mast,*nn.* (III)	MAHSST	mast	mina,*nn.* (I)	MEE-*nah*	mine (explosive)
mästare,*nn.* (V)	MESS-*tah-reh*	champion	mindre	MIN-*dreh*	minor (lesser)
"	"	master (great artist)	"	"	less (*adj.*, *adv.*)
måste (4)	MOHSS-*teh*	must (*v.*)	mineral,*n.* (V)	*min-eh-*RAWL	mineral
mäta (2)	MAI-*tah*	measure (find size of), to	ministär,*nn.* (III)	*min-iss-*TAIR	cabinet (*govt.*)
matematik,*nn.*	*mah-teh-mah-*TEEK	mathematics	minister,*nn.* (II)	*min-*ISS-*tehr*	minister (cabinet member)
material,*n.* (V)	*mah-teh-ree-*AWL	material (substance)	minnas (2)	MIN-*ahs*	remember (recollect), to
matiné,*nn.* (III)	*mah-tin-*NAY	matinee (theater performance)	minne,*n.*	MIN-*eh*	remembrance
matsal,*nn.* (II)	MAWT-*sawl*	dining room	minne,*n.* (IV)	MIN-*eh*	memory (recollection)
matsedel,*nn.* (II)	MAWT-*say-dell*	menu	minnesmärke,*n.* (IV)	MIN-*ess-mairr-keh*	memorial (*n.*)
matsked,*nn.* (II)	MAWT-*shayd*	spoon (tablespoon)			
mått,*n.* (V)	MOHT	measure (dimensions)	minoritet,*nn.* (III)	*min-oh-ree-*TAYT	minority (smaller number)
matta,*nn.* (I)	MAHT-*ah*	carpet			
"	"	rug			
med	MAYD	with			
medalj,*nn.*(III)	*meh-*DAHLḺ-*yuh*	medal			
medan	MAY-*dahn*	as (while, *conj.*)			
"	"	while (during the time that, *conj.*)			

Swedish	Pronunciation	English
minska (1)	MIN-*skah*	lessen (make less), to
"	"	reduce (diminish), to
minskning,*nn.*	MINSK-*ning*	decrease
"	"	reduction (lessening)
minst	MINST	least (*adj., adv.*)
minsta, (det),*n.*	(*deh-*)MIN-*stah*	least (*n.*)
minus	MEE-*nuhs*	less (minus, *prep.*)
minut,*nn.* (III)	*min-*UH_T	minute (unit of time)
missa (1)	MISS-*ah*	miss (fail to do), to
missionär,*nn.* (III)	*mish-oo-*NAIR	missionary
misslyckande,*n.* (IV)	MISS-*lück-ahn-deh*	failure (lack of success)
misslyckas (1)	MISS-*lück-ahs*	fail (be unsuccessful), to
misstag,*n.* (V)	MISS-*tawg*	mistake
missta(ga) sig (9)	MISS-*taw* (*-gah*) *say*	err, to
misstänka (2)	MISS-*tenk-ah*	suspect (distrust), to
misstanke,*nn.* (II)	MISS-*tahnk-eh*	suspicion
mitt,*nn.*	MIT	middle (center)
mitt emot	MIT *eh-*MOOT	opposite (*prep.*)
mitt ibland	MIT *ee-*BLAHND	amid
mjöl,*n.*	M_YÖL	flour
mjölk,*nn.*	M_YÖLK	milk
mjölnare,*nn.* (V)	M_YÖL-*nah-reh*	miller
mjuk	M_YUK	soft (not hard)
mö,*nn.* (III)	MÖ	maiden
möbler,*nn.pl.*	MÖ_B-*lehr*	furniture
möblera (1)	*möb-*LAY-*rah*	furnish (put furniture in), to
mockaskinn,*n.* (V)	MOHCK-*ah-shinn*	suede (*n.*)
mod,*n.*	MOOD	courage
mod,*n.* (III, V)	MOOD	fashion (current style)
möda,*nn.* (I)	MÖ-*dah*	labor (exertion)
"	"	struggle (great effort)
"	"	trouble (exertion)
modell,*nn.* (III)	*moh-*DELL	model (small copy)
mo(de)r,*nn.* (*pl.* mödrar)	MOO(*-deh*)RR	mother
modern	*moh-*DAIRN	modern
"	"	contemporary
modifiera (1)	*moo-dee-fee-*AYR-*ah*	qualify (modify), to
modig	MOO-*dig*	brave
mogen	MOO_G-*en*	ripe
möglig	MÖ_G-*lig*	moldy
mogna (1)	MOO_G-*nah*	mature (ripen), to
möjlig	MÖY-*lig*	possible
möjliggöra (11)	MÖY-*lig-yö-rah*	enable (make able), to
möjlighet,*nn.* (III)	MÖY-*lig-hayt*	chance
"	"	possibility
moln,*n.* (V)	MOHLN	cloud
monark,*nn.* (III)	*moo-*NAHRRK	monarch
mönster,*n.* (V)	MÖN-*stehr*	design
"	"	model (exemplar)
"	"	pattern
Montevideo,*n.*	*mohn-teh-vid-*DAY-*oo*	Montevideo
monument,*n.* (V)	*moh-nuh-*MENT	monument
moral,*nn.*	*moo-*RAWL	morals
moralisk	*moo-*RAW-*lisk*	moral (ethical)
morbro(de)r,*nn.* (*pl.* -bröder)	MOORR-*broo*(*-deh*)*rr*	uncle (maternal)
mord,*n.* (V)	MOORD	murder
mördare,*nn.* (V)	MÖRD-*ah-reh*	murderer
morfa(de)r,*nn.* (*pl.* -fäder)	MOORR-*fah*(*-deh*)*rr*	grandfather (maternal)
morgon,*nn.* (*pl.* morgnar)	MOHRR-*ohn*	morning
morgon, i	*ee-*MOHRR-*ohn*	tomorrow
morgonrock,*nn.* (II)	MOHRR-*ohn-rohck*	robe (dressing gown)
mörk	MÖRRK	dark (in color, *adj.*)
"	"	dark (without light, *adj.*)
mörker,*n.*	MÖRRK-*ehr*	darkness
mormo(de)r,*nn.* (*pl.* -mödrar)	MOORR-*moo*(*deh*)*rr*	grandmother (maternal)
morot,*nn.* (*pl.* -rötter)	MOO-*roo_t*	carrot
morra (1)	MOHRR-*ah*	growl, to
Moskva,*n.*	*mohss-*KVAW	Moscow
mossa,*nn.* (I)	MOHSS-*ah*	moss
mössa,*nn.* (I)	MÖSS-*ah*	cap (hat)
moster,*nn.* (II)	MOOSS-*tehr*	aunt (maternal)

Swedish	Pronunciation	English
mot	MOOT	toward
möta (2)	MÖ-*tah*	encounter, to
"	"	meet, to
möte,*n.* (IV)	MÖ-*teh*	meeting (assembly)
mötessal,*nn.* (II)	MÖ-*tess-sawl*	auditorium
motion,*nn.*	*moht-*SHOON	exercise (physical exertion)
motiv,*n.* (V)	*moo-*TEEV	motive (*n.*)
motor,*nn.* (III)	MOO-*tor*	motor (engine)
motsats,*nn.* (III)	MOOT-*sahts*	opposite (*n.*)
"	"	reverse (contrary, *n.*)
motsatt	MOOT-*saht*	contrary
"	"	opposite (*adj.*)
motstå (10)	MOOT-*stoh*	resist, to
motstånd,*n.*	MOOT-*stohnd*	opposition
"	"	resistance
motståndare,*nn.* (V)	MOOT-*stohn-dah-reh*	opponent (*n.*)
motsvara (1)	MOOT-*svaw-rah*	match (equal), to
motta(ga) (9)	MOOT-*taw*(*-gah*)	receive, to
mottagande,*n.*	MOOT-*taw-gahn-deh*	receipt (receiving)
"	"	reception
mottagande,*n.* (IV)	MOOT-*taw-gahn-deh*	acceptance (receipt)
mottagare,*nn.* (V)	MOOT-*taw-gah-reh*	consignee (*bus.*)
motto,*n.* (IV)	MOHT-*oo*	motto
motvilja,*nn.*	MOOT-*vill-yah*	dislike
mulåsna,*nn.* (I)	MUH_L-*oh_s-nah*	mule
mulen	MUH-*len*	cloudy (overcast)
mullvad,*nn.* (II)	MUHLL-*vawd*	mole (animal)
multiplicera (1)	*muhll-tip-lis-*SAY-*rah*	multiply (*arith.*), to
mumla (1)	MUHM-*lah*	murmur, to
mun,*nn.* (II)	MUHN	mouth (*anat.*)
munk,*nn.* (II)	MUHNK	monk
munter	MUHN-*tehr*	merry
munterhet,*nn.*	MUHN-*tehr-hayt*	glee (joy)
"	"	mirth
muntlig	MUHNT-*lig*	oral (spoken)
murare,*nn.* (V)	MUH-*rah-reh*	mason (stonelayer)
murbruk,*n.*	MUHR-*bru_k*	plaster (wall coating)
murgröna,*nn.*	MUHR-*grö-nah*	ivy
mus,*nn.* (*pl.* möss)	MUH_S	mouse
museum,*n.* (III)	*muh-*SAY-*uhm*	museum
musik,*nn.*	*muh-*SEEK	music
musikalisk	*muh-sih-*KAW-*lisk*	musical
musiker,*nn.* (V)	MUH-*sick-ehr*	musician
muskel,*nn.* (III)	MUHSS-*kell*	muscle
muskot,*nn.*	MUHSS-*koht*	nutmeg
mussla,*nn.* (I)	MUHSS-*lah*	clam
mustasch,*nn.* (III)	*muhss-*TAWSH	mustache
muta (1)	MUH-*tah*	bribe, to
muttra (1)	MUHT-*rah*	mutter (mumble), to
mycket	MÜCK-*eh*	much
"	"	very (extremely)
mycket liten	MÜCK-*eh* LEE-*ten*	wee
mygga,*nn.* (I)	MÜG-*ah*	mosquito
myndighet,*nn.*	MÜN-*dig-hayt*	authority (power)
mynt,*n.* (V)	MÜNT	coin
myra,*nn.* (I)	MÜ-*rah*	ant
mysterium,*n.* (III)	*müss-*TAY-*ree-uhm*	mystery (enigma)
mystisk	MÜSS-*tisk*	mysterious
myt,*nn.* (III)	MÜ_T	myth (legend)
nå	NOH	well (and then?, *interj.*)
näbb,*nn.* (II)	NEB	bill (beak)
nacke,*nn.* (II)	NAHCK-*eh*	nape
nagel,*nn.* (II)	NAWG-*el*	nail (*anat.*)
någon	NOH-*gohn*	any (any one, *adj.*)
"	"	any (a quantity of, *adj.*)
"	"	any (*pron.*)
"	"	anybody (not...anybody)
"	"	anybody (somebody)
någon	NOH-*gohn*	anyone (not...anyone)
"	"	anyone (someone)
"	"	some (unspecified, *adj.*)
"	"	some (a quantity of, *adj.*)
"	"	somebody
"	"	someone

Swedish	Pronunciation	English
någon alls	NOH-*gohn* AHLLS	any (any at all, *adj.*)
	"	anybody (anybody whosoever)
"	"	anyone (anyone whosoever)
någonsin	NOH-*gohn-sin*	ever (at any time)
någonstans	NOH-*gohn-*STAHNS	anywhere (not...anywhere)
"	"	somewhere
någonting	NOH-*gohn-ting*	something
något	NOH-*goht*	anything (not...anything)
"	"	anything (something)
"	"	some (a quantity, *pron.*)
"	"	somewhat (*adv.*)
något alls	NOH-*goht* AHLLS	anything (anything whatever)
några	NOH‿G-*rah*	few, a
"	"	some (a few, *adj.*)
naken	NAW-*ken*	naked
näktergal, *nn.* (II)	NECK-*tehr-gawl*	nightingale
nalkas (1)	NAHLL-*kahss*	approach (come near to), to
nämligen	NEM-*lig-en*	namely
namn, *n.* (V)	NAHMN	name
nämna (2)	NEM-*nah*	mention, to
nämnd, *nn.* (III)	NEMD	jury
namnteckning, *nn.* (II)	NAHMN-*teck-ning*	signature (name)
när	NAIR	when
nära	NAI-*rah*	close (*adv.*)
"	"	near (not far, *adv.*)
"	"	near (*prep.*)
nära (2)	NAI-*rah*	nourish, to
närhelst	*nair-*HELST	whenever
näring, *nn.*	NAIR-*ing*	nourishment
narkotika, *nn.pl.*	*nahr-*KOH-*tick-ah*	drug (narcotic)
närvarande	NAIR-*vaw-rahn-deh*	present (current, *adj.*)
närvarande tid, *nn.*	NAIR-*vaw-rahn-deh* TEED	present (present time, *n.*)
närvaro, *nn.*	NAIR-*vaw-roo*	attendance
"	"	presence (being present)
näsa, *nn.* (I)	NAI-*sah*	nose (*anat.*)
näsborre, *nn.* (II)	NAIS-*bohrr-eh*	nostril
näsduk, *nn.* (II)	NAIS-*duh‿k*	handkerchief
näst	NEST	next (*adv.*)
näst(a)	NEST(-*ah*)	next (following, *adj.*)
nästan	NESS-*tahn*	almost
"	"	nearly
näst intill	NEST *in-*TILL	next to (alongside of, *prep.*)
nät, *n.* (V)	NAIT	net (mesh)
nation, *nn.* (III)	*naht-*SHOON	nation
nationalekonomi, *nn.*	*naht-shoo-*NAWL-*eh-koh-noh-*MEE	economics
nationell	*naht-shoo-*NELL	national (*adj.*)
natt, *nn.* (*pl.* nätter)	NAHT	night
nattdräkt, *nn.* (III)	NAHT-*dreckt*	nightgown
natur, *nn.*	*nah-*TU‿R	nature (physical world)
natur, *nn.* (III)	*nah-*TU‿R	nature (character)
naturlig	*nah-*TU‿R-*lig*	natural
naturligtvis	*nah-*TU‿R-*lickt-vees*	course, of
näve, *nn.* (II)	NAI-*veh*	fist
navigation, *nn.*	*nah-vig-ah-*SHOON	navigation
Neapel, *n.*	*nay-*AW-*pel*	Naples
nedanför	NAY-*dahn-för*	below (lower down, *adv.*)
"	"	beneath (below, *adv.*)
nedåt	NAYD-*oht*	downward (*adv.*)
nederlag, *n.* (V)	NAY-*dehr-lawg*	defeat
Nederländerna, *def. pl.*	NAY-*dehr-len-dehr-nah*	Netherlands, The
nedför trappan	NAYD-*för* TRAHP-*ahn*	downstairs (downward)
nedgång, *nn.*	NAYD-*gohng*	decline (deterioration)
nedslagenhet, *nn.*	NAYD-*slawg-en-hayt*	depression (sadness)
neger, *nn.* (III)	NAY-*gehr*	Negro
nej	NAY	no (nay)
nejlika, *nn.* (I)	NAY-*lick-ah*	carnation

Swedish	Pronunciation	English
nere	NAY-*reh*	down (in lower place, *adv.*)
nerv, *nn.* (III)	NAIRRV	nerve (*anat.*)
nervös	*nehr-*VÖ‿S	nervous (highstrung)
netto	NET-*oo*	net (*adj.*)
neutral	*nay-uh-*TRAWL	neutral
New Delhi, *n.*	*new-*DELL-*ih*	New Delhi
New York, *n.*	*new-*YORK	New York
ni	NEE	you (formal)
"	"	you (plural)
Nicaragua, *n.*	*nih-kah-*RAW-*guh-ah*	Nicaragua
nicka (1)	NICK-*ah*	nod, to
nickel, *nn.*	NICK-*el*	nickel (*chem.*)
Nilen, *nn.*	NEE-*len*	Nile
njure, *nn.* (II)	N‿YU-*reh*	kidney (*anat.*)
njuta av (6)	N‿YU-*tah awv*	enjoy (derive joy from), to
nöd, *nn.*	NÖ‿D	distress
nödfall, *n.*	NÖ‿D-*fahll*	emergency (*n.*)
nödvändig	NÖ‿D-*ven-dig*	necessary
nödvändighet, *nn.* (III)	NÖ‿D-*ven-dig-hayt*	necessity
nog	NOO‿G	enough (*adv.*)
noggrann	NOO-*grahn*	accurate
nöjd	NÖYD	content (satisfied)
nöje, *n.* (IV)	NÖY-*eh*	amusement
"	"	fun
"	"	pleasure
nolla, *nn.* (I)	NOHLL-*ah*	zero (*n.*)
nominellt värde, *n.* (IV)	*noh-min-*NELT VAIRD-*eh*	face value (*bus.*)
nord, *nn.*	NOORD	north (*n.*)
Nordamerika, *n.*	NOORD-*ah-may-rick-ah*	North America
nordlig	NOORD-*lig*	northern
nordöstlig	*noord-*ÖST-*lig*	northeast (*adj.*)
nordvästlig	*noord-*VEST-*lig*	northwest (*adj.*)
Norge, *n.*	NOHRR-*yeh*	Norway
normal	*nohrr-*MAWL	normal (*adj.*)
"	"	sane
norr	NOHRR	north (*adv.*)
norsk	NOHSHK	Norwegian (*adj.*)
not, *nn.* (III)	NOOT	note (*mus.*)
nöt, *nn.* (*pl.* nötter)	NÖ‿T	nut (food)
notarie, *nn.* (III)	*noh-*TAR-*ee-eh*	notary
notering, *nn.* (II)	*noo-*TAY-*ring*	quotation (price)
nötkött, *n.*	NÖ‿T-*chöt*	beef
novell, *nn.* (III)	*noh-*VELL	short story
nu	NU	now (*adv.*)
nummerskiva, *nn.* (I)	NUHM-*ehr-shee-vah*	dial (graduated face)
numrera (1)	*nuhm-*RAY-*rah*	number (assign numbers to), to
nunna, *nn.* (I)	NUHN-*ah*	nun
ny	NÜ	fresh
"	"	new
"	"	recent
nyårsdag, *nn.* (II)	NÜ-*ohsh-dawg*	New Year's Day
nybyggare, *nn.* (V)	NÜ-*büg-ah-reh*	colonist
"		settler
nybygge, *n.* (IV)	NÜ-*büg-eh*	settlement (colony)
nyckel, *nn.* (II)	NÜCK-*el*	key (for lock)
nyfiken	NÜ-*fee-ken*	curious (inquisitive)
nyfikenhet, *nn.*	NÜ-*fee-ken-hayt*	curiosity (inquisitiveness)
nyligen	NÜ-*lig-en*	recently
nylon, *n., nn.*	*nü-*LOH‿N	nylon (*n.*)
nypa (2, 7)	NÜ-*pah*	pinch (squeeze), to
nysa (2)	NÜ-*sah*	sneeze, to
nytta, *nn.*	NÜT-*ah*	use (usefulness)
"	"	utility (usefulness)
nyttig	NÜT-*ig*	helpful
"		useful
ö, *nn.* (II)	ö	island (*geog.*)
oändlig	*oo-*END-*lig*	infinite
oas, *nn.* (III)	*oo-*AWS	oasis
oavbruten	*oo-awv-bru-ten*	continuous
obehaglig	*oo-beh-hawg-lig*	disagreeable
"	"	unpleasant
oberoende	*oo-beh-roo-en-deh*	independent
oberoende, *n.*	*oo-beh-roo-en-deh*	independence

Swedish	Pronunciation	English	Swedish	Pronunciation	English
obestämd	oo-beh-stemd	vague (not precise)	oliv,*nn.* (III)	*oh*-LEEV	olive (fruit)
			olivolja,*nn.*	*oh*-LEEV-*ohll-yah*	olive oil
obetald	oo-beh-tawld	unpaid (due)	olja,*nn.* (I)	OHLL-*yah*	oil
obetänksam	oo-beh-tenk-sahm	rash (*adj.*)			
obetydlig	oo-beh-tü̲d-lig	insignificant (trivial)	olycklig	oo-*lück-lig*	miserable
"	"	petty (minor)	"	"	unfortunate
		slight (*adj.*)	"	"	unhappy (sorrowful)
			"	"	unlucky
obligation,*nn.* (III)	ohb-lig-ah-SHOON	bond	olyckshändelse,*nn.*	oo-*lüx-hen-dell-seh*	accident (mishap)
"	"	debenture	(III)		
obligatorisk	ohb-lig-ah-TOO-*risk*	obligatory (binding)	om	OHM	about (concerning)
oboe,*nn.* (III)	OH-*boh*(-*eh*)	oboe	"	"	if
ocean,*nn.* (III)	oo-seh-AWN	ocean	"	"	in (during, *prep.*)
oceanbåt,*nn.* (II)	oo-seh-AWN-*boh̲t*	liner, ocean	"	"	whether (*conj.*)
och	OH(CK)	and			
			öm	ÖM	sore (*adj.*)
också	OHCK-*soh*	also	"	"	tender (loving)
"	"	likewise	ombord	ohm-BOORD	aboard
"	"	so (*adv.*)	ombud,*n.* (V)	OHM-*buh̲d*	commissioner (dep-
"	"	too			utized person)
ockupation,*nn.*	ohck-uh-pah-SHOON	occupation (*mil.*)	"	"	delegate
(III)			omdöme,*n.* (IV)	OHM-*döm-eh*	judgment (estima-
öde,*n.* (IV)	ö-*deh*	destiny			tion)
"	"	fate	omedelbar	oo-*may-dell-bar*	direct
ödesdiger	ö-*des-deeg-ehr*	fatal (fateful)	"	"	immediate (instant)
odjur,*n.* (V)	oo-*yu̲r*	monster (beast)	omedelbart	oo-*may-dell-bart*	immediately (in-
odla (1)	OOD-*lah*	cultivate, to			stantly)
"	"	grow, to	omfamna (1)	OHM-*fahm-nah*	clasp, to
"	"	till (cultivate), to	"	"	embrace, to
					hug, to
ödmjuk	ö̲D-*m̲yu̲k*	humble (lowly)	omge (10)	OHM-*yay*	enclose, to
ödmjukhet,*nn.*	ö̲D-*m̲yu̲k-hayt*	humility			surround, to
odödlig	oo-*dö̲d-lig*	immortal (*adj.*)			
oerhörd	oo-*ehr-hörd*	enormous	omgivning,*nn.* (II)	OHM-*yeev-ning*	surroundings
ofantlig	oo-FAHNT-*lig*	immense	ömhet,*nn.*	ÖM-*hayt*	tenderness (love)
ofärdig	oo-*faird-ig*	lame	omhulda (1)	OHM-*huhll-dah*	cherish, to
offer,*n.* (V)	OHFF-*ehr*	victim	om inte	ohm-IN-*teh*	but (if not, *conj.*)
officer,*nn.* (*pl.*	oh-*fiss*-SAYR	officer (*mil.*)			
-are)			omintetgöra (11)	ohm-IN-*tet-yö-rah*	defeat (thwart), to
officiell	oh-*fiss-ee*-ELL	official (*adj.*)	"	"	foil (frustrate), to
ofog,*n.*	oo-*foog*	mischief (harm)	ömka (1)	ÖM-*kah*	pity, to
oförnuftg	oo-*för-nuhff-tig*	unreasonable (un-	omkomma (10)	OHM-*kohm-ah*	perish, to
		reasoning)	omkostnad,*nn.*	OHM-*kohst-nahd*	expense (cost)
ofruktbar	oo-*fruhkt-bawr*	barren	(III)		
ofta	OFF-*tah*	often	omkrets,*nn.*	OHM-*krets*	circumference
ofullständig	oo-*fuhll-sten-dig*	partial (incomplete)	omkring	*ohm*-KRING	around (*prep.*)
öga,*n.* (*pl.* ögon)	ö-*gah*	eye (*anat.*)	omöjlig	oo-*möy-lig*	impossible
ogift	oo-*yift*	single (unmarried)	omöjlighet,*nn.*	oo-*möy-lig-hayt*	impossibility
ogiltig	oo-*yill-tig*	void (null)	område,*n.* (IV)	OHM-*roh-deh*	field
ögonblick,*n.* (V)	ö-*gohn-blick*	instant (*n.*)	"	"	range (scope)
"	"	moment	"	"	sphere (range)
ögonbryn,*n.* (V)	ö-*gohn-brü̲n*	eyebrow	ömsesidig	ÖM-*seh-see-dig*	mutual
ögonfrans,*nn.* (II)	ö-*gohn-frahns*	eyelash	omsorg,*nn.* (III)	OHM-*sohrr̲_yuh*	care (heed)
"	"	lash	omständighet,*nn.*	OHM-*sten-dig-hayt*	circumstance (ex-
ögonlock,*n.* (V)	ö-*gohn-lohck*	eyelid	(III)		ternal condition)
			omväg,*nn.* (II)	OHM-*vaig*	detour
ögräs,*n.* (V)	oo-*grais*	weed	omvänd,*nn.* (*pl.* -a)	OHM-*vend*	convert (proselyte)
ohövlig	oo-*hö̲v-lig*	rude (impolite)	ond	OOND	evil (*adj.*)
ojämn	oo-*yemn*	rough (uneven)	ondska,*nn.*	OOND-*skah*	spite (ill will)
ok,*n.* (V)	OO̲K	yoke (wooden frame)	onödig	oo-*nö-dig*	needless
öka (1)	ö-*kah*	increase (add to), to	"	"	unnecessary
okänd	oo-*chend*	obscure (unre-			
		nowned)	önska (1)	ÖN-*skah*	desire (long for), to
"	"	unknown	"	"	want, to
ökänd	ö-*chend*	notorious	önska (sig)	ÖN-*skah* (*say*)	wish for, to
ökas (1)	ö-*kahs*	increase (grow), to	önskan,*nn.*	ÖN-*skahn*	wish
"	"	multiply (grow			
		numerous), to	önskvärd	ÖNSK-*vaird*	desirable
"	"	rise (increase), to	ont,*n.*	OONT	evil (*n.*)
öken,*nn.* (II)	ö-*ken*	desert	ont i halsen,*n.*	*oont-ee*-HAHLL-*sen*	sore throat
oklar	oo-*klawr*	dim	onyttig	oo-*nüt-ig*	idle
öknamn,*n.* (V)	ö̲K-*nahmn*	nickname	"	"	useless
ökning,*nn.* (II)	ö̲K-*ning*	gain			
"	"	increase (increment)	oordning,*nn.* (II)	oo-*ord-ning*	disorder (confusion)
			opera,*nn.* (I)	oo-*peh-rah*	opera
okunnig	oo-*kuhn-ig*	ignorant	operation,*nn.* (III)	oo-*peh-rah*-SHOON	operation (*med.*)
okunnighet,*nn.*	oo-*kuhn-ig-hayt*	ignorance	operera (1)	oo-*peh*-RAY-*rah*	operate (perform
öl,*n.*	Ö̲L	beer			surgery), to
olägenhet,*nn.* (III)	oo-*laig-en-hayt*	inconvenience	öppen	ÖP-*en*	open (*adj.*)
olaglig	oo-*lawg-lig*	illegal	öppna (1)	ÖP-*nah*	open (make open), to
			öppnande,*n.* (IV)	ÖP-*nahn-deh*	opening (beginning,
olik	oo-*leek*	distinct (different)			*n.*)
"	"	unlike (*adj.*)	öppning,*nn.* (II)	ÖP-*ning*	gap
olika	oo-*lee-kah*	different	"	"	opening (aperture)
"	"	unequal	optimistisk	ohp-*tih*-MISS-*tisk*	optimistic
"	"	various	öra,*n.* (*pl.* öron)	ö-*rah*	ear (organ of hear-
olikhet,*nn.* (III)	oo-*leek-hayt*	difference (dissimi-			ing)
		larity)	orange	*oh*-RAHNSH	orange (color)

Swedish	Pronunciation	English
orättfärdig	oo-ret-faird-ig	unjust (inequitable)
orättvis	oo-ret-vees	wrong (unjust, adj.)
orättvisa,nn. (I)	oo-ret-vee-sah	injustice
"	"	wrong (n.)
ord,n. (V)	OORD	word
ordbok,nn. (pl. -böcker)	OORD-boo_k	dictionary
order,nn. (V)	ORD-ehr	command
"	"	order
"	"	order (purchase)
ordförande,nn. (V)	OORD-fö-rahn-deh	chairman
ordförteckning,nn. (II)	OORD-för-teck-ning	glossary
ordna (1)	ORD-nah	arrange (place), to
"	"	fix, to
"	"	settle, to
"	"	straighten (put in order), to
ordning,nn.	ORD-ning	order (orderliness)
"	"	order (sequence)
ordning,nn (II)	ORD-ning	arrangement
ordspråk,n. (V)	OORD-sproh_k	proverb
oregelbunden	oo-rayg-el-buhn-den	irregular
oren	oo-rayn	impure
organ,n. (V)	or-GAWN	organ (anat.)
organisation,nn. (III)	or-gah-niss-ah-SHOON	organization (association)
organisera (1)	or-gah-niss-SAY-rah	organize (systematize), to
orgel,nn. (II)	ORR-yell	organ (mus.)
örhänge,n. (IV)	ÖR-heng-eh	earring
Orienten,nn.def.	or-ee-ENT-en	Orient
oriktig	oo-rick-lig	incorrect
orkester,nn. (II)	or-KESS-tehr	band (instrumental group)
"	"	orchestra (mus.)
orkidé,nn. (III)	or-kid-DAY	orchid (flower)
orm,nn. (II)	OORRM	serpent
"	"	snake
ormbunke,nn. (II)	OORRM-buhnk-eh	fern
örn,nn. (II)	ÖRN	eagle
ornament,n. (V)	orn-ah-MENT	ornament
oro,nn.	oo-roo	alarm (fear)
"	"	worry (anxiety)
oroa (1)	oo-roo-ah	trouble (disquiet), to
oroa sig	oo-roo-ah (say)	fret, to
"	"	worry (feel anxious), to
orolig	oo-roo-lig	anxious
"	"	restless
"	"	uneasy
orsak,nn. (III)	oo-shawk	reason (ground)
örsprång,n.	ö-shprohng	earache
ört,nn. (III)	ÖRRT	herb
osanning,nn. (II)	oo-sahn-ing	falsehood (lie)
oskyldig	oo-shüll-dig	innocent (guiltless)
Oslo,n.	OOSS-loo	Oslo
oss	OHSS	us
ost,nn. (II)	OOST	cheese
öster,nn.	ÖSS-tehr	east
Österrike,n.	ÖSS-tehr-ree-keh	Austria
österrikisk	ÖSS-tehr-ree-kisk	Austrian (adj.)
östlig	ÖST-lig	eastern
ostron,n. (V)	OOST-rohn	oyster
osynlig	oo-sü_n-lig	invisible
otålig	oo-toh-lig	impatient
otålighet,nn.	oo-toh-lig-hayt	impatience
otillräcklig	oo-till-reck-lig	inadequate
"	"	insufficient
Ottawa,n.	OHT-tah-vah	Ottawa
otur,nn.	oo-tuhr	misfortune
otvivelaktig	oo-tvee-vel-ahck-tig	doubtless
otvivelaktigt	oo-tvee-vel-ahck-tickt	undoubtedly
oundviklig	oo-uhnd-veek-lig	inevitable (adj.)
oväntad	oo-ven-tahd	unexpected (adj.)
ovärdig	oo-vaird-ig	unworthy
över	ö-vehr	above (higher than, prep.)
"	"	across (to the other side)
"	"	over (prep.)
överallt	ö-vehr-AHLLT	everywhere

Swedish	Pronunciation	English
överallt i	ö-vehr-AHLLT ee	throughout (in every part of, prep.)
överdriva (5)	ö-vehr-dree-vah	exaggerate, to
överdriven	ö-vehr-dree-ven	excessive
överenskommelse, nn. (III)	ö-vehr-ens-kohm-el-seh	bargain (agreement)
överensstämma (2)	ö-vehr-ens-stem-ah	agree (concur), to
"	"	correspond, to
överensstämmelse, nn. (III)	ö-vehr-ens-stem-el-seh	accord (agreement)
"	"	sympathy
överfall,n. (V)	ö-vehr-fahll	attack (personal assault)
överfalla (10)	ö-vehr-fahll-ah	assault, to
"	"	attack, to
överflöd,n.	ö-vehr-flö_d	abundance
"	"	plenty (n.)
övergå (10)	ö-vehr-goh	exceed, to
överge (10)	ö-vehr-yay	forsake, to
överklaga (1)	ö-vehr-KLAW-gah	appeal (ask reconsideration of), to
överlämna (1)	ö-vehr-lem-nah	deliver (hand over), to
överlämnande,n. (IV)	ö-vehr-lem-nahn-deh	delivery (handing over)
överlåtelse,nn. (III)	ö-vehr-loh-tell-seh	assignment (legal transfer)
överleva (2)	ö-vehr-lay-vah	survive (remain alive), to
övermått,n.	ö-vehr-moht	excess
övernaturlig	ö-vehr-nah-TU_R-lig	weird (unearthly)
överraska (1)	ö-vehr-rahs-kah	surprise (come upon suddenly), to
överresa,nn. (I)	ö-vehr-ray-sah	crossing (ocean voyage)
överrock,nn. (II)	ö-vehr-rohck	coat (man's overcoat)
översända	ö-veh-shen-dah	remit (send payment), to
översätta (11)	ö-veh-shet-ah	translate, to
översida,nn. (I)	ö-veh-shee-dah	top (upper surface)
överskott,n. (V)	ö-veh-shkoht	surplus (n.)
överste,nn. (II)	ö-vesh-teh	colonel
översvämning,nn. (II)	ö-veh-shvem-ning	flood
övertala (1)	ö-vehr-taw-lah	induce, to
"	"	persuade, to
övertid,nn.	ö-vehr-teed	overtime (bus., n.)
överträda (2)	ö-vehr-trai-dah	violate (infringe upon), to
överträdelse,nn. (III)	ö-vehr-trai-dell-seh	offense (transgression)
överträffa (1)	ö-vehr-tref-ah	surpass, to
övertyga (1)	ö-vehr-tü-gah	convince, to
övertygelse,nn. (III)	ö-vehr-tü_g-el-seh	conviction (belief)
överväga (2)	ö-vehr-vai-gah	consider (reflect on), to
övervinna (8)	ö-vehr-vin-ah	overcome (conquer), to
övning,nn. (II)	ö_v-ning	exercise (drill)
oxe,nn. (II)	OOX-eh	ox
på	POH	at (by)
"	"	at (on)
"	"	on (prep.)
"	"	upon
på andra sidan	poh AHN-drah SEE-dahn	across (beyond)
packa in (1)	pahck-ah-IN	pack (wrap), to
packe,nn. (II)	PAHCK-eh	bundle (parcel)
packning,nn.	PAHCK-ning	packing (n.)
padda,nn. (I)	PAHDD-ah	toad
paddel,nn. (II)	PAHDD-el	paddle (oar)
påfågel,nn. (II)	POH-foh_g-el	peacock
på grund av	poh-GRUHND awv	because of (adv.)
paj,nn. (III)	PIE	pie
paket,n. (V)	pah-KAYT	package
"	"	parcel
paketpost,nn.	pah-KAYT-pohsst	parcel post
Pakistan,n.	pah-kih-STAWN	Pakistan
pakistansk	pah-kih-STAWNSK	Pakistani (adj.)
palats,n. (V)	pah-LAHTS	palace
Palestina,n.	pah-leh-STEE-nah	Palestine
pålitlig	POH-leet-lig	reliable
pall,nn. (II)	PAHLL	stool (seat)
palm,nn. (III)	PAHLLM	palm (tree)

Swedish	Pronunciation	English
palmsöndagen,*nn.* *def.*	PAHLLM-*sön-dawg-en*	Palm Sunday
pälsverk,*n.* (V)	PELLS-*vairk*	fur
påminna (2)	POH-*min-ah*	remind, to
på något sätt	*poh*-NOH-*goht* SET	somehow
Panama,*n.*	*pah-nah*-MAW	Panama
panik,*nn.*	*pah*-NEEK	panic (fear)
panna,*nn.* (I)	PAHN-*ah*	forehead
panter,*nn.* (II)	PAHN-*tehr*	panther
pantlånekontor,*nn.* (V)	PAHNT-*loh-neh-kohn*-TOOR	pawnshop
pantsätta (11)	PAHNT-*set-ah*	pawn, to
papegoja,*nn.* (I)	*pah-peh*-GOY-*ah*	parrot
papp,*nn.*	PAHP	cardboard
pappa,*nn.* (I)	PAHP-*pah*	dad
papper,*n.* (V)	PAHP-*ehr*	paper
par,*n.* (V)	PAR	couple (*n.*)
"	"	pair
para (1)	PAR-*ah*	mate (find mate for), to
para *nn.* (III)	*pah*-RAWD	parade (procession)
paradis,*n.* (V)	PAW-*rah-dees*	paradise
paragraf,*nn.* (III)	*pah-rah*-GRAWF	paragraph
Paraguay,*n.*	*pah-rah-guh*-AY	Paraguay
parallell	*pah-rah*-LELL	parallel (*adj.*)
paraply,*n.*, *nn.* (III)	*pah-rah*-PLÜ	umbrella
parentes,*nn.* (III)	*pah-ren*-TAYS	parentheses
parfym,*nn.* (III)	*pahr*-FÜ_M	perfume (fragrance)
Paris,*n.*	*pah*-REES	Paris
park,*nn.* (III)	PAHRRK	park
parkera (1)	*pahr*-KAY-*rah*	park (put in place), to
pärla,*nn.* (I)	PAIR-*lah*	bead (jewelry)
"	"	pearl (gem)
parlament,*n.* (V)	*pahr-lah*-MENT	parliament
päron,*n.* (V)	PAIR-*ohn*	pear
parti-...	*pahr*-TEE-...	wholesale (*adj.*, *bus.*)
parti,*n.* (III)	*pahr*-TEE	lot (salable items, *bus.*)
"	"	party (*pol.*)
på samma sätt	*poh*-SAHM-*ah* SET	like (*adv.*)
påse,*nn.* (II)	POH-*seh*	bag (sack)
påsk,*nn.* (II)	POHSSK	Easter
påskynda (1)	POH-*shün-dah*	hasten (expedite), to
"	"	quicken, to
pass,*n.* (V)	PAHSS	passport
passa (1)	PAHSS-*ah*	apply (be fitting), to
passagerare,*nn.* (V)	*pah-sah*-SHAY-*rah-reh*	passenger
passande	PAHSS-*ahn-deh*	fit (suitable)
"	"	proper (acceptable)
passare,*nn.* (V)	PAHSS-*ah-reh*	compass (drawing instrument)
passera (1)	*pah*-SAY-*rah*	pass (go by), to
påssjuka,*nn.*	POH_S-*shu-kah*	mumps
påstå (10)	POH-*stoh*	argue (maintain), to
pastor,*nn.* (III)	PAHSS-*tor*	pastor
påteckning,*nn.* (II)	POH-*teck-ning*	endorsement (signature)
patent,*n.* (V)	*pah*-TENT	patent (*n.*)
patient,*nn.* (III)	*pah-see*-ENT	patient (invalid)
patriot,*nn.* (III)	*pah-tree*-OOT	patriot
påve,*nn.* (II)	POH-*veh*	pope
påverka (1)	POH-*vairrk-ah*	affect (influence), to
peka (1)	PAY-*kah*	point (indicate), to
Peking,*n.*	PAY-*king*	Peiping
pelare,*nn.* (V)	PAY-*lah-reh*	pillar (column)
pengar,*nn.pl.*	PENG-*ahr*	money
penicillin,*n.*	*peh-niss-sill*-LEEN	penicillin
penna,*nn.* (I)	PEN-*ah*	pen
pensé,*nn.* (III)	*pahng*-SAY	pansy
pensionat,*n.* (V)	*pahng-shoo*-NAWT	boarding house
peppar,*nn.*	PEP-*ahr*	pepper (seasoning)
per	PEHR	per (for each)
period,*nn.* (III)	*peh-ree*-OOD	period (of time)
permanent	*pehr-mah*-NENT	permanent (*adj.*)
persika,*nn.* (I)	PASH-*ick-ah*	peach
person,*nn.* (III)	*peh*-SHOON	character
"	"	person
personal,*nn.*	*pesh-oh*-NAWL	staff (personnel)
personlig	*peh*-SHOON-*lig*	personal
personlighet,*nn.* (III)	*peh*-SHOON-*lig-hayt*	personality

Swedish	Pronunciation	English
personvagn,*nn.* (II)	*peh*-SHOON-*vahngn*	coach, railroad
Peru,*n.*	*peh*-RU	Peru
peruansk	*peh-ru*-AWNSK	Peruvian (*adj.*)
pessimistisk	*pess-im*-MISS-*tisk*	pessimistic
petition,*nn.* (III)	*peh-tih*-SHOON	petition (written request)
piano,*n.* (IV)	*pih*-AW-*noo*	piano (*n.*)
picknick,*nn.* (II, III)	PICK-*nick*	picnic
pil,*nn.* (II)	PEEL	arrow
piller,*n.* (V)	PILL-*ehr*	pill
pilot,*nn.* (III)	*pee*-LOOT	pilot (flier)
pina,*nn.* (I)	PEE-*nah*	torment
pinne,*nn.* (II)	PIN-*eh*	peg (pin)
"	"	stick
pionjär,*nn.* (III)	*pee-ohn*-YAIR	pioneer
pipa,*nn.* (I)	PEE-*pah*	pipe (tobacco pipe)
pirat,*nn.* (III)	*pee*-RAWT	pirate
piska (1)	PISS-*kah*	lash, to
"	"	whip (flog), to
piska,*nn.* (I)	PISS-*kah*	whip
pistol,*nn.* (III)	*pih*-STOOL	pistol
pittoresk	*pit-oh*-RESK	picturesque
pjäs,*nn.* (III)	P_YAIS	play (stage presentation)
pladdra (1)	PLAHDD-*rah*	chatter, to
plåga (1)	PLOH-*gah*	torment, to
plågoris,*n.* (V)	PLOH-*goo-rees*	pest (nuisance)
plan,*n.* (V)	PLAWN	level (plane, *n.*)
plan,*nn.* (III)	PLAWN	plan
"	"	scheme
planera (1)	*plah*-NAY-*rah*	plan (prearrange), to
planet,*nn.* (III)	*plah*-NAYT	planet
planka,*nn.* (I)	PLAHNK-*ah*	plank (timber)
plantera (1)	*plahn*-TAY-*rah*	plant (sow), to
plast,*nn.*	PLAHSST	plastic (*n.*)
platå,*nn.* (III)	*plah*-TOH	plateau (tableland)
platina,*nn.*	*plah*-TEE-*nah*	platinum
plats,*nn.* (III)	PLAHTS	locality
"	"	place
plattform,*nn.* (II)	PLAHT-*fohrm*	platform, railroad
plikt,*nn.* (III)	PLICKT	duty (obligation)
plocka (1)	PLOHCK-*ah*	pluck (pull off), to
plog,*nn.* (II)	PLOOG	plow (*n.*)
plöja (2)	PLÖY-*ah*	plow (till), to
plommon,*n.* (V)	PLOOMM-*ohn*	plum (fruit)
plötslig	PLÖTS-*lig*	sudden (unexpected)
plural	PLU-*rawl*	plural (*adj.*)
plus	PLUHSS	plus (*prep.*)
pöbel,*nn.*	PÖ-*bell*	mob (disorderly crowd)
poesi,*nn.*	*poo-eh*-SEE	poetry
pojke,*nn.* (II)	POY-*keh*	boy
"	"	lad
pol,*nn.* (III)	POOL	pole (end of axis)
pöl,*nn.* (II)	PÖ_L	pool (standing water)
Polen,*n.*	POH-*len*	Poland
polera (1)	*poh*-LAY-*rah*	polish, to
polis,*nn.*	*poh*-LEES	police
polis,*nn.* (III)	*poh*-LEES	policeman
politik,*nn.*	*poh-lit*-TEEK	policy (course)
"	"	politics
politiker,*nn.* (V)	*poh*-LEE-*tick-ehr*	politician
politisk	*poh*-LEE-*tisk*	political
polityr,*nn.*	*poh-lit*-TÜ_R	polish
polsk	POHLSK	Polish (*adj.*)
ponny,*nn.* (III)	POHNN-*ih*	pony (animal)
populär	*poh-puh*-LAIR	popular (well-liked)
porslin,*n.*	*ponsh*-LEEN	porcelain (*n.*)
port,*nn.* (II)	POORT	gate
portfölj,*nn.* (III)	*pohrt*-FÖLL_*yuh*	briefcase
portmonnä,*nn.* (III)	*pohrt-moh*-NAY	purse (coin pouch)
porto,*n.* (IV)	POHRT-*oo*	postage (postal charge)
porträtt,*n.* (V)	*pohrt*-RET	portrait
Portugal,*n.*	POHRT-*uh-gawl*	Portugal
post,*nn.*	POHSST	mail (letters exchanged)
"	"	mail (postal system)
post,*nn.* (III)	POHSST	entry (*acctg.*)
"	"	item (detail)
"	"	post (position)

Swedish	Pronunciation	English
posta (1)	POHSS-*tah*	mail (post), to
postanvisning,*nn.* (II)	POHSST-*ahn-vees-ning*	money order
postkontor,*n.* (V)	POHSST-*kohn*-TOOR	post office
postskriptum,*n.* (*pl.* -skripta)	*pohss*-SKRIP-*tuhm*	postscript
potatis,*nn.*, *n.* (II)	*poo*-TAW-*tis*	potato (white)
prakt,*nn.*	PRAHKT	splendor
praktfull	PRAHKT-*full*	gorgeous
praktisk	PRAHCK-*lisk*	practical (not theo-retical)
prärie,*nn.* (III)	PRAI-*ree-eh*	prairie
prassel,*n.*	PRAHSS-*el*	rustle
präst,*nn.* (III)	PREST	minister (clergyman)
"	"	priest
prata (1)	PRAW-*tah*	chat, to
precis	*preh*-SEES	precise
predika (1)	*preh*-DEE-*kah*	preach, to
predikan,*nn.*	*preh*-DEE-*kahn*	sermon
predikant,*nn.* (III)	*preh-dick*-KAHNT	preacher
premie,*nn.* (III)	PRAY-*mee-yeh*	premium (payment)
preposition,*nn.* (III)	*preh-poh-see*-SHOON	preposition (*gram.*)
presentation,*nn.* (III)	*preh-sen-tah*-SHOON	introduction (presen-tation)
presentera (1)	*preh-sen*-TAY-*rah*	introduce (make ac-quainted), to
"	"	present, to
president,*nn.* (III)	*preh-sid*-DENT	president
press,*nn.*	PRESS	press (newspapers and periodicals)
pressa (1)	PRESS-*ah*	press (bear upon), to
"	"	press (iron), to
prick,*nn.* (II)	PRICK	dot (point)
primitiv	*prim-it*-TEEV	primitive (early)
prins,*nn.* (II)	PRINS	prince
prinsessa,*nn.* (I)	*prin*-SESS-*ah*	princess
pris,*n.* (III)	PREES	charge (price)
"	"	price (*bus.*)
"	"	prize (trophy)
"	"	rate (price)
privat	*pree*-VAWT	private (personal)
privilegium,*n.* (III)	*pree-vee*-LAYG-*ee-uhm*	privilege
problem,*n.* (V)	*prohb*-LAYM	problem
procedur,*nn.* (III)	*proh-seh*-DUR	process (set of opera-tions)
procent,*nn.* (V)	*proh*-SENT	percent (*n.*)
"	"	percentage
procession,*nn.* (III)	*proh-seh*-SHOON	procéssion (parade)
producera (1)	*proh-duh*-SAY-*rah*	produce (make), to
produkt,*nn.* (III)	*proh*-DUHKT	product
produktion,*nn.*	*proh-duhk*-SHOON	output
"	"	production (manu-facture)
produktiv	*proh-duhk*-TEEV	productive
profan	*proh*-FAWN	profane (blasphe-mous)
professionell	*proh-fesh-oh*-NELL	professional
professor,*nn.* (III)	*proo*-FESS-*or*	professor (teacher)
profet,*nn.* (III)	*proh*-FAYT	prophet (religious teacher)
program,*n.* (V)	*proo*-GRAHM	program (plan)
projekt,*n.* (V)	*proo*-SHECKT	project
promemoria,*nn.* (I)	*proh-meh*-MOO-*ree-ah*	memorandum
promenad,*nn.* (III)	*proo-meh*-NAWD	walk (stroll)
propp,*nn.* (II)	PROHP	fuse (*elec.*)
"	"	plug (stopper)
prosa,*nn.*	PROO-*sah*	prose
protest,*nn.* (III)	*proo*-TEST	protest
protestera (1)	*proo-tess*-TAY-*rah*	protest, to
protokoll,*n.* (V)	*proh-toh*-KOHLL	minutes (record)
prov,*n.* (V)	PROOV	sample
"	"	test (*educ.*)
"	"	test (trial)
pröva (1)	PRÖ-*vah*	test, to
"	"	try, to
provins,*nn.* (III)	*proo*-VINS	province (*pol.*)
provision,*nn.* (III)	*proo-vih*-SHOON	commission (fee)
prövning,*nn.* (II)	PRÖ_V-*ning*	examination (test)
pryda (2)	PRÜ-*dah*	adorn (beautify), to
"	"	decorate, to

Swedish	Pronunciation	English
psalm,*nn.* (III)	SAHLLM	hymn (religious song)
psykiatri,*nn.*	*p_sü-kee-ah*-TREE	psychiatry
psykologi,*nn.*	*p_sü-koh-log*-EE	psychology
publicera (1)	*puhb-liss*-SAY-*rah*	publish, to
publicitet,*nn.*	*puhb-liss-it*-TAYT	publicity (notoriety)
publik,*nn.*	*puhb*-LEEK	audience
publikation,*nn.* (III)	*puhb-lick-ah*-SHOON	publication (pub-lished work)
puckel,*nn.* (II)	PUHCK-*el*	hump
pudding,*nn.* (II)	PUHD-*ing*	pudding (dessert)
puder,*n.*	PUH-*dehr*	powder (cosmetic)
puls,*nn.* (II)	PUHLS	pulse (*physiol.*)
pulsåder,*nn.* (I)	PUHLS-*oh-dehr*	artery (*anat.*)
pump,*nn.* (II)	PUHMP	pump
punkt,*nn.* (III)	PUHNKT	period (*punct.*)
"	"	point (item)
punktlig	PUHNKT-*lig*	prompt (punctual)
"	"	punctual
pupill,*nn.* (III)	*puh*-PILL	pupil (of eye)
purpurfärgad	PUHR-*puhr-fairr-yahd*	purple (color)
pussel,*n.* (V)	PUHSS-*el*	puzzle (game)
pyjamas,*nn.* (V)	*pü*-YAW-*mahss*	pajamas
Quito,*n.*	KEE-*toh*	Quito
rå	ROH	crude
"	"	raw (in natural state)
rabatt,*nn.* (III)	*rah*-BAHT	discount (*n.*)
rabbin,*nn.*	*rah*-BEEN	rabbi
rad,*nn.* (III)	RAWD	line
"	"	rank (row)
"	"	row (series)
råd,*n.* (V)	ROH_D	advice
"	"	council
"	"	counsel
råda (2)	ROH-*dah*	advise, to
"	"	counsel, to
"	"	prevail (exist widely), to
radar,*nn.*	RAW-*dahr*	radar (*n.*)
rädd	RED	afraid
"	"	fearful
rädda (1)	RED-*ah*	rescue, to
"	"	save, to
räddning,*nn.*	RED-*ning*	rescue
"	"	salvation
radergummi,*n.* (IV)	*rah*-DAYR-*guhm-ih*	eraser (rubber eraser)
rådfråga (1)	ROH_D-*froh-gah*	consult (seek pro-fessional advice of), to
radio,*nn.*	RAW-*dee-oo*	radio (receiving set)
radioaktivitet,*nn.*	RAW-*dih-oo-ahck-tih-vih*-TAYT	radioactivity
radiosignal,*nn.* (III)	RAW-*dee-oo-sing*-NAWL	beam (radio signal)
radioutsändning,*nn.* (II)	RAW-*dee-oo-uh_t*-SEND-*ning*	broadcasting (*rad.*)
rådjur,*n.* (V)	ROH-*yu_r*	deer
råg,*nn.*	ROH_G	rye (grain)
rak	RAWK	straight (not crooked, *adj.*)
räka,*nn.* (I)	RAI-*kah*	shrimp
raka sig (1)	RAW-*kah say*	shave (oneself), to
rakblad,*n.* (V)	RAWK-*blawd*	razor blade
raket,*nn.* (III)	*rah*-KAYT	rocket
rakkniv,*nn.* (II)	RAWK-*k_neev*	razor
rakkräm,*nn.* (III)	RAWK-*kraim*	shaving cream
räkna (1)	RAIK-*nah*	count (enumerate), to
räkna på	RAIK-*nah* POH	count (rely) on, to
räknemaskin,*nn.* (III)	RAIK-*neh-mah*-SHEEN	adding machine
räkning,*nn.* (II)	RAIK-*ning*	arithmetic
"	"	bill (invoice)
ramla (1)	RAHM-*lah*	tumble (fall), to
råna (1)	ROH-*nah*	rob (steal from), to
rånare,*nn.* (V)	ROH-*nah-reh*	robber
rand,*nn.*	RAHND	brink (verge)
rang,*nn.*	RAHNG	rank (standing)
rännsten,*nn.* (II)	REN-*stayn*	gutter (of street)
ranson,*nn.* (III)	*rahn*-SOON	ration (allotment)
ränta,*nn.* (I)	REN-*tah*	interest (money rate)

Swedish	Pronunciation	English
ränta på ränta,*nn.*	REN-*tah poh* REN-*tah*	compound interest
rapport,*nn.* (III)	*rah*-POHRRT	dispatch (communication)
"	"	report (account)
rapportera (1)	*rah-pohrrt*-TAY-*rah*	report (account formally), to
ras,*nn.* (III)	RAWS	breed (stock)
"	"	race (*anthrop.*)
rasa (1)	RAW-*sah*	rage (rave), to
rasande	RAW-*sahn-deh*	furious
raseri,*n.*	*raw-seh*-REE	fury
"	"	rage (wrath)
rast,*nn.* (III)	RAHSST	recess (school intermission)
rätt	RET	right (correct, *adj.*)
rätt,*nn.*	RET	right (claim)
rätt,*nn.* (III)	RET	dish (food)
råtta,*nn.* (I)	ROHT-*ah*	rat
rättegång,*nn.* (II)	RET-*eh-gohng*	trial (court proceeding)
rättskipning,*nn.*	RET-*sheep-ning*	justice (administration of law)
rättstvist,*nn.* (III)	RETS-*tvist*	litigation
rättvis	RET-*vees*	fair (impartial)
"	"	just (equitable, *adj.*)
rättvisa,*nn.*	RET-*vee-sah*	justice (rightfulness)
rättvist	RET-*veest*	fairly (impartially)
räv,*nn.* (II)	RAIV	fox
reagera (1)	*reh-ah*-GAY-*rah*	respond (react), to
reaktion,*nn.* (III)	*reh-ahck*-SHOON	reaction
reaktionsmotor,*nn.* (III)	*reh-ahck*-SHOONS-*moo-tor*	jet engine
rebell,*nn.* (III)	*reh*-BELL	rebel (*n.*)
recension,*nn.* (III)	*reh-sen*-SHOON	review (critique)
recept,*n.* (V)	*reh*-SEPT	prescription (*med.*)
"	"	recipe
redaktör,*nn.* (III)	*reh-dahck*-TÖR	editor
redan	RAY-*dahn*	already
redogöra för (11)	RAY-*doo-yö-rah* FÖR	account for, to
"	"	explain, to
redogörelse,*nn.* (III)	RAY-*doo-yö-rel-seh*	account (report)
redovisning,*nn.* (II)	RAY-*doo-vees-ning*	statement (accounting, *bus.*)
reform,*nn.* (III)	*reh*-FOHRRM	reform (*n.*)
regel,*nn.*	RAYG-*el*	rule (usual case)
regel,*nn.* (II)	RAYG-*el*	bolt (lock)
regel,*nn.* (III)	RAYG-*el*	rule (regulation)
regelbundenhet,*nn.*	RAYG-*el-buhn-den-hayt*	regularity
regemente,*n.* (IV)	*rehg-eh*-MEN-*teh*	regiment (*n.*)
regera över (1)	*reh*-YAY-*rah* ö-*vehr*	govern, to
regering,*nn.* (II)	*reh*-YAY-*ring*	government
regeringstid,*nn.* (III)	*reh*-YAY-*rings-teed*	reign (period of rule)
register,*n.* (V)	*reh*-YISS-*tehr*	index (list)
registrera (1)	*reh-yih*-STRAY-*rah*	register, to
regn,*n.* (V)	RENGN	rain
regna (1)	RENG-*nah*	rain, to
regnbåge,*nn.* (II)	RENGN-*boh_g-eh*	rainbow
regnig	RENG-*nig*	rainy
regnrock,*nn.* (II)	RENGN-*rohck*	raincoat
rekommendation,*nn.* (III)	*reh-koh-men-dah*-SHOON	recommendation
rekommenderad	*reh-koh-men*-DAY-*rahd*	registered (postal designation)
rektangel,*nn.* (II)	*reck*-TAHNG-*el*	rectangle
relativ	RAY-*lah-teev*	comparative
"	"	relative
religion,*nn.* (III)	*reh-lee*-YOON	religion
religiös	*reh-lee*-SHÖ_S	religious (*adj.*)
rem,*nn.* (II)	REM	strap
remissa,*nn.* (I)	*reh*-MISS-*ah*	remittance
remsa,*nn.* (I)	REM-*sah*	strip (band)
ren	RAYN	clean
"	"	pure (unadulterated)
"	"	sheer (pure)
ren,*nn.* (II)	RAYN	reindeer
rena (1)	RAY-*nah*	refine (purify), to
rengöra (11)	RAYN-*yöh-rah*	clean, to
renhet,*nn.*	RAYN-*hayt*	purity (cleanness)
rep,*n.* (V)	RAYP	cord
"	"	rope

Swedish	Pronunciation	English
reparation,*nn.* (III)	*reh-pah-rah*-SHOON	repair (*n.*)
reparera (1)	*reh-pah*-RAY-*rah*	repair (fix), to
repetition,*nn.* (III)	*reh-pet-ee*-SHOON	rehearsal
reporter,*nn.* (*pl.* -s)	*reh*-PORT-*ehr*	reporter (journalist)
representant,*nn.* (III)	*reh-preh-sen*-TAHNT	representative (deputy)
representation,*nn.*	*reh-preh-sen-tah*-SHOON	representation (*pol.*)
representera (1)	*reh-preh-sen*-TAY-*rah*	represent (act for), to
republik,*nn.* (III)	*reh-puhb*-LEEK	republic
republikansk	*reh-puhb-lick*-KAWNSK	republican (*adj.*)
resa (2)	RAY-*sah*	leave (depart), to
"	"	travel, to
resa,*nn.* (I)	RAY-*sah*	journey
(sjö)resa,*nn.* (I)	(SHÖ-)RAY-*sah*	voyage
resande,*nn.* (V)	RAY-*sahn-deh*	traveler
resa sig	RAY-*sah say*	stand up, to
reservera (1)	*reh-sehr*-VAY-*rah*	reserve (withhold), to
reservfond,*nn.* (III)	*reh*-SAIRRV-*fohnd*	reserve (*bus.*)
reservoar,*nn.* (III)	*reh-sehr-voo*-ARR	reservoir (water reserve)
reservoarpenna,*nn.* (I)	*reh-sehr-voo*-AHR-*pen-ah*	pen, fountain
resolution,*nn.* (III)	*reh-soh-lu*-SHOON	resolution (formal expression)
respekt,*nn.*	*reh*-SPECKT	respect (esteem)
respektabel	*reh-speck*-TAW-*bell*	respectable
respektera (1)	*reh-speck*-TAY-*rah*	respect (esteem), to
respektive	*reh-speck*-TEE-*veh*	respective (*adj.*)
rest,*nn.* (III)	REST	rest (remainder)
restaurang,*nn.* (III)	*reh-stoh*-RAHNG	restaurant
restaurangvagn,*nn.* (II)	*reh-stoh*-RAHNG-*vahngn*	diner (railway dining car)
resultat,*n.* (V)	*reh-suhll*-TAWT	result (consequence)
resumé,*nn.* (III)	*reh-su*-MAY	summary (synopsis)
reta (1)	RAY-*tah*	tease, to
reträtt,*nn.* (III)	*reh*-TRET	retreat (*mil.*)
reumatism,*nn.*	*rö-mah*-TISSM	rheumatism
revben,*n.* (V)	RAYV-*bayn*	rib (*anat.*)
revers,*nn.* (III)	*reh*-VASH	note (promise to pay, *bus.*)
revision,*nn.* (III)	*reh-vee*-SHOON	audit (*n.*)
revisor,*nn.* (III)	*reh*-VEE-*sohr*	auditor
revolution,*nn.* (III)	*reh-voh-luh*-SHOON	revolution (*pol.*)
revolver,*nn.* (II)	*reh*-VOHLL-*vehr*	revolver (weapon)
Rhen,*nn.*	RAYN	Rhine
riddare,*nn.* (V)	RID-*ah-reh*	knight
rik	REEK	rich
rike,*n.* (IV)	REE-*keh*	realm (kingdom)
rikedom,*nn.* (II)	REE-*keh-doomm*	riches
"	"	treasure
"	"	wealth
riklig	REEK-*lig*	abundant
"	"	ample
"	"	full
"	"	plentiful
rikta (1)	RICK-*tah*	beam (direct, *rad.*), to
"	"	direct (aim), to
riktig	RICK-*tig*	correct
riktigt	RICK-*tikt*	quite (considerably)
riktning,*nn.* (II)	RICKT-*ning*	direction (course)
rim,*n.* (V)	RIM	rhyme
ring,*nn.* (II)	RING	ring (circle)
"	"	ring (jewelry)
ringa (2)	RING-*ah*	ring (resound)
"	"	sound (make heard), to
rinna (8)	RIN-*ah*	run (flow), to
Rio de Janeiro,*n.*	REE-*oh deh shah*-NAY-*roh*	Rio de Janeiro
ris,*n.*	REES	rice
risk,*nn.* (III)	RISK	risk (danger)
rit,*nn.* (III)	REET	rite
riva	REE-*vah*	scratch, to
riva (sönder)	REE-*vah* (SÖN-*dehr*)	tear (rip), to
rival,*nn.* (III)	*ree*-VAWL	rival (competitor)
roa (1)	ROO-*ah*	amuse, to
röd	RÖ_D	red
rödbeta,*nn.* (I)	RÖ_D-*bay-tah*	beet (red root)

Swedish	Pronunciation	English
roder,*n.* (V)	ROO-*dehr*	rudder (of a boat)
rödhakesångare, *nn.* (V)	RÖ̱D-*hawk-eh-sohng-ah-reh*	robin
rodna (1)	ROH̲D-*nah*	blush, to
röja (2)	RÖY-*ah*	betray (reveal), to
rök,*nn.*	RÖ̲K	smoke
röka (2)	RÖ-*kah*	smoke, to
rökt fläsk,*n.*	RÖ̲KT FLESK	bacon
rolig	ROO-*lig*	funny (comical)
roll,*nn.* (III)	ROHLL	role
Rom,*n.*	ROOMM	Rome
rom,*nn.*	ROHM	rum
roman,*nn.* (III)	*roo*-MAWN	novel (book)
romantisk	*roo*-MAHN-*tisk*	romantic
romersk	ROOMM-*eshk*	Roman (*adj.*)
röntga (1)	RÖNT-*gah*	X-ray (examine), to
röntgen,*nn.* (V)	RÖNT-*ghen*	X-ray (X-ray picture)
rop,*n.* (V)	ROOP	call
"	"	shout (cry)
ropa (1)	ROO-*pah*	call, to
"	"	shout (say loudly), to
ropa bifall	*roo-pah*-BEE-*fahll*	cheer (applaud), to
rör,*n.* (V)	RÖR	pipe
"	"	tube
röra,*nn.*	RÖ-*rah*	mess (muddle)
röra om (2)	*rö-rah*-OHM	stir (mix), to
rörelse,*nn.* (III)	RÖ-*rel-seh*	emotion
"	"	motion
"	"	movement
ros,*nn.* (I)	ROOS	rose (flower)
rost,*nn.*	ROHSST	rust
röst,*nn.* (III)	RÖSST	voice
"	"	vote
rösta (1)	RÖSS-*tah*	vote, to
rostat bröd,*n.*	ROHSS-*taht* BRÖ̲D	toast (bread)
rostfritt stål,*n.*	ROHSST-*frit* STOHL	stainless steel
rostig	ROHSS-*tig*	rusty
röstning,*nn.* (II)	RÖSST-*ning*	poll (survey)
rot,*nn.* (*pl.* rötter)	ROO̲T	root (*bot.*)
rouge,*n.*	ROUGE	rouge
rova,*nn.* (I)	ROO-*vah*	turnip (white)
royalty,*nn.* (*pl.* -ties)	ROY-*ahll-tih*	royalty (fee)
rubin,*nn.* (III)	*ruh*-BEEN	ruby (gem)
rubrik,*nn.* (III)	*ruh*-BREEK	heading (title)
ruin,*nn.* (III)	*ruh*-EEN	ruins (remains)
ruinera (1)	*ruh-in*-NAY-*rah*	ruin, to
rulla (1)	RUHLL-*ah*	roll (impel), to
rulle,*nn.* (II)	RUHLL-*eh*	roll (cylinder)
rullgardin,*nn.* (III)	RUHLL-*gar*-DEEN	shade (window blind)
rum,*n.* (V)	RUHM	room (of house)
Rumänien,*n.*	*ruh*-MAI-*nih-en*	Rumania
rund	RUHND	round (*adj.*)
rusa (1)	RU-*sah*	dash, to
"	"	rush, to
rusning,*nn.*	RU̲S-*ning*	rush (rapid motion)
russin,*n.* (V)	RUHSS-*in*	raisin
rustning,*nn.* (II)	RUHST-*ning*	armor
rutt,*nn.* (III)	RUHT	route
rutten	RUHT-*en*	rotten (decayed)
ruttna (1)	RUHT-*nah*	rot, to
rycka till sig (2)	*rück-ah*-TILL *say*	snatch, to
rygg,*nn.* (II)	RÜG	back (*anat.*)
ryggrad,*nn.* (III)	RÜG-*rawd*	spine (*anat.*)
ryktbarhet,*nn.*	RÜCKT-*bar-hayt*	fame
"	"	glory (renown)
rykte,*n.* (IV)	RÜCK-*teh*	rumor
rynka,*nn.* (I)	RÜNK-*ah*	wrinkle (fold)
rynka pannan (1)	RÜNK-*ah* PAHN-*ahn*	frown, to
rysa (2)	RÜ-*sah*	shudder, to
rysk	RÜSK	Russian (*adj.*)
rysning,*nn.* (II)	RÜ̲S-*ning*	chill (shivering sensation)
Ryssland,*n.*	RÜSS-*lahnd*	Russia
ryta (7)	RÜ-*tah*	bellow (roar), to
rytande,*n.* (IV)	RÜ-*tahn-deh*	roar (*n.*)
ryttare,*nn.* (V)	RÜT-*ah-reh*	rider (horseman)
så	SOH	so (therefore, *adv.*)
"	"	thus (in this way)
så (3)	SOH	sow, to
så att	*soh*-AHT	so (in order that, *conj.*)
säck,*nn.* (II)	SECK	sack (bag)
säd,*nn.*	SAI̲D	grain (cereal)
sådan	SOH-*dahn*	such (of that kind, *adj.*)
sadel,*nn.* (II)	SAW-*dell*	saddle (seat)
sädesslag,*n.* (V)	SAI-*des-slawg*	cereal (grain)
safir,*nn.* (III)	*sah*-FEER	sapphire (gem)
saft,*nn.* (III)	SAHFFT	juice
såg,*nn.* (II)	SOH̲G	saw (tool)
saga,*nn.* (I)	SAW-*gah*	fairy tale
säga (11)	SAY-*ah*	say, to
sak,*nn.* (III)	SAWK	article
"	"	matter (affair)
"	"	thing (material object)
säker	SAI-*kehr*	certain
"	"	safe (unharmed)
"	"	secure
"	"	sure
säkerhet,*nn.*	SAI-*kehr-hayt*	safety (*n.*)
"	"	security
säkerhetsnål,*nn.* (II)	SAI-*kehr-hayts-noh̲l*	safety pin
säkert	SAI-*kehrt*	certainly (surely, *adv.*)
sakna (1)	SAWK-*nah*	lack (be without), to
"	"	miss (feel the loss of), to
sal,*nn.* (II)	SAWL	hall (meeting room)
säl,*nn.* (II)	SAIL	seal (animal)
således	SOH-*lay-des*	thus (therefore)
sälja (11)	SELL-*yah*	sell, to
säljare,*nn.* (V)	SELL-*yah-reh*	vendor (seller)
säljbar	SELL-*yuh-bar*	negotiable (*bus.*)
sålla (1)	SOHLL-*ah*	sift (separate), to
sallad,*nn.* (III)	SAHLL-*ahd*	salad
(grön)sallad,*nn.* (III)	(GRÖ̲N-)SAHLL-*ahd*	lettuce
salladsås,*nn.* (III)	SAHLL-*ahd-soh̲s*	dressing (sauce)
sällan	SELL-*ahn*	seldom
sällhet,*nn.*	SELL-*hayt*	bliss
sällsam	SELL-*sahm*	quaint (unusual)
sällskaplig	SELL-*skawp-lig*	sociable (companionable)
sällsynt	SELL-*sü̲nt*	rare (uncommon)
salt,*n.* (III)	SAHLLT	salt
salva,*nn.* (I)	SAHLL-*vah*	ointment
Salvador,*n.*	*sahl-vah*-DOR	Salvador, El
samarbete,*n.*	SAHM-*ahr*-BAY-*teh*	cooperation
samband,*n.* (V)	SAHM-*bahnd*	connection (relationship)
samhälle,*n.* (IV)	SAHM-*hell-eh*	community (the public)
"	"	society (the public)
samla (1)	SAHM-*lah*	assemble (bring together), to
"	"	collect (bring together), to
"	"	gather (bring together), to
samlas (1)	SAHM-*lahss*	assemble (meet), to
"	"	gather (congregate), to
samling,*nn.* (II)	SAHM-*ling*	collection
samma	SAHM-*ah*	same (*adj.*)
sammandra(ga) (9)	SAHM-*ahn-draw*(-*gah*)	contract (make shrink), to
sammankomst,*nn.* (III)	SAHM-*ahn-kohmst*	assembly (meeting)
"	"	convention (meeting)
sammansättning, *nn.* (II)	SAHM-*ahn-set-ning*	composition (make-up)
"	"	compound (mixture)
sammanträde,*n.* (IV)	SAHM-*ahn-trai-deh*	session
sammet,*nn.*	SAHM-*et*	velvet (*n.*)
sämre	SEM-*reh*	inferior (mediocre)
"	"	worse (*adj.*)
sämst	SEMST	worst (*adj.*)
samtal,*n.* (V)	SAHM-*tawl*	conversation
"	"	talk

Swedish	Pronunciation	English
samtycka (2)	SAHM-*tück-ah*	agree, to
"	"	assent, to
		comply (acquiesce), to
"	"	consent, to
samvete,*n.* (IV)	SAHM-*vay-teh*	conscience
sand,*nn.*	SAHNND	sand
sända (2)	SEN-*dah*	send, to
"	"	ship (send goods), to
sandig	SAHN-*dig*	sandy
sändning,*nn.* (II)	SEND-*ning*	consignment (*bus.*)
	"	shipment (goods)
säng,*nn.* (II)	SENG	bed
sång,*nn.* (III)	SONG	song
sångare,*nn.* (V)	SONG-*ah-reh*	singer
sänka (2)	SENG-*kah*	lower, to
sann	SAHN	true
sannerligen	SAHN-*ehr-lig-en*	indeed (*adv.*)
sanning,*nn.* (II)	SAHN-*ing*	truth
sannolik	SAHN-*oo-leek*	likely (probable, *adj.*)
Santiago,*n.*	*sahn-tih-*AW-*goo*	Santiago
sår,*n.* (V)	SOR	wound (injury)
såra (1)	SOR-*ah*	wound, to
sardin,*nn.* (III)	*sahr-*DEEN	sardine
säregen	SAIR-*ayg-en*	singular (peculiar)
särskild	SAIR-*shilld*	individual (*adj.*)
"	"	particular (specific, *adj.*)
"	"	separate
särskilja (2)	SAIR-*shill-yah*	distinguish (differentiate), to
särskilt	SAIR-*shilt*	especially
sås,*nn.* (III)	SOH_S	gravy
"	"	sauce
satäng,*nn.*	*sah-*TENG	satin (*n.*)
sätt,*n.* (V)	SET	fashion
"	"	manner
"	"	means (method)
"	"	mode
"	"	style
"	"	way
sätta (11)	SET-*ah*	put (place), to
"	"	set, to
sätta i gång	*set-ah-ee-*GOHNG	launch (start), to
sätta i stället	*set-ah-ee-*STELL-*et*	substitute (put in place of), to
sätta sig	SET-*ah say*	sit down, to
sav,*nn.*	SAWV	sap (fluid)
såvida inte	*soh-*VEE-*dah* IN-*teh*	unless (*conj.*)
sax,*nn.* (II)	SAHX	scissors
saxofon,*nn.* (III)	*sahx-oo-*FOH_N	saxophone
scen,*nn.* (III)	SAYN	scene (dramatic unit)
"	"	stage (dais)
scenario,*n.* (III, IV)	*seh-*NAW-*ree-oh*	scenario
schack,*nn.*	SHAHCK	chess
scharlakansfeber, *nn.*	SHAR-*law-kahns-fay-behr*	scarlet fever
scharlakansröd	SHAR-*law-kahns-rö_d*	scarlet (*adj.*)
Schweiz,*n.*	SHVAYTS	Switzerland
schweizisk	SHVAYT-*sisk*	Swiss (*adj.*)
se (10)	SAY	see, to
sebra,*nn.* (I)	SAY-*brah*	zebra
sed,*nn.* (III)	SAYD	custom (habit)
sedan	SAY-*dahn*	after (*conj.*)
"	"	since (after, *prep.*)
"	"	then (subsequently)
sedan, för...	*för...*SAY-*dahn*	ago (past, *adj.*)
sedan dess	*say-dahn-*DESS	since (from then to now, *adv.*)
sedel,*nn.* (II)	SAY-*dell*	bill (currency)
seg	SAYG	tough (resistant)
seger,*nn.* (II)	SAYG-*ehr*	victory
segerrik	SAYG-*ehr-reek*	victorious
segrare,*nn.* (V)	SAYG-*rah-reh*	victor
sekreterare,*nn.* (V)	*seh-kreh-*TAY-*rah-reh*	secretary (stenographer)
sekund,*nn.* (III)	*seh-*KUHND	second (time unit)
sele,*nn.* (II)	SAY-*leh*	harness
selleri,*nn., n.*	SELL-*eh-rih*	celery
semester,*nn.* (II)	*seh-*MESS-*tehr*	vacation (work holidays)
semikolon,*n.* (V)	SAY-*mih-koo-lohn*	semicolon

Swedish	Pronunciation	English
sen	SAYN	tardy
sen(färdig)	SAYN-(*faird-dig*)	slow (tardy)
senap,*nn.*	SAY-*nahp*	mustard
senare	SAY-*nah-reh*	latter (second of two, *adj.*)
senast	SAY-*nahst*	last (most recent, *adj.*)
"	"	last (most recently, *adv.*)
senat,*nn.* (III)	*say-*NAWT	senate
senator,*nn.* (III)	*seh-*NAW-*tor*	senator
sent	SAYNT	late (at relative time, *adv.*)
sent, för	*fö-*SHAYNT	late (tardily, *adv.*)
sergeant,*nn.* (III)	*sehr-*SHAHNT	sergeant
serie,*nn.* (III)	SAY-*rih-eh*	series
servett,*nn.* (III)	*sehr-*VET	napkin
servis,*nn.* (III)	*sehr-*VEES	dishes (tableware)
sida,*nn.* (I)	SEE-*dah*	page (leaf)
"	"	side
sidan, åt	*oht-*SEE-*dahn*	aside (away)
siffra,*nn.* (I)	SIF-*rah*	figure (numeral)
"	"	number (numeral)
sig (själv)	SAY (SHELV)	itself
sigill,*n.* (V)	*sih-*YILL	seal (mark)
signal,*nn.* (III)	*sing-*NAWL	signal
signalhorn,*n.* (V)	*sing-*NAWL-*hoorn*	horn (*auto.*)
sikta (1)	SICK-*tah*	aim (direct), to
sila (1)	SEE-*lah*	strain (filter), to
silke,*n.*	SILL-*keh*	silk (*n.*)
sill,*nn.* (II)	SILL	herring
silver,*n.*	SILL-*vehr*	silver (metal, *n.*)
simma (1, 8)	SIM-*ah*	swim, to
simpel	SIM-*pell*	common (vulgar)
sin, sitt, sina	SIN, SIT, SEE-*nah*	his (*poss. adj., poss. pron.*)
"	"	her, hers
"	"	its (*poss. adj., poss. pron.*)
"	"	their, theirs
singularis,*n.*	SING-*guh-lar-is*	singular (*gram., n.*)
sist	SIST	final
"	"	last (after all others, *adv.*)
"	"	last (final, *adj.*)
sitta (8)	SIT-*ah*	sit (be sitting), to
sitta fast	*sit-ah-*FAHSST	stick (adhere), to
sitta uppflugen	*sit-ah* UHP-*flu_g-en*	perch (sit), to
sittplats,*nn.* (III)	SIT-*plahts*	seat
situation,*nn.* (III)	*sit-uh-ah-*SHOON	situation (circumstances)
själ,*nn.* (II)	SHAIL	soul
själskval,*n.* (V)	SHAILS-*kvawl*	agony (mental pain)
själslig	SHAILS-*lig*	mental
själv	SHELV	self (*pron.*)
självbiografi,*nn.* (III)	SHELV-*bih-oo-grah-*FEE	autobiography
självisk	SHELL-*visk*	selfish
självmord,*n.* (V)	SHELV-*moord*	suicide
självsäker	SHELV-*say-kehr*	confident (self-assured)
sjö,*nn.* (II)	SHÖ	lake
sjöman,*nn.* (*pl.* -män)	SHÖ-*mahn*	sailor
sjösätta (11)	SHÖ-*set-ah*	launch (set afloat), to
sjuk	SHU_K	ill
"	"	sick (ailing)
sjukdom,*nn.* (II)	SHU_K-*doomm*	disease
"	"	illness
"	"	sickness
sjukhus,*n.* (V)	SHUH_K-*huh_s*	hospital
sjuksal,*nn.* (II)	SHU_K-*sawl*	ward (sickroom)
sjuksköterska,*nn.* (I)	SHU_K-*shö-tesh-kah*	nurse (medical assistant)
sjunga (6)	SHUHNG-*ah*	sing, to
sjunka (6)	SHUHNK-*ah*	sink, to
skada (1)	SKAW-*dah*	damage, to
"	"	harm, to
"	"	hurt (inflict pain upon), to
"	"	injure, to
skada,*nn.* (I)	SKAW-*dah*	damage
"	"	injury
skåda (1)	SKOH-*dah*	behold, to
skådespel,*n.* (V)	SKOH-*deh-spayl*	spectacle (pageant)

Swedish	Pronunciation	English
skådespelare,*m.* (V)	SKOH-*deh-spay-lah-reh*	actor (player)
skådespelerska,*f.* (I)	SKOH-*deh-spay-lesh-kah*	actress
skadestånd,*n.* (V)	SKAW-*deh-stohnd*	damages (indemnification)
"	"	indemnity (compensation)
skaffa (1)	SKAHFF-*ah*	furnish (supply), to
"	"	procure (obtain), to
"	"	secure (obtain), to
skaft,*n.* (V)	SKAHFFT	shaft (*mech.*)
skägg,*n.* (V)	SHEG	beard
skaka (1)	SKAW-*kah*	shake, to
skal,*n.* (V)	SKAWL	shell (covering)
skål,*nn.* (II)	SKOHL	bowl (dish)
skala,*nn.* (I)	SKAW-*lah*	scale (graduated measure)
"	"	scale (proportion)
skala (1)	SKAW-*lah*	peel (take skin from), to
skalbagge,*nn.* (II)	SKAWL-*bahg-eh*	beetle
skall (4)	SKAHLL	shall (*v.*)
"	"	will (*v.*)
skalla (1)	SKAHLL-*ah*	peal, to
skälla (2)	SHELL-*ah*	bark (bay), to
skalle,*nn.* (II)	SKAHLL-*eh*	skull
skallig	SKAHLL-*ig*	bald (hairless)
skälva (2)	SHELL-*vah*	quake (shake), to
"	"	quiver, to
skam,*nn.*	SKAHM	disgrace
"	"	shame
skamlig	SKAHM-*lig*	shameful
skamsen	SKAHM-*sen*	ashamed (mortified)
skämt,*n.* (V)	SHEMT	jest
"	"	joke
skämta (1)	SHEM-*tah*	jest, to
"	"	joke, to
skämtserie,*nn.* (III)	SHEMT-*say-rih-eh*	comic strip
skandal,*nn.* (III)	*skahn*-DAWL	scandal
skänka (2)	SHENK-*ah*	bestow, to
"	"	donate, to
"	"	present (give), to
skåp,*n.* (V)	SKOH P	cupboard
skapa (1)	SKAW-*pah*	create, to
skapande,*n.*	SKAW-*pahn-deh*	creation
skaplig	SKAWP-*lig*	fair (passable)
skär	SHAIR	pink (color)
skära (10)	SHAI-*rah*	cut (divide into parts), to
skära (10)	SHAI-*rah*	cut (wound), to
skärm,*nn.* (II)	SHAIRRM	screen (partition)
skarp	SKAHRRP	keen
"	"	sharp
skatt,*nn.* (III)	SKAHT	tax (*n.*)
"	"	treasure
skede,*n.* (IV)	SHAY-*deh*	phase (stage)
skelett,*n.* (V)	*skeh*-LET	skeleton (*anat.*)
skena,*nn.* (I)	SHAY-*nah*	rail (bar on track)
skepp,*n.* (V)	SHEP	ship
skeppsvarv,*n.* (V)	SHEPS-*vahrrv*	shipyard
skicklig	SHICK-*lig*	clever
"	"	skilful
skicklighet,*nn.*	SHICK-*lig-hayt*	skill (proficiency)
skift,*n.* (V)	SHIFT	shift (crew)
skifta (1)	SHIFF-*tah*	vary (undergo change), to
skilja (11)	SHILL-*yah*	separate (disconnect), to
"	"	sever, to
skiljande,*n.*	SHILL-*yahn-deh*	separation
skiljas (11)	SHILL-*yahs*	part (leave each other), to
"	"	separate (come apart), to
skillnad,*nn.* (III)	SHILL-*nahd*	difference (*math.*)
skilsmässa,*nn.* (I)	SHILLS-*mess-ah*	divorce (*law*)
skina (5)	SHEE-*nah*	shine (gleam), to
skinka,*nn.* (I)	SHINK-*ah*	ham (food)
skinn,*n.* (V)	SHIN	skin (animal hide)

Swedish	Pronunciation	English
skiss,*nn.* (III)	SKISS	sketch (rough drawing)
skiva,*nn.* (I)	SHEE-*vah*	slice
skjorta,*nn.* (I)	SHOORT-*ah*	shirt
skjul,*n.* (V)	SHU L	shed (shelter)
skjuta (6)	SHU-*tah*	shoot (fire at), to
sko,*nn.* (III)	SKOO	shoe (footwear)
skog,*nn.* (II)	SKOOG	forest
"	"	wood
skola,*nn.* (I)	SKOO-*lah*	school
sköldpadda,*nn.* (I)	SHÖLLD-*pahd-ah*	turtle
skolhus,*n.* (V)	SKOOL-*huh s*	schoolhouse
skolning,*nn.*	SKOOL-*ning*	discipline (training)
skolrum,*n.* (V)	SKOOL-*ruhm*	schoolroom
skolundervisning,*nn.*	SKOOL-*uhn-dehr-vees-ning*	schooling (instruction)
skomakare,*nn.* (V)	SKOO-*maw-kah-reh*	shoemaker
skona (1)	SKOO-*nah*	spare (not harm), to
skönhet,*nn.*	SHÖ N-*hayt*	beauty
skönhetsmedel,*n.* (V)	SHÖ N-*hayts-may-dell*	cosmetic (*n.*)
skör	SHÖR	brittle
"	"	crisp
skörd,*nn.* (II)	SHÖRD	crop (produce)
"	"	harvest
skörda (1)	SHÖRD-*ah*	reap, to
skorpa,*nn.* (I)	SKOHRR-*pah*	crust
skorsten,*nn.* (II)	SKOHSH-*ten*	chimney
sköta (2b)	SHÖ-*tah*	manage (administer), to
"	"	operate (handle), to
skotsk	SKOHTSK	Scotch (*adj.*)
skott,*n.* (V)	SKOHT	shot (from firearm)
Skottland,*n.*	SKOHT-*lahnd*	Scotland
skovel,*nn.* (II)	SKOHV-*el*	shovel (tool)
skräck,*nn.*	SKRECK	fright (alarm)
"	"	horror
"	"	terror
skräddare,*nn.* (V)	SKRED-*ah-reh*	tailor
skramla (1)	SKRAHM-*lah*	rattle, to
skrämma (2)	SKREM-*ah*	frighten (make afraid), to
skrämma	SKREM-*ah*	scare, to
"	"	terrify, to
skrank,*n.* (V)	SKRAHNK	barrier
skräp,*n.*	SKRAIP	rubbish (litter)
skrapa (1)	SKRAW-*pah*	scrape (make smooth or clean), to
skratt,*n.* (V)	SKRAHT	laughter
skratta (1)	SKRAHT-*ah*	laugh, to
skridsko,*nn.* (III)	SKRISS-*skoo*	skate, ice
skrik,*n.* (V)	SKREEK	cry (utterance)
skrika (5)	SKREE-*kah*	cry (shout), to
"	"	scream, to
"	"	shriek, to
"	"	yell, to
skriva (5)	SKREE-*vah*	write, to
skriva maskin	SKREE-*vah mah*-SHEEN	type (typewrite), to
skrivbord,*n.* (V)	SKREEV-*boord*	desk
skrivmaskin,*nn.* (III)	SKREEV-*mah*-SHEEN	typewriter
skrivpapper,*n.* (V)	SKREEV-*pahp-ehr*	stationery (writing paper)
skruv,*nn.* (II)	SKRU V	screw (threaded nail)
skruvmejsel,*nn.* (II)	SKRU V-*may-sel*	screw driver
skruvmutter,*nn.* (II)	SKRU V-*muht-ehr*	nut (*mech.*)
skryta (7)	SKRÜ-*tah*	boast, to
skugga,*nn.* (I)	SKUHG-*ah*	shade
"	"	shadow
skuggig	SKUHG-*ig*	shady
skuld,*nn.*	SKUHLLD	blame
"	"	guilt
skuld,*nn.* (III)	SKUHLLD	debt
skuldra,*nn.* (I)	SKUHLL-*drah*	shoulder (*anat.*)
skulle (4)	SKUHLL-*eh*	should (*v.*)
"	"	would (*v.*)
skulptör,*nn.* (III)	*skuhlp*-TÖR	sculptor
skum,*n.*	SKUHM	foam
skumgummi,*n.*	SKUHM-*guhm-ih*	foam rubber
skur,*nn.* (II)	SKU R	shower (rainfall)
skura (1)	SKU-*rah*	scrub, to

Swedish	Pronunciation	English
skurk,*nn.* (II)	SKUHRRK	villain
skutta (1)	SKUHT-*ah*	skip (caper), to
skvaller,*n.*	SKVAHLL-*ehr*	gossip (idle talk)
skydd,*n.* (V)	SHÜD	shelter
skydda (1)	SHÜDD-*ah*	protect, to
"	"	shelter, to
		shield, to
skyldig	SHÜLL-*dig*	guilty
skyldighet,*nn.* (III)	SHÜLL-*dig-hayt*	obligation (duty)
skylta med (1)	SHÜLL-*tah mayd*	display (exhibit), to
skymfa (1)	SHÜM-*fah*	abuse (misuse), to
skymning,*nn.* (II)	SHÜM-*ning*	twilight
skynda (sig) (1)	SHÜN-*dah* (*say*)	hasten, to
"	"	hurry, to
skyskrapa,*nn.* (I)	SHÜ-*skraw-pah*	skyscraper
skyttegrav,*nn.* (II)	SHÜT-*eh-grawv*	trench (*mil.*)
slå (10)	SLOH	beat (thrash), to
"	"	hit, to
"	"	knock, to
"	"	strike, to
släcka (2)	SLECK-*ah*	quench, to
slå dank	*sloh*-DAHNK	loaf, to
släde,*nn.* (II)	SLAI-*deh*	sleigh
slag,*n.* (V)	SLAWG	blow
"	"	cuff (of trouser)
"	"	kind (*n.*)
"	"	punch
"	"	stroke (*n.*)
"	"	type
slagskepp,*n.* (V)	SLAWG-*shep*	battleship
slagträ,*n.* (IV)	SLAWG-*trai*	bat (club)
slå ihjäl	*sloh-ee*-YAIL	slay, to
slå in	*sloh*-IN	wrap (envelop)
slakt,*nn.* (III)	SLAHKT	slaughter
slaktare,*nn.* (V)	SLAHCK-*tah-reh*	butcher
släkting,*nn.* (II)	SLECK-*ting*	relative (kinsman)
slang,*nn.*	SLAHNG	slang (*n.*)
slang,*nn.* (II)	SLAHNG	hose (tube)
slänga (2)	SLENG-*ah*	fling, to
"	"	toss (throw), to
släpa (1)	SLAI-*pah*	drag (pull), to
slapp	SLAHP	limp (flaccid)
släppa (2)	SLEP-*ah*	drop (let fall)
släppa lös	SLEP-*ah*-LÖ_S	release (let go of), to
slå sig	SLOH *say*	warp (become misshapen), to
slå sig ned	*sloh-say*-NAYD	settle (make one's home), to
slå sönder	*sloh*-SÖN-*dehr*	break (make smash), to
slät	SLAIT	smooth (*adj.*)
slätt,*nn.* (III)	SLET	plain (level land)
slav,*nn.* (II)	SLAWV	slave
slå vad om	*sloh*-VAWD *ohm*	bet, to
slaveri,*n.*	*slaw-veh*-REE	slavery
slavisk	SLAW-*visk*	Slavic (*adj.*)
slicka (1)	SLICK-*ah*	lick (lap), to
slips,*nn.* (II)	SLIPS	tie (necktie)
slita (5)	SLEE-*tah*	rip (tear away), to
slö	SLÖ	blunt
"	"	dull
slösa (1)	SLÖ-*sah*	waste (squander), to
slöseri,*n.* (III)	*slö-seh*-REE	waste (squandering)
slott,*n.* (V)	SLOHT	castle
slug	SLU_G	shrewd
"	"	sly (crafty)
sluka (1)	SLU-*kah*	devour (eat), to
slummer,*nn.*	SLUHM-*ehr*	slumber
slump,*nn.*	SLUHMP	accident (chance)
slunga (1)	SLUHNG-*ah*	hurl, to
slut,*n.* (V)	SLU_T	conclusion
"		end
"		ending
sluta (1)	SLU-*tah*	cease, to
"	"	close (finish), to
"	"	end, to
slutligen	SLU_T-*lig-en*	finally
slutrealisation,*nn.* (III)	SLU_T-*ray-ah-liss-ah*-SHOON	clearance sale
slutsumma,*nn.* (I)	SLU_T-*suhm-ah*	total (sum)

Swedish	Pronunciation	English
slutta (1)	SLUHTT-*ah*	slant (slope), to
sluttning,*nn.* (II)	SLUHTT-*ning*	hillside
"	"	slope (slant)
smak,*nn.*	SMAWK	flavor (savor)
"	"	taste
smaka (1)	SMAW-*kah*	taste (sample), to
smal	SMAWL	narrow
smälla (2)	SMELL-*ah*	snap (crackle), to
smälta (2)	SMELL-*tah*	digest, to
"	"	melt (become liquid), to
smal väg,*nn.* (II)	SMAWL VAIG	lane (narrow path)
smaragd,*nn.* (III)	*smah*-RAHGD	emerald
smärt	SMAIRRT	slender (lean)
smärta,*nn.* (I)	SMAIRRT-*ah*	pain (ache)
smärtsam	SMAIRRT-*sahm*	painful
småsak,*nn.* (III)	SMOH-*sawk*	trifle
småsten,*nn.* (II)	SMOH-*stayn*	pebble
smed,*nn.* (III)	SMAYD	blacksmith
smet,*nn.* (III)	SMAYT	batter (flour mixture)
smickra (1)	SMICK-*rah*	flatter (praise insincerely), to
smida (2)	SMEE-*dah*	forge (shape), to
smiska (1)	SMISS-*kah*	spank, to
smittkoppor,*nn. pl.*	SMIT-*kohp-or*	smallpox
smör,*n.*	SMÖR	butter
smörgås,*nn.* (II)	SMÖRR-*gohs*	sandwich
smörja,*nn.*	SMÖRR-*yah*	mud
smula,*nn.* (I)	SMU-*lah*	bit (small part)
"	"	crumb
"	"	little (small amount, *n.*)
"	"	morsel (small bit)
smuts,*nn.*	SMUHTS	dirt (unclean matter)
smutsa ned (1)	*smuht-sah*-NAYD	soil (make dirty), to
smutsig	SMUHT-*sig*	dirty (soiled)
"	"	foul (filthy)
smutta på (1)	SMUHT-*ah poh*	sip, to
smycka (1)	SMÜCK-*ah*	dress (decorate), to
smycken,*n.pl.*	SMÜCK-*en*	jewelry
snabb	SNAHBB	fast
"	"	prompt
"	"	quick
"	"	rapid (*adj.*)
"	"	swift
snål	SNOH_L	stingy
snäll	SNELL	kind (*adj.*)
snår,*n.* (V)	SNOR	thicket
snara,*nn.* (I)	SNAW-*rah*	snare (trap)
snarare	SNAW-*rah-reh*	rather (preferably)
snart	SNART	soon (shortly)
snärt,*nn.* (II)	SNAIRRT	lash (whip)
snava (1)	SNAW-*vah*	stumble, to
"	"	trip, to
snickare,*nn.* (V)	SNICK-*ah-reh*	carpenter
snida (1)	SNEE-*dah*	carve (cut designs), to
snigel,*nn.* (II)	SNEEG-*el*	snail
snö,*nn.*	SNÖ	snow
snörband,*n.* (V)	SNÖR-*bahnd*	lace (shoelace)
snöre,*n.* (IV)	SNÖ-*reh*	string (cord)
snöstorm,*nn.* (II)	SNÖ-*storrm*	blizzard
snurra (1)	SNUHRR-*ah*	spin (revolve), to
"	"	turn (make rotate), to
"	"	whirl (make revolve), to
snyfta (1)	SNÜFF-*tah*	sob, to
snygg	SNÜG	neat (tidy)
social	*soh-sih*-AWL	social (societal)
socialism,*nn.*	*soh-sih-ah*-LISSM	socialism
socialist,*nn.* (III)	*soh-sih-ah*-LIST	socialist (*n.*)
sociologi,*nn.*	*soh-sih-oh-lohg*-EE	sociology
sockel,*nn.* (II)	SOHCK-*el*	base (foundation)
socken,*nn.* (II)	SOOCK-*en*	parish
socker,*n.*	SOHCK-*ehr*	sugar
sockersjuka,*nn.*	SOHCK-*ehr-shuh-kah*	diabetes
söder,*nn.*	SÖ-*dehr*	south (*n.*)
soffa,*nn.* (I)	SOHFF-*ah*	couch
"	"	sofa
sökande,*n.*	sö-*kahn-deh*	quest
"	"	search (hunt)

Swedish	Pronunciation	English
sol,*nn.* (II)	SOOL	sun
solbränna,*nn.*	SOOL-*bren-ah*	sunburn
soldat,*nn.* (III)	*sohll*-DAWT	soldier
solglasögon (*pl.*)	SOOL-*glaws-ö-gohn*	sunglasses
solid	*soh*-LEED	solid (compact)
solig	SOO-*lig*	sunny
solljus,*n.*	SOOL-*yu͟s*	sunlight
solnedgång,*nn.* (II)	SOOL-*nayd-gohng*	sunset
solsken,*n.*	SOOL-*shayn*	sunshine
soluppgång,*nn.* (II)	SOOL-*uhp-gohng*	sunrise
som	SOHM	as (in the role of, *prep.*)
"	"	as (in the same way, *conj.*)
som	SOHM	that (*rel. pron.*)
"	"	which (*rel. pron.*)
"	"	who (*rel. pron.*)
"	"	whom (*rel. pron.*)
söm,*nn.* (II)	SÖM	seam (line of stitches)
somliga	SOHM-*lig-ah*	some (certain ones, *pron.*)
sommar,*nn.* (*pl.* somrar)	SOHM-*ahr*	summer (*n.*)
sömn,*nn.*	SÖMN	sleep
son,*nn.* (*pl.* söner)	SOH͟N	son
söndersmula (1)	SÖN-*desh-muh-lah*	crumble, to
sondotter,*nn.* (*pl.* -döttrar)	SOH͟N-*doht-ehr*	granddaughter
sonson,*nn.* (*pl.* -söner)	SOH͟N-*soh͟n*	grandson
sopa (1)	SOO-*pah*	sweep (clean), to
soppa,*nn.* (I)	SOHP-*ah*	soup
sorg,*nn.* (III)	SOHRR͟_*yuh*	grief
"	"	sorrow (sadness)
sorglig	SOHRR͟_*yuh-lig*	mournful (saddening)
sorgsen	SOHRR͟_*yuh-sen*	sad (sorrowful)
sorgsenhet,*nn.*	SOHRR͟_*yuh-sen-hayt*	sadness
sörja (2)	SÖRR-*yah*	grieve, to
"	"	mourn (feel grief), to
sort,*nn.* (III)	SOHRRT	sort
sortering,*nn.* (II)	*sohr*-TAY-*ring*	variety (assortment)
söt	SÖ͟T	sweet (pleasant tasting)
sötma,*nn.*	SÖT-*mah*	sweetness
sötsaker,*nn.pl.*	SÖ͟T-*saw-kehr*	candy
sova (10)	SOH-*vah*	sleep, to
sovande	SOH-*vahn-deh*	asleep (sleeping)
sovrum,*n.* (V)	SOHV-*ruhm*	bedroom
spädbarn,*n.* (V)	SPAID-*barn*	baby
"	"	infant (*n.*)
spade,*nn.* (II)	SPAW-*deh*	spade (tool)
spak,*nn.* (II)	SPAWK	lever
spalt,*nn.* (III)	SPAHLT	column (*print.*)
spanare,*nn.* (V)	SPAW-*nah-reh*	scout (lookout)
spänd	SPEND	tight (taut)
Spanien,*n.*	SPAHN-*ih-en*	Spain
spänning,*nn.*	SPEN-*ing*	tension
spännvidd,*nn.*	SPEN-*vid*	span (spread)
spansk	SPAHNSK	Spanish (*adj.*)
spår,*n.* (V)	SPOR	mark (evidence)
"	"	trace (vestige)
"	"	track (rails)
spara (1)	SPAW-*rah*	save (store up), to
spark,*nn.* (II)	SPAHRRK	kick (boot)
sparka (1)	SPAHRR-*kah*	kick (boot), to
sparkasseräkning, *nn.* (II)	SPAWR-*kahss-eh-raik-ning*	savings account
spärra (1)	SPAIRR-*ah*	bar, to
"	"	block (obstruct), to
sparris,*nn.*	SPAHRR-*iss*	asparagus
sparsam	SPAW-*shahm*	economical (thrifty)
sparsamhet,*nn.*	SPAW-*shahm-hayt*	economy (thrift)
sparv,*nn.* (II)	SPAHRRV	sparrow
spårvagn,*nn.* (II)	SPOR-*vahngn*	trolley (street car)
speceriaffär,*nn.* (III)	*speh-seh*-REE-*ah*-FAIR	grocery
speciell	*speh-sih*-ELL	special
speditör,*nn.* (III)	*speh-dit*-TÖR	shipping agent
spegel,*nn.* (II)	SPAYG-*el*	mirror
spegelbild,*nn.* (III)	SPAYG-*el-billd*	reflection (image)
spekulant,*nn.* (III)	*speh-kuh*-LAHNT	bidder (*bus.*)

Swedish	Pronunciation	English
spel,*n.* (V)	SPAYL	game (contest)
spela (1)	SPAY-*lah*	play (perform music upon), to
spela	SPAY-*lah*	play (take the role of), to
spelare,*nn.* (V)	SPAY-*lah-reh*	player (in a game)
spelkort,*n.* (V)	SPAYL-*koort*	card, playing
spenat,*nn.*	*speh*-NAWT	spinach
spetälska,*nn.*	SPAY-*tell-skah*	leprosy
spets,*nn.* (II)	SPETS	lace (fabric)
"	"	point (sharp end)
"	"	tip
spetsig	SPET-*sig*	pointed (tapered)
spik,*nn.* (II)	SPEEK	nail (hardware)
spilla (2)	SPILL-*ah*	spill (let pour out), to
spillror,*nn.pl.*	SPILL-*roor*	wreck (ruins)
spindel,*nn.* (II)	SPIN-*dell*	spider
spinna (8)	SPIN-*ah*	spin (form thread), to
spion,*nn.* (III)	*spih*-OON	spy
spionage,*n.* (III)	*spih-oo*-NAWSH	espionage
spis,*nn.* (II)	SPEES	stove (for cooking)
spjut,*n.* (V)	SPYU͟T	spear (weapon)
splittra (1)	SPLIT-*rah*	shatter (smash in pieces), to
"	"	split (rend), to
spöke,*n.* (IV)	SPÖ-*keh*	ghost
spole,*nn.* (II)	SPOO-*leh*	coil (*elec.*)
sporre,*nn.* (II)	SPOHRR-*eh*	spur (spike)
sport,*nn.* (III)	SPOHRRT	sport (game)
spotta (1)	SPOHT-*ah*	spit, to
spräcka (2)	SPRECK-*ah*	crack (make split), to
språk,*n.* (V)	SPROH͟K	language
språng,*n.* (V)	SPROHNG	leap (bound)
spränga (2)	SPRENG-*ah*	blast (explode), to
sprängämne,*n.* (IV)	SPRENG-*em-neh*	explosive (*n.*)
spricka,*nn.* (I)	SPRICK-*ah*	crack (fissure)
sprida (5)	SPREE-*dah*	spread (diffuse), to
spridning,*nn.*	SPREED-*ning*	circulation (dissemination)
springa (8)	SPRING-*ah*	run (sprint), to
sprit,*nn.*	SPREET	liquor (alcoholic beverage)
spruta (1)	SPRU-*tah*	squirt, to
spruta,*nn.* (I)	SPRU-*tah*	syringe
stå (10)	STOH	stand (be upright), to
stackare,*nn.* (V)	STAHCK-*ah-reh*	wretch (hapless person)
stackars	STAHCK-*ahsh*	poor (unfortunate)
stad,*nn.* (*pl.* städer)	STAWD	city
"	"	town
stadga,*nn.* (I)	STAHD-*gah*	by-law
stadig	STAW-*dig*	stable (steadfast)
"	"	steady (firm)
stadion,*n.* (V)	STAW-*dih-ohn*	stadium
stadium,*n.* (III)	STAW-*dih-uhm*	stage (period)
stads-...	STAHDS-...	urban
stake,*nn.* (II)	STAW-*keh*	stake (post)
stål,*n.*	STOH͟L	steel
stall,*n.* (V)	STAHLL	stable (shelter)
ställe,*n.* (IV)	STELL-*eh*	spot (place)
"	"	stead (place)
stället för, i	*ee*-STELL-*et för*	instead of
stam,*nn.* (II)	STAHM	stem (*bot.*)
"	"	tribe
"	"	trunk
stämjärn,*n.* (V)	STEM-*yairn*	chisel (tool)
stamma (1)	STAHM-*ah*	stammer, to
"	"	stutter, to
stämma (2)	STEM-*ah*	sue (bring action against), to
stampa (1)	STAHM-*pah*	stamp (tread heavily), to
stämpla (1)	STEMP-*lah*	stamp (mark), to
standard-...	STAHN-*dard*-...	standard (regular)
ständig	STEN-*dig*	constant
"	"	continual
"	"	perpetual
stång,*nn.* (*pl.* stänger)	STOHNG	bar
"	"	pole
"	"	rod

Swedish	Pronunciation	English
stänga (2)	STENG-*ah*	close, to
"	"	shut (make close), to
stängsel,*n.* (V)	STENG-*sel*	fence (barrier)
stänka (2)	STENK-*ah*	splash, to
stanna (1)	STAHN-*ah*	abide, to
"	"	halt (come to a stop), to
"	"	remain (stay behind), to
"	"	stall (stop going), to
"	"	stay, to
"	"	stop (come to a standstill), to
stark	STAHRRK	strong
stärka (2)	STAIRR-*kah*	strengthen, to
stärkelse,*nn.*	STAIRR-*kel-seh*	starch (in food)
starta (1)	START-*ah*	start (set out), to
stat,*nn.* (III)	STAWT	state (nation)
station,*nn.* (III)	*stah*-SHOON	depot
"	"	station, railroad
statsförbund,*n.* (V)	STAHTS-*för-buhnd*	commonwealth
statsinkomster,*nn.* *pl.*	STAHTS-*in-kohm-stehr*	revenue (*govt.*)
statsman,*nn.* (*pl.* -män)	STAHTS-*mahn*	statesman
statsvetenskap,*nn.*	STAHTS-*vay-ten-skawp*	political science
staty,*nn.* (III)	*stah*-TÜ	statue
stå ut med	*stoh*-UH_T *mayd*	stand (bear), to
stav,*nn.* (II)	STAWV	staff (stick)
stava (1)	STAW-*vah*	spell, to
stavelse,*nn.* (III)	STAW-*vel-seh*	syllable
steg,*n.* (V)	STAYG	step (stride)
stege,*nn.* (II)	STAYG-*eh*	ladder
stek,*nn.* (II)	STAYK	roast
steka (2)	STAY-*kah*	fry (be cooked in fat), to
stekpanna,*nn.* (I)	STAYK-*pahn-ah*	pan, frying
sten,*nn.* (II)	STAYN	stone (piece of rock)
stenblock,*n.* (V)	STAYN-*blohck*	rock (large stone)
stencil,*nn.* (III)	*sten*-SEEL	stencil
stenlägga (11)	STAYN-*leg-ah*	pave, to
stenläggning,*nn.* (II)	STAYN-*leg-ning*	pavement
stenograf,*nn.* (III)	*steh-noh*-GRAWF	stenographer
stenografi,*nn.*	*steh-noh-grah*-FEE	shorthand (stenography,*n.*)
steward,*nn.* (II)	ST_YU-*ahrd*	steward (attendant on ship)
sticka (1)	STICK-*ah*	knit, to
sticka (8)	STICK-*ah*	prick, to
"	"	stab, to
"	"	stick (thrust), to
"	"	sting (pierce skin); to
stickkontakt,*nn.* (III)	STICK-*kohn*-TAHKT	plug (*elec.*)
stickning,*nn.*	STICK-*ning*	knitting
stig,*nn.* (II)	STEEG	path
"	"	trail
stiga (5)	STEE-*gah*	climb, to
"	"	rise (ascend), to
"	"	soar, to
"	"	step, to
stiga upp	*stee-gah*-UHP	rise (stand up), to
stilig	STEE-*lig*	smart (chic)
stilla	STILL-*ah*	peaceful (tranquil)
"	"	quiet (without motion, *adj.*)
stilla	STILL-*ah*	still (motionless, *adj.*)
Stilla havet,*n.def.*	*still-ah*-HAW-*vet*	Pacific (*n.*)
stillastående	STILL-*ah-stoh-en-deh*	stationary (unmoving)
stillhet,*nn.*	STILL-*hayt*	quiet (stillness)
stimulera (1)	*stim-uh*-LAY-*rah*	stimulate (incite), to
stinka (8)	STINK-*ah*	stink, to
stirra (1)	STIHRR-*ah*	gaze, to
"	"	glare, to
"	"	peer (look intently), to
"	"	stare, to
stjäla (10)	SHAI-*lah*	steal, to
stjälk,*nn.* (II)	SHELK	stalk (stem)
stjälpa (2)	SHELL-*pah*	upset (knock over), to
stjärna,*nn.* (I)	SHAIRN-*ah*	star (*astron.*)
sto,*n.* (IV)	STOO	mare
stock,*nn.* (II)	STOHCK	log (rough timber)

Swedish	Pronunciation	English
Stockholm,*n.*	STOHCK-*hohllm*	Stockholm
stöd,*n.*	STÖ_D	support (approval)
stödja (11)	STÖ_D-*yah*	support (hold up), to
stoft,*n.*	STOHFT	powder (dust)
stol,*nn.* (II)	STOOL	chair
stolpe,*nn.* (II)	STOHLL-*peh*	post (pole)
stolt	STOHLLT	proud (taking pride in)
stolthet,*nn.*	STOHLLT-*hayt*	pride (self-esteem)
stöna (1)	STÖ-*nah*	groan, to
"	"	moan, to
stoppa (1)	STOHP-*ah*	darn (mend), to
stoppa in	*stohp-ah*-IN	tuck (slip inside), to
stor	STOOR	big
"	"	great
"	"	large
störa (2)	STÖ-*rah*	disturb, to
storartad	STOOR-*art-ahd*	grand (imposing)
"	"	magnificent
Storbritannien,*n.*	STOOR-*brit-tahn-ih-en*	Great Britain
storhet,*nn.*	STOOR-*hayt*	greatness (eminence)
stork,*nn.* (II)	STORRK	stork
storlek,*nn.* (II)	STOOR-*layk*	size
storm,*nn.* (II)	STORRM	storm
"	"	tempest
stormig	STORRM-*ig*	stormy
större	STÖRR-*eh*	major (larger)
störta (sig) (1)	STÖRT-*ah* (*say*)	plunge (hurl oneself), to
störta in	*stört-ah*-IN	collapse (cave in), to
stöta (2)	STÖ-*tah*	thrust (push), to
stöta mot	*stö-tah*-MOOT	ram (butt), to
stövel,*nn.* (II)	STÖ-*vel*	boot (footgear)
sträcka (2)	STRECK-*ah*	stretch (draw out), to
sträcka sig	STRECK-*ah say*	reach (extend to), to
"	"	run (extend), to
"	"	stretch, to
straff,*n.* (V)	STRAHFF	penalty
"	"	punishment
straffa (1)	STRAHFF-*ah*	punish, to
stråla (1)	STROH-*lah*	beam (shine), to
strålande	STROH-*lahn-deh*	radiant
stråle,*nn.* (II)	STROH-*leh*	beam
"	"	ray
strand,*nn.* (*pl.* stränder)	STRAHND	bank
"	"	shore
(sand)strand,*nn.* (*pl.* stränder)	(SAHND-)STRAHNND	beach (strand)
sträng	STRENG	harsh (severe)
"	"	severe (strict)
sträng	STRENG	stern (*adj.*)
"	"	strict (stringent)
sträng,*nn.* (II)	STRENG	strand (thread)
stränghet,*nn.*	STRENG-*hayt*	severity (sternness)
sträv	STRAIV	harsh (grating)
sträva (1)	STRAI-*vah*	endeavor, to
"	"	strive (exert oneself), to
strävan,*nn.*	STRAI-*vahn*	endeavor
streck,*n.* (V)	STRECK	line (mark)
strejk,*nn.* (III)	STRAYK	strike (work stoppage)
strejka (1)	STRAY-*kah*	strike (stop work), to
strid,*nn.* (III)	STREED	battle
"	"	conflict (struggle)
strimma,*nn.* (I)	STRIM-*ah*	streak
"	"	stripe
strö (3)	STRÖ	sprinkle (scatter), to
strö (ut)	STRÖ (UH_T)	scatter (strew), to
ström,*nn.* (II)	STRÖMM	current (of electricity)
"	"	stream (rivulet)
"	"	torrent
strömbrytare,*nn.* (V)	STRÖMM-*brü-tah-reh*	switch (*elec.*)
strömdrag,*n.* (V)	STRÖMM-*drawg*	current (of water)
strömma (1)	STRÖMM-*ah*	stream, to
ströva (1)	STRÖ-*vah*	roam, to
"	"	stray, to

Swedish	Pronunciation	English
ströva omkring	strö-vah-ohm-KRING	rove, to
struktur,*nn.* (III)	struhck-TU_R	structure (arrangement of parts)
strumpa,*nn.* (I)	STRUHM-*pah*	stocking
strumpa, (kort),*nn.* (I)	(KOHRRT) STRUHM-*pah*	sock (garment)
strumpeband,*n.* (V)	STRUHM-*peh-bahnd*	garter
stryka (7)	STRÜ-*kah*	stroke (rub gently), to
strykjärn,*n.* (V)	STRÜ_K-*yairn*	iron, electric
stubbe,*nn.* (II)	STUHB-*eh*	stump (of tree)
student,*nn.* (III)	stuh-DENT	student
studera (1)	stuh-DAY-*rah*	study, to
studium,*n.* (III)	STUH-*dih-uhm*	study (active learning)
studsa (1)	STUHT-*sah*	bounce, to
stuga,*nn.* (I)	STU-*gah*	lodge (cabin)
stum	STUHM	dumb (mute)
"	"	mute (silent)
stund,*nn.* (III)	STUHND	while (short time, *n.*)
stycke,*n.* (IV)	STÜCK-*eh*	piece (bit)
styckevis	STÜCK-*eh-vees*	piecemeal (*adv.*)
stygg	STÜG	naughty (disobedient)
stygn,*n.* (V)	STÜNGN	stitch (of sewing)
styra (2)	STÜ-*rah*	control (direct), to
"	"	steer, to
styrbar projektil, *nn.* (III)	STÜR-*bar proh-sheck-*TEEL	guided missile
styrelse,*nn.* (III)	STÜ-*rell-seh*	board
styrka,*nn.*	STÜRR-*kah*	strength
styv	STÜ_V	stiff (inflexible)
styvdotter,*nn.* (*pl.* -döttrar)	STÜ_V-*doht-ehr*	stepdaughter
styvfa(de)r,*nn.* (*pl.* -fäder)	STÜ_V-*fa(-deh)r*	stepfather
styvmo(de)r,*nn.* (*pl.* -mödrar)	STÜ_V-*moo(-deh)r*	stepmother
styvson,*nn.* (*pl.* -söner)	STÜ_V-*soh_n*	stepson
subjektiv	suhb-yeck-TEEV	subjective
subskribentsamlare,*nn.* (V)	suhb-skrib-ENT-*sahm-lah-reh*	canvasser (*bus.*)
substans,*nn.* (III)	suhb-STAHNS	substance (matter)
substantiv,*n.* (V)	SUHB-*stahn-teev*	noun
subtrahera (1)	suhb-trah-HAY-*rah*	subtract, to
sucka (1)	SUHCK-*ah*	sigh, to
suga (6)	SUH-*gah*	suck, to
sula,*nn.* (I)	SU-*lah*	sole (of shoe)
summa,*nn.* (I)	SUHM-*ah*	amount
"	"	sum (quantity)
sund,*n.* (V)	SUHND	channel (strait)
sur	SU_R	sour (tart)
Surinam,*n.*	su-rih-NAHM	Surinam
surr,*n.*	SUHRR	hum (murmur)
surra (1)	SUHRR-*ah*	lash (fasten), to
surrogat,*n.* (V)	suhrr-oo-GAWT	substitute (thing replacing another)
suspendera (1)	suhs-pen-DAY-*rah*	suspend (terminate), to
suvenir,*nn.* (III)	suh-veh-NEER	souvenir
suverän,*nn.* (III)	suh-veh-RAIN	sovereign (ruler)
svag	SVAWG	faint (dim, *adj.*)
"	"	feeble
"	"	weak (not firm)
svåger,*nn.* (II)	SVOH-*gehr*	brother-in-law
svägerska,*nn.* (I)	SVAIG-*esh-kah*	sister-in-law
svaghet,*nn.* (III)	SVAWG-*hayt*	weakness
sval	SVAWL	cool (having low temperature)
svala,*nn.* (I)	SVAW-*lah*	swallow (bird)
svälja (2)	SVELL-*yah*	swallow, to
svälla (2)	SVELL-*ah*	swell (bulge), to
svälta (10)	SVELL-*tah*	starve (die of hunger), to
svamp,*nn.* (II)	SVAHMP	mushroom (*n.*)
"	"	sponge
svan,*nn.* (I,II)	SVAWN	swan
svänga (2)	SVENG-*ah*	sway, to
"	"	swing (oscillate), to
svans,*nn.* (II)	SVAHNS	tail (of animal)
svår	SVOR	difficult
"	"	hard (difficult)

Swedish	Pronunciation	English
svar,*n.* (V)	SVAWR	answer
"	"	reply
"	"	response
svara (1)	SVAW-*rah*	answer (address reply to), to
"	"	reply, to
"	"	respond, to
svära (10)	SVAI-*rah*	curse, to
"	"	swear, to
"	"	swear (vow), to
svärd,*n.* (V)	SVAIRD	sword
svärdotter,*nn.* (*pl.* -döttrar)	SVAIR-*doht-ehr*	daughter-in-law
svärfa(de)r,*nn.* (*pl.* -fäder)	SVAIR-*fa(-deh)r*	father-in-law
svårighet,*nn.* (III)	SVOR-*ig-hayt*	difficulty (obstacle)
svärmo(de)r,*nn.* (*pl.* -mödrar)	SVAIR-*moo(-deh)r*	mother-in-law
svärson,*nn.* (*pl.* -söner)	SVAI-*shoh_n*	son-in-law
svart	SVAHRRT	black
svart tavla,*nn.* (I)	SVAHRRT TAWV-*lah*	blackboard
svavel,*n.*	SVAW-*vel*	sulphur
svensk	SVENSK	Swedish (*adj.*)
Sverige,*n.*	SVAIRR-*yeh*	Sweden
svett,*nn.*	SVET	sweat
svettas (1)	SVET-*ahs*	perspire, to
svika (5)	SVEE-*kah*	betray (deceive), to
svimma (1)	SVIM-*ah*	faint, to
svimning,*nn.* (II)	SVIM-*ning*	faint (swoon, *n.*)
svin,*n.* (V)	SVEEN	hog (animal)
"	"	swine
sy (3)	SÜ	sew, to
Sydamerika,*n.*	SÜ_D-*ah-meh-rick-ah*	South America
sydlig	SÜ_D-*lig*	southern
sydöstlig	sü_d-ÖST-*lig*	southeast (*adj.*)
sydvästlig	sü_d-VEST-*lig*	southwest (*adj.*)
syfta (1)	SÜF-*tah*	refer (allude), to
syfte,*n.* (IV)	SÜF-*teh*	object (aim)
"	"	purpose (aim)
sylt,*nn.* (III)	SÜLT	jam (preserve)
symaskin,*nn.* (III)	SÜ-*mah*-SHEEN	sewing machine
symfoni,*nn.* (III)	süm-foh-NEE	symphony
symptom,*n.* (V)	sümp-TOH_M	symptom
syn,*nn.*	SÜ_N	outlook (attitude)
"	"	sight (eyesight)
"	"	vison (eyesight)
syn,*nn.* (III)	SÜ_N	sight (spectacle)
synål,*nn.* (II)	SÜ-*noh_l*	needle
synas (2)	SÜ-*nahs*	appear (seem), to
"	"	look (seem), to
synd,*nn.* (III)	SÜND	sin
synda (1)	SÜN-*dah*	sin, to
syndare,*nn.* (V)	SÜN-*dah-reh*	sinner
synhåll,*n.*	SÜ_N-*hohll*	sight (range of view)
synlig	SÜ_N-*lig*	visible
synvinkel,*nn.* (II)	SÜN-*vink-el*	aspect (phase)
syra,*nn.* (I)	SÜ-*rah*	acid
syre,*n.*	SÜ-*reh*	oxygen
syren,*nn.* (III)	sü-RAYN	lilac (flower)
syrsa,*nn.* (I)	SÜSH-*ah*	cricket (*insect*)
sysselsätta (11)	SÜSS-*el-set-ah*	occupy (make busy), to
sysslolös	SÜSS-*loo-lö_s*	idle (not busy)
sysslolöshet,*nn.*	SÜSS-*loo-lö_s-hayt*	idleness (inactivity)
system,*n.* (V)	sü-STAYM	system (method)
syster,*nn.* (II)	SÜSS-*tehr*	sister (*n.*)
systerdotter,*nn.* (*pl.* -döttrar)	SÜSS-*tehr-doht-ehr*	niece (sister's daughter)
systerson,*nn.* (*pl.* -söner)	SÜSS-*teh-shoh_n*	nephew (sister's son)
tå,*nn.* (III)	TOH	toe
tabell,*nn.* (III)	tah-BELL	chart (graph)
"	"	table (tabulation)
tack,*nn.*, *n.* (V)	TAHCK	thanks (gratitude)
tacka (1)	TAHCK-*ah*	thank, to
täcka (2)	TECK-*ah*	cover, to
täcke,*n.* (IV)	TECK-*eh*	quilt (bedcover)
tacksam	TAHCK-*sahm*	grateful
"	"	thankful
tacksamhet,*nn.*	TAHCK-*sahm-hayt*	gratitude
tafatt	TAW-*faht*	awkward

Swedish	Pronunciation	English
tåg,*n.* (V)	TOH_G	train, railroad
ta(ga) (9)	TAW(-*gah*)	take, to
ta(ga) med	*taw*(-*gah*) MAYD	bring, to
ta(ga) sin tillflykt	*taw*(-*gah*) sin-TILL-*flückt*	resort (have recourse), to
ta(ga) tillbaka	*taw*(-*gah*)-till-BAW-*kah*	withdraw (take back), to
ta(ga) upp	*taw*(-*gah*)-UHP	pick up (lift), to
tagg,*nn.* (II)	TAHG	thorn
tak,*n.* (V)	TAWK	roof
"	"	ceiling (of room)
tal,*n.* (V)	TAWL	speech (address)
tala (1)	TAW-*lah*	speak, to
"	"	talk, to
tålamod,*n.*	TOH-*lah-mood*	patience
talang,*nn.* (III)	*tah*-LAHNG	talent
tala om	*taw-lah*-OHM	tell (inform), to
talare,*nn.* (V)	TAW-*lah-reh*	speaker (orator)
tålig	TOH-*lig*	patient (forbearing)
tall,*nn.* (II)	TAHLL	pine (tree)
tallrik,*nn.* (II)	TAHLL-*rick*	plate (shallow·dish)
talrik	TAWL-*reek*	numerous
tält,*n.* (V)	TELT	tent
tam	TAWM	tame
tand,*nn.* (*pl.* tänder)	TAHND	tooth
tända (2)	TEN-*dah*	light (set fire to), to
tandborste,*nn.* (II)	TAHND-*bosh-teh*	toothbrush
tandkött,*n.*	TAHND-*chöt*	gum (*anat.*)
tandkräm,*nn.* (III)	TAHND-*kraim*	tooth paste
tandläkare,*nn.* (V)	TAHND-*lai-kah-reh*	dentist
tändsticka,*nn.* (I)	TEND-*stick-ah*	match (lucifer)
tandvärk,*nn.*	TAHND-*vairk*	toothache
tank,*nn.* (II)	TAHNK	tank (container)
tänka (2)	TENK-*ah*	think (reason), to
tankar,*nn. pl.*	TAHNK-*ahr*	thought (contemplation)
tänka sig	TENK-*ah say*	conceive (imagine), to
tanke,*nn.* (II)	TAHNG-*keh*	thought (idea)
tankfull	TAHNK-*fuhll*	thoughtful (reflective)
tappa ur (1)	*tahp-ah*-UHR	drain (make dry), to
tår,*nn.* (II)	TOR	tear (teardrop)
tärningar,*nn. pl.*	TAIRN-*ing-ahr*	dice (marked cubes)
tårta,*nn.* (I)	TORT-*ah*	cake (dessert)
tass,*nn.* (II)	TAHSS	paw
tät	TAIT	dense
tävlan,*nn.*	TAIV-*lahn*	contest
tävling,*nn.* (II)	TAIV-*ling*	race
taxera (1)	*tahck*-SAY-*rah*	assess (impose tax), to
taxi,*nn.* (V)	TAHCK-*sih*	cab
"	"	taxi
te,*n.* (III)	TAY	tea
teater,*nn.* (II)	*tay*-AW-*tehr*	theater
tecken,*n.* (V)	TECK-*en*	evidence
"	"	sign (indication)
teckna (1)	TECK-*nah*	draw (sketch), to
teckning,*nn.* (II)	TECK-*ning*	drawing (sketch)
tefat,*n.* (V)	TAY-*fawt*	saucer
tegel,*n.*	TAYG-*el*	brick (building material)
Tel Aviv,*n.*	*tell-ah*-VEEV	Tel Aviv
telefon,*nn.* (III)	*teh-leh*-FOH_N	telephone
telefonera (1)	*teh-leh-foh*-NAY-*rah*	telephone, to
telegrafera (1)	*teh-leh-grah*-FAY-*rah*	telegraph, to
		cable, to
telegram,*n.* (V)	*teh-leh*-GRAHM	telegram
"	"	wire
teleskop,*n.* (V)	*teh-leh*-SKOH_P	telescope
television,*nn.*	*teh-leh-vih*-SHOON	television
tema,*n.* (IV)	TAY-*mah*	theme (subject)
tempel,*n.* (V)	TEM-*pell*	temple (place of worship)
temperatur,*nn.* (III)	*tem-peh-rah*-TU_R	temperature
tendens,*nn.* (III)	*ten*-DENS	tendency
tendera (1)	*ten*-DAY-*rah*	tend (be apt), to
tenn,*n.*	TEN	tin (metal)
tennis,*nn.*	TEN-*iss*	tennis
teori,*nn.* (III)	*tay-oh*-REE	theory

Swedish	Pronunciation	English
term,*nn.* (III)	TAIRRM	term (expression)
termin,*nn.* (III)	*tairr*-MEEN	term (duration)
termometer,*nn.* (II)	*tehr-moo*-MAY-*tehr*	thermometer
terrass,*nn.* (III)	*teh*-RAHSS	terrace
territorium,*n.* (III)	*teh-rih*-TOO-*rih-uhm*	territory
tesked,*nn.* (II)	TAY-*shayd*	spoon (teaspoon)
testamente,*n.* (IV)	*tes-tah*-MEN-*teh*	will (document)
text,*nn.* (III)	TEXT	text
tid,*nn.* (III)	TEED	time
tidig	TEE-*dig*	early (before-time, *adj.*)
tidigt	TEE-*dickt*	soon
"	"	early (ahead of time, *adv.*)
tidning,*nn.* (II)	TEED-*ning*	newspaper
tidningskiosk,*nn.* (III)	TEED-*nings-chohssk*	newsstand
tidsfördriv,*n.* (V)	TEEDS-*för-dreev*	pastime
tidskrift,*nn.* (III)	TEED-*skrift*	journal (magazine)
tidtabell,*nn.* (III)	TEED-*tah*-BELL	schedule
		timetable
tiger,*nn.* (II)	TEEG-*ehr*	tiger
tigga (2)	TIG-*ah*	beg (solicit alms), to
tiggare,*nn.* (V)	TIG-*ah-reh*	beggar
till	TILL	at (to, toward)
"	"	to (indicating destination, *prep.*)
"	"	to (indicating direction, *prep.*)
"	"	to (used with indirect object, *prep.*)
"	"	until (up to the time of, *prep.*)
tillägg,*n.* (V)	TILL-*leg*	addition (supplement)
"	"	amendment (enacted change)
tilläggsavgift,*nn.* (III)	TILL-*legs-awv*-YIFT	surcharge (*bus.*)
tillämpa (1)	TILL-*lem-pah*	apply (put to use), to
tillåta (10)	TILL-*loh-tah*	allow, to
"	"	permit, to
"	"	tolerate, to
tillåtelse,*nn.* (III)	TILL-*loh-tell-seh*	permission
tillbe (10)	TILL-*bay*	adore, to
tillbedjare,*nn.* (V)	TILL-*bayd-yah-reh*	lover
tillbringare,*nn* (V)	TILL-*bring-ah-reh*	pitcher (container)
tilldela (1)	TILL-*day-lah*	confer (bestow), to
tilldra(ga) (9)	TILL-*draw*(-*gah*)	attract, to
tilldragande	TILL-*draw-gahn-deh*	attractive (pleasing)
tillfälle,*n.* (IV)	TILL-*fell-eh*	chance
"	"	occasion
"	"	opportunity
tillfällig	TILL-*fell-ig*	occasional
"	"	temporary
tillfällighet,*nn.* (III)	TILL-*fell-ig-hayt*	chance (fate)
tillflykt,*nn.*	TILL-*flückt*	refuge
tillfredsställa (2)	TILL-*freds-stell-ah*	please, to
"		satisfy, to
tillfredsställande	TILL-*freds-stell-ahn-deh*	satisfactory
tillfredsställelse, *nn.*	TILL-*freds-stell-el-seh*	satisfaction (gratification)
tillfriskna (1)	TILL-*frisk-nah*	recover (get well), to
tillgång,*nn.* (II)	TILL-*gohng*	supply (amount available)
tillgångar,*nn. pl.*	TILL-*gohng-ahr*	asset (*bus.*)
"	"	resources (wealth)
tillgänglig	TILL-*yeng-lig*	available
tillgiven	TILL-*yee-ven*	affectionate (loving)
tillgivenhet,*nn.*	TILL-*yee-ven-hayt*	affection (love)
till hands	*till*-HAHNDS	handy (near at hand)
till höger	*till*-HÖ_G-*ehr*	right (to the right, *adv.*)
tillhöra (2)	TILL-*hö-rah*	belong to (be the property of), to
"	"	belong (be a part of), to
tillkalla (1)	TILL-*kahll-ah*	summon (send for), to
"	"	call, to
tillkännage (10)	*till*-CHEN-*ah-yay*	advertise (give notice of), to
"	"	announce, to
"	"	proclaim, to

Swedish	Pronunciation	English
tillkännagivande, n. (IV)	*till*-CHEN-*ah-yee-vahn-deh*	announcement
"	"	declaration
"	"	notice (notification)
tillnamn,*n.* (V)	TILL-*nahmn*	surname
tillönska (1)	TILL-*ön-skah*	wish (desire on behalf of), to
tillräcklig	TILL-*reck-lig*	adequate
"	"	enough (*adj.*)
"	"	sufficient
tillräcklig mängd, *nn.* (III)	TILL-*reck-lig* MENGD	enough (*n.*)
tillråda (2)	TILL-*roh-dah*	recommend (advise), to
tills	TILLS	until (*conj.*)
tillsammans	*till*-SAHM-*ahns*	together
tillstånd,*n.* (V)	TILL-*stohnd*	condition
"	"	state
tillta(ga) (9)	TILL-*taw(-gah)*	grow (expand), to
tillträde,*n.*	TILL-*trai-deh*	admission (right to enter)
till vänster	*till*-VEN-*stehr*	left (*adv.*)
tillvaro,*nn.*	TILL-*vaw-roo*	existence
tillverka (1)	TILL-*vairr-kah*	manufacture, to
timme,*nn.* (II)	TIM-*eh*	hour
timmer,*n.*	TIM-*ehr*	lumber
timmerskog,*nn.* (II)	TIM-*eh-shkoo_g*	timber (standing trees)
tindra (1)	TIN-*drah*	twinkle, to
tinning,*nn.* (II)	TIN-*ing*	temple (*anat.*)
titel,*nn.* (II)	TIT-*el*	title (name)
titta (1)	TIT-*ah*	look (gaze), to
tjäna (1)	CHAI-*nah*	earn (be paid), to
"	"	serve, to
tjänare,*nn.* (V)	CHAI-*nah-reh*	servant (in a household)
tjänst,*nn.* (III)	CHENST	service
tjänsteman,*nn.* (*pl.* -män)	CHEN-*steh-mahn*	official (*n.*)
tjära,*nn.*	CHAIR-*ah*	tar
Tjeckoslovakien,*n.*	*check-oo-sloo*-VAW-*kih-en*	Czechoslovakia
tjock	CHOHCK	thick (not thin)
tjocklek,*nn.*	CHOHCK-*layk*	thickness (dimension)
tjur,*nn.* (II)	CHUH_R	bull (male bovine)
tjuta (6)	CHU-*tah*	howl (wail), to
tjuv,*nn.* (II)	CHU_V	thief
töa (1)	TÖ-*ah*	thaw, to
toalett,*nn.* (III)	*too-ah*-LET	toilet (water closet)
toalettbyrå,*nn.* (II)	*too-ah*-LET-*bü-roh*	dresser (bureau)
tobak,*nn.*	TOO-*bahck*	tobacco
toffel,*nn.* (I)	TOHF-*el*	slipper
tok,*nn.* (II)	TOO_K	fool
tokig	TOO-*kig*	crazy
Tokyo,*n.*	TOH_K-*yoh*	Tokyo
tolka (1)	TOHLL-*kah*	interpret (explain), to
tom	TOOMM	empty
tomat,*nn.* (III)	*too*-MAWT	tomato
tömma (2)	TÖM-*ah*	empty (remove contents of), to
ton,*nn.* (III)	TOON	tone (quality of sound)
topp,*nn.* (II)	TOHP	summit
"	"	top
torg,*n.* (V)	TOHRR_*yuh*	square (plaza)
torka (1)	TOHRR-*kah*	dry, to
"	"	wipe (make dry by wiping), to
torn,*n.* (V)	TOORN	tower
torped,*nn.* (III)	*tohrr*-PAYD	torpedo
torr	TOHRR	dry
törst,*nn.*	TÖSHT	thirst
törstig	TÖSH-*tig*	thirsty
tortyr,*nn.*	*tohrr*-TÜ_R	torture
tös,*nn.* (III)	TÖ_S	lass
total	*too*-TAWL	total (complete)
trä,*n.*	TRAI	wood (lumber)
tråd,*nn.* (II)	TROH_D	thread (sewing thread)
träd,*n.* (V)	TRAID	tree
trädgård,*nn.* (II)	TRAI-*gord*	garden
trädgårdsmästare, *nn.* (V)	TRAI-*gordsh-mess-tah-reh*	gardener
tradition,*nn.* (III)	*trah-dih*-SHOON	tradition

Swedish	Pronunciation	English
träffa (1)	TREF-*ah*	meet (be introduced to), to
träffas (1)	TREF-*ahs*	meet (come together), to
trafik,*nn.*	*trah*-FEEK	traffic (flow of vehicles)
tragedi,*nn.* (III)	*trah-sheh*-DEE	tragedy
tragisk	TRAWG-*isk*	tragic
tråkig	TROH-*kig*	dull (boring)
tråkighet,*nn.*	TROH-*kig-hayt*	boredom
trakt,*nn.* (III)	TRAHKT	area
"	"	land
"	"	region
traktor,*nn.* (III)	TRAHK-*tor*	tractor (farm machine)
trampa sönder (1)	*trahm-pah*-SÖN-*dehr*	trample, to
träna (1)	TRAI-*nah*	coach (train), to
trång	TROHNG	tight (close-fitting)
transmarin	*trahns-mah*-REEN	oversea(s) (*adj.*)
transport,*nn.* (III)	*trahn*-SPOHRRT	transit (passage)
"	"	transportation (conveying)
transportera (1)	*trahn-spohrrt*-TAY-*rah*	transport, to
transportör,*nn.* (III)	*trahn-spohrrt*-TÖR	carrier (*bus.*)
transportvagn,*nn.* (II)	*trahn*-SPOHRRT-*vahngn*	van (vehicle)
trappa,*nn.* (I)	TRAHP-*ah*	stairway
trappsteg,*n.* (V)	TRAHP-*stayg*	step (stair)
trasa,*nn.* (I)	TRAW-*sah*	rag (piece of cloth)
träsk,*n.* (V)	TRESK	swamp (*n.*)
tratta,*nn.* (I)	TRAHT-*ah*	draft (check)
trav,*n.*	TRAWV	trot
treva efter (1)	TRAY-*vah* EF-*tehr*	feel (grope) for, to
trevlig	TRAYV-*lig*	nice (agreeable)
triangel,*nn.* (II)	*trih*-AHNG-*el*	triangle (*geom.*)
tribut,*nn.* (III)	*trih*-BUH_T	tribute (money)
triumf,*nn.* (III)	*trih*-UHMF	triumph
tro,*nn.*	TROO	faith (creed)
"	"	belief (opinion)
tro (3)	TROO	believe (accept), to
trogen	TROOG-*en*	faithful (loyal)
trolig	TROO-*lig*	probable (likely)
trollkarl,*nn.* (II)	TROHLL-*kawr*	magician
"	"	wizard (sorcerer)
tron,*nn.* (III)	TROON	throne
tro och lydnad	TROO *ohck* LÜ_D-*nahd*	allegiance
tröst,*nn.*	TRÖST	comfort (solace)
"	"	consolation
trösta (1)	TRÖSS-*tah*	comfort (console), to
trots	TROHTS	despite (*prep.*)
trotsa (1)	TROHT-*sah*	defy, to
trött	TRÖT	tired
"	"	weary
trötta (1)	TRÖT-*ah*	tire (make weary), to
trötthet,*nn.*	TRÖT-*hayt*	fatigue
tröttna (1)	TRÖT-*nah*	tire (become weary), to
trottoar,*nn.* (III)	*troo-too*-AWR	sidewalk
trottoarkant,*nn.* (III)	*troo-too*-AWR-*kahnt*	curb (edge of street)
trumma,*nn.* (I)	TRUHM-*ah*	drum (*mus.*)
trumpet,*nn.* (III)	*truhm*-PAYT	trumpet (*mus.*)
trupper,*nn.pl.*	TRUHP-*ehr*	troops (*mil.*)
trust,*nn.* (III)	TRUHST	trust (cartel)
tryck,*n.*	TRÜCK	pressure (force)
"	"	stress (physical tension)
tryck,*n.* (V)	TRÜCK	print (printed reproduction)
trycka (2)	TRÜCK-*ah*	print, to
tryckare,*nn.* (V)	TRÜCK-*ah-reh*	printer
trygg	TRÜG	safe (without risk)
tuberkulos,*nn.*	*tuh-behr-kuh*-LOH_S	tuberculosis
tugga (1)	TUHG-*ah*	chew, to
tuggummi,*n.* (IV)	TUHG-*guhm-ih*	gum (chewing gum)
tull,*nn.* (II)	TUHLL	customs (tax)
"	"	duty (tax)
tullfri	TUHLL-*free*	duty-free
tullkammare,*nn.* (V)	TUHLL-*kahm-ah-reh*	customhouse
tullklarering,*nn.* (II)	TUHLL-*klah*-RAY-*ring*	clearance (customs clearance)

Swedish	Pronunciation	English
tulltariff,*nn.* (III)	TUHLL-*tah*-RIFF	tariff (duty)
tulpan,*nn.* (III)	*tuhll*-PAWN	tulip
tumme,*nn.* (II)	TUHM-*eh*	thumb
tumör,*nn.* (III)	*tuh*-MÖR	tumor
tumult,*n.* (V)	*tuh*-MUHLLT	riot (disturbance)
tung	TUHNG	heavy
tunga,*nn.* (I)	TUHNG-*ah*	tongue (*anat.*)
tunn	TUHNN	thin (not thick)
tunnel,*nn.* (II)	TUHNN-*el*	tunnel
tunnelbana,*nn.* (I)	TUHNN-*el-baw-nah*	subway (underground railway)
tupp,*nn.* (II)	TUHP	cock
"	"	rooster
tur,*nn.*	TUHR	fortune
"	"	luck
tur,*nn.* (III)	TUHR	tour
"	"	trip (journey)
turist,*nn.* (III)	*tuh*-RIST	tourist (*n.*)
turistsäng,*nn.* (II)	*tuh*-RIST-*seng*	cot (bed)
Turkiet,*n.*	*tuhr*-KEE-*et*	Turkey
turkisk	TUHRR-*kisk*	Turkish (*adj.*)
tusensköna,*nn.* (I)	TUH-*sen-shö-nah*	daisy
två gånger	TVOH GOHNG-*ehr*	twice
tvål,*nn.* (II)	TVOH_L	soap
tvång,*n.*	TVOHNG	force (coercion)
tvärs över	TVASH Ö-*vehr*	across (from side to side)
tvätt,*nn.*	TVET	laundry (articles laundered)
tvätta (1)	TVET-*ah*	wash (cleanse), to
tvätta sig	TVET-*ah say*	wash (cleanse oneself), to
tvättinrättning,*nn.* (II)	TVET-*in-ret-ning*	laundry (commercial plant)
tveka (1)	TVAY-*kah*	hesitate, to
tvilling,*nn.* (II)	TVILL-*ing*	twin (*n.*)
tvinga (1, 8)	TVING-*ah*	compel, to
"	"	force, to
"	"	oblige, to
tvinna (1)	TVIN-*ah*	twist (wind), to
tvivel,*n.* (V)	TVEE-*vel*	doubt
tvivelaktig	TVEE-*vel-ahck-tig*	doubtful
tvivla på (1)	TVEEV-*lah poh*	doubt (be uncertain about), to
tweed,*nn.*	TWEED	tweed (cloth)
tycka illa om (2)	*tück-ah*-ILL-*ah ohm*	dislike, to
tycka om	*tück-ah*-OHM	like (be fond of), to
tyckas (2)	TÜCK-*ahs*	seem (appear), to
tydlig	TÜ_D-*lig*	apparent
"	"	distinct (unmistakable)
"	"	obvious
"	"	plain (clear)
tyfus,*nn.*	TÜ-*fuhss*	typhoid fever
tyg,*n.* (III)	TÜ_G	cloth
"	"	fabric
tygel,*nn.* (II)	TÜ_G-*el*	rein (strap)
tygla (1)	TÜ_G-*lah*	curb (restrain), to
typisk	TÜ-*pisk*	typical
tyrann,*nn.* (III)	*tü*-RAHN	tyrant
tysk	TÜSK	German (*adj.*)
Tyskland,*n.*	TÜSK-*lahnd*	Germany
tyst	TÜST	quiet
"	"	silent
tysta ned (1)	*tüss-tah*-NAYD	hush (make quiet), to
tystnad,*nn.*	TÜST-*nahd*	silence (stillness)
udda	UHD-*ah*	odd (not even)
udde,*nn.* (II)	UHD-*eh*	cape (headland)
"	"	point (in space)
uggla,*nn.* (I)	UHG-*lah*	owl
ugn,*nn.* (II)	UHNGN	oven
ugnsteka (2)	UHNGN-*stay-kah*	roast (be roasted), to
ull,*nn.*	UHLL	wool (fleece)
umbärande,*n.* (IV)	UHM-*bair-ahn-deh*	hardship (privation)
undantag,*n.* (V)	UHN-*dahn-tawg*	exception (unusual case)
under	UHN-*dehr*	below (*prep.*)
"	"	beneath
"	"	during
"	"	under
"	"	underneath (*prep.*)

Swedish	Pronunciation	English
under,*n.* (V)	UHN-*dehr*	marvel
"	"	miracle
underbar	UHN-*dehr-bar*	marvelous
"	"	wonderful
undergång,*nn.*	UHN-*dehr-gohng*	doom (ruin)
underhålla (10)	UHN-*dehr-hohll-ah*	entertain (amuse), to
underhållning,*nn.*	UHN-*dehr-hohll-ning*	entertainment
underhandla om (1)	UHN-*dehr-hahnd-lah ohm*	negotiate, to
underhandling,*nn.* (II)	UHN-*dehr-hahnd-ling*	negotiation
underjordisk	UHN-*dehr-yoord-isk*	underground (belowground, *adj.*)
underkjol,*nn.* (II)	UHN-*dehr-chool*	petticoat
		slip
underkläder,*nn.pl.*	UHN-*dehr-klai-dehr*	underwear
underkuva (1)	UHN-*dehr-kuh-vah*	subdue (conquer), to
underlåta (10)	UHN-*dehr-loh-tah*	fail (neglect) to, to
underlig	UHN-*dehr-lig*	strange (peculiar)
underrätta (1)	UHN-*dehr-ret-ah*	acquaint, to
"	"	inform (apprise), to
"	"	notify, to
undersåte,*nn.* (II)	UHN-*deh-shoh-teh*	subject (citizen)
underskott,*n.* (V)	UHN-*deh-shkoht*	deficit (*bus.*)
undersöka (2)	UHN-*deh-shö-kah*	examine, to
"	"	investigate, to
undersökning,*nn.* (II)	UHN-*deh-shö_k-ning*	investigation
understöd,*n.* (V)	UHN-*deh-shtö_d*	relief (aid)
underteckna (1)	UHN-*dehr-teck-nah*	sign (endorse), to
under tiden	*uhn-dehr*-TEE-*den*	meanwhile (*adv.*)
undertrycka (2)	UHN-*dehr-trück-ah*	suppress (subdue), to
undervattensbåt,*nn.* (II)	UHN-*dehr-vaht-ens*-BOH_T	submarine
undervisa (1)	UHN-*dehr-vee-sah*	instruct (teach), to
undervisning,*nn.*	UHN-*dehr-vees-ning*	instruction (teaching)
undgå (10)	UHND-*goh*	escape, to
undra (1)	UHN-*drah*	wonder (ask oneself), to
undvika (5)	UHND-*vee-kah*	avoid, to
ung	UHNG	young (*adj.*)
ungdom,*nn.*	UHNG-*doomm*	youth (period of life)
ungdomlig	UHNG-*doomm-lig*	youthful
ungdomlighet,*nn.*	UHNG-*doomm-lig-hayt*	youthfulness
unge,*nn.* (II)	UHNG-*eh*	youngster
ungefär	*uhn-yeh*-FAIR	about (approximately)
Ungern,*n.*	UHNG-*ern*	Hungary
ungkarl,*nn.* (II)	UHNG-*kawr*	bachelor (unmarried man)
uniform,*nn.* (III)	*uhn-if*-FOHRRM	uniform (*n.*)
universitet,*n.* (V)	*uh-nih-vesh-ih*-TAYT	university
universum,*n.*	*uh-nih*-VASH-*uhm*	universe
upp	UHP	upstairs (to upper story, *adv.*)
upp(e)	UHP(-*eh*)	up (*adv.*)
uppåt	UHP-*oht*	upward (to a higher level, *adv.*)
uppegga (1)	UHP-*egg-ah*	excite, to
uppehåll,*n.* (V)	UHP-*eh-hohll*	stop (halt)
uppehålla (10)	UHP-*eh-hohll-ah*	sustain (maintain), to
uppehälle,*n.*	UHP-*eh-hell-eh*	living (livelihood)
"	"	support (livelihood)
uppenbar	UHP-*en-bar*	evident
"	"	manifest (*adj.*)
uppfinna (8)	UHP-*fin-ah*	invent, to
uppfinning,*nn.* (II)	UHP-*fin-ing*	invention
uppföra (2)	UHP-*för-ah*	erect (build), to
uppförande,*n.*	UHP-*för-ahn-deh*	behavior
uppföra sig	UHP-*för-ah say*	behave (conduct oneself), to
uppfostra (1)	UHP-*foosst-rah*	educate, to
uppfriska (1)	UHP-*friss-kah*	refresh, to
uppfylla (2)	UHP-*füll-ah*	fulfill, to
uppgå till (10)	UHP-*goh till*	number (amount to), to
uppge (10)	UHP-*yay*	abandon (give up), to
"	"	renounce (give up), to
"	"	state (say), to
"	"	surrender (relinquish), to

Swedish	Pronunciation	English
uppgift,*nn.* (III)	UHP-*yift*	task
uppgörelse,*nn.* (III)	UHP-*yö-rell-seh*	settlement (compromise, *bus.*)
upphäva (2)	UHP-*hai-vah*	annul, to
upphöja (2)	UHP-*höy-ah*	elevate (lift up), to
upphöjning,*nn.* (II)	UHP-*höy-ning*	ridge (raised area)
upphöra (2)	UHP-*hö-rah*	cease (desist), to
"	"	stop, to
upphöra med	UHP-*hö-rah mayd*	quit, to
upplaga,*nn.* (I)	UHP-*law-gah*	edition
upplevelse,*nn.* (III)	UHP-*lay-vel-seh*	experience (conscious event)
upplösa (2)	UHP-*lö-sah*	dissolve, to
"	"	dissolve (make liquefy), to
upplysa (2)	UHP-*lü-sah*	illuminate, to
"	"	light, to
upplysning,*nn.* (II)	UHP-*lü_s-ning*	information (news)
uppmana (1)	UHP-*maw-nah*	urge (try to persuade), to
uppmärksam	UHP-*mairrk-sahm*	attentive (heedful)
uppmärksamhet, *nn.*	UHP-*mairrk-sahm-hayt*	attention (heed)
"	"	notice
uppmuntra (1)	UHP-*muhn-trah*	encourage, to
"	"	cheer (gladden), to
uppnå (3)	UHP-*noh*	achieve (attain), to
"	"	attain (arrive at), to
uppoffra (1)	UHP-*ohf-rah*	sacrifice (forego), to
uppoffrande,*n.*	UHP-*ohf-rahn-deh*	sacrifice (giving up)
upprätt	UHP-*ret*	erect (*adj.*)
upprepa (1)	UHP-*ray-pah*	repeat (reiterate), to
uppriktig	UHP-*rick-tig*	frank (*adj.*)
"	"	sincere
uppror,*n.* (V)	UHP-*roor*	rebellion
"	"	revolt
uppskatta (1)	UHP-*skaht-ah*	appreciate (be grateful for), to
"	"	esteem, to
"	"	estimate (calculate), to
uppskjuta (6)	UHP-*shu-tah*	delay, to
"	"	postpone, to
uppstå (10)	UHP-*stoh*	arise (come about), to
uppståndelse,*nn.*	UHP-*stohn-dell-seh*	excitement
upptäcka (2)	UHP-*teck-ah*	detect, to
"	"	discover, to
upptäckt,*nn.* (III)	UHP-*teckt*	discovery
uppta(ga) (9)	UHP-*taw(-gah)*	occupy (fill), to
uppta(ga) illa	UHP-*taw(-gah)* ILL-*ah*	resent, to
upptagen	UHP-*tawg-en*	busy (occupied)
uppteckna (1)	UHP-*teck-nah*	record (set down), to
uppväcka (2)	UHP-*veck-ah*	arouse (excite), to
uppvärma (2)	UHP-*vairr-mah*	heat, to
uran,*n.* or *nn.*	*uh*-RAWN	uranium
urkund,*nn.* (III)	UHR-*kuhnd*	charter (act of incorporation)
ursäkta (1)	UH-*sheck-tah*	excuse (pardon), to
ursprung,*n.* (V)	UH-*shpruhng*	origin (source)
ursprunglig	UH-*shpruhng-lig*	original (first)
Uruguay,*n.*	*uhr-uh-guh*-AY	Uruguay
urval,*n.* (V)	UHR-*vawl*	selection (things chosen)
ut	UH_T	out (forth, *adv.*)
utan	UH-*tahn*	without (lacking, *prep.*)
utan att	UH-*tahn aht*	without (failing to, *prep.*)
utan hopp	UH-*tahn* HOHP	hopeless
utbetalning,*nn.* (II)	UH_T-*beh-tawl-ning*	disbursement (*bus.*)
utbildning,*nn.*	UH_T-*billd-ning*	education (schooling process)
"	"	training (instruction)
utbyta (2)	UH_T-*bü-tah*	exchange (interchange), to
utbyte,*n.* (IV)	UH_T-*bü-teh*	exchange (barter)
ute	UH_T-*eh*	out (not in, *adv.*)
"	"	outside (*adv.*)
utelämna (1)	UH_T-*eh-lem-nah*	omit (leave out), to
utesluta (6)	UH_T-*eh-slu-tah*	exclude, to
uteslutande	UH_T-*eh-slu-tahn-deh*	exclusive (not including)

Swedish	Pronunciation	English
utföra (2)	UH_T-*för-ah*	accomplish, to
"	"	perform (do), to
utförande,*n.* (IV)	UH_T-*för-ahn-deh*	performance (action)
utforska (1)	UH_T-*fohsh-kah*	explore, to
utgång,*nn.* (II)	UH_T-*gohng*	exit
"	"	outlet
utgift,*nn.* (III)	UH_T-*yift*	expenditure (outlay)
uthärda (1)	UH_T-*haird-ah*	bear, to
"	"	endure, to
utkast,*n.* (V)	UH_T-*kahst*	draft (sketch)
"	"	outline (rough draft)
utländsk	UH_T-*lensk*	foreign
utlänning,*nn.* (II)	UH_T-*len-ing*	foreigner
utlöpa (2)	UH_T-*lö-pah*	expire (become void, *bus.*), to
utmaning,*nn.* (II)	UH_T-*maw-ning*	challenge
utmärkt	UH_T-*mairrkt*	excellent
"	"	superior
utnämna (2)	UH_T-*nem-nah*	appoint, to
utnämning,*nn.* (II)	UH_T-*nem-ning*	appointment (nomination)
utom	UH_T-*ohm*	beside (other than, *prep.*)
"	"	except (*prep.*)
utomhus	UH_T-*ohm-huh_s*	outdoors (*adv.*)
utomlands	UH_T-*ohm-lahnds*	abroad (in foreign land)
utomordentlig	UH_T-*ohm-or-dent-lig*	extraordinary
utöva (1)	UH_T-*ö-vah*	exercise (employ), to
"	"	practice (put to practice), to
utövning,*nn.*	UH_T-*ö_v-ning*	practice (performance)
utplåna (1)	UH_T-*ploh-nah*	blot out (efface), to
"	"	erase, to
utrop,*n.* (V)	UH_T-*roop*	exclamation (*n.*)
utropa (1)	UH_T-*roop-ah*	exclaim, to
utrustning,*nn.*	UH_T-*ruhst-ning*	equipment
"	"	outfit
utrymme,*n.* (IV)	UH_T-*rüm-eh*	room (space)
"	"	space (area)
utsätta (11)	UH_T-*set-ah*	expose (lay open), to
utseende,*n.* (IV)	UH_T-*say-en-deh*	appearance (aspect)
"	"	look (aspect)
utsida,*nn.* (I)	UH_T-*see-dah*	outside (*n.*)
utsikt,*nn.*	UH_T-*sickt*	view (scene)
utsikt,*nn.* (III)	UH_T-*sickt*	prospect (thing expected)
utskjutande	UH_T-*shu-tahn-deh*	prominent (jutting)
utsökt	UH_T-*sö_kt*	dainty
"	"	exquisite
utställa (2)	UH_T-*stell-ah*	exhibit, to
utställning,*nn.* (II)	UH_T-*stell-ning*	exhibit
"	"	exhibition (exposition)
"	"	show
utsträckning,*nn.*	UH_T-*streck-ning*	extent (magnitude)
utta(ga) till värnplikt (9)	UH_T-*taw(-gah) till* VAIRN-*plickt*	draft (conscript), to
uttala (1)	UH_T-*taw-lah*	pronounce (enunciate), to
uttryck,*n.* (V)	UH_T-*trück*	expression
uttrycka (2)	UH_T-*trück-ah*	express (state), to
utveckla (1)	UH_T-*veck-lah*	develop, to
utveckling,*nn.*	UH_T-*veck-ling*	development
utvidga (1)	UH_T-*vid-gah*	expand (make larger), to
"	"	extend (enlarge), to
utvidgning,*nn.*	UH_T-*vid-g_ning*	extension (enlargement)
vaccination,*nn.* (III)	*vahck-sin-ah*-SHOON	vaccination
väcka (2)	VECK-*ah*	awaken (make awaken), to
"	"	rouse, to
"	"	wake (make awaken), to
vacker	VAHCK-*ehr*	beautiful
"	"	handsome (attractive)
"	"	pretty
vackla (1)	VAHCK-*lah*	reel, to
"	"	stagger (totter), to

Swedish	Pronunciation	English
vad	VAW(D)	what (*interrog. pron.*)
vad,*n.* (V)	VAWD	bet
vad,*nn.* (III)	VAWD	calf (*anat.*)
vad (som)	VAW(D) (*sohm*)	what (*rel. pron.*)
vada (1)	VAW-*dah*	wade, to
vad än	VAWD EN	whatever (*pron.*)
vada över	VAW-*dah ö-vehr*	ford, to
väder,*n.*	VAI-*dehr*	weather
vädja till (1)	VAID-*yah till*	appeal to (entreat), to
vädjan,*nn.*	VAID-*yahn*	appeal (entreaty)
vädra (1)	VAID-*rah*	sniff, to
våg,*nn.* (I)	VOH_G	wave (billow)
våg,*nn.* (II)	VOH_G	scales (balance)
väg,*nn.* (II)	VAIG	road
"	"	way (route)
våga (1)	VOH-*gah*	dare, to
"	"	venture (dare), to
väga (2)	VAI-*gah*	weigh, to
vägg,*nn.* (II)	VEG	wall
vagga,*nn.* (I)	VAHGG-*ah*	cradle
vagn,*nn.* (II)	VAHNGN	car, railroad
"	"	carriage (horse-drawn vehicle)
vagnslast,*nn.* (III)	VAHNGS-*lahsst*	carload (*bus.*)
vägra (1)	VAIG-*rah*	deny, to
"	"	refuse (make a refusal), to
vågrät	VOH_G-*rait*	horizontal (*adj.*)
vågstycke,*n.* (IV)	VOH_G-*stück-eh*	venture
vaja (1)	VAH-*yah*	wave (flutter), to
vaken	VAW-*ken*	awake
vakna (1)	VAWK-*nah*	awaken (rouse oneself), to
"	"	wake (rouse oneself), to
vakt,*nn.* (III)	VAHKT	guard (watcher)
"	"	keeper
vakta (1)	VAHCK-*tah*	guard (watch over), to
val,*n.* (V)	VAWL	choice (act of choosing)
"	"	election
val,*nn.* (II)	VAWL	whale
välbekant	VAIL-*beh-kahnt*	familiar (well-known)
vald	VAWLD	chosen
våld,*n.*	VOHLLD	violence
välde,*n.* (IV)	VELL-*deh*	dominion (rule)
väldig	VELL-*dig*	huge
"	"	mighty (vast)
våldsam	VOHLLD-*sahm*	fierce
"	"	violent
välfärd,*nn.*	VAIL-*faird*	welfare (well-being)
valfri	VAWL-*free*	optional
välgörenhet,*nn.*	VAIL-*yö-ren-hayt*	charity (philanthropy)
välja (11)	VELL-*yah*	choose, to
"	"	elect, to
"	"	pick, to
"	"	select, to
väljare,*nn.* (V)	VELL-*yah-reh*	voter
välkommen,*n.*	VAIL-*kohm-en*	welcome (*n.*)
välkomna (1)	VAIL-*kohm-nah*	welcome (receive hospitably), to
valnöt,*nn.* (*pl.* -nötter)	VAWL-*nö_t*	walnut (*n.*)
vals,*nn.* (III)	VAHLLS	roller (cylinder)
"	"	waltz (dance step)
valsedel,*nn.* (II)	VAWL-*say-dell*	ballot
välsigna (1)	*vell*-SING-*nah*	bless, to
välsignelse,*nn.* (III)	*vell*-SING-*nel-seh*	blessing (boon)
välstånd,*n.*	VAIL-*stohnd*	prosperity
välta (II)	VELL-*tah*	overturn (upset), to
vältalig	VAIL-*taw-lig*	eloquent
valuta,*nn.* (I)	*vah*-LU-*tah*	currency (money)
valv,*n.* (V)	VAHLLV	arch (curved structure)
vän,*nn.* (III)	VEN	friend
vana,*nn.* (I)	VAW-*nah*	habit (custom)
vanära,*nn.*	VAWN-*air-ah*	dishonor
vånda,*nn.*	VOHN-*dah*	anguish
vända sig (2)	VEN-*dah say*	turn (face about), to

Swedish	Pronunciation	English
vändning,*nn.* (II)	VEND-*ning*	turn (change of direction)
vandra (1)	VAHN-*drah*	wander, to
vandra omkring	VAHN-*drah ohm*-KRING	stroll, to
(fot)vandring,*nn.* (II)	(FOO_T)VAHND-*ring*	hike (march)
våning,*nn.* (II)	VOH-*ning*	floor
"	"	story (floor)
våningen under, i	*ee*-VOH-*ning-en* UHN-*dehr*	downstairs (on a lower floor)
vänja sig (11)	VEN-*yah say*	accustom oneself, to
vanlig	VAWN-*lig*	common
"	"	frequent
"	"	ordinary
"	"	regular (normal)
"	"	usual
vänlig	VEN-*lig*	friendly
vänlighet,*nn.*	VEN-*lig-hayt*	kindness (favor)
vanpryda (2)	VAWN-*prü-dah*	mar (disfigure), to
vansinne,*n.*	VAWN-*sin-eh*	madness (insanity)
vansinnig	VAWN-*sin-ig*	mad (insane)
vänskap,*nn.*	VEN-*skawp*	friendship
vänster	VEN-*stehr*	left (*adj.*)
vänster hand	VEN-*stehr* HAHND	left (*n.*)
vänta (1)	VEN-*tah*	wait (defer action), to
vänta på	VEN-*tah poh*	wait for, to
vänta sig	VEN-*tah say*	expect, to
vante,*nn.* (II)	VAHN-*teh*	mitten
vapen,*n.* (V)	VAW-*pen*	weapon
var	VAWR	each (apiece, *adv.*)
"	"	where (in, at what place, *adv.*)
vår,*nn.* (II)	VOR	spring (season)
vår, vårt, våra	VOR, VORT, VOH-*rah*	our
"	"	ours
vara,*nn.* (I)	VAW-*rah*	commodity
vara (1)	VAW-*rah*	last (continue), to
vara (4)	VAW-*rah*	be, to
vara böjd	*vaw-rah*-BÖYD	incline (tend), to
vara ense med	*vaw-rah*-EN-*seh mayd*	agree with, to
vara hungrig	*vaw-rah*-HUHNG-*rig*	hungry, to be
varaktighet,*nn.*	VAWR-*ahck-tig-hayt*	duration
vara ledsen	*vaw-rah*-LESS-*en*	sorry, to be
vara ledsen över	*vaw-rah*-LESS-*en ö-vehr*	regret, to
var...än	VAWR...EN	wherever (no matter where)
vara oense	*vaw-rah*-OO-*en-seh*	disagree (differ), to
vara olik	*vaw-rah*-OO-*leek*	differ (be unlike), to
"	"	vary (differ), to
vara olydig mot	*vaw-rah*-OO-*lü-dig moot*	disobey, to
vara skyldig	*vaw-rah*-SHÜLL-*dig*	owe, to
vård,*nn.*	VORD	care (custody)
värd,*nn.* (II)	VAIRD	host
vårda (1)	VORD-*ah*	nurse (give treatment to), to
vardaglig	VAWR-*dawg-lig*	homely (everyday)
vardagsrum,*n.* (V)	VAWR-*dahx-ruhm*	parlor (living room)
värde,*n.* (IV)	VAIRD-*eh*	value
"	"	worth
värdefull	VAIRD-*eh-fuhll*	valuable (precious)
värdelös	VAIRD-*eh-lö_s*	worthless (valueless)
värdepapper,*n.pl.*	VAIRD-*eh-pahp-ehr*	securities (stocks, etc.)
värdera (1)	*vaird*-DAY-*rah*	value (appraise), to
värdering,*nn.* (II)	*vaird*-DAY-*ring*	appraisal (*bus.*)
"	"	rating (evaluation)
värdig	VAIRD-*ig*	worthy (deserving)
värdighet,*nn.* (III)	VAIRD-*ig-hayt*	dignity
värdshus,*n.* (V)	VAIRDS-*huh_s*	inn
vårdslös	VORDS-*lö_s*	careless (negligent)
varelse,*nn.* (III)	VAWR-*el-seh*	creature (living being)
vare sig	VAWR-*eh-say*	whether (either, *conj.*)
varför	VAHRR-*för*	why
varg,*nn.* (II)	VAHRR_*yuh*	wolf
varhelst	*vahr*-HELST	wherever (at, in whatever place)
varje	VAHRR-*yeh*	any (*adj.*)
"	"	each (*adj.*)
"	"	every

Swedish	Pronunciation	English
varje fall, i "	*ee* VAHRR-*yeh* FAHLL "	anyhow (in any case) anyway (in any case)
värk,*nn.*	VAIRRK	ache
värka (2)	VAIRRK-*ah*	ache, to
varken...eller	VAHRR-*ken*...ELL-*ehr*	neither...nor (*conj.*)
värld,*nn.* (II)	VAIRD	world
varm	VAHRRM	warm
värma (2)	VAIRR-*mah*	warm, to
värme,*nn.* "	VAIRR-*meh* "	heat warmth
värmeelement,*n.* (V)	VAIRR-*meh-el-eh*-MENT	radiator (heater)
värmepanna,*nn.* (I)	VAIRR-*meh-pahn-ah*	furnace (home heater)
varna (1) "	VARN-*ah* "	caution, to warn, to
värnplikt,*nn.*	VAIRN-*plickt*	draft (conscription)
var och en " "	VAWR-*oh*-EN " "	each one (*pron.*) everybody everyone
varor,*nn.pl.* " "	VAW-*ror* " "	goods merchandise wares
värre	VAIRR-*eh*	worse (*adv.*)
vars	VAHSH	whose (*rel. pron.*)
var som helst	VAWR *sohm* HELST	anywhere (whereso-ever)
värst	VASHT	worst (*adv.*)
värsta, (det),*n.*	(*deh*) VASH-*tah*	worst (*n.*)
vart	VAHRRT	where (to what place, *adv.*)
varuhus,*n.* (V)	VAW-*ruh-hu̱ s*	department store
varumärke,*n.* (IV)	VAW-*ruh-mairrk-eh*	trade mark
varuupplag,*n.* (V)	VAW-*ruh-uhp*-LAWG	warehouse
vas,*nn.* (III)	VAWS	vase
väsa (2)	VAI-*sah*	hiss, to
väsentlig "	*veh*-SENT-*lig* "	essential (*adj.*) vital
vask,*nn.* (II)	VAHSSK	sink (*n.*)
väsnas (1)	VAIS-*nahs*	rave (rant), to
vass,*nn.*	VAHSS	reed (grass)
vässa (1)	VESS-*ah*	sharpen, to
väst,*nn.* (II)	VEST	vest
väster,*nn.*	VESS-*tehr*	west (*n.*)
västlig	VEST-*lig*	western
våt	VOH̱T	wet
väta (2)	VAI-*tah*	wet, to
vätska,*nn.* (I)	VET-*skah*	liquid (*n.*)
vatten,*n.* (V)	VAHT-*en*	water
vattenfall,*n.* (V)	VAHT-*en-fahll*	falls (waterfalls)
vattenkoppor,*nn.pl.*	VAHT-*en-kohp-or*	chicken pox
vattenkran,*nn.* (II)	VAHT-*en-krawn*	faucet
vattentät	VAHT-*en-tait*	waterproof
väva (2)	VAI-*vah*	weave, to
vävnad,*nn.* (III) "	VAIV-*nahd* "	textile (*n.*) tissue (*biol.*)
vävstol,*nn.* (II)	VAIV-*stool*	loom
vax,*n.*	VAHX	wax (beeswax)
växa (2)	VEX-*ah*	grow, to (*biol.*)
växa upp	*vex-ah*-UHP	grow up (mature), to
växel,*nn.* (II) "	VEX-*el* "	bill of exchange gear (*mech.*)
växt,*nn.*	VEXT	growth (develop-ment)
växt,*nn.* (III)	VEXT	plant (flora)
ve,*n.*	VAY	woe
veck,*nn.* (V)	VECK	fold (plait, *n.*)
vecka,*nn.* (I)	VECK-*ah*	week
vecko-...	VECK-*oo*-...	weekly (*adj.*)
veckoslut,*n.* (V)	VECK-*oo-slu̱t*	weekend (*n.*)
vederbörlig	VAY-*dehr-bör-lig*	due (proper)
vederlägga (11)	VAY-*dehr-leg-ah*	refute, to
vem "	VEM "	who (*interrog. pron.*) whom (*interrog. pron.*)
vem än	VEM EN	whoever
vems	VEMS	whose (*interrog. pron.*)
Venedig,*n.*	*veh*-NAY-*dig*	Venice
Venezuela,*n.*	*veh-neh-suh*-AYL-*ah*	Venezuela
veranda,*nn.* (I)	*vehr*-AHN-*dah*	porch
verb,*n.* (V)	VAIRRB	verb
verk,*n.* (V)	VAIRRK	work (opus)
verkan,*nn.*	VAIRR-*kahn*	effect
verklig "	VAIRRK-*lig* "	actual real
verkligen	VAIRRK-*lig-en*	really (actually)
verklighet,*nn.*	VAIRRK-*lig-hayt*	reality
verksam	VAIRRK-*sahm*	effective (effectual)
verksamhet,*nn.*	VAIRRK-*sahm-hayt*	activity (exertion of energy)
verkställa (2)	VAIRRK-*stell-ah*	execute (carry out), to
verkställande	VAIRRK-*stell-ahn-deh*	executive (*adj.*)
verktyg,*n.* (V)	VAIRRK-*tü̱ g*	tool
vers,*nn.* (III)	VAISH	verse (poetic writing)
vertikal	*vairr-tih*-KAWL	vertical (*adj.*)
veta (11)	VAY-*tah*	know (have knowl-edge), to
vete,*n.*	VAY-*teh*	wheat
vetenskap,*nn.* (III)	VAY-*ten-skawp*	science
vetenskaplig	VAY-*ten-skawp-lig*	scientific
vetenskapsman,*nn.* (*pl.* -män)	VAY-*ten-skawps-mahn*	scholar (savant)
(natur)vetenskaps-man,*nn.* (*pl.* -män)	(*nah*-TU̱ R-)VAY-*ten-skawps-mahn*	scientist
veteran,*nn.* (III)	*veh-teh*-RAWN	veteran (*mil., n.*)
vetskap,*nn.*	VAYT-*skawp*	knowledge (informa-tion)
vi	VEE	we
via	VEE-*ah*	by (via, *prep.*)
vid " " "	VEED " " "	at (by) at (near) by (near, *prep.*) wide (not narrow)
vidare	VEE-*dah-reh*	further (to greater extent, *adv.*)
vidarebefordra (1)	VEE-*dah-reh-beh-foord-rah*	forward (send by mail), to
vide,*n.* (IV)	VEE-*deh*	willow
vidhålla (10)	VEED-*hohll-ah*	contend (maintain), to
vidskepelse,*nn.* (III)	VEED-*shay-pell-seh*	superstition
vidskeplig	VEED-*shayp-lig*	superstitious
vidsträckt " "	VEED-*streckt* " "	extensive vast wide (comprehen-sive)
vig	VEEG	nimble (agile)
vik,*nn.* (II)	VEEK	bay (inlet)
vika (5)	VEE-*kah*	fold (lap over), to
vikt,*nn.* "	VICKT "	importance weight (scale weight)
viktig "	VICK-*tig* "	important urgent
vila,*nn.*	VEE-*lah*	rest (repose)
vila (1)	VEE-*lah*	rest (repose), to
vild "	VILLD "	savage (*adj.*) wild (undomesti-cated)
vildmark,*nn.* (III)	VILLD-*mahrrk*	wilderness
vilja,*nn.* (I)	VILL-*yah*	will (power of choice)
vilken, vilket, vilka "	VILL-*ken*, VILL-*ket*, VILL-*kah* "	what (*interrog. adj.*) which (*interrog. adj., pron.*)
" "	" "	who whom
vilken, vilket, vilka ...än "	VILL-*ken*, VILL-*ket*, VILL-*kah*...EN "	whatever (*adj.*) whichever (*adj.*)
vilken, vilket, vilka som helst	VILL-*ken*, VILL-*ket*, VILL-*kah sohm* HELST	either (either one, *pron.*)
vilkens	VILL-*kens*	whose
villig	VILL-*ig*	willing (favorably disposed)
villkor,*n. pl.* (V) "	VILL-*kor* "	condition (stipula-tion) terms
vin,*n.* (III)	VEEN	wine (beverage)
vind,*nn.* (II) "	VINND "	attic wind

Swedish	Pronunciation	English
vindruta,*nn.* (I)	VINND-*ru-tah*	windshield
vindruva,*nn.* (I)	VEEN-*dru-vah*	grape
vingård,*nn.* (II)	VEEN-*gord*	vineyard
vinge,*nn.* (II)	VING-*eh*	wing (*zool.*)
vink,*nn.* (II)	VINK	hint (inkling)
vinkel,*nn.* (II)	VING-*kel*	angle (*geom.*)
vinna (8)	VIN-*ah*	gain (get), to
"	"	win (be victor in), to
vinna poäng	*vin-ah-poh*-ENG	score (gain points), to
vinranka,*nn.* (I)	VEEN-*rahnk-ah*	vine (grapevine)
vinst,*nn.* (III)	VINST	profit (*bus.*)
vinter,*nn.* (II)	VIN-*tehr*	winter (*n.*)
viol,*nn.* (III)	*vee*-OOL	violet (flower)
vis	VEES	sage (*adj.*)
visa (1)	VEE-*sah*	indicate (point out), to
"	"	instruct (direct), to
"	"	show (make visible), to
visa sig	VEE-*sah say*	show (be visible), to
vision,*nn.* (III)	*vih*-SHOON	vision (foresight)
visit,*nn.* (III)	*vih*-SEET	visit (social call)
visitkort,*n.* (V)	*viss*-SEET-*koort*	card, calling
viska (1)	VISS-*kah*	whisper (utter softly), to
viskning,*nn.* (II)	VISK-*ning*	whisper
visky,*nn.*	VISS-*kü*	whiskey
viss	VISS	certain (particular)
vissla (1)	VISS-*lah*	whistle, to
vissna (1)	VISS-*nah*	wilt, to
"	"	wither, to
vistelse,*nn.* (III)	VISS-*tell-seh*	stay (sojourn)
vit	VEET	white (*adj.*)
vitamin,*nn.* (III)	*vih-tah*-MEEN	vitamin
vitlök,*nn.* (II)	VEET-*lö_k*	garlic
vittne,*n.* (IV)	VIT-*neh*	witness (one who testifies)
vittnesmål,*n.* (V)	VIT-*nes-moh_l*	testimony
volym,*nn.* (III)	*voh*-LÜ_M	volume (quantity)
"	"	volume (space occupied)

Swedish	Pronunciation	English
vördnad,*nn.*	VÖRD-*nahd*	awe
"	"	reverence (respect)
vrede,*nn.*	V_RAY-*deh*	anger
		wrath
vricka (1)	V_RICK-*ah*	sprain, to
vrida (5)	V_REE-*dah*	wrench (wrest), to
vulgär	*vuhll*-GAIR	vulgar (ill-bred)
vulkan,*nn.* (III)	*vuhll*-KAWN	volcano
Wales,*n.*	*oo*-AILS	Wales
Warszawa,*n.*	*vahr*-SHAW-*vah*	Warsaw
Wien,*n.*	VEEN	Vienna
wiensk	VEENSK	Viennese (*adj.*)
ylle,*n.*	ÜLL-*eh*	wool (cloth)
ylletröja,*nn.* (I)	ÜLL-*eh-tröy-ah*	sweater
yngling,*nn.* (II)	ÜNG-*ling*	youth (young man)
yngre	ÜNG-*reh*	junior (younger)
yr	ÜR	dizzy (unsteady)
yrka (1)	ÜRR-*kah*	insist, to
yrke,*n.* (IV)	ÜRR-*keh*	occupation (calling)
"	"	profession
"	"	trade (craft)
yta,*nn.* (I)	Ü-*tah*	area (extent)
"	"	surface
yta, plan,*nn.*	*plawn* Ü-*tah*	plane (surface)
ytterlig	ÜT-*ehr-lig*	utter (*adj.*)
ytterligare	ÜT-*ehr-lig-ah-reh*	additional
"	"	further (*adj.*)
ytterrock,*nn.* (II)	ÜT-*ehr-rohck*	overcoat
ytterst	ÜT-*esht*	extreme (farthest)
		utmost (*adj.*)
yttra (1)	ÜT-*rah*	remark (say), to
yttrande,*n.* (IV)	ÜT-*rahn-deh*	remark (comment)
yttre	ÜT-*reh*	exterior (*adj.*)
"	"	outer
"	"	outside (*adj.*)
yxa,*nn.* (I)	ÜX-*ah*	axe
"	"	hatchet
zigenare,*nn.* (V)	*sih*-YAYN-*ah-reh*	gypsy
zink,*nn.*	SINK	zinc
zon,*nn.* (III)	SOON	zone
zoologi,*nn.*	*soo-log*-EE	zoology

Swedish Special Lists

Alphabet

a	AW	i	EE	r	AIRR
å	OH	j	YEE	s	ESS
ä	AI	k	KOH	t	TAY
b	BAY	l	ELL	u	UH
c	SAY	m	EM	v	VAY
d	DAY	n	EN	w	DUHB-*ell-vay*
e	EH	o	OO	x	ECKS
f	EF	ö	Ö	y	Ü
g	GAY	p	PAY	z	SAY-*tah*
h	HOH	q	KUH		

Cardinal Numbers

Swedish	Pronunciation	English	Swedish	Pronunciation	English
en, ett	EN, ETT	one	tjugoen	*chu-goo*-EN	twenty-one
två	TVOH	two	tjugotvå	*chu-goo*-TVOH	twenty-two
tre	TRAY	three	trettio	TRET-*tih*	thirty
fyra	FÜ-*rah*	four	fyrtio	FÖRT-*tih*	forty
fem	FEM	five	femtio	FEM-*tih*	fifty
sex	SEX	six	sextio	SEX-*tih*	sixty
sju	SHU	seven	sjuttio	SHUHT-*tih*	seventy
åtta	OHT-*ah*	eight	åttio	OHT-*tih*	eighty
nio	NEE-*eh*	nine	nittio	NIT-*tih*	ninety
tio	TEE-*eh*	ten	hundra	HUHN-*drah*	one hundred
elva	ELL-*vah*	eleven	hundraen	*huhn-drah*-EN	one hundred one
tolv	TOHLLV	twelve	tvåhundra	TVOH-*huhn-drah*	two hundred
tretton	TRET-*tohn*	thirteen	tvåhundraen	*tvoh-huhn-drah*-EN	two hundred one
fjorton	F_YOORT-*tohn*	fourteen	tusen	TUH-*sen*	one thousand
femton	FEM-*tohn*	fifteen	ett tusen en	ETT TUH-*sen en*	one thousand one
sexton	SEX-*tohn*	sixteen	två tusen	TVOH TUH-*sen*	two thousand
sjutton	SHUHT-*tohn*	seventeen	två tusen en	TVOH TUH-*sen en*	two thousand one
arton	ART-*tohn*	eighteen	en miljon	EN *mill*-YOON	one million
nitton	NIT-*tohn*	nineteen	en miljard	EN *mill*-YARD	one billion
tjugo	CHU-*goo*	twenty			

Ordinal Numbers

Swedish	Pronunciation	English	Swedish	Pronunciation	English
första	FÖSH-*tah*	first	sjunde	SHUHN-*deh*	seventh
andra	AHN-*drah*	second	åttonde	OHT-*ohn-deh*	eighth
tredje	TRAYD-*yeh*	third	nionde	NEE-*ohn-deh*	ninth
fjärde	F_YAIRD-*eh*	fourth	tionde	TEE-*ohn-deh*	tenth
femte	FEM-*teh*	fifth	elfte	ELF-*teh*	eleventh
sjätte	SHET-*eh*	sixth	tolfte	TOHLLF-*teh*	twelfth

Days of the Week

Swedish	Pronunciation	English	Swedish	Pronunciation	English
söndag, *nn.*	SÖN-*dah*(g)	Sunday	torsdag, *nn.*	TOOSH-*dah*(g)	Thursday
måndag, *nn.*	MOHN-*dah*(g)	Monday	fredag, *nn.*	FRAY-*dah*(g)	Friday
tisdag, *nn.*	TEES-*dah*(g)	Tuesday	lördag, *nn.*	LÖRD-*dah*(g)	Saturday
onsdag, *nn.*	OONS-*dah*(g)	Wednesday			

Months of the Year

Swedish	Pronunciation	English	Swedish	Pronunciation	English
januari, *nn.*	*yah-nuh*-AW-*rih*	January	juli, *nn.*	U-*lih*	July
februari, *nn.*	*feb-ruh*-AW-*rih*	February	augusti, *nn.*	*aw*-GUHS-*tih*	August
mars, *nn.*	MAHSH	March	september, *nn.*	*sep*-TEM-*behr*	September
april, *nn.*	*ah*-PRILL	April	oktober, *nn.*	*ohck*-TOO-*behr*	October
maj, *nn.*	MY	May	november, *nn.*	*noo*-VEM-*behr*	November
juni, *nn.*	U-*nih*	June	december, *nn.*	*deh*-SEM-*behr*	December

First Names

Swedish	Pronunciation	English	Swedish	Pronunciation	English
Abraham	AW-*brah-hahm*	Abraham	Bernhard	BAIRN-*hahrd*	Bernard
Adam	AW-*dahm*	Adam	Berta	BAIRT-*ah*	Bertha
Agnes	AHNG-*nes*	Agnes	Charlotta	*shah*-LOHT-*ah*	Charlotte
Albert	AHLL-*behrt*	Albert	Daniel	DAW-*nih-el*	Daniel
Alexander	*ah-leck*-SAHN-*dehr*	Alexander			
Alfred	AHLL-*fred*	Alfred	David	DAW-*vid*	David
Alice	AHLL-*iss*	Alice	Dorotea	*doh-roh*-TAY-*ah*	Dorothy
Anders	AHN-*desh*	Andrew	Edit	AYD-*it*	Edith
Anna	AHN-*ah*	Ann, Anne	Edmund	AYD-*muhnd*	Edmund
Anton	AHN-*tohn*	Anthony	Edvard	AYD-*vahrd*	Edward
Arnold	ARN-*ohlld*	Arnold	Eleonora	*eh-leh-oh*-NOO-*rah*	Eleanor
Artur	AHRT-*uhr*	Arthur			
			Elisabet	*eh*-LEE-*sah-bet*	Elizabeth
Barbara	BAR-*bah-rah*	Barbara	Emilia	*eh*-MEE-*lih-ah*	Emily
Benjamin	BAYN-*yah-min*	Benjamin	Emma	EM-*ah*	Emma

Swedish	Pronunciation	English	Swedish	Pronunciation	English
Ernst	AIRNSHT	Ernest	Leopold	LAY-*oo-pohlld*	Leopold
Eugen	*eh-uh-*SHAYN	Eugene	Lisa	LEE-*sah*	Elizabeth
Felix	FAY-*lix*	Felix			
			Lovisa	*loo-*VEE-*sah*	Louise
Ferdinand	FAIRD-*ih-nahnd*	Ferdinand	Ludvig	LUHD-*vig*	Louis
Filip	FEE-*lip*	Philip	Margareta	*mahr-gah-*RAY-*tah*	Margaret
Frans	FRAHNS	Francis	Maria	*mah-*REE-*ah*	Marie
Fredrik	FRAY-*drick*	Frederick	"	"	Mary
Georg	YAY-*or_yuh*	George	Markus	MAHRR-*kuhs*	Mark
Gertrud	YAIRT-*ruhd*	Gertrude			
			Marta	MAHRRT-*ah*	Martha
Greta	GRAY-*tah*	Margaret	Märta	MAIRRT-*ah*	Martha
Gustav	GUHS-*tahv*	Gustav	Martin	MAHRRT-*in*	Martin
Harald	HAW-*rahld*	Harold	Matteus	*mah-*TAY-*uhs*	Matthew
Harry	HAHRR-*ü*	Harry	Mikael	MEE-*kah-el*	Michael
Helena	*heh-*LAY-*nah*	Helen	Nicklas	NICK-*lahs*	Nicholas
Henrietta	*hen-rih-*ET-*ah*	Henrietta			
			Nikolaus	*nick-oo-*LAW-*uhs*	Nicholas
Henrik	HEN-*rick*	Henry	Olga	OHLL-*gah*	Olga
Herbert	HAIRR-*behrt*	Herbert	Otto	OHT-*oo*	Otto
Herman	HAIRR-*mahn*	Herman	Patrik	PAW-*trick*	Patrick
Horatius	*hoo-*RAWT-*sih-uhs*	Horace	Paul	PAW-*uhll*	Paul
Hugo	HUH-*goo*	Hugh	Paula	PAW-*uh-lah*	Paula
Isabella	*ee-sah-*BELL-*ah*	Isabel			
			Per	PAIR	Peter
Isak	EE-*sahck*	Isaac	Petrus	PAY-*truhs*	Peter
Jakob	YAW-*kohp*	Jacob	Petter	PET-*ehr*	Peter
"	"	James	Rebecka	*reh-*BECK-*ah*	Rebecca
Johan	YOO-*hahn*	John	Rickard	RICK-*ahrd*	Richard
John	YOHN	John	Robert	ROH-*behrt*	Robert
Josef	YOO-*sef*	Joseph			
			Rolf	ROHLLF	Ralph
Josefina	*yoo-seh-*FEE-*nah*	Josephine	Rosa	ROO-*sah*	Rose
Judit	YU-*dit*	Judith	Rudolf	RU-*dohllf*	Rudolph
Karin	KAW-*rin*	Katharine	Rut	RU_T	Ruth
Karl	KAWL	Charles	Samuel	SAW-*muh-el*	Samuel
Karolina	*kah-roo-*LEE-*nah*	Caroline	Sara	SAW-*rah*	Sarah
Katarina	*kah-tah-*REE-*nah*	Katharine			
Klara	KLAW-*rah*	Clara	Saul	SAW-*uhll*	Saul
"	"	Clare	Stefan	STAY-*fahn*	Stephen
Konrad	KOHN-*rahd*	Conrad	Susanna	*suh-*SAHN-*ah*	Susan
Kristina	*krih-*STEE-*nah*	Christine	Sylvia	SÜLL-*vih-ah*	Sylvia
Kristofer	KRISS-*stohf-ehr*	Christopher	Teresia	*teh-*RAY-*sih-ah*	Theresa
Laura	LAW-*uh-rah*	Laura	Tomas	TOO-*mahs*	Thomas
			Valter	VAHLL-*tehr*	Walter
Lena	LAY-*nah*	Helen	Viktor	VICK-*tor*	Victor
Leo	LAY-*oo*	Leo	Vilhelm	VILL-*helm*	William
Leon	LAY-*ohn*	Leon	Vincent	VIN-*sent*	Vincent
Leonard	LAY-*oo-nahrd*	Leonard	Virginia	*vihrg-*EE-*nih-ah*	Virginia

USEFUL EXPRESSIONS

Greetings

English	Pronunciation	Swedish
How are you?	*huh-shtor deh* TILL?	Hur står det till?
Well, thanks, and you?	TAHCK, BRAW. *oh* NEE (DU)?	Tack, bra. Och ni (du)?
Good morning.	*goo-*MOHRR-*ohn.*	God morgon.
Good afternoon.	*goo-*DAWG.	Goddag.
Good evening.	*goo-*AHF-*tohn.*	God afton.
Good night.	*goo-*NAHT.	God natt.
See you again.	*ah-*YÖ *soh* LENG-*eh.*	Adjö så länge.
So long.	HAY *soh* LENG-*eh.*	Hej så länge.
Good luck.	*lück-ah* TILL.	Lycka till.
Good-by.	*ah-*YÖ.	Adjö.
Glad to meet you.	*deh vah* TRAYV-*lit aht* TREF-*ahs.*	Det var trevligt att träffas.
Congratulations.	*grah-tuh-*LAY-*rahr.*	Gratulerar.
Happy Birthday.	*hawr den* AIR-*ahn poh* FÖ-*dell-seh-dawg-en.*	Har den äran på födelsedagen.
Merry Christmas.	GOO_D YU_L.	God jul.
Happy New Year.	GOHT *nüt* OR.	Gott nytt år.

Ordinary Conversation

English	Pronunciation	Swedish
Thank you.	TAHCK (*soh* MÜCK-*eh*).	Tack (så mycket).
Please.	*vaw-*SHNELL *oh...*	Var snäll och...
You're welcome.	VAW-*shoh-*GOO_D.	Varsågod.
Pardon me.	UH-*sheck-tah.*	Ursäkta.
What do you call this?	*vah* HAY-*tehr deh-*HAIR?	Vad heter det här?
I'm sorry.	*soh* TROH-*kit.*	Så tråkigt.
Allow me.	*for yah* LOHV?	Får jag lov?
I would like...	*yah skuhll-eh* VILL-*yah...*	Jag skulle vilja...

English	Pronunciation	Swedish
Come in.	*steeg* IN.	Stig in.
May I introduce...	*for yah preh-sen-*TAY-*rah...*	Får jag presentera...
What is your name?	*vah eh* NAHM-*net?*	Vad är namnet?
My name is...	*mit* NAHMN *eh...*	Mitt namn är...
I don't know.	*yah* VAYT *in-teh.*	Jag vet inte.
I'm thirsty.	*yah eh* TÖSH-*tig.*	Jag är törstig.
I'm hungry.	*yah eh* HUHNG-*rig.*	Jag är hungrig.
I'm an American.	*yah eh ah-meh-rih-*KAWN.	Jag är amerikan.
Where can I find...?	VAWR AIR...?	Var är...?
What is this?	*vah eh deh* HAIR?	Vad är det här?

Foreign Languages

English	Pronunciation	Swedish
Do you speak...?	TAW-*lahr nee...?*	Talar ni...?
I speak (understand) a little...	*yah* TAW-*lahr (fö-*SHTOHR) *lee-teh...*	Jag talar (förstår) lite...
I do not speak...	*yah* TAW-*lahr in-teh...*	Jag talar inte...
Is there someone here who speaks English?	FINNS *deh noh-gohn* HAIR, *sohm taw-lahr* ENG-*el-skah?*	Finns det någon här, som talar engelska?
I understand you.	*yah fö-*SHTOHR *ehr.*	Jag förstår er.
I don't understand.	*yah fö-*SHTOHR IN-*teh.*	Jag förstår inte.
Please speak more slowly.	*vah-*SHNELL *oh* TAW-*lah* LOHNG-*sahm-ah-reh.*	Var snäll och tala långsammare.
Please repeat.	*vah-*SHNELL *oh say* OHM *deh.*	Var snäll och säg om det.

Asking Directions

English	Pronunciation	Swedish
In which direction is...?	*oht vill-ket* HOHLL *eh...?*	Åt vilket håll är...?
Please take me to...	*vah-*SHNELL *oh* TAW *may till...*	Var snäll och tag mig till...
Please take me there.	*vah-*SHNELL *oh* TAW *may* DEET.	Var snäll och tag mig dit.
Where can I mail this?	VAWR *kahn yah* POHSS-*tah deh hair?*	Var kan jag posta det här?
Please direct me to...	*vah-*SHNELL *oh* VEE-*sah may till...*	Var snäll och visa mig till...
...the telephone.	*...tell-eh-*FOHN-*en.*	...telefonen.
...the toilet.	*...too-ah-*LET-*en.*	...toaletten.
...the post office.	*...*POHSST-*kohn-*TOO-*ret.*	...postkontoret.
...the bank.	*...*BAHNK-*en.*	...banken.
...the police station.	*...poo-*LEES-*stah-*SHOON-*en.*	...polisstationen.
...the U.S. consulate.	*...ah-meh-rih-*KAWN-*skah kohn-suh-*LAW-*tet.*	...amerikanska konsulatet.
Please point.	*vah-*SHNELL *oh* VEE-*sah may.*	Var snäll och visa mig.

The Hotel

English	Pronunciation	Swedish
I would like a room...	*yah skuhll-eh vill-yah* HAW *et* RUHM...	Jag skulle vilja ha ett rum...
...with a single bed.	*...mayd* EN SENG.	...med en säng.
...with two beds.	*...mayd* TVOH SENG-*ahr.*	...med två sängar.
...with bath.	*...mayd* BAWD.	...med bad.
...without meals.	*...uh-tahn* MOH L-*tee-dehr.*	...utan måltider.
Please, the key for Room...	*for yah bay ohm* NÜCK-*eln till ruhm...*	Får jag be om nyckeln till rum...
Please call me at...o'clock.	*vah-*SHNELL *oh* VECK *may klohck-ahn...*	Var snäll och väck mig klockan...
I want this...	*yah skuhll-eh vill-yah haw den* HAIR...	Jag skulle vilja ha den här...
...pressed.	*...*PRESS-*ahd.*	...pressad.
...cleaned.	*...*CHAY-*miskt* TVET-*ahd.*	...kemiskt tvättad.
...washed.	*...*TVET-*ahd.*	...tvättad.
...repaired.	*...*LAW-*gahd.*	...lagad.
When will (my suit) be returned?	NAIR *for yah (min koh-*STÜ_M) *till-*BAW-*kah?*	När får jag (min kostym) tillbaka?
Please return (my suit) at...	*vah-*SHNELL *oh shick-ah till-*BAW-*kah (min koh-*STÜ_M) *klohck-ahn...*	Var snäll och skicka tillbaka (min kostym) klockan...

The Restaurant

English	Pronunciation	Swedish
A table for two please.	*yah skuhll-eh vill-yah haw et* BOORD *för* TVOH.	Jag skulle vilja ha ett bord för två.
I would like to see the menu.	*for yah* BAY *om* MAWT-*say-deln.*	Får jag be om matsedeln.
I want it...	*yah skuhll-eh vill-yah* HAW *deh...*	Jag skulle vilja ha det...
...rare.	*...*LET STAYKT.	...lätt stekt.
...medium.	*...*LAW-*gohm* STAYKT.	...lagom stekt.
...well-done.	*...*VAIL STAYKT.	...väl stekt.
Check, please!	*for yah* BAY *ohm* NOO-*tahn!*	Får jag be om notan!

Telephoning

English	Pronunciation	Swedish
I wish to telephone.	*yah skuhll-eh vill-yah tell-eh-foh-*NAY-*rah.*	Jag skulle vilja telefonera.
Please get me this number.	*vah-*SHNELL *oh beh-*STELL *det-ah* NUHM-*ehr.*	Var snäll och beställ detta nummer.
Please give me the number of...	*vah-*SHNELL *oh* YAY *may* NUHM-*ret till...*	Var snäll och ge mig numret till...
What did you say?	*fö-*LOH T, *yah* HÖRD-*eh in-teh.*	Förlåt, jag hörde inte.
The line is busy.	UHP-*tawg-et.*	Upptaget.

English	Pronunciation	Swedish
What is the charge?	*vah* KOHSS-*tahr deh?*	Vad kostar det?

Time

English	Pronunciation	Swedish
What time is it?	*vah eh* KLOHCK-*ahn?*	Vad är klockan?
It is...	KLOHCK-*ahn eh...*	Klockan är...
...five o'clock.	...FEM.	...fem.
...ten past eight.	...TEE-*eh min-*UH-*tehr ö-vehr* OHT-*ah.*	...tio minuter över åtta.
...a quarter past six.	...*en* KVAHRRT *ö-vehr* SEX.	...en kvart över sex.
...half past five.	...HAHLLV SEX.	...halv sex.
...five to seven.	...FEM *min-*UH-*tehr ee* SHU.	...fem minuter i sju.
The day before yesterday	*ee* FÖRR-*gohr*	I förrgår
Yesterday evening	*ee* GOHR KVELL	I går kväll
This morning	*ee* MOHSH-*eh*	I morse
At noon	*klohck-ahn* TOHLLV	Klockan tolv
In the afternoon	*poh* EFF-*tehr-mid-*DAWG-*en*	På eftermiddagen
In the evening	*poh* KVELL-*en*	På kvällen
At night	*poh* NAHTT-*en*	På natten
At midnight	*veed* MEED-*nahtt*	Vid midnatt
Tomorrow morning	*ee mohrr-ohn* BIT-*tih*	I morgon bitti
Tomorrow evening	*ee mohrr-ohn* KVELL	I morgon kväll
The day after tomorrow	*ee ö-vehr-mohrr-ohn*	I övermorgon

Weather

English	Pronunciation	Swedish
It's hot.	*deh eh* VAHRRMT.	Det är varmt.
It's cold.	*deh eh* KAHLLT.	Det är kallt.
It's raining.	*deh* RENG-*nahr.*	Det regnar.
It's snowing.	*deh* SNÖ-*ahr.*	Det snöar.
What fine weather!	*sohnt* FEENT VAI-*dehr!*	Sådant fint väder!

Postal Information

English	Pronunciation	Swedish
How much is the postage on this?	*vah eh* POHRRT-*oht för deh-*HAIR?	Vad är porto för det här?
Give me...worth of stamps.	*vah-*SHNELL *oh yay may* FREE-*mairr-ken för...*	Var snäll och ge mig frimärken för...
Please send this letter...	*vah-*SHNELL *oh* SHICK-*ah deh-hair* BRAY-*vet...*	Var snäll och skicka det här brevet...
...airmail.	...LUHFT-*pohsst.*	...luftpost.
...special delivery.	...*ex-*SPRESS.	...express.
...registered.	...*reh-kohm-en-*DAY-*raht.*	...rekommenderat.
Please send this parcel post.	*vah-*SHNELL *oh* SHICK-*ah deh-*HAIR *sohm pah-*KAYT-*pohsst.*	Var snäll och skicka det här som paketpost.

Barber and Beauty Shop

English	Pronunciation	Swedish
I want a haircut.	*yah skuhll-eh vill-yah haw* KLIP-*ning.*	Jag skulle vilja ha klippning.
Not too short.	IN-*teh för* KOHRRT.	Inte för kort.
No hair oil, thank you.	NAY *tahck, ing-et* HOHR-*vaht-en.*	Nej tack, inget hårvatten.
I want a shave.	*yah skuhll-eh vill-yah haw* RAWK-*ning.*	Jag skulle vilja ha rakning.
I want a shampoo.	*yah skuhll-eh vill-yah haw shahm-poo-*NAY-*ring.*	Jag skulle vilja ha schamponering.
I want my hair set.	*yah skuhll-eh vill-yah haw ohn-duh-*LAY-*ring.*	Jag skulle vilja ha ondulering.

Transportation

English	Pronunciation	Swedish
Where is the ticket office?	*vawr eh bill-*YET-*luhck-ahn?*	Var är biljettluckan?
When does...arrive?	*nair* KOHM-*ehr...*	När kommer...
...the train...	...TOH-*get?*	...tåget?
...the plane...	...PLAW-*net?*	...planet?
...the bus...	...BUHSS-*en?*	...bussen?
At what time does the train leave for...?	NAIR *gor* TOH-*get till...?*	När går tåget till...?
From which track does the train for... leave?	*frohn vill-ken* PLAHT-*fohrrm gor* TOH-*get till...?*	Från vilken plattform går tåget till...?
Is this the right train for...?	*eh deh-*HAIR *ret-ah* TOH-*get till...?*	Är det här rätta tåget till...?
Where is my baggage?	VAWR *eh mit bah-*GAWSH?	Var är mitt bagage?
Where is the baggage room?	VAWR *eh* RAYS-*goots-in-*LEM-*ning-en?*	Var är resgodsinlämningen?
Please call a taxi.	*vah-*SHNELL *oh* RING *ef-tehr en* BEEL.	Var snäll och ring efter en bil.

Auto Travel

English	Pronunciation	Swedish
What place is this?	*vah* HAY-*tehr den-hair* PLAHT-*sen?*	Vad heter den här platsen?
Where is the town?	VAWR *eh* STAWN?	Var är stan?

English	Pronunciation	Swedish
Which is the best road for...?	*vill-ken eh den* BES-*tah* VAIG-*en till...?*	Vilken är den bästa vägen till...?
Turn to the right.	*tah* AWV *till* HÖ_G-*ehr.*	Tag av till höger.
Turn to the left.	*tah* AWV *till* VEN-*stehr.*	Tag av till vänster.
Go straight on.	FOORT-*set* RAWKT *frahm.*	Fortsätt rakt fram.
Go back.	FOORT-*set till-*BAW-*kah.*	Fortsätt tillbaka.
This way.	*den-*HAIR VAIG-*en.*	Den här vägen.
That way.	*den-*DAIR VAIG-*en.*	Den där vägen.
How far is it to...?	*huh_r* LOHNGT *eh deh till...?*	Hur långt är det till...?
Is this the road to...?	*eh deh-*HAIR VAIG-*en till...?*	Är det här vägen till...?
Is it...	*eh deh...*	Är det...
...near?	...NAIR-*ah?*	...nära?
...far?	...LOHNGT?	...långt?
...very far?	...MÜCK-*eh* LOHNGT?	...mycket långt?
Which way is...	*oht vill-ket* HOHLL *eh...*	Åt vilket håll är...
...north?	...NOHRR?	...norr?
...south?	...SÖ-*dehr?*	...söder?
...east?	...ÖSS-*tehr?*	...öster?
...west?	...VESS-*tehr?*	...väster?
Is the road...?	*eh* VAIG-*en...?*	Är vägen...?
Is there a detour?	*eh deh noh-gohn* OHM-*vaig?*	Är det någon omväg?
What is the speed limit?	*vah eh* HÖCK-*stah* TILL-*loh_t-nah* HAHSS-*tig-hayt-en?*	Vad är högsta tillåtna hastigheten?
Where is the nearest gas station?	VAWR *eh* NAIRR-*mah-steh ben-*SEEN-*stah-*SHOON?	Var är närmaste bensinstation?
Where can I find a garage (for repairs)?	VAWR *fins deh noh-gohn* BEEL-*vairrk-stahd?*	Var finns det någon bilverkstad?
I need...	*yah be-*HÖ-*vehr...*	Jag behöver...
...oil.	...OHLL-*yah.*	...olja.
...gasoline.	...*ben-*SEEN.	...bensin.
...a tire.	...*ett* BEEL-*deck.*	...ett bildäck.

Public Signs

English	Pronunciation	Swedish
Keep Out	TILL-*trai-deh för-*B_YU-*det*	Tillträde förbjudet
For Hire	*aht* HÜ-*rah*	Att hyra
No Parking	*pahrr-*KAY-*ring för-*B_YU-*den*	Parkering förbjuden
No Smoking	RÖK-*ning för-*B_YU-*den*	Rökning förbjuden
Sale	*till* SAW-*luh*	Till salu
Women	DAW-*mehr*	Damer
Men	HAIRR-*ahr*	Herrar
No Spitting	SPOHT-*ning för-*B_YU-*den*	Spottning förbjuden
Railroad	YAIRN-*vaig*	Järnväg
Dangerous Curve	FAR-*lig* KUHRR-*vah*	Farlig kurva
Keep to the Right (Left)	HOHLL *till* HÖ_G-*ehr* (VEN-*stehr*)	Håll till höger (vänster)
Dead End	OH-*tehr-vends-*GREND	Återvändsgränd
Men Working	VAIG-*ahr-bay-teh* POH-*gohr*	Vägarbete pågår
No Thoroughfare	YAY-*nohm-fart för-*B_YU-*den*	Genomfart förbjuden
One-way Street	ENK-*el-rick-tahd* GAW-*tah*	Enkelriktad gata
Go Slow	CHÖR LOHNG-*sahmt*	Kör långsamt
Toilet	*too-ah-*LET	Toalett
Entrance	IN-*gohng*	Ingång
Exit	UH_T-*gohng*	Utgång

Swedish Grammar

ARTICLES

Definite article

In Swedish, the definite article is an ending, attached to the noun. It has the following forms:

Nonneuter   -en after most nouns ending in a consonant

       plane*n*   the plan

     -n after nouns ending in a vowel or -el, -er, -or

       flicka*n*   the girl

       sedel*n*   the bill

       neger*n*   the Negro

       doktor*n*   the doctor

Neuter   -et after nouns ending in a consonant

       hus*et*   the house

     -t after most nouns ending in a vowel

       ställe*t*   the place

Pl.   -na for nouns belonging to the first three declensions and those of the fifth declension ending in -ande and -are

       flickor*na*   the girls

       resande*na*   the travelers

     -a for nouns of the fourth declension

       ställen*a*   the places

-en (in the spoken language -ena) for neuter nouns of the fifth declension

       huse*n(a)*   the houses

Neuter nouns ending in -el, -en, -er drop the e before the article in the singular and in the plural.

   fönster   window

   fönstr*et*   the window

   fönstr*en*   the windows

Nonneuter nouns which end in -an and a number of those ending in -en remain unchanged in the definite singular.

   fruktan   fear; the fear

   fröken   miss; the miss

Latin loan words ending in -eum, -ium drop the -um before adding the definite article.

   mus*eum*   mus*eet*   the museum

Nouns containing a short vowel followed by m or n double the nasal in the definite form.

kam	comb	ka*mm*en	the comb
man	man	ma*nn*en	the man

Indefinite article

Nonneuter	*en*	a, an	en flicka	a girl
			en pojke	a boy
			en plan	a plan
Neuter	*ett*	a, an	ett hus	a house

Plural of nouns

In Swedish, there are five declensions of nouns:

(I) Plural ending -*or*

flicka	girl	flick*or*	girls

(II) Plural ending -*ar*

pojke	boy	pojk*ar*	boys

(III) Plural ending -*er*

plan	plan	plan*er*	plans

(IV) Plural ending -*n*

ställe	place	ställe*n*	places

(V) No plural ending

hus	house	hus	houses

Nouns of the first three declensions ending in unstressed -*a* or -*e* drop these vowels before the ending, as in flick*or*, pojk*ar*.

Nouns of the first three declensions ending in unstressed -*el*, -*en* or -*er* drop the *e* before the ending:

regel	rule	regl*er*	rules
socken	parish	sockn*ar*	parishes
vinter	winter	vintr*ar*	winters

A few nouns belonging to the third declension and ending in a vowel take the plural ending -*r* instead of -*er*; e.g.:

hustru	wife	hustru*r*	wives
ko	cow	ko*r*	cows
sko	shoe	sko*r*	shoes

Nouns borrowed from the Latin and ending in -*eum* or -*ium* drop the -*um* before the ending:

mus*eum*		mus*eer*	museums

Loan words ending in -*or* shift the stress to that ending in the plural.

Nouns containing a short vowel followed by *m* or *n* double the nasal before the plural ending:

dröm	dream	drö*mm*ar	dreams
vän	friend	vä*nn*er	friends

Personal pronouns

Subject of the verb

jag	I	vi	we
du, ni	you	ni	you
han	he	de	they
hon	she		
den	it		
det	it		

Object of the verb

mig	me	oss	us
dig, er (eder)	you	er (eder)	you
honom	him	dem	them
henne	her		
den	it		
det	it		

The pronoun *du* is used with children, relatives and close friends. *Ni* is the pronoun of formal address; the object form *eder* is used in formal style.

The pronoun *den* refers to a nonneuter noun denoting an animal or an inanimate object. *Det* refers to a neuter noun.

Det is sometimes also used corresponding to English "there," "so," "he," "she," "they":

Det är en man här.	*There* is a man here.
Han tycker *det*.	He thinks *so*.
Det är min syster.	*She* is my sister.

Possessive pronouns and adjectives *

The possessives agree in gender and number with the object possessed. Pronouns ending in -*s* are indeclinable.

Sing.			*Pl.*
Nonneuter	*Neuter*		
min	mitt	my, mine	mina

---

* For convenience, possessive, interrogative, demonstrative and indefinite adjectives are treated in this section on pronouns.

Prepositive article

If the noun in the definite form is qualified by an adjective, it is preceded by a prepositive article which in the singular is *den* for nonneuter, *det* for neuter and *de* in the plural.

den vackra flickan	the pretty girl
det stora huset	the big house
de små pojkarna	the small boys

NOUNS

Irregular plural forms are given in the word list.

Gender of nouns

Swedish nouns are either neuter or nonneuter. Nonneuter includes the genders masculine, feminine and common. There are no simple, general rules for determining the gender. In the English list the gender is indicated by the letters *n.* (= neuter) and *nn.* (= nonneuter). In the Swedish-to-English list nouns are followed by numbers referring to the appropriate declension.

Case of nouns

Swedish nouns have two case forms: nominative (also used as objective case) and genitive. The genitive is formed by adding *s* (without apostrophe) to the nominative, both in the indefinite and definite form, in the singular and in the plural:

flicka*s*	girl's	flickor*s*	girls'
flickan*s*	the girl's	flickorna*s*	the girls'

With inanimate nouns the possessive is also expressed by use of a preposition. This is particularly common in the spoken language:

taket på huset   the roof of the house

Declension patterns

Most Swedish nouns are declined according to the following patterns:

	Indefinite Sing.	*Definite Sing.*	*Indefinite Pl.*	*Definite Pl.*
(I)	en flicka (a girl)	flicka*n*	flick*or*	flickor*na*
(II)	en pojke (a boy)	pojke*n*	pojk*ar*	pojkar*na*
(III)	en plan (a plan)	plan*en*	plan*er*	planer*na*
(IV)	ett ställe (a place)	ställe*t*	ställe*n*	ställe*na*
(V)	Neuter: ett hus (a house)	hus*et*	hus	hus*en*(*a*)
	Nonneuter: en bagare (a baker)	bagare*n*	bagare	bagar*na*

PRONOUNS

din	ditt	your, yours (informal)	dina
er (eder)	ert (edert)	your, yours (formal)	era (edra)
hans	hans	his	hans
hennes	hennes	her, hers	hennes
dess	dess	its	dess
vår	vårt	our, ours	våra
er (eder)	ert (edert)	your, yours	era (edra)
deras	deras	their, theirs	deras

The reflexive possessive *sin* (neuter *sitt*, plural *sina*) is used instead of *hans, hennes, dess, deras* when the owner is the subject of the clause. For example:

Hon leker med *sitt* barn.	She plays with *her* (*own*) child.
Hon leker med *hennes* barn.	She plays with *her* (*someone else's*) child.

Reflexive pronouns

The reflexive pronoun *sig* is used in the third person singular and plural corresponding to "himself," "herself," "itself," "themselves." It is indeclinable. In the first and second persons the objective forms of the personal pronouns are used as reflexives. For a discussion of the use of reflexive pronouns with certain verbs, see *Reflexive Verbs*, p. 3078.

Relative pronouns

Who, whom

Som, the commonest relative pronoun, is used in all genders and numbers. If used with a preposition, the preposition must be placed at the end of the clause. It is indeclinable.

Jag såg mannen, *som* du talade *med*.	I saw the man *with whom* you talked.

Vilken (nonneuter), *vilket* (neuter), *vilka* (plural). This pronoun agrees in gender and number with the noun it refers to. It may be preceded by a preposition.

Jag såg mannen, *med vilken* du talade.	I saw the man *with whom* you talked.

Whose
Vars, the commonest possessive relative. It refers to all genders, singular and plural.
Vilkens (vilkets, vilkas). Cf. *vilken* above.

Which
Som or *vilken*. Cf. above.

What
Vad, used as object.
Vad som, used as subject.

Note: When used in the objective case, *som* and *vilken* are often omitted as in English.

Interrogative pronouns and adjectives *

Who, whom
Vem, used only as a pronoun and only in the singular.
Vilken (nonneuter), *vilket* (neuter), *vilka* (plural), used both as a pronoun and an adjective.

Whose
Vems. Cf. *vem* above.
Vilkens (vilkets, vilkas). Cf. *vilken* above.

What
Vad, used both as a pronoun and an adjective.
Vilken, etc. Cf. above.

Which one
Vilken, etc. Cf. above.
Vilkendera (nonneuter), *vilketdera* (neuter), used in the singular only. It stresses the meaning "which one of two."

Note: When the interrogative pronouns are used as the subject in a dependent question, they are followed by *som*. Example:

Såg du *vem som* kom?	Did you see *who* came?

Demonstrative pronouns and adjectives *

This, these
Denna, denne (nonneuter), *detta* (neuter), *dessa* (plural).

Den här (nonneuter), *det här* (neuter), *de här* (plural).
The form *denne* is used when referring to a masculine noun.

That, those
Den (nonneuter), *det* (neuter), *de* (plural).
Den där (nonneuter), *det där* (neuter), *de där* (plural).
Den här and *den där* are the forms generally used in spoken Swedish. After a demonstrative adjective the noun takes the definite article, except after *denna (detta, dessa.)*

Indefinite pronouns and adjectives *

One
Man, possessive *ens*, objective *en*. This pronoun is often used when English has "they," "you," "we," "people."

Man kan se det härifrån.	*One (you)* can see it from here.
Säga vad *man* vill.	Say what *people (you)* will.

Some, any, somebody, anybody, something, anything
Någon (nonneuter), *något* (neuter), *några* (plural).

No, nobody, nothing
Ingen (nonneuter), *intet, inget* (neuter), *inga* (plural).

Other, else
Annan (nonneuter), *annat* (neuter), *andra* (plural).
The definite forms are: *den andra (andre,* masculine) (nonneuter), *det andra* (neuter), *de andra* (plural).

Each, every
Var or *varje* (nonneuter), *vart* or *varje* (neuter).
Varenda (nonneuter), *vartenda* (neuter).
Var, varje, varenda are used only as adjectives and only in the singular.

All
All (nonneuter), *allt* (neuter), *alla* (plural).

Note: hel (nonneuter), *helt* (neuter), *hela* (plural) is used when "all" in English means "whole."

alla dagar	*all* days
hela dagen	*all* the day

* For convenience, possessive, interrogative, demonstrative and indefinite adjectives are treated in this section on pronouns.

ADJECTIVES *

Declension of adjectives

In Swedish, adjectives agree in gender and number with the nouns they modify. There are two declensions, the indefinite and the definite.

Indefinite declension. The adjective takes no ending in the singular when modifying a nonneuter indefinite noun. When referring to a neuter noun it takes *-t* and to plural nouns *-a*. For example:

Nonneuter	en stor pojke	a big boy
Neuter	ett stort hus	a big house
Pl.	stora pojkar	big boys

Definite declension. The definite declension is used after the prepositive articles (*den, det, de*), after a genitive and after demonstrative and possessive adjectives. In this declension the adjective takes the ending *-a*. For example:

Nonneuter	den stora pojken	the big boy
Neuter	hans nya hus	his new house
Pl.	dessa snälla flickor	these nice girls

Adjectives ending in *-ad* (past participles of the first conjugation) and *-ast* (superlatives) take *-e* instead of *-a* in the definite form and in the plural.

Adjectives ending in *-al, -el, -en, -er* drop the vowel of the ending before adding the *-a* of the definite and the plural forms. For example:

gammal	old	den gamla staden	the old city
enkel	simple	den enkla regeln	the simple rule
trogen	faithful	den trogna vännen	the faithful friend
vacker	pretty	vackra flickor	pretty girls

Before adding the neuter ending *-t*, adjectives ending in *-en* drop the *n;* those ending in *-d* preceded by a consonant or an unstressed vowel drop the *d;* those ending in *-nn* drop one *n.* Adjectives ending in a stressed vowel or in *-d* and *-t* preceded by a long vowel get double *t* and shorten the vowel in the neuter; those ending in *-dd* substitute *tt* for *dd;* those ending in *-t* preceded by a consonant remain unchanged. For example:

Nonneuter	*Neuter*		*Nonneuter*	*Neuter*	
mogen	moget	ripe	röd	rött	red
värd	värt	worth	vit	vitt	white
sann	sant	true	född	fött	born
blå	blått	blue	tyst	tyst	silent

* For convenience, possessive, interrogative, demonstrative and indefinite adjectives are treated in the section on pronouns.

The adjective *liten* (little) has the definite form *lilla* in the singular and the form *små* in the plural.

In the masculine singular the ending *-e* is sometimes used instead of *-a*.

Indeclinable are adjectives ending in *-a*, such as *bra* (good), *stackars* (poor) and a few others.

Comparison of adjectives

The comparative of most adjectives is formed by adding *-are* and the superlative by adding *-ast* to the nonneuter positive form.

Positive	*Comparative*	*Superlative*
varm (warm)	varmare (warmer)	varmast (warmest)

If the positive ends in unstressed *-el, -en* or *-er*, the *e* is dropped before *-are* and *-ast*. For example:

enkel (simple)	enklare	enklast
mogen (ripe)	mognare	mognast
vacker (pretty)	vackrare	vackrast

A few adjectives take the endings *-re* in the comparative and *-st* in the superlative, usually also mutating the stem vowel:

hög (high)	högre	högst
låg (low)	lägre	lägst
lång (long)	längre	längst
stor (big, great)	större	störst
tung (heavy)	tyngre	tyngst
ung (young)	yngre	yngst

Irregular comparison

bra, god (good, well)	bättre	bäst
dålig (bad, ill)	sämre	sämst
gammal (old)	äldre	äldst
liten (little)	mindre	minst
mycken (much)	mera	mest
många (many)	flera	flest
nära (near)	närmare	närmast
ond (evil)	värre	värst

Comparison with *mera* (more) and *mest* (most). Adjectives ending in *-ad, -e, -isk* as well as present and past participles form their comparison by using *mera* (more) and *mest* (most).

kritisk (critical)	mera kritisk	mest kritisk
aktad (respected)	mera aktad	mest aktad

ADVERBS

Various types of adverbs

Many adverbs are formed from adjectives by adding -*t*. Thus, adjectives of this type are identical with the neuter forms of the adjectives.

Han är *sen*. (adj.)	He is *late*.
Han kom *sent*. (adv.)	He came *late*.

Present participles are often used as adverbs without change.

Hon var *förtjusande* vacker.   She was *exceedingly* pretty.

Comparison of adverbs

Adverbs derived from adjectives are compared in the same way as the corresponding adjectives.

A few other adverbs may also be compared:

bra, väl (well)	bättre	bäst
fort (quickly)	fortare	fortast
gärna (gladly)	hellre	helst
illa (badly)	värre	värst
nära (near)	närmare	närmast

Adverbs with double forms

Some adverbs have double forms, one indicating direction and the other indicating position:

Han går *dit*.	He goes *there*.	Han är *där*.	He is *there*.
Han kommer *hit*.	He comes *here*.	Han är *här*.	He is *here*.
Han kommer *in*.	He comes *in*.	Han är *inne*.	He is *in*.
Han går *ut*.	He goes *out*.	Han är *ute*.	He is *out*.
Han går *hem*.	He goes *home*.	Han är *hemma*.	He is *at home*.
Han far *bort*.	He goes *away*.	Han stannar *borta*.	He stays *away*.
Vart far han?	*Where* does he go?	*Var* bor han?	*Where* does he live?
Han går *upp*.	He gets *up*.	Han är *uppe*.	He is *up*.

VERBS

Numbering of verbs

Each verb in the Swedish-to-English list is followed by a number in parentheses. These numbers correspond to groups (1) through (11) in this grammar section.

Weak verbs. There are three conjugations of weak verbs. They are numbered (1), (2) and (3) in the Swedish-to-English list. Sample verbs have been conjugated under *Present Tense*, *Past Tense* and so forth. These may be used as models for the conjugation of all verbs numbered (1) through (3) in the word list. Irregular weak verbs are numbered (11) and are conjugated in the section *Irregular Weak Verbs*, p. 3079.

Strong verbs. Most strong verbs are numbered in classes (5) through (9). A sample for each of these classes has been conjugated in the section *Models of Strong Verbs*, pp. 3078–79. Strong verbs which do not belong to any of these groups are numbered (10) and their main forms are given in the same section.

Auxiliary verbs. Auxiliary verbs are used to help other verbs form their tenses and moods. They are numbered (4) and are conjugated in the section on *Auxiliary Verbs*, p. 3078.

Infinitive and verb stem

Each verb in the lists appears in its infinitive form. The infinitive in most cases consists of the verb stem and an ending, -*a*. Monosyllabic verbs have no ending. For example:

Infinitive	*Stem*	*Ending*
tal*a*	tal-	-*a*
tro	tro	—

Present tense

Weak verbs. In Swedish, the verbs usually have the same form for all persons, singular and plural. Therefore only the first person singular will be given in the following. To form the present tense of the weak verbs use the stem of the infinitive and add the following endings: -*ar* (1), -*er* (2), -*r* (3). For example:

(1) tala (to speak)
   jag tal*ar*   I speak
(2) äga (to own)
   jag äg*er*   I own
(3) tro (to believe)
   jag tro*r*   I believe

Note: In elevated and formal style the present plural has the same form as the infinitive; e.g., *vitala, äga*, etc. (we talk, own).

Note: Verbs of the 2nd conjugation do not add the -*er* if the stem ends in -*r*; e.g., *jag för* (*föra*, to lead).

Strong verbs. To form the present tense of strong verbs (5) through (10) use the stem of the infinitive and add the ending -*er*:

skriva (to write)
   jag skriv*er*   I write

Note: Monosyllabic strong verbs add only -*r*; e.g., *jag går* (*gå*, to walk).

Note: No ending is added if the stem ends in -*r* or -*l*; e.g., *jag bär* (*bära*, to carry).

Past tense

Weak verbs (1). To form the past of weak verbs (1), use the stem of the infinitive and add the ending -*ade*. For example: *jag tal*ade*   I spoke

Weak verbs (2). To form the past of weak verbs (2), use the stem of the infinitive and add the ending -*de* after voiced and -*te* after voiceless consonants. For example:
   jag äg*de*   I owned

   jag läs*te*   I read

Note: If the stem ends in a *d* or a *t* preceded by a consonant, only *e* is added in the 2nd conjugation; e.g., *jag vände* (*vända*, to turn).

Note: If the stem ends in double *m* or *n*, one *m* or *n* is dropped before adding the ending in the 2nd conjugation; e.g., *jag glömde* (*glömma*, to forget), *jag kände* (*känna*, to feel).

Weak verbs (3). To form the past of weak verbs (3), use the stem of the infinitive and add the ending -*dde*. For example:
   jag tro*dde*   I believed

Strong verbs. The verbs of this group form their past tense by a change of the stem vowel. No endings are added to the stem except in elevated and formal style, where the plural ending -*o* might be used. For example:
   jag skrev   I wrote
   vi skrev(*o*)   we wrote
Models for the strong verbs are given on pp. 1950–51.

Present and past perfect

These tenses are formed by using the present and past tenses of the auxiliary *ha* (*hava*), to have, together with a form of the main verb, called the supine. For example:
   jag *har* skrivit   I *have* written
   jag *hade* skrivit   I *had* written

Supine

Weak verbs. To form the supine of weak verbs (1) through (3), use the stem and add the endings below:

Conjugation	*Supine ending*	*Example*
(1)	-at	tal*at* (spoken)
(2)	-t	äg*t* (owned)
(3)	-tt	tro*tt* (believed)

Strong verbs. The supine forms of the strong verbs are normally formed by adding -*it* to the appropriate stem which is found under models for these verbs, below. Monosyllabic verbs, however, form their supine by adding -*tt* to the infinitive. Examples:
   skriv*it* written   gå*tt* gone

Future tense

Future is expressed in the following ways:
By the present tense, particularly if the clause contains an expression of time.

Han *skriver* idag.   He *will write* today.

By the present tense of the verb *komma* (to come), plus *att* (to) and the infinitive of the verb.

Han *kommer att skriva*.   He *will write*.

By the present tense of the auxiliary *skola* (shall, will), plus the infinitive of the verb. This form generally implies promise, intention, decision or command.

Han lovar, att han *skall skriva*.   He promises that he *will write*.

Imperative mood

The imperative of verbs of the 1st conjugation (1) is identical with the infinitive. In the other conjugations it is identical with the stem of the verb. For example:

(1) tala	speak!
(2) läs	read!
(3) tro	believe!
(5) skriv	write!

Subjunctive mood

The subjunctive forms are rarely used in spoken Swedish.

Present subjunctive. To form the present subjunctive, drop the *-a* of the infinitive and add *-e*. For example:

Infinitive	*Subjunctive*
läsa	läse

Past subjunctive. The past subjunctive of the weak verbs is identical with the indicative. That of the strong verbs is formed by substituting *-e* for *-o* of the past plural indicative.

Past Pl. Indicative	*Past Subjunctive*
läste	läste
sprungo (ran)	sprunge

Present participle

The present participle ends in *-ande* if the infinitive ends in *-a*. If the infinitive ends in another vowel *-ende* is added.

tala	
tal*ande*	speaking
gå	
gå*ende*	walking

Past participle

The past participle is used in Swedish only as an adjective or together with the verbs *bliva* (to become, to be) and *vara* (to be). The past participle of the weak verbs has the same form as the past tense without the final *-e*. The past participle of the strong verbs is formed by adding *-en* to the stem of the supine.

The past participles are inflected like adjectives. Cf. *Declension of Adjectives*, p. 3076.

	Sing.		*Pl.*	
	Nonneuter	*Neuter*		
(1)	uttalad	uttalat	uttalade	pronounced
(2)	ägd	ägt	ägda	owned
(3)	trodd	trott	trodda	believed
(5)	skriven	skrivet	skrivna	written

Reflexive verbs

When the subject and the object of a verb are the same person or the same thing, the verb is called reflexive. The object is always a pronoun (see *Reflexive Pronouns*, p. 3075). For example:

Jag slår mig.   I hurt myself.

In Swedish, reflexive verbs are commoner than in English. For example:

förlova sig	to become engaged	lägga sig	to go to bed
förkyla sig	to get a cold	lära sig	to learn
gifta sig	to get married	raka sig	to shave
kläda sig	to get dressed	skynda sig	to hurry
känna sig	to feel	sätta sig	to sit down

Verbs which are used only reflexively are indicated as follows in the vocabulary list:

gifta sig   to get married

For verbs which are used both reflexively and unreflexively, the reflexive pronoun appears in parentheses after the verb in the vocabulary list:

raka (sig)   to shave

Passive voice

In Swedish, the passive voice, which has a more restricted use than in English, is formed in two ways:

By adding *-s* to the active forms of the verb, dropping the final *-r* in the present tense.

jag kalla*s*	I am called
jag kallade*s*	I was called
jag har kallat*s*	I have been called

By the use of the auxiliary *bli(va)* (to become) plus the past participle of the verb.

jag blir kallad	I am called
jag blev kallad	I was called
jag har blivit kallad	I have been called

The periphrastic passive is commoner than the *s*-passive in the spoken language.

Note: The participle which is an adjective must agree with the subject in gender and number; cf. *Declension of Adjectives*, p. 3076.

Note: The verb forms in *-s* are also used to express a reciprocal action:

de möttes   they met

Note: Some verbs have passive form but active meaning. For example: *hoppas* (to hope), *minnas* (to remember), *lyckas* (to succeed), *synas* (to seem), *tyckas* (to seem).

Auxiliary verbs

Listed below are the Swedish auxiliary verbs which have been numbered (4) in the Swedish-to-English list.

Infinitive	*Present*	*Past Sing.*	*Past Pl.*	*Supine*
bli(va) (to become, be, get)	blir	blev	blevo	blivit
böra	bör (ought to)	borde	borde	bort
få (be allowed to)	får	fick	fingo	fått
ha(va) (to have)	har	hade	hade	haft
kunna (be able to)	kan	kunde	kunde	kunnat
—	måste (must)	måste	måste	måst
—	må (may)	måtte	måtte	—
skola	skall	skulle	skulle	skolat
—	tör (is likely)	torde	torde	—
vara (to be)	är	var	voro	varit
vilja (be willing)	vill	ville	ville	velat

Strong verbs

The strong verbs are numbered (5) through (10) in the Swedish-to-English word list. Most of the strong verbs included in that list follow the patterns of the groups (5) through (9) in respect to the change of the stem vowel. Thus, the forms of those strong verbs can be completed by the following two steps:

Finding the appropriate stem vowels from the model verb to which reference is made in the list.

Following the rules given in the previous sections for the formation of the various forms.

Models of strong verbs

	Past Sing.	*Past Pl.*	*Supine*
(5) Vowel change *i - e - i*: skriva (to write)			
	skrev	skrevo	skrivit
(6) Vowel change *u - ö - u*: bjuda (to offer)			
	bjöd	bjödo	bjudit
(7) Vowel change *y - ö - u*: flyga (to fly)			
	flög	flögo	flugit
(8) Vowel change *i - a - u*: finna (to find)			
	fann	funno	funnit
(9) Vowel change *a - o - a*: fara (to travel)			
	for	foro	farit

(10) Strong verbs which do not belong to any of the previous groups are listed below in alphabetical order. The conjugation forms are given under the uncompounded verbs. The forms given are the past singular, past plural and supine, in that order.

Angå (to concern): see *gå*.
Ankomma (to arrive): see *komma.*
Anse (to consider): see *se.*
Äta (to eat): åt, åto, ätit
Återfå (to recover): see *få.*
Återfalla (to relapse): see *falla.*
Återstå (to remain): see *stå.*
Avgå (to resign): see *gå.*
Avskära (to cut off): see *skära.*
Avslå (to decline): see *slå.*
Bära (to carry): bar, buro, burit
Be (to ask): bad, bådo, bett
Begå (to commit): see *gå.*
Behålla (to keep): see *hålla.*
Beskära (to cut): see *skära.*
Bestå (to consist): see *stå.*
Bibehålla (to maintain): see *hålla.*
Bistå (to assist): see *stå.*
Bönfalla (to beg): see *falla.*
Dö (to die): dog, dogo, dött
Dyka (to dive): dök, döko, dykt
Erhålla (to obtain): see *hålla.*
Få (to get): fick, fingo, fått
Falla (to fall): föll, föllo, fallit
Fastslå (to establish): see *slå.*
Föreslå (to propose): see *slå.*
Förlåta (to forgive): see *låta.*
Förse (to provide): see *se.*
Förstå (to understand): see *stå.*
Framhålla (to point out): see *hålla.*
Frige (to release): see *ge.*
Gå (to go): gick, gingo, gått
Ge (to give): gav, gåvo, givit

Genomgå (to suffer): see *gå*.
Gråta (to cry): grät, gräto, gråtit
Hålla (to hold): höll, höllo, hållit
Infalla (to invade): see *falla*.
Innehålla (to contain): see *hålla*.
Inse (to realize): see *se*.
Komma (to come): kom, kommo, kommit
Köpslå (to bargain): see *slå*.
Låta (to let): lät, läto, låtit
Le (to smile): log, logo, lett
Ligga (to lie): låg, lågo, legat
Medge (to admit): see *ge*.
Motstå (to resist): see *stå*.
Omge (to surround): see *ge*.
Omkomma (to perish): see *komma*.
Overfalla (to attack): see *falla*.
Övergå (to exceed): see *gå*.
Överge (to forsake): see *ge*.
Se (to see): såg, sågo, sett
Skära (to cut): skar, skuro, skurit
Slå (to strike): slog, slogo, slagit
Sova (to sleep): sov, sovo, sovit
Stå (to stand): stod, stodo, stått
Stjäla (to steal): stal, stulo, stulit
Svälta (to starve): svalt, svulto, svultit
Svära (to swear): svor, svuro, svurit
Tillåta (to allow): see *låta*.
Tillbe (to adore): see *be*.
Tillkännage (to announce): see *ge*.
Underhålla (to entertain): see *hålla*.
Underlåta (to fail): see *låta*.
Undgå (to escape): see *gå*.
Uppbära (to support): see *bära*.
Uppehålla (to sustain): see *hålla*.
Uppgå (to amount): see *gå*.
Uppge (to state): see *ge*.

Uppstå (to arise): see *stå*.
Vidhålla (to insist): see *hålla*.

Irregular weak verbs

Listed below are irregular weak verbs which have been numbered (11) in the Swedish-to-English list. The forms given are the past and the supine, in that order.

Ålägga (to impose): see *lägga*.
Dölja (to conceal): dolde, dolt
Ersätta (to replace): see *sätta*.
Förlägga (to mislay): see *lägga*.
Fortsätta (to continue): see *sätta*.
Förutsäga (to predict): see *säga*.
Förutsätta (to assume): see *sätta*.
Framlägga (to present): see *lägga*.
Glädja (to rejoice): gladde, glatt
Göra (to do): gjorde, gjort
Insätta (to insert): see *sätta*.
Lägga (to lay): lade, lagt
Möjliggöra (to enable): see *göra*.
Omintetgöra (to thwart): see *göra*.
Pantsätta (to pawn): see *sätta*.
Redogöra (to account): see *göra*.
Rengöra (to clean): see *göra*.
Säga (to say): sade, sagt
Sätta (to set): satte, satt
Sjösätta (to launch): see *sätta*.
Skilja(s) (to separate): skilde(s), skilts
Stödja (to support): stödde, stött
Sysselsätta (to occupy): see *sätta*.
Utsätta (to subject): see *sätta*.
Välja (to choose): valde, valt
Vänja (to accustom): vande, vant
Vederlägga (to refute): see *lägga*.
Veta (to know): vet (*bres. tense*); visste, vetat

Swedish Pronunciation

VOWELS

Vowels are long or short. All unstressed vowels are short. Stressed vowels are long if final and, as a rule, if followed by one consonant.

Swedish Vowel	Closest English Equivalent	Swedish Example	Swedish Vowel	Closest English Equivalent	Swedish Example
long a	a as in bar	hat, av	short o (1)	oo as in book	ost, blomma
short a	a as in aha	arv, all	short o (2)	o as in boy	om, bort
long å	o as in or	år, mål	long ö	i as in fir	för, slö
short å	o as in boy	åtta, håll	short ö	i as in fir but shorter	dörr, föll
long ä	ai as in air	äga, äta	long u	similar to u in Yule, French lui, but pronounced with more rounded lips	jul, ut
short ä	e as in best	sätta, snäll			
short ä before r	a as in hat	ärm, ärta			
long e	e as in they but closer and long like German e, French é	se, ben	short u	more open than long u, similar to u in put, but more rounded	upp, full
short e	e as in best	hem, eld	long y	like English ee, but pronounced with rounded lips; like German ü and French u in vue	sy, fyra
short e before r	a as in hat	vers, herr			
long i	ee as in see	bil, dit			
short i	i as in bit	in, sist			
long o (1)	oo as in moon	stol, sko	short y	same as long y, but shorter	synd, fylla
long o (2)	o as in or	son, sova			

CONSONANTS

Consonants which do not appear in the list below are to be given approximately the same sound as in English.

Swedish Consonant	Closest English Equivalent	Swedish Example	Swedish Consonant	Closest English Equivalent	Swedish Example
dj	y as in yes	djur	kj	ch as in child	kjol
g	g as in go before a, o, u, å; also at end of a syllable (except after l and r) and before e in a final unstressed syllable (often like k before s and t)	gata, dag, fågel (högst)	lj	y as in yes	ljus
			ng	ng as in singer, not as in finger	ängel, länge
			r	usually trilled, resembling r in through	ro, bra
	y as in yes before e, i, y, ä, ö (except before e in a final unstressed syllable); also after l and r in a final syllable	ge, helg, varg	rd, rn, rt	as in lord, barn, short in American English	bord, barn, bort
			rs	similar to sh in shoe	fors, förstå
			s	s as in so, never voiced as in his	så, gas
gj	y as in yes	gjuta	sj, skj, stj	sh as in shoe	sjö, skjul, stjärna
gn	ng as in sing before an n in the same root syllable	vagn	sk	sk as in sky before a consonant and before a, o, u, å; also before e and i in an unstressed syllable	skrika, sko, ruskig
hj	y as in yes	hjul			
j	y as in yes (or sh in a few words of French origin)	jag (journalist)		sh as in shoe before e, i, y, ä, ö (except before e and i in an unstressed syllable)	ske, skydd
k	k as in kind before a, o, u, å; also at the end of a syllable and before e and i in an unstressed syllable	kall, lik, tråkig	ti	as sh or tsh in the ending -tion in loan words	station, nation
				as tsi before e and a in loan words	aktier, initiativ
	ch as in child before e, i, y, ä, ö (except before e and i in an unstressed syllable and in a few loan words)	kedja (monarki)	tj	ch as in child	tjock
			x	ks as in six	exempel
			z	s as in so	zon

Yiddish

to English

CONTENTS

Note on Symbols. For a list of abbreviations used in the main word list, see p. 2674. The number indicated for each Yiddish verb in the word list is the key to its inflection. Verbs numbered (1) are regular and are inflected according to models found under *Present Tense, Past Tense, Future Tense*, etc., p. 3134 of the Yiddish grammar. Verbs numbered (2) through (30) are irregular; for their patterns of inflection, see the corresponding

numbers, p. 3134 of the Yiddish grammar. Letters (a) through (e), which appear in combination with certain verb numbers, are discussed on p. 3133.

Notes on Pronunciation. The pronunciation of words in the following list is indicated wherever possible by words or syllables easily recognized by English-speaking persons. Thus *meydl* is rendered MAY-*dil*. (N.B.: *g* is always hard as in "go"; the *i* sound [as in "light"] is rendered either as *i* [VIBE for *veib*] or *y* [FRY for *frei*] or *ye* [EYE-*zin* for *ayzn*]; *s* as in "measure" is rendered as *zh*.) The Yiddish sound rendered as *kh* has no standard English equivalent; it resembles the *ch* as in the Scottish word *loch*. Readers who are interested in more detailed rules of Yiddish pronunciation are referred to "Basic Key to Yiddish Pronunciation," p. 3136.

Note on Spelling. Yiddish adjectives which form compounds with the nouns they modify are indicated in the lists as prefixes; for example, oysfir-..., executive (*adj.*).

Yiddish	Pronunciation	English
a, an	AH, AHN	a (an)
"	"	per (for each)
abi velkher	*ah*-BEE VELL-*khehr*	any (any at all, *adj.*)
"	"	any (any one, *adj.*)
abi ver	*ah*-BEE VEHR	anybody (anybody whosoever)
abi vos	*ah*-BEE VAWSS	anything (anything whatever)
abonement, *m.*	*ah-baw-neh-*MENT	subscription (for periodicals)
absolut	*ahb-so-*LUTE	absolute (complete)
aderabe, yo	YAW AH-*deh-rah-beh*	yes (after negative question)
aderoyf, *m.*	AH-*deh-royf*	down payment (*bus.*)
adl, *m.*	AH-*dil*	nobility
administratsye, *f.*	*ahd-mee-nis-*TRAHTS-*yeh*	administration (*bus.*)
admiral, *m.*	*ahd-mee-*RAHL	admiral
adres, *m.*	AHD-*ress*	address (postal directions)
adresat, *m.*	*ahd-reh-*SAHT	addressee
adverb, *m.*	*ahd-*VEHRB	adverb
advokat, *m.*	*ahd-vo-*KAHT	attorney
"	"	counsel
"	"	lawyer
adyektiv, *m.*	*ahd-yeck-*TEEV	adjective
aeroplan, *m.*	*ah-eh-ro-*PLAHN	airplane
"	"	plane
afrikanish	*ahf-ree-*KAH-*nish*	African (*adj.*)
Afrike, *n.*	AHF-*ree-keh*	Africa
agent, *m.*	*ah-*G ENT	agent (representative)
agentur, *f.*	*ahg-en-*TOOR	agency (business firm)
agrikultur, *f.*	*ah-gree-kool-*TOOR	agriculture
aher	*ah-*HEHR	here (to this place, *adv.*)
aheym	*ah-*HAME	homeward
aker, *m.*	AH-*kehr*	plow (*n.*)
akern (1)	AH-*keh-rin*	plow (till), to
akhdes, *f.*	AH KH-*dess*	unity (accord)
akhrayes, *f.*	*ah kh-*RAH-*yes*	charge
"	"	liability
"	"	responsibility (accountability)
akht, *f.*	AH KHT	attention (heed)
"		notice
akht, nemen in (8)	NEH-*men in* AH KHT	heed (mind), to
akht, nit leygn genug oyf (1)	*nit* LAYG-*in g eh-*NOOG *oyf* AH KHT	neglect (slight), to
akhtleygung, *f.*	AH KHT-*lay-goon g*	care (heed)
akhzoryesdik	*ah kh-*ZOR-*yess-dik*	cruel
aksl, *m.*	AHX-*il*	shoulder (*anat.*)
akt, *m.*	AHKT	act (dramatic unit)
"	"	deed
aktiv	*ahk-*TEEV	active
aktivitet, *f.*	*ahk-tee-vee-*TEHT	activity (exertion of energy)

Yiddish	Pronunciation	English
aktivn, *pl.*	*ahk-*TEE-*vin*	asset (*bus.*)
aktn, *pl.*	AHK-*tin*	file (collection of papers)
"	"	records (files)
aktrise, *f.*	*ahk-*TREE-*seh*	actress
aktsent, *m.*	*ahk-*TSENT	accent (speech)
aktsie, *f.*	AHK-*tsee-eh*	action (deed)
aktsye, *f.*	AHKTS-*yeh*	share
aktsyes, *pl.*	AHKTS-*yess*	stock (shares)
aktsyoner, *m.*	*ahkts-yaw-*NEHR	stockholder
aktyor, *m.*	*ahk-*T YORE	actor (player)
akumulator, *m.*	*ah-koo-moo-*LAH-*tor*	battery (storage)
Alaske, *f.*	*ah-*LAHSS-*keh*	Alaska
Albanye, *f.*	*ahl-*BAHN-*yeh*	Albania
ale	AH-*leh*	all (every, *adj.*)
alef-beys, *m.*	AH-*lef-base*	alphabet
alergye, *f.*	*ah-*LEHRG-*yeh*	allergy (*med.*)
aleyn	*ah-*LANE	alone
ale yor	AH-*leh* YORE	yearly (*adv.*)
algemeyn	AHL-*g eh-mane*	general (*adj.*)
aliirter, *m.*	*ah-lee-*EER-*tehr*	ally
al-keyn	*ahl-*CANE	thus (therefore)
alkohol, *m.*	*ahl-ko-*HAWL	alcohol
"	"	liquor (alcoholic beverage)
almen, *m.*	AHL-*men*	widower
almone, *f.*	*ahl-*MAW-*neh*	widow
alt	AHLT	old
altar, *m.*	*ahl-*TAHR	altar
alt-frenkish	*ahlt-*FREN-*kish*	quaint (unusual)
alt-gebakn	AHLT-*g eh-*BAH-*kin*	stale
alts	AHLTS	all (everything, *n.*)
altsding	*ahlts-*DEEN G	everything (*pron.*)
aluminyum, *n.*	*ah-loo-*MEEN-*yoom*	aluminum
alyants, *f.*	*ahl-*YAHNTS	alliance
ambasador, *m.*	*ahm-bah-*SAH-*dor*	ambassador
ambitsye, *f.*	*ahm-*BEETS-*yeh*	ambition
ambitsyez	*ahm-beets-*YEHZ	ambitious (aspiring)
ambulans, *m.*	*ahm-boo-*LAHNSS	ambulance
amerikanish	*ah-meh-ree-*KAH-*nish*	American (*adj.*)
Amerike, *f.*	*ah-*MEH-*ree-keh*	America
amortizatsye, *f.*	*ah-mor-tee-*ZAHTS-*yeh*	amortization (*bus.*)
amortizirn (1b)	*ah-mor-tee-*ZEE-*rin*	amortize, to
Amsterdam, *n.*	AHM-*stehr-dahm*	Amsterdam
amstl, *m.*	AHMS-*til*	blackbird
amt, *m.*	AHMT	office (position)
an (see a)		
ander	AHN-*dehr*	different (unlike)
"	"	other (*adj.*)
ander, an	*ahn* AHN-*dehr*	another (*adj.*)
andere, an	*ahn* AHN-*deh-reh*	another (different one, *pron.*)
anderer	AHN-*deh-rehr*	other (*pron.*)
anderer, an	*ahn* AHN-*deh-rehr*	another (different one, *pron.*)

Yiddish	Pronunciation	English
andersh	AHN-*dehrsh*	else (different, *adj.*)
"	"	otherwise (contrarily)
andersh, zayn (18d)	*zine* AHN-*dehrsh*	differ (be unlike), to
"	"	vary (differ), to
andersh vu	AHN-*dehrsh voo*	elsewhere
anit	*ah-*NEET	else (if not, *adv.*)
"	"	else (instead, *adv.*)
"	"	otherwise (under other conditions)
anives,*f.*	*ah-*NEE-*vess*	humility
anker,*m.*	AHN-*kehr*	anchor
anons,*m.*	*ah-*NAWNSS	advertisement
anonsirn (1b)	*ah-nawn-*SEE-*rin*	advertise (give notice of), to
anshtalt,*f.*	*ahn-*SHTAHLT	asylum (institution)
anshtot	*ahn-*SHTAWT	instead of
antene,*f.*	*ahn-*TEH-*neh*	aerial (antenna)
antibiotik,*m.*	*ahn-tee-bee-*AW-*tick*	antibiotic
antipatye,*f.*	*ahn-tee-*PAHT-*yeh*	dislike
antkegn	*ahnt-*KEG-*in*	opposite (*prep.*)
antkegnshteln zikh (1a)	*ahnt-*K EG-*in-shteh-lin zikh*	oppose (combat), to
"	"	resist, to
antlayen (9b)	*ahnt-*LYE-*en*	borrow, to
antlayer,*m.*	*ahnt-*LYE-*ehr*	borrower (*bus.*)
antloyfn (7bd)	*ahnt-*LOY-*fin*	escape, to
"	"	flee (run from), to
antloyfn,*n.*	*ahnt-*LOY-*fin*	flight (hasty departure)
antmutikn (1b)	*ahnt-*MOO-*tee-kin*	discourage (dishearten), to
antologye,*f.*	*ahn-toh-*LAWG-*yeh*	anthology
antplekn (1b)	*ahnt-*PLEH-*kin*	expose (lay open), to
antropologye,*f.*	*ahn-tro-po-*LAWG-*yeh*	anthropology
antshedikung,*f.*	*ahnt-*SHEH-*dee-koon_g*	damages (indemnification)
"	"	indemnity (compensation)
antshlosnkayt,*f.*	*ahnt-*SHLAW-*sin-kite*	determination (fixed intent)
antshuldikn (1b)	*ahnt-*SHOOL-*dee-kin*	excuse, to
"	"	pardon (forgive), to
anttoyshn (1b)	*ahnt-*TOY-*shin*	disappoint, to
anttoyshung,*f.*	*ahnt-*TOY-*shoon_g*	disappointment
antviklen (1b)	*ahnt-*VEEK-*len*	develop, to
antviklung,*f.*	*ahnt-*VEEK-*loon_g*	development
anulirn (1b)	*ah-noo-*LEE-*rin*	cancel (revoke), to
anumlt	*ah-*NOO-*milt*	recently
anumltik	*ah-*NOO-*mil-tick*	recent
aparat,*m.*	*ah-pah-*RAHT	camera
apelirn (1b)	*ah-peh-*LEE-*rin*	appeal (ask reconsideration of), to
apenditsit,*m.*	*ah-pen-dee-*TSEET	appendicitis
apetit,*m.*	*ah-peh-*TEET	appetite
aplikatsye,*f.*	*ah-plee-*KAHTS-*yeh*	application (request)
aplodirn (1b)	*ah-plo-*DEE-*rin*	cheer (applaud), to
"	"	clap (applaud), to
aplodisment,*m.*	*ah-plo-diss-*MENT	applause
apostol,*m.*	*ah-pawss-*TAWL	apostle
aprikos,*m.*	*ahp-ree-*KAWSS.	apricot
apteyk,*f.*	*ahp-*TAKE.	pharmacy (drug store)
apteyker,*m.*	*ahp-*TAY-*kehr*	pharmacist
araynfir,*m.*	*ah-*RINE-*fear*	introduction (preliminary part)
araynfirn (1a)	*ah-*RINE-*fee-rin*	introduce (bring in) to
arayngang,*m.*	*ah-*RINE-*gahn_g*	entrance
arayngeton	*ah-*RINE-*g_eh-tawn*	intent (engrossed)
arayngeyn in (14ad)	*ah-*RINE-*gain een*	enter (come or go into), to
"	"	enter (join), to
araynlozn (1a)	*ah-*RINE-*law-zin*	admit (permit to enter), to
araynmishn zikh (1a)	*ah-*RINE-*mee-shin zikh*	interfere (meddle), to
araynnem,*m.*	*ah-*RINE-*nem*	capacity (volume)
araynnemen (8a)	*ah-*RINE-*neh-men*	contain, to
"	"	embrace, to
"	"	include, to
araynraysn zikh in (9a)	*ah-*RINE-*rye-sin zikh een*	invade, to (*mil.*)
araynshraybn (9a)	*ah-*RINE-*shrye-bin*	enter (make record of), to
araynshraybung,*f.*	*ah-*RINE-*shrye-boon_g*	entry (*acctg.*)
araynshtekn (1a)	*ah-*RINE-*shteh-kin*	stick (thrust), to
araynton (22a)	*ah-*RINE-*tawn*	insert, to
arayntrit,*m.*	*ah-*RINE-*treet*	admission (right to enter)
araynvarfn zikh (7a)	*ah-*RINE-*var-fin zikh*	plunge (hurl oneself), to
arbes,*m.*	AR-*bess*	pea
arbet,*f.*	AR-*bet*	work (labor)
arbeter,*m.*	AR-*beh-tehr*	worker
arbet-geber,*m.*	AR-*bet-g_eh-behr*	employer (boss)
arbet-hoytsoes,*pl.*	AR-*bet-hoy-tsaw-ess*	operating expenses (*bus.*)
arbetkraft,*f.*	AR-*bet-krahft*	labor (labor force)
arbetn (1)	AR-*beh-tin*	work (labor), to
arbetn bay	AR-*beh-tin bye*	operate (handle), to
arbetsloz	AR-*bets-laws*	unemployed
arbetslozikayt,*f.*	AR-*bets-law-zee-kite*	unemployment
arbl,*m.*	AR-*bil*	sleeve
arestant,*m.*	*ah-res-*TAHNT	prisoner
arestirn (1b)	*ah-ress-*TEE-*rin*	arrest (take into custody), to
Argentine,*f.*	*arg-en-*TEE-*neh*	Argentina
argentinish	*arg-en-*TEE-*nish*	Argentinian (*adj.*)
ariber	*ah-*REE-*behr*	across (from side to side)
"	"	across (to the other side)
"	"	over (across, *prep.*)
ariberfirer,*m.*	*ah-*REE-*behr-fee-rehr*	carrier (*bus.*)
ariberfirn (1a)	*ah-*REE-*behr-fee-rin*	convey, to
"	"	transport, to
ariberfirn,*n.*	*ah-*REE-*behr-fee-rin*	transit (passage)
"	"	transportation (conveying)
ariberforn,*n.*	*ah-*REE-*behr-faw-rin*	crossing (ocean voyage)
aribergeyn (14ad)	*ah-*REE-*behr-gain*	cross (traverse), to
"	"	exceed, to
ariberklaybn zikh (9a)	*ah-*REE-*behr-*KLYE-*bin zikh*	move (change residence), to
aribershtaygn (9a)	*ah-*REE-*behr-shtye-g_in*	surpass, to
aritmetik,*f.*	*ah-rit-*MEH-*tick*	arithmetic
arkhitekt,*m.*	*ar-khee-*TEKT	architect
armey,*f.*	*ar-*MAY	army
arn (1)	AH-*rin*	care (be concerned), to
aromat,*m.*	*ah-ro-*MAHT	flavor (savor)
arop	*ah-*RAWP	down (downward, *adv.*)
aroplozn (1a)	*ah-*RAWP-*law-zin*	launch (set afloat), to
"	"	lower, to
aropnemen (8a)	*ah-*RAWP-*neh-men*	subtract, to
aropnidern (1a)	*ah-*RAWP-*nee-deh-rin*	descend (move downward), to
aroprekhenen (3a)	*ah-*RAWP-*reh-kheh-nen*	debit, to
"	"	deduct, to
aroptsien (23a)	*aw-*RAWP-*tsee-en*	strip (denude), to
aropvarfn (7a)	*ah-*RAWP-*var-fin*	shed (cast off), to
aroyf	*ah-*ROYF	upward (to a higher level, *adv.*)
aroyf di trep	*ah-*ROYF *dee* TREP	upstairs (to upper story, *adv.*)
aroyfkrikhn (7ad)	*ah-*ROYF-*kree-khin*	ascend (go upward along), to
aroyfkrikhn oyf	*ah-*ROYF-*kree-khin oyf*	mount (climb upon), to
aroys	*ah-*ROYSS	out (forth, *adv.*)
aroysgang,*m.*	*ah-*ROYSS-*gahn_g*	exit
aroysgeber,*m.*	*ah-*ROYSS-*g_eh-behr*	publisher
aroysgebn (13a)	*ah-*ROYSS-*g_eh-bin*	betray (reveal), to
"	"	publish, to
aroysgebn a psak	*ah-*ROYSS-*g_eh-bin ah* PSAHK	pronounce (declare), to
aroysgerufn vern (7cd)	*ah-*ROYSS-*g_eh-roo-fin veh-rin*	recite (repeat something learned), to
aroysgevorfn	*ah-*ROYSS-*g_eh-*VOR-*fin*	idle (useless)
"	"	vain (futile)
aroyskrign (7a)	*ah-*ROYSS-*kreeg-in*	derive (get), to
aroyskuk,*m.*	*ah-*ROYSS-*cook*	expectation
aroyskumen (5ad)	*ah-*ROYSS-*koo-men*	emerge, to
"	"	follow (result), to
aroyslozn zikh (1a)	*ah-*ROYSS-*law-zin zikh*	start (set out), to
aroysraysn (9a)	*ah-*ROYSS-*rye-sin*	wrench (wrest), to

Yiddish	Pronunciation	English
aroysredn (1a)	*ah*-ROYSS-*reh-din*	pronounce (enunciate), to
aroysruf,*m.*	*ah*-ROYSS-*roof*	challenge
aroysrufn (5a)	*ah*-ROYSS-*roo-fin*	summon (send for), to
aroysshtartsndik	*ah*-ROYSS-*shtart-sin-dick*	prominent (jutting)
aroystraybn (9a)	*ah*-ROYSS-*try-bin*	expel (eject), to
aroyszogn (1a)	*ah*-ROYSS-*zawg-in*	express (state), to
arterye,*f.*	*ar*-TEHR-*yeh*	artery (*anat.*)
artikl,*m.*	*ar*-TEE-*kil*	article (literary composition)
artrit,*m.*	*ar*-TREET	arthritis
arts,*n.*	ARTS	ore
arum	*ah*-ROOM	around (*prep.*)
arum,*m.*	*ah*-ROOM	surroundings
arumforn (5ad,	*ah*-ROOM-*faw-rin*	travel, to
arumnem,*m.*	*ah*-ROOM-*nem*	circumference
arumnemen (8a)	*ah*-ROOM-*neh-men*	clasp, to
"	"	embrace (hug), to
arumredn (1a)	*ah*-ROOM-*reh-din*	discuss, to
arumringlen (1a)	*ah*-ROOM-*rin-glen*	surround (enclose), to
arumtsamen (1a)	*ah*-ROOM-*tsah-men*	enclose (surround), to
arumvandern (1a)	*ah*-ROOM-*vahn-deh-rin*	rove, to
arunter	*ah*-ROON-*tehr*	downward (*adv.*)
a sakh, merer, merste	*ah* SAH_KH, MEH-*rehr*, MEHR-*steh*	many, more, most
asekuratsye,*f.*	*ah-seh-koo*-RAHTS-*yeh*	insurance
asekurirn (1b)	*ah-seh-koo*-REE-*rin*	insure (buy insurance on), to
ash,*n.*	AHSH	ashes
ashires,*f.*	*ah*-SHEE-*ress*	fortune
"	"	riches
"	"	wealth
ashmitvokh,*m.*	AHSH-*mit-vukh*	Ash Wednesday
ashtetsl,*n.*	AHSH-*teh-tsil*	ash tray
asistent,*m.*	*ah-sis*-TENT	assistant
aspekt,*m.*	*ahss*-PEHKT	aspect (phase)
aspirin,*f.*	*ahss-pee*-REEN	aspirin
atake,*f.*	*ah*-TAH-*keh*	offense (attack)
Aten,*n.*	*ah*-TEHN	Athens
Atlantik,*m.*	*aht*-LAHN-*tick*	Atlantic (*n.*)
atlas,*m.*	AHT-*lahss*	atlas
atles,*m.*	AHT-*less*	satin (*n.*)
atlet,*m.*	*aht*-LEHT	athlete
atletish	*aht*-LEH-*lish*	athletic
atmosfer,*f.*	*aht-moss*-FEHR	atmosphere
atom,*m.*	*ah*-TAWM	atom
atomishe bombe,*f.*	*ah*-TAW-*mee-sheh* BAWM-*beh*	atomic bomb
atraktsye,*f.*	*ah*-TRAHK_TS-*yeh*	attraction
atsind	*ah*-TSEEND	now (*adv.*)
avade	*ah*-VAH-*deh*	certainly (*interj.*)
"	"	course, of
avanture,*f.*	*ah-vahn*-TOO-*reh*	adventure
avek	*ah*-VECK	away (from a place, *adv.*)
avekforn (5ad)	*ah*-VECK-*faw-rin*	depart (leave), to
avekgeyn (14ad)	*ah*-VECK-*gain*	leave (depart), to
avekshikn (1a)	*ah*-VECK-*shee-kin*	mail (post), to
avekvarfn (7a)	*ah*-VECK-*var-fin*	abandon (give up), to
avle,*f.*	AHV-*leh*	wrong (injustice)
aylenish,*f.*	EYE-*leh-nish*	haste
"	"	hurry
aylik	EYE-*lick*	hasty (hurried)
ayln zikh (1)	EYE-*lin zikh*	hurry (hasten), to
"	"	rush (dash), to
aynbrekher,*m.*	INE-*breh-khehr*	burglar
ayndreyen (1a)	INE-*dray-en*	twist (wind), to
aynengen (1a)	INE-*en-g_en*	qualify (modify), to
aynfal,*m.*	INE-*fahl*	fancy
"	"	notion (idea)
aynfaln (5ad)	INE-*fah-lin*	collapse (cave in), to
ayngeboyrn	INE-*g_eh-boy-rin*	native (indigenous)
ayngegleybt	INE-*g_eh-glabe_t*	superstitious
ayngemakhts,*n.*	INE-*g_eh-mah_khts*	jam (preserve)
ayngenem	INE-*g_eh-nem*	pleasant
ayngeshlofn	INE-*g_eh-shlaw-fin*	asleep
ayngleybenish,*f.*	INE-*glay-beh-nish*	superstition

Yiddish	Pronunciation	English
ayngos,*m.*	INE-*gawss*	bay (inlet)
"	"	gulf (large bay)
aynhaltn (5a)	INE-*hahl-tin*	restrain (check), to
aynhern zikh (1a)	INE-*heh-rin zikh*	listen (hearken), to
aynkasirn (1a)	INE-*kah-see-rin*	cash (receive cash for), to
aynkneln (1a)	INE-*k_neh-lin*	coach (train), to
aynkoyf,*m.*	INE-*koyf*	purchase (act of buying)
aynkoyfn (1a)	INE-*koy-fin*	shop, to
aynkukn zikh (1a)	INE-*koo-kin zikh*	gaze, to
"	"	peer (look intently), to
aynmonen (1a)	INE-*maw-nen*	collect, to (*bus.*)
aynnemen (8a)	INE-*neh-men*	conquer, to
aynnemen,*n.*	INE-*neh-men*	conquest
aynnetsn (1a)	INE-*net-sin*	wet, to
aynordenen (3a)	INE-*or-deh-nen*	accommodate (have room for), to
"	"	arrange (plan), to
aynpakn (1a)	INE-*pah-kin*	pack, to
aynpakung,*f.*	INE-*pah-koon_g*	packing (*n.*)
aynrikhtn (1a)	INE-*reekh-tin*	soil (make dirty), to
aynshafn (5a)	INE-*shah-fin*	secure (obtain), to
aynshpritsung,*f.*	INE-*sphree-tsoon_g*	injection (*med.*)
aynshrift,*f.*	INE-*shrift*	inscription
aynshtelenish,*f.*	INE-*shteh-leh-nish*	venture
aynshteln (1a)	INE-*shteh-lin*	venture (dare), to
aynshteyn (17ad)	INE-*shtane*	lodge (reside), to
aynshtiln (1a)	INE-*shtee-lin*	appease (calm), to
"	"	hush (make quiet), to
"	"	lull (quiet), to
ayntsien (23a)	INE-*tsee-en*	contract (make shrink), to
ayntsien zikh	INE-*tsee-en zikh*	shrink (become contracted), to
ayntsoler,*m.*	INE-*tsaw-lehr*	depositor (*fin.*)
ayntsoln (1a)	INE-*tsaw-lin*	deposit, to (*fin.*)
ayntsolung,*f.*	INE-*tsaw-loon_g*	deposit (money deposited)
aynvendn (1a)	INE-*ven-din*	object, to
aynvendung,*f.*	INE-*ven-doon_g*	objection
aynveykn (1a)	INE-*vay-kin*	soak (saturate), to
aynviklen (1a)	INE-*vick-len*	wrap (envelop), to
aynvoyner,*m.*	INE-*voy-nehr*	inhabitant
"	"	resident (*n.*)
aynzapn (1a)	INE-*zah-pin*	absorb (suck up), to
aynzeenish,*n.*	INE-*zeh-eh-nish*	consideration (regard)
aynzeenish, on	AWN INE-*zeh-eh-nish*	unreasonable (unreasoning)
aynzen (6a)	INE-*zen*	realize, to
aynzinken (8ad)	INE-*zin-ken*	sink (become submerged), to
ayz,*n.*	IZE	ice (frozen water)
ayzik	EYE-*zick*	icy
ayzkastn,*m.*	IZE-*kah-stin*	icebox
ayzkrem,*m.*	IZE-*krem*	ice-cream
ayzn,*n.*	EYE-*zin*	iron (metal)
ayznvarg,*n.*	EYE-*zin-varg*	hardware
az	AHZ	that (*conj.*)
aza	*ah*-ZAH	such (of that kind, *adj.*)
azoy	*ah*-ZOY	so (to such a degree, *adv.*)
"	"	thus (in this way)
azoy vi	*ah*-ZOY *vee*	as (equally, *adv.*)
"	"	as (in the same way, *conj.*)
azyatish	*ahz*-YAH-*tish*	Asiatic (*adj.*)
Azye,*f.*	AHZ-*yeh*	Asia
baamter,*m.*	*bah*-AHM-*tehr*	official (*n.*)
baarbetn (1b)	*bah*-AR-*beh-tin*	till (cultivate), to
badarfn (1be)	*bah*-DAR-*fin*	require (need), to
baderfenish,*f.*	*bah*-DEHR-*feh-nish*	want (need)
bading,*m.*	*bah*-DEEN_G	provision (stipulation)
badoyern (1b)	*bah*-DAW-*yeh-rin*	regret, to
"	"	sorry, to be
badoyern,*n.*	*bah*-DAW-*yeh-rin*	regret (sorrow)
badrikn (1b)	*bah*-DREEK-*in*	oppress (tyrannize), to
"	"	oppress (weigh down), to

Yiddish	Pronunciation	English
bafaln (5bd)	bah-FAH-lin	assault, to
"	"	attack (assault physically), to
bafel, m.	bah-FELL	command
"	"	order
bafelkerung, f.	bah-FELL-keh-roon_g	population (number of people)
bafeln (10b)	bah-FEH-lin	command, to
"	"	order, to
bafrayen (1b)	bah-FRY-en	free, to
"	"	liberate, to
"	"	relieve, to
"	"	rid, to
bafridikn (1b)	bah-FREE-dee-kin	satisfy, to
bafridikndik	bah-FREE-dee-kin-dick	satisfactory
bafridikt	bah-FREE-dikt	content
"	"	satisfied
bafridikung, f.	bah-FREE-dee-koon_g	satisfaction (content-ment)
"	"	satisfaction (grati-fication)
baganvenen (4b)	bah-GAHN-veh-nen	rob (steal from), to
bagazh, m.	bah-GAH_ZH	baggage
"	"	luggage
bager, m.	bah-G_EHR	desire
"	"	wish
bagern (1b)	bah-G_EH-rin	desire (long for), to
bageyn (14bd)	bah-GAIN	commit (perpetrate), to
bagleyter, m.	bah-GLAY-tehr	escort (social com-panion)
bagleytn (1b)	bah-GLAY-tin	accompany (go along with); to
bagnedikung, f.	bah-GNEH-dee-koon_g	pardon (law)
bagrayfn (9b)	bah-GRYE-fin	comprehend (under-stand), to
bagrenetsn (1b)	bah-GREH-neh-tsin	confine, to
"	"	limit, to
bagrisn (1b)	bah-GREE-sin	greet (salute), to
"	"	welcome (receive hospitably), to
bagrisung, f.	bah-GREE-soon_g	greeting
bagrobn (5b)	bah-GRAW-bin	bury (entomb), to
bahaltn (5b)	bah-HAHL-tin	hide (conceal), to
bahandlen (1b)	bah-HAHND-len	treat (behave to-ward), to
bahandlen, shlekht	shlekht bah-HAHND-len	abuse (misuse), to
bahandlung, f.	bah-HAHND-loon_g	treatment (behavior toward)
"	"	treatment (medical care)
bahershn (1b)	bah-HEHR-shin	control, to
"	"	master (learn), to
bak, f.	BAHK	cheek
bak, m.	BAHK	tank (container)
bakant	bah-KAHNT	familiar (well-known)
bakanter, m.	bah-KAHN-tehr	acquaintance (person known)
bakemfn (1b)	bah-KEM-fin	contest (dispute), to
"	"	fight (struggle against), to
bakenen (1b)	bah-KEH-nen	acquaint (inform), to
"	"	introduce (make ac-quainted), to
bakenen zikh mit	bah-KEH-nen zikh mit	meet (be introduced to) to
baklogn zikh (1b)	bah-KLAWG-in zikh	complain to
bakn zikh (5)	BAH-kin zikh	bake (be cooking), to
bakoshe, f.	bah-KAW-sheh	appeal (entreaty)
"	"	request
bakumen, n.	bah-KOO-men	receipt (receiving)
bakumen (5b)	bah-KOO-men	receive, to
bakvem	bahk-VEM	comfortable (afford-ing comfort)
"	"	convenient
bakvemkayt, f.	bahk-VEM-kite	comfort (ease)
"	"	convenience
balagan, m.	bah-lah-GAHN	mess (muddle)
balaybt	bah-LIBE_T	stout (corpulent)
balaykhtn (10b)	bah-LYE_KH-tin	illuminate (eluci-date), to
"	"	illuminate (light up), to
"	"	light, to
bald	BAHLD	soon (shortly)
balebatishkayt, f.	bah-leh-BAH-tish-kite	household

Yiddish	Pronunciation	English
balebos, m.	bah-leh-BOSS	master (one in authority)
baleboste, f.	bah-leh-BOSS-teh	housewife
balegerung, f.	bah-LEG-eh-roon_g	siege (mil.)
baleydikn (1b)	bah-LAY-dee-kin	offend (affront), to
baleydikung, f.	bah-LAY-dee-koon_g	insult
balibt	bah-LEEBT	beloved (adj.)
"	"	favorite (adj.)
"	"	popular (well-liked)
bal-khoyv, m.	bahl-KHOYV	debtor (bus.)
balkn, m.	BAHL-kin	beam (rafter)
bal-nitsokhn, m.	bahl-nee-TSAW-khin	victor
balon, m.	bah-LAWN	balloon
baloynen (1b)	bah-LOY-nen	reward, to
bal-pe	bahl-PEH	oral (spoken)
bamerkn (1b)	bah-MEHR-kin	note (perceive), to
"	"	notice (see), to
"	"	observe, to
"	"	remark (say), to
bamerkung, f.	bah-MEHR-koon_g	comment
"	"	remark
bamien zikh (1b)	bah-MEE-en zikh	endeavor, to
bamiung, f.	bah-MEE-oon_g	endeavor
ban, f.	BAHN	railroad
banane, f.	bah-NAH-neh	banana
banayen (1b)	bah-NAH-yen	renew, to
band, m.	BAHND	bond (emotional tie)
"	"	volume (book)
bandazh, m.	bahn-DAH_ZH	bandage
bandazhirn (1b)	bahn-dah-ZHEE-rin	dress, to (med.)
bande, f.	BAHN-deh	band
"	"	gang
bandit, m.	bahn-DEET	bandit
band-rekordirer, m.	BAHND-rek-kor-dee-rehr	tape recorder
bandzho, m.	BAHN-jo	banjo
bank, f.	BAHNK	bench (long seat)
bank, m.	BAHNK	bank (treasury)
banket, m.	bahn-KET	banquet
bankir, m.	bahn-KEER	banker
bankireray, f.	bahn-KEE-reh-rye	banking
banknot, m.	bahnk-NAWT	bill (currency)
bankrot, m.	bahnk-RAWT	bankruptcy
"	"	failure (bus.)
banuts, m.	bah-NOOTS	use (utilization)
baputsn (1b)	bah-POO-tsin	decorate (adorn), to
"	"	dress, to
"	"	trim, to
baputsung, f.	bah-POO-tsoon_g	decoration
baputsungen, on	AWN bah-POO-tsoon_g-en	severe (austere)
bar, m.	BAR	bar (barroom)
baran, m.	BAH-rahn	ram (animal)
barekhtikn (1b)	bah-REH_KH-tee-kin	entitle (give a right to), to
"	"	justify (defend), to
"	"	warrant, to
barg, m.	BARG	mountain
bargik	BARG-ick	mountainous
bargkeyt, f.	BARG-kate	range (of mountains)
"	"	ridge (of mountains)
barikht, m.	bah-REEKHT	account
"	"	report
barimen zikh (1b)	bah-REE-men zikh	boast, to
barimt	bah-REEMT	famous
barminen, m.	BAR-mee-nen	corpse
barne, f.	BAR-neh	pear
barometer, m.	bah-ro-MEH-tehr	barometer
barsht, f.	BARSHT	brush (scrubbing utensil)
baruikn (1b)	bah-ROO-ee-kin	soothe (calm), to
bashafn (5b)	bah-SHAH-fin	create, to
bashafung, f.	bah-SHAH-foon_g	creation
bashaymperlekh	bah-SHIME-pehr-lukh	apparent (obvious)
"	"	manifest (adj.)
bashefenish, n.	bah-SHEH-feh-nish	creature (living being)
basheftikn (1)	bah-SHEF-tee-kin	occupy (make busy), to
basheftikung, f.	bah-SHEF-tee-koon_g	employment (work)
bashenken (7b)	bah-SHEN-kin	bestow, to
basheydn	bah-SHAY-din	modest
bashitser, m.	bah-SHEE-tsehr	guardian (protector)

Yiddish	Pronunciation	English
bashitsn (1b)	*bah*-SHEE-*tsin*	protect, to / shield, to
bashitsung, *f.*	*bah*-SHEE-*tsoon_g*	protection
bashlisn (7b)	*bah*-SHLEE-*sin*	decide (make up one's mind), to
bashlisn bay zikh	*bah*-SHLEE-*sin bye zikh*	determine (make up one's mind), to
bashlus, *m.*	*bah*-SHLOOSS	decision (judgment)
bashonken	*bah*-SHAWN-*ken*	gifted (talented)
bashprenklen (1b)	*bah*-SHPRENK-*len*	sprinkle (scatter), to / spray, to
bashraybn (9b)	*bah*-SHRYE-*bin*	describe (portray), to
bashraybung, *f.*	*bah*-SHRYE-*boon_g*	description (account)
bashtayern (1b)	*bah*-SHTYE-*eh-rin*	assess (impose tax), to
bashteln (1b)	*bah*-SHTEH-*lin*	book (engage space), to / order (purchase), to
bashtelung, *f.*	*bah*-SHTEH-*loon_g*	appointment (meeting) / date / engagement / order (purchase)
bashtetikn (1b)	*bah*-SHTEH-*tee-kin*	acknowledge (note receipt of), to / approve (sanction), to / certify, to / confirm (corroborate), to
bashtetikung, *f.*	*bah*-SHTEH-*tee-koon_g*	certificate / confirmation (corroboration)
bashteyn (17bd)	*bah*-SHTANE	insist, to
bashteyn fun	*bah*-SHTANE *foon*	consist of (comprise), to
bashtimen (1b)	*bah*-SHTEE-*men*	appoint, to / fix (settle), to / resolve (determine), to
bashtimt	*bah*-SHTEEMT	definite
bashtimung, *f.*	*bah*-SHTEE-*moon_g*	appointment (nomination)
bashuldikn (1b)	*bah*-SHOOL-*dee-kin*	accuse, to / blame, to / charge, to
bashuldikung, *f.*	*bah*-SHOOL-*dee-koon_g*	accusation / charge
bataamt	*bah*-TAHMT	delicious
batayt, *m.*	*bah*-TIGHT	meaning (sense) / significance (importance)
bataytik	*bah*-TIE-*tick*	significant (meaningful)
bataytn (1b)	*bah*-TIE-*tin*	signify (denote), to
batereyke, *f.*	*bah-tah-*RAY-*keh*	flashlight
baterye, *f.*	*bah*-TEHR-*yeh*	battery (artillery) / battery (primary cell)
batrakhtn (1b)	*bah*-TRAH_KH-*tin*	consider (reflect on), to / regard, to / watch (observe), to
batrakhtung, *f.*	*bah*-TRAH_KH-*toon_g*	consideration (thought)
batrefn (7b)	*bah*-TREH-*fin*	amount to, to
batseykhenen (3b)	*bah*-TSAY-*kheh-nen*	mark (designate), to
batsirn (1b)	*bah*-TSEE-*rin*	adorn (beautify), to
bavakhn (1b)	*bah*-VAH-*khin*	watch (guard), to
bavaserung, *f.*	*bah*-VAH-*seh-roon_g*	irrigation
bavayz, *m.*	*bah*-VIZE	demonstration / evidence / proof
bavayzn (9b)	*bah*-VYE-*zin*	demonstrate (show), to
bavayzn zikh	*bah*-VYE-*zin zikh*	appear (come in sight), to
bavegung, *f.*	*bah*-VEH-*goon_g*	motion / movement
bavilikn (1b)	*bah*-VEE-*lee-kin*	grant (bestow), to
bavl, *m.*	BAH-*vil*	cotton
bavofenen (3b)	*bah*-VAW-*feh-nen*	arm, to
bavorenish, *f.*	*bah*-VAW-*reh-nish*	reservation (mental qualification)
bavoynen (1b)	*bah*-VOY-*nen*	inhabit, to
bavundern (1b)	*bah*-VOON-*deh-rin*	admire, to
bavunderung, *f.*	*bah*-VOON-*deh-roon_g*	admiration
bavust	*bah*-VOOST	known (familiar)
bay	BYE	at (by) / at (in) / by (near, *prep.*)
Bayern, *n.*	BYE-*eh-rin*	Bavaria
baykumen (5ad)	BYE-*koo-men*	overcome (conquer), to
baylage, *f.*	BYE-*lahg-eh*	enclosure (addition)
bayleygn (1a)	BYE-*layg-in*	enclose (include in envelope), to
baym zinen	*bime* ZEE-*nen*	sane
bayprodukt, *m.*	BYE-*pro-dookt*	by-product
bayshpil, *m.*	BYE-*shpil*	instance (example)
baysn (9)	BYE-*sin*	bite, to
bayt, *m.*	BITE	change (alteration)
baytl, *n.*	BYE-*til*	purse (coin pouch)
baytn (9)	BYE-*lin*	alter, to / change (make different), to
baytn zikh	BYE-*tin zikh*	change (become different), to / vary (undergo change), to
baytsh, *f.*	BYE_CH	lash / whip
bayzayn, *n.*	BYE-*zine*	presence (being present)
bayzayn (18ad)	BYE-*zine*	attend (be present at), to
bazaytikung, *f.*	*bah*-ZYE-*tee-koon_g*	disposition (disposal)
baze, *f.*	BAH-*zeh*	base (foundation)
bazetsn zikh (1b)	*bah*-ZEH-*tsin zikh*	settle (make one's home), to
bazign (1b)	*bah*-ZEEG-*in*	defeat (conquer), to
bazirn (1b)	*bah*-ZEE-*rin*	base (found), to
bazitser, *m.*	*bah*-ZEE-*tsehr*	owner
Bazl, *n.*	BAH-*zil*	Basle
bazukh, *m.*	*bah*-ZOOKH	attendance (presence) / visit (stay)
bazukher, *m.*	*bah*-ZOO-*khehr*	visitor
bazukhn (1b)	*bah*-ZOO-*khin*	visit (go to view), to
bazunder	*bah*-ZOON-*dehr*	apart / separate
bedeye hobn (25)	*beh*-DEH-*yeh haw-bin*	intend (propose), to
beemes	*beh*-EH-*mess*	really (actually) / really (indeed)
beerakh	*beh*-EH-*rukh*	about (approximately)
befeyresh	*beh*-FAY-*resh*	positive (decisive)
behadrogedik	*beh-hah-*DRAWG-*eh-dick*	gradual
behole, *f.*	*beh*-HAW-*leh*	confusion (disorder)
beker, *m.*	BEH-*kehr*	baker
bekheyn	*beh*-KHAYN	consequently / hence
bekivndik	*beh*-KEE-*vin-dick*	deliberate (intentional)
bekovedik	*beh*-KAW-*veh-dick*	honorable (upright)
belgish	BEHL-*g_ish*	Belgian (*adj.*)
Belgye, *f.*	BEHLG-*yeh*	Belgium
benken nokh (1)	BEN-*ken* NUH_KH	long for, to / miss (feel the loss of), to
benoygeye	*beh-noy-*GAY-*eh*	concerning (regarding)
bentshn (1)	BEN-*chin*	bless, to
ber, *m.*	BEHR	bear (animal)
bergele, *n.*	BEHRG-*eh-leh*	mound (hill)
bergl, *n.*	BEHRG-*il*	hill
Berlin, *n.*	*behr*-LEEN	Berlin
Bern, *n.*	BEH-*rin*	Berne
beryesh	BEHR-*yesh*	efficient (competent)
beryeshaft, *f.*	BEHR-*yeh-shahft*	dexterity / skill (proficiency)
beryoze, *f.*	*behr*-YAW-*zeh*	birch (tree)
berze, *f.*	BEHR-*zeh*	exchange, stock
beser	BEH-*sehr*	better (*adj.*) / better (*adv.*)
beshas	*beh*-SHAHSS	as (*conj.*) / during / while (during the time that, *conj.*)
beshefe	*beh*-SHEH-*feh*	ample
besholem	*beh*-SHAW-*lem*	safe (unharmed)

Yiddish	Pronunciation	English
beshutfesdik	*beh*-SHOOT-*fess-dick*	joint (combined)
best	BEHSST	best (*adj.*)
bestye, *f.*	BEST-*yeh*	brute (animal, *n.*)
bet, *f.*	BET	bed
betl, *n.*	BEH-*til*	berth (train bunk)
"	"	cot
betlen (1)	BET-*len*	beg (solicit alms), to
betler, *m.*	BET-*lehr*	beggar
betn (5)	BEH-*tin*	ask, to
"	"	request, to
betn zikh	BEH-*tin zikh*	plead (appeal earnestly), to
betn zikh bay	BEH-*tin zikh bye*	appeal to (entreat), to
"	"	beg (entreat), to
beton, *m.*	*beh*-TAWN	concrete (artificial stone)
beyde	BAY-*deh*	both (*adj.*)
"	"	both (*pron.*)
beygn (10)	BEYG-*in*	bend (make bend), to
beygn zikh	BEYG-*in zikh*	bend (be bent), to
"	"	lean, to
"	"	slant (slope), to
beykon, *m.*	BAY-*kin*	bacon
beyn, *m.*	BANE	bone
beyn-hashmoshes, *m.*	*bane-hah-*SHMAW-*shess*	twilight
beysbol, *m.*	BASE-*bawl*	baseball
beysbol-bet, *m.*	BASE-*bawl-bat*	bat (club)
beys-oylem, *m.*	*bay-*SOY-*lem*	cemetery
beyz	BAZE	evil (*adj.*)
beyz, *n.*	BAZE	evil (*n.*)
bez, *m.*	BEZ	lilac (flower)
bezem, *m.*	BEH-*zem*	broom
biber, *m.*	BEE-*behr*	beaver (animal)
bibl, *f.*	BEE-*bil*	Bible
bibliografye, *f.*	*beeb-lee-o-*GRAHF-*yeh*	bibliography
bibliotek, *f.*	*bib-lee-o-*TECK	library
bibliotekar, *m.*	*bib-lee-o-teh-*CAR	librarian
bikher-revizye, *f.*	BEE-*khehr-reh-veez-yeh*	audit (*n.*)
biks, *f.*	BEEX	gun
"	"	rifle
bild, *n.*	BEELD	picture (depiction)
bilderish	BEEL-*deh-rish*	picturesque
bildershtreyf, *m.*	BEEL-*dehr-shtrafe*	comic strip
bildung, *f.*	BEEL-*doon_g*	education (schooling process)
bilet, *m.*	*bee-*LETT	ticket (entitling card)
biln (1)	BEE-*lin*	bark (bay), to
bilyard, *m.*	*bill-*YARD	billiards
bimkem, *m.*	BEEM-*kem*	substitute (thing replacing another)
bin, *f.*	BEAN	bee
bindglid, *m.*	BEEND-*gleed*	link (connecting part)
bindn (8)	BEEN-*din*	bind, to
"	"	tie (fasten), to
binshtok, *m.*	BEEN-*shtawk*	hive (beehive)
binyen, *m.*	BEEN-*yen*	building
"	"	structure (thing built)
biografye, *f.*	*bee-o-*GRAHF-*yeh*	biography
biologye, *f.*	*bee-o-*LAWG-*yeh*	biology
bir, *n.*	BEER	beer
birger, *m.*	BEERG-*ehr*	citizen
birger-mayster, *m.*	BEERG-*ehr-my-stehr*	mayor
bis, *m.*	BEESS	bite
biskup, *m.*	BEESS-*koop*	bishop
bisl, a	*ah-*BEE-*sil*	some (a quantity of, *adj.*)
"	"	some (a quantity, *pron.*)
"	"	somewhat (*adv.*)
bisl, *n.*	BEE-*sil*	bit (small part)
bistre	BEE-*streh*	swift
biter	BEE-*tehr*	bitter
bitl, *m.*	BEE-*til*	contempt
"	"	scorn
bitl, hobn (25)	HAW-*bin* BEE-*til*	scorn (despise), to
bitokhn, *m.*	*bee-*TAW-*khin*	faith (trust)

Yiddish	Pronunciation	English
biz	BEEZ	by (prior to, *prep.*)
"	"	until (before, *prep.*)
"	"	until (*conj.*)
"	"	until (up to the time of, *prep.*)
blakirn (1b)	*blah-*KEE-*rin*	fade (lose color), to
blas	BLAHSS	pale (wan)
blat, *n.*	BLAHT	leaf (*bot.*)
blay, *n.*	BLYE	lead (metal)
blaybn (9d)	BLYE-*bin*	abide, to
"	"	remain (be left), to
"	"	remain (continue unchanged), to
"	"	remain (stay behind), to
"	"	stay, to
blaybn lebn	BLYE-*bin* LEH-*bin*	survive (remain alive), to
blaybn shteyn	BLYE-*bin* SHTANE	pause (wait), to
blayer, *m.*	BLAH-*yehr*	pencil
bleykhn (1)	BLAY-*khin*	bleach (make white), to
blezlen (1)	BLEZ-*len*	bubble, to
blien (1)	BLEE-*en*	bloom, to
"	"	flourish, to
"	"	thrive (succeed), to
bliendik	BLEE-*en-dick*	prosperous
blik, *m.*	BLEEK	glance (quick look)
"	"	glimpse
blik ton, a (22)	*ah* BLEEK *tawn*	glance, to
blind	BLEEND	blind (lacking sight)
blind makhn (1)	BLEEND *mah-khin*	blind, to
blishtshen (2)	BLEESH-*chen*	shine (gleam), to
bli-sofek	*blee-*SAW-*feck*	undoubtedly
blits, *m.*	BLEATS	flash (burst of light)
"	"	lightning
blok, *m.*	BLAWK	block (solid piece)
blond	BLAWND	blond
blondzhen (2)	BLAWN-*jen*	stray (roam), to
blote, *f.*	BLAW-*teh*	mud
bloy	BLOY	blue
bloyz	BLOYZ	mere
"	"	merely
bloyz, *m.*	BLOYZ	gap
blozn (5)	BLAW-*zin*	blow (breathe out), to
"	"	blow (make move), to
blum, *f.*	BLOOM	flower (blossom)
blut, *n.*	BLOOT	blood
blutikn (1)	BLOO-*tee-kin*	bleed (lose blood), to
blutoysgos, *m.*	BLOOT-*oyss-gawss*	hemorrhage
bluze, *f.*	BLOO-*zeh*	blouse (shirtwaist)
bobe, *f.*	BAW-*beh*	grandmother
bodkostyum, *m.*	BAWD-*kost-yoom*	bathing suit
bodn, *m.*	BAW-*din*	soil (ground)
bodn zikh (1)	BAW-*din zikh*	bathe (take a bath), to
bodtsimer, *m.*	BAWD-*tsee-mehr*	bathroom
bokher, *m.*	BAW-*khehr*	bachelor (unmarried man)
"	"	chap (fellow)
bokherl, *n.*	BAW-*kheh-ril*	youngster
boksn zikh (1)	BAWK-*sin zikh*	box (fight), to
Bolivye, *f.*	*baw-*LEAVE-*yeh*	Bolivia
bolpoynt-feder, *f.*	BAWL-*point-feh-dehr*	ball-point pen
bombe, *f.*	BAWM-*beh*	bomb (projectile)
bord, *f.*	BOARD	beard
botanik, *f.*	*baw-*TAH-*nick*	botany
boydem, *m.*	BOY-*dem*	attic
boyen (1)	BOY-*en*	build, to
"	"	construct, to
boygn, *m.*	BOYG-*in*	arch (curved structure)
"	"	curve
"	"	sheet (of paper)
boykh, *m.*	BOY_KH	abdomen
"	"	belly
boykhtifus, *m.*	BOYKH-*tee-fooss*	typhoid fever
boylet	BOY-*let*	distinct (unmistakable)
boym, *m.*	BOYM	tree
boyml, *m.*	BOY-*mil*	olive oil
branfn, *m.*	BRAHM-*fin*	whiskey
braslet, *m.*	*brahss-*LET	bracelet

Yiddish	Pronunciation	English
brazgen (2)	BRAHZG-*en*	clang, to
Brazil,*n.*	*brah*-ZEEL	Brazil
brazilish	*brah*-ZEE-*lish*	Brazilian (*adj.*)
breg,*m.*	BREG	bank
"	"	border (edge)
		shore
brekhik	BREH-*khick*	brittle
brekhn (7)	BREH-*khin*	break (make divide), to
brekhn zikh	BREH-*khin zikh*	break (come apart), to
brekl,*n.*	BREH-*kil*	crumb
"	"	scrap (fragment)
brem,*f.*	BREM	eyebrow
bren,*m.*	BREN	zeal
brenen	BREN-*en*	burn (be on fire), to
brengen (21)	BREN_G-*en*	bring, to
brenger,*m.*	BREHNG-*ehr*	bearer (*banking*)
brenvarg,*n.*	BREN-*varg*	fuel
bret,*f.*	BRET	board (plank)
breyt	BRATE	broad
"	"	extensive
"	"	wide (not narrow)
"	"	wide (of specified width)
breyt,*f.*	BRATE	breadth
"	"	width
breythartsik	BRATE-*hart-sick*	generous
bridzh,*m.*	BRIDGE	bridge, contract
brik,*f.*	BREEK	bridge (span)
brike,*m.*	BREE-*keh*	kick (boot)
briken (2)	BREE-*ken*	kick (boot), to
bril,*m.*	BREEL	roar (*n.*)
briln,*pl.*	BREE-*lin*	glasses
"	"	spectacles
brilyant,*m.*	*bril*-YAHNT	jewel
Brisl,*n.*	BREE-*sil*	Brussels
british	BREE-*tish*	British (*adj.*)
britve,*f.*	BREET-*veh*	razor blade
briv,*m.*	BREEV	letter (epistle)
brivl,*n.*	BREE-*vil*	note (letter)
brivn-treger,*m.*	BREE-*vin-treg-ehr*	postman
brodzhen (2)	BRAW-*jen*	wade, to
brokh,*m.*	BRAWKH	fracture (*med.*)
brokhe,*f.*	BRAW-*kheh*	blessing (boon)
brondz,*n.*	BRAWNDS	bronze (*n.*)
bronkhit,*m.*	*brawn*-KHEET	bronchitis
brosh,*f.*	BRAWSH	brooch
broshur,*f.*	*braw*-SHOOR	booklet
brotn zikh (5)	BRAW-*tin zikh*	roast (be roasted), to
broygez	BROYG-*ezz*	angry
broyn	BROYN	brown
broyt,*n.*	BROYT	bread
bruder,*m.*	BROO-*dehr*	brother
brudik	BROO-*dick*	foul (filthy)
bruk,*m.*	BROOK	pavement
brukhteyl,*m.*	BROOKH-*tale*	fraction (part)
brukirn (1b)	*broo*-KEE-*rin*	pave, to
brukve,*f.*	BROOK-*veh*	turnip (white)
brum,*m.*	BROOM	hum (murmur)
brunem,*m.*	BROO-*nem*	well (oil, gas shaft, *n.*)
"	"	well (water pit, *n.*)
brunet	*broo*-NET	brunette (*adj.*)
brust,*f.*	BROOST	breast
"	"	chest (*anat.*)
bruto	BROO-*taw*	gross (before deductions, *adj.*)
bsule,*f.*	BSOO-*leh*	maiden
"	"	virgin (*n.*)
budzhet,*m.*	*boo*-JET	budget (*n.*)
Buenos Aires,*n.*	*boo*-EH-*nos* EYE-*ress*	Buenos Aires
bufloks,*m.*	BOOF-*lawx*	buffalo
buk,*m.*	BOOK	beech (tree)
bukh,*n.*	BOOKH	book
bukhhalter,*m.*	*bookh*-HAHL-*tehr*	bookkeeper (*bus.*)
bukhhalterye,*f.*	*bookh-hahl*-TEHR-*yeh*	bookkeeping (*bus.*)
Bulgarye,*n.*	*bool*-GAR-*yeh*	Bulgaria
bund,*m.*	BOOND	tie (bond)
burik,*m.*	BOO-*rick*	beet (red root)
burshtinen	*boor*-SHTEE-*nen*	amber (*adj.*)

Yiddish	Pronunciation	English
burtshen (2)	BOOR-*chen*	grumble, to
busheven (2)	BOO-*sheh-ven*	rage (rave), to
bushl,*m.*	BOO-*shil*	stork
buzem,*m.*	BOO-*zem*	bosom
byuro,*n.*	*bew*-RAW	bureau
"	"	office (place of business)
byust,*m.*	BEWST	bust (statue)
dakh,*m.*	DAH_KH	roof
dakh ibern kop, gebn a (13)	G_EH-*bin a* DAH_KH *ee-beh-rin* KAWP	shelter, to
dales,*m.*	DAH-*less*	poverty
dambe,*f.*	DAHM-*beh*	dam (dike)
dame,*f.*	DAH-*meh*	lady
dank,*m.*	DAHNK	thanks (gratitude)
dankbar	DAHNK-*bar*	grateful
"	"	thankful
dankbarkayt,*f.*	DAHNK-*bar-kite*	gratitude
danken (1)	DAHN-*ken*	thank, to
dar	DAR	thin (not fat)
darfn (le)	DAR-*fin*	need (require), to
"	"	ought (*v.*)
date,*f.*	DAH-*teh*	date (calendar designation)
dayge,*f.*	DYE-*g_eh*	worry (anxiety)
daygen (2)	DYE-*g_en*	worry (feel anxious), to
dayn	DINE	your
dayner	DIE-*nehr*	yours
daytsh	DIE_CH	German (*adj.*)
daytshland,*n.*	DIE_CH-*lahnd*	Germany
debate,*f.*	*deh*-BAH-*teh*	debate
definirn (1b)	*deh-fee*-NEE-*rin*	define, to
defitsit,*m.*	*deh-fee*-TSEET	deficit (*bus.*)
dehayne	*deh*-HI-*neh*	namely
dek,*f.*	DECK	bottom
"	"	lid (cover)
dek,*m.*	DECK	deck (of ship)
dekl,*n.*	DEH-*kil*	cover (lid)
deklaratsye,*f.*	*deh-klah*-RAHTS-*yeh*	declaration (announcement)
dekret,*m.*	*deh*-KRET	decree (edict)
delegat,*m.*	*deh-leh*-GAHT	delegate
delikat	*deh-lee*-KAHT	dainty
"	"	delicate
demb,*m.*	DEMB	oak
demokrat,*m.*	*deh-mo*-KRAHT	democrat
demokratish	*deh-mo*-KRAH-*tish*	democratic
demokratye,*f.*	*deh-mo*-KRAHT-*yeh*	democracy
demolt	DEH-*mawlt*	then (at that time)
demolt on, fun	*foon* DEH-*mawlt* AWN	since (from then to now, *adv.*)
Denemark,*n.*	DEH-*neh-mark*	Denmark
denervirn (1b)	*deh-nehr*-VEE-*rin*	vex (anger), to
denish	DEH-*nish*	Danish (*adj.*)
denken (1)	DEN-*ken*	meditate (reflect), to
denkmol,*m.*	DENK-*mawl*	memorial (*n.*)
"	"	monument
depesh,*f.*	*deh*-PESH	dispatch (communication)
"	"	wire (telegram)
depresye,*f.*	*deh*-PRESS-*yeh*	depression (*econ.*)
der	DEHR	the
"	"	this (*adj.*)
derekh-erets,*m.*	*deh-rekh*-EH-*rets*	respect (esteem)
derendikn (1b)	*dehr*-EN-*dee-kin*	complete (finish), to
derforn biz (5bd)	*dehr*-FAW-*rin* BIZ	reach (arrive at), to
derfreyen (1b)	*dehr*-FRAY-*en*	cheer (gladden), to
derfun	*dehr*-FOON	thereof
dergeyn (14bd)	*dehr*-GAIN	achieve (attain), to
dergeyn biz	*dehr*-GAIN *beez*	attain (arrive at), to
dergreykhn (1b)	*dehr*-GRAY-*khin*	reach (extend to), to
derhargenen (4b)	*dehr*-HARG-*eh-nen*	kill, to
derheybn (10b)	*dehr*-HAY-*bin*	exalt, to
deriber	*deh*-REE-*behr*	therefore
der iker	*dehr* EE-*kehr*	chiefly (mainly)
derkenen,*n.*	*dehr*-KEH-*nen*	recognition (identification)
derkenen (1b)	*dehr*-KEH-*nen*	recognize (identify), to

Yiddish	Pronunciation	English	Yiddish	Pronunciation	English
derklern (1b)	*dehr*-KLEH-*rin*	assert, to	dingen zikh	DEEN-*g*_*en zikh*	bargain (negotiate), to
"	"	declare, to	dinst,*f.*	DEENST	maid (servant)
"	"	explain (clarify), to	dinst,*n.*	DEENST	service
		state (say), to			
derklerung,*f.*	*dehr*-KLEH-*roon_g*	assertion (declaration)	dire,*f.*	DEE-*reh*	apartment
			dire-gelt,*n.*	DEE-*reh-g_elt*	rent (payment)
"	"	explanation	direkt	*dee*-REKT	direct (immediate)
"	"	statement (declaration)	direktor,*m.*	*dee*-RECK-*tor*	director
derlangen (1b)	*dehr*-LAHNG-*en*	give (deliver), to	dirigent,*m.*	*dee*-*reeg*-ENT	conductor (*mus.*)
"	"	present, to	disenterye,*f.*	*dee*-*sen*-TEHR-*yeh*	dysentery
derloybenish,*f.*	*dehr*-LOY-*beh-nish*	permission	dishen (2)	DEE-*shen*	gasp, to
derloybn (1b)	*dehr*-LOY-*bin*	allow, to	diskontirn (1b)	*dis*-*kawn*-TEE-*rin*	discount, to (*bus.*)
"	"	permit, to	diskusye,*f.*	*diss*-KOOSS-*yeh*	discussion
derlozn (1b)	*dehr*-LAW-*zin*	tolerate (permit), to	dispozitsye,*f.*	*dis*-*paw*-ZEETS-*yeh*	disposition (arrangement)
dermit	*dehr*-MEET	thereby	distrikt,*m.*	*dis*-TREEKT	district (locality)
dermonen (1b)	*dehr*-MAW-*nen*	mention, to	distsiplin,*f.*	*dist*-*see*-PLEEN	discipline (training)
"	"	note, to	divan,*m.*	*dee*-VAHN	rug
"	"	remind, to	dividend,*m.*	*dee*-*vee*-DEND	dividend (*bus.*)
"	"	suggest (bring to mind), to	divizye,*f.*	*dee*-VEEZ-*yeh*	division (*mil.*)
dermonen zikh	*dehr*-MAW-*nen zikh*	recall, to	dlonye,*f.*	DLAWN-*yeh*	palm (of hand)
"	"	remember (recollect), to	dlot,*m.*	DLAWT	chisel (tool)
			dok,*m.*	DAWK	dock
dermonung,*f.*	*dehr*-MAW-*noon_g*	remembrance (recollection)	dokh	DAW_KH	still (nevertheless, *conj.*)
derneentern zikh tsu (1b)	*dehr*-NEH-*en-teh-rin zikh tsoo*	approach (come near to), to	"	"	yet (nevertheless, *adv.*)
dernern (1b)	*dehr*-NEH-*rin*	nourish, to	dokter,*m.*	DAWK-*tehr*	doctor
dernerung,*f.*	*dehr*-NEH-*roon_g*	nourishment	"	"	physician
dernokhdem	*dehr*-NAW_KH-*dem*	afterward (later)	dokument,*m.*	*daw*-*koo*-MENT	document
"	"	thereafter	Dominikaner Republik,*f.*	*daw*-*mee*-*nee*-KAH-*nehr reh-poo*-BLEEK	Dominican Republic
dershatsn (1b)	*dehr*-SHAH-*tsin*	appreciate (perceive fully), to	dor,*m.*	DAWR	generation (period of time)
dershpirn (1b)	*dehr*-SHPEE-*rin*	detect, to	dorem,*m.*	DAW-*rem*	south (*n.*)
"	"	perceive, to	dorem-amerike,*f.*	DAW-*rem-ah*-MEH-*ree-keh*	South America
dershrokn	*dehr*-SHRAW-*kin*	afraid			
"	"	fearful	doremdik	DAW-*rem-dick*	southern
			dorem-mayrevdik	DAW-*rem-MY-rev-dick*	southwest (*adj.*)
dershtekhn (7b)	*dehr*-SHTEH-*khin*	stab, to	dorem-mizrakhdik	DAW-*rem-MEEZ-rukh-dick*	southeast (*adj.*)
dershtikn (1b)	*dehr*-SHTEE-*kin*	suppress (subdue), to			
dertrinken (8b)	*dehr*-TREEN-*ken*	drown (kill by drowning), to	dorf,*n.*	DORF	village
			dorfish	DOR-*fish*	rural
dertrunken vern (7cd)	*dehr*-TROON-*ken veh-rin*	drown (die by drowning), to	dorn,*m.*	DAW-*rin*	thorn
			dorsht,*m.*	DORSHT	thirst
dertseyln (1b)	*dehr*-TSAY-*lin*	tell (narrate), to	dorshtik	DORSH-*lick*	thirsty
dertseylung,*f.*	*dehr*-TSAY-*loon_g*	tale (narrative)	dortn	DOR-*tin*	there (at that place)
dertsu	*dehr*-TSOO	futher (to greater extent)	dos	DAWSS	that (*dem. pron.*)
"	"	moreover	"	"	the
derunterdik	*deh*-ROON-*tehr-dick*	inferior (mediocre)	"	"	this (*dem. pron.*)
dervayl	*dehr*-VILE	meanwhile (*adv.*)	"	"	this (*adj.*)
dervaylik	*dehr*-VIE-*lick*	temporary	doyer,*m.*	DAW-*yehr*	duration
dervayzn (9b)	*dehr*-VIE-*zin*	establish, to			
"	"	prove (verify), to	doykhek,*m.*	DOY-*khek*	lack (deficiency)
dervegn zikh (1b)	*dehr*-VEG-*in zikh*	dare (venture), to	"	"	shortage
dervisn zikh (27)	*der*-VEE-*sin zikh*	learn (find out), to	"	"	want
derzen (6b)	*dehr*-ZEHN	behold, to	doze,*f.*	DAW-*zeh*	dose (*med.*)
desert,*m.*	*deh*-SEHRT	dessert	drame,*f.*	DRAH-*meh*	drama
destroyer,*m.*	*deh*-STRAW-*yehr*	destroyer (ship)	drayek,*m.*	DRY-*eck*	triangle (*geom.*)
deye,*f.*	DEH-*yeh*	sway (influence)	drayst	DRY_ST	bold (courageous)
deyfek,*m.*	DAY-*fick*	pulse (*physiol.*)	dreml,*m.*	DREH-*mil*	slumber
di	DEE	the	dreyen (1)	DRAY-*en*	turn (make rotate), to
"	"	these (*adj.*)			
"	"	these (*pron.*)	dreyen zikh	DREH-*yen zikh*	spin (revolve), to
"	"	this (*adj.*)	drey ton, a (22)	*ah* DRAY *tawn*	whirl (make revolve), to
diagram,*f.*	*dee-ah*-GRAHM	chart (graph)			
diameter,*m.*	*dee*-AH-*meh-tehr*	diameter	drikn (1)	DREE-*kin*	press (bear upon), to
diete,*f.*	*dee*-EH-*teh*	diet	driml,*m.*	DREE-*mil*	nap (doze, *n.*)
diferents,*f.*	*dee-feh*-RENTS	difference (*math.*)	dringlekh	DREEN_G-*lukh*	urgent
			drobne	DRAWB-*neh*	fine (very small)
difterit,*m.*	*diff-teh*-REET	diphtheria	drong,*m.*	DRAWN_G	pole (rod)
dik	DEEK	thick (not thin)			
dikh,*f.*	DEEKH	thigh	drot,*m.*	DRAWT	wire (metal thread)
diktirn (1b)	*dick*-TEE-*rin*	dictate, to	droysn,*m.*	DROY-*sin*	face (surface)
diment,*m.*	DEE-*ment*	diamond (gem)			outside (*n.*)
din	DEEN	thin (not thick)	droysn, in	*in* DROY-*sin*	outdoors (*adv.*)
dinen (1)	DEE-*nen*	serve, to	"	"	outside (*adv.*)
		worship, to (*rel.*)			
dinen, nemen (8)	NEH-*men* DEE-*nen*	draft (conscript), to	droysndik	DROY-*sin-dick*	exterior (*adj.*)
diner,*m.*	DEE-*nehr*	servant (in a household)	"	"	outer
			"	"	outside (*adj.*)
dingen (8)	DEEN-*g_en*	engage (employ), to	druk,*m.*	DROOK	pressure (force)
"	"	hire (employ), to	"	"	stress (physical tension)
"	"	lease (hold by lease), to			
"	"	rent (pay rent for), to			

Yiddish	Pronunciation	English	Yiddish	Pronunciation	English
druker, *m.*	DROO-*kehr*	printer	elokvent	*eh-lo-*KVENT	eloquent
drukn (1)	DROO-*kin*	print, to	elter	ELL-*tehr*	senior (older)
drukrekht, *n.*	DROOK-*rekht*	copyright (*n.*)	elter, *m.*	EHL-*tehr*	age (accumulated years)
du	DOO	you			
Dunay, *m.*	DOO-*nay*	Danube	emer, *m.*	EH-*mehr*	bucket
			"	"	pail
duner, *m.*	DOO-*nehr*	thunder	emes	EH-*mess*	true
duplikat, *m.*	*doo-plee-*KAHT	duplicate (copy, *n.*)	emes, *m.*	EH-*mess*	truth
durkh	DOORKH	by (via, *prep.*)	emetser	EH-*met-sehr*	somebody
"	"	through (by means of, *prep.*)	"	"	someone
"	"	through (from end to end of, *prep.*)	emotsye, *f.*	*eh-*MAWTS-*yeh*	emotion
"	"	throughout (from start to finish of, *prep.*)	emune, *f.*	*eh-*MOO-*neh*	faith (creed)
			endikn (1)	EN-*dee-kin*	end (bring to an end), to
durkhbrodyen (2a)	DOORKH-*broad-yen*	ford, to	"	"	finish (complete), to
durkhdringen (8a)	DOORKH-*dreen_g-en*	penetrate (pierce), to	endikn zikh	END-*ee-kin zikh*	end (come to an end), to
durkhfal, *m.*	DOORKH-*fahl*	failure (lack of success)	"	"	finish (reach the end), to
durkhfaln (5ad)	DOORKH-*fah-lin*	fail (be unsuccessful), to	energye, *f.*	*eh-*NEHRG-*yeh*	energy
			eng	EN_G	tight (close-fitting)
durkhfirn (1a)	DOORKH-*fee-rin*	perform (do), to	England, *n.*	EN-*glahnd*	England
durkhgang, *m.*	DOORKH-*gahn_g*	aisle (passageway)	english	EN-*glish*	English (*adj.*)
"	"	passage (passageway)	enlekh	ENN-*lukh*	alike
durkhhaltn (5a)	DOORKH-*hahl-tin*	persist (persevere), to	"	"	like (*adj.*)
durkhkukn (1a)	DOORKH-*koo-kin*	examine (investigate), to	"	"	similar
durkhkumen (5ad)	DOORKH-*koo-men*	settle (agree on), to	enlekh, zayn (18d)	ZINE EN-*lukh*	resemble, to
durkhlaykhtn (10a)	DOORKH-*lye_kh-tin*	X-ray (examine), to	enlekhkayt, *f.*	EN-*lukh-kite*	similarity
durkhshnit, *m.*	DOORKH-*shnit*	average (mean, *n.*)	ensayn, *m.*	EN-*sign*	ensign (*Nav.*)
durkhshnitlekh	DOORKH-*shnit-lukh*	average (ordinary, *adj.*)	entfer, *m.*	ENT-*fehr*	answer
			"	"	response (reply)
durkhshtekhn (7a)	DOORKH-*shteh-khin*	pierce, to	entfern (1)	ENT-*feh-rin*	answer (address reply to), to
durkh un durkh	DOORKH un DOORKH	thoroughly	"	"	reply, to
durkhzeevdik	DOORKH-*zeh-ev-dick*	transparent	"	"	respond, to
dzhentlman, *m.*	JEN-*til-mahn*	gentleman	entfern oyf	ENT-*feh-rin oyf*	answer (give answer to), to
dzhet-motor, *m.*	JET-*mo-tore*	jet engine			
dzhez, *m.*	JAZZ	jazz	entsiklopedye, *f.*	*en-tsee-klo-*PED-*yeh*	encyclopaedia
			entuzyazm, *m.*	*en-tooz-*YAH-*zim*	enthusiasm
Edinburg, *n.*	EH-*din-boorg*	Edinburgh	epes	EH-*pess*	something
efekt, *m.*	*eh-*FEKT	effect	epes a	EH-*pess ah*	some (unspecified, *adj.*)
efektiv	*eh-fek-*TEEV	effective (effectual)	epidemye, *f.*	*eh-pee-*DEM-*yeh*	epidemic
"	"	efficient (producing desired results)	epl, *m.*	EH-*pil*	apple
efenen (3)	EH-*feh-nen*	open (make open), to	er	EHR	he
efenung, *f.*	EH-*feh-noon_g*	opening (aperture)	erd, *f.*	EHRD	dirt (soil)
efntlekh	EH-*fint-lukh*	public (common, *adj.*)	"	"	earth
			"	"	earth (planet)
efsher	EF-*shehr*	maybe	"	"	land (property)
"	"	perhaps	erd-tsiternish, *f.*	EHRD-*tsee-tehr-nish*	earthquake
egoistish	*eh-go-*EES-*tish*	selfish	Erets-Yisroel, *n.*	*eh-rets-yis-*RAW-*ell*	Palestine
ek, *m.*	ECK	tail (of animal)			
ekbern (1)	ECK-*beh-rin*	drill (bore), to	erger	EHRG-*ehr*	worse
ekht	EH_KHT	genuine	ergets	EHRG-*ets*	somewhere
ekl, *m.*	EH-*kil*	disgust	ergets nit, in	*in* EHRG-*ets neet*	anywhere (not...anywhere)
ekonomik, *f.*	*eh-ko-*NAW-*mik*	economics	"	"	nowhere
ekran, *m.*	*eh-*KRAHN	screen (for movies)	ergst	EHRGST	worst (*adj.*)
eksistents, *f.*	*ek-sis-*TENTS	existence	ergste, *n.*	EHRG-*steh*	worst (*n.*)
eksistirn (1b)	*ek-sis-*TEE-*rin*	exist, to	erlekh	EHR-*lukh*	honest
ekspeditsye, *f.*	*ex-peh-*DEETS-*yeh*	expedition (journey)	erlekhkayt, *f.*	EHR-*lukh-kite*	honesty
eksperiment, *m.*	*ex-peh-ree-*MENT	experiment	erntst	EH-*rintst*	earnest
eksport, *m.*	*ex-*PORT	exportation	"	"	grave
eksportirer, *m.*	*ex-por-*TEE-*rehr*	exporter	"	"	serious
eksportirn (1b)	*ex-por-*TEE-*rin*	export, to	ersht	EHRSHT	first (*adj.*)
ekst	EXT	extreme (farthest)	"	"	prime
"	"	utmost	ershtik	EHR-*shtick*	primary (first, *adj.*)
			es	ESS	it (*pers. pron.*)
ekstre	EX-*treh*	extra (additional)			
ekstrem	*ex-*TREMM	extreme (intense)	esik, *m.*	EH-*sick*	vinegar
Ekvador, *n.*	EHK-*vah-dor*	Ecuador	eslefl, *m.*	ESS-*leh-fil*	spoon (tablespoon)
ekzamen, *m.*	*ek-*ZAH-*men*	examination (test)	esn (20)	EH-*sin*	eat, to
ekzemplar, *m.*	*ek-zem-*PLAR	copy (of a publication)	esn mitik	EH-*sin* MEE-*tik*	dine, to
elastish	*eh-*LAHSS-*tish*	elastic (springy)	esnvarg, *n.*	EH-*sin-varg*	food
elektre, *f.*	*eh-*LEK-*treh*	electricity	Estraykh, *n.*	EST-*rye_kh*	Austria
elektrish	*eh-*LEK-*trish*	electric	estraykhish	EST-*rye-khish*	Austrian (*adj.*)
elektronik, *f.*	*eh-lek-*TRAW-*nik*	electronics	estsimer, *m.*	ESS-*tsee-mehr*	dining room
element, *m.*	*eh-leh-*MENT	element	etiket, *m.*	*eh-tee-*KET	etiquette
elementar	*eh-leh-men-*TAR	elementary (rudimentary)	"	"	label
			etlekhe	ET-*lukh-eh*	several (a few, *adj.*)
eln-boygn, *m.*	EH-*lin-boyg-in*	elbow	"	"	some (a few, *adj.*)
elnt	EH-*lint*	lonely			
"	"	lonely (unfrequented)	evenyu, *f.*	EH-*veh-new*	avenue (street)
"	"	lonesome			

Yiddish	Pronunciation	English
ey, n.	AY	egg
eyberflakh, f.	AY-behr-flah_kh	surface
eyberhar, m.	AY-behr-har	sovereign (ruler)
eybik	AY-bik	eternal
"	"	everlasting
"	"	perpetual
eybike feder, f.	AY-bee-keh FEH-dehr	pen, fountain
eydem, m.	AY-dem	son-in-law
eyder	AY-dehr	before (prior to the time when, conj.)
"	"	than
eydes, m.	AY-dess	witness (one who testifies)
eydes zogn (1)	AY-dess zawg-in	testify, to
eydl	AY-dil	civil
"	"	courteous
"	"	frail (fragile)
"	"	noble (adj.)
"	"	polite
eydlkayt, f.	AY-dil-kite	courtesy
eydlshteyn, m.	AY-dil-shtane	gem
eyferdik	AY-fehr-dick	keen (eager)
eyferzikhtik	AY-fehr-zikh-tick	jealous
eygn	AYG-in	own (adj.)
eygnshaft, f.	AYG-in-shahft	attribute (characteristic)
"	"	quality
eyl, m.	ALE	oil
eyme, f.	AY-meh	dread
eymedik	AY-meh-dik	dreadful
eynhaytlekh	ANE-hite-lukh	uniform (adj.)
eynikl, n.	AY-nee-kil	granddaughter
"	"	grandson
eyn-leshaer	ANE-leh-SHAH-ehr	immense
eyn mol	ANE mawl	once (one time, adv.)
eyntsik	ANE-tsick	lone (solitary)
"	"	only
"	"	single
"	"	sole
eyntsol, f.	AINT-sawl	singular (gram., n.)
eynzamkayt, f.	ANE-zahm-kite	solitude
Eyrope, m.	ay-RAW-peh	Europe
eyropeish	ay-raw-PEH-ish	European (adj.)
eytse, f.	AY-tseh	advice
"	"	counsel
eytsen (2)	ATE-sen	advise, to
"	"	counsel, to
eyver, m.	AY-vehr	limb (anat.)
eyzl, m.	AY-zil	donkey
fabrik, f.	fah-BREEK	factory
"	"	plant
fabrikant, m.	fah-bree-KAHNT	manufacturer
fakh, m.	FAH_KH	occupation (calling)
fakt, m.	FAH_KT	fact
faktish	FAHK-tish	actual (real)
faktor, m.	FAH_K-tor	factor (element)
fal, m.	FAHL	case (instance)
"	"	drop (sudden fall)
"	"	fall
falk, m.	FAHLK	hawk
faln (5d)	FAH-lin	drop, to
"	"	fall, to
"	"	succumb (yield), to
"	"	tumble, to
faln, lozn (1)	LAW-zin FAH-lin	drop (let fall), to
falsh	FAHLSH	counterfeit (adj.)
"	"	false (deceitful)
"	"	false (erroneous)
"	"	wrong (erroneous, adj.)
falshe shvue, f.	FAHL-sheh SHVOO-eh	perjury
familye, f.	fah-MEEL-yeh	surname
fantazye, f.	fahn-TAHZ-yeh	fancy (fantasy)
"	"	imagination
far	FAR	before (earlier than, prep.)
"	"	before (in front of, prep.)
"	"	for (prep.)

Yiddish	Pronunciation	English
farakbtn (1b)	far-AH_KH-tin	despise, to
farakshnt	far-AHK-shint	stubborn
farantvortlekh	far-AHNT-vort-lukh	responsible (answerable)
farb, f.	FARB	paint
farband, m.	far-BAHND	association (body of persons)
"	"	union (league)
farbay	far-BYE	past (beyond, prep.)
"	"	past (bygone, adj.)
farbaygeyn (14ad)	far-BYE-gain	pass (go by), to
farbaytn (9b)	far-BYE-tin	replace, to
"	"	substitute (put in place of), to
farbenkt	far-BENKT	homesick
farbesern (1b)	far-BEH-seh-rin	improve (make better), to
farbeserung, f.	far-BEH-seh-roon_g	amendment (enacted change)
"	"	improvement (betterment)
farbetn (5b)	far-BEH-tin	invite, to
farbetung, f.	far-BEH-toon_g	invitation
farbindn (8b)	far-BEEN-din	associate (relate), to
farbisn	far-BEE-sin	grim (stern)
farblendn (1b)	far-BLEN-din	dazzle, to
farbn (7)	FAR-bin	dye, to
"	"	paint (spread color), to
farborgn (5b)	far-BORG-in	conceal, to
farbrekh, m.	far-BREKH	crime
farbrekher, m.	far-BREH-khehr	criminal (n.)
farbrekherish	far-BREH-kheh-rish	criminal (adj.)
farbrenen (1b)	far-BREH-nen	burn (set fire to), to
farbreytern (1b)	far-BRAY-teh-rin	expand (make larger), to
"	"	extend (enlarge), to
"	"	involve (entail), to
farbundn mit, zayn (18d)	ZINE far-BOON-din mit	
fardamen (1b)	far-DAH-men	condemn (censure), to
fardayen (1b)	far-DIE-en	digest, to
fardinen (1b)	far-DEE-nen	deserve, to
"	"	earn (be paid), to
"	"	earn, to
"	"	merit, to
fardingen (8b)	far-DEEN_G-en	rent (charge rent for), to
farendikn (1b)	far-EN-dee-kin	conclude (make end), to
farentfern (1b)	far-ENT-feh-rin	account for (explain), to
"	"	explain, to
"	"	solve, to
farentferung, f.	far-ENT-feh-roon_g	solution (solving)
fareyn, m.	far-ANE	union (trade union)
fareynikn (1b)	far-AY-nee-kin	join (bring together), to
"	"	unite (make one), to
fareynikn zikh	far-AY-nee-kin zikh	combine (coalesce), to
Fareynikte Natsyes, pl.	far-AY-nick-teh NAHTS-yess	United Nations
Fareynikte Shtatn, pl.	far-AY-nick-teh SHTAH-tin	United States
farfeln, n.	far-FEH-lin	failure (neglect)
farfeln (1b)	far-FEH-lin	fail (neglect), to
"	"	miss (fail to do), to
farflekhtn (7b)	far-FLEKH-tin	braid (plait), to
farfleytsung, f.	far-FLAY-tsoon_g	food
farforn (5bd)	far-FAW-rin	ram (butt), to
farfoylt	far-FOILT	rotten (decayed)
farfroyrn	far-FROY-rin	frozen
farfroyrn vern (7cd)	far-FROY-rin veh-rin	freeze (turn to ice), to
fargafn (1b)	far-GAH-fin	amaze, to
fargafung, f.	far-GAH-foon_g	amazement
fargangen	far-GAHN_G-en	last (most recent, adj.)
fargebn (13b)	far-G_EH-bin	assign (prescribe lesson), to
fargebung, f.	far-GEH-boon_g	assignment (educ.)
fargenign, m.	far-g_eh-NEEG-in	pleasure
fargesn	far-G_EH-sin	forgotten
fargesn (5b)	far-G_EH-sin	forget, to
fargetern (1b)	far-G_EH-teh-rin	adore, to
fargeterung, f.	far-GET-eh-roon_g	worship (rel.)

Yiddish	Pronunciation	English
fargeyn in trogn, *n.*	*far*-GAIN *in* TRAWG-*in*	conception (*physiol.*)
fargikhern (1)	*far*-G_EE-*kheh-rin*	quicken, to
farginen zikh (8b)	*far*-G_EE-*nen zikh*	afford (have the means), to
fargisn (7b)	*far*-GEESE-*in*	spill (let pour out), to
farglaykh, *m.*	*far*-GLYE_KH	comparison
farglaykhik	*far*-GLYE-*khik*	comparative
farglaykhn (9b)	*far*-GLYE-*khin*	compare (consider relatively), to
fargleybt in zikh	*far*-GLABE_T *in* ZEEKH	vain (conceited)
fargresern (1b)	*far*-GREH-*seh-rin*	enlarge (make larger), to
fargringern (1b)	*far*-GREEN-*g_eh-rin*	ease, to
		relieve, to
fargringerung, *f.*	*far*-GREEN-*g_eh-roong*	relief (alleviation)
farhakn zikh (1b)	*far*-HAH-*kin zikh*	stall (stop going), to
farhandlen vegn (1b)	*far*-HAHND-*len veg-in*	negotiate, to
farhandlung, *f.*	*far*-HAHND-*loon_g*	negotiation
farheltenish, *f.*	*far*-HELL-*teh-nish*	proportion
"	"	ratio
farhitn (1b)	*far*-HEE-*tin*	avert, to
		prevent (stop), to
faribl hobn (25c)	*fah*-REE-*bil* HAW-*bin*	resent, to
fariken zikh (2b)	*far*-EE-*ken zikh*	stammer, to
farker, *m.*	*far*-KEHR	traffic (flow of vehicles)
farkert	*far*-KEHRT	backward (in reverse, *adv.*)
"	"	contrary
"	"	opposite (*adj.*)
farkhideshn (1b)	*far*-KHEE-*deh-shin*	astonish, to
"	"	surprise, to
farkilung, *f.*	*far*-KEE-*loon_g*	cold (disease)
farkishefn (1b)	*far*-KEE-*sheh-fin*	charm (delight), to
farklenern (1b)	*far*-KLEH-*nehrn*	diminish (make smaller), to
farknasung, *f.*	*far*-K_NAH-*soon_g*	engagement (betrothal)
farkoyf, *m.*	*far*-KOYF	sale (exchange)
farkoyfer, *m.*	*far*-KOY-*fehr*	clerk (salesperson)
"	"	salesman
		vendor (seller)
farkoyfevdik	*far*-KOY-*fev-dick*	negotiable (*bus.*)
farkoyfn (1b)	*far*-KOY-*fin*	sell, to
farkoyf-tsetl, *n.*	*far*-KOYF-*tseh-til*	bill of sale
farkrimen (1b)	*far*-KREE-*men*	pervert (distort), to
farkukn (1b)	*far*-KOO-*kin*	overlook (disregard), to
farlegnhayt, *f.*	*far*-LEG-*in-hite*	embarrassment
"	"	quandary
farlengern (1b)	*far*-LEN_G-*eh-rin*	extend (stretch out), to
"	"	prolong, to
farlengerung, *f.*	*far*-LEN_G-*eh-roong_g*	extension (enlargement)
farleygn (1b)	*far*-LAYG-*in*	mislay, to
farlozlekh	*far*-LAWZ-*lukh*	reliable
farlozn (1b)	*far*-LAW-*zin*	forsake, to
farlozn zikh	*far*-LAW-*zin zikh*	depend (rely) on, to
farm, *f.*	FAH-*rim*	farm
farmakhn (1b)	*far*-MAH-*khin*	close, to
"	"	shut (make close), to
farmatern (1b)	*far*-MAH-*teh-rin*	tire (make weary), to
farmatert	*far*-MAH-*tehrt*	tired
"	"	weary
farmegn, *n.*	*far*-MEG-*in*	holdings (possessions)
"	"	property (possession)
farmer, *m.*	FAR-*mehr*	farmer
farmern (1b)	*far*-MEH-*rin*	increase (add to), to
farmest, *m.*	*far*-MEST	race (contest)
farminern (1b)	*far*-MEE-*neh-rin*	lessen (make less), to
farminerung, *f.*	*far*-MEE-*neh-roon_g*	decrease
farmishpetn (1b)	*far*-MEESH-*peh-tin*	doom (condemn), to
		sentence, to
farmogn, *n.*	*far*-MAWG-*in*	possession (ownership)
farmogn (1b)	*far*-MAWG-*in*	own, to
"	"	possess, to
farnarekhts, *n.*	*far*-NAH-*rekhts*	bait (for animals)
farnem, *m.*	*far*-NEM	volume (space occupied)
farnemen (8b)	*far*-NEH-*men*	occupy (fill), to

Yiddish	Pronunciation	English
farnemen zikh mit	*far*-NEH-*men zikh mit*	engage (be occupied) in, to
farneyg, *m.*	*far*-NAYG	bow (nod)
farneygn zikh (1b)	*far*-NAYG-*in zikh*	bow (in greeting), to
farnits, *m.*	*far*-NEETS	consumption (using up)
farnitsn (1b)	*far*-NEE-*tsin*	consume, to
farnumen	*far*-NOO-*men*	busy (occupied)
farrat, *m.*	*far*-RAHT	treason
farrekhenen (3b)	*far*-REH-*kheh-nen*	charge (debit), to
farrekhn-konte, *f.*	*far*-REH-*khin-kawn-teh*	charge account
farreter, *m.*	*far*-REH-*tehr*	traitor
farrikhtn (1b)	*far*-REEKH-*tin*	fix, to
"	"	mend, to
"	"	repair, to
farrufn zikh (5b)	*far*-ROO-*fin zikh*	refer (allude), to
farrufn zikh, *n.*	*far*-ROO-*fin zikh*	reference (allusion)
farsamen (1b)	*far*-SAH-*men*	poison, to
farshafn (1b)	*far*-SHAH-*fin*	procure (obtain), to
farshayt	*far*-SHYE_T	shrewd
farsheltn (7b)	*far*-SHEL-*tin*	damn, to
farshemt	*far*-SHEMT	ashamed (mortified)
farsheydn	*far*-SHAY-*din*	distinct (different)
"	"	miscellaneous
		various
farsheydn-farbik	*far*-SHAY-*din-far-bick*	motley (diverse)
farsheydnkayt, *f.*	*far*-SHAY-*din-kite*	variety (diversity)
farshikn (1b)	*far*-SHEE-*kin*	banish (exile), to
farshimlt	*far*-SHEE-*milt*	moldy
farshlingen (8b)	*far*-SHLEEN-*g_en*	devour (eat), to
farshlisn (7b)	*far*-SHLEE-*sin*	lock (fasten with key), to
farshparn (1b)	*far*-SHPAH-*rin*	block (obstruct), to
farshpetikt	*far*-SHPEH-*tick_t*	late (overdue, *adj.*)
"	"	slow (tardy)
farshpreytn (1b)	*far*-SHPRAY-*tin*	spread (diffuse), to
farshpreytung, *f.*	*far*-SHPRAY-*toon_g*	circulation (dissemination)
"	"	distribution (*bus.*)
farshtekl, *n.*	*far*-SHTEH-*kil*	plug (stopper)
farshtekn (1b)	*far*-SHTEH-*kin*	tuck (slip inside), to
farshteln (1b)	*far*-SHTEH-*lin*	bar (block), to
farshtelung, *f.*	*far*-SHTEH-*loon_g*	disguise
farshtendenish, *n.*	*far*-SHTEN-*deh-nish*	understanding (comprehension)
farshteyn (17b)	*far*-SHTANE	understand (comprehend), to
farshtorbn	*far*-SHTOR-*bin*	late (deceased, *adj.*)
farshverung, *f.*	*far*-SHVEH-*roon_g*	plot (conspiracy)
farshvundn vern (7cd)	*far*-SHVOON-*din veh-rin*	disappear, to
"	"	fade, to
"	"	vanish (cease to be), to
fartekh, *m.*	FAR-*tukh*	apron (garment)
farteydikn (1b)	*far*-TAY-*dee-kin*	defend (protect), to
farteydikung, *f.*	*far*-TAY-*dee-koon_g*	defense
farteyln (1b)	*far*-TAY-*lin*	distribute (allot), to
farteylung, *f.*	*far*-TAY-*loon_g*	distribution (allotment)
fartrakht	*far*-TRAH_KHT	thoughtful (reflective)
fartrogn (5b)	*far*-TRAWG-*in*	bear, to
"	"	endure, to
"	"	stand, to
fartsaytik	*far*-TSYE-*tick*	ancient
fartsaytikayt, *f.*	*far*-TSYE-*tee-kite*	antiquity (ancientness)
fartseykhenen (3b)	*far*-TSAY-*kheh-nen*	record (set down), to
fartsveyflt	*far*-TSVAY-*filt*	desperate
fartunklen (1b)	*far*-TOONK-*len*	darken (make dark), to
farumert	*far*-OO-*mehrt*	gloomy (melancholy)
farvalter, *m.*	*far*-VAHL-*tehr*	manager (administrator)
farvandlen (1b)	*far*-VAHND-*len*	convert (transform), to
"	"	turn, to
farvayln (1b)	*far*-VIE-*lin*	amuse, to
"	"	entertain, to
farvaylung, *f.*	*far*-VIE-*loon_g*	amusement
		entertainment
farvelkn (1b)	*far*-VEL-*kin*	wither, to

Yiddish	Pronunciation	English
farver, *m.*	*far*-VEHR	prohibition
farvern (1b)	*far*-VEH-*rin*	forbid, to
farvert	*far*-VEHRT	forbidden
farveykhern (1b)	*far*-VAY-*kheh-rin*	soften (mitigate), to
far vos	*far* VAWSS	why
farvundn (1b)	*far*-VOON-*din*	wound, to
farvyanet vern (7cd)	*far-vee*-AH-*net-veh-rin*	wilt, to
farzamlung, *f.*	*far*-ZAHM-*loon_g*	assembly
"	"	meeting
farze, *m.*	*far*-ZEH	oversight (error)
farzeenish, *f.*	*far*-ZEH-*eh-nish*	monster (beast)
farzetsn (1b)	*far*-ZET-*sin*	pawn, to
"	"	plant (sow), to
farzhavert	*far*-ZHAH-*vehrt*	rusty
farzikhern (1b)	*far*-ZEE-*kheh-rin*	assure, to
farzikhern zikh	*far*-ZEE-*kheh-rin zikh*	insure (make sure), to
farzorgn (1b)	*far*-ZORG-*in*	furnish, to
"	"	provide (supply), to
farzukhn (1b)	*far*-ZOO-*khin*	taste (sample), to
fas, *f.*	FAHSS	barrel (cask)
fashizm, *m.*	*fah*-SHEE-*zim*	fascism
fasolye, *f.*	*fah*-SAWL-*yeh*	bean (string bean)
fasttsayt, *f.*	FAHST-*tsyte*	Lent
fatal	*fah*-TAHL	fatal (fateful)
fayer, *n.*	FAH-*yehr*	fire
fayerlekh	FAH-*yehr-lukh*	solemn (grave)
fayer-lesher, *m.*	FAH-*yehr-leh-shehr*	fireman
fayershteyn, *m.*	FAH-*yehr-shtane*	flint
fayfn (1)	FY-*fin*	whistle, to
fayg, *f.*	FYE_G	fig
faykht	FYE_KHT	damp
"	"	moist
faykhtkayt, *f.*	FYE_KHT-*kite*	moisture
fayl, *f.*	FILE	file (tool)
fayl, *m.*	FILE	arrow
faylkhl, *n.*	FILE-*khil*	violet (flower)
fayn	FINE	fine (good)
faynd, *m.*	FYE_ND	foe
faynkukhn, *m.*	FINE-*koo-khin*	scrambled eggs
faynt hobn (25c)	FINE_T *haw-bin*	hate, to
fayntlekh	FINE_T-*lukh*	hostile
faze, *f.*	FAH-*zeh*	phase (stage)
feder, *f.*	FEH-*dehr*	feather
federal	*feh-deh*-RAHL	federal
federgroz, *n.*	FEH-*dehr-grawz*	fern
fefer, *m.*	FEH-*fehr*	pepper (green vegetable)
"	"	pepper (seasoning)
feik	FEH-*ick*	able
"	"	capable (competent)
feikayt, *f.*	FEH-*ee-kite*	ability
"	"	faculty
fel, *f.*	FELL	fleece
"	"	hide
"	"	skin (animal hide)
feld, *n.*	FELD	field (cleared land)
feldz, *m.*	FELDS	cliff
"	"	rock (large stone)
feler, grober, *m.*	GRAW-*behr* FEH-*lehr*	blunder
felik	FEH-*lik*	due (payable)
felik vern (7cd)	FEH-*lick veh-rin*	mature (fall due), to
feln, *n.*	FEH-*lin*	absence
feln (1)	FEH-*lin*	lack (be without), to
felndik	FEH-*lin-dick*	absent
fentster, *m.*	FENTS-*tehr*	window
ferd, *n.*	FEHRD	horse
ferdkraft, *f.*	FEHRD-*krahft*	horsepower
fershke, *f.*	FEHRSH-*keh*	peach
fertl, *n.*	FEHR-*til*	quarter (one-fourth)
fertl-yorik	FEHR-*til-yaw-rick*	quarterly (four times a year)
ferzn, *pl.*	FEHR-*zin*	verse (poetic writing)
fest	FEST	fast
"	"	firm (*adj.*)
"	"	stationary (unmoving)
"	"	steady
festshteln (1a)	FEST-*shteh-lin*	determine (ascertain), to

Yiddish	Pronunciation	English
festung, *f.*	FESS-*toon_g*	fortress
fet	FETT	fat (obese, *adj.*)
feter, *m.*	FEH-*tehr*	uncle
fets, *n.*	FETTS	fat (fatty tissue, *n.*)
"	"	grease (melted fat)
feye, *f.*	FEH-*yeh*	fairy (*n.*)
fidl, *m.*	FEE-*dil*	violin
figur, *f.*	*fee*-GOOR	figure (human form)
fikh, *n.*	FEEKH	cattle
"	"	stock (livestock)
Filipinen, *pl.*	*fee-lee*-PEE-*nen*	Philippines
film, *m.*	FEE-*lim*	film (*photog.*)
filosofye, *f.*	*fee-lo*-SAWF-*yeh*	philosophy
finantsn, *pl.*	*fee*-NAHNT-*sin*	finances
finantsyel	*fee-nahnts*-YELL	financial
finger, *m.*	FEEN_G-*ehr*	finger
finger (fun fus), *m.*	FEEN_G-*ehr (foon* FOOSS)	toe
fingerl, *n.*	FEEN_G-*eh-ril*	ring (jewelry)
finish	FEE-*nish*	Finnish (*adj.*)
finklen (1)	FEENK-*len*	glitter, to
"	"	sparkle, to
"	"	twinkle, to
Finland, *n.*	FEEN-*lahnd*	Finland
fintster	FEENTS-*tehr*	dark (without light, *adj.*)
fintsternish, *f.*	FEENTS-*tehr-nish*	darkness
firer, *m.*	FEE-*rehr*	driver (of automobile)
"	"	guide (one who guides)
firme, *f.*	FEER-*meh*	company (*bus.*)
"	"	concern (business firm)
"	"	establishment
"	"	firm (business company)
firn (1)	FEE-*rin*	drive (a vehicle), to
"	"	lead, to
"	"	operate (handle), to
firn zikh	FEE-*rin zikh*	act (behave), to
firung, *f.*	FEE-*roon_g*	practice (custom)
fish, *m.*	FEESH	fish
fisher, *m.*	FEE-*shehr*	fisherman
fishn (1)	FEE-*shin*	fish, to
fistashke, *f.*	*fee*-STAHSH-*keh*	peanut
fizik, *f.*	*fee*-ZEEK	physics (science)
fizish	FEE-*zish*	physical (bodily)
"	"	physical (material)
flakh	FLAH_KH	flat (level, *adj.*)
"	"	shallow
flakh, *f.*	FLAH_KH	plane (surface)
flaks, *m.*	FLAHX	flax
flam, *m.*	FLAHM	flame
flamen (1)	FLAH-*men*	blaze (burn brightly), to
flash, *f.*	FLAHSH	bottle
flaterl, *n.*	FLAH-*teh-ril*	butterfly
flatern (1)	FLAH-*teh-rin*	wave (flutter), to
flaysik	FLY-*sick*	diligent
"	"	industrious
fledermoyz, *f.*	FLEH-*dehr-moyz*	bat (animal)
flek, *m.*	FLECK	blot (stain)
"	"	spot (stain)
flekl, *n.*	FLEH-*kil*	peg (pin)
fleysh, *n.*	FLAYSH	flesh
"	"	meat
fleyt, *f.*	FLATE	flute (*mus.*)
fli, *m.*	FLEE	flight (journey by air)
flien (23d)	FLEE-*en*	fly, to
flier, *m.*	FLEE-*ehr*	aviator
flig, *f.*	FLEEG	fly (housefly)
fligl, *m.*	FLEEG-*il*	wing (*zool.*)
flikn (1)	FLEE-*kin*	pluck (pull off), to
fliplats, *m.*	FLEE-*plahts*	airport
flishlang, *f.*	FLEE-*shlahn_g*	kite
flisikayt, *f.*	FLEE-*see-kite*	liquid (*n.*)
flisn (7d)	FLEE-*sin*	flow (circulate), to
"	"	run, to
flokn, *m.*	FLAW-*kin*	club (cudgel)

Yiddish	Pronunciation	English
flot, *m.*	FLAWT	fleet (group of vessels)
floym, *f.*	FLOYM	plum (fruit)
floym, getriknte, *f.*	g_eh-TREE-kin-teh FLOYM	prune
fodem, *m.*	FAW-*dem*	thread (sewing thread)
fodern (1)	FAW-*deh-rin*	demand (ask for), to
foderung, *f.*	FAW-*deh-roon_g*	demand (request)
fokhen (2)	FAW-*khen*	flutter (flap), to
folgevdik	FAWLG-*ev-dick*	obedient
folgn (1)	FAWLG-*in*	obey, to
folgn, *n.*	FAWLG-*in*	obedience (compliance)
folgn, nit	*neet* FAWL-g_in	disobey, to
folk, *n.*	FAWL_K	people (populace)
folkstseylung, *f.*	FAWLX-*tsay-loon_g*	census
fon, *f.*	FAWN	banner
"		flag
fond, *m.*	FAWND	fund
fondn, *pl.*	FAWN-*din*	funds
fonograf, *m.*	*faw-no*-GRAHF	phonograph
fontan, *m.*	*fawn*-TAHN	fountain
for, *m.*	FOR	ride (in a car)
forel, *f.*	*faw*-RELL	trout
forgelt, *n.*	FOR-*g_elt*	fare (*transp.*)
forhang, *m.*	FOR-*hahn_g*	curtain (drape)
forleygn (1a)	FOR-*layg-in*	propose (suggest), to
"	"	submit (offer), to
forleygn khasene tsu hobn	FOR-*layg-in* KHAH-*seh-neh tsoo haw-bin*	propose (offer marriage), to
form, *f.*	FAW-*rim*	form (shape)
formelkayt, *f.*	*for*-MEL-*kite*	formality
formitl, *n.*	FOR-*mee-til*	vehicle (conveyance)
forml, *f.*	FOR-*mil*	formula (prescribed guide)
forn (5d)	FAW-*rin*	go, to
"	"	ride (in a car), to
fornt	FAW-*rint*	ahead (in front)
fornt, *m.*	FAW-*rint*	bow (of ship)
		front (forward part)
fornt, fun	*foon* FAW-*rint*	before (ahead, *adv.*)
foroys	*faw*-ROYSS	ahead
"	"	forward (*adv.*)
"	"	onward (*adv.*)
foroyszogn (1a)	*faw*-ROYSS-*zawg-in*	predict, to
forplan, *m.*	FOR-*plahn*	timetable
forshlog, *m.*	FOR-*shlawg*	proposal
"	"	suggestion
forshlogn (5a)	FOR-*shlawg-in*	suggest (recommend), to
forshn (1)	FOR-*shin*	explore, to
forshteln, *n.*	FOR-*shteh-lin*	introduction (presentation)
forshteln (1a)	FOR-*shteh-lin*	present (introduce), to
forshtelung, *f.*	FOR-*shteh-loon_g*	performance (stage presentation)
forshteyer, *m.*	FOR-*shteh-yehr*	representative (deputy)
forshung, *f.*	FOR-*shoon_g*	research
fort, *m.*	FORT	fort
forurteyl, *m.*	FOR-*oor-tale*	prejudice
forzitser, *m.*	FOR-*zee-tsehr*	chairman
foter, *m.*	FAW-*tehr*	father
fotografye, *f.*	*faw-taw*-GRAHF-*yeh*	photograph
foygl, *m.*	FOYG-*il*	bird
foyl	FOIL	lazy
foyln (1)	FOY-*lin*	rot, to
foylung, *f.*	FOY-*loon_g*	decay (rottenness)
foyst, *f.*	FOIST	fist
frage, *f.*	FRAHG-*eh*	question (query)
fragment, *m.*	*frahg*-MENT	fragment
frakht, *f.*	FRAH_KHT	cargo
"	"	freight
frakhttsetl, *n.*	FRAH_KHT-*tseh-til*	bill of lading
frandz, *m.*	FRAHNDZ	fringe
Frankraykh, *n.*	FRAHNK-*rye_kh*	France
frantseyzish	*frahnt*-SAY-*zish*	French (*adj.*)
fray	FRY	free (independent)
frayhayt, *f.*	FRY-*hite*	freedom
"	"	liberty
frayleydik	FRY-*lay-dick*	single (unmarried)
frayln, *n.*	FRY-*lin*	Miss
fraynd, guter, *m.*	*goo-tehr* FRYE_ND	friend
frayndlekh	FRYE_ND-*lukh*	friendly
frayndlekhkayt, *f.*	FRYE_ND-*lukh-kite*	kindness (favor)
fraytsayt, *f.*	FRY-*tsyte*	leisure
fraze, *f.*	FRAH-*zeh*	phrase (*gram.*)
fregn (1)	FREHG-*in*	ask (put question to), to
fregn vegn	FREHG-*in* VEG-*in*	ask about, to
fregn zikh	FREHG-*in zikh*	wonder (ask oneself), to
fremder, *m.*	FREM-*dehr*	stranger (unknown person)
frestl, *n.*	FREHSS-*til*	chill (coldness)
freyd, *f.*	FRADE	joy
freydik	FRAY-*dick*	joyful
freyen zikh (1)	FREH-*yen zikh*	rejoice, to
freylekh	FRAY-*lukh*	cheerful (joyful)
"	"	gay
"	"	jolly
"	"	merry
fri	FREE	early (ahead of time, *adv.*)
"	"	soon
fridlekh	FREED-*lekh*	peaceful (tranquil)
fridzhider, *m.*	*free-jee*-DEHR	refrigerator
frier	FREE-*ehr*	before (earlier, *adv.*)
"	"	before (in the past, *adv.*)
"	"	beforehand (*adv.*)
frierdik	FREE-*ehr-dik*	former (*adj.*)
"	"	previous
friik	FREE-*ik*	early (before-time, *adj.*)
friling, *m.*	FREE-*lin_g*	spring (season)
frimorgn, *m.*	*free*-MORG-*in*	morning
frish	FREESH	fresh (new)
"	"	fresh (not stale)
front, *m.*	FRAWNT	front (battle front)
frost, *m.*	FRAWST	frost
froy, *f.*	FROY	Mrs. (Mistress)
"	"	wife
"	"	woman
frukhperdik	FROOKH-*pehr-dick*	fertile
frukht, *f.*	FROOKHT	fruit
fuks, *m.*	FOOX	fox
ful	FOOL	full
fulmakht, *f.*	FOOL-*mah_kht*	power of attorney
fulshtendik	FOOL-*shten-dik*	complete (entire)
"	"	utter (*adj.*)
fun	FOON	from
"	"	of
funanderlozn (1a)	*foo*-NAHN-*dehr-law-zin*	dissolve (make end), to
funandersheydn (1a)	*foo*-NAHN-*dehr-shay-din*	distinguish (differentiate), to
fundament, *m.*	*foon-dah*-MENT	foundation (base)
fundamental	*foon-dah-men*-TAHL	fundamental
fun dest vegn	*foon* DEST *vehg-in*	however
"	"	nevertheless
funk, *m.*	FOONK	spark
funktsye, *f.*	FOONK_TS-*yeh*	function
funktsyonirung, *f.*	*foonkts-yo*-NEE-*roon_g*	performance (action)
furemen (1)	FOO-*reh-men*	form (shape), to
furemung, *f.*	FOO-*reh-moon_g*	formation (creation)
fus, *m.*	FOOSS	foot (*anat.*)
"	"	leg (*anat.*)
fusbol, *m.*	FOOSS-*ball*	soccer
futer, *m.*	FOO-*tehr*	fur
gadles, *f.*	GAHD-*less*	vanity (self-conceit)
galaret, *m.*	*ga-lah*-RETT	jelly
galerye, *f.*	*ga*-LEHR-*yeh*	gallery (balcony)
galop, *m.*	*ga*-LAWP	gallop (*n.*)
gandz, *f.*	GAHNDZ	goose
ganev, *m.*	GAH-*nev*	thief
ganeydn, *m.*	*gah*-NAY-*din*	heaven
"		paradise
gang, *m.*	GAHN_G	gear (*mech.*)
"	"	operation (functioning)
gang, lozn in (1)	LAW-*zin in* GAHN_G	launch (start), to

Yiddish	Pronunciation	English
gang foroys,*m.*	*gahn g faw*-ROYSS	advance (progress)
ganik,*m.*	GAH-*nick*	porch
gants	GAHNTS	all
"	"	entire
"	"	fairly (somewhat)
"	"	quite (considerably)
"	"	rather (somewhat)
"	"	total (complete)
"	"	whole (entire, *adj.*)
gantse,*n.*	GAHNT-*seh*	whole (entirety, *n.*)
gantsn, in	*in* GAHN-*tsin*	all (entirely, *adv.*)
"	"	altogether (entirely)
ganvenen (4)	GAHN-*veh-nen*	steal, to
garantirn (1b)	*gah-rahn*-TEE-*rin*	guarantee, to
garantye,*f.*	*gah*-RAHNT-*yeh*	guarantee (warrant)
garazh,*m.*	*ga*-RAH ZH	garage
garderob,*m.*	*gar-deh*-RAWB	wardrobe (apparel)
gare,*f.*	GAH-*reh*	furrow (*agric.*)
garn,*m.*	GAH-*rin*	yarn (fiber)
garn (1)	GAH-*rin*	crave (desire), to
garniter,*m.*	*gar*-NEE-*tehr*	suit, man's
garnizon,*m.*	*gar-nee*-ZAWN	garrison
gartl,*m.*	GAR-*til*	belt (article of clothing)
gas,*f.*	GAHSS	street
gast,*m.*	GAHST	guest (visitor)
gastgeber,*m.*	GAHST-*g eh-behr*	host
gayst,*m.*	GUY ST	ghost
"	"	mind (intellect)
"	"	spirit
gaystik	GUY-*stick*	mental
"	"	spiritual (*adj.*)
gaystlekher,*m.*	GUY ST-*lukh-ehr*	minister (clergyman)
"	"	parson
gaz,*m.*	GAHZ	gas
gazlen,*m.*	GAHZ-*len*	robber
gazolin,*f.*	*gah-zo*-LEEN	gasoline
gebn (13)	G EH-*bin*	give (bestow), to
gebn tsu farshteyn	G EH-*bin tsoo far*-SHTANE	indicate (suggest), to
geboyrener,*m.*	*g eh*-BOY-*reh-nehr*	native (*n.*)
geboyrn,*n.*	*g eh*-BOY-*rin*	birth
geboyrn-tog,*m.*	*g eh*-BOY-*rin-tawg*	birthday
geboyrn vern (7cd)	*g eh*-BOY-*rin veh-rin*	born, to be
gebrotns,*n.*	*g eh*-BRAW-*linss*	roast
gedank,*m.*	*g eh*-DAHNK	thought (idea)
gedayen (1b)	*g eh*-DIE-*en*	thrive (grow vigorously), to
gederem,*pl.*	*g eh*-DEH-*rem*	bowels (*anat.*)
gedikht	*g eh*-DEEKHT	dense
gedikhtenish,*f.*	*g eh*-DEEKH-*teh-nish*	thicket
gedoyern (1b)	*g eh*-DAW-*yeh-rin*	last (continue), to
gedrang,*m.*	*g eh*-DRAHN G	throng
geduld,*f.*	*g eh*-DOOLD	patience
geduldik	*g eh*-DOOL-*dick*	patient (forbearing)
gefangener,*m.*	*g eh*-FAHN-*g eh-nehr*	captive (prisoner)
gefil,*n.*	*g eh*-FEEL	feeling (emotion)
"	"	sensation
gefinen (8b)	*g eh*-FEE-*nen*	find (discover), to
"	"	locate, to
gegnt,*f.*	G EHG-*int*	area (region)
gehenem,*n.*	*g eh*-HEH-*nem*	hell
geherik	*g eh*-HEH-*rik*	due (proper)
"	"	respective (*adj.*)
gehern (1b)	*g eh*-HEH-*rin*	belong (be a part of), to
gehern tsu	*g eh*-HEH-*rin tsoo*	belong to (be the property of), to
geheym	*g eh*-HAME	secret (*adj.*)
gehilf,*m.*	*g eh*-HEELF	helper
gehilts,*n.*	*g eh*-HEELTS	lumber
"	"	timber (standing trees)
gehoybn	*g eh*-HOY-*bin*	lofty (high)
gekereveter proyektil,*m.*	*g eh*-KEH-*reh-veh-tehr praw-yeck*-TEEL	guided missile
gel	G EL	yellow (*adj.*)
gelegnhayt,*f.*	*g eh*-LEHG-*in-hite*	chance
"	"	occasion
"	"	opportunity
gelekhter,*n.*	*g eh*-LEKH-*tehr*	laughter
geler fiber,*m.*	G EH-*lehr* FEE-*behr*	yellow fever

Yiddish	Pronunciation	English
gelernter,*m.*	*g eh*-LEH-*rin-tehr*	scholar (savant)
geleymt	*g eh*-LAME T	numb
gelibte,*f.*	*g eh*-LEEB-*teh*	sweetheart
gelibter,*m.*	*g eh*-LEEB-*tehr*	sweetheart
gelt,*n.*	G ELT	currency
"	"	money
gelt-onvayzung,*f.*	G ELT-*awn-vie-zoon g*	money order
geltshikung,*f.*	G ELT-*shee-koon g*	remittance
geltshtrof,*f.*	G ELT-*shtrawf*	fine (penalty, *n.*)
gemel,*n.*	*g eh*-MEHL	illustration (pictorial representation)
"	"	painting (picture)
gemish,*m.*	*g eh*-MEESH	blend
"	"	compound
"	"	mixture
general,*m.*	*g eh-neh*-RAHL	general (officer)
genetsn (1)	G EH-*net-sin*	yawn, to
genit	*g eh*-NEET	veteran (experienced)
genitung,*f.*	*g eh*-NEE-*toon g*	exercise (drill)
genoy	*g eh*-NOY	exact (precise)
genug	*g eh*-NOOG	enough (*adj.*)
"	"	enough (*adv.*)
"	"	enough (*n.*)
genugik	*g eh*-NOOG-*ick*	adequate
"	"	sufficient
genugik, nit	NEET *g eh*-NOOG-*ick*	insufficient
geografye,*f.*	*g eh-o*-GRAHF-*yeh*	geography
geologye,*f.*	*g eh-o*-LAWG-*yeh*	geology
ger,*m.*	G EHR	convert (*to Judaism*)
gerangl,*m.*	*g eh*-RAN-*g ill*	struggle (great effort)
gerekhtik	*g eh*-REKH-*tick*	just (equitable, *adj.*)
gerekhtikayt,*f.*	*g eh*-REKH-*tee-kite*	justice (administration of law)
"	"	justice (rightfulness)
gerikht,*n.*	*g eh*-REE KHT	court (of law)
gern	G EH-*rin*	willing (favorably disposed)
gerotn (5bd)	*g eh*-RAW-*tin*	manage (contrive), to
gershtn,*pl.*	G EHRSH-*tin*	barley
gertner,*m.*	G EHRT-*nehr*	gardener
gesheenish,*f.*	*g eh*-SHEH-*eh-nish*	event (happening)
gesheft,*n.*	*g eh*-SHEFT	bargain (agreement)
"	"	business (commerce)
gesheftsman,*m.*	*g eh*-SHEFTS-*mahn*	businessman
geshen (6bd)	*g eh*-SHEN	happen, to
"	"	occur, to
geshikhte,*f.*	*g eh*-SHEEKH-*teh*	history
geshikt	*g eh*-SHEEKT	skilful
geshlekht,*n.*	*g eh*-SHLE KHT	sex
geshmelts,*n.*	*g eh*-SHMELLTS	alloy (metal)
geshpan,*n.*	*g eh*-SHPAHN	harness
geshrey,*m.*	*g eh*-SHRAY	cry (utterance)
"	"	shout
geshtalt,*n.*	*g eh*-SHTAHLT	shape (contour)
geshtroykhlt vern (7cd)	*g eh*-SHTROY-*khilt veh-rin*	stumble (trip), to
geshvind	*g eh*-SHVEEND	rapid (*adj.*)
gest,*pl.*	GUEST	company (guests)
get,*m.*	GET	divorce (*law*)
getlekh	GET-*lukh*	divine (*adj.*)
getrank,*m.*	*g eh*-TRAHNK	drink (beverage)
getray	*g eh*-TRY	faithful (loyal)
getrayshaft,*f.*	*g eh*-TRY-*shahft*	allegiance
"	"	devotion (loyal attachment)
getrog,*n.*	*g eh*-TRAWG	yield (product)
getroyen (1b)	*g eh*-TRAW-*yen*	trust (rely on), to
gets,*m.*	GETS	idol
getsatsket	*g eh*-TSAH TS-*ket*	fancy (ornamental, *adj.*)
getselt,*n.*	*g eh*-TSELT	tent
geule,*f.*	*g eh*-OO-*leh*	salvation
geveb,*n.*	*g eh*-VEB	fabric (cloth)
"	"	tissue (*biol.*)
gevet,*n.*	*g eh*-VEHT	bet
geveyntlekh	*g eh*-VAINT-*lukh*	common
"	"	ordinary
"	"	usual
geviks,*n.*	*g eh*-VEEKS	plant (flora)
gevinen (8b)	*g eh*-VEE-*nen*	bear (give birth to), to
"	"	gain (get), to

Yiddish	Pronunciation	English
gevinen	g_eh-VEE-nen	win (be victor in), to
gevinen punktn	g_eh-VEE-nen POONK-tin	score (gain points), to
gevins, n.	g_eh-VEENSS	gain (increase)
gevirts, n.	g_eh-VEERTS	spice
gevis	g_eh-VEESS	certain (particular)
gevisn, n.	g_eh-VEE-sin	conscience
gevoynhayt, f.	g_eh-VOYN-hite	habit (custom)
geyeg, n.	g_eh-YEGG	hunt (sport)
geyn (14d)	GAIN	go, to
"	"	walk, to
geyn brengen	GAIN BREN_G-en	fetch (bring), to
geyn foroys	GAIN faw-ROYSS	advance (go forward), to
gezegenung, f.	g_eh-ZEG-eh-noon_g	farewell (leave-taking)
gezelshaft, f.	g_eh-ZELL-shahft	society (association)
"	"	society (the public)
gezelshaftlekh	g_eh-ZELL-shahft-lukh	sociable (companionable)
gezets, n.	g_eh-ZETS	law (governing code)
"	"	law (statute)
gezets-gebung, f.	g_eh-ZETS-g_eh-boon_g	legislation
gezetslekh	g_eh-ZETS-lukh	lawful
gezunt	g_eh-ZOONT	healthy
"	"	sound
"	"	well (in health, *adj.*)
"	"	wholesome (beneficial)
gezunt, n.	g_eh-ZOONT	health
gezunt, zay(t)	ZIE(T) g_eh-ZOONT	good-by
gikh	G_EEKH	fast (quick)
"	"	fast (quickly)
gikhkayt, f.	G_EEKH-kite	speed (rapidity)
gilyen, m.	G_EEL-yen	margin (edge)
gimnastik, f.	g_im-NAHSS-tik	exercise (physical exertion)
gimnastisher zal, m.	g_im-NAHSS-tee-shehr ZAHL	gymnasium (athletic arena)
gintsik	G_EEN-tsik	favorable
girik	G_EE-rick	greedy
gisn (7)	G_EE-sin	pour (make flow), to
gitare, f.	g_ee-TAH-reh	guitar
glants, m.	GLAHNTS	luster (sheen)
"	"	splendor
glantsik	GLAHN-tsick	bright (shining)
glantsn (1)	GLAHNT-sin	gleam (shine), to
glat	GLAHT	smooth (*adj.*)
glaykh	GLYE_KH	equal (*adj.*)
"	"	erect (*adj.*)
"	"	level (flat)
"	"	straight (directly, *adv.*)
"	"	straight (not crooked, *adj.*)
glaykher, m.	GLYE-khehr	peer (equal)
glaykhgiltik	GLYE_KH-g_il-tick	indifferent (unconcerned)
glaykhn, des	dess GLYE-khin	likewise (also)
glaykhvog, f.	GLYE_KH-vawg	balance (equilibrium)
glentsndik	GLEN-tsin-dick	brilliant (remarkable)
"	"	splendid
glet-khayele, n.	GLET-khah-yeh-leh	pet (animal)
gletn (1)	GLEH-tin	stroke (rub gently), to
gleybn (1)	GLAY-bin	believe (accept), to
glien (1)	GLEE-en	glow (shine), to
glik, n.	GLEEK	happiness
glik, tsum	tsoom GLEEK	happily (luckily)
gliklekh	GLEEK-lukh	happy (glad)
glikzelikayt, f.	GLEEK-zeh-lee-kite	bliss
glitsher, m.	GLEE-chehr	skate, ice
glitshik	GLEE-chick	slippery
glitshn zikh (1)	GLEE-chin zikh	glide, to
"	"	slide, to
globus, m.	GLAW-boos	globe
glok, m.	GLAWK	bell
glorraykh	GLOR-rye_kh	glorious (resplendent)
glorye, f.	GLOR-yeh	glory (renown)
glosar, m.	glo-SAR	glossary
glotsn (1)	GLAWT-sin	stare, to
gloz, f.	GLAWZ	glass (vessel)
gloz, n.	GLAWZ	glass (material)

Yiddish	Pronunciation	English
goen, m.	GAW-en	genius
gold, n.	GAWLD	gold
goldn	GAWL-din	golden
gole	GAW-leh	sheer (pure)
goles, m.	GAW-less	exile (banishment)
golf, m.	GAWLF	golf
golmeser, n.	GAWL-meh-sehr	razor
gombe, f.	GAWM-beh	chin
gopl, m.	GAW-pil	fork (eating utensil)
"	"	plug (*elec.*)
gorn, m.	GAW-rin	floor
"	"	story
gornit	GOR-nit	nothing (*n.*)
gortn, m.	GOR-tin	garden
Got, m.	GAWT	God
goyel, m.	GAW-yell	savior
goyrem zayn (18c)	GOY-rem zine	cause, to
goyrl, m.	GOY-ril	fate
"	"	destiny
goyver zayn (18c)	GOY-vehr zine	beat, to
"	"	defeat (thwart), to
grable, f.	GRAHB-leh	rake (tool)
grad, m.	GRAHD	degree (unit of measurement)
gragern (1)	GRAHG-eh-rin	rattle, to
gram, m.	GRAHM	rhyme
gramatik, f.	grah-MAH-tick	grammar
grandyez	grahnd-YEHZ	grand (imposing)
granit, m.	grah-NEET	granite
grate, f.	GRAH-teh	grate (of furnace)
gratsye, f.	GRAHTS-yeh	grace (gracefulness)
gratsyez	grahts-YEHZ	graceful
gratulirn (1b)	grah-too-LEE-rin	congratulate, to
grayzl, n.	GRYE-zil	curl (ringlet)
greb, f.	GREB	thickness (dimension)
greber, m.	GREH-behr	miner
grenets, m.	GREH-nets	border
"	"	boundary (limit)
"	"	frontier
greser	GREH-sehr	major (larger)
greykh, m.	GRAY_KH	range (scope)
greys, f.	GRACE	extent (magnitude)
"	"	size (magnitude)
greyt	GREAT	ready (prepared)
grikhish	GREE-khish	Greek (*adj.*)
Grikhnland, n.	GREE-khin-lahnd	Greece
gril, f.	GREEL	cricket (insect)
griltsndik	GREEL-tsin-dick	harsh (grating)
grin	GREEN	green (color)
grinder, m.	GREEN-dehr	founder (*n.*)
grindn (1)	GREEN-din	establish (found), to
"	"	found (originate), to
grindung, f.	GREEN-doon_g	establishment (founding)
gring	GREEN_G	easy (not difficult)
"	"	light (of little weight)
gringkayt, f.	GREEN_G-kite	ease (comfort)
"	"	ease (effortlessness)
grins, n.	GREENS	vegetable
gripe, f.	GREE-peh	influenza
grive, f.	GREE-veh	mane (of horse)
grizhen (2)	GREE-zhen	gnaw (bite), to
grob	GRAWB	coarse
"	"	crude
"	"	gross (flagrant)
"	"	profane (blasphemous)
"	"	rough (harsh)
"	"	rude (impolite)
grober finger, m.	GRAW-behr FEEN-g_ehr	thumb
grobn (5)	GRAW-bin	dig (excavate), to
"	"	mine, to
grod	GRAWD	even (level, *adj.*)
grodek, m.	GRAW-deck	rectangle
gros, m.	GRAWSS	gross (twelve dozen)
groy	GROY	gray
groyl, m.	GROYL	horror (dread)
groylik	GROY-lick	horrible
groys	GROYSS	big
"	"	great
"	"	large
Groys-Britanye, f.	GROYSS-bree-TAHN-yeh	Great Britain

Yiddish	Pronunciation	English
groyskayt, *f.*	GROYSS-*kite*	greatness (eminence)
groz, *n.*	GRAWZ	grass
grub, *f.*	GROOB	mine
"	"	pit (hole)
grund, *m.*	GROOND	ground (basis)
grunt, *m.*	GROONT	ground (earth)
grunteygns, *n.*	GROONT-*ayg-inss*	real estate
gruntik	GROON-*tick*	thorough (complete)
grupe, *f.*	GROO-*peh*	group
gubernator, *m.*	*goo-behr-*NAH-*tor*	governor
guf, *m.*	GOOF	body (*anat.*)
gume, *f.*	GOO-*meh*	rubber
gut	GOOT	good
"	"	well (commendably, *adv.*)
gute mides, *pl.*	*goo-teh* MEE-*dess*	virtue (moral excellence)
guter fraytik, *m.*	GOO-*tehr* FRY-*tick*	Good Friday
gutfrayndshaft, *f.*	*goot-*FRYE ND-*shahft*	friendship
gutskayt, *f.*	GOOTS-*kite*	goodness
"	"	kindness
gvald, *f.*	GVAHLD	force (coercion)
"	"	violence
gvald-...	GVAHLD-...	violent
gvaldeven (2)	GVAHL-*deh-ven*	rave (rant), to
"	"	scream, to
gvaldik	GVAHL-*dick*	mighty (vast)
Gvatemala, *f.*	*gvah-teh-*MAH-*lah*	Guatemala
gvias-eydes, *m.*	*gvee-ahss-A-dess*	testimony
gvul, *m.*	GVOOL	limit
gvure, *f.*	GVOO-*reh*	feat
gvuredik	GVOO-*re-dick*	manly
hafsoke, *f.*	*hahf-*SAW-*keh*	lull (calm)
"	"	recess (school intermission)
Haiti, *n.*	*hah-*EE-*tee*	Haiti
hak, *f.*	HAHK	axe
"	"	hatchet
hakdome, *f.*	*hahk-*DAW-*meh*	preface
hakhnose, *f.*	*hah kh-*NAW-*seh*	income
"	"	revenue (*govt.*)
hakhnose-shtayer, *m.*	*hah kh-*NAW-*seh-shtye-ehr*	income tax
halb	HAHLB	half (*adj.*)
halbe levones, *pl.*	HAHL-*beh leh-*VAW-*ness*	parentheses
halber tog, *m.*	HAHL-*behr* TAWG	noon
halbindzl, *m.*	HAHL-*bind-zil*	peninsula
halbkaylekh, *m.*	HAHLB-*kye-lukh*	hemisphere (*geog.*)
halboshe, *f.*	*hahl-*BAW-*sheh*	attire (apparel)
"	"	clothing
haldz, *m.*	HAHLDZ	throat
haldzband, *m.*	HAHLDZ-*bahnd*	necklace
haldzn (1)	HAHLD-*zin*	hug, to
haldzveytik, *m.*	HAHLDZ-*vay-tick*	sore throat
halibut, *m.*	*hah-lee-*BOOT	halibut
haltn (5)	HAHL-*tin*	contend (maintain), to
"	"	hold, to
"	"	reckon (consider), to
haltn far	HAHL-*tin far*	deem (regard), to
haltn fun	HAHL-*tin foon*	advocate, to
"	"	approve (think well of), to
haltn in eyn	HAHL-*tin in* ANE	keep (continue), to
haltn zikh	HAHL-*tin zikh*	last (withstand use), to
haltn zikh oyfn vaser	HAHL-*tin zikh oy-fin* VAH-*sehr*	float (be buoyant), to
haltung, *f.*	HAHL-*toon g*	attitude (manner)
"	"	carriage (posture)
halvoe, *f.*	*hahl-*VAW-*eh*	loan
hamer, *m.*	HAH-*mehr*	hammer (tool)
hamoyn, *m.*	*hah-*MOYN	mob (disorderly crowd)
handl, *m.*	HAHN-*dill*	trade (commerce)
handlen (1)	HAHND-*len*	act (do), to
"	"	deal (trade), to
handls-...	HAHN-*dils-...*	mercantile
handls-kamer, *f.*	HAHN-*dilss-kah-mehr*	chamber of commerce
handls-marke, *f.*	HAHN-*dils-mar-keh*	trade mark
hanoe, *f.*	*hah-*NAW-*eh*	fun
hanoe hobn fun (25c)	*hah-*NAW-*eh haw-bin foon*	enjoy (derive joy from), to
hanoe-nesie, *f.*	*hah-*NAW-*eh-neh-see-eh*	cruise (voyage)
hanokhe, *f.*	*hah-*NAW-*kheh*	discount (*n.*)

Yiddish	Pronunciation	English
hant, *f.*	HAHNT	hand (*anat.*)
"	"	handful
hant, tsu der	*tsoo dehr* HAHNT	handy (near at hand)
hant-...	HAHNT-...	manual (by hand)
hantbukh, *n.*	HAHNT-*bookh*	manual (small book)
hantekh, *n.*	HAHN-*tukh*	towel, hand
hantgelenk, *n.*	HAHNT-*g eh-lenk*	wrist
har, *m.*	HAR	lord (master)
harbst, *m.*	HARBST	autumn
"	"	fall
harf, *f.*	HARF	harp
harmat, *m.*	*har-*MAHT	cannon
harmonye, *f.*	*har-*MAWN-*yeh*	accordion
"	"	harmony (*mus.*)
hart	HART	hard (not soft)
"	"	tough (resistant)
harteven (2)	HAR-*teh-ven*	harden (make hard), to
harts, *n.*	HEARTS	heart
hartsik	HAR-*tsik*	cordial (*adj.*)
"	"	hearty
hashpoe, *f.*	*hah-*SHPAW-*eh*	influence
haskhole, *f.*	*hahss-*KHAW-*leh*	opening (beginning, *n.*)
haskome, *f.*	*hahss-*KAW-*meh*	approval
hasmode, *f.*	*hahss-*MAW-*deh*	diligence
hasoge, *f.*	*hah-*SAWG-*eh*	conception (notion)
hatslokhe, *f.*	*hahts-*LAW-*kheh*	success (attainment)
Havai, *n.*	*hah-*VAH-*ee*	Hawaii
havtokhe, *f.*	*hahv-*TAW-*kheh*	pledge (vow)
haynt	HINE T	today
haynt in ovnt	HINE T *in* AW-*vint*	tonight
haynttsaytik	HYE NT-*tsye-tick*	contemporary (modern)
haytl, *n.*	HYE-*til*	film (thin coating)
hayzl, *n.*	HYE-*zil*	lodge (cabin)
hazhgokhe, *f.*	*hah zh-*GAW-*kheh*	care (custody)
hebreish	*heh-*BREH-*ish*	Hebrew (*adj.*)
hefkerdik	HEF-*kehr-dick*	reckless
heft, *f.*	HEFT	notebook
hekher	HEH-*khehr*	up (*adv.*)
hekhern (1a)	HEH-*kheh-rin*	promote (raise in rank), to
hekherung, *f.*	HEH-*kheh-roon g*	promotion (advance)
hekhst	HEKH ST	supreme
"	"	top (highest, *adj.*)
hel	HELL	fair (blond)
held, *m.*	HELD	hero
heldin, *f.*	HELL-*din*	heroine
heldish	HELL-*dish*	brave
helfant, *m.*	HELL-*fahnt*	elephant
helfantbeyn, *m.*	HELL-*fahnt-bane*	ivory
helfn (7)	HELL-*fin*	aid, to
"	"	help, to
helft, *f.*	HELFT	half (*n.*)
helikopter, *m.*	*heh-lee-kawp-*TEHR	helicopter
Helsingfors, *n.*	HELL-*sin g-force*	Helsinki
helter hobn (25c)	HELL-*tehr* HAW-*bin*	prefer (like better), to
hemd, *n.*	HEMD	shirt
hemshekh, *m.*	HEM-*shukh*	continuation
hengen (24d)	HEN G-*en*	hang (be suspended), to
"	"	hang (suspend), to
hentl, *n.*	HEN-*til*	handle
hentshke, *f.*	HENCH-*keh*	glove
hentshke on finger, *f.*	HENCH-*keh awn* FEEN G-*ehr*	mitten
her, *m.*	HEHR	Mr. (Mister)
hering, *m.*	HEH-*rin g*	herring
hern (1)	HEH-*rin*	hear, to
hershaft, *f.*	HEHR-*shahft*	rule (political control)
hersher, *m.*	HEHR-*shehr*	ruler (sovereign)
hershn (1)	HEHR-*shin*	prevail (exist widely), to
"	"	rule (govern), to
heskem, *m.*	HESS-*kehm*	accord
"	"	agreement (mutual understanding)
hetsn (1)	HET-*sin*	bait (harass), to
hey, *n.*	HAY	hay
heyber, *m.*	HAY-*behr*	lever
heybn (10)	HAY-*bin*	heave, to
"	"	lift (raise), to

Yiddish	Pronunciation	English
heybn zikh	HAY-*bin zikh*	climb, to
"	"	rise (increase), to
heykh,*f.*	HAY_KH	height (highness)
"	"	stature
heyl,*f.*	HALE	cave
heylik	HAY-*lick*	holy
"	"	sacred
heyliker,*m.*	HAY-*lee-kehr*	saint
heyln (1)	HAY-*lin*	heal (cure), to
heym,*f.*	HAME	home
heymbrand,*m.*	HAME-*brahnd*	hearth
heymish	HAY-*mish*	homely (everyday)
heypekh,*m.*	HAY-*pukh*	opposite (*n.*)
"	"	reverse (contrary, *n.*)
heys	HACE	hot
heytsn (1)	HATE-*sin*	heat, to
heyvn,*pl.*	HAY-*vin*	yeast
hilf,*f.*	HEELF	aid
"	"	assistance
"	"	help
"	"	relief
hilf, gikhe,*f.*	GEE-*kheh* HEELF	first aid (*med.*)
himl,*m.*	HEE-*mil*	sky
hinken (8)	HEEN-*ken*	limp, to
hinter	HEEN-*tehr*	behind (*prep.*)
hintersht	HEEN-*tehrsht*	hind (posterior, *adj.*)
"	"	rear (*adj.*)
hintershtelik	HEEN-*tehr-shteh-lick*	behind (late, *adv.*)
hintershte zayt,*f.*	HIN-*tehrsh-teh-*ZITE	back (reverse side)
hintervaylekhts	HEEN-*tehr-vie-leh-khts*	backward (rearward, *adv.*)
hintn	HEEN-*tin*	behind (in the rear, *adv.*)
hipotek,*f.*	*hee-po-*TECK	mortgage
hipsh	HEEPSH	substantial (sizable)
hirsh,*m.*	HEERSH	buck (male deer)
hirzhen (2)	HEER-*zhen*	neigh, to
hiskhayves,*f.*	*hiss-*KHYE-*vess*	commitment (*bus.*)
"	"	obligation (duty)
hispayles,*f.*	*hiss-*PIE-*less*	rapture
historish	*hiss-*TAW-*rish*	historical
hitl,*n.*	HEE-*til*	cap (hat)
hitn (1)	HEE-*tin*	guard (watch over), to
hitn zikh far	HEE-*tin zikh far*	beware of, to
hits,*f.*	HEETS	fever
"	"	heat
hober,*m.*	HAW-*behr*	oats
hobn (25)	HAW-*bin*	have, to
hodeven (2)	HAW-*deh-ven*	grow (cultivate), to
hofenung,*f.*	HAW-*feh-noon_g*	hope
hofenung, ful mit	FOOL *mit* HAW-*feh-noon_g*	hopeful
hofenung, on	AWN HAW-*feh-noon_g*	hopeless
hofn (1)	HAW-*fin*	hope, to
hogl,*m.*	HAWG-*il*	hail (ice)
hoglen (1)	HAWG-*len*	hail (precipitate hail), to
Holand,*n.*	HAW-*lahnd*	Holland
holendish	HAW-*len-dish*	Dutch (*adj.*)
holts,*n.*	HAWLTS	wood (lumber)
homar,*m.*	*haw-*MAR	lobster
hon,*m.*	HAWN	cock
"	"	rooster
Honduras,*n.*	*hawn-*DOO-*rahss*	Honduras
honik,*m.*	HAW-*nick*	honey
honorar,*m.*	*haw-no-*RAR	royalty (fee)
hopken (2)	HAWP-*ken*	skip (caper), to
hor,*m.*	HORE	hair
horizont,*m.*	*ho-ree-*ZAWNT	horizon
horizontal	*haw-ree-zawn-*TAHL	horizontal (*adj.*)
horn,*m.*	HAW-*rin*	horn (*anat.*)
"	"	horn (*mus.*)
hotel,*m.*	*ho-*TELL	hotel
hoyf,*m.*	HOYF	court (of ruler)
"	"	yard (enclosure near house)
hoyker,*m.*	HOY-*kehr*	hump
hoykh	HOYKH	aloud
"	"	high
"	"	loud (resounding)
"	"	tall

Yiddish	Pronunciation	English
hoyl	HOYL	hollow (*adj.*)
hoypt-...	HOYPT-...	chief (leading)
"	"	main
"	"	principal
hoyptkvartir,*f.*	HOYPT-*kvar-teer*	headquarters
hoyptshtot,*f.*	HOYPT-*shtawt*	capital (city)
hoyt,*f.*	HOYT	skin (human skin)
hoytsoe,*f.*	*hoy-*TSAW-*eh*	expenditure (outlay)
"	"	expense (cost)
hoytsoes, generale, *pl.*	*g_eh-neh-*RAH-*leh hoy-*TSAW-*ess*	overhead (expenses, *bus.*)
hoyz,*n.*	HOYZ	house
hoyzn,*pl.*	HOY-*zin*	trousers
hoz,*m.*	HAWZ	hare
humor,*m.*	*hoo-*MORE	humor (drollery)
hun,*f.*	HOON	chicken
"	"	hen
hunger,*m.*	HOON-*g_ehr*	hunger
hungerik	HOON-*g_eh-rick*	hungry
hungerik, zayn (18d)	ZINE HOON-*g_eh-rick*	hungry, to be
hunt,*m.*	HOONT	dog
hurt-...	HOORT-...	wholesale (*adj., bus.*)
hurtovnik,*m.*	*hoor-*TAWV-*nick*	wholesaler (*bus.*)
hust,*m.*	HOOST	cough
hut,*m.*	HOOT	hat
iber	EE-*ber*	above (higher than, *prep.*)
"	"	over
iberbaysn,*m.*	EE-*behr-bye-sin*	breakfast
iberblik,*m.*	EE-*behr-bleek*	survey (inspection)
iberentfern (1a)	EE-*behr-ent-feh-rin*	surrender (relinquish), to
ibergebn,*n.*	EE-*behr-g_eh-bin*	delivery (handing over).
ibergebn (13a)	EE-*behr-g_eh-bin*	convey (communicate), to
"	"	deliver (hand over), to
"	"	relate (tell), to
iberhipern (1a)	EE-*behr-hee-peh-rin*	skip (omit), to
iberik	EE-*beh-rick*	excessive
iberkern (1a)	EE-*behr-keh-rin*	overturn, to
"	"	upset (knock over), to
iberkhazern (1a)	EE-*behr-khah-zeh-rin*	repeat (reiterate), to
iberkukn (1a)	EE-*behr-koo-kin*	review (look over again), to
iberlebung,*f.*	EE-*behr-leh-boon_g*	experience (conscious event)
iberlozn (1a)	EE-*behr-law-zin*	leave (let remain), to
iberlozn zikh	EE-*behr-law-zin zikh*	reserve (withhold), to
ibermakhn (1a)	EE-*behr-mah-khin*	transform, to
iberraysn (9a)	EE-*behr-rye-sin*	interrupt, to
iberredn (1a)	EE-*behr-reh-din*	persuade, to
iberrukn (1a)	EE-*behr-roo-kin*	move (shift the position of), to
iberrukn zikh	EE-*behr-roo-kin zikh*	move (shift one's position), to
ibershiker,*m.*	EE-*behr-shee-kehr*	shipping agent
ibershikn (1a)	EE-*behr-shee-kin*	forward (send by mail), to
"	"	remit (send payment), to
"	"	ship (send goods), to
ibershoen,*pl.*	EE-*behr-shaw-en*	overtime (*bus., n.*)
ibershraybn,*n.*	EE-*behr-shrye-bin*	assignment (legal transfer)
ibershrek,*m.*	EE-*behr-shreck*	fright (alarm)
ibershrekn (7a)	EE-*behr-shreh-kin*	frighten (make afraid), to
"	"	scare, to
ibertsaygung,*f.*	*ee-behr-*TSYE-*goon_g*	conviction (belief)
iberzetsn (1a)	EE-*behr-zet-sin*	translate, to
ideal,*m.*	*ee-deh-*AHL	ideal (*n.*)
idee,*f.*	*ee-*DAY-*eh*	idea
identifitsirn (1b)	*ee-den-tee-feet-*SEE-*rin*	identify, to
ikerdik	EE-*kehr-dik*	essential (*adj.*)
ikh	EEKH	I
ilustratsye,*f.*	*ee-loo-*STRAHTS-*yeh*	illustration (example)
ilustrirn (1b)	*ee-loo-*STREE-*rin*	illustrate (exemplify), to
iluzye,*f.*	*ee-*LOOZ-*yeh*	illusion
im	EEM	him

Yiddish	Pronunciation	English	Yiddish	Pronunciation	English
imperye, *f.*	*im*-PEHR-*yeh*	empire	ir	EER	her
imponirn (1b)	*eem-po*-NEE-*rin*	impress (affect deeply), to	irer	EE-*rehr*	hers
			irish	EE-*rish*	Irish (*adj.*)
import, *m.*	*eem*-PORT	importation	Irland, *n.*	EER-*lahnd*	Ireland
importirer, *m.*	*eem-por*-TEE-*rehr*	importer			
importirn (1b)	*eem-por*-TEE-*rin*	import, to (*bus.*)	istmos, *m.*	EAST-*moss*	isthmus
in	IN	in (during, *prep.*)	Italye, *f.*	*ee*-TAHL-*yeh*	Italy
"	"	in (inside, *prep.*)	italyenish	*ee-tahl*-YEH-*nish*	Italian (*adj.*)
"	"	inside (within, *prep.*)	itst	EETST	now (*adv.*)
in...arayn	*in...ah*-RINE	in (into, *prep.*)	itstik	EETS-*tick*	present (current, *adj.*)
"	"	into (to the inside)			
in a zayt	*in ah* ZITE	aside (away)	itstikayt, *f.*	EETS-*tee-kite*	present (present time, *n.*)
indik, *m.*	EEN-*dick*	turkey			
individuel	*een-dee-vee-doo*-ELL	individual (particular, *adj.*)	itst on, fun	*foon* EETST AWN	henceforth
			"	"	hereafter (after this, *adv.*)
indorsirn (1b)	*in-dor*-SEE-*rin*	endorse (sign), to			
			iz	EEZ	so (therefore, *adv.*)
indorsirung, *f.*	*in-dor*-SEE-*roon_g*	endorsement (signature)	kaas, *m.*	KAHSS	anger
			kabinet, *m.*	*kah-bee*-NET	cabinet (*govt.*)
industriel	*in-doo-stree*-ELL	industrial	kabl, *m.*	KAH-*bil*	cable (rope)
industrye, *f.*	*in*-DOO-*stree-eh*	industry (trade)			
Indyaner, *m.*	*eend*-YAH-*nehr*	Indian, American	kablen (1)	KAHB-*len*	cable, to
Indye, *f.*	EEND-*yeh*	India	kablgram, *f.*	*kah-bil*-GRAHM	cablegram
			kabolas-ponem, *m.*	*kah*-BAW-*lahss*-PAW-*nem*	welcome (*n.*)
indzl, *m.*	EEND-*zil*	island (*geog.*)			
infektsye, *f.*	*een*-FECK-*tsee-yeh*	infection	kabole, *f.*	*kah*-BAW-*leh*	receipt (voucher)
inflatsye, *f.*	*in*-FLAHTS-*yeh*	inflation (*econ.*)	Kairo, *n.*	KAH-*ee-ro*	Cairo
informatsye, *f.*	*in-for*-MAHTS-*yeh*	information	kakao, *m.*	*kah*-KAH-*aw*	cocoa
ingber, *m.*	EEN_G-*behr*	ginger (spice)	kalb, *n.*	KAHLB	calf (animal)
in gor	*in* GORE	throughout (in every part of, *prep.*)	kale, *f.*	KAH-*leh*	bride
			kalendar, *m.*	*kah-len*-DAR	calendar
inhalt, *m.*	EEN-*hahlt*	contents			
			kalifyor, *m.*	*kah-leef*-YOR	cauliflower
initsyal, *m.*	*ee-nits*-YAHL	initial (letter)	kalike, *m., f.*	KAH-*lee-keh*	cripple
inlendish	EEN-*len-dish*	domestic (not foreign)	kalkhshteyn, *m.*	KAHL_KH-*shtane*	limestone
			kalorye, *f.*	*kah*-LOR-*yeh*	calorie
in oysland	*in* OYSS-*lahnd*	abroad (in foreign land)	kaloshn, *pl.*	*kah*-LAW-*shin*	galoshes
			"	"	rubbers (overshoes)
insekt, *m.*	*in*-SECT	insect			
inspiratsye, *f.*	*in-spee*-RAHTS-*yeh*	inspiration	kalt	KAHLT	cold (*adj.*)
			kaluzhe, *f.*	*kah*-LOO-*zhuh*	pool (standing water)
inspirirn (1b)	*in-spee*-REE-*rin*	inspire, to	kalye	KAHL-*yeh*	wrong (amiss, *adv.*)
instalirn (1b)	*in-stah*-LEE-*rin*	install (set up for use), to	kalye makhn (1)	KAHL-*yeh mah-khin*	spoil (mar), to
			kam, *m.*	KAHM	comb (for hair)
instinkt, *m.*	*in*-STEENKT	instinct	"	"	crest (summit)
institut, *m.*	*in-stee*-TOOT	institute			
institutsye, *f.*	*in-stee*-TOOTS-*yeh*	institution (establishment)	kamf, *m.*	KAHM_F	combat
			"	"	fight
instrument, *m.*	*in-stroo*-MENT	instrument (implement)	kamin, *m.*	*kah*-MEEN	fireplace
			kampanye, *f.*	*kahm*-PAHN-*yeh*	campaign (*mil.*)
intelektuel	*in-teh-leck-too*-ELL	intellectual (*adj.*)	kamtsn, *m.*	KAHM-*tsin*	miser
			Kanade, *f.*	*kah*-NAH-*deh*	Canada
inteligent	*in-teh-lee*-G_ENT	intelligent			
inteligents, *f.*	*in-teh-lee*-G_ENTS	intelligence (understanding)	kanadish	*kah*-NAH-*dish*	Canadian (*adj.*)
			kanal, *m.*	*kah*-NAHL	canal
intensiv	*in-ten*-SEEV	intense	"	"	channel (strait)
interes, *m.*	*in-teh*-RESS	interest (attention)	"	"	sewer (conduit)
"	"	interest (engaging quality)	kanape, *f.*	*kah*-NAH-*peh*	couch
interesant	*in-teh-reh*-SAHNT	interesting	kanarik, *m.*	*kah*-NAH-*rik*	canary
interesirn (1b)	*in-teh-reh*-SEE-*rin*	interest, to	kandidat, *m.*	*kahn-dee*-DAHT	candidate
			kane, *f.*	KAH-*neh*	enema
internatsyonal	EEN-*tehr-nahts-yaw*-NAHL	international	kant, *m.*	KAHNT	edge (border)
			kantshaft, *f.*	KAHNT-*shahft*	acquaintance (knowledge)
intervyu, *m.*	*in-tehr*-VIEW	interview			
intim	*in*-TEEM	intimate (personal)	kanu, *m.*	*kah*-NOO	canoe
intsident, *m.*	*een-tsee*-DENT	incident (event)	kap, *m.*	KAHP	cape (headland)
intuitsye, *f.*	*in-too*-EETS-*yeh*	intuition			
inventar, *m.*	*in-ven*-TAR	inventory (*bus.*)	kapelye, *f.*	*kah*-PEHL-*yeh*	band (instrumental group)
			"	"	chapel
investirn (1b)	*in-vess*-TEE-*rin*	invest, to (*bus.*)	kapen (2)	KAH-*pen*	drip, to
investitsye, *f.*	*in-vess*-TEETS-*yeh*	investment (*bus.*)	kapital, *m.*	*kah-pee*-TAHL	capital (wealth)
inveynik	EEN-*vay-nick*	indoors (*adv.*)	kapitan, *m.*	*kah-pee*-TAHN	captain (officer)
"	"	inside (within, *adv.*)	kapitl, *m.*	*kah*-PEE-*til*	chapter (of book)
"	"	within (on the inside, *adv.*)			
			kapitulatsye, *f.*	*kah-pee-too*-LAHTS-*yeh*	surrender (*mil.*)
inveynik, *m.*	EEN-*vay-nick*	inside (interior, *n.*)	kapral, *m.*	*cahp*-RAHL	corporal (*mil.*)
"	"	interior (inside, *n.*)	kaptur, *m.*	KAHP-*toor*	hood (cowl)
inveynik in	ENN-*vay-nick in*	within (inside, *prep.*)	Karatshi, *n.*	*kah*-RAH-*chee*	Karachi
			karete, *f.*	KAH-*reh-teh*	carriage (horse-drawn vehicle)
inveynikst	EEN-*vay-nixt*	inner			
"	"	inside (*adj.*)	karg	KARG	stingy
"	"	internal	karikatur, *f.*	*kah-ree-kah*-TOOR	cartoon (caricature)
inyen, *m.*	EEN-*yen*	affair	kark, *m.*	KARK	neck (*anat.*)
"	"	issue (question)	karlik, *m.*	KAR-*lik*	dwarf
inyen, *m.*	EEN-*yen*	matter	karnaval, *m.*	*kar-nah*-VAHL	carnival
inzhenir, *m.*	*een-zheh*-NEER	engineer (professional engineer)	karsh, *f.*	KARSH	cherry (fruit)
			karte, *f.*	KAR-*teh*	map

Yiddish	Pronunciation	English
kartl, *n.*	KAR-*til*	card, calling
"	"	card, postal
kartofl, *m.*	*kar*-TAW-*fil*	potato (white)
karton, *m.*	*kar*-TAWN	cardboard
karyere, *f.*	*kar*-YEH-*reh*	career
kashe, *f.*	KAH-*sheh*	cereal (prepared food)
kasirer, *m.*	*kah*-SEE-*rehr*	cashier
kaske, *f.*	KAHSS-*keh*	helmet
kastn, *m.*	KAHSS-*tin*	chest (box)
katalog, *m.*	*kah-tah*-LAWG	catalogue
katastrofe, *f.*	*kah-tah*-STRAW-*feh*	disaster
katedral, *m.*	*kah-ted*-RAHL	cathedral
katoves, *m.*	*kah*-TAW-*vess*	jest (joke)
katoves, traybn (9)	TRY-*bin kah*-TAW-*vess*	jest (joke), to
katoylish	*kah*-TOY-*lish*	Catholic (*adj.*)
kats, *f.*	KAHTS	cat
katsev, *m.*	KAH-*tsev*	butcher
katshke, *f.*	KAH_CH-*keh*	duck
kave, *f.*	KAH-*veh*	coffee
kavenik, *m.*	KAH-*veh-nik*	coffee pot
kavone, *f.*	*kah*-VAW-*neh*	design
"	"	intention
kayen (1)	KYE-*en*	chew, to
kaygume, *f.*	KYE-*goo-meh*	gum (chewing gum)
kaykhhust, *m.*	KYE_KH-*hoost*	whooping cough
kayklen (1)	KIKE-*len*	roll (impel), to
kaylekh, *m.*	KYE-*lukh*	sphere (globe)
kaylekhdik	KYE-*lukh-dik*	circular (*adj.*)
"	"	round (*adj.*)
kayor, *m.*	*kah*-YOR	dawn (daybreak)
kayute, *f.*	*kah*-YOO-*teh*	cabin (of ship)
kedey	*keh*-DAY	so (in order that, *conj.*)
"	"	to (in order to, *prep.*)
kedey nit	*keh*-DAY NEET	lest
kegener, *m.*	KEG-*eh-nehr*	opponent (*n.*)
kegn	KEG-*in*	against
kegnshtel, *m.*	KEG-*in-shtel*	opposition
"	"	resistance
kegn-untershrift, *f.*	KEG-*in-oon-tehr-shrift*	countersignature (*bus.*)
kegnzaytik	KEG-*in-zye-tick*	mutual
kelberner kotlet, *m.*	KEL-*behr-nehr kawt*-LET	veal chop
kelberns, *n.*	KEL-*beh-rinse*	veal
keler, *m.*	KEH-*lehr*	basement
"	"	cellar
kelishek, *m.*	KEH-*lee-sheck*	tumbler (glass)
kelner, *m.*	KEL-*nehr*	waiter
kelt, *f.*	KELT	cold (low temperature)
kemerl, *n.*	KEH-*meh-ril*	cell (biol.)
kemfn (1)	KEM-*fin*	fight (contend), to
keml, *m.*	KEH-*mil*	camel
kenen (1e)	KEN-*en*	can (*v.*)
"	"	know (be acquainted with), to
kentenish, *f.*	KEN-*teh-nish*	knowledge (understanding)
kentik	KEN-*tik*	evident
"	"	visible
kepl, *n.*	KEH-*pil*	heading (title)
ker, *m.*	KEHR	turn (change of direction)
kereven (2)	KEH-*reh-ven*	steer, to
kerme, *f.*	KEHR-*meh*	rudder (of a boat)
kerndl, *n.*	KEH-*rin-dil*	kernel
keseyderdik	*keh*-SAY-*dehr-dik*	constant
"	"	continual
"	"	continuous
keshene, *f.*	KEH-*sheh-neh*	pocket
kesl, *m.*	KEH-*sil*	kettle
kestl, *n.*	KESS-*til*	box (container)
kestnboym, *m.*	KEHSS-*tin-boym*	chestnut (tree)
ketsl, *n.*	KETS-*il*	kitten
keyflen (1)	KAFE-*len*	multiply, to (*arith.*)
keyle, *f.*	KAY-*leh*	vessel (receptacle)
keylim, *pl.*	KAY-*lim*	dishes (tableware)
keyn	KANE	no (not any, *adj.*)
"	"	to (indicating direction, *prep.*)

Yiddish	Pronunciation	English
keyne	KAY-*neh*	any (*pron.*)
keyner nit	KAY-*nehr neet*	anybody (not...anybody)
"	"	anyone (not...anyone)
"	"	nobody (*pron.*)
"	"	none (*pron.*)
keyn mol nit	KANE *mawl nit*	never
keyn zakh nit	KANE *zah_kh neet*	anything (not...anything)
keyser, *m.*	KAY-*sehr*	emperor
keyserin, *f.*	KAY-*seh-rin*	empress
keyserlekh	KAY-*sehr-lukh*	imperial
keyt, *f.*	KATE	chain
keyver, *m.*	KAY-*vehr*	grave
"	"	tomb
kez, *m.*	KEZZ	cheese
khakhomish	*kh_ah*-KHAW-*mish*	sage (*adj.*)
khaleshn (1)	KHAH-*leh-shin*	faint, to
khaloshes, *f.*	*khah*-LAW-*shess*	faint (swoon, *n.*)
khaneles eygele, *n.*	KHAH-*neh-less* AIG-*eh-leh*	pansy
khanfenen (4)	KHAHN-*feh-nen*	flatter (praise insincerely), to
khap, *m.*	KHAHP	grip (grasp)
khapn (1)	KHAH-*pin*	capture, to
"	"	catch (nab), to
"	"	grab, to
"	"	seize, to
"	"	snatch, to
kharakter, *m.*	*khah*-RAHK-*tehr*	character (nature)
kharakteristish	*khah-rahk-teh*-REESS-*tish*	characteristic (typical)
kharote hobn (25c)	*khah*-RAW-*teh haw-bin*	repent, to
kharpe, *f.*	KHAR-*peh*	disgrace
"	"	shame
khasene, *f.*	KHAH-*seh-neh*	wedding
khasene gehat	KHAH-*seh-neh g_eh*-HAHT	married
khasene hobn (mit) (25c)	KHAH-*seh-neh haw-bin* (*mit*)	marry, to
khate, *f.*	KHAH-*teh*	hut
khaver, *m.*	KHAH-*vehr*	companion
"	"	comrade
"	"	pal
khaye, *f.*	KHAH-*yeh*	animal
"	"	beast
khazer, *m.*	KHAH-*zehr*	hog (animal)
"	"	pig (animal)
khazer, *m.*	KHAH-*zehr*	swine
khazer-fleysh, *n.*	KHAH-*zehr-flaysh*	pork
khazerish nisl, *n.*	KHAH-*zeh-rish* NEE-*sil*	acorn
khazer-kotlet, *m.*	KHAH-*zehr-kawt-lett*	pork chop
khazer-shmalts, *n.*	KHAH-*zehr-shmahlts*	lard
khemye, *f.*	KHEM-*yeh*	chemistry
khet, *m.*	KHET	offense (transgression)
khevre-man, *m.*	KHEV-*reh-mahn*	fellow (person)
"	"	guy
kheyfets, *m.*	KHAY-*fets*	article (thing)
kheylek, *m.*	KHAY-*lek*	division
"	"	interest
"	"	portion (part)
"	"	share (part)
kheyn, *m.*	KHAYN	charm (attraction)
kheynevdik	KHAY-*nev-dik*	charming
khezhbenen (3)	KHE_ZH-*beh-nen*	reckon (compute), to
khezhbn, *m.*	KHEZH-*bin*	account (calculation)
"	"	bill
"	"	invoice
khezhbn-firer, *m.*	KHE_ZH-*bin-fee-rehr*	accountant
khidesh, *m.*	KHEE-*desh*	astonishment
"	"	surprise
"	"	wonder
khilek, *m.*	KHEE-*lek*	difference (dissimilarity)
Khine, *f.*	KHEE-*neh*	China
khinezish	*khee*-NEH-*zish*	Chinese (*adj.*)
khirurg, *m.*	*khee*-ROORG	surgeon
khisorn, *m.*	*khee*-SAW-*rin*	fault (defect)
khitre	KHEET-*reh*	cunning
"	"	sly (crafty)
khiyune, *f.*	*khee*-YOO-*neh*	support (livelihood)

Yiddish	Pronunciation	English
khlipen (2)	KHLEE-*pen*	sob, to
khokhme,*f.*	KHAW_KH-*meh*	wisdom
kholem,*m.*	KHAW-*lem*	dream
kholemen (1)	KHAW-*leh-men*	dream, to
kholere,*f.*	*kho*-LEH-*reh*	cholera
khor,*m.*	KHAWR	choir
khorev makhn (1c)	KHAW-*rev mah-khin*	ruin, to
khosn,*m.*	KHAW-*sin*	groom (bridegroom)
khotsh	KHAW_CH	although
"	"	though (*conj.*)
khoydesh,*m.*	KHOY-*desh*	month
khoydeshlekh	KHOY-*desh-lukh*	monthly (every month, *adj.*)
khoylek zayn (18c)	KHOY-*lek zine*	disagree (differ), to
khoyshed zayn (18c)	KHOY-*shed zine*	suspect (distrust), to
khoyv,*m.*	KHOYV	debt
"	"	duty (obligation)
khoyzek,*m.*	KHOY-*zek*	ridicule
khoyzekn fun (1)	KHOY-*zeh-kin* FOON	mock (deride), to
khrom,*m.*	KH_RAWM	chromium
khronik,*f.*	KH_RAW-*nik*	chronicle
khshad,*m.*	KH_SHAHD	suspicion
khshad, hobn a (25)	HAW-*bin ah* KH_SHAHD	suspect (surmise), to
khshives,*f.*	KH_SHEE-*vess*	importance
khsime,*f.*	KH_SEE-*meh*	signature (name)
khurbn,*m.*	KHOOR-*bin*	destruction (demolition)
khurve,*f.*	KHOOR-*veh*	ruins (remains)
khuts	KHOOTS	beside (other than *prep.*)
"	"	except (*prep.*)
khuts dem	KHOOTS *dehm*	besides (moreover, *adv.*)
khvalye,*f.*	KH_VAHL-*yeh*	wave (billow)
kibed,*m.*	KEE-*bed*	refreshments
kibets,*m.*	KEE-*bets*	community (neighborhood)
kikh,*f.*	KEEKH	kitchen
kil	KEEL	chilly
"	"	cool (having low temperature)
kilakharyad	*ki-lah-khar*-YAHD	casual (offhand)
kiln (1)	KEE-*lin*	cool (make less hot), to
kimat	*kee*-MAHT	almost
"	"	nearly
kin,*f.*	KIN	jaw
kind,*n.*	KEEND	child
kinder-gortn,*m.*	KEEN-*dehr-gor-tin*	kindergarten
kinder-paraliz,*m.*	KEEN-*dehr-pah-rah-liz*	infantile paralysis
kinder-tsimer,*m.*	KEEN-*dehr-tsee-mehr*	nursery (children's room)
kindhayt,*f.*	KEEND-*hite*	childhood
kinds kind,*n.*	KEENDS KEEND	descendant (offspring)
kine,*f.*	KEE-*neh*	envy
kinig,*m.*	KEE-*nig*	king
kinigin,*f.*	KEE-*nig-in*	queen
kinigl,*n.*	KEE-*neeg-il*	rabbit
kiniglekh	KEE-*nig-lukh*	regal
"	"	royal
kinigraykh,*n.*	KEE-*nig-rye_kh*	kingdom
kino,*m.*	KEE-*no*	movies
kinstlekh	KEENST-*lukh*	artificial (synthetic)
kinstler,*m.*	KEENST-*lehr*	artist
kinstlerish	KEENST-*leh-rish*	artistic (tasteful)
kiosk,*m.*	*kee*-AWSK	newsstand
kirtsung,*f.*	KEER-*tsoon_g*	abbreviation
kishef,*m.*	KEE-*sheff*	magic (*n.*)
"	"	spell (charm)
kishef-makher,*m.*	KEE-*shef-mah-khehr*	magician
kishele,*n.*	KEE-*sheh-leh*	pad (cushion)
kishke,*f.*	KEESH-*keh*	hose (tube)
kishn,*f.*	KEE-*shin*	cushion
"	"	pillow
Kito,*n.*	KEE-*taw*	Quito
kitser,*m.*	KEET-*sehr*	summary (synopsis)
kitslen (1)	KEETS-*len*	tickle (touch lightly), to
klal,*m.*	KLAHL	community (the public)
"	"	rule (usual case)

Yiddish	Pronunciation	English
klang,*m.*	KLAHN_G	noise (sound)
"	"	rumor
klap,*m.*	KLAHP	blow
"	"	stroke
klap, laykhter,*m.*	LYE_KH-*tehr* KLAHP	pat (tap)
klapn (1)	KLAH-*pin*	knock (hit), to
klapn, laykht	LYE_KHT KLAH-*pin*	pat (tap), to
klarnet,*m.*	*klar*-NET	clarinet
klas,*m.*	KLAHSS	class (kind)
"	"	grade (school division)
klasish	KLAH-*sish*	classic (first-class, *adj.*)
klasish verk,*n.*	KLAH-*sish* VEHRK	classic (first-class work)
klastsimer,*m.*	KLAHSS-*tsee-mehr*	classroom
klatshe,*f.*	KLAHT-*sheh*	mare
klaybn (9)	KLYE-*bin*	collect (bring together), to
"	"	gather (bring together), to
"	"	pick (choose), to
klaybn zikh	KLYE-*bin zikh*	gather (congregate), to
klekn (1)	KLEH-*kin*	blot (stain), to
klem,*f.*	KLEM	plight (predicament)
klem,*m.*	CLAM	clam
klener	KLEH-*nehr*	minor (lesser)
kleplen (1)	KLEP-*len*	tap (rap), to
klepn zikh (1)	KLEH-*pin zikh*	stick (adhere), to
klern (1)	KLEH-*rin*	muse (meditate), to
klern vegn	KLEH-*rin* VEG-*in*	brood over, to
kley,*f.*	CLAY	glue
kleyd,*n.*	KLADE	dress (frock)
"	"	gown
kleyn	KLANE	little (*adj.*)
"	"	small
kleynikayt,*f.*	KLAY-*nee-kite*	trifle
kley-zayin,*n.*	*clay*-ZAH-*yin*	weapon
klimat,*m.*	KLEE-*maht*	climate (weather)
kling,*f.*	KLEEN_G	blade (cutting tool)
klingen (8)	KLEEN_G-*en*	peal, to
"	"	ring (resound), to
"	"	sound (make heard), to
klole,*f.*	KLAW-*leh*	curse
klon,*m.*	KLAWN	maple (tree)
klor	KLORE	clear
"	"	plain
klor vi der tog	KLOR *vee dehr* TAWG	obvious
klots,*m.*	KLAWTS	log (rough timber)
kloyster,*m.*	KLOYSS-*tehr*	church
kloysterlid,*n.*	KLOY-*stehr-leed*	hymn (religious song)
kloyster-turem,*m.*	KLOY-*stehr-too-rem*	steeple
klozet,*m.*	*klaw*-ZET	toilet (water closet)
klub,*m.*	KLOOB	club (association)
klug	KLOOG	clever
"	"	smart
"	"	wise
knakn (1)	K_NAH-*kin*	snap (crackle), to
knap	K_NAHP	scarce
"	"	slight (*adj.*)
knapkayt,*f.*	K_NAHP-*kite*	scarcity
knaypn (1)	K_NYE-*pin*	pinch (squeeze), to
knekhl,*n.*	K_NEH-*khil*	ankle
knepl,*n.*	K_NEH-*pil*	button
kneytsh,*m.*	K_NAY_CH	fold (plait, *n.*)
"	"	wrinkle
kni,*m.*	K_NEE	knee
knien (1)	K_NEE-*en*	kneel, to
knobl,*m.*	K_NAW-*bil*	garlic
knosp,*m.*	K_NAWSP	bud (*bot.*)
knup,*m.*	K_NOOP	knot
kodeks,*m.*	KAW-*dex*	code (law)
kokhn (1)	KAW-*khin*	boil (bubble up), to
"	"	cook, to
kokosnus,*m.*	KAW-*kawss-noose*	coconut
koks,*m.*	KAWX	coke
kokteyl,*m.*	KAWK-*tale*	cocktail
kol,*n.*	CALL	voice

Yiddish	Pronunciation	English
koldre, *f.*	KAWLD-*reh*	blanket
koldre, geshtepte *f.*	g_*eh*-SHTEP-*teh* KAWLD-*reh*	quilt (bedcover)
kolir, *m.*	ko-LEER	color
kolner, *m.*	KAWL-*nehr*	collar
Kolombye, *f.*	ko-LAWMB-*yeh*	Colombia
kolonel, *m.*	ko-*lo*-NELL	colonel
kolonist, *m.* "	ko-*lo*-NEEST	colonist settler
kolonyal	ko-LAWN-*yahl*	colonial
kolonye, *f.*	ko-LAWN-*yeh*	colony
komande, *f.*	ko-MAHN-*deh*	command (author- ity)
komandir, *m.*	ko-*mahn*-DEER	commander (officer)
komar, *m.*	kaw-MAR	mosquito
kombinatsye, *f.*	kawn-bee-NAHTS-*yeh*	combination
kombinirn (1b)	kawm-bee-NEE-*rin*	combine (make join), to
kome, *f.*	KAW-*meh*	comma
komedye, *f.*	ko-MED-*yeh*	comedy (comic play)
komentirn (1b)	ko-men-TEE-*rin*	comment, to
komertsyel	ko-*mehrts*-YEHL	commercial
komish	KAW-*mish*	funny (comical)
komisye, *f.* "	ko-MEESS-*yeh*	commission (fee) commission (group)
komisyoner, *m.*	ko-*meess*-yo-NEHR	commissioner (dep- utized person)
komitet, *m.*	ko-*mee*-TET	committee
komivoyazhor, *m.*	kaw-mee-vaw-yah-ZHOR	traveling salesman
komod, *m.* "	ko-MAWD	bureau (chest) dresser
komonvelt, *m.*	COM-*mon*-*welth*	commonwealth
kompakt "	kawm-PAHKT	compact (brief) compact (packed firmly)
kompanye, *f.*	kawm-PAHN-*yeh*	company (*mil.*)
kompas, *m.*	KAWM-*pahss*	compass (magnetic instrument)
kompensatsye, *f.*	kawm-pen-SAHTS-*yeh*	compensation (*bus.*)
kompetent	kawm-*peh*-TENT	competent (able)
kompliment, *m.*	kawm-*plee*-MENT	compliment
komplitsirt	kawm-*plee*-TSEERT	complex (compli- cated)
komponirn (1b)	kawm-*po*-NEE-*rin*	compose, to (*mus.*)
komunikatsye, *f.*	ko-*moo*-nee-KAHTS-*yeh*	communication (intercourse)
komunizm, *m.*	ko-*moo*-NEE-*zim*	communism
kon, *m.*	KAWN	stake (thing wa- gered)
kondensirn (1b)	kawn-den-SEE-*rin*	condense (compress), to
kondukter, *m.*	kawn-DOOK-*tehr*	conductor (ticket collector)
konfidentsyel	kawn-fee-dents-YELL	confidential (private)
konfiskatsye, *f.*	kawn-fiss-KAHTS-*yeh*	attachment (legal seizure)
konflikt, *m.*	kawn-FLEEKT	conflict (opposition)
kongregatsye, *f.*	kawn-greh-GAHTS-*yeh*	congregation (reli- gious community)
kongres, *m.*	kawn-GRESS	congress (legislature)
konishine, *f.*	kaw-nee-SHEE-*neh*	clover
konkret	kawn-KRETT	concrete (real)
konkurent, *m.* "	kawn-*koo*-RENT	competitor (*bus.*) rival
konkurents, *f.*	kawn-koo-RENTS	competition (*bus.*)
konkurs, *m.*	KAWN-*koorss*	contest
konsekvents, *f.*	kawn-*seh*-KVENTS	consequence
konservativ	kawn-*sehr*-vah-TEEV	conservative (cau- tious)
konstitutsye, *f.*	kawn-*stee*-TOOTS-*yeh*	constitution (law)
konstruktsye, *f.*	kawn-STROOKTS-*yeh*	construction (fabri- cation)
konsul, *m.*	KAWN-*sool*	consul
kontakt, *m.*	kawn-TAHKT	contact (meeting)
konte, *n.*	KAWN-*teh*	account (bank ac- count)
konte-barikht, *m.*	KAWN-*teh*-*bah*-*reekht*	statement (account- ing, *bus.*)
kontinent, *m.*	kawn-*tee*-NENT	continent (*geog.*)
kontrabande, *f.*	kawn-*trah*-BAHN-*deh*	contraband
kontrakt-bre- khung, *f.*	kawn-TRAHKT-*breh*- *khoon_g*	breach of contract (*bus.*)
kontrast, *m.*	kawn-TRAHST	contrast
kontrol, *f.*	kawn-TRAWL	check (examination)

Yiddish	Pronunciation	English
kontrolirn (1b)	kawn-*tro*-LEE-*rin*	check (test), to
kontsentrirn (1b)	kawn-*tsen*-TREE-*rin*	concentrate (make converge), to
kontsert, *m.*	kawn-TSEHRT	concert (musical performance)
konvert, *m.*	kawn-VEHRT	envelope (folded wrapper)
konvoy, *m.*	kawn-VOY	convoy (*mil.*)
konyak, *m.*	KAWN-*yahk*	brandy
konyunktsye, *f.*	kawn-YOONK_TS-*yeh*	conjunction (*gram.*)
kooperativ, *m.*	kaw-*o*-*peh*-*rah*-TEEV	cooperative (*n.*)
kooperatsye, *f.*	kaw-*o*-*peh*-RAHTS-*yeh*	cooperation
kop, *m.*	KAWP	head (*anat.*)
kopete, *f.*	KAW-*peh*-*teh*	hoof
Kopnhavn, *n.*	kaw-*pin*-HAH-*vin*	Copenhagen
kopveytik, *m.*	KAWP-*vay*-*tick*	headache
kopye, *f.* "	KAWP-*yeh*	carbon copy copy (duplicate)
korb, *m.*	KAWRB	basket
korbn, *m.*	CORE-*bin*	victim
kore, *f.*	KAW-*reh*	bark (of tree)
korek, *m.* "	KAW-*rek*	cork (stopper) fuse (*elec.*)
korespondent, *m.*	kaw-*res*-*pawn*-DENT	correspondent (letter writer)
korespondents, *f.*	kaw-*res*-*pawn*-DENTS	correspondence (letters)
korespondents- shul, *f.*	kaw-*res*-*pawn*-DENTS- *shool*	correspondence school
korespondirn (1b)	kaw-*res*-*pawn*-DEE-*rin*	correspond with (write to), to
korev, *m.*	KAW-*rev*	relative (kinsman)
koridor, *m.*	ko-*ree*-DOR	hall (corridor)
kormen (2)	KOR-*men*	feed (give food to), to
korn, *m.*	KAW-*rin*	rye (grain)
korporatsye, *f.*	kor-*po*-RAHTS-*yeh*	corporation
korset, *m.*	kor-SET	girdle (corset)
kort, *f.*	KORT	card, playing
kosmetik, *f.*	kaw-SMEH-*tik*	cosmetic (*n.*)
Kostarike, *f.*	kawss-*tah*-REE-*keh*	Costa Rica
kostn (1)	KAWSS-*tin*	cost, to
kostyum, *m.* "	cost-YOOM	costume suit, woman's
koved, *m.*	KAW-*ved*	honor
koved, leygn (1)	LAYG-*in* KAW-*ved*	esteem, to
koved, opgebn (13a)	AWP-g_*eh*-*bin* KAW-*ved*	honor (respect), to
koyakh, *m.* "	KOY-*ukh*	force (power) strength
koyfer, *m.*	KOY-*fehr*	buyer
koyfn (1)	KOY-*fin*	buy, to
koyl, *f.*	COIL	bullet
koyleldik	KOY-*lel*-*dick*	wide (comprehen- sive)
koyln, *pl.*	KOY-*lin*	coal
koylnshtof, *m.*	KOY-*lin*-*shtawf*	carbon (*chem.*)
koym	KOYM	hardly (barely)
koymen, *m.*	KOY-*men*	chimney
koyne, *m.*	KOY-*neh*	customer (buyer)
koyne, shtendiker *m.*	SHTEN-*dee*-*kehr* KOY- *neh*	patron
koyshbol, *m.*	KOYSH-*bawl*	basketball
krab, *m.*	KRAHB	crab (shellfish)
kraft, *f.*	KRAHFT	vigor (strength)
kraftik	KRAHF-*lick*	vigorous
krakh, *m.*	KRAH_KH	crash (loud noise)
krakhn (1)	KRAH-*khin*	crash (be smashed), to
kran, *m.* "	KRAHN	faucet tap
krank "	KRAHNK	ill sick (ailing)
krankayt, *f.* "	KRAHN-*kite*	disease illness
krankn-shvester, *f.*	KRAHN-*kin*-*shves*-*tehr*	nurse (medical as- sistant)
krants, *m.*	KRAHNTS	wreath
kratsn (1)	KRAHT-*sin*	scratch, to
krayd, *f.*	KRIDE	chalk
kraytekhts, *n.*	CRY-*tukh*_*ts*	herb
krayz, *m.*	KRIZE	circle (*geom.*)
kredit, *m.*	kreh-DEET	credit (*bus.*)
kreditirn (1b)	kreh-*dee*-TEE-*rin*	credit, to (*bus.*)
kreditor, *m.*	kreh-DEE-*tor*	creditor (*bus.*)

Yiddish	Pronunciation	English
kreftik	KREF-*tick*	sturdy
krekhtsn (1)	KREH_KH-*tsin*	groan (moan), to
krel, *f.*	KREHL	bead (jewelry)
krenk, *f.*	KRENK	sickness
kretshme, *f.*	KRECH-*meh*	inn
kreynen (1)	KRAY-*nen*	crown, to
kreytser, *m.*	CRAY-*tsehr*	cruiser (ship)
kreytsn (1)	KRAY-*tsin*	cross (crossbreed), to
kreytsung, *f.*	KRAY-*tsoon_g*	crossing (intersection)
krig, *f.*	KREEG	quarrel (dispute)
krign (7)	KREEG-*in*	acquire, to
"	"	get, to
"	"	obtain, to
krign, tsu	*tsoo* KREEG-*in*	available
krign zikh (1)	KREEG-*in zikh*	quarrel (dispute), to
krigsflot, *m.*	KREEGS-*flawt*	navy (*n.*)
krikhn (7d)	KREE-*khin*	creep, to
krikhn oyf	KREE-*khin oyf*	climb (scale), to
krimen zikh (1)	KREE-*men zikh*	frown, to
krishtol, *n.*	*kree*-SHTAWL	crystal (*min.*)
Krist, *m.*	KREEST	Christian (*n.*)
kristikung, *f.*	KREESS-*tee-koon_g*	baptism
Kristus, *m.*	KREESS-*toos*	Christ
kritik, *f.*	*kree*-TEEK	criticism (censure)
"	"	criticism (judgment)
kritiker, *m.*	KREE-*tee-kehr*	critic
krizis, *m.*	KREE-*ziss*	crisis
kro, *f.*	CRAW	crow (bird)
krokhmal, *m.*	KRAW_KH-*mahl*	starch (in food)
krom, *f.*	KRAWM	shop
"	"	store
krot, *m.*	KRAWT	mole (animal)
kroyn, *f.*	KROYN	crown (headdress)
"	"	crown (sovereignty)
kroyt, *n.*	KROYT	cabbage
kroyvish	KROY-*vish*	related (connected)
krug, *m.*	KROOG	jug
"	"	pitcher (container)
kruk, *m.*	KROOK	hook
krukhle	KROOKH-*leh*	crisp (brittle)
krum	KROOM	crooked
krume, *f.*	KROO-*meh*	graph
ksav, *m.*	KSAHV	writing (handwriting)
kshak, *m.*	K_SHAHK	shrub
ku, *f.*	KOO	cow
kub, *m.*	KOOB	cube (*geom.*)
Kuba, *f.*	KOO-*bah*	Cuba
kubik, *m.*	KOO-*bik*	cup
kufert, *m.*	KOO-*fehrt*	trunk (baggage)
kuk, *m.*	COOK	look (glance)
"	"	outlook (attitude)
kukavke, *f.*	*koo*-KAHV-*keh*	cuckoo (bird)
kukher, *m.*	KOO-*khehr*	cook
kukhn, *m.*	KOO-*khin*	cake (dessert)
kukn (1)	KOO-*kin*	look (gaze), to
kukuruze, *f.*	*koo-koo*-ROO-*zeh*	corn (maize)
kule, *f.*	KOO-*leh*	crutch
kultivirn (1b)	*kool-tee*-VEE-*rin*	cultivate (till), to
kultur, *f.*	*kool*-TOOR	culture (refinement)
"	"	culture (stage of civilization)
kumedik	KOO-*meh-dick*	future (*adj.*)
kumen (5d)	KOO-*men*	come, to
kumen (1)	KOO-*men*	owe, to
kumendik	KOO-*men-dick*	next (following, *adj.*)
kumen nokh (5d)	KOO-*men nawkh*	succeed (follow), to
kumen tsu gast tsu	KOO-*men tsoo* GAHST *tsoo*	visit (call on), to
kumen tsu zikh (5d)	KOO-*men tsoo* ZEEKH	recover (get well), to
kunst, *f.*	KOONST	art
"	"	trick (knack)
kunstzayd, *n.*	KOONST-*zide*	rayon
kupe, *f.*	KOO-*peh*	heap
"	"	pile
kupe, *m.*	*koo*-PEH	compartment (of train)
kuper, *n.*	KOO-*pehr*	copper
kuplung, *f.*	KOOP-*loon_g*	clutch (automotive device)

Yiddish	Pronunciation	English
kupol, *m.*	*koo*-PAWL	dome (cupola)
kupon, *m.*	*koo*-PAWN	coupon (detachable certificate)
kurator, *m.*	*koo*-RAH-*tor*	curator
kurort, *n.*	KOO-*rort*	resort (spa)
kurs, *m.*	KOORSS	conversion rate (*bus.*)
"	"	rate (exchange)
kurts	KOORTS	brief (fleeting)
"	"	short
kurtsh, *m*	KOORCH	cramp (*med.*)
kush, *m.*	KOOSH	kiss
kushn (1)	KOO-*shin*	kiss, to
kust, *m.*	KOOST	bush (plant)
kvadratish	*kvah*-DRAH-*tish*	square (*adj.*)
kvartir, *f.*	*kvar*-TEER	lodging (temporary quarters)
kvekzilber, *n.*	KVECK-*zil-behr*	mercury
kvenklen zikh (1)	KVENK-*len zikh*	hesitate, to
kvetshn (1)	KVEH-*chin*	squeeze, to
kveyt, *f.*	KVATE	blossom
kvitirn (1b)	*kvee*-TEE-*rin*	receipt, to (*bus.*)
kvitshen (2)	KVEE-*chen*	shriek, to
kvote, *f.*	KVAW-*teh*	quota
kvure, *f.*	KVOO-*reh*	burial
labn, *m.*	LAH-*bin*	loaf
laboratorye, *f.*	*lah-bo-rah*-TOR-*yeh*	laboratory
lager, *m.*	LAHG-*ehr*	camp (encampment, *mil.*)
lager, haltn oyfn (5)	HAHL-*tin oyfn* LAHG-*ehr*	store (accumulate), to
lager, lign in, *n.*	LEEG-*in in* LAHG-*ehr*	storage
lakhn (1)	LAH-*khin*	laugh, to
lakhodim-handl, *m.*	*lah*-KHAW-*dim-hahn-dil*	retail (*bus., n.*)
lakhodim-hendler, *m.*	*lah*-KHAW-*dim-hend-lehr*	retailer (*bus.*)
laks, *m.*	LAHX	salmon
lalke, *f.*	LAHL-*keh*	doll
lam, *f.*	LAHM	lamb
lamtern, *m.*	*lahm*-TEH-*rin*	lantern
land, *n.*	LAHND	country
"	"	land (region)
landn (1)	LAHN-*din*	land (an airplane), to
"	"	land (from a ship), to
landshaft, *f.*	LAHND-*shahft*	landscape (scenery)
lang	LAHN_G	long
langvayl, *f.*	LAHN_G-*vile*	boredom
lape, *f.*	LAH-*peh*	paw
larem, *m.*	LAH-*rem*	din
lastoyto, *m.*	LAHST-*oy-taw*	truck (automobile)
lataynish	*la*-TIE-*nish*	Latin (*adj.*)
late, *f.*	LAH-*leh*	patch (repair)
laydn (11)	LIE-*din*	suffer (undergo), to
laydn, *n.*	LIE-*din*	suffering
laydnshaft, *f.*	LIE-*din-shahft*	passion (emotion)
laydnshaftlekh	LIE-*din-shahft-lukh*	passionate
layen (12)	LIE-*en*	lend, to
laylekh, *m.*	LIE-*lukh*	sheet (bedding)
laym, *m.*	LIME	lime (fruit)
layt, *pl.*	LITE	people (persons)
laytish	LIE-*tish*	respectable
laytzelik	LITE-*zeh-lick*	gracious
layvnt, *m.*	LYE-*vint*	canvas (cloth)
"	"	linen (fabric)
lebedik	LEH-*beh-dick*	alive
"	"	live (*adj.*)
"	"	vivid
leber, *f.*	LEH-*behr*	liver (*anat.*)
lebn	LEH-*bin*	at
"	"	beside
"	"	near (*prep.*)
"	"	next (alongside of, *prep.*)
lebn, *n.*	LEH-*bin*	life
lebn (1)	LEH-*bin*	live (be alive), to
leder, *f.*	LEH-*dehr*	leather (*n.*)
ledl, *n.*	LEH-*dil*	eyelid
legal	*leh*-GAHL	legal
legende, *f.*	*lehg*-EN-*deh*	legend (story)
legislatur, *f.*	*lehg-iss-lah*-TOOR	legislature
lehakhes, *m.*	*leh*-HAH-*khess*	spite (ill will)

Yiddish	Pronunciation	English
lekhatkhiledik	*leh-khaht-*KHEE-*leh-dick*	original (first)
lekherlekh	LEH-*khehr-lukh*	ridiculous
lekn (1)	LEH-*kin*	lick (lap), to
lektsye,*f.*	LEKTS-*yeh*	lecture (speech)
"	"	lesson (assignment)
lempert,*m.*	LEM-*pehrt*	leopard
lempl,*n.*	LEM-*pil*	bulb (light bulb)
lend,*f.*	LEND	hip
leng,*f.*	LEN_G	length
lengoys	*len-*GOYSS	along (lengthwise of)
lente,*f.*	LEN-*teh*	ribbon
lerer,*m.*	LEH-*rehr*	teacher
lernbukh,*n.*	LEH-*rin-bookh*	textbook
lernen,*n.*	LEHR-*nen*	instruction (teaching)
"	"	study (active learning)
lernen (1)	LEHR-*nen*	instruct, to
"	"	study, to
"	"	teach, to
lernen zikh	LEHR-*nen zikh*	learn (acquire knowledge), to
lernyingl,*m.*	LEH-*rin-yin-g_il*	apprentice (trade student)
lesate	*leh-*SAH-*teh*	hitherto (thus far)
letst	LETST	final
"	"	last (final, *adj.*)
letst, tsu	*tsoo* LETST	last (after all others, *adv.*)
"	"	last (most recently, *adv.*)
letster	LETS-*tehr*	latter (second of two)
levaye,*f.*	*leh-*VAH-*yeh*	funeral
levone,*f.*	*le-*VAW-*neh*	moon
levone-likht,*n.*	*le-*VAW-*neh-likht*	moonlight
leyb,*m.*	LABE	lion
leydik	LAY-*dick*	vacant (untenanted)
leydik, geyn (14d)	GAIN LAY-*dick*	loaf, to
leyenen (1)	LAY-*eh-nen*	read, to
leyener,*m.*	LAY-*eh-nehr*	reader
leygn (1)	LAYG-*in*	lay (put down), to
"	"	place, to
leygn zikh	LAYG-*in zikh*	lie down, to
leykenen (3)	LAY-*keh-nen*	deny (contradict), to
leym,*f.*	LAME	clay
leytenant,*m.*	*lay-teh-*NAHNT	lieutenant
leyter,*m.*	LAY-*tehr*	ladder
leytse,*f.*	LATE-*seh*	rein (strap)
lib	LEEB	dear (beloved, *adj.*)
"	"	kind (*adj.*)
liberal	*lee-beh-*RAHL	liberal (*polit.*, *adj.*)
libersht	LEE-*behrsht*	rather (preferably)
libhober,*m.*	LEEB-*haw-behr*	lover
lib hobn (25c)	LEEB *haw-bin*	like (be fond of), to
"	"	love, to
lib hobn, nit	*neet* LEEB *haw-bin*	dislike, to
libshaft,*f.*	LEEB-*shahft*	affection
"	"	love
lid,*n.*	LEED	song
lidke,*f.*	LEED-*keh*	calf (*anat.*)
lift,*m.*	LEEFT	elevator (passenger lift)
lige,*f.*	LEEG-*eh*	league
lign,*m.*	LEEG-*in*	lie
lign (29)	LEEG-*in*	lie (be located), to
"	"	lie (be prone), to
ligner,*m.*	LEEG-*nehr*	liar
lign zogn (1c)	LEEG-*in zawg-in*	lie (prevaricate), to
liker,*m.*	*lee-*KEHR	liqueur
likht,*f.*	LEEKHT	candle
likht,*n.*	LEEKHT	light (illumination)
likhtik	LEEKH-*tick*	light (bright)
lila	LEE-*lah*	purple (color)
lilye,*f.*	LEEL-*yeh*	lily
Lima,*n.*	LEE-*mah*	Lima
limene,*f.*	LEE-*meh-neh*	lemon
limonad,*m.*	*lee-mo-*NAHD	lemonade
link	LINK	left (*adj.*)
links	LEENX	left (*adv.*)
"	"	left (*n.*)
linoleum,*n.*	*lee-no-*LEH-*oom*	linoleum
linye,*f.*	LEEN-*yeh*	line (mark)

Yiddish	Pronunciation	English
lip,*f.*	LEEP	lip (*anat.*)
lipnshtift,*m.*	LEE-*pin-shtift*	lipstick
lise	LEE-*seh*	bald (hairless)
literarish	*lee-teh-*RAH-*rish*	literary
literatur,*f.*	*lee-teh-rah-*TOOR	literature (belles-lettres)
litografye,*f.*	*lee-to-*GRAHF-*yeh*	lithography
litsents,*f.*	*leet-*SENTS	license (permit)
litsitatsye,*f.*	*lee-tsee-*TAHTS-*yeh*	auction (sale)
liverant,*m.*	*lee-veh-*RAHNT	supplier (*bus.*)
lodenish,*f.*	LAW-*deh-nish*	litigation
lodn (5)	LAW-*din*	sue (bring action against), to
lohet	LAW-*het*	eager
lokal	*lo-*KAHL	local (regional)
lokator,*m.*	*law-*KAH-*tor*	tenant
lokh,*f.*	LAWKH	hole (cavity)
lokomotiv,*m.*	*law-ko-mo-*TEEV	engine
"	"	locomotive
lom	LAWM	lame
lombard,*m.*	LAWM-*bard*	pawnshop
lomp,*m.*	LAWMP	lamp
London,*n.*	LAWN-*dawn*	London
lonke,*f.*	LAWN-*keh*	lawn
"	"	meadow
lopete,*f.*	LAW-*peh-teh*	spade (tool)
loyal	*lo-*YAHL	loyal
loyalkayt,*f.*	*lo-*YAHL-*kite*	loyalty
loybn (1)	LOY-*bin*	praise, to
loyfik	LOY-*fik*	current (contemporary, *adj.*)
loyfn (7d)	LOY-*fin*	run (sprint), to
loyn,*m.*	LOYN	wages
loyt	LOYT	according to (in accordance with)
loyz	LOYZ	loose (unbound)
lozn (1)	LAW-*zin*	let (permit), to
lozn bay zikh	LAW-*zin bye* ZIKH	keep, to
"	"	retain, to
loz ton zikh, a (22)	*ah* LAWZZ *tawn zikh*	dash (rush), to
luft,*f.*	LOOFT	air (atmosphere)
luftl,*n.*	LOOF-*til*	dandelion
luftpost,*f.*	LOOFT-*pawst*	air mail
luft-regulirung,*f.*	LOOFT-*reh-goo-lee-roon_g*	air conditioning
luksus,*m.*	LOOX-*ooss*	luxury
lulke,*f.*	LOOL-*keh*	pipe (tobacco pipe)
lung,*f.*	LOON_G	lung
lungen-ontsindung,*f.*	LOON_G-*en-awn-tsin-doon_g*	pneumonia
lyubenyu,*n.*	LEW-*behr-new*	darling
madreyge,*f.*	*mahd-*RAYG-*eh*	grade (relative position)
"	"	level (plane, *n.*)
Madrid,*n.*	*mahd-*REED	Madrid
magemase,*m.*	*mahg-eh-*MAH-*seh*	dealings (relations)
magnet,*m.*	*mahg-*NET	magnet
makef,*m.*	MAH-*kef*	hyphen
makhmes	MAH_KH-*mess*	because of (*adv.*)
makhn (1)	MAH-*khin*	make, to
makhn far	MAH-*khin far*	render (cause to become), to
makhsheyfe,*f.*	*mah_kh-*SHAY-*feh*	witch
makhshir,*m.*	MAH_KH-*sheer*	tool
makht,*f.*	MAH_KHT	authority
"	"	might (*n.*)
"	"	power
makhtik	MAH_KH-*lick*	powerful
makriv zayn,*n.*	MAHK-*riv zine*	sacrifice (giving up)
malakh,*m.*	MAH-*lukh*	angel
malarye,*f.*	*mah-*LAR-*yeh*	malaria
malbush,*n.*	MAHL-*boosh*	garment
maline,*f.*	MAH-*lee-neh*	raspberry
maline, shvartse,*f.*	SHVAR-*tseh* MAH-*lee-neh*	blackberry
malpe,*f.*	MAHL-*peh*	monkey
mamshikh zayn (18c)	MAHM-*shikh zine*	continue, to
mamshole,*f.*	*mahm-*SHAW-*leh*	dominion (rule)
"	"	reign (period of rule)
man,*m.*	MAHN	husband
"	"	man
mandl,*m.*	MAHN-*dil*	almond

Yiddish	Pronunciation	English
mandl-ontsindung, *f.*	MAHN-*dil-awn-tsin-doon_g*	tonsillitis
manirn, *pl.*	mah-NEE-*rin*	manners (polite behavior)
manket, *m.*	mahn-KETT	cuff (of clothing)
manshaft, *f.*	MAHN-*shahft*	crew
"		team (in sports)
mantl, *m.*	MAHN-*til*	cloak (apparel)
"	"	overcoat
mapole, *f.*	mah-PAW-*leh*	defeat
marants, *m.*	mah-RAHNTS	orange (fruit)
margarin, *m.*	mar-gah-REEN	margarine
margeritke, *f.*	marg-eh-REET-*keh*	daisy
mark, *m.*	MARK	market (trading center)
"	"	outlet
marke, *f.*	MAR-*keh*	brand (trade mark)
"	"	stamp, postage
markh, *m.*	MARKH	brain (*anat.*)
marshirn (1b)	mar-SHEE-*rin*	march, to
marshrut, *m.*	marsh-ROOT	route
mase, *f.*	MAH-*seh*	burden
"	"	load
"	"	mass (matter)
"	"	multitude
mashin, *f.*	mah-SHEEN	machine
mashinerye, *f.*	mah-shee-NEHR-*yuh*	machinery
mashinist, *m.*	mah-shee-NEEST	engineer (railroad engineman)
mashmoes	mahsh-MAW-*ess*	likely
"	"	probable
masig zayn (18c)	MAH-*sig zine*	conceive (imagine), to
maske, *f.*	MAHSS-*keh*	mask (face covering)
maskim zayn (18c)	MAHSS-*kim zine*	agree, to
"	"	assent, to
"	"	consent, to
maskim zayn mit	MAHSS-*kim zine mit*	agree with, to
masline, *f.*	MAHSS-*lee-neh*	olive (fruit)
masshtab, *m.*	mahs-SHTAHB	scale (proportion)
mastboym, *m.*	MAHST-*boym*	mast
matbeye, *f.*	maht-BEH-*yeh*	coin
matematik, *f.*	mah-teh-MAH-*tick*	mathematics
matern (1)	MAH-*teh-rin*	torment, to
maternish, *f.*	MAH-*tehr-nish*	torment
materyal, *m.*	mah-tehr-YAHL	material (substance)
materye, *f.*	mah-TEHR-*yeh*	matter (substance)
matine, *m.*	mah-tee-NEH	matinee (theater performance)
matone, *f.*	mah-TAW-*neh*	gift (present)
matrats, *m.*	maht-RAHTS	mattress
matriakh zayn (18c)	mah-TREE-*ukh zin*	trouble (inconvenience), to
matroz, *m.*	maht-RAWZ	sailor
matsdik zayn (18c)	MAHTS-*dick zine*	justify (exonerate), to
matsev, *m.*	MAH-*tsev*	condition
"	"	state
matsliakhdik	mahts-LEE-*ukh-dick*	successful
matsliakh zayn (18d)	mahts-LEE-*ukh zine*	prosper, to
"	"	succeed (attain goal), to
mayestet, *f.*	mah-yes-TETT	majesty
maykhl, *m.*	MY-*khil*	dish (food)
mayle, *f.*	MY-*leh*	advantage
"		merit
mayn	MINE	my
mayner	MY-*nehr*	mine (*poss. pron.*)
mayontik, *m.*	mah-YAWN-*tick*	estate (total possessions)
mayrev, *m.*	MY-*rev*	west (*n.*)
mayrevdik	MY-*rev-dick*	western
mayse, *f.*	MY-*seh*	story (account)
maysele, *n.*	MY-*seh-leh*	fairy tale
mayster, *m.*	MY-*stehr*	master (great artist)
mazl, *n.*	MAH-*zil*	fortune
"	"	luck
mazldik	MAH-*zil-dik*	fortunate
"	"	lucky
mebl, *pl.*	MEH-*bil*	furniture
meblfur, *f.*	MEH-*bil-foor*	van (vehicle)
medal, *m.*	meh-DAHL	medal
meditsin, *f.*	meh-dee-TSEEN	drug
"	"	medicine
meditsinish	meh-dee-TSEE-*nish*	medical
medyum, *n.*	MED-*yoom*	medium (means)
meeyver-leyam	meh-AY-*vehr* leh-YAHM	oversea(s) (*adj.*)
megazem zayn (18c)	meh-GAH-*zim zine*	exaggerate, to
mehalekh, *m.*	meh-HAH-*lukh*	distance
mehuderdik	meh-HOO-*dehr-dick*	exquisite
mehume, *f.*	meh-HOO-*meh*	riot (disturbance)
mekane zayn (18c)	meh-KAH-*neh zine*	envy, to
mekayem zayn (18c)	meh-KAH-*yem zine*	fulfil, to
"	"	realize (accomplish) to
meken (2)	MEH-*ken*	bleat, to
meker, *m.*	MEH-*kehr*	eraser (rubber eraser)
mekhaber, *m.*	meh-KHAH-*behr*	author
mekhaniker, *m.*	meh-KHAH-*nee-kehr*	mechanic
mekhanish	meh-KHAH-*nish*	mechanical
mekhashef, *m.*	meh-KHAH-*shef*	wizard (sorcerer)
mekhayedik	meh-KHAH-*yeh-dik*	delightful
mekhaye zayn (18c)	meh-KHAH-*yeh zine*	delight (give pleasure to), to
mekhile, *f.*	meh-KHEE-*leh*	forgiveness
"	"	pardon
mekhile, betn (5)	BEH-*tin* meh-KHEE-*leh*	apologize, to
mekhtik	MEKH-*tick*	mighty (powerful)
mekler, *m.*	MECK-*lehr*	broker (*bus.*)
meklergelt, *n.*	MECK-*lehr-g_elt*	brokerage (fee)
mekn (1)	MEH-*kin*	erase, to
meksikanish	mehk-see-KAH-*nish*	Mexican (*adj.*)
Meksike, *f.*	MEX-*ee-keh*	Mexico
Meksike, Shtot, *f.*	SHTAWT MEX-*ee-keh*	Mexico City
mel, *f.*	MELL	flour
melankholye, *f.*	meh-lahn-KHAWL-*yeh*	melancholy (dejection)
meldung, *f.*	MEL-*doon_g*	notice (notification)
melokhe, *f.*	meh-LAW-*kheh*	craft
"	"	trade
melukhe, *f.*	meh-LOO-*kheh*	realm (kingdom)
"	"	state (nation)
melukhe-man, *m.*	meh-LOO-*kheh-mahn*	statesman
melukhe-oytser, *m.*	meh-LOO-*kheh-oyt-sehr*	treasury (*govt.*)
memorandum, *m.*	meh-mo-RAHN-*doom*	memorandum
menie, *f.*	meh-NEE-*yeh*	difficulty (obstacle)
menlekh	MEN-*lukh*	male (*adj.*)
"	"	masculine
mentshhayt, *f.*	MENCH-*hite*	humanity
"	"	mankind
mentshlekh	MENCH-*lukh*	human (*adj.*)
menukhe, *f.*	meh-NOO-*kheh*	repose (calm)
menyu, *m.*	meh-NEW	menu
mer, *f.*	MEHR	carrot
merakhemdik	meh-RAH-*khem-dick*	merciful
merder, *m.*	MEHR-*dehr*	murderer
merer	MEH-*rehr*	more (*adj.*)
merhayt, *f.*	MEHR-*hite*	majority (greater number)
meride, *f.*	meh-REE-*deh*	rebellion
merkverdik	MEHRK-*vehr-dick*	notable (*adj.*)
"	"	remarkable (extraordinary)
mern zikh (1)	MEH-*rin zikh*	multiply (grow numerous), to
merste	MEHR-*steh*	most (greatest quantity, *adj.*)
merste, (dos), *n.*	(*dawss*) MEHR-*steh*	most (*n.*)
merstns	MEHR-*stinss*	mostly
merstn, tsum	*tsoom* MEHR-*stin*	most (*adv.*)
mertsol-...	MEHRT-*sawl*-...	plural (*adj.*)
mese, *f.*	MEH-*seh*	mass (*rel.*)
meser, *n.*	MEH-*sehr*	knife
mesh, *m.*	MESH	brass (metal, *n.*)
meshaer zayn (18c)	meh-SHAH-*ehr zine*	assume (take for granted), to
"	"	guess, to
"	"	presume, to
"	"	suppose, to
meshekh fun, in	*in* MEH-*shukh foon*	within (in less time than, *prep.*)
meshugaas, *f.*	meh-shoo-GAHSS	madness (insanity)
meshuge	meh-SHOOG-*eh*	crazy
"	"	mad (insane)

Yiddish	Pronunciation	English
mesik	MEH-*sick*	moderate (not extreme)
mesles, *m.*	*mes*-LESS	day (24-hour period)
mestn (7)	MESS-*tin*	measure (find size of), to
metal, *m.*	*meh*-TAHL	metal (*n.*)
metod, *m.*	*meh*-TAWD	method
metrese, *f.*	*met*-REH-*seh*	mistress (paramour)
metsie, *f.*	*meh*-TSEE-*eh*	bargain (advantageous purchase)
metushtesh	*meh*-TOOSH-*tesh*	vague (not precise)
meuyemdik	*meh-oo-yem*-dick	monstrous (horrible)
mevater zayn oyf (18c)	*meh*-VAH-*tehr zine oyf*	sacrifice (forego), to
mevatl zayn (18c)	*meh*-VAH-*til zine*	annul, to
meyashev zayn zikh mit (18c)	*meh*-YAH-*shev zine zikh mit*	consult (seek professional advice of), to
meydl, *f.*	MAY-*dil*	girl
meydlsher nomen, *m.*	MAY-*dil-shehr* NAW-*men*	maiden name
meynen (1)	MAY-*nen*	mean (have in mind), to
meynung, *f.*	MAY-*noon g*	belief
"	"	mind
"	"	opinion
"	"	view
mezumen, *n.*	*meh*-ZOO-*men*	cash (money)
mi, *f.*	MEE	labor (exertion)
midkayt, *f.*	MEED-*kite*	fatigue
midber, *f.*	MEED-*behr*	desert
mid vern (7c)	MEED *veh-rin*	tire (become weary), to
mies	MEE-*ess*	ugly
miglekh	MEEG-*lukh*	possible
miglekhkayt, *f.*	MEEG-*lukh-kite*	possibility
miglekhkayt, gebn di (13)	G_EH-*bin dee* MEEG-*lukh-kite*	enable (make able), to
mikh	MEEKH	me
mikhshl, *m.*	MEEKH-*shil*	obstacle
mikoyakh	*mee*-KAW-*yukh*	regarding (concerning)
mikrob, *m.*	*meek*-RAWB	germ (microorganism)
militer, *n.*	*mee-lee*-TEHR	troops (*mil.*)
militerish	*mee-lee*-TEH-*rish*	military (*adj.*)
milkh, *f.*	MEELKH	milk
milkhikeray, *f.*	*mil-khee-keh*-RYE	dairy
milkhome, *f.*	*mil*-KHAW-*meh*	war
milner, *m.*	MEEL-*nehr*	miller
min, *m.*	MEEN	kind (*n.*)
minderhayt, *f.*	MEEN-*dehr-hite*	minority (smaller number)
mindst	MEENDST	least (*adj.*)
mindste, (dos), *n.*	(*dawss*) MEEND-*steh*	least (*n.*)
mindstn, tsum	*tsoom* MEEND-*stin*	least (*adv.*)
mine, *f.*	MEE-*neh*	mine (explosive)
mineral, *m.*	*mee-neh*-RAHL	mineral
minern (1)	MEE-*neh-rin*	reduce, to
minerung, *f.*	MEE-*neh-roon g*	reduction (lessening)
minheg, *m.*	MEEN-*heg*	custom (habit)
minister, *m.*	*mee*-NEES-*tehr*	minister (cabinet member)
minus	MEE-*nooss*	less (minus, *prep.*)
minut, *f.*	*mee*-NOOT	minute (unit of time)
mir	MEER	we
mir	MEER	me
mirmlshteyn, *m.*	MEER-*mil-shtane*	marble (mineral)
mishn (1)	MEE-*shin*	blend, to
"	"	mix (make blend), to
"	"	stir, to
mishn zikh	MEE-*shin zikh*	meddle, to
mishpetn (1)	MEESH-*peh-tin*	judge, to
mishpokhe, *f.*	*mish*-PAW-*kheh*	family
miskher, *m.*	MEESS-*khehr*	commerce (trade)
mispalel zayn (18c)	*mis*-PAH-*lel zine*	pray, to
mist, *n.*	MEEST	rubbish (litter)
misyoner, *m.*	*miss-yo*-NEHR	missionary
mit	MEET	with
mitbazitser, *m.*	MEET-*bah-zee-tsehr*	co-owner (*bus.*)
mitgefil, *n.*	MEET-*g_eh-feel*	sympathy (compassion)
mitglid, *m.*	MEET-*gleed*	member (one of a group)
mitik, *m.*	MEE-*tik*	dinner

Yiddish	Pronunciation	English
mitl, *n.*	MEE-*til*	agency (instrumentality)
"	"	device (apparatus)
"	"	means (method)
Mitllendisher Yam, *m.*	MEE-*til-len-dee-sher* YAHM	Mediterranean Sea
mitlshul, *f.*	MEE-*til-shool*	high school
mitn, *m.*	MEE-*tin*	middle (center)
mitn, in	*in* MEE-*tin*	amid
mitos, *m.*	MEE-*toss*	myth (legend)
Mitsraim, *n.*	*mits*-RAH-*yim*	Egypt
mitsrish	MEETS-*rish*	Egyptian (*adj.*)
mit...tsurik	*mit...tsoo*-REEK	ago (past, *adj.*)
mizrakh, *m.*	MEEZ-*rukh*	east
mizrakhdik	MEEZ-*rukh-dik*	eastern
mode, *f.*	MAW-*deh*	fashion (current style)
model, *m.*	*mo*-DELL	model
modern	*mo*-DEH-*rin*	modern
modish	MAW-*dish*	smart (chic)
modne	MAWD-*neh*	funny
"	"	odd (queer)
"	"	peculiar
modne	MAWD-*neh*	singular
"	"	strange
moger	MAWG-*ehr*	lean (thin)
mogn, *m.*	MAWG-*in*	stomach
mogn-geshvir, *m.*	MAWG-*in-g_eh*-SHVEER	ulcer
mokem-miklet, *m.*	*maw-kem*-MEEK-*let*	refuge
moker, *m.*	MAW-*kehr*	origin
"	"	source
mokh, *m.*	MAWKH	moss
mol, *m.*	MAWL	moth
mol, a	*ah* MAWL	once (formerly, *adv.*)
moler, *m.*	MAW-*lehr*	painter (artist)
moln (5)	MAW-*lin*	paint (represent), to
moln zikh	MAW-*lin zikh*	fancy, to
"	"	imagine (picture mentally), to
moltsayt, *m.*	MAWL-*tsyte*	meal (repast)
moment, *m.*	*mo*-MENT	moment (instant)
monakh, *m.*	*mo*-NAH_KH	monk
monarkh, *m.*	*mo*-NAR_KH	monarch
monashke, *f.*	*mo*-NAHSH-*keh*	nun
monastir, *m.*	*mo-nahss*-TEER	monastery
monoton	*mo-no*-TAWN	monotonous (boring)
Montevideo, *n.*	*mawn-teh-vee*-DEH-*o*	Montevideo
montshinker	MAWN-*chin-kehr*	tiny
moral, *f.*	*mo*-RAHL	morale
"	"	morals
moralish	*mo*-RAH-*lish*	moral (ethical)
mord, *m.*	MORD	murder
more-shkhoyre, *f.*	*mo-reh*-SH_KHOY-*reh*	depression (sadness)
morgn	MORG-*in*	tomorrow
morgn, *m.*	MORG-*in*	morrow
mos, *f.*	MOSS	measure (dimensions)
moshl, *m.*	MAW-*shil*	fable
"	"	example
Moskve, *f.*	MOSS-*kveh*	Moscow
motike, *f.*	*maw*-TEE-*keh*	hoe
motikeven (2)	*maw*-TEE-*keh-ven*	hoe, to
motiv, *m.*	*mo*-TEEV	motive (*n.*)
moto, *m.*	MAW-*taw*	motto
motor, *m.*	*mo*-TOR	motor (engine)
motordek, *f.*	*mo*-TOR-*deck*	hood (*auto.*)
moyd, *f.*	MOYD	lass
moyde zayn (18c)	MOY-*deh zine*	acknowledge (admit), to
"	"	admit (concede), to
moyde zayn zikh	MOY-*deh zine zikh*	confess (admit), to
moydie zayn	*moy*-DEE-*eh zine*	announce, to
moydoe, *f.*	*moy*-DAW-*eh*	announcement
moykhl zayn (18c)	MOY-*khil zine*	forgive, to
moyl, *n.*	MOYL	mouth (*anat.*)
moyleyzl, *m.*	MOYL-*ay-zil*	mule
moyre, *f.*	MOY-*reh*	fear
"	"	terror
moyredik	MOY-*reh-dik*	fearful (terrible)
moyre hobn far (25c)	MOY-*reh haw-bin far*	fear (be afraid of), to
moyz, *f.*	MOYZ	mouse
mozlen, *pl.*	MAWZ-*len*	measles
muler, *m.*	MOO-*lehr*	mason (stonelayer)

Yiddish	Pronunciation	English
mume, *f.*	MOO-*meh*	aunt
mumkhe, *m.*	MOOM-*kheh*	expert (*n.*)
mundir, *m.*	moon-DEER	uniform (*n.*)
murashke, *f.*	moo-RAHSH-*keh*	ant
murmlen (1)	MOOR-*m_len*	murmur, to
musern (1)	MOO-*seh-rin*	scold, to
mushkat, *m.*	MOOSH-*kaht*	nutmeg
muskl, *m.*	MOOSS-*kil*	muscle
muster, *m.*	MOOSS-*tehr*	design
"	"	pattern
"	"	sample
mut, *m.*	MOOT	courage
mut, tsugebn (13)	TSOO-*g_eh-bin* MOOT	encourage, to
muter, *f.*	MOO-*tehr*	mother
"	"	nut (*mech.*)
mutershif, *f.*	MOO-*tehr-shif*	aircraft carrier
muzey, *m.*	moo-ZAY	museum
muzik, *f.*	moo-ZEEK	music
muzikalish	moo-zee-KAH-*leesh*	musical
muziker, *m.*	MOO-*zee-kehr*	musician
muzn (1e)	MOO-*zin*	must (*v.*)
nafke-mine, *f.*	NAHF-*keh-mee-neh*	distinction (difference)
naft, *m.*	NAHFT	kerosene
naket	NAH-*ket*	bare (nude)
"	"	naked
nakht, *f.*	NAH_KHT	night
nakht, halbe, *f.*	HAHL-*beh* NAH_KHT	midnight
nakhthemd, *n.*	NAH_KHT-*hemd*	nightgown
nar, *m.*	NAR	fool
narish	NAH-*rish*	dumb
"	"	foolish
"	"	silly
"	"	stupid
narkotik, *m.*	nar-KAW-*tick*	drug (narcotic)
nartlen zikh (1)	NART-*len zikh*	ski, to
nas	NAHSS	wet
natirlekh	nah-TEER-*lukh*	natural
natsye, *f.*	NAHTS-*yeh*	nation
natsyonal	nahts-yo-NAHL	national (*adj.*)
natur, *f.*	nah-TOOR	nature (physical world)
navigatsye, *f.*	nah-vee-GAHTS-*yeh*	navigation
nay	NYE	new
Nay-Delhi, *n.*	NYE-DELL-*hee*	New Delhi
naygerik	NYE-*g_eh-rik*	curious (inquisitive)
naygerikayt, *f.*	NYE-*g_eh-ree-kite*	curiosity (inquisitiveness)
naylon, *m.*	NYE-*lawn*	nylon (*n.*)
naysfilm, *m.*	NICE-*fee-lim*	newsreel
nayyor-tog, *m.*	NYE-*yor-tawg*	New Year's Day
Neapl, *n.*	neh-AH-*pil*	Naples
nebekh	NEH-*bukh*	poor (unfortunate)
negele, *n.*	NEHG-*eh-leh*	carnation
"	"	clove
Neger, *m.*	NEGG-*ehr*	Negro
nekeyve, *f.*	neh-KAY-*veh*	female (*zool.*, *n.*)
nekhome, *f.*	neh-KHAW-*meh*	consolation (comfort)
nekhtn	NEKH-*tin*	yesterday
nekome, *f.*	neh-KAW-*meh*	revenge
"	"	vengeance
nekrolog, *m.*	nek-ro-LAWG	obituary (*n.*)
nelm vern (7c)	NEH-*lim veh-rin*	vanish (go out of sight), to
nemen (8)	NEH-*men*	take, to
nepl, *m.*	NEH-*pil*	fog
"	"	mist
nerv, *m.*	NEHRV	nerve (*anat.*)
nervez	nehr-VEZ	nervous (high-strung)
nes, *m.*	NESS	miracle
neshome, *f.*	neh-SHAW-*meh*	soul
nesie, *f.*	neh-SEE-*eh*	journey
"	"	trip
"	"	voyage
nest, *f.*	NEST	nest (bird home)
netie, *f.*	neh-TEE-*yeh*	bent (penchant)
"	"	inclination (tendency)
neto	NEH-*taw*	net (*adj.*)
nets, *f.*	NETS	net (mesh)
neyder, *m.*	NAY-*dehr*	vow

Yiddish	Pronunciation	English
neyen (1)	NEH-*yen*	sew, to
neymashin, *f.*	NAY-*mah-shin*	sewing machine
neyn	NANE	no (nay)
neytik	NAY-*tick*	necessary
neytikayt, *f.*	NAY-*tee-kite*	necessity
"	"	need
neytik in lebn	NAY-*tick in* LEH-*bin*	vital (essential)
neytn (1)	NAY-*lin*	compel, to
"	"	force, to
"	"	oblige, to
neytral	nay-TRAHL	neutral
niderik	NEE-*deh-rick*	low
Niderland, *n.*	NEE-*dehr-lahnd*	Netherlands, The
nign, *m.*	NEEG-*in*	tune (melody)
Nikaragva, *f.*	nee-kah-RAHG-*vah*	Nicaragua
nikhter	NEEKH-*tehr*	sober (serious)
nikl, *n.*	NEE-*kil*	nickel (*chem.*)
Nilus, *m.*	NEE-*loose*	Nile
nir, *f.*	NEAR	kidney (*anat.*)
nishkoshedik	nish-KAW-*sheh-dik*	considerable (*adj.*)
"	"	fair (passable)
nisht	NEESHT	not
nishtik	NEESH-*tick*	insignificant (trivial)
"	"	petty (minor)
nisn (7)	NEE-*sin*	sneeze, to
nisoyen, *m.*	nee-SAW-*yen*	temptation
nit	NEET	no (not any, *adv.*)
"	"	not
nit-batsolt	*nit-bah*-TSAWLT	unpaid (due)
nit der; nit yener	*nit* DEHR, *nit* YEH-*nehr*	neither (*adj.*)
"	"	neither (*pron.*)
nit-enlekh	*nit*-EN-*lukh*	unlike (*adj.*)
nit-fardayung, *f.*	*nit-far*-DIE-*oon_g*	indigestion
nit inveynik	NEET EEN-*vay-nick*	out (not in, *adv.*)
nit kukndik oyf	*nit* KOO-*kin-dik oyf*	despite (*prep.*)
nitl, *m.*	NEE-*til*	Christmas
nit ...-ndik	NEET ...-*in-dick*	without (failing to, *prep.*)
nit...nit	*nit...nit*	neither...nor (*conj.*)
nito	nee-TAW	away (absent, *adj.*)
nit-obligatorish	NEET-*awb-lee-gah*-TAW-*rish*	optional
nit-rikhtik	*nit*-REEKH-*tick*	incorrect
nitsn (1)	NEET-*sin*	employ (use), to
nitsokhn, *m.*	nee-TSAW-*khin*	victory
nitsokhndik	nee-TSAW-*khin-dick*	victorious
nodl, *f.*	NAW-*dil*	needle
noent	NAW-*ent*	close (*adj.*, *adv.*)
"	"	familiar (intimate)
"	"	near (not far, *adv.*)
nogl, *m.*	NAWG-*il*	claw (of animal)
"	"	claw (of bird)
"	"	nail (*anat.*)
nokh	NAW_KH	after (*prep.*)
"	"	else (in addition, *adj.*)
"	"	still (as yet, *adv.*)
"	"	still (even more, *adv.*)
"	"	yet (now, until now, *adv.*)
nokh a	NAW_KH *ah*	another (one more, *adj.*)
nokh dem vi	NAW_KH *dem vee*	after (*conj.*)
nokh eyner, nokh eyne	NAW_KH *ay-neh(r)*	another (one more, *pron.*)
nokhfreg, *m.*	NAW_KH-*freg*	demand (*econ.*)
nokhgebn (13a)	NAW_KH-*g_eh-bin*	yield (give in), to
nokhgeyn (14ad)	NAW_KH-*gain*	follow (go or come after), to
nokhkumen (5ad)	NAW_KH-*koo-men*	comply (acquiesce), to
nokhmakhn (1a)	NAW_KH-*mah-khin*	copy, to
"	"	forge (counterfeit), to
"	"	imitate, to
nokhmitik, *m.*	*naw_kh*-MEE-*tick*	afternoon
nokhvort, *n.*	NAW_KH-*vort*	postscript
nokhyogn (1a)	NAW_KH-*yawg-in*	chase, to
"	"	pursue, to
nomen, *m.*	NAW-*men*	name
nominatsye, *f.*	naw-mee-NAHTS-*yeh*	nomination
nominirn (1b)	naw-mee-NEE-*rin*	nominate, to

Yiddish	Pronunciation	English
nor	NOR	just (merely)
"	"	only (merely)
nore,*f.*	NAW-*reh*	den (animal lair)
normal	nor-MAHL	normal (*adj.*)
norvegish	nor-VEG-*ish*	Norwegian (*adj.*)
Norvegye,*f.*	nor-VEG-*yeh*	Norway
not,*f.*	NAWT	seam (line of stitches)
notar,*m.*	no-TAR	notary
note,*f.*	NAW-*teh*	note (*mus.*)
novele,*f.*	naw-VEH-*leh*	short story
novi,*m.*	NAW-*vee*	prophet (religious teacher)
noyt,*f.*	NOYT	distress
"	"	hardship (privation)
noyte zayn (18c)	NOY-*teh* zine	incline, to
"	"	tend (be apt), to
noytfal,*m.*	NOYT-*fahl*	emergency (*n.*)
noz,*f.*	NAWZ	nose (*anat.*)
nozlokh,*f.*	NAWZ-*lawkh*	nostril
noztikhl,*n.*	NAWZ-*tee-khil*	handerkerchief
nu	NOO	well (and then?, *interj.*)
nudne	NOOD-*neh*	dull (boring)
nul,*m.*	NOOL	zero (*n.*)
numer,*m.*	NOO-*mehr*	number (numeral)
"	"	size (garment measure)
numerirn (1b)	noo-meh-REE-*rin*	number (assign numbers to), to
nus,*m.*	NOOSE	nut (food)
nuts,*m.*	NOOTS	use (usefulness)
nutsik	NOOT-*sick*	helpful
"	"	useful
nutsikayt,*f.*	NOOT-*see-kite*	utility (usefulness)
nutsn (1)	NOOT-*sin*	use (utilize), to
nutsn, on a	AWN *ah* NOOT-*sin*	useless
Nyu-York,*n.*	new-YORK	New York
oaze,*f.*	aw-AH-*zeh*	oasis
ober	AW-*behr*	but (yet, *conj.*)
obligatorish	awb-lee-gah-TAW-*rish*	obligatory (binding)
obligatsye,*f.*	awb-lee-GAHTS-*yeh*	bond (debenture)
oboe,*f.*	aw-BAW-*eh*	oboe
observator,*m.*	awb-sehr-VAH-*tor*	observer
observatsye,*f.*	owb-sehr-VAHTS-*yeh*	observation (watching)
observirn (1b)	awb-sehr-VEE-*rin*	observe (watch), to
obyekt,*m.*	awb-YEKT	object (thing)
oder	AW-*dehr*	or
oder der oder yener	AW-*dehr* DEHR AW-*dehr* YEH-*nehr*	either (one or the other, *adj.*)
"	"	either (either one, *pron.*)
oder...oder	AW-*dehr*...AW-*dehr*	either...or (*conj.*)
odler,*m.*	AWD-*lehr*	eagle
of,*n.*	AWF	fowl (poultry)
ofitsir,*m.*	aw-fee-TSEER	officer (*mil.*)
ofitsyel	aw-feets-YEHL	official (*adj.*)
ofn	AW-*fin*	frank (*adj.*)
"	"	open (*adj.*)
oft	AWFT	frequent
"	"	often
oger,*m.*	AWG-*ehr*	stallion
okean,*m.*	aw-keh-AHN	ocean
okean-shif,*f.*	aw-keh-AHN-*shif*	liner, ocean
okhtsn (1)	AWKH-*tsin*	moan, to
oks,*m.*	AWX	bull (male bovine)
"	"	ox
okupatsye,*f.*	aw-koo-PAHTS-*yeh*	occupation (*mil.*)
olel	AW-*lel*	liable (responsible)
olel tsu	AW-*lil* tsoo	apt to (prone to)
omed,*m.*	AW-*med*	column (*print.*)
on	AWN	without (lacking, *prep.*)
onbaysn,*m.*	AWN-*bye-sin*	lunch (midday meal)
onbeygn zikh (10a)	AWN-*bayg-in zikh*	stoop (bend forward), to
onbot,*m.*	AWN-*bawt*	bid (amount offered)
"	"	offer
onboter,*m.*	AWN-*baw-tehr*	bidder (*bus.*)
onbotn (5a)	AWN-*baw-tin*	offer (tender), to
ondenk,*m.*	AWN-*denk*	souvenir
onerkenung,*f.*	aw-nehr-KEH-*noon_g*	credit (commendation)
"	"	recognition (acknowledgment)

Yiddish	Pronunciation	English
onfal,*m.*	AWN-*fahl*	attack (personal assault)
onfiln (1a)	AWN-*fee-lin*	fill (make full), to
onfirn mit (1a)	AWN-*fee-rin mit*	conduct (manage), to
"	"	direct (manage), to
"	"	manage (administer), to
onfirung,*f.*	AWN-*fee-roon_g*	management (administration)
onfli,*m.*	AWN-*flee*	air raid
onfreg,*m.*	AWN-*freg*	inquiry (question)
onfregn (1a)	AWN-*freg-in*	inquire (ask), to
ongeleygt	AWN-*g_eh-laygt*	desirable
ongenem	AWN-*g_eh-nem*	agreeable (pleasing)
ongeshtelter,*m.*	AWN-*g_eh-shtehl-tehr*	employee
ongeyn (14ad)	AWN-*gain*	concern (affect), to
ongezen	AWN-*g_eh-zen*	distinguished (notable)
onhenger,*m.*	AWN-*hen-g_ehr*	follower (adherent)
onhengershaft,*f.*	AWN-*hen-g_ehr-shahft*	following (followers)
onheyb,*m.*	AWN-*habe*	beginning
"	"	start
onheybn (10a)	AWN-*hay-bin*	begin (start to do), to
"	"	start (initiate), to
onheybn zikh	AWN-*hay-bin zikh*	begin (come into being), to
"	"	commence (make a start), to
onkhapn (1a)	AWN-*khah-pin*	grasp (grip), to
"	"	seize (clutch), to
onklapn (1a)	AWN-*klah-pin*	rap, to
onklaybn (9a)	AWN-*klye-bin*	accumulate (amass), to
onkukn,*n.*	AWN-*koo-kin*	inspection (scrutiny)
onkukn (1a)	AWN-*koo-kin*	inspect, to
onkum,*m.*	AWN-*koom*	arrival
onkumen (5ad)	AWN-*koo-men*	arrive, to
"	"	resort (have recourse), to
onlodn (5a)	AWN-*law-din*	charge, to (*elec.*)
"	"	load (fill), to
onnemen,*n.*	AWN-*neh-men*	acceptance (approval)
"	"	acceptance (receipt)
onnemen (8a)	AWN-*neh-men*	accept, to
"	"	adopt (embrace), to
onrirn (1a)	AWN-*ree-rin*	touch, to
onshlisn zikh in (7a)	AWN-*shlee-sin zikh in*	join (become a member of), to
onshtel,*m.*	AWN-*shtel*	pretense (pretending)
onshtel, makhn dem (1)	MAH-*khin dem* AWN-*shtel*	pretend (feign), to
onshtel fun, makhn dem	MAH-*khin dem* AWN-*shtel foon*	affect (pretend), to
onshteln (1a)	AWN-*shteh-lin*	beam (shine), to
"	"	employ (hire), to
onshtrengung,*f.*	AWN-*shtren-goon_g*	strain (exertion)
onteyl nemen (8c)	AWN-*tale neh-men*	participate, to
onton (22a)	AWN-*tawn*	clothe, to
"	"	dress (clothe), to
"	"	impose (inflict), to
onton zikh	AWN-*tawn zikh*	dress (get dressed), to
ontshepenish,*f.*	AWN-*cheh-peh-nish*	pest (nuisance)
ontsindn (8a)	AWN-*tsin-din*	light (set fire to), to
ontsindung,*f.*	AWN-*tsin-doon_g*	inflammation
ontsuherenish,*f.*	AWN-*tsoo-heh-reh-nish*	hint (inkling)
onvarfn (7a)	AWN-*var-fin*	draft (sketch), to
onvayzn (9a)	AWN-*vie-zin*	indicate (point out), to
"	"	point (indicate), to
onvayzung,*f.*	AWN-*vie-zoon_g*	draft (check)
onvendn (1a)	AWN-*ven-din*	apply (put to use), to
onvendung,*f.*	AWN-*ven-doon_g*	application (use)
onver,*m.*	AWN-*vehr*	loss
onvern (10a)	AWN-*veh-rin*	lose, to
onvorf,*m.*	AWN-*vorf*	outline (rough draft)
onzogn (1a)	AWN-*zawg-in*	inform (apprise), to
"	"	instruct (direct), to
"	"	notify, to
opbren,*m.*	AWP-*bren*	sunburn
opdakh,*m.*	AWP-*dahkh*	shelter
opdruk,*m.*	AWP-*drook*	print (printed reproduction)

Yiddish	Pronunciation	English
operatsye, *f.*	*aw-peh-*RAHTS*-yeh*	operation (*med.*)
opere, *f.*	AW-*peh-reh*	opera
operirn (1b)	AW-*peh-ree-rin*	operate (perform surgery), to
opfal, *m.*	AWP-*fahl*	garbage
opfaln (5ad)	AWP-*fah-lin*	decline (deteriorate), to
opflisrer, *f.*	AWP-*flis-rehr*	drain (conduit)
opflus, *m.*	AWP-*flooss*	tide, low
opfor, *m.*	AWP-*for*	departure (setting out)
opfregn (1a)	AWP-*freg-in*	dispute (oppose by argument), to
"	"	refute, to
opgebn zikh (13a)	AWP-*g̱ eh-bin zikh*	devote oneself, to
opgehit	AWP-*g̱ eh-heet*	careful (cautious)
opgehitkayt, *f.*	AWP-*g̱ eh-heet-kite*	caution (heed)
opgelozn	AWP-*g̱ eh-law-zin*	careless (negligent)
opgezundert	AWP-*g̱ eh-zoon-dehrt*	solitary (unaccompanied)
opgos, *m.*	AWP-*gawss*	sink (*n.*)
ophalt, *m.*	AWP-*hahlt*	check (restraint)
"	"	delay
ophaltn (5a)	AWP-*hahl-tin*	check (stop), to
"	"	delay (retard), to
"	"	keep (prevent), to
ophengik	AWP-*hen-g̱ ick*	dependent (reliant)
opleygn (1a)	AWP-*layg-in*	delay (postpone), to
"	"	postpone, to
oplozn (1a)	AWP-*law-zin*	release (let go of), to
oplozn, nit	NEET AWP-*law-zin*	haunt (visit often), to
opmakh, *m.*	AWP-*maẖ kh*	contract
opnar, *m.*	AWP-*nar*	deceit
opnarn (1a)	AWP-*nah-rin*	betray, to
"	"	cheat (defraud), to
"	"	deceive (delude), to
opnemer, *n.*	AWP-*neh-mehr*	consignee (*bus.*)
opraysn (9a)	AWP-*rye-sin*	sever, to
opredn (1a)	AWP-*reh-din*	settle (arrange), to
oprikhtn (1a)	AWP-*rikh-tin*	celebrate, to
opruf, *m.*	AWP-*roof*	reaction
oprufn zikh (5a)	AWP-*roo-fin zikh*	respond (react), to
opshafn (1a)	AWP-*shah-fin*	abolish, to
opshatsn (1a)	AWP-*shah-tsin*	appreciate (be grateful for), to
opshatsung, *f.*	AWP-*shaht-sooṉ g*	judgment (estimation)
opshay, *m.*	AWP-*shy*	reverence (respect)
opshpiglen (1a)	AWP-*shpeeg-len*	reflect (throw back), to
opshpiglung, *f.*	AWP-*shpeeg-looṉ g*	reflection (image)
opshporung, *f.*	AWP-*shpaw-rooṉ g*	savings (money)
opshpringen (8ad)	AWP-*shpreen-g̱ en*	bounce, to
opshtel, *m.*	AWP-*shtel*	stop (halt)
opshteln (1a)	AWP-*shteh-lin*	arrest, to
"	"	halt (come to a stop), to
"	"	stop (make halt), to
"	"	suspend (terminate), to
opshteln zikh	AWP-*shteh-lin zikh*	stop (come to a standstill), to
opshteyn (17ad)	AWP-*shtane*	lag (fall behind), to
opshvakhn (1a)	AWP-*shvah-khin*	weaken (make weak), to
opteyl, *m.*	AWP-*tail*	section (part)
opteyln (1a)	AWP-*tay-lin*	separate (disconnect), to
opteylung, *f.*	AWP-*tay-looṉ g*	department (administrative unit)
optimistish	*awp-tee-*MEES*-tish*	optimistic
optretn (7a)	AWP-*treh-tin*	cede, to
optsol, *m.*	AWP-*tsawl*	charge (price)
"	"	fee
optsoln (1a)	AWP-*tsaw-lin*	repay (reimburse), to
opvarfn (7a)	AWP-*var-fin*	reject, to
opvaykh, *m.*	AWP-*vye̱ kh*	departure (deviation)
opvaykhn (1a)	AWP-*vie-khin*	deviate (diverge), to
opzog, *m.*	AWP-*zawg*	discharge (dismissal)
opzogn (1a)	AWP-*zawg-in*	deny, to
opzogn zikh	AWP-*zawg-in zikh*	refuse, to

Yiddish	Pronunciation	English
opzogn zikh fun	AWP-*zawg-in zikh foon*	decline, to
"	"	renounce (give up), to
oranzh	*aw-*RAHṈ ZH	orange (color)
ordenung, *f.*	OR-*deh-nooṉ g*	order (orderliness)
orem	AW-*rem*	poor (needy)
orem, *m.*	AW-*rim*	arm (*anat.*)
orev, *m.*	AW-*rev*	guarantor
organ, *m.*	*or-*GAHN	organ (*anat.*)
organizatsye, *f.*	*or-gah-nee-*ZAHTS*-yeh*	organization (association)
organizirn (1b)	*or-gah-nee-*ZEE*-rin*	organize (systematize), to
orgl, *f.*	ORG-*il*	organ (*mus.*)
orkester, *m.*	*or-*KESS*-tehr*	orchestra (*mus.*)
orkhidee, *f.*	*or-khee-*DAY*-eh*	orchid (flower)
orn, *m.*	AW-*rin*	coffin (Jewish)
ornament, *m.*	*or-nah-*MENT	ornament
orntlekh	AW-*rint-lukh*	decent
"	"	proper (acceptable)
ort, *n.*	ORT	locality (place)
"	"	location
"	"	room (space)
"	"	site
"	"	stead (place)
Oryent, *m.*	*or-*YENT	Orient
os, *m.*	AWSS	letter (character)
Oslo, *n.*	OSS-*lo*	Oslo
Otava, *n.*	AW-*ta-vah*	Ottawa
otem, *m.*	AW-*tem*	breath
otemen (1)	AW-*teh-men*	breathe (draw breath), to
over, *m.*	AW-*vehr*	past (*n.*)
oves, *pl.*	AW-*vess*	ancestor
ovnt, *m.*	AW-*vint*	evening
oyb	OYB	if (supposing that)
oyb azoy	OYB *ah-*ZOY	then (in that case)
oybn	OY-*bin*	above (overhead, *adv.*)
oybn, *m.*	OY-*bin*	top (upper surface)
"	"	upstairs (at upper story, *adv.*)
oydef, *m.*	OY-*def*	excess
"	"	margin
"	"	surplus (*n.*)
oyer, *m.*	OY-*ehr*	ear
oyer-veytik, *m.*	AW-*yehr-vay-tick*	earache
oyf	OYF	at (on)
"	"	at (to, toward)
"	"	by (*prep., math.*)
"	"	on (*prep.*)
"	"	upon
oyfbli, *m.*	OYF-*blee*	boom (*bus.*)
oyfblozn zikh (5a)	OYF-*blaw-zin zikh*	swell (bulge), to
oyfdekn (1a)	OYF-*deh-kin*	discover, to
"	"	expose (disclose), to
oyfdekung, *f.*	OYF-*deh-kooṉ g*	discovery
oyfele, *n.*	OY-*feh-leh*	baby
"	"	infant (*n.*)
oyfes, *pl.*	OY-*fess*	poultry
oyffir, *m.*	OYF-*fear*	behavior
oyffirn zikh (1a)	OYF-*fee-rin zikh*	behave (conduct oneself), to
oyffrishn (1a)	OYF-*free-shin*	refresh, to
oyfgebrakhtkayt, *f.*	OYF-*g̱ eh-braẖ kht-kite*	indignation
oyfgekokht	OYF-*g̱ eh-kawkht*	furious
oyfgeyn (14ad)	OYF-*gain*	rise (in the sky), to
oyfhalt, *m.*	OYF-*hahlt*	stay (sojourn)
oyfhern (1a)	OYF-*heh-rin*	cease, to
"	"	quit, to
"	"	stop, to
oyfheybn (10a)	OYF-*hay-bin*	elevate, to
"	"	pick up (lift), to
"	"	raise (lift up), to
oyfhitn (1a)	OYF-*hee-tin*	maintain, to
"	"	preserve, to
oyfkumen (5ad)	OYF-*koo-men*	arise (come about), to
oyflebn (1a)	OYF-*leh-bin*	revive, to
oyfmerkzam	OYF-*mehrk-zahm*	attentive (heedful)
oyfn, *m.*	OY-*fin*	fashion
"	"	manner

Yiddish	Pronunciation	English	Yiddish	Pronunciation	English
oyfn, *m.*	OY-*fin*	mode	oysgletn (1a)	OYSS-*gleh-tin*	smooth (level), to
"	"	way	oysglitshn zikh (1)	OYSS-*glee-chin zikh*	slip (slide), to
oyfnem, *m.*	OYF-*nem*	reception	oyshaltn (5a)	OYSS-*hahl-tin*	pass (not fail in), to
oyfnemen (8a)	OYF-*neh-men*	entertain (be host to), to	"	"	sustain (maintain), to
oyfrays-materyal, *m.*	OYF-*rice-mah-tehr-yahl*	explosive (*n.*)	oyshelfik	OYSS-*hell-fick*	helpful (volunteering help)
oyfraysn (9a)	OYF-*rye-sin*	blast (explode), to	oysheyln (1a)	OYSS-*hay-lin*	cure (heal), to
oyfregn (1a)	OYF-*rehg-in*	excite, to	oyskern (1a)	OYSS-*keh-rin*	sweep (clean), to
oyfregung, *f.*	OYF-*reh-goon_g*	excitement	oysklayb, *m.*	OYSS-*klybe*	choice (act of choosing)
oyfrikhtik	OYF-*rikh-tick*	sincere	"	"	selection
oyfrudern (1a)	OYF-*roo-deh-rin*	arouse (excite), to	"	"	variety (assortment)
oyfshoydern (1a)	OYF-*shoy-deh-rin*	shudder, to	oysklaybn (9a)	OYSS-*klye-bin*	choose, to
oyfshteln (1a)	OYF-*shteh-lin*	erect (build), to	"	"	elect, to
oyfshteln, tsurik	tsoo-REEK OYF-*shteh-lin*	restore (reestablish), to	"	"	select, to
oyfshteyn (17ad)	OYF-*shtane*	rise, to	oyskoyfn (1a)	OYSS-*koy-fin*	redeem (buy back), to
"	"	stand up, to	oyskrimen zikh (1a)	OYSS-*kree-men zikh*	warp (become misshapen), to
oyfton (22a)	OYF-*tawn*	accomplish, to	oyskuk, *m.*	OYSS-*cook*	prospect (thing expected)
oyftsikind, *n.*	OYF-*tsee-kind*	foster child	oyslender, *m.*	OYSS-*len-dehr*	foreigner
oyfvaksn (5ad)	OYF-*vahk-sin*	grow up (mature), to	oyslendish	OYSS-*len-dish*	foreign
oyfvekn (1a)	OYF-*veh-kin*	awaken (make awaken), to	oysleydikn (1a)	OYSS-*ley-dee-kin*	empty (remove contents of), to
"	"	rouse, to	oysleygn (1a)	OYSS-*layg-in*	spell, to
"	"	wake (make awaken), to	oysleyzgelt, *n.*	OYSS-*laze-g_elt*	ransom (*n.*)
oyfvekn zikh	OYF-*veh-kin zikh*	awaken (become awake), to	oyslinken (8a)	OYSS-*lin-ken*	sprain, to
"	"	wake (rouse oneself), to	oyslodn (5a)	OYSS-*law-din*	unload, to
oyfzeer, *m.*	OYF-*zeh-ehr*	foreman (overseer)	oysloyfn (7ad)	OYSS-*loy-fin*	lapse (become void), to
oyg, *n.*	OYG	eye (*anat.*)	oysloz, *m.*	OYSS-*lawz*	conclusion (end)
oygngreykh, *m.*	OYG-*in-gray_kh*	sight (range of sight)	"	"	ending
oygn, oyfshteln a por (1a)	OYF-*shteh-lin ah pore* OYG-*in*	glare (stare), to	oyslozn (1a)	OYSS-*law-zin*	omit (leave out), to
oykh	OYKH	also	oysmaydn (11a)	OYS-*my-din*	avoid, to
"	"	so	oysmekn (1a)	OYSS-*meh-kin*	blot out (efface), to
"	"	too	oysnem, *m.*	OYSS-*nem*	exception (unusual case)
oykh nit	OYKH *nit*	either (not... either, *adv.*)	oysnitsn (1a)	OYSS-*neet-sin*	exercise (employ), to
"	"	nor	oyspoyshn (1a)	OYSS-*poy-shin*	puff (inflate), to
oylem, *m.*	OY-*lem*	audience	oyspruvn (1a)	OYSS-*proo-vin*	test, to
"	"	crowd	"	"	try, to
"	"	public (populace, *n.*)	oysrekhenen (3a)	OYS-*reh-kheh-nen*	calculate (compute), to
oyringl, *n.*	OY-*rin-g_il*	earring	oysseydern (1a)	OYSS-*say-deh-rin*	arrange (place), to
oysarbetn (1a)	OYSS-*ar-beh-tin*	manufacture, to	oysshepn (1a)	OYSS-*sheh-pin*	exhaust (use up), to
oysbayt, *m.*	OYSS-*bite*	exchange (barter)	oysshliser, *m.*	OYSS-*shlee-sehr*	switch (*elec.*)
oysbaytn (9a)	OYSS-*bye-tin*	exchange (interchange), to	oysshlisn (7a)	OYSS-*shlee-sin*	exclude, to
oysbildn (1a)	OYSS-*bil-din*	educate, to	oysshlisndik	OYSS-*shlee-sin-dick*	exclusive (not including)
oysblik, *m.*	OYSS-*blick*	view (scene)	oysshpirer, *m.*	OYSS-*shpee-rehr*	scout (lookout)
oysbrekhn (7a)	OYSS-*breh-khin*	vomit, to	oysshrayen (12a)	OYSS-*shrye-en*	exclaim, to
oysbrien (1a)	OYSS-*bree-en*	hatch, to	oysshtayer, *m.*	OYSS-*shtye-ehr*	equipment
oysderveylt	OYSS-*dehr-vaylt*	chosen	"	"	outfit
oysdreyen zikh (1a)	OYSS-*dray-en zikh*	turn (face about), to	oysshtayern (1a)	OYSS-*shtye-eh-rin*	furnish (put furniture in), to
oysdruk, *m.*	OYSS-*drook*	expression	oysshteln (1a)	OYSS-*shteh-lin*	display, to
oysergeveyntlekh	OY-*sehr-g_eh*-VAINT-*lukh*	extraordinary	"	"	exhibit, to
oysesn zikh dos harts (20a)	OYSS-*eh-sin zikh dawss* HARTS	fret (worry), to	oysshtelung, *f.*	OYSS-*shteh-loon_g*	exhibit
oysfarkoyf, *m.*	OYSS-*far-koyf*	clearance sale	"	"	exhibition (exposition)
oysfir, *m.*	OYSS-*feer*	conclusion (decision)	"	"	show
oysfir-...	OYSS-*feer-...*	executive (*adj.*)	oysshulung, *f.*	OYSS-*shoo-loon_g*	schooling (instruction)
oysfirn (1a)	OYSS-*fee-rin*	execute (carry out), to	"	"	training (instruction)
oysforshn (1a)	OYSS-*for-shin*	investigate, to	oystaytshn (1a)	OYSS-*tie-chin*	interpret (explain), to
oysforshung, *f.*	OYSS-*for-shoon_g*	investigation	oyster, *m.*	OYSS-*tehr*	oyster
oysfreg, *m.*	OYSS-*fregg*	poll (survey)	oysterlish	OYSS-*tehr-lish*	queer
oysfregn (1a)	OYSS-*fregg-in*	question (query), to	oysteyln (1a)	OYSS-*tay-lin*	confer (bestow), to
oysgabe, *f.*	OYSS-*gah-beh*	edition	oystrakhtn (1a)	OYSS-*trah_kh-tin*	devise (contrive), to
oysgebn	OYSS-*g_eh-bin*	spend (pay out), to	oystralish	*oys*-TRAH-*lish*	Australian (*adj.*)
oysgeboygn	OYS-*g_eh-boyg-in*	bent (curved)	Oystralye, *n.*	*oys*-TRAHL-*yeh*	Australia
oysgefinen (8ab)	OYSS-*g_eh-fee-nen*	invent, to	oystrikenen (3a)	OYSS-*tree-keh-nen*	drain (make dry), to
oysgefins, *n.*	OYSS-*g_eh-finss*	invention	oystseykhenung, *f.*	OYSS-*tsay-kheh-noon_g*	distinction (eminence)
oysgepashet	OYS-*g_eh-pah-shet*	plump (chubby)	oystsien (23a)	OYSS-*tsee-en*	stretch (draw out), to
oysgeshrey, *m.*	OYS-*g_eh-shray*	exclamation (*n.*)	oystsolung, *f.*	OYSS-*tsaw-loon_g*	disbursement (*bus.*)
oysgetseykhnt	OYS-*g_eh-tsay-khint*	excellent	oysveg, *m.*	OYSS-*veg*	outlet (exit)
"	"	superior	oysze, *m.*	OYSS-*zeh*	appearance (aspect)
oysgeyn (14ad)	OYSS-*gain*	expire (become void, *bus.*), to	"	"	look (aspect)
oysglaykhn (9a)	OYSS-*glye-khin*	straighten (put in order), to	oyszen (6a)	OYSS-*zen*	appear, to
			"	"	look, to
			"	"	seem, to

Yiddish	Pronunciation	English
oyszogn (1a)	OYSS-*zawg-in*	reveal (divulge), to
oyto, *m.*	OY-*taw*	car (auto)
oytobiografye, *f.*	OY-*taw-bee-o-*GRAHF-*yeh*	autobiography
oytobus, *m.*	*oy-taw-*BOOSS	bus
oytomobil, *m.*	*oy-taw-mo-*BEEL	automobile
oytoritet, *m.*	*oy-taw-ree-*TEHT	authority (person with power)
oytorizirung, *f.*	*oy-taw-ree-*ZEE-*roon_g*	authorization
oytser, *m.*	OYT-*sehr*	treasure
oytsres, *pl.*	OYTS-*ress*	resources (wealth)
oyver zayn oyf (18cd)	OY-*vehr zine oyf*	violate (infringe upon), to
oyvn, *m.*	OY-*vin*	furnace (home heater)
"	"	oven
"	"	stove (for heating)
ozere, *f.*	AW-*zeh-reh*	lake
padeshve, *f.*	*pah-*DESH-*veh*	sole (of shoe)
pakhdn, *m.*	PAH_KH-*din*	coward
Pakistan, *n.*	*pah-kee-*STAHN	Pakistan
pakistanish	*pah-kee-*STAH-*nish*	Pakistani (*adj.*)
palate, *f.*	*pah-*LAH-*teh*	ward (sickroom)
palats, *m.*	PAH-*lahts*	palace
palme, *f.*	PAHL-*meh*	palm (tree)
palmen-zuntik, *m.*	PAHL-*men-zoon-tik*	Palm Sunday
pamelekh	*pah-*MEH-*lukh*	slow (not fast)
Paname, *f.*	*pah-*NAH-*meh*	Panama
panik, *f.*	PAH-*neek*	panic (fear)
pansyon, *m.*	*pahnss-*YAWN	boarding house
pantere, *f.*	*pahn-*TEH-*reh*	panther
pantser, *m.*	PAHN-*tsehr*	armor (protective clothing)
pantsershif, *f.*	PAHN-*tsehr-sheef*	battleship
pap, *m.*	PAHP	paste (adhesive)
papir, *n.*	*pah-*PEER	paper
papiros, *m.*	*pah-pee-*ROSS	cigarette
papugay, *m.*	*pah-poo-*GUY	parrot
parad, *m.*	*pah-*RAHD	parade (procession)
parafye, *f.*	*pah-*RAHF-*yeh*	parish
paragraf, *m.*	*pah-rah-*GRAHF	clause (stipulation)
"	"	paragraph
Paragvay, *n.*	PAH-*rahg-vie*	Paraguay
paralel	*pah-rah-*LELL	parallel (*adj.*)
paraliz, *m.*	*pah-*RAH-*leez*	paralysis
parashut, *m.*	*pah-rah-*SHOOT	parachute
pare, *f.*	PAH-*reh*	steam
"	"	vapor
parfum, *m.*	*par-*FOOM	perfume (fragrance)
Pariz, *n.*	*pah-*REEZ	Paris
park, *m.*	PARK	park
parkan, *m.*	PAR-*kahn*	fence (barrier)
parkn (1)	PAR-*kin*	park (put in place), to
parlament, *m.*	*par-lah-*MENT	parliament
parnose, *f.*	*par-*NAW-*seh*	living (livelihood)
parom, *m.*	*pah-*RAWM	ferry (boat)
parshoyn, *m.*	*par-*SHOYN	character (person portrayed)
partey, *f.*	*par-*TAY	party (*pol.*)
pas, *m.*	PAHSS	passport
"	"	streak
"	"	stripe
pasazhir, *m.*	*pah-sah-*ZHEER	passenger
pashe, *f.*	PAH-*sheh*	pasture (grassland)
pashen zikh (2)	PAH-*shen zikh*	graze (feed), to
pashtes, *f.*	PAHSH-*tess*	simplicity
pasik	PAH-*sick*	fit
"	"	suitable
paskhe, *f.*	PAHSS-*kheh*	Easter
pasn (1)	PAH-*sin*	apply (be fitting), to
pasn zikh	PAH-*sin zikh*	match (equal), to
pastekh, *m.*	PAHS-*tukh*	shepherd
pastke, *f.*	PAHST-*keh*	trap (snare)
pastor, *m.*	PAHSS-*tor*	pastor
patent, *m.*	*pah-*TENT	patent (*n.*)
patern, *n.*	PAH-*teh-rin*	waste (squandering)
patern (1)	PAH-*teh-rin*	waste (squander), to
patike, *f.*	PAH-*tee-keh*	molasses
patilnitse, *f.*	*pah-*TEEL-*nee-tseh*	nape
patriot, *m.*	*paht-ree-*AWT	patriot

Yiddish	Pronunciation	English
patsifik, *m.*	*pah-*TSEE-*fick*	Pacific (*n.*)
patsyent, *m.*	*pahts-*YENT	patient (invalid)
pave, *f.*	PAH-*veh*	peacock
pay, *m.*	PIE	pie
payn, *f.*	PINE	anguish
paynikung, *f.*	PIE-*nee-koon_g*	torture
pekl, *n.*	PEH-*kil*	bundle
"	"	package
"	"	parcel
peklpost, *f.*	PEH-*kil-pawst*	parcel post
pen, *f.*	PEN	pen
penets, *m.*	PEH-*nets*	slice
penitsilin, *m.*	*peh-neet-see-*LEEN	penicillin
penkher, *m.*	PEN-*khehr*	bladder (*anat.*)
"	"	blister
perfekt	*pehr-*FEKT	perfect (flawless)
period, *m.*	*peh-*REE-*awd*	term (duration)
perl, *m.*	PEH-*ril*	pearl (gem)
peron, *m.*	*peh-*RAWN	platform, railroad
Peru, *n.*	*peh-*ROO	Peru
peruanish	*peh-roo-*AH-*nish*	Peruvian (*adj.*)
peryod, *m.*	*pehr-*YAWD	period (of time)
perzenlekh	*pehr-*ZEN-*lukh*	personal
perzenlekhkayt, *f.*	*pehr-*ZEN-*lukh-kite*	personality
perzon, *f.*	*pehr-*ZAWN	person
peshl, *n.*	PEH-*shil*	deck (of cards)
pesimistish	*peh-see-*MEES-*tish*	pessimistic
petitsye, *f.*	*peh-*TEETS-*yeh*	petition (written request)
Peyping, *n.*	*pay-*PEEN_G	Peiping
Peysakh, *m.*	PAY-*sukh*	Passover
pgam, *m.*	P_GAHM	defect (flaw)
pgimedik	PG_EE-*meh-dick*	imperfect (defective)
pikn (1)	PEE-*kin*	peck, to
piknik, *m.*	PEEK-*nick*	picnic
pil, *f.*	PEEL	pill
pileven (2)	PEE-*leh-ven*	nurse (give treatment to), to
pilke, *f.*	PEEL-*keh*	ball (sphere)
pilot, *m.*	*pee-*LAWT	pilot (flier)
pinktlekh	PEENKT-*lukh*	accurate
"	"	prompt
"	"	punctual
pintele, *n.*	PEEN-*teh-leh*	dot (point)
piper-noter, *m.*	*pee-pehr-*NAW-*tehr*	dragon
pirat, *m.*	*pee-*RAHT	pirate
pirsum, *m.*	PEER-*sum*	publicity (notoriety)
pistoyl, *m.*	*pis-*TOYL	pistol
pitsl	PEET-*sil*	wee
pizhame, *f.*	*pee-*ZHAH-*meh*	pajamas
plame, *f.*	PLAH-*meh*	stain
plan, *m.*	PLAHN	blueprint
"	"	plan
"	"	scheme
planet, *m.*	*plah-*NET	planet
planeven (2)	PLAH-*neh-ven*	plan (prearrange), to
plankn, *m.*	PLAHN-*kin*	plank (timber)
plaplen (1)	PLAHP-*lin*	chatter, to
plastik, *m.*	PLAHSS-*tick*	plastic (*n.*)
platin, *n.*	*plah-*TEEN	platinum
plato, *m.*	*plah-*TAW	plateau (tableland)
plats, *m.*	PLAHTS	place (locality)
"	"	spot
"	"	square (plaza)
platsn (1)	PLAH-*tsin*	burst, to
plazh, *m.*	PLAH_ZH	beach (strand)
plimenik, *m.*	*plee-*MEH-*nick*	nephew
plimenitse, *f.*	*plee-*MEH-*neet-seh*	niece
plis, *m.*	PLEESS	velveteen (*n.*)
plite, *f.*	PLEE-*teh*	stove (for cooking)
ployn, *m.*	PLOYN	plain (level land)
ployt, lebediker, *m.*	LEH-*beh-dee-kehr* PLOYT	hedge (bushes)
plus	PLOOSS	plus (*prep.*)
plutsemdik	PLOO-*tsem-dick*	sudden (unexpected)
pnyak, *m.*	*pnee-*AHK	stump (of tree)
podloge, *f.*	*pawd-*LAWG-*eh*	floor (bottom surface)
poeme, *f.*	*po-*EH-*meh*	poem
poet, *m.*	*po-*EHT	poet

Yiddish	Pronunciation	English
poezye,*f.*	*po-*EZZ*-yeh*	poetry
pokn,*pl.*	PAW*-kin*	smallpox
pokost,*m.*	PAW*-kost*	varnish
polir,*m.*	*paw-*LEER	polish
polirn (1b)	*po-*LEE*-rin*	polish, to
"	"	shine, to
polis,*m.*	*po-*LEASE	policy (contract of insurance)
polit,*m.*	PAW*-lit*	refugee
politik,*f.*	*po-lee-*TEEK	policy (course)
"	"	politics
politikant,*m.*	*po-lee-tee-*KAHNT	politician
politish	*po-*LEE*-tish*	political
politishe visnshaft, *f.*	*po-*LEE*-tee-sheh* VEE*-sin-shahft*	political science
politse,*f.*	PAW*-leet-seh*	shelf
politsey,*f.*	*po-lee-*TSAY	police
politsyant,*m.*	*po-leets-*YAHNT	policeman
polus,*m.*	PAW*-loose*	pole (end of axis)
pomidor,*m.*	*paw-mee-*DOR	tomato
pompe,*f.*	PAWM*-peh*	pump
poni,*m.*	PAW*-nee*	pony (animal)
ponim,*n.*	PAW*-nim*	countenance
"	"	face (*anat.*)
populer	*po-poo-*LEHR	popular (prevalent)
por,*f.*	POR	couple
"	"	pair
por, a	*ah* POR	few, a
port,*m.*	PORT	harbor
"	"	port
portret,*m.*	*port-*RETT	portrait
portselay,*n.*	*port-seh-*LIE	porcelain (*n.*)
Portugal,*n.*	POR*-too-gahl*	Portugal
poshet	PAW*-shet*	simple (uninvolved)
posl	PAW*-sil*	void (null)
post,*f.*	PAWST	mail (letters received)
postamt,*m.*	PAWST*-ahmt*	post office
postgelt,*n.*	PAWST*-g elt*	postage (postal charge)
postn,*m.*	PAWSS*-tin*	post (position)
poter	PAW*-tehr*	exempt
poter vern fun (7cd)	PAW*-tehr veh-rin foon*	dispose of (put away), to
"	"	eliminate, to
poyeln (1)	POY*-eh-lin*	convince, to
"	"	induce (persuade), to
poyer,*m.*	PAW*-yehr*	peasant
poyk,*f.*	POYK	drum (*mus.*)
poylish	POY*-lish*	Polish (*adj.*)
Poyln,*n.*	POY*-lin*	Poland
poyps,*m.*	POYPS	pope
poysht,*m.*	POYSHT	felt (*n.*)
poyzen (2)	POY*-zen*	crawl (creep), to
pozitsye,*f.*	*po-*ZEETS*-yeh*	position (location)
prakhtik	PRAH KH*-lick*	magnificent
praktik,*f.*	PRAHK*-tik*	experience (skill)
"	"	practice (performance)
praktish	PRAHK*-tish*	practical (not theoretical)
praktitsirn (1b)	*prahk-tee-*TSEE*-rin*	practice (put to practice), to
praln (1)	PRAH*-lin*	thrust (push), to
prat,*m.*	PRAHT	detail (minor item)
"	"	item (detail)
"	"	particular
prayz,*m.*	PRIZE	cost
"	"	price (*bus.*)
"	"	rate
prayz-notirung,*f.*	PRIZE*-naw-tee-roon g*	quotation (price)
preglen zikh (1)	PREG*-len zikh*	fry (be cooked in fat), to
prekhtik	PREH KH*-lick*	gorgeous
preliminar	*preh-lee-mee-*NAR	preliminary (*adj.*)
premye,*f.*	PREHM*-yeh*	bonus (extra wages)
"	"	premium (payment)
prent,*m.*	PRENT	rod (bar)
preplen (1)	PREP*-len*	mutter (mumble), to
prepozitsye,*f.*	*preh-po-*ZEETS*-yeh*	preposition (*gram.*)
prerye,*f.*	PREHR*-yeh*	prairie
presayzn,*n.*	PRESS*-eye-zin*	iron, electric

Yiddish	Pronunciation	English
prese,*f.*	PREH*-seh*	press (newspapers and periodicals)
presn (1)	PREH*-sin*	press (iron), to
pretendirn (1b)	*preh-ten-*DEE*-rin*	claim, to
pretenzye,*f.*	*preh-*TEN*-zee-yeh*	claim
pretsiz	*pret-*SEEZ	precise (exact)
preydik,*f.*	PRAY*-dick*	sermon
preydiker,*m.*	PRAY*-dee-kehr*	preacher
preydikn (1)	PRAY*-dee-kin*	preach, to
prezentirn (1b)	*preh-zen-*TEE*-rin*	present (set forth), to
prezident,*m.*	*preh-zee-*DENT	president
prikre	PREEK*-reh*	disagreeable
primitiv	*pree-mee-*TEEV	primitive (early)
prints,*m.*	PREENTS	prince
printsesin,*f.*	*preent-*SEH*-sin*	princess
printsip,*m.*	*print-*SEEP	principle (basic truth)
prister,*m.*	PREES*-tehr*	priest
privat	*pree-*VAHT	private (personal)
privilegye,*f.*	*pree-vee-*LEG*-yeh*	privilege
priz,*m.*	PREEZE	prize (trophy)
probe,*f.*	PRAW*-beh*	test (trial)
problem,*f.*	*prawb-*LEM	problem
produkt,*m.*	*praw-*DOOKT	crop
"	"	produce (yield)
"	"	product
produktiv	*pro-dook-*TEEV	productive
produktsye,*f.*	*pro-*DOOKTS*-yeh*	output
"	"	production (manufacture)
produtsirn (1b)	*pro-doot-*SEE*-rin*	produce (make), to
profesor,*m.*	*pro-*FEH*-sore*	professor (teacher)
profesornshaft,*f.*	*pro-feh-*SAW*-rin-shahft*	faculty (teaching staff)
profesye,*f.*	*pro-*FESS*-yeh*	profession (occupation)
profesyonel	*pro-fess-yaw-*NELL	professional
program,*f.*	*pro-*GRAHM	program (plan)
progres,*m.*	*pro-*GRESS	progress
progresiv	*pro-greh-*SEEV	progressive
proklamirn (1b)	*pro-klah-*MEE*-rin*	proclaim, to
prominent	*pro-mee-*NENT	prominent (eminent)
proports,*f.*	*pro-*PORTS	proportion (part)
proshik,*m.*	PRAW*-shick*	powder (dust)
prosperitet,*f.*	*prawss-peh-ree-*TETT	prosperity
prost	PRAWST	common (vulgar)
protest,*m.*	*pro-*TEST	protest
protestirn (1b)	*pro-tes-*TEE*-rin*	protest, to
protezhirn (1b)	*pro-teh-*ZHEE*-rin*	promote (further), to
protokol,*m.*	*pro-taw-*CALL	minutes (record)
protsent,*m.*	*pro-*TSENT	interest (money rate)
"	"	percent (*n.*)
"	"	percentage
protsent oyf protsent,*m.*	*pro-*TSENT *oyf pro-*TSENT	compound interest
protses,*m.*	*prawt-*SESS	process (set of operations)
"	"	suit (lawsuit)
"	"	trial (court proceeding)
protsesye,*f.*	*prawt-*SESS*-yeh*	procession (parade)
provints,*f.*	*pro-*VEENTS	province (*pol.*)
proyekt,*m.*	*pro-*YEKT	project
proze,*f.*	PRAW*-zeh*	prose
pruv,*m.*	PROVE	attempt
pruvn (1)	PROO*-vin*	attempt, to
"	"	tempt, to
"	"	try, to
psak-din,*m.*	*p sahk-*DEEN	judgment (*law*)
psak, mekayem zayn dem (18)	*meh-*KAH*-yem zine dem* P SAHK	execute (put to death), to
pshat,*m*	P SHAHT	sense (signification)
pshore,*f.*	P SHAW*-reh*	compromise (mutual concessions)
psikhologye,*f.*	*p see-khaw-*LAWG*-yeh*	psychology
psikhyatrye,*f.*	*p see-khee-*AHT*-ree-yeh*	psychiatry
publikatsye,*f.*	*poob-lee-*KAHTS*-yeh*	publication (published work)
puder,*m.*	POO*-dehr*	powder (cosmetic)
puding,*m.*	POO*-din g*	pudding (dessert)
punkt,*m.*	POONKT	period (*punct.*)
"	"	point (in space)
"	"	point (item)

Yiddish	Pronunciation	English
punktkome, *f.*	*poonkt-*KAW*-meh*	semicolon
purpl	POOR*-pil*	crimson
"	"	scarlet (*adj.*)
pushke, *f.*	POOSH*-keh*	can (tin)
pust	POOST	blank (unmarked)
"	"	empty
pust un pas	POOST *oon* PAHSS	idle (not busy)
pust-un-paskayt, *f.*	*poost-oon-*PAHSS*-kite*	idleness (inactivity)
puter, *f.*	POO*-tehr*	butter
pyane, *f.*	*pee-*AH*-neh*	piano (*n.*)
pyate, *f.*	*pee-*AH*-teh*	heel (*anat.*)
pyese, *f.*	*pee-*EH*-seh*	play (stage presentation)
pyoner, *m.*	*pee-*AW*-nehr*	pioneer
radar, *m.*	RAH*-dar*	radar (*n.*)
radikal	*rah-dee-*KAHL	radical (basic)
radioaktivkayt, *f.*	*rahd-yaw-ahk-*TEEV*-kite*	radioactivity
radyator, *m.*	*rahd-*YAH*-tor*	radiator (heater)
radyo, *m.*	RAHD*-yaw*	radio (receiving set)
radyoshtral, *m.*	RAHD*-yaw-shtrahl*	beam (radio signal)
radyo-transmiti-rung, *f.*	RAHD*-yaw-trahnss-mee-tee-roon_g*	broadcasting (*rad.*)
rafinirn (1b)	*rah-fee-*NEE*-rin*	refine (purify), to
rak, *m.*	RAHK	cancer
rakete, *f.*	*rah-*KEH*-teh*	rocket
rakhmim, *pl.*	RAH_KH*-mim*	mercy
rakhmones, *n.*	*rah_kh-*MAW*-ness*	pity (compassion)
rakhmones hobn oyf (25d)	*rah_kh-*MAW*-ness haw-bin oyf*	pity, to
rakl, *n.*	RAH*-kil*	shrimp
rand, *m.*	RAHND	brink (verge)
"	"	ledge
"	"	rim
rang, *m.*	RAHN_G	rank (standing)
ranglen zikh (1)	RAHN*-glen zikh*	wrestle, to
rase, *f.*	RAH*-seh*	breed (stock)
"	"	race (*anthrop.*)
rate, *f.*	RAH*-teh*	installment (payment, *bus.*)
rateven (2)	RAH*-teh-ven*	rescue, to
"	"	save, to
ratsye, *f.*	RAHTS*-yeh*	ration (allotment)
raybn (9)	RYE*-bin*	rub, to
raykh	RYE_KH	rich
"	"	wealthy
rayon, *m.*	*rah-*YAWN	region (area)
raysn (9)	RYE*-sin*	rip, to
"	"	tear, to
rayter, *m.*	RYE*-tehr*	rider (horseman)
rayz, *m.*	RIZE	rice
rayznder, *m.*	RYE*-zin-dehr*	traveler
razirer, elektri-sher, *m.*	*eh-*LEK*-tree-shehr rah-*ZEE*-rehr*	electric shaver
razirn zikh (1b)	*rah-*ZEE*-rin zikh*	shave (oneself), to
razirzeyf, *f.*	*rah-*ZEER*-zafe*	shaving cream
real	*reh-*AHL	real (actual)
rebel, *m.*	*reh-*BELL	rebel (*n.*)
redaktor, *m.*	*reh-*DAHK*-tor*	editor
rede, *f.*	REH*-deh*	address
"	"	speech
redn (1)	REH*-din*	speak (talk), to
"	"	talk, to
redner, *m.*	RED*-nehr*	speaker (orator)
referirn (1b)	*reh-feh-*REE*-rin*	report (account formally), to
reform, *f.*	*reh-*FAW*-rim*	reform (*n.*)
refue, *f.*	*reh-*FOO*-eh*	cure
rege, *f.*	REG*-eh*	instant (*n.*)
regenen (3)	REG*-eh-nen*	rain, to
regiment, *m.*	*rehg-ee-*MENT	regiment (*n.*)
regirn (1b)	*reh-*G_EE*-rin*	govern, to
regirung, *f.*	*reh-*G_EE*-roon_g*	government
register, *m.*	*rehg-*EESS*-tehr*	register (record)
registrirn (1b)	*rehg-iss-*TREE*-rin*	register, to
registrirt	*rehg-iss-*TREERT	registered (postal designation)
regn, *m.*	REG*-in*	rain
regn-boygn, *m.*	REG*-in-boyg-in*	rainbow
regndik	REG*-in-dick*	rainy
regndl, *n.*	REG*-in-dil*	shower (rainfall)
regn-mantl, *m.*	REG*-in-mahn-til*	raincoat
reguler	*reh-goo-*LEHR	regular (normal)

Yiddish	Pronunciation	English
regulerkayt, *f.*	*reh-goo-*LEHR*-kite*	regularity
regulirn (1b)	*reh-goo-*LEE*-rin*	adjust (regulate), to
rekhenen (3)	REH*-kheh-nen*	mean (intend), to
rekhenen oyf	REH*-kheh-nen oyf*	count (rely) on, to
rekhiles, *f.*	*reh-*KHEE*-less*	gossip (idle talk)
rekhn-mashin, *f.*	REH*-khin-mah-sheen*	adding machine
rekht	REKHT	right (on the right, *adj.*)
rekht, *n.*	REKHT	right (claim)
rekhts	REKHTS	right (to the right, *adv.*)
"	"	right (right-hand side)
rekl, *n.*	REH*-kil*	skirt (garment)
reklamirn (1b)	*reh-klah-*MEE*-rin*	advertise (sponsor advertising), to
rekomendatsye, *f.*	*reh-kaw-men-*DAHTS*-yeh*	recommendation
rekomendirn (1b)	*reh-kaw-men-*DEE*-rin*	recommend (advise), to
rekord, *m.*	*reh-*CORD	record (disk)
relativ	*reh-lah-*TEEV	relative (comparative)
religye, *f.*	*reh-*LEEG*-yeh*	religion
religyez	*reh-lig-*YEZZ	religious (*adj.*)
rels, *m.*	RELSS	rail (bar on track)
relsveg, *m.*	RELSS*-veg*	track (rails)
renifer, *m.*	*reh-nee-*FEHR	reindeer
rentgen-bild, *n.*	RENT*-g_en-bild*	X-ray (X-ray picture)
rentgen-shtral, *m.*	RENT*-g_en-shtrahl*	X-ray (Roentgen ray)
reparatur, *f.*	*reh-pah-rah-*TOOR	repair (*n.*)
repetitsye, *f.*	*reh-peh-*TEETS*-yeh*	rehearsal
reporter, *m.*	*reh-*POR*-tehr*	reporter (journalist)
reprezentirn (1b)	*reh-preh-zen-*TEE*-rin*	represent, to
reprezentirung, *f.*	*reh-preh-zen-*TEE*-roon_g*	representation (*pol.*)
republik, *f.*	*reh-poo-*BLEEK	republic
republikanish	*reh-poo-blee-*KAH*-nish*	republican (*adj.*)
rer, *f.*	REHR	pipe
"	"	tube
reshime, *f.*	*reh-*SHEE*-meh*	list
resht, *m.*	RESHT	remainder
"	"	rest (remainder)
respektirn (1b)	*ress-peck-*TEE*-rin*	respect (esteem), to
restoran, *m.*	*res-taw-*RAHN	restaurant
retenish, *f.*	REH*-teh-nish*	mystery (enigma)
"	"	riddle (*n.*)
retsenzye, *f.*	*reh-*TSENZ*-yeh*	review (critique)
retsept, *m.*	*reh-*TSEPT	prescription (*med.*)
"	"	recipe
retsikhedik	*reh-*TSEE*-kheh-dik*	fierce
retung, *f.*	REH*-toon_g*	rescue
revakh, *m.*	REH*-vah_kh*	profit (*bus.*)
revmatizm, *m.*	*rev-mah-*TEE*-zim*	rheumatism
revokhimdik	*reh-*VAW*-khim-dick*	profitable
revolt, *m.*	*reh-*VAWLT	revolt
revolutsye, *f.*	*reh-vo-*LOOTS*-yeh*	revolution (*pol.*)
revolver, *m.*	*reh-*VAWL*-vehr*	revolver (weapon)
rey, *f.*	RAY	rank (row)
reyakh, *m.*	RAY*-ukh*	odor
"	"	scent
"	"	smell
reyd, *pl.*	RAID	speech (oral expression)
reyf, *m.*	RAFE	tire
reykhern (1)	RAY*-kheh-rin*	smoke, to
reyn	RANE	clean
"	"	pure (unadulterated)
Reyn, *m.*	RANE	Rhine
reynikn (1)	RAY*-nee-kin*	clean, to
reynkayt, *f.*	RAIN*-kite*	purity (cleanness)
reytlen zikh (1)	RATE*-lin zikh*	blush, to
reytsn zikh mit (1)	RATE*-sin zikh mit*	irritate (annoy), to
"	"	tease, to
rezerv, *m.*	*re-*ZEHRV	reserve (*bus.*)
rezervatsye, *f.*	*reh-zehr-*VAHTS*-yeh*	reservation (advance order)
rezervirn (1b)	*reh-zehr-*VEE*-rin*	reserve (order in advance), to
rezervuar, *m.*	*reh-zehr-voo-*ARE	reservoir (water reserve)

Yiddish	Pronunciation	English
rezignirn (1b)	reh-zig-NEE-rin	resign (from a job), to
rezolutsye, f.	reh-zo-LOOTS-yeh	resolution (formal expression)
rezultat, m.	reh-zool-TAHT	result (consequence)
rigl, m.	REEG-il	bolt (lock)
rikhter, m.	RIKH-tehr	judge
rikhtik	REEKH-tik	correct
"	"	right (adj.)
rikhtn zikh oyf (1)	RIKH-tin zikh oyf	anticipate, to
"	"	expect, to
rikhtung, f.	REEKH-toon_g	direction (course)
rimen, m.	REE-men	strap
rinderns, n.	RIN-deh-rins	beef
ring, m.	REEN_G	ring (circle)
rinshtok, m.	REEN-shtawk	gutter (of street)
Rio de Zhaneyro, n.	REE-aw deh zhah-NAY-raw	Rio de Janeiro
rip, f.	REEP	rib (anat.)
rirevdik	REE-rev-dick	lively (adj.)
rishes, f.	REE-shess	malice
rishesdik	REE-shes-dick	mean (malicious)
riter, m.	REE-tehr	knight
ritshen (2)	REE-chen	bellow (roar), to
ritshke, f.	REACH-keh	brook
ritus, m.	REE-toos	rite
riye, f.	REE-yeh	sight (eyesight)
"	"	vision (eyesight)
riz, m.	REEZ	giant
rizik	REEZ-ick	huge
"	"	vast
rizike, f.	REE-zee-keh	risk (danger)
rod, n.	RAWD	wheel
roe	RAW-eh	worthy (deserving)
rog, m.	RAWG	corner (street inter-section)
role, f.	RAW-leh	role
rolke, f.	RAWL-keh	roll (cylinder)
rom, m.	RAWM	rum
roman, m.	ro-MAHN	novel (book)
romantish	ro-MAHN-tish	romantic
ror, m.	ROR	reed (grass)
rosh, m.	RAWSH	head (leader)
roshe, m.	RAW-sheh	villain
rot, m.	RAWT	board
"	"	council
rov, m.	RAWV	ditch
"	"	rabbi
rov, n.	RAWV	bulk (largest part)
rov, s'	SRAWV	most (almost all, adj.)
roy	ROY	harsh (severe)
"	"	raw (in natural state)
"	"	rough (uneven)
royb, m.	ROYB	prey (victim)
roye-khezbn, m.	raw-yeh-KHE_ZH-bin	auditor
roykh, m.	ROYKH	smoke
Roym, n.	ROYM	Rome
roymish	ROY-mish	Roman (adj.)
royshem, m.	ROY-shem	impression (effect)
royt	ROYT	red
roytheldzl, n.	ROYT-held-zil	robin
royz, f.	ROYZ	rose (flower)
rozeve	RAW-zeh-veh	pink (color)
rozhinke, f.	RAW-zhin-keh	raisin
ru, f.	ROO	rest (repose)
rubin, m.	roo-BEEN	ruby (gem)
ruder, f.	ROO-dehr	oar (n.)
"	"	paddle
ruen (1)	ROO-en	rest (repose), to
ruf, m.	ROOF	call (shout)
rufn (5)	ROO-fin	call, to
ruik	ROO-ik	calm (adj.)
"	"	quiet (without motion, adj.)
"	"	still (motionless, adj.)
ruker, m.	ROO-kehr	latch
rukn, m.	ROO-kin	back (anat.)
"	"	ridge (raised area)
ruknbeyn, m.	ROO-kin-bane	spine (anat.)

Yiddish	Pronunciation	English
Rumenye, f.	roo-MEN-yeh	Rumania
runtsl, n.	ROONT-sil	ripple
rusish	ROO-sish	Russian (adj.)
Rusland, n.	ROOSS-lahnd	Russia
sakh, a	ah SAH_KH	many
"	"	much
sakhakl, m.	sah-KHAH-kil	total (sum)
sakone, f.	sah-KAW-neh	danger
"	"	peril
sakonesdik	sah-KAW-nes-dik	dangerous
saksofon, m.	sahck-saw-FAWN	saxophone
salat, m.	sah-LAHT	lettuce
"	"	salad
salon, m.	sah-LAWN	parlor (living room)
salutirn (1b)	sah-loo-TEE-rin	salute, to
Salvador, m.	sahl-vah-DOR	Salvador, El
sam, m.	SAHM	poison
samet, m.	SAH-met	velvet (n.)
Santyago, n.	sahnt-YAH-gaw	Santiago
saray, m.	sah-RYE	shed (shelter)
sardinke, f.	sahr-DEEN-keh	sardine
sarne, f.	SAR-neh	deer
saydn	SYE-din	but (if not, conj.)
"	"	unless (conj.)
say vi say	SYE vee sye	anyhow (in any case)
"	"	anyway (in any case)
sekretarshe, m.	seck-reh-TAR-sheh	secretary (stenographer)
sekunde, f.	seh-KOON-deh	second (time unit)
selerye, f.	seh-LEHR-yeh	celery
senat, m.	seh-NAHT	senate
senator, m.	seh-NAH-tor	senator
sendvitsh, m.	SEND-vitch	sandwich
sentiment, m.	sen-tee-MENT	sentiment
ser, m.	SEHR	sir
servetke, f.	sehr-VET-keh	napkin
serye, f.	SEHR-yeh	series
serzhant, m.	sehr-ZHAHNT	sergeant
sesye, f.	SESS-yeh	session
seyder, m.	SAY-dehr	arrangement
"	"	order (sequence)
seykhl, m.	SAY-khil	reason (intellect)
"	"	sense (intelligence)
seykhldik	SAY-khil-dick	reasonable (rational)
"	"	sensible
sfere, f.	SFEH-reh	realm (field)
"	"	sphere (range)
sgule, f.	SGOO-leh	remedy
shablon, m.	shahb-LAWN	stencil
shadkhenen zikh tsu (3)	SHAHD-kheh-nen zikh tsoo	woo, to
shafir, m.	shah-FEER	sapphire (gem)
shafn (5)	SHAH-fin	raise (collect), to
shaneven (2)	SHAH-neh-ven	spare (not harm), to
shans, m.	SHAHNSS	chance (possibility)
sharbn, m.	SHAR-bin	skull
sharf	SHARF	keen
"	"	sharp
sharf, f.	SHARF	edge (sharp side)
"	"	scarf (neck cloth)
shatirung, f.	shah-TEE-roon_g	hue
shatn (1)	SHAH-tin	harm (damage), to
shatsn (1)	SHAHT-sin	estimate (calculate), to
"	"	value (appraise), to
shatsung, f.	SHAH-tsoon_g	appraisal (bus.)
"	"	rating (evaluation)
shayekh, zayn (18d)	ZINE SHAH-yukh	relate (pertain) to, to
shayern (1)	SHYE-eh-rin	scrub, to
shaykhes, f.	SHY-khess	connection (relationship)
"	"	relation
shef, m.	SHEF	boss (master)
shefe, f.	SHEH-feh	abundance
"	"	plenty (n.)
shefedik	SHEH-feh-dick	abundant
"	"	plentiful
sheker, m.	SHEH-kehr	falsehood (lie)
sheltn (7)	SHEHL-tin	curse (damn), to
shem, m.	SHEM	fame
"	"	reputation

Yiddish	Pronunciation	English
shemevdik	SHEH-*mev-dick*	bashful
"	"	shy
shendlekh	SHEND-*lukh*	shameful
shenken (7)	SHEN-*ken*	donate, to
shepsener kotlet, *m.*	SHEP-*seh-nehr kawt-*LET	lamb chop
shepsnfleysh, *n.*	SHEP-*sin-flaysh*	mutton
sheptsh, *m.*	SHEP_CH	whisper
sheptshen (2)	SHEP-*chen*	whisper (utter softly), to
sher, *f.*	SHEHR	scissors
sherer, *m.*	SHEH-*rehr*	barber
shern (10)	SHEH-*rin*	shear, to
shetakh, *m.*	SHEH-*takh*	area (extent)
"	"	field (sphere of action)
"	"	space
sheydn zikh (1)	SHAY-*din zikh*	part (leave each other), to
sheydveg, *m.*	SHEYD-*vehg*	crossroads
sheyln (1)	SHAY-*lin*	peel (take skin from), to
sheyn	SHANE	beautiful
"	"	fair (not cloudy)
"	"	handsome (attractive)
"	"	pretty
sheynkayt, *f.*	SHANE-*kite*	beauty
sheyvet, *m.*	SHAY-*vet*	tribe
shif, *f.*	SHEEF	craft
"	"	ship
"	"	vessel
shif, oyf der	*oyf dair* SHEEF	aboard
shifboy-hoyf, *m.*	SHEEF-*boy-hoyf*	shipyard
shifl, *n.*	SHEE-*fil*	boat
shigoen, *m.*	*shee-*GAW-*en*	craze (fad)
shiker	SHEE-*kehr*	drunk (intoxicated)
shikht, *f.*	SHEE_KHT	layer (thickness)
"	"	shift (crew)
shikn (1)	SHEE-*kin*	send, to
shikres, *f.*	SHEEK-*ress*	intoxication (drunkenness)
shikung, *f.*	SHEE-*koon_g*	consignment (*bus.*)
"	"	shipment (goods)
shiltn (7)	SHEEL-*lin*	swear (curse), to
shinke, *f.*	SHEEN-*keh*	ham (food)
shipue, *m.*	*shee-*POO-*eh*	slope (slant)
shirem, *m.*	SHEE-*rem*	umbrella
shirme, *f.*	SHEER-*meh*	screen (partition)
shisl, *f.*	SHEE-*sil*	bowl (dish)
shisn (7)	SHEE-*sin*	shoot (fire at), to
shite, *f.*	SHEE-*teh*	doctrine
shkheynes, *f.*	SH_KHAY-*ness*	vicinity
shkheyneshaft, *f.*	SH_KHAY-*neh-shahft*	neighborhood
shkhite, *f.*	SH_KHEE-*teh*	slaughter
shklaf, *m.*	SHKLAHF	slave
shklaferay, *f.*	*shklah-feh-*RAY	slavery
shlaberik	SHLAH-*beh-rick*	limp (flaccid)
shlak, *m.*	SHLAHK	stroke (attack of paralysis)
shlakht, *f.*	SHLAHKHT	battle
shlang, *f.*	SHLAHN_G	serpent
"	"	snake
shlank	SHLAHNK	slender (lean)
shlaydern (1)	SHLYE-*deh-rin*	fling, to
"	"	hurl, to
shlayfn (9)	SHLYE-*fin*	sharpen, to
shlekht	SHLEKHT	bad
shlepn (1)	SHLEH-*pin*	drag (pull), to
"	"	haul (pull), to
"	"	tug, to
shlesl, *n.*	SHLEH-*sil*	zipper
shleyer, *m.*	SHLEH-*yehr*	veil (*n.*)
shleyerl, *n.*	SHLEH-*yeh-ril*	caterpillar
shleyf, *f.*	SHLAFE	temple (*anat.*)
shleykes, *pl.*	SHLAY-*kess*	suspenders
shleymes, *f.*	SHLAY-*mess*	perfection (flawlessness)
shlikhes, *f.*	SHLEE-*khess*	errand (commission)
shlimazldik	*shlee-*MAH-*zil-dick*	unlucky
shlingen (8)	SHLEEN_G-*en*	swallow, to
shlisl, *m.*	SHLEE-*sil*	key (for lock)
shlisn (7)	SHLEE-*sin*	close (finish), to

Yiddish	Pronunciation	English
shlitn, *m.*	SHLEE-*lin*	sled
"	"	sleigh
shlof, *m.*	SHLAWF	sleep
shlofn (5d)	SHLAW-*fin*	sleep, to
shlofrok, *m.*	SHLAWF-*rawk*	robe (dressing gown)
shloftsimer, *m.*	SHLAWF-*tsee-mehr*	bedroom
shlogn (5)	SHLAWG-*in*	beat (thrash), to
"	"	hit, to
"	"	strike, to
shlos, *m.*	SHLAWSS	castle
"	"	lock (fastening)
shmant, *m.*	SHMAHNT	cream
shmaragd, *m.*	*shmah-*RAHGD	emerald
shmate, *f.*	SHMAH-*teh*	rag (piece of cloth)
shmaydik	SHMYE-*dick*	nimble (agile)
shmaysn (9)	SHMYE-*sin*	lash, to
"	"	spank, to
"	"	whip (flog), to
shmekn (1)	SHMEH-*kin*	smell (perceive odor), to
shmeykhl, *m.*	SHMAY-*khil*	smile
shmeykhlen (1)	SHMAY_KH-*len*	smile, to
shmeykhlen, breyt	BRATE SHMAY_KH-*len*	grin, to
shmid, *m.*	SHMEED	blacksmith
shmidn (1)	SHMEE-*din*	forge (shape), to
shminke, *f.*	SHMEEN-*keh*	rouge
shmol	SHMAWL	narrow
shmues, *m.*	SHMOO-*ess*	conversation
"	"	talk
shmuesn (1)	SHMOO-*eh-sin*	chat, to
shmuts, *n.*	SHMOOTS	dirt (unclean matter)
shmutsik	SHMOO-*tsik*	dirty (soiled)
shnayder, *m.*	SHNYE-*dehr*	tailor
shnaydn (11)	SHNYE-*din*	cut (reduce), to
"	"	reap, to
shnek, *m.*	SHNECK	snail
shnel	SHNELL	quick (rapid)
shney, *m.*	SHNAY	snow
shnips, *m.*	SHNEEPS	tie (necktie)
shnirl, *n.*	SHNEE-*ril*	lace (shoelace)
"	"	strand (thread)
shnit, *m.*	SHNEET	harvest
shnitsn (1)	SHNEE-*tsin*	carve (cut designs), to
shnobl, *m.*	SHNAW-*bil*	bill (beak)
shnur, *f.*	SHNOOR	daughter-in-law
shnur, *m.*	SHNOOR	string (cord)
sho, *f.*	SHAW	hour
shobn (1)	SHAW-*bin*	scrape (make smooth or clean), to
shodn, *m.*	SHAW-*din*	damage (injury)
"	"	mischief (harm)
shoen-plan, *m.*	SHAW-*en-plahn*	schedule (timetable)
shof, *f.*	SHAWF	sheep
shofl	SHAW-*fil*	humble (lowly)
shok, *m.*	SHAWK	shock (mental jolt)
shokh, *m.*	SHAW_KH	chess
shokhn, *m.*	SHAW-*khin*	neighbor
shokirn (1b)	*shaw-*KEE-*rin*	shock (jar), to
shoklen (1)	SHAWK-*len*	nod, to
"	"	shake, to
shokolad, *m.*	*shaw-ko-*LAHD	chocolate
sholekhts, *f.*	SHAW-*lukhts*	shell (covering)
sholem, *m.*	SHAW-*lem*	peace
sholiakh, *m.*	*shaw-*LEE-*ukh*	messenger (courier)
shorkh, *m.*	SHORE_KH	rustle
shos, *m.*	SHAWSS	shot (from firearm)
shosey, *m.*	*shaw-*SAY	highway
shotish	SHAW-*tish*	Scotch (*adj.*)
Shotland, *n.*	SHAWT-*lahnd*	Scotland
shotn, *m.*	SHAW-*tin*	shade
"	"	shadow
shotndik	SHAW-*tin-dick*	shady
shoyb, *f.*	SHOYB	pane, window
shoym, *m.*	SHOYM	foam
shoymer, *m.*	SHOY-*mehr*	guard (watcher)
"	"	keeper
shoymgume, *f.*	SHOYM-*goo-meh*	foam rubber
shoyn	SHOYN	already
shoys, *f.*	SHOYSS	lap (of seated person)
shpagat, *m.*	*shpah-*GAHT	cord (rope)

Yiddish	Pronunciation	English
shpalt, *m.*	SHPAHLT	crack (fissure)
shpaltn (7)	SHPAHL-*lin*	crack, to
"	"	split (rend), to
shpan, *m.*	SHPAHN	span (spread)
shpanen (1)	SHPAH-*nen*	stride (walk), to
shpanish	SHPAH-*nish*	Spanish (*adj.*)
shpanung, *f.*	SHPAH-*noon_g*	tension (anxiety)
Shpanye, *f.*	SHPAHN-*yeh*	Spain
shpatsir, *m.*	*shpah*-TSEER	hike (march)
"	"	walk (stroll)
shpatsirn (1b)	*shpah*-TSEE-*rin*	stroll, to
shpayen (12)	SHPYE-*en*	spit, to
shpayzkrom, *f.*	SHPYE_Z-*krawm*	grocery
shperl, *m.*	SHPEH-*ril*	sparrow
shpet	SHPET	late (at relative time, *adv.*)
"	"	tardy (*adj.*)
shpeter	SHPEH-*tehr*	then (subsequently)
shpeterdik	SHPEH-*tehr-dick*	subsequent
shpigl, *m.*	SHPEEG-*il*	mirror
shpil, *f.*	SHPEEL	game (contest)
shpiler, *m.*	SHPEE-*lehr*	player (in a game)
shpilke, *f.*	SHPEEL-*keh*	pin (sewing accessory)
shpil-khaver, *m.*	SHPEEL-*khah-vehr*	playmate
shpilkhl, *n.*	SHPEEL-*khil*	toy
shpiln (1)	SHPEE-*lin*	play (perform music upon), to
"	"	play (take the role of), to
shpiln zikh	SHPEE-*lin zikh*	play (engage in recreation), to
shpilplats, *m.*	SHPEEL-*plahts*	playground
shpin, *f.*	SHPEEN	spider
shpinat, *m.*	*shpee*-NAHT	spinach
shpinen (8)	SHPEE-*nen*	spin (form thread), to
shpirevdik	SHPEE-*rev-dick*	sensitive (susceptible)
shpirhunt, *m.*	SHPEER-*hoont*	hound
shpirn (1)	SHPEE-*rin*	feel (experience), to
shpitol, *m.*	*shpee*-TAWL	hospital
shpits, *m.*	SHPEETS	peak (mountain top)
"	"	point (sharp end)
"	"	summit
shpits, *m.*	SHPEETS	tip
"	"	top
shpitsik	SHPEET-*sick*	pointed (tapered)
shpitsl, *n.*	SHPEET-*sil*	trick (ruse)
shpitsn, *pl.*	SHPEET-*sin*	lace (fabric)
shpiz, *f.*	SHPEEZ	spear (weapon)
shpor, *m.*	SHPORE	spur (spike)
shporevdik	SHPAW-*rev-dik*	economical (thrifty)
shporevdikayt, *f.*	SHPAW-*rev-dee-kite*	economy (thrift)
shporkonte, *f.*	SHPOR-*kawn-teh*	savings account
shporn (1)	SHPAW-*rin*	save (store up), to
shprakh, *f.*	SHPRAH_KH	language
shprikhvort, *n.*	SHPREEKH-*vort*	proverb
shpringen (8d)	SHPREEN_G-*en*	jump (bound), to
"	"	leap, to
shpringen dem kop foroys	SHPRIN_G-*en dem* KAWP *foh*-ROYSS	dive, to
shpringer, *m.*	SHPREEN-*g_ehr*	grasshopper
shprits, *f.*	SHPREETS	syringe
shprits, *m.*	SHPREETS	shower (bath)
shpritsn (1)	SHPREET-*sin*	splash, to
"	"	squirt, to
shprung, *m.*	SHPROON_G	bound
"	"	jump
"	"	leap
shprung ton, a (22)	*ah* SHPROON_G *tawn*	spring (leap), to
shpul, *f.*	SHPOOL	coil (*elec.*)
shpur, *f.*	SHPOOR	trace (vestige)
shpyon, *m.*	*shpee*-AWN	spy
shpyonazh, *m.*	*shpee-aw*-NAH_ZH	espionage
shram, *m.*	SHRAHM	scar
shrank, *m.*	SHRAHNK	cupboard
shrayber, *m.*	SHRYE-*behr*	writer (author)
shraybmashin, *f.*	SHRIBE-*mah-shin*	typewriter
shraybn, *n.*	SHRYE-*bin*	writing (art of writing)
shraybn (9)	SHRYE-*bin*	write, to

Yiddish	Pronunciation	English
shraybpapir, *n.*	SHRIBE-*pah-peer*	stationery (writing paper)
shraybtish, *m.*	SHRIBE-*tish*	desk
shrayen (12)	SHRYE-*en*	cry, to
"	"	shout (say loudly), to
"	"	yell, to
shrayik	SHRYE-*ick*	shrill
shrek, *m.*	SHRECK	alarm (fear)
"	"	dismay
shrekevdik	SHREH-*kev-dick*	timid
shreklekh	SHRECK-*lukh*	awful
"		terrible
shrekn (7)	SHREH-*kin*	terrify, to
shroyf, *m.*	SHROYF	bolt (long metal fastener)
"	"	screw (threaded nail)
shroyfn-tsier, *m.*	SHROY-*fin-tsee-ehr*	screw driver
shtab, *m.*	SHTAHB	staff (personnel)
"		staff (stick)
shtal, *m.*	SHTAHL	barn
"	"	stable (shelter)
shtam, *m.*	SHTAHM	trunk (stem)
shtamlen (1)	SHTAHM-*len*	stutter, to
shtang, *m.*	SHTAHN_G	bar (pole)
shtar, *m.*	SHTAR	deed (transfer agreement)
shtarbn (7d)	SHTAR-*bin*	die, to
shtarbn fun hunger	SHTAHR-*bin foon* HOON-*g_ehr*	starve (die of hunger), to
shtark	SHTARK	stout
"	"	strong
shtar-khoyv, *m.*	*shtar*-KHOYV	debenture
shtarkn (1)	SHTAR-*kin*	strengthen, to
shtayer, *m.*	SHTY-*ehr*	tax (*n.*)
shtayer, gebn tsu (13)	G_EH-*bin tsoo* SHTYE-*ehr*	contribute, to
shtayf	SHTIFE	stiff (inflexible)
"	"	tight (taut)
shtayg, *f.*	SHTYE_G	cage
shtaygn (9d)	SHTYE_G-*in*	rise (ascend), to
shteg, *m.*	SHTEG	path
shtegl, *n.*	SHTEG-*il*	lane (narrow path)
shtekhn (7)	SHTEH-*khin*	prick, to
"	"	sting (pierce skin), to
shtekn, *m.*	SHTEH-*kin*	cane (walking stick)
"		stick (small branch)
shtekshukh, *m.*	SHTEK-*shoo_kh*	slipper
shtele, *f.*	SHTEH-*leh*	job (employment)
shteln (1)	SHTEH-*lin*	put (place), to
"		set, to
shtemplen (1)	SHTEMP-*len*	stamp (mark), to
shtendik	SHTENN-*dick*	always
"	"	permanent (*adj.*)
"	"	steady (regular)
shtengl, *n.*	SHTEN_G-*il*	stalk (stem)
"	"	stem (*bot.*)
shtepsl, *m.*	SHTEP-*sil*	outlet (*elec.*)
shterblekh	SHTERB-*lukh*	mortal (*adj.*)
shtern, *m.*	SHTEH-*rin*	forehead
"	"	star (*astron.*)
shtern (1)	SHTEH-*rin*	bother (annoy), to
"	"	disturb, to
"	"	foil (frustrate), to
"	"	hinder, to
shterung, *f.*	SHTEH-*roon_g*	barrier
shtetl, *n.*	SHTEH-*til*	town
shteyn, *m.*	SHTANE	stone (piece of stone)
shteyn (17d)	SHTANE	stand (be upright), to
shteyn berosh	SHTANE *beh*-RAWSH	head (lead), to
shteyndl, *n.*	SHTANE-*dil*	pebble
shteynerdik	SHTAY-*nehr-dick*	rocky (rock-covered)
shtiferish	SHTEE-*feh-rish*	naughty (disobedient)
shtifmame, *f.*	SHTEEF-*mah-meh*	stepmother
shtiftate, *m.*	SHTEEF-*tah-teh*	stepfather
shtiftokhter, *f.*	SHTEEF-*tawkh-tehr*	stepdaughter
shtifzun, *m.*	SHTEEF-*zoon*	stepson
shtik, *n.*	SHTEEK	lump (shapeless piece)
"	"	piece (bit)
shtikarbet, *f.*	SHTEEK-*ahr-bet*	piecework (*n.*)

Yiddish	Pronunciation	English
shtikl, *n.*	SHTEE-*kil*	morsel (small bit)
shtiklekhvayz	SHTEEK-*lukh-vize*	piecemeal (*adv.*)
shtikn (1)	SHTEE-*kin*	choke, to
shtil	SHTEEL	quiet (silent, *adj.*)
"	"	silent (mute)
shtil,*f.*	SHTEEL	shaft (*mech.*)
shtilet,*m.*	*shtee*-LET	dagger
shtilkayt,*f.*	SHTEEL-*kite*	quiet (stillness)
"	"	silence (stillness)
shtiln (1)	SHTEE-*lin*	quench, to
shtim,*f.*	SHTEEM	vote
shtimen (1)	SHTEE-*men*	correspond (agree), to
"	"	vote, to
shtimtsetl, *n.*	SHTEEM-*tseh-til*	ballot
shtimung,*f.*	SHTEE-*moon_g*	mood (humor)
shtinken (8)	SHTEEN-*ken*	stink, to
shtitsn (1)	SHTEET-*sin*	foster (encourage), to
shtivl,*m.*	SHTEE-*vil*	boot (footgear)
shtof,*m.*	SHTAWF	cloth
"	"	stuff (substance)
shtokh,*m.*	SHTAW_KH	stitch (of sewing)
Shtokholm,*n.*	SHTAWK-*haw-lim*	Stockholm
shtol,*n.*	SHTAWL	steel
shtolts	SHTAWLTS	proud (taking pride in)
shtolts,*m.*	SHTAWLTS	pride (self-esteem)
shtore,*f.*	SHTAW-*reh*	shade (window blind)
shtot,*f.*	SHTAWT	city
shtotish	SHTAW-*tish*	urban
shtotsik	SHTAWT-*sick*	steep (*adj.*)
shtoyb,*m.*	SHTOYB	dust
shtoybik	SHTOY-*bik*	dusty
shtoybzoyger,*m.*	SHTOYB-*zoyg-ehr*	vacuum cleaner
shtoys,*m.*	SHTOYSS	impulse (sudden incitement)
shtral,*m.*	SHTRAHL	ray (beam)
shtraln (1)	SHTRAH-*lin*	beam (direct, *rad.*), to
shtralndik	SHTRAH-*lin-dick*	radiant
shtrebn (1)	SHTREH-*bin*	strive (exert oneself), to
shtreng	SHTREN_G	severe
"	"	stern (*adj.*)
"	"	strict (stringent)
shtrengkayt,*f.*	SHTREN_G-*kite*	severity (sternness)
shtreyf,*m.*	SHTRAFE	strip (band)
shtrik,*m.*	SHTREEK	line (cord)
"	"	rope
shtrikeray,*f.*	*shtree-keh*-RYE	knitting
shtrikh,*m.*	SHTREEKH	feature (attribute)
"	"	feature (part of face)
shtrikn (1)	SHTREE-*kin*	knit, to
shtrof,*f.*	SHTRAWF	penalty
"	"	punishment
shtrofn (1)	SHTRAW-*fin*	punish, to
shtrom,*m.*	SHTRAWM	current (of electricity)
"	"	current (of water)
"	"	torrent
shtromen (1)	SHTRAW-*men*	stream, to
shtroy,*f.*	SHTROY	straw (dry grain stalks)
shtshur,*m.*	SH_TSHOOR	rat
shtubik	SHTOO-*bick*	domestic (household, *adj.*)
"	"	tame
shtul,*m.*	SHTOOL	chair
shtum	SHTOOM	dumb
"	"	mute (silent)
shtup,*m.*	SHTOOP	push (shove)
shtupn (1)	SHTOO-*pin*	push (shove), to
shturem,*m.*	SHTOO-*rem*	storm
shturemdik	SHTOO-*rem-dick*	stormy
shturemvint,*m.*	SHTOO-*rem-vint*	gale (wind)
"	"	tempest
shturkats,*m.*	*shtoor*-KAHTS	torch
shufl,*f.*	SHOO-*fil*	shovel (tool)
shuflod,*m.*	SHOOF-*lawd*	drawer (sliding box)
shukh,*m.*	SHOOKH	shoe (footwear)
shul,*f.*	SHOOL	school
"	"	schoolhouse

Yiddish	Pronunciation	English
shuld,*f.*	SHOOLD	blame
"	"	fault (cause for blame)
"	"	guilt
shuldik	SHOOL-*dick*	guilty
shultsimer,*m.*	SHOOL-*tsee-mehr*	schoolroom
shure,*f.*	SHOO-*reh*	line
"	"	row (series)
shuster,*m.*	SHOO-*stehr*	shoemaker
shutef,*m.*	SHOO-*tef*	partner (*bus.*)
shutfeshaft glaykh oyf glaykh,*f.*	SHOOT-*feh-shahft* GLYE_KH *oyf* GLYE_KH	copartnership (*bus.*)
shvakh	SHVAH_KH	faint (dim, *adj.*)
"	"	feeble
"	"	weak
shvakh,*m.*	SHVAH_KH	praise
shvakhkayt,*f.*	SHVAH_KH-*kite*	weakness
shvalb,*f.*	SHVAHLB	swallow (bird)
shvan,*m.*	SHVAHN	swan
shvarts	SHVARTS	black
shvartsapl,*n.*	SHVARTS-*ah-pil*	pupil (of eye)
shvarts-arbeter,*m.*	SHVARTS-AR-*beh-tehr*	laborer
shvebele,*n.*	SHVEH-*beh-leh*	match (lucifer)
shvebl,*m.*	SHVEH-*bil*	sulphur
shvebn (1)	SHVEH-*bin*	soar (rise), to
shvedish	SHVEH-*dish*	Swedish (*adj.*)
shvedish leder,*n.*	SHVEH-*dish* LEH-*dehr*	suede (*n.*)
Shvedn,*n.*	SHVEH-*din*	Sweden
shvegerin,*f.*	SHVEG-*eh-rin*	sister-in-law
shveml,*n.*	SHVEH-*mil*	mushroom (*n.*)
shver	SHVEHR	difficult
"	"	hard
"	"	heavy
shver,*m.*	SHVEHR	father-in-law
shverd,*f.*	SHVEHRD	sword
shverkayt,*f.*	SHVEHR-*kite*	difficulty (hardness)
shver makhn dos harts (1)	SHVEHR *mah-khin dawss* HARTS	trouble (disquiet), to
shvern (10)	SHVEH-*rin*	swear (vow), to
shvester,*f.*	SHVES-*tehr*	sister (*n.*)
shvesterkind,*n.*	*shves-tehr*-KEEND	cousin
shveys,*m.*	SHVACE	sweat
Shveyts,*f.*	SHVATES	Switzerland
shveytserish	SHVAY-*tseh-rish*	Swiss (*adj.*)
shviger,*f.*	SHVEEG-*ehr*	mother-in-law
shvimen (8d)	SHVEE-*men*	swim, to
shvindl,*m.*	SHVEEN-*dil*	fraud (deception)
shvindldik	SHVEEN-*dil-dick*	dizzy (unsteady)
shvitsn (1)	SHVEET-*sin*	perspire, to
shvoger,*m.*	SHVAWG-*ehr*	brother-in-law
shvom,*m.*	SHVAWM	sponge
shvue,*f.*	SHVOO-*eh*	oath (vow)
sibe,*f.*	SEE-*beh*	cause
signal,*m.*	*sig*-NAHL	signal
sikhsekh,*m.*	SEEKH-*sukh*	conflict (struggle)
silek,*m.*	SEE-*leck*	settlement (compromise, *bus.*)
siltse,*f.*	SEELT-*seh*	snare (trap)
simen,*m.*	SEE-*men*	mark (evidence)
"	"	sign (indication)
simfonye,*f.*	*sim*-FAWN-*yeh*	symphony
simkhe,*f.*	SEEM-*kheh*	glee (joy)
"	"	mirth
"	"	party (social gathering)
simpatye,*f.*	*sim*-PAHT-*yeh*	sympathy (accord)
simptom,*m.*	*simp*-TAWM	symptom
sine,*f.*	SEE-*neh*	hate (hatred)
sinyak,*m.*	*seen*-YAHK	bruise
sistem,*f.*	*siss*-TEM	system (method)
situatsye,*f.*	*see-too*-AHTS-*yeh*	situation (circumstances)
skale,*f.*	SKAH-*leh*	scale (graduated measure)
skandal,*m.*	*skahn*-DAHL	scandal
skarlatin,*m.*	*scar-lah*-TEEN	scarlet fever
skarpet,*m.*	*scar*-PET	sock (garment)
skelet,*m.*	*skeh*-LET	skeleton (*anat.*)
skhar,*m.*	S_KHAHR	reward (recompense)
skhar-limud,*m.*	*s_khahr*-LEE-*mood*	tuition (school fee)
skhires,*pl.*	S_KHEE-*ress*	salary

Yiddish	Pronunciation	English
skhoyre, *f.*	S_KHOY-*reh*	commodity
"	"	goods
"	"	merchandise
"	"	wares
skhum, *m.*	S_KHOOM	amount
"	"	lot (salable items, *bus.*)
"	"	quantity
"	"	volume
skitse, *f.*	SKEET-*seh*	draft
"	"	sketch (rough drawing)
sklad, *m.*	SKLAHD	warehouse
skorinke, *f.*	SKAW-*rin-keh*	crust
skovrode, *f.*	SKAWV-*ro-deh*	pan, frying
skoyt, *m.*	SKOYT	Boy Scout
skoytin, *f.*	SKOY-*tin*	girl scout
skulptor, *m.*	SKOOLP-*tor*	sculptor
slavish	SLAH-*vish*	Slavic (*adj.*)
sleng, *m.*	SLANG	slang (*n.*)
sloy, *m.*	SLOY	jar (vessel)
slup, *m.*	SLOOP	post (pole)
"	"	stake
smole, *f.*	SMAW-*leh*	pitch
"	"	tar
snop likht, *m.*	SNAWP LIH_KHT	beam (ray)
sod, *m.*	SAWD	orchard
"	"	secret (*n.*)
sof, *m.*	SAWF	end (conclusion)
sof, on a	AWN *ah* SAWF	endless
sofe, *f.*	SAW-*feh*	sofa
sofek, *m.*	SAW-*fek*	doubt
sofek, on	AWN SAW-*fek*	doubtless
sofekdik	SAW-*fek-dick*	doubtful
sofekn (1)	SAW-*feh-kin*	question, to
sofekn in	SAW-*feh-kin een*	doubt (be uncertain about), to
sofklsof	*sawf-kil-*SAWF	finally
sof-vokh, *m.*	*sawf-*VAWKH	weekend (*n.*)
sok, *m.*	SAWK	sap (fluid)
soldat, *m.*	*sawl-*DAHT	private (*mil.*)
solid	*saw-*LEED	solid (compact)
solovey, *m.*	*so-lo-*VAY	nightingale
sopen (2)	SAW-*pen*	pant (puff), to
sort, *m.*	SORT	sort
sosne, *f.*	SAWSS-*neh*	pine (tree)
sotsyal	*sawts-*YAHL	social (societal)
sotsyalist, *m.*	*sawts-yah-*LEEST	socialist (*n.*)
sotsyalizm, *m.*	*sawts-yah-*LEE-*zim*	socialism
sotsyologye, *f.*	*sawts-yaw-*LAWG-*yeh*	sociology
sous, *m.*	SO-*ooss*	dressing
"	"	sauce
sove, *f.*	SAW-*veh*	owl
soydesdik	SOY-*dess-dick*	mysterious
soykher, *m.*	SOY-*khehr*	dealer
"	"	merchant
"	"	trader
soyne, *m.*	SOY-*neh*	enemy
soyser zayn (18c)	SOYS-*sehr zine*	contradict (deny), to
sparzhe, *f.*	SPAR-*zheh*	asparagus
spektakl, *m.*	*speck-*TAH-*kil*	sight
"	"	spectacle (pageant)
spetsifish	*speh-*TSEE-*fish*	particular (specific, *adj.*)
spetsyel	*spets-*YEHL	especially
"	"	special
sport, *m.*	SPORT	sport (game)
spotiken zikh (2b)	*spaw-*TEE-*ken zikh*	trip (stumble), to
sprunzhine, *f.*	*sproon-*ZHEE-*neh*	spring (coil)
stabil	*stah-*BEEL	stable (steadfast)
stade, *f.*	STAH-*deh*	herd (of animals)
"	"	flock
stadye, *f.*	STAHD-*yeh*	stage (period)
stadyon, *m.*	STAHD-*yawn*	stadium
standard-...	STAHN-*dahrd-*...	standard (regular)
stanik, *m.*	STAH-*nick*	brassiere
stantsye, *f.*	STAHNTS-*yeh*	station, railroad
statue, *f.*	STAH-*too-eh*	statue
statut, *m.*	*stah-*TOOT	by-law
stav, *m.*	STAHV	pond
stele, *f.*	STEH-*leh*	ceiling (of room)

Yiddish	Pronunciation	English
stenge, *f.*	STEHN_G-*eh*	band (ribbon)
stenografin, *m.*	*steh-naw-*GRAHF-*in*	stenographer
stenografye, *f.*	*steh-naw-*GRAHF-*yeh*	shorthand (stenography, *n.*)
stil, *m.*	STEEL	style (manner)
stimulirn (1b)	*stee-moo-*LEE-*rin*	stimulate (incite), to
stoler, *m.*	STAW-*lehr*	carpenter
strakhirung, *f.*	*strah-*KHEE-*roon_g*	fire insurance
strashen (2)	STRAH-*shen*	threaten, to
strashunik, *m.*	*strah-*SHOO-*nick*	threat
strayk, *m.*	STRIKE	strike (work stoppage)
straykn (1)	STRY-*kin*	strike (stop work), to
struktur, *f.*	*strook-*TOOR	structure (arrangement of parts)
stsenar, *m.*	*stseh-*NAR	scenario
stsene, *f.*	STSEH-*neh*	scene (dramatic unit)
"	"	stage (dais)
styuard, *m.*	STEW-*ard*	steward (attendant on ship)
substantiv, *m.*	*soob-stahn-*TEEV	noun
substants, *f.*	*soob-*STAHNTS	substance (matter)
subyektiv	*soob-yeck-*TEEV	subjective
sude, *f.*	SOO-*deh*	feast (meal)
sume, *f.*	SOO-*meh*	sum (quantity)
Surinam, *n.*	*soo-ree-*NAHM	Surinam
sveter, *m.*	SVEH-*tehr*	sweater
svinke, *f.*	SVEEN-*keh*	mumps
taam, *m.*	TAHM	taste (flavor)
"	"	reason (ground)
tabak, *m.*	TAH-*bahk*	tobacco
tabele, *f.*	*tah-*BEH-*leh*	table (tabulation)
taburet, *m.*	*tah-boo-*RET	stool (seat)
take	TAH-*keh*	indeed (*adv.*)
takone, *f.*	*tah-*KAW-*neh*	regulation
"	"	rule
taks, *m.*	TAHX	badger (animal)
taksi, *m.*	TAHK-*see*	cab
"	"	taxi
talant, *m.*	*tah-*LAHNT	talent
talmid, *m.*	TAHL-*mid*	pupil
"	"	student
talye, *f.*	TAHL-*yeh*	waist (*anat.*)
tants, *m.*	TAHNTS	dance (movement to music)
"	"	dance (party)
tantsn (1)	TAHN-*tsin*	dance, to
tapn (1)	TAH-*pin*	feel (grope) for, to
"	"	feel (touch), to
taretam, *m.*	*tah-reh-*RAHM	fuss (ado)
tash, *f.*	TAHSH	bag (purse)
tate, *m.*	TAH-*teh*	dad
tate-mame, *pl.*	*tah-teh-*MAH-*meh*	parents
tats, *f.*	TAHTS	tray
tayer	TYE-*ehr*	adorable
"	"	costly
"	"	expensive
"	"	precious
tayer haltn (5c)	TYE-*ehr hahl-tin*	cherish, to
"	"	value (prize), to
taykh, *m.*	TYE_KH	river
taykhl, *n.*	TYE-*khil*	creek
"	"	stream (rivulet)
tayne, *f.*	TYE-*neh*	complaint
"	"	reproach
tayneg, *m.*	TYE-*neg*	delight
taynen (2)	TYE-*nen*	argue (maintain), to
taynes, hobn (25)	HAW-*bin* TYE-*ness*	reproach, to
tayve, *f.*	TYE-*veh*	lust (desire)
tayvl, *m.*	TYE-*vil*	devil
teater, *m.*	*teh-*AH-*tehr*	theater
teke, *f.*	TEH-*keh*	briefcase
tekst, *m.*	TEXT	text
tekstil, *m.*	*tex-*TEEL	textile (*n.*)
Tel-Aviv, *n.*	*tehl-ah-*VEEV	Tel Aviv
telefon, *m.*	*teh-leh-*FAWN	telephone
telefonirn (1b)	*teh-leh-fo-*NEE-*rin*	phone, to
"	"	telephone, to
telegrafirn (1b)	*teh-leh-grah-*FEE-*rin*	telegraph, to
telegram, *f.*	*teh-leh-*GRAHM	telegram

Yiddish	Pronunciation	English
teler, *m.*	TEH-*lehr*	plate (shallow dish)
teleskop, *m.*	*teh-leh*-SKAWP	telescope
televizye, *f.*	*teh-leh*-VEEZ-*yeh*	television
teme, *f.*	TEH-*meh*	subject
"	"	theme
"	"	topic
temp	TEMP	blunt
"	"	dull
temperament, *m.*	*tem-peh-rah*-MENT	disposition (temperament)
"	"	temper (mood)
temperatur, *f.*	*tem-peh-rah*-TOOR	temperature
templ, *m.*	TEM-*pil*	temple (place of worship)
tempo, *m.*	TEM-*paw*	pace (degree of speed)
"	"	rate
tendents, *f.*	*ten*-DENTS	tendency
tenenboym, *m.*	TEH-*nen-boym*	fir
tenis, *m.*	TEH-*niss*	tennis
teorye, *f.*	*teh*-OR-*yeh*	theory
tepekh, *m.*	TEH-*pekh*	carpet
terase, *f.*	*teh*-RAH-*seh*	terrace
terets, *m.*	TEH-*rets*	excuse
"	"	pretext
teritorye, *f.*	*teh-ree*-TOR-*yeh*	territory
Terkay, *f.*	*tehr*-KYE	Turkey
terkish	TEHR-*kish*	Turkish (*adj.*)
termin, *m.*	*tehr*-MEEN	maturity (due date, *bus.*)
"	"	term (expression)
termin, ariber dem	*ah*-REE-*behr dem tehr*-MEEN	overdue (in arrears)
termometer, *m.*	*tehr-maw*-MEH-*tehr*	thermometer
test, *m.*	TEST	test (*educ.*)
tetsl, *n.*	TEHT-*sil*	saucer
teve, *f.*	TEH-*veh*	nature (character)
tey, *f.*	TAY	tea
teyg, *n.*	TAYG	batter (flour mixture)
teykef	TAY-*kef*	immediately (instantly)
teykefdik	TAY-*kef-dick*	immediate (instant)
"	"	prompt (quick)
teyl, *m.*	TAIL	part (portion)
teyl	TAIL	some (certain, *adj.*)
teyl, a	*ah* TAIL	some (certain ones, *pron.*)
teyl, tsum	*tsoom* TAIL	partly
teylefl, *m.*	TAY-*leh-fil*	spoon (teaspoon)
teyl mol	TAIL-*mawl*	sometimes
teyln (1)	TAY-*lin*	divide (make separate), to
"	"	divide, to (*arith.*)
teyln zikh	TAY-*lin zikh*	divide (become separate), to
teyln zikh mit	TAY-*lin zikh mit*	share, to
teylvayz	TAIL-*vize*	partial (incomplete)
teytl, *m.*	TAY-*til*	date (fruit)
teytn (1)	TAY-*lin*	slay, to
tfile, *f.*	TFEE-*leh*	prayer (petition)
thom, *m.*	T_HAWM	precipice
tif, *f.*	TEEF	depth (deepness)
tif	TEEF	deep
"	"	profound
tiger, *m.*	TEEG-*ehr*	tiger
tink, *m.*	TEENK	plaster (wall coating)
tint, *f.*	TEENT	ink
tip, *m.*	TEEP	type (kind)
tipirn (1b)	*tee*-PEE-*rin*	type (typewrite), to
tipish	TEE-*pish*	typical
tipist, *m.*	*tee*-PEEST	typist
tipshes, *f.*	TEEP-*shess*	folly
tir, *f.*	TEER	door
tiran, *m.*	*lee*-RAHN	tyrant
tirkhe, *f.*	TEER-*kheh*	effort
"	"	trouble (exertion)
tish, *m.*	TEESH	table (furniture)
tishtekh, *m.*	TEESH-*tukh*	tablecloth
titl, *m.*	TEE-*til*	title (name)

Yiddish	Pronunciation	English
tkhilesdik	T_KHEE-*less-dick*	initial (first, *adj.*)
tlis, *m.*	TLEESS	trot
tnay, *m.*	T_NYE	condition (stipulation)
tnoyim, *pl.*	TNAW-*im*	terms (conditions)
tnue, *f.*	TNOO-*eh*	gesture (motion)
toes, *m.*	TAW-*ess*	error
"	"	mistake
tog, *m.*	TAWG	day (daytime)
toglikht, *n.*	TAWG-*likht*	daylight
togteglekh	*tawg*-TEHG-*lukh*	daily (*adj.*)
tokhter, *f.*	TAWKH-*tehr*	daughter
Tokyo, *n.*	TAWK-*yaw*	Tokyo
tol, *m.*	TAWL	valley
tombank, *m.*	TAWM-*bahnk*	counter (table)
tomid	TAW-*mid*	ever (at all times)
tomid, oyf	*oyf* TAW-*mid*	forever
ton, *m.*	TAWN	tone (quality of sound)
ton (22)	TAWN	do, to
ton antkegn	TAWN *ahnt*-KEG-*in*	defy, to
top, *m.*	TAWP	pot (container)
topl	TAW-*pil*	double (*adj.*)
toplpunkt, *m.*	TAW-*pil-poonkt*	colon (*punct.*)
toplshteyner, *pl.*	TAW-*pil-shtay-nehr*	dice (marked cubes)
tormoz, *m.*	TOR-*mawz*	brake
torpede, *f.*	*tor*-PEH-*deh*	torpedo
toust, *m.*	TOAST	toast (bread)
tovl, *m.*	TAW-*vil*	blackboard
toy, *m.*	TOY	dew
toyb	TOYB	deaf
toyb, *f.*	TOYB	dove
"	"	pigeon
toyer, *m.*	TAW-*yehr*	gate
toye zayn zikh (18c)	TAW-*yeh zine zikh*	err, to
toyfes zayn (18c)	TOY-*fess zine*	grasp (understand), to
toyt, *m.*	TOYT	death
toyt	TOYT	dead
toyt-...	TOYT-...	deadly
"	"	fatal
toyve, *f.*	TOY-*veh*	benefit (advantage)
"	"	favor (kindness)
traditsye, *f.*	*trah*-DEETS-*yeh*	tradition
traf, *m.*	TRAHF	syllable
tragedye, *f.*	*trah*-G_ED-*yeh*	tragedy
tragish	TRAHG-*ish*	tragic
trakht, *f.*	TRAH_KHT	womb
trakhtn (1)	TRAH_KH-*tin*	think (reason), to
trakhtn, *n.*	TRAH_KH-*tin*	thought (contemplation)
traktat, *m.*	*trahk*-TAHT	treaty
traktor, *m.*	TRAHK-*tor*	tractor (farm machine)
tramvay, *m.*	*trahm*-VYE	trolley (street car)
transhee, *f.*	*trahn*-SHAY-*eh*	trench (*mil.*)
traybn (9)	TRY-*bin*	drive (propel), to
trefn (7)	TREH-*fin*	encounter, to
"	"	guess (divine), to
"	"	meet (encounter), to
trefn zikh	TREH-*fin zikh*	meet (come together), to
trefshpil, *f.*	TREFF-*shpeel*	puzzle (game)
treger, *m.*	TREG-*ehr*	porter (baggage carrier)
trep, *pl.*	TREP	stairway
trep, arop di	*ah*-RAWP *dee* TREP	downstairs (downward)
trepl, *n.*	TREH-*pil*	step (stair)
trer, *f.*	TREHR	tear (teardrop)
tretn (7)	TREH-*lin*	step, to
treyst, *f.*	TRAYST	comfort (solace)
treystn (1)	TRACE-*tin*	comfort (console), to
trib	TREEB	dreary
tribut, *m.*	*tree*-BOOT	tribute (money)
trikenen (3)	TREE-*keh-nen*	dry (make dry), to
trikenen zikh	TREE-*keh-nen zikh*	dry (become dry), to
trilerl, *n.*	TREE-*leh-ril*	lark (bird)
trinken (8)	TREEN-*ken*	drink, to
trinkgelt, *n.*	TREENK-*g_elt*	tip (gratuity)

Yiddish	Pronunciation	English
triumf, *m.*	*tree*-OOMPH	triumph
trogbetl, *n.*	TRAWG-*beh-til*	litter (stretcher)
trogn (5)	TRAWG-*in*	bear, to
"	"	carry, to
"	"	wear (have on), to
trogn zikh	TRAWG-*in zikh*	drift (float), to
trombon, *m.*	*trawm*-BAWN	trombone
tron, *m.*	TRAWN	throne
trop, *m.*	TRAWP	accent (stress)
tropn, *m.*	TRAW-*pin*	drop (droplet)
trost, *m.*	TRAWST	trust (cartel)
trot, *m.*	TRAWT	step (stride)
trotuar, *m.*	*traw-too*-AR	sidewalk
trotuar-shvel, *f.*	*traw-too*-AR-*shvel*	curb (edge of street)
troyer, *m.*	TRAW-*yehr*	sorrow (sadness)
troyerik	TRAW-*yeh-rick*	mournful (saddening)
troyerik barimt	TRAW-*yeh-rick bah-*REEMT	notorious
troyern (1)	TRAW-*yeh-rin*	grieve, to
"	"	mourn, to
trukn	TROO-*kin*	dry
trumeyt, *m.*	*troo*-MATE	bugle
"	"	horn (*auto.*)
"	"	trumpet (*mus.*)
truskavke, *f.*	*troos*-KAHV-*keh*	strawberry
tsaar, *m.*	TSAR	grief
tsam, *f.*	TSAHM	curb (restraint)
tsamen (1)	TSAH-*men*	curb (restrain), to
tsart	TSART	gentle (soothing)
tsavoe, *f.*	*tsah*-VAW-*eh*	will (document)
tsayml, *n.*	TSYE-*mil*	bridle (harness)
tsayt, *f.*	TSYTE	time (interval)
tsayt, fun tsayt tsu	*foon* TSYTE *tsoo* TSYTE	occasional
"	"	occasionally
tsaytfartrayb, *m.*	TSYTE-*far-tribe*	pastime
tsayt fun yor, *f.*	TSYTE *foon* YOR	season (of year)
tsaytik	TSYE-*tick*	ripe
tsaytik vern (7d)	TSYE-*tick veh-rin*	mature (ripen), to
tsaytung, *f.*	TSYE-*toon_g*	newspaper
tsdoke, *f.*	TS_DAW-*keh*	charity (philanthropy)
tsebrekhn (7b)	*tseh*-BREH-*khin*	break (make smash), to
tsebreklen (1b)	*tseh*-BREHK-*len*	crumble, to
tsederboym, *m.*	TSEH-*dehr-boym*	cedar (tree)
tsefal, *m.*	*tseh*-FAHL	decay (decline)
tsegeyn (14bc)	*tseh*-GAIN	thaw, to
tsekaletshen (2b)	*tseh-kah*-LEH-*chen*	injure, to
tsekrimen (1b)	*tseh*-KREE-*men*	mar (disfigure), to
tselozn (1b)	*tseh*-LAW-*zin*	dissolve (liquefy), to
tsement, *m.*	*tseh*-MENT	cement
tsemishn (1b)	*tseh*-MEE-*shin*	confuse (mix up), to
"	"	distract (divert), to
tsemoln (1b)	*tseh*-MAW-*lin*	grind (crush), to
tsenter, *m.*	TSEN-*tehr*	center
tsentral	TSEN-*trahl*	central
tsepitslen (1b)	*tseh*-PEETS-*len*	shatter (smash in pieces), to
tseremonye, *f.*	*tseh-reh*-MAWN-*yeh*	ceremony
tsertlekh	TSEHRT-*lukh*	tender (loving)
tsertlekhkayt, *f.*	TSEHRT-*lukh-kite*	tenderness (love)
tseshedikn (1b)	*tseh*-SHEH-*dee-kin*	damage (injure), to
tseshitn (7b)	*tseh*-SHEE-*tin*	scatter (strew), to
tseshmetern (1b)	*tseh*-SHMEH-*teh-rin*	crush, to
"	"	smash, to
tseshmoltsn vern (7d)	*tseh*-SHMAWLT-*sin veh-rin*	melt (become liquid), to
tseshnaydn (11b)	*tseh*-SHNYE-*din*	cut (divide into parts), to
"	"	cut (wound), to
tseshtern (1b)	*tseh*-SHTEH-*rin*	destroy (demolish), to
"	"	wreck, to
tseshtoysn (5b)	*tseh*-SHTOY-*sin*	pound (pummel), to
tseteyln zikh (1b)	*tseh*-TAY-*lin zikh*	separate (come apart), to
tseteylung, *f.*	*tseh*-TAY-*loon_g*	separation
tsetretn (7b)	*tseh*-TREH-*tin*	trample, to
tsetumlen (1b)	*tseh*-TOOM-*len*	bewilder, to
tseveytikt	*tseh*-VAY-*tickt*	sore (*adj.*)
tseykhenen (3)	TSAY-*kheh-nen*	draw (sketch), to
tseykhenung, *f.*	TSAY-*kheh-noon_g*	drawing (sketch)

Yiddish	Pronunciation	English
tseykhn, *m.*	TSAY-*khin*	grade (academic rating)
tseykhnshtift, *m.*	TSAY-*khin-shtift*	crayon
tseylem, *m.*	TSAY-*lem*	cross (crucifix)
tseyln (1)	TSAY-*lin*	count (enumerate), to
"	"	number (amount to), to
tsharter, *m.*	CHAR-*tehr*	charter (act of incorporation)
tshek, *m.*	CHECK	check (bank check)
Tshekhoslovakay, *f.*	*cheh-khaw-slaw-vah*-KIE	Czechoslovakia
tshempyon, *m.*	*chemp*-YAWN	champion
tshepen (2)	CHEH-*pen*	annoy (irk), to
tshepen zikh tsu	CHEH-*pen zikh* TSOO	pester, to
tsherepakhe, *f.*	*cheh-reh*-PAH-*kheh*	turtle
Tshile, *n.*	CHEE-*leh*	Chile
tshilenish	*chee*-LEH-*nish*	Chilean (*adj.*)
tshudne	CHOOD-*neh*	weird (unearthly)
tshuve, *f.*	TSHOO-*veh*	reply
tshvok, *m.*	CH_VAWK	nail (hardware)
tsi	TSEE	if
"	"	whether (either, *conj.*)
"	"	whether (if, *conj.*)
tsibele, *f.*	TSEE-*beh-leh*	onion
tsien (23)	TSEE-*en*	draw (pull along), to
"	"	pull, to
tsien mit der noz	TSEE-*en mit dehr* NAWZ	sniff, to
tsien zikh	TSEE-*en zikh*	run (extend), to
"	"	stretch (extend), to
tsifer, *f.*	TSEE-*fehr*	figure (numeral)
tsiferblat, *n.*	TSEE-*fehr-blaht*	dial (graduated face)
tsig, *f.*	TSEEG	goat
tsigar, *m.*	*tsee*-GAR	cigar
Tsigayner, *m.*	*tsee*-GYE-*nehr*	gypsy
tsigele, *n.*	TSEEG-*eh-leh*	kid (goat)
tsigl, *m.*	TSEEG-*il*	brick (building material)
tsikhtik	TSEE_KH-*tick*	neat (tidy)
tsil, *m.*	TSEEL	aim
"	"	destination
"	"	end
"	"	goal
"	"	object
tsil, *m.*	TSEEL	objective
"	"	purpose
tsilinder, *m.*	*tsee*-LEEN-*dehr*	cylinder (*geom.*)
tsiln (1)	TSEE-*lin*	aim, to
"	"	direct, to
tsimer, *m.*	TSEE-*mehr*	room (chamber)
tsimering, *m.*	TSEE-*meh-rin_g*	cinnamon
tsin, *n.*	TSEEN	tin (metal)
tsink, *n.*	TSEENK	zinc
tsireven (2)	TSEE-*reh-ven*	darn (mend), to
tsirk, *m.*	TSEERK	circus
tsirkl, *m.*	TSEER-*kil*	compass (drawing instrument)
tsirkular, *m.*	*tseer-koo*-LAR	circular (letter or brochure, *bus.*)
tsirung, *f.*	TSEE-*roon_g*	jewelry
tsishen (2)	TSEE-*shen*	hiss, to
tsitat, *m.*	*tsee*-TAHT	quotation (selection)
tsiter, *m.*	TSEE-*tehr*	chill (shivering sensation)
tsitern (1)	TSEE-*teh-rin*	quake (shake), to
"	"	quiver, to
"	"	shiver, to
"	"	tremble, to
tsitirn (1b)	*tsee*-TEE-*rin*	quote (cite), to
tsivil	*tsee*-VEEL	civil (secular)
tsivilizatsye, *f.*	*tsee-vee-lee*-ZAHTS-*yeh*	civilization
tsniesdik	TS_NEE-*ess-dik*	chaste
tsofn, *m.*	TSAW-*fin*	north (*n.*)
Tsofn-Amerike, *f.*	TSAW-*fin-ah*-MEH-*ree-keh*	North America
tsofndik	TSAW-*fin-dick*	northern
tsofn-mayrevdik	TSAW-*fin-*MY-*rev-dick*	northwest (*adj.*)
tsofn-mizrakhdik	TSAW-*fin-*MEEZ-*rukh-dick*	northeast (*adj.*)
tsol, *f.*	TSAWL	number (quantity)
tsol, *m.*	TSAWL	customs (tax)
"	"	duty (tax)
"	"	tariff

Yiddish	Pronunciation	English
tsolamt, *n.*	TSAWL-*ahmt*	customhouse
tsolfray	TSAWL-*frye*	duty-free
tsoln (1)	TSAW-*lin*	pay, to
tsoln, tsu	*tsoo* TSAW-*lin*	payable (due)
tsolraykh	TSAWL-*rye_kh*	numerous
tsol-silek, *m.*	TSAWL-*see-lek*	clearance (customs clearance)
tsolung, *f.*	TSAW-*loon_g*	payment
tson, *m.*	TSAWN	tooth
tsonbershtl, *n.*	TSAWN-*behrsh-til*	toothbrush
tsondokter, *m.*	TSAWN-*dawk-tehr*	dentist
tsonpaste, *f.*	TSAWN-*pahss-teh*	tooth paste
tsonveytik, *m.*	TSAWN-*vay-tick*	toothache
tsoraas, *f.*	*tsaw-*RAH-*ahss*	leprosy
tsore, *f.*	TSAW-*reh*	trouble (distress)
"	"	woe
tsores, *pl.*	TSAW-*ress*	misery (grief)
tsores, oyf	*oyf* TSAW-*ress*	miserable (unhappy)
tsorn, *m.*	TSAW-*rin*	fury
"	"	rage
"	"	wrath
tsu	TSOO	at (for the price of)
"	"	to (indicating destination, *prep.*)
"	"	to (used with indirect object, *prep.*)
"	"	too (overly)
"	"	toward
tsuayln (1a)	TSOO-*eye-lin*	hasten (expedite), to
tsuayln zikh	TSOO-*eye-lin zikh*	hasten (hurry), to
tsubindn (8a)	TSOO-*bin-din*	lash (fasten), to
tsudekn (1a)	TSOO-*deh-kin*	cover, to
tsufal, *m.*	TSOO-*fahl*	accident
"	"	chance
tsufestikn (1a)	TSOO-*fes-tee-kin*	fasten, to
tsuflus, *m.*	TSOO-*flooss*	tide, high
tsufridn	*tsoo-*FREE-*din*	glad
tsufridnkayt, *f.*	*tsoo-*FREE-*din-kite*	gladness
tsufridn shteln (1c)	*tsoo-*FREE-*din shteh-lin*	please (satisfy), to
tsug, *m.*	TSOOG	train, railroad
tsugeaylt	TSOO-*geh-eye_lt*	hasty (rash)
tsugebn, *n.*	TSOO-*geh-bin*	addition (process of adding)
tsugebn (13a)	TSOO-*geh-bin*	add (find sum of), to
"	"	add (include), to
tsugevoynen zikh (1a)	TSOO-*geh-voy-nen zikh*	accustom oneself, to
tsugob-...	TSOO-*gawb-..*	additional
tsugob, *m.*	TSOO-*gawb*	addition (supplement)
tsugob-optsol, *m.*	TSOO-*gawb-awp-tsawl*	surcharge (*bus.*)
tsugreytn (1a)	TSOO-*gray-tin*	prepare (make ready), to
tsugreytung, *f.*	TSOO-*gray-toon_g*	arrangement
"	"	preparation (preparatory act)
tsugvint, *m.*	TSOOG-*vint*	draft (air current)
tsuhelfn (7a)	TSOO-*hell-fin*	assist, to
tsuker, *m.*	TSOO-*kehr*	sugar
tsuker-krankayt, *f.*	TSOO-*kehr-krahn-kite*	diabetes
tsukerl, *n.*	TSOO-*keh-ril*	candy
tsukuker, *m.*	TSOO-*koo-kehr*	spectator
tsukum, *m.*	TSOO-*koom*	increase (increment)
tsukunft, *f.*	TSOO-*koonft*	future (*n.*)
tsunemen (8a)	TSOO-*neh-men*	deprive (divest), to
"	"	remove (take away), to
tsunemenish, *n.*	TSOO-*neh-meh-nish*	nickname
tsung, *f.*	TSOON_G	tongue (*anat.*)
tsunoyfbindn (8a)	*tsoo-*NOYF-*been-din*	connect (link), to
tsunoyfklaybn (9a)	*tsoo-*NOYF-*klye-bin*	assemble (bring together), to
tsunoyfklaybn zikh	*tsoo-*NOYF-*klye-bin zikh*	assemble (meet), to
tsunoyfleygn (1a)	*tsoo-*NOYF-*layg-in*	fold (lap over), to
tsunoyfporn (1a)	*tsoo-*NOYF-*paw-rin*	mate (find mate for), to
tsunoyfshtel, *m.*	*tsoo-*NOYF-*shtel*	composition (make-up)
"	"	constitution (nature)
tsunoyfshteln (1a)	*tsoo-*NOYF-*shteh-lin*	constitute (make up), to
tsupasn (1a)	TSOO-*pah-sin*	adapt, to

Yiddish	Pronunciation	English
tsuredn (1a)	TSOO-*reh-din*	urge (try to persuade), to
tsurik	*tsoo-*REEK	back (rearward, *adv.*)
tsurikfaln (5ad)	*tsoo-*REEK-*fah-lin*	relapse, to
tsurikker, *m.*	*tsoo-*REEK-*kehr*	return (coming or going back)
tsurikkrign (7a)	*tsoo-*REEK-*kreeg-in*	recover (get back), to
tsuriktsi, *m.*	*tsoo-*REEK-*tsee*	retreat (*mil.*)
tsuriktsien (23a)	*tsoo-*REEK-*tsee-en*	withdraw (take back), to
tsuriktsien zikh	*tsoo-*REEK-*tsee-en zikh*	retire (stop working), to
"	"	withdraw (depart), to
tsuriktsolung, *f.*	*tsoo-*REEK-*tsaw-loon_g*	rebate (*bus.*)
"	"	refund (*bus.*)
tsushtayer, *m.*	*tsoo-*SHTYE-*ehr*	contribution
tsushteln (1a)	TSOO-*shteh-lin*	supply (provide), to
tsushtimung, *f.*	TSOO-*shtee-moon_g*	favor (approval)
tsutroy, *m.*	TSOO-*troy*	confidence
"	"	trust
tsutshepen (2a)	TSOO-*cheh-pen*	attach (join), to
tsutsien (23a)	TSOO-*tsee-en*	attract, to
tsutsiendik	TSOO-*tsee-en-dick*	attractive (pleasing)
tsuzamen	*tsoo-*ZAH-*men*	together
tsuzamenfor, *m.*	*tsoo-*ZAH-*men-for*	convention (meeting)
tsuzog, *m.*	TSOO-*zawg*	promise (pledge)
tsuzogn (1a)	TSOO-*zawg-in*	promise (pledge), to
tsvangdinst, *n.*	TSVAHN_G-*deenst*	draft (conscription)
tsvayg, *m.*	TSVYE_G	bough
"	"	branch
tsvaygl, *n.*	TSVYE-*g_il*	twig
tsvey mol	TSVAY *mawl*	twice
tsveyt	TSVATE	second (*adj.*)
tsviling, *m.*	TSVEE-*lin_g*	twin (*n.*)
tsvishn	TSVEE-*shin*	among
"	"	between (*prep.*)
tsvishntsayt, *f.*	TSVEE-*shin-tsyte*	interval (period of time)
"	"	meantime (*n.*)
tuberkuloz, *m.*	*too-behr-koo-*LAWZ	tuberculosis
tulpan, *m.*	*tool-*PAHN	tulip
tuml, *m.*	TOO-*mil*	noise (din)
tumldik	TOO-*mil-dick*	noisy
tumor, *m.*	TOO-*more*	tumor
tunel, *m.*	*too-*NEL	tunnel
tunken (1)	TOON-*ken*	dip (immerse), to
tunkl	TOON-*kil*	dark (in color, *adj.*)
"	"	dim
"	"	obscure (unclear)
tunkshif, *f.*	TOONK-*shif*	submarine
tupen (2)	TOO-*pen*	stamp (tread heavily), to
tur, *m.*	TOOR	tour
turem, *m.*	TOO-*rem*	tower
turist, *m.*	*too-*REEST	tourist (*n.*)
turme, *f.*	TOOR-*meh*	jail
"	"	prison
tuts, *m.*	TOOTS	dozen
tuung, *f.*	TOO-*oon_g*	act (deed)
tvan, *m.*	TVAHN	mire (bog)
tvidshtof, *m.*	TVEED-*shtawf*	tweed (cloth)
tvue, *f.*	TVOO-*eh*	cereal
"	"	grain
ugerke, *f.*	OOG-*ehr-keh*	cucumber
ulme, *f.*	OOL-*meh*	elm
umadekvat	OOM-*ah-deh-*KVAHT	inadequate
umayngenem	OOM-*ine-geh-nem*	unpleasant
umbaholfn	OOM-*bah-*HAWL-*fin*	helpless
umbakant	OOM-*bah-kahnt*	obscure (unrenowned)
"	"	unknown
umbakvemkayt, *f.*	OOM-*bah-kvem-kite*	inconvenience
umbatrakht	OOM-*bah-*TRAH_KHT	rash (*adj.*)
umdirekt	OOM-*dee-rekt*	indirect
umendlekh	OOM-END-*lukh*	infinite
umer, *m.*	*oo-*mehr	gloom (depression)
umet, *m.*	*oo-*met	sadness
umetik	*oo-*meh-tick	sad (sorrowful)
umetum	*oo-*meh-*TOOM	everywhere
umfarmaydlekh	OOM-*far-*MIDE-*lukh*	inevitable (*adj.*)

Yiddish	Pronunciation	English
umfeikayt tsu tsoln, *f.*	OOM-*feh-ee-kite tsoo* TSAW-*lin*	insolvency (*bus.*)
umfrukhperdik	OOM-*frookh-pehr-dick*	barren
umgeduld, *f.*	OOM-*g_eh-doold*	impatience
umgeduldik	OOM-*g_eh-dool-dick*	impatient
umgehayer	OOM-*g_eh-hye-ehr*	enormous
umgelumpert	OOM-*g_eh-*LOOM-*pehrt*	awkward
umgenoy	OOM-*g_eh-noy*	inaccurate
umgerekht	OOM-*g_eh-rekht*	wrong (unjust, *adj.*)
umgerikht	OOM-*g_eh-*REEKHT	unexpected (*adj.*)
umgerikht on-kumen (5ac)	OOM-*g_eh-rikht* AWN-*koo-men*	surprise (come upon suddenly), to
umgern	OOM-*g_eh-rin*	unwilling
umgeveyntlekh	OOM-*g_eh-*VANE_T-*lukh*	unusual
umglaykh	OOM-*glye_kh*	unequal
umglik, *n.*	OOM-*gleek*	accident (mishap)
"	"	misfortune
umgliklekh	OOM-*gleek-lukh*	unfortunate
"	"	unhappy (sorrowful)
umgliklekher, *m.*	OOM-GLEEK-*lukh-ehr*	wretch (hapless person)
umgrod	OOM-*grawd*	odd (not even)
umkern (1a)	OOM-*keh-rin*	return (give back), to
umkern di hoyt-tsoes	OOM-*keh-rin dee hoyt-*SAW-*ess*	reimburse, to
umkern zikh	OOM-*keh-rin zikh*	return (go back), to
umkoved, *m.*	OOM-*kaw-ved*	dishonor
umkumen (5ad)	OOM-*koo-men*	perish, to
umlegal	OOM-*leh-gahl*	illegal
umloyalkayt, *f*	OOM-*law-*YAHL-*kite*	disloyalty
ummiglekh	OOM-MEEG-*lukh*	impossible
ummiglekhkayt, *f.*	OOM-MEEG-*lukh-kite*	impossibility
umneytik	OOM-*nay-tick*	needless
"	"	unnecessary
umophengik	OOM-*awp-hen_g-ick*	independent
umophengikayt, *f.*	OOM-*awp-*HEN_G-*ee-kite*	independence
umordenung, *f.*	OOM-*or-deh-noon_g*	disorder (confusion)
umreguler	OOM-*reh-goo-*LEHR	irregular (asymmetrical)
umreyn	OOM-*rain*	impure
umru, *f.*	OOM-*roo*	anxiety
umruik	OOM-*roo-ick*	anxious
"	"	restless
"	"	uneasy
umshtand, *m.*	OOM-*shtahnd*	circumstance (external condition)
umshterblekh	OOM-SHTEHRB-*lukh*	immortal (*adj.*)
umshuldik	OOM-*shool-dick*	innocent (guiltless)
umveg, *m.*	OOM-*veg*	detour
umverdik	OOM-*vehr-dick*	unworthy
umvisn, *n.*	OOM-*vee-sin*	ignorance
umvisndik	OOM-*vee-sin-dick*	ignorant
umyoysher, *m.*	OOM-*yoy-shehr*	injustice
umzikhtbar	OOM-*zikht-bar*	invisible
umzin, *m.*	OOM-*zin*	nonsense
umzist	*oom-*ZEEST	free (gratuitous)
un	OON	and
undz	OONDS	us
undzer	OOND-*zehr*	our
undzerer	OOND-*zeh-rehr*	ours
Ungern, *n.*	OON-*g_eh-rin*	Hungary
univers, *m.*	*oo-nee-*VEHRSS	universe
universal	*oo-nee-vehr-*SAHL	universal (*adj.*)
universal-krom, *f.*	*oo-nee-vehr-*SAHL-*krawm*	department store
universitet, *m.*	*oo-nee-vehr-see-*TET	university
unter	OON-*tehr*	below (less than, *prep.*)
"	"	below (lower than, *prep.*)
"	"	beneath (*prep.*)
"	"	under (beneath, *prep.*)
"	"	under (subject to, *prep.*)
"	"	underneath (*prep.*)
unterban, *f.*	OON-*tehr-bahn*	subway (underground railway)
unterdrikn (1a)	OON-*tehr-dree-kin*	subdue (conquer), to
untererdish	OON-*tehr-*EHR-*dish*	underground (belowground, *adj.*)
untergang, *m.*	OON-*tehr-gahn_g*	doom (ruin)

Yiddish	Pronunciation	English
untergebn zikh (13a)	OON-*tehr-g_eh-bin zikh*	surrender (give oneself up), to
untergeyn (14ad)	OON-*tehr-gain*	set (in sky), to
unterhaltn (5a)	OON-*tehr-hahl-tin*	support (hold up), to
unterkleyd, *n.*	OON-*tehr-klade*	petticoat
"	"	slip
unterkoyfn (1a)	OON-*tehr-koy-fin*	bribe, to
unternemen zikh (8a)	OON-*tehr-neh-men zikh*	undertake (attempt), to
unternemung, *f.*	*oon-tehr-*NEH-*moon_g*	enterprise
"	"	undertaking
untershlok, *m.*	OON-*tehr-shlawk*	lining
untershpringen (8ad)	OON-*tehr-shpreen-g_en*	hop, to
untershraybn (9a)	OON-*tehr-shrye-bin*	sign (endorse), to
untershtitsung, *f.*	OON-*tehr-shteet-soon_g*	support (approval)
untertaner, *m.*	OON-*tehr-tah-nehr*	subject (citizen)
untervesh, *pl.*	OON-*tehr-vesh*	underwear
untn	OON-*tin*	below (lower down, *adv.*)
"	"	beneath (*adv.*)
"	"	down (in lower place, *adv.*)
"	"	downstairs (on a lower floor)
uranyum, *n.*	*oo-*RAHN-*yoom*	uranium
Urugvay, *n.*	*oo-roog-vye*	Uruguay
uvde, *f.*	OOV-*deh*	job
"	"	task
vagon, *m.*	*vah-*GAWN	car, railroad
"	"	carload (*bus.*)
vagon-restoran, *m.*	*vah-*GAWN-*res-to-*RAHN	diner (railway dining car)
vakatsye, *f.*	*vah-*KAHTS-*yeh*	vacation (work holidays)
vakh	VAH_KH	awake
vaklen zikh (1)	VAHK-*len zikh*	stagger (totter), to
vaks, *m.*	VAHX	wax (beeswax)
vaksn (5d)	VAHK-*sin*	grow, to (*biol.*)
"	"	grow (expand), to
"	"	increase, to
vaktsinirung, *f.*	*vahk-tsee-*NEE-*roon_g*	vaccination
vald, *m.*	VAHLD	forest
"	"	wood
valfish, *m.*	VAHL-*fish*	whale
valn, *pl.*	VAH-*lin*	election
vals, *m.*	VAHLSS	waltz (dance step)
valts, *m.*	VAHLTS	roller (cylinder)
vandern (1)	VAHN-*deh-rin*	wander, to
vane, *f.*	VAH-*neh*	bath
"	"	bathtub
"	"	tub
vant, *f.*	VAHNT	wall
varem	VAH-*rim*	affectionate (loving)
"	"	warm
varemen (1)	VAH-*reh-men*	warm, to
varemkayt, *f.*	VAH-*rem-kite*	warmth
varfn (7)	VAR-*fin*	cast, to
"	"	pitch, to
"	"	throw, to
"	"	toss, to
Varshe, *f.*	VAR-*sheh*	Warsaw
vartn (1)	VAR-*tin*	wait (defer action), to
vartn oyf	VAR-*tin oyf*	await, to
"	"	wait for, to
vaser, *n.*	VAH-*sehr*	water
vaserfal, *m.*	VAH-*sehr-fahl*	falls (waterfall)
vaser-zikher	VAH-*sehr-zee-khehr*	waterproof
vashn (5)	VAH-*shin*	wash (cleanse), to
vashn zikh	VAH-*shin zikh*	wash (cleanse oneself), to
vayblekh	VIBE-*lukh*	female (*adj.*)
"	"	feminine
vayl	VILE	because (*conj.*)
"	"	since (*conj.*)
vayle, *f.*	VYE-*leh*	while (short time, *n.*)
vayle, a	*ah* VYE-*leh*	awhile (*adv.*)
vayn, *m.*	VINE	wine (beverage)
vayngortn, *m.*	VINE-*gor-tin*	vineyard
vaynshtok, *m.*	VINE-*shtawk*	vine (grapevine)
vayntroyb, *f.*	VINE-*troyb*	grape

Yiddish	Pronunciation	English
vayn, vilder, *m.*	VEEL-*dehr* VINE	ivy
vays	VICE	white (*adj.*)
vayt	VITE	distant (far-off)
"	"	far (*adj.*)
"	"	far (afar, *adv.*)
"	"	remote
vayter	VIE-*tehr*	farther (*adj., adv.*)
"	"	next (*adv.*)
"	"	further (additional, *adj.*)
vayter fun	VYE-*tehr foon*	beyond
vayzn (9)	VYE-*zin*	show (make visible), to
vayzn zikh	VYE-*zin zikh*	show (be visible), to
vaze, *f.*	VAH-*zeh*	vase
vebn (1)	VEH-*bin*	weave, to
vebshtul, *m.*	VEB-*shtool*	loom
veg, *m.*	VEG	road
"	"	trail (path)
"	"	way (route)
vegele, *n.*	VEHG-*eh-leh*	carriage (baby buggy)
vegn	VEG-*in*	about (concerning)
vegn (10)	VEG-*in*	weigh, to
veksl, *m.*	VEHK-*sil*	bill of exchange
"	"	note (promise to pay, *bus.*)
vel (29)	VEL	will (*v.*)
veldl, *n.*	VELL-*dil*	grove (small woods)
velisher nus, *m.*	VEH-*lee-shehr* NOOSE	walnut (*n.*)
velkhe(r) es iz	VELL-*kheh(r) ess* EEZ	any (a quantity of, *adj.*)
velkher	VEL-*khehr*	what (*interrog. adj.*)
"	"	which (*interrog. adj.*)
"	"	which (*interrog. pron.*)
velkher nor	VEL-*khehr nor*	whatever (*adj.*)
"	"	whichever (*adj.*)
veln (28e)	VEH-*lin*	want (desire), to
"	"	wish for, to
velosiped, *m.*	*veh-lo-see-*PEHD	bicycle
velt, *f.*	VELT	world
vemen	VEH-*men*	whom (*interrog. pron.*)
vemes	VEH-*mess*	whose (*interrog. pron.*)
"	"	whose (*rel. pron.*)
ven	VEN	when (any time that, *conj.*)
"	"	when (at the time that, *conj.*)
"	"	when (at what time, *adv.*)
"	"	when (which time, *pron.*)
vendn zikh (1)	VEN-*din zikh*	depend (be contingent) on, to
"	"	solicit (ask for), to
vene, *f.*	VEH-*neh*	vein (*anat.*)
ven es iz	VEHN *ess* EEZ	ever (at any time)
Venetsuele, *f.*	*veh-neh-tsoo-*EH-*leh*	Venezuela
venetsuelish	*veh-neh-tsoo-*EH-*lish*	Venezuelan (*adj.*)
Venetsye, *f.*	*veh-*NETS-*yeh*	Venice
venger, *m.*	VEN-*g͏ehr*	eel
ven nor	VEN *nor*	whenever
ventilator, *m.*	*ven-tee-*LAH-*tor*	fan, electric
ver	VEHR	who (*interrog. pron.*)
verb, *m.*	VEHRB	verb
verbe, *f.*	VEHR-*beh*	willow
verbirer, *m.*	*vehr-*BEE-*rehr*	canvasser (*bus.*)
verde, *f.*	VEHR-*deh*	dignity
ver es iz	VEHR *ess* EEZ	anybody
"	"	anyone (someone)
verk, *n.*	VEHRK	work (composition)
vern (7d)	VEH-*rin*	become, to
vern fun	VEH-*rin foon*	become of (happen to), to
ver nor	VEHR *nor*	whoever (any person who)
ver s'zol nit zayn	VEHR *s-zawl nit* ZINE	whoever (no matter who)

Yiddish	Pronunciation	English
vert, *f.*	VEHRT	value
"	"	worth
vert, nominale, *f.*	*naw-mee-*NAH-*leh* VEHRT	face value (*bus.*)
vert, on a	AWN *ah* VEHRT	worthless (valueless)
verterbukh, *n.*	VEHR-*tehr-bookh*	dictionary
vertful	VEHRT-*full*	valuable (precious)
vertikal	*vehr-tee-*KAHL	vertical (*adj.*)
vertpapirn, *pl.*	VEHRT-*pah-pee-rin*	securities (stocks, etc.)
vesh, *f.*	VESH	laundry (articles laundered)
vesheray, *f.*	*veh-sheh-*RYE	laundry (commercial plant)
vesp, *f.*	VESP	wasp
vest, *f.*	VEST	vest
veter, *n.*	VEH-*tehr*	weather
veteran, *m.*	*veh-teh-*RAHN	veteran (*mil., n.*)
vetn zikh (1)	VEH-*tin zikh*	bet, to
vetshere, *f.*	VEH-*cheh-reh*	supper (light evening meal)
veverke, *f.*	VEH-*vehr-keh*	squirrel
veykh	VAY_KH	soft (not hard)
veyler, *m.*	VAY-*lehr*	voter
Veylz, *n.*	VALES	Wales
veynen (1)	VAY-*nen*	cry, to
"	"	weep, to
veytik, *m.*	VAY-*tick*	ache
"	"	pain
veytikdik	VAY-*tick-dick*	painful
vey ton (22)	VAY *tawn*	ache, to
"	"	hurt, to
veyts, *m.*	VAITS	wheat
vi	VEE	as (in the role of, *prep.*)
"	"	how
"	"	like (*adv.*)
vider	VEE-*dehr*	again
viderfarkoyf, *m.*	VEE-*dehr-far-koyf*	resale (*bus.*)
viderkol, *m.*	VEE-*dehr-kawl*	echo
vider nemen (8)	VEE-*dehr* NEH-*men*	resume (recommence), to
vie, *f.*	VEE-*eh*	eyelash
"	"	lash
vi es iz	VEE *ess* EEZ	somehow
vig, *f.*	VEEG	cradle
vign zikh (1)	VEEG-*in zikh*	reel (stagger), to
"	"	sway, to
"	"	swing (oscillate), to
vikhtik	VEEKH-*tick*	important
vikuakh, *m.*	*vee-*KOO-*ukh*	argument
"	"	dispute
vild	VEELD	savage (*adj.*)
"	"	wild (undomesticated)
vildgroz, *n.*	VEELD-*grawz*	weed
vildland, *n.*	VEELD-*lahnd*	wilderness
viln, *m.*	VEE-*lin*	will (power of choice)
Vin, *n.*	VEEN	Vienna
viner	VEE-*nehr*	Viennese (*adj.*)
vinken (8)	VEEN-*ken*	wink, to
vinkl, *m.*	VEEN-*kil*	angle (*geom.*)
"	"	corner
vint, *m.*	VEENT	wind
vinter, *m.*	VEEN-*tehr*	winter (*n.*)
vintik	VEEN-*tick*	windy (windswept)
vintl, *n.*	VEEN-*til*	breeze
vintpokn, *pl.*	VEENT-*paw-kin*	chicken-pox
vintshn (8)	VEEN-*chin*	wish (desire on behalf of), to
vintshoyb, *f.*	VEENT-*shoyb*	windshield
vintsik	VEENT-*sick*	few
"	"	little (not much, *adj.*)
"	"	little (slightly, *adv.*)
"	"	little (small amount, *n.*)
vintsiker	VEENT-*see-kehr*	less
viole, *f.*	*vee-*AW-*leh*	viola
violontshel, *m.*	*vee-aw-lawn-*CHELL	cello
vire, *f.*	VEE-*reh*	ruler (measuring instrument)
virkn oyf (1)	VEER-*kin oyf*	affect (influence), to
vishn (1)	VEE-*shin*	wipe (make dry by wiping), to

Yiddish	Pronunciation	English
visik	VEE-*sick*	conscious (aware)
visn,*n.*	VEE-*sin*	knowledge (information)
visn (26e)	VEE-*sin*	know (have knowledge), to
visndik	VEE-*sin-dick*	aware
visnshaft,*f.*	VEE-*sin-shahft*	science
visnshaftlekh	VEE-*sin-shahft-lukh*	scientific
visnshaftler,*m.*	VEE-*sin-shahft-lehr*	scientist
vist	VEEST	dismal
viste-onvayzung,*f.*	VEE-*steh-awn-vie-zoon_g*	sight draft (*bus.*)
vitamin,*m.*	*vee-tah-*MEEN	vitamin
vits,*m.*	VEETS	joke (jest)
vitsik	VEET-*sick*	witty
vitsikayt,*f.*	VEET-*see-kite*	wit (humor)
vitslen zikh (1)	VEETS-*len zikh*	joke (jest), to
vizit,*m.*	*vee-*ZEET	visit (social call)
vizye,*f.*	VEEZ-*yeh*	vision (foresight)
vog,*f.*	VAWG	scales (balance)
"	"	weight (scale weight)
voglen (1)	VAWG-*len*	roam, to
vogn,*m.*	VAWG-*in*	cart
vokh,*f.*	VAWKH	week
vokhn-...	VAW-*khin-*...	weekly (*adj.*)
vokzal,*m.*	*vawk-*ZAHL	depot (station)
vol,*f.*	VAWL	wool
volf,*m.*	VAWLF	wolf
volkn,*m.*	VAWL-*kin*	cloud
volkndik	VAWL-*kin-dik*	cloudy (overcast)
volkn-kratser,*m.*	VAWL-*kin-kraht-sehr*	skyscraper
volontir,*m.*	*vaw-lawn-*TEER	volunteer (*mil.*)
volt (30)	VAULT	would (*v.*)
volt gekent	VAULT *g_eh-*KENT	could (*v.*)
"	"	might (*v.*)
volvl	VAWL-*vil*	cheap (inexpensive)
vontses,*pl.*	VAWNT-*sess*	mustache
vor,*f.*	VORE	reality
vorem	VAW-*rem*	for (*conj.*)
vorem,*m.*	VAW-*rem*	worm
vorenen (3)	VAW-*reh-nen*	caution, to
"	"	warn, to
vort,*n.*	VORT	word
vortshen (2)	VOR-*chen*	growl, to
vortsl,*m.*	VORT-*sil*	root (*bot.*)
vos	VAWSS	that (*rel. pron.*)
"	"	what (*interrog. pron.*)
"	"	what (*rel. pron.*)
"	"	which (*rel. pron.*)
"	"	who (*rel. pron.*)
"	"	whom (*rel. pron.*)
vos es iz	VAWSS *ess* EEZ	anything (something)
vos nor	VAWSS *nor*	whatever (*pron.*)
voyen (2)	VAW-*yen*	howl (wail), to
voyl	VOYL	nice (agreeable)
voylshtand,*m.*	VOYL-*shtahnd*	welfare (well-being)
voynen (1)	VOY-*nen*	dwell (reside), to
"	"	live, to
voynen in	VOY-*nen in*	occupy (live in), to
voynort,*n.*	VOY-*nort*	residence (abode)
voynung,*f.*	VOY-*noon_g*	dwelling
vrak,*m.*	VRAHK	wreck (ruins)
vu	VOO	where (in, at the place that, *conj.*)
"	"	where (in, at what place, *adv.*)
vu es iz	VOO *ess* EEZ	anywhere (wheresoever)
vuhin	*voo-*HEEN	where (to what place, *adv.*)
vuks,*m.*	VOOX	growth (development)
vulgar	*vool-*GAHR	vulgar (ill-bred)
vulkan,*m.*	*vool-*KAHN	volcano
vund,*f.*	VOOND	injury
"	"	wound
vunder,*m.*	VOON-*dehr*	marvel
vunderlekh	VOON-*dehr-lukh*	marvelous
"	"	wonderful

Yiddish	Pronunciation	English
vu nor	VOO *nor*	wherever (at, in whatever place)
vursht,*f.*	VOORSHT	sausage
vu s'zol nit zayn	VOO *s-zawl nit* ZINE	wherever (no matter where)
yaboshe,*f.*	*yah-*BAW-*sheh*	land (ground)
yagde,*f.*	YAHG-*deh*	berry (fruit)
yagde, shvartse,*f.*	SHVAR-*tseh* YAHG-*deh*	blueberry
yak,*m.*	YAHK	jacket (short coat)
yam-...	YAHM-...	marine (oceanic)
yam,*m.*	YAHM	sea
yam-breg,*m.*	YAHM-*breg*	coast (seaboard)
yam-hunt,*m.*	YAHM-*hoont*	seal (animal)
Yapan,*n.*	*yah-*PAHN	Japan
yapanish	*yah-*PAH-*nish*	Japanese (*adj.*)
yarshenen (3)	YAR-*sheh-nen*	inherit, to
yasle,*f.*	YAHSS-*leh*	gum (*anat.*)
yeder	YEH-*dehr*	any (*adj.*)
"	"	each (*adj.*)
"	"	every
yederer	YEH-*deh-rehr*	each (apiece, *adv.*)
"	"	each one (*pron.*)
yeder eyner	YEH-*dehr* AY-*nehr*	everybody
"	"	everyone
yedie,*f.*	*yeh-*DEE-*eh*	communication
"	"	message
yeger,*m.*	YEGG-*ehr*	hunter
yeloles, makhn (1)	MAH-*khin yeh-*LAW-*less*	wail, to
yene	YEH-*neh*	those (*adj.*)
"	"	those (*pron.*)
yener	YEH-*nehr*	that (*dem. adj.*)
yeride,*f.*	*yeh-*REE-*deh*	decline (deterioration)
yerlekh	YEHR-*lukh*	annual
yerushedikayt,*f.*	*yeh-*ROO-*sheh-dee-kite*	heredity
Yerusholaim,*n.*	*yeh-roo-shaw-*LAH-*im*	Jerusalem
yesod,*m.*	*yeh-*SAWD	basis
yesurim, *pl.*	*ye-*SOO-*rim*	agony (mental pain)
Yezus	YEH-*zooss*	Jesus
Yid,*m.*	YEED	Jew (*n.*)
yidish	YEE-*dish*	Jewish (*adj.*)
yinger	YEEN_G-*ehr*	junior (younger)
yingl,*m.*	YEEN-*g_il*	boy (lad)
yiras-hakoved,*m.*	YEE-*rahss-hah-*KAW-*vehd*	awe
yishev,*m.*	YEE-*shev*	reflection (meditation)
"	"	settlement (colony)
Yisroel,*n.*	*yis-*RAW-*ell*	Israel
yisroeylish	*yis-ro-*AY-*lish*	Israeli (*adj.*)
yiush,*m.*	YEE-*oosh*	despair (hopelessness)
yiush, zayn in	ZINE *in* YEE-*oosh*	despair, to
yo	YAW	yes
yod,*m.*	YAWD	iodine (antiseptic)
yog,*f.*	YAWG	pursuit (chase)
yog,*m.*	YAWG	rush (rapid motion)
yokh,*m.*	YAWKH	yoke (wooden frame)
yokhid,*m.*	YAW-*khid*	individual (person, *n.*)
yontev,*m.*	YAWN-*tev*	festival
"	"	holiday
yor,*n.*	YORE	year
yorgelt,*n.*	YORE-*g_elt*	annuity
yorhundert,*m.*	*yor-*HOON-*dehrt*	century
yorik	YAW-*rick*	yearly (*adj.*)
yortog,*m.*	YORE-*tawg*	anniversary
yosem,*m.*	YAW-*sem*	orphan (*n.*)
yoykh,*f.*	YOY_KH	gravy
yoyresh,*m.*	YOY-*resh*	heir
yoysherdik	YOY-*shehr-dick*	fair (impartial)
"	"	fairly (impartially)
Yugoslavye,*f.*	*yoo-gaw-*SLAHV-*yeh*	Yugoslavia
yugnt,*f.*	YOOG-*int*	youthfulness
yugntlekh	YOOG-*int-lukh*	youthful
yung	YOON_G	young (*adj.*)
yung,*m.*	YOON_G	lad
yunger-man,*m.*	*yoon-g_ehr-*MAHN	youth (young man)
zaft,*m.*	ZAHFT	juice
zak,*m.*	ZAHK	sack (bag)
zakh,*f.*	ZAH_KH	thing (material object)

Yiddish	Pronunciation	English
zal,m.	ZAHL	auditorium
"		hall (meeting room)
zalb,f.	ZAHLB	ointment
zalts,f.	ZAHLTS	salt
zamd,n.	ZAHMD	sand
zamdik	ZAHM-dick	sandy
zamen zikh (1)	ZAH-men zikh	linger (tarry), to
zamlung,f.	ZAHM-loon_g	collection
zapas,m.	zah-PAHSS	stock
"	"	supply (amount available)
zats,m.	ZAHTS	sentence (gram.)
zaverukhe,f.	zah-veh-ROO-kheh	blizzard
zayd,n.	ZIDE	silk (n.)
zayen (1)	ZIE-en	strain (filter), to
zayern (1)	ZAH-yeh-rin	pickle (preserve), to
zayers,n.	ZYE-ehrss	acid
zayl,m.	ZILE	column
"	"	pillar
zayn	ZINE	his (poss. adj.)
"	"	its (poss. adj.)
zayn (18d)	ZINE	be, to
zayner	ZYE-nehr	his (poss. pron.)
"	"	its (poss. pron.)
zayt,f.	ZITE	page (leaf)
"	"	side
zayt fun bergl,f.	ZITE foon BEHRG-il	hillside
zebre,f.	ZEB-reh	zebra
zeg,f.	ZEGG	saw (tool)
zekl,n.	ZEH-kil	bag (sack)
zelbik	ZEL-bick	same (adj.)
zelbstmord,m.	ZELBST-mord	suicide
zelner,m.	ZELL-nehr	soldier
zeltn	ZELL-tin	rare (uncommon)
"	"	seldom
zeml,f.	ZEH-mil	roll (bread)
zen (6)	ZEN	see, to
zeneft,m.	ZEH-neft	mustard
zets,m.	ZETS	punch (blow)
zetsn zikh (1)	ZET-sin zikh	sit down, to
zey	ZAY	them
"	"	they
zeyde,m.	ZAY-deh	grandfather
zeyen (1)	ZAY-en	sow, to
zeyer	ZAY-ehr	their
"	"	very (extremely)
zeyerer	ZAY-eh-rehr	theirs
zeyf,f.	ZAFE	soap
zeyger,m.	ZAY-gehr	clock
"	"	time (hour determined by clock)
"	"	watch (timepiece)
zhabe,f.	ZHAH-beh	frog
"	"	toad
zhaver,m.	ZHAH-vehr	rust
zhaverfray shtol, n.	ZHAH-vehr-fry SHTAWL	stainless steel
zhedne	ZHED-neh	anxious (wanting very much)
Zhenev,n.	zheh-NEV	Geneva
zhrebtshik,m.	ZHREB-chik	colt
zhuk,m.	ZHOOK	beetle
"	"	bug (insect)
zhuri,f.	zhoo-REE	jury
zhurnal,m.	zhoor-NAHL	journal
"	"	magazine (periodical)
zhvir,m.	ZHVEER	gravel
zi	ZEE	she
zidlen zikh (1)	ZEED-len zikh	curse (swear), to
ziftsn (1)	ZEEFT-sin	sigh, to
zigl,m.	ZEEG-il	seal (mark)
zikh	ZIKH	herself
"	"	himself
"	"	itself
"	"	myself
"	"	ourselves
"	"	self (pron.)
"	"	themselves
"	"	yourself
"	"	yourselves
zikher	ZEE-khehr	certain
"	"	certainly (surely, adv.)
"	"	safe (without risk)
"	"	secure
"	"	sure
zikher bay zikh	ZEE-khehr bay zikh	confident (self-assured)
zikherkayt,f.	ZEE-khehr-kite	safety (n.)
"	"	security
zikher-nodl,f.	ZEE-khehr-naw-dil	safety pin
zikhroynes,pl.	zeekh-ROY-ness	memory (recollection)
zikorn,m.	zee-KAW-rin	memory (ability to recall)
zilber,n.	ZEEL-behr	silver (metal, n.)
zind,f.	ZEEND	sin
zindiker,m.	ZEEN-dee-kehr	sinner
zindikn (1)	ZEEN-dee-kin	sin, to
zingen (8d)	ZEEN_G-en	sing, to
zinger,m.	ZEEN_G-ehr	singer
zinken (8d)	ZEEN-ken	sink (fall slowly), to
zint	ZEENT	since (after, prep.)
zipn (1)	ZEE-pin	sift (separate), to
zis	ZEESS	sweet (pleasant tasting)
ziskayt,f.	ZEESS-kite	sweetness
zitsn (15d)	ZEET-sin	perch, to
"	"	sit (be sitting), to
zitsort,n.	ZEETS-ort	seat
zitsung,f.	ZEE-tsoon_g	conference (meeting)
zitsvagon,m.	ZEETS-vah-gawn	coach, railroad
zivegshaft,f.	ZEE-veg-shahft	marriage
zogn (1)	ZAWG-in	say, to
"	"	tell (inform), to
zok,m.	ZAWK	stocking
zokher,m.	ZAW-khehr	male (n.)
zoknbendl,n.	ZAW-kin-ben-dil	garter
zoln (1e)	ZAW-lin	should (v.)
zomen,m.	ZAW-men	seed (ovule)
zone,f.	ZAW-neh	zone
zoologisher gortn, m.	zaw-oh-LAWG-ee-shehr GOR-tin	zoo
zoologye,f.	zaw-oh-LAWG-yeh	zoology
zorg,f.	ZORG	care (concern)
zotl,m.	ZAW-til	saddle (seat)
zoyer	ZOY-ehr	sour (tart)
zoyershtof,m.	ZAW-yehr-shtawf	oxygen
zoygn (5)	ZOYG-in	suck, to
zoym,m.	ZOYM	hem
zukhenish,f.	zoo-kheh-nish	search (hunt)
zukhn (1)	zoo-khin	look for, to
zukhn,n.	zoo-khin	quest (search)
zukhtsetl,n.	zookh-tseh-til	index (list)
zumer,m.	zoo-mehr	summer (n.)
zump,m.	zoomp	marsh
"	"	moor (waste land)
zump,m.	zoomp	swamp (n.)
zun,f.	zoon	sun
zun,m.	zoon	son
zunbriln,pl.	zoon-bree-lin	sunglasses
zunenshayn,f.	zoo-nen-shine	sunshine
zunik	zoo-nick	sunny
zunlikht,f.	zoon-leekht	sunlight
zunoyfgang,m.	zoon-oyf-gan_g	sunrise
zun-untergang,m.	zoon-oon-tehr-gan_g	sunset
zup,f.	zoop	soup
zupn (1)	zoo-pin	sip, to

Yiddish Special Lists

Alphabet

Yiddish is normally written in a modified Hebrew alphabet. The names of the Yiddish letters in their standard order, the pronunciation of those names and the usual phonetic values of the letters follow.

alef	AH-*lef*	(mute)	pasakh tsvey yudn	PAH-*sukh* TSVAY YOO-*din*	ay
pasakh alef	PAH-*sukh* AH-*lef*	a	kof	KAWF	k
komets alef	KAW-*mets* AH-*lef*	o	khof	KH_AWF	kh
beyz	BAZE	b	lamed	LAH-*med*	l
veyz	VAZE	v	mem	MEM	m
giml	G_EE-*mil*	g	nun	NOON	n
daled	DAH-*led*	d	samekh	SAH-*mekh*	s
hey	HAY	h	ayen	AH-*yen*	e
vov	VAWV	u	pey	PAY	p
melupm vov	meh-LOO-*pim* VAWV	u	fay	FAY	f
tsvey vovn	TSVAY VAW-*vin*	v	tsadik	TSAH-*dick*	ts
zayen	ZAH-*yen*	z	kuf	KOOF	k
khes	KHESS	kh	reysh	RAYSH	r
tes	TESS	t	shin	SHEEN	sh
yud	YOOD	i, y	sin	SEEN	s
khirik yud	KHEE-*rick* YOOD	i	tof	TAWF	t
tsvey yudn	TSVAY YOO-*din*	ey	sof	SAWF	s

For the designation of letters of the Latin alphabet when the need arises, it is customary in Yiddish to adopt the names used in the country where the speakers or writers live; thus, the Latin letter *h* might in Yiddish be called AYCH in English-speaking countries, AHSH in France, HAH in Poland, etc.

Cardinal Numbers

Yiddish	Pronunciation	English	Yiddish	Pronunciation	English
eyns	ANE_SS	one	tsvey un tsvantsik	TSVAY *oon* TSVAHN-*tsick*	twenty-two
tsvey	TSVAY	two	draysik	DRY-*sick*	thirty
dray	DRY	three	fertsik	FEHR-*tsick*	forty
fir	FEER	four	fuftsik	FOOF-*tsick*	fifty
finf	FEENF	five	zekhtsik	ZEKH-*tsick*	sixty
zeks	ZEX	six	zibetsik	ZEE-*beh-tsick*	seventy
zibn	ZEE-*bin*	seven	akhtsik	AH_KH-*tsick*	eighty
akht	AH_KHT	eight	nayntsik	NINE-*tsick*	ninety
nayn	NINE	nine	hundert	HOON-*dehrt*	one hundred
tsen	TSEN	ten	hundert eyns	HOON-*dehrt* ANE_SS	one hundred one
elf	ELF	eleven	tsvey hundert	TSVAY HOON-*dehrt*	two hundred
tsvelf	TSVELF	twelve	tsvey hundert eyns	TSVAY HOON-*dehrt* ANE_SS	two hundred one
draytsn	DRY-*tsin*	thirteen			
fertsn	FEHR-*tsin*	fourteen	toyznt	TOY-*zint*	one thousand
fuftsn	FOOF-*tsin*	fifteen	toyznt un eyns	TOY-*zint oon* ANE_SS	one thousand and one
zekhtsn	ZEKH-*tsin*	sixteen	tsvey toyznt	TSVAY TOY-*zint*	two thousand
zibetsn	ZEE-*beh-tsin*	seventeen	tsvey toyznt un eyns	TSVAY TOY-*zint oon* ANE_SS	two thousand one
akhtsn	AH_KH-*tsin*	eighteen			
nayntsn	NINE-*tsin*	nineteen	eyn milyon	ANE *mil*-YAWN	one million
tsvantsik	TSVAHN-*tsick*	twenty	eyn milyard	ANE *mil*-YARD	one billion
eyn un tsvantsik	ANE *oon* TSVAHN-*tsick*	twenty-one			

Ordinal Numbers

Yiddish	Pronunciation	English	Yiddish	Pronunciation	English
ershter	EHR-*shtehr*	first	zibeter	ZEE-*beh-tehr*	seventh
tsveyter	TSVAY-*tehr*	second	akhter	AH_KH-*tehr*	eighth
driter	DREE-*tehr*	third	naynter	NINE-*tehr*	ninth
ferter	FEHR-*tehr*	fourth	tsenter	TSEN-*tehr*	tenth
finfter	FEENF-*tehr*	fifth	elfter	ELF-*tehr*	eleventh
zekster	ZEX-*tehr*	sixth	tsvelfter	TSVELF-*tehr*	twelfth

Days of the Week

Yiddish	Pronunciation	English	Yiddish	Pronunciation	English
zuntik,*m.*	ZOON-*tick*	Sunday	donershtik,*m.*	DAW-*nehrsh-tick*	Thursday
montik,*m.*	MAWN-*tick*	Monday	fraytik,*m.*	FRY-*tick*	Friday
dinstik,*m.*	DEEN-*stick*	Tuesday	shabes,*m.*	SHAH-*bess*	Saturday
mitvokh,*m.*	MEET-*vawkh*	Wednesday			

Months of the Year

Yiddish	Pronunciation	English	Yiddish	Pronunciation	English
Yanuar,*m.*	YAH-*noo-ahr*	January	Yuli,*m.*	YOO-*lee*	July
Februar,*m.*	FEB-*roo-ahr*	February	Oygust,*m.*	*oy*-GOOST	August
Marts,*m.*	MARTS	March	September,*m.*	*sep*-TEM-*behr*	September
April,*m.*	*ahp*-REEL	April	Oktober,*m.*	*awk*-TAW-*behr*	October
May,*m.*	MY	May	November,*m.*	*naw*-VEM-*behr*	November
Yuni,*m.*	YOO-*nee*	June	Detsember,*m.*	*det*-SEM-*behr*	December

First Names

Yiddish	Pronunciation	English	Yiddish	Pronunciation	English
Aleksander	*ah-leck-*SAHN*-dehr*	Alexander	Rivke	REEV*-keh*	Rebecca
Avrohom	*ahv-*RAW*-hum*	Abraham	Shmuel	SHMOO*-el*	Samuel
Ayzik	EYE*-zick*	Isaac	Shoul	SHAW*-ool*	Saul
Binyomin	*bin-*YAW*-min*	Benjamin			
Doniel	*daw-*NEE*-el*	Daniel	Sore	SAW*-reh*	Sarah
Dovid	DAW*-vid*	David	Yankev	YAHN*-kev*	Jacob
			Yehudis	*yeh-*HOO*-diss*	Judith
Khane	KHAH*-neh*	Anna	Yitskhok	YITS*-khawk*	Isaac
Leyb	LABE	Leo	Yoysef	YOY*-sef*	Joseph
Mikhoel	*mee-*KHAW*-el*	Michael			

USEFUL EXPRESSIONS

Greetings

English	Pronunciation	Yiddish
How are you?	*vawss* MAH_KHT *eer?*	Vos makht ir?
Well, thanks, and you?	GOOT, *ah* DAHNK, *oon* EER?	Gut, a dank, un ir?
Good morning.	*goot* MOR*-g_in.*	Gut morgn.
Good afternoon.	*gawt* HELF.	Got helf.
Good evening.	*goo-tin* AW*-vint.*	Gutn ovnt.
Good night.	*ah* GOO*-teh* NAH_KHT.	A gute nakht.
See you again.	*meh vet zikh* ZEN.	Me vet zikh zen.
So long.	ZITE *geh-*ZOONT.	Zayt gezunt.
Good luck!	*zawl* ZINE *mit* MAH*-zil!*	Zol zayn mit mazl!
Good-by.	*ah* GOO*-tin.*	A gutn.
Glad to meet you.	*tsoo-*FREE*-din eye_kh tsoo* KEH*-nen.*	Tsufridn aykh tsu kenen.
Congratulations.	MAH*-zil-tawv.*	Mazl-tov.
Happy Birthday!	MAH*-zil-tawv (tsoom g_eh-*BOY*-rin-tawg)!*	Mazl-tov (tsum geboyrn-tog)!
Merry Christmas.	*ah* FRAY*-luh-khin* NEE*-til.*	A freylekhn nitl.
Happy New Year.	*a* GLEEK*-lukh-khin* NY*-yor.*	A gliklekhn nay-yor.

Ordinary Conversation

English	Pronunciation	Yiddish
Thank you.	*ah* DAHNK.	A dank.
Please.	ZITE *ah-*ZOY GOOT.	Zayt azoy gut.
You're welcome.	*nee-*TAW *far* VAWSS.	Nito far vos.
Pardon me.	ZITE MOY*-khil.*	Zayt moykhl.
What do you call this?	*vee* HASTE *dawss?*	Vi heyst dos?
I'm sorry.	*ess* TOOT *meer* LAID.	Es tut mir leyd.
Allow me.	ZITE MOY*-khil.*	Zayt moykhl.
I would like...	*ikh vawlt* VEH*-lin...*	Ikh volt veln...
Come in.	*ah-*RINE.	Arayn.
May I introduce...	*bah-*KENT *zikh mit...*	Bakent zikh mit...
What is your name?	*vee* HASTE *eer?*	Vi heyst ir?
My name is...	*ikh* HACE...	Ikh heys...
I don't know.	*ikh* VACE *nit.*	Ikh veys nit.
I'm thirsty.	*ikh bin* DORSH*-tick.*	Ikh bin dorshtik.
I'm hungry.	*ikh bin* HOON*-g_eh-rick.*	Ikh bin hungerik.
I'm an American.	*ikh bin ahn ah-meh-ree-*KAH*-nehr.*	Ikh bin an Amerikaner.
Where can I find...?	VOO *ken ikh g_eh-*FEE*-nen...?*	Vu ken ikh gefinen...?
What is this?	VAWSS *iz* DAWSS?	Vos iz dos?

Foreign Languages

English	Pronunciation	Yiddish
Do you speak...?	*tsee* RET *eer...?*	Tsi redt ir...?
I speak(understand) a little...	*ikh* RED *(far-*SHTAY*) ah* BEE*-sil...*	Ikh red (farshtey) a bisl...
I do not speak...	*ikh* RED *nit kane...*	Ikh red nit keyn...
Is there someone here who speaks English?	*tsee* RET *daw* EH*-meh-tsehr* ENG*-lish?*	Tsi redt do emetser english?
I understand you.	*ikh far-*SHTAY *eye_kh.*	Ikh farshtey aykh.
I don't understand.	*ikh far-*SHTAY *nit.*	Ikh farshtey nit.
Please speak more slowly.	RET *pah-*MEH*-luh-khehr,* ZITE *ah-*ZOY GOOT.	Redt pamelekher, zayt azoy gut.
Please repeat.	KHAH*-zehrt* EE*-behr,* ZITE *ah-zoy* GOOT.	Khazert iber, zayt azoy gut.

Asking Directions

English	Pronunciation	Yiddish
In which direction is...?	*in* VEL*-khehr* REEKH*-toon_g iz...?*	In velkher rikhtung iz...?
Please take me to...	FEERT *mikh* TSOO, *ikh bet eye_kh, tsoo...*	Firt mikh tsu, ikh bet aykh, tsu...
Please take me there.	FEERT *mikh* TSOO *ah-*HEEN, *ikh* BET *eye_kh.*	Firt mikh tsu ahin, ikh bet aykh.
Where can I mail this?	VOO *ken ikh dawss* AWP*-shee-kin?*	Vu ken ikh dos opshikn?
Please direct me to...	VIZE_T *meer, ikh* BET *eye_kh, voo iz...*	Vayzt mir, ikh bet aykh, vu iz...
...the telephone.	*...dehr teh-leh-*FAWN.	...der telefon.
...the toilet.	*...dehr klaw-*ZET.	...der klozet.
...the post office.	*...dee* PAWST.	...di post.

English	Pronunciation	Yiddish
...the bank.	...*dee* BAHNK.	...di bank.
...the police station.	...*dee* paw-lee-TSAY-*stahnts-yeh.*	...di politsey-stantsye.
...the U. S. consulate.	...*dehr* kawn-soo-LAHT *foon dee* fah-RAY-*nick-teh* SHTAH-*tin.*	...der konsulat fun di Fareynikte Shtatn.
Please point.	VIZE_T, ZITE *ah-zoy* GOOT.	Vayzt, zayt azoy gut.

The Hotel

English	Pronunciation	Yiddish
I would like a room...	*ikh vawlt* VEH-*lin ah* TSEE-*mehr...*	Ikh volt veln a tsimer...
...with a single bed.	...*mit ahn* ANE-*tsick* BET.	...mit an eynstik bet.
...with two beds.	...*mit* TSVAY BEH-*tin.*	...mit tsvey betn.
...with bath.	...*mit ah* VAH-*neh.*	...mit a vane.
...without meals.	...AWN MAWL-*tsye-tin.*	...on moltsaytn.
Please, the key for Room...	ZITE *ah-zoy* GOOT, *dem* SHLEE-*sil tsoom* TSEE-*mehr...*	Zayt azoy gut, dem shlisl tsum tsimer...
Please call me at...o'clock.	KLEENGT *meer, ikh* BET *eye_kh,...ah-*ZAYG-*ehr.*	Klingt mir, ikh bet aykh,...a zeyger.
I want this...	*ikh vawlt* VEH-*lin men zawl dawss..*	Ikh volt veln men zol dos...
...pressed.	...OYSS-*preh-sin.*	...oyspresn.
...cleaned.	...OYSS-*ray-nee-kin.*	...oysreynikn.
...washed.	...EE-*behr-vah-shin.*	...ibervashn.
...repaired.	...*far-*REEKH-*tin.*	...farrikhtn.
When will (my suit) be returned?	VEN *vet men* OOM-*keh-rin (mine kawst-*YOOM)?	Ven vet men umkern (mayn kostyum)?
Please return (my suit) at...	ZITE *ah-zoy* GOOT, BRENG_T AWP *(mine kawst-*YOOM)...*ah-*ZAY-*g_ehr.*	Zayt azoy gut, brengt op (mayn kostyum)... a zeyger.

The Restaurant

English	Pronunciation	Yiddish
A table for two, please.	*ah* TEESH *far* TSVAY-*en,* ZITE *ah-zoy* GOOT.	A tish far tsveyen, zayt azoy gut.
I would like to see the menu.	*ikh vawlt* VEH-*lin zen dem meh-*NEW.	Ikh volt veln zen dem menyu.
I want it...	*ikh* VEEL *ess...*	Ikh vil es...
...rare.	...NEET *dehr-*KAW_KHT.	...nit derkokht.
...medium.	...HAHLB-DOORKH-*g_eh-kaw_kht.*	...halb-durkhgekokht.
...well-done.	...GOOT DOORKH-*g_eh-kaw_kht.*	...gut durkhgekokht.
Check, please!	*dem* KHEZH-*bin,* ZITE *ah-*ZOY GOOT!	Dem khezhbn, zayt azoy gut!

Telephoning

English	Pronunciation	Yiddish
I wish to telephone.	*ikh* VEEL *tel-leh-faw-*NEE-*rin.*	Ikh vil telefonirn.
Please get me this number.	ZITE *ah-*ZOY GOOT *oon far-*BINT *mikh mit* DEM NOO-*mehr.*	Zayt azoy gut un farbindt mikh mit dem numer.
Please give me the number of...	ZITE *ah-*ZOY GOOT *oon* G_EET *meer dem* NOO-*mehr foon...*	Zayt azoy gut un git mir dem numer fun...
What did you say?	VAWSS *hawt eer g_eh-*ZAWGT?	Vos hot ir gezogt?
The line is busy.	*dee* LEEN-*yeh iz far-*NOO-*men.*	Di linye iz farnumen.
What is the charge?	VEE-*fil bah-*TREFT *der* AWP-*tsawl?*	Vifl batreft der optsol?

Time

English	Pronunciation	Yiddish
What time is it?	VEE-*fil iz dehr* ZAYG-*ehr?*	Vifl iz der zeyger?
It is...	*ess iz...*	Es iz...
...five o'clock.	...FEENF *ah* ZAYG-*ehr.*	...finf a zeyger.
...ten past eight.	...TSEN *nawkh* AH_KHT.	...tsen nokh akht.
...a quarter past six.	...*ah* FEHR-*til nawkh* ZEX.	...a fertl nokh zeks.
...half past five.	...HAHLB *nawkh* FEENF.	...halb nokh finf.
...five to seven.	...FEENF *tsoo* ZEE-*bin.*	...finf tsu zibn.
The day before yesterday	AY-*ehr-nekh-tin*	Eyernekhtn
Yesterday evening	NEKH-*tin in* AW-*vint*	Nekhtn in ovnt
This morning	HINE_T *in dehr* FREE	Haynt in der fri
At noon	MEE-*lawg-tsite*	Mitogtsayt
In the afternoon	NAWKH MEE-*tawg*	Nokh mitog
In the evening	*in* AW-*vint*	In ovnt
At night	*by* NAH_KHT	Bay nakht
At midnight	*oom* HAHL-*beh* NAH_KHT	Um halbe nakht
Tomorrow morning	MORG-*in in dehr* FREE	Morgn in der fri
Tomorrow evening	MORG-*in in* AW-*vint*	Morgn in ovnt
The day after tomorrow	EE-*behr morg-in*	Iber morgn

Weather

English	Pronunciation	Yiddish
It's hot.	*siz* HACE.	S'iz heys.
It's cold.	*siz* KAHLT.	S'iz kalt.
It's raining.	*ess* REG-*int.*	Es regnt.
It's snowing.	*ess* SHNATE.	Es shneyt.
What fine weather!	*sah-rah* SHANE VEH-*tehr!*	Sara sheyn veter!

Postal Information

English	Pronunciation	Yiddish
How much is the postage on this?	VEE-*fil* MAR-*kess* oyf DEM?	Vifl markes oyf dem?
Give me...worth of stamps.	G_EET *meer far*...MAR-*kess*.	Git mir far...markes.
Please send this letter...	ZITE *ah*-ZOY GOOT *oon* SHEEKT *dem* BREEV...	Zayt azoy gut un shikt dem briv...
...airmail.	...*mit* LOOFT-*pawst*.	...mit luftpost.
...special delivery.	...*ex*-PRESS.	...ekspres.
...registered.	...*reg-iss*-TREERT.	...registrirt.
Please send this parcel post.	ZITE *ah*-ZOY GOOT *oon* SHEEKT *dawss vee a* PEH-*kil*.	Zayt azoy gut un shikt dos vi a pekl.

Barber and Beauty Shop

English	Pronunciation	Yiddish
I want a haircut.	*ikh* VEEL *zikh* AWP-*sheh-rin*.	Ikh vil zikh opshern.
Not too short.	NEET *tsoo* KOORTS.	Nit tsu kurts.
No hair oil, thank you.	*ah* DAHNK, AWN *paw*-MAH-*duh*.	A dank, on pomade.
I want a shave.	*ikh* VEEL *zikh* AWP-*rah-zee-rin*.	Ikh vil zikh oprazirn.
I want a shampoo.	*ikh* VEEL *zikh* OYSS-*vah-shin dee* HORE.	Ikh vil zikh oysvashn di hor.
I want my hair set.	*ikh* VEEL *ah* HORE-*free-zoor*.	Ikh vil a hor-frizur.

Transportation

English	Pronunciation	Yiddish
Where is the ticket office?	VOO *iz dee* KAH-*seh*?	Vu iz di kase?
When does the...arrive?	VENN *koomt* AWN DEHR...	Ven kumt on der...
...train...	...TSOOG?	...tsug?
...plane...	... *ah-eh-raw*-PLAHN?	...aeroplan?
...bus...	... *oy-taw*-BOOSS?	...oytobus?
At what time does the train leave for...?	VEE-*fil ah* ZAYG-*ehr fort* AWP *dehr* TSOOG *kane*...?	Vifl a zeyger fort op der tsug keyn...?
From which track does the train for... leave?	*foon* VEL-*khin peh*-RAWN *fort* AWP *dehr* TSOOG *kane*...?	Fun velkhn peron fort op der tsug keyn...?
Is this the right train for...?	*tsee iz* DAWSS *dehr* REEKH-*tee-kehr* TSOOG *kane*...?	Tsi iz dos der rikhtiker tsug keyn...?
Where is my baggage?	VOO *iz mine bah*-GAH_ZH?	Vu iz mayn bagazh?
Where is the baggage room?	VOO *iz dehr bah*-GAH_ZH-*tsee-mehr*?	Vu iz der bagazh-tsimer?
Please call a taxi.	ZITE *ah-zoy* GOOT *oon* ROOFT *ah* TAHK-*see*.	Zayt azoy gut un ruft a taksi.

Auto Travel

English	Pronunciation	Yiddish
What place is this?	VEE HASTE *dawss* ORT?	Vi heyst dos ort?
Where is the town?	VOO *iz dawss* SHTEH-*til*?	Vu iz dos shtetl?
Which is the best road for...?	VEL-*khehr iz dehr* BESS-*tehr shaw*-SAY *kane*...?	Velkher iz der bester shosey keyn...?
Turn to the right.	*far*-KEH-*reh-vet zikh oyf* REKHTS.	Farkerevet zikh oyf rekhts.
Turn to the left.	*far*-KEH-*reh-vet zikh oyf* LINX.	Farkerevet zikh oyf links.
Go straight on.	FORT GLYE_KH.	Fort glaykh.
Go back.	FORT *tsoo*-REEK.	Fort tsurik.
This way.	*doorkh* DAH-*nen*.	Durkh danen.
That way.	*doorkh* DOR-*tin*.	Durkh dortn.
How far is it to...?	*vee* VITE *iz biz*...?	Vi vayt iz biz...?
Is this the road to...?	*tsee iz* DAWSS *dehr* VEG *kane*...?	Tsi iz dos der veg keyn...?
Is it...	*tsee* EEZ *ess*...	Tsi iz es...
...near?	...NAW-*ent*?	...noent?
...far?	...VITE?	...vayt?
...very far?	...ZAY-*ehr* VITE?	...zeyer vayt?
Which way is...	VOO *iz*...	Vu iz...
...north?	...TSAW-*fin*?	...tsofn?
...south?	...DAW-*rem*?	...dorem?
...east?	...MEEZ-*rukh*?	...mizrakh?
...west?	...MY-*rev*?	...mayrev?
Is the road...?	*tsee* EEZ *dehr shaw*-SAY...?	Tsi iz der shosay...?
Is there a detour?	*tsee iz fah*-RAHN *ahn* OOM-*veg*?	Tsi iz faran an umveg?
What is the speed limit?	VEE-*fil iz dee mahk-see*-MAH-*leh* G_EEKH-*kite*?	Vifl iz di maksimale gikhkayt?
Where is the nearest gas station?	VOO *iz dee* NEH-*ents-teh gah-zaw*-LEEN-*stahnts-yeh*?	Vu iz di neentste gazolin-stantsye?
Where can I find a garage (for repairs)?	VOO *ken ikh g_eh*-FEE-*nen ah gah*-RAHZH?	Vu ken ikh gefinen a garazh?
I need...	*ikh darf*...	Ikh darf...
...oil.	...ALE.	...eyl.
...gasoline.	...*gah-zaw*-LEEN.	...gazolin.
...a tire.	...*ah* RAFE.	...a reyf.

Public Signs

English	Pronunciation	Yiddish
Keep Out	NEET *ah*-RINE-*gain*	Nit arayngeyn
For Hire	*tsoom far*-DEENG-*en*	Tsum fardingen

English	Pronunciation	Yiddish
No Parking	NEET PAR-*kin*	Nit parkn
No Smoking	NEET RAY-*kheh-rin*	Nit reykhern
Sale	OYSS-*far-koyf*	Oysfarkoyf
Women	FROY-*en*	Froyen
Men	MEH-*nehr*	Mener
No Spitting	NEET SHPAH-*yen*	Nit shpayen
Railroad	EYE-*zin-bahn*	Ayznban
Dangerous Curve	*g_eh*-FEHR-*lukh-ehr* OYSS-*bayg*	Geferlekher oysbeyg
Keep to the Right (Left)	HAHLT *zikh* REKHTS (LINX)	Halt zikh rekhts (links)
Dead End	BLEEND G_EH-*sil*	Blind gesl
Men Working	MENT-*shin* AR-*beh-tin*	Mentshn arbetn
No Thoroughfare	NEET *tsoom* DOORKH-*faw-rin*	Nit tsum durkhforn
One-way Street	ANE-REEKH-*toon_g-gahss*	Eyn-rikhtung-gas
Go slow	*pah*-VAWL-*yeh*	Pavolye
Toilet	AWP-*tret*	Optret
Entrance	*ah*-RINE-*gahn_g*	Arayngang
Exit	*ah*-ROYSS-*gahn_g*	Aroysgang

Yiddish Grammar

ARTICLES

Definite article

The definite article, "the," has the same gender, number and case as the noun with which it is used.

	Masc. Sing.	Fem. Sing.	Neuter Sing.	Masc., Fem., Neuter Pl.
Nominative	der	di	dos	di
Accusative	dem	di	dos	di
Dative and Possessive	dem	der	dem	di

Contractions of the definite article. The masculine and neuter definite article is commonly contracted with a preceding preposition, thus: *bay dem = baym, biz dem = bizn, far dem = farn, fun dem = funem, iber dem = ibern, in dem = inem, mit dem = mitn, nokh dem = nokhn, oyf dem = oyfn, tsu dem = tsum, unter dem = untern.*

Indefinite article

The indefinite article is usually *a*, but it is *an* if the following word begins with a vowel.

NOUNS

Plural of nouns

Yiddish nouns differ in the way they form their plurals. The nouns contained in this dictionary, if they form plurals at all, belong to the following categories:

Plural ending in -s, or in -es if so indicated

administratsye
aker
aktrise
aktsye
alergye
almen
almone
ambitsye
amortizatsye
anker
antene
antipatye
antlayer
antologye
aplikatsye
apteyker
arbeter
arbet-geber
ariberfirer
aroysgeber
arterye
asekuratsye
atake
atraktsye
avanture
avle
aynbrekher
ayntsoler
aynvoyner
ayzkastn
ayzn
bagleyter
bakoshe
baleboste
balkn
britve
brokhe
brukve
brunetin
bsule
bukhhalter
burik (es)
buzem
dambe
date
dayge
debate
deklaratsye
demb
demokratye
depresye
deye
diameter
diete
diner
dire
diskusye
dispozitsye
divizye
dlonye
doze
drame
droysn
druker
ekspeditsye
ekzamen

eln-boygn
elter
emer
emotsye
emune
energye
entfer
entsiklopedye
epidemye
evenyu
eydem
eytse
falshe shvue
familye
fantazye
farbrekher
fargenign
farkoyfer
farmegn
farmer
farreter
farvalter
fasolye
fayer-lesher
faynkukhn
faze
fershke
feter
feye
filosofye
firer
firme
fisher
fistashke
flier
flokn
forshteyer
forzitser
foter
fotografye
frage
frayln
frimorgn
funktsye
futer
galerye
ganeydn
ganik (es)
garantye
gare
garn
garniter
gehenem
gelekhter
gertner
geshikhte
geule
gevisn
glitsher
glorye
golmeser
gombe
gorn
grable
grate
greber

grinder
gripe
grive
grub (mine)
grupe
gvure
hafsoke
hakdome
hakhnose
halvoe
hamer
hanokhe
harmonye
hashpoe
haskhole
haskome
hasoge
hatslokhe
havtokhe
heldin
hentshke
hersher
heyber
hoyker
hoytsoe
idee
ilustratsye
iluzye
imperye
importirer
indik (es)
industrye
informatsye
inspiratsye
institutsye
intuitsye
investitsye
kabole
kale
kalike
kalorye
kaluzhe
kampanye
kanape
kanarik (es)
kane
kapelye
karete
kark (es)
karlik (es)
karte
kartofl (es)
karyere
kashe
kasirer
kaske
kastn
katastrofe
katshke
kavenik (es)
kavone
kayute

kegener
keler
kelner
kerme
keshene
keyserin
kharpe
khasene
khate
khaye
khezhbn-firer
khokhme
khoyv (es)
khronik (es)
khsime
khurve
khvalye
kinigin
kino
kinstler
kishef-makher
kishke
kishn
klatshe
klem (clam)
klole
kloyster
kloyster-turem
kokteyl
koldre
kolonye
komande
kombinatsye
kome
komedye
komisye
kompanye
kompensatsye
konfiskatsye
kongregatsye
konstitutsye
konstruktsye
konte
kontrabande
konyunktsye
kopete
kopye
kore
korporatsye
koyfer
koymen
kretshme
kritiker
kruk (es)
krume
kshak (es)
kubik
kukavke
kukher
kukhn
kule
kupe (heap, pile)
kust
kvote
kvure

labn
laboratorye
lakhodim-hendler
lalke
lamtern
lape
lastoyto
late
lebn
legende
lektsye
lente
lerer
levaye
levone
leyener
leyter
leytse
libhober
lidke
lige
lign
ligner
lilye
limene
linoleum
linye
litografye
litsitatsye
lonke
lopete
lulke
lyubenyu
madreyge
maline
mamshole
mapole
margeritke
marke
mashinerye
maske
masline
matbeye
materye
matone
mayle
mayse
mayster
medyum
mehume
meker
mekhaniker
mekler
melokhe
melukhe
memorandum
menie
merder
meride
mese
meser
metsie
milkhome
milner
mine
mishpokhe
mitbazitser
mitn
mode
mogn
moler

monashke
morgn
motike
moto
moydoe
moyre
muler
mume
murashke
muter
muziker
nafke-mine
natsye
nekhome
nekome
neshome
nesie
netie
nominatsye
nore
note
novele
oaze
obligatsye
oboe
observatsye
odler
oger
okupatsye
onbaysn
onboter
onhenger
operatsye
opere
opnemer
orem
organizatsye
orkester
orkhidee
otem
oybn
oyfzeer
oylem
oysgabe
oysshpirer
oysshtayer
oyster
oyto
oytobiografye
oyvn
ozere
padeshve
palate
palme
pantere
pantser
parafye
pare
parkan (es)
parnose
pastke
patilnitse
pave
penkher
petitsye
pilke
piper-noter
pizhame
plame
plankn
plimenik (es)
plimenitse

plite
pnyak (es)
podloge
poeme
politse
pompe
poni
postn
pozitsye
premye
prent (es)
prepozitsye
prerye
presayzn
pretenzye
preydiker
printsesin
prister
privilegye
probe
produktsye
profesye
proshik (es)
protsesye
pshore
publikatsye
punktkome
pushke
pyane
pyate
pyese
radyator
radyo
rakete
rase
rate
ratsye
rayter
razirer
rede
redner
refue
rege
register
regn
regn-boygn
rekomendatsye
religye
repetitsye
reporter
reshime
retsenzye
revolutsye
rezervatsye
rezolutsye
rikhter
rimen
riter
ritshke
rizike
role
rolke
roye-khezhbn
royshem
rozhinke
ruder
ruker
rukn
sakone
sarne
sekretarshe

sekunde
servetke
serye
sesye
sfere
sgule
sharbn
sherer
shipue
shirem
shirme
shite
shkhite
shleyer
shlitn
shmate
shminke
shnayder
shodn
shotn
shpiler
shpilke
shpringer
shrayber
shroyfn-tsier
shtar-khoyv (es)
shtekn
shtele
shtern (fore-head)
shtiftate
shtore
shtshur (es)
shturem
shure
shuster
shviger
shvoger
shvue
sibe
siltse
simfonye
simkhe
simpatye
sine
sinyak (es)
situatsye
skale
skhoyre
skitse
skorinke
skovrode
skoytin
sloy (es)
slup (es)
sofe
sosne
sove
sprunzhine
stade
stadye
stanik (es)
stantsye
statue
stele
stenge
stenografin
stoler
stsene
sude
sume

sveter	toyve	tvue	visnshaftler
tabele	traditsye	ugerke	vizye
takone	tragedye	ulme	vogn
taksi	transhee	untertaner	volkn
talye	treger	uvde	volkn-kratser
tate	tropn	vakatsye	yagde
tayne	truskavke	vane	yasle
tayve	tsavoe	vayle	yedie
teater	tsenter	vaze	yeger
teke	tseremonye	vene	yeride
televizye	tseykhn	venger	zaverukhe
teme	tsharter	verbe	zayers
tempo	tsherepakhe	verbirer	zebre
teorye	tshuve	verde	zelner
terase	tsibele	vetshere	zeyde
teritorye	tsilinder	veverke	zeyger
termometer	tsivilizatsye	veyler	zhabe
teve	tsonpaste	vie	zhrebtshik (es)
tfile	tsore	viln	zhuk (es)
tiger	tsukuker	vinter	zinger
tirkhe	tsushtayer	viole	zone
tnue	turem	vire	zumer
torpede	turme		

Sing.	Pl.	Sing.	Pl.
tsederboym	tsederbeymer	verterbukh	verterbikher
tsiferblat	tsiferbleter	vort	verter
tsung	tsinger	voynort	voynerter
vald	velder	zitsort	zitserter
vayngortn	vayngertner		

Plural without an ending (same form as singular; example: *der arbl*, "the sleeve," *di arbl*, "the sleeves")

arbes	finger	lefl	teler
arbl	fish	likht	teylefl
briv	fraynd	mol	trop
drukrekht	hering	perl	tsigl
epl	hor	rekht	verk
eslefl	Indyaner	shof	vunder
eydes	kley-zayin	shtern (star)	yor
faynd	kni	shtivl	zeml
fentster	krankn-	shtrik	zind
ferd	shvester	shvester	zomen

Plural without an ending, but with a change in vowel as indicated

Sing.	Pl.	Sing.	Pl.
arayngang	arayngeng	mark	merk
aroysgang	aroysgeng	moyz	mayz
band (volume)	bend	nakht	nekht
bank	benk	nayyor-tog	nayyor-teg
barg	berg	nogl	negl
barsht	bersht	nomen	nemen
bord	berd	not	net
bruder	brider	nus	nis
brust	brist	shlak	shlek
durkhgang	durkhgeng	shlofrok	shlofrek
fledermoyz	fledermayz	shnur	shnir
fodem	fedem	shpirhunt	shpirhint
foygl	feygl	shrank	shrenk
frandz	frendz	shtekshukh	shtekshikh
frost	frest	shtiftokhter	shtiftekhter
fus	fis	shtifzun	shtifzin
gandz	gendz	shtokh	shtekh
gang	geng	shtot	shtet
gast	gest	shukh	shikh
geboyrn-tog	geboyrn-teg	tants	tents
hak	hek	tog	teg
hant	hent	tokhter	tekhter
hoyptshtot	hoyptshtet	top	tep
hund	hint	trot	trit
hut	hit	tson	tseyn
kats	kets	untershlok	untershlek
klap	klep	vant	vent
kokosnus	kokosnis	volf	velf
kolner	kelner	vorem	verem
kop	kep	yam-hunt	yam-hint
korb	kerb	yortog	yorteg
krants	krents	zak	zek
krug	krig	zun (son)	zin
ku	ki		

Plural ending in –s or –es and a change in vowel as indicated

Sing.	Pl.	Sing.	Pl.
bal-khoyv	bale-khoyves	mayontik	mayontkes
bal-nitsokhn	bale-nit-skhoynes	midber	midboryes
dor	doyres	nisoyen	nisyoynes
gilyen	gilyoynes	nitsokhn	nitskhoynes
goyrl	goyroles	of	oyfes
kelishek	kelishkes	orn	aroynes
khezhbn	khezhboynes	os	oysyes
khisorn	khesroynes	oytser	oytsres
kholem	khaloymes	reyakh	reykhes
kol	koyles	shtar	shtores
korbn	korbones	sod (secret)	soydes
korek	korkes	sofek	sfeykes
koyakh	koykhes	strashunik	strashunkes
mase (burden, load)	masoes	tshvok	tshvekes
		viderkol	viderkoyles
		yesod	yesoydes

Plural ending in –er (example: *beyn*, "bone," *beyner*, "bones")

beyn	gelt	laylekh	shteyn
bezem	hantekh	lid	shtik
bild	hemd	midglid	shvesterkind
bindglid	hundert	nakhthemd	tepekh
bret	kern	oyftsikind	tishtekh
ey	kind	pastekh	toyznt
fartekh	kleyd	protsent	unterkleyd
feld	kloysterlid	rentgen-bild	yorhundert
gayst	kraytekhts	ruknbeyn	

Plural ending in –er and a change in the vowel as indicated

Sing.	Pl.	Sing.	Pl.
band	bender	hun	hiner
blat	bleter	kalb	kelber
boydem	beydemer	kestnboym	kestnbeymer
boykh	baykher	kinder-gortn	kinder-gertner
boym	beymer	klots	kletser
brunem	brinimer	kurort	kurerter
bukh	bikher	lam	lemer
dakh	dekher	land	lender
dorf	derfer	lernbukh	lernbikher
dorn	derner	lokh	lekher
fas	feser	man	mener
flash	flesher	mastboym	mastbeymer
fliplats	flipletser	moyl	mayler
folk	felker	nokhvort	nokhverter
fon	fener	noz	nezer
forplan	forplener	ort	erter
glok	gleker	pas (passport)	peser
gloz	glezer	plan	plener
gortn	gertner	plats	pletser
got	geter	ponem	penemer
groz	grezer	rod	reder
grub (pit)	griber	shlos	shleser
haldz	heldzer	shoen-plan	shoen-plener
haldzband	haldzbender	shpilplats	shpilpletser
hantbukh	hantbikher	shpitol	shpiteler
harts	hertser	shprikhvort	shprikhverter
hon	hener	sod (orchard)	seder
horn	herner	tenenboym	tenenbeymer
hoyz	hayzer	ton	tener

Plural ending –im

bokher	guf	min	poyer
goyel			

Plural ending –im and a change in stem as indicated

Sing.	Pl.	Sing.	Pl.
balebos	balebatim	khilek	khilukim
beged	bgodim	khosn	khasanim
binyen	binyonim	khoydesh	khadoshim
dokter	doktoyrim	khshad	khshodim
eyver	eyvrim	kibed	kibudim
ganev	ganovim	kibets	kibutsim
gazlen	gazlonim	kishef	kishufim
ger	geyrim	kitser	kitsurim
goen	geoynim	klal	klolim
hemshekh	hemsheykhim	korev	kroyvim
heypekh	heypukhim	koved	kibudim
kamtsn	kamtsonim	koyne	koynim
katsev	katsovim	malakh	malokhim
keyle	keylim	malbesh	malbushim
keyser	keysorim	maykhl	maykholim
keyver	kvorim	mekhaber	mekhabrim
khaver	khaveyrim	mekhashef	mekhashfim
khazer	khazeyrim	mikhshl	mikhshoylim
khet	khatoim	minheg	minhogim
kheyfets	khfeytsim	moker	mekoyrim
kheylek	khalokim	moshl	mesholim
khidesh	khidushim	mumkhe	mumkhim

Sing.	Pl.	Sing.	Pl.
nar	naronim	shutef	shutfim
nes	nisim	sikhsekh	sikhsukhim
neyder	nedorim	silek	silukim
nign	nigunim	simen	simonim
novi	neviim	soykher	sokhrim
omed	amudim	soyne	sonim
orev	orvim	talmid	talmidim
oyfn	oyfanim	tayneg	taynugim
pakhdn	pakhdonim	tayvl	tayvolim
polit	pleytim	terets	terutsim
prat	protim	tnay	tnoyim
revakh	rvokhim	toes	tousim
roshe	reshoim	tseylem	tseylomim
rov (rabbi)	rabonim	tsondokter	tsondoktoy-
seyder	sdorim		rim
shabes	shabosim	vikuakh	vikukhim
sheker	shkorim	yishev	yishuvim
shetakh	shtokhim	yokhid	yekhidim
sheyvet	shvotim	yontev	yontoyvim
shokhn	shkheynim	yosem	yesoymim
sholiakh	shlikhim	yoyresh	yorshim
shoymer	shomrim	zokher	zkhorim
shpil-khaver	shpil-		
	khaveyrim		

Plural ending in -ekh or -kh (example: *bergele*, "mound," *bergelekh*, "mounds"; *yingl*, "boy," *yinglekh*, "boys")

ashtetsl	haybl	luftl	shtengl
bergele	haytl	maysele	shtetl
bergl	hayzl	meydl	shteyndl
betl	hentl	negele	shvebele
bintl	kapitl	noztikhl	shveml
bisl	kartl	oyfele	taykhl
bokherl (bok-	kemerl	oyringl	tetsl
herimlekh)	kepl	pekl	trepl
brekl	kerndl	pintele	trilerl
brivl	kestl	rakl	trogbetl
dekl	ketsl	regndl	tsayml
eynikl	khaneles	rekl	tsigele
farshtekl	eygele	roytheldzl	tsonbershtl
faylkhl	khazerish nisl	runtsl	tsukerl
fertl	kinigl	shifl	tsvaygl
fingerl	kishele	shlesl	vegele
flaterl	knekhl	shleyerl	veldl
flekl	knepl	shnirl	vintl
frestl	ledl	shpilkhl	yingl
glet-khayele	lempl	shpitsl	zekl
grayzl	lernyingl	shtegl	zoknbendl

Plural formed by dropping final -r (example: *gelernter*, "scholar," *gelernte*, "scholars")

aliirter	fremder	gelernter	ongeshtelter
ayngeboyrener	gaystlekher	gelibter	umgliklekher
baamter	geboyrener	glaykher	zindiker
bakanter	gefangener	heyliker	

Irregular plurals

Sing.	Pl.	Sing.	Pl.
dzhentlman	dzhentllayt	melukhe-man	melukhe-layt
gesheftsman	gesheftslayt	yunger-man	yunge-layt
khevre-man	khevre-layt		

Plural ending in -n or -en

All nouns not listed in the preceding groups belong to this category. If the singular form ends in *m*, *n*, *ng*, *nk*, *y*, stressed vowel or consonant plus *l*, the ending is *-en*; otherwise it is *-n*. Examples:

Sing.	Pl.	Sing.	Pl.
bin	binen	mitl	mitlen
gedank	gedanken	partey	parteyen
krom	kromen	rekhenung	rekhenungen
menyu	menyuen		

But:

zats	zatsn
etc.	

Gender of nouns

Every Yiddish noun in the singular is either masculine, feminine or neuter in gender. The article and adjectives, if any, which are used with a noun must be of the same gender as the noun. The gender of a noun may be found in the dictionary, where *m.* stands for masculine, *f.* for feminine and *n.* for neuter. With reference to women Yiddish usually employs special feminine nouns even where English does not do this; for example, *shokhn* means "neighbor," but for a girl or woman neighbor the feminine *shokhnte* is used. For some nouns, the suffix which makes them feminine is *-in*; for others it is *-te* or *-ke*.

Case of nouns

Names of persons

Nominative	Moyshe	Moses	Sore	Sarah
Accusative and				
Dative	Moyshen		Soren	
Possessive	Moyshes		Sores	

Common nouns. The vast majority of Yiddish nouns have only two case forms, one for the possessive and one for the other cases.

	Sing.		Pl.	
Nominative,				
Accusative				
and Dative	shokhn	neighbor	shkheynim	neighbors
Possessive	shokhns	neighbor's	shkheynims	neighbors'

A few nouns have special forms for the nominative and for the accusative and dative:

Nominative	tate	father	zeyde	grandfather
Accusative and				
Dative	tatn		zeydn	
Possessive	tatns		zeydns	

PRONOUNS

Yiddish has two pronouns meaning "you": *du*, which is used in the singular with a child, a relative or a close friend; and *ir*, which is used always in the plural and in the singular with persons with whom one is not on sufficiently familiar terms to say *du*.

Personal pronouns

Subject of the verb

ikh	I	mir	we
du	you	ir	you
er	he	zey	they
zi	she		
es	it		

Ikh leyen.　　　　*I* am reading.

Direct object of the verb

mikh	me	undz	us
dikh	you	aykh	you
im	him	zey	them
zi	her		
es	it		

Er zet *mikh*.　　　　He sees *me*.

Indirect object of the verb

mir	me	undz	us
dir	you	aykh	you
im	him	zey	them

ir	her	
im	it	

Er helft *mir*.　　　　He helps *me*.

These forms of the personal pronoun are also used after prepositions.

far *mir*　　　　for *me*

Possessive pronouns

Forms

mayn	my	undzer	our
dayn	your	ayer	your
zayn	his	zeyer	their
ir	her		
zayn	its		

Inflection. In the singular the possessive pronoun remains uninflected regardless of gender or case. In the plural, the ending *-e* is added in all genders and cases.

mayn tate un *mayn* mame　*my* father and *my* mother
mayne eltern　　　　　　*my* parents

Reflexive pronoun

The reflexive pronoun *zikh* may be used for all persons and genders.

ikh vash *zikh*	I wash *myself*
ir vasht *zikh*	you wash *yourselves*

See also section on *Reflexive Verbs*, p. 3134.

Relative pronouns

Who, which, that

The Yiddish word corresponding to these English relative pronouns is *vos*.

di froy *vos* farkoyft grins	the woman *who* (*that*) sells vegetables

Whose

Where English uses "whose" in a relative sense, Yiddish uses *vos* followed by the possessive adjective of the gender and number which agrees with the antecedent:

di froy *vos ir* krom	the woman *whose* store
di kinder *vos zeyer* lerer	the children *whose* teacher

Whom, that

Where English uses "whom" in a relative sense, Yiddish uses *vos*, sometimes followed by the appropriate personal pronoun in its direct-object or indirect-object form.

der mentsh *vos im* hot er geholfn	the man *whom* he helped

Interrogative pronouns

Who, whom, whose (*living things*)

Who—subject of a verb: *ver*

Ver iz dos?	*Who* is this?

Whom—object of a verb or preposition: *vemen.*

Vemen zet er?	*Whom* does he see?
Far *vemen* iz dos?	For *whom* is this?

Whose—possessive: *vemens*

Vemens hut iz dos?	*Whose* hat is this?

What (*inanimate things*): *vos*

Vos iz dos?	*What* is this?

See also the section on *Interrogative Adjectives*, below.

Demonstrative pronouns

This: *dos*

Gib mir *dos.*	Give me *this.*

That: *yens*

Yens darf ikh nit.	*That* I don't need.

See also the section on *Demonstrative Adjectives*, below.

ADJECTIVES

Declension of adjectives

In Yiddish adjectives agree in number, gender and case with the nouns with which they are used. In addition, with neuter nouns in the singular, the form of the adjective differs depending on whether it is or is not preceded by a definite article.

	Masc. Sing.	Fem. Sing.	Neuter Sing. Preceded by definite article	Neuter Sing. Not preceded by definite article	Pl.	
Nominative	guter	gute	gute	gut	gute	good
Accusative	gutn	gute	gute	gut	gute	good
Dative and Possessive	gutn	guter	gutn	gut	gute	good

a *guter* briv	a *good* letter
di *gute* shif	the *good* ship
mit a *gut* vort	with a *good* word

Comparison of adjectives

Regular endings

Positive	Comparative	Superlative
reyn (clean)	reyner	reynst

Change of vowel. A number of adjectives, in the comparative and superlative, undergo a change in vowel in addition to taking on an ending. Among the adjectives in this dictionary, the following belong to this group:

Positive	Comparative	Superlative
alt	elter	eltst
frum	frimer	frimst
gezunt	gezinter	gezintst
grob	greber	grebst
groys	greser	grest
hoykh	hekher	hekhst
kalt	kelter	keltst
kleyn	klener	klenst
klor	klerer	klerst
klug	kliger	kligst
kurts	kirtser	kirtst

Positive	Comparative	Superlative
lang	lenger	lengst
noent	neenter	neentst
oft	efter	eftst
sheyn	shener	shenst
shmol	shmeler	shmelst
tunkl	tinkeler	tinklst
yung	yinger	yingst

Irregular comparison. Several adjectives have irregular comparisons:

Positive	Comparative	Superlative
a sakh	merer	merste
gut	beser	best
shlekht	erger	ergst

Interrogative adjective

The interrogative adjective "which" is *velkher*. It is inflected like a regular adjective.

in *velkhn* bukh?	in *which* book?
velkhe bikher?	*which* books?

Like any other adjective, it can also be used without a noun.

Velkher is dayner?	*Which* is yours?

Demonstrative adjectives

The demonstrative adjectives are *der* (this) and *yener* (that). The former is inflected like the definite article, but when used as a demonstrative it is stressed. *Yener* is inflected like a regular adjective.

der tog	*this* day
in *dem* bukh	in *this* book
yene gas	*that* street

Like other adjectives, *der* and *yener* can also be used without nouns.

Git mir *di.*	Give me *these.*
Vos tut er mit *yenem?*	What does he do with *that* one?

VERBS

Numbering of verbs

Each verb in the Yiddish to English list is followed by a number in parentheses. These numbers correspond to models (1) through (30) in this Yiddish grammar section.

Verbs with certain peculiarities are indicated in the main Yiddish word list by lower-case letters following the verb group number. Explanations of these may be found as follows below: "a" in the section on *Complemented Verbs;* "b" in the section on *Past Participle;* "c" in the section on *Periphrastic Verbs;* "d" in the section on *Past Tense;* and "e" in the section on *Present Tense.*

Infinitive and verb root

Each verb in the main word list appears in its infinitive form. The infinitive is made up of a verb root and an infinitive ending. In most groups the infinitive ending is *-n* or *-en*, depending on the final sound of the verb root; but in verbs numbered (2) the ending is always *-n*, in verbs numbered (3) it is always *-en* and in verbs numbered (4) it is *-nen*. Examples:

Group	Infinitive	Root	Ending
All but (2)—(4)	krign	krig-	-n
" " "	kayen	kay-	-en
(2)	taynen	tayne-	-n

Group	Infinitive	Root	Ending
(3)	efenen	efn-	-en
(4)	hargenen	harge-	-nen

Present tense

Regular verbs form the present tense by adding endings to the verb root as follows:

ikh klayb	I collect	mir klaybn	we collect
du klaybst	you collect	ir klaybt	you collect
er klaybt	he collects	zey klaybn	they collect

If the verb root ends in *m, n, ng, nk,* consonant plus *l* or a stressed vowel or diphthong, the ending in the first and third persons plural of the present tense is *-en* instead of *-n.*

ikh kum	I come	mir kumen	we come
du kumst	you come	ir kumt	you come
er kumt	he comes	zey kumen	they come

Verbs in groups (12), (18), (22), (25), (26), (28), (29) and (30) have irregularities in the present tense. See the section on *Irregularities of Verb Inflection,* below.

In verbs indicated in the word list by "e" following the group number, the third person singular of the present tense does not take the ending *-t.* Example: *darfn* (1e), "to need."

ikh darf	I need	mir darfn	we need
du darfst	you need	ir darft	you need
er darf	he needs	zey darfn	they need

Past participle

The past participle of most verbs is formed from the verb root by the addition of a suffix and a prefix, and sometimes by a change in the root itself.

The past participles of nearly all Yiddish verbs are formed with the prefix *ge-.* Those verbs whose participles do not take the prefix *ge-* are identified in the word list by the letter "b" following the group number.

Verbs of groups (1) to (4) add the suffix *-t* to the root of the verb in forming the past participle. In verbs of group (5) the suffix *-n* or *-en* is added. Verbs whose past participles have irregular endings are listed in the section *Irregularities of Verb Inflection,* below.

Past participles of verbs in groups (1) to (5) are formed with no change in the root. Root changes in other groups of verbs are explained in *Irregularities of Verb Inflection,* below.

(1)	zogn	
	gezogt	said
(1b)	marshirn	
	marshirt	marched
(5)	trogn	
	getrogn	borne
(5b)	bahaltn	
	bahaltn	hidden

Past tense

The past tense is formed by means of the past participle and an auxiliary verb, usually *hobn* (to have). Certain verbs (identified in the word list by the letter "d" following the group number of the verb) take the auxiliary *zayn* (to be).

(5) trogn

ikh hob getrogn	I carried	mir hobn getrogn	we carried
du host getrogn	you carried	ir hot getrogn	you carried
er hot getrogn	he carried	zey hobn getrogn	they carried

(5d) kumen

ikh bin gekumen	I came	mir zaynen gekumen	we came
du bist gekumen	you came	ir zayt gekumen	you came
er iz gekumen	he came	zey zaynen gekumen	they came

Future tense

The future tense is formed by using the infinitive and a special auxiliary verb, whose inflection is as follows:

ikh *vel* kumen	I *will* come	mir *veln* kumen	we *will* come
du *vest* kumen	you *will* come	ir *vet* kumen	you *will* come
er *vet* kumen	he *will* come	zey *veln* kumen	they *will* come

Imperative

The singular of the imperative is identical with the first person singular of the present tense. The only exception is the verb *zayn* (to be), whose singular imperative is *zay* (be).

The plural of the imperative is identical with the second person plural of the present tense.

shrayb (*sing.*)	shraybt (*pl.*)	write!

Present participle

The present participle is formed by adding *-ndik* or *-endik* to the verb root.

lakhn	
lakh*ndik*	laughing
kumen	
kum*endik*	coming

Conditional tense

The conditional is formed by means of the past participle and a special auxiliary verb, whose inflection is as follows:

ikh *volt* gekumen	I *would* come
du *voltst* gekumen	you *would* come
er *volt* gekumen	he *would* come
mir *voltn* gekumen	we *would* come
ir *volt* gekumen	you *would* come
zey *voltn* gekumen	they *would* come

Reflexive verbs

When the subject and the object of a verb are the same, the verb is called reflexive. Reflexive verbs are commoner in Yiddish than in English. All reflexives are formed by the use of the word *zikh,* in all persons and genders.

ikh rikht *zikh*	I expect	mir rikhtn *zikh*	we expect
du rikhtst *zikh*	you expect	ir rikht *zikh*	you expect
er rikht *zikh*	he expects	zey rikhtn *zikh*	they expect

Reflexive verbs are indicated in the vocabulary list by the word *zikh.*

Complemented verbs

Verbs that in the word list are identified by the letter "a" following the group number consist of a verb root and a "complement." The complement is attached to the infinitive, the past participle and the present participle. In the present tense and in the imperative, it is detached and follows the verb. For example:

(1a) *op*leygn	to postpone	(*infinitive*)
*op*geleygt	postponed	(*past participle*)
*op*leygndik	postponing	(*present participle*)

But:

ikh leyg *op,* etc.	I postpone, etc.	(*present tense*)
leyg *op*	postpone	(*imperative*)

The most frequently used complements are the following: *antkegn, arayn, ariber, arop, aroyf, aroys, arum, avek, ayn, bay, durkh, for, foroys, funander, iber, mit, nokh, on, op, oyf, oys, tsu, tsunoyf, tsurik, tsuzamen, um* and *unter.*

Periphrastic verbs

Certain verbs, called "periphrastic," are indicated in the word list by the letter "c" following the group number. These verbs consist of an invariant part, which is always stressed, and an inflected auxiliary verb. In the infinitive, the past participle and the present participle, the invariant part usually precedes the auxiliary. In the present tense and the imperative, it usually follows the auxiliary, sometimes with one or several words between them. For example:

(25c) moyre hobn	to fear	(*infinitive*)
moyre gehat	feared	(*past participle*)
moyre hobndik	fearing	(*present participle*)
ikh hob moyre	I fear	(*present tense*)
hob nisht moyre	do not fear	(*imperative*)

Irregularities of verb inflection

Group **(1)** has no irregularities in its inflection.

(2)–(4)—see section on *Infinitive and Verb Root,* p. 3133.

(5)—see section on *Past Participle,* above.

(6) Zen (to see)
   Past Participle: gezen

(7) Change in verb root. Past participle has vowel *o.* Example: trefn, getrofn

(8) Change in verb root. Past participle has vowel *u.* Example: nemen, genumen

(9) Change in verb root. Past participle has vowel *i.* Example: blaybn, geblibn

(10) Change in verb root. Past participle has vowel *oy.* Example: heybn, gehoybn

(11) Vowel and consonant change in past participle. Example: shnaydn, geshnitn

(12) Gebn (to give)
   Present: ikh gib, du gist, er git, mir gibn, ir git, zey gibn

Past Participle: gegebn

(13) Vowel and consonant change in past participle. Example: shpayen, geshpign

(14) Geyn (to walk)
Past Participle: gegangen

(15) Zitsn (to sit)
Past Participle: gezesn

(16) Lign (to lie)
Past Participle: gelegn

(17) Shteyn (to stand)
Past Participle: geshtanen

(18) Zayn (to be)
Present: ikh bin, du bist, er iz, mir zaynen, ir zayt, zey zaynen
Past Participle: geven
Singular Imperative: zay
Plural Imperative: zayt

(19) Vowel and consonant change in past participle. Example: zidn, gezotn

(20) Esn (to eat)
Past Participle: gegesn

(21) Brengen (to bring)
Past Participle: gebrakht

(22) Ton (to do)
Present: ikh tu, du tust, er tut, mir tuen, ir tut, zey tuen

Past Participle: geton

(23) Vowel and consonant change in past participle. Example: tsien, getsoygn

(24) Vowel change in past participle. Example: hengen, gehangen

(25) Hobn (to have)
Present: ikh hob, du host, er hot, mir hobn, ir hot, zey hobn
Past Participle: gehat

(26) Visn (to know)
Present: ikh veys, du veyst, er veys, mir veysn, ir veyst, zey veysn
Past Participle: gevust

(27) Dervisn zikh (to learn)
Past Participle: dervust zikh

(28) Veln (to want)
Present: ikh vil, du vilst, er vil, mir viln, ir vilt, zey viln
Past Participle: gevolt

(29) Vel (will): Auxiliary used to form future tense. Has no past participle. For inflection, see section on *Future Tense,* above.

(30) Volt (would): Auxiliary used to form conditional. Has no past participle. For inflection, see section on *Conditional Tense,* above.

Yiddish Pronunciation

Yiddish is normally written in a modified Hebrew alphabet. The pronunciation given here is that of standard Yiddish, the literary language as taught in Yiddish schools and several American colleges and universities. The transliteration into Roman characters is that recommended by the Yiddish Scientific Institute (Yivo) and often used in elementary college-level instruction.

VOWELS

Most Yiddish vowels are of medium length, as distinguished from the long and short vowels in English and German:

Yiddish Vowel	Closest English Equivalent	Yiddish Example	Yiddish Vowel	Closest English Equivalent	Yiddish Example
a	a as in father	varm, tate	u	oo as in look	klug
e	e as in bed	gel, ver	ay	i as in line	vayn, ayzn
e (unstressed)	e as in the	koyfer, libe	ey	ay as in say	shevn, eydl
i	ee as in beer	mir	oy	oy as in toy	royt
o	aw as in law, but shorter	zorg, vos, sholem			

CONSONANTS

Many consonants (for example, b, f) have approximately the same values in English and Yiddish. Those Yiddish consonants whose pronunciations differ from English are listed below:

Yiddish Consonant	Closest English Equivalent	Yiddish Example	Yiddish Consonant	Closest English Equivalent	Yiddish Example
g	g as in go	gut	r	no English equivalent; trilled and not omitted	barsht
kh	ch as in the Scottish loch	ikh	s	s as in soft	sof
l	l as in let (includes a silent e when it follows certain consonants)	aleyn (aydl, vinkl)	ts	ts as in cats	hits
			tsh	ch as in church	patshn
n	n as in no	nokh	y	y as in yet	yetst
	includes a silent e when it follows certain consonants	loyfn, zetsn	zh	s as in measure	begazh